CollegeBoard

2013

College Handbook

College Handbook

2013

CollegeBoard

Fiftieth Edition

The College Board, New York

About the College Board

The College Board is a mission-driven not-for-profit organization that connects students to college success and opportunity. Founded in 1900, the College Board was created to expand access to higher education. Today, the membership association is made up of over 6,000 of the world's leading educational institutions and is dedicated to promoting excellence and equity in education. Each year, the College Board helps more than seven million students prepare for a successful transition to college through programs and services in college readiness and college success — including the SAT® and the Advanced Placement Program®. The organization also serves the education community through research and advocacy on behalf of students, educators and schools.

For further information, visit www.collegeboard.org.

Editorial inquiries concerning this book should be directed to Guidance Publications, The College Board, 45 Columbus Avenue, New York, NY 10023-6992; or telephone 800-323-7155.

Copies of this book are available from your local bookseller or may be ordered from College Board Publications, P.O. Box 4699, Mount Vernon, IL 62864. The book may also be ordered online through the College Board Store at www.collegeboard.org. The price is $29.99.

ISBN: 978-0-87447-980-5

Printed in the United States of America

Contents

Preface

When the *College Handbook* first appeared in 1941, students and parents had little access to college information of any kind. Now, in this Internet age, many find the amount of available information to be overwhelming.

What's needed is a single, trusted source where the key facts about colleges can be compared and contrasted on a consistent basis. From its inception, the *Handbook* has met this need by providing college-bound students and their advisers with the authoritative, reliable and up-to-date facts necessary to make informed college decisions.

This edition of the *Handbook* presents facts about 3,952 colleges, universities and technical schools. To be included, an institution must be accredited by a national or regional accrediting association recognized by the U.S. Department of Education and offer some undergraduate degree programs — at least an associate degree.

Throughout the *Handbook*, information is presented in accordance with the Common Data Set initiative, in which the College Board has taken a leading role. The goal of this collaborative effort with other publishers and college administrators is to provide students with the most accurate, consistently comparable data available.

The college descriptions are based primarily on information supplied by the colleges themselves in response to the College Board's Annual Survey of Colleges 2012, with some data supplied by federal and state agencies. The survey was completed by participating colleges in spring 2012. Several thousand college administrators across the country participated in this effort. Without their continued cooperation, publication of the *Handbook* would not be possible.

A staff of data editors verified the facts to be certain that all descriptions are as complete and accurate as possible. Although the College Board makes every effort to ensure that the information about colleges is correct and up to date, we urge students to confirm facts with the colleges themselves.

The enormous task of data collection, management and verification was directed by Connie Betterton and Stan Bernstein, with the assistance of Cathy Serico, Andrew Costello, Roger Harris and Doris Chow. Susan Bailey, Mary Anne Blazier, May Cooper, Christina Latimer, Diana McDermott, Randy Peery, Leah Swaggerty and Jenny Xie compiled, edited and verified the data. Technical support was provided by Joe Antonellis, Sherry Chen, Robert Hargrove, Mairead Holly, Ajay Kumar, Wayne Lau, Janis Linkov-Johnson, Jason Robertson and Elizabeth Shroyer.

We thank our readers — you and the many students, parents and counselors whose comments and suggestions over the years have helped to make this the most widely used college directory in the nation. We welcome your suggestions on how the *Handbook* can continue to meet the ever-changing needs of future generations of college-bound students.

Tom Vanderberg
Senior Editor, Guidance Publishing

What's in this book

If you're beginning your college search feeling a bit overwhelmed and intimidated by the sheer number of choices, you're not alone. Just about everyone starts out feeling that way. But even the most daunting job can be easily handled with the right tools and a plan, and the *College Handbook* gives you both.

Getting Started

The *College Handbook* is the best place to begin your college search, and you will no doubt find yourself returning to this source as your search progresses and evolves. You should not, however, rely on this book exclusively. Take advantage of the other resources available to you — the Internet, campus visits and interviews, college fairs and viewbooks, your school counselor, family and friends — before you make your final decision. Don't be dismayed if you find that you must change directions more than once as you learn about the colleges. This only means that you are learning more about yourself as well.

The *Handbook* is divided into four major sections. The first (where you are now) contains guidance materials to help you plan for college. Four-year college descriptions are in the second section, two-year college descriptions are in the third, and the last section contains tables and indexes. Margin tabs help you to quickly move from section to section.

Although you might be eager to dive right into the college descriptions, it is far better to start your college search with a basic idea of what you want to look for. Take the time to go through the guidance materials in the first section to get on the right track. Read the articles, ranging from college admission and placement tests to dorm life. The valuable insights you gain will give you confidence as you continue your college search.

Once you can identify your needs and preferences with regard to college size and type and have an idea of what other characteristics are important to you, the indexes at the end of the book will help you locate colleges that fit the bill.

KNOW THE LINGO

You'll find sidebars like this throughout the first part of this book highlighting and defining key terms. There's also a comprehensive glossary beginning on page 39.

For a complete explanation of the various index categories, see "Tables and Indexes" beginning on page 7.

The heart and soul of the *Handbook*, of course, are the descriptions of four-year and two-year colleges. These follow standard formats to make it easy to find a particular item of information in any description and to compare one college with another. Read "The College Descriptions" below to see what the descriptions contain and how the information is presented. If you are not sure of the meaning of a term found in the *Handbook* descriptions or guidance materials, check the glossary beginning on page 39.

GOOD TO KNOW

The chapter "Selecting colleges" has broad advice on using the college profiles and indexes to find colleges you're interested in and assess your chances of being admitted when you apply. The information in this chapter, on the other hand, defines exactly what's covered in every college description.

The College Descriptions

The college. Each description begins with the college's official name — which isn't always the one in popular use. The heading also includes the college's city, state and website address. Most colleges now have websites that are invaluable resources in your college search. The designation "CB member" after the college's name indicates that the college is a member of the College Board; the four-digit CB code should be used when requesting that SAT® scores or Advanced Placement® (AP®) scores be sent to the college.

Key facts. The bulleted list highlights information that you may want to compare across colleges and that you'll need if you decide to apply. This information includes:

- Type of institution (e.g., liberal arts college, university) and whether it has a religious affiliation.

- Whether the campus is urban, suburban or rural, and whether it is primarily a residential or a commuter campus.

- Total number of undergraduate students; profile of the undergraduate student body (percent part-time, women, minority breakdown, international); total number of graduate students on campus. *Two-year undergraduate data are included under Student Profile.*

- Percentage of applicants admitted to the freshman class, which gives you some idea of how competitive the college is. *Four-year colleges only.*

- Admission requirements for fall 2013: tests, essay, interview (if required of all applicants).

- Percentage of students who graduate within six years (most students take more than four years to earn a bachelor's degree). Caveat: This figure is based on students who enrolled as freshmen and remained to graduate; it does not include students who transferred into or out of the college during that period.

General information. The date the college was founded, the type of institutional accreditation it has, the number and type of degrees awarded in 2010-11, and whether the college has an ROTC program, will give you a sense of the academic life on campus. Whether the college organizes its calendar

GOOD TO KNOW

The College Board's **Web-based College Search** (www.collegeboard.org/collegesearch) is a powerful, fast and easy tool for creating your list of colleges to investigate. The intuitive interface helps you find colleges that match your requirements, do side-by-side comparisons and find additional colleges that may also fit the bill. You can also go directly to any college's website. With the *College Handbook* as your companion desk reference, you can quickly cut your college search down to size.

on a semester, trimester, quarter or some other schedule indicates the way the college structures its courses.

Pay particular attention to the faculty information. The total number of faculty and its makeup are important to your everyday experience at an institution. Class size information, showing percentages of classes with few or many students, is another indication of a college's learning environment. Colleges were also invited to provide a list of special facilities (from arboretums to zoos) or additional unique information about their institutions in this section.

For two-year colleges only: This is where you will find total enrollment figures for both degree-seeking and non-degree-seeking students, and information about partnerships with other schools or organizations.

Freshman class profile. (*Four-year colleges*) This provides a snapshot of the college's fall 2011 freshman class and is presented in tabular format to make it easily accessible. This is the best source of information about whether your own profile fits in with that of students currently attending the college, and whether you'd be comfortable if admitted.

- Number who applied, were admitted and enrolled.

- Mid-50 percent of enrolled freshmen's SAT/ACT test scores. This is the score range for half the freshman class. (Remember that 25 percent of enrolled freshmen scored below and 25 percent above the reported figures.)

- Information about high school GPA and class rank.

- Percentage who completed the year in good standing and returned as sophomores.

- Percentage who come from out of state, live on campus, are international students, and join fraternities or sororities.

Student profile. (*Two-year colleges*) This is similar to the freshman class profile for four-year colleges, but the data presented covers the entire undergraduate student body.

- Percentage enrolled in transfer or vocational programs. Number admitted and enrolled as first-time, first-year students. Percentage who already have a bachelor's degree or higher. Number who transferred from other institutions.

- Percentage of the total undergraduate student body who are part-time students, live on campus, are women, come from out of state, are minorities and are international students.

Transfer out. (*Two-year colleges*)

- Percentage of students in transfer programs who go on to four-year colleges.

- Colleges to which most students transferred in 2011.

Basis for selection. This is where you can find the details of a college's admission policies, including factors the college considers most important in deciding whether or not to offer you admission. If it says "Open admission,"

that means the college accepts anyone with a high school or GED diploma, space permitting. Special requirements for homeschooled and learning-disabled students are also reported here.

High school preparation. Almost all colleges listed in the *Handbook* require a high school diploma or its equivalent. Some colleges have very specific requirements in terms of education background and high school courses taken. The required and recommended number of course units that applicants should have taken in high school is listed here. Where a range is given, the lower number represents the required units; the higher number is a recommendation.

2012-13 annual costs. You should estimate and anticipate the total annual costs for each college you are considering. In doing so, the elements listed below need to be considered. Unless otherwise noted, the reported figures reflect the costs for the 2012-13 academic year.

- *Tuition/fees* include the cost of instruction and mandated fees for all students. For public colleges, both in-state and out-of-state costs are listed. If the college combines tuition, fees, and room and board expenses, that single figure is given as a comprehensive fee.

- *Room/board* figures are for a student living on campus in a double room with a full meal plan. Single rooms or rooms for three or more could cost a lot more or less than the figure reported here. Many colleges have a range of meal plans with fewer meals per week, which would lower your board cost.

- *Books/supplies* expenses can vary depending on the program you take. Some fields, such as art or architecture, may require more expensive supplies.

- *Personal expenses* include items such as clothing, laundry, entertainment and furnishings. Personal expenses will vary widely depending on your lifestyle. Transportation costs are not included.

- *Per-credit-hour tuition* (two-year colleges only) is of particular interest to students planning to attend college part time.

Financial aid. This information provides a summary of financial aid awarded for the academic year(s) indicated, and describes financial aid award policies for need-based and non-need-based aid. This information will give you an idea of how first-year and undergraduate student assistance has been awarded and will help you compare financial aid policies among the colleges. You should always contact the admission or financial aid office for complete information and for answers to any questions you might have regarding eligibility and award policies.

Application procedures. This is where you can find out about the college's application procedures and deadlines for both admission and financial aid.

- *Admission.* Most colleges require an application fee, noted here, but will waive it for applicants with need. Take note of any "priority dates" — after which qualified applicants are considered on a first-come, first-served basis, and only for as long as slots are available.

- *Financial aid.* Required forms plus priority, closing, notification and reply dates are listed for fall-term financial aid applications. The Free Application for Federal Student Aid (FAFSA) is required by every college offering federal financial aid. If the college requires the CSS/Financial Aid PROFILE® to determine your eligibility for nonfederal funds, it is noted here. "Institutional form" means the college has a form of its own. Pay special attention to priority dates and deadlines; if the college indicates "no deadline" for financial aid, it means it will continue to process requests as long as funds are available. You should always apply as early as possible to obtain the best consideration for financial aid awards.

Academics. Many colleges offer a range of special study options that can enrich or enhance your education experience. Special academic programs are listed in this section. Check the glossary for brief descriptions of each of the programs listed.

College policies on granting credit or advanced placement through the College Board's AP Program, College-Level Examination Program® (CLEP®), SAT Subject Tests™, and/or other placement programs and institutional tests are listed next. Most colleges have a maximum number of credit hours by examination that may be counted toward a degree, which is also listed.

Academic support services list the programs the college provides to assist students in succeeding academically. Preadmission summer programs, special counselors, tutoring, learning disabled programs and study skills assistance are some of the options offered.

Honors college/program. If a college has a separate undergraduate honors college or a program with different admission and academic offerings from those available to regular students, this section will tell you what's available and how to apply.

Majors. Only majors leading to a bachelor's degree (for four-year colleges) or an associate degree (for two-year colleges) are included here. They are listed alphabetically by general category. The majors listed here are based on the U.S. Department of Education's Classification of Instructional Programs; colleges were asked to match the majors they offer to this list. Many colleges additionally offer concentrations within a major, which are not reflected here.

Most popular majors. This will give you an idea of whether a substantial number of students are completing a major in an area that is of interest to you. This list is based on the percentage of students who were awarded degrees in each of the general categories listed in the 2010-11 academic year.

Computing on campus. Whether you bring your own computer to campus, or plan on using college-provided workstations, you'll want to know what technological support the college provides for student use, and whether the college requires you to bring your own PC or laptop. This section lists the number of workstations available for student use and where they're located; whether dorms are wired for high-speed Internet access and/or linked to the campus network; if there is a wireless network; if there's

online course registration, an online library or student Web hosting; and whether commuter students can link to the campus network.

Student life. If you attend the college, you will need to know if it requires enrollees to attend freshman orientation, and if it has policies and regulations governing student behavior.

If on-campus housing is available — whether it's in the form of dormitories, apartments, fraternity/sorority housing or cooperative housing — it will be indicated here. Most dormitories today are coeducational, but many colleges offer single-sex accommodations either in separate buildings or separate floors. Some colleges are now also offering "substance-free" or "wellness" dormitories, whose residents pledge not to use alcohol, tobacco or any illegal drugs. This section also indicates if on-campus housing is guaranteed for freshmen, or for all four years; and the policies and deadlines for deposits.

Most colleges have provided a selective list of student activities sponsored by the institution. Read the list carefully to see if it reflects the type of student organizations and opportunities of interest to you.

Athletics. Intercollegiate and intramural sports available at the college are listed here, along with the team name. Sports offered for men or women only are indicated by (M) or (W). The athletic association to which the college belongs also is indicated. If you want to know which colleges play in the NCAA and at what division level, see the index at the back of this book titled "NCAA sports by division," where you'll see each college listed by sport.

Student services. This section lists the college's basic range of services for students. Among these are health, personal counseling, services for adult students, student employment services, placement service for graduates, veterans' counseling and on-campus day care. This section also lists special services/facilities for learning disabled students and those with visual, speech or hearing impairments.

Contact. The last item in each description provides the admission office's address, telephone and fax numbers, the name and/or title of the admission director, and the mailing address of the college office to contact for further information and applications.

Brief Descriptions

The 271 colleges that did not respond to our Annual Survey of Colleges are described in brief with the following information: name, city, state, college type, accreditation, location and calendar. Annual costs and financial aid information are provided, if available. The addresses to contact for further information are also listed.

Tables and Indexes

The tables and indexes in the back of this book are a useful tool to find colleges quickly and zero in on the schools that interest you.

Early Application and Wait List Outcomes

If you are considering applying to a college early, the Early Decision and Early Action table (that follows the Two-year section) shows application deadlines and notification dates for early application programs, as well as the number of students who applied and were admitted last year under those policies.

If you find that you have been placed on a college's wait list for acceptance, consult the Wait List table that appears next. It will give you a sense of your chances, by showing how many students were placed on the wait list last year, how many accepted their place on the list, and how many were eventually admitted from the list.

College Indexes

You can use the college indexes to quickly find schools that interest you. In most of the indexes, colleges are listed alphabetically by state because, for many students, geographic location is a primary requirement. Colleges that are part of a system are listed alphabetically under the system name.

The following explanation of index terms may help you decide whether a certain type of college or a special program or policy interests you.

College type

Liberal arts. Sometimes known as arts and sciences. The study of liberal arts is intended to develop general knowledge and reasoning ability as opposed to specific preparation for a career. Most liberal arts colleges are privately controlled. They generally don't offer as many majors in the technical or scientific disciplines as comprehensive colleges or universities.

Upper-division. Offer the last two years of undergraduate study (junior and senior courses only), usually in specialized programs leading to the bachelor's degree. Students generally transfer to upper-division colleges after completing an associate degree or after finishing their second year of study at a four-year college.

Specialized. Concentrate their offerings in one or two specific areas, such as business or engineering. Students who enroll at specialized colleges generally have a precise idea of what they want to study.

KNOW THE LINGO

There are so many **types of specialized colleges** that we didn't have room to describe them all here. If you'd like to know more about a specific type of college, see the glossary that begins on page 39.

Special characteristics

Colleges for men/women. Some of these colleges may enroll a few women or men, but their student bodies are predominantly of one sex.

Colleges with religious affiliations. Lists each college under the official name of the denomination with which it is affiliated. Student life at some colleges is greatly influenced by the religious affiliation. At other colleges, the affiliation may be historic only, having little influence on college life.

Historically black colleges. Identifies historically or predominantly black colleges that are committed to educating African American students. The information was obtained from the National Association for Equal Opportunity in Higher Education and the U.S. government.

Hispanic-serving colleges. Identifies colleges where Hispanic students comprise at least 25 percent of the total full-time undergraduate enrollment. The information was obtained from the Hispanic Association of Colleges and Universities (HACU).

Tribal colleges. Identifies colleges committed to serving geographically isolated populations of Native Americans. The information was obtained from the Carnegie Classification of Institutions of Higher Education.

Undergraduate enrollment size

The number of students at a college helps determine its environment.

Very small. Fewer than 750 undergraduates.

Small. 750 to 1,999 undergraduates.

Medium to large. 2,000 to 7,499 undergraduates.

Large. 7,500 to 14,999 undergraduates.

Very large. 15,000 or more undergraduates.

Admission selectivity

Admit under 50%, 50%–75%, over 75%. Colleges in three categories of selectivity that limit admission to applicants who meet specific requirements.

Open admission. Colleges that admit virtually all applicants with a high school diploma or its equivalent, as long as space is available.

Many public institutions offer open admission to state residents but have selective admission requirements for out-of-state students or to selected programs; check the college descriptions to see what applies.

Admission/placement policies

No closing date. These colleges will accept applications up to the time of registration.

SAT Subject Test required/recommended. These two indexes list colleges that require or recommend that applicants take one or more

SAT Subject Tests for admission. The college descriptions provide more detailed information.

Colleges that offer ROTC

The U.S. armed forces offer Reserve Officers' Training Corps programs that prepare candidates for commissions in the Air Force, Army and Navy (Naval ROTC includes the Marine Corps). These programs are offered either at the colleges listed in the index or at cooperating institutions. ROTC programs may take either two or four years to complete. Use this index, organized by branch of service, to find colleges that offer the ROTC program of interest to you.

Colleges with NCAA sports

Lists National Collegiate Athletic Association (NCAA) championship sports by division level and the colleges, state by state, that offer them. Also indicates whether each sport is available for men only or for women only. (Crew is an NCAA sport for women only; use the college search on collegeboard.org to find colleges that offer crew for men.) To be an NCAA member, colleges must offer at least four sports and have at least one in each season (fall, winter and spring).

Alphabetical index of colleges

Lists the name and state abbreviation for every institution in the *Handbook*. If a name has changed, the old name is cross-referenced to the new name.

KEEP IN MIND

The **NCAA sports indexes** only list colleges that offer sports for which the NCAA holds a championship. There are NCAA sports that don't have a championship, such as men's rowing. And remember that many colleges offer sports through a different association (NAIA or NJCAA), or offer intramural play.

About accreditation

Every college and university in this book is accredited by an agency recognized by the U.S. Department of Education. That means you can trust that any of them will give you an education that meets basic standards for college-level study, that your studies will qualify for federal need-based financial aid and/or federal education tax breaks, and that the degree you will earn at the end of your studies will be recognized by future employers.

What Is Accreditation?

Accreditation is a voluntary process of peer review and self-regulation. The standards for each accrediting agency are slightly different but, generally, each agency ensures that its members meet basic standards in their administrative procedures, physical facilities and the quality of their academic programs.

The agencies listed on page 12 are *regional* and *national* agencies that accredit entire institutions. In majors that lead to a professional certification — such as nursing, engineering or teacher education — there may also be *specialized* agencies that accredit just one program, department or school at the college. For example, the Accreditation Board for Engineering and Technology (ABET) accredits engineering and engineering technology programs. In addition to guaranteeing the academic quality of programs, these specialized agencies often have a guidance component that helps university students make the transition to professional careers. You can find more information about specialized accrediting agencies in the College Board's *Book of Majors*, or at the Council for Higher Education Accreditation's website (www.chea.org).

What Does Accreditation Mean to Me?

If you attend an accredited college, you can be sure that:

- You will be able to use federal student aid (Title IV money) to help pay for your costs if you qualify based on financial need.

- Your tuition will qualify you for federal income tax deductions and/or credits (if you meet other conditions).

- Academic credits you earn there are eligible to transfer to another accredited college.

- Employers and professional licensing boards will recognize the degree you earn as an academic credential, as will graduate schools and other academic institutions to which you may apply.

You should, however, understand what accreditation *doesn't* mean:

- There's no guarantee that you will receive federal need-based financial aid just by attending any college, even if it's accredited.

- Regional and national accreditation ensures that every academic program at the college meets standards, but that doesn't mean that the quality of every program at the college is equal.

- If you're applying for transfer from one undergraduate institution to another, there's no guarantee that all your credits will count toward the graduation requirements of the college where you plan to finish your degree. If you plan to attend a lower-division college for your first two years of study and then go on to earn a bachelor's degree, be sure to talk to the transfer counselor there before enrolling in courses.

- Similarly, there's no guarantee that graduate schools or employers will see your undergraduate course of study as appropriate preparation for the demands of their program or job requirements.

REGIONAL
ACCREDITING ASSOCIATIONS

Middle States Commission on Higher Education

3624 Market Street
Philadelphia, PA 19104
www.msche.org

Delaware, District of Columbia, Maryland, New Jersey, New York, Pennsylvania, Puerto Rico, Virgin Islands

**New England Association
of Schools and Colleges**

209 Burlington Road, Suite 201
Bedford, MA 01730-1433
www.neasc.org

Connecticut, Maine, Massachusetts, New Hampshire, Rhode Island, Vermont

**North Central Association
of Colleges and Schools**

30 North LaSalle Street, Suite 2400
Chicago, IL 60602-2504
www.ncahigherlearningcommission.org

Arizona, Arkansas, Colorado, Illinois, Indiana, Iowa, Kansas, Michigan, Minnesota, Missouri, Nebraska, New Mexico, North Dakota, Ohio, Oklahoma, South Dakota, West Virginia, Wisconsin, Wyoming

Northwest Association of Accredited Schools

1510 Robert Street, Suite 103
Boise, ID 83705-5194
www.northwestaccreditation.org

Alaska, Idaho, Montana, Nevada, Oregon, Utah, Washington

Southern Association of Colleges and Schools

1866 Southern Lane
Decatur, GA 30033-4097
www.sacs.org

Alabama, Florida, Georgia, Kentucky, Louisiana, Mississippi, North Carolina, South Carolina, Tennessee, Texas, Virginia

Western Association of Schools and Colleges

Accrediting Commission for Senior Colleges and Universities
985 Atlantic Avenue, Suite 100
Alameda, CA 94501
www.wascsenior.org

Accrediting Commission for Community and Junior Colleges
10 Commercial Boulevard, Suite 204
Novato, CA 94949
www.accjc.org

American Samoa, California, Guam, Hawaii, Trust Territory of the Pacific

New York Board of Regents

Office of College and University Evaluation
New York State Education Department
89 Washington Avenue
Albany, NY 12234
www.regents.nysed.gov

NATIONAL
ACCREDITING ASSOCIATIONS

ACICS   **Accrediting Council for Independent Colleges and Schools**
Washington, DC
www.acics.org

ACCSC   **Accrediting Commission of Career Schools and Colleges**
Arlington, VA
www.accsc.org

ABHE   **Association for Biblical Higher Education**
Orlando, FL
www.abhe.org

AARTS   **Association of Advanced Rabbinical and Talmudic Schools**
11 Broadway, Suite 405
New York, NY 10004

ATS   **Association of Theological Schools in the United States and Canada**
Pittsburgh, PA
www.ats.edu

DETC   **Distance Education and Training Council**
Washington, DC
www.detc.org

TRACS   **Transnational Association of Christian Colleges and Schools**
Forest, VA
www.tracs.org

Selecting colleges

There are more than 3,900 accredited colleges in the United States. This book will help you get an idea of the types of colleges you're interested in attending and learn more about colleges that fall into those categories. From there, you can create a list of colleges you would like to learn more about, and start requesting information from them, visiting their websites, and (if you can) visiting their campuses. By December of your senior year, you should have your choices narrowed down to a final list of four to eight colleges to which you want to apply.

KNOW THE LINGO

"Target" school — a college you'd like to attend that will be somewhat difficult for you to get in. Usually a college where your GPA and standardized test scores would be about average. Most students apply to between two and four target schools.

"Reach" school — a college you'd like to attend, but will be difficult for you to get in. Your GPA and test scores may be below average for this school, but some other aspect of your application may make up for that. You should apply to one or two reach schools.

"Safety" school — a college you'd like to attend that's also sure to accept you. You should apply to at least one safety school.

Finding Your Fit

Every college is unique in some way. And everybody has different interests, ambitions and needs. When investigating colleges, you will probably look for different things than your friends, parents and siblings did when they applied. But there are some "big picture" elements that everyone, including you, should consider.

Colleges fall into broad categories — small and large, liberal arts and professionally oriented, academically selective, and open admission. There are also personal criteria you need to consider, such as whether a college is in your hometown or a thousand miles away.

Type of Institution

This will give you a sense of how the college organizes its academic departments. Different types of institutions include:

Liberal arts colleges offer a broad base of courses in the humanities, social sciences and natural sciences. Most are private and focus mainly on undergraduate students. Classes tend to be small, and personal attention is available. An education at a liberal arts college will prepare you for a broad range of career and graduate school options.

Community and junior colleges offer a degree after the completion of two years of full-time study. They frequently offer technical programs that prepare you for immediate entry into the job market. To learn more about the benefits of attending a community college, read "About Community Colleges" on page 20.

Agricultural colleges, technical schools and professional institutes emphasize preparation for specific careers. Examples include art institutes and music conservatories, Bible colleges, business colleges, schools of health science, seminaries and rabbinical yeshivas, and teachers colleges.

Universities are generally bigger than colleges and offer more majors and research facilities. Classes in introductory subjects may have hundreds of students, and some classes may be taught by graduate students.

Most universities are subdivided into colleges or schools. For example, a state university might have a large college of liberal arts, a school of engineering and applied sciences, a small school of nursing, a teachers college and several graduate schools all on the same campus.

Different universities have different rules for whether you can, for example, take a computer science course offered by the engineering school while enrolled in the liberal arts college. Generally, the different colleges of a university share campus facilities (such as dorms and dining halls) and some research facilities (such as libraries), and a university-wide administration handles admission, financial aid and similar services for the various colleges.

Size of the Student Body and Faculty

Size will affect many of your opportunities and experiences, including:

- the range of academic majors offered;
- the possibilities for extracurricular activities and athletics;
- the amount of personal attention you'll receive from faculty, administrators and other students; and
- the availability and size of academic facilities such as laboratories, libraries and art studios.

When considering size, be sure to look beyond the raw number of students attending. For example, perhaps you're considering a large university, but you'll be applying to its much smaller school of health sciences.

Also remember to investigate not just the number of faculty, but also how accessible faculty members are to students. You can get a rough sense of this from the "class size" entry in the *Handbook* descriptions, but if you are already interested in a particular major or department, it really helps to visit the campus and talk to students who are enrolled in that program.

Location

Do you want to go home frequently, or do you see this as a time to experience a new part of the country? Perhaps you like an urban environment with access to museums, ethnic food or major league ball games. Or maybe you hope for easy access to the outdoors or the serenity of a small town.

Academic Quality

The easiest way to measure a school's quality and the satisfaction of its students is to learn the percentage of students who return after the first year and the percentage of entering students who remain to graduate. Comparatively good retention and graduation rates are indicators that responsible academic, social and financial support systems exist for most students. These figures are reported in the *Handbook* descriptions. On average nationwide, 59 percent of four-year college students graduate from the same institution within six years or less.

One of the best ways to research a college's reputation is by talking to people who are familiar with colleges or the fields that interest you. Ask your parents if anyone they know went to one of the colleges on your short list. Talk to your school counselor — he or she probably knows quite a bit about local colleges and nationally known universities. Talk to your teachers — they might know the academic reputations of departments that relate to their teaching field. You can also research the reputations of colleges on the Internet, but beware — not everyone on the Internet is an expert, and sometimes rumors get passed along as fact.

If you already know what subjects you want to study, research the strengths of those schools or departments at the colleges and universities in which you're interested. One way to do this is to look at their departmental websites for the following:

- Are there a lot of courses offered, or just a few?

- Do the courses offered concentrate on one subfield within the major? This is not necessarily a bad thing, but it could tell you that the department is strong in some areas and weak in others.

- Do most of the professors have terminal degrees in their field? Usually the Ph.D. is the terminal degree, but in some fields, it's another graduate degree.

- The website may also tell you about research and scholarship that professors are doing, work that undergraduate students are doing, or the careers of recent alumni.

These are general questions that would apply to any department. For questions to ask colleges about a specific major, see the College Board's *Book of Majors*. It contains profiles of undergraduate majors, and each profile has a list of things to look for in a department offering that major.

Campus Life

Consider what your college life will be like beyond the classroom. Aim for a balance between academics, activities and social life. In your research, try to learn the answers to these questions:

- What extracurricular activities, athletics and special activities are available?
- Does the community around the college offer interesting outlets for students?
- Are students welcomed by the surrounding community?
- Is there a congregation of my faith on campus? Are there student groups based around my ethnic group or national culture?
- Is the college religiously affiliated? If so, how does that affiliation affect student life — for example, is attendance at services required?
- How do fraternities and sororities influence campus life?
- Is housing guaranteed? How are dorms assigned? (For more about housing options, see page 37.)

You can learn the answers to many of these questions by reading the college profiles in this book, but for others, you may have to do more in-depth research, such as visiting the college's website or its campus.

Can I Afford This College?

Today's college price tags make cost an important consideration for most students. At the same time, most colleges work to ensure that academically qualified students from every economic circumstance can find financial aid. Be sure to look beyond the price tag in considering cost. The *Handbook* descriptions give you a general idea of the college's cost and its financial aid packages. For more detailed "cost profiles" of the colleges, and for general advice about financial aid, see the College Board's *Getting Financial Aid*, which is a companion volume to this book.

Where Can I Get In?

Of course, finding a college that's the right fit for you is only half of the equation. Unless you're applying to a college with an open admission policy, you also have to convince the admission reviewers that you really are a good fit.

What Are Colleges Looking For?

When they review your application, college admission officers want to see, foremost, "students who have challenged themselves academically," says Martha Pitts, the director of admission at the University of Oregon. But they don't just want to see good grades; they also want to make sure that candidates will add something positive to the campus community. Mike Sexton, the

Where to Find More Information

Once you've created a list of colleges you'd like to learn more about, you should try to get information from as many sources as possible. Different people will tell you different things about colleges, so the more the merrier!

- ✔ **Your school counselor** can tell you about colleges and let you know when college fairs or visits from admission recruiters are coming to your school. He or she may also have a file of college course catalogs, viewbooks and other literature.

- ✔ **Visiting admission staff** who come to your school — either by themselves or as part of a large college fair — can tell you more about the college they represent and its application process.

- ✔ **College websites and guidebooks** offer a wealth of information about majors offered, activities and life on campus.

- ✔ **Returning graduates** who went to your school and come home for breaks will probably be eager to tell you all about their experiences.

- ✔ **Campus visits** are a chance to see the campus and its dorms, libraries and other facilities in person; talk to admission officers (whether informally or in an interview); observe classes and talk to students; and much more. Try to visit the campus while classes are in session. For tips on planning a visit, read the articles in the "Find a College" section of www.collegeboard.org, or get the latest edition of *Campus Visits & College Interviews* by Zola Dincin Schneider (College Board, 2012).

vice president of enrollment management at Santa Clara University, puts it this way: He looks at the applications for "a spark that tells us they'll be good roommates, good lab partners, good to have in class."

One thing you should never do is try to guess what the admission committee is looking for and try to tailor your application to it. Admission officers read thousands of applications every year, and they can almost instantly tell feigned interest in a college or a false presentation of oneself from the real thing.

Your transcript is the most important thing

There it is, in large type, but it bears repeating: Your high school transcript is the most important thing for your application success. Colleges want to see that you've challenged yourself academically throughout high school and that you are willing to put academics first for the next two to four years.

Be aware that admission staff won't just look at the grades on your transcript. They will look at which courses you took, and the grade trend over four years. For example, if you barely passed Intro to Biology as a freshman, but then turned around and got a B in AP Biology as a junior, colleges will consider that a plus. On the other hand, if you've been getting steady C's in English for the last three years, colleges may wonder why you haven't improved.

A related factor that admission officers look for is an upward trend in the difficulty of your course work. Sexton says he becomes concerned when students "start taking a lighter load senior year. I can see why they would do it sometimes, but for some people, it's going to close doors." Don't feel you need to suffocate yourself with too many courses and extracurriculars, but don't try to cruise through your senior year either.

Test scores are just part of the picture

Your scores on the admission tests can be important, but generally they're not as important as your high school transcript. Most often, admission officers will use your test scores to supplement your transcript or help them interpret it.

Although grades earned in high school courses are very important, they don't always mean the same thing. An A earned in the same course taught by different teachers in your school may not represent exactly the same amount of work, the same teaching or the same level of learning. Likewise, an A earned in the same course but in different schools and different parts of the country may not really be the same. That's where standardized tests can help.

If you've already taken an admission test (e.g., the SAT), look at your scores the same way the admission committee will look at them — objectively. They don't represent all that you've achieved or will achieve. The scores are one indicator of how far along you are right now in developing the skills you need for college and a career. In deciding where to apply to college, it's helpful to compare your scores to those of the mid-50 percent score range of freshmen who enrolled the previous year in the colleges you're considering. You'll find this information in the section titled "freshman class profile" of each four-year college description. If your scores compare favorably, you're on your way to finding the right match. But if your scores are higher or lower, it's not necessarily a mismatch. Only 50 out of every 100 freshmen had scores in that range, which means 25 had higher scores and 25 had lower scores. You may be well suited for this college in other important ways. You'll be better able to decide after reading the entire college description, visiting the college's website and (if possible) visiting the campus.

Personality can go a long way

Very few colleges assess applications using just transcripts and test scores. Most will ask for information about your involvement in extracurricular activities, recommendations from your teachers, a recommendation from your counselor, and a brief application essay. Some will ask for an interview as well. A few will ask for recommendations from someone who is not on your school faculty, for example, a minister, employer or friend.

What all of these application components have in common is that they help admission officers look "beyond the numbers" and see what kind of person you are, and how you might contribute to their campus community. They won't be the first, or most important, thing the college looks at, but they

"**The first thing most colleges and universities will consider** will be the high school courses a student chose. Are they challenging? Are they college-prep, honors or AP courses?"

— *Mary Ellen Anderson, Director of Admissions, Indiana University–Bloomington*

can help round out your application and may help the admission committee decide between you and several equally qualified candidates.

Here's a closer look at each of the personal factors colleges usually look at:

Recommendations. Recommendations will give the college a sense of your overall attitude toward learning, your character and the context for the grades on your transcript. Do you have a real passion for mathematics? Did you try really hard and improve over the year to get that "B" in U.S. History? Or could you have been an "A" student if you had taken the class more seriously? For tips on choosing which teachers to ask for recommendations, and how to ask them, see pages 27 and 28.

Extracurriculars. Your involvement in extracurricular activities — whether they're sports, a part-time job, volunteering in your community, the school play, the yearbook or something entirely different — will tell the college about how active you are in your community. From that, they'll have a good picture of your leadership potential and how likely you are to contribute to their own campus community. They'll also have a sense of how much time you spend on nonschool work, which gives them a context for reading your grades. Generally, it's best to dedicate yourself to a few extracurricular activities in which you're really interested. Making minor contributions to 10 different activities doesn't look as impressive as becoming a leader of one club that you're passionate about. Similarly, changing activities every semester makes you look fickle; it's better to show some consistency.

Essays. Admission officers use application essays to learn how creative you are, how well you can write and, sometimes, whether you're truly interested in attending their college. They are the most subjective of all the components of an application, but they are also the one component over which you have total control. For more about how applications are used by admission officials, and tips on writing your essays, read the latest edition of *The College Application Essay* by Sarah Myers McGinty (College Board, 2012).

Interviews. Interviews are rarely required and usually don't carry a great deal of weight in the overall application. If you are asked to come to an interview, you should look at it as an opportunity to put a personal face on your application, tell the college more about yourself, and learn more about whether the college would be a good fit for you. If you are shy, don't worry — no one ever gets rejected by a college because of a bad interview. For more about interviews, including checklists of questions to expect and questions you should ask, read *Campus Visits & College Interviews* by Zola Dincin Schneider (College Board, 2012).

How "interested" are you?

As college admissions have become more competitive, colleges have begun to weigh an additional factor along with the other parts of the application: "demonstrated interest." What this means is that admission officials try to determine whether, if they accept you, you will enroll at their college.

GOOD TO KNOW

You can use the college descriptions in this *Handbook* to learn their course requirements and what they recommend beyond these requirements. **This is your best indication of whether you can get in:** Do you have the lab science courses and foreign language study they require? Have you settled for the required minimum of history and social sciences, or have you taken their full recommendation? You can also learn about the high school GPAs of last year's entering class, and how those students were ranked in their high schools.

GOOD TO KNOW

Your school counselor will send the colleges to which you apply a **profile of your high school**, which will list what courses are offered, describe high school diploma requirements and generally give admission officers an overview of the academic program at your school. From this, **colleges will know whether you haven't taken the most rigorous courses available** — or, for that matter, if you've done extremely well despite a gap in your school's academic program.

Interest in a college is not something you should try to fake — if you have to pretend to want to go to a college, you won't be happy going there, so your application is a waste of time. If you really want to go to a college, your interest will show itself naturally, and colleges will be able to tell. That said, here are some things that colleges usually look for when they try to gauge your level of interest:

- Is your application essay customized to the college, or does it seem like a generic essay that you could have sent to any college?

- Did you write the college asking for information about its programs?

- Have you talked to any admission officers from the college — at your high school, via email or when visiting the campus?

- If you interview with the college, do you ask basic questions that you could have answered by reading its website, or do you ask in-depth questions that show that you've already researched the college?

Like the personal factors, your level of interest in the college isn't nearly as important as the courses you've taken, your grades or your test scores. But if the admission committee is trying to decide between you and another equally qualified candidate, it could tip your application one way or the other.

About Community Colleges

Do you want a quick start to a career path? Do you need to cut the cost of a four-year college degree? Do you want to sharpen your study skills before enrolling at a university? Do you need to attend classes at night or on weekends? Do you want to attend a college close to home?

If you said yes to even one question above, check out your options at a community college (CC). You won't be alone — 45 percent of all first-time freshmen go to two-year colleges. One reason: These institutions offer two kinds of learning.

- If your goal is a four-year degree, you can earn a two-year associate degree at a low-cost community college, then transfer to a four-year college as a junior.

- If your goal is career training, you can earn an occupational degree or certificate in two years or less, then start working immediately in many high-demand fields (like health care or computer technology).

Fit Your Education to Your Needs

A community college offers many advantages in terms of academic preparation for upper-division university work.

If you need more academic preparation, a community college can offer a leg up to achieving your goals. New students usually take placement tests in reading, writing and math. Those who need to build skills can take catch-up courses, then — over time — move into a regular academic program.

If your high school grades aren't the greatest, but a four-year college is your goal, taking community college courses — and building a record of good grades — can polish your academic record. Then you can transfer. (But don't expect it to be easy — community college courses are no different than four-year college courses.)

If you're achievement oriented, community colleges offer challenging honors courses. Honors programs not only stimulate you but also offer mentoring and networking opportunities. They will also make you a strong candidate for transfer to a four-year college.

If English is your second language, community colleges have special programs that will help you build your English skills.

Keep on Track at a Community College

If you go to a community college or junior college, it's important for you to keep your goals in mind as you choose courses.

PLANNING TO TRANSFER TO A FOUR-YEAR COLLEGE?

✔ Talk to advisers at the community college. Most public CCs offer two-year course plans that fulfill requirements at nearby colleges. To transfer without losing credits, follow those plans!

✔ Talk to advisers at the four-year college you hope to attend, too. They may have inside info.

✔ Make sure you've fulfilled requirements to declare a major at the four-year college — not just the general admission requirements. For example, Biology 101 at your CC may transfer, but might not be enough preparation for you to take the junior-level courses in the chemistry major.

✔ Don't self-advise! If you're not sure whether a course will transfer, ask. Wrong courses waste your time and money, and that's discouraging.

✔ Keep going. Don't "gap" your education, taking time out between semesters or colleges. Once you begin, keep at it — that's the path to getting your four-year degree.

TRAINING FOR AN OCCUPATION?

Make sure your degree or certificate can lead to employment.

✔ Talk to advisers at your community college, but don't just accept claims that when you graduate, you'll get a job.

✔ Ask how many students have gone straight from the college to the workforce in recent years, what jobs they got, and with which employers.

✔ Before you enroll, talk to potential employers in the outside world, too.

Learn on Your Schedule

Many CC students have jobs and family responsibilities. Scheduling classes may be a big challenge. So community colleges tend to offer day, night and weekend courses. They have pioneered new teaching methods, too. Some offer online courses (distance learning), combine Internet and classroom learning, give interactive TV courses, condense semester courses into a shorter time frame, and more.

Community College Can Be a Ticket to Hot Job Markets

With two years or less of community college training, you can earn an occupational degree or certificate in

- Fast-growing health fields
- The computer world
- New and emerging fields

A community college may be the best route to many high-demand jobs that require two-year degrees not available at four-year colleges. Look for CC courses in construction technology, culinary arts, law enforcement and biotechnology. With homeland security in the news, colleges are training many first responders.

Many community colleges also have certificate options that provide intensive training in a specialized field like computer-assisted drafting, food service technology or paralegal studies. These certificates usually take six months to a year to complete.

CCs often focus on preparing people to work in local industries.

Do you want work in your area? Look for programs like these in local community colleges:

Joliet, Ill. Joliet Junior College is nationally known for its agriculture and horticulture programs. Farming is big business in the Midwest, and Joliet grads have job offers waiting. Students learn at a 100-acre college farm and do paid internships for credit.

Tucson, Ariz. Home to many air-industry businesses, Pima Community College boasts an FAA-certified aviation tech program that prepares students to repair the structure, "airframe" and power plants of commercial jetliners. Pima's job placement record for successful grads of the program is over 95 percent.

Not bad! But also, not the case at every CC or in every field. So research your CC and your local job markets like crazy — just as you'd research a four-year college.

Applying to colleges

After you've gone through some exploration and preliminary research, it's time to sit down and apply! In order to successfully apply, you'll need to budget and manage your time, follow each college's instructions to a tee and, most important, take a good hard look at yourself and your interests.

Managing Your Time

Most deadlines for regular admission applications are due in early January or February, and most early application deadlines are in November. For any application, you'll need to fill out forms and request that your transcript and standardized test scores be sent to the college. For most applications to selective colleges, you'll also need to ask teachers and your counselor for recommendations, write an essay or personal statement, and maybe even schedule an interview with the admission office. You may also want to take the SAT or SAT Subject Tests in November or December. Meanwhile, you'll be in the middle of your senior year, with academic, extracurricular and social commitments all over your calendar.

The first thing you should do once you decide to which colleges you're applying is to make a checklist of all the deadlines and tasks you'll have to accomplish for the applications. Remember to budget time for other people to do things. Teachers won't write recommendations overnight, and testing organizations will need a few weeks to send official score reports to colleges.

For some sample checklists and a college application calendar, read the articles in the "Apply to College" section of www.collegeboard.org. For more help, use the My Organizer feature of the site, which will help you plan and remind you of upcoming deadlines, or read *Get It Together for College: A Planner to Help You Get Organized and Get In, 2nd Edition* (College Board, 2011).

JUNIOR YEAR CALENDAR

THE SUMMER BEFORE

- **Read** interesting books — no matter what you select as a major in college, you'll need a good vocabulary and strong reading comprehension skills. Reading is also one of the best ways to get ready.
- **Get a Social Security number** if you don't already have one — you'll need it for your college applications.

- **Think about yourself.** What are you curious about — nature and animals? People and places? Math and science? What do you like to do — working with your hands or with computers? Helping people? Being outdoors? Knowing the basics about yourself will help you make the right college choices.
- **Talk to your family and friends** about college and your goals. They know you best and will have good insights.

SEPTEMBER

- **Meet with your school counselor** to make sure you are taking the courses that colleges look for.
- **Resolve to get the best grades** you can this year. The payoff will be more colleges to choose from, and a better chance for scholarship money.
- **Pick up the *Official Student Guide to the PSAT/NMSQT®*** from your guidance office and take the practice test (you'll take the real test in October).
- Get involved in an **extracurricular activity**.
- Find out if your school will have a **college night**.

OCTOBER

- Take the **PSAT/NMSQT**.
- Attend a **college fair**.
- Begin looking through the *College Handbook* — **start a preliminary list of colleges** that might interest you.
- Start to **learn about financial aid**. Use the College Board's *Getting Financial Aid* to learn how it works, and the financial aid calculators at **www.collegeboard.org** to estimate how much aid you might receive.

NOVEMBER

- Begin to **research scholarships** — use the College Board's *Scholarship Handbook* to find out about deadlines and eligibility requirements.
- **Learn about the SAT.** Go to sat.collegeboard.org to learn how to get ready and when to register.
- If you are planning to major in the arts (drama, music, fine art), ask your teachers about requirements for a **portfolio or audition**.

DECEMBER

- Review your **PSAT/NMSQT Score Report Plus** with your school counselor. Sign up for your free My College QuickStart™ account on collegeboard.org/quickstart.
- Spend time over the holidays to **think about what kind of college** you want. Big or small? Far away or close to home? **Make a list** of the college features that are important to you.
- **Begin preparing for the SAT.** Learn more about **SAT** practice tools on sat.collegeboard.org.

JANUARY

- **Meet with your school counselor** to talk about the colleges in which you are interested, what entrance exams you should take, and when you should take them.
- If English is not your primary language, decide when to take the **TOEFL** test.
- Start thinking about **what you want to study in college**. Use resources like the College Board's *Book of Majors* and My College QuickStart.
- **Register for the SAT** if you want to take it in **March**.

FEBRUARY

- Think about which teachers you will ask to write **letters of recommendation**.
- **Register for AP Exams** given in May.
- Ask your counselor or teacher about taking the **SAT Subject Tests** in the spring. You should take them while course material is still fresh in your mind.

MARCH

- **Register for the SAT and/or SAT Subject Tests** if you want to take them in **late spring**.
- **Narrow your college list** to a reasonable number. Explore the colleges' websites, read their brochures and catalogs, and talk to your family and friends.
- **Practice the SAT**. Try a full-length practice test and more at **sat.collegeboard.org**.

APRIL

- **Register for the SAT and/or SAT Subject Tests** if you want to take them **before fall**.
- **Plan courses for your senior year.** Make sure you are going to meet the high school course requirements for your top-choice colleges.
- **Plan campus visits.** It's best to go when classes are in session. Start with colleges that are close by.

MAY

- AP Exams are given.
- If you are considering **military academies or ROTC** scholarships, contact your counselor before leaving school for the summer.
- Talk to your counselor about **NCAA requirements** if you want to play Division I or II sports in college.
- Start looking for a **summer job or volunteer work** — the good ones go fast.

SENIOR YEAR CALENDAR

THE SUMMER BEFORE

- **Register for the SAT and/or SAT Subject Tests** if you want to take them in **the fall**.
- If you want to play a NCAA Division I or II sport in college, **register with the NCAA Eligibility Center (www.ncaaclearinghouse.net)**.
- **Visit colleges** on your list. Call ahead for the campus tour schedule.

- Begin working on your **college application essays**.
- Find out about **local scholarships** offered by church groups, civic associations and businesses in your area.
- **Write a résumé** (accomplishments, activities and work experiences) to help you later with your college applications.
- **Request college application forms** if you aren't going to apply online.

SEPTEMBER

- Meet with your school counselor to **finalize your list of colleges**. Be sure your list includes "safety," "reach" and "target" schools.
- **Start a checklist** of all application requirements, deadlines, fees, etc.
- If you can't afford SAT or SAT Subject Test application fees, your counselor can help you request a **fee waiver**.
- Set up **final campus visits and interviews**; attend open houses at colleges that interest you.
- Find out if there will be a **family financial aid night** at your school or elsewhere in your area this fall, and put it on your calendar.

OCTOBER

- **Register for the SAT and/or SAT Subject Tests** if you want to take them in **the winter**.
- If you are going to apply under an **Early Decision or Early Action** plan, get started now.
- **Ask for letters of recommendation** from your counselor, teachers, coaches or employers.
- Write **first drafts of your college essays** and ask your parents and teachers to review them.
- If you need to fill out the **CSS/Financial Aid PROFILE®**, you can do so on collegeboard.org starting Oct. 1.

NOVEMBER

- **Finish your application essays**. Proofread them rigorously for mistakes.
- **Apply to colleges with rolling admission** (first-come, first-served) as early as possible. Keep hard copies.
- Make sure your **admission test (e.g., SAT) scores** will be sent by the testing agency to each one of your colleges.
- Give your school counselor the proper **forms to send transcripts** to your colleges at least two weeks in advance.
- **Get PINs for the FAFSA** for both yourself and for one of your parents from **www.pin.ed.gov**.

DECEMBER

- Try to **wrap up college applications** before winter break. Make copies for yourself and your school counselor.
- If you applied for **Early Decision**, you should have an answer by Dec. 15. If you are denied or deferred, submit applications now to other colleges.
- **Apply for scholarships** in time to meet application deadlines.
- Start gathering what you need to complete the FAFSA. **Visit FAFSA on the Web** for a list of needed documents.
- **Contact the financial aid office** at the colleges on your list to see if they require any **other financial aid forms**.

JANUARY

- **Submit your FAFSA** as soon as you can. If a college to which you're applying has a financial aid priority date of Feb. 1, use estimates based on your end-of-year pay stubs and last year's tax returns.
- **Submit other financial aid forms** that may be required — such as PROFILE or the college's own forms. Keep copies.
- If a college wants to see your **midyear grades**, give the form to your school counselor.
- If you have any **new honors or accomplishments** that were not in your original application, let your colleges know.

FEBRUARY

- **Contact your colleges** to confirm that all application materials have been received.
- Correct or update your **Student Aid Report (SAR)** that follows the FAFSA.
- If any **special circumstances** affect your family's financial situation, alert each college's financial aid office.
- **File income tax returns early.** Some colleges want copies of your family's returns before finalizing financial aid offers.
- **Register for AP Exams** you want to take. (If you are homeschooled or your school does not offer AP, you must contact AP Services by March 1.)

MARCH

- **Admission decisions start arriving.** Read everything you receive carefully, as some documents may require prompt action on your part.
- **Revisit colleges** that accepted you if it's hard to make a choice.
- **Don't get senioritis!** Colleges want to see strong grades in the second half of your senior year.

APRIL

- **Carefully compare financial aid award letters** from the colleges that accept you — it might not be clear which is the better offer. If you have questions, contact the college's financial aid office or talk to your school counselor.
- **If you don't get enough aid**, consider your options, which include appealing the award.
- Make a final decision, **accept the aid package, and mail a deposit check** to the college you select before May 1 (the acceptance deadline for most schools).
- **Notify the other colleges** that you won't be attending (so another student can have your spot).

MAY

- AP Exams are given. Make sure your **AP score report** is sent to your college.
- **Study hard for final exams.** Most admission offers are contingent on your final grades.
- **Thank everyone** who wrote you recommendations or otherwise helped with your college applications.
- If you plan on playing a Division I or II college sport, have your school counselor send your **final transcript to the NCAA Eligibility Center**.
- **If you weren't accepted** anywhere, don't give up — you still have options. Talk to your school counselor about them.

Filling Out the Application

A typical application will ask you to provide some personal information; a list of schools you have attended; brief descriptions of your extracurricular activities, jobs and any academic honors you have earned; and standardized test scores. They will also ask for information about your family and their education background, which colleges may use to determine whether you merit special consideration as a first-generation college student or a "legacy" applicant. Finally, most applications give you the option of affiliating yourself with a race or ethnic group. If you choose to do so, colleges may take that into consideration when reviewing your application; however, your answer won't hurt your chances of admission.

Finally, all applications will ask whether and when you plan to file for financial aid. Checking this box does not mean you have applied for financial aid! It just lets the admission office know that they should coordinate with the financial aid office later on. For more information on financial aid and how to apply for it, read the articles in the "Pay for College" section of www.collegeboard.org, or get the College Board's book, *Getting Financial Aid*.

What Goes with Your Application

Besides the application form, there are several things that need to be included with your application. You will have to send some of them with the form; others will be sent to the college by other people.

Application fee

The average college application fee is around $25. (Some colleges charge up to $60, while others don't have an application fee at all.) The fee is usually nonrefundable, even if you're not offered admission. Many colleges offer fee waivers for applicants from low-income families. If you need a fee waiver, call the college's admission office for more information.

High school transcript

This form is filled out by an official of your high school. If it comes with your admission materials, you should give it to the guidance office to complete as early as possible. Some colleges send this form directly to your school after receiving your application.

Admission test scores

If you need to submit standardized test scores, you must make sure the testing agency itself sends an official score report. Writing your scores on your application or sending a photocopy of your own personal score report will not suffice. When you take the SAT, you are entitled to four free official score reports, which are sent to the colleges you choose. This service is included in the fee you pay to take the test.

PLANNING AHEAD

In addition to the traditional typed or handwritten application, many schools today accept **online applications** (if they do, it will say so in their *Handbook* description). You may also be able to fill out the **Common Application** and send it to several schools — though you should be aware that some Common Application subscribers also require a supplementary form of their own.

KEEP IN MIND

If you apply online, remember to print your applications and proofread them before you submit them, just as you would with a printed application. Also, be sure to tell your school counselor that you've applied online — your school will still need to send your transcript to the college.

Letters of recommendation

Some colleges ask you to submit one or more letters of recommendation from a teacher, counselor or other adult who knows you well. Usually the person writing the letter will send it directly to the college, though sometimes your school counselor will assemble the letters and send them with your transcript.

Essays short and long

If you're applying to selective colleges, your essay often plays a very important role. Whether you're writing an autobiographical statement or an essay on a specific theme, take the opportunity to express your individuality in a way that sets you apart from other applicants.

Some applications will ask you to attach a separate essay of one or two pages, others will ask you to fill in some one-paragraph short responses directly on the application form, and others will ask for both. Whichever type of question you're answering, give it some thought. Draft, revise and edit your response before putting it with the application, and be sure to type or (if you must) print legibly. (The "fun" fonts that came with your word processor are usually not legible.)

Your parents, school counselors and teachers may have some helpful insights into things you should talk about in your essays. For tips and strategies on how to approach different types of essay questions, general advice on the writing process, and information about how admission officers evaluate essays, obtain a copy of Sarah Myers McGinty's *The College Application Essay* (College Board, 2012).

Interview

An interview is required or recommended by some colleges. Even if it's not required, it's a good idea to set up an interview because it gives you a chance to make a personal connection with someone who will have a voice in deciding whether or not you'll be offered admission. If you're too far away for an on-campus interview, try to arrange to meet with an alumnus in your community.

Try to schedule interviews early in your senior year — if you wait until December you may not have time to make the appointment before the application is due. Also, scheduling an interview late in the year may make the college think that your decision to apply was an afterthought. Many students feel most comfortable scheduling their first interviews with colleges they feel confident about getting into. That way, they can experience interview situations and build their confidence before going to "high stakes" interviews with their "reach" schools.

For tips on preparing for interviews and getting the most out of them, obtain a copy of Zola Dincin Schneider's *Campus Visits & College Interviews* (College Board, 2012), or read the articles in the "Apply to College" section of the College Board website.

How to Ask for Recommendations

The key to getting a great recommendation is to be a great student. But showing good manners helps.

✔ Be sure to *ask* for a recommendation — don't demand one.

✔ Respect the time constraints of those you're asking for this favor. Mary Lee Hoganson, a former counselor at Homewood-Flossmoor High School in Illinois, says that "teachers should always receive a minimum of two weeks' notice."

✔ Provide teachers and counselors with a deadline for each recommendation that you are requesting, especially noting the earliest deadline.

✔ Offer them a "brag sheet" or résumé reminding them of your accomplishments over the years. They might know your work in their classes very well, but they might not remember that you were also responsible for organizing the school talent show your junior year.

✔ Include addressed and stamped envelopes for each school to which you're applying.

✔ On the application form, waive your right to view recommendation letters. This makes the recommendation more credible in the eyes of the college.

✔ Follow up with your recommendation writers a week or so before your first deadline.

✔ Once you have decided which college to attend, write thank-you notes to everyone who provided a recommendation and tell them where you've decided to go to college. Be sure to do this before you leave high school.

EXPERT ADVICE

"Be sure to **ask for recommendations in a way that allows a teacher to decline** comfortably if he or she does not have time to do an adequate job. For example: 'Do you feel you know me well enough, and do you have enough time to write a supportive letter of recommendation?'"

— *Mary Lee Hoganson, former counselor, Homewood-Flossmoor High School, Flossmoor, Ill.*

Auditions, portfolios and other supplementary materials

If you're applying for a fine or performing arts program in music, studio art or graphic design, you may have to document prior work by auditioning on campus or submitting an audiotape, slides or some other sample of your work to demonstrate your ability. Talk to a teacher or mentor in your subject for advice on both how to assemble a portfolio and which of your pieces to include. Be sure to check the deadlines for auditions — they are often different from the deadlines for applications.

In some cases, a college will ask all students to submit an academic writing sample, either instead of or in addition to a personal statement. You should send a graded essay, presentation or lab report that you did well on, preferably a copy that has your teacher's comments and the grade you received on it.

Taking college admission and placement tests

In your junior or senior year of high school, you will probably have to take a college admission test to satisfy the admission requirements at the colleges you are considering.

You may also want to take college-level exams in specific subjects in order to strengthen your application portfolio, place out of introductory college courses, get college credit for your high school work, or all three. At the end of this chapter, you'll find an introduction to the two most widely recognized college credit-by-exam programs.

College Admission Tests: Why You Should Take Them

This chapter will give you advice on how to get ready and register for the standardized tests that satisfy the admission requirements at the colleges you are considering. You may also want to take the college-level exams in specific subjects in order to strengthen your application portfolio, place out of introductory college courses, get college credit for your high school work, or all three.

Some colleges also require one or more SAT Subject Tests. These requirements are all spelled out in the *Handbook* descriptions for each college.

The SAT®

The SAT is a globally recognized college admission test that lets you show colleges what you know and how well you can apply that knowledge. It tests your knowledge of reading, writing and mathematics — subjects that are taught every day in high school classrooms. All colleges and universities accept the SAT, and the SAT can connect you to scholarship opportunities.

Taking the SAT is an important step in finding the right college for you. But SAT scores are just one of many factors that colleges consider when making their admission decisions. High school grades are also very important. In fact, the combination of high school grades and SAT scores is the best predictor of your academic success in college.

What Are SAT Subject Tests™?

The SAT Subject Tests are one-hour exams that give you the opportunity to demonstrate your knowledge and showcase your achievement in specific subjects. There are 20 SAT Subject Tests, so you can select the tests that best showcase your achievements and interests.

By taking the tests, you can:

- Differentiate yourself by providing a more complete picture of your academic interests.

- Highlight your strength in particular subjects or areas of study, such as science, mathematics, the humanities or foreign languages.

- Fulfill admission requirements for colleges that require or recommend SAT Subject Tests, especially if you are interested in specific programs or majors.

- Satisfy basic requirements for certain majors or programs of study.

The SAT Subject Tests can also:

- Provide an opportunity for ESL (English as a Second Language) and international students to demonstrate achievement in subject areas that are not as reliant on English language mastery, such as mathematics, science and foreign languages.

- Allow home-schooled students or distance learners to show mastery in specific subjects.

Colleges use SAT Subject Tests to:

- Help put other admission factors, such as grades and course choices, into context.

- Help place students into the right courses, based on how well they've learned the material in specific subjects.

- Connect with or recruit students who are interested in specific majors/programs based on their strengths highlighted by SAT Subject Tests.

KNOW THE LINGO

The SAT — A college entrance exam that measures the academic skills you'll need for success in college. The SAT assesses how well you analyze and solve problems — skills you learned in high school that you'll need in college. It consists of three sections: mathematics, critical reading and writing. The writing section includes both multiple-choice questions and a short essay.

SAT Subject Tests — Tests designed to measure knowledge of specific subjects like English, history, mathematics, science and language for college admission purposes. These multiple-choice tests are based on high school subject material and are independent of any particular textbook or method of instruction.

2012–2013 SAT PROGRAM TEST CALENDAR

Test Dates	Oct. 6*	Nov. 3	Dec. 1	Jan. 26†	Mar. 9	May 4†	June 1
Registration Deadlines*							
Regular	Sept. 7	Oct. 4	Nov. 1	Dec. 28	Feb. 8	Apr. 5	May 2
Late	Sept. 21	Oct. 19	Nov. 16	Jan. 11	Feb. 22	Apr. 19	May 17
SAT	■	■	■	■	■	■	■
SAT Subject Tests							
Literature	■	■	■	■		■	■
United States (U.S.) History	■	■	■	■		■	■
World History			■				■
Mathematics Level 1††	■	■	■	■		■	■
Mathematics Level 2††	■	■	■	■		■	■
Biology E/M (Ecological/Molecular)	■	■	■	■		■	■
Chemistry	■	■	■	■		■	■
Physics	■	■	■	■		■	■
Languages: Reading Only							
French	■		■	■			■
German							■
Modern Hebrew							■
Italian			■				
Latin			■				■
Spanish			■				■
Languages: Reading and Listening							
Chinese		■					
French		■					
German		■					
Japanese		■					
Korean		■					
Spanish		■					

*Please note that all registration deadlines are subject to change. Visit sat.collegeboard.org for the most up-to-date listings.
†Question-and-Answer Service available.
††Calculator required.
NOTE: Sunday test dates follow each Saturday test date for students who cannot test on Saturday because of a religious observance.

Services for Students with Disabilities

Students may receive accommodations (extended time, large print, etc.) on College Board exams if they submit an eligibility form and meet the eligibility requirements. **Students must: 1)** have a disability that requires testing accommodations; **2)** have documentation on file that supports the need for accommodations; **and 3)** receive and use the requested accommodations for school-based tests. (See program material regarding the Guidelines for Documentation, and for exceptions to the above requirements.)

SSD Contacts
(all College Board programs):

Voice   609-771-7137
TTY   609-882-4118
Fax   609-771-7944
Email   sat.ssd@ets.org
www.collegeboard.com/ssd

Getting Ready for the SAT

The best way to get ready for the SAT is to take challenging courses, study hard and familiarize yourself with the test. College admission staff are more impressed by an academic record that shows real effort and achievement than they are by test scores alone.

Before taking the SAT, you should:

- Take the PSAT/NMSQT.

- Become familiar with the test's format, directions, answer sheet and question types, with free tools on sat.collegeboard.org.

- Understand the skills tested on the SAT using the Skills Insight™ tool on sat.collegeboard.org.

- Review algebra and geometry.

- Practice reading critically.

- Read and write as much as possible, in and out of school.

The PSAT/NMSQT®

Taking the PSAT/NMSQT (Preliminary SAT/National Merit Scholarship Qualifying Test) is the best way to practice for the SAT. For many students, the PSAT/NMSQT is also the first official step on the road to college. It assesses skills developed through years of study in a wide range of courses. Students taking the test in their junior year also may be eligible to enter National Merit Scholarship Corporation competitions and other scholarship programs.

All students who take the test receive free online access to My College QuickStart™ until they graduate from high school. This personalized planning kit, based on your test results, features:

- My Online Score Report — an enhanced score report that allows students to review each test question, their answers, and the correct answers with answer explanations

- My SAT Study Plan™ — a customized SAT study plan based on students' PSAT/NMSQT test performance, highlighting skills for review and practice

- My Personality — a detailed personality test that helps students learn about themselves and discover majors and careers that fit their strengths and interests

- My Major & Career Matches — extensive information about majors and careers, including insights about what to expect and what courses to take now

- My College Matches — a starter list of colleges based on students' home state and indicated choice of major

PLANNING AHEAD

Most students take the SAT in the spring of their junior year and again in the fall of their senior year. Students who take SAT Subject Tests usually do so near the end of the course taken in the subject area for each exam.

When you know which test(s) to take, you'll find a schedule of registration and administration dates on page 31. Your school counselor can tell you where the SAT will be administered close to your home and school. You can also find SAT information and practice tools at **www.sat.collegeboard.org**.

Practice Materials

To help students get ready for the SAT and college success, the College Board offers many free and affordable online test practice tools. Available at sat.collegeboard.org/practice, these resources can help you get familiar with and practice for the SAT.

- **The Official SAT Question of the Day™:** Make practice a daily routine by signing up for the College Board's popular SAT Question of the Day. It is available for free online, via email, or download the mobile app from iTunes.

- **The Official SAT Practice Test:** Taking the free SAT Practice Test online is a stress-free way to find your strengths and weaknesses on the SAT.

- **SAT Skills Insight:** Use this free online tool to help you understand and improve your skills. It identifies the types of skills that are tested on the SAT with sample test questions so that you can do your best if you're taking the SAT for the first time or want to improve your scores.

- *The Official SAT Study Guide™:* This best-seller is the only guide from the creators of the SAT. It features:
  - 10 official practice tests with targeted practice questions for all SAT question types.
  - Practice essay questions, along with sample essays and annotations.
  - A review of concepts and helpful test-taking approaches.
  - Exclusive access to free online score reports and answer explanations.

- *The Official SAT Study Guide™ with DVD:* The SAT Study Guide enhanced with a companion DVD featuring:
  - Bonus SAT test with online answer explanations
  - Virtual proctor for a timed SAT test-taking experience
  - Math Review video with step-by-step problem-solving instructions

- **The Official SAT Online Course™:** This interactive, online tool is available anytime from any computer with Internet access. It features:
  - 18 lessons with interactive activities and multimedia content.
  - 10 practice tests and over 600 practice questions.
  - Personalized score reports.
  - Detailed answer explanations and immediate essay scoring.

Taking the Test

When's the best time to take the SAT?

The SAT is offered several times a year. Most students take the SAT for the first time during the spring of their junior year and a second time during the fall of their senior year. At least half of all students take the SAT twice and most students improve their scores the second time around.

How many times should I take the test?

Research shows that many students see modest increases in their score upon taking the test a second time. Taking the test more than twice will probably not lead to significant gains.

Remember: All of the work you've done in school — including your reading, writing and math — is what really helps you do your best on the test and be better prepared for college.

How to register

The best way to register is online. It's fast and easy, and it helps you avoid late fees or missed postmark deadlines. You can even register for next year's tests over the summer. SAT registration may be completed at sat.collegeboard.org.

To register for the SAT by mail, complete the paper registration form included with the *SAT Registration Guide* and send it with your test fee payment. You can get a *Registration Guide* in your school's guidance office. Registration deadlines are about four and a half weeks before the test date. There are also late registration deadlines, and it's possible to register on a standby basis. Both of these involve an additional fee.

Score Choice™

Score Choice™ is a feature that gives you the option to choose the SAT scores you send to colleges by test date — in accordance with each college's or university's score-use practice. Designed to reduce your stress and improve the test-day experience, Score Choice gives you an opportunity to show colleges the scores you feel best represent your abilities.

Score Choice is optional, so if you don't choose to use it, all of your scores will be sent automatically. Since most colleges only consider your best scores, you should feel comfortable reporting scores from all of your test dates.

Each college and scholarship program has different score-use practices. Our score-reporting process displays score-use practices for each participating institution, but you should also check with colleges to ensure that you are following their requirements. Email reminders will be sent to you if you have not sent SAT scores to any colleges by the usual deadlines.

Remember:

- Scores from an entire SAT test (critical reading, writing and mathematics sections) will be sent — scores of individual sections from different test dates cannot be selected independently.

- You can send any or all scores to a college on a single report — it will not cost more to send one, multiple or all test scores.

- You receive four free score reports with your registration. We continue to recommend that you take full advantage of these reports.

- Score Choice is available via the Web or by calling Customer Service (toll free within the United States).

Earning College Credit by Examination

Most colleges allow you to place out of introductory courses in subject areas where you have already done college-level work, either in high school or through your own life experiences. For example, you might be able to skip the first year of college Spanish and go straight to intermediate-level courses. In order to demonstrate your knowledge, the college usually requires you to either take a nationally offered standardized test, such as an AP Exam, a CLEP exam or an SAT Subject Test, or to take an exam offered by the college on campus. (You often have a choice of doing either — that is, if you haven't taken the AP Spanish Language Exam, you can take the college's Spanish placement test as an alternative.)

If you take an AP Exam or CLEP exam, many colleges also allow you to earn credit based on your exam score. To use the same example as above, you wouldn't just place into second-year Spanish; you would also earn credits toward graduation as if you had taken first-year Spanish there on campus. If you have qualifying scores on enough exams, some colleges will even grant you "sophomore standing," meaning you are treated as a sophomore for academic purposes such as when you get to register for courses. (You still have to obey the college's other rules for freshmen, though, so don't expect to be given a single dorm room and a parking permit just because you have sophomore standing through AP.)

AP Course Calendar

Spring before starting an AP course	Well ahead of time, you need to start thinking about what AP courses you might want to take. Discuss your plans with your parents, teachers and school counselor.
Summer	Some AP teachers require you to complete work (like reading) during the summer months to prepare for their courses. For example, for AP English Literature and Composition you may be given a reading list. Make sure you complete these assignments so that you're up to speed when the class begins.
January	Talk to your AP teachers and/or AP Coordinator about taking the exams. Contact the disabilities (SSD) coordinator at your school if you will need testing accommodations.
February	Deadline for requests for testing accommodations.
March	Deadlines for homeschooled students and students whose schools do not offer AP to arrange for testing at a nearby school.
May 6–10 and May 13–17, 2013	Exam dates.
June 15, 2013	Deadline for receipt of requests for score withholding, score cancellation or a change in a college score report recipient.
July	AP score reports released to designated colleges, and to students and their high schools.

More About AP®

AP offers a wide range of college-level courses that are taught in high schools by high school teachers; a standardized exam is given for each subject every May. AP courses give you a chance to do college-level work while still in high school. Research studies have shown that students with AP experience succeed in college at a rate significantly higher than the average student.

In all, there are 34 courses in a wide variety of subject areas. Even if an AP course is not offered at your school, you may still be able to take the exam if you make arrangements with your school's AP Coordinator (usually a school counselor or a teacher). If your school doesn't offer AP at all, or you are home-schooled, you may be able to make arrangements to take an AP Exam at a nearby school that offers AP.

AP courses are challenging — after all, you're doing college-level work in high school! They can also be very rewarding. If you're not sure whether you should take an AP course, talk to your teachers, your school counselor and your parents. You might also want to look at the College Board publications *Choose AP* or the bilingual *Elige AP*. Your school should be able to order copies of these for you and your parents.

More About the College-Level Examination Program® (CLEP®)

CLEP is the most widely accepted college-based credit-by-examination program in the country. Over 2,900 accredited colleges and universities award credit for qualifying scores on CLEP exams. You can take a CLEP exam at over 1,700 test centers.

CLEP offers 33 exams in the areas of business, English composition and literature, world languages, history and social sciences, and science and mathematics. You can take a CLEP exam at any time during your college career, and the exams are offered year-round. Find out if your college grants credit for CLEP exams by using the CLEP college search at clep.collegeboard.org/search/colleges.

CLEP is computer based, allowing for instant score reports, so you know that day if you will be awarded credit for your performance. To find out more about CLEP exams, to see a list of suggested textbooks and online resources for each exam, and to download study guides, visit clep.collegeboard.org.

GOOD TO KNOW

Many colleges grant credit or advanced placement to incoming freshmen who have qualifying scores on AP Exams. Some even grant sophomore standing if you've earned qualifying scores on a requisite number of exams. You can find out specific AP policies for each exam at more than 1,000 colleges at **www.collegeboard.org/apcreditpolicy**.

Life on campus

A college isn't just a place where you'll take classes for two or four years. You'll also be spending most of your time there — and, if you're a residential student, you'll even be living there. When you're deciding where to go, academics should come first, but you should also consider how comfortable the campus feels. Some things to take into account are the housing options, local transit, whether the campus feels safe, and the social life of the campus.

Housing Options

At most colleges, you'll have lots of choices about where to live. You may live in an on-campus dorm, an off-campus house or apartment building, or a fraternity/sorority house. At some colleges, you won't have as many choices your freshman year, but even then you may have a choice of several freshman dorms.

Typically, after you accept an offer of admission, the college's housing office will ask you to submit a form stating your housing preferences. You should use this form not only to state your preference of what dorm in which they will place you, but also to help them find you a roommate who will be compatible. Are you a quiet person? What times do you usually wake up and go to bed? Are you messy or neat? Do you smoke? The housing office will try to find someone whose answers to those questions were similar to your own.

Living in Dorms

College dormitories have changed a lot over the years. While they were once bare-bones facilities that offered little more than a place to sleep, today most dorms offer a complete living and learning environment. It's not uncommon to find study areas, TV lounges, computer labs, small kitchens or even fast-food take-out restaurants built into modern dorms. While some dorms are still built on the traditional floor plan of a hallway of double rooms sharing a bathroom, others are based around suites or apartments.

Some colleges offer theme-related residences for both freshmen and upper-classmen. These programs give you the opportunity to live with other students who share similar interests in a field of study, culture, hobby or personal value. Students in theme residences not only live together, but often they also eat together and participate in social events related around the dorm's theme. Some theme residences will also have a member of the faculty who lives in the dorm and advises its students. Examples of theme residences include:

- *Diversity programs,* where the residents come from a wide variety of cultural backgrounds

- *Honors residences,* where all the students are on merit scholarships

- *Discipline-based residences,* such as a dorm for engineering and science majors

- *Foreign language immersion dorms,* where all the residents study and speak a particular foreign language

- *Substance-free housing* (a.k.a. "wellness" or "positive choice" housing), where all the residents pledge not to drink, smoke or do drugs

Roommate issues

Most roommate situations work out OK; often, freshman roommates become good friends. But there are cases when roommates just don't get along.

The best way to avoid this is to communicate with your roommates. At the beginning of the semester, tell them what you expect in terms of when you'll go to bed, when you'll get up in the mornings, when it's OK to have friends visit the room, and whether you'll be able to sleep while they work on their computer. Remember that communication is a two-way street: You should also ask your roommates about their own expectations, and listen to what they tell you.

As the semester goes on, be sure to let your roommates know if something is bothering you. Don't ignore problems or obnoxious behavior — they will only get worse if you don't speak up. Similarly, if your roommate complains about your own habits, try to correct them.

If worse comes to worst, it's not unknown for colleges to reassign roommates in midsemester. But because of space issues, this isn't always possible, and when it is possible, it's not always ideal. You'll probably find yourself living in a new dorm, away from all the friends you've already made. You might also find yourself as the new third roommate who is squeezed into a room that had previously slept two.

Glossary

Definitions of commonly used terms vary from college to college. Consult specific college catalogs or their websites for more detailed information.

Accelerated study. A college program of study completed in less time than is usually required, most often by attending classes in the summer or by taking extra courses during the regular academic terms. Completion of a bachelor's degree program in three years is an example of acceleration.

Accreditation. Recognition by an accrediting organization or agency that a college meets certain acceptable standards in its education programs, services and facilities. Regional accreditation applies to a college as a whole and not to any particular programs or courses of study. Accreditation of specific types of schools, such as Bible colleges or trade and technical schools, may also be determined by a national organization. Institutional accreditation by regional accrediting associations and by national accrediting organizations is included in the *Handbook*'s descriptions of colleges. See pages 10–12 for more information about accreditation and the names and addresses of the national and regional accrediting associations.

ACT. A college admission examination given at test centers on specified dates. Please visit the organization's website for further information.

Advanced placement. Admission or assignment of a first-year student to an advanced course in a certain subject on the basis of evidence that the student has already completed the equivalent of the college's freshman course in that subject.

Advanced Placement Program (AP). An academic program of the College Board that provides high school students with the opportunity to study and learn at the college level. AP offers courses in 34 subjects, each culminating in a rigorous exam. High schools offer the courses and administer the exams to interested students. Most colleges and universities in the United States accept qualifying AP Exam scores for credit, advanced placement or both.

Agricultural college. A college or university that primarily trains students in the agricultural sciences and agribusiness operations.

Articulation agreement. A formal agreement between two higher education institutions, stating specific policies relating to transfer and recognition of academic achievement in order to facilitate the successful transfer of students without duplication of course work.

Associate degree. A degree granted by a college or university after the satisfactory completion of the equivalent of a two-year, full-time program of study. In general, the associate of arts (A.A.) or associate of science (A.S.) degree is granted after completing a program of study similar to the first two years of a four-year college curriculum. The associate in applied science (A.A.S.) is awarded by many colleges on completion of technological or vocational programs of study.

Bachelor's, or baccalaureate, degree. A degree received after the satisfactory completion of a four- or five-year, full-time program of study (or its part-time equivalent) at a college or university. The bachelor of arts (B.A.), bachelor of science (B.S.) and bachelor of fine arts (B.F.A.) are the most common baccalaureates. Policies concerning their award vary from college to college.

Bible college. An undergraduate institution whose program, in addition to a general education in the liberal arts, includes a significant element of Bible study. Most Bible colleges seek to prepare their students for vocational or lay Christian ministry.

Branch campus. A part of a college, university or community college that is geographically separate from the main campus, has its own faculty and administration, and may have separate admission requirements and degree programs.

Business college. A college that primarily prepares students to work in an office or entrepreneurial setting. The curriculum may focus on management, clerical positions or both.

Campus. The physical location of a college or university. Includes classroom buildings, libraries, research facilities, dormitories, dining halls and administration buildings.

Calendar. The system by which an institution divides its year into shorter periods for instruction and awarding credit. The most common calendars are those based on the semester, trimester, quarter and 4-1-4.

Candidates Reply Date Agreement (CRDA). A college subscribing to this College Board–sponsored agreement will not require any applicants offered admission as freshmen to notify the college of their decision to attend (or to accept an offer of financial aid) before May 1 of the year the applicants apply. The purpose of the agreement is to give applicants time to hear from all the colleges to which they have applied before having to make a commitment to any of them.

CB code. A four-digit College Board code number that students use to designate colleges or scholarship programs to receive their SAT score reports.

Certificate. An award for completing a particular program or course of study, usually given by two-year colleges or vocational or technical schools for nondegree programs of a year or less.

College. The generic term for an institution of higher education. Also a term used to designate divisions within a university.

College-Level Examination Program (CLEP). A program in which students receive college credit by earning a qualifying score in any of 33 examinations in business, composition and literature, world languages, history and social sciences, and science and mathematics. Sponsored by the College Board, exams are administered at over 1,700 test centers. Over 2,900 colleges and universities grant credit for passing a CLEP exam.

College-preparatory subjects. A term used to describe subjects required for admission to, or recommended as preparation for, college. It is usually understood to mean subjects from the fields of English, history and social studies, foreign languages, mathematics, science and the arts.

College Scholarship Service (CSS). A unit of the College Board that assists postsecondary institutions, state scholarship programs and private scholarship organizations in the equitable and efficient distribution of student financial aid funds, mainly through its stewardship of the CSS/Financial Aid PROFILE and the Institutional Methodology.

Combined bachelor's/graduate degree. A program in which students complete a bachelor's degree and a master's degree or first-professional degree in less than the usual amount of time. In most programs, students apply to the graduate program during their first three years of undergraduate study, and begin the graduate program in their fourth year of college. Successful completion results in awarding of both a bachelor's degree and a graduate degree. At some colleges, this option is called a joint degree program.

Common Application. The standard application form distributed by the National Association of Secondary School Principals to colleges who are subscribers to the Common Application Group.

Community/junior college. A college that offers only the first two years of undergraduate study. Community colleges are public institutions, whereas junior colleges are privately operated on a not-for-profit basis. Both usually offer terminal (or "vocational") programs and transfer programs.

Consortium. A group of colleges and universities that share a common geographic location. Consortiums of colleges in the same town often allow students at one institution to take classes at other consortium colleges and use facilities (such as libraries) at the member colleges. Larger consortiums, on the state or regional level, may allow for "visiting semesters" or offer in-state tuition to out-of-state students.

Cooperative education (co-op). A program that provides for alternative class attendance and employment in business, industry or government. Students are typically paid for their work. Under a cooperative plan, five years are normally required to complete a bachelor's degree, but graduates have the advantage of about a year's practical work experience in addition to their studies.

Cooperative housing. College-owned, operated or affiliated housing in which students share room and board expenses and participate in household chores to reduce their living expenses.

Credit hour. A unit of measure representing an hour (50 minutes) of instruction over a 15-week period in a semester or trimester system, or over a 10-week period in a quarter system. It is applied toward the total number of hours needed for completing the requirements of a degree, diploma, certificate or other formal award.

Credit/placement by examination. Academic credit or placement out of introductory courses granted by a college to entering students who have demonstrated proficiency in college-level studies through examinations such as those administered by the College Board's AP and CLEP programs.

Cross-registration. The practice, through agreements between colleges, of permitting students enrolled at one college or university to enroll in courses at another institution without formally applying for admission to the second institution.

CSS code. A four-digit College Board number that students use to designate colleges or scholarship programs to receive their CSS/Financial Aid PROFILE information. A complete list of all CSS codes can be viewed at the CSS/Financial Aid PROFILE section on collegeboard.org.

CSS/Financial Aid PROFILE®. An application and service offered by the College Board, which is used by some colleges, universities and private scholarship programs to award their own private financial aid funds. Students pay a fee to send reports to institutions and programs that use PROFILE. Students register for PROFILE on www.collegeboard.org. PROFILE provides a customized application for each registrant based on the individual's information and the requirements of the colleges and programs from which she or he is seeking aid. Students complete and submit the customized application to the College Board for processing and reporting to institutions. The PROFILE is not a federal form and may not be used to apply for federal student aid.

Culinary school. A vocational college that primarily prepares students to work as chefs or caterers.

Deferred admission. The practice of permitting students to postpone enrollment, usually for one year, after acceptance to the college.

Degree. An award given by a college or university certifying that a student has completed a course of study. *See* bachelor's degree, associate degree, graduate degree. *See also* Certificate.

Distance learning. An option for earning course credit off campus via cable television, the Internet, satellite classes, videotapes, correspondence courses or other means. *See also* Virtual university.

Doctoral degree (doctorate). *See* Graduate degree.

Dormitory. *See* Residence hall.

Double major. Any program in which a student concurrently completes the requirements of two majors.

Dual enrollment. The practice of students enrolling in college courses while still in high school.

Early Action (EA). Students who apply under a college's Early Action plan receive a decision earlier than the standard response date but are not required to accept the admission offer or to make a deposit prior to May 1. See the Early Decision/Early Action table for a list of colleges that offer Early Action plans, including application deadlines and notification dates.

Early admission. The policy of some colleges of admitting certain students who have not completed high school — usually students of exceptional ability who have completed their junior year. These students are enrolled full-time in college.

Early Decision (ED). Students who apply under Early Decision make a commitment to enroll at the college if admitted and offered a satisfactory financial aid package. Application deadlines are usually in November or December with a mid-to-late-December notification date. Some colleges have two rounds of Early Decision. See the Early Decision/Early Action table for details.

Engineering college/institute/school. An institution of higher education that primarily prepares students for careers as licensed professional engineers or engineering technologists.

Exchange student program. Any arrangement that permits a student to study for a semester or more at another college in the United States without extending the amount of time required for a degree.

External degree program. A system of study whereby a student earns credit toward a degree through independent study, college courses, proficiency examinations and personal experience. External degree colleges generally have no campus or classroom facilities.

FAFSA. *See* Free Application for Federal Student Aid (FAFSA).

For-profit college. A private institution operated by its owners as a profit-making enterprise.

4-1-4 calendar. A variation of the semester calendar system, the 4-1-4 calendar consists of two terms of about 16 weeks each, separated by a one-month intersession used for intensive short courses, independent study, off-campus work or other types of instruction.

Free Application for Federal Student Aid (FAFSA). A form completed by all applicants for federal student aid. In many states, completion of the FAFSA is also sufficient to establish eligibility for state-sponsored aid programs. There is no charge to students for completing the FAFSA. The online form may be filed any time after Jan. 1 of the year for which one is seeking aid (e.g., after Jan. 1, 2013, for academic year 2013-14 assistance).

General Educational Development (GED). A series of tests that individuals who did not complete high school may take through their state education system to qualify for a high school equivalency certificate.

Grade point average (GPA) or ratio. A system used by many schools for evaluating the overall scholastic performance of students. Grade points are determined by first multiplying the number of hours given for a course by the numerical value of the grade and then dividing the sum of all grade points by the total number of hours carried. The most common system of numerical values for grades is A = 4, B = 3, C = 2, D = 1, and E or F = 0. Also called quality point average or ratio.

Graduate degree. A degree pursued after a student has earned a bachelor's degree. The master's degree, which requires one to three years of study, is usually the degree earned after the bachelor's. The doctoral degree requires further study. First-professional degrees are also graduate degrees.

Health sciences college. An institution of higher education that primarily prepares students to enter work in a clinic, hospital or private medical practice.

Hispanic-serving college. A college where Hispanic students comprise at least 25 percent of the total of full-time undergraduate enrollment.

Historically black college. An institution founded before 1964 whose mission was historically, and remains, the education of African Americans.

Homeschooled. For purposes of the application requirements described in the "basis for selection" entries of the college descriptions, this refers to homeschooling during the four years of secondary school (grades 9–12).

Honors program. Any special program for very able students that offers the opportunity for education enrichment, independent study, acceleration or some combination of these.

Independent student. For financial aid purposes, a student who is not dependent on financial support from his or her parents. Also called a self-supporting student.

Independent study. Academic work chosen or designed by the student under an instructor's supervision. This work is usually undertaken outside of the regular classroom structure.

International Baccalaureate (IB). A high school curriculum offered by some schools in the United States and other countries. Some colleges award credit for completion of this curriculum. Please visit the organization's website for further information.

Internship. A short-term, supervised work experience, usually related to a student's major field, for which the student earns academic credit. The work can be full or part time, on or off campus, paid or unpaid. Student teaching and apprenticeships are examples.

Intersession term. A short term offered between semesters. *See also* 4-1-4 calendar.

Junior college. *See* Community/junior college.

Liberal arts. The study of the humanities (literature, the arts and philosophy), history, foreign languages, social sciences, mathematics and natural sciences. Study of the liberal arts and humanities prepares students to develop general knowledge and reasoning ability rather than specific skills.

Liberal arts/career combination. A program of study in which a student typically completes three years of study in a liberal arts field followed by two years of professional/technical study (for example, engineering) at the end of which the student is awarded bachelor of arts and bachelor of science degrees. The combination is also referred to as a 3+2 program.

Liberal arts college. A college that emphasizes the liberal arts in its core curriculum and academic offerings and does not offer vocational or professional programs.

Lower division. The freshman and sophomore years of college study.

Major. A student's academic field of specialization. In general, most courses in the major are taken during the junior and senior years.

Maritime college/institute/academy. An institution of higher education that prepares students to operate commercial shipping or fishing vessels. Upon graduation, students of most maritime academies are commissioned as officers in the United States Merchant Marine, and simultaneously commissioned as officers in the U.S. Navy Reserve.

Master's degree. *See* Graduate degree.

Military college/institute/academy. An institution of higher education that prepares students (who are called "cadets" while enrolled) to become active-duty officers in the armed services. The curriculum usually combines a study of the liberal arts, military science and engineering. Cadets usually participate in military training assignments during the summer term in addition to attending the college in the fall and spring semesters.

Minor. Course work that is not as extensive as that in a major but gives students some specialized knowledge of a second field.

NAIA. The National Association of Intercollegiate Athletics. NAIA members are mostly small colleges. Championships are offered in 13 sports.

NCAA. The National Collegiate Athletic Association. The largest collegiate athletic association, it oversees the most athletic scholarship money. The NCAA governs league play in 23 championship sports.

NCCAA. National Christian College Athletic Association. NCCAA sponsors league play among Bible colleges and other Christian-oriented institutions.

NJCAA. The National Junior College Athletic Association. NJCAA members are two-year junior or community colleges.

Need-based financial aid. Financial aid given to students who have demonstrated financial need, which is calculated by subtracting the student's expected family contribution from a college's total costs. The expected family contribution is derived from a need analysis of the family's overall financial circumstances.

Nondegree study. A college-level course of study that does not lead to a degree. Nondegree study may or may not be part of a program leading to a certificate.

Nursing college. An institution of higher education that primarily prepares students to become registered nurses (RNs) or licensed practical nurses (LPNs).

Open admission. The college admission policy of admitting high school graduates and other adults generally without regard to conventional academic qualifications, such as high school subjects, high school grades and admission test scores. Virtually all applicants with high school diplomas or their equivalent are accepted, space permitting.

Placement by examination. *See* Credit/placement by examination.

Private college. Institutions described in this book as "private" are operated on a not-for-profit basis. They may be independent or church affiliated. *See also* Proprietary college.

Professional degree. A degree granted upon completion of academic requirements to become licensed in a recognized profession. The programs of study require at least two years of previous college work for entrance, and at least six years of total college work for completion. The medical doctorate (M.D.) is one kind of first-professional degree.

PROFILE. *See* CSS/Financial Aid PROFILE.

Priority date. The date by which an application, whether for admission, housing or financial aid, must be received to be given the strongest possible consideration. After that date, applicants are considered on a first-come, first-served basis.

Proprietary college. *See* For-profit college.

PSAT/NMSQT (Preliminary SAT/ National Merit Scholarship Qualifying Test). A comprehensive program that helps schools put students on the path to college. The PSAT/NMSQT is administered by high schools to sophomores and juniors each year in October and serves as the qualifying test for scholarships awarded by the National Merit Scholarship Corporation.

Public college/university. An institution that is supported by taxes and other public revenue and governed by a county, state or federal government agency.

Quality point average. *See* Grade point average (GPA) or ratio.

Quarter. An academic calendar period of about 12 weeks. Four quarters make up an academic year, but at colleges using the quarter system, students make normal academic progress by attending three quarters each year. In some colleges, students can accelerate their programs by attending all four quarters in one or more years.

Rabbinical college. *See* Seminary/rabbinical college.

Regional accreditation. *See* Accreditation.

Regular admission. Admission during the college's normal calendar for admission, as opposed to Early Decision or Early Action admission.

Reserve Officers' Training Corps (ROTC). Programs conducted by certain colleges in cooperation with the United States Air Force, Army and Navy. Navy ROTC includes the Marine Corps (the Coast Guard and Merchant Marine do not sponsor ROTC programs). Local recruiting offices of the services themselves can supply detailed information about these programs, as can participating colleges.

Residence hall. An on-campus living facility. Also known as a dormitory (or "dorm").

Residency requirement. The minimum number of terms that a student must spend taking courses on campus (as opposed to independent study, transfer credits from other colleges, or credit by examination) to be eligible for graduation. Can also refer to the minimum amount of time a student must have lived in-state in order to qualify for the in-state tuition rate at a public college or university.

Rolling admission. An admission procedure by which the college considers each student's application as soon as all the required credentials, such as school records and test scores, have been received. The college usually notifies an applicant of its decision without delay. At many colleges, rolling admission allows for early notification and works much like nonbinding Early Action programs.

Room and board. The cost of housing and meals for students who reside on campus and/or dine in college-operated meal halls.

SAT. A college entrance exam that tests critical reading, writing and mathematics skills, given on specified dates throughout the year at test centers in the United States and other countries. The SAT is used by most colleges and sponsors of financial aid programs.

SAT Subject Tests. Admission tests in specific subjects given at test centers in the United States and other countries on specified dates throughout the year. The tests are used by colleges for help in both evaluating applicants for admission and determining course placement, and exemption of enrolled first-year students.

Semester. A period of about 16 weeks. Colleges on a semester system offer two semesters of instruction a year; there may be an additional summer session.

Semester at sea. A program for credit, usually for students with majors in oceanography or marine-related fields, in which students live on a ship, frequently a research vessel, for part of a semester. Academic courses are generally taken in conjunction with the sea experience.

Seminary/rabbinical college. An institution that prepares its student for professional religious ministry. Most seminaries are graduate-only institutions that offer first-professional degrees in divinity or rabbinical studies. The seminaries described in this book also offer undergraduate programs in philosophy, theology, Bible studies or other related liberal arts.

Sophomore standing. Consideration of a student as a sophomore for academic purposes such as registering for classes and declaring a major. A college may grant sophomore standing to incoming freshmen if they have enough credits from AP, CLEP or IB exams.

Student Aid Report (SAR). A report produced by the U.S. Department of Education and sent to students in response to their having filed the Free Application for Federal Student Aid (FAFSA). The SAR contains information the student provided on the FAFSA as well as the federally calculated result, which the financial aid office will use in determining the student's eligibility for a Federal Pell Grant and other federal student aid programs.

Student-designed major. An academic program that allows a student to construct a major field of study not formally offered by the college. Often nontraditional and interdisciplinary in nature, the major is developed by the student with the approval of a designated college officer or committee.

Study abroad. Any arrangement by which a student completes part of the college program — typically the junior year but sometimes only a semester or a summer — by studying in another country. A college may operate a campus abroad, or it may have a cooperative agreement with some other U.S. college or an institution of the other country.

Teacher certification. A college program designed to prepare students to meet the requirements for certification as teachers in elementary and secondary schools.

Teachers college. A college that specializes in preparing students to teach in elementary or secondary schools. Most teachers colleges offer a curriculum that combines a study of the liberal arts with the study of pedagogy.

Technical college/school. A college that offers a wide variety of vocational programs to students.

Term. The shorter period into which colleges divide the school year. *See* Calendar.

Terminal degree. The highest degree level attainable in a particular field. For most teaching faculty this is a doctoral degree. In certain fields, however, a master's degree is the highest level.

Terminal program. An education program designed to prepare students for immediate employment. These programs usually can be completed in less than four years beyond high school and are available in most community colleges and vocational-technical institutes.

Test of English as a Foreign Language (TOEFL). A test generally used by international students to demonstrate their English language proficiency at the advanced level required for study at colleges and universities worldwide. Please visit the organization's website for further information.

Transcript. A copy of a student's official academic record listing all courses taken and grades received.

Transfer program. An education program in a two-year college (or a four-year college that offers associate degrees), primarily for students who plan to continue their studies in a four-year college or university.

Transfer student. A student who has attended another college for any period, which may be defined by various colleges as any time from a single term up to three years. A transfer student may receive credit for all or some of the courses successfully completed before the transfer.

Trimester. An academic calendar period of about 15 weeks. Three trimesters make up one year. Students normally progress by attending two of the trimesters each year and in some colleges can accelerate their programs by attending all three trimesters in one or more years.

Tuition. The price of instruction at a college. Tuition may be charged per term or per credit hour.

Two-year college. *See* Community/junior college; Upper-division college.

United Nations semester. A program in which students take courses at a college in New York City while interning at the United Nations.

University. An institution of higher education that is divided into several colleges, schools or institutes. When applying to a university, students typically have to apply for admission to a specific college, which may have its own admission requirements. Not all colleges within a university will admit applicants who are high school graduates — some may be for graduate study only, and some may be upper-division colleges. Generally, university students take classes in the college to which they were accepted, but they may be allowed to take some courses offered by other colleges within the university and can use shared facilities such as libraries and laboratories.

Upper division. The junior and senior years of study.

Upper-division college. A college offering bachelor's degree programs that begin with the junior year. Entering students must have completed their freshman and sophomore years at other colleges.

Urban semester. A program for credit in which students spend a semester in a major city and experience the complexities of an urban center through course work, seminars and/or internships related to their major.

USCAA. United States Collegiate Athletic Association. USCAA's members are primarily very small colleges.

Virtual university. A degree-granting, accredited institution wherein all courses are delivered by distance learning, with no physical campus.

Vocational program. *See* Terminal program.

Wait list. A list of students who meet the admission requirements, but will only be offered a place in the class if space becomes available. See the wait-list table in the back of this book for a list of colleges that placed students on a wait list last year, along with the number of students who were eventually accepted from that list.

Washington semester. A program in which students intern with a government agency or department in the Washington, D.C., metropolitan area. Students earn field service credit for their work and frequently take courses at area colleges.

Weekend college. A program that allows students to take a complete course of study and attend classes only on weekends. These programs are generally restricted to a few areas of study at a college and require more than the traditional number of years to complete.

Work-study. An arrangement by which a student combines employment and college study. The employment may be an integral part of the academic program (as in cooperative education and internships) or simply a means of paying for college (as in the Federal Work-Study Program).

Four-year colleges

Alabama

Alabama Agricultural and Mechanical University
Huntsville, Alabama   **CB member**
www.aamu.edu   **CB code: 1003**

- Public 4-year university and agricultural college
- Residential campus in large city
- 4,285 degree-seeking undergraduates: 8% part-time, 52% women
- 785 degree-seeking graduate students
- 50% of applicants admitted
- SAT or ACT (ACT writing optional) required
- 32% graduate within 6 years

General. Founded in 1875. Regionally accredited. Campus located near Redstone Arsenal-Defense Research/Space Research Center. **Degrees:** 619 bachelor's awarded; master's, doctoral offered. **ROTC:** Army. **Location:** 2 miles from downtown, 95 miles from Birmingham. **Calendar:** Semester, extensive summer session. **Full-time faculty:** 315 total. **Part-time faculty:** 70 total. **Class size:** 41% < 20, 46% 20-39, 9% 40-49, 3% 50-99, less than 1% >100. **Special facilities:** State black archives research center and museum.

Freshman class profile. 7,156 applied, 3,585 admitted, 872 enrolled.

Mid 50% test scores			
SAT critical reading:	370-450	**ACT composite:**	16-19
SAT math:	360-450	**Return as sophomores:**	67%
SAT writing:	370-440	**Out-of-state:**	36%

Basis for selection. 2.0 GPA required. Test scores important, but may be waived dependent upon evaluation of GPA and other achievements. Interview, essay recommended. **Home schooled:** Must meet Alabama State Department of Education requirements.

High school preparation. Required units include English 4, mathematics 4 and science 2.

2011-2012 Annual costs. Tuition/fees: $7,455; $14,115 out-of-state. Room/board: $6,980.

2011-2012 Financial aid. Need-based: Average need met was 8%. Average scholarship/grant was $7,570; average loan $3,289. 47% of total undergraduate aid awarded as scholarships/grants, 53% as loans/jobs. **Non-need-based:** Scholarships awarded for athletics, minority status.

Application procedures. Admission: Priority date 5/1; deadline 7/15 (receipt date). $25 fee, may be waived for applicants with need. Admission notification on a rolling basis. **Financial aid:** Priority date 3/1; no closing date. FAFSA, institutional form required. Applicants notified on a rolling basis starting 4/15; must reply within 2 week(s) of notification.

Academics. Bachelor of Technical Studies available to adult learners in nontraditional fields. **Special study options:** Cooperative education, distance learning, double major, dual enrollment of high school students, exchange student, honors, independent study, internships, study abroad, teacher certification program, Washington semester, weekend college. **Credit/placement by examination:** AP, CLEP, SAT, ACT, institutional tests. 9 credit hours maximum toward bachelor's degree. Scores from DANTES, CLEP, ACE, and similar tests, and work experiences considered for credit toward degree. **Support services:** Learning center, reduced course load, remedial instruction, study skills assistance, tutoring.

Honors college/program. Second semester freshmen with 20-21 ACT (SAT 1030) may be considered with 3.5 college GPA, 12 credit hours completed at the university, and 3.3 high school GPA.

Majors. Architecture: Urban/community planning. **Biology:** General. **Business:** General, accounting, business admin, finance, marketing, office management, public finance. **Communications:** Journalism. **Communications technology:** General, graphic/printing. **Computer sciences:** General. **Education:** General, business, early childhood, elementary, music, physical, school counseling, secondary, special ed, speech impaired. **Engineering:** Civil, mechanical. **English:** English lit. **General:** Economics. **Human services:** Social work. **Math:** General. **Physical sciences:** Chemistry, physics. **Psychology:** General. **Social sciences:** Political science, sociology. **Visual/performing arts:** Art, conducting, music, music performance. **Work/family studies:** General.

Most popular majors. Agriculture 6%, biology 9%, business/marketing 19%, education 16%, engineering/engineering technologies 13%, psychology 7%, public administration/social services 6%, social sciences 6%.

Computing on campus. 928 workstations in dormitories, library, computer center, student center, student center. Dormitories linked to campus network. Commuter students can connect to campus network. Helpline available.

Student life. Freshman orientation: Mandatory, $100 fee. Preregistration for classes offered. **Housing:** Guaranteed on-campus for all undergraduates. Single-sex dorms available. $250 deposit, deadline 8/1. **Activities:** Bands, choral groups, dance, drama, literary magazine, music ensembles, radio station, student government, student newspaper, TV station, Christian student organization, honor society, service clubs, NAACP, African-American political club, Baptist student union, Islamic association, Caribbean students association, International Association of Nigerian Students.

Athletics. NCAA. **Intercollegiate:** Baseball M, basketball, bowling W, cross-country, football (tackle) M, golf, soccer W, softball W, tennis, track and field, volleyball W. **Intramural:** Basketball, football (tackle) M, soccer W, softball, volleyball. **Team name:** Bulldogs.

Student services. Adult student services, career counseling, student employment services, health services, personal counseling, placement for graduates, veterans' counselor. **Physically disabled:** Services for visually, speech, hearing impaired.

Contact. E-mail: admissions@aamu.edu
Phone: (256) 372-5245 Toll-free number: (256) 372-5245
Fax: (256) 372-5249
Venita King, Director of Admissions, Alabama Agricultural and Mechanical University, Box 908, Normal, AL 35762

Alabama State University
Montgomery, Alabama
www.alasu.edu   **CB code: 1006**

- Public 4-year university
- Residential campus in small city
- 4,703 degree-seeking undergraduates: 8% part-time, 59% women, 96% African American, 1% Hispanic American
- 659 degree-seeking graduate students
- 46% of applicants admitted
- SAT or ACT (ACT writing recommended), interview required

General. Founded in 1867. Regionally accredited. **Degrees:** 570 bachelor's awarded; master's, professional, doctoral offered. **ROTC:** Army, Air Force. **Location:** 91 miles from Birmingham, 162 miles from Atlanta. **Calendar:** Semester, limited summer session. **Full-time faculty:** 256 total; 71% minority, 53% women. **Part-time faculty:** 167 total; 80% minority, 49% women. **Class size:** 51% < 20, 48% 20-39, 1% 40-49, less than 1% 50-99, less than 1% >100. **Special facilities:** Black history collection, E. D. Nixon papers from civil rights movement of 1960's.

Freshman class profile. 7,592 applied, 3,495 admitted, 1,104 enrolled.

Mid 50% test scores			
SAT critical reading:	370-460	GPA 2.0-2.99:	67%
SAT math:	360-480	Rank in top quarter:	27%
ACT composite:	15-19	Rank in top tenth:	10%
GPA 3.75 or higher:	3%	Return as sophomores:	55%
GPA 3.50-3.74:	5%	Out-of-state:	36%
GPA 3.0-3.49:	23%	Live on campus:	67%
		International:	1%

Basis for selection. School record and GPA very important; 2.2 GPA from accredited high school required. Interview and essay recommended. Audition required of music majors. Portfolio recommended for art majors. **Home schooled:** Transcript of courses and grades required. 20 ACT required. **Learning Disabled:** Must submit appropriate documentation in order to be given special consideration.

High school preparation. College-preparatory program recommended. 15 units required. Required units include English 4, mathematics 3, social studies 3, science 3, foreign language 1 and computer science 1.

2011-2012 Annual costs. Tuition/fees: $7,932; $14,244 out-of-state. Room/board: $5,366. Books/supplies: $1,600. Personal expenses: $1,380.

2011-2012 Financial aid. Need-based: 1,090 full-time freshmen applied for aid; 1,003 were judged to have need; 982 of these received aid. Average need met was 86%. Average scholarship/grant was $5,411; average loan $3,423. 61% of total undergraduate aid awarded as scholarships/grants, 39% as loans/jobs. **Non-need-based:** Scholarships awarded for academics, alumni affiliation, art, athletics, leadership, music/drama, religious affiliation, ROTC.

Application procedures. Admission: Closing date 7/31 (postmark date). $25 fee, may be waived for applicants with need. Admission notification on a rolling basis. **Financial aid:** Priority date 4/1; no closing date. FAFSA required. Applicants notified on a rolling basis starting 5/1.

Academics. Special study options: Combined bachelor's/graduate degree, cooperative education, cross-registration, distance learning, double major, honors, independent study, internships, teacher certification program. Enrollment with Auburn University Montgomery and Troy University Montgomery. **Credit/placement by examination:** AP, CLEP, SAT, ACT, institutional tests. 45 credit hours maximum toward bachelor's degree. Students must have approval of the academic advisor, department head, dean and vice president for academic affairs prior to taking CLEP exam. **Support services:** Learning center, remedial instruction, study skills assistance, tutoring, writing center.

Honors college/program. 3.3 GPA and 24 ACT or 1100 SAT required; 34 freshmen admitted.

Majors. Biology: General, marine. **Business:** Accounting, business admin, finance, marketing. **Communications:** Communications/speech/rhetoric. **Computer sciences:** Computer science, information systems. **Education:** Early childhood, elementary, music, physical, secondary, special ed. **English:** English lit. **Health services:** Medical records admin. **History:** General. **Human services:** Social work. **Math:** General. **Parks/recreation:** Facilities management. **Physical sciences:** Chemistry, physics. **Protective services:** Criminal justice. **Psychology:** General. **Social sciences:** Political science, sociology. **Visual/performing arts:** Art, dramatic, music.

Most popular majors. Biology 11%, business/marketing 12%, communications/journalism 8%, computer/information sciences 6%, education 13%, health sciences 6%, psychology 9%, public administration/social services 13%, science technologies 9%, security/protective services 10%.

Computing on campus. 405 workstations in library, computer center. Dormitories wired for high-speed internet access. Online course registration, online library, helpline, repair service, wireless network available.

Student life. Freshman orientation: Mandatory, $55 fee. Preregistration for classes offered. **Housing:** Single-sex dorms, special housing for disabled, apartments available. $200 fully refundable deposit, deadline 5/31. Living-learning communities available. **Activities:** Bands, campus ministries, choral groups, dance, drama, international student organizations, music ensembles, Model UN, musical theater, radio station, student government, student newspaper, Student Christian Association.

Athletics. NCAA. **Intercollegiate:** Baseball M, basketball, bowling W, cross-country, football (tackle) M, golf, soccer W, softball W, tennis, track and field, volleyball W. **Intramural:** Baseball M, basketball, softball, swimming, tennis, track and field, volleyball W. **Team name:** Hornets.

Student services. Adult student services, alcohol/substance abuse counseling, career counseling, services for economically disadvantaged, student employment services, financial aid counseling, health services, minority student services, personal counseling, placement for graduates, veterans' counselor. **Physically disabled:** Services for visually impaired.

Contact. E-mail: admissions@alasu.edu
Phone: (334) 229-4291 Toll-free number: (800) 253-5037
Fax: (334) 229-4984
Feddie Williams, Director of Admissions and Recruitment, Alabama State University, PO Box 271, Montgomery, AL 36101-0271

Amridge University
Montgomery, Alabama
www.amridgeuniversity.edu   CB code: 7001

- Private 4-year virtual university affiliated with Church of Christ
- Commuter campus in small city
- 361 degree-seeking undergraduates: 39% part-time, 56% women, 18% African American, 1% Asian American, 3% Hispanic American
- 419 degree-seeking graduate students

General. Founded in 1967. Regionally accredited. **Degrees:** 102 bachelor's, 3 associate awarded; master's, doctoral offered. **Location:** 100 miles from Birmingham, 150 miles from Atlanta. **Calendar:** Semester, extensive summer session. **Full-time faculty:** 58 total. **Part-time faculty:** 37 total.

Basis for selection. Open admission, but selective for some programs. Students admitted under conditional admission must earn a 2.0 during the first 24 semester hours attempted. **Home schooled:** Transcript of courses and grades, interview required.

High school preparation. 15 units recommended.

2011-2012 Annual costs. $330 per-semester-hour charge; full-time students receive a $150 credit per semester. New students receive an additional one-time $150 credit their first semester. Required fees $400 per term. Books/supplies: $800. Personal expenses: $1,739.

2011-2012 Financial aid. Need-based: 29% of total undergraduate aid awarded as scholarships/grants, 71% as loans/jobs. **Non-need-based:** Scholarships awarded for academics, leadership.

Application procedures. Admission: No deadline. $75 fee. Admission notification on a rolling basis. **Financial aid:** Priority date 5/1, closing date 6/30. FAFSA, institutional form required. Must reply by 8/15 or within 2 week(s) of notification.

Academics. Special study options: Accelerated study, distance learning, double major, independent study, internships. Participant in the U.S. Department of Education's Distance Education Demonstration Program and in GoArmyEd initiative. **Credit/placement by examination:** AP, CLEP. 36 credit hours maximum toward bachelor's degree. **Support services:** Tutoring, writing center.

Majors. Business: Business admin. **Computer sciences:** General. **Liberal arts:** Arts/sciences. **Theology:** Bible.

Most popular majors. Communication technologies 9%, liberal arts 73%, theological studies 23%.

Computing on campus. PC or laptop required. 25 workstations in library, computer center. Online course registration, online library, helpline available.

Student life. Freshman orientation: Available. Preregistration for classes offered. Online orientation available at any time.

Student services. Financial aid counseling, placement for graduates, veterans' counselor.

Contact. E-mail: admissions@amridgeuniversity.edu
Phone: (334) 387-7524 Toll-free number: (800) 351-4040 ext. 7524
Fax: (334) 387-3878
Ora Davis, Admissions Officer, Amridge University, PO Box 240240, Montgomery, AL 36124-0240

Athens State University
Athens, Alabama
www.athens.edu   CB code: 0706

- Public two-year upper-division liberal arts and teachers college
- Commuter campus in large town
- 91% of applicants admitted

General. Founded in 1822. Regionally accredited. **Degrees:** 961 bachelor's awarded. **Articulation:** Agreements with state schools through the Alabama

Articulation and General Studies Committee. **Location:** 14 miles from Decatur, 24 miles from Huntsville. **Calendar:** Semester, extensive summer session. **Full-time faculty:** 80 total; 12% minority, 45% women. **Part-time faculty:** 115 total; 10% minority, 57% women. **Class size:** 44% < 20, 44% 20-39, 4% 40-49, 3% 50-99, 5% >100.

Student profile. 3,287 degree-seeking undergraduates. 697 applied as first time-transfer students, 634 admitted, 434 enrolled. 81% transferred from two-year, 19% transferred from four-year institutions.

Women:	65%	Out-of-state:	4%
Part-time:	53%	25 or older:	90%

Basis for selection. College transcript required. Transfer accepted as juniors, seniors.

2011-2012 Annual costs. Tuition/fees: $5,340; $9,930 out-of-state. Books/supplies: $800.

Financial aid. Non-need-based: Scholarships awarded for academics, alumni affiliation, art, athletics, leadership, minority status.

Application procedures. Admission: Rolling admission. $30 fee. **Financial aid:** FAFSA required.

Academics. Special study options: Cooperative education, distance learning, double major, dual enrollment of high school students, honors, independent study, internships, liberal arts/career combination, study abroad, teacher certification program, weekend college. **Credit/placement by examination:** AP, CLEP.

Majors. Biology: General. **Business:** Accounting, business admin, human resources, information resources management. **Computer sciences:** General. **Education:** General, biology, chemistry, early childhood, elementary, English, history, mathematics, middle, physical, physics, science, secondary, social science, social studies, special ed, trade/industrial. **English:** English lit. **History:** General. **Liberal arts:** Arts/sciences. **Math:** General. **Philosophy/religion:** Religion. **Physical sciences:** Chemistry, physics. **Protective services:** Criminal justice. **Psychology:** General. **Social sciences:** Political science, sociology. **Visual/performing arts:** Art.

Most popular majors. Business/marketing 31%, computer/information sciences 6%, education 34%, interdisciplinary studies 6%, liberal arts 6%.

Computing on campus. 341 workstations in library, computer center, student center. Commuter students can connect to campus network. Online library available.

Student life. Activities: Campus ministries, drama, literary magazine, student government, student newspaper, African-American history association, Centurions, Athenian hosts/hostesses, TKE, Tau Kappa Epsilon, Wesley Fellowship campus ministries, Pi tau Chi, pre-law society, council for exceptional children.

Student services. Career counseling, student employment services, financial aid counseling, minority student services, placement for graduates, veterans' counselor. **Physically disabled:** Services for visually, speech, hearing impaired.

Contact. E-mail: admissions@athens.edu
Phone: (256) 233-8220 Toll-free number: (800) 522-0272
Fax: (256) 233-6565
Necedah Henderson, Coordinator of Admissions, Athens State University, 300 North Beaty Street, Athens, AL 35611

Auburn University
Auburn, Alabama
www.auburn.edu

CB member
CB code: 1005

- Public 4-year university
- Commuter campus in large town
- 20,436 degree-seeking undergraduates: 9% part-time, 49% women, 7% African American, 2% Asian American, 3% Hispanic American, 1% Native American, 1% international
- 4,978 degree-seeking graduate students
- 70% of applicants admitted
- SAT or ACT with writing, application essay required
- 66% graduate within 6 years

General. Founded in 1856. Regionally accredited. **Degrees:** 4,157 bachelor's awarded; master's, professional, doctoral offered. **ROTC:** Army, Naval, Air Force. **Location:** 55 miles from Montgomery, 110 miles from Atlanta. **Calendar:** Semester, extensive summer session. **Full-time faculty:** 1,177

total; 2% have terminal degrees, 18% minority, 34% women. **Part-time faculty:** 181 total; 2% have terminal degrees, 4% minority, 44% women. **Class size:** 26% < 20, 51% 20-39, 6% 40-49, 10% 50-99, 7% >100. **Special facilities:** Nuclear science center, hybridoma facility, herbarium, art museum, hypervelocity impact facility, advanced microscopy and imaging laboratory, microelectronics science and technology center, water resources research institute, airport with aircraft and flight simulators, forest sustainability center, governmental services center, pharmacy operations and designs center, drug information and learning resources center, economic and community development institute, fish molecular genetics and biotechnology laboratory, forest policy center, forest products development center, fusion lab, early learning center, health behavior assessment center, highway research center, marriage and family therapy center, microfibrous materials manufacturing center, biomechanics lab, motor behavior center, plasma sciences lab, veterinary medicine radiology clinic, raptor rehabilitation center, animal health clinics.

Freshman class profile. 18,323 applied, 12,827 admitted, 4,202 enrolled.

Mid 50% test scores			
SAT critical reading:	550-680	GPA 2.0-2.99:	4%
SAT math:	570-680	Rank in top quarter:	68%
SAT writing:	530-650	Rank in top tenth:	46%
ACT composite:	24-30	Return as sophomores:	89%
GPA 3.75 or higher:	57%	Out-of-state:	45%
GPA 3.50-3.74:	18%	Live on campus:	67%
GPA 3.0-3.49:	21%	Fraternities:	25%
		Sororities:	43%

Basis for selection. Each student evaluated based on combination of standardized test scores, GPA, and additional information required on application.

High school preparation. College-preparatory program required. 12 units required; 15 recommended. Required and recommended units include English 4, mathematics 3, social studies 3-4, science 2 (laboratory 1-2) and foreign language 1. Math must include algebra I, algebra II, and either geometry, trigonometry, calculus or analysis. Science must include biology and a physical science.

2011-2012 Annual costs. Tuition/fees: $8,298; $22,890 out-of-state. Room/board: $9,992.

2010-2011 Financial aid. Need-based: 2,515 full-time freshmen applied for aid; 1,511 were judged to have need; 1,511 of these received aid. Average need met was 62%. Average scholarship/grant was $8,071; average loan $3,389. 44% of total undergraduate aid awarded as scholarships/grants, 56% as loans/jobs. **Non-need-based:** Awarded to 3,821 full-time undergraduates, including 1,415 freshmen. **Additional information:** State of Alabama has pre-paid college tuition plan for residents.

Application procedures. Admission: Closing date 2/1 (postmark date). $50 fee, may be waived for applicants with need. Admission notification on a rolling basis beginning on or about 10/15. Must reply by May 1 or within 4 week(s) if notified thereafter. **Financial aid:** Priority date 3/1; no closing date. FAFSA required. Applicants notified on a rolling basis starting 10/2.

Academics. Special study options: Accelerated study, cooperative education, distance learning, double major, dual enrollment of high school students, ESL, honors, independent study, internships, liberal arts/career combination, study abroad, teacher certification program, Washington semester. DVM-Master's in veterinary specialty, dual option program in education/subject areas. **Credit/placement by examination:** AP, CLEP, institutional tests. **Support services:** Learning center, reduced course load, study skills assistance, tutoring, writing center.

Honors college/program. 29 ACT/1280 SAT (exclusive of Writing) and 3.5 GPA required (3.4 GPA may be considered). Approximately 1000 freshmen accepted last year.

Majors. Architecture: Architecture, environmental design, interior. **Biology:** Bacteriology, biochemistry, biomedical sciences, botany, marine, molecular, zoology. **Business:** Accounting, business admin, entrepreneurial studies, finance, human resources, international, logistics, management information systems, management science, managerial economics, marketing, training/development. **Communications:** Journalism, media studies, public relations, radio/TV. **Computer sciences:** General. **Conservation:** General, environmental science, forest sciences, wildlife/wilderness. **Education:** Agricultural, business, early childhood, early childhood special, elementary, English, foreign languages, French, German, health, mathematics, music, physical, science, social science, Spanish, special ed, voc/tech. **Engineering:** Aerospace, agricultural, architectural, biological, chemical, civil, computer, electrical, manufacturing, materials, mechanical, polymer, software. **English:** English lit. **Foreign languages:** French, German, Spanish. **General:** Animal sciences, aquaculture, economics, food science, horticultural science, plant sciences, poultry, soil science. **Health services:** Audiology/speech pathology, clinical lab science, communication disorders, health care admin, nursing (RN), predental, premedicine, prenursing, prepharmacy, preveterinary. **History:** General. **Human services:** General, social work. **Math:** General, applied. **Parks/recreation:** Exercise sciences. **Philosophy/religion:** Philosophy, religion.

Physical sciences: Chemistry, geology, physics. **Psychology:** General. **Social sciences:** Anthropology, criminology, economics, geography, political science, sociology. **Visual/performing arts:** Art history/conservation, design, dramatic, industrial design, music, studio arts. **Work/family studies:** Apparel marketing, family studies.

Most popular majors. Biology 6%, business/marketing 22%, communications/journalism 6%, education 10%, engineering/engineering technologies 15%.

Computing on campus. 1,722 workstations in dormitories, library, computer center, student center. Dormitories linked to campus network. Commuter students can connect to campus network. Online course registration, online library, helpline, repair service, wireless network available.

Student life. Freshman orientation: Available, $75 fee. Preregistration for classes offered. **Housing:** Coed dorms, single-sex dorms, special housing for disabled, apartments, fraternity/sorority housing, wellness housing available. $300 partly refundable deposit. Honors housing available. **Activities:** Bands, campus ministries, choral groups, dance, drama, film society, international student organizations, literary magazine, music ensembles, musical theater, opera, radio station, student government, student newspaper, symphony orchestra, TV station, over 300 student organizations.

Athletics. NCAA. **Intercollegiate:** Baseball M, basketball, cross-country, diving, equestrian W, football (tackle) M, golf, gymnastics W, soccer W, softball W, swimming, tennis, track and field, volleyball W. **Intramural:** Badminton, basketball, bowling, cheerleading, football (non-tackle), golf, racquetball, soccer, softball, swimming, table tennis, tennis, track and field, volleyball. **Team name:** Tigers.

Student services. Adult student services, alcohol/substance abuse counseling, career counseling, student employment services, financial aid counseling, health services, minority student services, personal counseling, placement for graduates, veterans' counselor, women's services. **Physically disabled:** Services for visually, speech, hearing impaired.

Contact. E-mail: admissions@auburn.edu
Phone: (334) 844-4080 Toll-free number: (800) 282-8769
Fax: (334) 844-6436
Cindy Singley, Director of University Recruitment, Auburn University, Quad Center, Auburn, AL 36849-5111

Auburn University at Montgomery
Montgomery, Alabama
www.aum.edu **CB code: 1036**

- Public 4-year university
- Commuter campus in small city
- 4,310 degree-seeking undergraduates: 31% part-time, 62% women, 30% African American, 3% Asian American, 2% Hispanic American, 3% international
- 885 degree-seeking graduate students
- 74% of applicants admitted
- ACT (writing optional) required

General. Founded in 1967. Regionally accredited. **Degrees:** 643 bachelor's awarded; master's, doctoral offered. **ROTC:** Army, Air Force. **Location:** 100 miles from Auburn, 90 miles from Birmingham. **Calendar:** Semester, extensive summer session. **Full-time faculty:** 197 total; 4% have terminal degrees, 20% minority, 43% women. **Part-time faculty:** 124 total; less than 1% have terminal degrees, 14% minority, 56% women. **Class size:** 53% < 20, 43% 20-39, 2% 40-49, 2% 50-99, less than 1% >100.

Freshman class profile. 1,739 applied, 1,286 admitted, 930 enrolled.

Mid 50% test scores			
ACT composite:	21-24	Rank in top quarter:	41%
GPA 3.75 or higher:	16%	Rank in top tenth:	16%
GPA 3.50-3.74:	12%	Return as sophomores:	50%
GPA 3.0-3.49:	31%	Out-of-state:	7%
GPA 2.0-2.99:	40%	Live on campus:	24%

Basis for selection. GPA and ACT/SAT scores considered. Provisional admission may be available for students who do not meet requirements for regular admission during summer semester only. C average after 18 hours of academic courses required for provisional students to become regular students. SAT recommended. **Learning Disabled:** Student must establish eligibility for services by providing documentation that meets institutional standards.

High school preparation. College-preparatory program recommended. 4 units recommended. Recommended units include English 3, mathematics

3, social studies 2, history 2, science 2 (laboratory 2), foreign language 2 and academic electives 2.

2011-2012 Annual costs. Tuition/fees: $7,580; $21,440 out-of-state. Room only: $3,820. Books/supplies: $1,000. Personal expenses: $1,170.

2010-2011 Financial aid. Need-based: Average scholarship/grant was $4,738; average loan $3,320. 39% of total undergraduate aid awarded as scholarships/grants, 61% as loans/jobs. **Non-need-based:** Scholarships awarded for academics, alumni affiliation, art, athletics, job skills, leadership, minority status, music/drama, religious affiliation, ROTC.

Application procedures. Admission: Closing date 8/1. No application fee. Admission notification on a rolling basis. **Financial aid:** Priority date 3/1; no closing date. FAFSA required. Applicants notified on a rolling basis starting 6/1; must reply within 2 week(s) of notification.

Academics. Interdisciplinary Master of Liberal Arts available. **Special study options:** Accelerated study, cooperative education, cross-registration, distance learning, double major, dual enrollment of high school students, ESL, honors, independent study, internships, liberal arts/career combination, study abroad, teacher certification program, weekend college. Joint Ph.D. in public administration with Auburn University; cooperative doctoral program in educational leadership with Auburn University (Ed.D.). **Credit/placement by examination:** AP, CLEP, IB, SAT, ACT, institutional tests. 64 credit hours maximum toward bachelor's degree. **Support services:** Learning center, reduced course load, remedial instruction, tutoring.

Majors. Biology: General. **Business:** General, accounting, business admin, finance, human resources, management information systems, managerial economics, marketing. **Communications:** Communications/speech/rhetoric. **Education:** Elementary, secondary. **English:** English lit. **Foreign languages:** General. **Health services:** Nursing (RN). **History:** General. **Liberal arts:** Arts/sciences. **Math:** General. **Physical sciences:** General. **Protective services:** Criminal justice. **Psychology:** General. **Social sciences:** Political science, sociology. **Visual/performing arts:** Art.

Most popular majors. Biology 9%, business/marketing 31%, education 15%, health sciences 15%, psychology 6%.

Computing on campus. 685 workstations in dormitories, library, computer center, student center. Dormitories wired for high-speed internet access and linked to campus network. Commuter students can connect to campus network. Online course registration, online library, helpline, repair service, student web hosting, wireless network available.

Student life. Freshman orientation: Mandatory, $75 fee. Preregistration for classes offered. **Policies:** Students required to conform to all policies and regulations by October registration. **Housing:** Coed dorms, special housing for disabled, apartments available. **Activities:** Campus ministries, drama, film society, international student organizations, musical theater, radio station, student government, student newspaper, Baptist campus ministries, Landmark campus ministries, Disney college program, Young African Americans Against Media, green alliance, American Humanics student association.

Athletics. NAIA. **Intercollegiate:** Baseball M, basketball, soccer, softball W, tennis. **Intramural:** Baseball, basketball M, bowling, football (non-tackle), softball, tennis, volleyball. **Team name:** Warhawks.

Student services. Adult student services, career counseling, student employment services, financial aid counseling, health services, personal counseling, placement for graduates, veterans' counselor, women's services. **Physically disabled:** Services for visually, speech, hearing impaired.

Contact. E-mail: admitme@aum.edu
Phone: (334) 244-3615 Toll-free number: (800) 227-2649
Fax: (334) 244-3795
Valerie Crawford, Director of Admissions, Auburn University at Montgomery, 7400 East Drive, Room 139 Taylor Center, Montgomery, AL 36124-4023

Birmingham-Southern College
Birmingham, Alabama **CB member**
www.bsc.edu **CB code: 1064**

- Private 4-year liberal arts college affiliated with United Methodist Church
- Residential campus in very large city
- 1,305 degree-seeking undergraduates: 1% part-time, 49% women, 7% African American, 5% Asian American, 3% Hispanic American, 1% Native American
- 64% of applicants admitted
- SAT or ACT (ACT writing recommended), application essay required
- 61% graduate within 6 years

General. Founded in 1856. Regionally accredited. **Degrees:** 324 bachelor's awarded; master's offered. **ROTC:** Army, Air Force. **Location:** 3 miles from downtown. **Calendar:** 4-1-4, limited summer session. **Full-time faculty:** 81 total; 99% have terminal degrees, 37% women. **Part-time faculty:** 26 total; 46% have terminal degrees, 4% minority, 58% women. **Class size:** 63% < 20, 35% 20-39, 2% 40-49, less than 1% 50-99. **Special facilities:** Planetarium, Southern environmental center and interactive museum, urban environmental park.

Freshman class profile. 1,798 applied, 1,155 admitted, 278 enrolled.

Mid 50% test scores			
SAT critical reading:	500-620	**GPA 2.0-2.99:**	23%
SAT math:	490-630	**Rank in top quarter:**	57%
SAT writing:	490-630	**Rank in top tenth:**	31%
ACT composite:	23-29	**Return as sophomores:**	79%
GPA 3.75 or higher:	36%	**Out-of-state:**	42%
GPA 3.50-3.74:	14%	**Live on campus:**	93%
GPA 3.0-3.49:	27%	**Fraternities:**	42%
		Sororities:	52%

Basis for selection. High school record most important, followed by test scores, recommendations, and required essay. Interview required for early admission, recommended for borderline applicants. Auditions required for music, theatre, dance majors. **Home schooled:** Interviews recommended.

High school preparation. College-preparatory program required. 16 units required. Required and recommended units include English 4, mathematics 4, social studies 2, history 2, science 4 (laboratory 2), foreign language 2 and academic electives 10.

2011-2012 Annual costs. Tuition/fees: $29,290. Room/board: $9,620. Books/supplies: $1,260. Personal expenses: $500.

2011-2012 Financial aid. **Need-based:** 233 full-time freshmen applied for aid; 177 were judged to have need; 177 of these received aid. Average need met was 81%. Average scholarship/grant was $5,032; average loan $3,426. 68% of total undergraduate aid awarded as scholarships/grants, 32% as loans/jobs. **Non-need-based:** Awarded to 1,117 full-time undergraduates, including 234 freshmen. Scholarships awarded for academics, alumni affiliation, art, job skills, leadership, minority status, music/drama, religious affiliation, ROTC, state residency. **Additional information:** Auditions required for music, theatre, dance applicants seeking scholarships. Portfolios required for art applicants seeking scholarships, and essays recommended for all applicants seeking scholarships.

Application procedures. **Admission:** Priority date 1/1; no deadline. $40 fee, may be waived for applicants with need. Admission notification on a rolling basis beginning on or about 7/1. **Financial aid:** Priority date 3/1; no closing date. FAFSA required. Applicants notified on a rolling basis starting 3/1; must reply by 8/21.

Academics. **Special study options:** Combined bachelor's/graduate degree, cooperative education, cross-registration, double major, dual enrollment of high school students, exchange student, honors, independent study, internships, semester at sea, student-designed major, study abroad, teacher certification program, Washington semester. 4-1-4 in nursing with Vanderbilt; 3-2 in engineering with Washington University, Columbia University, University of Alabama, and Auburn University; 3-2 in environment studies with Duke University. **Credit/placement by examination:** AP, CLEP, IB, SAT, ACT, institutional tests. 64 credit hours maximum toward bachelor's degree. **Support services:** Learning center, pre-admission summer program, reduced course load, study skills assistance, tutoring, writing center.

Majors. **Biology:** General. **Business:** General, accounting, business admin, finance, international, marketing. **Computer sciences:** General, computer science. **Conservation:** Environmental studies. **Education:** General, art, early childhood, elementary, music, secondary, special ed. **English:** English lit. **Foreign languages:** French, German, Spanish. **History:** General. **Math:** General. **Philosophy/religion:** Philosophy, religion. **Physical sciences:** Chemistry, physics. **Psychology:** General. **Social sciences:** Economics, political science, sociology. **Theology:** Sacred music. **Visual/performing arts:** General, art, art history/conservation, dance, dramatic, drawing, music, music history, music theory/composition, painting, photography, piano/keyboard, sculpture, voice/opera.

Most popular majors. Biology 10%, business/marketing 21%, education 6%, English 10%, interdisciplinary studies 9%, psychology 10%, social sciences 8%, visual/performing arts 10%.

Computing on campus. 252 workstations in dormitories, library, computer center, student center. Dormitories wired for high-speed internet access and linked to campus network. Commuter students can connect to campus network. Online course registration, online library, helpline, student web hosting, wireless network available.

Student life. **Freshman orientation:** Mandatory. Preregistration for classes offered. One-day mini-session in June and 4-day session prior to

beginning of fall classes. **Housing:** Guaranteed on-campus for all undergraduates. Single-sex dorms, special housing for disabled, apartments, fraternity/sorority housing, wellness housing available. $200 nonrefundable deposit, deadline 5/1. Handicapped students accommodated on individual basis. **Activities:** Bands, campus ministries, choral groups, dance, drama, international student organizations, literary magazine, music ensembles, musical theater, opera, student government, student newspaper, Fellowship of Christian Athletes, Young Republicans, Young Democrats, Black student union, Allies, Students Offering Support, conservancy, Wesley Fellowship, Intervarsity Christian Fellowship.

Athletics. NCAA. **Intercollegiate:** Baseball M, basketball, cheerleading, cross-country, football (tackle) M, golf, lacrosse, rifle W, soccer, softball W, tennis, track and field, volleyball W. **Intramural:** Basketball, football (non-tackle), racquetball, soccer, softball, table tennis, volleyball, water polo. **Team name:** Panthers.

Student services. Alcohol/substance abuse counseling, chaplain/spiritual director, career counseling, student employment services, financial aid counseling, health services, personal counseling, placement for graduates, veterans' counselor.

Contact. E-mail: admission@bsc.edu
Phone: (205) 226-4696 Toll-free number: (800) 523-5793
Fax: (205) 226-3074
Sheri Salmon, Dean for Enrollment Management, Birmingham-Southern College, 900 Arkadelphia Road, Birmingham, AL 35254

Columbia Southern University
Orange Beach, Alabama
www.columbiasouthern.edu   **CB code: 3878**

▸ For-profit 4-year virtual university
▸ Commuter campus in small town
▸ 13,136 degree-seeking undergraduates: 62% part-time, 35% women
▸ 4,780 degree-seeking graduate students
▸ 35% graduate within 6 years

General. Accredited by DETC. **Degrees:** 1,290 bachelor's, 417 associate awarded; master's, doctoral offered. **Location:** 60 miles from Mobile; 30 miles from Pensacola, FL. **Calendar:** Differs by program. **Full-time faculty:** 40 total. **Part-time faculty:** 245 total.

Basis for selection. Open admission.

High school preparation. College-preparatory program recommended.

2011-2012 Annual costs. Tuition/fees: $6,020. Personal expenses: $3,720.

Application procedures. **Admission:** No deadline. No application fee. **Financial aid:** FAFSA, institutional form required.

Academics. **Special study options:** Distance learning. **Credit/placement by examination:** AP, CLEP. 45 credit hours maximum toward associate degree, 90 toward bachelor's. May transfer CLEP credit up to maximum transfer limit. **Support services:** Learning center, tutoring, writing center.

Majors. **Business:** Business admin, hospitality admin, human resources, marketing, organizational leadership. **Computer sciences:** Information technology. **Conservation:** Environmental studies. **Health services:** Health care admin. **Protective services:** Firefighting, police science.

Most popular majors. Business/marketing 37%, engineering/engineering technologies 21%, natural resources/environmental science 6%, security/protective services 29%.

Computing on campus. PC or laptop required. Commuter students can connect to campus network. Online course registration, online library available.

Student life. **Freshman orientation:** Mandatory, $600 fee. Preregistration for classes offered. Online course. **Activities:** Student newspaper.

Student services. Career counseling, financial aid counseling.

Contact. E-mail: admissions@columbiasouthern.edu
Phone: (800) 977-8449 ext. 1521
Toll-free number: (800) 977-8449 ext. 1521 Fax: (251) 981-3815
Bonnie Lader, Director of Admissions/Enrollments, Columbia Southern University, 21982 University Lane, Orange Beach, AL 36561

Concordia College
Selma, Alabama
www.concordiaselma.edu

CB code: 1989

- Private 4-year liberal arts college affiliated with Lutheran Church - Missouri Synod
- Residential campus in large town

General. Founded in 1922. Regionally accredited. **Location:** 50 miles from Montgomery. **Calendar:** Semester.

Annual costs/financial aid. Tuition/fees (2011-2012): $8,090. Room/board: $4,150. Books/supplies: $1,000. Need-based financial aid available to full-time and part-time students.

Contact. Phone: (334) 874-5700
Director of Admissions, 1804 Green Street, Selma, AL 36701

Faulkner University
Montgomery, Alabama
www.faulkner.edu

CB code: 1034

- Private 4-year university and liberal arts college affiliated with Church of Christ
- Residential campus in large city
- 2,695 degree-seeking undergraduates: 24% part-time, 64% women
- 569 degree-seeking graduate students
- 58% of applicants admitted
- SAT or ACT (ACT writing optional) required
- 35% graduate within 6 years

General. Founded in 1942. Regionally accredited. Additional extended campuses (non-residential) in Birmingham, Huntsville and Mobile. **Degrees:** 602 bachelor's, 23 associate awarded; master's, professional offered. **ROTC:** Army, Air Force. **Location:** 10 miles from downtown. **Calendar:** Semester, limited summer session. **Full-time faculty:** 94 total; 63% have terminal degrees, 44% women. **Part-time faculty:** 193 total; 26% have terminal degrees, 39% women. **Class size:** 77% < 20, 18% 20-39, 3% 40-49, 1% 50-99, less than 1% >100.

Freshman class profile. 1,215 applied, 705 admitted, 323 enrolled.

Mid 50% test scores			
SAT critical reading:	280-480	GPA 3.50-3.74:	5%
SAT math:	250-470	GPA 3.0-3.49:	20%
SAT writing:	260-450	GPA 2.0-2.99:	60%
ACT composite:	17-25	Rank in top quarter:	31%
GPA 3.75 or higher:	10%	Rank in top tenth:	10%
		Live on campus:	69%

Basis for selection. Academic record, test scores, and personal or career goals most important. Interview and essay strongly recommended. **Home schooled:** Statement describing home school structure and mission, transcript of courses and grades, letter of recommendation (nonparent) required. **Learning Disabled:** After admission, students with disabilities are eligible to apply for services on campus.

High school preparation. College-preparatory program recommended. 15 units required. Required units include English 3, mathematics 3, history 3 and science 3.

2011-2012 Annual costs. Tuition/fees: $15,880. Room/board: $6,650. Books/supplies: $1,600. Personal expenses: $1,350.

Financial aid. Non-need-based: Scholarships awarded for academics, alumni affiliation, art, athletics, leadership, music/drama, religious affiliation, ROTC, state residency.

Application procedures. Admission: Priority date 2/15; no deadline. $25 fee, may be waived for applicants with need. Admission notification on a rolling basis beginning on or about 8/15. **Financial aid:** Priority date 5/1; no closing date. FAFSA, institutional form required. Applicants notified on a rolling basis starting 6/1; must reply within 3 week(s) of notification.

Academics. Full-time students required to take Bible course each semester. **Special study options:** Accelerated study, cross-registration, distance learning, double major, dual enrollment of high school students, ESL, honors, independent study, internships, liberal arts/career combination, study abroad, teacher certification program, weekend college. **Credit/placement by examination:** AP, CLEP, IB, SAT, ACT, institutional tests. 16 credit hours maximum toward associate degree, 32 toward bachelor's. **Support services:** Learning center, pre-admission summer program, reduced course load, remedial instruction, study skills assistance, tutoring, writing center.

Honors college/program. 27 ACT English/640 SAT verbal and 3.0 GPA required. Students must take five Great Books courses and complete thesis.

Majors. Biology: General, biomedical sciences. **Business:** General, accounting/finance, business admin, human resources, management information systems, management science, marketing. **Communications:** Journalism. **Computer sciences:** General, computer science, information systems. **Education:** Biology, drama/dance, elementary, English, history, mathematics, multi-level teacher, physical, science, secondary, social science, social studies. **English:** Creative writing, English lit, rhetoric/composition. **Health services:** Community health services, marriage/family therapy, mental health counseling, predental, premedicine, prenursing, prepharmacy, preveterinary. **History:** General. **Liberal arts:** Arts/sciences, humanities. **Math:** General. **Parks/recreation:** Health/fitness, sports admin. **Philosophy/religion:** Christian, religion. **Protective services:** Criminal justice. **Psychology:** General. **Social sciences:** General. **Theology:** Bible, missionary, theology, youth ministry. **Visual/performing arts:** Dramatic, music, theater arts management, theater design. **Work/family studies:** Communication, family/community services.

Most popular majors. Business/marketing 73%.

Computing on campus. 250 workstations in dormitories, library, computer center, student center. Dormitories wired for high-speed internet access and linked to campus network. Commuter students can connect to campus network. Online library, helpline, wireless network available.

Student life. Freshman orientation: Mandatory. Preregistration for classes offered. **Policies:** Religious observance required. **Housing:** Guaranteed on-campus for freshmen. Single-sex dorms, special housing for disabled, apartments, wellness housing available. $50 nonrefundable deposit, deadline 7/31. **Activities:** Bands, campus ministries, choral groups, drama, international student organizations, literary magazine, music ensembles, musical theater, student government, student newspaper, minister's club, service organizations, religious organizations.

Athletics. NAIA, NCCAA. **Intercollegiate:** Baseball M, basketball, cheerleading, cross-country, football (tackle) M, golf, softball W, volleyball W. **Intramural:** Badminton, basketball, bowling, football (non-tackle), racquetball, softball, table tennis, tennis, track and field, volleyball. **Team name:** Eagles.

Student services. Adult student services, alcohol/substance abuse counseling, chaplain/spiritual director, career counseling, services for economically disadvantaged, student employment services, financial aid counseling, health services, personal counseling, placement for graduates, veterans' counselor. **Physically disabled:** Services for visually, speech, hearing impaired.

Contact. E-mail: admissions@faulkner.edu
Phone: (334) 386-7200 Toll-free number: (800) 879-9816 ext. 7200
Fax: (334) 386-7137
Keith Mock, Vice President of Enrollment Management, Director of Admissions, Faulkner University, 5345 Atlanta Highway, Montgomery, AL 36109-3398

Heritage Christian University
Florence, Alabama
www.hcu.edu

CB code: 0805

- Private 4-year Bible college affiliated with Church of Christ
- Commuter campus in large town
- 83 degree-seeking undergraduates: 45% part-time, 17% women
- 26 degree-seeking graduate students

General. Founded in 1971. Accredited by ABHE. **Degrees:** 10 bachelor's, 2 associate awarded; master's offered. **Location:** 125 miles from Birmingham, 50 miles from Huntsville. **Calendar:** Semester, limited summer session. **Full-time faculty:** 3 total. **Part-time faculty:** 15 total. **Class size:** 96% < 20, 4% 20-39.

Freshman class profile.

Out-of-state:	40%	Live on campus:	10%

Basis for selection. Religious affiliation and recommendations very important; school achievement considered. Interview recommended.

2011-2012 Annual costs. Tuition/fees: $11,670. Meal plan covers 10 meals per week. Room/board: $3,850. Books/supplies: $1,000. Personal expenses: $600.

Application procedures. Admission: Closing date 7/1. $25 fee. Admission notification on a rolling basis. **Financial aid:** Priority date 6/1; no closing date. FAFSA required. Applicants notified on a rolling basis starting 6/1; must reply by 7/28 or within 2 week(s) of notification.

Academics. Special study options: Accelerated study, distance learning, dual enrollment of high school students, independent study, internships. **Credit/placement by examination:** AP, CLEP, institutional tests. 24 credit hours maximum toward associate degree, 24 toward bachelor's. **Support services:** Reduced course load, remedial instruction, study skills assistance, tutoring.

Majors. Theology: Bible.

Computing on campus. 12 workstations in library, computer center. Wireless network available.

Student life. Freshman orientation: Mandatory. Preregistration for classes offered. **Housing:** Guaranteed on-campus for freshmen. Single-sex dorms, apartments, wellness housing available. **Activities:** Student government, Christian service program, mission club.

Student services. Career counseling, student employment services, personal counseling, placement for graduates, veterans' counselor.

Contact. E-mail: hcu@hcu.edu
Phone: (256) 766-6610 Toll-free number: (800) 367-3565
Fax: (256) 766-9289
Larry Davenport, Director of Enrollment Services, Heritage Christian University, 3625 Helton Drive, Florence, AL 35630

Herzing University: Birmingham
Birmingham, Alabama
www.herzing.edu   **CB code: 2851**

- For-profit 4-year business and technical college
- Very large city
- 330 degree-seeking undergraduates

General. Regionally accredited. **Degrees:** 24 bachelor's, 115 associate awarded. **Calendar:** Semester, extensive summer session. **Full-time faculty:** 8 total. **Part-time faculty:** 24 total.

Basis for selection. Students must submit high school transcript or GED, interview with admissions representative, pass admissions exam or have 1275 SAT/17 ACT. TEAS test required for nursing applicants.

2011-2012 Annual costs. Tuition/fees: $13,800. Reported annual tuition is representative. Actual costs vary by program with nursing programs somewhat more expensive.

Financial aid. All financial aid based on need.

Application procedures. Admission: No deadline. No application fee. **Financial aid:** FAFSA required.

Academics. Credit/placement by examination: AP, CLEP.

Majors. Computer sciences: General, information systems, LAN/WAN management.

Contact. E-mail: admiss@bhm.herzing.edu
Phone: (205) 916-2800 Fax: (205) 916-2807
Tommy Dennis, Director of Admissions, Herzing University: Birmingham, 280 West Valley Avenue, Birmingham, AL 35209

Huntingdon College
Montgomery, Alabama
www.huntingdon.edu   **CB code: 1303**

- Private 4-year liberal arts college affiliated with United Methodist Church
- Residential campus in small city
- 1,110 degree-seeking undergraduates: 20% part-time, 51% women, 17% African American, 1% Asian American, 2% Hispanic American, 1% international
- 62% of applicants admitted

- SAT or ACT (ACT writing optional) required
- 52% graduate within 6 years; 39% enter graduate study

General. Founded in 1854. Regionally accredited. Adult Degree Completion Program offered in Montgomery, Bay Minette, Brewton, Center Point, Clanton, Daphne, Enterprise, Gadsden, Pell City and Shelby. **Degrees:** 239 bachelor's awarded. **ROTC:** Army, Air Force. **Location:** 90 miles from Birmingham, 180 miles from Atlanta. **Calendar:** Semester, limited summer session. **Full-time faculty:** 48 total; 81% have terminal degrees, 4% minority, 46% women. **Part-time faculty:** 67 total; 42% have terminal degrees, 21% minority, 45% women. **Class size:** 62% < 20, 36% 20-39, 2% 40-49. **Special facilities:** Ecological center, music facility with recital hall, studios, rehearsal rooms and modern electronic music laboratory, sports medicine and athletic training facilities, United Methodist Church archives.

Freshman class profile. 1,407 applied, 868 admitted, 256 enrolled.

Mid 50% test scores			
SAT critical reading:	440-600	Rank in top quarter:	35%
SAT math:	450-560	Rank in top tenth:	10%
SAT writing:	410-540	End year in good standing:	85%
ACT composite:	19-23	Return as sophomores:	60%
GPA 3.75 or higher:	20%	Out-of-state:	24%
GPA 3.50-3.74:	19%	Live on campus:	78%
GPA 3.0-3.49:	33%	International:	1%
GPA 2.0-2.99:	27%	Fraternities:	16%
		Sororities:	44%

Basis for selection. AP, CLEP, IB and dual enrollment credits are considered for acceptance. Important factors in the admission decision are advanced placement or honors courses, evidence of special talent and a leadership record. Interview, essay recommended. Audition required of music majors; portfolio recommended for art majors. **Home schooled:** Transcript of courses and grades required. **Learning Disabled:** Student must self-identify to Disabilities Intake Coordinator and provide appropriate and current documentation to verify disability. Documentation should include diagnosis and description of functional limitations that may affect student's academic performance.

High school preparation. College-preparatory program recommended. 17 units recommended. Recommended units include English 4, mathematics 3, social studies 3, history 3, science 2 and foreign language 2.

2011-2012 Annual costs. Tuition/fees: $21,990. Full-time students in the traditional program are provided a laptop computer for use during all four years of study and is theirs to keep. The cost of the laptop is included in the Annual Student Fee. Room/board: $8,000. Books/supplies: $1,000. Personal expenses: $1,035.

2011-2012 Financial aid. Need-based: 239 full-time freshmen applied for aid; 208 were judged to have need; 208 of these received aid. Average need met was 65%. Average scholarship/grant was $7,811; average loan $3,308. 53% of total undergraduate aid awarded as scholarships/grants, 47% as loans/jobs. **Non-need-based:** Awarded to 391 full-time undergraduates, including 240 freshmen. Scholarships awarded for academics, alumni affiliation, leadership, music/drama, religious affiliation, ROTC, state residency.

Application procedures. Admission: Priority date 5/15; deadline 8/15 (receipt date). No application fee. Admission notification on a rolling basis beginning on or about 9/6. Must reply by May 1 or within 2 week(s) if notified thereafter. **Financial aid:** Priority date 4/15; no closing date. FAFSA required. Applicants notified on a rolling basis starting 3/1; must reply by 5/1 or within 2 week(s) of notification.

Academics. Special study options: Combined bachelor's/graduate degree, cross-registration, distance learning, double major, honors, independent study, internships, liberal arts/career combination, student-designed major, study abroad, teacher certification program, Washington semester. Adult Degree Completion Program in which students take classes year long only in the evening; dual engineering degree with Auburn University and exchange student program with universities Ireland; travel opportunities to all full-time junior and seniors within regular educational costs or for nominal additional fees. **Credit/placement by examination:** AP, CLEP, IB, SAT, ACT, institutional tests. **Support services:** Learning center, reduced course load, study skills assistance, tutoring, writing center.

Majors. Biology: General, biochemistry, cellular/anatomical. **Business:** General, accounting, business admin. **Communications:** General. **Education:** Biology, chemistry, elementary, English, history, mathematics, music, physical. **English:** English lit. **Health services:** Athletic training. **History:** General. **Math:** General. **Parks/recreation:** Exercise sciences, sports admin. **Philosophy/religion:** Religion. **Physical sciences:** Chemistry. **Psychology:** General. **Social sciences:** Political science. **Theology:** Religious ed, youth ministry. **Visual/performing arts:** Music performance, studio arts.

Most popular majors. Biology 12%, business/marketing 49%, education 6%, parks/recreation 6%.

Computing on campus. PC or laptop required. 12 workstations in library. Dormitories wired for high-speed internet access and linked to campus network. Commuter students can connect to campus network. Online library, repair service, student web hosting, wireless network available.

Student life. Freshman orientation: Mandatory. Preregistration for classes offered. Two day, overnight program where students stay on campus. Generally held in June and July with a one day option in August. **Policies:** Students expected to abide by the Student Honor Code. **Housing:** Guaranteed on-campus for all undergraduates. Coed dorms, single-sex dorms available. $250 nonrefundable deposit, deadline 5/1. **Activities:** Bands, campus ministries, choral groups, dance, international student organizations, literary magazine, music ensembles, student government, student newspaper, hosts/ambassadors, campus activities board, environmental club, business club, freshman forum, College Democrats, accounting club, commuter student organizations.

Athletics. NCAA. **Intercollegiate:** Baseball M, basketball, cross-country, football (tackle) M, golf, lacrosse M, soccer, softball W, tennis, track and field, volleyball W. **Intramural:** Basketball, bowling, football (non-tackle), softball, tennis, volleyball. **Team name:** Hawks.

Student services. Adult student services, alcohol/substance abuse counseling, chaplain/spiritual director, career counseling, student employment services, financial aid counseling, health services, personal counseling, placement for graduates.

Contact. E-mail: admiss@huntingdon.edu
Phone: (334) 833-4497 Toll-free number: (800) 763-0313
Fax: (334) 833-4347
Joseph Miller, Director, Office of Admission, Huntingdon College, 1500 East Fairview Avenue, Montgomery, AL 36106-2148

Huntsville Bible College
Huntsville, Alabama
www.hbc1.edu

- Private 4-year Bible college
- Small city
- 98 degree-seeking undergraduates

General. Accredited by ABHE. **Degrees:** 2 bachelor's, 2 associate awarded. **Location:** 87 miles from Birmingham; 100 miles from Nashville, TN. **Calendar:** Semester. **Part-time faculty:** 13 total; 15% minority, 23% women.

Freshman class profile. 36 enrolled.

Basis for selection. Open admission.

2011-2012 Annual costs. Tuition/fees: $3,980. Books/supplies: $550.

Application procedures. Admission: Closing date 9/1. $10 fee. **Financial aid:** Priority date 4/1, closing date 6/30.

Academics. Credit/placement by examination: AP, CLEP.

Majors. Theology: Bible, theology.

Student life. Freshman orientation: Mandatory. Preregistration for classes offered.

Contact. E-mail: students@hbc1.edu
Phone: (256) 539-0834 Fax: (256) 539-0854
Jermaine Turner, Dean of Instruction, Huntsville Bible College, 904 Oakwood Avenue, Huntsville, AL 35811-1632

ITT Technical Institute: Birmingham
Bessemer, Alabama
www.itt-tech.edu   CB code: 2696

- For-profit 4-year technical college
- Commuter campus in very large city
- 1,020 undergraduates
- Interview required

General. Accredited by ACICS. **Degrees:** 44 bachelor's, 243 associate awarded. **Calendar:** Quarter, extensive summer session. **Full-time faculty:** 14 total. **Part-time faculty:** 72 total.

Basis for selection. Satisfactory scores from on-site tests in English and mathematics required.

2011-2012 Annual costs. Estimated costs as of June 2011: per-credit-hour charge, $493, depending upon level and course of study; academic fee, $200. Certain programs of study require purchase of tools, which could cost an additional $100 to $500. All costs are subject to change.

Application procedures. Admission: No deadline. No application fee. Admission notification on a rolling basis. **Financial aid:** No deadline. FAFSA, institutional form required. Applicants notified on a rolling basis.

Academics. Credit/placement by examination: AP, CLEP. **Support services:** Learning center, tutoring.

Majors. Business: Business admin, construction management. **Communications technology:** Animation/special effects. **Computer sciences:** Programming, security. **Protective services:** Law enforcement admin.

Most popular majors. Business/marketing 7%, communication technologies 31%, computer/information sciences 29%, engineering/engineering technologies 16%, security/protective services 16%.

Computing on campus. Online library available.

Student life. Freshman orientation: Available. Preregistration for classes offered.

Student services. Career counseling, student employment services.

Contact. Phone: (205) 991-5410 Toll-free number: (800) 488-7033
Jesse Johnson, Director of Recruitment, ITT Technical Institute: Birmingham, 6270 Park South Drive, Bessemer, AL 35022

Jacksonville State University
Jacksonville, Alabama
www.jsu.edu   CB code: 1736

- Public 4-year university
- Commuter campus in small town
- 7,810 degree-seeking undergraduates: 22% part-time, 58% women
- 1,291 degree-seeking graduate students
- 84% of applicants admitted
- SAT or ACT (ACT writing optional) required
- 33% graduate within 6 years

General. Founded in 1883. Regionally accredited. **Degrees:** 1,217 bachelor's awarded; master's, doctoral offered. **ROTC:** Army. **Location:** 75 miles from Birmingham, 100 miles from Atlanta. **Calendar:** Semester, extensive summer session. **Full-time faculty:** 321 total; 13% minority, 46% women. **Part-time faculty:** 163 total; 9% minority, 70% women. **Class size:** 38% < 20, 47% 20-39, 8% 40-49, 7% 50-99, less than 1% >100. **Special facilities:** Space observatory, Little River Canyon field school.

Freshman class profile. 3,400 applied, 2,844 admitted, 1,414 enrolled.

Mid 50% test scores		Rank in top quarter:	42%
SAT critical reading:	410-520	Rank in top tenth:	19%
SAT math:	420-510	Out-of-state:	20%
ACT composite:	18-25	Live on campus:	66%
GPA 3.75 or higher:	14%	International:	2%
GPA 3.50-3.74:	11%	Fraternities:	10%
GPA 3.0-3.49:	31%	Sororities:	14%
GPA 2.0-2.99:	39%		

Basis for selection. High school record and test scores very important. 17 ACT or 830 SAT (exclusive of Writing) required for conditional admission. 20 ACT or 950 SAT (exclusive of Writing) required for unconditional admission. SAT/ACT scores must be submitted by beginning of term.

High school preparation. 15 units required. Required units include English 3 and academic electives 4. 8 units required in math, science, foreign language, social studies/history.

2011-2012 Annual costs. Tuition/fees: $7,650; $15,300 out-of-state. Room/board: $6,162. Books/supplies: $1,238. Personal expenses: $3,178.

2010-2011 Financial aid. Need-based: Average scholarship/grant was $3,251; average loan $3,217. 52% of total undergraduate aid awarded as scholarships/grants, 48% as loans/jobs. **Non-need-based:** Scholarships awarded for academics, alumni affiliation, art, athletics, music/drama, ROTC.

Application procedures. Admission: No deadline. $30 fee. Admission notification on a rolling basis beginning on or about 9/1. **Financial aid:** Priority date 3/15; no closing date. FAFSA, institutional form required.

Applicants notified on a rolling basis starting 4/16; must reply within 2 week(s) of notification.

Academics. Special study options: Accelerated study, combined bachelor's/graduate degree, cooperative education, distance learning, double major, dual enrollment of high school students, ESL, honors, independent study, internships, teacher certification program. **Credit/placement by examination:** AP, CLEP, SAT, ACT, institutional tests. 46 credit hours maximum toward bachelor's degree. Maximum credit hours awarded through CLEP examinations: 31 for general tests, 15 through subject tests. **Support services:** Learning center, pre-admission summer program, remedial instruction, tutoring.

Majors. Biology: General. **Business:** Accounting, business admin, finance, managerial economics, marketing. **Communications:** Radio/TV. **Computer sciences:** General. **Education:** Elementary, health, physical, secondary, special ed. **English:** English lit. **Foreign languages:** General. **Health services:** Nursing (RN). **History:** General. **Human services:** Social work. **Liberal arts:** Arts/sciences. **Math:** General. **Parks/recreation:** General. **Physical sciences:** Chemistry, physics. **Protective services:** Criminal justice. **Psychology:** General. **Social sciences:** Economics, geography, political science, sociology. **Visual/performing arts:** Art, dramatic, music. **Work/family studies:** General.

Most popular majors. Business/marketing 16%, education 19%, health sciences 18%, public administration/social services 6%, security/protective services 6%.

Computing on campus. 400 workstations in library, student center. Dormitories linked to campus network. Commuter students can connect to campus network. Online course registration, online library, helpline, wireless network available.

Student life. Freshman orientation: Available, $40 fee. Preregistration for classes offered. **Housing:** Coed dorms, single-sex dorms, apartments, fraternity/sorority housing, wellness housing available. $100 fully refundable deposit. **Activities:** Bands, campus ministries, choral groups, drama, international student organizations, music ensembles, musical theater, opera, radio station, student government, student newspaper, symphony orchestra, TV station, Panhellenic council, adult learners forum, peer counselors, African American association, book club.

Athletics. NCAA. **Intercollegiate:** Baseball M, basketball, cross-country, football (tackle) M, golf, rifle, soccer W, softball W, tennis, track and field, volleyball W. **Intramural:** Basketball, bowling, football (tackle) M, racquetball, rugby M, softball, tennis, track and field, volleyball. **Team name:** Gamecocks.

Student services. Career counseling, student employment services, financial aid counseling, health services, minority student services, on-campus daycare, personal counseling, placement for graduates, veterans' counselor. **Physically disabled:** Services for visually, speech, hearing impaired.

Contact. E-mail: info@jsu.edu
Phone: (256) 782-5268 Toll-free number: (800) 231-5291
Fax: (256) 782-5121
Andy Green, Director of Admissions, Jacksonville State University, 700 Pelham Road North, Jacksonville, AL 36265-1602

Judson College
Marion, Alabama
www.judson.edu   CB code: 1349

- Private 4-year liberal arts college for women affiliated with Baptist faith
- Residential campus in small town
- 341 degree-seeking undergraduates: 20% part-time, 98% women, 16% African American, 1% Asian American, 2% Hispanic American, 1% Native American
- 74% of applicants admitted
- SAT or ACT (ACT writing optional) required
- 38% graduate within 6 years; 18% enter graduate study

General. Founded in 1838. Regionally accredited. Men accepted for distance learning program only. **Degrees:** 40 bachelor's awarded. **ROTC:** Army. **Location:** 75 miles from Birmingham and Montgomery. **Calendar:** Semester, limited summer session. **Full-time faculty:** 27 total; 82% have terminal degrees, 11% minority, 48% women. **Part-time faculty:** 17 total; 35% have terminal degrees, 6% minority, 65% women. **Class size:** 87% < 20, 12% 20-39, less than 1% 40-49. **Special facilities:** Alabama Women's Hall of Fame, Baptist missionary memorabilia, equine studies center, Perry Lakes Park.

Freshman class profile. 270 applied, 201 admitted, 75 enrolled.

Mid 50% test scores			
SAT critical reading:	430-560	GPA 2.0-2.99:	22%
SAT math:	410-510	Rank in top quarter:	28%
SAT writing:	420-540	Rank in top tenth:	26%
ACT composite:	19-25	End year in good standing:	88%
GPA 3.75 or higher:	32%	Return as sophomores:	65%
GPA 3.50-3.74:	16%	Out-of-state:	18%
GPA 3.0-3.49:	30%	Live on campus:	92%

Basis for selection. Academic record, recommendations, test scores considered. **Learning Disabled:** Provide current copy of doctor's evaluation containing recommended accommodations.

High school preparation. College-preparatory program recommended. 16 units required; 20 recommended. Required and recommended units include English 4, mathematics 2-4, social studies 3-4, science 2-4, foreign language 2 and academic electives 5.

2012-2013 Annual costs. Tuition/fees (projected): $15,090. Room/board: $8,700. Books/supplies: $1,250. Personal expenses: $1,600.

2011-2012 Financial aid. Need-based: 74 full-time freshmen applied for aid; 61 were judged to have need; 61 of these received aid. Average need met was 66%. Average loan was $3,378. 56% of total undergraduate aid awarded as scholarships/grants, 44% as loans/jobs. **Non-need-based:** Awarded to 135 full-time undergraduates, including 33 freshmen. Scholarships awarded for academics, alumni affiliation, art, athletics, music/drama, religious affiliation, ROTC, state residency.

Application procedures. Admission: Priority date 8/1; no deadline. $35 fee, may be waived for applicants with need. Admission notification on a rolling basis beginning on or about 7/1. **Financial aid:** Priority date 3/1; no closing date. FAFSA, institutional form required. Applicants notified on a rolling basis starting 3/15; must reply within 2 week(s) of notification.

Academics. Special study options: Accelerated study, cross-registration, distance learning, double major, dual enrollment of high school students, external degree, honors, independent study, internships, student-designed major, study abroad, teacher certification program, Washington semester. **Credit/placement by examination:** AP, CLEP, IB, SAT, ACT, institutional tests. 30 credit hours maximum toward bachelor's degree. No student may receive more than 30 semester hours of non-attendance credit from all sources, or more than six semester hours in any one department. Maximum permitted from CLEP General Examinations is 15 of 30 hours. **Support services:** Reduced course load, remedial instruction, study skills assistance, tutoring, writing center.

Majors. Biology: General. **Business:** Business admin. **Education:** Elementary, English, mathematics, music, science, social science. **English:** English lit. **Foreign languages:** General, Spanish. **General:** Equestrian studies. **History:** General. **Human services:** Social work. **Math:** General. **Philosophy/religion:** Religion. **Physical sciences:** Chemistry. **Protective services:** Law enforcement admin. **Psychology:** General. **Visual/performing arts:** Art, music.

Most popular majors. Biology 30%, education 10%, English 10%, psychology 20%, security/protective services 17%, visual/performing arts 10%.

Computing on campus. 54 workstations in library, computer center. Dormitories wired for high-speed internet access. Commuter students can connect to campus network. Online library, helpline, wireless network available.

Student life. Freshman orientation: Mandatory, $120 fee. Preregistration for classes offered. Orientation includes placement tests, academic registration. **Housing:** Guaranteed on-campus for all undergraduates. Wellness housing available. $130 nonrefundable deposit, deadline 8/15. **Activities:** Campus ministries, choral groups, drama, literary magazine, music ensembles, student government, student newspaper, Students in Free Enterprise, College Democrats, College Republicans, psych-key club, Cahaba River society, Judson Ambassadors, science club, art club.

Athletics. USCAA. **Intercollegiate:** Basketball W, equestrian W, soccer W, softball W, volleyball W. **Intramural:** Basketball W, field hockey W, soccer W, softball W, tennis W, volleyball W. **Team name:** Lady Eagles.

Student services. Adult student services, alcohol/substance abuse counseling, chaplain/spiritual director, career counseling, student employment services, financial aid counseling, health services, personal counseling.

Contact. E-mail: admissions@judson.edu
Phone: (334) 683-5110 Toll-free number: (800) 447-9472
Fax: (334) 683-5282
Charlotte Clements, Vice President for Admissions and Financial Aid, Judson College, 302 Bibb Street, Marion, AL 36756

Miles College
Birmingham, Alabama
www.miles.edu

CB member
CB code: 1468

- Private 4-year liberal arts college affiliated with Christian Methodist Episcopal Church
- Commuter campus in very large city
- 1,700 degree-seeking undergraduates

General. Founded in 1905. Regionally accredited. **Degrees:** 197 bachelor's awarded. **ROTC:** Army, Air Force. **Location:** 6 miles from downtown. **Calendar:** Semester, limited summer session. **Full-time faculty:** 97 total. **Part-time faculty:** 33 total. **Special facilities:** African-American materials center, learning research center.

Basis for selection. Open admission, but selective for some programs. 3 letters of recommendation required. Admission to education program based on 2.0 GPA, 16 ACT and recommendations.

High school preparation. 20 units recommended. Recommended units include English 4, mathematics 4, social studies 4, history 4 and science 4. 4 units math and science recommended, particularly, for natural science applicants.

2011-2012 Annual costs. Tuition/fees: $10,490. Room/board: $6,552. Books/supplies: $1,200. Personal expenses: $800.

Financial aid. All financial aid based on need.

Application procedures. Admission: Closing date 7/15. No application fee. Admission notification on a rolling basis. **Financial aid:** Priority date 4/15; no closing date. FAFSA required. Applicants notified on a rolling basis starting 7/15; must reply within 2 week(s) of notification.

Academics. Special study options: Cooperative education, cross-registration, double major, dual enrollment of high school students, exchange student, honors, independent study, internships, teacher certification program. **Credit/placement by examination:** AP, CLEP, institutional tests. **Support services:** Reduced course load, remedial instruction, study skills assistance, tutoring, writing center.

Majors. Biology: General. **Business:** Accounting, business admin, purchasing. **Communications:** Communications/speech/rhetoric. **Computer sciences:** General. **Conservation:** Environmental science. **Education:** Educational technology, elementary, English, mathematics, science, secondary, social science, social studies. **English:** English lit. **History:** General. **Human services:** Social work. **Math:** General. **Physical sciences:** Chemistry. **Social sciences:** Political science. **Visual/performing arts:** Music, music pedagogy, music performance.

Computing on campus. 150 workstations in dormitories, library, computer center. Commuter students can connect to campus network.

Student life. Freshman orientation: Available, $100 fee. Preregistration for classes offered. Week-long program held week prior to start of classes. **Policies:** Students must maintain 2.0 GPA to participate in student activities that are not co-curricular on campus. **Housing:** Single-sex dorms, apartments, wellness housing available. $150 nonrefundable deposit. **Activities:** Marching band, choral groups, dance, drama, music ensembles, musical theater, radio station, student government, student newspaper, TV station, interdenominational ministerial association.

Athletics. NCAA. **Intercollegiate:** Baseball M, basketball, cross-country, football (tackle) M, softball W, volleyball. **Intramural:** Badminton, basketball, softball, tennis, volleyball. **Team name:** Golden Bears.

Student services. Adult student services, chaplain/spiritual director, career counseling, services for economically disadvantaged, student employment services, financial aid counseling, health services, personal counseling, placement for graduates.

Contact. E-mail: admissions@miles.edu
Phone: (205) 929-1655 Fax: (205) 923-9292
Christopher Robertson, Director of Admissions and Recruitment, Miles College, 5500 Myron-Massey Boulevard, Fairfield, AL 35064

New Charter University
Birmingham, Alabama
www.new.edu

CB code: 3877

- For-profit 4-year virtual liberal arts college
- Very large city

General. Accredited by DETC. **Calendar:** Differs by program.

Annual costs/financial aid. Undergraduates pay $499 for one online course; $796 for up to four online courses. Books/supplies: $750.

Contact. Director of Admissions, 2919 John Hawkins Parkway, Birmingham, AL 35244

Oakwood University
Huntsville, Alabama
www.oakwood.edu

CB member
CB code: 1586

- Private 4-year liberal arts college affiliated with Seventh-day Adventists
- Residential campus in small city
- 1,953 degree-seeking undergraduates
- SAT or ACT (ACT writing optional) required

General. Founded in 1896. Regionally accredited. **Degrees:** 272 bachelor's, 2 associate awarded; master's offered. **Location:** 5 miles from Huntsville. **Calendar:** Semester, limited summer session. **Full-time faculty:** 106 total. **Part-time faculty:** 69 total. **Class size:** 56% < 20, 36% 20-39, 6% 40-49, 3% 50-99.

Freshman class profile.

GPA 3.75 or higher:	13%	Rank in top quarter:	26%
GPA 3.50-3.74:	13%	Rank in top tenth:	8%
GPA 3.0-3.49:	26%	Out-of-state:	89%
GPA 2.0-2.99:	44%	Live on campus:	90%

Basis for selection. 2.0 GPA required. **Home schooled:** Transcript of courses and grades, letter of recommendation (nonparent) required.

High school preparation. College-preparatory program recommended. 18 units recommended. Recommended units include English 4, mathematics 2, social studies 1, history 1, science 2 (laboratory 1) and foreign language 2.

2011-2012 Annual costs. Tuition/fees: $14,966. Room/board: $9,510.

Financial aid. Non-need-based: Scholarships awarded for academics, leadership, religious affiliation, state residency.

Application procedures. Admission: Priority date 4/15; no deadline. $25 fee, may be waived for applicants with need. Admission notification on a rolling basis beginning on or about 12/1. **Financial aid:** Closing date 4/15. FAFSA required. Applicants notified on a rolling basis starting 4/1.

Academics. Special study options: Double major, honors, internships, study abroad, teacher certification program. **Credit/placement by examination:** AP, CLEP, SAT, ACT, institutional tests. **Support services:** Learning center, reduced course load, remedial instruction, study skills assistance, tutoring, writing center.

Majors. Biology: General, biochemistry, biomedical sciences. **Business:** Accounting, business admin, finance, marketing. **Communications:** Communications/speech/rhetoric. **Computer sciences:** General, computer science, information technology. **Education:** Biology, business, chemistry, elementary, English, family/consumer sciences, history, mathematics, music, physical, science, social science. **English:** English lit. **Foreign languages:** French, Spanish. **Health services:** Cytotechnology. **History:** General. **Human services:** Social work. **Liberal arts:** Arts/sciences. **Math:** General, applied. **Parks/recreation:** Health/fitness. **Philosophy/religion:** Religion. **Physical sciences:** Chemistry. **Psychology:** General. **Theology:** Religious ed, theology. **Work/family studies:** General, family studies, food/nutrition.

Most popular majors. Biology 16%, business/marketing 13%, communications/journalism 7%, education 7%, health sciences 7%, psychology 10%, theological studies 9%.

Computing on campus. 300 workstations in dormitories, library. Dormitories wired for high-speed internet access and linked to campus network. Commuter students can connect to campus network. Helpline, wireless network available.

Student life. Freshman orientation: Mandatory. Preregistration for classes offered. **Policies:** Students sit on most faculty and administrative committees. Religious observance required. **Housing:** Single-sex dorms, apartments available. **Activities:** Choral groups, music ensembles, radio station, student government, student newspaper, Outreach, NAACP.

Athletics. Intramural: Baseball M, basketball, golf, gymnastics, soccer, softball, tennis, volleyball. **Team name:** Ambassadors.

Student services. Adult student services, chaplain/spiritual director, career counseling, student employment services, financial aid counseling, health services, on-campus daycare, personal counseling, placement for graduates, veterans' counselor.

Contact. E-mail: admission@oakwood.edu
Phone: (256) 726-7030 Toll-free number: (800) 824-5312
Fax: (256) 726-7154
Joyce Smith, Director of Admissions, Oakwood University, 7000 Adventist Boulevard, NW, Huntsville, AL 35896

Samford University
Birmingham, Alabama
www.samford.edu

CB member
CB code: 1302

- Private 4-year university affiliated with Southern Baptist Convention
- Residential campus in small city
- 2,927 degree-seeking undergraduates: 6% part-time, 64% women
- 1,789 degree-seeking graduate students
- 83% of applicants admitted
- SAT or ACT (ACT writing optional) required

General. Founded in 1841. Regionally accredited. Students taught to integrate Christian faith with learning and living. **Degrees:** 598 bachelor's, 5 associate awarded; master's, professional, doctoral offered. **ROTC:** Army, Air Force. **Location:** 4 miles from downtown. **Calendar:** 4-1-4, extensive summer session. **Full-time faculty:** 294 total; 93% have terminal degrees, 8% minority, 46% women. **Part-time faculty:** 145 total; 59% have terminal degrees, 8% minority, 52% women. **Class size:** 68% < 20, 27% 20-39, 3% 40-49, 1% 50-99. **Special facilities:** Observatory, field house, global center, planetarium, conservatory, informational hub center, law library.

Freshman class profile. 2,623 applied, 2,166 admitted, 686 enrolled.

Mid 50% test scores			
SAT critical reading:	510-630	Rank in top tenth:	33%
SAT math:	530-640	End year in good standing:	90%
ACT composite:	23-29	Return as sophomores:	84%
GPA 3.75 or higher:	50%	Out-of-state:	67%
GPA 3.50-3.74:	16%	Live on campus:	95%
GPA 3.0-3.49:	25%	International:	1%
GPA 2.0-2.99:	9%	Fraternities:	34%
Rank in top quarter:	61%	Sororities:	47%

Basis for selection. Rigor of high school curriculum, GPA, test scores, and recommendations considered. Separate application, audition, and interview required for admission to School of the Arts. **Home schooled:** Statement describing home school structure and mission, transcript of courses and grades, letter of recommendation (nonparent) required. Leadership resume required.

High school preparation. College-preparatory program required. Required units include English 4, mathematics 3, history 2, science 2 (laboratory 2) and foreign language 2.

2011-2012 Annual costs. Tuition/fees: $23,963. Room/board: $7,775. Books/supplies: $1,000. Personal expenses: $4,603.

2010-2011 Financial aid. Need-based: 518 full-time freshmen applied for aid; 347 were judged to have need; 347 of these received aid. Average need met was 69%. Average scholarship/grant was $13,881; average loan $3,063. 56% of total undergraduate aid awarded as scholarships/grants, 44% as loans/jobs. **Non-need-based:** Awarded to 930 full-time undergraduates, including 233 freshmen. Scholarships awarded for academics, alumni affiliation, art, athletics, leadership, minority status, music/drama, religious affiliation, ROTC, state residency.

Application procedures. Admission: Priority date 12/1; no deadline. $35 fee, may be waived for applicants with need. Admission notification on a rolling basis beginning on or about 10/1. **Financial aid:** Priority date 3/1; no closing date. FAFSA required.

Academics. Special study options: Accelerated study, combined bachelor's/graduate degree, cooperative education, cross-registration, distance learning, double major, dual enrollment of high school students, ESL, exchange student, honors, independent study, internships, liberal arts/career combination, study abroad, teacher certification program, weekend college. **Credit/placement by examination:** AP, CLEP, IB, institutional tests. 30 credit hours maximum toward associate degree. **Support services:** Learning center, reduced course load, study skills assistance, tutoring, writing center.

Majors. Area/ethnic studies: Asian, Latin American. **Biology:** General, biochemistry, marine. **Business:** Accounting, business admin, entrepreneurial studies, finance, international, managerial economics, marketing, training/

development. **Communications:** Communications/speech/rhetoric, journalism. **Computer sciences:** Computer science. **Conservation:** Environmental science. **Education:** English, history, multi-level teacher, music, physical, social science. **Engineering:** Applied physics. **English:** English lit. **Foreign languages:** General, ancient Greek, classics, French, German, Latin, Spanish. **Health services:** Athletic training, nursing (RN), premedicine. **History:** General. **Human services:** General. **Math:** General. **Parks/recreation:** Exercise sciences, health/fitness, sports admin. **Philosophy/religion:** Philosophy, religion. **Physical sciences:** Chemistry, physics. **Psychology:** General, counseling. **Social sciences:** Geography, GIS/cartography, international relations, political science, sociology. **Theology:** Sacred music. **Visual/performing arts:** Art, dramatic, graphic design, interior design, music pedagogy, music performance, music theory/composition, musical theater, piano/keyboard, voice/opera. **Work/family studies:** Family studies.

Most popular majors. Biology 9%, business/marketing 19%, communications/journalism 7%, education 6%, health sciences 14%, social sciences 6%, visual/performing arts 11%.

Computing on campus. Dormitories wired for high-speed internet access and linked to campus network. Commuter students can connect to campus network. Online library, helpline, repair service, wireless network available.

Student life. Freshman orientation: Mandatory, $175 fee. Preregistration for classes offered. Two-day session held in June. **Policies:** Student code of values observed. **Housing:** Guaranteed on-campus for freshmen. Single-sex dorms, special housing for disabled, apartments, fraternity/sorority housing, wellness housing available. $250 nonrefundable deposit, deadline 5/1. **Activities:** Bands, campus ministries, choral groups, dance, drama, international student organizations, literary magazine, music ensembles, Model UN, musical theater, radio station, student government, student newspaper, symphony orchestra, TV station, Catholic student association, dance ministry, In His Hands, Nurses Christian Fellowship, RANSOM, gospel choir, WordPlayers, College Republicans, Samford Democrats, black student union.

Athletics. NCAA. **Intercollegiate:** Baseball M, basketball, cross-country, football (tackle) M, golf, soccer W, softball W, tennis, track and field, volleyball W. **Intramural:** Basketball, football (non-tackle), racquetball, soccer, softball, table tennis, tennis, volleyball. **Team name:** Bulldogs.

Student services. Adult student services, alcohol/substance abuse counseling, chaplain/spiritual director, career counseling, student employment services, financial aid counseling, health services, on-campus daycare, personal counseling, placement for graduates. **Physically disabled:** Services for visually, speech, hearing impaired.

Contact. E-mail: admiss@samford.edu
Phone: (205) 726-3673 Toll-free number: (800) 888-7218
Fax: (205) 726-2171
Jason Black, Dean of Admission, Samford University, 800 Lakeshore Drive, Birmingham, AL 35229

Selma University
Selma, Alabama
www.selmauniversity.org

CB code: 1792

- Private 4-year university affiliated with Baptist faith
- Large town
- 440 degree-seeking undergraduates

General. Founded in 1878. Candidate for regional accreditation; also accredited by ABHE. **Degrees:** 3 bachelor's, 14 associate awarded; master's offered. **Location:** 50 miles from Montgomery. **Calendar:** Semester, limited summer session. **Full-time faculty:** 9 total. **Part-time faculty:** 32 total.

Basis for selection. Open admission. Students with deficient high school record or low test scores must take remedial courses.

2011-2012 Annual costs. Tuition/fees: $5,375. Room/board: $4,600. Books/supplies: $1,000. Personal expenses: $650.

Financial aid. All financial aid based on need.

Application procedures. Admission: No deadline. $20 fee, may be waived for applicants with need. Admission notification on a rolling basis beginning on or about 8/1. **Financial aid:** Priority date 5/1, closing date 6/30. FAFSA, institutional form required. Applicants notified on a rolling basis starting 8/23; must reply within 2 week(s) of notification.

Academics. Credit/placement by examination: AP, CLEP, institutional tests. **Support services:** Reduced course load, remedial instruction, tutoring.

Majors. Theology: Bible.

Student life. Freshman orientation: Mandatory. Preregistration for classes offered. **Housing:** Single-sex dorms available. **Activities:** Campus ministries, choral groups, music ensembles, student government, Ministerial union.

Athletics. USCAA. **Intercollegiate:** Baseball M. **Team name:** Bulldogs.

Student services. Career counseling, financial aid counseling, personal counseling, veterans' counselor.

Contact. E-mail: selmau.admissions@bellsouth.net
Phone: (334) 872-2533 ext. 18 Fax: (334) 872-7746
Angela Stewart, Registrar, Selma University, 1501 Lapsley Street, Selma, AL 36701

South University: Montgomery
Montgomery, Alabama
www.southuniversity.edu   **CB code: 3947**

- For-profit 4-year university
- Commuter campus in small city
- 681 degree-seeking undergraduates
- Interview required

General. Founded in 1887. Regionally accredited. **Degrees:** 39 bachelor's, 70 associate awarded; master's offered. **Location:** 100 miles from Birmingham, 160 miles from Atlanta. **Calendar:** Quarter, extensive summer session. **Full-time faculty:** 11 total. **Part-time faculty:** 71 total.

Freshman class profile. 73 enrolled.

Basis for selection. High school diploma or GED required. School-administered entrance test may be provided in place of SAT/ACT. SAT or ACT recommended. **Home schooled:** Students must provide evidence that home schooling was conducted in accordance with state laws.

2011-2012 Annual costs. Tuition/fees: $15,735.

Financial aid. All financial aid based on need.

Application procedures. Admission: No deadline. $50 fee. Admission notification on a rolling basis. **Financial aid:** No deadline. FAFSA required. Applicants notified on a rolling basis starting 6/1.

Academics. Special study options: Distance learning, internships. **Credit/placement by examination:** AP, CLEP, institutional tests. **Support services:** Remedial instruction, study skills assistance, tutoring.

Majors. Business: Business admin. **Computer sciences:** Information technology. **Health services:** Health care admin, nursing (RN). **Protective services:** Law enforcement admin. **Psychology:** General.

Most popular majors. Business/marketing 35%, computer/information sciences 18%, health sciences 33%, legal studies 15%, security/protective services 18%.

Computing on campus. Online library, repair service, wireless network available.

Student life. Freshman orientation: Mandatory. Preregistration for classes offered.

Student services. Career counseling, financial aid counseling, placement for graduates, veterans' counselor.

Contact. E-mail: apearson@southuniversity.edu
Phone: (334) 395-8800 Fax: (334) 395-8859
Anna Pearson, Director of Admissions, South University: Montgomery, 5355 Vaughn Road, Montgomery, AL 36116-1120

Southeastern Bible College
Birmingham, Alabama
www.sebc.edu   **CB code: 1723**

- Private 4-year Bible college affiliated with nondenominational tradition
- Commuter campus in very large city
- 174 degree-seeking undergraduates: 22% part-time, 40% women, 32% African American, 1% Hispanic American, 1% Native American, 1% international

- 100% of applicants admitted
- SAT or ACT (ACT writing optional), application essay required

General. Founded in 1935. Accredited by ABHE. **Degrees:** 28 bachelor's, 2 associate awarded. **Calendar:** Semester, limited summer session. **Full-time faculty:** 6 total; 100% have terminal degrees, 17% women. **Part-time faculty:** 14 total; 36% have terminal degrees, 50% women. **Class size:** 78% < 20, 20% 20-39, 2% 40-49.

Freshman class profile. 24 applied, 24 admitted, 14 enrolled.

Mid 50% test scores			
SAT critical reading:	370-470	GPA 3.0-3.49:	23%
SAT math:	270-680	GPA 2.0-2.99:	23%
SAT writing:	210-440	Return as sophomores:	70%
ACT composite:	19-24	Out-of-state:	8%
GPA 3.75 or higher:	24%	Live on campus:	64%
GPA 3.50-3.74:	15%	International:	7%

Basis for selection. High school GPA and SAT or ACT test scores important. Christian character evaluated through 2 recommendations, one from church and the other a personal recommendation. Autobiography and statement of agreement with college's principle doctrines required. **Learning Disabled:** Students should meet with equity coordinator if desired.

High school preparation. College-preparatory program recommended. 24 units recommended. Recommended units include English 4, mathematics 4, social studies 4, science 4, computer science .5, academic electives 7.5.

2011-2012 Annual costs. Tuition/fees: $11,600. Room only: $2,550.

Financial aid. Non-need-based: Scholarships awarded for academics, leadership.

Application procedures. Admission: No deadline. $30 fee, may be waived for applicants with need. Admission notification on a rolling basis beginning on or about 1/1. **Financial aid:** Priority date 4/1; no closing date. FAFSA, institutional form required. Applicants notified on a rolling basis starting 1/1.

Academics. Special study options: Double major, dual enrollment of high school students, internships. **Credit/placement by examination:** AP, CLEP, IB, SAT, ACT, institutional tests. **Support services:** Reduced course load, study skills assistance.

Majors. Theology: Bible, lay ministry.

Computing on campus. 25 workstations in library, computer center. Dormitories wired for high-speed internet access. Wireless network available.

Student life. Freshman orientation: Mandatory. Preregistration for classes offered. One-day session held the day before registration. **Policies:** Religious observance required. **Housing:** Single-sex dorms, special housing for disabled available. $100 nonrefundable deposit, deadline 8/15. **Activities:** Campus ministries, music ensembles, student government, student missions fellowship.

Athletics. Team name: Sabers.

Student services. Adult student services, chaplain/spiritual director, financial aid counseling, personal counseling. **Physically disabled:** Services for speech, hearing impaired.

Contact. E-mail: info@sebc.edu
Phone: (205) 970-9210 Fax: (205) 970-9207
Jonathan Barber, Director of Admissions, Southeastern Bible College, 2545 Valleydale Road, Birmingham, AL 35244-2083

Spring Hill College
Mobile, Alabama   **CB member**
www.shc.edu   **CB code: 1733**

- Private 4-year liberal arts college affiliated with Roman Catholic Church
- Residential campus in large city
- 1,279 degree-seeking undergraduates: 8% part-time, 63% women, 19% African American, 1% Asian American, 8% Hispanic American, 1% Native American, 1% international
- 163 degree-seeking graduate students
- 49% of applicants admitted
- SAT or ACT (ACT writing recommended), application essay required
- 61% graduate within 6 years

General. Founded in 1830. Regionally accredited. **Degrees:** 252 bachelor's awarded; master's offered. **ROTC:** Army, Air Force. **Location:** 140 miles from New Orleans. **Calendar:** Semester, limited summer session. **Full-time faculty:** 84 total; 90% have terminal degrees, 13% minority, 50% women. **Part-time faculty:** 51 total; 35% have terminal degrees, 4% minority, 53% women. **Class size:** 55% < 20, 41% 20-39, 3% 40-49, less than 1% 50-99. **Special facilities:** National historic buildings, 450-acre wooded campus, 18-hole golf course.

Freshman class profile. 6,048 applied, 2,936 admitted, 335 enrolled.

Mid 50% test scores			
SAT critical reading:	500-610	GPA 2.0-2.99:	21%
SAT math:	470-590	Rank in top quarter:	47%
SAT writing:	480-580	Rank in top tenth:	23%
ACT composite:	21-26	Return as sophomores:	76%
GPA 3.75 or higher:	34%	Out-of-state:	60%
GPA 3.50-3.74:	19%	Live on campus:	86%
GPA 3.0-3.49:	26%	International:	1%

Basis for selection. Grades, scores and achievements/accomplishments outside the classroom considered. Interview recommended; portfolio recommended of art majors. **Home schooled:** Statement describing home school structure and mission, transcript of courses and grades required. Comprehensive portfolio should be submitted and should include thorough explanation of all coursework, how it was graded, comprehensive reading list, documentation of any program affiliation, and personal assessments provided by both the student and the primary teacher. Information on any independent research project, community outreach, or unique experience that enriched the home-schooling experience may be included.

High school preparation. College-preparatory program recommended. 16 units recommended. Recommended units include English 4, mathematics 3, social studies 2, history 1, science 3 (laboratory 1), foreign language 2 and academic electives 1.

2011-2012 Annual costs. Tuition/fees: $28,060. Room/board: $10,760.

2011-2012 Financial aid. Need-based: 302 full-time freshmen applied for aid; 254 were judged to have need; 254 of these received aid. Average need met was 88%. Average scholarship/grant was $9,892; average loan $4,282. 71% of total undergraduate aid awarded as scholarships/grants, 29% as loans/jobs. **Non-need-based:** Awarded to 1,248 full-time undergraduates, including 363 freshmen. Scholarships awarded for academics, alumni affiliation, athletics, job skills, leadership, minority status, ROTC, state residency.

Application procedures. Admission: Priority date 1/15; deadline 7/15 (postmark date). $25 fee, may be waived for applicants with need, free for online applicants. Admission notification on a rolling basis beginning on or about 11/1. Must reply by May 1 or within 2 week(s) if notified thereafter. **Financial aid:** Priority date 3/1; no closing date. FAFSA required. Applicants notified on a rolling basis starting 2/15; must reply by 5/1 or within 2 week(s) of notification.

Academics. Special study options: Accelerated study, distance learning, double major, dual enrollment of high school students, honors, independent study, internships, student-designed major, study abroad, teacher certification program, Washington semester. Marine biology courses at the Dauphin Island Sea Laboratory in conjunction with the Marine Environmental Sciences Consortium; 3-2 engineering with Auburn University, University of Alabama in Birmingham, Marquette University, University of Florida, and Texas A&M University. **Credit/placement by examination:** AP, CLEP, IB, SAT, ACT, institutional tests. 30 credit hours maximum toward bachelor's degree. **Support services:** Learning center, remedial instruction, study skills assistance, tutoring, writing center.

Majors. Biology: General, biochemistry. **Business:** Business admin, organizational leadership. **Communications:** General. **Education:** Biology, chemistry, early childhood, elementary, English, history, mathematics, social studies, Spanish. **Engineering:** Pre-engineering. **English:** English lit, writing. **Foreign languages:** Spanish. **Health services:** Nursing (RN). **History:** General. **Liberal arts:** Humanities. **Math:** General. **Philosophy/religion:** Philosophy, religion. **Physical sciences:** Chemistry. **Psychology:** General. **Social sciences:** General, international relations, political science. **Visual/performing arts:** Dramatic, graphic design, studio arts, studio arts management.

Most popular majors. Biology 12%, business/marketing 23%, communications/journalism 8%, English 9%, health sciences 8%, psychology 8%, social sciences 6%, visual/performing arts 7%.

Computing on campus. 200 workstations in library, computer center, student center. Dormitories wired for high-speed internet access and linked to campus network. Commuter students can connect to campus network. Online course registration, online library, helpline, student web hosting, wireless network available.

Student life. Freshman orientation: Mandatory, $250 fee. Preregistration for classes offered. Two-day program held in summer for students and parents.

Housing: Guaranteed on-campus for all undergraduates. Coed dorms, apartments available. $150 fully refundable deposit, deadline 6/1. **Activities:** Jazz band, campus ministries, choral groups, dance, drama, literary magazine, student government, student newspaper.

Athletics. NAIA. **Intercollegiate:** Baseball M, basketball, cross-country, golf, soccer, softball W, tennis, volleyball W. **Intramural:** Basketball, football (non-tackle), racquetball, soccer, softball, volleyball, weight lifting. **Team name:** Badgers.

Student services. Adult student services, alcohol/substance abuse counseling, chaplain/spiritual director, career counseling, student employment services, financial aid counseling, health services, minority student services, personal counseling, placement for graduates.

Contact. E-mail: admit@shc.edu
Phone: (251) 380-3030 Toll-free number: (800) 742-6704
Fax: (251) 460-2186
Brian Studebaker, Director of Admissions, Spring Hill College, 4000 Dauphin Street, Mobile, AL 36608-1791

Stillman College
Tuscaloosa, Alabama
www.stillman.edu

CB member
CB code: 1739

- Private 4-year liberal arts college affiliated with Presbyterian Church (USA)
- Residential campus in small city
- 1,072 degree-seeking undergraduates
- 46% of applicants admitted
- SAT or ACT (ACT writing optional) required

General. Founded in 1876. Regionally accredited. **Degrees:** 103 bachelor's awarded. **ROTC:** Army, Naval, Air Force. **Location:** 60 miles from Birmingham. **Calendar:** Semester, limited summer session. **Full-time faculty:** 54 total. **Part-time faculty:** 7 total. **Class size:** 64% < 20, 24% 20-39, 5% 40-49, 7% 50-99.

Freshman class profile. 3,555 applied, 1,635 admitted, 311 enrolled.

Mid 50% test scores			
SAT critical reading:	380-440	GPA 3.50-3.74:	6%
SAT math:	420-480	GPA 3.0-3.49:	25%
ACT composite:	16-19	GPA 2.0-2.99:	65%
GPA 3.75 or higher:	4%	Rank in top quarter:	28%
		Rank in top tenth:	8%

Basis for selection. Applicants must submit admissions packet, high school transcript, 2 letters of recommendation, and ACT/SAT. 19 ACT/900 SAT (exclusive of Writing) and 2.5 GPA required. All decisions based on overall admissions file. **Home schooled:** Students unable to present a high school transcript may enroll upon presentation of satisfactory passing score on GED.

High school preparation. 24 units required. Required units include English 4, mathematics 2, social studies 2 and science 1.

2011-2012 Annual costs. Tuition/fees: $15,088. Room/board: $6,785.

Financial aid. All financial aid based on need.

Application procedures. Admission: Priority date 5/1; no deadline. $15 fee, may be waived for applicants with need. Admission notification on a rolling basis. Admitted applicants must reply within 5 days of notification of acceptance. **Financial aid:** Priority date 4/15; no closing date. FAFSA, institutional form required. Applicants notified on a rolling basis; must reply within 4 week(s) of notification.

Academics. Special study options: Combined bachelor's/graduate degree, cooperative education, double major, dual enrollment of high school students, honors, independent study, internships, study abroad, teacher certification program. **Credit/placement by examination:** AP, CLEP, SAT, ACT, institutional tests. 30 credit hours maximum toward bachelor's degree. **Support services:** Learning center, reduced course load, remedial instruction, tutoring, writing center.

Honors college/program. High school average of A-, demonstrated success in arts, 1075 SAT (exclusive of Writing)/23 ACT, demonstrated leadership activity, strong performance in sciences, and original essay required.

Majors. Biology: General. **Business:** Business admin. **Computer sciences:** General. **Education:** Elementary, health. **English:** English lit. **History:** General. **Math:** General. **Visual/performing arts:** Art, music.

Computing on campus. PC or laptop required. 225 workstations in dormitories, library, computer center, student center. Dormitories wired for high-speed internet access and linked to campus network. Commuter students can connect to campus network. Online course registration, online library, helpline, student web hosting, wireless network available.

Student life. Freshman orientation: Available, $50 fee. Preregistration for classes offered. **Policies:** Religious observance required. **Housing:** Guaranteed on-campus for freshmen. Single-sex dorms available. $200 nonrefundable deposit, deadline 7/1. **Activities:** Bands, choral groups, drama, music ensembles, radio station, student government, student newspaper, Christian Student Association, Chancellorettes, Chancellors.

Athletics. NCAA. **Intercollegiate:** Baseball M, basketball, cross-country, football (tackle) M, softball W, tennis, track and field, volleyball W. **Intramural:** Basketball, softball, track and field W, volleyball. **Team name:** Tigers.

Student services. Chaplain/spiritual director, career counseling, student employment services, financial aid counseling, health services, personal counseling, placement for graduates, veterans' counselor.

Contact. E-mail: vbowen@stillman.edu
Phone: (205) 366-8814 Toll-free number: (800) 841-5722
Fax: (205) 366-8941
Victoria Boman, Director of Admissions, Stillman College, 3600 Stillman Boulevard, Tuscaloosa, AL 35403

Talladega College
Talladega, Alabama
www.talladega.edu
CB member
CB code: 1800

- Private 4-year liberal arts college affiliated with United Church of Christ
- Residential campus in large town
- 706 degree-seeking undergraduates
- Application essay required

General. Founded in 1867. Regionally accredited. **Degrees:** 134 bachelor's awarded. **ROTC:** Army. **Location:** 55 miles from Birmingham, 120 miles from Atlanta. **Calendar:** Semester, limited summer session. **Full-time faculty:** 36 total. **Part-time faculty:** 10 total. **Class size:** 60% < 20, 28% 20-39, 7% 40-49, 4% 50-99, less than 1% >100. **Special facilities:** Amistad murals.

Basis for selection. Open admission, but selective for some programs. SAT/ACT recommended for bachelor's program in education. Test scores considered for scholarships. Audition required of music majors. **Home schooled:** Transcript of courses and grades, state high school equivalency certificate required.

High school preparation. 22 units recommended. Recommended units include English 4, mathematics 2, social studies 3, science 2 and academic electives 2. 2 units recommended in health/physical education.

2011-2012 Annual costs. Tuition/fees: $12,112. Room/board: $5,885. Books/supplies: $1,178. Personal expenses: $2,402.

Financial aid. All financial aid based on need.

Application procedures. Admission: No deadline. $25 fee, may be waived for applicants with need. Admission notification on a rolling basis. **Financial aid:** Closing date 4/15. FAFSA, institutional form required. Applicants notified on a rolling basis; must reply within 2 week(s) of notification.

Academics. Special study options: Combined bachelor's/graduate degree, cooperative education, double major, dual enrollment of high school students, independent study, internships, teacher certification program. Dual degree linkage programs with other colleges in nursing, engineering, pharmacy, veterinary sciences, geology, and allied health. **Credit/placement by examination:** AP, CLEP, institutional tests. 12 credit hours maximum toward bachelor's degree. **Support services:** Learning center, pre-admission summer program, reduced course load, remedial instruction, study skills assistance, tutoring, writing center.

Majors. Area/ethnic studies: African-American. **Biology:** General. **Business:** Accounting, business admin, finance, managerial economics, marketing. **Communications:** Journalism, media studies. **Computer sciences:** General. **Education:** Biology, English, history, mathematics, music, secondary. **English:** English lit. **History:** General. **Human services:** General, social work. **Math:** General. **Physical sciences:** Chemistry. **Psychology:** General. **Social sciences:** Sociology. **Visual/performing arts:** Piano/keyboard, studio arts, voice/opera.

Most popular majors. Biology 9%, business/marketing 52%, psychology 9%, visual/performing arts 6%.

Computing on campus. 200 workstations in dormitories, library, computer center. Dormitories wired for high-speed internet access and linked to campus network. Commuter students can connect to campus network. Online library available.

Student life. Freshman orientation: Mandatory, $50 fee. Preregistration for classes offered. Held one week prior to school opening. **Policies:** Religious observance required. **Housing:** Guaranteed on-campus for freshmen. Single-sex dorms, wellness housing available. $200 deposit. Dorms for honors students, seniors, athletes. **Activities:** Concert band, choral groups, dance, drama, student government, Arna Bontemps historical society, biology club, business and economics club, chemistry club, debate club, Faith Outreach campus ministry, foreign language club, math club, National Association of Negro Musicians, psychology club.

Athletics. USCAA. **Intercollegiate:** Baseball M, basketball, cheerleading W, golf M, volleyball W. **Intramural:** Softball W, table tennis, tennis, volleyball W. **Team name:** Tornadoes.

Student services. Alcohol/substance abuse counseling, chaplain/spiritual director, career counseling, student employment services, financial aid counseling, health services, personal counseling, placement for graduates, veterans' counselor. **Physically disabled:** Services for visually, hearing impaired.

Contact. E-mail: admissions@talladega.edu
Phone: (256) 761-6235 Toll-free number: (866) 540-3956
Fax: (256) 362-0274
Jacqueline Paddio, Director of Admissions, Talladega College, 627 West Battle Street, Talladega, AL 35160

Troy University
Troy, Alabama
www.troy.edu
CB member
CB code: 1738

- Public 4-year university
- Residential campus in large town
- 20,384 degree-seeking undergraduates: 47% part-time, 63% women, 40% African American, 1% Asian American, 3% Hispanic American, 1% Native American, 2% international
- 5,512 degree-seeking graduate students
- 62% of applicants admitted
- SAT or ACT (ACT writing optional) required
- 35% graduate within 6 years

General. Founded in 1887. Regionally accredited. **Degrees:** 2,694 bachelor's, 497 associate awarded; master's, professional offered. **ROTC:** Army, Air Force. **Location:** 50 miles from Montgomery. **Calendar:** Semester, extensive summer session. **Full-time faculty:** 486 total; 72% have terminal degrees, 18% minority, 48% women. **Part-time faculty:** 992 total; 37% have terminal degrees, 16% minority, 45% women. **Class size:** 53% < 20, 39% 20-39, 4% 40-49, 3% 50-99, less than 1% >100. **Special facilities:** Rosa Parks library and museum, planetarium, performing arts theatre.

Freshman class profile. 6,269 applied, 3,905 admitted, 2,486 enrolled.

Mid 50% test scores			
ACT composite:	18-24	Rank in top quarter:	47%
GPA 3.75 or higher:	21%	End year in good standing:	65%
GPA 3.50-3.74:	11%	Return as sophomores:	71%
GPA 3.0-3.49:	24%	Out-of-state:	32%
GPA 2.0-2.99:	41%	Live on campus:	62%
		International:	1%

Basis for selection. 2.0 GPA and 18 ACT required. Audition required of music education majors.

High school preparation. 15 units required. Required units include English 3.

2011-2012 Annual costs. Tuition/fees: $7,990; $15,040 out-of-state. Room/board: $6,360. Books/supplies: $1,082. Personal expenses: $2,422.

2011-2012 Financial aid. Need-based: 1,278 full-time freshmen applied for aid; 1,278 were judged to have need; 1,278 of these received aid. Average scholarship/grant was $4,590; average loan $3,484. 21% of total undergraduate aid awarded as scholarships/grants, 79% as loans/jobs. **Non-need-based:** Awarded to 4,321 full-time undergraduates, including 977 freshmen. Scholarships awarded for academics, alumni affiliation, art, athletics, leadership, minority status, music/drama, ROTC.

Application procedures. Admission: No deadline. $30 fee. Admission notification on a rolling basis. **Financial aid:** Closing date 5/1. FAFSA, institutional form required. Applicants notified on a rolling basis starting 5/1; must reply within 2 week(s) of notification.

Academics. **Special study options:** Combined bachelor's/graduate degree, distance learning, double major, dual enrollment of high school students, ESL, external degree, honors, independent study, internships, study abroad, teacher certification program, weekend college. **Credit/placement by examination:** AP, CLEP, SAT, ACT, institutional tests. 45 credit hours maximum toward associate degree, 90 toward bachelor's. **Support services:** Learning center, pre-admission summer program, reduced course load, remedial instruction, study skills assistance, tutoring, writing center.

Majors. **Biology:** General, marine. **Business:** General, accounting, business admin, finance, management information systems, marketing. **Communications:** Communications/speech/rhetoric, radio/TV. **Computer sciences:** General. **Conservation:** Environmental science. **Education:** Early childhood, elementary, health, multi-level teacher, secondary. **English:** English lit. **Foreign languages:** General, translation. **Health services:** Athletic training, nursing (RN). **History:** General. **Human services:** Social work. **Liberal arts:** Arts/sciences. **Math:** General. **Parks/recreation:** Sports admin. **Physical sciences:** General, chemistry. **Protective services:** Criminal justice. **Psychology:** General. **Social sciences:** General, political science, sociology. **Visual/performing arts:** Art, music.

Most popular majors. Business/marketing 40%, education 9%, psychology 18%, security/protective services 13%, social sciences 8%.

Computing on campus. 1,945 workstations in library, computer center, student center. Online course registration, online library, helpline available.

Student life. **Freshman orientation:** Mandatory, $55 fee. Preregistration for classes offered. Two-day sessions held during summer. **Housing:** Coed dorms, single-sex dorms, apartments, fraternity/sorority housing, wellness housing available. $100 partly refundable deposit. Substance-abuse-free housing, honor student housing available. **Activities:** Bands, campus ministries, choral groups, dance, drama, international student organizations, music ensembles, musical theater, student government, student newspaper, TV station, religious organizations, service organizations, professional organizations, honor societies, Young Democrats, Young Republicans.

Athletics. NCAA. **Intercollegiate:** Baseball M, basketball, cheerleading, cross-country, football (tackle) M, golf, rodeo, soccer W, softball W, tennis, track and field, volleyball W. **Intramural:** Basketball, cross-country, diving, field hockey W, golf, softball, swimming, tennis, track and field, volleyball W. **Team name:** Trojans.

Student services. Chaplain/spiritual director, career counseling, student employment services, financial aid counseling, health services, on-campus daycare, personal counseling, placement for graduates, veterans' counselor, women's services. **Physically disabled:** Services for visually, hearing impaired.

Contact. E-mail: bstar@troy.edu
Phone: (334) 670-3179 Toll-free number: (800) 551-9716
Fax: (334) 670-3733
Buddy Starling, Dean of Enrollment Management, Troy University, University Avenue, Adams Administration 111, Troy, AL 36082

Tuskegee University
Tuskegee, Alabama   **CB member**
www.tuskegee.edu   **CB code: 1813**

- Private 4-year university
- Residential campus in small town
- 2,683 degree-seeking undergraduates: 3% part-time, 57% women, 87% African American, 1% international
- 468 degree-seeking graduate students
- 65% of applicants admitted
- SAT or ACT (ACT writing optional) required
- 43% graduate within 6 years; 75% enter graduate study

General. Founded in 1881. Regionally accredited. **Degrees:** 395 bachelor's awarded; master's, professional, doctoral offered. **ROTC:** Army, Air Force. **Location:** 30 miles from Montgomery, 162 miles from Atlanta. **Calendar:** Semester, limited summer session. **Full-time faculty:** 271 total; 78% have terminal degrees, 66% minority, 35% women. **Part-time faculty:** 26 total; 35% have terminal degrees, 65% minority, 46% women. **Class size:** 55% < 20, 27% 20-39, 8% 40-49, 10% 50-99, less than 1% >100. **Special facilities:** George Washington Carver museum, aerospace science and health education center, bioethics center.

Freshman class profile. 2,815 applied, 1,816 admitted, 819 enrolled.

Mid 50% test scores			
SAT critical reading:	400-490	Rank in top quarter:	60%
SAT math:	390-500	Rank in top tenth:	20%
ACT composite:	17-22	End year in good standing:	66%
GPA 3.75 or higher:	13%	Return as sophomores:	71%
GPA 3.50-3.74:	16%	Out-of-state:	67%
GPA 3.0-3.49:	38%	Live on campus:	98%
GPA 2.0-2.99:	33%	International:	1%

Basis for selection. School achievement record and test scores important. 800 SAT (exclusive of Writing) or equivalent ACT required for engineering and nursing applicants, 700 for other applicants. National League for Nursing Guidance Examination required of nursing applicants. Essay recommended; interview recommended for veterinary medicine majors.

High school preparation. College-preparatory program recommended. 16 units required. Required units include English 4, mathematics 3, social studies 3, science 2 and academic electives 4.

2011-2012 Annual costs. Tuition/fees: $17,870. $490 per-credit hour charge for students taking over 19 hours. Cost for undergraduate part-time (less than 12 hours): first 2 credit hours $1,890; each additional credit hour $705. Room/board: $7,950. Books/supplies: $1,109. Personal expenses: $1,596.

2011-2012 Financial aid. **Need-based:** 758 full-time freshmen applied for aid; 678 were judged to have need; 572 of these received aid. Average need met was 75%. Average scholarship/grant was $8,000; average loan $3,500. 33% of total undergraduate aid awarded as scholarships/grants, 67% as loans/jobs. **Non-need-based:** Awarded to 1,310 full-time undergraduates, including 483 freshmen. Scholarships awarded for academics, athletics, ROTC, state residency.

Application procedures. **Admission:** Priority date 5/15; deadline 7/15. $25 fee. Admission notification on a rolling basis beginning on or about 3/1. Must reply by May 1 or within 2 week(s) if notified thereafter. **Financial aid:** Closing date 3/31. FAFSA, institutional form required. Applicants notified on a rolling basis starting 5/15; must reply within 2 week(s) of notification.

Academics. **Special study options:** Combined bachelor's/graduate degree, cooperative education, double major, honors, independent study, internships, liberal arts/career combination, teacher certification program. Engineering program with 2-year colleges. **Credit/placement by examination:** AP, CLEP, SAT, ACT. Credit-by-examination policies determined individually by dean. **Support services:** Learning center, pre-admission summer program, reduced course load, remedial instruction, study skills assistance, tutoring, writing center.

Majors. **Architecture:** Architecture. **Biology:** General, ecology. **Business:** Accounting, business admin, finance, hospitality admin, management science. **Computer sciences:** General. **Conservation:** General, forestry. **Education:** General, biology, early childhood, elementary, mathematics, mentally handicapped, physical, science, voc/tech. **Engineering:** Aerospace, chemical, electrical, mechanical. **English:** English lit. **General:** Animal sciences, plant sciences, poultry, soil science. **Health services:** Clinical lab science. **History:** General. **Human services:** Social work. **Math:** General. **Physical sciences:** Chemistry, physics. **Psychology:** General. **Social sciences:** Economics, political science, sociology. **Work/family studies:** Food/nutrition.

Most popular majors. Agriculture 13%, biology 11%, business/marketing 20%, engineering/engineering technologies 27%, psychology 8%.

Computing on campus. 1,000 workstations in dormitories, library, computer center, student center. Dormitories wired for high-speed internet access and linked to campus network. Commuter students can connect to campus network. Online course registration, online library, helpline, repair service, wireless network available.

Student life. **Freshman orientation:** Available. Preregistration for classes offered. **Housing:** Single-sex dorms, apartments. $300 deposit. Honors dormitories available. Freshmen and sophomores not living with parents or guardians required to reside on campus. **Activities:** Bands, choral groups, dance, drama, film society, student government, student newspaper.

Athletics. NCAA. **Intercollegiate:** Baseball M, basketball, cross-country, football (tackle) M, softball W, tennis, track and field, volleyball W. **Intramural:** Basketball M, rifle. **Team name:** Golden Tigers.

Student services. Chaplain/spiritual director, career counseling, financial aid counseling, health services, on-campus daycare, personal counseling, placement for graduates, veterans' counselor.

Contact. E-mail: adm@tuskegee.edu
Phone: (334) 727-8500 Toll-free number: (800) 622-6531
Fax: (334) 724-4402
Cynthia Sellers, Vice President, Student Affairs & Enrollment
Management, Tuskegee University, 102 Old Administration Building,
Tuskegee, AL 36088

United States Sports Academy
Daphne, Alabama
www.ussa.edu

- Private two-year upper-division university
- Large town
- Application essay required

General. Regionally accredited. **Degrees:** 10 bachelor's awarded; master's, doctoral offered. **Articulation:** Agreements with Alabama Southern CC, American River College, Andrew College, Barstow CC, Bishop State CC, Camden County College, City College of San Francisco, Columbus State CC, Consumes River College, Cuyahoga CC, Dakota County Technical College, Dallas County CC, East Mississippi CC, Eastern Iowa CC, Eastern Oklahoma State College, Faulkner State CC, Finger Lakes CC, Gadsden State CC, Hagerstown CC, Herkimer County CC, Hillsborough CC, Hiwassee College, Hudson Valley CC, Jamestown CC, Jones County Junior College, Jefferson Davis CC, Manatee CC, Monroe CC, Northern Virginia CC, Ocean County CC, Pensacola Junior College, Saddleback CC, Sufolk County CC. **Location:** 9 miles from Mobile. **Calendar:** Semester, extensive summer session. **Full-time faculty:** 10 total. **Part-time faculty:** 20 total. **Special facilities:** American sports art museum and archives.

Student profile. 125 degree-seeking undergraduates, 364 degree-seeking graduate students.

Women:	18%	Part-time:	82%

Basis for selection. College transcript, application essay required. Transfer accepted as juniors, seniors.

2011-2012 Annual costs. Tuition/fees: $10,650. Tuition includes cost of books.

Application procedures. Admission: Rolling admission. $50 fee. Application must be submitted online.

Academics. Special study options: Distance learning, internships, student-designed major. **Credit/placement by examination:** AP, CLEP.

Majors. Parks/recreation: Sports admin.

Computing on campus. PC or laptop required. Commuter students can connect to campus network. Online library, wireless network available.

Student services. Adult student services, financial aid counseling. **Physically disabled:** Services for visually, speech, hearing impaired.

Contact. E-mail: admissions@ussa.edu
Phone: (251) 626-3303 Toll-free number: (800) 223-2668
Fax: (251) 625-1035
Tim Foley, Director of Student Services, United States Sports Academy, One Academy Drive, Daphne, AL 36526

University of Alabama
Tuscaloosa, Alabama   **CB member**
www.ua.edu   **CB code: 1830**

- Public 4-year university
- Residential campus in small city
- 25,613 degree-seeking undergraduates: 8% part-time, 53% women, 13% African American, 1% Asian American, 2% Hispanic American, 1% Native American, 2% international
- 5,288 degree-seeking graduate students
- 44% of applicants admitted
- SAT or ACT with writing required
- 66% graduate within 6 years; 25% enter graduate study

General. Founded in 1831. Regionally accredited. Services available for learning impaired students. **Degrees:** 4,463 bachelor's awarded; master's, professional, doctoral offered. **ROTC:** Army, Air Force. **Location:** 60 miles from Birmingham. **Calendar:** Semester, extensive summer session. **Full-time faculty:** 1,171 total; 86% have terminal degrees, 16% minority, 42%

women. **Part-time faculty:** 419 total; 53% have terminal degrees, 8% minority, 52% women. **Class size:** 45% < 20, 31% 20-39, 7% 40-49, 10% 50-99, 7% >100. **Special facilities:** Museum of natural history, arboretum, marine science laboratory, archeological park, observatory, access to CRAY X-UP/24 supercomputer in Huntsville, simulated coal mine setting, concert hall.

Freshman class profile. 22,134 applied, 9,636 admitted, 5,728 enrolled.

Mid 50% test scores		Rank in top quarter:	62%
SAT critical reading:	500-620	Rank in top tenth:	43%
SAT math:	500-640	End year in good standing:	88%
SAT writing:	490-610	Return as sophomores:	87%
ACT composite:	22-29	Out-of-state:	50%
GPA 3.75 or higher:	38%	Live on campus:	92%
GPA 3.50-3.74:	16%	International:	2%
GPA 3.0-3.49:	29%	Fraternities:	28%
GPA 2.0-2.99:	17%	Sororities:	43%

Basis for selection. Admissions based on ACT/SAT (Writing essay score required), GPA, and course schedule. Typically, students with 21 ACT or 1000 SAT (exclusive of Writing) and 3.0 GPA will be admitted. Interview required of any student who appeals admission type or rejection. Audition required for some performance programs. **Home schooled:** Statement describing home school structure and mission, state high school equivalency certificate required. Students who do not present certified transcripts must submit GED and meet GED admission policy. **Learning Disabled:** Documentation concerning disability should be submitted to Office of Disability Services upon admission.

High school preparation. College-preparatory program required. 15 units required. Required units include English 4, mathematics 3, social studies 4, history 1, science 3 (laboratory 2), foreign language 1 and academic electives 5.

2011-2012 Annual costs. Tuition/fees: $8,600; $21,900 out-of-state. Room/board: $8,564. Books/supplies: $1,100. Personal expenses: $2,300.

2010-2011 Financial aid. Need-based: 3,218 full-time freshmen applied for aid; 2,343 were judged to have need; 2,266 of these received aid. Average need met was 57%. Average scholarship/grant was $8,500; average loan $3,488. 44% of total undergraduate aid awarded as scholarships/grants, 56% as loans/jobs. **Non-need-based:** Awarded to 8,782 full-time undergraduates, including 2,810 freshmen. Scholarships awarded for academics, alumni affiliation, art, athletics, leadership, minority status, music/drama, ROTC, state residency.

Application procedures. Admission: Priority date 2/1; no deadline. $40 fee, may be waived for applicants with need. Admission notification on a rolling basis beginning on or about 8/1. Freshman enrollment deposit ($200 prepaid tuition) due 5/1. **Financial aid:** Priority date 3/1; no closing date. FAFSA required. Applicants notified on a rolling basis starting 4/1; must reply within 3 week(s) of notification.

Academics. Special study options: Accelerated study, combined bachelor's/graduate degree, cooperative education, cross-registration, distance learning, double major, dual enrollment of high school students, ESL, exchange student, external degree, honors, independent study, internships, liberal arts/career combination, student-designed major, study abroad, teacher certification program, Washington semester, weekend college. **Credit/placement by examination:** AP, CLEP, IB, institutional tests. **Support services:** Learning center, pre-admission summer program, remedial instruction, study skills assistance, tutoring, writing center.

Honors college/program. Students with 3.3 GPA and 28 ACT/1250 SAT (exclusive of Writing) eligible to apply.

Majors. **Area/ethnic studies:** African-American, American, Latin American. **Biology:** General, marine, microbiology. **Business:** Accounting, business admin, finance, management information systems, management science, managerial economics, marketing, restaurant/food services. **Communications:** Advertising, communications/speech/rhetoric, journalism, public relations, radio/TV. **Computer sciences:** General. **Conservation:** Environmental science. **Education:** Early childhood, elementary, music, physical, secondary, special ed. **Engineering:** Aerospace, chemical, civil, construction, electrical, mechanical, metallurgical. **English:** English lit. **Foreign languages:** General, Spanish. **Health services:** Athletic training, audiology/speech pathology, dietetics, facilities admin, nursing (RN). **History:** General. **Human services:** Social work. **Math:** General. **Philosophy/religion:** Philosophy, religion. **Physical sciences:** Chemistry, geology, physics. **Protective services:** Criminal justice. **Psychology:** General. **Social sciences:** Anthropology, geography, international relations, political science, sociology. **Visual/performing arts:** Art history/conservation, dance, dramatic, interior design, music, studio arts. **Work/family studies:** General, clothing/textiles, family resources, family studies.

Most popular majors. Business/marketing 29%, communications/journalism 9%, education 6%, engineering/engineering technologies 7%, family/consumer sciences 7%, health sciences 10%.

Computing on campus. 2,200 workstations in dormitories, library, computer center, student center. Dormitories wired for high-speed internet access and linked to campus network. Commuter students can connect to campus network. Online course registration, online library, helpline, repair service, student web hosting, wireless network available.

Student life. Freshman orientation: Mandatory, $120 fee. Preregistration for classes offered. **Policies:** Academic integrity policies guided by Capstone Creed and administered through Academic Honors Council. Living/learning program offered. **Housing:** Guaranteed on-campus for freshmen. Coed dorms, single-sex dorms, special housing for disabled, apartments, fraternity/sorority housing available. $200 partly refundable deposit, deadline 2/1. Apartments for visiting scholars available. **Activities:** Bands, campus ministries, choral groups, dance, drama, film society, international student organizations, literary magazine, music ensembles, Model UN, musical theater, opera, radio station, student government, student newspaper, symphony orchestra, TV station, College Republicans, College Democrats, NAACP, black student union, Baptist student association, National Society of Black Engineers, Up til Dawn, Hillel House.

Athletics. NAIA, NCAA. **Intercollegiate:** Baseball M, basketball, cheerleading, cross-country, diving, football (tackle) M, golf, gymnastics W, rowing (crew) W, soccer W, softball W, swimming, tennis, track and field, volleyball W. **Intramural:** Badminton, basketball, bowling, football (nontackle), golf, racquetball, rowing (crew) W, soccer, swimming, table tennis, tennis, volleyball. **Team name:** Crimson Tide.

Student services. Adult student services, alcohol/substance abuse counseling, chaplain/spiritual director, career counseling, services for economically disadvantaged, student employment services, financial aid counseling, health services, legal services, minority student services, on-campus daycare, personal counseling, placement for graduates, veterans' counselor, women's services. **Physically disabled:** Services for visually, speech, hearing impaired.

Contact. E-mail: admissions@ua.edu
Phone: (205) 348-5666 Toll-free number: (800) 933-2262
Fax: (205) 348-9046
Mary Spiegel, Executive Director of Enrollment Services, University of Alabama, Box 870132, Tuscaloosa, AL 35487-0132

University of Alabama at Birmingham
Birmingham, Alabama   **CB member**
www.uab.edu   **CB code: 1856**

- Public 4-year university
- Residential campus in very large city
- 10,854 degree-seeking undergraduates: 25% part-time, 58% women, 27% African American, 4% Asian American, 2% Hispanic American, 2% international
- 6,103 degree-seeking graduate students
- 72% of applicants admitted
- SAT or ACT (ACT writing optional) required

General. Founded in 1969. Regionally accredited. **Degrees:** 1,997 bachelor's awarded; master's, professional, doctoral offered. **ROTC:** Army, Air Force. **Location:** Downtown. **Calendar:** Semester, extensive summer session. **Full-time faculty:** 862 total; 86% have terminal degrees, 22% minority, 45% women. **Part-time faculty:** 69 total; 72% have terminal degrees, 9% minority, 48% women. **Class size:** 39% < 20, 38% 20-39, 8% 40-49, 11% 50-99, 4% >100. **Special facilities:** Alabama Museum of Health Sciences.

Freshman class profile. 5,575 applied, 4,027 admitted, 1,605 enrolled.

Mid 50% test scores		End year in good standing:	85%
ACT composite:	21-27	Return as sophomores:	80%
GPA 3.75 or higher:	37%	Out-of-state:	10%
GPA 3.50-3.74:	17%	Live on campus:	67%
GPA 3.0-3.49:	28%	International:	2%
GPA 2.0-2.99:	18%	Fraternities:	7%
Rank in top quarter:	52%	Sororities:	8%
Rank in top tenth:	27%		

Basis for selection. Admissions based on ACT/SAT, GPA, and college preparatory curriculum. **Home schooled:** Statement describing home school structure and mission, transcript of courses and grades required.

High school preparation. College-preparatory program required. 17 units required. Required units include English 4, mathematics 3, social studies 3, science 3 (laboratory 2), foreign language 1 and academic electives 3.

2011-2012 Annual costs. Tuition/fees: $7,470; $17,730 out-of-state. Room/board: $9,714. Books/supplies: $1,000. Personal expenses: $2,000.

2010-2011 Financial aid. Need-based: 1,220 full-time freshmen applied for aid; 902 were judged to have need; 885 of these received aid. Average need met was 46%. Average scholarship/grant was $5,183; average loan $3,589. 44% of total undergraduate aid awarded as scholarships/grants, 56% as loans/jobs. **Non-need-based:** Awarded to 2,961 full-time undergraduates, including 947 freshmen. Scholarships awarded for academics, alumni affiliation, art, athletics, leadership, minority status, music/drama, ROTC.

Application procedures. Admission: Priority date 5/1; no deadline. $30 fee, may be waived for applicants with need. Application must be submitted online. Admission notification on a rolling basis beginning on or about 9/1. Housing deposit refundable if requested by June 1. **Financial aid:** Priority date 3/1; no closing date. FAFSA required. Applicants notified on a rolling basis starting 4/1; must reply within 4 week(s) of notification.

Academics. Special study options: Combined bachelor's/graduate degree, cooperative education, cross-registration, distance learning, double major, dual enrollment of high school students, ESL, honors, independent study, internships, student-designed major, study abroad, teacher certification program. **Credit/placement by examination:** AP, CLEP, IB, SAT, ACT, institutional tests. 45 credit hours maximum toward bachelor's degree. **Support services:** Learning center, reduced course load, remedial instruction, study skills assistance, tutoring, writing center.

Honors college/program. Additional application required; 200 admitted.

Majors. Area/ethnic studies: African-American. **Biology:** General. **Business:** Accounting, business admin, finance, management information systems, managerial economics, marketing, sales/distribution. **Communications:** Communications/speech/rhetoric. **Computer sciences:** General. **Education:** Early childhood, elementary, health, physical, secondary, special ed. **Engineering:** Biomedical, civil, electrical, materials, mechanical. **English:** English lit. **Foreign languages:** General. **Health services:** Clinical lab science, cytotechnology, medical radiologic technology/radiation therapy, medical records admin, nuclear medical technology, nursing (RN), respiratory therapy technology. **History:** General. **Human services:** Social work. **Math:** General. **Philosophy/religion:** Philosophy. **Physical sciences:** Chemistry, physics. **Protective services:** Criminal justice. **Psychology:** General. **Social sciences:** Anthropology, political science, sociology. **Visual/performing arts:** Art, dramatic, music.

Most popular majors. Biology 8%, business/marketing 19%, education 12%, health sciences 21%, psychology 6%.

Computing on campus. Dormitories wired for high-speed internet access and linked to campus network. Commuter students can connect to campus network. Online course registration, online library, helpline, student web hosting, wireless network available.

Student life. Freshman orientation: Mandatory, $150 fee. Preregistration for classes offered. Two-day program offered various times between May and August. **Housing:** Coed dorms, special housing for disabled, apartments available. $250 fully refundable deposit, deadline 5/1. **Activities:** Bands, campus ministries, choral groups, dance, drama, international student organizations, literary magazine, music ensembles, musical theater, opera, radio station, student government, student newspaper, Young Democrats, College Republicans, campus civitan club, veterans student organization, Catholic student association, Muslim student association, Chinese student association, African student association.

Athletics. NCAA. **Intercollegiate:** Baseball M, basketball, bowling W, cross-country W, football (tackle) M, golf, rifle W, soccer, softball W, synchronized swimming W, tennis, track and field W, volleyball W. **Intramural:** Badminton, basketball, bowling, football (non-tackle), racquetball, skiing, soccer, softball, squash, swimming, table tennis, tennis, track and field, volleyball, water polo, wrestling M. **Team name:** Blazers.

Student services. Adult student services, career counseling, student employment services, financial aid counseling, health services, minority student services, on-campus daycare, personal counseling, placement for graduates, veterans' counselor, women's services. **Physically disabled:** Services for visually, speech, hearing impaired.

Contact. E-mail: undergradadmit@uab.edu
Phone: (205) 934-8221 Toll-free number: (800) 421-8743
Fax: (205) 975-7114
Kirk Kluver, Director of Admission, University of Alabama at Birmingham, HUC 260, 1530 Third Avenue South, Birmingham, AL 35294-1150

University of Alabama in Huntsville
Huntsville, Alabama   **CB member**
www.uah.edu   **CB code: 1854**

- Public 4-year university
- Commuter campus in small city

- 5,755 degree-seeking undergraduates: 23% part-time, 46% women, 14% African American, 3% Asian American, 3% Hispanic American, 2% Native American, 3% international
- 1,549 degree-seeking graduate students
- 64% of applicants admitted
- SAT or ACT (ACT writing optional) required
- 45% graduate within 6 years

General. Founded in 1950. Regionally accredited. **Degrees:** 1,028 bachelor's awarded; master's, professional, doctoral offered. **ROTC:** Army. **Location:** 100 miles from Birmingham; 100 miles from Nashville, TN. **Calendar:** Semester, extensive summer session. **Full-time faculty:** 306 total; 86% have terminal degrees, 22% minority, 37% women. **Part-time faculty:** 180 total; 40% have terminal degrees, 9% minority, 41% women. **Class size:** 39% < 20, 39% 20-39, 10% 40-49, 10% 50-99, 1% >100. **Special facilities:** Optical observatory, radio telescope.

Freshman class profile. 1,952 applied, 1,243 admitted, 677 enrolled.

Mid 50% test scores			
SAT critical reading:	500-630	Rank in top tenth:	29%
SAT math:	520-670	End year in good standing:	83%
ACT composite:	22-29	Return as sophomores:	79%
GPA 3.75 or higher:	45%	Out-of-state:	15%
GPA 3.50-3.74:	18%	Live on campus:	52%
GPA 3.0-3.49:	26%	International:	2%
GPA 2.0-2.99:	11%	Fraternities:	14%
Rank in top quarter:	50%	Sororities:	21%

Basis for selection. School achievement record and test scores most important. Conditional admission may be available for applicants with evidence of serious commitment to academic pursuits who do not meet requirements for regular admission. Auditions required for majoring or minoring in music. **Home schooled:** Official high school record should contain titles of courses, annotation of general content in academic courses, and textbooks used. Teaching credentials of home school teacher should be included with application.

High school preparation. College-preparatory program required. 20 units required; 26 recommended. Required and recommended units include English 4, mathematics 3-4, social studies 4, science 3-4 (laboratory 2), foreign language 2 and academic electives 6. Social studies requirements may include history. Computer science and visual/performing arts counted in academic electives requirements.

2011-2012 Annual costs. Tuition/fees: $8,094; $19,424 out-of-state. Each college has required course fees which vary by college. The average of all colleges' course fees at 15 hours per semester for 2 semesters is $741. Room/board: $7,930. Books/supplies: $1,567. Personal expenses: $1,959.

2011-2012 Financial aid. Need-based: 590 full-time freshmen applied for aid; 356 were judged to have need; 355 of these received aid. Average need met was 65%. Average scholarship/grant was $8,195; average loan $5,384. 38% of total undergraduate aid awarded as scholarships/grants, 62% as loans/jobs. **Non-need-based:** Awarded to 992 full-time undergraduates, including 250 freshmen. Scholarships awarded for academics, art, athletics, leadership, minority status, music/drama, ROTC.

Application procedures. Admission: Closing date 8/22 (receipt date). $30 fee, may be waived for applicants with need. Admission notification on a rolling basis. Must reply by May 1 or within 3 week(s) if notified thereafter. **Financial aid:** Priority date 4/1, closing date 7/31. FAFSA required. Applicants notified on a rolling basis starting 4/1; must reply within 2 week(s) of notification.

Academics. All Academic Support Services are housed within a dedicated Student Success Center. This center includes 25 sections of supplemental instruction for historically difficult classes, tutoring in over 100 subjects, evening tutoring in math and writing in the residence halls, academic coaching, grade recovery, early alert, Honors program and First Year Experience program which includes mandatory 1 credit hour class. **Special study options:** Combined bachelor's/graduate degree, cooperative education, cross-registration, distance learning, double major, dual enrollment of high school students, ESL, honors, independent study, internships, student-designed major, study abroad, teacher certification program. 3-2 program in engineering. Research centers employ undergraduate students on campus and in the community. Co-op program with U.S. Army Redstone Arsenal, NASA Marshall Space Flight Center, U.S. Army Missile Command, over 50 Fortune 500 companies. Intensive English Program (IEP) for nonnative speakers of English available prior to enrollment in a degree program. **Credit/placement by examination:** AP, CLEP, IB, SAT, ACT, institutional tests. 32 credit hours maximum toward bachelor's degree. **Support services:** Learning center, reduced course load, remedial instruction, study skills assistance, tutoring, writing center.

Majors. Biology: General. **Business:** Accounting, business admin, finance, management information systems, marketing. **Communications:** Communications/speech/rhetoric. **Computer sciences:** General. **Education:** Elementary. **Engineering:** Chemical, civil, computer, electrical, industrial, mechanical. **English:** English lit. **Foreign languages:** General. **Health services:** Nursing (RN). **History:** General. **Math:** General. **Philosophy/religion:** Philosophy. **Physical sciences:** Chemistry, physics. **Psychology:** General. **Social sciences:** Political science, sociology. **Visual/performing arts:** Art, music.

Most popular majors. Biology 7%, business/marketing 23%, engineering/engineering technologies 25%, health sciences 18%.

Computing on campus. 1,227 workstations in dormitories, library, computer center, student center. Dormitories wired for high-speed internet access and linked to campus network. Commuter students can connect to campus network. Online course registration, online library, helpline, repair service, student web hosting, wireless network available.

Student life. Freshman orientation: Mandatory, $150 fee. Preregistration for classes offered. Two-day program offered throughout summer. **Housing:** Guaranteed on-campus for freshmen. Coed dorms, special housing for disabled, apartments, cooperative housing, fraternity/sorority housing available. $125 partly refundable deposit, deadline 6/1. Athletic team housing. **Activities:** Bands, campus ministries, choral groups, dance, drama, international student organizations, literary magazine, music ensembles, Model UN, student government, student newspaper, black student association, Campus Crusade for Christ, Chinese student & scholar association, Muslim students association, College Democrats, Indian student organization, Invisible Children United, National Society of Black Engineers, Reformed University Fellowship.

Athletics. NCAA. **Intercollegiate:** Baseball M, basketball, cross-country, ice hockey M, soccer, softball W, tennis, track and field, volleyball W. **Intramural:** Basketball, football (non-tackle), racquetball, soccer, softball, tennis, volleyball. **Team name:** Chargers.

Student services. Adult student services, alcohol/substance abuse counseling, career counseling, student employment services, financial aid counseling, health services, minority student services, personal counseling, placement for graduates, veterans' counselor, women's services. **Physically disabled:** Services for visually, speech, hearing impaired.

Contact. E-mail: admitme@uah.edu
Phone: (256) 824-2773 Toll-free number: (800) 824-2255
Fax: (256) 824-6073
Sandra Barinowski, Director of Admissions, University of Alabama in Huntsville, UAH Office of Undergraduate Admissions, Huntsville, AL 35899

University of Mobile
Mobile, Alabama
www.umobile.edu   **CB code: 1515**

- Private 4-year university and liberal arts college affiliated with Baptist faith
- Commuter campus in small city
- 1,543 degree-seeking undergraduates: 13% part-time, 67% women, 24% African American, 1% Asian American, 1% Hispanic American, 2% Native American, 3% international
- 186 degree-seeking graduate students
- 81% of applicants admitted
- SAT or ACT (ACT writing optional) required
- 43% graduate within 6 years

General. Founded in 1961. Regionally accredited. **Degrees:** 262 bachelor's, 26 associate awarded; master's offered. **ROTC:** Army, Air Force. **Location:** 12 miles from downtown, 140 miles from New Orleans. **Calendar:** Semester, limited summer session. **Full-time faculty:** 83 total; 58% have terminal degrees, 4% minority, 51% women. **Part-time faculty:** 95 total; 22% have terminal degrees, 13% minority, 46% women. **Class size:** 54% < 20, 44% 20-39, 1% 40-49, less than 1% 50-99. **Special facilities:** Forest resource learning center, nature trails.

Freshman class profile. 620 applied, 500 admitted, 251 enrolled.

Mid 50% test scores			
SAT critical reading:	440-560	GPA 2.0-2.99:	26%
SAT math:	430-550	Rank in top quarter:	47%
ACT composite:	20-25	Rank in top tenth:	16%
GPA 3.75 or higher:	26%	Return as sophomores:	72%
GPA 3.50-3.74:	18%	Out-of-state:	33%
GPA 3.0-3.49:	29%	Live on campus:	81%
		International:	3%

Basis for selection. Admission decisions based on test scores, high school record. SAT Subject Tests recommended. Interview recommended for nursing majors, audition recommended for music majors, portfolio recommended for art majors. **Home schooled:** Statement describing home school structure and mission required.

High school preparation. College-preparatory program recommended. 22 units recommended. Recommended units include English 4, mathematics 3, social studies 3 and foreign language 2.

2011-2012 Annual costs. Tuition/fees: $17,130. Room/board: $8,076. Books/supplies: $1,550. Personal expenses: $1,700.

2011-2012 Financial aid. **Need-based:** 219 full-time freshmen applied for aid; 194 were judged to have need; 194 of these received aid. Average need met was 74%. Average scholarship/grant was $5,332; average loan $3,688. 66% of total undergraduate aid awarded as scholarships/grants, 34% as loans/jobs. **Non-need-based:** Scholarships awarded for academics, alumni affiliation, athletics, music/drama, religious affiliation.

Application procedures. **Admission:** Closing date 8/1. $50 fee. Admission notification on a rolling basis. **Financial aid:** No deadline. FAFSA, institutional form required. Applicants notified on a rolling basis starting 2/1; must reply within 2 week(s) of notification.

Academics. **Special study options:** Accelerated study, combined bachelor's/graduate degree, double major, honors, independent study, internships, teacher certification program. **Credit/placement by examination:** AP, CLEP, IB, SAT, ACT, institutional tests. 30 credit hours maximum toward associate degree, 30 toward bachelor's. **Support services:** Learning center, pre-admission summer program, reduced course load, remedial instruction, study skills assistance, tutoring, writing center.

Majors. **Biology:** General, marine. **Business:** Accounting, business admin. **Communications:** General. **Computer sciences:** General. **Conservation:** Environmental science. **Education:** Biology, early childhood, elementary, English, history, mathematics, music, physical, social science. **English:** English lit. **Health services:** Athletic training, nursing (RN). **History:** General. **Liberal arts:** Humanities. **Math:** General. **Parks/recreation:** Health/fitness. **Philosophy/religion:** Religion. **Psychology:** General. **Social sciences:** General, political science, sociology. **Theology:** Sacred music. **Visual/performing arts:** Art, music, musical theater, voice/opera.

Most popular majors. Business/marketing 20%, education 20%, health sciences 17%, liberal arts 9%, philosophy/religious studies 6%, psychology 6%, theological studies 7%.

Computing on campus. 120 workstations in dormitories, library, computer center. Dormitories wired for high-speed internet access and linked to campus network. Commuter students can connect to campus network. Online course registration, online library, helpline, wireless network available.

Student life. **Freshman orientation:** Mandatory, $100 fee. Preregistration for classes offered. **Policies:** Religious observance required. **Housing:** Guaranteed on-campus for freshmen. Single-sex dorms available. $250 nonrefundable deposit, deadline 4/30. **Activities:** Bands, campus ministries, choral groups, music ensembles, musical theater, opera, student government, campus activities board, student government association, ministerial association, honor societies, academic clubs, Fellowship of Christian Athletes.

Athletics. NAIA. **Intercollegiate:** Baseball M, basketball, cheerleading M, cross-country, golf, soccer, softball W, tennis, volleyball W. **Intramural:** Basketball, football (non-tackle), softball, volleyball. **Team name:** Rams.

Student services. Adult student services, chaplain/spiritual director, career counseling, student employment services, financial aid counseling, health services, personal counseling, placement for graduates, veterans' counselor.

Contact. E-mail: adminfo@umobile.edu
Phone: (251) 442-2273 Toll-free number: (800) 946-7267
Fax: (251) 442-2498
Kim Leousis, Vice President for Enrollment Services and Campus Life, University of Mobile, 5735 College Parkway, Mobile, AL 36613-2842

University of Montevallo
Montevallo, Alabama
www.montevallo.edu

CB member
CB code: 1004

‣ Public 4-year university and liberal arts college
‣ Residential campus in small town
‣ 2,525 degree-seeking undergraduates: 11% part-time, 66% women, 15% African American, 3% Hispanic American, 1% Native American, 2% international

‣ 481 degree-seeking graduate students
‣ 78% of applicants admitted
‣ SAT or ACT (ACT writing optional) required
‣ 41% graduate within 6 years

General. Founded in 1896. Regionally accredited. **Degrees:** 437 bachelor's awarded; master's offered. **ROTC:** Army, Air Force. **Location:** 35 miles from Birmingham. **Calendar:** Semester, extensive summer session. **Full-time faculty:** 131 total; 13% minority, 49% women. **Part-time faculty:** 80 total; 6% minority, 69% women. **Special facilities:** Ecological preserve, observatory, anagama kiln, speech and hearing center, foreign language laboratory, child development center, mass communication production center, traffic safety center.

Freshman class profile. 1,315 applied, 1,022 admitted, 507 enrolled.

Mid 50% test scores			
ACT composite:	20-26	Return as sophomores:	77%
GPA 3.75 or higher:	23%	Out-of-state:	6%
GPA 3.50-3.74:	15%	Live on campus:	78%
GPA 3.0-3.49:	40%	International:	4%
GPA 2.0-2.99:	21%	Fraternities:	22%
		Sororities:	28%

Basis for selection. High school record and test scores essential factors in individual evaluation. Interview recommended. Audition required of music majors; portfolio required of art majors. **Home schooled:** Transcript of courses and grades required. **Learning Disabled:** Conditional admission may be granted if standard requirements not met. Reasonable accommodations will be provided as necessary. Enrolled students needing disability accommodations and services must provide current documentation and make requests through the Services for Students with Disabilities Office.

High school preparation. College-preparatory program recommended. 16 units required. Required and recommended units include English 4, mathematics 2-3, social studies 2, history 2, science 2-3, foreign language 2 and academic electives 4.

2011-2012 Annual costs. Tuition/fees: $8,520; $16,560 out-of-state. Room/board: $5,192. Books/supplies: $1,155. Personal expenses: $2,310.

Financial aid. **Non-need-based:** Scholarships awarded for academics, art, athletics, job skills, leadership, minority status, music/drama, religious affiliation, ROTC.

Application procedures. **Admission:** Closing date 8/20. $30 fee, may be waived for applicants with need. Admission notification on a rolling basis beginning on or about 9/1. **Financial aid:** Priority date 4/1; no closing date. FAFSA required. Applicants notified on a rolling basis starting 4/20; must reply within 2 week(s) of notification.

Academics. Academic support programs available to all first-generation college students from low-income families and students with disabilities through the ASPIRE program. Tutoring, study-skills classes, academic counseling, career exploration, course advisement and registration, computer lab access, computer-assisted instruction, and cultural and social enrichment activities provided. **Special study options:** Accelerated study, combined bachelor's/graduate degree, cross-registration, double major, dual enrollment of high school students, exchange student, honors, independent study, internships, study abroad, teacher certification program. **Credit/placement by examination:** AP, CLEP, IB, institutional tests. 45 credit hours maximum toward bachelor's degree. **Support services:** Learning center, pre-admission summer program, reduced course load, remedial instruction, study skills assistance, tutoring, writing center.

Majors. **Biology:** General. **Business:** Accounting, business admin, finance. **Communications:** Radio/TV. **Education:** Elementary. **English:** English lit, rhetoric/composition. **Foreign languages:** General. **Health services:** Audiology/hearing, speech pathology. **History:** General. **Human services:** Social work. **Math:** General. **Parks/recreation:** Health/fitness. **Physical sciences:** Chemistry. **Psychology:** General. **Social sciences:** General, political science, sociology. **Visual/performing arts:** Art, dramatic, music. **Work/family studies:** General.

Most popular majors. Biology 6%, business/marketing 18%, education 13%, English 8%, family/consumer sciences 7%, history 6%, visual/performing arts 15%.

Computing on campus. 340 workstations in dormitories, library, computer center. Dormitories wired for high-speed internet access and linked to campus network. Commuter students can connect to campus network. Online course registration, online library, helpline, wireless network available.

Student life. **Freshman orientation:** Mandatory. Preregistration for classes offered. Two preregistration sessions during the summer and orientation immediately prior to beginning of fall semester. **Housing:** Guaranteed on-campus for freshmen. Coed dorms, single-sex dorms, apartments available. $100 fully refundable deposit. Several rooms are handicapped accessible.

Activities: Bands, campus ministries, choral groups, dance, drama, international student organizations, literary magazine, music ensembles, Model UN, musical theater, student government, student newspaper, TV station, African American Society, Young Republicans, Young Democrats, campus outreach, Episcopal Student Fellowship, Feminine Majority Leadership Alliance.

Athletics. NCAA. Intercollegiate: Baseball M, basketball, cross-country W, golf, soccer, tennis W, volleyball W. **Intramural:** Basketball, soccer, softball, volleyball. **Team name:** Falcons.

Student services. Adult student services, alcohol/substance abuse counseling, chaplain/spiritual director, career counseling, student employment services, financial aid counseling, health services, minority student services, personal counseling, placement for graduates, veterans' counselor. **Physically disabled:** Services for visually, speech, hearing impaired.

Contact. E-mail: admissions@montevallo.edu
Phone: (205) 665-6030 Toll-free number: (800) 292-4349
Fax: (205) 665-6032
Ira Gurganus, Director of Admissions, University of Montevallo, Palmer Hall, Station 6030, Montevallo, AL 35115-6000

University of North Alabama
Florence, Alabama   CB member
www.una.edu   CB code: 1735

- Public 4-year university
- Commuter campus in large town
- 5,681 degree-seeking undergraduates: 14% part-time, 58% women, 13% African American, 1% Asian American, 2% Hispanic American, 1% Native American, 4% international
- 960 degree-seeking graduate students
- 81% of applicants admitted
- SAT or ACT required

General. Founded in 1830. Regionally accredited. **Degrees:** 912 bachelor's awarded; master's offered. **ROTC:** Army. **Location:** 116 miles from Birmingham. **Calendar:** Semester, extensive summer session. **Full-time faculty:** 231 total; 76% have terminal degrees, 19% minority, 48% women. **Part-time faculty:** 100 total; 27% have terminal degrees, 8% minority, 49% women. **Class size:** 39% < 20, 46% 20-39, 10% 40-49, 4% 50-99, less than 1% >100. **Special facilities:** Planetarium-observatory, laboratory school.

Freshman class profile. 2,381 applied, 1,924 admitted, 889 enrolled.

Mid 50% test scores		GPA 2.0-2.99:	38%
SAT critical reading:	420-530	Return as sophomores:	65%
SAT math:	430-540	Out-of-state:	13%
ACT composite:	18-25	Live on campus:	49%
GPA 3.75 or higher:	20%	International:	2%
GPA 3.50-3.74:	12%	Fraternities:	4%
GPA 3.0-3.49:	26%	Sororities:	7%

Basis for selection. 18 ACT or 700 SAT (exclusive of Writing), or rank in upper 50% of class required. If submitting GED, 35 on each section or average of 45 on all GED test sections required. Auditions required of music majors. Interviews recommended for education, nursing, social work, preprofessional programs. Portfolios recommended for art majors.

High school preparation. College-preparatory program recommended. 13 units required. Required units include English 4, mathematics 2, social studies 3, science 2 and foreign language 2.

2011-2012 Annual costs. Tuition/fees: $7,458; $13,578 out-of-state. Room/board: $5,490. Books/supplies: $1,100. Personal expenses: $900.

2010-2011 Financial aid. Need-based: 936 full-time freshmen applied for aid; 852 were judged to have need; 811 of these received aid. Average need met was 66%. Average scholarship/grant was $4,345; average loan $3,001. 48% of total undergraduate aid awarded as scholarships/grants, 52% as loans/jobs. **Non-need-based:** Awarded to 1,698 full-time undergraduates, including 547 freshmen. Scholarships awarded for academics, alumni affiliation, art, athletics, job skills, leadership, minority status, music/drama, religious affiliation, ROTC, state residency.

Application procedures. Admission: Priority date 8/1; no deadline. $25 fee. Admission notification on a rolling basis beginning on or about 6/15. **Financial aid:** Priority date 3/1; no closing date. FAFSA required. Applicants notified on a rolling basis starting 3/30.

Academics. Special study options: Accelerated study, cooperative education, distance learning, double major, dual enrollment of high school students, ESL, honors, independent study, internships, student-designed major, study abroad, teacher certification program, weekend college. **Credit/placement by examination:** AP, CLEP, institutional tests. 34 credit hours maximum toward bachelor's degree. **Support services:** Learning center, pre-admission summer program, reduced course load, remedial instruction, study skills assistance, tutoring, writing center.

Majors. Biology: General, marine. **Business:** Accounting, business admin, finance, management information systems, managerial economics, marketing. **Communications:** Communications/speech/rhetoric, media studies. **Computer sciences:** General. **Education:** Elementary, multi-level teacher, secondary. **English:** English lit. **Foreign languages:** General. **Health services:** Nursing (RN). **History:** General. **Human services:** Social work. **Math:** General. **Parks/recreation:** General. **Physical sciences:** Chemistry, physics. **Protective services:** Law enforcement admin. **Psychology:** General. **Social sciences:** General, geography, political science, sociology. **Visual/performing arts:** Art, music. **Work/family studies:** General.

Most popular majors. Business/marketing 24%, education 14%, English 10%, health sciences 16%, social sciences 7%.

Computing on campus. 600 workstations in dormitories, library, computer center, student center. Dormitories wired for high-speed internet access and linked to campus network. Commuter students can connect to campus network. Online course registration, online library, helpline, wireless network available.

Student life. Freshman orientation: Mandatory, $25 fee. Preregistration for classes offered. Two-day sessions in June and July include academic advisement. **Housing:** Coed dorms, single-sex dorms, apartments, fraternity/sorority housing, wellness housing available. $100 nonrefundable deposit. **Activities:** Bands, campus ministries, choral groups, drama, international student organizations, literary magazine, music ensembles, musical theater, radio station, student government, student newspaper, Young Democrats, Young Republicans, Circle-K, Gold Triangle, black student alliance, Christian student fellowship.

Athletics. NCAA. Intercollegiate: Baseball M, basketball, cross-country, football (tackle) M, golf M, soccer W, softball W, tennis, volleyball W. **Intramural:** Badminton, baseball M, basketball, bowling, cross-country, football (tackle) M, golf M, racquetball, softball W, swimming, table tennis, tennis, volleyball. **Team name:** Lions.

Student services. Adult student services, alcohol/substance abuse counseling, chaplain/spiritual director, career counseling, student employment services, financial aid counseling, health services, minority student services, on-campus daycare, personal counseling, placement for graduates, veterans' counselor, women's services. **Physically disabled:** Services for visually, speech, hearing impaired.

Contact. E-mail: admissions@una.edu
Phone: (256) 765-4608 Toll-free number: (800) 825-5862
Fax: (256) 765-4329
Kim Mauldin, Director of Admissions, University of North Alabama, One Harrison Plaza, UNA Box 5011, Florence, AL 35632-0001

University of Phoenix: Birmingham
Birmingham, Alabama
www.phoenix.edu

- For-profit 4-year university
- Commuter campus in small city
- 478 degree-seeking undergraduates

General. Regionally accredited. **Degrees:** 17 bachelor's awarded; master's offered. **Calendar:** Differs by program. **Full-time faculty:** 7 total. **Part-time faculty:** 65 total.

Basis for selection. Open admission.

2011-2012 Annual costs. Estimated costs as of August 2011: per-credit-hour charge, $420 to $450, depending upon level and course of study; electronic course materials fee, $95, if applicable. Book and material charges may vary by course and program. All fees are subject to change.

Application procedures. Admission: No deadline. No application fee. **Financial aid:** No deadline.

Academics. Credit/placement by examination: AP, CLEP.

Majors. Business: Accounting, business admin, credit management, e-commerce, entrepreneurial studies, human resources, marketing, operations. **Health services:** Health care admin, long term care admin, medical records technology. **Human services:** General. **Protective services:** Disaster management, law enforcement admin.

Contact. Toll-free number: (866) 766-0766
Marc Booker, Director of Admissions and Evaluation, University of Phoenix: Birmingham, 100 Corporate Drive, Suite 150, Birmingham, AL 35242-2982

University of South Alabama
Mobile, Alabama
www.southalabama.edu   **CB code: 1880**

- Public 4-year university
- Commuter campus in small city
- 11,403 degree-seeking undergraduates: 24% part-time, 56% women, 21% African American, 3% Asian American, 2% Hispanic American, 1% Native American, 4% international
- 3,191 degree-seeking graduate students
- 87% of applicants admitted
- 39% graduate within 6 years

General. Founded in 1963. Regionally accredited. **Degrees:** 1,713 bachelor's awarded; master's, professional, doctoral offered. **ROTC:** Army, Air Force. **Location:** 10 miles from downtown, 150 miles from New Orleans. **Calendar:** Semester, extensive summer session. **Full-time faculty:** 759 total; 76% have terminal degrees, 43% women. **Part-time faculty:** 347 total; 62% women. **Special facilities:** Sea laboratory.

Freshman class profile. 4,473 applied, 3,903 admitted, 1,944 enrolled.

Mid 50% test scores			
SAT critical reading:	440-570	Return as sophomores:	65%
SAT math:	420-560	International:	2%
SAT writing:	420-560	Fraternities:	10%
ACT composite:	19-25	Sororities:	10%

Basis for selection. School achievement record and test scores important. Auditions required of music majors. **Learning Disabled:** Students should submit required documentation to special student services office if requesting services.

High school preparation. 16 units recommended. Recommended units include English 4, mathematics 3, social studies 2, science 2 and academic electives 2.

2011-2012 Annual costs. Tuition/fees: $7,380; $14,760 out-of-state. Room/board: $6,270. Books/supplies: $1,200.

Financial aid. Non-need-based: Scholarships awarded for academics, alumni affiliation, art, athletics, job skills, leadership, minority status, music/drama, ROTC, state residency.

Application procedures. Admission: Closing date 8/10. $35 fee. Application must be submitted on paper. Admission notification on a rolling basis. **Financial aid:** Priority date 5/1; no closing date. FAFSA, institutional form required. Applicants notified on a rolling basis starting 5/15.

Academics. Students in entry-level programming courses must own a laptop. **Special study options:** Accelerated study, combined bachelor's/graduate degree, cooperative education, distance learning, double major, ESL, honors, independent study, internships, student-designed major, study abroad, teacher certification program, weekend college. **Credit/placement by examination:** AP, CLEP, institutional tests. Maximum of 32 credit hours can be awarded under any combination of AP and CLEP examination credits. **Support services:** Learning center, remedial instruction, study skills assistance, tutoring, writing center.

Majors. Biology: General, biomedical sciences. **Business:** General, accounting, business admin, e-commerce, finance, marketing. **Communications:** Communications/speech/rhetoric. **Computer sciences:** General. **Education:** Early childhood, elementary, health, physical, secondary, special ed. **Engineering:** Chemical, civil, computer, electrical, mechanical. **English:** English lit. **Foreign languages:** General. **Health services:** Audiology/speech pathology, clinical lab science, EMT paramedic, medical radiologic technology/radiation therapy, nursing (RN), respiratory therapy technology. **History:** General. **Human services:** Social work. **Math:** Statistics. **Parks/recreation:** General. **Philosophy/religion:** Philosophy. **Physical sciences:** Atmospheric science, chemistry, geology, physics. **Protective services:** Criminal justice. **Psychology:** General. **Social sciences:** Anthropology, geography, political science, sociology. **Visual/performing arts:** Art, dramatic, music.

Most popular majors. Biology 6%, business/marketing 15%, education 12%, engineering/engineering technologies 7%, health sciences 24%, interdisciplinary studies 6%.

Computing on campus. 500 workstations in library, computer center, student center. Dormitories wired for high-speed internet access and linked to campus network. Commuter students can connect to campus network. Online course registration, online library, helpline available.

Student life. Freshman orientation: Mandatory, $75 fee. Preregistration for classes offered. **Housing:** Coed dorms, special housing for disabled, apartments, fraternity/sorority housing available. $150 deposit. **Activities:** Bands, choral groups, dance, drama, film society, literary magazine, music ensembles, musical theater, opera, radio station, student government, student newspaper, TV station.

Athletics. NCAA. **Intercollegiate:** Baseball M, basketball, cross-country, football (tackle) M, golf, soccer W, softball W, tennis, track and field, volleyball W. **Intramural:** Basketball, bowling, football (non-tackle), golf, racquetball, soccer, softball, table tennis, tennis, volleyball, water polo. **Team name:** Jaguars.

Student services. Adult student services, alcohol/substance abuse counseling, chaplain/spiritual director, career counseling, services for economically disadvantaged, student employment services, financial aid counseling, health services, minority student services, personal counseling, placement for graduates, veterans' counselor. **Physically disabled:** Services for visually, speech, hearing impaired.

Contact. E-mail: admiss@usouthal.edu
Phone: (251) 460-6141 Toll-free number: (800) 872-5247
Fax: (251) 460-7876
Norma Tanner, Director of Admissions, University of South Alabama, Meisler Hall, Suite 2500, Mobile, AL 36688-0002

University of West Alabama
Livingston, Alabama
www.uwa.edu   **CB code: 1737**

- Public 4-year university
- Residential campus in small town
- 2,066 degree-seeking undergraduates: 14% part-time, 60% women, 46% African American, 1% Hispanic American, 3% international
- 3,178 degree-seeking graduate students
- 49% of applicants admitted
- SAT or ACT (ACT writing optional) required
- 44% graduate within 6 years

General. Founded in 1835. Regionally accredited. **Degrees:** 199 bachelor's, 51 associate awarded; master's offered. **ROTC:** Army, Air Force. **Location:** 60 miles from Tuscaloosa; 35 miles from Meridian, MS. **Calendar:** Semester, limited summer session. **Full-time faculty:** 123 total; 79% have terminal degrees, 17% minority, 54% women. **Part-time faculty:** 149 total; 17% minority, 65% women. **Class size:** 56% < 20, 39% 20-39, 3% 40-49, 3% 50-99, less than 1% >100. **Special facilities:** Nature trail, herbarium, greenhouses, wildflower gardens, bluebird trail, lake, Center for the Study of the Black Belt, Black Belt museum, movie theater.

Freshman class profile. 937 applied, 455 admitted, 354 enrolled.

Mid 50% test scores			
		Out-of-state:	18%
ACT composite:	18-23	International:	2%
Return as sophomores:	56%		

Basis for selection. School achievement record and test scores most important.

High school preparation. 15 units required. Required units include English 3, mathematics 3, social studies 3, science 3 and academic electives 3.

2012-2013 Annual costs. Tuition/fees (projected): $6,918; $12,766 out-of-state. Room/board: $5,840. Personal expenses: $3,800.

2010-2011 Financial aid. Need-based: 324 full-time freshmen applied for aid; 295 were judged to have need; 292 of these received aid. Average need met was 31%. Average scholarship/grant was $4,658. 57% of total undergraduate aid awarded as scholarships/grants, 43% as loans/jobs. **Non-need-based:** Scholarships awarded for academics, alumni affiliation, art, athletics, leadership, music/drama, state residency.

Application procedures. Admission: No deadline. $50 fee. Admission notification on a rolling basis. **Financial aid:** Priority date 4/1; no closing date. FAFSA, institutional form required. Applicants notified on a rolling basis starting 4/1; must reply within 2 week(s) of notification.

Academics. Tutoring and counseling services are also available for online students. **Special study options:** Accelerated study, combined bachelor's/

graduate degree, cooperative education, distance learning, double major, dual enrollment of high school students, ESL, honors, independent study, internships, teacher certification program. **Credit/placement by examination:** AP, CLEP, SAT, ACT, institutional tests. 15 credit hours maximum toward associate degree, 30 toward bachelor's. **Support services:** Learning center, pre-admission summer program, reduced course load, remedial instruction, study skills assistance, tutoring, writing center.

Honors college/program. 22 ACT with 24 ACT English, reading or science reasoning, or 23 ACT math with appropriate placement scores required.

Majors. Biology: General, marine. **Business:** Accounting, business admin, management information systems. **Conservation:** General. **Education:** Early childhood, elementary, physical, secondary, special ed. **English:** English lit. **Health services:** Athletic training. **History:** General. **Math:** General. **Physical sciences:** Chemistry. **Psychology:** General. **Social sciences:** Sociology.

Most popular majors. Biology 7%, business/marketing 17%, education 39%, English 7%, history 6%.

Computing on campus. 310 workstations in dormitories, library, computer center, student center. Dormitories wired for high-speed internet access and linked to campus network. Commuter students can connect to campus network. Online course registration, online library, helpline, repair service, wireless network available.

Student life. Freshman orientation: Mandatory, $40 fee. Preregistration for classes offered. Two-day summer session. **Housing:** Guaranteed on-campus for all undergraduates. Coed dorms, single-sex dorms, apartments, wellness housing available. $100 partly refundable deposit, deadline 4/9. **Activities:** Bands, campus ministries, choral groups, dance, drama, international student organizations, music ensembles, musical theater, student government, student newspaper, TV station, campus outreach, Fellowship of Christian Athletes, student support services club, African-American cultural association, Baptist campus ministries, Wesley Foundation ministries.

Athletics. NCAA. **Intercollegiate:** Baseball M, basketball, cheerleading, cross-country, football (tackle) M, rodeo, soccer W, softball W, tennis, volleyball W. **Intramural:** Basketball, football (non-tackle), soccer, softball, table tennis, tennis, volleyball. **Team name:** Tigers.

Student services. Alcohol/substance abuse counseling, career counseling, student employment services, financial aid counseling, health services, on-campus daycare, personal counseling, placement for graduates, veterans' counselor. **Physically disabled:** Services for visually, hearing impaired.

Contact. E-mail: admissions@uwa.edu
Phone: (205) 652-3578 Toll-free number: (888) 636-8800
Fax: (205) 652-3708
Olivier Charles, Director of Admissions, University of West Alabama, Station 4, Livingston, AL 35470

Virginia College at Birmingham
Birmingham, Alabama
www.vc.edu
CB code: 2596

▸ For-profit 4-year technical college
▸ Commuter campus in very large city
▸ 1,768 degree-seeking undergraduates
▸ Interview required

General. Founded in 1975. Regionally accredited; also accredited by ACICS. **Degrees:** 139 bachelor's, 872 associate awarded; master's offered. **Calendar:** Quarter, extensive summer session. **Full-time faculty:** 91 total. **Part-time faculty:** 89 total. **Special facilities:** Full service restaurant and bakery operated by Culinary Institute.

Basis for selection. Open admission, but selective for some programs. High school record, interview and essay evaluated. **Home schooled:** Diploma and transcript required. **Learning Disabled:** Documentation for untimed testing required.

2011-2012 Annual costs. Tuition/fees: $21,900. Tuition is typical for full-time attendance for four quarters and depends on program, hours attempted, and other factors. Tuition includes textbooks and fees. Personal expenses: $100.

Application procedures. Admission: No deadline. $100 fee. Admission notification on a rolling basis. **Financial aid:** No deadline.

Academics. Special study options: Accelerated study, distance learning, independent study, internships. **Credit/placement by examination:** AP,

CLEP, institutional tests. 45 credit hours maximum toward associate degree. **Support services:** Learning center, study skills assistance, tutoring.

Majors. Business: Business admin. **Visual/performing arts:** Graphic design, interior design.

Computing on campus. 1,000 workstations in library, computer center. Online library, repair service available.

Student life. Freshman orientation: Mandatory. Preregistration for classes offered.

Student services. Career counseling, student employment services, financial aid counseling, placement for graduates, veterans' counselor.

Contact. Phone: (205) 802-1200 Fax: (205) 802-7045
Bevin Yeskevicz, Director of Admissions, Virginia College at Birmingham, 488 Palisades Boulevard, Birmingham, AL 35209

Virginia College at Huntsville
Huntsville, Alabama
www.vc.edu
CB code: 3451

▸ For-profit 4-year business and technical college
▸ Commuter campus in small city
▸ 750 undergraduates

General. Accredited by ACICS. **Degrees:** 23 bachelor's, 167 associate awarded. **Calendar:** Quarter. **Full-time faculty:** 25 total. **Part-time faculty:** 65 total.

Basis for selection. Open admission. Accuplacer or SAT/ACT used for placement. **Home schooled:** Transcript of courses and grades required.

2011-2012 Annual costs. Tuition/fees: $21,900. Tuition is typical for full-time attendance for four quarters and depends on program, hours attempted, and other factors. Tuition includes textbooks and fees. Personal expenses: $2,978.

Application procedures. Admission: No deadline. $100 fee. **Financial aid:** No deadline. FAFSA, institutional form required. Applicants notified on a rolling basis.

Academics. Special study options: Distance learning. **Credit/placement by examination:** AP, CLEP. **Support services:** Learning center, tutoring.

Majors. Computer sciences: LAN/WAN management, modeling/simulation, system admin. **Protective services:** Law enforcement admin.

Contact. E-mail: daryl.coleman@vc.edu
Phone: (256) 533-7387 Fax: (256) 533-7785
Daryl Coleman, Director of Admissions, Virginia College at Huntsville, 2800 Bob Wallace Avenue, Huntsville, AL 35805

Alaska

Alaska Bible College
Glennallen, Alaska
www.akbible.edu
CB code: 1237

- Private 4-year Bible college affiliated with nondenominational tradition
- Residential campus in rural community
- 29 degree-seeking undergraduates: 17% part-time, 38% women
- SAT or ACT, application essay required

General. Founded in 1966. Accredited by ABHE. **Degrees:** 7 bachelor's, 4 associate awarded. **Location:** 187 miles from Anchorage, 250 miles from Fairbanks. **Calendar:** Semester. **Full-time faculty:** 4 total; 25% have terminal degrees. **Part-time faculty:** 5 total. **Class size:** 100% < 20. **Special facilities:** Largest theological library collection in Alaska, Alaskan book collection.

Freshman class profile. 16 applied, 15 admitted, 15 enrolled.

Basis for selection. Open admission, but selective for some programs. Applicants considered on a case-by-case basis. References and indications of religious commitment most important, followed by school grade record. Test scores and extracurricular activities also considered. **Home schooled:** Transcript of courses and grades required. Applicants must have documentation of high school equivalence.

High school preparation. Recommended units include English 4, mathematics 4, social studies 4, history 4, science 4 and foreign language 2.

2012-2013 Annual costs. Tuition/fees (projected): $6,985. Room/board: $5,400. Books/supplies: $200.

2010-2011 Financial aid. Need-based: 5 full-time freshmen applied for aid; 2 were judged to have need; 1 of these received aid. Average need met was 63%. Average scholarship/grant was $2,750. **Non-need-based:** Scholarships awarded for academics.

Application procedures. Admission: Closing date 7/1 (postmark date). $35 fee. Application must be submitted on paper. Admission notification on a rolling basis beginning on or about 7/1. Must reply by 7/15. **Financial aid:** Priority date 5/30, closing date 7/1. FAFSA, institutional form required. Applicants notified by 8/1; must reply within 2 week(s) of notification.

Academics. Special study options: Double major, dual enrollment of high school students, independent study, internships. **Credit/placement by examination:** AP, CLEP, institutional tests. **Support services:** Reduced course load, remedial instruction, tutoring.

Majors. Theology: Bible.

Computing on campus. 11 workstations in library, computer center, student center. Dormitories linked to campus network. Online library, repair service, wireless network available.

Student life. Freshman orientation: Mandatory. Preregistration for classes offered. 4-5 day program held immediately before beginning of school year. **Policies:** Religious observance required. **Housing:** Guaranteed on-campus for freshmen. Single-sex dorms, apartments, wellness housing available. $150 fully refundable deposit, deadline 7/1. **Activities:** Radio station, student government.

Student services. Chaplain/spiritual director, financial aid counseling, health services, personal counseling.

Contact. E-mail: info@akbible.edu
Phone: (907) 822-3201 ext. 224 Toll-free number: (800) 478-7884
Fax: (907) 822-5027
Nikki Palmer, Director of Admissions, Alaska Bible College, Box 289, Glennallen, AK 99588-0289

Alaska Pacific University
Anchorage, Alaska
www.alaskapacific.edu
CB code: 4201

- Private 4-year university and liberal arts college affiliated with United Methodist Church
- Commuter campus in large city

General. Founded in 1957. Regionally accredited. **Calendar:** Semester.

Annual costs/financial aid. Tuition/fees (2011-2012): $27,160. Room/board: $9,300. Books/supplies: $1,000. Personal expenses: $1,000. Need-based financial aid available to full-time and part-time students.

Contact. Phone: (907) 564-8248
Director of Admissions, 4101 University Drive, Anchorage, AK 99508-3051

Charter College
Anchorage, Alaska
www.chartercollege.edu
CB code: 3453

- For-profit 4-year junior and technical college
- Commuter campus in large city

General. Accredited by ACICS. **Calendar:** Differs by program.

Annual costs/financial aid. Books/supplies: $700. Need-based financial aid available to full-time and part-time students.

Contact. Phone: (907) 277-1000
Admissions Director, 2221 East Northern Lights Boulevard, Suite 120, Anchorage, AK 99508

University of Alaska Anchorage
Anchorage, Alaska
www.uaa.alaska.edu
CB member
CB code: 4896

- Public 4-year university
- Commuter campus in large city
- 13,492 degree-seeking undergraduates: 44% part-time, 58% women, 4% African American, 7% Asian American, 7% Hispanic American, 13% Native American
- 1,008 degree-seeking graduate students
- 80% of applicants admitted

General. Founded in 1954. Regionally accredited. **Degrees:** 1,001 bachelor's, 756 associate awarded; master's offered. **ROTC:** Army, Air Force. **Location:** 3 miles from downtown. **Calendar:** Semester, extensive summer session. **Full-time faculty:** 667 total; 50% have terminal degrees, 14% minority, 52% women. **Part-time faculty:** 707 total; 2% have terminal degrees, 10% minority, 59% women. **Class size:** 53% < 20, 38% 20-39, 6% 40-49, 4% 50-99, less than 1% >100. **Special facilities:** Institutes of environment and natural resources, circumpolar health studies, North Pacific fisheries observer training center, planetarium and visualization theater.

Freshman class profile. 4,312 applied, 3,433 admitted, 2,017 enrolled.

Mid 50% test scores			
SAT critical reading:	470-620	GPA 3.0-3.49:	28%
SAT math:	450-570	GPA 2.0-2.99:	46%
ACT composite:	18-25	Rank in top quarter:	29%
GPA 3.75 or higher:	10%	Rank in top tenth:	11%
GPA 3.50-3.74:	11%	Return as sophomores:	73%
		Out-of-state:	8%

Basis for selection. For acceptance into bachelor's program, applicants must have high school GPA of at least 2.5 and either SAT, ACT or UAA-approved test scores; high school graduates with GPAs between 2.0 and 2.49 will be admitted on probation. Alternatively, applicants must have successful completion of the GED and either SAT, ACT or UAA-approved test scores. Interviews and essays vary according to program. **Home schooled:** Transcript of courses and grades required. **Learning Disabled:** Make an appointment with DSS, provide current diagnostic and evaluative reports, and request reasonable accommodations that are supported by documentation.

High school preparation. Requirements vary by program.

2011-2012 Annual costs. Tuition/fees: $5,396; $17,036 out-of-state. Room/board: $9,427. Books/supplies: $1,214. Personal expenses: $1,523.

Financial aid. Non-need-based: Scholarships awarded for academics, athletics.

Application procedures. Admission: Closing date 7/1. $50 fee, may be waived for applicants with need. Application must be submitted online. Admission notification on a rolling basis. Freshman early admission plan allows students to apply early but wait as long as 2 years to enroll. **Financial aid:** Priority date 4/1, closing date 8/1. FAFSA, institutional form required. Applicants notified on a rolling basis starting 3/15; must reply within 4 week(s) of notification.

Academics. Many programs to assist nontraditional and/or at-risk students for college success. **Special study options:** Combined bachelor's/graduate degree, cooperative education, cross-registration, distance learning, double major, dual enrollment of high school students, ESL, exchange student, honors, independent study, internships, liberal arts/career combination, semester at sea, student-designed major, study abroad, teacher certification program, Washington semester. **Credit/placement by examination:** AP, CLEP, IB, institutional tests. Credit by examination is considered non-resident credit, and non-resident credit policies apply. **Support services:** Learning center, reduced course load, remedial instruction, study skills assistance, tutoring, writing center.

Honors college/program. Students must submit a completed University Honors College application, high school transcript, SAT or ACT scores, essay on personal goals, and a completed reference form from two teachers.

Majors. Biology: General. **Business:** Accounting, business admin, construction management, entrepreneurial studies, finance, hospitality admin, hospitality/recreation, logistics, management information systems, management science, marketing, restaurant/food services. **Communications:** Journalism. **Computer sciences:** Computer science. **Education:** Early childhood, elementary. **Engineering:** General, civil. **English:** English lit. **Foreign languages:** General, French, German, Japanese, Russian, Spanish. **History:** General. **Human services:** General. **Liberal arts:** Arts/sciences. **Math:** General. **Parks/recreation:** Health/fitness. **Philosophy/religion:** Philosophy. **Physical sciences:** Chemistry. **Psychology:** General. **Social sciences:** Anthropology, economics, political science, sociology. **Visual/performing arts:** Art, dramatic, music, studio arts. **Work/family studies:** General.

Most popular majors. Engineering/engineering technologies 6%, health sciences 14%, history 18%, psychology 9%, social sciences 6%.

Computing on campus. Dormitories wired for high-speed internet access and linked to campus network. Commuter students can connect to campus network. Online course registration, online library, helpline, repair service, student web hosting, wireless network available.

Student life. Freshman orientation: Available. Preregistration for classes offered. **Housing:** Coed dorms, special housing for disabled, apartments, wellness housing available. $200 fully refundable deposit. Separate floors for Alaska natives studying engineering, nursing students, honor students, language and cultures, first-year students under age 20, healthy lifestyle, quiet lifestyle, WWAMI program, Far East exchange program. **Activities:** Jazz band, campus ministries, choral groups, dance, drama, film society, international student organizations, literary magazine, music ensembles, Model UN, musical theater, opera, radio station, student government, student newspaper, Alaska Native student organization, African American student associations, Baha'i club, College Republicans, Korean Campus Crusade for Christ, Intervarsity Christian Fellowship, disability awareness club, Student Organization Against Racism.

Athletics. NCAA. **Intercollegiate:** Basketball, cross-country, gymnastics W, ice hockey M, skiing, track and field, volleyball W. **Intramural:** Basketball, ice hockey, soccer, volleyball. **Team name:** Seawolves.

Student services. Adult student services, alcohol/substance abuse counseling, career counseling, services for economically disadvantaged, student employment services, financial aid counseling, health services, legal services, minority student services, on-campus daycare, personal counseling, veterans' counselor. **Physically disabled:** Services for visually, speech, hearing impaired.

Contact. E-mail: enroll@uaa.alaska.edu
Phone: (907) 786-1480 Fax: (907) 786-4888
Cecile Mitchell, Director of Admissions, University of Alaska Anchorage, PO Box 141629, Anchorage, AK 99514-1629

University of Alaska Fairbanks

Fairbanks, Alaska   **CB member**
www.uaf.edu   **CB code: 4866**

- Public 4-year university
- Commuter campus in small city

- 5,896 degree-seeking undergraduates: 37% part-time, 57% women, 2% African American, 1% Asian American, 5% Hispanic American, 15% Native American, 1% international
- 1,156 degree-seeking graduate students
- 79% of applicants admitted
- 31% graduate within 6 years; 29% enter graduate study

General. Founded in 1917. Regionally accredited. Public broadcasting TV and radio stations headquartered on UAF campus; extensive ski and multiuse trail system located on campus; University of the Arctic participating institution. **Degrees:** 523 bachelor's, 233 associate awarded; master's, doctoral offered. **ROTC:** Army. **Location:** 4 miles from downtown. **Calendar:** Semester, limited summer session. **Full-time faculty:** 344 total; 58% have terminal degrees, 20% minority, 43% women. **Part-time faculty:** 698 total; 41% have terminal degrees, 14% minority, 47% women. **Class size:** 65% < 20, 28% 20-39, 3% 40-49, 3% 50-99, 1% >100. **Special facilities:** Museum of the North, geophysical institute, bioscience library, institute of arctic biology, arctic region supercomputing center, international arctic research center, boreal forest research range, Alaska native language center, institute of marine sciences, institute of northern engineering, rocketry research range, agricultural and forestry experiment station, botanical garden.

Freshman class profile. 2,034 applied, 1,610 admitted, 1,072 enrolled.

Mid 50% test scores			
SAT critical reading:	460-590	GPA 2.0-2.99:	31%
SAT math:	450-590	Rank in top quarter:	39%
SAT writing:	430-550	Rank in top tenth:	17%
ACT composite:	19-25	End year in good standing:	68%
GPA 3.75 or higher:	22%	Return as sophomores:	76%
GPA 3.50-3.74:	14%	Out-of-state:	9%
GPA 3.0-3.49:	30%	Live on campus:	43%
		International:	1%

Basis for selection. GED not accepted. Minimum 2.5 GPA in 16 core classes; minimum 3.0 overall GPA or at least 2.5 overall GPA and ACT score of at least 18 or SAT score of at least 1290 for bachelor's degree-seeking students. Open admissions for associate degree applicants over age 18. Some students may be required to take ASSET and/or COMPASS tests for additional course placement. Students with high school GPA of 2.5 or higher but less than 3.0 must have ACT composite score of at least 18 or total SAT score of at least 1290 for entry into baccalaureate program. Students with high school GPA below 3.0 and ACT composite score below 18 or total SAT score below 1290 are admitted as pre-majors. Regardless of GPA, ACT and SAT scores are used for placement in English and math classes. **Home schooled:** Transcript of courses and grades, state high school equivalency certificate required. Students who have completed a state-recognized program and have a valid high school diploma may be admitted to a baccalaureate program. All others admitted via individual review by the UAF admissions office. **Learning Disabled:** Disability services program provides assistance for students with documented disabilities.

High school preparation. College-preparatory program required. 16 units required. Required and recommended units include English 4, mathematics 3, social studies 3, science 3 (laboratory 1) and foreign language 2. Mathematics should include 3 from algebra, geometry and trigonometry, precalculus or calculus.

2012-2013 Annual costs. Tuition/fees (projected): $5,907; $18,357 out-of-state. Room/board: $6,960. Books/supplies: $1,400. Personal expenses: $2,250.

Financial aid. Non-need-based: Scholarships awarded for academics, art, athletics, music/drama, state residency.

Application procedures. Admission: Priority date 2/15; deadline 7/1 (postmark date). $50 fee, may be waived for applicants with need. Admission notification by 9/1. Admission notification on a rolling basis beginning on or about 1/1. Students must have completed 75% of their high school academic core curriculum and have a 3.0 GPA. ACT or SAT (including Writing portions) required prior to enrolling at UAF. Upon receipt of high school diploma, students may change major from General Studies to another program offered at UAF. **Financial aid:** Priority date 2/15, closing date 7/1. FAFSA required. Applicants notified on a rolling basis starting 3/1; must reply within 2 week(s) of notification.

Academics. Student support services program (federally funded) for students with qualified at-risk status. **Special study options:** Accelerated study, combined bachelor's/graduate degree, cooperative education, distance learning, double major, dual enrollment of high school students, ESL, exchange student, external degree, honors, independent study, internships, semester at sea, student-designed major, study abroad, teacher certification program. Legislative aide intern program; excellent undergraduate research opportunities. **Credit/placement by examination:** AP, CLEP, IB, institutional tests. Credit awarded for AP scores of 3 or greater, International Baccalaureate scores of 4 or better, CLEP, DANTES-DSST, or local credit by exam. Credit by exam is considered neither UAF residence credit nor part of semester

course load for classification as full-time student. For bachelor's degree, students required to complete a minimum of 30 residence credits;15 residence credits required for associate degree. **Support services:** Learning center, preadmission summer program, remedial instruction, study skills assistance, tutoring, writing center.

Majors. Area/ethnic studies: Native American, Russian/Slavic. **Biology:** General. **Business:** Accounting, business admin. **Communications:** Communications/speech/rhetoric, journalism. **Computer sciences:** General, computer science. **Conservation:** Fisheries, forestry, management/policy, wildlife/wilderness. **Education:** Elementary, music. **Engineering:** Civil, computer, electrical, geological, mechanical, mining, petroleum. **English:** English lit. **Foreign languages:** General, Japanese, linguistics, Native American. **History:** General. **Human services:** Community org/advocacy, social work. **Liberal arts:** Arts/sciences. **Math:** General. **Philosophy/religion:** Philosophy. **Physical sciences:** Chemistry, geology, physics. **Protective services:** Criminal justice. **Psychology:** General. **Social sciences:** Anthropology, economics, geography, political science, sociology. **Visual/performing arts:** Art, dramatic, film/cinema/video, music, music performance, theater design. **Work/family studies:** Child development.

Most popular majors. Biology 8%, business/marketing 9%, education 6%, engineering/engineering technologies 17%, psychology 9%, social sciences 10%.

Computing on campus. 125 workstations in dormitories, library, computer center. Dormitories wired for high-speed internet access and linked to campus network. Commuter students can connect to campus network. Online course registration, online library, helpline, repair service, student web hosting, wireless network available.

Student life. Freshman orientation: Mandatory, $75 fee. Preregistration for classes offered. Held over three days immediately before start of classes each fall and spring term. **Policies:** Student organizations must be officially recognized on an annual basis by the Student Activities Office. **Housing:** Coed dorms, special housing for disabled, apartments, wellness housing available. $350 partly refundable deposit, deadline 8/1. Alaska native cultural housing. **Activities:** Bands, campus ministries, choral groups, dance, drama, international student organizations, literary magazine, music ensembles, Model UN, radio station, student government, student newspaper, symphony orchestra, TV station, Muslim student association, UAF Zen club, Inu-Yupiaq dance group, UAF Coalition for Peace and Justice, American Indian science and engineering society, Alaska native social workers association, Circle K UAF chapter, Filipino-American society of UAF.

Athletics. NCAA. **Intercollegiate:** Basketball, cross-country, ice hockey M, rifle, skiing, swimming W, volleyball W. **Intramural:** Basketball, bowling, football (non-tackle), soccer, volleyball. **Team name:** Nanooks.

Student services. Alcohol/substance abuse counseling, chaplain/spiritual director, career counseling, services for economically disadvantaged, student employment services, financial aid counseling, health services, legal services, minority student services, personal counseling, placement for graduates, women's services. **Physically disabled:** Services for visually, speech, hearing impaired.

Contact. E-mail: admissions@uaf.edu
Phone: (907) 474-7500 Toll-free number: (800) 478-1823
Fax: (907) 474-5379
Mike Earnest, Director of Admissions, University of Alaska Fairbanks, PO Box 757480, Fairbanks, AK 99775-7480

University of Alaska Southeast

Juneau, Alaska   **CB member**
www.uas.alaska.edu   **CB code: 4897**

- Public 4-year university and liberal arts college
- Commuter campus in large town
- 1,641 degree-seeking undergraduates: 50% part-time, 66% women, 1% African American, 2% Asian American, 3% Hispanic American, 12% Native American
- 341 degree-seeking graduate students
- 62% of applicants admitted

General. Founded in 1972. Regionally accredited. All University of Alaska Southeast campuses (Juneau, Ketchikan, Sitka) are accessible only by ferry or air. **Degrees:** 24 bachelor's, 34 associate awarded; master's offered. **Location:** 11 miles from downtown Juneau. **Calendar:** Semester, limited summer session. **Full-time faculty:** 101 total; 48% have terminal degrees, 7% minority, 48% women. **Part-time faculty:** 131 total; 8% have terminal degrees, 7% minority, 58% women. **Class size:** 70% < 20, 27% 20-39, less than 1% 40-49, 2% 50-99. **Special facilities:** Ice field, glacier, national forest, raptor center.

Freshman class profile. 510 applied, 316 admitted, 270 enrolled.

Mid 50% test scores			
SAT critical reading:	420-550	GPA 3.0-3.49:	26%
SAT math:	410-560	GPA 2.0-2.99:	45%
SAT writing:	390-540	Rank in top quarter:	23%
GPA 3.75 or higher:	7%	Rank in top tenth:	9%
GPA 3.50-3.74:	14%	Return as sophomores:	57%
		Out-of-state:	7%

Basis for selection. High school record most important. Students not meeting BA requirements counseled to AA or certificate program with possibility of later transfer to BA program. Some BA programs admit students as pre-majors and upon satisfying prerequisites may be admitted to major. Financial statement and immunization records required of international applicants, as well as statement of educational equivalency written in English. **Home schooled:** Student must graduate from accredited home school program or obtain GED.

High school preparation. College-preparatory program recommended.

2011-2012 Annual costs. Tuition/fees: $5,477; $17,117 out-of-state. Upper division per-credit-hour charge, $187. Room/board: $7,100. Books/supplies: $1,253. Personal expenses: $1,575.

2010-2011 Financial aid. Need-based: 176 full-time freshmen applied for aid; 112 were judged to have need; 109 of these received aid. Average need met was 66%. Average scholarship/grant was $5,341; average loan $5,678. 47% of total undergraduate aid awarded as scholarships/grants, 53% as loans/jobs. **Non-need-based:** Awarded to 106 full-time undergraduates, including 40 freshmen. Scholarships awarded for academics, job skills, leadership, music/drama, state residency. **Additional information:** Transfer, continuing, and freshman scholarship deadline March 1.

Application procedures. Admission: Closing date 8/1 (receipt date). $50 fee, may be waived for applicants with need. Admission notification on a rolling basis beginning on or about 9/1. Housing deposit required if letter of cancellation provided prior to July 1. **Financial aid:** Priority date 4/15; no closing date. FAFSA required. Applicants notified on a rolling basis starting 3/1; must reply within 3 week(s) of notification.

Academics. Special study options: Combined bachelor's/graduate degree, distance learning, double major, dual enrollment of high school students, exchange student, independent study, internships, student-designed major, study abroad, teacher certification program. **Credit/placement by examination:** AP, CLEP, institutional tests. 15 credit hours maximum toward associate degree, 30 toward bachelor's. **Support services:** Learning center, preadmission summer program, remedial instruction, study skills assistance, tutoring, writing center.

Majors. Biology: General, marine. **Business:** General, accounting, management science, marketing. **Communications:** Communications/speech/rhetoric. **Conservation:** Environmental science, environmental studies. **Education:** Elementary. **English:** English lit. **Liberal arts:** Arts/sciences. **Math:** General. **Social sciences:** General, political science. **Visual/performing arts:** Art.

Most popular majors. Biology 15%, business/marketing 21%, education 12%, interdisciplinary studies 7%, liberal arts 16%, mathematics 7%, social sciences 12%.

Computing on campus. 225 workstations in dormitories, library, computer center, student center. Dormitories wired for high-speed internet access and linked to campus network. Commuter students can connect to campus network. Online course registration, online library, helpline, repair service, student web hosting, wireless network available.

Student life. Freshman orientation: Mandatory, $75 fee. Preregistration for classes offered. Three-day orientation includes outdoor experiences. **Housing:** Coed dorms, special housing for disabled, apartments available. $300 fully refundable deposit, deadline 9/1. **Activities:** Campus ministries, choral groups, dance, drama, international student organizations, radio station, student government, student newspaper, global connections club, Amnesty International, LBGI organization, English club, Wooch Een Native student organization.

Athletics. Intramural: Basketball, softball, tennis, volleyball, weight lifting.

Student services. Adult student services, alcohol/substance abuse counseling, career counseling, student employment services, financial aid counseling, health services, minority student services, personal counseling, placement for graduates, veterans' counselor, women's services. **Physically disabled:** Services for visually, hearing impaired.

Contact. E-mail: admissions@uas.alaska.edu
Phone: (907) 796-6100 Toll-free number: (877) 465-4827
Fax: (907) 796-6365
Joe Nelson, Admissions Director, University of Alaska Southeast, 11120 Glacier Highway, Juneau, AK 99801-8681

Arizona

American Indian College of the Assemblies of God
Phoenix, Arizona
www.aicag.edu   CB code: 2597

♦ Private 4-year Bible and teachers college affiliated with Assemblies of God
♦ Residential campus in very large city
♦ 85 degree-seeking undergraduates
♦ SAT or ACT (ACT writing optional), application essay required

General. Founded in 1957. Regionally accredited. **Degrees:** 6 bachelor's, 7 associate awarded. **Location:** 15 miles from downtown. **Calendar:** Semester. **Full-time faculty:** 7 total. **Part-time faculty:** 15 total.

Freshman class profile.

Out-of-state:	45%	Live on campus:	78%

Basis for selection. Applicants must show Christian commitment, willingness to abide by Student Handbook, favorable reference from home pastor, and ability to complete college-level instruction through SAT/ACT score and transcripts. ACT/SAT requirement may be waived by approval of Academic Dean when other evidence of student ability available. **Home schooled:** Favorable pastoral reference required.

2011-2012 Annual costs. Tuition/fees: $10,500. Room/board: $6,202. Books/supplies: $500. Personal expenses: $2,570.

Application procedures. Admission: No deadline. No application fee. Admission notification on a rolling basis. Students admitted with proper paperwork through first week of semester. **Financial aid:** Priority date 4/1; no closing date. FAFSA required. Applicants notified on a rolling basis starting 7/15.

Academics. Special study options: Accelerated study, double major, ESL, independent study, internships, liberal arts/career combination, teacher certification program. **Credit/placement by examination:** AP, CLEP, institutional tests. **Support services:** Learning center, pre-admission summer program, reduced course load, remedial instruction, study skills assistance, tutoring.

Majors. Education: Elementary. **Theology:** Theology.

Most popular majors. Education 27%, theological studies 73%.

Computing on campus. 39 workstations in library, computer center, student center.

Student life. Freshman orientation: Mandatory. Preregistration for classes offered. Pre-registration orientation session. **Policies:** Religious observance required. **Housing:** Guaranteed on-campus for freshmen. Single-sex dorms, special housing for disabled available. Pets allowed in dorm rooms. **Activities:** Choral groups, music ensembles, student government, associated student body, campus missions fellowship.

Athletics. Intercollegiate: Basketball. **Intramural:** Basketball. **Team name:** Warriors.

Student services. Adult student services, chaplain/spiritual director, career counseling, student employment services, financial aid counseling, personal counseling, placement for graduates.

Contact. E-mail: aicadm@aicag.edu
Phone: (602) 943-335 ext. 232 Toll-free number: (800) 933-3828 ext. 232
Fax: (602) 943-8299
Sandra Gonzales, Director of Enrollment Management, American Indian College of the Assemblies of God, 10020 North 15th Avenue, Phoenix, AZ 85021-2199

Argosy University: Online
Phoenix, Arizona
www.online.argosy.edu

♦ For-profit 4-year virtual university
♦ Very large city
♦ 8,125 degree-seeking undergraduates

General. Regionally accredited. **Degrees:** 201 bachelor's awarded; master's, doctoral offered. **Calendar:** Differs by program. **Full-time faculty:** 104 total. **Part-time faculty:** 1,670 total.

Basis for selection. Open admission.

2011-2012 Annual costs. Tuition/fees: $16,200.

Application procedures. Admission: Closing date 9/13. $50 fee. **Financial aid:** No deadline.

Academics. Credit/placement by examination: AP, CLEP.

Majors. Business: Business admin. **Liberal arts:** Arts/sciences. **Protective services:** Law enforcement admin. **Psychology:** General.

Contact. Phone: (866) 427-4679
Matt Gavlik, Senior Director of Admissions, Argosy University: Online, 2233 West Dunlap Avenue, Phoenix, AZ 85021

Argosy University: Phoenix
Phoenix, Arizona
www.argosy.edu/phoenix

♦ For-profit 4-year university
♦ Very large city
♦ 180 degree-seeking undergraduates

General. Regionally accredited. **Degrees:** 14 bachelor's awarded; master's, professional, doctoral offered. **Calendar:** Differs by program. **Full-time faculty:** 18 total. **Part-time faculty:** 69 total.

Basis for selection. Open admission.

2011-2012 Annual costs. Tuition/fees: $17,962.

Application procedures. Admission: Closing date 9/13. $50 fee. **Financial aid:** No deadline.

Academics. Credit/placement by examination: AP, CLEP.

Majors. Business: Business admin. **Liberal arts:** Arts/sciences. **Protective services:** Law enforcement admin. **Psychology:** General.

Contact. Phone: (602) 216-2600
Lori Smith, Senior Director of Admissions, Argosy University: Phoenix, 2233 West Dunlap Avenue, Phoenix, AZ 85021

Arizona Christian University
Phoenix, Arizona
www.arizonachristian.edu   CB code: 4736

♦ Private 4-year university and liberal arts college affiliated with nondenominational tradition
♦ Residential campus in very large city
♦ 486 degree-seeking undergraduates
♦ 57% of applicants admitted
♦ SAT or ACT (ACT writing optional), application essay required
♦ 51% graduate within 6 years

General. Founded in 1960. Regionally accredited. **Degrees:** 79 bachelor's, 1 associate awarded. **ROTC:** Air Force. **Calendar:** Semester, limited summer session. **Full-time faculty:** 17 total. **Part-time faculty:** 60 total.

Freshman class profile. 293 applied, 166 admitted, 100 enrolled.

Mid 50% test scores		SAT math:	450-560
SAT critical reading:	460-570	ACT composite:	19-24

Basis for selection. School achievement record and recommendations very important. Written testimony of conversion experience required for admission. **Home schooled:** Statement describing home school structure and mission, transcript of courses and grades required.

High school preparation. Recommended units include English 4, mathematics 3, social studies 3, history 2, science 2, foreign language 2 and computer science 1.

2011-2012 Annual costs. Tuition/fees: $18,868. Room/board: $7,374. Books/supplies: $1,168. Personal expenses: $6,115.

Financial aid. Non-need-based: Scholarships awarded for academics, alumni affiliation, athletics, leadership, minority status, music/drama, religious affiliation.

Application procedures. Admission: Priority date 4/1; deadline 8/15. $30 fee, may be waived for applicants with need. Admission notification on a rolling basis. **Financial aid:** Priority date 3/15, closing date 8/31. FAFSA, institutional form required. Applicants notified on a rolling basis.

Academics. Off-campus, noncredit Christian internship work required during each semester. **Special study options:** Double major, dual enrollment of high school students, independent study, internships, teacher certification program. **Credit/placement by examination:** AP, CLEP, SAT, ACT, institutional tests. 30 credit hours maximum toward bachelor's degree. **Support services:** Reduced course load, remedial instruction, study skills assistance, tutoring.

Majors. Education: Elementary, music, secondary. **Health services:** Health behavior. **Philosophy/religion:** Religion. **Psychology:** Family. **Theology:** Bible, missionary, religious ed, sacred music, theology.

Computing on campus. 60 workstations in dormitories, library, computer center. Dormitories wired for high-speed internet access and linked to campus network. Online library, wireless network available.

Student life. Freshman orientation: Mandatory. Preregistration for classes offered. **Policies:** Religious observance required. **Housing:** Guaranteed on-campus for freshmen. Single-sex dorms, special housing for disabled, apartments available. $100 nonrefundable deposit, deadline 5/1. **Activities:** Bands, campus ministries, choral groups, drama, music ensembles, musical theater, student government, student newspaper, symphony orchestra.

Athletics. NAIA, NCCAA. **Intercollegiate:** Baseball M, basketball, cross-country, golf, soccer, volleyball W. **Intramural:** Football (tackle) M, table tennis, tennis, volleyball. **Team name:** Firestorm.

Student services. Chaplain/spiritual director, student employment services, financial aid counseling, health services, personal counseling, veterans' counselor, women's services.

Contact. E-mail: admissions@arizonachristian.edu
Phone: (602) 386-5300 ext. 100 Toll-free number: (800) 247-2697
Fax: (602) 404-2159
Nate Bradley, Director of Admissions, Arizona Christian University, 2625 East Cactus Road, Phoenix, AZ 85032-7042

Arizona State University
Tempe, Arizona
www.asu.edu

CB member
CB code: 4007

- Public 4-year university
- Commuter campus in very large city
- 58,184 degree-seeking undergraduates: 13% part-time, 50% women, 5% African American, 6% Asian American, 19% Hispanic American, 2% Native American, 3% international
- 13,039 degree-seeking graduate students
- 89% of applicants admitted
- 58% graduate within 6 years; 15% enter graduate study

General. Founded in 1885. Regionally accredited. Four sites: downtown Phoenix, Tempe, Polytechnic campus in Mesa, West campus in northwest Phoenix. **Degrees:** 12,194 bachelor's awarded; master's, professional, doctoral offered. **ROTC:** Army, Naval, Air Force. **Calendar:** Semester, extensive summer session. **Full-time faculty:** 2,513 total; 87% have terminal degrees, 22% minority, 43% women. **Part-time faculty:** 185 total; 66% have terminal degrees, 13% minority, 50% women. **Class size:** 39% < 20, 38% 20-39, 6% 40-49, 12% 50-99, 5% >100. **Special facilities:** Biodesign institute, global institute of sustainability, arboretum, creative writing center, museums, galleries.

Freshman class profile. 29,722 applied, 26,425 admitted, 9,254 enrolled.

Mid 50% test scores			
SAT critical reading:	480-610	Rank in top quarter:	58%
SAT math:	490-630	Rank in top tenth:	28%
ACT composite:	21-27	End year in good standing:	91%
GPA 3.75 or higher:	29%	Return as sophomores:	84%
GPA 3.50-3.74:	20%	Out-of-state:	32%
GPA 3.0-3.49:	33%	Live on campus:	70%
GPA 2.0-2.99:	18%	International:	4%

Basis for selection. Applicants must successfully complete competency requirement and must meet at least one of the following: top 25% in high school graduating class, 3.0 GPA in competency courses, 22 ACT (24 nonresidents), 1040 SAT Reasoning (1110 nonresidents). Some colleges/schools have higher requirements. SAT or ACT recommended. SAT/ACT required for honors college and for some majors. Auditions, interviews and/or portfolios required in certain majors. **Home schooled:** Evaluation of Laboratory Science Courses, Affidavit of Completion of Secondary School Education, and SAT/ACT required.

High school preparation. College-preparatory program recommended. 16 units required. Required units include English 4, mathematics 4, social studies 1, history 1, science 3 (laboratory 3) and foreign language 2. One unit fine arts required; 2 foreign language units must be from same language. Additional requirements vary by program.

2011-2012 Annual costs. Tuition/fees: $9,720; $22,319 out-of-state. Room/board: $11,436. Books/supplies: $1,290. Personal expenses: $2,052.

2010-2011 Financial aid. Need-based: 6,088 full-time freshmen applied for aid; 4,995 were judged to have need; 4,995 of these received aid. Average need met was 70%. Average scholarship/grant was $9,760; average loan $2,865. 56% of total undergraduate aid awarded as scholarships/grants, 44% as loans/jobs. **Non-need-based:** Awarded to 7,570 full-time undergraduates, including 2,212 freshmen. Scholarships awarded for academics, art, athletics, leadership, music/drama, ROTC.

Application procedures. Admission: $50 fee ($65 out-of-state), may be waived for applicants with need. Admission notification on a rolling basis beginning on or about 9/15. Must reply by May 1 or within 2 week(s) if notified thereafter. **Financial aid:** Priority date 3/1; no closing date. FAFSA required. Applicants notified on a rolling basis.

Academics. Special study options: Accelerated study, combined bachelor's/graduate degree, cooperative education, distance learning, double major, ESL, honors, independent study, internships, liberal arts/career combination, semester at sea, student-designed major, study abroad, teacher certification program, Washington semester. Work-study, continuing education, programs for high school students. **Credit/placement by examination:** AP, CLEP, IB, SAT, ACT, institutional tests. 60 credit hours maximum toward bachelor's degree. **Support services:** Learning center, study skills assistance, tutoring, writing center.

Honors college/program. Separate application required. High school GPA (Arizona Board of Regents GPA based on 16 competency courses), class rank, SAT/ACT, talents that contribute to leadership and community service considered. Over 1,000 freshmen admitted in Fall 2011.

Majors. Architecture: Architecture, interior, landscape, urban/community planning. **Area/ethnic studies:** General, African-American, American, Asian, Asian-American, Chicano/Hispanic-American/Latino, Native American, women's. **Biology:** General, biochemistry, conservation, microbiology, molecular. **Business:** Accounting, business admin, construction management, finance, marketing, nonprofit/public, operations, purchasing, real estate, tourism/travel. **Communications:** Communications/speech/rhetoric, journalism. **Communications technology:** Graphics. **Computer sciences:** General, computer science, informatics, information systems, systems analysis. **Education:** Early childhood, elementary, music, secondary, special ed. **Engineering:** General, aerospace, biomedical, chemical, civil, computer, construction, electrical, environmental, industrial, materials, mechanical, software. **English:** English lit, technical writing. **Foreign languages:** General, East Asian, French, German, Italian, Russian, Spanish. **General:** Business. **Health services:** Clinical lab science, communication disorders, music therapy, nursing (RN). **History:** General. **Human services:** Public policy, social work. **Liberal arts:** Arts/sciences. **Math:** General, applied, computational, statistics. **Parks/recreation:** General, exercise sciences. **Philosophy/religion:** General, Judaic, philosophy, religion. **Physical sciences:** General, chemistry, geology, physics. **Protective services:** Law enforcement admin. **Psychology:** General, applied. **Social sciences:** General, anthropology, economics, geography, political science, sociology, urban studies. **Visual/performing arts:** General, art, dance, design, dramatic, film/cinema/video, graphic design, industrial design, music, music performance, music theory/composition. **Work/family studies:** Family resources, food/nutrition.

Most popular majors. Biology 6%, business/marketing 16%, communications/journalism 7%, education 8%, engineering/engineering technologies

6%, interdisciplinary studies 8%, psychology 6%, social sciences 8%, visual/performing arts 6%.

Computing on campus. 4,250 workstations in dormitories, library, computer center, student center. Dormitories wired for high-speed internet access and linked to campus network. Commuter students can connect to campus network. Online course registration, online library, helpline, repair service, student web hosting, wireless network available.

Student life. Freshman orientation: Mandatory. Preregistration for classes offered. One-day programs held between March and August. **Policies:** First-time freshmen expected to live on-campus. **Housing:** Guaranteed on-campus for freshmen. Coed dorms, apartments, fraternity/sorority housing available. Honors housing, freshmen housing, residential colleges available. **Activities:** Bands, campus ministries, choral groups, dance, drama, film society, international student organizations, literary magazine, music ensembles, Model UN, musical theater, radio station, student government, student newspaper, symphony orchestra, TV station, over 800 organizations available.

Athletics. NCAA. **Intercollegiate:** Baseball M, basketball, cross-country, diving, football (tackle) M, golf, gymnastics W, soccer W, softball W, swimming, tennis W, track and field, volleyball W, water polo M, wrestling M. **Intramural:** Badminton, basketball, bowling, football (non-tackle), racquetball, soccer, table tennis, tennis, volleyball. **Team name:** Sun Devils.

Student services. Adult student services, career counseling, student employment services, financial aid counseling, health services, legal services, minority student services, on-campus daycare, personal counseling, placement for graduates, veterans' counselor. **Physically disabled:** Services for visually, speech, hearing impaired.

Contact. E-mail: admissions@asu.edu
Phone: (480) 965-7788 Fax: (480) 965-3610
David Burge, Executive Director of Undergraduate Admissions, Arizona State University, Box 870112, Tempe, AZ 85287-0112

Art Institute of Phoenix
Phoenix, Arizona
www.artinstitutes.edu/phoenix   **CB code: 4003**

- For-profit 3-year culinary school and visual arts college
- Residential campus in very large city
- 1,200 degree-seeking undergraduates
- Application essay, interview required

General. Accredited by ACICS. **Degrees:** 193 bachelor's, 79 associate awarded. **Calendar:** Quarter, extensive summer session. **Full-time faculty:** 50 total. **Part-time faculty:** 50 total. **Special facilities:** Culinary labs, video studio, computer labs, editing suites, sound lab, herb garden.

Basis for selection. High school diploma or GED required; high school GPA considered.

2011-2012 Annual costs. Tuition/fees: $22,002. Room/board: $8,628.

Application procedures. Admission: Closing date 11/11 (receipt date). $50 fee. Admission notification on a rolling basis. **Financial aid:** No deadline. FAFSA required.

Academics. Special study options: Distance learning, independent study, internships. **Credit/placement by examination:** AP, CLEP, IB, SAT, ACT, institutional tests. **Support services:** Learning center, reduced course load, remedial instruction, study skills assistance, tutoring.

Majors. BACHELOR'S. Business: Apparel. **Communications technology:** Animation/special effects. **Computer sciences:** Computer graphics, web page design, webmaster. **Visual/performing arts:** Cinematography, commercial photography, commercial/advertising art, graphic design, interior design. **ASSOCIATE. Visual/performing arts:** Graphic design.

Most popular majors. Health sciences 92%, personal/culinary services 8%.

Student life. Freshman orientation: Mandatory. Preregistration for classes offered. **Housing:** Apartments available. $150 fully refundable deposit, deadline 10/13. **Activities:** Film society.

Student services. Adult student services, career counseling, student employment services, financial aid counseling, personal counseling, placement for graduates.

Contact. E-mail: aipxadm@aii.edu
Phone: (602) 331-7500 Toll-free number: (800) 474-2479
Fax: (602) 331-5301
Stacey Till, Senior Director of Admissions, Art Institute of Phoenix, 2233 West Dunlap Avenue, Phoenix, AZ 85021-2859

Art Institute of Tucson
Tucson, Arizona
www.artinstitutes.edu/tucson   **CB code: 7551**

- For-profit 4-year culinary school and visual arts college
- Commuter campus in very large city
- 374 degree-seeking undergraduates
- Application essay, interview required

General. Accredited by ACICS. Selected online courses offered through consortium agreement with the Art Institute of Pittsburg online division. **Degrees:** 22 bachelor's, 20 associate awarded. **Location:** 115 miles from Phoenix. **Calendar:** Quarter, limited summer session. **Full-time faculty:** 10 total. **Part-time faculty:** 35 total. **Special facilities:** Fully equipped fashion design lab with industrial sewing machines, sergers, dress forms, computer pattern making software; fully stocked interior design resource room; MAC lab; PC lab; digital video editing suite; green screen lab; audio lab; video production, audio, and film editing suites; two kitchens and student-run dining labs.

Basis for selection. GPA, school record, and talent most important. Applicants to Media Arts & Animation and Game Art & Design bachelor's programs must submit a portfolio. Artwork portfolio required. **Home schooled:** Transcript of courses and grades, interview required.

Application procedures. Admission: No deadline. $50 fee. Application must be submitted on paper. Admission notification on a rolling basis.

Academics. Special study options: Accelerated study. **Credit/placement by examination:** AP, CLEP. **Support services:** Tutoring.

Majors. Business: Fashion. **Communications:** Advertising. **Communications technology:** Animation/special effects. **Computer sciences:** Web page design. **Visual/performing arts:** Cinematography, fashion design, graphic design, interior design, photography.

Computing on campus. Online library available.

Student life. Freshman orientation: Mandatory, $100 fee. Preregistration for classes offered. **Housing:** Apartments available. **Activities:** Film society, international student organizations, American Society of Interior Designers student chapter, fashion club.

Student services. Career counseling, student employment services, financial aid counseling, personal counseling, placement for graduates, veterans' counselor.

Contact. Phone: (520) 881-2900 Toll-free number: (866) 690-8850
Fax: (520) 881-4794
Brande McClellan, Senior Director of Admissions, Art Institute of Tucson, 5099 East Grant Road, #100, Tucson, AZ 85712

Brown Mackie College: Tucson
Tucson, Arizona
www.brownmackie.edu   **CB code: 3458**

- For-profit 4-year career college
- Commuter campus in very large city
- 800 degree-seeking undergraduates
- Interview required

General. Accredited by ACICS. **Degrees:** 10 bachelor's, 140 associate awarded. **Location:** 117 miles from Phoenix. **Calendar:** Differs by program, extensive summer session. **Full-time faculty:** 20 total; 25% have terminal degrees, 55% minority, 50% women. **Part-time faculty:** 19 total; 21% have terminal degrees, 63% minority, 74% women. **Special facilities:** Labs for medical, surgical technology, computer networking, and occupational therapy assistant programs.

Basis for selection. Open admission, but selective for some programs. Additional admissions criteria for Occupational Therapy Assistant program. **Home schooled:** Transcript of courses and grades, state high school equivalency certificate, interview required.

2011-2012 Annual costs. Books/supplies: $1,275.

Application procedures. Admission: No deadline. No application fee. Admission notification on a rolling basis.

Academics. Special study options: Internships, liberal arts/career combination. **Credit/placement by examination:** AP, CLEP. **Support services:** Learning center, remedial instruction, study skills assistance, tutoring, writing center.

Majors. Business: Accounting, business admin. **Computer sciences:** Computer science.

Computing on campus. 24 workstations in library. Online library, wireless network available.

Student life. Freshman orientation: Mandatory. Preregistration for classes offered. Conducted prior to first class.

Student services. Career counseling, financial aid counseling, personal counseling, placement for graduates, veterans' counselor.

Contact. E-mail: stklein@brownmackie.edu
Phone: (520) 391-3300 Fax: (520) 319-3495
Stacy Klein, Senior Director of Admissions, Brown Mackie College: Tucson, 4585 East Speedway Boulevard, Tucson, AZ 85712

Chamberlain College of Nursing: Phoenix
Phoenix, Arizona
www.chamberlain.edu   **CB code: 5768**

- For-profit 4-year nursing college
- Large city
- 406 degree-seeking undergraduates
- SAT or ACT required

General. Degrees: 69 bachelor's awarded. **Calendar:** Semester. **Full-time faculty:** 15 total. **Part-time faculty:** 52 total.

Basis for selection. Test scores, GPA, class rank very important.

2011-2012 Annual costs. Tuition/fees: $15,600. Books/supplies: $1,400. Personal expenses: $2,218.

Application procedures. Admission: No deadline. $95 fee. Admission notification on a rolling basis. **Financial aid:** No deadline.

Academics. Special study options: Accelerated study, distance learning. **Credit/placement by examination:** AP, CLEP.

Majors. Health services: Nursing (RN).

Contact. Chamberlain College of Nursing: Phoenix, 2149 West Dunlap Avenue, Phoenix, AZ 85021

Collins College
Phoenix, Arizona
www.collinscollege.edu   **CB code: 2174**

- For-profit 4-year visual arts and technical college
- Commuter campus in small city
- 907 full-time, degree-seeking undergraduates
- Application essay, interview required

General. Founded in 1978. Accredited by ACICS, ACCSC. Satellite campus in west Phoenix. **Degrees:** 197 bachelor's, 127 associate awarded. **Location:** 5 miles from Phoenix. **Calendar:** Differs by program, extensive summer session. **Full-time faculty:** 24 total. **Part-time faculty:** 78 total. **Special facilities:** Photography and video studio with 2 full edit bays.

Basis for selection. Open admission.

Application procedures. Admission: No deadline. $50 fee. Admission notification on a rolling basis.

Academics. Special study options: Liberal arts/career combination. **Credit/placement by examination:** AP, CLEP. **Support services:** Tutoring.

Majors. Communications technology: Animation/special effects. **Computer sciences:** LAN/WAN management, system admin, web page design. **Visual/performing arts:** Commercial/advertising art.

Student life. Freshman orientation: Mandatory. Preregistration for classes offered. **Activities:** TV station.

Student services. Career counseling, student employment services, placement for graduates.

Contact. Phone: (480) 966-3000 Toll-free number: (888) 574-6777 Fax: (480) 902-0663
Admissions and Marketing, Collins College, 4750 South 44th Place, Phoenix, AZ 85040

DeVry University: Phoenix
Phoenix, Arizona
www.devry.edu   **CB code: 4277**

- For-profit 4-year university
- Commuter campus in large city
- 1,362 degree-seeking undergraduates
- Interview required

General. Founded in 1967. Regionally accredited. Additional locations: Glendale, Mesa, Northeast Phoenix, Henderson (NV). **Degrees:** 205 bachelor's, 43 associate awarded; master's offered. **ROTC:** Air Force. **Calendar:** Semester, extensive summer session. **Full-time faculty:** 34 total. **Part-time faculty:** 99 total.

Basis for selection. Applicants must have high school diploma or equivalent or a degree from accredited postsecondary institution, demonstrate proficiency in basic college-level skills through SAT or ACT scores or institution-administered placement exams, and be at least 17 years of age on the first day of classes. New students may enter at beginning of any semester. CPT accepted.

High school preparation. College-preparatory program recommended. Required units include mathematics 1.

2011-2012 Annual costs. Tuition/fees: $15,294. Books/supplies: $1,310. Personal expenses: $3,574.

Financial aid. All financial aid based on need.

Application procedures. Admission: No deadline. $50 fee. Admission notification on a rolling basis. **Financial aid:** No deadline. FAFSA required. Applicants notified on a rolling basis.

Academics. Special study options: Accelerated study, distance learning. **Credit/placement by examination:** AP, CLEP, institutional tests. **Support services:** Learning center, remedial instruction, tutoring.

Majors. Business: Business admin. **Computer sciences:** Networking, systems analysis, web page design. **Engineering:** Software. **Health services:** Clinical lab science.

Most popular majors. Business/marketing 40%, computer/information sciences 25%, engineering/engineering technologies 34%.

Computing on campus. 436 workstations in library, computer center. Online course registration, online library, helpline available.

Student life. Freshman orientation: Mandatory. Preregistration for classes offered. **Activities:** Institute of Electrical and Electronics Engineers, Campus Crusaders for Christ, travel club, Sigma Beta Delta, computer society, inventors club, sports compact car club, Tau Alpha Pi, hockey league.

Athletics. Intramural: Field hockey M, golf, softball.

Student services. Career counseling, student employment services, financial aid counseling, placement for graduates, veterans' counselor. **Physically disabled:** Services for visually, hearing impaired.

Contact. E-mail: admissions@phx.devry.edu
Phone: (602) 870-9201 Toll-free number: (800) 528-0250
Fax: (602) 331-1494
Jerry Driskill, Director of Admissions, DeVry University: Phoenix, 2149 West Dunlap Avenue, Phoenix, AZ 85021-2995

Dunlap-Stone University
Phoenix, Arizona
www.dunlap-stone.edu

- For-profit 4-year virtual career college
- Commuter campus in very large city

- 50 degree-seeking undergraduates
- 65% graduate within 6 years; 20% enter graduate study

General. Accredited by DETC. **Degrees:** 8 bachelor's awarded. **Calendar:** Differs by program, extensive summer session. **Part-time faculty:** 50 total; 20% have terminal degrees.

Freshman class profile.

End year in good standing:	95%	Return as sophomores:	95%

Basis for selection. Open admission. **Learning Disabled:** Learning disability accommodations reviewed on case by case basis.

2011-2012 Annual costs. Tuition/fees: $9,300.

Application procedures. Admission: No deadline. $50 fee. Admission notification on a rolling basis.

Academics. Special study options: Accelerated study, distance learning. **Credit/placement by examination:** AP, CLEP, IB. 15 credit hours maximum toward associate degree, 20 toward bachelor's.

Majors. Business: International.

Computing on campus. PC or laptop required. Online library, helpline available.

Student life. Activities: Student newspaper.

Contact. E-mail: info@dunlap-stone.edu
Phone: (602) 648-5750 Toll-free number: (800) 474-8013
Fax: (602) 648-5755
Caulyne Barron, Dunlap-Stone University, 11225 North 28th Drive Suite B201, Phoenix, AZ 85029

Embry-Riddle Aeronautical University: Prescott Campus
Prescott, Arizona
www.embryriddle.edu

CB member
CB code: 4305

- Private 4-year university
- Residential campus in large town
- 1,655 degree-seeking undergraduates: 5% part-time, 18% women, 2% African American, 5% Asian American, 11% Hispanic American, 1% Native American, 4% international
- 51 degree-seeking graduate students
- 82% of applicants admitted
- SAT or ACT (ACT writing optional) required
- 57% graduate within 6 years; 24% enter graduate study

General. Founded in 1978. Regionally accredited. Eastern residential campus in Daytona Beach, Florida. More than 170 continuing education centers located throughout the United States and Europe. **Degrees:** 347 bachelor's awarded; master's offered. **ROTC:** Army, Air Force. **Location:** 100 miles from Phoenix. **Calendar:** Semester, extensive summer session. **Full-time faculty:** 85 total; 75% have terminal degrees, 14% minority, 19% women. **Part-time faculty:** 42 total; 19% have terminal degrees, 12% minority, 43% women. **Class size:** 38% < 20, 52% 20-39, 7% 40-49, 3% 50-99. **Special facilities:** Machine vision laboratory, supersonic wind tunnel, fleet of 40 aircraft, engineering and technical center, aviation safety center.

Freshman class profile. 1,319 applied, 1,086 admitted, 349 enrolled.

Mid 50% test scores			
SAT critical reading:	500-600	Rank in top quarter:	61%
SAT math:	520-580	Rank in top tenth:	26%
ACT composite:	23-28	Return as sophomores:	78%
GPA 3.75 or higher:	39%	Out-of-state:	88%
GPA 3.50-3.74:	21%	Live on campus:	97%
GPA 3.0-3.49:	26%	International:	4%
GPA 2.0-2.99:	14%	Fraternities:	3%
		Sororities:	2%

Basis for selection. High school GPA, class rank, test scores most important. Specific requirements vary by degree program. Flight program applicants must pass medical examination for Class I or II Federal Aviation Administration Medical Certificate at least 60 calendar days prior to enrollment. Interview and essay recommended.

High school preparation. College-preparatory program recommended. 16 units required; 18 recommended. Required and recommended units include English 4, mathematics 3-4, social studies 2, history 1, science 2-3 (laboratory 2-3), foreign language 2 and academic electives 2.

2012-2013 Annual costs. Tuition/fees (projected): $30,420. Room/board: $9,340. Books/supplies: $1,400. Personal expenses: $1,504.

2011-2012 Financial aid. Need-based: 304 full-time freshmen applied for aid; 262 were judged to have need; 261 of these received aid. Average scholarship/grant was $11,392; average loan $3,459. 56% of total undergraduate aid awarded as scholarships/grants, 44% as loans/jobs. **Non-need-based:** Awarded to 74 full-time undergraduates, including 23 freshmen. Scholarships awarded for academics, alumni affiliation, athletics, leadership, ROTC.

Application procedures. Admission: Priority date 1/15; no deadline. $50 fee, may be waived for applicants with need. Admission notification on a rolling basis beginning on or about 11/1. Must reply by May 1 or within 2 week(s) if notified thereafter. Application closing date 60 days prior to start of term. Early application encouraged; available facilities limit enrollment in some programs. **Financial aid:** No deadline. FAFSA required. Applicants notified on a rolling basis starting 3/1; must reply within 4 week(s) of notification.

Academics. Special study options: Accelerated study, cooperative education, distance learning, double major, dual enrollment of high school students, ESL, honors, independent study, internships, study abroad. Flight training. **Credit/placement by examination:** AP, CLEP, IB, SAT, ACT, institutional tests. 15 credit hours maximum toward associate degree, 30 toward bachelor's. **Support services:** Remedial instruction, study skills assistance, tutoring, writing center.

Majors. Engineering: General, aerospace, computer, electrical, software. **Physical sciences:** Physics. **Social sciences:** International relations.

Most popular majors. Business/marketing 8%, engineering/engineering technologies 32%, social sciences 14%, trade and industry 35%.

Computing on campus. 475 workstations in library, computer center, student center. Dormitories wired for high-speed internet access and linked to campus network. Commuter students can connect to campus network. Online library, helpline, wireless network available.

Student life. Freshman orientation: Available. Preregistration for classes offered. Held in August. **Policies:** Free tutoring available. **Housing:** Guaranteed on-campus for freshmen. Coed dorms, apartments available. $250 fully refundable deposit, deadline 6/15. **Activities:** Campus ministries, international student organizations, music ensembles, radio station, student government, student newspaper, Rangers, student activities association, Angel Flight/Silver Wings, residence halls association, Arnold Air Society, Golden Eagles flight team, Greeks, aerobatic club, Japanese anime/manga.

Athletics. NAIA. **Intercollegiate:** Soccer, volleyball W, wrestling M. **Intramural:** Basketball, bowling, football (non-tackle), racquetball, soccer, softball, table tennis, tennis, volleyball, weight lifting W. **Team name:** Eagles.

Student services. Adult student services, career counseling, student employment services, financial aid counseling, health services, personal counseling, placement for graduates, veterans' counselor, women's services. **Physically disabled:** Services for visually, speech, hearing impaired.

Contact. E-mail: pradmit@erau.edu
Phone: (928) 777-6600 Toll-free number: (800) 888-3728
Fax: (928) 777-6606
Bryan Dougherty, Director of Admissions, Embry-Riddle Aeronautical University: Prescott Campus, 3700 Willow Creek Road, Prescott, AZ 86301-3720

Grand Canyon University
Phoenix, Arizona
www.gcu.edu/clgbrd

CB code: 4331

- For-profit 4-year university
- Commuter campus in very large city
- 3,855 full-time, degree-seeking undergraduates
- 15,495 graduate students
- 37% of applicants admitted

General. Founded in 1949. Regionally accredited. **Degrees:** 1,575 bachelor's awarded; master's, doctoral offered. **ROTC:** Army. **Calendar:** Semester, limited summer session. **Full-time faculty:** 188 total; 19% have terminal degrees, 14% minority, 53% women. **Part-time faculty:** 1,529 total; 8% minority, 63% women. **Class size:** 66% < 20, 33% 20-39, less than 1% 40-49, less than 1% 50-99. **Special facilities:** Cadaver laboratory.

Freshman class profile. 7,136 applied, 2,628 admitted, 2,122 enrolled.

Basis for selection. Admissions based on graduation from high school (or GED) and academic potential demonstrated by 2.25 GPA or standardized test scores. Any student willing to uphold the University's vision and mission and who is open to possibility of spiritual as well as intellectual development is encouraged to apply. SAT or ACT recommended. **Home schooled:** Transcript of courses and grades required.

High school preparation. Recommended units include English 4, mathematics 4, social studies 2, science 3 (laboratory 1) and foreign language 1.

2011-2012 Annual costs. Tuition/fees: $16,900. Room/board: $12,400. Books/supplies: $1,200. Personal expenses: $2,400.

2011-2012 Financial aid. Non-need-based: Scholarships awarded for academics, alumni affiliation, art, athletics, leadership, minority status, music/drama, religious affiliation, ROTC, state residency.

Application procedures. Admission: No deadline. No application fee. Admission notification on a rolling basis. **Financial aid:** No deadline. FAFSA required. Applicants notified on a rolling basis.

Academics. Special study options: Accelerated study, combined bachelor's/graduate degree, cooperative education, distance learning, double major, dual enrollment of high school students, exchange student, honors, independent study, internships, liberal arts/career combination, study abroad, teacher certification program. **Credit/placement by examination:** AP, CLEP, IB, institutional tests. 30 credit hours maximum toward bachelor's degree. **Support services:** Learning center, reduced course load, remedial instruction, study skills assistance, tutoring, writing center.

Majors. Biology: General, exercise physiology. **Business:** Accounting, business admin, entrepreneurial studies, finance, information resources management, marketing. **Communications:** Broadcast journalism, communications/speech/rhetoric, journalism. **Education:** Biology, chemistry, drama/dance, early childhood, elementary, English, mathematics, music, physical, secondary, special ed. **English:** English lit. **Health services:** Athletic training, clinical lab science, facilities admin, health care admin, nursing (RN), respiratory therapy technology, substance abuse counseling. **History:** General. **Parks/recreation:** Sports admin. **Philosophy/religion:** Christian. **Protective services:** Disaster management, firefighting, forensics, law enforcement admin. **Social sciences:** Sociology. **Theology:** Bible, pastoral counseling, youth ministry. **Visual/performing arts:** Cinematography, digital arts, dramatic, piano/keyboard, voice/opera.

Most popular majors. Business/marketing 16%, education 11%, health sciences 58%.

Computing on campus. 95 workstations in library, computer center, student center. Dormitories wired for high-speed internet access and linked to campus network. Commuter students can connect to campus network. Online course registration, online library, helpline, wireless network available.

Student life. Freshman orientation: Mandatory. Preregistration for classes offered. Held the week before start of Fall semester. **Policies:** No alcohol, drugs, weapons, drug paraphernelia, spice or candles allowed. Smoking allowed outdoors only. **Housing:** Guaranteed on-campus for all undergraduates. Coed dorms, special housing for disabled, apartments available. **Activities:** Bands, campus ministries, choral groups, dance, drama, international student organizations, literary magazine, music ensembles, musical theater, student government, student newspaper, international student organizations, honors organizations, professional clubs, Christ-purposed relationships, ethnic diversity in Christ, wildlife society, student health advocates, law society, Latino student organization, Adopt-A-Block.

Athletics. NCAA. **Intercollegiate:** Baseball M, basketball, cheerleading, cross-country, diving, golf, soccer, softball W, swimming, tennis, track and field, volleyball, wrestling M. **Intramural:** Basketball, bowling, football (non-tackle), softball, volleyball. **Team name:** Lopes.

Student services. Adult student services, alcohol/substance abuse counseling, chaplain/spiritual director, career counseling, student employment services, financial aid counseling, health services, on-campus daycare, personal counseling, placement for graduates, veterans' counselor, women's services. **Physically disabled:** Services for visually, speech, hearing impaired.

Contact. E-mail: campusadmissions@gcu.edu
Phone: (877) 533-7017 Toll-free number: (888) 261-2393
Fax: (602) 589-2017
Kim Naig, Director of Admissions, Grand Canyon University, 3300 West Camelback Road, Phoenix, AZ 85017-8562

Harrison Middleton University
Tempe, Arizona
www.hmu.edu

⯈ For-profit 4-year liberal arts college
⯈ Small city

General. Accredited by DETC. **Location:** 12 miles from Phoenix. **Calendar:** Differs by program.

Annual costs/financial aid. Undergraduates complete one course at a time and pay $1,000 per 4-credit course. Payment, which may be made in four installments of $250 each over a 4-month period, must be made in full prior to enrolling in a subsequent course.

Contact. Phone: (877) 248-6724
Registrar, 1105 East Broadway Road, Tempe, AZ 85282

International Baptist College
Chandler, Arizona
www.ibconline.edu   **CB code: 5461**

⯈ Private 4-year Bible and seminary college affiliated with Baptist faith
⯈ Very large city
⯈ 58 degree-seeking undergraduates: 19% part-time, 55% women
⯈ 9 degree-seeking graduate students
⯈ Application essay required

General. Regionally accredited; also accredited by TRACS. **Degrees:** 10 bachelor's awarded; master's, doctoral offered. **Location:** 20 miles from Phoenix. **Calendar:** 4-1-4, limited summer session. **Full-time faculty:** 5 total. **Part-time faculty:** 15 total.

Freshman class profile. 12 enrolled.

Basis for selection. Open admission, but selective for some programs.

2011-2012 Annual costs. Tuition/fees: $10,450. Room/board: $5,350. Books/supplies: $1,000.

Application procedures. Admission: No deadline. $35 fee. Admission notification on a rolling basis. **Financial aid:** Priority date 8/18; no closing date.

Academics. Credit/placement by examination: AP, CLEP.

Majors. Theology: Missionary, pastoral counseling, religious ed, sacred music.

Most popular majors. Education 30%, theological studies 70%.

Student life. Freshman orientation: Mandatory. Preregistration for classes offered. **Housing:** Single-sex dorms available. **Activities:** Campus ministries, choral groups, drama, music ensembles, student newspaper.

Contact. E-mail: info@ibconline.edu
Phone: (480) 245-7903 Toll-free number: (800) 422-4858 ext. 7970
Fax: (480) 245-7908
Nicole Teachout, Director of Public Relations, International Baptist College, 2211 West Germann Road, Chandler, AZ 85286

ITT Technical Institute: Tempe
Tempe, Arizona
www.itt-tech.edu

⯈ For-profit 4-year technical college
⯈ Commuter campus in small city
⯈ 829 undergraduates
⯈ Interview required

General. Accredited by ACICS. **Degrees:** 72 bachelor's, 170 associate awarded. **Calendar:** Quarter. **Full-time faculty:** 10 total. **Part-time faculty:** 56 total.

Basis for selection. Satisfactory scores from on-site tests in English and math required.

2011-2012 Annual costs. Estimated costs as of July 2011: per-credit-hour charge, $493, depending upon level and course of study; academic fee, $200. Certain programs of study require purchase of tools, which could cost an additional $100 to $500. All costs are subject to change.

Application procedures. Admission: No deadline. No application fee. Admission notification on a rolling basis.

Academics. Credit/placement by examination: AP, CLEP.

Majors. Business: Accounting/business management, business admin, construction management, e-commerce. **Communications technology:** Animation/special effects. **Computer sciences:** Networking, security. **Protective services:** Law enforcement admin.

Contact. Phone: (602) 437-7500 Toll-free number: (800) 879-4881 Fax: (602) 267-8727
Gene McWhorter, Director of Recruitment, ITT Technical Institute: Tempe, 5005 South Wendler Drive, Tempe, AZ 85282

ITT Technical Institute: Tucson
Tucson, Arizona
www.itt-tech.edu   **CB code: 3598**

- For-profit 4-year technical college
- Commuter campus in large city
- 521 undergraduates
- Interview required

General. Founded in 1984. Accredited by ACICS. Classes begin in March, June, September and December. **Degrees:** 45 bachelor's, 119 associate awarded. **Calendar:** Quarter, extensive summer session. **Full-time faculty:** 10 total. **Part-time faculty:** 24 total.

Basis for selection. Satisfactory scores on institutional tests in English and math required.

2011-2012 Annual costs. Estimated costs as of July 2011: per-credit-hour charge, $493, depending upon level and course of study; academic fee, $200. Certain programs of study require purchase of tools, which could cost an additional $100 to $500. All costs are subject to change.

Application procedures. Admission: No deadline. No application fee. Admission notification on a rolling basis. **Financial aid:** No deadline. FAFSA, institutional form required. Applicants notified on a rolling basis.

Academics. Credit/placement by examination: AP, CLEP. **Support services:** Learning center, tutoring.

Majors. Business: Business admin, construction management, e-commerce. **Communications technology:** Animation/special effects. **Computer sciences:** Networking, security. **Protective services:** Law enforcement admin. **Visual/performing arts:** Game design.

Computing on campus. Online library available.

Student life. Freshman orientation: Available. Preregistration for classes offered.

Student services. Career counseling, student employment services, placement for graduates.

Contact. Phone: (520) 408-7488 Toll-free number: (800) 950-2944
Linda Lemken, Director of Recruitment, ITT Technical Institute: Tucson, 1455 West River Road, Tucson, AZ 85704

Northcentral University
Prescott Valley, Arizona
www.ncu.edu   **CB code: 3883**

- For-profit 4-year virtual university
- Commuter campus in large town
- 458 degree-seeking undergraduates: 66% part-time, 59% women, 2% African American, 1% Asian American
- 9,204 degree-seeking graduate students

General. Regionally accredited. All courses and programs offered via distance education. **Degrees:** 104 bachelor's awarded; master's, doctoral offered. **Location:** 12 miles from Prescott, 92 miles from Phoenix. **Calendar:** Differs by program, extensive summer session. **Full-time faculty:** 8 total. **Part-time faculty:** 411 total.

Basis for selection. Open admission.

2012-2013 Annual costs. Tuition/fees: $11,910.

Application procedures. Admission: No deadline. $75 fee. Application must be submitted online. Admission notification on a rolling basis. **Financial aid:** No deadline. FAFSA required. Applicants notified on a rolling basis; must reply within 4 week(s) of notification.

Academics. Programs are online, with one-to-one faculty mentoring and no physical residency required. Marriage and Family Therapy's practicum, internship require client contact and supervision. **Special study options:** Distance learning. **Credit/placement by examination:** AP, CLEP, IB. **Support services:** Reduced course load, writing center.

Majors. Business: General, accounting, business admin, e-commerce, international, management science, marketing. **Computer sciences:** General. **Health services:** Health care admin. **Human services:** General. **Protective services:** Homeland security, law enforcement admin. **Psychology:** General.

Most popular majors. Business/marketing 88%, education 6%, psychology 6%.

Computing on campus. Online course registration, online library, helpline available.

Student life. Freshman orientation: Available. Preregistration for classes offered.

Student services. Adult student services, financial aid counseling.

Contact. E-mail: admissions@ncu.edu
Phone: (866) 776-0331 Toll-free number: (866) 776-0331
Fax: (928) 541-7817
Bob Hanks, Director of Admissions, Northcentral University, 8667 East Hartford Drive, Scottsdale, AZ 85255

Northern Arizona University
Flagstaff, Arizona   **CB member**
www.nau.edu   **CB code: 4006**

- Public 4-year university
- Residential campus in small city
- 20,648 degree-seeking undergraduates: 15% part-time, 58% women, 3% African American, 2% Asian American, 17% Hispanic American, 4% Native American, 4% international
- 4,476 degree-seeking graduate students
- 65% of applicants admitted
- 52% graduate within 6 years

General. Founded in 1899. Regionally accredited. Additional 34 sites across Arizona and online. **Degrees:** 4,020 bachelor's awarded; master's, professional, doctoral offered. **ROTC:** Army, Air Force. **Location:** 140 miles from Phoenix. **Calendar:** Semester, extensive summer session. **Class size:** 32% < 20, 42% 20-39, 12% 40-49, 12% 50-99, 3% >100. **Special facilities:** 400-acre forest, observatory, skydome.

Freshman class profile. 31,995 applied, 20,727 admitted, 3,872 enrolled.

Mid 50% test scores			
SAT critical reading:	470-590	GPA 2.0-2.99:	19%
SAT math:	480-590	Rank in top quarter:	48%
SAT writing:	460-570	Rank in top tenth:	19%
ACT composite:	20-25	Return as sophomores:	72%
GPA 3.75 or higher:	30%	Out-of-state:	33%
GPA 3.50-3.74:	16%	Live on campus:	87%
GPA 3.0-3.49:	35%	International:	3%

Basis for selection. Applicants will be considered with one of the following: 1) 3.0 GPA or top 25% class rank with no deficiencies in required college preparatory courses; 2) 2.5 core GPA or top 50% class rank with no more than one deficiency in any two subjects in the college reparatory courses. Students with a combination of math and lab science deficiencies are not admissible. Audition required of music, music education majors. **Home schooled:** 22 ACT or 1040 SAT required for Arizona residents. 24 ACT or 1110 SAT required for non-residents. SAT scores are exclusive of writing.

High school preparation. College-preparatory program required. 16 units required. Required units include English 4, mathematics 4, social studies 1,

history 1, science 3 (laboratory 3), foreign language 2 and visual/performing arts 1.

2011-2012 Annual costs. Tuition/fees: $8,830; $21,184 out-of-state. Room/board: $8,474.

2010-2011 Financial aid. Need-based: 3,272 full-time freshmen applied for aid; 2,453 were judged to have need; 2,363 of these received aid. Average need met was 64%. Average scholarship/grant was $7,664; average loan $3,216. 48% of total undergraduate aid awarded as scholarships/grants, 52% as loans/jobs. **Non-need-based:** Awarded to 6,434 full-time undergraduates, including 1,879 freshmen. Scholarships awarded for academics, alumni affiliation, art, athletics, leadership, minority status, music/drama, ROTC, state residency. **Additional information:** Guaranteed gift aid for 4 years.

Application procedures. Admission: Priority date 3/1; no deadline. $25 fee, may be waived for applicants with need. Admission notification on a rolling basis. **Financial aid:** Priority date 2/14; no closing date. FAFSA required. Applicants notified on a rolling basis starting 3/15.

Academics. Special study options: Accelerated study, cooperative education, distance learning, double major, dual enrollment of high school students, ESL, exchange student, honors, independent study, internships, study abroad, teacher certification program. **Credit/placement by examination:** AP, CLEP, IB, SAT, ACT, institutional tests. 60 credit hours maximum toward bachelor's degree. **Support services:** Learning center, pre-admission summer program, reduced course load, remedial instruction, study skills assistance, tutoring, writing center.

Honors college/program. 29 ACT or 1290 SAT (exclusive of writing) or rank in top 5% of high school class required.

Majors. Area/ethnic studies: Native American, women's. **Biology:** General, biomedical sciences, microbiology. **Business:** Accounting, business admin, construction management, fashion, finance, hospitality admin, management information systems, managerial economics, marketing. **Communications:** Advertising, journalism, public relations, radio/TV. **Computer sciences:** Computer science, systems analysis. **Conservation:** Environmental science, environmental studies, forest sciences. **Education:** Early childhood, elementary, music, secondary, special ed. **Engineering:** Civil, electrical, environmental, mechanical. **English:** English lit, rhetoric/composition. **Foreign languages:** General, Spanish. **Health services:** Athletic training, dental hygiene, nursing (RN). **History:** General. **Human services:** Social work. **Liberal arts:** Arts/sciences. **Math:** General. **Parks/recreation:** General, exercise sciences. **Philosophy/religion:** Philosophy. **Physical sciences:** Astronomy, chemistry, geology, physics. **Psychology:** General. **Social sciences:** Anthropology, criminology, geography, international relations, political science, sociology, U.S. government. **Visual/performing arts:** Art, design, dramatic, interior design, music, music performance, photography.

Most popular majors. Business/marketing 18%, communications/journalism 6%, education 16%, health sciences 9%, liberal arts 9%, social sciences 8%.

Computing on campus. 1,600 workstations in dormitories, library, computer center, student center. Dormitories wired for high-speed internet access and linked to campus network. Commuter students can connect to campus network. Online course registration, online library, helpline, repair service, student web hosting, wireless network available.

Student life. Freshman orientation: Mandatory. Preregistration for classes offered. Two-day session held in June and July. Enrollment deposit of $325 must be paid prior to registering for orientation session. **Policies:** All new student organizations must submit roster of at least five student members, a full-time faculty or staff member willing to be organization adviser, and organization constitution or governing document. **Housing:** Guaranteed on-campus for freshmen. Coed dorms, single-sex dorms, special housing for disabled, apartments, fraternity/sorority housing available. $100 partly refundable deposit, deadline 4/1. Honor halls, floors for students 21 years of age and older available. **Activities:** Bands, campus ministries, choral groups, dance, drama, international student organizations, literary magazine, music ensembles, musical theater, opera, radio station, student government, student newspaper, symphony orchestra, TV station, Catholic Newman club, Christian Challenge, Native American Church of Northern Arizona University, Younglife, Arizona Students Count, People Representing Individuals and Sexual Minorities, black student union, Chinese student and scholar association, Kayettes, Blue Key honor society.

Athletics. NCAA. **Intercollegiate:** Basketball, cheerleading, cross-country, diving W, football (tackle) M, golf W, soccer W, swimming W, tennis, track and field, volleyball W. **Intramural:** Basketball, football (non-tackle), racquetball, soccer, volleyball, weight lifting. **Team name:** Lumberjacks.

Student services. Alcohol/substance abuse counseling, chaplain/spiritual director, career counseling, student employment services, financial aid counseling, health services, minority student services, personal counseling, placement for graduates, veterans' counselor. **Physically disabled:** Services for visually, speech, hearing impaired.

Contact. E-mail: undergraduate.admissions@nau.edu
Phone: (928) 523-5511 Toll-free number: (888) 628-2968
Fax: (928) 523-0226
Paul Orscheln, Director of Admissions, Northern Arizona University, PO Box 4084, Flagstaff, AZ 86011-4084

Prescott College
Prescott, Arizona
www.prescott.edu

CB member
CB code: 0484

- Private 4-year liberal arts college
- Commuter campus in large town
- 721 degree-seeking undergraduates: 20% part-time, 59% women, 2% African American, 1% Asian American, 7% Hispanic American, 1% Native American, 2% international
- 360 degree-seeking graduate students
- 83% of applicants admitted
- SAT or ACT (ACT writing optional), application essay required

General. Founded in 1966. Regionally accredited. **Degrees:** 196 bachelor's awarded; master's, doctoral offered. **Location:** 100 miles from Phoenix. **Calendar:** Semester, limited summer session. **Full-time faculty:** 75 total; 63% have terminal degrees, 9% minority, 52% women. **Part-time faculty:** 15 total; 40% have terminal degrees, 7% minority, 93% women. **Class size:** 98% < 20, 1% 20-39, less than 1% >100. **Special facilities:** Visual arts center, experimental agroecology farm, field station on the Gulf of California, equine-assisted learning center.

Freshman class profile. 424 applied, 350 admitted, 66 enrolled.

Mid 50% test scores			
SAT critical reading:	510-650	GPA 2.0-2.99:	46%
SAT math:	470-630	Rank in top quarter:	40%
SAT writing:	500-610	Rank in top tenth:	30%
ACT composite:	21-26	Return as sophomores:	62%
GPA 3.75 or higher:	7%	Out-of-state:	81%
GPA 3.50-3.74:	19%	Live on campus:	20%
GPA 3.0-3.49:	26%	International:	5%

Basis for selection. Essay and GPA most important. Letters of recommendation, any personal additions important. College visit, interview recommended. **Home schooled:** Must submit portfolio that includes course titles, course descriptions, and bibliography; minimum length is 5-10 pages.

High school preparation. 16 units recommended. Recommended units include English 4, mathematics 3, social studies 3, history 2, science 2, foreign language 1 and visual/performing arts 1.

2011-2012 Annual costs. Tuition/fees: $26,819. Health insurance is required; cost of school's health insurance is $788 for fall term and $1,103 for spring term. Room only: $4,400. Books/supplies: $720. Personal expenses: $2,650.

2011-2012 Financial aid. Need-based: 49 full-time freshmen applied for aid; 41 were judged to have need; 41 of these received aid. Average need met was 67%. Average scholarship/grant was $15,332; average loan $3,707. 51% of total undergraduate aid awarded as scholarships/grants, 49% as loans/jobs. **Non-need-based:** Awarded to 126 full-time undergraduates, including 12 freshmen. Scholarships awarded for academics, leadership.

Application procedures. Admission: Priority date 3/1; deadline 8/15 (postmark date). $25 fee, may be waived for applicants with need. Admission notification on a rolling basis beginning on or about 4/1. Must reply by May 1 or within 4 week(s) if notified thereafter. **Financial aid:** Priority date 3/1; no closing date. FAFSA required. Applicants notified on a rolling basis starting 3/15; must reply within 12 week(s) of notification.

Academics. Special study options: Cross-registration, double major, dual enrollment of high school students, exchange student, external degree, independent study, internships, liberal arts/career combination, student-designed major, teacher certification program. Adult degree program designed for working adults to obtain degree on year-round, part-time basis. Master of arts self-study program available. Programs also available at center in Tucson. **Credit/placement by examination:** AP, CLEP, IB, institutional tests. 20 credit hours maximum toward bachelor's degree. **Support services:** Learning center, reduced course load, tutoring, writing center.

Majors. Architecture: Environmental design. **Area/ethnic studies:** Regional, women's. **Biology:** Conservation, marine. **Business:** Business admin. **Communications:** Photojournalism. **Conservation:** Environmental studies. **Education:** Early childhood, elementary, learning disabled, mentally handicapped, physical, secondary. **English:** Creative writing. **General:** Sustainable agriculture. **Health services:** General. **Liberal arts:** Humanities.

Parks/recreation: Outdoor education. **Physical sciences:** Geology. **Psychology:** General, comparative, counseling, environmental, industrial, medical. **Social sciences:** Cultural anthropology. **Visual/performing arts:** General, documentaries.

Most popular majors. Education 24%, natural resources/environmental science 16%, parks/recreation 9%, psychology 14%.

Computing on campus. 50 workstations in dormitories, library, computer center, student center. Dormitories wired for high-speed internet access and linked to campus network. Online library, helpline, wireless network available.

Student life. Freshman orientation: Mandatory, $950 fee. Preregistration for classes offered. Wilderness backpacking orientation offered. Water-based wilderness orientations and community-based orientations offered to those who cannot participate in backpacking session. **Housing:** Coed dorms available. $225 fully refundable deposit, deadline 4/1. Coed housing. **Activities:** Dance, drama, film society, international student organizations, literary magazine, radio station, student government, student newspaper, student environmental network, student chapter of Amnesty International, gender and sexuality alliance, peace and justice center, Aztlan center, service learning program, Maasai community project, student arts council, African-inspired dance gatherings.

Student services. Adult student services, career counseling, financial aid counseling, personal counseling, placement for graduates. **Physically disabled:** Services for visually, speech, hearing impaired.

Contact. E-mail: admissions@prescott.edu
Phone: (877) 350-2100 ext. 2100
Toll-free number: (877) 350-2100 ext. 2100 Fax: (928) 776-5242
Michelle Tissot, Director of Admissions, Prescott College, 220 Grove Avenue, Prescott, AZ 86301

Southwest University of Visual Arts
Tucson, Arizona
www.suva.edu   **CB code: 3037**

- For-profit 4-year visual arts college
- Commuter campus in very large city
- 255 degree-seeking undergraduates: 45% part-time, 61% women
- 90% of applicants admitted
- SAT or ACT with writing, application essay, interview required

General. **Degrees:** 42 bachelor's awarded; master's offered. **ROTC:** Army. **Calendar:** Semester, extensive summer session. **Full-time faculty:** 32 total. **Part-time faculty:** 22 total. **Class size:** 3% < 20, 97% 20-39.

Freshman class profile. 31 applied, 28 admitted, 27 enrolled.

Basis for selection. High school transcripts, ACT/SAT, essay, interview, personal statement form required. Admissions based on evaluation of strengths, academic preparedness and communication skills. Art work required for illustration, fine arts, animation and graphic design programs.

High school preparation. College-preparatory program recommended.

2011-2012 Annual costs. Tuition/fees: $18,360. Books/supplies: $1,250. Personal expenses: $3,204.

Financial aid. All financial aid based on need.

Application procedures. Admission: No deadline. $25 fee. Admission notification on a rolling basis. **Financial aid:** No deadline. FAFSA required.

Academics. Special study options: Double major, independent study, internships, liberal arts/career combination. **Credit/placement by examination:** AP, CLEP, IB, SAT, ACT, institutional tests. **Support services:** Learning center, reduced course load, remedial instruction, study skills assistance, tutoring, writing center.

Majors. Architecture: Landscape. **Business:** Marketing. **Communications:** Advertising. **Communications technology:** Animation/special effects. **Visual/performing arts:** Graphic design, illustration, interior design, photography, studio arts.

Computing on campus. 125 workstations in library, computer center, student center. Online course registration, online library, helpline, student web hosting, wireless network available.

Student life. Freshman orientation: Mandatory, $100 fee. Preregistration for classes offered.

Student services. Adult student services, career counseling, student employment services, financial aid counseling, personal counseling, placement for graduates, veterans' counselor.

Contact. E-mail: inquire@suva.edu
Phone: (520) 325-0123 Toll-free number: (800) 825-8753
Fax: (520) 325-5535
Adrian Smith, Director of Admissions, Southwest University of Visual Arts, 2525 North Country Club Road, Tucson, AZ 85716

University of Advancing Technology
Tempe, Arizona
www.uat.edu   **CB code: 3608**

- For-profit 4-year university
- Residential campus in very large city
- 980 degree-seeking undergraduates
- 60 graduate students
- 78% of applicants admitted

General. Founded in 1983. Accredited by ACICS. Bachelor's degree can be earned in 2 2/3 years. **Degrees:** 192 bachelor's, 16 associate awarded; master's offered. **Location:** 7 miles from Phoenix. **Calendar:** Semester, extensive summer session. **Full-time faculty:** 31 total; 16% have terminal degrees, 36% women. **Part-time faculty:** 29 total; 3% have terminal degrees, 21% women. **Class size:** 68% < 20, 27% 20-39, 2% 40-49, 3% 50-99. **Special facilities:** Technology lab, motion capture studio, robotics lab, digital video studio, network security lab.

Freshman class profile. 845 applied, 659 admitted, 99 enrolled.

Basis for selection. Academic achievements, leadership experience, career aspirations, hobbies and community and extra-curricular involvement considered. Acceptance based on previous education, ACT/SAT, student's match with university culture and a passion for technology. SAT or ACT recommended. Test scores considered during admissions process, but not required unless GPA is not satisfactory. **Home schooled:** Transcript of courses and grades, state high school equivalency certificate required.

2011-2012 Annual costs. Tuition/fees: $19,400. Room/board: $10,926. Books/supplies: $1,000. Personal expenses: $3,000.

Application procedures. Admission: No deadline. No application fee. Admission notification on a rolling basis. **Financial aid:** Priority date 4/15; no closing date. FAFSA required. Applicants notified on a rolling basis; must reply within 2 week(s) of notification.

Academics. Special study options: Accelerated study, distance learning, double major, independent study, internships, student-designed major. **Credit/placement by examination:** AP, CLEP, IB, institutional tests. **Support services:** Learning center, tutoring.

Majors. Communications technology: Animation/special effects. **Computer sciences:** Artificial intelligence, LAN/WAN management, networking, security, web page design, webmaster. **Engineering:** Software. **Protective services:** Computer forensics. **Visual/performing arts:** Game design.

Computing on campus. 400 workstations in dormitories, library, computer center, student center. Dormitories wired for high-speed internet access and linked to campus network. Commuter students can connect to campus network. Online course registration, online library, helpline, student web hosting, wireless network available.

Student life. Freshman orientation: Mandatory. Preregistration for classes offered. **Housing:** Guaranteed on-campus for freshmen. Coed dorms, apartments available. $550 partly refundable deposit. **Activities:** Dance, film society, student government, student newspaper, Bible study club.

Athletics. Intercollegiate: Fencing.

Student services. Career counseling, student employment services, financial aid counseling, personal counseling, placement for graduates.

Contact. E-mail: admissions@uat.edu
Phone: (602) 383-8228 Toll-free number: (800) 658-5744
Fax: (602) 383-8222
Michelle Wilcox, Manager of Enrollment, University of Advancing Technology, 2625 West Baseline Road, Tempe, AZ 85283-1056

University of Arizona
Tucson, Arizona
www.arizona.edu

CB member
CB code: 4832

- Public 4-year university
- Residential campus in very large city
- 30,445 degree-seeking undergraduates: 11% part-time, 52% women, 3% African American, 5% Asian American, 22% Hispanic American, 1% Native American, 4% international
- 8,081 degree-seeking graduate students
- 69% of applicants admitted
- Application essay required
- 61% graduate within 6 years

General. Founded in 1885. Regionally accredited. Sierra Vista campus offers credit-bearing classes in general studies and education. **Degrees:** 6,195 bachelor's awarded; master's, professional, doctoral offered. **ROTC:** Army, Naval, Air Force. **Location:** 111 miles from Phoenix. **Calendar:** Semester, extensive summer session. **Full-time faculty:** 1,530 total; 18% minority, 37% women. **Part-time faculty:** 490 total; 13% minority, 52% women. **Special facilities:** Geological museum, state anthropological museum, planetarium, observatory, center for creative photography.

Freshman class profile. 32,227 applied, 22,116 admitted, 7,300 enrolled.

Mid 50% test scores			
SAT critical reading:	480-600	GPA 3.50-3.74:	19%
SAT math:	490-620	GPA 3.0-3.49:	35%
SAT writing:	480-600	GPA 2.0-2.99:	20%
ACT composite:	21-27	Return as sophomores:	77%
GPA 3.75 or higher:	26%	Out-of-state:	36%
		International:	3%

Basis for selection. Applicants must be in top 25% of class or have 3.0 GPA. In-state applicants must have 1040 SAT (exclusive of Writing) or 22 ACT. 1110 SAT (exclusive of Writing) or 24 ACT required of out-of-state applicants. Conditional admission may be offered to in-state applicants who meet 1 or more of the following: top half of class or 2.5 GPA and no more than 1 deficiency in any 2 required subjects, (deficiency not allowed in both math and science). SAT or ACT recommended. Auditions required of applied music and all performance majors. Portfolios required for studio art majors. **Home schooled:** Course work completion information required. **Learning Disabled:** Separate application for fee-based program (SALT).

High school preparation. College-preparatory program recommended. 16 units required. Required units include English 4, mathematics 4, social studies 1, history 1, science 3 (laboratory 3), foreign language 2 and visual/performing arts 1. One unit fine arts required.

2011-2012 Annual costs. Tuition/fees: $9,299; $25,509 out-of-state. Room/board: $8,540. Books/supplies: $1,000. Personal expenses: $1,500.

2010-2011 Financial aid. Need-based: 4,919 full-time freshmen applied for aid; 3,733 were judged to have need; 3,611 of these received aid. Average need met was 66%. Average scholarship/grant was $10,669; average loan $3,172. 57% of total undergraduate aid awarded as scholarships/grants, 43% as loans/jobs. **Non-need-based:** Awarded to 6,886 full-time undergraduates, including 2,027 freshmen. Scholarships awarded for academics, art, music/drama. **Additional information:** Arizona Assurance Program; provides housing, books, and tuition for all new, incoming resident freshmen; must be Pell-eligible with combined family income less than $42,500; funding provided as grants, scholarships, and federal work-study.

Application procedures. Admission: Closing date 5/1 (postmark date). $50 fee ($65 out-of-state), may be waived for applicants with need. Admission notification on a rolling basis beginning on or about 11/1. Must reply by May 1 or within 4 week(s) if notified thereafter. **Financial aid:** Priority date 3/1; no closing date. FAFSA required. Applicants notified on a rolling basis starting 4/1; must reply within 3 week(s) of notification.

Academics. Special study options: Accelerated study, combined bachelor's/graduate degree, cooperative education, cross-registration, distance learning, double major, dual enrollment of high school students, ESL, exchange student, external degree, honors, independent study, internships, liberal arts/career combination, semester at sea, student-designed major, study abroad, teacher certification program, weekend college. **Credit/placement by examination:** AP, CLEP, IB, SAT, ACT, institutional tests. 60 credit hours maximum toward bachelor's degree. **Support services:** Learning center, pre-admission summer program, reduced course load, study skills assistance, tutoring, writing center.

Majors. Architecture: Architecture, landscape, urban/community planning. **Area/ethnic studies:** Chicano/Hispanic-American/Latino, East Asian, Latin American, Near/Middle Eastern, women's. **Biology:** General, animal physiology, bacteriology, biochemistry, cell/histology, ecology. **Business:** General,

accounting, entrepreneurial studies, finance, human resources, management information systems, managerial economics, marketing, operations. **Communications:** Communications/speech/rhetoric, journalism, radio/TV. **Computer sciences:** General. **Conservation:** General, environmental studies, wildlife/wilderness. **Education:** Agricultural, art, biology, drama/dance, elementary, English, family/consumer sciences, French, history, kindergarten/preschool, mathematics, music, physical, science, social science, social studies, Spanish, special ed. **Engineering:** General, aerospace, agricultural, applied physics, chemical, civil, computer, electrical, geological, industrial, mechanical, mining, systems, water resource. **English:** Creative writing, English lit. **Foreign languages:** Classics, French, German, Italian, linguistics, Russian, Spanish. **General:** Agronomy, animal sciences, economics, plant sciences, range science, soil science. **Health services:** Clinical lab science, communication disorders, health care admin, nursing (RN), preveterinary, speech pathology. **History:** General. **Human services:** General. **Math:** General. **Philosophy/religion:** Judaic, religion. **Physical sciences:** Astronomy, atmospheric science, chemistry, geology, hydrology, materials science, optics, physics. **Protective services:** Law enforcement admin. **Psychology:** General. **Social sciences:** Anthropology, applied economics, economics, geography, political science, sociology. **Visual/performing arts:** General, art history/conservation, dance, dramatic, music, music performance, musical theater, studio arts, theater design. **Work/family studies:** Consumer economics, family resources, family studies.

Most popular majors. Biology 9%, business/marketing 16%, engineering/engineering technologies 6%, psychology 7%, social sciences 10%.

Computing on campus. 2,500 workstations in dormitories, library, computer center, student center. Dormitories wired for high-speed internet access and linked to campus network. Commuter students can connect to campus network. Online course registration, online library, helpline, repair service, student web hosting, wireless network available.

Student life. Freshman orientation: Mandatory, $100 fee. Preregistration for classes offered. 2 day program. **Housing:** Coed dorms, single-sex dorms, special housing for disabled, apartments, fraternity/sorority housing available. $350 partly refundable deposit, deadline 5/1. Special housing for honors students available. **Activities:** Bands, campus ministries, choral groups, dance, drama, international student organizations, literary magazine, music ensembles, Model UN, musical theater, opera, radio station, student government, student newspaper, symphony orchestra, TV station, over 400 clubs and organizations available.

Athletics. NCAA. **Intercollegiate:** Baseball M, basketball, cross-country, diving, football (tackle) M, golf, gymnastics W, lacrosse M, soccer W, softball W, swimming, tennis, track and field, volleyball W. **Intramural:** Basketball, cross-country, diving, football (non-tackle), golf, racquetball, soccer, softball, swimming, table tennis, tennis, track and field, volleyball. **Team name:** Wildcats.

Student services. Adult student services, alcohol/substance abuse counseling, chaplain/spiritual director, career counseling, services for economically disadvantaged, student employment services, financial aid counseling, health services, legal services, minority student services, personal counseling, placement for graduates, veterans' counselor, women's services. **Physically disabled:** Services for visually, speech, hearing impaired.

Contact. E-mail: admissions@arizona.edu
Phone: (520) 621-3237 Fax: (520) 621-9799
Kasey Urguidez, Assistant Dean of Admissions, University of Arizona, Robert L. Nugent Building, Tucson, AZ 85721-0073

University of Phoenix: Phoenix-Hohokam
Phoenix, Arizona
www.phoenix.edu

CB member
CB code: 1024

- For-profit 4-year university
- Commuter campus in large town
- 4,270 degree-seeking undergraduates

General. Founded in 1976. Regionally accredited. **Degrees:** 849 bachelor's awarded; master's offered. **Calendar:** Differs by program, extensive summer session. **Full-time faculty:** 103 total. **Part-time faculty:** 620 total.

Basis for selection. Open admission, but selective for some programs.

2011-2012 Annual costs. Estimated costs as of August 2011: per-credit-hour charge, $405 to $435, depending upon level and course of study; electronic course materials fee, $95, if applicable. Book and material charges may vary by course and program. All fees are subject to change.

Application procedures. Admission: No deadline. No application fee. Admission notification on a rolling basis. **Financial aid:** No deadline. FAFSA, institutional form required. Applicants notified on a rolling basis.

Academics. Online library. **Special study options:** Accelerated study, combined bachelor's/graduate degree, cooperative education, distance learning, independent study, teacher certification program. **Credit/placement by examination:** AP, CLEP, IB. 30 credit hours maximum toward associate degree, 30 toward bachelor's. **Support services:** Learning center, remedial instruction, tutoring, writing center.

Majors. Business: Accounting, accounting/business management, business admin, communications, e-commerce, entrepreneurial studies, finance, hospitality admin, international, logistics, management information systems, management science, marketing, nonprofit/public, office management, retailing. **Communications:** General. **Computer sciences:** General, database management, information technology, networking, programming, security, systems analysis, web page design, webmaster. **Education:** Elementary, secondary. **Engineering:** Software. **Health services:** Facilities admin, health care admin, medical records technology, nursing (RN). **Protective services:** Law enforcement admin, security services.

Most popular majors. Business/marketing 65%, computer/information sciences 8%, health sciences 8%, security/protective services 7%.

Computing on campus. PC or laptop required. Commuter students can connect to campus network. Online course registration, online library, helpline, wireless network available.

Student life. Freshman orientation: Mandatory. Preregistration for classes offered.

Student services. Adult student services, career counseling, financial aid counseling, personal counseling. **Physically disabled:** Services for visually, speech, hearing impaired.

Contact. E-mail: chris.alvarado@phoenix.edu
Toll-free number: (866) 766-0766
Marc Booker, Director of Admissions and Evaluation, University of Phoenix: Phoenix-Hohokam, 4035 South Riverpoint Parkway, Phoenix, AZ 85040-0723

University of Phoenix: Southern Arizona
Tucson, Arizona
www.phoenix.edu

▶ For-profit 4-year university
▶ Very large city
▶ 1,810 degree-seeking undergraduates

General. Regionally accredited. **Degrees:** 376 bachelor's awarded; master's offered. **Calendar:** Differs by program. **Full-time faculty:** 26 total. **Part-time faculty:** 284 total.

Basis for selection. Open admission, but selective for some programs.

2011-2012 Annual costs. Estimated costs as of August 2011: per-credit-hour charge, $405 to $435, depending upon level and course of study; electronic course materials fee, $95, if applicable. Book and material charges may vary by course and program. All fees are subject to change.

Application procedures. Admission: No deadline. No application fee. **Financial aid:** No deadline.

Academics. Credit/placement by examination: AP, CLEP.

Majors. Business: Accounting, business admin. **Computer sciences:** Information technology. **Education:** General. **Protective services:** Law enforcement admin.

Contact. Marc Booker, Director of Admission and Evaluation, University of Phoenix: Southern Arizona, 300 South Craycroft Road, Tucson, AZ 85711-4574

Western International University
Phoenix, Arizona
www.west.edu   CB code: 1316

▶ For-profit 4-year university and business college
▶ Commuter campus in very large city
▶ 2,249 degree-seeking undergraduates: 65% women, 18% African American, 1% Asian American, 12% Hispanic American, 2% Native American, 1% international
▶ 671 graduate students

General. Founded in 1978. Regionally accredited. Adult student body. Portfolio evaluation of relevant experience for course credit. **Degrees:** 332 bachelor's, 50 associate awarded; master's offered. **Calendar:** Differs by program, extensive summer session. **Part-time faculty:** 408 total; 9% have terminal degrees, 28% minority, 43% women. **Class size:** 94% < 20, 6% 20-39.

Basis for selection. Open admission. Interview and essay recommended.

2011-2012 Annual costs. Tuition/fees: $12,900. Books/supplies: $1,068.

2011-2012 Financial aid. All financial aid based on need. 32% of total undergraduate aid awarded as scholarships/grants, 68% as loans/jobs.

Application procedures. Admission: No deadline. $25 fee. Admission notification on a rolling basis. **Financial aid:** No deadline. FAFSA, institutional form required. Applicants notified on a rolling basis.

Academics. Special study options: Accelerated study, distance learning, independent study, internships. Evening courses. **Credit/placement by examination:** AP, CLEP, IB, institutional tests. 24 credit hours maximum toward associate degree, 60 toward bachelor's. Maximum of 60 credits by examination and/or assessment may be counted toward degree; 36 hour residency requirement. **Support services:** Learning center, tutoring, writing center.

Majors. Business: General, accounting, business admin, finance, management information systems, marketing. **Computer sciences:** General. **Liberal arts:** Arts/sciences.

Most popular majors. Business/marketing 77%, computer/information sciences 8%, liberal arts 15%.

Computing on campus. 195 workstations in library, computer center. Commuter students can connect to campus network. Online course registration, online library, helpline, wireless network available.

Student life. Freshman orientation: Mandatory. Preregistration for classes offered. **Policies:** Cultural activities and special seminars/workshops available. **Activities:** International student organizations, Delta Mu Delta, Upsilon Pi Epsilon, Golden Key honor societies.

Student services. Adult student services, career counseling, financial aid counseling, veterans' counselor.

Contact. Phone: (602) 943-2311 Toll-free number: (866) 943-2311 Fax: (602) 371-8637
Hue Haslim, Senior Director of University Student Services, Western International University, 9215 North Black Canyon Highway, Phoenix, AZ 85021-2718

Arkansas

Arkansas Baptist College
Little Rock, Arkansas
www.arkansasbaptist.edu   CB code: 7301

‣ Private 4-year liberal arts college affiliated with American Baptist Churches in the USA
‣ Residential campus in small city
‣ 1,189 degree-seeking undergraduates: 20% part-time, 40% women, 95% African American, 1% international

General. Founded in 1884. Regionally accredited. **Degrees:** 62 bachelor's, 13 associate awarded. **Calendar:** Semester, limited summer session. **Full-time faculty:** 39 total; 8% have terminal degrees, 15% minority, 51% women. **Part-time faculty:** 27 total; 7% have terminal degrees, 15% minority, 26% women. **Class size:** 41% < 20, 56% 20-39, 2% 40-49, 1% 50-99. **Special facilities:** African American leadership institute, literacy writing center.

Basis for selection. Open admission. Applicants with test scores or GPA below our requirement may be admitted provisionally but must earn 2.0 GPA by end of first semester to continue in good academic standing. **Home schooled:** Statement describing home school structure and mission, interview required.

High school preparation. 18 units recommended. Recommended units include English 4, mathematics 4, social studies 1 and science 2. Vocational and agriculture courses also recommended.

2011-2012 Annual costs. Tuition/fees: $7,705. Incoming freshman may purchase a laptop computer if so desired but not mandatory; the laptop fee is $325. Room/board: $7,950. Books/supplies: $1,325. Personal expenses: $2,600.

Financial aid. All financial aid based on need.

Application procedures. Admission: No deadline. $25 fee, may be waived for applicants with need. Admission notification on a rolling basis beginning on or about 6/30. **Financial aid:** Closing date 4/1. FAFSA required. Applicants notified on a rolling basis starting 6/15.

Academics. Special study options: Double major, independent study, internships. **Credit/placement by examination:** AP, CLEP, institutional tests. **Support services:** Remedial instruction, tutoring, writing center.

Majors. Business: Business admin. **Education:** Elementary. **Social sciences:** General.

Most popular majors. Business/marketing 27%, interdisciplinary studies 10%, philosophy/religious studies 15%, public administration/social services 27%.

Computing on campus. PC or laptop required. 61 workstations in dormitories, library, computer center. Dormitories wired for high-speed internet access. Commuter students can connect to campus network. Helpline, wireless network available.

Student life. Freshman orientation: Mandatory, $10 fee. Preregistration for classes offered. Held in August and in January each year. **Policies:** Religious observance required. **Housing:** Single-sex dorms available. $150 nonrefundable deposit. **Activities:** Marching band, choral groups, student government, student newspaper, Baptist student union, student teacher organization.

Athletics. NJCAA. **Intercollegiate:** Baseball M, basketball, cheerleading M, football (tackle) M, softball W, track and field, wrestling M. **Team name:** Buffaloes.

Student services. Career counseling, student employment services, health services, on-campus daycare, personal counseling, placement for graduates, veterans' counselor.

Contact. E-mail: admissions@arkansasbaptist.edu
Phone: (501) 244-5186 Toll-free number: (866) 920-4222
Fax: (501) 372-0321
Jocelyn Spriggs, Director of Admissions and Recruitment, Arkansas Baptist College, 1621 Dr. Martin Luther King Drive, Little Rock, AR 72202

Arkansas State University
State University, Arkansas   CB member
www.astate.edu   CB code: 6011

‣ Public 4-year university
‣ Commuter campus in small city
‣ 9,455 degree-seeking undergraduates: 20% part-time, 58% women, 16% African American, 1% Asian American, 2% Hispanic American, 5% international
‣ 3,699 degree-seeking graduate students
‣ 63% of applicants admitted
‣ SAT or ACT (ACT writing optional) required
‣ 38% graduate within 6 years; 16% enter graduate study

General. Founded in 1909. Regionally accredited. **Degrees:** 1,582 bachelor's, 601 associate awarded; master's, professional, doctoral offered. **ROTC:** Army. **Location:** 70 miles from Memphis. **Calendar:** Semester, extensive summer session. **Full-time faculty:** 485 total; 72% have terminal degrees, 14% minority, 50% women. **Part-time faculty:** 169 total; 6% have terminal degrees, 9% minority, 58% women. **Class size:** 46% < 20, 42% 20-39, 7% 40-49, 4% 50-99, less than 1% >100. **Special facilities:** Environmental ecotoxicology research facility, electron microscope facility, geographic information center facility, equine center, plantation, center for health sciences, museum.

Freshman class profile. 4,806 applied, 3,040 admitted, 1,562 enrolled.

Mid 50% test scores			
SAT critical reading:	410-480	Rank in top quarter:	44%
SAT math:	440-580	Rank in top tenth:	23%
SAT writing:	410-500	End year in good standing:	85%
ACT composite:	20-26	Return as sophomores:	71%
GPA 3.75 or higher:	25%	Out-of-state:	10%
GPA 3.50-3.74:	19%	Live on campus:	64%
GPA 3.0-3.49:	31%	International:	6%
GPA 2.0-2.99:	25%	Fraternities:	10%
		Sororities:	9%

Basis for selection. 21 ACT and 2.5 GPA required; 525 GED required of applicants without high school diploma/transcripts. Proof of immunization required. Proof of registration with selective service required for all males 18 to 25. Students without SAT/ACT may submit ASSET or Compass. SAT, SAT Subject Tests, ACT must be received by first day of classes for fall term admission. Auditions required of music majors; portfolios required of art majors.

High school preparation. College-preparatory program recommended. 14 units required. Required and recommended units include English 4, mathematics 4, social studies 1, history 2, science 3 (laboratory 3) and foreign language 2.

2011-2012 Annual costs. Tuition/fees: $6,934; $12,238 out-of-state. Annual tuition for returning undergraduates through the 2011-12 academic year is $13,854; per-credit-hour charge is $461.80. Room/board: $6,920. Books/supplies: $1,000. Personal expenses: $3,781.

2011-2012 Financial aid. Need-based: 1,485 full-time freshmen applied for aid; 1,301 were judged to have need; 1,300 of these received aid. Average need met was 61%. Average scholarship/grant was $7,000; average loan $5,900. 63% of total undergraduate aid awarded as scholarships/grants, 37% as loans/jobs. **Non-need-based:** Awarded to 3,450 full-time undergraduates, including 845 freshmen. Scholarships awarded for academics, alumni affiliation, art, athletics, leadership, minority status, music/drama, ROTC, state residency.

Application procedures. Admission: Closing date 8/20 (receipt date). $15 fee. Admission notification on a rolling basis. **Financial aid:** Priority date 2/15, closing date 7/1. FAFSA, institutional form required. Applicants notified on a rolling basis starting 6/1; must reply within 2 week(s) of notification.

Academics. Of the first 59 hours completed in college, students allowed to repeat courses with final grade of less than C. No more than 18 semester hours of course work may be repeated. **Special study options:** Accelerated study, distance learning, double major, dual enrollment of high school students, ESL, exchange student, honors, independent study, internships, study abroad, teacher certification program. **Credit/placement by examination:** AP, CLEP, SAT, ACT, institutional tests. 15 credit hours maximum toward associate degree, 30 toward bachelor's. **Support services:** Learning center, reduced course load, remedial instruction, study skills assistance, tutoring.

Honors college/program. 27 ACT or 3.5 GPA required.

Majors. Biology: General. **Business:** Accounting, business admin, finance, international, managerial economics, marketing. **Communications:** General,

journalism, radio/TV. **Computer sciences:** General, data processing. **Conservation:** Wildlife/wilderness. **Education:** Biology, business, chemistry, early childhood, English, foreign languages, mathematics, middle, music, physical, physics, social science. **Engineering:** General, civil, electrical, mechanical. **English:** English lit. **Foreign languages:** General. **General:** Agribusiness operations, animal sciences, plant sciences. **Health services:** Athletic training, audiology/speech pathology, clinical lab science, dietetics, medical radiologic technology/radiation therapy, nursing (RN). **History:** General. **Human services:** Social work. **Math:** General. **Parks/recreation:** Exercise sciences, health/fitness, sports admin. **Philosophy/religion:** Philosophy. **Physical sciences:** Chemistry, physics. **Protective services:** Forensics. **Psychology:** General. **Social sciences:** Criminology, economics, geography, political science, sociology. **Visual/performing arts:** Art, commercial/advertising art, dramatic, music, music performance.

Most popular majors. Business/marketing 15%, education 20%, health sciences 13%, liberal arts 10%.

Computing on campus. 177 workstations in dormitories, library, computer center, student center. Dormitories wired for high-speed internet access and linked to campus network. Commuter students can connect to campus network. Online course registration, online library, helpline, wireless network available.

Student life. Freshman orientation: Mandatory. Preregistration for classes offered. All-day session held on various dates. **Policies:** Smoking is prohibited on campus. **Housing:** Coed dorms, single-sex dorms, apartments, fraternity/sorority housing, wellness housing available. $100 fully refundable deposit. Honors, STEM, and ROTC living/learning community available. **Activities:** Bands, campus ministries, choral groups, dance, drama, international student organizations, music ensembles, Model UN, musical theater, opera, radio station, student government, student newspaper, symphony orchestra, TV station, Ambassadors for Christ, Arkansas State Rugby, Black Student Association, Brother-to-Brother, Circle of Trust, Gay-Straight Alliance, honors college association, student activities board, student association of radiology and imaging sciences, student government association.

Athletics. NCAA. **Intercollegiate:** Baseball M, basketball, bowling W, cross-country, football (tackle) M, golf, soccer W, tennis W, track and field, volleyball W. **Intramural:** Badminton, basketball, bowling, football (non-tackle), soccer, softball, table tennis, tennis, volleyball. **Team name:** Red Wolves.

Student services. Adult student services, alcohol/substance abuse counseling, career counseling, student employment services, financial aid counseling, health services, minority student services, on-campus daycare, personal counseling, placement for graduates, veterans' counselor. **Physically disabled:** Services for visually, speech, hearing impaired.

Contact. E-mail: admissions@astate.edu
Phone: (870) 972-3024 Toll-free number: (800) 382-3030
Fax: (870) 972-3406
Tammy Fowler, Director of Admissions, Arkansas State University, PO Box 1630, State University, AR 72467-1630

Arkansas Tech University
Russellville, Arkansas
www.atu.edu   **CB code: 6010**

◆ Public 4-year university and liberal arts college
◆ Commuter campus in large town
◆ 8,369 degree-seeking undergraduates: 16% part-time, 55% women, 6% African American, 2% Asian American, 4% Hispanic American, 2% Native American, 2% international
◆ 742 degree-seeking graduate students
◆ 90% of applicants admitted
◆ SAT or ACT (ACT writing optional) required
◆ 44% graduate within 6 years

General. Founded in 1909. Regionally accredited. **Degrees:** 1,149 bachelor's, 263 associate awarded; master's offered. **ROTC:** Army. **Location:** 75 miles from Little Rock, 85 miles from Fort Smith. **Calendar:** Semester, extensive summer session. **Full-time faculty:** 307 total; 63% have terminal degrees, 9% minority, 45% women. **Part-time faculty:** 496 total; 42% have terminal degrees, 8% minority, 51% women. **Class size:** 36% < 20, 50% 20-39, 7% 40-49, 8% 50-99, less than 1% >100. **Special facilities:** Energy center, observatory, technology center.

Freshman class profile. 3,741 applied, 3,380 admitted, 1,859 enrolled.

Mid 50% test scores			
SAT critical reading:	410-470	Rank in top quarter:	36%
SAT math:	430-540	Rank in top tenth:	15%
ACT composite:	19-25	Return as sophomores:	67%
GPA 3.75 or higher:	20%	Out-of-state:	4%
GPA 3.50-3.74:	15%	Live on campus:	57%
GPA 3.0-3.49:	25%	International:	1%
GPA 2.0-2.99:	38%	Fraternities:	9%
		Sororities:	9%

Basis for selection. Secondary school record and standardized test scores very important; class rank considered. **Home schooled:** Documentation of 2.0 GPA and completion of university's secondary school core curriculum, or 450 GED required. 19 ACT, 910 SAT (math and critical reading), or 68 COMPASS also required.

High school preparation. College-preparatory program recommended. 4 units required; 18 recommended. Required and recommended units include English 4, mathematics 4, social studies 3, history 1, science 3 (laboratory 3), foreign language 2, visual/performing arts .5 and academic electives 4. .5 PE, .5 Health, and .5 Oral communications.

2011-2012 Annual costs. Tuition/fees: $6,258; $11,658 out-of-state. Room/board: $5,560. Books/supplies: $1,410. Personal expenses: $1,568.

2010-2011 Financial aid. Need-based: 1,655 full-time freshmen applied for aid; 1,166 were judged to have need; 1,141 of these received aid. Average need met was 70%. Average scholarship/grant was $4,958; average loan $2,773. 60% of total undergraduate aid awarded as scholarships/grants, 40% as loans/jobs. **Non-need-based:** Awarded to 2,981 full-time undergraduates, including 1,029 freshmen. Scholarships awarded for academics, athletics, leadership, music/drama, ROTC, state residency.

Application procedures. Admission: No deadline. No application fee. Admission notification on a rolling basis. Students can postpone their enrollment for one semester. **Financial aid:** Priority date 4/15; no closing date. FAFSA, institutional form required. Applicants notified on a rolling basis starting 5/1; must reply within 2 week(s) of notification.

Academics. Special study options: Accelerated study, distance learning, double major, dual enrollment of high school students, ESL, honors, independent study, internships, study abroad, teacher certification program, weekend college. **Credit/placement by examination:** AP, CLEP, IB, SAT, ACT, institutional tests. 30 credit hours maximum toward associate degree, 30 toward bachelor's. **Support services:** Learning center, reduced course load, remedial instruction, study skills assistance, tutoring, writing center.

Honors college/program. 3.5 GPA and 28 ACT required.

Majors. Biology: General. **Business:** Accounting, business admin, hospitality admin, managerial economics. **Communications:** Communications/speech/rhetoric, journalism. **Computer sciences:** General, information technology, systems analysis. **Conservation:** Wildlife/wilderness. **Education:** Agricultural, art, biology, business, early childhood, English, foreign languages, mathematics, middle, music, physical, science, social studies, speech. **Engineering:** Applied physics, electrical, mechanical. **English:** Creative writing, English lit. **Foreign languages:** General. **General:** Agribusiness operations. **Health services:** Clinical lab science, medical records admin, nursing (RN), rehabilitation science. **History:** General, applied. **Math:** General. **Parks/recreation:** Facilities management. **Physical sciences:** General, chemistry, geology, nuclear physics, physics. **Protective services:** Disaster management. **Psychology:** General. **Social sciences:** Political science, sociology. **Visual/performing arts:** Art, music.

Most popular majors. Business/marketing 10%, education 19%, engineering/engineering technologies 6%, health sciences 12%, interdisciplinary studies 10%.

Computing on campus. 1,124 workstations in dormitories, library, computer center, student center. Dormitories wired for high-speed internet access and linked to campus network. Commuter students can connect to campus network. Online course registration, online library, helpline, wireless network available.

Student life. Freshman orientation: Mandatory. Preregistration for classes offered. **Housing:** Guaranteed on-campus for freshmen. Coed dorms, single-sex dorms, special housing for disabled, apartments, cooperative housing, fraternity/sorority housing available. $50 fully refundable deposit, deadline 6/1. **Activities:** Bands, campus ministries, choral groups, dance, drama, international student organizations, literary magazine, music ensembles, Model UN, musical theater, opera, radio station, student government, student newspaper, TV station.

Athletics. NCAA. **Intercollegiate:** Baseball M, basketball, cross-country W, football (tackle) M, golf, softball W, tennis W, volleyball W. **Intramural:** Basketball, bowling, cheerleading, football (non-tackle), racquetball, soccer,

softball, table tennis, tennis, volleyball. **Team name:** Wonder Boys, Golden Suns.

Student services. Adult student services, alcohol/substance abuse counseling, career counseling, services for economically disadvantaged, student employment services, financial aid counseling, health services, minority student services, personal counseling, placement for graduates, veterans' counselor. **Physically disabled:** Services for visually, speech, hearing impaired.

Contact. E-mail: tech.enroll@atu.edu
Phone: (479) 968-0343 Toll-free number: (800) 582-6953
Fax: (479) 964-0522
Shauna Donnell, Assistant Vice President for Enrollment Management, Arkansas Tech University, 1605 Coliseum Drive, Suite 141, Russellville, AR 72801-2222

Central Baptist College
Conway, Arkansas
www.cbc.edu   CB code: 0788

- Private 4-year Bible and junior college affiliated with Baptist faith
- Commuter campus in large town
- 818 degree-seeking undergraduates: 14% part-time, 48% women
- 74% of applicants admitted
- SAT or ACT (ACT writing optional) required

General. Founded in 1952. Regionally accredited. **Degrees:** 82 bachelor's, 18 associate awarded. **ROTC:** Army. **Location:** 30 miles from Little Rock. **Calendar:** Semester, limited summer session. **Full-time faculty:** 24 total; 50% have terminal degrees, 4% minority, 42% women. **Part-time faculty:** 44 total; 16% have terminal degrees, 7% minority, 34% women.

Freshman class profile. 316 applied, 235 admitted, 159 enrolled.

GPA 3.75 or higher:	19%	GPA 2.0-2.99:	33%
GPA 3.50-3.74:	13%	Out-of-state:	15%
GPA 3.0-3.49:	35%	Live on campus:	25%

Basis for selection. ACT and transfer GPA most important. **Home schooled:** Statement describing home school structure and mission, transcript of courses and grades required.

High school preparation. College-preparatory program recommended. 15 units recommended. Recommended units include English 4, mathematics 2, social studies 2 and science 2.

2011-2012 Annual costs. Tuition/fees: $11,610. Room/board: $6,000. Books/supplies: $600. Personal expenses: $800.

2011-2012 Financial aid. Non-need-based: Scholarships awarded for academics, athletics, music/drama, religious affiliation.

Application procedures. Admission: Closing date 8/15 (postmark date). $25 fee, may be waived for applicants with need. Admission notification on a rolling basis. **Financial aid:** Priority date 7/1, closing date 8/1. FAFSA required. Applicants notified on a rolling basis starting 4/1.

Academics. Special study options: Accelerated study, distance learning, internships, study abroad. **Credit/placement by examination:** AP, CLEP, ACT, institutional tests. 15 credit hours maximum toward associate degree, 27 toward bachelor's. **Support services:** Learning center, reduced course load, remedial instruction, study skills assistance, tutoring.

Majors. Biology: General, biotechnology. **Business:** Accounting, business admin, marketing, organizational behavior. **Communications:** Journalism. **Computer sciences:** Data processing. **Human services:** Social work. **Liberal arts:** Arts/sciences. **Parks/recreation:** Health/fitness. **Psychology:** General. **Theology:** Bible, sacred music. **Visual/performing arts:** Music.

Most popular majors. Business/marketing 39%, computer/information sciences 11%, liberal arts 13%, public administration/social services 10%, theological studies 22%.

Computing on campus. 52 workstations in library, computer center. Online library, wireless network available.

Student life. Freshman orientation: Mandatory, $50 fee. Preregistration for classes offered. **Policies:** Religious observance required. **Housing:** Guaranteed on-campus for freshmen. Single-sex dorms, wellness housing available. $100 partly refundable deposit, deadline 8/15. **Activities:** Choral groups, international student organizations, music ensembles, student government, student newspaper, Association of Baptist Students, College Republicans.

Athletics. NAIA, NCCAA. **Intercollegiate:** Baseball M, basketball, golf, soccer, softball W, volleyball W. **Intramural:** Basketball, football (non-tackle), softball, table tennis, tennis, volleyball. **Team name:** Mustangs.

Student services. Career counseling, financial aid counseling, health services, personal counseling, veterans' counselor.

Contact. E-mail: rjohnson@cbc.edu
Phone: (501) 329-6872 Fax: (501) 329-2941
Ryan Johnson, Director of Admissions, Central Baptist College, 1501 College Avenue, Conway, AR 72034

Ecclesia College
Springdale, Arkansas
www.ecollege.edu   CB code: 6442

- Private 4-year Bible and liberal arts college affiliated with interdenominational tradition
- Residential campus in large town
- 215 degree-seeking undergraduates
- 89% of applicants admitted
- SAT or ACT (ACT writing optional), application essay required

General. Accredited by ABHE. **Degrees:** 17 bachelor's, 1 associate awarded. **Location:** 10 miles from Fayetteville. **Calendar:** Semester, limited summer session. **Full-time faculty:** 8 total. **Part-time faculty:** 28 total.

Freshman class profile. 75 applied, 67 admitted, 58 enrolled.

Out-of-state:	25%	Live on campus:	75%

Basis for selection. Recommendations and personal character very important. **Home schooled:** Interview required.

High school preparation. College-preparatory program recommended. Recommended units include English 4, mathematics 3, social studies 3, science 3 and foreign language 1.

2011-2012 Annual costs. Tuition/fees: $15,240. Room/board: $5,010. Books/supplies: $1,400. Personal expenses: $2,102.

Financial aid. Non-need-based: Scholarships awarded for academics, athletics, leadership, music/drama.

Application procedures. Admission: Closing date 8/22 (receipt date). $35 fee. Application must be submitted on paper. Admission notification on a rolling basis. **Financial aid:** No deadline. FAFSA required. Applicants notified on a rolling basis starting 7/1.

Academics. Special study options: Double major, dual enrollment of high school students, independent study, internships. **Credit/placement by examination:** AP, CLEP, institutional tests. **Support services:** Remedial instruction, tutoring.

Majors. Business: Business admin. **Parks/recreation:** Sports admin. **Theology:** Bible, missionary, pastoral counseling, preministerial, religious ed, sacred music, theology, youth ministry.

Most popular majors. Theological studies 95%.

Computing on campus. 15 workstations in library, computer center. Dormitories wired for high-speed internet access. Online library, wireless network available.

Student life. Freshman orientation: Mandatory. Preregistration for classes offered. **Policies:** Religious observance required. **Housing:** Single-sex dorms, apartments, wellness housing available. **Activities:** Campus ministries, choral groups, drama, music ensembles, student government, Circle K.

Athletics. NCCAA. **Intercollegiate:** Baseball M, basketball. **Team name:** Royals.

Student services. Alcohol/substance abuse counseling, chaplain/spiritual director, career counseling, financial aid counseling, personal counseling, placement for graduates. **Physically disabled:** Services for visually impaired.

Contact. E-mail: admissions@ecollege.edu
Phone: (479) 248-7236 ext. 223 Fax: (479) 248-1455
Barry Landon, Director of Admissions, Ecclesia College, 9653 Nations Drive, Springdale, AR 72762

Harding University
Searcy, Arkansas
www.harding.edu

CB code: 6267

- Private 4-year university affiliated with Church of Christ
- Residential campus in large town
- 4,228 degree-seeking undergraduates: 5% part-time, 53% women, 4% African American, 1% Asian American, 3% Hispanic American, 1% Native American, 7% international
- 1,531 degree-seeking graduate students
- 72% of applicants admitted
- SAT or ACT (ACT writing optional) required
- 63% graduate within 6 years; 30% enter graduate study

General. Founded in 1924. Regionally accredited. **Degrees:** 798 bachelor's awarded; master's, professional, doctoral offered. **Location:** 50 miles from Little Rock, 105 miles from Memphis. **Calendar:** Semester, extensive summer session. **Full-time faculty:** 263 total; 70% have terminal degrees, 4% minority, 33% women. **Part-time faculty:** 222 total; 31% have terminal degrees, 4% minority, 37% women. **Class size:** 48% < 20, 34% 20-39, 9% 40-49, 9% 50-99, less than 1% >100.

Freshman class profile. 2,121 applied, 1,531 admitted, 1,013 enrolled.

Mid 50% test scores			
SAT critical reading:	500-620	Rank in top tenth:	28%
SAT math:	500-640	End year in good standing:	90%
ACT composite:	22-28	Return as sophomores:	81%
GPA 3.75 or higher:	38%	Out-of-state:	73%
GPA 3.50-3.74:	21%	Live on campus:	97%
GPA 3.0-3.49:	28%	International:	4%
GPA 2.0-2.99:	12%	Fraternities:	40%
Rank in top quarter:	53%	Sororities:	47%

Basis for selection. Test scores, academic record, references, interview important. Selective admission with limited openings, students must apply early. Students are encouraged to take rigorous classes in high school. Audition recommended for music majors, portfolio for art majors.

High school preparation. College-preparatory program recommended. 15 units required; 20 recommended. Required and recommended units include English 4, mathematics 3-4, social studies 3-4, science 2-4, foreign language 2 and academic electives 3.

2011-2012 Annual costs. Tuition/fees: $14,610. Room/board: $6,031. Books/supplies: $900. Personal expenses: $1,600.

Financial aid. Non-need-based: Scholarships awarded for academics, alumni affiliation, art, athletics, leadership, music/drama, religious affiliation, ROTC, state residency.

Application procedures. Admission: No deadline. $40 fee. Admission notification on a rolling basis. Early application encouraged. **Financial aid:** Priority date 4/15; no closing date. FAFSA required. Applicants notified on a rolling basis starting 2/15; must reply within 2 week(s) of notification.

Academics. Special study options: Accelerated study, combined bachelor's/graduate degree, cooperative education, distance learning, double major, dual enrollment of high school students, ESL, honors, independent study, internships, liberal arts/career combination, student-designed major, study abroad, teacher certification program. **Credit/placement by examination:** AP, CLEP, IB, SAT, ACT, institutional tests. 32 credit hours maximum toward bachelor's degree. **Support services:** Learning center, reduced course load, remedial instruction, study skills assistance, tutoring, writing center.

Honors college/program. ACT score of 27 or higher, or SAT of 1220 (exclusive of Writing) or higher. About 200 students admitted each fall.

Majors. Biology: General, biochemistry, Biochemistry/molecular biology. **Business:** Accounting, business admin, fashion, finance, international, marketing, sales/distribution. **Communications:** Advertising, broadcast journalism, communications/speech/rhetoric, digital media, journalism, public relations. **Computer sciences:** Computer science, information technology, web page design. **Education:** Art, biology, early childhood, early childhood special, elementary, English, family/consumer sciences, French, health, mathematics, middle, multi-level teacher, music, science, social studies, Spanish, special ed, speech. **Engineering:** Biomedical, computer, electrical, mechanical. **English:** English lit. **Foreign languages:** French, Spanish. **Health services:** Athletic training, clinical lab science, communication disorders, dietetics, health care admin, nursing (RN), prepharmacy, speech pathology. **History:** General. **Human services:** General, social work. **Liberal arts:** Humanities. **Math:** General. **Parks/recreation:** Exercise sciences, sports admin. **Physical sciences:** Chemistry, physics. **Protective services:** Criminal

justice. **Psychology:** General. **Social sciences:** General, economics, international economic development, political science. **Theology:** Bible, missionary, religious ed, theology, youth ministry. **Visual/performing arts:** Dramatic, graphic design, interior design, music, painting, studio arts. **Work/family studies:** General, child development, family/community services, housing.

Most popular majors. Business/marketing 19%, communications/journalism 6%, education 12%, health sciences 13%, liberal arts 9%.

Computing on campus. 482 workstations in library, computer center, student center. Dormitories wired for high-speed internet access and linked to campus network. Commuter students can connect to campus network. Online course registration, online library, helpline, repair service, wireless network available.

Student life. Freshman orientation: Available, $95 fee. Preregistration for classes offered. Held the 3 days before start of fall semester. Fee includes all activities, meals, t-shirt and academic planner. **Policies:** Religious observance required. **Housing:** Guaranteed on-campus for freshmen. Single-sex dorms, special housing for disabled, apartments, wellness housing available. $130 fully refundable deposit, deadline 5/1. Approved off-campus housing. **Activities:** Bands, campus ministries, choral groups, drama, international student organizations, music ensembles, radio station, student government, student newspaper, symphony orchestra, TV station, College Republicans, College Democrats, Good News Singers, Timothy Club, religious mission campaigns, Multi-cultural Student Action Committee, Harding Athletes as Role Models, Harding in Action.

Athletics. NCAA. **Intercollegiate:** Baseball M, basketball, cheerleading M, cross-country, football (tackle) M, golf, soccer, tennis, track and field, volleyball W. **Intramural:** Archery M, basketball, cross-country M, football (non-tackle), racquetball M, soccer, softball, swimming, table tennis M, tennis, track and field, volleyball. **Team name:** Bisons.

Student services. Adult student services, chaplain/spiritual director, career counseling, student employment services, financial aid counseling, health services, minority student services, personal counseling, placement for graduates. **Physically disabled:** Services for visually, speech, hearing impaired.

Contact. E-mail: admissions@harding.edu
Phone: (501) 279-4407 Toll-free number: (800) 477-4407
Fax: (501) 279-4129
Glenn Dillard, Assistant Vice President for Enrollment Management, Harding University, 915 East Market Avenue, Searcy, AR 72149-2255

Henderson State University
Arkadelphia, Arkansas
www.getreddie.com

CB member
CB code: 6272

- Public 4-year university and liberal arts college
- Commuter campus in large town
- 3,365 degree-seeking undergraduates: 10% part-time, 56% women, 23% African American, 1% Asian American, 3% Hispanic American, 1% international
- 345 degree-seeking graduate students
- 61% of applicants admitted
- SAT or ACT (ACT writing optional) required

General. Founded in 1890. Regionally accredited. **Degrees:** 447 bachelor's awarded; master's offered. **ROTC:** Army. **Location:** 67 miles from Little Rock. **Calendar:** Semester, limited summer session. **Full-time faculty:** 166 total; 69% have terminal degrees, 13% minority, 42% women. **Part-time faculty:** 74 total; 20% have terminal degrees, 8% minority, 68% women. **Class size:** 53% < 20, 40% 20-39, 5% 40-49, 2% 50-99, less than 1% >100. **Special facilities:** Planetarium.

Freshman class profile. 3,222 applied, 1,981 admitted, 826 enrolled.

Mid 50% test scores			
SAT critical reading:	380-580	GPA 3.0-3.49:	33%
SAT math:	450-520	GPA 2.0-2.99:	35%
SAT writing:	430-520	Rank in top quarter:	39%
ACT composite:	18-24	Rank in top tenth:	13%
GPA 3.75 or higher:	15%	Return as sophomores:	58%
GPA 3.50-3.74:	15%	Out-of-state:	12%
		Live on campus:	73%

Basis for selection. Applicants must have 19 ACT and 2.5 GPA for unconditional admission. Those not meeting GPA requirement admitted conditionally. Applicants who do not meet minimum test score standards may be admitted through appeal process. Deadline for applying for appeal is July 15. Test scores must be on file with Admissions prior to registering for classes. Audition recommended for music and theater arts majors. **Home

schooled: Transcript of courses and grades required. 18 ACT required. Completion of college prep curriculum encouraged. **Learning Disabled:** Student Support Disability Services assesses needs of students with learning disabilities.

High school preparation. 14 units required; 22 recommended. Required and recommended units include English 4, mathematics 4, social studies 2, history 1 and science 3. Required: 1/2 oral comm, 1/2 fine art, 6 career focus.

2011-2012 Annual costs. Tuition/fees: $6,714; $12,324 out-of-state. Room/board: $5,816. Books/supplies: $1,200. Personal expenses: $2,200.

Financial aid. Non-need-based: Scholarships awarded for academics, alumni affiliation, art, athletics, leadership, minority status, music/drama, state residency.

Application procedures. Admission: Closing date 7/15 (receipt date). No application fee. Admission notification on a rolling basis. Application closing date July 15 for applicants with ACT score under 18. **Financial aid:** Priority date 4/15; no closing date. FAFSA required. Applicants notified on a rolling basis starting 3/1; must reply within 2 week(s) of notification.

Academics. Special study options: Cross-registration, distance learning, honors, internships, liberal arts/career combination, teacher certification program. **Credit/placement by examination:** AP, CLEP, SAT, ACT, institutional tests. 30 credit hours maximum toward bachelor's degree. **Support services:** Learning center, remedial instruction, study skills assistance, tutoring, writing center.

Honors college/program. 26 ACT required; approximately 90 admitted.

Majors. Biology: General. **Business:** General, accounting, management information systems. **Communications:** Journalism. **Computer sciences:** General. **Education:** Art, business, early childhood, middle, physical, social science. **English:** English lit, rhetoric/composition. **Foreign languages:** Spanish. **Health services:** Athletic training, clinical lab science, nursing (RN), radiologic technology/medical imaging. **History:** General. **Human services:** General, social work. **Math:** General. **Parks/recreation:** Facilities management. **Physical sciences:** Chemistry, physics. **Psychology:** General. **Social sciences:** Political science, sociology. **Visual/performing arts:** Art, dramatic, music, music performance. **Work/family studies:** General.

Most popular majors. Business/marketing 17%, education 19%, health sciences 6%, liberal arts 11%, psychology 8%.

Computing on campus. 125 workstations in dormitories, library, computer center, student center. Dormitories linked to campus network. Commuter students can connect to campus network. Online library, helpline, wireless network available.

Student life. Freshman orientation: Mandatory. Preregistration for classes offered. 1.5 day program for students and parents, held several times during July, again in August if necessary. **Housing:** Guaranteed on-campus for freshmen. Coed dorms, single-sex dorms, cooperative housing available. $50 nonrefundable deposit. Special hall for Honors College participants, special floor for freshman interest groups available. On-campus apartments leased by outside firm available. Two residence halls are co-ed. **Activities:** Bands, campus ministries, choral groups, dance, drama, literary magazine, music ensembles, radio station, student government, student newspaper, TV station, College Republicans, Young Democrats, Student Foundation, Heart and Key service organization, several religious organizations.

Athletics. NCAA. **Intercollegiate:** Baseball M, basketball, cross-country W, football (tackle) M, golf, softball W, swimming, tennis W, volleyball W. **Team name:** Reddies.

Student services. Career counseling, student employment services, health services, personal counseling, placement for graduates, veterans' counselor. **Physically disabled:** Services for visually, speech, hearing impaired.

Contact. E-mail: admissions@hsu.edu
Phone: (870) 230-5028 Toll-free number: (800) 228-7333
Fax: (870) 230-5066
Vikita Hardwrick, Director of Admissions, Henderson State University, 1100 Henderson Street, Arkadelphia, AR 71999-0001

Hendrix College
Conway, Arkansas
www.hendrix.edu

CB member
CB code: 6273

- Private 4-year liberal arts college affiliated with United Methodist Church
- Residential campus in small city

- 1,413 degree-seeking undergraduates: 1% part-time, 58% women, 3% African American, 3% Asian American, 5% Hispanic American, 4% international
- 11 degree-seeking graduate students
- 83% of applicants admitted
- SAT or ACT (ACT writing optional), application essay required
- 73% graduate within 6 years; 62% enter graduate study

General. Founded in 1876. Regionally accredited. **Degrees:** 286 bachelor's awarded; master's offered. **ROTC:** Army. **Location:** 30 miles from Little Rock. **Calendar:** Semester. **Full-time faculty:** 109 total; 90% have terminal degrees, 12% minority, 43% women. **Part-time faculty:** 30 total; 53% have terminal degrees, 50% women. **Class size:** 63% < 20, 35% 20-39, 2% 40-49, less than 1% 50-99. **Special facilities:** Teaching theater, two pipe organs, access to elephant farm for research and volunteer service, arboretum, ring laser, hybrid rocket lab, climbing wall.

Freshman class profile. 1,528 applied, 1,261 admitted, 375 enrolled.

Mid 50% test scores			
SAT critical reading:	570-690	Rank in top quarter:	80%
SAT math:	550-670	Rank in top tenth:	59%
ACT composite:	27-32	End year in good standing:	3%
GPA 3.75 or higher:	69%	Return as sophomores:	80%
GPA 3.50-3.74:	12%	Out-of-state:	54%
GPA 3.0-3.49:	16%	Live on campus:	99%
GPA 2.0-2.99:	3%	International:	4%

Basis for selection. Academic competence, scholastic potential, motivation, character, and high school leadership important. High school transcript, application, and school report required. Interview may be required. **Home schooled:** Interview required. Portfolio required.

High school preparation. College-preparatory program required. 14 units recommended. Recommended units include English 4, mathematics 3, social studies 3, science 2 and foreign language 2.

2011-2012 Annual costs. Tuition/fees: $34,230. Room/board: $9,714. Books/supplies: $1,100. Personal expenses: $860.

2011-2012 Financial aid. Need-based: 313 full-time freshmen applied for aid; 256 were judged to have need; 256 of these received aid. Average need met was 87%. Average scholarship/grant was $26,165; average loan $4,226. 82% of total undergraduate aid awarded as scholarships/grants, 18% as loans/jobs. **Non-need-based:** Awarded to 821 full-time undergraduates, including 214 freshmen. Scholarships awarded for academics, art, leadership, music/drama.

Application procedures. Admission: Priority date 2/1; deadline 6/1 (postmark date). $40 fee, may be waived for applicants with need, free for online applicants. Admission notification on a rolling basis beginning on or about 12/15. Must reply by May 1 or within 4 week(s) if notified thereafter. Second Early Action plan: deadline 2/1, decision notification begins 3/1. **Financial aid:** Priority date 3/1; no closing date. FAFSA required. Applicants notified on a rolling basis starting 3/1; must reply by 5/1 or within 4 week(s) of notification.

Academics. Special study options: Combined bachelor's/graduate degree, cooperative education, double major, ESL, independent study, internships, student-designed major, study abroad, teacher certification program, Washington semester. Hendrix-in-Brussels (Belgium), Hendrix-in-Costa Rica, Hendrix-in-Heilongjiang (China), Hendrix-in-Graz (Austria), Hendrix-in-London (UK), Hendrix-in-Madrid (Spain), Hendrix-in-Oxford (UK), Hendrix-in-Shangai, Hendrix-in-Uganda/Rwanda, Hendrix-in-Florence, Hendrix-in-Turkey, Academia dell 'Arte, other programs with 140 colleges and universities on 6 continents including countries such as Australia, Finland, France, Ghana, Japan. **Credit/placement by examination:** AP, CLEP, IB, SAT, ACT, institutional tests. 6 credit hours maximum toward bachelor's degree. **Support services:** Pre-admission summer program, study skills assistance, tutoring, writing center.

Majors. Area/ethnic studies: American. **Biology:** General, Biochemistry/molecular biology. **Business:** Accounting. **Computer sciences:** Computer science. **Conservation:** Environmental studies. **English:** English lit. **Foreign languages:** Classics, French, German, Spanish. **History:** General. **Math:** General. **Philosophy/religion:** Philosophy, religion. **Physical sciences:** Chemical physics, chemistry, physics. **Psychology:** General. **Social sciences:** Anthropology, economics, international relations, political science, sociology. **Visual/performing arts:** Art, dramatic, music.

Most popular majors. Biology 15%, English 8%, interdisciplinary studies 6%, psychology 12%, social sciences 22%.

Computing on campus. 75 workstations in dormitories, library, computer center, student center. Dormitories wired for high-speed internet access and

linked to campus network. Commuter students can connect to campus network. Online course registration, helpline, repair service, student web hosting, wireless network available.

Student life. Freshman orientation: Mandatory. Preregistration for classes offered. 7 day program held prior to fall term. **Housing:** Guaranteed on-campus for freshmen. Coed dorms, single-sex dorms, special housing for disabled, apartments, wellness housing available. $350 nonrefundable deposit, deadline 5/1. Suite-style small houses. **Activities:** Bands, campus ministries, choral groups, dance, drama, film society, international student organizations, literary magazine, music ensembles, Model UN, radio station, student government, student newspaper, Students for Black Culture, College Republicans, Young Democrats, environmental group, Amnesty International, BACCHUS, Hendrix Peace Links, religious life council, volunteer action center, Students Promoting the Education of Asian Cultures.

Athletics. NCAA. **Intercollegiate:** Baseball M, basketball, cross-country, diving, field hockey W, golf, lacrosse M, soccer, softball W, swimming, tennis, track and field, volleyball W. **Intramural:** Basketball, football (non-tackle), racquetball, soccer, softball, table tennis, tennis. **Team name:** Warriors.

Student services. Alcohol/substance abuse counseling, chaplain/spiritual director, career counseling, student employment services, financial aid counseling, health services, minority student services, personal counseling, placement for graduates. **Physically disabled:** Services for visually impaired.

Contact. E-mail: adm@hendrix.edu
Phone: (501) 450-1362 Toll-free number: (800) 277-9017
Fax: (501) 450-3843
Fred Baker, Director of Admission, Hendrix College, 1600 Washington Avenue, Conway, AR 72032-3080

ITT Technical Institute: Little Rock
Little Rock, Arkansas
www.itt-tech.edu   CB code: 2721

- For-profit 4-year technical college
- Commuter campus in small city
- 638 undergraduates
- Interview required

General. Accredited by ACICS. **Degrees:** 31 bachelor's, 134 associate awarded. **Calendar:** Quarter, extensive summer session. **Full-time faculty:** 11 total. **Part-time faculty:** 39 total.

Basis for selection. Satisfactory scores from on-site tests in English and mathematics required.

2011-2012 Annual costs. Estimated costs as of July 2011: per-credit-hour charge, $493, depending upon level and course of study; academic fee, $200. Certain programs of study require purchase of tools, which could cost an additional $100 to $600. All costs are subject to change.

Application procedures. Admission: No deadline. No application fee. Admission notification on a rolling basis. **Financial aid:** No deadline. FAFSA, institutional form required. Applicants notified on a rolling basis.

Academics. Credit/placement by examination: AP, CLEP. **Support services:** Learning center, tutoring.

Majors. Business: Business admin, construction management. **Communications technology:** Animation/special effects. **Computer sciences:** Security. **Protective services:** Law enforcement admin.

Most popular majors. Communication technologies 56%, computer/information sciences 44%, security/protective services 18%.

Computing on campus. Online library available.

Student life. Freshman orientation: Available. Preregistration for classes offered.

Student services. Career counseling, student employment services, placement for graduates.

Contact. Phone: (501) 565-5550 Toll-free number: (800) 359-4429
Reed Thompson, Director of Recruitment, ITT Technical Institute: Little Rock, 12200 Westhaven Drive, Little Rock, AR 72211

John Brown University
Siloam Springs, Arkansas
www.jbu.edu   CB code: 6321

- Private 4-year university and liberal arts college affiliated with interdenominational tradition
- Residential campus in large town
- 1,264 degree-seeking undergraduates: 2% part-time, 53% women, 2% African American, 1% Asian American, 4% Hispanic American, 1% Native American, 8% international
- 439 degree-seeking graduate students
- 70% of applicants admitted
- SAT or ACT (ACT writing optional), application essay required
- 66% graduate within 6 years; 18% enter graduate study

General. Founded in 1919. Regionally accredited. **Degrees:** 492 bachelor's awarded; master's offered. **ROTC:** Army, Air Force. **Location:** 30 miles from Fayetteville; 75 miles from Tulsa, OK. **Calendar:** Semester, limited summer session. **Full-time faculty:** 68 total; 76% have terminal degrees, 9% minority, 24% women. **Part-time faculty:** 55 total; 11% have terminal degrees, 4% minority, 51% women. **Class size:** 55% < 20, 39% 20-39, 6% 40-49. **Special facilities:** Cadaver lab, outdoor renewable energy lab, indoor high-bay construction management work area, historical cathedral.

Freshman class profile. 1,093 applied, 765 admitted, 360 enrolled.

Mid 50% test scores			
SAT critical reading:	520-680	GPA 3.0-3.49:	20%
SAT math:	510-620	GPA 2.0-2.99:	10%
SAT writing:	490-630	Rank in top quarter:	69%
ACT composite:	22-29	Rank in top tenth:	37%
GPA 3.75 or higher:	49%	Return as sophomores:	78%
GPA 3.50-3.74:	21%	International:	6%

Basis for selection. Test scores, secondary school record, recommendations, essay, interview most important. Special talents, class rank considered. Combined SAT score of 950 (exclusive of Writing), ACT score of 20 or above. Interview recommended. Audition required of music majors; portfolio recommended for art majors. **Home schooled:** Transcript of courses and grades required.

High school preparation. College-preparatory program recommended. Recommended units include English 4, mathematics 3, social studies 2, history 1, science 2 (laboratory 1) and foreign language 2. 4 units of math, 3 science for science and engineering majors; 2 foreign language recommended for home educated students.

2011-2012 Annual costs. Tuition/fees: $20,766. Room/board: $7,562. Books/supplies: $800. Personal expenses: $1,350.

2011-2012 Financial aid. Need-based: 321 full-time freshmen applied for aid; 277 were judged to have need; 277 of these received aid. Average need met was 76%. Average scholarship/grant was $16,422; average loan $1,954. 72% of total undergraduate aid awarded as scholarships/grants, 28% as loans/jobs. **Non-need-based:** Awarded to 358 full-time undergraduates, including 141 freshmen. Scholarships awarded for academics, alumni affiliation, art, athletics, leadership, music/drama, ROTC.

Application procedures. Admission: Priority date 5/1; no deadline. $25 fee, may be waived for applicants with need. Admission notification on a rolling basis beginning on or about 11/1. Must reply by May 1 or within 2 week(s) if notified thereafter. **Financial aid:** Priority date 3/1; no closing date. FAFSA required. Applicants notified on a rolling basis starting 3/1; must reply by 5/1 or within 4 week(s) of notification.

Academics. Special study options: Accelerated study, distance learning, double major, dual enrollment of high school students, ESL, exchange student, honors, independent study, internships, liberal arts/career combination, student-designed major, study abroad, teacher certification program, Washington semester. **Credit/placement by examination:** AP, CLEP, IB. 15 credit hours maximum toward associate degree, 30 toward bachelor's. **Support services:** Learning center, reduced course load, remedial instruction, study skills assistance, tutoring, writing center.

Honors college/program. Selected by admissions office/honors committee; based on GPA, SAT/ACT and interview.

Majors. Biology: General, biochemistry. **Business:** Accounting, business admin, construction management, international, management information systems, marketing. **Communications:** Broadcast journalism, communications/speech/rhetoric, digital media, journalism, public relations, radio/TV. **Conservation:** Environmental science. **Education:** Early childhood, English, mathematics, middle, music, social studies. **Engineering:** General. **English:** English lit. **Foreign languages:** Spanish. **Health services:** Athletic training.

History: General. **Math:** General. **Parks/recreation:** Exercise sciences, sports admin. **Physical sciences:** Chemistry. **Psychology:** General. **Social sciences:** Political science. **Theology:** Missionary, sacred music, theology, youth ministry. **Visual/performing arts:** Graphic design, illustration, music, music performance, photography. **Work/family studies:** Family/community services.

Most popular majors. Business/marketing 47%, education 10%, theological studies 6%, visual/performing arts 6%.

Computing on campus. 200 workstations in dormitories, library, computer center, student center. Dormitories wired for high-speed internet access and linked to campus network. Commuter students can connect to campus network. Online course registration, online library, helpline, wireless network available.

Student life. Freshman orientation: Mandatory, $75 fee. Preregistration for classes offered. **Policies:** No alcohol, drugs, or tobacco allowed on campus; all applicants required to sign community covenant each year. Religious observance required. **Housing:** Guaranteed on-campus for freshmen. Coed dorms, single-sex dorms, special housing for disabled, apartments available. $100 fully refundable deposit. **Activities:** Bands, campus ministries, choral groups, dance, drama, film society, international student organizations, literary magazine, music ensembles, musical theater, radio station, student government, student newspaper.

Athletics. NAIA. **Intercollegiate:** Basketball, cheerleading, cross-country, golf M, soccer, tennis, volleyball W. **Intramural:** Baseball M, basketball, football (non-tackle), football (tackle) M, racquetball, soccer, softball, tennis, volleyball. **Team name:** Golden Eagles.

Student services. Chaplain/spiritual director, career counseling, student employment services, financial aid counseling, health services, personal counseling, placement for graduates. **Physically disabled:** Services for visually, hearing impaired.

Contact. E-mail: jbuinfo@jbu.edu
Phone: (479) 524-7157 Toll-free number: (877) 528-4636
Fax: (479) 524-4196
Don Crandall, Vice President for Enrollment Management, John Brown University, 2000 West University Street, Siloam Springs, AR 72761-2121

Lyon College
Batesville, Arkansas — **CB member**
www.lyon.edu — **CB code: 6009**

- Private 4-year liberal arts college affiliated with Presbyterian Church (USA)
- Residential campus in small town
- 586 degree-seeking undergraduates: 3% part-time, 54% women, 4% African American, 2% Asian American, 5% Hispanic American, 1% Native American, 3% international
- 62% of applicants admitted
- SAT or ACT (ACT writing optional) required
- 48% graduate within 6 years

General. Founded in 1872. Regionally accredited. **Degrees:** 99 bachelor's awarded. **Location:** 90 miles from Little Rock. **Calendar:** Semester, limited summer session. **Full-time faculty:** 42 total; 98% have terminal degrees, 10% minority, 29% women. **Part-time faculty:** 28 total; 4% minority, 64% women. **Class size:** 70% < 20, 28% 20-39, 2% 40-49, 1% 50-99. **Special facilities:** Ozark Regional Studies Center.

Freshman class profile. 970 applied, 605 admitted, 158 enrolled.

Mid 50% test scores			
SAT critical reading:	490-670	GPA 2.0-2.99:	8%
SAT math:	510-620	Rank in top quarter:	64%
SAT writing:	530-590	Rank in top tenth:	32%
ACT composite:	23-29	End year in good standing:	86%
GPA 3.75 or higher:	42%	Return as sophomores:	61%
GPA 3.50-3.74:	21%	Out-of-state:	18%
GPA 3.0-3.49:	29%	Live on campus:	89%
		International:	1%

Basis for selection. High school academic performance and standardized test scores most important. Personal essays and letters of recommendation considered on case by case basis. Math proficiency and placement judged with ACT math subscores. Auditions or portfolios required for fine arts.

High school preparation. College-preparatory program recommended. 16 units required; 18 recommended. Required and recommended units include English 4, mathematics 3-4, social studies 1, history 2, science 3-4 (laboratory 2), foreign language 2 and academic electives 1.

2011-2012 Annual costs. Tuition/fees: $22,906. Room/board: $7,340. Books/supplies: $1,000. Personal expenses: $1,000.

2011-2012 Financial aid. Need-based: 150 full-time freshmen applied for aid; 136 were judged to have need; 136 of these received aid. Average need met was 83%. Average scholarship/grant was $18,682; average loan $3,177. 73% of total undergraduate aid awarded as scholarships/grants, 27% as loans/jobs. **Non-need-based:** Awarded to 226 full-time undergraduates, including 61 freshmen. Scholarships awarded for academics, art, athletics, leadership, minority status, music/drama, religious affiliation, state residency.

Application procedures. Admission: Priority date 1/15; no deadline. $25 fee, may be waived for applicants with need. Admission notification on a rolling basis. Must reply by May 1 or within 2 week(s) if notified thereafter. **Financial aid:** Priority date 3/15; no closing date. FAFSA required. Applicants notified on a rolling basis starting 3/1; must reply by 8/15.

Academics. Academic honor code administered by peer-elected student honor council. **Special study options:** Accelerated study, combined bachelor's/graduate degree, cross-registration, double major, dual enrollment of high school students, independent study, internships, student-designed major, study abroad, teacher certification program, Washington semester. **Credit/placement by examination:** AP, CLEP, IB, SAT, ACT, institutional tests. 33 credit hours maximum toward bachelor's degree. **Support services:** Learning center, study skills assistance, tutoring, writing center.

Majors. Biology: General. **Business:** Accounting, business admin. **Education:** Early childhood. **English:** English lit. **Foreign languages:** Spanish. **History:** General. **Math:** General. **Philosophy/religion:** Philosophy, religion. **Physical sciences:** Chemistry. **Psychology:** General. **Social sciences:** Economics, political science. **Visual/performing arts:** Art, dramatic, music.

Most popular majors. Biology 15%, business/marketing 17%, English 9%, history 15%, psychology 12%, social sciences 8%, visual/performing arts 11%.

Computing on campus. 100 workstations in dormitories, library, computer center, student center. Dormitories wired for high-speed internet access and linked to campus network. Commuter students can connect to campus network. Online course registration, online library, helpline, repair service, wireless network available.

Student life. Freshman orientation: Mandatory, $150 fee. Preregistration for classes offered. **Policies:** Social code administered by peer-elected student social council. **Housing:** Guaranteed on-campus for all undergraduates. Coed dorms, single-sex dorms, apartments, wellness housing available. $100 fully refundable deposit. Limited college-owned off-campus housing is available. **Activities:** Concert band, campus ministries, choral groups, drama, international student organizations, literary magazine, music ensembles, Model UN, student government, student newspaper, black student association, Fellowship of Christian Athletes.

Athletics. NAIA. **Intercollegiate:** Baseball M, basketball, cheerleading, cross-country, golf, soccer, softball W, volleyball W. **Intramural:** Badminton, basketball, football (non-tackle), softball, table tennis, tennis, volleyball. **Team name:** Scots.

Student services. Chaplain/spiritual director, career counseling, financial aid counseling, health services, personal counseling, placement for graduates.

Contact. E-mail: admissions@lyon.edu
Phone: (870) 307-7250 Toll-free number: (800) 423-2542
Fax: (870) 307-7542
Josh Manning, Director of Admissions, Lyon College, PO Box 2317, Batesville, AR 72503-2317

Ouachita Baptist University
Arkadelphia, Arkansas
www.obu.edu — **CB code: 6549**

- Private 4-year liberal arts college affiliated with Southern Baptist Convention
- Residential campus in large town
- 1,571 degree-seeking undergraduates: 1% part-time, 53% women, 6% African American, 1% Asian American, 3% Hispanic American, 1% Native American, 3% international
- 64% of applicants admitted
- SAT or ACT (ACT writing optional) required
- 62% graduate within 6 years; 50% enter graduate study

General. Founded in 1886. Regionally accredited. **Degrees:** 258 bachelor's awarded. **ROTC:** Army. **Location:** 65 miles from Little Rock. **Calendar:**

Semester, extensive summer session. **Full-time faculty:** 108 total; 82% have terminal degrees, 2% minority, 35% women. **Part-time faculty:** 31 total; 19% have terminal degrees, 3% minority, 64% women. **Class size:** 55% < 20, 41% 20-39, 4% 40-49.

Freshman class profile. 1,953 applied, 1,245 admitted, 459 enrolled.

Mid 50% test scores			
SAT critical reading:	470-590	Rank in top tenth:	32%
SAT math:	500-610	End year in good standing:	92%
ACT composite:	21-27	Return as sophomores:	82%
GPA 3.75 or higher:	42%	Out-of-state:	39%
GPA 3.50-3.74:	21%	Live on campus:	99%
GPA 3.0-3.49:	24%	International:	1%
GPA 2.0-2.99:	13%	Fraternities:	33%
Rank in top quarter:	62%	Sororities:	40%

Basis for selection. Test scores and school achievement record most important. 2.75 GPA, 20 ACT required. Interview recommended. Portfolio recommended for studio art majors.

High school preparation. College-preparatory program recommended. 15 units required; 19 recommended. Required and recommended units include English 4, mathematics 2-3, social studies 1, history 2, science 2-3, foreign language 2 and academic electives 4.

2011-2012 Annual costs. Tuition/fees: $20,630. Room/board: $6,040. Books/supplies: $1,100. Personal expenses: $1,500.

2011-2012 Financial aid. Need-based: 418 full-time freshmen applied for aid; 314 were judged to have need; 314 of these received aid. Average need met was 85%. Average scholarship/grant was $12,732; average loan $4,859. 76% of total undergraduate aid awarded as scholarships/grants, 24% as loans/jobs. **Non-need-based:** Awarded to 992 full-time undergraduates, including 268 freshmen. Scholarships awarded for academics, alumni affiliation, art, athletics, job skills, leadership, minority status, music/drama, religious affiliation, ROTC, state residency.

Application procedures. Admission: Priority date 1/15; no deadline. No application fee. Admission notification on a rolling basis. Deferred admission up to one year. **Financial aid:** Priority date 1/15, closing date 6/1. FAFSA required. Applicants notified on a rolling basis starting 11/1; must reply by 6/1.

Academics. Classes in Arkansas Folkways taught at Old Washington State Park. International exchange programs in Australia, Austria, China, Costa Rica, England, France, Germany, Hong Kong, Indonesia, Japan, Morocco, New Zealand, Russia, Scotland, and South Africa. **Special study options:** Cross-registration, distance learning, double major, ESL, honors, independent study, internships, study abroad, teacher certification program. **Credit/placement by examination:** AP, CLEP, IB, ACT, institutional tests. 24 credit hours maximum toward bachelor's degree. **Support services:** Learning center, reduced course load, remedial instruction, study skills assistance, tutoring, writing center.

Majors. Biology: General. **Business:** Accounting, business admin. **Communications:** Communications/speech/rhetoric, media studies. **Computer sciences:** Computer science. **Education:** Art, biology, business, chemistry, drama/dance, early childhood, English, foreign languages, French, health, history, mathematics, middle, music, physical, physics, science, secondary, social studies, Spanish, speech. **English:** English lit. **Foreign languages:** French, Spanish. **Health services:** Communication disorders, dietetics, predental, premedicine, prenursing, prepharmacy, prephysical therapy, preveterinary. **History:** General. **Math:** General. **Parks/recreation:** Exercise sciences. **Philosophy/religion:** Philosophy. **Physical sciences:** Chemistry, physics. **Psychology:** General. **Social sciences:** Political science, sociology. **Theology:** Bible, missionary, pastoral counseling, sacred music, theology. **Visual/performing arts:** Dramatic, graphic design, music, music history, music performance, music theory/composition, musical theater, piano/keyboard, studio arts, voice/opera.

Most popular majors. Biology 8%, business/marketing 15%, communications/journalism 7%, education 9%, health sciences 8%, psychology 6%, theological studies 19%, visual/performing arts 8%.

Computing on campus. 275 workstations in dormitories, library, computer center, student center. Dormitories wired for high-speed internet access and linked to campus network. Commuter students can connect to campus network. Online library, helpline, student web hosting, wireless network available.

Student life. Freshman orientation: Mandatory. Preregistration for classes offered. 3-day weekend program prior to registration with one session for parents; optional 3-day summer retreat. **Policies:** Students under 22 must live in campus housing unless commuting. Only local fraternities and sororities are permitted. Religious observance required. **Housing:** Guaranteed on-campus for all undergraduates. Single-sex dorms, special housing for disabled, apartments, wellness housing available. $50 fully refundable deposit, deadline 6/1. **Activities:** Bands, campus ministries, choral groups, drama, international

student organizations, literary magazine, music ensembles, Model UN, musical theater, opera, student government, student newspaper, Fellowship of Christian Athletes, Ouachita student foundation, Pew College Society, ROMS, Young Democrats, College Republicans.

Athletics. NCAA. **Intercollegiate:** Baseball M, basketball, cheerleading, cross-country W, diving, football (tackle) M, golf, soccer, softball W, swimming, tennis, volleyball W, wrestling M. **Intramural:** Basketball, football (non-tackle), handball, racquetball, soccer, softball, table tennis, volleyball. **Team name:** Tigers.

Student services. Alcohol/substance abuse counseling, chaplain/spiritual director, career counseling, services for economically disadvantaged, student employment services, financial aid counseling, health services, minority student services, personal counseling, placement for graduates, veterans' counselor. **Physically disabled:** Services for visually, speech, hearing impaired.

Contact. E-mail: motll@obu.edu
Phone: (870) 245-5110 Toll-free number: (800) 342-5628
Fax: (870) 245-5500
Lori Motl, Director of Admissions Counseling, Ouachita Baptist University, OBU Box 3776, Arkadelphia, AR 71998-0001

Philander Smith College
Little Rock, Arkansas
www.philander.edu

CB member
CB code: 6578

- Private 4-year liberal arts college affiliated with United Methodist Church
- Commuter campus in small city
- 729 degree-seeking undergraduates: 7% part-time, 65% women, 92% African American, 1% Hispanic American, 5% international
- 68% of applicants admitted
- SAT or ACT (ACT writing optional) required

General. Founded in 1877. Regionally accredited. **Degrees:** 98 bachelor's awarded. **Calendar:** Semester, limited summer session. **Full-time faculty:** 44 total; 64% have terminal degrees, 73% minority, 39% women. **Part-time faculty:** 29 total; 10% have terminal degrees, 86% minority, 45% women. **Class size:** 73% < 20, 27% 20-39.

Freshman class profile. 2,906 applied, 1,976 admitted, 197 enrolled.

Mid 50% test scores			
SAT critical reading:	360-510	GPA 2.0-2.99:	51%
SAT math:	350-510	Rank in top quarter:	32%
SAT writing:	390-490	Rank in top tenth:	16%
ACT composite:	16-20	Return as sophomores:	60%
GPA 3.75 or higher:	10%	Out-of-state:	66%
GPA 3.50-3.74:	9%	Live on campus:	84%
GPA 3.0-3.49:	25%	International:	2%

Basis for selection. High school GPA of 2.5 and ACT Composite of 19 along with rigor of high school record for unconditional admission. Students not meeting that criteria can be admitted on probation. Students admitted without ACT scores are administered COMPASS test for placement purposes. Students who score below placement cut-off scores in writing, English, or math also required to take COMPASS test.

High school preparation. College-preparatory program recommended. Recommended units include English 4, mathematics 3, social studies 2, science 2 (laboratory 1), foreign language 2 and academic electives 6.

2011-2012 Annual costs. Tuition/fees: $11,760. Tuition only for incoming freshman is $11,350. Returning undergraduates pay $9,500 for full-time tuition; all other fees are the same for all students. Room/board: $7,600. Books/supplies: $1,000. Personal expenses: $1,620.

2011-2012 Financial aid. All financial aid based on need. 181 full-time freshmen applied for aid; 177 were judged to have need; 177 of these received aid. Average need met was 60%. Average scholarship/grant was $10,210; average loan $3,380. 50% of total undergraduate aid awarded as scholarships/grants, 50% as loans/jobs.

Application procedures. Admission: Priority date 3/1; deadline 7/1. $25 fee, may be waived for applicants with need. Admission notification on a rolling basis. Must reply by May 1 or within 2 week(s) if notified thereafter. **Financial aid:** Priority date 3/1; no closing date. FAFSA required. Applicants notified on a rolling basis starting 3/1; must reply within 2 week(s) of notification.

Academics. Special study options: Accelerated study, double major, dual enrollment of high school students, independent study, internships, study abroad, teacher certification program, weekend college. **Credit/placement by examination:** AP, CLEP, SAT, ACT. 30 credit hours maximum toward

bachelor's degree. **Support services:** Learning center, reduced course load, remedial instruction, tutoring.

Majors. Biology: General. **Business:** Administrative services, business admin. **Computer sciences:** Computer science. **Education:** Business. **English:** English lit. **Human services:** Social work. **Math:** General. **Philosophy/religion:** Philosophy, religion. **Physical sciences:** Chemistry. **Psychology:** General. **Social sciences:** Political science, sociology. **Visual/performing arts:** Music.

Most popular majors. Biology 10%, business/marketing 30%, computer/information sciences 6%, parks/recreation 9%, public administration/social services 9%, social sciences 19%.

Computing on campus. 72 workstations in dormitories, library, computer center. Dormitories wired for high-speed internet access and linked to campus network. Commuter students can connect to campus network. Online library, wireless network available.

Student life. Freshman orientation: Mandatory, $150 fee. Preregistration for classes offered. **Housing:** Coed dorms available. $245 nonrefundable deposit, deadline 7/15. Honors housing. **Activities:** Campus ministries, choral groups, dance, drama, international student organizations, student government, student newspaper.

Athletics. Intercollegiate: Baseball M, basketball, volleyball W. **Intramural:** Badminton, basketball, tennis. **Team name:** Panthers.

Student services. Career counseling, student employment services, health services, personal counseling, veterans' counselor. **Physically disabled:** Services for visually, hearing impaired.

Contact. E-mail: admissions@philander.edu
Phone: (501) 370-5221 Toll-free number: (800) 446-6772
Fax: (501) 370-5225
David Page, Director of Admissions, Philander Smith College, 900 Daisy Bates Drive, Little Rock, AR 72202-3718

Southern Arkansas University
Magnolia, Arkansas
www.saumag.edu   **CB code: 6661**

▶ Public 4-year university
▶ Residential campus in large town
▶ 2,782 degree-seeking undergraduates: 9% part-time, 57% women, 30% African American, 1% Asian American, 3% Hispanic American, 1% Native American, 3% international
▶ 460 graduate students
▶ 67% of applicants admitted
▶ SAT or ACT (ACT writing optional) required
▶ 33% graduate within 6 years

General. Founded in 1909. Regionally accredited. **Degrees:** 376 bachelor's, 63 associate awarded; master's offered. **Location:** 53 miles from Texarkana, TX; 70 miles from Shreveport, LA. **Calendar:** Semester, extensive summer session. **Full-time faculty:** 171 total; 59% have terminal degrees, 17% minority, 47% women. **Class size:** 51% < 20, 40% 20-39, 6% 40-49, 2% 50-99. **Special facilities:** University farm.

Freshman class profile. 2,499 applied, 1,671 admitted, 646 enrolled.

Mid 50% test scores		GPA 3.0-3.49:	29%
SAT critical reading:	420-550	GPA 2.0-2.99:	35%
SAT math:	450-610	Return as sophomores:	60%
ACT composite:	18-25	Out-of-state:	23%
GPA 3.75 or higher:	19%	Live on campus:	83%
GPA 3.50-3.74:	15%	International:	2%

Basis for selection. For unconditional admission, applicants must have ACT of 19 or higher. ACT of 16 to 18 allows conditional admission. Interview required of nursing majors.

High school preparation. Recommended units include English 4, mathematics 4, social studies 3, science 3 (laboratory 3) and foreign language 2. 0.5 computer science also recommended.

2011-2012 Annual costs. Tuition/fees: $6,786; $9,666 out-of-state. Room/board: $4,700. Books/supplies: $1,000. Personal expenses: $2,200.

2010-2011 Financial aid. Need-based: 50% of total undergraduate aid awarded as scholarships/grants, 50% as loans/jobs. **Non-need-based:** Scholarships awarded for academics, alumni affiliation, art, athletics, leadership, minority status, music/drama, state residency.

Application procedures. Admission: Closing date 8/30 (receipt date). No application fee. Admission notification on a rolling basis. **Financial aid:** Priority date 7/1; no closing date. FAFSA required. Applicants notified on a rolling basis starting 4/15; must reply within 2 week(s) of notification.

Academics. Special study options: Combined bachelor's/graduate degree, cross-registration, distance learning, double major, dual enrollment of high school students, honors, independent study, internships, teacher certification program. **Credit/placement by examination:** AP, CLEP, SAT, ACT. 15 credit hours maximum toward associate degree, 30 toward bachelor's. **Support services:** Learning center, reduced course load, remedial instruction, tutoring, writing center.

Honors college/program. 26 ACT required.

Majors. Biology: General. **Business:** General, accounting. **Communications:** Journalism. **Computer sciences:** General. **Education:** Agricultural, early childhood, middle, music, physical. **English:** English lit. **Foreign languages:** Spanish. **General:** Business. **Health services:** Athletic training, clinical lab science, nursing (RN). **History:** General. **Human services:** Community org/advocacy, social work. **Math:** General. **Parks/recreation:** Exercise sciences. **Physical sciences:** Chemistry, physics. **Protective services:** Criminal justice. **Psychology:** General. **Social sciences:** General, political science, sociology. **Visual/performing arts:** Dramatic, music, studio arts.

Most popular majors. Agriculture 6%, biology 6%, business/marketing 23%, education 21%, liberal arts 9%.

Computing on campus. 202 workstations in dormitories, library, computer center. Dormitories wired for high-speed internet access and linked to campus network. Commuter students can connect to campus network. Online library, helpline, wireless network available.

Student life. Freshman orientation: Mandatory, $25 fee. Preregistration for classes offered. **Policies:** Freshmen required to live on campus unless commuting or living with parents. **Housing:** Guaranteed on-campus for all undergraduates. Coed dorms, single-sex dorms, apartments, wellness housing available. $50 fully refundable deposit. **Activities:** Bands, choral groups, drama, international student organizations, music ensembles, musical theater, radio station, student government, student newspaper, more than 80 student organizations available.

Athletics. NCAA. Intercollegiate: Baseball M, basketball, cross-country, football (tackle) M, golf M, softball W, tennis W, track and field W, volleyball W. **Intramural:** Badminton, basketball, football (tackle) M, golf M, softball, table tennis, tennis, volleyball. **Team name:** Muleriders.

Student services. Alcohol/substance abuse counseling, career counseling, services for economically disadvantaged, student employment services, financial aid counseling, health services, minority student services, personal counseling, placement for graduates, veterans' counselor, women's services. **Physically disabled:** Services for visually, hearing impaired.

Contact. E-mail: sejennings@saumag.edu
Phone: (870) 235-4040 Toll-free number: (800) 332-7286
Fax: (870) 235-4931
Sarah Jennings, Dean of Enrollment Services, Southern Arkansas University, Box 9382, Magnolia, AR 71754-9382

University of Arkansas
Fayetteville, Arkansas   **CB member**
www.uark.edu   **CB code: 6866**

▶ Public 4-year university
▶ Residential campus in small city
▶ 18,617 degree-seeking undergraduates: 11% part-time, 49% women, 5% African American, 3% Asian American, 5% Hispanic American, 1% Native American, 3% international
▶ 4,016 degree-seeking graduate students
▶ 61% of applicants admitted
▶ SAT or ACT (ACT writing optional) required
▶ 59% graduate within 6 years

General. Founded in 1871. Regionally accredited. Arkansas Center for Space and Planetary Sciences, GENESIS Technology Incubator program provides tech-based companies with research and development support. **Degrees:** 2,958 bachelor's awarded; master's, professional, doctoral offered. **ROTC:** Army, Air Force. **Location:** 192 miles from Little Rock; 120 miles from Tulsa, Oklahoma. **Calendar:** Semester, limited summer session. **Full-time faculty:** 989 total; 86% have terminal degrees, 14% minority, 35% women. **Part-time faculty:** 98 total; 47% have terminal degrees, 6% minority, 46% women. **Class size:** 29% < 20, 46% 20-39, 7% 40-49, 12% 50-99, 6%

>100. **Special facilities:** Arts center, poultry science center, equine pavilion, animal science center.

Freshman class profile. 16,633 applied, 10,146 admitted, 4,464 enrolled.

Mid 50% test scores			
SAT critical reading:	500-610	Rank in top quarter:	56%
SAT math:	520-630	Rank in top tenth:	27%
ACT composite:	23-28	Return as sophomores:	83%
GPA 3.75 or higher:	36%	Out-of-state:	45%
GPA 3.50-3.74:	22%	Live on campus:	89%
GPA 3.0-3.49:	30%	International:	1%
GPA 2.0-2.99:	12%	Fraternities:	21%
		Sororities:	41%

Basis for selection. Secondary school record, class rank, test scores, evidence of commitment to success most important. As mandated by state law, those with ACT subscore of 18 or less in English, mathematics or reading assigned developmental coursework or required to take institutional placement test. University policies more restrictive than state of Arkansas' policies.

High school preparation. College-preparatory program required. 16 units required. Required and recommended units include English 4, mathematics 4, social studies 3, science 3 (laboratory 2), foreign language 2 and academic electives 2. Mathematics must include algebra I or 2 units applied math, and 3 units chosen from algebra II, geometry, calculus/trigonometry, and statistics. 2 foreign languages strongly recommended.

2011-2012 Annual costs. Tuition/fees: $7,174; $17,606 out-of-state. Room/board: $8,330.

2011-2012 Financial aid. Need-based: Average need met was 68%. Average scholarship/grant was $7,989; average loan $3,394. 52% of total undergraduate aid awarded as scholarships/grants, 48% as loans/jobs. **Non-need-based:** Scholarships awarded for academics, alumni affiliation, art, athletics, leadership, minority status, music/drama, ROTC, state residency.

Application procedures. Admission: Priority date 11/15; deadline 8/1 (receipt date). $40 fee, may be waived for applicants with need. Admission notification on a rolling basis beginning on or about 9/1. **Financial aid:** Priority date 3/15; no closing date. FAFSA required. Applicants notified on a rolling basis starting 4/1; must reply within 4 week(s) of notification.

Academics. Special study options: Accelerated study, combined bachelor's/graduate degree, cooperative education, distance learning, double major, dual enrollment of high school students, ESL, honors, independent study, internships, liberal arts/career combination, student-designed major, study abroad, teacher certification program, United Nations semester. **Credit/placement by examination:** AP, CLEP, IB, SAT, ACT, institutional tests. **Support services:** Learning center, reduced course load, remedial instruction, study skills assistance, tutoring, writing center.

Honors college/program. 28 ACT/SAT equivalent, 3.5 GPA required. College of Business requires 28 ACT/SAT equivalent and 3.75 GPA.

Majors. Architecture: Architecture, landscape. **Area/ethnic studies:** American. **Biology:** General, bacteriology. **Business:** General, accounting, business admin, finance, international, logistics, managerial economics, marketing. **Communications:** Communications/speech/rhetoric, journalism. **Computer sciences:** General, data processing. **Conservation:** Environmental science. **Education:** Agricultural, elementary, kindergarten/preschool, middle, trade/industrial. **Engineering:** Agricultural, chemical, civil, computer, electrical, industrial, mechanical. **English:** English lit. **Foreign languages:** Classics, French, German, Spanish. **General:** Agribusiness operations, agronomy, animal sciences, food science, ornamental horticulture, poultry. **Health services:** Audiology/speech pathology, nursing (RN). **History:** General. **Human services:** General, social work. **Math:** General. **Parks/recreation:** General, health/fitness. **Philosophy/religion:** Philosophy. **Physical sciences:** Chemistry, geology, physics. **Protective services:** Criminal justice. **Psychology:** General. **Social sciences:** Anthropology, economics, geography, international relations, political science, sociology. **Visual/performing arts:** Art, dramatic, music performance. **Work/family studies:** Clothing/textiles, family studies, food/nutrition, housing.

Most popular majors. Business/marketing 24%, communications/journalism 7%, engineering/engineering technologies 9%, health sciences 6%, social sciences 8%.

Computing on campus. 3,335 workstations in dormitories, library, computer center, student center. Dormitories wired for high-speed internet access and linked to campus network. Commuter students can connect to campus network. Online course registration, online library, helpline, repair service, student web hosting, wireless network available.

Student life. Freshman orientation: Mandatory, $140 fee. Preregistration for classes offered. 2 day program held in summer for students and parents; $50 for guest/parents. **Housing:** Coed dorms, single-sex dorms, special housing for disabled, apartments, fraternity/sorority housing available. $235 partly refundable deposit. Living/learning communities, suites with private bedrooms. Several residences remain open over holiday and winter breaks. **Activities:** Bands, campus ministries, choral groups, dance, drama, film society, international student organizations, literary magazine, music ensembles, musical theater, opera, radio station, student government, student newspaper, symphony orchestra, TV station, over 300 organizations available.

Athletics. NCAA. Intercollegiate: Baseball M, basketball, cheerleading, cross-country, diving W, football (tackle) M, golf, gymnastics W, soccer W, softball W, swimming W, tennis, track and field, volleyball W. **Intramural:** Badminton, basketball, bowling, racquetball, soccer, softball, tennis, volleyball W. **Team name:** Razorbacks.

Student services. Adult student services, alcohol/substance abuse counseling, chaplain/spiritual director, career counseling, student employment services, financial aid counseling, health services, legal services, minority student services, personal counseling, placement for graduates, veterans' counselor. **Physically disabled:** Services for visually, speech, hearing impaired.

Contact. E-mail: uofa@uark.edu
Phone: (479) 575-5346 Toll-free number: (800) 377-8632
Fax: (479) 575-7515
Suzanne McCray, Vice Provost for Enrollment, University of Arkansas, 232 Silas Hunt Hall, Fayetteville, AR 72701

University of Arkansas at Fort Smith
Fort Smith, Arkansas CB member
www.uafs.edu CB code: 6220

- Public 4-year university
- Commuter campus in small city
- 6,817 degree-seeking undergraduates: 24% part-time, 58% women, 4% African American, 4% Asian American, 7% Hispanic American, 3% Native American, 1% international

General. Founded in 1928. Regionally accredited. Arboretum. **Degrees:** 531 bachelor's, 402 associate awarded. **ROTC:** Army, Air Force. **Location:** 150 miles from Little Rock, AR; 120 miles from Tulsa, OK. **Calendar:** Semester, limited summer session. **Full-time faculty:** 241 total; 54% have terminal degrees, 19% minority, 50% women. **Part-time faculty:** 207 total; 21% have terminal degrees, 9% minority, 49% women. **Class size:** 38% < 20, 53% 20-39, 3% 40-49, 6% 50-99.

Freshman class profile. 3,989 applied, 2,237 admitted, 1,357 enrolled.

Mid 50% test scores			
ACT composite:	19-24	End year in good standing:	65%
GPA 3.75 or higher:	16%	Return as sophomores:	62%
GPA 3.50-3.74:	16%	Out-of-state:	8%
GPA 3.0-3.49:	28%	Live on campus:	24%
GPA 2.0-2.99:	37%	International:	1%
Rank in top quarter:	31%	Fraternities:	4%
Rank in top tenth:	10%	Sororities:	5%

Basis for selection. Open admission, but selective for some programs. Special criteria for health career and education programs. Pre-admission exams are required for all health science programs. Teacher education applicants must take PRAXIS I exam, have grade of C or B in specific English and Rhetoric courses. COMPASS required for placement if ACT/SAT not submitted, or if scores below acceptable minimum (18 on ACT). Interview required of nursing, radiology, surgical technology, paramedic, and dental hygiene majors, as well as teacher education programs. **Home schooled:** Any private school, homeschool, or GED student who graduates after May 1, 2002, must have achieved a composite score of 19 on the ACT or the equivalent score on the SAT or COMPASS for unconditional admission. **Learning Disabled:** In order to be considered for accommodations, a student must first submit verification of his or her condition based on Student ADA Services' guidelines and meet with the Student ADA Services coordinator to discuss an accommodation request.

High school preparation. College-preparatory program recommended. 14 units recommended. Recommended units include English 4, mathematics 4, social studies 3, science 3 (laboratory 3).

2011-2012 Annual costs. Tuition/fees: $5,267; $11,717 out-of-state. Room only: $5,100. Books/supplies: $1,330. Personal expenses: $2,025.

2010-2011 Financial aid. Need-based: 1,274 full-time freshmen applied for aid; 1,097 were judged to have need; 1,086 of these received aid. Average need met was 68%. Average scholarship/grant was $4,721; average loan $3,060. 64% of total undergraduate aid awarded as scholarships/grants, 36% as loans/jobs. **Non-need-based:** Awarded to 2,060 full-time undergraduates,

including 817 freshmen. Scholarships awarded for academics, athletics, job skills, leadership, music/drama.

Application procedures. Admission: No deadline. No application fee. Admission notification on a rolling basis. Early applications advised for financial aid. **Financial aid:** Priority date 6/15; no closing date. FAFSA required. Applicants notified on a rolling basis starting 3/1; must reply within 4 week(s) of notification.

Academics. Special study options: Distance learning, double major, dual enrollment of high school students, ESL, external degree, honors, independent study, internships, liberal arts/career combination, student-designed major, study abroad, teacher certification program, weekend college. Associate of Art through distance learning. **Credit/placement by examination:** AP, CLEP, institutional tests. 30 credit hours maximum toward associate degree, 30 toward bachelor's. Prior work/life experience credits awarded for military transcripts only; maximum 30 hours. **Support services:** Learning center, pre-admission summer program, reduced course load, remedial instruction, study skills assistance, tutoring, writing center.

Majors. Biology: General. **Business:** Business admin, organizational leadership. **Communications:** General. **Communications technology:** Animation/special effects. **Computer sciences:** General. **Education:** Biology, chemistry, early childhood, English, history, mathematics, middle, music, Spanish. **English:** English lit, technical writing. **Foreign languages:** Spanish. **Health services:** Nursing (RN), radiologic technology/medical imaging. **History:** General. **Liberal arts:** Arts/sciences. **Math:** General. **Physical sciences:** Chemistry. **Protective services:** Law enforcement admin. **Psychology:** General. **Visual/performing arts:** Art, dramatic, graphic design, music.

Most popular majors. Business/marketing 21%, education 21%, health sciences 11%, history 6%, interdisciplinary studies 15%, psychology 6%.

Computing on campus. 1,075 workstations in library, computer center, student center. Dormitories wired for high-speed internet access and linked to campus network. Online course registration, online library, helpline, repair service, wireless network available.

Student life. Freshman orientation: Available. Preregistration for classes offered. **Housing:** Coed dorms, apartments, wellness housing available. $75 nonrefundable deposit. **Activities:** Bands, campus ministries, choral groups, drama, international student organizations, literary magazine, music ensembles, student government, student newspaper, symphony orchestra, Future Educators Association, math club, drama club, cultural network, Students Together Effectively Progressing (STEP), Sigma Tau Delta, Lions for Christ, Sebastian Commons Organization for Protecting the Environment, transfer student organization, non-traditional students.

Athletics. NCAA. **Intercollegiate:** Baseball M, basketball, cross-country, golf, tennis, volleyball W. **Intramural:** Basketball, bowling, football (non-tackle), soccer, softball, table tennis, volleyball. **Team name:** Lions.

Student services. Adult student services, career counseling, services for economically disadvantaged, student employment services, financial aid counseling, health services, personal counseling, placement for graduates, veterans' counselor. **Physically disabled:** Services for visually, speech, hearing impaired.

Contact. E-mail: information@uafortsmith.edu
Phone: (479) 788-7120 Toll-free number: (888) 512-5466
Fax: (479) 788-7108
Mark Lloyd, Director of Admissions, University of Arkansas at Fort Smith, PO Box 3649, Fort Smith, AR 72913-3649

University of Arkansas at Little Rock
Little Rock, Arkansas
www.ualr.edu

CB member
CB code: 6368

- Public 4-year university
- Commuter campus in small city
- 9,041 degree-seeking undergraduates: 37% part-time, 60% women, 26% African American, 2% Asian American, 2% Hispanic American, 2% international
- 2,656 degree-seeking graduate students
- 57% of applicants admitted
- ACT (writing optional) required

General. Founded in 1927. Regionally accredited. **Degrees:** 1,177 bachelor's, 209 associate awarded; master's, professional, doctoral offered. **ROTC:** Army. **Calendar:** Semester, limited summer session. **Full-time faculty:** 486 total; 64% have terminal degrees, 43% women. **Part-time faculty:** 334 total;

18% have terminal degrees, 55% women. **Class size:** 46% < 20, 45% 20-39, 5% 40-49, 4% 50-99, less than 1% >100. **Special facilities:** Planetarium, observatory, government documents depository.

Freshman class profile. 2,192 applied, 1,252 admitted, 923 enrolled.

Mid 50% test scores		Rank in top quarter:	36%
ACT composite:	19-25	Rank in top tenth:	16%
GPA 3.75 or higher:	15%	Return as sophomores:	62%
GPA 3.50-3.74:	12%	Out-of-state:	3%
GPA 3.0-3.49:	34%	Live on campus:	43%
GPA 2.0-2.99:	37%	International:	3%

Basis for selection. Unconditional admission based on 21 ACT, 990 SAT (exclusive of Writing), 2.5 GPA, and completion of college preparatory curriculum. Students must meet 2 of 3 basic criteria. All students born after January 1, 1957 required to show Arkansas Certificate of Immunization for Institutions of Higher Education. Interview recommended for academically weak applicants.

High school preparation. College-preparatory program required. 16 units required. Required units include English 4, mathematics 4, social studies 3, science 3, foreign language 2 and academic electives 2. Social studies should include 1 unit each of American history, world history, and civics or American government.

2011-2012 Annual costs. Tuition/fees: $7,041; $16,551 out-of-state. Room only: $3,358. Books/supplies: $1,574. Personal expenses: $2,146.

Financial aid. Non-need-based: Scholarships awarded for academics, art, athletics, leadership, music/drama.

Application procedures. Admission: Closing date 8/1 (postmark date). $40 fee, may be waived for applicants with need. Application must be submitted online. Admission notification on a rolling basis. **Financial aid:** Priority date 3/1, closing date 11/1. FAFSA required. Applicants notified on a rolling basis starting 5/1.

Academics. Special study options: Accelerated study, cooperative education, distance learning, double major, dual enrollment of high school students, ESL, exchange student, honors, independent study, internships, student-designed major, study abroad, teacher certification program, weekend college. **Credit/placement by examination:** AP, CLEP, IB, ACT, institutional tests. 30 credit hours maximum toward associate degree, 30 toward bachelor's. Credit obtained through examination is recorded as approved hours on the official permanent record without grade or grade points. **Support services:** Learning center, reduced course load, remedial instruction, tutoring, writing center.

Honors college/program. Factors in the selection process are GPA, community involvement, test scores, recommendations, written essays and personal interviews. Although all factors are considered, a student's GPA carries the most weight.

Majors. Biology: General. **Business:** Accounting, business admin, finance, international, management information systems, managerial economics, marketing. **Communications:** Advertising, communications/speech/rhetoric, journalism. **Computer sciences:** General, information systems. **Education:** Early childhood, elementary, middle. **Engineering:** Construction, systems. **English:** English lit, technical writing. **Foreign languages:** French, German, sign language interpretation, Spanish. **Health services:** Audiology/speech pathology, environmental health, nursing (RN). **History:** General. **Human services:** Social work. **Liberal arts:** Arts/sciences, humanities. **Math:** General. **Philosophy/religion:** Philosophy. **Physical sciences:** Chemistry, geology, physics. **Protective services:** Criminal justice. **Psychology:** General. **Social sciences:** Anthropology, economics, international relations, political science, sociology. **Visual/performing arts:** Art, art history/conservation, dance, dramatic, music.

Most popular majors. Business/marketing 18%, engineering/engineering technologies 9%, health sciences 15%, psychology 6%.

Computing on campus. 500 workstations in dormitories, library, computer center. Dormitories wired for high-speed internet access and linked to campus network. Commuter students can connect to campus network. Online library, wireless network available.

Student life. Freshman orientation: Mandatory. Preregistration for classes offered. **Housing:** Coed dorms available. $100 fully refundable deposit, deadline 7/1. **Activities:** Bands, campus ministries, choral groups, dance, drama, literary magazine, music ensembles, musical theater, opera, radio station, student government, student newspaper, TV station, Baptist student union, University Republicans, Methodist student club, Muslim students association, Young Democrats, Association for Minority Students Education Needs and Development, Advocates for People with Disabilities.

Athletics. NCAA. **Intercollegiate:** Baseball M, basketball, cross-country, golf, soccer, swimming, tennis, track and field, volleyball W. **Intramural:**

Badminton, basketball, bowling, football (tackle) M, golf, softball, swimming, table tennis M, tennis, volleyball. **Team name:** Trojans.

Student services. Adult student services, alcohol/substance abuse counseling, career counseling, student employment services, health services, minority student services, personal counseling, placement for graduates, veterans' counselor. **Physically disabled:** Services for visually, speech, hearing impaired.

Contact. E-mail: admissions@ualr.edu
Phone: (501) 569-3127 Toll-free number: (800) 482-8892
Fax: (501) 569-8956
Tammy Harrison, Director of Admissions and Financial Aid, University of Arkansas at Little Rock, 2801 South University Avenue, Little Rock, AR 72204

University of Arkansas at Monticello
Monticello, Arkansas
www.uamont.edu   CB code: 6007

- Public 4-year university and technical college
- Commuter campus in large town
- 3,278 degree-seeking undergraduates: 19% part-time, 60% women, 37% African American, 2% Hispanic American
- 118 degree-seeking graduate students

General. Founded in 1909. Regionally accredited. **Degrees:** 309 bachelor's, 153 associate awarded; master's offered. **ROTC:** Army. **Location:** 100 miles from Little Rock, 50 miles from Pine Bluff. **Calendar:** Semester, extensive summer session. **Full-time faculty:** 172 total; 41% have terminal degrees, 9% minority, 48% women. **Part-time faculty:** 68 total; 12% minority, 65% women. **Class size:** 55% < 20, 37% 20-39, 4% 40-49, 4% 50-99, less than 1% >100. **Special facilities:** Museum of natural history, extensive research forest, planetarium, farm.

Freshman class profile. 2,977 applied, 1,277 admitted, 822 enrolled.

Mid 50% test scores		Return as sophomores:	37%
ACT composite:	15-22	Out-of-state:	11%
GPA 3.75 or higher:	6%	Live on campus:	38%
GPA 3.50-3.74:	8%	Fraternities:	10%
GPA 3.0-3.49:	21%	Sororities:	10%
GPA 2.0-2.99:	51%		

Basis for selection. Open admission, but selective for some programs. ACT, SAT, ASSET, or COMPASS scores may be requested for placement. **Home schooled:** Transcript of courses and grades required. ACT/SAT required for placement.

High school preparation. Recommended units include English 4, mathematics 4, social studies 3, science 3 and foreign language 2.

2011-2012 Annual costs. Tuition/fees: $5,290; $10,510 out-of-state. Room/board: $4,640. Books/supplies: $1,000. Personal expenses: $2,250.

2011-2012 Financial aid. Need-based: 68% of total undergraduate aid awarded as scholarships/grants, 32% as loans/jobs. **Non-need-based:** Scholarships awarded for academics, athletics, job skills, leadership, music/drama, ROTC, state residency.

Application procedures. Admission: Priority date 8/1; no deadline. No application fee. Admission notification on a rolling basis. **Financial aid:** Priority date 5/1; no closing date. FAFSA required. Applicants notified on a rolling basis starting 5/1; must reply within 2 week(s) of notification.

Academics. Special study options: Combined bachelor's/graduate degree, cross-registration, distance learning, double major, dual enrollment of high school students, independent study, internships, liberal arts/career combination, study abroad, teacher certification program. **Credit/placement by examination:** AP, CLEP, IB, institutional tests. 9 credit hours maximum toward bachelor's degree. **Support services:** Learning center, pre-admission summer program, reduced course load, remedial instruction, study skills assistance, tutoring, writing center.

Majors. Biology: General. **Business:** Accounting, business admin, management information systems. **Communications:** Communications/speech/rhetoric. **Conservation:** Forestry, wildlife/wilderness. **Education:** Kindergarten/preschool, middle, music, physical. **English:** English lit. **Foreign languages:** General. **General:** Agribusiness operations. **Health services:** Nursing (RN). **History:** General. **Human services:** Social work. **Math:** General. **Parks/recreation:** Health/fitness. **Physical sciences:** Chemistry. **Protective services:** Criminal justice. **Psychology:** General. **Social sciences:** General, political science. **Visual/performing arts:** Art, music.

Most popular majors. Agriculture 6%, business/marketing 24%, education 7%, health sciences 10%, liberal arts 8%, parks/recreation 10%.

Computing on campus. 400 workstations in dormitories, library, computer center, student center. Dormitories wired for high-speed internet access and linked to campus network. Commuter students can connect to campus network. Online course registration, wireless network available.

Student life. Freshman orientation: Mandatory. Preregistration for classes offered. One-day program held at beginning of semester. **Housing:** Guaranteed on-campus for all undergraduates. Single-sex dorms, special housing for disabled, apartments, wellness housing available. $60 fully refundable deposit, deadline 8/1. **Activities:** Bands, choral groups, drama, literary magazine, music ensembles, musical theater, student government, student newspaper, Baptist student union, Missionary Baptist student fellowship, Wesley Foundation, Christians in Action, Catholic Weevils, Chi Alpha.

Athletics. NCAA. **Intercollegiate:** Baseball M, basketball, cross-country, football (tackle) M, golf, rodeo, softball W, tennis W, volleyball W. **Intramural:** Archery, badminton, baseball M, basketball, bowling, boxing M, cross-country, football (tackle) M, golf, handball, racquetball, soccer, softball, swimming, table tennis, tennis, track and field, volleyball. **Team name:** Boll Weevils.

Student services. Alcohol/substance abuse counseling, chaplain/spiritual director, career counseling, student employment services, financial aid counseling, health services, personal counseling, placement for graduates, veterans' counselor. **Physically disabled:** Services for visually, speech, hearing impaired.

Contact. E-mail: whitingm@uamont.edu
Phone: (870) 460-1026 Toll-free number: (800) 844-1826
Fax: (870) 460-1926
Mary Whiting, Director of Admissions, University of Arkansas at Monticello, Box 3600, Monticello, AR 71656

University of Arkansas at Pine Bluff
Pine Bluff, Arkansas   CB member
www.uapb.edu   CB code: 6004

- Public 4-year university
- Commuter campus in small city
- 3,000 full-time, degree-seeking undergraduates
- SAT or ACT (ACT writing optional) required

General. Founded in 1873. Regionally accredited. **Degrees:** 359 bachelor's awarded; master's offered. **ROTC:** Army. **Location:** 42 miles from Little Rock. **Calendar:** Semester, limited summer session. **Full-time faculty:** 171 total; 62% have terminal degrees, 47% women. **Part-time faculty:** 63 total; 22% have terminal degrees, 46% women. **Class size:** 42% < 20, 47% 20-39, 6% 40-49, 5% 50-99. **Special facilities:** 220-acre farm, aquaculture fisheries.

Freshman class profile.

Out-of-state:	45%	Live on campus:	77%

Basis for selection. Admission credentials for entering freshmen must include formal application, high school transcript, ACT test information and scores (SAT is accepted) and immunization record.

High school preparation. 21 units required. Required units include English 4, mathematics 3, social studies 1, history 2, science 3 (laboratory 2), foreign language 2 and academic electives 4.

2011-2012 Annual costs. Tuition/fees: $5,330; $10,595 out-of-state. Room/board: $6,710. Books/supplies: $1,000. Personal expenses: $1,750.

Financial aid. Non-need-based: Scholarships awarded for academics, alumni affiliation, art, athletics, leadership, minority status, music/drama, religious affiliation, ROTC, state residency.

Application procedures. Admission: Priority date 8/1; no deadline. No application fee. Admission notification on a rolling basis. **Financial aid:** Priority date 4/15; no closing date. FAFSA required. Applicants notified on a rolling basis starting 3/1.

Academics. Special study options: Cooperative education, cross-registration, distance learning, double major, dual enrollment of high school students, honors, internships, study abroad, teacher certification program. **Credit/placement by examination:** AP, CLEP, IB, SAT, ACT. **Support services:** Learning center, pre-admission summer program, reduced course load, remedial instruction, study skills assistance, tutoring, writing center.

Majors. Biology: General. **Business:** Accounting, business admin. **Communications:** Journalism. **Computer sciences:** General. **Conservation:** Fisheries. **Education:** Agricultural, art, business, early childhood, English, family/consumer sciences, mathematics, middle, physical, science, social science, special ed, trade/industrial. **English:** English lit. **General:** Agribusiness operations. **Health services:** Nursing (RN). **History:** General. **Human services:** Social work. **Math:** General, applied. **Parks/recreation:** General. **Physical sciences:** Chemistry, physics. **Protective services:** Criminal justice. **Psychology:** General. **Social sciences:** Political science, sociology. **Visual/performing arts:** Art, music. **Work/family studies:** General, aging.

Most popular majors. Business/marketing 18%, education 8%, family/consumer sciences 10%, liberal arts 10%, psychology 6%, security/protective services 12%.

Computing on campus. 1,000 workstations in dormitories, library, computer center, student center. Dormitories linked to campus network. Commuter students can connect to campus network. Online library, helpline, repair service available.

Student life. Freshman orientation: Mandatory. Preregistration for classes offered. **Housing:** Single-sex dorms available. $100 partly refundable deposit. **Activities:** Bands, campus ministries, choral groups, drama, international student organizations, music ensembles, radio station, student government, student newspaper, TV station, Baptist student union, political science/pre-law club, Church of God in Christ, Wesley Foundation, criminal justice club, accounting club, agriculture club, English club, Student Nurses Association, Students in Free Enterprise.

Athletics. NCAA. **Intercollegiate:** Baseball M, basketball, bowling W, cross-country, football (tackle) M, golf, soccer W, softball W, tennis, track and field, volleyball W. **Intramural:** Baseball M, basketball, bowling, cross-country M, football (tackle), golf, gymnastics, handball, racquetball, softball, swimming, table tennis, tennis, volleyball, weight lifting. **Team name:** Golden Lions.

Student services. Adult student services, alcohol/substance abuse counseling, chaplain/spiritual director, career counseling, services for economically disadvantaged, student employment services, financial aid counseling, health services, on-campus daycare, personal counseling, placement for graduates, veterans' counselor.

Contact. E-mail: jonesm@uapb.edu
Phone: (870) 575-8492 Toll-free number: (800) 264-6585
Fax: (870) 575-4607
Mary Jones, Director of Admissions, University of Arkansas at Pine Bluff, 1200 North University Drive, Mail Slot 4981, Pine Bluff, AR 71601-2799

University of Arkansas for Medical Sciences
Little Rock, Arkansas
www.uams.edu   CB code: 0424

▸ Public 4-year university and health science college
▸ Commuter campus in large city
▸ 928 degree-seeking undergraduates
▸ SAT or ACT required

General. Founded in 1876. Regionally accredited. University has 5 colleges: medicine, nursing, pharmacy, health-related professions, graduate. **Degrees:** 326 bachelor's, 116 associate awarded; master's offered. **Location:** One mile from downtown. **Calendar:** Semester, limited summer session. **Full-time faculty:** 1,352 total.

Basis for selection. Most incoming students must have prior college credit.

High school preparation. College-preparatory program recommended.

2011-2012 Annual costs. In-state students pay $233 per-credit-hour for the following programs: dental hygiene, diagnostic medical sonography, nuclear medicine imaging sciences and radiologic technology. In-state students pay $220 per-credit-hour for the following programs: cytotechnology, health information management, medical dosimetry, medical technology, ophthalmic medical technology, radiation therapy, respiratory care and surgical technology. All out-of-state students pay tuition of $534 per-credit-hour for programs. Emergency medical sciences/paramedic students pay according to program: 4-semester program, $1,108 tuition per semester; 5-semester program, $886 tuition per semester. Additional required fees vary by program. Books/supplies: $500. Personal expenses: $1,800.

Application procedures. Admission: $47 fee. Admission notification on a rolling basis. Must reply by May 1 or within 2 week(s) if notified thereafter. Application closing dates vary by program. **Financial aid:** No deadline.

FAFSA required. Applicants notified on a rolling basis starting 5/1; must reply within 2 week(s) of notification.

Academics. Special study options: Combined bachelor's/graduate degree, distance learning, double major, dual enrollment of high school students, independent study. **Credit/placement by examination:** AP, CLEP.

Majors. Health services: Clinical lab science, cytotechnology, dental hygiene, medical radiologic technology/radiation therapy, nuclear medical technology, nursing (RN).

Student life. Freshman orientation: Mandatory. Preregistration for classes offered. **Housing:** Coed dorms, special housing for disabled, apartments available. **Activities:** Campus ministries, student government.

Student services. Alcohol/substance abuse counseling, chaplain/spiritual director, career counseling, financial aid counseling, health services, minority student services, personal counseling. **Physically disabled:** Services for visually, hearing impaired.

Contact. Phone: (501) 686-5000 Fax: (501) 686-5905
University of Arkansas for Medical Sciences, 4301 West Markham Street, Little Rock, AR 72205

University of Central Arkansas
Conway, Arkansas   CB member
www.uca.edu   CB code: 6012

▸ Public 4-year university
▸ Residential campus in small city
▸ 8,956 degree-seeking undergraduates: 11% part-time, 57% women, 17% African American, 2% Asian American, 3% Hispanic American, 1% Native American, 4% international
▸ 1,497 degree-seeking graduate students
▸ 93% of applicants admitted
▸ SAT or ACT (ACT writing optional) required
▸ 42% graduate within 6 years

General. Founded in 1907. Regionally accredited. **Degrees:** 1,499 bachelor's, 1,886 associate awarded; master's, professional offered. **ROTC:** Army. **Location:** 30 miles from Little Rock. **Calendar:** Semester, extensive summer session. **Full-time faculty:** 527 total; 67% have terminal degrees, 7% minority, 48% women. **Part-time faculty:** 188 total; 25% have terminal degrees, 9% minority, 67% women. **Class size:** 44% < 20, 49% 20-39, 5% 40-49, 2% 50-99, less than 1% >100. **Special facilities:** Observatory, greenhouse, honors center, visual arts center, nature preserve, 24-hour study center, fitness center, human anatomy lab, herbarium, planetarium.

Freshman class profile. 3,370 applied, 3,131 admitted, 1,960 enrolled.

Mid 50% test scores		GPA 2.0-2.99:	31%
ACT composite:	20-26	Return as sophomores:	70%
GPA 3.75 or higher:	21%	Out-of-state:	6%
GPA 3.50-3.74:	16%	Live on campus:	77%
GPA 3.0-3.49:	31%	International:	3%

Basis for selection. Test scores, GPA, and class rank important. **Learning Disabled:** Eligibility for services determined individually based on documentation of need. Prospective students encouraged to meet with DSS staff.

High school preparation. College-preparatory program recommended. Recommended units include English 4, mathematics 4, social studies 1, history 2, science 3 and academic electives 10.

2011-2012 Annual costs. Tuition/fees: $7,183; $12,569 out-of-state. Room/board: $5,180. Books/supplies: $1,100. Personal expenses: $1,791.

2010-2011 Financial aid. Non-need-based: Scholarships awarded for academics, art, athletics, leadership, minority status, music/drama, ROTC, state residency. **Additional information:** Room and board may be paid monthly.

Application procedures. Admission: Priority date 5/1; no deadline. $25 fee, may be waived for applicants with need. Admission notification on a rolling basis. **Financial aid:** Priority date 4/15, closing date 7/1. FAFSA required. Applicants notified on a rolling basis starting 5/4.

Academics. Special study options: Accelerated study, combined bachelor's/graduate degree, cooperative education, distance learning, double major, dual enrollment of high school students, ESL, honors, independent study, internships, liberal arts/career combination, study abroad, teacher certification program. 5-year professional programs in physical therapy and occupational

therapy. **Credit/placement by examination:** AP, CLEP, IB, SAT, institutional tests. 30 credit hours maximum toward associate degree, 30 toward bachelor's. **Support services:** Learning center, pre-admission summer program, remedial instruction, study skills assistance, tutoring, writing center.

Honors college/program. Special honors courses and minor in interdisciplinary studies offered. 27 ACT and 3.6 GPA minimum.

Majors. Area/ethnic studies: African-American. **Biology:** General. **Business:** General, accounting, business admin, finance, insurance, management information systems, marketing. **Communications:** Advertising, journalism, public relations. **Computer sciences:** General. **Conservation:** Environmental studies. **Education:** Business, family/consumer sciences, kindergarten/preschool, mathematics, middle, physical, science, social studies. **English:** English lit, rhetoric/composition, writing. **Foreign languages:** French, Spanish. **Health services:** Athletic training, audiology/speech pathology, clinical lab science, community health services, medical radiologic technology/radiation therapy, nuclear medical technology, nursing (RN), substance abuse counseling. **History:** General. **Human services:** General. **Liberal arts:** Arts/sciences. **Math:** General. **Parks/recreation:** Exercise sciences. **Philosophy/religion:** Philosophy, religion. **Physical sciences:** Chemistry, physics. **Psychology:** General. **Social sciences:** Economics, geography, political science, sociology. **Visual/performing arts:** Art, cinematography, dramatic, interior design, music, music performance. **Work/family studies:** General, food/nutrition.

Most popular majors. Biology 6%, business/marketing 19%, education 8%, health sciences 21%, psychology 6%, social sciences 6%, visual/performing arts 8%.

Computing on campus. 608 workstations in dormitories, library, computer center, student center. Dormitories wired for high-speed internet access and linked to campus network. Commuter students can connect to campus network. Online course registration, online library, helpline, repair service, wireless network available.

Student life. Freshman orientation: Available. Preregistration for classes offered. **Housing:** Guaranteed on-campus for freshmen. Coed dorms, single-sex dorms, special housing for disabled, apartments, fraternity/sorority housing available. $100 deposit. **Activities:** Bands, campus ministries, choral groups, dance, drama, film society, international student organizations, literary magazine, music ensembles, Model UN, radio station, student government, student newspaper, symphony orchestra, TV station, Baptist student union, Methodist student union, Newman Club, Young Democrats, College Republicans, Students for Propagation of Black Culture, Association of Baptist Students, Catholic Campus Ministries, ORBIS.

Athletics. NCAA. **Intercollegiate:** Baseball M, basketball, cross-country, football (tackle) M, golf, soccer, softball W, tennis W, track and field, volleyball W. **Intramural:** Badminton, basketball, bowling, cross-country, football (non-tackle), golf, racquetball, soccer, softball, table tennis, tennis, volleyball. **Team name:** Bears.

Student services. Alcohol/substance abuse counseling, chaplain/spiritual director, career counseling, student employment services, financial aid counseling, health services, minority student services, on-campus daycare, personal counseling, placement for graduates, veterans' counselor, women's services. **Physically disabled:** Services for visually, speech, hearing impaired.

Contact. E-mail: admissions@uca.edu
Phone: (501) 450-3128 Toll-free number: (800) 243-8245
Fax: (501) 450-5228
Penny Hatfield, Director of Admissions, University of Central Arkansas, 201 Donaghey Avenue, Conway, AR 72035

University of Phoenix: Little Rock
Little Rock, Arkansas
www.phoenix.edu

- For-profit 4-year university
- Commuter campus in small city
- 919 degree-seeking undergraduates

General. Regionally accredited. **Degrees:** 55 bachelor's awarded; master's offered. **Calendar:** Differs by program. **Full-time faculty:** 27 total. **Part-time faculty:** 174 total.

Basis for selection. Open admission, but selective for some programs.

2011-2012 Annual costs. Estimated costs as of August 2011: per-credit-hour charge, $380 to $415, depending upon level and course of study; electronic course materials fee, $95, if applicable. Book and material charges may vary by course and program. All fees are subject to change.

Application procedures. Admission: No deadline. No application fee. **Financial aid:** No deadline.

Academics. Credit/placement by examination: AP, CLEP.

Majors. Business: Accounting, business admin, human resources, marketing. **Computer sciences:** General, networking, programming, security, systems analysis, web page design, webmaster. **Protective services:** Law enforcement admin. **Psychology:** General.

Most popular majors. Business/marketing 80%, computer/information sciences 9%, security/protective services 9%.

Contact. Toll-free number: (866) 766-0766
Marc Booker, Director of Admission and Evaluation, University of Phoenix: Little Rock, 10800 Financial Center Parkway, Little Rock, AR 72211-3552

University of Phoenix: Northwest Arkansas
Rogers, Arkansas
www.phoenix.edu

- For-profit 4-year university
- Commuter campus in small city
- 671 degree-seeking undergraduates

General. Regionally accredited. **Degrees:** 74 bachelor's awarded; master's offered. **Calendar:** Differs by program. **Full-time faculty:** 8 total. **Part-time faculty:** 120 total.

Basis for selection. Open admission, but selective for some programs.

2011-2012 Annual costs. Estimated costs as of August 2011: per-credit-hour charge, $380 to $415, depending upon level and course of study; electronic course materials fee, $95, if applicable. Book and material charges may vary by course and program. All fees are subject to change.

Application procedures. Admission: No deadline. No application fee. **Financial aid:** No deadline.

Academics. Credit/placement by examination: AP, CLEP.

Majors. Business: Accounting, business admin, human resources, marketing. **Computer sciences:** General, networking, programming, security, systems analysis, web page design, webmaster. **Health services:** Health care admin. **Human services:** General. **Protective services:** Law enforcement admin. **Psychology:** General.

Most popular majors. Business/marketing 71%, computer/information sciences 14%, security/protective services 7%.

Student services. Career counseling.

Contact. Toll-free number: (866) 766-0766
Marc Booker, Director of Admission and Evaluation, University of Phoenix: Northwest Arkansas, 903 North 47th Street, Rogers, AR 72756-9615

University of the Ozarks
Clarksville, Arkansas
www.ozarks.edu   CB code: 6111

- Private 4-year university and liberal arts college affiliated with Presbyterian Church (USA)
- Residential campus in small town
- 595 full-time, degree-seeking undergraduates
- 7 graduate students
- SAT or ACT (ACT writing optional), application essay required
- 46% graduate within 6 years

General. Founded in 1834. Regionally accredited. **Degrees:** 101 bachelor's awarded. **Location:** 100 miles from Little Rock, 65 miles from Fort Smith. **Calendar:** Semester, limited summer session. **Full-time faculty:** 49 total; 49% have terminal degrees, 8% minority, 37% women. **Part-time faculty:** 12 total. **Class size:** 79% < 20, 21% 20-39.

Freshman class profile.

GPA 3.75 or higher:	21%	Rank in top tenth:	18%
GPA 3.50-3.74:	24%	Return as sophomores:	59%
GPA 3.0-3.49:	26%	Out-of-state:	26%
GPA 2.0-2.99:	28%	Live on campus:	90%
Rank in top quarter:	44%		

Basis for selection. School achievement record and test scores most important. Interview required of those with marginal grades, recommended for all applicants.

High school preparation. College-preparatory program recommended. 18 units recommended. Recommended units include English 4, mathematics 4, social studies 1, history 2, science 3 (laboratory 2) and foreign language 2.

2011-2012 Annual costs. Tuition/fees: $22,050. Room/board: $6,500. Books/supplies: $800. Personal expenses: $2,965.

Financial aid. Non-need-based: Scholarships awarded for academics, alumni affiliation, art, leadership, minority status, music/drama, religious affiliation, state residency. **Additional information:** Walton International Scholarship Program provides full scholarships to selected Central American and Mexican residents.

Application procedures. Admission: Priority date 4/1; no deadline. $30 fee, may be waived for applicants with need, free for online applicants. Admission notification on a rolling basis. **Financial aid:** Priority date 2/15; no closing date. FAFSA required. Applicants notified on a rolling basis starting 3/1; must reply within 2 week(s) of notification.

Academics. Special study options: Cooperative education, double major, dual enrollment of high school students, independent study, internships, liberal arts/career combination, study abroad, teacher certification program. **Credit/placement by examination:** AP, CLEP, SAT, ACT, institutional tests. 30 credit hours maximum toward bachelor's degree. **Support services:** Learning center, remedial instruction, study skills assistance, tutoring.

Majors. Biology: General. **Business:** Accounting, business admin, marketing. **Communications:** Broadcast journalism, media studies. **Conservation:** Environmental studies. **Education:** Biology, business, early childhood, elementary, middle, physical, science, special ed. **English:** English lit. **Health services:** Predental, premedicine, prepharmacy, preveterinary. **History:** General. **Human services:** General. **Math:** General. **Parks/recreation:** Health/fitness. **Philosophy/religion:** Philosophy, religion. **Physical sciences:** Chemistry, physics. **Psychology:** General. **Social sciences:** General, political science, sociology. **Visual/performing arts:** General, art, dramatic, music.

Most popular majors. Biology 8%, business/marketing 47%, communications/journalism 10%, education 6%, liberal arts 6%, visual/performing arts 6%.

Computing on campus. 150 workstations in dormitories, library, computer center, student center. Dormitories wired for high-speed internet access and linked to campus network. Commuter students can connect to campus network. Online course registration, online library, helpline, wireless network available.

Student life. Freshman orientation: Mandatory. Preregistration for classes offered. **Housing:** Guaranteed on-campus for freshmen. Coed dorms, single-sex dorms, apartments available. $100 partly refundable deposit, deadline 8/15. **Activities:** Campus ministries, choral groups, drama, film society, international student organizations, literary magazine, radio station, student government, TV station, Ozarks Area Mission, Alpha & Omega, various religious/ethnic/social service organizations.

Athletics. NCAA. **Intercollegiate:** Baseball M, basketball, cheerleading, cross-country, soccer, softball W, tennis. **Intramural:** Badminton, basketball, bowling, football (non-tackle), racquetball, soccer, softball, tennis, volleyball. **Team name:** Eagles.

Student services. Chaplain/spiritual director, career counseling, student employment services, financial aid counseling, health services, personal counseling, placement for graduates, veterans' counselor.

Contact. E-mail: admiss@ozarks.edu
Phone: (479) 979-1227 Toll-free number: (800) 264-8636
Fax: (479) 979-1417
Kim Myrick, Dean of Enrollment, University of the Ozarks, 415 North College Avenue, Clarksville, AR 72830-2880

Williams Baptist College
Walnut Ridge, Arkansas
www.wbcoll.edu   CB code: 6658

- Private 4-year liberal arts college affiliated with Southern Baptist Convention
- Residential campus in small town
- 547 degree-seeking undergraduates: 4% part-time, 58% women, 3% African American, 5% Hispanic American, 1% international
- 59% of applicants admitted
- SAT or ACT (ACT writing optional) required
- 36% graduate within 6 years

General. Founded in 1941. Regionally accredited. **Degrees:** 97 bachelor's, 3 associate awarded. **ROTC:** Army. **Location:** 30 miles from Jonesboro, 100 miles from Memphis. **Calendar:** Semester, limited summer session. **Full-time faculty:** 28 total; 61% have terminal degrees, 39% women. **Part-time faculty:** 16 total; 6% have terminal degrees, 6% minority, 75% women. **Class size:** 52% < 20, 47% 20-39, less than 1% 40-49.

Freshman class profile. 535 applied, 313 admitted, 140 enrolled.

GPA 3.75 or higher:	28%	Return as sophomores:	55%
GPA 3.50-3.74:	16%	Out-of-state:	10%
GPA 3.0-3.49:	31%	Live on campus:	85%
GPA 2.0-2.99:	25%	International:	3%
End year in good standing:	91%		

Basis for selection. 19 ACT and 2.5 GPA required in order to be admitted unconditionally.

High school preparation. College-preparatory program recommended. Recommended units include English 4, mathematics 4, social studies 3, science 3 (laboratory 3) and foreign language 2.

2011-2012 Annual costs. Tuition/fees: $12,620. Room/board: $5,800. Books/supplies: $1,140. Personal expenses: $1,326.

2010-2011 Financial aid. Need-based: 133 full-time freshmen applied for aid; 113 were judged to have need; 113 of these received aid. Average scholarship/grant was $4,769; average loan $2,610. 67% of total undergraduate aid awarded as scholarships/grants, 33% as loans/jobs. **Non-need-based:** Scholarships awarded for academics, art, athletics, leadership, minority status, music/drama, religious affiliation, state residency. **Additional information:** Art scholarship applicants must submit portfolio.

Application procedures. Admission: No deadline. $20 fee. Admission notification on a rolling basis. **Financial aid:** Priority date 5/1; no closing date. FAFSA required. Applicants notified on a rolling basis starting 4/1; must reply within 2 week(s) of notification.

Academics. Special study options: Double major, dual enrollment of high school students, independent study, internships, study abroad. **Credit/placement by examination:** AP, CLEP, IB, ACT. 30 credit hours maximum toward bachelor's degree. **Support services:** Learning center, reduced course load, remedial instruction, study skills assistance, tutoring.

Majors. Biology: General. **Business:** Business admin, finance. **Computer sciences:** General. **Education:** General, art, early childhood, elementary, English, music, physical, secondary, social studies. **English:** English lit. **History:** General. **Psychology:** General. **Theology:** Bible, missionary, religious ed, sacred music, theology, youth ministry. **Visual/performing arts:** Studio arts.

Most popular majors. Biology 8%, business/marketing 11%, education 36%, liberal arts 10%, psychology 12%, theological studies 14%.

Computing on campus. 70 workstations in library, computer center, student center. Dormitories wired for high-speed internet access and linked to campus network. Commuter students can connect to campus network. Online library, wireless network available.

Student life. Freshman orientation: Mandatory, $75 fee. Preregistration for classes offered. 2 day program held at beginning of fall semester. **Policies:** Religious observance required. **Housing:** Guaranteed on-campus for all undergraduates. Single-sex dorms, apartments available. $75 fully refundable deposit, deadline 5/1. All full-time students under 21 required to live in college housing, unless commuting. **Activities:** Campus ministries, choral groups, drama, international student organizations, music ensembles, student government, Fellowship of Christian Athletes, student activities board, student Ambassadors.

Athletics. NAIA. **Intercollegiate:** Baseball M, basketball, cheerleading, soccer M, softball W, volleyball W. **Intramural:** Baseball M, basketball, football (non-tackle), softball, volleyball. **Team name:** Eagles.

Student services. Alcohol/substance abuse counseling, chaplain/spiritual director, career counseling, financial aid counseling, health services, personal counseling, veterans' counselor.

Contact. E-mail: admissions@wbcoll.edu
Phone: (870) 759-4121 Toll-free number: (800) 722-4434
Fax: (870) 886-3924
Aaron Abbott, Director of Admissions, Williams Baptist College, PO Box 3665, Walnut Ridge, AR 72476

California

Academy of Art University
San Francisco, California
www.academyart.edu   **CB code: 1981**

- For-profit 4-year university and visual arts college
- Commuter campus in very large city
- 11,877 degree-seeking undergraduates: 42% part-time, 56% women, 6% African American, 9% Asian American, 9% Hispanic American, 1% Native American, 17% international
- 5,928 degree-seeking graduate students

General. Founded in 1929. Equal emphasis on both fine and applied arts. **Degrees:** 794 bachelor's, 121 associate awarded; master's offered. **Calendar:** Semester, extensive summer session. **Full-time faculty:** 233 total; 16% have terminal degrees, 10% minority, 43% women. **Part-time faculty:** 1,114 total. **Class size:** 80% < 20, 19% 20-39, less than 1% 40-49, less than 1% 50-99. **Special facilities:** 3 nonprofit galleries, photography darkrooms, Bosch Telecen, green screen stage, interior design resource room, foundry, sculpture center, Final Cut Pro, soundstages, Cintiq lab, Media and Avid Express editing stations.

Freshman class profile. 4,452 applied, 4,452 admitted, 1,880 enrolled.

End year in good standing:	70%	Live on campus:	38%
Return as sophomores:	64%	International:	18%
Out-of-state:	45%		

Basis for selection. Open admission. Continuing education program offered. Interview recommended, and can be in person or over the phone. **Learning Disabled:** Reasonable accommodations made for students with disabilities.

High school preparation. Art and design courses recommended.

2012-2013 Annual costs. Tuition/fees (projected): $23,240. Room/board: $13,400. Books/supplies: $1,656. Personal expenses: $2,277.

2010-2011 Financial aid. Need-based: 709 full-time freshmen applied for aid; 645 were judged to have need; 635 of these received aid. Average need met was 21%. Average scholarship/grant was $5,228; average loan $3,112. 24% of total undergraduate aid awarded as scholarships/grants, 76% as loans/jobs. **Non-need-based:** Awarded to 742 full-time undergraduates, including 216 freshmen. Scholarships awarded for academics, art, athletics. **Additional information:** Numerous summer grant programs available.

Application procedures. Admission: No deadline. $100 fee. Admission notification on a rolling basis. Accepted applicants may preregister in mid March. **Financial aid:** Priority date 7/10; no closing date. FAFSA, institutional form required. Applicants notified on a rolling basis.

Academics. Special study options: Combined bachelor's/graduate degree, distance learning, ESL, honors, independent study, internships. **Credit/placement by examination:** AP, CLEP, IB. Interview, essay recommended for placement. Portfolio recommended for bachelor of arts applicants. **Support services:** Learning center, pre-admission summer program, reduced course load, remedial instruction, study skills assistance, tutoring, writing center.

Majors. Architecture: Architecture, landscape. **Communications:** Advertising, media studies. **Communications technology:** Animation/special effects, desktop publishing. **Computer sciences:** Web page design. **Education:** Art. **Visual/performing arts:** Cinematography, commercial photography, commercial/advertising art, design, drawing, fashion design, fiber arts, game design, graphic design, illustration, industrial design, interior design, metal/jewelry, multimedia, painting, photography, printmaking, sculpture, studio arts.

Most popular majors. Communication technologies 16%, visual/performing arts 78%.

Computing on campus. 800 workstations in dormitories, library, computer center. Dormitories wired for high-speed internet access. Commuter students can connect to campus network. Online course registration, online library, helpline, student web hosting, wireless network available.

Student life. Freshman orientation: Mandatory. Preregistration for classes offered. 5-day session week before start of classes. **Housing:** Guaranteed on-campus for freshmen. Coed dorms, single-sex dorms, special housing for disabled, wellness housing available. $500 nonrefundable deposit. **Activities:** Dance, drama, film society, international student organizations, student government, Christian student fellowship, Korean students association, Indian students association, Chinese students association, Taiwanese students association, Outloud (LGBT club), Veteran's club.

Athletics. NCAA. **Intercollegiate:** Baseball M, basketball, cross-country, golf, soccer, softball W, tennis W, track and field, volleyball W. **Team name:** Urban Knights.

Student services. Alcohol/substance abuse counseling, career counseling, student employment services, financial aid counseling, personal counseling. **Physically disabled:** Services for visually, hearing impaired.

Contact. E-mail: info@academyart.edu
Phone: (415) 274-2200 Toll-free number: (800) 544-2787
Fax: (415) 618-6287
Admissions, Academy of Art University, 79 New Montgomery Street, San Francisco, CA 94105-3410

Academy of Couture Art
Los Angeles, California
www.academyofccoutureart.edu   **CB code: 6454**

- Private 4-year visual arts and career college
- Commuter campus in very large city

General. Regionally accredited. **Location:** Located on the Miracle Mile with inspirations from the Los Angeles County Museum of Art, the ACA campus including entertainment leaders E!, Style, NBCUniversal, and the high end fashion home of Beverly Hills, Academy of Couture Art offers innovative, challenging, and flexible fashion education programs that prepare a diverse student population for professional excellence in design, fashion, and business. **Calendar:** Quarter.

Annual costs/financial aid. Full-time tuition and required fees for four quarters, which is the academic calendar mandatory for all students: associate-degree level, $28,451; bachelor's-degree level $28,951. Textbooks and supplies not included. Need-based financial aid available to full-time and part-time students.

Contact. Phone: (310) 360-8888 ext. 120
Director of Admissions, 5700 Wilshire Boulevard, Suite 275, Los Angeles, CA 90036

Alliant International University
San Diego, California
www.alliant.edu   **CB code: 4039**

- Private two-year upper-division university
- Commuter campus in very large city

General. Founded in 1952. Regionally accredited. Focuses on preparing students for professional careers in applied social sciences. Students may enter as transfers after 2 years of undergraduate study at San Diego, and as freshmen or transfers at Mexico City. **Degrees:** 62 bachelor's awarded; master's, professional, doctoral offered. **Articulation:** Agreements with Cuyamaca College, Glendale College, Grossmont College, Imperial Valley College, MiraCosta College, Mt. San Antonio College, Mt. San Jacinto College, Palomar College, Pasadena College, Riverside Community College, Saddleback College, San Diego City College, San Diego Mesa College, San Diego Miramar College, Santa Monica College, Southwestern College, Ventura College. **Location:** 16 miles from downtown. **Calendar:** Semester, limited summer session. **Full-time faculty:** 249 total; 100% have terminal degrees. **Part-time faculty:** 383 total. **Class size:** 99% < 20, less than 1% 20-39.

Student profile. 165 degree-seeking undergraduates. 45% transferred from two-year, 55% transferred from four-year institutions.

Out-of-state:	14%	25 or older:	54%
Live on campus:	35%		

Basis for selection. High school transcript, college transcript required. Transfer accepted as sophomores, juniors, seniors.

2011-2012 Annual costs. Tuition/fees: $16,870. Room only: $7,270. Books/supplies: $1,620. Personal expenses: $2,214.

Financial aid. **Non-need-based:** Scholarships awarded for academics, alumni affiliation, athletics, leadership.

Application procedures. **Admission:** Priority date 3/2. $45 fee, may be waived for applicants with need. **Financial aid:** FAFSA required.

Academics. **Special study options:** Combined bachelor's/graduate degree, ESL, independent study, internships, liberal arts/career combination, study abroad. **Credit/placement by examination:** AP, CLEP, IB, institutional tests. 27 credit hours maximum toward bachelor's degree.

Majors. **Area/ethnic studies:** Latin American. **Business:** Business admin, hospitality/recreation, international, management information systems, tourism promotion. **Communications:** Journalism. **Conservation:** Environmental studies. **Education:** ESL. **Protective services:** Law enforcement admin. **Psychology:** General, forensic. **Social sciences:** International relations.

Most popular majors. Business/marketing 52%, liberal arts 13%, psychology 17%, social sciences 15%.

Computing on campus. 100 workstations in library, computer center. Dormitories wired for high-speed internet access and linked to campus network. Commuter students can connect to campus network. Online library, student web hosting available.

Student life. **Housing:** Guaranteed on-campus for all undergraduates. Coed dorms available. $265 deposit. **Activities:** International student organizations, Model UN, student government, student newspaper, Indian student association, Latino student organization, Alliant Turk Society.

Athletics. **Intramural:** Basketball, bowling, soccer, softball, tennis, volleyball.

Student services. Adult student services, alcohol/substance abuse counseling, career counseling, student employment services, financial aid counseling, health services, personal counseling, placement for graduates, veterans' counselor, women's services. **Physically disabled:** Services for visually, speech, hearing impaired.

Contact. E-mail: admissions3@alliant.edu
Phone: (866) 825-5426 Toll-free number: (866) 825-5426
Fax: (858) 635-4555
Alliant International University, 10455 Pomerado Road, San Diego, CA 92131-1799

American Jewish University
Los Angeles, California
www.ajula.edu
CB code: 4876

- Private 4-year university and liberal arts college affiliated with Jewish faith
- Residential campus in very large city
- 131 degree-seeking undergraduates: 2% part-time, 50% women, 2% African American, 2% Asian American, 4% Hispanic American, 2% Native American, 5% international
- 131 degree-seeking graduate students
- 95% of applicants admitted
- SAT or ACT (ACT writing optional), application essay required
- 38% graduate within 6 years

General. Founded in 1947. Regionally accredited. **Degrees:** 28 bachelor's awarded; master's offered. **Location:** 5 miles from Los Angeles. **Calendar:** Semester. **Full-time faculty:** 12 total; 100% have terminal degrees, 42% women. **Part-time faculty:** 58 total; 45% have terminal degrees, 3% minority, 38% women. **Class size:** 86% < 20, 14% 20-39. **Special facilities:** Outdoor basketball court, sculpture garden.

Freshman class profile. 39 applied, 37 admitted, 11 enrolled.

Mid 50% test scores			
SAT critical reading:	470-600	GPA 2.0-2.99:	37%
SAT math:	450-580	Rank in top quarter:	50%
SAT writing:	490-580	Rank in top tenth:	50%
ACT composite:	20-22	End year in good standing:	93%
GPA 3.75 or higher:	18%	Return as sophomores:	63%
GPA 3.0-3.49:	45%	Out-of-state:	18%
		Live on campus:	100%

Basis for selection. An applicant's aspirations, goals, personal experience, ability to connect with others, interpersonal skills, and involvement with leadership activities weigh heavily in the application process. On-campus visit highly encouraged. If an applicant shows a lot of promise but has a truly low GPA and/or test scores, his/her file is brought to the Dean of the College of Arts and Sciences for further examination. Interview recommended.

2012-2013 Annual costs. Tuition/fees (projected): $25,788. Room/board: $12,764. Books/supplies: $1,656. Personal expenses: $2,852.

2011-2012 Financial aid. **Need-based:** 5 full-time freshmen applied for aid; 5 were judged to have need; 5 of these received aid. Average need met was 87%. Average scholarship/grant was $10,600; average loan $3,500. 54% of total undergraduate aid awarded as scholarships/grants, 46% as loans/jobs. **Non-need-based:** Awarded to 117 full-time undergraduates, including 13 freshmen. Scholarships awarded for leadership, minority status, music/drama, state residency.

Application procedures. **Admission:** Closing date 5/31 (postmark date). $35 fee, may be waived for applicants with need. Application must be submitted online. Admission notification on a rolling basis beginning on or about 9/15. Varies due to rolling admissions. **Financial aid:** Priority date 3/2; no closing date. FAFSA, institutional form required. Applicants notified on a rolling basis starting 1/1; must reply by 6/30.

Academics. In addition to majors and general education requirements, students take core curriculum of Jewish and Western Civilization classes. **Special study options:** Combined bachelor's/graduate degree, cross-registration, double major, independent study, internships, student-designed major, study abroad. **Credit/placement by examination:** AP, CLEP, IB, institutional tests. **Support services:** Reduced course load, study skills assistance, tutoring, writing center.

Majors. **Business:** General. **Communications:** Media studies. **Health services:** Ethics. **Liberal arts:** Arts/sciences. **Philosophy/religion:** Judaic. **Psychology:** General. **Social sciences:** International relations, political science, U.S. government.

Most popular majors. Business/marketing 38%, communications/journalism 10%, health sciences 10%, philosophy/religious studies 10%, psychology 17%, social sciences 14%.

Computing on campus. 38 workstations in dormitories, library, computer center. Dormitories wired for high-speed internet access and linked to campus network. Commuter students can connect to campus network. Online library, helpline, wireless network available.

Student life. **Freshman orientation:** Mandatory. Preregistration for classes offered. Held 1-2 weeks before the start of the traditional Fall semester. **Policies:** All Freshman and Sophomore students (i.e. those with less than 60 college credits) who are under the age of 21 must live on-campus. Junior and Senior students (i.e. those with 60 or more college credits) and those students over the age of 21 may live off-campus. **Housing:** Guaranteed on-campus for all undergraduates. Coed dorms, special housing for disabled, apartments available. $100 nonrefundable deposit. **Activities:** Choral groups, dance, drama, literary magazine, student government, student newspaper, Hillel, Israel Action Committee, National Council for Jewish Women, Giving Tree.

Athletics. **Team name:** Lions.

Student services. Alcohol/substance abuse counseling, chaplain/spiritual director, career counseling, student employment services, financial aid counseling, health services.

Contact. E-mail: admissions@ajula.edu
Phone: (310) 476-9777 ext. 247 Fax: (310) 471-3657
Matt Spooner, Director of Admissions, American Jewish University, Office of Undergraduate Admissions, Bel Air, CA 90077

Antioch University Los Angeles
Culver City, California
www.antiochla.edu
CB code: 1862

- Private two-year upper-division branch campus and liberal arts college
- Commuter campus in very large city
- 81% of applicants admitted
- Application essay required

General. Founded in 1972. Regionally accredited. Bachelor of Arts Degree Completion program offered on-campus with various attendance options available. **Degrees:** 48 bachelor's awarded; master's offered. **Articulation:** Agreements with UCLA Extension, Santa Monica College, West Los Angeles College, Compton City College. **Location:** 15 miles from Los Angeles. **Calendar:** Quarter, extensive summer session. **Full-time faculty:** 26 total. **Part-time faculty:** 136 total.

Student profile. 200 degree-seeking undergraduates. 52 applied as first time-transfer students, 42 admitted, 34 enrolled.

Basis for selection. High school transcript, college transcript, application essay required. Admission decision of full or provisional acceptance made by program chair. Transfer accepted as sophomores, juniors, seniors.

2011-2012 Annual costs. Tuition/fees: $18,285. Books/supplies: $1,644.

Application procedures. Admission: Priority date 7/22; deadline 8/17. $60 fee, may be waived for applicants with need. **Must reply by 9/7. AULA does not accept freshman. Applicants are required to have at least 30 quarter/20 semester units of college-level learning from a regionally accredited institution of higher learning. **Financial aid:** FAFSA, institutional form required.

Academics. Prior experiential learning credits. **Special study options:** Accelerated study, combined bachelor's/graduate degree, cooperative education, cross-registration, double major, independent study, internships, liberal arts/career combination, student-designed major, study abroad, teacher certification program, weekend college. **Credit/placement by examination:** AP, CLEP. 40 credit hours maximum toward bachelor's degree. DANTES examination scores accepted.

Majors. Liberal arts: Arts/sciences.

Computing on campus. 12 workstations in library, computer center. Commuter students can connect to campus network. Online library, helpline, wireless network available.

Student life. Activities: Radio station, student government, student newspaper, TV station.

Athletics. Team name: Radicals.

Student services. Adult student services, career counseling, student employment services, financial aid counseling, personal counseling, veterans' counselor. **Physically disabled:** Services for visually, speech, hearing impaired.

Contact. E-mail: admissions.aula@antioch.edu
Phone: (310) 578-1080 ext. 411 Toll-free number: (800) 726-8462
Fax: (310) 822-4824
Antioch University Los Angeles, 400 Corporate Pointe, Culver City, CA 90230-7615

Antioch University Santa Barbara
Santa Barbara, California
www.antiochsb.edu   **CB code: 3071**

▶ Private two-year upper-division university and liberal arts college
▶ Commuter campus in small city
▶ Application essay, interview required

General. Founded in 1852. Regionally accredited. **Degrees:** 74 bachelor's awarded; master's, doctoral offered. **Articulation:** Agreements with Santa Barbara City College, University of California: Santa Barbara, Ventura Community College, Cuesta Community College, Allan Hancock Community College. **Location:** Downtown. **Calendar:** Quarter, extensive summer session. **Full-time faculty:** 12 total; 75% women. **Part-time faculty:** 52 total; 50% women. **Class size:** 92% < 20, 8% 20-39.

Student profile. 148 degree-seeking undergraduates, 188 degree-seeking graduate students.

Women:	70%	**25 or older:**	70%
Part-time:	53%		

Basis for selection. Open admission. High school transcript, college transcript, application essay, interview required. Grade averages and the quality and content of previous academic work are evaluated, recognizing that an adult's present capacities may not be reflected in grades earned long before or in fields unrelated to present interests. Transfer accepted as juniors, seniors.

2011-2012 Annual costs. Tuition/fees: $20,685.

Application procedures. Admission: Rolling admission. $60 fee. **Financial aid:** Priority date 4/1, no deadline. FAFSA, institutional form required.

Academics. Special study options: Cross-registration, independent study, internships, liberal arts/career combination, student-designed major, teacher certification program. **Credit/placement by examination:** AP, CLEP, IB.

Majors. Liberal arts: Arts/sciences.

Computing on campus. 12 workstations in computer center. Online library, helpline, wireless network available.

Student life. Activities: Student newspaper.

Student services. Adult student services, financial aid counseling, personal counseling, veterans' counselor.

Contact. Phone: (805) 962-8179 Fax: (805) 962-4786
Steve Weir, Director of Enrollment and Financial Aid, Antioch University Santa Barbara, 602 Anacapa Street, Santa Barbara, CA 93101

Argosy University: Inland Empire
Ontario, California
www.argosy.edu/inlandempire   **CB code: 6239**

▶ For-profit 4-year university
▶ Very large city
▶ 344 degree-seeking undergraduates

General. Degrees: 13 bachelor's awarded; master's, doctoral offered. **Calendar:** Differs by program. **Full-time faculty:** 1 total. **Part-time faculty:** 65 total.

Basis for selection. Open admission.

2011-2012 Annual costs. Tuition/fees: $17,962.

Application procedures. Admission: Closing date 9/13. $50 fee. **Financial aid:** No deadline.

Academics. Credit/placement by examination: AP, CLEP.

Majors. Business: Business admin. **Liberal arts:** Arts/sciences. **Protective services:** Police science. **Psychology:** General.

Student life. Freshman orientation: Available. Preregistration for classes offered.

Contact. Phone: (909) 915-3800
Wendy Vasquez-Osborn, Senior Director of Admissions, Argosy University: Inland Empire, 3401 Centre Lake Drive, Suite 200, Ontario, CA 91761

Argosy University: Los Angeles
Los Angeles, California
www.argosy.edu/losangeles   **CB code: 6237**

▶ For-profit 4-year university
▶ Small city
▶ 200 degree-seeking undergraduates

General. Regionally accredited. **Degrees:** 13 bachelor's awarded; master's, doctoral offered. **Calendar:** Differs by program. **Full-time faculty:** 1 total. **Part-time faculty:** 67 total.

Basis for selection. Open admission.

2011-2012 Annual costs. Tuition/fees: $17,962.

Application procedures. Admission: Closing date 9/13. $50 fee. **Financial aid:** No deadline.

Academics. Credit/placement by examination: AP, CLEP.

Majors. Business: Business admin. **Liberal arts:** Arts/sciences. **Protective services:** Police science. **Psychology:** General.

Student life. Freshman orientation: Available. Preregistration for classes offered.

Contact. E-mail: ausmadms@argosy.edu
Daniel Banyai, Senior Director of Admissions, Argosy University: Los Angeles, 5230 Pacific Concourse, Suite 200, Los Angeles, CA 90045

Argosy University: Orange County
Orange, California
www.argosy.edu/orangecounty   CB code: 7910

- For-profit 4-year university
- Very large city
- 230 degree-seeking undergraduates

General. Regionally accredited. **Degrees:** 9 bachelor's awarded; master's, professional, doctoral offered. **Calendar:** Differs by program. **Full-time faculty:** 8 total. **Part-time faculty:** 152 total.

Basis for selection. Open admission.

2011-2012 Annual costs. Tuition/fees: $17,962.

Application procedures. Admission: Closing date 9/13. $50 fee. **Financial aid:** No deadline.

Academics. Credit/placement by examination: AP, CLEP.

Majors. Business: Business admin. **Liberal arts:** Arts/sciences. **Protective services:** Police science. **Psychology:** General.

Student life. Freshman orientation: Available. Preregistration for classes offered.

Contact. Phone: (714) 620-3715 Toll-free number: (800) 716-9598
Leisa Ruiz, Senior Director of Admissions, Argosy University: Orange County, 601 South Lewis Street, Orange, CA 92868

Argosy University: San Diego
San Diego, California
www.argosy.edu/sandiego

- For-profit 4-year university
- Very large city
- 166 degree-seeking undergraduates

General. Degrees: 10 bachelor's awarded; master's, doctoral offered. **Calendar:** Differs by program. **Part-time faculty:** 73 total.

Basis for selection. Open admission.

2011-2012 Annual costs. Tuition/fees: $17,962.

Application procedures. Admission: Closing date 9/13. $50 fee. **Financial aid:** No deadline.

Academics. Credit/placement by examination: AP, CLEP.

Majors. Business: Business admin. **Liberal arts:** Arts/sciences. **Protective services:** Police science. **Psychology:** General.

Student life. Freshman orientation: Available. Preregistration for classes offered.

Contact. E-mail: ausdadmissions@argosy.edu
Detroit Whiteside, Senior Director of Admissions, Argosy University: San Diego, 1615 Murray Canyon Road, San Diego, CA 92108

Argosy University: San Francisco Bay Area
Alameda, California
www.argosy.edu/sanfrancisco

- For-profit 4-year university
- Small city
- 124 degree-seeking undergraduates

General. Regionally accredited. **Degrees:** 19 bachelor's awarded; master's, professional, doctoral offered. **Calendar:** Differs by program. **Full-time faculty:** 17 total. **Part-time faculty:** 75 total.

Basis for selection. Open admission.

2011-2012 Annual costs. Tuition/fees: $17,962.

Application procedures. Admission: Closing date 9/13. $50 fee. **Financial aid:** No deadline.

Academics. Credit/placement by examination: AP, CLEP.

Majors. Business: Business admin. **Liberal arts:** Arts/sciences. **Protective services:** Police science. **Psychology:** General.

Student life. Freshman orientation: Available. Preregistration for classes offered.

Contact. E-mail: ausfadmissions@argosy.edu
Phone: (510) 217-4777
John Stofan, Senior Director of Admissions, Argosy University: San Francisco Bay Area, 1005 Atlantic Avenue, Alameda, CA 94501

Art Center College of Design
Pasadena, California   CB member
www.artcenter.edu   CB code: 4009

- Private 4-year visual arts college
- Commuter campus in small city
- 1,641 degree-seeking undergraduates: 17% part-time, 48% women, 2% African American, 37% Asian American, 11% Hispanic American, 20% international
- 188 degree-seeking graduate students
- Application essay required

General. Founded in 1930. Regionally accredited. **Degrees:** 319 bachelor's awarded; master's offered. **Location:** 15 miles from Los Angeles. **Calendar:** Trimester, extensive summer session. **Full-time faculty:** 93 total. **Part-time faculty:** 279 total. **Class size:** 91% < 20, 9% 20-39, less than 1% 40-49, less than 1% 50-99. **Special facilities:** 3 galleries; 3-D modelling and industrial design facilities.

Freshman class profile.

Out-of-state:	23%	International:	24%

Basis for selection. Strength of specific portfolio for one major, academic record, standardized test scores. Interviews recommended for local applicants. **Home schooled:** Transcript of courses and grades required.

High school preparation. College-preparatory program recommended. Art classes recommended.

2011-2012 Annual costs. Tuition/fees: $34,044. Books/supplies: $4,000. Personal expenses: $4,198.

Financial aid. Additional information: Students may apply for scholarships after they enroll while progressing through the program.

Application procedures. Admission: Priority date 2/15; no deadline. $50 fee, may be waived for applicants with need. Admission notification on a rolling basis beginning on or about 1/1. **Financial aid:** Priority date 3/1; no closing date. FAFSA required. Applicants notified on a rolling basis starting 5/15.

Academics. Special study options: Cross-registration, independent study, internships, study abroad. **Credit/placement by examination:** AP, CLEP, institutional tests. **Support services:** Reduced course load, remedial instruction, writing center.

Majors. Architecture: Environmental design. **Communications:** Advertising. **Communications technology:** Animation/special effects, graphics. **Visual/performing arts:** Cinematography, commercial photography, commercial/advertising art, graphic design, illustration, industrial design, interior design, painting, photography, sculpture, studio arts.

Most popular majors. Computer/information sciences 20%, visual/performing arts 67%.

Computing on campus. 250 workstations in library, computer center. Commuter students can connect to campus network. Online library, wireless network available.

Student life. Freshman orientation: Mandatory. Preregistration for classes offered. 3-day program including through peer mentor program. **Activities:** Film society, international student organizations, literary magazine, radio station, student government, Chroma, Eco Council, Out Network, Girls of ID, Marathoner's club, Trails of Escape adventure club, Art Center Christian Fellowship, Industrial Designers Society of America, "Yo" Japanese student association.

Student services. Alcohol/substance abuse counseling, career counseling, student employment services, financial aid counseling, personal counseling,

placement for graduates. **Physically disabled:** Services for hearing impaired.

Contact. E-mail: admissions@artcenter.edu
Phone: (626) 396-2373 Fax: (626) 795-0578
Kit Baron, Vice President, Admissions, Art Center College of Design, 1700 Lida Street, Pasadena, CA 91103

Art Institute of California: Hollywood
North Hollywood, California
www.artinstitutes.edu/hollywood   CB code: 3463

- For-profit 4-year culinary school and visual arts college
- Commuter campus in very large city
- 2,100 degree-seeking undergraduates
- 51% of applicants admitted
- Application essay, interview required

General. Accredited by ACICS. **Degrees:** 119 bachelor's, 62 associate awarded. **Location:** 10 miles from downtown. **Calendar:** Quarter, extensive summer session. **Full-time faculty:** 19 total; 42% have terminal degrees, 10% minority, 53% women. **Part-time faculty:** 108 total; 44% have terminal degrees, 39% minority, 56% women. **Class size:** 71% < 20, 29% 20-39. **Special facilities:** Sewing and construction rooms, interior design resource room, TV studio, video editing labs, photo studio.

Freshman class profile. 499 applied, 254 admitted, 196 enrolled.

2012-2013 Annual costs. Tuition/fees (projected): $18,948. Room/board: $11,190. Books/supplies: $1,656.

Application procedures. Admission: No deadline. $50 fee. Admission notification on a rolling basis.

Academics. Special study options: Distance learning, internships, weekend college. **Credit/placement by examination:** AP, CLEP, IB, institutional tests. **Support services:** Reduced course load, study skills assistance, tutoring, writing center.

Majors. Business: Fashion. **Communications technology:** Animation/special effects. **Computer sciences:** Web page design. **Visual/performing arts:** Fashion design, graphic design, industrial design, interior design, photography.

Most popular majors. Business/marketing 30%, visual/performing arts 70%.

Computing on campus. 289 workstations in library, computer center. Online course registration, online library, helpline, wireless network available.

Student life. Freshman orientation: Mandatory. Preregistration for classes offered. **Housing:** Single-sex dorms available. $250 fully refundable deposit, deadline 10/5. **Activities:** Student newspaper.

Student services. Career counseling, student employment services, financial aid counseling, personal counseling, placement for graduates. **Physically disabled:** Services for hearing impaired.

Contact. E-mail: aicahadm@aii.edu
Phone: (818) 299-5100 Toll-free number: (877) 468-6232
Fax: (877) 299-5151
Melissa Huen, Senior Director of Admissions, Art Institute of California: Hollywood, 5250 Lankershim Boulevard, North Hollywood, CA 91601

Art Institute of California: Inland Empire
San Bernardino, California
www.artinstitutes.edu/inland-empire/

- For-profit 4-year culinary school and visual arts college
- Large city
- 1,938 degree-seeking undergraduates
- 64% of applicants admitted

General. Regionally accredited; also accredited by ACCSC. **Degrees:** 95 bachelor's, 132 associate awarded. **Calendar:** Quarter. **Full-time faculty:** 42 total. **Part-time faculty:** 62 total.

Freshman class profile. 550 applied, 352 admitted, 285 enrolled.

Basis for selection. Admission requirements vary by programs.

2011-2012 Annual costs. Tuition/fees: $23,185. Room/board: $10,872. Books/supplies: $1,566.

Application procedures. Admission: $50 fee. **Financial aid:** Closing date 3/2.

Academics. Special study options: Distance learning, internships, study abroad. **Credit/placement by examination:** AP, CLEP.

Majors. Business: Apparel. **Communications technology:** Animation/special effects, recording arts. **Computer sciences:** Computer graphics, web page design. **Visual/performing arts:** Fashion design, graphic design, interior design.

Most popular majors. Communication technologies 10%, computer/information sciences 12%, personal/culinary services 48%, visual/performing arts 30%.

Contact. Toll-free number: (800) 353-0812
Matt Madrid, Senior Director of Admissions, Art Institute of California: Inland Empire, 674 East Brier Drive, San Bernardino, CA 92408-2800

Art Institute of California: Orange County
Santa Ana, California
www.artinstitutes.edu/orangecounty   CB code: 3831

- For-profit 3-year culinary school and visual arts college
- Commuter campus in very large city
- 2,227 degree-seeking undergraduates
- Application essay, interview required

General. Accredited by ACICS. **Degrees:** 265 bachelor's, 108 associate awarded. **Location:** 40 miles from Los Angeles, 90 miles from San Diego. **Calendar:** Quarter, extensive summer session. **Full-time faculty:** 51 total. **Part-time faculty:** 61 total. **Special facilities:** 4 professional skills kitchens, 11 computer labs, interior design resource library, interior design studio, industrial design workshop, student dining lab, fashion lab.

Basis for selection. Open admission. Proof of high school graduation, or equivalent from a foreign institution, required. International students require proof of English proficiency. Acceptance determined by committee of faculty members.

2011-2012 Annual costs. Tuition/fees: $23,510. Room only: $2,997. Books/supplies: $1,100. Personal expenses: $2,280.

Financial aid. Non-need-based: Scholarships awarded for academics, art, minority status.

Application procedures. Admission: No deadline. $50 fee. Admission notification on a rolling basis. **Financial aid:** No deadline. FAFSA required. Applicants notified on a rolling basis; must reply within 2 week(s) of notification.

Academics. Special study options: Cooperative education, distance learning, internships. Online courses. **Credit/placement by examination:** AP, CLEP, IB, institutional tests. 3 credit hours maximum toward associate degree, 3 toward bachelor's. **Support services:** Learning center, pre-admission summer program, reduced course load, study skills assistance, tutoring.

Majors. BACHELOR'S. Business: Apparel. **Communications:** Digital media. **Communications technology:** Animation/special effects. **Computer sciences:** Computer graphics, web page design, webmaster. **Visual/performing arts:** Commercial/advertising art, fashion design, graphic design, industrial design, interior design. **ASSOCIATE. Communications:** Digital media. **Computer sciences:** Computer graphics, web page design, webmaster. **Visual/performing arts:** Commercial/advertising art, graphic design, interior design.

Computing on campus. 312 workstations in library, computer center, student center. Online course registration, online library, helpline, repair service, wireless network available.

Student life. Freshman orientation: Mandatory. Preregistration for classes offered. **Housing:** Special housing for disabled, apartments available. School-sponsored housing available. **Activities:** Film society, student newspaper.

Student services. Career counseling, student employment services, financial aid counseling, personal counseling, placement for graduates, veterans' counselor. **Physically disabled:** Services for visually, speech, hearing impaired.

Contact. E-mail: aicaocadm@aii.edu
Phone: (888) 549-3055 Toll-free number: (888) 549-3055
Fax: (714) 556-1923
Harry Ramos, Senior Director of Admissions, Art Institute of California: Orange County, 3601 West Sunflower Avenue, Santa Ana, CA 92704-7931

Art Institute of California: Sacramento
Sacramento, California
www.artinstitutes.edu/sacramento   CB code: 5737

- For-profit 3-year culinary school and visual arts college
- Large city
- 1,293 degree-seeking undergraduates
- 49% of applicants admitted

General. Regionally accredited; also accredited by ACICS. **Degrees:** 43 bachelor's, 24 associate awarded. **Calendar:** Quarter. **Full-time faculty:** 17 total. **Part-time faculty:** 60 total.

Freshman class profile. 256 applied, 125 admitted, 115 enrolled.

Basis for selection. High school diploma required and GED accepted.

2011-2012 Annual costs. Tuition/fees: $23,310. Required fees vary by program. Room only: $6,525. Books/supplies: $1,692.

Application procedures. Admission: No deadline. $50 fee.

Academics. Credit/placement by examination: AP, CLEP.

Majors. BACHELOR'S. Communications technology: Animation/special effects. **Visual/performing arts:** Cinematography, game design, graphic design, interior design, multimedia. **ASSOCIATE. Visual/performing arts:** Graphic design, multimedia.

Student life. Freshman orientation: Available, $100 fee. Preregistration for classes offered.

Contact. Phone: (800) 477-1957
Courtney Amos, Director of Admissions, Art Institute of California: Sacramento, 2850 Gateway Oaks Drive, Suite 100, Sacramento, CA 95833

Art Institute of California: San Diego
San Diego, California
www.artinstitutes.edu/sandiego   CB code: 3036

- For-profit 3-year visual arts college
- Residential campus in very large city
- 2,101 degree-seeking undergraduates
- 44% of applicants admitted
- Application essay, interview required

General. Accredited by ACCSC. **Degrees:** 344 bachelor's, 131 associate awarded. **Calendar:** Quarter. **Full-time faculty:** 54 total. **Part-time faculty:** 88 total. **Special facilities:** Dining lab run by culinary students.

Freshman class profile. 399 applied, 176 admitted, 164 enrolled.

Basis for selection. Submission of an essay, an official high school transcript with GPA and graduation date as well as an admissions interview are most important. A portfolio and standardized test scores may also be important in the admissions process. **Learning Disabled:** Students requiring assistance should notify Assistant Director of Admissions.

2011-2012 Annual costs. Tuition/fees: $23,310.

Application procedures. Admission: No deadline. $50 fee. Admission notification on a rolling basis. **Financial aid:** No deadline. FAFSA required.

Academics. Special study options: Accelerated study, distance learning, internships. **Credit/placement by examination:** AP, CLEP. **Support services:** Study skills assistance, tutoring.

Majors. BACHELOR'S. Communications: Advertising. **Computer sciences:** Computer graphics, web page design, webmaster. **Visual/performing arts:** Commercial/advertising art, fashion design, game design, graphic design, interior design, multimedia. **ASSOCIATE. Visual/performing arts:** Commercial/advertising art, design, graphic design.

Computing on campus. 300 workstations in library, computer center. Online library, wireless network available.

Student life. Freshman orientation: Mandatory. Preregistration for classes offered. **Housing:** Single-sex dorms, apartments available. **Activities:** Student government, student newspaper.

Student services. Alcohol/substance abuse counseling, career counseling, services for economically disadvantaged, student employment services, financial aid counseling, personal counseling. **Physically disabled:** Services for visually, speech, hearing impaired.

Contact. E-mail: aicaadmin@aii.edu
Phone: (866) 275-2422 Toll-free number: (866) 275-2422
John Kerns, Director of Admissions, Art Institute of California: San Diego, 7650 Mission Valley Road, San Diego, CA 92108-4423

Art Institute of California: San Francisco
San Francisco, California
www.artinstitutes.edu/sanfrancisco   CB code: 4421

- For-profit 4-year culinary school and visual arts college
- Commuter campus in very large city
- 1,500 degree-seeking undergraduates
- Application essay required

General. Founded in 1939. Accredited by ACICS. **Degrees:** 248 bachelor's, 268 associate awarded; master's offered. **Location:** Downtown. **Calendar:** Quarter, extensive summer session. **Full-time faculty:** 34 total. **Part-time faculty:** 93 total.

Basis for selection. High school record and general appropriateness of educational background to specific program applied for most important. Portfolio, interview, standardized test scores also important. Interview and portfolio recommended.

High school preparation. Recommended units include English 1, mathematics 1, social studies 1 and history 1. One art class recommended.

2011-2012 Annual costs. Tuition/fees: $23,360. Required fee, $50, is activity fee for students pursuing bachelor's degree. Associate degree activity fee is $35. Room only: $8,370. Books/supplies: $1,620.

Application procedures. Admission: No deadline. $50 fee. Admission notification on a rolling basis. **Financial aid:** No deadline. FAFSA required. Applicants notified on a rolling basis.

Academics. Special study options: Combined bachelor's/graduate degree, distance learning, honors, internships, study abroad. **Credit/placement by examination:** AP, CLEP, IB. **Support services:** Reduced course load, remedial instruction, study skills assistance, tutoring.

Majors. Business: Fashion. **Communications technology:** Animation/special effects. **Computer sciences:** Computer graphics, web page design. **Visual/performing arts:** Commercial/advertising art, fashion design, film/cinema/video, graphic design, interior design.

Computing on campus. Wireless network available.

Student life. Freshman orientation: Mandatory. Preregistration for classes offered. **Housing:** Coed dorms, apartments available. $300 deposit. **Activities:** International student organizations, student government, student newspaper, adLab, Society of Web Architects and Programmers, Design Innovation Club, Game Art & Design Club, Adventurous Appetites, Photo Club, Ai Production Workshop, Alpha Beta Kappa, Audio Club, Expressionz.

Student services. Career counseling, student employment services, financial aid counseling. **Physically disabled:** Services for hearing impaired.

Contact. E-mail: aisfadm@aii.edu
Phone: (415) 865-0198 Toll-free number: (888) 493-3261
Fax: (415) 863-6344
Louie Garcia, Senior Director of Admissions, Art Institute of California: San Francisco, 1170 Market Street, San Francisco, CA 94102

Azusa Pacific University
Azusa, California   CB member
www.apu.edu   CB code: 4596

- Private 4-year university affiliated with interdenominational tradition
- Residential campus in small city

♦ 5,998 degree-seeking undergraduates: 14% part-time, 64% women, 5% African American, 8% Asian American, 17% Hispanic American, 2% international

♦ 3,931 degree-seeking graduate students

♦ 49% of applicants admitted

♦ SAT or ACT (ACT writing optional), application essay required

♦ 63% graduate within 6 years

General. Founded in 1899. Regionally accredited. **Degrees:** 1,331 bachelor's awarded; master's, professional, doctoral offered. **ROTC:** Army, Air Force. **Location:** 30 miles from Los Angeles. **Calendar:** Semester, limited summer session. **Full-time faculty:** 351 total; 74% have terminal degrees. **Part-time faculty:** 42 total; 43% have terminal degrees.

Freshman class profile. 8,187 applied, 4,028 admitted, 1,180 enrolled.

Mid 50% test scores		GPA 2.0-2.99:	6%
SAT critical reading:	490-600	Rank in top quarter:	60%
SAT math:	490-610	Rank in top tenth:	60%
ACT composite:	21-27	Return as sophomores:	88%
GPA 3.75 or higher:	45%	Out-of-state:	25%
GPA 3.50-3.74:	19%	Live on campus:	92%
GPA 3.0-3.49:	30%	International:	2%

Basis for selection. GPA, test scores, references, statement of agreement, essay important. Auditions required for music applicants. Interviews recommended for borderline applicants. **Home schooled:** SAT or ACT and transcript from organization required.

High school preparation. College-preparatory program recommended. Recommended units include English 4, mathematics 3, social studies 1, history 2, science 2 and foreign language 3.

2011-2012 Annual costs. Tuition/fees: $29,940. Room/board: $8,488. Books/supplies: $1,656.

Financial aid. Non-need-based: Scholarships awarded for academics, athletics, leadership, minority status, music/drama, religious affiliation, ROTC.

Application procedures. Admission: Priority date 2/15; deadline 6/1 (postmark date). $45 fee, may be waived for applicants with need. Admission notification by 4/1. Admission notification on a rolling basis beginning on or about 10/1. Must reply by May 1 or within 2 week(s) if notified thereafter. **Financial aid:** Priority date 3/2, closing date 7/1. FAFSA, institutional form required. Applicants notified on a rolling basis starting 3/1; must reply within 3 week(s) of notification.

Academics. Special study options: Accelerated study, cooperative education, distance learning, double major, ESL, exchange student, honors, independent study, internships, study abroad, teacher certification program, urban semester, Washington semester. **Credit/placement by examination:** AP, CLEP, IB, SAT, ACT, institutional tests. Essays required for Analysis and Interpretation of Literature and Freshman College Composition. **Support services:** Learning center, reduced course load, remedial instruction, study skills assistance, tutoring, writing center.

Majors. Biology: General, biochemistry. **Business:** General, accounting, business admin, finance, management information systems, marketing. **Communications:** Communications/speech/rhetoric, journalism. **Computer sciences:** General, computer science. **Education:** Art, business, elementary, middle, multi-level teacher, physical, secondary. **English:** English lit. **Foreign languages:** Spanish. **Health services:** Nurse practitioner, nursing (RN), predental, premedicine. **History:** General. **Human services:** Social work. **Liberal arts:** Arts/sciences. **Math:** General. **Philosophy/religion:** Philosophy, religion. **Physical sciences:** General, chemistry, physics. **Psychology:** General. **Social sciences:** General, international relations, political science, sociology. **Theology:** Bible, religious ed, sacred music, theology. **Visual/performing arts:** Art, dramatic, music, music performance, music theory/composition, studio arts.

Most popular majors. Business/marketing 19%, communications/journalism 8%, health sciences 18%, liberal arts 12%, psychology 7%, theological studies 7%, visual/performing arts 6%.

Computing on campus. Dormitories wired for high-speed internet access and linked to campus network. Commuter students can connect to campus network. Online course registration, online library, helpline, repair service, wireless network available.

Student life. Freshman orientation: Mandatory. Preregistration for classes offered. Class taken during first semester. **Policies:** Students will refrain from activities which may be spiritually or morally destructive. Religious observance required. **Housing:** Coed dorms, single-sex dorms, apartments available. $250 fully refundable deposit, deadline 5/1. **Activities:**

Bands, campus ministries, choral groups, drama, international student organizations, music ensembles, musical theater, opera, radio station, student government, student newspaper, symphony orchestra, TV station, Multi-Ethnic Student Alliance, Japanese Christian Fellowship, Chinese Christian Fellowship.

Athletics. NAIA, NCCAA. **Intercollegiate:** Baseball M, basketball, cross-country, football (tackle) M, soccer, softball W, tennis M, track and field, volleyball W. **Intramural:** Basketball, football (tackle) M, skiing, volleyball. **Team name:** Cougars.

Student services. Chaplain/spiritual director, career counseling, student employment services, financial aid counseling, health services, minority student services, personal counseling, placement for graduates, veterans' counselor. **Physically disabled:** Services for visually, speech, hearing impaired.

Contact. E-mail: admissions@apu.edu
Phone: (626) 812-3016 Toll-free number: (800) 825-5278
Fax: (626) 812-3096
Dave Burke, Director of Undergraduate Admissions, Azusa Pacific University, 901 East Alosta Avenue, Azusa, CA 91702-7000

Bergin University of Canine Studies
Santa Rosa, California
www.berginu.edu

♦ Private 4-year university and agricultural college

♦ Very large city

♦ 32 degree-seeking undergraduates

General. Regionally accredited; also accredited by ACICS. **Degrees:** 1 bachelor's, 9 associate awarded; master's offered. **Calendar:** Semester. **Full-time faculty:** 3 total. **Part-time faculty:** 12 total.

Basis for selection. Open admission, but selective for some programs. One-year's continuous work experience in canine-related activity for Master of Science in Canine Life Sciences program in addition to educational requirements.

2011-2012 Annual costs. Tuition/fees: $7,386.

Application procedures. Admission: Closing date 8/17. $25 fee. **Financial aid:** Closing date 8/3.

Academics. Credit/placement by examination: AP, CLEP.

Contact. E-mail: info@berginu.edu
Phone: (707) 545-3647 ext. 21
Delores Ford, Director of Admissions, Bergin University of Canine Studies, 1215 Sebastopol Road, Santa Rosa, CA 95407

Bethesda University of California
Anaheim, California
www.bcu.edu　　　　　　　　　**CB code: 3895**

♦ Private 4-year university affiliated with Christian Church

♦ Commuter campus in large city

♦ 195 degree-seeking undergraduates

♦ 75% of applicants admitted

♦ Application essay, interview required

General. Accredited by ABHE. Extension office in South Korea. **Degrees:** 27 bachelor's awarded; master's offered. **Location:** 30 miles from Los Angeles. **Calendar:** Semester, limited summer session. **Full-time faculty:** 6 total. **Class size:** 33% < 20, 64% 20-39, 3% 40-49.

Freshman class profile. 155 applied, 116 admitted, 87 enrolled.

Basis for selection. GED not accepted. Admissions decision based on recommendations, essay and interview. Secondary school record also important. ESL placement test not required for students who have TOEFL score 550 or higher or have graduated from English-speaking high school. Auditions required for music majors. Portfolio required for design majors. Christian experience essay required. **Home schooled:** Transcript of courses and grades, state high school equivalency certificate, letter of recommendation (nonparent) required.

High school preparation. College-preparatory program required.

2011-2012 Annual costs. Tuition/fees: $7,160. Room/board: $3,200. Books/supplies: $1,000.

Financial aid. All financial aid based on need.

Application procedures. Admission: Priority date 2/1; deadline 3/1 (receipt date). $35 fee ($80 out-of-state). Application must be submitted on paper. Admission notification on a rolling basis. **Financial aid:** No deadline. FAFSA, institutional form required. Applicants notified on a rolling basis starting 6/30.

Academics. Special study options: Combined bachelor's/graduate degree, distance learning, dual enrollment of high school students, ESL, external degree, independent study, liberal arts/career combination, study abroad, teacher certification program. **Credit/placement by examination:** AP, CLEP, IB, institutional tests. **Support services:** Reduced course load.

Majors. Computer sciences: Information technology. **Education:** Early childhood. **Foreign languages:** Translation. **Philosophy/religion:** Religion. **Theology:** Bible, missionary, religious ed, sacred music, theology. **Visual/performing arts:** Conducting, design, fashion design, metal/jewelry, music, music management, music performance, music theory/composition, piano/keyboard, stringed instruments, voice/opera.

Computing on campus. PC or laptop required. 30 workstations in dormitories, library, computer center, student center. Dormitories wired for high-speed internet access. Online course registration, helpline, repair service, wireless network available.

Student life. Freshman orientation: Mandatory. Preregistration for classes offered. **Policies:** Religious observance required. **Housing:** Off-campus housing available. **Activities:** Student government.

Athletics. NCCAA.

Student services. Chaplain/spiritual director, financial aid counseling, personal counseling.

Contact. E-mail: registrar@bcu.edu
Phone: (714) 517-1945 Fax: (714) 517-1948
Jacqueline Ha, Director of Admissions, Bethesda University of California, 730 North Euclid Street, Anaheim, CA 92801

Biola University
La Mirada, California
www.biola.edu   **CB code: 4017**

- Private 4-year university and Bible college affiliated with interdenominational tradition
- Residential campus in large town
- 4,234 degree-seeking undergraduates: 6% part-time, 61% women, 2% African American, 13% Asian American, 16% Hispanic American, 1% international
- 1,902 degree-seeking graduate students
- 76% of applicants admitted
- SAT or ACT (ACT writing optional), application essay required
- 66% graduate within 6 years

General. Founded in 1908. Regionally accredited. Biblically centered Christian institution. Every undergraduate student graduates with Bible minor. Over 145 academic programs in seven schools located on one campus. **Degrees:** 906 bachelor's awarded; master's, doctoral offered. **ROTC:** Army, Air Force. **Location:** 20 miles from downtown Los Angeles. **Calendar:** 4-1-4, extensive summer session. **Full-time faculty:** 244 total; 74% have terminal degrees, 18% minority, 34% women. **Part-time faculty:** 253 total; 15% minority, 37% women. **Class size:** 46% < 20, 44% 20-39, 4% 40-49, 3% 50-99, 3% >100. **Special facilities:** Concert hall, electron microscope, recording studio, film studio, MIDI lab for music composition, electronic piano lab, archaeological dig site, art studio, on-campus olive grove, fitness center, computer labs.

Freshman class profile. 3,337 applied, 2,548 admitted, 935 enrolled.

Mid 50% test scores		GPA 2.0-2.99:	11%
SAT critical reading:	500-630	Rank in top quarter:	52%
SAT math:	500-620	Rank in top tenth:	25%
SAT writing:	500-620	Return as sophomores:	86%
ACT composite:	21-27	Out-of-state:	24%
GPA 3.75 or higher:	32%	Live on campus:	92%
GPA 3.50-3.74:	24%	International:	2%
GPA 3.0-3.49:	33%		

Basis for selection. Official transcripts, SAT/ACT, pastoral reference form required. Christian commitment most important; academic record, personal references, test scores next in importance. School, community, church activities helpful. Separate application for cinema & media arts program and Torrey Honors program. No exceptions to SAT/ACT requirement. If more than one SAT score, the best combination of scores accepted. Interview requested of some students. Auditions required for music applicants. Portfolios recommended for art applicants. Any body of work recommended for cinema & media arts applicants. **Home schooled:** Applicants advised to go through accreditation agency. **Learning Disabled:** Student must request the services of the ODS and provide documentation supporting the nature and limitations of a disability.

High school preparation. College-preparatory program recommended. 16 units recommended. Recommended units include English 4, mathematics 3, social studies 1, history 1, science 2 (laboratory 1) and foreign language 4. 1 algebra and 1 chemistry required of nursing applicants. 2 math, 1 physics, 1 chemistry required of biology applicants. Some deficiencies may be satisfied during freshman year.

2011-2012 Annual costs. Tuition/fees: $29,908. On-campus room and board rate reflects an average. Room/board: $8,990. Books/supplies: $1,656. Personal expenses: $2,277.

2010-2011 Financial aid. Need-based: 773 full-time freshmen applied for aid; 637 were judged to have need; 633 of these received aid. Average need met was 56%. Average scholarship/grant was $14,152; average loan $3,126. 64% of total undergraduate aid awarded as scholarships/grants, 36% as loans/jobs. **Non-need-based:** Awarded to 837 full-time undergraduates, including 238 freshmen. Scholarships awarded for academics, alumni affiliation, art, athletics, leadership, minority status, music/drama.

Application procedures. Admission: No deadline. $45 fee, may be waived for applicants with need. Admission notification by 4/1. Admission notification on a rolling basis beginning on or about 1/15. **Financial aid:** Priority date 3/1; no closing date. FAFSA required. Applicants notified on a rolling basis starting 3/1.

Academics. Most departments offer individualized academic help to students, scheduled according to need. **Special study options:** Combined bachelor's/graduate degree, distance learning, double major, ESL, exchange student, honors, independent study, internships, New York semester, study abroad, teacher certification program, Washington semester. 3-2 program with Los Angeles College of Chiropractic, 3-2 engineering program with University of Southern California. **Credit/placement by examination:** AP, CLEP, IB, SAT, ACT, institutional tests. Maximum of 32 credits from CLEP, AP, and IB can be counted toward degree. **Support services:** Learning center, reduced course load, remedial instruction, study skills assistance, tutoring, writing center.

Honors college/program. Admission by invitation after application to the university. Students trained in rigorous discussion group format through classical learning style, practicing high-level writing and critical thinking skills.

Majors. Biology: General, biochemistry. **Business:** Accounting, business admin, international, management information systems, marketing. **Communications:** Broadcast journalism, communications/speech/rhetoric, journalism, public relations, radio/TV. **Computer sciences:** Computer science. **Education:** General, elementary, music, physical, secondary. **Engineering:** General. **English:** Creative writing, English lit. **Foreign languages:** Spanish. **Health services:** Communication disorders, nursing (RN). **History:** General. **Liberal arts:** Arts/sciences. **Math:** General. **Parks/recreation:** Exercise sciences, health/fitness. **Philosophy/religion:** Philosophy, religion. **Physical sciences:** Chemistry, physics. **Psychology:** General. **Social sciences:** General, anthropology, sociology. **Theology:** Bible, religious ed, theology. **Visual/performing arts:** Art, cinematography, dramatic, drawing, multimedia, music, music performance, music theory/composition, painting, photography, sculpture, studio arts, theater arts management.

Most popular majors. Business/marketing 19%, communications/journalism 8%, education 6%, health sciences 6%, psychology 10%, social sciences 9%, theological studies 12%, visual/performing arts 13%.

Computing on campus. 225 workstations in library, computer center. Dormitories wired for high-speed internet access and linked to campus network. Commuter students can connect to campus network. Online course registration, online library, helpline, repair service, student web hosting, wireless network available.

Student life. Freshman orientation: Mandatory. Preregistration for classes offered. Week-long, held week before term begins. Led by current students. Various social activities hosted. **Policies:** Christian service assignment and regular church attendance encouraged. Students adhere to code of conduct and sign contract. Use and possession of drugs and/or alcohol not permitted. Freshmen and sophomores under 21 required to live on campus

unless living with relatives. Religious observance required. **Housing:** Guaranteed on-campus for freshmen. Coed dorms, single-sex dorms, special housing for disabled, apartments available. $250 partly refundable deposit, deadline 6/1. Flex-style dorms with single sex floors/wings available. **Activities:** Bands, campus ministries, choral groups, drama, film society, international student organizations, music ensembles, musical theater, opera, radio station, student government, student newspaper, symphony orchestra, TV station, Student Missionary Union, Korean student association, evangelism team, International Justice Mission, theology club, Society of Christian Philosophy, Tijuana Ministry, Bas Bleu (women's issues), Naturally Diverse.

Athletics. NAIA. **Intercollegiate:** Baseball M, basketball, cross-country, diving, golf, soccer, softball W, swimming, tennis, track and field, volleyball W. **Intramural:** Basketball, football (non-tackle), soccer, softball, volleyball. **Team name:** Eagles.

Student services. Alcohol/substance abuse counseling, chaplain/spiritual director, career counseling, student employment services, financial aid counseling, health services, minority student services, personal counseling, placement for graduates, veterans' counselor, women's services. **Physically disabled:** Services for speech, hearing impaired.

Contact. E-mail: admissions@biola.edu
Phone: (562) 903-4752 Toll-free number: (800) 652-4652
Fax: (562) 903-4709
Andre Stephens, Senior Director of Undergraduate Admissions, Biola University, 13800 Biola Avenue, La Mirada, CA 90639-0001

Brooks Institute
Santa Barbara, California
www.brooks.edu
CB code: 4228

- For-profit 3-year visual arts college
- Commuter campus in small city
- 787 degree-seeking undergraduates
- Application essay, interview required

General. Founded in 1945. Accredited by ACICS. Two facilities in Santa Barbara and one in Ventura. **Degrees:** 228 bachelor's awarded; master's offered. **Location:** 90 miles from Los Angeles. **Calendar:** Semester, extensive summer session. **Full-time faculty:** 32 total. **Part-time faculty:** 59 total. **Special facilities:** Digital labs, sounds stages, studio back-lot, prop house.

Basis for selection. School achievement record most important. Photographic experience not required for entrance. Advanced standing may be offered to those with 4X5 view camera experience. Evaluation consists of written examination portfolio and review. TOEFL required of students whose first language is not English. Different standards exist based on paper vs. computer scores and for undergraduate and graduate applicants. At time of matriculation, institution will assess English and math proficiencies for students who have not demonstrated proficiency in both at the college level or by receiving minimum standard scores in national tests. Interviews can be conducted via telephone. Interview and photography portfolio required for advanced standing in core courses. **Home schooled:** GED required if home schooling not recognized by state. **Learning Disabled:** Protocol for students seeking accommodation is mailed to accepted applicants with provisional acceptance letter.

High school preparation. College-preparatory program recommended. Recommended units include English 4, mathematics 2, social studies 1, science 1 and foreign language 2.

2011-2012 Annual costs. Tuition/fees: $17,880. Personal expenses: $1,896.

Application procedures. **Admission:** No deadline. $50 fee. Admission notification on a rolling basis. Students encouraged to apply at least 6 months in advance. **Financial aid:** Priority date 3/2; no closing date. FAFSA, institutional form required. Applicants notified on a rolling basis starting 5/1.

Academics. **Special study options:** Accelerated study, combined bachelor's/graduate degree, distance learning, double major, independent study, internships. Documentary courses in foreign countries, travel courses, water photography (for upper-division students). **Credit/placement by examination:** AP, CLEP, institutional tests. 54 credit hours maximum toward bachelor's degree. **Support services:** Remedial instruction, tutoring.

Majors. **Communications:** Photojournalism. **Visual/performing arts:** Cinematography, graphic design, photography.

Computing on campus. 20 workstations in library, computer center. Online library, helpline, wireless network available.

Student life. **Freshman orientation:** Mandatory. Preregistration for classes offered. Immediately prior to matriculation; normally 2-3 days of activities. **Policies:** Car necessary for travel between campuses and to assignment locations. **Activities:** Student government.

Student services. Career counseling, student employment services, financial aid counseling, personal counseling, placement for graduates.

Contact. E-mail: admissions@brooks.edu
Phone: (888) 304-3456 Toll-free number: (888) 304-3456
Fax: (805) 565-1386
Maggie Balderas, Vice President of Marketing and Admissions, Brooks Institute, 27 East Cota Street, Santa Barbara, CA 93101

California Baptist University
Riverside, California
www.calbaptist.edu
CB member
CB code: 4094

- Private 4-year university affiliated with Southern Baptist Convention
- Residential campus in large city
- 4,403 degree-seeking undergraduates: 12% part-time, 63% women, 9% African American, 5% Asian American, 24% Hispanic American, 1% Native American, 3% international
- 1,010 degree-seeking graduate students
- 74% of applicants admitted
- SAT or ACT (ACT writing optional), application essay required
- 56% graduate within 6 years

General. Founded in 1950. Regionally accredited. **Degrees:** 720 bachelor's awarded; master's offered. **ROTC:** Army, Air Force. **Location:** 60 miles from Los Angeles. **Calendar:** Semester, extensive summer session. **Full-time faculty:** 196 total; 68% have terminal degrees, 20% minority, 45% women. **Part-time faculty:** 264 total; 28% have terminal degrees, 29% minority, 54% women. **Class size:** 38% < 20, 42% 20-39, 8% 40-49, 9% 50-99, 3% >100. **Special facilities:** Music performance and recording studios, aquatic center, outdoor athletic center, student recreation center, holocaust collection, digital design and photography studio, theater arts stage production workshop facility, prayer chapel, hymnology collection, health/wellness center, counseling center, career services center, patient simulation laboratory.

Freshman class profile. 2,398 applied, 1,776 admitted, 790 enrolled.

Mid 50% test scores			
SAT critical reading:	430-560	GPA 2.0-2.99:	34%
SAT math:	440-570	Rank in top quarter:	45%
SAT writing:	440-550	Rank in top tenth:	15%
ACT composite:	19-24	Return as sophomores:	77%
GPA 3.75 or higher:	23%	Out-of-state:	7%
GPA 3.50-3.74:	16%	Live on campus:	82%
GPA 3.0-3.49:	27%	International:	2%

Basis for selection. School achievement record, test scores, essays, and recommendations very important. SAT and SAT Subject Tests or ACT recommended. Interviews recommended. Auditions required for music, drama applicants. **Home schooled:** Transcript of courses and grades, letter of recommendation (nonparent) required.

High school preparation. College-preparatory program recommended. 15 units required; 19 recommended. Required and recommended units include English 4, mathematics 3-4, social studies 2, history 2, science 2-3 (laboratory 1-2), foreign language 2-3 and academic electives 3.

2011-2012 Annual costs. Tuition/fees: $25,768. Room/board: $8,700. Books/supplies: $1,656. Personal expenses: $2,276.

2011-2012 Financial aid. **Need-based:** 574 full-time freshmen applied for aid; 486 were judged to have need; 485 of these received aid. Average need met was 71%. Average scholarship/grant was $12,296; average loan $3,449. 52% of total undergraduate aid awarded as scholarships/grants, 48% as loans/jobs. **Non-need-based:** Awarded to 1,873 full-time undergraduates, including 307 freshmen. Scholarships awarded for academics, art, athletics, leadership, music/drama, religious affiliation, ROTC.

Application procedures. **Admission:** Priority date 2/1; no deadline. $45 fee, may be waived for applicants with need. Admission notification on a rolling basis beginning on or about 11/9. **Financial aid:** Priority date 3/2; no closing date. FAFSA required. Applicants notified on a rolling basis starting 3/2; must reply by 5/1 or within 3 week(s) of notification.

Academics. **Special study options:** Accelerated study, distance learning, double major, ESL, exchange student, honors, internships, liberal arts/career combination, study abroad, teacher certification program, Washington semester, weekend college. **Credit/placement by examination:** AP, CLEP, IB,

SAT, ACT, institutional tests. 30 credit hours maximum toward bachelor's degree. Portfolio course available to assist students in documenting work that may be counted for credit for prior learning experiences. **Support services:** Learning center, reduced course load, remedial instruction, study skills assistance, tutoring, writing center.

Majors. Biology: General. **Business:** General, accounting, marketing. **Communications:** Communications/speech/rhetoric, digital media, journalism, public relations. **Communications technology:** Desktop publishing. **Education:** Early childhood. **Engineering:** General, civil, computer, mechanical. **English:** English lit. **Foreign languages:** Spanish. **Health services:** Nursing (RN). **History:** General. **Liberal arts:** Arts/sciences. **Math:** General. **Parks/recreation:** Exercise sciences. **Philosophy/religion:** Christian, philosophy. **Physical sciences:** Chemistry. **Protective services:** Law enforcement admin. **Psychology:** General. **Social sciences:** Anthropology, political science, sociology. **Theology:** Bible, missionary. **Visual/performing arts:** General, art, dramatic, film/cinema/video, music, music performance, music theory/composition, piano/keyboard, voice/opera.

Most popular majors. Business/marketing 13%, health sciences 11%, liberal arts 12%, parks/recreation 7%, psychology 8%, social sciences 6%.

Computing on campus. 279 workstations in library, computer center. Dormitories wired for high-speed internet access and linked to campus network. Commuter students can connect to campus network. Online course registration, online library, helpline available.

Student life. Freshman orientation: Mandatory, $310 fee. Preregistration for classes offered. Held prior to beginning of semester. **Policies:** Students receiving institutional scholarships required to live in student housing. Religious observance required. **Housing:** Guaranteed on-campus for freshmen. Single-sex dorms, apartments, cooperative housing available. $300 fully refundable deposit, deadline 8/1. **Activities:** Bands, campus ministries, choral groups, drama, international student organizations, music ensembles, musical theater, student government, student newspaper, symphony orchestra, Young Republicans, Young Democrats, Fellowship of Christian Athletes, black student union, Big Brother, Big Sister, Active Compassion, elderly ministry, homeless ministry, international service projects.

Athletics. NAIA. **Intercollegiate:** Baseball M, basketball, cheerleading, cross-country, diving, golf, soccer, softball W, swimming, track and field, volleyball, water polo, wrestling M. **Intramural:** Basketball, bowling, football (non-tackle), golf, softball, table tennis, volleyball. **Team name:** Lancers.

Student services. Adult student services, chaplain/spiritual director, career counseling, student employment services, financial aid counseling, personal counseling, placement for graduates, veterans' counselor.

Contact. E-mail: admissions@calbaptist.edu
Phone: (951) 343-4212 Toll-free number: (877) 228-8866
Fax: (951) 343-4525
Allen Johnson, Associate Dean of Enrollment Services, California Baptist University, 8432 Magnolia Avenue, Riverside, CA 92504-3297

California Christian College
Fresno, California
www.calchristiancollege.org   CB code: 4123

- Private 4-year Bible college affiliated with Free Will Baptists
- Residential campus in large city
- 22 degree-seeking undergraduates: 18% part-time, 50% women, 14% African American, 32% Hispanic American
- Application essay required

General. Regionally accredited; also accredited by TRACS. **Degrees:** 2 bachelor's awarded. **Location:** 190 miles from San Francisco, 220 miles from Los Angeles. **Calendar:** Semester. **Part-time faculty:** 7 total; 29% have terminal degrees, 29% women.

Freshman class profile. 12 applied, 11 admitted, 9 enrolled.

Basis for selection. Open admission. **Home schooled:** Transcript of courses and grades, state high school equivalency certificate, letter of recommendation (nonparent) required.

2011-2012 Annual costs. Tuition/fees: $9,380. Room/board: $4,150. Books/supplies: $700. Personal expenses: $2,052.

2010-2011 Financial aid. Need-based: 47% of total undergraduate aid awarded as scholarships/grants, 53% as loans/jobs.

Application procedures. Admission: No deadline. $40 fee, may be waived for applicants with need. Application must be submitted on paper.

Admission notification on a rolling basis. **Financial aid:** No deadline. FAFSA, institutional form required.

Academics. Special study options: Distance learning, honors, independent study. **Credit/placement by examination:** AP, CLEP, institutional tests.

Majors. Theology: Theology.

Computing on campus. PC or laptop required. Dormitories wired for high-speed internet access and linked to campus network. Commuter students can connect to campus network. Online course registration, online library, wireless network available.

Student life. Freshman orientation: Mandatory. Preregistration for classes offered. **Policies:** Religious observance required. **Housing:** Single-sex dorms available. **Activities:** Campus ministries, choral groups, music ensembles, student government.

Student services. Financial aid counseling, personal counseling.

Contact. E-mail: cccadmissions@sbcglobal.net
Phone: (559) 455-5571 Fax: (559) 251-4231
Jennifer Maxwell, Admissions, California Christian College, 4881 East University Avenue, Fresno, CA 93703

California Coast University
Santa Ana, California
www.calcoast.edu

- For-profit 4-year virtual university
- Large city
- 4,112 degree-seeking undergraduates

General. Accredited by DETC. **Degrees:** 320 bachelor's, 108 associate awarded; master's, doctoral offered. **Calendar:** Differs by program, extensive summer session. **Part-time faculty:** 26 total.

Basis for selection. Open admission.

2011-2012 Annual costs. Tuition/fees: $4,500. Textbooks can be rented from the University's rental library for $25 per text.

Application procedures. Admission: No deadline. $75 fee.

Academics. Special study options: Accelerated study, cross-registration, distance learning, external degree, honors, independent study. **Credit/placement by examination:** AP, CLEP.

Majors. Business: General, business admin. **Health services:** Health care admin. **Psychology:** General. **Social sciences:** Criminology.

Student life. Activities: Student newspaper.

Contact. E-mail: admissions@calcoast.edu
Phone: (714) 547-9625
Christi Okuma, Admissions Director, California Coast University, 925 North Spurgeon Street, Santa Ana, CA 92701

California College of the Arts
San Francisco, California   CB member
www.cca.edu   CB code: 4031

- Private 4-year visual arts college
- Commuter campus in very large city
- 1,476 degree-seeking undergraduates: 6% part-time, 61% women, 5% African American, 16% Asian American, 13% Hispanic American, 1% Native American, 15% international
- 490 degree-seeking graduate students
- 76% of applicants admitted
- Application essay required
- 49% graduate within 6 years

General. Founded in 1907. Regionally accredited. 2 campuses located in San Francisco and Oakland. **Degrees:** 258 bachelor's awarded; master's offered. **Location:** 3 miles from downtown. **Calendar:** Semester, limited summer session. **Full-time faculty:** 86 total; 70% have terminal degrees, 23% minority, 52% women. **Part-time faculty:** 438 total; 62% have terminal degrees, 18% minority, 44% women. **Class size:** 93% < 20, 7% 20-39, less

than 1% 40-49, less than 1% 50-99. **Special facilities:** Center for art and public life, contemporary arts institute, materials resource center.

Freshman class profile. 1,352 applied, 1,031 admitted, 234 enrolled.

Mid 50% test scores				
SAT critical reading:	470-620	GPA 3.0-3.49:	43%
SAT math:	480-610	GPA 2.0-2.99:	34%
SAT writing:	470-610	Return as sophomores:	79%
ACT composite:	21-26	Out-of-state:	48%
GPA 3.75 or higher:	10%	Live on campus:	80%
GPA 3.50-3.74:	13%	International:	22%

Basis for selection. High school achievement as evidenced by grade point average, portfolio of creative work, personal essay/statement of purpose, interview, and 2 letters of recommendation required. The college also reviews art/design activities and interests. SAT or ACT recommended. Test scores are primarily used for placement, but may be considered for admission. SAT or ACT scores with Writing highly recommended and used in English course placement. Portfolio of creative work and statement of artistic and professional goals required. **Home schooled:** Transcript of courses and grades required. Detailed syllabus of courses (equivalent to grades 10-12) and details of curriculum, including community college transcripts (if applicable) required.

High school preparation. College-preparatory program recommended.

2012-2013 Annual costs. Tuition/fees (projected): $37,310. Room only: $7,400. Books/supplies: $1,500. Personal expenses: $2,200.

2010-2011 Financial aid. Need-based: 168 full-time freshmen applied for aid; 155 were judged to have need; 155 of these received aid. Average need met was 62%. Average scholarship/grant was $19,788; average loan $3,537. 65% of total undergraduate aid awarded as scholarships/grants, 35% as loans/jobs. **Non-need-based:** Awarded to 622 full-time undergraduates, including 166 freshmen. Scholarships awarded for academics, art. **Additional information:** Application deadline for merit scholarships February 1.

Application procedures. Admission: Priority date 2/1; no deadline. $60 fee, may be waived for applicants with need. Admission notification on a rolling basis. Must reply by May 1 or within 2 week(s) if notified thereafter. Maximum period of postponement is one semester. **Financial aid:** Priority date 3/1; no closing date. FAFSA required. Applicants notified on a rolling basis starting 3/15; must reply by 5/1 or within 3 week(s) of notification.

Academics. Special study options: Combined bachelor's/graduate degree, cross-registration, double major, ESL, exchange student, independent study, internships, student-designed major, study abroad. Sponsored studios, community engagement with project-based learning, community service fellowships, annual career expo, summer English second language (ESL) program for international students, pre-college program, disability services. **Credit/placement by examination:** AP, CLEP, IB, SAT, ACT, institutional tests. **Support services:** Learning center, pre-admission summer program, reduced course load, remedial instruction, study skills assistance, tutoring, writing center.

Majors. Architecture: Architecture. **English:** Creative writing. **Visual/performing arts:** Art, ceramics, cinematography, crafts, drawing, fashion design, fiber arts, game design, graphic design, illustration, industrial design, interior design, metal/jewelry, painting, photography, printmaking, sculpture, studio arts.

Most popular majors. Architecture 11%, visual/performing arts 77%.

Computing on campus. PC or laptop required. 403 workstations in dormitories, library, computer center, student center. Dormitories wired for high-speed internet access and linked to campus network. Commuter students can connect to campus network. Online library, helpline, student web hosting, wireless network available.

Student life. Freshman orientation: Mandatory. Preregistration for classes offered. Educational and social programs are offered one week before classes start. **Policies:** Freshmen not permitted cars on campus. **Housing:** Coed dorms, apartments, wellness housing available. $750 partly refundable deposit, deadline 5/15. First-year community, transfer community, multicultural community service theme halls available. **Activities:** International student organizations, literary magazine, student government, Alliance for Multiculturalism in Architecture, American Institute of Architecture Students, Asian Student Association, basketball club, ceramics guild, Future Action Reclamation Mob (FARM), Glass League, International Interior Design association, CCA/UC Berkeley Queer Straight Alliance, Students of Color Coalition.

Athletics. Team name: Chimera.

Student services. Alcohol/substance abuse counseling, career counseling, student employment services, financial aid counseling, personal counseling, placement for graduates. **Physically disabled:** Services for visually, speech, hearing impaired.

Contact. E-mail: enroll@cca.edu
Phone: (415) 703-9523 Toll-free number: (800) 447-1278
Fax: (415) 703-9539
Robynne Royster, Director of Undergraduate Admission, California College of the Arts, 1111 Eighth Street, San Francisco, CA 94107-2247

California College San Diego
San Diego, California
www.cc-sd.edu
CB code: 3354

- For-profit 4-year business and health science college
- Commuter campus in very large city
- 1,438 degree-seeking undergraduates
- Interview required

General. Accredited by ACCSC. **Degrees:** 56 bachelor's, 221 associate awarded; master's offered. **Location:** 5 miles from downtown. **Calendar:** Differs by program, extensive summer session. **Full-time faculty:** 12 total. **Part-time faculty:** 22 total.

Basis for selection. Open admission. **Home schooled:** State high school equivalency certificate required.

2011-2012 Annual costs. Associate programs: Business Management & Accounting $40,385; Computer Programming $40,385; Computer Networking & Technology $40,385; Graphic Arts $40,385; Medical Specialties $40,385; Respiratory Therapy $47,165. Bachelor programs: Accounting $71,180; Business Administration $71,180; Computer Science $71,180; Graphic Arts $71,180; Health Science $30,155; Healthcare Administration $71,180; Nursing $40,385; Nursing Administration $30,155; Respiratory Therapy $78,070.

Application procedures. Admission: No deadline. No application fee. Application must be submitted on paper.

Academics. Special study options: Combined bachelor's/graduate degree. **Credit/placement by examination:** AP, CLEP. **Support services:** Remedial instruction, tutoring.

Majors. Business: Accounting, business admin. **Computer sciences:** Computer science. **Health services:** Health care admin, respiratory therapy technology.

Computing on campus. Commuter students can connect to campus network. Online library, helpline, repair service, wireless network available.

Student life. Freshman orientation: Mandatory. Preregistration for classes offered.

Athletics. Team name: Bulldogs.

Student services. Adult student services, career counseling, services for economically disadvantaged, student employment services, financial aid counseling, placement for graduates, veterans' counselor.

Contact. Phone: (619) 680-4430 Toll-free number: (800) 622-3188
Fax: (619) 295-5762
Erick Asero, Director of Admissions, California College San Diego, 2820 Camino del Rio South 300, San Diego, CA 92108

California Institute of Integral Studies
San Francisco, California
www.ciis.edu
CB code: 3609

- Private two-year upper-division liberal arts college
- Commuter campus in very large city
- 87% of applicants admitted
- Application essay required

General. Regionally accredited. **Degrees:** 69 bachelor's awarded; master's, doctoral offered. **Location:** Downtown. **Calendar:** Semester, extensive summer session. **Full-time faculty:** 60 total; 30% minority, 48% women. **Part-time faculty:** 142 total; 30% minority, 56% women. **Class size:** 100% < 20. **Special facilities:** Meditation room, Zen roof garden, art galleries in hallways, counseling centers.

Student profile. 79 degree-seeking undergraduates, 1,339 degree-seeking graduate students. 70 applied as first time-transfer students, 61 admitted, 53 enrolled.

Women:	24%	International:	1%
African American:	9%	Part-time:	9%
Asian American:	5%	Out-of-state:	5%
Hispanic American:	15%	25 or older:	95%
Native American:	3%		

Basis for selection. College transcript, application essay required. Transfer accepted as juniors.

2011-2012 Annual costs. Tuition/fees: $15,540. Cost quoted for 2 semesters; 3-semester attendance mandatory. Books/supplies: $1,722.

Financial aid. Need-based: 80 applied for aid; 68 were judged to have need; 68 of these received aid. Average need met was 16%. 28% of total undergraduate aid awarded as scholarships/grants, 72% as loans/jobs. **Non-need-based:** Awarded to 21 undergraduates. Scholarships awarded for academics, alumni affiliation, art, job skills, leadership, minority status, music/drama, ROTC, state residency.

Application procedures. Admission: Priority date 4/1. $65 fee, may be waived for applicants with need. Application priority dates differ by program. **Financial aid:** Priority date 4/15, no deadline.

Academics. Special study options: Distance learning, dual enrollment of high school students, independent study, internships, weekend college. Offers interdisciplinary, cross-cultural, and applied studies in psychology, philosophy, religion, cultural anthropology, transformative studies and leadership, integrative health, women's spirituality, master's in counseling psychology, community mental health, and the arts. **Credit/placement by examination:** AP, CLEP. 30 credit hours maximum toward bachelor's degree. **Support services:** Tutoring, writing center.

Computing on campus. 20 workstations in computer center. Commuter students can connect to campus network. Online library, helpline, wireless network available.

Student life. Activities: Choral groups, international student organizations, student government, People of Color, Queer at CIIS, Student Alliance, Interdisciplinary Dialog Group, UNITE!, AWARE (Awakening to Whiteness and Racism Everywhere), International Students & Friends, Zen Meditation Group, Theater for Change.

Student services. Career counseling, financial aid counseling, minority student services, personal counseling, placement for graduates.

Contact. E-mail: admissions@ciis.edu
Phone: (415) 575-6150
Allyson Werner, Associate Director of Admissions, California Institute of Integral Studies, 1453 Mission Street, San Francisco, CA 94103

California Institute of Technology
Pasadena, California   **CB member**
www.caltech.edu   **CB code: 4034**

♦ Private 4-year university
♦ Residential campus in small city
♦ 978 degree-seeking undergraduates: 39% women
♦ 1,253 degree-seeking graduate students
♦ 13% of applicants admitted
♦ SAT or ACT (ACT writing optional), SAT Subject Tests, application essay required
♦ 87% graduate within 6 years

General. Founded in 1891. Regionally accredited. Caltech is located in Pasadena, California, approximately 11 miles northeast of Los Angeles. The Institute's faculty and alumni have received 32 Nobel Prizes. **Degrees:** 235 bachelor's awarded; master's, doctoral offered. **ROTC:** Army, Air Force. **Location:** 10 miles from downtown Los Angeles. **Calendar:** Quarter. **Full-time faculty:** 322 total; 98% have terminal degrees, 18% minority, 19% women. **Part-time faculty:** 16 total; 50% have terminal degrees, 25% minority, 38% women. **Class size:** 63% < 20, 22% 20-39, 4% 40-49, 7% 50-99, 3% >100. **Special facilities:** Jet Propulsion Laboratory (JPL), observatories, wind and water tunnels, radio observatory, seismological laboratory, marine biological laboratory.

Freshman class profile. 5,225 applied, 667 admitted, 244 enrolled.

Mid 50% test scores			
SAT critical reading:	700-790	Rank in top quarter:	100%
SAT math:	760-800	Rank in top tenth:	97%
SAT writing:	700-790	Return as sophomores:	98%
ACT composite:	33-35	Live on campus:	100%
		International:	11%

Basis for selection. High school preparation and record (particularly in mathematics and science), test scores, extracurricular activities (science and nonscience-related), counselors' and teachers' recommendations, and demonstrated interest in mathematics and science are major considerations. SAT Subject Test requirements: Math level IIC and one science, either biology (environmental or molecular), chemistry, or physics.

High school preparation. College-preparatory program required. Required and recommended units include English 3-4, mathematics 4, social studies 1-3, history 1, science 2-4 (laboratory 1) and foreign language 3.

2012-2013 Annual costs. Tuition/fees: $39,588. Room/board: $12,084. Books/supplies: $1,323. Personal expenses: $3,387.

2011-2012 Financial aid. Need-based: 200 full-time freshmen applied for aid; 137 were judged to have need; 137 of these received aid. Average need met was 100%. Average scholarship/grant was $33,006; average loan $4,079. 87% of total undergraduate aid awarded as scholarships/grants, 13% as loans/jobs. **Non-need-based:** Awarded to 955 full-time undergraduates, including 5 freshmen. Scholarships awarded for academics.

Application procedures. Admission: Closing date 1/3 (postmark date). $65 fee, may be waived for applicants with need. Admission notification by 4/1. Must reply by 5/1. **Financial aid:** Priority date 3/2; no closing date. FAFSA, institutional form, CSS PROFILE required. Applicants notified on a rolling basis starting 4/1; must reply by 5/1 or within 2 week(s) of notification.

Academics. Remedial services not formally offered. Remediation available for students deficient in basic scientific knowledge or technical skills. **Special study options:** Combined bachelor's/graduate degree, cooperative education, cross-registration, double major, ESL, exchange student, independent study, liberal arts/career combination, student-designed major, study abroad. **Credit/placement by examination:** AP, CLEP, institutional tests. **Support services:** Reduced course load, tutoring.

Majors. Biology: General. **Business:** Managerial economics. **Computer sciences:** Computer science. **Engineering:** General, applied physics, chemical, computer, electrical, environmental, mechanical. **English:** English lit. **History:** General, science/technology. **Math:** General, applied. **Philosophy/religion:** Philosophy. **Physical sciences:** Astronomy, astrophysics, chemistry, geochemistry, geology, geophysics, materials science, physics, planetary. **Social sciences:** General, economics, political science.

Most popular majors. Biology 8%, computer/information sciences 11%, engineering/engineering technologies 41%, mathematics 18%, physical sciences 25%.

Computing on campus. 112 workstations in dormitories, library, computer center. Dormitories wired for high-speed internet access and linked to campus network. Commuter students can connect to campus network. Online course registration, online library, helpline, repair service, student web hosting, wireless network available.

Student life. Freshman orientation: Mandatory, $500 fee. Preregistration for classes offered. 3 day Frosh camp. **Policies:** Honor Code: "No member of the Caltech community shall take unfair advantage of any other member of the Caltech community.". **Housing:** Guaranteed on-campus for all undergraduates. Coed dorms, special housing for disabled, apartments available. Pets allowed in dorm rooms. Single-unit houses available. **Activities:** Bands, choral groups, dance, drama, film society, international student organizations, literary magazine, music ensembles, musical theater, opera, student government, student newspaper, symphony orchestra, Caltech Y, Christian fellowship, Newman Club, Hillel, Amnesty International, Caltech Center for Diversity.

Athletics. NCAA. **Intercollegiate:** Baseball M, basketball, cross-country, diving, fencing, soccer M, swimming, tennis, track and field, volleyball W, water polo. **Intramural:** Badminton, baseball M, basketball, cheerleading, cricket M, cross-country, football (tackle) M, soccer, softball, squash, swimming, table tennis, tennis, track and field, volleyball, water polo M. **Team name:** Beavers.

Student services. Alcohol/substance abuse counseling, chaplain/spiritual director, career counseling, student employment services, financial aid counseling, health services, minority student services, on-campus daycare, personal counseling, placement for graduates, women's services. **Physically disabled:** Services for visually, speech, hearing impaired.

Contact. E-mail: ugadmissions@caltech.edu
Phone: (626) 395-6341 Fax: (626) 683-3026
Jarrid Whitney, Director of Admissions, California Institute of
Technology, 383 South Hill Avenue, Mail Code 10-90, Pasadena, CA
91125

California Institute of the Arts
Valencia, California   **CB member**
www.calarts.edu   **CB code: 4049**

- Private 4-year visual arts and performing arts college
- Residential campus in small city
- 904 degree-seeking undergraduates: 1% part-time, 52% women, 7% African American, 11% Asian American, 11% Hispanic American, 1% Native American, 9% international
- 524 degree-seeking graduate students
- 26% of applicants admitted
- Application essay required
- 65% graduate within 6 years

General. Founded in 1961. Regionally accredited. Single complex of 6 professional schools: art, critical studies, dance, film/video, music and theater. **Degrees:** 161 bachelor's awarded; master's, doctoral offered. **Location:** 30 miles from Los Angeles. **Calendar:** Semester. **Full-time faculty:** 159 total; 64% have terminal degrees, 18% minority, 43% women. **Part-time faculty:** 164 total; 48% have terminal degrees, 19% minority, 41% women. **Class size:** 81% < 20, 18% 20-39, less than 1% 40-49, less than 1% 50-99, less than 1% >100. **Special facilities:** Art studios, galleries, animation studios, concert halls, 6 theaters (including a modular theater, a dance theater, and music pavillion).

Freshman class profile. 1,521 applied, 393 admitted, 133 enrolled.

End year in good standing:	85%	Live on campus:	90%
Return as sophomores:	85%	International:	12%
Out-of-state:	58%		

Basis for selection. Admission is talent based, evaluated by faculty via group review. Portfolio required for art/design, film/video, music composition majors, and theater design and production. Auditions required for acting, dance, music majors. Music applicants may submit audio tape recordings in lieu of live audition for some programs. Interview required for directing/performance/production studies majors. **Home schooled:** Transcript of courses and grades, state high school equivalency certificate, letter of recommendation (nonparent) required.

High school preparation. College-preparatory program recommended. Recommended units include English 4, mathematics 3, social studies 3, science 3, foreign language 2, computer science 1, visual/performing arts 3 and academic electives 2.

2011-2012 Annual costs. Tuition/fees: $38,260. Room/board: $9,626. Books/supplies: $1,545. Personal expenses: $1,700.

2011-2012 Financial aid. Need-based: 106 full-time freshmen applied for aid; 92 were judged to have need; 91 of these received aid. Average need met was 74%. Average scholarship/grant was $14,987; average loan $7,623. 56% of total undergraduate aid awarded as scholarships/grants, 44% as loans/jobs. **Non-need-based:** Awarded to 57 full-time undergraduates, including 11 freshmen. Scholarships awarded for academics, art, minority status, music/drama.

Application procedures. Admission: Priority date 12/1; deadline 1/5 (receipt date). $70 fee, may be waived for applicants with need. Application must be submitted online. Admission notification on a rolling basis beginning on or about 4/1. Must reply by May 1 or within 3 week(s) if notified thereafter. Some programs remain open after January 5. **Financial aid:** Priority date 3/2; no closing date. FAFSA required. Applicants notified on a rolling basis starting 4/1; must reply by 5/1 or within 3 week(s) of notification.

Academics. Special study options: Independent study, internships, student-designed major, study abroad. **Credit/placement by examination:** AP, CLEP, IB, institutional tests. 6 credit hours maximum toward bachelor's degree. **Support services:** Learning center, tutoring.

Majors. Visual/performing arts: Cinematography, dance, design, music performance, music theory/composition, photography, studio arts, theater design.

Computing on campus. 40 workstations in library. Dormitories wired for high-speed internet access. Helpline, wireless network available.

Student life. Freshman orientation: Mandatory. Preregistration for classes offered. Held the week before classes begin each semester. **Housing:** Coed dorms, special housing for disabled, apartments available. $350 fully refundable deposit, deadline 5/1. **Activities:** Jazz band, dance, drama, film society, literary magazine, music ensembles, opera, radio station, student government, student newspaper, TV station, black student union, Latino student union, GLBT student union, Asian club, political issues club.

Student services. Career counseling, student employment services, financial aid counseling, health services, personal counseling, placement for graduates, veterans' counselor. **Physically disabled:** Services for visually, speech, hearing impaired.

Contact. E-mail: admissions@calarts.edu
Phone: (661) 255-1050 ext. 2185 Toll-free number: (800) 545-2787
Fax: (661) 253-7710
Molly Ryan, Director of Admissions, California Institute of the Arts,
24700 McBean Parkway, Valencia, CA 91355

California Lutheran University
Thousand Oaks, California   **CB member**
www.callutheran.edu   **CB code: 4088**

- Private 4-year university and liberal arts college affiliated with Evangelical Lutheran Church in America
- Residential campus in small city
- 2,713 degree-seeking undergraduates
- 44% of applicants admitted
- SAT or ACT (ACT writing optional), application essay required

General. Founded in 1959. Regionally accredited. **Degrees:** 613 bachelor's awarded; master's, professional offered. **ROTC:** Army, Air Force. **Location:** 45 miles from Los Angeles. **Calendar:** Semester, limited summer session. **Full-time faculty:** 163 total; 76% have terminal degrees, 15% minority. **Part-time faculty:** 210 total; 41% have terminal degrees, 9% minority. **Class size:** 58% < 20, 38% 20-39, 2% 40-49, 2% 50-99. **Special facilities:** Sports and fitness center with dance studio, Olympic-size pool, television studio with editing room.

Freshman class profile. 7,245 applied, 3,188 admitted, 510 enrolled.

Mid 50% test scores			
SAT critical reading:	500-600	GPA 3.0-3.49:	30%
SAT math:	510-610	GPA 2.0-2.99:	5%
SAT writing:	490-590	Rank in top quarter:	70%
ACT composite:	22-27	Rank in top tenth:	33%
GPA 3.75 or higher:	41%	Out-of-state:	16%
GPA 3.50-3.74:	24%	Live on campus:	81%

Basis for selection. High school achievement record, rank in class, test scores, essay, letters of recommendation very important. Interview recommended. **Home schooled:** Transcript of courses and grades, letter of recommendation (nonparent) required. Encouraged to submit passing score on GED and complete interview with Admission Counselor. Transcript must include: brief description of courses, textbook (title and author) information for each course, how foreign language verbal component and natural science laboratory requirements were met; official transcripts from other school(s) attended. **Learning Disabled:** Meeting with the Accessibility Resource Coordinator is recommended.

High school preparation. College-preparatory program recommended. Required units include English 4, mathematics 3, social studies 2, science 2 (laboratory 2) and foreign language 2. Math must be through algebra II and preferably 4 years; 2 years of foreign language must be same language; highly recommend 3 years of science.

2011-2012 Annual costs. Tuition/fees: $32,850. Room/board: $11,070. Books/supplies: $1,450. Personal expenses: $2,100.

Financial aid. Non-need-based: Scholarships awarded for academics, alumni affiliation, art, leadership, minority status, music/drama, religious affiliation, state residency.

Application procedures. Admission: Priority date 11/15; deadline 1/15 (postmark date). $25 fee, may be waived for applicants with need. Admission notification by 4/15. Must reply by May 1 or within 2 week(s) if notified thereafter. **Financial aid:** Priority date 3/1; no closing date. FAFSA required. Applicants notified on a rolling basis starting 3/15; must reply within 2 week(s) of notification.

Academics. Special study options: Accelerated study, cooperative education, double major, dual enrollment of high school students, exchange student, honors, independent study, internships, New York semester, semester at sea, student-designed major, study abroad, teacher certification program,

Washington semester. **Credit/placement by examination:** AP, CLEP, IB, SAT, ACT, institutional tests. 30 credit hours maximum toward bachelor's degree. **Support services:** Learning center, reduced course load, study skills assistance, tutoring, writing center.

Majors. Biology: General, biochemistry, molecular. **Business:** General, accounting, business admin, finance, managerial economics, marketing. **Communications:** Advertising, broadcast journalism, communications/speech/rhetoric, journalism, public relations. **Computer sciences:** General, computer graphics, computer science, information systems, programming. **Conservation:** Environmental science. **Education:** General, art, early childhood, elementary, English, foreign languages, mathematics, middle, music, physical, reading, science, secondary, social science, social studies, special ed. **Engineering:** Biomedical. **English:** English lit, rhetoric/composition. **Foreign languages:** General, French, German, Spanish. **Health services:** Athletic training, predental, premedicine, prepharmacy, preveterinary. **History:** General. **Liberal arts:** Arts/sciences. **Math:** General. **Philosophy/religion:** Philosophy, religion. **Physical sciences:** Chemistry, geology, physics. **Protective services:** Police science. **Psychology:** General. **Social sciences:** Criminology, economics, international relations, political science, sociology. **Theology:** Religious ed, theology, youth ministry. **Visual/performing arts:** General, art, commercial/advertising art, dramatic, music.

Most popular majors. Biology 13%, business/marketing 31%, communications/journalism 11%, liberal arts 7%, psychology 8%, social sciences 9%.

Computing on campus. 200 workstations in library, computer center, student center. Dormitories wired for high-speed internet access and linked to campus network. Commuter students can connect to campus network. Online library, helpline, wireless network available.

Student life. Freshman orientation: Mandatory. Preregistration for classes offered. **Policies:** No alcohol on campus except in the chapel for communion, drug free campus. **Housing:** Coed dorms, special housing for disabled, apartments available. $195 fully refundable deposit, deadline 5/1. On campus houses available. **Activities:** Bands, campus ministries, choral groups, dance, drama, international student organizations, literary magazine, music ensembles, Model UN, musical theater, radio station, student government, student newspaper, symphony orchestra, TV station, Lutheran Church Congregation, multicultural and international clubs and organizations, Hillel, Habitat for Humanitiy.

Athletics. NCAA. **Intercollegiate:** Baseball M, basketball, cross-country, diving, football (tackle) M, golf M, soccer, softball W, swimming, tennis, track and field, volleyball W, water polo. **Intramural:** Basketball, football (non-tackle), soccer, softball, volleyball, water polo. **Team name:** Kingsmen/Regals.

Student services. Adult student services, alcohol/substance abuse counseling, chaplain/spiritual director, career counseling, services for economically disadvantaged, student employment services, financial aid counseling, health services, minority student services, personal counseling, placement for graduates, veterans' counselor, women's services. **Physically disabled:** Services for visually, hearing impaired.

Contact. E-mail: admissions@callutheran.edu
Phone: (805) 493-3135 Toll-free number: (877) 258-3678
Fax: (805) 493-3114
Michael Elgarico, Vice President for Enrollment Management, California Lutheran University, 60 West Olsen Road #1350, Thousand Oaks, CA 91360-2787

California Maritime Academy
Vallejo, California
www.csum.edu

CB member
CB code: 4035

- Public 4-year university and maritime college
- Residential campus in small city
- 886 degree-seeking undergraduates

General. Founded in 1929. Regionally accredited. All students participate in at least one 2-month training cruise around Pacific Ocean geared toward their major. **Degrees:** 154 bachelor's awarded. **ROTC:** Naval. **Location:** 30 miles from San Francisco. **Calendar:** Semester, limited summer session. **Full-time faculty:** 60 total. **Part-time faculty:** 18 total. **Special facilities:** 500-foot training ship, computer-aided radar simulators, bridge simulator, steam simulator.

Freshman class profile.

Out-of-state:	17%	Live on campus:	90%

Basis for selection. Applicants must meet California State University Eligibility Index requirements and have strong grades in mathematics and sciences. All accepted students must pass physical examination.

High school preparation. Required and recommended units include English 4, mathematics 3-4, social studies 1, history 1, science 2 (laboratory 2), foreign language 2-3 and academic electives 1. One additional mathematics course recommended for mechanical engineering applicants. Chemistry or physics required. One visual or performing arts elective required.

2011-2012 Annual costs. Tuition/fees: $5,948; $17,108 out-of-state. Room/board: $10,134. Books/supplies: $1,746. Personal expenses: $3,096.

Financial aid. All financial aid based on need. **Additional information:** US Maritime Administration provides annual incentive payment of $3,000 per student, with certain conditions. Tuition waiver for children of deceased or disabled California veterans.

Application procedures. Admission: Closing date 11/30 (postmark date). $55 fee, may be waived for applicants with need. Admission notification on a rolling basis beginning on or about 2/1. Must reply by May 1 or within 2 week(s) if notified thereafter. **Financial aid:** Closing date 3/2. FAFSA required. Applicants notified on a rolling basis starting 4/1.

Academics. Center for Excellence and Learning provides free tutoring/workshops hosted by professors. **Special study options:** Cooperative education, distance learning, double major, ESL, internships. International training cruise onboard ship "Golden Bear". **Credit/placement by examination:** AP, CLEP. 24 credit hours maximum toward bachelor's degree. **Support services:** Learning center, remedial instruction, tutoring.

Majors. Business: Business admin, logistics. **Engineering:** Marine, mechanical. **Social sciences:** Political science.

Computing on campus. 85 workstations in dormitories, library, computer center, student center. Dormitories wired for high-speed internet access and linked to campus network. Helpline, repair service available.

Student life. Freshman orientation: Mandatory, $350 fee. Preregistration for classes offered. Held last week of August. **Policies:** Students required to live on campus except those married or with children. **Housing:** Guaranteed on-campus for all undergraduates. Coed dorms available. $500 deposit, deadline 7/1. **Activities:** Student government, student newspaper.

Athletics. NAIA. **Intercollegiate:** Basketball, rowing (crew), rugby M, sailing, soccer, water polo. **Intramural:** Badminton, baseball M, basketball, boxing M, golf, racquetball, rowing (crew), rugby M, sailing, softball, tennis, volleyball, water polo. **Team name:** Keelhaulers.

Student services. Career counseling, student employment services, financial aid counseling, health services, minority student services, personal counseling, placement for graduates, veterans' counselor.

Contact. E-mail: admission@csum.edu
Phone: (707) 654-1330 Fax: (707) 654-1336
Marc McGee, Director of Admission, California Maritime Academy, 200 Maritime Academy Drive, Vallejo, CA 94590

California Miramar University
San Diego, California
www.calmu.edu

CB code: 6458

- Private 3-year university
- Very large city
- 125 degree-seeking undergraduates

General. Regionally accredited; also accredited by ACICS, DETC. **Degrees:** 57 bachelor's awarded; master's offered. **Calendar:** Semester. **Full-time faculty:** 6 total. **Part-time faculty:** 30 total.

Basis for selection. Open admission.

Academics. Credit/placement by examination: AP, CLEP.

Majors. BACHELOR'S. Business: Business admin. **Human services:** General. **ASSOCIATE. Business:** Business admin.

Contact. E-mail: admissions@calmu.edu
Phone: (858) 653-3000
Jean Van Slyke, Director of Admissions, California Miramar University, 9750 Miramar Road, Suite 180, San Diego, CA 92126

California National University for Advanced Studies
Northridge, California
www.cnuas.edu **CB code: 3894**

- For-profit 4-year virtual university
- Small city
- 89 degree-seeking undergraduates

General. Accredited by DETC. 100% distance learning university. **Degrees:** 29 bachelor's awarded; master's offered. **Calendar:** Differs by program. **Part-time faculty:** 53 total.

Basis for selection. Application/portfolio important.

2011-2012 Annual costs. Tuition/fees: $7,200. Books and supplies cost varies by program.

Application procedures. Admission: No deadline. $75 fee. **Financial aid:** No deadline.

Academics. Special study options: Distance learning. **Credit/placement by examination:** AP, CLEP.

Majors. Business: Business admin. **Computer sciences:** Computer science. **Engineering:** General.

Contact. E-mail: cnuadms@mail.cnuas.edu
Phone: (818) 830-2411 Toll-free number: (800) 782-2422
Fax: (818) 830-2418
Cynthia Speed, Director of Admissions, California National University for Advanced Studies, 8550 Balboa Boulevard, Suite 210, Northridge, CA 91325

California Polytechnic State University: San Luis Obispo
San Luis Obispo, California
CB member
www.calpoly.edu **CB code: 4038**

- Public 4-year university
- Residential campus in large town
- 17,652 degree-seeking undergraduates: 4% part-time, 45% women, 1% African American, 11% Asian American, 13% Hispanic American, 1% international
- 919 degree-seeking graduate students
- 37% of applicants admitted
- SAT or ACT (ACT writing optional) required
- 76% graduate within 6 years

General. Founded in 1901. Regionally accredited. **Degrees:** 4,081 bachelor's awarded; master's offered. **ROTC:** Army. **Location:** 200 miles from Los Angeles, 230 miles from San Francisco. **Calendar:** Quarter. **Full-time faculty:** 800 total; 80% have terminal degrees, 33% women. **Part-time faculty:** 444 total; 31% have terminal degrees, 44% women. **Class size:** 15% < 20, 57% 20-39, 14% 40-49, 10% 50-99, 4% >100. **Special facilities:** Printing press museum, university farm, dairy products technical center, architectural design institute.

Freshman class profile. 33,001 applied, 12,341 admitted, 4,316 enrolled.

Mid 50% test scores		GPA 2.0-2.99:	1%
SAT critical reading:	540-640	Rank in top quarter:	83%
SAT math:	580-690	Rank in top tenth:	46%
ACT composite:	25-29	Return as sophomores:	93%
GPA 3.75 or higher:	63%	Out-of-state:	10%
GPA 3.50-3.74:	21%	Live on campus:	97%
GPA 3.0-3.49:	15%	International:	1%

Basis for selection. Course work, high school GPA, test scores most important. Extracurricular activities considered. Portfolio required for art and design majors; audition required for music majors.

High school preparation. College-preparatory program required. 15 units required; 22 recommended. Required and recommended units include English 4-5, mathematics 3-5, social studies 1, history 1, science 2-4 (laboratory 2), foreign language 2-4, visual/performing arts 1-2 and academic electives 1. History must be U.S. history/government.

2011-2012 Annual costs. Tuition/fees: $7,921; $19,081 out-of-state. Room/board: $10,444. Books/supplies: $1,698. Personal expenses: $2,286.

2010-2011 Financial aid. Need-based: 2,651 full-time freshmen applied for aid; 1,487 were judged to have need; 1,309 of these received aid. Average need met was 60%. Average scholarship/grant was $2,453; average loan $3,207. 58% of total undergraduate aid awarded as scholarships/grants, 42% as loans/jobs. **Non-need-based:** Awarded to 1,102 full-time undergraduates, including 421 freshmen. Scholarships awarded for academics, alumni affiliation, art, athletics, job skills, leadership, music/drama, ROTC, state residency. **Additional information:** College-administered financial aid is not available for undergraduate international students.

Application procedures. Admission: Closing date 11/30 (postmark date). $55 fee, may be waived for applicants with need. Application must be submitted online. Admission notification by 4/1. Must reply by 5/1. Housing deposit due on first-come, first-served basis. **Financial aid:** Priority date 3/2; no closing date. FAFSA required. Applicants notified on a rolling basis starting 4/1.

Academics. Special study options: Cooperative education, distance learning, double major, ESL, exchange student, honors, internships, liberal arts/career combination, semester at sea, study abroad, teacher certification program. **Credit/placement by examination:** AP, CLEP, IB, SAT, ACT, institutional tests. 45 credit hours maximum toward bachelor's degree. **Support services:** Learning center, pre-admission summer program, reduced course load, remedial instruction, study skills assistance, tutoring, writing center.

Majors. Architecture: Architecture, landscape, urban/community planning. **Biology:** General, bacteriology, biochemistry. **Business:** Business admin. **Communications:** Journalism. **Communications technology:** Graphics. **Computer sciences:** Computer science, systems analysis. **Conservation:** Forestry. **Education:** Agricultural, kindergarten/preschool. **Engineering:** Aerospace, agricultural, architectural, biomedical, civil, computer, electrical, engineering science, environmental, industrial, manufacturing, materials, mechanical. **English:** English lit, rhetoric/composition. **Foreign languages:** General. **General:** Agronomy, animal sciences, business, dairy, food science, mechanization, soil science. **Health services:** Dietetics. **History:** General. **Liberal arts:** Arts/sciences. **Math:** General, statistics. **Parks/recreation:** General, health/fitness. **Philosophy/religion:** Philosophy. **Physical sciences:** Chemistry, geology, physics. **Psychology:** General. **Social sciences:** Economics, political science, sociology. **Visual/performing arts:** Dramatic, music, studio arts.

Most popular majors. Agriculture 14%, architecture 7%, business/marketing 13%, engineering/engineering technologies 25%.

Computing on campus. Dormitories wired for high-speed internet access and linked to campus network. Commuter students can connect to campus network. Online course registration, online library, helpline, student web hosting, wireless network available.

Student life. Freshman orientation: Available. Preregistration for classes offered. Held week prior to start of fall term. **Housing:** Coed dorms, special housing for disabled, apartments available. $1,125 fully refundable deposit. **Activities:** Bands, campus ministries, choral groups, dance, drama, international student organizations, literary magazine, music ensembles, Model UN, musical theater, opera, radio station, student government, student newspaper, symphony orchestra, TV station, MECHA, Society of Black Engineers and Scientists, Minority Engineering Program, Campus Crusade for Christ, Intervarsity Christian Fellowship, Engineering World Health.

Athletics. NCAA. **Intercollegiate:** Baseball M, basketball, cross-country, football (tackle) M, golf, soccer, softball W, swimming, tennis, track and field, volleyball W, wrestling M. **Intramural:** Basketball, football (tackle), racquetball, soccer, softball, tennis, volleyball. **Team name:** Mustangs.

Student services. Adult student services, alcohol/substance abuse counseling, career counseling, student employment services, financial aid counseling, health services, minority student services, on-campus daycare, personal counseling, placement for graduates, women's services. **Physically disabled:** Services for visually, speech, hearing impaired.

Contact. E-mail: admissions@calpoly.edu
Phone: (805) 756-2311 Fax: (805) 756-5400
James Maraviglia, Associate Vice Provost for Marketing & Enrollment Development, California Polytechnic State University: San Luis Obispo, Admissions Office, Cal Poly, San Luis Obispo, CA 93407-0031

California State Polytechnic University: Pomona
Pomona, California
CB member
www.csupomona.edu **CB code: 4082**

- Public 4-year university
- Commuter campus in small city

- 19,306 degree-seeking undergraduates: 13% part-time, 43% women, 3% African American, 26% Asian American, 34% Hispanic American, 4% international
- 1,699 degree-seeking graduate students
- 55% of applicants admitted
- SAT or ACT (ACT writing optional) required
- 51% graduate within 6 years

General. Founded in 1938. Regionally accredited. **Degrees:** 4,020 bachelor's awarded; master's offered. **ROTC:** Army. **Location:** 30 miles from downtown Los Angeles. **Calendar:** Quarter, extensive summer session. **Full-time faculty:** 515 total; 80% have terminal degrees, 36% minority, 41% women. **Part-time faculty:** 508 total; 31% have terminal degrees, 30% minority, 34% women. **Class size:** 14% < 20, 59% 20-39, 16% 40-49, 10% 50-99, 2% >100. **Special facilities:** Electron microscope center, international center, small ruminant center, Arabian horse center, equine research center, land laboratory, ecological reserve, center for regenerative studies, center for community affairs.

Freshman class profile. 23,946 applied, 13,191 admitted, 3,249 enrolled.

Mid 50% test scores			
SAT critical reading:	450-560	GPA 3.0-3.49:	44%
SAT math:	480-620	GPA 2.0-2.99:	22%
ACT composite:	19-25	Return as sophomores:	90%
GPA 3.75 or higher:	15%	Out-of-state:	1%
GPA 3.50-3.74:	19%	Live on campus:	45%
		International:	2%

Basis for selection. High school GPA, courses, and test scores important.

High school preparation. College-preparatory program required. 15 units required. Required and recommended units include English 4, mathematics 3-4, social studies 1, history 1, science 2 (laboratory 2), foreign language 2, visual/performing arts 1 and academic electives 1.

2011-2012 Annual costs. Tuition/fees: $6,099; $17,259 out-of-state. Room/board: $11,375. Books/supplies: $1,500. Personal expenses: $1,755.

2011-2012 Financial aid. Need-based: 2,659 full-time freshmen applied for aid; 2,114 were judged to have need; 1,942 of these received aid. Average need met was 64%. Average scholarship/grant was $8,902; average loan $3,454. 71% of total undergraduate aid awarded as scholarships/grants, 29% as loans/jobs. **Non-need-based:** Awarded to 728 full-time undergraduates, including 207 freshmen. Scholarships awarded for academics, alumni affiliation, athletics, leadership, state residency.

Application procedures. Admission: Priority date 11/30; deadline 5/1 (postmark date). $55 fee, may be waived for applicants with need. Admission notification on a rolling basis beginning on or about 10/2. Must reply by May 1 or within 3 week(s) if notified thereafter. Applications for first time freshmen accepted October 1 through November 30. **Financial aid:** Priority date 3/2; no closing date. FAFSA required. Applicants notified on a rolling basis starting 4/1; must reply within 2 week(s) of notification.

Academics. Special study options: Cooperative education, cross-registration, distance learning, double major, dual enrollment of high school students, ESL, exchange student, external degree, honors, internships, study abroad, teacher certification program. Ocean studies institute, desert studies consortium. **Credit/placement by examination:** AP, CLEP, SAT, ACT, institutional tests. 36 credit hours maximum toward bachelor's degree. **Support services:** Learning center, pre-admission summer program, remedial instruction, study skills assistance, tutoring, writing center.

Honors college/program. Incoming freshmen invited to apply to Honors College if they have scores of 550 or higher on both Math and Critical Reading SAT tests and GPA of 3.5 or higher. Incoming transfer students must have GPA of at least 3.5 at previous institution.

Majors. Architecture: Architecture, landscape, urban/community planning. **Biology:** General, biotechnology, environmental. **Business:** Business admin, hospitality admin. **Communications:** Communications/speech/rhetoric. **Computer sciences:** Computer science. **Education:** Agricultural. **Engineering:** General, aerospace, chemical, civil, computer, electrical, industrial, manufacturing, mechanical. **English:** English lit. **Foreign languages:** Spanish. **General:** Animal sciences, business, food science, plant protection. **Health services:** Dietetics. **History:** General. **Liberal arts:** Arts/sciences. **Math:** General. **Parks/recreation:** Health/fitness. **Philosophy/religion:** Philosophy. **Physical sciences:** Chemistry, geology, physics. **Psychology:** General. **Social sciences:** General, anthropology, economics, geography, political science, sociology. **Visual/performing arts:** Art, dramatic, graphic design, music. **Work/family studies:** Clothing/textiles.

Most popular majors. Business/marketing 34%, engineering/engineering technologies 18%, social sciences 6%.

Computing on campus. 280 workstations in library, computer center. Dormitories wired for high-speed internet access and linked to campus network. Commuter students can connect to campus network. Online course registration, helpline, student web hosting, wireless network available.

Student life. Freshman orientation: Mandatory, $40 fee. Preregistration for classes offered. Held between June to September (Freshman 3 days, 2 nights). **Housing:** Coed dorms, apartments available. $50 fully refundable deposit. **Activities:** Bands, campus ministries, choral groups, dance, drama, international student organizations, literary magazine, music ensembles, Model UN, musical theater, opera, student government, student newspaper, symphony orchestra, Campus Crusade for Christ, black student union, Hawaiian club, MECHA, Studies of the World, Newman Club, Hillel, Bahai club, Coptic-Orthodox Christian club.

Athletics. NCAA. **Intercollegiate:** Baseball M, basketball, cross-country, soccer, tennis, track and field, volleyball W. **Intramural:** Badminton, basketball, football (non-tackle) M, golf, racquetball, softball, swimming, table tennis, tennis, track and field, volleyball. **Team name:** Broncos.

Student services. Adult student services, career counseling, student employment services, health services, on-campus daycare, personal counseling, placement for graduates, veterans' counselor. **Physically disabled:** Services for visually, speech, hearing impaired.

Contact. E-mail: admissions@csupomona.edu
Phone: (909) 869-5299 Fax: (909) 869-4848
Deborah Brandon, Executive Director, Admissions and Outreach, California State Polytechnic University: Pomona, 3801 West Temple Avenue, Pomona, CA 91768-4019

California State University: Bakersfield
Bakersfield, California CB member
www.csub.edu CB code: 4110

- Public 4-year university and liberal arts college
- Commuter campus in small city
- 6,376 degree-seeking undergraduates: 11% part-time, 62% women, 7% African American, 7% Asian American, 45% Hispanic American, 1% Native American, 2% international
- 762 degree-seeking graduate students
- 68% of applicants admitted
- 41% graduate within 6 years

General. Founded in 1965. Regionally accredited. **Degrees:** 1,289 bachelor's awarded; master's offered. **Location:** 112 miles from Los Angeles. **Calendar:** Quarter, limited summer session. **Full-time faculty:** 284 total; 14% have terminal degrees, 26% minority, 50% women. **Part-time faculty:** 157 total; 26% minority, 60% women. **Special facilities:** 40-acre facility for wild animal care, archaeological information center, center for business and economic research, center for economic education, well-sample repository, center for physiological research.

Freshman class profile. 5,055 applied, 3,416 admitted, 1,060 enrolled.

Mid 50% test scores			
SAT critical reading:	390-500	GPA 3.50-3.74:	11%
SAT math:	400-520	GPA 3.0-3.49:	42%
ACT composite:	16-21	GPA 2.0-2.99:	40%
GPA 3.75 or higher:	7%	International:	1%

Basis for selection. GED not accepted. GPA, test scores, and certain honors courses must place applicant in upper third of California high school graduates (upper sixth for out-of-state applicants) using eligibility index table. Minimum test scores slightly higher for out-of-state students.

High school preparation. College-preparatory program required. 15 units required. Required units include English 4, mathematics 3, social studies 1, history 1, science 2 (laboratory 2), foreign language 2, visual/performing arts 1 and academic electives 1. Foreign language must be in same language; math must include algebra, geometry, and intermediate algebra; science must include biology and a physical science.

2011-2012 Annual costs. Tuition/fees: $6,682; $17,842 out-of-state. Room/board: $7,872. Books/supplies: $1,752. Personal expenses: $3,027.

2010-2011 Financial aid. All financial aid based on need. 2,587 full-time freshmen applied for aid; 2,413 were judged to have need; 2,336 of these received aid. Average need met was 9%. Average scholarship/grant was $3,511; average loan $1,405. 65% of total undergraduate aid awarded as scholarships/grants, 35% as loans/jobs.

Application procedures. Admission: Priority date 10/1; deadline 3/1. $55 fee, may be waived for applicants with need. Admission notification on a rolling basis beginning on or about 10/1. **Financial aid:** Priority date 3/2; no closing date. FAFSA required. Applicants notified on a rolling basis starting 4/15; must reply within 3 week(s) of notification.

Academics. Most courses are 5 quarter units. Students enrolled in 3 courses are carrying full unit load. **Special study options:** Accelerated study, cooperative education, cross-registration, distance learning, double major, dual enrollment of high school students, ESL, exchange student, external degree, honors, independent study, internships, liberal arts/career combination, student-designed major, study abroad, teacher certification program. 2+2 at specified locations for liberal studies (teaching) majors. **Credit/placement by examination:** AP, CLEP, SAT, ACT, institutional tests. Unlimited number of hours of credit by examination may be counted toward degree. **Support services:** Learning center, pre-admission summer program, reduced course load, remedial instruction, study skills assistance, tutoring.

Majors. Biology: General. **Business:** Business admin. **Communications:** Communications/speech/rhetoric. **Computer sciences:** Computer science. **Conservation:** Land use planning. **Education:** Early childhood. **English:** American lit, English lit. **Foreign languages:** Spanish. **Health services:** Nursing (RN). **History:** General. **Human services:** General. **Liberal arts:** Arts/sciences. **Math:** General. **Philosophy/religion:** Philosophy, religion. **Physical sciences:** Chemistry, geology, physics. **Protective services:** Criminal justice. **Psychology:** General. **Social sciences:** Anthropology, criminology, economics, political science, sociology. **Visual/performing arts:** General, art, dramatic, music.

Most popular majors. Business/marketing 18%, education 8%, liberal arts 15%, psychology 10%, security/protective services 8%, social sciences 9%.

Computing on campus. 600 workstations in library, computer center, student center. Dormitories linked to campus network. Commuter students can connect to campus network. Online course registration, online library, helpline, student web hosting available.

Student life. Freshman orientation: Available, $35 fee. Preregistration for classes offered. **Housing:** Guaranteed on-campus for all undergraduates. Coed dorms, special housing for disabled available. Nursing floor available. **Activities:** Bands, choral groups, drama, international student organizations, literary magazine, music ensembles, musical theater, opera, student government, student newspaper, Black student union, Movimiento Estudiantil Chicano de Aztlan, Christian union, student nursing association, Circle-K, Latinos United for Education.

Athletics. NCAA. **Intercollegiate:** Basketball, cheerleading, cross-country W, golf M, soccer, softball W, swimming, tennis W, track and field, volleyball W, water polo W, wrestling M. **Intramural:** Badminton, basketball, golf, handball, racquetball, soccer, softball, tennis, volleyball. **Team name:** Roadrunners.

Student services. Adult student services, alcohol/substance abuse counseling, career counseling, services for economically disadvantaged, student employment services, financial aid counseling, health services, minority student services, on-campus daycare, personal counseling, placement for graduates, veterans' counselor. **Physically disabled:** Services for visually, speech, hearing impaired.

Contact. E-mail: admissions@csub.edu
Phone: (661) 654-3036 Toll-free number: (800) 788-2782
Fax: (661) 654-3389
Jacqueline Mimms, Director of Admissions, California State University: Bakersfield, 9001 Stockdale Highway, Bakersfield, CA 93311-1099

California State University: Channel Islands
Camarillo, California   **CB member**
www.csuci.edu   **CB code: 4128**

- Public 4-year university
- Commuter campus in small city
- 3,976 degree-seeking undergraduates: 17% part-time, 65% women, 2% African American, 7% Asian American, 31% Hispanic American, 1% Native American
- 183 degree-seeking graduate students
- 71% of applicants admitted
- 53% graduate within 6 years

General. Regionally accredited. **Degrees:** 872 bachelor's awarded; master's offered. **Calendar:** Semester. **Full-time faculty:** 130 total; 87% have terminal degrees, 27% minority, 45% women. **Part-time faculty:** 146 total; 44% have terminal degrees, 18% minority, 52% women. **Class size:** 30% < 20, 61% 20-39, 5% 40-49, 4% 50-99, less than 1% >100.

Freshman class profile. 8,208 applied, 5,790 admitted, 613 enrolled.

Mid 50% test scores			
SAT critical reading:	430-540	GPA 3.50-3.74:	15%
SAT math:	420-530	GPA 3.0-3.49:	44%
SAT writing:	440-540	GPA 2.0-2.99:	32%
ACT composite:	18-23	End year in good standing:	85%
GPA 3.75 or higher:	9%	Return as sophomores:	81%
		Live on campus:	63%

Basis for selection. Academic GPA very important. Rigor of secondary school record and state residency important. Test scores required for students with less than 3.0 HS GPA.

High school preparation. College-preparatory program required. 15 units required. Required units include English 4, mathematics 3, social studies 1, history 1, science 2 (laboratory 2), foreign language 2, visual/performing arts 1 and academic electives 1.

2011-2012 Annual costs. Tuition/fees: $6,316; $17,476 out-of-state. Room/board: $11,844.

2010-2011 Financial aid. Non-need-based: Scholarships awarded for academics, leadership, state residency.

Application procedures. Admission: Priority date 11/30; deadline 1/15 (receipt date). $55 fee, may be waived for applicants with need. Admission notification on a rolling basis beginning on or about 1/2. Must reply by 5/1. **Financial aid:** Priority date 3/2; no closing date. FAFSA required. Applicants notified by 4/7.

Academics. Special study options: Double major, independent study, study abroad, teacher certification program. **Credit/placement by examination:** AP, CLEP, SAT, ACT, institutional tests. **Support services:** Pre-admission summer program, remedial instruction, tutoring, writing center.

Majors. Area/ethnic studies: Chicano/Hispanic-American/Latino. **Biology:** General, biotechnology. **Business:** General. **Communications:** Communications/speech/rhetoric. **Computer sciences:** General. **Conservation:** Environmental science, management/policy. **Education:** Early childhood. **English:** English lit. **Foreign languages:** Spanish. **History:** General. **Liberal arts:** Arts/sciences. **Math:** General. **Physical sciences:** Chemistry. **Psychology:** General. **Social sciences:** Economics, political science, sociology. **Visual/performing arts:** General, art.

Most popular majors. Biology 6%, business/marketing 19%, communications/journalism 9%, liberal arts 11%, psychology 16%, visual/performing arts 7%.

Computing on campus. Dormitories wired for high-speed internet access. Commuter students can connect to campus network. Online course registration, online library, helpline, wireless network available.

Student life. Freshman orientation: Mandatory, $120 fee. Preregistration for classes offered. Two-day session in July. **Housing:** Coed dorms, wellness housing available. $1,000 fully refundable deposit, deadline 6/1. **Activities:** Choral groups, student government, student newspaper.

Student services. Alcohol/substance abuse counseling, career counseling, services for economically disadvantaged, student employment services, financial aid counseling, health services, personal counseling, women's services. **Physically disabled:** Services for visually, speech, hearing impaired.

Contact. E-mail: admissionsandrecords@csuci.edu
Phone: (805) 437-8400
Jane Sweetland, Dean of Enrollment, California State University: Channel Islands, One University Drive, Camarillo, CA 93012

California State University: Chico
Chico, California   **CB member**
www.csuchico.edu   **CB code: 4048**

- Public 4-year university and liberal arts college
- Residential campus in small city
- 14,766 degree-seeking undergraduates: 8% part-time, 51% women, 2% African American, 5% Asian American, 18% Hispanic American, 1% Native American, 3% international
- 854 degree-seeking graduate students
- 78% of applicants admitted
- SAT or ACT (ACT writing optional) required
- 62% graduate within 6 years

General. Founded in 1887. Regionally accredited. 119-acre campus. **Degrees:** 3,603 bachelor's awarded; master's offered. **Location:** 90 miles

from Sacramento, 175 miles from San Francisco. **Calendar:** Semester, limited summer session. **Full-time faculty:** 465 total; 85% have terminal degrees, 17% minority, 43% women. **Part-time faculty:** 407 total; 28% have terminal degrees, 10% minority, 52% women. **Special facilities:** 1,000-acre farm, planetarium, instructional media center, biology field station, anthropology museum, intercultural studies center, computer graphics lab, assistive technology center, media prep lab, recording arts studio, hydrotherapy pool, echocardiography system, gas displacement chamber, two ecological preserves with nearly 4,100 acres, forensics lab, archaeology lab and research center, gateway science museum.

Freshman class profile. 14,509 applied, 11,285 admitted, 2,429 enrolled.

Mid 50% test scores			
SAT critical reading:	450-560	Rank in top quarter:	76%
SAT math:	460-570	Rank in top tenth:	35%
ACT composite:	19-24	End year in good standing:	81%
GPA 3.75 or higher:	11%	Return as sophomores:	87%
GPA 3.50-3.74:	15%	Out-of-state:	1%
GPA 3.0-3.49:	46%	Live on campus:	62%
GPA 2.0-2.99:	28%	International:	2%

Basis for selection. Eligibility index derived from high school GPA and test scores. First-time freshmen applicants rank order based on characteristics of applicant pool. GPA determined from 10th, and 11th grade college prep courses only, excluding physical education. Nursing program open only to state residents. All freshmen applicants must submit SAT or ACT test scores regardless of high school GPA. SAT or ACT must be taken by the December test date for admission consideration. Portfolio required for fine arts majors. **Home schooled:** Transcript of courses and grades required. Must be able to verify completion of required college preparatory subject requirements and meet institutional eligibility index. **Learning Disabled:** Students must meet established admission criteria.

High school preparation. College-preparatory program required. 15 units required. Required units include English 4, mathematics 3, social studies 2, science 2 (laboratory 2), foreign language 2, visual/performing arts 1 and academic electives 1.

2011-2012 Annual costs. Tuition/fees: $6,882; $18,042 out-of-state. Reduced out-of-state tuition for residents of AK, AZ, CO, HI, ID, MT, NV, NM, ND, OR, SD, UT, WA, WY may be available under the Western Undergraduate Exchange (WUE) program. Room/board: $11,118. Books/supplies: $1,746. Personal expenses: $3,326.

2010-2011 Financial aid. Need-based: 1,514 full-time freshmen applied for aid; 1,164 were judged to have need; 1,094 of these received aid. Average need met was 86%. Average scholarship/grant was $9,626; average loan $3,862. 61% of total undergraduate aid awarded as scholarships/grants, 39% as loans/jobs. **Non-need-based:** Awarded to 1,683 full-time undergraduates, including 430 freshmen. Scholarships awarded for academics, art, athletics, leadership, minority status, music/drama, religious affiliation.

Application procedures. Admission: Priority date 10/1; deadline 11/30 (postmark date). $55 fee, may be waived for applicants with need. Admission notification on a rolling basis beginning on or about 2/1. Must reply by May 1 or within 2 week(s) if notified thereafter. Applications for the following majors must be made during priority periods of October and August: nursing, media arts, graphic design, recording arts, and interior design. All first time freshmen fall applicants should apply between October 1 and November 30. **Financial aid:** Priority date 3/2; no closing date. FAFSA required. Applicants notified on a rolling basis starting 3/2.

Academics. Special study options: Cooperative education, cross-registration, distance learning, double major, dual enrollment of high school students, ESL, exchange student, external degree, honors, independent study, internships, student-designed major, study abroad, teacher certification program. **Credit/placement by examination:** AP, CLEP, IB, SAT, ACT, institutional tests. 30 credit hours maximum toward bachelor's degree. 6 semester hours awarded for each International Baccalaureate higher level exam passed with score of 4 to 7. **Support services:** Learning center, pre-admission summer program, reduced course load, remedial instruction, study skills assistance, tutoring, writing center.

Majors. Architecture: Urban/community planning. **Area/ethnic studies:** American, Asian, Latin American, women's. **Biology:** General, biochemistry, botany, ecology, microbiology. **Business:** Accounting, business admin, finance, human resources, management information systems, marketing. **Communications:** Journalism, organizational, public relations, radio/TV. **Computer sciences:** Computer graphics, computer science, information technology. **Conservation:** Environmental science, management/policy. **Education:** Agricultural, art, biology, chemistry, early childhood, educational technology, English, ESL, French, German, health, mathematics, music, physical, science, social science, Spanish. **Engineering:** Civil, computer, mechanical. **English:** English lit, rhetoric/composition. **Foreign languages:** French, German, linguistics, Spanish. **General:** Agronomy, animal sciences, business,

range science. **Health services:** Clinical lab science, communication disorders, dietetics, nursing (RN), predental, premedicine, prepharmacy, preveterinary, recreational therapy. **History:** General. **Human services:** General, social work. **Liberal arts:** Arts/sciences, humanities. **Math:** General, applied, statistics. **Parks/recreation:** General, exercise sciences, facilities management, health/fitness. **Philosophy/religion:** Judaic, philosophy, religion. **Physical sciences:** General, atmospheric science, chemistry, geology, hydrology, physics. **Protective services:** Criminal justice. **Psychology:** General. **Social sciences:** General, anthropology, economics, geography, international economics, international relations, political science, sociology. **Visual/performing arts:** Art, art history/conservation, design, dramatic, graphic design, interior design, music, music theory/composition, musical theater, piano/keyboard, studio arts.

Most popular majors. Business/marketing 17%, engineering/engineering technologies 8%, health sciences 8%, liberal arts 6%, parks/recreation 8%, psychology 6%, social sciences 9%, visual/performing arts 8%.

Computing on campus. 1,212 workstations in dormitories, library, student center. Dormitories wired for high-speed internet access and linked to campus network. Commuter students can connect to campus network. Online course registration, online library, helpline, repair service, student web hosting, wireless network available.

Student life. Freshman orientation: Available, $50 fee. Preregistration for classes offered. June and July sessions for students and parents. One-day session $50, two days $90. Free mini-orientation session in August, or online orientation also offered. **Housing:** Coed dorms, special housing for disabled, apartments, fraternity/sorority housing available. $1,000 fully refundable deposit, deadline 4/13. **Activities:** Bands, choral groups, dance, drama, film society, literary magazine, music ensembles, musical theater, opera, radio station, student government, student newspaper, symphony orchestra, over 200 organizations available.

Athletics. NCAA. **Intercollegiate:** Baseball M, basketball, cross-country, golf, soccer, softball W, track and field, volleyball W. **Intramural:** Badminton, basketball, bowling, football (non-tackle), soccer, softball, volleyball, water polo. **Team name:** Wildcats.

Student services. Adult student services, alcohol/substance abuse counseling, career counseling, services for economically disadvantaged, student employment services, financial aid counseling, health services, legal services, minority student services, on-campus daycare, personal counseling, placement for graduates, veterans' counselor, women's services. **Physically disabled:** Services for visually, speech, hearing impaired.

Contact. E-mail: info@csuchico.edu
Phone: (530) 898-4428 Toll-free number: (800) 542-4426
Fax: (530) 898-6456
Allan Bee, Director of Admissions, California State University: Chico, 400 West First Street, Chico, CA 95929-0722

California State University: Dominguez Hills
Carson, California — CB member
www.csudh.edu — CB code: 4098

- Public 4-year university
- Commuter campus in small city
- 11,052 degree-seeking undergraduates: 29% part-time, 64% women, 21% African American, 9% Asian American, 48% Hispanic American, 2% international
- 2,260 degree-seeking graduate students
- 84% of applicants admitted
- 31% graduate within 6 years

General. Founded in 1960. Regionally accredited. **Degrees:** 2,057 bachelor's awarded; master's offered. **ROTC:** Army, Air Force. **Location:** 13 miles from Los Angeles. **Calendar:** Semester, extensive summer session. **Full-time faculty:** 247 total; 89% have terminal degrees, 40% minority, 51% women. **Part-time faculty:** 496 total; 36% have terminal degrees, 44% minority, 54% women. **Class size:** 17% < 20, 54% 20-39, 16% 40-49, 12% 50-99, 1% >100. **Special facilities:** Nature preserve, greenhouse, observatory, urban community research center, Japanese garden, and theater complex.

Freshman class profile. 8,759 applied, 7,337 admitted, 1,173 enrolled.

Mid 50% test scores			
SAT critical reading:	370-460	GPA 3.0-3.49:	48%
SAT math:	370-470	GPA 2.0-2.99:	43%
SAT writing:	380-460	End year in good standing:	80%
ACT composite:	15-19	Return as sophomores:	80%
GPA 3.75 or higher:	3%	Out-of-state:	1%
GPA 3.50-3.74:	6%	Live on campus:	17%
		International:	1%

Basis for selection. Academic record and test scores are most important. SAT/ACT required of applicants who do not meet minimum requirement based on admissions eligibility index. Interview required of Educational Opportunity Program applicants. **Home schooled:** Statement describing home school structure and mission, transcript of courses and grades, state high school equivalency certificate required. **Learning Disabled:** Student must show proof of learning disability to Office of Disability Services.

High school preparation. College-preparatory program required. 15 units required. Required units include English 4, mathematics 3, social studies 1, history 1, science 2 (laboratory 2), foreign language 2, visual/performing arts 1 and academic electives 1.

2011-2012 Annual costs. Tuition/fees: $6,095; $17,255 out-of-state. Room/board: $10,320. Books/supplies: $1,656. Personal expenses: $2,800.

2010-2011 Financial aid. Need-based: 925 full-time freshmen applied for aid; 868 were judged to have need; 858 of these received aid. Average need met was 35%. Average scholarship/grant was $4,528; average loan $1,641. 68% of total undergraduate aid awarded as scholarships/grants, 32% as loans/jobs. **Non-need-based:** Awarded to 1,244 full-time undergraduates, including 159 freshmen. Scholarships awarded for academics, alumni affiliation, art, athletics, leadership, music/drama.

Application procedures. Admission: Priority date 11/30; no deadline. $55 fee, may be waived for applicants with need. Application must be submitted online. Admission notification on a rolling basis beginning on or about 10/15. **Financial aid:** Priority date 3/2; no closing date. FAFSA required. Applicants notified on a rolling basis starting 2/28; must reply within 4 week(s) of notification.

Academics. Special study options: Accelerated study, cross-registration, distance learning, double major, dual enrollment of high school students, external degree, honors, independent study, internships, student-designed major, study abroad, teacher certification program, weekend college. **Credit/placement by examination:** AP, CLEP, IB, SAT, ACT, institutional tests. **Support services:** Learning center, pre-admission summer program, reduced course load, remedial instruction, study skills assistance, tutoring, writing center.

Majors. Area/ethnic studies: African-American, Chicano/Hispanic-American/Latino. **Biology:** General, biochemistry, cell/histology, ecology, microbiology. **Business:** General, accounting, business admin, entrepreneurial studies, international, labor studies, logistics, marketing, operations, real estate. **Communications:** General, communications/speech/rhetoric, digital media, journalism. **Computer sciences:** Computer science, information technology. **English:** English lit. **Foreign languages:** Linguistics, Spanish. **Health services:** Clinical lab science, health care admin, nursing (RN), physics/radiologic health. **History:** General. **Human services:** General. **Liberal arts:** Arts/sciences. **Math:** General. **Parks/recreation:** Health/fitness. **Philosophy/religion:** Philosophy. **Physical sciences:** Chemistry, geology, physics. **Protective services:** Criminal justice. **Psychology:** General. **Social sciences:** Anthropology, geography, political science, sociology, urban studies. **Visual/performing arts:** Art, art history/conservation, dramatic, graphic design, music.

Most popular majors. Business/marketing 21%, communications/journalism 6%, health sciences 13%, liberal arts 10%, psychology 9%, public administration/social services 7%, social sciences 10%.

Computing on campus. 256 workstations in dormitories, library, computer center. Dormitories wired for high-speed internet access and linked to campus network. Commuter students can connect to campus network. Online course registration, online library, helpline, student web hosting, wireless network available.

Student life. Freshman orientation: Available, $55 fee. Preregistration for classes offered. Offered to incoming admitted freshmen and transfer students. **Housing:** Special housing for disabled, apartments available. $300 fully refundable deposit. **Activities:** Bands, choral groups, dance, drama, international student organizations, literary magazine, music ensembles, musical theater, radio station, student government, student newspaper, TV station, Accounting Society, African-American business student association, dance club, literary club, Phi Alpha Delta, political science club, Science Society, Hispanic Association of Natural and Social Science, Campus Crusade for Christ.

Athletics. NCAA. **Intercollegiate:** Baseball M, basketball, cross-country W, golf M, soccer, softball W, track and field W, volleyball W. **Intramural:** Basketball, cross-country, football (non-tackle), golf, soccer, softball, swimming, tennis, track and field, volleyball, water polo, weight lifting. **Team name:** Toros.

Student services. Career counseling, services for economically disadvantaged, student employment services, financial aid counseling, health services, on-campus daycare, personal counseling, placement for graduates, veterans'

counselor, women's services. **Physically disabled:** Services for visually, speech, hearing impaired.

Contact. E-mail: info@csudh.edu
Phone: (310) 243-3645 Fax: (310) 516-3609
Brandy McLelland, Director of Student Records & Student Information Services, California State University: Dominguez Hills, 1000 East Victoria Street, Carson, CA 90747

California State University: East Bay
Hayward, California   **CB member**
www.csueastbay.edu   **CB code: 4011**

- Public 4-year university
- Commuter campus in small city
- 9,788 degree-seeking undergraduates: 13% part-time, 60% women, 10% African American, 20% Asian American, 19% Hispanic American, 8% international
- 2,279 degree-seeking graduate students
- 36% of applicants admitted
- 43% graduate within 6 years

General. Founded in 1957. Regionally accredited. Branch campus in Concord and extensive online courses offered. **Degrees:** 2,537 bachelor's awarded; master's, doctoral offered. **Location:** 30 miles from San Francisco, 30 miles from San Jose. **Calendar:** Quarter, limited summer session. **Full-time faculty:** 322 total; 34% minority, 49% women. **Part-time faculty:** 361 total; 24% minority, 59% women. **Class size:** 18% < 20, 52% 20-39, 12% 40-49, 17% 50-99, 1% >100. **Special facilities:** Ecological field station, museum of anthropology, marine laboratory, geology summer field camp.

Freshman class profile. 10,749 applied, 3,838 admitted, 1,225 enrolled.

Mid 50% test scores			
SAT critical reading:	400-500	GPA 3.50-3.74:	10%
SAT math:	400-510	GPA 3.0-3.49:	37%
SAT writing:	410-500	GPA 2.0-2.99:	48%
ACT composite:	16-21	Return as sophomores:	76%
GPA 3.75 or higher:	5%	Out-of-state:	1%
		International:	5%

Basis for selection. Eligibility index based on GPA, test results, and 15 units of subject requirements to yield students in top third of California high school graduates. Out-of-state applicants should be in top sixth of high school class. Test scores not required for residents with high school GPA above 3.0, nonresidents with high school GPA above 3.61.

High school preparation. College-preparatory program required. 15 units required. Required units include English 4, mathematics 3, history 2, science 2 (laboratory 2), foreign language 2 and academic electives 1. One visual and performing arts. Math must be algebra, geometry, and intermediate algebra. Science must be biology and a physical science. Foreign language units must be in same language.

2011-2012 Annual costs. Tuition/fees: $6,333; $17,493 out-of-state. Room/board: $11,352. Books/supplies: $1,734. Personal expenses: $3,120.

Financial aid. Non-need-based: Scholarships awarded for athletics, music/drama.

Application procedures. Admission: Closing date 8/31 (postmark date). $55 fee, may be waived for applicants with need. Admission notification on a rolling basis beginning on or about 10/1. **Financial aid:** Priority date 3/2; no closing date. FAFSA required. Applicants notified on a rolling basis starting 3/30; must reply within 3 week(s) of notification.

Academics. Special study options: Accelerated study, cooperative education, cross-registration, distance learning, double major, dual enrollment of high school students, ESL, exchange student, honors, independent study, internships, liberal arts/career combination, student-designed major, study abroad, teacher certification program. **Credit/placement by examination:** AP, CLEP, IB, institutional tests. 45 credit hours maximum toward bachelor's degree. 45-unit limitation excludes advanced placement. **Support services:** Learning center, pre-admission summer program, reduced course load, remedial instruction, study skills assistance, tutoring.

Majors. Area/ethnic studies: African-American, Asian-American, Chicano/Hispanic-American/Latino, Latin American, Native American. **Biology:** General, biochemistry, biomedical sciences. **Business:** General, accounting, business admin, entrepreneurial studies, finance, human resources, management information systems, managerial economics, marketing, purchasing, real estate. **Communications:** Advertising, broadcast journalism, communications/speech/rhetoric, journalism, public relations. **Computer sciences:** General, computer science, information systems, networking. **Conservation:**

General, environmental studies. **Education:** Mathematics, physical, speech. **Engineering:** Software. **English:** American lit, British lit, English lit, rhetoric/composition. **Foreign languages:** French, Spanish. **Health services:** Athletic training, audiology/speech pathology, clinical lab technology, environmental health, prenursing, recreational therapy. **History:** General. **Human services:** General, public policy, social work. **Liberal arts:** Arts/sciences. **Math:** General, applied, statistics. **Parks/recreation:** General, exercise sciences, facilities management, health/fitness. **Philosophy/religion:** Philosophy, religion. **Physical sciences:** Chemistry, geology, physics. **Protective services:** Corrections, law enforcement admin. **Psychology:** General. **Social sciences:** Anthropology, archaeology, economics, geography, political science, sociology. **Visual/performing arts:** Art, art history/conservation, ceramics, commercial/advertising art, dance, dramatic, drawing, music, painting, photography, printmaking, sculpture, studio arts, studio arts management, theater design.

Most popular majors. Business/marketing 29%, family/consumer sciences 6%, health sciences 13%, social sciences 6%.

Computing on campus. 1,062 workstations in dormitories, library, computer center. Dormitories wired for high-speed internet access and linked to campus network. Commuter students can connect to campus network. Online course registration, helpline, student web hosting available.

Student life. Freshman orientation: Mandatory, $80 fee. Preregistration for classes offered. 2 day program with overnight lodging on campus optional. **Policies:** Community and campus-based volunteer programs available. **Housing:** Apartments available. $900 deposit, deadline 5/1. Private coeducational dormitory adjacent to campus. **Activities:** Bands, choral groups, dance, drama, literary magazine, music ensembles, musical theater, opera, radio station, student government, student newspaper, symphony orchestra, TV station, 90 campus organizations.

Athletics. NAIA, NCAA. **Intercollegiate:** Baseball M, basketball, cross-country, golf, soccer, softball W, swimming W, track and field, volleyball W, water polo W. **Intramural:** Badminton, basketball, golf, gymnastics M, racquetball, soccer, softball, swimming, tennis, volleyball. **Team name:** Pioneers.

Student services. Adult student services, career counseling, services for economically disadvantaged, student employment services, financial aid counseling, health services, legal services, minority student services, on-campus daycare, personal counseling, placement for graduates, veterans' counselor. **Physically disabled:** Services for visually, speech, hearing impaired.

Contact. E-mail: admissions@csueastbay.edu
Phone: (510) 885-2784 Fax: (510) 885-4059
Gregory Smith, Associate Vice President, Planning and Enrollment Management, California State University: East Bay, 25800 Carlos Bee Boulevard, Hayward, CA 94542-3095

California State University: Fresno

Fresno, California	**CB member**
www.csufresno.edu	**CB code: 4312**

▶ Public 4-year university
▶ Commuter campus in very large city
▶ 18,784 degree-seeking undergraduates: 12% part-time, 57% women, 5% African American, 15% Asian American, 38% Hispanic American, 1% Native American, 3% international
▶ 2,848 degree-seeking graduate students
▶ 60% of applicants admitted
▶ SAT or ACT (ACT writing optional) required
▶ 49% graduate within 6 years

General. Founded in 1911. Regionally accredited. Designated as an arboretum in 1978. **Degrees:** 3,551 bachelor's awarded; master's, doctoral offered. **ROTC:** Army, Air Force. **Location:** 217 miles from Los Angeles, 192 miles from San Francisco. **Calendar:** Semester, limited summer session. **Full-time faculty:** 624 total; 95% have terminal degrees, 29% minority, 42% women. **Part-time faculty:** 465 total; 24% have terminal degrees, 24% minority, 51% women. **Class size:** 17% < 20, 48% 20-39, 20% 40-49, 11% 50-99, 3% >100. **Special facilities:** 1,190-acre university farm, planetarium.

Freshman class profile. 15,482 applied, 9,352 admitted, 2,925 enrolled.

Mid 50% test scores		Rank in top quarter:	80%
SAT critical reading:	400-510	Rank in top tenth:	15%
SAT math:	410-530	End year in good standing:	81%
SAT writing:	400-510	Return as sophomores:	86%
ACT composite:	16-22	Live on campus:	22%
GPA 3.75 or higher:	19%	International:	2%
GPA 3.50-3.74:	17%	Fraternities:	7%
GPA 3.0-3.49:	42%	Sororities:	3%
GPA 2.0-2.99:	22%		

Basis for selection. Academic GPA, standardized test scores, and rigor of secondary school record very important. Tests recommended, but not required, if student has a high school GPA of 3.0 or higher. **Home schooled:** Transcript of courses and grades required. **Learning Disabled:** Contact Services for Students with Disabilities after submitting application for consideration.

High school preparation. College-preparatory program required. 15 units required. Required units include English 4, mathematics 3, social studies 1, history 1, science 1 (laboratory 1), foreign language 2, visual/performing arts 1 and academic electives 1.

2011-2012 Annual costs. Tuition/fees: $6,123; $17,283 out-of-state. Room/board: $12,000. Books/supplies: $1,256. Personal expenses: $2,162.

2011-2012 Financial aid. Need-based: 2,436 full-time freshmen applied for aid; 2,181 were judged to have need; 2,133 of these received aid. Average need met was 72%. Average scholarship/grant was $10,923; average loan $3,089. 80% of total undergraduate aid awarded as scholarships/grants, 20% as loans/jobs. **Non-need-based:** Awarded to 1,553 full-time undergraduates, including 171 freshmen. Scholarships awarded for academics, art, athletics, leadership, music/drama, ROTC, state residency.

Application procedures. Admission: Closing date 11/30 (receipt date). $55 fee, may be waived for applicants with need. Application must be submitted online. Admission notification on a rolling basis. **Financial aid:** Priority date 3/3; no closing date. FAFSA required. Applicants notified on a rolling basis starting 4/1; must reply within 3 week(s) of notification.

Academics. Special study options: Accelerated study, combined bachelor's/graduate degree, cooperative education, cross-registration, distance learning, double major, dual enrollment of high school students, ESL, exchange student, honors, independent study, internships, student-designed major, study abroad, teacher certification program. **Credit/placement by examination:** AP, CLEP, IB, institutional tests. 30 credit hours maximum toward bachelor's degree. **Support services:** Learning center, pre-admission summer program, reduced course load, remedial instruction, study skills assistance, tutoring, writing center.

Honors college/program. Admits 50-100 students each year. Criteria include intellectual/creative potential, SAT of 1800, top 10% of graduating class, or minimum GPA of 3.6 through end of junior year. Students participate in 2 general education honors courses and honors colloquium each semester during first 2 years; 3 upper division honors courses during junior and senior years. 30 hours of community service required freshmen year with yearly requirement thereafter.

Majors. Area/ethnic studies: African-American, Chicano/Hispanic-American/Latino, Latin American, women's. **Biology:** General, anatomy, bacteriology, botany, cell/histology, ecology, molecular, zoology. **Business:** Accounting, business admin, finance, financial planning, human resources, insurance, international, labor relations, logistics, management information systems, management science, managerial economics, marketing, office management, real estate. **Communications:** Advertising, journalism, media studies, public relations, radio/TV. **Computer sciences:** General, computer science. **Conservation:** Environmental studies. **Education:** General, agricultural, Deaf/hearing impaired, music, technology/industrial arts, trade/industrial. **Engineering:** General, civil, computer, electrical, environmental, mechanical. **English:** English lit, rhetoric/composition. **Foreign languages:** French, German, linguistics, Russian, Spanish. **General:** Agronomy, animal sciences, business, dairy, economics, food science, horticultural science, mechanization, ornamental horticulture, plant protection, plant sciences, poultry, products processing, range science, soil science. **Health services:** Athletic training, communication disorders, community health services, dietetics, environmental health, health care admin, nursing (RN), occupational health, prenursing, preveterinary, vocational rehab counseling. **History:** General. **Human services:** General, social work. **Liberal arts:** Arts/sciences. **Math:** General. **Parks/recreation:** General, exercise sciences, facilities management, health/fitness. **Philosophy/religion:** Philosophy, religion. **Physical sciences:** General, chemistry, geology, physics. **Protective services:** Corrections, criminal justice. **Psychology:** General. **Social sciences:** General, anthropology, criminology, economics, geography, political science, sociology. **Visual/performing arts:** Art, commercial/advertising art, dramatic, graphic design, interior design, music, music performance. **Work/family studies:** General, child development.

Most popular majors. Business/marketing 17%, engineering/engineering technologies 6%, health sciences 12%, liberal arts 8%, psychology 6%.

Computing on campus. 1,500 workstations in dormitories, library, computer center, student center. Dormitories linked to campus network. Commuter students can connect to campus network. Online course registration, online library, helpline, repair service, student web hosting, wireless network available.

Student life. Freshman orientation: Mandatory, $55 fee. Preregistration for classes offered. One day program held during June and July for fall

semester; November and December for spring semester. **Housing:** Coed dorms, single-sex dorms, fraternity/sorority housing available. $150 partly refundable deposit, deadline 4/1. **Activities:** Bands, choral groups, dance, drama, international student organizations, literary magazine, music ensembles, musical theater, radio station, student government, student newspaper, symphony orchestra, TV station, over 250 student organizations including religious and ethnic groups.

Athletics. NCAA. **Intercollegiate:** Baseball M, basketball, cross-country, diving W, equestrian W, football (tackle) M, golf, lacrosse W, soccer W, softball W, swimming W, tennis, track and field, volleyball W. **Intramural:** Basketball, football (non-tackle), racquetball, soccer, softball, tennis, volleyball. **Team name:** Bulldogs.

Student services. Adult student services, career counseling, services for economically disadvantaged, student employment services, financial aid counseling, health services, minority student services, on-campus daycare, personal counseling, placement for graduates, veterans' counselor, women's services. **Physically disabled:** Services for visually, speech, hearing impaired.

Contact. E-mail: admissions@csufresno.edu
Phone: (559) 278-2261 Fax: (559) 278-4812
Vivian Franco, Director, California State University: Fresno, 5150 North Maple Avenue, M/S JA 57, Fresno, CA 93740-8026

California State University: Fullerton

Fullerton, California — CB member
www.fullerton.edu — CB code: 4589

- Public 4-year university
- Commuter campus in small city
- 30,702 degree-seeking undergraduates: 21% part-time, 56% women, 3% African American, 22% Asian American, 34% Hispanic American, 3% international
- 5,359 degree-seeking graduate students
- 47% of applicants admitted
- SAT or ACT required
- 50% graduate within 6 years

General. Founded in 1957. Regionally accredited. **Degrees:** 6,875 bachelor's awarded; master's, doctoral offered. **ROTC:** Army. **Location:** 30 miles from Los Angeles. **Calendar:** Semester, extensive summer session. **Full-time faculty:** 848 total; 89% have terminal degrees, 26% minority, 47% women. **Part-time faculty:** 832 total; 89% have terminal degrees, 29% minority, 52% women. **Class size:** 22% < 20, 54% 20-39, 14% 40-49, 7% 50-99, 3% >100. **Special facilities:** Wildlife sanctuary, arboretum, desert studies center, twin studies center, center for children who stutter, south central coastal information center, demographic research center, institute of gerontology, center for oral and public history, center for study of religion in American life, center for study of economics of aging.

Freshman class profile. 35,235 applied, 16,452 admitted, 4,195 enrolled.

Mid 50% test scores			
SAT critical reading:	450-550	Rank in top quarter:	55%
SAT math:	460-570	Rank in top tenth:	16%
ACT composite:	19-24	End year in good standing:	85%
GPA 3.75 or higher:	14%	Return as sophomores:	85%
GPA 3.50-3.74:	21%	Out-of-state:	1%
GPA 3.0-3.49:	53%	Live on campus:	10%
GPA 2.0-2.99:	12%	International:	2%

Basis for selection. Eligibility index consisting of combination of high school GPA and SAT or ACT score. Audition required of music majors.

High school preparation. College-preparatory program required. 15 units required; 16 recommended. Required and recommended units include English 4, mathematics 3, social studies 1, history 1, science 2 (laboratory 2), foreign language 2-3, visual/performing arts 1 and academic electives 1. 1 unit U.S. history/government required.

2011-2012 Annual costs. Tuition/fees: $6,128; $17,288 out-of-state. Room/board: $10,587. Books/supplies: $1,656. Personal expenses: $2,900.

2010-2011 Financial aid. Need-based: 3,070 full-time freshmen applied for aid; 2,064 were judged to have need; 2,064 of these received aid. Average need met was 63%. Average scholarship/grant was $8,595; average loan $4,826. 67% of total undergraduate aid awarded as scholarships/grants, 33% as loans/jobs. **Non-need-based:** Awarded to 2,495 full-time undergraduates, including 650 freshmen. Scholarships awarded for academics. **Additional information:** Fee waiver for children of veterans killed in action or with service-connected disability whose annual income is $5,000 or less.

Application procedures. Admission: Closing date 11/30 (postmark date). $55 fee, may be waived for applicants with need. Application must be submitted online. Admission notification on a rolling basis beginning on or about 1/1. Must reply by 5/6. Reply date given on notification letter. **Financial aid:** Priority date 3/2, closing date 7/7. FAFSA required. Applicants notified by 4/22; Applicants notified on a rolling basis starting 4/22; must reply within 4 week(s) of notification.

Academics. Special study options: Cross-registration, distance learning, double major, dual enrollment of high school students, honors, independent study, internships, study abroad, teacher certification program. Service learning. **Credit/placement by examination:** AP, CLEP, IB, SAT, ACT, institutional tests. 30 credit hours maximum toward bachelor's degree. **Support services:** Learning center, pre-admission summer program, reduced course load, remedial instruction, study skills assistance, tutoring, writing center.

Majors. Area/ethnic studies: African-American, American, Asian-American, Chicano/Hispanic-American/Latino, European, Latin American, women's. **Biology:** General, biochemistry. **Business:** Accounting, business admin, entrepreneurial studies, finance, international, managerial economics, marketing. **Communications:** Advertising, communications/speech/rhetoric, journalism, public relations, radio/TV. **Computer sciences:** Computer science, information technology. **Education:** Early childhood, music. **Engineering:** Civil, computer, electrical, mechanical, operations research. **English:** English lit. **Foreign languages:** Comparative lit, French, Japanese, linguistics, Spanish. **Health services:** Athletic training, communication disorders, prenursing. **History:** General. **Human services:** General. **Liberal arts:** Arts/sciences. **Math:** General, applied, statistics. **Parks/recreation:** Health/fitness. **Philosophy/religion:** Philosophy, religion. **Physical sciences:** Chemistry, geology, physics. **Protective services:** Criminal justice. **Psychology:** General. **Social sciences:** Anthropology, economics, geography, political science, sociology. **Visual/performing arts:** Art, art history/conservation, dance, dramatic, music, music performance, studio arts.

Most popular majors. Business/marketing 25%, communications/journalism 15%, education 6%, health sciences 7%, psychology 6%, social sciences 7%, visual/performing arts 6%.

Computing on campus. 2,000 workstations in dormitories, library, computer center, student center. Dormitories wired for high-speed internet access and linked to campus network. Commuter students can connect to campus network. Online course registration, online library, helpline, repair service, wireless network available.

Student life. Freshman orientation: Mandatory. Preregistration for classes offered. **Housing:** Apartments, fraternity/sorority housing available. **Activities:** Bands, choral groups, dance, drama, international student organizations, music ensembles, Model UN, musical theater, radio station, student government, student newspaper, symphony orchestra, Chinese Christian Fellowship, Christian student association, disabled student association, Fellowship of Christian Athletes, Human Services Student Association, Movimiento Estudiantil Chicano de Atlan, New Democratic Movement, political science student association.

Athletics. NCAA. **Intercollegiate:** Baseball M, basketball, cross-country, golf, soccer, softball W, tennis W, track and field, volleyball W. **Intramural:** Badminton, basketball, bowling, football (non-tackle), racquetball, rugby M, skiing, soccer M, softball, swimming, table tennis, volleyball. **Team name:** Titans.

Student services. Adult student services, career counseling, student employment services, financial aid counseling, health services, legal services, on-campus daycare, personal counseling, placement for graduates, veterans' counselor, women's services. **Physically disabled:** Services for visually, speech, hearing impaired.

Contact. E-mail: admissions@fullerton.edu
Phone: (657) 278-2370 Fax: (657) 278-2356
Jessica Wagoner, Director of Admissions, California State University: Fullerton, 800 North State College Boulevard, Langsdorf Hall-114, Fullerton, CA 92831-6900

California State University: Long Beach

Long Beach, California — CB member
www.csulb.edu — CB code: 4389

- Public 4-year university
- Commuter campus in large city
- 29,287 degree-seeking undergraduates: 16% part-time, 58% women, 4% African American, 21% Asian American, 33% Hispanic American, 1% Native American, 5% international
- 4,393 degree-seeking graduate students
- 30% of applicants admitted

▶ SAT or ACT (ACT writing optional) required
▶ 54% graduate within 6 years

General. Founded in 1949. Regionally accredited. **Degrees:** 6,746 bachelor's awarded; master's, doctoral offered. **ROTC:** Army. **Location:** 25 miles from Los Angeles. **Calendar:** Semester, extensive summer session. **Full-time faculty:** 930 total; 86% have terminal degrees, 31% minority, 45% women. **Part-time faculty:** 1,066 total; 31% have terminal degrees, 26% minority, 53% women. **Class size:** 22% < 20, 54% 20-39, 12% 40-49, 7% 50-99, 5% >100. **Special facilities:** Japanese garden, performing arts center, media center.

Freshman class profile. 49,767 applied, 15,122 admitted, 3,987 enrolled.

Mid 50% test scores			
SAT critical reading:	440-560	GPA 2.0-2.99:	13%
SAT math:	460-590	Rank in top quarter:	82%
ACT composite:	18-24	End year in good standing:	87%
GPA 3.75 or higher:	23%	Return as sophomores:	89%
GPA 3.50-3.74:	24%	Out-of-state:	1%
GPA 3.0-3.49:	40%	Live on campus:	30%
		International:	3%

Basis for selection. Admission based on secondary school record and standardized test scores. Audition required of dance, music majors. Portfolio required of art, design majors.

High school preparation. College-preparatory program required. 15 units required. Required units include English 4, mathematics 3, social studies 1, history 1, science 2 (laboratory 2), foreign language 2 and academic electives 1. 1 unit fine arts required.

2011-2012 Annual costs. Tuition/fees: $6,240; $17,400 out-of-state. Room/board: $11,038. Books/supplies: $1,666. Personal expenses: $2,694.

2011-2012 Financial aid. Need-based: 3,312 full-time freshmen applied for aid; 2,716 were judged to have need; 2,513 of these received aid. Average need met was 80%. Average scholarship/grant was $6,892; average loan $2,863. 71% of total undergraduate aid awarded as scholarships/grants, 29% as loans/jobs. **Non-need-based:** Awarded to 3,617 full-time undergraduates, including 451 freshmen. Scholarships awarded for academics, art, athletics, job skills, leadership, music/drama, state residency.

Application procedures. Admission: Closing date 11/30 (postmark date). $55 fee, may be waived for applicants with need. Admission notification on a rolling basis beginning on or about 12/1. **Financial aid:** Priority date 3/2; no closing date. FAFSA required. Applicants notified on a rolling basis starting 4/1; must reply within 3 week(s) of notification.

Academics. Special study options: Accelerated study, cross-registration, distance learning, double major, dual enrollment of high school students, ESL, honors, independent study, internships, student-designed major, study abroad, teacher certification program, Washington semester. Concurrent enrollment at other CSU campuses. **Credit/placement by examination:** AP, CLEP, IB, SAT, ACT, institutional tests. **Support services:** Learning center, pre-admission summer program, reduced course load, remedial instruction, study skills assistance, tutoring, writing center.

Majors. Architecture: Interior. **Area/ethnic studies:** African-American, Asian, Chicano/Hispanic-American/Latino, women's. **Biology:** General, bacteriology, biochemistry, botany, cell/histology, molecular. **Business:** General, accounting, fashion, finance, human resources, international, management science, managerial economics, operations, real estate. **Communications:** Broadcast journalism, journalism, public relations. **Computer sciences:** General, computer science, information systems. **Education:** Art, bilingual, elementary, English, family/consumer sciences, foreign languages, physical, science, social science. **Engineering:** General, aerospace, biomedical, chemical, civil, computer, electrical, materials, mechanical. **English:** Creative writing, English lit, rhetoric/composition, writing. **Foreign languages:** Classics, comparative lit, French, German, Japanese, Spanish. **Health services:** Medical illustrating, medical radiologic technology/radiation therapy, nursing (RN), public health ed. **History:** General. **Human services:** Social work. **Liberal arts:** Arts/sciences. **Math:** General, applied, statistics. **Parks/recreation:** Facilities management. **Philosophy/religion:** Philosophy, religion. **Physical sciences:** Chemistry, geology, physics. **Protective services:** Criminal justice. **Psychology:** General. **Social sciences:** Anthropology, economics, geography, sociology. **Visual/performing arts:** Art, art history/conservation, ceramics, cinematography, commercial/advertising art, conducting, dance, design, dramatic, drawing, fiber arts, industrial design, interior design, jazz, metal/jewelry, music, music history, music performance, painting, photography, piano/keyboard, printmaking, sculpture, studio arts, theater design, voice/opera. **Work/family studies:** General, clothing/textiles, food/nutrition.

Most popular majors. Business/marketing 19%, English 9%, family/consumer sciences 6%, health sciences 8%, social sciences 7%, visual/performing arts 10%.

Computing on campus. 1,200 workstations in dormitories, library, computer center. Dormitories linked to campus network. Commuter students can connect to campus network. Online course registration available.

Student life. Freshman orientation: Available, $45 fee. Preregistration for classes offered. One-day pre-semester session. **Housing:** Coed dorms available. **Activities:** Bands, choral groups, dance, drama, film society, literary magazine, music ensembles, musical theater, opera, radio station, student government, student newspaper, symphony orchestra, TV station, more than 150 political, ethnic, and social service organizations.

Athletics. NCAA. **Intercollegiate:** Baseball M, basketball, cross-country, golf, soccer W, softball, tennis W, track and field, volleyball, water polo. **Intramural:** Basketball, handball, racquetball, rugby M, soccer, softball, tennis, volleyball. **Team name:** Forty-Niners.

Student services. Adult student services, alcohol/substance abuse counseling, chaplain/spiritual director, career counseling, services for economically disadvantaged, student employment services, financial aid counseling, health services, minority student services, on-campus daycare, personal counseling, placement for graduates, veterans' counselor, women's services. **Physically disabled:** Services for visually, speech, hearing impaired.

Contact. E-mail: eslb@csulb.edu
Phone: (562) 985-5471 Fax: (562) 985-4973
Thomas Enders, Assistant Vice President for Enrollment Services, California State University: Long Beach, 1250 Bellflower Boulevard, Long Beach, CA 90840-0106

California State University: Los Angeles
Los Angeles, California   CB member
www.calstatela.edu   CB code: 4399

▶ Public 4-year university
▶ Commuter campus in very large city
▶ 17,313 degree-seeking undergraduates: 17% part-time, 59% women, 6% African American, 17% Asian American, 59% Hispanic American, 4% international
▶ 3,971 degree-seeking graduate students
▶ 69% of applicants admitted
▶ 37% graduate within 6 years

General. Founded in 1947. Regionally accredited. **Degrees:** 3,742 bachelor's awarded; master's offered. **ROTC:** Army, Air Force. **Location:** 5 miles from downtown. **Calendar:** Quarter, extensive summer session. **Full-time faculty:** 727 total; 56% have terminal degrees, 45% minority, 48% women. **Part-time faculty:** 506 total; 26% have terminal degrees, 41% minority, 50% women. **Class size:** 32% < 20, 49% 20-39, 12% 40-49, 5% 50-99, 2% >100. **Special facilities:** Baroque pipe organ, 4 megavolt Van de Graaff accelerator.

Freshman class profile. 24,218 applied, 16,812 admitted, 2,473 enrolled.

Mid 50% test scores			
SAT critical reading:	380-480	GPA 3.0-3.49:	48%
SAT math:	380-500	GPA 2.0-2.99:	37%
SAT writing:	380-490	Rank in top quarter:	3%
ACT composite:	15-20	End year in good standing:	91%
GPA 3.75 or higher:	5%	Return as sophomores:	82%
GPA 3.50-3.74:	10%	Live on campus:	15%
		International:	3%

Basis for selection. Secondary school record and standardized test scores important. SAT/ACT not required if GPA is 3.0 or above. EPT/ELM required for placement; may be waived based on SAT score. **Home schooled:** Syllabi and written evaluation of courses completed may be required.

High school preparation. 15 units required. Required units include English 4, mathematics 3, social studies 1, history 1, science 2 (laboratory 2), foreign language 2, visual/performing arts 1 and academic electives 1.

2011-2012 Annual costs. Tuition/fees: $6,088; $17,248 out-of-state. Room/board: $9,264. Books/supplies: $1,656. Personal expenses: $3,054.

2010-2011 Financial aid. Need-based: 1,522 full-time freshmen applied for aid; 1,498 were judged to have need; 1,440 of these received aid. Average need met was 76%. Average scholarship/grant was $9,665; average loan $3,643. 73% of total undergraduate aid awarded as scholarships/grants, 27% as loans/jobs. **Non-need-based:** Awarded to 70 full-time undergraduates, including 8 freshmen.

Application procedures. Admission: Closing date 11/30 (postmark date). $55 fee, may be waived for applicants with need. Admission notification on a rolling basis beginning on or about 11/1. **Financial aid:** Priority date

3/2; no closing date. FAFSA required. Applicants notified on a rolling basis starting 4/1; must reply within 3 week(s) of notification.

Academics. Special study options: Accelerated study, combined bachelor's/graduate degree, cooperative education, cross-registration, distance learning, double major, dual enrollment of high school students, ESL, exchange student, honors, independent study, internships, student-designed major, study abroad, teacher certification program. **Credit/placement by examination:** AP, CLEP, institutional tests. **Support services:** Learning center, pre-admission summer program, reduced course load, remedial instruction, tutoring.

Majors. Area/ethnic studies: African-American, Chicano/Hispanic-American/Latino, Latin American. **Biology:** General, biochemistry, microbiology. **Business:** Business admin. **Communications:** Communications/speech/rhetoric, radio/TV. **Computer sciences:** General. **Education:** Kindergarten/preschool, physical, technology/industrial arts, trade/industrial. **Engineering:** General, civil, electrical, mechanical. **English:** English lit. **Foreign languages:** Chinese, French, Japanese, Spanish. **Health services:** Communication disorders, nursing (RN). **History:** General. **Human services:** Social work. **Liberal arts:** Arts/sciences. **Math:** General. **Philosophy/religion:** Philosophy. **Physical sciences:** Chemistry, geology, physics. **Protective services:** Fire services admin, law enforcement admin. **Psychology:** General. **Social sciences:** Anthropology, economics, geography, political science, sociology. **Visual/performing arts:** Art, commercial/advertising art, dramatic, music, music performance. **Work/family studies:** Food/nutrition.

Most popular majors. Business/marketing 22%, education 6%, health sciences 9%, psychology 7%, public administration/social services 7%, security/protective services 8%, social sciences 9%.

Computing on campus. 1,500 workstations in dormitories, library, computer center, student center. Commuter students can connect to campus network. Online library, helpline, repair service, student web hosting, wireless network available.

Student life. Freshman orientation: Available, $35 fee. Preregistration for classes offered. **Housing:** Coed dorms, apartments available. $100 fully refundable deposit, deadline 7/2. **Activities:** Jazz band, choral groups, dance, drama, literary magazine, music ensembles, musical theater, opera, student government, student newspaper, symphony orchestra, Chicanos for Creative Medicine, Hispanic business society, society of women engineers, Movimiento Estudiantil Chicanos de Aetlar, Asian student union, black student association, Sisters of the African Star, Vietnamese student association, Latin American society, Chinese American service club.

Athletics. NCAA. **Intercollegiate:** Baseball M, basketball, cross-country W, soccer, tennis W, track and field, volleyball W. **Intramural:** Basketball, bowling, gymnastics, handball, judo, racquetball, skiing, soccer, softball, swimming, synchronized swimming, tennis, track and field, volleyball, water polo, wrestling M. **Team name:** Golden Eagles.

Student services. Career counseling, student employment services, health services, on-campus daycare, personal counseling, placement for graduates, veterans' counselor. **Physically disabled:** Services for visually, speech, hearing impaired.

Contact. E-mail: admission@calstatela.edu
Phone: (323) 343-3901 Fax: (323) 343-3888
Joan Woosley, Director of Admissions and University Registrar, California State University: Los Angeles, 5151 State University Drive SA101, Los Angeles, CA 90032

California State University: Monterey Bay
Seaside, California   **CB member**
www.csumb.edu   **CB code: 1945**

♦ Public 4-year liberal arts and teachers college
♦ Residential campus in large town
♦ 4,814 degree-seeking undergraduates: 7% part-time, 61% women, 5% African American, 5% Asian American, 32% Hispanic American, 1% Native American, 1% international
♦ 197 degree-seeking graduate students
♦ 47% of applicants admitted
♦ SAT or ACT (ACT writing optional) required
♦ 38% graduate within 6 years

General. Founded in 1995. Regionally accredited. Dedicated to serving low-income, adult learner, first-generation, and underrepresented populations. **Degrees:** 702 bachelor's awarded; master's offered. **Location:** 108 miles from San Francisco, 68 miles from San Jose. **Calendar:** Semester, limited summer session. **Full-time faculty:** 124 total; 91% have terminal degrees,

44% minority, 47% women. **Part-time faculty:** 212 total; 20% have terminal degrees, 26% minority, 61% women. **Class size:** 16% < 20, 70% 20-39, 7% 40-49, 6% 50-99, less than 1% >100. **Special facilities:** Watershed facilities to complement environmental science major, seafloor mapping lab.

Freshman class profile. 11,607 applied, 5,455 admitted, 873 enrolled.

Mid 50% test scores			
SAT critical reading:	430-540	GPA 2.0-2.99:	29%
SAT math:	430-550	Rank in top quarter:	45%
SAT writing:	430-530	Rank in top tenth:	11%
ACT composite:	18-23	End year in good standing:	85%
GPA 3.75 or higher:	7%	Return as sophomores:	79%
GPA 3.50-3.74:	13%	Out-of-state:	2%
GPA 3.0-3.49:	51%	Live on campus:	88%
		International:	1%

Basis for selection. Students must be high school graduates or GED equivalents, complete 15-unit "a-g" course pattern of college preparatory study with grades of C or better and earn qualifying eligibility index. GPA below 3.0, requires SAT/ACT score. **Home schooled:** Applicants may be asked to provide supplemental information to document completion of CSU eligibility requirements. **Learning Disabled:** Reviewed case-by-case by Student Disability Resources department.

High school preparation. College-preparatory program required. 15 units required. Required units include English 4, mathematics 3, social studies 1, history 1, science 2 (laboratory 2), foreign language 2 and visual/performing arts 1. Science lab units must include 1 biological, 1 physical. Language must be the same language both years. History must include U.S. History.

2011-2012 Annual costs. Tuition/fees: $5,963; $17,123 out-of-state. Room/board: $9,152. Books/supplies: $1,386. Personal expenses: $2,520.

2011-2012 Financial aid. Need-based: 782 full-time freshmen applied for aid; 619 were judged to have need; 583 of these received aid. Average need met was 81%. Average scholarship/grant was $11,013; average loan $3,352. 72% of total undergraduate aid awarded as scholarships/grants, 28% as loans/jobs. **Non-need-based:** Awarded to 359 full-time undergraduates, including 127 freshmen. Scholarships awarded for academics, athletics, state residency.

Application procedures. Admission: Priority date 11/30; deadline 11/30 (receipt date). $55 fee, may be waived for applicants with need. Admission notification by 4/30. Admission notification on a rolling basis beginning on or about 1/1. Must reply by 5/1. **Financial aid:** Priority date 3/2, closing date 5/19. FAFSA required.

Academics. Special study options: Cross-registration, distance learning, double major, exchange student, independent study, internships, semester at sea, student-designed major, study abroad, teacher certification program. Service Learning. **Credit/placement by examination:** AP, CLEP, IB, SAT, ACT, institutional tests. 30 credit hours maximum toward bachelor's degree. **Support services:** Learning center, reduced course load, remedial instruction, study skills assistance, tutoring, writing center.

Majors. Biology: General. **Business:** Business admin. **Communications:** Radio/TV. **Conservation:** Environmental science, environmental studies. **Foreign languages:** Japanese, linguistics, Spanish. **Liberal arts:** Arts/sciences, humanities. **Math:** General. **Parks/recreation:** Health/fitness. **Psychology:** General. **Social sciences:** General, international relations. **Visual/performing arts:** Art, design, music.

Most popular majors. Business/marketing 16%, communications/journalism 6%, liberal arts 22%, parks/recreation 8%, psychology 9%, public administration/social services 6%, social sciences 9%, visual/performing arts 7%.

Computing on campus. 980 workstations in library, computer center. Dormitories wired for high-speed internet access and linked to campus network. Commuter students can connect to campus network. Online course registration, online library, helpline, student web hosting, wireless network available.

Student life. Freshman orientation: Mandatory, $65 fee. Preregistration for classes offered. **Housing:** Coed dorms, special housing for disabled, apartments, wellness housing available. $250 partly refundable deposit. Six-person suite-style living with living areas and kitchenette, substance-free residence hall available. **Activities:** Bands, campus ministries, choral groups, dance, drama, film society, international student organizations, music ensembles, radio station, student government, student newspaper, business club, Black Students United, First Year Council, M.E.Ch.A., Electronic Music Culture (E=MC2), CAMP Club.

Athletics. NCAA. **Intercollegiate:** Baseball M, basketball, cross-country, golf, sailing, soccer, softball W, volleyball W, water polo W. **Intramural:** Basketball, bowling, soccer, volleyball. **Team name:** Otters.

Student services. Adult student services, alcohol/substance abuse counseling, chaplain/spiritual director, career counseling, services for economically disadvantaged, student employment services, financial aid counseling, health services, minority student services, on-campus daycare, personal counseling, placement for graduates, veterans' counselor, women's services. **Physically disabled:** Services for visually, speech, hearing impaired.

Contact. E-mail: admissions@csumb.edu
Phone: (831) 582-3738 Fax: (831) 582-3783
David Linnevers, Director of Admissions, California State University: Monterey Bay, 100 Campus Center, Student Services Building, Seaside, CA 93955-8001

California State University: Northridge
Northridge, California
www.csun.edu   **CB code: 4707**

▸ Public 4-year university
▸ Commuter campus in very large city
▸ 31,504 degree-seeking undergraduates: 20% part-time, 55% women, 7% African American, 11% Asian American, 37% Hispanic American, 6% international
▸ 5,407 degree-seeking graduate students
▸ 62% of applicants admitted
▸ SAT or ACT (ACT writing recommended) required
▸ 46% graduate within 6 years

General. Founded in 1958. Regionally accredited. University center in Ventura. **Degrees:** 6,723 bachelor's awarded; master's, professional offered. **ROTC:** Army, Air Force. **Location:** 20 miles from Los Angeles. **Calendar:** Semester, limited summer session. **Full-time faculty:** 833 total; 33% minority, 46% women. **Part-time faculty:** 1,023 total; 23% minority, 52% women. **Class size:** 10% < 20, 58% 20-39, 15% 40-49, 12% 50-99, 5% >100. **Special facilities:** Anthropology museum, art botanical gardens, urban archives center, observatory, map library, center for the study of cancer and developmental biology, National Center on Deafness, planetarium.

Freshman class profile. 25,822 applied, 16,075 admitted, 5,269 enrolled.

Mid 50% test scores			
SAT critical reading:	400-510	Return as sophomores:	75%
SAT math:	410-530	Out-of-state:	1%
ACT composite:	16-22	International:	5%

Basis for selection. Index using high school GPA and test scores, and completion of subject requirements. In-state applicants should rank in top third of class; out-of-state in the top sixth. Business administration, economics, engineering, computer science, and physical therapy programs open to California residents only. SAT scores can be used to meet English/Math proficiency requirements. Audition required of music majors.

High school preparation. College-preparatory program required. 15 units required. Required units include English 4, mathematics 3, social studies 1, history 1, science 2 (laboratory 2), foreign language 2, visual/performing arts 1 and academic electives 1.

2011-2012 Annual costs. Tuition/fees: $6,448; $17,548 out-of-state. Room/board: $12,276. Books/supplies: $1,746. Personal expenses: $3,074.

Financial aid. Non-need-based: Scholarships awarded for academics, athletics, state residency.

Application procedures. Admission: Closing date 11/30. $55 fee, may be waived for applicants with need. Admission notification on a rolling basis beginning on or about 3/1. Must reply by May 1 or within 2 week(s) if notified thereafter. Applications must be completed by November 30 for business administration, economics and physical therapy programs. **Financial aid:** Priority date 3/2; no closing date. FAFSA required. Applicants notified on a rolling basis starting 4/1.

Academics. Special study options: Cross-registration, distance learning, double major, dual enrollment of high school students, ESL, exchange student, independent study, internships, student-designed major, study abroad, teacher certification program. Evening degree program, Saturday classes, extended studies, open university, Program for Adult College Education (PACE) available. **Credit/placement by examination:** AP, CLEP, SAT, ACT, institutional tests. **Support services:** Learning center, pre-admission summer program, remedial instruction, tutoring.

Majors. Area/ethnic studies: African-American, Chicano/Hispanic-American/Latino. **Biology:** General, bacteriology, biochemistry, cell/histology, molecular. **Business:** Banking/financial services, business admin, human

resources, management information systems, management science, managerial economics, real estate. **Communications:** Broadcast journalism, journalism. **Computer sciences:** General. **Education:** Art, business, English, family/consumer sciences, foreign languages, health, mathematics, music, physical, social science, social studies, speech impaired. **Engineering:** General, chemical, civil, computer, electrical, engineering mechanics, materials, mechanical. **English:** British lit, creative writing, English lit, rhetoric/composition. **Foreign languages:** Comparative lit, French, German, linguistics, Spanish. **Health services:** Nursing (RN), speech pathology. **History:** General. **Liberal arts:** Arts/sciences. **Math:** General, applied, statistics. **Parks/recreation:** General. **Philosophy/religion:** Philosophy, religion. **Physical sciences:** Chemistry, geology, geophysics, physics, planetary. **Psychology:** General. **Social sciences:** Anthropology, economics, geography, political science, sociology, urban studies. **Visual/performing arts:** Art, art history/conservation, ceramics, commercial/advertising art, crafts, dance, dramatic, drawing, metal/jewelry, music, music history, music performance, music theory/composition, painting, printmaking, sculpture. **Work/family studies:** General, business, child care management, clothing/textiles, family studies, family/community services, food/nutrition, housing.

Most popular majors. Business/marketing 20%, communications/journalism 8%, English 6%, liberal arts 7%, psychology 10%, social sciences 14%, visual/performing arts 7%.

Computing on campus. 723 workstations in library, computer center. Dormitories wired for high-speed internet access and linked to campus network. Commuter students can connect to campus network. Online course registration, online library, helpline, student web hosting, wireless network available.

Student life. Freshman orientation: Mandatory. Preregistration for classes offered. **Housing:** Apartments, fraternity/sorority housing available. Off campus housing choices available. **Activities:** Bands, choral groups, dance, drama, music ensembles, musical theater, radio station, student government, student newspaper, women's center, communities, various clubs and organizations.

Athletics. NCAA. **Intercollegiate:** Baseball M, basketball, cross-country, diving, golf, soccer, softball W, swimming, tennis W, track and field, volleyball, water polo W. **Intramural:** Badminton, baseball M, basketball, bowling, cross-country, diving, handball, ice hockey M, racquetball, rugby, sailing, skiing, soccer, softball, swimming, table tennis, tennis, track and field, volleyball. **Team name:** Matadors.

Student services. Adult student services, alcohol/substance abuse counseling, career counseling, services for economically disadvantaged, student employment services, financial aid counseling, health services, minority student services, on-campus daycare, personal counseling, placement for graduates, veterans' counselor, women's services. **Physically disabled:** Services for visually, speech, hearing impaired.

Contact. E-mail: admissions.records@csun.edu
Phone: (818) 677-3700 Fax: (818) 677-3766
Eric Forbes, Director of Admissions and Records, California State University: Northridge, 18111 Nordhoff Street, Northridge, CA 91330-8207

California State University: Sacramento
Sacramento, California   **CB member**
www.csus.edu   **CB code: 4671**

▸ Public 4-year university
▸ Commuter campus in very large city
▸ 24,701 degree-seeking undergraduates: 17% part-time, 57% women, 6% African American, 20% Asian American, 18% Hispanic American, 1% Native American, 1% international
▸ 3,315 degree-seeking graduate students
▸ 67% of applicants admitted
▸ SAT or ACT (ACT writing optional) required
▸ 42% graduate within 6 years

General. Founded in 1947. Regionally accredited. **Degrees:** 5,075 bachelor's awarded; master's, doctoral offered. **ROTC:** Army, Air Force. **Location:** 100 miles from San Francisco. **Calendar:** Semester, extensive summer session. **Full-time faculty:** 703 total; 84% have terminal degrees, 30% minority, 46% women. **Part-time faculty:** 697 total; 24% have terminal degrees, 19% minority, 52% women. **Class size:** 20% < 20, 46% 20-39, 16% 40-49, 13% 50-99, 5% >100. **Special facilities:** Aquatic center, anthropology museum, Hellenic collection.

Freshman class profile. 18,617 applied, 12,496 admitted, 4,671 enrolled.

Mid 50% test scores			
SAT critical reading:	410-520	GPA 2.0-2.99:	30%
SAT math:	420-540	Return as sophomores:	83%
ACT composite:	17-23	Out-of-state:	1%
GPA 3.75 or higher:	12%	Live on campus:	30%
GPA 3.50-3.74:	17%	International:	1%
GPA 3.0-3.49:	41%	Fraternities:	2%
		Sororities:	2%

Basis for selection. Admission requirements vary by programs. If high school GPA is 3.00+, test scores are not required to make an admission decision; if high school GPA is >3.00, either ACT or SAT (exclusive of Writing) is required. ACT and SAT are only used to exempt students from required placement tests in English and Math.

High school preparation. College-preparatory program required. 15 units required. Required units include English 4, mathematics 3, history 2, science 2 (laboratory 2), foreign language 2, visual/performing arts 1 and academic electives 1. History must be U.S. history/government.

2011-2012 Annual costs. Tuition/fees: $6,572; $17,732 out-of-state. Room/board: $11,518. Books/supplies: $1,734. Personal expenses: $3,838.

2010-2011 Financial aid. Need-based: 2,257 full-time freshmen applied for aid; 1,867 were judged to have need; 1,710 of these received aid. Average need met was 62%. Average scholarship/grant was $9,895; average loan $3,366. 67% of total undergraduate aid awarded as scholarships/grants, 33% as loans/jobs. Non-need-based: Awarded to 1,090 full-time undergraduates, including 292 freshmen.

Application procedures. Admission: Priority date 11/30; deadline 3/1 (receipt date). $55 fee, may be waived for applicants with need. Admission notification on a rolling basis beginning on or about 11/1. Must reply by May 1 or within 2 week(s) if notified thereafter. Financial aid: No deadline. FAFSA required. Applicants notified on a rolling basis starting 4/23; must reply within 4 week(s) of notification.

Academics. Special study options: Accelerated study, cooperative education, cross-registration, distance learning, double major, dual enrollment of high school students, ESL, honors, independent study, internships, student-designed major, study abroad, teacher certification program. Credit/placement by examination: AP, CLEP, IB, SAT, ACT, institutional tests. SAT/ACT may be used to exempt students from English/math placement tests. Support services: Learning center, remedial instruction, study skills assistance, tutoring, writing center.

Majors. Architecture: Interior. Area/ethnic studies: Asian. Biology: General, bacteriology, molecular. Business: Accounting, business admin, finance, human resources, insurance, international, marketing, operations, real estate. Communications: Communications/speech/rhetoric, journalism. Computer sciences: General, information systems. Conservation: General, environmental studies. Education: General, kindergarten/preschool, mathematics. Engineering: Civil, computer, electrical, mechanical. English: English lit. Foreign languages: American Sign Language, French, Spanish. Health services: Audiology/speech pathology, clinical lab technology, nursing (RN), prenursing. History: General. Human services: Social work. Liberal arts: Arts/sciences, humanities. Math: General. Parks/recreation: General, health/fitness. Philosophy/religion: Philosophy, religion. Physical sciences: General, chemistry, geology, physics. Protective services: Corrections, law enforcement admin. Psychology: General. Social sciences: General, anthropology, economics, geography, political science, sociology. Visual/performing arts: Art, cinematography, commercial/advertising art, dramatic, music, music management, music performance, music theory/composition, photography, voice/opera. Work/family studies: General.

Most popular majors. Business/marketing 21%, communications/journalism 8%, parks/recreation 6%, psychology 6%, security/protective services 8%.

Computing on campus. 700 workstations in dormitories, library, computer center, student center. Dormitories wired for high-speed internet access and linked to campus network. Commuter students can connect to campus network. Online course registration, online library, helpline, repair service, student web hosting, wireless network available.

Student life. Freshman orientation: Mandatory, $50 fee. Preregistration for classes offered. Housing: Coed dorms, special housing for disabled, apartments available. $175 deposit, deadline 7/1. Suites for single students available. Activities: Bands, campus ministries, choral groups, dance, drama, film society, international student organizations, literary magazine, music ensembles, musical theater, opera, radio station, student government, student newspaper, symphony orchestra, more than 250 clubs, organizations and special interest groups.

Athletics. NCAA. Intercollegiate: Baseball M, basketball, cross-country, football (tackle) M, golf, gymnastics W, rowing (crew) W, soccer, softball W, tennis, track and field, volleyball W. Intramural: Badminton, basketball, bowling, football (non-tackle), golf, racquetball, skiing, soccer, tennis, volleyball. Team name: Hornets.

Student services. Adult student services, alcohol/substance abuse counseling, career counseling, services for economically disadvantaged, student employment services, financial aid counseling, health services, legal services, on-campus daycare, personal counseling, placement for graduates, veterans' counselor, women's services. Physically disabled: Services for visually, speech, hearing impaired.

Contact. E-mail: outreach@csus.edu
Phone: (916) 278-7766 Fax: (916) 278-5603
Emiliano Diaz, Director of Outreach, Admissions & Records, California State University: Sacramento, 6000 J Street, Sacramento, CA 95819-6048

California State University: San Bernardino

San Bernardino, California — CB member
www.csusb.edu — CB code: 4099

- Public 4-year university and liberal arts college
- Commuter campus in small city
- 14,732 degree-seeking undergraduates: 12% part-time, 63% women, 9% African American, 7% Asian American, 49% Hispanic American, 4% international
- 1,883 degree-seeking graduate students
- 58% of applicants admitted
- SAT or ACT (ACT writing optional) required
- 48% graduate within 6 years

General. Founded in 1962. Regionally accredited. Palm Desert satellite campus offers day and evening courses in degree and credential programs. Degrees: 2,868 bachelor's awarded; master's, doctoral offered. ROTC: Army, Air Force. Location: 60 miles from Los Angeles. Calendar: Quarter, limited summer session. Full-time faculty: 434 total; 82% have terminal degrees, 31% minority, 43% women. Part-time faculty: 478 total; 19% have terminal degrees, 30% minority, 58% women. Class size: 27% < 20, 48% 20-39, 7% 40-49, 12% 50-99, 6% >100. Special facilities: Animal house, greenhouse, desert studies center, college-operated museum.

Freshman class profile. 10,908 applied, 6,353 admitted, 2,131 enrolled.

Mid 50% test scores			
SAT critical reading:	400-500	GPA 3.0-3.49:	52%
SAT math:	410-510	GPA 2.0-2.99:	26%
SAT writing:	400-500	Return as sophomores:	89%
ACT composite:	16-21	Out-of-state:	1%
GPA 3.75 or higher:	9%	International:	2%
GPA 3.50-3.74:	13%	Fraternities:	10%
		Sororities:	7%

Basis for selection. High school GPA and test scores most important. SAT/ACT not required if high school GPA is 3.0 or higher. Entering undergraduates, except those who qualify for exemption, must take CSU entry-level mathematics (ELM) examination and CSU English placement test (EPT) after admission and before enrolling in classes.

High school preparation. College-preparatory program required. 15 units required. Required units include English 4, mathematics 3, social studies 1, history 1, science 2 (laboratory 2), foreign language 2, visual/performing arts 1 and academic electives 1. One visual and performing arts unit also required. Students with disabilities may substitute alternate courses for specific subject requirements.

2011-2012 Annual costs. Tuition/fees: $6,433; $17,593 out-of-state. Room/board: $9,796. Books/supplies: $1,656. Personal expenses: $2,052.

2011-2012 Financial aid. Need-based: 1,666 full-time freshmen applied for aid; 1,519 were judged to have need; 1,483 of these received aid. Average need met was 67%. Average scholarship/grant was $9,777; average loan $2,845. 84% of total undergraduate aid awarded as scholarships/grants, 16% as loans/jobs. Non-need-based: Awarded to 803 full-time undergraduates, including 164 freshmen.

Application procedures. Admission: No deadline. $55 fee, may be waived for applicants with need. Admission notification on a rolling basis. Students may apply as late as 3 weeks into quarter. Financial aid: Priority date 3/2; no closing date. FAFSA required. Applicants notified on a rolling basis starting 4/1.

Academics. Special study options: Accelerated study, cooperative education, cross-registration, distance learning, double major, dual enrollment of high school students, exchange student, honors, independent study, internships, student-designed major, study abroad, teacher certification program. School of Social and Behavioral Sciences offers master's in National Security

Studies. **Credit/placement by examination:** AP, CLEP, IB, SAT, ACT, institutional tests. 40 credit hours maximum toward bachelor's degree. **Support services:** Learning center, pre-admission summer program, remedial instruction, tutoring, writing center.

Majors. Area/ethnic studies: African-American, American, Chicano/Hispanic-American/Latino. **Biology:** General, biochemistry. **Business:** Accounting, business admin, finance, human resources, international, management information systems, managerial economics, marketing, operations, organizational behavior, real estate. **Communications:** Communications/speech/rhetoric, radio/TV. **Computer sciences:** Computer science, systems analysis. **Conservation:** Environmental studies. **Education:** Physical, trade/industrial. **English:** Creative writing, English lit. **Foreign languages:** French, Spanish. **Health services:** Environmental health, kinesiotherapy, nursing (RN), premedicine. **History:** General. **Human services:** General, social work. **Liberal arts:** Arts/sciences, humanities. **Math:** General. **Parks/recreation:** Exercise sciences. **Philosophy/religion:** Philosophy. **Physical sciences:** Chemistry, geology, physics. **Protective services:** Law enforcement admin. **Psychology:** General. **Social sciences:** General, anthropology, economics, geography, political science, sociology. **Visual/performing arts:** Art, art history/conservation, commercial/advertising art, dramatic, music, music history, music performance, musicology, studio arts, theater design, theater history. **Work/family studies:** Child development, family studies, food/nutrition.

Most popular majors. Business/marketing 22%, health sciences 9%, liberal arts 9%, psychology 11%, security/protective services 7%, social sciences 9%.

Computing on campus. 600 workstations in dormitories, library, computer center, student center. Dormitories wired for high-speed internet access and linked to campus network. Commuter students can connect to campus network. Online course registration, online library, wireless network available.

Student life. Freshman orientation: Available. Preregistration for classes offered. **Housing:** Coed dorms, single-sex dorms, apartments, wellness housing available. **Activities:** Jazz band, choral groups, dance, drama, music ensembles, musical theater, radio station, student government, student newspaper, symphony orchestra, TV station, more than 80 clubs and organizations.

Athletics. NCAA. **Intercollegiate:** Baseball M, basketball, cross-country W, golf M, soccer, softball W, swimming, tennis W, volleyball W, water polo. **Intramural:** Basketball, field hockey W, soccer, softball M, volleyball. **Team name:** Coyotes.

Student services. Adult student services, career counseling, student employment services, financial aid counseling, health services, legal services, minority student services, on-campus daycare, personal counseling, placement for graduates, veterans' counselor, women's services. **Physically disabled:** Services for visually, speech, hearing impaired.

Contact. E-mail: moreinfo@mail.csusb.edu
Phone: (909) 537-5188 Fax: (909) 537-7034
Olivia Rosas, Director of Admissions and Student Recruitment, California State University: San Bernardino, 5500 University Parkway, San Bernardino, CA 92407-2397

California State University: San Marcos

San Marcos, California	CB member
www.csusm.edu	CB code: 5677

- Public 4-year university
- Commuter campus in large town
- 9,440 degree-seeking undergraduates: 23% part-time, 60% women
- 535 degree-seeking graduate students
- 59% of applicants admitted
- 55% graduate within 6 years

General. Founded in 1989. Regionally accredited. **Degrees:** 1,665 bachelor's awarded; master's offered. **ROTC:** Army, Naval, Air Force. **Location:** 30 miles from San Diego. **Calendar:** Semester, limited summer session. **Full-time faculty:** 249 total; 43% minority. **Part-time faculty:** 320 total; 26% minority. **Class size:** 18% < 20, 61% 20-39, 13% 40-49, 6% 50-99, 2% >100.

Freshman class profile. 9,978 applied, 5,841 admitted, 1,450 enrolled.

Mid 50% test scores		GPA 3.0-3.49:	47%
SAT critical reading:	420-530	GPA 2.0-2.99:	32%
SAT math:	440-540	Return as sophomores:	82%
GPA 3.75 or higher:	9%	Out-of-state:	1%
GPA 3.50-3.74:	12%	International:	1%

Basis for selection. Student eligibility index calculated on GPA and test score combination. **Learning Disabled:** C or better grades in all college preparatory classes -- Minimum GPA-2.0.

High school preparation. College-preparatory program required. 15 units required; 16 recommended. Required and recommended units include English 4, mathematics 3-4, social studies 2, science 2 (laboratory 2), foreign language 2 and academic electives 1.

2011-2012 Annual costs. Tuition/fees: $6,008; $17,168 out-of-state. Room only: $10,863.

Financial aid. Non-need-based: Scholarships awarded for academics, athletics, leadership, state residency.

Application procedures. Admission: $55 fee, may be waived for applicants with need. Admission notification on a rolling basis beginning on or about 12/1. Must reply by May 1 or within 3 week(s) if notified thereafter.

Academics. Special study options: Accelerated study, cross-registration, distance learning, double major, dual enrollment of high school students, ESL, independent study, internships, student-designed major, study abroad, teacher certification program, weekend college. Evening degree program, Saturday classes, Air Force ROTC, extended studies, open university, special sessions, including winter. **Credit/placement by examination:** AP, CLEP, IB, SAT, ACT, institutional tests. 30 credit hours maximum toward bachelor's degree. **Support services:** Learning center, pre-admission summer program, study skills assistance, tutoring, writing center.

Majors. Area/ethnic studies: Women's. **Biology:** General, biochemistry, biotechnology. **Business:** Business admin. **Communications:** Communications/speech/rhetoric. **Computer sciences:** General, computer science. **Engineering:** Applied physics. **English:** English lit. **Foreign languages:** Spanish. **History:** General. **Liberal arts:** Arts/sciences. **Math:** General. **Physical sciences:** Chemistry, physics. **Psychology:** General. **Social sciences:** General, economics, political science, sociology. **Visual/performing arts:** General. **Work/family studies:** Family studies.

Most popular majors. Business/marketing 23%, communications/journalism 12%, history 7%, liberal arts 17%, social sciences 7%.

Computing on campus. 1,400 workstations in library, computer center. Dormitories wired for high-speed internet access and linked to campus network. Commuter students can connect to campus network. Online course registration, helpline, wireless network available.

Student life. Freshman orientation: Mandatory, $70 fee. Preregistration for classes offered. One-day program. **Housing:** Special housing for disabled, apartments available. $50 nonrefundable deposit. **Activities:** Choral groups, drama, music ensembles, student newspaper, American Indian Science Engineering Society, Circle K, InterVarsity Christian Fellowship, Latter-day Saints student association, accounting society, Black Men on Campus, College Democrats, pre-health society, student housing asociation.

Athletics. NAIA. **Intercollegiate:** Baseball M, cross-country, golf, soccer, softball W, track and field. **Team name:** Cougars.

Student services. Adult student services, alcohol/substance abuse counseling, career counseling, services for economically disadvantaged, student employment services, financial aid counseling, health services, on-campus daycare, personal counseling, placement for graduates, veterans' counselor. **Physically disabled:** Services for visually, speech, hearing impaired.

Contact. E-mail: apply@csusm.edu
Phone: (760) 750-4848
Nathan Evans, Director of Admissions and Recruitment, California State University: San Marcos, 333 South Twin Oaks Valley Road, San Marcos, CA 92096-0001

California State University: Stanislaus

Turlock, California	CB member
www.csustan.edu	CB code: 4713

- Public 4-year business and liberal arts college
- Commuter campus in small city
- 7,911 degree-seeking undergraduates: 19% part-time, 64% women, 3% African American, 11% Asian American, 39% Hispanic American, 1% Native American, 1% international
- 1,325 degree-seeking graduate students
- 77% of applicants admitted
- 42% graduate within 6 years

General. Founded in 1957. Regionally accredited. **Degrees:** 1,442 bachelor's awarded; master's, doctoral offered. **Location:** 15 miles from Modesto. **Calendar:** Semester, extensive summer session. **Full-time faculty:** 266 total; 87% have terminal degrees, 25% minority, 47% women. **Part-time faculty:** 178 total; 21% have terminal degrees, 17% minority, 51% women. **Class size:** 20% < 20, 55% 20-39, 11% 40-49, 12% 50-99, 2% >100. **Special facilities:** Observatory, interactive television classrooms, laser laboratory, marine sciences station, greenhouse, mainstage theater, bio-ag eco building.

Freshman class profile. 5,387 applied, 4,128 admitted, 1,251 enrolled.

Mid 50% test scores			
SAT critical reading:	400-510	GPA 3.0-3.49:	43%
SAT math:	410-530	GPA 2.0-2.99:	28%
SAT writing:	410-510	Return as sophomores:	87%
ACT composite:	16-21	Out-of-state:	1%
GPA 3.75 or higher:	14%	Live on campus:	25%
GPA 3.50-3.74:	15%	International:	2%

Basis for selection. High school GPA, courses taken, and test scores. Special consideration for veterans, low-income, and minority applicants. For non-native English speakers, ELPT can be substituted for TOEFL for placement. Exemptions result from scoring well on other specified tests or completion of appropriate courses. Interview recommended for theatre arts and music majors. Audition recommended for music majors. Portfolio recommended for art majors. **Home schooled:** Transcript of courses and grades, interview required. Applicant must submit SAT or ACT scores. **Learning Disabled:** Students with diagnosed learning disability or neurological disorder that significantly impairs academic performance in specified area may be eligible for waiver of General Education Breadth (GEB) requirement. Additional coursework required in lieu of GEB. Contact Disabled Student Services or submit documentation of disability.

High school preparation. College-preparatory program required. 15 units required. Required units include English 4, mathematics 3, social studies 1, history 1, science 2 (laboratory 2), foreign language 2, visual/performing arts 1 and academic electives 1. History units include history/social studies.

2011-2012 Annual costs. Tuition/fees: $6,582; $17,742 out-of-state. Room/board: $8,368. Books/supplies: $1,700. Personal expenses: $2,482.

2011-2012 Financial aid. Non-need-based: Scholarships awarded for academics, alumni affiliation, art, athletics, leadership, minority status, music/drama, state residency.

Application procedures. Admission: Priority date 11/30; deadline 11/30 (receipt date). $55 fee, may be waived for applicants with need. Admission notification on a rolling basis beginning on or about 1/1. **Financial aid:** Priority date 3/2; no closing date. FAFSA required. Applicants notified on a rolling basis starting 3/15; must reply within 3 week(s) of notification.

Academics. First Year Programs, lecture series and cultural offerings, study abroad opportunities, University Honors Program, intensive learning experiences, ESL, community service and service learning opportunities, variety of internships, Cooperative Learning Program. **Special study options:** Accelerated study, cooperative education, cross-registration, distance learning, double major, dual enrollment of high school students, ESL, exchange student, honors, independent study, internships, liberal arts/career combination, student-designed major, study abroad, teacher certification program. Additional course offerings developed specifically for learners seeking professional or personal development are available through University Extended Education. **Credit/placement by examination:** AP, CLEP, IB, SAT, ACT, institutional tests. 24 credit hours maximum toward bachelor's degree. Credit by examination does not count toward residency requirement. **Support services:** Learning center, reduced course load, remedial instruction, study skills assistance, tutoring, writing center.

Majors. Biology: General. **Business:** Business admin. **Communications:** Communications/speech/rhetoric. **Education:** Early childhood. **English:** English lit. **Foreign languages:** Spanish. **History:** General. **Liberal arts:** Arts/sciences. **Math:** General. **Parks/recreation:** Health/fitness. **Philosophy/religion:** Philosophy. **Physical sciences:** General, chemistry, geology, physics. **Protective services:** Criminal justice. **Psychology:** General, cognitive. **Social sciences:** General, anthropology, economics, geography, political science, sociology. **Visual/performing arts:** Art, dramatic, music, music performance, studio arts.

Most popular majors. Business/marketing 19%, health sciences 6%, liberal arts 13%, psychology 8%, security/protective services 8%, social sciences 12%.

Computing on campus. 201 workstations in dormitories, library, computer center, student center. Dormitories wired for high-speed internet access and linked to campus network. Commuter students can connect to campus network. Online course registration, online library, helpline, wireless network available.

Student life. Freshman orientation: Available. Preregistration for classes offered. Held year-round. **Housing:** Coed dorms, apartments available. $200 partly refundable deposit, deadline 4/16. Summer housing available. **Activities:** Bands, choral groups, dance, drama, international student organizations, music ensembles, Model UN, musical theater, opera, radio station, student government, student newspaper, symphony orchestra, Over 90 clubs and organizations that range from political, pre-professional, social, fraternities & sororities, cultural, and religious available on campus.

Athletics. NCAA. **Intercollegiate:** Baseball M, basketball, cross-country, golf M, soccer, softball W, tennis W, track and field, volleyball W. **Intramural:** Basketball, football (non-tackle), soccer M, softball W, volleyball. **Team name:** Warriors.

Student services. Adult student services, alcohol/substance abuse counseling, career counseling, services for economically disadvantaged, student employment services, financial aid counseling, health services, minority student services, on-campus daycare, personal counseling, placement for graduates, veterans' counselor, women's services. **Physically disabled:** Services for visually, speech, hearing impaired.

Contact. E-mail: outreach_help_desk@csustan.edu
Phone: (209) 667-3070 Toll-free number: (800) 300-7420
Fax: (209) 667-3394
Lisa Bernardo, Dean of Admissions, California State University: Stanislaus, One University Circle, Turlock, CA 95382-0256

California University of Management and Sciences
Anaheim, California
www.calums.edu

- Private 4-year university and business college
- Commuter campus in very large city
- 26 degree-seeking undergraduates: 42% women, 4% Asian American, 96% international
- 162 degree-seeking graduate students
- Application essay, interview required

General. Regionally accredited; also accredited by ACICS. **Degrees:** 3 bachelor's, 5 associate awarded; master's offered. **Location:** 3 miles from Downtown. **Calendar:** Quarter. **Full-time faculty:** 7 total; 86% have terminal degrees, 14% women. **Part-time faculty:** 18 total; 72% have terminal degrees, 11% women. **Class size:** 100% < 20. **Special facilities:** Golf swing analysis room.

Freshman class profile.

Return as sophomores:	65%	International:	100%

Basis for selection. GED not accepted. School record, GPA, interview most important followed by class rank, test scores, essay and recommendations. TOEFL test scores, EPAT test scores, and Wonderlic Test scores are used for admission. Completion of high school education is required of applicants for Associate and Bachelor degree programs. Completion of bachelor degree is required of applicants for Master's programs. **Home schooled:** Transcript of courses and grades, interview required.

High school preparation. College-preparatory program recommended. 26 units required. Required units include English 4, mathematics 4, social studies 2, history 1, science 4 (laboratory 6), foreign language 1, computer science 2, visual/performing arts 1 and academic electives 1.

2012-2013 Annual costs. Tuition/fees: $7,400. Books/supplies: $1,500.

Application procedures. Admission: Priority date 8/15; deadline 9/15 (receipt date). $100 fee.

Academics. Special study options: ESL, independent study. **Credit/placement by examination:** AP, CLEP, institutional tests. **Support services:** Remedial instruction, tutoring.

Majors. Business: Business admin.

Computing on campus. 20 workstations in library, computer center. Online library, wireless network available.

Student life. Freshman orientation: Mandatory. Preregistration for classes offered. **Activities:** Student government, student newspaper.

Student services. Career counseling, financial aid counseling.

Contact. E-mail: info@calums.edu
Phone: (714) 533-3946 Fax: (714) 533-7778
Lisa Lee, Director of Admissions, California University of Management and Sciences, 721 North Euclid Streeet, Anaheim, CA 92801-4116

Carrington College: Emeryville
Emeryville, California
www.westerncollege.edu

- For-profit 4-year technical college
- Commuter campus in small town
- 205 degree-seeking undergraduates

General. Regionally accredited. **Degrees:** 33 associate awarded. **Calendar:** Differs by program, extensive summer session. **Full-time faculty:** 1 total. **Part-time faculty:** 9 total.

Basis for selection. Admission requirements vary by programs. CPAT required.

2011-2012 Annual costs. Tuition/fees: $14,280.

Application procedures. **Admission:** No deadline. No application fee. Admission notification on a rolling basis. **Financial aid:** FAFSA required. Applicants notified on a rolling basis.

Academics. **Credit/placement by examination:** AP, CLEP. **Support services:** Learning center, tutoring.

Majors. **Communications technology:** Animation/special effects, desktop publishing. **Computer sciences:** Computer graphics.

Student life. **Freshman orientation:** Mandatory. Preregistration for classes offered.

Student services. Student employment services, financial aid counseling.

Contact. Phone: (510) 601-0133 Toll-free number: (800) 750-5627 Carrington College: Emeryville, 6001 Shellmound, #145, Emeryville, CA 94608

Chapman University
Orange, California   **CB member**
www.chapman.edu   **CB code: 4047**

- Private 4-year university and liberal arts college affiliated with Christian Church (Disciples of Christ)
- Residential campus in very large city
- 5,264 degree-seeking undergraduates: 4% part-time, 57% women, 2% African American, 9% Asian American, 13% Hispanic American, 3% international
- 1,846 degree-seeking graduate students
- 45% of applicants admitted
- SAT or ACT with writing, application essay required
- 72% graduate within 6 years

General. Founded in 1861. Regionally accredited. **Degrees:** 1,147 bachelor's awarded; master's, professional, doctoral offered. **ROTC:** Army, Air Force. **Location:** 35 miles from Los Angeles, 60 miles from San Diego. **Calendar:** 4-1-4, limited summer session. **Full-time faculty:** 380 total; 42% women. **Part-time faculty:** 369 total; 40% women. **Class size:** 42% < 20, 53% 20-39, 3% 40-49, 1% 50-99, less than 1% >100.

Freshman class profile. 9,616 applied, 4,313 admitted, 1,272 enrolled.

Mid 50% test scores			
SAT critical reading:	550-650	Rank in top quarter:	91%
SAT math:	560-660	Rank in top tenth:	49%
SAT writing:	570-660	End year in good standing:	96%
ACT composite:	24-29	Return as sophomores:	91%
GPA 3.75 or higher:	51%	Out-of-state:	33%
GPA 3.50-3.74:	22%	Live on campus:	89%
GPA 3.0-3.49:	23%	International:	3%
GPA 2.0-2.99:	4%	Fraternities:	12%
		Sororities:	16%

Basis for selection. Academic course work plus GPA and test scores most important. Recommendations, essay, extracurricular activities also considered. SAT Subject Tests recommended. Audition required for music, dance, theater majors. Portfolio required for art, film majors. Supplemental application required for all talent-based majors. **Home schooled:** Statement describing home school structure and mission, transcript of courses and grades, state high school equivalency certificate required.

High school preparation. College-preparatory program recommended. 11 units required; 18 recommended. Required and recommended units include English 2-4, mathematics 2-4, social studies 3-4, science 2 (laboratory 1) and foreign language 2-4.

2011-2012 Annual costs. Tuition/fees: $40,234. Room/board: $12,957.

Financial aid. **Non-need-based:** Scholarships awarded for academics, alumni affiliation, art, music/drama, religious affiliation, ROTC.

Application procedures. **Admission:** Closing date 1/15 (postmark date). $60 fee, may be waived for applicants with need. Application must be submitted online. Admission notification on a rolling basis beginning on or about 3/15. Must reply by May 1 or within 2 week(s) if notified thereafter. **Financial aid:** Priority date 3/2; no closing date. FAFSA required. Applicants notified on a rolling basis starting 3/15; must reply within 3 week(s) of notification.

Academics. **Special study options:** Combined bachelor's/graduate degree, distance learning, double major, honors, independent study, internships, liberal arts/career combination, semester at sea, student-designed major, study abroad, teacher certification program, Washington semester. **Credit/placement by examination:** AP, CLEP, IB, SAT, ACT, institutional tests. 32 credit hours maximum toward bachelor's degree. **Support services:** Learning center, reduced course load, remedial instruction, study skills assistance, tutoring, writing center.

Majors. **Biology:** General, biochemistry. **Business:** Accounting, business admin, managerial economics. **Communications:** Broadcast journalism, communications/speech/rhetoric, public relations. **Computer sciences:** General, computer science. **Conservation:** Management/policy. **Education:** General, music. **English:** Creative writing, English lit. **Foreign languages:** French, Spanish. **Health services:** Athletic training, health services admin, predental, premedicine, preveterinary. **History:** General. **Human services:** Social work. **Liberal arts:** Arts/sciences. **Math:** General. **Philosophy/religion:** Philosophy, religion. **Physical sciences:** Chemistry, theoretical physics. **Psychology:** General. **Social sciences:** Political science, sociology. **Visual/performing arts:** Acting, art, art history/conservation, cinematography, conducting, dance, dramatic, film/cinema/video, graphic design, music, music performance, music theory/composition, piano/keyboard, play/screenwriting, studio arts, voice/opera.

Most popular majors. Business/marketing 24%, communications/journalism 18%, psychology 7%, visual/performing arts 27%.

Computing on campus. Dormitories wired for high-speed internet access and linked to campus network. Commuter students can connect to campus network. Online course registration, online library, helpline, repair service, student web hosting, wireless network available.

Student life. **Freshman orientation:** Mandatory. Preregistration for classes offered. 5-day summer program for new students and their parents immediately preceding the start of semester. **Housing:** Guaranteed on-campus for freshmen. Coed dorms, special housing for disabled, apartments, wellness housing available. $600 partly refundable deposit, deadline 5/1. Housing for students with dependents available. **Activities:** Bands, campus ministries, choral groups, dance, drama, film society, international student organizations, literary magazine, music ensembles, Model UN, musical theater, opera, radio station, student government, student newspaper, symphony orchestra.

Athletics. NCAA. **Intercollegiate:** Baseball M, basketball, cross-country, football (tackle) M, golf M, rowing (crew) W, soccer, softball W, swimming W, tennis, track and field W, volleyball W, water polo. **Intramural:** Basketball, soccer, volleyball. **Team name:** Panthers.

Student services. Adult student services, alcohol/substance abuse counseling, chaplain/spiritual director, career counseling, student employment services, financial aid counseling, health services, personal counseling, placement for graduates, veterans' counselor. **Physically disabled:** Services for visually, speech, hearing impaired.

Contact. E-mail: admit@chapman.edu
Phone: (714) 997-6711 Toll-free number: (888) 282-7759
Fax: (714) 997-6713
Michael Drummy, Assistant Vice President and Chief Admission Officer, Chapman University, One University Drive, Orange, CA 92866

Charles Drew University of Medicine and Science
Los Angeles, California
www.cdrewu.edu   CB code: 4982

- Private 4-year university and health science college
- Commuter campus in very large city
- 95 degree-seeking undergraduates: 64% part-time, 55% women
- 313 graduate students
- Application essay, interview required

General. Regionally accredited. **Degrees:** 30 bachelor's, 24 associate awarded; master's offered. **Location:** Downtown. **Calendar:** Semester, limited summer session. **Full-time faculty:** 30 total; 47% have terminal degrees, 40% minority. **Part-time faculty:** 49 total; 12% have terminal degrees, 29% minority. **Class size:** 77% < 20, 9% 20-39, 5% 40-49, 9% 50-99. **Special facilities:** Health sciences library, clinical and population-based research facilities.

Basis for selection. Open admission, but selective for some programs. Official transcripts of all schools attended, personal goal statement, three recommendations, SAT scores, evidence of prerequisite courses (if applicable), and participation in an interview with the admissions selection committee required.

High school preparation. College-preparatory program recommended.

2011-2012 Annual costs. Tuition/fees: $14,140. Books/supplies: $1,656. Personal expenses: $3,313.

Application procedures. Admission: No deadline. $35 fee. Application deadlines vary by program. **Financial aid:** Closing date 4/1.

Academics. Special study options: Cross-registration, distance learning, double major, dual enrollment of high school students, independent study, internships. **Credit/placement by examination:** AP, CLEP, IB, institutional tests. **Support services:** Tutoring.

Computing on campus. 35 workstations in library, computer center. Commuter students can connect to campus network. Online course registration, online library, helpline, wireless network available.

Student life. Freshman orientation: Mandatory. Preregistration for classes offered. **Activities:** Student government.

Student services. Financial aid counseling.

Contact. E-mail: admissionsinfo@cdrewu.edu
Phone: (323) 563-5886 Fax: (323) 569-0597
Rita Gloria Sawyer, Director of Admissions, Charles Drew University of Medicine and Science, 1731 East 120th Street, Los Angeles, CA 90059

Claremont McKenna College
Claremont, California   CB member
www.cmc.edu   CB code: 4054

- Private 4-year liberal arts college
- Residential campus in large town
- 1,292 degree-seeking undergraduates: 47% women, 3% African American, 11% Asian American, 8% Hispanic American, 9% international
- 20 degree-seeking graduate students
- 14% of applicants admitted
- SAT or ACT (ACT writing recommended), application essay required
- 91% graduate within 6 years

General. Founded in 1946. Regionally accredited. One of seven members of The Claremont Colleges, which includes five undergraduate liberal arts colleges (Claremont McKenna, Harvey Mudd, Pitzer, Pomona, and Scripps) and two graduate institutions (Claremont Graduate University and the Keck Graduate Institute for Applied Life Sciences). The campuses share some facilities and cross-enrollment is readily available. **Degrees:** 292 bachelor's awarded; master's offered. **ROTC:** Army, Air Force. **Location:** 35 miles from downtown Los Angeles. **Calendar:** Semester. **Full-time faculty:** 128 total; 97% have terminal degrees, 19% minority, 29% women. **Part-time faculty:** 24 total; 92% have terminal degrees, 8% minority, 33% women. **Class size:** 86% < 20, 11% 20-39, 1% 40-49, 1% 50-99. **Special facilities:** 10 research institutes, athenaeum.

Freshman class profile. 4,481 applied, 623 admitted, 305 enrolled.

Mid 50% test scores			
SAT critical reading:	630-720	Rank in top tenth:	85%
SAT math:	670-760	Return as sophomores:	97%
ACT composite:	29-32	Out-of-state:	61%
Rank in top quarter:	99%	Live on campus:	100%
		International:	16%

Basis for selection. Applications are reviewed on a holistic basis, taking into account academic and personal achievement in the context of each student's educational and home environment. SAT Subject Tests are only required for home schooled applicants; they will not be considered, even if submitted, for all other applicants. **Home schooled:** Interview required.

High school preparation. College-preparatory program recommended. Required and recommended units include English 4, mathematics 3-4, social studies 1, history 1, science 2-3 (laboratory 2) and foreign language 3.

2011-2012 Annual costs. Tuition/fees: $42,240. Room/board: $13,625.

2011-2012 Financial aid. Need-based: 151 full-time freshmen applied for aid; 122 were judged to have need; 122 of these received aid. Average need met was 100%. Average scholarship/grant was $36,530. 98% of total undergraduate aid awarded as scholarships/grants, 2% as loans/jobs. **Non-need-based:** Awarded to 153 full-time undergraduates, including 22 freshmen. Scholarships awarded for academics, leadership.

Application procedures. Admission: Closing date 1/2 (postmark date). $60 fee, may be waived for applicants with need. Admission notification by 4/1. Must reply by 5/1. **Financial aid:** Closing date 2/1. FAFSA, CSS PROFILE required. Applicants notified by 4/1; must reply by 5/1.

Academics. Special study options: Combined bachelor's/graduate degree, cross-registration, double major, ESL, exchange student, independent study, internships, student-designed major, study abroad, Washington semester. **Credit/placement by examination:** AP, CLEP, IB, institutional tests. 4 credit hours maximum toward bachelor's degree. **Support services:** Tutoring, writing center.

Majors. Area/ethnic studies: African, African-American, American, Asian, Asian-American, Chicano/Hispanic-American/Latino, European, gay/lesbian, Latin American, Pacific, regional, South Asian, Southeast Asian, Spanish/Iberian, Western European, women's. **Biology:** General, biochemistry, molecular, neuroscience. **Business:** Accounting, accounting/business management, finance, managerial economics. **Communications:** Media studies. **Computer sciences:** Computer science. **Conservation:** Environmental science, environmental studies. **Engineering:** General. **English:** English lit. **Foreign languages:** Chinese, classics, French, German, Italian, Japanese, Russian, Spanish. **Health services:** Premedicine. **History:** General. **Math:** General. **Philosophy/religion:** Philosophy, religion. **Physical sciences:** Chemistry, physics. **Psychology:** General. **Social sciences:** Economics, international relations, political science. **Visual/performing arts:** Art, dance, dramatic, music.

Most popular majors. Biology 6%, business/marketing 6%, psychology 10%, social sciences 41%.

Computing on campus. Dormitories wired for high-speed internet access and linked to campus network. Commuter students can connect to campus network. Online course registration, online library, helpline, repair service, student web hosting, wireless network available.

Student life. Freshman orientation: Mandatory. Preregistration for classes offered. 5-day program; parents invited for the first day. **Policies:** Freshmen not permitted cars on campus. **Housing:** Guaranteed on-campus for all undergraduates. Coed dorms, special housing for disabled, apartments, wellness housing available. $500 fully refundable deposit, deadline 7/1. **Activities:** Pep band, campus ministries, choral groups, dance, drama, international student organizations, music ensembles, Model UN, radio station, student government, student newspaper, symphony orchestra, debate/forensics, volunteer service, Young Republicans, Young Democrats, Pan-African Students Association, MECHA, Asian American Student Alliance, religious activities center, Intervarsity Faith Team, Hillel.

Athletics. NCAA. **Intercollegiate:** Baseball M, basketball, cross-country, diving, football (tackle) M, golf, lacrosse W, soccer, softball W, swimming, tennis, track and field, volleyball W, water polo. **Intramural:** Archery, badminton, basketball, bowling, fencing, racquetball, rugby, sailing, skiing, soccer, softball, squash, swimming, tennis, track and field, volleyball, water polo, weight lifting. **Team name:** Stags (M), Athenas (W).

Student services. Alcohol/substance abuse counseling, chaplain/spiritual director, career counseling, student employment services, financial aid counseling, health services, minority student services, personal counseling, placement for graduates, women's services. **Physically disabled:** Services for visually, speech, hearing impaired.

Contact. E-mail: admission@cmc.edu
Phone: (909) 621-8088 Fax: (909) 621-8516
Georgette DeVeres, Associate Vice President of Admission & Financial
Aid, Claremont McKenna College, 888 Columbia Avenue, Claremont, CA
91711

Cogswell Polytechnical College
Sunnyvale, California
www.cogswell.edu   CB code: 4057

- Private 4-year visual arts and engineering college
- Commuter campus in small city
- 279 degree-seeking undergraduates: 35% part-time, 16% women, 4%
  African American, 8% Asian American, 16% Hispanic American, 1%
  Native American, 1% international
- 54% of applicants admitted
- Application essay, interview required
- 43% graduate within 6 years

General. Founded in 1887. Regionally accredited. Program fusion of art
and engineering. **Degrees:** 48 bachelor's awarded; master's offered. **Location:**
45 miles from San Francisco, 4 miles from San Jose. **Calendar:** Semester,
extensive summer session. **Full-time faculty:** 11 total; 54% have terminal
degrees, 18% women. **Part-time faculty:** 41 total; 7% have terminal degrees,
20% women. **Class size:** 99% < 20, less than 1% 20-39. **Special facilities:**
Electronic music laboratories, sound/recording studio, video studio, editing
studio, computer imaging laboratories, SGI laboratory, MIDI laboratory, 2D
and 3D animation laboratories.

Freshman class profile. 146 applied, 79 admitted, 45 enrolled.

Mid 50% test scores			
SAT critical reading:	470-560	GPA 3.50-3.74:	7%
SAT math:	490-620	GPA 3.0-3.49:	31%
SAT writing:	440-540	GPA 2.0-2.99:	49%
ACT composite:	16-28	End year in good standing:	58%
GPA 3.75 or higher:	12%	Return as sophomores:	67%
		Out-of-state:	14%

Basis for selection. Motivation, 2.7 GPA in academic subjects, test scores
most important. Recommendations, art portfolio required for art programs,
personal essay. SAT or ACT recommended. Portfolio required for all digital
art programs. **Home schooled:** Transcript of courses and grades, state high
school equivalency certificate, interview, letter of recommendation (nonparent) required. **Learning Disabled:** Must be documented by medical/psycho-
logical professional.

High school preparation. College-preparatory program recommended.
7 units required. Required and recommended units include English 3, mathematics 3, science 1 (laboratory 1), computer science 1 and visual/performing
arts 1. 1 algebra, 1 geometry, 1 trigonometry required for engineering program; 1 algebra, 1 geometry required for art programs.

2012-2013 Annual costs. Tuition/fees (projected): $24,540. Room only:
$6,000. Books/supplies: $1,656. Personal expenses: $2,277.

2011-2012 Financial aid. Need-based: 57% of total undergraduate aid
awarded as scholarships/grants, 43% as loans/jobs. **Non-need-based:** Scholarships awarded for academics.

Application procedures. Admission: No deadline. No application fee.
Admission notification on a rolling basis. **Financial aid:** Priority date 3/2;
no closing date. FAFSA required. Applicants notified on a rolling basis
starting 4/30; must reply within 4 week(s) of notification.

Academics. Special study options: Distance learning, double major,
exchange student, independent study, internships, student-designed major,
study abroad. **Credit/placement by examination:** AP, CLEP, IB, SAT,
ACT, institutional tests. 18 credit hours maximum toward bachelor's degree.
Support services: Reduced course load, remedial instruction, tutoring.

Majors. Business: Entrepreneurial studies. **Engineering:** Software. **Protective services:** Fire safety technology, fire services admin.

Most popular majors. Engineering/engineering technologies 9%, secu-
rity/protective services 38%, visual/performing arts 57%.

Computing on campus. 164 workstations in library, computer center.
Commuter students can connect to campus network. Online course registration, online library, helpline, wireless network available.

Student life. Freshman orientation: Mandatory. Preregistration for
classes offered. **Housing:** Apartments available. $300 fully refundable
deposit, deadline 7/1. **Activities:** Radio station, student government.

Student services. Alcohol/substance abuse counseling, career counseling,
student employment services, financial aid counseling, personal counseling,
placement for graduates.

Contact. E-mail: admissions@cogswell.edu
Phone: (408) 541-0100 Toll-free number: (800) 264-7955
Fax: (408) 747-0764
Abraham Chacko, Executive Director of Admissions, Cogswell
Polytechnical College, 1175 Bordeaux Drive, Sunnyvale, CA 94089-1299

Coleman University
San Diego, California
www.coleman.edu   CB code: 0955

- Private 4-year technical college
- Commuter campus in very large city
- 583 degree-seeking undergraduates: 13% part-time, 11% women
- 95 degree-seeking graduate students
- Interview required
- 70% graduate within 6 years; 93% enter graduate study

General. Founded in 1963. Accredited by ACICS. **Degrees:** 78 bachelor's,
105 associate awarded; master's offered. **Calendar:** Differs by program. **Full-
time faculty:** 21 total; 14% have terminal degrees, 29% minority, 33%
women. **Part-time faculty:** 51 total; 6% have terminal degrees, 43% minority,
20% women. **Class size:** 96% < 20, 4% 20-39.

Freshman class profile. 80 applied, 80 admitted, 80 enrolled.

Basis for selection. Open admission, but selective for some programs.
Aside from the HS diploma or GED, applicants required to pass an aptitude
test of math and logic. Test scores recommended for placement and credit.
Institutionally administered aptitude test required. Skills test given during
interview.

2011-2012 Annual costs. Tuition/fees: $15,143. Tuition quoted is one
year cost for undergraduate study. Associate's: $35,000. Bachelor's: $58,500.
Master's: $23,100, for full programs.

2011-2012 Financial aid. All financial aid based on need. 67 full-time
freshmen applied for aid; 67 were judged to have need; 67 of these received
aid. Average need met was 84%. Average scholarship/grant was $3,464;
average loan $3,119. 56% of total undergraduate aid awarded as scholarships/
grants, 44% as loans/jobs.

Application procedures. Admission: No deadline. $100 fee. Admission
notification on a rolling basis. **Financial aid:** No deadline. FAFSA, institutional form required. Applicants notified on a rolling basis starting 1/2; must
reply within 1 week(s) of notification.

Academics. University uses inverted curriculum with major taken before
general curriculum. **Special study options:** Accelerated study, combined
bachelor's/graduate degree, cooperative education, distance learning, double
major. **Credit/placement by examination:** AP, CLEP. 36 credit hours maximum toward associate degree, 88 toward bachelor's. **Support services:**
Reduced course load, tutoring, writing center.

Majors. Computer sciences: Computer graphics, networking, programming, security, web page design.

Computing on campus. 390 workstations in library, computer center.
Helpline, wireless network available.

Student life. Freshman orientation: Available. Preregistration for classes
offered. Two sessions held before classes start for new students and international students. **Activities:** International student organizations, student activities committee.

Student services. Career counseling, financial aid counseling, personal
counseling, placement for graduates, veterans' counselor.

Contact. E-mail: admis@coleman.edu
Phone: (858) 499-0202 Toll-free number: (800) 430-2030
Fax: (858) 499-0233
Bobbie Strohm, Director of Admissions, Coleman University, 8888
Balboa Avenue, San Diego, CA 92123

Concordia University
Irvine, California
www.cui.edu

CB member
CB code: 4069

◆ Private 4-year university and liberal arts college affiliated with Lutheran Church - Missouri Synod
◆ Residential campus in small city
◆ 1,622 degree-seeking undergraduates: 5% part-time, 59% women, 3% African American, 5% Asian American, 18% Hispanic American, 4% international
◆ 1,572 degree-seeking graduate students
◆ 76% of applicants admitted
◆ SAT or ACT (ACT writing optional), application essay required
◆ 51% graduate within 6 years

General. Founded in 1972. Regionally accredited. **Degrees:** 362 bachelor's awarded; master's offered. **ROTC:** Army. **Location:** 40 miles from Los Angeles, 80 miles from San Diego. **Calendar:** Semester, limited summer session. **Full-time faculty:** 89 total; 10% minority, 42% women. **Part-time faculty:** 210 total; 14% minority, 43% women. **Class size:** 51% < 20, 45% 20-39, 2% 40-49, 2% 50-99, less than 1% >100. **Special facilities:** Spectroscopy lab.

Freshman class profile. 1,469 applied, 1,116 admitted, 294 enrolled.

Mid 50% test scores			
SAT critical reading:	450-560	GPA 3.0-3.49:	40%
SAT math:	460-570	GPA 2.0-2.99:	20%
SAT writing:	450-570	End year in good standing:	84%
ACT composite:	19-24	Return as sophomores:	72%
GPA 3.75 or higher:	25%	Out-of-state:	17%
GPA 3.50-3.74:	15%	Live on campus:	89%
		International:	6%

Basis for selection. Official secondary school transcript and standardized test scores are most important. Recommendations, involvement, and character/personal qualities are also important. Test scores (Dantes, AP, CLEP) are not used for placement but upon review may be accepted for credit. **Home schooled:** Each file reviewed on individual basis. Some documentation of home school structure, courses and grades, state high school equivalency, and/or personal recommendations may be requested.

High school preparation. College-preparatory program recommended. 12 units required; 6 recommended. Required and recommended units include English 4, mathematics 3, social studies 2, history 2, science 3 (laboratory 2) and foreign language 4. Algebra I and II and geometry specifically required.

2012-2013 Annual costs. Tuition/fees: $28,500. Room/board: $8,760. Books/supplies: $1,650. Personal expenses: $2,270.

2011-2012 Financial aid. Need-based: 267 full-time freshmen applied for aid; 225 were judged to have need; 225 of these received aid. Average need met was 66%. Average scholarship/grant was $14,747; average loan $3,320. 75% of total undergraduate aid awarded as scholarships/grants, 25% as loans/jobs. **Non-need-based:** Awarded to 405 full-time undergraduates, including 90 freshmen. Scholarships awarded for academics, athletics, music/drama, religious affiliation.

Application procedures. Admission: Priority date 12/1; no deadline. $50 fee, may be waived for applicants with need, free for online applicants. Admission notification on a rolling basis beginning on or about 12/15. Must reply by May 1 or within 4 week(s) if notified thereafter. **Financial aid:** Priority date 3/2, closing date 3/2. FAFSA required. Applicants notified on a rolling basis starting 3/15; must reply within 4 week(s) of notification.

Academics. Special study options: Accelerated study, distance learning, double major, exchange student, honors, independent study, internships, student-designed major, study abroad, teacher certification program. **Credit/placement by examination:** AP, CLEP, IB. 32 credit hours maximum toward bachelor's degree. **Support services:** Learning center, reduced course load, study skills assistance, tutoring, writing center.

Majors. Biology: General. **Business:** Business admin. **Communications:** General. **English:** English lit. **Foreign languages:** Biblical. **Health services:** Athletic training, health care admin, nursing (RN). **History:** General. **Liberal arts:** Arts/sciences, humanities. **Math:** General. **Parks/recreation:** Health/fitness. **Philosophy/religion:** Religion. **Physical sciences:** Chemistry. **Psychology:** General. **Social sciences:** Economics, political science. **Theology:** Religious ed, theology. **Visual/performing arts:** Art, dramatic, graphic design, music.

Most popular majors. Business/marketing 20%, communications/journalism 9%, health sciences 15%, liberal arts 20%, parks/recreation 9%, visual/performing arts 6%.

Computing on campus. 100 workstations in dormitories, library, computer center, student center. Dormitories wired for high-speed internet access and linked to campus network. Commuter students can connect to campus network. Online course registration, online library, helpline, wireless network available.

Student life. Freshman orientation: Mandatory, $100 fee. Preregistration for classes offered. Orientation events held in summer and fall before start of classes. **Housing:** Guaranteed on-campus for freshmen. Coed dorms, special housing for disabled, wellness housing available. $300 nonrefundable deposit, deadline 6/30. **Activities:** Bands, campus ministries, choral groups, drama, international student organizations, literary magazine, music ensembles, musical theater, student government, student newspaper, Nuestra Voz, Improve Club, Republican Club, math club, sports medicine club, Fellowship of Christian Athletes, ethics club, Cross Cultural Link.

Athletics. NAIA. **Intercollegiate:** Baseball M, basketball, cross-country, soccer, softball W, swimming, tennis, track and field, volleyball W, water polo. **Intramural:** Basketball, bowling, football (non-tackle), soccer, softball, track and field, volleyball. **Team name:** Eagles.

Student services. Adult student services, alcohol/substance abuse counseling, chaplain/spiritual director, career counseling, financial aid counseling, health services, minority student services, personal counseling.

Contact. E-mail: admission@cui.edu
Phone: (949) 214-3010 Toll-free number: (800) 229-1200 ext. 3010
Fax: (949) 854-6894
Rick Hardy, Associate Vice President for Enrollment Management, Concordia University, 1530 Concordia West, Irvine, CA 92612-3203

Design Institute of San Diego
San Diego, California
www.disd.edu

CB code: 3492

◆ For-profit 4-year career college
◆ Very large city
◆ 370 degree-seeking undergraduates
◆ Application essay, interview required

General. Accredited by ACICS. **Degrees:** 76 bachelor's awarded. **Calendar:** Semester, limited summer session. **Full-time faculty:** 6 total. **Part-time faculty:** 57 total.

Basis for selection. High school/college grades, 2 professional references considered.

2011-2012 Annual costs. Tuition/fees: $18,605.

Application procedures. Admission: No deadline. $25 fee. Admission notification on a rolling basis. **Financial aid:** No deadline. Applicants notified on a rolling basis.

Academics. Credit/placement by examination: AP, CLEP.

Majors. Visual/performing arts: Interior design.

Contact. Phone: (858) 566-1200 Toll-free number: (800) 619-4337
Fax: (858) 566-2711
Paula Parrish, Director of Admissions, Design Institute of San Diego, 8555 Commerce Avenue, San Diego, CA 92121

DeVry University: Pomona
Pomona, California
www.devry.edu

CB code: 4214

◆ For-profit 4-year university
◆ Commuter campus in small city
◆ 2,566 degree-seeking undergraduates
◆ Interview required

General. Founded in 1983. Regionally accredited. Additional locations: Colton, Alhambra, Long Beach, Anaheim, Irvine, Sherman Oaks, Palmdale, Fremont, Daly City, Oakland City, San Jose, Fresno, Bakersfield, Sacramento, San Diego. **Degrees:** 295 bachelor's, 77 associate awarded; master's offered. **Location:** 13 miles from Los Angeles. **Calendar:** Semester, extensive summer session. **Full-time faculty:** 21 total; 48% minority. **Part-time faculty:** 86 total; 58% minority.

Basis for selection. Applicant must have high school diploma or equivalent, degree from an accredited postsecondary institution, or submit acceptable test scores and be at least 17 years of age on the first day of classes. New students may enter at beginning of any semester. SAT/ACT considered but not required for admission. If applicant chooses not to submit either, must take an institution-administered admissions test.

High school preparation. College-preparatory program recommended.

2011-2012 Annual costs. Tuition/fees: $15,294. Books/supplies: $1,310. Personal expenses: $3,574.

Financial aid. All financial aid based on need.

Application procedures. Admission: No deadline. $50 fee. Admission notification on a rolling basis. **Financial aid:** No deadline. FAFSA required. Applicants notified on a rolling basis.

Academics. Special study options: Accelerated study, distance learning. **Credit/placement by examination:** AP, CLEP, institutional tests. **Support services:** Learning center, remedial instruction, tutoring.

Majors. Business: General. **Computer sciences:** General, networking. **Visual/performing arts:** Game design.

Most popular majors. Business/marketing 63%, computer/information sciences 22%, engineering/engineering technologies 15%.

Computing on campus. 517 workstations in library, computer center. Online course registration, online library, helpline available.

Student life. Freshman orientation: Mandatory. Preregistration for classes offered. **Housing:** Private apartments, student-plan housing, private rooms available. **Activities:** Gaming association, Institute for Electrical and Electronic Engineers, Living in Truth, National Society of Black Engineers, Phi Beta Lambda, Society of Hispanic Professional Engineers, networking professional association, Toastmasters.

Student services. Career counseling, student employment services, financial aid counseling, placement for graduates, veterans' counselor. **Physically disabled:** Services for visually, hearing impaired.

Contact. Phone: (909) 622-8866
Jere Thrasher, Director of Admissions, DeVry University: Pomona, 901 Corporate Center Drive, Pomona, CA 91768-2642

Dominican University of California
San Rafael, California   **CB member**
www.dominican.edu   **CB code: 4284**

- Private 4-year university
- Residential campus in small city
- 1,637 degree-seeking undergraduates: 17% part-time, 73% women, 4% African American, 19% Asian American, 19% Hispanic American, 1% Native American, 2% international
- 600 degree-seeking graduate students
- 54% of applicants admitted
- SAT or ACT with writing, application essay required
- 46% graduate within 6 years

General. Founded in 1890. Regionally accredited. **Degrees:** 305 bachelor's awarded; master's offered. **Location:** 12 miles from San Francisco. **Calendar:** Semester, limited summer session. **Full-time faculty:** 99 total; 74% have terminal degrees, 13% minority, 61% women. **Part-time faculty:** 272 total; 43% have terminal degrees, 12% minority, 64% women. **Class size:** 63% < 20, 35% 20-39, 1% 40-49, less than 1% 50-99. **Special facilities:** Heritage and alumni house, NORS-DUC (National Ornamental Research Site at Dominican University of California).

Freshman class profile. 3,093 applied, 1,662 admitted, 279 enrolled.

Mid 50% test scores			
SAT critical reading:	470-570	**Rank in top quarter:**	56%
SAT math:	480-590	**Rank in top tenth:**	29%
ACT composite:	22-25	**End year in good standing:**	6%
GPA 3.75 or higher:	27%	**Return as sophomores:**	84%
GPA 3.50-3.74:	29%	**Out-of-state:**	9%
GPA 3.0-3.49:	31%	**Live on campus:**	85%
GPA 2.0-2.99:	13%	**International:**	3%

Basis for selection. School achievement record, test scores, rigor of secondary school record, character/qualities most important. Interview recommended for borderline applicants. Audition recommended for music majors.

Portfolio recommended for art majors. **Home schooled:** State high school equivalency certificate required.

High school preparation. College-preparatory program recommended. 11 units required; 15 recommended. Required and recommended units include English 4, mathematics 2-3, history 1-2, science 1-2 (laboratory 1) and foreign language 2.

2011-2012 Annual costs. Tuition/fees: $37,350. Room/board: $14,460. Books/supplies: $1,656. Personal expenses: $2,277.

2010-2011 Financial aid. Need-based: 322 full-time freshmen applied for aid; 291 were judged to have need; 291 of these received aid. Average need met was 66%. Average scholarship/grant was $23,669; average loan $4,099. 67% of total undergraduate aid awarded as scholarships/grants, 33% as loans/jobs. **Non-need-based:** Awarded to 163 full-time undergraduates, including 49 freshmen. Scholarships awarded for academics, alumni affiliation, athletics, leadership, minority status, music/drama. **Additional information:** 4-year guarantee program.

Application procedures. Admission: Priority date 2/1; no deadline. $40 fee, may be waived for applicants with need, free for online applicants. Admission notification on a rolling basis beginning on or about 10/15. Must reply by May 1 or within 4 week(s) if notified thereafter. **Financial aid:** Priority date 3/2; no closing date. FAFSA, institutional form required. Applicants notified on a rolling basis starting 3/15; must reply within 2 week(s) of notification.

Academics. Special study options: Accelerated study, combined bachelor's/graduate degree, cross-registration, distance learning, double major, dual enrollment of high school students, exchange student, honors, independent study, internships, student-designed major, study abroad, teacher certification program, weekend college. Pathways program (evening/weekend degree program for working adults), semester available at Aquinas College (MI), St. Thomas Aquinas College (NY), Barry University (FL), cross-registration with University of California, Berkeley, (4+1 humanities, occupational therapy, BA - MBA), liberal studies + multiple subject credential. **Credit/placement by examination:** AP, CLEP, IB, SAT, ACT, institutional tests. No more than 30 units from one of the following sources: CLEP/Regents College Exams, ACE/PONSI review courses, experiential learning portfolios. No more than 12 units from challenging courses. No more than 38 units from NLN exams. **Support services:** Learning center, reduced course load, remedial instruction, study skills assistance, tutoring, writing center.

Majors. Area/ethnic studies: Women's. **Biology:** General, molecular. **Business:** Business admin. **Communications:** Communications/speech/rhetoric. **English:** Creative writing, English lit. **Health services:** Nursing (RN). **History:** General. **Liberal arts:** Arts/sciences, humanities. **Philosophy/religion:** Religion. **Physical sciences:** Chemistry. **Psychology:** General. **Social sciences:** Political science. **Visual/performing arts:** Art, art history/conservation, dance, graphic design, music.

Most popular majors. Biology 10%, business/marketing 13%, health sciences 36%, liberal arts 13%, psychology 10%, visual/performing arts 8%.

Computing on campus. 260 workstations in library, computer center, student center. Dormitories wired for high-speed internet access and linked to campus network. Commuter students can connect to campus network. Helpline, repair service, wireless network available.

Student life. Freshman orientation: Available. Preregistration for classes offered. Fall program held week prior to start of classes. **Housing:** Coed dorms, wellness housing available. $500 fully refundable deposit, deadline 5/1. **Activities:** Jazz band, campus ministries, choral groups, dance, drama, international student organizations, literary magazine, music ensembles, musical theater, radio station, student government, student newspaper, STAND, Dominican Republican Women, ASDU, black student union, Latinos of the Americas, Men's Bible Study, BASIC, Women's Bible Study.

Athletics. NCAA. **Intercollegiate:** Basketball, cross-country M, golf, lacrosse M, soccer, softball W, tennis W, volleyball W. **Intramural:** Cheerleading W. **Team name:** Penguins.

Student services. Adult student services, alcohol/substance abuse counseling, chaplain/spiritual director, career counseling, student employment services, financial aid counseling, health services, personal counseling, veterans' counselor, women's services. **Physically disabled:** Services for visually impaired.

Contact. E-mail: enroll@dominican.edu
Phone: (415) 485-3204 Toll-free number: (888) 323-6763
Fax: (415) 485-3214
Rebecca Finn Kenney, Assistant Vice President Undergraduate Admissions, Dominican University of California, 50 Acacia Avenue, San Rafael, CA 94901-2298

Ex'pression College for Digital Arts
Emeryville, California
www.expression.edu

- For-profit 4-year visual arts and technical college
- Commuter campus in large town
- 1,015 degree-seeking undergraduates
- 96% of applicants admitted

General. Accredited by ACCSC. The Ex'pression bachelor's degree is accelerated, and may be earned in 2½ years. **Degrees:** 280 bachelor's awarded. **Location:** 10 miles from San Francisco. **Calendar:** Semester, extensive summer session. **Full-time faculty:** 56 total. **Part-time faculty:** 57 total. **Special facilities:** 100,000 square foot facility of professional-grade equipment and studios.

Freshman class profile. 75 applied, 72 admitted, 66 enrolled.

Basis for selection. Applicants to visual arts programs (animation and visual effects, game art & design and motion graphic design) required to complete either on-site drawing test, or submit 3 sketches of their hand holding an object of their choice.

2012-2013 Annual costs. Tuition/fees: $23,072.

Application procedures. Admission: No deadline. $95 fee. **Financial aid:** No deadline.

Academics. Special study options: Accelerated study, liberal arts/career combination. **Credit/placement by examination:** AP, CLEP. **Support services:** Pre-admission summer program, study skills assistance, tutoring.

Majors. Communications technology: Animation/special effects, graphics, photo/film/video. **Computer sciences:** Computer graphics, modeling/simulation, web page design. **Visual/performing arts:** Cinematography, digital arts, game design, graphic design.

Computing on campus. Student web hosting available.

Student life. Freshman orientation: Mandatory. Preregistration for classes offered. Held 2 days before classes begin. **Housing:** Apartments available. **Activities:** Radio station, student government, student newspaper.

Student services. Career counseling, financial aid counseling, personal counseling. **Physically disabled:** Services for hearing impaired.

Contact. E-mail: admissions@expression.edu
Phone: (510) 654-2934 Toll-free number: (877) 833-8800
Chitvan Nayyar, Director of Admissions, Ex'pression College for Digital Arts, 6601 Shellmound Street, Emeryville, CA 94608

Fresno Pacific University
Fresno, California   **CB member**
www.fresno.edu   **CB code: 4616**

- Private 4-year university and liberal arts college affiliated with Mennonite Brethren Church
- Residential campus in large city
- 2,523 degree-seeking undergraduates
- 45% of applicants admitted
- SAT and SAT Subject Tests or ACT (ACT writing optional) required

General. Founded in 1944. Regionally accredited. **Degrees:** 741 bachelor's awarded; master's offered. **Location:** 150 miles from San Francisco. **Calendar:** Semester, limited summer session. **Full-time faculty:** 104 total; 47% have terminal degrees, 9% minority. **Part-time faculty:** 10 total. **Class size:** 72% < 20, 22% 20-39, 5% 40-49, less than 1% 50-99, less than 1% >100. **Special facilities:** Mennonite brethren studies center, conflict studies and peacemaking center.

Freshman class profile. 642 applied, 289 admitted, 248 enrolled.

Mid 50% test scores			
SAT critical reading:	430-530	GPA 3.0-3.49:	32%
SAT math:	450-560	GPA 2.0-2.99:	20%
SAT writing:	450-550	Rank in top quarter:	69%
ACT composite:	18-26	Rank in top tenth:	32%
GPA 3.75 or higher:	31%	Out-of-state:	5%
GPA 3.50-3.74:	16%	Live on campus:	66%

Basis for selection. School achievement record and test scores very important, minimum 3.1 high school GPA. Recommendations, autobiography

also considered. Interview recommended for academically weak applicants. Auditions for music, English (with drama emphasis) majors.

High school preparation. 13 units required. Required units include English 4, mathematics 3, social studies 2, science 1 (laboratory 1) and foreign language 2. One year of visual or performing arts.

2011-2012 Annual costs. Tuition/fees: $24,790. Room/board: $6,440. Books/supplies: $1,656. Personal expenses: $2,277.

Financial aid. Non-need-based: Scholarships awarded for academics, athletics, music/drama.

Application procedures. Admission: Priority date 12/1; deadline 7/31 (postmark date). $40 fee, may be waived for applicants with need. Admission notification on a rolling basis beginning on or about 12/1. **Financial aid:** Priority date 3/2; no closing date. FAFSA, institutional form required. Applicants notified on a rolling basis starting 3/2; must reply by 7/30 or within 3 week(s) of notification.

Academics. Special study options: Accelerated study, distance learning, double major, dual enrollment of high school students, ESL, exchange student, independent study, internships, student-designed major, study abroad, teacher certification program, Washington semester. **Credit/placement by examination:** AP, CLEP, IB. 30 credit hours maximum toward associate degree, 30 toward bachelor's. **Support services:** Learning center, reduced course load, remedial instruction, study skills assistance, tutoring, writing center.

Majors. Biology: General. **Business:** General, accounting, business admin, human resources, international, management information systems, marketing, nonprofit/public, organizational behavior. **Communications:** Communications/speech/rhetoric. **Computer sciences:** Computer science. **Conservation:** Environmental science, environmental studies. **Education:** Biology, business, elementary, English, mathematics, music, physical, science, social science. **English:** Creative writing. **Foreign languages:** Spanish. **Health services:** Athletic training, premedicine. **History:** General. **Human services:** Social work. **Liberal arts:** Arts/sciences. **Math:** General, applied. **Parks/recreation:** Health/fitness, sports admin. **Philosophy/religion:** Philosophy. **Physical sciences:** Chemistry. **Protective services:** Criminalistics. **Psychology:** General. **Social sciences:** General, political science, sociology. **Theology:** Bible. **Visual/performing arts:** Art, dramatic, music, music performance, music theory/composition.

Most popular majors. Business/marketing 38%, education 36%.

Computing on campus. 90 workstations in dormitories, library, computer center, student center. Dormitories wired for high-speed internet access and linked to campus network. Commuter students can connect to campus network. Online course registration, helpline, student web hosting, wireless network available.

Student life. Freshman orientation: Mandatory. Preregistration for classes offered. 4-day fall orientation, 1-day spring. **Housing:** Single-sex dorms, special housing for disabled, apartments, wellness housing available. $200 nonrefundable deposit, deadline 6/1. Several college-rented apartments available nearby. Resident freshmen under age 23 required to live on campus. **Activities:** Bands, choral groups, dance, drama, international student organizations, music ensembles, student government, student newspaper, Summer Harvest, Shalom Covenant, Kids Klub, Amigos Unidos, Students In Free Enterprise, student chaplains, Daughters of Christ, Faith Project, social work club.

Athletics. NAIA. **Intercollegiate:** Baseball M, basketball, cross-country, soccer, swimming, tennis, track and field, volleyball W, water polo. **Intramural:** Basketball, bowling, football (non-tackle), racquetball, soccer, table tennis, volleyball. **Team name:** Sunbirds.

Student services. Adult student services, alcohol/substance abuse counseling, chaplain/spiritual director, career counseling, student employment services, financial aid counseling, health services, personal counseling. **Physically disabled:** Services for visually, hearing impaired.

Contact. E-mail: ugadmis@fresno.edu
Phone: (559) 453-2039 Toll-free number: (800) 660-6089
Fax: (559) 453-2007
Rina Campbell, Director of Undergraduate Admissions, Fresno Pacific University, 1717 South Chestnut Avenue, Fresno, CA 93702-4709

Golden Gate University
San Francisco, California
www.ggu.edu   **CB code: 4329**

- Private 4-year university
- Commuter campus in very large city

♦ 436 degree-seeking undergraduates
♦ 3,095 graduate students

General. Founded in 1853. Regionally accredited. Evening and weekend degree programs available in San Francisco, Silicon Valley, Los Angeles, and Seattle. Program length differs by location. **Degrees:** 132 bachelor's awarded; master's, professional, doctoral offered. **Calendar:** Trimester, extensive summer session. **Full-time faculty:** 71 total; 35% women. **Part-time faculty:** 313 total; 27% women. **Class size:** 96% < 20, 4% 20-39.

Basis for selection. School achievement record most important. Work history or military service factor in determining admission of adult students. SAT recommended. Interviews recommended for undecided major applicants.

High school preparation. 14 units recommended. Recommended units include English 4, mathematics 3, social studies 1, history 1, science 2 (laboratory 1) and foreign language 2.

2011-2012 Annual costs. Tuition/fees: $17,400.

Financial aid. All financial aid based on need.

Application procedures. Admission: Priority date 7/1; no deadline. $55 fee. Admission notification on a rolling basis. Students may be admitted up to 1 year (3 trimesters) before they intend to enroll. **Financial aid:** Priority date 1/2; no closing date. FAFSA, institutional form required. Applicants notified on a rolling basis; must reply within 3 week(s) of notification.

Academics. Professional degree, certification, and lifelong learning programs in business, law, tax, technology and related professions. **Special study options:** Accelerated study, distance learning, ESL, independent study, internships, study abroad. **Credit/placement by examination:** AP, CLEP, IB, institutional tests. **Support services:** Reduced course load, tutoring, writing center.

Majors. Business: Accounting, business admin, finance, human resources, information resources management, international, marketing, operations. **Computer sciences:** Information technology.

Computing on campus. 300 workstations in library, computer center. Commuter students can connect to campus network. Online course registration, online library, wireless network available.

Student life. Activities: Student government, student newspaper, Phi Alpha Delta law fraternity, Chi Pi Alpha, Indonesian students organization, Malayan students association, Chinese students club, Indian student association, Korean student association, American Marketing Association, Toastmasters.

Student services. Adult student services, career counseling, student employment services, personal counseling, veterans' counselor. **Physically disabled:** Services for visually, speech, hearing impaired.

Contact. E-mail: info@ggu.edu
Phone: (415) 442-7800 Fax: (415) 442-7807
Louis Riccardi, Director of Enrollment Services, Golden Gate University, 536 Mission Street, San Francisco, CA 94105-2968

Harvey Mudd College
Claremont, California
www.hmc.edu

CB member
CB code: 4341

♦ Private 4-year engineering and liberal arts college
♦ Residential campus in small city
♦ 777 degree-seeking undergraduates: 42% women, 1% African American, 21% Asian American, 6% Hispanic American, 1% Native American, 7% international
♦ 22% of applicants admitted
♦ SAT or ACT with writing, SAT Subject Tests, application essay required
♦ 84% graduate within 6 years; 35% enter graduate study

General. Founded in 1955. Regionally accredited. Member of consortium of 5 undergraduate and 2 graduate schools on adjoining campuses. Campuses share facilities and cross-enrollment is available within the 5 undergraduate colleges, which include Claremont-McKenna, Harvey Mudd, Pitzer, Pomona, and Scripps. **Degrees:** 181 bachelor's awarded. **ROTC:** Army, Air Force. **Location:** 35 miles from Los Angeles. **Calendar:** Semester, limited summer session. **Full-time faculty:** 87 total; 100% have terminal degrees, 23% minority, 38% women. **Part-time faculty:** 20 total; 100% have terminal degrees, 15% minority, 45% women. **Class size:** 62% < 20, 26% 20-39, 4% 40-49, 6% 50-99, 2% >100. **Special facilities:** Observatory, biological field station, high performance parallel processor.

Freshman class profile. 2,957 applied, 660 admitted, 194 enrolled.

Mid 50% test scores		Rank in top tenth:	95%
SAT critical reading:	690-770	Return as sophomores:	98%
SAT math:	740-800	Out-of-state:	60%
SAT writing:	690-770	Live on campus:	100%
ACT composite:	32-35	International:	10%
Rank in top quarter:	100%		

Basis for selection. School achievement record important, especially in mathematics and science. Test scores, recommendations, school and community activities important. Students required to take SAT or ACT with writing; must also submit SAT Subject Tests in Math Level 2 and another subject of their choice. Interviews highly recommended. **Home schooled:** Portfolio suggested describing texts used, curriculum format, how instruction was given. Recommend lab science and foreign language courses be taken at high school or college.

High school preparation. College-preparatory program required. Required and recommended units include English 4, mathematics 3-4, social studies 2, history 1-2, science 3-4 (laboratory 2) and foreign language 2. 1 year calculus, 1 year chemistry, 1 year physics required.

2011-2012 Annual costs. Tuition/fees: $42,410. Room/board: $13,858. Books/supplies: $800. Personal expenses: $900.

2010-2011 Financial aid. Need-based: 134 full-time freshmen applied for aid; 100 were judged to have need; 100 of these received aid. Average need met was 100%. Average scholarship/grant was $32,835; average loan $3,333. 82% of total undergraduate aid awarded as scholarships/grants, 18% as loans/jobs. **Non-need-based:** Awarded to 405 full-time undergraduates, including 90 freshmen. Scholarships awarded for academics. **Additional information:** Students can use 100% of their outside awards toward first reducing the need-based portion of their student loans and/or Federal Work Study award. Once need-based student loans and/or Federal Work Study award have been completely eliminated, any additional outside scholarships may reduce need-based Harvey Mudd Scholarship only. However, to maximize financial aid eligibility, students may retain need-based student loans and/or Federal Work Study award up to their federal need.

Application procedures. Admission: Closing date 1/2 (postmark date). $60 fee, may be waived for applicants with need. Admission notification by 4/1. Must reply by May 1 or within 2 week(s) if notified thereafter. **Financial aid:** Closing date 2/1. FAFSA, CSS PROFILE required. Applicants notified by 4/1; must reply by 5/1 or within 2 week(s) of notification.

Academics. Course work divided equally between technical core, major, and humanities and social sciences. **Special study options:** Combined bachelor's/graduate degree, cross-registration, double major, exchange student, independent study, internships, liberal arts/career combination, student-designed major, study abroad. Applied engineering, mathematics and computer science clinics, 4+1 BS/MBA with Claremont Graduate University. **Credit/placement by examination:** AP, CLEP, institutional tests. **Support services:** Learning center, reduced course load, study skills assistance, tutoring, writing center.

Majors. Biology: General, computational. **Computer sciences:** General. **Engineering:** General. **Math:** General, applied. **Physical sciences:** Chemistry, physics.

Most popular majors. Computer/information sciences 12%, engineering/engineering technologies 42%, mathematics 12%, physical sciences 22%.

Computing on campus. Dormitories wired for high-speed internet access and linked to campus network. Commuter students can connect to campus network. Online course registration, online library, helpline, repair service, student web hosting, wireless network available.

Student life. Freshman orientation: Mandatory. Preregistration for classes offered. 5-day residential introduction. **Policies:** Student-directed honor code governs academic and nonacademic life on campus. Freshmen not permitted cars on campus. **Housing:** Guaranteed on-campus for freshmen. Coed dorms, apartments available. $150 partly refundable deposit, deadline 5/1. Pets allowed in dorm rooms. **Activities:** Bands, campus ministries, choral groups, dance, drama, film society, international student organizations, literary magazine, music ensembles, musical theater, radio station, student government, student newspaper, symphony orchestra, TV station, InterVarsity Christian Fellowship, Hillel, Society of Women Engineers, PRISM, API-SPAM, Muslim student association, Society of Hispanic Engineers, National Society of Black Engineers, Mudders Making A Difference, Engineers for a Sustainable World.

Athletics. NCAA. **Intercollegiate:** Baseball M, basketball, cross-country, diving, football (tackle) M, golf, lacrosse W, soccer, softball W, swimming, tennis, track and field, volleyball W, water polo. **Intramural:** Basketball, football (tackle), soccer, softball, table tennis, tennis, volleyball, water polo. **Team name:** Athenas/Stags.

Student services. Alcohol/substance abuse counseling, chaplain/spiritual director, career counseling, student employment services, financial aid counseling, health services, minority student services, personal counseling, placement for graduates, women's services.

Contact. E-mail: admission@hmc.edu
Phone: (909) 621-8011 Fax: (909) 607-7046
Peter Osgood, Director of Admission, Harvey Mudd College, 301 Platt Boulevard, Claremont, CA 91711-5901

Holy Names University
Oakland, California   **CB member**
www.hnu.edu   **CB code: 4059**

- Private 4-year university affiliated with Roman Catholic Church
- Commuter campus in large city
- 728 degree-seeking undergraduates: 21% part-time, 72% women, 25% African American, 10% Asian American, 23% Hispanic American, 1% Native American, 4% international
- 486 degree-seeking graduate students
- 64% of applicants admitted
- SAT or ACT (ACT writing optional), application essay required
- 39% graduate within 6 years

General. Founded in 1868. Regionally accredited; master's offered. **Degrees:** 103 bachelor's awarded; master's offered. **ROTC:** Army, Air Force. **Location:** 14 miles from San Francisco. **Calendar:** Semester, limited summer session. **Full-time faculty:** 42 total; 76% have terminal degrees, 14% minority, 64% women. **Part-time faculty:** 109 total; 11% have terminal degrees, 14% minority, 60% women. **Class size:** 70% < 20, 30% 20-39. **Special facilities:** Folk music collection, institute for learning disabled.

Freshman class profile. 669 applied, 428 admitted, 126 enrolled.

Mid 50% test scores			
SAT critical reading:	410-500	GPA 3.0-3.49:	43%
SAT math:	420-500	GPA 2.0-2.99:	38%
SAT writing:	400-510	End year in good standing:	90%
ACT composite:	17-21	Return as sophomores:	72%
GPA 3.75 or higher:	9%	Out-of-state:	10%
GPA 3.50-3.74:	10%	Live on campus:	85%
		International:	7%

Basis for selection. Overall strength of high school preparation, SAT or ACT scores, personal essay, letter of recommendation, extracurricular activities and individual talents and achievements. For non-native English speakers, ESL Center proficiency report certifying completion of Level 107 or higher may be substituted for TOEFL. Proficiency exams in theory, sight-singing, dictation and piano are required of all students entering the music program. Exams offered during week prior to beginning of each semester. Music major applicant must also audition for faculty jury. **Home schooled:** Transcript of courses and grades, letter of recommendation (nonparent) required. Transcript demonstrating completion of basic credit hours for high school along with short evaluation from primary instructor. May require additional portfolio or performance-based assessments to document competency.

High school preparation. College-preparatory program recommended. 15 units required. Required and recommended units include English 4, mathematics 3, history 1-2, science 1-2 (laboratory 1), foreign language 2-3 and academic electives 3. U.S. history or government required, plus 1 additional year of math, foreign language, or lab science.

2011-2012 Annual costs. Tuition/fees: $30,390. Room/board: $10,260.

2010-2011 Financial aid. Non-need-based: Scholarships awarded for academics, athletics, leadership, music/drama, religious affiliation.

Application procedures. Admission: Priority date 3/2; deadline 8/15 (postmark date). No application fee. Admission notification on a rolling basis beginning on or about 10/1. Must reply by May 1 or within 2 week(s) if notified thereafter. **Financial aid:** Priority date 3/2; no closing date. FAFSA required. Applicants notified on a rolling basis starting 9/1; must reply by 5/1 or within 2 week(s) of notification.

Academics. All undergraduate students must satisfy general education requirements. First component is Foundation in Critical Thinking and Communication. Remaining components use thematic and disciplinary approaches to learning. **Special study options:** Accelerated study, combined bachelor's/graduate degree, cross-registration, distance learning, double major, ESL, exchange student, independent study, internships, liberal arts/career combination, student-designed major, study abroad, teacher certification program, weekend college. **Credit/placement by examination:** AP, CLEP, IB, institutional tests. 6 credit hours maximum toward bachelor's degree. Maximum of 6 credit hours per general exam awarded. **Support services:** Learning

center, reduced course load, remedial instruction, study skills assistance, tutoring, writing center.

Majors. Biology: General. **Business:** Business admin, communications, human resources, international, marketing. **Communications:** Digital media. **English:** English lit. **Foreign languages:** Spanish. **Health services:** Nursing (RN). **History:** General. **Liberal arts:** Arts/sciences, humanities. **Parks/recreation:** Sports admin. **Philosophy/religion:** Philosophy, religion. **Psychology:** General, psychobiology. **Social sciences:** Criminology, international relations, sociology. **Visual/performing arts:** Music, music pedagogy, music performance.

Most popular majors. Business/marketing 33%, health sciences 12%, liberal arts 11%, psychology 14%, social sciences 9%.

Computing on campus. 100 workstations in dormitories, library, computer center, student center. Dormitories wired for high-speed internet access and linked to campus network. Online course registration, online library, helpline, wireless network available.

Student life. Freshman orientation: Mandatory, $50 fee. Preregistration for classes offered. 2-3 day weekend event prior to start of term. **Housing:** Guaranteed on-campus for all undergraduates. Coed dorms, wellness housing available. $100 fully refundable deposit, deadline 8/18. **Activities:** Campus ministries, choral groups, drama, film society, music ensembles, Model UN, student government, symphony orchestra, Asian Pacific International, Black Student Union, drama club, speech and debate team, Holy Names Construction, Global Outlook, International Village, Latinos Unidos, social justice club.

Athletics. NAIA. **Intercollegiate:** Baseball, basketball, cross-country, golf M, soccer, softball W, tennis, volleyball. **Team name:** Hawks.

Student services. Adult student services, chaplain/spiritual director, career counseling, student employment services, financial aid counseling, personal counseling. **Physically disabled:** Services for visually impaired.

Contact. E-mail: admission@hnu.edu
Phone: (510) 436-1351 Toll-free number: (800) 430-1321
Fax: (510) 436-1325
Brian O'Rourke, Director of Admissions and Recruitment, Holy Names University, 3500 Mountain Boulevard, Oakland, CA 94619-1699

Hope International University
Fullerton, California
www.hiu.edu   **CB code: 4614**

- Private 4-year university and liberal arts college affiliated with Christian Church
- Residential campus in small city
- 964 degree-seeking undergraduates: 23% part-time, 57% women, 7% African American, 3% Asian American, 15% Hispanic American, 1% Native American
- 401 degree-seeking graduate students
- SAT or ACT (ACT writing optional), application essay required
- 31% graduate within 6 years; 15% enter graduate study

General. Founded in 1928. Regionally accredited; also accredited by ABHE. In addition to the campus in Fullerton, CA, there is an extension site in Everett, Washington and we offer over 200 classes online. **Degrees:** 132 bachelor's, 2 associate awarded; master's offered. **Location:** 35 miles from Los Angeles. **Calendar:** Semester, limited summer session. **Full-time faculty:** 36 total; 75% have terminal degrees, 6% minority, 36% women. **Part-time faculty:** 152 total; 41% have terminal degrees, 8% minority, 42% women. **Class size:** 75% < 20, 22% 20-39, 3% 40-49.

Freshman class profile.

GPA 3.75 or higher:	20%	Rank in top tenth:	17%
GPA 3.50-3.74:	8%	End year in good standing:	90%
GPA 3.0-3.49:	37%	Return as sophomores:	67%
GPA 2.0-2.99:	35%	Out-of-state:	20%
Rank in top quarter:	38%	Live on campus:	77%

Basis for selection. Prior academic achievement, standardized test scores, statement of purpose essays, commitment to the mission of the institution and recommendations are important. Extracurricular activities are also considered along with all other factors bearing on potential success. Interviews recommended for academically borderline applicants. **Home schooled:** If schooled under the auspices of an organization that can offer transcripts, the university will accept these transcripts and SAT/ACT scores. If not, a GED score and SAT/ACT scores are required. **Learning Disabled:** All documentation must be recent, within the past three years of enrollment, and must have been

completed by an appropriate professional, e.g., State licensed psychologist or school psychologist. Documentation shall include both appropriate tests of learning abilities as well as interview material.

High school preparation. College-preparatory program recommended. 13.5 units recommended. Recommended units include English 4, mathematics 2, history 1, science 1 (laboratory 1), foreign language 1, computer science .5 and academic electives 3. One half-unit speech and one-half unit computer science or literacy is recommended.

2011-2012 Annual costs. Tuition/fees: $24,080. Room/board: $7,900. Books/supplies: $1,620. Personal expenses: $2,250.

2011-2012 Financial aid. Need-based: 128 full-time freshmen applied for aid; 128 were judged to have need; 124 of these received aid. Average need met was 67%. Average scholarship/grant was $7,530; average loan $4,750. 47% of total undergraduate aid awarded as scholarships/grants, 53% as loans/jobs. **Non-need-based:** Awarded to 578 full-time undergraduates, including 177 freshmen. Scholarships awarded for academics, job skills, leadership, music/drama, state residency.

Application procedures. Admission: Priority date 12/1; deadline 2/1. $40 fee, may be waived for applicants with need. Admission notification on a rolling basis. **Financial aid:** Closing date 3/2. FAFSA, institutional form required. Applicants notified by 3/2; Applicants notified on a rolling basis starting 3/15; must reply within 2 week(s) of notification.

Academics. Emphasis on field-based interactive learning combined with direct professional involvement with students. **Special study options:** Combined bachelor's/graduate degree, distance learning, double major, ESL, exchange student, external degree, internships, liberal arts/career combination, study abroad, teacher certification program. **Credit/placement by examination:** AP, CLEP, IB, institutional tests. The amount of credit for examinations depends upon the applicability of the exam(s) to the specific degree program requirements. **Support services:** Reduced course load, remedial instruction, study skills assistance, tutoring.

Majors. Business: Business admin. **Education:** Elementary, music, social science. **Health services:** Athletic training. **Psychology:** General. **Social sciences:** General. **Theology:** Bible, missionary, sacred music, theology, youth ministry. **Work/family studies:** Family studies.

Most popular majors. Business/marketing 20%, family/consumer sciences 17%, psychology 8%, theological studies 35%.

Computing on campus. 53 workstations in library, computer center. Dormitories wired for high-speed internet access. Online library, helpline, repair service, wireless network available.

Student life. Freshman orientation: Mandatory, $75 fee. Preregistration for classes offered. Fall and spring new student orientation held 3 days before beginning of term. **Policies:** No alcohol permitted, smoking discouraged. Religious observance required. **Housing:** Guaranteed on-campus for freshmen. Single-sex dorms, wellness housing available. $100 partly refundable deposit, deadline 7/1. Single students required to live on campus until age 21 or reaching junior standing, unless living at home or given special approval. **Activities:** Choral groups, drama, international student organizations, music ensembles, musical theater, student government, student newspaper, school outreach, minority students association, business club, counseling center, fitness center, University Praise.

Athletics. NAIA. **Intercollegiate:** Basketball, cheerleading, soccer, softball W, tennis, volleyball. **Intramural:** Badminton, basketball, football (non-tackle) W, soccer, volleyball. **Team name:** Royals.

Student services. Adult student services, chaplain/spiritual director, career counseling, student employment services, financial aid counseling, health services, personal counseling, veterans' counselor.

Contact. E-mail: PCCAdmissions@hiu.edu
Phone: (714) 879-3901 ext. 2215 Toll-free number: (866) 722-4673
Fax: (714) 681-7423
Butch Ellis, Director of Undergraduate Admissions, Hope International University, 2500 East Nutwood Avenue, Fullerton, CA 92831-3199

Horizon College of San Diego
San Diego, California
www.horizoncollege.org

- Private 4-year Bible and liberal arts college affiliated with nondenominational tradition
- Commuter campus in very large city
- 28 degree-seeking undergraduates: 54% part-time, 29% women

General. Candidate for regional accreditation; also accredited by ABHE. Christ-centered instruction. ADA approved single-story campus. **Degrees:** 4 bachelor's awarded. **Calendar:** Semester, limited summer session. **Part-time faculty:** 11 total; 73% have terminal degrees, 36% minority, 18% women.

Basis for selection. Open admission, but selective for some programs.

2012-2013 Annual costs. Tuition/fees (projected): $6,300. Books/supplies: $500.

Academics. Special study options: Distance learning. **Credit/placement by examination:** AP, CLEP.

Majors. Theology: Bible.

Computing on campus. 2 workstations in library. Wireless network available.

Student life. Freshman orientation: Mandatory. Preregistration for classes offered. **Policies:** Religious observance required. **Activities:** Campus ministries.

Student services. Financial aid counseling, personal counseling.

Contact. E-mail: info@horizoncollege.org
Phone: (858) 695-8587 Fax: (858) 695-9527
Horizon College of San Diego, 5331 Mount Alifan Drive, San Diego, CA 92111

Humboldt State University
Arcata, California — CB member
www.humboldt.edu — CB code: 4345

- Public 4-year university and liberal arts college
- Residential campus in large town
- 7,323 degree-seeking undergraduates: 7% part-time, 53% women, 4% African American, 3% Asian American, 21% Hispanic American, 1% Native American, 1% international
- 583 degree-seeking graduate students
- 93% of applicants admitted
- 40% graduate within 6 years

General. Founded in 1913. Regionally accredited. **Degrees:** 1,364 bachelor's awarded; master's offered. **Location:** 275 miles from San Francisco. **Calendar:** Semester, limited summer session. **Full-time faculty:** 231 total; 99% have terminal degrees, 14% minority, 38% women. **Part-time faculty:** 286 total; 18% have terminal degrees, 13% minority, 62% women. **Class size:** 35% < 20, 42% 20-39, 9% 40-49, 9% 50-99, 4% >100. **Special facilities:** Marine lab, observatory, marsh and wildlife sanctuary, small lakes and ponds, 280-acre sand dune preserve, research vessel, freshwater fish hatchery, small-game animal pen, fungal genetic stock center, 360-acre experimental forest, 170,000 specimen herbarium, center for appropriate technology, energy research center.

Freshman class profile. 9,466 applied, 8,770 admitted, 1,282 enrolled.

Mid 50% test scores			
SAT critical reading:	450-580	GPA 2.0-2.99:	37%
SAT math:	450-560	Rank in top quarter:	39%
SAT writing:	440-570	Rank in top tenth:	11%
ACT composite:	18-24	End year in good standing:	76%
GPA 3.75 or higher:	11%	Return as sophomores:	74%
GPA 3.50-3.74:	12%	Out-of-state:	10%
GPA 3.0-3.49:	40%	Live on campus:	84%

Basis for selection. High school GPA and test scores most important. In-state residents with high school GPA of 3.0 or higher or out-of-state applicants with high school GPA over 3.61 do not have to submit test scores for admission. Essay recommended for academically weak, special consideration applicants. **Home schooled:** Transcript of courses and grades required.

High school preparation. College-preparatory program required. 15 units required. Required units include English 4, mathematics 3, social studies 1, history 1, science 2 (laboratory 2), foreign language 2, visual/performing arts 1 and academic electives 1.

2011-2012 Annual costs. Tuition/fees: $7,084; $18,244 out-of-state. Room/board: $10,486. Books/supplies: $1,544. Personal expenses: $2,744.

Financial aid. Non-need-based: Scholarships awarded for academics, athletics.

Application procedures. Admission: Priority date 10/31; deadline 11/30 (postmark date). $55 fee, may be waived for applicants with need. Admission notification on a rolling basis beginning on or about 12/1. Must reply by 5/1. **Financial aid:** Priority date 3/2; no closing date. FAFSA required. Applicants notified on a rolling basis starting 4/15; must reply within 6 week(s) of notification.

Academics. Indian Teacher and Educational Personnel Program, Indian Natural Resources, Sciences and Engineering Program available. **Special study options:** Cross-registration, distance learning, double major, dual enrollment of high school students, ESL, exchange student, independent study, internships, study abroad, teacher certification program. **Credit/placement by examination:** AP, CLEP, IB, SAT, ACT, institutional tests. 30 credit hours maximum toward bachelor's degree. Humboldt grants undergraduate degree credit for successful completion of non-collegiate instruction, either military or civilian, appropriate to the baccalaureate degree. Credit must be recommended by the Commission on Educational Credit and Credentials of the American Council on Education. **Support services:** Learning center, pre-admission summer program, reduced course load, remedial instruction, study skills assistance, tutoring, writing center.

Majors. Area/ethnic studies: Native American, women's. **Biology:** General, botany, zoology. **Business:** General, business admin. **Communications:** Communications/speech/rhetoric, journalism. **Computer sciences:** Computer science, information technology. **Conservation:** Environmental studies, fisheries, forestry, management/policy, wildlife/wilderness. **Education:** Early childhood, elementary, physical. **Engineering:** Environmental. **English:** English lit, writing. **Foreign languages:** French, Spanish. **General:** Range science. **Health services:** Kinesiotherapy. **History:** General. **Human services:** Social work. **Liberal arts:** Arts/sciences. **Math:** General. **Parks/recreation:** Health/fitness. **Philosophy/religion:** Philosophy, religion. **Physical sciences:** Chemistry, geology, oceanography, physics. **Psychology:** General. **Social sciences:** General, anthropology, economics, geography, political science, sociology. **Visual/performing arts:** Art, dance, dramatic, music.

Most popular majors. Biology 9%, business/marketing 7%, liberal arts 9%, natural resources/environmental science 12%, social sciences 10%, visual/performing arts 11%.

Computing on campus. 1,098 workstations in dormitories, library, computer center, student center. Dormitories wired for high-speed internet access and linked to campus network. Commuter students can connect to campus network. Online course registration, online library, helpline, student web hosting, wireless network available.

Student life. Freshman orientation: Mandatory, $50 fee. Preregistration for classes offered. Student-directed program held in August. **Housing:** Coed dorms, wellness housing available. $500 partly refundable deposit, deadline 4/17. **Activities:** Bands, choral groups, dance, drama, film society, international student organizations, literary magazine, music ensembles, musical theater, radio station, student government, student newspaper, symphony orchestra, Newman Club, Campus Crusade for Christ, Youth Educational Services, black student union, MECHA, Gay, Lesbian and Bisexual Students Association, Native American club, Jewish student union, multicultural center, veterans organization.

Athletics. NCAA. **Intercollegiate:** Basketball, cross-country, football (tackle) M, rowing (crew) W, soccer, softball W, track and field, volleyball W. **Intramural:** Badminton, basketball, football (tackle) M, soccer, softball, volleyball. **Team name:** Lumberjacks.

Student services. Adult student services, alcohol/substance abuse counseling, career counseling, student employment services, financial aid counseling, health services, minority student services, on-campus daycare, personal counseling, placement for graduates, veterans' counselor, women's services. **Physically disabled:** Services for visually, speech, hearing impaired.

Contact. E-mail: hsuinfo@humboldt.edu
Phone: (707) 826-4402 Toll-free number: (866) 850-9556
Fax: (707) 826-6190
Scott Hagg, Director of Admissions and Student Recruitment, Humboldt State University, One Harpst Street, Arcata, CA 95521-8299

Humphreys College
Stockton, California
www.humphreys.edu   CB code: 4346

- Private 4-year business and liberal arts college
- Residential campus in large city
- 995 degree-seeking undergraduates
- 42% of applicants admitted
- Interview required

General. Founded in 1896. Regionally accredited. **Degrees:** 137 bachelor's, 52 associate awarded; master's, professional, doctoral offered. **Location:** 35 miles from Sacramento, California. **Calendar:** Quarter, extensive summer session. **Full-time faculty:** 69 total. **Part-time faculty:** 121 total. **Class size:** 80% < 20, 20% 20-39.

Freshman class profile. 398 applied, 167 admitted, 159 enrolled.

Out-of-state: 3%   **Live on campus:**   25%

Basis for selection. High school diploma or GED required. ACT used for placement only. **Home schooled:** State high school equivalency certificate required.

2011-2012 Annual costs. Tuition/fees: $10,620. Books/supplies: $1,620. Personal expenses: $3,096.

Financial aid. Non-need-based: Scholarships awarded for academics.

Application procedures. Admission: No deadline. $35 fee, may be waived for applicants with need. Application must be submitted on paper. Admission notification on a rolling basis. **Financial aid:** No deadline. FAFSA required. Applicants notified on a rolling basis starting 8/15; must reply within 2 week(s) of notification.

Academics. Special study options: Combined bachelor's/graduate degree, cooperative education, cross-registration, double major, honors, independent study, internships. **Credit/placement by examination:** AP, CLEP, IB, institutional tests. 4 credit hours maximum toward associate degree, 45 toward bachelor's. **Support services:** Learning center, pre-admission summer program, remedial instruction, tutoring, writing center.

Majors. Business: General, accounting, administrative services, business admin, office technology, office/clerical. **Computer sciences:** General. **Education:** General. **Health services:** Medical secretary. **Human services:** Community org/advocacy. **Liberal arts:** Arts/sciences. **Social sciences:** General.

Computing on campus. 25 workstations in library, computer center. Online library, helpline, wireless network available.

Student life. Freshman orientation: Available. Preregistration for classes offered. Held on campus the first week of each academic term. **Housing:** Apartments available. $200 partly refundable deposit, deadline 8/20. **Activities:** Student government, student newspaper, business club.

Student services. Career counseling, student employment services, financial aid counseling, on-campus daycare, personal counseling, placement for graduates, veterans' counselor.

Contact. E-mail: ugadmission@humphreys.edu
Phone: (209) 478-0800 Fax: (209) 478-8721
Santa Lopez-Minarte, Admissions Director, Humphreys College, 6650 Inglewood Avenue, Stockton, CA 95207-3896

Interior Designers Institute
Newport Beach, California
www.idi.edu   CB code: 2318

- For-profit 4-year visual arts college
- Commuter campus in large city
- 216 degree-seeking undergraduates

General. Accredited by ACCSC. **Degrees:** 28 bachelor's, 60 associate awarded; master's offered. **Calendar:** Quarter. **Part-time faculty:** 30 total.

Basis for selection. Open admission.

2011-2012 Annual costs. 12-week certificate program: $1,995. 2-year associate degree program: $15,950. Bachelor's degree program: $14,950. Books/supplies: $1,500.

Application procedures. Admission: No deadline. $95 fee. Application must be submitted on paper.

Academics. Credit/placement by examination: AP, CLEP.

Majors. Visual/performing arts: Interior design.

Contact. E-mail: contact@idi.edu
Phone: (949) 675-4451 Fax: (949) 759-0667
Interior Designers Institute, 1061 Camelback Road, Newport Beach, CA 92660-3228

International Academy of Design and Technology: Sacramento
Sacramento, California
www.iadtsacramento.com

- For-profit 4-year technical and career college
- Very large city
- 443 degree-seeking undergraduates

General. Regionally accredited; also accredited by ACICS. **Degrees:** 77 bachelor's, 70 associate awarded. **Calendar:** Quarter, extensive summer session. **Full-time faculty:** 10 total; 10% have terminal degrees, 40% minority, 70% women. **Part-time faculty:** 45 total; 9% have terminal degrees, 18% minority, 71% women. **Class size:** 71% < 20, 29% 20-39.

Freshman class profile.

End year in good standing: 80%   Return as sophomores: 55%

Basis for selection. Open admission.

2012-2013 Annual costs. Tuition/fees (projected): $17,200. Student tuition recovery fund: $80.50 for associate degrees and $157.50 for bachelor degrees. Books/supplies: $1,260. Personal expenses: $335.

Application procedures. Admission: No deadline. $50 fee. Admission notification on a rolling basis. **Financial aid:** No deadline.

Academics. Special study options: Distance learning, independent study, internships, study abroad. **Credit/placement by examination:** AP, CLEP. **Support services:** Learning center, reduced course load, remedial instruction, study skills assistance, tutoring, writing center.

Majors. Visual/performing arts: Fashion design, interior design.

Student life. Activities: Student government.

Contact. Phone: (916) 285-9468 Fax: (916) 285-6986 Director of Admissions, International Academy of Design and Technology: Sacramento, 2450 Del Paso Road, Sacramento, CA 95834

ITT Technical Institute: Lathrop
Lathrop, California
www.itt-tech.edu   CB code: 2720

- For-profit 4-year technical college
- Commuter campus in small town
- 723 undergraduates
- Interview required

General. Accredited by ACICS. **Degrees:** 74 bachelor's, 159 associate awarded. **Calendar:** Quarter, extensive summer session. **Full-time faculty:** 13 total. **Part-time faculty:** 49 total.

Basis for selection. Satisfactory scores from on-site tests in English and mathematics required.

2011-2012 Annual costs. Estimated costs as of July 2011: per-credit-hour charge, $493, depending upon level and course of study; academic fee, $200. Certain programs of study require purchase of tools, which could cost an additional $100 to $500. All costs are subject to change.

Application procedures. Admission: No deadline. No application fee. Admission notification on a rolling basis. **Financial aid:** No deadline. FAFSA, institutional form required. Applicants notified on a rolling basis.

Academics. Credit/placement by examination: AP, CLEP. **Support services:** Learning center, tutoring.

Majors. Business: Business admin, construction management, project management. **Communications technology:** Animation/special effects. **Computer sciences:** Security, system admin. **Protective services:** Law enforcement admin.

Computing on campus. Online library available.

Student life. Freshman orientation: Available. Preregistration for classes offered.

Student services. Career counseling, student employment services, placement for graduates.

Contact. Phone: (209) 858-0077 Toll-free number: (800) 346-1786 Kathy Paradis, Director of Recruitment, ITT Technical Institute: Lathrop, 16916 South Harlan Road, Lathrop, CA 95330

ITT Technical Institute: Oxnard
Oxnard, California
www.itt-tech.edu   CB code: 2744

- For-profit 4-year technical college
- Commuter campus in small city
- 474 undergraduates
- Interview required

General. Accredited by ACICS. **Degrees:** 53 bachelor's, 100 associate awarded. **Location:** 34 miles from Santa Barbara, 52 miles from Los Angeles. **Calendar:** Quarter, extensive summer session. **Full-time faculty:** 11 total. **Part-time faculty:** 30 total.

Basis for selection. Satisfactory scores from on-site tests in English and mathematics required.

2011-2012 Annual costs. Estimated costs as of June 2011: per-credit-hour charge, $493, depending upon level and course of study; academic fee, $200. Certain programs of study require purchase of tools, which could cost an additional $100 to $500. All costs are subject to change.

Application procedures. Admission: No deadline. No application fee. Admission notification on a rolling basis. **Financial aid:** No deadline. FAFSA, institutional form required. Applicants notified on a rolling basis.

Academics. Credit/placement by examination: AP, CLEP. **Support services:** Learning center, tutoring.

Majors. Business: Business admin, construction management, e-commerce, project management. **Communications technology:** Animation/special effects. **Computer sciences:** Security. **Protective services:** Law enforcement admin.

Computing on campus. Online library available.

Student life. Freshman orientation: Available. Preregistration for classes offered.

Student services. Career counseling, student employment services, placement for graduates.

Contact. Phone: (805) 988-0143 Toll-free number: (800) 530-1582 Claudia Wilroy, Director of Recruitment, ITT Technical Institute: Oxnard, 2051 Solar Drive, Suite 150, Oxnard, CA 93036

ITT Technical Institute: Rancho Cordova
Rancho Cordova, California
www.itt-tech.edu   CB code: 3597

- For-profit 4-year technical college
- Commuter campus in large city
- 755 undergraduates
- Interview required

General. Founded in 1954. Accredited by ACICS. **Degrees:** 46 bachelor's, 192 associate awarded. **Location:** 11 miles from Sacramento, 87 miles from San Francisco. **Calendar:** Quarter, extensive summer session. **Full-time faculty:** 14 total. **Part-time faculty:** 61 total.

Basis for selection. Satisfactory scores from on-site tests in English and mathematics required.

2011-2012 Annual costs. Estimated costs as of July 2011: per-credit-hour charge, $493, depending upon level and course of study; academic fee, $200. Certain programs of study require purchase of tools, which could cost an additional $100 to $500. All costs are subject to change.

Application procedures. Admission: No deadline. No application fee. Admission notification on a rolling basis. **Financial aid:** No deadline. FAFSA, institutional form required. Applicants notified on a rolling basis.

Academics. Credit/placement by examination: AP, CLEP. **Support services:** Learning center, tutoring.

Majors. Business: Business admin, construction management, project management. **Communications technology:** Animation/special effects. **Computer sciences:** Security, system admin. **Protective services:** Law enforcement admin.

Computing on campus. Online library available.

Student life. Freshman orientation: Available. Preregistration for classes offered.

Student services. Career counseling, student employment services, placement for graduates.

Contact. Phone: (916) 366-3900 Toll-free number: (800) 488-8466 Bob Menszer, Director of Recruitment, ITT Technical Institute: Rancho Cordova, 10863 Gold Center Drive, Rancho Cordova, CA 95670

ITT Technical Institute: San Bernardino
San Bernardino, California
www.itt-tech.edu   CB code: 7103

- For-profit 4-year technical college
- Commuter campus in very large city
- 1,513 undergraduates
- Interview required

General. Accredited by ACICS. **Degrees:** 129 bachelor's, 355 associate awarded. **Location:** 60 miles from Los Angeles. **Calendar:** Quarter, extensive summer session. **Full-time faculty:** 22 total. **Part-time faculty:** 66 total.

Basis for selection. Satisfactory scores from on-site tests in English and mathematics required.

2011-2012 Annual costs. Estimated costs as of June 2011: per-credit-hour charge, $493, depending upon level and course of study; academic fee, $200. Certain programs of study require purchase of tools, which could cost an additional $100 to $500. All costs are subject to change.

Application procedures. Admission: No deadline. No application fee. Admission notification on a rolling basis. **Financial aid:** No deadline. FAFSA, institutional form required. Applicants notified on a rolling basis.

Academics. Credit/placement by examination: AP, CLEP. **Support services:** Learning center, tutoring.

Majors. Business: Business admin, construction management, project management. **Communications technology:** Animation/special effects. **Computer sciences:** Security, system admin. **Protective services:** Law enforcement admin.

Computing on campus. Online library available.

Student life. Freshman orientation: Available. Preregistration for classes offered.

Student services. Career counseling, student employment services, placement for graduates.

Contact. Phone: (800) 888-3801 Fax: (909) 888-6970 Tyron Cooley, Director of Recruitment, ITT Technical Institute: San Bernardino, 670 East Carnegie Drive, San Bernardino, CA 92408-2800

ITT Technical Institute: San Diego
San Diego, California
www.itt-tech.edu   CB code: 0206

- For-profit 4-year technical college
- Commuter campus in very large city
- 1,654 undergraduates
- Interview required

General. Founded in 1981. Accredited by ACICS. **Degrees:** 109 bachelor's, 325 associate awarded. **Calendar:** Quarter, extensive summer session. **Full-time faculty:** 15 total. **Part-time faculty:** 94 total.

Basis for selection. Satisfactory scores from on-site English and mathematics tests required.

2011-2012 Annual costs. Estimated costs as of July 2011: per-credit-hour charge, $493, depending upon level and course of study; academic fee,

$200. Certain programs of study require purchase of tools, which could cost an additional $100 to $500. All costs are subject to change.

Application procedures. Admission: No deadline. No application fee. Admission notification on a rolling basis. **Financial aid:** No deadline. FAFSA, institutional form required. Applicants notified on a rolling basis.

Academics. Credit/placement by examination: AP, CLEP. **Support services:** Learning center, tutoring.

Majors. Business: Business admin, construction management, project management. **Communications technology:** Animation/special effects. **Computer sciences:** Security. **Protective services:** Law enforcement admin.

Computing on campus. Online library available.

Student life. Freshman orientation: Available. Preregistration for classes offered.

Student services. Career counseling, student employment services, placement for graduates.

Contact. Phone: (858) 571-8500 Toll-free number: (800) 883-0380 Robert Dutton, Director of Recruitment, ITT Technical Institute: San Diego, 9680 Granite Ridge Drive, San Diego, CA 92123

ITT Technical Institute: Sylmar
Sylmar, California
www.itt-tech.edu   CB code: 3571

- For-profit 4-year technical college
- Commuter campus in very large city
- 1,046 undergraduates
- Interview required

General. Founded in 1982. Accredited by ACICS. **Degrees:** 102 bachelor's, 219 associate awarded. **Calendar:** Quarter, extensive summer session. **Full-time faculty:** 15 total. **Part-time faculty:** 50 total.

Basis for selection. Satisfactory scores from on-site English and mathematics tests required.

2011-2012 Annual costs. Estimated costs as of June 2011: per-credit-hour charge, $493, depending upon level and course of study; academic fee, $200. Certain programs of study require purchase of tools, which could cost an additional $100 to $500. All costs are subject to change.

Application procedures. Admission: No deadline. No application fee. Admission notification on a rolling basis. **Financial aid:** No deadline. FAFSA, institutional form required. Applicants notified on a rolling basis.

Academics. Credit/placement by examination: AP, CLEP. **Support services:** Learning center, tutoring.

Majors. Business: Business admin, construction management, project management. **Communications technology:** Animation/special effects. **Computer sciences:** Programming, security, system admin. **Protective services:** Law enforcement admin.

Computing on campus. Online library available.

Student life. Freshman orientation: Available. Preregistration for classes offered.

Student services. Career counseling, student employment services, placement for graduates.

Contact. Phone: (818) 364-5151 Toll-free number: (800) 363-2086 Fax: (818) 364-5150 Kelly Christensen, Director of Recruitment, ITT Technical Institute: Sylmar, 12669 Encinitas Avenue, Sylmar, CA 91342-3664

ITT Technical Institute: Torrance
Torrance, California
www.itt-tech.edu   CB code: 7104

- For-profit 4-year technical college
- Commuter campus in small city
- 905 undergraduates
- Interview required

General. Accredited by ACICS. **Degrees:** 70 bachelor's, 209 associate awarded. **Calendar:** Quarter, extensive summer session. **Full-time faculty:** 11 total. **Part-time faculty:** 52 total.

Basis for selection. Satisfactory from on-site tests in English and mathematics required.

2011-2012 Annual costs. Estimated costs as of June 2011: per-credit-hour charge, $493, depending upon level and course of study; academic fee, $200. Certain programs of study require purchase of tools, which could cost an additional $100 to $500. All costs are subject to change.

Application procedures. Admission: No deadline. No application fee. Admission notification on a rolling basis. **Financial aid:** No deadline. FAFSA, institutional form required. Applicants notified on a rolling basis.

Academics. Credit/placement by examination: AP, CLEP. **Support services:** Learning center, tutoring.

Majors. Business: Business admin, construction management, project management. **Communications technology:** Animation/special effects. **Computer sciences:** Security, system admin. **Protective services:** Law enforcement admin.

Computing on campus. Online library available.

Student services. Career counseling, student employment services, placement for graduates.

Contact. Phone: (310) 380-1555
Freddie Polk, Director of Recruitment, ITT Technical Institute: Torrance, 20050 South Vermont Avenue, Torrance, CA 90502

John F. Kennedy University
Pleasant Hill, California
www.jfku.edu   CB code: 1362

- Private two-year upper-division university
- Commuter campus in large town

General. Founded in 1964. Regionally accredited. **Location:** 35 miles from San Francisco. **Calendar:** Quarter.

Annual costs/financial aid. Tuition/fees (2011-2012): $19,095. Books/supplies: $1,100. Need-based financial aid available to full-time and part-time students.

Contact. Phone: (925) 969-3535
Director of Admissions, 100 Ellinwood Way, Pleasant Hill, CA 94523-4817

The King's University
Van Nuys, California
www.kingsuniversity.edu   CB code: 3896

- Private 4-year Bible and seminary college affiliated with nondenominational tradition
- Commuter campus in very large city
- 280 degree-seeking undergraduates
- 74% of applicants admitted
- Application essay required

General. Regionally accredited; also accredited by ABHE, TRACS. Evangelical Charismatic institution. **Degrees:** 11 bachelor's, 8 associate awarded; master's, professional offered. **Location:** 20 miles from downtown Los Angeles. **Calendar:** Quarter, extensive summer session. **Full-time faculty:** 10 total. **Part-time faculty:** 41 total.

Freshman class profile. 23 applied, 17 admitted, 16 enrolled.

Basis for selection. Demonstration of commitment to Christian faith required, essays, references important. SAT or ACT recommended. **Home schooled:** Statement describing home school structure and mission, transcript of courses and grades required.

2011-2012 Annual costs. Tuition/fees: $9,375. Books/supplies: $1,200.

Financial aid. Non-need-based: Scholarships awarded for academics. **Additional information:** Specific scholarships may require specific essays.

Application procedures. Admission: No deadline. $75 fee. Admission notification on a rolling basis. Must reply by May 1 or within 4 week(s) if notified thereafter. Must reply within 30 days. **Financial aid:** No deadline. FAFSA required. Applicants notified on a rolling basis; must reply within 4 week(s) of notification.

Academics. Special study options: Accelerated study, distance learning, external degree, independent study, internships, study abroad. **Credit/placement by examination:** AP, CLEP, IB, institutional tests. 45 credit hours maximum toward associate degree, 45 toward bachelor's. **Support services:** Pre-admission summer program, reduced course load, remedial instruction, study skills assistance.

Majors. Theology: Bible.

Computing on campus. Commuter students can connect to campus network. Online course registration, online library, helpline available.

Student life. Freshman orientation: Mandatory. Preregistration for classes offered. **Policies:** Drug- and alcohol-free campus. Religious observance required. **Activities:** Campus ministries, choral groups, music ensembles, student government, student newspaper, C.S. Lewis club, women in ministry group, Delta Epsilon, National Association of Evangelicals.

Student services. Adult student services, alcohol/substance abuse counseling, chaplain/spiritual director, career counseling, student employment services, financial aid counseling, personal counseling, placement for graduates, veterans' counselor, women's services.

Contact. E-mail: admissions@kingsuniversity.edu
Phone: (818) 779-8040 Toll-free number: (888) 779-8040
Fax: (818) 779-8429
Marilyn Chappell, Director of Admissions, The King's University, 14800 Sherman Way, Van Nuys, CA 91405-2233

LA College International
Los Angeles, California
www.lac.edu   CB code: 3046

- For-profit 4-year business and technical college
- Commuter campus in very large city
- 348 degree-seeking undergraduates

General. Accredited by ACICS. **Degrees:** 3 bachelor's, 162 associate awarded. **Calendar:** Differs by program. **Full-time faculty:** 5 total. **Part-time faculty:** 97 total.

Basis for selection. Open admission. ATB required if no high school diploma.

2011-2012 Annual costs. Associate programs: $390 per-credit-hour for the first 24 credits and $265 per-credit-hour for the remaining credits. Bachelor programs: $390 per-credit-hour for the first 24 credits and $235 per-credit-hour for the remaining credits. Books and supplies included in per-credit-hour charge. Technology fee: $25 per-credit-hour for all campus students.

2010-2011 Financial aid. Need-based: 69% of total undergraduate aid awarded as scholarships/grants, 31% as loans/jobs.

Application procedures. Admission: No deadline. $35 fee. **Financial aid:** FAFSA, institutional form required.

Academics. Credit/placement by examination: AP, CLEP.

Majors. Business: Business admin. **Computer sciences:** General.

Student life. Freshman orientation: Available. Preregistration for classes offered. 4 days before start date. **Activities:** Student government.

Contact. Phone: (213) 381-3333 Toll-free number: (800) 574-6428
Fax: (213) 383-9369
Brian Jeanette, Senior Director of Marketing and Admissions, LA College International, 3200 Wilshire Boulevard, Suite 400, Los Angeles, CA 90010-1308

La Sierra University
Riverside, California   CB member
www.lasierra.edu   CB code: 4380

- Private 4-year university and liberal arts college affiliated with Seventh-day Adventists
- Residential campus in large city

- 1,841 degree-seeking undergraduates: 8% part-time, 55% women, 7% African American, 16% Asian American, 35% Hispanic American, 16% international
- 297 degree-seeking graduate students
- 46% of applicants admitted
- SAT or ACT (ACT writing optional), application essay required
- 35% graduate within 6 years

General. Founded in 1922. Regionally accredited. Affiliated with the Seventh-day Adventist Church. **Degrees:** 163 bachelor's awarded; master's, doctoral offered. **Location:** 55 miles from Los Angeles. **Calendar:** Quarter, limited summer session. **Full-time faculty:** 94 total; 82% have terminal degrees, 15% minority, 40% women. **Part-time faculty:** 151 total; 9% minority, 47% women. **Class size:** 66% < 20, 26% 20-39, 5% 40-49, 3% 50-99, less than 1% >100. **Special facilities:** Natural history museum, mineral spheres collection, arboretum, observatory, woman's resource center, archeology center.

Freshman class profile. 2,662 applied, 1,237 admitted, 437 enrolled.

Mid 50% test scores		GPA 2.0-2.99:	30%
SAT critical reading:	410-520	Rank in top quarter:	39%
SAT math:	410-520	Rank in top tenth:	13%
SAT writing:	420-540	End year in good standing:	76%
ACT composite:	16-20	Return as sophomores:	76%
GPA 3.75 or higher:	21%	Out-of-state:	8%
GPA 3.50-3.74:	13%	Live on campus:	49%
GPA 3.0-3.49:	36%	International:	13%

Basis for selection. Secondary school record and GPA, test scores, recommendations, and religious affiliation or commitment important. **Home schooled:** Transcript of courses and grades required. **Learning Disabled:** Applicants and parents are highly recommended to attend orientation program; incentives given to students who attend.

High school preparation. 15 units required. Required and recommended units include English 4, mathematics 3-4, social studies 2, science 2-3 (laboratory 2-3), foreign language 2-3, visual/performing arts 1 and academic electives 1.

2012-2013 Annual costs. Tuition/fees (projected): $28,547. Room/board: $9,265. Books/supplies: $1,656. Personal expenses: $2,277.

Financial aid. Non-need-based: Scholarships awarded for academics, leadership, music/drama, religious affiliation.

Application procedures. Admission: Priority date 2/1; no deadline. $30 fee, may be waived for applicants with need. Admission notification on a rolling basis. **Financial aid:** Priority date 3/2; no closing date. FAFSA required. Applicants notified on a rolling basis starting 4/15; must reply by 9/1.

Academics. Special study options: Accelerated study, combined bachelor's/graduate degree, cross-registration, distance learning, double major, dual enrollment of high school students, ESL, honors, independent study, internships, student-designed major, study abroad, teacher certification program. **Credit/placement by examination:** AP, CLEP, IB, institutional tests. 24 credit hours maximum toward bachelor's degree. **Support services:** Learning center, pre-admission summer program, reduced course load, remedial instruction, study skills assistance, tutoring, writing center.

Honors college/program. High school GPA above 3.25 and ACT above 60th percentile. 25 freshmen admitted per year. Offers chance to study in special classroom settings, travel internationally, and engage in advanced research. Honors scholarship also available.

Majors. Biology: General, biochemistry, biomedical sciences, biometrics, biophysics. **Business:** Accounting, business admin, finance, human resources, marketing. **Communications:** Advertising, communications/speech/rhetoric, persuasive communications. **Computer sciences:** Computer science, information systems. **English:** English lit, writing. **Foreign languages:** Spanish. **History:** General. **Human services:** Social work. **Liberal arts:** Arts/sciences, humanities. **Math:** General. **Parks/recreation:** Exercise sciences, health/fitness. **Philosophy/religion:** Religion. **Physical sciences:** General, chemistry. **Protective services:** Law enforcement admin. **Psychology:** General, psychobiology. **Social sciences:** Political economy, sociology. **Visual/performing arts:** Art, graphic design, music, music performance, music technology, studio arts, studio arts management.

Most popular majors. Biology 20%, business/marketing 25%, liberal arts 7%, parks/recreation 9%, psychology 10%, visual/performing arts 6%.

Computing on campus. 300 workstations in dormitories, library, computer center, student center. Dormitories wired for high-speed internet access and linked to campus network. Commuter students can connect to campus network. Online course registration, online library, helpline, repair service, wireless network available.

Student life. Freshman orientation: Mandatory. Preregistration for classes offered. $200 credit is given to all the freshmen for attending orientation in summer. **Policies:** Smoke- and alcohol-free campus. Religious observance required. **Housing:** Guaranteed on-campus for all undergraduates. Single-sex dorms, apartments, wellness housing available. $100 fully refundable deposit. Honors residence hall available. **Activities:** Bands, campus ministries, choral groups, drama, international student organizations, literary magazine, music ensembles, student government, student newspaper, symphony orchestra, Accounting and Finance Society, Active Minds at LSU, Amnesty International, Best Buddies International, biology club, biophysics club, black student association, business club, Chemistry Society, Chinese cultural club.

Athletics. NAIA. **Intercollegiate:** Baseball M, basketball, soccer M, softball W, volleyball W. **Intramural:** Basketball, softball W, volleyball W. **Team name:** Golden Eagles.

Student services. Adult student services, alcohol/substance abuse counseling, chaplain/spiritual director, career counseling, student employment services, financial aid counseling, health services, personal counseling, placement for graduates, women's services.

Contact. E-mail: admissions@lasierra.edu
Phone: (951) 785-2176 Toll-free number: (800) 874-5587
Fax: (951) 785-2477
Faye Swayze, Director of Admissions & Registrar, La Sierra University, 4500 Riverwalk Parkway, Riverside, CA 92515-8247

Laguna College of Art and Design
Laguna Beach, California
www.lagunacollege.edu — CB code: 7248

- Private 4-year visual arts college
- Commuter campus in large town
- 420 degree-seeking undergraduates
- 39% of applicants admitted
- SAT or ACT (ACT writing optional) required

General. Founded in 1961. Regionally accredited. **Degrees:** 78 bachelor's awarded; master's offered. **Location:** 50 miles from Los Angeles, 75 miles from San Diego. **Calendar:** Semester, limited summer session. **Full-time faculty:** 14 total. **Part-time faculty:** 86 total.

Freshman class profile. 380 applied, 148 admitted, 65 enrolled.

Basis for selection. Selection based on academic record and overall merit of 10-piece portfolio which includes minimum of 4 observational drawings. Application fee waived for online applications. Portfolios required.

High school preparation. 14 units recommended. Recommended units include English 2, mathematics 2, social studies 2, history 2, science 2, foreign language 2 and academic electives 2. 3 units of studio art, drawing and painting recommended.

2011-2012 Annual costs. Tuition/fees: $22,890. Books/supplies: $2,400. Personal expenses: $2,826.

Financial aid. Additional information: Need- and merit-based scholarship deadline March 20.

Application procedures. Admission: Priority date 2/2; no deadline. $45 fee, may be waived for applicants with need, free for online applicants. Admission notification on a rolling basis. **Financial aid:** No deadline. FAFSA, institutional form required. Applicants notified on a rolling basis; must reply within 2 week(s) of notification.

Academics. Special study options: Cooperative education, double major, exchange student, independent study, internships, New York semester, study abroad. **Credit/placement by examination:** AP, CLEP. **Support services:** Pre-admission summer program, reduced course load, remedial instruction, tutoring.

Majors. Visual/performing arts: Commercial/advertising art, drawing, painting.

Computing on campus. 26 workstations in library, computer center.

Student life. Freshman orientation: Available. Preregistration for classes offered. **Policies:** Very strong student government promoting activities on and off campus. Many art-related social gatherings. **Activities:** Student government, student newspaper, foreign student organization, cultural diversity organization.

Student services. Career counseling, personal counseling, veterans' counselor.

Contact. E-mail: admissions@lagunacollege.edu
Phone: (949) 376-6000 Toll-free number: (800) 255-0762
Fax: (949) 376-6009
Mike Rivas, Vice President of Admissions, Laguna College of Art and Design, 2222 Laguna Canyon Road, Laguna Beach, CA 92651-1136

Life Pacific College
San Dimas, California
www.lifepacific.edu   CB code: 4264

- Private 4-year Bible college affiliated with Christian - The Foursquare Church
- Residential campus in large town
- 459 degree-seeking undergraduates
- 96% of applicants admitted
- SAT or ACT with writing, application essay required

General. Founded in 1925. Candidate for regional accreditation; also accredited by ABHE. Chapel twice each week. **Degrees:** 90 bachelor's, 4 associate awarded; master's offered. **Location:** 30 miles from Los Angeles. **Calendar:** Continuous, limited summer session. **Full-time faculty:** 18 total; 22% have terminal degrees, 11% minority. **Part-time faculty:** 11 total; 54% have terminal degrees. **Class size:** 75% < 20, 20% 20-39, less than 1% 40-49, 5% 50-99. **Special facilities:** Recording studio.

Freshman class profile. 136 applied, 131 admitted, 89 enrolled.

Mid 50% test scores		ACT composite:	16-22
SAT critical reading:	420-550	Out-of-state:	26%
SAT math:	390-500	Live on campus:	84%
SAT writing:	390-520		

Basis for selection. Christian character, ministry motivation, and ability to accord with college's program. Cumulative GPA in last school attended and SAT or ACT scores also considered. **Home schooled:** Must present official transcript with graduation date. SAT or ACT required. **Learning Disabled:** The LIFE Challenges Program is available to students with documented learning disabilities.

2011-2012 Annual costs. Tuition/fees: $12,500. Room/board: $6,000. Books/supplies: $1,682.

Financial aid. Non-need-based: Scholarships awarded for academics, alumni affiliation.

Application procedures. Admission: Priority date 4/1; deadline 5/3 (postmark date). $35 fee. Application must be submitted on paper. Admission notification on a rolling basis. **Financial aid:** No deadline. FAFSA required. Applicants notified on a rolling basis starting 6/1.

Academics. Bible studies taught from Charismatic/Pentecostal perspective training leaders for ministry. **Special study options:** Cooperative education, distance learning, dual enrollment of high school students, external degree, independent study, internships, study abroad. **Credit/placement by examination:** AP, CLEP, SAT, ACT, institutional tests. 16 credit hours maximum toward associate degree, 32 toward bachelor's. Credit limited by the number of subjects accepted, course by course basis. **Support services:** Reduced course load, remedial instruction, study skills assistance, writing center.

Majors. Theology: Bible, pastoral counseling.

Computing on campus. 10 workstations in dormitories, library. Dormitories wired for high-speed internet access and linked to campus network. Online course registration, online library, helpline, wireless network available.

Student life. Freshman orientation: Mandatory, $100 fee. Preregistration for classes offered. One full day (meal provided), includes testing. **Policies:** Religious observance required. **Housing:** Guaranteed on-campus for freshmen. Single-sex dorms, wellness housing available. $200 nonrefundable deposit, deadline 6/1. **Activities:** Campus ministries, choral groups, drama, music ensembles, student government.

Athletics. Team name: Warriors.

Student services. Adult student services, chaplain/spiritual director, career counseling, student employment services, financial aid counseling, minority student services, personal counseling, placement for graduates, veterans' counselor. **Physically disabled:** Services for speech, hearing impaired.

Contact. E-mail: admissions@lifepacific.edu
Phone: (909) 599-5433 ext. 314
Toll-free number: (877) 886-5433 ext. 314 Fax: (909) 706-3070
Amber Coffey, Registrar and Enrollment Manager, Life Pacific College, Attn: Admissions, San Dimas, CA 91773

Lincoln University
Oakland, California
www.lincolnuca.edu   CB code: 4386

- Private 4-year university and business college
- Commuter campus in very large city
- 74 degree-seeking undergraduates

General. Founded in 1919. Accredited by ACICS. Institution primarily serves international students. **Degrees:** 2 bachelor's, 12 associate awarded; master's, professional offered. **Location:** 12 miles from San Francisco. **Calendar:** Semester, limited summer session. **Full-time faculty:** 9 total; 33% women. **Part-time faculty:** 22 total.

Basis for selection. High school achievement record is most important. Prior to enrollment, students take following tests and procedures in English placement: 1) Michigan Test of English Language Proficiency (MTELP), 2) Comprehensive English Language Test Structure (CELT-SA), 3) Comprehensive English Language Test Listening (CELT-LA), 4) a writing sample, and 5) a personal interview. Interview recommended and personal statements encouraged. **Home schooled:** Transcript of courses and grades, state high school equivalency certificate required.

2011-2012 Annual costs. Tuition/fees: $9,160. Tuition for Intensive English program is $3,000 per 16 weeks. Books/supplies: $760. Personal expenses: $2,520.

2011-2012 Financial aid. All financial aid based on need.

Application procedures. Admission: No deadline. $75 fee. Admission notification on a rolling basis. **Financial aid:** Priority date 3/22, closing date 8/22. FAFSA required. Applicants notified by 12/1; must reply by 1/2.

Academics. Special study options: Cross-registration, double major, ESL, internships. **Credit/placement by examination:** AP, CLEP. **Support services:** Reduced course load, tutoring.

Majors. Business: Business admin, international, management information systems, managerial economics.

Computing on campus. 34 workstations in library, computer center. Online library, repair service, wireless network available.

Student life. Freshman orientation: Mandatory. Preregistration for classes offered. One hour discussion of procedures, event announcements. Student government provides information on banking, transportation and other related materials. **Activities:** Student government.

Student services. Career counseling, financial aid counseling, personal counseling.

Contact. E-mail: admissions@lincolnuca.edu
Phone: (510) 628-8010 Toll-free number: (888) 810-9998
Fax: (510) 628-8012
Peggy Au, Director of Admissions and Records, Lincoln University, 401 15th Street, Oakland, CA 94612

Loma Linda University
Loma Linda, California
www.llu.edu   CB code: 4062

- Private 3-year university and health science college affiliated with Seventh-day Adventists
- Commuter campus in large town
- 1,101 degree-seeking undergraduates: 16% part-time, 72% women, 4% African American, 22% Asian American, 23% Hispanic American, 5% international
- 3,230 degree-seeking graduate students

General. Founded in 1905. Regionally accredited. Two undergraduate schools: School of Allied Health and School of Nursing, offering sophomore, junior, senior year study. All LLU programs require previous college credit, thus no first-time freshman applicants accepted. **Degrees:** 318 bachelor's, 173 associate awarded; master's, professional, doctoral offered. **Location:**

60 miles from Los Angeles, 50 miles from Palm Springs. **Calendar:** Quarter, limited summer session. **Full-time faculty:** 353 total; 35% minority, 53% women. **Part-time faculty:** 57 total; 28% minority, 40% women. **Class size:** 59% < 20, 18% 20-39, 15% 40-49, 8% 50-99.

Basis for selection. No first-time freshman accepted, only transfer students. All programs require prior college credits for admission, which varies by program; typically minimum of 48 credit units. Application is made to specific programs, rather than to the University in general. Some programs require interviews or essays.

2011-2012 Annual costs. Tuition/fees: $26,772. Tuition quoted for nursing program. Full-time tuition for dental hygiene program: $27,846 plus $2,073 fees. For allied health program $497/credit hour; for certificate programs, $373/credit. Application fee may vary by program; tuition may vary by grade level in program. Room only: $2,580. Books/supplies: $1,200.

Application procedures. Admission: No deadline. $60 fee. Application must be submitted online. Admission notification on a rolling basis. Varies by program. Each program is applied to separately and has its own requirements and dates. Student must give at least a two-week notice prior to housing entry date in order to receive a full refund; otherwise no refund will be given. **Financial aid:** FAFSA required.

Academics. Special study options: Combined bachelor's/graduate degree, distance learning, double major, independent study, internships. **Credit/placement by examination:** AP, CLEP. **Support services:** Study skills assistance.

Majors. BACHELOR'S. Conservation: Environmental science. **Health services:** Clinical lab science, cytotechnology, dental hygiene, dietetics, EMT paramedic, health care admin, medical records admin, nursing (RN), radiologic technology/medical imaging, respiratory therapy technology, speech pathology. **Physical sciences:** Geology. **ASSOCIATE. Health services:** Dental hygiene, medical radiologic technology/radiation therapy, physical therapy assistant.

Computing on campus. 482 workstations in library, computer center, student center. Dormitories wired for high-speed internet access and linked to campus network. Commuter students can connect to campus network. Online library, helpline, wireless network available.

Student life. Policies: Students are not allowed to smoke, use alcohol or drugs. Religious observance required. **Housing:** Guaranteed on-campus for all undergraduates. Single-sex dorms, apartments, wellness housing available. $145 fully refundable deposit. **Activities:** Campus ministries, choral groups, international student organizations, music ensembles, student government, student newspaper, Black Health Professional Student Association, Association of Latin American Students, Social Action Corps, Students for International Mission Service.

Athletics. Intramural: Basketball, football (non-tackle), soccer M, softball, tennis, volleyball.

Student services. Alcohol/substance abuse counseling, chaplain/spiritual director, financial aid counseling, health services, on-campus daycare, personal counseling. **Physically disabled:** Services for hearing impaired.

Contact. E-mail: admissions.app@llu.edu
Phone: (909) 651-5029 Toll-free number: (800) 422-4558
Fax: (909) 558-4879
Loma Linda University, Admissions Processing, Loma Linda, CA 92350

Loyola Marymount University

Los Angeles, California	CB member
www.lmu.edu	CB code: 4403

- Private 4-year university affiliated with Roman Catholic Church
- Residential campus in very large city
- 5,951 degree-seeking undergraduates: 2% part-time, 57% women, 6% African American, 10% Asian American, 21% Hispanic American, 4% international
- 3,015 degree-seeking graduate students
- 53% of applicants admitted
- SAT or ACT (ACT writing recommended), application essay required
- 77% graduate within 6 years; 25% enter graduate study

General. Founded in 1911. Regionally accredited. **Degrees:** 1,314 bachelor's awarded; master's, professional, doctoral offered. **ROTC:** Army, Naval, Air Force. **Location:** 15 miles from downtown. **Calendar:** Semester, extensive summer session. **Full-time faculty:** 521 total; 96% have terminal degrees, 26% minority, 43% women. **Part-time faculty:** 532 total; 22% minority,

47% women. **Class size:** 48% < 20, 50% 20-39, 1% 40-49, 2% 50-99, less than 1% >100. **Special facilities:** Fine arts complex with recital hall and recording arts facilities, marine station.

Freshman class profile. 11,309 applied, 6,043 admitted, 1,288 enrolled.

Mid 50% test scores		Rank in top quarter:	65%
SAT critical reading:	540-630	Rank in top tenth:	34%
SAT math:	560-650	End year in good standing:	97%
SAT writing:	550-650	Return as sophomores:	92%
ACT composite:	24-28	Out-of-state:	23%
GPA 3.75 or higher:	48%	Live on campus:	94%
GPA 3.50-3.74:	26%	International:	4%
GPA 3.0-3.49:	24%	Fraternities:	12%
GPA 2.0-2.99:	2%	Sororities:	37%

Basis for selection. High school GPA, curriculum, test scores, recommendations, essays, activities important. Portfolio required for some arts majors.

High school preparation. College-preparatory program recommended. 18 units recommended. Recommended units include English 4, mathematics 3, social studies 3, science 2 (laboratory 2), foreign language 3 and academic electives 1. 4 math required of engineering, math, and science majors; physics and chemistry required of engineering and science majors; biology and chemistry required (physics recommended) of biology majors.

2011-2012 Annual costs. Tuition/fees: $37,825. Freshmen generally stay in the less expensive dorms. Room/board: $13,025.

2010-2011 Financial aid. Need-based: 1,130 full-time freshmen applied for aid; 817 were judged to have need; 815 of these received aid. Average need met was 72%. Average scholarship/grant was $20,698; average loan $4,621. 69% of total undergraduate aid awarded as scholarships/grants, 31% as loans/jobs. **Non-need-based:** Awarded to 1,444 full-time undergraduates, including 597 freshmen. Scholarships awarded for academics, alumni affiliation, art, athletics, music/drama, religious affiliation, ROTC.

Application procedures. Admission: Closing date 1/15. $60 fee, may be waived for applicants with need. Admission notification on a rolling basis beginning on or about 11/1. Must reply by 5/1. Applicants who desire housing or financial aid should apply by January 15. **Financial aid:** Priority date 2/1, closing date 5/15. FAFSA required. Applicants notified on a rolling basis starting 3/15; must reply by 5/1 or within 4 week(s) of notification.

Academics. Special study options: Accelerated study, combined bachelor's/graduate degree, cross-registration, distance learning, double major, dual enrollment of high school students, ESL, exchange student, honors, independent study, internships, liberal arts/career combination, semester at sea, student-designed major, study abroad, teacher certification program, Washington semester, weekend college. Encore program for adult students. **Credit/placement by examination:** AP, CLEP, IB, institutional tests. **Support services:** Learning center, reduced course load, study skills assistance, tutoring.

Majors. Area/ethnic studies: African-American, Asian, Chicano/Hispanic-American/Latino, European, women's. **Biology:** General, biochemistry. **Business:** Accounting, entrepreneurial studies, finance, human resources, management information systems, marketing. **Communications:** Communications/speech/rhetoric. **Communications technology:** Animation/special effects, recording arts. **Computer sciences:** General. **Conservation:** Environmental science. **Engineering:** Applied physics, civil, electrical, mechanical. **English:** English lit. **Foreign languages:** Ancient Greek, classics, French, Latin, modern Greek, Spanish. **Health services:** Kinesiotherapy. **History:** General. **Liberal arts:** Arts/sciences, humanities. **Math:** General, applied. **Philosophy/religion:** Philosophy. **Physical sciences:** Chemistry, physics. **Psychology:** General. **Social sciences:** Economics, political science, sociology, urban studies. **Theology:** Theology. **Visual/performing arts:** Art history/conservation, cinematography, dance, dramatic, music, play/screenwriting, studio arts.

Most popular majors. Biology 6%, business/marketing 25%, communications/journalism 10%, English 6%, social sciences 13%, visual/performing arts 15%.

Computing on campus. 650 workstations in dormitories, library, computer center, student center. Dormitories wired for high-speed internet access and linked to campus network. Commuter students can connect to campus network. Online course registration, online library, helpline, repair service, student web hosting, wireless network available.

Student life. Freshman orientation: Available, $220 fee. Preregistration for classes offered. **Housing:** Guaranteed on-campus for freshmen. Coed dorms, single-sex dorms, special housing for disabled, apartments, wellness housing available. $400 nonrefundable deposit. **Activities:** Pep band, campus ministries, choral groups, dance, drama, film society, international student organizations, literary magazine, music ensembles, radio station, student government, student newspaper, TV station, more than 130 student organizations, clubs, and associations.

Athletics. NCAA. **Intercollegiate:** Baseball M, basketball, cross-country, golf M, rowing (crew) W, soccer, softball W, swimming W, tennis, track and field, volleyball W, water polo. **Intramural:** Basketball, football (non-tackle), soccer, volleyball. **Team name:** Lions.

Student services. Adult student services, alcohol/substance abuse counseling, chaplain/spiritual director, career counseling, services for economically disadvantaged, student employment services, financial aid counseling, health services, minority student services, personal counseling, placement for graduates, veterans' counselor. **Physically disabled:** Services for visually, speech, hearing impaired.

Contact. E-mail: admissions@lmu.edu
Phone: (310) 338-2750 Toll-free number: (800) 568-4636
Fax: (310) 338-2797
Matthew Fissinger, Director of Admissions, Loyola Marymount University, Office of Undergraduate Admission, Los Angeles, CA 90045-8350

The Master's College
Santa Clarita, California
www.masters.edu | **CB code: 4411**

- Private 4-year liberal arts and seminary college affiliated with Conservative Evangelical Christian Church
- Residential campus in small city
- 1,156 degree-seeking undergraduates: 10% part-time, 47% women
- 419 degree-seeking graduate students
- 66% of applicants admitted
- SAT or ACT with writing, application essay required
- 60% graduate within 6 years

General. Founded in 1927. Regionally accredited. Branch Campus in Israel; strong overseas summer missions program. **Degrees:** 226 bachelor's awarded; master's, professional, doctoral offered. **ROTC:** Army, Air Force. **Location:** 40 miles from Los Angeles. **Calendar:** Semester, limited summer session. **Full-time faculty:** 54 total; 87% have terminal degrees, 13% minority. **Class size:** 76% < 20, 14% 20-39, 4% 40-49, 6% 50-99, less than 1% >100. **Special facilities:** Family and consumer sciences center.

Freshman class profile. 822 applied, 541 admitted, 231 enrolled.

Mid 50% test scores			
SAT critical reading:	480-610	GPA 2.0-2.99:	10%
SAT math:	460-580	Rank in top quarter:	57%
ACT composite:	21-27	Rank in top tenth:	31%
GPA 3.75 or higher:	47%	Return as sophomores:	84%
GPA 3.50-3.74:	19%	Out-of-state:	35%
GPA 3.0-3.49:	24%	Live on campus:	90%
		International:	5%

Basis for selection. School achievement record, references, religious commitment most important. Applications from all individuals who have placed their faith in Jesus Christ as Lord and Savior are welcome. Audition required of music majors. **Home schooled:** Transcript of courses and grades, letter of recommendation (nonparent) required. **Learning Disabled:** Must speak with human resources department before attending.

High school preparation. College-preparatory program recommended. Required and recommended units include English 4, mathematics 3, history 2, science 2 and academic electives 3.

2012-2013 Annual costs. Tuition/fees: $27,690. Room/board: $9,010. Books/supplies: $1,665. Personal expenses: $2,277.

2011-2012 Financial aid. Need-based: 192 full-time freshmen applied for aid; 165 were judged to have need; 165 of these received aid. Average need met was 73%. Average scholarship/grant was $18,265; average loan $3,916. 67% of total undergraduate aid awarded as scholarships/grants, 33% as loans/jobs. **Non-need-based:** Awarded to 267 full-time undergraduates, including 57 freshmen. Scholarships awarded for academics, alumni affiliation, art, athletics, leadership, music/drama.

Application procedures. Admission: Priority date 3/2; no deadline. $40 fee, may be waived for applicants with need. Admission notification on a rolling basis beginning on or about 3/15. Must reply by May 1 or within 2 week(s) if notified thereafter. **Financial aid:** Priority date 3/2; no closing date. FAFSA, institutional form required. Applicants notified on a rolling basis starting 2/18; must reply by 5/1 or within 2 week(s) of notification.

Academics. Students who attend 4 years earn a minor in Biblical studies upon graduation. **Special study options:** Accelerated study, cooperative education, distance learning, double major, independent study, internships, liberal arts/career combination, study abroad, teacher certification program, Washington semester. Israel semester. **Credit/placement by examination:** AP, CLEP, IB, SAT, ACT, institutional tests. 32 credit hours maximum toward bachelor's degree. **Support services:** Reduced course load, remedial instruction, study skills assistance, tutoring.

Majors. Biology: General, environmental. **Business:** Accounting, actuarial science, business admin, finance, international, management information systems, marketing. **Communications:** Media studies, public relations, radio/TV. **Computer sciences:** General. **Education:** General, elementary, ESL, middle, music, physical, science, secondary. **English:** English lit, rhetoric/composition. **Foreign languages:** Biblical. **Health services:** Premedicine. **History:** General. **Liberal arts:** Arts/sciences. **Math:** General, applied. **Parks/recreation:** Health/fitness. **Philosophy/religion:** Religion. **Physical sciences:** General. **Social sciences:** Political science, U.S. government. **Theology:** Bible, pastoral counseling, religious ed, sacred music, theology. **Visual/performing arts:** Music, music management, piano/keyboard, voice/opera. **Work/family studies:** General, food/nutrition.

Most popular majors. Biology 7%, business/marketing 19%, communications/journalism 8%, liberal arts 20%, theological studies 25%.

Computing on campus. PC or laptop required. 57 workstations in library, computer center. Dormitories wired for high-speed internet access and linked to campus network. Commuter students can connect to campus network. Online course registration, online library, helpline, repair service, wireless network available.

Student life. Freshman orientation: Mandatory. Preregistration for classes offered. 5-day program before start of classes. **Policies:** Emphasis on Godly lifestyle, character and leadership development, service, learning, cross-cultural education. Religious observance required. **Housing:** Single-sex dorms, wellness housing available. $200 fully refundable deposit, deadline 5/2. **Activities:** Bands, campus ministries, choral groups, drama, music ensembles, opera, student government, symphony orchestra, summer missions, outreach teams.

Athletics. NAIA, NCCAA. **Intercollegiate:** Baseball M, basketball, cross-country, golf M, soccer, tennis W, track and field, volleyball W. **Intramural:** Basketball, football (non-tackle), soccer, volleyball. **Team name:** Mustangs.

Student services. Adult student services, chaplain/spiritual director, career counseling, student employment services, financial aid counseling, health services, personal counseling, placement for graduates, veterans' counselor. **Physically disabled:** Services for visually, speech impaired.

Contact. E-mail: admissions@masters.edu
Phone: (661) 259-3540 ext. 3362
Toll-free number: (800) 568-6248 ext. 3362 Fax: (661) 288-1037
Hollie Gorsh, Director of Admissions, The Master's College, 21726 Placerita Canyon Road, Santa Clarita, CA 91321-1200

Menlo College
Atherton, California
www.menlo.edu | **CB member** / **CB code: 4483**

- Private 4-year business and liberal arts college
- Residential campus in small city
- 642 degree-seeking undergraduates: 2% part-time, 36% women, 6% African American, 7% Asian American, 19% Hispanic American, 12% international
- 37% of applicants admitted
- SAT or ACT (ACT writing optional), application essay required
- 44% graduate within 6 years

General. Founded in 1927. Regionally accredited. **Degrees:** 111 bachelor's awarded. **ROTC:** Army, Air Force. **Location:** 30 miles from San Francisco, 30 miles from San Jose. **Calendar:** Semester, limited summer session. **Full-time faculty:** 28 total; 82% have terminal degrees, 25% minority, 46% women. **Part-time faculty:** 45 total; 38% have terminal degrees, 33% minority, 60% women. **Class size:** 49% < 20, 48% 20-39, 3% 40-49.

Freshman class profile. 4,105 applied, 1,526 admitted, 148 enrolled.

Mid 50% test scores			
SAT critical reading:	430-520	GPA 3.0-3.49:	37%
SAT math:	440-550	GPA 2.0-2.99:	31%
SAT writing:	420-520	End year in good standing:	85%
ACT composite:	19-24	Return as sophomores:	74%
GPA 3.75 or higher:	19%	Out-of-state:	29%
GPA 3.50-3.74:	13%	Live on campus:	95%
		International:	11%

Basis for selection. High school record minimum GPA of 2.5, test scores (minimum 1200 SAT, or 16 ACT), 1 recommendation, essay, depth of achievement in cocurricular activities considered. **Home schooled:** Statement describing home school structure and mission, transcript of courses and grades, state high school equivalency certificate, letter of recommendation (nonparent) required. **Learning Disabled:** Direct queries to Academic Success Center.

High school preparation. College-preparatory program recommended. 15 units required; 24 recommended. Required and recommended units include English 4, mathematics 3, social studies 3, science 3 and foreign language 2.

2012-2013 Annual costs. Tuition/fees: $36,110. Room/board: $11,444. Books/supplies: $1,666. Personal expenses: $2,278.

2011-2012 Financial aid. Need-based: 121 full-time freshmen applied for aid; 117 were judged to have need; 117 of these received aid. Average need met was 42%. Average scholarship/grant was $26,604; average loan $3,300. 77% of total undergraduate aid awarded as scholarships/grants, 23% as loans/jobs. **Non-need-based:** Awarded to 213 full-time undergraduates, including 49 freshmen. Scholarships awarded for academics, athletics.

Application procedures. Admission: Priority date 2/1; no deadline. $40 fee, may be waived for applicants with need. Admission notification on a rolling basis beginning on or about 10/1. Must reply by May 1 or within 4 week(s) if notified thereafter. **Financial aid:** Priority date 3/2, closing date 8/1. FAFSA required. Applicants notified on a rolling basis starting 12/15; must reply by 5/1 or within 2 week(s) of notification.

Academics. Special study options: Accelerated study, double major, ESL, independent study, internships, student-designed major, study abroad. **Credit/placement by examination:** AP, CLEP, IB, institutional tests. 30 credit hours maximum toward bachelor's degree. **Support services:** Learning center, reduced course load, remedial instruction, study skills assistance, tutoring, writing center.

Majors. Business: Accounting, business admin, entrepreneurial studies, finance, international, management information systems, marketing. **Psychology:** General.

Most popular majors. Business/marketing 58%, communications/journalism 19%, liberal arts 23%.

Computing on campus. 185 workstations in library, computer center. Dormitories wired for high-speed internet access and linked to campus network. Commuter students can connect to campus network. Online course registration, online library, helpline, repair service, wireless network available.

Student life. Freshman orientation: Mandatory. Preregistration for classes offered. Five days before classes begin. Workshops for both parents and students, and overnight trip to off-campus location. **Housing:** Guaranteed on-campus for freshmen. Coed dorms, single-sex dorms, special housing for disabled, wellness housing available. $300 fully refundable deposit, deadline 7/1. **Activities:** Film society, international student organizations, radio station, student government, student newspaper, International Club, African-American student union, Latino student union, Asia club, Rotaract, Chinese culture research club, Women's club, Alpha Chi Honor Society, Delta Mu Delta Honor Society, Gay Straight Alliance.

Athletics. NAIA. **Intercollegiate:** Baseball M, basketball, cheerleading, cross-country, football (tackle) M, golf M, soccer, softball W, volleyball W, wrestling. **Intramural:** Basketball M, volleyball M. **Team name:** Oaks.

Student services. Adult student services, career counseling, student employment services, financial aid counseling, personal counseling, placement for graduates, women's services. **Physically disabled:** Services for visually, hearing impaired.

Contact. E-mail: admissions@menlo.edu
Phone: (650) 543-3753 Toll-free number: (800) 556-3656
Fax: (650) 543-4496
Priscila de Souza, Director of Admissions, Menlo College, 1000 El Camino Real, Atherton, CA 94027

Mills College
Oakland, California
www.mills.edu

CB member
CB code: 4485

- Private 4-year liberal arts college for women
- Residential campus in large city
- 924 degree-seeking undergraduates: 5% part-time, 100% women, 8% African American, 10% Asian American, 18% Hispanic American, 1% Native American, 2% international
- 612 degree-seeking graduate students
- 57% of applicants admitted
- SAT or ACT (ACT writing optional), application essay required
- 57% graduate within 6 years; 30% enter graduate study

General. Founded in 1852. Regionally accredited. Cross registration at University of California-Berkeley and California College of the Arts, and many local community colleges. Extensive Study Abroad opportunities. Institutional emphasis on social justice. **Degrees:** 222 bachelor's awarded; master's, doctoral offered. **ROTC:** Army. **Location:** 18 miles from San Francisco, 8 miles from Berkeley. **Calendar:** Semester, limited summer session. **Full-time faculty:** 100 total; 89% have terminal degrees, 30% minority, 66% women. **Part-time faculty:** 103 total; 64% have terminal degrees, 25% minority, 68% women. **Class size:** 75% < 20, 24% 20-39, less than 1% 40-49, less than 1% 50-99, less than 1% >100. **Special facilities:** Art museum, electronic collaborative learning center, center for contemporary music, laboratory children's school for student teachers, institute for civic leadership, center for the book.

Freshman class profile. 2,251 applied, 1,284 admitted, 168 enrolled.

Mid 50% test scores			
SAT critical reading:	530-660	GPA 2.0-2.99:	1%
SAT math:	520-620	Rank in top quarter:	79%
SAT writing:	520-630	Rank in top tenth:	40%
ACT composite:	24-29	End year in good standing:	95%
GPA 3.75 or higher:	51%	Return as sophomores:	78%
GPA 3.50-3.74:	21%	Out-of-state:	23%
GPA 3.0-3.49:	27%	Live on campus:	94%
		International:	3%

Basis for selection. Minimum 3.0 GPA required, school achievement record most important. All credentials considered. SAT Subject Tests recommended. Interview recommended. **Home schooled:** Statement describing home school structure and mission, state high school equivalency certificate, letter of recommendation (nonparent) required. Must submit SAT Reasoning Test and two Subject Tests, or ACT.

High school preparation. College-preparatory program recommended. Required and recommended units include English 4, mathematics 3-4, social studies 2-4, history 2-4, science 2-4 (laboratory 2), foreign language 2-4 and visual/performing arts 2.

2012-2013 Annual costs. Tuition/fees: $40,080. Room/board: $11,580. Books/supplies: $1,430. Personal expenses: $2,000.

2010-2011 Financial aid. Need-based: 151 full-time freshmen applied for aid; 137 were judged to have need; 137 of these received aid. Average need met was 85%. Average scholarship/grant was $21,891; average loan $6,109. 74% of total undergraduate aid awarded as scholarships/grants, 26% as loans/jobs. **Non-need-based:** Awarded to 142 full-time undergraduates, including 43 freshmen. Scholarships awarded for academics, leadership, minority status, music/drama.

Application procedures. Admission: Priority date 2/1; deadline 8/1 (postmark date). $50 fee, may be waived for applicants with need. Admission notification on a rolling basis beginning on or about 12/1. Must reply by May 1 or within 2 week(s) if notified thereafter. **Financial aid:** Priority date 2/15; no closing date. FAFSA, institutional form required. Applicants notified on a rolling basis starting 3/1; must reply by 5/1 or within 2 week(s) of notification.

Academics. Cooperative bachelor of science in nursing program with Samuel Merritt College; pre-nursing students in this program receive a pre-nursing certificate from Mills upon completion of two years of study. Certificate premedicine program available to postbaccalaureate students. BA/MA in Infant Mental Health, BA/Teaching Credential/MA, and BA/MPP (Public Policy) offered. **Special study options:** Combined bachelor's/graduate degree, cross-registration, double major, exchange student, independent study, internships, liberal arts/career combination, student-designed major, study abroad, teacher certification program, Washington semester. **Credit/placement by examination:** AP, CLEP, IB, institutional tests. 8 credit hours maximum toward bachelor's degree. **Support services:** Learning center, pre-admission summer program, reduced course load, remedial instruction, study skills assistance, tutoring, writing center.

Majors. Area/ethnic studies: General, American, Chicano/Hispanic-American/Latino, French, gay/lesbian, Latin American, women's. **Biology:** General, biochemistry, molecular biochemistry. **Business:** General, managerial economics. **Computer sciences:** General, computer science. **Conservation:** Environmental science, environmental studies. **Engineering:** General. **English:** British lit, creative writing, English lit. **Foreign languages:** Comparative lit, French, Spanish. **History:** General, American. **Human services:** Public policy. **Math:** General. **Philosophy/religion:** Philosophy. **Physical sciences:** Chemistry. **Psychology:** General. **Social sciences:** General, anthropology, economics, international relations, political science, sociology, U.S. government. **Visual/performing arts:** Art, art history/conservation, dance, multimedia, music, studio arts. **Work/family studies:** Child development.

Most popular majors. Area/ethnic studies 11%, biology 6%, English 18%, psychology 11%, social sciences 18%, visual/performing arts 10%.

Computing on campus. 319 workstations in dormitories, library, computer center, student center. Dormitories wired for high-speed internet access and linked to campus network. Commuter students can connect to campus network. Online course registration, online library, helpline, student web hosting, wireless network available.

Student life. Freshman orientation: Mandatory. Preregistration for classes offered. 5 days prior to the start of classes. **Policies:** Individual integrity and mutual respect form foundation of learning community. Responsibility of every student to know and abide by standards set forth in the Honor Code, which also obliges students to report any violations of its standards. **Housing:** Guaranteed on-campus for all undergraduates. Special housing for disabled, apartments, cooperative housing, wellness housing available. $150 fully refundable deposit, deadline 6/1. **Activities:** Campus ministries, choral groups, dance, literary magazine, music ensembles, Model UN, radio station, student government, student newspaper, Black Women's Collective, Mujeres Unidas, Asian Pacific Islander Sisterhood Alliance, Muslim Student Association, Pagan Alliance, Fem Dems, Anime Alliance, Mills Earth CORPS, Mills Disability Alliance.

Athletics. NCAA. **Intercollegiate:** Cross-country W, rowing (crew) W, soccer W, swimming W, tennis W, track and field W, volleyball W. **Intramural:** Badminton W, basketball W. **Team name:** Cyclones.

Student services. Adult student services, alcohol/substance abuse counseling, chaplain/spiritual director, career counseling, student employment services, financial aid counseling, health services, minority student services, personal counseling, placement for graduates, women's services. **Physically disabled:** Services for visually, speech, hearing impaired.

Contact. E-mail: admission@mills.edu
Phone: (510) 430-2135 Toll-free number: (800) 876-4557
Fax: (510) 430-3314
Giulietta Aquino, Dean of Undergraduate Admission, Mills College, 5000 MacArthur Boulevard, Oakland, CA 94613

Mount St. Mary's College
Los Angeles, California
CB member
www.msmc.la.edu
CB code: 4493

- Private 4-year liberal arts college for women affiliated with Roman Catholic Church
- Residential campus in very large city
- 2,265 degree-seeking undergraduates: 22% part-time, 93% women, 10% African American, 18% Asian American, 50% Hispanic American, 1% Native American
- 647 degree-seeking graduate students
- 68% of applicants admitted
- SAT or ACT (ACT writing optional), application essay required
- 62% graduate within 6 years; 21% enter graduate study

General. Founded in 1925. Regionally accredited. Primarily a women's college at the undergraduate level, although men are admitted to undergraduate nursing and music programs, graduate division, weekend college and some summer courses. **Degrees:** 410 bachelor's, 143 associate awarded; master's, professional offered. **Location:** 2 miles from Los Angeles. **Calendar:** Semester, limited summer session. **Full-time faculty:** 99 total; 61% have terminal degrees, 21% minority, 75% women. **Part-time faculty:** 260 total; 30% have terminal degrees, 39% minority, 72% women. **Class size:** 56% < 20, 40% 20-39, 3% 40-49, 1% 50-99.

Freshman class profile. 1,822 applied, 1,237 admitted, 383 enrolled.

Mid 50% test scores			
SAT critical reading:	410-520	GPA 3.0-3.49:	39%
SAT math:	400-520	GPA 2.0-2.99:	23%
SAT writing:	420-530	End year in good standing:	86%
ACT composite:	17-22	Return as sophomores:	84%
GPA 3.75 or higher:	22%	Out-of-state:	2%
GPA 3.50-3.74:	16%	Live on campus:	74%

Basis for selection. Primary emphasis on school academic record, then test scores, essay, and letters of recommendation. School and community activities also considered. Interview important. Admission requirements considered very competitive in baccalaureate program. Interviews recommended. Auditions recommended of music majors. Portfolios recommended of art majors. **Home schooled:** Statement describing home school structure and mission, transcript of courses and grades, state high school equivalency certificate, letter of recommendation (nonparent) required. **Learning Disabled:** Documentation of learning disability required.

High school preparation. College-preparatory program recommended. Recommended units include English 4, mathematics 3, history 2, science 3 (laboratory 2), foreign language 2 and academic electives 1. For associate degree applicants, required courses include algebra, geometry, American history/government, and 4 units English.

2011-2012 Annual costs. Tuition/fees: $31,626. Room/board: $10,125.

2011-2012 Financial aid. Need-based: 380 full-time freshmen applied for aid; 368 were judged to have need; 367 of these received aid. Average need met was 63%. Average scholarship/grant was $19,911; average loan $2,596. 70% of total undergraduate aid awarded as scholarships/grants, 30% as loans/jobs. **Non-need-based:** Awarded to 219 full-time undergraduates, including 56 freshmen. Scholarships awarded for academics, alumni affiliation, music/drama.

Application procedures. Admission: Priority date 2/15; no deadline. $50 fee, may be waived for applicants with need. Admission notification on a rolling basis beginning on or about 11/30. Must reply by May 1 or within 2 week(s) if notified thereafter. **Financial aid:** Priority date 3/2; no closing date. FAFSA required. Applicants notified on a rolling basis starting 3/15; must reply by 5/1.

Academics. Special study options: Accelerated study, combined bachelor's/graduate degree, cross-registration, double major, exchange student, honors, independent study, internships, student-designed major, study abroad, teacher certification program, United Nations semester, Washington semester, weekend college. **Credit/placement by examination:** AP, CLEP, IB, SAT, ACT, institutional tests. 24 credit hours maximum toward associate degree, 30 toward bachelor's. **Support services:** Learning center, pre-admission summer program, reduced course load, remedial instruction, study skills assistance, tutoring, writing center.

Majors. Area/ethnic studies: American. **Biology:** General, biochemistry. **Business:** General, accounting, business admin, international. **Education:** Elementary, middle, secondary. **English:** English lit. **Foreign languages:** French, Spanish. **Health services:** Health care admin, nursing (RN), predental, premedicine, preveterinary. **History:** General. **Math:** General, applied. **Philosophy/religion:** Philosophy, religion. **Physical sciences:** Chemistry. **Psychology:** General. **Social sciences:** General, criminology, political science, sociology. **Theology:** Sacred music. **Visual/performing arts:** Music, music performance, music theory/composition, studio arts.

Most popular majors. Business/marketing 11%, health sciences 38%, psychology 10%, social sciences 22%.

Computing on campus. 300 workstations in dormitories, library, computer center, student center. Dormitories wired for high-speed internet access and linked to campus network. Commuter students can connect to campus network. Online course registration, helpline, student web hosting, wireless network available.

Student life. Freshman orientation: Available. Preregistration for classes offered. Occurs during a weekend, typically in late June. **Policies:** Student resident life largely self-regulated under direction of Residence Council. **Housing:** Guaranteed on-campus for freshmen. $200 fully refundable deposit, deadline 5/1. **Activities:** Campus ministries, choral groups, dance, literary magazine, music ensembles, student government, student newspaper, symphony orchestra, various academic, service, cultural and Greek organizations and student clubs available.

Athletics. Intramural: Basketball, soccer, softball, swimming, tennis, volleyball. **Team name:** Athenians.

Student services. Adult student services, chaplain/spiritual director, career counseling, student employment services, financial aid counseling, health services, personal counseling, placement for graduates.

Contact. E-mail: admissions@msmc.la.edu
Phone: (310) 954-4250 Toll-free number: (800) 999-9893
Fax: (310) 954-4259
Yvonne Berumen, Director of Admissions, Mount St. Mary's College, 12001 Chalon Road, Los Angeles, CA 90049

Mt. Sierra College
Monrovia, California
www.mtsierra.edu
CB code: 3090

- For-profit 3-year visual arts and business college
- Commuter campus in large city
- 614 degree-seeking undergraduates
- 40% of applicants admitted
- Application essay, interview required

General. Accredited by ACCSC. **Degrees:** 60 bachelor's awarded. **Location:** 20 miles from Los Angeles. **Calendar:** Quarter, extensive summer session. **Full-time faculty:** 12 total. **Part-time faculty:** 59 total. **Class size:** 98% < 20, 2% 20-39. **Special facilities:** Green-screen room for special effects video, sound room, mac and game arts computer labs.

Freshman class profile. 379 applied, 153 admitted, 133 enrolled.

Basis for selection. Must have high school diploma or equivalent and take a basic writing, math, online assessments. High school and/or college GPA are also considered. **Home schooled:** Transcript of courses and grades, state high school equivalency certificate, interview required.

2011-2012 Annual costs. Tuition/fees: $15,715. Mandatory STRF fee between $197.50 and $217.50 depending upon program and due upon enrollment; laptop expenses between $600 - $1,600 depending upon program. Books and supplies: $5,544 - $6,648 depending upon program.

Application procedures. Admission: No deadline. $50 fee, may be waived for applicants with need. Admission notification on a rolling basis. **Financial aid:** FAFSA required.

Academics. Special study options: Accelerated study, distance learning, independent study, weekend college. **Credit/placement by examination:** AP, CLEP, IB, institutional tests. **Support services:** Learning center, study skills assistance, tutoring.

Majors. Business: Business admin, entrepreneurial studies. **Computer sciences:** General, information technology, networking, security, web page design. **Visual/performing arts:** Digital arts, game design, graphic design, multimedia.

Most popular majors. Business/marketing 14%, computer/information sciences 39%, visual/performing arts 47%.

Computing on campus. PC or laptop required. 35 workstations in library, computer center. Commuter students can connect to campus network. Online library, wireless network available.

Student life. Freshman orientation: Available. Preregistration for classes offered. Held prior to class start dates. Date of orientations are announced. **Activities:** Student newspaper.

Student services. Placement for graduates.

Contact. E-mail: pazadian@mtsierra.edu
Phone: (626) 873-2100 Toll-free number: (888) 828-8800
Fax: (626) 359-1378
Patrick Azadian, Director of Admissions, Mt. Sierra College, 101 East Huntington Drive, Monrovia, CA 91016

National Hispanic University
San Jose, California
www.nhu.edu   CB code: 4593

- Private 4-year university
- Commuter campus in very large city
- 441 degree-seeking undergraduates
- 177 graduate students
- Application essay required

General. Regionally accredited. **Degrees:** 36 bachelor's, 1 associate awarded; master's offered. **Calendar:** Semester, limited summer session. **Full-time faculty:** 11 total; 46% have terminal degrees, 27% minority, 18% women. **Part-time faculty:** 65 total; 48% minority, 52% women.

Freshman class profile. 144 applied, 142 admitted, 85 enrolled.

Basis for selection. Open admission. High school GPA, transcript, two letters of recommendation required. **Home schooled:** State high school equivalency certificate required.

2011-2012 Annual costs. Tuition/fees: $10,110.

Application procedures. Admission: No deadline. $50 fee, may be waived for applicants with need. Application must be submitted online. Admission notification on a rolling basis. **Financial aid:** FAFSA required.

Academics. Special study options: Cross-registration, distance learning, independent study, teacher certification program. **Credit/placement by examination:** AP, CLEP, IB, institutional tests. **Support services:** Learning center, pre-admission summer program, remedial instruction, study skills assistance, tutoring.

Majors. Business: Business admin. **Computer sciences:** General. **Liberal arts:** Arts/sciences.

Computing on campus. Online course registration, online library, wireless network available.

Student life. Freshman orientation: Mandatory. Preregistration for classes offered. **Activities:** Student government.

Student services. Financial aid counseling, personal counseling.

Contact. Phone: (408) 729-2283 Fax: (408) 254-1369
National Hispanic University, 14271 Story Road, San Jose, CA 95127-3823

National University
La Jolla, California   CB member
www.nu.edu   CB code: 0470

- Private 4-year university
- Commuter campus in very large city
- 11,629 degree-seeking undergraduates: 67% part-time, 60% women, 12% African American, 10% Asian American, 22% Hispanic American, 1% Native American, 1% international
- 15,675 degree-seeking graduate students
- Interview required
- 36% graduate within 6 years

General. Founded in 1971. Regionally accredited. Campuses in 11 major cities throughout California; courses offered both on-site and online. **Degrees:** 1,234 bachelor's, 103 associate awarded; master's offered. **ROTC:** Army, Naval, Air Force. **Calendar:** Differs by program, limited summer session. **Full-time faculty:** 253 total; 74% have terminal degrees, 23% minority, 51% women. **Part-time faculty:** 2,853 total; 23% have terminal degrees, 30% minority, 52% women. **Class size:** 68% < 20, 30% 20-39, 1% 40-49, less than 1% 50-99. **Special facilities:** Nursing labs, forensics labs, e-book collection.

Freshman class profile. 3,793 applied, 3,793 admitted, 796 enrolled.

Out-of-state: 11%   **International:**   3%

Basis for selection. Open admission, but selective for some programs. Interview, previous business and work experience, academic record considered.

2011-2012 Annual costs. Tuition/fees: $11,436. Books/supplies: $1,440. Personal expenses: $2,504.

2010-2011 Financial aid. Need-based: 40% of total undergraduate aid awarded as scholarships/grants, 60% as loans/jobs.

Application procedures. Admission: No deadline. $60 fee. Admission notification on a rolling basis. **Financial aid:** No deadline. FAFSA, institutional form required. Applicants notified on a rolling basis.

Academics. Agreements with over 950 public and private schools to place students earning teaching credentials in practicums. **Special study options:** Accelerated study, cross-registration, distance learning, double major, ESL, independent study, internships, liberal arts/career combination, teacher certification program. **Credit/placement by examination:** AP, CLEP, institutional tests. 14 credit hours maximum toward associate degree, 23 toward bachelor's. **Support services:** Learning center, remedial instruction, tutoring, writing center.

Majors. Area/ethnic studies: Chinese, Near/Middle Eastern. **Business:** General, accounting, business admin, construction management, finance, hospitality admin, human resources, operations, organizational behavior. **Communications:** Broadcast journalism, digital media, journalism, media studies, radio/TV. **Computer sciences:** General, computer science, information systems, information technology, security, system admin, systems analysis. **Conservation:** Environmental science, management/policy. **Education:** Early childhood, mathematics, multi-level teacher, secondary. **Engineering:** Construction, systems. **English:** English lit. **Foreign languages:** American Sign Language, Arabic, Chinese, Iranian. **Health services:** Health care admin, nursing (RN), preop/surgical nursing. **History:** General. **Human services:** General. **Liberal arts:** Arts/sciences. **Math:** General. **Physical sciences:** General, geology. **Protective services:** Criminal justice, law enforcement admin, security services. **Psychology:** General. **Social sciences:** Economics, sociology. **Visual/performing arts:** Game design, multimedia. **Work/family studies:** Child development.

Most popular majors. Business/marketing 24%, education 8%, health sciences 16%, legal studies 7%, liberal arts 6%, psychology 10%.

Computing on campus. 3,100 workstations in library, computer center, student center. Commuter students can connect to campus network. Online course registration, online library, helpline, wireless network available.

Student life. Freshman orientation: Available. Preregistration for classes offered.

Student services. Adult student services, career counseling, services for economically disadvantaged, student employment services, financial aid counseling, minority student services, placement for graduates, veterans' counselor. **Physically disabled:** Services for visually, speech, hearing impaired.

Contact. E-mail: advisor@nu.edu
Phone: (800) 628-8648 Toll-free number: (800) 628-8648
Fax: (858) 541-7792
Mark Moses, Associate Regional Dean - San Diego, National University, 11255 North Torrey Pines Road, La Jolla, CA 92037-1011

NewSchool of Architecture & Design
San Diego, California
www.newschoolarch.edu   CB code: 2419

- For-profit 5-year visual arts and liberal arts college
- Commuter campus in very large city
- 613 degree-seeking undergraduates
- Interview required

General. Founded in 1980. Accredited by ACICS. **Degrees:** 55 bachelor's awarded; master's offered. **Location:** 90 miles from Los Angeles, 17 miles from Tijuana, Mexico. **Calendar:** Quarter, extensive summer session. **Full-time faculty:** 23 total. **Part-time faculty:** 72 total. **Special facilities:** Design clinic.

Basis for selection. Resume considered if submitted. Portfolio review required.

2011-2012 Annual costs. Tuition/fees: $22,995. Books/supplies: $2,885. Personal expenses: $2,754.

Financial aid. Non-need-based: Scholarships awarded for academics.

Application procedures. Admission: No deadline. $75 fee, may be waived for applicants with need. Admission notification on a rolling basis. Must reply by May 1 or within 4 week(s) if notified thereafter. **Financial aid:** No deadline. FAFSA required. Applicants notified on a rolling basis.

Academics. Special study options: Accelerated study, cooperative education, double major, internships, liberal arts/career combination. Cooperative program available at nearby U.S. International University, where students can take ESL and general education classes. **Credit/placement by examination:** AP, CLEP. **Support services:** Pre-admission summer program, tutoring.

Majors. Architecture: Architecture.

Computing on campus. 17 workstations in library, computer center.

Student life. Freshman orientation: Available. Preregistration for classes offered. Held 1-2 days before start of classes in fall. **Housing:** Some housing through US International University. **Activities:** Literary magazine, student government, student newspaper, American Institute of Architects student chapter.

Student services. Career counseling, student employment services, health services, personal counseling, placement for graduates, veterans' counselor.

Contact. E-mail: admissions@newschoolarch.edu
Phone: (619) 684-8841 Fax: (619) 235-4651
Meg Booth, Director of Admissions, NewSchool of Architecture & Design, 1249 F Street, San Diego, CA 92101

Northwestern Polytechnic University
Fremont, California
www.npu.edu   CB code: 4335

- Private 4-year business and engineering college
- Commuter campus in small city
- 222 degree-seeking undergraduates

General. Accredited by ACICS. **Degrees:** 41 bachelor's awarded; master's, professional offered. **Location:** 42 miles from San Francisco, 7 miles from

San Jose. **Calendar:** Trimester, extensive summer session. **Full-time faculty:** 19 total. **Part-time faculty:** 58 total. **Class size:** 62% < 20, 38% 20-39.

Basis for selection. High school record, pre-calculus required. Recommendations and test scores as reference. Interview recommended. English placement exams are given to international students who do not provide standardized English test scores. On-campus English placement exam may replace TOEFL; on-campus freshman exam may replace SAT. Standardized test administered by ETS or on-campus equivalent assessment test acceptable. The test score does not affect the student's admission to the program.

High school preparation. College-preparatory program required. Required and recommended units include English 3, mathematics 2, social studies 1 and science 1. 1 math required for business programs.

2012-2013 Annual costs. Tuition/fees: $9,250. Books/supplies: $800.

Financial aid. Additional information: Work-study, co-op program, internships available. Employment opportunities with local firms help defray costs.

Application procedures. Admission: Priority date 8/1; deadline 8/29 (postmark date). $60 fee. Admission notification on a rolling basis. Must reply by 9/7.

Academics. Curricula designed to meet needs of high-tech industries and global businesses. **Special study options:** ESL. **Credit/placement by examination:** AP, CLEP, IB, institutional tests. 15 credit hours maximum toward bachelor's degree. **Support services:** Learning center, tutoring.

Majors. Business: Business admin. **Engineering:** Electrical, software, systems.

Most popular majors. Business/marketing 63%, engineering/engineering technologies 37%.

Computing on campus. 250 workstations in library, computer center, student center. Dormitories wired for high-speed internet access. Commuter students can connect to campus network. Online library, helpline, repair service, student web hosting, wireless network available.

Student life. Freshman orientation: Mandatory. Preregistration for classes offered. One-day program before the semester start date. **Policies:** Students are required to join student association, and encouraged to join student clubs. **Housing:** Apartments, wellness housing available. $300 fully refundable deposit, deadline 8/1. **Activities:** Dance, international student organizations, literary magazine, music ensembles, Model UN, student government, student newspaper.

Athletics. Intercollegiate: Table tennis. **Intramural:** Table tennis.

Student services. Adult student services, career counseling, services for economically disadvantaged, student employment services, personal counseling, placement for graduates, veterans' counselor.

Contact. E-mail: admission@npu.edu
Phone: (510) 592-9688 ext. 8 Fax: (510) 657-8975
Monica Sinha, Director of Admission, Northwestern Polytechnic University, 47671 Westinghouse Drive, Fremont, CA 94539

Notre Dame de Namur University
Belmont, California   CB member
www.ndnu.edu   CB code: 4063

- Private 4-year university and liberal arts college affiliated with Roman Catholic Church
- Residential campus in large town
- 1,146 degree-seeking undergraduates: 35% part-time, 66% women, 7% African American, 11% Asian American, 26% Hispanic American, 1% Native American, 3% international
- 582 degree-seeking graduate students
- 71% of applicants admitted
- SAT or ACT (ACT writing recommended), application essay required
- 51% graduate within 6 years

General. Founded in 1851. Regionally accredited. **Degrees:** 196 bachelor's awarded; master's offered. **ROTC:** Air Force. **Location:** 19 miles from San Francisco. **Calendar:** Semester, limited summer session. **Full-time faculty:** 56 total; 89% have terminal degrees, 27% minority, 55% women. **Part-time faculty:** 146 total; 14% minority, 64% women. **Class size:** 69% < 20, 30% 20-39, 1% 40-49. **Special facilities:** Gymnasium, gallery.

Freshman class profile. 1,789 applied, 1,270 admitted, 177 enrolled.

Mid 50% test scores				
SAT critical reading:	420-530	Rank in top quarter:	41%
SAT math:	420-530	Rank in top tenth:	15%
ACT composite:	18-23	End year in good standing:	86%
GPA 3.75 or higher:	12%	Return as sophomores:	77%
GPA 3.50-3.74:	9%	Out-of-state:	8%
GPA 3.0-3.49:	33%	Live on campus:	94%
GPA 2.0-2.99:	46%	International:	3%

Basis for selection. High school record and GPA most important; test scores also important. Essay, recommendation, and school and community activities considered. Audition for music students. Audition required for music programs. **Home schooled:** Statement describing home school structure and mission, transcript of courses and grades, state high school equivalency certificate, interview, letter of recommendation (nonparent) required.

High school preparation. College-preparatory program recommended. 15 units required; 18 recommended. Required and recommended units include English 4, mathematics 2-3, social studies 2, history 1, science 1-2 (laboratory 1), foreign language 2-3 and academic electives 3. Electives: 3 units from fine arts, advanced laboratory science, advanced mathematics, advanced social science, computer science, or advanced foreign language recommended.

2012-2013 Annual costs. Tuition/fees (projected): $30,522. Room/board: $11,970. Books/supplies: $1,656. Personal expenses: $3,150.

2011-2012 Financial aid. Non-need-based: Scholarships awarded for academics, alumni affiliation, athletics, leadership, music/drama, religious affiliation.

Application procedures. **Admission:** Priority date 2/1; no deadline. $50 fee, may be waived for applicants with need. Admission notification on a rolling basis. Must reply by May 1 or within 3 week(s) if notified thereafter. **Financial aid:** Priority date 3/2; no closing date. FAFSA required. CSS PROFILE accepted but not required. Applicants notified on a rolling basis starting 1/15.

Academics. **Special study options:** Accelerated study, double major, dual enrollment of high school students, ESL, exchange student, independent study, internships, liberal arts/career combination, student-designed major, study abroad, teacher certification program. **Credit/placement by examination:** AP, CLEP, IB, institutional tests. Units earned by examination cannot be used in satisfying the 30-unit residency requirement. **Support services:** Learning center, reduced course load, remedial instruction, study skills assistance, tutoring, writing center.

Majors. **Biology:** General, biochemistry, exercise physiology. **Business:** Business admin. **Communications:** Communications/speech/rhetoric. **Computer sciences:** General. **English:** English lit. **Health services:** Premedicine, prenursing. **History:** General. **Liberal arts:** Arts/sciences. **Philosophy/religion:** Philosophy, religion. **Psychology:** General. **Social sciences:** General, political science, sociology. **Visual/performing arts:** Art, dramatic, graphic design, music, music performance, studio arts, voice/opera.

Most popular majors. Biology 9%, business/marketing 24%, liberal arts 7%, psychology 10%, public administration/social services 21%, social sciences 7%, visual/performing arts 10%.

Computing on campus. 90 workstations in library, computer center. Dormitories wired for high-speed internet access and linked to campus network. Commuter students can connect to campus network. Online library, helpline, student web hosting, wireless network available.

Student life. **Freshman orientation:** Mandatory, $175 fee. Preregistration for classes offered. Held 1 week before classes begin in fall. **Housing:** Guaranteed on-campus for freshmen. Coed dorms, apartments available. $200 nonrefundable deposit. **Activities:** Campus ministries, choral groups, dance, drama, international student organizations, musical theater, student government, student newspaper, Isang Lahi, Latino Unidos, business/career club, black student union, Roteract, Toastmasters, Students for Sustainability, Amnesty International, science and medical careers club.

Athletics. NCAA. **Intercollegiate:** Basketball, cross-country, golf M, lacrosse M, soccer, softball W, tennis W, volleyball W. **Team name:** Argonauts.

Student services. Adult student services, alcohol/substance abuse counseling, chaplain/spiritual director, career counseling, student employment services, financial aid counseling, health services, personal counseling, placement for graduates.

Contact. E-mail: admiss@ndnu.edu
Phone: (650) 508-3600 Toll-free number: (800) 263-0545
Fax: (650) 508-3426
Jason Murray, Director of Admissions, Notre Dame de Namur University, 1500 Ralston Avenue, Belmont, CA 94002-1908

Occidental College

Los Angeles, California
www.oxy.edu

CB member
CB code: 4581

- Private 4-year liberal arts college affiliated with nondenominational tradition
- Residential campus in very large city
- 2,107 degree-seeking undergraduates: 1% part-time, 57% women
- 2 degree-seeking graduate students
- 39% of applicants admitted
- SAT or ACT with writing, application essay required
- 84% graduate within 6 years; 22% enter graduate study

General. Founded in 1887. Regionally accredited. **Degrees:** 448 bachelor's awarded; master's offered. **ROTC:** Army, Air Force. **Location:** 5 miles from downtown. **Calendar:** Semester. **Full-time faculty:** 184 total; 28% minority, 48% women. **Part-time faculty:** 81 total; 24% minority, 43% women. **Class size:** 69% < 20, 30% 20-39, less than 1% 40-49, less than 1% 50-99, less than 1% >100. **Special facilities:** Marine biology program with scuba access, plasma physics and fluid dynamics labs, paleomagnetic lab, dark matter detector, geochemical/environmental lab, ornithology collection, geological collection, astronomical instruments collection, vivarium, greenhouses, print studio, film lab, student garden, student-run coffee lounge.

Freshman class profile. 6,120 applied, 2,369 admitted, 537 enrolled.

Mid 50% test scores				
SAT critical reading:	600-700	GPA 2.0-2.99:	3%
SAT math:	610-690	Rank in top quarter:	91%
SAT writing:	600-700	Rank in top tenth:	60%
ACT composite:	27-31	Return as sophomores:	90%
GPA 3.75 or higher:	41%	Out-of-state:	53%
GPA 3.50-3.74:	23%	Live on campus:	100%
GPA 3.0-3.49:	33%	International:	4%

Basis for selection. Primary consideration given to academic credentials and holistic qualities such as intellectual curiosity, out-of-class interests, and personal character. SAT subject tests may be used for some foreign language placement. SAT Subject Tests recommended. Interview recommended. **Home schooled:** Statement describing home school structure and mission, transcript of courses and grades, state high school equivalency certificate, letter of recommendation (nonparent) required. At least 2 SAT Subject Tests recommended.

High school preparation. College-preparatory program recommended. 20 units recommended. Recommended units include English 4, mathematics 4, social studies 2, history 2, science 3 (laboratory 2), foreign language 3 and academic electives 2.

2011-2012 Annual costs. Tuition/fees: $42,960. Room/board: $11,990. Books/supplies: $1,180. Personal expenses: $1,440.

Financial aid. Non-need-based: Scholarships awarded for academics, leadership, music/drama, state residency. **Additional information:** Work-study programs are available during the day when students are not in class.

Application procedures. **Admission:** Closing date 1/10 (postmark date). $60 fee, may be waived for applicants with need. Application must be submitted online. Admission notification by 4/1. Must reply by May 1 or within 2 week(s) if notified thereafter. **Financial aid:** Closing date 2/1. FAFSA, CSS PROFILE required. Applicants notified by 4/1; must reply by 5/1.

Academics. **Special study options:** Combined bachelor's/graduate degree, cross-registration, double major, honors, independent study, internships, student-designed major, study abroad, United Nations semester. Richter Fellowships for funded international research, summer research program, endowment investment management program (Blyth Fund). **Credit/placement by examination:** AP, CLEP, IB, institutional tests. **Support services:** Learning center, pre-admission summer program, study skills assistance, tutoring, writing center.

Majors. **Area/ethnic studies:** American, Asian. **Biology:** General, biochemistry. **English:** English lit. **Foreign languages:** General, French, Spanish. **History:** General. **Math:** General. **Parks/recreation:** Exercise sciences. **Philosophy/religion:** Philosophy, religion. **Physical sciences:** Chemistry, geology, geophysics, physics. **Psychology:** General. **Social sciences:** Economics, international relations, political science, sociology. **Visual/performing arts:** Art, art history/conservation, dramatic, music.

Most popular majors. Biology 9%, English 6%, foreign language 6%, natural resources/environmental science 6%, psychology 8%, social sciences 32%, visual/performing arts 10%.

Computing on campus. 300 workstations in dormitories, library, computer center. Commuter students can connect to campus network. Online course registration, online library, helpline, wireless network available.

Student life. Freshman orientation: Mandatory. Preregistration for classes offered. Held one week in August before the start of classes. Prior to orientation, students can participate in a wilderness trip, community service work, or an arts and culture experience. **Policies:** All residence halls student-run; freshmen, sophomores and juniors are required to live on campus. **Housing:** Guaranteed on-campus for freshmen. Coed dorms, single-sex dorms, fraternity/sorority housing, wellness housing available. **Activities:** Bands, campus ministries, choral groups, dance, drama, film society, international student organizations, literary magazine, music ensembles, musical theater, radio station, student government, student newspaper, symphony orchestra, TV station, 100 clubs and organizations available.

Athletics. NCAA. **Intercollegiate:** Baseball M, basketball, cross-country, diving, football (tackle) M, golf, lacrosse W, soccer, softball W, swimming, tennis, track and field, volleyball W, water polo. **Intramural:** Basketball, football (non-tackle), soccer, volleyball. **Team name:** Tigers.

Student services. Alcohol/substance abuse counseling, chaplain/spiritual director, career counseling, services for economically disadvantaged, financial aid counseling, health services, minority student services, on-campus daycare, personal counseling, women's services. **Physically disabled:** Services for hearing impaired.

Contact. E-mail: admission@oxy.edu
Phone: (323) 259-2700 Toll-free number: (800) 825-5262
Fax: (323) 341-4875
Sally Richmond, Director of Admission, Occidental College, 1600 Campus Road, Los Angeles, CA 90041

Otis College of Art and Design
Los Angeles, California
www.otis.edu

CB member
CB code: 4394

- Private 4-year visual arts college
- Commuter campus in very large city
- 1,138 degree-seeking undergraduates: 2% part-time, 68% women, 4% African American, 35% Asian American, 14% Hispanic American, 1% Native American, 15% international
- 68 degree-seeking graduate students
- 51% of applicants admitted
- SAT or ACT (ACT writing optional), application essay required
- 57% graduate within 6 years

General. Founded in 1918. Regionally accredited. **Degrees:** 235 bachelor's awarded; master's offered. **Calendar:** Semester, limited summer session. **Full-time faculty:** 55 total; 49% have terminal degrees, 14% minority, 56% women. **Part-time faculty:** 360 total; 17% have terminal degrees, 20% minority, 44% women. **Class size:** 78% < 20, 20% 20-39, 2% 50-99. **Special facilities:** Rare art books collection, full foundry and casting facilities, photographic darkroom, fully equipped printmaking studio, fine art book press room, wood and metal working shops, toy design department, digital imaging studio.

Freshman class profile. 1,458 applied, 745 admitted, 185 enrolled.

Mid 50% test scores			
SAT critical reading:	430-570	GPA 3.0-3.49:	34%
SAT math:	460-550	GPA 2.0-2.99:	38%
ACT composite:	21-27	Return as sophomores:	78%
GPA 3.75 or higher:	14%	Out-of-state:	32%
GPA 3.50-3.74:	14%	Live on campus:	58%
		International:	11%

Basis for selection. Portfolio most important, followed by school achievement record, essay and test scores. Activities, leadership, motivation also considered. Portfolio required. Interview recommended. **Home schooled:** Documentation that student has solid academic foundation, is socially and intellectually mature, and has passion for the arts.

High school preparation. Required and recommended units include English 4, mathematics 3-4, social studies 1-2, history 2-3, science 2-4 (laboratory 1-4) and foreign language 2. Drawing and as much art as possible recommended.

2011-2012 Annual costs. Tuition/fees: $35,354. Books/supplies: $1,400. Personal expenses: $1,300.

2011-2012 Financial aid. Need-based: 146 full-time freshmen applied for aid; 134 were judged to have need; 134 of these received aid. Average need met was 45%. Average scholarship/grant was $19,852; average loan

$3,470. 66% of total undergraduate aid awarded as scholarships/grants, 34% as loans/jobs. **Non-need-based:** Awarded to 179 full-time undergraduates, including 37 freshmen. Scholarships awarded for academics, art.

Application procedures. Admission: Priority date 2/15; no deadline. $60 fee, may be waived for applicants with need. Admission notification on a rolling basis beginning on or about 12/15. Must reply by May 1 or within 2 week(s) if notified thereafter. **Financial aid:** Priority date 2/15; no closing date. FAFSA required. Applicants notified on a rolling basis starting 3/1; must reply within 2 week(s) of notification.

Academics. Approximately one-third of curriculum consists of liberal arts classes. **Special study options:** Cooperative education, ESL, exchange student, honors, internships, study abroad, teacher certification program. **Credit/placement by examination:** AP, CLEP, IB, institutional tests. **Support services:** Learning center, pre-admission summer program, reduced course load, remedial instruction, study skills assistance, tutoring.

Majors. Architecture: Architecture, environmental design, interior, landscape. **Communications technology:** Animation/special effects. **Visual/performing arts:** Art, design, fashion design, graphic design, illustration, industrial design, interior design, multimedia, painting, photography, sculpture, studio arts.

Most popular majors. Architecture 8%, visual/performing arts 92%.

Computing on campus. 350 workstations in library, computer center. Helpline, wireless network available.

Student life. Freshman orientation: Mandatory. Preregistration for classes offered. Held in January, July and August. **Housing:** Apartments available. $550 nonrefundable deposit, deadline 6/1. Otis sponsored off-campus apartments available. **Activities:** International student organizations, student government, literary organization, Campus Crusade.

Student services. Adult student services, alcohol/substance abuse counseling, career counseling, student employment services, financial aid counseling, personal counseling, placement for graduates. **Physically disabled:** Services for hearing impaired.

Contact. E-mail: admissions@otis.edu
Phone: (310) 665-6820 Toll-free number: (800) 527-6847
Fax: (310) 665-6821
Yvette Sobky Shaffer, Assistant Dean and Director of Admissions, Otis College of Art and Design, 9045 Lincoln Boulevard, Los Angeles, CA 90045-9785

Pacific Oaks College
Pasadena, California
www.pacificoaks.edu

CB code: 0482

- Private two-year upper-division teachers college
- Commuter campus in small city
- Application essay required

General. Founded in 1951. Regionally accredited. College and children's school founded by Quaker families as community education center. **Degrees:** 48 bachelor's awarded; master's offered. **Articulation:** Agreements with De Anza College, Glendale City College, College of the Canyons, Pasadena City College, Rio Hondo College, Santa Monica College, Santa Barbara College, East Los Angeles College, El Camino College, Mt. San Antonio College, Citrus College. **Location:** 10 miles from downtown Los Angeles. **Calendar:** Semester, limited summer session. **Full-time faculty:** 11 total. **Part-time faculty:** 100 total. **Class size:** 72% < 20, 28% 20-39.

Student profile. 129 degree-seeking undergraduates.

Out-of-state:	19%	25 or older:	94%

Basis for selection. College transcript, application essay required. Must have completed equivalent of GED. Transfer accepted as juniors, seniors.

2011-2012 Annual costs. Tuition/fees: $22,040. Books/supplies: $1,638. Personal expenses: $3,096.

Application procedures. Admission: Priority date 4/15; deadline 6/1. $50 fee, may be waived for applicants with need. Application must be submitted on paper.

Academics. Special study options: Accelerated study, distance learning, independent study, internships, teacher certification program, weekend college. **Credit/placement by examination:** AP, CLEP. 30 credit hours maximum toward bachelor's degree. Students age 30-35 without a bachelor's degree may earn credit based on life experience.

Majors. Work/family studies: Family studies.

Computing on campus. 17 workstations in library, computer center. Online library available.

Student life. Activities: Teacher education student association; marriage, family therapy student association.

Student services. Adult student services, career counseling, financial aid counseling. **Physically disabled:** Services for visually, speech, hearing impaired.

Contact. E-mail: admissions@pacificoaks.edu
Phone: (626) 397-1349 Toll-free number: (800) 684-0900
Fax: (626) 666-1220
Crystal Miller, Director of Admissions, Pacific Oaks College, 5 Westmoreland Place, Pasadena, CA 91103

Pacific States University
Los Angeles, California
www.psuca.edu   CB code: 3547

- Private 4-year university
- Commuter campus in very large city
- 16 degree-seeking undergraduates: 25% women, 62% international
- 139 degree-seeking graduate students

General. Accredited by ACICS. **Degrees:** 5 bachelor's awarded; master's, doctoral offered. **Location:** 5 miles from downtown. **Calendar:** Quarter, limited summer session. **Full-time faculty:** 7 total; 57% have terminal degrees, 100% minority, 14% women. **Part-time faculty:** 23 total; 44% have terminal degrees, 100% minority, 17% women.

Basis for selection. Open admission, but selective for some programs. High school diploma and English proficiency required. TOEFL required of students whose native language is not English. **Home schooled:** Transcript of courses and grades, state high school equivalency certificate required.

2012-2013 Annual costs. Tuition/fees (projected): $19,340. Room/board: $12,600. Books/supplies: $2,160.

Financial aid. Non-need-based: Scholarships awarded for academics.

Application procedures. Admission: No deadline. $100 fee. Application must be submitted on paper. Admission notification on a rolling basis. **Financial aid:** No deadline. FAFSA, institutional form required.

Academics. Special study options: Combined bachelor's/graduate degree, distance learning, double major, ESL, liberal arts/career combination. **Credit/placement by examination:** AP, CLEP, IB. 8 credit hours maximum toward bachelor's degree.

Majors. Business: Accounting, management information systems, marketing. **Computer sciences:** General.

Computing on campus. 40 workstations in dormitories, library, computer center. Online course registration, online library, wireless network available.

Student life. Freshman orientation: Available. Preregistration for classes offered. Held 2 weeks after each quarter starts, lasting 2 hours. **Housing:** Guaranteed on-campus for all undergraduates. Coed dorms, wellness housing available. **Activities:** Literary magazine, TV station.

Student services. Student employment services, financial aid counseling, personal counseling.

Contact. E-mail: admissions@psuca.edu
Phone: (323) 731-2383 ext. 203 Toll-free number: (888) 200-0383
Fax: (323) 731-7276
Seohee Yang, Admission Advisor, Pacific States University, 3450 Wilshire Boulevard, Suite 500, Los Angeles, CA 90010

Pacific Union College
Angwin, California
www.puc.edu   CB code: 4600

- Private 4-year liberal arts college affiliated with Seventh-day Adventists
- Residential campus in small town

- 1,487 degree-seeking undergraduates: 9% part-time, 54% women, 6% African American, 20% Asian American, 22% Hispanic American, 1% Native American, 5% international
- 1 degree-seeking graduate students
- 47% of applicants admitted
- SAT or ACT (ACT writing recommended) required
- 49% graduate within 6 years

General. Founded in 1882. Regionally accredited. **Degrees:** 199 bachelor's, 98 associate awarded; master's offered. **Location:** 30 miles from Napa, 75 miles from San Francisco. **Calendar:** Quarter, limited summer session. **Full-time faculty:** 94 total; 55% have terminal degrees, 26% minority, 48% women. **Part-time faculty:** 41 total; 22% have terminal degrees, 22% minority, 46% women. **Class size:** 56% < 20, 34% 20-39, 5% 40-49, 4% 50-99, less than 1% >100. **Special facilities:** Observatory, airport/flight training, biology museum, Pitcairn Island study center, 1500-acre nature preserve.

Freshman class profile. 2,524 applied, 1,182 admitted, 363 enrolled.

Mid 50% test scores			
SAT critical reading:	440-560	GPA 3.0-3.49:	26%
SAT math:	430-590	GPA 2.0-2.99:	27%
SAT writing:	440-560	End year in good standing:	77%
ACT composite:	18-25	Return as sophomores:	71%
GPA 3.75 or higher:	27%	Out-of-state:	19%
GPA 3.50-3.74:	20%	Live on campus:	98%
		International:	3%

Basis for selection. Minimum GPA of 2.3 and acceptable recommendations. **Home schooled:** Transcript of courses and grades, state high school equivalency certificate, letter of recommendation (nonparent) required. **Learning Disabled:** Documentation if available.

High school preparation. College-preparatory program recommended. 10 units required. Required and recommended units include English 4, mathematics 2-3, history 2, science 2-3 and foreign language 2. Computer literacy, religion (if offered).

2012-2013 Annual costs. Tuition/fees: $26,040. $600 health insurance. Room/board: $7,350. Books/supplies: $1,665. Personal expenses: $2,277.

2011-2012 Financial aid. Need-based: 364 full-time freshmen applied for aid; 294 were judged to have need; 294 of these received aid. Average need met was 52%. Average scholarship/grant was $19,390; average loan $3,101. 77% of total undergraduate aid awarded as scholarships/grants, 23% as loans/jobs. **Non-need-based:** Awarded to 826 full-time undergraduates, including 145 freshmen. Scholarships awarded for academics, art, athletics, leadership, minority status, music/drama, religious affiliation.

Application procedures. Admission: No deadline. $30 fee, may be waived for applicants with need, free for online applicants. Admission notification on a rolling basis beginning on or about 1/15. **Financial aid:** Priority date 3/2; no closing date. FAFSA, institutional form required. Applicants notified on a rolling basis starting 4/1; must reply within 3 week(s) of notification.

Academics. Special study options: Combined bachelor's/graduate degree, cooperative education, double major, external degree, honors, independent study, internships, study abroad, teacher certification program. **Credit/placement by examination:** AP, CLEP, IB, SAT, ACT, institutional tests. 24 credit hours maximum toward associate degree, 45 toward bachelor's. **Support services:** Learning center, remedial instruction, study skills assistance, tutoring, writing center.

Majors. Biology: General, biochemistry, bioinformatics, biophysics. **Business:** General. **Communications:** General, intercultural. **Computer sciences:** Computer science. **Conservation:** Environmental studies. **Education:** Early childhood, elementary, music, physical, social science. **English:** English lit. **Foreign languages:** Spanish. **Health services:** Nursing (RN), prechiropractic, predental, premedicine, preoptometry, prepharmacy, preveterinary. **History:** General. **Human services:** Social work. **Math:** General. **Parks/recreation:** Health/fitness. **Philosophy/religion:** Religion. **Physical sciences:** Chemistry, physics. **Psychology:** General. **Theology:** Theology. **Visual/performing arts:** Cinematography, graphic design, music, music performance, photography, studio arts.

Most popular majors. Biology 15%, business/marketing 18%, communications/journalism 6%, education 7%, foreign language 6%, health sciences 17%, public administration/social services 6%, visual/performing arts 8%.

Computing on campus. 150 workstations in dormitories, library. Dormitories wired for high-speed internet access and linked to campus network. Commuter students can connect to campus network. Online course registration, online library, helpline, repair service, wireless network available.

Student life. Freshman orientation: Mandatory. Preregistration for classes offered. **Policies:** Religious observance required. **Housing:** Guaranteed on-campus for freshmen. Single-sex dorms, apartments, wellness housing available. $150 fully refundable deposit. **Activities:** Bands, campus ministries, choral groups, drama, film society, literary magazine, music ensembles, musical theater, student government, student newspaper, symphony orchestra.

Athletics. NAIA. **Intercollegiate:** Basketball, cross-country, soccer M, volleyball W. **Intramural:** Basketball, football (non-tackle) M, softball, volleyball. **Team name:** Pioneers.

Student services. Adult student services, alcohol/substance abuse counseling, chaplain/spiritual director, career counseling, student employment services, financial aid counseling, health services, on-campus daycare, personal counseling, placement for graduates. **Physically disabled:** Services for visually, speech, hearing impaired.

Contact. E-mail: enroll@puc.edu
Phone: (707) 965-6336 Toll-free number: (800) 862-7080
Fax: (707) 965-6432
Craig Philpott, Associate Director, Admissions, Pacific Union College, One Angwin Avenue, Angwin, CA 94508-9707

Patten University
Oakland, California
www.patten.edu

CB member
CB code: 4620

- Private 4-year university and liberal arts college affiliated with interdenominational tradition
- Residential campus in large city
- 489 degree-seeking undergraduates
- SAT or ACT (ACT writing optional), application essay, interview required

General. Founded in 1944. Regionally accredited. **Degrees:** 62 bachelor's, 18 associate awarded; master's offered. **Location:** 18 miles from San Francisco, 30 miles from San Jose. **Calendar:** Semester, limited summer session. **Full-time faculty:** 14 total; 86% have terminal degrees, 43% minority. **Part-time faculty:** 55 total; 58% have terminal degrees, 66% minority.

Basis for selection. Open admission, but selective for some programs. Christian commitment most important. High school record, interview, essay, test scores, recommendation important.

High school preparation. 22 units required. Required units include English 4, mathematics 2, social studies 4, history 2, science 2 (laboratory 1), foreign language 1 and academic electives 6.

2011-2012 Annual costs. Tuition/fees: $13,440. Room/board: $7,090. Books/supplies: $1,638. Personal expenses: $2,250.

Financial aid. Non-need-based: Scholarships awarded for academics, athletics, state residency.

Application procedures. Admission: Priority date 3/31; deadline 7/31. $30 fee, may be waived for applicants with need. Admission notification on a rolling basis. **Financial aid:** Priority date 3/31; no closing date. FAFSA, institutional form required. Applicants notified on a rolling basis starting 5/31.

Academics. Special study options: Accelerated study, double major, dual enrollment of high school students, independent study, teacher certification program, weekend college. **Credit/placement by examination:** AP, CLEP, institutional tests. **Support services:** Learning center, remedial instruction, tutoring, writing center.

Majors. Business: Business admin. **Education:** Adult/continuing, early childhood. **Liberal arts:** Arts/sciences. **Philosophy/religion:** Religion. **Psychology:** General. **Theology:** Religious ed, sacred music.

Most popular majors. Business/marketing 15%, communications/journalism 10%, liberal arts 13%, psychology 23%, theological studies 40%.

Computing on campus. 30 workstations in library, computer center. Dormitories wired for high-speed internet access. Online library, wireless network available.

Student life. Freshman orientation: Mandatory. Preregistration for classes offered. 3-day overview held week before start of classes. **Policies:** Christian service program designed to involve students in practical ministry. Religious observance required. **Housing:** Guaranteed on-campus for all undergraduates. Single-sex dorms, apartments available. $150 deposit, deadline 7/31. **Activities:** Concert band, choral groups, drama, music ensembles,

student government, student newspaper, symphony orchestra, Community of Faith groups, prison ministry.

Athletics. NAIA. **Intercollegiate:** Baseball M, softball W. **Team name:** Lions.

Student services. Adult student services, career counseling, student employment services, personal counseling, placement for graduates, veterans' counselor.

Contact. E-mail: admissions@patten.edu
Phone: (510) 261-8500 ext. 7764 Toll-free number: (877) 472-8836
Fax: (510) 534-4344
Kim Guerra, Director of Admissions, Patten University, 2433 Coolidge Avenue, Oakland, CA 94601-2699

Pepperdine University
Malibu, California
www.pepperdine.edu

CB member
CB code: 4630

- Private 4-year university and liberal arts college affiliated with Church of Christ
- Residential campus in small city
- 3,461 degree-seeking undergraduates: 12% part-time, 56% women, 7% African American, 11% Asian American, 14% Hispanic American, 1% Native American, 7% international
- 4,021 degree-seeking graduate students
- 32% of applicants admitted
- SAT or ACT (ACT writing recommended), application essay required
- 81% graduate within 6 years

General. Founded in 1937. Regionally accredited. Education, psychology, business graduate campuses in Los Angeles. Educational centers in Long Beach, Irvine, Encino, West Los Angeles, Westlake Village. **Degrees:** 874 bachelor's awarded; master's, professional, doctoral offered. **ROTC:** Army, Air Force. **Location:** 14 miles from Santa Monica, 30 miles from Los Angeles. **Calendar:** Semester, limited summer session. **Full-time faculty:** 386 total; 91% have terminal degrees, 13% minority, 39% women. **Part-time faculty:** 309 total; 52% have terminal degrees, 12% minority, 44% women. **Class size:** 68% < 20, 28% 20-39, 2% 40-49, 1% 50-99, 1% >100.

Freshman class profile. 9,384 applied, 2,962 admitted, 676 enrolled.

Mid 50% test scores			
SAT critical reading:	540-650	GPA 2.0-2.99:	2%
SAT math:	560-680	Rank in top quarter:	77%
SAT writing:	560-660	Rank in top tenth:	39%
ACT composite:	25-31	Return as sophomores:	93%
GPA 3.75 or higher:	43%	Out-of-state:	47%
GPA 3.50-3.74:	27%	International:	7%
GPA 3.0-3.49:	28%	Fraternities:	16%
		Sororities:	27%

Basis for selection. School achievement record and test scores most important. Special talents, school and community activities, letters of recommendation, personal qualities also considered. Audition required for music, theater majors. Portfolio recommended for art majors. **Home schooled:** Transcript of courses and grades, state high school equivalency certificate required. **Learning Disabled:** Proper documentation from doctor diagnosing learning disability required.

High school preparation. College-preparatory program recommended.

2011-2012 Annual costs. Tuition/fees: $40,752. Room/board: $11,844. Books/supplies: $1,200. Personal expenses: $900.

2011-2012 Financial aid. Need-based: 546 full-time freshmen applied for aid; 409 were judged to have need; 403 of these received aid. Average need met was 78%. Average scholarship/grant was $37,813; average loan $3,758. 78% of total undergraduate aid awarded as scholarships/grants, 22% as loans/jobs. **Non-need-based:** Awarded to 2,101 full-time undergraduates, including 461 freshmen. Scholarships awarded for academics, art, athletics, leadership, music/drama, religious affiliation.

Application procedures. Admission: Closing date 1/5 (postmark date). $65 fee, may be waived for applicants with need. Admission notification by 4/1. Must reply by 5/1. **Financial aid:** Priority date 2/15; no closing date. FAFSA required. Applicants notified by 4/15; must reply by 5/1.

Academics. Great books colloquium, freshman seminars and first year faculty mentor program for all students. **Special study options:** Combined bachelor's/graduate degree, double major, honors, independent study, internships, student-designed major, study abroad, teacher certification program, Washington semester. 3/2 Engineering program with University of Southern

California School of Engineering, or Washington University School of Engineering in St. Louis. 5-year BS/MBA program which allows select Seaver College business majors to earn their bachelor's and MBA or International MBA degrees in five years. Academic Year residential program offered in Heidelberg, Germany; London, United Kingdom; Florence, Italy; Buenos Aires, Argentina; Lausanne, Switzerland; and Shanghai, China. Part-time, evening, weekend classes for business undergrad programs. **Credit/placement by examination:** AP, CLEP, IB, SAT, ACT, institutional tests. 32 credit hours maximum toward bachelor's degree. IB credit awarded for higher level exams only: 4 credits for each score of 5 and above; maximum 16. **Support services:** Pre-admission summer program, remedial instruction, tutoring, writing center.

Majors. Area/ethnic studies: Asian, European, Latin American. **Biology:** General, biochemistry. **Business:** Accounting, business admin, finance, international, marketing. **Communications:** Advertising, broadcast journalism, communications/speech/rhetoric, journalism, organizational, public relations, radio/TV. **Computer sciences:** General. **Education:** General, chemistry, English, music, physical, speech. **Engineering:** General. **English:** Creative writing, English lit. **Foreign languages:** French, German, Spanish. **Health services:** Athletic training. **History:** General. **Liberal arts:** Arts/sciences, humanities. **Math:** General. **Parks/recreation:** Exercise sciences, sports admin. **Philosophy/religion:** Philosophy, religion. **Physical sciences:** Chemistry, physics. **Psychology:** General. **Social sciences:** Economics, political science, sociology. **Visual/performing arts:** Acting, art, art history/conservation, dramatic, multimedia, music, music history, music theory/composition, studio arts, theater design. **Work/family studies:** Food/nutrition.

Most popular majors. Business/marketing 27%, communications/journalism 22%, interdisciplinary studies 8%, social sciences 10%.

Computing on campus. 292 workstations in dormitories, library, computer center, student center. Dormitories wired for high-speed internet access and linked to campus network. Commuter students can connect to campus network. Online library, helpline, repair service, wireless network available.

Student life. Freshman orientation: Mandatory. Preregistration for classes offered. Orientation held week before official start of Fall semester. **Policies:** Students required to attend weekly convocation. Freshmen and sophomores live on campus or at home with parent or guardian if single and under 21. **Housing:** Guaranteed on-campus for freshmen. Single-sex dorms, special housing for disabled, apartments available. **Activities:** Bands, campus ministries, choral groups, dance, drama, film society, international student organizations, literary magazine, music ensembles, Model UN, musical theater, opera, radio station, student government, student newspaper, symphony orchestra, TV station, Campus Crusade for Christ, College Republicans, Young Democrats, volunteer center, Black student union, Latin student association, Hawaiian club, Korean student association, Japan club.

Athletics. NCAA. **Intercollegiate:** Baseball M, basketball, cross-country, golf, soccer W, swimming W, tennis, track and field W, volleyball, water polo M. **Intramural:** Basketball, football (non-tackle), handball, soccer, swimming, tennis, volleyball. **Team name:** Waves.

Student services. Alcohol/substance abuse counseling, chaplain/spiritual director, career counseling, student employment services, financial aid counseling, health services, personal counseling, placement for graduates, veterans' counselor. **Physically disabled:** Services for visually, hearing impaired.

Contact. E-mail: admission-seaver@pepperdine.edu
Phone: (310) 506-4392 Fax: (310) 506-4861
Mike Trushke, Director of Admission, Pepperdine University, 24255 Pacific Coast Highway, Malibu, CA 90263-4392

Pitzer College
Claremont, California
www.pitzer.edu

CB member
CB code: 4619

- Private 4-year liberal arts college
- Residential campus in large town
- 1,099 degree-seeking undergraduates: 4% part-time, 62% women, 6% African American, 8% Asian American, 16% Hispanic American, 1% Native American, 3% international
- 24% of applicants admitted
- Application essay required
- 81% graduate within 6 years; 14% enter graduate study

General. Founded in 1963. Regionally accredited. One of 5 undergraduate and 2 graduate institutions on adjoining campuses which share facilities. Cross-enrollment available at Claremont-McKenna, Harvey Mudd, Pitzer, Pomona, and Scripps. Interdisciplinary curriculum with social responsibility requirement, intercultural education objective; no academic departments. **Degrees:** 244 bachelor's awarded. **ROTC:** Army, Air Force. **Location:** 35 miles from Los Angeles. **Calendar:** Semester, limited summer session. **Full-time faculty:** 74 total; 100% have terminal degrees, 36% minority, 46% women. **Part-time faculty:** 42 total; 81% have terminal degrees, 29% minority, 43% women. **Class size:** 69% <20, 30% 20-39, 2% 40-49. **Special facilities:** Ecology center, nature reserve, arboretum, organic garden, women's studies center, restored arts and crafts home with poetry reading room.

Freshman class profile. 3,743 applied, 903 admitted, 272 enrolled.

Mid 50% test scores			
SAT critical reading:	610-690	Rank in top quarter:	89%
SAT math:	600-690	Rank in top tenth:	55%
ACT composite:	26-31	End year in good standing:	99%
GPA 3.75 or higher:	58%	Return as sophomores:	93%
GPA 3.50-3.74:	21%	Out-of-state:	58%
GPA 3.0-3.49:	19%	Live on campus:	100%
GPA 2.0-2.99:	2%	International:	3%

Basis for selection. School record, essays, 3 recommendations, test scores, leadership, community service, work experience, talent, involvement in sports considered. SAT/ACT not required of students graduating in top 10% of class, or those with unweighted cumulative GPA of 3.50 or higher in academic subjects. Otherwise, 1 of the following required: ACT or SAT scores; 2 SAT Subject Tests (1 in math); 2 or more AP test scores of at least 4 (1 English or English Language and 1 math or science); 2 International Baccalaureate exams (English 1A and math); or 1 recent junior or senior year graded analytical writing sample from humanities or social science course and 1 recent graded exam from advanced math course. Samples must include teacher's comments, grades, and the assignment. Interview recommended.

High school preparation. College-preparatory program recommended. 21 units required. Required units include English 4, mathematics 3, social studies 3, history 1, science 3 (laboratory 3), foreign language 3 and visual/performing arts 1.

2011-2012 Annual costs. Tuition/fees: $42,550. Room/board: $12,438. Books/supplies: $1,000. Personal expenses: $1,000.

2011-2012 Financial aid. Need-based: 140 full-time freshmen applied for aid; 94 were judged to have need; 94 of these received aid. Average need met was 100%. Average scholarship/grant was $32,873; average loan $2,946. 84% of total undergraduate aid awarded as scholarships/grants, 16% as loans/jobs. **Non-need-based:** Awarded to 28 full-time undergraduates, including 1 freshmen. Scholarships awarded for academics, leadership.

Application procedures. Admission: Closing date 1/1 (postmark date). $60 fee, may be waived for applicants with need. Admission notification by 4/1. Must reply by 5/1. **Financial aid:** Closing date 2/1. FAFSA, CSS PROFILE required. Applicants notified by 4/1; must reply by 5/1.

Academics. Students may take up to one-third of courses at other Claremont campuses (and more for shared majors) and must take 32 courses for graduation. Can create independent study courses and special majors. **Special study options:** Combined bachelor's/graduate degree, cooperative education, cross-registration, double major, ESL, exchange student, honors, independent study, internships, liberal arts/career combination, student-designed major, study abroad, urban semester. New Resources (for students over age 25 and nontraditional students), joint science program, joint BA/DO program. **Credit/placement by examination:** AP, CLEP, IB. **Support services:** Tutoring, writing center.

Majors. Area/ethnic studies: African-American, American, Asian, Asian-American, Caribbean, Chicano/Hispanic-American/Latino, European, Latin American, women's. **Biology:** General, biochemistry, biophysics, microbiology, neuroscience. **Business:** Organizational behavior. **Conservation:** Environmental science, environmental studies. **English:** Creative writing, English lit. **Foreign languages:** General, Chinese, classics, French, German, Italian, Japanese, linguistics, Russian, Spanish. **History:** General, American, European. **Math:** General. **Philosophy/religion:** Philosophy, religion. **Physical sciences:** Chemistry, organic chemistry, physics. **Psychology:** General. **Social sciences:** General, anthropology, economics, international relations, political science, sociology. **Visual/performing arts:** Art, art history/conservation, cinematography, dance, dramatic, film/cinema/video, studio arts.

Most popular majors. Communications/journalism 9%, English 7%, foreign language 6%, interdisciplinary studies 12%, natural resources/environmental science 6%, psychology 12%, social sciences 21%, visual/performing arts 9%.

Computing on campus. 100 workstations in dormitories, library, computer center, student center. Dormitories wired for high-speed internet access and linked to campus network. Commuter students can connect to campus network. Online course registration, online library, helpline, student web hosting, wireless network available.

Student life. Freshman orientation: Mandatory. Preregistration for classes offered. Held the week prior to start of fall semester. **Policies:** Strong

philosophical framework of social responsibility and self-governance. Freshmen not permitted cars on campus. **Housing:** Guaranteed on-campus for freshmen. Coed dorms, special housing for disabled, apartments, cooperative housing, wellness housing available. **Activities:** Campus ministries, choral groups, dance, drama, international student organizations, literary magazine, music ensembles, Model UN, radio station, student government, student newspaper, symphony orchestra, over 75 social service, religious, political, and ethnic organizations.

Athletics. NCAA. **Intercollegiate:** Badminton, baseball M, basketball, cross-country, diving, football (tackle) M, golf, lacrosse, soccer, softball W, swimming, tennis, track and field, volleyball W, water polo. **Intramural:** Archery, badminton, basketball, golf, racquetball, sailing, soccer, softball W, squash, tennis. **Team name:** Sagehens.

Student services. Adult student services, alcohol/substance abuse counseling, chaplain/spiritual director, career counseling, student employment services, financial aid counseling, health services, minority student services, personal counseling, women's services. **Physically disabled:** Services for visually, speech, hearing impaired.

Contact. E-mail: admission@pitzer.edu
Phone: (909) 621-8129 Toll-free number: (800) 748-9371
Fax: (909) 621-8770
Angel Perez, Vice President of Admission and Financial Aid, Pitzer College, 1050 North Mills Avenue, Claremont, CA 91711-6101

Platt College: Ontario
Ontario, California
www.plattcollege.edu
CB code: 3015

- For-profit 4-year branch campus and technical college
- Commuter campus in small city
- 411 degree-seeking undergraduates
- Application essay, interview required

General. Accredited by ACCSC. Branch of Los Angeles campus. **Degrees:** 31 bachelor's, 130 associate awarded. **Location:** 20 miles from Los Angeles. **Calendar:** Differs by program. **Full-time faculty:** 20 total; 20% have terminal degrees, 15% minority. **Part-time faculty:** 18 total; 56% have terminal degrees, 67% minority. **Class size:** 71% < 20, 29% 20-39. **Special facilities:** Motion capture lab.

Basis for selection. Students admitted based on interview, high school diploma or GED, entrance test and essay, and completion of the admissions process. Math and English workshops available to students upon entrance if desired or recommended. **Learning Disabled:** Students with learning disabilities may request consideration for extra time to complete entrance test.

2011-2012 Annual costs. Cost varies by program. Associate degree cost ranges from $26,967 to $37,995. Bachelor's degree cost ranges from $73,082.50 to $79,097.50.

Application procedures. Admission: No deadline. $75 fee. Admission notification on a rolling basis. **Financial aid:** Priority date 3/2; no closing date. FAFSA, institutional form required. Applicants notified on a rolling basis starting 1/1.

Academics. Special study options: Accelerated study, cooperative education, internships. **Credit/placement by examination:** AP, CLEP. 48 credit hours maximum toward associate degree, 48 toward bachelor's. **Support services:** Tutoring.

Majors. Communications technology: Animation/special effects, graphics. **Computer sciences:** Computer graphics, web page design. **Visual/performing arts:** General, commercial/advertising art, design.

Computing on campus. 12 workstations in library.

Student life. Freshman orientation: Mandatory. Preregistration for classes offered. Held on first day of classes. **Activities:** Various student clubs and activities available.

Student services. Adult student services, career counseling, student employment services, financial aid counseling, placement for graduates.

Contact. Phone: (909) 941-9410 Toll-free number: (866) 752-8846
Fax: (909) 941-9660
Admissions Director, Platt College: Ontario, 3700 Inland Empire Boulevard, Ontario, CA 91764

Platt College: San Diego
San Diego, California
www.platt.edu
CB code: 3020

- For-profit 4-year visual arts and technical college
- Commuter campus in very large city
- 380 degree-seeking undergraduates: 25% women
- Application essay, interview required

General. Accredited by ACCSC. **Degrees:** 70 bachelor's, 149 associate awarded. **Calendar:** Differs by program. **Full-time faculty:** 6 total. **Part-time faculty:** 23 total; 26% have terminal degrees, 17% minority, 39% women. **Class size:** 91% < 20, 9% 20-39.

Basis for selection. Open admission, but selective for some programs and for out-of-state students. Aptitude test used to measure academic preparedness to undertake college-level courses; SAT considered in lieu of test. **Learning Disabled:** Documentation of the disability required to ensure reasonable accommodation.

2012-2013 Annual costs. Tuition/fees (projected): $15,310. Books/supplies: $1,870.

Application procedures. Admission: No deadline. No application fee. Application must be submitted on paper. **Financial aid:** Closing date 3/2. FAFSA, institutional form required. Applicants notified on a rolling basis; must reply within 1 week(s) of notification.

Academics. Special study options: Accelerated study, internships, liberal arts/career combination. **Credit/placement by examination:** AP, CLEP, institutional tests. **Support services:** Study skills assistance, tutoring.

Majors. Visual/performing arts: General, commercial/advertising art.

Computing on campus. 200 workstations in library, computer center. Online library available.

Student life. Freshman orientation: Mandatory. Preregistration for classes offered.

Student services. Career counseling, services for economically disadvantaged, student employment services, financial aid counseling, personal counseling, placement for graduates.

Contact. E-mail: info@platt.edu
Phone: (619) 265-0107 Toll-free number: (866) 752-8826
Fax: (619) 308-0570
Kimberly Harbert, Director of Admissions, Platt College: San Diego, 6250 El Cajon Boulevard, San Diego, CA 92115

Point Loma Nazarene University
San Diego, California
www.pointloma.edu
CB member
CB code: 4605

- Private 4-year university and liberal arts college affiliated with Church of the Nazarene
- Residential campus in very large city
- 2,366 degree-seeking undergraduates: 2% part-time, 61% women, 3% African American, 7% Asian American, 16% Hispanic American, 2% Native American, 1% international
- 922 degree-seeking graduate students
- 52% of applicants admitted
- SAT or ACT (ACT writing optional), application essay, interview required
- 72% graduate within 6 years

General. Founded in 1902. Regionally accredited. **Degrees:** 533 bachelor's awarded; master's offered. **ROTC:** Army, Naval, Air Force. **Location:** 5 miles from downtown. **Calendar:** Semester, limited summer session. **Full-time faculty:** 143 total; 81% have terminal degrees, 14% minority, 40% women. **Class size:** 51% < 20, 35% 20-39, 12% 40-49, 2% 50-99. **Special facilities:** Historical Greek amphitheater.

Freshman class profile. 3,671 applied, 1,924 admitted, 532 enrolled.

Mid 50% test scores			
SAT critical reading:	510-620	GPA 2.0-2.99:	5%
SAT math:	520-630	Rank in top quarter:	67%
ACT composite:	23-28	Rank in top tenth:	36%
GPA 3.75 or higher:	53%	End year in good standing:	90%
GPA 3.50-3.74:	19%	Return as sophomores:	81%
GPA 3.0-3.49:	23%	Out-of-state:	19%
		Live on campus:	95%

Basis for selection. Moral character, maturity, intellectual ability, and academic achievement important. Preference given to self-directed applicants who appear to share ideals and objectives of college. SAT recommended.

High school preparation. College-preparatory program recommended. 18 units recommended. Recommended units include English 4, mathematics 3, social studies 2, history 1, science 3 (laboratory 2), foreign language 2 and academic electives 1.

2011-2012 Annual costs. Tuition/fees: $28,310. Room/board: $8,800. Books/supplies: $1,656. Personal expenses: $2,277.

2010-2011 Financial aid. Need-based: 486 full-time freshmen applied for aid; 404 were judged to have need; 404 of these received aid. Average need met was 61%. Average scholarship/grant was $14,890; average loan $3,851. 63% of total undergraduate aid awarded as scholarships/grants, 37% as loans/jobs. **Non-need-based:** Awarded to 562 full-time undergraduates, including 100 freshmen. Scholarships awarded for academics, art, athletics, leadership, music/drama, religious affiliation.

Application procedures. Admission: Closing date 2/15 (receipt date). $50 fee, may be waived for applicants with need. Admission notification on a rolling basis beginning on or about 3/15. Must reply by May 1 or within 2 week(s) if notified thereafter. **Financial aid:** Priority date 3/2; no closing date. FAFSA, institutional form required. Applicants notified on a rolling basis starting 3/1; must reply by 5/1.

Academics. Special study options: Double major, honors, independent study, internships, semester at sea, study abroad, teacher certification program, United Nations semester, Washington semester. **Credit/placement by examination:** AP, CLEP, IB, SAT, ACT, institutional tests. 32 credit hours maximum toward bachelor's degree. Some restrictions apply in special majors. **Support services:** Learning center, reduced course load, remedial instruction, study skills assistance, tutoring, writing center.

Majors. Biology: General, biochemistry. **Business:** Accounting, business admin, communications, fashion, management information systems. **Communications:** Broadcast journalism, communications/speech/rhetoric, journalism, media studies. **Computer sciences:** Computer science. **Conservation:** Environmental science. **Education:** Art, music. **Engineering:** Applied physics. **English:** English lit, writing. **Foreign languages:** Romance, Spanish. **Health services:** Athletic training, clinical nurse leader, dietetics, nursing (RN). **History:** General. **Human services:** Social work. **Liberal arts:** Arts/sciences. **Math:** General. **Parks/recreation:** Exercise sciences, health/fitness. **Philosophy/religion:** Philosophy. **Physical sciences:** Chemistry, physics. **Psychology:** General, industrial. **Social sciences:** General, international economic development, political science, sociology. **Theology:** Bible, preministerial, sacred music, youth ministry. **Visual/performing arts:** Art history/conservation, dramatic, fashion design, graphic design, interior design, music, music performance, music theory/composition, piano/keyboard, studio arts, voice/opera. **Work/family studies:** General, child development, food/nutrition, institutional food production.

Most popular majors. Business/marketing 23%, communications/journalism 6%, health sciences 11%, psychology 8%, visual/performing arts 8%.

Computing on campus. 520 workstations in dormitories, library, computer center, student center. Dormitories wired for high-speed internet access and linked to campus network. Commuter students can connect to campus network. Online course registration, online library, helpline, repair service, wireless network available.

Student life. Freshman orientation: Mandatory. Preregistration for classes offered. Held Friday through Sunday before classes begin. **Policies:** Students are expected to exercise self-discipline, sound judgment and manage conduct both on and off campus consistent with agreements made upon application and with University catalog and Student Handbook. Religious observance required. Freshmen not permitted cars on campus. **Housing:** Guaranteed on-campus for freshmen. Single-sex dorms, apartments, wellness housing available. $425 nonrefundable deposit, deadline 5/1. **Activities:** Bands, campus ministries, choral groups, drama, international student organizations, literary magazine, music ensembles, musical theater, opera, radio station, student government, student newspaper, symphony orchestra, TV station, Students for Social Justice, social work club, College Democrats, College Republicans, Brothers and Sisters United, Association of Latin American Students, Asian student union, black student union.

Athletics. NAIA, NCCAA. **Intercollegiate:** Baseball M, basketball, cross-country, golf, soccer, tennis, track and field, volleyball W. **Intramural:** Basketball, football (non-tackle), golf, soccer, softball, tennis, track and field, volleyball. **Team name:** Sea Lions.

Student services. Chaplain/spiritual director, career counseling, student employment services, financial aid counseling, health services, minority student services, on-campus daycare, personal counseling, veterans' counselor. **Physically disabled:** Services for visually, speech, hearing impaired.

Contact. E-mail: admissions@pointloma.edu
Phone: (619) 849-2273 Toll-free number: (800) 733-7770
Fax: (619) 849-2601
Eric Groves, Director of Undergraduate Admissions, Point Loma Nazarene University, 3900 Lomaland Drive, San Diego, CA 92106-2899

Pomona College
Claremont, California
www.pomona.edu

CB member
CB code: 4607

- Private 4-year liberal arts college
- Residential campus in large town
- 1,567 degree-seeking undergraduates: 51% women, 6% African American, 10% Asian American, 13% Hispanic American, 5% international
- 14% of applicants admitted
- SAT and SAT Subject Tests or ACT (ACT writing recommended), application essay required
- 95% graduate within 6 years

General. Founded in 1887. Regionally accredited. One of 5 undergraduate and 2 graduate schools on adjoining campuses. Campuses share facilities. Cross-enrollment available at any of the 5 colleges, which include Claremont-McKenna, Harvey Mudd, Pitzer, Pomona, and Scripps. Extensive overseas studies. **Degrees:** 394 bachelor's awarded. **ROTC:** Army, Air Force. **Location:** 35 miles from Los Angeles, 20 miles from Pasadena. **Calendar:** Semester. **Full-time faculty:** 189 total; 98% have terminal degrees, 30% minority, 41% women. **Part-time faculty:** 37 total; 73% have terminal degrees, 8% minority, 43% women. **Class size:** 70% < 20, 27% 20-39, 3% 40-49, 1% 50-99. **Special facilities:** Science center, center for modern language and international relations, observatory, biological field station, ecological preserve, botanic garden, social sciences center, Greek theater, multimedia labs, foreign language resource center, college-operated museum.

Freshman class profile. 7,207 applied, 1,011 admitted, 394 enrolled.

Mid 50% test scores			
SAT critical reading:	680-780	Rank in top tenth:	90%
SAT math:	690-770	Return as sophomores:	99%
SAT writing:	680-780	Out-of-state:	66%
ACT composite:	31-34	Live on campus:	100%
Rank in top quarter:	100%	International:	7%

Basis for selection. School achievement record, test scores, essays, 3 recommendations most important. Special skills in music, art, drama, or athletics; leadership, motivation, and diversity of background also important. Some preference to children of alumni; special consideration for underrepresented groups. School and community activities also considered. Students submitting SAT must also submit 2 SAT Subject Tests in different subject areas. Interviews recommended for all; expected of Southern California applicants. Audition recommended for music, dance, and theater majors. Portfolio recommended for studio art majors. **Home schooled:** SAT and at least 3 SAT Subject Tests required, more recommended. Detailed description of curriculum required.

High school preparation. College-preparatory program required. 20 units required. Required and recommended units include English 4, mathematics 3-4, social studies 2, history 3, science 3-4 (laboratory 2-3) and foreign language 2-3. 3-4 laboratory sciences recommended for science applicants. Mathematics through calculus recommended for all applicants.

2011-2012 Annual costs. Tuition/fees: $39,883. Room/board: $13,227. Books/supplies: $1,000.

2010-2011 Financial aid. All financial aid based on need. 252 full-time freshmen applied for aid; 210 were judged to have need; 210 of these received aid. Average need met was 100%. Average scholarship/grant was $37,639. 96% of total undergraduate aid awarded as scholarships/grants, 4% as loans/jobs. **Additional information:** Financial aid awards loan-free for all elligible students.

Application procedures. Admission: Closing date 1/2 (receipt date). $65 fee, may be waived for applicants with need. Admission notification by 4/1. Must reply by May 1 or within 1 week(s) if notified thereafter. **Financial aid:** Closing date 2/1. FAFSA, CSS PROFILE required. Applicants notified by 4/1; must reply by 5/1.

Academics. Special study options: Combined bachelor's/graduate degree, cross-registration, double major, exchange student, independent study, internships, student-designed major, study abroad, Washington semester. 3-2 program in engineering with California Institute of Technology and Washington University in St. Louis, 4-1 education certification program with Claremont Graduate University. **Credit/placement by examination:** AP, CLEP, IB,

SAT, ACT, institutional tests. 8 credit hours maximum toward bachelor's degree. **Support services:** Tutoring, writing center.

Majors. Area/ethnic studies: African-American, American, Asian, Asian-American, Chicano/Hispanic-American/Latino, German, Latin American, Russian/Eastern European/Eurasian, women's. **Biology:** General, molecular, neuroscience. **Communications:** Media studies. **Computer sciences:** Computer science. **Conservation:** Environmental studies. **English:** English lit. **Foreign languages:** Chinese, classics, French, Japanese, linguistics, Romance, Russian, Spanish. **History:** General. **Human services:** Public policy. **Math:** General. **Philosophy/religion:** Philosophy, religion. **Physical sciences:** Astronomy, chemistry, geology, physics. **Psychology:** General. **Social sciences:** Anthropology, economics, international relations, political science, sociology. **Visual/performing arts:** Art history/conservation, dance, dramatic, music, studio arts.

Most popular majors. Biology 8%, interdisciplinary studies 8%, mathematics 7%, natural resources/environmental science 9%, physical sciences 7%, psychology 6%, social sciences 26%, visual/performing arts 8%.

Computing on campus. 180 workstations in dormitories, library, computer center, student center. Dormitories wired for high-speed internet access and linked to campus network. Commuter students can connect to campus network. Online library, helpline, wireless network available.

Student life. Freshman orientation: Mandatory. Preregistration for classes offered. Held immediately prior to fall semester. **Housing:** Guaranteed on-campus for all undergraduates. Coed dorms available. $500 nonrefundable deposit, deadline 5/1. **Activities:** Bands, campus ministries, choral groups, dance, drama, film society, international student organizations, literary magazine, music ensembles, Model UN, musical theater, radio station, student government, student newspaper, symphony orchestra, TV station, center for religious activities, international peace, Asian students association, Mortar Board (service organization), women's coalition, gay and lesbian student union, Office of Black Student Affairs, Chicano/Latino Student Association.

Athletics. NCAA. **Intercollegiate:** Baseball M, basketball, cross-country, diving, football (tackle) M, golf, lacrosse W, soccer, softball W, swimming, tennis, track and field, volleyball W, water polo. **Intramural:** Badminton, basketball, equestrian, handball, racquetball, skiing, soccer, softball, squash, table tennis, track and field, volleyball, water polo. **Team name:** Sagehens.

Student services. Chaplain/spiritual director, career counseling, services for economically disadvantaged, student employment services, financial aid counseling, health services, minority student services, personal counseling, placement for graduates. **Physically disabled:** Services for visually, hearing impaired.

Contact. E-mail: admissions@pomona.edu
Phone: (909) 621-8134 Fax: (909) 621-8952
Art Rodriguez, Dean of Admissions, Pomona College, 333 North College Way, Claremont, CA 91711-6312

Providence Christian College
Pasadena, California
www.providencecc.net
CB code: 7893

- Private 4-year liberal arts college
- Residential campus in very large city
- 71 degree-seeking undergraduates: 3% part-time, 62% women
- 48% of applicants admitted
- Application essay, interview required
- 59% graduate within 6 years; 10% enter graduate study

General. Regionally accredited. **Degrees:** 10 bachelor's awarded. **Calendar:** Semester. **Full-time faculty:** 6 total; 50% have terminal degrees, 17% women. **Part-time faculty:** 13 total; 15% have terminal degrees, 23% women. **Class size:** 91% < 20, 9% 20-39.

Freshman class profile. 62 applied, 30 admitted, 24 enrolled.

GPA 3.75 or higher:	27%	GPA 2.0-2.99:	9%
GPA 3.50-3.74:	30%	Return as sophomores:	91%
GPA 3.0-3.49:	34%		

Basis for selection. Admission is granted to applicants who provide evidence of qualities of mind and purpose required for a liberal arts college education, and whose personal qualifications provide assurance they will be responsible and contributing members of a college community committed to the lordship of Jesus Christ. Qualities of mind are demonstrated by breadth and quality of high school preparation. Among considerations are the application essay and/or an interview. **Home schooled:** Transcript of courses and grades required.

High school preparation. College-preparatory program recommended. 16 units required. Required units include English 3, mathematics 3, social studies 1, history 2, science 2 (laboratory 1) and foreign language 2.

2011-2012 Annual costs. Tuition/fees: $19,994. Room/board: $7,592.

2010-2011 Financial aid. Need-based: 54% of total undergraduate aid awarded as scholarships/grants, 46% as loans/jobs.

Application procedures. Admission: No deadline. $200 fee. Admission notification on a rolling basis. **Financial aid:** Closing date 2/1.

Academics. Special study options: Dual enrollment of high school students, internships. **Credit/placement by examination:** AP, CLEP. **Support services:** Learning center, remedial instruction, study skills assistance, tutoring, writing center.

Majors. Business: Business admin. **Communications:** General. **English:** English lit. **History:** General. **Liberal arts:** Arts/sciences. **Theology:** Bible, theology.

Most popular majors. Business/marketing 22%, liberal arts 44%, theological studies 33%.

Computing on campus. Commuter students can connect to campus network. Online course registration, helpline, wireless network available.

Student life. Freshman orientation: Mandatory, $200 fee. Preregistration for classes offered. **Policies:** Religious observance required. **Housing:** Guaranteed on-campus for all undergraduates. Single-sex dorms available. $200 nonrefundable deposit, deadline 5/1. **Activities:** Campus ministries, choral groups, dance, drama, literary magazine, student government, student newspaper.

Athletics. Intercollegiate: Cross-country. **Intramural:** Basketball M, soccer. **Team name:** Sea Beggars.

Student services. Chaplain/spiritual director, career counseling, student employment services, financial aid counseling.

Contact. E-mail: admissions@providencecc.net
Phone: (626) 696-4000
Larissa Kamps, Director of Admissions, Providence Christian College, 1539 East Howard Street, Pasadena, CA 91104

Samuel Merritt University
Oakland, California
www.samuelmerritt.edu
CB member
CB code: 4750

- Private two-year upper-division health science and nursing college
- Commuter campus in large city
- Application essay required

General. Founded in 1909. Regionally accredited. Part of Alta Bates Summit Medical Center, a nonprofit, community-based health care organization. **Degrees:** 381 bachelor's awarded; master's, professional offered. **ROTC:** Army, Naval, Air Force. **Location:** 15 miles from San Francisco. **Calendar:** Continuous, limited summer session. **Full-time faculty:** 88 total; 72% have terminal degrees, 26% minority. **Part-time faculty:** 141 total; 16% have terminal degrees, 28% minority. **Class size:** 8% < 20, 62% 20-39, 30% 40-49. **Special facilities:** Nursing resource laboratory, health education center, health science library, anatomy laboratory, therapeutic exercise laboratory, living skills laboratory, human occupations laboratory, health sciences simulation lab.

Student profile. 514 degree-seeking undergraduates. 3% entered as juniors. 100% transferred from two-year institutions.

Out-of-state:	2%	25 or older:	65%

Basis for selection. College transcript, application essay required. Must have UC transferable college-level coursework in chemistry, anatomy, physiology, multicultural psychology, English (2) and humanities (2). Letter of recommendation and experience in health care environment required. Transfer accepted as juniors.

2011-2012 Annual costs. Tuition/fees: $37,648. $3,960 per semester health insurance mandatory unless student covered by existing insurance. Books/supplies: $1,370.

Financial aid. Non-need-based: Scholarships awarded for academics, leadership, minority status. **Additional information:** Ongoing private scholarships available. Students eligible to work in Medical Center (associated with college).

Application procedures. Admission: Priority date 3/1. $50 fee, may be waived for applicants with need. Application must be submitted on paper. Admission notification 4/1. Must reply by 5/1. **Financial aid:** Priority date 3/2, no deadline. Applicants notified on a rolling basis; must reply within 3 weeks of notification.

Academics. Special study options: Accelerated study, combined bachelor's/graduate degree, cooperative education, cross-registration, distance learning, ESL, independent study, internships, liberal arts/career combination. **Credit/placement by examination:** AP, CLEP. 80 credit hours maximum toward bachelor's degree.

Majors. Health services: Nursing (RN).

Computing on campus. 78 workstations in library, computer center. Online course registration, online library, helpline, wireless network available.

Student life. Activities: Student government, student newspaper, multicultural committee, American Physical Therapy Association, California Nursing Students Association, Christian Fellowship, American Occupational Therapy Association, Chi Eta Phi, gay, lesbian, bisexual and transgender group.

Student services. Career counseling, financial aid counseling, health services, personal counseling. **Physically disabled:** Services for visually, speech, hearing impaired.

Contact. E-mail: admission@samuelmerritt.edu
Phone: (510) 869-6576 Toll-free number: (800) 607-6377
Fax: (510) 869-6576
Anne Seed, Director of Admissions, Samuel Merritt University, 370 Hawthorne Avenue, Oakland, CA 94609-9954

San Diego Christian College
El Cajon, California
www.sdcc.edu   **CB code: 4150**

- Private 4-year liberal arts college affiliated with nondenominational tradition
- Residential campus in small city
- 616 degree-seeking undergraduates: 11% part-time, 52% women, 12% African American, 1% Asian American, 17% Hispanic American, 1% Native American, 1% international
- 8 degree-seeking graduate students
- 39% of applicants admitted
- SAT or ACT (ACT writing optional), application essay required
- 30% graduate within 6 years

General. Founded in 1970. Regionally accredited. **Degrees:** 110 bachelor's awarded. **ROTC:** Army, Naval, Air Force. **Location:** 15 miles from downtown San Diego. **Calendar:** Semester, limited summer session. **Full-time faculty:** 16 total; 44% have terminal degrees, 12% minority, 44% women. **Part-time faculty:** 62 total; 11% have terminal degrees, 8% minority, 47% women. **Class size:** 78% < 20, 18% 20-39, 3% 40-49, less than 1% 50-99. **Special facilities:** Museum supporting creationist view, flight school.

Freshman class profile. 585 applied, 226 admitted, 87 enrolled.

Mid 50% test scores				
SAT critical reading:	430-550	GPA 2.0-2.99:	26%
SAT math:	410-540	Rank in top quarter:	42%
SAT writing:	430-540	Rank in top tenth:	20%
ACT composite:	19-23	End year in good standing:	93%
GPA 3.75 or higher:	24%	Return as sophomores:	64%
GPA 3.50-3.74:	12%	Out-of-state:	24%
GPA 3.0-3.49:	38%	Live on campus:	71%
		International:	1%

Basis for selection. Academic abilities as indicated by school achievement record and test scores. Personal and spiritual qualities as indicated by essays, recommendations, and interview.

High school preparation. College-preparatory program recommended. 15 units recommended. Recommended units include English 4, mathematics 3, social studies 3, science 3 and foreign language 2.

2011-2012 Annual costs. Tuition/fees: $23,824. Room/board: $8,322. Books/supplies: $1,656. Personal expenses: $2,277.

2011-2012 Financial aid. Need-based: 83 full-time freshmen applied for aid; 80 were judged to have need; 80 of these received aid. Average need met was 55%. Average scholarship/grant was $4,292; average loan $3,344. 56% of total undergraduate aid awarded as scholarships/grants, 44% as loans/jobs. **Non-need-based:** Awarded to 299 full-time undergraduates, including

74 freshmen. Scholarships awarded for academics, alumni affiliation, athletics, leadership, music/drama, state residency.

Application procedures. Admission: Priority date 7/1; deadline 8/1 (postmark date). $25 fee, may be waived for applicants with need. Admission notification on a rolling basis. Must reply by May 1 or within 4 week(s) if notified thereafter. **Financial aid:** Priority date 3/2, closing date 7/15. FAFSA, institutional form required. Applicants notified on a rolling basis starting 4/1; must reply by 5/1 or within 4 week(s) of notification.

Academics. Special study options: Accelerated study, distance learning, double major, ESL, honors, independent study, internships, liberal arts/career combination, student-designed major, study abroad, teacher certification program, Washington semester. **Credit/placement by examination:** AP, CLEP, IB, SAT, ACT, institutional tests. 9 credit hours maximum toward bachelor's degree. **Support services:** Learning center, reduced course load, remedial instruction, study skills assistance, tutoring, writing center.

Majors. Biology: General. **Business:** Business admin. **Communications:** Communications/speech/rhetoric. **Education:** General, early childhood, elementary, English, history, mathematics, middle, music, physical, secondary, social science. **English:** English lit. **Health services:** Athletic training. **History:** General. **Math:** General. **Parks/recreation:** Exercise sciences. **Psychology:** General. **Social sciences:** General. **Theology:** Bible, missionary. **Visual/performing arts:** Dramatic, music, music performance. **Work/family studies:** Family studies.

Most popular majors. Business/marketing 19%, communications/journalism 7%, family/consumer sciences 7%, interdisciplinary studies 15%, parks/recreation 9%, theological studies 12%, trade and industry 7%.

Computing on campus. 48 workstations in library, computer center, student center. Dormitories wired for high-speed internet access and linked to campus network. Commuter students can connect to campus network. Online library, helpline, repair service, wireless network available.

Student life. Freshman orientation: Mandatory, $100 fee. Preregistration for classes offered. Takes place within 2 weeks of start of classes in fall. **Policies:** Religious observance required. **Housing:** Guaranteed on-campus for all undergraduates. Single-sex dorms available. $250 deposit, deadline 7/1. **Activities:** Concert band, campus ministries, choral groups, drama, music ensembles, musical theater, student government, student newspaper, student senate, flight team, missions club, art club.

Athletics. NAIA. **Intercollegiate:** Baseball M, basketball, cross-country, golf M, soccer, volleyball W. **Intramural:** Basketball, football (non-tackle) M, soccer, softball, tennis, volleyball. **Team name:** Hawks.

Student services. Adult student services, chaplain/spiritual director, career counseling, student employment services, financial aid counseling, health services, personal counseling, placement for graduates.

Contact. E-mail: admissions@sdcc.edu
Phone: (619) 201-8787 Toll-free number: (800) 676-2242
Fax: (619) 201-8749
Mitchell Fisk, Vice President for Enrollment & Marketing, San Diego Christian College, 2100 Greenfield Drive, El Cajon, CA 92019-1157

San Diego State University
San Diego, California
www.sdsu.edu   **CB member**   **CB code: 4682**

- Public 4-year university
- Commuter campus in very large city
- 26,371 degree-seeking undergraduates: 13% part-time, 56% women, 4% African American, 7% Asian American, 29% Hispanic American, 4% international
- 4,932 degree-seeking graduate students
- 33% of applicants admitted
- SAT or ACT (ACT writing optional) required
- 66% graduate within 6 years

General. Founded in 1897. Regionally accredited. Branch campus at Calexico in Imperial Valley. **Degrees:** 6,892 bachelor's awarded; master's, doctoral offered. **ROTC:** Army, Naval, Air Force. **Location:** 8 miles from downtown. **Calendar:** Semester, extensive summer session. **Full-time faculty:** 783 total; 86% have terminal degrees, 26% minority, 45% women. **Part-time faculty:** 630 total; 11% have terminal degrees, 25% minority, 54% women. **Class size:** 28% < 20, 41% 20-39, 7% 40-49, 16% 50-99, 9% >100. **Special facilities:** Observatory, electron microscope facility, open-air theater, aquatic center, international student center, American Language Institute, recital hall, field studies stations (off-campus), multimedia interactive fine arts lab.

Freshman class profile. 45,027 applied, 14,805 admitted, 4,019 enrolled.

Mid 50% test scores		GPA 2.0-2.99:	2%
SAT critical reading:	480-580	Return as sophomores:	89%
SAT math:	500-610	Out-of-state:	8%
ACT composite:	21-26	Live on campus:	66%
GPA 3.75 or higher:	37%	International:	3%
GPA 3.50-3.74:	32%	Fraternities:	16%
GPA 3.0-3.49:	29%	Sororities:	17%

Basis for selection. High school GPA and test scores most important; 20% of those admitted selected using faculty-defined criteria, such as socioeconomic status and San Diego and Imperial County residency. **Home schooled:** Transcript of courses and grades required. In cases where the Lab Science courses are not completed at regular high school or community college, course descriptions requested to ensure lab component meets CSU requirement for admission.

High school preparation. College-preparatory program recommended. 15 units required. Required and recommended units include English 4, mathematics 3-4, social studies 1, history 1, science 2 (laboratory 2), foreign language 2, visual/performing arts 1 and academic electives 1. One visual and performing arts required. History must be US history or US government. Science must be 1 biology, 1 physical science.

2011-2012 Annual costs. Tuition/fees: $6,578; $17,738 out-of-state. Room/board: $11,549. Books/supplies: $1,661. Personal expenses: $2,694.

2011-2012 Financial aid. **Need-based:** 3,100 full-time freshmen applied for aid; 2,200 were judged to have need; 2,000 of these received aid. Average need met was 71%. Average scholarship/grant was $9,700; average loan $3,000. 58% of total undergraduate aid awarded as scholarships/grants, 42% as loans/jobs. **Non-need-based:** Awarded to 4,200 full-time undergraduates, including 990 freshmen. Scholarships awarded for academics, alumni affiliation, art, athletics, leadership, music/drama, ROTC, state residency.

Application procedures. Admission: Closing date 11/30 (postmark date). $55 fee, may be waived for applicants with need. Application must be submitted online. Admission notification by 3/1. Must reply by 5/1. **Financial aid:** Priority date 4/1, closing date 3/2. FAFSA required. Applicants notified on a rolling basis starting 2/14.

Academics. Special study options: Combined bachelor's/graduate degree, distance learning, double major, ESL, exchange student, external degree, honors, independent study, internships, liberal arts/career combination, semester at sea, study abroad, teacher certification program. **Credit/placement by examination:** AP, CLEP, IB, SAT, ACT, institutional tests. 30 credit hours maximum toward bachelor's degree. Must be registered in at least 1 course, matriculated and in good standing. Approval of department chair and dean of college required. Restricted to regular undergraduate courses. Does not count toward 30-unit minimum residency requirement. **Support services:** Pre-admission summer program, reduced course load, remedial instruction, tutoring.

Majors. Area/ethnic studies: African-American, American, Asian, Chicano/Hispanic-American/Latino, European, Latin American, Native American, Russian/Eastern European/Eurasian, Russian/Slavic, women's. **Biology:** General, microbiology. **Business:** General, accounting, business admin, finance, financial planning, hospitality admin, international, marketing, real estate. **Communications:** Advertising, journalism, public relations, radio/TV. **Computer sciences:** General, computer science, information systems, information technology. **Conservation:** General, environmental studies. **Education:** Early childhood, music, trade/industrial. **Engineering:** General, aerospace, civil, computer, electrical, environmental, mechanical. **English:** English lit, rhetoric/composition. **Foreign languages:** Classics, comparative lit, French, German, Japanese, linguistics, Russian, Spanish. **General:** Business. **Health services:** Communication disorders, nursing (RN). **History:** General. **Human services:** General, social work. **Liberal arts:** Arts/sciences, humanities. **Math:** General, applied, statistics. **Parks/recreation:** General, health/fitness. **Philosophy/religion:** Judaic, philosophy, religion. **Physical sciences:** General, astronomy, chemistry, geology, molecular physics, physics, theoretical physics. **Protective services:** Law enforcement admin. **Psychology:** General. **Social sciences:** General, anthropology, economics, geography, international relations, political science, sociology, urban studies. **Visual/performing arts:** Art history/conservation, dance, design, dramatic, graphic design, interior design, music performance, studio arts. **Work/family studies:** Child development.

Most popular majors. Business/marketing 23%, English 7%, health sciences 7%, parks/recreation 6%, psychology 8%, social sciences 12%.

Computing on campus. 400 workstations in dormitories, library, computer center, student center. Dormitories wired for high-speed internet access and linked to campus network. Commuter students can connect to campus network. Online course registration, online library, helpline, repair service, wireless network available.

Student life. Freshman orientation: Mandatory, $55 fee. Preregistration for classes offered. One-day academic orientation in July and August. Student life orientation held in August. **Housing:** Guaranteed on-campus for freshmen. Coed dorms, apartments, fraternity/sorority housing available. $800 partly refundable deposit, deadline 5/1. Quiet study environment, living/learning center available. **Activities:** Bands, campus ministries, choral groups, dance, drama, film society, international student organizations, literary magazine, music ensembles, musical theater, opera, radio station, student government, student newspaper, symphony orchestra, TV station, more than 300 academic, recreational, sports, ethnic, political, honor, and service clubs on campus.

Athletics. NCAA. **Intercollegiate:** Baseball M, basketball, cross-country W, diving W, football (tackle) M, golf, lacrosse W, rowing (crew) W, soccer, softball W, swimming W, tennis, track and field W, volleyball W, water polo W. **Intramural:** Basketball, bowling, football (non-tackle), golf, racquetball, soccer, softball, swimming, tennis, volleyball. **Team name:** Aztecs.

Student services. Alcohol/substance abuse counseling, chaplain/spiritual director, career counseling, services for economically disadvantaged, student employment services, financial aid counseling, health services, on-campus daycare, personal counseling, placement for graduates, veterans' counselor, women's services. **Physically disabled:** Services for visually, speech, hearing impaired.

Contact. E-mail: admissions@sdsu.edu
Phone: (619) 594-6336
Beverly Arata, Director of Admissions, San Diego State University, 5500 Campanile Drive, San Diego, CA 92182-7455

San Francisco Art Institute
San Francisco, California
www.sfai.edu

CB member
CB code: 4036

- Private 4-year visual arts college
- Commuter campus in very large city
- 397 degree-seeking undergraduates: 9% part-time, 56% women, 3% African American, 8% Asian American, 13% Hispanic American, 1% Native American, 6% international
- 261 degree-seeking graduate students
- 99% of applicants admitted
- Application essay required
- 45% graduate within 6 years

General. Founded in 1871. Regionally accredited. **Degrees:** 63 bachelor's awarded; master's offered. **Location:** Downtown. **Calendar:** Semester, limited summer session. **Full-time faculty:** 22 total; 73% have terminal degrees, 23% minority, 32% women. **Part-time faculty:** 92 total; 72% have terminal degrees, 15% minority, 44% women. **Class size:** 86% < 20, 12% 20-39, 1% 50-99, less than 1% >100. **Special facilities:** Art galleries, production facilities for photography, printmaking, media, digital imaging, and sound, a special collection of rare books, periodicals, and limited-edition artists' books.

Freshman class profile. 245 applied, 243 admitted, 86 enrolled.

Mid 50% test scores		GPA 3.0-3.49:	37%
SAT critical reading:	460-580	GPA 2.0-2.99:	43%
SAT math:	450-560	Return as sophomores:	53%
SAT writing:	460-550	Out-of-state:	50%
ACT composite:	20-25	Live on campus:	89%
GPA 3.75 or higher:	7%	International:	5%
GPA 3.50-3.74:	10%		

Basis for selection. Admission is based on the evaluation of the portfolio, academic credentials based on transcripts and standardized test scores, letters of recommendation, and the personal statement. Institutional exam used for writing placement. SAT or ACT recommended. Portfolio of artwork required. Interviews recommended, but not required. **Home schooled:** State high school equivalency certificate, letter of recommendation (nonparent) required.

High school preparation. College-preparatory program recommended. Recommended units include English 4, mathematics 2, social studies 3, history 2, science 2, foreign language 2 and visual/performing arts 4. A strong background in English, humanities, and social sciences is recommended along with an extensive high school or extracurricular art education.

2011-2012 Annual costs. Tuition/fees: $34,916. Room/board: $13,185. Books/supplies: $1,701. Personal expenses: $2,238.

2010-2011 Financial aid. **Need-based:** 71 full-time freshmen applied for aid; 71 were judged to have need; 71 of these received aid. 54% of total undergraduate aid awarded as scholarships/grants, 46% as loans/jobs. **Non-need-based:** Scholarships awarded for academics, art.

Application procedures. Admission: Priority date 2/1; no deadline. $65 fee, may be waived for applicants with need. Admission notification on a rolling basis. Must reply by May 1 or within 3 week(s) if notified thereafter. **Financial aid:** Priority date 3/1, closing date 5/31. FAFSA required. Applicants notified on a rolling basis starting 4/15; must reply within 3 week(s) of notification.

Academics. Special study options: Double major, ESL, exchange student, independent study, internships, study abroad. **Credit/placement by examination:** AP, CLEP, IB, institutional tests. 30 credit hours maximum toward bachelor's degree. **Support services:** Learning center, remedial instruction, study skills assistance, tutoring, writing center.

Majors. Social sciences: Urban studies. **Visual/performing arts:** Art, art history/conservation, ceramics, cinematography, film/cinema/video, multimedia, painting, photography, printmaking, sculpture, studio arts.

Most popular majors. Visual/performing arts 98%.

Computing on campus. 40 workstations in library, computer center. Dormitories wired for high-speed internet access. Online library, wireless network available.

Student life. Freshman orientation: Mandatory. Preregistration for classes offered. Held one week prior to the start of fall and spring semesters; includes overview of services and resources available, and planned social events. **Housing:** Coed dorms available. $450 nonrefundable deposit, deadline 6/1. **Activities:** Film society, international student organizations, radio station, student government, student newspaper, Indigenous Arts Coalition.

Student services. Career counseling, student employment services, financial aid counseling, personal counseling, placement for graduates, veterans' counselor. **Physically disabled:** Services for visually, speech, hearing impaired.

Contact. E-mail: admissions@sfai.edu
Phone: (415) 749-4500 Toll-free number: (800) 345-7324
Fax: (415) 749-4592
Elizabeth O'Brien, Vice President of Enrollment, San Francisco Art Institute, SFAI - Admissions, San Francisco, CA 94133-2299

San Francisco Conservatory of Music
San Francisco, California
www.sfcm.edu   CB code: 4744

- Private 4-year music college
- Commuter campus in very large city
- 185 degree-seeking undergraduates: 1% part-time, 47% women, 3% African American, 9% Asian American, 6% Hispanic American, 1% Native American, 22% international
- 194 degree-seeking graduate students
- 41% of applicants admitted
- Application essay required
- 73% graduate within 6 years

General. Founded in 1917. Regionally accredited. **Degrees:** 42 bachelor's awarded; master's offered. **Location:** Downtown. **Calendar:** Semester. **Full-time faculty:** 32 total; 28% have terminal degrees, 16% minority, 25% women. **Part-time faculty:** 78 total; 17% have terminal degrees, 9% minority, 33% women. **Class size:** 72% <20, 22% 20-39, 2% 40-49, 2% 50-99, less than 1% >100. **Special facilities:** Three concert performance halls, recording studios, listening lab, music library, soundproof practice rooms, percussion suite, reed-making room, baroque studio, electronic music studio.

Freshman class profile. 271 applied, 111 admitted, 39 enrolled.

End year in good standing:	88%	Live on campus:	77%
Return as sophomores:	81%	International:	36%
Out-of-state:	34%		

Basis for selection. Most important criterion is music audition, followed by school achievement record, letters of recommendation, and test scores. Musical needs of institution also influence admission decisions. Audition required. **Home schooled:** Transcript of courses and grades, state high school equivalency certificate, letter of recommendation (nonparent) required. SAT or ACT required.

High school preparation. Recommended units include English 3 and foreign language 3.

2011-2012 Annual costs. Tuition/fees: $37,046. Room/board: $11,250. Books/supplies: $620.

2011-2012 Financial aid. Need-based: 38 full-time freshmen applied for aid; 34 were judged to have need; 34 of these received aid. Average need met was 66%. Average scholarship/grant was $22,131; average loan $4,637. 72% of total undergraduate aid awarded as scholarships/grants, 28% as loans/jobs. **Non-need-based:** Awarded to 49 full-time undergraduates, including 13 freshmen. Scholarships awarded for music/drama.

Application procedures. Admission: Closing date 12/1 (receipt date). $100 fee. Application must be submitted online. Admission notification on a rolling basis beginning on or about 4/1. Must reply by May 1 or within 2 week(s) if notified thereafter. **Financial aid:** Priority date 3/1; no closing date. FAFSA, institutional form required. Applicants notified on a rolling basis starting 3/15; must reply by 5/1 or within 2 week(s) of notification.

Academics. Special study options: Independent study, internships. **Credit/placement by examination:** AP, CLEP, institutional tests. 36 credit hours maximum toward bachelor's degree. **Support services:** Remedial instruction, study skills assistance, tutoring.

Majors. Visual/performing arts: Music performance, music theory/composition, piano/keyboard, stringed instruments, voice/opera.

Computing on campus. 25 workstations in library, computer center. Dormitories wired for high-speed internet access. Student web hosting, wireless network available.

Student life. Freshman orientation: Mandatory. Preregistration for classes offered. **Housing:** Coed dorms available. $600 deposit. **Activities:** Choral groups, music ensembles, musical theater, opera, student government, symphony orchestra.

Student services. Financial aid counseling, health services, personal counseling.

Contact. E-mail: admit@sfcm.edu
Phone: (415) 864-7326 Toll-free number: (800) 899-7326
Fax: (415) 503-6299
Melissa Cocco-Mitten, Director of Admission, San Francisco Conservatory of Music, 50 Oak Street, San Francisco, CA 94102

San Francisco State University
San Francisco, California   CB member
www.sfsu.edu   CB code: 4684

- Public 4-year university
- Commuter campus in very large city
- 25,053 degree-seeking undergraduates: 15% part-time, 57% women, 5% African American, 28% Asian American, 21% Hispanic American, 7% international
- 4,057 degree-seeking graduate students
- 65% of applicants admitted
- SAT or ACT (ACT writing optional) required
- 48% graduate within 6 years

General. Founded in 1899. Regionally accredited. **Degrees:** 5,967 bachelor's awarded; master's, professional, doctoral offered. **ROTC:** Army, Air Force. **Location:** 10 miles from downtown. **Calendar:** Semester, limited summer session. **Full-time faculty:** 863 total; 71% have terminal degrees, 40% minority, 48% women. **Part-time faculty:** 730 total; 21% have terminal degrees, 34% minority, 57% women. **Class size:** 19% <20, 46% 20-39, 13% 40-49, 14% 50-99, 7% >100. **Special facilities:** Marine laboratories, environmental studies center, Sierra Nevada field campus, anthropology museum, astronomy facility.

Freshman class profile. 30,096 applied, 19,569 admitted, 3,537 enrolled.

Mid 50% test scores		GPA 3.0-3.49:	48%
SAT critical reading:	440-560	GPA 2.0-2.99:	34%
SAT math:	450-560	Return as sophomores:	81%
ACT composite:	19-25	Out-of-state:	1%
GPA 3.75 or higher:	5%	Live on campus:	48%
GPA 3.50-3.74:	13%	International:	4%

Basis for selection. School achievement record and score on SAT or ACT most important. Students with GPA over 3.0 may be exempted from SAT/ACT. SAT or ACT scores required if high school GPA does not reach a standard of 3.0 for California residents or 3.61 for non-residents. All applicants for admission are urged to take the SAT or ACT. **Home schooled:** Local school district verification of completion of secondary schooling; SAT or ACT scores.

High school preparation. College-preparatory program required. 14 units required; 15 recommended. Required and recommended units include English

4, mathematics 3, social studies 1, history 1, science 2 (laboratory 2), foreign language 2 and visual/performing arts 1.

2011-2012 Annual costs. Tuition/fees: $6,276; $17,436 out-of-state. Room/board: $12,414. Books/supplies: $1,754. Personal expenses: $3,288.

2011-2012 Financial aid. All financial aid based on need. 2,862 full-time freshmen applied for aid; 2,357 were judged to have need; 2,258 of these received aid. Average need met was 61%. Average scholarship/grant was $10,642; average loan $2,506. 61% of total undergraduate aid awarded as scholarships/grants, 39% as loans/jobs.

Application procedures. Admission: Priority date 10/1; deadline 11/30. $55 fee, may be waived for applicants with need. Admission notification on a rolling basis beginning on or about 10/1. Must reply by May 1 or within 2 week(s) if notified thereafter. **Financial aid:** Priority date 3/2; no closing date. FAFSA required. Applicants notified on a rolling basis starting 2/1; must reply within 2 week(s) of notification.

Academics. Special study options: Cooperative education, cross-registration, distance learning, double major, dual enrollment of high school students, ESL, honors, independent study, internships, liberal arts/career combination, student-designed major, study abroad, teacher certification program, Washington semester. **Credit/placement by examination:** AP, CLEP, IB, SAT, ACT, institutional tests. 30 credit hours maximum toward bachelor's degree. **Support services:** Learning center, pre-admission summer program, remedial instruction, study skills assistance, tutoring, writing center.

Majors. Area/ethnic studies: African-American, American, Asian-American, Chicano/Hispanic-American/Latino, Native American, women's. **Biology:** General, biochemistry. **Business:** Business admin, hospitality admin, labor studies. **Communications:** Journalism, radio/TV. **Computer sciences:** Computer science. **Conservation:** Environmental studies. **Education:** Early childhood. **Engineering:** Civil, computer, electrical, mechanical. **English:** English lit, rhetoric/composition, technical writing. **Foreign languages:** Chinese, classics, comparative lit, French, German, Italian, Japanese, Spanish. **Health services:** Communication disorders, dietetics, nursing (RN), public health ed. **History:** General. **Human services:** Social work. **Liberal arts:** Arts/sciences, humanities. **Math:** General, applied, statistics. **Parks/recreation:** Exercise sciences, facilities management. **Philosophy/religion:** Judaic, philosophy. **Physical sciences:** Atmospheric science, chemistry, geology, physics. **Protective services:** Criminal justice. **Psychology:** General. **Social sciences:** Anthropology, economics, geography, international relations, political science, sociology, urban studies. **Visual/performing arts:** Art, dance, design, dramatic, film/cinema/video, industrial design, interior design, music, music performance. **Work/family studies:** General, clothing/textiles.

Most popular majors. Business/marketing 22%, communications/journalism 10%, health sciences 6%, psychology 7%, social sciences 9%, visual/performing arts 9%.

Computing on campus. 2,800 workstations in library, computer center. Dormitories wired for high-speed internet access and linked to campus network. Online course registration, online library, helpline, repair service, student web hosting, wireless network available.

Student life. Freshman orientation: Mandatory, $35 fee. Preregistration for classes offered. **Housing:** Coed dorms, single-sex dorms, special housing for disabled, apartments, wellness housing available. $200 fully refundable deposit. Women-only floors available. **Activities:** Bands, campus ministries, choral groups, dance, drama, film society, international student organizations, literary magazine, music ensembles, Model UN, musical theater, opera, radio station, student government, student newspaper, symphony orchestra, TV station, College Democrats, College Republicans, Muslim Student Association, Hillel, Korean Student Association, Filipino American Collegiate Endeavor, Environmentally Concerned Organization of Students.

Athletics. NCAA. **Intercollegiate:** Baseball M, basketball, cross-country, soccer, softball W, track and field W, volleyball W, wrestling M. **Intramural:** Basketball, soccer, volleyball. **Team name:** Gators.

Student services. Adult student services, alcohol/substance abuse counseling, career counseling, services for economically disadvantaged, student employment services, financial aid counseling, health services, legal services, minority student services, on-campus daycare, personal counseling, placement for graduates, veterans' counselor, women's services. **Physically disabled:** Services for visually, speech, hearing impaired.

Contact. E-mail: ugadmit@sfsu.edu
Phone: (415) 338-1113 Fax: (415) 338-3880
John Pliska, Director, Undergraduate Admissions, San Francisco State University, 1600 Holloway Avenue, San Francisco, CA 94132

San Jose State University
San Jose, California **CB member**
www.sjsu.edu **CB code: 4687**

- Public 4-year university and liberal arts college
- Commuter campus in very large city
- 24,804 degree-seeking undergraduates: 19% part-time, 51% women, 4% African American, 34% Asian American, 22% Hispanic American, 4% international
- 5,432 degree-seeking graduate students
- 75% of applicants admitted
- 46% graduate within 6 years

General. Founded in 1857. Regionally accredited. **Degrees:** 4,832 bachelor's awarded; master's offered. **ROTC:** Army, Air Force. **Location:** 50 miles from San Francisco. **Calendar:** Semester, limited summer session. **Full-time faculty:** 627 total; 30% minority, 48% women. **Part-time faculty:** 1,104 total; 27% minority, 52% women. **Class size:** 25% < 20, 54% 20-39, 12% 40-49, 7% 50-99, 1% >100. **Special facilities:** Marine laboratory, natural history living museum, nuclear science lab, center for Beethoven studies, Chicano resource center, art metal foundry, deep-sea research ship, electro-acoustic and recording studio.

Freshman class profile. 22,978 applied, 17,265 admitted, 3,947 enrolled.

Mid 50% test scores			
SAT critical reading:	430-540	GPA 3.0-3.49:	47%
SAT math:	460-580	GPA 2.0-2.99:	30%
SAT writing:	440-540	Return as sophomores:	87%
ACT composite:	18-24	Out-of-state:	1%
GPA 3.75 or higher:	10%	Live on campus:	54%
GPA 3.50-3.74:	13%	International:	2%

Basis for selection. High school record and test scores most important. SAT or ACT required for applicants with less than 3.0 GPA.

High school preparation. College-preparatory program recommended. 15 units required. Required and recommended units include English 4, mathematics 3-4, social studies 1, history 1, science 2-3 (laboratory 2), foreign language 2, visual/performing arts 1 and academic electives 1. History is 2 units in history/social science.

2011-2012 Annual costs. Tuition/fees: $6,828; $17,988 out-of-state. Room/board: $10,733. Books/supplies: $1,746. Personal expenses: $3,096.

2010-2011 Financial aid. All financial aid based on need. 1,979 full-time freshmen applied for aid; 1,614 were judged to have need; 1,521 of these received aid. Average need met was 82%. Average scholarship/grant was $9,979; average loan $2,037. 54% of total undergraduate aid awarded as scholarships/grants, 46% as loans/jobs.

Application procedures. Admission: Closing date 11/30. $55 fee, may be waived for applicants with need. Application must be submitted online. Admission notification on a rolling basis beginning on or about 2/25. Must reply by May 1 or within 2 week(s) if notified thereafter. **Financial aid:** Priority date 3/2, closing date 6/15. Applicants notified on a rolling basis starting 4/1.

Academics. Special study options: Distance learning, double major, dual enrollment of high school students, honors, independent study, internships, student-designed major, study abroad, teacher certification program. **Credit/placement by examination:** AP, CLEP. **Support services:** Learning center, pre-admission summer program, remedial instruction, study skills assistance, tutoring, writing center.

Majors. Area/ethnic studies: African-American. **Biology:** General, biochemistry, conservation, marine, microbiology, molecular, physiology. **Business:** Accounting, business admin, finance, hospitality admin, human resources, international, marketing. **Communications:** Advertising, journalism, public relations, radio/TV. **Computer sciences:** Computer science, information systems, information technology, systems analysis. **Conservation:** Environmental studies. **Education:** Early childhood. **Engineering:** General, aerospace, chemical, civil, computer, electrical, industrial, materials, mechanical, software. **English:** English lit, rhetoric/composition. **Foreign languages:** Chinese, French, German, Japanese, linguistics, Spanish. **Health services:** Communication disorders, dietetics, health care admin, nursing (RN). **History:** General. **Human services:** Social work. **Liberal arts:** Arts/sciences, humanities. **Math:** General, applied. **Parks/recreation:** General, health/fitness. **Philosophy/religion:** Philosophy, religion. **Physical sciences:** Chemistry, geology, physics. **Protective services:** Criminal justice, forensics. **Psychology:** General. **Social sciences:** General, anthropology, economics, geography, international relations, political science, sociology. **Visual/performing arts:** General, art, art history/conservation, dance, dramatic, graphic design, industrial design, interior design, music, music performance, studio arts.

Four-Year Colleges

Most popular majors. Business/marketing 31%, engineering/engineering technologies 7%, health sciences 8%, psychology 7%, social sciences 6%, visual/performing arts 8%.

Computing on campus. Dormitories wired for high-speed internet access and linked to campus network. Commuter students can connect to campus network. Online course registration, online library, helpline, repair service, wireless network available.

Student life. Freshman orientation: Mandatory, $130 fee. Preregistration for classes offered. Mandatory overnight program for all first-time freshmen. **Housing:** Coed dorms, single-sex dorms, special housing for disabled, apartments, cooperative housing, fraternity/sorority housing available. $600 fully refundable deposit. **Activities:** Bands, campus ministries, choral groups, dance, drama, film society, international student organizations, literary magazine, music ensembles, musical theater, radio station, student government, student newspaper, symphony orchestra, TV station.

Athletics. NCAA. Intercollegiate: Baseball M, basketball, cheerleading, cross-country, diving W, football (tackle) M, golf, gymnastics W, soccer, softball W, swimming W, tennis W, volleyball W, water polo W. **Intramural:** Archery, badminton, baseball M, basketball, bowling, field hockey W, football (non-tackle), lacrosse, racquetball, soccer, softball, swimming, table tennis, tennis, volleyball W, water polo. **Team name:** Spartans.

Student services. Adult student services, alcohol/substance abuse counseling, chaplain/spiritual director, career counseling, services for economically disadvantaged, student employment services, financial aid counseling, health services, legal services, minority student services, on-campus daycare, personal counseling, placement for graduates, veterans' counselor, women's services. **Physically disabled:** Services for visually, speech, hearing impaired.

Contact. E-mail: admissions@sjsu.edu
Phone: (408) 283-7500 Fax: (408) 924-2050
Deanna Gonzales, Director of Undergraduate/Graduate Admissions Manager, San Jose State University, One Washington Square, San Jose, CA 95192-0011

Santa Clara University
Santa Clara, California
www.scu.edu

CB member
CB code: 4851

- Private 4-year university affiliated with Roman Catholic Church
- Residential campus in small city
- 5,182 degree-seeking undergraduates: 2% part-time, 51% women, 3% African American, 14% Asian American, 18% Hispanic American, 3% international
- 3,442 degree-seeking graduate students
- 54% of applicants admitted
- SAT or ACT (ACT writing optional), application essay required
- 85% graduate within 6 years; 25% enter graduate study

General. Founded in 1851. Regionally accredited. **Degrees:** 1,259 bachelor's awarded; master's, professional, doctoral offered. **ROTC:** Army, Air Force. **Location:** 40 miles from San Francisco. **Calendar:** Continuous, limited summer session. **Full-time faculty:** 483 total; 92% have terminal degrees, 23% minority, 42% women. **Part-time faculty:** 349 total; 66% have terminal degrees, 24% minority, 42% women. **Special facilities:** California mission, archeology lab, center for nanostructures, robotics, systems lab, satellite mission control room, three interdisciplinary centers of distinction: center for science, technology, and society, Ignatian center for Jesuit education, center for applied ethics, centers of academic outreach in the business and legal disciplines.

Freshman class profile. 13,342 applied, 7,263 admitted, 1,283 enrolled.

Mid 50% test scores			
SAT critical reading:	570-680	Rank in top quarter:	75%
SAT math:	600-690	Rank in top tenth:	42%
ACT composite:	27-31	Return as sophomores:	94%
GPA 3.75 or higher:	37%	Out-of-state:	39%
GPA 3.50-3.74:	32%	Live on campus:	94%
GPA 3.0-3.49:	29%	International:	2%
GPA 2.0-2.99:	2%		

Basis for selection. Rigor of high school curriculum, GPA and test scores most important, followed by recommendation, personal essay, and class rank. Extracurricular activities, ethnicity and alumni affiliations given special consideration. Audition recommended for music, theater arts majors. **Home schooled:** Statement describing home school structure and mission required. **Learning Disabled:** Need-blind admissions policy.

High school preparation. College-preparatory program required. 15 units required; 19 recommended. Required and recommended units include English 4, mathematics 3-4, social studies 3, science 2-3 (laboratory 2-3), foreign language 2-3, visual/performing arts 1 and academic electives 1. Social studies includes history units.

2011-2012 Annual costs. Tuition/fees: $39,048. Room/board: $11,997.

2011-2012 Financial aid. Need-based: 871 full-time freshmen applied for aid; 600 were judged to have need; 580 of these received aid. Average need met was 69%. Average scholarship/grant was $18,274; average loan $3,388. 82% of total undergraduate aid awarded as scholarships/grants, 18% as loans/jobs. **Non-need-based:** Awarded to 2,511 full-time undergraduates, including 641 freshmen. Scholarships awarded for academics, alumni affiliation, athletics, music/drama.

Application procedures. Admission: Closing date 1/7 (postmark date). $55 fee, may be waived for applicants with need. Application must be submitted online. Admission notification by 4/1. Must reply by 5/1. **Financial aid:** Priority date 2/1; no closing date. FAFSA, CSS PROFILE required. Applicants notified by 4/1; must reply by 5/1 or within 2 week(s) of notification.

Academics. Special study options: Combined bachelor's/graduate degree, cooperative education, double major, honors, independent study, internships, liberal arts/career combination, student-designed major, study abroad, teacher certification program, Washington semester. **Credit/placement by examination:** AP, CLEP, IB, institutional tests. No credit by examination awarded to new students. Number of credit hours awarded for International Baccalaureate determined on case-by-case basis. **Support services:** Learning center, study skills assistance, tutoring, writing center.

Majors. Area/ethnic studies: Women's. **Biology:** General, biochemistry. **Business:** Accounting, accounting/business management, finance, management information systems, managerial economics, marketing, organizational behavior. **Communications:** Communications/speech/rhetoric. **Computer sciences:** Web page design. **Conservation:** Environmental science, environmental studies. **Engineering:** General, applied physics, biomedical, civil, computer, electrical, mechanical. **English:** English lit. **Foreign languages:** Ancient Greek, classics, French, German, Italian, Latin, Spanish. **History:** General. **Liberal arts:** Arts/sciences. **Math:** General. **Philosophy/religion:** Philosophy, religion. **Physical sciences:** Chemistry, physics. **Psychology:** General. **Social sciences:** Anthropology, economics, political science, sociology. **Visual/performing arts:** Art history/conservation, dramatic, music, studio arts.

Most popular majors. Biology 6%, business/marketing 33%, communications/journalism 7%, engineering/engineering technologies 11%, psychology 6%, social sciences 13%.

Computing on campus. 826 workstations in dormitories, library, computer center, student center. Dormitories wired for high-speed internet access and linked to campus network. Commuter students can connect to campus network. Online course registration, online library, helpline, repair service, student web hosting, wireless network available.

Student life. Freshman orientation: Mandatory, $285 fee. Preregistration for classes offered. 2-day session in summer and 2-day session on weekend before school starts. Parents attend separate program. **Policies:** 100% of freshmen participate in residential learning communities. Freshmen not permitted cars on campus. **Housing:** Guaranteed on-campus for freshmen. Coed dorms, special housing for disabled, apartments available. $250 fully refundable deposit, deadline 5/1. **Activities:** Bands, campus ministries, choral groups, dance, drama, international student organizations, literary magazine, music ensembles, Model UN, musical theater, opera, radio station, student government, student newspaper, symphony orchestra, Asian Pacific Student Union, Ka Mana'o O Hawaii, community action program, Barkada, MECHA, Chinese student association, CORE Christian Fellowship, Engineers Without Borders, political science student association.

Athletics. NCAA. Intercollegiate: Baseball M, basketball, cross-country, golf, rowing (crew), soccer, softball W, tennis, track and field, volleyball W, water polo. **Intramural:** Badminton, basketball, football (non-tackle), soccer, softball, table tennis, tennis, volleyball. **Team name:** Broncos.

Student services. Alcohol/substance abuse counseling, chaplain/spiritual director, career counseling, student employment services, financial aid counseling, health services, legal services, minority student services, on-campus daycare, personal counseling, placement for graduates, veterans' counselor. **Physically disabled:** Services for visually, speech, hearing impaired.

Contact. E-mail: admissions@scu.edu
Phone: (408) 554-4700 Fax: (408) 554-5255
Sandra Hayes, Dean of Undergraduate Admissions, Santa Clara University, 500 El Camino Real, Santa Clara, CA 95053

School of Urban Missions: Oakland
Oakland, California
www.sum.edu

♦ Private 4-year Bible college affiliated with Assemblies of God
♦ Residential campus in very large city
♦ 313 degree-seeking undergraduates
♦ Application essay, interview required

General. Regionally accredited; also accredited by ABHE. Extensive hands-on ministry training with 8 hours per week of ministry. Additional campus in New Orleans. **Degrees:** 25 bachelor's, 1 associate awarded. **Location:** Downtown. **Calendar:** Trimester, limited summer session. **Full-time faculty:** 7 total; 29% have terminal degrees. **Part-time faculty:** 26 total; 12% have terminal degrees. **Class size:** 37% < 20, 63% 20-39.

Basis for selection. Open admission, but selective for some programs. Recommendations, interview, character/personal qualities are very important. 2 1-page essays, academic transcripts, and a photo are required. Pastor's recommendation and one general recommendation required. **Home schooled:** Transcript of courses and grades, state high school equivalency certificate, letter of recommendation (nonparent) required.

High school preparation. Required and recommended units include English 4, mathematics 3-4, history 2, science 2-3, foreign language 2-3, visual/performing arts 1 and academic electives 1. No academic requirement for high school diploma. Minimum 2.0 GPA preferred. If student is below 2.0, the student may be enrolled but with academic probation.

2011-2012 Annual costs. Tuition/fees: $8,100. Room only: $2,400. Books/supplies: $1,500.

Financial aid. Non-need-based: Scholarships awarded for academics, leadership, religious affiliation.

Application procedures. Admission: Closing date 7/20. $20 fee. Application must be submitted on paper. Admission notification on a rolling basis beginning on or about 1/1. **Financial aid:** Closing date 7/2. FAFSA required.

Academics. Special study options: Distance learning. **Credit/placement by examination:** AP, CLEP. No credit for life experience in the academic courses. Field ministry credits can be considered life experience. **Support services:** Reduced course load, remedial instruction, tutoring.

Majors. Theology: Bible.

Computing on campus. 5 workstations in library. Dormitories wired for high-speed internet access and linked to campus network. Online course registration, online library, wireless network available.

Student life. Freshman orientation: Mandatory. Preregistration for classes offered. **Policies:** 2 hours of Christian service required per week. Religious observance required. **Housing:** Guaranteed on-campus for all undergraduates. Single-sex dorms, apartments available. **Activities:** Campus ministries, student government.

Student services. Chaplain/spiritual director, financial aid counseling, health services, personal counseling.

Contact. E-mail: sum@sum.edu
Phone: (510) 567-6174 Toll-free number: (888) 567-6171
Fax: (510) 568-1024
Michael Savage, Academic Dean, School of Urban Missions: Oakland, 735 105th Avenue, Oakland, CA 94603

Scripps College
Claremont, California   **CB member**
www.scrippscollege.edu   **CB code: 4693**

♦ Private 4-year liberal arts college for women
♦ Residential campus in large town
♦ 956 degree-seeking undergraduates: 1% part-time, 100% women, 5% African American, 17% Asian American, 8% Hispanic American, 1% Native American, 4% international
♦ 17 degree-seeking graduate students
♦ 36% of applicants admitted
♦ SAT or ACT with writing, application essay required
♦ 88% graduate within 6 years

General. Founded in 1926. Regionally accredited. One of cluster of 5 undergraduate and 2 graduate schools on adjoining campuses. Campuses share facilities. Cross-enrollment available at any of the Claremont colleges: Claremont-McKenna, Harvey Mudd, Pitzer, Pomona, and Scripps. **Degrees:** 217 bachelor's awarded. **ROTC:** Army, Air Force. **Location:** 35 miles from Los Angeles. **Calendar:** Semester, limited summer session. **Full-time faculty:** 85 total; 100% have terminal degrees, 21% minority, 55% women. **Part-time faculty:** 30 total; 90% have terminal degrees, 3% minority, 70% women. **Class size:** 70% < 20, 24% 20-39, 3% 40-49, 2% 50-99, less than 1% >100. **Special facilities:** Art slide library, biological field station, humanities museum, field house.

Freshman class profile. 2,163 applied, 785 admitted, 257 enrolled.

Mid 50% test scores		GPA 2.0-2.99:	1%
SAT critical reading:	640-740	Rank in top quarter:	93%
SAT math:	640-710	Rank in top tenth:	79%
SAT writing:	660-740	Return as sophomores:	91%
ACT composite:	29-32	Out-of-state:	48%
GPA 3.75 or higher:	64%	Live on campus:	100%
GPA 3.50-3.74:	29%	International:	5%
GPA 3.0-3.49:	6%		

Basis for selection. Rigor of high school curriculum, GPA, class rank, aptitude as reflected in standardized testing most important. Essays, recommendations, required graded writing assignment significant. SAT Subject Tests used for placement in language only; institutional language and math exam used for placement. Interviews recommended. Audition recommended for music, dance majors. Portfolio recommended for art majors. **Home schooled:** Statement describing home school structure and mission, transcript of courses and grades, letter of recommendation (nonparent) required. Interview highly recommended. **Learning Disabled:** Documentation of learning disability required.

High school preparation. College-preparatory program recommended. 16 units required. Required units include English 4, mathematics 3, social studies 3, science 3 and foreign language 3.

2011-2012 Annual costs. Tuition/fees: $41,950. Room/board: $12,950. Books/supplies: $800. Personal expenses: $1,000.

2010-2011 Financial aid. Need-based: 116 full-time freshmen applied for aid; 92 were judged to have need; 92 of these received aid. Average need met was 100%. Average scholarship/grant was $33,717; average loan $2,924. 91% of total undergraduate aid awarded as scholarships/grants, 9% as loans/jobs. **Non-need-based:** Awarded to 155 full-time undergraduates, including 18 freshmen. Scholarships awarded for academics, leadership.

Application procedures. Admission: Closing date 1/2 (postmark date). $60 fee, may be waived for applicants with need. Admission notification by 4/1. Must reply by 5/1. **Financial aid:** Priority date 2/1, closing date 2/1. FAFSA, CSS PROFILE required. Applicants notified by 4/1; must reply by 5/1.

Academics. Almost half of junior class elects to study abroad for semester or year. **Special study options:** Accelerated study, combined bachelor's/graduate degree, cross-registration, double major, dual enrollment of high school students, exchange student, independent study, internships, New York semester, student-designed major, study abroad, United Nations semester, Washington semester. Post-baccalaureate pre-medical certificate program, humanities internship program, 3-2 engineering program with Harvey Mudd College. **Credit/placement by examination:** AP, CLEP, IB, institutional tests. 16 credit hours maximum toward bachelor's degree. SAT Subject Test in foreign languages may meet foreign language graduation requirement. **Support services:** Reduced course load, tutoring, writing center.

Majors. Area/ethnic studies: African-American, American, Asian, Asian-American, Chicano/Hispanic-American/Latino, European, French, German, Italian, Latin American, Near/Middle Eastern, Russian/Eastern European/Eurasian, Spanish/Iberian, women's. **Biology:** General, biochemistry, molecular, neuroscience. **Business:** Accounting, organizational behavior. **Communications:** Media studies. **Computer sciences:** Computer science. **English:** English lit. **Foreign languages:** General, Chinese, classics, French, German, Italian, Japanese, linguistics, Russian, Spanish. **History:** General. **Human services:** Public policy. **Liberal arts:** Humanities. **Math:** General. **Philosophy/religion:** Judaic, philosophy, religion. **Physical sciences:** Chemistry, geology, physics. **Psychology:** General. **Social sciences:** Anthropology, econometrics, economics, political science, sociology. **Visual/performing arts:** Art history/conservation, dance, dramatic, music, studio arts.

Most popular majors. Area/ethnic studies 13%, biology 12%, English 7%, psychology 7%, social sciences 18%, visual/performing arts 10%.

Computing on campus. 87 workstations in dormitories, library, computer center, student center. Dormitories wired for high-speed internet access and linked to campus network. Commuter students can connect to campus network. Online course registration, online library, helpline, repair service, student web hosting, wireless network available.

Student life. Freshman orientation: Mandatory. Preregistration for classes offered. 5-day orientation begins last Thursday in August. **Housing:** Guaranteed on-campus for freshmen. Special housing for disabled, apartments, wellness housing available. Off-campus houses for single students available. **Activities:** Campus ministries, choral groups, dance, drama, international student organizations, literary magazine, music ensembles, Model UN, radio station, student government, student newspaper, symphony orchestra, Asian American student union, Cafe Con Leche, Wanawake Weusi, Criminal Justice Network, Economic Society, international club, Office of Black Student Affairs, On The Loose.

Athletics. NCAA. **Intercollegiate:** Basketball W, cross-country W, diving W, golf W, lacrosse W, soccer W, softball W, swimming W, tennis W, track and field W, volleyball W, water polo W. **Intramural:** Basketball W, soccer W, softball W, volleyball W, water polo W. **Team name:** Athenas.

Student services. Adult student services, alcohol/substance abuse counseling, chaplain/spiritual director, career counseling, student employment services, financial aid counseling, health services, minority student services, personal counseling, placement for graduates, women's services.

Contact. E-mail: admission@scrippscollege.edu
Phone: (909) 621-8149 Toll-free number: (800) 770-1333
Fax: (909) 607-7508
Laura Stratton, Director of Admission, Scripps College, 1030 Columbia Avenue, Claremont, CA 91711-3905

Shasta Bible College and Graduate School
Redding, California
www.shasta.edu   **CB code: 4717**

- Private 4-year Bible and seminary college affiliated with Baptist faith
- Residential campus in small city
- 55 degree-seeking undergraduates
- 10 graduate students
- Application essay required

General. Regionally accredited; also accredited by TRACS. A strong emphasis on inductive Bible Study, hermeneutics (Bible Interpretation), biblical languages, evangelism, apologetics, and homiletics (preaching and teaching), along with general education requirements. **Degrees:** 7 bachelor's, 2 associate awarded; master's offered. **Calendar:** Semester, limited summer session. **Full-time faculty:** 7 total. **Part-time faculty:** 31 total. **Special facilities:** Vernal pool containing a variety of endangered species, creation museum.

Freshman class profile.

Out-of-state:	10%	Live on campus:	90%

Basis for selection. An essay on Psalms 23, an autobiography, and 4 references required. All applicable transcripts from high school and colleges attended required. **Home schooled:** Transcript of courses and grades required.

2011-2012 Annual costs. Tuition/fees: $9,670. Room only: $2,400. Books/supplies: $3,240.

Financial aid. Non-need-based: Scholarships awarded for music/drama.

Application procedures. Admission: Closing date 8/26 (receipt date). $50 fee. Admission notification on a rolling basis. **Financial aid:** No deadline. FAFSA required. Applicants notified on a rolling basis.

Academics. Special study options: Distance learning, dual enrollment of high school students, independent study, teacher certification program. Association of Christian Schools International certificates, standard and temporary. **Credit/placement by examination:** AP, CLEP, institutional tests. 30 credit hours maximum toward associate degree, 30 toward bachelor's.

Majors. Theology: Theology.

Computing on campus. 10 workstations in library. Dormitories wired for high-speed internet access and linked to campus network. Commuter students can connect to campus network. Online course registration, online library, wireless network available.

Student life. Freshman orientation: Mandatory. Preregistration for classes offered. **Policies:** Lifestyle commitment must be signed annually by each student. Dress code. Religious observance required. **Housing:** Single-sex dorms available. $100 nonrefundable deposit. **Activities:** Campus ministries, choral groups, student government.

Student services. Chaplain/spiritual director, career counseling, financial aid counseling, personal counseling.

Contact. E-mail: admissions@shasta.edu
Phone: (530) 221-4275 Toll-free number: (800) 800-4722
Fax: (530) 221-6929
George Gunn, Dean of Admissions, Shasta Bible College and Graduate School, 2951 Goodwater Avenue, Redding, CA 96002

Silicon Valley University
San Jose, California
www.svuca.edu   **CB code: 3600**

- Private 4-year business and engineering college
- Commuter campus in very large city
- 50 degree-seeking undergraduates

General. Accredited by ACICS. **Degrees:** 11 bachelor's awarded; master's, doctoral offered. **Calendar:** Trimester. **Full-time faculty:** 2 total. **Part-time faculty:** 27 total.

Basis for selection. Admission requirements vary by programs. **Home schooled:** Transcript of courses and grades, state high school equivalency certificate, interview, letter of recommendation (nonparent) required.

High school preparation. College-preparatory program recommended.

2012-2013 Annual costs. Tuition/fees: $9,175. Books/supplies: $700.

Application procedures. Admission: Closing date 7/1. $75 fee. Application must be submitted online.

Academics. Special study options: Accelerated study, ESL, independent study, internships, weekend college. **Credit/placement by examination:** AP, CLEP.

Majors. Business: Business admin. **Computer sciences:** Computer science.

Computing on campus. 12 workstations in library, computer center. Commuter students can connect to campus network. Online library, wireless network available.

Student life. Freshman orientation: Mandatory. Preregistration for classes offered. **Activities:** International student organizations, student government.

Student services. Minority student services, personal counseling.

Contact. E-mail: studentoffice@svuca.edu
Phone: (408) 435-8989 ext. 106
Seiko Cheng, Admissions Director, Silicon Valley University, 2160 Lundy Avenue Suite #110, San Jose, CA 95131

Simpson University
Redding, California
www.simpsonu.edu   **CB code: 4698**

- Private 4-year liberal arts college affiliated with Christian and Missionary Alliance
- Residential campus in small city
- 1,015 degree-seeking undergraduates: 3% part-time, 67% women, 3% African American, 6% Asian American, 8% Hispanic American, 3% Native American
- 276 degree-seeking graduate students
- 81% of applicants admitted
- SAT or ACT (ACT writing optional), application essay required
- 43% graduate within 6 years; 31% enter graduate study

General. Founded in 1921. Regionally accredited. Christ-centered educational community. **Degrees:** 300 bachelor's, 1 associate awarded; master's offered. **ROTC:** Army. **Location:** 170 miles from Sacramento. **Calendar:** Semester, limited summer session. **Full-time faculty:** 47 total; 60% have terminal degrees, 13% minority, 32% women. **Part-time faculty:** 81 total; 28% have terminal degrees, 1% minority, 57% women. **Class size:** 63% < 20, 30% 20-39, 3% 40-49, 3% 50-99, less than 1% >100. **Special facilities:** Climbing wall, ropes course, outdoor recreation.

Freshman class profile. 378 applied, 308 admitted, 146 enrolled.

Mid 50% test scores			
SAT critical reading:	470-590	GPA 2.0-2.99:	14%
SAT math:	460-570	Rank in top quarter:	56%
SAT writing:	460-570	Rank in top tenth:	27%
ACT composite:	20-26	End year in good standing:	77%
GPA 3.75 or higher:	38%	Return as sophomores:	63%
GPA 3.50-3.74:	14%	Out-of-state:	20%
GPA 3.0-3.49:	34%	Live on campus:	83%
		International:	1%

Basis for selection. Commitment to Jesus Christ as reflected in personal statement and required references, academic achievement, other recommendations, and standardized test scores important. SAT and SAT Subject Tests or ACT recommended. **Home schooled:** Transcript of courses and grades required.

High school preparation. College-preparatory program recommended. Recommended units include English 4, mathematics 2, social studies 2, history 1, science 2, foreign language 2 and visual/performing arts 1. College-preparatory program highly recommended.

2011-2012 Annual costs. Tuition/fees: $21,600. Room/board: $7,300.

2011-2012 Financial aid. Need-based: 132 full-time freshmen applied for aid; 124 were judged to have need; 124 of these received aid. Average need met was 69%. Average scholarship/grant was $13,000; average loan $3,233. 57% of total undergraduate aid awarded as scholarships/grants, 43% as loans/jobs. **Non-need-based:** Awarded to 128 full-time undergraduates, including 40 freshmen. Scholarships awarded for academics, alumni affiliation, athletics, leadership, minority status, music/drama, religious affiliation. **Additional information:** Work-study programs available.

Application procedures. Admission: No deadline. $25 fee, may be waived for applicants with need. Admission notification on a rolling basis. **Financial aid:** Priority date 3/2; no closing date. FAFSA, institutional form required. Applicants notified on a rolling basis starting 3/15; must reply within 4 week(s) of notification.

Academics. 34-semester-hour teacher credential program permits students to earn California Clear Credential for grades K-8 (multiple subjects) or for grades 7-12 (single subject). **Special study options:** Combined bachelor's/graduate degree, distance learning, double major, honors, independent study, internships, student-designed major, study abroad, teacher certification program, Washington semester, weekend college. **Credit/placement by examination:** AP, CLEP, SAT, ACT, institutional tests. 30 credit hours maximum toward bachelor's degree. Credit by examination granted only to enrolled students. Students may take challenge exam for particular course only once. **Support services:** Reduced course load, remedial instruction, study skills assistance, tutoring, writing center.

Majors. Biology: General. **Business:** Accounting, business admin, organizational behavior. **Communications:** Communications/speech/rhetoric. **Education:** English, mathematics, music, social science. **English:** English lit. **Health services:** Health care admin, nursing practice. **History:** General. **Liberal arts:** Arts/sciences. **Math:** General. **Parks/recreation:** General. **Philosophy/religion:** Christian, religion. **Psychology:** General. **Social sciences:** General. **Theology:** Bible, missionary, pastoral counseling, theology, youth ministry. **Visual/performing arts:** Music.

Most popular majors. Business/marketing 23%, health sciences 11%, liberal arts 11%, psychology 20%, theological studies 12%.

Computing on campus. 50 workstations in dormitories, library, computer center. Dormitories wired for high-speed internet access and linked to campus network. Commuter students can connect to campus network. Online course registration, online library, helpline, repair service, wireless network available.

Student life. Freshman orientation: Mandatory. Preregistration for classes offered. Sessions include placement tests. **Policies:** All single undergraduates under 22 required to live on campus. Request for off-campus living must be approved by Vice President for Student Development. Religious observance required. **Housing:** Guaranteed on-campus for all undergraduates. Single-sex dorms, special housing for disabled, apartments, wellness housing available. **Activities:** Jazz band, campus ministries, choral groups, dance, drama, film society, music ensembles, student government, student newspaper, symphony orchestra, Asian Fellowship, Hispanic Fellowship, summer missions teams, chapel worship team, spiritual action committee, psychology club, Missionary Kids Association, commuter student association.

Athletics. NAIA, NCCAA. **Intercollegiate:** Baseball M, basketball, cross-country, golf, soccer, softball W, volleyball W. **Intramural:** Basketball, football (non-tackle), soccer. **Team name:** Red Hawks.

Student services. Adult student services, alcohol/substance abuse counseling, chaplain/spiritual director, career counseling, student employment services, financial aid counseling, health services, minority student services, personal counseling, veterans' counselor. **Physically disabled:** Services for visually, speech, hearing impaired.

Contact. E-mail: admissions@simpsonu.edu
Phone: (530) 226-4606 Toll-free number: (888) 974-6776
Fax: (530) 226-4861
Kendell Kluttz, Director of Admissions, Simpson University, 2211 College View Drive, Redding, CA 96003-8606

Soka University of America
Aliso Viejo, California   **CB member**
www.soka.edu   **CB code: 4066**

- Private 4-year university and liberal arts college
- Residential campus in large town
- 438 degree-seeking undergraduates: 65% women, 4% African American, 22% Asian American, 10% Hispanic American, 42% international
- 3 graduate students
- 49% of applicants admitted
- SAT or ACT with writing, application essay required
- 88% graduate within 6 years; 35% enter graduate study

General. Study abroad is mandatory and included in tuition. Learning Clusters occur in 3.5-week block periods provide for field and service learning, traveling to places such as South Africa, China, the Amazon, Panama and India. **Degrees:** 89 bachelor's awarded; master's offered. **Location:** 70 miles from Los Angeles, 75 miles from San Diego. **Calendar:** Semester. **Full-time faculty:** 42 total; 95% have terminal degrees, 33% minority, 38% women. **Part-time faculty:** 19 total; 53% have terminal degrees, 53% minority, 63% women. **Class size:** 96% < 20, 4% 20-39. **Special facilities:** Performing arts center complex, black box theater, dance studio, writing center, language lab, darkroom, aquatic center.

Freshman class profile. 364 applied, 179 admitted, 110 enrolled.

Mid 50% test scores			
SAT critical reading:	470-620	GPA 2.0-2.99:	3%
SAT math:	540-680	Rank in top quarter:	80%
SAT writing:	530-610	Rank in top tenth:	43%
ACT composite:	23-27	End year in good standing:	97%
GPA 3.75 or higher:	44%	Return as sophomores:	94%
GPA 3.50-3.74:	28%	Out-of-state:	60%
GPA 3.0-3.49:	25%	Live on campus:	99%
		International:	33%

Basis for selection. High school curriculum, test scores, essay, and recommendations very important. Commitment to service, active leadership, and extracurricular activities important. Applications will be evaluated only when all required materials have been received. Official SAT or ACT scores must be sent directly by the testing agency. Applicants with prior college experience are also required to take the SAT Test or the ACT with its associated Writing Test, regardless of how many college credits they may have earned. SAT Subject Tests not required. **Home schooled:** Transcript of courses and grades, state high school equivalency certificate required. Program must be accredited by regional, state, or national agency. **Learning Disabled:** Admission decisions do not consider learning disabilities. Special needs discussed only after student has been admitted and has identified need.

High school preparation. 16 units recommended. Recommended units include English 4, mathematics 3, social studies 1, history 2, science 2 (laboratory 2) and foreign language 2.

2012-2013 Annual costs. Tuition/fees: $27,214. Room/board: $10,628. Books/supplies: $1,000. Personal expenses: $1,500.

2011-2012 Financial aid. Need-based: 104 full-time freshmen applied for aid; 92 were judged to have need; 92 of these received aid. Average need met was 67%. Average scholarship/grant was $22,074; average loan $3,379. 79% of total undergraduate aid awarded as scholarships/grants, 21% as loans/jobs. **Non-need-based:** Awarded to 430 full-time undergraduates, including 124 freshmen. Scholarships awarded for academics, athletics, leadership. **Additional information:** All admitted students whose annual family income is $60,000 or less qualify for Soka Opportunity Scholarships which covers full tuition. All admitted students to the BA in Liberal Arts program will be considered for additional scholarship opportunities for higher income levels. The scholarship is awarded based on family income.

Application procedures. Admission: Closing date 1/15 (receipt date). $45 fee, may be waived for applicants with need. Admission notification by 3/1. Must reply by 5/1. **Financial aid:** Closing date 3/2. FAFSA, institutional form required. Applicants notified on a rolling basis starting 3/15; must reply within 4 week(s) of notification.

Academics. Study abroad required of all students during one semester of their junior year. **Special study options:** Double major, ESL, independent study, internships, liberal arts/career combination, study abroad. **Credit/ placement by examination:** AP, CLEP. **Support services:** Study skills assistance, tutoring, writing center.

Majors. Liberal arts: Arts/sciences.

Computing on campus. PC or laptop required. 100 workstations in dormitories, library, computer center, student center. Dormitories wired for high-speed internet access and linked to campus network. Commuter students can connect to campus network. Online course registration, online library, helpline, repair service, wireless network available.

Student life. Freshman orientation: Mandatory. Preregistration for classes offered. 4-day orientation session held before upperclassmen arrive. **Housing:** Guaranteed on-campus for all undergraduates. Coed dorms, wellness housing available. Students required to live on campus. **Activities:** Bands, choral groups, dance, film society, international student organizations, literary magazine, music ensembles, Model UN, student government, student newspaper, symphony orchestra, Amnesty International, Global Brigades, Chinese club, Green Planet, Humanism in Action, Orchestra club, Activist Collective, French club, Ohana Volleyball club, Hip Hop Congress.

Athletics. NAIA. **Intercollegiate:** Cross-country, diving, soccer, swimming, track and field. **Intramural:** Badminton, basketball, football (non-tackle), handball, racquetball, soccer, softball, tennis, volleyball, weight lifting. **Team name:** Lions.

Student services. Alcohol/substance abuse counseling, career counseling, student employment services, financial aid counseling, health services, personal counseling, placement for graduates. **Physically disabled:** Services for visually, hearing impaired.

Contact. E-mail: admission@soka.edu
Phone: (949) 480-4150 Toll-free number: (888) 600-7652
Fax: (949) 480-4151
Andrew Woolsey, Director of Enrollment Services, Soka University of America, One University Drive, Aliso Viejo, CA 92656-8081

Sonoma State University
Rohnert Park, California
www.sonoma.edu   CB code: 4723

- Public 4-year university and liberal arts college
- Commuter campus in large town
- 7,704 degree-seeking undergraduates: 9% part-time, 60% women, 2% African American, 4% Asian American, 15% Hispanic American, 1% Native American, 1% international
- 554 degree-seeking graduate students
- 85% of applicants admitted
- SAT or ACT (ACT writing optional) required
- 53% graduate within 6 years

General. Founded in 1960. Regionally accredited. **Degrees:** 1,695 bachelor's awarded; master's offered. **ROTC:** Army, Naval, Air Force. **Location:** 50 miles from San Francisco, 10 miles from Santa Rosa. **Calendar:** Semester. **Full-time faculty:** 259 total; 93% have terminal degrees, 18% minority, 49% women. **Part-time faculty:** 208 total; 39% have terminal degrees, 14% minority. **Class size:** 35% < 20, 48% 20-39, 8% 40-49, 6% 50-99, 2% >100. **Special facilities:** Observatory, performing arts center, nature preserves, information technology center.

Freshman class profile. 12,151 applied, 10,317 admitted, 1,810 enrolled.

Mid 50% test scores		GPA 2.0-2.99:	33%
SAT critical reading:	450-560	Return as sophomores:	80%
SAT math:	450-560	Out-of-state:	1%
ACT composite:	18-24	Live on campus:	90%
GPA 3.75 or higher:	8%	International:	1%
GPA 3.50-3.74:	12%	Fraternities:	16%
GPA 3.0-3.49:	47%	Sororities:	22%

Basis for selection. School GPA and test scores most important. SAT, ACT, SAT Subject Tests must be received before start of term. Audition required of music majors. Portfolio required of art majors. RN required for graduate nursing. **Learning Disabled:** Applicants with disabilities strongly encouraged to complete college preparatory course requirements if at all possible. If applicant judged unable to fulfill specific course requirement because of disability, alternative college preparatory courses may be substituted for specific subject requirements.

High school preparation. College-preparatory program required. 15 units required. Required units include English 4, mathematics 3, history 2, science 2 (laboratory 1), foreign language 2, visual/performing arts 1 and academic electives 1. One visual and performing arts, US government required.

2011-2012 Annual costs. Tuition/fees: $6,862; $16,942 out-of-state. Room/board: $10,961. Books/supplies: $1,746. Personal expenses: $3,096.

2010-2011 Financial aid. Need-based: 747 full-time freshmen applied for aid; 516 were judged to have need; 456 of these received aid. Average need met was 87%. Average scholarship/grant was $9,996; average loan $3,003. 66% of total undergraduate aid awarded as scholarships/grants, 34% as loans/jobs. **Non-need-based:** Awarded to 491 full-time undergraduates, including 84 freshmen. Scholarships awarded for academics, alumni affiliation, art, athletics, leadership, minority status, music/drama.

Application procedures. Admission: Priority date 11/30; deadline 11/30 (postmark date). $55 fee, may be waived for applicants with need. Admission notification by 3/1. Admission notification on a rolling basis. Must reply by 5/1. **Financial aid:** Priority date 1/31; no closing date. FAFSA required. Applicants notified on a rolling basis starting 3/25; must reply within 2 week(s) of notification.

Academics. Special study options: Accelerated study, combined bachelor's/graduate degree, cross-registration, distance learning, double major, dual enrollment of high school students, ESL, exchange student, external degree, honors, independent study, internships, liberal arts/career combination, New York semester, semester at sea, student-designed major, study abroad, teacher certification program, United Nations semester, urban semester, Washington semester. Combined degree programs: bachelor's/MBA; bachelor's/MPA. **Credit/placement by examination:** AP, CLEP, SAT, ACT, institutional tests. 30 credit hours maximum toward bachelor's degree. **Support services:** Learning center, pre-admission summer program, reduced course load, remedial instruction, study skills assistance, tutoring, writing center.

Majors. Area/ethnic studies: African-American, Chicano/Hispanic-American/Latino, women's. **Biology:** General, biochemistry. **Business:** Business admin. **Communications:** Communications/speech/rhetoric. **Computer sciences:** Computer science, programming. **Conservation:** General, environmental studies. **Engineering:** Computer. **English:** English lit. **Foreign languages:** French, German, Spanish. **Health services:** Nursing (RN). **History:** General. **Liberal arts:** Arts/sciences. **Math:** General. **Philosophy/religion:** Philosophy. **Physical sciences:** Chemistry, geology, physics. **Protective services:** Law enforcement admin. **Psychology:** General. **Social sciences:** Anthropology, economics, geography, political science, sociology. **Visual/performing arts:** General, art history/conservation, dramatic, music, studio arts. **Work/family studies:** Family studies.

Most popular majors. Business/marketing 17%, liberal arts 12%, psychology 14%, social sciences 9%.

Computing on campus. PC or laptop required. 400 workstations in library, computer center. Dormitories wired for high-speed internet access and linked to campus network. Commuter students can connect to campus network. Online course registration, online library, helpline, student web hosting, wireless network available.

Student life. Freshman orientation: Available. Preregistration for classes offered. 2-day residential program in June. Parents invited. **Housing:** Guaranteed on-campus for freshmen. Coed dorms, apartments, wellness housing available. $1,000 partly refundable deposit. Focus learning communities, freshman seminar, healthy living, women in math/science dorms available. **Activities:** Jazz band, choral groups, dance, drama, literary magazine, music ensembles, Model UN, musical theater, opera, radio station, student government, student newspaper, symphony orchestra, Student Advocates for Education, College Republicans, Asian Pacific Islander Organization, Raza Native American Council, El Movimiento Estudiantil Chicano/a de Aztlán, InterVarsity Christian Fellowship, Hillel, Best Buddies, Student Ambassadors.

Athletics. NCAA. **Intercollegiate:** Baseball M, basketball, golf, soccer, softball W, tennis, track and field W, volleyball W, water polo W. **Intramural:** Basketball, football (non-tackle), soccer, softball, volleyball. **Team name:** Sea Wolves.

Student services. Adult student services, alcohol/substance abuse counseling, career counseling, services for economically disadvantaged, student employment services, financial aid counseling, health services, minority student services, on-campus daycare, personal counseling, placement for graduates, veterans' counselor, women's services. **Physically disabled:** Services for visually, speech, hearing impaired.

Contact. Phone: (707) 664-2778 Fax: (707) 664-2060
Gustavo Flores, Director, Admissions, Sonoma State University, 1801 East Cotati Avenue, Rohnert Park, CA 94928-3609

Southern California Institute of Architecture
Los Angeles, California
www.sciarc.edu   CB code: 1575

- Private 5-year visual arts college
- Commuter campus in very large city
- 241 degree-seeking undergraduates: 4% part-time, 29% women, 26% Asian American, 22% Hispanic American, 1% Native American, 22% international
- 201 degree-seeking graduate students
- 81% of applicants admitted
- SAT or ACT (ACT writing optional), application essay required
- 79% graduate within 6 years

General. Founded in 1972. Regionally accredited. **Degrees:** 37 bachelor's awarded; master's offered. **Location:** Downtown. **Calendar:** Semester, limited summer session. **Full-time faculty:** 28 total; 32% women. **Part-time faculty:** 39 total; 20% women. **Special facilities:** Wood and metal shop, on-site print center, robotics lab.

Freshman class profile. 43 applied, 35 admitted, 5 enrolled.

End year in good standing:	96%	Return as sophomores:	83%

Basis for selection. Portfolio, statement of purpose, letters of recommendation, academic transcripts and test scores are considered. Applicants that have completed previous architectural design studios are eligible to apply for advanced placement. Applicants that have no previous architectural design studio work must apply for first year placement. SAT/ACT test scores are only required for applicants that have completed less than 24 undergraduate credit hours at the time of their application. Portfolio of creative work required.

High school preparation. Art, design or architecture courses are recommended.

2011-2012 Annual costs. Tuition/fees: $30,700. Books/supplies: $8,048.

2010-2011 Financial aid. Need-based: 2 full-time freshmen applied for aid; 2 were judged to have need; 2 of these received aid. Average need met was 100%. Average scholarship/grant was $4,500; average loan $5,500. 18% of total undergraduate aid awarded as scholarships/grants, 82% as loans/jobs. **Non-need-based:** Scholarships awarded for academics, state residency.

Application procedures. Admission: Closing date 1/15 (postmark date). $85 fee, may be waived for applicants with need. Application must be submitted online. Admission notification on a rolling basis beginning on or about 3/31. Must reply by 4/23. **Financial aid:** Priority date 3/2, closing date 3/2. FAFSA, institutional form required. Applicants notified on a rolling basis starting 3/30; must reply within 3 week(s) of notification.

Academics. Special study options: Exchange student, internships, study abroad. SCI-Arc study abroad programs in Milan, Mexico, Korea, Vienna and Tokyo; exchange programs in Australia, Denmark, Paris, Jerusalem, Netherlands. **Credit/placement by examination:** AP, CLEP, institutional tests. **Support services:** Pre-admission summer program.

Majors. Architecture: Architecture.

Computing on campus. PC or laptop required. 60 workstations in library, computer center. Commuter students can connect to campus network. Online course registration, online library, helpline, wireless network available.

Student life. Freshman orientation: Mandatory. Preregistration for classes offered. Held for the three consecutive days prior to the first day of classes; opportunity to visit alumni architectural firms on last day of orientation. **Policies:** Informal weekly gathering of entire school sponsored by student government. **Activities:** Student government, Architects, Designers, and Planners for Social Responsibility, American Institute of Architects student affiliation, Women in Architecture.

Student services. Career counseling, financial aid counseling, personal counseling, veterans' counselor. **Physically disabled:** Services for speech, hearing impaired.

Contact. E-mail: admissions@sciarc.edu
Phone: (213) 356-5320 Fax: (213) 613-2260
Sandy Frigo, Admissions Manager, Southern California Institute of Architecture, 960 E 3rd Street, Los Angeles, CA 90013

Southern California Institute of Technology
Anaheim, California
www.scitech.edu   CB code: 3034

- For-profit 4-year business and engineering college
- Residential campus in large city
- 675 degree-seeking undergraduates: 8% African American, 21% Asian American, 47% Hispanic American
- Interview required

General. Accredited by ACCSC. Strong focus on applying theoretical concepts to real world projects and lab work. **Degrees:** 75 bachelor's, 4 associate awarded. **Calendar:** Differs by program, extensive summer session. **Full-time faculty:** 16 total.

Basis for selection. Open admission, but selective for some programs. Interview required. High School Diploma, GED, official transcripts from other schools attended, standardized entrance exam required. Wonderlic required. **Home schooled:** Transcript of courses and grades, interview required.

2011-2012 Annual costs. Electronic Engineering associate degree program tuition $15,440, fees $750; bachelor's degree program tuition $14,325, fees $860. Electrical Engineering bachelor's degree program tuition $13,875, fees $375. Accounting bachelor's program tuition $13,670, fees $800. Business Management bachelor's program tuition $13,820, fees $750. Books/supplies: $2,500.

Application procedures. Admission: No deadline. $100 fee. Application must be submitted on paper. **Financial aid:** FAFSA required.

Academics. Special study options: Accelerated study, combined bachelor's/graduate degree, cooperative education, double major, ESL, liberal arts/career combination. **Credit/placement by examination:** AP, CLEP. **Support services:** Tutoring.

Majors. Business: Business admin. **Engineering:** Electrical.

Most popular majors. Business/marketing 68%, engineering/engineering technologies 29%.

Student life. Freshman orientation: Available. Preregistration for classes offered.

Student services. Adult student services, career counseling, student employment services, financial aid counseling, placement for graduates.

Contact. E-mail: admissions@scitech.edu
Phone: (714) 300-0300 Fax: (714) 300-0311
Parviz Shams, School Director, Southern California Institute of Technology, 222 South Harbor Boulevard, Suite 200, Anaheim, CA 92805-3758

Southern California Seminary
El Cajon, California
www.socalsem.edu

- Private 4-year Bible and seminary college
- Commuter campus in small city
- 97 degree-seeking undergraduates
- Application essay, interview required

General. Regionally accredited; also accredited by TRACS. **Degrees:** 13 bachelor's, 1 associate awarded; master's, professional offered. **Location:** 10 miles from San Diego. **Calendar:** Trimester, extensive summer session. **Full-time faculty:** 1 total. **Part-time faculty:** 34 total.

Basis for selection. Open admission, but selective for some programs. Application requirements include a standard background check. MMPI (Minnesota Multiphasic Personality Inventory) and interview required of MA in Counseling Psychology and PsyD degree programs applicants. **Home schooled:** Transcript of courses and grades, state high school equivalency certificate, letter of recommendation (nonparent) required. 2 essays on specific content.

High school preparation. College-preparatory program recommended.

2011-2012 Annual costs. Tuition/fees: $12,552. Room only: $5,110. Books/supplies: $1,700. Personal expenses: $1,700.

Application procedures. Admission: No deadline. $32 fee. **Financial aid:** Closing date 3/2.

Academics. Credit/placement by examination: AP, CLEP, institutional tests.

Majors. Theology: Bible.

Computing on campus. Commuter students can connect to campus network. Online library, helpline, wireless network available.

Student life. Freshman orientation: Mandatory. Preregistration for classes offered. **Housing:** Coed dorms, apartments available.

Student services. Chaplain/spiritual director, financial aid counseling, personal counseling, veterans' counselor.

Contact. E-mail: admissions@socalsem.edu
Phone: (619) 201-8959 Toll-free number: (888) 389-7244
Fax: (619) 201-8975
Thomas Pittman, Admissions Officer, Southern California Seminary, 2075 East Madison Avenue, El Cajon, CA 92019

St. Mary's College of California
Moraga, California **CB member**
www.stmarys-ca.edu **CB code: 4675**

- Private 4-year liberal arts college affiliated with Roman Catholic Church
- Residential campus in large town
- 2,985 degree-seeking undergraduates: 7% part-time, 62% women, 5% African American, 10% Asian American, 23% Hispanic American, 1% Native American, 2% international
- 1,103 degree-seeking graduate students
- 69% of applicants admitted
- SAT or ACT (ACT writing optional), application essay required
- 61% graduate within 6 years; 40% enter graduate study

General. Founded in 1863. Regionally accredited. **Degrees:** 516 bachelor's, 20 associate awarded; master's, doctoral offered. **ROTC:** Army. **Location:** 20 miles from San Francisco. **Calendar:** 4-1-4, limited summer session. **Full-time faculty:** 196 total; 95% have terminal degrees, 18% minority, 53% women. **Part-time faculty:** 299 total; 90% have terminal degrees, 11% minority, 64% women. **Class size:** 42% < 20, 57% 20-39, less than 1% 40-49, less than 1% 50-99. **Special facilities:** Observatory, college-operated museum.

Freshman class profile. 4,874 applied, 3,355 admitted, 648 enrolled.

Mid 50% test scores		Rank in top quarter:	62%
SAT critical reading:	500-600	Rank in top tenth:	28%
SAT math:	500-610	End year in good standing:	93%
ACT composite:	22-26	Return as sophomores:	87%
GPA 3.75 or higher:	21%	Out-of-state:	15%
GPA 3.50-3.74:	24%	Live on campus:	99%
GPA 3.0-3.49:	46%	International:	1%
GPA 2.0-2.99:	9%		

Basis for selection. School achievement record most important. Interview recommended. **Home schooled:** Transcript of courses and grades, letter of recommendation (nonparent) required.

High school preparation. College-preparatory program required. 16 units required; 19 recommended. Required and recommended units include English 4, mathematics 3-4, social studies 1, history 1, science 2-3 (laboratory 1), foreign language 2-3 and academic electives 2. One unit each of chemistry, physics, advanced algebra, and trigonometry required for applicants to school of science.

2012-2013 Annual costs. Tuition/fees (projected): $38,450. Room/board: $12,840. Books/supplies: $1,656. Personal expenses: $2,277.

2010-2011 Financial aid. Need-based: 547 full-time freshmen applied for aid; 501 were judged to have need; 501 of these received aid. Average need met was 77%. Average scholarship/grant was $23,072; average loan $3,384. 70% of total undergraduate aid awarded as scholarships/grants, 30% as loans/jobs. **Non-need-based:** Awarded to 328 full-time undergraduates, including 104 freshmen. Scholarships awarded for academics, art, athletics, leadership, music/drama, religious affiliation.

Application procedures. Admission: Priority date 11/15; deadline 2/1 (postmark date). $55 fee, may be waived for applicants with need. Admission notification by 3/15. Admission notification on a rolling basis. Must reply by May 1 or within 2 week(s) if notified thereafter. **Financial aid:** Priority date 2/15; no closing date. FAFSA required. Applicants notified on a rolling basis starting 3/15; must reply by 5/1 or within 2 week(s) of notification.

Academics. Academic support services are available on Sunday evenings or by appointment. **Special study options:** Combined bachelor's/graduate degree, cross-registration, double major, exchange student, honors, independent study, internships, liberal arts/career combination, student-designed major, study abroad, teacher certification program. 4-year interdisciplinary program with Great Books orientation. **Credit/placement by examination:** AP, CLEP, IB, SAT, ACT, institutional tests. 30 credit hours maximum toward bachelor's degree. **Support services:** Learning center, study skills assistance, tutoring, writing center.

Majors. Area/ethnic studies: European, Latin American, women's. **Biology:** General, biochemistry. **Business:** General, accounting, business admin, finance, international. **Communications:** Communications/speech/rhetoric. **Conservation:** Environmental science, environmental studies. **English:** English lit. **Foreign languages:** General, classics, French, German, Italian, Japanese, Spanish. **Health services:** Health care admin. **History:** General. **Liberal arts:** Arts/sciences. **Math:** General. **Parks/recreation:** Exercise sciences, health/fitness, sports admin. **Philosophy/religion:** Philosophy, religion. **Physical sciences:** Chemistry, physics. **Psychology:** General, developmental, experimental, industrial, social. **Social sciences:** Anthropology, archaeology, economics, political science, sociology. **Visual/performing arts:** General, art, dance, dramatic, music.

Most popular majors. Business/marketing 31%, communications/journalism 10%, liberal arts 10%, psychology 7%, social sciences 13%.

Computing on campus. 244 workstations in computer center. Dormitories wired for high-speed internet access and linked to campus network. Commuter students can connect to campus network. Online course registration, online library, helpline, repair service, student web hosting, wireless network available.

Student life. Freshman orientation: Mandatory, $250 fee. Preregistration for classes offered. 4 sessions plus separate transfer session. Freshmen attend 1 session plus 4-day welcome weekend. **Housing:** Guaranteed on-campus for freshmen. Coed dorms, apartments available. $350 nonrefundable deposit, deadline 5/1. Honors, Science, Lasallian Community, Santiago Community housing available. **Activities:** Bands, campus ministries, choral groups, dance, drama, international student organizations, literary magazine, music ensembles, musical theater, radio station, student government, student newspaper, symphony orchestra, TV station, Catholic Institute for Lasallian Social Action, Habitat for Humanity, Amnesty International, Lasallian Collegians, Asian Pacific American Student Association, Black Student Union, Dante, Gay Straight Alliance, Hermanas Unidas, Humans Actively Practicing Aloha Club.

Athletics. NCAA. **Intercollegiate:** Baseball M, basketball, cheerleading M, cross-country, golf M, lacrosse W, rowing (crew) W, soccer, softball W, tennis, track and field M, volleyball W. **Intramural:** Badminton, basketball, football (non-tackle), skiing, soccer, softball, volleyball. **Team name:** Gaels.

Student services. Alcohol/substance abuse counseling, chaplain/spiritual director, career counseling, services for economically disadvantaged, student employment services, financial aid counseling, health services, minority student services, personal counseling, placement for graduates, veterans' counselor, women's services. **Physically disabled:** Services for visually, speech, hearing impaired.

Contact. E-mail: smcadmit@stmarys-ca.edu
Phone: (925) 631-4224 Toll-free number: (800) 800-4762
Fax: (925) 376-7193
Michael McKeon, Dean of Admissions, St. Mary's College of California, Box 4800, Moraga, CA 94575-4800

Stanbridge College
Irvine, California
www.stanbridge.edu

- For-profit 4-year technical college
- Large city
- 724 degree-seeking undergraduates

General. Regionally accredited; also accredited by ACCSC. **Degrees:** 3 associate awarded. **Calendar:** Quarter, extensive summer session. **Full-time faculty:** 4 total. **Part-time faculty:** 37 total.

Freshman class profile. 400 applied, 260 admitted, 133 enrolled.

Basis for selection. Open admission, but selective for some programs.

2011-2012 Annual costs. Vocational Nursing: tuition $31,190, books and supplies $1,805, 12 months. Information Technology: Diploma tuition $9,910, books and supplies $3,085, 11 months; Associate degree tuition $24,352, books and supplies $5,643, 23 months. Occupational Therapy Assistant: tuition $38,100, books and supplies $1,895, 16 months.

Academics. **Credit/placement by examination:** AP, CLEP.

Majors. **Business:** Accounting. **Computer sciences:** Information technology.

Contact. E-mail: info@stanbridge.edu
Phone: (949) 794-9090 ext. 5116 Fax: (949) 794-9094
Edward Riepma, Director of Admissions, Stanbridge College, 2041 Business Center Drive, Suite 107, Irvine, CA 92612

Stanford University
Stanford, California
www.stanford.edu

CB member
CB code: 4704

- Private 4-year university and liberal arts college
- Residential campus in small city
- 6,927 degree-seeking undergraduates: 1% part-time, 48% women, 7% African American, 18% Asian American, 17% Hispanic American, 1% Native American, 8% international
- 8,883 degree-seeking graduate students
- 7% of applicants admitted
- SAT or ACT with writing, application essay required
- 96% graduate within 6 years; 31% enter graduate study

General. Founded in 1885. Regionally accredited. Research university with seven schools: Business, Earth Sciences, Education, Engineering, Humanities and Sciences, Law and Medicine. **Degrees:** 1,670 bachelor's awarded; master's, professional, doctoral offered. **ROTC:** Army, Naval, Air Force. **Location:** 29 miles from San Francisco, 22 miles from San Jose. **Calendar:** Quarter, extensive summer session. **Full-time faculty:** 1,027 total; 99% have terminal degrees, 20% minority, 26% women. **Part-time faculty:** 15 total; 93% have terminal degrees, 7% minority, 13% women. **Class size:** 69% < 20, 15% 20-39, 4% 40-49, 7% 50-99, 5% >100. **Special facilities:** Linear accelerator, nature preserve, marine research center, Rodin sculpture garden, observatory, medical center, arts center.

Freshman class profile. 34,348 applied, 2,437 admitted, 1,707 enrolled.

Mid 50% test scores			
SAT critical reading:	670-770	Rank in top quarter:	98%
SAT math:	690-780	Rank in top tenth:	92%
SAT writing:	680-780	Return as sophomores:	98%
ACT composite:	30-34	Out-of-state:	57%
GPA 3.75 or higher:	91%	Live on campus:	100%
GPA 3.50-3.74:	6%	International:	8%
GPA 3.0-3.49:	3%		

Basis for selection. Academic excellence is the primary criterion. Prospective students should have challenged themselves throughout high school and done very well. Transcript most important; personal qualities considered. SAT Subject Tests recommended. Official scores from all test dates must be sent to Stanford directly from ACT or the College Board or both if the applicant has taken the ACT and the SAT. Score reports must arrive by the appropriate application deadline.Test of English as a Foreign Language (TOEFL) recommended for non-native speakers of English. Arts students may submit supplementary materials for review. Submissions should have previously received significant recognition at regional, state, national or international level. **Home schooled:** Statement describing home school structure and mission required. Standardized test scores important. Subject tests recommended. **Learning Disabled:** Prospective students with disabilities are encouraged to meet with Disability Resource Center.

High school preparation. College-preparatory program recommended. 20 units recommended. Recommended units include English 4, mathematics 4, social studies 3, history 3, science 3 (laboratory 3) and foreign language 3.

2011-2012 Annual costs. Tuition/fees: $40,050. Room/board: $12,291. Books/supplies: $1,500. Personal expenses: $2,400.

2010-2011 Financial aid. All financial aid based on need. 987 full-time freshmen applied for aid; 827 were judged to have need; 821 of these received aid. Average need met was 100%. Average scholarship/grant was $39,429; average loan $2,138. 93% of total undergraduate aid awarded as scholarships/grants, 7% as loans/jobs. **Additional information:** For parents with total annual income below $60,000 and typical assets for this income range, parent contribution toward educational costs not expected. Students will still be expected to contribute from their income and savings. For parents with total annual income below $100,000 and typical assets for this income range, the

expected parent contribution will be low enough to ensure that all tuition charges are covered with need-based scholarship, federal and state grants, and/or outside scholarship funds. Families with incomes at higher levels (typically up to $200,000) may also qualify for assistance, especially if more than one family member is enrolled in college.

Application procedures. **Admission:** Closing date 1/1 (postmark date). $90 fee, may be waived for applicants with need. Admission notification by 4/1. Must reply by 5/1. Early action candidates may not apply to other schools under any type of early action, early decision, or early notification program, but may apply under regular admissions. **Financial aid:** Priority date 2/15; no closing date. FAFSA, CSS PROFILE required. Applicants notified on a rolling basis starting 4/1; must reply by 5/1.

Academics. Undergraduate academic offerings stress access to senior faculty through small-group learning experiences and research opportunities. **Special study options:** Combined bachelor's/graduate degree, distance learning, double major, ESL, exchange student, honors, independent study, internships, student-designed major, study abroad, Washington semester. **Credit/placement by examination:** AP, CLEP, IB, institutional tests. 45 Advanced Placement units allowed. **Support services:** Learning center, pre-admission summer program, reduced course load, study skills assistance, tutoring, writing center.

Majors. **Area/ethnic studies:** African-American, American, Asian-American, Chicano/Hispanic-American/Latino, East Asian, German, Native American, Spanish/Iberian, women's. **Biology:** General. **Communications:** General. **Computer sciences:** General, computer science. **Conservation:** Environmental science. **Engineering:** General, chemical, civil, electrical, environmental, materials, mechanical, petroleum. **English:** British lit, English lit, writing. **Foreign languages:** Chinese, classics, comparative lit, French, German, Italian, Japanese, linguistics, Slavic, Spanish. **History:** General. **Human services:** Public policy. **Liberal arts:** Humanities. **Math:** General. **Philosophy/religion:** Philosophy, religion. **Physical sciences:** Chemistry, geology, geophysics, materials science, physics. **Psychology:** General. **Social sciences:** Anthropology, archaeology, economics, international relations, political science, sociology, urban studies. **Visual/performing arts:** Art, dramatic, music, studio arts.

Most popular majors. Biology 7%, engineering/engineering technologies 19%, interdisciplinary studies 16%, social sciences 21%.

Computing on campus. 1,000 workstations in dormitories, library, computer center, student center. Dormitories wired for high-speed internet access and linked to campus network. Commuter students can connect to campus network. Online course registration, online library, helpline, repair service, student web hosting, wireless network available.

Student life. **Freshman orientation:** Mandatory, $438 fee. Preregistration for classes offered. 6-day academically oriented program held in late September. **Policies:** Students are expected to abide by the Fundamental Standard and the Honor Code. Freshmen not permitted cars on campus. **Housing:** Guaranteed on-campus for all undergraduates. Coed dorms, single-sex dorms, special housing for disabled, apartments, cooperative housing, fraternity/sorority housing available. **Activities:** Bands, campus ministries, choral groups, dance, drama, film society, international student organizations, literary magazine, music ensembles, Model UN, musical theater, opera, radio station, student government, student newspaper, symphony orchestra, TV station, approximately 650 student groups available.

Athletics. NCAA. **Intercollegiate:** Baseball M, basketball, cross-country, diving, fencing, field hockey W, football (tackle) M, golf, gymnastics, lacrosse W, rowing (crew), sailing, soccer, softball W, squash W, swimming, synchronized swimming W, tennis, track and field, volleyball, water polo, wrestling M. **Intramural:** Badminton, basketball, football (non-tackle), golf, racquetball, soccer, softball, squash, table tennis, tennis, volleyball. **Team name:** Cardinal.

Student services. Alcohol/substance abuse counseling, chaplain/spiritual director, career counseling, student employment services, financial aid counseling, health services, legal services, minority student services, on-campus daycare, personal counseling, placement for graduates, women's services. **Physically disabled:** Services for visually, speech, hearing impaired.

Contact. E-mail: admission@stanford.edu
Phone: (650) 723-2091 Fax: (650) 723-6050
Richard Shaw, Dean of Undergraduate Admission and Financial Aid, Stanford University, Montag Hall, Stanford, CA 94305-6106

Thomas Aquinas College
Santa Paula, California
www.thomasaquinas.edu

CB member
CB code: 4828

- Private 4-year liberal arts college affiliated with Roman Catholic Church
- Residential campus in rural community

- 358 degree-seeking undergraduates: 51% women, 1% Asian American, 13% Hispanic American, 6% international
- 79% of applicants admitted
- SAT or ACT (ACT writing optional), application essay required
- 68% graduate within 6 years; 20% enter graduate study

General. Founded in 1971. Regionally accredited. **Degrees:** 81 bachelor's awarded. **Location:** 5 miles from Santa Paula, 12 miles from Ojai. **Calendar:** Semester. **Full-time faculty:** 30 total; 70% have terminal degrees, 10% women. **Part-time faculty:** 7 total; 71% have terminal degrees. **Class size:** 100% < 20.

Freshman class profile. 171 applied, 135 admitted, 92 enrolled.

Mid 50% test scores		GPA 2.0-2.99:	4%
SAT critical reading:	610-710	Rank in top quarter:	40%
SAT math:	550-660	Rank in top tenth:	40%
SAT writing:	580-690	End year in good standing:	93%
ACT composite:	25-29	Return as sophomores:	90%
GPA 3.75 or higher:	59%	Out-of-state:	69%
GPA 3.50-3.74:	20%	Live on campus:	100%
GPA 3.0-3.49:	17%	International:	3%

Basis for selection. Application essays, 3 letters of reference, academic records, and test scores required. Test scores are accepted on a rolling basis throughout the year. Interview recommended for applicants whose academic preparation is non-traditional, and for those out of high school for significant period of time. **Home schooled:** Those applicants who are not home schooled through formal programs must provide written records of all their studies from grades 9 through 12.

High school preparation. College-preparatory program recommended. 13 units required; 16 recommended. Required and recommended units include English 4, mathematics 3-4, history 2, science 2-3 (laboratory 2), foreign language 2 and academic electives 3.

2012-2013 Annual costs. Tuition/fees: $23,600. Room/board: $7,800. Books/supplies: $450. Personal expenses: $2,316.

2011-2012 Financial aid. All financial aid based on need. 65% of total undergraduate aid awarded as scholarships/grants, 35% as loans/jobs.

Application procedures. Admission: No deadline. No application fee. Admission notification on a rolling basis beginning on or about 10/1. Must reply by May 1 or within 2 week(s) if notified thereafter. **Financial aid:** Closing date 3/2. FAFSA, institutional form required. Applicants notified on a rolling basis starting 2/1; must reply by 5/1 or within 2 week(s) of notification.

Academics. Special study options: Cross-disciplinary curriculum of liberal education through reading and analyzing the "Great Books," with special emphasis on theology, philosophy, math, laboratory science, and literature. **Credit/placement by examination:** AP, CLEP. **Support services:** Tutoring.

Majors. Liberal arts: Arts/sciences.

Computing on campus. PC or laptop required. 19 workstations in dormitories, library, computer center, student center. Dormitories linked to campus network. Helpline available.

Student life. Freshman orientation: Mandatory. Preregistration for classes offered. 2-day program immediately before classes begin. **Housing:** Guaranteed on-campus for all undergraduates. Single-sex dorms available. **Activities:** Campus ministries, choral groups, dance, drama, literary magazine, music ensembles, musical theater, student newspaper, Medical Society, Pro-life group, Legion of Mary, Third Order Dominican, Tocqueville Political Forum.

Athletics. Intramural: Basketball, football (non-tackle) M, soccer, softball, table tennis, tennis, volleyball.

Student services. Alcohol/substance abuse counseling, chaplain/spiritual director, career counseling, student employment services, financial aid counseling, health services, personal counseling, placement for graduates.

Contact. E-mail: admissions@thomasaquinas.edu
Phone: (805) 525-4417 Toll-free number: (800) 634-9797
Fax: (805) 421-5905
Jonathan Daly, Director of Admissions, Thomas Aquinas College, 10000 Ojai Road, Santa Paula, CA 93060-9621

Touro College Los Angeles
West Hollywood, California
www.touro.edu/losangeles   CB code: 4753

- Private 4-year liberal arts college
- Very large city
- 77 degree-seeking undergraduates

General. Regionally accredited. **Degrees:** 22 bachelor's awarded; master's offered. **Calendar:** Semester. **Full-time faculty:** 4 total; 100% have terminal degrees, 50% women. **Part-time faculty:** 12 total; 67% have terminal degrees, 42% women.

Basis for selection. Admission requirements vary by programs.

2011-2012 Annual costs. Tuition/fees: $15,900. Books/supplies: $975. Personal expenses: $2,306.

2010-2011 Financial aid. Need-based: 89% of total undergraduate aid awarded as scholarships/grants, 11% as loans/jobs.

Application procedures. Admission: Closing date 5/15.

Academics. Credit/placement by examination: AP, CLEP.

Majors. Business: General. **Philosophy/religion:** Judaic. **Psychology:** General.

Student life. Freshman orientation: Mandatory. Preregistration for classes offered.

Contact. E-mail: tourolaadmissions@touro.edu
Phone: (323) 822-9700 ext. 85155 Fax: (323) 654-2086
Samira Miller, Director of Admissions, Touro College Los Angeles, 1317 North Crescent Heights Boulevard, West Hollywood, CA 90046

Trident University International
Cypress, California
www.trident.edu   CB code: 6332

- For-profit 4-year virtual university
- Very large city
- 2,730 degree-seeking undergraduates: 43% part-time, 32% women, 14% African American, 3% Asian American, 5% Hispanic American
- 2,845 degree-seeking graduate students
- Interview required

General. Regionally accredited. **Degrees:** 1,260 bachelor's awarded; master's, doctoral offered. **Location:** 30 Miles from Los Angeles. **Calendar:** Differs by program, extensive summer session. **Full-time faculty:** 69 total; 20% minority, 45% women. **Part-time faculty:** 410 total; 8% minority, 39% women.

Freshman class profile. 302 enrolled.

Basis for selection. Open admission. Student must present official high school transcript or equivalent and possess high school diploma or equivalent. **Home schooled:** Transcript of courses and grades required. Transcripts from State Department of Education or local school board.

2011-2012 Annual costs. Tuition/fees: $9,514. 100% online institution, no room and board. Course materials CDs included in cost of tuition. Additional $74 fee for Anatomy and Physiology Labs, $12.99 fee for Microbiology Lab.

2010-2011 Financial aid. Need-based: 25 full-time freshmen applied for aid; 25 were judged to have need; 25 of these received aid. Average scholarship/grant was $2,774. 35% of total undergraduate aid awarded as scholarships/grants, 65% as loans/jobs.

Application procedures. Admission: No deadline. No application fee. **Financial aid:** No deadline. FAFSA, institutional form required.

Academics. Special study options: Distance learning, independent study. **Credit/placement by examination:** AP, CLEP.

Majors. Business: Business admin. **Computer sciences:** General, information technology. **Conservation:** Environmental science. **Health services:** Health care admin.

Most popular majors. Business/marketing 50%, computer/information sciences 10%, health sciences 40%.

Computing on campus. PC or laptop required. Online course registration, online library available.

Student life. Freshman orientation: Available. Preregistration for classes offered. **Activities:** Student newspaper.

Contact. E-mail: admissions@tuiu.edu
Phone: (800) 579-3170 Fax: (800) 403-9024
Robert Givenrod, Director of Admissions, Trident University International, Attn: Office of the Registrar, Cypress, CA 90630

University of California: Berkeley

Berkeley, California	CB member
www.berkeley.edu	CB code: 4833

- Public 4-year university
- Residential campus in small city
- 25,885 degree-seeking undergraduates: 3% African American, 39% Asian American, 12% Hispanic American, 1% Native American, 9% international
- 10,257 graduate students
- 22% of applicants admitted
- SAT or ACT with writing, application essay required
- 90% graduate within 6 years

General. Founded in 1868. Regionally accredited. **Degrees:** 7,466 bachelor's awarded; master's, professional, doctoral offered. **ROTC:** Army, Naval, Air Force. **Location:** 10 miles from San Francisco. **Calendar:** Semester, extensive summer session. **Full-time faculty:** 1,578 total; 99% have terminal degrees, 20% minority, 32% women. **Part-time faculty:** 512 total; 99% have terminal degrees, 19% minority, 45% women. **Special facilities:** Museums of art, anthropology, archaeology, paleontology and vertebrate zoology, film archive, science museum and research center for K-12 education, botanical garden, libraries of rare books, Western and Latin Americana, seismographic station, herbacia, performing arts facilities.

Freshman class profile. 52,786 applied, 11,440 admitted, 4,443 enrolled.

Mid 50% test scores		GPA 2.0-2.99:	1%
SAT critical reading:	600-720	Rank in top quarter:	100%
SAT math:	650-770	Rank in top tenth:	98%
SAT writing:	620-740	Return as sophomores:	97%
ACT composite:	28-33	Out-of-state:	25%
GPA 3.75 or higher:	78%	Live on campus:	95%
GPA 3.50-3.74:	15%	International:	14%
GPA 3.0-3.49:	6%		

Basis for selection. Thorough review of academic performance; likely contribution to the intellectual and cultural vitality of the campus; diversity in personal background and experience; demonstrated qualities in leadership, motivation, concern for others and community; non-academic achievement in the performing arts, athletics or employment; demonstrated interest in major. SAT Subject Tests recommended. SAT Subject tests recommended only for applicants to colleges of chemistry or engineering.

High school preparation. College-preparatory program required. 15 units required; 18 recommended. Required and recommended units include English 4, mathematics 3-4, history 2, science 2-3 (laboratory 2-3), foreign language 2-3, visual/performing arts 1 and academic electives 1. 2 units in history or social sciences are required.

2011-2012 Annual costs. Tuition/fees: $12,835; $35,713 out-of-state. Room and board rate is based on a weighted average of all on-campus housing. Room/board: $14,990. Books/supplies: $1,202. Personal expenses: $3,014.

Financial aid. Non-need-based: Scholarships awarded for academics.

Application procedures. Admission: Closing date 11/30. $70 fee, may be waived for applicants with need. Admission notification by 3/31. Must reply by 5/1. **Financial aid:** Closing date 3/2. FAFSA required. Applicants notified by 4/15.

Academics. All students required to pass one American cultures class. **Special study options:** Accelerated study, cross-registration, double major, dual enrollment of high school students, ESL, exchange student, honors, independent study, internships, student-designed major, study abroad. Freshman seminar, undergraduate research apprenticeship, university research expeditions. **Credit/placement by examination:** AP, CLEP, institutional tests. **Support services:** Learning center, pre-admission summer program, reduced course load, study skills assistance, tutoring.

Majors. Architecture: Architecture, landscape. **Area/ethnic studies:** African-American, American, Asian, Asian-American, Chicano/Hispanic-American/Latino, Latin American, Native American, Near/Middle Eastern, Southeast Asian, women's. **Biology:** General, botany, cellular/molecular, microbiology, toxicology. **Business:** Business admin. **Communications:** Media studies. **Computer sciences:** Computer science. **Conservation:** General, forest management, forestry, management/policy. **Engineering:** Applied physics, biomedical, chemical, civil, electrical, engineering science, environmental, geological, manufacturing, mechanical, nuclear, operations research. **English:** English lit, rhetoric/composition. **Foreign languages:** Ancient Greek, Celtic, Chinese, classics, comparative lit, Dutch/Flemish, French, German, Italian, Japanese, Latin, linguistics, Scandinavian, Slavic, Spanish. **History:** General. **Human services:** Social work. **Math:** General, applied, statistics. **Philosophy/religion:** Philosophy, religion. **Physical sciences:** General, astrophysics, atmospheric science, chemistry, geology, geophysics, materials science, oceanography, physics. **Psychology:** General. **Social sciences:** Anthropology, economics, geography, political science, sociology, urban studies. **Visual/performing arts:** Art, art history/conservation, dance, dramatic, film/cinema/video, music.

Most popular majors. Biology 13%, engineering/engineering technologies 11%, social sciences 20%.

Computing on campus. Dormitories wired for high-speed internet access and linked to campus network. Commuter students can connect to campus network. Online course registration, online library, helpline, repair service, wireless network available.

Student life. Freshman orientation: Available, $295 fee. Preregistration for classes offered. Cost varies by term and entry status. **Housing:** Guaranteed on-campus for freshmen. Coed dorms, single-sex dorms, special housing for disabled, apartments, cooperative housing, fraternity/sorority housing available. $300 partly refundable deposit, deadline 5/25. Apartments for students with children. **Activities:** Bands, choral groups, dance, drama, film society, international student organizations, literary magazine, music ensembles, Model UN, musical theater, radio station, student government, student newspaper, symphony orchestra, TV station, Asian American Christian fellowship, black recruitment and retention center, hiking and outdoor society, Americorps, forensics, Chabad, Lesbian and Gay alliance, Raza recruitment and retention center, College Democrats, College Republicans.

Athletics. NCAA. **Intercollegiate:** Baseball M, basketball, cross-country, diving, field hockey W, football (tackle) M, golf, gymnastics, rowing (crew), rugby M, soccer, softball W, swimming, tennis, track and field, volleyball W, water polo. **Intramural:** Basketball, bowling, fencing, field hockey M, football (tackle), handball, ice hockey, lacrosse, racquetball, rowing (crew), sailing, skiing, soccer, softball, squash, tennis, volleyball M. **Team name:** Bears.

Student services. Adult student services, alcohol/substance abuse counseling, chaplain/spiritual director, career counseling, services for economically disadvantaged, student employment services, financial aid counseling, health services, legal services, minority student services, on-campus daycare, personal counseling, placement for graduates, veterans' counselor, women's services. **Physically disabled:** Services for visually, speech, hearing impaired.

Contact. Phone: (510) 642-6000
University of California: Berkeley, 110 Sproul Hall, #5800, Berkeley, CA 94720-5800

University of California: Davis

Davis, California	CB member
www.ucdavis.edu	CB code: 4834

- Public 4-year university
- Residential campus in small city
- 24,913 degree-seeking undergraduates: 1% part-time, 55% women, 2% African American, 37% Asian American, 16% Hispanic American, 3% international
- 6,636 degree-seeking graduate students
- 46% of applicants admitted
- SAT or ACT with writing, application essay required
- 82% graduate within 6 years

General. Founded in 1905. Regionally accredited. **Degrees:** 6,511 bachelor's awarded; master's, professional, doctoral offered. **ROTC:** Army, Naval, Air Force. **Location:** 15 miles from Sacramento, 72 miles from San Francisco. **Calendar:** Continuous, extensive summer session. **Full-time faculty:** 1,471 total; 98% have terminal degrees, 23% minority, 36% women. **Part-time faculty:** 149 total; 98% have terminal degrees, 20% minority, 48% women. **Class size:** 36% < 20, 35% 20-39, 5% 40-49, 13% 50-99, 11% >100. **Special**

facilities: 150-acre arboretum, equestrian center, craft center, marine laboratory, nuclear laboratory, California Regional Primate Research Center, natural reserves, raptor center.

Freshman class profile. 45,806 applied, 21,085 admitted, 4,705 enrolled.

Mid 50% test scores			
SAT critical reading:	520-650	GPA 3.0-3.49:	9%
SAT math:	570-690	Rank in top quarter:	100%
SAT writing:	540-670	Rank in top tenth:	100%
ACT composite:	24-30	Return as sophomores:	93%
GPA 3.75 or higher:	72%	Out-of-state:	5%
GPA 3.50-3.74:	19%	Live on campus:	92%
		International:	4%

Basis for selection. Scholastic achievement most important, followed by school and community activities, academic interests, special circumstances, special achievements and awards. Two SAT Subject Tests in different subject areas of student's choice required: history/social science, English literature, mathematics (Level 2), laboratory science or language other than English.

High school preparation. 15 units required; 18 recommended. Required and recommended units include English 4, mathematics 3-4, social studies 1, history 1, science 2-3 (laboratory 2-3), foreign language 2-3, visual/performing arts 1 and academic electives 1. History/social science (social studies above) requirement is one year of U.S. history, or one-half year of U.S. history and one-half year of civics or U.S. government; and one year of world history, cultures and geography. For academic elective ("g" requirement): two semesters chosen from the following areas: visual and performing arts (non-introductory-level courses), history, social science, English, advanced mathematics, laboratory science and language other than English.

2011-2012 Annual costs. Tuition/fees: $13,860; $36,738 out-of-state. Estimated personal expenses include $1,263 for our student health insurance plan. Although this is a mandatory fee, if a student is covered through private insurance, he or she can waive out. Room/board: $12,697. Books/supplies: $1,589. Personal expenses: $2,489.

Financial aid. All financial aid based on need.

Application procedures. Admission: Closing date 11/30. $70 fee, may be waived for applicants with need. Admission notification by 3/31. Must reply by 5/1. **Financial aid:** Priority date 3/2; no closing date. FAFSA required. Applicants notified on a rolling basis starting 3/24.

Academics. Seventy percent of undergraduates participate in full- and part-time internships. **Special study options:** Accelerated study, cross-registration, double major, dual enrollment of high school students, ESL, honors, independent study, internships, student-designed major, study abroad, teacher certification program, Washington semester. **Credit/placement by examination:** AP, CLEP. 10 credit hours maximum toward bachelor's degree. **Support services:** Learning center, pre-admission summer program, reduced course load, remedial instruction, study skills assistance, tutoring, writing center.

Majors. Architecture: Landscape, urban/community planning. **Area/ethnic studies:** African, African-American, American, Asian-American, Chicano/Hispanic-American/Latino, East Asian, Native American, women's. **Biology:** General, biotechnology, botany, cell/histology, entomology, environmental toxicology, evolutionary, exercise physiology, genetics, microbiology, molecular biochemistry, neurobiology/anatomy, zoology. **Communications:** Communications/speech/rhetoric. **Computer sciences:** Computer science. **Conservation:** General, environmental studies, urban forestry. **Engineering:** Aerospace, applied physics, biomedical, chemical, civil, computer, electrical, materials, mechanical. **English:** English lit. **Foreign languages:** Chinese, comparative lit, French, German, Italian, Japanese, linguistics, Russian, Spanish. **General:** Agronomy, animal sciences, food science, international, range science, soil science. **History:** General. **Math:** General, applied, computational, statistics. **Philosophy/religion:** Philosophy, religion. **Physical sciences:** Atmospheric science, chemistry, geology, hydrology, physics. **Psychology:** General. **Social sciences:** Anthropology, economics, international relations, political science, sociology. **Visual/performing arts:** Art history/conservation, design, dramatic, film/cinema/video, music, studio arts. **Work/family studies:** Clothing/textiles, family studies.

Most popular majors. Agriculture 9%, biology 19%, engineering/engineering technologies 7%, philosophy/religious studies 11%, psychology 11%, social sciences 19%.

Computing on campus. 1,500 workstations in dormitories, library, computer center, student center. Dormitories wired for high-speed internet access and linked to campus network. Commuter students can connect to campus network. Online course registration, online library, helpline, repair service, wireless network available.

Student life. Freshman orientation: Available, $265 fee. Preregistration for classes offered. Summer advising June-August. **Policies:** Residents and visitors must abide by state and university regulations relating to alcohol. Alcohol delivery by outside vendors is prohibited. Behavioral problems while under the influence of alcohol or any other substance will not be tolerated and may be subject to disciplinary action. **Housing:** Guaranteed on-campus for freshmen. Coed dorms, single-sex dorms, special housing for disabled, apartments, cooperative housing, wellness housing available. $500 fully refundable deposit, deadline 6/9. Special interest housing available. **Activities:** Bands, campus ministries, choral groups, dance, drama, film society, international student organizations, literary magazine, music ensembles, Model UN, musical theater, radio station, student government, student newspaper, symphony orchestra, TV station, 316 student organizations.

Athletics. NCAA. **Intercollegiate:** Baseball M, basketball, cross-country, diving W, field hockey W, football (tackle) M, golf, gymnastics W, lacrosse W, soccer, softball W, swimming W, tennis, track and field, volleyball W, water polo. **Intramural:** Badminton, basketball, bowling, golf, racquetball, soccer, softball, squash, table tennis, tennis, volleyball, water polo. **Team name:** Aggies.

Student services. Adult student services, alcohol/substance abuse counseling, chaplain/spiritual director, career counseling, services for economically disadvantaged, student employment services, financial aid counseling, health services, legal services, minority student services, on-campus daycare, personal counseling, placement for graduates, veterans' counselor, women's services. **Physically disabled:** Services for visually, speech, hearing impaired.

Contact. E-mail: undergraduateadmissions@ucdavis.edu
Phone: (530) 752-2971 Fax: (530) 752-1280
Walter Robinson, Director, University of California: Davis, One Shields Ave, Davis, CA 95616

University of California: Irvine
Irvine, California   **CB member**
www.uci.edu   **CB code: 4859**

- Public 4-year university
- Residential campus in small city
- 22,004 degree-seeking undergraduates: 2% part-time, 54% women, 2% African American, 49% Asian American, 18% Hispanic American, 4% international
- 5,083 degree-seeking graduate students
- 47% of applicants admitted
- SAT or ACT with writing, application essay required
- 82% graduate within 6 years

General. Founded in 1965. Regionally accredited. **Degrees:** 6,720 bachelor's awarded; master's, professional, doctoral offered. **ROTC:** Army, Air Force. **Location:** 40 miles from Los Angeles. **Calendar:** Quarter, extensive summer session. **Full-time faculty:** 1,463 total; 98% have terminal degrees, 30% minority, 35% women. **Part-time faculty:** 460 total; 98% have terminal degrees, 26% minority, 44% women. **Class size:** 47% < 20, 29% 20-39, 4% 40-49, 8% 50-99, 12% >100. **Special facilities:** Outdoor laboratory, ecological preserve, freshwater marsh reserve, arboretum, center for art and technology, observatory.

Freshman class profile. 49,287 applied, 23,391 admitted, 5,115 enrolled.

Mid 50% test scores			
SAT critical reading:	500-630	Rank in top tenth:	96%
SAT math:	560-680	End year in good standing:	98%
SAT writing:	510-640	Return as sophomores:	94%
GPA 3.75 or higher:	73%	Out-of-state:	2%
GPA 3.50-3.74:	18%	Live on campus:	81%
GPA 3.0-3.49:	9%	International:	5%
Rank in top quarter:	100%	Fraternities:	8%
		Sororities:	10%

Basis for selection. Demonstrated record of academic preparation, educational engagement, talent and skills important. SAT Subject Tests recommended. Students need only submit scores for the ACT With Writing or SAT. SAT Subject Test scores no longer required. However, submission of SAT Subject Test scores may add positively to review of student's application.

High school preparation. College-preparatory program required. 15 units required; 18 recommended. Required and recommended units include English 4, mathematics 3-4, history 2, science 2-3 (laboratory 2-3), foreign language 2-3, visual/performing arts 1 and academic electives 1.

2011-2012 Annual costs. Tuition/fees: $13,122; $36,000 out-of-state. Room/board: $11,611. Books/supplies: $1,553. Personal expenses: $1,338.

2010-2011 Financial aid. Need-based: 3,785 full-time freshmen applied for aid; 2,884 were judged to have need; 2,793 of these received aid. Average need met was 86%. Average scholarship/grant was $14,807; average loan $5,942. 79% of total undergraduate aid awarded as scholarships/grants, 21% as loans/jobs. **Non-need-based:** Awarded to 835 full-time undergraduates,

including 127 freshmen. **Additional information:** Blue and Gold opportunity plan guarantees needy in-state students from families earning less than $70,000/yr that their system-wide fees & tuition will be paid through scholarships and grants.

Application procedures. Admission: Closing date 11/30 (receipt date). $70 fee, may be waived for applicants with need. Application must be submitted online. Admission notification by 3/31. Must reply by 5/1. **Financial aid:** Priority date 3/2, closing date 5/1. FAFSA required. Applicants notified on a rolling basis starting 4/1.

Academics. Special study options: Accelerated study, distance learning, double major, dual enrollment of high school students, ESL, honors, independent study, internships, semester at sea, study abroad, teacher certification program, Washington semester. **Credit/placement by examination:** AP, CLEP, IB, institutional tests. **Support services:** Learning center, preadmission summer program, reduced course load, remedial instruction, study skills assistance, tutoring, writing center.

Majors. Area/ethnic studies: African-American, Asian-American, Chicano/Hispanic-American/Latino, Chinese, East Asian, European, German, women's. **Biology:** General, Biochemistry/molecular biology, bioinformatics, botany, cellular/molecular, ecology/evolutionary, genetics, microbiology/immunology, neurobiology/anatomy. **Business:** Business admin, information resources management, managerial economics. **Computer sciences:** General, computer science, informatics. **Conservation:** Environmental studies. **Education:** Biology. **Engineering:** General, aerospace, biomedical, chemical, civil, computer, electrical, environmental, materials, mechanical. **English:** English lit. **Foreign languages:** Classics, comparative lit, French, Japanese, Korean, Spanish. **Health services:** Pharmaceutical sciences. **History:** General. **Liberal arts:** Humanities. **Math:** General. **Philosophy/religion:** Philosophy, religion. **Physical sciences:** Chemistry, geology, physics. **Psychology:** General, social. **Social sciences:** General, anthropology, criminology, econometrics, economics, political science, sociology, urban studies. **Visual/performing arts:** Art history/conservation, dance, dramatic, film/cinema/video, game design, music, music performance, musical theater, studio arts.

Most popular majors. Biology 16%, business/marketing 8%, engineering/engineering technologies 8%, interdisciplinary studies 7%, psychology 11%, social sciences 24%, visual/performing arts 6%.

Computing on campus. 1,500 workstations in dormitories, library, computer center, student center. Dormitories wired for high-speed internet access and linked to campus network. Commuter students can connect to campus network. Online course registration, online library, helpline, repair service, student web hosting, wireless network available.

Student life. Freshman orientation: Mandatory, $185 fee. Preregistration for classes offered. A two-day program held during summer. Orientation for parents is available on Day 2. **Housing:** Guaranteed on-campus for freshmen. Coed dorms, single-sex dorms, special housing for disabled, apartments, fraternity/sorority housing available. $350 partly refundable deposit. **Activities:** Bands, campus ministries, choral groups, dance, drama, film society, international student organizations, literary magazine, music ensembles, Model UN, musical theater, opera, radio station, student government, student newspaper, symphony orchestra.

Athletics. NCAA. **Intercollegiate:** Baseball M, basketball, cross-country, golf, soccer, tennis, track and field, volleyball, water polo. **Intramural:** Basketball, bowling, football (non-tackle), racquetball, soccer, softball, swimming, table tennis, tennis, track and field, volleyball, water polo, wrestling. **Team name:** Anteaters.

Student services. Adult student services, alcohol/substance abuse counseling, career counseling, services for economically disadvantaged, student employment services, financial aid counseling, health services, minority student services, on-campus daycare, personal counseling, placement for graduates, veterans' counselor, women's services. **Physically disabled:** Services for visually, speech, hearing impaired.

Contact. E-mail: admissions@uci.edu
Phone: (949) 824-6703 Fax: (949) 824-2951
Brent Yunek, Director of Admissions, University of California: Irvine, 260 Aldrich Hall, Irvine, CA 92697-1075

University of California: Los Angeles

Los Angeles, California   **CB member**
www.ucla.edu   **CB code: 4837**

◗ Public 4-year university
◗ Residential campus in very large city

◗ 27,189 degree-seeking undergraduates: 3% part-time, 55% women, 3% African American, 34% Asian American, 17% Hispanic American, 7% international
◗ 12,072 degree-seeking graduate students
◗ 25% of applicants admitted
◗ SAT or ACT with writing, application essay required
◗ 90% graduate within 6 years

General. Founded in 1919. Regionally accredited. **Degrees:** 7,503 bachelor's awarded; master's, professional, doctoral offered. **ROTC:** Army, Naval, Air Force. **Location:** 10 miles from downtown Los Angeles. **Calendar:** Quarter, extensive summer session. **Full-time faculty:** 2,014 total; 98% have terminal degrees, 25% minority, 35% women. **Part-time faculty:** 563 total; 98% have terminal degrees, 23% minority, 36% women. **Class size:** 52% < 20, 22% 20-39, 4% 40-49, 10% 50-99, 12% >100. **Special facilities:** Museums with specialized collections, centers for cancer research, plasma physics research labs, film and television archive, high power auroral simulation observatory, lab for embedded collaborative systems, research centers for molecular and neuroscience, graphic and animation labs, nanoscience research labs and centers, cell mimetic space exploration center, particle beam physics lab, particle center, ranch for ecological studies, ethnomusicology archive.

Freshman class profile. 61,528 applied, 15,689 admitted, 5,825 enrolled.

Mid 50% test scores			
SAT critical reading:	560-690	Rank in top quarter:	100%
SAT math:	610-740	Rank in top tenth:	97%
SAT writing:	590-710	Return as sophomores:	97%
ACT composite:	25-31	Out-of-state:	11%
GPA 3.75 or higher:	92%	Live on campus:	94%
GPA 3.50-3.74:	5%	International:	10%
GPA 3.0-3.49:	3%	Fraternities:	11%
		Sororities:	11%

Basis for selection. GPA, test scores, course work, number of and performance in honors and AP courses most important. Essay considered. Strong senior program important. Extracurricular activities, honors and awards also reviewed. SAT Subject Tests not required of Fall Quarter 2012, or later, freshmen applicants. Will review if submitted; certain SAT subject exams may be recommended for some majors. Audition required of music, dance, theater majors. Portfolio required of art majors.

High school preparation. College-preparatory program required. 15 units required; 18 recommended. Required and recommended units include English 4, mathematics 3-4, history 2, science 2-3 (laboratory 2-3), foreign language 2-3, visual/performing arts 1 and academic electives 1.

2011-2012 Annual costs. Tuition/fees: $12,686; $35,564 out-of-state. Estimated personal expenses include $1,225 for our student health insurance plan. Although this is a mandatory fee, if a student is covered through private insurance, he or she can waive out. Room/board: $13,979. Books/supplies: $1,509. Personal expenses: $2,593.

2010-2011 Financial aid. Need-based: 76% of total undergraduate aid awarded as scholarships/grants, 24% as loans/jobs. **Non-need-based:** Scholarships awarded for academics, alumni affiliation, athletics, ROTC.

Application procedures. Admission: Closing date 11/30 (postmark date). $70 fee, may be waived for applicants with need. Admission notification by 3/31. Must reply by 5/1. **Financial aid:** Priority date 3/2; no closing date. FAFSA required. Applicants notified on a rolling basis starting 3/15; must reply within 3 week(s) of notification.

Academics. Special study options: Accelerated study, distance learning, double major, honors, independent study, internships, student-designed major, study abroad, urban semester, Washington semester. **Credit/placement by examination:** AP, CLEP, SAT, ACT. **Support services:** Learning center, study skills assistance, tutoring, writing center.

Majors. Architecture: Architecture. **Area/ethnic studies:** African-American, Asian, Asian-American, Chicano/Hispanic-American/Latino, East Asian, European, Latin American, Native American, Russian/Slavic, Scandinavian, Southeast Asian, women's. **Biology:** General, bacteriology, biochemistry, biophysics, biotechnology, cellular/molecular, ecology, immunology, marine, molecular genetics, neuroscience, physiology. **Business:** Managerial economics. **Computer sciences:** General. **Conservation:** Environmental science. **Engineering:** Aerospace, agricultural, chemical, civil, computer, electrical, geological, materials, mechanical. **English:** American lit, English lit. **Foreign languages:** African, ancient Greek, Arabic, Chinese, comparative lit, East Asian, French, German, Hebrew, Italian, Japanese, Korean, Latin, linguistics, Portuguese, Russian, Scandinavian, Slavic, Spanish. **History:** General. **Math:** General, applied, statistics. **Philosophy/religion:** Judaic, philosophy, religion. **Physical sciences:** Astrophysics, chemistry, geology, geophysics, materials science, physics. **Psychology:** General, psychobiology. **Social sciences:** Anthropology, economics, geography, international economic development, international economics, political science, sociology.

Visual/performing arts: Art, art history/conservation, dramatic, film/cinema/video, music, music history, musicology.

Most popular majors. Biology 13%, engineering/engineering technologies 9%, history 7%, psychology 10%, social sciences 27%, visual/performing arts 6%.

Computing on campus. Dormitories wired for high-speed internet access and linked to campus network. Commuter students can connect to campus network. Online course registration, online library, helpline, repair service, student web hosting, wireless network available.

Student life. Freshman orientation: Available, $340 fee. Preregistration for classes offered. 3-day, 2-night program. **Housing:** Guaranteed on-campus for freshmen. Coed dorms, special housing for disabled, apartments, cooperative housing, fraternity/sorority housing, wellness housing available. **Activities:** Bands, campus ministries, choral groups, dance, drama, film society, international student organizations, literary magazine, music ensembles, Model UN, musical theater, opera, radio station, student government, student newspaper, symphony orchestra, TV station.

Athletics. NCAA. **Intercollegiate:** Baseball M, basketball, cross-country, diving W, football (tackle) M, golf, gymnastics W, rowing (crew) W, soccer, softball W, swimming W, tennis, track and field, volleyball, water polo. **Intramural:** Badminton, basketball, football (non-tackle), golf, racquetball, soccer, squash, swimming, table tennis, tennis, track and field, volleyball. **Team name:** Bruins.

Student services. Alcohol/substance abuse counseling, chaplain/spiritual director, career counseling, services for economically disadvantaged, student employment services, financial aid counseling, health services, legal services, minority student services, on-campus daycare, personal counseling, placement for graduates, veterans' counselor, women's services. **Physically disabled:** Services for visually, speech, hearing impaired.

Contact. E-mail: ugadm@saonet.ucla.edu
Phone: (310) 825-3101 Fax: (310) 206-1206
Vu Tran, Director of Undergraduate Admissions, University of California: Los Angeles, 1147 Murphy Hall, Los Angeles, CA 90095-1436

University of California: Merced

Merced, California
www.ucmerced.edu

CB member
CB code: 4129

- Public 4-year university
- Commuter campus in small city
- 4,938 degree-seeking undergraduates: 1% part-time, 50% women, 7% African American, 29% Asian American, 37% Hispanic American, 1% international
- 260 degree-seeking graduate students
- 80% of applicants admitted
- SAT or ACT with writing, application essay required
- 58% graduate within 6 years

General. Candidate for regional accreditation. **Degrees:** 401 bachelor's awarded; master's, doctoral offered. **Location:** 120 miles from San Francisco, 60 miles from Fresno. **Calendar:** Semester, limited summer session. **Full-time faculty:** 220 total; 79% have terminal degrees, 16% minority, 40% women. **Part-time faculty:** 44 total; 36% have terminal degrees, 9% minority, 54% women. **Class size:** 18% < 20, 50% 20-39, 7% 40-49, 15% 50-99, 10% >100. **Special facilities:** Sierra Nevada research institute, Yosemite National Park research station, computational biology center, energy research center.

Freshman class profile. 15,205 applied, 12,160 admitted, 1,443 enrolled.

Mid 50% test scores			
SAT critical reading:	440-550	GPA 3.0-3.49:	57%
SAT math:	460-590	GPA 2.0-2.99:	3%
SAT writing:	440-550	End year in good standing:	72%
GPA 3.75 or higher:	18%	Return as sophomores:	85%
GPA 3.50-3.74:	22%	Live on campus:	75%
		International:	1%

Basis for selection. Academic record and test scores determine eligibility. **Home schooled:** If school is not accredited by a regional association, student must meet eligibility by examination alone.

High school preparation. College-preparatory program required. 15 units required; 18 recommended. Required and recommended units include English 4, mathematics 3-4, history 2, science 2-3 (laboratory 2-3), foreign language 2-3, visual/performing arts 1 and academic electives 1. History is 2 units in history/social science.

2011-2012 Annual costs. Tuition/fees: $13,070; $35,948 out-of-state. Estimated personal expenses include $1,298 for our student health insurance plan. Although this is a mandatory fee, if a student is covered through private insurance, he or she can waive out. Room/board: $13,720. Books/supplies: $1,385. Personal expenses: $1,578.

Financial aid. Non-need-based: Scholarships awarded for academics, leadership.

Application procedures. Admission: Closing date 11/30 (postmark date). $70 fee, may be waived for applicants with need. Admission notification by 3/1. Must reply by May 1 or within 3 week(s) if notified thereafter. **Financial aid:** Priority date 3/2; no closing date. FAFSA required. Applicants notified on a rolling basis starting 3/2.

Academics. Special study options: Accelerated study, double major, independent study, internships, study abroad, Washington semester. Research opportunities and internships at Lawrence Livermore National Laboratories and Yosemite National Park. **Credit/placement by examination:** AP, CLEP, IB, institutional tests. Credit by examination with the approval of instructor giving examination and dean of school involved. Some courses may not be deemed appropriate for obtaining credit by examination. **Support services:** Learning center, study skills assistance, tutoring, writing center.

Majors. Biology: General. **Business:** Business admin. **Engineering:** Biomedical, computer, environmental, materials, mechanical. **Foreign languages:** Comparative lit. **History:** General. **Math:** Applied. **Physical sciences:** Chemistry, geology, physics. **Psychology:** General. **Social sciences:** General, anthropology, economics, political science, sociology.

Most popular majors. Biology 22%, business/marketing 12%, engineering/engineering technologies 14%, psychology 22%, social sciences 11%.

Computing on campus. 157 workstations in dormitories, library, computer center. Dormitories wired for high-speed internet access and linked to campus network. Commuter students can connect to campus network. Online course registration, online library, helpline, wireless network available.

Student life. Freshman orientation: Available, $49 fee. Preregistration for classes offered. **Housing:** Guaranteed on-campus for freshmen. Coed dorms, special housing for disabled, wellness housing available. $300 partly refundable deposit, deadline 5/3. **Activities:** Marching band, choral groups, dance, film society, radio station, student government, student newspaper, African American student union, Liberal activism club, student government advisory committee, Latino students alliance, Filipino student alliance, Circle K International, American Red Cross club, Jewish student union.

Athletics. NAIA. **Intercollegiate:** Basketball, cross-country, soccer W, volleyball W. **Intramural:** Basketball, football (non-tackle), racquetball, soccer, softball, tennis, volleyball. **Team name:** Golden Bobcats.

Student services. Alcohol/substance abuse counseling, career counseling, services for economically disadvantaged, student employment services, financial aid counseling, health services, minority student services, on-campus daycare, personal counseling, veterans' counselor, women's services. **Physically disabled:** Services for visually, hearing impaired.

Contact. E-mail: admissions@ucmerced.edu
Phone: (209) 228-4682 Toll-free number: (866) 270-7301
Fax: (209) 228-4244
Encarnacion Ruiz, Director, Admissions and Relations with Schools & Colleges, University of California: Merced, 5200 North Lake Road, Merced, CA 95343-5603

University of California: Riverside

Riverside, California
www.ucr.edu/

CB member
CB code: 4839

- Public 4-year university
- Residential campus in large city
- 18,517 degree-seeking undergraduates: 3% part-time, 52% women, 6% African American, 37% Asian American, 34% Hispanic American, 2% international
- 2,326 degree-seeking graduate students
- 69% of applicants admitted
- SAT or ACT with writing, application essay required
- 65% graduate within 6 years; 35% enter graduate study

General. Founded in 1954. Regionally accredited. **Degrees:** 3,615 bachelor's awarded; master's, doctoral offered. **ROTC:** Army, Air Force. **Location:** 60 miles from Los Angeles. **Calendar:** Quarter, limited summer session. **Full-time faculty:** 754 total; 98% have terminal degrees, 32% minority, 34%

women. **Part-time faculty:** 128 total; 98% have terminal degrees, 42% minority, 43% women. **Class size:** 37% < 20, 36% 20-39, 3% 40-49, 13% 50-99, 11% >100. **Special facilities:** Botanical gardens, air pollution research center, photography museum, 8 nature preserves, citrus research center and agricultural experiment station, institute of geophysics and planetary physics, water resources center, salinity lab.

Freshman class profile. 28,101 applied, 19,389 admitted, 3,664 enrolled.

Mid 50% test scores			
SAT critical reading:	460-580	GPA 3.0-3.49:	40%
SAT math:	490-630	GPA 2.0-2.99:	2%
SAT writing:	470-580	Rank in top quarter:	100%
ACT composite:	19-25	Rank in top tenth:	94%
GPA 3.75 or higher:	29%	Live on campus:	77%
GPA 3.50-3.74:	29%	International:	2%

Basis for selection. Uses a fixed weight point system comprehensive review model that culminates in an Academic Index Score to determine admission for incoming freshmen. SAT Subject scores are not required but if submitted, official scores must be received by 7/15. All tests must be taken by December of the student's senior year. A personal statement is required as part of the application process. **Home schooled:** Portfolio describing subjects studied and methods of study is required. **Learning Disabled:** No special admission requirements; students should mention disability in either personal statement or the additional information section of application.

High school preparation. College-preparatory program required. Required and recommended units include English 4, mathematics 3-4, science 3-4 (laboratory 3-4), foreign language 2-3, computer science 2, visual/performing arts 1 and academic electives 1.

2011-2012 Annual costs. Tuition/fees: $12,923; $35,801 out-of-state. Estimated personal expenses include $684 for our student health insurance plan. Although this is a mandatory fee, if a student is covered through private insurance, he or she can waive out. Room/board: $12,093. Books/supplies: $1,800. Personal expenses: $1,700.

2011-2012 Financial aid. Need-based: 3,277 full-time freshmen applied for aid; 2,896 were judged to have need; 2,863 of these received aid. Average need met was 91%. Average scholarship/grant was $18,714; average loan $5,189. 78% of total undergraduate aid awarded as scholarships/grants, 22% as loans/jobs. **Non-need-based:** Awarded to 409 full-time undergraduates, including 141 freshmen. Scholarships awarded for academics, art, athletics, job skills, leadership, music/drama, state residency.

Application procedures. Admission: Closing date 11/30 (receipt date). $70 fee ($80 out-of-state), may be waived for applicants with need. Application must be submitted online. Admission notification by 3/23. Admission notification on a rolling basis beginning on or about 2/1. Must reply by 5/1. **Financial aid:** Closing date 3/2. FAFSA required. Applicants notified on a rolling basis starting 3/1; must reply by 5/1 or within 3 week(s) of notification.

Academics. Special study options: Accelerated study, combined bachelor's/graduate degree, cross-registration, double major, ESL, honors, independent study, internships, study abroad, teacher certification program, Washington semester. **Credit/placement by examination:** AP, CLEP, IB, institutional tests. **Support services:** Learning center, pre-admission summer program, reduced course load, study skills assistance, tutoring, writing center.

Majors. Area/ethnic studies: General, African-American, Asian, Asian-American, Chicano/Hispanic-American/Latino, German, Latin American, Native American, Russian/Slavic, women's. **Biology:** General, biochemistry, botany, entomology, neuroscience. **Business:** Business admin, managerial economics. **Computer sciences:** Computer science. **Conservation:** Environmental science. **Engineering:** Biomedical, chemical, computer, electrical, environmental, materials, mechanical. **English:** Creative writing, English lit. **Foreign languages:** General, classics, comparative lit, French, linguistics, Spanish. **History:** General. **Human services:** Public policy. **Liberal arts:** Arts/sciences, humanities. **Math:** General, applied, statistics. **Philosophy/religion:** Philosophy, religion. **Physical sciences:** General, chemistry, geology, geophysics, materials science, physics. **Psychology:** General. **Social sciences:** Anthropology, economics, political science, sociology. **Visual/performing arts:** Art, art history/conservation, dramatic, music, studio arts.

Most popular majors. Biology 12%, business/marketing 18%, interdisciplinary studies 7%, psychology 11%, social sciences 19%.

Computing on campus. 556 workstations in dormitories, library, computer center, student center. Dormitories wired for high-speed internet access and linked to campus network. Commuter students can connect to campus network. Online course registration, online library, helpline, repair service, student web hosting, wireless network available.

Student life. Freshman orientation: Mandatory, $250 fee. Preregistration for classes offered. Nine two-day mandatory orientation sessions from July 11 through August 10. **Housing:** Guaranteed on-campus for freshmen. Coed dorms, special housing for disabled, apartments available. $250 fully refundable deposit, deadline 5/10. **Activities:** Bands, campus ministries, choral groups, dance, drama, film society, international student organizations, literary magazine, music ensembles, musical theater, radio station, student government, student newspaper, 350 clubs and organizations available.

Athletics. NCAA. **Intercollegiate:** Baseball M, basketball, cross-country, golf, rugby, soccer, softball W, tennis, track and field, volleyball W. **Intramural:** Badminton, baseball M, basketball, football (non-tackle), golf, soccer, softball W, table tennis, tennis, volleyball W. **Team name:** Highlanders.

Student services. Adult student services, alcohol/substance abuse counseling, career counseling, student employment services, financial aid counseling, health services, minority student services, on-campus daycare, personal counseling, placement for graduates, veterans' counselor, women's services. **Physically disabled:** Services for visually, speech, hearing impaired.

Contact. E-mail: admit@ucr.edu
Phone: (951) 827-3411 Fax: (951) 827-6344
Merlyn Campos, Director of Undergraduate Admissions, University of California: Riverside, Admissions Office, Riverside, CA 92521

University of California: San Diego

La Jolla, California **CB member**
www.ucsd.edu **CB code: 4836**

- Public 4-year university
- Residential campus in large town
- 23,046 degree-seeking undergraduates
- 4,529 graduate students
- 38% of applicants admitted
- SAT or ACT with writing, application essay required
- 81% graduate within 6 years

General. Founded in 1959. Regionally accredited. Includes 6 undergraduate colleges, each with different housing and general education requirements. **Degrees:** 6,336 bachelor's awarded; master's, doctoral offered. **Location:** 12 miles from San Diego. **Calendar:** Quarter, extensive summer session. **Full-time faculty:** 943 total; 98% have terminal degrees, 24% minority. **Part-time faculty:** 219 total; 100% have terminal degrees, 17% minority. **Class size:** 44% < 20, 22% 20-39, 4% 40-49, 11% 50-99, 20% >100. **Special facilities:** Performing arts centers, student-run co-ops, supercomputer center, nature preserves, electron beam lithography facility, center for music experiment, structural engineering lab, aquarium, additional specialty research centers.

Freshman class profile. 48,098 applied, 18,272 admitted, 4,021 enrolled.

Mid 50% test scores			
SAT critical reading:	540-670	GPA 3.0-3.49:	4%
SAT math:	610-720	Rank in top quarter:	100%
SAT writing:	560-690	Rank in top tenth:	100%
ACT composite:	25-31	Out-of-state:	4%
GPA 3.75 or higher:	80%	Live on campus:	92%
GPA 3.50-3.74:	16%	Fraternities:	10%
		Sororities:	10%

Basis for selection. High school course pattern, GPA, essay and test scores most important. Admission for out-of-state applicants more selective than for residents. If not native English speaker, one of following is required: Test of English as a Foreign Language (TOEFL) examination, International English Language Testing System (IELTS) examination (academic modules).

High school preparation. College-preparatory program required. 17 units required. Required and recommended units include English 4, mathematics 3-4, history 2, science 2-3 (laboratory 2-3), foreign language 2-3, visual/performing arts 1 and academic electives 1. History is 2 units in history/social science.

2011-2012 Annual costs. Tuition/fees: $13,202; $36,080 out-of-state. Estimated personal expenses include $930 for our student health insurance plan. Although this is a mandatory fee, if a student is covered through private insurance, he or she can waive out. Room/board: $11,684. Books/supplies: $1,427. Personal expenses: $1,341.

Financial aid. Non-need-based: Scholarships awarded for academics, art, athletics, leadership, minority status, music/drama.

Application procedures. Admission: Closing date 11/30 (postmark date). $70 fee, may be waived for applicants with need. Application must be submitted online. Admission notification by 3/31. Admission notification on a rolling basis. Must reply by 5/1. **Financial aid:** Priority date 3/2, closing date 6/1. FAFSA required. Applicants notified on a rolling basis starting 3/15; must reply within 3 week(s) of notification.

Academics. Special study options: Combined bachelor's/graduate degree, cross-registration, double major, dual enrollment of high school students, ESL, exchange student, honors, independent study, internships, liberal arts/career combination, semester at sea, student-designed major, study abroad, teacher certification program, Washington semester. In-depth academic assignments working in small groups or one-to-one with faculty; research programs. **Credit/placement by examination:** AP, CLEP, IB, SAT, institutional tests. **Support services:** Learning center, pre-admission summer program, reduced course load, study skills assistance, tutoring, writing center.

Majors. Architecture: Urban/community planning. **Area/ethnic studies:** Chinese, German, Italian, Japanese, Latin American, Russian/Slavic, women's. **Biology:** General, animal physiology, bacteriology, biochemistry, bioinformatics, biophysics, biotechnology, cell/histology, ecology, evolutionary, molecular, neuroscience. **Business:** Management science. **Communications:** Communications/speech/rhetoric, digital media. **Computer sciences:** General, computer science, information systems, systems analysis. **Conservation:** Environmental science, environmental studies. **Engineering:** Aerospace, applied physics, biomedical, chemical, computer, electrical, engineering mechanics, engineering science, mechanical, structural, systems. **English:** American lit, British lit, English lit, writing. **Foreign languages:** General, classics, French, German, Italian, Japanese, linguistics, Russian, Spanish. **History:** General. **Human services:** Public policy. **Math:** General, applied. **Philosophy/religion:** Judaic, philosophy, religion. **Physical sciences:** Chemical physics, chemistry, molecular physics, physics, planetary. **Psychology:** General. **Social sciences:** Anthropology, archaeology, economics, political science, sociology, U.S. government, urban studies. **Visual/performing arts:** Art history/conservation, dance, dramatic, music, studio arts. **Work/family studies:** Family studies.

Most popular majors. Biology 17%, engineering/engineering technologies 14%, psychology 8%, social sciences 32%.

Computing on campus. 1,500 workstations in library, computer center, student center. Dormitories wired for high-speed internet access and linked to campus network. Commuter students can connect to campus network. Online course registration, online library, helpline, repair service, student web hosting, wireless network available.

Student life. Freshman orientation: Mandatory, $170 fee. Preregistration for classes offered. One- to two-day programs for freshmen and transfers; additional one-day program for international students. **Housing:** Guaranteed on-campus for freshmen. Coed dorms, single-sex dorms, special housing for disabled, apartments, cooperative housing, fraternity/sorority housing available. $650 fully refundable deposit, deadline 6/30. Language, cultural interest and international houses available. **Activities:** Bands, campus ministries, choral groups, dance, drama, film society, international student organizations, literary magazine, music ensembles, Model UN, musical theater, opera, radio station, student government, student newspaper, symphony orchestra, TV station, 550 student organizations available.

Athletics. NCAA. **Intercollegiate:** Baseball M, basketball, cross-country, diving, fencing, golf M, rowing (crew), soccer, softball W, swimming, tennis, track and field, volleyball, water polo. **Intramural:** Basketball, bowling, football (non-tackle), football (tackle), soccer, softball, tennis, volleyball, water polo. **Team name:** Tritons.

Student services. Alcohol/substance abuse counseling, career counseling, services for economically disadvantaged, student employment services, financial aid counseling, health services, legal services, minority student services, on-campus daycare, personal counseling, placement for graduates, veterans' counselor, women's services. **Physically disabled:** Services for visually, speech, hearing impaired.

Contact. E-mail: admissionsreply@ucsd.edu
Phone: (858) 534-4831 Fax: (858) 534-5629
Mae Brown, Assistant Vice Chancellor and Director of Admissions, University of California: San Diego, 9500 Gilman Drive, 0021, La Jolla, CA 92093-0021

University of California: Santa Barbara
Santa Barbara, California   **CB member**
www.ucsb.edu   **CB code: 4835**

- Public 4-year university
- Residential campus in small city
- 18,617 degree-seeking undergraduates: 2% part-time, 52% women
- 3,065 degree-seeking graduate students
- 46% of applicants admitted
- SAT or ACT with writing, application essay required

General. Founded in 1909. Regionally accredited. **Degrees:** 5,812 bachelor's awarded; master's, doctoral offered. **ROTC:** Army. **Location:** 10 miles from downtown, 100 miles from Los Angeles. **Calendar:** Quarter, extensive summer session. **Full-time faculty:** 884 total; 100% have terminal degrees, 18% minority, 34% women. **Part-time faculty:** 176 total; 100% have terminal degrees, 12% minority, 48% women. **Class size:** 45% < 20, 31% 20-39, 4% 40-49, 11% 50-99, 9% >100. **Special facilities:** Nature preserves with research facilities, seawater laboratories, robotics laboratory, free electron laser laboratory; institutes for polymers and organic solids, neuroscience research, quantum, nuclear particle astrophysics and cosmology, marine science, theoretical physics.

Freshman class profile. 49,008 applied, 22,379 admitted, 4,107 enrolled.

Mid 50% test scores			
SAT critical reading:	550-670	GPA 2.0-2.99:	1%
SAT math:	570-690	Rank in top quarter:	98%
SAT writing:	550-670	Rank in top tenth:	96%
ACT composite:	24-30	Out-of-state:	5%
GPA 3.75 or higher:	75%	Live on campus:	94%
GPA 3.50-3.74:	18%	Fraternities:	7%
GPA 3.0-3.49:	6%	Sororities:	12%

Basis for selection. Eligibility established by high school GPA, course requirement, and SAT scores. Special consideration for disadvantaged students. SAT Subject Tests recommended. All applicants must take 2 SAT Subject Tests in different subject areas. If Math SAT Subject Test is taken, must be Level 2. Audition required of music, dance, drama majors. Portfolio required of art majors.

High school preparation. College-preparatory program required. Required and recommended units include English 4, mathematics 3-4, history 3, (laboratory 2-3), foreign language 2-3, visual/performing arts 1 and academic electives 1.

2011-2012 Annual costs. Tuition/fees: $13,595; $36,473 out-of-state. Room/board: $13,345. Books/supplies: $1,414. Personal expenses: $2,741.

2011-2012 Financial aid. Non-need-based: Scholarships awarded for academics, athletics.

Application procedures. Admission: Closing date 11/30 (postmark date). $60 fee, may be waived for applicants with need. Admission notification by 3/31. Must reply by 5/1. **Financial aid:** Priority date 3/2, closing date 5/31. FAFSA required. Must reply within 2 week(s) of notification.

Academics. Special study options: Accelerated study, cross-registration, distance learning, double major, dual enrollment of high school students, ESL, exchange student, honors, independent study, internships, student-designed major, study abroad, teacher certification program, Washington semester. Graduate-level classes, off-campus study, freshman seminars, pre-professional programs and advising, academic minors, and undergraduate research, professional studies in school of environmental science and management and school of education. **Credit/placement by examination:** AP, CLEP, institutional tests. **Support services:** Learning center, pre-admission summer program, reduced course load, study skills assistance, tutoring, writing center.

Majors. Area/ethnic studies: African-American, Asian, Chicano/Hispanic-American/Latino, Latin American, women's. **Biology:** General, aquatic, bacteriology, biochemistry, cell/histology, ecology, marine, molecular, pharmacology, zoology. **Communications:** Communications/speech/rhetoric. **Computer sciences:** General. **Conservation:** Environmental studies. **Engineering:** Chemical, computer, electrical, mechanical. **English:** English lit. **Foreign languages:** Chinese, classics, comparative lit, French, German, Italian, Japanese, linguistics, Portuguese, Russian, Slavic, Spanish. **History:** General. **Math:** General, statistics. **Philosophy/religion:** Philosophy, religion. **Physical sciences:** Chemistry, geology, geophysics, physics. **Psychology:** General. **Social sciences:** Anthropology, econometrics, economics, geography, political science, sociology. **Visual/performing arts:** General, art, art history/conservation, cinematography, dance, dramatic, film/cinema/video, music, studio arts.

Most popular majors. Biology 7%, business/marketing 11%, communications/journalism 7%, interdisciplinary studies 8%, psychology 8%, social sciences 20%, visual/performing arts 7%.

Computing on campus. 255 workstations in dormitories, library, computer center, student center. Dormitories wired for high-speed internet access and linked to campus network. Online library, repair service, student web hosting, wireless network available.

Student life. Freshman orientation: Available. Preregistration for classes offered. Two-day program; includes sessions for parents. **Housing:** Guaranteed on-campus for freshmen. Coed dorms, apartments, cooperative housing, fraternity/sorority housing, wellness housing available. $100 nonrefundable deposit, deadline 9/1. **Activities:** Bands, campus ministries, choral groups, dance, drama, film society, international student organizations, literary magazine, music ensembles, Model UN, musical theater, opera, radio station, student government, student newspaper, symphony orchestra, TV station,

Hillel, Catholic Student Organization, Democratic and Republican student organizations, El Congreso, Persian Student Association, Habitat for Humanity.

Athletics. NCAA. **Intercollegiate:** Baseball M, basketball, cross-country, golf M, gymnastics, soccer, softball W, swimming, tennis, track and field, volleyball, water polo. **Intramural:** Badminton, basketball, bowling, cross-country, football (non-tackle), golf, gymnastics, racquetball, rowing (crew), soccer, softball, squash, tennis, volleyball, water polo. **Team name:** Gauchos.

Student services. Adult student services, alcohol/substance abuse counseling, career counseling, services for economically disadvantaged, student employment services, financial aid counseling, health services, minority student services, on-campus daycare, personal counseling, placement for graduates, veterans' counselor, women's services. **Physically disabled:** Services for visually, speech, hearing impaired.

Contact. E-mail: admissions@sa.ucsb.edu
Phone: (805) 893-2881 Fax: (805) 893-2676
Christine Van Gieson, Director of Admissions, University of California: Santa Barbara, 1210 Cheadle Hall, Santa Barbara, CA 93106-2014

University of California: Santa Cruz

Santa Cruz, California	CB member
www.ucsc.edu	CB code: 4860

- Public 4-year university
- Residential campus in small city
- 15,945 degree-seeking undergraduates: 2% part-time, 52% women, 2% African American, 20% Asian American, 23% Hispanic American, 1% Native American
- 1,509 degree-seeking graduate students
- 68% of applicants admitted
- SAT or ACT with writing, application essay required
- 74% graduate within 6 years

General. Founded in 1965. Regionally accredited. **Degrees:** 3,661 bachelor's awarded; master's, doctoral offered. **ROTC:** Army, Naval, Air Force. **Location:** 75 miles from San Francisco, 30 miles from San Jose. **Calendar:** Quarter, limited summer session. **Full-time faculty:** 554 total; 95% have terminal degrees, 21% minority, 34% women. **Part-time faculty:** 237 total; 95% have terminal degrees, 13% minority, 53% women. **Class size:** 40% < 20, 33% 20-39, 5% 40-49, 9% 50-99, 14% >100. **Special facilities:** Observatories, arboretum, agroecology farm, campus preserve, nonlinear science center, music center, bilingual research center, institutes of marine sciences, tectonics, particle physics, center for adaptive optics.

Freshman class profile. 28,236 applied, 19,228 admitted, 3,606 enrolled.

Mid 50% test scores			
SAT critical reading:	500-630	GPA 3.0-3.49:	30%
SAT math:	520-640	GPA 2.0-2.99:	1%
SAT writing:	510-630	Rank in top quarter:	100%
ACT composite:	22-29	Rank in top tenth:	96%
GPA 3.75 or higher:	33%	Out-of-state:	3%
GPA 3.50-3.74:	36%	Live on campus:	99%

Basis for selection. Test scores, GPA in required subjects most important. Personal statement very important. All applicants must take 2 SAT Subject Tests in different subject areas. Math SAT Subject Test must be Level 2. SAT Subject Tests not required for admission, but may be required for specific majors. Audition required for music majors. Portfolio recommended for art majors. **Home schooled:** Eligibility appraised on basis of entrance examination or previous college-level work. **Learning Disabled:** Any extenuating circumstances should be included in the personal statement.

High school preparation. College-preparatory program required. 15 units required; 18 recommended. Required and recommended units include English 4, mathematics 3-4, social studies 1, history 1, science 2-3 (laboratory 2-3), foreign language 2-3, visual/performing arts 1 and academic electives 1. History is 2 units in history/social science. 2 semesters of approved arts courses from single visual and performing arts discipline: dance, drama/theater, music, or visual art. Required elective includes 2 semesters from following areas: visual and performing arts, history, social science, English, advanced mathematics, laboratory science, foreign language.

2011-2012 Annual costs. Tuition/fees: $13,416; $36,294 out-of-state. Estimated personal expenses include $1,443 for our student health insurance plan. Although this is a mandatory fee, if a student is covered through private insurance, he or she can waive out. Room/board: $14,727. Books/supplies: $1,401. Personal expenses: $1,350.

Financial aid. Non-need-based: Scholarships awarded for academics, alumni affiliation, art, leadership, music/drama. **Additional information:** Blue and Gold Opportunity Plan covers the educational and student services fees for CA residents whose family earns less than $80,000 a year. Blue and Gold students with sufficient financial need can qualify for more grant aid to reduce the cost of attendance.

Application procedures. Admission: Closing date 11/30 (postmark date). $60 fee, may be waived for applicants with need. Admission notification by 4/30. Must reply by 5/1. **Financial aid:** Closing date 3/2. FAFSA required. Applicants notified on a rolling basis starting 4/1; must reply within 4 week(s) of notification.

Academics. Special study options: Combined bachelor's/graduate degree, cooperative education, double major, dual enrollment of high school students, exchange student, independent study, internships, student-designed major, study abroad, teacher certification program, Washington semester. **Credit/placement by examination:** AP, CLEP, IB, institutional tests. **Support services:** Learning center, reduced course load, remedial instruction, study skills assistance, tutoring, writing center.

Majors. Area/ethnic studies: American, German, Italian, women's. **Biology:** General, bioinformatics, cellular/molecular, ecology, marine, molecular biochemistry, neuroscience. **Business:** Managerial economics. **Computer sciences:** General, web page design. **Conservation:** Environmental studies. **Engineering:** Biomedical, computer, electrical. **English:** English lit. **Foreign languages:** General, classics, linguistics. **General:** Plant sciences. **History:** General. **Human services:** Community org/advocacy. **Math:** General. **Philosophy/religion:** Judaic, philosophy. **Physical sciences:** Astrophysics, chemistry, geology, physics. **Psychology:** General, cognitive. **Social sciences:** Anthropology, economics, political science, sociology. **Visual/performing arts:** Art, art history/conservation, dramatic, game design, music.

Most popular majors. Biology 13%, business/marketing 9%, English 6%, natural resources/environmental science 6%, psychology 11%, social sciences 17%, visual/performing arts 10%.

Computing on campus. Dormitories wired for high-speed internet access and linked to campus network. Commuter students can connect to campus network. Online course registration, online library, helpline, repair service, student web hosting, wireless network available.

Student life. Freshman orientation: Available, $110 fee. Preregistration for classes offered. One-day orientation sessions held fall and winter terms for students and family. **Policies:** Student Organization Advising and Resources (SOARS) helps students create their own organizations. Freshmen not permitted cars on campus. **Housing:** Guaranteed on-campus for freshmen. Coed dorms, single-sex dorms, apartments, cooperative housing, wellness housing available. $150 partly refundable deposit, deadline 5/1. **Activities:** Jazz band, choral groups, dance, drama, film society, international student organizations, literary magazine, music ensembles, Model UN, musical theater, opera, radio station, student government, student newspaper, symphony orchestra, TV station, more than 100 student organizations.

Athletics. NCAA. **Intercollegiate:** Basketball, cross-country, diving, golf W, soccer, swimming, tennis, volleyball. **Intramural:** Basketball, football (non-tackle), soccer, softball, volleyball, water polo. **Team name:** Banana Slugs.

Student services. Adult student services, alcohol/substance abuse counseling, career counseling, services for economically disadvantaged, student employment services, financial aid counseling, health services, minority student services, on-campus daycare, personal counseling, veterans' counselor, women's services. **Physically disabled:** Services for visually, speech, hearing impaired.

Contact. E-mail: admissions@ucsc.edu
Phone: (831) 459-4008 Fax: (831) 459-4452
Michael McCawley, Director of Admissions, University of California: Santa Cruz, Cook House, 1156 High Street, Santa Cruz, CA 95064

University of La Verne

La Verne, California	CB member
www.laverne.edu	CB code: 4381

- Private 4-year university and liberal arts college
- Commuter campus in large town
- 2,155 degree-seeking undergraduates: 3% part-time, 59% women, 5% African American, 5% Asian American, 50% Hispanic American, 3% international
- 2,504 degree-seeking graduate students
- 40% of applicants admitted

◗ SAT or ACT with writing, application essay required
◗ 57% graduate within 6 years

General. Founded in 1891. Regionally accredited. Satellite campuses throughout California provide graduate and professional programs to adult students. **Degrees:** 321 bachelor's awarded; master's, professional, doctoral offered. **ROTC:** Army. **Location:** 35 miles from Los Angeles. **Calendar:** 4-1-4, limited summer session. **Full-time faculty:** 211 total; 87% have terminal degrees, 22% minority, 49% women. **Part-time faculty:** 244 total; 14% minority, 45% women. **Class size:** 62% < 20, 37% 20-39, less than 1% 50-99. **Special facilities:** Natural science field station.

Freshman class profile. 5,734 applied, 2,286 admitted, 506 enrolled.

Mid 50% test scores		GPA 2.0-2.99:	13%
SAT critical reading:	450-550	Rank in top quarter:	62%
SAT math:	470-560	Rank in top tenth:	24%
SAT writing:	460-540	Return as sophomores:	85%
ACT composite:	19-23	Out-of-state:	5%
GPA 3.75 or higher:	26%	Live on campus:	53%
GPA 3.50-3.74:	20%	International:	2%
GPA 3.0-3.49:	41%		

Basis for selection. Secondary school record, recommendations, standardized test scores, and essay very important; extracurricular activities, character or personal qualities also important. Class rank, interview, special talents or abilities, alumni relationships, volunteer work, work experience may also be considered. Individual departments may require interview, audition, or portfolio.

High school preparation. College-preparatory program required. 14 units required; 19 recommended. Required and recommended units include English 4, mathematics 3-4, social studies 2, history 3, science 2 (laboratory 1-2), foreign language 2 and academic electives 2.

2011-2012 Annual costs. Tuition/fees: $31,300. Room/board: $11,280. Books/supplies: $1,656. Personal expenses: $2,377.

2011-2012 Financial aid. **Need-based:** 479 full-time freshmen applied for aid; 449 were judged to have need; 449 of these received aid. Average need met was 40%. Average scholarship/grant was $11,270; average loan $3,882. 76% of total undergraduate aid awarded as scholarships/grants, 24% as loans/jobs. **Non-need-based:** Awarded to 1,929 full-time undergraduates, including 497 freshmen. Scholarships awarded for academics, alumni affiliation, art, leadership, minority status, music/drama.

Application procedures. **Admission:** Priority date 2/1; no deadline. $50 fee, may be waived for applicants with need. Admission notification on a rolling basis beginning on or about 12/1. Must reply by May 1 or within 2 week(s) if notified thereafter. **Financial aid:** Priority date 3/2; no closing date. FAFSA required. Applicants notified on a rolling basis starting 4/1; must reply within 2 week(s) of notification.

Academics. Main Campus offers a traditional-age undergraduate program and an accelerated program for adults in school of continuing education. Off-campus centers available for degree-seeking students in selected majors. **Special study options:** Distance learning, double major, ESL, exchange student, honors, independent study, internships, liberal arts/career combination, semester at sea, student-designed major, study abroad, teacher certification program, weekend college. **Credit/placement by examination:** AP, CLEP, institutional tests. 44 credit hours maximum toward bachelor's degree. **Support services:** Learning center, reduced course load, remedial instruction, study skills assistance, tutoring, writing center.

Majors. **Biology:** General, environmental. **Business:** Accounting, business admin, e-commerce, international, managerial economics. **Communications:** Communications/speech/rhetoric, journalism, radio/TV. **Computer sciences:** General. **Conservation:** Environmental science. **Education:** General, early childhood, elementary, physical, secondary. **English:** English lit. **Foreign languages:** Comparative lit, French, German, Spanish. **Health services:** Athletic training, health care admin. **History:** General. **Human services:** General. **Liberal arts:** Arts/sciences. **Math:** General. **Philosophy/religion:** Philosophy, religion. **Physical sciences:** Chemistry, physics. **Psychology:** General. **Social sciences:** General, anthropology, criminology, economics, international relations, political science, sociology. **Visual/performing arts:** Art, art history/conservation, dramatic, music, photography. **Work/family studies:** Child care management.

Most popular majors. Business/marketing 21%, communications/journalism 8%, education 7%, liberal arts 17%, psychology 10%, social sciences 14%.

Computing on campus. Dormitories wired for high-speed internet access and linked to campus network. Commuter students can connect to campus network. Online course registration, online library, helpline, student web hosting, wireless network available.

Student life. **Freshman orientation:** Available, $50 fee. Preregistration for classes offered. All-day events for both students and parents. Held primarily in August. **Policies:** Students must be in good academic standing to participate in clubs or organizations, including fraternities/sororities. Freshmen not permitted to join fraternities during the Fall term. **Housing:** Coed dorms, single-sex dorms, special housing for disabled available. $250 fully refundable deposit, deadline 5/1. **Activities:** Campus ministries, choral groups, dance, drama, international student organizations, literary magazine, music ensembles, Model UN, musical theater, radio station, student government, student newspaper, TV station, African American student alliance, Latino student forum, Brothers Forum, Sisters Circle, Rainbow Alliance.

Athletics. NCAA. **Intercollegiate:** Baseball M, basketball, cross-country, diving, football (tackle) M, golf M, soccer, softball W, swimming, tennis W, track and field, volleyball W, water polo. **Intramural:** Basketball, soccer, softball, table tennis, volleyball. **Team name:** Leopards.

Student services. Adult student services, alcohol/substance abuse counseling, chaplain/spiritual director, career counseling, services for economically disadvantaged, student employment services, financial aid counseling, health services, minority student services, personal counseling, placement for graduates, veterans' counselor. **Physically disabled:** Services for visually, speech, hearing impaired.

Contact. E-mail: admission@laverne.edu
Phone: (909) 392-2800 Toll-free number: (800) 876-4858
Fax: (909) 392-2714
Ana Liza Zell, Associate Dean of Undergraduate Admissions, University of La Verne, 1950 Third Street, La Verne, CA 91750

University of Phoenix: Bay Area
San Jose, California
www.phoenix.edu

◗ For-profit 4-year university
◗ Very large city
◗ 1,824 degree-seeking undergraduates

General. Regionally accredited. **Degrees:** 458 bachelor's, 1 associate awarded; master's offered. **Calendar:** Differs by program. **Full-time faculty:** 30 total. **Part-time faculty:** 400 total.

Basis for selection. Open admission, but selective for some programs.

2011-2012 Annual costs. Estimated costs as of August 2011: per-credit-hour charge, $420 to $520, depending upon level and course of study; electronic course materials fee, $95, if applicable. Book and material charges may vary by course and program. All fees are subject to change.

Application procedures. **Financial aid:** No deadline.

Academics. **Credit/placement by examination:** AP, CLEP.

Majors. **Business:** General, accounting, finance. **Health services:** Health care admin. **Protective services:** Law enforcement admin. **Psychology:** General.

Contact. Marc Booker, Director of Admission and Evaluation, University of Phoenix: Bay Area, 3590 North First Street, San Jose, CA 95134-1805

University of Phoenix: Central Valley
Fresno, California
www.phoenix.edu

◗ For-profit 4-year university
◗ Large city
◗ 2,314 degree-seeking undergraduates

General. Regionally accredited. **Degrees:** 377 bachelor's awarded; master's offered. **Calendar:** Differs by program. **Full-time faculty:** 37 total. **Part-time faculty:** 299 total.

Basis for selection. Open admission, but selective for some programs.

2011-2012 Annual costs. Estimated costs as of August 2011: per-credit-hour charge, $420 to $520, depending upon level and course of study; electronic course materials fee, $95, if applicable. Book and material charges may vary by course and program. All fees are subject to change.

Application procedures. Admission: No deadline. No application fee. **Financial aid:** No deadline.

Academics. Credit/placement by examination: AP, CLEP.

Majors. Business: General, accounting, management information systems. **Communications:** General. **Computer sciences:** Information technology. **Health services:** Health care admin. **Protective services:** Law enforcement admin. **Psychology:** General.

Contact. Marc Booker, Director of Admission and Evaluation, University of Phoenix: Central Valley, 45 River Park Place West, Fresno, CA 93720-1562

University of Phoenix: Sacramento Valley
Sacramento, California
www.phoenix.edu

- For-profit 4-year university
- Large city
- 3,463 degree-seeking undergraduates

General. Regionally accredited. **Degrees:** 659 bachelor's awarded; master's offered. **Calendar:** Differs by program. **Full-time faculty:** 50 total. **Part-time faculty:** 550 total.

Basis for selection. Open admission, but selective for some programs.

2011-2012 Annual costs. Estimated costs as of August 2011: per-credit-hour charge, $420 to $520, depending upon level and course of study; electronic course materials fee, $95, if applicable. Book and material charges may vary by course and program. All fees are subject to change.

Application procedures. Admission: No deadline. No application fee. **Financial aid:** No deadline.

Academics. Credit/placement by examination: AP, CLEP.

Majors. Business: Accounting, business admin. **Communications:** General. **Computer sciences:** Information technology. **Human services:** General. **Protective services:** Law enforcement admin. **Psychology:** General.

Contact. Marc Booker, Director of Admission and Evaluation, University of Phoenix: Sacramento Valley, 2860 Gateway Oaks Drive, Suite 200, Sacramento, CA 95833-4334

University of Phoenix: San Diego
San Diego, California
www.phoenix.edu

- For-profit 4-year university
- Very large city
- 5,874 degree-seeking undergraduates

General. Regionally accredited. **Degrees:** 674 bachelor's, 2 associate awarded; master's offered. **Calendar:** Differs by program. **Full-time faculty:** 39 total. **Part-time faculty:** 466 total.

Basis for selection. Open admission, but selective for some programs.

2011-2012 Annual costs. Estimated costs as of August 2011: per-credit-hour charge, $435 to $480, depending upon level and course of study; electronic course materials fee, $95, if applicable. Book and material charges may vary by course and program. All fees are subject to change.

Application procedures. Admission: No deadline. No application fee. **Financial aid:** No deadline.

Academics. Credit/placement by examination: AP, CLEP.

Majors. Computer sciences: Information technology. **Psychology:** General.

Contact. Marc Booker, Director of Admission and Evaluation, University of Phoenix: San Diego, 3890 Murphy Canyon Road, Suite 100, San Diego, CA 92123-4403

University of Phoenix: Southern California
Costa Mesa, California
www.phoenix.edu

- For-profit 4-year university
- Very large city
- 9,204 degree-seeking undergraduates

General. Regionally accredited. **Degrees:** 2,078 bachelor's, 1 associate awarded; master's offered. **Calendar:** Differs by program. **Full-time faculty:** 67 total. **Part-time faculty:** 1,410 total.

Basis for selection. Open admission, but selective for some programs.

2011-2012 Annual costs. Estimated costs as of August 2011: per-credit-hour charge, $495 to $520, depending upon level and course of study; electronic course materials fee, $95, if applicable. Book and material charges may vary by course and program. All fees are subject to change.

Application procedures. Admission: No deadline. No application fee. **Financial aid:** No deadline.

Academics. Credit/placement by examination: AP, CLEP.

Majors. Business: Business admin. **Health services:** Health care admin. **Protective services:** Law enforcement admin. **Psychology:** General.

Contact. Marc Booker, Director of Admission and Evaluation, University of Phoenix: Southern California, 3100 Bristol Street, Suite 500, Costa Mesa, CA 92626-3099

University of Redlands
Redlands, California   **CB member**
www.redlands.edu   **CB code: 4848**

- Private 4-year university and liberal arts college
- Residential campus in small city
- 3,175 degree-seeking undergraduates: 24% part-time, 56% women, 4% African American, 4% Asian American, 19% Hispanic American, 1% Native American
- 1,463 degree-seeking graduate students
- 65% of applicants admitted
- SAT or ACT (ACT writing recommended), application essay required
- 63% graduate within 6 years; 25% enter graduate study

General. Founded in 1907. Regionally accredited. NASM accredited School of Music within College of Arts & Sciences. **Degrees:** 599 bachelor's awarded; master's, professional offered. **ROTC:** Army, Naval, Air Force. **Location:** 65 miles from Los Angeles, 40 miles from Palm Springs. **Calendar:** 4-1-4, limited summer session. **Full-time faculty:** 202 total; 89% have terminal degrees, 19% minority, 48% women. **Part-time faculty:** 280 total. **Class size:** 65% < 20, 32% 20-39, 2% 40-49, less than 1% 50-99, less than 1% >100. **Special facilities:** Center for the arts, black box theater, community garden.

Freshman class profile. 4,125 applied, 2,674 admitted, 645 enrolled.

Mid 50% test scores			
SAT critical reading:	520-620	GPA 2.0-2.99:	11%
SAT math:	520-620	Rank in top quarter:	37%
SAT writing:	500-610	Rank in top tenth:	35%
ACT composite:	22-27	Return as sophomores:	87%
GPA 3.75 or higher:	36%	Out-of-state:	26%
GPA 3.50-3.74:	20%	Live on campus:	93%
GPA 3.0-3.49:	33%	International:	1%

Basis for selection. Course selection and grades important. Recommendations, test scores, essays, extracurricular activities are also considered. Interview required of Johnston Center for Integrated Studies applicants, strongly recommended for others. Audition required of music majors. Portfolio recommended of art (slides only), creative writing majors. **Home schooled:** Statement describing home school structure and mission required. Common application homeschool supplement required.

High school preparation. College-preparatory program required. 15 units required; 17 recommended. Required and recommended units include English 4, mathematics 3, social studies 2, history 1, science 2-3 (laboratory 2) and foreign language 2.

2011-2012 Annual costs. Tuition/fees: $37,302. Room/board: $11,206. Books/supplies: $1,650. Personal expenses: $3,100.

2011-2012 Financial aid. Need-based: 598 full-time freshmen applied for aid; 496 were judged to have need; 496 of these received aid. Average need met was 90%. Average scholarship/grant was $29,025; average loan $4,259. 73% of total undergraduate aid awarded as scholarships/grants, 27% as loans/jobs. **Non-need-based:** Awarded to 544 full-time undergraduates, including 204 freshmen. Scholarships awarded for academics, art, music/drama.

Application procedures. Admission: Priority date 11/15; deadline 3/1 (postmark date). $30 fee, may be waived for applicants with need. Admission notification on a rolling basis beginning on or about 12/1. Must reply by 5/1. **Financial aid:** Priority date 2/15; no closing date. FAFSA required. Applicants notified on a rolling basis starting 2/28; must reply by 5/1.

Academics. Special study options: Cross-registration, double major, exchange student, honors, independent study, internships, liberal arts/career combination, New York semester, student-designed major, study abroad, teacher certification program, United Nations semester, Washington semester. Nontraditional study programs available through Johnston Center for Integrated Studies and Schools of Business and Education. **Credit/placement by examination:** AP, CLEP, IB, SAT, ACT, institutional tests. 16 credit hours maximum toward bachelor's degree. **Support services:** Learning center, pre-admission summer program, reduced course load, study skills assistance, tutoring, writing center.

Majors. Area/ethnic studies: Asian, Latin American, women's. **Biology:** General, biochemistry. **Business:** General, accounting, business admin, management information systems, managerial economics. **Computer sciences:** General. **Conservation:** Environmental science, environmental studies, management/policy. **Education:** Elementary, middle, music, secondary, speech impaired. **English:** British lit, creative writing, English lit. **Foreign languages:** French, German, Spanish. **Health services:** Audiology/speech pathology. **History:** General. **Liberal arts:** Arts/sciences. **Math:** General. **Philosophy/religion:** Philosophy, religion. **Physical sciences:** Chemistry, physics. **Psychology:** General. **Social sciences:** Anthropology, economics, international relations, political science, sociology. **Visual/performing arts:** Art, art history/conservation, dramatic, music, music history, music performance, music theory/composition.

Most popular majors. Business/marketing 47%, health sciences 6%, natural resources/environmental science 6%, psychology 6%, social sciences 8%, visual/performing arts 6%.

Computing on campus. 655 workstations in dormitories, library, computer center, student center. Dormitories wired for high-speed internet access and linked to campus network. Commuter students can connect to campus network. Online library, helpline, repair service, student web hosting, wireless network available.

Student life. Freshman orientation: Mandatory. Preregistration for classes offered. One full week preceding academic school year. **Housing:** Guaranteed on-campus for freshmen. Coed dorms, single-sex dorms, special housing for disabled, apartments, fraternity/sorority housing, wellness housing available. **Activities:** Bands, choral groups, dance, drama, literary magazine, music ensembles, musical theater, opera, radio station, student government, student newspaper, symphony orchestra, Associated Students, Intervarsity Christian Fellowship, African American association, Gay, Lesbian, Bisexual student union, women's center, College Republicans, College Democrats, Asian Pacific Islander Association, Theater Association, Students for Environmental Action.

Athletics. NCAA. **Intercollegiate:** Baseball M, basketball, cross-country, diving, football (tackle) M, golf, lacrosse W, soccer, softball W, swimming, tennis, track and field, volleyball W, water polo. **Intramural:** Basketball, football (non-tackle), racquetball, soccer, softball, table tennis, tennis, volleyball, water polo. **Team name:** Bulldogs.

Student services. Adult student services, alcohol/substance abuse counseling, chaplain/spiritual director, career counseling, student employment services, financial aid counseling, health services, minority student services, personal counseling, placement for graduates, veterans' counselor, women's services. **Physically disabled:** Services for visually, speech, hearing impaired.

Contact. E-mail: admissions@redlands.edu
Phone: (909) 748-8074 Toll-free number: (800) 455-5064
Fax: (909) 335-4089
Paul Driscoll, Dean of Admissions, University of Redlands, 1200 East Colton Avenue, Redlands, CA 92373-0999

University of San Diego
San Diego, California
www.sandiego.edu

CB member
CB code: 4849

- Private 4-year university affiliated with Roman Catholic Church
- Residential campus in very large city

- 5,409 degree-seeking undergraduates: 3% part-time, 55% women, 2% African American, 6% Asian American, 17% Hispanic American, 5% international
- 2,792 degree-seeking graduate students
- 48% of applicants admitted
- SAT or ACT with writing, application essay required
- 75% graduate within 6 years

General. Founded in 1949. Regionally accredited. **Degrees:** 1,188 bachelor's awarded; master's, professional, doctoral offered. **ROTC:** Army, Naval, Air Force. **Location:** 5 miles from downtown. **Calendar:** 4-1-4, extensive summer session. **Full-time faculty:** 402 total; 94% have terminal degrees, 18% minority, 46% women. **Part-time faculty:** 443 total; 59% have terminal degrees, 18% minority, 50% women. **Class size:** 39% < 20, 57% 20-39, 4% 40-49, less than 1% 50-99.

Freshman class profile. 13,867 applied, 6,590 admitted, 1,143 enrolled.

Mid 50% test scores			
SAT critical reading:	560-650	GPA 2.0-2.99:	1%
SAT math:	570-670	Rank in top quarter:	81%
SAT writing:	570-660	Rank in top tenth:	41%
ACT composite:	26-30	End year in good standing:	84%
GPA 3.75 or higher:	69%	Return as sophomores:	87%
GPA 3.50-3.74:	18%	Out-of-state:	46%
GPA 3.0-3.49:	12%	Live on campus:	96%
		International:	4%

Basis for selection. School achievement record, test scores, recommendations, and extracurricular activities are important. Out-of-state and international applicants encouraged. Audition required of choral scholarship applicants. **Home schooled:** Letter of recommendation (nonparent) required. **Learning Disabled:** Must contact Director of Disability Services.

High school preparation. College-preparatory program recommended. 15 units required; 19 recommended. Required and recommended units include English 4, mathematics 3-4, social studies 2-3, science 3-4 (laboratory 2-3) and foreign language 3-4.

2011-2012 Annual costs. Tuition/fees: $38,582. Room/board: $11,752.

2010-2011 Financial aid. Need-based: 807 full-time freshmen applied for aid; 653 were judged to have need; 636 of these received aid. Average need met was 72%. Average scholarship/grant was $23,605; average loan $6,419. 71% of total undergraduate aid awarded as scholarships/grants, 29% as loans/jobs. **Non-need-based:** Awarded to 2,012 full-time undergraduates, including 574 freshmen. Scholarships awarded for academics, athletics, leadership, music/drama, religious affiliation, ROTC.

Application procedures. Admission: Priority date 1/15; deadline 3/1 (postmark date). $55 fee, may be waived for applicants with need. Admission notification by 4/15. Must reply by May 1 or within 2 week(s) if notified thereafter. **Financial aid:** Priority date 3/2; no closing date. FAFSA required. Applicants notified on a rolling basis starting 3/1; must reply by 5/1 or within 3 week(s) of notification.

Academics. Special study options: Double major, ESL, honors, independent study, internships, liberal arts/career combination, semester at sea, study abroad, teacher certification program, Washington semester. **Credit/placement by examination:** AP, CLEP, IB, institutional tests. **Support services:** Pre-admission summer program, reduced course load, study skills assistance, tutoring, writing center.

Majors. Architecture: History/criticism. **Area/ethnic studies:** General. **Biology:** General, biochemistry, biophysics, marine. **Business:** Accounting, business admin, finance, international, managerial economics, marketing, real estate. **Communications:** General. **Computer sciences:** Computer science. **Conservation:** Environmental studies. **Engineering:** Electrical, industrial, mechanical. **English:** English lit. **Foreign languages:** French, Spanish. **History:** General. **Liberal arts:** Arts/sciences, humanities. **Math:** General. **Philosophy/religion:** Philosophy, religion. **Physical sciences:** Chemistry, physics. **Psychology:** General. **Social sciences:** Anthropology, economics, international relations, political science, sociology. **Visual/performing arts:** Art, art history/conservation, dramatic, music.

Most popular majors. Biology 7%, business/marketing 41%, communications/journalism 10%, psychology 6%, social sciences 15%.

Computing on campus. 1,283 workstations in dormitories, library, computer center, student center. Dormitories wired for high-speed internet access and linked to campus network. Commuter students can connect to campus network. Online course registration, helpline, repair service, student web hosting, wireless network available.

Student life. Freshman orientation: Mandatory. Preregistration for classes offered. 4-day program that starts at the beginning of the semester. **Policies:** Freshmen required to live on campus unless living with parents.

Housing: Guaranteed on-campus for freshmen. Coed dorms, single-sex dorms, special housing for disabled, apartments available. $200 partly refundable deposit, deadline 5/1. **Activities:** Bands, campus ministries, choral groups, dance, drama, international student organizations, literary magazine, music ensembles, Model UN, musical theater, radio station, student government, student newspaper, TV station, over 75 organizations available.

Athletics. NCAA. **Intercollegiate:** Baseball M, basketball, cross-country, diving W, football (tackle) M, golf M, rowing (crew), soccer, softball W, swimming W, tennis, track and field W, volleyball W. **Intramural:** Basketball, football (non-tackle), soccer, softball, tennis, volleyball. **Team name:** Toreros.

Student services. Alcohol/substance abuse counseling, chaplain/spiritual director, career counseling, services for economically disadvantaged, student employment services, financial aid counseling, health services, legal services, minority student services, on-campus daycare, personal counseling, placement for graduates, veterans' counselor, women's services. **Physically disabled:** Services for visually impaired.

Contact. E-mail: admissions@sandiego.edu
Phone: (619) 260-4506 Toll-free number: (800) 248-4873
Fax: (619) 260-6836
Minh-Ha Hoang, Director of Admissions and Enrollment, University of San Diego, 5998 Alcala Park, San Diego, CA 92110-2492

University of San Francisco
San Francisco, California   **CB member**
www.usfca.edu   **CB code: 4850**

- Private 4-year university affiliated with Roman Catholic Church
- Residential campus in very large city
- 5,571 degree-seeking undergraduates: 3% part-time, 64% women, 3% African American, 19% Asian American, 18% Hispanic American, 13% international
- 3,679 degree-seeking graduate students
- 58% of applicants admitted
- SAT or ACT with writing, application essay required
- 70% graduate within 6 years

General. Founded in 1855. Regionally accredited. **Degrees:** 1,283 bachelor's awarded; master's, professional, doctoral offered. **ROTC:** Army, Air Force. **Location:** 3 miles from downtown. **Calendar:** 4-1-4, extensive summer session. **Full-time faculty:** 406 total; 92% have terminal degrees, 24% minority, 48% women. **Part-time faculty:** 558 total; 42% have terminal degrees, 19% minority, 60% women. **Class size:** 53% < 20, 37% 20-39, 8% 40-49, 2% 50-99, less than 1% >100. **Special facilities:** Rare book room, institute for Chinese Western cultural history, electron microscope, law library.

Freshman class profile. 12,029 applied, 6,973 admitted, 1,190 enrolled.

Mid 50% test scores			
SAT critical reading:	510-620	Rank in top quarter:	63%
SAT math:	520-630	Rank in top tenth:	29%
SAT writing:	520-630	Return as sophomores:	86%
ACT composite:	23-27	Out-of-state:	37%
GPA 3.75 or higher:	37%	Live on campus:	92%
GPA 3.50-3.74:	25%	International:	15%
GPA 3.0-3.49:	34%	Fraternities:	1%
GPA 2.0-2.99:	4%	Sororities:	1%

Basis for selection. Rigor of secondary school record, academic GPA, standardized test scores, and application essay very important. Require TOEFL for non-native speakers of English. Interviews required for nursing students. **Home schooled:** Statement describing home school structure and mission, letter of recommendation (nonparent) required. Statement from parents on curriculum required if student not evaluated through high school homeschooling program or agency that evaluates home school programs. **Learning Disabled:** After acceptance, students with disabilities must contact Office of Disability Related Services to request accommodations.

High school preparation. College-preparatory program recommended. 20 units required. Required units include English 4, mathematics 3, social studies 3, science 2 (laboratory 2), foreign language 2 and academic electives 6. One chemistry and 1 biology or physics required of nursing and science applicants.

2012-2013 Annual costs. Tuition/fees: $38,884. Room/board: $12,640. Books/supplies: $1,500. Personal expenses: $2,500.

Financial aid. **Non-need-based:** Scholarships awarded for academics, athletics, ROTC. **Additional information:** Most aid to international students is for athletics.

Application procedures. **Admission:** Priority date 1/15; no deadline. $55 fee, may be waived for applicants with need. Notification begins approximately 4 weeks after all materials submitted including fall grades. Must reply by May 1 or within 2 week(s) if notified thereafter. **Financial aid:** Priority date 2/1; no closing date. FAFSA required. Applicants notified on a rolling basis starting 4/1; must reply within 4 week(s) of notification.

Academics. **Special study options:** Combined bachelor's/graduate degree, cooperative education, cross-registration, double major, ESL, exchange student, external degree, honors, independent study, internships, liberal arts/career combination, study abroad, teacher certification program, Washington semester. College of Professional Studies for adult degree-seeking students coming back to school to earn undergraduate bachelor's degree; cooperative work study in Computer Science courses. **Credit/placement by examination:** AP, CLEP, IB, SAT, ACT, institutional tests. 30 credit hours maximum toward bachelor's degree. Credit for experiential learning limited to maximum of 30 undergraduate semester units for Degree Completion students in the School of Management's undergraduate Mclaren School of Management. **Support services:** Learning center, pre-admission summer program, reduced course load, study skills assistance, tutoring, writing center.

Majors. **Architecture:** Architecture. **Area/ethnic studies:** American. **Biology:** General. **Business:** General, accounting, business admin, entrepreneurial studies, finance, hotel/motel admin, international, marketing, organizational behavior, restaurant/food services. **Communications:** Advertising, communications/speech/rhetoric, media studies. **Computer sciences:** General, information systems. **Conservation:** Environmental science, environmental studies. **English:** English lit. **Foreign languages:** Comparative lit, French, Japanese, Spanish. **Health services:** Nursing (RN). **History:** General. **Human services:** General. **Liberal arts:** Arts/sciences. **Math:** General. **Parks/recreation:** Exercise sciences. **Philosophy/religion:** Philosophy. **Physical sciences:** Chemistry, physics. **Psychology:** General. **Social sciences:** Economics, international economics, political science, sociology. **Theology:** Theology. **Visual/performing arts:** General, art history/conservation, commercial/advertising art, studio arts, studio arts management.

Most popular majors. Business/marketing 29%, communications/journalism 7%, computer/information sciences 6%, health sciences 8%, psychology 8%, social sciences 14%, visual/performing arts 6%.

Computing on campus. 320 workstations in dormitories, library, computer center, student center. Dormitories wired for high-speed internet access and linked to campus network. Commuter students can connect to campus network. Online course registration, online library, helpline, student web hosting, wireless network available.

Student life. **Freshman orientation:** Mandatory. Preregistration for classes offered. Two-day session including placement tests. **Policies:** Freshman and sophomores under 21 required to live in residence halls unless they have permanent address within 20-mile radius of campus. **Housing:** Guaranteed on-campus for freshmen. Coed dorms, single-sex dorms, special housing for disabled, apartments available. $300 nonrefundable deposit, deadline 5/1. **Activities:** Pep band, choral groups, dance, drama, international student organizations, literary magazine, music ensembles, musical theater, radio station, student government, student newspaper, TV station, St. Ignatius Institute, People Advocating Cultural Endeavors, Phelan multicultural community.

Athletics. NCAA. **Intercollegiate:** Baseball M, basketball, cross-country, golf, rifle, soccer, tennis, track and field, volleyball W. **Intramural:** Basketball, football (non-tackle), racquetball, soccer, softball, swimming, table tennis, tennis, volleyball. **Team name:** Dons.

Student services. Adult student services, alcohol/substance abuse counseling, chaplain/spiritual director, career counseling, student employment services, financial aid counseling, health services, minority student services, personal counseling, placement for graduates. **Physically disabled:** Services for visually, speech, hearing impaired.

Contact. E-mail: admissions@usfca.edu
Phone: (415) 422-6563 Toll-free number: (800) 225-5873
Fax: (415) 422-2217
Michael Hughes, Director of Admissions, University of San Francisco, 2130 Fulton Street, San Francisco, CA 94117-1046

University of Southern California
Los Angeles, California   **CB member**
www.usc.edu   **CB code: 4852**

- Private 4-year university
- Residential campus in very large city

- 17,090 degree-seeking undergraduates: 3% part-time, 51% women, 5% African American, 23% Asian American, 14% Hispanic American, 12% international
- 19,933 degree-seeking graduate students
- 23% of applicants admitted
- SAT or ACT with writing, application essay required
- 90% graduate within 6 years

General. Founded in 1880. Regionally accredited. Permanent facilities for study in Sacramento available. **Degrees:** 4,915 bachelor's awarded; master's, professional, doctoral offered. **ROTC:** Army, Naval, Air Force. **Location:** 3 miles from downtown. **Calendar:** Semester, limited summer session. **Full-time faculty:** 1,723 total; 90% have terminal degrees, 26% minority, 36% women. **Part-time faculty:** 1,400 total; 65% have terminal degrees, 28% minority, 43% women. **Class size:** 61% < 20, 20% 20-39, 8% 40-49, 8% 50-99, 4% >100. **Special facilities:** 3 art/architecture galleries, 2 museums, 2 sculpture gardens, marine science center, Gamble House (designed by Greene and Greene), Freeman House (designed by Frank Lloyd Wright), technical theater laboratory, recording studio, cinematic arts complex, integrated media systems center, center for digital arts, engineering undergraduate fabrication laboratory, image processing and informatics laboratory, sun- and wind-simulation labs, rocket propulsion laboratory, geographic information systems laboratory, cognitive neuroscience imaging center.

Freshman class profile. 37,210 applied, 8,566 admitted, 2,931 enrolled.

Mid 50% test scores		Rank in top quarter:	97%
SAT critical reading:	610-720	Rank in top tenth:	88%
SAT math:	670-770	Return as sophomores:	97%
SAT writing:	650-740	Out-of-state:	43%
ACT composite:	29-33	Live on campus:	98%
GPA 3.75 or higher:	55%	International:	15%
GPA 3.50-3.74:	29%	Fraternities:	30%
GPA 3.0-3.49:	15%	Sororities:	19%
GPA 2.0-2.99:	1%		

Basis for selection. GED not accepted. Academic achievement, curriculum and test scores most important. Recommendations, activities, essays/writing samples are also very important. Audition required of music and theater majors. Portfolio required of fine arts and architecture majors. **Home schooled:** 3 SAT Subject tests (1 must be in math) and detailed syllabi of courses, names of textbooks, names and applicable credentials of instructors, details of assistance received or curriculum followed through any public or private agency, and any additional information that may be helpful.

High school preparation. College-preparatory program required. 16 units required; 20 recommended. Required and recommended units include English 4, mathematics 3-4, social studies 2-3, history 3, science 2-3 (laboratory 2-3), foreign language 2-3 and academic electives 3.

2011-2012 Annual costs. Tuition/fees: $42,818. Room/board: $12,078.

2010-2011 Financial aid. Need-based: 1,957 full-time freshmen applied for aid; 1,184 were judged to have need; 1,183 of these received aid. Average need met was 100%. Average scholarship/grant was $27,217; average loan $4,452. 78% of total undergraduate aid awarded as scholarships/grants, 22% as loans/jobs. **Non-need-based:** Awarded to 6,446 full-time undergraduates, including 1,470 freshmen. Scholarships awarded for academics, alumni affiliation, art, athletics, leadership, music/drama, ROTC.

Application procedures. Admission: Priority date 12/1; deadline 1/10 (postmark date). $70 fee, may be waived for applicants with need. Admission notification by 4/1. Must reply by 5/1. Students may defer admission for up to one year. **Financial aid:** Priority date 2/2; no closing date. FAFSA, CSS PROFILE required. Applicants notified on a rolling basis; must reply by 5/1.

Academics. Special study options: Combined bachelor's/graduate degree, cooperative education, distance learning, double major, ESL, exchange student, honors, independent study, internships, liberal arts/career combination, student-designed major, study abroad, Washington semester. Learning communities, thematic option, undergraduate research, freshman seminars. **Credit/placement by examination:** AP, CLEP, IB, institutional tests. 32 credit hours maximum toward bachelor's degree. **Support services:** Learning center, reduced course load, study skills assistance, tutoring, writing center.

Majors. Architecture: Architecture, landscape. **Area/ethnic studies:** African-American, American, Asian-American, Chicano/Hispanic-American/Latino, East Asian, Near/Middle Eastern. **Biology:** General, biochemistry, biophysics, neuroscience. **Business:** Accounting, business admin. **Communications:** Broadcast journalism, communications/speech/rhetoric, journalism, public relations, radio/TV. **Computer sciences:** Computer science. **Conservation:** Environmental science, environmental studies. **Engineering:** Aerospace, biomedical, chemical, civil, computer, construction, electrical, environmental, industrial, mechanical, polymer, structural. **English:** Creative writing, English lit. **Foreign languages:** Classics, comparative lit, East Asian, French, German, Italian, linguistics, Russian, Spanish. **Health services:** Dental

hygiene, health behavior, international public health, occupational therapy. **History:** General. **Human services:** General. **Math:** General, applied, computational/applied, financial. **Parks/recreation:** Exercise sciences. **Philosophy/religion:** Judaic, philosophy, religion. **Physical sciences:** General, astronomy, chemistry, geology, physics. **Psychology:** General. **Social sciences:** General, anthropology, archaeology, economics, geography, international relations, political science, sociology. **Visual/performing arts:** General, acting, art, art history/conservation, brass instruments, cinematography, digital arts, dramatic, film/cinema/video, game design, jazz, music, music management, music performance, music theory/composition, percussion instruments, piano/keyboard, play/screenwriting, stringed instruments, studio arts, theater arts management, theater design, voice/opera, woodwind instruments.

Most popular majors. Biology 6%, business/marketing 26%, communications/journalism 9%, engineering/engineering technologies 8%, social sciences 14%, visual/performing arts 13%.

Computing on campus. 2,500 workstations in dormitories, library, computer center, student center. Dormitories wired for high-speed internet access and linked to campus network. Commuter students can connect to campus network. Online course registration, online library, helpline, repair service, student web hosting, wireless network available.

Student life. Freshman orientation: Available, $180 fee. Preregistration for classes offered. **Policies:** Every incoming student required to take online alcohol education course and pass final exam. **Housing:** Guaranteed on-campus for freshmen. Coed dorms, special housing for disabled, apartments, fraternity/sorority housing, wellness housing available. $400 fully refundable deposit. African-American, Jewish, Latino, LGBT, and Muslim floors, faculty-in-residence programs and residential colleges available. **Activities:** Bands, campus ministries, choral groups, dance, drama, film society, international student organizations, literary magazine, music ensembles, Model UN, musical theater, opera, radio station, student government, student newspaper, symphony orchestra, TV station, academic honors assembly, emerging leaders program, minority consortium, religious council, residential community council, student program board, student volunteer center.

Athletics. NCAA. **Intercollegiate:** Baseball M, basketball, cross-country W, diving, football (tackle) M, golf, rowing (crew) W, soccer W, swimming, tennis, track and field, volleyball, water polo. **Intramural:** Badminton, basketball, cross-country, football (non-tackle), golf, racquetball, soccer, softball, tennis, volleyball. **Team name:** Trojans.

Student services. Alcohol/substance abuse counseling, chaplain/spiritual director, career counseling, services for economically disadvantaged, student employment services, financial aid counseling, health services, legal services, minority student services, on-campus daycare, personal counseling, placement for graduates, veterans' counselor, women's services. **Physically disabled:** Services for visually, speech, hearing impaired.

Contact. E-mail: admitusc@usc.edu
Phone: (213) 740-1111 Fax: (213) 821-0200
Timothy Brunold, Dean of Admission, University of Southern California, Office of Admission, Los Angeles, CA 90089-0911

University of the Pacific
Stockton, California — **CB member**
www.pacific.edu — **CB code: 4065**

- Private 4-year university
- Residential campus in large city
- 3,872 degree-seeking undergraduates: 2% part-time, 55% women
- 2,815 degree-seeking graduate students
- 36% of applicants admitted
- SAT or ACT (ACT writing optional), application essay required
- 69% graduate within 6 years

General. Founded in 1851. Regionally accredited. School of Dentistry in San Francisco. McGeorge School of Law in Sacramento. **Degrees:** 659 bachelor's awarded; master's, professional, doctoral offered. **ROTC:** Air Force. **Location:** 80 miles from San Francisco, 40 miles from Sacramento. **Calendar:** Semester, limited summer session. **Full-time faculty:** 453 total; 92% have terminal degrees, 20% minority, 41% women. **Part-time faculty:** 359 total; 39% have terminal degrees, 26% minority, 41% women. **Class size:** 63% < 20, 31% 20-39, 3% 40-49, 4% 50-99, less than 1% >100. **Special facilities:** Recital facilities, center for western studies, John Muir papers collection, music conservatory.

Freshman class profile. 21,230 applied, 7,608 admitted, 927 enrolled.

Mid 50% test scores				
SAT critical reading:	510-630		GPA 2.0-2.99:	13%
SAT math:	540-690		Rank in top quarter:	69%
SAT writing:	500-630		Rank in top tenth:	38%
ACT composite:	23-29		Return as sophomores:	85%
GPA 3.75 or higher:	29%		Out-of-state:	10%
GPA 3.50-3.74:	23%		Live on campus:	78%
GPA 3.0-3.49:	35%		International:	7%

Basis for selection. Secondary school record, standardized test scores, recommendations, essay, extracurricular activities important. SAT Subject Tests recommended. Audition required of music/conservatory majors. **Home schooled:** Standardized test scores weighted heavily.

High school preparation. College-preparatory program recommended. 16 units required. Required and recommended units include English 4, mathematics 3, social studies 2, history 1, (laboratory 2), foreign language 2, visual/performing arts 1 and academic electives 1. 1 fine/performing arts required.

2011-2012 Annual costs. Tuition/fees: $36,290. Room/board: $11,688. Books/supplies: $1,656. Personal expenses: $2,783.

Financial aid. Non-need-based: Scholarships awarded for academics, athletics, leadership, music/drama, religious affiliation.

Application procedures. Admission: Priority date 11/15; deadline 1/15. $60 fee, may be waived for applicants with need, free for online applicants. Admission notification on a rolling basis beginning on or about 3/15. Must reply by 5/1. Housing deposit refundable if canceled by May 1. **Financial aid:** Priority date 2/15; no closing date. FAFSA required. Applicants notified on a rolling basis starting 4/1.

Academics. Special study options: Accelerated study, combined bachelor's/graduate degree, cooperative education, double major, dual enrollment of high school students, ESL, exchange student, honors, independent study, internships, liberal arts/career combination, student-designed major, study abroad, teacher certification program, United Nations semester, Washington semester. Practicum, minors, undergraduate research, combination, ethnic studies, environmental science, gender studies, service learning, thematic minors. **Credit/placement by examination:** AP, CLEP, IB, SAT, ACT, institutional tests. 20 credit hours maximum toward bachelor's degree. **Support services:** Learning center, pre-admission summer program, reduced course load, remedial instruction, tutoring, writing center.

Majors. Area/ethnic studies: Asian. **Biology:** General, biochemistry. **Business:** Business admin, organizational behavior. **Communications:** Communications/speech/rhetoric. **Computer sciences:** Computer science, information systems. **Conservation:** Environmental science, environmental studies. **Education:** General, music. **Engineering:** General, applied physics, biomedical, civil, computer, electrical, mechanical. **English:** English lit. **Foreign languages:** French, Spanish. **Health services:** Athletic training, dental hygiene, music therapy, speech pathology. **History:** General. **Liberal arts:** Arts/sciences. **Math:** General, applied. **Philosophy/religion:** Philosophy, religion. **Physical sciences:** Chemistry, geology, physics. **Psychology:** General. **Social sciences:** General, economics, international relations, political science, sociology. **Visual/performing arts:** Art, commercial/advertising art, dramatic, graphic design, jazz, music, music history, music management, music performance, music theory/composition, piano/keyboard, studio arts, voice/opera.

Most popular majors. Biology 16%, business/marketing 24%, engineering/engineering technologies 10%, health sciences 8%, parks/recreation 7%, social sciences 7%, visual/performing arts 6%.

Computing on campus. 325 workstations in dormitories, library, computer center. Dormitories wired for high-speed internet access and linked to campus network. Commuter students can connect to campus network. Online course registration, online library, helpline, wireless network available.

Student life. Freshman orientation: Mandatory, $120 fee. Preregistration for classes offered. Offered in January, June, July & August, 2-4 days each. **Policies:** Freshmen and sophomores required to live on campus unless living with parents. **Housing:** Guaranteed on-campus for freshmen. Coed dorms, apartments, fraternity/sorority housing available. $200 fully refundable deposit. **Activities:** Bands, campus ministries, choral groups, dance, drama, film society, international student organizations, literary magazine, music ensembles, Model UN, musical theater, opera, radio station, student government, student newspaper, symphony orchestra, 100 student organizations and clubs.

Athletics. NCAA. **Intercollegiate:** Baseball M, basketball, cross-country W, field hockey W, golf M, soccer M, softball W, swimming, tennis, volleyball, water polo. **Intramural:** Badminton, basketball, bowling, football (tackle), golf, racquetball, soccer, softball, swimming, tennis, volleyball, water polo. **Team name:** Tigers.

Student services. Adult student services, alcohol/substance abuse counseling, chaplain/spiritual director, career counseling, services for economically disadvantaged, student employment services, financial aid counseling, health services, personal counseling, placement for graduates, veterans' counselor. **Physically disabled:** Services for visually, speech, hearing impaired.

Contact. E-mail: admissions@pacific.edu
Phone: (209) 946-2211 Toll-free number: (800) 959-2867
Fax: (209) 946-2413
Rich Toledo, Director of Admissions, University of the Pacific, 3601 Pacific Avenue, Stockton, CA 95211-0197

University of the West
Rosemead, California
www.uwest.edu

- Private 4-year business and liberal arts college affiliated with Buddhist faith
- Commuter campus in small city
- 40 degree-seeking undergraduates
- Application essay required

General. WASC-accredited, private, non-profit campus, Buddhist-founded institution. **Degrees:** 5 bachelor's awarded; master's, doctoral offered. **Location:** 5 miles from Pasadena, 10 miles from Los Angeles. **Calendar:** Semester, extensive summer session. **Full-time faculty:** 12 total. **Part-time faculty:** 45 total. **Special facilities:** Investment lab, meditation hall.

Basis for selection. Standardized tests not required, but English placement tests administered. Admission decision based on recommendation of department chair after transcript review. SAT scores are not required for admission, however a score does help in consideration for admission and for determination of scholarship awards. **Home schooled:** Handled on case-by-case basis.

2011-2012 Annual costs. Tuition/fees: $10,310. Room/board: $6,290. Books/supplies: $1,314. Personal expenses: $2,826.

Financial aid. Non-need-based: Scholarships awarded for academics, leadership.

Application procedures. Admission: No deadline. $75 fee, may be waived for applicants with need. Application must be submitted on paper. Admission notification on a rolling basis. **Financial aid:** No deadline. FAFSA, institutional form required.

Academics. Special study options: Combined bachelor's/graduate degree, ESL, exchange student, independent study, internships, study abroad. **Credit/placement by examination:** AP, CLEP. 15 credit hours maximum toward bachelor's degree. **Support services:** Learning center, remedial instruction, study skills assistance, tutoring, writing center.

Majors. Business: Accounting, international. **English:** English lit. **History:** General. **Philosophy/religion:** Religion. **Psychology:** General.

Most popular majors. Business/marketing 40%, philosophy/religious studies 40%, psychology 8%.

Computing on campus. 30 workstations in dormitories, library, computer center. Dormitories wired for high-speed internet access and linked to campus network. Commuter students can connect to campus network. Online course registration, online library, student web hosting, wireless network available.

Student life. Freshman orientation: Mandatory. Preregistration for classes offered. **Housing:** Guaranteed on-campus for all undergraduates. Coed dorms, apartments available. $200 fully refundable deposit. **Activities:** Campus ministries, international student organizations, literary magazine, student government.

Student services. Chaplain/spiritual director, career counseling, financial aid counseling.

Contact. E-mail: admission@uwest.edu
Phone: (626) 677-3311 Fax: (626) 571-1413
Grace Hsiao, Admissions Officer, University of the West, 1409 North Walnut Grove Avenue, Rosemead, CA 91770

Vanguard University of Southern California
Costa Mesa, California
www.vanguard.edu

CB code: 4701

- Private 4-year university and liberal arts college affiliated with Assemblies of God
- Residential campus in small city
- 1,872 degree-seeking undergraduates
- 74% of applicants admitted
- SAT or ACT (ACT writing optional), application essay required

General. Founded in 1920. Regionally accredited. **Degrees:** 406 bachelor's awarded; master's offered. **ROTC:** Army, Air Force. **Location:** 45 miles from Los Angeles, 70 miles from San Diego. **Calendar:** Semester, limited summer session. **Full-time faculty:** 63 total; 84% have terminal degrees, 19% minority. **Part-time faculty:** 140 total; 18% have terminal degrees, 16% minority. **Class size:** 57% < 20, 34% 20-39, 4% 40-49, 5% 50-99, less than 1% >100.

Freshman class profile. 1,244 applied, 921 admitted, 414 enrolled.

Mid 50% test scores			
SAT critical reading:	440-540	GPA 3.0-3.49:	34%
SAT math:	430-540	GPA 2.0-2.99:	21%
SAT writing:	450-540	Rank in top quarter:	29%
ACT composite:	18-25	Rank in top tenth:	22%
GPA 3.75 or higher:	26%	Out-of-state:	18%
GPA 3.50-3.74:	18%	Live on campus:	86%

Basis for selection. Priority given to students with GPA of 2.8 or higher, Christian commitment essay, academic reference, reference from pastor. Applications from Christian students who desire an education that integrates Christian faith with learning and living encouraged. Interview recommended for borderline applicants. Audition recommended for music, theater majors. **Home schooled:** Should take GED to qualify for federal financial aid.

High school preparation. Recommended units include English 4, mathematics 2, social studies 3 and science 2.

2011-2012 Annual costs. Tuition/fees: $27,400. Room/board: $8,434. Books/supplies: $1,656. Personal expenses: $2,277.

Financial aid. **Non-need-based:** Scholarships awarded for academics, athletics, music/drama, religious affiliation.

Application procedures. **Admission:** Priority date 12/1; deadline 3/2. $45 fee, may be waived for applicants with need. Admission notification on a rolling basis beginning on or about 1/15. Must reply by May 1 or within 3 week(s) if notified thereafter. **Financial aid:** Priority date 3/2, closing date 3/2. FAFSA required. Applicants notified on a rolling basis starting 4/1; must reply within 3 week(s) of notification.

Academics. **Special study options:** Accelerated study, combined bachelor's/graduate degree, double major, internships, liberal arts/career combination, study abroad, teacher certification program, Washington semester, weekend college. **Credit/placement by examination:** AP, CLEP, IB, SAT, ACT. 24 credit hours maximum toward bachelor's degree. **Support services:** Learning center, reduced course load, study skills assistance, tutoring, writing center.

Majors. **Biology:** General, biochemistry. **Business:** General, accounting, business admin, finance, international, marketing. **Communications:** Communications/speech/rhetoric, digital media. **Computer sciences:** Information technology. **Education:** Music, physical. **English:** English lit. **Health services:** Athletic training, nursing (RN), premedicine. **History:** General. **Liberal arts:** Arts/sciences. **Math:** General. **Parks/recreation:** Exercise sciences, health/fitness. **Philosophy/religion:** Christian, religion. **Physical sciences:** Chemistry. **Psychology:** General. **Social sciences:** General, anthropology, political science, sociology. **Theology:** Bible, missionary, pastoral counseling, religious ed, theology, youth ministry. **Visual/performing arts:** Cinematography, dramatic, music, music history, music performance, theater design. **Work/family studies:** Family studies.

Most popular majors. Business/marketing 24%, communications/journalism 16%, education 8%, psychology 13%, social sciences 6%, visual/performing arts 10%.

Computing on campus. 76 workstations in dormitories, library. Dormitories wired for high-speed internet access and linked to campus network. Commuter students can connect to campus network. Online course registration, online library, helpline, wireless network available.

Student life. **Freshman orientation:** Mandatory, $125 fee. Preregistration for classes offered. 4-day program prior to first day of fall semester. **Policies:** Students must be in good standing to live on campus. Religious observance required. **Housing:** Guaranteed on-campus for all undergraduates. Coed dorms, single-sex dorms, apartments, wellness housing available. $400 deposit, deadline 8/9. **Activities:** Bands, campus ministries, choral groups, drama, film society, international student organizations, literary magazine, music ensembles, musical theater, student government, student newspaper, Students for Social Action, Live 2 Free, Club Mosaic, El Puente, Students in Free Enterprise, Invisible Children Club, Acting on AIDS, Prayer Movement, Hands Across the Border.

Athletics. NAIA. **Intercollegiate:** Baseball M, basketball, cross-country, soccer, softball W, swimming, tennis, track and field, volleyball W. **Intramural:** Basketball. **Team name:** Lions.

Student services. Adult student services, alcohol/substance abuse counseling, chaplain/spiritual director, career counseling, student employment services, financial aid counseling, health services, minority student services, personal counseling, placement for graduates, veterans' counselor, women's services.

Contact. E-mail: admissions@vanguard.edu
Phone: (714) 966-5496 ext. 3901 Toll-free number: (800) 722-6279
Fax: (714) 966-5471
Vanguard University of Southern California, 55 Fair Drive, Costa Mesa, CA 92626-9601

West Coast University
North Hollywood, California
www.westcoastuniversity.edu

CB code: 6184

- For-profit 4-year health science college
- Commuter campus in very large city
- 1,101 degree-seeking undergraduates
- 56% of applicants admitted
- Interview required

General. Accredited by ACICS. **Degrees:** 17 bachelor's, 214 associate awarded; master's offered. **Location:** Downtown. **Calendar:** Semester, extensive summer session. **Full-time faculty:** 16 total. **Part-time faculty:** 39 total. **Special facilities:** Simulation labs.

Freshman class profile. 147 applied, 82 admitted, 54 enrolled.

Basis for selection. Incoming students must pass entrance exams for any program where it is required for entry. Academic record is important but not definitive. Interview with admissions and academic dean is required. **Learning Disabled:** Students with disabilities should request accommodations through Student Services Department.

2011-2012 Annual costs. Tuition/fees: $33,923. Room/board: $16,530. Books/supplies: $1,566.

Application procedures. **Admission:** No deadline. $75 fee. Application must be submitted on paper. **Financial aid:** FAFSA required.

Academics. **Special study options:** Accelerated study, distance learning, internships. **Credit/placement by examination:** AP, CLEP, institutional tests. May challenge test-out of 12 semester credits, maximum. Must achieve score of 75% or higher, one attempt only. Must be taken before enrolling in the course in which equivalency is sought. **Support services:** Study skills assistance, tutoring.

Majors. **Health services:** Nursing (RN).

Computing on campus. 1,250 workstations in library. Online library, wireless network available.

Student life. **Freshman orientation:** Mandatory. Preregistration for classes offered. **Activities:** Student government.

Student services. Adult student services, career counseling, services for economically disadvantaged, student employment services, financial aid counseling, placement for graduates.

Contact. Phone: (877) 505-4928 Toll-free number: (877) 505-4928
Herman Whitaker, Admissions Director, West Coast University, 12215 Victory Boulevard, North Hollywood, CA 91606

Westmont College
Santa Barbara, California
www.westmont.edu

CB member
CB code: 4950

- Private 4-year liberal arts college affiliated with nondenominational tradition
- Residential campus in small city
- 1,333 degree-seeking undergraduates
- 61% of applicants admitted
- SAT or ACT with writing, application essay required

General. Founded in 1937. Regionally accredited. **Degrees:** 333 bachelor's awarded. **ROTC:** Army, Air Force. **Location:** 90 miles from Los Angeles. **Calendar:** Semester, limited summer session. **Full-time faculty:** 97 total; 91% have terminal degrees, 11% minority. **Part-time faculty:** 56 total; 27% have terminal degrees, 7% minority. **Class size:** 59% < 20, 31% 20-39, 8% 40-49, 2% 50-99. **Special facilities:** Visual arts building with gallery, theater, observatory, electronic music lab, physiology lab, organic garden, Cosmic Muon Detector Array (CMDA), vivarium.

Freshman class profile. 2,318 applied, 1,414 admitted, 325 enrolled.

Mid 50% test scores			
SAT critical reading:	540-650	GPA 3.50-3.74:	17%
SAT math:	540-650	GPA 3.0-3.49:	35%
SAT writing:	540-660	GPA 2.0-2.99:	11%
ACT composite:	23-29	Rank in top quarter:	73%
GPA 3.75 or higher:	37%	Rank in top tenth:	42%
		Live on campus:	100%

Basis for selection. Personal Christian statement, college preparatory high school curriculum, high school rank, test scores, 1 academic recommendation, and essay important. Personal interview, teacher, pastor, and other recommendations may enhance chances. Test scores must be received by November 1 for Early Action applicants. Personal interviews recommended. **Home schooled:** Applicants encouraged. Evaluation based on individual merit as well as high school achievement. Greater emphasis may be given to SAT or ACT scores.

High school preparation. College-preparatory program required. 16 units required. Required and recommended units include English 4, mathematics 3, social studies 2, science 3 (laboratory 2), foreign language 2-3 and academic electives 4. Three math credits required, one of which must include Algebra 2.

2011-2012 Annual costs. Tuition/fees: $35,650. Room/board: $11,340. Books/supplies: $1,600. Personal expenses: $3,840.

Financial aid. **Non-need-based:** Scholarships awarded for academics, art, athletics, leadership, minority status, music/drama.

Application procedures. **Admission:** Priority date 2/20; no deadline. $50 fee, may be waived for applicants with need. Admission notification on a rolling basis beginning on or about 3/1. Must reply by May 1 or within 2 week(s) if notified thereafter. Candidates not accepted for Early Action may be considered for admission under Regular Decision. This allows time for submission of additional materials that may strengthen overall application. **Financial aid:** Priority date 3/1; no closing date. FAFSA required. Applicants notified on a rolling basis starting 3/15; must reply by 5/1 or within 2 week(s) of notification.

Academics. **Special study options:** Accelerated study, double major, exchange student, honors, independent study, internships, New York semester, semester at sea, student-designed major, study abroad, teacher certification program, urban semester, Washington semester. Cross-cultural studies in Western and Eastern Europe, England, Africa, East Asia, South America and Egypt; semester study available in San Francisco, Los Angeles, Mexico and at one of 12 other member colleges of the Christian College Consortium. **Credit/placement by examination:** AP, CLEP, IB, SAT, ACT, institutional tests. 32 credit hours maximum toward bachelor's degree. **Support services:** Learning center, pre-admission summer program, study skills assistance, tutoring, writing center.

Majors. **Area/ethnic studies:** European. **Biology:** General. **Business:** General. **Communications:** Communications/speech/rhetoric. **Computer sciences:** Computer science. **Education:** General. **Engineering:** Applied physics. **English:** English lit. **Foreign languages:** French, Spanish. **Health services:** Predental, premedicine, prenursing, prepharmacy, preveterinary. **History:** General. **Math:** General. **Parks/recreation:** Exercise sciences. **Philosophy/religion:** Philosophy, religion. **Physical sciences:** Chemistry, physics. **Psychology:** General. **Social sciences:** General, anthropology, economics, political science, sociology. **Visual/performing arts:** Art, dramatic, music.

Most popular majors. Biology 7%, business/marketing 15%, communications/journalism 9%, English 11%, parks/recreation 7%, philosophy/religious studies 8%, psychology 6%, social sciences 11%, visual/performing arts 8%.

Computing on campus. 100 workstations in library, computer center. Dormitories wired for high-speed internet access and linked to campus network. Commuter students can connect to campus network. Online course registration, online library, helpline, repair service, student web hosting, wireless network available.

Student life. Freshman orientation: Mandatory. Preregistration for classes offered. Held 4 days before Fall semester begins. **Policies:** Chapel attendance required on Mondays, Wednesdays, and Fridays. Dry, tobacco-free campus. Men and women do not share hallways and bathrooms in dorms. Selected visiting hours for members of opposite sex. Religious observance required. **Housing:** Guaranteed on-campus for all undergraduates. Coed dorms, single-sex dorms, apartments, wellness housing available. $500 nonrefundable deposit, deadline 5/1. **Activities:** Jazz band, campus ministries, choral groups, dance, drama, film society, international student organizations, literary magazine, music ensembles, Model UN, musical theater, radio station, student government, student newspaper, symphony orchestra, Amnesty International, Habitat for Humanity, Leadership Development Program, political organizations, Fellowship of Christian Athletes, community service organizations.

Athletics. NAIA. **Intercollegiate:** Baseball M, basketball, cross-country, soccer, tennis, track and field, volleyball W. **Intramural:** Badminton, basketball, football (non-tackle), golf, lacrosse, racquetball, soccer, swimming, table tennis, tennis, volleyball. **Team name:** Warriors.

Student services. Alcohol/substance abuse counseling, chaplain/spiritual director, career counseling, student employment services, financial aid counseling, health services, minority student services, personal counseling, placement for graduates. **Physically disabled:** Services for visually, speech, hearing impaired.

Contact. E-mail: admissions@westmont.edu
Phone: (805) 565-6200 Toll-free number: (800) 777-9011
Fax: (805) 565-6234
Joyce Luy, Dean of Admission, Westmont College, 955 La Paz Road, Santa Barbara, CA 93108-1089

Westwood College: Anaheim
Anaheim, California
www.westwood.edu

- For-profit 4-year technical college
- Very large city

General. Regionally accredited. **Calendar:** Differs by program.

Annual costs/financial aid. Tuition/fees (2011-2012): $15,020. Books/supplies: $1,106.

Contact. Phone: (714) 938-6140 ext. 60100
Director of Admissions, 1551 South Douglass Road, Anaheim, CA 92806

Westwood College: Inland Empire
Upland, California
www.westwood.edu

- For-profit 3-year business and technical college
- Commuter campus in small city

General. Regionally accredited. **Location:** 45 miles from Los Angeles, 22 miles from Riverside. **Calendar:** Differs by program.

Annual costs/financial aid. Tuition/fees (2011-2012): $15,020. Books/supplies: $1,106. Need-based financial aid available to full-time and part-time students.

Contact. Phone: (909) 931-7550
Director of Admissions, 20 West Seventh Street, Upland, CA 91786

Westwood College: South Bay
Torrance, California
www.westwood.edu

- For-profit 4-year technical college
- Large city

General. Regionally accredited. **Calendar:** Differs by program.

Annual costs/financial aid. Tuition/fees (2011-2012): $15,020. Books/supplies: $1,106.

Contact. Phone: (310) 965-0888
Admissions Director, 19700 South Vermont Avenue #100, Torrance, CA 90502

Whittier College
Whittier, California
www.whittier.edu

CB member
CB code: 4952

- Private 4-year liberal arts college
- Residential campus in small city
- 1,626 degree-seeking undergraduates: 2% part-time, 54% women, 5% African American, 10% Asian American, 33% Hispanic American, 3% international
- 41 degree-seeking graduate students
- 71% of applicants admitted
- SAT or ACT with writing, application essay required
- 55% graduate within 6 years

General. Founded in 1887. Regionally accredited. Historic affiliation with the Quakers. **Degrees:** 268 bachelor's awarded; master's, professional offered. **ROTC:** Army. **Location:** 18 miles from Los Angeles. **Calendar:** 4-1-4, limited summer session. **Full-time faculty:** 106 total; 99% have terminal degrees, 26% minority, 51% women. **Part-time faculty:** 46 total; 85% have terminal degrees, 35% minority, 65% women. **Class size:** 58% < 20, 39% 20-39, 2% 40-49, less than 1% 50-99, less than 1% >100. **Special facilities:** Quaker books and materials collection, John Greenleaf Whittier collection including manuscripts, letters and furniture, collection of Richard M. Nixon gifts, Keck image processing laboratory.

Freshman class profile. 2,989 applied, 2,137 admitted, 430 enrolled.

Mid 50% test scores			
SAT critical reading:	470-570	Rank in top quarter:	34%
SAT math:	470-580	Rank in top tenth:	24%
SAT writing:	460-570	End year in good standing:	81%
ACT composite:	20-26	Out-of-state:	71%
GPA 3.75 or higher:	8%	Live on campus:	80%
GPA 3.50-3.74:	10%	International:	3%
GPA 3.0-3.49:	42%	Fraternities:	9%
GPA 2.0-2.99:	40%	Sororities:	19%

Basis for selection. GPA, course selection, and class rank most important followed by essays, references, interviews, test scores, activities, and geographic considerations. Interview recommended. **Home schooled:** Statement describing home school structure and mission, transcript of courses and grades, letter of recommendation (nonparent) required.

High school preparation. College-preparatory program required. Required and recommended units include English 3-4, mathematics 2-3, social studies 1-2, science 1-2 (laboratory 1) and foreign language 2-3.

2012-2013 Annual costs. Tuition/fees: $38,640. Room/board: $10,948. Books/supplies: $1,110. Personal expenses: $1,730.

2011-2012 Financial aid. Need-based: 372 full-time freshmen applied for aid; 333 were judged to have need; 332 of these received aid. Average need met was 79%. Average scholarship/grant was $28,304; average loan $7,051. 69% of total undergraduate aid awarded as scholarships/grants, 31% as loans/jobs. **Non-need-based:** Awarded to 372 full-time undergraduates, including 101 freshmen. Scholarships awarded for academics, alumni affiliation, art, leadership, minority status. **Additional information:** Auditions required for talent scholarship applicants in art, music, and theater.

Application procedures. Admission: Priority date 2/1; no deadline. $50 fee, may be waived for applicants with need. Admission notification on a rolling basis beginning on or about 12/30. Must reply by May 1 or within 2 week(s) if notified thereafter. **Financial aid:** Priority date 3/1, closing date 6/30. FAFSA required. Applicants notified on a rolling basis starting 2/15; must reply within 2 week(s) of notification.

Academics. Special study options: Combined bachelor's/graduate degree, double major, independent study, internships, liberal arts/career combination, semester at sea, student-designed major, study abroad, teacher certification program, Washington semester. **Credit/placement by examination:** AP, CLEP, IB, SAT, ACT, institutional tests. 30 credit hours maximum toward bachelor's degree. **Support services:** Learning center, study skills assistance, tutoring, writing center.

Majors. Area/ethnic studies: Latin American. **Biology:** General. **Business:** General. **Conservation:** General. **Education:** General, early childhood.

English: American lit, British lit, English lit. **Foreign languages:** General, comparative lit, French, Spanish. **Health services:** Athletic training, predental, premedicine, prepharmacy, preveterinary, recreational therapy. **History:** General. **Human services:** Social work. **Liberal arts:** Arts/sciences. **Math:** General. **Philosophy/religion:** Philosophy, religion. **Physical sciences:** Chemistry, physics. **Psychology:** General. **Social sciences:** Anthropology, international relations, political science, sociology, urban studies. **Visual/performing arts:** Art, art history/conservation, dramatic, music, music history, theater history.

Most popular majors. Biology 7%, business/marketing 17%, English 6%, history 6%, parks/recreation 8%, psychology 8%, social sciences 22%, visual/performing arts 6%.

Computing on campus. 165 workstations in dormitories, library, computer center. Dormitories wired for high-speed internet access and linked to campus network. Online course registration, helpline, wireless network available.

Student life. Freshman orientation: Mandatory, $200 fee. Preregistration for classes offered. Orientation begins over Labor Day weekend. **Housing:** Guaranteed on-campus for freshmen. Coed dorms, single-sex dorms, special housing for disabled, wellness housing available. $200 nonrefundable deposit, deadline 5/1. Multicultural hall, honors floor, living and learning community available. **Activities:** Jazz band, campus ministries, choral groups, dance, drama, film society, international student organizations, literary magazine, music ensembles, Model UN, musical theater, radio station, student government, student newspaper, national honor societies.

Athletics. NCAA. **Intercollegiate:** Baseball M, basketball, cross-country, diving, football (tackle) M, golf, lacrosse, soccer, softball W, swimming, tennis, track and field, volleyball W, water polo. **Intramural:** Basketball, softball, volleyball. **Team name:** Poets.

Student services. Career counseling, student employment services, health services, on-campus daycare, personal counseling, placement for graduates.

Contact. E-mail: admission@whittier.edu
Phone: (562) 907-4238 Fax: (562) 907-4870
Kieron Miller, Director of Admission, Whittier College, 13406 East Philadelphia Street, Whittier, CA 90608-0634

William Jessup University
Rocklin, California
www.jessup.edu

CB code: 4756

- Private 4-year Bible and liberal arts college affiliated with nondenominational tradition
- Residential campus in small city
- 859 degree-seeking undergraduates: 19% part-time, 59% women, 6% African American, 3% Asian American, 10% Hispanic American, 2% Native American
- 27 degree-seeking graduate students
- 65% of applicants admitted
- SAT or ACT (ACT writing optional), application essay required
- 53% graduate within 6 years

General. Founded in 1939. Regionally accredited; also accredited by ABHE. **Degrees:** 141 bachelor's awarded. **Location:** 20 miles from Sacramento. **Calendar:** Semester, limited summer session. **Full-time faculty:** 27 total; 78% have terminal degrees, 11% minority, 33% women. **Part-time faculty:** 87 total; 22% have terminal degrees, 10% minority, 47% women. **Class size:** 64% < 20, 28% 20-39, 4% 40-49, 3% 50-99, less than 1% >100.

Freshman class profile. 389 applied, 251 admitted, 121 enrolled.

Mid 50% test scores			
SAT critical reading:	470-580	GPA 3.0-3.49:	24%
SAT math:	440-540	GPA 2.0-2.99:	30%
SAT writing:	460-560	Rank in top quarter:	44%
ACT composite:	20-25	Rank in top tenth:	15%
GPA 3.75 or higher:	26%	Return as sophomores:	78%
GPA 3.50-3.74:	20%	Out-of-state:	9%
		Live on campus:	71%

Basis for selection. Academic records, supporting documents, moral character, willingness to comply with standards and values of university strongly considered. Interview strongly recommended, and may be required. Audition required for music performance scholarship. **Home schooled:** Statement describing home school structure and mission required. Extra emphasis placed on SAT/ACT; professional/third-party home educators transcript provider preferred over in-home development of transcripts. **Learning Disabled:** Once voluntarily disclosed, student is asked to provide documentation of learning disability and to meet with academic support advisor regularly.

High school preparation. College-preparatory program recommended. 17 units required; 23 recommended. Required and recommended units include English 4, mathematics 3-4, social studies 1, history 2-3, science 3 (laboratory 2), foreign language 2-3, computer science 1, visual/performing arts 1 and academic electives 2-3. Religion taken for credit at accredited parochial/Christian high school may be given academic consideration.

2011-2012 Annual costs. Tuition/fees: $21,800. Room/board: $8,640. Books/supplies: $1,620. Personal expenses: $2,250.

2011-2012 Financial aid. Need-based: 113 full-time freshmen applied for aid; 103 were judged to have need; 103 of these received aid. Average need met was 71%. Average scholarship/grant was $15,287; average loan $3,337. 76% of total undergraduate aid awarded as scholarships/grants, 24% as loans/jobs. **Non-need-based:** Awarded to 155 full-time undergraduates, including 24 freshmen. Scholarships awarded for academics, athletics, leadership, minority status, music/drama, religious affiliation, state residency.

Application procedures. Admission: Priority date 4/1; deadline 8/25 (postmark date). $45 fee, may be waived for applicants with need. Admission notification on a rolling basis beginning on or about 11/1. Must reply by June 1 or by date in acceptance letter thereafter. **Financial aid:** Priority date 3/2; no closing date. FAFSA required. Applicants notified on a rolling basis starting 3/2; must reply within 3 week(s) of notification.

Academics. All church vocation/ministry-based degrees offer dual major in Bible and Theology. Emphasis placed on pastoral training, missions, youth ministry, and family and children ministry. **Special study options:** Accelerated study, double major, independent study, internships, liberal arts/career combination, study abroad, teacher certification program, urban semester, Washington semester. School of Professional Studies (adult degree completion program). **Credit/placement by examination:** AP, CLEP, IB, SAT, ACT, institutional tests. 16 credit hours maximum toward associate degree, 16 toward bachelor's. A maximum of 30 units will be awarded for AP, IB, or CLEP. **Support services:** Learning center, reduced course load, study skills assistance, tutoring, writing center.

Majors. Business: Business admin. **Education:** Elementary. **English:** English lit. **History:** General. **Math:** General. **Psychology:** General. **Theology:** Missionary, pastoral counseling, theology, youth ministry. **Visual/performing arts:** Music.

Most popular majors. Business/marketing 22%, education 7%, psychology 31%, social sciences 6%, theological studies 28%.

Computing on campus. 35 workstations in library, computer center. Dormitories wired for high-speed internet access and linked to campus network. Commuter students can connect to campus network. Online course registration, online library, helpline, repair service, wireless network available.

Student life. Freshman orientation: Mandatory. Preregistration for classes offered. Combination mini new student orientation with summer registration dates; 4-day new student orientation leading up to first day of classes for Fall (in August), 3-day session leading up to first day of classes for Spring (in January). **Policies:** Dry campus. Quiet hours, but no curfew. No formal dress code, but appropriate dress recommended. Chapel attendance required. Religious observance required. **Housing:** Guaranteed on-campus for freshmen. Coed dorms, single-sex dorms, apartments available. Local hotel arrangement for upper classmen available. **Activities:** Campus ministries, choral groups, film society, literary magazine, music ensembles, student government, student newspaper, spiritual formation groups.

Athletics. NAIA. **Intercollegiate:** Basketball, cross-country, golf M, soccer, softball W, track and field, volleyball W. **Team name:** Warriors.

Student services. Alcohol/substance abuse counseling, chaplain/spiritual director, career counseling, financial aid counseling, personal counseling. **Physically disabled:** Services for visually, hearing impaired.

Contact. E-mail: admissions@jessup.edu
Phone: (916) 577-2222 Fax: (916) 577-2220
Vance Pascua, Director of Admission, William Jessup University, 333 Sunset Boulevard, Rocklin, CA 95765

Woodbury University
Burbank, California
www.woodbury.edu

CB member
CB code: 4955

- Private 4-year university
- Commuter campus in very large city
- 1,261 degree-seeking undergraduates: 14% part-time, 53% women, 4% African American, 9% Asian American, 33% Hispanic American, 13% international

- 282 degree-seeking graduate students
- 72% of applicants admitted
- SAT or ACT (ACT writing optional), application essay required
- 53% graduate within 6 years

General. Founded in 1884. Regionally accredited. **Degrees:** 248 bachelor's awarded; master's offered. **Location:** 15 miles from downtown Los Angeles. **Calendar:** Semester, limited summer session. **Full-time faculty:** 71 total; 97% have terminal degrees, 10% minority, 45% women. **Part-time faculty:** 220 total; 69% have terminal degrees, 20% minority, 33% women. **Class size:** 81% < 20, 19% 20-39, less than 1% 40-49. **Special facilities:** Design galleries.

Freshman class profile. 416 applied, 299 admitted, 194 enrolled.

Mid 50% test scores			
SAT critical reading:	420-520	GPA 3.0-3.49:	33%
SAT math:	420-530	GPA 2.0-2.99:	36%
ACT composite:	17-23	Return as sophomores:	72%
GPA 3.75 or higher:	16%	Out-of-state:	5%
GPA 3.50-3.74:	15%	Live on campus:	32%
		International:	15%

Basis for selection. Primary emphasis placed on applicant's prior academic record and standardized test scores. Interview recommended. **Home schooled:** State high school equivalency certificate required.

High school preparation. College-preparatory program recommended. 13 units recommended. Recommended units include English 4, mathematics 3, social studies 2, science 1 and foreign language 3.

2011-2012 Annual costs. Tuition/fees: $29,709. Room/board: $10,124. Books/supplies: $1,750. Personal expenses: $2,340.

2011-2012 Financial aid. Need-based: 90 full-time freshmen applied for aid; 85 were judged to have need; 85 of these received aid. Average need met was 61%. Average scholarship/grant was $20,007; average loan $3,364. 64% of total undergraduate aid awarded as scholarships/grants, 36% as loans/jobs. **Non-need-based:** Awarded to 84 full-time undergraduates, including 19 freshmen. Scholarships awarded for academics.

Application procedures. Admission: Priority date 3/1; no deadline. $50 fee, may be waived for applicants with need. Admission notification on a rolling basis beginning on or about 11/1. **Financial aid:** Priority date 3/1; no closing date. FAFSA, institutional form required. Applicants notified on a rolling basis starting 4/1; must reply within 2 week(s) of notification.

Academics. Combines professional programs in design, architecture, and business with liberal arts components. **Special study options:** Accelerated study, double major, dual enrollment of high school students, ESL, exchange student, independent study, internships, liberal arts/career combination, student-designed major, study abroad, weekend college. **Credit/placement by examination:** AP, CLEP, IB, institutional tests. Institutional/departmental examinations used for placement or counseling. **Support services:** Learning center, reduced course load, remedial instruction, tutoring, writing center.

Majors. Architecture: Architecture, interior. **Business:** Accounting, business admin, fashion, marketing, organizational behavior. **Communications:** Media studies. **Computer sciences:** General. **Psychology:** General. **Visual/performing arts:** Commercial/advertising art, fashion design, graphic design.

Most popular majors. Architecture 42%, business/marketing 35%, visual/performing arts 15%.

Computing on campus. 169 workstations in library, computer center, student center. Commuter students can connect to campus network. Online course registration, online library, helpline, wireless network available.

Student life. Freshman orientation: Mandatory, $75 fee. Preregistration for classes offered. **Housing:** Coed dorms, special housing for disabled available. $250 fully refundable deposit, deadline 5/1. Pets allowed in dorm rooms. Quiet study wing. **Activities:** International student organizations, student government, Armenian Student Association, La Voz Unida.

Athletics. Intramural: Basketball, soccer.

Student services. Adult student services, alcohol/substance abuse counseling, career counseling, services for economically disadvantaged, student employment services, financial aid counseling, health services, personal counseling, placement for graduates. **Physically disabled:** Services for visually, speech, hearing impaired.

Contact. E-mail: admissions@woodbury.edu
Phone: (818) 767-0888 ext. 221 Toll-free number: (800) 784-9663
Fax: (818) 767-7520
Ruth Lorenzana, Director of Admissions, Woodbury University, 7500 Glenoaks Boulevard, Burbank, CA 91510-7846

World Mission University
Los Angeles, California
www.wmu.edu

- Private 4-year Bible and seminary college affiliated with nondenominational tradition
- Very large city
- 150 degree-seeking undergraduates
- 64% of applicants admitted

General. Accredited by ABHE. All programs taught in Korean language. **Degrees:** 35 bachelor's awarded; master's, professional offered. **Location:** Downtown. **Calendar:** Semester, limited summer session. **Full-time faculty:** 3 total. **Part-time faculty:** 5 total.

Freshman class profile. 67 applied, 43 admitted, 32 enrolled.

Basis for selection. Admissions criteria include sense of calling for Christian ministry, participation in church community, academic performance, test results, recommendations. Audition and additional supplementary application required for music programs. **Home schooled:** Statement describing home school structure and mission, transcript of courses and grades, letter of recommendation (nonparent) required.

2011-2012 Annual costs. Tuition/fees: $5,500.

Application procedures. Admission: No deadline. $100 fee. Application must be submitted on paper. Admission notification on a rolling basis.

Academics. Special study options: Distance learning, dual enrollment of high school students, ESL. **Credit/placement by examination:** AP, CLEP, IB, institutional tests.

Majors. Theology: Bible. **Visual/performing arts:** Music.

Computing on campus. Online library, wireless network available.

Student life. Freshman orientation: Mandatory. Preregistration for classes offered.

Contact. E-mail: wmuoffice@gmail.com
Phone: (213) 385-2322 Fax: (213) 385-2332
John Park, Admissions Director, World Mission University, 500 Shatto Place, Los Angeles, CA 90020

Yeshiva Ohr Elchonon Chabad/West Coast Talmudical Seminary
Los Angeles, California
CB code: 1331

- Private 4-year rabbinical college for men affiliated with Jewish faith
- Residential campus in very large city
- 136 degree-seeking undergraduates: 11% international
- 71% of applicants admitted
- Interview required

General. Founded in 1953. Accredited by AARTS. Ordination available. **Degrees:** 12 bachelor's awarded. **Calendar:** Semester, limited summer session. **Full-time faculty:** 6 total; 100% have terminal degrees. **Part-time faculty:** 4 total.

Freshman class profile. 51 applied, 36 admitted, 36 enrolled.

Out-of-state:	57%	International:	19%
Live on campus:	100%		

Basis for selection. Interview, recommendations, religious affiliation or commitment, and test scores most important. Priority given to California residents. **Home schooled:** Statement describing home school structure and mission, interview, letter of recommendation (nonparent) required.

High school preparation. Recommended units include English 3, mathematics 3, social studies 3, history 2, science 3 and foreign language 2.

2012-2013 Annual costs. Tuition/fees: $12,400. Room/board: $7,450. Books/supplies: $200. Personal expenses: $100.

Financial aid. All financial aid based on need.

Application procedures. Admission: No deadline. No application fee. Admission notification on a rolling basis. **Financial aid:** Priority date 1/15, closing date 6/30. FAFSA, institutional form required. Applicants notified by 5/1; must reply by 7/1.

Academics. Special study options: Independent study, weekend college. **Credit/placement by examination:** AP, CLEP, institutional tests. 90 credit hours maximum toward bachelor's degree. For transfer students. **Support services:** Pre-admission summer program, remedial instruction, tutoring.

Majors. Theology: Religious ed, Talmudic.

Most popular majors. Liberal arts 50%, theological studies 50%.

Computing on campus. 18 workstations in dormitories, computer center.

Student life. Freshman orientation: Available. Preregistration for classes offered. **Policies:** Religious observance required. **Housing:** Guaranteed on-campus for all undergraduates. $300 fully refundable deposit. **Activities:** Literary magazine, student government, student newspaper.

Student services. Career counseling, services for economically disadvantaged, financial aid counseling, minority student services, personal counseling. **Physically disabled:** Services for visually, speech impaired.

Contact. E-mail: MSpalter@yoec.edu
Phone: (323) 937-3763 Fax: (323) 937-9456
Rabbi Chaim Citron, Director of Admissions, Yeshiva Ohr Elchonon Chabad/West Coast Talmudical Seminary, 7215 Waring Avenue, Los Angeles, CA 90046

Colorado

Adams State College
Alamosa, Colorado
www.adams.edu

CB code: 4001

- Public 4-year liberal arts college
- Residential campus in small town
- 2,422 degree-seeking undergraduates: 17% part-time, 55% women, 6% African American, 1% Asian American, 32% Hispanic American, 1% Native American
- 798 degree-seeking graduate students
- 64% of applicants admitted
- SAT or ACT (ACT writing optional) required

General. Founded in 1921. Regionally accredited. Hispanic-serving institution. **Degrees:** 331 bachelor's, 40 associate awarded; master's offered. **Location:** 225 miles from Denver; 200 miles from Albuquerque, New Mexico. **Calendar:** Semester, limited summer session. **Full-time faculty:** 111 total; 70% have terminal degrees, 19% minority, 47% women. **Part-time faculty:** 63 total; 11% minority, 70% women. **Class size:** 63% < 20, 29% 20-39, 5% 40-49, 2% 50-99. **Special facilities:** Observatory, planetarium, natural history museum, geology museum, community partnerships.

Freshman class profile. 2,534 applied, 1,613 admitted, 599 enrolled.

Mid 50% test scores			
SAT critical reading:	430-550	GPA 3.0-3.49:	27%
SAT math:	450-550	GPA 2.0-2.99:	44%
SAT writing:	410-520	Rank in top quarter:	24%
ACT composite:	17-22	Rank in top tenth:	9%
GPA 3.75 or higher:	12%	End year in good standing:	83%
GPA 3.50-3.74:	13%	Return as sophomores:	55%
		Out-of-state:	22%

Basis for selection. Open admissions for associate degree programs only. Bachelor's degree candidates must have either 2.0 GPA, or rank in top two-thirds of class with average or above average score on ACT or SAT. ACCUPLACER tests for math and English required if SAT or ACT not available. Audition required of music majors. Portfolio required of art majors. **Home schooled:** Transcript of courses and grades required.

High school preparation. College-preparatory program recommended. 17 units required. Required and recommended units include English 4, mathematics 4, social studies 2, history 1, science 3 (laboratory 2), foreign language 1 and academic electives 2. Computer applications: .5 units recommended. Math should include Algebra I and one advanced math course.

2011-2012 Annual costs. Tuition/fees: $5,627; $15,875 out-of-state. Room/board: $7,120. Books/supplies: $1,312. Personal expenses: $1,270.

2010-2011 Financial aid. Need-based: 535 full-time freshmen applied for aid; 451 were judged to have need; 450 of these received aid. Average need met was 60%. Average scholarship/grant was $5,196; average loan $2,837. 67% of total undergraduate aid awarded as scholarships/grants, 33% as loans/jobs. **Non-need-based:** Scholarships awarded for academics, alumni affiliation, art, athletics, leadership, minority status, music/drama, state residency.

Application procedures. Admission: Priority date 8/1; no deadline. $30 fee, may be waived for applicants with need. Admission notification on a rolling basis. **Financial aid:** Priority date 3/1, closing date 4/15. FAFSA required. Applicants notified on a rolling basis starting 4/30; must reply within 4 week(s) of notification.

Academics. Special study options: Accelerated study, distance learning, double major, dual enrollment of high school students, exchange student, external degree, independent study, internships, student-designed major, study abroad, teacher certification program, weekend college. **Credit/placement by examination:** AP, CLEP, IB, SAT, ACT, institutional tests. 15 credit hours maximum toward associate degree, 30 toward bachelor's. **Support services:** Learning center, pre-admission summer program, remedial instruction, study skills assistance, tutoring, writing center.

Majors. Biology: General, bacteriology, biochemistry, cellular/molecular, wildlife. **Business:** General, accounting, business admin, finance, international, management information systems, marketing, small business admin.

Communications: Advertising, media studies. **Computer sciences:** Computer science. **Conservation:** Management/policy. **Education:** General, art, biology, business, chemistry, drama/dance, elementary, English, history, mathematics, middle, multi-level teacher, music, physical, science, secondary, social science, social studies, Spanish, special ed, speech. **Engineering:** Applied physics. **English:** Creative writing, English lit. **Foreign languages:** Spanish. **General:** Business. **Health services:** Health care admin, nursing (RN), predental, premedicine, prenursing, prepharmacy, preveterinary. **History:** General. **Human services:** Social work. **Liberal arts:** Arts/sciences. **Math:** General. **Parks/recreation:** Exercise sciences, health/fitness. **Physical sciences:** Chemical physics, chemistry, geology, physics. **Psychology:** General. **Social sciences:** Criminology, economics, sociology. **Visual/performing arts:** Art, ceramics, dramatic, drawing, metal/jewelry, music, music performance, music theory/composition, painting, photography, printmaking, sculpture, studio arts, voice/opera.

Most popular majors. Business/marketing 29%, liberal arts 19%, parks/recreation 9%, social sciences 15%, visual/performing arts 9%.

Computing on campus. 336 workstations in library, student center. Dormitories wired for high-speed internet access and linked to campus network. Commuter students can connect to campus network. Online course registration, online library, helpline, repair service, student web hosting, wireless network available.

Student life. Freshman orientation: Mandatory, $50 fee. Preregistration for classes offered. Program held weekend before start of semester. **Housing:** Guaranteed on-campus for freshmen. Coed dorms, single-sex dorms, special housing for disabled, apartments, wellness housing available. $150 partly refundable deposit. Learning community house, freshman interest-group housing, drug and alcohol-free learning community, outdoor adventure community, making the grade community (must maintain 3.5 GPA). **Activities:** Bands, campus ministries, choral groups, dance, drama, international student organizations, literary magazine, music ensembles, Model UN, musical theater, radio station, student government, student newspaper, Circle K, College Republicans, Newman club, student ambassadors, teacher education association, associated students and faculty, gay straight alliance, Semillas de la Tierra, El Parnaso.

Athletics. NCAA. **Intercollegiate:** Basketball, cross-country, football (tackle) M, golf, lacrosse, soccer, softball W, swimming, track and field, volleyball W, wrestling M. **Intramural:** Basketball, bowling, football (non-tackle), racquetball, skiing, soccer, softball, volleyball, water polo. **Team name:** Grizzlies.

Student services. Adult student services, alcohol/substance abuse counseling, chaplain/spiritual director, career counseling, services for economically disadvantaged, student employment services, financial aid counseling, health services, minority student services, on-campus daycare, personal counseling, veterans' counselor. **Physically disabled:** Services for visually, hearing impaired.

Contact. E-mail: ascadmit@adams.edu
Phone: (719) 587-7712 Toll-free number: (800) 824-6494
Fax: (719) 587-7522
Eric Carpio, Assistant Vice President for Enrollment Management, Adams State College, 208 Edgemont Boulevard, Alamosa, CO 81101

American Sentinel University
Aurora, Colorado
www.americansentinel.edu

CB code: 3806

- For-profit 4-year virtual university
- Commuter campus in very large city
- 1,400 degree-seeking undergraduates
- 600 graduate students

General. Accredited by DETC. **Degrees:** 140 bachelor's, 11 associate awarded; master's, professional offered. **Calendar:** Differs by program, extensive summer session. **Full-time faculty:** 15 total. **Part-time faculty:** 86 total.

Basis for selection. Open admission.

2011-2012 Annual costs. Online university. Cost of bachelor's program varies depending on number of credits completed or transferred. $350 per-credit hour for bachelor's in business and technology; $370 per-credit-hour for bachelor's in nursing.

Application procedures. Admission: No deadline. No application fee. Admission notification on a rolling basis.

Academics. Special study options: Accelerated study, combined bachelor's/graduate degree, distance learning, honors, independent study, liberal

arts/career combination. **Credit/placement by examination:** AP, CLEP. 45 credit hours maximum toward associate degree, 90 toward bachelor's. **Support services:** Learning center, reduced course load, study skills assistance, tutoring, writing center.

Majors. Business: Business admin, e-commerce, human resources, management information systems, marketing. **Computer sciences:** General, computer science, information systems, information technology, security, system admin, web page design. **Health services:** Medical records technology, nursing (RN). **Protective services:** Law enforcement admin. **Visual/performing arts:** Game design.

Computing on campus. PC or laptop required.

Student life. Freshman orientation: Mandatory. Preregistration for classes offered. **Activities:** Student newspaper.

Student services. Adult student services, career counseling, financial aid counseling.

Contact. E-mail: admissions@americansentinel.edu
Phone: (866) 922-5690 Toll-free number: (866) 922-5690
Fax: (866) 505-2450
Natalie Nixon, Vice President, Admissions, American Sentinel University, 500 Century Park South, Suite 202, Birmingham, AL 35226

Argosy University: Denver
Denver, Colorado
www.argosy.edu/denver

- For-profit 4-year university
- Very large city
- 133 degree-seeking undergraduates

General. Degrees: 16 bachelor's awarded; master's, professional, doctoral offered. **Calendar:** Differs by program. **Full-time faculty:** 5 total. **Part-time faculty:** 79 total.

Basis for selection. Open admission.

2011-2012 Annual costs. Tuition/fees: $17,962.

Application procedures. Admission: Closing date 9/13. $50 fee. **Financial aid:** No deadline.

Academics. Credit/placement by examination: AP, CLEP.

Majors. Business: Business admin. **Liberal arts:** Arts/sciences. **Protective services:** Law enforcement admin. **Psychology:** General.

Contact. Phone: (303) 248-2700
Diane Rotondo, Senior Director of Admissions, Argosy University: Denver, 1200 Lincoln Street, Denver, CO 80203

The Art Institute of Colorado
Denver, Colorado
www.artinstitutes.edu/denver   CB code: 7150

- For-profit 4-year culinary school and visual arts college
- Commuter campus in very large city
- 2,050 degree-seeking undergraduates
- SAT or ACT (ACT writing optional), application essay, interview required

General. Founded in 1952. **Degrees:** 274 bachelor's, 138 associate awarded. **Location:** Downtown. **Calendar:** Differs by program, extensive summer session. **Full-time faculty:** 67 total; 25% have terminal degrees, 12% minority, 43% women. **Part-time faculty:** 67 total; 13% have terminal degrees, 12% minority, 42% women. **Class size:** 17% < 20, 83% 20-39. **Special facilities:** Teaching restaurant open to the public at the International School of Culinary Arts.

Basis for selection. Commitment to career most important; essay, interview important; high school transcript considered with GPA. Portfolio required of advanced standing applicants. **Home schooled:** Documentation of grades and official graduation date required. **Learning Disabled:** Discussion with Dean of Student Affairs required.

2011-2012 Annual costs. Tuition/fees: $22,065. Supply kit $590-$2,260 depending on program. Books/supplies: $3,487.

Application procedures. Admission: No deadline. $50 fee. Admission notification on a rolling basis. **Financial aid:** No deadline. FAFSA, institutional form required. Applicants notified on a rolling basis.

Academics. Special study options: Distance learning, independent study, internships. **Credit/placement by examination:** AP, CLEP, IB, institutional tests. 30 credit hours maximum toward associate degree. **Support services:** Reduced course load, remedial instruction, study skills assistance, tutoring, writing center.

Majors. Business: Apparel. **Communications technology:** Animation/special effects. **Computer sciences:** Computer graphics, web page design. **Visual/performing arts:** Cinematography, graphic design, industrial design, interior design, multimedia, photography.

Most popular majors. Personal/culinary services 6%, visual/performing arts 94%.

Computing on campus. 500 workstations in dormitories, library, computer center. Dormitories wired for high-speed internet access and linked to campus network. Commuter students can connect to campus network. Online course registration, online library, helpline, repair service, wireless network available.

Student life. Freshman orientation: Mandatory. Preregistration for classes offered. **Policies:** Pets allowed in apartment living with specific restrictions in contract. **Housing:** Coed dorms, special housing for disabled, wellness housing available. $300 fully refundable deposit. **Activities:** Film society, international student organizations, student government, student newspaper.

Student services. Adult student services, alcohol/substance abuse counseling, career counseling, services for economically disadvantaged, student employment services, financial aid counseling, minority student services, personal counseling, placement for graduates, veterans' counselor. **Physically disabled:** Services for visually, speech, hearing impaired.

Contact. E-mail: aicadm@aii.edu
Phone: (303) 837-0825 Toll-free number: (800) 275-2420
Fax: (303) 860-8520
Sarah Johnson, Senior Director of Admissions, The Art Institute of Colorado, 1200 Lincoln Street, Denver, CO 80203-2172

Aspen University
Denver, Colorado
www.aspen.edu

- For-profit 4-year virtual university
- Very large city
- 15 full-time, degree-seeking undergraduates
- 655 graduate students
- Application essay required

General. Accredited by DETC. **Degrees:** 19 bachelor's awarded; master's, doctoral offered. **Calendar:** Differs by program, extensive summer session.

Basis for selection. Open admission, but selective for some programs. **Home schooled:** State high school equivalency certificate required.

2011-2012 Annual costs. Tuition/fees: $7,600.

Application procedures. Admission: No deadline. No application fee. Admission notification on a rolling basis. **Financial aid:** No deadline.

Academics. Special study options: Accelerated study, distance learning. **Credit/placement by examination:** AP, CLEP. **Support services:** Reduced course load, remedial instruction.

Majors. Business: Business admin, restaurant/food services. **Education:** Early childhood. **Protective services:** Law enforcement admin.

Computing on campus. PC or laptop required. Online library available.

Contact. E-mail: admissions@aspen.edu
Phone: (303) 333-4224 Toll-free number: (800) 441-4746
Fax: (303) 336-1144
Angela Siegel, Executive Vice President, Marketing & Enrollment, Aspen University, 720 South Colorado Boulevard, Suite 1150N, Denver, CO 80246

CollegeAmerica: Colorado Springs
Colorado Springs, Colorado
www.collegeamerica.edu

▶ For-profit 4-year career college
▶ Commuter campus in large city

General. Accredited by ACCSCT. **Calendar:** Differs by program.

Annual costs/financial aid. Tuition ranges from $324 to $408 per quarter credit depending on program. Need-based financial aid available to full-time and part-time students.

Contact. Phone: (719) 637-0600
Director of Admissions, 3645 Citadel Drive South, Colorado Springs, CO 80909

CollegeAmerica: Fort Collins
Fort Collins, Colorado
www.collegeamerica.edu

▶ For-profit 4-year health science and technical college
▶ Commuter campus in small city
▶ 300 degree-seeking undergraduates

General. Accredited by ACCSC. **Degrees:** 6 bachelor's, 5 associate awarded; master's offered. **Calendar:** Differs by program, extensive summer session. **Full-time faculty:** 3 total; 100% women. **Part-time faculty:** 10 total; 40% women.

Basis for selection. Open admission. **Home schooled:** Transcript of courses and grades required.

2011-2012 Annual costs. Tuition ranges from $324 to $408 per quarter credit depending on program.

Application procedures. Admission: No deadline. No application fee. **Financial aid:** No deadline.

Academics. Special study options: Accelerated study, combined bachelor's/graduate degree, distance learning, independent study. **Credit/placement by examination:** AP, CLEP. **Support services:** Learning center, remedial instruction, study skills assistance, tutoring.

Majors. Business: General, accounting. **Computer sciences:** General.

Computing on campus. 50 workstations in library, computer center, student center. Online library, helpline, repair service, wireless network available.

Student life. Freshman orientation: Mandatory. Preregistration for classes offered. **Activities:** Student government.

Student services. Adult student services, career counseling, services for economically disadvantaged, student employment services, financial aid counseling, personal counseling, placement for graduates, veterans' counselor.

Contact. Phone: (970) 223-6060 Toll-free number: (800) 622-2894
Kristy McNear, Director of Admissions, CollegeAmerica: Fort Collins, 4601 South Mason Street, Fort Collins, CO 80525

Colorado Christian University
Lakewood, Colorado   **CB member**
www.ccu.edu   **CB code: 4659**

▶ Private 4-year university and liberal arts college affiliated with nondenominational tradition
▶ Residential campus in large city
▶ 2,822 degree-seeking undergraduates: 54% part-time, 65% women, 6% African American, 1% Asian American, 10% Hispanic American, 1% Native American, 1% international
▶ 356 degree-seeking graduate students
▶ 71% of applicants admitted
▶ SAT or ACT (ACT writing optional), application essay required
▶ 43% graduate within 6 years

General. Founded in 1914. Regionally accredited. Adult and graduate programs available online and at Colorado Springs, Grand Junction, Loveland,

Northglenn, Sterling, Denver (multiple locations), and Lakewood campuses. **Degrees:** 410 bachelor's, 36 associate awarded; master's offered. **ROTC:** Army, Air Force. **Location:** 10 miles from Denver. **Calendar:** Semester, extensive summer session. **Full-time faculty:** 61 total. **Part-time faculty:** 1 total.

Freshman class profile. 1,153 applied, 817 admitted, 290 enrolled.

Mid 50% test scores		GPA 3.0-3.49:	24%
SAT critical reading:	470-610	GPA 2.0-2.99:	17%
SAT math:	490-600	Rank in top quarter:	45%
SAT writing:	470-580	Rank in top tenth:	20%
ACT composite:	21-27	Return as sophomores:	71%
GPA 3.75 or higher:	39%	International:	2%
GPA 3.50-3.74:	20%		

Basis for selection. Applicants should exemplify vital Christian experience. Decisions based on high academic ability, personal integrity, and desire for Christ-centered community. Applicant's course selection, academic performance, test scores, essays, spiritual recommendation, activities, and work experience carefully considered. Audition required of music and theater majors.

High school preparation. College-preparatory program recommended. 19 units recommended. Recommended units include English 4, mathematics 3, social studies 3, history 2, science 2 (laboratory 2) and foreign language 2. Recommend 1 unit of computer science.

2012-2013 Annual costs. Tuition/fees (projected): $23,870. Room/board: $9,490.

Financial aid. Non-need-based: Scholarships awarded for academics, athletics, leadership, music/drama.

Application procedures. Admission: Priority date 3/1; deadline 9/1 (receipt date). $30 fee, may be waived for applicants with need. Application must be submitted online. Admission notification on a rolling basis beginning on or about 11/1. **Financial aid:** Priority date 3/15; no closing date. FAFSA required. Applicants notified on a rolling basis starting 4/1; must reply by 5/1 or within 4 week(s) of notification.

Academics. Special study options: Accelerated study, combined bachelor's/graduate degree, cooperative education, distance learning, double major, honors, independent study, internships, semester at sea, student-designed major, study abroad, teacher certification program, urban semester, Washington semester, weekend college. American studies program (Washington, DC), host university for Institute for Family Studies; China studies program at various sites in China, Latin American program (Costa Rica), Los Angeles film studies center, Middle East studies (Cairo, Egypt), Oxford honors program (University of Oxford, England), Russian studies program at various sites in Russia, Summer Institute of Journalism (Washington, DC). **Credit/placement by examination:** AP, CLEP, IB, SAT, ACT, institutional tests. 15 credit hours maximum toward associate degree, 45 toward bachelor's. **Support services:** Learning center, reduced course load, remedial instruction, study skills assistance, tutoring, writing center.

Majors. Biology: General. **Business:** Accounting, business admin, human resources, management information systems, management science, organizational behavior. **Communications:** Communications/speech/rhetoric. **Computer sciences:** General. **Education:** General, adult/continuing, early childhood, elementary, English, history, mathematics, music, science, secondary. **English:** English lit. **Health services:** Nursing (RN). **History:** General. **Liberal arts:** Arts/sciences. **Math:** General. **Protective services:** Law enforcement admin. **Psychology:** General, psychobiology. **Social sciences:** General. **Theology:** Bible, sacred music, theology, youth ministry. **Visual/performing arts:** Music, music performance, studio arts.

Most popular majors. Business/marketing 53%, education 19%, theological studies 7%.

Computing on campus. 186 workstations in dormitories, library, computer center, student center. Dormitories wired for high-speed internet access and linked to campus network. Commuter students can connect to campus network. Online course registration, online library, helpline, wireless network available.

Student life. Freshman orientation: Mandatory. Preregistration for classes offered. Seminars for students and parents held 4 days prior to beginning of classes. **Policies:** Use of alcoholic beverages, illegal drugs, and tobacco prohibited on campus and at college-sponsored activities. Premarital sexual relationships prohibited. Religious observance required. **Housing:** Guaranteed on-campus for freshmen. Coed dorms, single-sex dorms, special housing for disabled, apartments, wellness housing available. $200 nonrefundable deposit, deadline 9/1. **Activities:** Bands, campus ministries, choral groups, drama, literary magazine, music ensembles, musical theater, student government, student newspaper, symphony orchestra, world missions, discipleship groups, Fat Boys, Footprints, prayer ministry, refugee family ministry, SALT, Snappers, Westside.

Athletics. NCAA, NCCAA. **Intercollegiate:** Baseball M, basketball, cross-country, golf, soccer, softball W, tennis, volleyball W. **Intramural:** Basketball, football (non-tackle), soccer, softball, tennis, volleyball. **Team name:** Cougars.

Student services. Adult student services, chaplain/spiritual director, career counseling, student employment services, financial aid counseling, health services, personal counseling, placement for graduates, veterans' counselor, women's services. **Physically disabled:** Services for visually, speech, hearing impaired.

Contact. E-mail: admission@ccu.edu
Phone: (303) 963-3200 Toll-free number: (800) 443-2484
Fax: (303) 963-3201
Derry Ebert, Dean of Enrollment, Colorado Christian University, 8787 West Alameda Avenue, Lakewood, CO 80226

Colorado College
Colorado Springs, Colorado
www.coloradocollege.edu
CB member
CB code: 4072

- Private 4-year liberal arts college
- Residential campus in large city
- 2,008 degree-seeking undergraduates: 54% women, 1% African American, 4% Asian American, 8% Hispanic American, 5% international
- 17 degree-seeking graduate students
- 26% of applicants admitted
- Application essay required
- 88% graduate within 6 years

General. Founded in 1874. Regionally accredited. Mountain cabin located about 35 minutes from campus for class and retreat use. Baca campus in Southern Colorado available for intensive study. **Degrees:** 540 bachelor's awarded; master's offered. **ROTC:** Army. **Location:** 70 miles from Denver. **Calendar:** Semester, extensive summer session. **Full-time faculty:** 171 total; 99% have terminal degrees, 15% minority, 42% women. **Part-time faculty:** 31 total. **Class size:** 65% < 20, 35% 20-39, less than 1% 40-49. **Special facilities:** Electronic music studio, telescope dome, multimedia computer lab, press, herbarium, environmental science van equipped for field research, petrographic microscopes, X-ray diffractometer, Fourier transform nuclear magnetic resonance spectrometer, sedimentology lab, metabolic equipment, hydrostatic weighing equipment, cadaver study in sports science, scanning electron microscope, transmission electron microscope.

Freshman class profile. 4,916 applied, 1,267 admitted, 490 enrolled.

Mid 50% test scores		Return as sophomores:	96%
SAT critical reading:	630-720	Out-of-state:	82%
SAT math:	630-700	Live on campus:	100%
SAT writing:	620-710	International:	6%
ACT composite:	29-32	Fraternities:	1%
Rank in top quarter:	89%	Sororities:	7%
Rank in top tenth:	70%		

Basis for selection. Personal essays, school achievement record most important. Counselor and teacher recommendations, extracurricular activities and test scores also important. Special talents, geographic, socioeconomic, ethnic diversity considered. Challenging curriculum, including honors, AP, IB, recommended when available. Institutional exams used for placement in foreign languages. SAT or ACT or 3 exams of student's choice required. Choice of exams must include one quantitative test, one verbal or writing test, and a third test of the student's choice; required exams selected from SAT and/or ACT subsections, Advanced Placement exams, SAT Subject Tests, and/or International Baccalaureate exams. Interview optional. **Home schooled:** Letter of recommendation (nonparent) required. Three letters of recommendation from outside the family required. Reading lists, curriculum information, teacher narratives about courses of study, and copies of papers or projects can be used in place of traditional transcript.

High school preparation. College-preparatory program recommended. 16 units required; 20 recommended. Required and recommended units include English 4.

2011-2012 Annual costs. Tuition/fees: $40,250. Room/board: $10,200. Books/supplies: $1,182. Personal expenses: $952.

Financial aid. **Non-need-based:** Scholarships awarded for academics, athletics.

Application procedures. **Admission:** Closing date 1/15 (postmark date). $50 fee, may be waived for applicants with need. Admission notification by 4/1. Must reply by May 1 or within 2 week(s) if notified thereafter. Campus

visit recommended. **Financial aid:** Closing date 2/15. FAFSA, CSS PROFILE required. Applicants notified by 3/15; must reply by 5/1.

Academics. Cooperative programs available with other schools in engineering, which require that students spend 3 years in residence pursuing a liberal arts foundation before transferring to cooperative university for 2 years of engineering. Students receive 2 bachelor degrees upon completion. **Special study options:** Combined bachelor's/graduate degree, double major, ESL, independent study, internships, liberal arts/career combination, semester at sea, student-designed major, study abroad, urban semester, Washington semester. Teacher licensure program, urban studies, urban arts and urban education (Chicago); science semester (Oak Ridge, Tennessee); tropical field research (Costa Rica); wilderness field station (Wisconsin); ACM London-Florence program; ACM program in Tanzania and Zimbabwe. **Credit/placement by examination:** AP, CLEP, IB, institutional tests. **Support services:** Learning center, pre-admission summer program, study skills assistance, tutoring, writing center.

Majors. **Area/ethnic studies:** Asian, Chicano/Hispanic-American/Latino, French, Italian, regional, Russian/Slavic, women's. **Biology:** General, biochemistry, neuroscience. **Computer sciences:** Computer science. **Conservation:** Environmental science. **English:** Creative writing, English lit. **Foreign languages:** Classics, comparative lit, French, German, Italian, Russian, Spanish. **History:** General. **Liberal arts:** Arts/sciences. **Math:** General. **Philosophy/religion:** Philosophy, religion. **Physical sciences:** Chemistry, geology, physics. **Psychology:** General. **Social sciences:** Anthropology, econometrics, economics, international economics, political science, sociology. **Visual/performing arts:** Art history/conservation, dance, dramatic, film/cinema/video, music, studio arts.

Most popular majors. Biology 15%, English 7%, natural resources/environmental science 7%, physical sciences 6%, social sciences 29%, visual/performing arts 9%.

Computing on campus. 400 workstations in dormitories, library, computer center, student center. Dormitories wired for high-speed internet access and linked to campus network. Commuter students can connect to campus network. Online course registration, helpline, wireless network available.

Student life. **Freshman orientation:** Mandatory. Preregistration for classes offered. One-week program held prior to beginning of fall classes; includes service trip. Parents welcome for first 3 days. **Policies:** Fish/crustaceans that live in water at all times are the only pets permitted in dorm rooms. Exceptions made for service animals. **Housing:** Guaranteed on-campus for all undergraduates. Coed dorms, single-sex dorms, apartments, fraternity/sorority housing, wellness housing available. $200 nonrefundable deposit, deadline 6/30. Pets allowed in dorm rooms. **Activities:** Bands, campus ministries, choral groups, dance, drama, film society, international student organizations, literary magazine, music ensembles, musical theater, radio station, student government, student newspaper, Asian American students union, black student union, Chaverim/Hillel, gay/lesbian/bisexual alliance, community kitchen, environmental action, chapel council, Chicano/Latino organization, victim's assistance team.

Athletics. NCAA. **Intercollegiate:** Basketball, cross-country, ice hockey M, lacrosse, soccer, swimming, tennis, track and field, volleyball W. **Intramural:** Basketball, football (non-tackle), ice hockey, racquetball, soccer, softball, volleyball, water polo. **Team name:** Tigers.

Student services. Alcohol/substance abuse counseling, chaplain/spiritual director, career counseling, financial aid counseling, health services, minority student services, on-campus daycare, personal counseling, women's services. **Physically disabled:** Services for visually, speech, hearing impaired.

Contact. E-mail: admission@coloradocollege.edu
Phone: (719) 389-6344 Toll-free number: (800) 542-7214
Fax: (719) 389-6816
Roberto Garcia, Director of Admission, Colorado College, 14 East Cache La Poudre Street, Colorado Springs, CO 80903-9854

Colorado Heights University
Denver, Colorado
www.chu.edu
CB code: 4878

- Private 4-year business and liberal arts college
- Residential campus in very large city
- 77 degree-seeking undergraduates
- Application essay required

General. Accredited by ACICS. Member of the Teikyo University Group of 50 campuses in Asia, Europe, and North America; all students complete part of their studies abroad. **Degrees:** 6 bachelor's awarded; master's offered. **Calendar:** Semester, limited summer session. **Full-time faculty:** 25 total. **Part-time faculty:** 8 total.

Basis for selection. 18 ACT/720 SAT and 2.5 GPA required. Provisional admission may be granted to students who do not meet requirements.

Application procedures. Admission: No deadline. $50 fee, may be waived for applicants with need, free for online applicants. Admission notification on a rolling basis. **Financial aid:** No deadline. FAFSA required.

Academics. Special study options: Combined bachelor's/graduate degree, double major, dual enrollment of high school students, ESL, independent study, internships, liberal arts/career combination, study abroad. **Credit/placement by examination:** AP, CLEP, IB.

Majors. Business: International.

Computing on campus. PC or laptop required. Dormitories wired for high-speed internet access and linked to campus network. Online library available.

Student life. Freshman orientation: Available. Preregistration for classes offered. **Policies:** Students under 21 required to live in dorms; exceptions may be made if living with a family member and for those who live on-campus for 1 year and then meet the waiver requirements to move off-campus. **Housing:** Guaranteed on-campus for all undergraduates. Coed dorms available. $230 nonrefundable deposit.

Athletics. Team name: Voyagers.

Student services. Career counseling, student employment services, financial aid counseling, placement for graduates.

Contact. E-mail: admissions@chu.edu
Phone: (303) 937-4280 Fax: (303) 937-4224
Jason Johnson, Assistant Director of Recruiting, Colorado Heights University, 3001 South Federal Boulevard, Denver, CO 80236

Colorado Mesa University
Grand Junction, Colorado
www.coloradomesa.edu   **CB code: 4484**

- Public 4-year community and liberal arts college
- Commuter campus in small city
- 8,221 degree-seeking undergraduates
- SAT or ACT (ACT writing optional) required

General. Founded in 1925. Regionally accredited. **Degrees:** 639 bachelor's, 170 associate awarded; master's offered. **Location:** 250 miles from Denver, 300 miles from Salt Lake City. **Calendar:** Semester, limited summer session. **Full-time faculty:** 245 total. **Part-time faculty:** 286 total. **Class size:** 49% < 20, 38% 20-39, 5% 40-49, 7% 50-99, 1% >100. **Special facilities:** Electron microscope laboratory, herbarium, computer-aided drafting laboratory, technical training facility, environmental restoration laboratory.

Freshman class profile.

GPA 3.75 or higher:	13%	Rank in top quarter:	22%
GPA 3.50-3.74:	11%	Rank in top tenth:	7%
GPA 3.0-3.49:	25%	Out-of-state:	13%
GPA 2.0-2.99:	44%	Live on campus:	51%

Basis for selection. Admission based on GPA, ACT/SAT, class rank and satisfaction of HEAR requirements. Open admissions to most technical, associates and certificate programs. Audition required of music, music theater, theater majors. Interview recommended for nursing, allied health, teacher certification majors. **Home schooled:** Statement describing home school structure and mission, transcript of courses and grades required.

High school preparation. College-preparatory program recommended. 17 units required. Required units include English 4, mathematics 4, social studies 3, science 3 (laboratory 2), foreign language 1 and academic electives 2.

2011-2012 Annual costs. Tuition/fees: $6,548; $16,726 out-of-state. Room/board: $8,657. Books/supplies: $1,748. Personal expenses: $2,858.

Financial aid. Non-need-based: Scholarships awarded for academics, art, athletics, leadership, music/drama.

Application procedures. Admission: No deadline. $30 fee, may be waived for applicants with need. Admission notification on a rolling basis beginning on or about 9/1. **Financial aid:** Priority date 3/1; no closing date. FAFSA required. Applicants notified on a rolling basis starting 4/1; must reply within 5 week(s) of notification.

Academics. Special study options: Accelerated study, combined bachelor's/graduate degree, distance learning, double major, dual enrollment of high school students, exchange student, honors, independent study, internships, study abroad, teacher certification program. Area vocational school provides training in technical skills. **Credit/placement by examination:** AP, CLEP, IB, SAT, ACT, institutional tests. 12 credit hours maximum toward associate degree, 20 toward bachelor's. **Support services:** Learning center, pre-admission summer program, reduced course load, remedial instruction, study skills assistance, tutoring, writing center.

Majors. Biology: General. **Business:** General, accounting, management information systems. **Communications:** Media studies. **Computer sciences:** General. **Conservation:** Environmental science. **English:** English lit. **Foreign languages:** Spanish. **Health services:** Athletic training, nursing (RN), radiologic technology/medical imaging. **History:** General. **Human services:** General. **Liberal arts:** Arts/sciences. **Math:** General. **Parks/recreation:** Exercise sciences, sports admin. **Physical sciences:** General. **Protective services:** Criminal justice. **Psychology:** General. **Social sciences:** General, political science, sociology. **Visual/performing arts:** Art, dramatic, graphic design, music.

Most popular majors. Biology 6%, business/marketing 22%, health sciences 12%, liberal arts 6%, parks/recreation 11%, psychology 7%, social sciences 6%, visual/performing arts 8%.

Computing on campus. 625 workstations in dormitories, library, computer center, student center. Dormitories wired for high-speed internet access and linked to campus network. Commuter students can connect to campus network. Online course registration, online library, helpline, student web hosting, wireless network available.

Student life. Freshman orientation: Available, $15 fee. Preregistration for classes offered. **Housing:** Coed dorms, single-sex dorms, special housing for disabled, apartments, wellness housing available. $150 partly refundable deposit. **Activities:** Bands, choral groups, dance, drama, film society, literary magazine, music ensembles, musical theater, radio station, student government, student newspaper, symphony orchestra, TV station, black student alliance, La Raza, Christian student fellowship, Native American student council, Polynesian club, cultral diversity board, dance society, drama society, sustainability council.

Athletics. NCAA. **Intercollegiate:** Baseball M, basketball, cross-country, football (tackle) M, golf, lacrosse, soccer, softball W, swimming, tennis, track and field, volleyball W, wrestling M. **Intramural:** Basketball, football (non-tackle), soccer, softball, volleyball. **Team name:** Mavericks.

Student services. Adult student services, alcohol/substance abuse counseling, chaplain/spiritual director, career counseling, services for economically disadvantaged, student employment services, financial aid counseling, health services, minority student services, on-campus daycare, personal counseling, veterans' counselor. **Physically disabled:** Services for visually, speech, hearing impaired.

Contact. E-mail: admissions@mesastate.edu
Phone: (970) 248-1875 Toll-free number: (800) 982-6372
Fax: (970) 248-1973
Jared Meier, Director of Admissions, Colorado Mesa University, 1100 North Avenue, Grand Junction, CO 81501

Colorado School of Mines
Golden, Colorado   **CB member**
www.mines.edu   **CB code: 4073**

- Public 4-year university and engineering college
- Residential campus in large town
- 3,876 degree-seeking undergraduates: 4% part-time, 26% women, 1% African American, 5% Asian American, 8% Hispanic American, 5% international
- 1,343 degree-seeking graduate students
- 45% of applicants admitted
- SAT or ACT (ACT writing recommended) required
- 72% graduate within 6 years; 24% enter graduate study

General. Founded in 1874. Regionally accredited. Curriculum and research program geared towards responsible stewardship of the earth and its resources; broad expertise in resource exploration, extraction, production and utilization. **Degrees:** 669 bachelor's awarded; master's, doctoral offered. **ROTC:** Army, Air Force. **Location:** 20 miles from Denver. **Calendar:** Semester, limited summer session. **Full-time faculty:** 238 total; 96% have terminal degrees, 18% minority, 21% women. **Part-time faculty:** 99 total; 31% have terminal degrees, 11% minority, 29% women. **Class size:** 36% < 20, 36% 20-39, 12% 40-49, 11% 50-99, 6% >100. **Special facilities:** Geology museum, geological

survey and earthquake center, experimental mine, graduate research laboratory, center for technology and learning media.

Freshman class profile. 10,145 applied, 4,520 admitted, 879 enrolled.

Mid 50% test scores		Rank in top quarter:	85%
SAT critical reading:	570-680	Rank in top tenth:	52%
SAT math:	630-710	Return as sophomores:	89%
SAT writing:	530-640	Out-of-state:	38%
ACT composite:	27-31	Live on campus:	94%
GPA 3.75 or higher:	61%	International:	4%
GPA 3.50-3.74:	25%	Fraternities:	17%
GPA 3.0-3.49:	14%	Sororities:	17%

Basis for selection. Applicants should rank in top third of class. Both test scores and academic record considered with heavier weight given to academic record. Rigor of coursework and strong and consistent results in all coursework important. Applicants encouraged to apply early in fall of senior year and take SAT/ACT by September or October of senior year. **Home schooled:** Transcript of courses and grades required. More weight given to SAT/ACT.

High school preparation. College-preparatory program required. 17 units required. Required units include English 4, mathematics 4, social studies 3, science 3 (laboratory 3), foreign language 1 and academic electives 2. Math units should include 2 algebra, 1 geometry, 1 advanced math (including trigonometry). Science units should include 1 chemistry and/or physics.

2011-2012 Annual costs. Tuition/fees: $14,454; $29,139 out-of-state. Room/board: $8,995. Books/supplies: $1,500. Personal expenses: $1,125.

2010-2011 Financial aid. Need-based: 722 full-time freshmen applied for aid; 435 were judged to have need; 435 of these received aid. Average need met was 66%. Average scholarship/grant was $4,965; average loan $3,393. 44% of total undergraduate aid awarded as scholarships/grants, 56% as loans/jobs. **Non-need-based:** Awarded to 2,059 full-time undergraduates, including 656 freshmen. Scholarships awarded for academics, athletics, music/drama.

Application procedures. Admission: Priority date 4/1; deadline 5/1 (receipt date). $45 fee, may be waived for applicants with need, free for online applicants. Admission notification on a rolling basis beginning on or about 10/1. Must reply by May 1 or within 2 week(s) if notified thereafter. **Financial aid:** Priority date 2/14; no closing date. FAFSA required. Applicants notified on a rolling basis starting 3/1.

Academics. Special study options: Accelerated study, combined bachelor's/graduate degree, cooperative education, double major, dual enrollment of high school students, exchange student, honors, independent study, internships, study abroad. **Credit/placement by examination:** AP, CLEP, IB, institutional tests. **Support services:** Pre-admission summer program, reduced course load, study skills assistance, tutoring, writing center.

Majors. Computer sciences: Computer science. **Engineering:** General, applied physics, biochemical, chemical, civil, electrical, environmental, geological, mechanical, metallurgical, mining, petroleum. **Math:** Applied, probability, statistics. **Physical sciences:** Chemistry, geology, geophysics, physics. **Social sciences:** Economics.

Most popular majors. Engineering/engineering technologies 89%, mathematics 7%.

Computing on campus. 450 workstations in dormitories, library, computer center, student center. Dormitories wired for high-speed internet access and linked to campus network. Commuter students can connect to campus network. Online course registration, online library, helpline, repair service, student web hosting, wireless network available.

Student life. Freshman orientation: Mandatory, $122 fee. Preregistration for classes offered. Held weekend prior to start of fall semester; optional parent/student orientation offered on 4 separate days in summer. **Policies:** First-year students required to live-on campus for first two semesters. **Housing:** Guaranteed on-campus for freshmen. Coed dorms, apartments, fraternity/sorority housing available. $150 partly refundable deposit, deadline 5/1. **Activities:** Bands, campus ministries, choral groups, dance, drama, international student organizations, literary magazine, music ensembles, musical theater, radio station, student government, student newspaper, symphony orchestra, Society of Women Engineers, American Indian Science and Engineering Society, Professional Asian Society of Engineers and Scientists, National Society of Black Engineers, Society of Hispanic Professional Engineers, Blue Key, Alpha Phi Omega, Circle K International, Engineers Without Borders.

Athletics. NCAA. **Intercollegiate:** Baseball M, basketball, cross-country, diving, football (tackle) M, golf M, soccer, softball W, swimming, track and field, volleyball W, wrestling M. **Intramural:** Badminton, basketball, bowling, cross-country, diving, equestrian, field hockey, football (non-tackle),

golf, handball, lacrosse, racquetball, rugby M, skiing, soccer, softball, swimming, table tennis, tennis, track and field, volleyball, water polo, wrestling M. **Team name:** Orediggers.

Student services. Alcohol/substance abuse counseling, career counseling, student employment services, financial aid counseling, health services, minority student services, personal counseling, placement for graduates, veterans' counselor, women's services. **Physically disabled:** Services for visually, hearing impaired.

Contact. E-mail: admit@mines.edu
Phone: (303) 273-3220 Toll-free number: (888) 446-9489
Fax: (303) 273-3509
Bruce Goetz, Director of Admissions, Colorado School of Mines, Undergraduate Admissions, Golden, CO 80401-6114

Colorado State University
Fort Collins, Colorado
www.colostate.edu

CB member
CB code: 4075

- Public 4-year university
- Residential campus in small city
- 22,300 degree-seeking undergraduates: 7% part-time, 51% women, 2% African American, 2% Asian American, 8% Hispanic American, 2% international
- 4,435 degree-seeking graduate students
- 76% of applicants admitted
- SAT or ACT (ACT writing optional), application essay required
- 64% graduate within 6 years

General. Founded in 1870. Regionally accredited. Land grant university. **Degrees:** 4,436 bachelor's awarded; master's, professional, doctoral offered. **ROTC:** Army, Air Force. **Location:** 60 miles from Denver. **Calendar:** Semester, extensive summer session. **Full-time faculty:** 924 total; 100% have terminal degrees, 17% minority, 34% women. **Part-time faculty:** 37 total; 100% have terminal degrees, 5% minority, 11% women. **Class size:** 37% < 20, 38% 20-39, 7% 40-49, 10% 50-99, 7% >100. **Special facilities:** Concert hall, thrust theater, music hall, art museum, engineering research center, equine center, veterinary teaching hospital, environmental learning center, plant environmental research center, behavioral science building.

Freshman class profile. 16,559 applied, 12,564 admitted, 4,504 enrolled.

Mid 50% test scores		Rank in top tenth:	22%
SAT critical reading:	510-620	End year in good standing:	83%
SAT math:	520-630	Return as sophomores:	84%
ACT composite:	22-27	Out-of-state:	22%
GPA 3.75 or higher:	37%	Live on campus:	96%
GPA 3.50-3.74:	24%	International:	1%
GPA 3.0-3.49:	34%	Fraternities:	5%
GPA 2.0-2.99:	5%	Sororities:	8%
Rank in top quarter:	53%		

Basis for selection. Priority consideration given to applicants with 3.25 GPA and successful completion of 18 recommended high school units. Applicants with GPA below 3.25 and/or fewer than the 18 recommended high school units encouraged to apply since many factors are considered in the holistic review process. Letter of recommendation required, preferably from teacher or school counselor.

High school preparation. College-preparatory program required. 15 units required; 18 recommended. Required and recommended units include English 4, mathematics 4, social studies 2, history 1, science 3 (laboratory 2), foreign language 1-2 and academic electives 2. Individual programs may have additional requirements.

2011-2012 Annual costs. Tuition/fees: $8,042; $23,742 out-of-state. Room/board: $9,172. Books/supplies: $1,126. Personal expenses: $2,232.

2010-2011 Financial aid. Need-based: 3,539 full-time freshmen applied for aid; 2,214 were judged to have need; 2,214 of these received aid. Average need met was 73%. Average scholarship/grant was $10,114; average loan $5,156. 45% of total undergraduate aid awarded as scholarships/grants, 55% as loans/jobs. **Non-need-based:** Awarded to 2,210 full-time undergraduates, including 563 freshmen. Scholarships awarded for academics, art, athletics, leadership, music/drama, state residency. **Additional information:** Land Grant Award guarantees that all full-time Colorado residents who are Pell eligible will be funded with grant aid at a minimum of tuition and general fees.

Application procedures. Admission: Closing date 2/1 (receipt date). $50 fee, may be waived for applicants with need. Admission notification on a rolling basis beginning on or about 10/1. Must reply by May 1 or within 2 week(s) if notified thereafter. Early application (once 6th semester transcript

is available) encouraged. **Financial aid:** Priority date 3/1; no closing date. FAFSA required. Applicants notified on a rolling basis starting 3/1.

Academics. **Special study options:** Accelerated study, combined bachelor's/graduate degree, cooperative education, distance learning, double major, dual enrollment of high school students, ESL, honors, independent study, internships, liberal arts/career combination, semester at sea, study abroad, teacher certification program. **Credit/placement by examination:** AP, CLEP, IB, SAT, ACT, institutional tests. **Support services:** Learning center, study skills assistance, tutoring, writing center.

Majors. **Architecture:** Landscape. **Area/ethnic studies:** General. **Biology:** General, biochemistry, biomedical sciences, microbiology, wildlife, zoology. **Business:** Accounting, business admin, construction management, finance, management information systems, marketing, real estate, restaurant/food services. **Communications:** Communications/speech/rhetoric, journalism, public relations, radio/TV. **Computer sciences:** General, information systems, information technology. **Conservation:** General, forest sciences, management/policy, water/wetlands/marine. **Education:** General, agricultural, art, biology, business, chemistry, early childhood, English, family/consumer sciences, French, German, mathematics, music, physics, sales/marketing, science, social studies, Spanish, speech, technology/industrial arts, trade/industrial. **Engineering:** Applied physics, chemical, civil, computer, electrical, engineering science, environmental, mechanical. **English:** Creative writing, English lit. **Foreign languages:** General, French, German, Spanish. **General:** Agribusiness operations, agronomy, animal sciences, economics, education services, equestrian studies, horticultural science, horticulture, landscaping, nursery operations, range science, soil science. **Health services:** Athletic training, environmental health, music therapy. **History:** General. **Human services:** Social work. **Liberal arts:** Arts/sciences. **Math:** General. **Parks/recreation:** Exercise sciences, facilities management. **Philosophy/religion:** Philosophy. **Physical sciences:** Chemistry, geology, physics. **Protective services:** Fire services admin. **Psychology:** General. **Social sciences:** Anthropology, economics, political science, sociology. **Visual/performing arts:** Art, art history/conservation, conducting, dance, dramatic, graphic design, interior design, music, music performance, music theory/composition, studio arts. **Work/family studies:** General, apparel marketing, family studies, food/nutrition, human nutrition.

Most popular majors. Biology 8%, business/marketing 15%, communications/journalism 8%, engineering/engineering technologies 10%, family/consumer sciences 10%, parks/recreation 7%, social sciences 8%.

Computing on campus. 2,500 workstations in dormitories, library, computer center, student center. Dormitories wired for high-speed internet access and linked to campus network. Commuter students can connect to campus network. Online course registration, online library, helpline, repair service, student web hosting, wireless network available.

Student life. **Freshman orientation:** Available. Preregistration for classes offered. 19 sessions offered from mid-June to mid-July for freshmen, family members, and guests. Lodging provided for student. **Housing:** Guaranteed on-campus for freshmen. Coed dorms, special housing for disabled, apartments, wellness housing available. $150 partly refundable deposit. Special interest floors, residential learning communities (curricular, academic, themed). **Activities:** Bands, campus ministries, choral groups, dance, drama, international student organizations, literary magazine, music ensembles, musical theater, opera, radio station, student government, student newspaper, symphony orchestra, TV station, Asian/American student services, black student services, El Centro student services, GLBT student services, Native American student services, Campus Crusade for Christ, Chabad Jewish student alliance, Habitat for Humanity, College Republicans, Young Democrats.

Athletics. NCAA. **Intercollegiate:** Basketball, cross-country, diving W, football (tackle) M, golf, softball W, swimming W, tennis W, track and field, volleyball W, water polo W. **Intramural:** Basketball, bowling, football (nontackle), golf, racquetball, soccer, softball, tennis M, volleyball. **Team name:** Rams.

Student services. Adult student services, alcohol/substance abuse counseling, chaplain/spiritual director, career counseling, services for economically disadvantaged, student employment services, financial aid counseling, health services, legal services, minority student services, on-campus daycare, personal counseling, placement for graduates, veterans' counselor, women's services. **Physically disabled:** Services for visually, speech, hearing impaired.

Contact. E-mail: admissions@colostate.edu
Phone: (970) 491-6909 Fax: (970) 491-7799
James Rawlins, Executive Director of Admissions, Colorado State University, Office of Admissions/Colorado State University, Fort Collins, CO 80523-1062

Colorado State University: Pueblo
Pueblo, Colorado
www.colostate-pueblo.edu   **CB code: 4611**

◗ Public 4-year university
◗ Commuter campus in small city
◗ 4,977 degree-seeking undergraduates
◗ SAT or ACT (ACT writing optional) required

General. Founded in 1933. Regionally accredited. **Degrees:** 714 bachelor's awarded; master's offered. **ROTC:** Army. **Location:** 42 miles from Colorado Springs, 100 miles from Denver. **Calendar:** Semester, extensive summer session. **Full-time faculty:** 186 total. **Part-time faculty:** 188 total. **Class size:** 42% < 20, 44% 20-39, 6% 40-49, 6% 50-99, 2% >100. **Special facilities:** 3 electron microscopes, golf course, river trail system, automotive service, ropes course, music amphitheater, 1+ megawatt solar system, 6 kilowatt solar system.

Freshman class profile.

GPA 3.75 or higher:	15%	**Rank in top tenth:**	2%
GPA 3.50-3.74:	12%	**Out-of-state:**	8%
GPA 3.0-3.49:	25%	**Live on campus:**	54%
GPA 2.0-2.99:	48%	**Fraternities:**	1%
Rank in top quarter:	7%	**Sororities:**	1%

Basis for selection. High school achievement record and test scores most important. Auditions for music, portfolios for art required for scholarships.

High school preparation. College-preparatory program required. 17 units required. Required units include English 4, mathematics 4, social studies 2, history 1, science 3 (laboratory 2), foreign language 1 and academic electives 2.

2011-2012 Annual costs. Tuition/fees: $6,269; $16,969 out-of-state. Room/board: $8,970. Books/supplies: $1,200. Personal expenses: $2,079.

Financial aid. **Non-need-based:** Scholarships awarded for academics, alumni affiliation, art, athletics, job skills, leadership, minority status, music/drama, ROTC, state residency. **Additional information:** Resident undergraduates with a family adjusted gross income of $50,000 or less and who receive a Pell grant will have tuition or mandatory fess covered by grant and institutional aid.

Application procedures. **Admission:** Closing date 8/1 (receipt date). $25 fee, may be waived for applicants with need. Admission notification on a rolling basis beginning on or about 9/15. **Financial aid:** Closing date 3/1. FAFSA, institutional form required. Applicants notified on a rolling basis starting 3/13; must reply within 3 week(s) of notification.

Academics. Tutoring center provides face-to-face tutoring for all general education courses and skill-building math courses. **Special study options:** Accelerated study, combined bachelor's/graduate degree, cooperative education, cross-registration, distance learning, double major, dual enrollment of high school students, ESL, exchange student, external degree, honors, independent study, internships, semester at sea, study abroad, teacher certification program, weekend college. **Credit/placement by examination:** AP, CLEP, IB, SAT, ACT, institutional tests. 30 credit hours maximum toward bachelor's degree. **Support services:** Learning center, reduced course load, remedial instruction, study skills assistance, tutoring, writing center.

Majors. **Biology:** General. **Business:** Accounting, managerial economics. **Communications:** Media studies. **Computer sciences:** Information systems. **Engineering:** General, industrial. **English:** English lit. **Foreign languages:** General. **Health services:** Nursing (RN). **History:** General. **Human services:** Social work. **Liberal arts:** Arts/sciences. **Math:** General. **Parks/recreation:** Exercise sciences. **Physical sciences:** Chemistry, physics. **Psychology:** General. **Social sciences:** Political science, sociology. **Visual/performing arts:** Music, studio arts.

Most popular majors. Biology 6%, business/marketing 18%, communications/journalism 6%, health sciences 10%, liberal arts 8%, social sciences 18%.

Computing on campus. 702 workstations in dormitories, library, computer center, student center. Dormitories wired for high-speed internet access and linked to campus network. Commuter students can connect to campus network. Online library, helpline, student web hosting, wireless network available.

Student life. **Freshman orientation:** Available. Preregistration for classes offered. Three-day program in August before classes begin. New students placed in small groups led by upperclass peer. **Housing:** Guaranteed on-campus for all undergraduates. Coed dorms, special housing for disabled,

apartments, wellness housing available. $250 partly refundable deposit, deadline 7/1. **Activities:** Bands, campus ministries, choral groups, dance, international student organizations, literary magazine, music ensembles, radio station, student government, student newspaper, symphony orchestra, TV station, Amnesty International, Benefiting the Education of Latinas in Leadership/Academics/Sisterhood, Black student organization, Bold And Beautiful Educated Sisters, Campus Crusade for Christ, Christian Challenge, Fellowship of Christian Athletes, Movimiento Estudiantil Chicano de Aztln, PRIZM.

Athletics. NCAA. **Intercollegiate:** Baseball M, basketball, cross-country W, football (tackle) M, golf, soccer, softball W, tennis, track and field W, volleyball W, wrestling M. **Intramural:** Badminton, basketball, football (non-tackle), golf, soccer, softball, squash, table tennis, volleyball. **Team name:** Thunderwolves.

Student services. Alcohol/substance abuse counseling, chaplain/spiritual director, career counseling, services for economically disadvantaged, student employment services, financial aid counseling, health services, minority student services, on-campus daycare, personal counseling, placement for graduates, veterans' counselor. **Physically disabled:** Services for visually, speech, hearing impaired.

Contact. E-mail: info@colostate-pueblo.edu
Phone: (719) 549-2461 Fax: (719) 549-2419
Dana Trujillo, Director of Admissions, Colorado State University: Pueblo, 2200 Bonforte Boulevard, Pueblo, CO 81001-4901

Colorado Technical University
Colorado Springs, Colorado
www.coloradotech.edu   CB code: 4133

▶ For-profit 4-year university and technical college
▶ Commuter campus in large city
▶ 989 full-time, degree-seeking undergraduates
▶ Interview required

General. Founded in 1965. Regionally accredited. **Degrees:** 170 bachelor's, 113 associate awarded; master's, doctoral offered. **ROTC:** Army. **Location:** 63 miles from Denver. **Calendar:** Quarter, extensive summer session. **Full-time faculty:** 24 total. **Part-time faculty:** 318 total. **Class size:** 69% < 20, 31% 20-39. **Special facilities:** Extensive laboratories and computer facilities.

Basis for selection. Open admission, but selective for some programs. Certain programs require successful performance on one or more entrance assessments.

2011-2012 Annual costs. Tuition/fees: $10,700. Books/supplies: $1,300. Personal expenses: $1,215.

Financial aid. Non-need-based: Scholarships awarded for academics, ROTC.

Application procedures. Admission: No deadline. $50 fee. Admission notification on a rolling basis. **Financial aid:** No deadline. FAFSA required. Applicants notified on a rolling basis starting 6/30.

Academics. Special study options: Accelerated study, cooperative education, distance learning, double major, internships, weekend college. **Credit/placement by examination:** AP, CLEP, institutional tests. 30 credit hours maximum toward associate degree, 60 toward bachelor's. Course challenge test offered. Credit for life experience based on evaluation by faculty. **Support services:** Learning center, reduced course load, remedial instruction, tutoring.

Majors. Business: Business admin, e-commerce, human resources, information resources management, logistics, management information systems. **Computer sciences:** General, computer science, information systems, information technology, system admin, systems analysis. **Engineering:** Computer, electrical, software.

Most popular majors. Business/marketing 34%, computer/information sciences 32%, engineering/engineering technologies 34%.

Computing on campus. 154 workstations in library, computer center. Commuter students can connect to campus network. Online library, helpline, wireless network available.

Student life. Freshman orientation: Mandatory. Preregistration for classes offered. **Policies:** Students must comply with university's standards of conduct. **Housing:** Apartments available. **Activities:** Student government.

Student services. Career counseling, student employment services, financial aid counseling, personal counseling, placement for graduates, veterans' counselor.

Contact. E-mail: cosadmissions@coloradotech.edu
Phone: (719) 598-0200 Toll-free number: (800) 599-9287
Fax: (719) 598-3740
Beth Braaten, Vice President of Admissions, Colorado Technical University, 4435 North Chestnut Street, Colorado Springs, CO 80907

Denver School of Nursing
Denver, Colorado
www.denverschoolofnursing.edu

▶ For-profit 4-year nursing college
▶ Very large city
▶ 545 degree-seeking undergraduates

General. Regionally accredited. **Degrees:** 176 bachelor's, 84 associate awarded. **Calendar:** Quarter. **Full-time faculty:** 18 total. **Part-time faculty:** 54 total.

Basis for selection. Admissions based on number of factors including personal statement, previous health care and or volunteer experience and cumulative/science GPA. BSN applicants who appear best qualified for the program will receive invitation for application interview. SAT or ACT recommended.

Financial aid. All financial aid based on need.

Application procedures. Admission: Closing date 4/1. $50 fee. Admission notification on a rolling basis. **Financial aid:** No deadline. FAFSA required.

Academics. Credit/placement by examination: AP, CLEP.

Majors. Health services: Nursing (RN).

Computing on campus. 46 workstations in library, computer center. Online library, wireless network available.

Contact. E-mail: j.johnson@denverschoolofnursing.edu
Phone: (303) 292-0015
Jeff Johnson, Director of Admissions, Denver School of Nursing, 1401 19th Street, Denver, CO 80202

DeVry University: Westminster
Westminster, Colorado
www.devry.edu   CB code: 1327

▶ For-profit 4-year university
▶ Commuter campus in very large city
▶ 812 degree-seeking undergraduates
▶ Interview required

General. Founded in 1945. Regionally accredited. Additional locations: Colorado Springs, Denver South, Sandy (UT). **Degrees:** 118 bachelor's, 23 associate awarded; master's offered. **Calendar:** Semester, extensive summer session. **Full-time faculty:** 13 total. **Part-time faculty:** 74 total.

Basis for selection. Applicants must have high school diploma or equivalent or a degree from an accredited postsecondary institution, demonstrate proficiency in basic college-level skills through SAT or ACT scores or institutional-administered placement exams, and be at least 17 years of age.

High school preparation. College-preparatory program recommended. Math unit must be algebra or higher.

2011-2012 Annual costs. Tuition/fees: $15,294. Books/supplies: $1,310. Personal expenses: $3,574.

Financial aid. All financial aid based on need.

Application procedures. Admission: No deadline. $50 fee. Admission notification on a rolling basis. **Financial aid:** No deadline. FAFSA required. Applicants notified on a rolling basis.

Academics. Special study options: Accelerated study, distance learning. **Credit/placement by examination:** AP, CLEP, institutional tests. **Support services:** Learning center, tutoring.

Majors. Business: Business admin. **Computer sciences:** Networking, systems analysis, web page design. **Engineering:** Software.

Most popular majors. Business/marketing 61%, computer/information sciences 23%, engineering/engineering technologies 16%.

Computing on campus. 308 workstations in library, computer center. Online course registration, online library, helpline available.

Student life. Freshman orientation: Mandatory. Preregistration for classes offered.

Athletics. Intramural: Basketball, volleyball.

Student services. Career counseling, student employment services, financial aid counseling, placement for graduates, veterans' counselor.

Contact. E-mail: denver-admissions@den.devry.edu
Phone: (303) 280-7600 Toll-free number: (888) 212-1857
Fax: (303) 280-7606
Rick Rodman, Director of Admissions, DeVry University: Westminster, 1870 West 122 Avenue, Westminster, CO 80234-2010

Fort Lewis College
Durango, Colorado **CB member**
www.fortlewis.edu **CB code: 4310**

◗ Public 4-year liberal arts college
◗ Residential campus in large town
◗ 3,748 degree-seeking undergraduates: 8% part-time, 48% women, 1% African American, 8% Hispanic American, 21% Native American, 1% international
◗ 71% of applicants admitted
◗ SAT or ACT (ACT writing optional) required
◗ 38% graduate within 6 years; 20% enter graduate study

General. Regionally accredited. **Degrees:** 635 bachelor's awarded. **Location:** 220 miles from Albuquerque, NM; 342 miles from Denver. **Calendar:** Semester, extensive summer session. **Full-time faculty:** 166 total; 89% have terminal degrees, 11% minority, 48% women. **Part-time faculty:** 63 total; 49% have terminal degrees, 5% minority, 52% women. **Class size:** 49% < 20, 44% 20-39, 5% 40-49, 2% 50-99, less than 1% >100. **Special facilities:** Southwest studies center, nuclear magnetic resonance spectrometer, archaeological dig site, community concert hall, separations and spectroscopy lab, mass spectrometer facilities, tissue culture facility, atomic force microscope.

Freshman class profile. 2,792 applied, 1,974 admitted, 777 enrolled.

Mid 50% test scores			
SAT critical reading:	460-570	GPA 2.0-2.99:	37%
SAT math:	460-560	Rank in top quarter:	28%
SAT writing:	430-550	Rank in top tenth:	11%
ACT composite:	20-25	End year in good standing:	77%
GPA 3.75 or higher:	12%	Out-of-state:	36%
GPA 3.50-3.74:	18%	Live on campus:	90%
GPA 3.0-3.49:	33%	International:	1%

Basis for selection. Colorado Commission on Higher Education index score comprised of high school GPA and test scores utilized as part of admission criteria. Essay recommended. **Home schooled:** Official copy of high school completion records; 1010 SAT (exclusive of Writing), 22 ACT.

High school preparation. College-preparatory program required. 17 units required. Required units include English 4, mathematics 4, social studies 2, history 1, science 3 (laboratory 2), foreign language 1 and academic electives 2.

2012-2013 Annual costs. Tuition/fees: $6,462; $17,734 out-of-state. Room/board: $8,310. Books/supplies: $1,680. Personal expenses: $2,296.

2010-2011 Financial aid. Need-based: 699 full-time freshmen applied for aid; 682 were judged to have need; 675 of these received aid. Average need met was 67%. Average scholarship/grant was $3,884; average loan $3,620. 52% of total undergraduate aid awarded as scholarships/grants, 48% as loans/jobs. **Non-need-based:** Awarded to 2,068 full-time undergraduates, including 814 freshmen. Scholarships awarded for academics, alumni affiliation, art, athletics, leadership, minority status, music/drama, state residency. **Additional information:** Tuition waived for Native Americans of federally recognized tribes; census number and Certificate of Indian Blood must accompany application.

Application procedures. Admission: Closing date 8/1 (postmark date). $40 fee, may be waived for applicants with need. Admission notification on a rolling basis beginning on or about 10/15. **Financial aid:** Priority date 2/15; no closing date. FAFSA required. Applicants notified on a rolling basis starting 3/15; must reply within 2 week(s) of notification.

Academics. Special study options: Accelerated study, combined bachelor's/graduate degree, cooperative education, distance learning, double major, dual enrollment of high school students, ESL, exchange student, honors, independent study, internships, liberal arts/career combination, semester at sea, student-designed major, study abroad, teacher certification program. **Credit/placement by examination:** AP, CLEP, IB, SAT, ACT, institutional tests. 24 credit hours maximum toward bachelor's degree. Up to 24 credits may be granted based on CLEP general exam scores. IB diploma holders will receive a minimum of 24 semester credits. **Support services:** Learning center, remedial instruction, study skills assistance, tutoring, writing center.

Majors. Area/ethnic studies: Chicano/Hispanic-American/Latino, Native American, women's. **Biology:** General, ecology. **Business:** General, accounting, business admin, marketing, operations. **Computer sciences:** General. **Conservation:** Environmental studies. **Education:** Multicultural. **Engineering:** General, applied physics. **English:** English lit. **Foreign languages:** Spanish. **General:** Business, economics. **Health services:** Athletic training. **History:** General. **Liberal arts:** Arts/sciences, humanities. **Math:** General. **Parks/recreation:** General, exercise sciences. **Philosophy/religion:** Philosophy. **Physical sciences:** Chemistry, geology, physics. **Psychology:** General, counseling, industrial. **Social sciences:** Anthropology, economics, political science, sociology. **Visual/performing arts:** Dramatic, music, studio arts.

Most popular majors. Biology 7%, business/marketing 27%, English 6%, liberal arts 7%, parks/recreation 7%, physical sciences 6%, psychology 10%, social sciences 10%, visual/performing arts 7%.

Computing on campus. 769 workstations in dormitories, library, computer center, student center. Dormitories wired for high-speed internet access and linked to campus network. Commuter students can connect to campus network. Online course registration, online library, helpline, repair service, student web hosting, wireless network available.

Student life. Freshman orientation: Mandatory, $50 fee. Preregistration for classes offered. **Housing:** Guaranteed on-campus for all undergraduates. Coed dorms, special housing for disabled, apartments available. $100 partly refundable deposit, deadline 7/15. **Activities:** Bands, campus ministries, choral groups, drama, literary magazine, musical theater, radio station, student government, student newspaper, Newman Club, Circle-K, business club, American Indian business leaders, American Indian science and engineering society, sociology club, Native American club, Habitat for Humanity.

Athletics. NCAA. Intercollegiate: Basketball, cross-country, football (tackle) M, golf M, soccer, softball W, volleyball W. **Intramural:** Badminton, basketball, football (tackle), racquetball, soccer, softball, volleyball. **Team name:** Skyhawks.

Student services. Adult student services, alcohol/substance abuse counseling, chaplain/spiritual director, career counseling, services for economically disadvantaged, student employment services, financial aid counseling, health services, legal services, minority student services, on-campus daycare, personal counseling, placement for graduates, veterans' counselor, women's services. **Physically disabled:** Services for visually, speech, hearing impaired.

Contact. E-mail: admission@fortlewis.edu
Phone: (970) 247-7184 Fax: (970) 247-7179
Andrew Burns, Director of Admission, Fort Lewis College, 1000 Rim Drive, Durango, CO 81301-3999

ITT Technical Institute: Westminster
Westminster, Colorado
www.itt-tech.edu **CB code: 3605**

◗ For-profit 4-year technical college
◗ Commuter campus in large city
◗ 568 undergraduates
◗ Interview required

General. Founded in 1984. Accredited by ACICS. **Degrees:** 41 bachelor's, 141 associate awarded. **Calendar:** Quarter, extensive summer session. **Full-time faculty:** 11 total. **Part-time faculty:** 55 total.

Basis for selection. Satisfactory scores from on-site tests in English and math required.

2011-2012 Annual costs. Estimated costs as of June 2011: per-credit-hour charge, $493, depending upon level and course of study; academic fee, $200. Certain programs of study require purchase of tools, which could cost an additional $100 to $500. All costs are subject to change.

Application procedures. Admission: No deadline. No application fee. Admission notification on a rolling basis. **Financial aid:** No deadline. FAFSA, institutional form required. Applicants notified on a rolling basis.

Academics. **Credit/placement by examination:** AP, CLEP. **Support services:** Learning center, tutoring.

Majors. **Business:** Business admin, construction management. **Computer sciences:** Programming, security. **Protective services:** Law enforcement admin.

Computing on campus. Online library available.

Student life. **Freshman orientation:** Available. Preregistration for classes offered.

Student services. Career counseling, student employment services, placement for graduates.

Contact. Phone: (303) 288-4488 Toll-free number: (800) 395-4488 Niki Donahue, Director of Recruitment, ITT Technical Institute: Westminster, 500 East 84th Avenue, Thornton, CO 80229-5338

Johnson & Wales University: Denver
Denver, Colorado
www.jwu.edu   CB code: 3567

- Private 4-year university
- Residential campus in large city
- 1,672 degree-seeking undergraduates: 8% part-time, 59% women, 5% African American, 3% Asian American, 11% Hispanic American, 1% Native American, 1% international
- 70% of applicants admitted
- 48% graduate within 6 years

General. Regionally accredited. **Degrees:** 231 bachelor's, 265 associate awarded. **Calendar:** Quarter, limited summer session. **Full-time faculty:** 54 total; 37% women. **Part-time faculty:** 45 total; 49% women. **Class size:** 53% < 20, 42% 20-39, 5% 40-49. **Special facilities:** Community leadership institute.

Freshman class profile. 2,520 applied, 1,754 admitted, 420 enrolled.

GPA 3.75 or higher:	14%	Out-of-state:	66%
GPA 3.50-3.74:	13%	Live on campus:	79%
GPA 3.0-3.49:	35%	International:	1%
GPA 2.0-2.99:	37%		

Basis for selection. Academic record important, including secondary school curriculum, GPA, class rank, test scores. Student motivation and interest given strong consideration. SAT or ACT required for students entering honors program only. **Home schooled:** Transcript of courses and grades, state high school equivalency certificate required. SAT or ACT required.

High school preparation. College-preparatory program recommended. Required units include English 4, mathematics 3, social studies 2 and science 3.

2011-2012 Annual costs. Tuition/fees: $25,107. Room/board: $9,261. Books/supplies: $1,800. Personal expenses: $1,065.

Financial aid. **Non-need-based:** Scholarships awarded for academics, alumni affiliation, job skills, leadership, state residency.

Application procedures. **Admission:** No deadline. No application fee. Admission notification on a rolling basis beginning on or about 11/1. Must reply by May 1 or within 2 week(s) if notified thereafter. **Financial aid:** No deadline. FAFSA required. Applicants notified on a rolling basis starting 3/1; must reply within 2 week(s) of notification.

Academics. **Special study options:** Accelerated study, cooperative education, dual enrollment of high school students, ESL, exchange student, honors, independent study, internships, study abroad. **Credit/placement by examination:** AP, CLEP, institutional tests. **Support services:** Learning center, remedial instruction, study skills assistance, tutoring, writing center.

Majors. **Business:** Business admin, entrepreneurial studies, fashion, hospitality admin, hotel/motel admin, international, marketing. **Parks/recreation:** Facilities management, sports admin. **Protective services:** Law enforcement admin. **Work/family studies:** Food/nutrition.

Most popular majors. Business/marketing 34%, family/consumer sciences 52%, parks/recreation 12%.

Computing on campus. Dormitories wired for high-speed internet access and linked to campus network. Commuter students can connect to campus network. Online course registration, online library, helpline, repair service, wireless network available.

Student life. **Freshman orientation:** Mandatory, $250 fee. Preregistration for classes offered. **Housing:** Coed dorms, apartments, wellness housing available. $200 deposit. **Activities:** Campus ministries, dance, international student organizations, student government, student newspaper.

Athletics. NAIA. **Intercollegiate:** Basketball, cross-country, volleyball. **Intramural:** Basketball, football (non-tackle), softball, volleyball. **Team name:** Wildcats.

Student services. Adult student services, alcohol/substance abuse counseling, career counseling, student employment services, financial aid counseling, health services, minority student services, personal counseling, placement for graduates. **Physically disabled:** Services for visually, speech, hearing impaired.

Contact. E-mail: den@admissions.jwu.edu
Phone: (303) 256-9300 Toll-free number: (877) 598-3368
Kim Ostrowski, Director of Admissions, Johnson & Wales University: Denver, 7150 Montview Boulevard, Denver, CO 80220

Jones International University
Centennial, Colorado
www.jiu.edu   CB code: 2785

- For-profit 4-year virtual college
- Large city

General. Regionally accredited. **Location:** 20 miles from Denver. **Calendar:** Differs by program.

Annual costs/financial aid. Tuition is $1,560 per course for bachelor's degrees. Books are approximately $170 per course. Books/supplies: $1,360. Need-based financial aid available to full-time and part-time students.

Contact. Phone: (303) 784-8904
Registrar, 9697 East Mineral Avenue, Centennial, CO 80112

Metropolitan State College of Denver
Denver, Colorado   CB member
www.mscd.edu   CB code: 4505

- Public 4-year liberal arts college
- Commuter campus in very large city
- 22,751 degree-seeking undergraduates: 39% part-time, 53% women, 6% African American, 3% Asian American, 18% Hispanic American, 1% Native American, 1% international
- 251 degree-seeking graduate students
- 63% of applicants admitted
- SAT or ACT (ACT writing optional) required

General. Founded in 1963. Regionally accredited. Library, student center, physical education facilities, child care center shared with Community College of Denver and University of Colorado at Denver. Degree completion programs offered at off-campus sites in North Glen and Englewood. **Degrees:** 2,899 bachelor's awarded; master's offered. **ROTC:** Army, Air Force. **Location:** Downtown. **Calendar:** Semester, extensive summer session. **Full-time faculty:** 527 total; 23% minority, 48% women. **Part-time faculty:** 887 total; 15% minority, 52% women. **Class size:** 33% < 20, 60% 20-39, 6% 40-49, 2% 50-99. **Special facilities:** Art galleries, CAD/CAM laboratory, world indoor airport.

Freshman class profile. 5,942 applied, 3,744 admitted, 2,016 enrolled.

Mid 50% test scores			
SAT critical reading:	450-560	GPA 3.0-3.49:	30%
SAT math:	440-540	GPA 2.0-2.99:	51%
ACT composite:	18-23	Rank in top quarter:	21%
GPA 3.75 or higher:	8%	Rank in top tenth:	6%
GPA 3.50-3.74:	9%	Return as sophomores:	66%
		Out-of-state:	3%

Basis for selection. ACT/SAT, GPA, and class rank important. ACT/SAT not required of those submitting GED. Open admission for applicants 20 years of age and older who are high school graduates, have GED, or have 30 transferable credits. Students 19 years of age or younger with a CCHE index score between 76-91 must apply by April 6.

High school preparation. College-preparatory program recommended. 17 units recommended. Recommended units include English 4, mathematics 4, social studies 3, science 3, foreign language 1 and academic electives 2.

2011-2012 Annual costs. Tuition/fees: $4,834; $15,690 out-of-state. Books/supplies: $1,656. Personal expenses: $1,125.

Application procedures. Admission: Closing date 7/29 (receipt date). $25 fee, may be waived for applicants with need. Admission notification on a rolling basis. **Financial aid:** No deadline. FAFSA required.

Academics. Special study options: Accelerated study, cooperative education, cross-registration, distance learning, double major, dual enrollment of high school students, honors, independent study, internships, liberal arts/career combination, student-designed major, study abroad, teacher certification program, Washington semester. **Credit/placement by examination:** AP, CLEP, IB, SAT, ACT. 64 credit hours maximum toward bachelor's degree. **Support services:** Pre-admission summer program, study skills assistance, tutoring, writing center.

Majors. Area/ethnic studies: African-American, Chicano/Hispanic-American/Latino. **Biology:** General. **Business:** Accounting, business admin, finance, hospitality admin, hospitality/recreation, marketing, tourism promotion, tourism/travel. **Communications:** Broadcast journalism, communications/speech/rhetoric, journalism. **Computer sciences:** General, computer science. **Conservation:** General, environmental studies, land use planning. **Education:** Art, music. **English:** English lit, rhetoric/composition. **Foreign languages:** General, Spanish. **Health services:** Health care admin, nursing (RN). **History:** General. **Human services:** Social work. **Math:** General. **Parks/recreation:** General, exercise sciences. **Philosophy/religion:** Philosophy. **Physical sciences:** Atmospheric science, chemistry, physics. **Protective services:** Criminal justice, law enforcement admin. **Psychology:** General. **Social sciences:** Anthropology, economics, political science, sociology. **Visual/performing arts:** Art, industrial design, music performance.

Most popular majors. Business/marketing 21%, English 8%, interdisciplinary studies 9%, psychology 8%, security/protective services 7%, visual/performing arts 6%.

Computing on campus. 700 workstations in library, computer center, student center. Commuter students can connect to campus network. Online course registration, online library, helpline, repair service, wireless network available.

Student life. Freshman orientation: Mandatory. Preregistration for classes offered. Several sessions held preceding each semester. **Housing:** Off-campus apartments in area. **Activities:** Bands, choral groups, dance, drama, international student organizations, literary magazine, music ensembles, musical theater, radio station, student government, student newspaper, TV station, approximately 100 student organizations and clubs available.

Athletics. NCAA. **Intercollegiate:** Baseball M, basketball, cross-country, diving, soccer, swimming, tennis, volleyball W. **Intramural:** Basketball, handball, lacrosse M, racquetball, rugby M, skiing, softball W, tennis, volleyball. **Team name:** Roadrunners.

Student services. Adult student services, alcohol/substance abuse counseling, chaplain/spiritual director, career counseling, services for economically disadvantaged, student employment services, financial aid counseling, health services, legal services, on-campus daycare, personal counseling, placement for graduates, veterans' counselor, women's services. **Physically disabled:** Services for visually, speech, hearing impaired.

Contact. E-mail: askmetro@mscd.edu
Phone: (303) 556-3058 Fax: (303) 556-6345
Elena Sandoval-Lucero, Director of Admissions, Metropolitan State College of Denver, Campus Box 16, Denver, CO 80217

Naropa University
Boulder, Colorado
www.naropa.edu

CB member
CB code: 0908

- Private 4-year university and liberal arts college
- Commuter campus in small city
- 414 degree-seeking undergraduates: 6% part-time, 59% women
- 646 degree-seeking graduate students
- 91% of applicants admitted
- Application essay, interview required
- 42% graduate within 6 years

General. Founded in 1974. Regionally accredited. Uses contemplative education. **Degrees:** 111 bachelor's awarded; master's offered. **Location:** 35 miles from Denver. **Calendar:** Semester, limited summer session. **Full-time**

faculty: 48 total; 54% have terminal degrees, 21% minority, 52% women. **Part-time faculty:** 127 total; 31% have terminal degrees, 10% minority, 58% women. **Class size:** 89% < 20, 11% 20-39, less than 1% 50-99. **Special facilities:** Meditation halls, maitri rooms, consciousness laboratory, greenhouse, tea house, Chogyam Trungpa Rinpoche archives, performing arts center, dance studios, music studio, art studio, art exhibits, audio archives.

Freshman class profile. 137 applied, 125 admitted, 54 enrolled.

Out-of-state: 72%	**Live on campus:**	82%

Basis for selection. Assessment of academic background, community service, mission, and readiness important. Determination based on fit with unique mission, as well as academic background and readiness. Supplemental applications and/or art samples required for applicants to performance, environmental studies, interdisciplinary studies, music, visual arts, and writing and literature programs. **Home schooled:** Portfolio of work completed during high school required, including subjects studied and modes of learning for each subject; extracurricular/community activities; academic achievements that support academic preparedness for college, such as internship positions; parent or teacher narrative; self-evaluation of work and how it contributed to intellectual growth; and transcripts from mainstream high schools or colleges (if applicable).

High school preparation. College-preparatory program recommended. 23 units recommended. Recommended units include English 4, mathematics 3, social studies 3, history 3, science 3 (laboratory 2), foreign language 3 and academic electives 4. Art, dance, theater and/or creative writing recommended.

2012-2013 Annual costs. Tuition/fees (projected): $26,520. Room only: $8,442. Books/supplies: $1,200.

2011-2012 Financial aid. All financial aid based on need. Average need met was 75%. Average scholarship/grant was $15,646; average loan $7,969. 58% of total undergraduate aid awarded as scholarships/grants, 42% as loans/jobs.

Application procedures. Admission: Priority date 1/15; no deadline. $50 fee, may be waived for applicants with need. Admission notification on a rolling basis. Must reply by May 1 or within 3 week(s) if notified thereafter. **Financial aid:** Priority date 3/1; no closing date. FAFSA required. Applicants notified on a rolling basis starting 3/1; must reply within 3 week(s) of notification.

Academics. Special study options: Double major, independent study, internships, student-designed major. Consortium agreement with University of Colorado allows degree-seeking students to take courses at University of Colorado at an in-state tuition rate. **Credit/placement by examination:** AP, CLEP, IB. 30 credit hours maximum toward bachelor's degree. **Support services:** Reduced course load, study skills assistance, tutoring, writing center.

Majors. Conservation: Environmental studies. **Education:** Early childhood. **English:** English lit. **Philosophy/religion:** Religion. **Psychology:** General. **Visual/performing arts:** General, music, studio arts.

Most popular majors. English 12%, interdisciplinary studies 19%, natural resources/environmental science 8%, parks/recreation 10%, psychology 29%, visual/performing arts 20%.

Computing on campus. 77 workstations in library, computer center. Online course registration, online library, helpline, wireless network available.

Student life. Freshman orientation: Mandatory. Preregistration for classes offered. Week-long session in August. 1- or 2-day orientations offered for parents and families. **Policies:** Code of Conduct enforced. **Housing:** Guaranteed on-campus for freshmen. Apartments, wellness housing available. $300 nonrefundable deposit, deadline 7/1. **Activities:** Jazz band, campus ministries, choral groups, dance, drama, international student organizations, literary magazine, music ensembles, musical theater, student government, student newspaper, Allies in Action, gender discussion group, students for peace and justice, healers, laughter club, Tibetan debate club, Reconnecting on Outer Terrain, Japanese tea ceremony club.

Student services. Alcohol/substance abuse counseling, chaplain/spiritual director, career counseling, financial aid counseling, minority student services, personal counseling. **Physically disabled:** Services for visually, hearing impaired.

Contact. E-mail: admissions@naropa.edu
Phone: (303) 546-3572 Toll-free number: (800) 772-6951
Fax: (303) 546-3583
Naropa University, 2130 Arapahoe Avenue, Boulder, CO 80302-6697

National American University: Denver
Denver, Colorado
www.national.edu
CB code: 5354

- For-profit 4-year university and branch campus college
- Commuter campus in very large city

General. Founded in 1941. Regionally accredited. **Calendar:** Quarter.

Annual costs/financial aid. Books/supplies: $1,200.

Contact. Phone: (303) 876-7100
Director of Admissions, 1325 South Colorado Boulevard, Suite 100, Denver, CO 80222-3308

Nazarene Bible College
Colorado Springs, Colorado
www.nbc.edu
CB code: 0476

- Private 4-year Bible college affiliated with Church of the Nazarene
- Commuter campus in very large city
- 816 undergraduates
- Application essay required

General. Founded in 1964. Accredited by ABHE. Extensive online program for most majors. **Degrees:** 83 bachelor's, 7 associate awarded. **Location:** 60 miles from Denver. **Calendar:** Trimester, limited summer session. **Full-time faculty:** 9 total; 89% have terminal degrees, 11% minority, 11% women. **Part-time faculty:** 110 total; 68% have terminal degrees, 9% minority, 18% women.

Basis for selection. Open admission. **Home schooled:** Transcript of courses and grades, letter of recommendation (nonparent) required.

2011-2012 Annual costs. Tuition/fees: $10,605. Books/supplies: $900.

Financial aid. Non-need-based: Scholarships awarded for religious affiliation. **Additional information:** Tuition waiver available to students serving as student body officers.

Application procedures. Admission: No deadline. No application fee. Admission notification on a rolling basis beginning on or about 5/1. **Financial aid:** Priority date 6/1; no closing date. FAFSA required. Applicants notified on a rolling basis starting 6/15; must reply within 2 week(s) of notification.

Academics. Full programs offered in evening classes, cater to adult students. Extensive online degree programs offered. Degree completion program offered online and on campus. **Special study options:** Accelerated study, cross-registration, distance learning, double major, dual enrollment of high school students, independent study, internships. **Credit/placement by examination:** AP, CLEP, institutional tests. 24 credit hours maximum toward associate degree, 24 toward bachelor's. **Support services:** Learning center, reduced course load, remedial instruction, study skills assistance, tutoring.

Majors. Theology: Bible, pastoral counseling, religious ed, sacred music.

Computing on campus. 20 workstations in library. Online library, wireless network available.

Student life. Freshman orientation: Mandatory. Preregistration for classes offered. **Policies:** Religious observance required. **Activities:** Concert band, campus ministries, choral groups, music ensembles, student government, student newspaper.

Student services. Adult student services, alcohol/substance abuse counseling, chaplain/spiritual director, career counseling, services for economically disadvantaged, student employment services, financial aid counseling, personal counseling, placement for graduates, women's services. **Physically disabled:** Services for visually, hearing impaired.

Contact. E-mail: campusadmissions@nbc.edu
Phone: (719) 884-5000 ext. 5096
Toll-free number: (800) 873-3873 ext. 5096 Fax: (719) 884-5199
Jay Ott, Vice President for Campus Academic Services, Nazarene Bible College, 1111 Academy Park Loop, Colorado Springs, CO 80910-3704

Platt College: Aurora
Aurora, Colorado
www.plattcolorado.edu
CB code: 3012

- For-profit 4-year visual arts and nursing college
- Commuter campus in very large city
- 182 degree-seeking undergraduates
- Application essay, interview required

General. Accredited by ACCSC. **Degrees:** 37 bachelor's, 12 associate awarded. **Calendar:** Quarter. **Full-time faculty:** 12 total. **Part-time faculty:** 24 total.

Basis for selection. Open admission, but selective for some programs. Background check, letter of recommendation, Test of Essential Academic Skills (TEAS) required for nursing applicants. **Home schooled:** State high school equivalency certificate required.

High school preparation. College-preparatory program recommended.

2011-2012 Annual costs. Associate degree program, Website Design: $35,510; bachelor's degree program, Media Arts: $53,132; bachelor's program, Nursing: $73,445.

Financial aid. All financial aid based on need.

Application procedures. Admission: No deadline. $75 fee. Admission notification on a rolling basis. **Financial aid:** No deadline. FAFSA, institutional form required. Applicants notified on a rolling basis.

Academics. Credit/placement by examination: AP, CLEP. **Support services:** Learning center, study skills assistance, writing center.

Majors. Health services: Nursing (RN). **Visual/performing arts:** Commercial/advertising art.

Most popular majors. Health sciences 76%, visual/performing arts 24%.

Computing on campus. PC or laptop required.

Student life. Freshman orientation: Mandatory. Preregistration for classes offered.

Contact. E-mail: admissions@plattcolorado.edu
Phone: (303) 369-5151 Toll-free number: (877) 369-5151
Fax: (303) 745-1433
Hollie Campanella, Director of Admissions, Platt College: Aurora, 3100 South Parker Road, Aurora, CO 80014-3141

Regis University
Denver, Colorado
www.regis.edu
CB member
CB code: 4656

- Private 4-year university and liberal arts college affiliated with Roman Catholic Church
- Residential campus in very large city
- 5,345 degree-seeking undergraduates: 53% part-time, 65% women, 6% African American, 5% Asian American, 14% Hispanic American, 1% Native American, 1% international
- 5,062 degree-seeking graduate students
- 76% of applicants admitted
- SAT or ACT (ACT writing optional), application essay required
- 61% graduate within 6 years

General. Founded in 1877. Regionally accredited. **Degrees:** 1,318 bachelor's awarded; master's, professional offered. **ROTC:** Army. **Location:** 10 miles from downtown. **Calendar:** Semester, limited summer session. **Full-time faculty:** 268 total; 9% minority, 60% women. **Part-time faculty:** 825 total; 10% minority, 56% women. **Class size:** 91% < 20, 8% 20-39, less than 1% 40-49, 1% 50-99, less than 1% >100. **Special facilities:** Arboretum, Santos collection (Hispanic religious art), center for the study of war experience, recorder music center.

Freshman class profile. 3,027 applied, 2,297 admitted, 514 enrolled.

Mid 50% test scores			
SAT critical reading:	480-590	GPA 2.0-2.99:	15%
SAT math:	460-590	Rank in top quarter:	64%
SAT writing:	480-590	Rank in top tenth:	34%
ACT composite:	22-27	End year in good standing:	87%
GPA 3.75 or higher:	42%	Return as sophomores:	82%
GPA 3.50-3.74:	15%	Out-of-state:	42%
GPA 3.0-3.49:	28%	Live on campus:	75%

Basis for selection. High school record, test scores, recommendations, essay, school and community activities most important. Interview, campus visit recommended. Audition recommended of music majors.

High school preparation. College-preparatory program required. 15 units required. Required and recommended units include English 4, mathematics 3, social studies 2, science 2 (laboratory 1), foreign language 2 and academic electives 1.

2012-2013 Annual costs. Tuition/fees (projected): $31,800. Room/board: $9,220. Books/supplies: $2,000. Personal expenses: $1,269.

2010-2011 Financial aid. **Need-based:** 430 full-time freshmen applied for aid; 308 were judged to have need; 307 of these received aid. Average need met was 79%. Average scholarship/grant was $20,389; average loan $2,164. 25% of total undergraduate aid awarded as scholarships/grants, 75% as loans/jobs. **Non-need-based:** Awarded to 1,032 full-time undergraduates, including 278 freshmen. Scholarships awarded for academics, athletics, leadership, music/drama, religious affiliation, ROTC, state residency.

Application procedures. **Admission:** Priority date 3/1; deadline 8/1 (postmark date). $40 fee, may be waived for applicants with need, free for online applicants. Admission notification on a rolling basis beginning on or about 9/1. Must reply by May 1 or within 2 week(s) if notified thereafter. **Financial aid:** Priority date 5/31; no closing date. FAFSA required. Applicants notified on a rolling basis starting 3/15.

Academics. School of Professional Studies offers part-time undergraduate, graduate, certificate and corporate education programs to adult students on 6 campuses and online. **Special study options:** Accelerated study, combined bachelor's/graduate degree, distance learning, double major, dual enrollment of high school students, honors, independent study, internships, liberal arts/career combination, student-designed major, study abroad, teacher certification program, weekend college. **Credit/placement by examination:** AP, CLEP, IB, SAT, ACT, institutional tests. 30 credit hours maximum toward bachelor's degree. Regis, CLEP, DANTES, Challenge exams offered. **Support services:** Learning center, pre-admission summer program, reduced course load, remedial instruction, study skills assistance, tutoring, writing center.

Majors. **Area/ethnic studies:** Women's. **Biology:** General, biochemistry, neuroscience. **Business:** General, accounting, business admin, finance, human resources, managerial economics, marketing, organizational behavior. **Communications:** Communications/speech/rhetoric. **Computer sciences:** General, computer science. **Conservation:** Environmental science. **Education:** General, autistic, biology, chemistry, elementary, English, history, mathematics, middle, physical, science, secondary, special ed. **English:** English lit. **Foreign languages:** French, Spanish. **Health services:** Medical records admin, nursing (RN), predental, premedicine, preveterinary. **History:** General. **Human services:** General. **Liberal arts:** Arts/sciences. **Math:** General. **Philosophy/religion:** Philosophy, religion. **Physical sciences:** Chemistry. **Psychology:** General. **Social sciences:** General, criminology, economics, political science, sociology. **Theology:** Religious ed. **Visual/performing arts:** General, art history/conservation, cinematography, music.

Most popular majors. Business/marketing 29%, computer/information sciences 6%, health sciences 32%, liberal arts 8%.

Computing on campus. 547 workstations in dormitories, library, computer center, student center. Dormitories wired for high-speed internet access and linked to campus network. Commuter students can connect to campus network. Online course registration, online library, helpline, wireless network available.

Student life. **Freshman orientation:** Mandatory, $75 fee. Preregistration for classes offered. Held weekend before classes begin. **Policies:** Freshmen required to live on campus unless residing with parent, guardian or spouse in Denver metropolitan area. **Housing:** Guaranteed on-campus for freshmen. Coed dorms, special housing for disabled, wellness housing available. $150 nonrefundable deposit, deadline 5/1. **Activities:** Bands, campus ministries, choral groups, dance, literary magazine, music ensembles, musical theater, radio station, student government, student newspaper, peer education, environmental action program, Christian Fellowship, Jewish student group, Asian awareness association, black student alliance, Mi Gente, multicultural awareness committee, Romero House, Young Democrats and Republicans.

Athletics. NCAA. **Intercollegiate:** Baseball M, basketball, cross-country, golf, lacrosse W, soccer, softball W, volleyball W. **Intramural:** Tennis. **Team name:** Rangers.

Student services. Adult student services, alcohol/substance abuse counseling, chaplain/spiritual director, career counseling, student employment services, financial aid counseling, health services, minority student services, personal counseling, placement for graduates, veterans' counselor. **Physically disabled:** Services for visually, speech, hearing impaired.

Contact. E-mail: regisadm@regis.edu
Phone: (303) 458-4900 Toll-free number: (800) 388-2366 ext. 4900
Fax: (303) 964-5534
Victor Davolt, Director of Admissions, Regis College, Regis University, 3333 Regis Boulevard, Mail Code B20, Denver, CO 80221-1099

Rocky Mountain College of Art & Design
Denver, Colorado
www.rmcad.edu   CB code: 1943

- For-profit 4-year visual arts college
- Commuter campus in very large city
- 620 degree-seeking undergraduates: 13% part-time, 62% women, 3% African American, 3% Asian American, 9% Hispanic American, 2% Native American, 1% international
- Interview required
- 56% graduate within 6 years

General. Founded in 1963. Regionally accredited. **Degrees:** 113 bachelor's awarded. **Location:** 5 miles from downtown. **Calendar:** Semester, extensive summer session. **Full-time faculty:** 49 total; 8% have terminal degrees, 47% minority, 47% women. **Part-time faculty:** 65 total; 14% have terminal degrees, 54% minority, 54% women. **Class size:** 94% < 20, 6% 20-39. **Special facilities:** Fine arts center exhibition space, outdoor exhibition space, photography lab and darkroom, documentation room for digitally recording student work for portfolios and assessment.

Freshman class profile. 375 applied, 375 admitted, 106 enrolled.

Return as sophomores:	59%	Live on campus:	43%
Out-of-state:	29%		

Basis for selection. Open admission. SAT/ACT required of all first-time freshmen applicants under the age of 24 for academic counseling and placement. **Home schooled:** State high school equivalency certificate required.

2011-2012 Annual costs. Tuition/fees: $27,648. Flat fee of $13,824 per term for students taking 12 to 18 credits. Books/supplies: $1,749. Personal expenses: $2,896.

2011-2012 Financial aid. **Need-based:** 86 full-time freshmen applied for aid; 77 were judged to have need; 77 of these received aid. Average need met was 75%. Average scholarship/grant was $5,205; average loan $3,337. 46% of total undergraduate aid awarded as scholarships/grants, 54% as loans/jobs. **Non-need-based:** Scholarships awarded for academics, art, state residency.

Application procedures. **Admission:** No deadline. $50 fee, may be waived for applicants with need. Admission notification on a rolling basis beginning on or about 9/1. **Financial aid:** Priority date 3/15; no closing date. FAFSA required. Applicants notified on a rolling basis starting 4/1; must reply within 2 week(s) of notification.

Academics. **Special study options:** Accelerated study, distance learning, double major, honors, independent study, internships, study abroad, teacher certification program. **Credit/placement by examination:** AP, CLEP, IB, SAT, ACT. **Support services:** Learning center, reduced course load, remedial instruction, study skills assistance, tutoring, writing center.

Majors. **Communications technology:** Animation/special effects. **Computer sciences:** Computer graphics. **Education:** Art. **Visual/performing arts:** Design, graphic design, illustration, interior design, painting, photography, sculpture, studio arts.

Most popular majors. Communication technologies 20%, visual/performing arts 75%.

Computing on campus. Online course registration, online library, wireless network available.

Student life. **Freshman orientation:** Mandatory. Preregistration for classes offered. Three-day program held before start of term. **Housing:** Coed dorms available. **Activities:** Dance, film society, student government, student newspaper.

Student services. Career counseling, student employment services, financial aid counseling, personal counseling, placement for graduates, veterans' counselor. **Physically disabled:** Services for visually, speech, hearing impaired.

Contact. E-mail: admissions@rmcad.edu
Phone: (303) 753-6046 Toll-free number: (800) 888-2787
Fax: (303) 759-4970
Joe Leonhardt, Vice President of Admissions, Rocky Mountain College of Art & Design, 1600 Pierce Street, Denver, CO 80214

United States Air Force Academy
USAF Academy, Colorado
www.academyadmissions.com

CB member
CB code: 4830

- Public 4-year liberal arts and military college
- Residential campus in large city
- 4,413 degree-seeking undergraduates: 22% women, 7% African American, 7% Asian American, 9% Hispanic American, 1% Native American, 1% international
- 11% of applicants admitted
- SAT or ACT (ACT writing optional), application essay, interview required
- 76% graduate within 6 years; 9% enter graduate study

General. Founded in 1954. Regionally accredited. **Degrees:** 1,030 bachelor's awarded. **Location:** 8 miles from Colorado Springs, 60 miles from Denver. **Calendar:** Semester, limited summer session. **Full-time faculty:** 524 total; 54% have terminal degrees, 13% minority, 20% women. **Part-time faculty:** 5 total; 40% have terminal degrees, 20% women. **Class size:** 70% <20, 29% 20-39, less than 1% 40-49, less than 1% 50-99. **Special facilities:** 3 airfields, tri-sonic wind tunnel, aeronautics lab, instrumentation lab, research lab, radio-frequency systems lab, training facility, meteorology lab, engineering mechanics lab, laser optics center.

Freshman class profile. 12,732 applied, 1,372 admitted, 1,127 enrolled.

Mid 50% test scores			
SAT critical reading:	590-680	Rank in top quarter:	80%
SAT math:	630-710	Rank in top tenth:	55%
ACT composite:	28-32	End year in good standing:	78%
GPA 3.75 or higher:	79%	Return as sophomores:	89%
GPA 3.50-3.74:	12%	Out-of-state:	93%
GPA 3.0-3.49:	9%	Live on campus:	100%
		International:	1%

Basis for selection. Must be a citizen of the United States, unmarried with no dependents, between the ages of 17 and not past the 23rd birthday on July 1 of the year of entry, and of good moral character. Legal nomination from member of Congress, US President or Vice President or other selected sources required. Secondary school record, test scores, leadership ability, extracurricular activities, character most important. Satisfactory completion of medical exam and fitness test, and personal interview required. Admissions counselors available to assist in the admission process.

High school preparation. College-preparatory program required. Recommended units include English 4, mathematics 4, social studies 3, history 3, science 4 (laboratory 4), foreign language 2 and computer science 1. English should include college preparatory composition and speech courses. Math should include algebra, geometry, trigonometry, calculus, and functional analysis (if available). Science should include biology, chemistry, physics, computers, and additional science courses. Foreign language instruction should be in a modern language.

2012-2013 Annual costs. Tuition, room, board, medical and dental care paid by U.S. Government. Each cadet receives monthly salary to pay for uniforms, supplies and personal expenses. A government loan is advanced to each member of the freshman class.

Application procedures. Admission: Closing date 12/31 (postmark date). No application fee. Application must be submitted online. Admission notification on a rolling basis beginning on or about 10/15. Must reply by 5/1. Several stages of application process; begin junior year.

Academics. Special study options: Double major, ESL, exchange student, honors, independent study, internships, study abroad. Academically at-risk, hospital instruction, extra instruction, and summer programs available. **Credit/placement by examination:** AP, CLEP, IB, institutional tests. **Support services:** Learning center, reduced course load, study skills assistance, tutoring, writing center.

Majors. Biology: General. **Business:** Business admin. **Computer sciences:** Computer science. **Engineering:** General, aerospace, civil, computer, electrical, engineering mechanics, environmental, mechanical, operations research, systems. **English:** English lit. **History:** General. **Liberal arts:** Humanities. **Math:** General. **Physical sciences:** Atmospheric science, chemistry, physics. **Social sciences:** General, economics, geography, political science.

Most popular majors. Biology 6%, business/marketing 11%, engineering/engineering technologies 35%, interdisciplinary studies 14%, social sciences 19%.

Computing on campus. PC or laptop required. 150 workstations in library, computer center. Dormitories wired for high-speed internet access and linked to campus network. Commuter students can connect to campus network. Online library, helpline, repair service, wireless network available.

Student life. Policies: Freshmen not permitted cars on campus. **Housing:** Guaranteed on-campus for all undergraduates. Coed dorms available. **Activities:** Bands, campus ministries, choral groups, dance, drama, international student organizations, music ensembles, Model UN, musical theater, radio station, student government, symphony orchestra, multicultural council, women's forums, women's aircrew issues, premarital/relationship enhancement workshop, cultural clubs/organizations, Way of Life committee, Native American heritage committee, international club, Tuskegee airmen club, interfaith council.

Athletics. NCAA. **Intercollegiate:** Baseball M, basketball, boxing M, cheerleading, cross-country, diving, fencing, football (tackle) M, golf M, gymnastics, ice hockey M, lacrosse M, rifle, soccer, swimming, tennis, track and field, volleyball W, water polo M, wrestling M. **Intramural:** Basketball, boxing M, cross-country, football (non-tackle), handball, racquetball, rugby M, soccer, softball, tennis, volleyball. **Team name:** Falcons.

Student services. Alcohol/substance abuse counseling, chaplain/spiritual director, career counseling, health services, legal services, personal counseling, women's services.

Contact. E-mail: rr_webmail@usafa.edu
Phone: (800) 443-9266 Toll-free number: (800) 443-9266
Fax: (719) 333-3647
Col. Carolyn Benyshek, Director of Admissions, United States Air Force Academy, HQ USAF/RRS, 2304 Cadet Drive, Suite 2400, USAF Academy, CO 80840

University of Colorado Boulder
Boulder, Colorado
www.colorado.edu

CB member
CB code: 4841

- Public 4-year university
- Residential campus in small city
- 25,774 degree-seeking undergraduates: 7% part-time, 47% women, 2% African American, 6% Asian American, 8% Hispanic American, 1% Native American, 2% international
- 5,497 degree-seeking graduate students
- 87% of applicants admitted
- SAT or ACT (ACT writing optional), application essay required
- 68% graduate within 6 years; 20% enter graduate study

General. Founded in 1876. Regionally accredited. **Degrees:** 5,642 bachelor's awarded; master's, professional, doctoral offered. **ROTC:** Army, Naval, Air Force. **Location:** 30 miles from Denver. **Calendar:** Semester, extensive summer session. **Full-time faculty:** 1,241 total; 91% have terminal degrees, 17% minority, 36% women. **Part-time faculty:** 770 total; 36% have terminal degrees, 10% minority, 44% women. **Class size:** 39% <20, 38% 20-39, 6% 40-49, 9% 50-99, 7% >100. **Special facilities:** Natural history museum, art museum and galleries, heritage center, observatory, planetarium and science center, electron microscopes, outdoor theater, video interactive foreign language laboratory, mountain research station, centrifuge laboratory, engineering lab, multipurpose conference center, concert hall, multi-disciplinary information technology center.

Freshman class profile. 20,506 applied, 17,828 admitted, 5,700 enrolled.

Mid 50% test scores			
SAT critical reading:	520-630	Rank in top quarter:	54%
SAT math:	540-650	Rank in top tenth:	24%
ACT composite:	24-28	Return as sophomores:	84%
GPA 3.75 or higher:	37%	Out-of-state:	43%
GPA 3.50-3.74:	20%	Live on campus:	92%
GPA 3.0-3.49:	35%	International:	2%
GPA 2.0-2.99:	8%	Fraternities:	15%
		Sororities:	27%

Basis for selection. Rigor of secondary school record, academic GPA, class rank, test scores most important; personal statement, talents, abilities important; recommendations considered. Audition required of music majors.

High school preparation. College-preparatory program required. 17 units required. Required units include English 4, mathematics 4, social studies 3, science 3 (laboratory 2) and foreign language 3. English must include 2 composition for College of Arts and Science, School of Business. Math must

include 2 algebra, 1 geometry, and 1 college preparatory math such as trigonometry, analytic geometry, or elementary functions. Physics or chemistry with lab required for College of Arts and Sciences, School of Business. For College of Engineering, science includes 1 of physics and 1 of chemistry or biology, or 2 of chemistry and 1 of physics or biology, or 2 of biology and 1 of chemistry or physics. Social Studies includes 1 of U.S. or world history and 1 of geography for College of Arts and Sciences, School of Business. 3 single foreign language required for College of Arts & Sciences, College of Engineering, School of Business; 2 single foreign language required for Colleges of Music and Architecture and Planning. 1 elective required for College of Architecture and Planning; 2 art electives required for College of Music.

2011-2012 Annual costs. Tuition/fees: $9,152; $30,330 out-of-state. Tuition varies by program. Room/board: $11,278. Books/supplies: $1,992. Personal expenses: $3,518.

2011-2012 Financial aid. Need-based: 3,697 full-time freshmen applied for aid; 2,553 were judged to have need; 2,483 of these received aid. Average need met was 87%. Average scholarship/grant was $7,600; average loan $5,389. 46% of total undergraduate aid awarded as scholarships/grants, 54% as loans/jobs. **Non-need-based:** Awarded to 5,416 full-time undergraduates, including 1,490 freshmen. Scholarships awarded for academics, alumni affiliation, art, athletics, leadership, music/drama, ROTC, state residency.

Application procedures. Admission: Priority date 12/1; deadline 1/15 (postmark date). $50 fee, may be waived for applicants with need. Admission notification by 4/1. Must reply by May 1 or within 2 week(s) if notified thereafter. **Financial aid:** Priority date 4/1; no closing date. FAFSA required. Applicants notified on a rolling basis starting 3/1; must reply within 3 week(s) of notification.

Academics. Residential academic programs offered in leadership, natural and environmental sciences, humanities and cultural studies, the arts, honors, international and global affairs, communication and society, the health professions, business, engineering, environmental sustainability, and history, culture, and society. **Special study options:** Accelerated study, combined bachelor's/graduate degree, cooperative education, cross-registration, distance learning, double major, dual enrollment of high school students, ESL, exchange student, honors, independent study, internships, liberal arts/career combination, semester at sea, student-designed major, study abroad, teacher certification program. Undergraduate research opportunities; concurrent bachelor's/master's programs; small group academic programs. **Credit/placement by examination:** AP, CLEP, IB, institutional tests. Policies vary by department. **Support services:** Learning center, pre-admission summer program, reduced course load, study skills assistance, tutoring, writing center.

Majors. Architecture: Environmental design. **Area/ethnic studies:** General, Asian, Russian/Slavic, women's. **Biology:** Biochemistry, cellular/molecular, ecology/evolutionary, physiology. **Business:** Accounting, business admin, entrepreneurial studies, finance, international, management information systems, marketing, real estate, small business admin. **Communications:** Communications/speech/rhetoric, journalism. **Computer sciences:** Computer science. **Conservation:** Environmental studies. **Education:** Music. **Engineering:** Aerospace, applied physics, architectural, biochemical, chemical, civil, computer, electrical, environmental, mechanical. **English:** English lit. **Foreign languages:** Chinese, classics, French, Germanic, Italian, Japanese, linguistics, Spanish. **Health services:** Communication disorders. **History:** General. **Liberal arts:** Humanities. **Math:** General, applied. **Philosophy/religion:** Philosophy, religion. **Physical sciences:** Astronomy, chemistry, geology, physics. **Psychology:** General. **Social sciences:** Anthropology, economics, geography, political science, sociology. **Visual/performing arts:** Art history/conservation, dance, dramatic, film/cinema/video, music, music performance, studio arts.

Most popular majors. Biology 10%, business/marketing 12%, communications/journalism 8%, engineering/engineering technologies 8%, psychology 10%, social sciences 16%, visual/performing arts 7%.

Computing on campus. 1,879 workstations in dormitories, library, computer center, student center. Dormitories wired for high-speed internet access and linked to campus network. Commuter students can connect to campus network. Online course registration, online library, helpline, repair service, student web hosting, wireless network available.

Student life. Freshman orientation: Mandatory. Preregistration for classes offered. Two-day programs for students and parents held throughout summer. **Policies:** Honor code, student conduct code, and alcohol and drug policy. **Housing:** Guaranteed on-campus for freshmen. Coed dorms, special housing for disabled, apartments, fraternity/sorority housing, wellness housing available. $300 nonrefundable deposit. Residential academic programs within specific dorms. **Activities:** Bands, campus ministries, choral groups, dance, drama, film society, international student organizations, literary magazine, music ensembles, Model UN, musical theater, opera, radio station, student government, student newspaper, symphony orchestra, TV station, volunteer resource center, Rocky Mountain Rescue Group student chapter,

multicultural business students association, student emergency medical services, religious campus organizations, gay-straight alliance, ethical and civic engagement institute, Student Veterans Association, College Democrats, College Republicans.

Athletics. NCAA. **Intercollegiate:** Basketball, cross-country, football (tackle) M, golf, skiing, soccer W, tennis W, track and field, volleyball W. **Intramural:** Badminton, basketball, football (non-tackle), ice hockey, soccer, table tennis, tennis, volleyball, water polo. **Team name:** Colorado Buffaloes.

Student services. Adult student services, alcohol/substance abuse counseling, chaplain/spiritual director, career counseling, services for economically disadvantaged, student employment services, financial aid counseling, health services, legal services, minority student services, on-campus daycare, personal counseling, placement for graduates, veterans' counselor, women's services. **Physically disabled:** Services for visually, speech, hearing impaired.

Contact. E-mail: apply@colorado.edu
Phone: (303) 492-6301 Fax: (303) 492-7115
Kevin McLennan, Director of Admissions, University of Colorado Boulder, 552 UCB, Boulder, CO 80309-0552

University of Colorado Colorado Springs
Colorado Springs, Colorado
www.uccs.edu   CB code: 4874

- Public 4-year university
- Commuter campus in large city
- 7,620 degree-seeking undergraduates: 20% part-time, 53% women, 4% African American, 4% Asian American, 12% Hispanic American, 1% Native American, 1% international
- 1,612 degree-seeking graduate students
- 68% of applicants admitted
- SAT or ACT (ACT writing optional) required
- 41% graduate within 6 years; 33% enter graduate study

General. Founded in 1965. Regionally accredited. **Degrees:** 1,328 bachelor's awarded; master's, professional, doctoral offered. **ROTC:** Army. **Location:** 60 miles from Denver. **Calendar:** Semester, extensive summer session. **Full-time faculty:** 343 total; 14% minority, 52% women. **Part-time faculty:** 333 total; 8% minority, 52% women. **Class size:** 40% < 20, 37% 20-39, 13% 40-49, 8% 50-99, 2% >100.

Freshman class profile. 5,203 applied, 3,549 admitted, 1,352 enrolled.

Mid 50% test scores			
SAT critical reading:	480-580	GPA 2.0-2.99:	29%
SAT math:	490-600	Rank in top quarter:	36%
ACT composite:	21-25	Rank in top tenth:	14%
GPA 3.75 or higher:	22%	End year in good standing:	85%
GPA 3.50-3.74:	16%	Return as sophomores:	71%
GPA 3.0-3.49:	33%	Out-of-state:	11%
		Live on campus:	42%

Basis for selection. Priority given to applicants who rank in top 40% of graduating class with 1080 SAT (exclusive of Writing) or 24 ACT, 2.8 GPA, and all high school course units are required. **Home schooled:** Transcript of courses and grades, state high school equivalency certificate required. **Learning Disabled:** Students with disabilities may register with Disability Services Office for assistance with accommodations.

High school preparation. College-preparatory program recommended. 15 units required; 16 recommended. Required and recommended units include English 4, mathematics 3-4, social studies 2, science 3 (laboratory 2), foreign language 2 and academic electives 1. Course requirements may vary by college.

2011-2012 Annual costs. Tuition/fees: $7,894; $17,414 out-of-state. Tuition varies by program and level. Room/board: $7,990.

2010-2011 Financial aid. Need-based: 908 full-time freshmen applied for aid; 477 were judged to have need; 472 of these received aid. Average need met was 77%. Average scholarship/grant was $5,705; average loan $3,061. 54% of total undergraduate aid awarded as scholarships/grants, 46% as loans/jobs. **Non-need-based:** Awarded to 1,251 full-time undergraduates, including 440 freshmen. Scholarships awarded for academics, alumni affiliation, athletics.

Application procedures. Admission: Priority date 4/1; no deadline. $50 fee. Admission notification on a rolling basis. **Financial aid:** Priority date 3/1; no closing date. FAFSA required. Applicants notified on a rolling basis starting 4/15.

Academics. Special study options: Accelerated study, combined bachelor's/graduate degree, distance learning, double major, dual enrollment of high school students, exchange student, honors, independent study, internships, liberal arts/career combination, student-designed major, study abroad, teacher certification program, weekend college. **Credit/placement by examination:** AP, CLEP, IB, SAT, ACT, institutional tests. 30 credit hours maximum toward bachelor's degree. **Support services:** Learning center, remedial instruction, study skills assistance, tutoring, writing center.

Honors college/program. 25 ACT or 1200 SAT (exclusive of Writing), 3.75 GPA and completion of Honors application (including the essay and statement of objectives) required.

Majors. Area/ethnic studies: General, women's. **Biology:** General, biochemistry. **Business:** Business admin. **Communications:** General. **Computer sciences:** General, computer science, modeling/simulation, security. **Engineering:** General, computer, electrical, mechanical. **English:** English lit. **Foreign languages:** Spanish. **Health services:** Nursing (RN). **History:** General. **Math:** General. **Philosophy/religion:** Philosophy. **Physical sciences:** Chemistry, physics. **Protective services:** Law enforcement admin. **Psychology:** General. **Social sciences:** Anthropology, economics, geography, political science, sociology. **Visual/performing arts:** General.

Most popular majors. Biology 7%, business/marketing 23%, communications/journalism 8%, English 6%, health sciences 11%, psychology 8%, social sciences 14%.

Computing on campus. 600 workstations in dormitories, library, computer center, student center. Dormitories wired for high-speed internet access and linked to campus network. Commuter students can connect to campus network. Online course registration, online library, helpline, repair service, wireless network available.

Student life. Freshman orientation: Mandatory, $50 fee. Preregistration for classes offered. Several 1-day sessions throughout summer; online version available for students who cannot travel to campus. **Housing:** Coed dorms, single-sex dorms, special housing for disabled, apartments available. $100 partly refundable deposit. **Activities:** Pep band, choral groups, dance, drama, film society, international student organizations, literary magazine, music ensembles, musical theater, radio station, student government, student newspaper, TV station, advocating woman's assistance resources education club, students pushing the limits of advanced technology club, El Circulo de Espanol, Spectrum, Catholic student community, Hillel, Campus Crusade.

Athletics. NCAA. **Intercollegiate:** Basketball, cross-country, golf M, soccer, softball W, track and field, volleyball W. **Intramural:** Badminton, basketball, bowling, cricket, field hockey, football (non-tackle), soccer, table tennis, volleyball, water polo. **Team name:** Mountain Lions.

Student services. Adult student services, alcohol/substance abuse counseling, career counseling, student employment services, financial aid counseling, health services, minority student services, on-campus daycare, personal counseling, veterans' counselor. **Physically disabled:** Services for visually, speech, hearing impaired.

Contact. E-mail: admrec@uccs.edu
Phone: (719) 255-3383 Toll-free number: (800) 990-8227 ext. 3383
Fax: (719) 255-3116
John Salnaitis, Admissions Director, University of Colorado Colorado Springs, 1420 Austin Bluffs Parkway, Colorado Springs, CO 80918

University of Colorado Denver
Denver, Colorado
www.ucdenver.edu   CB code: 4875

- Public 4-year university
- Commuter campus in very large city
- 10,299 degree-seeking undergraduates: 27% part-time, 54% women, 6% African American, 11% Asian American, 13% Hispanic American, 1% Native American, 6% international
- 8,521 degree-seeking graduate students
- 60% of applicants admitted
- SAT or ACT (ACT writing optional), application essay required
- 42% graduate within 6 years

General. Founded in 1912. Regionally accredited. Library, student center, and classrooms shared with Metropolitan State College and Community College of Denver. **Degrees:** 2,034 bachelor's awarded; master's, professional, doctoral offered. **ROTC:** Army, Air Force. **Calendar:** Semester, extensive summer session. **Full-time faculty:** 2,602 total; 79% have terminal degrees, 12% minority, 50% women. **Part-time faculty:** 556 total; 39% have terminal degrees, 11% minority, 54% women. **Class size:** 29% < 20, 48% 20-39, 12% 40-49, 8% 50-99, 3% >100. **Special facilities:** Computational math centers, applied psychology center, environmental science center, transportation research center, Fourth World center for study of indigenous law and politics.

Freshman class profile. 5,413 applied, 3,235 admitted, 1,086 enrolled.

Mid 50% test scores			
SAT critical reading:	470-610	GPA 2.0-2.99:	23%
SAT math:	480-620	Rank in top quarter:	44%
ACT composite:	20-25	Rank in top tenth:	19%
GPA 3.75 or higher:	26%	Out-of-state:	9%
GPA 3.50-3.74:	15%	Live on campus:	25%
GPA 3.0-3.49:	36%	International:	6%

Basis for selection. Previous academic performance including high school course work and GPA; evidence of academic ability and accomplishments as indicated by test scores; and evidence of maturity, motivation, potential for academic success most important. Audition required of music majors.

High school preparation. College-preparatory program recommended. 17 units required; 18 recommended. Required and recommended units include English 4, mathematics 4, social studies 3, science 3 (laboratory 2), foreign language 1-2 and academic electives 2. 4 math required for engineering and business students.

2011-2012 Annual costs. Tuition/fees: $7,702; $22,064 out-of-state. Tuition varies by level. Room/board: $9,890. Books/supplies: $2,076. Personal expenses: $2,214.

Financial aid. Non-need-based: Scholarships awarded for academics, alumni affiliation, art, job skills, leadership, music/drama, ROTC, state residency.

Application procedures. Admission: Priority date 7/22; deadline 9/1. $50 fee, may be waived for applicants with need. Admission notification on a rolling basis. **Financial aid:** Priority date 4/1; no closing date. FAFSA, institutional form required. Applicants notified on a rolling basis starting 5/1.

Academics. Learning opportunities through center for internships and cooperative education. **Special study options:** Accelerated study, combined bachelor's/graduate degree, cooperative education, cross-registration, distance learning, double major, ESL, honors, independent study, internships, student-designed major, study abroad, teacher certification program. **Credit/placement by examination:** AP, CLEP, IB, institutional tests. 30 credit hours maximum toward bachelor's degree. **Support services:** Learning center, study skills assistance, tutoring, writing center.

Majors. Biology: General, biomedical sciences. **Business:** Business admin, human resources. **Communications:** Communications/speech/rhetoric. **Computer sciences:** General. **Engineering:** Civil, electrical, mechanical. **English:** English lit, writing. **Foreign languages:** French, Spanish. **Health services:** Nursing (RN). **History:** General. **Math:** General. **Philosophy/religion:** Philosophy. **Physical sciences:** Chemistry, physics. **Protective services:** Law enforcement admin. **Psychology:** General, psychobiology. **Social sciences:** Anthropology, economics, geography, political science, sociology. **Visual/performing arts:** Dramatic, music, studio arts.

Most popular majors. Biology 8%, business/marketing 17%, communications/journalism 7%, health sciences 11%, psychology 11%, social sciences 13%, visual/performing arts 11%.

Computing on campus. 205 workstations in library, computer center, student center. Dormitories wired for high-speed internet access. Commuter students can connect to campus network. Online course registration, online library, helpline, student web hosting, wireless network available.

Student life. Freshman orientation: Mandatory. Preregistration for classes offered. **Housing:** Coed dorms, wellness housing available. **Activities:** Jazz band, campus ministries, choral groups, dance, drama, film society, international student organizations, music ensembles, musical theater, student government, more than 60 groups available.

Athletics. Intramural: Basketball, racquetball, tennis, volleyball.

Student services. Alcohol/substance abuse counseling, career counseling, student employment services, financial aid counseling, health services, legal services, minority student services, on-campus daycare, personal counseling, placement for graduates, veterans' counselor, women's services. **Physically disabled:** Services for visually, speech, hearing impaired.

Contact. E-mail: admissions@ucdenver.edu
Phone: (303) 556-2704 Fax: (303) 556-4838
Barbara Edwards, Director of Admissions, University of Colorado Denver, Box 173364, Campus Box 167, Denver, CO 80217-3364

University of Denver
Denver, Colorado
www.du.edu

CB member
CB code: 4842

- Private 4-year university
- Residential campus in very large city
- 5,424 degree-seeking undergraduates: 8% part-time, 56% women, 3% African American, 4% Asian American, 9% Hispanic American, 1% Native American, 8% international
- 6,134 degree-seeking graduate students
- 68% of applicants admitted
- SAT or ACT (ACT writing optional), application essay required
- 79% graduate within 6 years

General. Founded in 1864. Regionally accredited. **Degrees:** 1,299 bachelor's awarded; master's, professional, doctoral offered. **ROTC:** Army, Air Force. **Location:** 8 miles from downtown. **Calendar:** Quarter, limited summer session. **Full-time faculty:** 630 total; 90% have terminal degrees, 14% minority, 42% women. **Part-time faculty:** 669 total; 4% have terminal degrees, 8% minority, 48% women. **Class size:** 60% < 20, 31% 20-39, 3% 40-49, 6% 50-99, less than 1% >100. **Special facilities:** Observatory, high-altitude research laboratory, mechanical engineering testing facility, early learning center, center for gifted children.

Freshman class profile. 10,504 applied, 7,160 admitted, 1,240 enrolled.

Mid 50% test scores			
SAT critical reading:	550-660	Rank in top quarter:	81%
SAT math:	560-670	Rank in top tenth:	44%
SAT writing:	540-640	Return as sophomores:	89%
ACT composite:	25-30	Out-of-state:	54%
GPA 3.75 or higher:	57%	Live on campus:	93%
GPA 3.50-3.74:	20%	International:	10%
GPA 3.0-3.49:	19%	Fraternities:	23%
GPA 2.0-2.99:	4%	Sororities:	27%

Basis for selection. GPA, test scores and strength of curriculum most important. Interview, academic maturity, contributions to school and community activities, leadership also important. Recommendations from teacher and counselor, and personal essay considered. Interview strongly encouraged. Audition required of music majors. Portfolio recommended of art majors. **Home schooled:** Letter of recommendation (nonparent) required.

High school preparation. College-preparatory program recommended. Recommended units include English 4, mathematics 3, social studies 3, science 3 (laboratory 2) and foreign language 3.

2012-2013 Annual costs. Tuition/fees: $39,177. Room/board: $10,818. Books/supplies: $2,000. Personal expenses: $1,287.

2011-2012 Financial aid. Need-based: 768 full-time freshmen applied for aid; 567 were judged to have need; 566 of these received aid. Average need met was 82%. Average scholarship/grant was $24,024; average loan $3,373. 77% of total undergraduate aid awarded as scholarships/grants, 23% as loans/jobs. **Non-need-based:** Awarded to 2,360 full-time undergraduates, including 592 freshmen. Scholarships awarded for academics, art, athletics, leadership, music/drama.

Application procedures. Admission: Closing date 1/15 (postmark date). $50 fee, may be waived for applicants with need. Admission notification by 3/15. Must reply by 5/1. **Financial aid:** Priority date 2/15, closing date 5/1. FAFSA, CSS PROFILE required. Must reply by 5/1 or within 4 week(s) of notification.

Academics. Special 3-week inter-term courses available for focused concentration. **Special study options:** Accelerated study, combined bachelor's/graduate degree, cooperative education, distance learning, double major, dual enrollment of high school students, ESL, honors, independent study, internships, semester at sea, student-designed major, study abroad, teacher certification program, Washington semester, weekend college. Learning disability services. **Credit/placement by examination:** AP, CLEP, IB, institutional tests. 45 credit hours maximum toward bachelor's degree. **Support services:** Learning center, pre-admission summer program, reduced course load, study skills assistance, tutoring, writing center.

Majors. Area/ethnic studies: Asian-American, women's. **Biology:** General, biochemistry, bioinformatics, ecology, molecular. **Business:** General, accounting, business admin, construction management, finance, hospitality admin, international, management information systems, managerial economics, marketing, organizational behavior, real estate, statistics. **Communications:** Communications/speech/rhetoric, digital media, journalism. **Computer sciences:** Computer science, information technology, systems analysis. **Conservation:** Environmental science. **Engineering:** General, computer, electrical, mechanical. **English:** English lit. **Foreign languages:** French,

German, Italian, Russian, Spanish. **General:** Animal sciences. **History:** General. **Human services:** Public policy. **Liberal arts:** Arts/sciences. **Math:** General. **Philosophy/religion:** Philosophy, religion. **Physical sciences:** General, chemistry, physics. **Psychology:** General. **Social sciences:** General, anthropology, criminology, economics, geography, international relations, political science, sociology. **Visual/performing arts:** Art, art history/conservation, dramatic, graphic design, music, music performance, musicology.

Most popular majors. Biology 6%, business/marketing 42%, communications/journalism 7%, psychology 6%, social sciences 13%, visual/performing arts 8%.

Computing on campus. PC or laptop required. 200 workstations in dormitories, library, computer center, student center. Dormitories wired for high-speed internet access and linked to campus network. Commuter students can connect to campus network. Online course registration, online library, helpline, repair service, student web hosting, wireless network available.

Student life. Freshman orientation: Mandatory. Preregistration for classes offered. Held first week of September for 5 days; includes programs for parents/families. **Policies:** Code of conduct, honor code in effect. **Housing:** Guaranteed on-campus for freshmen. Coed dorms, apartments, fraternity/sorority housing, wellness housing available. $200 nonrefundable deposit, deadline 5/1. **Activities:** Bands, campus ministries, choral groups, dance, drama, film society, international student organizations, literary magazine, music ensembles, Model UN, musical theater, opera, radio station, student government, student newspaper, symphony orchestra, Campus Crusade for Christ, Chabad, Fellowship of Catholic University Students, Hillel, College Democrats, College Republicans, Students for a Democratic Society, Students for a Free Tibet, environmental team, volunteer club.

Athletics. NCAA. **Intercollegiate:** Basketball, diving, golf, gymnastics W, ice hockey M, lacrosse, skiing, soccer, swimming, tennis, volleyball W. **Intramural:** Basketball, football (non-tackle), ice hockey M, soccer, softball. **Team name:** Pioneers.

Student services. Adult student services, alcohol/substance abuse counseling, chaplain/spiritual director, career counseling, student employment services, financial aid counseling, health services, minority student services, personal counseling, placement for graduates, women's services. **Physically disabled:** Services for visually, speech, hearing impaired.

Contact. E-mail: admission@du.edu
Phone: (303) 871-2036 Toll-free number: (800) 525-9495
Fax: (303) 871-3301
Todd Rinehart, Director of Admission, University of Denver, 2197 South University Boulevard, Denver, CO 80208

University of Northern Colorado
Greeley, Colorado
www.unco.edu

CB member
CB code: 4074

- Public 4-year university
- Residential campus in small city
- 10,118 degree-seeking undergraduates: 9% part-time, 62% women, 5% African American, 2% Asian American, 13% Hispanic American, 1% Native American, 1% international
- 2,148 degree-seeking graduate students
- 73% of applicants admitted
- 49% graduate within 6 years

General. Founded in 1889. Regionally accredited. **Degrees:** 1,997 bachelor's awarded; master's, professional, doctoral offered. **ROTC:** Army, Air Force. **Location:** 50 miles from Denver; 50 miles from Cheyenne, Wyoming. **Calendar:** Semester, extensive summer session. **Full-time faculty:** 491 total; 13% minority, 51% women. **Part-time faculty:** 191 total; 10% minority, 66% women. **Class size:** 21% < 20, 55% 20-39, 8% 40-49, 14% 50-99, 2% >100. **Special facilities:** African-American cultural center, Hispanic cultural center, Native American and Asian Pacific cultural center.

Freshman class profile. 8,169 applied, 5,949 admitted, 2,280 enrolled.

Mid 50% test scores			
SAT critical reading:	470-590	GPA 3.0-3.49:	33%
SAT math:	470-580	GPA 2.0-2.99:	34%
ACT composite:	19-25	Rank in top quarter:	38%
GPA 3.75 or higher:	18%	Rank in top tenth:	14%
GPA 3.50-3.74:	15%	Out-of-state:	10%
		Live on campus:	88%

Basis for selection. Expected 2.9 GPA; 21 ACT or 970 SAT (exclusive of Writing). Higher ACT/SAT score can compensate for lower GPA and higher GPA can compensate for lower test score. SAT or ACT recommended.

High school preparation. College-preparatory program required. 17 units required. Required units include English 4, mathematics 4, social studies 3, science 3 (laboratory 2), foreign language 1 and academic electives 2. Math should include 2 algebra, additional higher level math unit.

2011-2012 Annual costs. Tuition/fees: $6,623; $18,145 out-of-state. Costs reflect student share of tuition after the Colorado College Opportunity Fund. Room/board: $9,750. Books/supplies: $1,325. Personal expenses: $619.

2010-2011 Financial aid. Need-based: 1,287 full-time freshmen applied for aid; 1,277 were judged to have need; 1,277 of these received aid. Average need met was 61%. Average scholarship/grant was $2,097; average loan $1,659. 54% of total undergraduate aid awarded as scholarships/grants, 46% as loans/jobs. **Non-need-based:** Awarded to 3,664 full-time undergraduates, including 1,428 freshmen. Scholarships awarded for academics, art, athletics.

Application procedures. Admission: Closing date 8/1 (receipt date). $45 fee, may be waived for applicants with need. Admission notification on a rolling basis. **Financial aid:** Priority date 3/1; no closing date. FAFSA required. Applicants notified on a rolling basis starting 4/15; must reply within 4 week(s) of notification.

Academics. Special study options: Accelerated study, cooperative education, cross-registration, distance learning, double major, dual enrollment of high school students, ESL, exchange student, external degree, honors, independent study, internships, semester at sea, student-designed major, study abroad, teacher certification program, urban semester. **Credit/placement by examination:** AP, CLEP, IB, SAT, ACT, institutional tests. 30 credit hours maximum toward bachelor's degree. **Support services:** Learning center, reduced course load, remedial instruction, study skills assistance, tutoring, writing center.

Majors. Area/ethnic studies: African-American, Asian, Chicano/Hispanic-American/Latino. **Biology:** General. **Business:** Business admin. **Communications:** Communications/speech/rhetoric, journalism. **Conservation:** Environmental studies. **Education:** Music, special ed. **English:** English lit. **Foreign languages:** General, sign language interpretation, Spanish. **Health services:** Athletic training, audiology/hearing, audiology/speech pathology, dietetics, health care admin, nursing (RN), public health ed, speech pathology, vocational rehab counseling. **History:** General. **Math:** General. **Parks/recreation:** Exercise sciences, facilities management. **Philosophy/religion:** Philosophy. **Physical sciences:** Chemistry, geology, physics. **Protective services:** Criminal justice. **Psychology:** General. **Social sciences:** General, anthropology, economics, geography, international relations, political science, sociology. **Visual/performing arts:** Dramatic, music, music management, studio arts. **Work/family studies:** Aging.

Most popular majors. Business/marketing 12%, communications/journalism 8%, health sciences 14%, interdisciplinary studies 14%, parks/recreation 7%, social sciences 9%, visual/performing arts 7%.

Computing on campus. 1,671 workstations in dormitories, library, computer center, student center. Dormitories wired for high-speed internet access and linked to campus network. Commuter students can connect to campus network. Online course registration, online library, helpline, repair service, wireless network available.

Student life. Freshman orientation: Mandatory. Preregistration for classes offered. Two-day sessions that correspond with intended major. **Housing:** Guaranteed on-campus for freshmen. Coed dorms, single-sex dorms, special housing for disabled, apartments, fraternity/sorority housing, wellness housing available. $200 nonrefundable deposit. **Activities:** Bands, campus ministries, choral groups, dance, drama, film society, international student organizations, literary magazine, music ensembles, musical theater, opera, radio station, student government, student newspaper, symphony orchestra, TV station, African-American student union, Hispanic students organization, Native American student services, Asian/Pacific American student services.

Athletics. NCAA. **Intercollegiate:** Baseball M, basketball, cross-country W, diving W, football (tackle) M, golf, soccer W, softball W, swimming W, tennis, track and field, volleyball W, wrestling M. **Intramural:** Basketball, football (non-tackle), golf, racquetball, soccer, softball, table tennis, tennis, volleyball, water polo. **Team name:** Bears.

Student services. Adult student services, alcohol/substance abuse counseling, chaplain/spiritual director, career counseling, student employment services, financial aid counseling, health services, legal services, minority student services, personal counseling, placement for graduates, veterans' counselor, women's services. **Physically disabled:** Services for visually, speech, hearing impaired.

Contact. E-mail: admissions@unco.edu
Phone: (970) 351-2881 Toll-free number: (888) 700-4862
Fax: (970) 351-2984
Sean Broghammer, Director of Admissions, University of Northern Colorado, 501 20th Street, Campus Box 10, Greeley, CO 80639

University of Phoenix: Denver
Lone Tree, Colorado
www.phoenix.edu

- For-profit 4-year university
- Commuter campus in rural community
- 1,343 degree-seeking undergraduates

General. Regionally accredited. **Degrees:** 344 bachelor's awarded; master's offered. **Calendar:** Differs by program. **Full-time faculty:** 41 total. **Part-time faculty:** 332 total.

Basis for selection. Open admission, but selective for some programs.

2011-2012 Annual costs. Estimated costs as of August 2011: per-credit-hour charge, $380 to $415, depending upon level and course of study; electronic course materials fee, $95, if applicable. Book and material charges may vary by course and program. All fees are subject to change.

Application procedures. Admission: No deadline. No application fee. **Financial aid:** No deadline.

Academics. Credit/placement by examination: AP, CLEP.

Majors. Business: Accounting, business admin, credit management, e-commerce, entrepreneurial studies, management information systems, marketing, operations. **Communications:** Media studies. **Computer sciences:** General, database management, information technology, networking, programming, security, systems analysis, web page design, webmaster. **Education:** Early childhood. **Health services:** Facilities admin, long term care admin, medical records technology, nursing (RN). **Human services:** General. **Protective services:** Disaster management, law enforcement admin, security management. **Psychology:** General.

Contact. Marc Booker, Director of Admission and Evaluation, University of Phoenix: Denver, 10004 Park Meadows Drive, Lone Tree, CO 80124-5453

University of Phoenix: Southern Colorado
Colorado Springs, Colorado
www.phoenix.edu

- For-profit 4-year university
- Commuter campus in large city
- 591 degree-seeking undergraduates

General. Regionally accredited. **Degrees:** 86 bachelor's awarded; master's offered. **Calendar:** Differs by program. **Full-time faculty:** 12 total. **Part-time faculty:** 84 total.

Basis for selection. Open admission, but selective for some programs.

2011-2012 Annual costs. Estimated costs as of August 2011: per-credit-hour charge, $380 to $415, depending upon level and course of study; electronic course materials fee, $95, if applicable. Book and material charges may vary by course and program. All fees are subject to change.

Application procedures. Admission: No deadline. No application fee. **Financial aid:** No deadline.

Academics. Credit/placement by examination: AP, CLEP.

Majors. Business: Accounting, business admin, credit management, e-commerce, entrepreneurial studies, human resources, marketing, operations. **Communications:** Media studies. **Computer sciences:** General. **Health services:** Long term care admin, medical records technology. **Human services:** General. **Protective services:** Disaster management, law enforcement admin, security management.

Contact. Marc Booker, Director of Admission and Evaluation, University of Phoenix: Southern Colorado, 5725 Mark Dabling Boulevard, Colorado Springs, CO 80919-2221

Western State College of Colorado
Gunnison, Colorado
www.western.edu
CB code: 4946

- Public 4-year liberal arts college
- Residential campus in small town

- 1,958 degree-seeking undergraduates: 6% part-time, 39% women, 2% African American, 6% Hispanic American, 1% international
- 144 degree-seeking graduate students
- 93% of applicants admitted
- SAT or ACT (ACT writing optional) required

General. Founded in 1901. Regionally accredited. College-based mountain search and rescue team. **Degrees:** 396 bachelor's awarded. **Location:** 200 miles from Denver. **Calendar:** Semester, limited summer session. **Full-time faculty:** 134 total; 63% have terminal degrees, 2% minority, 44% women. **Part-time faculty:** 32 total; 75% have terminal degrees, 12% minority, 56% women. **Class size:** 52% < 20, 42% 20-39, 5% 40-49, less than 1% 50-99, less than 1% >100. **Special facilities:** Botanical gardens, archaeological site, dinosaur reconstruction lab.

Freshman class profile. 1,495 applied, 1,383 admitted, 436 enrolled.

Mid 50% test scores			
SAT critical reading:	460-580	GPA 2.0-2.99:	43%
SAT math:	480-560	Rank in top quarter:	20%
ACT composite:	19-24	Rank in top tenth:	2%
GPA 3.75 or higher:	10%	Return as sophomores:	64%
GPA 3.50-3.74:	12%	Out-of-state:	27%
GPA 3.0-3.49:	33%	Live on campus:	93%

Basis for selection. School achievement record, test scores very important; recommendations considered. Essay recommended. Interview recommended for academically weak applicants.

High school preparation. College-preparatory program required. 17 units required. Required and recommended units include English 4, mathematics 4, social studies 2, history 1, science 3 (laboratory 2), foreign language 1-2 and academic electives 2.

2011-2012 Annual costs. Tuition/fees: $5,473; $15,087 out-of-state. In-state tuition based upon assumption of Colorado Opportunity Fund waiver. Room/board: $8,472. Books/supplies: $1,400. Personal expenses: $1,269.

2011-2012 Financial aid. Need-based: 347 full-time freshmen applied for aid; 210 were judged to have need; 210 of these received aid. Average need met was 50%. Average scholarship/grant was $2,935; average loan $3,900. 49% of total undergraduate aid awarded as scholarships/grants, 51% as loans/jobs. **Non-need-based:** Awarded to 773 full-time undergraduates, including 225 freshmen. Scholarships awarded for academics, alumni affiliation, art, athletics, leadership, music/drama.

Application procedures. Admission: Priority date 6/1; no deadline. $30 fee, may be waived for applicants with need. Admission notification on a rolling basis beginning on or about 10/21. Must reply by May 1 or within 2 week(s) if notified thereafter. **Financial aid:** Priority date 3/1; no closing date. FAFSA required. Applicants notified on a rolling basis starting 4/1; must reply by 5/1 or within 4 week(s) of notification.

Academics. Special study options: Combined bachelor's/graduate degree, distance learning, double major, dual enrollment of high school students, honors, independent study, internships, liberal arts/career combination, semester at sea, study abroad, teacher certification program. **Credit/placement by examination:** AP, CLEP, IB, SAT, ACT, institutional tests. 30 credit hours maximum toward bachelor's degree. **Support services:** Study skills assistance, tutoring, writing center.

Majors. Biology: General. **Business:** Accounting, business admin, management information systems, resort management. **Communications:** Communications/speech/rhetoric. **Conservation:** Environmental studies. **Education:** Art, elementary, English, foreign languages, mathematics, music, physical, science, social science, social studies, special ed. **English:** English lit. **Foreign languages:** Spanish. **History:** General. **Math:** General. **Parks/recreation:** Exercise sciences. **Physical sciences:** Chemistry, geology. **Protective services:** Criminal justice, police science. **Psychology:** General. **Social sciences:** Anthropology, economics, political science, sociology. **Visual/performing arts:** Art, music, music management, studio arts.

Most popular majors. Biology 7%, business/marketing 28%, natural resources/environmental science 6%, parks/recreation 17%, social sciences 13%, visual/performing arts 7%.

Computing on campus. 168 workstations in dormitories, library, student center. Dormitories linked to campus network. Commuter students can connect to campus network. Online course registration available.

Student life. Freshman orientation: Available, $65 fee. Preregistration for classes offered. Wilderness-based orientation available. **Housing:** Guaranteed on-campus for freshmen. Coed dorms, single-sex dorms, apartments available. $100 nonrefundable deposit, deadline 4/9. **Activities:** Bands, campus ministries, choral groups, dance, drama, international student organizations, literary magazine, music ensembles, radio station, student government, student newspaper, symphony orchestra, TV station, Hillel, Black student alliance, Amigos, Campus Crusade, Hui-O-Ka-Aina, lesbian-gay-bisexual alliance, Newman club, Baptist student union, Christian athletes fellowship, women's action coalition.

Athletics. NCAA. **Intercollegiate:** Basketball, cross-country, football (tackle) M, skiing, track and field, volleyball W, wrestling M. **Intramural:** Baseball M, basketball, golf, ice hockey M, lacrosse, rugby, skiing, soccer, softball, swimming, tennis, track and field, volleyball, wrestling M. **Team name:** Mountaineers.

Student services. Adult student services, career counseling, health services, on-campus daycare, personal counseling, veterans' counselor. **Physically disabled:** Services for visually, hearing impaired.

Contact. E-mail: discover@western.edu
Phone: (970) 943-2119 Toll-free number: (800) 876-5309
Fax: (970) 943-2212
Tim Albers, Director of Admissions, Western State College of Colorado, 600 North Adams Street, Gunnison, CO 81231

Westwood College: Denver North
Denver, Colorado
www.westwood.edu/locations/colorado/denver-north-campus
CB code: 3948

- For-profit 4-year technical college
- Commuter campus in very large city
- 797 degree-seeking undergraduates
- Interview required

General. Founded in 1953. Regionally accredited; also accredited by ACCSC. **Degrees:** 105 bachelor's, 88 associate awarded. **Location:** 5 miles from downtown. **Calendar:** 5 ten-week terms per year. Extensive summer session. **Full-time faculty:** 23 total. **Part-time faculty:** 57 total.

Basis for selection. SAT/ACT/ACCUPLACER and interview most important. Developmental courses may be required for those who do not pass entrance examination. SAT or ACT recommended. ACCUPLACER waived for students with sufficient SAT/ACT scores.

High school preparation. At least 1 algebra required for electronics, drafting and surveying programs. General math required for all other programs.

2011-2012 Annual costs. Tuition/fees: $15,020. Books/supplies: $1,106. Personal expenses: $2,000.

Financial aid. Non-need-based: Scholarships awarded for academics, state residency.

Application procedures. Admission: No deadline. $50 fee. Admission notification on a rolling basis. **Financial aid:** No deadline. FAFSA, institutional form required. Applicants notified on a rolling basis starting 1/1; must reply within 2 week(s) of notification.

Academics. Instruction and emphasis on laboratory work and practical application. **Special study options:** Accelerated study, cooperative education, distance learning, independent study, internships, liberal arts/career combination. **Credit/placement by examination:** AP, CLEP, institutional tests. 69 credit hours maximum toward associate degree, 140 toward bachelor's. **Support services:** Learning center, remedial instruction, study skills assistance, tutoring.

Majors. Architecture: Interior. **Business:** General, accounting, business admin, e-commerce, management information systems, marketing. **Communications:** Communications/speech/rhetoric. **Communications technology:** Graphic/printing. **Computer sciences:** General, computer graphics, information systems, networking, security, web page design, webmaster. **Engineering:** Electrical. **Protective services:** Law enforcement admin. **Visual/performing arts:** Commercial/advertising art, design, graphic design.

Most popular majors. Business/marketing 20%, computer/information sciences 44%, engineering/engineering technologies 15%, visual/performing arts 21%.

Computing on campus. 50 workstations in library, computer center. Online library available.

Student life. Freshman orientation: Mandatory. Preregistration for classes offered. **Policies:** No-tolerance drug/alcohol policy.

Student services. Career counseling, student employment services, financial aid counseling, placement for graduates, veterans' counselor. **Physically disabled:** Services for visually impaired.

Contact. E-mail: rdejong@westwood.edu
Phone: (303) 650-5050 Fax: (303) 487-0214
Ron DeJong, Director of Admissions, Westwood College: Denver North, 7350 North Broadway, Denver, CO 80221

Westwood College: Denver South
Denver, Colorado
www.westwood.edu/locations/colorado/denver-south-campus

- For-profit 4-year technical and career college
- Commuter campus in very large city
- 427 degree-seeking undergraduates
- Interview required

General. Regionally accredited; also accredited by ACCSC. **Degrees:** 36 bachelor's, 58 associate awarded. **Calendar:** Differs by program, extensive summer session. **Full-time faculty:** 4 total. **Part-time faculty:** 48 total.

Basis for selection. Institutional test (ACCUPLACER) and interview most important. Developmental courses may be required for those who do not pass entrance examination.

2011-2012 Annual costs. Tuition/fees: $15,020. Books/supplies: $1,106. Personal expenses: $2,534.

Application procedures. Admission: No deadline. $50 fee. Admission notification on a rolling basis. **Financial aid:** No deadline. FAFSA, institutional form required. Applicants notified on a rolling basis; must reply within 2 week(s) of notification.

Academics. Special study options: Accelerated study, distance learning, independent study, weekend college. **Credit/placement by examination:** AP, CLEP, institutional tests. 67 credit hours maximum toward associate degree, 135 toward bachelor's. **Support services:** Reduced course load, remedial instruction, study skills assistance, tutoring, writing center.

Majors. Architecture: Interior. **Business:** E-commerce, fashion. **Communications technology:** Animation/special effects, desktop publishing, graphics. **Computer sciences:** Computer graphics, LAN/WAN management, networking, security, system admin, web page design, webmaster. **Protective services:** Law enforcement admin. **Visual/performing arts:** Commercial/advertising art, design, graphic design, interior design.

Computing on campus. 300 workstations in library, computer center, student center. Commuter students can connect to campus network. Online course registration, online library, wireless network available.

Student life. Freshman orientation: Mandatory. Preregistration for classes offered.

Student services. Adult student services, career counseling, student employment services, financial aid counseling, placement for graduates.

Contact. Phone: (303) 934-1122 Fax: (303) 934-2583
Daniel Vopat, Director of Admissions, Westwood College: Denver South, 3150 South Sheridan Boulevard, Denver, CO 80227-5507

Westwood College: Online
Broomfield, Colorado
www.westwood.edu

- For-profit 3-year virtual career college
- Very large city

General. Regionally accredited. **Calendar:** Quarter.

Annual costs/financial aid. Tuition/fees (2011-2012): $15,020.

Contact. Phone: (800) 281-2978
Vice President of Admissions, 10249 Church Ranch Way, Broomfield, CO 80021

Connecticut

Albertus Magnus College

New Haven, Connecticut
www.albertus.edu

CB member
CB code: 3001

- Private 4-year liberal arts college affiliated with Roman Catholic Church
- Residential campus in small city
- 1,598 degree-seeking undergraduates: 14% part-time, 66% women, 22% African American, 1% Asian American, 11% Hispanic American, 1% Native American
- 392 degree-seeking graduate students
- 67% of applicants admitted
- SAT or ACT (ACT writing optional), application essay required
- 62% graduate within 6 years

General. Founded in 1925. Regionally accredited. Majority of students enrolled in adult education and graduate programs. Approximately 500 undergraduates are traditional age and are able to live on campus. **Degrees:** 333 bachelor's, 101 associate awarded; master's offered. **Location:** 90 miles from New York City. **Calendar:** Semester, limited summer session. **Full-time faculty:** 42 total; 71% have terminal degrees, 5% minority, 43% women. **Part-time faculty:** 206 total. **Class size:** 82% < 20, 18% 20-39.

Freshman class profile. 722 applied, 484 admitted, 130 enrolled.

Mid 50% test scores		GPA 3.0-3.49:	26%
SAT critical reading:	440-490	GPA 2.0-2.99:	62%
SAT math:	390-460	Rank in top quarter:	28%
SAT writing:	440-490	Rank in top tenth:	10%
GPA 3.75 or higher:	4%	Return as sophomores:	76%
GPA 3.50-3.74:	6%	Live on campus:	38%

Basis for selection. School achievement record most important. Recommendations, test scores, interview, school and community activities also considered. **Home schooled:** Letter of recommendation (nonparent) required. GED preferred.

High school preparation. 16 units required. Required and recommended units include English 4, mathematics 2-3, social studies 2-3, science 2-3 (laboratory 1) and foreign language 3.

2011-2012 Annual costs. Tuition/fees: $26,174. Room/board: $11,088. Books/supplies: $984. Personal expenses: $3,140.

2010-2011 Financial aid. **Need-based:** 159 full-time freshmen applied for aid; 149 were judged to have need; 146 of these received aid. Average need met was 66%. Average scholarship/grant was $15,162; average loan $2,893. 42% of total undergraduate aid awarded as scholarships/grants, 58% as loans/jobs. **Non-need-based:** Scholarships awarded for academics, art, job skills, leadership, music/drama, religious affiliation.

Application procedures. **Admission:** No deadline. $35 fee, may be waived for applicants with need. Admission notification on a rolling basis beginning on or about 12/1. Must reply by May 1 or within 4 week(s) if notified thereafter. **Financial aid:** Priority date 2/28; no closing date. FAFSA required. Applicants notified on a rolling basis starting 3/1; must reply within 2 week(s) of notification.

Academics. **Special study options:** Accelerated study, double major, honors, independent study, internships, liberal arts/career combination, student-designed major, teacher certification program. **Credit/placement by examination:** AP, CLEP, SAT, institutional tests. 21 credit hours maximum toward associate degree, 45 toward bachelor's. **Support services:** Learning center, reduced course load, study skills assistance, tutoring, writing center.

Majors. **Biology:** General. **Business:** Accounting, business admin, finance, international, management information systems, managerial economics. **Communications:** Advertising, communications/speech/rhetoric, media studies, sports. **Computer sciences:** Information systems. **Education:** General, art, biology, business, chemistry, English, history, mathematics, middle, science, secondary, social studies, Spanish. **English:** British lit, creative writing, English lit. **Foreign languages:** Spanish. **Health services:** Art therapy, premedicine. **History:** General. **Liberal arts:** Arts/sciences. **Math:** General. **Parks/recreation:** Sports admin. **Philosophy/religion:** Philosophy, religion. **Physical sciences:** Chemistry. **Protective services:** Criminal justice. **Psychology:** General. **Social sciences:** General, political science, sociology.

Visual/performing arts: General, art, art history/conservation, commercial/advertising art, studio arts.

Most popular majors. Business/marketing 63%, psychology 9%, social sciences 9%.

Computing on campus. 146 workstations in library, computer center, student center. Dormitories wired for high-speed internet access and linked to campus network. Commuter students can connect to campus network. Helpline, repair service, wireless network available.

Student life. **Freshman orientation:** Mandatory. Preregistration for classes offered. **Housing:** Coed dorms, single-sex dorms, wellness housing available. $400 nonrefundable deposit, deadline 7/1. **Activities:** Campus ministries, choral groups, dance, drama, literary magazine, musical theater, student government, Students United for a Better World.

Athletics. NCAA. **Intercollegiate:** Baseball M, basketball, cross-country, lacrosse, soccer, softball W, tennis, volleyball. **Intramural:** Basketball, racquetball, soccer, table tennis. **Team name:** Falcons.

Student services. Adult student services, chaplain/spiritual director, career counseling, student employment services, financial aid counseling, health services, personal counseling, placement for graduates, veterans' counselor.

Contact. E-mail: admissions@albertus.edu
Phone: (203) 773-8501 Toll-free number: (800) 578-9160
Fax: (203) 773-5248
Richard LoLatte, Dean of Admissions and Enrollment Management, Albertus Magnus College, 700 Prospect Street, New Haven, CT 06511-1189

Central Connecticut State University

New Britain, Connecticut
www.ccsu.edu

CB member
CB code: 3898

- Public 4-year university
- Commuter campus in small city
- 9,763 degree-seeking undergraduates: 20% part-time, 48% women, 10% African American, 3% Asian American, 9% Hispanic American, 1% international
- 2,199 degree-seeking graduate students
- 63% of applicants admitted
- SAT or ACT (ACT writing optional), application essay required
- 48% graduate within 6 years

General. Founded in 1849. Regionally accredited. **Degrees:** 1,752 bachelor's awarded; master's, professional offered. **ROTC:** Army, Air Force. **Location:** 9 miles from Hartford. **Calendar:** Semester, extensive summer session. **Full-time faculty:** 440 total; 90% have terminal degrees, 18% minority, 42% women. **Part-time faculty:** 528 total; 16% have terminal degrees, 13% minority, 44% women. **Class size:** 43% < 20, 54% 20-39, 1% 40-49, 2% 50-99, less than 1% >100. **Special facilities:** Observatory, planetarium.

Freshman class profile. 6,473 applied, 4,087 admitted, 1,387 enrolled.

Mid 50% test scores		GPA 2.0-2.99:	49%
SAT critical reading:	460-540	Rank in top quarter:	21%
SAT math:	460-550	Rank in top tenth:	9%
SAT writing:	460-550	Return as sophomores:	76%
GPA 3.75 or higher:	6%	Out-of-state:	5%
GPA 3.50-3.74:	8%	Live on campus:	57%
GPA 3.0-3.49:	37%		

Basis for selection. High school record, class rank, SAT scores most important. Letters of recommendation, optional student essay, and resume of activities to assess applicant's attitude toward future success considered. School of Business, social work program, communication program, and School of Education programs require acceptance into majors after admission to the university. Interview optional but would be considered. Audition required for music. **Home schooled:** Statement describing home school structure and mission, transcript of courses and grades, state high school equivalency certificate required.

High school preparation. 13 units required. Required and recommended units include English 4, mathematics 3, social studies 2, history 1, science 2 (laboratory 1) and foreign language 3. Social science should include US history; math should include algebra I and II and geometry.

2011-2012 Annual costs. Tuition/fees: $8,055; $18,679 out-of-state. Room/board: $9,814. Books/supplies: $1,200. Personal expenses: $2,000.

2010-2011 Financial aid. Need-based: 1,205 full-time freshmen applied for aid; 947 were judged to have need; 919 of these received aid. Average need met was 67%. Average scholarship/grant was $4,420; average loan $3,454. 45% of total undergraduate aid awarded as scholarships/grants, 55% as loans/jobs. **Non-need-based:** Awarded to 942 full-time undergraduates, including 202 freshmen. Scholarships awarded for academics, athletics, minority status.

Application procedures. Admission: Priority date 10/1; deadline 6/1 (receipt date). $50 fee, may be waived for applicants with need. Admission notification on a rolling basis beginning on or about 12/1. Must reply by May 1 or within 2 week(s) if notified thereafter. **Financial aid:** Priority date 3/1, closing date 9/15. FAFSA required. Applicants notified on a rolling basis starting 4/1; must reply within 2 week(s) of notification.

Academics. Special study options: Cooperative education, cross-registration, distance learning, double major, dual enrollment of high school students, ESL, exchange student, honors, independent study, internships, student-designed major, study abroad, teacher certification program. Undergraduates may take graduate classes. **Credit/placement by examination:** AP, CLEP, IB, SAT, institutional tests. 30 credit hours maximum toward bachelor's degree. **Support services:** Learning center, pre-admission summer program, reduced course load, remedial instruction, study skills assistance, tutoring, writing center.

Majors. Biology: General, biochemistry, molecular. **Business:** Accounting, business admin, construction management, finance, management information systems, marketing, organizational behavior, travel services. **Communications:** Communications/speech/rhetoric, journalism. **Computer sciences:** General. **Education:** Art, elementary, music, secondary, technology/industrial arts. **Engineering:** Civil, electrical, mechanical. **English:** English lit. **Foreign languages:** French, German, Italian, Spanish. **Health services:** Athletic training, nursing (RN). **History:** General. **Human services:** Social work. **Math:** General. **Philosophy/religion:** Philosophy. **Physical sciences:** Chemistry, geology, physics. **Psychology:** General. **Social sciences:** General, anthropology, criminology, economics, geography, political science, sociology. **Visual/performing arts:** Art, design, dramatic, music.

Most popular majors. Business/marketing 30%, communications/journalism 6%, education 10%, engineering/engineering technologies 6%, psychology 10%, social sciences 14%.

Computing on campus. 400 workstations in dormitories, library, computer center, student center. Dormitories wired for high-speed internet access and linked to campus network. Commuter students can connect to campus network. Online course registration, online library, helpline, repair service, wireless network available.

Student life. Freshman orientation: Available, $65 fee. Preregistration for classes offered. One-day program in late June or early July. **Housing:** Coed dorms, single-sex dorms available. $250 nonrefundable deposit, deadline 5/1. **Activities:** Bands, campus ministries, choral groups, dance, drama, film society, international student organizations, literary magazine, music ensembles, musical theater, radio station, student government, student newspaper, TV station, Newman club, Union of Jewish Students, Christian Fellowship, Christian Science organization, Afro-American and African students, Latin American student association.

Athletics. NCAA. **Intercollegiate:** Baseball M, basketball, cross-country, diving W, football (tackle) M, golf, lacrosse W, soccer, softball W, swimming W, track and field, volleyball W. **Intramural:** Badminton, basketball, field hockey W, football (tackle) M, gymnastics W, lacrosse M, rugby, soccer, softball W, tennis, volleyball, water polo M. **Team name:** Blue Devils.

Student services. Adult student services, alcohol/substance abuse counseling, chaplain/spiritual director, career counseling, student employment services, financial aid counseling, health services, minority student services, on-campus daycare, personal counseling, placement for graduates, veterans' counselor, women's services. **Physically disabled:** Services for visually, speech, hearing impaired.

Contact. E-mail: admissions@ccsu.edu
Phone: (860) 832-2278 Fax: (860) 832-2295
Lawrence Hall, Director of Admissions, Central Connecticut State University, 1615 Stanley Street, New Britain, CT 06050

Charter Oak State College
New Britain, Connecticut

CB member
CB code: 0870

www.charteroak.edu

- Public 4-year virtual liberal arts college
- Commuter campus in small city
- 2,051 degree-seeking undergraduates

General. Founded in 1973. Regionally accredited. Nearly all courses are on-line. **Degrees:** 472 bachelor's, 78 associate awarded. **Location:** 5 miles from Hartford. **Calendar:** Differs by program, limited summer session. **Part-time faculty:** 153 total. **Class size:** 71% < 20, 18% 20-39, 4% 40-49, 7% 50-99.

Basis for selection. 9 college-level credits must be completed before enrolling. May be earned through college courses, testing, or ACE/PONSI recommendations for noncollege-sponsored instruction.

2011-2012 Annual costs. Per-credit-hour charge, in-state: $236; out-of-state, $310. College Fee: In-state associate degree or bachelor's degree, $165 per semester; out-of-state $220 per semester. Cost of education varies due to students having option to take courses at other institutions. Books/supplies: $1,000.

Financial aid. All financial aid based on need.

Application procedures. Admission: No deadline. $75 fee, may be waived for applicants with need. Admission notification on a rolling basis. **Financial aid:** No deadline. FAFSA, institutional form required. Applicants notified on a rolling basis starting 8/23.

Academics. Tutoring and writing center available online free to students. **Special study options:** Accelerated study, distance learning, dual enrollment of high school students, external degree, independent study, liberal arts/career combination, student-designed major. Students can take courses at any regionally accredited institution. **Credit/placement by examination:** AP, CLEP, institutional tests. 60 credit hours maximum toward associate degree, 120 toward bachelor's. Unlimited number of hours of credit by examination may be counted toward degree. **Support services:** Tutoring, writing center.

Majors. Liberal arts: Arts/sciences.

Computing on campus. Commuter students can connect to campus network. Online course registration, online library, helpline, wireless network available.

Student life. Activities: Student government.

Student services. Adult student services, financial aid counseling, veterans' counselor.

Contact. E-mail: info@charteroak.edu
Phone: (860) 832-3800 Fax: (860) 832-3999
Lori Pendleton, Director of Admission, Charter Oak State College, 55 Paul Manafort Drive, New Britain, CT 06053-2150

Connecticut College
New London, Connecticut

CB member
CB code: 3284

www.connecticutcollege.edu

- Private 4-year liberal arts college
- Residential campus in large town
- 1,781 degree-seeking undergraduates: 61% women, 4% African American, 3% Asian American, 7% Hispanic American, 4% international
- 7 degree-seeking graduate students
- 34% of applicants admitted
- Application essay required
- 84% graduate within 6 years; 25% enter graduate study

General. Founded in 1911. Regionally accredited. **Degrees:** 451 bachelor's awarded; master's offered. **Location:** 105 miles from Boston, 124 miles from New York City. **Calendar:** Semester, limited summer session. **Full-time faculty:** 178 total; 92% have terminal degrees, 24% minority, 48% women. **Part-time faculty:** 62 total; 21% have terminal degrees, 6% minority, 48% women. **Class size:** 63% < 20, 31% 20-39, 4% 40-49, 1% 50-99, less than 1% >100. **Special facilities:** 750-acre arboretum, greenhouse, ion accelerator, refracting telescope and observatory, scanning and transmission electron microscopes, nuclear magnetic resonance spectrometer, tunable diode laser spectroscopy laboratory, center for electronic and digital sound, neuroscience and animal behavior laboratories, clinical and social psychology research observation suites.

Freshman class profile. 5,241 applied, 1,804 admitted, 509 enrolled.

Mid 50% test scores		Rank in top tenth:	55%
SAT critical reading:	620-710	Return as sophomores:	90%
SAT math:	630-700	Out-of-state:	84%
SAT writing:	630-720	Live on campus:	100%
Rank in top quarter:	91%	International:	4%

Basis for selection. School achievement record most important. Recommendations, personal qualities, personal essay, special talents, extracurricular activities also significant. Applicants have option of submitting no test scores, SAT Critical Reading only, ACT only, or 2 SAT Subject Tests only. Interview recommended. Audition recommended for dance or music majors. Portfolio recommended for art majors. **Home schooled:** State high school equivalency certificate, letter of recommendation (nonparent) required. Extracurricular activities encouraged.

High school preparation. College-preparatory program recommended.

2011-2012 Annual costs. Tuition/fees: $43,990. Room/board: $10,980. Books/supplies: $1,000. Personal expenses: $500.

2011-2012 Financial aid. All financial aid based on need. 307 full-time freshmen applied for aid; 264 were judged to have need; 264 of these received aid. Average need met was 100%. Average scholarship/grant was $32,993; average loan $3,384. 86% of total undergraduate aid awarded as scholarships/grants, 14% as loans/jobs.

Application procedures. Admission: Closing date 1/1 (postmark date). $60 fee, may be waived for applicants with need. Admission notification by 3/31. Must reply by 5/1. **Financial aid:** Closing date 2/1. FAFSA, CSS PROFILE required. Applicants notified by 4/1; must reply by 5/1.

Academics. Four interdisciplinary centers through which students may earn a certificate to complement their major; competitive application process for acceptance into these programs. Students may also earn Connecticut teacher certification or museum studies certificates in addition to their majors. **Special study options:** Cross-registration, double major, dual enrollment of high school students, exchange student, independent study, internships, student-designed major, study abroad, teacher certification program, Washington semester. 12-college exchange, National Theater Institute, Mystic Seaport Program in American Maritime Studies, Institute for Architecture and Urban Studies, American Academy in Rome, Associated Kyoto Program, cross-registration with US Coast Guard Academy, Trinity College and Wesleyan University, study away-teach away opportunities, specially funded student research opportunities. **Credit/placement by examination:** AP, CLEP, IB, institutional tests. 32 credit hours maximum toward bachelor's degree. Students may use AP credit to repair credit deficiencies that arise from voluntary course withdrawals or failing grades, or to accelerate. **Support services:** Pre-admission summer program, reduced course load, study skills assistance, tutoring, writing center.

Majors. Architecture: Architecture. **Area/ethnic studies:** African, American, Chicano/Hispanic-American/Latino, East Asian, Latin American, women's. **Biology:** General, biochemistry, Biochemistry/molecular biology, botany, cellular/molecular, neuroscience. **Computer sciences:** Computer science. **Conservation:** Environmental studies. **English:** English lit. **Foreign languages:** Chinese, classics, French, German, Italian, Japanese, Slavic, Spanish. **History:** General. **Math:** General. **Philosophy/religion:** Philosophy, religion. **Physical sciences:** Astrophysics, chemistry, physics. **Psychology:** General. **Social sciences:** Anthropology, economics, international relations, political science, sociology, urban studies. **Visual/performing arts:** Art history/conservation, dance, dramatic, film/cinema/video, music, studio arts. **Work/family studies:** Family studies.

Most popular majors. Area/ethnic studies 6%, biology 15%, psychology 7%, social sciences 33%, visual/performing arts 11%.

Computing on campus. 500 workstations in library, computer center, student center. Dormitories wired for high-speed internet access and linked to campus network. Commuter students can connect to campus network. Online course registration, online library, helpline, repair service, student web hosting, wireless network available.

Student life. Freshman orientation: Mandatory. Preregistration for classes offered. Held the weekend prior to start of classes; optional outdoor program prior to full orientation offered for additional fee. **Policies:** Student-adjudicated honor code that governs both academic and social activities and behavior. Freshmen not permitted cars on campus. **Housing:** Guaranteed on-campus for all undergraduates. Coed dorms, special housing for disabled, apartments, wellness housing available. $500 nonrefundable deposit, deadline 5/1. Quiet housing, men's and women's floors, substance-free housing, living-and-learning housing, gender-neutral housing available. **Activities:** Bands, campus ministries, choral groups, dance, drama, film society, international student organizations, literary magazine, music ensembles, radio station, student government, student newspaper, symphony orchestra, College Democrats, College Republicans, Hillel, Intervarsity Christian Fellowship, multi-faith student council, Muslim student association, Asian/Asian American student association, Latino American student association, Sexual Orientations United for Liberation, African/African American student association.

Athletics. NCAA. **Intercollegiate:** Basketball, cross-country, diving, field hockey W, ice hockey, lacrosse, rowing (crew), sailing, soccer, squash, swimming, tennis, track and field, volleyball W, water polo. **Intramural:** Baseball M, basketball, football (non-tackle) M, racquetball, soccer, softball, squash, tennis, volleyball. **Team name:** Camels.

Student services. Adult student services, alcohol/substance abuse counseling, chaplain/spiritual director, career counseling, services for economically disadvantaged, student employment services, financial aid counseling, health services, minority student services, on-campus daycare, personal counseling, placement for graduates, women's services. **Physically disabled:** Services for visually, speech, hearing impaired.

Contact. E-mail: admission@conncoll.edu
Phone: (860) 439-2200 Fax: (860) 439-4301
Martha Merrill, Dean of Admission and Financial Aid, Connecticut College, 270 Mohegan Avenue, New London, CT 06320-4196

Eastern Connecticut State University
Willimantic, Connecticut CB member
www.easternct.edu CB code: 3966

- Public 4-year university and liberal arts college
- Residential campus in large town
- 5,047 degree-seeking undergraduates: 12% part-time, 53% women, 7% African American, 1% Asian American, 8% Hispanic American, 1% international
- 206 degree-seeking graduate students
- 70% of applicants admitted
- SAT or ACT (ACT writing optional) required
- 49% graduate within 6 years

General. Founded in 1889. Regionally accredited. Connecticut's public liberal arts college. **Degrees:** 1,057 bachelor's, 13 associate awarded; master's offered. **ROTC:** Army, Air Force. **Location:** 30 miles from Hartford, 90 miles from Boston. **Calendar:** Semester, extensive summer session. **Full-time faculty:** 193 total; 97% have terminal degrees, 22% minority, 46% women. **Part-time faculty:** 276 total; 34% have terminal degrees, 10% minority, 46% women. **Class size:** 37% < 20, 56% 20-39, 6% 40-49, less than 1% 50-99. **Special facilities:** Child and family development complex, sustainable energy institute, free enterprise institute, arboretum, planetarium, farm, 2 electron microscopes, bell carillon.

Freshman class profile. 3,095 applied, 2,180 admitted, 951 enrolled.

Mid 50% test scores			
SAT critical reading:	450-550	GPA 3.0-3.49:	38%
SAT math:	450-540	GPA 2.0-2.99:	46%
SAT writing:	460-560	Rank in top quarter:	24%
ACT composite:	19-23	Rank in top tenth:	6%
GPA 3.75 or higher:	6%	Return as sophomores:	76%
GPA 3.50-3.74:	9%	Out-of-state:	5%
		Live on campus:	87%

Basis for selection. Applicants should be in top half of class and recommended by high school. Quality of course work very important; 2.5 GPA in college preparatory program required. SAT score also important. Extracurricular activities considered. Interview and essay recommended.

High school preparation. College-preparatory program recommended. Required and recommended units include English 4, mathematics 3-4, social studies 2, science 1 (laboratory 1) and foreign language 2-3.

2011-2012 Annual costs. Tuition/fees: $8,555; $19,179 out-of-state. Room/board: $10,339. Books/supplies: $1,554. Personal expenses: $2,158.

2010-2011 Financial aid. Need-based: 818 full-time freshmen applied for aid; 656 were judged to have need; 629 of these received aid. Average need met was 53%. Average scholarship/grant was $7,386; average loan $3,747. 40% of total undergraduate aid awarded as scholarships/grants, 60% as loans/jobs. **Non-need-based:** Awarded to 117 full-time undergraduates, including 19 freshmen. Scholarships awarded for academics. **Additional information:** Tuition waiver for veterans and members of National Guard.

Application procedures. Admission: Priority date 5/1; no deadline. $50 fee, may be waived for applicants with need. Admission notification on a rolling basis beginning on or about 12/1. Must reply by May 1 or within 2 week(s) if notified thereafter. **Financial aid:** Priority date 3/15; no closing date. FAFSA required. Applicants notified on a rolling basis starting 2/15; must reply within 2 week(s) of notification.

Academics. Life learning portfolio class available. **Special study options:** Accelerated study, cooperative education, cross-registration, distance learning, double major, dual enrollment of high school students, exchange student, external degree, honors, independent study, internships, student-designed major, study abroad, teacher certification program, weekend college. **Credit/placement by examination:** AP, CLEP, institutional tests. 30 credit hours

maximum toward associate degree, 60 toward bachelor's. Institutional placement test required for all entering freshmen. **Support services:** Learning center, pre-admission summer program, reduced course load, remedial instruction, study skills assistance, tutoring, writing center.

Majors. Biology: General, biochemistry. **Business:** Accounting, business admin, management information systems. **Communications:** Communications/speech/rhetoric. **Computer sciences:** General. **Conservation:** Environmental science. **Education:** Early childhood, elementary, middle, physical, secondary. **English:** English lit. **Foreign languages:** Spanish. **History:** General. **Human services:** Social work. **Math:** General. **Parks/recreation:** Sports admin. **Psychology:** General. **Social sciences:** Economics, political science, sociology. **Visual/performing arts:** General, studio arts.

Most popular majors. Business/marketing 17%, communications/journalism 8%, education 7%, English 6%, liberal arts 10%, psychology 10%, social sciences 16%.

Computing on campus. 637 workstations in dormitories, library, computer center. Dormitories wired for high-speed internet access and linked to campus network. Commuter students can connect to campus network. Online library, helpline, repair service, student web hosting, wireless network available.

Student life. Freshman orientation: Mandatory. Preregistration for classes offered. **Policies:** No alcohol permitted on campus; all halls are smoke-free; sign-in guest policy for all first-year halls from 7pm-12am. **Housing:** Coed dorms, apartments available. $250 nonrefundable deposit, deadline 5/1. **Activities:** Bands, campus ministries, choral groups, dance, drama, international student organizations, literary magazine, music ensembles, musical theater, radio station, student government, student newspaper, TV station, over 60 organizations.

Athletics. NCAA. **Intercollegiate:** Baseball M, basketball, cheerleading M, cross-country, field hockey W, lacrosse, soccer, softball W, swimming W, track and field, volleyball W. **Intramural:** Badminton, basketball, bowling, cross-country, football (tackle) M, gymnastics W, racquetball, rugby, skiing, soccer, softball, swimming, tennis, track and field, volleyball, water polo. **Team name:** Warriors.

Student services. Adult student services, alcohol/substance abuse counseling, chaplain/spiritual director, career counseling, services for economically disadvantaged, student employment services, financial aid counseling, health services, minority student services, on-campus daycare, personal counseling, placement for graduates, veterans' counselor, women's services. **Physically disabled:** Services for visually, speech, hearing impaired.

Contact. E-mail: admissions@easternct.edu
Phone: (860) 465-5286 Toll-free number: (877) 353-3278
Fax: (860) 465-5544
Kimberly Crone, Director of Admissions and Enrollment Planning, Eastern Connecticut State University, 83 Windham Street, Willimantic, CT 06226-2295

Fairfield University
Fairfield, Connecticut
www.fairfield.edu

CB member
CB code: 3390

- Private 4-year university affiliated with Roman Catholic Church
- Residential campus in small city
- 3,655 degree-seeking undergraduates: 8% part-time, 58% women
- 1,126 degree-seeking graduate students
- 69% of applicants admitted
- Application essay required
- 81% graduate within 6 years

General. Founded in 1942. Regionally accredited. **Degrees:** 856 bachelor's, 7 associate awarded; master's, professional offered. **ROTC:** Army, Air Force. **Location:** 55 miles from New York City. **Calendar:** Semester, limited summer session. **Full-time faculty:** 262 total; 92% have terminal degrees, 11% minority, 51% women. **Part-time faculty:** 279 total; 7% minority, 53% women. **Class size:** 52% < 20, 47% 20-39, 1% 40-49, less than 1% 50-99. **Special facilities:** Fine arts center containing 2 theaters, campus ministry center, art galleries, Japanese meditation garden, business experimental center, simulation and trading floor, nursing simulation lab, art museum.

Freshman class profile. 8,486 applied, 5,892 admitted, 909 enrolled.

Mid 50% test scores			
SAT critical reading:	530-620		
SAT math:	540-630		
SAT writing:	540-630		
ACT composite:	24-27		
GPA 3.75 or higher:	22%		
GPA 3.50-3.74:	20%		
GPA 3.0-3.49:	36%		
GPA 2.0-2.99:		22%
Rank in top quarter:		69%
Rank in top tenth:		28%
End year in good standing:		99%
Return as sophomores:		88%
Out-of-state:		74%
Live on campus:		96%
International:		1%

Basis for selection. GED not accepted. School achievement record, recommendations, school activities, personal statement important. Special consideration given to children/siblings of alumni and students with special talents, diverse or unique backgrounds. Interview recommended. Portfolio highly recommended for music majors, resume for theater majors. **Home schooled:** Statement describing home school structure and mission, transcript of courses and grades required.

High school preparation. College-preparatory program required. 16 units required; 20 recommended. Required and recommended units include English 4, mathematics 3-4, social studies 2, history 2, science 2-3 (laboratory 2), foreign language 2-4 and academic electives 1. 1 additional math and 2 science recommended for math, business and science major.

2011-2012 Annual costs. Tuition/fees: $40,580. 12- and 14-meal plans available. Proof of health insurance required in order to waive health insurance fee. Room/board: $12,680. Books/supplies: $1,100. Personal expenses: $900.

2011-2012 Financial aid. Need-based: 704 full-time freshmen applied for aid; 588 were judged to have need; 579 of these received aid. Average need met was 82%. Average scholarship/grant was $18,651; average loan $4,034. 76% of total undergraduate aid awarded as scholarships/grants, 24% as loans/jobs. **Non-need-based:** Awarded to 1,484 full-time undergraduates, including 616 freshmen. Scholarships awarded for academics, alumni affiliation, art, athletics, leadership, music/drama. **Additional information:** Veteran's Pride Program provides tuition discounts for children of qualified veterans. Bridgeport Tuition Program provides free tuition to qualified students from City of Bridgeport with family income under $50,000.

Application procedures. Admission: Closing date 1/15 (postmark date). $60 fee, may be waived for applicants with need. Admission notification by 4/1. Must reply by 5/1. **Financial aid:** Closing date 2/15. FAFSA, CSS PROFILE required. Applicants notified by 4/1; must reply by 5/1.

Academics. Special study options: Combined bachelor's/graduate degree, cross-registration, double major, exchange student, honors, independent study, internships, liberal arts/career combination, student-designed major, study abroad, teacher certification program, Washington semester. 3-2 engineering program with University of Connecticut, Rensselaer Polytechnic Institute, Columbia University, and Stevens Institute of Technology. **Credit/placement by examination:** AP, CLEP, IB, institutional tests. 15 credit hours maximum toward bachelor's degree. **Support services:** Reduced course load, study skills assistance, tutoring, writing center.

Majors. Area/ethnic studies: American. **Biology:** General, biochemistry. **Business:** Accounting, business admin, finance, international, management information systems, marketing. **Communications:** Communications/speech/rhetoric. **Computer sciences:** General. **Engineering:** Computer, electrical, mechanical, software. **English:** English lit. **Foreign languages:** French, German, Italian, Spanish. **Health services:** Nursing (RN). **History:** General. **Math:** General. **Philosophy/religion:** Philosophy, religion. **Physical sciences:** Chemistry, physics. **Psychology:** General. **Social sciences:** Economics, international relations, political science, sociology. **Visual/performing arts:** General, art history/conservation, dramatic, music, studio arts.

Most popular majors. Business/marketing 33%, communications/journalism 8%, English 7%, health sciences 13%, psychology 7%, social sciences 12%.

Computing on campus. 220 workstations in dormitories, library, computer center, student center. Dormitories wired for high-speed internet access and linked to campus network. Commuter students can connect to campus network. Online course registration, online library, helpline, repair service, student web hosting, wireless network available.

Student life. Freshman orientation: Available, $230 fee. Preregistration for classes offered. 2 day program held in late June, early July for students and parents. **Policies:** Juniors and seniors may enter lottery to move off-campus. Freshmen not permitted cars on campus. **Housing:** Guaranteed on-campus for all undergraduates. Coed dorms, special housing for disabled, apartments available. $400 nonrefundable deposit, deadline 5/1. Extensive theme based living-learning options for sophomores. **Activities:** Bands, campus ministries, choral groups, dance, drama, film society, international student organizations, literary magazine, music ensembles, Model UN, radio station, student government, student newspaper, TV station, College Democrats, College Republicans, Circle K, Asian student association, Jewish cultural organization, Spanish and Latino student association, African-American and Caribbean student association, Colleges Against Cancer, student environmental association.

Athletics. NCAA. **Intercollegiate:** Baseball M, basketball, cross-country, diving, field hockey W, golf, lacrosse, rowing (crew), soccer, softball W, swimming, tennis, volleyball W. **Intramural:** Basketball, field hockey W, football (non-tackle) M, golf, lacrosse, racquetball, soccer, softball, table tennis, tennis, volleyball. **Team name:** Stags.

Student services. Adult student services, alcohol/substance abuse counseling, chaplain/spiritual director, career counseling, student employment services, financial aid counseling, health services, minority student services, on-campus daycare, personal counseling, placement for graduates. **Physically disabled:** Services for visually, hearing impaired.

Contact. E-mail: admis@fairfield.edu
Phone: (203) 254-4100 Fax: (203) 254-4199
Karen Pellegrino, Director of Admission, Fairfield University, 1073 North Benson Road, Fairfield, CT 06824-5195

Holy Apostles College and Seminary
Cromwell, Connecticut
www.holyapostles.edu   CB code: 0921

- Private 4-year liberal arts and seminary college affiliated with Roman Catholic Church
- Commuter campus in large town
- 26 full-time, degree-seeking undergraduates
- Interview required

General. Founded in 1956. Regionally accredited. 75% of students are lay students, 25% are seminarians. **Degrees:** 13 bachelor's awarded; master's offered. **Location:** 13 miles from Hartford. **Calendar:** Semester, limited summer session. **Full-time faculty:** 15 total; 73% have terminal degrees, 20% minority, 33% women. **Part-time faculty:** 21 total; 67% have terminal degrees, 19% women.

Basis for selection. Interview, level of interest and recommendations most important. 1050 SAT and 3.0 GPA in core courses recommended. SAT recommended. **Home schooled:** State high school equivalency certificate, interview, letter of recommendation (nonparent) required.

2011-2012 Annual costs. Tuition/fees: $9,840. Books/supplies: $400. Personal expenses: $580.

Financial aid. Non-need-based: Scholarships awarded for religious affiliation.

Application procedures. Admission: Priority date 8/15; no deadline. $50 fee, may be waived for applicants with need. Application must be submitted on paper. Admission notification on a rolling basis. Applications accepted up to one week before beginning of semester. **Financial aid:** Priority date 6/1; no closing date. FAFSA, institutional form required. Applicants notified on a rolling basis starting 8/25; must reply within 2 week(s) of notification.

Academics. 85-credit core curriculum required of all undergraduates. **Special study options:** ESL, independent study. **Credit/placement by examination:** AP, CLEP. 30 credit hours maximum toward bachelor's degree. **Support services:** Reduced course load, remedial instruction, tutoring.

Majors. Liberal arts: Humanities. **Philosophy/religion:** Philosophy, religion. **Social sciences:** General. **Theology:** Theology.

Most popular majors. Liberal arts 8%, philosophy/religious studies 92%.

Computing on campus. 10 workstations in library.

Student life. Freshman orientation: Available. Preregistration for classes offered. **Policies:** Men's dorms for seminarians only; other students must commute. **Housing:** Single-sex dorms available. **Activities:** Choral groups, Life League, Toastmasters.

Student services. Chaplain/spiritual director, financial aid counseling, personal counseling.

Contact. E-mail: registrar@holyapostles.edu
Phone: (860) 632-3033 Toll-free number: (800) 330-7272
Fax: (860) 632-3075
V. Rev. Douglas Mosey, President-Rector, Holy Apostles College and Seminary, 33 Prospect Hill Road, Cromwell, CT 06416-2005

Lyme Academy College of Fine Arts
Old Lyme, Connecticut
www.lymeacademy.edu   CB code: 1791

- Private 4-year visual arts college
- Residential campus in small town
- 64 full-time, degree-seeking undergraduates
- SAT or ACT (ACT writing recommended), application essay, interview required

General. Founded in 1976. Regionally accredited. **Degrees:** 19 bachelor's awarded. **Location:** 40 miles from Hartford, 20 miles from New London. **Calendar:** Semester, limited summer session. **Full-time faculty:** 10 total. **Part-time faculty:** 17 total. **Class size:** 89% < 20, 11% 20-39.

Freshman class profile.

GPA 3.75 or higher:	11%	GPA 2.0-2.99:	23%
GPA 3.50-3.74:	33%	Out-of-state:	56%
GPA 3.0-3.49:	33%		

Basis for selection. Admissions based on portfolio, interview, essay, GPA. SAT/ACT used primarily for placement. Portfolio, campus visit highly recommended. **Home schooled:** Statement describing home school structure and mission, transcript of courses and grades, state high school equivalency certificate, interview, letter of recommendation (nonparent) required. **Learning Disabled:** Students should disclose their disabilities to Student Services so that modifications and assistance can be offered.

2011-2012 Annual costs. Tuition/fees: $28,252. Books/supplies: $1,500. Personal expenses: $500.

Financial aid. Non-need-based: Scholarships awarded for academics, art, leadership.

Application procedures. Admission: Priority date 2/15; no deadline. $55 fee, may be waived for applicants with need. Admission notification on a rolling basis beginning on or about 2/15. Must reply by May 1 or within 2 week(s) if notified thereafter. **Financial aid:** Priority date 2/15, closing date 4/15. FAFSA required. Applicants notified on a rolling basis starting 3/1; must reply by 5/1 or within 2 week(s) of notification.

Academics. Special study options: Cross-registration, independent study. Student/alumni mentorship program. **Credit/placement by examination:** AP, CLEP, SAT, ACT. **Support services:** Pre-admission summer program, reduced course load, remedial instruction, study skills assistance, tutoring.

Majors. Visual/performing arts: Drawing, illustration, painting, sculpture.

Computing on campus. 6 workstations in library. Online library, wireless network available.

Student life. Freshman orientation: Mandatory. Preregistration for classes offered. Usually held several days before start of fall classes. **Activities:** Student government.

Student services. Alcohol/substance abuse counseling, career counseling, financial aid counseling, personal counseling, veterans' counselor, women's services.

Contact. E-mail: Admissionsl@lymeacademy.edu
Phone: (860) 434-5232 ext. 120 Fax: (860) 434-8725
Sarah Churchill, Assistant Dean of Admissions, Lyme Academy College of Fine Arts, 84 Lyme Street, Old Lyme, CT 06371

Mitchell College
New London, Connecticut   CB member
www.mitchell.edu   CB code: 3528

- Private 4-year liberal arts college
- Residential campus in small city
- 864 degree-seeking undergraduates: 6% part-time, 47% women, 12% African American, 2% Asian American, 11% Hispanic American, 2% Native American, 1% international
- Application essay, interview required
- 47% graduate within 6 years

General. Founded in 1938. Regionally accredited. **Degrees:** 140 bachelor's, 16 associate awarded. **Location:** 100 miles from New York City and Boston. **Calendar:** Semester, limited summer session. **Full-time faculty:** 36 total; 69% have terminal degrees, 6% minority, 50% women. **Part-time faculty:** 74 total; 28% have terminal degrees, 3% minority, 49% women. **Class size:** 79% < 20, 21% 20-39, less than 1% 40-49. **Special facilities:** Two beaches, dock with sailboat fleet, learning resource center for students with learning disabilities, hiking trails, nature preserve.

Freshman class profile.

GPA 3.75 or higher:	1%	Return as sophomores:	61%
GPA 3.50-3.74:	7%	Out-of-state:	49%
GPA 3.0-3.49:	24%	Live on campus:	85%
GPA 2.0-2.99:	68%		

Basis for selection. High school achievement, recommendations, motivation and interview very important. **Learning Disabled:** Students applying to Learning Resource Center should submit results of complete psychoeducational evaluation, testing accommodation recommendations made by professional who completed the evaluation, definitive diagnosis of learning disability or ADHD, and standardized achievement testing (reading, writing and math). All documentation should be less than 3 years old; testing must be administered by certified or licensed psychologist.

High school preparation. College-preparatory program recommended. 16 units required. Required units include English 4, mathematics 3, social studies 2, history 1, science 2 (laboratory 1) and academic electives 3.

2011-2012 Annual costs. Tuition/fees: $27,714. Room/board: $12,492. Books/supplies: $1,500. Personal expenses: $1,300.

2011-2012 Financial aid. Need-based: 171 full-time freshmen applied for aid; 157 were judged to have need; 157 of these received aid. Average need met was 59%. Average scholarship/grant was $19,030; average loan $3,642. 69% of total undergraduate aid awarded as scholarships/grants, 31% as loans/jobs. **Non-need-based:** Awarded to 648 full-time undergraduates, including 172 freshmen. Scholarships awarded for academics, alumni affiliation, art, leadership.

Application procedures. Admission: Priority date 4/1; no deadline. $30 fee, may be waived for applicants with need, free for online applicants. Admission notification on a rolling basis beginning on or about 12/15. Must reply by May 1 or within 2 week(s) if notified thereafter. **Financial aid:** Priority date 3/1; no closing date. FAFSA required. Applicants notified on a rolling basis starting 2/15; must reply within 3 week(s) of notification.

Academics. Free professional tutoring offered in most disciplines. **Special study options:** Independent study, internships, liberal arts/career combination, student-designed major, teacher certification program. **Credit/placement by examination:** AP, CLEP, institutional tests. 30 credit hours maximum toward associate degree. **Support services:** Learning center, preadmission summer program, reduced course load, study skills assistance, tutoring, writing center.

Majors. Biology: Environmental. **Business:** Accounting/business management, business admin, hospitality admin, hotel/motel admin, restaurant/food services, small business admin, tourism/travel. **Communications:** Broadcast journalism, digital media, journalism, media studies, organizational, public relations, radio/TV. **Communications technology:** Graphics. **Conservation:** Environmental studies. **Education:** Early childhood, kindergarten/preschool. **Liberal arts:** Arts/sciences, humanities. **Math:** General. **Parks/recreation:** Sports admin. **Protective services:** Criminal justice, homeland security, juvenile corrections. **Psychology:** General, community, developmental. **Social sciences:** Criminology, international economic development. **Visual/performing arts:** Graphic design. **Work/family studies:** Family studies.

Most popular majors. Business/marketing 20%, communications/journalism 6%, family/consumer sciences 6%, liberal arts 18%, parks/recreation 19%, psychology 9%, security/protective services 16%.

Computing on campus. Dormitories wired for high-speed internet access and linked to campus network. Commuter students can connect to campus network. Helpline, repair service, wireless network available.

Student life. Freshman orientation: Available. Preregistration for classes offered. Held in September prior to start of classes; concurrent program specific to parent issues. **Housing:** Guaranteed on-campus for all undergraduates. Coed dorms, single-sex dorms, apartments available. **Activities:** Dance, drama, film society, musical theater, radio station, student government, multicultural club, Hillel, spirituality club, African American alliance, communication club, improv club, Bible study club, peer educators, gay straight alliance.

Athletics. NCAA. **Intercollegiate:** Baseball M, basketball, cross-country, golf, lacrosse M, sailing, soccer, softball W, tennis, volleyball W. **Intramural:** Basketball, sailing, soccer, softball, tennis, volleyball. **Team name:** Mariners.

Student services. Adult student services, career counseling, services for economically disadvantaged, student employment services, financial aid counseling, health services, minority student services, personal counseling, veterans' counselor. **Physically disabled:** Services for visually, speech, hearing impaired.

Contact. E-mail: admissions@mitchell.edu
Phone: (860) 701-5037 Toll-free number: (800) 443-2811
Fax: (860) 444-1209
Susan Bibeau, Director of Admissions, Mitchell College, 437 Pequot Avenue, New London, CT 06320-4498

Paier College of Art
Hamden, Connecticut
www.paiercollegeofart.edu

CB code: 3699

- For-profit 4-year visual arts college
- Commuter campus in small city
- 172 degree-seeking undergraduates: 22% part-time, 71% women, 5% African American, 2% Asian American, 6% Hispanic American
- 67% of applicants admitted
- SAT or ACT, interview required
- 58% graduate within 6 years; 2% enter graduate study

General. Founded in 1946. Accredited by ACCSC. **Degrees:** 29 bachelor's, 1 associate awarded. **Location:** 2 miles from New Haven, 30 miles from Hartford. **Calendar:** Semester. **Full-time faculty:** 10 total; 40% have terminal degrees, 10% women. **Part-time faculty:** 28 total; 50% have terminal degrees, 18% women. **Class size:** 89% < 20, 11% 20-39.

Freshman class profile. 42 applied, 28 admitted, 19 enrolled.

Mid 50% test scores		Rank in top quarter:	20%
SAT critical reading:	400-540	End year in good standing:	93%
SAT math:	410-560	Return as sophomores:	91%
GPA 3.0-3.49:	30%	Out-of-state:	10%
GPA 2.0-2.99:	70%		

Basis for selection. Artistic ability, interest, and potential, as demonstrated in admission interview and portfolio review most important elements. Portfolio of 8 to 10 works of art required; essay recommended. **Home schooled:** Statement describing home school structure and mission, transcript of courses and grades, interview, letter of recommendation (nonparent) required. Notification from school district required stating that student is being home schooled.

High school preparation. 21 units required. Required and recommended units include English 4, mathematics 3, social studies 3, history 1, science 2, computer science 1 and visual/performing arts 2-4. Art classes recommended. All students must pass all state requirements.

2012-2013 Annual costs. Tuition/fees (projected): $12,960. Books/supplies: $2,700. Personal expenses: $600.

2010-2011 Financial aid. Need-based: 18 full-time freshmen applied for aid; 17 were judged to have need; 17 of these received aid. Average need met was 54%. Average scholarship/grant was $4,813; average loan $2,817. 59% of total undergraduate aid awarded as scholarships/grants, 41% as loans/jobs.

Application procedures. Admission: No deadline. $25 fee, may be waived for applicants with need. Application must be submitted on paper. Admission notification on a rolling basis beginning on or about 2/15. **Financial aid:** Priority date 4/15, closing date 8/1. FAFSA required. Applicants notified on a rolling basis starting 6/1; must reply within 3 week(s) of notification.

Academics. Academics required for BFA degrees include: 4 art histories, English I and II, 1 requirement each in the humanities, math, physical and social sciences, and 1 academic elective. **Special study options:** Independent study. **Credit/placement by examination:** AP, CLEP, IB, SAT, ACT. 6 credit hours maximum toward associate degree, 12 toward bachelor's. **Support services:** Reduced course load, remedial instruction, study skills assistance, tutoring.

Majors. Visual/performing arts: Graphic design, illustration, interior design, photography, studio arts.

Computing on campus. 75 workstations in library, computer center. Wireless network available.

Student life. Freshman orientation: Available. Preregistration for classes offered. Open to incoming students and their parents/guardians. Separate 1-hour library orientation. **Activities:** Student government, student newspaper.

Student services. Career counseling, student employment services, financial aid counseling, personal counseling, placement for graduates, veterans' counselor.

Contact. E-mail: paier.admission@snet.net
Phone: (203) 287-3031 Fax: (203) 287-3021
Daniel Paier, Dean of Admissions, Paier College of Art, 20 Gorham
Avenue, Hamden, CT 06514-3902

Post University
Waterbury, Connecticut
www.post.edu

CB member
CB code: 3698

- For-profit 4-year university and business college
- Residential campus in small city
- 794 degree-seeking undergraduates: 3% part-time, 50% women, 18% African American, 1% Asian American, 7% Hispanic American, 2% international
- 69% of applicants admitted
- SAT or ACT with writing required

General. Founded in 1890. Regionally accredited. **Degrees:** 59 bachelor's, 2 associate awarded; master's offered. **Location:** 32 miles from Hartford, 80 miles from New York City. **Calendar:** Semester, limited summer session. **Full-time faculty:** 21 total; 57% have terminal degrees, 14% minority, 38% women. **Part-time faculty:** 105 total; 11% have terminal degrees, 18% minority, 61% women. **Class size:** 66% < 20, 33% 20-39, less than 1% 40-49.

Freshman class profile. 1,861 applied, 1,280 admitted, 239 enrolled.

Mid 50% test scores			
SAT critical reading:	370-470	GPA 3.50-3.74:	3%
SAT math:	360-470	GPA 3.0-3.49:	17%
SAT writing:	360-470	GPA 2.0-2.99:	70%
ACT composite:	16-21	Return as sophomores:	52%
GPA 3.75 or higher:	2%	Out-of-state:	32%
		Live on campus:	57%

Basis for selection. Secondary school transcript, results of SAT/ACT most important. Guidance counselor's recommendation required. School and community activities and test scores also reviewed and considered. Interview recommended. **Home schooled:** Statement describing home school structure and mission, transcript of courses and grades, interview, letter of recommendation (nonparent) required. **Learning Disabled:** Students must submit documentation once enrolled to receive services; documentation not used for admissions.

High school preparation. College-preparatory program recommended. 13 units required. Required and recommended units include English 4, mathematics 3, social studies 1, history 2, science 3 (laboratory 1) and foreign language 2.

2011-2012 Annual costs. Tuition/fees: $25,800. Room/board: $9,850. Books/supplies: $1,000. Personal expenses: $1,200.

2011-2012 Financial aid. Need-based: Average need met was 54%. Average scholarship/grant was $15,943; average loan $3,561. 78% of total undergraduate aid awarded as scholarships/grants, 22% as loans/jobs. **Additional information:** Academic merit scholarships available based on GPA and test scores. Renewable contingent upon maintaining specific GPA.

Application procedures. Admission: Priority date 3/1; no deadline. $40 fee, may be waived for applicants with need, free for online applicants. Admission notification on a rolling basis beginning on or about 11/15. Must reply by May 1 or within 2 week(s) if notified thereafter. **Financial aid:** Priority date 3/15; no closing date. FAFSA required. Applicants notified on a rolling basis starting 4/15; must reply by 5/1 or within 3 week(s) of notification.

Academics. Special study options: Accelerated study, cooperative education, cross-registration, distance learning, double major, dual enrollment of high school students, ESL, honors, independent study, internships, liberal arts/career combination, student-designed major, study abroad, weekend college. **Credit/placement by examination:** AP, CLEP, IB, institutional tests. 15 credit hours maximum toward associate degree, 30 toward bachelor's. **Support services:** Learning center, pre-admission summer program, reduced course load, remedial instruction, study skills assistance, tutoring, writing center.

Majors. Biology: General. **Business:** General, accounting, business admin, finance, marketing. **Computer sciences:** General. **Conservation:** General, environmental studies. **General:** Equestrian studies. **Protective services:** Law enforcement admin. **Psychology:** General. **Social sciences:** Sociology.

Most popular majors. Agriculture 8%, business/marketing 45%, legal studies 16%, public administration/social services 11%.

Computing on campus. 150 workstations in library, computer center. Dormitories wired for high-speed internet access and linked to campus network. Commuter students can connect to campus network. Online course registration, online library, helpline, repair service, wireless network available.

Student life. Freshman orientation: Mandatory, $100 fee. Preregistration for classes offered. Held 2 days prior and international students the week prior to start of semester. **Housing:** Guaranteed on-campus for freshmen. Coed dorms available. $150 fully refundable deposit, deadline 5/1. **Activities:** Dance, drama, literary magazine, musical theater, student government, Phi Theta Kappa, student ambassadors, peer mentors, peer health educators, Newman club.

Athletics. NCAA. **Intercollegiate:** Baseball M, basketball, cross-country, football (tackle) M, golf M, lacrosse W, soccer, softball W, swimming, tennis, volleyball W. **Intramural:** Basketball. **Team name:** Eagles.

Student services. Adult student services, alcohol/substance abuse counseling, career counseling, student employment services, financial aid counseling, health services, minority student services, personal counseling, placement for graduates, veterans' counselor. **Physically disabled:** Services for visually impaired.

Contact. E-mail: admissions@post.edu
Phone: (203) 596-4520 Toll-free number: (800) 345-2562
Fax: (203) 756-5810
Jay Murray, Director of Admissions, Post University, 800 Country Club Road, Waterbury, CT 06723-2540

Quinnipiac University
Hamden, Connecticut
www.quinnipiac.edu

CB member
CB code: 3712

- Private 4-year university
- Residential campus in small city
- 6,155 degree-seeking undergraduates: 3% part-time, 62% women, 4% African American, 1% Asian American, 7% Hispanic American, 1% international
- 2,058 degree-seeking graduate students
- 63% of applicants admitted
- SAT or ACT (ACT writing recommended), application essay required
- 77% graduate within 6 years; 40% enter graduate study

General. Founded in 1929. Regionally accredited. **Degrees:** 1,306 bachelor's awarded; master's, professional offered. **ROTC:** Army, Naval, Air Force. **Location:** 8 miles from New Haven. **Calendar:** Semester, limited summer session. **Full-time faculty:** 308 total; 85% have terminal degrees, 15% minority, 51% women. **Part-time faculty:** 529 total; 7% minority, 52% women. **Class size:** 46% < 20, 51% 20-39, 2% 40-49, 2% 50-99. **Special facilities:** Financial technology center, polling institute, community health education institute, diagnostic imaging suite, critical care simulation laboratories for neonatal/pediatric and adult patients, motion analysis laboratory, Irish Famine museum, fully-digital high-definition production TV studio, audio production studio, news technology center.

Freshman class profile. 18,642 applied, 11,768 admitted, 1,513 enrolled.

Mid 50% test scores			
SAT critical reading:	520-590	Rank in top quarter:	68%
SAT math:	540-610	Rank in top tenth:	26%
SAT writing:	540-610	End year in good standing:	95%
GPA 3.75 or higher:	13%	Return as sophomores:	87%
GPA 3.50-3.74:	31%	Out-of-state:	75%
GPA 3.0-3.49:	48%	Live on campus:	95%
GPA 2.0-2.99:	8%	International:	2%

Basis for selection. Primary emphasis placed on high school transcript, grades, grade pattern, level of difficulty. Test scores, essay and recommendation(s) also important. Interview recommended, extracurricular activities, evidence of leadership, and employment also considered. Must send official test scores for all SAT and/or ACT tests taken. Highest SAT (individual scores) or ACT (composite) scores used when reviewing applications for admission and for scholarships. Campus visit recommended. **Home schooled:** Statement describing home school structure and mission, transcript of courses and grades, letter of recommendation (nonparent) required. Evaluation of completed education required.

High school preparation. College-preparatory program recommended. 16 units required. Required and recommended units include English 4, mathematics 3, social studies 2, science 3 (laboratory 2), foreign language 2-3 and academic electives 2. 4 lab science and 4 math required for students applying

to physical therapy, occupational therapy, nursing and physician assistant programs. Physics highly recommended for physical therapy applicants.

2011-2012 Annual costs. Tuition/fees: $36,130. Room/board: $13,430. Books/supplies: $800. Personal expenses: $900.

2011-2012 Financial aid. Need-based: 1,187 full-time freshmen applied for aid; 954 were judged to have need; 935 of these received aid. Average need met was 62%. Average scholarship/grant was $15,692; average loan $3,577. 52% of total undergraduate aid awarded as scholarships/grants, 48% as loans/jobs. **Non-need-based:** Awarded to 2,791 full-time undergraduates, including 813 freshmen. Scholarships awarded for academics, athletics.

Application procedures. Admission: Priority date 11/1; deadline 2/1 (postmark date). $45 fee, may be waived for applicants with need. Admission notification on a rolling basis beginning on or about 12/15. Must reply by May 1 or within 2 week(s) if notified thereafter. Students encouraged to apply early since applications reviewed in order they're received. Students applying for Nursing, BS/DPT in Physical Therapy or BS/MHS in Physician Assistant programs should apply by November 1. Students applying early decision must file the application by October 15 and provide all supporting materials by December 1. **Financial aid:** Priority date 3/1; no closing date. FAFSA, CSS PROFILE required. Applicants notified on a rolling basis starting 2/15; must reply by 5/1 or within 2 week(s) of notification.

Academics. Special study options: Combined bachelor's/graduate degree, distance learning, double major, honors, independent study, internships, liberal arts/career combination, semester at sea, student-designed major, study abroad, teacher certification program, Washington semester. **Credit/placement by examination:** AP, CLEP, IB, institutional tests. 32 credit hours maximum toward bachelor's degree. **Support services:** Learning center, study skills assistance, tutoring.

Majors. Biology: General, biochemistry, biomedical sciences, biotechnology, molecular, neuroscience. **Business:** General, accounting, business admin, communications, entrepreneurial studies, finance, human resources, international, international marketing, management information systems, management science, managerial economics, marketing, nonprofit/public, office management. **Communications:** Advertising, broadcast journalism, communications/speech/rhetoric, digital media, journalism, public relations. **Computer sciences:** General, applications programming, computer graphics, computer science. **Education:** Biology, chemistry, elementary, English, foreign languages, history, mathematics, middle, multi-level teacher, science, secondary, social studies, Spanish. **Engineering:** Civil, industrial, mechanical, software. **English:** English lit, writing. **Foreign languages:** Spanish. **Health services:** Athletic training, health care admin, nursing (RN), predental, premedicine, preveterinary, radiologic technology/medical imaging. **History:** General. **Math:** General. **Physical sciences:** Chemistry. **Protective services:** Criminal justice. **Psychology:** General. **Social sciences:** General, criminology, economics, political science, sociology. **Visual/performing arts:** Dramatic, game design.

Most popular majors. Business/marketing 25%, communications/journalism 19%, health sciences 27%, psychology 6%, social sciences 6%.

Computing on campus. PC or laptop required. 500 workstations in library, computer center. Dormitories wired for high-speed internet access and linked to campus network. Commuter students can connect to campus network. Online course registration, online library, helpline, repair service, student web hosting, wireless network available.

Student life. Freshman orientation: Mandatory. Preregistration for classes offered. 3 Friday/Saturday sessions offered in June; 2-day session offered prior to start of fall classes. **Policies:** Freshmen not permitted cars on campus. **Housing:** Guaranteed on-campus for all undergraduates. Coed dorms, apartments, wellness housing available. $350 partly refundable deposit, deadline 5/1. **Activities:** Pep band, campus ministries, choral groups, dance, drama, international student organizations, literary magazine, radio station, student government, student newspaper, TV station, Hillel, Catholic services, black student union, Latino cultural society, Greenpeace, Amnesty International, SADD, women's center, Asian and Pacific Islander club, Christian Fellowship.

Athletics. NCAA. **Intercollegiate:** Baseball M, basketball, cross-country, field hockey W, golf W, ice hockey, lacrosse, rugby W, soccer, softball W, tennis, track and field W, volleyball W. **Intramural:** Archery, badminton, baseball M, basketball, bowling, field hockey W, soccer, softball, tennis, volleyball. **Team name:** Bobcats.

Student services. Adult student services, alcohol/substance abuse counseling, chaplain/spiritual director, career counseling, student employment services, financial aid counseling, health services, minority student services, personal counseling, placement for graduates.

Contact. E-mail: admissions@quinnipiac.edu
Phone: (203) 582-8600 Toll-free number: (800) 462-1944
Fax: (203) 582-8906
Carla Knowlton, Director of Admissions, Quinnipiac University, 275 Mount Carmel Avenue, Hamden, CT 06518-1908

Sacred Heart University
Fairfield, Connecticut
www.sacredheart.edu

CB member
CB code: 3780

- Private 4-year university and liberal arts college affiliated with Roman Catholic Church
- Residential campus in large town
- 4,067 degree-seeking undergraduates: 14% part-time, 63% women
- 2,234 degree-seeking graduate students
- 54% of applicants admitted
- Application essay required
- 67% graduate within 6 years; 57% enter graduate study

General. Founded in 1963. Regionally accredited. **Degrees:** 868 bachelor's, 5 associate awarded; master's, professional offered. **ROTC:** Army. **Location:** 55 miles from New York City. **Calendar:** Semester, extensive summer session. **Full-time faculty:** 234 total; 84% have terminal degrees, 14% minority, 55% women. **Part-time faculty:** 336 total; 37% have terminal degrees, 9% minority, 48% women. **Class size:** 44% < 20, 55% 20-39, 2% 40-49. **Special facilities:** Performing arts center, multipurpose communication studios, 36-hole golf course, rehabilitation clinics for occupational and physical therapies, fashion design studio, chapel.

Freshman class profile. 8,321 applied, 4,470 admitted, 986 enrolled.

Mid 50% test scores			
SAT critical reading:	500-580	Rank in top quarter:	39%
SAT math:	510-600	Rank in top tenth:	6%
SAT writing:	510-590	End year in good standing:	95%
ACT composite:	22-25	Return as sophomores:	74%
GPA 3.75 or higher:	18%	Out-of-state:	70%
GPA 3.50-3.74:	17%	Live on campus:	93%
GPA 3.0-3.49:	43%	International:	1%
GPA 2.0-2.99:	22%	Fraternities:	7%
		Sororities:	14%

Basis for selection. High school record and college preparatory curriculum most important. Applicants may submit SAT/ACT if they desire the scores to be evaluated as part of their overall academic profile. SAT/ACT required upon deposit to the University for course placement purposes. Interview required for early decision candidates, recommended for all others. **Home schooled:** Statement describing home school structure and mission, transcript of courses and grades required. SAT/ACT required.

High school preparation. College-preparatory program required. 22 units required; 30 recommended. Required and recommended units include English 4, mathematics 3-4, social studies 3-4, history 3-4, science 3-4 (laboratory 1-2), foreign language 2-4 and academic electives 3-4.

2012-2013 Annual costs. Tuition/fees (projected): $33,956. Room/board: $13,462. Books/supplies: $1,400. Personal expenses: $1,000.

2011-2012 Financial aid. Need-based: 913 full-time freshmen applied for aid; 741 were judged to have need; 737 of these received aid. Average need met was 56%. Average scholarship/grant was $13,381; average loan $4,983. 57% of total undergraduate aid awarded as scholarships/grants, 43% as loans/jobs. **Non-need-based:** Awarded to 917 full-time undergraduates, including 296 freshmen. Scholarships awarded for academics, alumni affiliation, art, athletics, leadership, minority status, music/drama.

Application procedures. Admission: Priority date 2/1; no deadline. $50 fee, may be waived for applicants with need. Admission notification on a rolling basis beginning on or about 1/1. Must reply by May 1 or within 2 week(s) if notified thereafter. **Financial aid:** Priority date 2/15; no closing date. FAFSA, CSS PROFILE required. Applicants notified on a rolling basis starting 3/1; must reply within 2 week(s) of notification.

Academics. Special study options: Accelerated study, combined bachelor's/graduate degree, cooperative education, cross-registration, distance learning, double major, dual enrollment of high school students, ESL, honors, independent study, internships, liberal arts/career combination, student-designed major, study abroad, teacher certification program, United Nations semester, Washington semester, weekend college. Service-learning. **Credit/placement by examination:** AP, CLEP, IB, SAT, ACT, institutional tests. 30 credit hours maximum toward bachelor's degree. **Support services:** Learning center, study skills assistance, tutoring, writing center.

Majors. Biology: General. **Business:** General, accounting, fashion, finance, managerial economics, marketing. **Communications:** Media studies. **Communications technology:** General. **Computer sciences:** General, computer science, information technology. **English:** English lit. **Foreign languages:** Spanish. **Health services:** Athletic training, kinesiotherapy, nursing (RN), predental, premedicine, preoccupational therapy, preop/surgical nursing, prepharmacy, prephysical therapy, preveterinary. **History:** General. **Human services:** Social work. **Liberal arts:** Arts/sciences. **Math:** General. **Parks/**

recreation: Sports admin. **Philosophy/religion:** Philosophy, religion. **Physical sciences:** Chemistry. **Protective services:** Law enforcement admin. **Psychology:** General. **Social sciences:** Political science, sociology. **Visual/performing arts:** Art, fashion design, game design, graphic design.

Most popular majors. Business/marketing 36%, communications/journalism 6%, health sciences 16%, psychology 15%, security/protective services 6%, social sciences 6%.

Computing on campus. PC or laptop required. 78 workstations in dormitories, library, computer center, student center. Dormitories wired for high-speed internet access and linked to campus network. Commuter students can connect to campus network. Online course registration, online library, helpline, repair service, student web hosting, wireless network available.

Student life. Freshman orientation: Mandatory. Preregistration for classes offered. 2-day program in late spring for both parents and students. **Policies:** Freshman Convocation required for all first-year students; held in September. **Housing:** Guaranteed on-campus for all undergraduates. Coed dorms, special housing for disabled, apartments, wellness housing available. $1,500 nonrefundable deposit, deadline 5/1. Living and learning communities available for specific academic programs, honors floors. **Activities:** Bands, campus ministries, choral groups, dance, drama, film society, international student organizations, literary magazine, music ensembles, musical theater, radio station, student government, student newspaper, TV station, ONE Campaign, La Hispanidad, Habitat for Humanity, Circle K, Read Aloud, UMOJA, Active Minds, gay/straight alliance, College Democrats, College Republicans.

Athletics. NCAA. **Intercollegiate:** Baseball M, basketball, bowling W, cheerleading, cross-country, equestrian W, fencing, field hockey W, football (tackle) M, golf, ice hockey, lacrosse, rowing (crew) W, soccer, softball W, swimming W, tennis, track and field, volleyball, wrestling M. **Intramural:** Basketball, bowling, field hockey W, football (non-tackle), golf, skiing, soccer, softball, table tennis, tennis, volleyball. **Team name:** Pioneers.

Student services. Adult student services, alcohol/substance abuse counseling, chaplain/spiritual director, career counseling, services for economically disadvantaged, student employment services, financial aid counseling, health services, minority student services, personal counseling, placement for graduates, women's services. **Physically disabled:** Services for visually, speech, hearing impaired.

Contact. E-mail: enroll@sacredheart.edu
Phone: (203) 371-7880 Fax: (203) 365-7607
Jamie Romeo, Associate Dean of Undergraduate Admissions, Sacred Heart University, 5151 Park Avenue, Fairfield, CT 06825

Saint Joseph College
West Hartford, Connecticut
CB member
www.sjc.edu
CB code: 3754

- Private 4-year liberal arts college for women affiliated with Roman Catholic Church
- Residential campus in small city
- 1,001 degree-seeking undergraduates: 19% part-time, 99% women, 10% African American, 2% Asian American, 11% Hispanic American
- 1,438 degree-seeking graduate students
- 78% of applicants admitted
- SAT or ACT (ACT writing optional) required
- 56% graduate within 6 years

General. Founded in 1932. Regionally accredited. Coeducational programs available for adults seeking to complete a bachelor's degree, master's degree, or Pharm.D. **Degrees:** 204 bachelor's awarded; master's, professional offered. **Location:** 3 miles from Hartford. **Calendar:** Semester. **Full-time faculty:** 108 total; 92% have terminal degrees, 16% minority, 71% women. **Part-time faculty:** 182 total; 8% minority, 78% women. **Class size:** 71% < 20, 28% 20-39, less than 1% 40-49.

Freshman class profile. 1,335 applied, 1,047 admitted, 158 enrolled.

Mid 50% test scores			
SAT critical reading:	450-550	GPA 2.0-2.99:	19%
SAT math:	450-540	Rank in top quarter:	49%
ACT composite:	22-23	Rank in top tenth:	17%
GPA 3.75 or higher:	18%	Return as sophomores:	75%
GPA 3.50-3.74:	15%	Out-of-state:	10%
GPA 3.0-3.49:	48%	Live on campus:	70%

Basis for selection. Academic record, standardized test scores, and supplemental application materials should display evidence of sufficient college-level ability and potential. **Home schooled:** Statement describing home school structure and mission, transcript of courses and grades, state high school

---

equivalency certificate, interview, letter of recommendation (nonparent) required.

High school preparation. College-preparatory program required. 16 units required.

2011-2012 Annual costs. Tuition/fees: $30,310. Room/board: $13,200.

2011-2012 Financial aid. Need-based: 149 full-time freshmen applied for aid; 142 were judged to have need; 142 of these received aid. Average need met was 72%. Average scholarship/grant was $19,320; average loan $3,988. 65% of total undergraduate aid awarded as scholarships/grants, 35% as loans/jobs. **Non-need-based:** Awarded to 125 full-time undergraduates, including 27 freshmen. Scholarships awarded for academics.

Application procedures. Admission: Priority date 3/1; no deadline. $50 fee, may be waived for applicants with need, free for online applicants. Admission notification on a rolling basis. **Financial aid:** Priority date 2/15; no closing date. FAFSA required. Applicants notified on a rolling basis starting 2/15.

Academics. Special study options: Accelerated study, combined bachelor's/graduate degree, cross-registration, distance learning, double major, honors, independent study, internships, liberal arts/career combination, student-designed major, study abroad, teacher certification program, weekend college. **Credit/placement by examination:** AP, CLEP, institutional tests. **Support services:** Learning center, reduced course load, study skills assistance, tutoring, writing center.

Majors. Area/ethnic studies: Women's. **Biology:** General, biochemistry. **Business:** Accounting, business admin. **Education:** Special ed. **English:** English lit. **Foreign languages:** Spanish. **Health services:** Nursing (RN). **History:** General. **Human services:** Social work. **Math:** General. **Philosophy/religion:** Philosophy, religion. **Physical sciences:** Chemistry. **Psychology:** General. **Visual/performing arts:** Art history/conservation. **Work/family studies:** General, child development, food/nutrition.

Most popular majors. Business/marketing 6%, family/consumer sciences 12%, health sciences 26%, interdisciplinary studies 11%, psychology 15%, public administration/social services 11%.

Computing on campus. Dormitories wired for high-speed internet access and linked to campus network. Online course registration, online library, helpline, wireless network available.

Student life. Freshman orientation: Mandatory, $30 fee. Preregistration for classes offered. **Housing:** Special housing for disabled, wellness housing available. $250 nonrefundable deposit, deadline 6/15. Single rooms available for nontraditional students. Medical singles with private bathrooms available on a limited basis. **Activities:** Campus ministries, choral groups, dance, drama, international student organizations, music ensembles, student government.

Athletics. NCAA. **Intercollegiate:** Basketball W, cross-country W, diving W, lacrosse W, soccer W, softball W, swimming W, tennis W, volleyball W. **Team name:** Blue Jays.

Student services. Adult student services, alcohol/substance abuse counseling, chaplain/spiritual director, career counseling, student employment services, financial aid counseling, health services, personal counseling, placement for graduates, women's services. **Physically disabled:** Services for visually, hearing impaired.

Contact. E-mail: admissions@sjc.edu
Phone: (860) 231-5216 Toll-free number: (866) 442-8752
Fax: (860) 231-5744
Director of Admissions, Saint Joseph College, 1678 Asylum Avenue, West Hartford, CT 06117

Southern Connecticut State University
New Haven, Connecticut
CB member
www.southernct.edu
CB code: 3662

- Public 4-year university
- Commuter campus in small city
- 8,696 degree-seeking undergraduates: 13% part-time, 61% women, 14% African American, 2% Asian American, 10% Hispanic American
- 2,837 degree-seeking graduate students
- 72% of applicants admitted
- SAT or ACT with writing, application essay required
- 42% graduate within 6 years

General. Founded in 1893. Regionally accredited. **Degrees:** 1,581 bachelor's awarded; master's, doctoral offered. **ROTC:** Army, Air Force. **Location:** 75 miles from New York City. **Calendar:** Semester, extensive summer session. **Full-time faculty:** 433 total; 78% have terminal degrees, 16% minority, 49% women. **Part-time faculty:** 613 total; 12% minority, 58% women. **Class size:** 37% < 20, 56% 20-39, 5% 40-49, 1% 50-99, less than 1% >100. **Special facilities:** Planetarium, photonics laboratory, geospatial technology laboratory.

Freshman class profile. 5,332 applied, 3,831 admitted, 1,334 enrolled.

Mid 50% test scores		GPA 2.0-2.99:	68%
SAT critical reading:	420-510	Rank in top quarter:	6%
SAT math:	420-520	Rank in top tenth:	1%
SAT writing:	430-530	Return as sophomores:	76%
ACT composite:	17-22	Out-of-state:	6%
GPA 3.75 or higher:	3%	Live on campus:	66%
GPA 3.50-3.74:	3%	Fraternities:	1%
GPA 3.0-3.49:	25%	Sororities:	1%

Basis for selection. School achievement record, test scores most important. Special consideration to culturally disadvantaged students. **Home schooled:** Statement describing home school structure and mission, transcript of courses and grades, letter of recommendation (nonparent) required.

High school preparation. College-preparatory program required. 16 units required; 21 recommended. Required and recommended units include English 4, mathematics 3-4, social studies 2-3, history 2-3, science 2-3 (laboratory 1) and foreign language 2-4. One unit of algebra II required.

2011-2012 Annual costs. Tuition/fees: $8,248; $18,872 out-of-state. Room/board: $10,231. Books/supplies: $1,400. Personal expenses: $150.

2011-2012 Financial aid. Need-based: 1,210 full-time freshmen applied for aid; 898 were judged to have need; 869 of these received aid. Average need met was 83%. Average scholarship/grant was $6,215; average loan $6,117. 58% of total undergraduate aid awarded as scholarships/grants, 42% as loans/jobs. **Non-need-based:** Awarded to 932 full-time undergraduates, including 227 freshmen. Scholarships awarded for academics, alumni affiliation, athletics, ROTC, state residency.

Application procedures. Admission: Closing date 4/1 (postmark date). $50 fee, may be waived for applicants with need. Admission notification on a rolling basis beginning on or about 12/1. Must reply by May 1 or within 2 week(s) if notified thereafter. **Financial aid:** Priority date 3/5, closing date 3/9. FAFSA required. Applicants notified on a rolling basis starting 4/11; must reply within 2 week(s) of notification.

Academics. Special study options: Accelerated study, cooperative education, cross-registration, distance learning, double major, dual enrollment of high school students, exchange student, external degree, honors, independent study, internships, liberal arts/career combination, student-designed major, study abroad, teacher certification program. **Credit/placement by examination:** AP, CLEP, SAT, institutional tests. 30 credit hours maximum toward bachelor's degree. **Support services:** Learning center, pre-admission summer program, reduced course load, remedial instruction, study skills assistance, tutoring, writing center.

Majors. Biology: General. **Business:** Accounting, business admin, finance, management science, managerial economics, marketing. **Communications:** Communications/speech/rhetoric, journalism. **Computer sciences:** General. **Education:** General, art, biology, chemistry, elementary, English, history, mathematics, physical, physics, science, secondary, social science, social studies, Spanish. **English:** English lit, writing. **Foreign languages:** General, French, German, Italian, Spanish. **Health services:** Nursing (RN), predental, premedicine, prepharmacy, preveterinary. **History:** General. **Human services:** Social work. **Liberal arts:** Arts/sciences, library science. **Math:** General. **Parks/recreation:** General, exercise sciences. **Philosophy/religion:** Philosophy. **Physical sciences:** Chemistry, geology, physics. **Psychology:** General. **Social sciences:** Geography, political science, sociology. **Visual/performing arts:** Art, art history/conservation, dramatic, music.

Most popular majors. Business/marketing 14%, communications/journalism 8%, education 10%, health sciences 12%, liberal arts 10%, psychology 14%, social sciences 6%.

Computing on campus. 750 workstations in dormitories, library, computer center, student center. Dormitories wired for high-speed internet access and linked to campus network. Commuter students can connect to campus network. Online course registration, online library, helpline, student web hosting, wireless network available.

Student life. Freshman orientation: Mandatory. Preregistration for classes offered. **Policies:** Freshmen not permitted cars on campus. **Housing:** Coed dorms, special housing for disabled, apartments available. $250 nonrefundable deposit, deadline 3/30. **Activities:** Pep band, campus ministries, choral groups, dance, drama, international student organizations, literary magazine, music ensembles, musical theater, radio station, student government, student newspaper, TV station, Christian Fellowship, Newman club, Latin American students organization, black student union, People to People, Students for Disability Rights, veterans club.

Athletics. NCAA. **Intercollegiate:** Baseball M, basketball, cross-country, field hockey W, football (tackle) M, gymnastics W, lacrosse W, soccer, softball W, swimming, track and field, volleyball M. **Intramural:** Basketball, football (non-tackle), soccer, softball, tennis, volleyball. **Team name:** Owls.

Student services. Adult student services, alcohol/substance abuse counseling, chaplain/spiritual director, career counseling, student employment services, financial aid counseling, health services, personal counseling, placement for graduates, veterans' counselor, women's services. **Physically disabled:** Services for visually, speech, hearing impaired.

Contact. Phone: (203) 392-5644 Toll-free number: (888) 500-7278 Fax: (203) 392-5727
Kimberly Crone, Associate Vice President for Academic Student Services, Southern Connecticut State University, 131 Farnham Avenue, New Haven, CT 06515-1202

Trinity College
Hartford, Connecticut
www.trincoll.edu

CB member
CB code: 3899

- Private 4-year liberal arts college
- Residential campus in large city
- 2,254 degree-seeking undergraduates: 2% part-time, 49% women, 6% African American, 5% Asian American, 8% Hispanic American, 7% international
- 77 degree-seeking graduate students
- 30% of applicants admitted
- SAT or ACT (ACT writing recommended), application essay required
- 86% graduate within 6 years

General. Founded in 1823. Regionally accredited. **Degrees:** 554 bachelor's awarded; master's offered. **ROTC:** Army. **Location:** 125 miles from New York City, 100 miles from Boston. **Calendar:** Semester, limited summer session. **Full-time faculty:** 174 total; 92% have terminal degrees, 25% minority, 38% women. **Part-time faculty:** 70 total; 71% have terminal degrees, 16% minority, 44% women. **Class size:** 62% < 20, 32% 20-39, 3% 40-49, 3% 50-99. **Special facilities:** Library collections on Native Americans, maritime history, early American texts, nuclear magnetic spectrometer, mass spectrometer, electronic microscope, plasma spectrometer, optical diagnostics and communications laboratory, natural science field station.

Freshman class profile. 6,967 applied, 2,118 admitted, 591 enrolled.

Mid 50% test scores		Rank in top tenth:	55%
SAT critical reading:	580-680	Return as sophomores:	92%
SAT math:	600-690	Out-of-state:	84%
SAT writing:	610-700	Live on campus:	99%
ACT composite:	26-29	International:	9%
Rank in top quarter:	77%		

Basis for selection. School record and recommendations most important. Test scores used for math and writing placement. One of the following required: SAT, ACT, or 2 SAT Subject Tests. Interview recommended.

High school preparation. College-preparatory program recommended. 16 units required. Required units include English 4, mathematics 3, history 2, science 2 (laboratory 2) and foreign language 3.

2011-2012 Annual costs. Tuition/fees: $44,070. One-time $25 transcript fee for new students only. Room/board: $11,380. Books/supplies: $1,000. Personal expenses: $1,000.

2011-2012 Financial aid. Need-based: 263 full-time freshmen applied for aid; 225 were judged to have need; 225 of these received aid. Average need met was 100%. Average scholarship/grant was $37,457; average loan $3,784. 89% of total undergraduate aid awarded as scholarships/grants, 11% as loans/jobs. **Non-need-based:** Awarded to 74 full-time undergraduates, including 39 freshmen. Scholarships awarded for academics, leadership.

Application procedures. Admission: Closing date 1/1 (postmark date). $60 fee, may be waived for applicants with need. Admission notification by 4/1. Must reply by May 1 or within 2 week(s) if notified thereafter. **Financial aid:** Priority date 2/1, closing date 3/1. FAFSA, CSS PROFILE required. Applicants notified by 4/1; must reply by 5/1 or within 2 week(s) of notification.

Academics. Math center available. **Special study options:** Accelerated study, combined bachelor's/graduate degree, cross-registration, double major, exchange student, honors, independent study, internships, liberal arts/career combination, New York semester, semester at sea, student-designed major, study abroad, teacher certification program, United Nations semester, urban semester, Washington semester. Community Learning Initiative (courses with community-based components) available. **Credit/placement by examination:** AP, CLEP, IB, SAT, ACT, institutional tests. **Support services:** Study skills assistance, tutoring, writing center.

Majors. **Area/ethnic studies:** African, African-American, American, Asian, gay/lesbian, Latin American, Near/Middle Eastern, Russian/Slavic, women's. **Biology:** General, biochemistry, neuroscience. **Computer sciences:** General, computer science. **Conservation:** Environmental science. **Education:** General. **Engineering:** General, biomedical, electrical, mechanical. **English:** Creative writing, English lit. **Foreign languages:** General, Chinese, classics, comparative lit, French, German, Italian, Japanese, Russian, Spanish. **Health services:** Premedicine. **History:** General. **Human services:** Public policy. **Math:** General. **Philosophy/religion:** Judaic, philosophy, religion. **Physical sciences:** Chemistry, physics. **Psychology:** General. **Social sciences:** General, anthropology, economics, international relations, political science, sociology, urban studies. **Visual/performing arts:** General, art, art history/conservation, dance, dramatic, film/cinema/video, music, studio arts.

Most popular majors. Area/ethnic studies 10%, biology 6%, English 7%, history 7%, psychology 6%, social sciences 30%.

Computing on campus. 327 workstations in library, computer center. Dormitories wired for high-speed internet access and linked to campus network. Commuter students can connect to campus network. Online course registration, online library, helpline, student web hosting, wireless network available.

Student life. **Freshman orientation:** Available. Preregistration for classes offered. 4 day session beginning Thursday before Labor Day. Advising days held in June to begin registration process; optional outdoor challenge program in early August. **Policies:** All dorms are non-smoking. **Housing:** Guaranteed on-campus for freshmen. Coed dorms, fraternity/sorority housing available. Community service dorm, quiet dorm, alternative social programming dorm, cooking units available. **Activities:** Jazz band, campus ministries, choral groups, dance, drama, film society, international student organizations, literary magazine, music ensembles, Model UN, musical theater, radio station, student government, student newspaper, TV station, Asian-American student association, Intervarsity Christian Fellowship, Encouraging Respect of Sexualities, Friends Active in Civic Engagement and Service, Hillel, Imani, La Voz Latina, Promoting Healthy Awareness of the Body, Promoting Respect for Inclusive Diversity in Education, black women's organization.

Athletics. NCAA. **Intercollegiate:** Baseball M, basketball, cross-country, diving, field hockey W, football (tackle) M, golf M, ice hockey, lacrosse, rowing (crew), soccer, softball W, squash, swimming, tennis, track and field, volleyball W, wrestling M. **Intramural:** Badminton, basketball, football (non-tackle), ice hockey, soccer, softball, squash, tennis. **Team name:** Bantams.

Student services. Adult student services, alcohol/substance abuse counseling, chaplain/spiritual director, career counseling, services for economically disadvantaged, student employment services, financial aid counseling, health services, minority student services, on-campus daycare, personal counseling, placement for graduates, women's services.

Contact. E-mail: admissions.office@trincoll.edu
Phone: (860) 297-2180 Fax: (860) 297-2287
Larry Dow, Dean of Admissions and Financial Aid, Trinity College, 300 Summit Street, Hartford, CT 06106

United States Coast Guard Academy
New London, Connecticut   **CB member**
www.uscga.edu   **CB code: 5807**

- Public 4-year engineering and military college
- Residential campus in small city
- 1,045 degree-seeking undergraduates: 30% women, 3% African American, 4% Asian American, 10% Hispanic American, 1% Native American, 2% international
- 16% of applicants admitted
- SAT or ACT with writing, application essay required
- 83% graduate within 6 years

General. Founded in 1876. Regionally accredited. Cadets devote themselves to honor concept, and go directly into leadership positions in the United States Coast Guard. As a federal military service academy, The Coast Guard Academy is a tuition-free degree-granting institution. All students earn a modest stipend while enrolled, and receive medical and dental benefits at no charge. **Degrees:** 235 bachelor's awarded. **Location:** 120 miles from New York City, 130 miles from Boston. **Calendar:** Semester, limited summer session. **Full-time faculty:** 133 total; 51% have terminal degrees, 14% minority, 32% women. **Part-time faculty:** 10 total; 40% have terminal degrees, 10% minority, 40% women. **Class size:** 66% < 20, 34% 20-39. **Special facilities:** Museum, 295-foot-tall ship, ship navigation simulation facilities with bridge simulator, 10,000 gallon circulating water channel, ship model towing tank, observatory with reflector telescope.

Freshman class profile. 2,374 applied, 383 admitted, 297 enrolled.

Mid 50% test scores			
SAT critical reading:	550-640	GPA 2.0-2.99:	2%
SAT math:	590-670	Rank in top quarter:	85%
SAT writing:	540-630	Rank in top tenth:	52%
ACT composite:	25-29	End year in good standing:	89%
GPA 3.75 or higher:	56%	Return as sophomores:	89%
GPA 3.50-3.74:	24%	Out-of-state:	96%
GPA 3.0-3.49:	18%	Live on campus:	100%
		International:	2%

Basis for selection. Test scores, high school class rank, recommendations, essay, leadership potential as demonstrated by extracurricular activities, athletics, community affairs, and part-time employment considered. Congressional nomination not required. Applicants required to pass medical and physical fitness exams. SAT/ACT must be taken without accommodations. Interview recommended. **Home schooled:** AP and SAT Subject Tests recommended. Application should include detailed account of curriculum and course content. Students advised to take courses in math and science at a local college and have professor submit a recommendation. Recommendations from instructors other than parent recommended. Essay should include reasons for undertaking homeschooling, benefits realized, and how experience prepared student to succeed in college.

High school preparation. College-preparatory program recommended. Required units include English 4, mathematics 4, science 3 (laboratory 3). Math units should include algebra, quadratics, plane or coordinate geometry, or equivalent. Calculus and pre-calculus recommended. Sciences should include chemistry and physics.

2012-2013 Annual costs. All tuition, room and board for U.S. residents paid for by U.S. Government. All cadets are paid a monthly gross salary of $974.40 and an average monthly net salary of $800-$850 from which the cost of uniforms, books, supplies and a standard personal computer issued to them will be deducted. Cost of instruction for nonresident alien cadets is $77,594 per year. Before an international cadet is enrolled at the Academy, sponsoring country must agree to reimburse the U.S. Coast Guard for cost of instruction. Countries not listed on World Bank list would be eligible for partial tuition costs.

Application procedures. **Admission:** Priority date 11/1; deadline 2/1 (postmark date). No application fee. Application must be submitted online. Admission notification by 4/15. Admission notification on a rolling basis beginning on or about 11/15. Must reply by May 1 or within 2 week(s) if notified thereafter. **Financial aid:** No deadline.

Academics. Each student issued a laptop computer. Summers involve introductory and advanced Coast Guard/professional training including opportunities to sail aboard Eagle, fly Coast Guard aircraft, become small arms qualified (rifle and pistol), learn basic shipboard fire fighting and flooding control, and perform actual search and rescue coordination at Coast Guard units. Summer between junior and senior years typically involves piloting and navigation of Coast Guard Cutters and integration into all aspects of operational afloat Coast Guard missions. All graduates commissioned as officers in U.S Coast Guard with a 5-year obligatory military service after graduation. **Special study options:** Cross-registration, double major, ESL, exchange student, independent study, internships. **Credit/placement by examination:** AP, CLEP, institutional tests. **Support services:** Learning center, pre-admission summer program, reduced course load, remedial instruction, study skills assistance, tutoring, writing center.

Majors. **Business:** Business admin. **Engineering:** Civil, electrical, marine, mechanical. **Physical sciences:** Oceanography. **Social sciences:** Political science.

Most popular majors. Biology 17%, business/marketing 15%, engineering/engineering technologies 33%, mathematics 13%, social sciences 23%.

Computing on campus. PC or laptop required. 325 workstations in dormitories, library, computer center. Dormitories wired for high-speed internet access and linked to campus network. Online course registration, online library, helpline, repair service, student web hosting, wireless network available.

Student life. **Freshman orientation:** Mandatory. Preregistration for classes offered. 7-week military orientation, including one week onboard the

Coast Guard Cutter Eagle. **Policies:** Students part of corps of cadets. On-campus residence mandatory. Freshmen not permitted cars on campus. **Housing:** Guaranteed on-campus for all undergraduates. Coed dorms, wellness housing available. **Activities:** Bands, campus ministries, choral groups, dance, drama, music ensembles, Model UN, musical theater, student government, Officers Christian Fellowship, multicultural club, Fellowship of Christian Athletes, Big Brothers and Big Sisters, Boy Scouts, Genesis club.

Athletics. NCAA. **Intercollegiate:** Baseball M, basketball, cheerleading M, cross-country, diving, football (tackle) M, rifle, rowing (crew), sailing, soccer, softball W, swimming, tennis M, track and field, volleyball W, wrestling M. **Intramural:** Basketball, football (non-tackle), golf, racquetball, soccer, softball, tennis, volleyball. **Team name:** Bears.

Student services. Alcohol/substance abuse counseling, chaplain/spiritual director, career counseling, health services, legal services, minority student services, on-campus daycare, personal counseling, placement for graduates, veterans' counselor.

Contact. E-mail: admissions@uscga.edu
Phone: (860) 444-8500 Toll-free number: (800) 883-8724
Fax: (860) 701-6700
Capt. Stephan Finton, Director of Admissions, United States Coast Guard Academy, 31 Mohegan Avenue, New London, CT 06320

University of Bridgeport
Bridgeport, Connecticut
www.bridgeport.edu

CB member
CB code: 3914

- Private 4-year university
- Residential campus in small city
- 2,503 degree-seeking undergraduates: 33% part-time, 68% women, 37% African American, 3% Asian American, 19% Hispanic American, 9% international
- 2,302 degree-seeking graduate students
- 57% of applicants admitted
- SAT or ACT (ACT writing optional), application essay required

General. Founded in 1927. Regionally accredited. Off-campus facilities in Stamford and Waterbury. **Degrees:** 365 bachelor's, 71 associate awarded; master's, professional, doctoral offered. **ROTC:** Army. **Location:** 60 miles from New York City. **Calendar:** Semester, extensive summer session. **Full-time faculty:** 124 total; 75% have terminal degrees, 22% minority, 39% women. **Part-time faculty:** 349 total; 16% minority, 46% women. **Class size:** 68% < 20, 29% 20-39, 2% 40-49, 2% 50-99. **Special facilities:** Theater, recital halls, studios, exhibit rooms.

Freshman class profile. 5,595 applied, 3,171 admitted, 403 enrolled.

Mid 50% test scores		Rank in top quarter:	30%
SAT critical reading:	410-510	Rank in top tenth:	7%
SAT math:	420-510	End year in good standing:	62%
SAT writing:	400-500	Return as sophomores:	53%
ACT composite:	17-22	Out-of-state:	61%
GPA 3.75 or higher:	9%	Live on campus:	67%
GPA 3.50-3.74:	11%	International:	9%
GPA 3.0-3.49:	25%	Fraternities:	1%
GPA 2.0-2.99:	55%	Sororities:	1%

Basis for selection. School achievement record most important, followed by test scores, activities, trend of grades and curriculum in high school. Audition required of music majors. Portfolio required of fine and applied arts majors. Interview recommended of dental hygiene, basic studies majors.

High school preparation. College-preparatory program recommended. 16 units required. Required units include English 4, mathematics 3, social studies 2, science 2 (laboratory 2) and academic electives 5. 4 math required for math, science, computer science and engineering applicants. Chemistry required for dental hygiene.

2011-2012 Annual costs. Tuition/fees: $27,330. Room/board: $11,700. Books/supplies: $1,500. Personal expenses: $3,043.

Financial aid. Non-need-based: Scholarships awarded for academics, athletics, leadership, music/drama, state residency.

Application procedures. Admission: Priority date 4/1; no deadline. $25 fee, may be waived for applicants with need. Admission notification on a rolling basis. Must reply by May 1 or within 2 week(s) if notified thereafter. **Financial aid:** Priority date 4/1; no closing date. FAFSA required. Applicants notified on a rolling basis starting 4/1; must reply within 4 week(s) of notification.

Academics. Special study options: Accelerated study, combined bachelor's/graduate degree, cooperative education, cross-registration, distance learning, double major, dual enrollment of high school students, ESL, exchange student, honors, independent study, internships, liberal arts/career combination, New York semester, semester at sea, student-designed major, study abroad, teacher certification program, United Nations semester, Washington semester, weekend college. **Credit/placement by examination:** AP, CLEP, IB, SAT, ACT, institutional tests. 30 credit hours maximum toward associate degree, 30 toward bachelor's. **Support services:** Learning center, pre-admission summer program, reduced course load, remedial instruction, study skills assistance, tutoring, writing center.

Majors. Area/ethnic studies: East Asian. **Biology:** General. **Business:** General, accounting, fashion, finance, international, labor relations, management information systems, marketing. **Communications:** Advertising, communications/speech/rhetoric, journalism, media studies, public relations. **Computer sciences:** General. **Engineering:** Computer. **English:** Creative writing, English lit. **Health services:** Clinical lab science, dental hygiene. **Human services:** Community org/advocacy. **Liberal arts:** Arts/sciences, humanities. **Math:** General. **Philosophy/religion:** Religion. **Protective services:** Criminal justice. **Psychology:** General. **Social sciences:** General, criminology, international relations, political science, sociology. **Visual/performing arts:** Graphic design, illustration, industrial design, interior design, music.

Most popular majors. Business/marketing 20%, health sciences 8%, liberal arts 24%, psychology 14%, public administration/social services 11%, visual/performing arts 10%.

Computing on campus. 200 workstations in dormitories, library, computer center, student center. Dormitories wired for high-speed internet access and linked to campus network. Commuter students can connect to campus network. Online course registration, online library, helpline, repair service, student web hosting, wireless network available.

Student life. Freshman orientation: Mandatory, $150 fee. Preregistration for classes offered. Placement listing, registration, and orientation held during the summer with final program just prior to class. **Policies:** Student and dormitory governments plan student life activities. **Housing:** Guaranteed on-campus for all undergraduates. Coed dorms, wellness housing available. $200 nonrefundable deposit, deadline 5/1. Dormitories have special facilities. **Activities:** Choral groups, film society, international student organizations, literary magazine, music ensembles, Model UN, student government, student newspaper, interfaith center, black student alliance, social service sorority, Protestant fellowship, community service project.

Athletics. NCAA. **Intercollegiate:** Baseball M, basketball, cross-country, gymnastics W, lacrosse W, soccer, softball W, swimming, volleyball W. **Intramural:** Basketball, racquetball, soccer, softball, tennis, volleyball. **Team name:** Purple Knights.

Student services. Adult student services, alcohol/substance abuse counseling, chaplain/spiritual director, career counseling, services for economically disadvantaged, student employment services, financial aid counseling, health services, minority student services, personal counseling, placement for graduates, veterans' counselor. **Physically disabled:** Services for visually, speech, hearing impaired.

Contact. E-mail: admit@bridgeport.edu
Phone: (203) 576-4552 Toll-free number: (800) 392-3582
Fax: (203) 576-4941
Bryan Gross, Associate Vice President for Enrollment Management, University of Bridgeport, 126 Park Avenue, Bridgeport, CT 06604

University of Connecticut
Storrs, Connecticut
www.uconn.edu

CB member
CB code: 3915

- Public 4-year university
- Residential campus in large town
- 17,450 degree-seeking undergraduates: 3% part-time, 49% women, 6% African American, 8% Asian American, 7% Hispanic American, 2% international
- 7,348 degree-seeking graduate students
- 47% of applicants admitted
- SAT or ACT with writing, application essay required
- 83% graduate within 6 years

General. Founded in 1881. Regionally accredited. Students may take courses at nonresidential campuses in Groton, Hartford, Stamford, Waterbury, and Torrington. **Degrees:** 4,747 bachelor's, 29 associate awarded; master's, professional, doctoral offered. **ROTC:** Army, Air Force. **Location:** 26 miles from Hartford, 80 miles from Boston. **Calendar:** Semester, extensive summer

session. **Full-time faculty:** 1,036 total; 94% have terminal degrees, 21% minority, 37% women. **Part-time faculty:** 327 total; 26% have terminal degrees, 6% minority, 53% women. **Class size:** 42% < 20, 34% 20-39, 7% 40-49, 9% 50-99, 9% >100. **Special facilities:** Puppetry museum, contemporary art galleries, archaeology center, natural history museum, sports museum, conservatory, greenhouses, horse barn tours, art museum, performing arts center, repertory theater.

Freshman class profile. 27,247 applied, 12,894 admitted, 3,327 enrolled.

Mid 50% test scores			
SAT critical reading:	550-640	Return as sophomores:	92%
SAT math:	580-670	Out-of-state:	31%
SAT writing:	550-650	Live on campus:	96%
ACT composite:	25-29	International:	4%
Rank in top quarter:	82%	Fraternities:	6%
Rank in top tenth:	43%	Sororities:	8%

Basis for selection. Curriculum, grades, rank in class most important, followed by test scores. Particular consideration given to first generation college and/or socio-economically disadvantaged applicants and applicants with special talents. Audition required of music, acting, puppetry majors. Portfolio required for art major. Interview required for design/technical theater and theater studies majors. **Home schooled:** Statement describing home school structure and mission, transcript of courses and grades required. **Learning Disabled:** Students may submit disability documentation to Center for Students with Disabilities upon admission.

High school preparation. College-preparatory program required. 16 units required. Required and recommended units include English 4, mathematics 3, social studies 2, science 2 (laboratory 2), foreign language 2-3 and academic electives 3. Some programs may require additional units.

2012-2013 Annual costs. Tuition/fees: $11,242; $29,074 out-of-state. Room/board: $11,380. Books/supplies: $850. Personal expenses: $1,650.

2011-2012 Financial aid. Need-based: 2,823 full-time freshmen applied for aid; 1,935 were judged to have need; 1,893 of these received aid. Average need met was 67%. Average scholarship/grant was $8,392; average loan $3,452. 50% of total undergraduate aid awarded as scholarships/grants, 50% as loans/jobs. **Non-need-based:** Awarded to 6,683 full-time undergraduates, including 1,750 freshmen. Scholarships awarded for academics, art, athletics, leadership, minority status, music/drama. **Additional information:** Institution offers variety of need-based financial aid programs. Financial assistance packages may include grants, loans and work-study awards.

Application procedures. Admission: Closing date 2/1. $70 fee, may be waived for applicants with need. Admission notification on a rolling basis beginning on or about 1/1. Must reply by May 1 or within 2 week(s) if notified thereafter. **Financial aid:** Priority date 3/1; no closing date. FAFSA required. Applicants notified on a rolling basis starting 3/1; must reply within 4 week(s) of notification.

Academics. 5-year Eurotech Program program combining engineering and German language, including 6-month internship in Germany. **Special study options:** Accelerated study, combined bachelor's/graduate degree, cooperative education, distance learning, double major, dual enrollment of high school students, ESL, exchange student, external degree, honors, independent study, internships, liberal arts/career combination, New York semester, semester at sea, student-designed major, study abroad, teacher certification program, urban semester, Washington semester. Winter inter-session, summer session, urban semester. **Credit/placement by examination:** AP, CLEP, IB, SAT, institutional tests. 30 credit hours maximum toward bachelor's degree. **Support services:** Learning center, pre-admission summer program, study skills assistance, tutoring, writing center.

Majors. Architecture: Landscape. **Area/ethnic studies:** American, Latin American, Near/Middle Eastern, women's. **Biology:** General, animal physiology, biophysics, cellular/molecular, ecology, marine, pathology. **Business:** General, accounting, actuarial science, business admin, finance, insurance, management information systems, marketing, real estate. **Communications:** Communications/speech/rhetoric, journalism. **Computer sciences:** Computer science. **Conservation:** General, environmental studies. **Education:** Agricultural, elementary, music, physical, special ed. **Engineering:** Applied physics, biomedical, chemical, civil, computer, electrical, environmental, industrial, materials, mechanical. **English:** English lit. **Foreign languages:** Classics, French, German, Italian, linguistics, Spanish. **General:** Agronomy, animal sciences, economics, horticultural science. **Health services:** Athletic training, clinical lab science, cytotechnology, dietetics, gene therapy, health care admin, nursing (RN), prepharmacy, prephysical therapy. **History:** General. **Math:** General, applied, statistics. **Parks/recreation:** Facilities management. **Philosophy/religion:** Philosophy. **Physical sciences:** Chemistry, geology, materials science, physics. **Psychology:** General, cognitive. **Social sciences:** Anthropology, economics, geography, political science, sociology, urban studies. **Visual/performing arts:** Acting, art history/conservation, dramatic, music, studio arts, theater design. **Work/family studies:** Family studies.

Most popular majors. Biology 7%, business/marketing 13%, communications/journalism 6%, engineering/engineering technologies 8%, health sciences 9%, liberal arts 6%, psychology 7%, social sciences 14%.

Computing on campus. 1,318 workstations in dormitories, library, computer center, student center. Dormitories wired for high-speed internet access and linked to campus network. Commuter students can connect to campus network. Online course registration, online library, helpline, repair service, wireless network available.

Student life. Freshman orientation: Available, $60 fee. Preregistration for classes offered. Twelve 2-day sessions extending from late May to early July. **Policies:** Freshmen not permitted cars on campus. **Housing:** Coed dorms, single-sex dorms, special housing for disabled, apartments, fraternity/sorority housing available. $150 nonrefundable deposit, deadline 5/1. Living and learning communities. **Activities:** Bands, campus ministries, choral groups, dance, drama, film society, international student organizations, literary magazine, music ensembles, Model UN, musical theater, opera, radio station, student government, student newspaper, symphony orchestra, TV station, over 400 organizations available.

Athletics. NCAA. **Intercollegiate:** Baseball M, basketball, cross-country, diving, field hockey W, football (tackle) M, golf M, ice hockey, lacrosse W, rowing (crew) W, soccer, softball W, swimming, tennis, track and field, volleyball W. **Intramural:** Badminton, baseball M, basketball, bowling, cross-country, diving, equestrian, fencing, football (non-tackle), football (tackle) M, ice hockey, lacrosse, racquetball, rowing (crew), rugby, sailing, skiing, soccer, softball, squash, swimming, table tennis, tennis, track and field, volleyball, water polo, weight lifting M. **Team name:** Huskies.

Student services. Adult student services, alcohol/substance abuse counseling, chaplain/spiritual director, career counseling, student employment services, financial aid counseling, health services, minority student services, on-campus daycare, personal counseling, placement for graduates, veterans' counselor, women's services. **Physically disabled:** Services for visually, speech, hearing impaired.

Contact. E-mail: beahusky@uconn.edu
Phone: (860) 486-3137 Fax: (860) 486-1476
Nathan Fuerst, Director of Undergraduate Admissions, University of Connecticut, 2131 Hillside Road, Unit 3088, Storrs, CT 06269-3088

University of Hartford
West Hartford, Connecticut
www.hartford.edu

CB member
CB code: 3436

- Private 4-year university
- Residential campus in small city
- 5,141 degree-seeking undergraduates: 11% part-time, 51% women
- 1,609 degree-seeking graduate students
- 71% of applicants admitted
- SAT or ACT with writing required
- 59% graduate within 6 years

General. Founded in 1877. Regionally accredited. **Degrees:** 1,058 bachelor's, 160 associate awarded; master's, professional, doctoral offered. **ROTC:** Army, Air Force. **Location:** 4 miles from downtown. **Calendar:** Semester, extensive summer session. **Full-time faculty:** 347 total; 86% have terminal degrees, 16% minority, 39% women. **Part-time faculty:** 501 total. **Class size:** 61% < 20, 37% 20-39, less than 1% 40-49, less than 1% 50-99, less than 1% >100. **Special facilities:** Engineering applications center, humanities center, performing arts center, center for professional development, entrepreneurial center, construction institute.

Freshman class profile. 11,997 applied, 8,534 admitted, 1,331 enrolled.

Mid 50% test scores			
SAT critical reading:	470-570	Return as sophomores:	72%
SAT math:	480-590	Out-of-state:	65%
ACT composite:	19-25	Live on campus:	89%
		International:	3%

Basis for selection. Quality of academic program, school achievement record, class rank important. Test scores secondary. Employment, extracurricular activities, and community service considered. Writing samples and interview also considered. Admission committee can offer admission to alternative program. Interview and essay recommended. Audition required of music, dance, acting majors. Portfolio required of art majors. **Home schooled:** Statement describing home school structure and mission, transcript of courses and grades required.

High school preparation. 16 units required. Required and recommended units include English 4, mathematics 2-3, social studies 2, history 2, science 2-3, foreign language 3 and academic electives 4. Physics, chemistry, and

3.5 math (including trigonometry) recommended for engineering and science applicants.

2012-2013 Annual costs. Tuition/fees (projected): $32,172. Room/board: $12,104. Books/supplies: $860. Personal expenses: $1,350.

2010-2011 Financial aid. Need-based: 1,350 full-time freshmen applied for aid; 1,177 were judged to have need; 1,176 of these received aid. Average need met was 80%. Average scholarship/grant was $8,970; average loan $3,202. 86% of total undergraduate aid awarded as scholarships/grants, 14% as loans/jobs. **Non-need-based:** Awarded to 934 full-time undergraduates, including 175 freshmen. Scholarships awarded for academics, art, athletics, music/drama.

Application procedures. Admission: No deadline. $40 fee, may be waived for applicants with need. Admission notification on a rolling basis beginning on or about 10/1. Must reply by May 1 or within 2 week(s) if notified thereafter. **Financial aid:** Priority date 2/1; no closing date. FAFSA, institutional form required. Applicants notified on a rolling basis starting 3/1; must reply by 5/1.

Academics. Special study options: Combined bachelor's/graduate degree, cooperative education, cross-registration, distance learning, double major, dual enrollment of high school students, ESL, exchange student, honors, independent study, internships, liberal arts/career combination, student-designed major, study abroad, teacher certification program, Washington semester, weekend college. Saturday term. **Credit/placement by examination:** AP, CLEP, SAT, institutional tests. 30 credit hours maximum toward associate degree, 60 toward bachelor's. **Support services:** Learning center, reduced course load, tutoring, writing center.

Majors. Area/ethnic studies: Women's. **Biology:** General. **Business:** Accounting, business admin, entrepreneurial studies, finance, insurance, management information systems, marketing. **Communications:** Communications/speech/rhetoric. **Computer sciences:** General, information systems. **Education:** Early childhood, elementary, music, secondary, special ed. **Engineering:** General, civil, computer, electrical, mechanical. **English:** English lit, technical writing. **Foreign languages:** General. **Health services:** Clinical lab science, medical radiologic technology/radiation therapy, nursing (RN), respiratory therapy technology. **History:** General. **Human services:** Community org/advocacy. **Liberal arts:** Arts/sciences. **Math:** General. **Philosophy/religion:** Judaic, philosophy. **Physical sciences:** Chemistry, physics. **Protective services:** Police science. **Psychology:** General. **Social sciences:** Economics, international economics, political science, sociology. **Theology:** Sacred music. **Visual/performing arts:** General, acting, art history/conservation, ceramics, cinematography, commercial/advertising art, dance, design, dramatic, drawing, film/cinema/video, jazz, music, music history, music management, music performance, music theory/composition, painting, photography, printmaking, sculpture.

Most popular majors. Business/marketing 16%, communications/journalism 8%, education 7%, engineering/engineering technologies 12%, health sciences 12%, psychology 6%, visual/performing arts 19%.

Computing on campus. 300 workstations in dormitories, library, computer center. Dormitories wired for high-speed internet access and linked to campus network. Commuter students can connect to campus network. Online course registration, online library, helpline, repair service, student web hosting, wireless network available.

Student life. Freshman orientation: Mandatory. Preregistration for classes offered. **Housing:** Guaranteed on-campus for freshmen. Coed dorms, single-sex dorms, special housing for disabled, apartments, wellness housing available. $200 deposit, deadline 5/1. Dormitories with resident faculty members, international residential college, residential college for the arts available. **Activities:** Bands, choral groups, dance, drama, international student organizations, literary magazine, music ensembles, musical theater, opera, radio station, student government, student newspaper, symphony orchestra, TV station, Hillel, Protestant student organization, Newman club, African American students association, academic department clubs, prelaw and premedical societies, Brothers and Sisters United, Global Friends Association, Malaysian student association, Turkish student association.

Athletics. NCAA. **Intercollegiate:** Baseball M, basketball, cross-country, golf, lacrosse M, soccer, softball W, tennis, track and field, volleyball W. **Intramural:** Basketball, football (non-tackle), handball, racquetball, soccer, softball, tennis, volleyball, water polo. **Team name:** Hawks.

Student services. Chaplain/spiritual director, career counseling, student employment services, financial aid counseling, health services, minority student services, personal counseling, placement for graduates, veterans' counselor.

Contact. E-mail: admission@hartford.edu
Phone: (860) 768-4296 Fax: (860) 768-4961
Richard Zeiser, Dean of Admission, University of Hartford, Bates House, West Hartford, CT 06117-1599

University of New Haven
West Haven, Connecticut
www.newhaven.edu

CB member
CB code: 3663

- Private 4-year university
- Residential campus in small city
- 4,546 degree-seeking undergraduates: 9% part-time, 51% women, 8% African American, 2% Asian American, 5% Hispanic American, 5% international
- 1,740 degree-seeking graduate students
- 64% of applicants admitted
- SAT or ACT (ACT writing optional), application essay required
- 53% graduate within 6 years

General. Founded in 1920. Regionally accredited. Experiential learning emphasized. **Degrees:** 688 bachelor's, 38 associate awarded; master's, doctoral offered. **ROTC:** Army, Air Force. **Location:** 3 miles from downtown New Haven, 75 miles from New York City. **Calendar:** 4-1-4, limited summer session. **Full-time faculty:** 203 total; 78% have terminal degrees, 11% minority, 31% women. **Part-time faculty:** 298 total; 29% have terminal degrees, 41% women. **Class size:** 36% < 20, 59% 20-39, 2% 40-49, 3% 50-99, less than 1% >100. **Special facilities:** Theater, music and sound recording studio, shoreline environmental study preserve, institute of forensic science, learning center for finance and technology.

Freshman class profile. 11,181 applied, 7,129 admitted, 1,296 enrolled.

Mid 50% test scores			
SAT critical reading:	470-570	GPA 3.0-3.49:	37%
SAT math:	490-580	GPA 2.0-2.99:	19%
SAT writing:	470-570	Return as sophomores:	75%
ACT composite:	20-26	Out-of-state:	68%
GPA 3.75 or higher:	18%	Live on campus:	85%
GPA 3.50-3.74:	26%	International:	4%

Basis for selection. Academic record, recommendations, test scores, personal essay, advanced placement or honor courses, and extracurricular activities reviewed. **Learning Disabled:** Students required to meet with Disability Services Office to receive accommodations and/or services.

High school preparation. College-preparatory program recommended. Required and recommended units include English 4, mathematics 3, social studies 2, science 2 (laboratory 2), foreign language 2, computer science 1 and visual/performing arts 1.

2011-2012 Annual costs. Tuition/fees: $31,750. Room/board: $13,200. Books/supplies: $1,000. Personal expenses: $1,340.

Financial aid. Non-need-based: Scholarships awarded for academics, alumni affiliation, athletics, leadership.

Application procedures. Admission: No deadline. $75 fee, may be waived for applicants with need. Admission notification on a rolling basis beginning on or about 12/1. Must reply by May 1 or within 2 week(s) if notified thereafter. **Financial aid:** Closing date 3/1. FAFSA required. Applicants notified on a rolling basis starting 3/1; must reply by 5/1 or within 2 week(s) of notification.

Academics. Special study options: Accelerated study, combined bachelor's/graduate degree, cooperative education, distance learning, double major, ESL, honors, independent study, internships, study abroad, teacher certification program, weekend college. **Credit/placement by examination:** AP, CLEP, IB, SAT, ACT, institutional tests. **Support services:** Learning center, reduced course load, remedial instruction, study skills assistance, tutoring, writing center.

Majors. Architecture: Interior. **Biology:** General, ecology, marine. **Business:** Accounting, business admin, finance, hospitality admin, hotel/motel admin, international, marketing. **Communications:** Communications/speech/rhetoric. **Computer sciences:** General, computer science, information systems. **Conservation:** General. **Education:** Mathematics. **Engineering:** General, chemical, civil, computer, electrical, mechanical, systems. **English:** English lit. **Health services:** Dental hygiene, dietetics. **History:** General. **Human services:** General. **Liberal arts:** Arts/sciences. **Math:** General, applied. **Parks/recreation:** Sports admin. **Physical sciences:** Chemistry. **Protective services:** Corrections, criminalistics, fire safety technology, firefighting, forensics, juvenile corrections, law enforcement admin. **Psychology:** General, forensic. **Social sciences:** Political science. **Visual/performing arts:** Dramatic, graphic design, interior design, music, music management, studio arts.

Most popular majors. Biology 6%, business/marketing 15%, engineering/engineering technologies 7%, health sciences 6%, security/protective services 44%, visual/performing arts 11%.

Computing on campus. Dormitories wired for high-speed internet access and linked to campus network. Online course registration, helpline, repair service, wireless network available.

Student life. Freshman orientation: Mandatory. Preregistration for classes offered. **Housing:** Guaranteed on-campus for freshmen. Coed dorms, special housing for disabled, apartments available. $200 nonrefundable deposit, deadline 5/1. Living/learning communities available for freshmen majoring in business, engineering, forensic science, or music. Some dorm rooms are handicapped accessible. **Activities:** Bands, campus ministries, choral groups, dance, drama, international student organizations, literary magazine, Model UN, radio station, student government, student newspaper, symphony orchestra.

Athletics. NCAA. **Intercollegiate:** Baseball M, basketball, cheerleading M, cross-country, football (tackle) M, golf M, lacrosse W, soccer, softball W, tennis W, track and field, volleyball W. **Intramural:** Basketball, cricket, football (non-tackle), racquetball, soccer, softball, swimming, table tennis, volleyball. **Team name:** Chargers.

Student services. Career counseling, student employment services, financial aid counseling, health services, minority student services, personal counseling, placement for graduates, veterans' counselor, women's services. **Physically disabled:** Services for visually, speech, hearing impaired.

Contact. E-mail: adminfo@newhaven.edu
Phone: (203) 932-7319 Toll-free number: (800) 342-5864
Fax: (203) 931-6093
Kevin Phillips, Associate Vice President for Enrollment Management, University of New Haven, 300 Boston Post Road, West Haven, CT 06516

University of Phoenix: Fairfield County
Norwalk, Connecticut
www.phoenix.edu

- For-profit 4-year university
- Commuter campus in small city
- 34 degree-seeking undergraduates

General. Regionally accredited. **Degrees:** 10 bachelor's awarded; master's offered. **Calendar:** Differs by program. **Full-time faculty:** 9 total. **Part-time faculty:** 33 total.

Basis for selection. Open admission, but selective for some programs.

2011-2012 Annual costs. Estimated costs as of August 2011: per-credit-hour charge, $380 to $520, depending upon level and course of study; electronic course materials fee, $95, if applicable. Book and material charges may vary by course and program. All fees are subject to change.

Application procedures. Admission: No deadline. No application fee. **Financial aid:** No deadline.

Academics. Credit/placement by examination: AP, CLEP.

Majors. Business: Accounting, business admin, marketing, training/development. **Health services:** Health care admin.

Contact. Marc Booker, Director of Admission and Evaluation, University of Phoenix: Fairfield County, 535 Connecticut Avenue, Norwalk, CT 06854-1700

Wesleyan University
Middletown, Connecticut   **CB member**
www.wesleyan.edu   **CB code: 3959**

- Private 4-year university and liberal arts college
- Residential campus in large town
- 2,870 degree-seeking undergraduates: 51% women, 7% African American, 8% Asian American, 10% Hispanic American, 8% international
- 262 degree-seeking graduate students
- 24% of applicants admitted
- SAT and SAT Subject Tests or ACT (ACT writing recommended), application essay required
- 94% graduate within 6 years

General. Founded in 1831. Regionally accredited. **Degrees:** 719 bachelor's awarded; master's, doctoral offered. **ROTC:** Army, Air Force. **Location:** 15 miles from Hartford, 25 miles from New Haven. **Calendar:** Semester, limited

summer session. **Full-time faculty:** 339 total; 94% have terminal degrees, 18% minority, 45% women. **Part-time faculty:** 36 total; 69% have terminal degrees, 31% minority, 56% women. **Class size:** 68% < 20, 24% 20-39, 3% 40-49, 3% 50-99, 2% >100. **Special facilities:** 11-building arts center, observatory, science center with electron microscopes and nuclear magnetic resonance spectrometers, film studies center, center for humanities, East Asian studies center, African-American studies center.

Freshman class profile. 9,658 applied, 2,340 admitted, 808 enrolled.

Mid 50% test scores			
SAT critical reading:	640-740	Rank in top quarter:	88%
SAT math:	660-740	Rank in top tenth:	66%
SAT writing:	660-750	Return as sophomores:	94%
ACT composite:	29-33	Out-of-state:	91%
GPA 3.75 or higher:	61%	Live on campus:	100%
GPA 3.50-3.74:	26%	International:	8%
GPA 3.0-3.49:	12%	Fraternities:	1%
GPA 2.0-2.99:	1%	Sororities:	1%

Basis for selection. High school transcript, class rank, test scores, extracurricular activities, 2 teacher evaluations, personal statement, and other evidence of outstanding accomplishments are considered. 2 SAT Subject Test scores required with SAT score. Interview recommended. **Home schooled:** Campus interview, statement describing home school structure and mission, transcript of courses and grades, third-party recommendation, and home-school instructor recommendation strongly recommended. Financial aid applicants should be prepared to submit GED.

High school preparation. College-preparatory program recommended. Recommended units include English 4, mathematics 4, social studies 4, history 4, science 4 (laboratory 3) and foreign language 4.

2011-2012 Annual costs. Tuition/fees: $43,974. Reported fees for incoming freshmen include one-time matriculation fee of $300. Returning students pay $270 in required fees. Room/board: $12,032. Books/supplies: $1,333. Personal expenses: $1,332.

Financial aid. All financial aid based on need. **Additional information:** Most families whose income is below $40,000 will not be packaged with loans; grant aid will replace the standard loan in the package. Other students demonstrating significant need will graduate with 4-year packaged loan debt of $10,000 or $14,000 depending on need level. All other students will have their 4-year packaged loan debt reduced by about 30%.

Application procedures. Admission: Closing date 1/1 (postmark date). $55 fee, may be waived for applicants with need. Admission notification by 4/1. Must reply by May 1 or within 2 week(s) if notified thereafter. **Financial aid:** Closing date 2/15. FAFSA, CSS PROFILE required. Applicants notified by 4/1; must reply by 5/1.

Academics. Students expected to complete 3 classes in each of following areas before graduation: natural sciences and math, arts and humanities, social and behavioral sciences. **Special study options:** Combined bachelor's/graduate degree, cross-registration, double major, dual enrollment of high school students, exchange student, honors, independent study, internships, semester at sea, student-designed major, study abroad, urban semester, Washington semester. 12-college exchange, semester in environmental science at the Marine Biological Laboratory-Woods Hole, Wesleyan-Trinity-Connecticut College Consortium, 3-2 program in science and engineering, teaching apprentice program. **Credit/placement by examination:** AP, CLEP, IB, institutional tests. 2 credit hours maximum toward bachelor's degree. **Support services:** Reduced course load, tutoring, writing center.

Majors. Area/ethnic studies: African-American, American, East Asian, French, gay/lesbian, German, Latin American, Russian/Eastern European/Eurasian, Russian/Slavic. **Biology:** General, biochemistry, molecular, molecular biochemistry, neuroscience. **Computer sciences:** General. **Conservation:** Environmental science. **English:** English lit. **Foreign languages:** Chinese, classics, East Asian, French, German, Italian, Japanese, Romance, Russian, Spanish. **History:** General. **Liberal arts:** Arts/sciences. **Math:** General. **Philosophy/religion:** Philosophy, religion. **Physical sciences:** Astronomy, chemistry, geology, physics, planetary. **Psychology:** General. **Social sciences:** Anthropology, archaeology, economics, political science, sociology. **Visual/performing arts:** Art history/conservation, dance, dramatic, film/cinema/video, music, studio arts.

Most popular majors. Area/ethnic studies 12%, biology 6%, English 8%, psychology 11%, social sciences 24%, visual/performing arts 14%.

Computing on campus. 300 workstations in library, computer center, student center. Dormitories wired for high-speed internet access and linked to campus network. Commuter students can connect to campus network. Online course registration, online library, helpline, repair service, student web hosting, wireless network available.

Student life. Freshman orientation: Mandatory. Preregistration for classes offered. Held one week before start of fall classes. **Housing:** Guaranteed on-campus for all undergraduates. Coed dorms, special housing for disabled, apartments, fraternity/sorority housing, wellness housing available. **Activities:** Bands, campus ministries, choral groups, dance, drama, film society, literary magazine, music ensembles, musical theater, radio station, student government, student newspaper, symphony orchestra, more than 230 organizations.

Athletics. NCAA. **Intercollegiate:** Baseball M, basketball, cross-country, diving, field hockey W, football (tackle) M, golf M, ice hockey, lacrosse, rowing (crew), soccer, softball W, squash, swimming, tennis, track and field, volleyball W, wrestling M. **Intramural:** Basketball, ice hockey M, soccer, softball, squash, volleyball. **Team name:** Cardinals.

Student services. Adult student services, alcohol/substance abuse counseling, chaplain/spiritual director, career counseling, student employment services, financial aid counseling, health services, minority student services, on-campus daycare, personal counseling, placement for graduates, women's services. **Physically disabled:** Services for visually, speech, hearing impaired.

Contact. E-mail: admissions@wesleyan.edu
Phone: (860) 685-3000 Fax: (860) 685-3001
Nancy Meislahn, Dean of Admission and Financial Aid, Wesleyan University, 70 Wyllys Avenue, Middletown, CT 06459-0260

Western Connecticut State University
Danbury, Connecticut
www.wcsu.edu   CB code: 3350

- Public 4-year university
- Commuter campus in small city
- 5,467 degree-seeking undergraduates: 13% part-time, 55% women, 8% African American, 3% Asian American, 12% Hispanic American
- 511 degree-seeking graduate students
- 62% of applicants admitted
- SAT or ACT with writing required
- 40% graduate within 6 years

General. Founded in 1903. Regionally accredited. **Degrees:** 918 bachelor's, 12 associate awarded; master's, professional offered. **ROTC:** Army, Air Force. **Location:** 65 miles from New York City, 50 miles from Hartford. **Calendar:** Semester, extensive summer session. **Full-time faculty:** 226 total; 84% have terminal degrees, 13% minority, 51% women. **Part-time faculty:** 302 total; 6% minority, 39% women. **Class size:** 31% < 20, 60% 20-39, 5% 40-49, 3% 50-99, less than 1% >100. **Special facilities:** Weather station, observatory, nature preserve.

Freshman class profile. 4,157 applied, 2,593 admitted, 887 enrolled.

Mid 50% test scores		Rank in top quarter:	20%
SAT critical reading:	450-540	Rank in top tenth:	5%
SAT math:	450-540	Return as sophomores:	72%
GPA 3.75 or higher:	14%	Out-of-state:	8%
GPA 3.50-3.74:	9%	Live on campus:	58%
GPA 3.0-3.49:	19%	Fraternities:	7%
GPA 2.0-2.99:	54%	Sororities:	6%

Basis for selection. Limited freshman class spaces given to students with strongest academic and extracurricular backgrounds, including test results. Essay and interview recommended. Audition required of music majors. Portfolio recommended of graphic design majors. **Home schooled:** Transcript of courses and grades required. **Learning Disabled:** To receive services or accommodations, students must provide appropriate documentation by contacting the coordinator of disability services.

High school preparation. College-preparatory program required. 13 units required. Required units include English 4, mathematics 3, social studies 1, history 1, science 2 (laboratory 2) and foreign language 2. Additional credits in fine arts and computer science recommended. Academic course work in computer science, visual arts, theater, music or dance may be substituted for one of the required areas.

2011-2012 Annual costs. Tuition/fees: $8,104; $18,728 out-of-state. Room/board: $10,223. Books/supplies: $1,300. Personal expenses: $2,325.

2011-2012 Financial aid. **Need-based:** Average need met was 64%. Average scholarship/grant was $5,101; average loan $3,382. 39% of total undergraduate aid awarded as scholarships/grants, 61% as loans/jobs. **Non-need-based:** Scholarships awarded for academics.

Application procedures. **Admission:** Priority date 4/1; no deadline. $50 fee, may be waived for applicants with need. Admission notification on a rolling basis beginning on or about 12/1. Must reply by May 1 or within 2 week(s) if notified thereafter. **Financial aid:** Priority date 3/15, closing date 4/15. FAFSA, institutional form required. Applicants notified on a rolling basis starting 4/15; must reply by 5/1 or within 2 week(s) of notification.

Academics. **Special study options:** Cooperative education, cross-registration, distance learning, dual enrollment of high school students, honors, independent study, internships, student-designed major, study abroad, teacher certification program. **Credit/placement by examination:** AP, CLEP, IB, SAT, institutional tests. 30 credit hours maximum toward associate degree, 60 toward bachelor's. **Support services:** Learning center, pre-admission summer program, reduced course load, remedial instruction, study skills assistance, tutoring, writing center.

Majors. Area/ethnic studies: American. **Biology:** General. **Business:** Accounting, business admin, finance, management information systems, marketing. **Communications:** Communications/speech/rhetoric, media studies. **Computer sciences:** General. **Education:** Elementary, health, music, secondary. **English:** Creative writing, English lit, writing. **Foreign languages:** Spanish. **Health services:** Clinical lab science, community health services, nursing (RN). **History:** General. **Human services:** Social work. **Liberal arts:** Arts/sciences. **Math:** General. **Physical sciences:** Atmospheric science, chemistry, geology. **Protective services:** Police science. **Psychology:** General. **Social sciences:** General, economics, political science, sociology. **Visual/performing arts:** Art, dramatic, music, music theory/composition.

Most popular majors. Business/marketing 27%, communications/journalism 8%, education 8%, health sciences 6%, history 7%, psychology 8%, security/protective services 11%, visual/performing arts 8%.

Computing on campus. 1,021 workstations in dormitories, library, computer center, student center. Dormitories wired for high-speed internet access and linked to campus network. Commuter students can connect to campus network. Online course registration, online library, helpline, student web hosting, wireless network available.

Student life. Freshman orientation: Available. Preregistration for classes offered. 2-day program for students and parents held the weekend before classes start. **Policies:** Hazing and smoking inside all buildings prohibited. Honor code applies. **Housing:** Coed dorms, single-sex dorms, apartments available. $250 nonrefundable deposit. **Activities:** Bands, campus ministries, choral groups, dance, drama, international student organizations, literary magazine, music ensembles, musical theater, opera, radio station, student government, student newspaper, symphony orchestra, Black student alliance, Habitat for Humanity, justice and law club, Newman club, College Republicans, College Democrats.

Athletics. NCAA. **Intercollegiate:** Baseball M, basketball, field hockey W, football (tackle) M, lacrosse, soccer, softball W, swimming W, tennis, volleyball W. **Intramural:** Basketball M, football (non-tackle) M. **Team name:** Colonials.

Student services. Adult student services, alcohol/substance abuse counseling, chaplain/spiritual director, career counseling, student employment services, financial aid counseling, health services, minority student services, on-campus daycare, personal counseling, placement for graduates, veterans' counselor, women's services. **Physically disabled:** Services for visually, speech, hearing impaired.

Contact. E-mail: admissions@wcsu.edu
Phone: (203) 837-9000 Toll-free number: (877) 837-9278
Fax: (203) 837-8338
Steven Goetsch, Director, Admissions, Western Connecticut State University, 181 White Street, Danbury, CT 06810-6826

Yale University
New Haven, Connecticut   CB member
www.yale.edu   CB code: 3987

- Private 4-year university
- Residential campus in small city
- 5,342 degree-seeking undergraduates: 50% women, 6% African American, 15% Asian American, 10% Hispanic American, 1% Native American, 10% international
- 6,427 degree-seeking graduate students
- 8% of applicants admitted
- SAT and SAT Subject Tests or ACT with writing, application essay required
- 96% graduate within 6 years; 14% enter graduate study

General. Founded in 1701. Regionally accredited. **Degrees:** 1,281 bachelor's awarded; master's, professional, doctoral offered. **ROTC:** Army, Naval,

Air Force. **Location:** 75 miles from New York City. **Calendar:** Semester, limited summer session. **Full-time faculty:** 817 total; 93% have terminal degrees, 19% minority, 33% women. **Part-time faculty:** 11 total; 100% have terminal degrees, 27% minority, 9% women. **Class size:** 79% < 20, 12% 20-39, 2% 40-49, 4% 50-99, 3% >100. **Special facilities:** Two art museums, natural history museum, clean room, wind tunnel, engine testing facility, graphic workstations, robotics labs, crystal growth, nuclear accelerators, nuclear magnetic resonance spectrometers, optical spectroscopy instruments, high-resolution mass spectrometer, x-ray diffraction instruments, electron microscopes, observatories, marine studies field station, biospheric studies institute.

Freshman class profile. 27,283 applied, 2,109 admitted, 1,351 enrolled.

Mid 50% test scores			
SAT critical reading:	700-790	Rank in top tenth:	96%
SAT math:	700-800	Return as sophomores:	99%
SAT writing:	710-790	Out-of-state:	94%
ACT composite:	31-35	Live on campus:	100%
Rank in top quarter:	100%	International:	10%

Basis for selection. Honors work at secondary level, standardized test scores, and high degree of accomplishment in one or more nonacademic areas important, followed by diversity of interests, background and special talents. Interview recommended. Music and art submissions accepted digitally via Yale web portal. **Home schooled:** Letter of recommendation (nonparent) required. Require 2 recommendations from teachers of courses taken outside home, such as community college courses.

High school preparation. College-preparatory program recommended. Students recommended to take richest possible mix of demanding academic offerings.

2011-2012 Annual costs. Tuition/fees: $40,500. Room/board: $12,200. Books/supplies: $1,000.

2010-2011 Financial aid. All financial aid based on need. 871 full-time freshmen applied for aid; 802 were judged to have need; 802 of these received aid. Average need met was 100%. Average scholarship/grant was $39,303; average loan $2,154. 95% of total undergraduate aid awarded as scholarships/grants, 5% as loans/jobs. **Additional information:** All scholarships based on demonstrated need.

Application procedures. Admission: Closing date 12/31 (postmark date). $75 fee, may be waived for applicants with need. Admission notification by 4/1. Must reply by 5/1. **Financial aid:** Closing date 3/1. FAFSA, CSS PROFILE required. Applicants notified by 4/1; must reply by 5/1 or within 1 week(s) of notification.

Academics. Special study options: Accelerated study, combined bachelor's/graduate degree, double major, ESL, honors, independent study, internships, liberal arts/career combination, student-designed major, study abroad, teacher certification program. **Credit/placement by examination:** AP, CLEP, IB, institutional tests. **Support services:** Study skills assistance, tutoring, writing center.

Majors. Architecture: Architecture. **Area/ethnic studies:** African, African-American, American, East Asian, European, Latin American, Russian/Slavic, women's. **Biology:** General, biochemistry, Biochemistry/molecular biology, molecular. **Computer sciences:** General, applications programming. **Conservation:** Environmental studies. **Engineering:** Applied physics, biomedical, chemical, electrical, engineering science, environmental, mechanical. **English:** English lit. **Foreign languages:** Ancient Greek, Biblical, Chinese, classics, French, German, Italian, Japanese, Latin, linguistics, Portuguese, Russian, Spanish. **History:** General, science/technology. **Liberal arts:** Humanities. **Math:** General, applied, statistics. **Philosophy/religion:** Judaic, philosophy, religion. **Physical sciences:** Astronomy, astrophysics, chemistry, geology, physics. **Psychology:** General. **Social sciences:** Anthropology, archaeology, economics, international relations, political science, sociology. **Visual/performing arts:** Art, art history/conservation, dramatic, film/cinema/video, music.

Most popular majors. Area/ethnic studies 7%, biology 8%, English 7%, history 9%, interdisciplinary studies 8%, psychology 6%, social sciences 27%, visual/performing arts 6%.

Computing on campus. 400 workstations in dormitories, library, computer center, student center. Dormitories wired for high-speed internet access and linked to campus network. Commuter students can connect to campus network. Online course registration, online library, helpline, repair service, student web hosting, wireless network available.

Student life. Freshman orientation: Mandatory. Preregistration for classes offered. **Housing:** Guaranteed on-campus for freshmen. Coed dorms, special housing for disabled available. **Activities:** Bands, choral groups, dance, drama, film society, international student organizations, literary magazine, music ensembles, musical theater, opera, radio station, student government, student newspaper, symphony orchestra, TV station, over 135 organizations available.

Athletics. NCAA. **Intercollegiate:** Baseball M, basketball, cross-country, diving, fencing, field hockey W, football (tackle) M, golf, gymnastics W, ice hockey, lacrosse, rowing (crew), sailing, soccer, softball W, squash, swimming, tennis, track and field, volleyball W. **Intramural:** Badminton, baseball M, basketball, bowling, cross-country, field hockey W, football (tackle), golf, ice hockey, racquetball, rowing (crew), soccer, softball, squash, swimming, table tennis, tennis, volleyball, water polo, wrestling M. **Team name:** Bulldogs.

Student services. Alcohol/substance abuse counseling, chaplain/spiritual director, career counseling, student employment services, financial aid counseling, health services, minority student services, personal counseling, placement for graduates, women's services. **Physically disabled:** Services for visually, speech, hearing impaired.

Contact. E-mail: student.questions@yale.edu
Phone: (203) 432-9300 Fax: (203) 432-9392
Jeffrey Brenzel, Dean of Undergraduate Admissions, Yale University, Box 208234, New Haven, CT 06520-8234

Delaware

Delaware State University

Dover, Delaware
www.desu.edu

CB member
CB code: 5153

- Public 4-year university
- Residential campus in large town
- 3,744 degree-seeking undergraduates: 7% part-time, 62% women, 76% African American, 5% Hispanic American, 2% Native American, 1% international
- 196 degree-seeking graduate students
- 43% of applicants admitted
- SAT or ACT with writing required
- 35% graduate within 6 years; 30% enter graduate study

General. Founded in 1891. Regionally accredited. University has its own fleet of planes. **Degrees:** 500 bachelor's awarded; master's, doctoral offered. **ROTC:** Army, Air Force. **Location:** 46 miles from Wilmington, 100 miles from Washington DC. **Calendar:** Semester, extensive summer session. **Full-time faculty:** 211 total; 93% have terminal degrees, 59% minority, 40% women. **Part-time faculty:** 146 total; 52% minority, 49% women. **Class size:** 53% < 20, 40% 20-39, 5% 40-49, 3% 50-99. **Special facilities:** Science center, observatory, herbarium.

Freshman class profile. 9,221 applied, 3,933 admitted, 1,086 enrolled.

Mid 50% test scores			
SAT critical reading:	400-470	GPA 2.0-2.99:	54%
SAT math:	400-470	Rank in top quarter:	28%
SAT writing:	380-460	Rank in top tenth:	8%
ACT composite:	16-20	End year in good standing:	71%
GPA 3.75 or higher:	7%	Return as sophomores:	71%
GPA 3.50-3.74:	9%	Out-of-state:	60%
GPA 3.0-3.49:	30%	Live on campus:	81%
		International:	1%

Basis for selection. High school curriculum and GPA most important. Test scores only used in conjunction with GPA. Class rank considered. Interviews upon invitation; band students audition for scholarships.

High school preparation. College-preparatory program recommended. 19 units required. Required units include English 4, mathematics 3, social studies 1, history 2, science 3 (laboratory 3), foreign language 2 and academic electives 4. Math units must include 2 algebra and 1 geometry.

2011-2012 Annual costs. Tuition/fees: $7,056; $15,052 out-of-state. Room/board: $10,248. Books/supplies: $1,500. Personal expenses: $1,600.

2010-2011 Financial aid. All financial aid based on need. 855 full-time freshmen applied for aid; 794 were judged to have need; 790 of these received aid. Average need met was 48%. Average scholarship/grant was $6,772; average loan $2,813. 49% of total undergraduate aid awarded as scholarships/grants, 51% as loans/jobs. **Additional information:** Students must file FAFSA by March 15 every year.

Application procedures. Admission: Priority date 4/1; no deadline. $35 fee, may be waived for applicants with need. Admission notification on a rolling basis beginning on or about 9/1. May enroll in an Early Bird program. **Financial aid:** Priority date 3/1, closing date 7/1. FAFSA required. Applicants notified on a rolling basis starting 4/1; must reply by 8/20.

Academics. Special study options: Accelerated study, cooperative education, distance learning, double major, dual enrollment of high school students, ESL, exchange student, honors, independent study, internships, study abroad, teacher certification program. **Credit/placement by examination:** AP, CLEP, SAT, ACT, institutional tests. 30 credit hours maximum toward bachelor's degree. **Support services:** Learning center, pre-admission summer program, reduced course load, remedial instruction, study skills assistance, tutoring, writing center.

Majors. Biology: General. **Business:** Accounting, business admin, finance, hospitality admin, marketing, nonprofit/public. **Communications:** Broadcast journalism, journalism, media studies, radio/TV. **Computer sciences:** General, computer science, data processing, systems analysis. **Conservation:**

Environmental science, fisheries, forestry, management/policy, wildlife/wilderness. **Education:** General, art, biology, business, chemistry, early childhood, elementary, English, French, German, gifted/talented, health, mathematics, middle, music, physical, physics, science, social science, Spanish, special ed, trade/industrial. **Engineering:** Aerospace, applied physics, biomedical, civil, electrical, mining. **English:** English lit, writing. **Foreign languages:** French, German, Spanish. **General:** Business, food science, plant sciences, poultry, soil science. **Health services:** Nursing (RN), prenursing, preveterinary, public health nursing. **History:** General. **Human services:** Social work. **Math:** General. **Parks/recreation:** Health/fitness, sports admin. **Philosophy/religion:** Philosophy. **Physical sciences:** Chemistry, forensic chemistry, physics. **Protective services:** Criminal justice, fire safety technology. **Psychology:** General. **Social sciences:** Criminology, political science, sociology, urban studies. **Visual/performing arts:** General, art, music, studio arts, studio arts management. **Work/family studies:** Clothing/textiles, consumer economics, food/nutrition.

Most popular majors. Biology 6%, business/marketing 15%, communications/journalism 12%, health sciences 10%, parks/recreation 8%, psychology 13%, public administration/social services 6%, social sciences 10%.

Computing on campus. 400 workstations in library, computer center, student center. Dormitories wired for high-speed internet access and linked to campus network. Online course registration, online library, helpline, wireless network available.

Student life. Freshman orientation: Mandatory, $150 fee. Preregistration for classes offered. 2-day program during June, July and August. **Policies:** First-time, first-year freshmen must submit written request for parking permit. **Housing:** Guaranteed on-campus for freshmen. Coed dorms, single-sex dorms, special housing for disabled, apartments, cooperative housing, wellness housing available. $200 nonrefundable deposit, deadline 4/15. Suite style accommodations available for upper class students and honor students; residence hall available for honors students. **Activities:** Bands, campus ministries, choral groups, dance, drama, international student organizations, music ensembles, musical theater, radio station, student government, student newspaper, TV station, Wesley Foundation, commuters club, NAACP, Black studies club, honor societies, Greek letter organizations, student ambassadors.

Athletics. NCAA. **Intercollegiate:** Baseball M, basketball, bowling W, cheerleading, cross-country, equestrian W, football (tackle) M, soccer W, softball W, tennis W, track and field, volleyball W. **Intramural:** Basketball, football (non-tackle), soccer, softball, swimming, table tennis, tennis, track and field, volleyball. **Team name:** Hornets.

Student services. Adult student services, alcohol/substance abuse counseling, chaplain/spiritual director, career counseling, student employment services, financial aid counseling, health services, on-campus daycare, personal counseling, placement for graduates, veterans' counselor. **Physically disabled:** Services for visually, speech, hearing impaired.

Contact. E-mail: admissions@desu.edu
Phone: (302) 857-6351 Toll-free number: (800) 845-2544
Fax: (302) 857-6352
Erin Hill, Director of Admissions, Delaware State University, 1200 North DuPont Highway, Dover, DE 19901

Goldey-Beacom College

Wilmington, Delaware
www.gbc.edu

CB member
CB code: 5255

- Private 4-year business college
- Commuter campus in small city
- 681 degree-seeking undergraduates: 26% part-time, 53% women, 23% African American, 5% Asian American, 8% Hispanic American, 7% international
- 446 degree-seeking graduate students
- 56% of applicants admitted
- SAT required
- 46% graduate within 6 years

General. Founded in 1886. Regionally accredited. **Degrees:** 139 bachelor's, 26 associate awarded; master's offered. **ROTC:** Air Force. **Location:** 8 miles from Wilmington, 36 miles from Philadelphia. **Calendar:** Semester, extensive summer session. **Full-time faculty:** 19 total; 100% have terminal degrees, 16% minority, 37% women. **Part-time faculty:** 35 total; 26% have terminal degrees, 14% minority, 34% women. **Class size:** 31% < 20, 46% 20-39, 22% 40-49. **Special facilities:** Non-denominational chapel, athletic facilities and fields, fitness center, computer lab.

Freshman class profile. 709 applied, 395 admitted, 138 enrolled.

Basis for selection. Bachelor degree candidates must submit SAT scores and official transcripts from high school(s) and or college(s) attended. High school performance is evaluated. When necessary, interviews are requested. Interview recommended. **Home schooled:** Statement describing home school structure and mission, transcript of courses and grades, state high school equivalency certificate, interview required. **Learning Disabled:** Evaluation of disability and submission of documentation regarding disability.

High school preparation. 16 units recommended. Recommended units include English 4, mathematics 3 and science 3. 3 math units required for bachelor's degree applicants.

2012-2013 Annual costs. Tuition/fees: $21,120. Room only: $5,248. Books/supplies: $1,147. Personal expenses: $2,617.

2011-2012 Financial aid. Non-need-based: Scholarships awarded for academics, athletics.

Application procedures. Admission: No deadline. No application fee. Admission notification on a rolling basis. SAT not required but recommended for associate degree applicants for placement and counseling. **Financial aid:** Priority date 4/15, closing date 7/15. FAFSA required. Applicants notified on a rolling basis starting 3/1; must reply within 2 week(s) of notification.

Academics. Special study options: Accelerated study, combined bachelor's/graduate degree, cooperative education, double major, dual enrollment of high school students, honors, internships. **Credit/placement by examination:** AP, CLEP, SAT, ACT, institutional tests. **Support services:** Learning center, pre-admission summer program, reduced course load, remedial instruction, study skills assistance, tutoring, writing center.

Majors. Business: General, accounting, business admin, finance, international, management information systems, management science, marketing. **Computer sciences:** Information technology. **English:** English lit. **Psychology:** General. **Social sciences:** Economics.

Most popular majors. Business/marketing 95%.

Computing on campus. 159 workstations in library, computer center, student center. Dormitories linked to campus network. Commuter students can connect to campus network. Online library, wireless network available.

Student life. Freshman orientation: Mandatory. Preregistration for classes offered. **Housing:** Coed dorms, special housing for disabled, apartments, wellness housing available. $400 fully refundable deposit. Apartment-style residence halls. **Activities:** International student organizations, student government, student newspaper.

Athletics. NCAA. **Intercollegiate:** Basketball, cross-country, golf M, soccer, softball W, tennis W, volleyball W. **Team name:** Lightning.

Student services. Career counseling, student employment services, financial aid counseling, placement for graduates. **Physically disabled:** Services for visually, speech, hearing impaired.

Contact. E-mail: admissions@gbc.edu
Phone: (302) 225-6248 Toll-free number: (800) 833-4877
Fax: (302) 996-5408
Larry Eby, Director of Admissions, Goldey-Beacom College, 4701 Limestone Road, Wilmington, DE 19808

University of Delaware
Newark, Delaware
www.udel.edu

CB member
CB code: 5811

- Public 4-year university
- Residential campus in large town
- 16,340 degree-seeking undergraduates: 5% part-time, 57% women, 4% African American, 4% Asian American, 6% Hispanic American, 4% international
- 3,504 degree-seeking graduate students
- 58% of applicants admitted
- SAT or ACT with writing, application essay required
- 78% graduate within 6 years

General. Founded in 1743. Regionally accredited. **Degrees:** 3,621 bachelor's, 252 associate awarded; master's, doctoral offered. **ROTC:** Army, Air Force. **Location:** 12 miles from Wilmington, 30 miles from Philadelphia. **Calendar:** 4-1-4, limited summer session. **Full-time faculty:** 1,190 total; 86% have terminal degrees, 18% minority, 39% women. **Part-time faculty:** 295 total; 41% have terminal degrees, 14% minority, 54% women. **Class**

size: 36% < 20, 42% 20-39, 6% 40-49, 10% 50-99, 5% >100. **Special facilities:** Science development center, human performance laboratory, greenhouse, preschool lab, nutrition clinic, engineering research centers, 400-acre agriculture research complex, center for composites manufacturing and research, apparel design laboratory, simulated hospital rooms for nursing, physical therapy clinic, applied coastal research, Delaware biotechnology institute.

Freshman class profile. 23,647 applied, 13,768 admitted, 3,914 enrolled.

Mid 50% test scores			
SAT critical reading:	540-640	GPA 2.0-2.99:	7%
SAT math:	560-660	Rank in top quarter:	79%
SAT writing:	550-650	Rank in top tenth:	38%
ACT composite:	25-29	Return as sophomores:	93%
GPA 3.75 or higher:	41%	Out-of-state:	68%
GPA 3.50-3.74:	24%	Live on campus:	94%
GPA 3.0-3.49:	28%	International:	3%

Basis for selection. High school record, program of study, test scores most important. References, essay, extracurricular accomplishments considered. SAT Subject scores required for home-schooled applicants; strongly recommended for honors program. SAT Subject Tests recommended. Audition or portfolio required for music or art. **Home schooled:** Transcript of courses and grades required. Students should provide reading lists for courses they have completed. Sample portfolio of work or sample research paper recommended. Applicants should submit at least 2 SAT Subject Tests of their choice. In lieu of SAT and SAT Subject Tests, students may submit ACT with Writing score.

High school preparation. 18 units required; 22 recommended. Required and recommended units include English 4, mathematics 3-4, social studies 2, history 2, science 3-4 (laboratory 2-3), foreign language 2-4 and academic electives 2. 4 math strongly recommended for engineering, business, science or math applicants. 4 laboratory science strongly recommended for science, nursing, and engineering applicants.

2011-2012 Annual costs. Tuition/fees: $11,192; $27,462 out-of-state. Room/board: $10,470. Books/supplies: $800. Personal expenses: $1,500.

2011-2012 Financial aid. All financial aid based on need. 3,461 full-time freshmen applied for aid; 2,194 were judged to have need; 2,147 of these received aid. Average need met was 75%. Average scholarship/grant was $8,225; average loan $6,439. 43% of total undergraduate aid awarded as scholarships/grants, 57% as loans/jobs. **Additional information:** December 15 application deadline to receive scholarship consideration. Sibling/parent tuition credit plan. Senior citizen tuition credit for state residents over 60.

Application procedures. Admission: Priority date 12/1; deadline 1/15 (postmark date). $75 fee, may be waived for applicants with need. Admission notification by 3/15. Must reply by May 1 or within 3 week(s) if notified thereafter. **Financial aid:** Priority date 2/1, closing date 3/15. FAFSA required. Applicants notified on a rolling basis starting 3/15; must reply by 5/1 or within 3 week(s) of notification.

Academics. Special study options: Accelerated study, cooperative education, distance learning, double major, dual enrollment of high school students, ESL, honors, independent study, internships, liberal arts/career combination, student-designed major, study abroad, teacher certification program, Washington semester. Research program, minors in 68 disciplines, five-year engineering/liberal arts option. **Credit/placement by examination:** AP, CLEP, IB, SAT, institutional tests. For credit/placement to be awarded for International Baccalaureate, applicant must have taken higher level courses and have minimum score of 4 on exams. **Support services:** Pre-admission summer program, reduced course load, remedial instruction, study skills assistance, tutoring, writing center.

Honors college/program. Program emphasizes small classes, undergraduate research, honors housing, special scholarship opportunities. Special application required.

Majors. Area/ethnic studies: Latin American, women's. **Biology:** General, biochemistry, biotechnology, entomology, plant pathology. **Business:** Accounting, business admin, fashion, finance, management information systems, operations. **Communications:** Communications/speech/rhetoric, journalism. **Computer sciences:** General. **Conservation:** General, management/policy, wildlife/wilderness. **Education:** General, agricultural, biology, chemistry, early childhood, elementary, English, ESL, family/consumer sciences, foreign languages, French, geography, German, health, history, mathematics, middle, music, physical, physics, psychology, science, secondary, social science, Spanish, special ed. **Engineering:** Aerospace, agricultural, biomedical, chemical, civil, computer, electrical, environmental, mechanical, operations research. **English:** English lit. **Foreign languages:** General, Biblical, classics, comparative lit, French, German, Italian, Latin, Russian, Spanish. **General:** Agribusiness operations, agronomy, animal sciences, business, economics, food science, ornamental horticulture, plant sciences, soil science. **Health**

services: Athletic training, clinical lab science, clinical lab technology, nursing (RN), predental, premedicine, prepharmacy, preveterinary. **History:** General. **Liberal arts:** Arts/sciences. **Math:** General, statistics. **Parks/recreation:** Exercise sciences, facilities management, health/fitness, sports admin. **Philosophy/religion:** Philosophy. **Physical sciences:** Astronomy, chemistry, geology, geophysics, physics, planetary. **Protective services:** Criminal justice. **Psychology:** General. **Social sciences:** Anthropology, economics, geography, international relations, political science, sociology. **Visual/performing arts:** Art, art history/conservation, commercial/advertising art, fashion design, music, music performance, music theory/composition, piano/keyboard, studio arts, theater design, theater history, voice/opera. **Work/family studies:** General, child care management, family studies, family/community services, food/nutrition.

Most popular majors. Business/marketing 20%, education 9%, engineering/engineering technologies 8%, health sciences 8%, parks/recreation 6%, social sciences 12%.

Computing on campus. 900 workstations in dormitories, library, computer center. Dormitories wired for high-speed internet access and linked to campus network. Commuter students can connect to campus network. Online course registration, online library, helpline, repair service, student web hosting, wireless network available.

Student life. Freshman orientation: Mandatory, $65 fee. Preregistration for classes offered. One-day summer program, plus 3-day program before start of classes. **Housing:** Guaranteed on-campus for all undergraduates. Coed dorms, single-sex dorms, special housing for disabled, apartments, fraternity/sorority housing, wellness housing available. $200 partly refundable deposit, deadline 5/1. **Activities:** Bands, campus ministries, choral groups, dance, drama, film society, international student organizations, literary magazine, music ensembles, Model UN, musical theater, opera, radio station, student government, student newspaper, symphony orchestra, TV station, Black student union, Asian student association, Cosmopolitan Club, Hillel, Hispanic student association, Indian student association, lesbian/gay/bisexual student union, returning adult student association.

Athletics. NCAA. **Intercollegiate:** Baseball M, basketball, cheerleading, cross-country W, diving, field hockey W, football (tackle) M, golf M, lacrosse, rowing (crew) W, soccer, softball W, swimming, tennis, track and field W, volleyball W. **Intramural:** Badminton, basketball, cross-country, fencing, field hockey W, golf, lacrosse, racquetball, soccer, softball, table tennis, tennis, volleyball, water polo M. **Team name:** Fightin' Blue Hens.

Student services. Adult student services, alcohol/substance abuse counseling, chaplain/spiritual director, career counseling, services for economically disadvantaged, student employment services, financial aid counseling, health services, minority student services, personal counseling, placement for graduates, veterans' counselor, women's services. **Physically disabled:** Services for visually, speech, hearing impaired.

Contact. E-mail: admissions@udel.edu
Phone: (302) 831-8123 Fax: (302) 831-6905
Louis Hirsh, Director of Admission, University of Delaware, 210 South College Avenue, Newark, DE 19716

University of Phoenix: Delaware
Wilmington, Delaware
www.phoenix.edu

♦ For-profit 4-year university
♦ Small city
♦ 17 degree-seeking undergraduates

General. Calendar: Differs by program.

Basis for selection. Open admission.

Application procedures. Admission: No deadline. No application fee.

Academics. Credit/placement by examination: AP, CLEP.

Contact. Marc Booker, Director of Admission and Evaluation, University of Phoenix: Delaware, 900 Justison Street, Suite 920, Wilmington, DE 19801

Wesley College
Dover, Delaware
www.wesley.edu

CB member
CB code: 5894

♦ Private 4-year liberal arts college affiliated with United Methodist Church
♦ Residential campus in large town

♦ 1,734 degree-seeking undergraduates
♦ 150 graduate students
♦ 59% of applicants admitted
♦ SAT or ACT (ACT writing optional) required

General. Founded in 1873. Regionally accredited. **Degrees:** 241 bachelor's, 51 associate awarded; master's offered. **ROTC:** Army. **Location:** 75 miles from Philadelphia. **Calendar:** Semester, limited summer session. **Full-time faculty:** 71 total. **Part-time faculty:** 91 total. **Class size:** 55% < 20, 43% 20-39, less than 1% 40-49, 1% 50-99.

Freshman class profile. 3,693 applied, 2,165 admitted, 600 enrolled.

Mid 50% test scores			
SAT critical reading:	360-490	GPA 2.0-2.99:	58%
SAT math:	370-490	Rank in top quarter:	56%
SAT writing:	390-470	Rank in top tenth:	24%
GPA 3.75 or higher:	6%	Out-of-state:	66%
GPA 3.50-3.74:	9%	Live on campus:	87%
GPA 3.0-3.49:	27%	Sororities:	6%

Basis for selection. High school performance most important. Campus interview very important. Extracurricular activities important.

High school preparation. 20 units recommended. Recommended units include English 4, mathematics 4, social studies 2, history 2, science 4, foreign language 2 and academic electives 2.

2011-2012 Annual costs. Tuition/fees: $21,565. Room/board: $9,940. Books/supplies: $1,000. Personal expenses: $750.

Financial aid. All financial aid based on need.

Application procedures. Admission: Priority date 4/1; no deadline. $25 fee. Admission notification on a rolling basis. Must reply by May 1 or within 4 week(s) if notified thereafter. **Financial aid:** Priority date 2/1; no closing date. FAFSA, institutional form required. Applicants notified on a rolling basis starting 1/1; must reply within 2 week(s) of notification.

Academics. Credit requirement for bachelor's degree varies according to program. **Special study options:** Double major, ESL, exchange student, independent study, internships, liberal arts/career combination, study abroad, teacher certification program. **Credit/placement by examination:** AP, CLEP, SAT, ACT, institutional tests. 15 credit hours maximum toward associate degree, 33 toward bachelor's. **Support services:** Learning center, reduced course load, remedial instruction, study skills assistance, tutoring, writing center.

Majors. Area/ethnic studies: American. **Biology:** General. **Business:** Accounting, business admin, sales/distribution. **Communications:** Communications/speech/rhetoric. **Conservation:** Environmental studies. **Education:** General, elementary, physical. **English:** English lit. **Health services:** Clinical lab science, nursing (RN). **History:** General. **Liberal arts:** Arts/sciences. **Math:** General. **Parks/recreation:** Health/fitness. **Psychology:** General. **Social sciences:** Economics, political science. **Visual/performing arts:** Music.

Most popular majors. Business/marketing 30%, communications/journalism 7%, education 16%, parks/recreation 6%, psychology 16%, social sciences 8%.

Computing on campus. 225 workstations in library. Dormitories wired for high-speed internet access and linked to campus network. Commuter students can connect to campus network. Online course registration, online library, helpline, repair service, wireless network available.

Student life. Freshman orientation: Mandatory. Preregistration for classes offered. **Housing:** Coed dorms, single-sex dorms, apartments, wellness housing available. $250 fully refundable deposit, deadline 5/1. Floors in coed dorms are single-sex. **Activities:** Jazz band, choral groups, drama, literary magazine, music ensembles, student government, student newspaper, TV station, community action, Christian student associations, student activity board, National Coed Community Service Organization, Black student union.

Athletics. NCAA. **Intercollegiate:** Baseball M, basketball, cheerleading, cross-country, field hockey W, football (tackle) M, golf, lacrosse, soccer, softball W, tennis, volleyball W. **Intramural:** Basketball, cross-country, soccer M, volleyball. **Team name:** Wolverines.

Student services. Chaplain/spiritual director, career counseling, student employment services, financial aid counseling, health services, personal counseling, placement for graduates. **Physically disabled:** Services for speech impaired.

Contact. E-mail: admissions@wesley.edu
Phone: (302) 736-2400 Toll-free number: (800) 937-5398
Fax: (302) 736-2382
Susan Houser, Director of Enrollment Operations, Wesley College, 120
North State Street, Dover, DE 19901-3875

Wilmington University
New Castle, Delaware
CB member
www.wilmu.edu
CB code: 5925

♦ Private 4-year liberal arts college
♦ Commuter campus in large town
♦ 7,449 degree-seeking undergraduates: 50% part-time, 64% women
♦ 4,678 degree-seeking graduate students

General. Founded in 1967. Regionally accredited. Two 7-week sessions
within each trimester in addition to regular trimester sessions and weekend
modules. **Degrees:** 1,349 bachelor's, 51 associate awarded; master's, doctoral
offered. **ROTC:** Army, Air Force. **Location:** 7 miles from Wilmington.
Calendar: Trimester, limited summer session. **Full-time faculty:** 95 total.
Part-time faculty: 1,015 total. **Class size:** 76% < 20, 24% 20-39.

Freshman class profile. 1,434 applied, 1,432 admitted, 492 enrolled.

Basis for selection. Open admission. Interview recommended. **Home
schooled:** GED recommended for nonaccredited programs.

2011-2012 Annual costs. Tuition/fees: $9,470. Books/supplies: $1,000.
Personal expenses: $165.

Financial aid. **Non-need-based:** Scholarships awarded for academics, athletics.

Application procedures. Admission: No deadline. $25 fee, may be
waived for applicants with need. Admission notification on a rolling basis.
Financial aid: Priority date 4/30; no closing date. FAFSA required. Applicants notified on a rolling basis starting 8/5; must reply within 2 week(s)
of notification.

Academics. Mentoring program for all interested incoming freshmen. **Special study options:** Accelerated study, distance learning, double major, dual
enrollment of high school students, honors, independent study, internships,
liberal arts/career combination, teacher certification program, weekend college. **Credit/placement by examination:** AP, CLEP, institutional tests. 15
credit hours maximum toward associate degree, 15 toward bachelor's. **Support services:** Learning center, remedial instruction, tutoring, writing center.

Majors. Business: Accounting, finance, human resources, information
resources management, marketing. **Computer sciences:** General, programming, web page design. **Education:** Early childhood, elementary. **Health
services:** Preop/surgical nursing. **Liberal arts:** Arts/sciences. **Protective
services:** Criminal justice. **Psychology:** General.

Most popular majors. Business/marketing 29%, computer/information
sciences 12%, education 13%, liberal arts 18%, psychology 11%, social
sciences 10%.

Computing on campus. 516 workstations in library, computer center.

Student life. Freshman orientation: Available. Preregistration for classes
offered. Videotaped orientation distributed to all new students. Two new
student orientations offered in the fall. **Policies:** Adherence to student handbook expected. **Activities:** Student government, professional fraternities/
organizations, Sigma Theta Tau Nursing Society, Business Professionals of
America, Alpha Delta Chi, criminal justice club.

Athletics. NCAA. **Intercollegiate:** Baseball M, basketball, cross-country,
golf M, lacrosse W, soccer, softball W, volleyball W. **Team name:** Wildcats.

Student services. Career counseling, student employment services, financial aid counseling, placement for graduates.

Contact. E-mail: inquire@wilmu.edu
Phone: (302) 356-4636 Toll-free number: (877) 967-5464
Fax: (302) 328-5902
Laura Morris, Director of Admissions, Wilmington University, 320
Dupont Highway, New Castle, DE 19720

District of Columbia

American University
Washington, District of Columbia
www.american.edu

CB member
CB code: 5007

- Private 4-year university affiliated with United Methodist Church
- Residential campus in very large city
- 6,793 degree-seeking undergraduates: 3% part-time, 59% women, 5% African American, 6% Asian American, 8% Hispanic American, 7% international
- 5,320 degree-seeking graduate students
- 42% of applicants admitted
- SAT or ACT with writing, application essay required
- 77% graduate within 6 years

General. Founded in 1893. Regionally accredited. **Degrees:** 1,613 bachelor's, 3 associate awarded; master's, professional, doctoral offered. **ROTC:** Army, Air Force. **Location:** 2 miles from downtown. **Calendar:** Semester, extensive summer session. **Full-time faculty:** 712 total; 94% have terminal degrees, 18% minority, 46% women. **Part-time faculty:** 573 total; 7% minority, 45% women. **Class size:** 43% < 20, 50% 20-39, 4% 40-49, 2% 50-99, less than 1% >100. **Special facilities:** Arts center, museum, theater, spiritual life center, arboretum.

Freshman class profile. 18,706 applied, 7,788 admitted, 1,541 enrolled.

Mid 50% test scores			
SAT critical reading:	600-700	GPA 2.0-2.99:	3%
SAT math:	570-670	Rank in top quarter:	81%
SAT writing:	580-680	Rank in top tenth:	45%
ACT composite:	26-30	Return as sophomores:	90%
GPA 3.75 or higher:	57%	Out-of-state:	87%
GPA 3.50-3.74:	21%	Live on campus:	98%
GPA 3.0-3.49:	19%	International:	4%

Basis for selection. High school record, GPA, test scores, writing sample, recommendations, rigor of secondary school record very important. Extracurricular activities, class rank, leadership roles considered. SAT Subject Tests recommended. Interview optional, non-evaluative and informational in scope. Audition/interview required of music and music theater majors. **Home schooled:** Statement describing home school structure and mission, transcript of courses and grades required. At least two SAT Subject Tests and letter of recommendation are recommended but not required. If curriculum has been supplemented by formal coursework either at the secondary or postsecondary level, official transcripts from the school(s) or college(s) are required. **Learning Disabled:** Supplementary application, diagnostic reports, and high school transcript required for freshman learning services program.

High school preparation. College-preparatory program recommended. 16 units required; 18 recommended. Required and recommended units include English 4, mathematics 3-4, social studies 2-4, science 3-4 (laboratory 2), foreign language 2-3 and academic electives 3-4.

2012-2013 Annual costs. Tuition/fees: $39,499. Room/board: $13,920.

2011-2012 Financial aid. All financial aid based on need. Average need met was 82%. Average scholarship/grant was $21,486; average loan $4,471. 75% of total undergraduate aid awarded as scholarships/grants, 25% as loans/jobs. **Additional information:** Early decision applicants must submit estimated AU institutional financial aid application by 11/15 and a FASFA as soon as possible after Jan 1.

Application procedures. Admission: Closing date 1/15 (postmark date). $65 fee, may be waived for applicants with need. Admission notification by 4/1. Must reply by May 1 or within 4 week(s) if notified thereafter. **Financial aid:** Closing date 2/15. FAFSA, institutional form required. Applicants notified by 4/1; must reply by 5/1 or within 4 week(s) of notification.

Academics. Special study options: Accelerated study, combined bachelor's/graduate degree, double major, honors, independent study, internships, liberal arts/career combination, student-designed major, study abroad, teacher certification program, Washington semester, weekend college. One-semester, full-year, alternative spring break and language-immersion options are available. **Credit/placement by examination:** AP, CLEP, IB, institutional tests. 30 credit hours maximum toward bachelor's degree. Credit awarded for some international high school learning programs such as British A Levels or

German Arbitur; Advanced Placement, International Baccalaureate higher level tests only. **Support services:** Learning center, pre-admission summer program, reduced course load, study skills assistance, tutoring, writing center.

Majors. Area/ethnic studies: American, French, German, Latin American, Russian/Slavic, women's. **Biology:** General, biochemistry, environmental, marine. **Business:** Accounting, business admin, finance, management information systems. **Communications:** Journalism, media studies, public relations, radio/TV. **Communications technology:** Animation/special effects, recording arts. **Computer sciences:** General, computer graphics, computer science. **Conservation:** Environmental studies. **Education:** Elementary, secondary. **English:** English lit. **Foreign languages:** French, German, Russian, Spanish. **Health services:** Predental, premedicine, prenursing, prepharmacy, preveterinary. **History:** General. **Liberal arts:** Arts/sciences. **Math:** General, applied, statistics. **Parks/recreation:** Health/fitness, sports admin. **Philosophy/religion:** Judaic, philosophy. **Physical sciences:** Acoustics, chemistry, physics. **Protective services:** Criminal justice, police science. **Psychology:** General. **Social sciences:** Anthropology, economics, international relations, political science, sociology. **Visual/performing arts:** General, art, art history/conservation, cinematography, design, dramatic, film/cinema/video, graphic design, multimedia, music, music history, music performance, music theory/composition, studio arts.

Most popular majors. Business/marketing 14%, communications/journalism 9%, social sciences 44%, visual/performing arts 6%.

Computing on campus. 650 workstations in dormitories, library, computer center, student center. Dormitories wired for high-speed internet access and linked to campus network. Commuter students can connect to campus network. Online course registration, online library, helpline, repair service, student web hosting, wireless network available.

Student life. Freshman orientation: Available, $110 fee. Preregistration for classes offered. 2-day programs in late June and early July. Students take placement exams and meet advisors. Parents may attend. **Policies:** Academic integrity code. Freshmen not permitted cars on campus. **Housing:** Guaranteed on-campus for freshmen. Coed dorms, special housing for disabled available. $200 nonrefundable deposit, deadline 5/1. Housing for handicapped students handled individually; community service floor available. Some single-sex floors in coed dorms. **Activities:** Bands, campus ministries, choral groups, dance, drama, film society, international student organizations, literary magazine, music ensembles, musical theater, opera, radio station, student government, student newspaper, symphony orchestra, TV station, NAACP, Kennedy Political Union, Amnesty International, Habitat for Humanity, Asian students association, concert choir, Hillel, Latin American student organization.

Athletics. NCAA. **Intercollegiate:** Basketball, cross-country, diving, field hockey W, lacrosse W, soccer, swimming, track and field, volleyball W, wrestling M. **Intramural:** Basketball, football (non-tackle), soccer, softball, tennis, volleyball, weight lifting M. **Team name:** Eagles.

Student services. Alcohol/substance abuse counseling, chaplain/spiritual director, career counseling, student employment services, financial aid counseling, health services, minority student services, on-campus daycare, personal counseling, placement for graduates, women's services.

Contact. E-mail: admissions@american.edu
Phone: (202) 885-6000 Fax: (202) 885-6014
Greg Grauman, Director of Admissions, American University, 4400 Massachusetts Avenue NW, Washington, DC 20016-8001

Catholic University of America
Washington, District of Columbia
www.cua.edu

CB member
CB code: 5104

- Private 4-year university affiliated with Roman Catholic Church
- Residential campus in very large city
- 3,544 degree-seeking undergraduates: 5% part-time, 55% women, 5% African American, 3% Asian American, 8% Hispanic American, 4% international
- 3,159 degree-seeking graduate students
- 75% of applicants admitted
- SAT or ACT with writing, application essay required
- 68% graduate within 6 years; 30% enter graduate study

General. Founded in 1887. Regionally accredited. Internship and study opportunities with Congress, federal agencies, and international embassies. **Degrees:** 724 bachelor's, 9 associate awarded; master's, professional, doctoral offered. **ROTC:** Army, Naval, Air Force. **Location:** Downtown. **Calendar:** Semester, extensive summer session. **Full-time faculty:** 394 total; 96% have terminal degrees, 12% minority, 39% women. **Part-time faculty:** 403 total; 10% minority, 40% women. **Class size:** 63% < 20, 28% 20-39, 3% 40-49,

5% 50-99, less than 1% >100. **Special facilities:** Vitreous state laboratory, rare book collection.

Freshman class profile. 6,617 applied, 4,971 admitted, 904 enrolled.

Mid 50% test scores		GPA 2.0-2.99:	23%
SAT critical reading:	510-620	Return as sophomores:	80%
SAT math:	500-610	Out-of-state:	98%
ACT composite:	22-27	Live on campus:	90%
GPA 3.75 or higher:	25%	International:	3%
GPA 3.50-3.74:	21%	Fraternities:	1%
GPA 3.0-3.49:	31%	Sororities:	1%

Basis for selection. School achievement record, including strength of curriculum and test scores. SAT Subject Tests recommended. Students admitted to School of Arts and Sciences or School of Philosophy are recommended to submit SAT Subject Test scores in foreign languages for placement purposes. Audition required for music. **Home schooled:** Statement describing home school structure and mission, transcript of courses and grades, letter of recommendation (nonparent) required. **Learning Disabled:** Matriculated students with learning disabilities are asked to submit documentation to Office of Disability Support Services.

High school preparation. College-preparatory program recommended. 17 units recommended. Recommended units include English 4, mathematics 3, social studies 4, science 3 (laboratory 1) and foreign language 2. 1 fine arts or humanities recommended.

2011-2012 Annual costs. Tuition/fees: $35,460. Room/board: $13,824. Books/supplies: $1,400. Personal expenses: $1,500.

2011-2012 Financial aid. Need-based: 748 full-time freshmen applied for aid; 627 were judged to have need; 626 of these received aid. Average need met was 82%. Average scholarship/grant was $20,657; average loan $3,652. 64% of total undergraduate aid awarded as scholarships/grants, 36% as loans/jobs. **Non-need-based:** Awarded to 914 full-time undergraduates, including 208 freshmen. Scholarships awarded for academics, alumni affiliation, music/drama, religious affiliation.

Application procedures. Admission: Closing date 2/15 (postmark date). $55 fee, may be waived for applicants with need. Admission notification on a rolling basis beginning on or about 3/15. Must reply by May 1 or within 2 week(s) if notified thereafter. **Financial aid:** Priority date 2/15, closing date 4/10. FAFSA required. Applicants notified on a rolling basis starting 4/1; must reply by 5/1 or within 2 week(s) of notification.

Academics. Special study options: Accelerated study, combined bachelor's/graduate degree, cross-registration, distance learning, double major, dual enrollment of high school students, ESL, honors, independent study, internships, study abroad, teacher certification program, Washington semester. **Credit/placement by examination:** AP, CLEP, IB, institutional tests. All credit-by-examination awarded on case-by-case basis. No credit by outside examination given to matriculated students. **Support services:** Learning center, pre-admission summer program, reduced course load, study skills assistance, tutoring, writing center.

Honors college/program. Applicants with a combined SAT score of 1300 exclusive of Writing and a high school GPA of 3.5 or above are offered admission; students not meeting these requirements may petition for admission after their first semester. About 1 in 10 matriculated students belong to the University Honors Program.

Majors. Architecture: Architecture. **Biology:** General, biochemistry. **Business:** General, accounting, finance, human resources, international, international finance, management science. **Communications:** Communications/speech/rhetoric. **Computer sciences:** General. **Education:** General, early childhood, elementary, English, ESL, French, German, history, secondary, Spanish. **Engineering:** General, biomedical, civil, electrical, mechanical. **English:** English lit. **Foreign languages:** Classics, French, German, Latin, Spanish. **Health services:** Clinical lab science, nursing (RN). **History:** General. **Human services:** Social work. **Liberal arts:** Arts/sciences. **Math:** General. **Philosophy/religion:** Philosophy, religion. **Physical sciences:** Chemistry, physics. **Psychology:** General. **Social sciences:** Anthropology, economics, political science, sociology. **Visual/performing arts:** Art, art history/conservation, dramatic, music, music history, music performance, music theory/composition, piano/keyboard, voice/opera.

Most popular majors. Architecture 12%, business/marketing 11%, communications/journalism 6%, engineering/engineering technologies 7%, health sciences 9%, psychology 8%, social sciences 16%, visual/performing arts 6%.

Computing on campus. 500 workstations in dormitories, library, computer center, student center. Dormitories wired for high-speed internet access and linked to campus network. Commuter students can connect to campus network. Online course registration, online library, helpline, repair service, student web hosting, wireless network available.

Student life. Freshman orientation: Available. Preregistration for classes offered. Held Thursday-Sunday before start of fall semester. **Policies:** Code of Student Conduct is the guiding behavioral document; medical insurance is required for all full-time students and all full and part-time international students; immunization requirement for students under 26 years of age. Freshmen not permitted cars on campus. **Housing:** Guaranteed on-campus for freshmen. Coed dorms, single-sex dorms, special housing for disabled, apartments, wellness housing available. **Activities:** Jazz band, campus ministries, choral groups, dance, drama, international student organizations, literary magazine, music ensembles, Model UN, musical theater, opera, radio station, student government, student newspaper, symphony orchestra, College Republicans, College Democrats, Filipino Organization of Catholic University Students, Alpha Phi Omega service fraternity, Habitat for Humanity, Latin Alliance, Arab American Association.

Athletics. NCAA. **Intercollegiate:** Baseball M, basketball, cross-country, field hockey W, football (tackle) M, lacrosse, soccer, softball W, swimming, tennis, track and field, volleyball W. **Intramural:** Badminton, basketball, football (non-tackle), soccer, softball, tennis, volleyball. **Team name:** Cardinals.

Student services. Adult student services, alcohol/substance abuse counseling, chaplain/spiritual director, career counseling, student employment services, financial aid counseling, health services, legal services, minority student services, personal counseling, placement for graduates, veterans' counselor. **Physically disabled:** Services for visually, speech, hearing impaired.

Contact. E-mail: cua-admissions@cua.edu
Phone: (202) 319-5305 Toll-free number: (800) 673-2772
Fax: (202) 319-6533
Christine Mica, Dean, University Admissions, Catholic University of America, 102 McMahon Hall, Washington, DC 20064

Corcoran College of Art and Design
Washington, District of Columbia   **CB member**
www.corcoran.edu   **CB code: 5705**

- Private 4-year visual arts college
- Commuter campus in very large city

General. Founded in 1890. Regionally accredited. **Location:** Downtown. **Calendar:** Semester.

Annual costs/financial aid. Tuition/fees (2011-2012): $29,940. Room: $9,970. Books/supplies: $2,600. Personal expenses: $1,334. Need-based financial aid available to full-time and part-time students.

Contact. Phone: (202) 639-1814
Director of Admissions, 500 17th Street, NW, Washington, DC 20006-4804

Gallaudet University
Washington, District of Columbia
www.gallaudet.edu   **CB code: 5240**

- Private 4-year university and liberal arts college
- Residential campus in very large city
- 1,078 degree-seeking undergraduates: 5% part-time, 53% women, 11% African American, 4% Asian American, 8% Hispanic American, 5% international
- 410 degree-seeking graduate students
- 69% of applicants admitted
- SAT or ACT (ACT writing recommended), application essay required
- 41% graduate within 6 years

General. Founded in 1857. Regionally accredited. Only liberal arts university in the world designed exclusively for deaf and hard of hearing students. Bilingual (English/American Sign Language), multicultural environment, assistive devices (TTY's or campus phones, closed captioned television and campus films), specially-designed classrooms and dormitories available. **Degrees:** 194 bachelor's awarded; master's, doctoral offered. **Location:** Downtown. **Calendar:** Semester, limited summer session. **Full-time faculty:** 185 total; 89% have terminal degrees, 21% minority, 66% women. **Class size:** 97% < 20, 3% 20-39. **Special facilities:** Gallaudet Interpreting Services provides interpreters for university-related events.

Freshman class profile. 413 applied, 284 admitted, 201 enrolled.

Mid 50% test scores			
SAT critical reading:	310-470	Return as sophomores:	70%
SAT math:	330-440	Out-of-state:	97%
ACT composite:	15-21	Live on campus:	83%

Basis for selection. Applicants with hearing loss who show evidence of academic ability and motivation considered. Test scores, grades, class rank, essay, recommendation important. ACT recommended. Interview recommended. **Learning Disabled:** Untimed tests, psychological evaluations confirming disabilities required.

High school preparation. College-preparatory program recommended. 16 units recommended. Recommended units include English 4, mathematics 4, social studies 4, history 4, science 4 (laboratory 2).

2012-2013 Annual costs. Tuition/fees (projected): $12,806. Room/board: $10,760. Books/supplies: $1,020. Personal expenses: $4,908.

2010-2011 Financial aid. Need-based: 158 full-time freshmen applied for aid; 149 were judged to have need; 149 of these received aid. Average need met was 91%. Average scholarship/grant was $13,640; average loan $1,692. 85% of total undergraduate aid awarded as scholarships/grants, 15% as loans/jobs. **Non-need-based:** Awarded to 274 full-time undergraduates, including 49 freshmen. Scholarships awarded for academics, leadership, minority status. **Additional information:** Institution receives substantial aid from state vocational rehabilitation agencies, supplemented by institutional grants when needed.

Application procedures. Admission: No deadline. $50 fee, may be waived for applicants with need. Admission notification on a rolling basis. **Financial aid:** Priority date 7/1; no closing date. FAFSA, institutional form required. Applicants notified on a rolling basis starting 3/1; must reply within 4 week(s) of notification.

Academics. Undergraduate degree program open to deaf and hard of hearing students and a limited number of hearing students; visiting and exchange student programs available to any qualified student. **Special study options:** Accelerated study, combined bachelor's/graduate degree, cross-registration, distance learning, double major, ESL, honors, independent study, internships, student-designed major, study abroad, teacher certification program. Experiential programs off-campus including orientation program for employers of deaf students and paraprofessional jobs on campus, programs for interpreter-assisted mainstreaming of students into area colleges such as Georgetown University, George Mason University, Catholic University, Howard University. **Credit/placement by examination:** AP, CLEP, ACT, institutional tests. **Support services:** Learning center, pre-admission summer program, reduced course load, remedial instruction, study skills assistance, tutoring, writing center.

Majors. Biology: General. **Business:** General, accounting, business admin, entrepreneurial studies, management information systems. **Communications:** Communications/speech/rhetoric. **Computer sciences:** General, computer science, information systems. **Education:** General, art, Deaf/hearing impaired, early childhood, elementary, family/consumer sciences, multiple handicapped, physical, secondary. **English:** English lit. **Foreign languages:** American Sign Language, French, Spanish. **Health services:** Recreational therapy. **History:** General. **Human services:** Social work. **Math:** General. **Parks/recreation:** General, health/fitness. **Philosophy/religion:** Philosophy. **Physical sciences:** Chemistry, physics. **Psychology:** General. **Social sciences:** Criminology, economics, political science, sociology. **Visual/performing arts:** General, art history/conservation, commercial/advertising art, dramatic, studio arts. **Work/family studies:** Child development.

Most popular majors. Business/marketing 12%, communications/journalism 14%, education 15%, mathematics 6%, psychology 7%, visual/performing arts 10%.

Computing on campus. 352 workstations in dormitories, library, computer center, student center. Dormitories wired for high-speed internet access and linked to campus network. Commuter students can connect to campus network. Online course registration, online library, helpline, repair service, student web hosting, wireless network available.

Student life. Freshman orientation: Mandatory. Preregistration for classes offered. Held 1 week before beginning of semester. **Policies:** No alcohol allowed in freshman dorms; no smoking in residence halls. Only full-time students may reside in dorms. All dormitories equipped for deaf and hard of hearing students. **Housing:** Guaranteed on-campus for freshmen. Coed dorms, special housing for disabled, apartments available. $150 fully refundable deposit, deadline 7/18. **Activities:** Campus ministries, dance, drama, film society, international student organizations, literary magazine, student government, student newspaper, Asian Pacific association, Black deaf student union, Hispanic student association, literary society.

Athletics. NCAA. **Intercollegiate:** Baseball M, basketball, cross-country, football (tackle) M, soccer, softball W, swimming, track and field, volleyball

W. Intramural: Basketball, football (non-tackle), racquetball, volleyball. **Team name:** Bisons.

Student services. Adult student services, alcohol/substance abuse counseling, chaplain/spiritual director, career counseling, student employment services, health services, minority student services, on-campus daycare, personal counseling, placement for graduates. **Physically disabled:** Services for visually, speech, hearing impaired.

Contact. E-mail: admissions@gallaudet.edu
Phone: (202) 651-5750 Toll-free number: (800) 995-0550
Fax: (202) 651-5774
Charity Reedy Hines, Director of Admissions, Gallaudet University, 800 Florida Avenue, NE, Washington, DC 20002

George Washington University
Washington, District of Columbia **CB member**
www.gwu.edu/explore **CB code: 5246**

- Private 4-year university
- Residential campus in very large city
- 10,184 degree-seeking undergraduates: 5% part-time, 56% women, 7% African American, 10% Asian American, 7% Hispanic American, 7% international
- 14,854 graduate students
- 33% of applicants admitted
- SAT or ACT (ACT writing recommended), application essay required
- 81% graduate within 6 years

General. Founded in 1821. Regionally accredited. **Degrees:** 2,172 bachelor's, 169 associate awarded; master's, professional, doctoral offered. **ROTC:** Army, Naval, Air Force. **Calendar:** Semester, extensive summer session. **Full-time faculty:** 960 total; 93% have terminal degrees, 21% minority, 40% women. **Part-time faculty:** 1,260 total; 16% minority, 44% women. **Class size:** 54% < 20, 27% 20-39, 9% 40-49, 7% 50-99, 3% >100. **Special facilities:** Observatory.

Freshman class profile. 21,591 applied, 7,124 admitted, 2,241 enrolled.

Mid 50% test scores			
SAT critical reading:	600-690	Return as sophomores:	94%
SAT math:	610-690	Out-of-state:	99%
SAT writing:	620-710	Live on campus:	99%
ACT composite:	27-31	International:	7%
Rank in top quarter:	95%	Fraternities:	22%
Rank in top tenth:	78%	Sororities:	21%

Basis for selection. GED not accepted. Strong college-preparatory program, 3.0 GPA and class rank in top third important. Teacher and counselor recommendation and personal statement required. SAT and SAT Subject Tests or ACT recommended. SAT Subject Tests required for applicants to 7-year BA/MD and integrated engineering/MD programs (any math and any science); early admission applicants (any math, student's choice); and recommended for all for admission and placement. Interview recommended for all, required of early admission applicants. Audition required of bachelor of music applicants.

High school preparation. College-preparatory program required. Required and recommended units include English 4, mathematics 2-4, social studies 2-4, science 2-4 (laboratory 1) and foreign language 2-4. One physics, 1 chemistry, and additional 1 unit in math required for School of Engineering and Applied Science.

2012-2013 Annual costs. Tuition/fees: $45,780. Room/board: $10,530. Books/supplies: $1,275. Personal expenses: $1,400.

2011-2012 Financial aid. Need-based: 1,615 full-time freshmen applied for aid; 1,227 were judged to have need; 1,207 of these received aid. Average need met was 94%. Average scholarship/grant was $28,085; average loan $4,347. 80% of total undergraduate aid awarded as scholarships/grants, 20% as loans/jobs. **Non-need-based:** Awarded to 2,699 full-time undergraduates, including 1,080 freshmen. Scholarships awarded for academics, art, athletics, music/drama, ROTC. **Additional information:** Auditions required for performing arts scholarships.

Application procedures. Admission: Closing date 1/10. $75 fee, may be waived for applicants with need. Admission notification on a rolling basis. Admission notification by 4/1. Must reply by May 1 or within 2 week(s) if notified thereafter. Applications received after 2/1 reviewed on space-available basis. Supplemental applications required for honors program, 7-year BA/MD and integrated engineering/law program, integrated engineering/MD program. **Financial aid:** Closing date 2/1. FAFSA, CSS PROFILE required. Applicants notified on a rolling basis starting 3/24; must reply by 5/1.

Academics. **Special study options:** Accelerated study, cooperative education, cross-registration, distance learning, double major, dual enrollment of high school students, honors, independent study, internships, liberal arts/ career combination, student-designed major, study abroad. 7-year integrated BA/MD liberal arts program, 8-year integrated engineering/JD and engineering/MD programs. **Credit/placement by examination:** AP, CLEP, IB, institutional tests. 30 credit hours maximum toward bachelor's degree. **Support services:** Pre-admission summer program, reduced course load, tutoring.

Majors. **Area/ethnic studies:** American, European, Latin American, Near/ Middle Eastern. **Biology:** General, biomedical sciences, biophysics, pharmacology. **Business:** Accounting, business admin, finance, international, management information systems, tourism promotion. **Communications:** Communications/speech/rhetoric, journalism, political. **Computer sciences:** General, information systems. **Conservation:** General, environmental studies. **Education:** Physical. **Engineering:** General, biomedical, civil, computer, electrical, mechanical. **English:** English lit. **Foreign languages:** General, Arabic, Chinese, classics, French, German, Hebrew, Italian, Japanese, Latin, Portuguese, Romance, Russian, Spanish. **Health services:** Audiology/speech pathology, clinical lab technology, cytotechnology, physician assistant, sonography. **History:** General. **Human services:** Public policy. **Liberal arts:** Arts/sciences. **Math:** General, applied, statistics. **Parks/recreation:** Exercise sciences. **Philosophy/religion:** Judaic, philosophy, religion. **Physical sciences:** Chemistry, geology, physics. **Protective services:** Criminal justice, police science. **Psychology:** General. **Social sciences:** Anthropology, archaeology, economics, geography, international relations, political science, sociology. **Visual/performing arts:** General, art history/conservation, dance, dramatic, interior design, music, studio arts, theater history.

Most popular majors. Business/marketing 18%, psychology 6%, social sciences 38%.

Computing on campus. 600 workstations in dormitories, library, computer center, student center. Dormitories linked to campus network. Commuter students can connect to campus network. Repair service available.

Student life. **Housing:** Guaranteed on-campus for freshmen. Coed dorms, apartments, fraternity/sorority housing available. $800 nonrefundable deposit, deadline 5/1. **Activities:** Bands, choral groups, dance, drama, film society, international student organizations, literary magazine, music ensembles, Model UN, musical theater, radio station, student government, student newspaper, symphony orchestra, TV station, religious groups, national political party organizations, ethnic, social action, public affairs groups.

Athletics. NCAA. **Intercollegiate:** Baseball M, basketball, cross-country, diving, golf M, gymnastics W, lacrosse W, rowing (crew), soccer, softball W, squash, swimming, tennis, volleyball W, water polo. **Intramural:** Basketball, football (tackle) M, golf, racquetball, soccer, softball, table tennis, tennis, volleyball. **Team name:** Colonials.

Student services. Alcohol/substance abuse counseling, career counseling, student employment services, financial aid counseling, health services, on-campus daycare, personal counseling, placement for graduates, veterans' counselor. **Physically disabled:** Services for visually, speech, hearing impaired.

Contact. E-mail: gwadm@gwu.edu
Phone: (202) 994-6040 Fax: (202) 994-0325
Kathryn Napper, Dean for Undergraduate Admissions, George Washington University, 2121 I Street NW, Suite 201, Washington, DC 20052

Georgetown University
Washington, District of Columbia   **CB member**
www.georgetown.edu   **CB code: 5244**

- Private 4-year university affiliated with Roman Catholic Church
- Residential campus in very large city
- 7,232 degree-seeking undergraduates: 3% part-time, 55% women, 6% African American, 9% Asian American, 8% Hispanic American, 8% international
- 9,221 degree-seeking graduate students
- 18% of applicants admitted
- SAT or ACT (ACT writing optional), application essay, interview required
- 94% graduate within 6 years

General. Founded in 1789. Regionally accredited. **Degrees:** 1,817 bachelor's awarded; master's, professional, doctoral offered. **ROTC:** Army, Naval, Air Force. **Location:** 1.5 miles from downtown. **Calendar:** Semester, extensive summer session. **Full-time faculty:** 918 total; 91% have terminal degrees, 12% minority, 42% women. **Part-time faculty:** 838 total; 64% have terminal

degrees, 10% minority, 34% women. **Class size:** 59% < 20, 27% 20-39, 7% 40-49, 5% 50-99, 2% >100. **Special facilities:** Observatory, language learning technology lab with satellite link, library with special collections including archives, rare books, prints, manuscripts dealing with medieval and early modern periods, and American history.

Freshman class profile. 19,254 applied, 3,480 admitted, 1,599 enrolled.

Mid 50% test scores			
SAT critical reading:	640-740	Rank in top tenth:	90%
SAT math:	650-750	Return as sophomores:	96%
ACT composite:	29-33	Out-of-state:	99%
Rank in top quarter:	97%	Live on campus:	100%
		International:	8%

Basis for selection. School academic record most important, in addition to test scores, essays, extracurricular activities, interview, and recommendations. Special consideration given to qualified minorities, athletes, internationals, and alumni relatives. SAT Subject Tests recommended. Interview required unless not possible to assign based on geographic area; portfolio recommended for fine arts majors.

High school preparation. College-preparatory program required. Required units include English 4, mathematics 2, social studies 2, history 2, science 1 and foreign language 2. Additional units in science, math, and foreign language recommended for some programs.

2011-2012 Annual costs. Tuition/fees: $41,393. Room/board: $13,543. Books/supplies: $1,270. Personal expenses: $1,620.

2010-2011 Financial aid. **Need-based:** 944 full-time freshmen applied for aid; 703 were judged to have need; 703 of these received aid. Average need met was 100%. Average scholarship/grant was $29,961; average loan $3,492. 85% of total undergraduate aid awarded as scholarships/grants, 15% as loans/jobs. **Non-need-based:** Awarded to 1,094 full-time undergraduates, including 329 freshmen. Scholarships awarded for athletics.

Application procedures. **Admission:** Closing date 1/10 (receipt date). $65 fee, may be waived for applicants with need. Admission notification by 4/1. Must reply by May 1 or within 2 week(s) if notified thereafter. Early Action plan limits students from applying to binding Early Decision programs. **Financial aid:** Closing date 2/1. FAFSA, CSS PROFILE required. Applicants notified by 4/1; must reply by 5/1 or within 2 week(s) of notification.

Academics. Early assurance program to university's medical and law schools. **Special study options:** Combined bachelor's/graduate degree, cross-registration, double major, ESL, honors, independent study, internships, student-designed major, study abroad, Washington semester. **Credit/placement by examination:** AP, CLEP, IB, institutional tests. **Support services:** Learning center, pre-admission summer program, study skills assistance, tutoring, writing center.

Majors. **Area/ethnic studies:** American, women's. **Biology:** General, biochemistry, biomedical sciences, neurobiology/anatomy. **Business:** Accounting, business admin, finance, information resources management, international, marketing. **Computer sciences:** Computer science. **English:** English lit. **Foreign languages:** Arabic, Chinese, classics, comparative lit, French, German, Italian, Japanese, linguistics, Portuguese, Russian, Spanish. **Health services:** Health care admin, international public health, nursing (RN). **History:** General. **Liberal arts:** Arts/sciences. **Math:** General. **Philosophy/religion:** Philosophy, religion. **Physical sciences:** Chemistry, physics. **Psychology:** General. **Social sciences:** Anthropology, economics, international economics, international relations, political science, sociology. **Visual/performing arts:** Art, art history/conservation, music, studio arts.

Most popular majors. Business/marketing 26%, English 7%, foreign language 6%, health sciences 7%, social sciences 30%.

Computing on campus. Dormitories wired for high-speed internet access and linked to campus network. Commuter students can connect to campus network. Online course registration, online library, helpline, repair service, student web hosting, wireless network available.

Student life. **Freshman orientation:** Mandatory, $160 fee. Preregistration for classes offered. Student volunteer-led program. **Policies:** Freshmen and sophomores required to live on campus. Upperclass students obtain housing via lottery process. Freshmen not permitted cars on campus. **Housing:** Guaranteed on-campus for freshmen. Coed dorms, special housing for disabled, apartments, wellness housing available. Pets allowed in dorm rooms. **Activities:** Bands, campus ministries, choral groups, dance, drama, film society, international student organizations, literary magazine, music ensembles, musical theater, radio station, student government, student newspaper, symphony orchestra, TV station, over 170 student organizations available.

Athletics. NCAA. **Intercollegiate:** Baseball M, basketball, cross-country, diving, field hockey W, football (tackle) M, golf, lacrosse, rowing (crew), sailing, soccer, softball W, swimming, tennis, track and field, volleyball W. **Intramural:** Basketball, cross-country, football (non-tackle), golf, handball,

racquetball, skiing, soccer, softball, squash, table tennis, tennis, volleyball. **Team name:** Hoyas.

Student services. Alcohol/substance abuse counseling, chaplain/spiritual director, career counseling, student employment services, financial aid counseling, health services, minority student services, on-campus daycare, personal counseling, placement for graduates, women's services. **Physically disabled:** Services for visually, hearing impaired.

Contact. E-mail: guadmiss@georgetown.edu
Phone: (202) 687-3600 Fax: (202) 687-5084
Charles Deacon, Dean of Admissions, Georgetown University, 103 White-Gravenor, Washington, DC 20057-1002

Howard University
Washington, District of Columbia
www.howard.edu

CB member
CB code: 5297

- Private 4-year university
- Residential campus in very large city
- 7,119 degree-seeking undergraduates
- 54% of applicants admitted
- SAT or ACT with writing required

General. Founded in 1867. Regionally accredited. 5 campuses. 25 major research centers and several special programs. **Degrees:** 1,300 bachelor's awarded; master's, professional, doctoral offered. **ROTC:** Army, Air Force. **Location:** Downtown. **Calendar:** Semester, extensive summer session. **Full-time faculty:** 986 total. **Part-time faculty:** 223 total. **Class size:** 62% < 20, 29% 20-39, 5% 40-49, 3% 50-99, less than 1% >100. **Special facilities:** Research center, including museum and archives, with collections on Africa and persons of African descent; international affairs center.

Freshman class profile. 9,015 applied, 4,857 admitted, 1,546 enrolled.

Mid 50% test scores		GPA 3.0-3.49:	42%
SAT critical reading:	490-580	GPA 2.0-2.99:	26%
SAT math:	480-580	Rank in top quarter:	55%
SAT writing:	470-570	Rank in top tenth:	26%
ACT composite:	21-26	Out-of-state:	98%
GPA 3.75 or higher:	14%	Live on campus:	92%
GPA 3.50-3.74:	18%		

Basis for selection. High school achievement record, test scores most important. Requirements vary from college to college. SAT Subject Tests recommended. Dental Hygiene Aptitude Test required of dental hygiene applicants. Essay recommended; required of Early Action applicants. Audition required of music, drama majors. Portfolio required of art, architecture majors. Interview recommended for pharmacy and pharmaceutical programs, physician assistant majors. **Home schooled:** Must have GED.

High school preparation. 16 units required; 21 recommended. Required and recommended units include English 4, mathematics 2-3, social studies 2, science 2, foreign language 2 and academic electives 4. Academic electives must count toward graduation.

2011-2012 Annual costs. Tuition/fees: $20,171. Room/board: $11,601. Books/supplies: $2,509. Personal expenses: $1,216.

Financial aid. **Non-need-based:** Scholarships awarded for academics, art, athletics, music/drama.

Application procedures. Admission: Priority date 11/1; deadline 2/15 (receipt date). $45 fee. Admission notification on a rolling basis beginning on or about 4/15. Must reply by May 1 or within 4 week(s) if notified thereafter. Fall term procedures for applicants do not differ from spring, however spring term applicants stand better chance of acceptance. **Financial aid:** Priority date 2/15, closing date 8/15. FAFSA, institutional form required. Applicants notified on a rolling basis starting 4/1; must reply by 8/1 or within 4 week(s) of notification.

Academics. Special study options: Accelerated study, combined bachelor's/graduate degree, cooperative education, cross-registration, distance learning, double major, dual enrollment of high school students, exchange student, honors, independent study, internships, student-designed major, study abroad, teacher certification program. **Credit/placement by examination:** AP, CLEP, IB, SAT, ACT, institutional tests. 60 credit hours maximum toward bachelor's degree. **Support services:** Learning center, pre-admission summer program, reduced course load, remedial instruction, study skills assistance, tutoring, writing center.

Majors. Architecture: Architecture. **Area/ethnic studies:** African, African-American. **Biology:** General. **Business:** Accounting, business admin,

fashion, finance, hospitality admin, hospitality/recreation, insurance, international, management information systems, market research. **Communications:** Broadcast journalism, communications/speech/rhetoric, journalism, radio/TV. **Computer sciences:** Information systems, systems analysis. **Education:** Art, English, health, music, physical. **Engineering:** Chemical, civil, computer, electrical, mechanical, systems. **English:** English lit. **Foreign languages:** Ancient Greek, classics, French, German, modern Greek, Russian, Spanish. **Health services:** Clinical lab science, medical radiologic technology/radiation therapy, music therapy, physician assistant, recreational therapy. **History:** General. **Math:** General. **Parks/recreation:** General. **Philosophy/religion:** Philosophy. **Physical sciences:** Chemistry, physics. **Psychology:** General. **Social sciences:** Anthropology, economics, political science, sociology. **Visual/performing arts:** General, art, art history/conservation, conducting, dance, design, interior design, jazz, music history, music management, music theory/composition, piano/keyboard, studio arts management, theater arts management, theater design, theater history, voice/opera.

Most popular majors. Biology 7%, business/marketing 18%, communications/journalism 16%, health sciences 22%, psychology 6%, social sciences 6%.

Computing on campus. 7,006 workstations in dormitories, library, computer center, student center. Dormitories wired for high-speed internet access and linked to campus network. Commuter students can connect to campus network. Online course registration, online library, helpline, student web hosting, wireless network available.

Student life. Freshman orientation: Mandatory. Preregistration for classes offered. Held during the summer. **Housing:** Guaranteed on-campus for freshmen. Coed dorms, single-sex dorms, apartments, wellness housing available. $200 nonrefundable deposit, deadline 4/1. **Activities:** Bands, campus ministries, choral groups, dance, drama, film society, international student organizations, literary magazine, music ensembles, musical theater, opera, radio station, student government, student newspaper, symphony orchestra, TV station, Absalom Jones student association, Adventist committee, Baptist student union, Christian Science organization, Christian Fellowship-Igbimo Otito, Lutheran student organization, Muslim students, Wesley Foundation Methodist Fellowship, William J. Seymour Pentacostal Fellowship, academic honorary societies.

Athletics. NCAA. **Intercollegiate:** Baseball M, basketball, bowling, cross-country, diving, football (tackle) M, golf W, gymnastics, lacrosse W, soccer, softball W, swimming, tennis, track and field, volleyball W, wrestling M. **Intramural:** Badminton W, basketball, bowling, soccer W, softball, table tennis. **Team name:** Bison.

Student services. Alcohol/substance abuse counseling, chaplain/spiritual director, career counseling, student employment services, financial aid counseling, health services, on-campus daycare, personal counseling, placement for graduates, veterans' counselor, women's services. **Physically disabled:** Services for visually, speech impaired.

Contact. E-mail: admissions@howard.edu
Phone: (202) 806-2700 Toll-free number: (800) 469-2738
Fax: (202) 806-4467
Linda Saunders-Hawkins, Associate Director of Admissions, Howard University, 2400 Sixth Street NW, Washington, DC 20059

Potomac College
Washington, District of Columbia
www.potomac.edu

CB code: 3569

- For-profit 3-year business college
- Commuter campus in very large city
- 267 degree-seeking undergraduates
- Interview required

General. Regionally accredited. Additional campus in Herndon, Va. **Degrees:** 43 bachelor's, 36 associate awarded. **Calendar:** Differs by program, extensive summer session. **Full-time faculty:** 7 total. **Part-time faculty:** 30 total.

Basis for selection. Open admission.

2011-2012 Annual costs. Books/supplies: $630.

Application procedures. Admission: No deadline. No application fee. Admission notification on a rolling basis beginning on or about 2/1. **Financial aid:** No deadline. FAFSA, institutional form required. Applicants notified on a rolling basis; must reply within 4 week(s) of notification.

Academics. Credit earned for work-related research projects. **Special study options:** Accelerated study, distance learning, independent study, internships, weekend college. **Credit/placement by examination:** AP,

CLEP, institutional tests. 15 credit hours maximum toward associate degree, 30 toward bachelor's. **Support services:** Learning center, remedial instruction, tutoring.

Majors. BACHELOR'S. Business: Accounting, accounting/business management, management science, purchasing. **Computer sciences:** General, LAN/WAN management, security. **ASSOCIATE. Business:** Accounting, management science. **Computer sciences:** LAN/WAN management, security.

Most popular majors. Business/marketing 73%, computer/information sciences 27%.

Computing on campus. 30 workstations in library, computer center, student center. Online library, wireless network available.

Student life. Freshman orientation: Mandatory. Preregistration for classes offered. **Activities:** Student government.

Student services. Adult student services, financial aid counseling.

Contact. E-mail: admissions@potomac.edu
Phone: (202) 686-0876 Fax: (202) 686-0818
Angeliqua Wesley, Director of Admissions, Potomac College, 4000 Chesapeake Street NW, Washington, DC 20016

Strayer University
Washington, District of Columbia
www.strayer.edu — **CB code: 5632**

- For-profit 4-year university
- Commuter campus in very large city

General. Founded in 1892. Regionally accredited. **Location:** Downtown. **Calendar:** Quarter.

Annual costs/financial aid. Books/supplies: $1,200.

Contact. Phone: (202) 408-2400
Vice President, 1133 15th Sreet NW, Washington, DC 20005

Trinity Washington University
Washington, District of Columbia — **CB member**
www.trinitydc.edu — **CB code: 5796**

- Private 4-year liberal arts college affiliated with Roman Catholic Church
- Residential campus in very large city
- 1,761 degree-seeking undergraduates
- 51% of applicants admitted
- Application essay required

General. Founded in 1897. Regionally accredited. **Degrees:** 109 bachelor's, 15 associate awarded; master's offered. **ROTC:** Army. **Calendar:** Semester, extensive summer session. **Full-time faculty:** 77 total. **Part-time faculty:** 191 total. **Class size:** 70% < 20, 30% 20-39.

Freshman class profile. 1,346 applied, 680 admitted, 266 enrolled.

Out-of-state:	50%	Live on campus:	53%

Basis for selection. School achievement record, essay, recommendations, interview, school and community activities important. 3.0 GPA preferred. Test scores considered. SAT and SAT Subject Tests or ACT recommended. Interview recommended. **Home schooled:** Transcript of courses and grades required.

High school preparation. 16 units required. Required and recommended units include English 4, mathematics 3-4, social studies 3-4, history 2, science 2-3 (laboratory 1-2) and foreign language 2.

2011-2012 Annual costs. Tuition/fees: $20,310. Mandatory health insurance. Room/board: $9,210. Books/supplies: $1,000. Personal expenses: $1,500.

Financial aid. Non-need-based: Scholarships awarded for academics, alumni affiliation, leadership.

Application procedures. Admission: Priority date 2/1; deadline 9/1 (receipt date). $40 fee, may be waived for applicants with need, free for online applicants. Admission notification by 9/1. Admission notification on a rolling basis. Must reply by May 1 or within 3 week(s) if notified thereafter.

After August 1, must reply within 1 week. **Financial aid:** Priority date 3/1, closing date 4/1. FAFSA required. Applicants notified on a rolling basis starting 2/1; must reply within 2 week(s) of notification.

Academics. Special study options: Accelerated study, cross-registration, distance learning, double major, dual enrollment of high school students, honors, independent study, internships, student-designed major, study abroad, teacher certification program, Washington semester, weekend college. **Credit/placement by examination:** AP, CLEP, institutional tests. **Support services:** Learning center, pre-admission summer program, reduced course load, remedial instruction, tutoring.

Majors. Biology: General, biochemistry. **Business:** Business admin. **Communications:** Communications/speech/rhetoric. **Conservation:** Environmental science. **English:** English lit. **Foreign languages:** General. **History:** General. **Liberal arts:** Arts/sciences. **Math:** General. **Physical sciences:** General, chemistry. **Protective services:** Law enforcement admin. **Psychology:** General. **Social sciences:** Economics, international relations, political science, sociology. **Visual/performing arts:** Art history/conservation.

Most popular majors. Biology 7%, business/marketing 17%, communications/journalism 10%, English 6%, psychology 34%, social sciences 13%.

Computing on campus. 70 workstations in dormitories, library, computer center.

Student life. Freshman orientation: Available. Preregistration for classes offered. **Policies:** Student life mostly self-governed. Honor code exists. **Housing:** Guaranteed on-campus for all undergraduates. Single-sex dorms available. $100 fully refundable deposit. **Activities:** Choral groups, dance, drama, film society, international student organizations, literary magazine, student government, student newspaper, Young Democrats, Young Republicans, Black Student Alliance, Inter-American Club, peer ministry.

Athletics. NCAA. **Intercollegiate:** Basketball W, lacrosse W, soccer W, tennis W, volleyball W. **Team name:** Tigers.

Student services. Adult student services, alcohol/substance abuse counseling, chaplain/spiritual director, career counseling, student employment services, financial aid counseling, health services, on-campus daycare, personal counseling, placement for graduates, veterans' counselor. **Physically disabled:** Services for visually, speech, hearing impaired.

Contact. E-mail: admissions@trinitydc.edu
Phone: (202) 884-9400 Toll-free number: (800) 492-6882
Fax: (202) 884-9229
Kelly Gosnell, Director of Admissions, Trinity Washington University, 125 Michigan Avenue, NE, Washington, DC 20017

University of Phoenix: Washington DC
Washington, District of Columbia
www.phoenix.edu

- For-profit 4-year university
- Large city
- 167 degree-seeking undergraduates

General. Regionally accredited. **Degrees:** 1 bachelor's awarded; master's offered. **Calendar:** Differs by program. **Full-time faculty:** 5 total. **Part-time faculty:** 15 total.

Basis for selection. Open admission, but selective for some programs.

2011-2012 Annual costs. Estimated costs as of August 2011: per-credit-hour charge, $380 to $480, depending upon level and course of study; electronic course materials fee, $95, if applicable. Book and material charges may vary by course and program. All fees are subject to change.

Application procedures. Admission: No deadline. No application fee. **Financial aid:** No deadline.

Academics. Credit/placement by examination: AP, CLEP.

Majors. Business: Business admin. **Computer sciences:** Information technology.

Contact. Marc Booker, Director of Admission and Evaluation, University of Phoenix: Washington DC, 25 Massachusetts Avenue NW, Washington, DC 20001-1431

University of the District of Columbia
Washington, District of Columbia
www.udc.edu

CB member
CB code: 5929

- Public 4-year university and liberal arts college
- Commuter campus in very large city
- 4,658 degree-seeking undergraduates
- 28% of applicants admitted

General. Founded in 1976. Regionally accredited. **Degrees:** 366 bachelor's, 157 associate awarded; master's offered. **ROTC:** Army, Naval, Air Force. **Location:** Downtown. **Calendar:** Semester, limited summer session. **Full-time faculty:** 222 total; 47% have terminal degrees, 42% women. **Part-time faculty:** 75 total.

Freshman class profile. 3,268 applied, 924 admitted, 924 enrolled.

Out-of-state:	24%	Sororities:	2%
Fraternities:	1%		

Basis for selection. Special requirements for nursing, art, and music programs. Interview recommended for nursing majors. Audition recommended for music majors. Portfolio recommended for art majors. **Home schooled:** Transcript of courses and grades, state high school equivalency certificate required.

High school preparation. College-preparatory program required. Recommended units include English 4, mathematics 2, social studies 2, history 1, science 2, foreign language 2 and academic electives 3.

2011-2012 Annual costs. Tuition/fees: $7,000; $14,000 out-of-state. Books/supplies: $1,100. Personal expenses: $1,900.

Financial aid. All financial aid based on need.

Application procedures. Admission: Closing date 6/14 (postmark date). $75 fee ($100 out-of-state). Admission notification on a rolling basis. **Financial aid:** Priority date 3/15; no closing date. FAFSA required. Applicants notified on a rolling basis starting 5/1; must reply within 2 week(s) of notification.

Academics. Special study options: Combined bachelor's/graduate degree, cooperative education, cross-registration, double major, dual enrollment of high school students, ESL, honors, independent study, internships, teacher certification program, weekend college. **Credit/placement by examination:** AP, CLEP, IB, institutional tests. Upon successful completion of the examination, the credit must be approved by the department chairperson and the dean. Credit earned by examination will apear on the students' transcripts as 'CR" and will not be included in computing the grade point average. **Support services:** Learning center, pre-admission summer program, remedial instruction, study skills assistance, tutoring.

Majors. Architecture: Architecture, urban/community planning. **Biology:** General. **Business:** Accounting, business admin, finance, office management. **Communications technology:** Graphic/printing. **Computer sciences:** General, computer science. **Conservation:** General. **Education:** Art, business, early childhood, elementary, health, physical. **Engineering:** Civil, electrical, mechanical. **English:** English lit. **Foreign languages:** French, Spanish. **Health services:** Nursing (RN), speech pathology. **History:** General. **Human services:** Social work. **Math:** General. **Philosophy/religion:** Philosophy. **Physical sciences:** General, chemistry, physics. **Protective services:** Fire services admin. **Psychology:** General. **Social sciences:** Anthropology, economics, political science, sociology, urban studies. **Visual/performing arts:** Dramatic, music, studio arts. **Work/family studies:** General, family studies, food/nutrition.

Most popular majors. Business/marketing 8%, visual/performing arts 14%.

Computing on campus. PC or laptop required. 2 workstations in library, computer center. Helpline, repair service, wireless network available.

Student life. Freshman orientation: Mandatory. Preregistration for classes offered. **Activities:** Bands, choral groups, dance, drama, music ensembles, student government, student newspaper, symphony orchestra, TV station.

Athletics. NCAA. **Intercollegiate:** Basketball, cross-country, soccer, tennis, track and field, volleyball W. **Intramural:** Basketball, softball, swimming, tennis, volleyball W. **Team name:** Firebirds.

Student services. Career counseling, student employment services, financial aid counseling, health services, on-campus daycare, personal counseling, placement for graduates, veterans' counselor. **Physically disabled:** Services for visually, speech, hearing impaired.

Contact. E-mail: UDCadmissions@udc.edu
Phone: (202) 274-6110 Fax: (202) 274-5552
Director of Enrollment Services, University of the District of Columbia, 4200 Connecticut Avenue NW, Washington, DC 20008

Florida

Argosy University: Sarasota
Sarasota, Florida
www.argosy.edu/sarasota

- For-profit 4-year university
- Small city
- 137 degree-seeking undergraduates

General. Regionally accredited. **Degrees:** 8 bachelor's awarded; master's, professional, doctoral offered. **Calendar:** Differs by program. **Full-time faculty:** 11 total. **Part-time faculty:** 124 total.

Basis for selection. Open admission.

2011-2012 Annual costs. Tuition/fees: $17,962.

Application procedures. Admission: Closing date 9/13. $50 fee.

Academics. Credit/placement by examination: AP, CLEP.

Majors. Business: Business admin. **Liberal arts:** Arts/sciences. **Protective services:** Police science. **Psychology:** General.

Contact. E-mail: ausradmissions@argosy.edu
Phone: (877) 331-4480 Toll-free number: (800) 331-5995
Rachel Malone, Senior Director of Admissions, Argosy University: Sarasota, 5250 17th Street, Sarasota, FL 34235

Argosy University: Tampa
Tampa, Florida
www.argosy.edu/tampa

- For-profit 4-year university
- Large city
- 98 degree-seeking undergraduates

General. Regionally accredited. **Degrees:** 11 bachelor's awarded; master's, professional, doctoral offered. **Calendar:** Differs by program. **Full-time faculty:** 10 total. **Part-time faculty:** 77 total.

Basis for selection. Open admission.

2011-2012 Annual costs. Tuition/fees: $17,962.

Application procedures. Admission: Closing date 9/13. $50 fee.

Academics. Credit/placement by examination: AP, CLEP.

Majors. Business: Business admin. **Liberal arts:** Arts/sciences. **Protective services:** Police science. **Psychology:** General.

Contact. E-mail: autaadmis@argosy.edu
Phone: (866) 357-4426 Toll-free number: (800) 850-6488
Ken Jaco, Senior Director of Admissions, Argosy University: Tampa, 1403 North Howard Avenue, Tampa, FL 33607

Art Institute of Fort Lauderdale
Fort Lauderdale, Florida
www.aifl.edu   CB code: 5040

- For-profit 4-year visual arts and technical college
- Commuter campus in large city
- 2,541 degree-seeking undergraduates: 46% part-time, 53% women, 19% African American, 1% Asian American, 29% Hispanic American, 14% international
- 33% of applicants admitted
- Application essay, interview required

General. Founded in 1968. Accredited by ACICS. **Degrees:** 322 bachelor's, 273 associate awarded. **Location:** 25 miles from Miami, 30 miles from West Palm Beach. **Calendar:** Quarter, extensive summer session. **Full-time faculty:** 87 total; 39% have terminal degrees, 14% minority, 49% women. **Part-time faculty:** 49 total; 33% have terminal degrees, 35% minority, 45% women. **Special facilities:** Broadcasting studio, full culinary kitchens, full service print center, visual effects studio, imac labs.

Freshman class profile. 1,259 applied, 421 admitted, 392 enrolled.

Out-of-state:	10%	**International:**	13%
Live on campus:	9%		

Basis for selection. Interview, essay important. Portfolio recommended; required for game art design and illustration majors. **Home schooled:** State high school equivalency certificate required. **Learning Disabled:** Documentation must be submitted if student needs accommodations.

2012-2013 Annual costs. Tuition/fees (projected): $22,680. Books/supplies: $1,275. Personal expenses: $1,980.

2010-2011 Financial aid. Need-based: 32% of total undergraduate aid awarded as scholarships/grants, 68% as loans/jobs. **Non-need-based:** Scholarships awarded for academics. **Additional information:** Internal scholarships available. Financial planning program allows personalized service to budget and meet college costs through individualized payment plans.

Application procedures. Admission: No deadline. $50 fee. Admission notification on a rolling basis. **Financial aid:** No deadline. FAFSA required.

Academics. Academic program designed to simulate working environment. After completion of associate degree, students may continue to earn bachelor of science. **Special study options:** Distance learning, ESL, honors, independent study, internships, study abroad. **Credit/placement by examination:** AP, CLEP, IB, SAT, ACT. SAT or ACT preferred for placement but ACCUPLACER accepted. **Support services:** Remedial instruction, tutoring, writing center.

Majors. Business: Fashion. **Communications:** Advertising. **Communications technology:** Animation/special effects. **Computer sciences:** Computer graphics, web page design. **Visual/performing arts:** Cinematography, commercial photography, fashion design, game design, graphic design, illustration, industrial design, interior design.

Most popular majors. Business/marketing 12%, computer/information sciences 12%, visual/performing arts 65%.

Computing on campus. Dormitories wired for high-speed internet access and linked to campus network. Online course registration, online library, helpline, repair service, student web hosting, wireless network available.

Student life. Freshman orientation: Mandatory. Preregistration for classes offered. Held at the beginning of each quarter and midquarter. **Housing:** Guaranteed on-campus for all undergraduates. Coed dorms, special housing for disabled available. $275 deposit. **Activities:** Drama, film society, international student organizations, music ensembles, radio station, student government, culinary club, Industrial Design Society of America, American Society of Interior Design, fashion club, Future Video Producers and Broadcasters, illustration club, Toastmasters International, actor's club, music club.

Student services. Adult student services, alcohol/substance abuse counseling, career counseling, services for economically disadvantaged, student employment services, financial aid counseling, personal counseling, placement for graduates, veterans' counselor. **Physically disabled:** Services for visually, speech, hearing impaired.

Contact. Phone: (954) 463-3000 ext. 2434
Toll-free number: (800) 275-7603 ext. 2434 Fax: (954) 728-8637
Claude Toland, President, Art Institute of Fort Lauderdale, 1799 SE 17th Street, Fort Lauderdale, FL 33316

Ave Maria University
Ave Maria, Florida
www.avemaria.edu   CB code: 4249

- Private 4-year university and liberal arts college affiliated with Roman Catholic Church
- Residential campus in small town
- 745 degree-seeking undergraduates
- 48% of applicants admitted
- SAT or ACT (ACT writing optional), application essay required

General. Regionally accredited. **Degrees:** 123 bachelor's awarded; master's, doctoral offered. **Location:** 20 miles from Naples. **Calendar:** Semester,

limited summer session. **Full-time faculty:** 55 total. **Part-time faculty:** 10 total. **Class size:** 61% < 20, 37% 20-39, 1% 40-49, less than 1% 50-99.

Freshman class profile. 1,271 applied, 610 admitted, 220 enrolled.

Mid 50% test scores			
SAT critical reading:	500-620	GPA 3.50-3.74:	16%
SAT math:	490-600	GPA 3.0-3.49:	32%
SAT writing:	500-620	GPA 2.0-2.99:	12%
ACT composite:	21-26	Out-of-state:	55%
GPA 3.75 or higher:	39%	Live on campus:	92%

Basis for selection. For regular admission, 2.8 GPA and 1580 SAT or 22 ACT required. Students who do not meet all requirements may attain admission by special recommendation of the Admissions Committee. **Home schooled:** Transcript of courses and grades, letter of recommendation (non-parent) required.

High school preparation. College-preparatory program recommended. 15 units required; 22 recommended. Required and recommended units include English 3-4, mathematics 3-4, social studies 1-3, history 1, science 3 (laboratory 3), foreign language 2, visual/performing arts 1-2 and academic electives 1-3.

2011-2012 Annual costs. Tuition/fees: $20,160. Room/board: $9,450. Books/supplies: $1,000. Personal expenses: $1,800.

Financial aid. **Non-need-based:** Scholarships awarded for academics, athletics, leadership, music/drama, religious affiliation, state residency.

Application procedures. **Admission:** No deadline. No application fee. Admission notification on a rolling basis. **Financial aid:** Priority date 4/1; no closing date. FAFSA required. Applicants notified on a rolling basis starting 10/1.

Academics. **Special study options:** Double major, dual enrollment of high school students, independent study, internships, study abroad. **Credit/placement by examination:** AP, CLEP, IB, SAT, ACT, institutional tests. **Support services:** Pre-admission summer program, reduced course load, study skills assistance, tutoring, writing center.

Majors. **Biology:** General. **English:** English lit. **Foreign languages:** Classics. **History:** General. **Liberal arts:** Arts/sciences. **Math:** General. **Philosophy/religion:** Philosophy. **Psychology:** General. **Social sciences:** Economics, political science. **Theology:** Sacred music, theology.

Most popular majors. Biology 6%, English 13%, history 7%, philosophy/religious studies 16%, social sciences 20%, theological studies 21%, visual/performing arts 9%.

Computing on campus. 150 workstations in dormitories, library, computer center, student center. Dormitories wired for high-speed internet access and linked to campus network. Commuter students can connect to campus network. Online library, helpline, wireless network available.

Student life. **Freshman orientation:** Mandatory. Preregistration for classes offered. 3-day program held at beginning of the fall and spring semesters. **Policies:** Policies and procedures aligned with Catholic moral teaching. Students required to live on campus unless living with a parent or legal guardian, are 23 years of age or older, or receive special permission in certain unusual cases. **Housing:** Guaranteed on-campus for all undergraduates. Single-sex dorms, apartments available. $200 deposit. **Activities:** Bands, campus ministries, choral groups, dance, drama, film society, international student organizations, music ensembles, Model UN, musical theater, radio station, student government, student newspaper, Knights of Columbus, College Republicans, Global Awareness and Activism in Politics, World Youth Alliance, Students for Life, Faith in Action Today, Chastity Team, Communion and Liberation University.

Athletics. NAIA. **Intercollegiate:** Baseball M, basketball, cross-country, football (tackle) M, golf, rowing (crew) W, soccer, softball W, tennis, track and field, volleyball W. **Intramural:** Basketball, football (non-tackle), soccer, volleyball. **Team name:** Gyrene.

Student services. Alcohol/substance abuse counseling, chaplain/spiritual director, career counseling, student employment services, financial aid counseling, health services, personal counseling, veterans' counselor. **Physically disabled:** Services for visually, hearing impaired.

Contact. E-mail: admissions@avemaria.edu
Phone: (239) 280-2556 Toll-free number: (877) 283-8648
Fax: (239) 280-2559
Jason Fabaz, Director of Admissions, Ave Maria University, 5050 Ave Maria Boulevard, Ave Maria, FL 34142-9505

Baptist College of Florida
Graceville, Florida
www.baptistcollege.edu   **CB code: 5209**

- Private 4-year Bible and teachers college affiliated with Southern Baptist Convention
- Residential campus in small town
- 584 degree-seeking undergraduates: 25% part-time, 39% women, 7% African American, 3% Hispanic American
- 10 degree-seeking graduate students
- 44% of applicants admitted
- SAT or ACT (ACT writing optional), application essay required
- 42% graduate within 6 years

General. Founded in 1943. Regionally accredited. **Degrees:** 115 bachelor's, 9 associate awarded; master's offered. **Location:** 90 miles from Tallahassee, 60 miles from Panama City. **Calendar:** Semester, limited summer session. **Full-time faculty:** 22 total; 86% have terminal degrees, 18% women. **Part-time faculty:** 43 total; 65% have terminal degrees, 2% minority, 26% women. **Class size:** 80% < 20, 16% 20-39, 2% 40-49, 2% 50-99.

Freshman class profile. 144 applied, 64 admitted, 57 enrolled.

Mid 50% test scores			
SAT critical reading:	450-640	Return as sophomores:	70%
SAT math:	390-540	Out-of-state:	40%
ACT composite:	17-22	Live on campus:	90%

Basis for selection. Applicant must be member in good standing of church affiliated with Southern Baptist Convention or other evangelical body. Recommendations very important. Audition required of music applicants. Interview recommended. **Home schooled:** Transcript of courses and grades required. 2.5 GPA; 20 academic units with at least 14 units from fields of English, math, social and natural sciences required.

High school preparation. Recommended units include English 4, mathematics 4, social studies 1, history 2 and science 3.

2011-2012 Annual costs. Tuition/fees: $9,050. Room/board: $4,138. Books/supplies: $900. Personal expenses: $2,000.

2010-2011 Financial aid. **Need-based:** 164 full-time freshmen applied for aid; 152 were judged to have need; 75 of these received aid. Average need met was 26%. Average scholarship/grant was $5,382; average loan $2,659. 59% of total undergraduate aid awarded as scholarships/grants, 41% as loans/jobs. **Non-need-based:** Awarded to 14 full-time undergraduates, including 3 freshmen. Scholarships awarded for academics, minority status, music/drama, religious affiliation.

Application procedures. **Admission:** Closing date 8/15 (receipt date). $25 fee, may be waived for applicants with need. Admission notification on a rolling basis. **Financial aid:** Priority date 4/1, closing date 4/15. FAFSA, institutional form required. Applicants notified on a rolling basis starting 6/15; must reply within 4 week(s) of notification.

Academics. **Special study options:** Distance learning, double major, independent study, internships, liberal arts/career combination, teacher certification program. **Credit/placement by examination:** AP, CLEP, IB, SAT, ACT, institutional tests. **Support services:** Learning center, reduced course load, remedial instruction, study skills assistance, tutoring, writing center.

Majors. **Education:** Elementary, history, music. **Philosophy/religion:** Religion. **Theology:** Bible, pastoral counseling, religious ed, sacred music, theology. **Visual/performing arts:** Music, music performance.

Most popular majors. Education 8%, psychology 9%, theological studies 70%, visual/performing arts 11%.

Computing on campus. 25 workstations in library, computer center. Commuter students can connect to campus network. Online course registration, online library, wireless network available.

Student life. **Freshman orientation:** Mandatory. Preregistration for classes offered. Held week before classes begin for 1-2 days depending on major. **Policies:** Religious observance required. **Housing:** Single-sex dorms, apartments available. $100 fully refundable deposit. **Activities:** Bands, campus ministries, choral groups, drama, music ensembles, musical theater, radio station, Baptist Collegiate Ministry.

Athletics. NCCAA. **Intercollegiate:** Golf M, volleyball W. **Intramural:** Basketball, football (non-tackle), golf, soccer, softball, table tennis, volleyball. **Team name:** Eagles.

Student services. Career counseling, student employment services, financial aid counseling, personal counseling, veterans' counselor. **Physically disabled:** Services for visually, speech, hearing impaired.

Contact. E-mail: admissions@baptistcollege.edu
Phone: (850) 263-3261 ext. 460
Toll-free number: (800) 328-2660 ext. 460 Fax: (850) 263-9026
Sandra Richards, Director of Marketing, Baptist College of Florida, 5400 College Drive, Graceville, FL 32440-3306

Barry University
Miami Shores, Florida
www.barry.edu

CB member
CB code: 5053

- Private 4-year university affiliated with Roman Catholic Church
- Residential campus in large town
- 4,639 degree-seeking undergraduates: 15% part-time, 66% women
- 4,207 degree-seeking graduate students
- 59% of applicants admitted
- SAT or ACT (ACT writing optional) required
- 39% graduate within 6 years

General. Founded in 1940. Regionally accredited. 22 off-campus sites for adult and continuing education and some graduate degrees. Center for Dominican Studies. **Degrees:** 1,257 bachelor's awarded; master's, professional, doctoral offered. **ROTC:** Army, Air Force. **Location:** 14 miles from Fort Lauderdale, 7 miles from Miami. **Calendar:** Semester, limited summer session. **Full-time faculty:** 370 total; 30% minority, 57% women. **Part-time faculty:** 468 total; 34% minority, 48% women. **Class size:** 68% < 20, 31% 20-39, less than 1% 40-49, less than 1% 50-99, less than 1% >100. **Special facilities:** Human performance laboratory, athletic training room, cell biology/biotechnology lab, classroom of tomorrow, photography facilities, lighting studio, dark room, imaging lab, performing arts center, biomechanics lab.

Freshman class profile. 6,918 applied, 4,060 admitted, 662 enrolled.

Mid 50% test scores			
SAT critical reading:	420-510	GPA 3.0-3.49:	36%
SAT math:	420-500	GPA 2.0-2.99:	38%
ACT composite:	17-21	Out-of-state:	52%
GPA 3.75 or higher:	12%	Live on campus:	75%
GPA 3.50-3.74:	14%	International:	7%

Basis for selection. Test scores and school record important. Higher test score, GPA, and course requirements for certain majors. Interviews highly recommended. **Home schooled:** Statement describing home school structure and mission, transcript of courses and grades, state high school equivalency certificate required. Academic portfolio or GED, copy of home school rules of the state which home school is chartered required. **Learning Disabled:** Students must apply directly to comprehensive service program.

High school preparation. 13 units required; 16 recommended. Required and recommended units include English 4, mathematics 3, social studies 3 and science 3. For nursing program, 1 chemistry, 1 biology, algebra II required. For biology and allied health programs, 2 laboratory science including biology and chemistry, 3.5 math required. For math program, 4 math including algebra, geometry, trigonometry, required. For chemistry program, 3 math, 1 chemistry with lab required.

2011-2012 Annual costs. Tuition/fees: $28,160. Room/board: $9,300. Books/supplies: $1,200. Personal expenses: $2,000.

Financial aid. **Non-need-based:** Scholarships awarded for academics, art, athletics, music/drama.

Application procedures. **Admission:** No deadline. $30 fee. Admission notification on a rolling basis beginning on or about 9/8. Students are allowed to postpone enrollment after admissions for up to 1 year. **Financial aid:** No deadline. FAFSA required. Applicants notified on a rolling basis starting 1/25.

Academics. **Special study options:** Accelerated study, combined bachelor's/graduate degree, double major, ESL, honors, internships, study abroad, teacher certification program. **Credit/placement by examination:** AP, CLEP, IB, SAT, ACT, institutional tests. 30 credit hours maximum toward bachelor's degree. All credit by examination should be completed prior to junior status. **Support services:** Learning center, reduced course load, remedial instruction, study skills assistance, tutoring, writing center.

Majors. **Biology:** General. **Business:** Accounting, business admin, finance, international, marketing. **Communications:** Advertising, communications/speech/rhetoric, public relations, radio/TV. **Computer sciences:** General, computer science, information technology. **Education:** Early childhood, elementary, physical, special ed. **English:** English lit. **Foreign languages:**

French, Spanish. **Health services:** Athletic training, cardiovascular technology, clinical lab science, cytotechnology, health care admin, nuclear medical technology, nursing (RN), predental, premedicine, prepharmacy, preveterinary, sonography. **History:** General. **Human services:** General, social work. **Liberal arts:** Arts/sciences. **Math:** General. **Parks/recreation:** Exercise sciences, health/fitness, sports admin. **Philosophy/religion:** Philosophy. **Physical sciences:** Chemistry. **Psychology:** General. **Social sciences:** Criminology, political science, sociology. **Theology:** Theology. **Visual/performing arts:** Art, dramatic, music, photography.

Most popular majors. Computer/information sciences 9%, health sciences 44%, public administration/social services 18%.

Computing on campus. 165 workstations in dormitories, library, computer center. Dormitories wired for high-speed internet access and linked to campus network. Commuter students can connect to campus network. Online library, helpline, repair service, wireless network available.

Student life. **Freshman orientation:** Mandatory. Preregistration for classes offered. **Housing:** Coed dorms, single-sex dorms, special housing for disabled available. $200 nonrefundable deposit. **Activities:** Choral groups, dance, drama, literary magazine, music ensembles, musical theater, radio station, student government, student newspaper, TV station, Jamaican association, black student union, Habitat for Humanity, Caribbean student organization, Haitian intercultural association, Jewish/Christian/Muslim interfaith group, Latter-Day Saints student association, Best Buddies, Spanish club, Baptist dialogue group.

Athletics. NCAA. **Intercollegiate:** Baseball M, basketball, golf, rowing (crew) W, soccer, softball W, tennis, volleyball W. **Intramural:** Basketball, football (non-tackle), golf, skin diving, soccer, softball, volleyball. **Team name:** Buccaneers.

Student services. Adult student services, alcohol/substance abuse counseling, chaplain/spiritual director, career counseling, student employment services, financial aid counseling, health services, personal counseling, placement for graduates. **Physically disabled:** Services for visually, speech, hearing impaired.

Contact. E-mail: admissions@mail.barry.edu
Phone: (305) 899-3100 Toll-free number: (800) 695-2279
Fax: (305) 899-2971
Magda Castineyra, Director of Undergraduate Admissions, Barry University, 11300 NE Second Avenue, Miami Shores, FL 33161-6695

Beacon College
Leesburg, Florida
www.beaconcollege.edu

CB code: 3611

- Private 4-year liberal arts college
- Residential campus in large town
- 153 degree-seeking undergraduates
- Application essay required

General. Regionally accredited. College solely for students with learning disabilities. **Degrees:** 21 bachelor's, 11 associate awarded. **Location:** 50 miles from Orlando. **Calendar:** Semester, limited summer session. **Full-time faculty:** 13 total. **Part-time faculty:** 7 total. **Class size:** 100% < 20.

Freshman class profile.

GPA 3.0-3.49:	50%	Live on campus:	100%
GPA 2.0-2.99:	45%	Fraternities:	32%
Out-of-state:	72%	Sororities:	27%

Basis for selection. Selective but noncompetitive process. Recommendations, interview, character, level of interest very important; followed by rigor of secondary school record, GPA, test scores, essay, extracurricular activities, ability, volunteer work. Class rank, work experience considered. SAT or ACT recommended. Scores used noncompetitively for informational purposes only. Interview may be required. **Home schooled:** State high school equivalency certificate required. **Learning Disabled:** Students accepted by committee decision based on psychoeducational evaluation documenting learning disability, academic potential, evaluation of high school records, references, and campus interviews with assessments as part of admissions process. Students must provide current psychoeducational report (within 3 years) documenting learning disability as primary handicapping condition, including WAIS score.

High school preparation. College-preparatory program recommended. 12 units required. Required and recommended units include English 4, mathematics 1-2, social studies 1, history 2-3, science 1-2 and academic electives 3.

2011-2012 Annual costs. Tuition/fees: $29,050. Room/board: $8,350. Books/supplies: $900. Personal expenses: $2,565.

Financial aid. All financial aid based on need. **Additional information:** Work-study programs offered based on financial need.

Application procedures. Admission: Priority date 5/1; deadline 8/1 (receipt date). $50 fee. Application must be submitted on paper. Admission notification on a rolling basis. Must reply by May 1 or within 2 week(s) if notified thereafter. **Financial aid:** Priority date 4/1; no closing date. FAFSA, institutional form required. Applicants notified on a rolling basis starting 4/1; must reply within 2 week(s) of notification.

Academics. Provides remedial coursework in writing, reading, and math. **Special study options:** Double major, independent study, internships, liberal arts/career combination, study abroad. **Credit/placement by examination:** AP, CLEP, institutional tests. **Support services:** Learning center, reduced course load, remedial instruction, study skills assistance, tutoring, writing center.

Majors. Computer sciences: General. **Liberal arts:** Arts/sciences.

Most popular majors. Computer/information sciences 20%, liberal arts 44%, public administration/social services 36%.

Computing on campus. 32 workstations in library, computer center, student center. Dormitories wired for high-speed internet access and linked to campus network. Commuter students can connect to campus network. Online library, helpline, repair service, student web hosting, wireless network available.

Student life. Freshman orientation: Mandatory, $250 fee. Preregistration for classes offered. **Housing:** Guaranteed on-campus for all undergraduates. Apartments, wellness housing available. $750 nonrefundable deposit, deadline 5/1. **Activities:** Dance, literary magazine, student government, student newspaper.

Athletics. Team name: Bull Dogs.

Student services. Alcohol/substance abuse counseling, career counseling, student employment services, financial aid counseling, personal counseling, placement for graduates. **Physically disabled:** Services for visually, speech, hearing impaired.

Contact. E-mail: admissions@beaconcollege.edu
Phone: (352) 787-7249 Fax: (352) 787-0721
Betsy Stoutmorrill, Vice President of Enrollment Management and Academic Programs, Beacon College, 105 East Main Street, Leesburg, FL 34748

Bethune-Cookman University
Daytona Beach, Florida **CB member**
www.cookman.edu **CB code: 5061**

- Private 4-year liberal arts college affiliated with United Methodist Church
- Residential campus in small city
- 3,256 degree-seeking undergraduates: 6% part-time, 60% women, 91% African American, 2% Hispanic American, 2% international
- 51 degree-seeking graduate students
- 67% of applicants admitted
- SAT or ACT (ACT writing optional), application essay required
- 37% graduate within 6 years; 13% enter graduate study

General. Founded in 1904. Regionally accredited. **Degrees:** 561 bachelor's awarded; master's offered. **ROTC:** Army, Air Force. **Location:** 60 miles from Orlando. **Calendar:** Semester, limited summer session. **Full-time faculty:** 182 total; 56% have terminal degrees, 50% minority, 47% women. **Part-time faculty:** 48 total; 25% have terminal degrees, 52% minority, 56% women. **Class size:** 41% < 20, 54% 20-39, 2% 40-49, 2% 50-99, less than 1% >100. **Special facilities:** Art gallery/studio, audiologic recording studio, observatory.

Freshman class profile. 4,707 applied, 3,152 admitted, 896 enrolled.

Mid 50% test scores		GPA 2.0-2.99:	59%
SAT critical reading:	370-450	Rank in top quarter:	12%
SAT math:	360-450	Rank in top tenth:	4%
SAT writing:	360-440	End year in good standing:	90%
ACT composite:	16-19	Return as sophomores:	69%
GPA 3.75 or higher:	8%	Out-of-state:	32%
GPA 3.50-3.74:	8%	Live on campus:	93%
GPA 3.0-3.49:	24%	International:	1%

Basis for selection. School achievement record most important. Test scores and letters of recommendation important. Interview required of music majors.

High school preparation. 19 units required. Required and recommended units include English 4, mathematics 3, social studies 1, history 2, science 3 (laboratory 1), foreign language 2 and academic electives 6. 1 unit computer literacy.

2011-2012 Annual costs. Tuition/fees: $13,990. The Lee Rhyant Residential Center costs an additional $708 per year. Room/board: $8,300. Books/supplies: $1,400. Personal expenses: $2,800.

2010-2011 Financial aid. All financial aid based on need. 993 full-time freshmen applied for aid; 963 were judged to have need; 963 of these received aid. Average need met was 50%. Average scholarship/grant was $9,289; average loan $3,597. 51% of total undergraduate aid awarded as scholarships/grants, 49% as loans/jobs.

Application procedures. Admission: Priority date 6/30; no deadline. $25 fee, may be waived for applicants with need. Application must be submitted on paper. Admission notification on a rolling basis. **Financial aid:** Priority date 4/1; no closing date. FAFSA required. Applicants notified on a rolling basis starting 4/1; must reply within 3 week(s) of notification.

Academics. Special study options: Accelerated study, combined bachelor's/graduate degree, cooperative education, distance learning, double major, honors, independent study, internships, study abroad, teacher certification program, weekend college. **Credit/placement by examination:** AP, CLEP, IB, SAT, ACT, institutional tests. 30 credit hours maximum toward bachelor's degree. **Support services:** Learning center, reduced course load, remedial instruction, study skills assistance, tutoring, writing center.

Majors. Biology: General. **Business:** Accounting, business admin, hotel/motel admin, international. **Communications:** Communications/speech/rhetoric, media studies. **Computer sciences:** Computer science, information systems. **Conservation:** Environmental science. **Education:** General, biology, business, chemistry, elementary, English, learning disabled, music, physical, social studies. **Engineering:** Computer. **English:** English lit. **Health services:** Clinical lab science, nursing (RN). **History:** General. **Math:** General. **Parks/recreation:** General. **Philosophy/religion:** General. **Physical sciences:** Chemistry. **Protective services:** Law enforcement admin. **Psychology:** General. **Social sciences:** International relations, political science, sociology. **Visual/performing arts:** Music technology.

Most popular majors. Business/marketing 21%, communications/journalism 9%, education 12%, health sciences 11%, psychology 9%, security/protective services 14%, social sciences 7%.

Computing on campus. 558 workstations in dormitories, library, computer center, student center. Dormitories wired for high-speed internet access and linked to campus network. Commuter students can connect to campus network. Online course registration, online library, helpline, wireless network available.

Student life. Freshman orientation: Mandatory. Preregistration for classes offered. One-week program in beginning of fall and spring semster. **Housing:** Guaranteed on-campus for freshmen. Single-sex dorms, wellness housing available. $200 nonrefundable deposit, deadline 8/15. Scholarship housing available for honor students. **Activities:** Bands, choral groups, dance, drama, international student organizations, music ensembles, Model UN, radio station, student government, student newspaper, YM/YWCA, Religious Life fellowship, pre-seminarian club, Greek letter organization, Gamma Sigma Sigma national service sorority, Kappa Kappa Psi national band fraternity, Alpha Chi honor sorority, Alpha Kappa Mu honor sorority.

Athletics. NCAA. **Intercollegiate:** Baseball M, basketball, bowling W, cross-country, football (tackle) M, golf, softball W, tennis, track and field, volleyball W. **Intramural:** Basketball, football (tackle) M. **Team name:** Wildcats.

Student services. Adult student services, chaplain/spiritual director, career counseling, student employment services, financial aid counseling, health services, personal counseling, placement for graduates, veterans' counselor.

Contact. E-mail: admissions@cookman.edu
Phone: (386) 481-2600 Toll-free number: (800) 448-0228
Fax: (386) 481-2601
Frederick McCoy, Senior Assistant Director of Admissions, Bethune-Cookman University, Dr. Mary McLeod Bethune Boulevard, Daytona Beach, FL 32114-3099

Carlos Albizu University
Miami, Florida
www.albizu.edu   CB code: 2102

◆ Private 4-year university
◆ Commuter campus in very large city
◆ 331 degree-seeking undergraduates
◆ 61% of applicants admitted
◆ Application essay, interview required

General. Founded in 1980. Regionally accredited. **Degrees:** 108 bachelor's awarded; master's, professional offered. **Calendar:** Semester, extensive summer session. **Full-time faculty:** 24 total. **Part-time faculty:** 94 total. **Class size:** 39% < 20, 61% 20-39.

Freshman class profile. 36 applied, 22 admitted, 13 enrolled.

Basis for selection. 2.0 GPA required. **Home schooled:** State high school equivalency certificate required. **Learning Disabled:** Students requiring special accommodation must submit written request to Director of Student Affairs and attach documentary support.

2011-2012 Annual costs. Tuition/fees: $14,874. Reported tuition and fees are for bachelor's degree program in business. Other programs individually priced. Books/supplies: $690. Personal expenses: $1,800.

Financial aid. All financial aid based on need.

Application procedures. Admission: No deadline. $25 fee, may be waived for applicants with need. Admission notification on a rolling basis. **Financial aid:** Priority date 6/1; no closing date. FAFSA, institutional form required. Applicants notified on a rolling basis starting 2/1.

Academics. Special study options: Accelerated study, cooperative education, cross-registration, distance learning, double major, dual enrollment of high school students, ESL, honors, independent study, internships, study abroad, teacher certification program, weekend college. **Credit/placement by examination:** AP, CLEP, IB, institutional tests. 12 credit hours maximum toward bachelor's degree. 6 for foreign language, 6 for other foundation courses. **Support services:** Learning center, remedial instruction, study skills assistance, tutoring, writing center.

Majors. Business: General. **Education:** Elementary. **Psychology:** General.

Computing on campus. 50 workstations in library, computer center, student center. Commuter students can connect to campus network. Online course registration, online library, wireless network available.

Student life. Freshman orientation: Mandatory. Preregistration for classes offered. Two-hour program held before session. **Activities:** Student government, student newspaper.

Student services. Adult student services, career counseling, services for economically disadvantaged, student employment services, financial aid counseling, minority student services, placement for graduates.

Contact. E-mail: webmaster@albizu.edu
Phone: (305) 593-1223 ext. 137 Toll-free number: (888) 468-6228
Fax: (305) 593-1854
Phillip Fields, Director, Carlos Albizu University, 2173 NW 99th Avenue, Miami, FL 33172

Chamberlain College of Nursing: Jacksonville
Jacksonville, Florida
www.chamberlan.edu   CB code: 5968

◆ For-profit 4-year nursing college
◆ Commuter campus in small city

General. Regionally accredited. **Calendar:** Semester. **Full-time faculty:** 10 total. **Part-time faculty:** 8 total.

Basis for selection. Rigor of secondary school record, class rank, GPA, and recommendations very important.

2011-2012 Annual costs. Tuition/fees: $15,600. Books/supplies: $1,400. Personal expenses: $2,218.

Application procedures. Admission: No deadline. $60 fee. Admission notification on a rolling basis.

Academics. Special study options: Accelerated study, distance learning. **Credit/placement by examination:** AP, CLEP.

Majors. Health services: Nursing (RN).

Contact. Chamberlain College of Nursing: Jacksonville, 5200 Belfort Road, Jacksonville, FL 32256

Chamberlain College Of Nursing: Miramar
Miramar, Florida
www.chamberlain.edu   CB code: 7752

◆ For-profit 4-year nursing college
◆ Large town
◆ 69 degree-seeking undergraduates

General. Regionally accredited. **Calendar:** Semester. **Full-time faculty:** 3 total.

Basis for selection. GPA, secondary school record very important; standardized test scores recommended.

Application procedures. Admission: $95 fee. Admission notification on a rolling basis.

Academics. Credit/placement by examination: AP, CLEP.

Majors. Health services: Nursing (RN).

Contact. Chamberlain College Of Nursing: Miramar, 2300 Southwest 145th Avenue, Miramar, FL 33027

City College: Fort Lauderdale
Fort Lauderdale, Florida
www.citycollege.edu   CB code: 3578

◆ Private 4-year business and technical college
◆ Commuter campus in very large city

General. Accredited by ACICS. **Calendar:** Quarter.

Annual costs/financial aid. Tuition/fees (2011-2012): $12,375. Books/supplies: $1,044. Personal expenses: $2,931.

Contact. Phone: (954) 492-5353
Director of Admissions, 2000 West Commercial Boulevard, Fort Lauderdale, FL 33309

Clearwater Christian College
Clearwater, Florida
www.clearwater.edu   CB code: 5142

◆ Private 4-year liberal arts college affiliated with nondenominational tradition
◆ Residential campus in small city
◆ 506 degree-seeking undergraduates: 3% part-time, 49% women, 5% African American, 3% Hispanic American, 1% Native American, 1% international
◆ 10 degree-seeking graduate students
◆ 72% of applicants admitted
◆ SAT or ACT (ACT writing optional), application essay required
◆ 54% graduate within 6 years

General. Founded in 1966. Regionally accredited. **Degrees:** 110 bachelor's, 3 associate awarded; master's offered. **ROTC:** Army, Naval, Air Force. **Location:** 15 miles from Tampa, 15 miles from St. Petersburg. **Calendar:** Semester, limited summer session. **Full-time faculty:** 29 total; 72% have terminal degrees, 3% minority, 31% women. **Part-time faculty:** 14 total; 71% have terminal degrees, 29% women. **Class size:** 74% < 20, 21% 20-39, 3% 40-49, 2% 50-99.

Freshman class profile. 340 applied, 245 admitted, 151 enrolled.

Mid 50% test scores			
SAT critical reading:	480-570	GPA 2.0-2.99:	16%
SAT math:	450-550	Rank in top quarter:	24%
ACT composite:	20-26	Rank in top tenth:	11%
GPA 3.75 or higher:	29%	Out-of-state:	52%
GPA 3.50-3.74:	22%	Live on campus:	83%
GPA 3.0-3.49:	32%	International:	3%

Basis for selection. 2.0 GPA, 870 SAT (exclusive of Writing) or 18 ACT, recommendations, and Christian testimony important. Interview recommended. Audition recommended for music majors. **Home schooled:** Transcript of courses and grades required. GED required if transcript not available; liberal arts/college preparatory program recommended; academic placement testing may be administered.

High school preparation. College-preparatory program recommended. Recommended units include English 4, mathematics 3, social studies 3, history 1, science 3 and foreign language 2. Math units should include geometry; English units should emphasize grammar and writing.

2012-2013 Annual costs. Tuition/fees: $16,715. Room/board: $7,920. Books/supplies: $1,000. Personal expenses: $2,200.

2011-2012 Financial aid. Need-based: 108 full-time freshmen applied for aid; 94 were judged to have need; 94 of these received aid. Average need met was 58%. Average scholarship/grant was $9,765; average loan $3,515. 70% of total undergraduate aid awarded as scholarships/grants, 30% as loans/jobs. **Non-need-based:** Scholarships awarded for academics, alumni affiliation, leadership, music/drama, religious affiliation, ROTC. **Additional information:** Special consideration given to children of Christian service workers; need-based scholarships available to first-generation students; scholarships up to $3,000 available to dual-enrolled students.

Application procedures. Admission: Closing date 8/1 (receipt date). $35 fee, may be waived for applicants with need. Admission notification on a rolling basis. **Financial aid:** Priority date 3/1; no closing date. FAFSA, institutional form required. Applicants notified on a rolling basis starting 3/15; must reply within 2 week(s) of notification.

Academics. All students completing a bachelor's degree earn the equivalent of 20-credit minor in Bible. **Special study options:** Distance learning, double major, dual enrollment of high school students, honors, independent study, internships, liberal arts/career combination, student-designed major, study abroad, teacher certification program. International missions trips. **Credit/placement by examination:** AP, CLEP, IB, institutional tests. 24 credit hours maximum toward associate degree, 24 toward bachelor's. **Support services:** Reduced course load, remedial instruction, study skills assistance, tutoring.

Majors. Biology: General. **Business:** Accounting, business admin, office management. **Communications:** Communications/speech/rhetoric. **Computer sciences:** Information systems. **Education:** Biology, elementary, English, mathematics, music, physical, social studies. **English:** English lit. **Health services:** Premedicine. **History:** General. **Liberal arts:** Arts/sciences, humanities. **Math:** General. **Parks/recreation:** Exercise sciences, sports admin. **Psychology:** General. **Theology:** Bible, pastoral counseling. **Visual/performing arts:** Music.

Most popular majors. Biology 9%, business/marketing 14%, education 25%, liberal arts 18%, parks/recreation 10%, theological studies 8%.

Computing on campus. 38 workstations in dormitories, library, computer center. Dormitories wired for high-speed internet access and linked to campus network. Commuter students can connect to campus network. Online library, helpline, repair service, wireless network available.

Student life. Freshman orientation: Mandatory. Preregistration for classes offered. 2-day program held prior to start of fall semester. **Policies:** Convocation and Christian Life Conference; chapel 4 days per week; evening Bible studies and prayer meetings required of students in the residence halls. Religious observance required. **Housing:** Guaranteed on-campus for all undergraduates. Single-sex dorms available. $100 deposit. **Activities:** Bands, campus ministries, choral groups, drama, film society, music ensembles, musical theater, student government, student newspaper, symphony orchestra, political club, College Republicans, Fellowship of Preministerial Students, student missionary fellowship, China team, music ministry team, joy club, pro life club.

Athletics. NCCAA. **Intercollegiate:** Baseball M, basketball, golf, soccer, softball W, volleyball W. **Intramural:** Basketball, football (non-tackle) M, soccer, table tennis, tennis, volleyball. **Team name:** Cougars.

Student services. Chaplain/spiritual director, career counseling, student employment services, financial aid counseling, personal counseling, placement for graduates. **Physically disabled:** Services for visually, speech impaired.

Contact. E-mail: admissions@clearwater.edu
Phone: (727) 726-1153 ext. 220 Toll-free number: (800) 348-4463
Fax: (727) 726-8597
Bryan Johnson, Assistant Director of Admissions, Clearwater Christian College, 3400 Gulf-to-Bay Boulevard, Clearwater, FL 33759-4595

DeVry University: Miramar
Miramar, Florida
www.devry.edu   **CB code: 4134**

- For-profit 4-year university
- Commuter campus in large town
- Interview required

General. Additional locations: Fort Lauderdale, Miami. **Degrees:** 171 bachelor's, 28 associate awarded; master's offered. **Calendar:** Semester, extensive summer session. **Full-time faculty:** 18 total. **Part-time faculty:** 59 total.

Basis for selection. Applicants must have high school diploma or equivalent, or degree from accredited postsecondary institution; demonstrate proficiency in basic college-level skills through SAT, ACT or institution-administered placement exams; and be at least 17. New students may enter at beginning of any semester.

2011-2012 Annual costs. Tuition/fees: $15,294. Books/supplies: $1,100. Personal expenses: $1,816.

Financial aid. All financial aid based on need.

Application procedures. Admission: No deadline. $50 fee. Admission notification on a rolling basis. **Financial aid:** No deadline. FAFSA required. Applicants notified on a rolling basis.

Academics. Special study options: Accelerated study, distance learning. **Credit/placement by examination:** AP, CLEP. **Support services:** Learning center, remedial instruction, tutoring.

Majors. Business: Business admin. **Computer sciences:** Networking, systems analysis, web page design.

Most popular majors. Business/marketing 72%, computer/information sciences 18%, engineering/engineering technologies 10%.

Computing on campus. Online course registration, online library, helpline available.

Student life. Activities: Student government, student newspaper.

Student services. Career counseling, student employment services, financial aid counseling, placement for graduates, veterans' counselor. **Physically disabled:** Services for visually, hearing impaired.

Contact. E-mail: openhouse@mir.devry.edu
Phone: (954) 499-9700 Toll-free number: (866) 793-3879
Fax: (954) 499-9723
Aaron McCardell, Director of Admission, DeVry University: Miramar, 2300 SW 145th Avenue, Miramar, FL 33027

DeVry University: Orlando
Orlando, Florida
www.devry.edu   **CB code: 2881**

- For-profit 4-year university
- Commuter campus in very large city
- Interview required

General. Regionally accredited. Additional locations: Orlando North, Jacksonville, Tampa Bay, Tampa East. **Degrees:** 275 bachelor's, 48 associate awarded; master's offered. **Calendar:** Semester, extensive summer session. **Full-time faculty:** 22 total. **Part-time faculty:** 122 total.

Basis for selection. Applicants must have high school diploma or equivalent, or degree from an accredited postsecondary institution. New students may enter at the beginning of any semester. SAT or ACT or institution-administered placement examination used to determine proficiency in basic college-level skills.

High school preparation. Required units include mathematics 1. Math unit must be algebra or higher.

2011-2012 Annual costs. Tuition/fees: $15,294. Books/supplies: $1,300. Personal expenses: $3,152.

Financial aid. All financial aid based on need.

Application procedures. Admission: No deadline. $50 fee. Admission notification on a rolling basis. **Financial aid:** No deadline. FAFSA required. Applicants notified on a rolling basis.

Academics. Special study options: Accelerated study, distance learning. **Credit/placement by examination:** AP, CLEP, institutional tests. **Support services:** Learning center, remedial instruction, tutoring.

Majors. Business: Business admin. **Computer sciences:** Networking, systems analysis, web page design. **Engineering:** Software.

Most popular majors. Business/marketing 70%, computer/information sciences 12%, engineering/engineering technologies 18%.

Computing on campus. 303 workstations in library, computer center. Online course registration, online library, helpline available.

Student life. Freshman orientation: Mandatory. Preregistration for classes offered. **Activities:** Student newspaper, student activities council, National Society of Black Engineers, association for IT professionals, chess club, technology forum, Millennia Engineering Students Association.

Student services. Career counseling, student employment services, financial aid counseling, placement for graduates, veterans' counselor. **Physically disabled:** Services for visually, hearing impaired.

Contact. Phone: (407) 370-3131 Toll-free number: (866) 353-3879 Fax: (407) 370-3198
Jody Wasmer, Director of Admissions, DeVry University: Orlando, 4000 Millennia Boulevard, Orlando, FL 32839-2426

Digital Media Arts College
Boca Raton, Florida
www.dmac.edu   CB code: 5295

- For-profit 3-year visual arts college
- Commuter campus in large city
- 250 degree-seeking undergraduates: 37% part-time, 27% women
- 39 degree-seeking graduate students
- Application essay required
- 42% graduate within 6 years

General. Regionally accredited; also accredited by ACICS. **Degrees:** 65 bachelor's awarded; master's offered. **Calendar:** Semester, extensive summer session. **Full-time faculty:** 46 total. **Part-time faculty:** 14 total.

Basis for selection. Open admission. **Home schooled:** Transcript of courses and grades required.

2010-2011 Financial aid. Need-based: 52% of total undergraduate aid awarded as scholarships/grants, 48% as loans/jobs. **Non-need-based:** Scholarships awarded for art.

Application procedures. Admission: $100 fee. **Financial aid:** No deadline. FAFSA required. Applicants notified on a rolling basis starting 1/1; must reply within 4 week(s) of notification.

Academics. Special study options: Combined bachelor's/graduate degree, internships. **Credit/placement by examination:** AP, CLEP, IB. **Support services:** Reduced course load, tutoring.

Majors. Visual/performing arts: Digital arts, graphic design.

Computing on campus. PC or laptop required. Repair service available.

Student life. Freshman orientation: Mandatory. Preregistration for classes offered. **Activities:** Student government.

Student services. Career counseling, financial aid counseling, placement for graduates.

Contact. E-mail: admissions@dmac.edu
Phone: (866) 255-3622
Aylin Tito, Director of Admissions, Digital Media Arts College, 5400 Broken Sound Boulevard, Boca Raton, FL 33487

Eckerd College
St. Petersburg, Florida   CB member
www.eckerd.edu   CB code: 5223

- Private 4-year liberal arts college affiliated with Presbyterian Church (USA)
- Residential campus in large city
- 1,821 degree-seeking undergraduates: 1% part-time, 59% women, 3% African American, 1% Asian American, 7% Hispanic American, 3% international
- 53% of applicants admitted
- SAT or ACT (ACT writing optional), application essay required
- 63% graduate within 6 years

General. Founded in 1958. Regionally accredited. **Degrees:** 455 bachelor's awarded. **ROTC:** Army, Air Force. **Location:** 25 miles from Tampa. **Calendar:** 4-1-4, limited summer session. **Full-time faculty:** 110 total; 94% have terminal degrees, 16% minority, 41% women. **Part-time faculty:** 53 total; 49% have terminal degrees, 17% minority, 49% women. **Class size:** 48% < 20, 49% 20-39, 2% 40-49, less than 1% 50-99. **Special facilities:** Marine science laboratory, waterfront program.

Freshman class profile. 3,713 applied, 1,977 admitted, 502 enrolled.

Mid 50% test scores			
SAT critical reading:	510-620	GPA 3.0-3.49:	45%
SAT math:	500-610	GPA 2.0-2.99:	21%
SAT writing:	500-600	Return as sophomores:	81%
ACT composite:	22-28	Out-of-state:	84%
GPA 3.75 or higher:	15%	Live on campus:	98%
GPA 3.50-3.74:	19%	International:	3%

Basis for selection. School achievement record, school/community involvement, essay, student's character, test scores most important. **Home schooled:** Statement describing home school structure and mission, transcript of courses and grades, state high school equivalency certificate, letter of recommendation (nonparent) required. **Learning Disabled:** Students should provide proper documentation for any disability.

High school preparation. College-preparatory program recommended. 18 units recommended. Recommended units include English 4, mathematics 3, social studies 2, history 1, science 3 (laboratory 2), foreign language 2 and academic electives 3.

2011-2012 Annual costs. Tuition/fees: $34,546. Room/board: $9,652. Books/supplies: $1,200. Personal expenses: $1,440.

Financial aid. Non-need-based: Scholarships awarded for academics, art, athletics, music/drama, state residency.

Application procedures. Admission: No deadline. $40 fee, may be waived for applicants with need. Admission notification on a rolling basis beginning on or about 10/1. Must reply by May 1 or within 2 week(s) if notified thereafter. **Financial aid:** Priority date 3/1; no closing date. FAFSA required. Applicants notified on a rolling basis starting 2/20.

Academics. Special study options: Accelerated study, combined bachelor's/graduate degree, double major, ESL, honors, independent study, internships, liberal arts/career combination, semester at sea, student-designed major, study abroad. Semester, full year, and winter term international study programs, 3-2 (dual program) in engineering with Columbia University, Washington University (MO). **Credit/placement by examination:** AP, CLEP, IB, institutional tests. 32 credit hours maximum toward bachelor's degree. **Support services:** Reduced course load, study skills assistance, tutoring, writing center.

Majors. Area/ethnic studies: American, East Asian, women's. **Biology:** General, biochemistry. **Business:** Business admin, international, management science. **Communications:** General. **Computer sciences:** General. **Conservation:** Environmental studies. **English:** Creative writing, English lit. **Foreign languages:** Comparative lit, French, Spanish. **History:** General. **Liberal arts:** Humanities. **Math:** General. **Philosophy/religion:** Philosophy, religion. **Physical sciences:** Chemistry, physics. **Psychology:** General. **Social sciences:** Anthropology, economics, international relations, political science, sociology. **Visual/performing arts:** Dramatic, music, studio arts.

Most popular majors. Biology 18%, business/marketing 19%, communications/journalism 6%, natural resources/environmental science 12%, psychology 9%, social sciences 15%, visual/performing arts 6%.

Computing on campus. 300 workstations in dormitories, library, computer center, student center. Dormitories wired for high-speed internet access and linked to campus network. Commuter students can connect to campus

network. Online course registration, online library, helpline, repair service, student web hosting, wireless network available.

Student life. Freshman orientation: Mandatory. Preregistration for classes offered. 3-week session held in fall. **Housing:** Guaranteed on-campus for freshmen. Coed dorms, single-sex dorms, special housing for disabled, apartments, wellness housing available. Pets allowed in dorm rooms. Suite-style dorms, substance-free housing, pet dorms, community service dorms. **Activities:** Concert band, campus ministries, choral groups, dance, drama, international student organizations, literary magazine, music ensembles, Model UN, radio station, student government, student newspaper, TV station, Phi Beta Kappa, Afro-American society, Search and Rescue team, Circle-K, honor societies, Earth society.

Athletics. NCAA. **Intercollegiate:** Baseball M, basketball, golf, sailing, soccer, softball W, tennis, volleyball W. **Intramural:** Baseball M, basketball, bowling, sailing, soccer, softball, swimming, table tennis, tennis, volleyball. **Team name:** Tritons.

Student services. Adult student services, alcohol/substance abuse counseling, chaplain/spiritual director, career counseling, student employment services, financial aid counseling, health services, minority student services, personal counseling, placement for graduates, veterans' counselor, women's services.

Contact. E-mail: admissions@eckerd.edu
Phone: (727) 864-8331 Toll-free number: (800) 456-9009
Fax: (727) 866-2304
John Sullivan, Dean of Admission and Financial Aid, Eckerd College, 4200 54th Avenue South, St. Petersburg, FL 33711

Edward Waters College
Jacksonville, Florida — CB member
www.ewc.edu — CB code: 5182

- Private 4-year liberal arts college affiliated with African Methodist Episcopal Church
- Residential campus in very large city
- 751 degree-seeking undergraduates
- 23% of applicants admitted

General. Founded in 1866. Regionally accredited. **Degrees:** 81 bachelor's awarded. **Location:** 134 miles from Orlando. **Calendar:** Semester, extensive summer session. **Full-time faculty:** 32 total; 69% have terminal degrees, 97% minority, 41% women. **Part-time faculty:** 35 total; 11% have terminal degrees, 97% minority, 54% women. **Class size:** 57% < 20, 40% 20-39, 4% 40-49. **Special facilities:** African art collection, community resource center, community medical center.

Freshman class profile. 1,611 applied, 365 admitted, 228 enrolled.

Mid 50% test scores			
SAT critical reading:	330-420	ACT composite:	14-17
SAT math:	310-400	Return as sophomores:	54%
SAT writing:	360-390	Live on campus:	82%

Basis for selection. GPA and recommendations very important. SAT or ACT recommended. **Home schooled:** Statement describing home school structure and mission, transcript of courses and grades, state high school equivalency certificate, letter of recommendation (nonparent) required.

High school preparation. College-preparatory program recommended. 13 units recommended. Recommended units include English 4, mathematics 3, social studies 3 and science 3.

2011-2012 Annual costs. Tuition/fees: $10,994. Room/board: $6,592. Books/supplies: $500. Personal expenses: $750.

Application procedures. Admission: Priority date 4/15; no deadline. $25 fee, may be waived for applicants with need. Admission notification on a rolling basis. Must reply by May 1 or within 4 week(s) if notified thereafter. **Financial aid:** Closing date 4/15. FAFSA required. Applicants notified on a rolling basis starting 5/1; must reply within 2 week(s) of notification.

Academics. Special study options: Accelerated study, cooperative education, cross-registration, double major, dual enrollment of high school students, independent study, internships, liberal arts/career combination, teacher certification program. **Credit/placement by examination:** AP, CLEP, institutional tests. 30 credit hours maximum toward bachelor's degree. **Support services:** Learning center, pre-admission summer program, remedial instruction, study skills assistance, tutoring.

Majors. Biology: General. **Business:** Business admin. **Communications:** Communications/speech/rhetoric. **Education:** General, physical. **Liberal**

---

arts: Arts/sciences. **Math:** General. **Psychology:** General. **Social sciences:** Sociology. **Visual/performing arts:** Music.

Most popular majors. Business/marketing 37%, education 7%, mathematics 7%, psychology 16%.

Computing on campus. 120 workstations in dormitories, library, computer center. Dormitories wired for high-speed internet access and linked to campus network. Online library, repair service, wireless network available.

Student life. Freshman orientation: Mandatory. Preregistration for classes offered. **Policies:** Smoke-free campus. Religious observance required. **Housing:** Guaranteed on-campus for freshmen. Coed dorms, single-sex dorms, wellness housing available. $100 deposit, deadline 7/31. **Activities:** Bands, campus ministries, choral groups, international student organizations, music ensembles, student government, NAACP, ministerial alliance, debate club, Circle K.

Athletics. NAIA. **Intercollegiate:** Baseball M, basketball, cheerleading, cross-country M, football (tackle) M, golf, softball W, track and field M, volleyball W. **Intramural:** Table tennis, volleyball. **Team name:** Fighting Tigers.

Student services. Adult student services, career counseling, student employment services, financial aid counseling, health services, personal counseling, placement for graduates, veterans' counselor.

Contact. E-mail: admissions@ewc.edu
Phone: (904) 470-8000 Toll-free number: (888) 898-3191
Fax: (904) 470-8041
Edward Alexander, Director of Admissions, Edward Waters College, 1658 Kings Road, Jacksonville, FL 32209

Embry-Riddle Aeronautical University
Daytona Beach, Florida — CB member
www.embryriddle.edu — CB code: 5190

- Private 4-year university
- Residential campus in small city
- 4,496 degree-seeking undergraduates: 6% part-time, 15% women, 7% African American, 5% Asian American, 10% Hispanic American, 1% Native American, 14% international
- 607 degree-seeking graduate students
- 79% of applicants admitted
- SAT or ACT (ACT writing optional) required
- 55% graduate within 6 years; 31% enter graduate study

General. Founded in 1926. Regionally accredited. **Degrees:** 930 bachelor's, 26 associate awarded; master's offered. **ROTC:** Army, Naval, Air Force. **Location:** 50 miles from Orlando. **Calendar:** Semester, extensive summer session. **Full-time faculty:** 264 total; 69% have terminal degrees, 10% minority, 23% women. **Part-time faculty:** 101 total; 13% have terminal degrees, 18% minority, 43% women. **Class size:** 28% < 20, 67% 20-39, 3% 40-49, 2% 50-99, less than 1% >100. **Special facilities:** Aviation complex, air traffic control lab, airway science simulation lab, next generation advanced research lab, advanced vehicle green garage, FAA testing center, meteorology labs, weather center.

Freshman class profile. 4,176 applied, 3,280 admitted, 1,046 enrolled.

Mid 50% test scores			
SAT critical reading:	470-590	GPA 2.0-2.99:	25%
SAT math:	510-630	Rank in top quarter:	50%
ACT composite:	21-28	Rank in top tenth:	26%
GPA 3.75 or higher:	21%	Return as sophomores:	72%
GPA 3.50-3.74:	19%	Out-of-state:	74%
GPA 3.0-3.49:	34%	Live on campus:	93%
		International:	11%

Basis for selection. High school GPA, rank in class, and test scores important. Specific requirements vary by degree program. Interview and essay recommended.

High school preparation. 15 units required; 19 recommended. Required and recommended units include English 4, mathematics 3-4, social studies 2, history 1-2, science 2-3 (laboratory 2), foreign language 1 and academic electives 3.

2012-2013 Annual costs. Tuition/fees: $30,720. Room/board: $10,650. Books/supplies: $1,428. Personal expenses: $1,518.

2011-2012 Financial aid. Need-based: 1,044 full-time freshmen applied for aid; 867 were judged to have need; 766 of these received aid. Average

scholarship/grant was $10,837; average loan $3,688. 49% of total undergraduate aid awarded as scholarships/grants, 51% as loans/jobs. **Non-need-based:** Awarded to 2,393 full-time undergraduates, including 662 freshmen. Scholarships awarded for academics, alumni affiliation, athletics, leadership, ROTC.

Application procedures. Admission: Priority date 3/1; no deadline. $50 fee, may be waived for applicants with need. Admission notification on a rolling basis beginning on or about 11/1. Must reply by May 1 or within 4 week(s) if notified thereafter. Early application encouraged since available facilities limit enrollment in some programs. **Financial aid:** No deadline. FAFSA required. Applicants notified on a rolling basis starting 3/1; must reply within 4 week(s) of notification.

Academics. Special study options: Accelerated study, combined bachelor's/graduate degree, cooperative education, distance learning, double major, dual enrollment of high school students, ESL, honors, independent study, internships, student-designed major, study abroad. **Credit/placement by examination:** AP, CLEP, IB, SAT, ACT, institutional tests. 30 credit hours maximum toward bachelor's degree. **Support services:** Pre-admission summer program, remedial instruction, study skills assistance, tutoring, writing center.

Majors. Business: Business admin. **Communications:** Communications/speech/rhetoric. **Computer sciences:** General, computer science. **Engineering:** General, aerospace, applied physics, civil, computer, electrical, mechanical, software. **Physical sciences:** Atmospheric science, physics. **Protective services:** Homeland security.

Most popular majors. Engineering/engineering technologies 39%, trade and industry 44%.

Computing on campus. 1,049 workstations in library, computer center. Dormitories wired for high-speed internet access and linked to campus network. Commuter students can connect to campus network. Online library, helpline, student web hosting, wireless network available.

Student life. Freshman orientation: Mandatory. Preregistration for classes offered. **Housing:** Guaranteed on-campus for freshmen. Coed dorms available. $300 nonrefundable deposit, deadline 6/1. Special units available in regular coed dorms. **Activities:** Pep band, campus ministries, choral groups, dance, drama, international student organizations, music ensembles, Model UN, radio station, student government, student newspaper, more than 150 clubs and organizations available.

Athletics. NAIA. **Intercollegiate:** Baseball M, basketball M, cheerleading, cross-country, golf, soccer, tennis, track and field, volleyball W. **Intramural:** Basketball, bowling, football (non-tackle), golf, racquetball, soccer, softball, table tennis, tennis, volleyball. **Team name:** Eagles.

Student services. Alcohol/substance abuse counseling, chaplain/spiritual director, career counseling, student employment services, financial aid counseling, health services, personal counseling, placement for graduates, veterans' counselor, women's services. **Physically disabled:** Services for visually, speech, hearing impaired.

Contact. E-mail: dbadmit@erau.edu
Phone: (386) 226-6100 Toll-free number: (800) 862-2416
Fax: (386) 226-7070
Robert Adams, Director of Admissions, Embry-Riddle Aeronautical University, 600 South Clyde Morris Boulevard, Daytona Beach, FL 32114-3900

Embry-Riddle Aeronautical University: Worldwide Campus
Daytona Beach, Florida
www.embryriddle.edu
CB code: 5036

- Private 4-year university
- Commuter campus in small city
- 10,553 degree-seeking undergraduates: 74% part-time, 12% women, 6% African American, 2% Asian American, 11% Hispanic American, 1% international
- 5,313 degree-seeking graduate students

General. Regionally accredited. Campus is network of more than 150 campuses located in a mixture of military and civilian facilities across the United States, Europe, Asia and the Middle East, with virtual presence via distance learning covering every continent. **Degrees:** 1,993 bachelor's, 462 associate awarded; master's offered. **Calendar:** Semester, extensive summer session. **Full-time faculty:** 130 total; 45% have terminal degrees, 8% minority, 24% women. **Part-time faculty:** 2,520 total; 20% have terminal degrees, 18% minority, 24% women.

Basis for selection. High school GPA, rank in class, and test scores important. Specific requirements vary by degree program.

High school preparation. Required units include English 4, mathematics 3, social studies 2, science 2 (laboratory 1).

2011-2012 Annual costs. Per credit hour charges range from $290 - $335.

2011-2012 Financial aid. Need-based: 22 full-time freshmen applied for aid; 21 were judged to have need; 21 of these received aid. Average scholarship/grant was $4,891; average loan $2,808. 27% of total undergraduate aid awarded as scholarships/grants, 73% as loans/jobs. **Non-need-based:** Scholarships awarded for academics.

Application procedures. Admission: No deadline. $50 fee, may be waived for applicants with need. **Financial aid:** Priority date 4/15; no closing date. FAFSA required. Applicants notified on a rolling basis starting 3/1; must reply within 4 week(s) of notification.

Academics. Special study options: Distance learning. **Credit/placement by examination:** AP, CLEP, institutional tests.

Majors. Business: Business admin.

Most popular majors. Business/marketing 19%, trade and industry 81%.

Contact. E-mail: ecinfo@erau.edu
Phone: (386) 225-6910 Toll-free number: (800) 522-6787
Fax: (386) 226-6984
Linda Dammer, Director of Admissions, Embry-Riddle Aeronautical University: Worldwide Campus, 600 South Clyde Morris Boulevard, Daytona Beach, FL 32114-3900

Everglades University: Boca Raton
Boca Raton, Florida
www.EvergladesUniversity.edu
CB code: 3191

- Private 4-year university
- Commuter campus in small city

General. Regionally accredited. **Calendar:** Semester.

Annual costs/financial aid. Tuition/fees (2011-2012): $16,908. Online courses required fees, $2,000. Books/supplies: $1,125. Need-based financial aid available for full-time students.

Contact. Phone: (561) 912-1211
Director of Admissions, 5002 T-REX Avenue, Suite 100, Boca Raton, FL 33431

Everglades University: Orlando
Altamonte Springs, Florida
www.evergladesuniversity.edu

- Private 4-year branch campus and liberal arts college
- Very large city

General. Regionally accredited. **Calendar:** Differs by program.

Annual costs/financial aid. Tuition/fees (2011-2012): $16,553.

Contact. Phone: (407) 277-0311
887 East Altamonte Drive, Altamonte Springs, FL 32701

Flagler College
Saint Augustine, Florida
www.flagler.edu
CB member
CB code: 5235

- Private 4-year liberal arts college
- Residential campus in large town
- 2,878 degree-seeking undergraduates: 3% part-time, 58% women, 3% African American, 1% Asian American, 7% Hispanic American, 1% Native American, 2% international
- 40% of applicants admitted
- SAT or ACT (ACT writing recommended), application essay required
- 60% graduate within 6 years; 8% enter graduate study

General. Founded in 1968. Regionally accredited. Historic St. Augustine Research Institute is a joint partnership of St. Augustine Foundation, Flagler College and the University of Florida. **Degrees:** 642 bachelor's awarded. **Location:** 35 miles from Jacksonville. **Calendar:** Semester, limited summer session. **Full-time faculty:** 102 total; 71% have terminal degrees, 11% minority, 49% women. **Part-time faculty:** 121 total; 15% have terminal degrees, 7% minority, 43% women. **Class size:** 43% < 20, 57% 20-39, less than 1% 40-49.

Freshman class profile. 3,933 applied, 1,588 admitted, 671 enrolled.

Mid 50% test scores		GPA 2.0-2.99:	21%
SAT critical reading:	530-600	Rank in top quarter:	46%
SAT math:	520-580	Rank in top tenth:	16%
SAT writing:	510-580	End year in good standing:	84%
ACT composite:	22-26	Return as sophomores:	77%
GPA 3.75 or higher:	26%	Out-of-state:	39%
GPA 3.50-3.74:	17%	Live on campus:	94%
GPA 3.0-3.49:	36%	International:	2%

Basis for selection. Academic record, including pattern of courses most important, followed by test scores. Extracurricular activities, recommendations, and intended major also considered. Education applicants must score at or above 45th percentile on SAT or ACT. Interview required for early admission applicants; recommended for all others.

High school preparation. College-preparatory program required. 16 units required; 24 recommended. Required and recommended units include English 4, mathematics 3-4, social studies 3, history 1-2, science 2-3 (laboratory 1-2), foreign language 2, computer science 1, visual/performing arts 1 and academic electives 2.

2011-2012 Annual costs. Tuition/fees: $14,510. Room/board: $7,990. Books/supplies: $1,100. Personal expenses: $2,300.

2011-2012 Financial aid. Need-based: 555 full-time freshmen applied for aid; 397 were judged to have need; 395 of these received aid. Average need met was 60%. Average scholarship/grant was $8,807; average loan $3,223. 49% of total undergraduate aid awarded as scholarships/grants, 51% as loans/jobs. **Non-need-based:** Awarded to 316 full-time undergraduates, including 58 freshmen. Scholarships awarded for academics, art, athletics, job skills, leadership, minority status, music/drama, state residency.

Application procedures. Admission: Priority date 11/1; deadline 3/1 (postmark date). $40 fee, may be waived for applicants with need. Admission notification by 3/30. Must reply by May 1 or within 3 week(s) if notified thereafter. **Financial aid:** Priority date 4/1; no closing date. FAFSA, institutional form required. Applicants notified on a rolling basis starting 4/1; must reply within 2 week(s) of notification.

Academics. Freshmen must earn at least 24 semester hours credit for good academic standing. **Special study options:** Double major, external degree, independent study, internships, liberal arts/career combination, study abroad, teacher certification program. Deaf education majors work directly with faculty and students at nearby Florida School for the Deaf and Blind. **Credit/placement by examination:** AP, CLEP, IB, SAT, ACT. 30 credit hours maximum toward bachelor's degree. **Support services:** Learning center, reduced course load, study skills assistance, tutoring, writing center.

Majors. Area/ethnic studies: Latin American. **Business:** Accounting, business admin. **Communications:** Communications/speech/rhetoric. **Education:** Art, Deaf/hearing impaired, elementary, English, social science, social studies, special ed. **English:** English lit. **Foreign languages:** Spanish. **History:** General. **Human services:** General. **Liberal arts:** Arts/sciences. **Parks/recreation:** Sports admin. **Philosophy/religion:** Philosophy. **Psychology:** General. **Social sciences:** Economics, political science, sociology. **Visual/performing arts:** General, dramatic, studio arts.

Most popular majors. Business/marketing 22%, communications/journalism 13%, education 10%, English 7%, psychology 12%, public administration/social services 7%, social sciences 6%, visual/performing arts 10%.

Computing on campus. 265 workstations in library, computer center, student center. Dormitories wired for high-speed internet access and linked to campus network. Commuter students can connect to campus network. Online course registration, online library, helpline, student web hosting, wireless network available.

Student life. Freshman orientation: Mandatory. Preregistration for classes offered. 3-day program held each semester prior to classes; additional optional summer session. **Policies:** Male-female interdorm visitation not allowed in residence halls. Alcohol prohibited on campus. No smoking in buildings, including residence halls. **Housing:** Guaranteed on-campus for freshmen. Single-sex dorms available. $200 nonrefundable deposit, deadline 5/1. **Activities:** Campus ministries, choral groups, dance, drama, literary magazine, radio station, student government, student newspaper, Rotaract, Intervarsity Christian Fellowship, Catholic College Fellowship, Society for

Advancement of Management, Students in Free Enterprises, deaf awareness club, sport management club, Club Unity.

Athletics. NCAA. **Intercollegiate:** Baseball M, basketball, cross-country, golf, soccer, softball W, tennis, volleyball W. **Intramural:** Badminton, basketball, bowling, football (non-tackle), golf, soccer, softball, table tennis, tennis, volleyball, weight lifting. **Team name:** Saints.

Student services. Career counseling, student employment services, financial aid counseling, health services, personal counseling, veterans' counselor. **Physically disabled:** Services for visually, speech, hearing impaired.

Contact. E-mail: admiss@flagler.edu
Phone: (904) 829-6220 Toll-free number: (800) 304-4208
Fax: (904) 829-6838
Marc Williar, Director of Admissions, Flagler College, 74 King Street, St. Augustine, FL 32084

Florida Agricultural and Mechanical University

Tallahassee, Florida	CB member
www.famu.edu	CB code: 5215

- Public 4-year university
- Residential campus in small city
- 11,027 degree-seeking undergraduates: 8% part-time, 60% women, 95% African American, 1% Asian American, 1% Hispanic American, 1% international
- 1,987 degree-seeking graduate students
- 48% of applicants admitted
- SAT or ACT with writing, application essay required
- 40% graduate within 6 years; 15% enter graduate study

General. Founded in 1887. Regionally accredited. **Degrees:** 1,304 bachelor's, 67 associate awarded; master's, professional, doctoral offered. **ROTC:** Army, Naval, Air Force. **Location:** 169 miles from Jacksonville. **Calendar:** Semester, limited summer session. **Full-time faculty:** 538 total; 75% have terminal degrees, 82% minority, 46% women. **Part-time faculty:** 183 total; 3% have terminal degrees, 73% minority, 45% women. **Class size:** 29% < 20, 38% 20-39, 13% 40-49, 15% 50-99, 4% >100. **Special facilities:** Black archives research center, observatory, fine arts gallery, teaching gymnasium.

Freshman class profile. 7,322 applied, 3,540 admitted, 1,830 enrolled.

Mid 50% test scores		GPA 2.0-2.99:	37%
SAT critical reading:	430-510	Rank in top quarter:	34%
SAT math:	430-520	Rank in top tenth:	10%
SAT writing:	420-500	End year in good standing:	56%
ACT composite:	18-22	Return as sophomores:	79%
GPA 3.75 or higher:	9%	Out-of-state:	20%
GPA 3.50-3.74:	9%	Live on campus:	95%
GPA 3.0-3.49:	45%		

Basis for selection. School achievement record, test scores, recommendations, and essay very important. Audition required of music major applicants. **Home schooled:** Statement describing home school structure and mission, transcript of courses and grades, letter of recommendation (nonparent) required. Applicant may be asked to complete GED. **Learning Disabled:** May seek admission under alternate criteria, by requesting it in writing when applying. Current and appropriate documentation required.

High school preparation. College-preparatory program required. 18 units required. Required units include English 4, mathematics 4, social studies 3, science 3 (laboratory 2), foreign language 2 and academic electives 2.

2011-2012 Annual costs. Tuition/fees: $5,190; $17,130 out-of-state. Room/board: $8,754. Books/supplies: $1,138. Personal expenses: $2,052.

2010-2011 Financial aid. Need-based: 2,092 full-time freshmen applied for aid; 2,058 were judged to have need; 2,058 of these received aid. Average need met was 72%. Average scholarship/grant was $6,643; average loan $3,344. 62% of total undergraduate aid awarded as scholarships/grants, 38% as loans/jobs. **Non-need-based:** Awarded to 2,683 full-time undergraduates, including 961 freshmen. Scholarships awarded for academics, art, athletics, leadership, music/drama, ROTC.

Application procedures. Admission: Closing date 5/15 (receipt date). $30 fee. Admission notification on a rolling basis. **Financial aid:** Priority date 3/1; no closing date. FAFSA required. Applicants notified on a rolling basis starting 4/15.

Academics. Special study options: Accelerated study, combined bachelor's/graduate degree, cooperative education, distance learning, double major,

dual enrollment of high school students, honors, independent study, internships, study abroad, teacher certification program, weekend college. **Credit/placement by examination:** AP, CLEP, IB, SAT, ACT. 30 credit hours maximum toward bachelor's degree. Student must have passing scores (determined by state) for AP and CLEP exams. **Support services:** Learning center, pre-admission summer program, remedial instruction, study skills assistance, tutoring, writing center.

Majors. Architecture: Architecture. **Area/ethnic studies:** African-American. **Biology:** General. **Business:** Accounting, business admin. **Communications:** Journalism, public relations. **Computer sciences:** General, information technology. **Conservation:** Environmental science. **Education:** Early childhood, elementary, English, mathematics, music, physical, science, social science, trade/industrial. **Engineering:** Agricultural, chemical, civil, computer, electrical, industrial, mechanical. **English:** English lit. **General:** Agribusiness operations. **Health services:** Health care admin, medical records admin, nursing (RN), respiratory therapy technology. **History:** General. **Human services:** Social work. **Math:** General. **Physical sciences:** Chemistry, physics. **Protective services:** Criminal justice. **Psychology:** General. **Social sciences:** Economics, political science, sociology. **Visual/performing arts:** Dramatic, graphic design, music, studio arts.

Most popular majors. Business/marketing 14%, communications/journalism 6%, education 6%, health sciences 20%, psychology 6%, security/protective services 10%, social sciences 8%.

Computing on campus. 3,500 workstations in dormitories, library, computer center, student center. Dormitories wired for high-speed internet access and linked to campus network. Commuter students can connect to campus network. Online course registration, online library, helpline, repair service, wireless network available.

Student life. Freshman orientation: Mandatory, $35 fee. Preregistration for classes offered. 2.5 day session in fall. Cost contingent on whether student stays on campus. **Policies:** 2.5 GPA required for membership in social, service, honorary, and professional fraternities and sororities. 2.0 GPA and current enrollment required for active membership status in student organizations. Freshmen not permitted cars on campus. **Housing:** Guaranteed on-campus for freshmen. Coed dorms, single-sex dorms, special housing for disabled, apartments available. $350 partly refundable deposit, deadline 6/1. **Activities:** Bands, campus ministries, choral groups, dance, drama, international student organizations, literary magazine, music ensembles, musical theater, radio station, student government, student newspaper, symphony orchestra, TV station.

Athletics. NCAA. **Intercollegiate:** Baseball M, basketball, bowling W, cheerleading, cross-country, football (tackle) M, golf, softball W, swimming, tennis, track and field, volleyball W. **Intramural:** Badminton, basketball, bowling, cheerleading W, football (non-tackle), football (tackle) M, golf, gymnastics, racquetball, skiing, soccer, softball, swimming, table tennis, tennis, track and field, volleyball, weight lifting, wrestling. **Team name:** Rattlers.

Student services. Adult student services, alcohol/substance abuse counseling, career counseling, services for economically disadvantaged, student employment services, financial aid counseling, health services, minority student services, on-campus daycare, personal counseling, placement for graduates, veterans' counselor, women's services. **Physically disabled:** Services for visually, speech, hearing impaired.

Contact. E-mail: ugrdadmissions@famu.edu
Phone: (850) 599-3796 Toll-free number: (866) 642-1198
Fax: (850) 599-3069
Barbara Cox, Director of Admissions, Florida Agricultural and Mechanical University, Foote-Hilyer Adminstration Center, G-9, Tallahassee, FL 32307-3200

Florida Atlantic University
Boca Raton, Florida **CB member**
www.fau.edu **CB code: 5229**

- Public 4-year university
- Commuter campus in small city
- 23,613 degree-seeking undergraduates: 36% part-time, 57% women, 18% African American, 4% Asian American, 23% Hispanic American, 1% international
- 4,309 degree-seeking graduate students
- 35% of applicants admitted
- SAT or ACT (ACT writing recommended), application essay required
- 42% graduate within 6 years

General. Founded in 1961. Regionally accredited. Courses and degree programs offered at additional sites in Palm Beach, Broward, and St. Lucie counties. **Degrees:** 4,593 bachelor's, 220 associate awarded; master's, professional, doctoral offered. **ROTC:** Army, Air Force. **Location:** 17 miles from Fort Lauderdale. **Calendar:** Semester, extensive summer session. **Full-time faculty:** 800 total; 34% minority, 43% women. **Part-time faculty:** 532 total; 15% minority, 51% women. **Class size:** 29% < 20, 51% 20-39, 7% 40-49, 8% 50-99, 6% >100. **Special facilities:** Environmental center, native fish research center, ocean engineering laboratory, marine research facility, robotics laboratory, harbor branch research.

Freshman class profile. 28,197 applied, 9,805 admitted, 3,347 enrolled.

Mid 50% test scores			
SAT critical reading:	490-570	Rank in top quarter:	38%
SAT math:	490-580	Rank in top tenth:	12%
SAT writing:	480-560	Return as sophomores:	79%
ACT composite:	21-25	Out-of-state:	8%
GPA 3.75 or higher:	22%	Live on campus:	70%
GPA 3.50-3.74:	18%	International:	1%
GPA 3.0-3.49:	52%	Fraternities:	1%
GPA 2.0-2.99:	8%	Sororities:	1%

Basis for selection. Secondary school record, standardized test scores most important. Recommendation, talent, ability also important. Top 20% of state high school graduates guaranteed admission. Audition recommended for theater majors. Portfolio recommended for art majors. **Home schooled:** State high school equivalency certificate required.

High school preparation. College-preparatory program required. 18 units required; 19 recommended. Required and recommended units include English 4, mathematics 3-4, social studies 3, science 3 (laboratory 2), foreign language 2 and academic electives 3.

2011-2012 Annual costs. Tuition/fees: $5,330; $19,715 out-of-state. Room/board: $10,940. Books/supplies: $724. Personal expenses: $1,458.

2011-2012 Financial aid. Need-based: 2,940 full-time freshmen applied for aid; 2,101 were judged to have need; 2,085 of these received aid. Average need met was 65%. Average scholarship/grant was $6,138; average loan $5,025. 46% of total undergraduate aid awarded as scholarships/grants, 54% as loans/jobs. **Non-need-based:** Awarded to 849 full-time undergraduates, including 282 freshmen. Scholarships awarded for academics, athletics, music/drama, state residency.

Application procedures. Admission: Priority date 2/15; deadline 5/1 (receipt date). $30 fee, may be waived for applicants with need. Admission notification on a rolling basis beginning on or about 10/1. Must reply by May 1 or within 2 week(s) if notified thereafter. **Financial aid:** Priority date 3/1; no closing date. FAFSA required. Applicants notified on a rolling basis starting 4/1; must reply within 3 week(s) of notification.

Academics. Special study options: Accelerated study, combined bachelor's/graduate degree, cooperative education, cross-registration, distance learning, double major, dual enrollment of high school students, ESL, honors, independent study, internships, liberal arts/career combination, student-designed major, study abroad, teacher certification program, weekend college. **Credit/placement by examination:** AP, CLEP, IB. 45 credit hours maximum toward bachelor's degree. **Support services:** Learning center, pre-admission summer program, reduced course load, study skills assistance, tutoring, writing center.

Honors college/program. Most applicants have 3.5 GPA, 1280 SAT (exclusive of Writing) or 29 Enhanced ACT. Exceptional applicants who do not meet these criteria may be admitted on individual basis.

Majors. Architecture: Architecture, urban/community planning. **Biology:** General. **Business:** Accounting, business admin, finance, hospitality admin, human resources, international, management information systems, marketing, real estate. **Communications:** Communications/speech/rhetoric, digital media. **Computer sciences:** General. **Education:** General, elementary, English, mathematics, music, science, social science, special ed. **Engineering:** Civil, computer, electrical, mechanical, ocean, surveying. **English:** English lit. **Foreign languages:** French, linguistics, Spanish. **Health services:** Health care admin, nursing (RN). **History:** General. **Human services:** General, social work. **Liberal arts:** Arts/sciences. **Math:** General. **Parks/recreation:** Exercise sciences. **Philosophy/religion:** Judaic, philosophy. **Physical sciences:** Chemistry, geology, physics. **Protective services:** Criminal justice. **Psychology:** General, psychobiology. **Social sciences:** General, anthropology, economics, geography, political science, sociology. **Visual/performing arts:** Art, dramatic, music, music management.

Most popular majors. Biology 6%, business/marketing 26%, education 11%, health sciences 7%, psychology 6%, security/protective services 6%, social sciences 8%.

Computing on campus. 1,000 workstations in dormitories, library, computer center, student center. Dormitories wired for high-speed internet access

and linked to campus network. Commuter students can connect to campus network. Online course registration, online library, helpline, repair service, wireless network available.

Student life. Freshman orientation: Mandatory, $75 fee. Preregistration for classes offered. 2-day session. **Housing:** Guaranteed on-campus for freshmen. Coed dorms, single-sex dorms, apartments available. $200 partly refundable deposit, deadline 8/1. **Activities:** Bands, campus ministries, choral groups, dance, drama, film society, international student organizations, literary magazine, music ensembles, Model UN, musical theater, opera, radio station, student government, student newspaper, symphony orchestra, TV station, Circle K, College Democrats, College Republicans, B'nai B'rith Hillel, Neumann Club, Christian College Fellowship, human rights organization, European student association, NAACP, Peace Finders.

Athletics. NCAA. **Intercollegiate:** Baseball M, basketball, cheerleading, cross-country, football (tackle) M, golf, soccer, softball W, swimming, tennis, track and field W, volleyball W. **Intramural:** Basketball, diving, football (non-tackle), rugby, soccer M, softball, table tennis, volleyball M. **Team name:** Owls.

Student services. Adult student services, alcohol/substance abuse counseling, chaplain/spiritual director, career counseling, student employment services, financial aid counseling, health services, minority student services, on-campus daycare, personal counseling, placement for graduates, veterans' counselor, women's services. **Physically disabled:** Services for visually, speech, hearing impaired.

Contact. E-mail: Admissions@fau.edu
Phone: (561) 297-3040 Toll-free number: (800) 299-4328
Fax: (561) 297-2758
Barbara Pletcher, Director of Admissions, Florida Atlantic University, 777 Glades Road, Boca Raton, FL 33431

Florida Career College: Boynton Beach
Boynton Beach, Florida
www.careercollege.edu

- For-profit 4-year technical and career college
- Small city
- 904 degree-seeking undergraduates

General. Regionally accredited; also accredited by ACICS. **Calendar:** Quarter. **Full-time faculty:** 9 total. **Part-time faculty:** 16 total.

Basis for selection. Open admission.

2011-2012 Annual costs. Tuition ranges from $315 - $485 per credit hour, leading to a diploma, associate or bachelor's degree.

Application procedures. Admission: No deadline. $100 fee.

Academics. Credit/placement by examination: AP, CLEP.

Contact. Lauren Page, Director of Admissions, Florida Career College: Boynton Beach, 1749 North Congress Avenue, Boynton Beach, FL 33426

Florida Career College: Jacksonville
Jacksonville, Florida
www.careercollege.edu

- For-profit 4-year technical and career college
- Very large city
- 1,193 degree-seeking undergraduates

General. Regionally accredited; also accredited by ACICS. **Degrees:** 17 associate awarded. **Calendar:** Quarter. **Full-time faculty:** 10 total. **Part-time faculty:** 20 total.

Basis for selection. Open admission.

2011-2012 Annual costs. Tuition ranges from $315 - $485 per credit hour, leading to a diploma, associate or bachelor's degree.

Application procedures. Admission: No deadline. $100 fee.

Academics. Credit/placement by examination: AP, CLEP.

Contact. Jonathan Martin, Director of Admissions, Florida Career College: Jacksonville, 6600 Youngerman Circle, Jacksonville, FL 32244

Florida Career College: Lauderdale Lakes
Lauderdale Lakes, Florida
www.careercollege.edu

- For-profit 4-year technical and career college
- Large town
- 1,399 degree-seeking undergraduates

General. Accredited by ACICS. **Degrees:** 21 bachelor's, 45 associate awarded. **Calendar:** Quarter. **Full-time faculty:** 14 total. **Part-time faculty:** 18 total.

Basis for selection. Open admission.

2011-2012 Annual costs. Tuition ranges from $315 - $485 per credit hour, leading to a diploma, associate or bachelor's degree.

Application procedures. Admission: No deadline. $100 fee.

Academics. Credit/placement by examination: AP, CLEP.

Contact. Phone: (954) 535-8700
Djenny Narcisse, Associate Director of Admissions, Florida Career College: Lauderdale Lakes, 3383 North State Road 7, Lauderdale Lakes, FL 33319

Florida Career College: Riverview
Riverview, Florida
www.careercollege.edu

- For-profit 4-year technical and career college
- Large town
- 814 degree-seeking undergraduates

General. Regionally accredited; also accredited by ACICS. **Degrees:** 19 associate awarded. **Calendar:** Quarter. **Full-time faculty:** 8 total. **Part-time faculty:** 16 total.

Basis for selection. Open admission.

2011-2012 Annual costs. Tuition ranges from $315 - $485 per credit hour, leading to a diploma, associate or bachelor's degree.

Application procedures. Admission: No deadline. $100 fee.

Academics. Credit/placement by examination: AP, CLEP.

Majors. Business: General.

Contact. Jackie Conte, Director of Admissions, Florida Career College: Riverview, 2662 South Falkenburg Road, Riverview, FL 33578

Florida Christian College
Kissimmee, Florida
www.fcc.edu   CB code: 2167

- Private 4-year Bible and teachers college affiliated with Christian Churches/Churches of Christ
- Residential campus in small city
- 380 degree-seeking undergraduates
- 31% of applicants admitted
- SAT or ACT (ACT writing optional), application essay required

General. Founded in 1975. Candidate for regional accreditation; also accredited by ABHE. **Degrees:** 43 bachelor's, 4 associate awarded. **Location:** 20 miles from Orlando. **Calendar:** Semester, limited summer session. **Full-time faculty:** 12 total. **Part-time faculty:** 27 total. **Class size:** 69% < 20, 24% 20-39, 7% 40-49.

Freshman class profile. 361 applied, 111 admitted, 76 enrolled.

Mid 50% test scores		ACT composite:	17-26
SAT critical reading:	400-620	Out-of-state:	10%
SAT math:	350-520	Live on campus:	84%

Basis for selection. Autobiographical essays, personal recommendation, and church references required. **Home schooled:** State high school equivalency certificate, letter of recommendation (nonparent) required.

2011-2012 Annual costs. Tuition/fees: $12,960. Room only: $2,700. Books/supplies: $850. Personal expenses: $895.

Financial aid. Non-need-based: Scholarships awarded for academics, alumni affiliation, leadership, music/drama, religious affiliation, state residency.

Application procedures. Admission: Priority date 3/1; deadline 5/1 (postmark date). $35 fee, may be waived for applicants with need. Admission notification on a rolling basis. **Financial aid:** Priority date 5/1, closing date 7/15. FAFSA, institutional form required. Applicants notified on a rolling basis starting 3/1.

Academics. Online degree completion students must be 23 years or older and transfer in 60 credits. **Special study options:** Accelerated study, distance learning, dual enrollment of high school students, independent study, internships, student-designed major, teacher certification program. **Credit/placement by examination:** AP, CLEP, IB. 15 credit hours maximum toward associate degree, 30 toward bachelor's. **Support services:** Reduced course load, study skills assistance, tutoring.

Majors. Education: Elementary. **Philosophy/religion:** Philosophy, religion. **Theology:** Bible, missionary, pastoral counseling, sacred music, theology.

Computing on campus. 8 workstations in library, student center. Dormitories wired for high-speed internet access and linked to campus network. Online course registration, online library, helpline, repair service, student web hosting, wireless network available.

Student life. Freshman orientation: Mandatory. Preregistration for classes offered. **Policies:** Spiritual development and community involvement expected; students must attend chapel and small groups (or equivalent) and perform community service projects. Religious observance required. **Housing:** Special housing for disabled, apartments, wellness housing available. $100 fully refundable deposit, deadline 7/15. **Activities:** Choral groups, drama, music ensembles, student government, student newspaper, Christian service activities, mission group.

Athletics. NCCAA. **Intercollegiate:** Basketball M, volleyball W. **Intramural:** Football (non-tackle), racquetball M, soccer, softball, table tennis. **Team name:** Suns.

Student services. Career counseling, financial aid counseling, personal counseling, veterans' counselor. **Physically disabled:** Services for visually impaired.

Contact. E-mail: admissions@fcc.edu
Phone: (407) 569-1172 Toll-free number: (877) 468-6322
Fax: (321) 206-2007
Kellie Spencer, Director of Admission, Florida Christian College, 1011 Bill Beck Boulevard, Kissimmee, FL 34744-4402

Florida College
Temple Terrace, Florida
www.floridacollege.edu
CB code: 5216

- Private 4-year liberal arts college
- Residential campus in large town
- 511 degree-seeking undergraduates: 7% part-time, 52% women, 5% African American, 6% Hispanic American, 1% international
- 94% of applicants admitted
- SAT or ACT (ACT writing optional) required

General. Founded in 1944. Regionally accredited. **Degrees:** 47 bachelor's, 101 associate awarded. **ROTC:** Army, Air Force. **Location:** 2 miles from Tampa. **Calendar:** Semester, limited summer session. **Full-time faculty:** 37 total; 40% have terminal degrees, 3% minority, 19% women. **Part-time faculty:** 21 total; 19% have terminal degrees, 5% minority, 57% women. **Class size:** 75% < 20, 16% 20-39, 8% 40-49, less than 1% 50-99.

Freshman class profile. 378 applied, 356 admitted, 201 enrolled.

Mid 50% test scores			
SAT critical reading:	450-600	GPA 3.0-3.49:	16%
SAT math:	420-570	GPA 2.0-2.99:	42%
ACT composite:	20-26	Out-of-state:	67%
GPA 3.75 or higher:	28%	Live on campus:	95%
GPA 3.50-3.74:	14%	International:	1%

Basis for selection. 2 recommendations, 2.0 GPA required. Test scores, moral character important. Essay required for international students. **Home schooled:** Homeschool completion certification required. **Learning Disabled:** Provide voluntary declaration of disability form and documentation.

High school preparation. 16 units required. Required and recommended units include English 4, mathematics 3, social studies 2-3, science 2 (laboratory 2) and foreign language 2.

2012-2013 Annual costs. Tuition/fees (projected): $13,180. Room/board: $7,550. Books/supplies: $1,300. Personal expenses: $1,500.

2010-2011 Financial aid. Need-based: 170 full-time freshmen applied for aid; 143 were judged to have need; 143 of these received aid. Average need met was 54%. Average scholarship/grant was $5,892; average loan $3,477. 60% of total undergraduate aid awarded as scholarships/grants, 40% as loans/jobs. **Non-need-based:** Awarded to 401 full-time undergraduates, including 162 freshmen. Scholarships awarded for academics, athletics, music/drama, state residency.

Application procedures. Admission: Priority date 4/1; deadline 8/1 (postmark date). $30 fee, may be waived for applicants with need. Admission notification on a rolling basis. **Financial aid:** Closing date 9/30. FAFSA required. Applicants notified on a rolling basis starting 9/30; must reply within 2 week(s) of notification.

Academics. Special study options: Cross-registration, double major, independent study, teacher certification program. **Credit/placement by examination:** AP, CLEP, IB, SAT, ACT, institutional tests. 30 credit hours maximum toward associate degree, 30 toward bachelor's. **Support services:** Reduced course load, remedial instruction, study skills assistance, tutoring, writing center.

Majors. Business: Business admin. **Communications:** General. **Education:** Elementary. **Liberal arts:** Arts/sciences. **Theology:** Bible. **Visual/performing arts:** Music.

Most popular majors. Business/marketing 24%, education 19%, liberal arts 27%, philosophy/religious studies 8%, visual/performing arts 22%.

Computing on campus. 85 workstations in library, computer center. Dormitories wired for high-speed internet access and linked to campus network. Online library, wireless network available.

Student life. Freshman orientation: Mandatory. Preregistration for classes offered. **Policies:** All campus residents expected to attend Sunday worship services. **Housing:** Guaranteed on-campus for all undergraduates. Single-sex dorms, special housing for disabled, wellness housing available. $150 partly refundable deposit, deadline 8/1. **Activities:** Bands, choral groups, drama, literary magazine, music ensembles, musical theater, student government, honor society, social clubs, circle K. sowers club, LOVE.

Athletics. USCAA. **Intercollegiate:** Basketball M, cheerleading M, cross-country, soccer, volleyball W. **Intramural:** Basketball, football (non-tackle), soccer, softball, volleyball. **Team name:** Falcons.

Student services. Career counseling, financial aid counseling, health services, personal counseling, veterans' counselor.

Contact. E-mail: admission@floridacollege.edu
Phone: (813) 988-5131 Toll-free number: (800) 326-7655
Fax: (813) 899-1799
Paul Casebolt, Enrollment Management, Florida College, 119 North Glen Arven Avenue, Temple Terrace, FL 33617

Florida Gulf Coast University
Ft. Myers, Florida
www.fgcu.edu
CB member
CB code: 5221

- Public 4-year university
- Residential campus in small city
- 11,132 degree-seeking undergraduates: 18% part-time, 55% women, 6% African American, 2% Asian American, 17% Hispanic American, 1% international
- 1,091 degree-seeking graduate students
- 68% of applicants admitted
- SAT or ACT with writing required
- 47% graduate within 6 years

General. Regionally accredited. **Degrees:** 1,616 bachelor's, 122 associate awarded; master's, professional offered. **Location:** 100 miles from Tampa, 125 miles from Miami. **Calendar:** Semester, extensive summer session. **Full-time faculty:** 398 total; 74% have terminal degrees, 18% minority, 46% women. **Part-time faculty:** 232 total; 10% minority, 45% women. **Class size:** 21% < 20, 56% 20-39, 9% 40-49, 12% 50-99, 1% >100. **Special facilities:** Natural wetlands, observatory.

Freshman class profile. 9,199 applied, 6,248 admitted, 2,581 enrolled.

Mid 50% test scores		Rank in top quarter:	39%
SAT critical reading:	470-550	Rank in top tenth:	14%
SAT math:	470-550	Return as sophomores:	65%
SAT writing:	450-540	Out-of-state:	7%
ACT composite:	20-23	Live on campus:	72%
GPA 3.75 or higher:	20%	International:	1%
GPA 3.50-3.74:	15%	Fraternities:	10%
GPA 3.0-3.49:	42%	Sororities:	15%
GPA 2.0-2.99:	23%		

Basis for selection. Grades in academic units, test scores very important. **Home schooled:** Transcript of courses and grades required. 1010 SAT (exclusive of Writing) or 21 ACT required.

High school preparation. College-preparatory program recommended. 18 units required. Required units include English 4, mathematics 3, social studies 3, science 3 (laboratory 2), foreign language 2 and academic electives 3.

2011-2012 Annual costs. Tuition/fees: $5,533; $23,166 out-of-state. Room/board: $8,240. Books/supplies: $1,200. Personal expenses: $1,700.

2010-2011 Financial aid. Need-based: 1,893 full-time freshmen applied for aid; 995 were judged to have need; 995 of these received aid. Average need met was 66%. Average scholarship/grant was $5,033; average loan $6,472. 48% of total undergraduate aid awarded as scholarships/grants, 52% as loans/jobs. **Non-need-based:** Awarded to 2,840 full-time undergraduates, including 885 freshmen. Scholarships awarded for academics, alumni affiliation, athletics, leadership, minority status, music/drama, religious affiliation, state residency.

Application procedures. Admission: Priority date 2/15; deadline 5/1 (receipt date). $30 fee, may be waived for applicants with need. Admission notification on a rolling basis. **Financial aid:** Priority date 3/1, closing date 6/30. FAFSA, institutional form required. Applicants notified on a rolling basis starting 2/15.

Academics. Special study options: Accelerated study, combined bachelor's/graduate degree, cross-registration, distance learning, double major, dual enrollment of high school students, honors, independent study, internships, student-designed major, study abroad, teacher certification program, Washington semester. **Credit/placement by examination:** AP, CLEP, IB, SAT, ACT, institutional tests. 45 credit hours maximum toward bachelor's degree. Credit received from one exam program may not be duplicated by another, nor duplicated through dual enrollment credit. **Support services:** Learning center, reduced course load, remedial instruction, study skills assistance, tutoring, writing center.

Majors. Biology: General, biotechnology. **Business:** Accounting, business admin, finance, management information systems, marketing, resort management. **Communications:** Digital media, media studies. **Computer sciences:** General. **Conservation:** Environmental studies, water/wetlands/marine. **Education:** General, early childhood, elementary, special ed. **Engineering:** General, biomedical, civil, environmental. **English:** English lit. **Foreign languages:** Spanish. **Health services:** Athletic training, clinical lab science, community health, health care admin, nursing (RN). **History:** General. **Human services:** Social work. **Liberal arts:** Arts/sciences. **Math:** General. **Parks/recreation:** Exercise sciences. **Philosophy/religion:** Philosophy. **Physical sciences:** Chemistry. **Protective services:** Criminal justice, criminalistics. **Psychology:** General. **Social sciences:** Anthropology, economics, political science, sociology. **Visual/performing arts:** Art, dramatic, music performance.

Most popular majors. Business/marketing 29%, communications/journalism 9%, education 10%, health sciences 8%, psychology 6%, security/protective services 10%.

Computing on campus. 1,029 workstations in dormitories, library, computer center. Dormitories wired for high-speed internet access and linked to campus network. Commuter students can connect to campus network. Online course registration, online library, helpline, student web hosting, wireless network available.

Student life. Freshman orientation: Mandatory, $35 fee. Preregistration for classes offered. Two-day summer program prior to fall semester; families invited. **Policies:** Student code of conduct in effect. **Housing:** Coed dorms, special housing for disabled, apartments, wellness housing available. $50 partly refundable deposit, deadline 4/1. **Activities:** International student organizations, literary magazine, Model UN, student government, student newspaper, College Republicans, College Democrats, Christian Campus Fellowship, Intervarsity Christian Fellowship, Navigators, Colleges Against Cancer, American Association of University Women Student Affiliates, human services student organization.

Athletics. NCAA. **Intercollegiate:** Baseball M, basketball, cross-country, golf, softball W, tennis, volleyball W. **Intramural:** Basketball, cross-country, football (non-tackle), soccer, softball, table tennis, tennis, volleyball, water polo. **Team name:** Eagles.

Student services. Adult student services, alcohol/substance abuse counseling, career counseling, student employment services, financial aid counseling, health services, minority student services, on-campus daycare, personal counseling, placement for graduates, veterans' counselor, women's services. **Physically disabled:** Services for visually, speech, hearing impaired.

Contact. E-mail: admissions@fgcu.edu
Phone: (239) 590-7878 Toll-free number: (888) 889-1095
Fax: (239) 590-7894
Marc Laviolette, Director of Admissions and Records, Florida Gulf Coast University, 10501 FGCU Boulevard South, Ft. Myers, FL 33965-6565

Florida Hospital College of Health Sciences
Orlando, Florida
www.FHCHS.edu
CB code: 3614

- Private 4-year health science and nursing college affiliated with Seventh-day Adventists
- Commuter campus in large city
- 2,515 degree-seeking undergraduates
- 96% of applicants admitted
- Application essay required

General. Regionally accredited. Affiliated with Florida Hospital. **Degrees:** 437 bachelor's, 218 associate awarded; master's offered. **Calendar:** Trimester, limited summer session. **Full-time faculty:** 60 total. **Part-time faculty:** 185 total. **Class size:** 57% < 20, 32% 20-39, 9% 40-49, 2% 50-99. **Special facilities:** Human patient simulators.

Freshman class profile. 262 applied, 252 admitted, 83 enrolled.

Mid 50% test scores		GPA 3.75 or higher:	7%
SAT critical reading:	410-470	GPA 3.50-3.74:	6%
SAT math:	400-490	GPA 3.0-3.49:	39%
ACT composite:	17-20	GPA 2.0-2.99:	48%

Basis for selection. Standard high school diploma from regionally-accredited school required. 2.5 GPA, ACT/SAT and satisfactory recommendations required for general college admission. Professional program admission requirements vary and require essay explaining student's career choice. **Home schooled:** Curriculums must be regionally accredited. Applicants who have completed non-regionally accredited home school programs may submit passing GED scores or complete 12 hours of credit from regionally accredited college with 2.5 GPA.

High school preparation. 21 units recommended. Recommended units include English 4, mathematics 3, social studies 3, history 3, science 3 (laboratory 3) and foreign language 2.

2011-2012 Annual costs. Books/supplies: $1,950. Personal expenses: $1,296.

Financial aid. Non-need-based: Scholarships awarded for state residency.

Application procedures. Admission: Closing date 7/1 (postmark date). $20 fee, may be waived for applicants with need. Admission notification on a rolling basis. Students accepted to professional programs have reply dates in order to claim program seat. **Financial aid:** Priority date 4/12; no closing date. FAFSA, institutional form required. Applicants notified on a rolling basis starting 3/1.

Academics. Special study options: Distance learning, dual enrollment of high school students, independent study. **Credit/placement by examination:** AP, CLEP, SAT, ACT, institutional tests. **Support services:** Learning center, pre-admission summer program, remedial instruction, study skills assistance, tutoring.

Majors. Health services: Nursing (RN), radiologic technology/medical imaging, sonography.

Computing on campus. 45 workstations in dormitories, library, computer center. Commuter students can connect to campus network. Online library, repair service, wireless network available.

Student life. Freshman orientation: Mandatory. Preregistration for classes offered. One-day program. **Policies:** No-use policy for alcohol, drugs, smoking, and illegal substances. **Housing:** Apartments, wellness housing available. $200 fully refundable deposit, deadline 8/4. **Activities:** Campus ministries.

Athletics. Intramural: Basketball, football (non-tackle) M, soccer, volleyball.

Student services. Alcohol/substance abuse counseling, career counseling, student employment services, financial aid counseling, health services, personal counseling. **Physically disabled:** Services for visually, speech, hearing impaired.

Contact. E-mail: katie.shaw@fhchs.edu
Phone: (407) 303-7742 Toll-free number: (800) 500-7747
Fax: (407) 303-9408
Katie Shaw, Director of Admissions, Florida Hospital College of Health Sciences, 671 Winyah Drive, Orlando, FL 32803

Florida Institute of Technology
Melbourne, Florida   **CB member**
www.fit.edu   **CB code: 5080**

- Private 4-year university
- Residential campus in small city
- 5,225 degree-seeking undergraduates: 21% part-time, 47% women, 15% African American, 2% Asian American, 7% Hispanic American, 1% Native American, 14% international
- 3,575 degree-seeking graduate students
- 57% of applicants admitted
- SAT or ACT (ACT writing optional) required
- 56% graduate within 6 years; 38% enter graduate study

General. Founded in 1958. Regionally accredited. **Degrees:** 677 bachelor's, 73 associate awarded; master's, doctoral offered. **ROTC:** Army. **Location:** 76 miles from Orlando. **Calendar:** Semester, limited summer session. **Full-time faculty:** 234 total; 91% have terminal degrees, 14% minority, 24% women. **Part-time faculty:** 382 total; 54% have terminal degrees, 6% minority, 32% women. **Class size:** 54% < 20, 38% 20-39, 3% 40-49, 5% 50-99. **Special facilities:** Botanical garden, center for sports and recreation, center for textile arts, art museum, 0.8-m telescope, center for aviation training and research, center for autism treatment, center for science and engineering.

Freshman class profile. 6,841 applied, 3,925 admitted, 669 enrolled.

Mid 50% test scores		Rank in top tenth:	24%
SAT critical reading:	500-600	End year in good standing:	91%
SAT math:	540-650	Return as sophomores:	80%
ACT composite:	22-28	Out-of-state:	58%
GPA 3.75 or higher:	38%	Live on campus:	78%
GPA 3.50-3.74:	20%	International:	25%
GPA 3.0-3.49:	28%	Fraternities:	23%
GPA 2.0-2.99:	14%	Sororities:	19%
Rank in top quarter:	57%		

Basis for selection. Applications reviewed with reference to specific degree programs or for admission to first-year programs in engineering, science and general studies. High school curriculum, GPA, class rank, SAT/ACT, teachers' recommendations, experiential essay, special classes, clubs or teams that involve research projects/opportunities, and advanced problem-solving techniques important. Interview recommended. **Home schooled:** Transcript of courses and grades required. Self-descriptive 1-page essay, proof of research project participation required. SAT Subject Test strongly recommended (English composition, Math Level II, any sciences related to desired area of study).

High school preparation. College-preparatory program recommended. 16 units required; 22 recommended. Required and recommended units include English 4, mathematics 3-4, social studies 2, history 2, science 3-4 (laboratory 3), foreign language 2, computer science 2 and academic electives 2.

2011-2012 Annual costs. Tuition/fees: $34,990. Room/board: $11,820. Books/supplies: $1,200. Personal expenses: $1,500.

2011-2012 Financial aid. Need-based: 456 full-time freshmen applied for aid; 393 were judged to have need; 393 of these received aid. Average need met was 87%. Average scholarship/grant was $21,141; average loan $3,530. 70% of total undergraduate aid awarded as scholarships/grants, 30% as loans/jobs. **Non-need-based:** Scholarships awarded for academics, alumni affiliation, athletics, ROTC, state residency.

Application procedures. Admission: Priority date 2/1; no deadline. No application fee. Admission notification on a rolling basis beginning on or about 7/1. Must reply by May 1 or within 4 week(s) if notified thereafter. **Financial aid:** Priority date 3/1; no closing date. FAFSA required. Applicants notified on a rolling basis starting 2/15; must reply by 5/1 or within 4 week(s) of notification.

Academics. Special study options: Accelerated study, cooperative education, cross-registration, distance learning, double major, dual enrollment of high school students, ESL, independent study, internships, student-designed major, study abroad, teacher certification program. Dual degrees in computer engineering/electrical engineering, chemical engineering/chemistry, molecular/marine biology. **Credit/placement by examination:** AP, CLEP, IB, institutional tests. **Support services:** Learning center, remedial instruction, study skills assistance, tutoring, writing center.

Majors. Biology: General, aquatic, biochemistry, biomedical sciences, conservation, marine, molecular. **Business:** Accounting, accounting/business management, business admin, e-commerce, international, management information systems, marketing. **Communications:** General. **Computer sciences:** Computer science, information systems. **Conservation:** Environmental science. **Education:** Biology, chemistry, earth science, mathematics, middle, physics, science. **Engineering:** General, aerospace, biomedical, chemical, civil, computer, electrical, mechanical, ocean, software. **Health services:** Health care admin. **Liberal arts:** Humanities. **Math:** General, applied. **Parks/recreation:** Sports admin. **Physical sciences:** General, chemistry, meteorology, oceanography, physics, planetary. **Psychology:** General, forensic.

Most popular majors. Biology 12%, business/marketing 17%, engineering/engineering technologies 36%, physical sciences 7%, trade and industry 10%.

Computing on campus. 415 workstations in library, computer center, student center. Dormitories wired for high-speed internet access and linked to campus network. Commuter students can connect to campus network. Online course registration, online library, helpline, repair service, student web hosting, wireless network available.

Student life. Freshman orientation: Mandatory. Preregistration for classes offered. Three-day program in late August. **Policies:** Function in accordance with written constitution and bylaws approved by Dean of Students. **Housing:** Guaranteed on-campus for freshmen. Coed dorms, apartments, wellness housing available. $200 fully refundable deposit. **Activities:** Bands, campus ministries, choral groups, dance, drama, film society, international student organizations, literary magazine, music ensembles, radio station, student government, student newspaper, TV station, Newman Club, InterVarsity Christian Fellowship, Taiwanese student association, Saudi student house, National Society of Black Engineers, Society of Women Engineers, Korean student association, Caribbean students association, Chinese Student and Scholar Association, Muslim student association.

Athletics. NCAA. **Intercollegiate:** Baseball M, basketball, cross-country, golf, lacrosse M, rowing (crew) W, soccer, softball W, swimming M, tennis, track and field M, volleyball W. **Intramural:** Badminton, basketball, bowling, cricket, football (non-tackle), golf, ice hockey, soccer, softball, tennis, volleyball, water polo, weight lifting. **Team name:** Panthers.

Student services. Alcohol/substance abuse counseling, chaplain/spiritual director, career counseling, student employment services, financial aid counseling, health services, personal counseling, veterans' counselor. **Physically disabled:** Services for visually, speech, hearing impaired.

Contact. E-mail: admission@fit.edu
Phone: (321) 674-8030 Toll-free number: (800) 888-4348
Fax: (321) 674-8004
Michael Perry, Director of Undergraduate Admission, Florida Institute of Technology, 150 West University Boulevard, Melbourne, FL 32901-6975

Florida International University
Miami, Florida   **CB member**
www.fiu.edu   **CB code: 5206**

- Public 4-year university
- Commuter campus in very large city
- 35,006 degree-seeking undergraduates: 35% part-time, 55% women, 12% African American, 3% Asian American, 66% Hispanic American, 5% international
- 8,283 degree-seeking graduate students
- 39% of applicants admitted
- SAT or ACT (ACT writing optional) required
- 43% graduate within 6 years

General. Founded in 1965. Regionally accredited. **Degrees:** 7,077 bachelor's, 54 associate awarded; master's, professional, doctoral offered. **ROTC:** Army, Air Force. **Location:** 10 miles from downtown. **Calendar:** Semester, extensive summer session. **Full-time faculty:** 941 total; 90% have terminal degrees, 35% minority, 38% women. **Part-time faculty:** 842 total; 45% have terminal degrees, 46% minority, 52% women. **Class size:** 18% < 20, 46% 20-39, 14% 40-49, 16% 50-99, 7% >100. **Special facilities:** Nature preserve.

Freshman class profile. 16,626 applied, 6,545 admitted, 2,607 enrolled.

Mid 50% test scores			
SAT critical reading:	530-600	GPA 2.0-2.99:	4%
SAT math:	530-610	Rank in top quarter:	48%
SAT writing:	520-590	Rank in top tenth:	19%
ACT composite:	24-27	End year in good standing:	82%
GPA 3.75 or higher:	46%	Return as sophomores:	82%
GPA 3.50-3.74:	25%	Out-of-state:	4%
GPA 3.0-3.49:	25%	Live on campus:	20%
		International:	3%

Basis for selection. School record, class rank, GPA and test scores most important. SAT Subject Tests recommended. Audition required of music performance and theater majors. Portfolio required of art and architecture majors. Interview and essay recommended for academically marginal applicants. **Home schooled:** State high school equivalency certificate required. GED required if equivalency certificate is not available. **Learning Disabled:** The Florida International University Disability Resource Center will provide assistance to applicants with disabilities who do not meet standard admission criteria by seeking admission consideration based on disability when appropriate.

High school preparation. College-preparatory program required. 18 units required. Required units include English 4, mathematics 4, social studies 3, science 3 (laboratory 2), foreign language 2 and academic electives 2.

2011-2012 Annual costs. Tuition/fees: $5,678; $18,077 out-of-state. Room/board: $11,330.

2010-2011 Financial aid. Need-based: 2,991 full-time freshmen applied for aid; 2,932 were judged to have need; 2,892 of these received aid. Average need met was 21%. Average scholarship/grant was $7,018; average loan $8,654. 51% of total undergraduate aid awarded as scholarships/grants, 49% as loans/jobs. **Non-need-based:** Awarded to 8,065 full-time undergraduates, including 3,368 freshmen. Scholarships awarded for academics, art, athletics, minority status, music/drama, state residency.

Application procedures. Admission: Priority date 12/1; deadline 5/1 (receipt date). $30 fee, may be waived for applicants with need. Application must be submitted online. Admission notification on a rolling basis beginning on or about 1/16. Must reply by May 1 or within 2 week(s) if notified thereafter. **Financial aid:** Priority date 3/1, closing date 5/15. FAFSA required. Applicants notified on a rolling basis; must reply by 5/1 or within 4 week(s) of notification.

Academics. Special study options: Accelerated study, combined bachelor's/graduate degree, cooperative education, distance learning, double major, dual enrollment of high school students, exchange student, honors, independent study, internships, study abroad, teacher certification program, weekend college. **Credit/placement by examination:** AP, CLEP, IB, SAT, ACT, institutional tests. **Support services:** Learning center, pre-admission summer program, study skills assistance, tutoring.

Honors college/program. 3.5 weighted GPA and 1850 SAT/28 ACT required.

Majors. Area/ethnic studies: Asian, women's. **Biology:** General, marine. **Business:** Accounting, business admin, finance, hospitality admin, human resources, international, management information systems, marketing, real estate. **Communications:** Communications/speech/rhetoric, media studies. **Computer sciences:** General, information technology. **Conservation:** Environmental studies. **Education:** Art, early childhood, elementary, physical, special ed. **Engineering:** Biomedical, civil, computer, electrical, environmental, mechanical. **English:** English lit. **Foreign languages:** French, Portuguese, Spanish. **Health services:** Dietetics, health care admin, nursing (RN). **History:** General. **Human services:** General, social work. **Liberal arts:** Arts/sciences. **Math:** General, statistics. **Parks/recreation:** Facilities management. **Philosophy/religion:** Philosophy, religion. **Physical sciences:** Chemistry, geology, physics. **Protective services:** Criminal justice. **Psychology:** General. **Social sciences:** Economics, geography, international relations, political science, sociology. **Visual/performing arts:** Art, art history/conservation, dramatic, music, studio arts.

Most popular majors. Business/marketing 35%, engineering/engineering technologies 6%, psychology 8%, social sciences 8%.

Computing on campus. Dormitories wired for high-speed internet access and linked to campus network. Commuter students can connect to campus network. Online course registration, online library, helpline, repair service, wireless network available.

Student life. Freshman orientation: Mandatory, $90 fee. Preregistration for classes offered. Two-day overnight program. **Housing:** Coed dorms, apartments, fraternity/sorority housing available. $100 nonrefundable deposit. **Activities:** Bands, campus ministries, choral groups, drama, international student organizations, music ensembles, Model UN, opera, radio station, student government, student newspaper, symphony orchestra, over 150 student organizations available.

Athletics. NCAA. **Intercollegiate:** Baseball M, basketball, cross-country, diving W, football (tackle) M, golf W, soccer, softball, swimming W, tennis W, track and field, volleyball W. **Intramural:** Badminton, basketball, cross-country, football (non-tackle), golf W, racquetball, sailing, soccer, softball, swimming, table tennis, tennis, volleyball, weight lifting. **Team name:** Golden Panthers.

Student services. Adult student services, alcohol/substance abuse counseling, career counseling, student employment services, financial aid counseling, health services, minority student services, on-campus daycare, personal counseling, placement for graduates, veterans' counselor, women's services. **Physically disabled:** Services for visually, speech, hearing impaired.

Contact. E-mail: admiss@fiu.edu
Phone: (305) 348-2363 Fax: (305) 348-3648
Barry Taylor, Director, Florida International University, Modesto Maidique Campus, PC 140, Miami, FL 33199

Florida Memorial University
Miami Gardens, Florida **CB member**
www.fmuniv.edu **CB code: 5217**

♦ Private 4-year liberal arts college affiliated with American Baptist Churches in the USA
♦ Residential campus in very large city

General. Founded in 1879. Regionally accredited. **Location:** 15 miles from downtown Miami. **Calendar:** Semester.

Annual costs/financial aid. Tuition/fees (2011-2012): $14,604. Room/board: $6,112. Books/supplies: $1,500. Personal expenses: $3,500. Need-based financial aid available to full-time and part-time students.

Contact. Phone: (305) 626-3750
Director of Admissions, 15800 NW 42nd Avenue, Miami Gardens, FL 33054

Florida Southern College
Lakeland, Florida **CB member**
www.flsouthern.edu **CB code: 5218**

♦ Private 4-year liberal arts college affiliated with United Methodist Church
♦ Residential campus in small city
♦ 2,029 degree-seeking undergraduates: 1% part-time, 58% women, 6% African American, 2% Asian American, 8% Hispanic American, 1% Native American, 4% international
♦ 179 degree-seeking graduate students
♦ 65% of applicants admitted
♦ SAT or ACT (ACT writing optional), application essay required
♦ 55% graduate within 6 years; 27% enter graduate study

General. Founded in 1885. Regionally accredited. The campus also is home to the Roberts Center for Learning and Literacy and the Roberts Academy, a transitional school for gifted elementary-age students with dyslexia. **Degrees:** 478 bachelor's awarded; master's offered. **ROTC:** Army, Air Force. **Location:** 30 miles from Tampa, 40 miles from Orlando. **Calendar:** Semester, limited summer session. **Full-time faculty:** 116 total; 84% have terminal degrees, 16% minority, 42% women. **Part-time faculty:** 107 total; 19% have terminal degrees, 8% minority, 56% women. **Class size:** 50% < 20, 46% 20-39, 4% 40-49. **Special facilities:** Technology center.

Freshman class profile. 3,159 applied, 2,056 admitted, 525 enrolled.

Mid 50% test scores			
SAT critical reading:	490-590	Rank in top quarter:	51%
SAT math:	500-590	Rank in top tenth:	22%
SAT writing:	470-570	End year in good standing:	90%
ACT composite:	22-27	Return as sophomores:	77%
GPA 3.75 or higher:	37%	Out-of-state:	40%
GPA 3.50-3.74:	14%	Live on campus:	90%
GPA 3.0-3.49:	33%	International:	3%
GPA 2.0-2.99:	16%	Fraternities:	17%
		Sororities:	22%

Basis for selection. School achievement record most important, followed by test scores and recommendations. Character and motivation, demonstrated leadership and/or service, and extracurricular activities also important. Interview recommended. Audition required for music; audition recommended (required for scholarship consideration) for theater majors. Portfolio recommended (required for scholarship consideration) for art majors. **Home schooled:** Transcript of courses and grades required.

High school preparation. College-preparatory program required. 18 units required. Required and recommended units include English 4, mathematics 3, social studies 3, history 3, science 2 (laboratory 2), foreign language 2 and academic electives 1.

2011-2012 Annual costs. Tuition/fees: $26,112. Room/board: $8,808. Books/supplies: $1,150. Personal expenses: $1,180.

2011-2012 Financial aid. Need-based: 488 full-time freshmen applied for aid; 401 were judged to have need; 401 of these received aid. Average need met was 73%. Average scholarship/grant was $8,206; average loan $3,456. 69% of total undergraduate aid awarded as scholarships/grants, 31% as loans/jobs. **Non-need-based:** Awarded to 2,086 full-time undergraduates, including 579 freshmen. Scholarships awarded for academics, alumni affiliation, art, athletics, job skills, leadership, minority status, music/drama, religious affiliation, ROTC, state residency.

Application procedures. Admission: Priority date 3/1; no deadline. $30 fee, may be waived for applicants with need. Admission notification on a rolling basis beginning on or about 1/15. Must reply by May 1 or within 2 week(s) if notified thereafter. Housing deposit refundable through 5/1. **Financial aid:** Priority date 3/1, closing date 7/1. FAFSA, institutional form required. Applicants notified on a rolling basis starting 3/1; must reply within 3 week(s) of notification.

Academics. Special study options: Accelerated study, double major, dual enrollment of high school students, external degree, honors, independent study, internships, liberal arts/career combination, New York semester, student-designed major, study abroad, teacher certification program, United Nations semester, Washington semester. 3-2 Business Administration/MBA program and Pre-Med Honor's Program with USF. **Credit/placement by examination:** AP, CLEP, IB, SAT, ACT. 60 credit hours maximum toward bachelor's degree. **Support services:** Pre-admission summer program, reduced course load, study skills assistance, tutoring, writing center.

Majors. Biology: General, Biochemistry/molecular biology. **Business:** Accounting, business admin. **Communications:** Communications/speech/rhetoric, persuasive communications. **Computer sciences:** Computer science. **Conservation:** Environmental studies. **Education:** Art, elementary, music, physical. **English:** Creative writing, English lit. **Foreign languages:** Spanish. **General:** Business, landscaping, turf management. **Health services:** Athletic training, nursing (RN), predental, premedicine, preveterinary. **History:** General. **Liberal arts:** Humanities. **Math:** General. **Parks/recreation:** Exercise sciences. **Philosophy/religion:** Philosophy, religion. **Physical sciences:** Chemistry. **Psychology:** General. **Social sciences:** General, criminology, economics, political science, sociology. **Theology:** Youth ministry. **Visual/performing arts:** Art history/conservation, dramatic, graphic design, music, music management, music theory/composition, studio arts, theater design.

Most popular majors. Biology 6%, business/marketing 22%, communications/journalism 8%, education 12%, health sciences 12%, psychology 7%, social sciences 11%, visual/performing arts 8%.

Computing on campus. 435 workstations in dormitories, library, computer center. Dormitories wired for high-speed internet access and linked to campus network. Commuter students can connect to campus network. Online course registration, online library, helpline, wireless network available.

Student life. Freshman orientation: Mandatory, $100 fee. Preregistration for classes offered. Four-day program held prior to start of Fall classes. **Housing:** Guaranteed on-campus for all undergraduates. Coed dorms, single-sex dorms, special housing for disabled, apartments, fraternity/sorority housing, wellness housing available. $500 fully refundable deposit, deadline 5/1. Second Year Experience. **Activities:** Bands, campus ministries, choral groups, dance, drama, international student organizations, literary magazine, music ensembles, musical theater, opera, student government, student newspaper, symphony orchestra, TV station, Wesley Fellowship, Fellowship of Christian Athletes, Beyond Campus Ministries, TZeDeK, Shalom Friends, Sandwich Ministry to the homeless, multicultural student council, Catholic Student Ministries, Student Organization of Latinos.

Athletics. NCAA. **Intercollegiate:** Baseball M, basketball, cross-country, golf, lacrosse, soccer, softball W, swimming, tennis, track and field, volleyball W. **Intramural:** Basketball, bowling, field hockey, football (non-tackle), soccer, softball, swimming, tennis, volleyball. **Team name:** Moccasins.

Student services. Adult student services, alcohol/substance abuse counseling, chaplain/spiritual director, career counseling, student employment services, financial aid counseling, health services, minority student services, personal counseling, placement for graduates.

Contact. E-mail: fscadm@flsouthern.edu
Phone: (863) 680-4131 Toll-free number: (800) 274-4131
Fax: (863) 680-4120
Erin Ervin, Director of Admission, Florida Southern College, 111 Lake Hollingsworth Drive, Lakeland, FL 33801-5698

Florida State University
Tallahassee, Florida
www.fsu.edu

CB member
CB code: 5219

- Public 4-year university
- Residential campus in small city
- 31,594 degree-seeking undergraduates: 10% part-time, 55% women, 10% African American, 4% Asian American, 14% Hispanic American, 1% Native American, 1% international
- 8,466 degree-seeking graduate students
- 58% of applicants admitted
- SAT or ACT with writing, application essay required
- 74% graduate within 6 years

General. Founded in 1851. Regionally accredited. **Degrees:** 7,886 bachelor's awarded; master's, professional, doctoral offered. **ROTC:** Army, Naval, Air Force. **Location:** 191 miles from Pensacola, 163 miles from Jacksonville. **Calendar:** Semester, extensive summer session. **Full-time faculty:** 1,248 total; 92% have terminal degrees, 16% minority, 37% women. **Part-time faculty:** 366 total; 92% have terminal degrees, 12% minority, 54% women. **Special facilities:** Marine laboratory/aquarium, institute of molecular biophysics, national high magnetic field laboratory, music research center, accelerator, oceanographic institute, planetarium, reservation, golf course, Middle East center, institute of science and public affairs, center for the advancement of human rights.

Freshman class profile. 28,313 applied, 16,561 admitted, 6,145 enrolled.

Mid 50% test scores			
SAT critical reading:	550-650	Rank in top quarter:	76%
SAT math:	560-640	Rank in top tenth:	39%
ACT composite:	25-28	Return as sophomores:	93%
GPA 3.75 or higher:	53%	Out-of-state:	11%
GPA 3.50-3.74:	28%	Live on campus:	71%
GPA 3.0-3.49:	18%	Fraternities:	5%
GPA 2.0-2.99:	1%	Sororities:	8%

Basis for selection. Most Florida residents accepted have B+ average in academic subjects and 1100 SAT (exclusive of Writing) or 24 ACT. Out-of-state students must meet higher standards. Audition required of music, dance, BFA theater majors. Portfolio required of BFA art, interior design majors. Departmental application required for motion picture, television, and recording art programs. **Home schooled:** Statement describing home school structure and mission, transcript of courses and grades required. Must provide detailed course syllabi with complete course description and names of textbooks used.

High school preparation. 19 units required; 23 recommended. Required and recommended units include English 4, mathematics 4, social studies 1-2, history 2, science 3-4 (laboratory 2), foreign language 2-4 and academic electives 3. Math courses must be algebra I and above; 2 units of same foreign language required; at least 3 units English with substantial writing requirements; social studies must include history. Additional consideration given for completion of higher level courses (AP, IB, honors, dual enrollment, calculus and/or foreign language IV or V) and for completion of 4 or more senior academic courses.

2011-2012 Annual costs. Tuition/fees: $5,825; $20,992 out-of-state. Room/board: $8,900. Books/supplies: $1,000. Personal expenses: $3,462.

Financial aid. Non-need-based: Scholarships awarded for academics, athletics, state residency.

Application procedures. Admission: Priority date 10/17; deadline 1/18 (receipt date). $30 fee. Application must be submitted online. Notification on 12/14 and 3/21. Must reply by May 1 or within 2 week(s) if notified thereafter. Those applying before 10/17 who are denied admission are given additional opportunities to improve application standing. **Financial aid:** No deadline. FAFSA required. Applicants notified on a rolling basis starting 3/15.

Academics. 2+2 distance learning available in cooperation with selected Florida community colleges includes programs in computer science, interdisciplinary social sciences, and nursing (RN to BSN). **Special study options:** Accelerated study, combined bachelor's/graduate degree, cooperative education, cross-registration, distance learning, double major, dual enrollment of high school students, ESL, honors, independent study, internships, study abroad, teacher certification program. Cooperative programs with Florida Agricultural and Mechanical University and Tallahassee Community College; degree in three years; International year abroad, year-round study abroad in England, Italy, Panama, Spain; summer study abroad in Australia, Brazil, China, Costa Rica, Croatia, Czech Republic, Ecuador, England, France, Ireland, Italy, Japan, Netherlands, Russia, Switzerland. **Credit/placement by examination:** AP, CLEP, IB, SAT, ACT, institutional tests. 30 credit hours maximum toward associate degree, 45 toward bachelor's. English AP credit

not awarded for more than 1 exam. **Support services:** Learning center, reduced course load, study skills assistance, tutoring, writing center.

Majors. Area/ethnic studies: Asian, Russian/Eastern European/Eurasian, Russian/Slavic. **Biology:** General, biochemistry. **Business:** Accounting, actuarial science, business admin, finance, hospitality admin, human resources, insurance, international, management information systems, marketing, real estate. **Communications:** Advertising, public relations. **Computer sciences:** General, computer science, information technology. **Conservation:** Environmental studies. **Education:** Early childhood, elementary, English, music, physics, social science. **Engineering:** Chemical, civil, computer, electrical, environmental, industrial, materials, mechanical, software. **English:** Creative writing. **Foreign languages:** Ancient Greek, Chinese, French, German, Italian, Japanese, Latin, Russian, Spanish. **Health services:** Athletic training, audiology/speech pathology, dietetics, music therapy, nursing (RN), predental, premedicine, prepharmacy, preveterinary. **History:** General. **Human services:** Social work. **Liberal arts:** Humanities. **Math:** General, applied, computational, statistics. **Parks/recreation:** Facilities management, sports admin. **Philosophy/religion:** Philosophy, religion. **Physical sciences:** Atmospheric science, chemistry, physics. **Psychology:** General. **Social sciences:** General, applied economics, criminology, economics, geography, international relations, political science, sociology. **Visual/performing arts:** Acting, art history/conservation, cinematography, dance, dramatic, interior design, jazz, music, music theory/composition, piano/keyboard, stringed instruments, studio arts, theater design, voice/opera. **Work/family studies:** Merchandising.

Most popular majors. Business/marketing 20%, education 6%, family/consumer sciences 6%, social sciences 19%.

Computing on campus. PC or laptop required. 2,958 workstations in dormitories, library, computer center, student center. Dormitories wired for high-speed internet access and linked to campus network. Commuter students can connect to campus network. Online course registration, online library, helpline, repair service, student web hosting, wireless network available.

Student life. Freshman orientation: Mandatory, $90 fee. Preregistration for classes offered. Held during Summer. **Housing:** Coed dorms, single-sex dorms, special housing for disabled, apartments, fraternity/sorority housing, wellness housing available. $225 partly refundable deposit. Honor residences and living and learning communities available. **Activities:** Bands, campus ministries, choral groups, dance, drama, film society, literary magazine, music ensembles, musical theater, opera, radio station, student government, student newspaper, symphony orchestra, TV station, Hillel, Christian student association, Catholic student union, Campus Crusade for Christ, College Democrats, College Republicans, black student union, Hispanic student union, American civil liberties union.

Athletics. NCAA. **Intercollegiate:** Baseball M, basketball, cheerleading, cross-country, diving, football (tackle) M, golf, soccer W, softball W, swimming, tennis, track and field, volleyball W. **Intramural:** Basketball, bowling, field hockey, football (non-tackle), golf, racquetball, soccer, softball, swimming, table tennis, tennis, volleyball, wrestling. **Team name:** Seminoles.

Student services. Adult student services, alcohol/substance abuse counseling, career counseling, student employment services, financial aid counseling, health services, legal services, minority student services, on-campus daycare, personal counseling, placement for graduates, veterans' counselor, women's services. **Physically disabled:** Services for visually, speech, hearing impaired.

Contact. E-mail: admissions@admin.fsu.edu
Phone: (850) 644-6200 Fax: (850) 644-0197
Janice Finney, Director of Admissions, Florida State University, PO Box 3062400, Tallahassee, FL 32306-2400

Full Sail University
Winter Park, Florida
www.fullsail.edu   CB code: 3164

- For-profit 4-year visual arts and music college
- Commuter campus in very large city

General. Accredited by ACCSCT. **Location:** 8 miles from Orlando. **Calendar:** Differs by program.

Annual costs/financial aid. Tuition ranges from $29,500-$75,775 for the entire degree, including all books, lab fees, and other educational charges. Need-based financial aid available for full-time students.

Contact. Phone: (407) 679-6333
Vice President of Admissions, 3300 University Boulevard, Winter Park, FL 32792-7429

Hobe Sound Bible College
Hobe Sound, Florida
www.hsbc.edu   CB code: 5306

- Private 4-year Bible college affiliated with interdenominational tradition
- Residential campus in small town
- 291 degree-seeking undergraduates
- SAT or ACT (ACT writing optional) required

General. Founded in 1960. Accredited by ABHE. **Degrees:** 10 bachelor's, 5 associate awarded. **Location:** 25 miles from West Palm Beach. **Calendar:** 4-1-4, limited summer session. **Full-time faculty:** 5 total. **Part-time faculty:** 9 total.

Basis for selection. Recommendations, essay, religious commitment important. **Home schooled:** Must submit official transcripts from reputable organizations documenting completion of all academic coursework required for high school diploma.

2011-2012 Annual costs. Tuition/fees: $5,440. Room/board: $4,840. Books/supplies: $450. Personal expenses: $2,000.

Financial aid. Non-need-based: Scholarships awarded for academics, leadership.

Application procedures. Admission: Closing date 8/25. $25 fee, may be waived for applicants with need. Admission notification on a rolling basis beginning on or about 3/1. **Financial aid:** Closing date 8/1. FAFSA required.

Academics. Double major required of all students in 4-year programs. All students complete major in Bible as well as major in Christian vocational field. **Special study options:** Distance learning, double major, dual enrollment of high school students, ESL, external degree, internships, teacher certification program. **Credit/placement by examination:** AP, CLEP, institutional tests. **Support services:** Reduced course load, remedial instruction.

Majors. Education: Elementary, English, mathematics, music. **Philosophy/religion:** Religion. **Theology:** Bible, missionary, sacred music, theology. **Visual/performing arts:** Music performance, piano/keyboard.

Computing on campus. 10 workstations in computer center.

Student life. Freshman orientation: Mandatory. Preregistration for classes offered. **Policies:** Religious observance required. **Housing:** Guaranteed on-campus for all undergraduates. Single-sex dorms, apartments available. Unmarried students under 25 required to live in campus dormitories or with parents. **Activities:** Concert band, choral groups, music ensembles, student government, Christian service organizations.

Athletics. Intramural: Basketball, football (tackle) M, racquetball, soccer, softball, tennis, volleyball.

Student services. Health services, personal counseling.

Contact. E-mail: admissions@hsbc.edu
Phone: (772) 546-5534 ext. 1015 Toll-free number: (800) 881-5534
Fax: (772) 545-1422
Joanna Wetherald, Director of Admissions, Hobe Sound Bible College, Box 1065, Hobe Sound, FL 33475

Hodges University
Naples, Florida
www.hodges.edu   CB code: 5307

- Private 4-year university and business college
- Commuter campus in small city
- 2,158 degree-seeking undergraduates: 28% part-time, 67% women, 16% African American, 1% Asian American, 34% Hispanic American
- 267 degree-seeking graduate students
- 78% of applicants admitted

General. Founded in 1990. Regionally accredited. **Degrees:** 303 bachelor's, 202 associate awarded; master's offered. **Location:** 110 miles from Miami, 180 miles from Tampa. **Calendar:** Trimester, extensive summer session. **Full-time faculty:** 92 total; 50% have terminal degrees, 9% minority, 54% women. **Part-time faculty:** 76 total; 37% have terminal degrees, 21% minority, 50% women. **Class size:** 83% < 20, 17% 20-39.

Freshman class profile. 217 applied, 170 admitted, 162 enrolled.

Basis for selection. Essay and interview important; level of interest very important.

2011-2012 Annual costs. Tuition/fees: $14,600. Books/supplies: $1,200. Personal expenses: $2,144.

2011-2012 Financial aid. Need-based: 128 full-time freshmen applied for aid; 116 were judged to have need; 116 of these received aid. Average need met was 64%. Average scholarship/grant was $2,765; average loan $2,785. 2% of total undergraduate aid awarded as scholarships/grants, 98% as loans/jobs. **Non-need-based:** Awarded to 1,000 full-time undergraduates, including 126 freshmen. Scholarships awarded for academics.

Application procedures. Admission: No deadline. $20 fee. Admission notification on a rolling basis. **Financial aid:** Priority date 8/15; no closing date. FAFSA required. Applicants notified on a rolling basis starting 7/7.

Academics. Special study options: Accelerated study, cooperative education, distance learning, double major, ESL, independent study, internships, weekend college. **Credit/placement by examination:** AP, CLEP, IB, institutional tests. **Support services:** Remedial instruction, tutoring.

Majors. Business: Accounting, business admin. **Computer sciences:** Information technology. **Health services:** Health care admin. **Protective services:** Criminal justice.

Most popular majors. Business/marketing 49%, health sciences 18%, interdisciplinary studies 15%, legal studies 6%.

Computing on campus. 500 workstations in library, computer center. Wireless network available.

Student life. Freshman orientation: Mandatory. Preregistration for classes offered. **Activities:** Literary magazine.

Student services. Career counseling, financial aid counseling, personal counseling, placement for graduates.

Contact. E-mail: admit@hodges.edu
Phone: (239) 513-1122 Toll-free number: (800) 466-8017
Fax: (239) 513-9071
Rita Lampus, Vice President of Student Enrollment Management, Hodges University, 2655 Northbrooke Drive, Naples, FL 34119

International Academy of Design and Technology: Orlando
Orlando, Florida
www.iadt.edu   CB code: 4366

▸ For-profit 4-year career college
▸ Very large city
▸ 968 degree-seeking undergraduates

General. Accredited by ACICS. **Degrees:** 271 bachelor's, 112 associate awarded. **Location:** Downtown. **Calendar:** Quarter, extensive summer session. **Full-time faculty:** 10 total. **Part-time faculty:** 85 total.

Basis for selection. Open admission.

Application procedures. Admission: No deadline. $50 fee. **Financial aid:** No deadline. FAFSA required.

Academics. Special study options: Accelerated study. **Credit/placement by examination:** AP, CLEP. **Support services:** Learning center, remedial instruction, tutoring.

Majors. Business: Fashion, marketing. **Computer sciences:** Computer graphics, webmaster. **Visual/performing arts:** Game design, interior design.

Computing on campus. Online course registration, online library available.

Student life. Freshman orientation: Mandatory. Preregistration for classes offered.

Contact. Phone: (407) 857-2300
Dawn Wolff, Director of Admissions, International Academy of Design and Technology: Orlando, 6039 S Rio Grande Avenue, Orlando, FL 32809

International Academy of Design and Technology: Tampa
Tampa, Florida
www.academy.edu   CB code: 7114

▸ For-profit 4-year visual arts and technical college
▸ Commuter campus in very large city

General. Accredited by ACICS. **Calendar:** Quarter.

Annual costs/financial aid. Tuition/fees (2011-2012): $17,375. Need-based financial aid available to full-time and part-time students.

Contact. Phone: (813) 881-0007
Vice President of Admissions and Marketing, 5104 Eisenhower Boulevard, Tampa, FL 33634

ITT Technical Institute: Ft. Lauderdale
Ft. Lauderdale, Florida
www.itt-tech.edu   CB code: 2700

▸ For-profit 4-year technical college
▸ Commuter campus in small city
▸ 830 degree-seeking undergraduates
▸ Interview required

General. Accredited by ACICS. **Degrees:** 44 bachelor's, 210 associate awarded. **Calendar:** Quarter, extensive summer session. **Full-time faculty:** 13 total. **Part-time faculty:** 74 total.

Basis for selection. Satisfactory scores from on-site tests in English and mathematics required.

2011-2012 Annual costs. Estimated costs as of June 2011: per-credit-hour charge, $493, depending upon level and course of study; academic fee, $200. Certain programs of study require purchase of tools, which could cost an additional $100 to $655. All costs are subject to change.

Application procedures. Admission: No deadline. $100 fee. Admission notification on a rolling basis. **Financial aid:** No deadline. FAFSA, institutional form required. Applicants notified on a rolling basis.

Academics. Credit/placement by examination: AP, CLEP. **Support services:** Learning center, tutoring.

Majors. Business: Business admin, construction management. **Computer sciences:** Security. **Protective services:** Law enforcement admin.

Computing on campus. Online library available.

Student life. Freshman orientation: Available. Preregistration for classes offered.

Student services. Career counseling, student employment services, placement for graduates.

Contact. Phone: (954) 476-9300 Toll-free number: (800) 488-7797
Britt Carpenter, Director of Recruitment, ITT Technical Institute: Ft. Lauderdale, 3401 South University Drive, Ft. Lauderdale, FL 33328

ITT Technical Institute: Jacksonville
Jacksonville, Florida
www.itt-tech.edu   CB code: 2716

▸ For-profit 4-year technical college
▸ Commuter campus in very large city
▸ 700 degree-seeking undergraduates
▸ Interview required

General. Accredited by ACICS. **Degrees:** 37 bachelor's, 136 associate awarded. **Calendar:** Quarter, extensive summer session. **Full-time faculty:** 9 total. **Part-time faculty:** 656 total.

Basis for selection. Satisfactory scores from on-site tests in English and mathematics required.

2011-2012 Annual costs. Estimated costs as of June 2011: per-credit-hour charge, $493, depending upon level and course of study; academic fee,

$200. Certain programs of study require purchase of tools, which could cost an additional $100 to $655. All costs are subject to change.

Application procedures. Admission: No deadline. No application fee. Admission notification on a rolling basis. **Financial aid:** No deadline. FAFSA, institutional form required. Applicants notified on a rolling basis.

Academics. Credit/placement by examination: AP, CLEP. **Support services:** Learning center, tutoring.

Majors. Business: Business admin. **Computer sciences:** Security. **Protective services:** Law enforcement admin.

Computing on campus. Online library available.

Student life. Freshman orientation: Available. Preregistration for classes offered.

Student services. Career counseling, student employment services, placement for graduates.

Contact. Phone: (904) 573-9100 Toll-free number: (800) 318-1264 Jorge Torres, Director of Recruitment, ITT Technical Institute: Jacksonville, 7011 A.C. Skinner Parkway, Suite 140, Jacksonville, FL 32256

ITT Technical Institute: Lake Mary
Lake Mary, Florida
www.itt-tech.edu

- For-profit 4-year technical college
- Commuter campus in large town
- 670 degree-seeking undergraduates

General. Accredited by ACICS. **Degrees:** 42 bachelor's, 130 associate awarded. **Calendar:** Quarter. **Full-time faculty:** 9 total. **Part-time faculty:** 41 total.

Basis for selection. Additional requirements for some programs.

2011-2012 Annual costs. Estimated costs as of June 2011: per-credit-hour charge, $493, depending upon level and course of study; academic fee, $200. Certain programs of study require purchase of tools, which could cost an additional $100 to $655. All costs are subject to change.

Academics. Credit/placement by examination: AP, CLEP.

Majors. Business: Business admin, construction management. **Communications technology:** Animation/special effects. **Computer sciences:** Security. **Protective services:** Law enforcement admin.

Contact. Phone: (407) 660-2900 Toll-free number: (866) 489-8441 Fax: (407) 660-2566 Larry Johnson, Director of Recruitment, ITT Technical Institute: Lake Mary, 1400 International Parkway South, Lake Mary, FL 32746

ITT Technical Institute: Miami
Miami, Florida
www.itt-tech.edu   CB code: 2733

- For-profit 4-year technical college
- Commuter campus in large city
- 853 degree-seeking undergraduates
- Interview required

General. Accredited by ACICS. **Degrees:** 59 bachelor's, 181 associate awarded. **Calendar:** Quarter, extensive summer session. **Full-time faculty:** 11 total. **Part-time faculty:** 47 total.

Basis for selection. Satisfactory scores from on-site tests in English and mathematics required.

2011-2012 Annual costs. Estimated costs as of June 2011: per-credit-hour charge, $493, depending upon level and course of study; academic fee, $200. Certain programs of study require purchase of tools, which could cost an additional $100 to $655. All costs are subject to change.

Application procedures. Admission: No deadline. No application fee. Admission notification on a rolling basis. **Financial aid:** No deadline. FAFSA, institutional form required. Applicants notified on a rolling basis.

Academics. Credit/placement by examination: AP, CLEP. **Support services:** Learning center, tutoring.

Majors. Business: Accounting technology, business admin, construction management. **Computer sciences:** Security. **Protective services:** Law enforcement admin.

Computing on campus. Online library available.

Student life. Freshman orientation: Available. Preregistration for classes offered.

Student services. Career counseling, student employment services, placement for graduates.

Contact. Phone: (305) 477-3080 Alan Arellano, Director of Recruitment, ITT Technical Institute: Miami, 7955 NW 12th Street, Suite 119, Miami, FL 33126

ITT Technical Institute: Tampa
Tampa, Florida
www.itt-tech.edu   CB code: 2145

- For-profit 4-year technical college
- Commuter campus in large city
- Interview required

General. Founded in 1981. Accredited by ACICS. **Degrees:** 68 bachelor's, 185 associate awarded. **Calendar:** Quarter, extensive summer session. **Full-time faculty:** 16 total. **Part-time faculty:** 55 total.

Basis for selection. Satisfactory scores from on-site English and mathematics tests required.

2011-2012 Annual costs. Estimated costs as of June 2011: per-credit-hour charge, $493, depending upon level and course of study; academic fee, $200. Certain programs of study require purchase of tools, which could cost an additional $100 to $655. All costs are subject to change.

Application procedures. Admission: No deadline. No application fee. Admission notification on a rolling basis. **Financial aid:** No deadline. FAFSA, institutional form required. Applicants notified on a rolling basis.

Academics. Credit/placement by examination: AP, CLEP. **Support services:** Learning center, tutoring.

Majors. Business: Construction management. **Communications technology:** Animation/special effects. **Computer sciences:** Security. **Protective services:** Law enforcement admin.

Computing on campus. Online library available.

Student life. Freshman orientation: Available. Preregistration for classes offered.

Student services. Career counseling, student employment services, placement for graduates.

Contact. Phone: (813) 885-2244 Toll-free number: (800) 825-2831 Joe Rostkowski, Director of Recruitment, ITT Technical Institute: Tampa, 4809 Memorial Highway, Tampa, FL 33634

Jacksonville University
Jacksonville, Florida   CB member
www.ju.edu   CB code: 5331

- Private 4-year university and liberal arts college
- Residential campus in very large city
- 3,122 degree-seeking undergraduates: 30% part-time, 59% women, 19% African American, 4% Asian American, 7% Hispanic American, 1% Native American, 1% international
- 511 degree-seeking graduate students
- 42% of applicants admitted
- SAT or ACT (ACT writing optional) required
- 40% graduate within 6 years

General. Founded in 1934. Regionally accredited. **Degrees:** 772 bachelor's awarded; master's offered. **ROTC:** Naval. **Calendar:** Semester, limited summer session. **Full-time faculty:** 180 total; 79% have terminal degrees, 9%

minority, 43% women. **Part-time faculty:** 138 total; 36% have terminal degrees, 19% minority, 54% women. **Class size:** 64% < 20, 36% 20-39, less than 1% 40-49. **Special facilities:** Marine science research institute.

Freshman class profile. 8,096 applied, 3,369 admitted, 529 enrolled.

Mid 50% test scores			
SAT critical reading:	470-560	GPA 3.0-3.49:	33%
SAT math:	480-570	GPA 2.0-2.99:	18%
ACT composite:	20-26	Return as sophomores:	60%
GPA 3.75 or higher:	29%	Out-of-state:	34%
GPA 3.50-3.74:	19%	Live on campus:	72%
		International:	1%

Basis for selection. GPA and test scores very important, followed by rigor of secondary school record. Audition required of music, dance, theater majors. Portfolio required for art, computer art and design. **Home schooled:** Transcript of courses and grades, interview required. 2 letters of recommendation evaluating academic potential from qualified educator or evaluator outside of homeschool environment, portfolio that includes 2 writing samples of at least 100 words, bibliography of reading completed and texts used, and description of curriculum required.

High school preparation. College-preparatory program required. 13 units required; 16 recommended. Required and recommended units include English 4, mathematics 3-4, social studies 3, science 3 (laboratory 2) and foreign language 2. History units may be included for satisfaction of social studies requirement.

2011-2012 Annual costs. Tuition/fees: $27,900. $570 mandatory health insurance fee charged unless proof of other coverage is provided. Room/board: $9,540. Books/supplies: $800. Personal expenses: $1,178.

Financial aid. **Non-need-based:** Scholarships awarded for academics, art, athletics, job skills, leadership, music/drama, ROTC, state residency.

Application procedures. **Admission:** Priority date 3/1; no deadline. $30 fee, may be waived for applicants with need. Admission notification on a rolling basis beginning on or about 10/1. Must reply by May 1 or within 2 week(s) if notified thereafter. **Financial aid:** Priority date 3/15; no closing date. FAFSA, institutional form required. Applicants notified on a rolling basis starting 2/15.

Academics. **Special study options:** Accelerated study, combined bachelor's/graduate degree, cooperative education, distance learning, double major, dual enrollment of high school students, honors, independent study, internships, liberal arts/career combination, semester at sea, student-designed major, study abroad, teacher certification program, Washington semester. **Credit/placement by examination:** AP, CLEP, IB, SAT, ACT, institutional tests. 30 credit hours maximum toward associate degree, 30 toward bachelor's. **Support services:** Learning center, remedial instruction, study skills assistance, tutoring, writing center.

Majors. **Biology:** General, marine. **Business:** General, accounting, business admin, finance, international, marketing. **Communications:** Communications/speech/rhetoric. **Computer sciences:** General. **Education:** General, drama/dance, elementary, music, physical, secondary. **Engineering:** Applied physics, electrical, mechanical. **English:** English lit. **Foreign languages:** French, Spanish. **Health services:** Nursing (RN), predental, premedicine, prenursing, preveterinary. **History:** General. **Liberal arts:** Arts/sciences, humanities. **Math:** General. **Parks/recreation:** Exercise sciences. **Philosophy/religion:** Philosophy. **Physical sciences:** Chemistry, physics. **Psychology:** General. **Social sciences:** Economics, geography, political science, sociology. **Theology:** Sacred music. **Visual/performing arts:** Art, art history/conservation, dance, design, dramatic, music, music management, music performance, music theory/composition, studio arts, voice/opera.

Most popular majors. Business/marketing 16%, health sciences 47%, social sciences 8%, visual/performing arts 6%.

Computing on campus. 400 workstations in dormitories, library, computer center. Dormitories wired for high-speed internet access and linked to campus network. Commuter students can connect to campus network. Online course registration, online library, helpline, wireless network available.

Student life. **Freshman orientation:** Mandatory. Preregistration for classes offered. Spring program available for pre-registration; formal freshmen orientation occurs in the few days preceding first day of class. **Housing:** Guaranteed on-campus for freshmen. Coed dorms, single-sex dorms, special housing for disabled, apartments, fraternity/sorority housing available. $200 deposit, deadline 5/1. **Activities:** Bands, campus ministries, choral groups, dance, drama, international student organizations, literary magazine, music ensembles, musical theater, radio station, student government, student newspaper, symphony orchestra, TV station, political science society, Black student union, Baptist campus ministry, Hillel, Circle-K, Rotaract, Caribbean student group, Dolphin Diversity.

Athletics. NCAA. **Intercollegiate:** Baseball M, basketball, cross-country, football (tackle) M, golf, rowing (crew) W, soccer, softball W, tennis, track and field W, volleyball W. **Intramural:** Basketball, bowling, football (non-tackle), soccer, softball, table tennis, tennis, volleyball. **Team name:** Dolphins.

Student services. Adult student services, alcohol/substance abuse counseling, career counseling, student employment services, financial aid counseling, health services, minority student services, personal counseling, placement for graduates. **Physically disabled:** Services for visually, speech, hearing impaired.

Contact. E-mail: admissions@ju.edu
Phone: (904) 256-7000 Toll-free number: (800) 225-2027
Fax: (904) 256-7012
Yvonne Martel, Director of First Year Admissions and Enrollment, Jacksonville University, 2800 University Boulevard North, Jacksonville, FL 32211-3394

Johnson & Wales University: North Miami
North Miami, Florida
www.jwu.edu   CB code: 3441

- Private 4-year university
- Residential campus in large city
- 2,153 degree-seeking undergraduates: 4% part-time, 57% women, 24% African American, 1% Asian American, 21% Hispanic American, 1% Native American, 9% international
- 63% of applicants admitted
- 46% graduate within 6 years

General. Regionally accredited. **Degrees:** 215 bachelor's, 267 associate awarded. **Calendar:** Quarter, extensive summer session. **Full-time faculty:** 64 total; 34% women. **Part-time faculty:** 32 total; 50% women. **Class size:** 52% < 20, 39% 20-39, 8% 40-49. **Special facilities:** University-operated hotel.

Freshman class profile. 5,414 applied, 3,428 admitted, 652 enrolled.

Mid 50% test scores			
SAT critical reading:	400-500	GPA 3.0-3.49:	33%
SAT math:	400-500	GPA 2.0-2.99:	42%
SAT writing:	410-510	Return as sophomores:	67%
GPA 3.75 or higher:	14%	Out-of-state:	50%
GPA 3.50-3.74:	11%	Live on campus:	79%
		International:	8%

Basis for selection. Academic record, secondary school curriculum, GPA, class rank, and test scores important. Student motivation and interest given strong consideration. **Home schooled:** Transcript of courses and grades, state high school equivalency certificate required. SAT or ACT required.

High school preparation. College-preparatory program recommended. Required units include English 4, mathematics 3, social studies 2 and science 3.

2011-2012 Annual costs. Tuition/fees: $25,407. Room/board: $9,261. Books/supplies: $1,800. Personal expenses: $1,065.

Financial aid. **Non-need-based:** Scholarships awarded for academics, alumni affiliation, leadership, state residency.

Application procedures. **Admission:** No deadline. No application fee. Admission notification on a rolling basis. Must reply by May 1 or within 2 week(s) if notified thereafter. **Financial aid:** No deadline. FAFSA required. Applicants notified on a rolling basis starting 3/1; must reply within 2 week(s) of notification.

Academics. **Special study options:** Accelerated study, cooperative education, dual enrollment of high school students, ESL, exchange student, honors, independent study, internships, study abroad. **Credit/placement by examination:** AP, CLEP, institutional tests. **Support services:** Learning center, pre-admission summer program, reduced course load, remedial instruction, study skills assistance, tutoring, writing center.

Honors college/program. SAT/ACT required.

Majors. **Business:** Business admin, fashion, hospitality admin, hotel/motel admin, marketing, tourism/travel. **Parks/recreation:** Facilities management, sports admin. **Protective services:** Law enforcement admin. **Work/family studies:** Institutional food production.

Most popular majors. Business/marketing 45%, family/consumer sciences 23%, parks/recreation 12%, personal/culinary services 11%, security/protective services 9%.

Computing on campus. 60 workstations in library, computer center, student center. Dormitories wired for high-speed internet access and linked to campus network. Commuter students can connect to campus network. Online course registration, online library, helpline, repair service, wireless network available.

Student life. Freshman orientation: Mandatory, $255 fee. Preregistration for classes offered. **Housing:** Guaranteed on-campus for freshmen. Coed dorms, apartments, wellness housing available. All housing accessible for disabled students. **Activities:** Pep band, campus ministries, dance, international student organizations, music ensembles, student government, student newspaper.

Athletics. NAIA. **Intercollegiate:** Basketball, cheerleading, cross-country, golf M, soccer, track and field. **Intramural:** Basketball M, football (nontackle), soccer, softball, volleyball. **Team name:** Wildcats.

Student services. Adult student services, alcohol/substance abuse counseling, career counseling, student employment services, financial aid counseling, health services, personal counseling, placement for graduates, veterans' counselor. **Physically disabled:** Services for visually, speech, hearing impaired.

Contact. E-mail: mia@admissions.jwu.edu
Phone: (866) 598-3567 Fax: (305) 892-7020
Jeff Greenip, Director of Admissions, Johnson & Wales University: North Miami, 1701 Northeast 127th Street, North Miami, FL 33181

Jones College
Jacksonville, Florida
www.jones.edu   CB code: 5343

- Private 4-year business and teachers college
- Commuter campus in very large city
- 640 degree-seeking undergraduates: 86% part-time, 79% women, 72% African American, 4% Hispanic American
- Interview required

General. Founded in 1918. Accredited by ACICS. 2 campuses in Jacksonville. **Degrees:** 100 bachelor's, 25 associate awarded. **Calendar:** Trimester, extensive summer session. **Full-time faculty:** 10 total. **Part-time faculty:** 50 total. **Class size:** 91% < 20, 9% 20-39.

Basis for selection. Open admission. **Home schooled:** State high school equivalency certificate required.

2011-2012 Annual costs. Tuition/fees: $9,240. Books/supplies: $1,600. Personal expenses: $1,370.

Financial aid. All financial aid based on need.

Application procedures. Admission: No deadline. No application fee. Admission notification on a rolling basis. **Financial aid:** No deadline. FAFSA required. Applicants notified on a rolling basis.

Academics. Special study options: Accelerated study, distance learning, double major, dual enrollment of high school students, internships, weekend college. **Credit/placement by examination:** AP, CLEP, institutional tests. 15 credit hours maximum toward associate degree, 15 toward bachelor's. Life experience: 21 hours if in bachelor's degree programs, 9 hours if in associate degree programs. **Support services:** Reduced course load, remedial instruction, study skills assistance, tutoring.

Majors. Business: Business admin. **Computer sciences:** General. **Education:** Elementary. **Health services:** Medical assistant.

Most popular majors. Business/marketing 44%, computer/information sciences 11%, health sciences 18%, interdisciplinary studies 13%, legal studies 11%.

Computing on campus. 126 workstations in library, computer center. Commuter students can connect to campus network. Online library, wireless network available.

Student life. Freshman orientation: Mandatory. Preregistration for classes offered. **Activities:** Student government.

Student services. Career counseling, student employment services, financial aid counseling, personal counseling, placement for graduates, veterans' counselor.

Contact. E-mail: lvaughn@jones.edu
Phone: (904) 743-1122 ext. 112
Toll-free number: (800) 331-0176 ext. 112 Fax: (904) 743-4446
Linda Vaughn, Director of Admissions, Jones College, 5353 Arlington Expressway, Jacksonville, FL 32211

Lynn University
Boca Raton, Florida   **CB member**
www.lynn.edu   **CB code: 5437**

- Private 4-year university
- Residential campus in small city
- 1,577 degree-seeking undergraduates: 8% part-time, 48% women, 7% African American, 1% Asian American, 11% Hispanic American, 18% international
- 445 degree-seeking graduate students
- 63% of applicants admitted
- SAT or ACT (ACT writing recommended), application essay required
- 42% graduate within 6 years

General. Founded in 1962. Regionally accredited. **Degrees:** 437 bachelor's awarded; master's, doctoral offered. **ROTC:** Army, Air Force. **Location:** 20 miles from Fort Lauderdale, 20 miles from West Palm Beach. **Calendar:** Semester, extensive summer session. **Full-time faculty:** 89 total; 63% have terminal degrees, 11% minority, 39% women. **Part-time faculty:** 81 total; 32% have terminal degrees, 9% minority, 41% women. **Class size:** 61% < 20, 39% 20-39, less than 1% 50-99. **Special facilities:** University club (private dining room that serves as laboratory for hotel and restaurant management students), flight simulator, conservatory of music.

Freshman class profile. 2,953 applied, 1,862 admitted, 411 enrolled.

Mid 50% test scores		GPA 2.0-2.99:	65%
SAT critical reading:	410-490	Rank in top quarter:	16%
SAT math:	390-510	Rank in top tenth:	7%
ACT composite:	17-22	Return as sophomores:	60%
GPA 3.75 or higher:	6%	Out-of-state:	29%
GPA 3.50-3.74:	5%	Live on campus:	86%
GPA 3.0-3.49:	20%	International:	17%

Basis for selection. School achievement record, high school counselor's recommendation, test scores important; class rank, school and community activities considered. Special consideration given to foreign and minority applicants. Interview and essay recommended. Portfolio recommended for art and graphic design majors. **Learning Disabled:** Submit psychological testing in addition to other admission documents.

High school preparation. College-preparatory program recommended. 16 units required. Required units include English 4, mathematics 4, social studies 2, history 2 and science 4. Mathematics must include algebra I, algebra II, and either geometry, trigonometry, calculus, or analysis. Science must include biology and a physical science.

2011-2012 Annual costs. Tuition/fees: $31,700. Room/board: $10,900. Books/supplies: $1,000. Personal expenses: $2,900.

2011-2012 Financial aid. Need-based: 343 full-time freshmen applied for aid; 195 were judged to have need; 194 of these received aid. Average need met was 54%. Average scholarship/grant was $10,097; average loan $4,436. 63% of total undergraduate aid awarded as scholarships/grants, 37% as loans/jobs. **Non-need-based:** Awarded to 1,036 full-time undergraduates, including 334 freshmen. Scholarships awarded for academics, alumni affiliation, athletics, leadership, music/drama.

Application procedures. Admission: Priority date 3/31; no deadline. $45 fee, may be waived for applicants with need. Admission notification on a rolling basis beginning on or about 9/1. Must reply by May 1 or within 2 week(s) if notified thereafter. **Financial aid:** Priority date 3/1; no closing date. FAFSA required. Applicants notified on a rolling basis starting 2/1; must reply within 2 week(s) of notification.

Academics. Special study options: Accelerated study, cooperative education, distance learning, double major, dual enrollment of high school students, ESL, honors, independent study, internships, liberal arts/career combination, study abroad, teacher certification program, Washington semester. **Credit/placement by examination:** AP, CLEP, IB, institutional tests. 30 credit hours maximum toward associate degree, 30 toward bachelor's. **Support services:** Learning center, reduced course load, remedial instruction, tutoring, writing center.

Majors. Area/ethnic studies: American. **Biology:** General. **Business:** Business admin, hospitality admin. **Communications:** Broadcast journalism, digital media, journalism, media studies, persuasive communications. **Education:**

General, elementary. **English:** English lit. **Liberal arts:** Arts/sciences. **Parks/recreation:** Sports admin. **Protective services:** Law enforcement admin. **Psychology:** General. **Social sciences:** International relations, U.S. government. **Visual/performing arts:** Dramatic, film/cinema/video, graphic design, illustration, music performance, music theory/composition, photography.

Most popular majors. Business/marketing 54%, communications/journalism 9%, psychology 9%, visual/performing arts 8%.

Computing on campus. 220 workstations in dormitories, library, computer center, student center. Dormitories wired for high-speed internet access and linked to campus network. Online library, helpline, repair service, wireless network available.

Student life. Freshman orientation: Mandatory. Preregistration for classes offered. **Housing:** Guaranteed on-campus for all undergraduates. Coed dorms, single-sex dorms, special housing for disabled, wellness housing available. **Activities:** Campus ministries, choral groups, dance, drama, film society, international student organizations, literary magazine, music ensembles, musical theater, radio station, student government, student newspaper, symphony orchestra, TV station, black student union, debate team, gay-straight alliance, Hillel, honors colloquium, hospitality club, Knights of the Roundtable.

Athletics. NCAA. **Intercollegiate:** Baseball M, basketball, cross-country, golf, rowing (crew) M, soccer, softball W, tennis, volleyball W. **Intramural:** Basketball, bowling, cross-country, equestrian, golf, handball, ice hockey, lacrosse, rugby M, soccer, softball, swimming, table tennis, tennis, volleyball, water polo. **Team name:** Fighting Knights.

Student services. Adult student services, chaplain/spiritual director, career counseling, student employment services, health services, personal counseling, placement for graduates, veterans' counselor.

Contact. E-mail: admissions@lynn.edu
Phone: (561) 237-7900 Toll-free number: (800) 888-5966
Fax: (561) 237-7100
Stefano Papaleo, Director of Undergraduate Admission, Lynn University, 3601 North Military Trail, Boca Raton, FL 33431-5598

Miami International University of Art and Design
Miami, Florida
www.mymiu.edu   **CB code: 5327**

- For-profit 3-year university and visual arts college
- Commuter campus in very large city
- 3,966 degree-seeking undergraduates: 25% part-time, 56% women
- 102 graduate students
- 38% of applicants admitted
- Application essay, interview required
- 38% graduate within 6 years

General. Founded in 1965. Regionally accredited. **Degrees:** 538 bachelor's, 165 associate awarded; master's offered. **Location:** 2 miles from downtown. **Calendar:** Quarter, extensive summer session. **Full-time faculty:** 138 total. **Part-time faculty:** 174 total.

Freshman class profile. 2,186 applied, 838 admitted, 695 enrolled.

Basis for selection. Secondary school record, recommendations, and essay important. ACCUPLACER, SAT or ACT required for placement and to determine the need for developmental course work in English and/or math. Portfolio of work may be required depending on program and campus chosen. **Home schooled:** Require official GED certificate or evidence of completion of state home schooling requirements. **Learning Disabled:** Students who require accommodations should advise the Student Affairs department during application process.

2011-2012 Annual costs. Books/supplies: $1,500. Personal expenses: $1,200.

Application procedures. Admission: No deadline. $50 fee. Admission notification on a rolling basis. Admissions decisions are made on a rolling basis, and students are encouraged to apply as early as possible prior to their intended start date. **Financial aid:** Priority date 7/1; no closing date. FAFSA required. Applicants notified on a rolling basis starting 8/1.

Academics. Special study options: Distance learning, internships. **Credit/placement by examination:** AP, CLEP, IB, SAT, ACT, institutional tests. 22 credit hours maximum toward associate degree, 45 toward bachelor's. Official documents (CLEP or AP scores) related to transfer or proficiency

credit must be received by an Art Institutes school prior to the class start. No more than 25 percent of program credits will be considered for any type of proficiency credit. **Support services:** Learning center, reduced course load, remedial instruction, tutoring.

Majors. BACHELOR'S. Business: Apparel, fashion. **Communications:** Advertising. **Communications technology:** Animation/special effects, recording arts. **Computer sciences:** Computer graphics, web page design. **Visual/performing arts:** Cinematography, commercial photography, design, fashion design, game design, graphic design, interior design. **ASSOCIATE. Business:** Apparel, fashion. **Visual/performing arts:** Fashion design, graphic design.

Computing on campus. 87 workstations in library, computer center. Online library, student web hosting, wireless network available.

Student life. Freshman orientation: Mandatory. Preregistration for classes offered. Held the week before each quarter starts for approximately 4 hours. **Housing:** Coed dorms available. **Activities:** International student organizations, student government, student newspaper.

Student services. Career counseling, student employment services, financial aid counseling.

Contact. E-mail: kryan@aii.edu
Phone: (305) 428-5700 Toll-free number: (800) 225-9023
Fax: (305) 374-7946
Kevin Ryan, Senior Director of Admissions, Miami International University of Art and Design, 1501 Biscayne Boulevard, Suite 100, Miami, FL 33132-1418

New College of Florida
Sarasota, Florida   **CB member**
www.ncf.edu   **CB code: 5506**

- Public 4-year liberal arts college
- Residential campus in small city
- 845 degree-seeking undergraduates: 61% women, 1% African American, 3% Asian American, 13% Hispanic American
- 56% of applicants admitted
- SAT or ACT with writing, application essay required
- 68% graduate within 6 years; 57% enter graduate study

General. Founded in 1960. Regionally accredited. State legislatively-designated honors college for liberal arts and sciences. **Degrees:** 167 bachelor's awarded. **Location:** 50 miles from Tampa, 2 miles from Sarasota. **Calendar:** 4-1-4. **Full-time faculty:** 71 total; 99% have terminal degrees, 14% minority, 48% women. **Part-time faculty:** 32 total; 78% have terminal degrees, 9% minority, 53% women. **Class size:** 67% < 20, 29% 20-39, 2% 40-49, 2% 50-99. **Special facilities:** High-field nuclear magnetic resonance spectrometer, hardware/software system for brain function analysis, scanning electron microscope, UV-visible and infrared spectrophotometer, inert atmosphere glove box, fine arts center, laboratories for environmental studies, anthropology, psychology, marine biology research facility and laboratories, academic resource center.

Freshman class profile. 1,272 applied, 715 admitted, 237 enrolled.

Mid 50% test scores			
SAT critical reading:	630-740	GPA 3.0-3.49:	11%
SAT math:	570-680	GPA 2.0-2.99:	1%
SAT writing:	600-680	Rank in top quarter:	84%
ACT composite:	27-31	Rank in top tenth:	44%
GPA 3.75 or higher:	70%	End year in good standing:	79%
GPA 3.50-3.74:	18%	Out-of-state:	20%
		Live on campus:	98%

Basis for selection. Challenging courses and course loads, strong grades, writing ability, exam scores, and recommendations important. Class rank (if available) and extracurricular activities considered. SAT/ACT requirement waived for students with Florida College System AA degree. Portfolios and interviews considered, but not required. **Home schooled:** Transcript of courses and grades required. List of length and levels of study completed or planned for completion, textbook information and reading lists required. **Learning Disabled:** Applicants should contact Disabilities Services Coordinator to discuss resources and process for requesting accommodation.

High school preparation. College-preparatory program required. 18 units required; 20 recommended. Required and recommended units include English 4, mathematics 4, social studies 3-4, science 3-4 (laboratory 2), foreign language 2-4 and academic electives 2-4. History is included in social studies.

2011-2012 Annual costs. Tuition/fees: $6,060; $29,088 out-of-state. Room/board: $8,598. Books/supplies: $800. Personal expenses: $2,600.

2011-2012 Financial aid. Need-based: 230 full-time freshmen applied for aid; 138 were judged to have need; 138 of these received aid. Average need met was 100%. Average scholarship/grant was $10,742; average loan $3,402. 59% of total undergraduate aid awarded as scholarships/grants, 41% as loans/jobs. **Non-need-based:** Awarded to 277 full-time undergraduates, including 97 freshmen. Scholarships awarded for academics, state residency.

Application procedures. Admission: Priority date 11/1; deadline 4/15 (postmark date). $30 fee, may be waived for applicants with need. Admission notification by 4/25. Must reply by 5/1. **Financial aid:** Priority date 2/15; no closing date. FAFSA required. Applicants notified on a rolling basis starting 10/1; must reply by 5/1 or within 4 week(s) of notification.

Academics. All students required to complete three 4-week independent study projects, senior thesis, and oral baccalaureate exam before committee of faculty. **Special study options:** Cross-registration, double major, exchange student, honors, independent study, internships, semester at sea, student-designed major, study abroad, Washington semester. Academic contract, January Interterm (independent study), narrative evaluation/pass-fail, senior thesis, tutorials, undergraduate research. **Credit/placement by examination:** AP, CLEP, institutional tests. AP exam scores, IB higher-level exam scores, AICE A-level exam scores, and CLEP scores at certain levels may be used toward exemptions from Liberal Arts Curriculum requirements. **Support services:** Learning center, study skills assistance, tutoring, writing center.

Majors. Area/ethnic studies: European, French, German, Latin American, Spanish/Iberian. **Biology:** General, biochemistry, marine. **Conservation:** Environmental studies. **English:** English lit. **Foreign languages:** General, Chinese, classics, French, German, Russian, Spanish. **History:** General. **Human services:** Public policy. **Liberal arts:** Arts/sciences, humanities. **Math:** General, applied. **Philosophy/religion:** Philosophy, religion. **Physical sciences:** Chemistry, physics. **Psychology:** General. **Social sciences:** General, anthropology, economics, international relations, political science, sociology, urban studies. **Visual/performing arts:** Art history/conservation, music, studio arts.

Computing on campus. 41 workstations in library, computer center, student center. Dormitories wired for high-speed internet access and linked to campus network. Commuter students can connect to campus network. Online course registration, online library, helpline, student web hosting, wireless network available.

Student life. Freshman orientation: Mandatory, $125 fee. Preregistration for classes offered. Seven-day program. **Policies:** First-year students required to live on campus unless granted waiver by office of residential life. **Housing:** Guaranteed on-campus for freshmen. Coed dorms, special housing for disabled, apartments available. Specialized housing options may be arranged in response to student interest. **Activities:** Jazz band, campus ministries, choral groups, dance, drama, film society, literary magazine, music ensembles, radio station, student government, student newspaper, Amnesty International, China club, climate justice, origami club, Jesus club, service club, Best Buddies, Africa club, Food not Bombs, Hillel.

Athletics. Intercollegiate: Sailing. **Intramural:** Basketball, fencing, football (non-tackle), lacrosse, racquetball, swimming, table tennis, tennis, volleyball, weight lifting, wrestling.

Student services. Alcohol/substance abuse counseling, chaplain/spiritual director, career counseling, student employment services, financial aid counseling, health services, minority student services, on-campus daycare, personal counseling, women's services. **Physically disabled:** Services for visually, hearing impaired.

Contact. E-mail: admissions@ncf.edu
Phone: (941) 487-5000 Fax: (941) 487-5010
Kathleen Killion, Dean of Enrollment Services, New College of Florida, 5800 Bay Shore Road, Sarasota, FL 34243-2109

Northwood University: Florida
West Palm Beach, Florida
www.northwood.edu   CB code: 5162

- Private 4-year university and business college
- Residential campus in small city
- 520 degree-seeking undergraduates
- 50% of applicants admitted
- SAT or ACT (ACT writing optional), application essay required

General. Regionally accredited. Specialty university offering only business degrees in professional management. Additional residential campuses in Michigan and Texas; program centers across the United States; library center in Maine. **Degrees:** 197 bachelor's, 46 associate awarded; master's offered.

Location: 75 miles from Miami. **Calendar:** Semester, limited summer session. **Full-time faculty:** 16 total. **Part-time faculty:** 27 total. **Class size:** 51% < 20, 41% 20-39, 7% 40-49, 1% 50-99.

Freshman class profile. 844 applied, 418 admitted, 95 enrolled.

Mid 50% test scores			
SAT critical reading:	410-470	GPA 3.0-3.49:	34%
SAT math:	420-530	GPA 2.0-2.99:	39%
SAT writing:	380-490	Rank in top quarter:	17%
ACT composite:	17-21	Rank in top tenth:	7%
GPA 3.75 or higher:	11%	Out-of-state:	52%
GPA 3.50-3.74:	14%	Live on campus:	80%

Basis for selection. 2.0 GPA and strong interest in business or related field required. Test scores considered. Interview recommended. **Home schooled:** Transcript of courses and grades, state high school equivalency certificate required.

High school preparation. College-preparatory program recommended. 17 units recommended. Recommended units include English 4 and mathematics 3.

2011-2012 Annual costs. Tuition/fees: $20,140. Room/board: $9,284. Books/supplies: $1,182.

Financial aid. Non-need-based: Scholarships awarded for academics, athletics, leadership, minority status, state residency.

Application procedures. Admission: No deadline. $25 fee, may be waived for applicants with need, free for online applicants. Admission notification on a rolling basis beginning on or about 10/1. **Financial aid:** No deadline. FAFSA required. Applicants notified on a rolling basis starting 3/1.

Academics. Writing, math and accounting labs available. **Special study options:** Accelerated study, combined bachelor's/graduate degree, distance learning, double major, dual enrollment of high school students, external degree, honors, independent study, internships, study abroad, weekend college. **Credit/placement by examination:** AP, CLEP, IB, SAT, ACT, institutional tests. 12 credit hours maximum toward associate degree, 12 toward bachelor's. **Support services:** Learning center, reduced course load, remedial instruction, study skills assistance, tutoring.

Majors. Business: Accounting, banking/financial services, business admin, hotel/motel admin, international, management information systems, marketing, vehicle parts marketing. **Communications:** Advertising. **Computer sciences:** General. **Parks/recreation:** Sports admin.

Most popular majors. Business/marketing 96%.

Computing on campus. 89 workstations in dormitories, library, computer center, student center. Dormitories wired for high-speed internet access and linked to campus network. Commuter students can connect to campus network. Online course registration, online library, helpline, student web hosting, wireless network available.

Student life. Freshman orientation: Mandatory, $125 fee. Preregistration for classes offered. 3-day program in late August. **Policies:** Adheres to all federal and state laws concerning alcohol and drugs. Freshmen and sophomores not living at home must live on campus. **Housing:** Guaranteed on-campus for freshmen. Single-sex dorms, wellness housing available. $100 nonrefundable deposit, deadline 5/1. **Activities:** International student organizations, student government, residence hall association, ambassador club.

Athletics. NAIA. **Intercollegiate:** Baseball M, basketball, golf, soccer, softball W, tennis, volleyball W. **Intramural:** Basketball, bowling, football (non-tackle), racquetball, tennis. **Team name:** Seahawks.

Student services. Adult student services, alcohol/substance abuse counseling, career counseling, student employment services, financial aid counseling, health services, personal counseling, placement for graduates. **Physically disabled:** Services for hearing impaired.

Contact. E-mail: fladmit@northwood.edu
Phone: (561) 478-5500 Toll-free number: (800) 458-8325
Fax: (561) 640-3328
Emily Mass, Associate Director of Admissions, Northwood University: Florida, 2600 North Military Trail, West Palm Beach, FL 33409-2911

Nova Southeastern University
Fort Lauderdale, Florida   CB member
www.nova.edu   CB code: 5514

- Private 4-year university
- Commuter campus in small city

- 6,246 degree-seeking undergraduates: 33% part-time, 71% women, 24% African American, 6% Asian American, 32% Hispanic American, 4% international
- 21,801 degree-seeking graduate students
- 58% of applicants admitted
- 41% graduate within 6 years

General. Founded in 1964. Regionally accredited. Field-based programs offered throughout the nation and at selected international sites. **Degrees:** 1,307 bachelor's, 4 associate awarded; master's, professional, doctoral offered. **Location:** 10 miles from Fort Lauderdale. **Calendar:** Trimester, limited summer session. **Full-time faculty:** 814 total; 88% have terminal degrees, 30% minority, 48% women. **Part-time faculty:** 923 total; 74% have terminal degrees, 31% minority, 54% women. **Class size:** 76% < 20, 23% 20-39, less than 1% 40-49, less than 1% 50-99, less than 1% >100. **Special facilities:** Oceanographic center, university school (K-12).

Freshman class profile. 3,780 applied, 2,180 admitted, 675 enrolled.

Mid 50% test scores			
SAT critical reading:	460-570	GPA 3.0-3.49:	24%
SAT math:	470-590	GPA 2.0-2.99:	17%
ACT composite:	20-25	Return as sophomores:	70%
GPA 3.75 or higher:	45%	Out-of-state:	70%
GPA 3.50-3.74:	14%	International:	5%

Basis for selection. Test scores, GPA important. Career Development applicants (adult and evening/weekend) exempt from test score requirement; high school diploma or GED required. Interviews and essays recommended. **Home schooled:** Information about home school program of study and GED score to demonstrate high school equivalence required.

High school preparation. College-preparatory program recommended. Recommended units include English 4, mathematics 3, social studies 3 and science 3.

2011-2012 Annual costs. Tuition/fees: $23,200. Room/board: $9,516. Books/supplies: $1,500. Personal expenses: $2,862.

2010-2011 Financial aid. **Need-based:** 1,612 full-time freshmen applied for aid; 1,362 were judged to have need; 1,356 of these received aid. Average need met was 71%. Average scholarship/grant was $14,702; average loan $4,352. 44% of total undergraduate aid awarded as scholarships/grants, 56% as loans/jobs. **Non-need-based:** Awarded to 3,847 full-time undergraduates, including 1,932 freshmen. Scholarships awarded for academics, athletics, leadership, music/drama.

Application procedures. **Admission:** Closing date 8/1 (receipt date). $50 fee, may be waived for applicants with need. Admission notification on a rolling basis. **Financial aid:** Priority date 4/15; no closing date. FAFSA required. Applicants notified on a rolling basis starting 3/15.

Academics. 2 undergraduate programs: professional and liberal studies for traditional daytime students, career development for adult evening and weekend students. Core curriculum of liberal arts-based courses plus general education required. **Special study options:** Combined bachelor's/graduate degree, distance learning, double major, honors, independent study, internships, study abroad, teacher certification program. Dual admission with NSU graduate/professional programs. **Credit/placement by examination:** AP, CLEP, IB, institutional tests. 90 credit hours maximum toward bachelor's degree. **Support services:** Learning center, reduced course load, remedial instruction, study skills assistance, tutoring, writing center.

Majors. **Area/ethnic studies:** American. **Biology:** General, marine. **Business:** General, accounting, business admin, finance, marketing. **Communications:** Communications/speech/rhetoric. **Computer sciences:** General, computer science. **Conservation:** Environmental science, environmental studies. **Education:** Early childhood, elementary, kindergarten/preschool, secondary, special ed. **English:** English lit. **Health services:** Athletic training, nursing (RN), premedicine, sonography. **History:** General. **Liberal arts:** Arts/sciences, humanities. **Parks/recreation:** Sports admin. **Philosophy/religion:** Philosophy. **Physical sciences:** Chemistry. **Protective services:** Criminal justice. **Psychology:** General. **Social sciences:** Economics, international relations, sociology. **Visual/performing arts:** Dance, music, studio arts, theater arts management.

Most popular majors. Biology 15%, business/marketing 27%, education 7%, health sciences 24%, psychology 12%.

Computing on campus. 2,708 workstations in dormitories, library, computer center, student center. Dormitories wired for high-speed internet access and linked to campus network. Commuter students can connect to campus network. Online course registration, online library, helpline, student web hosting, wireless network available.

Student life. **Freshman orientation:** Mandatory. Preregistration for classes offered. Two-day sessions offered 3 times in summer. **Housing:** Guaranteed on-campus for freshmen. Coed dorms, special housing for disabled, apartments, fraternity/sorority housing, wellness housing available. $500 partly refundable deposit, deadline 5/14. **Activities:** Campus ministries, choral groups, dance, drama, international student organizations, literary magazine, radio station, student government, student newspaper, TV station, black student association, psychology club, Hillel, pre-med society, Alpha Phi Omega, Salsa, Indian student association, international Muslim association.

Athletics. NCAA. **Intercollegiate:** Baseball M, basketball, cheerleading M, cross-country, diving, golf, rowing (crew) W, soccer, softball W, swimming, tennis W, track and field, volleyball W. **Intramural:** Basketball, football (non-tackle), golf, racquetball, soccer, softball W, volleyball. **Team name:** Sharks.

Student services. Adult student services, career counseling, student employment services, financial aid counseling, health services, personal counseling, veterans' counselor, women's services. **Physically disabled:** Services for visually, speech, hearing impaired.

Contact. E-mail: admissions@nova.edu
Phone: (954) 262-8000 Toll-free number: (800) 338-4723 ext. 8000
Fax: (954) 262-3811
Maria Dillard, Director of Undergraduate Admissions, Nova Southeastern University, 3301 College Avenue, Fort Lauderdale, FL 33314

Palm Beach Atlantic University
West Palm Beach, Florida
www.pba.edu   CB code: 5553

- Private 4-year university and liberal arts college affiliated with nondenominational tradition
- Residential campus in large city
- 2,365 degree-seeking undergraduates: 6% part-time, 63% women, 16% African American, 2% Asian American, 12% Hispanic American, 4% international
- 824 degree-seeking graduate students
- 83% of applicants admitted
- SAT or ACT (ACT writing optional), application essay, interview required
- 58% graduate within 6 years

General. Founded in 1968. Regionally accredited. Distinctly Christian university with emphasis on student community service. University offers mission trips around the world, weekly worship services, and student-led prayer groups. **Degrees:** 490 bachelor's, 1 associate awarded; master's, professional offered. **ROTC:** Army. **Location:** 60 miles from Miami, 180 miles from Orlando. **Calendar:** Semester, limited summer session. **Full-time faculty:** 156 total; 80% have terminal degrees, 11% minority, 46% women. **Part-time faculty:** 187 total; 35% have terminal degrees, 14% minority, 48% women. **Class size:** 65% < 20, 32% 20-39, 2% 40-49, less than 1% 50-99.

Freshman class profile. 1,373 applied, 1,139 admitted, 478 enrolled.

Mid 50% test scores			
SAT critical reading:	470-590	End year in good standing:	84%
SAT math:	450-570	Return as sophomores:	72%
SAT writing:	450-570	Out-of-state:	43%
ACT composite:	21-25	Live on campus:	86%
		International:	4%

Basis for selection. Secondary school record, recommendations, test scores, interview, autobiographical essay important. Audition required of music, theater and dance majors. **Learning Disabled:** Students requesting accommodations advised to meet with Coordinator for Disability Services for initial interview.

High school preparation. Required and recommended units include English 4, mathematics 3, social studies 3, science 4 (laboratory 2).

2011-2012 Annual costs. Tuition/fees: $24,100. Room/board: $8,400. Books/supplies: $920. Personal expenses: $1,676.

2011-2012 Financial aid. **Need-based:** 437 full-time freshmen applied for aid; 341 were judged to have need; 341 of these received aid. Average need met was 64%. Average scholarship/grant was $14,309; average loan $3,264. 61% of total undergraduate aid awarded as scholarships/grants, 39% as loans/jobs. **Non-need-based:** Awarded to 647 full-time undergraduates, including 202 freshmen. Scholarships awarded for academics, art, athletics, leadership, minority status, music/drama, state residency.

Application procedures. **Admission:** No deadline. $50 fee, may be waived for applicants with need. Admission notification on a rolling basis

beginning on or about 9/1. **Financial aid:** Priority date 5/1; no closing date. FAFSA required. Applicants notified on a rolling basis starting 2/15; must reply within 4 week(s) of notification.

Academics. **Special study options:** Accelerated study, combined bachelor's/graduate degree, distance learning, double major, dual enrollment of high school students, honors, independent study, internships, student-designed major, study abroad, teacher certification program, Washington semester. **Credit/placement by examination:** AP, CLEP, IB, SAT, ACT, institutional tests. 32 credit hours maximum toward bachelor's degree. If enrolled in one of undergraduate evening adult programs, aggregate of credit by examinination or Professional Education Credit may not exceed 31 semester hours. **Support services:** Study skills assistance, tutoring, writing center.

Honors college/program. 3.5 GPA and 26 ACT/1200 SAT required; maximum of 50 students admitted annually.

Majors. **Biology:** General. **Business:** Accounting/finance, business admin, international, marketing. **Communications:** General, journalism, radio/TV. **Computer sciences:** Computer science. **Education:** General, art, biology, English, mathematics, music, physical. **English:** English lit. **Health services:** Athletic training, nursing (RN). **History:** General. **Math:** General. **Philosophy/religion:** Philosophy, religion. **Psychology:** General. **Social sciences:** Political science. **Theology:** Bible, missionary, theology. **Visual/performing arts:** General, dance, dramatic, graphic design, music, music performance, music theory/composition, piano/keyboard, studio arts, voice/opera.

Computing on campus. 585 workstations in dormitories, library, computer center, student center. Dormitories wired for high-speed internet access and linked to campus network. Commuter students can connect to campus network. Online course registration, online library, helpline, wireless network available.

Student life. **Freshman orientation:** Mandatory, $40 fee. Preregistration for classes offered. **Policies:** Undergraduate students required to donate 45 hours of community service for each year of attendance. Religious observance required. **Housing:** Guaranteed on-campus for freshmen. Coed dorms, single-sex dorms, apartments available. $200 fully refundable deposit, deadline 5/1. **Activities:** Bands, campus ministries, choral groups, dance, drama, international student organizations, literary magazine, music ensembles, musical theater, radio station, student government, student newspaper, symphony orchestra, TV station, Agora Club, Chariots of Jerusalem, Christian Pharmacists Fellowship International, College Democrats, College Republicans, Newman Club, NOW, Nu Delta Nu Men's social organization, Presidential Ambassadors, SALSA.

Athletics. NCAA, NCCAA. **Intercollegiate:** Baseball M, basketball, cheerleading, cross-country W, golf, soccer, softball W, tennis, volleyball W. **Intramural:** Basketball, bowling, football (non-tackle), golf, racquetball, soccer, softball, table tennis, volleyball. **Team name:** Sailfish.

Student services. Chaplain/spiritual director, career counseling, student employment services, financial aid counseling, health services, minority student services, personal counseling, veterans' counselor. **Physically disabled:** Services for visually, speech impaired.

Contact. E-mail: admit@pba.edu
Phone: (561) 803-2100 Toll-free number: (888) 468-6722
Fax: (561) 803-2115
James Zugelder, Director of Admission, Palm Beach Atlantic University, PO Box 24708, West Palm Beach, FL 33416-4708

Rasmussen College: Fort Myers
Fort Myers, Florida
www.rasmussen.edu

- For-profit 4-year technical college
- Small city
- 723 degree-seeking undergraduates

General. Regionally accredited. **Degrees:** 30 associate awarded. **Calendar:** Quarter. **Full-time faculty:** 5 total. **Part-time faculty:** 43 total.

Basis for selection. Open admission, but selective for some programs.

2011-2012 Annual costs. Tuition/fees: $15,750. Full-time tuition varies according to program of study. Examples of per-credit-hour charges include Early Childhood Education ($310), Medical Lab Technician, Surgical Technician, Practical Nursing ($395), Professional Nursing, Information Systems Mgmt, Multemedia Technician ($395).

Application procedures. **Admission:** No deadline. $20 fee. **Financial aid:** No deadline.

Academics. **Credit/placement by examination:** AP, CLEP.

Majors. **Business:** Accounting, business admin. **Communications technology:** Animation/special effects. **Health services:** Health care admin. **Protective services:** Police science. **Visual/performing arts:** Game design.

Contact. Phone: (239) 477-2100
Susan Hammerstrom, Director of Admissions, Rasmussen College: Fort Myers, 9160 Forum Corporate Parkway, Suite 100, Fort Myers, FL 33905-7805

Rasmussen College: Ocala
Ocala, Florida
www.rasmussen.edu   **CB code: 3502**

- For-profit 4-year career college
- Commuter campus in small city
- 1,255 degree-seeking undergraduates

General. Regionally accredited. **Degrees:** 31 bachelor's, 141 associate awarded. **Calendar:** Quarter, extensive summer session. **Full-time faculty:** 15 total. **Part-time faculty:** 365 total.

Basis for selection. Open admission, but selective for some programs. Some programs require entrance examinations and additional information. COMPASS used for placement.

2011-2012 Annual costs. Tuition/fees: $15,750. Full-time tuition varies according to program of study. Examples of per-credit-hour charges include Early Childhood Education ($310), Medical Lab Technician, Surgical Technician, Practical Nursing ($395), Professional Nursing, Information Systems Mgmt, Multemedia Technician ($395).

Application procedures. **Admission:** No deadline. $20 fee. Admission notification on a rolling basis. **Financial aid:** No deadline. FAFSA, institutional form required. Applicants notified on a rolling basis.

Academics. **Special study options:** Distance learning, double major, honors, independent study, internships. **Credit/placement by examination:** AP, CLEP, IB, institutional tests. 45 credit hours maximum toward associate degree, 90 toward bachelor's. Limited to specific programs, and to courses for which programs are available. **Support services:** Learning center, remedial instruction, study skills assistance, tutoring, writing center.

Majors. **Business:** Accounting, business admin. **Computer sciences:** Web page design. **Protective services:** Law enforcement admin.

Computing on campus. 100 workstations in library, computer center, student center. Online course registration, online library, helpline, wireless network available.

Student life. **Freshman orientation:** Mandatory. Preregistration for classes offered.

Student services. Adult student services, career counseling, services for economically disadvantaged, student employment services, financial aid counseling, placement for graduates.

Contact. E-mail: susan.hammerstrom@rasmussen.edu
Phone: (352) 629-1941 Fax: (352) 629-0926
Susan Hammerstrom, Director of Admissions, Rasmussen College: Ocala, 2221 Southwest 46th Court, Ocala, FL 34474

Rasmussen College: Pasco County
New Port Richey, Florida
www.rasmussen.edu   **CB code: 3503**

- For-profit 4-year career college
- Commuter campus in small city
- 895 degree-seeking undergraduates

General. Regionally accredited. **Degrees:** 26 bachelor's, 84 associate awarded. **Location:** 30 miles from Tampa. **Calendar:** Quarter, extensive summer session. **Full-time faculty:** 10 total. **Part-time faculty:** 26 total.

Basis for selection. Open admission, but selective for some programs. Some programs require entrance examinations and additional information. COMPASS used for placement.

2011-2012 Annual costs. Tuition/fees: $15,750. Full-time tuition varies according to program of study. Examples of per-credit-hour charges include

Early Childhood Education ($310), Medical Lab Technician, Surgical Technician, Practical Nursing ($395), Professional Nursing, Information Systems Mgmt, Multemedia Technician ($395).

Application procedures. Admission: No deadline. $20 fee. Admission notification on a rolling basis. **Financial aid:** No deadline. FAFSA, institutional form required. Applicants notified on a rolling basis.

Academics. Special study options: Distance learning, double major, honors, independent study, internships. **Credit/placement by examination:** AP, CLEP, IB, institutional tests. 45 credit hours maximum toward associate degree, 90 toward bachelor's. Limited to specific programs, and to courses. **Support services:** Learning center, remedial instruction, study skills assistance, tutoring, writing center.

Majors. Business: Accounting, business admin. **Computer sciences:** Web page design. **Health services:** Health care admin.

Computing on campus. 100 workstations in library, computer center, student center. Online course registration, online library, helpline, wireless network available.

Student life. Freshman orientation: Mandatory. Preregistration for classes offered.

Student services. Adult student services, career counseling, services for economically disadvantaged, student employment services, financial aid counseling, placement for graduates.

Contact. E-mail: susan.hammerstrom@rasmussen.edu
Phone: (727) 942-0069 Fax: (727) 938-5709
Susan Hammerstrom, Director of Admissions, Rasmussen College: Pasco County, 8661 Citizens Drive, New Port Richey, FL 34654

Rasmussen College: Tampa/Brandon
Tampa, Florida
www.rasmussen.edu

- For-profit 4-year branch campus and career college
- Large city

General. Regionally accredited. **Calendar:** Quarter.

Freshman class profile. 129 enrolled.

Basis for selection. Open admission, but selective for some programs.

Application procedures. Admission: $20 fee.

Academics. Credit/placement by examination: AP, CLEP.

Majors. Business: Accounting, business admin.

Contact. Phone: (813) 246-7600
Susan Hammerstrom, Director of Admissions, Rasmussen College: Tampa/Brandon, 4042 Park Oak Boulevard, Tampa, FL 33610

Remington College: Tampa
Tampa, Florida
www.remingtoncollege.edu　　　　**CB code: 0123**

- For-profit 4-year technical college
- Commuter campus in very large city
- 177 degree-seeking undergraduates
- Interview required

General. Founded in 1948. Accredited by ACCSC. **Degrees:** 3 bachelor's, 33 associate awarded. **Calendar:** Quarter, extensive summer session. **Full-time faculty:** 11 total. **Part-time faculty:** 14 total.

Basis for selection. Recommendations considered; Wonderlic test used.

2011-2012 Annual costs. Personal expenses: $1,200.

Financial aid. All financial aid based on need.

Application procedures. Admission: No deadline. $50 fee. Admission notification on a rolling basis. **Financial aid:** No deadline. FAFSA, institutional form required.

Academics. Special study options: Accelerated study, combined bachelor's/graduate degree, distance learning. **Credit/placement by examination:** AP, CLEP. **Support services:** Remedial instruction, tutoring.

Majors. Protective services: Law enforcement admin.

Computing on campus. 350 workstations in library, computer center. Online library, helpline, repair service, wireless network available.

Student life. Freshman orientation: Mandatory. Preregistration for classes offered.

Student services. Career counseling, student employment services, financial aid counseling, personal counseling, placement for graduates.

Contact. Phone: (813) 935-5700 Toll-free number: (800) 992-4850
Fax: (813) 935-7415
Gary Schwartz, Director of Recruiting, Remington College: Tampa, 6302 East Dr. Martin Luther King Jr. Boulevard, Tampa, FL 33619

Ringling College of Art and Design
Sarasota, Florida　　　　　　　　　　**CB member**
www.ringling.edu　　　　　　　　　　**CB code: 5573**

- Private 4-year visual arts college
- Residential campus in small city
- 1,376 degree-seeking undergraduates: 4% part-time, 60% women, 3% African American, 6% Asian American, 13% Hispanic American, 9% international
- 73% of applicants admitted
- Application essay required
- 66% graduate within 6 years; 8% enter graduate study

General. Founded in 1931. Regionally accredited. **Degrees:** 263 bachelor's awarded. **Location:** 50 miles from Tampa. **Calendar:** Semester. **Full-time faculty:** 92 total; 61% have terminal degrees, 5% minority, 30% women. **Part-time faculty:** 63 total; 35% have terminal degrees, 3% minority, 54% women. **Class size:** 68% < 20, 30% 20-39, less than 1% 40-49, 2% 50-99. **Special facilities:** Art library, art center, art galleries.

Freshman class profile. 1,313 applied, 963 admitted, 286 enrolled.

GPA 3.75 or higher:	15%	Return as sophomores:	83%
GPA 3.50-3.74:	13%	Out-of-state:	54%
GPA 3.0-3.49:	36%	Live on campus:	85%
GPA 2.0-2.99:	34%	International:	10%
End year in good standing:	91%		

Basis for selection. Portfolio, school achievement record, statement of purpose, and recommendations important. Interview recommended. Portfolio required. **Home schooled:** State high school equivalency certificate required. **Learning Disabled:** Students seeking special accommodations for learning disabilities must provide documentation of disability.

2011-2012 Annual costs. Tuition/fees: $34,840. Room/board: $11,750.

2011-2012 Financial aid. Need-based: Average need met was 41%. Average scholarship/grant was $11,426; average loan $5,491. 46% of total undergraduate aid awarded as scholarships/grants, 54% as loans/jobs. **Non-need-based:** Scholarships awarded for academics, art.

Application procedures. Admission: Priority date 3/1; no deadline. $70 fee, may be waived for applicants with need. Admission notification on a rolling basis beginning on or about 9/1. **Financial aid:** Priority date 3/1; no closing date. FAFSA required. Applicants notified on a rolling basis starting 4/1; must reply within 2 week(s) of notification.

Academics. Special study options: Dual enrollment of high school students, exchange student, independent study, internships, New York semester, study abroad. **Credit/placement by examination:** AP, CLEP, IB. 30 credit hours maximum toward bachelor's degree. **Support services:** Learning center, pre-admission summer program, remedial instruction, study skills assistance, tutoring, writing center.

Majors. Communications technology: Animation/special effects. **Visual/performing arts:** Commercial/advertising art, graphic design, illustration, interior design, painting, photography, printmaking, sculpture, studio arts.

Most popular majors. Communication technologies 16%, visual/performing arts 84%.

Computing on campus. 850 workstations in dormitories, library, computer center, student center. Dormitories wired for high-speed internet access

and linked to campus network. Commuter students can connect to campus network. Online course registration, helpline, repair service, student web hosting, wireless network available.

Student life. Freshman orientation: Mandatory. Preregistration for classes offered. Held the week prior to start of classes. **Housing:** Coed dorms, single-sex dorms, special housing for disabled, apartments, wellness housing available. $100 fully refundable deposit. All housing accommodations are ADA compliant. **Activities:** Campus ministries, dance, drama, international student organizations, student government.

Athletics. Intramural: Basketball, football (tackle), soccer, table tennis, volleyball, weight lifting.

Student services. Career counseling, student employment services, financial aid counseling, health services, minority student services, personal counseling, placement for graduates, veterans' counselor, women's services. **Physically disabled:** Services for visually, hearing impaired.

Contact. E-mail: admissions@ringling.edu
Phone: (941) 351-5100 Toll-free number: (800) 255-7695
Fax: (941) 359-7517
James Dean, Dean of Admissions, Ringling College of Art and Design, 2700 North Tamiami Trail, Sarasota, FL 34234-5895

Rollins College
Winter Park, Florida   **CB member**
www.rollins.edu   **CB code: 5572**

▸ Private 4-year liberal arts college
▸ Residential campus in large town
▸ 1,818 degree-seeking undergraduates: 59% women, 4% African American, 2% Asian American, 10% Hispanic American, 6% international
▸ 631 degree-seeking graduate students
▸ 54% of applicants admitted
▸ Application essay required
▸ 70% graduate within 6 years

General. Founded in 1885. Regionally accredited. **Degrees:** 610 bachelor's awarded; master's offered. **Location:** 5 miles from Orlando. **Calendar:** Semester, limited summer session. **Full-time faculty:** 174 total; 88% have terminal degrees, 11% minority, 45% women. **Class size:** 66% < 20, 34% 20-39, less than 1% 50-99. **Special facilities:** 2 performing arts theaters; 75,000-square foot sports center; fine arts museum; pool; boathouse, lakeside beach, and nature walk at Lake Virginia; child development center; greenhouse; high tech classrooms; outdoor classroom.

Freshman class profile. 4,416 applied, 2,378 admitted, 555 enrolled.

Mid 50% test scores		Rank in top tenth:	44%
SAT critical reading:	550-640	Return as sophomores:	81%
SAT math:	540-640	Out-of-state:	49%
ACT composite:	24-28	Live on campus:	88%
Rank in top quarter:	77%	International:	8%

Basis for selection. School achievement record and GPA most important, followed by test scores, activities, essay, recommendations, and interview (required for merit scholarships and certain academic programs only). Students considered for merit scholarships, 3/2 Accelerated Management Program, or Honors Program required to submit SAT/ACT. All other students have the option to apply for admission under Test Score Waived Option and must submit personal representation of their strengths, interests, and/or passions as well as a teacher recommendation from a junior or senior year core course. Auditions required for applicants seeking theater and/or music scholarships.

High school preparation. College-preparatory program recommended. 17 units required; 24 recommended. Required and recommended units include English 4, mathematics 3-4, social studies 2-3, history 2-3, science 2-4, foreign language 2-3 and academic electives 2-3.

2011-2012 Annual costs. Tuition/fees: $38,400. Room/board: $12,000. Books/supplies: $780. Personal expenses: $3,160.

2011-2012 Financial aid. Need-based: 384 full-time freshmen applied for aid; 302 were judged to have need; 300 of these received aid. Average need met was 80%. Average scholarship/grant was $28,392; average loan $4,431. 82% of total undergraduate aid awarded as scholarships/grants, 18% as loans/jobs. **Non-need-based:** Awarded to 507 full-time undergraduates, including 208 freshmen. Scholarships awarded for academics, art, athletics, leadership, music/drama, state residency. **Additional information:** Audition required for theater arts and music scholarship applicants. Portfolio required for art scholarships.

Application procedures. Admission: Closing date 2/15 (postmark date). $40 fee, may be waived for applicants with need. Admission notification by 4/1. Must reply by 5/1. **Financial aid:** Priority date 3/1; no closing date. FAFSA required. Applicants notified on a rolling basis starting 3/1.

Academics. International business major featuring language training, internships, and study abroad available; pre-professional support services. **Special study options:** Accelerated study, combined bachelor's/graduate degree, cross-registration, double major, dual enrollment of high school students, exchange student, honors, independent study, internships, semester at sea, student-designed major, study abroad, teacher certification program, Washington semester. **Credit/placement by examination:** AP, CLEP, IB, institutional tests. 76 credit hours maximum toward bachelor's degree. **Support services:** Learning center, reduced course load, study skills assistance, tutoring, writing center.

Honors college/program. Top 10% of entering freshman class admitted.

Majors. Area/ethnic studies: Latin American/Caribbean. **Biology:** General, biochemistry, Biochemistry/molecular biology, marine, molecular. **Business:** International, organizational behavior. **Communications:** Organizational. **Computer sciences:** General. **Conservation:** Environmental studies. **Education:** Elementary. **English:** English lit. **Foreign languages:** Classics, French, Spanish. **History:** General. **Math:** General. **Philosophy/religion:** Philosophy, religion. **Physical sciences:** Chemistry, physics. **Psychology:** General. **Social sciences:** Anthropology, economics, international relations, political science, sociology. **Visual/performing arts:** Art, art history/conservation, dramatic, music.

Most popular majors. Business/marketing 12%, communications/journalism 12%, English 8%, psychology 11%, social sciences 28%, visual/performing arts 8%.

Computing on campus. 170 workstations in library, computer center, student center. Dormitories wired for high-speed internet access and linked to campus network. Commuter students can connect to campus network. Online course registration, online library, helpline, repair service, student web hosting, wireless network available.

Student life. Freshman orientation: Mandatory. Preregistration for classes offered. Held just prior to fall semester. **Housing:** Guaranteed on-campus for freshmen. Coed dorms, special housing for disabled, apartments, fraternity/sorority housing available. **Activities:** Bands, campus ministries, choral groups, dance, drama, film society, international student organizations, literary magazine, music ensembles, Model UN, musical theater, opera, radio station, student government, student newspaper, symphony orchestra, TV station, Hillel, interfaith community club, Intervarsity Christian Fellowship, Muslim student association, College Democrats, College Republicans, Latin American student association, Spectrum, multi-ethnic student society.

Athletics. NCAA. **Intercollegiate:** Baseball M, basketball, cross-country, golf, lacrosse, rowing (crew), sailing, skiing, soccer, softball W, swimming, tennis, volleyball W. **Intramural:** Baseball M, basketball, bowling, football (non-tackle), soccer, softball, table tennis, tennis, volleyball W. **Team name:** Tars.

Student services. Alcohol/substance abuse counseling, chaplain/spiritual director, career counseling, financial aid counseling, health services, minority student services, personal counseling, veterans' counselor, women's services. **Physically disabled:** Services for visually, speech, hearing impaired.

Contact. E-mail: admission@rollins.edu
Phone: (407) 646-2161 Fax: (407) 646-1502
Holly Pohlig, Director of Admission, Rollins College, 1000 Holt Avenue, Campus Box 2720, Winter Park, FL 32789

Saint Leo University
Saint Leo, Florida   **CB member**
www.saintleo.edu   **CB code: 5638**

▸ Private 4-year university affiliated with Roman Catholic Church
▸ Residential campus in rural community
▸ 1,923 degree-seeking undergraduates: 3% part-time, 51% women, 10% African American, 1% Asian American, 13% Hispanic American, 9% international
▸ 2,848 degree-seeking graduate students
▸ 93% of applicants admitted
▸ 45% graduate within 6 years

General. Founded in 1889. Regionally accredited. **Degrees:** 293 bachelor's, 24 associate awarded; master's offered. **ROTC:** Army, Air Force. **Location:** 25 miles from Tampa. **Calendar:** Semester, limited summer session. **Full-time faculty:** 101 total; 83% have terminal degrees, 11% minority, 37%

women. **Part-time faculty:** 52 total; 19% have terminal degrees, 8% minority, 56% women. **Class size:** 52% < 20, 48% 20-39. **Special facilities:** Center for Catholic and Jewish studies.

Freshman class profile. 1,981 applied, 1,841 admitted, 544 enrolled.

Mid 50% test scores		GPA 2.0-2.99:	30%
SAT critical reading:	440-530	Rank in top quarter:	26%
SAT math:	440-520	Rank in top tenth:	5%
SAT writing:	410-510	End year in good standing:	77%
ACT composite:	19-23	Return as sophomores:	47%
GPA 3.75 or higher:	25%	Out-of-state:	30%
GPA 3.50-3.74:	20%	Live on campus:	78%
GPA 3.0-3.49:	25%	International:	7%

Basis for selection. High School GPA, guidance counselor's recommendation, high school curriculum important. SAT or ACT recommended. Interview recommended. **Home schooled:** Transcript of courses and grades, interview, letter of recommendation (nonparent) required. Bibliography of all high school reading material, 2 letters of recommendation, portfolio of sample work required.

High school preparation. College-preparatory program required. 16 units recommended. Recommended units include English 4, mathematics 3, social studies 3, science 2, foreign language 2 and academic electives 2. Algebra I and II, geometry strongly recommended. Those planning to study science should complete courses in biology and chemistry.

2011-2012 Annual costs. Tuition/fees: $18,570. First time in college freshmen are required to participate in Orientation. The fee for that is $300 and is not included in the tuition and fees reported elsewhere. Room/board: $9,120. Books/supplies: $1,200. Personal expenses: $1,300.

2011-2012 Financial aid. Need-based: 492 full-time freshmen applied for aid; 435 were judged to have need; 435 of these received aid. Average need met was 77%. Average scholarship/grant was $14,551; average loan $3,342. 61% of total undergraduate aid awarded as scholarships/grants, 39% as loans/jobs. **Non-need-based:** Awarded to 293 full-time undergraduates, including 125 freshmen. Scholarships awarded for academics, alumni affiliation, athletics, leadership, minority status, religious affiliation, state residency.

Application procedures. Admission: Priority date 3/1; deadline 8/15 (postmark date). $40 fee, may be waived for applicants with need. Admission notification on a rolling basis beginning on or about 10/15. Must reply by May 1 or within 2 week(s) if notified thereafter. **Financial aid:** Priority date 3/1; no closing date. FAFSA required. Applicants notified on a rolling basis starting 1/31.

Academics. Special study options: Combined bachelor's/graduate degree, distance learning, double major, honors, independent study, internships, liberal arts/career combination, study abroad, teacher certification program, weekend college. Opportunity to study abroad in Italy, France, Ecuador, Spain, United Kingdom, Ireland, Australia, Germany, Scotland and Greece. Freshman English Composition classes for non-native speakers of English available. **Credit/placement by examination:** AP, CLEP, IB, SAT, ACT, institutional tests. 40 credit maximum toward associate degree, 40 toward bachelor's. **Support services:** Learning center, pre-admission summer program, reduced course load, remedial instruction, study skills assistance, tutoring, writing center.

Honors college/program. 3.5 GPA and 1150 SAT (exclusive of Writing) or 25 ACT required. Full honors curriculum consists of integrated sequence of 6 courses plus 2 research courses.

Majors. Biology: General. **Business:** Accounting, business admin, communications, hospitality admin, human resources, management science, marketing. **Computer sciences:** General. **Conservation:** Environmental studies. **Education:** Elementary, middle. **English:** Creative writing, English lit. **Health services:** Clinical lab science, health care admin. **History:** General. **Human services:** Community org/advocacy, social work. **Liberal arts:** Arts/sciences. **Math:** General. **Parks/recreation:** Sports admin. **Philosophy/religion:** Religion. **Protective services:** Criminal justice, criminalistics, homeland security. **Psychology:** General. **Social sciences:** International relations, political science, sociology.

Most popular majors. Biology 10%, business/marketing 29%, education 8%, parks/recreation 6%, psychology 10%, security/protective services 13%, social sciences 6%.

Computing on campus. 1,264 workstations in dormitories, library, student center. Dormitories wired for high-speed internet access and linked to campus network. Commuter students can connect to campus network. Online course registration, online library, helpline, repair service, student web hosting, wireless network available.

Student life. Freshman orientation: Mandatory, $300 fee. Preregistration for classes offered. 4-day program in August includes team-building, personal

responsibility activities. Advising, testing, introduction to student life in mid-July. **Policies:** Fish aquariums allowed. **Housing:** Guaranteed on-campus for all undergraduates. Coed dorms, single-sex dorms, special housing for disabled, apartments available. $500 nonrefundable deposit, deadline 8/15. Freshmen-only housing. **Activities:** Campus ministries, choral groups, drama, international student organizations, literary magazine, musical theater, radio station, student government, student newspaper, Samaritans, intercultural student association, Student Chaplain program, Pi Sigma Alpha, social work club, La Familia, students for environmental awareness, Fellowship of Christian Athletes, salsa club, Progressive Black Men.

Athletics. NCAA. **Intercollegiate:** Baseball M, basketball, cross-country, golf, lacrosse, soccer, softball W, swimming, tennis, volleyball W. **Intramural:** Basketball, field hockey, football (non-tackle), soccer, softball, tennis, volleyball. **Team name:** Lions.

Student services. Adult student services, alcohol/substance abuse counseling, chaplain/spiritual director, career counseling, student employment services, financial aid counseling, health services, personal counseling, veterans' counselor. **Physically disabled:** Services for visually impaired.

Contact. E-mail: admissions@saintleo.edu
Phone: (352) 588-8283 Toll-free number: (800) 334-5532
Fax: (352) 588-8257
Scott Rhodes, Associate Vice President of Enrollment, Saint Leo University, Box 6665 MC2008, Saint Leo, FL 33574-6665

Saint Thomas University
Miami Gardens, Florida
www.stu.edu
CB code: 5076

- Private 4-year university affiliated with Roman Catholic Church
- Commuter campus in very large city
- 1,085 degree-seeking undergraduates: 7% part-time, 56% women, 26% African American, 41% Hispanic American, 13% international
- 1,387 degree-seeking graduate students
- 39% of applicants admitted
- SAT or ACT (ACT writing optional) required
- 38% graduate within 6 years

General. Founded in 1961. Regionally accredited. Multilocation institution. Affiliated with Archdiocese of Miami. **Degrees:** 320 bachelor's awarded; master's, professional, doctoral offered. **Location:** 10 miles from Miami. **Calendar:** Semester, extensive summer session. **Full-time faculty:** 102 total; 88% have terminal degrees, 30% minority, 47% women. **Part-time faculty:** 136 total; 25% have terminal degrees, 43% minority, 40% women. **Class size:** 62% < 20, 37% 20-39, less than 1% 40-49, less than 1% 50-99.

Freshman class profile. 681 applied, 268 admitted, 209 enrolled.

Mid 50% test scores		GPA 2.0-2.99:	55%
SAT critical reading:	400-480	Rank in top quarter:	19%
SAT math:	400-510	Rank in top tenth:	5%
SAT writing:	390-480	Return as sophomores:	67%
ACT composite:	17-21	Out-of-state:	14%
GPA 3.75 or higher:	2%	Live on campus:	42%
GPA 3.50-3.74:	7%	International:	14%
GPA 3.0-3.49:	35%		

Basis for selection. High school grades, test scores primary factors. Class rank, interview, school, community activities, recommendations also considered. Interview recommended.

High school preparation. College-preparatory program recommended. 18 units required. Required units include English 4, mathematics 3, social studies 3, science 2 and academic electives 6.

2011-2012 Annual costs. Tuition/fees: $23,910. Room/board: $7,140. Books/supplies: $1,000. Personal expenses: $1,870.

2011-2012 Financial aid. Need-based: 181 full-time freshmen applied for aid; 169 were judged to have need; 169 of these received aid. Average scholarship/grant was $2,928; average loan $3,622. 88% of total undergraduate aid awarded as scholarships/grants, 12% as loans/jobs. **Non-need-based:** Awarded to 1,071 full-time undergraduates, including 233 freshmen. Scholarships awarded for academics, athletics, leadership.

Application procedures. Admission: No deadline. $40 fee, may be waived for applicants with need. Admission notification on a rolling basis. Must reply by May 1 or within 2 week(s) if notified thereafter. Applicants needing on-campus housing strongly encouraged to apply before 5/15. **Financial aid:** Priority date 4/1; no closing date. FAFSA required. Applicants notified on a rolling basis starting 3/1.

Academics. Special study options: Combined bachelor's/graduate degree, distance learning, double major, dual enrollment of high school students, honors, independent study, internships, liberal arts/career combination, teacher certification program. **Credit/placement by examination:** AP, CLEP, SAT, ACT, institutional tests. 45 credit hours maximum toward bachelor's degree. **Support services:** Learning center, pre-admission summer program, reduced course load, remedial instruction, study skills assistance, tutoring, writing center.

Majors. Biology: General. **Business:** Accounting, business admin, finance, hospitality admin, international, organizational behavior, tourism/travel. **Communications:** Communications/speech/rhetoric, media studies. **Computer sciences:** General, computer science. **Conservation:** Environmental studies. **Education:** Elementary, secondary, social studies. **English:** English lit. **Health services:** Health care admin, premedicine, preveterinary. **History:** General. **Liberal arts:** Arts/sciences. **Parks/recreation:** Sports admin. **Philosophy/religion:** Religion. **Physical sciences:** Chemistry. **Protective services:** Criminal justice. **Psychology:** General. **Social sciences:** Political science. **Theology:** Religious ed.

Most popular majors. Business/marketing 47%, communications/journalism 6%, education 6%, psychology 7%, security/protective services 6%.

Computing on campus. 200 workstations in library, computer center. Dormitories linked to campus network. Online course registration, helpline, wireless network available.

Student life. Freshman orientation: Mandatory. Preregistration for classes offered. **Housing:** Single-sex dorms available. $225 fully refundable deposit. **Activities:** Campus ministries, choral groups, international student organizations, literary magazine, music ensembles, student government, TV station, Global Leadership Pax Romana student society, Caribbean students association, Kreyol Nation, Students Working for Equal Rights.

Athletics. NAIA. **Intercollegiate:** Baseball M, cross-country, golf, soccer, softball W, tennis, volleyball W. **Intramural:** Golf, soccer M, softball, tennis, volleyball. **Team name:** Bobcats.

Student services. Adult student services, alcohol/substance abuse counseling, career counseling, student employment services, financial aid counseling, health services, personal counseling, placement for graduates. **Physically disabled:** Services for visually, hearing impaired.

Contact. E-mail: signup@stu.edu
Phone: (305) 628-6546 Toll-free number: (800) 367-9010
Fax: (305) 628-6591
Andre Lightbourn, Dean, Enrollment Services, Saint Thomas University, 16401 Northwest 37th Avenue, Miami Gardens, FL 33054-6459

Schiller International University
Largo, Florida
www.schiller.edu   **CB code: 0835**

- For-profit 4-year university
- Residential campus in small city
- 102 degree-seeking undergraduates

General. Founded in 1964. Accredited by ACICS. Campuses located in Florida, Paris, London, Madrid, Heidelberg, as well as Schiller Online. Students may transfer between campuses without loss of time or credit. **Degrees:** 37 bachelor's, 3 associate awarded; master's offered. **Location:** 20 miles from Tampa. **Calendar:** Semester, extensive summer session. **Full-time faculty:** 12 total. **Part-time faculty:** 18 total.

Basis for selection. Open admission. Interviews recommended.

2011-2012 Annual costs. Books/supplies: $1,250.

Financial aid. Non-need-based: Scholarships awarded for academics, alumni affiliation, leadership, minority status, state residency. **Additional information:** Special scholarship program for US students studying abroad at European campuses of Schiller. Work-study available to students taking 2 or more courses.

Application procedures. Admission: No deadline. $20 fee. Application must be submitted on paper. Admission notification on a rolling basis. **Financial aid:** Closing date 4/1. FAFSA, institutional form required. Applicants notified on a rolling basis starting 5/1; must reply within 3 week(s) of notification.

Academics. Completion of intermediate level of at least one foreign language required for most undergraduate degree programs. **Special study options:** Accelerated study, cooperative education, distance learning, double

major, ESL, honors, independent study, internships, liberal arts/career combination, study abroad. **Credit/placement by examination:** AP, CLEP, IB, institutional tests. 16 credit hours maximum toward associate degree, 16 toward bachelor's. **Support services:** Learning center, reduced course load, study skills assistance, tutoring.

Majors. Business: General, banking/financial services, business admin, finance, hotel/motel admin, international, international marketing, management information systems, marketing, tourism/travel. **Foreign languages:** French, German. **Social sciences:** International economics, international relations.

Most popular majors. Business/marketing 77%.

Computing on campus. Online library, wireless network available.

Student life. Freshman orientation: Mandatory. Preregistration for classes offered. **Housing:** Coed dorms available. **Activities:** Model UN, student government.

Student services. Adult student services, career counseling, services for economically disadvantaged, student employment services, financial aid counseling, minority student services, personal counseling, placement for graduates.

Contact. E-mail: admissions@schiller.edu
Phone: (727) 736-5082 Toll-free number: (800) 261-9751
Fax: (727) 734-0359
David Reid, Director of Admissions, Schiller International University, 8560 Ulmerton Road, Largo, FL 33771

South University: Tampa
Tampa, Florida
www.southuniversity.edu   **CB code: 5734**

- For-profit 4-year university
- Commuter campus in large city
- 613 degree-seeking undergraduates
- 178 graduate students
- Interview required

General. Regionally accredited. **Degrees:** 84 bachelor's, 43 associate awarded; master's offered. **Calendar:** Quarter, extensive summer session. **Full-time faculty:** 22 total. **Part-time faculty:** 51 total.

Basis for selection. Test scores most important followed by rigor of secondary school record. SAT or ACT recommended. **Home schooled:** Students must provide evidence that home schooling was conducted in accordance with state laws.

2011-2012 Annual costs. Tuition/fees: $16,035. Tuition and fees are representative of most campus degree programs.

Application procedures. Admission: No deadline. $50 fee. Admission notification on a rolling basis.

Academics. Special study options: Distance learning, internships. **Credit/placement by examination:** AP, CLEP.

Majors. Business: Business admin. **Health services:** Health care admin, nursing (RN). **Psychology:** General.

Most popular majors. Health sciences 98%.

Computing on campus. Commuter students can connect to campus network. Online library available.

Student life. Freshman orientation: Mandatory. Preregistration for classes offered.

Student services. Career counseling, student employment services, financial aid counseling, placement for graduates.

Contact. Phone: (813) 393-3800
Michele D'Alessio, Director of Admissions, South University: Tampa, 4401 North Himes Avenue, Tampa, FL 33614

South University: West Palm Beach
Royal Palm Beach, Florida
www.southuniversity.edu   **CB code: 5321**

- For-profit 4-year university
- Commuter campus in large city

♦ 882 degree-seeking undergraduates

♦ Interview required

General. Regionally accredited. **Degrees:** 89 bachelor's, 74 associate awarded; master's offered. **Location:** 3 miles from downtown, 29 miles from Fort Lauderdale. **Calendar:** Quarter, extensive summer session. **Full-time faculty:** 21 total. **Part-time faculty:** 73 total.

Freshman class profile. 79 enrolled.

Basis for selection. 900 SAT (exclusive of Writing), 19 ACT, or satisfactory score on university-administered entrance exam required. SAT or ACT recommended. **Home schooled:** Students must provide evidence that home-schooling was conducted in accordance with state laws. Certificate of attendance or completion is not sufficient.

2011-2012 Annual costs. Tuition/fees: $16,035. Tuition and fees are representative of most campus degree programs.

Application procedures. Admission: No deadline. $50 fee. Admission notification on a rolling basis. **Financial aid:** No deadline. FAFSA required. Applicants notified on a rolling basis; must reply within 2 week(s) of notification.

Academics. Special study options: Distance learning, internships. **Credit/placement by examination:** AP, CLEP, SAT, ACT, institutional tests. **Support services:** Remedial instruction, study skills assistance, tutoring.

Majors. Business: Business admin. **Computer sciences:** Information technology. **Health services:** Health care admin, nursing (RN). **Protective services:** Police science. **Psychology:** General.

Most popular majors. Business/marketing 11%, health sciences 70%, legal studies 7%, security/protective services 9%.

Computing on campus. Commuter students can connect to campus network. Online library available.

Student life. Freshman orientation: Mandatory. Preregistration for classes offered.

Student services. Career counseling, student employment services, financial aid counseling, placement for graduates, veterans' counselor.

Contact. Phone: (561) 697-9200 Fax: (561) 273-6420
Sabrina Mohammed, Senior Director of Admissions, South University: West Palm Beach, 9801 Belvedere Road, Royal Palm Beach, FL 33411

Southeastern University
Lakeland, Florida
www.seuniversity.edu
CB code: 5621

♦ Private 4-year liberal arts and teachers college affiliated with Assemblies of God

♦ Residential campus in small city

♦ 2,159 degree-seeking undergraduates: 6% part-time, 57% women, 11% African American, 1% Asian American, 15% Hispanic American, 1% international

♦ 217 degree-seeking graduate students

♦ 70% of applicants admitted

♦ SAT or ACT (ACT writing optional), application essay required

♦ 42% graduate within 6 years

General. Founded in 1935. Regionally accredited. **Degrees:** 470 bachelor's awarded; master's offered. **ROTC:** Army. **Location:** 40 miles from Tampa, 50 miles from Orlando. **Calendar:** Semester, limited summer session. **Full-time faculty:** 97 total; 66% have terminal degrees, 16% minority, 33% women. **Part-time faculty:** 73 total; 20% have terminal degrees, 11% minority, 38% women. **Class size:** 60% < 20, 34% 20-39, 4% 40-49, 2% 50-99, less than 1% >100.

Freshman class profile. 1,234 applied, 859 admitted, 443 enrolled.

Mid 50% test scores			
SAT critical reading:	440-560	GPA 3.0-3.49:	28%
SAT math:	430-540	GPA 2.0-2.99:	26%
SAT writing:	430-540	Return as sophomores:	66%
ACT composite:	18-23	Out-of-state:	36%
GPA 3.75 or higher:	29%	Live on campus:	78%
GPA 3.50-3.74:	16%	International:	1%

Basis for selection. Christian character essay required. Interview recommended for academically weak applicants.

High school preparation. College-preparatory program recommended. Recommended units include English 4, mathematics 4, social studies 4, science 4 (laboratory 1) and foreign language 2.

2011-2012 Annual costs. Tuition/fees: $17,718. Room/board: $8,668. Books/supplies: $1,200. Personal expenses: $1,200.

2010-2011 Financial aid. Need-based: 464 full-time freshmen applied for aid; 403 were judged to have need; 402 of these received aid. Average need met was 63%. Average scholarship/grant was $10,124; average loan $3,190. 49% of total undergraduate aid awarded as scholarships/grants, 51% as loans/jobs. **Non-need-based:** Awarded to 409 full-time undergraduates, including 111 freshmen. Scholarships awarded for academics, athletics, leadership, music/drama, ROTC.

Application procedures. Admission: Closing date 5/1 (postmark date). $40 fee, may be waived for applicants with need. Admission notification on a rolling basis. Must reply by 6/1. **Financial aid:** Priority date 4/15; no closing date. FAFSA, institutional form required. Applicants notified on a rolling basis starting 1/1; must reply within 6 week(s) of notification.

Academics. Special study options: Distance learning, double major, dual enrollment of high school students, honors, independent study, internships, study abroad, teacher certification program, weekend college. **Credit/placement by examination:** AP, CLEP, IB, SAT, ACT, institutional tests. 45 credit hours maximum toward bachelor's degree. **Support services:** Reduced course load, remedial instruction, study skills assistance, tutoring, writing center.

Majors. Biology: General. **Business:** General, accounting, finance, international, management information systems, marketing, organizational leadership. **Communications:** General, journalism, radio/TV. **Education:** Biology, elementary, English, mathematics, music, social science, special ed. **English:** English lit. **Health services:** Premedicine. **History:** General. **Human services:** Public policy, social work. **Math:** General. **Parks/recreation:** Sports admin. **Protective services:** Law enforcement admin. **Psychology:** General. **Theology:** Missionary, preministerial, sacred music. **Visual/performing arts:** Dramatic, film/cinema/video, music, music performance, piano/keyboard, voice/opera.

Most popular majors. Business/marketing 24%, communications/journalism 7%, education 10%, psychology 6%, public administration/social services 13%, theological studies 24%.

Computing on campus. 145 workstations in library, computer center, student center. Dormitories wired for high-speed internet access and linked to campus network. Commuter students can connect to campus network. Online course registration, online library, helpline, wireless network available.

Student life. Freshman orientation: Mandatory. Preregistration for classes offered. **Policies:** Religious observance required. **Housing:** Guaranteed on-campus for freshmen. Single-sex dorms available. $200 fully refundable deposit, deadline 6/1. **Activities:** Bands, campus ministries, choral groups, drama, international student organizations, music ensembles, musical theater, opera, radio station, student government, student newspaper, TV station, College Republicans, Habitat for Humanity, international justice mission, social work club, Christian Medical and Dental Association, student missions organization.

Athletics. NAIA, NCCAA. **Intercollegiate:** Baseball M, basketball, cheerleading, golf M, soccer, tennis W, volleyball W. **Intramural:** Basketball, football (non-tackle), soccer, softball, tennis, volleyball. **Team name:** Fire.

Student services. Adult student services, chaplain/spiritual director, career counseling, student employment services, financial aid counseling, health services, personal counseling, placement for graduates.

Contact. E-mail: admission@seuniversity.edu
Phone: (863) 667-5018 Toll-free number: (800) 500-8760
Fax: (863) 667-5200
Chris Diaz, Director of Admission, Southeastern University, 1000 Longfellow Boulevard, Lakeland, FL 33801-6034

St. John Vianney College Seminary
Miami, Florida
www.sjvcs.edu
CB code: 5650

♦ Private 4-year liberal arts and seminary college for men affiliated with Roman Catholic Church

♦ Residential campus in very large city

♦ 81 degree-seeking undergraduates

• 100% of applicants admitted
• Interview required

General. Founded in 1959. Regionally accredited. **Degrees:** 14 bachelor's awarded. **Location:** 12 miles from downtown. **Calendar:** Semester, limited summer session. **Full-time faculty:** 6 total. **Part-time faculty:** 13 total. **Class size:** 100% < 20.

Freshman class profile. 9 applied, 9 admitted, 7 enrolled.

Out-of-state:	2%	Live on campus:	100%

Basis for selection. Interview, academic record, recommendations required. Those to be formed for priesthood should present evidence of vocation for priesthood and submit psychological and physical evaluations. Applicants referred by home (church) Diocesan Offices of Vocations.

High school preparation. 20 units required. Required units include English 4, mathematics 2, social studies 2, history 2, science 2, foreign language 2 and academic electives 6.

2011-2012 Annual costs. Tuition/fees: $17,000. Room/board: $9,500. Books/supplies: $600.

Application procedures. Admission: Priority date 6/30; deadline 7/15 (receipt date). No application fee. Admission notification on a rolling basis. **Financial aid:** No deadline. FAFSA required. Applicants notified on a rolling basis.

Academics. Fluency in both English and Spanish must be achieved. Students required to take at least 1 course in alternate language each semester. **Special study options:** Cross-registration, ESL, independent study. **Credit/ placement by examination:** AP, CLEP, institutional tests. **Support services:** Pre-admission summer program, reduced course load, remedial instruction, study skills assistance, tutoring.

Majors. Philosophy/religion: Philosophy.

Computing on campus. 12 workstations in library, computer center. Online library, wireless network available.

Student life. Freshman orientation: Mandatory, $2,000 fee. Preregistration for classes offered. 3 weeks during August. **Policies:** All sophomores and upperclassmen assigned weekly apostolic work at various locations. Religious observance required. **Housing:** Guaranteed on-campus for all undergraduates. **Activities:** Choral groups, drama, music ensembles, student government, student newspaper, apostolic works program.

Athletics. Intramural: Baseball M, basketball M, handball M, racquetball M, soccer M, softball M, swimming M, table tennis M, tennis M, volleyball M, weight lifting M.

Student services. Adult student services, career counseling, financial aid counseling, health services, personal counseling.

Contact. Phone: (305) 223-4561 ext. 115 Fax: (305) 223-0650 Ramon Santos, Academic Dean, St. John Vianney College Seminary, 2900 Southwest 87 Avenue, Miami, FL 33165-3244

Stetson University
DeLand, Florida
www.stetson.edu

CB member
CB code: 5630

• Private 4-year university
• Residential campus in large town
• 2,284 degree-seeking undergraduates: 2% part-time, 58% women, 7% African American, 2% Asian American, 14% Hispanic American, 4% international
• 1,533 degree-seeking graduate students
• 66% of applicants admitted
• Application essay required
• 64% graduate within 6 years; 33% enter graduate study

General. Founded in 1883. Regionally accredited. **Degrees:** 537 bachelor's awarded; master's, professional offered. **ROTC:** Army. **Location:** 20 miles from Daytona Beach, 40 miles from Orlando. **Calendar:** Semester, limited summer session. **Full-time faculty:** 232 total; 95% have terminal degrees, 14% minority, 41% women. **Part-time faculty:** 143 total; 66% have terminal degrees, 7% minority, 43% women. **Class size:** 63% < 20, 35% 20-39, 2% 40-49, less than 1% 50-99. **Special facilities:** Geological museum, greenhouse with growth chambers, digital arts laboratory, software development lab,

aquatic research station, art center, environmental learning classroom, political archives, native plant landscape/garden, neuroscience research lab, DNA sequencing lab, courtroom classrooms, trading room and investment lab, 6 Beckerath organs.

Freshman class profile. 3,454 applied, 2,295 admitted, 715 enrolled.

Mid 50% test scores			
SAT critical reading:	520-620	Rank in top quarter:	62%
SAT math:	510-610	Rank in top tenth:	28%
SAT writing:	500-610	Return as sophomores:	77%
ACT composite:	22-27	Out-of-state:	27%
GPA 3.75 or higher:	51%	Live on campus:	83%
GPA 3.50-3.74:	14%	International:	3%
GPA 3.0-3.49:	25%	Fraternities:	33%
GPA 2.0-2.99:	10%	Sororities:	23%

Basis for selection. High school record most important, followed by class rank, and secondary school's recommendation. Extracurricular activities and particular talents or abilities also important. Interview recommended. Audition required of music majors. Portfolio recommended for art majors.

High school preparation. College-preparatory program required. 14 units required. Required units include English 4, mathematics 3, social studies 2, science 3 and foreign language 2.

2012-2013 Annual costs. Tuition/fees: $36,644. Room/board: $10,688. Books/supplies: $1,200. Personal expenses: $1,000.

2011-2012 Financial aid. Need-based: 626 full-time freshmen applied for aid; 552 were judged to have need; 550 of these received aid. Average need met was 82%. Average scholarship/grant was $26,074; average loan $4,115. 75% of total undergraduate aid awarded as scholarships/grants, 25% as loans/jobs. **Non-need-based:** Awarded to 822 full-time undergraduates, including 263 freshmen. Scholarships awarded for academics, alumni affiliation, art, athletics, leadership, minority status, music/drama, religious affiliation, ROTC, state residency.

Application procedures. Admission: Priority date 3/15; no deadline. $25 fee, may be waived for applicants with need. Admission notification on a rolling basis beginning on or about 12/1. Must reply by May 1 or within 3 week(s) if notified thereafter. **Financial aid:** Priority date 3/15; no closing date. FAFSA, institutional form required. Applicants notified on a rolling basis starting 2/15; must reply within 2 week(s) of notification.

Academics. Special study options: Accelerated study, combined bachelor's/graduate degree, distance learning, double major, honors, independent study, internships, liberal arts/career combination, student-designed major, study abroad, teacher certification program, Washington semester, weekend college. **Credit/placement by examination:** AP, CLEP, IB, SAT, ACT, institutional tests. **Support services:** Reduced course load, study skills assistance, tutoring, writing center.

Majors. Area/ethnic studies: American, Russian/Slavic. **Biology:** General, aquatic, biochemistry, molecular. **Business:** Accounting, business admin, entrepreneurial studies, finance, international, management information systems, managerial economics, marketing. **Communications:** General. **Computer sciences:** General, computer science. **Conservation:** Environmental science. **Education:** Biology, elementary, English, foreign languages, French, German, mathematics, music, secondary, social science, Spanish. **English:** English lit. **Foreign languages:** French, German, Spanish. **History:** General. **Liberal arts: Math:** General. **Parks/recreation:** Sports admin. **Philosophy/religion:** Philosophy, religion. **Physical sciences:** Chemistry, physics. **Psychology:** General. **Social sciences:** General, economics, geography, international relations, political science, sociology. **Visual/performing arts:** Art, digital arts, dramatic, music, music performance, music technology, music theory/composition, piano/keyboard, stringed instruments, voice/opera.

Most popular majors. Business/marketing 34%, psychology 7%, social sciences 9%, visual/performing arts 12%.

Computing on campus. 488 workstations in dormitories, library, computer center, student center. Dormitories wired for high-speed internet access and linked to campus network. Commuter students can connect to campus network. Online course registration, online library, helpline, repair service, student web hosting, wireless network available.

Student life. Freshman orientation: Mandatory, $100 fee. Preregistration for classes offered. Held the 4 days prior to start of classes. **Housing:** Guaranteed on-campus for all undergraduates. Coed dorms, single-sex dorms, apartments, fraternity/sorority housing, wellness housing available. $200 nonrefundable deposit. Pets allowed in dorm rooms. Living-learning communities include First-Year Experience, Sophomore Experience, Women's Leadership, Global-Village, Wellness House and Honors House. **Activities:** Bands, campus ministries, choral groups, dance, drama, film society, international student organizations, literary magazine, music ensembles, Model UN, musical theater, opera, radio station, student government, student newspaper, symphony orchestra, black student association, Caribbean student organization, Habitat

for Humanity, Muslim student association, Jewish student organization, Hatter Harvest, National Organization for Women, College Democrats, College Republicans.

Athletics. NCAA. **Intercollegiate:** Baseball M, basketball, cross-country, golf, rowing (crew), soccer, softball W, tennis, volleyball W. **Intramural:** Baseball M, basketball, bowling, golf, soccer, softball, swimming, tennis, volleyball. **Team name:** Hatters.

Student services. Adult student services, alcohol/substance abuse counseling, chaplain/spiritual director, career counseling, student employment services, financial aid counseling, health services, minority student services, personal counseling, placement for graduates, women's services. **Physically disabled:** Services for visually, speech impaired.

Contact. E-mail: admissions@stetson.edu
Phone: (386) 822-7100 Toll-free number: (800) 688-0101
Fax: (386) 822-7112
Robert Stewart, Director of Admissions, Stetson University, Campus Box 8378, DeLand, FL 32723

Talmudic College of Florida
Miami Beach, Florida
www.talmudicu.edu   **CB code: 0514**

- Private 4-year rabbinical college for men affiliated with Jewish faith
- Very large city
- 48 degree-seeking undergraduates
- Interview required

General. Founded in 1974. Accredited by AARTS. **Degrees:** 5 bachelor's awarded; master's offered. **Location:** 3 miles from downtown. **Calendar:** Semester, extensive summer session. **Full-time faculty:** 5 total. **Class size:** 100% < 20. **Special facilities:** Rabbinical studies research library.

Freshman class profile.

Out-of-state:	60%	Live on campus:	100%

Basis for selection. Recommendations and personal interview most important. Essay recommended.

High school preparation. Recommended units include foreign language 2. Two Bible and Talmud, 1 Jewish thought recommended.

2011-2012 Annual costs. Tuition/fees: $10,500. Books/supplies: $900.

Financial aid. All financial aid based on need.

Application procedures. Admission: No deadline. $250 fee, may be waived for applicants with need. Admission notification on a rolling basis. **Financial aid:** No deadline. FAFSA, institutional form required. Applicants notified on a rolling basis.

Academics. Special study options: Cooperative education, distance learning, dual enrollment of high school students, honors, independent study, student-designed major, study abroad, weekend college. **Credit/placement by examination:** AP, CLEP. **Support services:** Remedial instruction, study skills assistance, tutoring.

Majors. Philosophy/religion: Judaic. **Theology:** Religious ed.

Computing on campus. 8 workstations in library, computer center. Online library available.

Student life. Freshman orientation: Available. Preregistration for classes offered. **Policies:** Students must be "Shomer Mitzvot". Religious observance required. **Housing:** Guaranteed on-campus for all undergraduates. Apartments available.

Student services. Adult student services, chaplain/spiritual director, career counseling, student employment services, financial aid counseling, health services, legal services, personal counseling.

Contact. Phone: (305) 534-0750 Toll-free number: (888) 825-6834
Fax: (305) 534-8444
Rabbi Yeshaya Greenberg, Dean of Students, Talmudic College of Florida, 1910 Alton Road, Miami Beach, FL 33139

Trinity Baptist College
Jacksonville, Florida
www.tbc.edu   **CB code: 5780**

- Private 4-year Bible and teachers college
- Very large city
- 264 degree-seeking undergraduates

General. Regionally accredited; also accredited by TRACS. **Degrees:** 32 bachelor's, 3 associate awarded; master's offered. **Calendar:** Semester. **Full-time faculty:** 11 total. **Part-time faculty:** 11 total.

Basis for selection. Meets school's high standard of Christian faith and academic rigor.

2011-2012 Annual costs. Tuition/fees: $8,730. Room/board: $5,200. Books/supplies: $1,500.

Application procedures. Admission: $30 fee.

Academics. Credit/placement by examination: AP, CLEP.

Majors. Education: Elementary, secondary, special ed. **Theology:** Missionary, pastoral counseling. **Visual/performing arts:** Music.

Contact. E-mail: admissions@tbc.edu
Phone: (800) 786-2206
Director of Enrollment Management, Trinity Baptist College, 800 Hammond Boulevard, Jacksonville, FL 32221

Trinity College of Florida
Trinity, Florida
www.trinitycollege.edu   **CB code: 1979**

- Private 4-year Bible college affiliated with interdenominational tradition
- Commuter campus in small city
- 192 degree-seeking undergraduates: 12% part-time, 43% women, 11% African American, 1% Asian American, 12% Hispanic American, 2% international
- 35% of applicants admitted
- SAT or ACT (ACT writing optional), application essay required

General. Regionally accredited; also accredited by ABHE. **Degrees:** 28 bachelor's awarded. **Location:** 25 miles from Tampa. **Calendar:** Semester, limited summer session. **Full-time faculty:** 7 total; 86% have terminal degrees, 29% women. **Part-time faculty:** 24 total; 33% have terminal degrees, 4% minority, 17% women. **Class size:** 77% < 20, 23% 20-39.

Freshman class profile. 243 applied, 85 admitted, 33 enrolled.

Mid 50% test scores			
SAT critical reading:	460-580	GPA 2.0-2.99:	38%
SAT math:	470-530	Rank in top quarter:	39%
SAT writing:	420-490	Rank in top tenth:	11%
ACT composite:	17-25	End year in good standing:	72%
GPA 3.75 or higher:	24%	Return as sophomores:	51%
GPA 3.50-3.74:	28%	Live on campus:	77%
GPA 3.0-3.49:	10%	International:	7%

Basis for selection. Applicants must provide evidence of Christian character and witness, GPA. **Home schooled:** Transcript of courses and grades required. GED may be required if student is not registered with local superintendent or umbrella school.

High school preparation. College-preparatory program recommended. 18 units required. Required units include English 4, mathematics 4, social studies 2, history 2, science 4 and foreign language 2.

2012-2013 Annual costs. Tuition/fees: $12,608. Room/board: $7,066. Books/supplies: $1,232. Personal expenses: $2,718.

2011-2012 Financial aid. Need-based: 28 full-time freshmen applied for aid; 27 were judged to have need; 24 of these received aid. Average need met was 51%. Average scholarship/grant was $7,396; average loan $3,391. 47% of total undergraduate aid awarded as scholarships/grants, 53% as loans/jobs. **Non-need-based:** Awarded to 4 full-time undergraduates, including 1 freshmen. Scholarships awarded for academics.

Application procedures. Admission: Closing date 8/2 (receipt date). $25 fee, may be waived for applicants with need, free for online applicants. Admission notification on a rolling basis. **Financial aid:** Priority date 3/15, closing date 9/15. FAFSA, institutional form required. Applicants notified

on a rolling basis starting 1/5; must reply within 2 week(s) of notification.

Academics. Special study options: Accelerated study, double major, dual enrollment of high school students, honors, independent study, internships, weekend college. **Credit/placement by examination:** AP, CLEP, SAT, ACT, institutional tests. 24 credit hours maximum toward associate degree, 24 toward bachelor's. **Support services:** Reduced course load, remedial instruction, tutoring, writing center.

Majors. Business: General. **Education:** Elementary. **Psychology:** Counseling. **Theology:** Missionary, pastoral counseling, preministerial, youth ministry.

Most popular majors. Education 7%, theological studies 93%.

Computing on campus. 14 workstations in library, computer center. Dormitories wired for high-speed internet access and linked to campus network. Online library, repair service, wireless network available.

Student life. Freshman orientation: Mandatory. Preregistration for classes offered. Held 4 days before classes begin. Includes social gathering, vehicle registration, student IDs, and assessment testing. **Policies:** Religious observance required. **Housing:** Guaranteed on-campus for all undergraduates. Single-sex dorms, special housing for disabled, apartments, wellness housing available. $150 fully refundable deposit, deadline 7/1. **Activities:** Campus ministries, choral groups, drama, literary magazine, student government.

Athletics. NCCAA. **Intercollegiate:** Basketball M, volleyball W. **Intramural:** Soccer M, softball M. **Team name:** Tigers.

Student services. Chaplain/spiritual director, career counseling, financial aid counseling, personal counseling.

Contact. E-mail: admissions@trinitycollege.edu
Phone: (727) 569-1411 Toll-free number: (800) 388-0869
Fax: (727) 569-1410
Mark Sawyer, Director of Admissions, Trinity College of Florida, 2430 Welbilt Boulevard, Trinity, FL 34655-4401

University of Central Florida
Orlando, Florida   **CB member**
www.ucf.edu   **CB code: 5233**

- Public 4-year university
- Residential campus in very large city
- 49,634 degree-seeking undergraduates: 25% part-time, 54% women, 10% African American, 6% Asian American, 19% Hispanic American, 1% international
- 8,122 degree-seeking graduate students
- 45% of applicants admitted
- SAT or ACT with writing required
- 62% graduate within 6 years

General. Founded in 1963. Regionally accredited. **Degrees:** 10,815 bachelor's, 338 associate awarded; master's, professional, doctoral offered. **ROTC:** Army, Air Force. **Location:** 13 miles from downtown. **Calendar:** Semester, extensive summer session. **Full-time faculty:** 1,307 total; 78% have terminal degrees, 24% minority, 40% women. **Part-time faculty:** 527 total; 34% have terminal degrees, 19% minority, 54% women. **Class size:** 26% < 20, 39% 20-39, 11% 40-49, 17% 50-99, 7% >100. **Special facilities:** Solar energy center, simulation and training institute, research/education in optics and lasers center, space education and research center, biomolecular sciences center, forensic science center, arboretum, observatory.

Freshman class profile. 33,968 applied, 15,303 admitted, 6,301 enrolled.

Mid 50% test scores			
SAT critical reading:	530-630	**Rank in top quarter:**	72%
SAT math:	560-650	**Rank in top tenth:**	34%
SAT writing:	510-610	**End year in good standing:**	97%
ACT composite:	24-28	**Return as sophomores:**	87%
GPA 3.75 or higher:	52%	**Out-of-state:**	7%
GPA 3.50-3.74:	28%	**Live on campus:**	68%
GPA 3.0-3.49:	19%	**International:**	1%
GPA 2.0-2.99:	1%	**Fraternities:**	9%
		Sororities:	11%

Basis for selection. Two-thirds of admission offers made via review of GPA and standardized test scores. One-third made via review of factors such as grades, strength of coursework, essays, letters of recommendation, special talents. Essay recommended. Audition required of music majors. Portfolio recommended for art majors. **Home schooled:** Provide detail about coursework and teaching process.

High school preparation. College-preparatory program required. 18 units required. Required units include English 4, mathematics 4, social studies 3, science 3 (laboratory 2), foreign language 2 and academic electives 2.

2011-2012 Annual costs. Tuition/fees: $5,584; $21,063 out-of-state. Room/board: $9,063. Books/supplies: $924. Personal expenses: $2,276.

2010-2011 Financial aid. Need-based: 4,865 full-time freshmen applied for aid; 4,009 were judged to have need; 3,966 of these received aid. Average need met was 63%. Average scholarship/grant was $6,022; average loan $3,462. 56% of total undergraduate aid awarded as scholarships/grants, 44% as loans/jobs. **Non-need-based:** Awarded to 15,326 full-time undergraduates, including 4,066 freshmen. Scholarships awarded for academics, alumni affiliation, athletics, leadership, ROTC, state residency.

Application procedures. Admission: Priority date 1/1; deadline 5/1 (postmark date). $30 fee, may be waived for applicants with need. Admission notification on a rolling basis beginning on or about 10/1. Must reply by May 1 or within 3 week(s) if notified thereafter. **Financial aid:** Priority date 3/1, closing date 6/30. FAFSA required. Applicants notified on a rolling basis starting 3/15; must reply within 3 week(s) of notification.

Academics. Special study options: Accelerated study, combined bachelor's/graduate degree, cooperative education, distance learning, double major, dual enrollment of high school students, ESL, honors, independent study, internships, study abroad, teacher certification program. Lead Scholars program. **Credit/placement by examination:** AP, CLEP, IB, SAT, ACT, institutional tests. 45 credit hours maximum toward bachelor's degree. **Support services:** Learning center, pre-admission summer program, reduced course load, study skills assistance, tutoring, writing center.

Honors college/program. Requires separate application, admission based on GPA, test scores, and class rank. Small general and specialized honors courses, honors building, and residence hall available. Accepts approximately 700 freshmen in the fall.

Majors. Architecture: Architecture. **Area/ethnic studies:** Latin American. **Biology:** General, biomedical sciences, biotechnology. **Business:** General, accounting, business admin, event planning, finance, hospitality admin, managerial economics, marketing, real estate, restaurant/food services. **Communications:** Advertising, communications/speech/rhetoric, journalism, radio/TV. **Computer sciences:** General, information technology. **Education:** Art, early childhood, elementary, English, foreign languages, mathematics, music, physical, science, social science, special ed, trade/industrial. **Engineering:** Aerospace, civil, computer, electrical, environmental, industrial, mechanical, structural. **English:** English lit. **Foreign languages:** General, French, Spanish. **Health services:** Athletic training, audiology/speech pathology, clinical lab science, health care admin, medical records admin, nursing (RN), predental, premedicine, prepharmacy, preveterinary. **History:** General. **Human services:** General, social work. **Liberal arts:** Humanities. **Math:** General, statistics. **Philosophy/religion:** Philosophy, religion. **Physical sciences:** Chemistry, physics. **Protective services:** Criminal justice, forensics. **Psychology:** General. **Social sciences:** General, anthropology, economics, political science, sociology. **Visual/performing arts:** Art, cinematography, digital arts, dramatic, music performance, photography, studio arts.

Most popular majors. Business/marketing 25%, education 9%, engineering/engineering technologies 6%, health sciences 11%, psychology 9%.

Computing on campus. 3,674 workstations in library, computer center, student center. Dormitories wired for high-speed internet access and linked to campus network. Commuter students can connect to campus network. Online course registration, online library, helpline, repair service, student web hosting, wireless network available.

Student life. Freshman orientation: Mandatory, $35 fee. Preregistration for classes offered. Ten sessions offered throughout spring and summer. 2-day event includes financial aid presentation, advising. **Housing:** Coed dorms, apartments, fraternity/sorority housing, wellness housing available. $250 non-refundable deposit. Affiliated student residence housing. Students under guidance of university housing resident assistants considered part of on-campus housing. **Activities:** Bands, campus ministries, choral groups, drama, film society, international student organizations, literary magazine, music ensembles, Model UN, musical theater, radio station, student government, student newspaper, symphony orchestra, TV station, campus activities board, African American student union, orientation team, Hispanic American student association, Korean student association, Indian student association, Christian student association, Jewish student union.

Athletics. NCAA. **Intercollegiate:** Baseball M, basketball, cheerleading, cross-country, football (tackle) M, golf, rowing (crew) W, soccer, softball W, tennis, track and field W, volleyball W. **Intramural:** Badminton, baseball M, basketball, bowling, football (non-tackle), golf, racquetball, soccer, softball, tennis, volleyball, weight lifting, wrestling M. **Team name:** Knights.

Student services. Adult student services, alcohol/substance abuse counseling, career counseling, student employment services, financial aid counseling, health services, legal services, minority student services, on-campus daycare, personal counseling, placement for graduates, veterans' counselor, women's services. **Physically disabled:** Services for visually, speech, hearing impaired.

Contact. E-mail: admissions@ucf.edu
Phone: (407) 823-3000 Fax: (407) 823-5625
Gordon Chavis, Associate Vice President, University of Central Florida, Box 160111, Orlando, FL 32816-0111

University of Florida
Gainesville, Florida   **CB member**
www.ufl.edu   **CB code: 5812**

- Public 4-year university
- Residential campus in small city
- 31,988 degree-seeking undergraduates: 6% part-time, 55% women, 9% African American, 8% Asian American, 18% Hispanic American, 1% international
- 12,341 degree-seeking graduate students
- 43% of applicants admitted
- SAT or ACT with writing, application essay required

General. Founded in 1853. Regionally accredited. **Degrees:** 8,685 bachelor's awarded; master's, professional, doctoral offered. **ROTC:** Army, Naval, Air Force. **Location:** 70 miles from Jacksonville. **Calendar:** Semester, limited summer session. **Full-time faculty:** 3,372 total. **Part-time faculty:** 224 total. **Special facilities:** Natural history museum, marine laboratory, wildlife sanctuary, citrus research center, bell carillon, pipe organ, center for performing arts, hyperbaric chamber, microkelvin laboratory, brain institute, nuclear reactor.

Freshman class profile. 27,295 applied, 11,786 admitted, 6,429 enrolled.

Mid 50% test scores			
SAT critical reading:	570-670	GPA 3.50-3.74:	6%
SAT math:	590-690	GPA 3.0-3.49:	2%
ACT composite:	24-30	Rank in top quarter:	93%
GPA 3.75 or higher:	92%	Rank in top tenth:	74%
		International:	1%

Basis for selection. High school grades, academic course selection, SAT/ACT scores, extracurricular activities, awards, honors, recognitions, special talents and recommendations considered. SAT Subject Tests used strictly for placement except for applicants from non-regionally accredited schools. **Home schooled:** Statement describing home school structure and mission, transcript of courses and grades, state high school equivalency certificate, letter of recommendation (nonparent) required. SAT Subject Test in math (level II-C) and letter from principal or guidance counselor required. **Learning Disabled:** Optional disclosure; students receive extra review by disability office.

High school preparation. College-preparatory program required. 18 units required. Required units include English 4, mathematics 4, social studies 3, science 3 (laboratory 2), foreign language 2 and academic electives 2. English units must include substantial writing; math units must include algebra I, formal geometry, algebra II; foreign language must be same language and must be sequential.

2011-2012 Annual costs. Tuition/fees: $5,657; $27,934 out-of-state. Room/board: $8,800. Books/supplies: $1,070. Personal expenses: $3,730.

Financial aid. Non-need-based: Scholarships awarded for academics, alumni affiliation, art, athletics, leadership, minority status, music/drama, ROTC, state residency.

Application procedures. Admission: Closing date 11/1 (postmark date). $30 fee, may be waived for applicants with need. Application must be submitted online. Admission notification on a rolling basis beginning on or about 2/12. Must reply by 5/1. $200 tuition deposit required by May 1. **Financial aid:** Priority date 3/15; no closing date. FAFSA required. Applicants notified on a rolling basis starting 4/1.

Academics. Special study options: Accelerated study, cooperative education, cross-registration, distance learning, double major, dual enrollment of high school students, ESL, exchange student, external degree, honors, independent study, internships, liberal arts/career combination, semester at sea, student-designed major, study abroad, teacher certification program, Washington semester, weekend college. TV-delivered credit-bearing courses. **Credit/placement by examination:** AP, CLEP, IB, SAT, ACT, institutional tests. 45 credit hours maximum toward bachelor's degree. **Support services:**

Learning center, reduced course load, study skills assistance, tutoring, writing center.

Majors. Architecture: Architecture, landscape. **Area/ethnic studies:** Asian, women's. **Biology:** General, bacteriology, botany, entomology, exercise physiology, zoology. **Business:** Accounting, business admin, finance, insurance, management science, marketing, real estate. **Communications:** Advertising, journalism, public relations, radio/TV. **Computer sciences:** General. **Conservation:** Environmental science, forestry, wildlife/wilderness. **Education:** Agricultural, art, elementary, music, special ed. **Engineering:** Aerospace, agricultural, chemical, civil, computer, electrical, environmental, materials, mechanical, nuclear, systems. **English:** English lit. **Foreign languages:** Classics, French, German, linguistics, Portuguese, Russian, Spanish. **General:** Animal sciences, economics, food science, horticultural science, ornamental horticulture, plant sciences, products processing, soil science. **Health services:** Athletic training, audiology/speech pathology, community health, nursing (RN). **History:** General. **Math:** General, statistics. **Parks/recreation:** Facilities management, sports admin. **Philosophy/religion:** Judaic, philosophy, religion. **Physical sciences:** Astronomy, chemistry, geology, physics. **Protective services:** Firefighting. **Psychology:** General. **Social sciences:** Anthropology, criminology, economics, geography, political science, sociology. **Visual/performing arts:** Art history/conservation, dance, digital arts, dramatic, graphic design, interior design, music, studio arts. **Work/family studies:** Family/community services.

Computing on campus. PC or laptop required. 1,512 workstations in library, student center. Dormitories wired for high-speed internet access and linked to campus network. Commuter students can connect to campus network. Online course registration, online library, helpline, student web hosting, wireless network available.

Student life. Freshman orientation: Mandatory, $120 fee. Preregistration for classes offered. Two-day program held various dates in May, June and July. **Policies:** Student code of conduct and honor code enforced. **Housing:** Coed dorms, special housing for disabled, apartments, fraternity/sorority housing available. $200 nonrefundable deposit. Pets allowed in dorm rooms. **Activities:** Bands, choral groups, dance, drama, film society, literary magazine, music ensembles, musical theater, radio station, student government, student newspaper, symphony orchestra, TV station, over 925 student groups available.

Athletics. NCAA. **Intercollegiate:** Baseball M, basketball, cheerleading, cross-country, diving, football (tackle) M, golf, gymnastics W, lacrosse W, soccer W, softball W, swimming, tennis, track and field, volleyball W. **Intramural:** Basketball, bowling, football (non-tackle), golf, racquetball, soccer, softball, swimming, table tennis, tennis, track and field, volleyball, wrestling. **Team name:** Gators.

Student services. Alcohol/substance abuse counseling, career counseling, services for economically disadvantaged, student employment services, financial aid counseling, health services, legal services, minority student services, on-campus daycare, personal counseling, placement for graduates, veterans' counselor. **Physically disabled:** Services for visually, speech, hearing impaired.

Contact. Phone: (352) 392-1365
Zina Evans, Vice President Enrollment Management, University of Florida, 201 Criser Hall-PO Box 114000, Gainesville, FL 32611-4000

University of Miami
Coral Gables, Florida   **CB member**
www.miami.edu   **CB code: 5815**

- Private 4-year university
- Residential campus in small city
- 10,144 degree-seeking undergraduates: 5% part-time, 51% women, 7% African American, 6% Asian American, 24% Hispanic American, 11% international
- 5,544 degree-seeking graduate students
- 38% of applicants admitted
- SAT or ACT (ACT writing optional), application essay required

General. Founded in 1925. Regionally accredited. **Degrees:** 2,383 bachelor's awarded; master's, professional, doctoral offered. **ROTC:** Army, Air Force. **Location:** 7 miles from downtown. **Calendar:** Semester, extensive summer session. **Full-time faculty:** 1,043 total; 87% have terminal degrees, 30% minority, 37% women. **Part-time faculty:** 359 total; 60% have terminal degrees, 40% minority, 38% women. **Class size:** 52% < 20, 37% 20-39, 5% 40-49, 5% 50-99, 2% >100. **Special facilities:** Cinema, observatory, palmetum, marine science research vessels, broadcasting studios, concert hall, arboretum, performing arts theater, film studios, sound stage.

Freshman class profile. 27,745 applied, 10,635 admitted, 2,172 enrolled.

Mid 50% test scores		GPA 2.0-2.99:	1%
SAT critical reading:	600-690	Rank in top quarter:	92%
SAT math:	630-710	Rank in top tenth:	72%
SAT writing:	600-690	End year in good standing:	95%
ACT composite:	28-32	Return as sophomores:	91%
GPA 3.75 or higher:	76%	Out-of-state:	62%
GPA 3.50-3.74:	13%	Live on campus:	84%
GPA 3.0-3.49:	10%	International:	12%

Basis for selection. Transcript, standardized test scores, letters of recommendation, extra-curricular activities, and essay most important. Portfolio, interviews, and/or audition may be required for some programs. SAT Subject Tests in math and science required for dual degree honors program in medicine. **Home schooled:** Transcript of courses and grades required.

High school preparation. College-preparatory program recommended. 20 units recommended. Recommended units include English 4, mathematics 4, social studies 3, history 2, science 3 (laboratory 2), foreign language 2, computer science 1 and visual/performing arts 1.

2011-2012 Annual costs. Tuition/fees: $39,654. Room/board: $11,528.

2011-2012 Financial aid. Need-based: 1,432 full-time freshmen applied for aid; 929 were judged to have need; 929 of these received aid. Average need met was 82%. Average scholarship/grant was $23,741; average loan $3,989. 70% of total undergraduate aid awarded as scholarships/grants, 30% as loans/jobs. **Non-need-based:** Awarded to 3,336 full-time undergraduates, including 950 freshmen. Scholarships awarded for academics, athletics, leadership, music/drama.

Application procedures. Admission: Closing date 1/1 (postmark date). $70 fee, may be waived for applicants with need. Application must be submitted online. Admission notification by 4/15. Must reply by 5/1. **Financial aid:** Priority date 2/1; no closing date. FAFSA required. Applicants notified on a rolling basis starting 3/1.

Academics. Special study options: Accelerated study, combined bachelor's/graduate degree, cooperative education, distance learning, double major, dual enrollment of high school students, ESL, honors, independent study, internships, liberal arts/career combination, student-designed major, study abroad, teacher certification program, Washington semester, weekend college. **Credit/placement by examination:** AP, CLEP, IB, SAT, ACT, institutional tests. **Support services:** Learning center, reduced course load, remedial instruction, study skills assistance, tutoring, writing center.

Majors. Architecture: Architecture. **Area/ethnic studies:** African-American, American, Latin American, women's. **Biology:** General, biochemistry, biophysics, exercise physiology, marine, microbiology/immunology, neuroscience. **Business:** Accounting, business admin, entrepreneurial studies, finance, human resources, international, management science, managerial economics, marketing, real estate. **Communications:** Advertising, broadcast journalism, communications/speech/rhetoric, digital media, journalism, media studies, organizational, photojournalism, public relations, radio/TV. **Computer sciences:** Computer graphics, computer science, data processing, information systems, security. **Conservation:** Management/policy. **Education:** Elementary, music, secondary, special ed. **Engineering:** Aerospace, architectural, biomedical, civil, computer, electrical, engineering science, environmental, industrial, manufacturing, mechanical. **English:** Creative writing, English lit. **Foreign languages:** Ancient Greek, classics, French, German, Italian, Latin, Spanish. **Health services:** Athletic training, health care admin, music therapy, nursing (RN), premedicine, prepharmacy. **History:** General. **Math:** General, applied, probability. **Parks/recreation:** Exercise sciences, sports admin. **Philosophy/religion:** Judaic, philosophy, religion. **Physical sciences:** Atmospheric science, chemistry, geology, meteorology, oceanography, physics. **Psychology:** General, community. **Social sciences:** Anthropology, criminology, economics, geography, international relations, political science, sociology. **Visual/performing arts:** General, acting, art, art history/conservation, ceramics, cinematography, design, directing/producing, dramatic, film/cinema/video, graphic design, jazz, multimedia, music, music performance, music theory/composition, musicology, painting, photography, piano/keyboard, printmaking, sculpture, studio arts, theater arts management, theater design, voice/opera. **Work/family studies:** Family/community services.

Most popular majors. Biology 15%, business/marketing 19%, communications/journalism 10%, engineering/engineering technologies 6%, health sciences 8%, psychology 7%, social sciences 9%, visual/performing arts 8%.

Computing on campus. Dormitories wired for high-speed internet access and linked to campus network. Commuter students can connect to campus network. Online course registration, online library, helpline, repair service, student web hosting, wireless network available.

Student life. Freshman orientation: Mandatory. Preregistration for classes offered. Three-day program held in August; designed for students, parents and families. **Policies:** Student initiated and administered honor code.

Freshmen not permitted cars on campus. **Housing:** Guaranteed on-campus for freshmen. Coed dorms, special housing for disabled, apartments, fraternity/sorority housing available. $250 nonrefundable deposit, deadline 5/1. Special interest housing (affinity communities). **Activities:** Bands, campus ministries, choral groups, dance, drama, film society, international student organizations, literary magazine, music ensembles, Model UN, musical theater, opera, radio station, student government, student newspaper, symphony orchestra, TV station, Campus Crusade for Christ, No Zebras, Canes Against Sexual Assault, National Gandhi Day of Service, Students Together Ending Poverty, National Pan Hellenic Council, Council for Democracy, United Black Students, Big Brothers Big Sisters and Dance Marathon.

Athletics. NCAA. **Intercollegiate:** Baseball M, basketball, cross-country, diving, football (tackle) M, golf W, rowing (crew) W, soccer W, swimming W, tennis, track and field, volleyball W. **Intramural:** Basketball, football (non-tackle), golf, racquetball, softball, tennis, track and field. **Team name:** Hurricanes.

Student services. Adult student services, alcohol/substance abuse counseling, career counseling, services for economically disadvantaged, student employment services, financial aid counseling, health services, minority student services, on-campus daycare, personal counseling, placement for graduates, veterans' counselor, women's services. **Physically disabled:** Services for visually, hearing impaired.

Contact. E-mail: admission@miami.edu
Phone: (305) 284-4323 Fax: (305) 284-6605
Deanna Voss, Director of Admission, University of Miami, PO Box 249117, Coral Gables, FL 33124-9117

University of North Florida
Jacksonville, Florida   **CB member**
www.unf.edu   **CB code: 5490**

- Public 4-year university
- Residential campus in very large city
- 14,103 degree-seeking undergraduates: 26% part-time, 56% women, 10% African American, 5% Asian American, 8% Hispanic American, 1% international
- 1,709 degree-seeking graduate students
- 49% of applicants admitted
- SAT or ACT with writing required
- 47% graduate within 6 years

General. Founded in 1965. Regionally accredited. **Degrees:** 2,995 bachelor's, 347 associate awarded; master's, professional, doctoral offered. **ROTC:** Army, Naval. **Location:** 12 miles from downtown. **Calendar:** Semester, extensive summer session. **Full-time faculty:** 537 total; 78% have terminal degrees, 13% minority, 46% women. **Part-time faculty:** 279 total; 28% have terminal degrees, 14% minority, 55% women. **Class size:** 30% < 20, 42% 20-39, 18% 40-49, 6% 50-99, 4% >100. **Special facilities:** Nature trails, designated bird sanctuary, fine arts center, skate park, museum of contemporay art.

Freshman class profile. 11,053 applied, 5,471 admitted, 1,777 enrolled.

Mid 50% test scores		Rank in top quarter:	60%
SAT critical reading:	530-620	Rank in top tenth:	27%
SAT math:	530-620	End year in good standing:	81%
ACT composite:	23-26	Return as sophomores:	82%
GPA 3.75 or higher:	45%	Out-of-state:	3%
GPA 3.50-3.74:	20%	Live on campus:	64%
GPA 3.0-3.49:	32%	International:	1%
GPA 2.0-2.99:	3%		

Basis for selection. SAT/ACT and GPA based on 19 academic units very important. High school academic courses (not including electives) used for calculating GPA. Summer program available for some students who do not meet fall admissions criteria; students admitted on probation. Audition required for music majors. **Home schooled:** Required to pass all sections of GED. **Learning Disabled:** Applicants should register with Disability Resource Center.

High school preparation. College-preparatory program required. 18 units required. Required units include English 4, mathematics 4, social studies 3, science 3 (laboratory 1), foreign language 2 and academic electives 2.

2011-2012 Annual costs. Tuition/fees: $5,627; $19,015 out-of-state. Room/board: $8,333. Books/supplies: $1,000. Personal expenses: $2,349.

2011-2012 Financial aid. Need-based: 1,620 full-time freshmen applied for aid; 1,040 were judged to have need; 1,030 of these received aid. Average need met was 90%. Average scholarship/grant was $6,714; average loan

$2,439. 52% of total undergraduate aid awarded as scholarships/grants, 48% as loans/jobs. **Non-need-based:** Awarded to 5,049 full-time undergraduates, including 1,164 freshmen. Scholarships awarded for academics, athletics, leadership, minority status, music/drama, state residency.

Application procedures. Admission: Priority date 11/18; no deadline. $30 fee, may be waived for applicants with need. Admission notification on a rolling basis beginning on or about 1/1. **Financial aid:** Priority date 4/1; no closing date. FAFSA required. Applicants notified on a rolling basis starting 3/15; must reply within 2 week(s) of notification.

Academics. Special study options: Accelerated study, combined bachelor's/graduate degree, cooperative education, distance learning, double major, dual enrollment of high school students, ESL, exchange student, honors, independent study, internships, New York semester, student-designed major, study abroad, teacher certification program, United Nations semester, Washington semester, weekend college. Living-Learning Communities (LLC) ,Transformational Learning Opportunities (TLO). **Credit/placement by examination:** AP, CLEP, IB, SAT, ACT, institutional tests. 30 credit hours maximum toward bachelor's degree. **Support services:** Learning center, pre-admission summer program, reduced course load, study skills assistance, tutoring, writing center.

Majors. Area/ethnic studies: French. **Biology:** General. **Business:** Accounting, banking/financial services, business admin, finance, international, managerial economics, marketing, transportation. **Communications:** Media studies. **Computer sciences:** General. **Education:** Art, early childhood, elementary, middle, music, physical, secondary, special ed. **Engineering:** Civil, electrical, mechanical. **English:** English lit. **Foreign languages:** Sign language interpretation, Spanish. **Health services:** Athletic training, dietetics, health care admin, nursing (RN). **History:** General. **Liberal arts:** Arts/sciences. **Math:** General, statistics. **Parks/recreation:** Sports admin. **Philosophy/religion:** Philosophy, religion. **Physical sciences:** Chemistry, physics. **Protective services:** Criminal justice. **Psychology:** General. **Social sciences:** Anthropology, economics, political science, sociology. **Visual/performing arts:** Art, jazz, music performance, studio arts.

Most popular majors. Business/marketing 21%, communications/journalism 9%, education 11%, engineering/engineering technologies 6%, health sciences 14%, psychology 9%.

Computing on campus. 850 workstations in library, computer center, student center. Dormitories wired for high-speed internet access and linked to campus network. Commuter students can connect to campus network. Online course registration, online library, helpline, student web hosting, wireless network available.

Student life. Freshman orientation: Mandatory, $35 fee. Preregistration for classes offered. One-and-one-half day program held several times during summer. **Policies:** Students must abide by drug/alcohol policy, student code of conduct, model bill of rights and responsibilities. **Housing:** Coed dorms, special housing for disabled, apartments available. $300 partly refundable deposit. Suite style housing available. **Activities:** Bands, campus ministries, choral groups, drama, international student organizations, literary magazine, music ensembles, radio station, student government, student newspaper, TV station, African American student union, Jewish student union, InterVarsity Christian Fellowship, College Republicans, Jeffersonian Society, The New Left, Muslim student association, Filipino student association, Golden Key international honor society.

Athletics. NCAA. **Intercollegiate:** Baseball M, basketball, cross-country, diving W, golf, soccer, softball W, swimming W, tennis, track and field, volleyball W. **Intramural:** Basketball, football (non-tackle), racquetball, soccer, softball, tennis, track and field, volleyball. **Team name:** Ospreys.

Student services. Adult student services, alcohol/substance abuse counseling, career counseling, student employment services, financial aid counseling, health services, minority student services, on-campus daycare, personal counseling, placement for graduates, veterans' counselor, women's services. **Physically disabled:** Services for visually, speech, hearing impaired.

Contact. E-mail: admissions@unf.edu
Phone: (904) 620-2624 Fax: (904) 620-2414
John Yancey, Director of Admissions, University of North Florida, 1 UNF Drive, Jacksonville, FL 32224-7699

University of Phoenix: Central Florida
Maitland, Florida
www.phoenix.edu

- For-profit 4-year university and health science college
- Small city
- 1,341 degree-seeking undergraduates

General. Regionally accredited. **Degrees:** 266 bachelor's awarded; master's offered. **Calendar:** Differs by program. **Full-time faculty:** 22 total. **Part-time faculty:** 199 total.

Basis for selection. Open admission, but selective for some programs.

2011-2012 Annual costs. Estimated costs as of August 2011: per-credit-hour charge, $420 to $450, depending upon level and course of study; electronic course materials fee, $95, if applicable. Book and material charges may vary by course and program. All fees are subject to change.

Application procedures. Admission: No deadline. No application fee. **Financial aid:** No deadline.

Academics. Credit/placement by examination: AP, CLEP.

Majors. Business: General, accounting, management science, marketing. **Computer sciences:** General, networking, security, web page design, webmaster. **Education:** Elementary. **Health services:** Facilities admin, nursing (RN). **Protective services:** Criminal justice.

Contact. Toll-free number: (866) 766-0766
Marc Booker, Director of Admission and Evaluation, University of Phoenix: Central Florida, 2290 Lucien Way, Suite 400, Maitland, FL 32751

University of Phoenix: North Florida
Jacksonville, Florida
www.phoenix.edu

- For-profit 4-year university and health science college
- Very large city
- 1,158 degree-seeking undergraduates

General. Regionally accredited. **Degrees:** 265 bachelor's awarded; master's offered. **Calendar:** Differs by program. **Full-time faculty:** 17 total. **Part-time faculty:** 192 total.

Basis for selection. Open admission, but selective for some programs.

2011-2012 Annual costs. Estimated costs as of August 2011: per-credit-hour charge, $420 to $450, depending upon level and course of study; electronic course materials fee, $95, if applicable. Book and material charges may vary by course and program. All fees are subject to change.

Application procedures. Admission: No deadline. No application fee. **Financial aid:** No deadline.

Academics. Credit/placement by examination: AP, CLEP.

Majors. Business: Accounting, business admin, human resources. **Computer sciences:** General, security, web page design, webmaster. **Education:** General, elementary. **Health services:** Health care admin. **Protective services:** Police science.

Contact. Marc Booker, Director of Admission and Evaluation, University of Phoenix: North Florida, 4500 Salisbury Road N, Suite 200, Jacksonville, FL 32216

University of Phoenix: South Florida
Plantation, Florida
www.phoenix.edu

- For-profit 4-year university
- Large city
- 1,786 degree-seeking undergraduates

General. Regionally accredited. **Degrees:** 349 bachelor's awarded; master's offered. **Calendar:** Differs by program. **Full-time faculty:** 25 total. **Part-time faculty:** 286 total.

Basis for selection. Open admission, but selective for some programs.

2011-2012 Annual costs. Estimated costs as of August 2011: per-credit-hour charge, $420 to $450, depending upon level and course of study; electronic course materials fee, $95, if applicable. Book and material charges may vary by course and program. All fees are subject to change.

Application procedures. Admission: No deadline. No application fee. **Financial aid:** No deadline.

Academics. Credit/placement by examination: AP, CLEP.

Majors. Business: Accounting, business admin. **Computer sciences:** General, webmaster. **Education:** Elementary, secondary. **Health services:** Facilities admin, health care admin, nursing (RN). **Protective services:** Law enforcement admin.

Contact. Marc Booker, Director of Admission and Evaluation, University of Phoenix: South Florida, 600 North Pine Island Road, Suite 500, Plantation, FL 33324

University of Phoenix: West Florida
Temple Terrace, Florida
www.phoenix.edu

▶ For-profit 4-year university and health science college
▶ Large city

General. Regionally accredited. **Degrees:** 192 bachelor's awarded; master's offered. **Calendar:** Differs by program. **Full-time faculty:** 20 total. **Part-time faculty:** 189 total.

Basis for selection. Open admission, but selective for some programs.

2011-2012 Annual costs. Estimated costs as of August 2011: per-credit-hour charge, $420 to $450, depending upon level and course of study; electronic course materials fee, $95, if applicable. Book and material charges may vary by course and program. All fees are subject to change.

Application procedures. Admission: No deadline. No application fee.

Academics. Credit/placement by examination: AP, CLEP.

Majors. Business: Accounting, business admin, e-commerce, management information systems, marketing. **Computer sciences:** General, networking, web page design, webmaster. **Education:** General, elementary. **Health services:** Facilities admin, nursing (RN). **Protective services:** Law enforcement admin. **Psychology:** General.

Contact. Marc Booker, Director of Admission and Evaluation, University of Phoenix: West Florida, 12802 Tampa Oaks Boulevard, Suite 200, Temple Terrace, FL 33637-1920

University of South Florida
Tampa, Florida   **CB member**
www.usf.edu   **CB code: 5828**

▶ Public 4-year university
▶ Commuter campus in very large city
▶ 29,232 degree-seeking undergraduates: 22% part-time, 56% women, 12% African American, 6% Asian American, 18% Hispanic American, 2% international
▶ 9,091 degree-seeking graduate students
▶ 38% of applicants admitted
▶ SAT or ACT with writing required
▶ 51% graduate within 6 years

General. Founded in 1956. Regionally accredited. Regional institutional campuses in St. Petersburg, Sarasota/Manatee, and Lakeland (Polytechnic). **Degrees:** 6,836 bachelor's, 146 associate awarded; master's, professional, doctoral offered. **ROTC:** Army, Naval, Air Force. **Location:** 10 miles from downtown. **Calendar:** Semester, extensive summer session. **Full-time faculty:** 1,106 total; 79% have terminal degrees, 26% minority, 43% women. **Part-time faculty:** 97 total; 53% have terminal degrees, 25% minority, 47% women. **Class size:** 27% < 20, 49% 20-39, 10% 40-49, 11% 50-99, 3% >100. **Special facilities:** Art museums, weather station, botanical garden, anthropology museum.

Freshman class profile. 29,194 applied, 11,107 admitted, 3,378 enrolled.

Mid 50% test scores		Rank in top quarter:	60%
SAT critical reading:	520-620	Rank in top tenth:	32%
SAT math:	540-630	Return as sophomores:	89%
SAT writing:	500-600	Out-of-state:	9%
ACT composite:	23-27	Live on campus:	76%
GPA 3.75 or higher:	55%	International:	2%
GPA 3.50-3.74:	19%	Fraternities:	10%
GPA 3.0-3.49:	24%	Sororities:	8%
GPA 2.0-2.99:	2%		

Basis for selection. GPA and test scores most important. On sliding scale, higher grades compensate for lower test scores. Requirements higher for several degree programs. Audition required of music majors. Portfolio required of art majors. **Home schooled:** State high school equivalency certificate required.

High school preparation. College-preparatory program required. 19 units required; 21 recommended. Required and recommended units include English 4, mathematics 4, social studies 3, science 3 (laboratory 2-3), foreign language 2-4 and academic electives 3. Foreign language units must be in 1 language.

2011-2012 Annual costs. Tuition/fees: $5,806; $14,994 out-of-state. Room/board: $9,190. Books/supplies: $1,500. Personal expenses: $4,100.

2010-2011 Financial aid. Need-based: 3,791 full-time freshmen applied for aid; 3,065 were judged to have need; 3,047 of these received aid. Average need met was 51%. Average scholarship/grant was $8,077; average loan $2,968. 57% of total undergraduate aid awarded as scholarships/grants, 43% as loans/jobs. **Non-need-based:** Awarded to 4,834 full-time undergraduates, including 3,913 freshmen. Scholarships awarded for academics, alumni affiliation, art, athletics, job skills, leadership, minority status, music/drama, religious affiliation, ROTC, state residency. **Additional information:** Deferred tuition payment plan available for late financial aid recipients.

Application procedures. Admission: Closing date 3/1 (postmark date). $30 fee, may be waived for applicants with need. Admission notification by 4/15. Admission notification on a rolling basis beginning on or about 10/1. Must reply by May 1 or within 2 week(s) if notified thereafter. **Financial aid:** Priority date 3/1; no closing date. FAFSA required. Applicants notified on a rolling basis starting 3/15.

Academics. Special study options: Accelerated study, combined bachelor's/graduate degree, cooperative education, cross-registration, distance learning, double major, dual enrollment of high school students, exchange student, honors, internships, study abroad, teacher certification program, Washington semester, weekend college. **Credit/placement by examination:** AP, CLEP, IB, SAT, ACT, institutional tests. **Support services:** Learning center, pre-admission summer program, remedial instruction, tutoring.

Majors. Area/ethnic studies: African-American, American, women's. **Biology:** General, bacteriology, biomedical sciences. **Business:** General, accounting, business admin, finance, hospitality admin, international, management information systems, managerial economics, marketing. **Computer sciences:** General, information systems, information technology. **Education:** General, art, business, drama/dance, early childhood, elementary, emotionally handicapped, English, foreign languages, learning disabled, mathematics, mentally handicapped, multi-level teacher, music, physical, science, social science, special ed, trade/industrial. **Engineering:** General, chemical, civil, computer, electrical, industrial, mechanical. **English:** English lit, rhetoric/composition. **Foreign languages:** Classics, French, German, Italian, Russian, Spanish. **Health services:** Athletic training, audiology/speech pathology, clinical lab science, health care admin, nursing (RN). **History:** General. **Human services:** Social work. **Liberal arts:** Arts/sciences, humanities. **Math:** General, statistics. **Philosophy/religion:** Philosophy, religion. **Physical sciences:** Chemistry, geology, physics. **Psychology:** General. **Social sciences:** General, anthropology, criminology, economics, geography, international relations, political science, sociology. **Visual/performing arts:** Art, art history/conservation, dance, dramatic, graphic design, music performance, studio arts.

Most popular majors. Biology 10%, business/marketing 21%, education 8%, engineering/engineering technologies 6%, health sciences 6%, psychology 9%, social sciences 17%.

Computing on campus. 500 workstations in dormitories, library, computer center, student center. Dormitories wired for high-speed internet access and linked to campus network. Commuter students can connect to campus network. Online course registration, helpline, wireless network available.

Student life. Freshman orientation: Mandatory, $35 fee. Preregistration for classes offered. **Housing:** Coed dorms, single-sex dorms, special housing for disabled, apartments, cooperative housing, fraternity/sorority housing, wellness housing available. $225 partly refundable deposit, deadline 8/1. Married students; medical students. **Activities:** Bands, choral groups, dance, drama, film society, international student organizations, literary magazine, music ensembles, musical theater, opera, radio station, student government, student newspaper, symphony orchestra, TV station, approximately 300 student organizations available.

Athletics. NCAA. **Intercollegiate:** Baseball M, basketball, cross-country, football (tackle) M, golf, sailing, soccer, softball W, tennis, track and field, volleyball W. **Intramural:** Badminton, basketball, bowling, cross-country, fencing, football (tackle) M, golf, handball, ice hockey, lacrosse, racquetball, rugby, sailing, soccer, softball W, swimming, table tennis, tennis, track and field, volleyball, wrestling M. **Team name:** Bulls.

Student services. Adult student services, career counseling, student employment services, financial aid counseling, health services, legal services,

minority student services, on-campus daycare, personal counseling, placement for graduates, veterans' counselor. **Physically disabled:** Services for visually, speech, hearing impaired.

Contact. E-mail: admissions@admin.usf.edu
Phone: (813) 974-3350 Fax: (813) 974-9689
J. Robert Spatig, Director of Admissions, University of South Florida, 4202 East Fowler Avenue, SVC 1036, Tampa, FL 33620-9951

University of Tampa
Tampa, Florida
www.ut.edu

CB member
CB code: 5819

- Private 4-year university and liberal arts college
- Residential campus in large city
- 6,025 degree-seeking undergraduates: 5% part-time, 57% women, 6% African American, 1% Asian American, 12% Hispanic American, 9% international
- 685 degree-seeking graduate students
- 53% of applicants admitted
- SAT or ACT (ACT writing recommended) required
- 57% graduate within 6 years; 19% enter graduate study

General. Founded in 1931. Regionally accredited. **Degrees:** 1,206 bachelor's, 2 associate awarded; master's offered. **ROTC:** Army, Naval, Air Force. **Location:** 20 miles from St. Petersburg, 70 miles from Orlando. **Calendar:** Semester, extensive summer session. **Full-time faculty:** 263 total; 91% have terminal degrees, 13% minority, 41% women. **Part-time faculty:** 301 total; 31% have terminal degrees, 15% minority, 55% women. **Class size:** 42% < 20, 55% 20-39, 1% 40-49, 1% 50-99. **Special facilities:** Art and furniture museum, dance studio, art studio, marine science research vessel, marine science research laboratory.

Freshman class profile. 13,690 applied, 7,245 admitted, 1,628 enrolled.

Mid 50% test scores			
SAT critical reading:	480-570	Rank in top quarter:	44%
SAT math:	490-580	Rank in top tenth:	16%
SAT writing:	480-570	End year in good standing:	90%
ACT composite:	21-25	Return as sophomores:	74%
GPA 3.75 or higher:	13%	Out-of-state:	73%
GPA 3.50-3.74:	17%	Live on campus:	90%
GPA 3.0-3.49:	46%	International:	7%
GPA 2.0-2.99:	24%	Fraternities:	9%
		Sororities:	18%

Basis for selection. Secondary school record, test scores most important. Recommendations, talent/ability, character/personal qualities considered. Interview recommended. Auditions required of music and performing arts majors. Portfolio recommended for art majors. **Home schooled:** Submit a copy of the 11th year annual pupil's educational progress evaluation or annual assessment test results, if available. **Learning Disabled:** Documentation required.

High school preparation. College-preparatory program required. 20 units required. Required units include English 4, mathematics 3, social studies 3, science 3 (laboratory 2), foreign language 2 and academic electives 3.

2011-2012 Annual costs. Tuition/fees: $23,976. Room/board: $8,830. Books/supplies: $1,050. Personal expenses: $1,849.

2010-2011 Financial aid. Need-based: 1,002 full-time freshmen applied for aid; 869 were judged to have need; 805 of these received aid. Average need met was 52%. Average scholarship/grant was $12,384; average loan $3,224. 60% of total undergraduate aid awarded as scholarships/grants, 40% as loans/jobs. **Non-need-based:** Awarded to 3,701 full-time undergraduates, including 1,007 freshmen. Scholarships awarded for academics, art, athletics, leadership, music/drama, state residency. **Additional information:** Early aid estimator service.

Application procedures. Admission: Priority date 11/15; no deadline. $40 fee, may be waived for applicants with need. Admission notification on a rolling basis beginning on or about 10/1. Must reply by May 1 or within 4 week(s) if notified thereafter. **Financial aid:** No deadline. Applicants notified on a rolling basis starting 3/1; must reply by 5/1 or within 3 week(s) of notification.

Academics. Special study options: Combined bachelor's/graduate degree, double major, dual enrollment of high school students, exchange student, honors, independent study, internships, liberal arts/career combination, semester at sea, study abroad, teacher certification program, Washington semester. Certificate of International Studies. **Credit/placement by examination:** AP, CLEP, IB, SAT, ACT, institutional tests. 30 credit hours maximum toward associate degree, 30 toward bachelor's. **Support services:** Learning center, reduced course load, study skills assistance, tutoring, writing center.

Majors. Biology: General, biochemistry, marine. **Business:** Accounting, business admin, entrepreneurial studies, finance, international, management information systems, management science, marketing. **Communications:** General, advertising, digital media, journalism, persuasive communications. **Computer sciences:** General. **Conservation:** Environmental studies. **Education:** Elementary, music, physical, secondary. **English:** English lit, writing. **Foreign languages:** Spanish. **Health services:** Athletic training, nursing (RN). **History:** General. **Liberal arts:** Arts/sciences. **Math:** General. **Parks/recreation:** Health/fitness, sports admin. **Philosophy/religion:** Philosophy. **Physical sciences:** Chemistry. **Protective services:** Forensics. **Psychology:** General. **Social sciences:** Criminology, economics, political science, sociology. **Visual/performing arts:** Art, digital arts, dramatic, film/cinema/video, graphic design, music, music performance, musical theater.

Most popular majors. Biology 7%, business/marketing 30%, communications/journalism 12%, parks/recreation 7%, social sciences 12%, visual/performing arts 8%.

Computing on campus. 795 workstations in dormitories, library, computer center, student center. Dormitories wired for high-speed internet access and linked to campus network. Commuter students can connect to campus network. Online course registration, online library, helpline, student web hosting, wireless network available.

Student life. Freshman orientation: Mandatory, $75 fee. Preregistration for classes offered. **Housing:** Coed dorms, special housing for disabled, apartments available. $200 fully refundable deposit, deadline 5/1. **Activities:** Bands, campus ministries, choral groups, dance, drama, film society, international student organizations, literary magazine, music ensembles, Model UN, musical theater, radio station, student government, student newspaper, symphony orchestra, TV station, over 140 student organizations.

Athletics. NCAA. **Intercollegiate:** Baseball M, basketball, cross-country, golf, lacrosse M, rowing (crew) W, soccer, softball W, swimming, tennis W, volleyball W. **Intramural:** Basketball, field hockey W, football (non-tackle) W, football (tackle) M, golf, soccer, softball, swimming, table tennis W, tennis, track and field, volleyball. **Team name:** Spartans.

Student services. Adult student services, career counseling, student employment services, financial aid counseling, health services, minority student services, personal counseling, placement for graduates, veterans' counselor, women's services. **Physically disabled:** Services for visually, hearing impaired.

Contact. E-mail: admissions@ut.edu
Phone: (813) 253-6211 Toll-free number: (888) 646-2738
Fax: (813) 258-7398
Dennis Nostrand, Vice President for Enrollment, University of Tampa, 401 West Kennedy Boulevard, Tampa, FL 33606-1490

University of West Florida
Pensacola, Florida
www.uwf.edu

CB code: 5833

- Public 4-year university
- Commuter campus in small city
- 9,472 degree-seeking undergraduates: 26% part-time, 58% women, 11% African American, 4% Asian American, 7% Hispanic American, 1% Native American, 1% international
- 1,790 degree-seeking graduate students
- 63% of applicants admitted
- SAT or ACT (ACT writing optional) required
- 48% graduate within 6 years

General. Founded in 1963. Regionally accredited. **Degrees:** 1,938 bachelor's, 161 associate awarded; master's, doctoral offered. **ROTC:** Army, Air Force. **Location:** 10 miles from downtown. **Calendar:** Semester, extensive summer session. **Full-time faculty:** 299 total; 79% have terminal degrees, 15% minority, 42% women. **Part-time faculty:** 244 total; 23% have terminal degrees, 9% minority, 48% women. **Class size:** 28% < 20, 51% 20-39, 12% 40-49, 7% 50-99, 1% >100. **Special facilities:** Archaeology museum, nature preserve, science and engineering complex with holodeck.

Freshman class profile. 5,744 applied, 3,616 admitted, 1,324 enrolled.

Mid 50% test scores			
SAT critical reading:	450-550	GPA 2.0-2.99:	26%
SAT math:	440-540	Rank in top quarter:	33%
SAT writing:	430-530	Rank in top tenth:	13%
ACT composite:	20-24	Return as sophomores:	74%
GPA 3.75 or higher:	14%	Out-of-state:	9%
GPA 3.50-3.74:	17%	Live on campus:	59%
GPA 3.0-3.49:	43%	International:	1%

Basis for selection. School achievement record, test scores, and school curriculum most important. **Home schooled:** Transcript of courses and grades required. **Learning Disabled:** If requesting special consideration due to disability, student must provide documentation.

High school preparation. College-preparatory program recommended. 19 units required. Required units include English 4, mathematics 3, social studies 3, science 3 (laboratory 2), foreign language 2 and academic electives 4. 4 academic electives includes courses chosen from list above. Social science includes history, economics, government, psychology, sociology and geography.

2011-2012 Annual costs. Tuition/fees: $5,425; $17,693 out-of-state. Room/board: $8,574. Books/supplies: $1,200. Personal expenses: $2,400.

2010-2011 Financial aid. Need-based: 84% of total undergraduate aid awarded as scholarships/grants, 16% as loans/jobs. **Non-need-based:** Scholarships awarded for academics, alumni affiliation, art, athletics, minority status, music/drama, ROTC.

Application procedures. Admission: Closing date 6/30 (postmark date). $30 fee, may be waived for applicants with need. Admission notification on a rolling basis beginning on or about 10/1. Must apply by January 1 for scholarship consideration. **Financial aid:** Priority date 3/1; no closing date. FAFSA, institutional form required. Applicants notified on a rolling basis starting 2/1.

Academics. Weekend program in nursing (BSN) available. **Special study options:** Cooperative education, distance learning, double major, dual enrollment of high school students, exchange student, honors, independent study, internships, study abroad, teacher certification program. **Credit/placement by examination:** AP, CLEP, IB, SAT, ACT, institutional tests. 30 credit hours maximum toward associate degree, 30 toward bachelor's. Up to 60 hours can be accepted, but academic department determines how credit counts toward degree. **Support services:** Learning center, remedial instruction, study skills assistance, tutoring, writing center.

Majors. Biology: General, marine. **Business:** General, accounting, business admin, finance, hospitality admin, management information systems, managerial economics, marketing. **Communications:** Media studies. **Computer sciences:** General, information technology. **Conservation:** Environmental science. **Education:** Art, early childhood, elementary, English, foreign languages, mathematics, mentally handicapped, middle, music, science, social science, special ed, trade/industrial. **Engineering:** Computer, electrical. **English:** English lit. **Foreign languages:** French, Spanish. **Health services:** Clinical lab science, community health services, nursing (RN). **History:** General. **Human services:** Social work. **Liberal arts:** Humanities. **Math:** General. **Parks/recreation:** Health/fitness. **Philosophy/religion:** Philosophy, religion. **Physical sciences:** Chemistry, oceanography, physics. **Protective services:** Criminal justice. **Psychology:** General. **Social sciences:** General, anthropology, economics, international relations, political science, sociology. **Visual/performing arts:** Art, art history/conservation, dramatic, music performance, studio arts.

Most popular majors. Business/marketing 17%, communications/journalism 7%, education 14%, health sciences 9%, psychology 7%, social sciences 7%.

Computing on campus. 300 workstations in dormitories, library, computer center, student center. Dormitories wired for high-speed internet access and linked to campus network. Commuter students can connect to campus network. Online course registration, online library, helpline, repair service, student web hosting, wireless network available.

Student life. Freshman orientation: Mandatory, $100 fee. Preregistration for classes offered. 2-day programs held throughout summer; includes parents. **Housing:** Coed dorms, apartments, fraternity/sorority housing, wellness housing available. $225 partly refundable deposit. **Activities:** Bands, campus ministries, choral groups, dance, drama, international student organizations, music ensembles, musical theater, radio station, student government, student newspaper, symphony orchestra, TV station, black student union, CLOVE, College Republicans.

Athletics. NCAA. **Intercollegiate:** Baseball M, basketball, cross-country, golf, soccer, softball W, tennis, track and field, volleyball W. **Intramural:** Badminton, basketball, bowling, fencing, football (non-tackle), handball, racquetball, soccer, swimming, table tennis, volleyball, water polo, weight lifting. **Team name:** Argonauts.

Student services. Alcohol/substance abuse counseling, career counseling, student employment services, financial aid counseling, health services, minority student services, on-campus daycare, personal counseling, placement for graduates, veterans' counselor. **Physically disabled:** Services for visually, speech, hearing impaired.

Contact. E-mail: admissions@uwf.edu
Phone: (850) 474-2230 Toll-free number: (800) 263-1074
Fax: (850) 474-3360
Steve McKellips, Director of Admissions, University of West Florida, 11000 University Parkway, Pensacola, FL 32514-5750

Warner University
Lake Wales, Florida
www.warner.edu   CB code: 5883

- Private 4-year liberal arts college affiliated with Church of God
- Commuter campus in large town
- 871 degree-seeking undergraduates
- 118 graduate students
- SAT or ACT (ACT writing optional), application essay required

General. Founded in 1968. Regionally accredited. Off-site locations including Lakeland Learning Center, Space Coast Learning Center in Melbourne, teaching site in Titusville. **Degrees:** 244 bachelor's, 37 associate awarded; master's offered. **Location:** 60 miles from Tampa, 55 miles from Orlando. **Calendar:** Semester, limited summer session. **Full-time faculty:** 32 total. **Part-time faculty:** 128 total. **Class size:** 72% < 20, 28% 20-39. **Special facilities:** Natural scrub brush preserve.

Freshman class profile.

GPA 3.75 or higher:	22%	Rank in top quarter:	27%
GPA 3.50-3.74:	13%	Rank in top tenth:	6%
GPA 3.0-3.49:	37%	Out-of-state:	18%
GPA 2.0-2.99:	28%	Live on campus:	79%

Basis for selection. Two of the following required: 2.25 GPA, top 50% of class, or 18 ACT/870 SAT (exclusive of Writing). ACT Residual test administered to those without scores or with scores too low. Interview recommended. Audition required of music majors. **Home schooled:** Statement describing home school structure and mission, transcript of courses and grades, interview, letter of recommendation (nonparent) required. GED or portfolio required of applicants without transcripts.

High school preparation. College-preparatory program recommended. Recommended units include English 4, mathematics 3, social studies 1, history 1, science 2, foreign language 2 and academic electives 2.

2011-2012 Annual costs. Tuition/fees: $16,560. Room/board: $7,204. Books/supplies: $1,000. Personal expenses: $1,792.

Financial aid. Non-need-based: Scholarships awarded for academics, alumni affiliation, art, athletics, leadership, music/drama, religious affiliation, state residency.

Application procedures. Admission: No deadline. $20 fee, may be waived for applicants with need. Admission notification on a rolling basis beginning on or about 9/15. **Financial aid:** Priority date 5/1; no closing date. FAFSA required. Applicants notified on a rolling basis starting 3/15; must reply within 2 week(s) of notification.

Academics. Special study options: Accelerated study, combined bachelor's/graduate degree, distance learning, double major, dual enrollment of high school students, ESL, independent study, internships, study abroad, teacher certification program, Washington semester. Online distance learning opportunities available for those interested in Organizational Management or Church Ministry. **Credit/placement by examination:** AP, CLEP, IB, SAT, ACT, institutional tests. **Support services:** Learning center, remedial instruction, study skills assistance, tutoring.

Majors. Biology: General. **Business:** Business admin. **Communications:** Communications/speech/rhetoric, journalism. **Education:** Elementary, English, music, physical, science, social science, special ed. **English:** English lit. **History:** General. **Human services:** Social work. **Parks/recreation:** Exercise sciences, sports admin. **Psychology:** General. **Social sciences:** General. **Theology:** Bible, sacred music, theology.

Most popular majors. Business/marketing 63%, education 18%.

Computing on campus. 69 workstations in library, computer center, student center. Dormitories wired for high-speed internet access. Commuter students can connect to campus network. Online library, helpline, repair service, wireless network available.

Student life. Freshman orientation: Mandatory. Preregistration for classes offered. Three-day program at start of fall semester. **Policies:** Student lifestyle agreement keeping with the moral and spiritual nature of the institution required. Religious observance required. **Housing:** Guaranteed on-campus for all undergraduates. Single-sex dorms, wellness housing available.

$50 nonrefundable deposit, deadline 8/15. **Activities:** Campus ministries, choral groups, drama, music ensembles, student government, student newspaper, star throwers, missions, Young Americans.

Athletics. NAIA. **Intercollegiate:** Baseball M, basketball, cheerleading, cross-country, golf, soccer, softball W, tennis, track and field, volleyball. **Intramural:** Basketball, football (non-tackle), soccer, volleyball W. **Team name:** Royals.

Student services. Alcohol/substance abuse counseling, career counseling, student employment services, financial aid counseling, health services, personal counseling, placement for graduates.

Contact. E-mail: admissions@warner.edu
Phone: (863) 638-7212 Toll-free number: (800) 309-9563
Fax: (863) 638-7290
Jason Roe, Director of Admissions, Warner University, 13895 Highway 27, Lake Wales, FL 33859

Webber International University
Babson Park, Florida
www.webber.edu
CB code: 5893

- Private 4-year university and business college
- Residential campus in rural community
- 664 degree-seeking undergraduates: 6% part-time, 33% women, 21% African American, 1% Asian American, 8% Hispanic American, 26% international
- 61 degree-seeking graduate students
- 55% of applicants admitted
- SAT or ACT (ACT writing recommended) required
- 34% graduate within 6 years

General. Founded in 1927. Regionally accredited. **Degrees:** 96 bachelor's, 3 associate awarded; master's offered. **Location:** 50 miles from Orlando, 60 miles from Tampa. **Calendar:** Semester, limited summer session. **Full-time faculty:** 21 total; 62% have terminal degrees, 10% minority, 43% women. **Part-time faculty:** 24 total; 25% have terminal degrees, 12% minority, 50% women. **Class size:** 45% < 20, 55% 20-39. **Special facilities:** Nature preserve.

Freshman class profile. 525 applied, 291 admitted, 141 enrolled.

Mid 50% test scores			
SAT critical reading:	410-500	GPA 2.0-2.99:	42%
SAT math:	440-520	Rank in top quarter:	15%
ACT composite:	17-21	Rank in top tenth:	5%
GPA 3.75 or higher:	9%	Return as sophomores:	51%
GPA 3.50-3.74:	11%	Out-of-state:	6%
GPA 3.0-3.49:	37%	Live on campus:	85%
		International:	19%

Basis for selection. GPA and standardized test scores very important, followed by school record. Interview recommended. **Home schooled:** Transcript of courses and grades required. Proof of graduation with 2.0 GPA required. **Learning Disabled:** Documentation of disability required in order to adequately assist student in studies.

High school preparation. College-preparatory program recommended. 15 units recommended. Required and recommended units include English 4, mathematics 2-3, social studies 2, history 2, science 1-3, foreign language 1 and academic electives 4. 2 business courses recommended.

2011-2012 Annual costs. Tuition/fees: $19,670. Room/board: $7,610. Books/supplies: $900. Personal expenses: $4,488.

2011-2012 Financial aid. Need-based: 140 full-time freshmen applied for aid; 96 were judged to have need; 96 of these received aid. Average need met was 55%. Average scholarship/grant was $2,846; average loan $3,837. 52% of total undergraduate aid awarded as scholarships/grants, 48% as loans/jobs. **Non-need-based:** Awarded to 624 full-time undergraduates, including 182 freshmen. Scholarships awarded for academics, alumni affiliation, athletics, leadership, minority status, state residency.

Application procedures. Admission: Priority date 5/1; deadline 8/1 (postmark date). $35 fee, may be waived for applicants with need. Admission notification on a rolling basis beginning on or about 12/1. Must reply by May 1 or within 4 week(s) if notified thereafter. **Financial aid:** Priority date 5/1, closing date 8/1. FAFSA required. Applicants notified on a rolling basis starting 4/1; must reply within 4 week(s) of notification.

Academics. Special study options: Combined bachelor's/graduate degree, cooperative education, cross-registration, distance learning, double major, dual enrollment of high school students, ESL, exchange student, external degree, independent study, internships, study abroad, weekend college.

Credit/placement by examination: AP, CLEP, IB, institutional tests. 30 credit hours maximum toward associate degree, 30 toward bachelor's. No more than 6 semester hours credit awarded in each of 5 areas (English, humanities, science, social science, mathematics). **Support services:** Reduced course load, remedial instruction, study skills assistance, tutoring.

Majors. Business: General, accounting, business admin, finance, hospitality admin, marketing. **Communications:** Communications/speech/rhetoric. **Computer sciences:** General. **Parks/recreation:** Facilities management. **Protective services:** Security management.

Most popular majors. Business/marketing 75%, parks/recreation 17%.

Computing on campus. 92 workstations in library, computer center. Dormitories wired for high-speed internet access and linked to campus network. Commuter students can connect to campus network. Online library, helpline available.

Student life. Freshman orientation: Mandatory. Preregistration for classes offered. Five-day program immediately preceding semester opening. **Housing:** Guaranteed on-campus for freshmen. Single-sex dorms available. $205 fully refundable deposit, deadline 8/28. **Activities:** Bands, student government, student newspaper, Fellowship of Christian Athletes, fishing club, international club, marketing club, Phi Beta Lambda, photography club, Society of Hosteurs.

Athletics. NAIA. **Intercollegiate:** Baseball M, basketball, bowling, cross-country, football (tackle) M, golf, soccer, softball W, tennis, track and field, volleyball W. **Intramural:** Basketball, bowling, football (non-tackle), soccer, softball, table tennis, tennis. **Team name:** Warriors.

Student services. Adult student services, alcohol/substance abuse counseling, career counseling, student employment services, financial aid counseling, health services, personal counseling, placement for graduates, veterans' counselor, women's services.

Contact. E-mail: admissions@webber.edu
Phone: (863) 638-2910 Toll-free number: (800) 741-1844
Fax: (863) 638-1591
Mike Mattison, Director of Admission, Webber International University, 1201 North Scenic Highway, Babson Park, FL 33827-0096

Yeshiva Gedolah Rabbinical College
Miami Beach, Florida

- Private 4-year rabbinical college for men affiliated with Jewish faith
- Very large city
- 47 degree-seeking undergraduates

General. Accredited by AARTS. **Calendar:** Semester. **Full-time faculty:** 4 total.

2011-2012 Annual costs. Tuition/fees: $8,800. Room/board: $8,500.

Academics. Credit/placement by examination: AP, CLEP.

Majors. Philosophy/religion: Judaic. **Theology:** Religious ed, Talmudic.

Contact. Phone: (305) 673-5664
Yeshiva Gedolah Rabbinical College, 1140 Alton Road, Miami Beach, FL 33139

Georgia

Agnes Scott College

Decatur, Georgia
www.agnesscott.edu

CB member
CB code: 5002

▸ Private 4-year liberal arts college for women affiliated with Presbyterian Church (USA)

▸ Residential campus in very large city

▸ 827 degree-seeking undergraduates: 100% women, 31% African American, 3% Asian American, 7% Hispanic American, 10% international

▸ 46% of applicants admitted

▸ Application essay required

▸ 65% graduate within 6 years; 24% enter graduate study

General. Founded in 1889. Regionally accredited. **Degrees:** 193 bachelor's awarded. **ROTC:** Army, Air Force. **Location:** 6 miles from downtown Atlanta. **Calendar:** Semester, limited summer session. **Full-time faculty:** 72 total; 97% have terminal degrees, 21% minority, 62% women. **Part-time faculty:** 23 total; 70% have terminal degrees, 35% minority, 65% women. **Class size:** 61% < 20, 38% 20-39, 1% 40-49. **Special facilities:** Observatory, planetarium, art collection, electron microscope, 30-inch Beck telescope, center for writing and speaking, interactive learning center, multi-media classrooms.

Freshman class profile. 2,284 applied, 1,048 admitted, 227 enrolled.

Mid 50% test scores		GPA 2.0-2.99:	3%
SAT critical reading:	520-630	Rank in top quarter:	71%
SAT math:	500-630	Rank in top tenth:	40%
SAT writing:	530-630	End year in good standing:	93%
ACT composite:	23-29	Return as sophomores:	84%
GPA 3.75 or higher:	47%	Out-of-state:	38%
GPA 3.50-3.74:	28%	Live on campus:	92%
GPA 3.0-3.49:	22%	International:	11%

Basis for selection. SAT/ACT scores are optional unless applicant is home-schooled. Applications must include at least ONE of the following: SAT/ACT scores; interview; analytical or critical writing sample including description of assignment, teacher comments and grade. Interview recommended. Audition required for music scholarship. **Home schooled:** Statement describing home school structure and mission, interview required. Must submit SAT (exclusive of Writing) or ACT scores and SAT Subject Tests.

High school preparation. College-preparatory program recommended. 16 units recommended. Recommended units include English 4, mathematics 3, social studies 2, history 2, science 2 (laboratory 2) and foreign language 2.

2011-2012 Annual costs. Tuition/fees: $32,195. Room/board: $10,150. Books/supplies: $1,000. Personal expenses: $1,000.

2011-2012 Financial aid. Need-based: 196 full-time freshmen applied for aid; 188 were judged to have need; 188 of these received aid. Average need met was 87%. Average scholarship/grant was $25,625; average loan $3,369. 83% of total undergraduate aid awarded as scholarships/grants, 17% as loans/jobs. **Non-need-based:** Awarded to 335 full-time undergraduates, including 83 freshmen. Scholarships awarded for academics, leadership, minority status, music/drama, religious affiliation. **Additional information:** Middle Income Assistance Grants available. Auditions required for music scholarship applicants.

Application procedures. Admission: $35 fee, may be waived for applicants with need, free for online applicants. Admission notification on a rolling basis. Must reply by May 1 or within 2 week(s) if notified thereafter. Scholarship applicants must apply for regular admission by 1/15. **Financial aid:** Priority date 2/15, closing date 5/1. FAFSA required. Applicants notified on a rolling basis starting 3/1; must reply within 3 week(s) of notification.

Academics. Special study options: Accelerated study, combined bachelor's/graduate degree, cross-registration, double major, dual enrollment of high school students, exchange student, independent study, internships, liberal arts/career combination, semester at sea, student-designed major, study abroad, United Nations semester, Washington semester. Global Awareness and Global Connections programs offer opportunities to visit other regions of the world. Internship opportunities guaranteed; over 250 internships and externships available in Atlanta and other cities. Atlanta Semester focuses on women, leadership and social change. Language Across the Curriculum links foreign languages to other disciplines. Opportunities to study at over 123 universities in 33 countries. **Credit/placement by examination:** AP, CLEP, IB, SAT, ACT, institutional tests. 32 credit hours maximum toward bachelor's degree. **Support services:** Learning center, reduced course load, study skills assistance, tutoring, writing center.

Majors. Area/ethnic studies: African, women's. **Biology:** General, biochemistry, neuroscience. **English:** Creative writing, English lit. **Foreign languages:** Classics, French, German, Spanish. **History:** General. **Math:** General. **Philosophy/religion:** Philosophy, religion. **Physical sciences:** Astrophysics, chemistry, physics. **Psychology:** General. **Social sciences:** Economics, international relations, political science. **Visual/performing arts:** Art history/conservation, dance, dramatic, music, studio arts.

Most popular majors. Biology 14%, English 12%, foreign language 6%, psychology 9%, social sciences 26%, visual/performing arts 9%.

Computing on campus. 458 workstations in dormitories, library, computer center, student center. Dormitories wired for high-speed internet access and linked to campus network. Commuter students can connect to campus network. Online course registration, online library, helpline, repair service, wireless network available.

Student life. Freshman orientation: Mandatory. Preregistration for classes offered. Held five days prior to start of semester; includes signing of honor code, breakfast with college president, introduction to Big/Little Sister program. **Housing:** Guaranteed on-campus for all undergraduates. Apartments, wellness housing available. $350 nonrefundable deposit, deadline 5/1. College-owned houses for nontraditional students available. **Activities:** Bands, campus ministries, choral groups, dance, drama, international student organizations, literary magazine, music ensembles, Model UN, musical theater, student government, student newspaper, symphony orchestra, TV station, religious life council, conservative forum, College Democrats, green earth organization, Circle-K, African American student group, Asian cultural awareness association, Amnesty International.

Athletics. NCAA. **Intercollegiate:** Basketball W, lacrosse W, soccer W, softball W, tennis W, volleyball W. **Team name:** Scotties.

Student services. Adult student services, alcohol/substance abuse counseling, chaplain/spiritual director, career counseling, student employment services, financial aid counseling, health services, minority student services, personal counseling, placement for graduates, women's services. **Physically disabled:** Services for visually, speech, hearing impaired.

Contact. E-mail: admission@agnesscott.edu
Phone: (404) 471-6285 Toll-free number: (800) 868-8602
Fax: (404) 471-6414
Alexa Gaeta, Director and Dean of Admission, Agnes Scott College, 141 East College Avenue, Decatur, GA 30030-3797

Albany State University

Albany, Georgia
www.asurams.edu

CB member
CB code: 5004

▸ Public 4-year university

▸ Residential campus in small city

▸ 4,173 degree-seeking undergraduates: 12% part-time, 66% women, 83% African American, 1% Hispanic American

▸ 456 degree-seeking graduate students

▸ 29% of applicants admitted

▸ SAT or ACT (ACT writing optional) required

▸ 41% graduate within 6 years

General. Founded in 1903. Regionally accredited. **Degrees:** 561 bachelor's awarded; master's offered. **ROTC:** Army. **Location:** 190 miles from Atlanta. **Calendar:** Semester, extensive summer session. **Full-time faculty:** 164 total; 77% have terminal degrees, 78% minority, 44% women. **Part-time faculty:** 106 total; 22% have terminal degrees, 81% minority, 67% women. **Class size:** 43% < 20, 43% 20-39, 9% 40-49, 4% 50-99, less than 1% >100. **Special facilities:** Natatorium, fitness center.

Freshman class profile. 6,554 applied, 1,878 admitted, 1,062 enrolled.

Mid 50% test scores		GPA 2.0-2.99:	51%
SAT critical reading:	390-450	Rank in top quarter:	30%
SAT math:	390-460	Rank in top tenth:	10%
ACT composite:	16-19	End year in good standing:	60%
GPA 3.75 or higher:	4%	Return as sophomores:	65%
GPA 3.50-3.74:	9%	Out-of-state:	4%
GPA 3.0-3.49:	35%	Live on campus:	84%

Basis for selection. 430 SAT Critical Reading and 400 SAT Math or 17 ACT English and Math, 2.22 GPA required. For joint enrollment students, 550 SAT Reading and 500 SAT Math or 21 ACT English and Math, parents and counselor approval required. **Home schooled:** Transcript of courses and grades, state high school equivalency certificate required. School must be accredited. **Learning Disabled:** Register with Office of Counseling and Disabllity, Student Support Services.

High school preparation. College-preparatory program required. 16 units required. Required units include English 4, mathematics 4, social studies 3, science 3 (laboratory 2) and foreign language 2. 2 foreign language units must be same language.

2011-2012 Annual costs. Tuition/fees: $5,802; $17,416 out-of-state. Room/board: $6,104.

Financial aid. Non-need-based: Scholarships awarded for academics, alumni affiliation, art, athletics, music/drama, ROTC.

Application procedures. Admission: Closing date 6/1. $20 fee, may be waived for applicants with need, free for online applicants. Admission notification by 9/30. Admission notification on a rolling basis. Must reply by orientation registration. Early admission high school students must have permission from their high school to attend; must also meet certain GPA and SAT/ACT test requirement. **Financial aid:** Priority date 4/15, closing date 4/30. FAFSA required. Applicants notified on a rolling basis starting 1/7; must reply within 2 week(s) of notification.

Academics. Special study options: Combined bachelor's/graduate degree, cooperative education, cross-registration, distance learning, double major, dual enrollment of high school students, honors, independent study, internships, liberal arts/career combination, study abroad, teacher certification program, weekend college. 3+2 and 2+2 engineering program with Georgia Institute of Technology. **Credit/placement by examination:** AP, CLEP, SAT, ACT, institutional tests. 45 credit hours maximum toward bachelor's degree. **Support services:** Learning center, pre-admission summer program, remedial instruction, study skills assistance, tutoring, writing center.

Majors. Biology: General. **Business:** Accounting, business admin, logistics, management information systems, marketing. **Communications:** Media studies. **Computer sciences:** General, information systems. **Education:** Early childhood, mathematics, middle, music, physical, science, social science, special ed. **English:** English lit, rhetoric/composition. **Foreign languages:** Spanish. **Health services:** Nursing (RN). **History:** General. **Human services:** Social work. **Math:** General. **Parks/recreation:** Health/fitness. **Physical sciences:** Chemistry. **Protective services:** Criminal justice, forensics. **Psychology:** General. **Social sciences:** Political science, sociology. **Visual/performing arts:** Drawing, music.

Most popular majors. Biology 7%, business/marketing 24%, education 26%, psychology 7%, security/protective services 11%.

Computing on campus. 400 workstations in dormitories, library, computer center, student center. Dormitories wired for high-speed internet access and linked to campus network. Commuter students can connect to campus network. Online course registration, online library, helpline, wireless network available.

Student life. Freshman orientation: Mandatory. Preregistration for classes offered. Held 5 times throughout academic year; fee varies. **Housing:** Coed dorms, single-sex dorms available. $250 partly refundable deposit, deadline 6/30. **Activities:** Bands, choral groups, dance, drama, music ensembles, Model UN, opera, radio station, student government, student newspaper, TV station, Annointed Gospel Choir, Annointed Students in Unity Fellowship Fraternity & Sorority, Divine Visions Outreach, Young Democrats, NAACP, Habitat for Humanity, peer educators, Relay for Life, HIV Aids peer educator.

Athletics. NCAA. **Intercollegiate:** Baseball M, basketball, cheerleading, cross-country, football (tackle) M, softball W, tennis W, track and field, volleyball W. **Intramural:** Basketball M, football (tackle) M, track and field. **Team name:** Rams.

Student services. Adult student services, alcohol/substance abuse counseling, career counseling, services for economically disadvantaged, student employment services, financial aid counseling, health services, minority student services, personal counseling, veterans' counselor. **Physically disabled:** Services for visually, speech, hearing impaired.

Contact. E-mail: enrollmentservices@asurams.edu
Phone: (229) 430-4646 Toll-free number: (800) 866-5793498
Fax: (229) 430-4105
James Burrell, Director of Enrollment Services, Albany State University, 504 College Drive, Albany, GA 31705-2796

American InterContinental University
Atlanta, Georgia
www.buckhead.aiuniv.edu/ CB code: 2486

- For-profit 4-year virtual university
- Commuter campus in very large city

General. Founded in 1977. Regionally accredited. **Calendar:** Quarter.

Annual costs/financial aid. Tuition/fees (2011-2012): $14,250. Tuition shown is for bachelor's of business administration program; cost of other programs may vary. Books/supplies: $1,500. Personal expenses: $960.

Contact. Phone: (404) 965-5700
Director of Admissions, 6600 Peachtree Dunwoody Road, 500 Embassy Row, Atlanta, GA 30328

Argosy University: Atlanta
Atlanta, Georgia
www.argosy.edu/atlanta

- For-profit 4-year university
- Very large city
- 390 degree-seeking undergraduates

General. Regionally accredited. **Degrees:** 25 bachelor's awarded; master's, professional, doctoral offered. **Calendar:** Differs by program. **Full-time faculty:** 38 total. **Part-time faculty:** 178 total.

Basis for selection. Open admission.

2011-2012 Annual costs. Tuition/fees: $17,962.

Application procedures. Admission: Closing date 9/13. $50 fee. **Financial aid:** No deadline.

Academics. Credit/placement by examination: AP, CLEP.

Majors. Business: Business admin. **Liberal arts:** Arts/sciences. **Protective services:** Police science. **Psychology:** General.

Contact. E-mail: auaadmissions@argosy.edu
Phone: (770) 671-1200 Toll-free number: (888) 671-4777
Johanna Collins, Senior Director of Admissions, Argosy University: Atlanta, 980 Hammond Drive, Suite 100, Atlanta, GA 30328

Armstrong Atlantic State University
Savannah, Georgia
www.armstrong.edu CB code: 5012

- Public 4-year university
- Commuter campus in small city
- 6,813 degree-seeking undergraduates: 29% part-time, 64% women, 24% African American, 3% Asian American, 6% Hispanic American, 2% international
- 680 degree-seeking graduate students
- 76% of applicants admitted
- SAT or ACT (ACT writing optional) required

General. Founded in 1935. Regionally accredited. **Degrees:** 908 bachelor's, 63 associate awarded; master's, doctoral offered. **ROTC:** Army, Naval. **Location:** 250 miles from Atlanta, 150 miles from Jacksonville, Florida. **Calendar:** Semester, extensive summer session. **Full-time faculty:** 258 total. **Part-time faculty:** 166 total. **Class size:** 33% < 20, 54% 20-39, 7% 40-49, 5% 50-99, less than 1% >100.

Freshman class profile. 2,856 applied, 2,158 admitted, 1,121 enrolled.

Mid 50% test scores			
SAT critical reading:	460-550	GPA 3.0-3.49:	35%
SAT math:	440-550	GPA 2.0-2.99:	35%
ACT composite:	19-24	Return as sophomores:	65%
GPA 3.75 or higher:	14%	Out-of-state:	9%
GPA 3.50-3.74:	16%	Live on campus:	50%
		International:	2%

Basis for selection. 430 SAT math, 460 SAT verbal and 2.0 GPA required for regular admissions. Conditional admission possible with 1.8 GPA and lower test scores. **Home schooled:** Applicants who do not complete an

accredited program must pass SAT Subject Tests to satisfy college prep requirements.

High school preparation. College-preparatory program required. Required units include English 4, mathematics 4, social studies 3, science 3 (laboratory 2) and foreign language 2.

2011-2012 Annual costs. Tuition/fees: $5,734; $17,348 out-of-state. Room/board: $9,342. Books/supplies: $1,000.

Financial aid. Non-need-based: Scholarships awarded for academics, alumni affiliation, art, athletics, leadership, minority status, music/drama, state residency.

Application procedures. Admission: Priority date 6/1; deadline 7/15. $25 fee, may be waived for applicants with need. Admission notification on a rolling basis beginning on or about 10/1. **Financial aid:** Priority date 3/15; no closing date. FAFSA required. Applicants notified on a rolling basis starting 2/1; must reply by 4/15 or within 6 week(s) of notification.

Academics. Special study options: Cooperative education, distance learning, double major, dual enrollment of high school students, honors, independent study, internships, study abroad, teacher certification program, weekend college. **Credit/placement by examination:** AP, CLEP, IB, SAT, ACT, institutional tests. 30 credit hours maximum toward associate degree, 30 toward bachelor's. **Support services:** Learning center, reduced course load, remedial instruction, study skills assistance, tutoring, writing center.

Majors. Biology: General. **Computer sciences:** General, information technology. **Education:** Art, business, early childhood, elementary, English, health, learning disabled, mathematics, middle, music, physical, science, secondary, social science, special ed, speech impaired. **English:** English lit. **Foreign languages:** Spanish. **Health services:** Clinical lab science, communication disorders, medical radiologic technology/radiation therapy, nuclear medical technology, nursing (RN), respiratory therapy technology, sonography. **History:** General. **Math:** Applied. **Physical sciences:** Chemistry, physics. **Protective services:** Police science. **Psychology:** General. **Social sciences:** Economics, political science. **Visual/performing arts:** Art, dramatic, music.

Most popular majors. Biology 6%, education 17%, health sciences 37%, liberal arts 9%.

Computing on campus. 300 workstations in dormitories, library, computer center, student center. Dormitories wired for high-speed internet access and linked to campus network. Commuter students can connect to campus network. Online course registration, online library, helpline, wireless network available.

Student life. Freshman orientation: Available, $45 fee. Preregistration for classes offered. One-day event prior to registration. **Housing:** Coed dorms, apartments available. $250 partly refundable deposit, deadline 7/16. **Activities:** Bands, campus ministries, choral groups, dance, drama, international student organizations, literary magazine, music ensembles, Model UN, musical theater, student government, student newspaper, NAACP, Baptist student union, Hispanic outreach and leadership, Cercle Francais, Newman Club, Wesley Foundation, College Democrats, College Republicans.

Athletics. NCAA. **Intercollegiate:** Baseball M, basketball, cheerleading, cross-country M, golf, soccer W, softball W, tennis, volleyball W. **Intramural:** Badminton, basketball, bowling, football (non-tackle), racquetball, soccer, softball, swimming, table tennis, tennis, volleyball. **Team name:** Pirates.

Student services. Adult student services, alcohol/substance abuse counseling, career counseling, student employment services, financial aid counseling, health services, minority student services, personal counseling, placement for graduates, veterans' counselor. **Physically disabled:** Services for visually, speech, hearing impaired.

Contact. E-mail: adm-info@armstrong.edu
Phone: (912) 344-2503 Toll-free number: (800) 633-2349
Fax: (912) 344-3417
Stephanie Whaley, Director of Admissions, Armstrong Atlantic State University, 11935 Abercorn Street, Savannah, GA 31419-1997

Art Institute of Atlanta
Atlanta, Georgia **CB member**
www.artinstitutes.edu/atlanta/ **CB code: 5429**

- For-profit 4-year culinary school and visual arts college
- Commuter campus in very large city

General. Founded in 1949. Regionally accredited. **Location:** 12 miles from city center. **Calendar:** Quarter.

Annual costs/financial aid. Tuition/fees (2011-2012): $23,535. Room: $8,868. Books/supplies: $1,700. Personal expenses: $7,692. Need-based financial aid available to full-time and part-time students.

Contact. Phone: (770) 394-8300
Senior Director of Admissions, 6600 Peachtree Dunwoody Road, NE, Atlanta, GA 30328

Augusta State University
Augusta, Georgia **CB member**
www.aug.edu **CB code: 5336**

- Public 4-year liberal arts and teachers college
- Commuter campus in small city
- 5,746 degree-seeking undergraduates: 28% part-time, 62% women, 27% African American, 2% Asian American, 4% Hispanic American, 1% international
- 747 degree-seeking graduate students
- 54% of applicants admitted
- SAT or ACT (ACT writing optional) required

General. Founded in 1925. Regionally accredited. **Degrees:** 656 bachelor's, 14 associate awarded; master's offered. **ROTC:** Army. **Location:** 145 miles from Atlanta. **Calendar:** Semester, extensive summer session. **Full-time faculty:** 241 total; 80% have terminal degrees, 16% minority, 50% women. **Part-time faculty:** 162 total; 47% have terminal degrees, 17% minority, 59% women. **Class size:** 34% < 20, 57% 20-39, 7% 40-49, 2% 50-99. **Special facilities:** History walk and museum, 18-hole golf course.

Freshman class profile. 2,423 applied, 1,316 admitted, 998 enrolled.

Mid 50% test scores			
SAT critical reading:	440-540	Return as sophomores:	67%
SAT math:	440-540	Out-of-state:	6%
GPA 3.75 or higher:	10%	Live on campus:	19%
GPA 3.50-3.74:	9%	International:	1%
GPA 3.0-3.49:	35%	Fraternities:	1%
GPA 2.0-2.99:	44%	Sororities:	1%

Basis for selection. 430 SAT verbal/17 ACT English and 400 SAT math/17 ACT math required. SAT Subject Tests required of GED recipients or graduates of non-accredited high schools.

High school preparation. College-preparatory program required. 18 units required. Required units include English 4, mathematics 4, social studies 3, science 3 and foreign language 2.

2011-2012 Annual costs. Tuition/fees: $5,742; $17,356 out-of-state. Limited meal plan available. Room only: $1,100. Books/supplies: $1,000. Personal expenses: $1,980.

2011-2012 Financial aid. Need-based: 680 full-time freshmen applied for aid; 575 were judged to have need; 554 of these received aid. Average scholarship/grant was $2,139; average loan $1,548. 46% of total undergraduate aid awarded as scholarships/grants, 54% as loans/jobs. **Non-need-based:** Awarded to 1,031 full-time undergraduates, including 141 freshmen. Scholarships awarded for academics, alumni affiliation, art, athletics, leadership, minority status, music/drama, ROTC, state residency.

Application procedures. Admission: Priority date 7/1; no deadline. $30 fee, may be waived for applicants with need. Admission notification on a rolling basis. **Financial aid:** Closing date 4/1. FAFSA required. Applicants notified on a rolling basis starting 4/1; must reply within 4 week(s) of notification.

Academics. Special study options: Cooperative education, crossregistration, distance learning, double major, dual enrollment of high school students, ESL, honors, independent study, internships, study abroad, teacher certification program. **Credit/placement by examination:** AP, CLEP, IB, institutional tests. 30 credit hours maximum toward associate degree, 30 toward bachelor's. **Support services:** Learning center, pre-admission summer program, reduced course load, remedial instruction, study skills assistance, tutoring, writing center.

Majors. Biology: General. **Business:** Accounting, business admin, finance, management information systems, marketing. **Communications:** General, communications/speech/rhetoric. **Computer sciences:** General. **Education:** Early childhood, middle, music, physical, special ed. **English:** English lit. **Foreign languages:** General. **Health services:** Clinical lab science, nursing (RN). **History:** General. **Human services:** Social work. **Math:** General. **Parks/recreation:** Exercise sciences. **Physical sciences:** Chemistry, physics. **Protective services:** Criminal justice. **Psychology:** General. **Social sciences:**

Political science, sociology. **Visual/performing arts:** Multimedia, music, music performance.

Most popular majors. Biology 7%, business/marketing 21%, communications/journalism 8%, education 18%, health sciences 7%, psychology 7%, social sciences 9%.

Computing on campus. 900 workstations in dormitories, library, computer center, student center. Dormitories wired for high-speed internet access and linked to campus network. Commuter students can connect to campus network. Online course registration, online library, helpline, student web hosting, wireless network available.

Student life. Freshman orientation: Available. Preregistration for classes offered. **Housing:** Coed dorms available. **Activities:** Bands, choral groups, dance, drama, international student organizations, literary magazine, music ensembles, Model UN, musical theater, opera, radio station, student government, student newspaper, symphony orchestra, black student union, Los Amigos Hispanos, Le Cercle Francais, Muslim student association, Amnesty International, Lambda Alliance, Baptist Collegiate Ministries, Campus Outreach, Model Arab League, Young Democrats of Georgia.

Athletics. NCAA. **Intercollegiate:** Baseball M, basketball, cross-country, golf, softball W, tennis, volleyball W. **Intramural:** Basketball, cheerleading W, golf, squash, table tennis. **Team name:** Jaguars.

Student services. Adult student services, alcohol/substance abuse counseling, career counseling, student employment services, financial aid counseling, minority student services, personal counseling, placement for graduates, veterans' counselor. **Physically disabled:** Services for visually, hearing impaired.

Contact. E-mail: admissions@aug.edu
Phone: (706) 737-1632 Toll-free number: (800) 341-4373
Fax: (706) 667-4355
Katherine Sweeney, Registrar and Director of Admissions, Augusta State University, 2500 Walton Way, Augusta, GA 30904-2200

Bauder College
Atlanta, Georgia
www.bauder.edu   CB code: 5070

- For-profit 4-year career college
- Commuter campus in very large city
- Application essay, interview required

General. Founded in 1964. Regionally accredited. Certified as a Pearson VUE Test Center. **Degrees:** 64 bachelor's, 190 associate awarded. **Location:** Downtown. **Calendar:** Quarter, extensive summer session. **Full-time faculty:** 40 total. **Part-time faculty:** 34 total.

Freshman class profile.

Out-of-state:	14%	Live on campus:	50%

Basis for selection. Open admission, but selective for some programs. Portfolio recommended for interior and fashion design majors. **Home schooled:** GED recommended.

2011-2012 Annual costs. Estimated tuition and fees ranges for entire programs as of July 2011: diploma programs, $16,293 -$31,521; associate degree programs, $32,545-$45,723; bachelor's degree programs, $67,026 -$79,840. Includes books, fees, and supplies. All costs subject to change at any time. Books/supplies: $900. Personal expenses: $1,100.

Financial aid. All financial aid based on need.

Application procedures. Admission: No deadline. $10 fee. Application must be submitted on paper. Admission notification on a rolling basis. **Financial aid:** No deadline. FAFSA, institutional form required. Applicants notified on a rolling basis starting 7/15.

Academics. Special study options: Double major, internships. **Credit/placement by examination:** AP, CLEP. **Support services:** Reduced course load, remedial instruction, tutoring.

Majors. Business: Business admin. **Protective services:** Law enforcement admin.

Computing on campus. 38 workstations in library, computer center, student center. Online library, helpline, wireless network available.

Student life. Freshman orientation: Mandatory. Preregistration for classes offered. **Housing:** Cooperative housing available. **Activities:** Student government, student newspaper.

Student services. Alcohol/substance abuse counseling, career counseling, services for economically disadvantaged, student employment services, financial aid counseling, personal counseling, placement for graduates.

Contact. E-mail: admissions@bauder.edu
Phone: (404) 237-7573 Toll-free number: (800) 241-3797
Fax: (404) 237-1619
Director of Admissions, Bauder College, 384 Northyards Boulevard NW, Ste 190, Atlanta, GA 30313

Berry College
Mount Berry, Georgia   CB member
www.berry.edu   CB code: 5059

- Private 4-year liberal arts college
- Residential campus in large town
- 1,928 degree-seeking undergraduates: 1% part-time, 67% women, 5% African American, 2% Asian American, 5% Hispanic American, 1% international
- 148 degree-seeking graduate students
- 62% of applicants admitted
- SAT or ACT (ACT writing optional), application essay required
- 57% graduate within 6 years; 24% enter graduate study

General. Founded in 1902. Regionally accredited. **Degrees:** 376 bachelor's awarded; master's offered. **Location:** 72 miles from Atlanta; 75 miles from Chattanooga, TN. **Calendar:** Semester, limited summer session. **Full-time faculty:** 146 total; 91% have terminal degrees, 7% minority, 38% women. **Part-time faculty:** 65 total; 40% have terminal degrees, 6% minority, 37% women. **Class size:** 60% < 20, 37% 20-39, 2% 40-49, less than 1% 50-99. **Special facilities:** Museum, waterwheel, wildlife management area and refuge, equine center with boarding facilities, dairy and beef cattle research center, on-campus elementary and middle schools, child development center, science center with 60-foot Foucault pendulum, student campsites.

Freshman class profile. 3,231 applied, 2,014 admitted, 557 enrolled.

Mid 50% test scores			
SAT critical reading:	520-650	GPA 2.0-2.99:	6%
SAT math:	520-620	Rank in top quarter:	70%
SAT writing:	520-620	Rank in top tenth:	32%
ACT composite:	23-29	End year in good standing:	94%
GPA 3.75 or higher:	53%	Return as sophomores:	79%
GPA 3.50-3.74:	16%	Out-of-state:	30%
GPA 3.0-3.49:	25%	Live on campus:	96%

Basis for selection. School achievement record and test scores most important. Class rank, recommendations and essays considered. Interview recommended; auditions required of music and theater majors; portfolio recommended for art majors. **Home schooled:** Transcript of courses and grades, letter of recommendation (nonparent) required. Must meet or exceed academic profile of previous freshman class.

High school preparation. College-preparatory program required. 20 units required. Required units include English 4, mathematics 4, social studies 3, science 3, foreign language 2 and academic electives 4. Algebra I, geometry or trigonometry, algebra II and fourth year higher than algebra II required.

2011-2012 Annual costs. Tuition/fees: $26,090. Room/board: $9,158. Books/supplies: $1,200. Personal expenses: $1,840.

2011-2012 Financial aid. Need-based: 528 full-time freshmen applied for aid; 417 were judged to have need; 417 of these received aid. Average need met was 79%. Average scholarship/grant was $18,339; average loan $3,772. 74% of total undergraduate aid awarded as scholarships/grants, 26% as loans/jobs. **Non-need-based:** Awarded to 809 full-time undergraduates, including 237 freshmen. Scholarships awarded for academics, art, leadership, minority status, music/drama. **Additional information:** All students are encouraged to work on-campus up to 16 hours per week.

Application procedures. Admission: Priority date 2/1; deadline 7/27 (receipt date). $50 fee, may be waived for applicants with need, free for online applicants. Admission notification on a rolling basis beginning on or about 11/1. Must reply by May 1 or within 4 week(s) if notified thereafter. **Financial aid:** Priority date 3/1; no closing date. FAFSA required. Applicants notified on a rolling basis starting 2/15.

Academics. Special study options: Combined bachelor's/graduate degree, cross-registration, double major, dual enrollment of high school students, honors, independent study, internships, student-designed major, study abroad, teacher certification program. 3-2 nursing with Emory University, 3-2 engineering with Georgia Institute of Technology. **Credit/placement by examination:** AP, CLEP, IB, SAT, ACT, institutional tests. No limit to credit by

examination that may be applied to degree. **Support services:** Study skills assistance, tutoring, writing center.

Majors. Biology: General, biochemistry. **Business:** Accounting, finance, marketing. **Computer sciences:** Computer science. **Conservation:** Environmental science. **Education:** Early childhood, mathematics, middle, music. **English:** English lit. **Foreign languages:** French, German, Spanish. **General:** Animal sciences. **Health services:** Nursing (RN). **History:** General. **Math:** General. **Parks/recreation:** Exercise sciences. **Philosophy/religion:** General. **Physical sciences:** Chemistry, physics. **Psychology:** General. **Social sciences:** General, economics, international relations, political science. **Visual/performing arts:** Art, music, music management, theater arts management.

Most popular majors. Agriculture 11%, biology 9%, business/marketing 12%, communications/journalism 8%, education 10%, psychology 10%, social sciences 6%, visual/performing arts 6%.

Computing on campus. 200 workstations in library, computer center, student center. Dormitories wired for high-speed internet access and linked to campus network. Commuter students can connect to campus network. Online library, helpline, repair service, wireless network available.

Student life. Freshman orientation: Mandatory, $90 fee. Preregistration for classes offered. Sessions for students and parents in June based on date of prepayment. Additional orientation 4 days prior to start of classes. **Policies:** Limited visitation hours. Dry campus. **Housing:** Guaranteed on-campus for freshmen. Coed dorms, single-sex dorms, apartments, wellness housing available. $100 fully refundable deposit, deadline 5/1. Special-interest housing for women in math and science and for students involved in environmental studies available. **Activities:** Bands, campus ministries, choral groups, dance, drama, international student organizations, literary magazine, music ensembles, Model UN, musical theater, student government, student newspaper, symphony orchestra, Amnesty International, Baptist collegiate ministries, Wesley Foundation, Catholic student association, Habitat for Humanity, Canterbury club, campus outreach, Fellowship of Christian Athletes, Young Democrats, College Republicans.

Athletics. NCAA. **Intercollegiate:** Baseball M, basketball, cross-country, diving, equestrian W, golf, lacrosse, soccer, softball W, swimming, tennis, volleyball W. **Intramural:** Badminton, basketball, bowling, cross-country, football (non-tackle), golf, racquetball, soccer, softball, swimming, table tennis, tennis, volleyball, water polo, weight lifting. **Team name:** Vikings.

Student services. Alcohol/substance abuse counseling, career counseling, student employment services, financial aid counseling, health services, minority student services, on-campus daycare, personal counseling, placement for graduates, veterans' counselor, women's services. **Physically disabled:** Services for visually, hearing impaired.

Contact. E-mail: admissions@berry.edu
Phone: (706) 236-2215 Toll-free number: (800) 237-7942
Fax: (706) 290-2178
Brett Kennedy, Director of Admissions, Berry College, PO Box 490159, Mount Berry, GA 30149-0159

Beulah Heights University
Atlanta, Georgia
www.beulah.org   CB code: 5082

▶ Private 5-year university and Bible college affiliated with interdenominational tradition
▶ Commuter campus in very large city
▶ 641 degree-seeking undergraduates: 54% part-time, 57% women
▶ 205 degree-seeking graduate students
▶ Application essay required
▶ 72% graduate within 6 years

General. Accredited by ABHE. **Degrees:** 81 bachelor's, 27 associate awarded; master's offered. **Location:** Downtown Atlanta. **Calendar:** Semester, extensive summer session. **Full-time faculty:** 11 total; 46% have terminal degrees, 64% minority, 18% women. **Part-time faculty:** 53 total; 58% have terminal degrees, 85% minority, 28% women. **Class size:** 20% < 20, 80% 20-39.

Freshman class profile. 99 applied, 99 admitted, 99 enrolled.

End year in good standing:	96%	**Live on campus:**	4%
Return as sophomores:	96%		

Basis for selection. Open admission. Qualitative faith important. Pastoral and personal references required. Applicants pursuing GED may be accepted prior to completion, but may not be eligible to receive degree until GED is

received. **Home schooled:** State high school equivalency certificate required. Program must be approved by state; 16 ACT/900 SAT (exclusive of Writing) required.

High school preparation. College-preparatory program recommended.

2011-2012 Annual costs. Tuition/fees: $7,480. Room only: $3,600. Books/supplies: $150.

2010-2011 Financial aid. Need-based: 50 full-time freshmen applied for aid; 50 were judged to have need; 50 of these received aid. Average need met was 85%. Average scholarship/grant was $2,000; average loan $5,000. 40% of total undergraduate aid awarded as scholarships/grants, 60% as loans/jobs.

Application procedures. Admission: No deadline. $35 fee. Application must be submitted on paper. Admission notification on a rolling basis. **Financial aid:** Priority date 2/1; no closing date. FAFSA required. Applicants notified on a rolling basis.

Academics. Special study options: Accelerated study, cross-registration, distance learning, double major, ESL, independent study, internships, weekend college. **Credit/placement by examination:** AP, CLEP. **Support services:** Learning center, reduced course load, remedial instruction, study skills assistance, tutoring, writing center.

Majors. Theology: Bible.

Computing on campus. Dormitories wired for high-speed internet access. Commuter students can connect to campus network. Online course registration, online library, student web hosting, wireless network available.

Student life. Freshman orientation: Mandatory. Preregistration for classes offered. **Policies:** Student are required to abide by the schools code of conduct and observe the schools rules and regulations. Religious observance required. **Housing:** Single-sex dorms, apartments, wellness housing available. $150 fully refundable deposit. **Activities:** Campus ministries, choral groups, international student organizations, student government, student newspaper, Club Give, international students association, Saturday Knight Live.

Student services. Adult student services, chaplain/spiritual director, career counseling, financial aid counseling, minority student services, personal counseling.

Contact. E-mail: admissions@beulah.org
Phone: (404) 627-2681 ext. 104 Toll-free number: (888) 777-2422
Fax: (404) 627-0702
John Dreher, Director of Admissions, Beulah Heights University, 892 Berne Street SE, Atlanta, GA 30316

Brenau University
Gainesville, Georgia   CB member
www.brenau.edu   CB code: 5066

▶ Private 4-year university and liberal arts college for women
▶ Residential campus in small city
▶ 790 degree-seeking undergraduates: 11% part-time, 100% women, 21% African American, 2% Asian American, 9% Hispanic American, 5% international
▶ 62 degree-seeking graduate students
▶ 34% of applicants admitted
▶ SAT or ACT (ACT writing optional) required
▶ 45% graduate within 6 years

General. Founded in 1878. Regionally accredited. Evening, weekend, performing arts, nursing and online colleges are coeducational. **Degrees:** 203 bachelor's awarded; master's offered. **Location:** 45 miles from Atlanta, GA. **Calendar:** Semester, limited summer session. **Full-time faculty:** 83 total; 76% have terminal degrees, 12% minority, 71% women. **Part-time faculty:** 64 total; 39% have terminal degrees, 12% minority, 69% women. **Class size:** 73% < 20, 25% 20-39, less than 1% 40-49, 2% 50-99. **Special facilities:** Regional history museum, visual arts center, performing arts center, Dian Fossey collection.

Freshman class profile. 3,696 applied, 1,263 admitted, 176 enrolled.

Mid 50% test scores			
		Return as sophomores:	69%
SAT critical reading:	450-560	**Out-of-state:**	6%
SAT math:	440-540	**Live on campus:**	85%
SAT writing:	440-540	**International:**	5%
ACT composite:	19-21	**Sororities:**	31%

Basis for selection. GPA and SAT/ACT weighted equally. Admission policies for Evening/Weekend College differ from Women's College. SAT/ACT used for placement into math courses. Auditions required of performing arts majors. **Home schooled:** Transcript of courses and grades required. **Learning Disabled:** Learning disability must be professionally diagnosed.

High school preparation. College-preparatory program recommended. 16 units required. Required units include English 4, mathematics 4, social studies 3, science 3 and foreign language 2.

2011-2012 Annual costs. Tuition/fees: $21,124. Room/board: $10,366.

Financial aid. **Non-need-based:** Scholarships awarded for academics, art, athletics, leadership, minority status, music/drama.

Application procedures. Admission: No deadline. $35 fee, may be waived for applicants with need. Admission notification on a rolling basis beginning on or about 10/1. **Financial aid:** Priority date 4/1; no closing date. FAFSA required. Applicants notified on a rolling basis starting 3/1.

Academics. Special study options: Combined bachelor's/graduate degree, cross-registration, distance learning, double major, dual enrollment of high school students, ESL, honors, independent study, internships, student-designed major, study abroad, teacher certification program, weekend college. **Credit/placement by examination:** AP, CLEP, IB, institutional tests. 27 credit hours maximum toward bachelor's degree. Total of 27 hours for non-traditional students allowed. **Support services:** Learning center, pre-admission summer program, reduced course load, remedial instruction, study skills assistance, tutoring, writing center.

Majors. Biology: General. **Business:** General, accounting, fashion, human resources, marketing, organizational leadership. **Communications:** Media studies. **Education:** Art, drama/dance, early childhood, early childhood special, elementary, elementary special ed, junior high special ed, mentally handicapped, middle, music, secondary, secondary special ed, special ed. **English:** English lit. **Health services:** Nursing practice, physician assistant. **History:** General. **Liberal arts:** Arts/sciences. **Psychology:** General. **Social sciences:** Political science. **Visual/performing arts:** Arts management, dance, dramatic, fashion design, graphic design, interior design, music, music performance, musical theater, studio arts, studio arts management, theater design.

Most popular majors. Biology 7%, business/marketing 12%, education 6%, health sciences 38%, psychology 6%, visual/performing arts 17%.

Computing on campus. 150 workstations in dormitories, library, computer center, student center. Dormitories wired for high-speed internet access and linked to campus network. Online course registration, online library, helpline, repair service, student web hosting, wireless network available.

Student life. Freshman orientation: Mandatory. Preregistration for classes offered. **Policies:** Single students under 22 years of age required to live on campus unless living with family or legal guardian; alcohol-free campus; required convocation attendance. **Housing:** Guaranteed on-campus for all undergraduates. Special housing for disabled, apartments, fraternity/sorority housing available. **Activities:** Campus ministries, choral groups, dance, drama, international student organizations, literary magazine, musical theater, radio station, student government, student newspaper, TV station, Brenau Fellowhip Association, Eco-Friends, Fellowship of Christian Athletes, College Republicans, College Democrats, Silhouettes, Greek letter service organizations, student activities board.

Athletics. NAIA. **Intercollegiate:** Basketball W, cheerleading M, cross-country W, soccer W, softball W, swimming W, tennis W, volleyball W. **Team name:** Golden Tigers.

Student services. Alcohol/substance abuse counseling, career counseling, student employment services, financial aid counseling, health services, minority student services, personal counseling, placement for graduates, women's services. **Physically disabled:** Services for visually, speech, hearing impaired.

Contact. E-mail: admissions@brenau.edu
Phone: (770) 534-6100 Toll-free number: (800) 252-5119
Fax: (770) 538-4701
Scott Briell, Senior Vice President for Enrollment Management & Student Services, Brenau University, 500 Washington Street SE, Gainesville, GA 30501

Brewton-Parker College
Mount Vernon, Georgia
www.bpc.edu

CB member
CB code: 5068

- Private 4-year liberal arts college affiliated with Southern Baptist Convention
- Residential campus in small town

- 512 degree-seeking undergraduates: 10% part-time, 51% women, 29% African American, 1% Asian American, 6% Hispanic American, 5% international
- 95% of applicants admitted
- SAT or ACT (ACT writing optional) required

General. Founded in 1904. Regionally accredited. **Degrees:** 124 bachelor's, 17 associate awarded. **Location:** 90 miles from Macon and Savannah. **Calendar:** Semester, limited summer session. **Full-time faculty:** 31 total; 45% have terminal degrees, 6% minority, 45% women. **Part-time faculty:** 54 total; 37% have terminal degrees, 15% minority, 48% women. **Class size:** 70% < 20, 30% 20-39, less than 1% 40-49. **Special facilities:** Living history museum, recital hall, greenhouse, nature trail.

Freshman class profile. 293 applied, 277 admitted, 130 enrolled.

Mid 50% test scores			
SAT critical reading:	400-510	GPA 2.0-2.99:	47%
SAT math:	390-500	Rank in top quarter:	40%
SAT writing:	380-490	Rank in top tenth:	24%
ACT composite:	15-20	Return as sophomores:	41%
GPA 3.75 or higher:	10%	Out-of-state:	12%
GPA 3.50-3.74:	13%	Live on campus:	75%
GPA 3.0-3.49:	29%	International:	7%

Basis for selection. Students evaluated on SAT/ACT and high school performance. Audition and interview required of music majors.

High school preparation. College-preparatory program recommended. 13 units required. Required units include English 4, mathematics 3, social studies 3 and science 3.

2011-2012 Annual costs. Tuition/fees: $12,290. Room/board: $7,464. Books/supplies: $2,000. Personal expenses: $1,700.

Financial aid. **Non-need-based:** Scholarships awarded for academics, athletics, music/drama, religious affiliation, state residency.

Application procedures. Admission: Closing date 8/1. $35 fee. Admission notification on a rolling basis beginning on or about 9/1. **Financial aid:** Closing date 4/15. FAFSA required. Applicants notified on a rolling basis starting 3/1; must reply within 2 week(s) of notification.

Academics. Special study options: Distance learning, double major, dual enrollment of high school students, external degree, honors, independent study, internships, teacher certification program. **Credit/placement by examination:** AP, CLEP, SAT, ACT, institutional tests. 30 credit hours maximum toward associate degree, 30 toward bachelor's. **Support services:** Learning center, reduced course load, remedial instruction, study skills assistance, tutoring.

Majors. Biology: General. **Business:** General, accounting, business admin. **Communications:** Communications/speech/rhetoric. **Computer sciences:** General. **Education:** General, biology, early childhood, English, history, mathematics, middle, music, science, social studies. **English:** English lit. **Foreign languages:** Spanish. **History:** General. **Math:** General. **Parks/recreation:** Sports admin. **Philosophy/religion:** Christian, religion. **Psychology:** General. **Social sciences:** General, political science, sociology. **Theology:** Sacred music, theology. **Visual/performing arts:** General, music, music performance.

Most popular majors. Business/marketing 21%, education 14%, English 6%, liberal arts 9%, parks/recreation 8%, philosophy/religious studies 8%, psychology 10%, public administration/social services 7%.

Computing on campus. 104 workstations in library, computer center. Dormitories wired for high-speed internet access. Online course registration, online library, wireless network available.

Student life. Freshman orientation: Available, $100 fee. Preregistration for classes offered. Held the week and/or weekend before classes start. **Policies:** All day students required to live on campus except seniors, students residing with parents, students 22 or older. Religious observance required. **Housing:** Guaranteed on-campus for freshmen. Single-sex dorms available. $125 nonrefundable deposit. **Activities:** Campus ministries, choral groups, film society, international student organizations, music ensembles, student government, student newspaper, ministerial association, Fellowship of Christian Athletes, Rotaract, Circle K, student activities council.

Athletics. NAIA. **Intercollegiate:** Baseball M, basketball, cheerleading, cross-country, soccer, softball W, volleyball W, wrestling M. **Intramural:** Basketball, football (non-tackle), softball, table tennis, tennis, volleyball. **Team name:** Barons.

Student services. Alcohol/substance abuse counseling, chaplain/spiritual director, career counseling, student employment services, financial aid counseling, health services, personal counseling, placement for graduates, veterans'

counselor. **Physically disabled:** Services for visually, speech, hearing impaired.

Contact. E-mail: admissions@bpc.edu
Phone: (912) 583-2241 ext. 265
Toll-free number: (800) 342-1087 ext. 265 Fax: (912) 583-3598
Sandra Clay, Director of Admissions, Brewton-Parker College, Brewton-Parker College # 2011, Mount Vernon, GA 30445

Carver Bible College
Atlanta, Georgia
www.carver.edu

- Private 4-year Bible college
- Commuter campus in very large city
- 104 degree-seeking undergraduates

General. Accredited by ABHE. **Degrees:** 5 bachelor's, 2 associate awarded. **Calendar:** Semester, limited summer session. **Full-time faculty:** 2 total. **Part-time faculty:** 17 total.

Basis for selection. Applicants assessed for admittance based on academic record, moral character and personal testimony of faith. Students who cannot meet the general entrance requirements may be given conditional admittance for probationary period.

2011-2012 Annual costs. Tuition/fees: $8,320.

Application procedures. Admission: No deadline.

Academics. Remedial instruction offered, particularly for those whose first language is not English. **Special study options:** Distance learning, independent study. **Credit/placement by examination:** AP, CLEP, institutional tests. Transfer credits offered for work done which may be same or similar to offered courses. **Support services:** Learning center, remedial instruction.

Majors. Theology: Bible.

Computing on campus. Wireless network available.

Student life. Freshman orientation: Mandatory. Preregistration for classes offered. **Policies:** Religious observance required. **Housing:** Single-sex dorms available.

Athletics. Intercollegiate: Basketball M. **Team name:** Carver Cougars.

Contact. Phone: (404) 527-4520 Fax: (404) 527-4524
Bertha Mack, Director of Admissions, Carver Bible College, 3837 Cascade Road, SW, Atlanta, GA 30313

Clark Atlanta University
Atlanta, Georgia   **CB member**
www.cau.edu   **CB code: 5110**

- Private 4-year university affiliated with United Methodist Church
- Residential campus in very large city
- 3,127 degree-seeking undergraduates: 6% part-time, 75% women, 91% African American, 1% international
- 716 degree-seeking graduate students
- 72% of applicants admitted
- SAT or ACT (ACT writing optional), application essay required
- 41% graduate within 6 years

General. Founded in 1869. Regionally accredited. Member of Atlanta University Center, a consortium of black private education institutions. **Degrees:** 547 bachelor's awarded; master's, doctoral offered. **ROTC:** Army, Naval. **Location:** 2 miles from downtown. **Calendar:** Semester, limited summer session. **Full-time faculty:** 171 total; 76% have terminal degrees, 89% minority, 40% women. **Part-time faculty:** 135 total; 40% have terminal degrees, 86% minority, 57% women. **Class size:** 42% <20, 44% 20-39, 8% 40-49, 5% 50-99, less than 1% >100. **Special facilities:** Exhibition gallery, research center for science and technology.

Freshman class profile. 5,261 applied, 3,772 admitted, 833 enrolled.

Mid 50% test scores			
SAT critical reading:	390-470	GPA 2.0-2.99:	46%
SAT math:	380-460	Rank in top quarter:	32%
ACT composite:	18-20	Rank in top tenth:	13%
GPA 3.75 or higher:	4%	End year in good standing:	80%
GPA 3.50-3.74:	9%	Return as sophomores:	65%
GPA 3.0-3.49:	40%	Out-of-state:	68%
		Live on campus:	32%

Basis for selection. Secondary school record most important. Test scores, recommendations, essay also important. Audition recommended for music and drama majors. **Home schooled:** Course work portfolio required.

High school preparation. College-preparatory program recommended. 18 units required. Required units include English 4, mathematics 3, social studies 3, science 3 (laboratory 1), foreign language 2 and academic electives 3.

2012-2013 Annual costs. Tuition/fees (projected): $18,912. Room/board: $9,285. Books/supplies: $2,200. Personal expenses: $1,803.

Financial aid. Non-need-based: Scholarships awarded for academics, art, athletics, leadership, minority status, music/drama, religious affiliation, ROTC, state residency.

Application procedures. Admission: Priority date 3/1; deadline 6/1 (postmark date). $35 fee, may be waived for applicants with need. Admission notification on a rolling basis beginning on or about 1/1. **Financial aid:** Priority date 3/1; no closing date. FAFSA required. Applicants notified on a rolling basis starting 4/1.

Academics. Special study options: Accelerated study, combined bachelor's/graduate degree, cooperative education, cross-registration, double major, dual enrollment of high school students, exchange student, honors, independent study, internships, study abroad, teacher certification program, Washington semester, weekend college. **Credit/placement by examination:** AP, CLEP, IB, institutional tests. 45 credit hours maximum toward bachelor's degree. **Support services:** Learning center, reduced course load, study skills assistance, tutoring, writing center.

Majors. Biology: General. **Business:** Accounting, business admin, managerial economics. **Computer sciences:** General, computer science. **Education:** General, early childhood. **English:** English lit, rhetoric/composition. **Foreign languages:** French, Spanish. **History:** General. **Human services:** Social work. **Math:** General. **Philosophy/religion:** Philosophy, religion. **Physical sciences:** Chemistry, physics. **Protective services:** Criminal justice. **Psychology:** General. **Social sciences:** Political science, sociology. **Visual/performing arts:** Art, fashion design, music, theater history.

Most popular majors. Business/marketing 21%, communications/journalism 26%, psychology 11%, security/protective services 6%, visual/performing arts 9%.

Computing on campus. 650 workstations in dormitories, library, computer center, student center. Dormitories wired for high-speed internet access and linked to campus network. Commuter students can connect to campus network. Online course registration, online library, helpline, repair service, wireless network available.

Student life. Freshman orientation: Mandatory, $150 fee. Preregistration for classes offered. **Policies:** Drug/alcohol policy, sanctions for violations, policies governing Greek and other student organizations. **Housing:** Guaranteed on-campus for freshmen. Coed dorms, single-sex dorms, apartments available. $325 partly refundable deposit, deadline 6/1. **Activities:** Bands, campus ministries, choral groups, dance, drama, film society, international student organizations, literary magazine, music ensembles, musical theater, opera, radio station, student government, student newspaper, symphony orchestra, TV station, NAACP, pan-Hellenic council, Anointed Students in Fellowship, Campus Crusade for Christ, Christian Fellowship, National Council of Negro Women, Forensic Society, Gamma Sigma Sigma, Caribbean-oriented student organization.

Athletics. NCAA. **Intercollegiate:** Baseball M, basketball, cross-country, football (tackle) M, softball W, tennis W, track and field, volleyball W. **Intramural:** Basketball, football (non-tackle), tennis W, track and field. **Team name:** Panthers.

Student services. Alcohol/substance abuse counseling, chaplain/spiritual director, career counseling, student employment services, financial aid counseling, health services, personal counseling, placement for graduates, veterans' counselor, women's services. **Physically disabled:** Services for visually, speech, hearing impaired.

Contact. E-mail: cauadmissions@cau.edu
Phone: (404) 880-6605 Toll-free number: (800) 688-3228
Fax: (404) 880-6174
Michelle Davis, Director of Admissions, Clark Atlanta University, 223 James P. Brawley Drive, SW, Atlanta, GA 30314-4391

Clayton State University
Morrow, Georgia   **CB member**
www.clayton.edu   **CB code: 5145**

- Public 4-year liberal arts and technical college
- Commuter campus in small city

- 6,564 degree-seeking undergraduates: 41% part-time, 71% women, 63% African American, 4% Asian American, 2% Hispanic American, 1% international
- 299 degree-seeking graduate students
- 37% of applicants admitted
- SAT or ACT (ACT writing optional) required

General. Founded in 1969. Regionally accredited. **Degrees:** 1,001 bachelor's, 84 associate awarded; master's offered. **ROTC:** Army, Naval, Air Force. **Location:** 12 miles from Atlanta. **Calendar:** Semester, extensive summer session. **Full-time faculty:** 225 total; 82% have terminal degrees, 38% minority, 51% women. **Part-time faculty:** 155 total; 53% minority, 56% women. **Class size:** 41% < 20, 51% 20-39, 4% 40-49, 4% 50-99, less than 1% >100. **Special facilities:** Concert hall.

Freshman class profile. 2,574 applied, 964 admitted, 499 enrolled.

Mid 50% test scores		GPA 2.0-2.99:	38%
SAT critical reading:	440-520	Return as sophomores:	66%
SAT math:	430-510	Out-of-state:	9%
ACT composite:	18-21	Live on campus:	30%
GPA 3.75 or higher:	13%	Fraternities:	8%
GPA 3.50-3.74:	12%	Sororities:	2%
GPA 3.0-3.49:	37%		

Basis for selection. 17 ACT or 400 SAT math and 430 verbal required. Secondary school record also very important for health sciences, music, teacher education, and business programs. Auditions recommended for music majors. **Home schooled:** Must validate the completion of a college prep curriculum. SAT tests may be used to do so.

High school preparation. 16 units required; 22 recommended. Required and recommended units include English 4, mathematics 4, social studies 3, history 2, science 3-4 (laboratory 3), foreign language 2-3 and academic electives 2. Students not meeting college-preparatory requirements must take remedial classes before entering any program.

2011-2012 Annual costs. Tuition/fees: $5,806; $17,419 out-of-state. Room/board: $9,028. Books/supplies: $1,000.

Financial aid. **Non-need-based:** Scholarships awarded for academics, athletics, music/drama.

Application procedures. **Admission:** Priority date 2/1; no deadline. $40 fee, may be waived for applicants with need. Admission notification on a rolling basis beginning on or about 1/1. **Financial aid:** Priority date 7/1; no closing date. FAFSA required. Applicants notified on a rolling basis.

Academics. **Special study options:** Cooperative education, cross-registration, distance learning, double major, dual enrollment of high school students, exchange student, honors, independent study, internships, liberal arts/career combination, student-designed major, study abroad, teacher certification program. **Credit/placement by examination:** AP, CLEP, IB, institutional tests. **Support services:** Learning center, reduced course load, remedial instruction, study skills assistance, tutoring, writing center.

Majors. **Biology:** General. **Business:** General, accounting, business admin, marketing, office management, operations. **Communications:** Communications/speech/rhetoric. **Computer sciences:** General, data processing, information systems, information technology, programming, systems analysis. **Education:** Middle. **English:** English lit. **Health services:** Dental assistant, dental hygiene, facilities admin, health care admin, nursing (RN). **History:** General. **Liberal arts:** Arts/sciences. **Math:** General. **Parks/recreation:** Sports admin. **Protective services:** Criminal justice. **Psychology:** Community. **Social sciences:** Political science. **Visual/performing arts:** Dramatic, music, music performance, music theory/composition.

Most popular majors. Business/marketing 22%, health sciences 25%, liberal arts 15%, psychology 12%.

Computing on campus. PC or laptop required. Dormitories wired for high-speed internet access and linked to campus network. Online course registration, online library, helpline, repair service, student web hosting, wireless network available.

Student life. **Freshman orientation:** Mandatory, $40 fee. Preregistration for classes offered. **Housing:** Coed dorms available. **Activities:** Jazz band, choral groups, drama, film society, literary magazine, music ensembles, musical theater, opera, radio station, student government, student newspaper, approximately 20 student groups.

Athletics. NAIA, NCAA. **Intercollegiate:** Basketball, cross-country, golf M, soccer, tennis W, track and field. **Team name:** Lakers.

Student services. Adult student services, alcohol/substance abuse counseling, career counseling, student employment services, financial aid counseling, health services, minority student services, personal counseling, placement for graduates, veterans' counselor. **Physically disabled:** Services for visually, speech, hearing impaired.

Contact. E-mail: csu-info@clayton.edu
Phone: (678) 466-4115 Fax: (678) 466-4149
Betty Momayezi, Director of Admissions, Clayton State University, 2000 Clayton State Boulevard, Morrow, GA 30260-0285

Columbus State University
Columbus, Georgia   **CB member**
www.columbusstate.edu/   **CB code: 5123**

- Public 4-year university and liberal arts college
- Commuter campus in small city
- 6,849 degree-seeking undergraduates: 27% part-time, 60% women, 36% African American, 2% Asian American, 5% Hispanic American, 1% Native American, 1% international
- 1,251 degree-seeking graduate students
- 56% of applicants admitted
- SAT or ACT (ACT writing optional) required
- 31% graduate within 6 years

General. Founded in 1958. Regionally accredited. **Degrees:** 905 bachelor's, 32 associate awarded; master's, doctoral offered. **ROTC:** Army. **Location:** 100 miles from Atlanta. **Calendar:** Semester, extensive summer session. **Full-time faculty:** 271 total; 76% have terminal degrees, 25% minority, 43% women. **Part-time faculty:** 198 total; 24% have terminal degrees, 15% minority, 46% women. **Class size:** 40% < 20, 48% 20-39, 6% 40-49, 6% 50-99, less than 1% >100. **Special facilities:** Environmental learning center, space science center, fine and performing arts center.

Freshman class profile. 3,843 applied, 2,144 admitted, 1,189 enrolled.

Mid 50% test scores		Rank in top quarter:	35%
SAT critical reading:	440-550	Rank in top tenth:	14%
SAT math:	420-530	End year in good standing:	68%
SAT writing:	420-530	Return as sophomores:	69%
ACT composite:	17-22	Out-of-state:	10%
GPA 3.75 or higher:	8%	Live on campus:	45%
GPA 3.50-3.74:	12%	Fraternities:	2%
GPA 3.0-3.49:	37%	Sororities:	2%
GPA 2.0-2.99:	43%		

Basis for selection. GED not accepted. 2.3 GPA, 440 SAT Critical Reading/17 ACT English, and 410 SAT math/17 ACT math required. Students must be on track to graduate with college preparatory seal. Students with college prep deficiencies will be considered on individual basis. Interviews and auditions required of music majors. Portfolio recommended for art majors. **Home schooled:** Statement describing home school structure and mission, transcript of courses and grades required. 1000 SAT (exclusive of Writing), Home School Credit Evaluation Table, letter from primary teacher certifying completion of high school and date of graduation and two letters of recommendation from non-family members required.

High school preparation. College-preparatory program required. 16 units required. Required units include English 4, mathematics 4, social studies 3, science 3 (laboratory 2) and foreign language 2. Social studies units required include U.S. history and world studies.

2011-2012 Annual costs. Tuition/fees: $6,404; $18,380 out-of-state. Room/board: $7,560. Books/supplies: $1,072. Personal expenses: $2,001.

2011-2012 Financial aid. **Need-based:** 966 full-time freshmen applied for aid; 769 were judged to have need; 766 of these received aid. Average need met was 74%. Average scholarship/grant was $4,777; average loan $3,331. 48% of total undergraduate aid awarded as scholarships/grants, 52% as loans/jobs. **Non-need-based:** Awarded to 1,534 full-time undergraduates, including 529 freshmen. Scholarships awarded for academics, alumni affiliation, art, athletics, job skills, leadership, minority status, music/drama, ROTC.

Application procedures. **Admission:** Priority date 5/15; deadline 6/30 (receipt date). $40 fee, may be waived for applicants with need. Admission notification on a rolling basis beginning on or about 9/1. **Financial aid:** Priority date 5/1; no closing date. FAFSA required. Applicants notified on a rolling basis starting 5/15; must reply within 4 week(s) of notification.

Academics. **Special study options:** Accelerated study, combined bachelor's/graduate degree, cooperative education, distance learning, double major, dual enrollment of high school students, ESL, honors, independent study, internships, liberal arts/career combination, study abroad, teacher certification

program. **Credit/placement by examination:** AP, CLEP, IB, institutional tests. 30 credit hours maximum toward associate degree, 60 toward bachelor's. **Support services:** Learning center, reduced course load, remedial instruction, study skills assistance, tutoring, writing center.

Majors. Biology: General. **Business:** General, accounting, business admin, finance, management information systems, marketing. **Computer sciences:** General, information technology. **Education:** Art, biology, chemistry, drama/dance, early childhood, English, mathematics, middle, music, physical, science, secondary, social science, social studies, special ed. **English:** English lit, rhetoric/composition. **Foreign languages:** General. **Health services:** Nursing (RN). **History:** General. **Liberal arts:** Arts/sciences. **Math:** General. **Parks/recreation:** Exercise sciences. **Physical sciences:** Chemistry, geology. **Protective services:** Criminal justice. **Psychology:** General. **Social sciences:** Political science, sociology. **Visual/performing arts:** Art, dramatic, music, music performance.

Most popular majors. Business/marketing 23%, education 17%, health sciences 17%, security/protective services 8%.

Computing on campus. 1,150 workstations in dormitories, library, computer center, student center. Dormitories wired for high-speed internet access and linked to campus network. Commuter students can connect to campus network. Online course registration, online library, helpline, repair service, student web hosting, wireless network available.

Student life. Freshman orientation: Mandatory, $85 fee. Preregistration for classes offered. **Policies:** Entering freshmen from outside local area must live in student housing. **Housing:** Special housing for disabled, apartments, fraternity/sorority housing, wellness housing available. $225 partly refundable deposit, deadline 5/1. Apartments take place of traditional dorms; weekday meals included in fee. **Activities:** Bands, campus ministries, choral groups, dance, drama, international student organizations, literary magazine, music ensembles, Model UN, musical theater, student government, student newspaper, symphony orchestra, College Republicans, Islamic association, Freethought Society, Cougars for Christ, CSU Democrats, minority student union, student political awareness, Westminster Fellowship, Baptist student union.

Athletics. NCAA. **Intercollegiate:** Baseball M, basketball, cross-country, golf, rifle, soccer W, softball W, tennis. **Intramural:** Badminton, basketball, football (tackle) M, skiing, soccer, softball, table tennis, tennis, volleyball. **Team name:** Cougars.

Student services. Adult student services, alcohol/substance abuse counseling, career counseling, student employment services, financial aid counseling, health services, minority student services, personal counseling, placement for graduates, veterans' counselor, women's services. **Physically disabled:** Services for visually, speech, hearing impaired.

Contact. E-mail: admissions@columbiastate.edu
Phone: (706) 507-8800 Toll-free number: (866) 264-2035
Fax: (706) 568-5091
Susan Lovell, Director of Enrollment Services, Columbus State University, 4225 University Avenue, Columbus, GA 31907-5645

Covenant College
Lookout Mountain, Georgia
www.covenant.edu   CB code: 6124

- Private 4-year liberal arts college affiliated with Presbyterian Church in America (PCA)
- Residential campus in small city
- 1,009 degree-seeking undergraduates: 1% part-time, 54% women, 3% African American, 2% Asian American, 2% Hispanic American, 2% international
- 64 degree-seeking graduate students
- 57% of applicants admitted
- SAT or ACT (ACT writing optional), application essay required
- 52% graduate within 6 years

General. Founded in 1955. Regionally accredited. **Degrees:** 202 bachelor's awarded; master's offered. **ROTC:** Army. **Location:** 120 miles from Atlanta, 5 miles from Chattanooga, TN. **Calendar:** Semester, limited summer session. **Full-time faculty:** 64 total; 88% have terminal degrees, 8% minority, 22% women. **Part-time faculty:** 29 total; 31% have terminal degrees, 10% minority, 45% women. **Class size:** 61% < 20, 37% 20-39, 2% 40-49, less than 1% 50-99, less than 1% >100.

Freshman class profile. 1,057 applied, 607 admitted, 286 enrolled.

Mid 50% test scores			
SAT critical reading:	550-660	GPA 2.0-2.99:	8%
SAT math:	520-630	Rank in top quarter:	46%
SAT writing:	520-630	Rank in top tenth:	18%
ACT composite:	23-29	Return as sophomores:	81%
GPA 3.75 or higher:	43%	Out-of-state:	77%
GPA 3.50-3.74:	26%	Live on campus:	98%
GPA 3.0-3.49:	23%	International:	1%

Basis for selection. 1000 SAT (exclusive of Writing) or 21 ACT, 2.5 GPA, academic evaluation, church evaluation, and personal testimony of faith important. Students that do not meet minimum scores may be asked to provide additional information. Auditions required for music and voice majors. **Home schooled:** Transcript of courses and grades, letter of recommendation (nonparent) required.

High school preparation. College-preparatory program recommended. 14 units required; 16 recommended. Required and recommended units include English 4, mathematics 3, social studies 2, science 2, foreign language 2 and academic electives 3.

2011-2012 Annual costs. Tuition/fees: $27,220. Room/board: $7,740. Books/supplies: $1,000. Personal expenses: $1,300.

2010-2011 Financial aid. Need-based: 209 full-time freshmen applied for aid; 170 were judged to have need; 170 of these received aid. Average need met was 85%. Average scholarship/grant was $16,354; average loan $5,225. 70% of total undergraduate aid awarded as scholarships/grants, 30% as loans/jobs. **Non-need-based:** Awarded to 257 full-time undergraduates, including 71 freshmen. Scholarships awarded for academics, alumni affiliation, art, job skills, leadership, minority status, music/drama, religious affiliation, state residency.

Application procedures. Admission: Priority date 3/1; no deadline. $35 fee, may be waived for applicants with need. Admission notification on a rolling basis beginning on or about 8/1. Must reply by May 1 or within 3 week(s) if notified thereafter. **Financial aid:** No deadline. FAFSA required. Applicants notified on a rolling basis starting 2/1; must reply within 3 week(s) of notification.

Academics. Special study options: Double major, dual enrollment of high school students, exchange student, independent study, internships, student-designed major, study abroad, teacher certification program, Washington semester. Dual engineering degree with Georgia Tech; cooperative nursing program with Emory University; bridge program for MSN with Vanderbilt University. **Credit/placement by examination:** AP, CLEP, IB, SAT, ACT, institutional tests. 30 credit hours maximum toward associate degree, 30 toward bachelor's. **Support services:** Reduced course load, remedial instruction, study skills assistance, tutoring, writing center.

Majors. Biology: General. **Business:** General. **Computer sciences:** General. **Education:** Elementary, English, history, mathematics, science. **English:** English lit. **Foreign languages:** French, Spanish. **History:** General. **Math:** General. **Philosophy/religion:** General, philosophy. **Physical sciences:** General, chemistry, physics. **Psychology:** General. **Social sciences:** General, economics, sociology. **Theology:** Bible. **Visual/performing arts:** Dramatic, music, music performance.

Most popular majors. Biology 7%, education 22%, English 12%, interdisciplinary studies 11%, social sciences 15%, visual/performing arts 6%.

Computing on campus. 130 workstations in dormitories, library, computer center. Dormitories linked to campus network. Commuter students can connect to campus network. Online library, helpline, repair service, wireless network available.

Student life. Freshman orientation: Mandatory, $355 fee. Preregistration for classes offered. Held the week prior to beginning of classes. **Policies:** Smoking, alcoholic beverages, and drugs prohibited. Students are to use wisdom and Christ-like discretion in applying Biblical principles to decisions regarding all areas of life. Religious observance required. **Housing:** Guaranteed on-campus for freshmen. Single-sex dorms, apartments available. **Activities:** Bands, campus ministries, choral groups, dance, drama, film society, international student organizations, literary magazine, music ensembles, musical theater, radio station, student government, student newspaper, Rotaract, Young Life, pre-law club, Psi Chi, Reformed University Fellowship, Evangelism club.

Athletics. NCAA. **Intercollegiate:** Baseball M, basketball, cross-country, golf, soccer, softball W, tennis, volleyball W. **Intramural:** Basketball, football (non-tackle), football (tackle) M, soccer, volleyball. **Team name:** Scots.

Student services. Adult student services, chaplain/spiritual director, career counseling, student employment services, financial aid counseling, health services, personal counseling, placement for graduates.

Contact. E-mail: admissions@covenant.edu
Phone: (706) 820-2398 Toll-free number: (888) 451-2683
Fax: (706) 820-0893
Matthew Bryant, Director of Admissions, Covenant College, 14049 Scenic
Highway, Lookout Mountain, GA 30750

Dalton State College
Dalton, Georgia
www.daltonstate.edu
CB code: 5167

- Public 4-year liberal arts and teachers college
- Commuter campus in large town
- 5,485 degree-seeking undergraduates: 41% part-time, 62% women
- 47% of applicants admitted
- SAT or ACT (ACT writing optional) required

General. Founded in 1963. Regionally accredited. **Degrees:** 225 bachelor's, 322 associate awarded. **Location:** 90 miles from Atlanta. **Calendar:** Semester, limited summer session. **Full-time faculty:** 167 total; 52% have terminal degrees, 10% minority, 53% women. **Part-time faculty:** 80 total; 15% have terminal degrees, 2% minority, 45% women. **Class size:** 28% < 20, 69% 20-39, 3% 40-49, less than 1% 50-99.

Freshman class profile. 3,592 applied, 1,676 admitted, 1,321 enrolled.

Mid 50% test scores			
SAT critical reading:	410-530	GPA 3.0-3.49:	33%
SAT math:	410-520	GPA 2.0-2.99:	36%
ACT composite:	17-22	Return as sophomores:	63%
GPA 3.75 or higher:	16%	Out-of-state:	1%
GPA 3.50-3.74:	14%	Live on campus:	8%

Basis for selection. 2.0 GPA in high school college preparatory curriculum and 2.2 GPA in Tech Prep curriculum required. SAT/ACT not required for certificate students. **Home schooled:** State high school equivalency certificate required.

High school preparation. College-preparatory program recommended. 16 units required. Required units include English 4, mathematics 4, social studies 1, history 2, science 3 and foreign language 2.

2011-2012 Annual costs. Tuition/fees: $3,622; $11,104 out-of-state. Room only: $4,070. Books/supplies: $1,000.

2010-2011 Financial aid. Need-based: 946 full-time freshmen applied for aid; 788 were judged to have need; 786 of these received aid. Average need met was 67%. Average scholarship/grant was $3,442; average loan $2,778. 63% of total undergraduate aid awarded as scholarships/grants, 37% as loans/jobs. **Non-need-based:** Awarded to 1,322 full-time undergraduates, including 543 freshmen. Scholarships awarded for academics, leadership, minority status, state residency.

Application procedures. Admission: Priority date 12/1; deadline 7/1. $30 fee, may be waived for applicants with need. Admission notification on a rolling basis beginning on or about 12/1. **Financial aid:** No deadline. FAFSA required. Applicants notified on a rolling basis starting 4/1.

Academics. Special study options: Double major, dual enrollment of high school students, ESL, internships, study abroad, teacher certification program, weekend college. **Credit/placement by examination:** AP, CLEP, SAT, ACT, institutional tests. Credit is awarded only to admitted students and recorded only for those who enroll for credit courses. Credit is awarded only for offered courses. **Support services:** Remedial instruction, study skills assistance, tutoring, writing center.

Majors. Biology: General. **Business:** Accounting, business admin, management information systems, management science, marketing, operations. **Computer sciences:** General. **Education:** Elementary. **English:** English lit. **History:** General. **Human services:** Social work. **Liberal arts:** Arts/sciences. **Math:** General. **Physical sciences:** Chemistry. **Protective services:** Police science.

Most popular majors. Business/marketing 44%, education 46%.

Computing on campus. 800 workstations in library, computer center, student center. Commuter students can connect to campus network. Online library, helpline available.

Student life. Freshman orientation: Mandatory. Preregistration for classes offered. **Housing:** Coed dorms, special housing for disabled, apartments available. $200 fully refundable deposit. **Activities:** Campus ministries, dance, drama, international student organizations, literary magazine, music ensembles, student government, student newspaper, social work club, LPN,

Baptist student union, psychology club, black student alliance, Phi The Kappa, Young Democrats, progressive student union.

Student services. Adult student services, career counseling, student employment services, financial aid counseling, personal counseling, placement for graduates, veterans' counselor. **Physically disabled:** Services for hearing impaired.

Contact. Phone: (706) 272-4436 Toll-free number: (800) 829-4436
Fax: (706) 272-2530
Jodi Johnson, Vice President for Enrollment Services, Dalton State College, 650 College Drive, Dalton, GA 30720

DeVry University: Decatur
Decatur, Georgia
www.devry.edu
CB code: 5715

- For-profit 4-year university
- Commuter campus in large town
- 2,720 degree-seeking undergraduates
- Interview required

General. Founded in 1969. Regionally accredited. Additional locations: Alpharetta, Atlanta Buckhead, Atlanta Cobb/Galleria, Atlanta Perimeter, Gwinnett, Henry County, Memphis, Nashville. **Degrees:** 359 bachelor's, 108 associate awarded; master's offered. **Location:** 15 miles from Atlanta. **Calendar:** Semester, extensive summer session. **Full-time faculty:** 37 total. **Part-time faculty:** 106 total.

Basis for selection. Applicants must have high school diploma or equivalent, or degree from accredited post-secondary institution, demonstrate proficiency in basic college-level skills through SAT/ACT or institution-administered placement exams, and be at least 17 years of age. New students may enter at beginning of any semester.

High school preparation. College-preparatory program recommended.

2011-2012 Annual costs. Tuition/fees: $15,294. Books/supplies: $1,310. Personal expenses: $3,574.

Financial aid. All financial aid based on need.

Application procedures. Admission: No deadline. $50 fee. Admission notification on a rolling basis. **Financial aid:** No deadline. FAFSA required. Applicants notified on a rolling basis.

Academics. Special study options: Accelerated study, distance learning. **Credit/placement by examination:** AP, CLEP, institutional tests. **Support services:** Learning center, remedial instruction, tutoring.

Majors. Business: Business admin, operations. **Computer sciences:** Information systems, networking, systems analysis. **Engineering:** Software.

Most popular majors. Business/marketing 75%, computer/information sciences 15%, engineering/engineering technologies 6%.

Computing on campus. 300 workstations in library, computer center. Online course registration, online library, helpline available.

Student life. Freshman orientation: Mandatory. Preregistration for classes offered. **Activities:** International student organizations, Toastmasters International, National Society of Black Engineers, Delta Pi Chi, Tau Alpha Pi, Sigma Beta Delta, Alpha Beta Kappa.

Athletics. Intramural: Basketball, football (non-tackle), softball, volleyball.

Student services. Career counseling, student employment services, financial aid counseling, placement for graduates, veterans' counselor. **Physically disabled:** Services for visually, hearing impaired.

Contact. E-mail: bsilva@admin.atl.devry.edu
Phone: (404) 292-2645 Toll-free number: (800) 221-4771
Fax: (404) 292-7011
Barbara Silva, Director of Admissions, DeVry University: Decatur, One West Court Square, Suite 100, Decatur, GA 30030-2556

Emmanuel College
Franklin Springs, Georgia **CB member**
www.ec.edu **CB code: 5184**

- Private 4-year liberal arts and teachers college affiliated with Pentecostal Holiness Church
- Residential campus in rural community
- 719 degree-seeking undergraduates: 4% part-time, 53% women
- 56% of applicants admitted
- SAT or ACT (ACT writing optional) required
- 35% graduate within 6 years

General. Founded in 1919. Regionally accredited. **Degrees:** 107 bachelor's, 22 associate awarded. **Location:** 30 miles from Athens, 90 miles from Atlanta. **Calendar:** Semester, limited summer session. **Full-time faculty:** 47 total; 55% have terminal degrees, 4% minority, 43% women. **Part-time faculty:** 40 total; 15% have terminal degrees, 5% minority, 50% women. **Class size:** 69% < 20, 29% 20-39, 2% 40-49.

Freshman class profile. 1,108 applied, 615 admitted, 189 enrolled.

Mid 50% test scores			
SAT critical reading:	420-540	Return as sophomores:	52%
SAT math:	420-520	Out-of-state:	17%
End year in good standing:	87%	Live on campus:	58%
		International:	3%

Basis for selection. High school record and SAT/ACT scores important. Recommendations considered. Audition required and interview recommended for music majors. **Learning Disabled:** Must submit professional documentation of disability.

High school preparation. College-preparatory program recommended.

2011-2012 Annual costs. Tuition/fees: $14,550. Room/board: $6,100. Books/supplies: $800. Personal expenses: $1,397.

2010-2011 Financial aid. Need-based: 182 full-time freshmen applied for aid; 167 were judged to have need; 167 of these received aid. Average need met was 70%. Average scholarship/grant was $9,867; average loan $3,070. 56% of total undergraduate aid awarded as scholarships/grants, 44% as loans/jobs. **Non-need-based:** Awarded to 155 full-time undergraduates, including 48 freshmen. Scholarships awarded for academics, art, athletics, job skills, leadership, music/drama, religious affiliation, state residency.

Application procedures. Admission: Closing date 8/1 (receipt date). $25 fee, may be waived for applicants with need, free for online applicants. Admission notification on a rolling basis beginning on or about 1/1. **Financial aid:** Priority date 5/1, closing date 6/15. FAFSA, institutional form required. Applicants notified on a rolling basis starting 3/1; must reply within 2 week(s) of notification.

Academics. Special study options: Dual enrollment of high school students, honors, independent study, internships, teacher certification program. **Credit/placement by examination:** AP, CLEP, IB, institutional tests. 24 credit hours maximum toward associate degree, 24 toward bachelor's. **Support services:** Remedial instruction, study skills assistance, tutoring, writing center.

Majors. Biology: General. **Business:** Business admin. **Communications:** Communications/speech/rhetoric. **Education:** Business, elementary, English, history, mathematics, middle, music. **English:** English lit. **Health services:** Premedicine. **History:** General. **Math:** General. **Parks/recreation:** Exercise sciences, sports admin. **Psychology:** General. **Theology:** Pastoral counseling, sacred music. **Visual/performing arts:** Music.

Most popular majors. Biology 7%, business/marketing 19%, education 27%, parks/recreation 13%, psychology 11%, theological studies 10%.

Computing on campus. 70 workstations in library, computer center. Dormitories wired for high-speed internet access and linked to campus network. Commuter students can connect to campus network. Online course registration, online library, repair service, wireless network available.

Student life. Freshman orientation: Mandatory. Preregistration for classes offered. Held first 2 days of semester. **Policies:** Chapel attendance required for all full-time students. Students not living at home must reside in college housing through junior year. Religious observance required. **Housing:** Guaranteed on-campus for all undergraduates. Single-sex dorms, apartments, wellness housing available. $150 fully refundable deposit, deadline 8/1. **Activities:** Bands, campus ministries, choral groups, dance, drama, international student organizations, literary magazine, music ensembles, musical theater, student government, student newspaper, ministerial fellowship, missions fellowship, Students in Free Enterprise.

Athletics. NAIA, NCCAA. **Intercollegiate:** Baseball M, basketball, cross-country, golf, soccer, softball W, tennis, track and field, volleyball W. **Intramural:** Basketball, soccer, softball, table tennis, tennis, track and field, volleyball. **Team name:** Lions.

Student services. Adult student services, chaplain/spiritual director, career counseling, financial aid counseling, personal counseling, veterans' counselor.

Contact. E-mail: admission@ec.edu
Phone: (706) 245-7226 ext. 2874 Toll-free number: (800) 860-8800
Fax: (706) 245-2876
Wendy Vinson, Dean of Enrollment Management, Emmanuel College, 181 Spring Street, Franklin Springs, GA 30639-0129

Emory University
Atlanta, Georgia **CB member**
www.emory.edu **CB code: 5187**

- Private 4-year university affiliated with United Methodist Church
- Residential campus in very large city
- 5,452 degree-seeking undergraduates: 10% African American, 24% Asian American, 5% Hispanic American, 11% international
- 6,452 graduate students
- 27% of applicants admitted
- SAT or ACT with writing, application essay required
- 90% graduate within 6 years

General. Founded in 1836. Regionally accredited. **Degrees:** 1,641 bachelor's, 377 associate awarded; master's, professional, doctoral offered. **ROTC:** Army, Naval, Air Force. **Location:** 5 miles from downtown. **Calendar:** Semester, limited summer session. **Full-time faculty:** 1,295 total; 99% have terminal degrees, 18% minority, 42% women. **Part-time faculty:** 239 total; 99% have terminal degrees, 11% minority, 44% women. **Class size:** 66% < 20, 24% 20-39, 3% 40-49, 6% 50-99, 2% >100. **Special facilities:** Art, architecture and archaeology museum; biological field station; primate research center; 185 acre park; planetarium; healthcare facilities; access to the Center for Disease Control; manuscript, archives and rare book library; Carter Center.

Freshman class profile. 17,027 applied, 4,548 admitted, 1,357 enrolled.

Mid 50% test scores			
SAT critical reading:	650-740	Rank in top quarter:	98%
SAT math:	670-770	Rank in top tenth:	87%
SAT writing:	660-750	Return as sophomores:	96%
ACT composite:	30-33	Out-of-state:	75%
GPA 3.75 or higher:	79%	Live on campus:	100%
GPA 3.50-3.74:	18%	International:	12%
GPA 3.0-3.49:	3%	Fraternities:	24%
		Sororities:	33%

Basis for selection. GED not accepted. Challenging curriculum and community involvement important. SAT/ACT important, but not deciding factor. Diversity, character and maturity, and indications of interest considered. Alumni interviews available in limited number of cities. Students may audition for music programs or scholarships on-campus or via recorded performance. Art and other portfolios should be sent directly to department of interest. **Home schooled:** Letter of recommendation (nonparent) required. 3 SAT Subject Tests required (1 math and 2 of student's choice).

High school preparation. College-preparatory program recommended. 16 units required. Required and recommended units include English 4, mathematics 4, social studies 3, history 2, science 4 (laboratory 2), foreign language 4 and visual/performing arts 1. History should include country/region other than U.S.

2011-2012 Annual costs. Tuition/fees: $41,164. Room/board: $11,628. Books/supplies: $1,100. Personal expenses: $1,200.

Financial aid. Non-need-based: Scholarships awarded for academics, art, leadership, music/drama, religious affiliation, state residency. **Additional information:** Loan replacement grant and loan cap program available to students from families with total annual incomes of $100,000 or less who demonstrate need for financial aid.

Application procedures. Admission: Closing date 1/15 (postmark date). $50 fee, may be waived for applicants with need. Admission notification by 4/1. Must reply by 5/1. **Financial aid:** Priority date 2/15, closing date 3/1. FAFSA, CSS PROFILE required. Applicants notified by 4/1; must reply by 5/1 or within 4 week(s) of notification.

Academics. Special study options: Combined bachelor's/graduate degree, cooperative education, cross-registration, double major, dual enrollment of

high school students, ESL, honors, independent study, internships, liberal arts/career combination, student-designed major, study abroad, teacher certification program, Washington semester. 3-2 dual-degree program in engineering with Georgia Institute of Technology. **Credit/placement by examination:** AP, CLEP, IB, institutional tests. **Support services:** Learning center, pre-admission summer program, remedial instruction, study skills assistance, tutoring, writing center.

Majors. Area/ethnic studies: African, African-American, American, Caribbean, Chinese, East Asian, French, German, Italian, Japanese, Latin American, Near/Middle Eastern, Russian/Slavic, South Asian, women's. **Biology:** General, neuroscience. **Business:** Accounting, business admin, finance, management information systems, management science, marketing, organizational behavior. **Communications:** Journalism. **Computer sciences:** Computer science. **Conservation:** Environmental studies. **Education:** General. **Engineering:** Applied physics. **English:** Creative writing, English lit. **Foreign languages:** Ancient Greek, Chinese, classics, comparative lit, French, German, Italian, Japanese, Latin, linguistics, Russian, Spanish. **Health services:** Nursing (RN). **History:** General. **Math:** General, applied. **Philosophy/religion:** Judaic, philosophy, religion. **Physical sciences:** Astronomy, chemistry, physics. **Psychology:** General. **Social sciences:** Anthropology, economics, international relations, political science, sociology. **Visual/performing arts:** Art history/conservation, dance, dramatic, film/cinema/video, music.

Most popular majors. Biology 14%, business/marketing 18%, health sciences 8%, psychology 8%, social sciences 27%.

Computing on campus. 1,000 workstations in dormitories, library, computer center, student center. Dormitories wired for high-speed internet access and linked to campus network. Commuter students can connect to campus network. Online course registration, online library, helpline, repair service, wireless network available.

Student life. Freshman orientation: Mandatory. Preregistration for classes offered. Five-day program held prior to start of classes. **Policies:** 2-year residency requirement. **Housing:** Guaranteed on-campus for freshmen. Coed dorms, special housing for disabled, apartments, fraternity/sorority housing, wellness housing available. $100 nonrefundable deposit, deadline 5/1. Gender-neutral housing available. **Activities:** Bands, campus ministries, choral groups, dance, drama, film society, international student organizations, literary magazine, music ensembles, Model UN, musical theater, opera, radio station, student government, student newspaper, symphony orchestra, TV station, over 220 student clubs and organizations.

Athletics. NCAA. **Intercollegiate:** Baseball M, basketball, cross-country, diving, golf M, soccer, softball W, swimming, tennis, track and field, volleyball W. **Intramural:** Basketball, football (non-tackle), racquetball, soccer, softball, swimming, tennis, track and field, volleyball. **Team name:** Eagles.

Student services. Alcohol/substance abuse counseling, chaplain/spiritual director, career counseling, student employment services, financial aid counseling, health services, legal services, minority student services, on-campus daycare, personal counseling, placement for graduates, women's services. **Physically disabled:** Services for visually, speech, hearing impaired.

Contact. E-mail: admiss@emory.edu
Phone: (404) 727-6036 Toll-free number: (800) 727-6036
Fax: (404) 727-4303
Jean Jordan, Dean of Admission, Emory University, 1390 Oxford Road NE, 3rd Floor, Atlanta, GA 30322

Fort Valley State University
Fort Valley, Georgia   **CB member**
www.fvsu.edu   **CB code: 5220**

- Public 4-year liberal arts and teachers college
- Residential campus in small town
- 3,751 degree-seeking undergraduates: 11% part-time, 58% women, 97% African American
- 257 degree-seeking graduate students
- 41% of applicants admitted
- SAT or ACT (ACT writing optional) required
- 32% graduate within 6 years

General. Founded in 1895. Regionally accredited. 1890 land-grant institution. **Degrees:** 288 bachelor's awarded; master's offered. **ROTC:** Army. **Location:** 30 miles from Macon. **Calendar:** Semester, limited summer session. **Full-time faculty:** 129 total; 72% have terminal degrees, 40% minority, 39% women. **Part-time faculty:** 84 total; 40% have terminal degrees, 27% minority, 63% women. **Class size:** 49% < 20, 37% 20-39, 10% 40-49, 4% 50-99.

Freshman class profile. 5,967 applied, 2,457 admitted, 1,030 enrolled.

Mid 50% test scores			
SAT critical reading:	370-450	GPA 3.0-3.49:	19%
SAT math:	370-450	GPA 2.0-2.99:	61%
SAT writing:	350-440	Rank in top quarter:	24%
ACT composite:	15-19	Rank in top tenth:	7%
GPA 3.75 or higher:	3%	Return as sophomores:	60%
GPA 3.50-3.74:	4%	Out-of-state:	3%
		Live on campus:	93%

Basis for selection. High school transcript, test scores, physical examination important. Audition recommended for music education majors.

High school preparation. College-preparatory program required. 16 units required. Required units include English 4, mathematics 4, social studies 1, history 2, science 3 and foreign language 2.

2011-2012 Annual costs. Tuition/fees: $6,030; $17,644 out-of-state. Room/board: $6,820. Books/supplies: $1,320. Personal expenses: $500.

2011-2012 Financial aid. Non-need-based: Scholarships awarded for academics, athletics, music/drama. **Additional information:** Financial aid transcripts must be received from former institutions before application for aid will be considered complete and reviewed for awards.

Application procedures. Admission: Closing date 7/15. $20 fee. Admission notification on a rolling basis. **Financial aid:** Priority date 3/1; no closing date. FAFSA required. Applicants notified on a rolling basis starting 3/15; must reply within 1 week(s) of notification.

Academics. Special study options: Distance learning, double major, dual enrollment of high school students, ESL, internships, teacher certification program. **Credit/placement by examination:** AP, CLEP, SAT, ACT, institutional tests. 20 credit hours maximum toward associate degree, 45 toward bachelor's. **Support services:** Learning center, reduced course load, remedial instruction, tutoring, writing center.

Majors. Biology: General. **Business:** General, accounting, business admin, marketing, office management. **Communications:** Journalism, public relations. **Computer sciences:** General, information systems. **Education:** Agricultural, elementary, English, family/consumer sciences, foreign languages, French, mathematics, middle, music, physical, secondary. **Engineering:** Agricultural. **English:** English lit. **General:** Animal sciences, economics, farm/ranch, horticultural science, plant sciences. **Health services:** Medical assistant, veterinary technology/assistant. **Human services:** Social work. **Liberal arts:** Arts/sciences. **Math:** General. **Physical sciences:** Chemistry. **Psychology:** General. **Social sciences:** Economics, political science, sociology. **Work/family studies:** General, child care management, child development, family studies, food/nutrition.

Most popular majors. Business/marketing 20%, education 8%, health sciences 8%, psychology 10%, public administration/social services 6%, security/protective services 10%.

Computing on campus. Dormitories linked to campus network. Commuter students can connect to campus network. Helpline available.

Student life. Freshman orientation: Mandatory. Preregistration for classes offered. **Housing:** Single-sex dorms available. $200 fully refundable deposit, deadline 8/5. **Activities:** Bands, campus ministries, choral groups, music ensembles, radio station, student government, student newspaper.

Athletics. NCAA. **Intercollegiate:** Basketball, cross-country, football (tackle) M, softball W, tennis, track and field, volleyball W. **Intramural:** Basketball, softball, swimming, tennis, track and field, volleyball. **Team name:** Wildcats.

Student services. Adult student services, career counseling, student employment services, health services, on-campus daycare, personal counseling, placement for graduates, veterans' counselor.

Contact. E-mail: admissap@fvsu.edu
Phone: (478) 825-6307 Toll-free number: (877) 462-3878
Fax: (478) 825-6394
Donovan Coley, Director of Admissions, Fort Valley State University, 1005 State University Drive, Fort Valley, GA 31030-4313

Georgia College and State University
Milledgeville, Georgia   **CB member**
www.gcsu.edu   **CB code: 5252**

- Public 4-year university and liberal arts college
- Residential campus in large town

- 5,557 degree-seeking undergraduates: 8% part-time, 60% women, 6% African American, 1% Asian American, 4% Hispanic American, 1% international
- 1,101 graduate students
- 70% of applicants admitted
- SAT or ACT with writing, application essay required
- 55% graduate within 6 years

General. Founded in 1889. Regionally accredited. Branch campuses in Macon and Warner Robins offering junior, senior, and graduate level options. **Degrees:** 1,139 bachelor's awarded; master's offered. **ROTC:** Army. **Location:** 95 miles from Atlanta, 30 miles from Macon. **Calendar:** Semester, limited summer session. **Full-time faculty:** 304 total. **Part-time faculty:** 132 total. **Class size:** 37% <20, 50% 20-39, 6% 40-49, 6% 50-99, less than 1% >100. **Special facilities:** Art galleries, greenhouse, challenge/ropes course, former Governor's mansion, Flannery O'Connor collection, Georgia education museum and archives.

Freshman class profile. 3,779 applied, 2,651 admitted, 1,209 enrolled.

Mid 50% test scores			
SAT critical reading:	520-610	GPA 3.0-3.49:	51%
SAT math:	520-610	GPA 2.0-2.99:	9%
SAT writing:	510-600	Return as sophomores:	83%
ACT composite:	22-26	Out-of-state:	1%
GPA 3.75 or higher:	17%	Live on campus:	99%
GPA 3.50-3.74:	23%	International:	1%

Basis for selection. Admissions based on total student portfolio, demonstrated potential for contribution to the university and probability for success. Test scores used in evaluating honors program candidates. Audition required of music and drama majors. **Home schooled:** Transcript of courses and grades required. Students from non-accredited home schools must have SAT/ACT equal to or above average of previous year's entering freshmen class; other documentation may be required. **Learning Disabled:** Students must identify themselves as disabled during admissions process.

High school preparation. College-preparatory program required. 17 units required. Required units include English 4, mathematics 4, social studies 3, science 4 (laboratory 2) and foreign language 2. Additional courses from the following areas strongly recommended: trigonometry, fine arts and computer technology.

2011-2012 Annual costs. Tuition/fees: $8,344; $25,382 out-of-state. Room/board: $8,998. Books/supplies: $1,000. Personal expenses: $2,304.

2010-2011 Financial aid. **Need-based:** 1,120 full-time freshmen applied for aid; 574 were judged to have need; 571 of these received aid. Average scholarship/grant was $4,043; average loan $3,113. 33% of total undergraduate aid awarded as scholarships/grants, 67% as loans/jobs. **Non-need-based:** Awarded to 2,082 full-time undergraduates, including 583 freshmen. Scholarships awarded for academics, alumni affiliation, art, athletics, job skills, leadership, minority status, music/drama, religious affiliation, ROTC, state residency.

Application procedures. **Admission:** Closing date 4/1 (postmark date). $40 fee. Admission notification on a rolling basis beginning on or about 1/1. Students encouraged to apply early to be considered for admission, university housing, scholarship funding, and financial aid. **Financial aid:** Priority date 3/1; no closing date. FAFSA, institutional form required. Applicants notified on a rolling basis starting 3/1; must reply within 2 week(s) of notification.

Academics. Advising sessions required for first-year students and new transfer students. In addition, academic advisors and students meet to review degree progress at completion of 30, 60, and 90 credit hours. **Special study options:** Accelerated study, distance learning, double major, ESL, external degree, honors, independent study, internships, liberal arts/career combination, semester at sea, student-designed major, study abroad, teacher certification program, Washington semester. 3-2 engineering program with Georgia Institute of Technology. **Credit/placement by examination:** AP, CLEP, IB, SAT, ACT, institutional tests. 30 credit hours maximum toward bachelor's degree. **Support services:** Learning center, pre-admission summer program, reduced course load, study skills assistance, tutoring, writing center.

Majors. **Biology:** General. **Business:** General, accounting, business admin, management science, managerial economics, marketing. **Communications:** Journalism. **Computer sciences:** General. **Conservation:** Environmental science. **Education:** Early childhood, health, middle, music, special ed. **English:** English lit, rhetoric/composition. **Foreign languages:** French, Spanish. **Health services:** Music therapy, nursing (RN). **History:** General. **Liberal arts:** Arts/sciences. **Math:** General. **Parks/recreation:** General. **Philosophy/religion:** Philosophy. **Physical sciences:** Chemistry. **Protective services:** Law enforcement admin. **Psychology:** General. **Social sciences:** Political science, sociology. **Visual/performing arts:** Art, dramatic, music.

Most popular majors. Business/marketing 24%, education 12%, English 7%, health sciences 10%, psychology 10%.

Computing on campus. 180 workstations in dormitories, library, computer center, student center. Dormitories wired for high-speed internet access and linked to campus network. Commuter students can connect to campus network. Online course registration, online library, helpline, wireless network available.

Student life. **Freshman orientation:** Available, $60 fee. Preregistration for classes offered. Several summer sessions available, with shorter programs held during the academic year. **Policies:** All first-year students under the age of 21 are required to live in university housing for 2 consecutive semesters. Meal plan required of incoming freshmen living in central campus housing. **Housing:** Guaranteed on-campus for freshmen. Coed dorms, apartments, wellness housing available. $235 partly refundable deposit, deadline 5/1. Pets allowed in dorm rooms. Living learning communities available. **Activities:** Bands, campus ministries, choral groups, dance, drama, international student organizations, literary magazine, music ensembles, Model UN, musical theater, radio station, student government, student newspaper, TV station, Baptist student alliance, student political movement, Young Democrats, AIDS Now Grasps Every Living Soul, Hillel Society, Sigma Alpha Omega.

Athletics. NCAA. **Intercollegiate:** Baseball M, basketball, cheerleading, cross-country, golf M, soccer W, softball W, tennis. **Intramural:** Basketball, bowling, football (non-tackle), golf, racquetball, soccer, softball, table tennis, tennis, volleyball. **Team name:** Bobcats.

Student services. Adult student services, alcohol/substance abuse counseling, career counseling, student employment services, financial aid counseling, health services, minority student services, personal counseling, placement for graduates, veterans' counselor, women's services. **Physically disabled:** Services for visually, hearing impaired.

Contact. E-mail: admissions@gcsu.edu
Phone: (478) 445-2774 Toll-free number: (800) 342-0471
Fax: (478) 445-1914
Suzanne Pittman, Assistant Vice President for Enrollment Management, Georgia College and State University, Campus Box 23, Milledgeville, GA 31061-0490

Georgia Gwinnett College
Lawrenceville, Georgia
www.ggc.edu   **CB code: 4796**

- Public 4-year liberal arts college
- Commuter campus in large town
- 7,508 degree-seeking undergraduates: 26% part-time, 54% women, 31% African American, 8% Asian American, 10% Hispanic American, 1% international
- 92% of applicants admitted

General. Regionally accredited. **Degrees:** 185 bachelor's awarded. **ROTC:** Army. **Calendar:** Semester, limited summer session. **Full-time faculty:** 124 total. **Part-time faculty:** 43 total. **Class size:** 31% <20, 69% 20-39, less than 1% 50-99.

Freshman class profile. 4,588 applied, 4,216 admitted, 2,364 enrolled.

Mid 50% test scores			
SAT critical reading:	410-520	GPA 2.0-2.99:	67%
SAT math:	420-530	Rank in top quarter:	13%
ACT composite:	16-21	Rank in top tenth:	3%
GPA 3.75 or higher:	2%	Return as sophomores:	68%
GPA 3.50-3.74:	5%	Live on campus:	22%
GPA 3.0-3.49:	23%	International:	1%

Basis for selection. 2.0 GPA required for college prep students; 2.2 GPA required for tech prep students. **Home schooled:** Transcript of courses and grades required.

High school preparation. College-preparatory program recommended. 16 units recommended. Recommended units include English 4, mathematics 4, social studies 3, science 3 and foreign language 2.

2011-2012 Annual costs. Tuition/fees: $4,842; $13,842 out-of-state. Books/supplies: $1,100. Personal expenses: $2,000.

2010-2011 Financial aid. **Need-based:** 43% of total undergraduate aid awarded as scholarships/grants, 57% as loans/jobs.

Application procedures. **Admission:** Closing date 6/1 (receipt date). $20 fee, may be waived for applicants with need. Application must be submitted online. Admission notification on a rolling basis. **Financial aid:** Priority date

7/1; no closing date. FAFSA required. Applicants notified on a rolling basis starting 6/1.

Academics. Special study options: Double major, dual enrollment of high school students, independent study, internships, study abroad. **Credit/placement by examination:** AP, CLEP, IB. 30 credit hours maximum toward bachelor's degree. **Support services:** Study skills assistance, tutoring, writing center.

Majors. Biology: General. **Business:** Business admin. **Computer sciences:** Information technology. **Education:** General. **English:** English lit. **Health services:** Nursing (RN). **History:** General. **Math:** General. **Parks/recreation:** Exercise sciences. **Protective services:** Police science. **Psychology:** General. **Social sciences:** Political science.

Most popular majors. Biology 16%, business/marketing 54%, computer/information sciences 11%, psychology 18%.

Computing on campus. 207 workstations in library, computer center, student center. Dormitories wired for high-speed internet access and linked to campus network. Commuter students can connect to campus network. Online course registration, online library, helpline, wireless network available.

Student life. Freshman orientation: Mandatory, $40 fee. Preregistration for classes offered. One-day sessions held prior to start of semester, with on-campus and online components. **Housing:** Coed dorms available. $408 partly refundable deposit. **Activities:** International student organizations, student government.

Athletics. Team name: Grizzlies.

Student services. Adult student services, alcohol/substance abuse counseling, career counseling, services for economically disadvantaged, student employment services, financial aid counseling, health services, minority student services, personal counseling, women's services. **Physically disabled:** Services for visually, speech, hearing impaired.

Contact. E-mail: ggcadmissions@ggc.edu
Phone: (678) 407-5313 Toll-free number: (877) 704-4422
Fax: (678) 407-5747
Tee Mitchell, Director of Admissions, Georgia Gwinnett College, 1000 University Center Lane, Lawrenceville, GA 30043

Georgia Health Sciences University
Augusta, Georgia   **CB member**
www.georgiahealth.edu   **CB code: 5406**

- Public two-year upper-division university
- Commuter campus in large city
- 29% of applicants admitted
- Test scores, application essay required

General. Founded in 1828. Regionally accredited. **Degrees:** 230 bachelor's awarded; master's, professional, doctoral offered. **Location:** 157 miles from Atlanta. **Calendar:** Semester. **Full-time faculty:** 633 total. **Part-time faculty:** 119 total. **Special facilities:** 478-bed medical center, children's medical center, outpatient clinics.

Student profile. 410 undergraduates, 2,027 graduate students. 882 applied as first time-transfer students, 258 admitted, 205 enrolled.

Out-of-state:	10%	25 or older:	31%
Live on campus:	9%		

Basis for selection. College transcript, application essay, standardized test scores required. Admission based on GPA, math and science test scores, 3 references, and statement of purpose. Interview required. 60 semester hours of transferable prescribed liberal arts courses required. Closing dates and score reports vary by program. Transfer accepted as juniors.

2011-2012 Annual costs. Tuition/fees: $8,908; $27,118 out-of-state. Declining balance account available for meals. Room only: $3,705.

Financial aid. Need-based: 59% of total undergraduate aid awarded as scholarships/grants, 41% as loans/jobs. **Non-need-based:** Scholarships awarded for academics, state residency. **Additional information:** State Hope scholarships only available to Georgia residents.

Application procedures. Admission: Rolling admission. $50 fee. **Financial aid:** Priority date 3/31, closing date 5/30. Applicants notified on a rolling basis; must reply within 2 weeks of notification. FAFSA, institutional form required.

Academics. Special study options: Combined bachelor's/graduate degree, distance learning. **Credit/placement by examination:** AP, CLEP.

Majors. Health services: Clinical lab science, dental hygiene, medical radiologic technology/radiation therapy, medical records admin, nursing (RN), physician assistant, preop/surgical nursing, respiratory therapy technology, sonography.

Computing on campus. 323 workstations in library, student center. Commuter students can connect to campus network. Online library, wireless network available.

Student life. Housing: Coed dorms, apartments available. **Activities:** Campus ministries, international student organizations, student government, Christian Medical Society, Black Student Medical Alliance.

Athletics. Intramural: Badminton, basketball, football (non-tackle), golf, racquetball, soccer, softball, table tennis, volleyball, weight lifting.

Student services. Career counseling, student employment services, health services, minority student services, on-campus daycare, personal counseling.

Contact. E-mail: admissions@georgiahealth.edu
Phone: (706) 721-2725 Toll-free number: (800) 519-3388
Fax: (706) 721-7279
John Engel, Director of Admissions, Georgia Health Sciences University, Office of Academic Admissions, Room 170 Kelly Building, Augusta, GA 30912-7310

Georgia Institute of Technology
Atlanta, Georgia   **CB member**
www.gatech.edu   **CB code: 5248**

- Public 4-year university
- Residential campus in large city
- 13,300 degree-seeking undergraduates: 5% part-time, 32% women, 6% African American, 17% Asian American, 6% Hispanic American, 7% international
- 6,936 degree-seeking graduate students
- 51% of applicants admitted
- SAT or ACT with writing, application essay required
- 79% graduate within 6 years; 26% enter graduate study

General. Founded in 1885. Regionally accredited. **Degrees:** 3,062 bachelor's awarded; master's, doctoral offered. **ROTC:** Army, Naval, Air Force. **Location:** Downtown. **Calendar:** Semester, extensive summer session. **Full-time faculty:** 936 total; 96% have terminal degrees, 26% minority, 22% women. **Part-time faculty:** 170 total; 58% have terminal degrees, 18% minority, 39% women. **Class size:** 41% < 20, 29% 20-39, 7% 40-49, 15% 50-99, 8% >100. **Special facilities:** Nuclear magnetic resonance spectroscopy center, research institute, paper museum, mechanical properties research laboratory with scanning electron microscope, virtual factory laboratory, trading floor, advanced computing building, nanotechnology research center, Aware home, compressible flow (high speed) wind tunnel, undergraduate learning commons.

Freshman class profile. 14,088 applied, 7,210 admitted, 2,695 enrolled.

Mid 50% test scores		GPA 2.0-2.99:	1%
SAT critical reading:	600-690	Rank in top quarter:	98%
SAT math:	660-760	Rank in top tenth:	83%
SAT writing:	600-700	End year in good standing:	96%
ACT composite:	28-32	Return as sophomores:	95%
GPA 3.75 or higher:	76%	Out-of-state:	33%
GPA 3.50-3.74:	17%	Live on campus:	97%
GPA 3.0-3.49:	6%	International:	9%

Basis for selection. Admission based on academic record, test scores, and evaluation of the applicant's essay, honors, extracurricular activities, and work experience. **Home schooled:** If home school program is not accredited by a recognized regional or state authority or the Accrediting Commission for Independent Study, student will need to submit the Home School Supplement form.

High school preparation. College-preparatory program required. 16 units required. Required units include English 4, mathematics 4, social studies 3, science 4 (laboratory 2) and foreign language 2.

2011-2012 Annual costs. Tuition/fees: $9,652; $27,862 out-of-state. Room/board: $8,826.

2010-2011 Financial aid. Need-based: 2,165 full-time freshmen applied for aid; 1,261 were judged to have need; 1,236 of these received aid. Average

need met was 67%. Average scholarship/grant was $11,802; average loan $3,306. 60% of total undergraduate aid awarded as scholarships/grants, 40% as loans/jobs. **Non-need-based:** Awarded to 4,480 full-time undergraduates, including 1,266 freshmen. Scholarships awarded for academics, athletics, leadership, music/drama, ROTC, state residency.

Application procedures. Admission: Priority date 10/1; deadline 1/10 (receipt date). $65 fee, may be waived for applicants with need. Admission notification by 3/15. Must reply by May 1 or within 2 week(s) if notified thereafter. **Financial aid:** Closing date 3/1. FAFSA, institutional form required. Applicants notified by 4/1; must reply by 5/1.

Academics. Special study options: Accelerated study, combined bachelor's/graduate degree, cooperative education, cross-registration, distance learning, double major, dual enrollment of high school students, ESL, honors, independent study, internships, student-designed major, study abroad, teacher certification program, weekend college. Undergraduate research opportunities program, dual degree program (3-2); Regent's engineering transfer program with 16 colleges in the University System of Georgia. **Credit/placement by examination:** AP, CLEP, IB, SAT, ACT, institutional tests. **Support services:** Learning center, pre-admission summer program, reduced course load, remedial instruction, tutoring, writing center.

Majors. Architecture: Architecture. **Biology:** General, biochemistry. **Business:** Business admin, management science, managerial economics, operations. **Communications:** Digital media. **Computer sciences:** General. **Engineering:** Aerospace, biomedical, chemical, civil, computer, electrical, environmental, industrial, materials, mechanical, nuclear, textile. **Foreign languages:** General. **History:** Science/technology. **Human services:** Public policy. **Math:** Applied. **Physical sciences:** Chemistry, geology, physics, polymer chemistry. **Psychology:** Industrial. **Social sciences:** International relations. **Visual/performing arts:** Industrial design.

Most popular majors. Business/marketing 14%, computer/information sciences 6%, engineering/engineering technologies 57%.

Computing on campus. PC or laptop required. 2,000 workstations in dormitories, library, computer center, student center. Dormitories wired for high-speed internet access and linked to campus network. Commuter students can connect to campus network. Online course registration, online library, helpline, student web hosting, wireless network available.

Student life. Freshman orientation: Available, $180 fee. Preregistration for classes offered. Two day program for freshmen and parents/guests; sessions offered throughout July and August. **Housing:** Guaranteed on-campus for freshmen. Coed dorms, single-sex dorms, special housing for disabled, apartments, fraternity/sorority housing available. $600 partly refundable deposit, deadline 5/1. **Activities:** Bands, campus ministries, choral groups, dance, drama, film society, international student organizations, literary magazine, music ensembles, Model UN, musical theater, radio station, student government, student newspaper, symphony orchestra, TV station, Campus Crusade for Christ, Wesley Foundation, College Democrats, College Republicans, environmental alliance, National Society of Black Engineers, Society of Women Engineers, Society of Hispanic Professional Engineers.

Athletics. NCAA. **Intercollegiate:** Baseball M, basketball, cross-country, diving, football (tackle) M, golf M, softball W, swimming, tennis, track and field, volleyball. **Intramural:** Basketball, bowling, football (non-tackle), racquetball, soccer, softball, volleyball. **Team name:** Yellow Jackets.

Student services. Alcohol/substance abuse counseling, career counseling, student employment services, financial aid counseling, health services, legal services, minority student services, on-campus daycare, personal counseling, placement for graduates, women's services. **Physically disabled:** Services for visually, speech, hearing impaired.

Contact. E-mail: admission@gatech.edu
Phone: (404) 894-4154 Fax: (404) 894-9511
Rick Clark, Director of Undergraduate Admissions, Georgia Institute of Technology, Office of Undergraduate Admissions, Atlanta, GA 30332-0320

Georgia Southern University
Statesboro, Georgia   **CB member**
www.georgiasouthern.edu   **CB code: 5253**

- Public 4-year university
- Residential campus in large town
- 16,757 degree-seeking undergraduates: 7% part-time, 49% women, 24% African American, 1% Asian American, 4% Hispanic American, 1% international
- 2,617 degree-seeking graduate students
- 49% of applicants admitted
- SAT or ACT with writing required
- 47% graduate within 6 years; 24% enter graduate study

General. Founded in 1906. Regionally accredited. Member of the University System of Georgia; Carnegie doctoral-research university. **Degrees:** 2,679 bachelor's awarded; master's, doctoral offered. **ROTC:** Army. **Location:** 50 miles from Savannah, 200 miles from Atlanta. **Calendar:** Semester, extensive summer session. **Full-time faculty:** 760 total; 82% have terminal degrees, 16% minority, 47% women. **Part-time faculty:** 110 total; 29% have terminal degrees, 6% minority, 62% women. **Class size:** 24% < 20, 56% 20-39, 9% 40-49, 7% 50-99, 4% >100. **Special facilities:** Planetarium, electron microscope, woodland nature preserve, museum, eagle sanctuary, national tick collection, wildlife education center, raptor center, botanical garden, family life center, international studies center, anthropology and parasitology institute, performing arts center, black box theater.

Freshman class profile. 11,032 applied, 5,456 admitted, 3,543 enrolled.

Mid 50% test scores			
SAT critical reading:	510-590	Rank in top quarter:	42%
SAT math:	520-590	Rank in top tenth:	17%
SAT writing:	480-560	End year in good standing:	80%
ACT composite:	21-24	Return as sophomores:	80%
GPA 3.75 or higher:	14%	Out-of-state:	4%
GPA 3.50-3.74:	15%	Live on campus:	93%
GPA 3.0-3.49:	38%	International:	1%
GPA 2.0-2.99:	32%	Fraternities:	8%
		Sororities:	14%

Basis for selection. GED not accepted. Test scores, high school GPA, and college preparatory curriculum considered. SAT and ACT not required for international or non-traditional applicants. Students may be required to take placement exams. Audition required for music majors. **Home schooled:** 1100 SAT (exclusive of Writing) or 24 ACT required. Per Board of Regents' policy, homeschooled students must take the SAT or ACT test and score at or above the average SAT score of the previous year's fall semester first-time freshman class. **Learning Disabled:** Admissions coordinated through student disability resource center.

High school preparation. College-preparatory program required. 17 units required. Required units include English 4, mathematics 4, social studies 3, science 4 (laboratory 2) and foreign language 2.

2011-2012 Annual costs. Tuition/fees: $6,606; $18,582 out-of-state. Room/board: $9,020. Books/supplies: $1,200. Personal expenses: $3,100.

2010-2011 Financial aid. Need-based: 3,386 full-time freshmen applied for aid; 2,359 were judged to have need; 2,314 of these received aid. Average need met was 59%. Average scholarship/grant was $8,224; average loan $3,283. 54% of total undergraduate aid awarded as scholarships/grants, 46% as loans/jobs. **Non-need-based:** Awarded to 995 full-time undergraduates, including 374 freshmen. Scholarships awarded for academics, alumni affiliation, art, athletics, leadership, minority status, music/drama, ROTC, state residency. **Additional information:** Majority of available scholarships are need-blind.

Application procedures. Admission: Priority date 4/1; deadline 5/1 (postmark date). $30 fee, may be waived for applicants with need. Admission notification on a rolling basis. **Financial aid:** Priority date 4/20; no closing date. FAFSA required. Applicants notified on a rolling basis starting 4/20.

Academics. Special study options: Accelerated study, combined bachelor's/graduate degree, cooperative education, distance learning, double major, ESL, honors, independent study, internships, student-designed major, study abroad, teacher certification program, Washington semester. **Credit/placement by examination:** AP, CLEP, IB, institutional tests. 30 credit hours maximum toward bachelor's degree. For AP exams, more credit hours will be awarded for higher-than-minimum scores. **Support services:** Learning center, pre-admission summer program, reduced course load, remedial instruction, study skills assistance, tutoring, writing center.

Majors. Biology: General, pharmacology. **Business:** Accounting, business admin, finance, hotel/motel admin, international, logistics, management information systems, managerial economics, marketing. **Communications:** Communications/speech/rhetoric, digital media, journalism, public relations. **Communications technology:** Graphic/printing. **Computer sciences:** Information systems. **Education:** Elementary, middle, music, physical, special ed. **Engineering:** Civil, electrical, mechanical. **English:** English lit, rhetoric/composition, writing. **Health services:** Athletic training, nursing (RN), nursing education, predental, premedicine, prepharmacy, preveterinary, public health ed. **History:** General. **Math:** General. **Parks/recreation:** General, exercise sciences, health/fitness, sports admin. **Philosophy/religion:** Philosophy. **Physical sciences:** Chemistry, geology, physics. **Protective services:** Criminal justice. **Psychology:** General. **Social sciences:** Anthropology, economics, geography, international economic development, international relations, political science, sociology. **Visual/performing arts:** Art, dramatic, graphic design, interior design, music, music performance, music theory/

composition. **Work/family studies:** Clothing/textiles, family studies, food/nutrition.

Most popular majors. Business/marketing 23%, education 10%, engineering/engineering technologies 7%, health sciences 7%, parks/recreation 6%.

Computing on campus. 3,320 workstations in dormitories, library, student center. Dormitories wired for high-speed internet access and linked to campus network. Commuter students can connect to campus network. Online course registration, online library, helpline, repair service, student web hosting, wireless network available.

Student life. Freshman orientation: Mandatory, $70 fee. Preregistration for classes offered. Freshman/parent program held for 2 days. **Policies:** Freshmen required to live on-campus. **Housing:** Guaranteed on-campus for freshmen. Coed dorms, special housing for disabled, apartments available. $250 partly refundable deposit. **Activities:** Bands, campus ministries, choral groups, dance, drama, film society, international student organizations, literary magazine, music ensembles, Model UN, musical theater, opera, radio station, student government, student newspaper, symphony orchestra, TV station, various ethnic/religious/political organizations available.

Athletics. NCAA. **Intercollegiate:** Baseball M, basketball, cheerleading, cross-country W, diving W, football (tackle) M, golf M, soccer, softball W, swimming W, tennis, track and field W, volleyball W. **Intramural:** Basketball, bowling, football (non-tackle), golf, racquetball, soccer, softball, swimming, table tennis, tennis, triathlon, volleyball, weight lifting. **Team name:** Eagles.

Student services. Adult student services, alcohol/substance abuse counseling, career counseling, services for economically disadvantaged, student employment services, financial aid counseling, health services, legal services, minority student services, on-campus daycare, personal counseling, veterans' counselor, women's services. **Physically disabled:** Services for visually, speech, hearing impaired.

Contact. E-mail: admissions@georgiasouthern.edu
Phone: (912) 478-5391 Fax: (912) 478-1156
Sarah Smith, Director of Admission, Georgia Southern University, PO Box 8024, Statesboro, GA 30460

Georgia Southwestern State University
Americus, Georgia — CB member
www.gsw.edu — CB code: 5250

- Public 4-year university and liberal arts college
- Residential campus in large town
- 2,743 degree-seeking undergraduates: 26% part-time, 63% women, 29% African American, 1% Asian American, 2% Hispanic American, 3% international
- 228 degree-seeking graduate students
- 68% of applicants admitted
- SAT or ACT (ACT writing optional) required
- 30% graduate within 6 years

General. Founded in 1906. Regionally accredited. **Degrees:** 523 bachelor's awarded; master's offered. **Location:** 135 miles from Atlanta. **Calendar:** Semester, limited summer session. **Full-time faculty:** 107 total; 71% have terminal degrees, 14% minority, 50% women. **Part-time faculty:** 53 total; 32% have terminal degrees, 6% minority, 64% women. **Class size:** 42% < 20, 44% 20-39, 9% 40-49, 4% 50-99. **Special facilities:** Observatory, glass blowing studio, golf course, indoor climbing wall.

Freshman class profile. 1,267 applied, 866 admitted, 413 enrolled.

Mid 50% test scores			
SAT critical reading:	450-530	Rank in top quarter:	36%
SAT math:	440-530	Rank in top tenth:	13%
SAT writing:	430-530	Return as sophomores:	65%
ACT composite:	17-20	Out-of-state:	3%
GPA 3.75 or higher:	20%	Live on campus:	66%
GPA 3.50-3.74:	13%	International:	6%
GPA 3.0-3.49:	34%	Fraternities:	20%
GPA 2.0-2.99:	33%	Sororities:	16%

Basis for selection. School achievement record, test scores most important. **Home schooled:** Statement describing home school structure and mission, transcript of courses and grades, letter of recommendation (nonparent) required. Must complete home schooled application or submit SAT along with 7 SAT Subject tests or a portfolio outlining work in 5 critical college preparatory areas.

High school preparation. College-preparatory program required. 16 units required. Required and recommended units include English 4, mathematics 4, social studies 1, history 2, science 3 (laboratory 2), foreign language 2 and academic electives 2.

2011-2012 Annual costs. Tuition/fees: $5,696; $17,310 out-of-state. Room/board: $6,334. Books/supplies: $1,000.

Financial aid. Non-need-based: Scholarships awarded for academics, athletics, leadership.

Application procedures. Admission: Closing date 7/21 (postmark date). $25 fee, may be waived for applicants with need. Admission notification on a rolling basis. Must reply by May 1 or within 3 week(s) if notified thereafter. **Financial aid:** Priority date 4/1, closing date 6/1. FAFSA, institutional form required. Applicants notified on a rolling basis starting 3/1.

Academics. Special study options: Accelerated study, distance learning, double major, dual enrollment of high school students, ESL, honors, independent study, internships, study abroad, teacher certification program. 3+2 program in engineering with Georgia Institute of Technology. **Credit/placement by examination:** AP, CLEP, IB, institutional tests. 30 credit hours maximum toward bachelor's degree. **Support services:** Learning center, reduced course load, remedial instruction, study skills assistance, tutoring, writing center.

Majors. Biology: General. **Business:** Accounting, business admin, human resources, marketing. **Computer sciences:** General, computer science. **Education:** Elementary, middle, physical, special ed. **English:** English lit. **Health services:** Nursing (RN). **History:** General. **Math:** General. **Parks/recreation:** Facilities management. **Physical sciences:** Chemistry, geology. **Psychology:** General. **Social sciences:** Political science, sociology. **Visual/performing arts:** Art, dramatic, music.

Most popular majors. Business/marketing 38%, education 25%, health sciences 11%, psychology 6%.

Computing on campus. 550 workstations in dormitories, library, computer center, student center. Dormitories wired for high-speed internet access and linked to campus network. Commuter students can connect to campus network. Online course registration, online library, wireless network available.

Student life. Freshman orientation: Mandatory, $70 fee. Preregistration for classes offered. Three sessions in summer; includes parents' program. **Housing:** Guaranteed on-campus for freshmen. Coed dorms, apartments, fraternity/sorority housing available. $200 nonrefundable deposit. **Activities:** Bands, campus ministries, choral groups, drama, international student organizations, literary magazine, music ensembles, musical theater, student government, student newspaper, TV station, Baptist Student Union, Wesley Foundation, Young Republicans, Young Democrats, SABU, Habitat for Humanity, campus activity board, ZEPHYR recruitment team, College Republicans.

Athletics. NCAA. **Intercollegiate:** Baseball M, basketball, cross-country W, golf M, soccer, softball W, tennis. **Intramural:** Badminton, basketball, football (non-tackle), racquetball, soccer, table tennis, tennis, volleyball, weight lifting, wrestling M. **Team name:** Hurricanes.

Student services. Career counseling, services for economically disadvantaged, student employment services, financial aid counseling, health services, personal counseling, veterans' counselor. **Physically disabled:** Services for visually, speech, hearing impaired.

Contact. E-mail: gswapps@canes.gsw.edu
Phone: (229) 928-1273 Toll-free number: (800) 338-0082
Fax: (229) 931-2059
Gaye Hayes, Vice President of Enrollment Management, Georgia Southwestern State University, 800 Georgia Southwestern State University Drive, Americus, GA 31709-9957

Georgia State University
Atlanta, Georgia — CB member
www.gsu.edu — CB code: 5251

- Public 4-year university
- Commuter campus in very large city
- 23,410 degree-seeking undergraduates: 26% part-time, 59% women, 38% African American, 11% Asian American, 8% Hispanic American, 2% international
- 7,598 degree-seeking graduate students
- 51% of applicants admitted

- SAT or ACT with writing required
- 48% graduate within 6 years

General. Founded in 1913. Regionally accredited. Courses offered at Alpharetta and Brookhaven Centers. Distance learning and web courses available in College of Health and Human Sciences and College of Education. **Degrees:** 4,196 bachelor's awarded; master's, professional, doctoral offered. **ROTC:** Army, Naval, Air Force. **Location:** Downtown. **Calendar:** Semester, extensive summer session. **Full-time faculty:** 1,127 total; 87% have terminal degrees, 24% minority, 47% women. **Part-time faculty:** 368 total; 18% minority, 51% women. **Class size:** 14% < 20, 47% 20-39, 23% 40-49, 11% 50-99, 5% >100. **Special facilities:** Viral immunology center, writing studio, advanced biotechnology center, Asian studies center, multi-media instructional lab, child development center, performing arts center, language acquisition and research centers, military science leadership lab, music media center, learning disorders center, speech and language center, hearing center, art galleries, observatory, business and marketing research centers, women's studies institute, Confucius institute, digital arts and entertainment laboratory, digital aquarium, cinefest, Indian Creek Lodge and Recreation Area, radio station.

Freshman class profile. 12,869 applied, 6,567 admitted, 2,758 enrolled.

Mid 50% test scores			
SAT critical reading:	500-590	GPA 2.0-2.99:	10%
SAT math:	500-600	End year in good standing:	88%
ACT composite:	21-25	Return as sophomores:	83%
GPA 3.75 or higher:	14%	Out-of-state:	3%
GPA 3.50-3.74:	24%	Live on campus:	58%
GPA 3.0-3.49:	52%	International:	1%

Basis for selection. GED not accepted. Grades achieved in 17 units of the required high school curriculum and SAT/ACT scores most important. Audition and interview required for music majors. Portfolio required for art majors. **Home schooled:** Transcript of courses and grades required. Portfolio outlining subjects studied, titles of text books, assignment descriptions, and examples of coursework, tests, assignments.

High school preparation. College-preparatory program required. 16 units required; 17 recommended. Required and recommended units include English 4, mathematics 4, social studies 3, science 3-4 (laboratory 2) and foreign language 2.

2011-2012 Annual costs. Tuition/fees: $9,410; $27,620 out-of-state. Room/board: $9,290. Books/supplies: $1,000. Personal expenses: $1,970.

2011-2012 Financial aid. **Need-based:** 2,538 full-time freshmen applied for aid; 2,081 were judged to have need; 2,039 of these received aid. Average need met was 30%. Average scholarship/grant was $3,991; average loan $3,913. 47% of total undergraduate aid awarded as scholarships/grants, 53% as loans/jobs. **Non-need-based:** Awarded to 14,139 full-time undergraduates, including 2,418 freshmen. Scholarships awarded for academics, alumni affiliation, art, athletics, minority status, music/drama, state residency.

Application procedures. **Admission:** Priority date 2/1; deadline 3/1 (receipt date). $60 fee, may be waived for applicants with need. Admission notification by 5/1. Must reply by 6/1. **Financial aid:** Priority date 4/1, closing date 11/1. FAFSA required. Applicants notified on a rolling basis starting 3/30.

Academics. **Special study options:** Combined bachelor's/graduate degree, cooperative education, cross-registration, distance learning, double major, dual enrollment of high school students, ESL, honors, independent study, internships, study abroad, teacher certification program. **Credit/placement by examination:** AP, CLEP, IB, institutional tests. 30 credit hours maximum toward bachelor's degree. Some credit awarded for DANTES subject examinations. **Support services:** Learning center, pre-admission summer program, reduced course load, remedial instruction, study skills assistance, tutoring, writing center.

Honors college/program. Applicants should have 3.5 GPA and 1200 SAT with 500 verbal and math; around 200 students admitted each year.

Majors. **Area/ethnic studies:** African-American, women's. **Biology:** General. **Business:** Accounting, actuarial science, business admin, finance, hospitality admin, insurance, managerial economics, marketing, real estate. **Communications:** Communications/speech/rhetoric, journalism. **Computer sciences:** General, computer science. **Education:** Art, kindergarten/preschool, physical. **English:** English lit. **Foreign languages:** French, German, linguistics, Spanish. **Health services:** Dietetics, nursing (RN), respiratory therapy technology. **History:** General. **Human services:** Public policy, social work. **Math:** General. **Philosophy/religion:** Philosophy, religion. **Physical sciences:** Chemistry, geology, physics. **Protective services:** Criminal justice. **Psychology:** General. **Social sciences:** Anthropology, economics, geography, international economics, political science, sociology. **Visual/performing arts:** Drawing, film/cinema/video, music management, music performance.

Most popular majors. Business/marketing 29%, communications/journalism 6%, education 8%, psychology 8%, social sciences 12%, trade and industry 7%.

Computing on campus. 574 workstations in library, computer center, student center. Dormitories wired for high-speed internet access and linked to campus network. Commuter students can connect to campus network. Online course registration, online library, helpline, student web hosting, wireless network available.

Student life. **Freshman orientation:** Mandatory, $56 fee. Preregistration for classes offered. Various types of orientation meetings available. **Policies:** Student code of conduct in effect. **Housing:** Coed dorms, special housing for disabled, apartments, fraternity/sorority housing available. $250 partly refundable deposit. **Activities:** Bands, campus ministries, choral groups, dance, drama, film society, international student organizations, literary magazine, music ensembles, Model UN, musical theater, opera, radio station, student government, student newspaper, symphony orchestra, TV station, African students association, Amnesty International, Bridge Builders, Catholic student association, Chinese student union, College Republicans, Christian legal society, Legal Society of Intimate Violence and Education, International Socialist Society, Alliance for Sexual and Gender Diversity.

Athletics. NCAA. **Intercollegiate:** Baseball M, basketball, cross-country, football (tackle) M, golf, soccer, softball W, tennis, track and field, volleyball W. **Intramural:** Badminton, boxing, cricket, equestrian, ice hockey M, lacrosse, racquetball, rowing (crew), rugby, soccer, swimming, table tennis, triathlon. **Team name:** Panthers.

Student services. Adult student services, alcohol/substance abuse counseling, career counseling, student employment services, financial aid counseling, health services, minority student services, on-campus daycare, personal counseling, veterans' counselor. **Physically disabled:** Services for visually, speech, hearing impaired.

Contact. E-mail: admissions@gsu.edu
Phone: (404) 413-2500 Fax: (404) 413-2002
Scott Burke, Director of Admissions, Georgia State University, Box 4009, Atlanta, GA 30302-4009

Herzing University: Atlanta
Atlanta, Georgia
www.herzing.edu   CB code: 2342

- For-profit 3-year business and technical college
- Commuter campus in very large city
- 467 degree-seeking undergraduates
- Interview required

General. Founded in 1949. Regionally accredited. **Degrees:** 92 bachelor's, 53 associate awarded. **Location:** 120 miles from Birmingham, AL; 70 miles from Chattanooga, TN. **Calendar:** Semester, extensive summer session. **Full-time faculty:** 10 total. **Part-time faculty:** 33 total. **Class size:** 84% < 20, 16% 20-39.

Basis for selection. Entrance test and evaluation required. Competitive admission to some programs based on score. SAT/ACT may be used for academic advising.

2011-2012 Annual costs. Tuition/fees: $11,760. Though reported costs are representative, costs may vary by program with nursing programs somewhat more expensive.

Financial aid. **Non-need-based:** Scholarships awarded for academics.

Application procedures. **Admission:** No deadline. No application fee. Admission notification on a rolling basis. **Financial aid:** No deadline. FAFSA, institutional form required. Applicants notified on a rolling basis.

Academics. Students train on types of equipment used in the field. **Special study options:** Distance learning, independent study, internships, liberal arts/career combination. **Credit/placement by examination:** AP, CLEP, IB, institutional tests. **Support services:** Learning center, study skills assistance, tutoring.

Majors. **BACHELOR'S. Business:** Accounting, accounting/business management, business admin, entrepreneurial studies, human resources, international. **Computer sciences:** Networking. **Health services:** Health care admin. **Protective services:** Criminal justice. **ASSOCIATE. Business:** Accounting, business admin. **Computer sciences:** Computer science. **Health services:** Massage therapy, medical assistant, surgical technology.

Most popular majors. Business/marketing 31%, computer/information sciences 41%.

Computing on campus. 157 workstations in library, computer center. Online library available.

Student life. Freshman orientation: Mandatory. Preregistration for classes offered. Orientation held beginning of each term for 2 hours. **Activities:** Student government.

Student services. Career counseling, student employment services, financial aid counseling, personal counseling, placement for graduates, veterans' counselor.

Contact. E-mail: info@atl.herzing.edu
Phone: (404) 816-4533 Toll-free number: (800) 573-4533
Fax: (404) 816-5576
Annisa Elder, Director of Admissions, Herzing University: Atlanta, 3393 Peachtree Road NE, Suite 1003, Atlanta, GA 30326

ITT Technical Institute: Duluth
Duluth, Georgia
www.itt-tech.edu

- For-profit 4-year technical college
- Commuter campus in large town
- 675 degree-seeking undergraduates

General. Accredited by ACICS. **Degrees:** 32 bachelor's, 162 associate awarded. **Calendar:** Quarter. **Full-time faculty:** 10 total. **Part-time faculty:** 45 total.

Basis for selection. Admission requirements will vary by program.

2011-2012 Annual costs. Estimated costs as of June 2011: per-credit-hour charge, $493, depending upon level and course of study; academic fee, $300. Certain programs of study require purchase of tools, which could cost an additional $100 to $500. All costs are subject to change.

Academics. Credit/placement by examination: AP, CLEP.

Majors. Business: Business admin, construction management, project management. **Communications technology:** Animation/special effects. **Computer sciences:** Security. **Protective services:** Law enforcement admin.

Contact. Phone: (866) 489-8818 Toll-free number: (866) 489-8818
Chip Hinton, Director of Recruitment, ITT Technical Institute: Duluth, 10700 Abbotts Bridge Road, Duluth, GA 30097

Kennesaw State University
Kennesaw, Georgia
www.kennesaw.edu
CB member
CB code: 5359

- Public 4-year university
- Commuter campus in large town
- 22,236 degree-seeking undergraduates: 25% part-time, 58% women, 15% African American, 3% Asian American, 6% Hispanic American, 2% international
- 1,766 degree-seeking graduate students
- 62% of applicants admitted
- SAT or ACT (ACT writing optional) required
- 41% graduate within 6 years

General. Founded in 1963. Regionally accredited. **Degrees:** 3,310 bachelor's awarded; master's, doctoral offered. **ROTC:** Army, Air Force. **Location:** 25 miles from Atlanta. **Calendar:** Semester, limited summer session. **Full-time faculty:** 738 total; 76% have terminal degrees, 22% minority, 53% women. **Part-time faculty:** 557 total; 28% have terminal degrees, 18% minority, 64% women. **Class size:** 21% < 20, 55% 20-39, 9% 40-49, 14% 50-99, 2% >100. **Special facilities:** Educational technology center, presentation technology department, teacher resource and activity center, 2 art galleries, performing arts library, rare book gallery.

Freshman class profile. 8,773 applied, 5,483 admitted, 2,988 enrolled.

Mid 50% test scores			
SAT critical reading:	500-580	Rank in top quarter:	53%
SAT math:	490-580	Rank in top tenth:	21%
SAT writing:	470-560	End year in good standing:	84%
ACT composite:	20-24	Return as sophomores:	77%
GPA 3.75 or higher:	11%	Out-of-state:	4%
GPA 3.50-3.74:	15%	Live on campus:	50%
GPA 3.0-3.49:	45%	International:	1%
GPA 2.0-2.99:	29%	Fraternities:	7%
		Sororities:	9%

Basis for selection. GED not accepted. 2.5 GPA in college prep courses and 490 SAT Critical Reading/460 SAT Math or 20 ACT English/19 ACT Math with a composite of 20 required. Applicants with test scores below minimum must take institutional placement exams in appropriate subject areas. Audition required of music majors. Portfolio required of art majors. **Home schooled:** Students considered based on portfolio, standardized tests scores, extra-curricular activities, and recommendations.

High school preparation. College-preparatory program required. 16 units required. Required units include English 4, mathematics 4, social studies 3, science 3 (laboratory 3) and foreign language 2.

2011-2012 Annual costs. Tuition/fees: $6,282; $18,258 out-of-state. Room/board: $7,694.

Financial aid. Non-need-based: Scholarships awarded for academics, alumni affiliation, art, athletics, job skills, leadership, minority status, music/drama, ROTC, state residency.

Application procedures. Admission: Closing date 5/14 (receipt date). $40 fee, may be waived for applicants with need. Admission notification on a rolling basis beginning on or about 1/1. **Financial aid:** Priority date 7/1; no closing date. FAFSA required. Applicants notified on a rolling basis starting 7/1.

Academics. Special study options: Cooperative education, cross-registration, distance learning, double major, ESL, honors, internships, study abroad, teacher certification program, weekend college. **Credit/placement by examination:** AP, CLEP, IB, institutional tests. 30 credit hours maximum toward bachelor's degree. **Support services:** Learning center, reduced course load, remedial instruction, study skills assistance, tutoring, writing center.

Honors college/program. 3.5 GPA and 1200 SAT (exclusive of Writing) required. Joint enrollment honors program for high school junior and seniors requires 3.0 GPA, 1100 SAT with 530 SAT verbal and math (exclusive of writing) or 25 ACT with 24 English and 20 math.

Majors. Area/ethnic studies: African. **Biology:** General, biochemistry, biotechnology. **Business:** Accounting, business admin, finance, international, managerial economics, marketing, sales/distribution. **Communications:** Communications/speech/rhetoric. **Computer sciences:** General, information systems, security. **Education:** Art, biology, early childhood, elementary, English, mathematics, middle, music, physical, social studies. **English:** English lit. **Health services:** Nursing (RN). **History:** General. **Math:** General. **Parks/recreation:** Exercise sciences, sports admin. **Philosophy/religion:** Philosophy. **Physical sciences:** Chemistry. **Protective services:** Criminal justice. **Psychology:** General. **Social sciences:** Anthropology, geography, GIS/cartography, international relations, political science, sociology. **Visual/performing arts:** Art, art history/conservation, dance, dramatic, music, music performance.

Most popular majors. Business/marketing 26%, communications/journalism 8%, education 17%, health sciences 7%, psychology 6%, social sciences 7%.

Computing on campus. 1,650 workstations in library, computer center, student center. Dormitories wired for high-speed internet access. Commuter students can connect to campus network. Online course registration, online library, helpline, wireless network available.

Student life. Freshman orientation: Mandatory, $25 fee. Preregistration for classes offered. Held prior to semester. **Housing:** Apartments available. $375 nonrefundable deposit. **Activities:** Bands, campus ministries, choral groups, dance, drama, international student organizations, literary magazine, music ensembles, Model UN, musical theater, radio station, student government, student newspaper, symphony orchestra, Baptist student union, Student Nurses Association, College Ambassadors, volunteer club, American Marketing Association, African American student alliance, Circle K, Catholic student association.

Athletics. NCAA. **Intercollegiate:** Baseball M, basketball, cross-country, golf, soccer W, softball W, tennis, track and field, volleyball W. **Intramural:** Basketball, bowling, football (non-tackle), golf, soccer, softball, tennis, volleyball. **Team name:** Fighting Owls.

Student services. Adult student services, alcohol/substance abuse counseling, career counseling, student employment services, financial aid counseling, health services, minority student services, personal counseling, placement for graduates, veterans' counselor. **Physically disabled:** Services for visually, speech, hearing impaired.

Contact. E-mail: ksuadmit@kennesaw.edu
Phone: (770) 423-6300 Fax: (770) 423-6541
Angela Evans, Director of Admissions, Kennesaw State University, 1000 Chastain Road, Kennesaw, GA 30144-5591

LaGrange College
LaGrange, Georgia
www.lagrange.edu

CB member
CB code: 5362

- Private 4-year liberal arts college affiliated with United Methodist Church
- Residential campus in large town
- 854 degree-seeking undergraduates: 23% African American, 1% Asian American, 3% Hispanic American, 2% international
- 99 graduate students
- 59% of applicants admitted
- SAT or ACT (ACT writing optional), application essay required
- 47% graduate within 6 years; 25% enter graduate study

General. Founded in 1831. Regionally accredited. Oldest private college in Georgia. **Degrees:** 166 bachelor's awarded; master's offered. **Location:** 70 miles from Atlanta, 45 miles from Columbus. **Calendar:** 4-1-4, limited summer session. **Full-time faculty:** 73 total; 82% have terminal degrees, 11% minority. **Part-time faculty:** 57 total; 12% have terminal degrees, 18% minority. **Class size:** 83% < 20, 14% 20-39, 2% 40-49, less than 1% 50-99. **Special facilities:** Performing arts auditorium, natatorium, art center.

Freshman class profile. 1,232 applied, 722 admitted, 226 enrolled.

Mid 50% test scores		Rank in top quarter:	43%
SAT critical reading:	450-540	Rank in top tenth:	16%
SAT math:	450-550	End year in good standing:	89%
ACT composite:	19-23	Return as sophomores:	64%
GPA 3.75 or higher:	18%	Out-of-state:	20%
GPA 3.50-3.74:	23%	Live on campus:	86%
GPA 3.0-3.49:	41%	Fraternities:	8%
GPA 2.0-2.99:	18%	Sororities:	28%

Basis for selection. School achievement record and test scores most important. Interview and recommendations considered. Separate application typically during sophomore year for nursing applicants. Students undergo a writing sample and math placement test prior to registration. **Home schooled:** Bibliography of high school readings, including textbooks, letter of recommendation from outside the home required.

High school preparation. College-preparatory program required. 14 units required; 16 recommended. Required and recommended units include English 4, mathematics 4, social studies 3, science 3 and foreign language 2.

2011-2012 Annual costs. Tuition/fees: $23,212. Room/board: $9,455.

2010-2011 Financial aid. Need-based: 162 full-time freshmen applied for aid; 136 were judged to have need; 136 of these received aid. Average need met was 80%. Average scholarship/grant was $14,493; average loan $3,280. 66% of total undergraduate aid awarded as scholarships/grants, 34% as loans/jobs. **Non-need-based:** Awarded to 209 full-time undergraduates, including 59 freshmen. Scholarships awarded for academics, art, leadership, music/drama, religious affiliation, state residency.

Application procedures. Admission: Priority date 3/1; no deadline. $30 fee, may be waived for applicants with need, free for online applicants. Admission notification on a rolling basis beginning on or about 9/15. Early admission candidates must be highly recommended by counselors and parents. **Financial aid:** Priority date 3/1; no closing date. FAFSA required. Applicants notified on a rolling basis starting 3/15; must reply by 8/15 or within 2 week(s) of notification.

Academics. Special study options: Accelerated study, combined bachelor's/graduate degree, double major, independent study, internships, student-designed major, study abroad, teacher certification program, Washington semester. Interim classes in January, Dual Engineering degree with Georgia Institute of Technology and Auburn University. **Credit/placement by examination:** AP, CLEP, IB, institutional tests. 6 credit hours maximum toward bachelor's degree. USAFI credit accepted. **Support services:** Reduced course load, remedial instruction, study skills assistance, tutoring, writing center.

Majors. Biology: General, biochemistry. **Business:** Accounting, business admin, organizational leadership. **Computer sciences:** General. **Education:** Elementary. **Engineering:** General. **English:** English lit. **Foreign languages:** Spanish. **Health services:** Nursing (RN). **History:** General. **Human services:** Social work. **Liberal arts:** Arts/sciences. **Math:** General. **Philosophy/religion:** General, religion. **Physical sciences:** Chemistry. **Psychology:** General. **Social sciences:** Political science, sociology. **Visual/performing arts:** General, dramatic, music.

Most popular majors. Business/marketing 19%, education 9%, health sciences 8%, history 7%, psychology 7%, social sciences 8%, visual/performing arts 15%.

Computing on campus. 141 workstations in dormitories, library, computer center. Dormitories wired for high-speed internet access and linked to campus network. Commuter students can connect to campus network. Online library, helpline, student web hosting, wireless network available.

Student life. Freshman orientation: Mandatory. Preregistration for classes offered. Three 2-day summer orientation sessions available. **Policies:** Honor code. **Housing:** Guaranteed on-campus for all undergraduates. Coed dorms, single-sex dorms, apartments, fraternity/sorority housing available. $100 fully refundable deposit, deadline 4/9. **Activities:** Pep band, campus ministries, choral groups, drama, international student organizations, literary magazine, music ensembles, musical theater, student government, student newspaper, symphony orchestra, Wesley Fellowship, Baptist student union, Rotaract, interfaith council, black collegiate student union, Reformed Bible Study, Servant Fellows, Panther Toy Store, bus project.

Athletics. NCAA. **Intercollegiate:** Baseball M, basketball, cheerleading M, cross-country, football (tackle) M, golf M, lacrosse W, soccer, softball W, swimming, tennis, volleyball W. **Intramural:** Basketball, football (non-tackle), softball, table tennis, water polo. **Team name:** Panthers.

Student services. Adult student services, chaplain/spiritual director, career counseling, student employment services, financial aid counseling, health services, personal counseling, placement for graduates.

Contact. E-mail: admission@lagrange.edu
Phone: (706) 880-8005 Toll-free number: (800) 593-2885
Fax: (706) 880-8010
Michael Thomas, Director of Admission, LaGrange College, 601 Broad Street, LaGrange, GA 30240-2999

Life University
Marietta, Georgia
www.life.edu

CB code: 7006

- Private 4-year university
- Very large city
- 862 degree-seeking undergraduates: 28% part-time, 53% women, 34% African American, 3% Asian American, 8% Hispanic American, 1% Native American, 4% international
- 231 degree-seeking graduate students
- 70% of applicants admitted
- SAT or ACT with writing required

General. Regionally accredited. **Degrees:** 77 bachelor's, 4 associate awarded; master's, professional offered. **Location:** 10 miles from downtown Atlanta. **Calendar:** Quarter, limited summer session. **Full-time faculty:** 118 total; 84% have terminal degrees, 25% minority, 41% women. **Part-time faculty:** 54 total; 61% have terminal degrees, 32% minority, 54% women. **Class size:** 81% < 20, 19% 20-39, less than 1% 40-49.

Freshman class profile. 775 applied, 544 admitted, 234 enrolled.

Return as sophomores:	71%	International:	2%
Out-of-state:	34%		

Basis for selection. Standardized test scores and high school record most important. 2.0 GPA and 1430 SAT (including Writing) or 18 ACT important. **Home schooled:** Transcript of courses and grades required. **Learning Disabled:** Letter from doctor required.

High school preparation. College-preparatory program recommended.

2011-2012 Annual costs. Tuition/fees: $8,967. Books/supplies: $1,650. Personal expenses: $2,187.

2011-2012 Financial aid. Need-based: Average scholarship/grant was $5,250; average loan $3,800. 54% of total undergraduate aid awarded as scholarships/grants, 46% as loans/jobs. **Non-need-based:** Scholarships awarded for academics.

Application procedures. Admission: Closing date 9/1 (postmark date). $50 fee, may be waived for applicants with need. Admission notification on a rolling basis. **Financial aid:** No deadline. FAFSA required. Applicants notified on a rolling basis starting 5/1.

Academics. Special study options: Accelerated study, double major, ESL, independent study, internships, study abroad. **Credit/placement by examination:** AP, CLEP, SAT, ACT. **Support services:** Learning center, reduced course load, remedial instruction, study skills assistance, tutoring, writing center.

Majors. Biology: General. **Business:** General, management information systems. **Health services:** Dietetics. **Parks/recreation:** Exercise sciences.

Most popular majors. Biology 52%, business/marketing 17%, psychology 10%.

Computing on campus. Dormitories linked to campus network. Commuter students can connect to campus network. Online course registration, online library, wireless network available.

Student life. Freshman orientation: Mandatory. Preregistration for classes offered. Two-day program usually held on Thursday and Friday before quarter begins. **Housing:** Apartments available. $250 partly refundable deposit. **Activities:** International student organizations, student newspaper.

Athletics. Intramural: Basketball, football (tackle), volleyball. **Team name:** Eagles.

Student services. Alcohol/substance abuse counseling, financial aid counseling, personal counseling.

Contact. E-mail: admissions@life.edu
Phone: (770) 426-2884 Toll-free number: (800) 543-3202
Fax: (770) 426-2895
Brian Gipson, Director of Admissions, Life University, 1269 Barclay Circle, Marietta, GA 30060

Luther Rice University
Lithonia, Georgia
www.lru.edu

- Private 4-year university and seminary college
- Very large city
- 484 degree-seeking undergraduates
- Application essay required

General. Regionally accredited; also accredited by TRACS. **Degrees:** 61 bachelor's awarded; master's, doctoral offered. **Location:** 19 miles from Atlanta. **Calendar:** Semester, extensive summer session. **Full-time faculty:** 14 total. **Part-time faculty:** 22 total.

Basis for selection. Open admission. **Home schooled:** Transcript of courses and grades, state high school equivalency certificate, letter of recommendation (nonparent) required. Bible knowledge test required.

2011-2012 Annual costs. Tuition/fees: $6,900.

Financial aid. Non-need-based: Scholarships awarded for alumni affiliation. **Additional information:** Financial aid department monitors satisfactory academic progress very closely. Must have financial aid applications submitted 30 days prior to start of semester.

Application procedures. Admission: No deadline. $50 fee, may be waived for applicants with need. Admission notification on a rolling basis. **Financial aid:** FAFSA, institutional form required. Applicants notified on a rolling basis; must reply within 2 week(s) of notification.

Academics. Special study options: Distance learning, independent study. **Credit/placement by examination:** AP, CLEP.

Student life. Activities: Campus ministries, student government, student newspaper.

Contact. E-mail: admissions@lru.edu
Toll-free number: (800) 442-1577
James Kinnebrew, Director of Admissions, Luther Rice University, 3038 Evans Mill Road, Lithonia, GA 30038

Macon State College
Macon, Georgia
www.maconstate.edu

CB member
CB code: 5439

- Public 4-year liberal arts and teachers college
- Commuter campus in small city
- 5,597 degree-seeking undergraduates: 42% part-time, 65% women, 31% African American, 2% Asian American, 4% Hispanic American, 1% international

General. Founded in 1968. Regionally accredited. **Degrees:** 518 bachelor's, 318 associate awarded. **Location:** 85 miles from Atlanta. **Calendar:** Semester, extensive summer session. **Full-time faculty:** 183 total. **Part-time faculty:** 104 total. **Class size:** 37% < 20, 57% 20-39, 5% 40-49, 2% 50-99, less than 1% >100. **Special facilities:** Botanical gardens.

Freshman class profile.

Mid 50% test scores		
SAT critical reading:	420-520	
SAT math:	410-510	
ACT composite:	17-21	
GPA 3.75 or higher:	6%	

GPA 3.50-3.74:	14%
GPA 3.0-3.49:	35%
GPA 2.0-2.99:	44%
Out-of-state:	2%

Basis for selection. Open admission. Interview required for respiratory therapy. May be required for RN-BSN completion program. **Home schooled:** SAT and portfolio with list of courses required.

High school preparation. 16 units recommended. Recommended units include English 4, mathematics 4, social studies 1, history 2, science 3 (laboratory 2) and foreign language 2.

2011-2012 Annual costs. Tuition/fees: $3,644; $11,126 out-of-state. Books/supplies: $1,040. Personal expenses: $5,168.

Financial aid. All financial aid based on need.

Application procedures. Admission: Closing date 7/16 (receipt date). $20 fee. Admission notification on a rolling basis. **Financial aid:** Priority date 4/1; no closing date. FAFSA required. Applicants notified on a rolling basis starting 4/15; must reply within 2 week(s) of notification.

Academics. Special study options: Combined bachelor's/graduate degree, distance learning, dual enrollment of high school students, honors, internships, liberal arts/career combination, study abroad, teacher certification program. **Credit/placement by examination:** AP, CLEP, IB, institutional tests. 40 credit hours maximum toward associate degree, 40 toward bachelor's. **Support services:** Learning center, pre-admission summer program, reduced course load, remedial instruction, study skills assistance, tutoring, writing center.

Majors. Biology: General. **Business:** Accounting, business admin, marketing, operations. **Communications:** Digital media. **Computer sciences:** Information technology. **Education:** Biology, early childhood, English, history, mathematics, middle. **English:** English lit. **Health services:** Health services admin, medical records admin, nursing (RN), respiratory therapy technology. **History:** General. **Math:** General. **Psychology:** General.

Most popular majors. Business/marketing 33%, computer/information sciences 10%, education 12%, health sciences 22%, public administration/social services 7%.

Computing on campus. 150 workstations in library, computer center, student center. Dormitories wired for high-speed internet access. Commuter students can connect to campus network. Online course registration, online library, helpline, wireless network available.

Student life. Freshman orientation: Mandatory, $25 fee. Preregistration for classes offered. **Housing:** Apartments available. $250 fully refundable deposit. **Activities:** Choral groups, drama, literary magazine, music ensembles, Model UN, musical theater, student government, student newspaper, TV station, Black student unification, association of nursing students, Spanish club, Baptist student union, astronomy club, pre-med club, honors student association, Amnesty International, information technology club.

Student services. Career counseling, student employment services, financial aid counseling, health services, minority student services, personal counseling, veterans' counselor. **Physically disabled:** Services for visually, speech, hearing impaired.

Contact. E-mail: admissions@maconstate.edu
Phone: (478) 471-2800 Toll-free number: (800) 272-7619
Fax: (478) 471-5343
Dee Minter, Associate Vice President for Enrollment Services, Macon State College, 100 College Station Drive, Macon, GA 31206-5145

Mercer University
Macon, Georgia
www.mercer.edu

CB member
CB code: 5409

- Private 4-year university affiliated with Baptist faith
- Residential campus in small city
- 2,284 degree-seeking undergraduates: 3% part-time, 52% women, 19% African American, 7% Asian American, 4% Hispanic American, 4% international
- 3,885 degree-seeking graduate students
- 83% of applicants admitted
- SAT or ACT (ACT writing optional) required
- 60% graduate within 6 years; 37% enter graduate study

General. Founded in 1833. Regionally accredited. Evening and weekend continuing education programs available at 4 regional academic centers and transfer degree programs offered at Atlanta campus. **Degrees:** 491 bachelor's awarded; master's, professional, doctoral offered. **ROTC:** Army. **Location:** 85 miles from Atlanta. **Calendar:** Semester, extensive summer session. **Full-time faculty:** 371 total; 90% have terminal degrees, 18% minority, 46% women. **Part-time faculty:** 306 total; 52% have terminal degrees, 24% minority, 51% women. **Class size:** 63% < 20, 36% 20-39, less than 1% 40-49, less than 1% 50-99. **Special facilities:** Opera house.

Freshman class profile. 2,582 applied, 2,137 admitted, 565 enrolled.

Mid 50% test scores			
SAT critical reading:	520-630	Rank in top quarter:	76%
SAT math:	540-630	Rank in top tenth:	44%
ACT composite:	24-29	Return as sophomores:	84%
GPA 3.75 or higher:	47%	Out-of-state:	16%
GPA 3.50-3.74:	25%	Live on campus:	92%
GPA 3.0-3.49:	24%	International:	2%
GPA 2.0-2.99:	4%	Fraternities:	19%
		Sororities:	23%

Basis for selection. Admissions based on academic merit. GPA, SAT and extracurricular activities important. Interview recommended. Audition recommended for music majors. **Home schooled:** Transcript of courses and grades, interview required. 1100 SAT (exclusive of Writing) and certified transcript indicating college-preparatory curriculum, including titles of textbooks, required. SAT Subject Tests or AP exams may be substituted for certified transcript. **Learning Disabled:** Documentation from licensed professional required.

High school preparation. College-preparatory program required. 16 units required. Required units include English 4, mathematics 4, social studies 1, history 2, science 3 and foreign language 2.

2011-2012 Annual costs. Tuition/fees: $31,548. Room/board: $10,408. Books/supplies: $1,200. Personal expenses: $1,526.

2011-2012 Financial aid. **Need-based:** 564 full-time freshmen applied for aid; 445 were judged to have need; 445 of these received aid. Average need met was 84%. Average scholarship/grant was $25,443; average loan $5,315. 67% of total undergraduate aid awarded as scholarships/grants, 33% as loans/jobs. **Non-need-based:** Awarded to 1,060 full-time undergraduates, including 255 freshmen. Scholarships awarded for academics, art, athletics, job skills, leadership, music/drama, religious affiliation, ROTC, state residency.

Application procedures. **Admission:** Priority date 4/1; deadline 7/1 (postmark date). $50 fee, may be waived for applicants with need, free for online applicants. Admission notification on a rolling basis beginning on or about 9/1. Must reply by May 1 or within 4 week(s) if notified thereafter. **Financial aid:** Priority date 4/1; no closing date. FAFSA, institutional form required. Applicants notified on a rolling basis starting 3/15; must reply within 2 week(s) of notification.

Academics. **Special study options:** Accelerated study, combined bachelor's/graduate degree, cooperative education, cross-registration, double major, dual enrollment of high school students, honors, independent study, internships, liberal arts/career combination, student-designed major, study abroad, teacher certification program. Students may satisfy general education requirements by completing either the Great Books Program or the Distributional Program. **Credit/placement by examination:** AP, CLEP, IB, SAT, ACT, institutional tests. 32 credit hours maximum toward bachelor's degree. **Support services:** Learning center, pre-admission summer program, reduced course load, study skills assistance, tutoring.

Majors. **Area/ethnic studies:** African, regional, women's. **Biology:** General, biochemistry, environmental. **Business:** General, accounting. **Communications:** Communications/speech/rhetoric, journalism, media studies. **Computer sciences:** Computer science, information systems. **Conservation:** Environmental studies. **Education:** Elementary, middle, music. **Engineering:** General. **English:** English lit. **Foreign languages:** Classics, French, German, Latin, Spanish. **Health services:** Nursing (RN), nursing practice, predental, premedicine, prenursing, prepharmacy, prephysical therapy. **History:** General. **Human services:** Community org/advocacy. **Liberal arts:** Arts/sciences. **Math:** General. **Philosophy/religion:** Christian, philosophy. **Physical sciences:** Chemistry, physics. **Protective services:** Criminal justice. **Psychology:** General. **Social sciences:** Economics, international relations, political science, sociology. **Visual/performing arts:** Art, dramatic, music, music performance.

Most popular majors. Biology 16%, business/marketing 20%, communications/journalism 6%, engineering/engineering technologies 13%, social sciences 9%.

Computing on campus. Dormitories wired for high-speed internet access and linked to campus network. Commuter students can connect to campus network. Online course registration, online library, helpline, repair service, wireless network available.

Student life. **Freshman orientation:** Mandatory. Preregistration for classes offered. One-day summer orientation and 4-day program in fall before semester begins. **Policies:** Alcohol not permitted on campus. **Housing:** Guaranteed on-campus for freshmen. Coed dorms, single-sex dorms, special housing for disabled, apartments, fraternity/sorority housing available. **Activities:** Bands, campus ministries, choral groups, dance, drama, film society, international student organizations, literary magazine, music ensembles, musical theater, opera, radio station, student government, student newspaper, TV station, Cooperative Student Fellowship, Habitat for Humanity, Alpha Phi Omega National Service Fraternity, College Republicans, College Democrats, Engineers without Borders, housing center, Indian cultural exchange, organization of black students, students for environmental action.

Athletics. NCAA. **Intercollegiate:** Baseball M, basketball, cross-country, football (tackle) M, golf, lacrosse M, soccer, softball W, tennis, volleyball W. **Intramural:** Basketball, football (non-tackle), soccer, softball, tennis, volleyball. **Team name:** Bears.

Student services. Adult student services, alcohol/substance abuse counseling, chaplain/spiritual director, career counseling, services for economically disadvantaged, student employment services, financial aid counseling, health services, minority student services, personal counseling, placement for graduates. **Physically disabled:** Services for visually, speech, hearing impaired.

Contact. E-mail: admissions@mercer.edu
Phone: (478) 301-2650 Toll-free number: (800) 840-8577
Fax: (478) 301-2828
Emory Dunn, Director of Freshman Admissions, Mercer University, 1400 Coleman Avenue, Macon, GA 31207-0001

Morehouse College
Atlanta, Georgia
www.morehouse.edu

CB member
CB code: 5415

▶ Private 4-year liberal arts college for men
▶ Residential campus in very large city
▶ 2,409 degree-seeking undergraduates: 6% part-time
▶ 62% of applicants admitted
▶ SAT or ACT (ACT writing recommended), application essay required
▶ 55% graduate within 6 years; 33% enter graduate study

General. Founded in 1867. Regionally accredited. One of 4 members of Atlanta University Center sharing facilities including library. **Degrees:** 444 bachelor's awarded. **ROTC:** Army, Naval, Air Force. **Location:** 3 miles from downtown. **Calendar:** Semester, limited summer session. **Full-time faculty:** 164 total; 88% have terminal degrees, 81% minority, 38% women. **Part-time faculty:** 50 total; 32% have terminal degrees, 86% minority, 30% women. **Class size:** 48% < 20, 49% 20-39, 2% 40-49, 1% 50-99. **Special facilities:** Chapels, meditation room.

Freshman class profile. 2,194 applied, 1,370 admitted, 505 enrolled.

Mid 50% test scores			
SAT critical reading:	460-590	GPA 2.0-2.99:	28%
SAT math:	470-580	Rank in top quarter:	48%
SAT writing:	450-570	Rank in top tenth:	20%
ACT composite:	19-25	End year in good standing:	80%
GPA 3.75 or higher:	18%	Return as sophomores:	86%
GPA 3.50-3.74:	16%	Out-of-state:	70%
GPA 3.0-3.49:	36%	Live on campus:	98%

Basis for selection. Academic record most important, followed by test scores, counselor recommendation(s), school and community activities, and student leadership. Interview recommended.

High school preparation. College-preparatory program recommended. 13 units required; 16 recommended. Required and recommended units include English 4, mathematics 3, social studies 2, science 2, foreign language 2 and academic electives 3.

2011-2012 Annual costs. Tuition/fees: $23,520. Room/board: $12,184. Books/supplies: $2,000. Personal expenses: $2,500.

2011-2012 Financial aid. All financial aid based on need. 496 full-time freshmen applied for aid; 496 were judged to have need; 480 of these received aid. Average need met was 59%. Average scholarship/grant was $18,456; average loan $4,016. 63% of total undergraduate aid awarded as scholarships/grants, 37% as loans/jobs.

Application procedures. **Admission:** Priority date 11/1; deadline 2/15 (postmark date). $50 fee, may be waived for applicants with need. Application must be submitted on paper. Admission notification by 4/1. Must reply by May 1 or within 2 week(s) if notified thereafter. Acceptance fee of $555

must be paid by 6/1; applied toward first semester tuition. **Financial aid:** Priority date 2/15, closing date 4/1. FAFSA, institutional form required. Applicants notified on a rolling basis starting 11/15; must reply by 5/1 or within 4 week(s) of notification.

Academics. **Special study options:** Combined bachelor's/graduate degree, cooperative education, cross-registration, double major, dual enrollment of high school students, exchange student, honors, internships, liberal arts/career combination, semester at sea, study abroad. Dual degree program in engineering and architecture with other institutions. **Credit/placement by examination:** AP, CLEP, SAT, ACT, institutional tests. 30 credit hours maximum toward bachelor's degree. **Support services:** Learning center, pre-admission summer program, reduced course load, remedial instruction, study skills assistance, tutoring, writing center.

Majors. **Area/ethnic studies:** African-American. **Biology:** General. **Business:** Business admin. **Computer sciences:** General. **Education:** Early childhood. **Engineering:** Applied physics, engineering science. **English:** English lit. **Foreign languages:** French, Spanish. **History:** General. **Math:** General. **Parks/recreation:** Exercise sciences. **Philosophy/religion:** Philosophy, religion. **Physical sciences:** Chemistry, physics. **Psychology:** General. **Social sciences:** Economics, international relations, political science, sociology, urban studies. **Visual/performing arts:** Art, dramatic, music.

Most popular majors. Biology 9%, business/marketing 29%, English 8%, psychology 7%, social sciences 22%.

Computing on campus. 300 workstations in dormitories, library, computer center. Dormitories wired for high-speed internet access and linked to campus network. Commuter students can connect to campus network. Online course registration, online library, helpline, repair service, wireless network available.

Student life. **Freshman orientation:** Mandatory, $668 fee. Preregistration for classes offered. Held several days before class begins each fall. **Housing:** Guaranteed on-campus for freshmen. Apartments, wellness housing available. $555 nonrefundable deposit, deadline 5/2. **Activities:** Bands, choral groups, drama, international student organizations, literary magazine, music ensembles, student government, student newspaper, Martin Luther King International Chapel Assistants, mentoring program, Frederick Douglass Tutorial Program, political science club, New Life Inspirational Gospel Choir, NAACP, Eagle Scout Association.

Athletics. NCAA. **Intercollegiate:** Baseball M, basketball M, cross-country M, football (tackle) M, golf M, tennis M, track and field M. **Intramural:** Baseball M, basketball M, football (non-tackle) M, soccer M, softball M, swimming M, table tennis M, tennis M, weight lifting M. **Team name:** Maroon Tigers.

Student services. Alcohol/substance abuse counseling, chaplain/spiritual director, career counseling, student employment services, financial aid counseling, health services, personal counseling, placement for graduates, veterans' counselor. **Physically disabled:** Services for visually, speech, hearing impaired.

Contact. E-mail: admissions@morehouse.edu
Phone: (404) 681-2800 ext. 2632 Toll-free number: (800) 851-1254
Fax: (404) 524-5635
Danny Bellinger, Associate Dean of Admissions and Recruitment, Morehouse College, 830 Westview Drive SW, Atlanta, GA 30314

North Georgia College & State University

Dahlonega, Georgia **CB member**
www.northgeorgia.edu **CB code: 5497**

- Public 4-year university and military college
- Commuter campus in small town
- 5,475 degree-seeking undergraduates: 16% part-time, 57% women, 3% African American, 1% Asian American, 4% Hispanic American, 1% international
- 474 degree-seeking graduate students
- 53% of applicants admitted
- SAT or ACT (ACT writing optional) required
- 52% graduate within 6 years

General. Founded in 1873. Regionally accredited. **Degrees:** 835 bachelor's, 126 associate awarded; master's, professional offered. **ROTC:** Army. **Location:** 70 miles from Atlanta. **Calendar:** Semester, extensive summer session. **Full-time faculty:** 247 total; 53% women. **Part-time faculty:** 101 total; 65% women. **Class size:** 39% < 20, 52% 20-39, 4% 40-49, 4% 50-99, less than 1% >100. **Special facilities:** Observatory, rappelling tower, planetarium, nature preserve.

Freshman class profile. 4,077 applied, 2,170 admitted, 995 enrolled.

Mid 50% test scores		
SAT critical reading:	510-600	
SAT math:	500-590	
ACT composite:	21-26	
GPA 3.75 or higher:	30%	
GPA 3.50-3.74:	25%	

GPA 3.0-3.49:	36%
GPA 2.0-2.99:	9%
Return as sophomores:	77%
Out-of-state:	6%
Live on campus:	72%

Basis for selection. GED not accepted. High school academic record, test scores important, disciplinary record considered. Students must provide certification of immunization against communicable diseases. Commuting students must apply for permission to commute. Audition recommended for music majors. Portfolio recommended for art majors. **Home schooled:** Must provide a high school summation exam showing scores that reflect at least average compared to national norm and must provide SAT or ACT scores that meet the average of previous Fall enrolled freshmen.

High school preparation. College-preparatory program required. 17 units required. Required units include English 4, mathematics 4, social studies 3, science 4 (laboratory 2) and foreign language 2.

2011-2012 Annual costs. Tuition/fees: $6,452; $18,428 out-of-state. Room/board: $6,510. Books/supplies: $500. Personal expenses: $1,000.

2011-2012 Financial aid. Need-based: 855 full-time freshmen applied for aid; 590 were judged to have need; 590 of these received aid. Average need met was 62%. Average scholarship/grant was $3,950; average loan $3,500. 50% of total undergraduate aid awarded as scholarships/grants, 50% as loans/jobs. **Non-need-based:** Awarded to 1,770 full-time undergraduates, including 555 freshmen. Scholarships awarded for academics, alumni affiliation, art, athletics, job skills, leadership, music/drama, religious affiliation, ROTC, state residency.

Application procedures. **Admission:** Closing date 7/1. $30 fee, may be waived for applicants with need. Admission notification on a rolling basis. Must reply by May 1 or within 2 week(s) if notified thereafter. **Financial aid:** Priority date 3/17; no closing date. FAFSA required. Applicants notified on a rolling basis starting 3/1; must reply within 4 week(s) of notification.

Academics. **Special study options:** Accelerated study, combined bachelor's/graduate degree, cooperative education, distance learning, double major, dual enrollment of high school students, external degree, honors, independent study, internships, liberal arts/career combination, study abroad, teacher certification program. Dual degree program in engineering with Georgia Institute of Technology and Clemson University. **Credit/placement by examination:** AP, CLEP, SAT, ACT, institutional tests. 30 credit hours maximum toward associate degree, 30 toward bachelor's. **Support services:** Learning center, pre-admission summer program, reduced course load, remedial instruction, study skills assistance, tutoring, writing center.

Honors college/program. Admission by application to program coordinator. 2 letters of recommendation and 1150 SAT or 3.5 GPA required.

Majors. **Biology:** General. **Business:** Accounting, business admin, finance, marketing. **Computer sciences:** General, information systems. **Education:** Art, early childhood, middle, music, physical, special ed. **English:** English lit. **Foreign languages:** French, Spanish. **Health services:** Athletic training, nursing (RN). **History:** General. **Math:** General. **Physical sciences:** Chemistry, physics. **Protective services:** Criminal justice. **Psychology:** General. **Social sciences:** General, international relations, political science, sociology. **Visual/performing arts:** Commercial/advertising art, music performance, studio arts.

Most popular majors. Business/marketing 26%, education 22%, health sciences 7%, history 6%, psychology 7%, security/protective services 8%, social sciences 8%.

Computing on campus. 850 workstations in dormitories, library, computer center, student center. Dormitories linked to campus network. Commuter students can connect to campus network. Online course registration, online library, helpline, repair service, student web hosting, wireless network available.

Student life. **Freshman orientation:** Available, $85 fee. Preregistration for classes offered. Two and 1/2-day program held at least 4 times during summer; students stay in residence halls. **Policies:** Cadets who have earned 90 semester hours may elect to leave Corps to become civilian students. Those leaving the Corps prior to earning 90 hours will be ineligible to enroll in courses for one year. **Housing:** Coed dorms, single-sex dorms, apartments available. $250 fully refundable deposit, deadline 5/1. Military housing. **Activities:** Bands, campus ministries, choral groups, dance, drama, international student organizations, literary magazine, music ensembles, student government, student newspaper, symphony orchestra, Commuter Council, Students of Caribbean Ancestry, Voices for Women, Habitat for Humanity, Wesley Foundation, Gay Straight Alliance, Graduate Student Senate.

Athletics. NCAA. **Intercollegiate:** Baseball M, basketball, cheerleading M, golf, rifle, soccer, softball W, tennis. **Intramural:** Basketball, football (non-tackle), softball, table tennis, volleyball, water polo. **Team name:** Saints.

Student services. Alcohol/substance abuse counseling, career counseling, student employment services, financial aid counseling, health services, minority student services, personal counseling, placement for graduates, veterans' counselor, women's services. **Physically disabled:** Services for visually, speech, hearing impaired.

Contact. E-mail: admissions@northgeorgia.edu
Phone: (706) 864-1800 Toll-free number: (800) 498-9581
Fax: (706) 864-1478
Jennifer Chadwick, Director of Admissions, North Georgia College & State University, 82 College Circle, Dahlonega, GA 30597

Oglethorpe University
Atlanta, Georgia   **CB member**
www.oglethorpe.edu   **CB code: 5521**

- Private 4-year liberal arts college
- Residential campus in very large city
- 1,068 degree-seeking undergraduates: 8% part-time, 59% women, 24% African American, 4% Asian American, 8% Hispanic American, 2% international
- 50 degree-seeking graduate students
- 85% of applicants admitted
- SAT or ACT (ACT writing recommended) required
- 48% graduate within 6 years

General. Founded in 1835. Regionally accredited. Professional Shakespeare repertory theater on campus, integrated with theater program. **Degrees:** 208 bachelor's awarded; master's offered. **ROTC:** Air Force. **Location:** 10 miles from downtown. **Calendar:** Semester, extensive summer session. **Full-time faculty:** 49 total; 98% have terminal degrees, 12% minority, 31% women. **Part-time faculty:** 53 total; 34% have terminal degrees, 24% minority, 53% women. **Class size:** 75% < 20, 25% 20-39. **Special facilities:** Art museum, performing arts center.

Freshman class profile. 2,376 applied, 2,027 admitted, 262 enrolled.

Mid 50% test scores			
SAT critical reading:	540-640	GPA 2.0-2.99:	10%
SAT math:	520-620	Rank in top quarter:	56%
SAT writing:	510-620	Rank in top tenth:	24%
ACT composite:	22-27	Return as sophomores:	73%
GPA 3.75 or higher:	32%	Out-of-state:	27%
GPA 3.50-3.74:	27%	Live on campus:	87%
GPA 3.0-3.49:	31%	International:	3%

Basis for selection. High school GPA and general academic record most important, followed by test scores. Recommendations required. Activities considered. Interview recommended.

High school preparation. College-preparatory program recommended. Required and recommended units include English 4, mathematics 3, social studies 3, science 2 and foreign language 2. Honors, AP, IB recommended where available.

2011-2012 Annual costs. Tuition/fees: $29,150. Room/board: $10,440. Books/supplies: $1,100. Personal expenses: $2,000.

2011-2012 Financial aid. Need-based: 220 full-time freshmen applied for aid; 210 were judged to have need; 210 of these received aid. Average need met was 79%. Average scholarship/grant was $23,431; average loan $3,131. 71% of total undergraduate aid awarded as scholarships/grants, 29% as loans/jobs. **Non-need-based:** Awarded to 251 full-time undergraduates, including 78 freshmen. Scholarships awarded for academics, music/drama.

Application procedures. Admission: Priority date 11/15; no deadline. $40 fee, may be waived for applicants with need. Admission notification on a rolling basis beginning on or about 12/5. Must reply by May 1 or within 3 week(s) if notified thereafter. **Financial aid:** No deadline. FAFSA, institutional form required. Applicants notified on a rolling basis starting 3/1; must reply by 5/1 or within 3 week(s) of notification.

Academics. Special study options: Accelerated study, cooperative education, cross-registration, double major, dual enrollment of high school students, honors, independent study, internships, liberal arts/career combination, student-designed major, study abroad. Dual engineering degree program with Auburn University, Georgia Institute of Technology, University of Florida, Auburn University, Mercer University, University of Southern California; dual degree program in environmental studies with Nicholas School of the Environment at Duke University; international partner degree program with Universite Catholique de Lille in France. **Credit/placement by examination:** AP, CLEP, IB, institutional tests. 32 credit hours maximum toward bachelor's degree. **Support services:** Learning center, tutoring, writing center.

Majors. Area/ethnic studies: American. **Biology:** General. **Business:** Accounting, business admin, managerial economics, organizational behavior, training/development. **Communications:** Communications/speech/rhetoric. **English:** English lit, rhetoric/composition. **Foreign languages:** French, Japanese, Spanish. **Health services:** Predental, premedicine, prepharmacy, preveterinary. **History:** General. **Human services:** Social work. **Liberal arts:** Arts/sciences. **Math:** General. **Philosophy/religion:** Philosophy. **Physical sciences:** Chemistry, physics. **Psychology:** General. **Social sciences:** Economics, international relations, political science, sociology. **Visual/performing arts:** Art, art history/conservation, studio arts, theater history.

Most popular majors. Business/marketing 25%, English 21%, history 7%, psychology 10%, social sciences 13%, visual/performing arts 6%.

Computing on campus. 64 workstations in library, computer center. Dormitories wired for high-speed internet access and linked to campus network. Commuter students can connect to campus network. Helpline, wireless network available.

Student life. Freshman orientation: Available. Preregistration for classes offered. **Housing:** Guaranteed on-campus for freshmen. Coed dorms, fraternity/sorority housing available. $200 fully refundable deposit, deadline 5/1. **Activities:** Pep band, campus ministries, choral groups, dance, drama, international student organizations, literary magazine, music ensembles, musical theater, radio station, student government, student newspaper, Catholic student association, black student caucus, Christian fellowship, environmentally concerned students, Jewish student union, Students Against Homophobia, APO service organization, Circle K.

Athletics. NCAA. **Intercollegiate:** Baseball M, basketball, cross-country, golf, soccer, tennis, track and field, volleyball W. **Intramural:** Badminton, basketball, softball, tennis, volleyball. **Team name:** Stormy Petrels.

Student services. Adult student services, career counseling, financial aid counseling, health services, personal counseling. **Physically disabled:** Services for visually, speech, hearing impaired.

Contact. E-mail: admission@oglethorpe.edu
Phone: (404) 364-8307 Toll-free number: (800) 428-4484
Fax: (404) 364-8491
Lucy Leusch, Vice President for Enrollment and Financial Aid, Oglethorpe University, 4484 Peachtree Road NE, Atlanta, GA 30319-2797

Paine College
Augusta, Georgia   **CB member**
www.paine.edu   **CB code: 5530**

- Private 4-year liberal arts college affiliated with Christian Methodist Episcopal Church
- Residential campus in large city
- 888 degree-seeking undergraduates: 8% part-time, 63% women, 94% African American, 1% Hispanic American
- 69% of applicants admitted
- SAT or ACT (ACT writing optional), application essay required

General. Founded in 1882. Regionally accredited. **Degrees:** 98 bachelor's awarded. **ROTC:** Army. **Location:** 72 miles from Columbia, SC; 150 miles from Atlanta. **Calendar:** Semester, limited summer session. **Full-time faculty:** 60 total; 73% have terminal degrees, 48% minority, 38% women. **Part-time faculty:** 22 total; 18% have terminal degrees, 73% minority, 54% women. **Class size:** 66% < 20, 33% 20-39, less than 1% 50-99. **Special facilities:** Frank Yerby house replica.

Freshman class profile. 1,923 applied, 1,335 admitted, 192 enrolled.

Mid 50% test scores			
SAT critical reading:	340-430	GPA 2.0-2.99:	56%
SAT math:	330-450	Rank in top quarter:	21%
SAT writing:	350-430	Rank in top tenth:	6%
ACT composite:	14-18	Return as sophomores:	62%
GPA 3.75 or higher:	2%	Out-of-state:	28%
GPA 3.50-3.74:	7%	Live on campus:	79%
GPA 3.0-3.49:	26%	International:	1%

Basis for selection. School achievement record, test scores, and recommendations considered. 2.0 GPA required. Two letters of recommendation required. Essay must be typed. Interview recommended. **Learning Disabled:**

Contact the Office of Disability Services to register with them and arrange an appointment.

High school preparation. College-preparatory program required. 16 units recommended. Recommended units include English 4, mathematics 3, social studies 2, history 1, science 3 and academic electives 3.

2011-2012 Annual costs. Tuition/fees: $12,502. Room/board: $6,093. Books/supplies: $800. Personal expenses: $1,940.

Financial aid. Non-need-based: Scholarships awarded for academics, alumni affiliation, athletics, music/drama, religious affiliation, ROTC.

Application procedures. Admission: Closing date 7/1 (receipt date). $35 fee, may be waived for applicants with need. Admission notification on a rolling basis. **Financial aid:** Priority date 3/1; no closing date. FAFSA required. Applicants notified on a rolling basis starting 5/1; must reply within 2 week(s) of notification.

Academics. Special study options: Combined bachelor's/graduate degree, cooperative education, cross-registration, distance learning, dual enrollment of high school students, honors, independent study, internships, liberal arts/career combination, study abroad, teacher certification program. Dual degree in engineering and mathematics with Tuskegee University; cross-registration with Augusta State University. **Credit/placement by examination:** AP, CLEP, SAT, ACT, institutional tests. **Support services:** Learning center, reduced course load, remedial instruction, study skills assistance, tutoring, writing center.

Majors. Biology: General. **Business:** Business admin. **Communications:** General. **Education:** Biology, elementary, English, history, mathematics, middle. **English:** English lit. **History:** General. **Math:** General. **Philosophy/religion:** General. **Physical sciences:** Chemistry. **Psychology:** General. **Social sciences:** Sociology.

Most popular majors. Biology 14%, business/marketing 19%, communications/journalism 16%, psychology 11%, social sciences 15%.

Computing on campus. 130 workstations in dormitories, library, computer center, student center. Dormitories wired for high-speed internet access and linked to campus network. Commuter students can connect to campus network. Online course registration, online library, helpline, repair service, wireless network available.

Student life. Freshman orientation: Mandatory, $117 fee. Preregistration for classes offered. Pre-testing and orientation held at the beginning of each semester. **Housing:** Single-sex dorms, wellness housing available. $100 nonrefundable deposit, deadline 7/1. Honors housing. **Activities:** Campus ministries, choral groups, dance, drama, international student organizations, literary magazine, music ensembles, student government, student newspaper, NAACP, pre-alumni club, National Pan Hellenic Council, Wesley Fellowship, Brother to Brother.

Athletics. NCAA. **Intercollegiate:** Baseball M, basketball, cross-country, golf M, softball W, track and field, volleyball W. **Intramural:** Badminton, baseball M, basketball, cross-country, football (non-tackle) M, softball, table tennis, tennis, track and field, volleyball, weight lifting. **Team name:** Lions.

Student services. Alcohol/substance abuse counseling, chaplain/spiritual director, career counseling, student employment services, financial aid counseling, health services, personal counseling, placement for graduates, veterans' counselor.

Contact. E-mail: jtinsley@paine.edu
Phone: (706) 821-8320 Toll-free number: (800) 476-7703
Fax: (706) 821-8648
Joseph Tinsley, Director of Admissions, Paine College, 1235 15th Street, Augusta, GA 30901-3182

Piedmont College
Demorest, Georgia   **CB member**
www.piedmont.edu   **CB code: 5537**

- Private 4-year liberal arts and teachers college affiliated with United Church of Christ
- Commuter campus in rural community
- 1,251 degree-seeking undergraduates: 11% part-time, 67% women, 11% African American, 1% Asian American, 2% Hispanic American, 1% Native American
- 1,522 graduate students
- 64% of applicants admitted

- SAT or ACT (ACT writing optional) required
- 46% graduate within 6 years

General. Founded in 1897. Regionally accredited. Comprehensive liberal arts institution. **Degrees:** 318 bachelor's awarded; master's, doctoral offered. **Location:** 30 miles from Gainesville, 75 miles from Atlanta. **Calendar:** Semester, limited summer session. **Full-time faculty:** 127 total. **Part-time faculty:** 147 total. **Class size:** 76% < 20, 23% 20-39, less than 1% 40-49, less than 1% 50-99. **Special facilities:** Athletic center, performing arts and communication center, pipe organ, worship and music center.

Freshman class profile. 876 applied, 563 admitted, 254 enrolled.

Mid 50% test scores		GPA 2.0-2.99:	16%
SAT critical reading:	460-560	Rank in top quarter:	44%
SAT math:	460-560	Rank in top tenth:	19%
ACT composite:	20-25	Return as sophomores:	82%
GPA 3.75 or higher:	24%	Out-of-state:	5%
GPA 3.50-3.74:	22%	Live on campus:	74%
GPA 3.0-3.49:	37%		

Basis for selection. GPA and standardized test scores most important. Essay recommended. Interview recommended for academically weak. **Home schooled:** Interview, letter of recommendation (nonparent) required. Transcript or portfolio detailing high school coursework completed, 2 letters of recommendation from sources outside home who have knowledge of student's academic/extracurricular achievements required. Interview with student and family may be required.

High school preparation. College-preparatory program recommended. 21 units recommended. Recommended units include English 4, mathematics 3, social studies 1, history 2, science 3 and foreign language 2.

2011-2012 Annual costs. Tuition/fees: $19,000. Room/board: $7,500. Books/supplies: $1,400. Personal expenses: $1,414.

2011-2012 Financial aid. Need-based: 205 full-time freshmen applied for aid; 182 were judged to have need; 182 of these received aid. Average need met was 73%. Average scholarship/grant was $10,329; average loan $3,336. 65% of total undergraduate aid awarded as scholarships/grants, 35% as loans/jobs. **Non-need-based:** Awarded to 268 full-time undergraduates, including 73 freshmen. Scholarships awarded for academics, alumni affiliation, art, leadership, music/drama, religious affiliation, state residency. **Additional information:** College meets 100% of unmet direct financial need for early applicants through grants, scholarships, and loan programs.

Application procedures. Admission: Closing date 7/1. No application fee. Admission notification on a rolling basis. **Financial aid:** Priority date 5/1; no closing date. FAFSA, institutional form required. Applicants notified on a rolling basis; must reply within 2 week(s) of notification.

Academics. Experiential learning credit allows students to document work experience for college credit as appropriate. **Special study options:** Accelerated study, combined bachelor's/graduate degree, distance learning, double major, dual enrollment of high school students, honors, independent study, internships, student-designed major, study abroad, teacher certification program. **Credit/placement by examination:** AP, CLEP. 30 credit hours maximum toward bachelor's degree. **Support services:** Study skills assistance, tutoring.

Majors. Biology: General. **Business:** Business admin. **Communications:** Media studies. **Conservation:** Environmental science. **Education:** Biology, chemistry, drama/dance, early childhood, English, history, middle, secondary, special ed. **English:** English lit. **Foreign languages:** Spanish. **Health services:** Nursing (RN). **History:** General. **Math:** General. **Philosophy/religion:** Philosophy, religion. **Physical sciences:** Chemistry. **Protective services:** Criminal justice. **Psychology:** General. **Social sciences:** General, political science, sociology. **Visual/performing arts:** Art, dramatic, music, studio arts.

Most popular majors. Business/marketing 21%, education 40%, health sciences 7%, psychology 7%, social sciences 8%.

Computing on campus. 240 workstations in dormitories, library, computer center, student center. Dormitories wired for high-speed internet access and linked to campus network. Commuter students can connect to campus network. Online library, wireless network available.

Student life. Freshman orientation: Mandatory. Preregistration for classes offered. Three-day weekend with activities for students, resident assistants, faculty and staff. **Policies:** Unmarried students under 21 must live in dormitories or with blood relatives. **Housing:** Guaranteed on-campus for all undergraduates. Coed dorms, single-sex dorms, special housing for disabled, apartments, wellness housing available. $250 nonrefundable deposit. **Activities:** Campus ministries, choral groups, drama, film society, literary magazine, music ensembles, musical theater, radio station, student government, student newspaper, symphony orchestra, TV station, psychology club,

Fellowhip of Christian Athletes, Green Giants, Student Association of Educators, literary society, science club, environmental club, Rotaract, history society.

Athletics. NCAA. **Intercollegiate:** Baseball M, basketball, cross-country, golf, lacrosse M, soccer, softball W, tennis, volleyball W. **Intramural:** Basketball, football (non-tackle), soccer, softball, table tennis, volleyball. **Team name:** Lions.

Student services. Chaplain/spiritual director, career counseling, financial aid counseling, health services, personal counseling, placement for graduates, veterans' counselor.

Contact. E-mail: ugrad@piedmont.edu
Phone: (706) 776-0103 Toll-free number: (800) 277-7020
Fax: (706) 776-6635
Cynthia Peterson, Director of Admissions, Piedmont College, 165 Central Avenue, Demorest, GA 30535-0010

Point University
East Point, Georgia
www.acc.edu
CB code: 5029

▶ Private 4-year Bible and liberal arts college affiliated with Christian Church
▶ Residential campus in small city
▶ 1,256 degree-seeking undergraduates: 7% part-time, 60% women, 67% African American, 3% Hispanic American
▶ 39% of applicants admitted
▶ SAT or ACT (ACT writing optional) required
▶ 35% graduate within 6 years

General. Founded in 1937. Regionally accredited. **Degrees:** 125 bachelor's, 44 associate awarded. **Location:** 10 miles from Atlanta. **Calendar:** Semester, limited summer session. **Full-time faculty:** 26 total; 65% have terminal degrees, 15% minority, 42% women. **Part-time faculty:** 88 total; 20% have terminal degrees, 17% minority, 52% women. **Class size:** 77% < 20, 20% 20-39, 2% 40-49, 2% 50-99.

Freshman class profile. 543 applied, 210 admitted, 151 enrolled.

Mid 50% test scores			
SAT critical reading:	420-500	GPA 2.0-2.99:	40%
SAT math:	410-520	Rank in top quarter:	28%
ACT composite:	17-21	Rank in top tenth:	14%
GPA 3.75 or higher:	14%	Return as sophomores:	63%
GPA 3.50-3.74:	11%	Out-of-state:	10%
GPA 3.0-3.49:	35%	Live on campus:	74%

Basis for selection. Recommendations, scholastic ability, and test scores are most important. **Home schooled:** Statement describing home school structure and mission, transcript of courses and grades, letter of recommendation (nonparent) required.

High school preparation. College-preparatory program recommended. 13 units required; 16 recommended. Required and recommended units include English 4, mathematics 3-4, science 3 (laboratory 2) and foreign language 3.

2011-2012 Annual costs. Tuition/fees: $16,226. Room/board: $5,980. Books/supplies: $2,000. Personal expenses: $500.

Application procedures. **Admission:** Priority date 8/1; deadline 8/15 (receipt date). $25 fee, may be waived for applicants with need. Admission notification on a rolling basis beginning on or about 9/1. **Financial aid:** Priority date 6/1, closing date 8/1. FAFSA required. Applicants notified on a rolling basis starting 3/1; must reply within 3 week(s) of notification.

Academics. **Special study options:** Double major, dual enrollment of high school students, teacher certification program. **Credit/placement by examination:** AP, CLEP, IB. 16 credit hours maximum toward associate degree, 32 toward bachelor's. **Support services:** Reduced course load, study skills assistance, tutoring, writing center.

Majors. Biology: General. **Business:** Business admin. **Education:** Early childhood, middle. **English:** English lit. **History:** General. **Liberal arts:** Humanities. **Protective services:** Criminal justice. **Psychology:** General. **Social sciences:** Sociology. **Theology:** Bible, theology. **Visual/performing arts:** Music. **Work/family studies:** Child development.

Computing on campus. 30 workstations in library, computer center, student center. Dormitories wired for high-speed internet access and linked to campus network. Commuter students can connect to campus network.

Online course registration, online library, helpline, repair service, wireless network available.

Student life. Freshman orientation: Mandatory. Preregistration for classes offered. **Policies:** Religious observance required. **Housing:** Guaranteed on-campus for freshmen. Single-sex dorms, special housing for disabled, apartments available. **Activities:** Pep band, campus ministries, choral groups, drama, literary magazine, music ensembles, student government, student newspaper, religious organizations, Christian service clubs, service-oriented fraternities and sororities.

Athletics. NAIA, NCCAA. **Intercollegiate:** Baseball M, basketball, soccer, softball W, volleyball W. **Intramural:** Basketball, football (non-tackle), softball W, table tennis, volleyball, weight lifting. **Team name:** Chargers.

Student services. Adult student services, alcohol/substance abuse counseling, chaplain/spiritual director, career counseling, services for economically disadvantaged, student employment services, financial aid counseling, health services, personal counseling, placement for graduates, veterans' counselor. **Physically disabled:** Services for hearing impaired.

Contact. E-mail: admissions@acc.edu
Phone: (404) 669-3202 Toll-free number: (800) 776-1222
Fax: (404) 460-2451
Stacy Bartlett, Director of Admission, Point University, 2605 Ben Hill Road, East Point, GA 30344

Reinhardt University
Waleska, Georgia
www.reinhardt.edu
CB member
CB code: 5568

▶ Private 4-year liberal arts and teachers college affiliated with United Methodist Church
▶ Commuter campus in rural community
▶ 980 degree-seeking undergraduates: 6% part-time, 55% women, 13% African American, 1% Asian American, 4% Hispanic American, 1% Native American
▶ 119 degree-seeking graduate students
▶ 59% of applicants admitted
▶ SAT or ACT (ACT writing optional) required
▶ 39% graduate within 6 years

General. Founded in 1883. Regionally accredited. Off-campus center in Alpharetta. Additional sites in Marietta, Cartersville, Cherokee County. **Degrees:** 239 bachelor's, 9 associate awarded; master's offered. **Location:** 50 miles from Atlanta. **Calendar:** Semester, extensive summer session. **Full-time faculty:** 62 total; 74% have terminal degrees, 11% minority, 48% women. **Part-time faculty:** 95 total; 45% have terminal degrees, 10% minority, 57% women. **Class size:** 83% < 20, 16% 20-39, less than 1% 40-49. **Special facilities:** Indian history museum, visual arts center, performing arts center.

Freshman class profile. 1,310 applied, 769 admitted, 233 enrolled.

Mid 50% test scores			
SAT critical reading:	410-540	GPA 3.0-3.49:	29%
SAT math:	430-530	GPA 2.0-2.99:	47%
ACT composite:	17-22	Return as sophomores:	56%
GPA 3.75 or higher:	12%	Out-of-state:	8%
GPA 3.50-3.74:	12%	Live on campus:	62%

Basis for selection. School achievement record and standardized test scores most important. Interview recommended. Audition required of music majors. Portfolio required of art majors. **Home schooled:** Transcript of courses and grades, state high school equivalency certificate required. **Learning Disabled:** Recommend that students be counseled by Academic Support Office.

High school preparation. College-preparatory program recommended. 14 units required. Required and recommended units include English 4, mathematics 4, social studies 3, science 3 and foreign language 2.

2011-2012 Annual costs. Tuition/fees: $17,840. Room/board: $6,626.

2010-2011 Financial aid. **Need-based:** 194 full-time freshmen applied for aid; 175 were judged to have need; 174 of these received aid. Average need met was 43%. Average scholarship/grant was $8,504; average loan $2,680. 61% of total undergraduate aid awarded as scholarships/grants, 39% as loans/jobs. **Non-need-based:** Awarded to 290 full-time undergraduates, including 68 freshmen. Scholarships awarded for academics, art, athletics, leadership, music/drama, religious affiliation, state residency.

Application procedures. Admission: No deadline. $25 fee, may be waived for applicants with need. Admission notification on a rolling basis beginning on or about 9/1. **Financial aid:** Priority date 5/1; no closing date. FAFSA required. Applicants notified on a rolling basis starting 2/1; must reply within 2 week(s) of notification.

Academics. Special study options: Accelerated study, cooperative education, distance learning, double major, dual enrollment of high school students, external degree, honors, independent study, internships, liberal arts/career combination, study abroad, teacher certification program, weekend college. **Credit/placement by examination:** AP, CLEP, SAT, ACT, institutional tests. 15 credit hours maximum toward associate degree, 30 toward bachelor's. **Support services:** Learning center, pre-admission summer program, reduced course load, remedial instruction, study skills assistance, tutoring, writing center.

Majors. Biology: General. **Business:** General, accounting, business admin. **Communications:** Communications/speech/rhetoric. **Education:** General, biology, early childhood, elementary, English, mathematics, middle, music, physical. **English:** English lit. **Foreign languages:** General. **History:** General. **Liberal arts:** Arts/sciences. **Math:** General. **Parks/recreation:** Sports admin. **Philosophy/religion:** Religion. **Protective services:** Police science. **Psychology:** General. **Social sciences:** Political science, sociology. **Visual/performing arts:** Art, music, studio arts.

Most popular majors. Business/marketing 15%, education 29%, liberal arts 23%, visual/performing arts 11%.

Computing on campus. 170 workstations in dormitories, library, computer center, student center. Dormitories wired for high-speed internet access and linked to campus network. Commuter students can connect to campus network. Online course registration, online library, helpline, student web hosting, wireless network available.

Student life. Freshman orientation: Mandatory, $100 fee. Preregistration for classes offered. One- or 2-day program. **Housing:** Guaranteed on-campus for freshmen. Coed dorms, single-sex dorms, special housing for disabled, apartments available. $200 fully refundable deposit, deadline 8/15. Honors house available. **Activities:** Bands, campus ministries, choral groups, drama, film society, international student organizations, literary magazine, music ensembles, musical theater, student government, student newspaper, symphony orchestra, TV station, Baptist collegiate ministry, Wesley Fellowship, Athletes for Christ Everyday, Phi Theta Kappa, Circle-K International, Habitat for Humanity, breast cancer awareness committee.

Athletics. NAIA. **Intercollegiate:** Baseball M, basketball, cheerleading, cross-country, golf M, lacrosse, soccer, softball W, tennis. **Intramural:** Basketball, football (non-tackle), soccer, softball, volleyball. **Team name:** Eagles.

Student services. Adult student services, alcohol/substance abuse counseling, chaplain/spiritual director, career counseling, student employment services, financial aid counseling, health services, personal counseling, placement for graduates, veterans' counselor. **Physically disabled:** Services for visually, speech, hearing impaired.

Contact. E-mail: admissions@mail.reinhardt.edu
Phone: (770) 720-5526 Toll-free number: (877) 343-4273
Fax: (770) 720-5602
Julie Fleming, Director of Admissions, Reinhardt University, 7300 Reinhardt Circle, Waleska, GA 30183-2981

Savannah College of Art and Design
Savannah, Georgia   **CB member**
www.scad.edu   **CB code: 5631**

- Private 4-year visual arts and performing arts college
- Commuter campus in small city
- 8,835 degree-seeking undergraduates: 13% part-time, 63% women, 8% African American, 4% Asian American, 5% Hispanic American, 1% Native American, 10% international
- 2,113 degree-seeking graduate students
- 63% of applicants admitted
- SAT or ACT (ACT writing optional) required
- 65% graduate within 6 years

General. Founded in 1978. Regionally accredited. Additional locations in Atlanta and Hong Kong. Study abroad program in Lacoste, France. **Degrees:** 1,750 bachelor's awarded; master's offered. **ROTC:** Army. **Location:** 250 miles from Atlanta; 150 miles from Jacksonville, FL. **Calendar:** Quarter, limited summer session. **Full-time faculty:** 524 total; 75% have terminal degrees, 17% minority, 40% women. **Part-time faculty:** 200 total; 64% have terminal degrees, 17% minority, 52% women. **Class size:** 81% < 20, 19% 20-39. **Special facilities:** Art museums, 2 vintage diners, amphitheater, restored 1943 theater.

Freshman class profile. 8,533 applied, 5,377 admitted, 1,789 enrolled.

Mid 50% test scores			
SAT critical reading:	480-600	GPA 2.0-2.99:	16%
SAT math:	460-580	Rank in top quarter:	42%
SAT writing:	470-590	Rank in top tenth:	16%
ACT composite:	21-26	Return as sophomores:	81%
GPA 3.75 or higher:	28%	Out-of-state:	81%
GPA 3.50-3.74:	20%	Live on campus:	87%
GPA 3.0-3.49:	36%	International:	10%

Basis for selection. Entrance test scores, 3 letters of recommendation, and high school transcript required. 540 SAT math/23 ACT math required for architecture regular acceptance; provisional status may be granted with lower scores. Interview, portfolio recommended. Essay recommended for historic preservation, art history, and architectural history programs. Portfolio or audition required for scholarship consideration. **Home schooled:** Statement describing home school structure and mission, transcript of courses and grades, state high school equivalency certificate required. **Learning Disabled:** Documentation of specific nature of disability required.

High school preparation. College-preparatory program recommended.

2012-2013 Annual costs. Tuition/fees: $32,405. Room/board: $12,945. Books/supplies: $2,496. Personal expenses: $1,872.

2011-2012 Financial aid. Non-need-based: Scholarships awarded for academics, alumni affiliation, art, athletics, music/drama, state residency. **Additional information:** Degree-seeking students awarded maximum of one scholarship from college, but may receive additional scholarships from other sources, as well as additional forms of financial aid. Scholarships based on academic achievement awarded through admission office.

Application procedures. Admission: Closing date 8/1 (receipt date). $70 fee. Admission notification on a rolling basis. Recommended deadline for reply is 5/1. Students encouraged to apply early to gain priority for housing. **Financial aid:** Priority date 2/15; no closing date. FAFSA required. Applicants notified on a rolling basis starting 3/1; must reply within 4 week(s) of notification.

Academics. Strong fine arts foundation along with strong liberal arts curriculum. **Special study options:** Combined bachelor's/graduate degree, distance learning, double major, dual enrollment of high school students, ESL, independent study, internships, New York semester, study abroad, teacher certification program, Washington semester. Off-campus programs in Europe and other art centers. Cross registration available at SCAD-Atlanta through membership in ARCHE. Teacher certification in art and drama available through MAT program. **Credit/placement by examination:** AP, CLEP, IB, SAT, ACT. 15 credit hours maximum toward bachelor's degree. **Support services:** Learning center, pre-admission summer program, reduced course load, study skills assistance, tutoring, writing center.

Majors. Architecture: Architecture, history/criticism. **Communications:** Digital media. **Communications technology:** Animation/special effects, recording arts. **English:** Creative writing. **General:** Equestrian studies. **Visual/performing arts:** Art history/conservation, cinematography, commercial/advertising art, dramatic, fashion design, fiber arts, game design, graphic design, illustration, industrial design, interior design, metal/jewelry, painting, photography, printmaking, sculpture, theater design. **Work/family studies:** Apparel marketing.

Most popular majors. Communication technologies 13%, visual/performing arts 74%.

Computing on campus. 2,859 workstations in dormitories, library, computer center, student center. Dormitories wired for high-speed internet access and linked to campus network. Commuter students can connect to campus network. Online course registration, online library, helpline, repair service, student web hosting, wireless network available.

Student life. Freshman orientation: Available. Preregistration for classes offered. Held before start of classes. Optional 2-day summer program, which includes parents, carries fee of $110. **Housing:** Coed dorms, single-sex dorms, apartments available. $250 nonrefundable deposit, deadline 6/1. Freshmen-only halls, case-by-case accommodations for disabled students available. **Activities:** Choral groups, dance, drama, international student organizations, music ensembles, musical theater, radio station, student government, student newspaper, TV station, American Institute of Architecture Students, American Society of Interior Designers, united student forum, inter-club council, student activities council, intercultural student association, Society of Illustrators, art history society, Society for Collegiate Journalists.

Athletics. NAIA. **Intercollegiate:** Baseball M, cross-country, equestrian, golf, lacrosse, soccer, softball W, swimming, tennis, volleyball W. **Intramural:** Basketball, football (non-tackle), soccer, softball, tennis, volleyball. **Team name:** Bees.

Student services. Adult student services, alcohol/substance abuse counseling, career counseling, student employment services, financial aid counseling, health services, personal counseling, placement for graduates. **Physically disabled:** Services for visually, speech, hearing impaired.

Contact. E-mail: admission@scad.edu
Phone: (912) 525-5100 Toll-free number: (800) 869-7223
Fax: (912) 525-5986
Sara Malbrough, Executive Director of Admission, Savannah College of Art and Design, PO Box 2072, Savannah, GA 31402-2072

Savannah State University
Savannah, Georgia   **CB member**
www.savannahstate.edu   **CB code: 5609**

- Public 4-year business and liberal arts college
- Commuter campus in small city
- 4,241 degree-seeking undergraduates: 12% part-time, 54% women, 91% African American, 1% Hispanic American, 1% international
- 166 degree-seeking graduate students
- SAT or ACT (ACT writing optional) required

General. Founded in 1890. Regionally accredited. **Degrees:** 369 bachelor's awarded; master's offered. **ROTC:** Army, Naval. **Location:** 250 miles from Atlanta; 120 miles from Jacksonville, FL. **Calendar:** Semester, extensive summer session. **Full-time faculty:** 163 total. **Part-time faculty:** 56 total. **Special facilities:** Marine biology dock, college archives, natural estuary.

Basis for selection. Test scores and high school GPA very important. Students lacking complete college-preparatory requirements admitted on provisional basis. **Home schooled:** Transcript of courses and grades, state high school equivalency certificate required. Declaration of Intent to Home School; Iowa TAP, SAT Subject Tests, California Achievement Test, Stanford Achievement Test or other national standardized high school summation exam; completion of collegiate preparatory curriculum; student and primary teacher certification of completion of high school and date of graduation required.

High school preparation. College-preparatory program required. 16 units required. Required units include English 4, mathematics 4, social studies 3, science 3 and foreign language 2.

2011-2012 Annual costs. Tuition/fees: $6,032; $17,646 out-of-state. Room/board: $6,604.

Financial aid. Non-need-based: Scholarships awarded for academics, alumni affiliation, music/drama.

Application procedures. Admission: Closing date 7/15. $20 fee, may be waived for applicants with need. Admission notification on a rolling basis beginning on or about 3/1. **Financial aid:** Closing date 4/1. FAFSA required. Applicants notified on a rolling basis starting 4/15; must reply within 2 week(s) of notification.

Academics. Special study options: Combined bachelor's/graduate degree, cooperative education, cross-registration, double major, dual enrollment of high school students, exchange student, honors, independent study, internships, study abroad. **Credit/placement by examination:** AP, CLEP, institutional tests. 45 credit hours maximum toward bachelor's degree. **Support services:** Learning center, pre-admission summer program, remedial instruction, study skills assistance, tutoring, writing center.

Majors. Area/ethnic studies: African. **Biology:** General, marine. **Business:** Accounting, business admin, marketing. **Communications:** Media studies. **Computer sciences:** General, computer science, information systems. **Conservation:** Environmental studies. **Education:** Early childhood. **English:** English lit. **History:** General. **Human services:** Social work. **Math:** General. **Physical sciences:** Chemistry. **Protective services:** Homeland security, law enforcement admin. **Social sciences:** Political science, sociology. **Visual/performing arts:** General.

Most popular majors. Biology 6%, business/marketing 20%, communications/journalism 11%, computer/information sciences 7%, engineering/engineering technologies 10%, psychology 10%, security/protective services 8%, social sciences 11%.

Computing on campus. 420 workstations in dormitories, library, computer center, student center. Dormitories wired for high-speed internet access and linked to campus network. Commuter students can connect to campus network. Online course registration, helpline, repair service, wireless network available.

Student life. Freshman orientation: Mandatory, $60 fee. Preregistration for classes offered. Available various times leading up to fall semester. Private appointments upon request. **Housing:** Single-sex dorms, apartments available. $100 deposit. **Activities:** Bands, campus ministries, choral groups, dance, drama, international student organizations, literary magazine, music ensembles, radio station, student government, student newspaper, Achievers of Today & Tomorrow, Caribbean student association, College Democrats, DC & Beyond, National Council of Negro Women, non-traditional student organization, Sisters Striving for Excellence, Way of Real Discovery.

Athletics. NCAA. **Intercollegiate:** Baseball M, basketball, bowling W, cross-country, football (tackle) M, golf, softball W, tennis W, track and field, volleyball W. **Intramural:** Baseball M, bowling, softball W, table tennis. **Team name:** Tigers.

Student services. Alcohol/substance abuse counseling, career counseling, student employment services, financial aid counseling, health services, personal counseling, placement for graduates, veterans' counselor. **Physically disabled:** Services for visually, speech, hearing impaired.

Contact. E-mail: admissions@savannahstate.edu
Phone: (912) 358-4338 Toll-free number: (800) 788-0478
Fax: (912) 358-3171
Carol Dolan, Assistant Director of Admission, Savannah State University, Office of Admissions and Recruitment, Savannah, GA 31404

Shorter University
Rome, Georgia   **CB member**
www.shorter.edu   **CB code: 5616**

- Private 4-year liberal arts college affiliated with Southern Baptist Convention
- Residential campus in large town
- 1,581 degree-seeking undergraduates: 5% part-time, 55% women, 17% African American, 1% Asian American, 4% Hispanic American, 3% international
- 54 degree-seeking graduate students
- 65% of applicants admitted
- SAT or ACT (ACT writing recommended), application essay required
- 43% graduate within 6 years

General. Founded in 1873. Regionally accredited. **Degrees:** 232 bachelor's awarded; master's offered. **Location:** 70 miles from Atlanta; 65 miles from Chattanooga, TN. **Calendar:** Semester, limited summer session. **Full-time faculty:** 92 total; 70% have terminal degrees, 9% minority, 50% women. **Part-time faculty:** 94 total; 6% have terminal degrees, 7% minority, 53% women. **Class size:** 50% < 20, 48% 20-39, 2% 40-49, less than 1% >100.

Freshman class profile. 1,944 applied, 1,263 admitted, 405 enrolled.

Mid 50% test scores		Rank in top quarter:	47%
SAT critical reading:	420-550	Rank in top tenth:	21%
SAT math:	430-550	Return as sophomores:	68%
SAT writing:	410-530	Out-of-state:	14%
ACT composite:	18-24	Live on campus:	74%
GPA 3.75 or higher:	31%	International:	4%
GPA 3.50-3.74:	10%	Fraternities:	7%
GPA 3.0-3.49:	28%	Sororities:	33%
GPA 2.0-2.99:	30%		

Basis for selection. High school achievement, curriculum most important. Test scores, essay, counselor recommendation considered. Auditions required of music and drama majors. Portfolios required of art majors. **Home schooled:** Interview may be required.

High school preparation. College-preparatory program required. 16 units required. Required units include English 4, mathematics 4, history 3, science 3 and foreign language 2. Math units should include 2 algebra, 1 geometry.

2011-2012 Annual costs. Tuition/fees: $17,870. Room/board: $8,600. Books/supplies: $1,200. Personal expenses: $1,770.

2011-2012 Financial aid. Need-based: 363 full-time freshmen applied for aid; 318 were judged to have need; 318 of these received aid. Average need met was 67%. Average scholarship/grant was $12,505; average loan $3,285. 61% of total undergraduate aid awarded as scholarships/grants, 39% as loans/jobs. **Non-need-based:** Awarded to 499 full-time undergraduates, including 159 freshmen. Scholarships awarded for academics, art, athletics, music/drama, religious affiliation, state residency. **Additional information:**

Four-Year Colleges

Cost is reduced for all in-state students by state tuition equalization grant program. College matches for out-of-state full-time students.

Application procedures. Admission: No deadline. $25 fee, may be waived for applicants with need. Admission notification on a rolling basis beginning on or about 1/1. Must reply by May 1 or within 2 week(s) if notified thereafter. **Financial aid:** Priority date 4/1; no closing date. FAFSA, institutional form required. Applicants notified on a rolling basis starting 3/1; must reply within 2 week(s) of notification.

Academics. Special study options: Combined bachelor's/graduate degree, cross-registration, distance learning, double major, dual enrollment of high school students, honors, independent study, internships, student-designed major, study abroad, teacher certification program, weekend college. **Credit/placement by examination:** AP, CLEP, IB, SAT, institutional tests. 30 credit hours maximum toward bachelor's degree. **Support services:** Learning center, pre-admission summer program, remedial instruction, study skills assistance, tutoring, writing center.

Majors. Biology: General. **Business:** Accounting, business admin, managerial economics. **Communications:** Communications/speech/rhetoric, public relations. **Computer sciences:** General. **Conservation:** General, environmental studies. **Education:** Art, elementary, mathematics, middle, music. **English:** English lit. **Foreign languages:** French, Spanish. **History:** General. **Liberal arts:** Arts/sciences. **Math:** General. **Parks/recreation:** Sports admin. **Philosophy/religion:** Religion. **Physical sciences:** Chemistry. **Psychology:** General. **Social sciences:** General, sociology. **Theology:** Sacred music, theology. **Visual/performing arts:** Dramatic, piano/keyboard, studio arts, voice/opera.

Most popular majors. Biology 7%, business/marketing 26%, education 17%, history 6%, liberal arts 8%, parks/recreation 6%, visual/performing arts 12%.

Computing on campus. 50 workstations in library, computer center. Dormitories wired for high-speed internet access and linked to campus network. Online course registration, online library, helpline, wireless network available.

Student life. Freshman orientation: Mandatory, $175 fee. Preregistration for classes offered. Several summer overnight sessions from June to August during which freshmen take placement exams. **Policies:** All housing is alcohol-, drug- and smoke-free. **Housing:** Guaranteed on-campus for freshmen. Single-sex dorms, apartments, wellness housing available. $200 fully refundable deposit, deadline 7/18. **Activities:** Bands, campus ministries, choral groups, dance, drama, film society, international student organizations, literary magazine, music ensembles, Model UN, musical theater, opera, radio station, student government, student newspaper, TV station, Baptist student union, relations society, Fellowship of Christian Athletes, optimist club.

Athletics. NAIA. **Intercollegiate:** Baseball M, basketball, cheerleading, cross-country, football (tackle) M, golf, lacrosse, soccer, softball W, tennis, track and field, volleyball W, wrestling M. **Intramural:** Basketball, bowling, football (non-tackle), soccer, softball, table tennis, tennis, track and field, volleyball. **Team name:** Hawks.

Student services. Adult student services, alcohol/substance abuse counseling, chaplain/spiritual director, career counseling, student employment services, financial aid counseling, health services, personal counseling, placement for graduates. **Physically disabled:** Services for visually, hearing impaired.

Contact. E-mail: admissions@shorter.edu
Phone: (706) 233-7319 Toll-free number: (800) 868-6980
Fax: (706) 233-7224
John Head, Vice President for Enrollment Management, Shorter University, 315 Shorter Avenue, Rome, GA 30165

South University: Savannah
Savannah, Georgia
www.southuniversity.edu   CB code: 5157

- For-profit 4-year university
- Commuter campus in small city
- 886 degree-seeking undergraduates
- Interview required

General. Founded in 1899. Regionally accredited. **Degrees:** 58 bachelor's, 78 associate awarded; master's, professional offered. **Location:** 225 miles from Atlanta; 165 miles from Jacksonville, FL. **Calendar:** Quarter, extensive summer session. **Full-time faculty:** 47 total. **Part-time faculty:** 62 total.

Basis for selection. Test scores and school achievement record considered. SAT or ACT recommended. Computerized placement test may be

submitted in place of test scores for admission. **Home schooled:** Students must provide evidence that homeschooling was conducted in accordance with state laws (certificate of attendance or completion is not sufficient).

2011-2012 Annual costs. Tuition/fees: $16,035.

Application procedures. Admission: No deadline. $50 fee. Admission notification on a rolling basis. **Financial aid:** No deadline. FAFSA required. Applicants notified on a rolling basis starting 9/1.

Academics. Special study options: Combined bachelor's/graduate degree, distance learning, internships. **Credit/placement by examination:** AP, CLEP, IB, SAT, ACT, institutional tests. **Support services:** Learning center, remedial instruction, study skills assistance, tutoring.

Majors. Business: Business admin. **Computer sciences:** Information technology. **Health services:** Health care admin, nursing (RN). **Protective services:** Law enforcement admin. **Psychology:** General.

Most popular majors. Business/marketing 17%, health sciences 69%, security/protective services 6%.

Computing on campus. Commuter students can connect to campus network. Online library, helpline, repair service, wireless network available.

Student life. Freshman orientation: Mandatory. Preregistration for classes offered. **Housing:** Apartments available.

Student services. Career counseling, student employment services, financial aid counseling, placement for graduates, veterans' counselor.

Contact. Phone: (912) 201-8100 Toll-free number: (866) 629-2901
Fax: (912) 201-8070
Danielle Maddox, Director of Admissions, South University: Savannah, 709 Mall Boulevard, Savannah, GA 31406

Southern Polytechnic State University
Marietta, Georgia   CB member
www.spsu.edu   CB code: 5626

- Public 4-year university
- Residential campus in small city
- 4,907 degree-seeking undergraduates: 27% part-time, 18% women, 22% African American, 6% Asian American, 7% Hispanic American, 5% international
- 759 degree-seeking graduate students
- 74% of applicants admitted
- SAT or ACT with writing required
- 35% graduate within 6 years

General. Founded in 1948. Regionally accredited. **Degrees:** 714 bachelor's, 9 associate awarded; master's offered. **ROTC:** Army, Naval, Air Force. **Location:** 15 miles from Atlanta. **Calendar:** Semester, extensive summer session. **Full-time faculty:** 206 total; 71% have terminal degrees, 28% minority, 31% women. **Part-time faculty:** 103 total; 38% have terminal degrees, 30% minority, 30% women. **Class size:** 49% < 20, 46% 20-39, 4% 40-49, less than 1% 50-99, less than 1% >100. **Special facilities:** Robotics labs.

Freshman class profile. 1,318 applied, 976 admitted, 601 enrolled.

Mid 50% test scores			
SAT critical reading:	500-590	Rank in top quarter:	41%
SAT math:	530-620	Rank in top tenth:	13%
SAT writing:	460-560	End year in good standing:	51%
ACT composite:	21-25	Return as sophomores:	69%
GPA 3.75 or higher:	13%	Out-of-state:	1%
GPA 3.50-3.74:	18%	Live on campus:	20%
GPA 3.0-3.49:	46%	International:	2%
GPA 2.0-2.99:	23%	Fraternities:	10%
		Sororities:	9%

Basis for selection. GED not accepted. SAT/ACT, high school college prep units earned, and GPA considered. **Home schooled:** 1130 SAT (exclusive of Writing)/24 ACT with 500 SAT Critical Reading/21 ACT English and 500 SAT Math/21 ACT Math required. Portfolio of high school level work that substantiates completion of required college preparatory courses also required.

High school preparation. College-preparatory program required. 19 units required. Required units include English 4, mathematics 4, social studies 3, science 4 (laboratory 2), foreign language 2 and academic electives 2.

2011-2012 Annual costs. Tuition/fees: $6,524; $19,644 out-of-state. Room/board: $6,892. Books/supplies: $1,700. Personal expenses: $1,700.

2010-2011 Financial aid. Need-based: 500 full-time freshmen applied for aid; 500 were judged to have need; 490 of these received aid. Average need met was 74%. Average scholarship/grant was $2,930; average loan $3,544. 50% of total undergraduate aid awarded as scholarships/grants, 50% as loans/jobs. **Non-need-based:** Awarded to 1,096 full-time undergraduates, including 338 freshmen. Scholarships awarded for academics, athletics, minority status.

Application procedures. Admission: Closing date 7/1 (postmark date). $20 fee, may be waived for applicants with need. Admission notification on a rolling basis beginning on or about 8/1. High school students on track to graduate may be conditionally admitted after completion of their junior year, pending receipt of final documentation after their senior year. **Financial aid:** Priority date 3/1; no closing date. FAFSA required. Applicants notified on a rolling basis starting 5/1.

Academics. 3-week workshop in July prior to Fall term required for architecture students. **Special study options:** Cooperative education, cross-registration, distance learning, double major, dual enrollment of high school students, honors, independent study, internships, liberal arts/career combination, study abroad, teacher certification program. **Credit/placement by examination:** AP, CLEP, IB, institutional tests. 20 credit hours maximum toward associate degree, 30 toward bachelor's. **Support services:** Learning center, reduced course load, study skills assistance, tutoring.

Majors. Architecture: Architecture. **Biology:** General. **Business:** Accounting, construction management, entrepreneurial studies. **Computer sciences:** Applications programming, computer science, information technology. **Education:** Biology, chemistry, mathematics, physics. **Engineering:** Civil, construction, electrical, mechanical, software, systems. **Math:** General. **Physical sciences:** Chemistry, physics. **Psychology:** General. **Social sciences:** International relations, political science. **Visual/performing arts:** General.

Most popular majors. Architecture 6%, business/marketing 20%, computer/information sciences 16%, engineering/engineering technologies 49%.

Computing on campus. 100 workstations in library, student center. Dormitories wired for high-speed internet access and linked to campus network. Commuter students can connect to campus network. Online course registration, online library, helpline, repair service, student web hosting, wireless network available.

Student life. Freshman orientation: Mandatory, $95 fee. Preregistration for classes offered. **Policies:** Student organization renewal and recognition; Greek housing policies; anti-hazing policies; social registration policy. Various policies, regulations, and requirements in place for travel and use of student activities fees. **Housing:** Guaranteed on-campus for all undergraduates. Coed dorms, special housing for disabled, apartments, fraternity/sorority housing, wellness housing available. $200 nonrefundable deposit. **Activities:** Bands, campus ministries, choral groups, drama, international student organizations, radio station, student government, student newspaper, Campus activities board, National Society of Black Engineers, Baptist Collegiate Ministries, Muslim student association, Indian Culture Exchange, Chinese Friendship Association, Gay Lesbian Straight Alliance, Campus Crusade for Christ, Alpha Omega, Talented 10th.

Athletics. NAIA. **Intercollegiate:** Baseball M, basketball, soccer M. **Intramural:** Badminton, basketball, football (non-tackle), golf, racquetball, soccer, softball, table tennis, volleyball. **Team name:** Runnin' Hornets.

Student services. Alcohol/substance abuse counseling, career counseling, student employment services, financial aid counseling, health services, minority student services, personal counseling, placement for graduates, veterans' counselor. **Physically disabled:** Services for visually, speech, hearing impaired.

Contact. E-mail: admiss@spsu.edu
Phone: (678) 915-4188 Toll-free number: (800) 635-3204
Fax: (678) 915-7292
Gary Bush, Director of Admissions, Southern Polytechnic State University, 1100 South Marietta Parkway, Marietta, GA 30060-2896

Spelman College
Atlanta, Georgia
www.spelman.edu

CB member
CB code: 5628

- Private 4-year liberal arts college for women
- Residential campus in very large city
- 2,170 degree-seeking undergraduates: 4% part-time, 100% women, 81% African American, 1% international
- 38% of applicants admitted
- SAT or ACT (ACT writing optional), application essay required
- 77% graduate within 6 years

General. Founded in 1881. Regionally accredited. One of 6 members of Atlanta University Center sharing facilities, resources, and activities. Students may take courses at other undergraduate schools in Atlanta University Consortium. **Degrees:** 426 bachelor's awarded. **ROTC:** Army, Naval, Air Force. **Location:** 2 miles from downtown. **Calendar:** Semester. **Full-time faculty:** 173 total; 87% have terminal degrees, 84% minority, 68% women. **Part-time faculty:** 77 total; 38% have terminal degrees, 79% minority, 73% women. **Class size:** 64% < 20, 30% 20-39, 2% 40-49, 3% 50-99, less than 1% >100. **Special facilities:** Women's research and resource center, fine arts museum.

Freshman class profile. 5,864 applied, 2,204 admitted, 531 enrolled.

Mid 50% test scores			
SAT critical reading:	480-570	GPA 2.0-2.99:	6%
SAT math:	460-560	Rank in top quarter:	70%
ACT composite:	20-24	Rank in top tenth:	33%
GPA 3.75 or higher:	38%	Return as sophomores:	89%
GPA 3.50-3.74:	30%	Out-of-state:	86%
GPA 3.0-3.49:	26%	Live on campus:	99%
		International:	1%

Basis for selection. School achievement record, letters of recommendation, test scores, leadership, activities, essay important. Portfolio required of art majors.

High school preparation. College-preparatory program required. 16 units required; 19 recommended. Required and recommended units include English 4, mathematics 3-4, social studies 3-4, history 2-3, science 3-4 (laboratory 2-3), foreign language 3-4 and academic electives 2. Math must include algebra and geometry. 2 years of same foreign language required. Social studies should include 2 years of history.

2011-2012 Annual costs. Tuition/fees: $23,254. Room/board: $10,986. Books/supplies: $1,150. Personal expenses: $2,100.

2010-2011 Financial aid. Need-based: 523 full-time freshmen applied for aid; 459 were judged to have need; 455 of these received aid. Average need met was 40%. Average scholarship/grant was $11,750; average loan $3,420. 62% of total undergraduate aid awarded as scholarships/grants, 38% as loans/jobs. **Non-need-based:** Scholarships awarded for academics, alumni affiliation, leadership, music/drama, state residency.

Application procedures. Admission: Closing date 2/1 (postmark date). $35 fee, may be waived for applicants with need. Admission notification by 4/1. Must reply by 5/1. **Financial aid:** Priority date 2/1; no closing date. FAFSA, institutional form required. Applicants notified on a rolling basis starting 2/15; must reply within 2 week(s) of notification.

Academics. Special study options: Cross-registration, double major, dual enrollment of high school students, exchange student, honors, independent study, internships, liberal arts/career combination, New York semester, student-designed major, study abroad, teacher certification program, Washington semester. **Credit/placement by examination:** AP, CLEP, IB, institutional tests. 16 credit hours maximum toward bachelor's degree. **Support services:** Learning center, pre-admission summer program, study skills assistance, tutoring, writing center.

Majors. Area/ethnic studies: Women's. **Biology:** General, biochemistry. **Computer sciences:** General. **Conservation:** Environmental science. **Education:** Early childhood. **Engineering:** General. **English:** English lit. **Foreign languages:** French, Spanish. **History:** General. **Math:** General. **Philosophy/religion:** Philosophy, religion. **Physical sciences:** Chemistry, physics. **Psychology:** General. **Social sciences:** Economics, political science, sociology, sociology/anthropology. **Visual/performing arts:** Dramatic, music, studio arts.

Most popular majors. Biology 14%, English 12%, psychology 20%, social sciences 24%, visual/performing arts 6%.

Computing on campus. 102 workstations in dormitories, library, computer center, student center. Dormitories wired for high-speed internet access and linked to campus network. Commuter students can connect to campus network. Online library, helpline, repair service, wireless network available.

Student life. Freshman orientation: Mandatory. Preregistration for classes offered. One-week program prior to registration. **Policies:** Freshmen not permitted cars on campus. **Housing:** Guaranteed on-campus for freshmen. **Activities:** Jazz band, campus ministries, choral groups, dance, drama, international student organizations, music ensembles, student government, student newspaper, subject-related clubs, community services office.

Athletics. NCAA. **Intercollegiate:** Basketball W, cross-country W, soccer W, softball W, tennis W, track and field W, volleyball W. **Intramural:** Basketball W, bowling W, golf W, soccer W, softball W, swimming W, tennis W, track and field W, volleyball W. **Team name:** Jaguars.

Student services. Adult student services, chaplain/spiritual director, career counseling, student employment services, financial aid counseling,

health services, on-campus daycare, personal counseling, placement for graduates, women's services. **Physically disabled:** Services for visually, speech, hearing impaired.

Contact. E-mail: admiss@spelman.edu
Phone: (404) 270-5193 Toll-free number: (800) 982-2411
Fax: (404) 270-5201
Erica Johnson, Director of Admission, Spelman College, 350 Spelman Lane SW, Campus Box 277, Atlanta, GA 30314-4399

Thomas University
Thomasville, Georgia
www.thomasu.edu CB code: 5072

- Private 4-year university and liberal arts college
- Commuter campus in large town
- 863 degree-seeking undergraduates
- 246 graduate students

General. Founded in 1950. Regionally accredited. **Degrees:** 140 bachelor's, 32 associate awarded; master's offered. **Location:** 60 miles from Albany; 35 miles from Tallahassee, Florida. **Calendar:** Semester, extensive summer session. **Full-time faculty:** 58 total; 45% have terminal degrees, 7% minority. **Part-time faculty:** 76 total; 26% have terminal degrees, 13% minority. **Class size:** 85% < 20, 14% 20-39, less than 1% 40-49.

Freshman class profile.

Out-of-state: 8%   Live on campus: 25%

Basis for selection. Open admission, but selective for some programs. Special requirements for nursing program. All students must take the Multiple Assessment Programs & Services examination and successfully complete remedial courses before enrolling in academic courses. **Home schooled:** Transcript of courses and grades, state high school equivalency certificate required.

2011-2012 Annual costs. Tuition/fees: $12,720. Room only: $3,150. Books/supplies: $1,100. Personal expenses: $1,500.

Financial aid. Non-need-based: Scholarships awarded for academics, athletics, leadership, state residency.

Application procedures. Admission: No deadline. $35 fee. Admission notification on a rolling basis. **Financial aid:** Priority date 5/1; no closing date. FAFSA required. Applicants notified on a rolling basis.

Academics. Special study options: Accelerated study, distance learning, dual enrollment of high school students, internships, liberal arts/career combination, teacher certification program. **Credit/placement by examination:** AP, CLEP, institutional tests. 40 credit hours maximum toward associate degree, 40 toward bachelor's. Total of 40 hours applies to credit by examination and prior work/life experience credit combined. **Support services:** Learning center, reduced course load, remedial instruction, study skills assistance, tutoring, writing center.

Majors. Biology: General. **Business:** General, accounting, management information systems, marketing. **Education:** Early childhood, elementary, middle, music, secondary. **English:** English lit. **Health services:** Nursing (RN), staff services technology. **History:** General. **Human services:** Social work. **Liberal arts:** Arts/sciences. **Protective services:** Criminal justice. **Psychology:** General. **Social sciences:** General, anthropology.

Most popular majors. Biology 6%, business/marketing 8%, education 21%, interdisciplinary studies 7%, science technologies 9%.

Computing on campus. 50 workstations in library, computer center. Dormitories wired for high-speed internet access and linked to campus network. Commuter students can connect to campus network. Online course registration, online library, helpline, wireless network available.

Student life. Freshman orientation: Available. Preregistration for classes offered. Half-day program held every semester. **Housing:** Guaranteed on-campus for freshmen. Coed dorms, apartments available. $250 deposit, deadline 8/1. **Activities:** Jazz band, choral groups, drama, literary magazine, music ensembles, student government, student newspaper.

Athletics. NAIA. **Intercollegiate:** Baseball M, golf, soccer, softball W. **Team name:** Night Hawks.

Student services. Adult student services, alcohol/substance abuse counseling, career counseling, student employment services, financial aid counseling, personal counseling, placement for graduates, veterans' counselor. **Physically disabled:** Services for visually, hearing impaired.

Contact. E-mail: admissions@thomasu.edu
Phone: (229) 226-1621 ext. 124
Toll-free number: (800) 538-9784 ext. 124 Fax: (229) 226-1679
Kerri Knight, Director of Admissions, Thomas University, 1501 Millpond Road, Thomasville, GA 31792-7499

Toccoa Falls College
Toccoa Falls, Georgia
www.tfc.edu CB member
CB code: 5799

- Private 4-year Bible and liberal arts college affiliated with Christian and Missionary Alliance
- Residential campus in large town
- 729 full-time, degree-seeking undergraduates
- SAT or ACT (ACT writing recommended), application essay required

General. Founded in 1907. Regionally accredited; also accredited by ABHE. **Degrees:** 166 bachelor's, 3 associate awarded. **Location:** 90 miles from Atlanta; 60 miles from Greenville, SC. **Calendar:** 4-1-4, limited summer session. **Full-time faculty:** 43 total. **Part-time faculty:** 24 total. **Special facilities:** 186-foot waterfall, 1898 hydroelectric generator, nature trails.

Freshman class profile.

Out-of-state: 62%   Live on campus: 87%

Basis for selection. Evidence of Christian commitment, character, capacity and desire to learn considered. Index score calculated by multiplying unweighted GPA by best total standardized test score. Students with score of 48 on GED also considered. Personal statement of Christian faith required.

High school preparation. College-preparatory program recommended. 19 units recommended. Recommended units include English 4, mathematics 3, social studies 3, science 3 and academic electives 6.

2011-2012 Annual costs. Tuition/fees: $16,910. Room/board: $6,300. Books/supplies: $1,000. Personal expenses: $2,270.

Financial aid. Non-need-based: Scholarships awarded for academics, alumni affiliation, leadership, music/drama, religious affiliation, state residency.

Application procedures. Admission: Priority date 5/1; deadline 8/1 (postmark date). $20 fee, may be waived for applicants with need. Admission notification on a rolling basis beginning on or about 3/1. Must reply by May 1 or within 2 week(s) if notified thereafter. **Financial aid:** Priority date 5/1, closing date 8/1. FAFSA, institutional form required. Applicants notified on a rolling basis starting 3/1; must reply within 2 week(s) of notification.

Academics. All students complete at least 30 credit hours of Bible courses (18 credit hours for associate degrees). **Special study options:** Distance learning, double major, dual enrollment of high school students, independent study, internships, teacher certification program. **Credit/placement by examination:** AP, CLEP, SAT, ACT, institutional tests. 30 credit hours maximum toward associate degree, 45 toward bachelor's. **Support services:** Learning center, reduced course load, study skills assistance, tutoring.

Majors. Biology: General. **Business:** Business admin, international. **Communications:** Media studies, organizational. **Education:** Early childhood, English, history, middle, music, science. **English:** English lit. **History:** General. **Philosophy/religion:** Philosophy. **Psychology:** General. **Theology:** Bible, missionary, pastoral counseling, sacred music, youth ministry. **Visual/performing arts:** Music, music performance.

Computing on campus. 60 workstations in library, computer center. Dormitories wired for high-speed internet access and linked to campus network. Commuter students can connect to campus network. Online course registration, online library, helpline, student web hosting, wireless network available.

Student life. Freshman orientation: Mandatory. Preregistration for classes offered. Held 1 week in fall and throughout spring semester. **Policies:** Students attend weekly church services and participate in student ministry field assignments. Religious observance required. **Housing:** Guaranteed on-campus for freshmen. Single-sex dorms, apartments, wellness housing available. $200 fully refundable deposit. **Activities:** Bands, campus ministries, choral groups, drama, international student organizations, music ensembles, radio station, student government, student newspaper, over 50 different ministry opportunities.

Athletics. NCCAA. **Intercollegiate:** Baseball M, basketball, cross-country, golf, soccer, volleyball W. **Intramural:** Basketball, football (non-tackle), soccer, softball, volleyball. **Team name:** Eagles.

Student services. Chaplain/spiritual director, career counseling, student employment services, financial aid counseling, health services, personal counseling. **Physically disabled:** Services for visually impaired.

Contact. E-mail: admissions@tfc.edu
Phone: (706) 886-6831 ext. 5380 Toll-free number: (888) 785-5264
Fax: (706) 282-6012
Joanna Bruce, Director of Admissions, Toccoa Falls College, PO Box 800899, Toccoa Falls, GA 30598-0368

Truett-McConnell College
Cleveland, Georgia   CB member
www.truett.edu   CB code: 5798

- Private 4-year liberal arts college affiliated with Southern Baptist Convention
- Residential campus in small town
- 598 degree-seeking undergraduates
- 83% of applicants admitted
- SAT or ACT (ACT writing optional) required

General. Founded in 1946. Regionally accredited. Associated with Baptist Convention of the State of Georgia. **Degrees:** 44 bachelor's, 9 associate awarded. **Location:** 75 miles from Atlanta, 25 miles from Gainesville. **Calendar:** Semester, limited summer session. **Full-time faculty:** 34 total. **Part-time faculty:** 55 total. **Class size:** 65% < 20, 31% 20-39, 2% 40-49, 2% 50-99. **Special facilities:** World Missions Center.

Freshman class profile. 400 applied, 332 admitted, 178 enrolled.

Mid 50% test scores			
SAT critical reading:	400-530	GPA 3.75 or higher:	23%
SAT math:	400-520	GPA 3.50-3.74:	17%
SAT writing:	390-520	GPA 3.0-3.49:	28%
ACT composite:	16-20	GPA 2.0-2.99:	32%

Basis for selection. 2.0 GPA in core classes and 710 SAT (exclusive of Writing) or 15 ACT required. Students with lower scores may apply and are reviewed by an appeal committee. Audition required of music majors. **Home schooled:** Transcript of courses and grades required. Letter from local school board stating that student has completed homeschool program requirements and placement exams required. **Learning Disabled:** Students may request accommodations upon presentation of appropriate documentation of disability. Determination of reasonable accommodations made on individual basis.

High school preparation. Recommended units include English 4, mathematics 3, social studies 3, science 3 and foreign language 2.

2011-2012 Annual costs. Tuition/fees: $15,010. Room/board: $6,180. Books/supplies: $1,200. Personal expenses: $3,500.

Financial aid. Non-need-based: Scholarships awarded for academics, alumni affiliation, athletics, leadership, music/drama, religious affiliation, state residency.

Application procedures. Admission: Closing date 8/1 (receipt date). $25 fee, may be waived for applicants with need, free for online applicants. Admission notification on a rolling basis. Must reply by May 1 or within 1 week(s) if notified thereafter. **Financial aid:** Priority date 4/1; no closing date. FAFSA, institutional form required. Applicants notified on a rolling basis starting 3/15; must reply within 2 week(s) of notification.

Academics. Special study options: Distance learning, double major, dual enrollment of high school students, independent study, teacher certification program. **Credit/placement by examination:** AP, CLEP, SAT, ACT, institutional tests. 30 credit hours maximum toward associate degree, 30 toward bachelor's. **Support services:** Remedial instruction, tutoring.

Majors. Business: General. **Education:** Early childhood. **English:** English lit. **History:** General. **Liberal arts:** Humanities. **Philosophy/religion:** Christian. **Visual/performing arts:** Music.

Most popular majors. Education 28%, history 16%, philosophy/religious studies 21%, visual/performing arts 13%.

Computing on campus. 45 workstations in library, computer center, student center. Dormitories linked to campus network. Online course registration, wireless network available.

Student life. Freshman orientation: Mandatory, $25 fee. Preregistration for classes offered. Several 1-day sessions held during summer prior to start of fall classes. **Policies:** Tobacco-free campus. Religious observance required. **Housing:** Single-sex dorms, apartments, wellness housing available. $100 fully refundable deposit. **Activities:** Bands, campus ministries, choral groups,

music ensembles, student government, Baptist collegiate ministries, Fellowship of Christian Athletes, ministerial association, campus activities board, Ambassadors club, Circle K, residence life staff.

Athletics. NAIA, NCCAA. **Intercollegiate:** Baseball M, basketball, cross-country, golf, soccer, softball W. **Intramural:** Basketball, football (non-tackle), soccer. **Team name:** Bears.

Student services. Chaplain/spiritual director, financial aid counseling, health services, veterans' counselor. **Physically disabled:** Services for visually, speech, hearing impaired.

Contact. E-mail: admissions@truett.edu
Phone: (706) 865-2134 Toll-free number: (800) 226-8621
Fax: (706) 865-3110
Nathan Raynor, Director of Admissions, Truett-McConnell College, 100 Alumni Drive, Cleveland, GA 30528

University of Georgia
Athens, Georgia   CB member
www.uga.edu   CB code: 5813

- Public 4-year university
- Commuter campus in small city
- 26,177 degree-seeking undergraduates: 6% part-time, 58% women, 7% African American, 8% Asian American, 4% Hispanic American, 1% international
- 8,186 degree-seeking graduate students
- 63% of applicants admitted
- SAT or ACT with writing, application essay required
- 83% graduate within 6 years; 29% enter graduate study

General. Founded in 1785. Regionally accredited. **Degrees:** 6,845 bachelor's awarded; master's, professional, doctoral offered. **ROTC:** Army, Air Force. **Location:** 70 miles from Atlanta. **Calendar:** Semester, extensive summer session. **Full-time faculty:** 1,796 total; 94% have terminal degrees, 20% minority, 36% women. **Part-time faculty:** 391 total; 68% have terminal degrees, 8% minority, 44% women. **Class size:** 39% < 20, 43% 20-39, 7% 40-49, 6% 50-99, 5% >100. **Special facilities:** Regional botanical garden, golf course, performing arts center, regional art museum.

Freshman class profile. 17,569 applied, 11,062 admitted, 5,482 enrolled.

Mid 50% test scores		Rank in top quarter:	89%
SAT critical reading:	560-650	Rank in top tenth:	47%
SAT math:	560-660	Return as sophomores:	94%
SAT writing:	560-650	Out-of-state:	11%
ACT composite:	25-30	Live on campus:	98%
GPA 3.75 or higher:	63%	International:	1%
GPA 3.50-3.74:	24%	Fraternities:	19%
GPA 3.0-3.49:	12%	Sororities:	33%
GPA 2.0-2.99:	1%		

Basis for selection. GPA in core academic courses, rigor of course selection, and best combination of SAT/ACT important. Applications reviewed for conduct issues, recommendations, and satisfactory completion of all courses including required college preparatory courses. Audition required of music majors.

High school preparation. College-preparatory program required. 18 units required; 21 recommended. Required and recommended units include English 4, mathematics 4, social studies 3, history 2, science 4 (laboratory 2), foreign language 2-3 and academic electives 1.

2011-2012 Annual costs. Tuition/fees: $9,472; $27,682 out-of-state. Room/board: $8,708.

2011-2012 Financial aid. Need-based: 4,524 full-time freshmen applied for aid; 2,233 were judged to have need; 2,233 of these received aid. Average need met was 73%. Average scholarship/grant was $9,711; average loan $3,345. 61% of total undergraduate aid awarded as scholarships/grants, 39% as loans/jobs. **Non-need-based:** Awarded to 2,846 full-time undergraduates, including 792 freshmen. Scholarships awarded for academics, athletics, ROTC, state residency.

Application procedures. Admission: Priority date 10/15; deadline 1/15 (postmark date). $60 fee, may be waived for applicants with need. Admission notification by 4/1. Must reply by May 1 or within 2 week(s) if notified thereafter. **Financial aid:** Priority date 3/1; no closing date. FAFSA required. Applicants notified on a rolling basis starting 5/15; must reply within 2 week(s) of notification.

Academics. Special study options: Accelerated study, combined bachelor's/graduate degree, cooperative education, cross-registration, distance learning, double major, dual enrollment of high school students, exchange student, external degree, honors, independent study, internships, liberal arts/career combination, student-designed major, study abroad, teacher certification program, Washington semester. **Credit/placement by examination:** AP, CLEP, IB, institutional tests. Unlimited number of hours of credit by examination may be counted toward bachelor's degree. **Support services:** Learning center, pre-admission summer program, reduced course load, remedial instruction, study skills assistance, tutoring, writing center.

Majors. Architecture: Landscape. **Area/ethnic studies:** African-American, Latin American/Caribbean; women's. **Biology:** General, Biochemistry/molecular biology, biotechnology, botany, cell/histology, ecology, entomology, genetics, microbiology. **Business:** General, accounting, business admin, fashion, finance, insurance, international, management information systems, managerial economics, marketing, real estate. **Communications:** Advertising, broadcast journalism, communications/speech/rhetoric, journalism, public relations. **Communications technology:** Radio/TV. **Computer sciences:** Computer science. **Conservation:** Environmental science, forestry, nature tourism, wildlife/wilderness. **Education:** Agricultural, early childhood, English, family/consumer sciences, foreign languages, kindergarten/preschool, mathematics, middle, music, science, social studies, special ed, voc/tech. **Engineering:** Agricultural, biochemical, biological, civil, computer, electrical, environmental, mechanical. **English:** English lit. **Foreign languages:** Ancient Greek, Arabic, Chinese, classics, comparative lit, French, German, Italian, Japanese, Latin, linguistics, Romance, Russian, Spanish. **General:** Agribusiness operations, animal health, animal sciences, communications, dairy, economics, food science, horticulture, poultry, soil science, turf management. **Health services:** Athletic training, communication disorders, dietetics, environmental health, music therapy, public health ed. **History:** General. **Human services:** Social work. **Liberal arts:** Arts/sciences. **Math:** General, statistics. **Parks/recreation:** Exercise sciences, health/fitness. **Philosophy/religion:** Philosophy, religion. **Physical sciences:** Astronomy, chemistry, environmental chemistry, geology, physics. **Protective services:** Law enforcement admin. **Psychology:** General. **Social sciences:** Anthropology, economics, geography, international relations, political science, sociology. **Visual/performing arts:** Art, art history/conservation, dance, dramatic, film/cinema/video, music, music performance, music theory/composition, studio arts. **Work/family studies:** Child development, communication, consumer economics, family resources, food/nutrition, housing.

Most popular majors. Biology 7%, business/marketing 23%, communications/journalism 9%, education 7%, psychology 6%, social sciences 9%.

Computing on campus. 3,096 workstations in dormitories, library, computer center, student center. Dormitories wired for high-speed internet access and linked to campus network. Commuter students can connect to campus network. Online course registration, online library, helpline, repair service, student web hosting, wireless network available.

Student life. Freshman orientation: Mandatory. Preregistration for classes offered. Two-day sessions offered during summer. **Housing:** Guaranteed on-campus for freshmen. Coed dorms, single-sex dorms, special housing for disabled, apartments, fraternity/sorority housing available. Honors and language focused housing available. **Activities:** Bands, campus ministries, choral groups, dance, drama, film society, international student organizations, literary magazine, music ensembles, Model UN, musical theater, opera, radio station, student government, student newspaper, symphony orchestra, TV station.

Athletics. NCAA. **Intercollegiate:** Baseball M, basketball, cross-country, diving, equestrian W, football (tackle) M, golf, gymnastics W, soccer W, softball W, swimming, tennis, track and field, volleyball W. **Intramural:** Basketball, football (non-tackle), football (tackle), golf, racquetball, soccer, softball, squash, tennis, track and field, volleyball. **Team name:** Bulldogs.

Student services. Adult student services, alcohol/substance abuse counseling, career counseling, student employment services, financial aid counseling, health services, legal services, minority student services, on-campus daycare, personal counseling, placement for graduates, veterans' counselor, women's services. **Physically disabled:** Services for visually, speech, hearing impaired.

Contact. E-mail: admproc@uga.edu
Phone: (706) 542-8776 Fax: (706) 542-1466
Nancy McDuff, Associate Vice President for Admissions and Enrollment Management, University of Georgia, Terrell Hall, Athens, GA 30602-1633

University of Phoenix: Atlanta
Sandy Springs, Georgia
www.phoenix.edu

- For-profit 4-year university
- Very large city
- 1,598 degree-seeking undergraduates

General. Regionally accredited. **Degrees:** 212 bachelor's awarded; master's offered. **Calendar:** Differs by program. **Full-time faculty:** 16 total. **Part-time faculty:** 208 total.

Basis for selection. Open admission.

2011-2012 Annual costs. Estimated costs as of August 2011: per-credit-hour charge, $380 to $480, depending upon level and course of study; electronic course materials fee, $95, if applicable. Book and material charges may vary by course and program. All fees are subject to change.

Application procedures. Admission: No deadline. No application fee. **Financial aid:** No deadline.

Academics. Credit/placement by examination: AP, CLEP.

Majors. Business: Accounting, business admin, e-commerce, marketing. **Computer sciences:** General, information technology, webmaster. **Health services:** Facilities admin, nursing (RN). **Protective services:** Law enforcement admin. **Psychology:** General.

Contact. Marc Booker, Director of Admission and Evaluation, University of Phoenix: Atlanta, 8200 Roberts Drive, Suite 300, Sandy Springs, GA 30350

University of Phoenix: Augusta
Augusta, Georgia
www.phoenix.edu

- For-profit 4-year university
- Small city
- 1,091 degree-seeking undergraduates

General. Regionally accredited. **Degrees:** 58 bachelor's awarded; master's offered. **Calendar:** Differs by program. **Full-time faculty:** 27 total. **Part-time faculty:** 166 total.

Basis for selection. Open admission.

2011-2012 Annual costs. Estimated costs as of August 2011: per-credit-hour charge, $380 to $450, depending upon level and course of study; electronic course materials fee, $95, if applicable. Book and material charges may vary by course and program. All fees are subject to change.

Application procedures. Admission: No deadline. No application fee.

Academics. Credit/placement by examination: AP, CLEP.

Majors. Business: Business admin.

Contact. Marc Booker, Director of Admission and Evaluation, University of Phoenix: Augusta, 3152 Perimeter Pkwy, Augusta, GA 30909-4583

University of Phoenix: Columbus Georgia
Columbus, Georgia
www.phoenix.edu

- For-profit 4-year university
- Small city
- 1,089 degree-seeking undergraduates

General. Regionally accredited. **Degrees:** 102 bachelor's awarded; master's offered. **Calendar:** Differs by program. **Full-time faculty:** 10 total. **Part-time faculty:** 106 total.

Basis for selection. Open admission.

2011-2012 Annual costs. Estimated costs as of August 2011: per-credit-hour charge, $420 to $450, depending upon level and course of study; electronic course materials fee, $95, if applicable. Book and material charges may vary by course and program. All fees are subject to change.

Application procedures. Admission: No deadline. No application fee. **Financial aid:** No deadline.

Academics. Credit/placement by examination: AP, CLEP.

Majors. Business: Business admin. **Computer sciences:** General. **Health services:** Facilities admin, health care admin. **Protective services:** Law enforcement admin.

Contact. Marc Booker, Director of Admission and Evaluation, University of Phoenix: Columbus Georgia, 4747 Hamilton Road, Columbus, GA 31904

University of Phoenix: Savannah
Savannah, Georgia
www.phoenix.edu

▶ For-profit 4-year university
▶ Small city
▶ 638 degree-seeking undergraduates

General. Regionally accredited. **Degrees:** 61 bachelor's awarded; master's offered. **Calendar:** Differs by program. **Full-time faculty:** 10 total. **Part-time faculty:** 93 total.

Basis for selection. Open admission.

2011-2012 Annual costs. Estimated costs as of August 2011: per-credit-hour charge, $420 to $450, depending upon level and course of study; electronic course materials fee, $95, if applicable. Book and material charges may vary by course and program. All fees are subject to change.

Application procedures. Admission: No deadline. No application fee. **Financial aid:** No deadline.

Academics. Credit/placement by examination: AP, CLEP.

Majors. Business: Accounting, business admin, operations. **Computer sciences:** General. **Health services:** Facilities admin, nursing (RN). **Protective services:** Law enforcement admin. **Psychology:** General.

Contact. Marc Booker, Director of Admission and Evaluation, University of Phoenix: Savannah, 8001 Chatham Center Drive, Suite 200, Savannah, GA 31405

University of West Georgia
Carrollton, Georgia
www.westga.edu
CB member
CB code: 5900

▶ Public 4-year university
▶ Commuter campus in large town
▶ 10,029 degree-seeking undergraduates: 18% part-time, 61% women, 29% African American, 1% Asian American, 4% Hispanic American, 1% international
▶ 1,617 degree-seeking graduate students
▶ 55% of applicants admitted
▶ SAT or ACT (ACT writing optional) required
▶ 38% graduate within 6 years

General. Founded in 1906. Regionally accredited. Off-campus undergraduate sites in Newnan. Advanced Academy of Georgia for academically accelerated high school juniors and seniors. **Degrees:** 1,467 bachelor's awarded; master's, doctoral offered. **ROTC:** Air Force. **Location:** 50 miles from Atlanta. **Calendar:** Semester, extensive summer session. **Full-time faculty:** 436 total; 72% have terminal degrees, 18% minority, 50% women. **Part-time faculty:** 166 total; 26% have terminal degrees, 9% minority, 68% women. **Class size:** 38% < 20, 44% 20-39, 7% 40-49, 8% 50-99, 2% >100. **Special facilities:** Observatory, performing arts center, archaeological laboratory, technology enhanced learning center, coliseum, football stadium, campus center.

Freshman class profile. 6,634 applied, 3,637 admitted, 1,991 enrolled.

Mid 50% test scores			
SAT critical reading:	450-540	GPA 2.0-2.99:	46%
SAT math:	440-530	Return as sophomores:	73%
SAT writing:	430-520	Out-of-state:	2%
ACT composite:	19-22	Live on campus:	72%
GPA 3.75 or higher:	10%	International:	2%
GPA 3.50-3.74:	12%	Fraternities:	13%
GPA 3.0-3.49:	32%	Sororities:	12%

Basis for selection. GED not accepted. Freshman admission based on SAT/ACT, GPA in college preparatory subjects, and system-mandated college preparatory curriculum. **Home schooled:** 430 SAT verbal and 410 SAT math or 17 ACT English and math required. Must submit academic portfolio booklets detailing all 16 high school college prep courses.

High school preparation. College-preparatory program required. 17 units required. Required units include English 4, mathematics 4, social studies 2, science 4 (laboratory 2) and foreign language 1. 1 math higher than algebra II required.

2011-2012 Annual costs. Tuition/fees: $6,592; $18,568 out-of-state. Room/board: $6,968. Books/supplies: $1,000. Personal expenses: $3,060.

Financial aid. Non-need-based: Scholarships awarded for academics, alumni affiliation, art, athletics, leadership, minority status, music/drama.

Application procedures. Admission: Closing date 6/1 (receipt date). $30 fee, may be waived for applicants with need. Admission notification on a rolling basis beginning on or about 6/1. **Financial aid:** Priority date 4/1; no closing date. FAFSA required. Applicants notified on a rolling basis starting 3/1.

Academics. Special study options: Accelerated study, cooperative education, distance learning, double major, dual enrollment of high school students, external degree, honors, independent study, internships, study abroad, teacher certification program. **Credit/placement by examination:** AP, CLEP, IB, SAT, ACT, institutional tests. 30 credit hours maximum toward bachelor's degree. **Support services:** Learning center, pre-admission summer program, reduced course load, remedial instruction, study skills assistance, tutoring, writing center.

Honors college/program. Two of the following recommended: 1200 SAT (exclusive of Writing)/26 ACT, 610 SAT Critical Reading/27 ACT English, 3.5 GPA.

Majors. Biology: General. **Business:** Accounting, business admin, finance, management information systems, managerial economics, marketing, real estate. **Communications:** Journalism. **Computer sciences:** General. **Conservation:** Environmental science, environmental studies. **Education:** Biology, business, chemistry, elementary, middle, music, physical, physics, secondary, special ed. **English:** English lit. **Foreign languages:** General. **Health services:** Nursing (RN), speech pathology. **History:** General. **Math:** General. **Parks/recreation:** Facilities management. **Philosophy/religion:** Philosophy. **Physical sciences:** Chemistry, geology, physics. **Psychology:** General. **Social sciences:** Anthropology, criminology, economics, geography, international economics, international relations, political science, sociology. **Visual/performing arts:** Art, dramatic, music performance, music theory/composition.

Most popular majors. Business/marketing 24%, education 19%, health sciences 14%, psychology 6%, social sciences 12%.

Computing on campus. 1,200 workstations in dormitories, library, computer center, student center. Dormitories wired for high-speed internet access and linked to campus network. Online course registration, online library, helpline, repair service, student web hosting, wireless network available.

Student life. Freshman orientation: Mandatory, $95 fee. Preregistration for classes offered. Held beginning of semester; includes registration assistance and presentation of available services. **Policies:** Freshmen required to reside on-campus unless married or living with parents, relatives, or legal guardians. **Housing:** Guaranteed on-campus for freshmen. Coed dorms, single-sex dorms, special housing for disabled, fraternity/sorority housing available. $150 nonrefundable deposit. **Activities:** Bands, campus ministries, choral groups, dance, drama, international student organizations, literary magazine, music ensembles, musical theater, opera, radio station, student government, student newspaper, TV station, Baptist Student Union, Catholic Student Life, Muslim student alliance, Latter-Day Saint student association, Jewish student group, Black student alliance, Democratic organization, Republican organization.

Athletics. NCAA. **Intercollegiate:** Baseball M, basketball, cheerleading, cross-country, football (tackle) M, golf, soccer W, softball W, tennis W, volleyball W. **Intramural:** Basketball, football (non-tackle), golf, soccer, softball, table tennis, tennis, track and field, volleyball, weight lifting. **Team name:** Wolves.

Student services. Adult student services, career counseling, student employment services, financial aid counseling, health services, minority student services, on-campus daycare, personal counseling, placement for graduates, veterans' counselor. **Physically disabled:** Services for visually, speech, hearing impaired.

Contact. E-mail: admiss@westga.edu
Phone: (678) 839-4000 Fax: (678) 839-4747
Justin Barlow, Director of Admissions, University of West Georgia, 1601 Maple Street, Carrollton, GA 30118

Valdosta State University

Valdosta, Georgia
www.valdosta.edu

CB member
CB code: 5855

- Public 4-year university
- Commuter campus in small city
- 10,638 degree-seeking undergraduates: 13% part-time, 60% women, 34% African American, 1% Asian American, 4% Hispanic American, 1% international
- 2,315 degree-seeking graduate students
- 58% of applicants admitted
- SAT or ACT (ACT writing optional) required
- 43% graduate within 6 years

General. Founded in 1906. Regionally accredited. **Degrees:** 1,662 bachelor's, 43 associate awarded; master's, doctoral offered. **ROTC:** Air Force. **Location:** 229 miles from Atlanta; 122 miles from Jacksonville, Florida. **Calendar:** Semester, extensive summer session. **Full-time faculty:** 489 total; 77% have terminal degrees, 15% minority, 48% women. **Part-time faculty:** 127 total; 24% have terminal degrees, 20% minority, 65% women. **Class size:** 40% < 20, 48% 20-39, 8% 40-49, 2% 50-99, 2% >100. **Special facilities:** Planetarium, herbarium, observatory, archives museum, pedestrian mall, camellia garden.

Freshman class profile. 7,950 applied, 4,648 admitted, 2,249 enrolled.

Mid 50% test scores			
SAT critical reading:	470-540	GPA 3.0-3.49:	34%
SAT math:	460-540	GPA 2.0-2.99:	43%
SAT writing:	450-530	Return as sophomores:	67%
ACT composite:	20-23	Out-of-state:	2%
GPA 3.75 or higher:	10%	Live on campus:	79%
GPA 3.50-3.74:	13%	Fraternities:	7%
		Sororities:	9%

Basis for selection. GED not accepted. 900 SAT (exclusive of Writing)/19 ACT, Board of Regents minimum requirements of 430 SAT Critical Reading/17 ACT English and 400 SAT Math/17 ACT Math, and freshman index of 2040 (calculated by multiplying GPA by 500 and adding to SAT Critical Reading and Math) required. Specific degree programs may require an interview, audition, essay, or personal statement for acceptance into the program. **Home schooled:** Letter of recommendation (nonparent) required. 1050 SAT with 440 Critical Reading/410 Math or 23 ACT with 18 English/17 math required; official transcripts from any high school and colleges attended; copy of Declaration of Intent to Home School as filed with your local Board of Education required. Portfolio must include information about each course used to satisfy CPC requirements and list of educational resources used, course outline or syllabus, and outcomes assessment. Also include any extracurricular activities and/or academic achievements, letter from primary teacher certifying completion of high school and a date of graduation, and two letters of recommendation from non-family members such as employer, clergy, civic leader, or tutor. **Learning Disabled:** Untimed SAT/ACT accepted.

High school preparation. College-preparatory program required. 16 units required. Required units include English 4, mathematics 4, social studies 3, science 3 (laboratory 2) and foreign language 2.

2011-2012 Annual costs. Tuition/fees: $6,644; $18,620 out-of-state. Room/board: $6,850. Books/supplies: $1,200. Personal expenses: $2,594.

2010-2011 Financial aid. **Need-based:** 2,276 full-time freshmen applied for aid; 1,879 were judged to have need; 1,879 of these received aid. Average need met was 91%. Average scholarship/grant was $7,410; average loan $3,280. 45% of total undergraduate aid awarded as scholarships/grants, 55% as loans/jobs. **Non-need-based:** Awarded to 476 full-time undergraduates, including 155 freshmen. Scholarships awarded for academics, art, athletics, minority status, music/drama, ROTC, state residency.

Application procedures. Admission: Closing date 6/1 (receipt date). $40 fee, may be waived for applicants with need. Admission notification on a rolling basis. **Financial aid:** Priority date 4/1; no closing date. FAFSA required. Applicants notified on a rolling basis starting 4/15.

Academics. Special study options: Accelerated study, cooperative education, distance learning, double major, dual enrollment of high school students, ESL, external degree, honors, independent study, internships, study abroad, teacher certification program, weekend college. **Credit/placement by examination:** AP, CLEP, IB, SAT, ACT, institutional tests. 30 credit hours maximum toward associate degree, 30 toward bachelor's. **Support services:** Study skills assistance, tutoring, writing center.

Honors college/program. 1130 SAT (exclusive of Writing)/15 ACT with 3.2 GPA required. Offers seminars, priority registration, honors center and state and national conference attendance options.

Majors. Biology: General. **Business:** Accounting, administrative services, business admin, finance, international, managerial economics, marketing. **Communications:** Media studies. **Computer sciences:** General, information systems. **Conservation:** Environmental science. **Education:** Art, business, Deaf/hearing impaired, early childhood, foreign languages, French, kindergarten/preschool, mentally handicapped, middle, music, physical, Spanish, special ed, trade/industrial. **English:** English lit, rhetoric/composition. **Foreign languages:** French, sign language interpretation, Spanish. **Health services:** Athletic training, nursing (RN), speech pathology. **History:** General. **Liberal arts:** Arts/sciences. **Math:** General, applied. **Parks/recreation:** Health/fitness. **Philosophy/religion:** Philosophy. **Physical sciences:** Astronomy, chemistry, physics. **Protective services:** Criminal justice. **Psychology:** General. **Social sciences:** Political science, sociology. **Visual/performing arts:** General, art, dance, interior design, music, music performance.

Most popular majors. Business/marketing 22%, education 18%, English 8%, health sciences 9%, social sciences 7%.

Computing on campus. 1,225 workstations in library, computer center, student center. Dormitories wired for high-speed internet access and linked to campus network. Commuter students can connect to campus network. Online course registration, online library, helpline, repair service, student web hosting, wireless network available.

Student life. Freshman orientation: Available, $35 fee. Preregistration for classes offered. One day programs held in summer. Provides students and parents with information about educational programs, support services, student life opportunities, and campus facilities. **Policies:** Student organizations must be registered with Student Life Office. **Housing:** Coed dorms, special housing for disabled, apartments available. $300 fully refundable deposit, deadline 4/15. Honors housing available. **Activities:** Bands, campus ministries, choral groups, dance, drama, international student organizations, literary magazine, music ensembles, Model UN, musical theater, opera, radio station, student government, student newspaper, symphony orchestra, TV station, Baptist College Ministries, black student league, Fellowship of Christian Athletes, Hillel, Latin American students association, Students Against Violating the Environment, Wesley Foundation.

Athletics. NCAA. **Intercollegiate:** Baseball M, basketball, cross-country, football (tackle) M, golf M, soccer W, softball W, tennis, volleyball W. **Intramural:** Badminton, basketball, bowling, cricket, football (non-tackle), golf, lacrosse, racquetball, soccer, softball, swimming, table tennis, tennis, volleyball, weight lifting. **Team name:** Blazers.

Student services. Adult student services, alcohol/substance abuse counseling, career counseling, student employment services, financial aid counseling, health services, minority student services, personal counseling, placement for graduates, veterans' counselor. **Physically disabled:** Services for visually, speech, hearing impaired.

Contact. E-mail: admissions@valdosta.edu
Phone: (229) 333-5791 Toll-free number: (800) 618-1878
Fax: (229) 333-5482
Walter Peacock, Director of Admissions, Valdosta State University, 1500 North Patterson Street, Valdosta, GA 31698-0170

Wesleyan College

Macon, Georgia
www.wesleyancollege.edu

CB member
CB code: 5895

- Private 4-year liberal arts college for women affiliated with United Methodist Church
- Residential campus in small city
- 615 degree-seeking undergraduates: 37% part-time, 100% women
- 50 degree-seeking graduate students
- 54% of applicants admitted
- SAT or ACT (ACT writing optional), application essay required
- 43% graduate within 6 years; 25% enter graduate study

General. Founded in 1836. Regionally accredited. **Degrees:** 94 bachelor's awarded; master's offered. **Location:** 75 miles from Atlanta. **Calendar:** Semester, limited summer session. **Full-time faculty:** 48 total; 96% have terminal degrees, 2% minority, 62% women. **Part-time faculty:** 40 total; 12% have terminal degrees, 8% minority, 38% women. **Class size:** 87% < 20, 12% 20-39, less than 1% 50-99. **Special facilities:** Equestrian facilities, arboretum, lake.

Freshman class profile. 516 applied, 280 admitted, 113 enrolled.

Mid 50% test scores			
SAT critical reading:	420-660	End year in good standing:	90%
SAT math:	400-690	Return as sophomores:	73%
ACT composite:	18-25	Out-of-state:	11%
		Live on campus:	90%

Basis for selection. Academic performance in college preparatory courses, standardized test scores, extra-curricular activities and recommendations most important. Interview recommended; required for scholarship competitions. Audition required of music or theater students interested in performance arts scholarship. Portfolio required of art majors. **Home schooled:** Statement describing home school structure and mission, transcript of courses and grades, letter of recommendation (nonparent) required. Diplomas issued by parents are recognized. Student may provide bibliography of high school literature and essay to evaluate exposure and thinking skills. Extra-curricular activities, counselor interviews considered. **Learning Disabled:** Student support team available through student services.

High school preparation. College-preparatory program recommended. 15 units required; 22 recommended. Required and recommended units include English 4, mathematics 3-4, social studies 3-4, science 3-4 (laboratory 2-3), foreign language 2-4 and academic electives 2.

2011-2012 Annual costs. Tuition/fees: $18,500. Room/board: $8,200. Books/supplies: $1,000. Personal expenses: $1,000.

Financial aid. Non-need-based: Scholarships awarded for academics, alumni affiliation, art, job skills, leadership, minority status, music/drama, religious affiliation, state residency.

Application procedures. Admission: Priority date 3/1; deadline 6/1 (postmark date). $30 fee, may be waived for applicants with need. Admission notification on a rolling basis beginning on or about 10/1. Must reply by 7/1. **Financial aid:** Priority date 2/15, closing date 6/3. FAFSA, institutional form required. Applicants notified on a rolling basis starting 3/1; must reply by 5/1 or within 3 week(s) of notification.

Academics. Special study options: Accelerated study, combined bachelor's/graduate degree, cross-registration, double major, dual enrollment of high school students, exchange student, honors, independent study, internships, liberal arts/career combination, student-designed major, study abroad, teacher certification program, urban semester, weekend college. **Credit/placement by examination:** AP, CLEP, IB, institutional tests. 30 credit hours maximum toward bachelor's degree. **Support services:** Learning center, pre-admission summer program, reduced course load, study skills assistance, tutoring, writing center.

Majors. Biology: General. **Business:** Business admin, international. **Communications:** Advertising, communications/speech/rhetoric. **Education:** Early childhood. **English:** English lit. **Foreign languages:** French, Spanish. **History:** General. **Liberal arts:** Arts/sciences. **Math:** General. **Philosophy/religion:** Philosophy, religion. **Physical sciences:** Chemistry, physics. **Psychology:** General. **Social sciences:** General, economics, international relations. **Theology:** Preministerial. **Visual/performing arts:** Art history/conservation, dramatic, music, studio arts.

Most popular majors. Biology 6%, business/marketing 24%, communications/journalism 8%, education 8%, psychology 16%, visual/performing arts 10%.

Computing on campus. PC or laptop required. 50 workstations in library, student center. Dormitories wired for high-speed internet access and linked to campus network. Commuter students can connect to campus network. Online course registration, online library, helpline, repair service, wireless network available.

Student life. Freshman orientation: Mandatory. Preregistration for classes offered. Summer orientation held in June; includes registration. Fall orientation held in August prior to start of classes. **Policies:** Students required to live on campus unless married or living with immediate family in the local area. Honor Code used. **Housing:** Guaranteed on-campus for all undergraduates. Special housing for disabled, apartments available. $150 deposit, deadline 7/1. **Activities:** Campus ministries, choral groups, dance, drama, international student organizations, literary magazine, music ensembles, Model UN, musical theater, student government, student newspaper, honor council, Mortar board, Young Democrats, Circle K, College Republicans, Council on Religions Concerns, American Chemical Society, Wesleyan Disciples.

Athletics. NCAA. **Intercollegiate:** Basketball W, cross-country W, equestrian W, soccer W, softball W, tennis W. **Intramural:** Basketball W, cross-country W, soccer W, softball W, volleyball W. **Team name:** Pioneers.

Student services. Adult student services, alcohol/substance abuse counseling, chaplain/spiritual director, career counseling, student employment services, financial aid counseling, health services, minority student services, personal counseling, women's services.

Contact. E-mail: admission@wesleyancollege.edu
Phone: (478) 757-5206 Toll-free number: (800) 447-6610
Fax: (478) 757-4030
C. Stephen Farr, Vice President for Enrollment Services, Wesleyan College, 4760 Forsyth Road, Macon, GA 31210-4462

Westwood College: Atlanta Midtown
Atlanta, Georgia
www.westwood.edu

❥ For-profit 3-year technical college
❥ Commuter campus in very large city

General. Regionally accredited. **Calendar:** Continuous.

Annual costs/financial aid. Tuition/fees (2011-2012): $15,020. Books/supplies: $1,106.

Contact. Phone: (404) 745-9096
Director of Admissions, 1100 Spring Street, Suite 200, Atlanta, GA 30309

Westwood College: Northlake
Atlanta, Georgia
www.westwood.edu

❥ For-profit 4-year visual arts and technical college
❥ Very large city

General. Regionally accredited. **Calendar:** Continuous.

Annual costs/financial aid. Tuition/fees (2011-2012): $15,020. Books/supplies: $1,106.

Contact. Phone: (404) 962-2998
Director of Admissions, 2220 Parklake Drive, Suite 175, Atlanta, GA 30345

Hawaii

Argosy University: Hawaii
Honolulu, Hawaii
www.argosy.edu/hawaii

- For-profit 4-year university
- Large city
- 145 degree-seeking undergraduates

General. Regionally accredited. **Degrees:** 4 bachelor's awarded; master's, professional, doctoral offered. **Calendar:** Differs by program. **Full-time faculty:** 5 total. **Part-time faculty:** 64 total.

Basis for selection. Open admission.

2011-2012 Annual costs. Tuition/fees: $17,962.

Application procedures. Admission: Closing date 9/13. $50 fee.

Academics. Credit/placement by examination: AP, CLEP.

Majors. Business: Business admin. **Liberal arts:** Arts/sciences. **Protective services:** Police science. **Psychology:** General.

Contact. E-mail: auhonadmissions@argosy.edu
Phone: (808) 791-5214 Toll-free number: (888) 323-2777
Paul Billington, Senior Director of Admissions, Argosy University: Hawaii, 400 ASB Tower, 1001 Bishop Street, Honolulu, HI 96813

Brigham Young University-Hawaii
Laie, Hawaii
www.byuh.edu   CB code: 4106

- Private 4-year university and liberal arts college affiliated with Church of Jesus Christ of Latter-day Saints
- Residential campus in small town
- 2,571 degree-seeking undergraduates
- 29% of applicants admitted
- Application essay, interview required

General. Founded in 1955. Regionally accredited. **Degrees:** 565 bachelor's, 51 associate awarded. **ROTC:** Army, Naval, Air Force. **Location:** 38 miles north of Honolulu. **Calendar:** Semester, limited summer session. **Full-time faculty:** 124 total. **Part-time faculty:** 126 total. **Class size:** 54% < 20, 40% 20-39, 4% 40-49, 2% 50-99, less than 1% >100. **Special facilities:** Center for Hawaiian language and cultural studies, museum of natural history, Polynesian cultural center, Pacific Islands collection housed in university archives, Pacific Islands research room.

Freshman class profile. 2,081 applied, 601 admitted, 459 enrolled.

Mid 50% test scores			
SAT critical reading:	460-580	GPA 3.50-3.74:	20%
SAT math:	490-580	GPA 3.0-3.49:	44%
ACT composite:	22-26	GPA 2.0-2.99:	15%
GPA 3.75 or higher:	21%	Out-of-state:	76%
		Live on campus:	90%

Basis for selection. GED not accepted. Interview, essay, recommendations very important. Test scores also important. 3.0 GPA required for domestic students. ACT recommended. Audition required for music majors. Portfolio required for art majors. Ecclesiastical interviews required for all students. Essays may make difference in admission.

High school preparation. Recommended units include English 4, mathematics 2, social studies 3, history 2 and science 2.

2011-2012 Annual costs. Tuition/fees: $4,450. 100% higher tuition and per-credit-hour charges for students who are not members of The Church of Jesus Christ of Latter-day Saints. Room/board: $4,900. Books/supplies: $1,300. Personal expenses: $2,148.

Financial aid. Non-need-based: Scholarships awarded for academics, art, athletics, leadership, music/drama, state residency.

Application procedures. Admission: Closing date 2/15 (receipt date). $30 fee. Admission notification on a rolling basis beginning on or about 4/1. Must reply by 8/25. **Financial aid:** Closing date 3/15. FAFSA required. Applicants notified by 5/1; must reply by 8/31.

Academics. Special study options: Cooperative education, double major, ESL, honors, independent study, internships, student-designed major, teacher certification program. **Credit/placement by examination:** AP, CLEP, IB, institutional tests. **Support services:** Learning center, remedial instruction, study skills assistance, tutoring, writing center.

Majors. Area/ethnic studies: Pacific. **Biology:** General, biochemistry. **Business:** Accounting, business admin. **Computer sciences:** Computer science, information systems, information technology. **Education:** Art, biology, business, chemistry, elementary, English, ESL, mathematics, music, physical, physics, science, secondary, social science, special ed. **English:** English lit. **History:** General. **Human services:** Social work. **Math:** General. **Parks/recreation:** Exercise sciences, health/fitness. **Psychology:** General. **Social sciences:** Political science. **Visual/performing arts:** Art, piano/keyboard, studio arts, voice/opera.

Most popular majors. Business/marketing 25%, computer/information sciences 7%, education 19%, interdisciplinary studies 13%, parks/recreation 6%, psychology 8%, public administration/social services 6%.

Computing on campus. 465 workstations in dormitories, library, computer center, student center. Dormitories wired for high-speed internet access and linked to campus network. Online course registration, online library, helpline, repair service, wireless network available.

Student life. Freshman orientation: Mandatory. Preregistration for classes offered. 2 weeks at the beginning of semester, includes luau, campus and island tour. **Policies:** Religious observance required. **Housing:** Guaranteed on-campus for freshmen. Single-sex dorms, apartments, wellness housing available. $50 deposit, deadline 4/30. All first-time, non-local freshmen required to live on campus until sophomore standing achieved. **Activities:** Bands, choral groups, dance, drama, film society, literary magazine, music ensembles, student government, student newspaper.

Athletics. NCAA. **Intercollegiate:** Basketball, cross-country, golf M, soccer, softball W, tennis, volleyball W. **Intramural:** Basketball, bowling, cross-country, golf, racquetball, rugby, soccer, softball, swimming, table tennis, tennis, volleyball, water polo M, weight lifting. **Team name:** Seasiders.

Student services. Chaplain/spiritual director, career counseling, student employment services, financial aid counseling, health services, personal counseling, placement for graduates, veterans' counselor, women's services. **Physically disabled:** Services for visually, speech, hearing impaired.

Contact. E-mail: admissions@byuh.edu
Phone: (808) 675-3738 Fax: (808) 675-3741
Arapata Meha, Dean of Admissions and Records, Brigham Young University-Hawaii, 55-220 Kulanui Street, #1973, Laie, HI 96762-1294

Chaminade University of Honolulu
Honolulu, Hawaii   CB member
www.chaminade.edu   CB code: 4105

- Private 4-year university affiliated with Roman Catholic Church
- Commuter campus in large city
- 1,217 degree-seeking undergraduates
- 90% of applicants admitted
- SAT or ACT (ACT writing optional), application essay required

General. Founded in 1955. Regionally accredited. Campus shared with St. Louis School. **Degrees:** 297 bachelor's, 78 associate awarded; master's offered. **ROTC:** Army, Air Force. **Location:** 2 miles from Waikiki. **Calendar:** Semester, limited summer session. **Full-time faculty:** 75 total. **Part-time faculty:** 54 total. **Class size:** 59% < 20, 41% 20-39. **Special facilities:** Montessori laboratory preschool, observatory, theater.

Freshman class profile. 1,008 applied, 907 admitted, 299 enrolled.

Mid 50% test scores			
SAT critical reading:	420-510	GPA 3.0-3.49:	36%
SAT math:	430-530	GPA 2.0-2.99:	35%
ACT composite:	19-22	Rank in top quarter:	34%
GPA 3.75 or higher:	14%	Rank in top tenth:	9%
GPA 3.50-3.74:	15%	Out-of-state:	42%
		Live on campus:	73%

Basis for selection. School achievement record, test scores, statement of purpose important. Interview recommended for marginal students.

High school preparation. Recommended units include English 4, mathematics 3, social studies 3, science 2 and academic electives 4.

2011-2012 Annual costs. Tuition/fees: $18,440. Room/board: $11,300. Books/supplies: $1,200. Personal expenses: $1,254.

Financial aid. **Non-need-based:** Scholarships awarded for academics, art, athletics, leadership, religious affiliation, ROTC, state residency. **Additional information:** For students whose eligibility for federal and institutional aid does not meet entire costs, alternative student loans may be secured for eligible applicants.

Application procedures. **Admission:** No deadline. $50 fee. Admission notification on a rolling basis. **Financial aid:** Priority date 2/15; no closing date. FAFSA required. Applicants notified on a rolling basis starting 2/15; must reply within 4 week(s) of notification.

Academics. **Special study options:** Accelerated study, distance learning, double major, exchange student, independent study, internships, semester at sea, student-designed major, study abroad, teacher certification program. **Credit/placement by examination:** AP, CLEP, IB, institutional tests. 30 credit hours maximum toward associate degree, 30 toward bachelor's. **Support services:** Learning center, pre-admission summer program, remedial instruction, study skills assistance, tutoring.

Majors. **Biology:** General. **Business:** Accounting, business admin, marketing. **Communications:** Broadcast journalism, communications/speech/rhetoric, media studies, public relations. **Computer sciences:** General, computer science. **Conservation:** Environmental studies. **Education:** Early childhood, elementary, secondary. **English:** English lit. **Health services:** Nursing (RN). **History:** General. **Liberal arts:** Arts/sciences. **Philosophy/religion:** Religion. **Protective services:** Criminalistics, forensics. **Psychology:** General. **Social sciences:** General, international relations, political science. **Visual/performing arts:** Interior design.

Most popular majors. Business/marketing 11%, communications/journalism 6%, education 17%, English 6%, history 8%, psychology 15%, security/protective services 20%.

Computing on campus. 100 workstations in dormitories, library, computer center, student center. Dormitories wired for high-speed internet access and linked to campus network. Online library, helpline, repair service, wireless network available.

Student life. **Freshman orientation:** Mandatory, $140 fee. Preregistration for classes offered. **Housing:** Guaranteed on-campus for freshmen. Coed dorms, single-sex dorms, special housing for disabled, apartments, wellness housing available. $300 deposit, deadline 5/1. **Activities:** Choral groups, drama, literary magazine, musical theater, student government, student newspaper, symphony orchestra, Samoan club, Hawaiian club, Rotaract club, accounting club, Black Student Union, Filipino club, CJ Sleuths, communications club.

Athletics. NCAA. **Intercollegiate:** Basketball M, cross-country, golf, softball W, tennis, volleyball W. **Intramural:** Cheerleading. **Team name:** Silverswords.

Student services. Adult student services, alcohol/substance abuse counseling, chaplain/spiritual director, career counseling, services for economically disadvantaged, student employment services, financial aid counseling, health services, personal counseling, placement for graduates. **Physically disabled:** Services for visually, speech, hearing impaired.

Contact. E-mail: admissions@chaminade.edu
Phone: (808) 735-4735 Toll-free number: (800) 735-3733
Fax: (808) 739-4647
Dan Yoshitake, Associate Director of Admissions, Chaminade University of Honolulu, 3140 Waialae Avenue, Honolulu, HI 96816

Hawaii Pacific University

Honolulu, Hawaii

www.hpu.edu

CB member

CB code: 4352

▶ Private 4-year university and liberal arts college
▶ Commuter campus in large city
▶ 6,171 degree-seeking undergraduates: 36% part-time, 55% women
▶ 1,268 degree-seeking graduate students
▶ 70% of applicants admitted
▶ SAT or ACT with writing required
▶ 39% graduate within 6 years

General. Founded in 1965. Regionally accredited. Two main campuses and an affiliate marine research facility (The Oceanic Institute) connected by free shuttle service. Programs offered for military personnel and their dependents and for older students. Satellite campus on six (6) military installations on Oahu. **Degrees:** 926 bachelor's, 150 associate awarded; master's offered. **ROTC:** Army, Air Force. **Calendar:** Semester, extensive summer session. **Full-time faculty:** 255 total; 73% have terminal degrees, 27% minority, 45% women. **Part-time faculty:** 384 total; 38% have terminal degrees, 41% minority, 47% women. **Class size:** 63% < 20, 37% 20-39, less than 1% 40-49. **Special facilities:** Oceanic Institute, research boat, theater, orchestra.

Freshman class profile. 4,367 applied, 3,038 admitted, 575 enrolled.

Mid 50% test scores			
SAT critical reading:	420-540	GPA 2.0-2.99:	25%
SAT math:	440-560	Rank in top quarter:	50%
SAT writing:	420-540	Rank in top tenth:	21%
ACT composite:	18-24	Return as sophomores:	66%
GPA 3.75 or higher:	21%	Out-of-state:	50%
GPA 3.50-3.74:	18%	Live on campus:	24%
GPA 3.0-3.49:	36%	International:	7%

Basis for selection. Academic record, test scores most important. Interview also important, recommendations considered. Essay recommended. **Home schooled:** Interview, letter of recommendation (nonparent) required.

High school preparation. 15 units recommended. Recommended units include English 4, mathematics 3, social studies 2, history 2, science 2 (laboratory 1) and foreign language 2. Additional science and mathematics required for nursing and marine science.

2011-2012 Annual costs. Tuition/fees: $16,610. Room/board: $12,230. Books/supplies: $1,300. Personal expenses: $800.

2010-2011 Financial aid. **Need-based:** 605 full-time freshmen applied for aid; 408 were judged to have need; 407 of these received aid. Average need met was 86%. Average scholarship/grant was $1,891; average loan $4,552. 20% of total undergraduate aid awarded as scholarships/grants, 80% as loans/jobs. **Non-need-based:** Awarded to 415 full-time undergraduates, including 86 freshmen. Scholarships awarded for academics, alumni affiliation, athletics, leadership, music/drama, ROTC.

Application procedures. **Admission:** Priority date 3/1; no deadline. $50 fee, may be waived for applicants with need. Admission notification on a rolling basis. Must reply by May 1 or within 4 week(s) if notified thereafter. **Financial aid:** Priority date 3/1; no closing date. FAFSA required. Applicants notified on a rolling basis starting 4/1; must reply within 3 week(s) of notification.

Academics. All students complete core requirements based on following themes: global systems, world cultures, communication skills, research/epistemology, values and choices. **Special study options:** Accelerated study, combined bachelor's/graduate degree, cooperative education, distance learning, double major, dual enrollment of high school students, ESL, honors, independent study, internships, liberal arts/career combination, student-designed major, study abroad, teacher certification program. 3-2 engineering program with University of Southern California (CA), Washington University, St. Louis (MO). **Credit/placement by examination:** AP, CLEP, IB, SAT, ACT, institutional tests. 36 credit hours maximum toward associate degree, 36 toward bachelor's. **Support services:** Learning center, reduced course load, study skills assistance, tutoring.

Majors. **Biology:** General, marine. **Business:** General, accounting, banking/financial services, business admin, communications, finance, human resources, international, international finance, management information systems, managerial economics, marketing, tourism/travel. **Communications:** Advertising, communications/speech/rhetoric, journalism, public relations. **Computer sciences:** General, computer science. **Conservation:** General, environmental science, environmental studies. **Education:** Elementary, ESL. **English:** English lit. **Foreign languages:** Comparative lit. **Health services:** Health care admin, nursing (RN), premedicine. **History:** General. **Human services:** General, social work. **Liberal arts:** Arts/sciences. **Math:** General, applied. **Physical sciences:** Oceanography. **Protective services:** Law enforcement admin. **Psychology:** General. **Social sciences:** General, anthropology, economics, international relations, political science, sociology. **Work/family studies:** Family studies.

Most popular majors. Business/marketing 33%, communications/journalism 6%, health sciences 28%, psychology 7%, social sciences 6%.

Computing on campus. 590 workstations in library, computer center, student center. Dormitories wired for high-speed internet access and linked to campus network. Commuter students can connect to campus network. Online course registration, online library, helpline, student web hosting, wireless network available.

Student life. **Freshman orientation:** Available, $120 fee. Preregistration for classes offered. Week of activities including on-campus sessions and off-campus activities. **Housing:** Coed dorms, apartments, wellness housing available. $500 nonrefundable deposit, deadline 3/31. **Activities:** Bands,

campus ministries, choral groups, dance, drama, film society, international student organizations, literary magazine, music ensembles, Model UN, musical theater, student government, student newspaper, symphony orchestra, Rotaract, President's Hosts, Christian Fellowship, American marketing association, hiking club, honors societies, computing club, Students In Free Enterprise.

Athletics. NCAA. **Intercollegiate:** Baseball M, basketball, cheerleading, cross-country, golf M, soccer, softball W, tennis, volleyball W. **Team name:** Sea Warriors.

Student services. Adult student services, alcohol/substance abuse counseling, chaplain/spiritual director, career counseling, student employment services, financial aid counseling, personal counseling, placement for graduates, veterans' counselor.

Contact. E-mail: admissions@hpu.edu
Phone: (808) 544-0238 Toll-free number: (866) 225-5478
Fax: (808) 544-1136
Sara Sato, Director of Admissions, Hawaii Pacific University, 1164 Bishop Street, Suite 200, Honolulu, HI 96813

University of Hawaii at Hilo

Hilo, Hawaii	CB member
www.uhh.hawaii.edu	CB code: 4869

- Public 4-year university and liberal arts college
- Commuter campus in large town
- 3,385 degree-seeking undergraduates: 17% part-time, 59% women, 1% African American, 19% Asian American, 10% Hispanic American, 1% Native American, 5% international
- 353 degree-seeking graduate students
- 72% of applicants admitted
- SAT or ACT (ACT writing optional) required
- 35% graduate within 6 years

General. Founded in 1970. Regionally accredited. **Degrees:** 581 bachelor's awarded; master's, professional, doctoral offered. **Location:** 200 miles from Honolulu. **Calendar:** Semester, limited summer session. **Full-time faculty:** 227 total. **Part-time faculty:** 73 total. **Class size:** 50% < 20, 44% 20-39, 4% 40-49, 2% 50-99, less than 1% >100. **Special facilities:** Active volcanoes study center, space science center, small business development center, marine education center, 110-acre farm laboratory.

Freshman class profile. 1,500 applied, 1,084 admitted, 474 enrolled.

Mid 50% test scores		GPA 2.0-2.99:	23%
SAT critical reading:	440-590	Rank in top quarter:	47%
SAT math:	440-600	Rank in top tenth:	17%
ACT composite:	17-24	Return as sophomores:	69%
GPA 3.75 or higher:	20%	Out-of-state:	23%
GPA 3.50-3.74:	17%	Live on campus:	64%
GPA 3.0-3.49:	40%	International:	3%

Basis for selection. High school GPA in academic subjects, SAT/ACT test scores, class rank, and school recommendation considered.

High school preparation. 17 units required. Required and recommended units include English 4, mathematics 3, social studies 2, history 2, science 3, foreign language 2 and academic electives 7. 3 mathematics beyond pre-algebra, 7 academic electives not including physical education or ROTC. 4 math and 4 science recommended for science and business majors.

2011-2012 Annual costs. Tuition/fees: $5,944; $17,416 out-of-state. Room/board: $7,182. Books/supplies: $1,017. Personal expenses: $1,166.

Financial aid. Additional information: Hawaii student incentive grants and tuition waivers (merit and need-based) available to Hawaii residents at participating institutions.

Application procedures. Admission: Priority date 3/1; deadline 7/1 (postmark date). $50 fee, may be waived for applicants with need. Admission notification on a rolling basis beginning on or about 10/1. Must reply by May 1 or within 2 week(s) if notified thereafter. **Financial aid:** Priority date 3/1; no closing date. FAFSA required. Applicants notified on a rolling basis starting 4/15; must reply within 2 week(s) of notification.

Academics. Special study options: Combined bachelor's/graduate degree, cross-registration, distance learning, double major, dual enrollment of high school students, ESL, exchange student, honors, independent study, internships, semester at sea, student-designed major, study abroad, teacher certification program. Marine sciences and astronomy summer programs. **Credit/placement by examination:** AP, CLEP, IB, institutional tests. 30 credit

hours maximum toward bachelor's degree. **Support services:** Learning center, tutoring, writing center.

Majors. Area/ethnic studies: Native American. **Biology:** General, marine. **Business:** General, accounting, business admin, finance, marketing. **Communications:** Communications/speech/rhetoric. **Computer sciences:** General. **English:** English lit, rhetoric/composition. **Foreign languages:** Japanese, linguistics. **General:** Agribusiness operations, agronomy, animal sciences, horticultural science, plant protection, soil science. **Health services:** Premedicine. **History:** General. **Human services:** General. **Liberal arts:** Arts/sciences. **Math:** General. **Parks/recreation:** Facilities management, health/fitness. **Philosophy/religion:** Philosophy, religion. **Physical sciences:** Astronomy, chemistry, geology, physics. **Psychology:** General. **Social sciences:** Anthropology, economics, geography, political science, sociology. **Visual/performing arts:** Art, music.

Most popular majors. Agriculture 6%, biology 14%, business/marketing 9%, communications/journalism 8%, health sciences 7%, social sciences 32%.

Computing on campus. 600 workstations in dormitories, library, computer center, student center. Commuter students can connect to campus network. Online course registration, online library, helpline, repair service, wireless network available.

Student life. Freshman orientation: Available, $25 fee. Preregistration for classes offered. 1-week program before start of classes. **Housing:** Coed dorms; special housing for disabled, apartments available. $20 deposit, deadline 7/15. Student housing units available for mobility-impaired students. **Activities:** Bands, choral groups, dance, drama, international student organizations, literary magazine, music ensembles, musical theater, radio station, student government, student newspaper, Samoan club, Delta Sigma Pi business fraternity, World Hope, Rotoract, Bayanihan club, Bahai Club, Chuukese Student Association, Earth Action, Nihon no kai.

Athletics. NCAA. **Intercollegiate:** Baseball M, basketball, cross-country W, golf, soccer, softball W, tennis, volleyball W. **Intramural:** Archery, badminton, basketball, bowling, cross-country, golf, softball, table tennis, tennis, volleyball. **Team name:** Vulcans.

Student services. Career counseling, services for economically disadvantaged, student employment services, financial aid counseling, health services, minority student services, personal counseling, placement for graduates, women's services. **Physically disabled:** Services for visually, speech, hearing impaired.

Contact. E-mail: uhhadm@hawaii.edu
Phone: (808) 974-7414 Toll-free number: (800) 897-4456
Fax: (808) 933-0861
James Cromwell, Director of Admissions, University of Hawaii at Hilo, 200 West Kawili Street, Hilo, HI 96720-4091

University of Hawaii at Manoa

Honolulu, Hawaii	CB member
www.manoa.hawaii.edu	CB code: 4867

- Public 4-year university
- Commuter campus in very large city
- 14,054 degree-seeking undergraduates: 19% part-time, 53% women, 1% African American, 41% Asian American, 2% Hispanic American, 3% international
- 5,475 degree-seeking graduate students
- 78% of applicants admitted
- SAT or ACT with writing required
- 50% graduate within 6 years

General. Founded in 1907. Regionally accredited. **Degrees:** 2,957 bachelor's awarded; master's, professional, doctoral offered. **ROTC:** Army, Air Force. **Location:** 3 miles from downtown. **Calendar:** Semester, extensive summer session. **Full-time faculty:** 1,164 total; 87% have terminal degrees, 39% minority, 43% women. **Part-time faculty:** 65 total; 62% have terminal degrees, 49% minority, 58% women. **Class size:** 60% < 20, 26% 20-39, 4% 40-49, 6% 50-99, 4% >100. **Special facilities:** Institute for astronomy, observatories, arboretum, East-West center, Japanese tea house and garden, Hawaiian studies center, Korean studies center.

Freshman class profile. 6,541 applied, 5,130 admitted, 2,010 enrolled.

Mid 50% test scores		Rank in top quarter:	63%
SAT critical reading:	480-580	Rank in top tenth:	28%
SAT math:	500-610	Return as sophomores:	77%
SAT writing:	470-560	Out-of-state:	30%
ACT composite:	21-26	Live on campus:	55%
GPA 3.75 or higher:	20%	International:	2%
GPA 3.50-3.74:	25%	Fraternities:	1%
GPA 3.0-3.49:	44%	Sororities:	1%
GPA 2.0-2.99:	11%		

Basis for selection. School achievement record, test scores, class rank important. **Home schooled:** State high school equivalency certificate required. In absence of official transcript from accredited school, students must submit GED results in addition to other requirements.

High school preparation. College-preparatory program required. 22 units required. Required units include English 4, mathematics 3, social studies 3, science 3 and academic electives 5.

2011-2012 Annual costs. Tuition/fees: $9,100; $23,932 out-of-state. Room/board: $10,279. Books/supplies: $1,170. Personal expenses: $1,522.

2010-2011 Financial aid. Need-based: 1,380 full-time freshmen applied for aid; 884 were judged to have need; 853 of these received aid. Average need met was 81%. Average scholarship/grant was $9,133; average loan $3,246. 63% of total undergraduate aid awarded as scholarships/grants, 37% as loans/jobs. **Non-need-based:** Awarded to 3,271 full-time undergraduates, including 663 freshmen. Scholarships awarded for academics, alumni affiliation, art, athletics, leadership, music/drama, ROTC. **Additional information:** Hawaii student incentive grants and tuition waivers (merit and need-based) available to Hawaii residents at participating institutions.

Application procedures. Admission: Priority date 1/5; deadline 5/1 (receipt date). $70 fee, may be waived for applicants with need. Admission notification on a rolling basis beginning on or about 12/1. Must reply by May 1 or within 2 week(s) if notified thereafter. **Financial aid:** Priority date 3/1; no closing date. FAFSA required. Applicants notified on a rolling basis starting 4/1; must reply by 5/1 or within 4 week(s) of notification.

Academics. Special study options: Cooperative education, distance learning, double major, ESL, exchange student, honors, independent study, internships, semester at sea, student-designed major, study abroad, teacher certification program. **Credit/placement by examination:** AP, CLEP, IB, SAT, ACT, institutional tests. 30 credit hours maximum toward bachelor's degree. **Support services:** Learning center, pre-admission summer program, remedial instruction, study skills assistance, tutoring, writing center.

Majors. Area/ethnic studies: American, Asian, Native American. **Biology:** General, botany, marine, microbiology, zoology. **Business:** General, accounting, business admin, finance, human resources, international, management information systems, marketing, tourism/travel. **Communications:** Communications/speech/rhetoric, journalism. **Computer sciences:** General, computer science. **Conservation:** Environmental science, management/policy. **Education:** Elementary, ESL, secondary. **Engineering:** Agricultural, civil, electrical, mechanical. **English:** English lit. **Foreign languages:** Chinese, classics, Filipino/Tagalog, French, German, Japanese, Korean, Russian, Spanish. **General:** Animal sciences, plant protection. **Health services:** Audiology/speech pathology, clinical lab science, dental hygiene, nursing (RN). **History:** General. **Human services:** Social work. **Liberal arts:** Arts/sciences. **Math:** General. **Parks/recreation:** Exercise sciences. **Philosophy/religion:** Philosophy, religion. **Physical sciences:** Chemistry, geology, meteorology, physics. **Psychology:** General. **Social sciences:** Anthropology, economics, geography, political science, sociology. **Visual/performing arts:** Art, dance, dramatic, music. **Work/family studies:** General, clothing/textiles.

Most popular majors. Business/marketing 21%, education 7%, psychology 6%, social sciences 11%.

Computing on campus. 1,400 workstations in dormitories, library, computer center, student center. Dormitories wired for high-speed internet access and linked to campus network. Commuter students can connect to campus network. Online course registration, online library, helpline, repair service, student web hosting, wireless network available.

Student life. Freshman orientation: Available, $80 fee. Preregistration for classes offered. 2-day program. **Housing:** Guaranteed on-campus for freshmen. Coed dorms, special housing for disabled, apartments available. $225 partly refundable deposit, deadline 5/1. **Activities:** Bands, campus ministries, choral groups, dance, drama, film society, international student organizations, literary magazine, music ensembles, musical theater, radio station, student government, student newspaper, symphony orchestra, over 150 registered organizations.

Athletics. NCAA. **Intercollegiate:** Baseball M, basketball, cheerleading, cross-country W, diving, football (tackle) M, golf, sailing, soccer W, softball W, swimming, tennis, track and field W, volleyball, water polo W. **Intramural:** Badminton, basketball, cross-country, golf, soccer, softball, table tennis, tennis, track and field W, volleyball, weight lifting. **Team name:** Warriors, Rainbow Warriors, Rainbows, Rainbow Wahine.

Student services. Adult student services, alcohol/substance abuse counseling, career counseling, services for economically disadvantaged, student employment services, financial aid counseling, health services, minority student services, on-campus daycare, personal counseling, placement for graduates, veterans' counselor, women's services. **Physically disabled:** Services for visually, speech, hearing impaired.

Contact. E-mail: ar-info@hawaii.edu
Phone: (808) 956-8975 Toll-free number: (800) 823-9771
Fax: (808) 956-4148
Alan Yang, Director of Admissions and Records, University of Hawaii at Manoa, 2600 Campus Road, QLC Rm 001, Honolulu, HI 96822

University of Hawaii: West Oahu
Pearl City, Hawaii   **CB member**
www.uhwo.hawaii.edu   **CB code: 1042**

> Public 4-year liberal arts and teachers college
> Commuter campus in large town
> 1,599 degree-seeking undergraduates: 69% part-time, 69% women, 1% African American, 40% Asian American, 2% Hispanic American
> 72% of applicants admitted

General. Founded in 1976. Regionally accredited. **Degrees:** 255 bachelor's awarded. **ROTC:** Army, Air Force. **Location:** 10 miles from Honolulu. **Calendar:** Semester, limited summer session. **Full-time faculty:** 49 total; 90% have terminal degrees, 51% minority, 41% women. **Part-time faculty:** 25 total; 32% have terminal degrees, 44% minority, 40% women. **Class size:** 34% < 20, 64% 20-39, 3% 40-49.

Freshman class profile. 448 applied, 324 admitted, 125 enrolled.

GPA 3.75 or higher:	9%	GPA 2.0-2.99:	27%
GPA 3.50-3.74:	13%	Return as sophomores:	37%
GPA 3.0-3.49:	51%	Out-of-state:	8%

Basis for selection. Students with 2.7 high school GPA and 22 credits of required high school coursework will be automatically accepted. **Home schooled:** State high school equivalency certificate required.

High school preparation. 22 units required. Required units include English 4, mathematics 3, social studies 3, science 3 and academic electives 5. Math credits must include Algebra II and Geometry. 4 credits of college prep coursework (language, fine arts, etc.) also required.

2011-2012 Annual costs. Tuition/fees: $5,146; $15,754 out-of-state. Books/supplies: $1,169. Personal expenses: $1,303.

2010-2011 Financial aid. Need-based: 16 full-time freshmen applied for aid; 16 were judged to have need; 16 of these received aid. Average need met was 50%. Average scholarship/grant was $4,547; average loan $2,403. 62% of total undergraduate aid awarded as scholarships/grants, 38% as loans/jobs. **Non-need-based:** Scholarships awarded for academics.

Application procedures. Admission: Priority date 3/1; deadline 8/1 (postmark date). $50 fee, may be waived for applicants with need. Application must be submitted on paper. Admission notification on a rolling basis beginning on or about 12/15. Must reply by May 1 or within 2 week(s) if notified thereafter. **Financial aid:** Priority date 5/1; no closing date. FAFSA required. Applicants notified on a rolling basis starting 5/1.

Academics. Special study options: Distance learning, double major, teacher certification program. **Credit/placement by examination:** AP, CLEP, IB, SAT, ACT, institutional tests. 42 credit hours maximum toward bachelor's degree. 21 lower division and 21 upper division credits may be earned through examination. **Support services:** Study skills assistance, tutoring, writing center.

Majors. Area/ethnic studies: Pacific. **Business:** Accounting, business admin. **Computer sciences:** LAN/WAN management. **Education:** Early childhood, elementary. **English:** English lit. **History:** General. **Human services:** General. **Philosophy/religion:** Philosophy. **Protective services:** Law enforcement admin. **Psychology:** General. **Social sciences:** General, anthropology, economics, political science, sociology.

Most popular majors. Business/marketing 29%, education 18%, health sciences 7%, psychology 10%, public administration/social services 6%, security/protective services 7%, social sciences 12%.

Computing on campus. 18 workstations in computer center. Commuter students can connect to campus network. Online course registration, online library, helpline, student web hosting, wireless network available.

Student life. Freshman orientation: Available. Preregistration for classes offered. **Activities:** Student government, accounting club, anthropology/sociology club, business club, economics club, Hawaiian-Pacific Club, humanities club, political science club, psychology association, students in free enterprise.

Student services. Career counseling, student employment services, financial aid counseling, veterans' counselor. **Physically disabled:** Services for visually, hearing impaired.

Contact. E-mail: admissions@uhwo.hawaii.edu
Phone: (808) 454-4700 Fax: (808) 453-6075
Robyn Oshiro, Admissions Specialist, University of Hawaii: West Oahu,
96-129 Ala Ike, Pearl City, HI 96782

University of Phoenix: Hawaii
Honolulu, Hawaii
www.phoenix.edu

▶ For-profit 4-year university
▶ Large city
▶ 1,228 degree-seeking undergraduates

General. Regionally accredited. **Degrees:** 130 bachelor's awarded; master's
offered. **Calendar:** Differs by program. **Full-time faculty:** 20 total. **Part-
time faculty:** 226 total.

Basis for selection. Open admission, but selective for some programs.

2011-2012 Annual costs. Estimated costs as of August 2011: per-credit-
hour charge, $435 to $480, depending upon level and course of study; electronic course materials fee, $95, if applicable. Book and material charges
may vary by course and program. All fees are subject to change.

Application procedures. Admission: No deadline. No application fee.

Academics. Credit/placement by examination: AP, CLEP.

Majors. Business: Accounting/business management, business admin, marketing. **Computer sciences:** General, web page design. **Health services:**
Facilities admin, nursing (RN). **Protective services:** Law enforcement admin,
security management. **Psychology:** General.

Contact. Marc Booker, Director of Admission and Evaluation,
University of Phoenix: Hawaii, 745 Fort Street, Suite 2000, Honolulu, HI
96813

Idaho

Boise Bible College
Boise, Idaho
www.boisebible.edu   CB code: 0891

- Private 4-year Bible college affiliated with nondenominational tradition
- Residential campus in small city
- 186 degree-seeking undergraduates
- 97% of applicants admitted
- SAT or ACT (ACT writing optional), application essay required

General. Founded in 1945. Accredited by ABHE. **Degrees:** 16 bachelor's, 7 associate awarded. **Location:** 4 miles from downtown. **Calendar:** Semester. **Full-time faculty:** 8 total. **Part-time faculty:** 5 total.

Freshman class profile. 93 applied, 90 admitted, 61 enrolled.

Mid 50% test scores			
SAT critical reading:	450-570	GPA 3.50-3.74:	11%
SAT math:	410-520	GPA 3.0-3.49:	39%
SAT writing:	430-540	GPA 2.0-2.99:	33%
ACT composite:	17-24	Rank in top quarter:	23%
GPA 3.75 or higher:	15%	Rank in top tenth:	3%

Basis for selection. Christian conduct or ethical code standards based on signed student statement, recommendation of home church minister, 1 employment/school reference, and 1 personal reference required. School achievement important. **Home schooled:** Transcript of courses and grades required. GED or transcripts from homeschooling agency recommended. Applicants submitting home-prepared transcripts advised to consult admissions office.

High school preparation. Recommended units include English 4, mathematics 2, history 2 and foreign language 1.

2011-2012 Annual costs. Tuition/fees: $9,985. Room/board: $5,850. Books/supplies: $605. Personal expenses: $1,210.

Financial aid. Non-need-based: Scholarships awarded for academics, leadership, music/drama, religious affiliation.

Application procedures. Admission: Priority date 5/1; deadline 8/1 (receipt date). $25 fee. Application must be submitted on paper. Admission notification on a rolling basis. Must reply by June 1 or 3 weeks after acceptance date if accepted after June 1. **Financial aid:** Priority date 5/1; no closing date. FAFSA, institutional form required. Applicants notified on a rolling basis starting 5/2; must reply by 8/1 or within 2 week(s) of notification.

Academics. Special study options: Distance learning, double major, independent study, internships. **Credit/placement by examination:** AP, CLEP, IB, SAT, ACT, institutional tests. ABHE Bible Knowledge Test. **Support services:** Reduced course load, remedial instruction.

Majors. Theology: Bible, missionary, pastoral counseling, religious ed, sacred music, theology, youth ministry.

Computing on campus. 7 workstations in library, computer center.

Student life. Freshman orientation: Mandatory, $50 fee. Preregistration for classes offered. 2 days of training and testing, followed by whitewater boat trip. **Policies:** Religious observance required. **Housing:** Guaranteed on-campus for freshmen. Single-sex dorms available. $150 deposit, deadline 7/1. Trailer hookups for married students. **Activities:** Choral groups, music ensembles, student government, student newspaper, Christian service missions club.

Athletics. Intramural: Basketball, football (non-tackle) M, soccer, volleyball. **Team name:** Lions.

Student services. Adult student services, career counseling, student employment services, financial aid counseling, health services, personal counseling, placement for graduates, veterans' counselor.

Contact. E-mail: boisebible@boisebible.edu
Phone: (208) 376-7731 Toll-free number: (800) 893-7755
Fax: (208) 376-7743
Martin Flaherty, Admissions Director, Boise Bible College, 8695 West Marigold Street, Boise, ID 83714-1220

Boise State University
Boise, Idaho   CB member
www.boisestate.edu   CB code: 4018

- Public 4-year university
- Commuter campus in small city
- 16,844 degree-seeking undergraduates: 25% part-time, 53% women, 2% African American, 3% Asian American, 7% Hispanic American, 1% Native American, 2% international
- 2,058 degree-seeking graduate students
- 81% of applicants admitted
- SAT or ACT (ACT writing optional) required

General. Founded in 1932. Regionally accredited. **Degrees:** 2,571 bachelor's, 219 associate awarded; master's, doctoral offered. **ROTC:** Army. **Location:** Downtown. **Calendar:** Semester, extensive summer session. **Full-time faculty:** 572 total; 74% have terminal degrees, 8% minority, 46% women. **Part-time faculty:** 679 total; 19% have terminal degrees, 7% minority, 54% women. **Class size:** 27% < 20, 52% 20-39, 10% 40-49, 7% 50-99, 4% >100. **Special facilities:** Performing arts center, technology center, natural area and world center for birds of prey research.

Freshman class profile. 5,298 applied, 4,291 admitted, 2,330 enrolled.

Mid 50% test scores			
SAT critical reading:	460-570	Rank in top quarter:	36%
SAT math:	480-580	Rank in top tenth:	12%
SAT writing:	450-550	End year in good standing:	88%
ACT composite:	20-25	Return as sophomores:	69%
GPA 3.75 or higher:	20%	Out-of-state:	31%
GPA 3.50-3.74:	19%	Live on campus:	48%
GPA 3.0-3.49:	40%	International:	3%
GPA 2.0-2.99:	21%	Fraternities:	1%
		Sororities:	1%

Basis for selection. Admission based on GPA and SAT/ACT. Applicants without high school diploma or GED may petition for admission. Interview required for nursing majors. **Home schooled:** State high school equivalency certificate required.

High school preparation. College-preparatory program recommended. 15 units recommended. Recommended units include English 4, mathematics 3, social studies 3, science 3 and foreign language 1. One unit foreign language, humanities, or fine arts and 1.5 units other college preparatory also recommended.

2011-2012 Annual costs. Tuition/fees: $5,566; $15,966 out-of-state. Room/board: $6,020. Books/supplies: $1,200. Personal expenses: $2,692.

2011-2012 Financial aid. Need-based: 1,604 full-time freshmen applied for aid; 1,555 were judged to have need; 1,555 of these received aid. Average need met was 20%. Average scholarship/grant was $4,267; average loan $5,253. 33% of total undergraduate aid awarded as scholarships/grants, 67% as loans/jobs. **Non-need-based:** Awarded to 1,735 full-time undergraduates, including 748 freshmen. Scholarships awarded for academics, athletics, music/drama, ROTC, state residency.

Application procedures. Admission: Closing date 5/15 (postmark date). $60 fee. Admission notification on a rolling basis beginning on or about 2/15. Strongly recommended that students apply January-March. **Financial aid:** Priority date 4/1; no closing date. FAFSA required. Applicants notified on a rolling basis starting 6/1; must reply within 2 week(s) of notification.

Academics. Basque studies program abroad. **Special study options:** Distance learning, double major, dual enrollment of high school students, exchange student, honors, independent study, internships, student-designed major, study abroad, teacher certification program, weekend college. **Credit/placement by examination:** AP, CLEP, SAT, ACT, institutional tests. 21 credit hours maximum toward associate degree, 42 toward bachelor's. **Support services:** Learning center, pre-admission summer program, reduced course load, remedial instruction, study skills assistance, tutoring, writing center.

Honors college/program. 3.5 GPA, 27 ACT or 1200 SAT required.

Majors. Area/ethnic studies: General. **Biology:** General. **Business:** Accounting, construction management, finance, human resources, international, management information systems, managerial economics, market

research, marketing, operations. **Communications:** Communications/speech/rhetoric, journalism, media studies. **Computer sciences:** Computer science, information systems. **Conservation:** Environmental studies. **Education:** General, art, bilingual, biology, chemistry, elementary, English, French, German, history, mathematics, music, physical, physics, science, social science, social studies, Spanish, special ed, speech. **Engineering:** Civil, electrical, mechanical. **English:** English lit. **Foreign languages:** French, German, Spanish. **Health services:** Athletic training, environmental health, medical radiologic technology/radiation therapy, medical records admin, nursing (RN), predental, premedicine, preveterinary, respiratory therapy technology. **History:** General. **Human services:** Social work. **Liberal arts:** Arts/sciences. **Math:** General, applied. **Parks/recreation:** Exercise sciences, health/fitness. **Philosophy/religion:** Philosophy. **Physical sciences:** Chemistry, geology, geophysics, materials science, physics. **Protective services:** Law enforcement admin. **Psychology:** General. **Social sciences:** General, anthropology, economics, political science, sociology. **Visual/performing arts:** Art, art history/conservation, commercial/advertising art, dramatic, music management, music performance, music theory/composition.

Most popular majors. Business/marketing 23%, communications/journalism 6%, education 9%, health sciences 15%, social sciences 6%.

Computing on campus. 900 workstations in dormitories, library, computer center. Dormitories wired for high-speed internet access and linked to campus network. Commuter students can connect to campus network. Online course registration, online library, helpline, wireless network available.

Student life. Freshman orientation: Mandatory, $75 fee. Preregistration for classes offered. **Housing:** Coed dorms, single-sex dorms, special housing for disabled, apartments, fraternity/sorority housing, wellness housing available. $225 fully refundable deposit, deadline 7/1. **Activities:** Bands, choral groups, dance, drama, international student organizations, literary magazine, music ensembles, musical theater, radio station, student government, student newspaper, symphony orchestra, TV station, black student union, Native American association, Organization de Estudiantes Latino-Americanos, Latter-day Saints student association, Alternative Mobility Adventure Seekers.

Athletics. NCAA. **Intercollegiate:** Basketball, cheerleading, cross-country, football (tackle) M, golf, gymnastics W, soccer W, softball W, swimming W, tennis, track and field, volleyball W, wrestling M. **Intramural:** Baseball M, basketball, bowling, handball, racquetball, rodeo, soccer M, softball W, swimming, tennis, volleyball W. **Team name:** Broncos.

Student services. Adult student services, alcohol/substance abuse counseling, career counseling, student employment services, financial aid counseling, health services, legal services, minority student services, on-campus daycare, personal counseling, placement for graduates, veterans' counselor, women's services. **Physically disabled:** Services for visually, speech, hearing impaired.

Contact. E-mail: bsuinfo@boisestate.edu
Phone: (208) 426-1156 Toll-free number: (800) 824-7017
Fax: (208) 426-3765
Jenny Cerda, Director of Admissions, Boise State University, 1910 University Drive, Boise, ID 83725

Brigham Young University-Idaho
Rexburg, Idaho
www.byui.edu   CB code: 4657

▶ Private 4-year university affiliated with Church of Jesus Christ of Latter-day Saints

▶ Residential campus in large town

▶ 14,999 degree-seeking undergraduates

▶ 97% of applicants admitted

▶ SAT or ACT (ACT writing optional), application essay required

General. Founded in 1888. Regionally accredited. **Degrees:** 2,976 bachelor's, 1,113 associate awarded. **ROTC:** Army. **Location:** 30 miles from Idaho Falls, 240 miles from Salt Lake City. **Calendar:** Semester, extensive summer session. **Full-time faculty:** 470 total. **Part-time faculty:** 165 total. **Special facilities:** Observatory, planetarium, livestock center, off-campus outdoor educational facility, leadership and service institute, arboretum, horticultural gardens.

Freshman class profile. 5,600 applied, 5,426 admitted, 3,024 enrolled.

Mid 50% test scores			
SAT critical reading:	470-570	GPA 3.75 or higher:	23%
SAT math:	480-580	GPA 3.50-3.74:	30%
ACT composite:	20-25	GPA 3.0-3.49:	40%
		GPA 2.0-2.99:	7%

Basis for selection. Religious affiliation, recommendations most important. High school record, test scores, personal essay, extracurricular activities also important. Interview with student's ecclesiastical leader required. Auditions required for music, dance, theater majors. **Home schooled:** GED or Compass test and ACT or SAT required.

2011-2012 Annual costs. Tuition/fees: $3,770. Tuition for students who are not members of The Church of Jesus Christ of Latter-day Saints is $6,940 for academic year. Room/board: $7,590. Books/supplies: $1,110. Personal expenses: $2,020.

Financial aid. Non-need-based: Scholarships awarded for academics, alumni affiliation, art, leadership, music/drama. **Additional information:** Application deadline for merit scholarships 3/1.

Application procedures. Admission: Priority date 12/1; deadline 2/1 (postmark date). $35 fee. Application must be submitted online. Admission notification by 4/1. Admission notification on a rolling basis beginning on or about 10/15. **Financial aid:** Priority date 5/1; no closing date. FAFSA required. Applicants notified on a rolling basis starting 2/1.

Academics. Special study options: Accelerated study, distance learning, double major, independent study, internships, student-designed major, study abroad, teacher certification program, urban semester. **Credit/placement by examination:** AP, CLEP, IB, institutional tests. **Support services:** Learning center, reduced course load, remedial instruction, study skills assistance, tutoring, writing center.

Majors. Architecture: Interior. **Biology:** General, zoology. **Business:** Accounting, business admin. **Communications:** Advertising, broadcast journalism, communications/speech/rhetoric, journalism, public relations. **Computer sciences:** General, computer science. **Conservation:** Environmental science, wildlife/wilderness. **Education:** Art, biology, chemistry, drama/dance, elementary, English, family/consumer sciences, history, mathematics, music, physics, science, social studies, Spanish. **Engineering:** Computer, mechanical. **English:** English lit, writing. **General:** Agronomy, animal sciences, horticulture. **Health services:** Nursing (RN), predental, premedicine, prepharmacy, preveterinary. **History:** General. **Liberal arts:** Arts/sciences. **Math:** General. **Parks/recreation:** General. **Physical sciences:** Chemistry, geology, physics. **Psychology:** General. **Social sciences:** Economics, international relations, political science, sociology. **Visual/performing arts:** Art, interior design, music, photography. **Work/family studies:** Food/nutrition.

Most popular majors. Agriculture 7%, biology 7%, education 20%, health sciences 7%, liberal arts 6%, social sciences 6%, visual/performing arts 10%.

Computing on campus. PC or laptop required. 2,500 workstations in dormitories, library, computer center, student center. Dormitories wired for high-speed internet access and linked to campus network. Commuter students can connect to campus network. Online course registration, online library, helpline, student web hosting, wireless network available.

Student life. Freshman orientation: Available. Preregistration for classes offered. **Policies:** Students encouraged to attend weekly devotional at which noted church leaders speak. Religious observance required. **Housing:** Single-sex dorms, apartments, wellness housing available. $175 deposit. **Activities:** Bands, choral groups, dance, drama, international student organizations, literary magazine, music ensembles, musical theater, radio station, student government, student newspaper, symphony orchestra, TV station, Lambda Delta Sigma, Sigma Gamma Chi, business club, married student association, outdoor club.

Athletics. Intramural: Archery, badminton, baseball, basketball, bowling, cheerleading, cross-country, diving, fencing, field hockey, football (nontackle), football (tackle), golf, ice hockey, lacrosse, racquetball, rodeo, skiing, skin diving, soccer, softball, swimming, table tennis, tennis, track and field, volleyball, water polo, wrestling M. **Team name:** Vikings.

Student services. Career counseling, student employment services, financial aid counseling, health services, personal counseling, placement for graduates, veterans' counselor. **Physically disabled:** Services for visually, hearing impaired.

Contact. E-mail: admissions@byui.edu
Phone: (208) 496-1300 Fax: (208) 496-1303
Tyler Williams, Director of Admissions, Brigham Young University-Idaho, 120 Kimball Building, Rexburg, ID 83460-1615

College of Idaho
Caldwell, Idaho   CB member
www.collegeofidaho.edu   CB code: 4060

▶ Private 4-year liberal arts college

▶ Residential campus in large town

- 1,007 degree-seeking undergraduates: 4% part-time, 58% women, 1% African American, 2% Asian American, 13% Hispanic American, 1% Native American, 10% international
- 18 degree-seeking graduate students
- 66% of applicants admitted
- SAT or ACT (ACT writing optional), application essay required
- 63% graduate within 6 years

General. Founded in 1891. Regionally accredited. **Degrees:** 207 bachelor's awarded; master's offered. **ROTC:** Army. **Location:** 30 miles from Boise. **Calendar:** 13-4-13. **Full-time faculty:** 74 total; 88% have terminal degrees, 5% minority, 43% women. **Part-time faculty:** 27 total; 11% have terminal degrees, 7% minority, 52% women. **Class size:** 62% < 20, 32% 20-39, 4% 40-49, 2% 50-99. **Special facilities:** Planetarium, herbarium, center for the performing and fine arts, art gallery, natural history museum.

Freshman class profile. 1,185 applied, 777 admitted, 246 enrolled.

Mid 50% test scores			
SAT critical reading:	440-630	Rank in top quarter:	68%
SAT math:	480-620	Rank in top tenth:	34%
SAT writing:	450-590	End year in good standing:	93%
ACT composite:	22-27	Return as sophomores:	80%
GPA 3.75 or higher:	48%	Out-of-state:	15%
GPA 3.50-3.74:	21%	International:	8%
GPA 3.0-3.49:	23%	Fraternities:	10%
GPA 2.0-2.99:	8%	Sororities:	20%

Basis for selection. Academic record, test scores, extracurricular activities, essay, teacher recommendation important. Interview and essay recommended. Audition required of music, theater majors. Portfolio required of art majors. **Home schooled:** Transcript of courses and grades, letter of recommendation (nonparent) required. Course descriptions required. **Learning Disabled:** Student must submit a request for accommodations, submit appropriate documentation of the diagnosed disability from a qualified treatment provider completed within the last 3 years; provide a signed release of information form with contact information to the Student Disability Services Office; and schedule an appointment with the Disability Services Coordinator.

High school preparation. College-preparatory program recommended. 15 units required; 20 recommended. Required and recommended units include English 4, mathematics 3-4, social studies 2, history 3, science 2-4, foreign language 4 and academic electives 3.

2012-2013 Annual costs. Tuition/fees: $22,975. Room/board: $8,113. Books/supplies: $1,200. Personal expenses: $700.

2011-2012 Financial aid. Need-based: 182 full-time freshmen applied for aid; 182 were judged to have need; 182 of these received aid. Average need met was 82%. Average scholarship/grant was $11,054; average loan $3,874. 62% of total undergraduate aid awarded as scholarships/grants, 38% as loans/jobs. **Non-need-based:** Awarded to 1,046 full-time undergraduates, including 237 freshmen. Scholarships awarded for academics, alumni affiliation, art, athletics, leadership, minority status, music/drama, religious affiliation, ROTC.

Application procedures. Admission: Priority date 2/15; deadline 8/1 (postmark date). No application fee. Admission notification on a rolling basis beginning on or about 10/15. **Financial aid:** Priority date 2/15; no closing date. FAFSA, institutional form required. Applicants notified on a rolling basis starting 2/1; must reply within 3 week(s) of notification.

Academics. Special study options: Combined bachelor's/graduate degree, cross-registration, double major, dual enrollment of high school students, ESL, honors, independent study, internships, study abroad, teacher certification program, Washington semester. BS/Pharm.D, Pharmacy - Idaho State University, BS/BS, Clinical Lab Science - Idaho State University, BS/BS, Nursing - Idaho State University, BS/BS, Speech Language Pathology & Audiology - Idaho State University, BS/BS, Environmental Architecture - St. John International University, BA or BS/JD, Law - University of Idaho. **Credit/placement by examination:** AP, CLEP, IB, SAT, ACT. **Support services:** Learning center, reduced course load, study skills assistance, tutoring, writing center.

Majors. Architecture: Environmental design. **Biology:** General. **Business:** Accounting, business admin. **Conservation:** Environmental studies. **Education:** Elementary, multi-level teacher, physical. **English:** Creative writing, English lit. **Foreign languages:** Spanish. **Health services:** Audiology/speech pathology, clinical lab science, prenursing, prepharmacy. **History:** General. **Math:** General, applied. **Parks/recreation:** Exercise sciences. **Philosophy/ religion:** Philosophy, religion. **Physical sciences:** Chemistry. **Psychology:** General. **Social sciences:** International relations, political science, sociology/ anthropology. **Visual/performing arts:** Dramatic, music, music theory/composition, studio arts.

Most popular majors. Biology 13%, business/marketing 15%, history 10%, psychology 7%, social sciences 10%, visual/performing arts 14%.

Computing on campus. 250 workstations in dormitories, library, computer center, student center. Dormitories wired for high-speed internet access and linked to campus network. Commuter students can connect to campus network. Online course registration, online library, helpline, repair service, student web hosting, wireless network available.

Student life. Freshman orientation: Mandatory. Preregistration for classes offered. One-day sessions to assist students and parents. **Policies:** Freshmen, sophomores and juniors under age 21 must live on campus unless living with parents or relatives. All buildings smoke-free. Honor Code has been implemented for all students. **Housing:** Guaranteed on-campus for freshmen. Coed dorms, special housing for disabled, apartments, fraternity/ sorority housing, wellness housing available. $300 fully refundable deposit, deadline 8/1. Academic communities (min GPA). **Activities:** Bands, campus ministries, choral groups, dance, drama, international student organizations, literary magazine, music ensembles, Model UN, musical theater, opera, student government, student newspaper, symphony orchestra, Over 75 activities or organizations.

Athletics. NAIA. **Intercollegiate:** Baseball M, basketball, cross-country, golf, skiing, soccer, softball W, swimming, tennis, track and field, volleyball W. **Intramural:** Badminton, basketball, football (non-tackle), soccer, softball, volleyball. **Team name:** Coyotes.

Student services. Alcohol/substance abuse counseling, chaplain/spiritual director, career counseling, student employment services, financial aid counseling, health services, minority student services, personal counseling, placement for graduates, women's services. **Physically disabled:** Services for hearing impaired.

Contact. E-mail: admissions@collegeofidaho.edu
Phone: (208) 459-5305 Toll-free number: (800) 224-3246
Fax: (208) 459-5757
Brian Bava, Dean of Enrollment, College of Idaho, 2112 Cleveland Boulevard, Caldwell, ID 83605-4432

Idaho State University
Pocatello, Idaho
www.isu.edu   CB code: 4355

- Public 4-year university
- Commuter campus in small city
- 10,275 degree-seeking undergraduates: 1% African American, 1% Asian American, 8% Hispanic American, 2% Native American, 3% international
- 2,051 graduate students
- 93% of applicants admitted
- SAT or ACT (ACT writing optional) required

General. Founded in 1901. Regionally accredited. Designated by State Board of Education as institution specializing in health-related programs. **Degrees:** 1,103 bachelor's, 348 associate awarded; master's, professional, doctoral offered. **ROTC:** Army. **Location:** 150 miles from Salt Lake City, 230 miles from Boise. **Calendar:** Semester, limited summer session. **Full-time faculty:** 599 total; 8% minority, 45% women. **Part-time faculty:** 247 total; 6% minority, 54% women. **Class size:** 52% < 20, 35% 20-39, 9% 40-49, 4% 50-99, less than 1% >100. **Special facilities:** Natural history museum, multi-purpose housing/classroom/meeting facility, accelerator center, geographical information systems center, performing arts center.

Freshman class profile. 3,253 applied, 3,035 admitted, 1,935 enrolled.

Mid 50% test scores			
		GPA 3.0-3.49:	27%
SAT critical reading:	450-570	GPA 2.0-2.99:	35%
SAT math:	480-630	Rank in top quarter:	28%
SAT writing:	450-560	Rank in top tenth:	10%
ACT composite:	18-24	Out-of-state:	7%
GPA 3.75 or higher:	19%	Live on campus:	24%
GPA 3.50-3.74:	16%	International:	6%

Basis for selection. For general admissions, predicted GPA of 1.5 (based on core GPA and test scores). Students not meeting those standards can be admitted conditionally or by petition or admission will be deferred. TOEFL, IELTS, Compass English, and SAT Critical Reading required for international students. US High School graduates with an "A" or "B" in English and students who completed ELS Language Centers level 112 are exempted. Students from countries where English is the official language can be exempted based on academic performance. ACT recommended. ACT preferred. Students 21 years or older are exempt from submitting ACT/SAT scores. Interview recommended. Audition recommended for music majors.

Portfolio recommended for experiential credit-seeking applicants. **Home schooled:** Students need to complete their GED along with taking the ACT or SAT test.

High school preparation. College-preparatory program required. 16 units required. Required units include English 4, mathematics 3, social studies 2.5, science 3 (laboratory 1) and foreign language 1. 1.5 Units in humanities,speech,studion/performing arts also required.

2011-2012 Annual costs. Tuition/fees: $5,796; $17,032 out-of-state. Room/board: $5,616. Books/supplies: $900. Personal expenses: $2,830.

2010-2011 Financial aid. Need-based: 1,291 full-time freshmen applied for aid; 1,114 were judged to have need; 1,093 of these received aid. Average need met was 53%. Average scholarship/grant was $4,671; average loan $3,188. 37% of total undergraduate aid awarded as scholarships/grants, 63% as loans/jobs. **Non-need-based:** Awarded to 1,968 full-time undergraduates, including 666 freshmen. Scholarships awarded for academics, alumni affiliation, art, athletics, leadership, minority status, music/drama, ROTC, state residency.

Application procedures. Admission: No deadline. $40 fee, may be waived for applicants with need. Admission notification on a rolling basis beginning on or about 3/1. High school students who graduate early may petition admissions committee to enroll full time. **Financial aid:** Priority date 3/1; no closing date. FAFSA required. Applicants notified on a rolling basis starting 4/1.

Academics. Special study options: Accelerated study, combined bachelor's/graduate degree, cooperative education, cross-registration, distance learning, double major, dual enrollment of high school students, ESL, exchange student, honors, independent study, internships, liberal arts/career combination, student-designed major, study abroad, teacher certification program, weekend college. **Credit/placement by examination:** AP, CLEP, IB, SAT, ACT, institutional tests. 32 credit hours maximum toward associate degree, 64 toward bachelor's. A student is unable to receive credit by challenge exam for courses already taken, or for courses that are prerequisites to courses already completed. **Support services:** Learning center, remedial instruction, study skills assistance, tutoring, writing center.

Majors. Area/ethnic studies: American. **Biology:** General, biochemistry, botany, ecology, microbiology, zoology. **Business:** General, accounting, business admin, finance, human resources, insurance, marketing. **Communications:** Communications/speech/rhetoric, media studies. **Computer sciences:** General, computer graphics, information systems. **Conservation:** Environmental science. **Education:** Early childhood, elementary, health, music, physical, secondary, special ed. **Engineering:** Civil, electrical, mechanical, nuclear. **English:** English lit. **Foreign languages:** French, German, sign language interpretation, Spanish. **Health services:** Audiology/speech pathology, clinical lab science, dental hygiene, dietetics, health care admin, medical radiologic technology/radiation therapy, nursing (RN). **History:** General. **Human services:** Social work. **Math:** General, statistics. **Philosophy/religion:** Philosophy. **Physical sciences:** Chemistry, geology, physics. **Protective services:** Firefighting. **Psychology:** General. **Social sciences:** Anthropology, economics, international relations, political science, sociology. **Visual/performing arts:** Art, dramatic, music, music performance. **Work/family studies:** General.

Most popular majors. Biology 8%, business/marketing 15%, education 14%, engineering/engineering technologies 6%, health sciences 24%, social sciences 7%.

Computing on campus. 697 workstations in dormitories, library, computer center, student center. Dormitories wired for high-speed internet access and linked to campus network. Commuter students can connect to campus network. Online course registration, online library, helpline, repair service, student web hosting, wireless network available.

Student life. Freshman orientation: Available. Preregistration for classes offered. Held several times before classes begin in both fall and spring semesters. **Policies:** In order for a student to be eligible for student housing he/she must be taking a minimum of 6 credits per semester and be working towards a degree. **Housing:** Coed dorms, single-sex dorms, special housing for disabled, apartments, fraternity/sorority housing, wellness housing available. $150 partly refundable deposit, deadline 8/23. Housing modified for disabled available on request, subject to waiting list. Graduate housing is also available. **Activities:** Bands, campus ministries, choral groups, dance, drama, international student organizations, literary magazine, music ensembles, musical theater, opera, radio station, student government, student newspaper, symphony orchestra, TV station, Newman Center, Latter-day Saints Institute, student ambassadors, Young Democrats, Young Republicans, Campus Crusade for Christ, Associated Black Students, Native Americans United, Cooperative Wilderness Handicapped Outdoor Group.

Athletics. NCAA. **Intercollegiate:** Basketball, cheerleading, cross-country, football (tackle) M, golf W, soccer W, softball W, tennis, track and field, volleyball W. **Intramural:** Badminton, basketball, bowling, fencing, football

(non-tackle) M, golf, judo, racquetball, soccer, softball, table tennis, tennis, volleyball. **Team name:** Bengals.

Student services. Adult student services, alcohol/substance abuse counseling, career counseling, student employment services, financial aid counseling, health services, legal services, minority student services, on-campus daycare, personal counseling, placement for graduates, veterans' counselor, women's services. **Physically disabled:** Services for visually, speech, hearing impaired.

Contact. E-mail: admiss@isu.edu
Phone: (208) 282-2475 Fax: (208) 282-4511
Laura McKenzie, Director, Idaho State University, 921 South 8th Stop 8270, Pocatello, ID 83209-8270

ITT Technical Institute: Boise
Boise, Idaho
www.itt-tech.edu   CB code: 3596

- For-profit 4-year technical college
- Commuter campus in small city
- 555 degree-seeking undergraduates
- Interview required

General. Founded in 1906. Accredited by ACICS. **Degrees:** 28 bachelor's, 117 associate awarded. **Calendar:** Quarter, extensive summer session. **Full-time faculty:** 14 total. **Part-time faculty:** 39 total.

Basis for selection. Satisfactory scores from on-site English and mathematics tests required.

2011-2012 Annual costs. Estimated costs as of June 2011: per-credit-hour charge, $493, depending upon level and course of study; academic fee, $200. Certain programs of study require purchase of tools, which could cost an additional $100 to $500. All costs are subject to change.

Application procedures. Admission: No deadline. $100 fee. Admission notification on a rolling basis. **Financial aid:** No deadline. FAFSA, institutional form required. Applicants notified on a rolling basis.

Academics. Credit/placement by examination: AP, CLEP. **Support services:** Tutoring.

Majors. Business: Business admin, construction management. **Communications technology:** Animation/special effects. **Computer sciences:** Programming, security. **Protective services:** Law enforcement admin.

Computing on campus. Online library available.

Student life. Freshman orientation: Available. Preregistration for classes offered.

Student services. Career counseling, student employment services, placement for graduates.

Contact. Phone: (208) 322-8844 Toll-free number: (800) 666-4888 Fax: (208) 322-0173
Terry Lowder, Director of Recruitment, ITT Technical Institute: Boise, 12302 West Explorer Drive, Boise, ID 83713-1529

Lewis-Clark State College
Lewiston, Idaho
www.lcsc.edu   CB code: 4385

- Public 4-year liberal arts and technical college
- Commuter campus in small city
- 3,477 degree-seeking undergraduates: 22% part-time, 60% women, 1% African American, 1% Asian American, 5% Hispanic American, 3% Native American, 3% international
- 63% of applicants admitted

General. Founded in 1893. Regionally accredited. Courses offered at outreach centers (Orofino, Grangeville, Coeur d'Alene, Kamiah, and Lapwai). **Degrees:** 420 bachelor's, 158 associate awarded. **ROTC:** Army, Naval, Air Force. **Location:** 300 miles from Boise, 100 miles from Spokane, Washington. **Calendar:** Semester, limited summer session. **Full-time faculty:** 159 total; 67% have terminal degrees, 3% minority, 56% women. **Part-time faculty:** 90 total; 68% women. **Class size:** 53% < 20, 45% 20-39, less than 1% 40-49, less than 1% 50-99, less than 1% >100. **Special facilities:**

Biodiversity museum and collection, geographical information systems center, observatory.

Freshman class profile. 1,365 applied, 866 admitted, 625 enrolled.

Mid 50% test scores			
SAT critical reading:	440-550	GPA 3.0-3.49:	28%
SAT math:	430-530	GPA 2.0-2.99:	42%
ACT composite:	17-22	Rank in top quarter:	14%
GPA 3.75 or higher:	12%	Rank in top tenth:	4%
GPA 3.50-3.74:	12%	Out-of-state:	19%
		International:	1%

Basis for selection. High school courses, GPA, test scores considered. Non-native speakers may be required to take ESL classes until they can pass TOEFL. ACT and SAT may be accepted for all students. Students may be asked to take COMPASS test under certain circumstances. **Home schooled:** Must have predicted college GPA of 2.0 based on ACT or SAT. Must have acceptable performance on 2 testing indicators: GED score of 500 (50 if tested before 2002) or higher, or other standardized diagnostic test such as ACT, SAT, COMPASS, ASSET, or CPT.

High school preparation. College-preparatory program required. 15 units required. Required units include English 4, mathematics 3, social studies 2.5, science 3 (laboratory 2), academic electives 1.5.

2011-2012 Annual costs. Tuition/fees: $5,348; $14,880 out-of-state. Room/board: $6,100. Books/supplies: $1,520. Personal expenses: $1,960.

2010-2011 Financial aid. Need-based: 557 full-time freshmen applied for aid; 494 were judged to have need; 486 of these received aid. Average need met was 6%. Average scholarship/grant was $4,525; average loan $2,938. 51% of total undergraduate aid awarded as scholarships/grants, 49% as loans/jobs. **Non-need-based:** Awarded to 690 full-time undergraduates, including 247 freshmen. Scholarships awarded for academics, alumni affiliation, art, athletics, leadership, minority status, music/drama.

Application procedures. Admission: No deadline. $35 fee. Admission notification on a rolling basis. **Financial aid:** Priority date 3/1; no closing date. FAFSA required. Applicants notified on a rolling basis starting 4/15; must reply within 2 week(s) of notification.

Academics. Communications/speech lab to help students prepare for speeches and presentations. **Special study options:** Accelerated study, cooperative education, distance learning, dual enrollment of high school students, ESL, independent study, internships, study abroad, teacher certification program. **Credit/placement by examination:** AP, CLEP, IB, SAT, ACT, institutional tests. 16 credit hours maximum toward associate degree, 32 toward bachelor's. **Support services:** Learning center, reduced course load, remedial instruction, study skills assistance, tutoring, writing center.

Majors. Biology: General. **Business:** Accounting technology, administrative services, business admin, hospitality admin, small business admin. **Communications:** Communications/speech/rhetoric. **Communications technology:** Graphic/printing. **Computer sciences:** General, computer science, webmaster. **Education:** Elementary, English, mathematics, physical, science, social science. **English:** Creative writing, English lit. **Health services:** Management/clinical assistant, nursing (RN), office assistant. **Human services:** Social work. **Math:** General. **Parks/recreation:** Exercise sciences. **Physical sciences:** Chemistry. **Protective services:** Corrections, criminal justice, firefighting. **Psychology:** General. **Social sciences:** General. **Work/family studies:** Child development.

Most popular majors. Business/marketing 22%, education 12%, health sciences 19%, parks/recreation 6%, public administration/social services 10%, security/protective services 7%.

Computing on campus. 455 workstations in dormitories, library, computer center, student center. Dormitories wired for high-speed internet access and linked to campus network. Commuter students can connect to campus network. Online course registration, helpline, student web hosting, wireless network available.

Student life. Freshman orientation: Available. Preregistration for classes offered. One-day session held in August. **Housing:** Coed dorms, apartments available. $200 partly refundable deposit. **Activities:** Jazz band, campus ministries, drama, international student organizations, literary magazine, radio station, student government, student newspaper, Native American Indian student organization, ambassadors' club, criminal justice society, Idaho student lobby, business students organization, Latter-day Saints student association, College Democrats, College Republicans.

Athletics. NAIA. **Intercollegiate:** Baseball M, basketball, cross-country, golf, tennis, track and field W, volleyball W. **Intramural:** Badminton, baseball, basketball, bowling, field hockey, football (non-tackle), golf, lacrosse, racquetball, rugby M, skiing, soccer, softball, table tennis, tennis, volleyball, weight lifting. **Team name:** Warriors.

Student services. Adult student services, alcohol/substance abuse counseling, career counseling, services for economically disadvantaged, student employment services, financial aid counseling, health services, minority student services, on-campus daycare, personal counseling, placement for graduates, veterans' counselor, women's services. **Physically disabled:** Services for visually, speech, hearing impaired.

Contact. E-mail: admissions@lcsc.edu
Phone: (208) 792-2210 Toll-free number: (800) 933-5272
Fax: (208) 792-2876
Diane Douglas, Registrar/Director of Admissions, Lewis-Clark State College, 500 Eighth Avenue, Lewiston, ID 83501-2698

New Saint Andrews College
Moscow, Idaho
www.nsa.edu   CB code: 3855

- Private 4-year liberal arts college
- Residential campus in large town
- 141 degree-seeking undergraduates: 9% part-time, 52% women
- 19 degree-seeking graduate students
- 77% of applicants admitted
- SAT or ACT (ACT writing optional), application essay required

General. Regionally accredited; also accredited by TRACS. **Degrees:** 15 bachelor's, 12 associate awarded; master's offered. **Calendar:** Quarter. **Full-time faculty:** 6 total; 67% have terminal degrees. **Part-time faculty:** 10 total; 40% have terminal degrees. **Class size:** 38% < 20, 48% 20-39, 5% 40-49, 10% 50-99.

Freshman class profile. 87 applied, 67 admitted, 44 enrolled.

Basis for selection. Academic achievement and test scores very important.

2012-2013 Annual costs. Tuition/fees (projected): $10,750. Books/supplies: $1,200.

Application procedures. Admission: Priority date 12/1; deadline 8/1 (postmark date). $40 fee, may be waived for applicants with need. Admission notification on a rolling basis beginning on or about 12/10. **Financial aid:** Priority date 2/15; no closing date. Institutional form required.

Academics. Special study options: Dual enrollment of high school students, independent study. **Credit/placement by examination:** AP, CLEP.

Majors. Liberal arts: Arts/sciences.

Computing on campus. Online course registration, wireless network available.

Student life. Freshman orientation: Mandatory. Preregistration for classes offered. **Housing:** Coed dorms available. **Activities:** Campus ministries, choral groups.

Contact. E-mail: admissions@nsa.edu
Phone: (208) 882-1566 ext. 113 Fax: (208) 882-4293
Brenda Schlect, Director of Admissions, New Saint Andrews College, PO Box 9025, Moscow, ID 83843

Northwest Nazarene University
Nampa, Idaho
www.nnu.edu   CB code: 4544

- Private 4-year university affiliated with Church of the Nazarene
- Residential campus in small city
- 1,256 degree-seeking undergraduates: 8% part-time, 58% women
- 730 graduate students
- SAT or ACT (ACT writing optional), application essay required

General. Founded in 1913. Regionally accredited. **Degrees:** 251 bachelor's awarded; master's offered. **ROTC:** Army, Air Force. **Location:** 18 miles from Boise. **Calendar:** Semester, limited summer session. **Full-time faculty:** 108 total; 71% have terminal degrees, 6% minority, 43% women. **Part-time faculty:** 4 total; 25% have terminal degrees, 25% women. **Class size:** 46% < 20, 40% 20-39, 9% 40-49, 5% 50-99. **Special facilities:** Depository for federal government publications.

Freshman class profile.

Mid 50% test scores			
SAT critical reading:	470-600	GPA 3.0-3.49:	23%
SAT math:	470-610	GPA 2.0-2.99:	17%
SAT writing:	460-590	Rank in top quarter:	47%
ACT composite:	20-27	Rank in top tenth:	24%
GPA 3.75 or higher:	37%	Out-of-state:	54%
GPA 3.50-3.74:	23%	Live on campus:	88%

Basis for selection. For unconditional admission 2 of following criteria must be met: minimum 2.5 high school GPA, class rank in top 50 percent, minimum ACT score of 18. Provisional admission available. Interview recommended for students with provisional admission.

High school preparation. College-preparatory program recommended. Recommended units include English 4, mathematics 3, history 3, science 3 and foreign language 2.

2012-2013 Annual costs. Tuition/fees (projected): $24,030. Room/board: $6,260. Books/supplies: $1,000. Personal expenses: $900.

Financial aid. Non-need-based: Scholarships awarded for academics, alumni affiliation, art, athletics, leadership, minority status, music/drama, religious affiliation, ROTC.

Application procedures. Admission: Priority date 3/1; deadline 8/15. $25 fee, may be waived for applicants with need. Admission notification on a rolling basis. **Financial aid:** Priority date 3/1; no closing date. FAFSA, institutional form required. Applicants notified on a rolling basis starting 3/1; must reply within 3 week(s) of notification.

Academics. Special study options: Accelerated study, combined bachelor's/graduate degree, cooperative education, cross-registration, distance learning, double major, ESL, exchange student, honors, independent study, internships, liberal arts/career combination, student-designed major, study abroad, teacher certification program. **Credit/placement by examination:** AP, CLEP, IB, SAT, ACT, institutional tests. 31 credit hours maximum toward bachelor's degree. **Support services:** Learning center, reduced course load, remedial instruction, study skills assistance, tutoring, writing center.

Majors. Biology: General, biochemistry, ecology, neuroscience. **Business:** Accounting, business admin, marketing, office management. **Communications:** Communications/speech/rhetoric, media studies. **Computer sciences:** Computer science. **Education:** General, art, biology, chemistry, elementary, English, health, history, mathematics, music, physical, physics, psychology, secondary, social science, Spanish. **Engineering:** Aerospace, applied physics, chemical, civil, electrical. **English:** English lit. **Foreign languages:** Spanish. **Health services:** Nursing (RN), physician assistant, predental, premedicine, prepharmacy, preveterinary. **History:** General. **Human services:** Social work. **Liberal arts:** Arts/sciences. **Math:** General. **Parks/recreation:** General, exercise sciences, health/fitness, sports admin. **Philosophy/religion:** Philosophy, religion. **Physical sciences:** Chemistry, physics. **Psychology:** General, industrial. **Social sciences:** General, international relations, political science. **Theology:** Bible, missionary, pastoral counseling, religious ed, sacred music, youth ministry. **Visual/performing arts:** Ceramics, graphic design, music, music performance, music theory/composition, piano/keyboard, voice/opera.

Most popular majors. Biology 7%, business/marketing 30%, education 13%, health sciences 11%, liberal arts 10%.

Computing on campus. 275 workstations in dormitories, library, computer center, student center. Dormitories wired for high-speed internet access and linked to campus network. Commuter students can connect to campus network. Online library, helpline, repair service, student web hosting, wireless network available.

Student life. Freshman orientation: Mandatory. Preregistration for classes offered. **Policies:** All students required to live on campus until senior year or age 21. Religious observance required. **Housing:** Guaranteed on-campus for all undergraduates. Single-sex dorms, apartments available. $50 fully refundable deposit. Some rental units available. **Activities:** Bands, campus ministries, choral groups, drama, international student organizations, literary magazine, music ensembles, musical theater, opera, student government, student newspaper, symphony orchestra, summer ministries, Circle-K, urban ministries club, social work clubs, Angels Ministry, PALS ministry, AIDS ministry, Fellowship of Christian Athletes, multicultural affairs club.

Athletics. NCAA. **Intercollegiate:** Baseball M, basketball, cross-country, golf M, soccer W, softball W, track and field, volleyball W. **Intramural:** Basketball, cross-country, football (non-tackle), softball, volleyball. **Team name:** Crusaders.

Student services. Adult student services, alcohol/substance abuse counseling, chaplain/spiritual director, career counseling, student employment services, financial aid counseling, health services, minority student services, personal counseling, placement for graduates. **Physically disabled:** Services for visually, hearing impaired.

Contact. E-mail: admissions@nnu.edu
Phone: (208) 467-8496 Toll-free number: (877) 668-4968
Fax: (208) 467-8645
Mike Marston, Director of Admissions, Northwest Nazarene University, 623 S. University Boulevard, Nampa, ID 83686-5897

University of Idaho
Moscow, Idaho
www.uidaho.edu   CB code: 4843

- Public 4-year university
- Residential campus in large town
- 9,221 degree-seeking undergraduates: 7% part-time, 47% women, 1% African American, 1% Asian American, 7% Hispanic American, 1% Native American, 2% international
- 2,522 degree-seeking graduate students
- 61% of applicants admitted
- SAT or ACT (ACT writing optional) required
- 51% graduate within 6 years

General. Founded in 1889. Regionally accredited. Residential land-grant university. **Degrees:** 1,681 bachelor's awarded; master's, professional, doctoral offered. **ROTC:** Army, Naval, Air Force. **Location:** 85 miles from Spokane, Washington. **Calendar:** Semester, extensive summer session. **Full-time faculty:** 544 total; 78% have terminal degrees, 13% minority, 33% women. **Part-time faculty:** 133 total; 20% have terminal degrees, 6% minority, 52% women. **Class size:** 41% < 20, 41% 20-39, 6% 40-49, 8% 50-99, 4% >100. **Special facilities:** Arboretum, CAVE IQ 3-D visualization image station, 18-hole golf course, art gallery, Lionel Hampton international jazz collection, indoor climbing facility.

Freshman class profile. 8,248 applied, 5,020 admitted, 1,631 enrolled.

Mid 50% test scores			
SAT critical reading:	480-600	Rank in top quarter:	44%
SAT math:	490-610	Rank in top tenth:	18%
SAT writing:	460-570	End year in good standing:	80%
ACT composite:	20-26	Return as sophomores:	80%
GPA 3.75 or higher:	23%	Out-of-state:	24%
GPA 3.50-3.74:	20%	Live on campus:	84%
GPA 3.0-3.49:	32%	International:	2%
GPA 2.0-2.99:	25%	Fraternities:	23%
		Sororities:	31%

Basis for selection. Applicants must have 3.0 GPA, or 2.2 to 3.0 GPA with high SAT/ACT scores. Recommendations, essay required of applicants with nonstandard high school diploma and adults long out of high school. **Home schooled:** Letter of recommendation (nonparent) required. Copy of GED test results, three signed letters of recommendation from individuals who know of and can attest to applicant's academic ability, a written statement from applicant including goals, education and/or professional objective, and explanation of past academic performance.

High school preparation. College-preparatory program recommended. 15 units required. Required units include English 4, mathematics 3, social studies 2.5, science 3 (laboratory 1), academic electives 1.5. Humanities and Foreign Language 1 unit: Courses should emphasize history, appreciation, theory, analysis, and/or critique; History courses beyond those required for state high school graduation may be counted, foreign language strongly recommended. For full course list, see http://www.uidaho.edu/futurestudents/admissions/admissionrequirements/corerequirements.

2011-2012 Annual costs. Tuition/fees: $5,856; $18,376 out-of-state. Room/board: $7,304. Books/supplies: $1,474. Personal expenses: $3,006.

2010-2011 Financial aid. Need-based: 1,521 full-time freshmen applied for aid; 1,188 were judged to have need; 1,165 of these received aid. Average need met was 79%. Average scholarship/grant was $4,544; average loan $5,618. 87% of total undergraduate aid awarded as scholarships/grants, 13% as loans/jobs. **Non-need-based:** Awarded to 6,934 full-time undergraduates, including 1,496 freshmen. Scholarships awarded for academics, alumni affiliation, art, athletics, leadership, minority status, music/drama, ROTC, state residency.

Application procedures. Admission: Priority date 2/15; deadline 8/1 (receipt date). $50 fee. Admission notification on a rolling basis. **Financial aid:** Priority date 2/15; no closing date. FAFSA required. Applicants notified on a rolling basis starting 3/30; must reply within 4 week(s) of notification.

Academics. Special study options: Accelerated study, combined bachelor's/graduate degree, cooperative education, cross-registration, distance

learning, double major, dual enrollment of high school students, ESL, exchange student, honors, independent study, internships, student-designed major, study abroad, teacher certification program. **Credit/placement by examination:** AP, CLEP, IB, SAT, ACT, institutional tests. 48 credit hours maximum toward bachelor's degree. **Support services:** Learning center, pre-admission summer program, reduced course load, remedial instruction, study skills assistance, tutoring, writing center.

Majors. Architecture: Interior, landscape. **Area/ethnic studies:** American, Latin American. **Biology:** General, biochemistry, conservation, microbiology, molecular. **Business:** Accounting, business admin, finance, human resources, management information systems, managerial economics, marketing. **Communications:** Advertising, digital media, journalism, organizational, public relations. **Communications technology:** Animation/special effects. **Computer sciences:** Computer science. **Conservation:** General, environmental science, fisheries, forest management, forest resources, forest sciences, management/policy, nature tourism, wildlife/wilderness, wood science. **Education:** General, agricultural, art, early childhood, elementary, English, music, physical, secondary. **Engineering:** Biological, chemical, civil, computer, electrical, materials, mechanical. **English:** Creative writing, English lit. **Foreign languages:** General, French, Spanish. **General:** Animal sciences, business, communications, economics, food science, horticultural science, mechanization, range science. **Health services:** Athletic training, clinical lab science. **History:** General. **Math:** General, applied. **Parks/recreation:** Exercise sciences, facilities management. **Philosophy/religion:** Philosophy. **Physical sciences:** Chemistry, geology, physics. **Psychology:** General. **Social sciences:** Anthropology, economics, geography, international relations, political science, sociology. **Visual/performing arts:** Art, dance, dramatic, interior design, music history, music management, music performance, music theory/composition, musical theater, studio arts, voice/opera. **Work/family studies:** Clothing/textiles, family studies, food/nutrition.

Most popular majors. Business/marketing 12%, communications/journalism 7%, education 9%, engineering/engineering technologies 8%, psychology 7%, social sciences 7%.

Computing on campus. 595 workstations in dormitories, library, computer center, student center. Dormitories wired for high-speed internet access and linked to campus network. Commuter students can connect to campus network. Online course registration, online library, helpline, repair service, student web hosting, wireless network available.

Student life. Freshman orientation: Available, $40 fee. Preregistration for classes offered. Two-day event held the week before classes start. **Policies:** First-year, first-time freshmen required to live on campus. **Housing:** Guaranteed on-campus for freshmen. Coed dorms, single-sex dorms, special housing for disabled, apartments, cooperative housing, fraternity/sorority housing available. $250 partly refundable deposit. **Activities:** Bands, campus ministries, choral groups, dance, drama, film society, international student organizations, literary magazine, music ensembles, Model UN, musical theater, opera, radio station, student government, student newspaper, symphony orchestra, TV station, Circle K International, environmental club, Engineers Without Borders, Intervarsity Christian Fellowship, Soil Stewards, Society of Professional Journalists, Moscow Pagan Society, Movimiento Activista Social.

Athletics. NCAA. **Intercollegiate:** Basketball, cross-country, diving W, football (tackle) M, golf, soccer W, swimming W, tennis, track and field, volleyball W. **Intramural:** Badminton, basketball, bowling, football (non-tackle), golf, racquetball, skiing, soccer, softball, swimming, table tennis, tennis, track and field, volleyball, weight lifting, wrestling M. **Team name:** Vandals.

Student services. Adult student services, alcohol/substance abuse counseling, chaplain/spiritual director, career counseling, services for economically disadvantaged, student employment services, financial aid counseling, health services, legal services, minority student services, on-campus daycare, personal counseling, placement for graduates, veterans' counselor, women's services. **Physically disabled:** Services for visually, speech, hearing impaired.

Contact. E-mail: admissions@uidaho.edu
Phone: (208) 885-6326 Toll-free number: (888) 884-3246
Fax: (208) 885-9119
Michael Loehring, Director of Admissions, University of Idaho, PO Box 444264, Moscow, ID 83844-4264

University of Phoenix: Idaho
Meridian, Idaho
www.phoenix.edu

- For-profit 4-year university
- Small city
- 486 degree-seeking undergraduates

General. Regionally accredited. **Degrees:** 75 bachelor's awarded; master's offered. **Calendar:** Differs by program. **Full-time faculty:** 24 total. **Part-time faculty:** 121 total.

Basis for selection. Open admission, but selective for some programs.

2011-2012 Annual costs. Estimated costs as of August 2011: per-credit-hour charge, $420 to $450, depending upon level and course of study; electronic course materials fee, $95, if applicable. Book and material charges may vary by course and program. All fees are subject to change.

Application procedures. Admission: No deadline. No application fee.

Academics. Credit/placement by examination: AP, CLEP.

Majors. Business: Accounting, business admin, marketing. **Computer sciences:** General, information technology, networking, webmaster. **Health services:** Facilities admin, health care admin. **Protective services:** Law enforcement admin. **Psychology:** General.

Contact. Marc Booker, Director of Admission and Evaluation, University of Phoenix: Idaho, 1422 South Tech Lane, Meridian, ID 83642-3014

Illinois

American Academy of Art
Chicago, Illinois
www.aaart.edu
CB code: 1013

- For-profit 4-year visual arts college
- Commuter campus in very large city
- 461 degree-seeking undergraduates
- Interview required

General. Founded in 1923. Accredited by ACCSC. **Degrees:** 54 bachelor's awarded; master's offered. **Location:** Downtown. **Calendar:** Semester, extensive summer session. **Full-time faculty:** 31 total. **Class size:** 76% < 20, 24% 20-39.

Freshman class profile. 349 applied, 318 admitted, 121 enrolled.

Basis for selection. Open admission.

2011-2012 Annual costs. Tuition/fees: $26,570. Books/supplies: $800.

Financial aid. Non-need-based: Scholarships awarded for art.

Application procedures. Admission: No deadline. $25 fee, may be waived for applicants with need. Admission notification on a rolling basis. Essay explaining desire to enter art school used for counseling purposes. **Financial aid:** No deadline. FAFSA, institutional form required. Applicants notified on a rolling basis.

Academics. Special study options: Accelerated study, independent study, internships, study abroad. **Credit/placement by examination:** AP, CLEP, institutional tests. **Support services:** Pre-admission summer program, tutoring.

Majors. Communications: Advertising. **Computer sciences:** Computer graphics. **Visual/performing arts:** General, commercial/advertising art, design, drawing, multimedia, painting, studio arts.

Computing on campus. 70 workstations in library, computer center.

Student life. Freshman orientation: Mandatory. Preregistration for classes offered. 1-day orientation held in week before classes start. **Activities:** Film society.

Student services. Career counseling, student employment services, personal counseling, placement for graduates, veterans' counselor.

Contact. E-mail: info@aaart.edu
Phone: (312) 461-0600 Toll-free number: (888) 461-0600
Fax: (312) 294-9570
Stuart Rosenbloom, Director of Admissions, American Academy of Art, 332 South Michigan Avenue, Suite 300, Chicago, IL 60604-4302

Argosy University: Chicago
Chicago, Illinois
www.argosy.edu/chicago
CB code: 3922

- For-profit 4-year university
- Very large city
- 209 degree-seeking undergraduates

General. Regionally accredited. Additional campuses in Northwest Chicago, Washington, D.C., Atlanta, Seattle, Tampa, Minneapolis/St. Paul, San Francisco Bay area, Dallas, Honolulu, Nashville, Phoenix, Sarasota, and Orange County, CA. **Degrees:** 27 bachelor's awarded; master's, professional, doctoral offered. **Calendar:** Differs by program, extensive summer session. **Full-time faculty:** 25 total. **Part-time faculty:** 128 total.

Basis for selection. 18 ACT, 850 SAT (exclusive of Writing) or passing score on institution's entrance exam required. Other requirements vary by program. SAT or ACT recommended.

2011-2012 Annual costs. Tuition/fees: $17,962.

Application procedures. Admission: Closing date 9/13. $50 fee. **Financial aid:** No deadline.

Academics. Special study options: Distance learning. **Credit/placement by examination:** AP, CLEP.

Majors. Business: Business admin. **Psychology:** General.

Most popular majors. Psychology 96%.

Computing on campus. Online library available.

Contact. Phone: (312) 201-0200 Toll-free number: (800) 626-4123
Christa Holton, Senior Director of Admissions, Argosy University: Chicago, 225 North Michigan Avenue, Suite 1300, Chicago, IL 60601

Argosy University: Schaumburg
Schaumburg, Illinois
www.argosy.edu/schaumburg
CB code: 6227

- For-profit 4-year university
- Small city
- 173 degree-seeking undergraduates

General. Regionally accredited. **Degrees:** 22 bachelor's awarded; master's, professional, doctoral offered. **Calendar:** Differs by program. **Full-time faculty:** 15 total. **Part-time faculty:** 78 total.

Basis for selection. Open admission.

2011-2012 Annual costs. Tuition/fees: $17,962.

Application procedures. Admission: No deadline. $50 fee.

Academics. Credit/placement by examination: AP, CLEP.

Majors. Business: Business admin. **Liberal arts:** Arts/sciences. **Protective services:** Police science. **Psychology:** General.

Contact. Phone: (847) 969-4910 Toll-free number: (866) 290-2777
Catherine Curran, Senior Director of Admissions, Argosy University: Schaumburg, 999 North Plaza Drive, Suite 111, Schaumburg, IL 60173-5403

Augustana College
Rock Island, Illinois
www.augustana.edu
CB member
CB code: 1025

- Private 4-year liberal arts college affiliated with Evangelical Lutheran Church in America
- Residential campus in large city
- 2,508 degree-seeking undergraduates: 1% part-time, 57% women, 3% African American, 2% Asian American, 6% Hispanic American, 1% international
- 62% of applicants admitted
- 76% graduate within 6 years

General. Founded in 1860. Regionally accredited. **Degrees:** 601 bachelor's awarded. **Location:** 165 miles from Chicago. **Calendar:** Quarter, limited summer session. **Full-time faculty:** 188 total; 90% have terminal degrees, 8% minority, 43% women. **Part-time faculty:** 119 total; 31% have terminal degrees, 8% minority, 56% women. **Class size:** 64% < 20, 33% 20-39, 1% 40-49, less than 1% 50-99. **Special facilities:** Educational technology center, planetarium/observatory, map library, geology museum, Swedish immigration research center, research foundation, 500 acres of environmental laboratories, scanning electron microscope, high-field NMR, x-ray diffractometer, scanning tunneling microscope, HeliFlux station magnetometer.

Freshman class profile. 4,609 applied, 2,838 admitted, 708 enrolled.

Mid 50% test scores		Rank in top quarter:	60%
ACT composite:	23-28	Rank in top tenth:	28%
GPA 3.75 or higher:	19%	Return as sophomores:	87%
GPA 3.50-3.74:	17%	Out-of-state:	15%
GPA 3.0-3.49:	36%	Live on campus:	97%
GPA 2.0-2.99:	27%	International:	1%

Basis for selection. GPA, class rank, test scores, high school curriculum most important. Extracurricular activities and essay important. Academic honors and special qualifications also considered. SAT or ACT recommended.

Test optional for those who interview and submit a photocopy of a graded high school paper. Interview and essay required of freshman honors program applicants, recommended for all applicants. Essay required of academically marginal applicants and for certain departmental programs. Portfolio required of applicants to some art programs. Audition recommended for music and theater majors.

High school preparation. College-preparatory program recommended. 16 units recommended. Required and recommended units include English 3-4, mathematics 3-4, social studies 1-2, history 1, science 3-4 (laboratory 2), foreign language 1-2 and academic electives 4.

2011-2012 Annual costs. Tuition/fees: $33,363. Room/board: $8,466. Books/supplies: $1,000.

Financial aid. Non-need-based: Scholarships awarded for academics, alumni affiliation, art, leadership, music/drama, religious affiliation.

Application procedures. Admission: Priority date 2/1; no deadline. $30 fee, may be waived for applicants with need. Admission notification on a rolling basis. **Financial aid:** Priority date 3/15; no closing date. FAFSA, institutional form required. Applicants notified on a rolling basis; must reply by 5/1.

Academics. Term-abroad programs in Asia, Europe, and South America. Internship programs in cities throughout United States and in South America, Europe, Asia, Africa, and Australia. Exchange programs with universities in People's Republic of China, Peru, and Sweden. Summer language study programs in Sweden, France, Ecuador and Israel. Team-taught, interdisciplinary honors sequence available. June registration for classes. **Special study options:** Accelerated study, combined bachelor's/graduate degree, double major, honors, independent study, internships, liberal arts/career combination, student-designed major, study abroad, teacher certification program. 3-2 forestry and environmental management program with Duke University, 3-2 landscape architecture program with University of Illinois at Urbana-Champaign, 3-2 engineering program with Washington University (MO), Iowa State University, University of Illinois at Urbana-Champaign, and Purdue University, 3-2 occupational therapy program with Washington University, early selection programs in dentistry with University of Iowa, study abroad programs in Asia, Europe, and South America. **Credit/placement by examination:** AP, CLEP, IB, ACT, institutional tests. More than 18 hours of credit by examination must be approved by the Dean of the College. **Support services:** Learning center, pre-admission summer program, reduced course load, study skills assistance, tutoring, writing center.

Majors. Area/ethnic studies: Asian, women's. **Biology:** General, biochemistry. **Business:** General, accounting, business admin, finance, international, management information systems, marketing. **Communications:** Communications/speech/rhetoric. **Computer sciences:** Computer science. **Conservation:** General. **Education:** General, art, biology, chemistry, elementary, English, foreign languages, French, German, history, mathematics, middle, music, physical, physics, science, secondary, social science, Spanish, speech. **Engineering:** Applied physics. **English:** English lit, rhetoric/composition. **Foreign languages:** Ancient Greek, classics, French, German, Latin, Scandinavian, Spanish. **Health services:** Audiology/speech pathology, predental, premedicine. **History:** General. **Human services:** General. **Liberal arts:** Arts/sciences. **Math:** General. **Philosophy/religion:** Philosophy, religion. **Physical sciences:** Chemistry, geology, physics, planetary. **Psychology:** General. **Social sciences:** Anthropology, economics, geography, political science, sociology. **Visual/performing arts:** Art, art history/conservation, dramatic, jazz, music, music performance, piano/keyboard, studio arts, voice/opera.

Most popular majors. Biology 21%, business/marketing 19%, education 12%, health sciences 8%, psychology 9%, social sciences 9%.

Computing on campus. 500 workstations in dormitories, library, computer center, student center. Dormitories wired for high-speed internet access and linked to campus network. Commuter students can connect to campus network. Online course registration, online library, helpline, repair service, student web hosting, wireless network available.

Student life. Freshman orientation: Mandatory. Preregistration for classes offered. Three-day program held before start of fall classes. **Policies:** Students represented on all major faculty/administrative committees and act as observers at Board of Trustees meetings. Student life governed by Bill of Student Rights and code of social conduct. Campus judiciary process includes student participation. Lower-division students not living with parents required to live on campus unless released to live off-campus by student services office. **Housing:** Guaranteed on-campus for all undergraduates. Coed dorms, single-sex dorms, apartments available. **Activities:** Bands, campus ministries, choral groups, dance, drama, international student organizations, literary magazine, music ensembles, Model UN, musical theater, opera, radio station, student government, student newspaper, symphony orchestra, black student union, Asian student organization, Latinos Unidos, Latin American council, multicultural programming board, feminist forum, Global Affect, Intervarsity Christian Fellowship, Catholic organization, Muslim student association, Viking Volunteers, College Republicans/Democrats, Habitat for Humanity, Amnesty International.

Athletics. NCAA. **Intercollegiate:** Baseball M, basketball, cross-country, diving, football (tackle) M, golf, lacrosse M, soccer, softball W, swimming, tennis, track and field, volleyball W, wrestling M. **Intramural:** Badminton, basketball, bowling, cross-country, fencing, football (non-tackle), golf, handball, racquetball, rowing (crew), skiing, soccer, softball, swimming M, table tennis, tennis, track and field, volleyball, water polo, wrestling M. **Team name:** Vikings.

Student services. Alcohol/substance abuse counseling, chaplain/spiritual director, career counseling, student employment services, financial aid counseling, health services, minority student services, personal counseling, placement for graduates, women's services. **Physically disabled:** Services for visually, speech, hearing impaired.

Contact. E-mail: admissions@augustana.edu
Phone: (309) 794-7341 Toll-free number: (800) 798-8100
Fax: (309) 794-8797
W. Kent Barnds, Vice President of Enrollment, Augustana College, 639 38th Street, Rock Island, IL 61201-2296

Aurora University
Aurora, Illinois
www.aurora.edu   CB code: 1027

- Private 4-year university
- Commuter campus in small city
- 2,778 degree-seeking undergraduates
- 74% of applicants admitted
- SAT or ACT required
- 54% graduate within 6 years

General. Founded in 1893. Regionally accredited. George Williams College of Aurora University is branch campus on shores of Geneva Lake in Williams Bay, Wisconsin. **Degrees:** 628 bachelor's awarded; master's, doctoral offered. **ROTC:** Army. **Location:** 40 miles from Chicago. **Calendar:** Semester, extensive summer session. **Full-time faculty:** 118 total; 85% have terminal degrees, 50% women. **Part-time faculty:** 372 total; 22% have terminal degrees, 59% women. **Class size:** 44% < 20, 56% 20-39. **Special facilities:** Native American cultures center, collection of adventual materials.

Freshman class profile. 1,803 applied, 1,334 admitted, 472 enrolled.

Mid 50% test scores		ACT composite:	20-24
SAT critical reading:	450-520	Out-of-state:	16%
SAT math:	480-540	Live on campus:	60%

Basis for selection. High school achievement record most important, followed by test scores. Recommendations considered. Interview and essay recommended. **Home schooled:** State high school equivalency certificate, interview required. Writing sample (graded paper or personal statement) required.

High school preparation. College-preparatory program required. 16 units required. Required units include English 4, mathematics 3, social studies 3, science 3 and academic electives 3.

2011-2012 Annual costs. Tuition/fees: $19,450. Course laboratory/clinical fees in lab sciences, photography, nursing, physical education, and student teaching. Tuition will vary for several adult degree completion programs. Room/board: $8,270. Books/supplies: $1,000. Personal expenses: $1,400.

2011-2012 Financial aid. Need-based: 445 full-time freshmen applied for aid; 394 were judged to have need; 393 of these received aid. Average need met was 85%. Average scholarship/grant was $7,395; average loan $3,374. 55% of total undergraduate aid awarded as scholarships/grants, 45% as loans/jobs. **Non-need-based:** Awarded to 2,249 full-time undergraduates, including 465 freshmen. Scholarships awarded for academics, alumni affiliation, art, music/drama, religious affiliation, ROTC, state residency.

Application procedures. Admission: Closing date 5/1 (receipt date). $25 fee, may be waived for applicants with need, free for online applicants. Admission notification on a rolling basis beginning on or about 9/1. Must reply by 6/20. Candidates may apply early and have until May 1 to have tuition and housing deposits refunded. **Financial aid:** Priority date 4/15; no closing date. FAFSA required. Applicants notified on a rolling basis starting 3/1; must reply by 5/1 or within 3 week(s) of notification.

Academics. Special study options: Accelerated study, cross-registration, double major, dual enrollment of high school students, honors, independent study, internships, liberal arts/career combination, student-designed major, study abroad, teacher certification program. 3-week May Term session offers

on-campus courses or travel/study abroad programs. **Credit/placement by examination:** AP, CLEP. 30 credit hours maximum toward bachelor's degree. **Support services:** Learning center, pre-admission summer program, reduced course load, remedial instruction, study skills assistance, tutoring, writing center.

Majors. **Biology:** General. **Business:** General, accounting, actuarial science, finance, management information systems, management science, marketing, operations. **Communications:** Communications/speech/rhetoric. **Computer sciences:** General, computer science. **Education:** Bilingual, elementary, physical, secondary, special ed. **English:** English lit. **Foreign languages:** Spanish. **Health services:** Athletic training, clinical lab science, nursing (RN). **History:** General. **Human services:** Social work. **Liberal arts:** Arts/sciences. **Math:** General. **Parks/recreation:** General. **Philosophy/religion:** Religion. **Protective services:** Criminal justice. **Psychology:** General. **Social sciences:** Political science, sociology. **Visual/performing arts:** Art, dramatic.

Most popular majors. Business/marketing 19%, education 21%, health sciences 18%, psychology 7%, public administration/social services 8%, security/protective services 8%.

Computing on campus. 90 workstations in library, computer center, student center. Dormitories wired for high-speed internet access and linked to campus network. Commuter students can connect to campus network. Online library, helpline, wireless network available.

Student life. Freshman orientation: Mandatory. Preregistration for classes offered. Day-long sessions held each May and June for admitted first-year students and their parents. **Policies:** Alcohol and smoke-free campus. **Housing:** Coed dorms available. $100 fully refundable deposit, deadline 5/1. **Activities:** Pep band, campus ministries, choral groups, drama, literary magazine, music ensembles, Model UN, radio station, student government, student newspaper, Black Student Association, Latin American Student Organization, Students for Wellness, Fellowship of Christian Athletes, Circle K International, Intervarsity Christian Fellowship, political science club, Future Leaders of the Work, Aurora University Human Rights Organization, A.R.I.S.E (Awareness, Responsibility, Integrity Sisterhood Empowerment).

Athletics. NCAA. **Intercollegiate:** Baseball M, basketball, cheerleading, cross-country, football (tackle) M, golf, lacrosse M, soccer, softball W, tennis, track and field, volleyball W. **Intramural:** Badminton, basketball, soccer, volleyball. **Team name:** Spartans.

Student services. Adult student services, alcohol/substance abuse counseling, chaplain/spiritual director, career counseling, student employment services, financial aid counseling, health services, minority student services, personal counseling, placement for graduates. **Physically disabled:** Services for visually, speech, hearing impaired.

Contact. E-mail: admission@aurora.edu
Phone: (630) 844-5533 Toll-free number: (800) 742-5281
Fax: (630) 844-5535
James Lancaster, Director of Freshman Admission, Aurora University, 347 South Gladstone Avenue, Aurora, IL 60506-4892

Benedictine University
Lisle, Illinois
www.ben.edu
CB code: 1707

- Private 4-year university and liberal arts college affiliated with Roman Catholic Church
- Commuter campus in large town
- 3,750 degree-seeking undergraduates: 21% part-time, 61% women, 10% African American, 13% Asian American, 7% Hispanic American, 1% international
- 2,899 degree-seeking graduate students
- 76% of applicants admitted
- SAT or ACT (ACT writing optional), application essay required
- 50% graduate within 6 years

General. Founded in 1887. Regionally accredited. **Degrees:** 859 bachelor's, 67 associate awarded; master's, doctoral offered. **ROTC:** Army. **Location:** 25 miles from Chicago. **Calendar:** Semester, extensive summer session. **Full-time faculty:** 144 total; 67% have terminal degrees, 13% minority, 51% women. **Part-time faculty:** 565 total; 19% have terminal degrees, 16% minority, 55% women. **Class size:** 61% < 20, 37% 20-39, 2% 40-49, less than 1% 50-99. **Special facilities:** Nature museum, Benedictine abbey, arboretum, Fermi nuclear accelerator laboratories, Argonne national laboratories.

Freshman class profile. 1,531 applied, 1,159 admitted, 502 enrolled.

Mid 50% test scores		Rank in top tenth:	13%
ACT composite:	19-25	End year in good standing:	82%
GPA 3.75 or higher:	27%	Return as sophomores:	81%
GPA 3.50-3.74:	14%	Out-of-state:	8%
GPA 3.0-3.49:	26%	Live on campus:	58%
GPA 2.0-2.99:	33%	International:	1%
Rank in top quarter:	37%		

Basis for selection. Require rank in top half of class and 21 ACT. Candidates falling below these criteria reviewed by admissions committee. Audition required of musical instrument and voice majors.

High school preparation. 16 units required. Required and recommended units include English 4, mathematics 3-4, social studies 3, history 1, science 2-3 (laboratory 1-2) and foreign language 2.

2011-2012 Annual costs. Tuition/fees: $24,650. Room/board: $7,410. Books/supplies: $1,260. Personal expenses: $2,200.

2011-2012 Financial aid. Need-based: 447 full-time freshmen applied for aid; 397 were judged to have need; 397 of these received aid. Average scholarship/grant was $7,707; average loan $3,503. 54% of total undergraduate aid awarded as scholarships/grants, 46% as loans/jobs. **Non-need-based:** Awarded to 2,082 full-time undergraduates, including 423 freshmen. Scholarships awarded for academics, alumni affiliation, athletics, leadership, music/drama, ROTC, state residency.

Application procedures. Admission: Priority date 8/30; no deadline. $40 fee, may be waived for applicants with need. Admission notification on a rolling basis. Must reply by May 1 or within 2 week(s) if notified thereafter. **Financial aid:** Priority date 4/15; no closing date. FAFSA required. Applicants notified on a rolling basis starting 2/15; must reply within 2 week(s) of notification.

Academics. Special study options: Accelerated study, combined bachelor's/graduate degree, cross-registration, distance learning, double major, dual enrollment of high school students, ESL, honors, independent study, internships, liberal arts/career combination, study abroad, teacher certification program, weekend college. Engineering degree program with Illinois Institute of Technology. **Credit/placement by examination:** AP, CLEP, institutional tests. 30 credit hours maximum toward bachelor's degree. **Support services:** Learning center, reduced course load, remedial instruction, study skills assistance, tutoring, writing center.

Majors. Biology: General, biochemistry, molecular. **Business:** Accounting, finance, international, managerial economics, marketing, organizational behavior. **Communications:** Communications/speech/rhetoric, publishing. **Computer sciences:** Computer science, information systems. **Conservation:** Environmental science. **Education:** Elementary, special ed. **Engineering:** Engineering science. **English:** English lit. **Foreign languages:** Spanish. **Health services:** Clinical lab science, health care admin, nuclear medical technology, sonography. **History:** General. **Math:** General. **Philosophy/religion:** Philosophy. **Physical sciences:** Chemistry, physics. **Psychology:** General. **Social sciences:** General, economics, international relations, political science, sociology. **Theology:** Theology. **Visual/performing arts:** Music, studio arts, studio arts management. **Work/family studies:** Food/nutrition.

Most popular majors. Business/marketing 45%, education 18%, health sciences 19%.

Computing on campus. 200 workstations in dormitories, library, computer center, student center. Dormitories wired for high-speed internet access and linked to campus network. Commuter students can connect to campus network. Online course registration, online library, helpline, wireless network available.

Student life. Freshman orientation: Mandatory, $75 fee. Preregistration for classes offered. Summer parent and student program. Student program 3 days prior to first day of classes. **Housing:** Coed dorms, single-sex dorms, apartments, wellness housing available. $125 deposit. **Activities:** Bands, campus ministries, choral groups, dance, drama, film society, international student organizations, literary magazine, music ensembles, Model UN, student government, student newspaper, symphony orchestra, TV station, Muslim student association, African-American student union, Knights of Columbus, Daughters of Isabella, Students for Life, Relay for Life, Best Buddies, South Asian student association, Democracy Matters, Hindu student association.

Athletics. NCAA. **Intercollegiate:** Baseball M, basketball, cross-country, football (tackle) M, golf, soccer, softball W, tennis W, track and field, volleyball W. **Intramural:** Basketball, bowling, football (non-tackle), softball, table tennis, volleyball. **Team name:** Eagles.

Student services. Adult student services, chaplain/spiritual director, career counseling, student employment services, financial aid counseling,

health services, personal counseling, placement for graduates. **Physically disabled:** Services for visually, speech, hearing impaired.

Contact. E-mail: admissions@ben.edu
Phone: (630) 829-6300 Toll-free number: (888) 829-6363
Fax: (630) 829-6301
Kari Gibbons, Dean of Enrollment, Benedictine University, 5700 College Road, Lisle, IL 60532

Blackburn College
Carlinville, Illinois
www.blackburn.edu

CB member
CB code: 1065

- Private 4-year liberal arts college affiliated with Presbyterian Church (USA)
- Residential campus in small town
- 549 degree-seeking undergraduates
- 70% of applicants admitted
- SAT or ACT (ACT writing optional) required

General. Founded in 1837. Regionally accredited. **Degrees:** 111 bachelor's awarded. **Location:** 40 miles from Springfield, 60 miles from St. Louis. **Calendar:** Semester, limited summer session. **Full-time faculty:** 38 total. **Part-time faculty:** 38 total. **Class size:** 72% < 20, 25% 20-39, 2% 40-49, less than 1% 50-99.

Freshman class profile. 660 applied, 462 admitted, 143 enrolled.

Mid 50% test scores		GPA 2.0-2.99:	28%
ACT composite:	18-23	Rank in top quarter:	43%
GPA 3.75 or higher:	32%	Rank in top tenth:	15%
GPA 3.50-3.74:	15%	Out-of-state:	9%
GPA 3.0-3.49:	25%	Live on campus:	87%

Basis for selection. High school academic record, substantiated by test scores, most important. Interview recommended. Audition recommended for music majors. Portfolio recommended for art majors. **Home schooled:** Statement describing home school structure and mission, transcript of courses and grades, state high school equivalency certificate required.

High school preparation. 16 units recommended. Recommended units include English 4, mathematics 3, social studies 2, history 2, science 3 and foreign language 2.

2011-2012 Annual costs. Tuition/fees: $16,296. All on-campus students participate in a work program which reduces net tuition costs. Room/board: $5,054. Books/supplies: $700. Personal expenses: $800.

Financial aid. **Non-need-based:** Scholarships awarded for academics, state residency. **Additional information:** Each resident student works 160 hours per semester.

Application procedures. **Admission:** No deadline. $20 fee, may be waived for applicants with need. Admission notification on a rolling basis beginning on or about 10/15. **Financial aid:** Priority date 4/1; no closing date. FAFSA required. Applicants notified on a rolling basis starting 3/1; must reply within 4 week(s) of notification.

Academics. **Special study options:** Accelerated study, cooperative education, double major, dual enrollment of high school students, independent study, internships, student-designed major, study abroad, teacher certification program, Washington semester. British studies semester, Mexico studies semester. **Credit/placement by examination:** AP, CLEP, SAT, ACT, institutional tests. 30 credit hours maximum toward bachelor's degree. **Support services:** Learning center, reduced course load, remedial instruction, study skills assistance, tutoring, writing center.

Majors. **Area/ethnic studies:** Latin American. **Biology:** General, biochemistry, environmental. **Business:** Accounting, marketing, organizational leadership. **Communications:** Communications/speech/rhetoric. **Computer sciences:** Computer science. **Education:** Art, biology, elementary, English, mathematics, physical, social science. **English:** English lit. **Foreign languages:** Spanish. **Health services:** Clinical lab science. **History:** General. **Human services:** General. **Math:** General. **Parks/recreation:** Health/fitness. **Physical sciences:** Chemistry. **Protective services:** Criminal justice. **Psychology:** General. **Social sciences:** Political science. **Visual/performing arts:** Art, music.

Most popular majors. Biology 9%, business/marketing 19%, communications/journalism 12%, education 24%, psychology 8%, security/protective services 7%.

Computing on campus. 75 workstations in library, computer center. Dormitories linked to campus network. Helpline available.

Student life. **Freshman orientation:** Mandatory. Preregistration for classes offered. One-day summer orientation and two-day fall orientation prior to beginning of semester. **Policies:** Participation in student-managed work program required for all resident students. Resident students work 160 hours per semester to reduce costs and gain valuable career skills. Alcohol allowed for students 21 and older. All residence halls are smoke-free. **Housing:** Guaranteed on-campus for all undergraduates. Coed dorms, single-sex dorms, wellness housing available. $150 fully refundable deposit, deadline 7/31. Quiet study housing available. **Activities:** Concert band, campus ministries, choral groups, dance, drama, literary magazine, music ensembles, musical theater, radio station, student government, student newspaper, Cultural Expressions, Habitat for Humanity chapter, Catacombs, Newman Club, Common Ground, Republican club, health and wellness club, fishing club, Beavers Against Destructive Decisions, psychology club.

Athletics. NCAA. **Intercollegiate:** Baseball M, basketball, cross-country, football (tackle) M, golf M, soccer, softball W, tennis W, volleyball W. **Intramural:** Badminton, basketball, racquetball, softball, swimming, table tennis, tennis, volleyball, water polo. **Team name:** Beavers.

Student services. Adult student services, alcohol/substance abuse counseling, career counseling, student employment services, financial aid counseling, minority student services, personal counseling, placement for graduates. **Physically disabled:** Services for visually, hearing impaired.

Contact. E-mail: jmali@blackburn.edu
Phone: (217) 854-3231 Toll-free number: (800) 233-3550
Fax: (217) 854-3713
Alisha Kapp, Director of Admissions, Blackburn College, 700 College Avenue, Carlinville, IL 62626

Blessing-Rieman College of Nursing
Quincy, Illinois
www.brcn.edu

CB code: 0139

- Private 4-year nursing college
- Commuter campus in small city
- 259 degree-seeking undergraduates
- 96% of applicants admitted
- SAT or ACT (ACT writing optional) required

General. Founded in 1891. Regionally accredited. Joint degree programs with Culver-Stockton College and Quincy University leading to BS in Nursing. General education classes held at partner campus, with nursing classes at BRCN campus and clinical experiences at Blessing Hospital, a regional medical facility and magnet hospital. **Degrees:** 61 bachelor's awarded; master's offered. **Location:** 120 miles from St. Louis, 100 miles from Springfield. **Calendar:** Semester, limited summer session. **Full-time faculty:** 20 total; 85% have terminal degrees, 100% women. **Part-time faculty:** 7 total; 100% women. **Class size:** 52% < 20, 48% 20-39.

Freshman class profile. 555 applied, 533 admitted, 147 enrolled.

Mid 50% test scores		GPA 3.0-3.49:	34%
ACT composite:	19-24	GPA 2.0-2.99:	28%
GPA 3.75 or higher:	14%	Out-of-state:	39%
GPA 3.50-3.74:	20%	Live on campus:	82%

Basis for selection. 3.0 GPA and 22 ACT required. **Home schooled:** Transcript of courses and grades required.

High school preparation. Required units include English 4, mathematics 2, social studies 3, science 4 (laboratory 2). Biology, chemistry, algebra suggested.

2011-2012 Annual costs. Tuition/fees: $23,325. Tuition and fees are average costs charged to freshman. Partnered with Quincy University and Culver-Stockton College. Freshmen and sophomores pay partnering school's tuition rate. Room/board: $8,395. Books/supplies: $1,000. Personal expenses: $1,775.

Financial aid. **Non-need-based:** Scholarships awarded for academics, alumni affiliation, leadership, state residency. **Additional information:** Financial aid for freshmen and sophomores administered by Culver-Stockton College and Quincy University. B-RCN does not have first time, full-time students, only junior and senior students.

Application procedures. **Admission:** No deadline. No application fee. Admission notification on a rolling basis. **Financial aid:** Priority date 3/1, closing date 9/1. FAFSA required.

Academics. **Special study options:** Accelerated study, combined bachelor's/graduate degree, internships. **Credit/placement by examination:** AP,

CLEP, SAT, ACT, institutional tests. **Support services:** Learning center, study skills assistance, tutoring.

Majors. Health services: Nursing (RN).

Computing on campus. 30 workstations in dormitories, library, computer center. Dormitories wired for high-speed internet access and linked to campus network. Online library, helpline, wireless network available.

Student life. Policies: Immunization and background check required for sophomore level and up. **Housing:** Apartments, wellness housing available. Men's and women's dormitories available at Culver-Stockton College and Quincy University. **Activities:** Student government, student nurses organization.

Student services. Alcohol/substance abuse counseling, career counseling, student employment services, financial aid counseling, health services, on-campus daycare, personal counseling, placement for graduates.

Contact. E-mail: admissions@brcn.edu
Phone: (217) 228-5520 ext. 6949
Toll-free number: (800) 877-9140 ext. 6949 Fax: (217) 223-4661
Ann O'Sullivan, Assistant Dean, Blessing-Rieman College of Nursing, PO Box 7005, Quincy, IL 62305-7005

Bradley University
Peoria, Illinois
www.bradley.edu

CB member
CB code: 1070

- Private 4-year university
- Residential campus in large city
- 4,948 degree-seeking undergraduates: 5% part-time, 53% women, 8% African American, 3% Asian American, 6% Hispanic American, 1% international
- 649 degree-seeking graduate students
- 70% of applicants admitted
- SAT or ACT (ACT writing optional), application essay required
- 73% graduate within 6 years; 14% enter graduate study

General. Founded in 1897. Regionally accredited. **Degrees:** 1,280 bachelor's awarded; master's, professional offered. **ROTC:** Army. **Location:** 157 miles from Chicago, 164 miles from St. Louis. **Calendar:** Semester, limited summer session. **Full-time faculty:** 349 total; 84% have terminal degrees, 17% minority, 38% women. **Part-time faculty:** 187 total; 6% minority, 52% women. **Class size:** 55% < 20, 39% 20-39, 3% 40-49, 2% 50-99, less than 1% >100. **Special facilities:** Global communications center, 2 art galleries.

Freshman class profile. 6,454 applied, 4,529 admitted, 1,018 enrolled.

Mid 50% test scores				
SAT critical reading:	530-630	Rank in top quarter:		58%
SAT math:	550-660	Rank in top tenth:		27%
SAT writing:	500-620	Return as sophomores:		86%
ACT composite:	22-28	Out-of-state:		14%
GPA 3.75 or higher:	38%	Live on campus:		91%
GPA 3.50-3.74:	18%	International:		1%
GPA 3.0-3.49:	35%	Fraternities:		47%
GPA 2.0-2.99:	9%	Sororities:		40%

Basis for selection. High school curriculum and achievement, test scores, special talents, co-curricular activities, letters of recommendation, personal statement, educational goals important. Student's academic interest, motivational level, and quality of secondary school education also considered. Interview recommended. Audition required of music majors, recommended for theater majors. Portfolio recommended for art majors. **Home schooled:** Transcript of courses and grades required. Record of courses taken, grades earned, personal statement, letter of recommendation and record of activities or club memberships required. Interview may be required and highly recommended.

High school preparation. College-preparatory program required. 16 units required; 22 recommended. Required and recommended units include English 4-5, mathematics 3-4, social studies 2-3, history 2, science 2-3 (laboratory 2-3) and foreign language 2. Additional requirements for business, science, engineering, music, nursing, and health science majors.

2011-2012 Annual costs. Tuition/fees: $26,704. Room/board: $8,200. Books/supplies: $1,200. Personal expenses: $1,876.

2010-2011 Financial aid. Need-based: 1,093 full-time freshmen applied for aid; 978 were judged to have need; 957 of these received aid. Average need met was 67%. Average scholarship/grant was $14,317; average loan $4,232. 72% of total undergraduate aid awarded as scholarships/grants, 28%

as loans/jobs. **Non-need-based:** Awarded to 1,441 full-time undergraduates, including 316 freshmen. Scholarships awarded for academics, alumni affiliation, art, athletics, leadership, minority status, music/drama, state residency.

Application procedures. Admission: Priority date 2/1; no deadline. $35 fee, may be waived for applicants with need, free for online applicants. Admission notification on a rolling basis beginning on or about 10/1. Must reply by May 1 or within 2 week(s) if notified thereafter. **Financial aid:** Priority date 3/1; no closing date. FAFSA required. Applicants notified on a rolling basis starting 2/15.

Academics. Academic Exploration Program assists undergraduates in choosing major. **Special study options:** Accelerated study, combined bachelor's/graduate degree, cooperative education, distance learning, double major, honors, independent study, internships, liberal arts/career combination, student-designed major, study abroad, teacher certification program, Washington semester. **Credit/placement by examination:** AP, CLEP, IB, SAT, ACT, institutional tests. 60 credit hours maximum toward bachelor's degree. **Support services:** Learning center, study skills assistance, tutoring, writing center.

Majors. Biology: General, biochemistry, cellular/molecular. **Business:** Accounting, actuarial science, business admin, entrepreneurial studies, finance, hospitality admin, human resources, insurance, international, management information systems, managerial economics, marketing, selling, small business admin. **Communications:** Advertising, communications/speech/rhetoric, journalism, organizational, photojournalism, public relations, radio/TV, sports. **Communications technology:** Animation/special effects. **Computer sciences:** Computer science, information systems. **Conservation:** Environmental science. **Education:** Art, biology, chemistry, drama/dance, early childhood, elementary, English, family/consumer sciences, French, German, history, learning disabled, mathematics, mentally handicapped, music, physics, psychology, science, social science, social studies, Spanish, speech. **Engineering:** Applied physics, civil, computer, construction, electrical, industrial, manufacturing, mechanical. **English:** English lit. **Foreign languages:** French, German, Spanish. **Health services:** Clinical lab science, dietetics, nursing (RN). **History:** General. **Human services:** Social work. **Liberal arts:** Arts/sciences, humanities. **Math:** General. **Philosophy/religion:** Philosophy, religion. **Physical sciences:** Chemistry, physics. **Protective services:** Law enforcement admin. **Psychology:** General. **Social sciences:** Economics, international relations, political science, sociology. **Visual/performing arts:** Acting, art, art history/conservation, ceramics, directing/producing, dramatic, drawing, game design, graphic design, music, music management, music performance, music theory/composition, painting, photography, printmaking, sculpture, studio arts. **Work/family studies:** General, merchandising.

Most popular majors. Business/marketing 21%, communications/journalism 11%, education 8%, engineering/engineering technologies 14%, health sciences 12%, social sciences 6%, visual/performing arts 6%.

Computing on campus. 900 workstations in dormitories, library, computer center. Dormitories wired for high-speed internet access and linked to campus network. Commuter students can connect to campus network. Online course registration, helpline, student web hosting, wireless network available.

Student life. Freshman orientation: Mandatory. Preregistration for classes offered. 13 sessions throughout summer. **Policies:** Freshmen not permitted cars on campus. **Housing:** Guaranteed on-campus for freshmen. Coed dorms, apartments, fraternity/sorority housing available. $100 partly refundable deposit, deadline 6/1. Service and leadership floor available. **Activities:** Bands, campus ministries, choral groups, dance, drama, film society, international student organizations, literary magazine, music ensembles, Model UN, musical theater, radio station, student government, student newspaper, symphony orchestra, TV station, Alpha Phi Omega, Hillel, InterVarsity Christian Fellowship, Cru, Newman Center, Amnesty International, Habitat for Humanity, Beyond Prejudice, Association of Latin American Students, NAACP student chapter.

Athletics. NCAA. **Intercollegiate:** Baseball M, basketball, cheerleading, cross-country, golf, soccer M, softball W, tennis, track and field, volleyball W. **Intramural:** Badminton, basketball, bowling, football (tackle) M, golf, handball, racquetball, soccer, softball, swimming, table tennis, tennis, volleyball, water polo, wrestling M. **Team name:** Braves.

Student services. Alcohol/substance abuse counseling, career counseling, student employment services, financial aid counseling, health services, minority student services, personal counseling, placement for graduates, veterans' counselor.

Contact. E-mail: admissions@bradley.edu
Phone: (309) 677-1000 Toll-free number: (800) 447-6460
Fax: (309) 677-2797
Rodney San Jose, Director of Admissions, Bradley University, 1501 West Bradley Avenue, Peoria, IL 61625

Chamberlain College of Nursing: Addison
Addison, Illinois
www.chamberlain.edu   CB code: 5759

- For-profit 4-year nursing college
- Large town
- 906 degree-seeking undergraduates
- SAT or ACT required

General. Regionally accredited. **Degrees:** 229 bachelor's awarded; master's offered. **Location:** 30 miles from Chicago. **Calendar:** Semester. **Full-time faculty:** 31 total. **Part-time faculty:** 69 total.

Basis for selection. ACT composite of 21 or SAT critical reading/mathematics score of 990, or admissions assessment score of 175; high school cumulative GPA of 2.75.

2011-2012 Annual costs. Tuition/fees: $15,600. Books/supplies: $1,400. Personal expenses: $3,718.

Application procedures. Admission: No deadline. $95 fee. Admission notification on a rolling basis.

Academics. Special study options: Accelerated study, distance learning. **Credit/placement by examination:** AP, CLEP.

Majors. Health services: Nursing (RN).

Contact. Chamberlain College of Nursing: Addison, 1221 North Swift Road, Addison, IL 60101-6106

Chamberlain College of Nursing: Chicago
Chicago, Illinois
www.chamberlain.edu/Locations/Chicago.aspx
CB code: 6504

- For-profit 4-year nursing college
- Very large city
- 450 degree-seeking undergraduates
- SAT or ACT, interview required

General. Regionally accredited. **Calendar:** Semester. **Full-time faculty:** 15 total. **Part-time faculty:** 14 total.

Basis for selection. Secondary school record, class rank, GPA most important; interview also important.

2011-2012 Annual costs. Tuition/fees: $15,600. Books/supplies: $1,400. Personal expenses: $3,718.

Application procedures. Admission: No deadline. $95 fee. Admission notification on a rolling basis.

Academics. Special study options: Accelerated study, distance learning. **Credit/placement by examination:** AP, CLEP.

Majors. Health services: Nursing (RN).

Contact. Chamberlain College of Nursing: Chicago, 3300 North Campbell Avenue, Chicago, IL 60618

Chicago State University
Chicago, Illinois
www.csu.edu   CB code: 1118

- Public 4-year university
- Commuter campus in very large city
- 5,252 degree-seeking undergraduates: 32% part-time, 72% women, 84% African American, 1% Asian American, 7% Hispanic American
- 1,472 degree-seeking graduate students
- 43% of applicants admitted
- ACT (writing optional) required

General. Founded in 1867. Regionally accredited. **Degrees:** 839 bachelor's awarded; master's, professional, doctoral offered. **ROTC:** Army. **Location:** 12 miles from downtown. **Calendar:** Semester, limited summer session. **Full-time faculty:** 325 total; 62% minority, 52% women. **Part-time faculty:**

174 total; 74% minority, 51% women. **Class size:** 48% < 20, 51% 20-39, less than 1% 40-49, less than 1% 50-99. **Special facilities:** Electron microscopy laboratory, video conference room, center of African heritage and culture.

Freshman class profile. 3,851 applied, 1,668 admitted, 486 enrolled.

Mid 50% test scores		Out-of-state:	4%
ACT composite:	16-19	Live on campus:	23%
Return as sophomores:	54%		

Basis for selection. High school GPA, standardized test scores, and subject/units completed important.

High school preparation. 15 units required. Required units include English 4, mathematics 3, social studies 3, science 3 and academic electives 2. 2 units foreign language, music, vocational education or art.

2011-2012 Annual costs. Tuition/fees: $9,721; $17,941 out-of-state. Room/board: $8,222. Books/supplies: $2,400. Personal expenses: $2,800.

2010-2011 Financial aid. Need-based: 34% of total undergraduate aid awarded as scholarships/grants, 66% as loans/jobs. **Non-need-based:** Scholarships awarded for academics, athletics, ROTC, state residency. **Additional information:** Freshmen of outstanding academic ability and talent eligible for Scholars Program full-tuition scholarship.

Application procedures. Admission: No deadline. $25 fee, may be waived for applicants with need. Admission notification on a rolling basis. **Financial aid:** Priority date 3/1; no closing date. FAFSA, institutional form required.

Academics. Special study options: Cooperative education, distance learning, double major, ESL, honors, independent study, internships, liberal arts/career combination, student-designed major, study abroad, teacher certification program. Programs for mature adults (University Without Walls, individualized curriculum, Board of Governors degree program). **Credit/placement by examination:** AP, CLEP, institutional tests. 60 credit hours maximum toward bachelor's degree. **Support services:** Learning center, remedial instruction, study skills assistance, tutoring, writing center.

Majors. Area/ethnic studies: African-American. **Biology:** General, bacteriology, biochemistry, environmental, molecular. **Business:** Accounting, business admin, fashion, finance, management information systems. **Communications:** Broadcast journalism. **Computer sciences:** General, data processing, information systems. **Education:** General, art, biology, business, chemistry, early childhood, elementary, English, health, history, mathematics, mentally handicapped, multi-level teacher, music, physical, secondary, technology/industrial arts. **English:** English lit, rhetoric/composition, technical writing. **Foreign languages:** Spanish. **Health services:** Medical records admin, nursing (RN). **History:** General. **Math:** General. **Parks/recreation:** Health/fitness. **Physical sciences:** Chemistry, physics. **Psychology:** General. **Social sciences:** Anthropology, economics, geography, political science, sociology. **Visual/performing arts:** Art, commercial/advertising art, music.

Most popular majors. Business/marketing 14%, education 7%, history 8%, liberal arts 31%, psychology 13%.

Computing on campus. 156 workstations in dormitories, library, computer center, student center. Dormitories wired for high-speed internet access. Commuter students can connect to campus network. Online course registration, online library available.

Student life. Freshman orientation: Mandatory. Preregistration for classes offered. One-day programs in July and August. **Housing:** Coed dorms available. $125 deposit, deadline 8/1. **Activities:** Bands, choral groups, dance, drama, literary magazine, music ensembles, radio station, student government, student newspaper, TV station, 47 clubs and organizations.

Athletics. NCAA. **Intercollegiate:** Baseball M, basketball, cross-country, golf, tennis, track and field, volleyball W. **Intramural:** Basketball, gymnastics, swimming, volleyball. **Team name:** Cougars.

Student services. Adult student services, alcohol/substance abuse counseling, chaplain/spiritual director, career counseling, student employment services, financial aid counseling, health services, minority student services, on-campus daycare, personal counseling, placement for graduates, veterans' counselor, women's services.

Contact. E-mail: ug-admissions@csu.edu
Phone: (773) 995-2513 Fax: (773) 995-3820
Matthew Harrison, Director of Admissions, Chicago State University, 9501 South King Drive, Chicago, IL 60628

Columbia College Chicago
Chicago, Illinois
www.colum.edu

CB member
CB code: 1135

- Private 4-year visual arts and liberal arts college
- Commuter campus in very large city
- 11,024 degree-seeking undergraduates: 10% part-time, 53% women
- 487 degree-seeking graduate students
- Application essay required
- 40% graduate within 6 years

General. Founded in 1890. Regionally accredited. **Degrees:** 2,096 bachelor's awarded; master's offered. **Location:** Downtown. **Calendar:** Semester, limited summer session. **Full-time faculty:** 341 total. **Part-time faculty:** 1,295 total. **Class size:** 74% < 20, 25% 20-39, 1% 40-49, less than 1% 50-99, less than 1% >100. **Special facilities:** Media production facility, film/video sound stage, contemporary photography museum, photography studios, dance performance space, theater, audio technology center, psychoacoustic classroom, animation facilities, reverb chamber, book and paper arts center, black music research center, community media workshop, international Latino cultural center, community arts partnership center, concert hall.

Freshman class profile. 7,132 applied, 5,973 admitted, 2,148 enrolled.

GPA 3.75 or higher:	12%	Rank in top tenth:	8%
GPA 3.50-3.74:	11%	Return as sophomores:	68%
GPA 3.0-3.49:	29%	Out-of-state:	48%
GPA 2.0-2.99:	43%	International:	1%
Rank in top quarter:	24%		

Basis for selection. Open admission, but selective for some programs. Proof of high school graduation (or earned GED), letter of recommendation, and essay required for placement/counseling. Students with less than 2.0 GPA may be required to attend special summer program. All freshmen take COMPASS placement test on campus. Interview recommended. **Home schooled:** Transcript of courses and grades required. **Learning Disabled:** Student must have regular earned GED or HS diploma and may have to complete BRIDGE program.

High school preparation. College-preparatory program recommended.

2011-2012 Annual costs. Tuition/fees: $20,544. Room/board: $13,120.

2010-2011 Financial aid. **Non-need-based:** Scholarships awarded for academics, art, leadership, music/drama, state residency.

Application procedures. **Admission:** Priority date 5/1; no deadline. $35 fee, may be waived for applicants with need. Application must be submitted online. Admission notification on a rolling basis beginning on or about 11/1. **Financial aid:** Priority date 5/1; no closing date. FAFSA, institutional form required. Applicants notified on a rolling basis.

Academics. **Special study options:** Cooperative education, distance learning, dual enrollment of high school students, ESL, independent study, internships, liberal arts/career combination, student-designed major, study abroad, teacher certification program. **Credit/placement by examination:** AP, CLEP, IB, institutional tests. 62 credit hours maximum toward bachelor's degree. **Support services:** Learning center, pre-admission summer program, reduced course load, remedial instruction, study skills assistance, tutoring, writing center.

Majors. **Architecture:** Interior. **Business:** Business admin, fashion, marketing. **Communications:** Advertising, broadcast journalism, journalism, public relations, radio/TV. **Communications technology:** Animation/special effects, recording arts. **Computer sciences:** Web page design. **Education:** Early childhood, kindergarten/preschool. **English:** Creative writing. **Foreign languages:** Sign language interpretation. **Liberal arts:** Arts/sciences. **Visual/performing arts:** General, acting, art, art history/conservation, cinematography, commercial/advertising art, dance, design, directing/producing, dramatic, fashion design, film/cinema/video, game design, graphic design, illustration, industrial design, interior design, jazz, multimedia, music, music management, music performance, photography, play/screenwriting, studio arts, studio arts management, theater design, voice/opera.

Most popular majors. Business/marketing 11%, communications/journalism 13%, visual/performing arts 62%.

Computing on campus. 851 workstations in dormitories, library, computer center, student center. Dormitories wired for high-speed internet access and linked to campus network. Commuter students can connect to campus network. Online course registration, helpline, wireless network available.

Student life. **Freshman orientation:** Mandatory, $70 fee. Preregistration for classes offered. Parent orientation and parent weekend program available. **Housing:** Coed dorms, apartments available. $500 deposit. Student housing available at nearby colleges and universities. **Activities:** Bands, campus ministries, choral groups, dance, drama, film society, international student organizations, literary magazine, music ensembles, musical theater, radio station, student government, student newspaper, TV station, Association of Black Journalists, Umoja, Black Actor's Guild, Black Ink, Latino Alliance, environmental campus organization, Hillel, Not In Our Name.

Athletics. **Intramural:** Baseball, basketball, soccer.

Student services. Adult student services, alcohol/substance abuse counseling, career counseling, services for economically disadvantaged, student employment services, financial aid counseling, health services, minority student services, personal counseling, placement for graduates, veterans' counselor, women's services. **Physically disabled:** Services for visually, speech, hearing impaired.

Contact. E-mail: admissions@colum.edu
Phone: (312) 369-7130 Fax: (312) 369-8024
Murphy Monroe, Executive Director of Admissions, Columbia College Chicago, 600 South Michigan Avenue, Chicago, IL 60605-1996

Concordia University Chicago
River Forest, Illinois
www.cuchicago.edu

CB member
CB code: 1140

- Private 4-year university and liberal arts college affiliated with Lutheran Church - Missouri Synod
- Residential campus in large town
- 1,413 degree-seeking undergraduates: 4% part-time, 59% women, 13% African American, 2% Asian American, 19% Hispanic American
- 3,399 degree-seeking graduate students
- 57% of applicants admitted
- SAT or ACT (ACT writing optional) required
- 60% graduate within 6 years

General. Founded in 1864. Regionally accredited. **Degrees:** 209 bachelor's awarded; master's, doctoral offered. **Location:** 10 miles from Chicago. **Calendar:** Semester, limited summer session. **Full-time faculty:** 152 total; 73% have terminal degrees. **Part-time faculty:** 274 total. **Class size:** 59% < 20, 41% 20-39, less than 1% 40-49, less than 1% 50-99. **Special facilities:** Early childhood education laboratory school, curriculum center (teacher's resource), human performance laboratory.

Freshman class profile. 3,309 applied, 1,873 admitted, 347 enrolled.

Mid 50% test scores		GPA 3.0-3.49:	30%
SAT critical reading:	460-570	GPA 2.0-2.99:	49%
SAT math:	450-560	End year in good standing:	70%
ACT composite:	19-25	Return as sophomores:	63%
GPA 3.75 or higher:	12%	Out-of-state:	30%
GPA 3.50-3.74:	8%		

Basis for selection. School achievement record is most important, particularly in college preparatory courses. Test scores considered (ACT or SAT), personal statement is optional. SAT Subject Test scores must be received before orientation for fall-term admission. Interview recommended. Essay and interview required for students who do not meet academic admission requirements. **Home schooled:** Statement describing home school structure and mission, transcript of courses and grades required. Syllabus for each course, personal statement or essay describing an important event or individual, certificate of completion from home school (if available), official transcripts of any college work completed required.

High school preparation. College-preparatory program required. 15 units required. Required and recommended units include English 4, mathematics 3, social studies 2, history 1, science 2-4 (laboratory 1) and foreign language 2.

2012-2013 Annual costs. Tuition/fees (projected): $26,656. Room/board: $8,580. Books/supplies: $1,200. Personal expenses: $800.

2010-2011 Financial aid. **Need-based:** 295 full-time freshmen applied for aid; 274 were judged to have need; 274 of these received aid. Average need met was 76%. Average scholarship/grant was $16,028; average loan $3,256. 80% of total undergraduate aid awarded as scholarships/grants, 20% as loans/jobs. **Non-need-based:** Awarded to 324 full-time undergraduates, including 57 freshmen. Scholarships awarded for academics, alumni affiliation, music/drama, religious affiliation, state residency.

Application procedures. **Admission:** No deadline. No application fee. Admission notification on a rolling basis beginning on or about 9/4. Must reply by May 1 or within specified timeframe if notified thereafter. **Financial aid:** Priority date 3/1; no closing date. FAFSA required. Applicants notified on a rolling basis starting 3/1; must reply within 4 week(s) of notification.

Academics. **Special study options:** Accelerated study, combined bachelor's/graduate degree, cross-registration, distance learning, double major, exchange student, honors, independent study, internships, study abroad, teacher certification program. Adult degree completion program. **Credit/placement by examination:** AP, CLEP, IB, ACT, institutional tests. 12 credit hours maximum toward bachelor's degree. **Support services:** Learning center, reduced course load, study skills assistance, tutoring, writing center.

Majors. **Area/ethnic studies:** Women's. **Biology:** General. **Business:** Accounting, business admin, communications, marketing, nonprofit/public. **Communications:** Communications/speech/rhetoric, journalism. **Computer sciences:** General. **Conservation:** Environmental science. **Education:** General, art, biology, chemistry, computer, early childhood, elementary, English, history, mathematics, multi-level teacher, music, physical, science, secondary, social science, special ed. **English:** English lit. **Foreign languages:** Biblical, Spanish. **Health services:** EMT paramedic. **History:** General. **Human services:** Social work. **Math:** General. **Parks/recreation:** Exercise sciences, sports admin. **Philosophy/religion:** Philosophy, religion. **Physical sciences:** General, chemistry, geology. **Psychology:** General. **Social sciences:** Criminology, geography, political science, sociology. **Theology:** Religious ed, sacred music, theology. **Visual/performing arts:** General, art, commercial/advertising art, dramatic, music.

Most popular majors. Business/marketing 7%, education 34%, social sciences 6%.

Computing on campus. 85 workstations in library, computer center, student center. Dormitories wired for high-speed internet access and linked to campus network. Commuter students can connect to campus network. Online course registration, helpline, repair service, student web hosting, wireless network available.

Student life. **Freshman orientation:** Mandatory. Preregistration for classes offered. Overnight sessions held over the summer that allow students to meet each other, finalize academic schedules, and learn about university resources. **Housing:** Guaranteed on-campus for freshmen. Coed dorms, apartments available. $200 nonrefundable deposit, deadline 7/1. **Activities:** Bands, campus ministries, choral groups, drama, literary magazine, music ensembles, musical theater, radio station, student government, student newspaper, TV station, Habitat for Humanity, Fellowship of Christian Athletes, Latin student union, Black student union, College Republicans, Human Rights Club, Green FCC Committee, history club.

Athletics. NCAA. **Intercollegiate:** Baseball M, basketball, cheerleading, cross-country, football (tackle) M, soccer, softball W, tennis, track and field, volleyball W. **Intramural:** Basketball, bowling, football (non-tackle), softball, tennis, volleyball. **Team name:** Cougars.

Student services. Adult student services, alcohol/substance abuse counseling, chaplain/spiritual director, career counseling, student employment services, financial aid counseling, health services, on-campus daycare, personal counseling, placement for graduates. **Physically disabled:** Services for visually, speech, hearing impaired.

Contact. E-mail: admission@cuchicago.edu
Phone: (708) 209-3100 Toll-free number: (877) 282-4422
Fax: (708) 209-3473
Gwen Kanelos, Assistant Vice President for Enrollment, Concordia University Chicago, 7400 Augusta Street, River Forest, IL 60305-1499

DePaul University
Chicago, Illinois
www.depaul.edu

CB member
CB code: 1165

- Private 4-year university affiliated with Roman Catholic Church
- Commuter campus in very large city
- 16,098 degree-seeking undergraduates: 17% part-time, 55% women, 9% African American, 7% Asian American, 16% Hispanic American, 2% international
- 8,793 degree-seeking graduate students
- 64% of applicants admitted
- Application essay required
- 66% graduate within 6 years

General. Founded in 1898. Regionally accredited. Largest Catholic university in the United States. **Degrees:** 3,463 bachelor's awarded; master's, professional, doctoral offered. **ROTC:** Army. **Location:** Downtown. **Calendar:** Quarter, extensive summer session. **Full-time faculty:** 956 total; 87% have terminal degrees, 26% minority, 44% women. **Part-time faculty:** 952 total; 18% have terminal degrees, 14% minority, 45% women. **Class size:** 38% < 20, 52% 20-39, 9% 40-49, 1% 50-99, less than 1% >100. **Special facilities:** Environmental science and chemistry building with greenhouse and green roof, digital cinema laboratory with motion-capture system, green-screen studio, converged newsroom, 10 specialized computer research labs including artificial intelligence, biomedics informatics & mobile e-commerce, 1,300-seat theatre.

Freshman class profile. 16,711 applied, 10,714 admitted, 2,458 enrolled.

Mid 50% test scores				
SAT critical reading:	530-640	GPA 2.0-2.99:	15%
SAT math:	520-620	Rank in top quarter:	54%
ACT composite:	23-28	Rank in top tenth:	25%
GPA 3.75 or higher:	37%	Return as sophomores:	86%
GPA 3.50-3.74:	19%	Out-of-state:	33%
GPA 3.0-3.49:	29%	Live on campus:	68%
		International:	2%

Basis for selection. Secondary school record most important; class rank, recommendations, test scores, essay, extracurricular activities, talent/ability, character, volunteer and work experience important. Interview, alumni/ae relation, geographical location, state residency, religious affiliation, racial or ethnic status considered. SAT and SAT Subject Tests or ACT recommended. Interview required of acting, theater technologies, and recording sound technology majors. Auditions required of music and theater majors. Portfolios required of theater technology and design majors. **Home schooled:** Transcript of courses and grades required. Official community college transcripts for any courses taken required. Listing of textbooks used, especially in math and science, recommended.

High school preparation. College-preparatory program required. 12 units required; 14 recommended. Required and recommended units include English 4, mathematics 3, science 3 (laboratory 2) and foreign language 2. 2 units social science/history.

2011-2012 Annual costs. Tuition/fees: $30,618. Room/board: $11,335. Books/supplies: $1,134. Personal expenses: $1,776.

2010-2011 Financial aid. **Need-based:** 1,916 full-time freshmen applied for aid; 1,686 were judged to have need; 1,673 of these received aid. Average need met was 67%. Average scholarship/grant was $13,931; average loan $3,437. 71% of total undergraduate aid awarded as scholarships/grants, 29% as loans/jobs. **Non-need-based:** Awarded to 5,252 full-time undergraduates, including 1,388 freshmen. Scholarships awarded for academics, art, athletics, leadership, music/drama, ROTC, state residency.

Application procedures. **Admission:** Priority date 11/15; deadline 2/1 (postmark date). $40 fee, may be waived for applicants with need. Admission notification by 3/15. Must reply by May 1 or within 2 week(s) if notified thereafter. Applications are accepted after 2/1 as space is available. Early action applicants receive early financial aid estimates, priority registration, priority housing and priority advising. **Financial aid:** Priority date 3/1; no closing date. FAFSA required. Applicants notified on a rolling basis starting 3/15.

Academics. Over 275 undergraduate and graduate degree programs offered. **Special study options:** Accelerated study, combined bachelor's/graduate degree, cooperative education, distance learning, double major, dual enrollment of high school students, ESL, honors, independent study, internships, student-designed major, study abroad, teacher certification program, weekend college. **Credit/placement by examination:** AP, CLEP, IB, SAT, ACT, institutional tests. Senior year residency requirement excludes CLEP, AP or IB credits. For transfer students, CLEP, IB or AP credits combined with transfer credits from 2-year institutions may total no more than 99 hours, and combined with transfer credits from 4-year institutions may total no more than 132 hours. **Support services:** Learning center, pre-admission summer program, reduced course load, remedial instruction, study skills assistance, tutoring, writing center.

Honors college/program. Admitted students who demonstrate strong academic motivation and seek a rigorous academic curriculum at the university level are encouraged to apply. Each Honors application individually reviewed, taking into consideration all components of student's academic profile, particularly content and quality of essay responses.

Majors. **Architecture:** History/criticism. **Area/ethnic studies:** African-American, American, East Asian, Latin American, women's. **Biology:** General. **Business:** General, accounting, business admin, e-commerce, finance, hospitality admin, human resources, management information systems, management science, managerial economics, marketing, operations, organizational behavior, real estate. **Communications:** Communications/speech/rhetoric. **Communications technology:** Animation/special effects. **Computer sciences:** General, applications programming, computer graphics, computer science, information systems, information technology, networking, programming, security, web page design. **Conservation:** Environmental science, environmental studies. **Education:** Art, early childhood, elementary, health, multi-level teacher, music, physical, secondary, special ed. **English:** English lit. **Foreign languages:** Arabic, Chinese, French, German, Italian, Spanish. **Health services:** Art therapy, clinical lab science, nursing (RN). **History:** General. **Human services:** Community org/advocacy, public policy. **Liberal**

arts: Humanities. **Math:** General. **Parks/recreation:** Health/fitness. **Philosophy/religion:** Islamic, Judaic, philosophy, religion. **Physical sciences:** Chemistry, physics. **Psychology:** General, educational. **Social sciences:** General, anthropology, economics, geography, international relations, political science, sociology, urban studies. **Visual/performing arts:** Acting, art, art history/conservation, cinematography, dramatic, jazz, music, music management, music performance, music theory/composition, play/screenwriting, studio arts management, theater design, theater history.

Most popular majors. Business/marketing 34%, communications/journalism 11%, computer/information sciences 6%, liberal arts 10%, psychology 6%, social sciences 10%, visual/performing arts 6%.

Computing on campus. 1,800 workstations in dormitories, library, computer center, student center. Dormitories wired for high-speed internet access and linked to campus network. Commuter students can connect to campus network. Online course registration, online library, helpline, repair service, student web hosting, wireless network available.

Student life. Freshman orientation: Mandatory, $170 fee. Preregistration for classes offered. Two-day summer program for students and their families. **Policies:** Student organizations must have a minimum of 4 DePaul students, agree to the abide by applicable policies and procedures as well as applicable city, state and federal laws. **Housing:** Coed dorms, special housing for disabled, apartments available. $200 fully refundable deposit, deadline 5/14. **Activities:** Bands, campus ministries, choral groups, dance, drama, film society, international student organizations, literary magazine, music ensembles, Model UN, musical theater, opera, radio station, student government, student newspaper, symphony orchestra, United Muslims Moving Ahead, Catholic Campus Ministries, Hillel, Global Brigades, Black Student Union, DePaul Community Service Association, Latinos Unidos, Spectrum, College Republicans, College Democrats.

Athletics. NCAA. **Intercollegiate:** Basketball, cross-country, golf M, soccer, softball W, tennis, track and field, volleyball W. **Intramural:** Badminton, basketball, football (non-tackle), racquetball, soccer, softball, table tennis, tennis, volleyball, water polo. **Team name:** Blue Demons.

Student services. Adult student services, alcohol/substance abuse counseling, chaplain/spiritual director, career counseling, services for economically disadvantaged, student employment services, financial aid counseling, health services, legal services, minority student services, personal counseling, placement for graduates, veterans' counselor, women's services. **Physically disabled:** Services for visually, speech, hearing impaired.

Contact. E-mail: admission@depaul.edu
Phone: (312) 362-8300 Toll-free number: (800) 433-7285
Fax: (312) 362-5749
Carlene Kennelly, Dean of Undergraduate Admission, DePaul University, One East Jackson Boulevard, Chicago, IL 60604-2287

DeVry University: Chicago
Chicago, Illinois
www.devry.edu   CB code: 1171

- For-profit 4-year university
- Commuter campus in very large city
- 2,006 degree-seeking undergraduates
- Interview required

General. Founded in 1931. Regionally accredited. Additional locations: Addison, Chicago Loop, Chicago O'Hare, Downers Grove, Elgin, Gurnee, Lincolnshire, Naperville, Schaumburg, Tinley Park; Merrillville (IN); Edina, St. Louis Park (MN); Milwaukee, Waukesha (WI). **Degrees:** 271 bachelor's, 182 associate awarded. **Location:** 6 miles from downtown. **Calendar:** Semester, extensive summer session. **Full-time faculty:** 37 total. **Part-time faculty:** 56 total.

Basis for selection. Applicants must have high school diploma or equivalent, or degree from an accredited postsecondary institution, demonstrate proficiency in basic college-level skills through ACT scores or institution-administered placement examinations, and be at least 17 years of age. New students may enter at beginning of any semester. SAT/ACT or DeVry-administered admissions test required for all.

High school preparation. College-preparatory program recommended.

2011-2012 Annual costs. Tuition/fees: $15,294. Books/supplies: $1,310. Personal expenses: $3,574.

Financial aid. All financial aid based on need.

Application procedures. Admission: No deadline. $50 fee. Admission notification on a rolling basis. **Financial aid:** No deadline. FAFSA required. Applicants notified on a rolling basis.

Academics. Special study options: Accelerated study, distance learning. **Credit/placement by examination:** AP, CLEP, institutional tests. **Support services:** Learning center, remedial instruction, tutoring.

Majors. Business: Business admin. **Computer sciences:** Networking, systems analysis, web page design. **Engineering:** Biomedical, electrical. **Health services:** Clinical lab science.

Most popular majors. Business/marketing 54%, computer/information sciences 25%, engineering/engineering technologies 20%.

Computing on campus. 600 workstations in library, computer center. Online course registration, online library, helpline available.

Student life. Freshman orientation: Mandatory. Preregistration for classes offered. **Housing:** Private apartments, student-plan housing, private rooms available. **Activities:** Student government, student newspaper, Muslim student association, Alpha Beta Gamma, Alpha Chi, Bible club, National Society of Black Engineers, Tau Alpha Pi.

Student services. Career counseling, student employment services, financial aid counseling, placement for graduates, veterans' counselor. **Physically disabled:** Services for visually, hearing impaired.

Contact. E-mail: admissions2@devry.edu
Phone: (773) 929-6550 Toll-free number: (800) 383-3879
Fax: (773) 697-2710
Christine Hierl, Director of Admissions, DeVry University: Chicago, 3300 North Campbell Avenue, Chicago, IL 60618-5994

DeVry University: Online
Addison, Illinois
www.devry.edu   CB code: 3816

- For-profit 4-year virtual college
- Small city
- 21,826 degree-seeking undergraduates

General. Regionally accredited. **Degrees:** 1,495 bachelor's, 860 associate awarded; master's offered. **Calendar:** Semester. **Full-time faculty:** 11 total. **Part-time faculty:** 3,141 total.

Basis for selection. Applicants must have high school diploma or equivalent, or degree from accredited post-secondary institution, demonstrate proficiency in basic college-level skills through SAT or ACT scores or institution-administered placement examinations, and be at least 17 years of age.

High school preparation. College-preparatory program recommended.

2011-2012 Annual costs. Tuition/fees: $15,294. Books/supplies: $1,300. Personal expenses: $3,574.

Financial aid. Non-need-based: Scholarships awarded for academics.

Application procedures. Admission: No deadline. $50 fee. Admission notification on a rolling basis. **Financial aid:** No deadline. FAFSA required. Applicants notified on a rolling basis.

Academics. Special study options: Accelerated study, distance learning. **Credit/placement by examination:** AP, CLEP.

Majors. Business: Accounting/finance, business admin, e-commerce. **Computer sciences:** Networking, systems analysis, web page design. **Engineering:** Software. **Visual/performing arts:** Game design.

Most popular majors. Business/marketing 88%, computer/information sciences 8%.

Contact. DeVry University: Online, One Tower Lane, Oakbrook Terrace, IL 60181

Dominican University
River Forest, Illinois   CB member
www.dom.edu   CB code: 1667

- Private 4-year university and liberal arts college affiliated with Roman Catholic Church
- Commuter campus in large town

- 1,802 degree-seeking undergraduates: 6% part-time, 67% women, 8% African American, 2% Asian American, 34% Hispanic American, 2% international
- 1,390 degree-seeking graduate students
- 59% of applicants admitted
- SAT or ACT (ACT writing optional), application essay required
- 63% graduate within 6 years

General. Founded in 1901. Regionally accredited. **Degrees:** 358 bachelor's awarded; master's, doctoral offered. **Location:** 10 miles from downtown Chicago. **Calendar:** Semester, extensive summer session. **Full-time faculty:** 159 total; 89% have terminal degrees, 59% women. **Part-time faculty:** 237 total; 61% women. **Class size:** 61% < 20, 38% 20-39, less than 1% 40-49, less than 1% 50-99. **Special facilities:** Food science laboratory.

Freshman class profile. 2,732 applied, 1,611 admitted, 416 enrolled.

Mid 50% test scores		GPA 3.0-3.49:	30%
SAT critical reading:	500-600	GPA 2.0-2.99:	23%
SAT math:	470-580	Rank in top quarter:	50%
SAT writing:	490-560	Rank in top tenth:	22%
ACT composite:	20-24	Return as sophomores:	82%
GPA 3.75 or higher:	31%	Out-of-state:	9%
GPA 3.50-3.74:	16%	Live on campus:	50%

Basis for selection. Rank in upper half of class, 2.75 GPA, ACT or SAT at or above national average, and 16 units college prep work. Interview recommended. **Home schooled:** Transcript of courses and grades required.

High school preparation. College-preparatory program required. 16 units required. Required and recommended units include English 4, mathematics 3, social studies 1, history 2, science 3 (laboratory 2) and foreign language 2. 14 credits must be in English, math, social science, laboratory science, and foreign languages.

2011-2012 Annual costs. Tuition/fees: $26,460. Room/board: $8,270. Books/supplies: $1,200. Personal expenses: $1,000.

2010-2011 Financial aid. Need-based: 401 full-time freshmen applied for aid; 380 were judged to have need; 380 of these received aid. Average need met was 83%. Average scholarship/grant was $19,032; average loan $3,151. 66% of total undergraduate aid awarded as scholarships/grants, 34% as loans/jobs. **Non-need-based:** Awarded to 288 full-time undergraduates, including 65 freshmen. Scholarships awarded for academics, alumni affiliation, art, leadership.

Application procedures. Admission: Priority date 6/1; no deadline. $25 fee, may be waived for applicants with need, free for online applicants. Admission notification on a rolling basis beginning on or about 10/1. Must reply by May 1 or within 2 week(s) if notified thereafter. **Financial aid:** Priority date 4/15; no closing date. FAFSA required. Applicants notified on a rolling basis starting 2/15; must reply within 2 week(s) of notification.

Academics. Special study options: Accelerated study, combined bachelor's/graduate degree, cross-registration, distance learning, double major, dual enrollment of high school students, ESL, honors, independent study, internships, liberal arts/career combination, study abroad, teacher certification program, Washington semester. 2+2 nursing with Rush University, 5-year BA/BS engineering program with Illinois Institute of Technology, license preparation in gerontology on-campus, 5 year program in occupational therapy with Rush University leading to master's degree. **Credit/placement by examination:** AP, CLEP, IB, institutional tests. 28 credit hours maximum toward bachelor's degree. **Support services:** Learning center, pre-admission summer program, reduced course load, remedial instruction, study skills assistance, tutoring, writing center.

Majors. Area/ethnic studies: African-American, American. **Biology:** General, neuroscience. **Business:** Accounting, business admin, fashion, international. **Communications:** Communications/speech/rhetoric, journalism, public relations. **Computer sciences:** Computer science, information systems. **Conservation:** Environmental science. **Education:** Early childhood. **English:** English lit. **Foreign languages:** French, Italian, Spanish. **General:** Food science. **Health services:** Dietetics, nursing (RN), occupational therapy, premedicine, prepharmacy. **History:** General. **Liberal arts:** Arts/sciences. **Math:** General. **Philosophy/religion:** Philosophy. **Physical sciences:** Chemistry. **Psychology:** General, clinical. **Social sciences:** Criminology, economics, international relations, political science, sociology. **Theology:** Pastoral counseling, theology. **Visual/performing arts:** Art, art history/conservation, commercial/advertising art, dramatic, fashion design, music, photography, sculpture, studio arts. **Work/family studies:** Food/nutrition, institutional food production.

Most popular majors. Business/marketing 27%, communications/journalism 7%, interdisciplinary studies 6%, psychology 10%, social sciences 16%, visual/performing arts 9%.

Computing on campus. 552 workstations in dormitories, library, computer center, student center. Dormitories wired for high-speed internet access and linked to campus network. Commuter students can connect to campus network. Online course registration, online library, helpline, wireless network available.

Student life. Freshman orientation: Mandatory. Preregistration for classes offered. Two-day program with overnight on campus. **Housing:** Guaranteed on-campus for freshmen. Coed dorms, apartments, wellness housing available. $200 partly refundable deposit. Pets allowed in dorm rooms. **Activities:** Campus ministries, choral groups, dance, drama, international student organizations, literary magazine, musical theater, student government, student newspaper, Students for Peace and Justice, Organization of Latino Americans, Eco Club, Black Student Union, Polish club, gospel choir, Team KIVA, Domestic Abuse Stops Here, Campus Crusade for Christ.

Athletics. NCAA. **Intercollegiate:** Baseball M, basketball, cross-country, golf M, soccer, softball W, tennis, volleyball W. **Intramural:** Basketball, bowling, cheerleading, racquetball, soccer, softball W, table tennis, volleyball. **Team name:** Stars.

Student services. Adult student services, alcohol/substance abuse counseling, career counseling, student employment services, financial aid counseling, health services, minority student services, on-campus daycare, personal counseling, placement for graduates, veterans' counselor. **Physically disabled:** Services for visually, hearing impaired.

Contact. E-mail: domadmis@dom.edu
Phone: (708) 524-6800 Toll-free number: (800) 828-8475
Fax: (708) 524-6864
Mary Ann Rowan, Vice President for Enrollment Management,
Dominican University, 7900 West Division Street, River Forest, IL 60305-1099

East-West University
Chicago, Illinois   CB member
www.eastwest.edu   CB code: 0798

- Private 4-year university
- Commuter campus in very large city
- 747 degree-seeking undergraduates
- Interview required

General. Founded in 1978. Regionally accredited. **Degrees:** 75 bachelor's, 58 associate awarded. **Calendar:** Quarter, limited summer session. **Full-time faculty:** 17 total. **Part-time faculty:** 53 total.

Freshman class profile.

Mid 50% test scores		Out-of-state:	10%
ACT composite:	16-22		

Basis for selection. Open admission, but selective for some programs. SAT or ACT recommended.

2011-2012 Annual costs. Tuition/fees: $16,695. Books/supplies: $1,200. Personal expenses: $2,100.

Financial aid. Non-need-based: Scholarships awarded for academics. **Additional information:** Foreign students eligible for institutional scholarship.

Application procedures. Admission: Priority date 5/1; no deadline. $50 fee, may be waived for applicants with need. Admission notification on a rolling basis. **Financial aid:** Closing date 3/31. FAFSA required. Applicants notified on a rolling basis starting 1/4; must reply within 4 week(s) of notification.

Academics. Special study options: Cooperative education, double major, ESL, honors, independent study, internships. **Credit/placement by examination:** AP, CLEP, institutional tests. Interview recommended for placement. **Support services:** Tutoring.

Majors. Business: Business admin. **Communications:** Communications/speech/rhetoric. **Computer sciences:** General. **Liberal arts:** Arts/sciences. **Math:** General.

Most popular majors. Business/marketing 32%, computer/information sciences 11%, engineering/engineering technologies 16%, liberal arts 40%.

Computing on campus. 10 workstations in computer center. Online library available.

Student life. Freshman orientation: Available. Preregistration for classes offered. **Activities:** Drama, student government, student newspaper.

Athletics. Team name: Phantom.

Student services. Career counseling.

Contact. E-mail: seeyou@eastwest.edu
Phone: (312) 939-0111 Toll-free number: (877) 398-9376
Fax: (312) 939-0083
Mettha Ross, Director of Admissions, East-West University, 816 South Michigan Avenue, Chicago, IL 60605-2185

Eastern Illinois University
Charleston, Illinois
www.eiu.edu   CB code: 1199

- Public 4-year university and teachers college
- Residential campus in large town
- 9,496 degree-seeking undergraduates: 10% part-time, 59% women, 15% African American, 1% Asian American, 4% Hispanic American, 1% international
- 1,438 degree-seeking graduate students
- 68% of applicants admitted
- SAT or ACT (ACT writing optional) required
- 62% graduate within 6 years; 27% enter graduate study

General. Founded in 1895. Regionally accredited. On-line courses and off-campus sites in Arlington Heights, Bridgeview, Carterville, Centralia, Champaign-Urbana, Chicago-American Indian Association of Illinois, Danville, Decatur, Effingham, Grayslake-University Center at College of Lake County, Mattoon, Olney, River Grove, Robinson and Vandalia. **Degrees:** 2,257 bachelor's awarded; master's offered. **ROTC:** Army. **Location:** 188 miles from Chicago, 127 miles from Indianapolis. **Calendar:** Semester, limited summer session. **Full-time faculty:** 599 total; 72% have terminal degrees, 13% minority, 46% women. **Part-time faculty:** 142 total; 11% have terminal degrees, 8% minority, 62% women. **Class size:** 36% < 20, 55% 20-39, 6% 40-49, 2% 50-99, less than 1% >100. **Special facilities:** Arts center, greenhouse, observatory, renewable energy center.

Freshman class profile. 7,076 applied, 4,808 admitted, 1,371 enrolled.

Mid 50% test scores		End year in good standing:	83%
ACT composite:	19-23	Return as sophomores:	79%
GPA 3.75 or higher:	13%	Out-of-state:	3%
GPA 3.50-3.74:	12%	Live on campus:	97%
GPA 3.0-3.49:	30%	International:	1%
GPA 2.0-2.99:	45%	Fraternities:	25%
Rank in top quarter:	30%	Sororities:	23%
Rank in top tenth:	11%		

Basis for selection. Applicants must meet one of following: Rank in top quarter of high school class six or more semesters or have GPA of 3.0 and ACT composite score of 18 (SAT 860); rank in top one half six or more semesters or have GPA of 2.50 and ACT composite score of 19 (SAT 910); rank in the top three quarters high school class six or more semesters or have a GPA of 2.25 and ACT composite score of 22 (SAT 1020). Gateway admissions program for students with at least 14 ACT and 2.0 GPA. Audition required of music majors. **Home schooled:** GED requirement may be waived with acceptable ACT score for students who present transcript of all courses completed with grades listed for each class.

High school preparation. College-preparatory program required. 17 units recommended. Recommended units include English 4, mathematics 3, social studies 3, science 3 (laboratory 3), foreign language 2 and academic electives 2. Significant science lab experience required.

2012-2013 Annual costs. New undergraduate students from bordering states of Indiana, Iowa, Kentucky, Missouri and Wisconsin will be billed at in-state tuition rate. Books/supplies: $120. Personal expenses: $1,470.

2011-2012 Financial aid. Need-based: 1,265 full-time freshmen applied for aid; 952 were judged to have need; 938 of these received aid. Average need met was 57%. Average scholarship/grant was $3,612; average loan $3,271. 42% of total undergraduate aid awarded as scholarships/grants, 58% as loans/jobs. **Non-need-based:** Awarded to 1,647 full-time undergraduates, including 390 freshmen. Scholarships awarded for academics, art, athletics, leadership, music/drama, ROTC.

Application procedures. Admission: Closing date 8/8 (postmark date). $30 fee, may be waived for applicants with need. Admission notification on a rolling basis. Must reply by May 1 or within 2 week(s) if notified thereafter. Consult university for possible early cut-off date. **Financial aid:** Priority

date 3/1; no closing date. FAFSA required. Applicants notified on a rolling basis starting 3/1; must reply within 2 week(s) of notification.

Academics. Special study options: Accelerated study, cooperative education, distance learning, double major, exchange student, honors, independent study, internships, study abroad, teacher certification program. **Credit/placement by examination:** AP, CLEP, IB, SAT, ACT, institutional tests. Credit will count toward graduation and may be used to fulfill graduation requirements but does not carry a grade. Credit by exam will only be applied toward degree if not used toward high school graduation. **Support services:** Learning center, reduced course load, remedial instruction, study skills assistance, tutoring, writing center.

Honors college/program. ACT composite score of 26 or higher, or SAT score of 1170/1600 (1760/2400) or higher; upper 10% of high school graduating class, or a 3.5 final high school GPA (on a 4.0 scale); permission of the Dean of the Honors College.

Majors. Area/ethnic studies: African-American. **Biology:** General. **Business:** Accounting, business admin, finance, management science, marketing. **Communications:** General, journalism. **Computer sciences:** General. **Education:** Elementary, health, kindergarten/preschool, science, social science, special ed, voc/tech. **Engineering:** General. **English:** English lit. **Foreign languages:** General. **Health services:** Athletic training, clinical lab science, communication disorders, nursing (RN). **History:** General. **Liberal arts:** Arts/sciences. **Math:** General. **Parks/recreation:** Exercise sciences, facilities management. **Philosophy/religion:** Philosophy. **Physical sciences:** Chemistry, geology, physics. **Psychology:** General. **Social sciences:** Economics, geography, political science, sociology. **Visual/performing arts:** Art, dramatic, music. **Work/family studies:** General.

Most popular majors. Business/marketing 14%, communications/journalism 9%, education 21%, family/consumer sciences 6%, liberal arts 9%, parks/recreation 8%, psychology 6%, social sciences 6%.

Computing on campus. 766 workstations in dormitories, library, computer center. Dormitories wired for high-speed internet access and linked to campus network. Commuter students can connect to campus network. Online course registration, online library, helpline, repair service, student web hosting, wireless network available.

Student life. Freshman orientation: Mandatory, $100 fee. Preregistration for classes offered. Offered for freshmen entering in the fall during June and July; includes advisement and registration. **Housing:** Guaranteed on-campus for all undergraduates. Coed dorms, single-sex dorms, apartments, fraternity/sorority housing available. **Activities:** Bands, campus ministries, choral groups, dance, drama, international student organizations, literary magazine, music ensembles, musical theater, radio station, student government, student newspaper, symphony orchestra, TV station, College Democrats, College Republicans, Christian Campus Fellowship, Newman Catholic Center, Unity Gospel Choir, Epsilon Sigma Alpha, Study Abroad Society, Black Student Union, College Against Cancer, Habitat for Humanity.

Athletics. NCAA. **Intercollegiate:** Baseball M, basketball, cross-country, football (tackle) M, golf, rugby W, soccer, softball W, swimming, tennis, track and field, volleyball W. **Intramural:** Badminton, basketball, bowling, football (non-tackle), racquetball, soccer, softball, table tennis, tennis, volleyball, weight lifting. **Team name:** Panthers.

Student services. Adult student services, alcohol/substance abuse counseling, career counseling, services for economically disadvantaged, student employment services, financial aid counseling, health services, legal services, minority student services, personal counseling, veterans' counselor, women's services. **Physically disabled:** Services for visually, speech, hearing impaired.

Contact. E-mail: admissions@eiu.edu
Phone: (217) 581-2223 Toll-free number: (877) 581-2348
Fax: (217) 581-7060
Brenda Major, Director of Admissions, Eastern Illinois University, 600 Lincoln Avenue, Charleston, IL 61920-3011

Elmhurst College
Elmhurst, Illinois   CB member
www.elmhurst.edu   CB code: 1204

- Private 4-year liberal arts college affiliated with United Church of Christ
- Commuter campus in large town
- 3,097 degree-seeking undergraduates: 5% part-time, 62% women, 4% African American, 4% Asian American, 10% Hispanic American, 1% Native American, 1% international
- 122 degree-seeking graduate students
- 72% of applicants admitted

- SAT or ACT (ACT writing optional) required
- 70% graduate within 6 years

General. Founded in 1871. Regionally accredited. **Degrees:** 794 bachelor's awarded; master's offered. **ROTC:** Army, Air Force. **Location:** 16 miles from Chicago. **Calendar:** 4-1-4, limited summer session. **Full-time faculty:** 141 total; 80% have terminal degrees, 11% minority. **Part-time faculty:** 233 total; 19% have terminal degrees, 10% minority. **Class size:** 62% < 20, 37% 20-39, less than 1% 40-49. **Special facilities:** 2 nuclear accelerators, 4 electron microscopes, Impressionist art collection, computer science and technology center, media center, sound studio, greenhouse.

Freshman class profile. 2,899 applied, 2,093 admitted, 608 enrolled.

Mid 50% test scores		Return as sophomores:	80%
SAT critical reading:	450-580	Out-of-state:	16%
SAT math:	490-590	Live on campus:	72%
SAT writing:	440-550	Fraternities:	7%
ACT composite:	21-26	Sororities:	11%

Basis for selection. School achievement record, including grades and course levels, most important, followed by test scores. Applicants should rank in top half of class. Activities and counselor recommendations also important. Interview and essay recommended for all applicants, required of academically marginal applicants. Audition required of music majors. Portfolio recommended for art majors. **Home schooled:** Interview strongly recommended.

High school preparation. College-preparatory program recommended. 16 units required; 21 recommended. Required and recommended units include English 4, mathematics 2-3, social studies 2-3, history 1-2, science 2-3 (laboratory 2-3), foreign language 1-2 and academic electives 4. Chemistry required for nursing applicants. 3 mathematics required for most business administration and computer-related specialties applicants.

2011-2012 Annual costs. Tuition/fees: $30,054. Room/board: $9,610. Books/supplies: $1,500. Personal expenses: $1,300.

Financial aid. Non-need-based: Scholarships awarded for academics, alumni affiliation, art, minority status, music/drama, religious affiliation, ROTC, state residency. **Additional information:** Must apply for admission by 1/15 for priority consideration for scholarships.

Application procedures. Admission: Priority date 4/15; no deadline. No application fee. Admission notification on a rolling basis beginning on or about 11/1. Must reply by May 1 or within 2 week(s) if notified thereafter. **Financial aid:** Priority date 4/15; no closing date. FAFSA required. Applicants notified on a rolling basis starting 3/1; must reply within 3 week(s) of notification.

Academics. Special study options: Accelerated study, combined bachelor's/graduate degree, cooperative education, double major, dual enrollment of high school students, honors, independent study, internships, liberal arts/career combination, study abroad, teacher certification program, Washington semester. 3+2 engineering with Illinois Institute of Technology, University of Illinois at Urbana-Champaign, and Washington University (MO). **Credit/placement by examination:** AP, CLEP, IB, institutional tests. 48 credit hours maximum toward bachelor's degree. **Support services:** Learning center, pre-admission summer program, reduced course load, study skills assistance, tutoring.

Majors. Area/ethnic studies: American. **Biology:** General. **Business:** Accounting, business admin, finance, international, logistics, marketing. **Communications:** Communications/speech/rhetoric. **Computer sciences:** Computer science, information systems. **Conservation:** Management/policy. **Education:** General, agricultural, art, biology, chemistry, early childhood, elementary, English, French, German, history, kindergarten/preschool, mathematics, music, physical, physics, secondary, Spanish, special ed. **English:** English lit. **Foreign languages:** French, German, Spanish. **Health services:** Nursing (RN), predental, premedicine, prepharmacy, preveterinary, speech pathology. **History:** General. **Liberal arts:** Arts/sciences. **Math:** General. **Parks/recreation:** Exercise sciences, health/fitness, sports admin. **Philosophy/religion:** Philosophy. **Physical sciences:** Chemistry, physics. **Protective services:** Criminal justice, law enforcement admin. **Psychology:** General. **Social sciences:** Criminology, economics, geography, political science, sociology, urban studies. **Theology:** Preministerial, theology. **Visual/performing arts:** Art, dramatic, music, music management.

Most popular majors. Business/marketing 20%, education 20%, health sciences 11%, psychology 9%.

Computing on campus. 800 workstations in library, computer center, student center. Dormitories wired for high-speed internet access and linked to campus network. Commuter students can connect to campus network. Online library, helpline, repair service, wireless network available.

Student life. Freshman orientation: Mandatory. Preregistration for classes offered. Three-day program held immediately prior to term. **Policies:** Each residence hall is self-governing. **Housing:** Coed dorms, apartments available. $300 nonrefundable deposit, deadline 4/1. **Activities:** Bands, campus ministries, choral groups, drama, international student organizations, literary magazine, music ensembles, musical theater, radio station, student government, student newspaper, over 90 organizations.

Athletics. NCAA. **Intercollegiate:** Baseball M, basketball, bowling W, cross-country, football (tackle) M, golf, lacrosse, soccer, softball W, tennis, track and field, volleyball W, wrestling M. **Intramural:** Basketball, football (tackle) M, golf, racquetball, softball, volleyball. **Team name:** Blue Jays.

Student services. Adult student services, career counseling, student employment services, financial aid counseling, health services, minority student services, on-campus daycare, personal counseling, placement for graduates.

Contact. E-mail: admit@elmhurst.edu
Phone: (630) 617-3400 Toll-free number: (800) 697-1871
Fax: (630) 617-5501
Stephanie Levenson, Director of Admission, Elmhurst College, 190 South Prospect Avenue, Elmhurst, IL 60126-3296

Eureka College
Eureka, Illinois **CB member**
www.eureka.edu **CB code: 1206**

- Private 4-year liberal arts college affiliated with Christian Church (Disciples of Christ)
- Residential campus in small town
- 755 degree-seeking undergraduates
- 72% of applicants admitted
- SAT or ACT (ACT writing recommended) required

General. Founded in 1855. Regionally accredited. **Degrees:** 163 bachelor's awarded. **Location:** 140 miles from Chicago. **Calendar:** Semester, limited summer session. **Full-time faculty:** 43 total. **Part-time faculty:** 29 total. **Class size:** 64% < 20, 36% 20-39. **Special facilities:** Ronald Reagan Museum, peace garden, lilac arboretum, labyrinth, fitness center.

Freshman class profile. 1,007 applied, 726 admitted, 160 enrolled.

Mid 50% test scores		Rank in top tenth:	23%
ACT composite:	19-26	Out-of-state:	4%
Rank in top quarter:	56%	Live on campus:	90%

Basis for selection. Class rank, high school GPA, ACT scores, and high school curriculum most important. Recommendations and interviews also important. Must have minimum ACT composite of 17 and high school GPA of 2.3. Audition required for music and drama scholarships. Portfolio required for art scholarship. **Home schooled:** Interview required.

High school preparation. 14 units recommended. Recommended units include English 4, mathematics 3, social studies 3, science 2 and foreign language 2.

2011-2012 Annual costs. Tuition/fees: $18,750. Room/board: $8,000. Books/supplies: $1,000. Personal expenses: $510.

Financial aid. Non-need-based: Scholarships awarded for academics, alumni affiliation, art, leadership, music/drama, religious affiliation.

Application procedures. Admission: Closing date 8/10 (postmark date). No application fee. Admission notification on a rolling basis. Must reply by May 1 or within 3 week(s) if notified thereafter. **Financial aid:** Priority date 4/15; no closing date. FAFSA required. Applicants notified on a rolling basis starting 2/15; must reply by 5/1 or within 3 week(s) of notification.

Academics. Special study options: Cooperative education, double major, dual enrollment of high school students, honors, independent study, internships, liberal arts/career combination, student-designed major, study abroad, teacher certification program, Washington semester. Students who began as freshmen, have a record of leadership and service, and hold a 3.5 GPA at the end of their sophomore year qualify for a mentorship paid for by the college. **Credit/placement by examination:** AP, CLEP, institutional tests. **Support services:** Learning center, reduced course load, remedial instruction, study skills assistance, tutoring, writing center.

Honors college/program. Admitted by invitation, includes advanced and special classes, advanced general education requirements along with thesis preparation and presentation, honors seminars on special topics.

Majors. Biology: General, environmental. **Business:** General, accounting, business admin, finance, management information systems, marketing. **Communications:** Communications/speech/rhetoric, media studies, public relations. **Computer sciences:** General, computer science. **Education:** General, elementary, middle, multi-level teacher, secondary, special ed. **Engineering:** General. **English:** Creative writing, English lit, writing. **Health services:** Predental, premedicine, prenursing, preveterinary. **History:** General. **Liberal arts:** Arts/sciences. **Math:** General. **Philosophy/religion:** Philosophy, religion. **Physical sciences:** Chemistry. **Protective services:** Law enforcement admin. **Psychology:** General. **Social sciences:** Political science. **Visual/performing arts:** Art, dramatic, music performance, studio arts management.

Computing on campus. 50 workstations in dormitories, library, computer center, student center. Dormitories wired for high-speed internet access and linked to campus network. Commuter students can connect to campus network. Online library, helpline, repair service available.

Student life. Freshman orientation: Mandatory. Preregistration for classes offered. Orientation for new students held at start of school year. **Policies:** All single students under 24 not living with parents required to live on campus. **Housing:** Guaranteed on-campus for all undergraduates. Coed dorms, single-sex dorms, special housing for disabled, fraternity/sorority housing, wellness housing available. $150 fully refundable deposit, deadline 8/14. **Activities:** Bands, choral groups, dance, drama, film society, literary magazine, music ensembles, musical theater, student government, student newspaper, Disciples on Campus, PRIDE, Young Republicans, Campus Democrats, Catholic Salve Regina Newman Center, Campus Crusade for Christ, Black student union, Habitat for Humanity, Student Foundation, International Healthcare Development Program.

Athletics. NCAA. **Intercollegiate:** Baseball M, basketball, cross-country, diving, football (tackle) M, golf, soccer, softball W, swimming, tennis, track and field, volleyball W. **Intramural:** Badminton, basketball, bowling, football (non-tackle), golf, softball, swimming, table tennis, tennis, volleyball. **Team name:** Red Devils.

Student services. Adult student services, alcohol/substance abuse counseling, chaplain/spiritual director, career counseling, student employment services, financial aid counseling, health services, personal counseling, placement for graduates.

Contact. E-mail: admissions@eureka.edu
Phone: (309) 467-6350 Toll-free number: (888) 438-7352
Fax: (309) 467-6576
Kurt Krile, Dean of Admissions and Financial Aid, Eureka College, 300 East College Avenue, Eureka, IL 61530-1500

Governors State University
University Park, Illinois
www.govst.edu   **CB code: 0807**

▶ Public two-year upper-division university
▶ Commuter campus in large town

General. Founded in 1969. Regionally accredited. Upper-division at the undergraduate-level, no freshmen or sophomores. **Degrees:** 908 bachelor's awarded; master's, professional, doctoral offered. **Articulation:** Agreements with Prairie State College, Joliet Junior College, Kankakee CC, Moraine Valley CC, South Suburban College of Cook County, College of DuPage, Morton College, City Colleges of Chicago, Waubonsee CC, Triton College, Parkland College, College of Lake County, Illinois Valley College, Ivy Tech State College (IN). **Location:** 30 miles from Chicago. **Calendar:** Semester, extensive summer session. **Full-time faculty:** 213 total; 68% have terminal degrees, 35% minority, 54% women. **Part-time faculty:** 177 total; 6% have terminal degrees, 24% minority, 55% women. **Class size:** 69% < 20, 29% 20-39, 1% 40-49, less than 1% 50-99, less than 1% >100. **Special facilities:** 750-acre campus, nature trails, 6 lakes, sculpture park, prairie restoration.

Student profile. 2,857 degree-seeking undergraduates, 2,241 degree-seeking graduate students. 63% transferred from two-year, 37% transferred from four-year institutions.

Women:	69%	Part-time:	61%
African American:	37%	Out-of-state:	16%
Asian American:	2%	25 or older:	69%
Hispanic American:	9%		

Basis for selection. Open admission. College transcript required. 60 semester hours or associate degree required. Transfer accepted as juniors, seniors.

2011-2012 Annual costs. Tuition/fees: $8,936; $16,226 out-of-state. Books/supplies: $1,200. Personal expenses: $800.

Financial aid. Non-need-based: Scholarships awarded for academics.

Application procedures. Admission: Rolling admission. $25 fee, may be waived for applicants with need.

Academics. Special study options: Distance learning, double major, dual enrollment of high school students, honors, independent study, internships, student-designed major, teacher certification program. Dual admission with several community colleges. **Credit/placement by examination:** AP, CLEP. 60 credit hours maximum toward bachelor's degree.

Majors. Biology: General. **Business:** Accounting, business admin, management information systems. **Communications:** Broadcast journalism, communications/speech/rhetoric, journalism. **Computer sciences:** General, computer science. **Education:** Biology, chemistry, early childhood, elementary, English, mathematics. **English:** English lit. **Health services:** Health care admin, nursing (RN), speech pathology. **Human services:** General, social work. **Liberal arts:** Arts/sciences. **Math:** General. **Physical sciences:** Chemistry. **Protective services:** Criminal justice. **Psychology:** General. **Social sciences:** General. **Visual/performing arts:** Art.

Most popular majors. Security/protective services 8%.

Computing on campus. 280 workstations in library, computer center, student center. Commuter students can connect to campus network. Online library, helpline, wireless network available.

Student life. Policies: A minimum of seven students can seek chartering as a student club or organization through the Office of Student Life. All organizations must renew their charters each academic year. **Activities:** Drama, international student organizations, literary magazine, student government, student newspaper, Art Forum, Association of Latin American Students, Black Student Union, Chinese students association, Japanese philosophy, art and culture club, Spanish reading club, table tennis club, wellness club, over 30 co-curricular professional service organizations.

Athletics. Intramural: Table tennis.

Student services. Career counseling, financial aid counseling, minority student services, on-campus daycare, personal counseling. **Physically disabled:** Services for visually, speech, hearing impaired.

Contact. Phone: (708) 534-4490 Fax: (708) 534-1640
Sharon Evans, Director of Admissions & Student Recruitment, Governors State University, One University Parkway, University Park, IL 60484

Greenville College
Greenville, Illinois
www.greenville.edu   **CB code: 1256**

▶ Private 4-year liberal arts college affiliated with Free Methodist Church of North America
▶ Residential campus in small town
▶ 1,254 degree-seeking undergraduates: 2% part-time, 49% women, 10% African American, 1% Asian American, 3% Hispanic American, 2% international
▶ 194 degree-seeking graduate students
▶ 74% of applicants admitted
▶ SAT or ACT (ACT writing optional), application essay required
▶ 52% graduate within 6 years

General. Founded in 1892. Regionally accredited. Academic and Christian values emphasized. **Degrees:** 379 bachelor's awarded; master's offered. **Location:** 50 miles from St. Louis, 190 miles from Indianapolis. **Calendar:** 4-1-4, limited summer session. **Full-time faculty:** 60 total; 78% have terminal degrees, 5% minority, 38% women. **Part-time faculty:** 101 total; 6% have terminal degrees, 1% minority, 54% women. **Class size:** 59% < 20, 31% 20-39, 5% 40-49, 5% 50-99, less than 1% >100. **Special facilities:** Sculpture collection, Frank Lloyd Wright architectural drawings, 140 acre field station and nature preserve, observatory, environmental education center.

Freshman class profile. 1,107 applied, 823 admitted, 276 enrolled.

Mid 50% test scores			
SAT critical reading:	450-580	GPA 2.0-2.99:	30%
SAT math:	450-610	Rank in top quarter:	35%
SAT writing:	440-560	Rank in top tenth:	12%
ACT composite:	19-25	Return as sophomores:	67%
GPA 3.75 or higher:	25%	Out-of-state:	45%
GPA 3.50-3.74:	15%	Live on campus:	95%
GPA 3.0-3.49:	28%	International:	1%

Basis for selection. Secondary school record, standardized test scores, application essay, and religious affiliation or commitment very important. Extracurricular activities, talent/ability and character considered. SAT, ACT,

SAT Subject Test scores must be received by institution's drop/add date. Interview required of academically weak applicants. Audition recommended for music majors. **Home schooled:** Transcript of courses and grades required.

High school preparation. College-preparatory program recommended. 11 units recommended. Recommended units include English 4, mathematics 2, history 1, science 1 (laboratory 1) and foreign language 2. Math recommendation includes algebra and geometry.

2011-2012 Annual costs. Tuition/fees: $22,198. Tuition includes textbook rental. Room/board: $7,338. Books/supplies: $250. Personal expenses: $2,000.

2010-2011 Financial aid. Need-based: 190 full-time freshmen applied for aid; 173 were judged to have need; 168 of these received aid. Average need met was 72%. Average scholarship/grant was $1,589; average loan $3,493. 65% of total undergraduate aid awarded as scholarships/grants, 35% as loans/jobs. **Non-need-based:** Awarded to 147 full-time undergraduates, including 36 freshmen. Scholarships awarded for academics, alumni affiliation, art, minority status, religious affiliation.

Application procedures. Admission: No deadline. $30 fee, may be waived for applicants with need. Admission notification on a rolling basis beginning on or about 7/10. Housing deposit refundable prior to May 1st. **Financial aid:** Priority date 3/1; no closing date. FAFSA required. Applicants notified on a rolling basis starting 3/31.

Academics. Special study options: Accelerated study, cooperative education, cross-registration, double major, external degree, honors, independent study, internships, liberal arts/career combination, semester at sea, student-designed major, study abroad, teacher certification program, urban semester, Washington semester. **Credit/placement by examination:** AP, CLEP, IB, SAT, ACT, institutional tests. 32 credit hours maximum toward bachelor's degree. **Support services:** Learning center, reduced course load, remedial instruction, study skills assistance, tutoring.

Majors. Biology: General, environmental. **Business:** Accounting, business admin, management information systems, marketing, organizational behavior. **Communications:** Media studies, public relations. **Computer sciences:** General. **Education:** Biology, chemistry, early childhood, elementary, English, history, mathematics, music, physical, physics, Spanish, special ed. **English:** English lit, rhetoric/composition. **Foreign languages:** Spanish. **Health services:** Predental, premedicine, prenursing, preveterinary. **History:** General. **Human services:** Social work. **Liberal arts:** Arts/sciences. **Math:** General. **Parks/recreation:** General, exercise sciences, sports admin. **Philosophy/religion:** Philosophy, religion. **Physical sciences:** Chemistry, physics. **Protective services:** Law enforcement admin. **Psychology:** General. **Social sciences:** Sociology. **Theology:** Pastoral counseling, youth ministry. **Visual/performing arts:** Art, dramatic, music, music management.

Most popular majors. Business/marketing 33%, education 26%, visual/performing arts 7%.

Computing on campus. 95 workstations in library, computer center. Dormitories wired for high-speed internet access and linked to campus network. Commuter students can connect to campus network. Online library, helpline, repair service, wireless network available.

Student life. Freshman orientation: Mandatory. Preregistration for classes offered. Service project conducted over orientation weekend. **Policies:** Signed statements of Christian values and academic honesty requested. Required chapel. All single students not living at home must live in college housing. Religious observance required. **Housing:** Guaranteed on-campus for all undergraduates. Single-sex dorms, apartments, wellness housing available. $200 fully refundable deposit, deadline 7/18. Upper division students may live in college-owned houses. **Activities:** Bands, campus ministries, choral groups, drama, music ensembles, musical theater, radio station, student government, student newspaper, Habitat for Humanity, Fellowship of Christian Athletes, Campus Activities Board, student outreach, Agape music festival, Circle K, E-cafe, Mosaic, Young Republicans, Big Brother/Big Sister.

Athletics. NCAA, NCCAA. **Intercollegiate:** Baseball M, basketball, cross-country, football (tackle) M, soccer, softball W, tennis, track and field, volleyball W. **Intramural:** Badminton, basketball, football (non-tackle), soccer, softball, table tennis, tennis, volleyball. **Team name:** Panthers.

Student services. Adult student services, career counseling, student employment services, financial aid counseling, personal counseling, placement for graduates.

Contact. E-mail: admissions@greenville.edu
Phone: (618) 664-7100 Toll-free number: (800) 345-4440
Fax: (618) 664-9841
Michael Ritter, Vice President for Enrollment, Greenville College, 315 East College Avenue, Greenville, IL 62246-0159

Harrington College of Design
Chicago, Illinois
www.harrington.edu   **CB code:** 0940

- For-profit 4-year visual arts college
- Commuter campus in very large city
- 640 degree-seeking undergraduates: 65% part-time, 76% women, 14% African American, 4% Asian American, 15% Hispanic American
- 128 degree-seeking graduate students
- Application essay, interview required
- 35% graduate within 6 years

General. Founded in 1931. Accredited by ACICS. **Degrees:** 162 bachelor's, 88 associate awarded; master's offered. **Location:** Downtown. **Calendar:** Semester, extensive summer session. **Full-time faculty:** 17 total; 18% have terminal degrees, 35% women. **Part-time faculty:** 60 total; 40% women. **Class size:** 86% < 20, 14% 20-39. **Special facilities:** Access to Chicago Merchandise Mart's wholesale showroom.

Freshman class profile. 77 applied, 69 admitted, 41 enrolled.

End year in good standing:	78%	**Out-of-state:**	17%
Return as sophomores:	64%		

Basis for selection. Open admission, but selective for some programs. Undergrad - Personal interview, personal statement of intent, commitment to career, standardized test scores, 2.0 GPA most important. **Home schooled:** Transcript of courses and grades, state high school equivalency certificate required.

High school preparation. College-preparatory program recommended. Recommended units include English 4, mathematics 3, science 3 and foreign language 1. 3 units social sciences recommended.

2011-2012 Annual costs. Tuition/fees: $19,300. Required fees vary by program. Some programs require laptop computer purchase. Books/supplies: $1,500. Personal expenses: $1,896.

Financial aid. Non-need-based: Scholarships awarded for academics, leadership.

Application procedures. Admission: No deadline. $60 fee. Admission notification on a rolling basis. **Financial aid:** Priority date 3/1, closing date 6/30. FAFSA required. Applicants notified on a rolling basis; must reply within 2 week(s) of notification.

Academics. Special study options: Cooperative education, internships, study abroad. **Credit/placement by examination:** AP, CLEP. **Support services:** Learning center, tutoring, writing center.

Majors. Visual/performing arts: Graphic design, interior design, photography.

Computing on campus. 293 workstations in library, computer center. Online course registration, online library, wireless network available.

Student life. Freshman orientation: Mandatory. Preregistration for classes offered. One-day program held 1 or 2 weeks before classes begin. **Activities:** Student government, American Society of Interior Design student chapter, IIDA student chapter.

Student services. Career counseling, student employment services, financial aid counseling, personal counseling, placement for graduates, veterans' counselor.

Contact. E-mail: admissions@interiordesign.edu
Phone: (312) 939-4975 Toll-free number: (877) 939-4975
Fax: (312) 939-8005
Jessie McEwen, Director of Admissions, Harrington College of Design, 200 West Madison Avenue, Chicago, IL 60606-3433

Hebrew Theological College
Skokie, Illinois
www.htc.edu   **CB code:** 0817

- Private 4-year liberal arts and rabbinical college affiliated with Jewish faith
- Residential campus in small city
- 473 degree-seeking undergraduates
- SAT or ACT (ACT writing optional), application essay, interview required

General. Regionally accredited. Co-ed on separate campuses. Program designated as master's level is Rabbinic Ordination. **Degrees:** 34 bachelor's awarded; master's offered. **Location:** 15 miles from downtown. **Calendar:** Semester, limited summer session. **Full-time faculty:** 11 total. **Part-time faculty:** 38 total. **Class size:** 94% < 20, 6% 20-39.

Basis for selection. Admissions decisions are reached by reviewing academic records, assessment data, and application materials in conjunction with input from personal interviews and recommendations.

2011-2012 Annual costs. Tuition/fees: $19,150. Room/board: $9,390.

Application procedures. Admission: No deadline. $100 fee, may be waived for applicants with need. Application must be submitted on paper. Admission notification on a rolling basis.

Academics. Special study options: Combined bachelor's/graduate degree, distance learning, double major, dual enrollment of high school students, independent study, teacher certification program. **Credit/placement by examination:** AP, CLEP, institutional tests. 15 credit hours maximum toward bachelor's degree. **Support services:** Remedial instruction, tutoring, writing center.

Majors. Business: General, accounting. **Education:** Elementary, special ed. **English:** English lit. **Liberal arts:** Arts/sciences. **Philosophy/religion:** Judaic. **Psychology:** General.

Most popular majors. Business/marketing 6%, philosophy/religious studies 66%, psychology 15%.

Computing on campus. 30 workstations in library, computer center. Dormitories wired for high-speed internet access.

Student life. Freshman orientation: Mandatory. Preregistration for classes offered. **Policies:** Religious observance required. **Housing:** Guaranteed on-campus for all undergraduates. Single-sex dorms, apartments available.

Contact. E-mail: admissions@htc.edu
Phone: (847) 982-2500 Fax: (847) 674-6381
Rabbi Joshua Zisook, Director of Admissions, Hebrew Theological College, 7135 North Carpenter Road, Skokie, IL 60077

Illinois College
Jacksonville, Illinois
www.ic.edu

CB member
CB code: 1315

- Private 4-year liberal arts college affiliated with Presbyterian Church (USA) and United Church of Christ
- Residential campus in large town
- 906 degree-seeking undergraduates: 47% women, 8% African American, 1% Asian American, 3% Hispanic American, 2% international
- 18 degree-seeking graduate students
- 65% of applicants admitted
- 56% graduate within 6 years

General. Founded in 1829. Regionally accredited. New England style quad and architecture. **Degrees:** 211 bachelor's awarded; master's offered. **Location:** 30 miles from Springfield, 90 miles from St. Louis. **Calendar:** Semester, limited summer session. **Full-time faculty:** 76 total; 83% have terminal degrees, 8% minority, 49% women. **Part-time faculty:** 17 total; 18% have terminal degrees, 59% women. **Class size:** 68% < 20, 29% 20-39, 2% 40-49, 2% 50-99. **Special facilities:** Biology station, observatory.

Freshman class profile. 1,626 applied, 1,054 admitted, 288 enrolled.

Mid 50% test scores			
SAT critical reading:	430-560	GPA 2.0-2.99:	27%
SAT math:	410-580	Rank in top quarter:	48%
SAT writing:	430-540	Rank in top tenth:	21%
ACT composite:	19-26	Return as sophomores:	83%
GPA 3.75 or higher:	24%	Out-of-state:	14%
GPA 3.50-3.74:	15%	Live on campus:	96%
GPA 3.0-3.49:	34%	International:	1%

Basis for selection. Core course GPA, rank in top half of class, test scores, 1 letter of recommendation from teacher, 1 letter of recommendation from guidance counselor important. Interview recommended, essay considered. **Home schooled:** Transcript of courses and grades, letter of recommendation (nonparent) required.

High school preparation. College-preparatory program recommended. 16 units required; 20 recommended. Required and recommended units include English 4, mathematics 3, social studies 1, history 1, science 2-3 (laboratory 2-3), foreign language 2 and academic electives 3.

2011-2012 Annual costs. Tuition/fees: $24,530. Room/board: $8,200. Books/supplies: $900. Personal expenses: $900.

2011-2012 Financial aid. Need-based: 253 full-time freshmen applied for aid; 231 were judged to have need; 231 of these received aid. Average need met was 86%. Average scholarship/grant was $17,153; average loan $4,284. 71% of total undergraduate aid awarded as scholarships/grants, 29% as loans/jobs. **Non-need-based:** Awarded to 257 full-time undergraduates, including 84 freshmen. Scholarships awarded for academics, art, minority status, music/drama.

Application procedures. Admission: Priority date 12/15; no deadline. No application fee. Admission notification on a rolling basis beginning on or about 11/1. Must reply by May 1 or within 3 week(s) if notified thereafter. **Financial aid:** Priority date 3/1; no closing date. FAFSA required. Applicants notified on a rolling basis starting 3/1; must reply within 2 week(s) of notification.

Academics. Special study options: Combined bachelor's/graduate degree, cross-registration, double major, dual enrollment of high school students, independent study, internships, liberal arts/career combination, student-designed major, study abroad, teacher certification program, Washington semester. 2 week BreakAway program for intensive study abroad or domestically. **Credit/placement by examination:** AP, CLEP, IB, SAT, ACT, institutional tests. 84 credit hours maximum toward bachelor's degree. **Support services:** Reduced course load, study skills assistance, tutoring, writing center.

Majors. Area/ethnic studies: American. **Biology:** General, environmental. **Business:** Accounting, finance, management information systems, managerial economics. **Computer sciences:** Computer science. **Education:** Early childhood, elementary, physical. **English:** English lit, rhetoric/composition. **Foreign languages:** French, German, Spanish. **History:** General. **Math:** General. **Philosophy/religion:** Philosophy, religion. **Physical sciences:** Chemistry, physics. **Psychology:** General. **Social sciences:** Economics, political science, sociology. **Visual/performing arts:** Art, dramatic, music, studio arts.

Most popular majors. Biology 14%, business/marketing 11%, education 10%, English 11%, history 6%, interdisciplinary studies 16%, psychology 8%, social sciences 12%.

Computing on campus. 125 workstations in library, computer center. Dormitories wired for high-speed internet access and linked to campus network. Commuter students can connect to campus network. Online course registration, online library, helpline, repair service, student web hosting, wireless network available.

Student life. Freshman orientation: Mandatory. Preregistration for classes offered. Overnight orientation program and several summer sessions are available. **Policies:** Student representation on faculty committees. **Housing:** Guaranteed on-campus for all undergraduates. Coed dorms, single-sex dorms, apartments available. Honors housing available. **Activities:** Campus ministries, choral groups, dance, drama, international student organizations, literary magazine, music ensembles, Model UN, radio station, student government, student newspaper, Young Republicans, Young Democrats, Alpha Phi Omega, men's and women's literary societies, debate club, Action Jacksonville.

Athletics. NCAA. **Intercollegiate:** Baseball M, basketball, cheerleading, cross-country, football (tackle) M, golf, soccer, softball W, tennis, track and field, volleyball W. **Intramural:** Basketball, cricket, football (non-tackle) M, handball, racquetball, softball, volleyball. **Team name:** Blueboys, Lady Blues.

Student services. Alcohol/substance abuse counseling, chaplain/spiritual director, career counseling, student employment services, financial aid counseling, health services, personal counseling, placement for graduates. **Physically disabled:** Services for visually, hearing impaired.

Contact. E-mail: admissions@ic.edu
Phone: (217) 245-3030 Toll-free number: (866) 464-5265
Fax: (217) 245-3034
Barb Lundberg, Vice President for Enrollment, Illinois College, 1101 West College Avenue, Jacksonville, IL 62650

Illinois Institute of Art: Chicago
Chicago, Illinois
www.ilic.artinstitutes.edu

CB code: 2908

- For-profit 4-year visual arts college
- Commuter campus in very large city

- 2,859 undergraduates
- Application essay required

General. Founded in 1916. Regionally accredited; also accredited by ACCSC. Branch campus at Woodfield in Schaumburg. **Degrees:** 434 bachelor's, 42 associate awarded. **Calendar:** Semester. **Full-time faculty:** 76 total. **Part-time faculty:** 145 total. **Special facilities:** Computer graphics laboratories, exhibit galleries, incentive studio.

Basis for selection. Secondary school record, interview, and personal statement most important. SAT or ACT recommended for placement and evaluation. Portfolio required for advertising design, illustration, photography, fashion design, fashion illustration majors.

High school preparation. Recommended units include English 4, mathematics 3, social studies 2, science 3 and foreign language 1. Recommend art, interior design, drafting, fashion.

2011-2012 Annual costs. Tuition/fees: $21,735. Room/board: $10,197. Books/supplies: $1,000.

Application procedures. Admission: No deadline. $150 fee. Admission notification on a rolling basis. **Financial aid:** Priority date 5/1; no closing date. FAFSA required. Applicants notified on a rolling basis.

Academics. Credit/placement by examination: AP, CLEP. **Support services:** Reduced course load.

Majors. Business: Fashion. **Communications:** Advertising. **Visual/performing arts:** Commercial/advertising art, fashion design, interior design.

Computing on campus. 25 workstations in computer center.

Student life. Activities: Student Positive Action Committee.

Contact. E-mail: antonj@aii.edu
Phone: (312) 280-3500 Toll-free number: (800) 351-3450
Janice Anton, Senior Director of Admissions, Illinois Institute of Art: Chicago, 350 North Orleans Street, Chicago, IL 60654

Illinois Institute of Art: Schaumburg
Schaumburg, Illinois
www.artinstitutes.edu/schaumburg   **CB code: 3043**

- For-profit 3-year visual arts and career college
- Commuter campus in small city
- 1,246 degree-seeking undergraduates
- 44% of applicants admitted
- Application essay, interview required

General. Regionally accredited; also accredited by ACCSC. **Degrees:** 200 bachelor's, 12 associate awarded. **Location:** 26 miles from Chicago. **Calendar:** Quarter, extensive summer session. **Full-time faculty:** 37 total. **Part-time faculty:** 48 total. **Special facilities:** Gallery, motion capture studio, lighting lab, sound lab, green room.

Freshman class profile. 540 applied, 238 admitted, 226 enrolled.

Basis for selection. SAT or ACT recommended. Portfolios required for some majors. **Home schooled:** Transcript of courses and grades required.

2011-2012 Annual costs. Tuition/fees: $23,184. Room/board: $7,470. Books/supplies: $987. Personal expenses: $1,788.

Financial aid. Non-need-based: Scholarships awarded for academics, art.

Application procedures. Admission: No deadline. $50 fee. Admission notification on a rolling basis. **Financial aid:** Priority date 3/1; no closing date. FAFSA required.

Academics. Special study options: Accelerated study, internships, liberal arts/career combination, study abroad. **Credit/placement by examination:** AP, CLEP. **Support services:** Learning center, pre-admission summer program, reduced course load, remedial instruction, study skills assistance, tutoring.

Majors. BACHELOR'S. Business: Fashion, hospitality admin, special products marketing. **Communications:** Advertising. **Communications technology:** Graphics, photo/film/video. **Computer sciences:** Webmaster. **Visual/performing arts:** General, art, commercial/advertising art, design, game design, interior design, multimedia. **ASSOCIATE. Communications technology:** Graphics. **Computer sciences:** Webmaster. **Visual/performing arts:** Design.

Student life. Freshman orientation: Mandatory. Preregistration for classes offered. Held the week before school begins. **Housing:** Single-sex dorms available. $200 deposit. Dormitory-style living in college-leased apartments. **Activities:** Literary magazine, student government, student newspaper.

Student services. Adult student services, career counseling, student employment services, financial aid counseling, personal counseling, placement for graduates, veterans' counselor.

Contact. E-mail: ILISadmissions@aii.edu
Phone: (847) 619-3450 Toll-free number: (800) 314-3450
Fax: (847) 619-3064
Jamie Carson, Senior Director of Admissions, Illinois Institute of Art: Schaumburg, 1000 North Plaza Drive, Schaumburg, IL 60173

Illinois Institute of Technology
Chicago, Illinois   **CB member**
www.iit.edu   **CB code: 1318**

- Private 4-year university and engineering college
- Residential campus in very large city
- 2,639 degree-seeking undergraduates: 5% part-time, 31% women, 7% African American, 11% Asian American, 11% Hispanic American, 21% international
- 4,873 degree-seeking graduate students
- 64% of applicants admitted
- SAT or ACT (ACT writing recommended), application essay required
- 64% graduate within 6 years

General. Founded in 1890. Regionally accredited. **Degrees:** 545 bachelor's awarded; master's, professional, doctoral offered. **ROTC:** Army, Naval, Air Force. **Location:** 3 miles from downtown. **Calendar:** Semester, extensive summer session. **Full-time faculty:** 397 total; 90% have terminal degrees, 2% minority, 23% women. **Part-time faculty:** 317 total; 2% minority, 29% women. **Class size:** 55% < 20, 33% 20-39, 6% 40-49, 5% 50-99, less than 1% >100. **Special facilities:** Prototyping shop.

Freshman class profile. 2,466 applied, 1,566 admitted, 448 enrolled.

Mid 50% test scores			
SAT critical reading:	530-640	Rank in top quarter:	75%
SAT math:	610-710	Rank in top tenth:	46%
SAT writing:	520-630	End year in good standing:	90%
ACT composite:	24-31	Return as sophomores:	95%
GPA 3.75 or higher:	64%	Out-of-state:	18%
GPA 3.50-3.74:	15%	Live on campus:	77%
GPA 3.0-3.49:	17%	International:	18%
GPA 2.0-2.99:	4%	Fraternities:	20%
		Sororities:	15%

Basis for selection. Admission decisions are based on the following: academic performance, strength of curriculum, test scores, counselor recommendations, and application essay. Class rank, interview, extracurricular activities, alumni relationship, volunteer and work experience also considered. Interview recommended. Portfolio optional for first-year freshmen entering College of Architecture. **Home schooled:** Statement describing home school structure and mission, letter of recommendation (nonparent) required.

High school preparation. College-preparatory program recommended. 15 units required; 19 recommended. Required and recommended units include English 4, mathematics 4, social studies 2, history 2, science 3 (laboratory 2), foreign language 2, computer science 1 and visual/performing arts 1. Technology and other courses recommended but not required.

2011-2012 Annual costs. Tuition/fees: $35,125. Room/board: $10,464. Books/supplies: $1,000. Personal expenses: $2,100.

Financial aid. Non-need-based: Scholarships awarded for academics, alumni affiliation, athletics, leadership, ROTC.

Application procedures. Admission: Priority date 2/1; no deadline. No application fee. Application must be submitted online. Admission notification on a rolling basis beginning on or about 10/1. **Financial aid:** Priority date 4/15; no closing date. FAFSA required. Applicants notified on a rolling basis starting 3/15.

Academics. Interprofessional Projects Program provides team-based learning environment in which students from various concentrations and disciplines work together to solve real-world problems. Research opportunities for undergraduates in science, engineering, technology and mathematics. **Special study options:** Combined bachelor's/graduate degree, cooperative education, cross-registration, distance learning, double major, ESL, independent study, internships, liberal arts/career combination, study abroad, teacher certification program. Joint enrollment at 2 institutions for 2 degrees. **Credit/placement by**

examination: AP, CLEP, IB, SAT, ACT, institutional tests. 18 credit hours maximum toward bachelor's degree. No limit for advanced placement credit. **Support services:** Learning center, study skills assistance, tutoring, writing center.

Majors. Architecture: Architecture. **Biology:** General, biochemistry, biophysics. **Business:** Business admin, operations. **Communications:** Journalism, technical/scientific. **Computer sciences:** General, computer science, information technology, web page design. **Education:** Physics. **Engineering:** Aerospace, architectural, biomedical, chemical, civil, computer, electrical, materials, mechanical. **Health services:** Prepharmacy. **Liberal arts:** Arts/sciences. **Math:** Applied. **Physical sciences:** Chemistry, physics. **Psychology:** General. **Social sciences:** General, political science, sociology.

Most popular majors. Architecture 20%, business/marketing 7%, computer/information sciences 8%, engineering/engineering technologies 53%.

Computing on campus. 500 workstations in dormitories, library, computer center, student center. Dormitories wired for high-speed internet access and linked to campus network. Online course registration, online library, helpline, student web hosting, wireless network available.

Student life. Freshman orientation: Mandatory, $150 fee. Preregistration for classes offered. Five summer sessions. Welcome Week held prior to start of classes. **Policies:** Student organizations register each semester, are nondiscriminatory and prohibit hazing. **Housing:** Guaranteed on-campus for all undergraduates. Coed dorms, apartments, fraternity/sorority housing available. Men's/women's floors in residence halls available. **Activities:** Concert band, campus ministries, choral groups, dance, drama, film society, international student organizations, literary magazine, music ensembles, musical theater, radio station, student government, student newspaper, TV station, Red Cross Club, Engineers Without Borders, Greek Council, Haiti Outreach, InterVarsity Christian Fellowship, Latinos Involved in Further Education, National Society of Black Engineers, Society of Women Engineers, Union Board.

Athletics. NAIA. **Intercollegiate:** Baseball M, cross-country, diving, soccer, swimming, volleyball W. **Intramural:** Badminton, basketball, bowling, field hockey, football (non-tackle), racquetball, soccer, softball, squash, table tennis, volleyball, wrestling. **Team name:** Scarlet Hawks.

Student services. Alcohol/substance abuse counseling, career counseling, student employment services, financial aid counseling, health services, legal services, minority student services, personal counseling, placement for graduates, women's services. **Physically disabled:** Services for visually, hearing impaired.

Contact. E-mail: admission@iit.edu
Phone: (312) 567-3025 Toll-free number: (800) 448-2329
Fax: (312) 567-6939
Alfred Nunez, Acting Director of Undergraduate Admission, Illinois Institute of Technology, 10 West 33rd Street, Chicago, IL 60616-3793

Illinois State University
Normal, Illinois
www.ilstu.edu

CB member
CB code: 1319

- Public 4-year university
- Residential campus in small city
- 18,526 degree-seeking undergraduates: 6% part-time, 55% women, 6% African American, 2% Asian American, 6% Hispanic American, 1% international
- 2,387 degree-seeking graduate students
- 63% of applicants admitted
- SAT or ACT (ACT writing optional), application essay required
- 71% graduate within 6 years

General. Founded in 1857. Regionally accredited. **Degrees:** 4,287 bachelor's awarded; master's, professional, doctoral offered. **ROTC:** Army. **Location:** 132 miles from Chicago, 168 miles from St. Louis. **Calendar:** Semester, limited summer session. **Full-time faculty:** 882 total; 84% have terminal degrees, 15% minority, 48% women. **Part-time faculty:** 326 total; 26% have terminal degrees, 6% minority, 56% women. **Class size:** 32% < 20, 54% 20-39, 3% 40-49, 7% 50-99, 4% >100. **Special facilities:** 310-acre farm, planetarium, museum of nations, laboratory school.

Freshman class profile. 13,156 applied, 8,339 admitted, 3,321 enrolled.

Mid 50% test scores		Return as sophomores:	85%
ACT composite:	22-26	Out-of-state:	1%
GPA 3.75 or higher:	20%	Live on campus:	97%
GPA 3.50-3.74:	17%	Fraternities:	15%
GPA 3.0-3.49:	41%	Sororities:	17%
GPA 2.0-2.99:	22%		

Basis for selection. School achievement record and test scores most important. Interview required of special admission applicants. Audition recommended for music majors. Portfolio recommended for art majors.

High school preparation. College-preparatory program required. 15 units required. Required units include English 4, mathematics 3, social studies 2, science 2 (laboratory 2), foreign language 2 and academic electives 2. 2 units required in foreign language and/or fine arts.

2011-2012 Annual costs. Tuition/fees: $11,832; $18,792 out-of-state. Room/board: $9,090. Books/supplies: $1,074. Personal expenses: $2,820.

2011-2012 Financial aid. Need-based: 2,871 full-time freshmen applied for aid; 2,217 were judged to have need; 2,108 of these received aid. Average need met was 75%. Average scholarship/grant was $9,114; average loan $5,692. 45% of total undergraduate aid awarded as scholarships/grants, 55% as loans/jobs. **Non-need-based:** Awarded to 2,767 full-time undergraduates, including 765 freshmen. Scholarships awarded for academics, art, athletics, music/drama.

Application procedures. Admission: Priority date 11/15; deadline 3/1 (receipt date). $40 fee, may be waived for applicants with need. Admission notification on a rolling basis beginning on or about 9/1. **Financial aid:** Priority date 3/1; no closing date. FAFSA required. Applicants notified on a rolling basis starting 4/1; must reply within 2 week(s) of notification.

Academics. Special study options: Accelerated study, combined bachelor's/graduate degree, cooperative education, distance learning, double major, dual enrollment of high school students, ESL, exchange student, honors, independent study, internships, student-designed major, study abroad, teacher certification program, Washington semester. **Credit/placement by examination:** AP, CLEP, SAT, ACT, institutional tests. 26 credit hours maximum toward bachelor's degree. **Support services:** Learning center, pre-admission summer program, tutoring.

Majors. Biology: General, biochemistry. **Business:** Accounting, business admin, construction management, finance, insurance, international, management science, marketing. **Communications:** Journalism, media studies, public relations. **Communications technology:** Graphics. **Computer sciences:** Computer science, information technology, networking. **Education:** Business, early childhood, elementary, health, middle, music, physical, social studies, special ed, technology/industrial arts. **English:** Rhetoric/composition. **Foreign languages:** General, French, German, Spanish. **General:** Agribusiness operations. **Health services:** Athletic training, audiology/speech pathology, clinical lab science, environmental health, medical records admin, nursing (RN), occupational health. **History:** General. **Human services:** Social work. **Liberal arts:** Arts/sciences. **Math:** General. **Parks/recreation:** Exercise sciences, facilities management. **Philosophy/religion:** Philosophy. **Physical sciences:** Chemistry, geology, physics. **Protective services:** Criminal justice. **Psychology:** General. **Social sciences:** Anthropology, economics, geography, political science, sociology. **Visual/performing arts:** Art, dramatic, music, music history, music performance, studio arts. **Work/family studies:** General.

Most popular majors. Business/marketing 18%, education 19%, health sciences 7%, social sciences 6%.

Computing on campus. PC or laptop required. 2,275 workstations in dormitories, library, computer center, student center. Dormitories wired for high-speed internet access and linked to campus network. Commuter students can connect to campus network. Online course registration, online library, helpline, repair service, student web hosting, wireless network available.

Student life. Freshman orientation: Mandatory, $50 fee. Preregistration for classes offered. Two-day sessions held each week from mid-June to end of July. **Housing:** Guaranteed on-campus for freshmen. Coed dorms, single-sex dorms, special housing for disabled, apartments, fraternity/sorority housing, wellness housing available. $300 partly refundable deposit. **Activities:** Bands, campus ministries, choral groups, dance, drama, film society, international student organizations, literary magazine, music ensembles, Model UN, musical theater, radio station, student government, student newspaper, symphony orchestra, TV station, over 250 student organizations.

Athletics. NCAA. **Intercollegiate:** Baseball M, basketball, cross-country, diving W, football (tackle) M, golf, gymnastics W, soccer W, softball W, swimming W, tennis, track and field, volleyball W. **Intramural:** Badminton, basketball, football (tackle), golf, racquetball, soccer, softball, volleyball. **Team name:** Redbirds.

Student services. Adult student services, alcohol/substance abuse counseling, career counseling, student employment services, financial aid counseling, health services, legal services, minority student services, on-campus daycare, personal counseling, placement for graduates, veterans' counselor. **Physically disabled:** Services for visually, speech, hearing impaired.

Contact. E-mail: admissions@ilstu.edu
Phone: (309) 438-2181 Toll-free number: (800) 366-2478
Fax: (309) 438-3932
Doris Groves, Director of Admissions, Illinois State University, Campus Box 2200, Normal, IL 61790-2200

Illinois Wesleyan University
Bloomington, Illinois — **CB member**
www.iwu.edu — **CB code: 1320**

- Private 4-year university and liberal arts college
- Residential campus in small city
- 2,083 degree-seeking undergraduates: 57% women, 4% African American, 5% Asian American, 5% Hispanic American, 4% international
- 61% of applicants admitted
- SAT or ACT (ACT writing optional), application essay required
- 82% graduate within 6 years

General. Founded in 1850. Regionally accredited. **Degrees:** 502 bachelor's awarded. **ROTC:** Army. **Location:** 125 miles from Chicago, 165 miles from St. Louis. **Calendar:** 4-4-1 (2 semesters plus May Term). **Full-time faculty:** 161 total; 92% have terminal degrees, 11% minority, 42% women. **Part-time faculty:** 65 total; 42% have terminal degrees, 9% minority, 62% women. **Class size:** 65% < 20, 33% 20-39, 1% 40-49, 1% 50-99, less than 1% >100. **Special facilities:** Observatory, natural sciences research labs, computerized music lab, social science research lab, visual anthropology lab, student-managed real-dollar investment portfolio program, nursing lab, lab theatre producing original works by undergraduates, Action Research Center (supporting community-based student research for academic credit).

Freshman class profile. 3,319 applied, 2,017 admitted, 510 enrolled.

Mid 50% test scores		Return as sophomores:	90%
SAT critical reading:	540-670	Out-of-state:	11%
SAT math:	490-760	Live on campus:	100%
ACT composite:	25-30	International:	5%
Rank in top quarter:	80%	Fraternities:	32%
Rank in top tenth:	45%	Sororities:	30%

Basis for selection. Test scores, class rank, high school record, and essay or personal statement most important. Interview strongly recommended. Audition required for bachelor of music or BFA in theater or music theater. Portfolio review required for BFA in art. **Home schooled:** Transcript of courses and grades required. **Learning Disabled:** Students welcome to submit information on learning disabilities as part of application review process.

High school preparation. College-preparatory program recommended. 15 units recommended. Recommended units include English 4, mathematics 3, social studies 2, science 3 (laboratory 2) and foreign language 3. Biology and chemistry are required for admission to nursing and biology.

2011-2012 Annual costs. Tuition/fees: $36,572. Room/board: $8,476. Books/supplies: $780. Personal expenses: $900.

2011-2012 Financial aid. Need-based: 430 full-time freshmen applied for aid; 360 were judged to have need; 360 of these received aid. Average need met was 90%. Average scholarship/grant was $20,627; average loan $3,801. 76% of total undergraduate aid awarded as scholarships/grants, 24% as loans/jobs. **Non-need-based:** Awarded to 730 full-time undergraduates, including 191 freshmen. Scholarships awarded for academics, art, music/drama.

Application procedures. Admission: No deadline. No application fee. Admission notification on a rolling basis beginning on or about 1/15. Must reply by May 1 or within 2 week(s) if notified thereafter. **Financial aid:** Priority date 3/1; no closing date. FAFSA, institutional form required. Applicants notified on a rolling basis starting 3/1; must reply by 5/1.

Academics. Optional 3-week May Term provides opportunities for students to pursue experimental courses, travel courses, interships, or independent research projects. Fall Term in London and Spring Term in Madrid led by Illinois Wesleyan faculty members where students may earn General Education credit during these terms. **Special study options:** Combined bachelor's/graduate degree, double major, exchange student, honors, independent study, internships, New York semester, student-designed major, study abroad, teacher certification program, United Nations semester, urban semester, Washington semester. 3-2 cooperative program in engineering with Washington University, Case Western Reserve University, and Northwestern University; 3-2 program in forestry and environmental management with Duke University; 3-2 program in occupational therapy with Washington University, 2-2 program in engineering with the University of Illinois, and a nonguaranteed cooperative program in engineering with Dartmouth College. **Credit/placement by examination:** AP, CLEP, IB, institutional tests. 32 credit

hours maximum toward bachelor's degree. Limit of 16 hours (equivalent to four courses) may count toward general education credit. Up to 16 additional hours (equivalent to four courses) can be awarded as elective credit. **Support services:** Reduced course load, study skills assistance, tutoring, writing center.

Majors. Area/ethnic studies: African, American, Asian, Latin American, Russian/Eastern European/Eurasian, Western European, women's. **Biology:** General. **Business:** Accounting, business admin, insurance, international. **Computer sciences:** General. **Conservation:** Environmental studies. **Education:** General, biology, chemistry, elementary, English, French, history, mathematics, music, physics, Spanish. **English:** English lit. **Foreign languages:** Classics, French, German, Spanish. **Health services:** Nursing (RN). **History:** General. **Math:** General. **Philosophy/religion:** Philosophy, religion. **Physical sciences:** Chemistry, physics. **Psychology:** General. **Social sciences:** Anthropology, economics, political science, sociology. **Visual/performing arts:** Acting, art, dramatic, music, music performance, music theory/composition, musical theater, piano/keyboard, stringed instruments, theater design, voice/opera.

Most popular majors. Biology 7%, business/marketing 20%, education 6%, English 7%, psychology 8%, social sciences 13%, visual/performing arts 8%.

Computing on campus. 400 workstations in dormitories, library, computer center, student center. Dormitories wired for high-speed internet access and linked to campus network. Commuter students can connect to campus network. Online course registration, online library, helpline, repair service, student web hosting, wireless network available.

Student life. Freshman orientation: Mandatory. Preregistration for classes offered. Orientation for parents held in June. New student orientation held 5-6 days prior to start of classes. **Policies:** No smoking permitted in residence halls. Beer and wine permitted in designated areas for students of legal age. **Housing:** Guaranteed on-campus for freshmen. Coed dorms, special housing for disabled, apartments, fraternity/sorority housing available. **Activities:** Bands, campus ministries, choral groups, dance, drama, film society, international student organizations, literary magazine, music ensembles, Model UN, musical theater, opera, radio station, student government, student newspaper, symphony orchestra, TV station, black student union, InterVarsity Christian Fellowship, Alpha Phi Omega, Council of Latin American Student Enrichment, Habitat for Humanity, several environmental concerns organizations, Amnesty International, Pan-Asian student association, College Democrats, College Republicans.

Athletics. NCAA. **Intercollegiate:** Baseball M, basketball, cross-country, diving, football (tackle) M, golf, soccer, softball W, swimming, tennis, track and field, volleyball W. **Intramural:** Badminton, basketball, football (non-tackle), golf, soccer, softball, tennis, volleyball. **Team name:** Titans.

Student services. Alcohol/substance abuse counseling, chaplain/spiritual director, career counseling, student employment services, financial aid counseling, health services, minority student services, personal counseling, placement for graduates. **Physically disabled:** Services for visually, speech, hearing impaired.

Contact. E-mail: iwuadmit@iwu.edu
Phone: (309) 556-3031 Toll-free number: (800) 332-2498
Fax: (309) 556-3820
Tony Bankston, Dean of Admissions, Illinois Wesleyan University, PO Box 2900, Bloomington, IL 61702-2900

International Academy of Design and Technology: Chicago
Chicago, Illinois
www.iadtchicago.edu — **CB code: 3363**

- For-profit 4-year visual arts and technical college
- Commuter campus in very large city

General. Founded in 1977. Accredited by ACICS. **Location:** Downtown. **Calendar:** Quarter.

Annual costs/financial aid. Tuition/fees (2011-2012): $18,225. Room: $8,170. Books/supplies: $1,800. Need-based financial aid available to full-time and part-time students.

Contact. Phone: (312) 980-9200
Vice President of Admissions, One North State Street, Suite 500, Chicago, IL 60602

ITT Technical Institute: Mount Prospect
Mount Prospect, Illinois
www.itt-tech.edu   CB code: 4271

- For-profit 4-year technical college
- Commuter campus in small city
- 513 degree-seeking undergraduates
- Interview required

General. Founded in 1986. Accredited by ACICS. **Degrees:** 43 bachelor's, 114 associate awarded. **Location:** 20 miles from Chicago. **Calendar:** Quarter, extensive summer session. **Full-time faculty:** 10 total. **Part-time faculty:** 53 total.

Basis for selection. Satisfactory scores required on English and math tests.

2011-2012 Annual costs. Estimated costs as of June 2011: per-credit-hour charge, $493, depending upon level and course of study; academic fee, $200. Certain programs of study require purchase of tools, which could cost an additional $100 to $500. All costs are subject to change.

Application procedures. Admission: No deadline. No application fee. Admission notification on a rolling basis. **Financial aid:** No deadline. FAFSA, institutional form required. Applicants notified on a rolling basis.

Academics. Credit/placement by examination: AP, CLEP, institutional tests. **Support services:** Learning center, tutoring.

Majors. Business: Construction management, e-commerce, retail management. **Computer sciences:** Security. **Protective services:** Law enforcement admin. **Visual/performing arts:** Game design.

Computing on campus. Online library available.

Student life. Freshman orientation: Available. Preregistration for classes offered.

Student services. Career counseling, student employment services.

Contact. Phone: (847) 375-8800
Cesar Rodriguez, Director of Recruitment, ITT Technical Institute: Mount Prospect, 1401 Feehanville Drive, Mount Prospect, IL 60056

Judson University
Elgin, Illinois
www.judsonu.edu   CB code: 1351

- Private 4-year university and liberal arts college affiliated with American Baptist Churches in the USA
- Residential campus in small city
- 933 degree-seeking undergraduates: 16% part-time, 52% women, 5% African American, 1% Asian American, 6% Hispanic American, 3% international
- 126 degree-seeking graduate students
- 64% of applicants admitted
- SAT or ACT (ACT writing optional) required
- 48% graduate within 6 years

General. Founded in 1963. Regionally accredited. **Degrees:** 272 bachelor's awarded; master's offered. **ROTC:** Army. **Location:** 40 miles from Chicago. **Calendar:** Continuous, limited summer session. **Full-time faculty:** 62 total; 82% have terminal degrees, 14% minority, 36% women. **Part-time faculty:** 138 total; 33% have terminal degrees, 14% minority, 51% women. **Class size:** 86% < 20, 13% 20-39, less than 1% 50-99. **Special facilities:** Gold LEED certified academic center.

Freshman class profile. 705 applied, 452 admitted, 161 enrolled.

Mid 50% test scores			
SAT critical reading:	440-580	Rank in top quarter:	29%
SAT math:	490-590	Rank in top tenth:	8%
ACT composite:	21-26	End year in good standing:	83%
GPA 3.75 or higher:	17%	Return as sophomores:	79%
GPA 3.50-3.74:	18%	Out-of-state:	22%
GPA 3.0-3.49:	41%	Live on campus:	86%
GPA 2.0-2.99:	24%	International:	5%

Basis for selection. School achievement record, class rank, and test scores are important. Audition recommended for performing arts majors. Portfolio recommended for art majors. Essay required for architecture majors. **Home schooled:** Transcript of courses and grades required. **Learning Disabled:**

Students need documentation, including medical, when requesting services.

High school preparation. College-preparatory program recommended. Recommended units include English 4, mathematics 3, social studies 2, science 2 (laboratory 2).

2011-2012 Annual costs. Tuition/fees: $26,120. Room/board: $8,800. Books/supplies: $1,500. Personal expenses: $2,000.

2011-2012 Financial aid. Need-based: 144 full-time freshmen applied for aid; 143 were judged to have need; 143 of these received aid. Average need met was 60%. Average scholarship/grant was $12,582; average loan $4,586. 61% of total undergraduate aid awarded as scholarships/grants, 39% as loans/jobs. **Non-need-based:** Awarded to 335 full-time undergraduates, including 74 freshmen. Scholarships awarded for academics, alumni affiliation, art, athletics, music/drama.

Application procedures. Admission: No deadline. $50 fee, may be waived for applicants with need. Admission notification on a rolling basis beginning on or about 10/1. **Financial aid:** Priority date 3/1, closing date 5/1. FAFSA required. Applicants notified on a rolling basis starting 3/15; must reply by 5/1 or within 4 week(s) of notification.

Academics. Special study options: Accelerated study, distance learning, double major, honors, independent study, internships, student-designed major, study abroad, teacher certification program, urban semester, Washington semester. **Credit/placement by examination:** AP, CLEP, IB, SAT, ACT, institutional tests. 30 credit hours maximum toward bachelor's degree. **Support services:** Learning center, reduced course load, remedial instruction, study skills assistance, tutoring.

Majors. Architecture: Architecture. **Biology:** General, biochemistry. **Business:** Accounting, business admin, human resources, management information systems, management science. **Communications:** Communications/speech/rhetoric. **Conservation:** Environmental studies. **Education:** Art, early childhood, elementary, music, physical, secondary. **English:** English lit. **History:** General. **Math:** General. **Parks/recreation:** Sports admin. **Physical sciences:** Chemistry. **Protective services:** Criminal justice. **Psychology:** General. **Social sciences:** Sociology. **Theology:** Bible, sacred music, theology, youth ministry. **Visual/performing arts:** Art, graphic design, interior design, music performance, studio arts.

Most popular majors. Architecture 7%, business/marketing 38%, education 16%, public administration/social services 11%, theological studies 6%.

Computing on campus. 150 workstations in dormitories, library, computer center, student center. Dormitories wired for high-speed internet access and linked to campus network. Commuter students can connect to campus network. Online course registration, online library, helpline, wireless network available.

Student life. Freshman orientation: Mandatory. Preregistration for classes offered. **Policies:** Chapel services held 3 mornings a week. **Housing:** Guaranteed on-campus for all undergraduates. Coed dorms, single-sex dorms, special housing for disabled, apartments, wellness housing available. $150 fully refundable deposit. **Activities:** Concert band, campus ministries, choral groups, drama, international student organizations, music ensembles, musical theater, student government, symphony orchestra, Judson Student Organization, University Ministries, B.A.S.I.C. (Brothers and Sisters in Christ), Fellowship of Christian Athletes, International Justice Mission-Judson Chapter, Student Sustainability Committee.

Athletics. NAIA, NCCAA. **Intercollegiate:** Baseball M, basketball, cheerleading, cross-country, golf, lacrosse M, soccer, softball W, tennis, track and field, volleyball W. **Intramural:** Basketball, football (tackle), soccer, volleyball. **Team name:** Eagles.

Student services. Adult student services, chaplain/spiritual director, career counseling, student employment services, financial aid counseling, health services, personal counseling, placement for graduates. **Physically disabled:** Services for visually, speech, hearing impaired.

Contact. E-mail: admissions@judsonu.edu
Phone: (847) 628-2510 Toll-free number: (800) 879-5376
Fax: (847) 628-2526
Nancy Binger, Director of Admissions, Judson University, 1151 North State Street, Elgin, IL 60123-1404

Kendall College
Chicago, Illinois
www.kendall.edu   CB code: 1366

- For-profit 4-year culinary school and teachers college
- Commuter campus in very large city

- 2,050 degree-seeking undergraduates
- 98% of applicants admitted
- Application essay, interview required

General. Founded in 1934. Regionally accredited. Internships required in every major. **Degrees:** 266 bachelor's, 149 associate awarded. **Location:** Downtown. **Calendar:** Quarter, extensive summer session. **Full-time faculty:** 45 total. **Part-time faculty:** 156 total. **Class size:** 60% < 20, 40% 20-39.

Freshman class profile. 376 applied, 368 admitted, 166 enrolled.

GPA 3.75 or higher:	5%	GPA 2.0-2.99:	55%
GPA 3.50-3.74:	7%	Out-of-state:	19%
GPA 3.0-3.49:	22%		

Basis for selection. High school record most important, followed by test scores, class rank, recommendations and interview. Placement test required.of all incoming students who do not transfer in composition and mathematics requirements. SAT or ACT recommended.

High school preparation. Recommended units include English 4, mathematics 2, social studies 2, science 2 and foreign language 2. Specific academic units required for certain majors.

2011-2012 Annual costs. Tuition/fees: $22,920. Board plan provides 15 meals per week. Room/board: $10,017. Books/supplies: $1,800.

Financial aid. Non-need-based: Scholarships awarded for academics, alumni affiliation, job skills.

Application procedures. Admission: No deadline. $50 fee, may be waived for applicants with need. Admission notification on a rolling basis. Must reply by May 1 or within 4 week(s) if notified thereafter. **Financial aid:** Priority date 4/15; no closing date. FAFSA required. Applicants notified on a rolling basis starting 1/1; must reply within 2 week(s) of notification.

Academics. Special study options: Accelerated study, combined bachelor's/graduate degree, distance learning, internships, study abroad, teacher certification program, weekend college. Hybrid coursework. **Credit/placement by examination:** AP, CLEP, IB, institutional tests. 24 credit hours maximum toward associate degree, 48 toward bachelor's. **Support services:** Learning center, reduced course load, remedial instruction, study skills assistance, tutoring, writing center.

Majors. Business: Business admin, hospitality admin. **Education:** Early childhood.

Most popular majors. Business/marketing 53%, education 41%, personal/culinary services 6%.

Computing on campus. 45 workstations in library, computer center, student center. Dormitories wired for high-speed internet access and linked to campus network. Commuter students can connect to campus network. Online library, helpline, wireless network available.

Student life. Freshman orientation: Mandatory. Preregistration for classes offered. One-day event held 1 week before start of quarter. **Policies:** Students are to have visible photo IDs at all times on campus. **Housing:** Coed dorms, wellness housing available. $350 nonrefundable deposit. **Activities:** International student organizations, student government, National Society for Minorities in Hospitality, Black Student Union, Latinos Juntos, Student Government Federation, Kendall HOPE, Kendall Pride.

Athletics. Team name: The Viking.

Student services. Adult student services, career counseling, student employment services, financial aid counseling, personal counseling, placement for graduates.

Contact. E-mail: admissions@kendall.edu
Phone: (312) 752-2020 Toll-free number: (866) 667-3344
Fax: (312) 752-2021
Steve Mulligan, Admissions Director, Kendall College, 900 N. North Branch Street, Chicago, IL 60642-4278

Knox College
Galesburg, Illinois CB member
www.knox.edu CB code: 1372

- Private 4-year liberal arts college
- Residential campus in large town
- 1,405 degree-seeking undergraduates: 58% women, 5% African American, 5% Asian American, 8% Hispanic American, 9% international

---

- 72% of applicants admitted
- Application essay required
- 78% graduate within 6 years; 22% enter graduate study

General. Founded in 1837. Regionally accredited. **Degrees:** 298 bachelor's awarded. **Location:** 200 miles from Chicago, 200 miles from St. Louis. **Calendar:** Trimester. **Full-time faculty:** 114 total; 94% have terminal degrees, 12% minority, 40% women. **Part-time faculty:** 16 total; 50% have terminal degrees, 6% minority, 50% women. **Class size:** 69% < 20, 30% 20-39, less than 1% 40-49, less than 1% 50-99. **Special facilities:** Electron microscope, greenhouse, studio and large-scale production theaters, 760-acre biological field station, ceramics, sculpture, painting and printmaking studios.

Freshman class profile. 2,385 applied, 1,706 admitted, 346 enrolled.

Mid 50% test scores			
SAT critical reading:	580-690	GPA 2.0-2.99:	22%
SAT math:	570-690	Rank in top quarter:	69%
SAT writing:	560-670	Rank in top tenth:	33%
ACT composite:	25-30	End year in good standing:	86%
GPA 3.75 or higher:	24%	Return as sophomores:	89%
GPA 3.50-3.74:	18%	Out-of-state:	43%
GPA 3.0-3.49:	36%	Live on campus:	99%
		International:	15%

Basis for selection. Course of study, grades, essay, and recommendations most important. Class rank, extracurricular activities, special skills, talents and personal qualities, interview also considered. Preference given to students who have taken advantage of academic opportunities offered by high school (honors, Advanced Placement, International Baccalaureate and/or college level courses) if available. Submission of ACT and SAT scores is optional for most applicants. Home schooled students or candidates from high schools that do not provide grades are asked to submit test results. Interviews are strongly recommended for all applicants; auditions or portfolios required for students applying for scholarships in the arts and writing. **Home schooled:** Statement describing home school structure and mission, transcript of courses and grades, state high school equivalency certificate required. Applicants should provide detailed documentation of coursework completed, including course syllabi as appropriate. SAT/ACT scores required. Interviews are strongly recommended. **Learning Disabled:** Students with learning disabilities who require accommodations can submit documentation for evaluation by the Center of Teaching and Learning.

High school preparation. College-preparatory program required. 20 units recommended. Recommended units include English 4, mathematics 4, social studies 2, history 2, science 4 (laboratory 2), foreign language 3 and academic electives 1.

2012-2013 Annual costs. Tuition/fees (projected): $36,492. Room/board: $7,932. Books/supplies: $900.

2011-2012 Financial aid. Need-based: 315 full-time freshmen applied for aid; 282 were judged to have need; 280 of these received aid. Average need met was 90%. Average scholarship/grant was $23,258; average loan $4,589. 80% of total undergraduate aid awarded as scholarships/grants, 20% as loans/jobs. **Non-need-based:** Awarded to 449 full-time undergraduates, including 108 freshmen. Scholarships awarded for academics, art, music/drama.

Application procedures. Admission: Closing date 2/1 (postmark date). $40 fee, may be waived for applicants with need. Admission notification by 3/31. Must reply by May 1 or within 2 week(s) if notified thereafter. **Financial aid:** Priority date 2/15; no closing date. FAFSA, institutional form required. Applicants notified on a rolling basis starting 3/15; must reply by 5/1.

Academics. Academic work conducted under an Honor Code. Peace Corps Preparatory Program featuring curriculum designed to prepare students to serve in the Peace Corps or other international service. **Special study options:** Combined bachelor's/graduate degree, double major, dual enrollment of high school students, honors, independent study, internships, liberal arts/career combination, student-designed major, study abroad, teacher certification program, Washington semester. More than 30 international and off-campus study programs. **Credit/placement by examination:** AP, CLEP, IB, SAT, ACT, institutional tests. 9 credit hours maximum toward bachelor's degree. **Support services:** Learning center, tutoring.

Majors. Area/ethnic studies: African-American, American, Asian, women's. **Biology:** General, biochemistry, neuroscience. **Computer sciences:** Computer science. **Conservation:** Environmental studies. **Education:** Elementary, secondary, social science. **English:** Creative writing, English lit. **Foreign languages:** General, ancient Greek, classics, French, German, Latin, Spanish. **History:** General. **Math:** General. **Philosophy/religion:** Philosophy. **Physical sciences:** Chemistry, physics. **Psychology:** General. **Social sciences:** Anthropology, economics, international relations, political science, sociology. **Visual/performing arts:** Art history/conservation, dramatic, music, studio arts.

Most popular majors. Biology 8%, education 10%, English 15%, psychology 10%, social sciences 28%, visual/performing arts 6%.

Computing on campus. 335 workstations in library, computer center, student center. Dormitories wired for high-speed internet access and linked to campus network. Commuter students can connect to campus network. Online course registration, online library, helpline, student web hosting, wireless network available.

Student life. Freshman orientation: Mandatory. Preregistration for classes offered. Held 1 week before beginning of fall term. Additional orientation for international students. **Housing:** Guaranteed on-campus for freshmen. Coed dorms, single-sex dorms, special housing for disabled, apartments, fraternity/sorority housing available. $300 nonrefundable deposit, deadline 5/1. Pets allowed in dorm rooms. **Activities:** Bands, choral groups, dance, drama, international student organizations, literary magazine, music ensembles, Model UN, musical theater, radio station, student government, student newspaper, symphony orchestra, Alliance for Peaceful Action, Amnesty International, Circle K, Food For Thought, Habitat For Humanity, Knox Democrats, Knox Republicans, Students Against Sexism In Society, Heath Advocacy Group.

Athletics. NCAA. **Intercollegiate:** Baseball M, basketball, cross-country, diving, football (tackle) M, golf, soccer, softball W, swimming, tennis, track and field, volleyball W, wrestling M. **Intramural:** Basketball, soccer, softball, volleyball. **Team name:** Prairie Fire.

Student services. Alcohol/substance abuse counseling, career counseling, services for economically disadvantaged, student employment services, financial aid counseling, health services, minority student services, personal counseling. **Physically disabled:** Services for visually, hearing impaired.

Contact. E-mail: admission@knox.edu
Phone: (309) 341-7100 Toll-free number: (800) 678-566
Fax: (309) 341-7070
Paul Steenis, Dean of Admission, Knox College, Two East South Street, Galesburg, IL 61401

Lake Forest College
Lake Forest, Illinois **CB member**
www.lakeforest.edu **CB code: 1392**

- Private 4-year liberal arts college
- Residential campus in large town
- 1,483 degree-seeking undergraduates: 1% part-time, 59% women, 6% African American, 4% Asian American, 12% Hispanic American, 12% international
- 19 degree-seeking graduate students
- 54% of applicants admitted
- Application essay required
- 68% graduate within 6 years; 30% enter graduate study

General. Founded in 1857. Regionally accredited. **Degrees:** 309 bachelor's awarded; master's offered. **Location:** 30 miles from Chicago. **Calendar:** Semester, limited summer session. **Full-time faculty:** 94 total; 98% have terminal degrees, 14% minority, 46% women. **Part-time faculty:** 67 total; 45% have terminal degrees, 10% minority, 60% women. **Class size:** 67% < 20, 30% 20-39, 2% 40-49, less than 1% 50-99. **Special facilities:** Rhetoric and production room, electronic music studio, technology resource center, Chicago programs center, vegetable garden.

Freshman class profile. 3,198 applied, 1,711 admitted, 406 enrolled.

Mid 50% test scores		GPA 2.0-2.99:	8%
SAT critical reading:	560-640	Rank in top quarter:	62%
SAT math:	530-670	Rank in top tenth:	33%
SAT writing:	550-630	Return as sophomores:	84%
ACT composite:	23-28	Out-of-state:	43%
GPA 3.75 or higher:	41%	Live on campus:	89%
GPA 3.50-3.74:	21%	International:	14%
GPA 3.0-3.49:	30%		

Basis for selection. Holistic approach to candidate review with emphasis on academic preparedness and character. ACT/SAT optional except for applicants for the highest academic scholarships and international students. Interviews are required for certain scholarships and for students who do not submit standardized test scores; highly recommended for all applicants. Audition required for theater and music scholarships. Portfolio required for art, foreign language, and writing scholarships. **Home schooled:** Statement describing home school structure and mission, transcript of courses and grades, interview, letter of recommendation (nonparent) required. SAT/ACT scores.

High school preparation. College-preparatory program required. 19 units required; 23 recommended. Required and recommended units include English 4, mathematics 3-4, social studies 2, history 2, science 3-4 (laboratory 3-4), foreign language 2-4 and academic electives 3. 1 honors or AP course recommended.

2011-2012 Annual costs. Tuition/fees: $36,920. Room/board: $8,660.

Financial aid. Non-need-based: Scholarships awarded for academics, alumni affiliation, art, leadership, music/drama, state residency.

Application procedures. Admission: Priority date 2/15; no deadline. No application fee. Application must be submitted online. Admission notification on a rolling basis beginning on or about 3/20. Must reply by May 1 or within 3 week(s) if notified thereafter. **Financial aid:** FAFSA, institutional form required.

Academics. Special study options: Accelerated study, combined bachelor's/graduate degree, double major, honors, independent study, internships, liberal arts/career combination, student-designed major, study abroad, teacher certification program, urban semester, Washington semester. **Credit/placement by examination:** AP, CLEP, IB. **Support services:** Learning center, study skills assistance, tutoring, writing center.

Majors. Area/ethnic studies: American, Asian, Latin American. **Biology:** General, neuroscience. **Business:** General, finance. **Communications:** Communications/speech/rhetoric. **Computer sciences:** Computer science. **Conservation:** Environmental studies. **Education:** General. **English:** English lit. **Foreign languages:** French, Spanish. **History:** General. **Math:** General. **Philosophy/religion:** Philosophy, religion. **Physical sciences:** Chemistry, physics. **Psychology:** General. **Social sciences:** Economics, international relations, political science. **Visual/performing arts:** Art, art history/conservation, music, studio arts, theater arts management.

Most popular majors. Biology 6%, business/marketing 9%, communications/journalism 8%, English 8%, foreign language 8%, social sciences 27%, visual/performing arts 6%.

Computing on campus. 130 workstations in library, computer center, student center. Dormitories wired for high-speed internet access and linked to campus network. Commuter students can connect to campus network. Online course registration, online library, helpline, repair service, student web hosting, wireless network available.

Student life. Freshman orientation: Mandatory. Preregistration for classes offered. 4-day program held on-campus in August. **Policies:** Freshmen not permitted cars on campus. **Housing:** Guaranteed on-campus for freshmen. Coed dorms, single-sex dorms, special housing for disabled, apartments, wellness housing available. $500 nonrefundable deposit, deadline 5/1. **Activities:** Bands, campus ministries, choral groups, dance, drama, film society, international student organizations, literary magazine, music ensembles, Model UN, musical theater, radio station, student government, student newspaper, symphony orchestra, Amnesty International, Habitat for Humanity, League for Environmental Awareness and Protection, United Black Association, Latinos Unidos, Asian Interest Group, Diversity Advocates (ALLY), Hillel, Bahai Campus Association, College Liberals, College Republicans, Muslim Student Association.

Athletics. NCAA. **Intercollegiate:** Basketball, cross-country, diving, football (tackle) M, handball, ice hockey, soccer, softball W, swimming, tennis, volleyball W. **Intramural:** Basketball, football (non-tackle), ice hockey, racquetball, soccer, softball, table tennis, tennis, volleyball. **Team name:** Foresters.

Student services. Alcohol/substance abuse counseling, career counseling, student employment services, financial aid counseling, health services, minority student services, personal counseling, placement for graduates, women's services. **Physically disabled:** Services for visually, hearing impaired.

Contact. E-mail: admissions@lakeforest.edu
Phone: (847) 735-5000 Toll-free number: (800) 828-4751
Fax: (847) 735-6271
William Motzer, Vice President for Admissions and Career Services, Lake Forest College, 555 North Sheridan Road, Lake Forest, IL 60045-2338

Lakeview College of Nursing
Danville, Illinois
www.lakeviewcol.edu **CB code: 0149**

- Private two-year upper-division nursing college
- Commuter campus in large town
- Application essay required

General. Founded in 1894. Regionally accredited. **Degrees:** 131 bachelor's awarded. **Articulation:** Agreements with Danville Area Community College, Eastern Illinois University. **Location:** 35 miles from Urbana-Champaign, 130 miles from Chicago. **Calendar:** Semester, limited summer session. **Full-time faculty:** 20 total. **Part-time faculty:** 8 total. **Special facilities:** Free clinic, nature preserve.

Student profile. 289 full-time, degree-seeking undergraduates.

Out-of-state:	2%	25 or older:	83%

Basis for selection. High school transcript, college transcript, application essay required. Based on interview, references, and transcripts. Applicant must have completed 33 credit hours of general course work with 2.5 GPA prior to admission. Transfer accepted as sophomores, juniors.

2011-2012 Annual costs. Tuition/fees: $13,200. Books/supplies: $582.

Application procedures. Admission: Rolling admission. $100 fee. Application must be submitted on paper. National League for Nursing examinations used to determine advanced placement for entering students who already have RN degree. **Financial aid:** Priority date 4/15, no deadline. FAFSA, institutional form required.

Academics. BS in nursing requires total of 125 credit hours. 95% of entering students complete degree in 5 years or less. **Special study options:** Distance learning, honors, independent study. **Credit/placement by examination:** AP, CLEP. **Support services:** Reduced course load, study skills assistance, tutoring.

Majors. Health services: Nursing (RN).

Computing on campus. 12 workstations in library, computer center.

Student life. Activities: Student government, student newspaper, Illinois Student Nurses Association, National Student Nurses Association.

Student services. Adult student services, career counseling, financial aid counseling, health services, personal counseling, veterans' counselor.

Contact. E-mail: admissions@lakeviewcol.edu
Phone: (217) 554-6899 Fax: (217) 477-2970
Connie Young, Director of Enrollment/Registrar, Lakeview College of Nursing, 903 North Logan Avenue, Danville, IL 61832

Lewis University
Romeoville, Illinois
www.lewisu.edu

CB member
CB code: 1404

- Private 4-year university affiliated with Roman Catholic Church
- Commuter campus in large town
- 4,376 degree-seeking undergraduates: 19% part-time, 57% women, 9% African American, 3% Asian American, 14% Hispanic American, 1% international
- 1,920 degree-seeking graduate students
- 62% of applicants admitted
- SAT or ACT (ACT writing optional) required
- 63% graduate within 6 years

General. Founded in 1932. Regionally accredited. Sponsored by De La Salle Christian Brothers. **Degrees:** 995 bachelor's, 16 associate awarded; master's, doctoral offered. **ROTC:** Army, Air Force. **Location:** 30 miles from Chicago. **Calendar:** Semester, extensive summer session. **Full-time faculty:** 205 total; 69% have terminal degrees, 12% minority, 51% women. **Part-time faculty:** 450 total; 14% have terminal degrees, 14% minority, 49% women. **Class size:** 64% < 20, 35% 20-39, 1% 40-49, less than 1% 50-99. **Special facilities:** Airport and aeronautical training center, all digital radio station.

Freshman class profile. 4,726 applied, 2,927 admitted, 736 enrolled.

Mid 50% test scores		Rank in top quarter:	41%
SAT critical reading:	460-540	Rank in top tenth:	13%
SAT math:	450-610	Return as sophomores:	77%
SAT writing:	420-500	Out-of-state:	6%
ACT composite:	20-25	Live on campus:	57%
GPA 3.75 or higher:	23%	International:	1%
GPA 3.50-3.74:	16%	Fraternities:	1%
GPA 3.0-3.49:	36%	Sororities:	2%
GPA 2.0-2.99:	25%		

Basis for selection. Applicants must graduate from approved high school with 2.0 GPA. Class rank and ACT/SAT scores must indicate strong likelihood of success in university studies. 20 ACT composite required for admission to nursing program. Interview recommended. **Home schooled:** Statement describing home school structure and mission required.

High school preparation. College-preparatory program required. 18 units required. Required and recommended units include English 3-4, mathematics 3, social studies 2, history 1, science 2 (laboratory 1), foreign language 2 and academic electives 4. 1 year chemistry and 2 years math at 2.0 level or above strongly recommended for nursing applicants.

2011-2012 Annual costs. Tuition/fees: $24,770. Room/board: $8,900. Books/supplies: $1,000. Personal expenses: $1,675.

2011-2012 Financial aid. Non-need-based: Scholarships awarded for academics, alumni affiliation, art, athletics, music/drama, religious affiliation, ROTC.

Application procedures. Admission: Priority date 4/15; no deadline. $40 fee, may be waived for applicants with need. Admission notification on a rolling basis beginning on or about 10/1. Must reply by May 1 or within 2 week(s) if notified thereafter. **Financial aid:** Closing date 5/1. FAFSA required. Applicants notified on a rolling basis starting 2/1; must reply by 5/1 or within 2 week(s) of notification.

Academics. Accelerated degree completion program available to students 24 years and older. **Special study options:** Accelerated study, distance learning, double major, dual enrollment of high school students, ESL, exchange student, honors, independent study, internships, liberal arts/career combination, student-designed major, study abroad, teacher certification program. **Credit/placement by examination:** AP, CLEP, IB, institutional tests. 60 credit hours maximum toward bachelor's degree. **Support services:** Learning center, pre-admission summer program, reduced course load, remedial instruction, study skills assistance, tutoring, writing center.

Majors. Biology: General, biochemistry. **Business:** General, accounting, business admin, finance, human resources, information resources management, international, management information systems, managerial economics, marketing, organizational behavior. **Communications:** Communications/speech/rhetoric, digital media, journalism, media studies, public relations, radio/TV. **Communications technology:** General. **Computer sciences:** Computer science, information systems, security. **Conservation:** Environmental science. **Education:** Elementary, secondary, special ed. **English:** English lit. **Health services:** Athletic training, dental hygiene, health care admin, nuclear medical technology, nursing (RN), radiation protection, sonography. **History:** General. **Human services:** General, community org/advocacy, social work. **Liberal arts:** Arts/sciences. **Math:** General. **Parks/recreation:** Sports admin. **Philosophy/religion:** Philosophy, religion. **Physical sciences:** Chemical physics, chemistry, physics. **Protective services:** Criminal justice, fire services admin, forensics, security services. **Psychology:** General. **Social sciences:** Political science, sociology. **Visual/performing arts:** Art, commercial/advertising art, design, dramatic, drawing, music, music management, painting.

Most popular majors. Business/marketing 25%, education 10%, health sciences 18%, psychology 6%, security/protective services 14%, trade and industry 7%.

Computing on campus. 350 workstations in library, computer center. Dormitories wired for high-speed internet access and linked to campus network. Commuter students can connect to campus network. Online course registration, online library, helpline, wireless network available.

Student life. Freshman orientation: Mandatory, $100 fee. Preregistration for classes offered. Two-day program includes transition seminars, assessment, and academic advising. Summer/winter orientations with overnight for freshman available, includes parent orientations and welcome weekend before first day of classes. **Housing:** Guaranteed on-campus for all undergraduates. Coed dorms, special housing for disabled available. $100 nonrefundable deposit, deadline 5/1. Handicapped accessibility available in most residence halls. **Activities:** Bands, campus ministries, choral groups, dance, drama, international student organizations, literary magazine, music ensembles, musical theater, radio station, student government, student newspaper, symphony orchestra, TV station, Peer Ministry, Latin American student organization, Black Student Union, Inter Fratority Council, National Pan Hellenic Council, American Association of Airline Executives, Fellowship of Justice, Student Nurses Association, Teachers of Tomorrow.

Athletics. NCAA. **Intercollegiate:** Baseball M, basketball, cheerleading, cross-country, golf, soccer, softball W, swimming, tennis, track and field, volleyball. **Intramural:** Badminton, basketball, bowling, football (non-tackle), rugby, softball, volleyball. **Team name:** Flyers.

Student services. Adult student services, alcohol/substance abuse counseling, chaplain/spiritual director, career counseling, student employment

services, financial aid counseling, health services, minority student services, personal counseling, placement for graduates, veterans' counselor.

Contact. E-mail: admissions@lewisu.edu
Phone: (815) 836-5250 Toll-free number: (800) 897-9000
Fax: (815) 836-5002
Ryan Cockerill, Director of Admission, Lewis University, One University Parkway, Romeoville, IL 60446-2200

Lexington College
Chicago, Illinois
www.lexingtoncollege.edu
CB code: 3843

- Private 4-year culinary school and business college for women affiliated with Roman Catholic Church
- Commuter campus in very large city
- 58 degree-seeking undergraduates: 100% women
- 32% of applicants admitted
- SAT or ACT (ACT writing recommended), application essay required

General. Founded in 1977. Regionally accredited. **Degrees:** 15 bachelor's awarded. **Location:** Downtown. **Calendar:** Semester. **Full-time faculty:** 6 total. **Part-time faculty:** 15 total. **Class size:** 100% < 20. **Special facilities:** Culinary laboratory, computer laboratory.

Freshman class profile. 125 applied, 40 admitted, 17 enrolled.

Basis for selection. School achievement record, essay, and interview most important. Work experience considered. **Home schooled:** Letter of recommendation (nonparent) required. Must submit GED with scores.

High school preparation. College-preparatory program recommended. 10 units recommended. Recommended units include English 4, mathematics 2, social studies 2 and science 2.

2012-2013 Annual costs. Tuition/fees (projected): $25,200. Books/supplies: $750. Personal expenses: $400.

Financial aid. All financial aid based on need. **Additional information:** Work-study is available.

Application procedures. Admission: No deadline. $30 fee, may be waived for applicants with need. Admission notification on a rolling basis. **Financial aid:** Closing date 5/15. FAFSA required. Applicants notified on a rolling basis starting 7/1; must reply within 2 week(s) of notification.

Academics. Special study options: Cooperative education, independent study, internships, study abroad. **Credit/placement by examination:** AP, CLEP, institutional tests. **Support services:** Remedial instruction, study skills assistance, tutoring.

Majors. Business: Business admin, hotel/motel admin, restaurant/food services. **Work/family studies:** Institutional food production.

Computing on campus. 30 workstations in library, computer center. Online library, wireless network available.

Student life. Freshman orientation: Mandatory. Preregistration for classes offered. 2-day program before classes begin. **Activities:** Student government, student newspaper.

Student services. Chaplain/spiritual director, career counseling, student employment services, financial aid counseling, personal counseling, placement for graduates.

Contact. E-mail: admissions@lexingtoncollege.edu
Phone: (312) 226-6294 ext. 225 Toll-free number: (866) 647-3093
Fax: (312) 226-6405
Veronica North, Director of Marketing and Enrollment, Lexington College, 310 South Peoria Street, Chicago, IL 60607-3534

Lincoln Christian University
Lincoln, Illinois
www.lincolnchristian.edu
CB code: 1405

- Private 4-year university and Bible college affiliated with Christian Church
- Residential campus in large town

- 671 degree-seeking undergraduates: 19% part-time, 53% women, 6% African American, 1% Asian American, 3% Hispanic American, 1% Native American, 1% international
- 414 degree-seeking graduate students
- 67% of applicants admitted
- SAT or ACT with writing, application essay required
- 51% graduate within 6 years

General. Founded in 1944. Regionally accredited; also accredited by ABHE, ATS. **Degrees:** 138 bachelor's, 11 associate awarded; master's, doctoral offered. **Location:** 30 miles from Springfield. **Calendar:** Semester, limited summer session. **Full-time faculty:** 39 total; 64% have terminal degrees, 8% minority, 20% women. **Part-time faculty:** 72 total; 25% have terminal degrees, 3% minority, 38% women. **Class size:** 77% < 20, 16% 20-39, 3% 40-49, 3% 50-99, less than 1% >100.

Freshman class profile. 327 applied, 219 admitted, 81 enrolled.

Mid 50% test scores		End year in good standing:	96%
ACT composite:	18-25	Return as sophomores:	68%
GPA 3.75 or higher:	26%	Out-of-state:	17%
GPA 3.50-3.74:	13%	Live on campus:	92%
GPA 3.0-3.49:	19%	International:	1%
GPA 2.0-2.99:	37%		

Basis for selection. Recommendation of applicant's church leaders as to suitability for church-related vocations very important. High school record (core courses) and ACT scores also considered. Subscores of writing and English, application essay also important. Interview recommended. Audition required of music majors. **Home schooled:** Transcript of courses and grades, interview, letter of recommendation (nonparent) required. List of involvement outside of education/academics required. **Learning Disabled:** Students with learning disabilities usually referred to Academic Resource Center.

High school preparation. College-preparatory program recommended. 17 units recommended. Recommended units include English 4, mathematics 3, social studies 3, history 3, science 2 and foreign language 2.

2011-2012 Annual costs. Tuition/fees: $14,580. Room/board: $6,679. Books/supplies: $600. Personal expenses: $1,700.

2010-2011 Financial aid. Need-based: Average need met was 56%. Average scholarship/grant was $6,139; average loan $3,092. 55% of total undergraduate aid awarded as scholarships/grants, 45% as loans/jobs. **Non-need-based:** Scholarships awarded for academics.

Application procedures. Admission: No deadline. $25 fee, may be waived for applicants with need. Admission notification on a rolling basis. **Financial aid:** Priority date 3/1; no closing date. FAFSA required. Applicants notified on a rolling basis starting 2/1; must reply within 4 week(s) of notification.

Academics. Special study options: Distance learning, double major, dual enrollment of high school students, honors, independent study, internships, study abroad, weekend college. Study abroad through the CCCU-BestSemester program. **Credit/placement by examination:** AP, CLEP, ACT, institutional tests. **Support services:** Learning center, reduced course load, remedial instruction, study skills assistance, tutoring, writing center.

Majors. Business: Organizational leadership. **Philosophy/religion:** Philosophy. **Psychology:** General. **Theology:** Bible, missionary, religious ed, sacred music, theology, youth ministry.

Most popular majors. Business/marketing 16%, psychology 7%, public administration/social services 12%, theological studies 63%.

Computing on campus. 51 workstations in library, computer center, student center. Dormitories wired for high-speed internet access and linked to campus network. Commuter students can connect to campus network. Online course registration, online library, helpline, repair service, wireless network available.

Student life. Freshman orientation: Mandatory, $300 fee. Preregistration for classes offered. **Policies:** Religious observance required. **Housing:** Guaranteed on-campus for all undergraduates. Single-sex dorms, apartments, wellness housing available. $150 fully refundable deposit, deadline 8/10. **Activities:** Campus ministries, choral groups, drama, international student organizations, music ensembles, musical theater, student government, student newspaper, volunteer groups in local health care institutions, missions interest groups, Christian service and outreach groups.

Athletics. NCCAA. **Intercollegiate:** Baseball M, basketball, soccer, volleyball W. **Intramural:** Badminton, basketball, soccer, volleyball. **Team name:** Red Lions.

Student services. Student employment services, financial aid counseling, health services, personal counseling. **Physically disabled:** Services for visually, hearing impaired.

Contact. E-mail: admissions@lincolnchristian.edu
Phone: (217) 732-3168 ext. 2251 Toll-free number: (888) 522-5228
Fax: (217) 732-4199
Krista Brooks, Vice President of Enrollment Management, Lincoln Christian University, 100 Campus View Drive, Lincoln, IL 62656-2111

Loyola University Chicago
Chicago, Illinois — **CB member**
www.luc.edu — **CB code: 1412**

- Private 4-year university affiliated with Roman Catholic Church
- Residential campus in very large city
- 9,483 degree-seeking undergraduates: 6% part-time, 63% women, 4% African American, 11% Asian American, 11% Hispanic American, 1% international
- 5,865 degree-seeking graduate students
- 55% of applicants admitted
- SAT or ACT (ACT writing optional), application essay required
- 70% graduate within 6 years

General. Founded in 1870. Regionally accredited. Lakefront and downtown campuses; extensive degree program for returning adults. **Degrees:** 2,705 bachelor's awarded; master's, professional, doctoral offered. **ROTC:** Army, Naval, Air Force. **Location:** Downtown Chicago. **Calendar:** Semester, extensive summer session. **Full-time faculty:** 683 total; 93% have terminal degrees, 12% minority, 46% women. **Part-time faculty:** 684 total; 14% minority, 51% women. **Class size:** 37% < 20, 41% 20-39, 14% 40-49, 6% 50-99, 2% >100. **Special facilities:** Theater, language learning resource center, wellness center, computer resource center, neuroscience labs, biodiesel lab, mock trial room, performance and specialized fine arts rooms, clinical nursing labs, Information commons, histology lab, green house, artificial stream research facility.

Freshman class profile. 17,828 applied, 9,793 admitted, 1,930 enrolled.

Mid 50% test scores			
SAT critical reading:	540-660	Rank in top quarter:	65%
SAT math:	540-650	Rank in top tenth:	32%
SAT writing:	530-640	End year in good standing:	98%
ACT composite:	25-29	Return as sophomores:	87%
GPA 3.75 or higher:	48%	Out-of-state:	40%
GPA 3.50-3.74:	24%	Live on campus:	85%
GPA 3.0-3.49:	24%	International:	2%
GPA 2.0-2.99:	4%	Fraternities:	6%
		Sororities:	13%

Basis for selection. High school GPA, rigor of high school curriculum, official test scores (ACT or SAT), recommendation letter and essay are important. Personal interviews recommended but not required.

High school preparation. College-preparatory program required. 15 units required; 20 recommended. Required and recommended units include English 4, mathematics 3-4, social studies 2, history 1-2, science 3, foreign language 2 and academic electives 3. Additional requirements for certain majors.

2012-2013 Annual costs. Tuition/fees: $34,938. Room/board: $12,010. Books/supplies: $1,200. Personal expenses: $1,600.

2011-2012 Financial aid. Need-based: 1,672 full-time freshmen applied for aid; 1,434 were judged to have need; 1,432 of these received aid. Average need met was 82%. Average scholarship/grant was $19,711; average loan $3,763. 64% of total undergraduate aid awarded as scholarships/grants, 36% as loans/jobs. **Non-need-based:** Awarded to 2,052 full-time undergraduates, including 529 freshmen. Scholarships awarded for academics, athletics, leadership, music/drama, religious affiliation.

Application procedures. Admission: Priority date 12/1; no deadline. No application fee. Admission notification on a rolling basis beginning on or about 10/15. Must reply by 5/1. Separate application, recommendation and essay required for admission to Interdisciplinary Honors Program. Must apply by March 1. **Financial aid:** Priority date 3/1; no closing date. FAFSA required. Applicants notified on a rolling basis starting 2/15; must reply within 3 week(s) of notification.

Academics. Special study options: Accelerated study, combined bachelor's/graduate degree, distance learning, double major, ESL, external degree, honors, independent study, internships, study abroad, teacher certification program, Washington semester. School of professional studies offers part-time evening programs leading to bachelor's degrees; cooperative programs with Erikson Institute for Early Education and St. Joseph's Seminary; study abroad in 55 countries. **Credit/placement by examination:** AP, CLEP, IB, SAT, ACT, institutional tests. 24 credit hours maximum toward bachelor's degree. **Support services:** Learning center, pre-admission summer program, reduced course load, study skills assistance, tutoring, writing center.

Majors. Area/ethnic studies: African-American, women's. **Biology:** General, biochemistry, bioinformatics, biophysics. **Business:** Accounting, finance, human resources, international, management information systems, managerial economics, marketing, office management, operations, organizational behavior, small business admin. **Communications:** Communications/speech/rhetoric, digital media, journalism. **Computer sciences:** General, information technology, security. **Conservation:** Environmental science. **Education:** Bilingual, early childhood, elementary, mathematics, science, secondary, special ed. **English:** English lit. **Foreign languages:** Ancient Greek, classics, French, Italian, Latin, Spanish. **Health services:** Clinical lab science, clinical nutrition, health care admin, nursing (RN). **History:** General. **Human services:** Social work. **Math:** General, statistics. **Philosophy/religion:** Philosophy. **Physical sciences:** Chemistry, physics. **Protective services:** Criminal justice, forensics. **Psychology:** General, applied. **Social sciences:** Anthropology, international relations, political science, sociology. **Theology:** Religious ed, theology. **Visual/performing arts:** Art history/conservation, dramatic, music, studio arts.

Most popular majors. Biology 11%, business/marketing 24%, communications/journalism 8%, health sciences 8%, psychology 10%, social sciences 12%.

Computing on campus. 1,363 workstations in library, computer center, student center. Dormitories wired for high-speed internet access and linked to campus network. Commuter students can connect to campus network. Online course registration, online library, helpline, repair service, student web hosting, wireless network available.

Student life. Freshman orientation: Mandatory, $350 fee. Preregistration for classes offered. 2-day orientation program at Lake Shore campus. **Housing:** Guaranteed on-campus for freshmen. Coed dorms, special housing for disabled, apartments, wellness housing available. $250 fully refundable deposit, deadline 5/1. Living learning community floors available. **Activities:** Bands, campus ministries, choral groups, dance, drama, film society, international student organizations, literary magazine, music ensembles, Model UN, musical theater, radio station, student government, student newspaper, TV station, Agape Christian Fellowship, College Republicans, College Democrats, student environmental alliance, Bible Fellowship, black cultural center, armed forces club, Graduate Students of Color Alliance.

Athletics. NCAA. **Intercollegiate:** Basketball, cheerleading, cross-country, golf, soccer, softball W, track and field, volleyball. **Intramural:** Badminton, basketball, football (non-tackle), racquetball, soccer, table tennis, tennis, volleyball. **Team name:** Ramblers.

Student services. Adult student services, alcohol/substance abuse counseling, chaplain/spiritual director, career counseling, student employment services, financial aid counseling, health services, minority student services, on-campus daycare, personal counseling, placement for graduates, veterans' counselor. **Physically disabled:** Services for visually, speech, hearing impaired.

Contact. E-mail: admission@luc.edu
Phone: (312) 915-6500 Toll-free number: (800) 262-2373
Fax: (312) 915-7216
Lori Greene, Director of Admissions, Loyola University Chicago, 820 North Michigan Avenue, Chicago, IL 60611-9810

MacMurray College
Jacksonville, Illinois — **CB member**
www.mac.edu — **CB code: 1435**

- Private 4-year liberal arts college affiliated with United Methodist Church
- Residential campus in large town
- 508 degree-seeking undergraduates
- 71% of applicants admitted
- SAT or ACT (ACT writing optional) required

General. Founded in 1846. Regionally accredited. **Degrees:** 106 bachelor's awarded. **Location:** 30 miles from Springfield. **Calendar:** Semester, limited summer session. **Full-time faculty:** 32 total. **Part-time faculty:** 29 total. **Class size:** 59% < 20, 39% 20-39, 2% 40-49, 1% 50-99.

Freshman class profile. 795 applied, 562 admitted, 126 enrolled.

Basis for selection. ACT composite 20, high school or college transfer GPA 2.5 required for unconditional acceptance. Application reviewed for ACT composite between 15 and 19, high school or college transfer GPA

less than 2.5. ACT of 20 required for nursing applicants. ACT composite less than 15 or GPA less than 1.5 is automatic denial. School, community, and church activities, and recommendations also considered. Interview recommended for academically deficient applicants. Portfolio recommended for art scholarship.

2011-2012 Annual costs. Tuition/fees: $20,400. Room/board: $7,650. Books/supplies: $1,000. Personal expenses: $960.

Financial aid. Non-need-based: Scholarships awarded for academics, alumni affiliation, art, leadership, religious affiliation. **Additional information:** Merit scholarships for accepted, enrolled freshman based on academic record. Need-based program meets 100% of direct tuition charges after family contribution and financial aid.

Application procedures. Admission: Priority date 4/9; no deadline. No application fee. Admission notification on a rolling basis beginning on or about 9/1. **Financial aid:** Priority date 3/1; no closing date. FAFSA required. Applicants notified on a rolling basis starting 2/1; must reply within 2 week(s) of notification.

Academics. Special study options: Combined bachelor's/graduate degree, cooperative education, distance learning, double major, dual enrollment of high school students, independent study, internships, liberal arts/career combination, student-designed major, study abroad, teacher certification program, weekend college. **Credit/placement by examination:** AP, CLEP, IB, institutional tests. 32 credit hours maximum toward bachelor's degree. **Support services:** Learning center, reduced course load, study skills assistance, tutoring, writing center.

Majors. Biology: General. **Business:** Accounting, business admin, finance, management information systems. **Communications:** Journalism. **Computer sciences:** General, computer science. **Education:** Biology, Deaf/hearing impaired, elementary, emotionally handicapped, English, history, learning disabled, mathematics, music, physical, secondary, Spanish, special ed. **Engineering:** General. **English:** English lit. **Foreign languages:** French, sign language interpretation, Spanish. **Health services:** Predental, premedicine, preveterinary. **History:** General. **Human services:** Social work. **Math:** General. **Parks/recreation:** Sports admin. **Philosophy/religion:** Philosophy, religion. **Physical sciences:** Chemistry, physics. **Psychology:** General. **Social sciences:** International relations, political science. **Visual/performing arts:** Art, dramatic, music.

Most popular majors. Security/protective services 9%.

Computing on campus. 75 workstations in dormitories, library, computer center. Dormitories wired for high-speed internet access and linked to campus network. Online library, helpline, wireless network available.

Student life. Freshman orientation: Mandatory. Preregistration for classes offered. Two-day acclimation to campus life held prior to start of classes. **Housing:** Guaranteed on-campus for all undergraduates. Coed dorms, single-sex dorms, special housing for disabled available. $150 fully refundable deposit. **Activities:** Campus ministries, choral groups, drama, international student organizations, literary magazine, student government.

Athletics. NCAA. **Intercollegiate:** Baseball M, basketball, football (tackle) M, golf, soccer, softball W, volleyball W. **Intramural:** Basketball, soccer, softball, volleyball. **Team name:** Highlanders.

Student services. Alcohol/substance abuse counseling, chaplain/spiritual director, career counseling, student employment services, financial aid counseling, health services, personal counseling, placement for graduates, veterans' counselor. **Physically disabled:** Services for visually, hearing impaired.

Contact. E-mail: admissions@mac.edu
Phone: (217) 479-7056 Toll-free number: (800) 252-7485
Fax: (217) 291-0702
Alicia Zeone, Director of Admissions, MacMurray College, 447 East College Avenue, Jacksonville, IL 62650-2590

McKendree University
Lebanon, Illinois
www.mckendree.edu   **CB code: 1456**

- Private 4-year university and liberal arts college affiliated with United Methodist Church
- Residential campus in small town
- 2,296 degree-seeking undergraduates: 28% part-time, 56% women, 9% African American, 1% Asian American, 2% Hispanic American, 1% international
- 952 degree-seeking graduate students
- 68% of applicants admitted

- SAT or ACT (ACT writing optional), application essay required
- 53% graduate within 6 years; 42% enter graduate study

General. Founded in 1828. Regionally accredited. **Degrees:** 521 bachelor's, 11 associate awarded; master's, doctoral offered. **ROTC:** Army, Air Force. **Location:** 12 miles from Belleville, 23 miles from St. Louis. **Calendar:** Semester, limited summer session. **Full-time faculty:** 98 total; 86% have terminal degrees, 6% minority, 43% women. **Part-time faculty:** 215 total; 25% have terminal degrees, 56% minority, 45% women. **Class size:** 67% < 20, 32% 20-39, less than 1% 40-49. **Special facilities:** Networked faculty and classroom buildings, fine arts center with theater.

Freshman class profile. 1,359 applied, 925 admitted, 290 enrolled.

Mid 50% test scores		GPA 2.0-2.99:	29%
SAT critical reading:	510-560	Rank in top quarter:	41%
SAT math:	490-580	Rank in top tenth:	13%
SAT writing:	450-530	End year in good standing:	99%
ACT composite:	19-28	Return as sophomores:	81%
GPA 3.75 or higher:	29%	Out-of-state:	11%
GPA 3.50-3.74:	14%	Live on campus:	82%
GPA 3.0-3.49:	28%	International:	3%

Basis for selection. Decisions based on high school records, including rigor of curriculum, test scores, recommendations, evidence of student leadership and desire to succeed in rigorous academic environment. Each application is reviewed holistically, and while not required for admission, college prep curriculum recommended. Interviews recommended. Audition required of music majors and minors. Portfolio recommended for art majors. **Home schooled:** Statement describing home school structure and mission, transcript of courses and grades, letter of recommendation (nonparent) required. Applicants must submit description of courses studied and 3 letters of recommendation from other than parents.

High school preparation. College-preparatory program recommended. 14 units recommended. Recommended units include English 4, mathematics 2, social studies 2, history 1, science 2 (laboratory 1) and foreign language 1. Two additional units from either Math or science also recommended.

2011-2012 Annual costs. Tuition/fees: $24,190. Room/board: $8,830. Books/supplies: $1,200. Personal expenses: $1,190.

2011-2012 Financial aid. Need-based: Average need met was 85%. Average scholarship/grant was $19,455; average loan $2,908. 72% of total undergraduate aid awarded as scholarships/grants, 28% as loans/jobs. **Non-need-based:** Scholarships awarded for academics, alumni affiliation, art, athletics, leadership, minority status, music/drama, religious affiliation.

Application procedures. Admission: No deadline. No application fee. Admission notification on a rolling basis beginning on or about 9/15. Must reply by May 1st or by August 1 if notified thereafter. **Financial aid:** Priority date 5/31; no closing date. FAFSA required. Applicants notified on a rolling basis starting 3/1; must reply within 4 week(s) of notification.

Academics. Special study options: Accelerated study, combined bachelor's/graduate degree, cooperative education, distance learning, double major, dual enrollment of high school students, external degree, honors, independent study, internships, liberal arts/career combination, student-designed major, study abroad, teacher certification program. 3-2 and 3-3 occupational therapy program with Washington University; 3-2 Engineering transfer option. **Credit/placement by examination:** AP, CLEP, IB, SAT, ACT, institutional tests. 36 credit hours maximum toward associate degree, 64 toward bachelor's. **Support services:** Learning center, reduced course load, remedial instruction, study skills assistance, tutoring, writing center.

Honors college/program. Admission requirements: 3.6 GPA and 27 composite ACT score; about 115 freshman admitted.

Majors. Biology: General. **Business:** Accounting, business admin, management science, marketing. **Communications:** Communications/speech/rhetoric. **Computer sciences:** General, computer science, information systems, information technology. **Conservation:** Environmental studies. **Education:** General, art, biology, business, chemistry, elementary, English, foreign languages, health, history, music, physical, science, secondary, social science. **English:** Creative writing, English lit, rhetoric/composition. **Health services:** Athletic training, nursing (RN). **History:** General. **Liberal arts:** Arts/sciences. **Math:** General, financial. **Philosophy/religion:** Philosophy, religion. **Physical sciences:** Chemistry. **Psychology:** General. **Social sciences:** General, economics, international relations, political science, sociology. **Visual/performing arts:** Music, studio arts.

Most popular majors. Business/marketing 33%, education 31%, health sciences 18%, psychology 6%.

Computing on campus. 338 workstations in dormitories, library, computer center, student center. Dormitories wired for high-speed internet access and linked to campus network. Commuter students can connect to campus

network. Online course registration, online library, helpline, repair service, student web hosting, wireless network available.

Student life. Freshman orientation: Mandatory, $50 fee. Preregistration for classes offered. Three day program held weekend before start of classes. **Policies:** Students required to live on campus unless 21 years of age, of senior class standing, married, commuting from the home of a parent or legal guardian, or a veteran with at least two years active military duty. **Housing:** Guaranteed on-campus for all undergraduates. Coed dorms, special housing for disabled, apartments, wellness housing available. $200 fully refundable deposit. Living learning communities based on interests, faculty in residence program available. **Activities:** Bands, campus ministries, choral groups, dance, drama, film society, international student organizations, literary magazine, music ensembles, Model UN, musical theater, radio station, student government, student newspaper, Campus Christian Fellowship, Students Against Social Injustice, black student organization, service organizations, resident hall association, Intergreek Council, Community Service Fellows.

Athletics. NCAA. Intercollegiate: Baseball M, basketball, bowling, cheerleading, cross-country, football (tackle) M, golf, ice hockey M, lacrosse M, soccer, softball W, tennis, track and field, volleyball W, wrestling M. **Intramural:** Basketball, football (non-tackle), softball, volleyball. **Team name:** Bearcats.

Student services. Adult student services, alcohol/substance abuse counseling, chaplain/spiritual director, career counseling, student employment services, financial aid counseling, health services, minority student services, personal counseling, placement for graduates, veterans' counselor. **Physically disabled:** Services for visually, speech, hearing impaired.

Contact. E-mail: inquiry@mckendree.edu
Phone: (618) 537-6400 Toll-free number: (800) 232-7228 ext. 6400
Fax: (618) 537-6496
Chris Hall, Vice President for Admission and Financial Aid, McKendree University, 701 College Road, Lebanon, IL 62254-1299

Midstate College
Peoria, Illinois
www.midstate.edu   CB code: 3329

- For-profit 4-year business college
- Commuter campus in small city
- 629 degree-seeking undergraduates
- Application essay, interview required

General. Founded in 1888. Regionally accredited. **Degrees:** 60 bachelor's, 72 associate awarded. **Location:** 165 miles from Chicago. **Calendar:** Quarter, extensive summer session. **Full-time faculty:** 30 total. **Part-time faculty:** 51 total.

Freshman class profile. 41 applied, 35 admitted, 30 enrolled.

Basis for selection. Open admission, but selective for some programs and for out-of-state students. Academic record, personal ability, and desire to succeed. Some programs have additional requirements. Entrance examination required of all applicants. To ensure compliance with state regulations, students from out-of-state must be approved to enroll.

2011-2012 Annual costs. Tuition/fees: $14,625.

Application procedures. Admission: No deadline. $25 fee. Admission notification on a rolling basis. **Financial aid:** No deadline. FAFSA, institutional form required. Applicants notified on a rolling basis; must reply within 4 week(s) of notification.

Academics. Special study options: Distance learning, dual enrollment of high school students, internships. **Credit/placement by examination:** AP, CLEP, institutional tests. 24 credit hours maximum toward associate degree, 46 toward bachelor's. **Support services:** Learning center, reduced course load, remedial instruction, study skills assistance, tutoring.

Majors. Business: Accounting, business admin. **Computer sciences:** Information systems. **Health services:** Medical records technology.

Computing on campus. 109 workstations in library, computer center. Commuter students can connect to campus network. Online library, helpline, repair service, wireless network available.

Student life. Freshman orientation: Mandatory. Preregistration for classes offered. Held first day of each quarter. **Activities:** Student government.

Student services. Career counseling, student employment services, financial aid counseling, personal counseling, placement for graduates, veterans' counselor.

Contact. E-mail: admissions@midstate.edu
Phone: (309) 692-4092 Toll-free number: (800) 251-4299
Fax: (309) 692-3893
Ashley Spain, Director of Enrollment Management, Midstate College, 411 West Northmoor Road, Peoria, IL 61614-3558

Millikin University
Decatur, Illinois   **CB member**
www.millikin.edu   **CB code: 1470**

- Private 4-year university affiliated with Presbyterian Church (USA)
- Residential campus in small city
- 2,196 degree-seeking undergraduates: 4% part-time, 61% women, 12% African American, 1% Asian American, 5% Hispanic American, 2% international
- 82 degree-seeking graduate students
- 56% of applicants admitted
- SAT or ACT (ACT writing optional) required
- 65% graduate within 6 years; 27% enter graduate study

General. Founded in 1901. Regionally accredited. **Degrees:** 463 bachelor's awarded; master's offered. **Location:** 180 miles from Chicago, 120 miles from St. Louis. **Calendar:** Semester, limited summer session. **Full-time faculty:** 159 total; 81% have terminal degrees, 9% minority, 52% women. **Part-time faculty:** 133 total; 22% have terminal degrees, 13% minority, 59% women. **Class size:** 61% < 20, 36% 20-39, 1% 40-49, 2% 50-99. **Special facilities:** Art museums, 32-track recording studio, computer imaging center, greenhouse, observatory, performance center, 24-hour computer labs, video-conferencing classroom, proscenium theater, science center, 3-D arts building, student-owned and operated publishing company, record label, business incubator, fine art press.

Freshman class profile. 3,285 applied, 1,856 admitted, 432 enrolled.

Mid 50% test scores			
SAT critical reading:	470-600	Rank in top quarter:	40%
SAT math:	460-550	Rank in top tenth:	17%
SAT writing:	470-560	End year in good standing:	89%
ACT composite:	20-26	Return as sophomores:	77%
GPA 3.75 or higher:	29%	Out-of-state:	14%
GPA 3.50-3.74:	13%	Live on campus:	85%
GPA 3.0-3.49:	30%	Fraternities:	23%
GPA 2.0-2.99:	27%	Sororities:	14%

Basis for selection. School achievement record most important. Class rank, GPA, recommendation, test scores important. Applicant should rank in top half of class. Character references considered. Interview recommended. Audition required of music, music/theater majors. Portfolio required of art majors.

High school preparation. College-preparatory program recommended. 15 units required; 16 recommended. Required and recommended units include English 4, mathematics 3, social studies 2, history 2, science 3 and foreign language 2.

2011-2012 Annual costs. Tuition/fees: $28,642. Freshman pay additional $100 First Week Fee. Room/board: $8,530. Books/supplies: $1,000. Personal expenses: $2,100.

2010-2011 Financial aid. Need-based: 486 full-time freshmen applied for aid; 455 were judged to have need; 453 of these received aid. Average need met was 90%. Average scholarship/grant was $9,840; average loan $3,520. 68% of total undergraduate aid awarded as scholarships/grants, 32% as loans/jobs. **Non-need-based:** Awarded to 1,771 full-time undergraduates, including 483 freshmen. Scholarships awarded for academics, alumni affiliation, art, leadership, minority status, music/drama.

Application procedures. Admission: Priority date 5/1; no deadline. No application fee. Admission notification on a rolling basis beginning on or about 9/15. **Financial aid:** Priority date 3/15; no closing date. FAFSA required. Applicants notified on a rolling basis starting 3/15; must reply within 4 week(s) of notification.

Academics. Small business consulting and accelerated adult education available. **Special study options:** Accelerated study, combined bachelor's/graduate degree, double major, ESL, exchange student, honors, independent study, internships, student-designed major, study abroad, teacher certification program, United Nations semester, urban semester, Washington semester. **Credit/placement by examination:** AP, CLEP, IB, ACT, institutional tests. 30 credit hours maximum toward bachelor's degree. To receive CLEP credit student must not have attended secondary school in the past 3 years; CLEP credit cannot count in the major and may not be used if the equivalent course

has been attempted. **Support services:** Learning center, reduced course load, study skills assistance, tutoring, writing center.

Majors. Biology: General, molecular. **Business:** Accounting, business admin, entrepreneurial studies, finance, international, management information systems, marketing, organizational leadership. **Communications:** Communications/speech/rhetoric. **Education:** Art, biology, chemistry, early childhood, elementary, English, mathematics, music, physical, social science. **English:** Creative writing, English lit. **Foreign languages:** Spanish. **Health services:** Art therapy, athletic training, nursing (RN), prechiropractic, predental, premedicine, preoccupational therapy, preoptometry, prepharmacy, prephysical therapy, preveterinary. **History:** General. **Math:** Applied. **Parks/recreation:** Sports admin. **Philosophy/religion:** Philosophy. **Physical sciences:** Chemistry, physics. **Psychology:** General. **Social sciences:** Political science, sociology. **Visual/performing arts:** Commercial/advertising art, dramatic, music, music performance, musical theater, piano/keyboard, studio arts, theater design, voice/opera.

Most popular majors. Biology 6%, business/marketing 18%, communications/journalism 7%, education 23%, health sciences 11%, visual/performing arts 12%.

Computing on campus. 200 workstations in dormitories, library, computer center, student center. Dormitories wired for high-speed internet access and linked to campus network. Commuter students can connect to campus network. Online course registration, online library, helpline, student web hosting, wireless network available.

Student life. Freshman orientation: Mandatory, $100 fee. Preregistration for classes offered. Held the 5 days before beginning of classes. **Housing:** Guaranteed on-campus for freshmen. Coed dorms, single-sex dorms, special housing for disabled, apartments, fraternity/sorority housing, wellness housing available. $150 fully refundable deposit, deadline 5/1. Learning communities available. **Activities:** Bands, choral groups, dance, drama, film society, international student organizations, literary magazine, music ensembles, Model UN, musical theater, opera, radio station, student government, student newspaper, symphony orchestra, Black Student Union, Latin American Student Organization, Amnesty International, Multicultural Voices of Praise, Multicultural Student Council, College Republicans, Inter-Varsity Christian Fellowship, Newman Catholic Community, Sister Circle, Up 'Til Dawn.

Athletics. NCAA. **Intercollegiate:** Baseball M, basketball, cheerleading, cross-country, football (tackle) M, golf, soccer, softball W, swimming, tennis W, track and field, volleyball W. **Intramural:** Basketball, bowling, football (non-tackle), soccer, softball, volleyball. **Team name:** Big Blue.

Student services. Adult student services, alcohol/substance abuse counseling, career counseling, services for economically disadvantaged, student employment services, financial aid counseling, health services, minority student services, personal counseling, placement for graduates, women's services. **Physically disabled:** Services for visually, speech impaired.

Contact. E-mail: admis@millikin.edu
Phone: (217) 424-6210 Toll-free number: (800) 373-7733
Fax: (217) 425-4669
Joseph Havis, Director of Admission, Millikin University, 1184 West Main Street, Decatur, IL 62522-2084

Monmouth College
Monmouth, Illinois
www.monmouthcollege.edu
CB member
CB code: 1484

- Private 4-year liberal arts college affiliated with Presbyterian Church (USA)
- Residential campus in large town
- 1,316 degree-seeking undergraduates: 3% part-time, 52% women, 9% African American, 1% Asian American, 7% Hispanic American, 1% Native American
- 65% of applicants admitted
- SAT or ACT (ACT writing optional), application essay required
- 56% graduate within 6 years; 26% enter graduate study

General. Founded in 1853. Regionally accredited. **Degrees:** 282 bachelor's awarded. **ROTC:** Army. **Location:** 180 miles from Chicago, 60 miles from Peoria. **Calendar:** Semester. **Full-time faculty:** 84 total; 84% have terminal degrees, 5% minority, 42% women. **Part-time faculty:** 27 total; 26% have terminal degrees, 11% minority, 74% women. **Special facilities:** Prairie-habitat biology field station, educational garden, nature preserve, art and antiquities collection, U.S. First Ladies letter collection, Native American artifacts collection and lab, federal government documents repository.

Freshman class profile. 2,170 applied, 1,401 admitted, 341 enrolled.

Mid 50% test scores			
ACT composite:	19-25	Rank in top tenth:	21%
GPA 3.75 or higher:	16%	Return as sophomores:	74%
GPA 3.50-3.74:	15%	Out-of-state:	5%
GPA 3.0-3.49:	33%	Live on campus:	97%
GPA 2.0-2.99:	35%	Fraternities:	23%
Rank in top quarter:	36%	Sororities:	32%

Basis for selection. Record of academic achievement is most important, followed by the recommendations of counselor and teachers, test scores, and interview. An Interview is highly recommended. Care should be taken in selecting authors of recommendation letters.

High school preparation. College-preparatory program required. 14 units required; 22 recommended. Required and recommended units include English 4, mathematics 3-4, social studies 2-3, history 1-2, science 2-3 (laboratory 1-2), foreign language 2-3 and academic electives 2.

2011-2012 Annual costs. Tuition/fees: $28,650. Room/board: $7,300. Books/supplies: $1,000. Personal expenses: $900.

2011-2012 Financial aid. Need-based: 336 full-time freshmen applied for aid; 307 were judged to have need; 307 of these received aid. Average need met was 89%. Average scholarship/grant was $21,611; average loan $3,670. 81% of total undergraduate aid awarded as scholarships/grants, 19% as loans/jobs. **Non-need-based:** Awarded to 198 full-time undergraduates, including 72 freshmen. Scholarships awarded for academics, art, leadership, music/drama, religious affiliation, ROTC.

Application procedures. Admission: No deadline. No application fee. Admission notification on a rolling basis beginning on or about 9/15. Must reply by May 1 or within 2 week(s) if notified thereafter. **Financial aid:** Priority date 3/1; no closing date. FAFSA required. Applicants notified on a rolling basis starting 3/1; must reply by 8/15 or within 2 week(s) of notification.

Academics. Special study options: Combined bachelor's/graduate degree, double major, ESL, exchange student, honors, independent study, internships, semester at sea, student-designed major, study abroad, teacher certification program, urban semester, Washington semester. Off-campus (domestic and study abroad) programs available in cooperation with Associated Colleges of the Midwest and other study-abroad organizations, plus institutional off-campus programs and student-exchange agreements with universities in Ireland, France, Greece, Mexico, Morocco, Senegal, Scotland and Sweden. Monmouth College belongs to the International Student Exchange Program (ISEP). **Credit/placement by examination:** AP, CLEP, IB, SAT, ACT, institutional tests. **Support services:** Learning center, pre-admission summer program, remedial instruction, study skills assistance, tutoring, writing center.

Majors. Biology: General, biochemistry. **Business:** Accounting, business admin, international, managerial economics. **Communications:** Communications/speech/rhetoric, public relations. **Computer sciences:** Computer science. **Conservation:** Environmental science. **Education:** General, elementary, physical. **English:** English lit, rhetoric/composition. **Foreign languages:** Ancient Greek, classics, French, Latin, Spanish. **History:** General. **Liberal arts:** Arts/sciences. **Math:** General. **Philosophy/religion:** Philosophy, religion. **Physical sciences:** Chemistry, physics. **Psychology:** General. **Social sciences:** Anthropology, economics, international relations, political science, sociology. **Visual/performing arts:** Art, dramatic, music, studio arts.

Most popular majors. Business/marketing 20%, communications/journalism 10%, education 19%, history 9%, social sciences 6%, visual/performing arts 6%.

Computing on campus. 140 workstations in dormitories, library, computer center, student center. Dormitories wired for high-speed internet access and linked to campus network. Commuter students can connect to campus network. Online course registration, online library, helpline, student web hosting, wireless network available.

Student life. Freshman orientation: Mandatory, $140 fee. Preregistration for classes offered. Occurs before the start of fall semester; includes introductions, activities, workshops, academic advising, and formal matriculation ceremony. **Housing:** Guaranteed on-campus for all undergraduates. Coed dorms, single-sex dorms, special housing for disabled, apartments, cooperative housing, fraternity/sorority housing, wellness housing available. $150 partly refundable deposit. **Activities:** Bands, campus ministries, choral groups, dance, drama, film society, international student organizations, literary magazine, music ensembles, musical theater, radio station, student government, student newspaper, symphony orchestra, TV station, Coalition for Ethnic Awareness, interdenominational religious groups, Students Organized for Service, PRISM: People Respecting Individual Sexualities at Monmouth, Students for Environmental Awareness, Liberal Legion, Conservative Club, Art Alliance.

Athletics. NCAA. **Intercollegiate:** Baseball M, basketball, cross-country, football (tackle) M, golf, soccer, softball W, swimming, tennis, track and field, volleyball W. **Intramural:** Badminton, basketball, cheerleading, football (non-tackle), golf, soccer, softball, tennis, volleyball. **Team name:** Fighting Scots.

Student services. Alcohol/substance abuse counseling, chaplain/spiritual director, career counseling, services for economically disadvantaged, student employment services, financial aid counseling, health services, minority student services, personal counseling, placement for graduates, veterans' counselor, women's services. **Physically disabled:** Services for visually, speech, hearing impaired.

Contact. E-mail: admit@monmouthcollege.edu
Phone: (309) 457-2131 Toll-free number: (800) 747-2687
Fax: (309) 457-2141
Omar Correa, Vice President for Enrollment Management, Monmouth College, 700 East Broadway, Monmouth, IL 61462-1998

Moody Bible Institute
Chicago, Illinois
www.moody.edu
CB code: 1486

▶ Private 4-year Bible and seminary college affiliated with interdenominational tradition

▶ Residential campus in very large city

▶ 2,786 degree-seeking undergraduates: 19% part-time, 44% women, 3% African American, 3% Asian American, 4% Hispanic American, 6% international

▶ 395 degree-seeking graduate students

▶ 88% of applicants admitted

▶ SAT or ACT with writing, application essay required

▶ 68% graduate within 6 years

General. Founded in 1886. Regionally accredited; also accredited by ABHE. **Degrees:** 343 bachelor's, 18 associate awarded; master's offered. **Location:** Downtown. **Calendar:** Semester, limited summer session. **Full-time faculty:** 85 total; 59% have terminal degrees, 11% minority, 24% women. **Part-time faculty:** 98 total; 26% have terminal degrees, 4% minority, 9% women. **Class size:** 33% < 20, 55% 20-39, 4% 40-49, 4% 50-99, 4% >100.

Freshman class profile. 924 applied, 813 admitted, 447 enrolled.

Mid 50% test scores		Return as sophomores:	78%
SAT critical reading:	490-620	Out-of-state:	81%
SAT math:	470-610	Live on campus:	98%
ACT composite:	20-26	International:	4%

Basis for selection. Rank in top half of graduating class and/or high school GPA above 2.0. Applicants must have been Christians for at least 1 year. Membership in Evangelical Protestant Church and recommendation from church leadership required. Interview recommended. Audition required of music majors. **Home schooled:** ACT plus GED or SAT required.

High school preparation. College-preparatory program recommended.

2011-2012 Annual costs. Tuition/fees: $8,796. Chicago students receive a scholarship to cover all tuition expenses. Room/board: $9,816. Books/supplies: $600. Personal expenses: $500.

Financial aid. All financial aid based on need. **Additional information:** Aid available to upperclassmen is based on private and not federal/state sources.

Application procedures. Admission: Priority date 12/1; deadline 3/1 (postmark date). $50 fee, may be waived for applicants with need. Admission notification by 4/1. Must reply by May 1 or within 6 week(s) if notified thereafter. **Financial aid:** No deadline. Institutional form required. Applicants notified on a rolling basis; must reply by 7/1.

Academics. Special study options: Distance learning, double major, dual enrollment of high school students, external degree, independent study, internships, student-designed major, study abroad. International Studies Program partnerships with Adelaide College of Ministries, Bible College of Queensland, Bible College of Victoria, Sydney Bible and Missionary College (Australia); All Nations College, London School of Theology, Moorlands College (England); Institut Biblique de Nogent (France); Ambex (Germany); Greek Bible Institute (Greece); IBEX, Israel College of the Bible (Israel); Jerusalem Evangelical Theological Seminary (Jordan); Laidlaw College, Mueller Colleg of Ministries, Pathways College of Bible and Missions (New Zealand); International Christian College (Spain); Spanish Bible Institute (Spain); Odessa Theological Seminary (Ukraine). **Credit/placement by examination:** AP, CLEP, IB, institutional tests. 9 credit hours maximum toward associate degree,

12 toward bachelor's. **Support services:** Learning center, pre-admission summer program, reduced course load, study skills assistance, tutoring.

Majors. Communications: Communications/speech/rhetoric. **Education:** General, ESL. **Foreign languages:** Ancient Greek, Hebrew, linguistics. **Philosophy/religion:** Judaic. **Theology:** Bible, missionary, pastoral counseling, religious ed, sacred music, theology. **Visual/performing arts:** Music performance, music theory/composition, piano/keyboard, voice/opera.

Most popular majors. Communications/journalism 7%, theological studies 89%.

Computing on campus. 50 workstations in dormitories, library, computer center. Dormitories wired for high-speed internet access and linked to campus network. Commuter students can connect to campus network. Online course registration, online library, helpline, repair service, wireless network available.

Student life. Freshman orientation: Mandatory. Preregistration for classes offered. Held for main and regional campus students at the beginning of fall term. **Policies:** Students are required to suscribe to and follow community life standards published in the student handbook. Religious observance required. **Housing:** Guaranteed on-campus for all undergraduates. Single-sex dorms, apartments available. $350 nonrefundable deposit, deadline 5/1. **Activities:** Concert band, campus ministries, choral groups, drama, international student organizations, music ensembles, radio station, student government, student newspaper, symphony orchestra, Student Missionary Fellowship, Gospel teams, Embrace, international student fellowship, Big Brother/Big Sister Program, married students fellowship, residence activities council, Hispanic student fellowship, student wives fellowship.

Athletics. NCCAA. **Intercollegiate:** Basketball, soccer M, volleyball. **Intramural:** Badminton, basketball, cross-country, football (non-tackle), racquetball, soccer, swimming, table tennis, tennis, volleyball, water polo. **Team name:** Archers.

Student services. Career counseling, student employment services, financial aid counseling, health services, minority student services, on-campus daycare, personal counseling, placement for graduates, veterans' counselor. **Physically disabled:** Services for visually impaired.

Contact. E-mail: admissions@moody.edu
Phone: (312) 329-4400 Toll-free number: (800) 967-4624
Fax: (312) 329-8987
Charles Dresser, Dean of Admissions, Moody Bible Institute, 820 N LaSalle Boulevard, Chicago, IL 60610

National University of Health Sciences
Lombard, Illinois
www.nuhs.edu
CB code: 1567

▶ Private 4-year university and health science college

▶ Commuter campus in large town

▶ 56 full-time, degree-seeking undergraduates

General. Regionally accredited. **Degrees:** 29 bachelor's awarded; master's, professional offered. **Location:** 20 miles from Chicago. **Calendar:** Trimester, extensive summer session. **Full-time faculty:** 59 total. **Part-time faculty:** 59 total. **Special facilities:** Learning resource center, medical library, onsite clinic.

Basis for selection. Associate degree and certificate programs require 2.0 GPA or GED; bachelor's completion program in biomedical science requires minimum of 60 semester hours of prerequisite courses. Must be 18 years of age and of good moral character.

2011-2012 Annual costs. Tuition/fees: $9,208. Room only: $7,480.

Application procedures. Admission: $55 fee, may be waived for applicants with need. **Financial aid:** No deadline.

Academics. College of Professional Studies offers doctor of chiropractic, doctor of naturopathy, and master's degrees in acupuncture and Oriental Medicine. Primary undergraduate enrollment is in bachelor of biomedical sciece completion progrm and certificate programs in massage therapy and chiropractic assistance. Accelerated prerequisite program available for students needing to complete science entrance requirements. **Special study options:** Internships. **Credit/placement by examination:** AP, CLEP. **Support services:** Learning center, reduced course load, study skills assistance, tutoring.

Majors. Biology: Biomedical sciences.

Computing on campus. 75 workstations in library. Dormitories wired for high-speed internet access and linked to campus network. Online course registration, helpline, student web hosting, wireless network available.

Student life. Freshman orientation: Mandatory. Preregistration for classes offered. 1/2 day program designed to familiarize new students with the campus, key people and where to go for help. **Policies:** Must be 21 to live on campus. **Housing:** Apartments available. Pets allowed in dorm rooms. **Activities:** Student government, student newspaper, student chiropractic organizations, professional sororities and fraternities, christian chiropractic association.

Athletics. Intramural: Basketball, golf, soccer, softball, tennis, volleyball.

Student services. Financial aid counseling, health services.

Contact. E-mail: admissions@nuhs.edu
Phone: (630) 889-6566 Toll-free number: (800) 826-6285
Fax: (630) 889-6554
Victoria Sweeney, Director of Communications and Enrollment Services, National University of Health Sciences, 200 East Roosevelt Road, Lombard, IL 60148-4583

National-Louis University
Chicago, Illinois **CB member**
www.nl.edu **CB code: 1551**

- Private 4-year university and teachers college
- Commuter campus in small city
- 1,378 degree-seeking undergraduates: 39% part-time, 79% women, 39% African American, 2% Asian American, 20% Hispanic American, 1% international
- 3,187 degree-seeking graduate students
- 30% of applicants admitted
- SAT or ACT required

General. Founded in 1886. Regionally accredited. Additional in-state locations in Skokie, Wheeling, Lisle and Elgin. Field programs available on and off campus. Out-of-state campuses located in Milwaukee/Beloit, and Tampa. **Degrees:** 586 bachelor's awarded; master's, doctoral offered. **Location:** 10 miles from Chicago. **Calendar:** Quarter, limited summer session. **Full-time faculty:** 213 total; 75% have terminal degrees, 11% minority, 66% women. **Part-time faculty:** 308 total; 15% minority, 69% women. **Special facilities:** Elementary demonstration school for practice teaching and observation.

Freshman class profile. 161 applied, 48 admitted, 26 enrolled.

Basis for selection. Rank in top half of high school class, score 19 ACT, 1150 SAT (exclusive of Writing) and 2 letters of recommendation from counselors or teachers. Interview and essay recommended.

High school preparation. Recommended units include English 4, mathematics 3, social studies 3, science 2 (laboratory 1) and foreign language 2. 1 unit U.S. government or U.S. history recommended.

2011-2012 Annual costs. Tuition/fees: $15,735. Books/supplies: $1,005.

Financial aid. Non-need-based: Scholarships awarded for academics.

Application procedures. Admission: No deadline. $40 fee, may be waived for applicants with need. Admission notification on a rolling basis. **Financial aid:** Priority date 4/15; no closing date. FAFSA, institutional form required. Applicants notified on a rolling basis starting 5/1; must reply within 2 week(s) of notification.

Academics. Degree-completion programs available in allied health leadership, management, and applied behavioral science. Field classes offered evenings/weekends. **Special study options:** Accelerated study, combined bachelor's/graduate degree, distance learning, double major, dual enrollment of high school students, ESL, honors, independent study, internships, liberal arts/career combination, teacher certification program. **Credit/placement by examination:** AP, CLEP. 132 credit hours maximum toward bachelor's degree. **Support services:** Learning center, pre-admission summer program, reduced course load, remedial instruction, study skills assistance, tutoring, writing center.

Majors. Biology: General. **Business:** Accounting, business admin. **Computer sciences:** Information systems. **Education:** Early childhood, elementary. **English:** English lit. **Health services:** Clinical lab science, health care admin, medical radiologic technology/radiation therapy, respiratory therapy technology, substance abuse counseling. **Liberal arts:** Arts/sciences. **Math:** General, applied. **Psychology:** General. **Social sciences:** General, anthropology, economics. **Visual/performing arts:** Art, dramatic.

Most popular majors. Business/marketing 36%, education 13%, health sciences 9%, interdisciplinary studies 33%.

Computing on campus. Commuter students can connect to campus network. Online course registration, online library, helpline, repair service available.

Student life. Freshman orientation: Available. Preregistration for classes offered. **Activities:** Drama, musical theater, student government, student newspaper, Chinese club, Polish club, educational club, social science club, school psychology club, drama club, educational honorary society.

Student services. Adult student services, career counseling, student employment services, financial aid counseling, health services, personal counseling, placement for graduates. **Physically disabled:** Services for visually, speech, hearing impaired.

Contact. E-mail: admissions@nl.edu
Phone: (847) 947-5718 Toll-free number: (800) 443-5522 ext. 5718
Fax: (847) 465-5730
Ken Kasprzak, National-Louis University, 122 South Michigan Avenue, Chicago, IL 60603

North Central College
Naperville, Illinois **CB member**
www.northcentralcollege.edu **CB code: 1555**

- Private 4-year liberal arts college affiliated with United Methodist Church
- Residential campus in small city
- 2,619 degree-seeking undergraduates: 5% part-time, 56% women, 4% African American, 2% Asian American, 7% Hispanic American, 1% international
- 248 degree-seeking graduate students
- 65% of applicants admitted
- SAT or ACT (ACT writing optional) required
- 64% graduate within 6 years

General. Founded in 1861. Regionally accredited. **Degrees:** 529 bachelor's awarded; master's offered. **ROTC:** Army, Air Force. **Location:** 25 miles from Chicago. **Calendar:** Quarter, limited summer session. **Full-time faculty:** 128 total; 88% have terminal degrees, 12% minority, 48% women. **Part-time faculty:** 119 total; 39% have terminal degrees, 6% minority, 54% women. **Class size:** 35% < 20, 63% 20-39, 2% 40-49. **Special facilities:** Fermi accelerator laboratory, Argonne laboratory, arboretum, aquarium.

Freshman class profile. 3,052 applied, 1,972 admitted, 574 enrolled.

Mid 50% test scores		Rank in top tenth:	22%
ACT composite:	22-27	End year in good standing:	91%
GPA 3.75 or higher:	38%	Return as sophomores:	82%
GPA 3.50-3.74:	19%	Out-of-state:	10%
GPA 3.0-3.49:	32%	Live on campus:	81%
GPA 2.0-2.99:	11%	International:	1%
Rank in top quarter:	52%		

Basis for selection. Academic record, SAT or ACT scores, and personal character all considered important. Interview and essay recommended for marginal students. **Home schooled:** Interview required. Review of the student's portfolio and curriculum, writing sample, interview with the Director of Freshman Admission, interview with a faculty member may be required. **Learning Disabled:** Students who self-identify are referred to the academic support center.

High school preparation. College-preparatory program required. 16 units required; 19 recommended. Required and recommended units include English 4, mathematics 3, social studies 2, history 1, science 3 (laboratory 1-3), foreign language 3 and academic electives 3.

2011-2012 Annual costs. Tuition/fees: $29,733. Room/board: $8,610. Books/supplies: $1,200. Personal expenses: $1,182.

2011-2012 Financial aid. Need-based: 510 full-time freshmen applied for aid; 455 were judged to have need; 455 of these received aid. Average need met was 81%. Average scholarship/grant was $18,733; average loan $3,552. 71% of total undergraduate aid awarded as scholarships/grants, 29% as loans/jobs. **Non-need-based:** Awarded to 726 full-time undergraduates, including 192 freshmen. Scholarships awarded for academics, art, leadership, minority status, music/drama, religious affiliation, ROTC, state residency.

Application procedures. Admission: Priority date 4/15; no deadline. $25 fee, may be waived for applicants with need, free for online applicants. Admission notification on a rolling basis beginning on or about 10/1. Must reply by May 1 or within 4 week(s) if notified thereafter. **Financial aid:** No

deadline. FAFSA, institutional form required. Applicants notified on a rolling basis starting 3/1; must reply within 4 week(s) of notification.

Academics. **Special study options:** Accelerated study, combined bachelor's/graduate degree, cross-registration, double major, dual enrollment of high school students, ESL, exchange student, honors, independent study, internships, New York semester, student-designed major, study abroad, teacher certification program, United Nations semester, urban semester, Washington semester. Independent study project grants; 3-2 engineering program with Universities of Illinois at Urbana-Champaign and Minnesota; 5-year bachelor's/master's degree programs. **Credit/placement by examination:** AP, CLEP, IB, SAT, ACT, institutional tests. 28 credit hours maximum toward bachelor's degree. Students must be tested or otherwise assessed in order for experiential credit to be awarded. **Support services:** Pre-admission summer program, reduced course load, remedial instruction, study skills assistance, tutoring, writing center.

Majors. **Area/ethnic studies:** East Asian. **Biology:** General, biochemistry. **Business:** Accounting, actuarial science, business admin, finance, human resources, international, management information systems, marketing, small business admin. **Communications:** Communications/speech/rhetoric, journalism, organizational, radio/TV. **Communications technology:** Animation/special effects. **Computer sciences:** Computer science. **Education:** General, art, elementary, music, physical. **English:** Creative writing, English lit. **Foreign languages:** Classics, French, German, Japanese, Spanish. **Health services:** Athletic training, medical radiologic technology/radiation therapy, nuclear medical technology. **History:** General. **Liberal arts:** Arts/sciences. **Math:** General, applied. **Parks/recreation:** Exercise sciences, health/fitness, sports admin. **Philosophy/religion:** Philosophy, religion. **Physical sciences:** Analytical chemistry, chemistry, physics. **Psychology:** General. **Social sciences:** General, anthropology, economics, political science, sociology, sociology/anthropology. **Visual/performing arts:** Art, art history/conservation, dramatic, graphic design, jazz, music, musical theater.

Most popular majors. Business/marketing 28%, communications/journalism 7%, education 13%, parks/recreation 7%, psychology 6%, social sciences 12%.

Computing on campus. 310 workstations in dormitories, library, computer center, student center. Dormitories wired for high-speed internet access and linked to campus network. Commuter students can connect to campus network. Online library, helpline, repair service, student web hosting, wireless network available.

Student life. **Freshman orientation:** Available, $125 fee. Preregistration for classes offered. Three orientations held in June, one in August. Session also held the week before beginning of term. **Housing:** Guaranteed on-campus for all undergraduates. Coed dorms, single-sex dorms, special housing for disabled, wellness housing available. $100 nonrefundable deposit, deadline 5/1. **Activities:** Bands, campus ministries, choral groups, dance, drama, international student organizations, literary magazine, music ensembles, Model UN, musical theater, opera, radio station, student government, student newspaper, United Methodist Student Organization, Black student organization, Fellowship of Christian Athletes, Raza Unida, Cardinals in Action, Green Scene, commuter student organization, Students in Free Enterprise.

Athletics. NCAA. **Intercollegiate:** Baseball M, basketball, cross-country, football (tackle) M, golf, lacrosse W, soccer, softball W, swimming, tennis, track and field, volleyball W, wrestling M. **Intramural:** Basketball, bowling, cheerleading, football (tackle) M, golf, softball, table tennis, volleyball. **Team name:** Cardinals.

Student services. Adult student services, alcohol/substance abuse counseling, career counseling, student employment services, financial aid counseling, health services, minority student services, personal counseling, placement for graduates. **Physically disabled:** Services for visually, hearing impaired.

Contact. E-mail: admissions@noctrl.edu
Phone: (630) 637-5800 Toll-free number: (800) 411-1861
Fax: (630) 637-5819
Martin Sauer, Dean of Admission and Financial Aid, North Central College, PO Box 3063, Naperville, IL 60566-7063

North Park University
Chicago, Illinois
www.northpark.edu

CB member
CB code: 1556

- Private 4-year university and liberal arts college affiliated with Evangelical Covenant Church of America
- Residential campus in very large city
- 2,305 degree-seeking undergraduates: 15% part-time, 64% women, 9% African American, 6% Asian American, 14% Hispanic American, 5% international

- 786 degree-seeking graduate students
- 47% of applicants admitted
- SAT or ACT (ACT writing recommended), application essay required
- 52% graduate within 6 years

General. Founded in 1891. Regionally accredited. Offers Christian, urban, multicultural educational experience. **Degrees:** 474 bachelor's awarded; master's, professional offered. **ROTC:** Army, Air Force. **Location:** 10 miles from downtown. **Calendar:** Semester, limited summer session. **Full-time faculty:** 122 total; 88% have terminal degrees, 16% minority, 53% women. **Part-time faculty:** 180 total; 56% have terminal degrees, 19% minority, 57% women. **Class size:** 56% < 20, 38% 20-39, 4% 40-49, 2% 50-99, less than 1% >100. **Special facilities:** Nursing simulation lab.

Freshman class profile. 3,503 applied, 1,634 admitted, 425 enrolled.

Mid 50% test scores			
SAT critical reading:	460-580	GPA 2.0-2.99:	38%
SAT math:	460-570	Rank in top quarter:	40%
ACT composite:	19-25	Rank in top tenth:	15%
GPA 3.75 or higher:	13%	Out-of-state:	39%
GPA 3.50-3.74:	16%	Live on campus:	74%
GPA 3.0-3.49:	33%	International:	1%

Basis for selection. Admission based on full review of student's record, and considers courses taken, GPA, class rank, test scores, recommendations, essay or writing sample, co-curricular involvements, and community service. Nursing has an early admission option available to high achieving students. An interview may be required for some applicants. All students who visit campus may schedule an appointment with an admission counselor. **Home schooled:** Transcript of courses and grades, letter of recommendation (non-parent) required. **Learning Disabled:** Provides and coordinates support services and reasonable accommodations to aid students with disabilities through Center for Academic Services.

High school preparation. College-preparatory program recommended. Recommended units include English 4, mathematics 3, social studies 1, history 1, science 3 and foreign language 2.

2012-2013 Annual costs. Tuition/fees: $22,090. Room/board: $8,660. Books/supplies: $1,000. Personal expenses: $2,100.

2011-2012 Financial aid. **Need-based:** 355 full-time freshmen applied for aid; 345 were judged to have need; 345 of these received aid. Average need met was 64%. Average scholarship/grant was $7,265; average loan $3,025. 64% of total undergraduate aid awarded as scholarships/grants, 36% as loans/jobs. **Non-need-based:** Scholarships awarded for academics, art, music/drama, religious affiliation.

Application procedures. **Admission:** Priority date 4/1; deadline 7/1 (receipt date). $40 fee, may be waived for applicants with need. Admission notification on a rolling basis beginning on or about 9/15. Must reply by May 1 or within 4 week(s) if notified thereafter. **Financial aid:** Priority date 5/1, closing date 8/1. FAFSA required. Applicants notified on a rolling basis starting 10/1; must reply by 5/1 or within 4 week(s) of notification.

Academics. **Special study options:** Accelerated study, combined bachelor's/graduate degree, distance learning, double major, ESL, exchange student, honors, independent study, internships, liberal arts/career combination, student-designed major, study abroad, teacher certification program, Washington semester. **Credit/placement by examination:** AP, CLEP, IB, SAT, ACT, institutional tests. 30 credit hours maximum toward bachelor's degree. **Support services:** Learning center, pre-admission summer program, reduced course load, remedial instruction, study skills assistance, tutoring, writing center.

Majors. **Area/ethnic studies:** African-American, Scandinavian. **Biology:** General. **Business:** General, business admin, nonprofit/public, organizational behavior. **Communications:** Advertising, communications/speech/rhetoric. **Computer sciences:** General. **Education:** Early childhood, elementary, middle, multi-level teacher. **English:** English lit. **Foreign languages:** French, Scandinavian, Spanish. **Health services:** Athletic training, clinical lab science, nursing (RN). **History:** General. **Math:** General. **Parks/recreation:** Exercise sciences. **Philosophy/religion:** Philosophy. **Physical sciences:** Chemistry, physics. **Protective services:** Law enforcement admin. **Psychology:** General. **Social sciences:** Political science, sociology. **Theology:** Bible, theology, youth ministry. **Visual/performing arts:** Art, music, music performance. **Work/family studies:** Family studies.

Most popular majors. Business/marketing 23%, communications/journalism 8%, education 8%, health sciences 22%.

Computing on campus. 100 workstations in dormitories, library, computer center, student center. Dormitories wired for high-speed internet access and linked to campus network. Commuter students can connect to campus network. Online course registration, online library, helpline, wireless network available.

Student life. Freshman orientation: Mandatory. Preregistration for classes offered. Begins 5 days before start of classes. **Policies:** Alcohol-free campus and smoke-free buildings. Visiting hours in residence halls for persons of opposite sex. Freshmen not permitted cars on campus. **Housing:** Guaranteed on-campus for all undergraduates. Coed dorms, single-sex dorms, apartments available. $250 nonrefundable deposit, deadline 5/1. **Activities:** Bands, campus ministries, choral groups, drama, literary magazine, music ensembles, musical theater, opera, student government, student newspaper, symphony orchestra, African student club, Black student association, Latino American student organization, Middle Eastern student association, East Asian student association, South Asian student association, Scandinavian student association, Urban Outreach.

Athletics. NCAA. **Intercollegiate:** Baseball M, basketball, cross-country, football (tackle) M, golf, rowing (crew) W, soccer, softball W, track and field, volleyball W. **Intramural:** Basketball, football (non-tackle), soccer, volleyball. **Team name:** Vikings.

Student services. Adult student services, alcohol/substance abuse counseling, chaplain/spiritual director, career counseling, services for economically disadvantaged, student employment services, financial aid counseling, health services, minority student services, personal counseling, placement for graduates.

Contact. E-mail: admission@northpark.edu
Phone: (773) 244-5500 Toll-free number: (800) 888-6728
Fax: (773) 244-5243
Mark Olson, Director, Undergraduate Recruitment and Enrollment, North Park University, 3225 West Foster Avenue Box 19, Chicago, IL 60625-4895

Northeastern Illinois University

Chicago, Illinois   **CB member**
www.neiu.edu   **CB code: 1090**

- Public 4-year university
- Commuter campus in very large city
- 9,282 degree-seeking undergraduates: 41% part-time, 56% women, 10% African American, 9% Asian American, 32% Hispanic American, 4% international
- 1,902 degree-seeking graduate students
- 64% of applicants admitted
- SAT or ACT (ACT writing optional) required

General. Founded in 1961. Regionally accredited. Two extension centers serve Hispanic and African-American communities. **Degrees:** 1,705 bachelor's awarded; master's offered. **ROTC:** Army, Air Force. **Calendar:** Semester, limited summer session. **Full-time faculty:** 416 total; 72% have terminal degrees, 26% minority, 51% women. **Part-time faculty:** 302 total; 24% have terminal degrees, 25% minority, 50% women. **Class size:** 41% < 20, 53% 20-39, 5% 40-49, 1% 50-99, less than 1% >100.

Freshman class profile. 5,118 applied, 3,291 admitted, 950 enrolled.

GPA 3.75 or higher:	12%	Rank in top quarter:	15%
GPA 3.50-3.74:	8%	Rank in top tenth:	10%
GPA 3.0-3.49:	20%	International:	3%
GPA 2.0-2.99:	49%		

Basis for selection. Rank in top half of graduating class or 19 ACT/equivalent SAT required. Audition recommended for dance and music majors. Portfolio recommended for art majors.

High school preparation. College-preparatory program required. 15 units required. Required units include English 4, mathematics 3, social studies 3 and science 3. 2 additional units in fine arts, music, art, foreign languages, or vocational education. (Only 1 vocational education course accepted.).

2011-2012 Annual costs. Tuition/fees: $9,939; $18,189 out-of-state. Books/supplies: $1,650. Personal expenses: $2,988.

2011-2012 Financial aid. Need-based: 801 full-time freshmen applied for aid; 704 were judged to have need; 638 of these received aid. Average need met was 34%. Average scholarship/grant was $7,392; average loan $3,219. 70% of total undergraduate aid awarded as scholarships/grants, 30% as loans/jobs. **Non-need-based:** Awarded to 562 full-time undergraduates, including 112 freshmen. Scholarships awarded for academics, art, leadership, music/drama.

Application procedures. Admission: Closing date 7/1 (receipt date). $30 fee, may be waived for applicants with need. Admission notification on a rolling basis beginning on or about 9/1. **Financial aid:** Priority date 2/15;

no closing date. FAFSA required. Applicants notified on a rolling basis starting 12/15; must reply within 2 week(s) of notification.

Academics. Special study options: Cooperative education, distance learning, double major, dual enrollment of high school students, exchange student, honors, independent study, student-designed major, study abroad, teacher certification program. **Credit/placement by examination:** AP, CLEP, IB, ACT, institutional tests. 30 credit hours maximum toward bachelor's degree. **Support services:** Learning center, pre-admission summer program, remedial instruction, study skills assistance, tutoring, writing center.

Majors. Area/ethnic studies: Women's. **Biology:** General. **Business:** General, accounting, business admin, finance, marketing. **Computer sciences:** Computer science. **Conservation:** Environmental studies. **Education:** Bilingual, early childhood, elementary, physical, special ed. **English:** English lit, rhetoric/composition. **Foreign languages:** French, linguistics, Spanish. **Health services:** Community health services. **History:** General. **Human services:** Social work. **Liberal arts:** Arts/sciences. **Math:** General. **Philosophy/religion:** Philosophy. **Physical sciences:** Chemistry, geology, physics. **Protective services:** Criminal justice. **Psychology:** General. **Social sciences:** General, anthropology, economics, geography, political science, sociology. **Visual/performing arts:** Art, music.

Most popular majors. Business/marketing 20%, communications/journalism 6%, education 14%, liberal arts 11%, security/protective services 10%, social sciences 9%.

Computing on campus. 520 workstations in library, computer center, student center. Commuter students can connect to campus network. Online course registration, helpline, wireless network available.

Student life. Freshman orientation: Mandatory, $65 fee. Preregistration for classes offered. Full day program to register for courses; held during summer for fall term and in December for spring term. **Activities:** Bands, campus ministries, choral groups, dance, drama, film society, literary magazine, music ensembles, musical theater, radio station, student government, student newspaper, Muslim student association, black heritage club, politics club, Chimexla student union, Indian student association, university bible association, program board, Union of Puerto Rican Students, Hillel, outdoor adventure club.

Athletics. Intramural: Badminton, basketball, cross-country, racquetball, soccer, softball, table tennis, tennis, volleyball, weight lifting. **Team name:** Eagles.

Student services. Adult student services, career counseling, student employment services, financial aid counseling, health services, minority student services, on-campus daycare, personal counseling, placement for graduates, veterans' counselor, women's services. **Physically disabled:** Services for visually, speech impaired.

Contact. E-mail: admrec@neiu.edu
Phone: (773) 442-4000 Fax: (773) 442-4020
Janice Harring-Hendon, Director of Admissions and Records, Northeastern Illinois University, 5500 North St. Louis Avenue, Chicago, IL 60625

Northern Illinois University

DeKalb, Illinois   **CB member**
www.niu.edu   **CB code: 1559**

- Public 4-year university
- Residential campus in large town
- 17,271 degree-seeking undergraduates: 12% part-time, 50% women, 15% African American, 5% Asian American, 11% Hispanic American, 1% international
- 4,752 degree-seeking graduate students
- 53% of applicants admitted
- SAT or ACT required
- 56% graduate within 6 years

General. Founded in 1895. Regionally accredited. Field campus in Oregon. **Degrees:** 3,921 bachelor's awarded; master's, professional, doctoral offered. **ROTC:** Army. **Location:** 65 miles from Chicago. **Calendar:** Semester, extensive summer session. **Full-time faculty:** 884 total; 84% have terminal degrees, 14% minority, 46% women. **Part-time faculty:** 261 total; 36% have terminal degrees, 6% minority, 49% women. **Class size:** 45% < 20, 38% 20-39, 5% 40-49, 8% 50-99, 3% >100. **Special facilities:** Observatory, Burma art collection, anthropology museum, historic scenic collection, history of education museum and research collection.

Freshman class profile. 17,586 applied, 9,239 admitted, 2,590 enrolled.

Mid 50% test scores			
ACT composite:	19-24	Rank in top tenth:	9%
GPA 3.75 or higher:	11%	End year in good standing:	92%
GPA 3.50-3.74:	10%	Return as sophomores:	71%
GPA 3.0-3.49:	34%	Out-of-state:	3%
GPA 2.0-2.99:	44%	Live on campus:	93%
Rank in top quarter:	29%	International:	1%

Basis for selection. 19 ACT required of applicants who rank in top half of class, 23 ACT required of applicants in top two-thirds of class or with high school equivalency certificate. Interview required of CHANCE program applicants. Audition required of music majors. Portfolio recommended for art majors.

High school preparation. 15 units required. Required and recommended units include English 4, mathematics 2-4, social studies 2-3, history 1, science 2-4 (laboratory 1-2) and foreign language 1-2. One unit of art, film, music, theater, or foreign language required. Mathematics must include algebra and/or geometry. Social sciences must include US history or a combination of US history and government.

2011-2012 Annual costs. Tuition/fees: $11,014; $19,505 out-of-state. Room/board: $10,246. Books/supplies: $1,400. Personal expenses: $2,396.

2010-2011 Financial aid. **Need-based:** 2,435 full-time freshmen applied for aid; 2,125 were judged to have need; 2,075 of these received aid. Average need met was 65%. Average scholarship/grant was $8,170; average loan $3,270. 49% of total undergraduate aid awarded as scholarships/grants, 51% as loans/jobs. **Non-need-based:** Awarded to 501 full-time undergraduates, including 100 freshmen. Scholarships awarded for academics, alumni affiliation, art, athletics, leadership, music/drama, ROTC. **Additional information:** Huskie Advantage Grant covers the remaining cost of tuition for freshman students who have the IL MAP Grant and Pell that does not cover 100% tuition.

Application procedures. **Admission:** Priority date 3/1; deadline 8/1. $40 fee, may be waived for applicants with need. Admission notification on a rolling basis. **Financial aid:** Priority date 3/1; no closing date. FAFSA required. Applicants notified on a rolling basis starting 4/15.

Academics. **Special study options:** Cooperative education, distance learning, double major, dual enrollment of high school students, honors, independent study, internships, student-designed major, study abroad, teacher certification program. **Credit/placement by examination:** AP, CLEP, institutional tests. Credit by examination not awarded for courses that are prerequisites for courses for which the student already has credit or is currently enrolled. **Support services:** Learning center, tutoring, writing center.

Majors. **Biology:** General. **Business:** General, accounting, business admin, finance, management science, marketing, nonprofit/public, operations. **Communications:** Communications/speech/rhetoric, journalism. **Computer sciences:** Computer science. **Conservation:** Environmental studies. **Education:** General, art, early childhood, elementary, family/consumer sciences, health, physical, special ed. **Engineering:** Electrical, industrial, mechanical. **English:** English lit. **Foreign languages:** French, German, Russian, Spanish. **Health services:** Athletic training, clinical lab science, communication disorders, community health services, dietetics, nursing (RN), public health nursing. **History:** General. **Liberal arts:** Arts/sciences. **Math:** General. **Parks/recreation:** Health/fitness. **Philosophy/religion:** Philosophy. **Physical sciences:** Atmospheric science, chemistry, geology, physics. **Psychology:** General. **Social sciences:** Anthropology, economics, geography, political science, sociology. **Visual/performing arts:** Art, art history/conservation, dramatic, music, studio arts. **Work/family studies:** Clothing/textiles, family studies, food/nutrition.

Most popular majors. Business/marketing 19%, communications/journalism 8%, education 9%, health sciences 15%, social sciences 11%.

Computing on campus. 1,500 workstations in dormitories, library, computer center, student center. Commuter students can connect to campus network. Helpline available.

Student life. **Freshman orientation:** Mandatory, $60 fee. Preregistration for classes offered. **Housing:** Guaranteed on-campus for freshmen. Coed dorms, special housing for disabled, apartments, fraternity/sorority housing available. $150 deposit. Quiet and alcohol-free lifestyle floors, 21 and over student floors, honors floors available. **Activities:** Bands, campus ministries, choral groups, dance, drama, film society, international student organizations, music ensembles, Model UN, musical theater, opera, radio station, student government, student newspaper, symphony orchestra, TV station, numerous organizations available.

Athletics. NCAA. **Intercollegiate:** Baseball M, basketball, cross-country W, football (tackle) M, golf, gymnastics W, soccer, softball W, swimming, tennis, track and field W, volleyball W, wrestling M. **Intramural:** Badminton, baseball M, basketball, football (tackle) M, golf, ice hockey M, racquetball,

sailing, soccer, softball, table tennis, tennis, volleyball, wrestling M. **Team name:** Huskies.

Student services. Career counseling, student employment services, health services, legal services, minority student services, on-campus daycare, personal counseling, placement for graduates, veterans' counselor, women's services. **Physically disabled:** Services for visually, speech, hearing impaired.

Contact. E-mail: admission-info@niu.edu
Phone: (815) 753-0446 Toll-free number: (800) 892-3050
Fax: (815) 753-8312
Kimberley Buster-Williams, Director of Admissions, Northern Illinois University, DeKalb, IL 60115-2854

Northwestern University
Evanston, Illinois
www.northwestern.edu

CB member
CB code: 1565

- Private 4-year university
- Residential campus in small city
- 8,991 degree-seeking undergraduates: 7% part-time, 51% women, 5% African American, 19% Asian American, 8% Hispanic American, 6% international
- 11,293 degree-seeking graduate students
- 18% of applicants admitted
- SAT or ACT with writing, application essay required
- 94% graduate within 6 years

General. Founded in 1851. Regionally accredited. **Degrees:** 2,135 bachelor's awarded; master's, professional, doctoral offered. **ROTC:** Army, Naval, Air Force. **Location:** 12 miles from downtown Chicago. **Calendar:** Quarter, limited summer session. **Full-time faculty:** 1,149 total. **Part-time faculty:** 126 total. **Class size:** 75% < 20, 14% 20-39, 3% 40-49, 4% 50-99, 3% >100. **Special facilities:** Nanotechnology center, fine-arts complex, dance center, observatory, engineering design center, tennis center.

Freshman class profile. 30,926 applied, 5,575 admitted, 2,108 enrolled.

Mid 50% test scores			
SAT critical reading:	680-760	Return as sophomores:	97%
SAT math:	700-780	Out-of-state:	80%
SAT writing:	680-770	Live on campus:	99%
ACT composite:	31-34	International:	7%
Rank in top quarter:	91%	Fraternities:	25%
Rank in top tenth:	91%	Sororities:	34%

Basis for selection. Academic record, essays, test scores, activity record, school recommendations most important. SAT Subject Tests recommended. SAT Subject Tests in Math Level 2 and Chemistry required of all applicants for Honors Program in Medical Education. Applicants to Integrated Science Program must take SAT Subject Tests in Chemistry or Physics, Math Level 2, plus second science. Audition required for music majors. **Home schooled:** 3 SAT Subject Tests required. Math Level 1 or 2 for students who plan to study sciences or engineering, Math Level 2 preferable, plus 2 other SAT Subject Tests of applicant's choice from different subject areas required.

High school preparation. College-preparatory program recommended. 16 units recommended. Recommended units include English 4, mathematics 3, social studies 2, science 2 (laboratory 2), foreign language 2 and academic electives 1. 4 units of mathematics recommended for engineering applicants. Applicants typically have 20 academic high school units.

2011-2012 Annual costs. Tuition/fees: $41,983. Room/board: $12,780. Books/supplies: $1,737. Personal expenses: $1,782.

2010-2011 Financial aid. **Need-based:** 1,276 full-time freshmen applied for aid; 1,091 were judged to have need; 1,091 of these received aid. Average need met was 100%. Average scholarship/grant was $31,777; average loan $3,873. 81% of total undergraduate aid awarded as scholarships/grants, 19% as loans/jobs. **Non-need-based:** Awarded to 691 full-time undergraduates, including 151 freshmen. Scholarships awarded for athletics, music/drama, ROTC.

Application procedures. **Admission:** Closing date 1/1 (postmark date). $65 fee, may be waived for applicants with need. Admission notification by 4/15. Must reply by May 1 or within 2 week(s) if notified thereafter. **Financial aid:** Closing date 2/15. FAFSA, CSS PROFILE required. Applicants notified by 4/15; must reply by 5/1 or within 2 week(s) of notification.

Academics. One unit of credit awarded for each course; 45-48 units required for graduation. **Special study options:** Accelerated study, combined bachelor's/graduate degree, cooperative education, double major, honors,

independent study, internships, liberal arts/career combination, student-designed major, study abroad, teacher certification program. 3-year integrated science program; 4-year mathematical methods in social sciences bachelor's program; honors programs in undergraduate research engineering, engineering and management, medical education; 7-year BA/MD program resulting in both an undergraduate degree and MD. **Credit/placement by examination:** AP, CLEP, IB, institutional tests. **Support services:** Study skills assistance, tutoring, writing center.

Majors. Area/ethnic studies: African-American, American, Asian, European, women's. **Biology:** General, ecology, neuroscience. **Business:** Organizational behavior. **Communications:** Broadcast journalism, communications/speech/rhetoric, journalism, radio/TV. **Computer sciences:** General, computer science, information systems. **Conservation:** Environmental science, environmental studies. **Education:** General, learning disabled, mathematics, music, secondary. **Engineering:** General, biomedical, chemical, civil, computer, electrical, engineering science, environmental, industrial, manufacturing, materials, mechanical. **English:** Creative writing, English lit. **Foreign languages:** Classics, comparative lit, East Asian, French, German, Italian, linguistics, Slavic, Spanish. **Health services:** Communication disorders, premedicine. **History:** General. **Human services:** Community org/advocacy, public policy. **Liberal arts:** Arts/sciences. **Math:** General, applied, statistics. **Philosophy/religion:** Philosophy, religion. **Physical sciences:** Chemistry, geology, materials science, physics. **Psychology:** General, cognitive, community. **Social sciences:** Anthropology, economics, geography, international relations, political science, sociology, urban studies. **Visual/performing arts:** General, art, art history/conservation, dance, dramatic, jazz, music, music performance, music theory/composition, musicology, piano/keyboard, stringed instruments, theater history, voice/opera.

Most popular majors. Communications/journalism 20%, engineering/engineering technologies 15%, psychology 8%, social sciences 17%, visual/performing arts 10%.

Computing on campus. Dormitories wired for high-speed internet access and linked to campus network. Commuter students can connect to campus network. Online course registration, online library, helpline, repair service, student web hosting, wireless network available.

Student life. Freshman orientation: Mandatory. Preregistration for classes offered. Held for 5 days prior to start of classes. **Housing:** Guaranteed on-campus for freshmen. Coed dorms, single-sex dorms, fraternity/sorority housing, wellness housing available. $200 nonrefundable deposit, deadline 5/25. Residential colleges available. **Activities:** Bands, campus ministries, choral groups, dance, drama, film society, international student organizations, literary magazine, music ensembles, musical theater, opera, radio station, student government, student newspaper, symphony orchestra, TV station, over 300 organizations.

Athletics. NCAA. **Intercollegiate:** Baseball M, basketball, cheerleading, cross-country W, diving, fencing W, field hockey W, football (tackle) M, golf, lacrosse W, soccer, softball W, swimming, tennis, volleyball W, wrestling M. **Intramural:** Basketball, football (non-tackle), ice hockey, soccer, softball, volleyball. **Team name:** Wildcats.

Student services. Adult student services, alcohol/substance abuse counseling, chaplain/spiritual director, career counseling, student employment services, financial aid counseling, health services, minority student services, personal counseling, placement for graduates, women's services. **Physically disabled:** Services for visually, speech, hearing impaired.

Contact. E-mail: ug-admission@northwestern.edu
Phone: (847) 491-7271
Christopher Watson, Dean of Undergraduate Admissions, Northwestern University, 1801 Hinman Avenue, Evanston, IL 60204-3060

Olivet Nazarene University

Bourbonnais, Illinois   **CB member**
www.olivet.edu   **CB code: 1596**

- Private 4-year university and liberal arts college affiliated with Church of the Nazarene
- Residential campus in small city
- 3,038 degree-seeking undergraduates: 14% part-time, 65% women, 10% African American, 2% Asian American, 3% Hispanic American, 1% international
- 1,143 degree-seeking graduate students
- 80% of applicants admitted
- ACT (writing optional) required
- 60% graduate within 6 years

General. Founded in 1907. Regionally accredited. Evangelical liberal arts institution emphasizing Christian values. **Degrees:** 733 bachelor's, 39 associate awarded; master's, doctoral offered. **ROTC:** Army. **Location:** 60 miles from Chicago. **Calendar:** Semester, extensive summer session. **Full-time faculty:** 118 total. **Part-time faculty:** 350 total. **Class size:** 39% < 20, 46% 20-39, 5% 40-49, 9% 50-99, 1% >100. **Special facilities:** Planetarium, observatory, science museum, distance learning classroom.

Freshman class profile. 2,705 applied, 2,165 admitted, 713 enrolled.

Mid 50% test scores		Out-of-state:	52%
ACT composite:	20-27	Live on campus:	92%
Return as sophomores:	73%		

Basis for selection. 2.0 GPA in college-preparatory subjects, ranking in top three-quarters of class, 18 ACT, 2 recommendations required. Interview recommended. Audition required of music majors. Portfolios required for art scholarship applicants.

High school preparation. College-preparatory program recommended. 15 units required. Required and recommended units include English 4, mathematics 3, social studies 4, history 2, science 3 and foreign language 2.

2012-2013 Annual costs. Tuition/fees (projected): $28,090. Room/board: $7,900. Books/supplies: $1,000. Personal expenses: $400.

2010-2011 Financial aid. Need-based: 695 full-time freshmen applied for aid; 634 were judged to have need; 633 of these received aid. Average need met was 87%. Average scholarship/grant was $17,864; average loan $3,478. 80% of total undergraduate aid awarded as scholarships/grants, 20% as loans/jobs. **Non-need-based:** Awarded to 1,019 full-time undergraduates, including 237 freshmen. Scholarships awarded for academics, art, athletics, leadership, music/drama, religious affiliation, ROTC, state residency.

Application procedures. Admission: Closing date 5/15 (postmark date). $25 fee, may be waived for applicants with need, free for online applicants. Admission notification on a rolling basis. **Financial aid:** Priority date 3/1; no closing date. FAFSA, institutional form required. Applicants notified on a rolling basis starting 1/15; must reply within 2 week(s) of notification.

Academics. Special study options: Accelerated study, distance learning, double major, honors, independent study, internships, liberal arts/career combination, student-designed major, study abroad, teacher certification program, Washington semester. Council of Christian Colleges and Universities study programs, adult studies degree program. **Credit/placement by examination:** AP, CLEP, IB, ACT, institutional tests. **Support services:** Learning center, pre-admission summer program, reduced course load, remedial instruction, tutoring.

Majors. Biology: General, zoology. **Business:** General, accounting, business admin, fashion, finance, international, marketing. **Communications:** Broadcast journalism, communications/speech/rhetoric, journalism. **Computer sciences:** General, computer science, information systems, programming. **Conservation:** Environmental studies. **Education:** Art, biology, chemistry, early childhood, elementary, English, family/consumer sciences, foreign languages, health, history, mathematics, music, physical, science, secondary, social science, social studies, Spanish. **Engineering:** General. **English:** English lit. **Foreign languages:** General, Spanish. **Health services:** Athletic training. **History:** General. **Human services:** Public policy, social work. **Liberal arts:** Arts/sciences. **Math:** General. **Parks/recreation:** Exercise sciences, sports admin. **Philosophy/religion:** Religion. **Physical sciences:** Chemistry, geology. **Protective services:** Criminal justice. **Psychology:** General. **Social sciences:** General, economics, political science, sociology. **Theology:** Bible, religious ed, sacred music, theology. **Visual/performing arts:** Art, music, music performance, piano/keyboard, voice/opera. **Work/family studies:** General, family/community services, housing.

Most popular majors. Business/marketing 16%, education 13%, foreign language 6%, health sciences 27%, parks/recreation 8%.

Computing on campus. 125 workstations in library, computer center, student center. Dormitories wired for high-speed internet access and linked to campus network. Commuter students can connect to campus network. Online library, helpline, repair service, student web hosting, wireless network available.

Student life. Freshman orientation: Mandatory. Preregistration for classes offered. Three-day program held on second and third weekends in June. Comprehensive for students and parents. **Policies:** Chapel convocations held twice weekly. Religious observance required. **Housing:** Guaranteed on-campus for all undergraduates. Single-sex dorms, special housing for disabled, apartments available. **Activities:** Bands, campus ministries, choral groups, drama, international student organizations, literary magazine, music ensembles, musical theater, radio station, student government, student newspaper, symphony orchestra, social service clubs, spiritual life groups.

Athletics. NAIA, NCCAA. **Intercollegiate:** Baseball M, basketball, cheerleading, cross-country, football (tackle) M, golf M, soccer, softball W, tennis,

track and field, volleyball W. **Intramural:** Badminton, basketball, bowling, cross-country, football (non-tackle) W, golf, handball, racquetball, soccer, softball, table tennis, tennis, track and field, volleyball. **Team name:** Tigers.

Student services. Adult student services, alcohol/substance abuse counseling, chaplain/spiritual director, career counseling, services for economically disadvantaged, student employment services, financial aid counseling, health services, personal counseling, placement for graduates, veterans' counselor.

Contact. E-mail: admissions@olivet.edu
Phone: (815) 939-5203 Toll-free number: (800) 648-1463
Fax: (815) 939-5069
Susan Wolff, Director of Admissions, Olivet Nazarene University, One University Avenue, Bourbonnais, IL 60914

Principia College
Elsah, Illinois
www.principiacollege.edu
CB member
CB code: 1630

- Private 4-year liberal arts college affiliated with First Church of Christ, Scientist (Christian Science)
- Residential campus in rural community
- 492 degree-seeking undergraduates: 1% part-time, 57% women, 1% African American, 4% Hispanic American, 13% international
- 79% of applicants admitted
- SAT or ACT with writing, application essay required
- 73% graduate within 6 years; 54% enter graduate study

General. Founded in 1910. Regionally accredited. All faculty, staff, and students are Christian Scientists. **Degrees:** 114 bachelor's awarded. **Location:** 35 miles from St. Louis. **Calendar:** Semester. **Full-time faculty:** 71 total; 54% have terminal degrees, 4% minority, 49% women. **Part-time faculty:** 5 total; 60% women. **Class size:** 88% < 20, 12% 20-39. **Special facilities:** School of Nations museum, astronomical observatory telescope, media center, tropical aviary, on-site mammoth excavation, Christian Science practitioner's office, athletic center with natatorium, 3,069-pipe organ, 39 bronze bell carillon.

Freshman class profile. 214 applied, 168 admitted, 103 enrolled.

Mid 50% test scores			
SAT critical reading:	440-620	GPA 2.0-2.99:	23%
SAT math:	460-620	Rank in top quarter:	69%
SAT writing:	450-610	Rank in top tenth:	23%
ACT composite:	20-29	End year in good standing:	91%
GPA 3.75 or higher:	30%	Return as sophomores:	81%
GPA 3.50-3.74:	22%	Out-of-state:	89%
GPA 3.0-3.49:	23%	Live on campus:	100%
		International:	11%

Basis for selection. High school transcript, admissions application and essay or personal statement most important. Test scores important as well. Applicant must be practicing Christian Scientist. Foreign language SAT Subject Test required for placement purposes. Interview recommended. Portfolio recommended for art majors. **Home schooled:** Must submit curricula program from accredited high school or accepted agency, plus GED.

High school preparation. 16 units required; 20 recommended. Required and recommended units include English 4, mathematics 3-4, social studies 1, history 1-2, science 3-4 (laboratory 2), foreign language 2-3 and academic electives 2.

2012-2013 Annual costs. Tuition/fees: $25,960. Room/board: $10,000. Books/supplies: $1,000. Personal expenses: $1,000.

2011-2012 Financial aid. **Need-based:** 86 full-time freshmen applied for aid; 77 were judged to have need; 77 of these received aid. Average need met was 91%. Average scholarship/grant was $23,168; average loan $6,254. 83% of total undergraduate aid awarded as scholarships/grants, 17% as loans/jobs. **Non-need-based:** Awarded to 252 full-time undergraduates, including 56 freshmen. Scholarships awarded for academics, alumni affiliation, leadership.

Application procedures. **Admission:** No deadline. No application fee. Application must be submitted online. Admission notification on a rolling basis beginning on or about 10/15. Must reply by May 1 or within 2 week(s) if notified thereafter. **Financial aid:** Closing date 3/1. Institutional form, CSS PROFILE required. Applicants notified by 4/1.

Academics. **Special study options:** Double major, independent study, internships, liberal arts/career combination, student-designed major, study abroad, teacher certification program. 3-2 engineering with Washington University, University of Southern California, Southern Illinois University at Edwardsville. **Credit/placement by examination:** AP, CLEP, IB, institutional tests. **Support services:** Learning center, study skills assistance, tutoring, writing center.

Majors. Biology: General. **Business:** Business admin. **Communications:** Media studies. **Computer sciences:** General, computer science. **Conservation:** General. **Education:** Elementary. **Engineering:** Engineering science. **English:** English lit. **Foreign languages:** General, French, Spanish. **History:** General. **Liberal arts:** Arts/sciences, humanities. **Math:** General. **Philosophy/religion:** Philosophy, religion. **Physical sciences:** Chemistry, physics. **Social sciences:** General, anthropology, economics, political science, sociology. **Visual/performing arts:** Art history/conservation, dramatic, music, studio arts.

Computing on campus. 250 workstations in dormitories, library, computer center, student center. Dormitories wired for high-speed internet access and linked to campus network. Online course registration, online library, helpline, student web hosting, wireless network available.

Student life. Freshman orientation: Mandatory. Preregistration for classes offered. One week orientation program offered each semester prior to start of classes in August and January. **Policies:** Students required to comply with standards of Christian Science. No alcoholic beverages, smoking, drugs. High moral standards and behavior expected. Standards maintained regarding abstinence from premarital sex or homosexual activity. Religious observance required. **Housing:** Guaranteed on-campus for all undergraduates. Coed dorms, single-sex dorms, apartments, wellness housing available. $100 nonrefundable deposit, deadline 5/1. Single-sex wings, 8 person cottages for non-traditional students available. **Activities:** Bands, choral groups, dance, drama, international student organizations, music ensembles, musical theater, radio station, student government, student newspaper, symphony orchestra, TV station, Christian Science organization, black student union, Latin American student organization, student volunteer program, public affairs conference.

Athletics. NCAA. **Intercollegiate:** Baseball M, basketball, cross-country, diving, soccer, swimming, tennis, track and field, volleyball W. **Intramural:** Basketball, soccer, softball, volleyball W. **Team name:** Panthers.

Student services. Adult student services, career counseling, student employment services, financial aid counseling, health services, on-campus daycare, personal counseling.

Contact. E-mail: collegeadmissions@principia.edu
Phone: (618) 374-5181 Toll-free number: (800) 277-4648 ext. 2802
Fax: (618) 374-4000
Brian McCauley, Dean of Enrollment Management, Principia College, One Maybeck Place, Elsah, IL 62028-9799

Quincy University
Quincy, Illinois
www.quincy.edu
CB code: 1645

- Private 4-year university and liberal arts college affiliated with Roman Catholic Church
- Residential campus in large town
- 1,225 degree-seeking undergraduates: 6% part-time, 57% women, 11% African American, 1% Asian American, 2% Hispanic American, 1% Native American, 1% international
- 375 degree-seeking graduate students
- 91% of applicants admitted
- SAT or ACT (ACT writing optional), application essay required
- 50% graduate within 6 years; 23% enter graduate study

General. Founded in 1860. Regionally accredited. **Degrees:** 249 bachelor's, 2 associate awarded; master's offered. **Location:** 300 miles from Chicago,120 miles from St. Louis. **Calendar:** Semester, limited summer session. **Full-time faculty:** 55 total; 71% have terminal degrees, 9% minority, 36% women. **Class size:** 66% < 20, 34% 20-39, less than 1% 40-49. **Special facilities:** National public radio station, 200-seat theater, multi-media and graphic design labs, environmental studies institute, TV production studio, rare books archive, hospital simulation lab, aviation facility with aviation simulator, university chapel and non-denominational praise/worship chapel.

Freshman class profile. 1,023 applied, 928 admitted, 276 enrolled.

Mid 50% test scores			
SAT critical reading:	410-520	Rank in top quarter:	31%
SAT math:	440-530	Rank in top tenth:	10%
ACT composite:	19-24	Return as sophomores:	72%
GPA 3.75 or higher:	20%	Out-of-state:	36%
GPA 3.50-3.74:	17%	Live on campus:	82%
GPA 3.0-3.49:	30%	International:	1%
GPA 2.0-2.99:	33%	Fraternities:	6%
		Sororities:	12%

Basis for selection. School achievement record is most important. Applicants for BS in nursing must have the minimum of a 22 ACT composite and 3.0 high school GPA and meet other requirements. May also require references and/or writing sample. Audition required of music majors. Portfolio recommended for art majors. **Home schooled:** Letter of recommendation (nonparent) required. Required documentation may vary. **Learning Disabled:** Must submit documentation of disability.

High school preparation. College-preparatory program recommended. 16 units recommended. Recommended units include English 4, mathematics 3, social studies 3, science 3 and foreign language 2. Courses in computers and the arts recommended.

2011-2012 Annual costs. Tuition/fees: $24,140. Room and board charges vary according to board plan and housing facility selected. Room/board: $9,420.

2011-2012 Financial aid. **Need-based:** 267 full-time freshmen applied for aid; 250 were judged to have need; 250 of these received aid. Average need met was 81%. Average scholarship/grant was $21,111; average loan $3,499. 73% of total undergraduate aid awarded as scholarships/grants, 27% as loans/jobs. **Non-need-based:** Awarded to 195 full-time undergraduates, including 30 freshmen. Scholarships awarded for academics, alumni affiliation, art, athletics, leadership, music/drama.

Application procedures. **Admission:** Priority date 4/15; no deadline. $25 fee. Admission notification on a rolling basis beginning on or about 9/1. **Financial aid:** Priority date 3/1; no closing date. FAFSA required. Applicants notified on a rolling basis starting 3/10; must reply by 5/1 or within 2 week(s) of notification.

Academics. **Special study options:** Accelerated study, distance learning, double major, dual enrollment of high school students, honors, independent study, internships, student-designed major, study abroad, teacher certification program, Washington semester. 3-2 program in engineering with Washington University resulting in 2 bachelors, can earn a master's with an additional year; 3-1 program in medical technology with various hospitals; learning communities. **Credit/placement by examination:** AP, CLEP, IB, ACT, institutional tests. 40 credit hours maximum toward bachelor's degree. Combined total of 40 semester hours of credit from nontraditional sources accepted toward a bachelor's degree, including a maximum of 30 semester hours of credit through CLEP. **Support services:** Learning center, pre-admission summer program, reduced course load, remedial instruction, study skills assistance, tutoring, writing center.

Majors. **Biology:** General. **Business:** Accounting, business admin, finance, management science, marketing. **Communications:** General. **Computer sciences:** Computer science, information systems. **Education:** Elementary, multi-level teacher, music, physical, special ed. **English:** English lit. **Foreign languages:** Sign language interpretation. **Health services:** Clinical lab science, nursing (RN). **History:** General. **Liberal arts:** Arts/sciences, humanities. **Math:** General. **Parks/recreation:** Health/fitness, sports admin. **Physical sciences:** Chemistry. **Protective services:** Criminal justice. **Psychology:** General. **Social sciences:** Political science. **Visual/performing arts:** Graphic design, music.

Most popular majors. Biology 7%, business/marketing 25%, communications/journalism 6%, education 12%, health sciences 11%, liberal arts 11%.

Computing on campus. 107 workstations in dormitories, library, computer center. Dormitories wired for high-speed internet access and linked to campus network. Commuter students can connect to campus network. Online library, helpline, wireless network available.

Student life. **Freshman orientation:** Mandatory, $135 fee. Preregistration for classes offered. Held 4 days prior to the beginning of fall semester and first day of spring semester for first-time/transfer students. **Policies:** All full-time regular undergraduate students who enter for the first time required to live on campus until they have attained senior standing unless living locally with immediate family who are permanent residents, or given permission from the Vice President for Student Affairs to live off campus. **Housing:** Guaranteed on-campus for all undergraduates. Coed dorms, single-sex dorms, special housing for disabled, apartments, fraternity/sorority housing available. Honors housing and on campus houses available. **Activities:** Bands, campus ministries, choral groups, dance, drama, film society, literary magazine, music ensembles, musical theater, radio station, student government, student newspaper, symphony orchestra, Circle K International, environmental club, minority student association, Peers 2 Peers, student senate, student programming board, Haiti Connection, Men of God Living with Integrity, Voices of Praise.

Athletics. NAIA, NCAA. **Intercollegiate:** Baseball M, basketball, cross-country, football (tackle) M, golf, soccer, softball W, tennis, volleyball. **Intramural:** Basketball, bowling, football (non-tackle), racquetball, soccer, softball, table tennis, volleyball. **Team name:** Hawks.

Student services. Alcohol/substance abuse counseling, chaplain/spiritual director, career counseling, student employment services, financial aid counseling, health services, minority student services, personal counseling, placement for graduates, women's services. **Physically disabled:** Services for visually, hearing impaired.

Contact. E-mail: admissions@quincy.edu
Phone: (217) 228-5210 Toll-free number: (800) 688-4295
Fax: (217) 228-5479
Syndi Peck, Director of Admissions, Quincy University, 1800 College Avenue, Quincy, IL 62301-2699

Rasmussen College: Mokena/Tinley Park
Mokena, Illinois
www.rasmussen.edu

- For-profit 4-year teachers and technical college
- Small town

General. Regionally accredited. **Calendar:** Quarter.

Basis for selection. Admission requirements vary by program.

Academics. Credit/placement by examination: AP, CLEP.

Contact. Rasmussen College: Mokena/Tinley Park, 8650 West Spring Lake Road, Mokena, IL 60448

Resurrection University
Oak Park, Illinois
www.wscn.edu   **CB code: 1927**

- Private two-year upper-division nursing college affiliated with Roman Catholic Church
- Commuter campus in very large city
- Test scores, application essay required

General. Founded in 1982. Regionally accredited. Facilities located in West Suburban Medical Center. **Degrees:** 172 bachelor's awarded; master's offered. **Location:** 10 miles from downtown Chicago. **Calendar:** Semester, limited summer session. **Full-time faculty:** 25 total. **Part-time faculty:** 11 total. **Class size:** 20% < 20, 23% 20-39, 26% 40-49, 31% 50-99. **Special facilities:** In-hospital location, health sciences library, nursing clinical skills laboratory.

Student profile. 395 degree-seeking undergraduates.

Basis for selection. College transcript, application essay, standardized test scores required. Natural and behavioral science grades more heavily weighted. Recommendation and essay required. Must have 2.75 science GPA. Satisfactory score on TEAS required. Transfer accepted as juniors.

2011-2012 Annual costs. Tuition/fees: $22,616. Books/supplies: $1,400. Personal expenses: $2,116.

Financial aid. **Non-need-based:** Scholarships awarded for academics, alumni affiliation.

Application procedures. **Admission:** $30 fee. Application must be submitted online. **Financial aid:** Priority date 4/1, no deadline. Applicants notified on a rolling basis starting 4/1; must reply within 3 weeks of notification. FAFSA required.

Academics. **Special study options:** Accelerated study, independent study. Evening and weekend BS completion program for registered nurses. **Credit/placement by examination:** AP, CLEP.

Majors. **Health services:** Nursing (RN).

Computing on campus. 10 workstations in library, computer center. Online library, wireless network available.

Student life. **Activities:** Student government.

Student services. Career counseling, student employment services, health services, personal counseling.

Contact. E-mail: admissions@wscn.edu
Phone: (708) 763-6530 Fax: (708) 763-1531
Scott Dunnell, Executive Director of Marketing & Admissions, Resurrection University, Three Erie Court, Oak Park, IL 60302

Robert Morris University: Chicago

Chicago, Illinois   **CB member**
www.robertmorris.edu   **CB code: 1670**

- Private 4-year university
- Commuter campus in very large city
- 3,630 degree-seeking undergraduates: 4% part-time, 55% women, 32% African American, 2% Asian American, 23% Hispanic American, 1% international
- 512 degree-seeking graduate students
- 33% of applicants admitted
- 78% graduate within 6 years

General. Founded in 1913. Regionally accredited. Branch campuses in Arlington Heights, Bensenville, DuPage, Elgin, Lake County, Orland Park, Peoria, Schaumburg, and Springfield. **Degrees:** 783 bachelor's, 886 associate awarded; master's offered. **ROTC:** Army. **Location:** Downtown. **Calendar:** Five 10-week sessions. Extensive summer session. **Full-time faculty:** 121 total; 27% have terminal degrees, 24% minority, 51% women. **Part-time faculty:** 154 total; 11% have terminal degrees, 22% minority, 49% women. **Class size:** 55% < 20, 42% 20-39, 2% 40-49, less than 1% 50-99.

Freshman class profile. 3,132 applied, 1,037 admitted, 902 enrolled.

Mid 50% test scores		Rank in top quarter:	18%
ACT composite:	16-22	Rank in top tenth:	5%
GPA 3.75 or higher:	5%	End year in good standing:	62%
GPA 3.50-3.74:	4%	Return as sophomores:	49%
GPA 3.0-3.49:	19%	Out-of-state:	13%
GPA 2.0-2.99:	60%	Live on campus:	19%

Basis for selection. Must submit high school transcript or GED for review. Secondary school record, class rank, GPA, and interview most important. Extra curricular activities and level of interest considered. Meeting with admissions counselor and campus visit strongly recommended. **Home schooled:** Transcript of courses and grades, state high school equivalency certificate required. Curriculum documentation, state certification, and standardized exam with acceptable achievement level required.

High school preparation. Recommended units include English 4, mathematics 3, social studies 2, history 3, science 2 (laboratory 1) and foreign language 2.

2011-2012 Annual costs. Tuition/fees: $21,600. Additional fees may apply, depending on program. Room/board: $10,326. Books/supplies: $1,500. Personal expenses: $2,334.

2010-2011 Financial aid. **Need-based:** 1,375 full-time freshmen applied for aid; 1,345 were judged to have need; 1,316 of these received aid. Average need met was 50%. Average scholarship/grant was $8,787; average loan $4,488. 45% of total undergraduate aid awarded as scholarships/grants, 55% as loans/jobs. **Non-need-based:** Awarded to 3,058 full-time undergraduates, including 622 freshmen. Scholarships awarded for academics, art, athletics, state residency.

Application procedures. **Admission:** No deadline. $20 fee, may be waived for applicants with need. Admission notification on a rolling basis. **Financial aid:** No deadline. FAFSA required. Applicants notified on a rolling basis.

Academics. **Special study options:** Accelerated study, combined bachelor's/graduate degree, double major, dual enrollment of high school students, honors, internships, study abroad. Master's Advantage and dual degree. **Credit/placement by examination:** AP, CLEP, institutional tests. 44 credit hours maximum toward associate degree, 44 toward bachelor's. **Support services:** Learning center, reduced course load, study skills assistance, tutoring, writing center.

Majors. **Business:** Business admin. **Computer sciences:** Information technology. **Visual/performing arts:** Graphic design.

Most popular majors. Business/marketing 73%, computer/information sciences 7%, interdisciplinary studies 12%, visual/performing arts 8%.

Computing on campus. 1,671 workstations in library, computer center, student center. Online library, helpline, repair service, student web hosting, wireless network available.

Student life. **Freshman orientation:** Mandatory. Preregistration for classes offered. Held 1-4 weeks prior to commencement of classes. Students required to attend one 2 1/2-hour session. **Policies:** Students required to abide by student code of conduct and housing policies. **Housing:** Coed dorms, apartments available. $300 fully refundable deposit, deadline 5/1. **Activities:** Bands, choral groups, dance, international student organizations, literary magazine, student newspaper, Students in Free Enterprise, volunteer club, Cooks for a Cause, mock trial club, Morris Men, Society of Human Resource Management, Techxperts.

Athletics. NAIA, USCAA. **Intercollegiate:** Baseball M, basketball, bowling, cross-country, diving W, equestrian W, football (tackle) M, golf, ice hockey, lacrosse, rowing (crew) W, soccer, softball W, swimming W, tennis W, track and field W, volleyball. **Intramural:** Bowling, cross-country, golf, softball. **Team name:** Eagles.

Student services. Adult student services, alcohol/substance abuse counseling, career counseling, services for economically disadvantaged, student employment services, financial aid counseling, personal counseling, placement for graduates. **Physically disabled:** Services for visually, speech, hearing impaired.

Contact. E-mail: ais@robertmorris.edu
Phone: (312) 935-4400 Toll-free number: (800) 762-5960
Fax: (312) 935-4440
Nicole Farinella, Senior Vice President for Enrollment Management,
Robert Morris University: Chicago, 401South State Street, Chicago, IL 60605

Rockford College

Rockford, Illinois   **CB member**
www.rockford.edu   **CB code: 1665**

- Private 4-year liberal arts college
- Residential campus in small city
- 985 degree-seeking undergraduates: 14% part-time, 62% women, 8% African American, 2% Asian American, 9% Hispanic American, 1% Native American
- 321 graduate students
- 44% of applicants admitted
- SAT or ACT (ACT writing optional) required
- 40% graduate within 6 years

General. Founded in 1847. Regionally accredited. **Degrees:** 207 bachelor's awarded; master's offered. **Location:** 90 miles from Chicago. **Calendar:** Semester, limited summer session. **Full-time faculty:** 71 total. **Part-time faculty:** 76 total. **Class size:** 80% < 20, 20% 20-39, less than 1% 50-99. **Special facilities:** Theater, nursing lab, center for civic engagement, center for ethics and entrepreneurship.

Freshman class profile. 1,245 applied, 550 admitted, 127 enrolled.

Mid 50% test scores		GPA 3.0-3.49:	32%
SAT critical reading:	410-530	GPA 2.0-2.99:	37%
SAT math:	450-540	Rank in top quarter:	39%
SAT writing:	430-520	Rank in top tenth:	17%
ACT composite:	18-23	Return as sophomores:	69%
GPA 3.75 or higher:	18%	Out-of-state:	37%
GPA 3.50-3.74:	13%	Live on campus:	69%

Basis for selection. School achievement record and test scores are most important. Recommendations and activities also are considered. Auditions required of theater arts and musical theater performance majors. Personal statements required of students who fall below standard admission criteria.

High school preparation. College-preparatory program recommended. 15 units recommended. Recommended units include English 4, mathematics 3, social studies 3, science 3 (laboratory 3) and academic electives 2.

2011-2012 Annual costs. Tuition/fees: $25,470. Room/board: $7,140. Books/supplies: $1,200. Personal expenses: $2,250.

2010-2011 Financial aid. **Need-based:** 145 full-time freshmen applied for aid; 135 were judged to have need; 134 of these received aid. Average need met was 71%. Average scholarship/grant was $14,709; average loan $3,345. 58% of total undergraduate aid awarded as scholarships/grants, 42% as loans/jobs. **Non-need-based:** Awarded to 153 full-time undergraduates, including 30 freshmen. Scholarships awarded for academics, alumni affiliation, leadership, minority status, music/drama, state residency.

Application procedures. **Admission:** No deadline. No application fee. Admission notification on a rolling basis beginning on or about 9/15. **Financial aid:** Priority date 3/1; no closing date. FAFSA required. Applicants notified on a rolling basis starting 3/1; must reply within 4 week(s) of notification.

Academics. Community-based learning opportunities available. **Special study options:** Accelerated study, distance learning, double major, dual

enrollment of high school students, ESL, exchange student, honors, independent study, internships, semester at sea, study abroad, teacher certification program, United Nations semester, Washington semester. Tutorial classes, special studies courses. **Credit/placement by examination:** AP, CLEP, SAT, ACT, institutional tests. **Support services:** Learning center, reduced course load, remedial instruction, study skills assistance, tutoring, writing center.

Majors. Biology: General, biochemistry. **Business:** Accounting, business admin. **Computer sciences:** General. **Education:** General, early childhood, elementary, physical, special ed. **English:** English lit. **Foreign languages:** Classics, French, Latin, Romance, Spanish. **Health services:** Nursing (RN). **History:** General. **Liberal arts:** Humanities. **Math:** General. **Philosophy/religion:** Philosophy. **Physical sciences:** Chemistry. **Psychology:** General. **Social sciences:** General, economics, international relations, political science. **Visual/performing arts:** Art, art history/conservation, dramatic, music, music history, musical theater.

Most popular majors. Biology 6%, business/marketing 28%, education 27%, health sciences 8%, psychology 9%, social sciences 6%, visual/performing arts 7%.

Computing on campus. 125 workstations in dormitories, library, computer center. Dormitories wired for high-speed internet access and linked to campus network. Commuter students can connect to campus network. Helpline, repair service, wireless network available.

Student life. Freshman orientation: Mandatory. Preregistration for classes offered. Four-day program held the week prior to beginning of fall classes, includes introduction to college resources. **Policies:** Alcohol and guest policies, Academic Honor Code in place. **Housing:** Guaranteed on-campus for all undergraduates. Coed dorms, special housing for disabled, wellness housing available. Special housing available for first-year students. **Activities:** Pep band, campus ministries, choral groups, dance, drama, international student organizations, literary magazine, music ensembles, musical theater, radio station, student government, student newspaper, multicultural club, ELITE Leadership Program.

Athletics. NCAA. Intercollegiate: Baseball M, basketball, cross-country, football (tackle) M, golf M, soccer, softball W, tennis, track and field, volleyball W. **Team name:** Regents.

Student services. Alcohol/substance abuse counseling, chaplain/spiritual director, career counseling, student employment services, financial aid counseling, health services, personal counseling. **Physically disabled:** Services for visually, hearing impaired.

Contact. E-mail: rcadmissions@rockford.edu
Phone: (815) 226-4050 Toll-free number: (800) 892-2984
Fax: (815) 226-2822
Jennifer Nordstrom, Associate Vice President for Undergraduate Admission and Strategic Marketing, Rockford College, 5050 East State Street, Rockford, IL 61108-2311

Roosevelt University
Chicago, Illinois
www.roosevelt.edu

CB member
CB code: 1666

- Private 4-year university
- Commuter campus in very large city
- 3,838 degree-seeking undergraduates: 28% part-time, 65% women, 15% Asian American, 22% Hispanic American, 2% international
- 2,695 degree-seeking graduate students
- 75% of applicants admitted
- SAT or ACT (ACT writing optional) required
- 49% graduate within 6 years

General. Founded in 1945. Regionally accredited. Additional campus in Schaumburg. **Degrees:** 950 bachelor's awarded; master's, professional, doctoral offered. **Location:** Downtown. **Calendar:** Semester, extensive summer session. **Full-time faculty:** 243 total; 22% minority, 43% women. **Part-time faculty:** 479 total; 13% minority, 43% women. **Class size:** 60% < 20, 36% 20-39, 3% 40-49, less than 1% 50-99, less than 1% >100.

Freshman class profile. 3,773 applied, 2,833 admitted, 448 enrolled.

Mid 50% test scores			
SAT critical reading:	510-600	Rank in top quarter:	10%
SAT math:	450-600	Rank in top tenth:	2%
SAT writing:	490-600	Return as sophomores:	65%
ACT composite:	20-25	Out-of-state:	21%
GPA 3.75 or higher:	15%	Live on campus:	71%
GPA 3.50-3.74:	14%	International:	3%
GPA 3.0-3.49:	31%	Fraternities:	1%
GPA 2.0-2.99:	38%	Sororities:	5%

Basis for selection. Recent secondary school performance most crucial. Personal statement and recommended interview can be used to communicate special circumstances. Placement evaluation required for all admitted, degree-seeking undergraduate students. Test results must be submitted by first year or transfer applicants with scores less than 2 years old. Interview recommended for early admission and borderline applicants. Audition required of music and theater majors. Portfolio recommended for art and theater majors. **Home schooled:** Statement describing home school structure and mission, letter of recommendation (nonparent) required.

High school preparation. College-preparatory program recommended. 11 units required; 24 recommended. Required and recommended units include English 4, mathematics 3-4, social studies 2-3, history 1-3, science 2-3 (laboratory 2-3), foreign language 2 and computer science 2. Extensive work in English, history, mathematics, foreign language, and science recommended.

2012-2013 Annual costs. Tuition/fees (projected): $25,950. Tuition for College of Performing Arts is $32,950 per year. Room/board: $12,100. Books/supplies: $1,200. Personal expenses: $4,400.

2010-2011 Financial aid. Need-based: 468 full-time freshmen applied for aid; 413 were judged to have need; 410 of these received aid. Average need met was 75%. Average scholarship/grant was $11,743; average loan $6,716. 40% of total undergraduate aid awarded as scholarships/grants, 60% as loans/jobs. **Non-need-based:** Awarded to 2,573 full-time undergraduates, including 470 freshmen. Scholarships awarded for academics, alumni affiliation, leadership, minority status, music/drama, state residency.

Application procedures. Admission: Priority date 8/15; no deadline. $25 fee, may be waived for applicants with need. Admission notification on a rolling basis beginning on or about 10/15. Admission deposit requested within two weeks of admission decision. Housing deposit fully refundable before 6/1. **Financial aid:** Priority date 4/1; no closing date. FAFSA, institutional form required. Applicants notified on a rolling basis starting 2/1; must reply within 3 week(s) of notification.

Academics. Special study options: Accelerated study, combined bachelor's/graduate degree, distance learning, double major, dual enrollment of high school students, ESL, exchange student, honors, independent study, internships, student-designed major, study abroad, teacher certification program. **Credit/placement by examination:** AP, CLEP, SAT, ACT, institutional tests. 30 credit hours maximum toward bachelor's degree. **Support services:** Learning center, pre-admission summer program, reduced course load, remedial instruction, study skills assistance, tutoring, writing center.

Majors. Area/ethnic studies: African-American, women's. **Biology:** General, biotechnology. **Business:** General, accounting, actuarial science, communications, finance, financial planning, hospitality admin, human resources, insurance, management science, marketing, office management, organizational behavior. **Communications:** Communications/speech/rhetoric, journalism, organizational. **Computer sciences:** Computer science, networking. **Education:** Early childhood, elementary, music, secondary, special ed. **English:** English lit. **Foreign languages:** General, comparative lit, Spanish. **Health services:** Clinical lab science, medical radiologic technology/radiation therapy, nuclear medical technology. **History:** General. **Liberal arts:** Arts/sciences. **Math:** General. **Philosophy/religion:** Philosophy. **Physical sciences:** Chemistry. **Protective services:** Criminal justice. **Psychology:** General. **Social sciences:** Economics, international relations, political science, sociology. **Visual/performing arts:** Acting, art history/conservation, dramatic, jazz, music, music performance, music theory/composition, musical theater, piano/keyboard, stringed instruments, voice/opera.

Most popular majors. Business/marketing 38%, education 7%, psychology 14%, social sciences 8%, visual/performing arts 8%.

Computing on campus. 250 workstations in dormitories, library, computer center, student center. Dormitories wired for high-speed internet access and linked to campus network. Commuter students can connect to campus network. Online course registration, online library, helpline, repair service available.

Student life. Freshman orientation: Mandatory, $35 fee. Preregistration for classes offered. Ongoing from mid-Spring through the summer; 1-2 days in duration, with coverage of academic and non-academic elements of student life. **Housing:** Guaranteed on-campus for all undergraduates. Coed dorms, apartments available. $500 fully refundable deposit, deadline 8/1. High-rise residence hall in cooperation with University Center of Chicago available. **Activities:** Dance, international student organizations, radio station, student government, student newspaper, Christian Bible groups, theater club, black student union, Hispanic organization, residence hall council, Asociacion de Latinos Unidos.

Athletics. Intercollegiate: Baseball M, basketball, cross-country, golf M, soccer, softball W, tennis, volleyball W. **Intramural:** Badminton, baseball M, basketball, table tennis. **Team name:** Lakers.

Student services. Adult student services, alcohol/substance abuse counseling, career counseling, student employment services, financial aid counseling, personal counseling, placement for graduates, veterans' counselor. **Physically disabled:** Services for visually, hearing impaired.

Contact. E-mail: applyru@roosevelt.edu
Phone: (312) 341-2101 Toll-free number: (877) 277-5978
Fax: (847) 619-8636
Asia Mitchell, Senior Director, Admissions, Roosevelt University, 430 South Michigan Avenue, Chicago, IL 60605-1394

Rush University
Chicago, Illinois
www.rushu.rush.edu   CB code: 3262

▶ Private two-year upper-division health science college
▶ Commuter campus in very large city

General. Founded in 1971. Regionally accredited. **Location:** 2 miles from downtown. **Calendar:** Quarter.

Annual costs/financial aid. Tuition/fees (2011-2012): $25,335. Tuition costs vary by program. Room charge based on 9 months occupancy of one-bedroom apartment. Room: $9,360. Need-based financial aid available to full-time and part-time students.

Contact. Phone: (312) 942-7100
Director of College Admission Services, College Admissions, Chicago, IL 60612

Saint Anthony College of Nursing
Rockford, Illinois
www.sacn.edu   CB code: 3923

▶ Private two-year upper-division nursing college affiliated with Roman Catholic Church
▶ Commuter campus in small city
▶ Application essay, interview required

General. Regionally accredited. MSN in Nurse Educator, Clinical Nurse Specialist (Adult Health) and Clinical Nurse Leader offered. **Degrees:** 55 bachelor's awarded; master's offered. **Articulation:** Agreements with Rock Valley College, McHenry County College, Sauk Valley Community College, Kishwaukee College, Elgin Community College, Blackhawk Technical College, Highland Community College. **Location:** 90 miles from of Chicago. **Calendar:** Semester, limited summer session. **Full-time faculty:** 18 total. **Part-time faculty:** 6 total. **Class size:** 12% < 20, 62% 20-39, 25% 40-49. **Special facilities:** Nursing labs, hospital facility.

Student profile. 183 degree-seeking undergraduates. 100% entered as juniors. 88% transferred from two-year, 12% transferred from four-year institutions.

Out-of-state:	6%	25 or older:	53%

Basis for selection. College transcript, application essay, interview required. 64 credits required in specific pre-nursing and general education courses. Transfer accepted as juniors.

2011-2012 Annual costs. Tuition/fees: $19,420. Required fees may vary by program. Books/supplies: $2,200. Personal expenses: $1,785.

Financial aid. Non-need-based: Scholarships awarded for academics, leadership, state residency.

Application procedures. Admission: Deadline 9/15. $50 fee. Admission notification 10/31. Must reply by 11/30. **Financial aid:** No deadline. Applicants notified on a rolling basis starting 8/18. FAFSA required.

Academics. Credit/placement by examination: AP, CLEP.

Majors. Health services: Adult health nursing.

Computing on campus. 37 workstations in library, computer center. Commuter students can connect to campus network. Online library, wireless network available.

Student life. Activities: Student government.

Student services. Alcohol/substance abuse counseling, chaplain/spiritual director, career counseling, financial aid counseling, health services, legal services, personal counseling, women's services.

Contact. E-mail: admissions@sacn.edu
Phone: (815) 227-2141 Fax: (815) 227-2730
Cheryl Delgado, Supervisor of Enrollment Management, Saint Anthony College of Nursing, 5658 East State Street, Rockford, IL 61108-2468

Saint Xavier University
Chicago, Illinois   CB member
www.sxu.edu   CB code: 1708

▶ Private 4-year university affiliated with Roman Catholic Church
▶ Commuter campus in very large city
▶ 2,963 degree-seeking undergraduates: 15% part-time, 69% women, 17% African American, 2% Asian American, 17% Hispanic American
▶ 1,696 degree-seeking graduate students
▶ SAT or ACT (ACT writing optional), application essay required
▶ 52% graduate within 6 years; 17% enter graduate study

General. Founded in 1847. Regionally accredited. Affiliated with Sisters of Mercy. **Degrees:** 724 bachelor's awarded; master's offered. **ROTC:** Air Force. **Location:** 20 miles from downtown. **Calendar:** Semester, limited summer session. **Full-time faculty:** 173 total; 87% have terminal degrees, 14% minority, 56% women. **Part-time faculty:** 258 total; 23% have terminal degrees, 12% minority, 65% women. **Class size:** 40% < 20, 56% 20-39, 2% 40-49, 1% 50-99. **Special facilities:** Music performance studio, reading clinic, speech clinic, learning disabilities clinic, mathematics laboratory.

Freshman class profile. 5,520 applied, 4,579 admitted, 583 enrolled.

Mid 50% test scores			
SAT critical reading:	440-590	GPA 3.0-3.49:	32%
SAT math:	480-610	GPA 2.0-2.99:	24%
SAT writing:	480-550	Rank in top quarter:	50%
ACT composite:	20-25	Rank in top tenth:	22%
GPA 3.75 or higher:	30%	Return as sophomores:	72%
GPA 3.50-3.74:	14%	Out-of-state:	7%
		Live on campus:	46%

Basis for selection. Open admission, but selective for some programs. GPA, test scores most important. Counselor recommendation, class rank considered. Interview recommended for borderline applicants. Audition required of music majors.

High school preparation. College-preparatory program recommended. 16 units recommended. Recommended units include English 4, mathematics 3, foreign language 2 and academic electives 3. 4 units of science and social studies combined.

2011-2012 Annual costs. Tuition/fees: $27,060. Room/board: $9,040. Books/supplies: $1,200. Personal expenses: $1,070.

2011-2012 Financial aid. Need-based: 566 full-time freshmen applied for aid; 539 were judged to have need; 539 of these received aid. Average need met was 84%. Average scholarship/grant was $18,515; average loan $3,544. 59% of total undergraduate aid awarded as scholarships/grants, 41% as loans/jobs. **Non-need-based:** Awarded to 518 full-time undergraduates, including 133 freshmen. Scholarships awarded for academics, athletics, music/drama.

Application procedures. Admission: No deadline. $25 fee, may be waived for applicants with need, free for online applicants. Admission notification on a rolling basis. Must reply by May 1 or within 4 week(s) if notified thereafter. **Financial aid:** Priority date 3/1; no closing date. FAFSA required. Applicants notified on a rolling basis starting 2/1; must reply by 5/1 or within 2 week(s) of notification.

Academics. Special study options: Accelerated study, cooperative education, distance learning, double major, dual enrollment of high school students, ESL, external degree, honors, independent study, internships, liberal arts/career combination, semester at sea, student-designed major, study abroad, teacher certification program. **Credit/placement by examination:** AP, CLEP, institutional tests. 27 credit hours maximum toward bachelor's degree. **Support services:** Learning center, pre-admission summer program, reduced course load, remedial instruction, study skills assistance, tutoring, writing center.

Majors. Biology: General. **Business:** General, accounting, international. **Communications:** Communications/speech/rhetoric, organizational. **Computer sciences:** General, computer science. **Education:** General, art, biology, history, mathematics, music, secondary, social science, Spanish. **English:** English lit. **Foreign languages:** Spanish. **Health services:** Nursing (RN),

premedicine, prepharmacy, speech pathology. **History:** General. **Liberal arts:** Arts/sciences. **Math:** General. **Philosophy/religion:** Philosophy, religion. **Physical sciences:** Chemistry. **Protective services:** Criminal justice. **Psychology:** General, industrial. **Social sciences:** General, international relations, political science, sociology. **Theology:** Pastoral counseling. **Visual/performing arts:** Music, studio arts, voice/opera.

Most popular majors. Business/marketing 25%, education 38%, health sciences 15%, security/protective services 6%.

Computing on campus. 700 workstations in dormitories, library, computer center, student center. Dormitories wired for high-speed internet access and linked to campus network. Commuter students can connect to campus network. Online course registration, online library, helpline, student web hosting, wireless network available.

Student life. Freshman orientation: Mandatory, $125 fee. Preregistration for classes offered. Two-day overnight orientation held in summer. **Housing:** Guaranteed on-campus for freshmen. Coed dorms, special housing for disabled, apartments available. $100 nonrefundable deposit, deadline 5/1. **Activities:** Bands, campus ministries, choral groups, film society, international student organizations, literary magazine, music ensembles, radio station, student government, student newspaper, symphony orchestra, Black student organization, Hispanic student organization, student activities board, student nurses association, Muslim student association, Celtic Connection, Fellowship of Christian Athletes, Xi Delta.

Athletics. NAIA. **Intercollegiate:** Baseball M, basketball, cross-country, football (tackle) M, soccer, softball W, volleyball W. **Intramural:** Basketball M, bowling, volleyball. **Team name:** Cougars.

Student services. Adult student services, alcohol/substance abuse counseling, chaplain/spiritual director, career counseling, services for economically disadvantaged, student employment services, financial aid counseling, health services, on-campus daycare, personal counseling, placement for graduates, veterans' counselor. **Physically disabled:** Services for speech impaired.

Contact. E-mail: admissions@sxu.edu
Phone: (773) 298-3050 Toll-free number: (800) 462-9288
Fax: (773) 298-3076
Brian Hotzfield, Director of Admission, Saint Xavier University, 3700 West 103rd Street, Chicago, IL 60655

School of the Art Institute of Chicago
Chicago, Illinois — CB member
www.saic.edu — CB code: 1713

- Private 4-year visual arts college
- Commuter campus in very large city
- 2,487 degree-seeking undergraduates: 6% part-time, 68% women, 4% African American, 12% Asian American, 6% Hispanic American, 1% Native American, 19% international
- 734 degree-seeking graduate students
- 77% of applicants admitted
- SAT or ACT (ACT writing optional), application essay required
- 61% graduate within 6 years

General. Founded in 1866. Regionally accredited. **Degrees:** 456 bachelor's awarded; master's offered. **Location:** Downtown Chicago. **Calendar:** Semester, extensive summer session. **Full-time faculty:** 106 total. **Part-time faculty:** 439 total. **Class size:** 82% < 20, 15% 20-39, 1% 40-49, less than 1% 50-99, less than 1% >100. **Special facilities:** Art collection, film center, video data bank, poetry center, art galleries, fashion resource center, artists' book collection, Roger Brown house museum and study collection.

Freshman class profile. 2,694 applied, 2,063 admitted, 455 enrolled.

Mid 50% test scores		Return as sophomores:	76%
SAT critical reading:	510-620	Out-of-state:	80%
SAT writing:	510-630	Live on campus:	89%
ACT composite:	22-27	International:	25%

Basis for selection. Portfolio very important, statement of purpose, 500 SAT Critical Reading or 20 ACT English, academic credentials, and recommendations also considered. Interview recommended. Portfolio required.

High school preparation. Advanced-level study of art recommended.

2011-2012 Annual costs. Tuition/fees: $37,560. Students required to have a notebook computer. If they don't own one already, it may be purchased from school. No charge for required software. Room only: $10,100. Books/supplies: $2,740. Personal expenses: $2,730.

2011-2012 Financial aid. Need-based: 279 full-time freshmen applied for aid; 231 were judged to have need; 231 of these received aid. Average need met was 76%. Average scholarship/grant was $15,778; average loan $3,391. 61% of total undergraduate aid awarded as scholarships/grants, 39% as loans/jobs. **Non-need-based:** Awarded to 932 full-time undergraduates, including 234 freshmen. Scholarships awarded for academics, art.

Application procedures. Admission: Priority date 2/15; deadline 6/1 (receipt date). $65 fee, may be waived for applicants with need. Application must be submitted online. Admission notification on a rolling basis beginning on or about 10/1. **Financial aid:** Priority date 3/15; no closing date. FAFSA required. Applicants notified on a rolling basis starting 3/1.

Academics. Interdisciplinary curriculum allows students to personalize education or concentrate on single discipline. **Special study options:** Cooperative education, cross-registration, double major, ESL, exchange student, independent study, internships, New York semester, student-designed major, study abroad, teacher certification program. Interdisciplinary curriculum with 6 credit off-campus study requirement,"credit/no-credit" grading system. **Credit/placement by examination:** AP, CLEP, IB. 18 credit hours maximum toward bachelor's degree. DANTES scores accepted. **Support services:** Learning center, pre-admission summer program, reduced course load, remedial instruction, study skills assistance, tutoring.

Majors. Architecture: Interior. **Communications:** Digital media. **Communications technology:** Animation/special effects, desktop publishing, graphics, photo/film/video, recording arts. **Education:** Art. **English:** Creative writing. **Visual/performing arts:** General, art, art history/conservation, ceramics, cinematography, design, digital arts, drawing, fashion design, fiber arts, graphic design, industrial design, interior design, multimedia, painting, photography, printmaking, sculpture, studio arts.

Computing on campus. PC or laptop required. 350 workstations in dormitories, library, computer center. Dormitories wired for high-speed internet access and linked to campus network. Commuter students can connect to campus network. Online library, helpline, repair service, student web hosting, wireless network available.

Student life. Freshman orientation: Mandatory, $100 fee. Preregistration for classes offered. 4 days prior to beginning of class. First day open to parents, family and friends. **Housing:** Coed dorms, special housing for disabled, wellness housing available. $550 nonrefundable deposit. **Activities:** Campus ministries, dance, drama, film society, international student organizations, literary magazine, radio station, student government, student newspaper, TV station, Black at SAIC, Hillel, InterVarsity, Korean Student Association, Latin American Student Organization, Oxfam, Taiwanese Student Organization.

Student services. Alcohol/substance abuse counseling, career counseling, student employment services, financial aid counseling, health services, minority student services, personal counseling, veterans' counselor. **Physically disabled:** Services for visually, speech, hearing impaired.

Contact. E-mail: admiss@saic.edu
Phone: (312) 629-6100 Toll-free number: (800) 232-7242
Fax: (312) 629-6101
Scott Ramon, Director, Undergraduate Admissions, School of the Art Institute of Chicago, 36 South Wabash Avenue, Chicago, IL 60603

Shimer College
Chicago, Illinois
www.shimer.edu — CB code: 1717

- Private 4-year liberal arts college
- Residential campus in very large city
- 125 degree-seeking undergraduates: 16% part-time, 47% women, 2% African American, 4% Asian American, 4% Hispanic American
- 48% of applicants admitted
- Application essay, interview required
- 63% graduate within 6 years

General. Founded in 1853. Regionally accredited. Located on campus of Illinois Institute of Technology. **Degrees:** 16 bachelor's awarded. **ROTC:** Army, Naval, Air Force. **Location:** 3 miles from downtown. **Calendar:** Semester, limited summer session. **Full-time faculty:** 10 total; 100% have terminal degrees, 20% minority, 30% women. **Part-time faculty:** 6 total; 67% have terminal degrees, 33% women. **Class size:** 100% < 20.

Freshman class profile. 119 applied, 57 admitted, 20 enrolled.

Mid 50% test scores			
SAT critical reading:	630-720	GPA 3.50-3.74:	6%
SAT math:	390-560	GPA 3.0-3.49:	18%
SAT writing:	580-680	GPA 2.0-2.99:	41%
ACT composite:	28-31	Return as sophomores:	85%
GPA 3.75 or higher:	29%	Out-of-state:	65%
		Live on campus:	90%

Basis for selection. Essays and interviews most important. Test scores, GPA, recommendations, motivation, maturity considered. Demonstrated writing skills and interest in and enthusiasm about Great Books curriculum and discussion method important. Early entrants and other applicants who do not have high school diplomas may be required to submit GED; applicants without high school diplomas who are too young to take GED may be required to complete additional approved testing in order to comply with financial aid regulations.

High school preparation. College-preparatory program recommended. 15 units recommended. Recommended units include English 4, mathematics 3, history 2, science 3, foreign language 2 and visual/performing arts 1.

2011-2012 Annual costs. Tuition/fees: $30,400. Room/board: $11,448. Books/supplies: $1,400. Personal expenses: $1,020.

2010-2011 Financial aid. **Need-based:** 18 full-time freshmen applied for aid; 13 were judged to have need; 13 of these received aid. Average need met was 63%. Average scholarship/grant was $14,070; average loan $3,500. 55% of total undergraduate aid awarded as scholarships/grants, 45% as loans/jobs. **Non-need-based:** Awarded to 29 full-time undergraduates, including 21 freshmen. Scholarships awarded for academics, alumni affiliation.

Application procedures. Admission: No deadline. $25 fee, may be waived for applicants with need. Admission notification on a rolling basis beginning on or about 9/15. Must reply by May 1 or within 2 week(s) if notified thereafter. **Financial aid:** No deadline. FAFSA, institutional form required. Applicants notified on a rolling basis starting 4/1.

Academics. Curriculum is based on The Great Books of Western Culture. **Special study options:** Combined bachelor's/graduate degree, cross-registration, double major, independent study, internships, study abroad, weekend college. 3+2 law school program. **Credit/placement by examination:** AP, CLEP, institutional tests. Shimer Institutional placement examinations may result in credit; no outside testing is accepted. **Support services:** Reduced course load, study skills assistance, tutoring, writing center.

Majors. **Liberal arts:** Arts/sciences, humanities. **Social sciences:** General.

Most popular majors. Liberal arts 88%, social sciences 13%.

Computing on campus. 25 workstations in dormitories, library, computer center, student center. Dormitories wired for high-speed internet access and linked to campus network. Commuter students can connect to campus network. Helpline, wireless network available.

Student life. **Freshman orientation:** Mandatory, $100 fee. Preregistration for classes offered. Held 3-4 days prior to start of classes. Includes demonstration class, placement exams, orientation to residence hall and Chicago. **Housing:** Guaranteed on-campus for freshmen. Coed dorms, special housing for disabled, apartments, wellness housing available. $300 fully refundable deposit, deadline 5/1. **Activities:** Bands, campus ministries, choral groups, dance, drama, international student organizations, literary magazine, music ensembles, radio station, student government, student newspaper, American Red Cross, Catholic campus ministry, gays/lesbians/allies and more, Hillel, Hindu student council, gospel choir, Muslim students association, chess club.

Athletics. **Intramural:** Basketball, football (non-tackle), soccer, softball, track and field, volleyball. **Team name:** Flaming Smelts.

Student services. Adult student services, alcohol/substance abuse counseling, career counseling, student employment services, financial aid counseling, health services, personal counseling, placement for graduates.

Contact. E-mail: admission@shimer.edu
Phone: (312) 235-3506 Toll-free number: (800) 215-7173
Fax: (312) 235-3501
Elaine Vincent, Director of Enrollment Services, Shimer College, 3424 South State Street, Chicago, IL 60616

Southern Illinois University Carbondale

Carbondale, Illinois

www.siuc.edu

CB member

CB code: 1726

▸ Public 4-year university
▸ Residential campus in large town

▸ 14,936 degree-seeking undergraduates: 13% part-time, 44% women, 22% African American, 2% Asian American, 5% Hispanic American, 2% international
▸ 4,768 degree-seeking graduate students·
▸ 44% of applicants admitted
▸ SAT or ACT (ACT writing optional) required
▸ 44% graduate within 6 years

General. Founded in 1869. Regionally accredited. **Degrees:** 3,761 bachelor's, 36 associate awarded; master's, professional, doctoral offered. **ROTC:** Army, Air Force. **Location:** 100 miles from St. Louis. **Calendar:** Semester, extensive summer session. **Full-time faculty:** 901 total; 81% have terminal degrees, 19% minority, 36% women. **Part-time faculty:** 153 total; 64% have terminal degrees, 10% minority, 47% women. **Class size:** 49% < 20, 40% 20-39, 4% 40-49, 5% 50-99, 1% >100. **Special facilities:** University press, coal research center, materials technology center, outdoor education laboratory, university farms, center for study of crime, electron microscopy center, cooperative wildlife research laboratory, cooperative fisheries research laboratory, vivarium, airport training facility, laboratory theater, child development laboratory, center for archaeological investigations, small business incubator, public policy institute, dental and medical clinics, environmental center, media center.

Freshman class profile. 14,511 applied, 6,402 admitted, 2,417 enrolled.

Mid 50% test scores			
SAT critical reading:	450-570	Rank in top tenth:	9%
SAT math:	440-610	Return as sophomores:	67%
ACT composite:	18-24	Out-of-state:	9%
Rank in top quarter:	27%	Live on campus:	90%
		International:	2%

Basis for selection. High school class rank and ACT scores most important. Holistic approach using these two items along with GPA, and core unit courses. Interviews required for major scholarships only, not for admission. **Home schooled:** Transcript of courses and grades required. **Learning Disabled:** Special requirements only apply for certain programs.

High school preparation. College-preparatory program required. 15 units required. Required units include English 4, mathematics 3, social studies 3, science 3 and academic electives 2.

2011-2012 Annual costs. Tuition/fees: $11,038; $22,729 out-of-state. Room/board: $8,648. Books/supplies: $900. Personal expenses: $1,218.

2010-2011 Financial aid. **Need-based:** 2,024 full-time freshmen applied for aid; 1,749 were judged to have need; 1,696 of these received aid. Average need met was 27%. Average scholarship/grant was $1,945; average loan $3,242. 47% of total undergraduate aid awarded as scholarships/grants, 53% as loans/jobs. **Non-need-based:** Awarded to 7,225 full-time undergraduates, including 1,441 freshmen. Scholarships awarded for academics, alumni affiliation, art, athletics, job skills, leadership, minority status, music/drama, ROTC, state residency. **Additional information:** Need-based financial aid available to part-time students enrolled in minimum of 6 semester hours.

Application procedures. Admission: Priority date 5/1; no deadline. $30 fee, may be waived for applicants with need. Admission notification on a rolling basis beginning on or about 9/1. Must reply by May 1 or within 6 week(s) if notified thereafter. **Financial aid:** Priority date 4/1; no closing date. FAFSA required. Applicants notified on a rolling basis starting 3/24.

Academics. Active production schedule in several theaters includes contemporary works, musicals, operas, original plays by faculty and students, and world drama from major periods in theater history. **Special study options:** Accelerated study, combined bachelor's/graduate degree, cooperative education, distance learning, double major, ESL, honors, independent study, internships, student-designed major, study abroad, teacher certification program. **Credit/placement by examination:** AP, CLEP, IB, SAT, ACT, institutional tests. 15 credit hours maximum toward associate degree, 30 toward bachelor's. **Support services:** Learning center, pre-admission summer program, reduced course load, remedial instruction, study skills assistance, tutoring, writing center.

Majors. **Architecture:** Architecture. **Biology:** General, botany, microbiology, physiology, zoology. **Business:** Accounting, business admin, finance, management science, managerial economics, marketing. **Communications:** Journalism, radio/TV. **Computer sciences:** Computer science, information systems. **Conservation:** Forestry. **Education:** Early childhood, elementary, health, physical, special ed, trade/industrial. **Engineering:** Civil, computer, electrical, mechanical, mining. **English:** English lit, rhetoric/composition. **Foreign languages:** Classics, French, German, linguistics, Spanish. **General:** Animal sciences, economics, plant sciences. **Health services:** Athletic training, communication disorders, dental hygiene, health care admin, medical radiologic technology/radiation therapy, physician assistant. **History:** General. **Human services:** Social work. **Liberal arts:** Arts/sciences. **Math:** General. **Parks/recreation:** General, exercise sciences, sports admin. **Philosophy/religion:** Philosophy. **Physical sciences:** Chemistry, geology, physics.

Protective services: Fire services admin, law enforcement admin. **Psychology:** General. **Social sciences:** General, anthropology, economics, geography, political science, sociology. **Visual/performing arts:** Art, cinematography, design, dramatic, interior design, music, studio arts. **Work/family studies:** Clothing/textiles, food/nutrition.

Most popular majors. Business/marketing 10%, education 20%, engineering/engineering technologies 11%, health sciences 8%.

Computing on campus. 1,820 workstations in dormitories, library, computer center, student center. Dormitories wired for high-speed internet access and linked to campus network. Commuter students can connect to campus network. Online course registration, online library, helpline, repair service, student web hosting, wireless network available.

Student life. Freshman orientation: Mandatory. Preregistration for classes offered. Several 1-day seminars offered April through July. Orientation cost included in one-time matriculation fee. **Housing:** Guaranteed on-campus for freshmen. Coed dorms, single-sex dorms, special housing for disabled, apartments, fraternity/sorority housing available. $650 partly refundable deposit, deadline 6/1. **Activities:** Bands, campus ministries, choral groups, dance, drama, film society, international student organizations, literary magazine, music ensembles, musical theater, opera, radio station, student government, student newspaper, symphony orchestra, TV station, over 400 student organizations.

Athletics. NCAA. **Intercollegiate:** Baseball M, basketball, cheerleading, cross-country, diving, football (tackle) M, golf, softball W, swimming, tennis, track and field, volleyball W. **Intramural:** Badminton, basketball, football (non-tackle), racquetball, soccer, softball, swimming, table tennis, tennis, track and field, volleyball. **Team name:** Salukis.

Student services. Adult student services, alcohol/substance abuse counseling, career counseling, services for economically disadvantaged, student employment services, financial aid counseling, health services, legal services, minority student services, on-campus daycare, personal counseling, placement for graduates, veterans' counselor, women's services. **Physically disabled:** Services for visually, speech, hearing impaired.

Contact. E-mail: joinsiuc@siu.edu
Phone: (618) 453-4381 Fax: (618) 453-3250
Katharine Suski, Director, Undergraduate Admissions, Southern Illinois University Carbondale, 425 Clocktower Drive, Carbondale, IL 62901

Southern Illinois University Edwardsville
Edwardsville, Illinois **CB member**
www.siue.edu **CB code: 1759**

- Public 4-year university
- Residential campus in very large city
- 11,385 degree-seeking undergraduates: 15% part-time, 53% women, 14% African American, 2% Asian American, 3% Hispanic American, 1% international
- 2,807 degree-seeking graduate students
- 80% of applicants admitted
- SAT or ACT (ACT writing optional) required
- 51% graduate within 6 years; 33% enter graduate study

General. Founded in 1957. Regionally accredited. 2,660-acre campus. **Degrees:** 2,208 bachelor's awarded; master's, professional, doctoral offered. **ROTC:** Army, Air Force. **Location:** 18 miles from St. Louis. **Calendar:** Semester, extensive summer session. **Full-time faculty:** 619 total; 81% have terminal degrees, 18% minority, 49% women. **Part-time faculty:** 282 total; 9% minority, 48% women. **Class size:** 40% < 20, 42% 20-39, 9% 40-49, 9% 50-99, less than 1% >100. **Special facilities:** Museum collections, arboretum, greenhouse, engineering labs, clinical nursing facility, observatory, applied research and technology park, corn-to-ethanol research center, biotechnology laboratory incubator, pharmaceutical care lab.

Freshman class profile. 7,540 applied, 6,069 admitted, 2,060 enrolled.

Mid 50% test scores		Return as sophomores:	70%
ACT composite:	19-25	Out-of-state:	8%
Rank in top quarter:	39%	Live on campus:	68%
Rank in top tenth:	15%		

Basis for selection. Meeting published deadlines; GPA; ACT and/or SAT composite score; high school course work; middle 50% range is 20-25 ACT (940-1160 SAT). Audition recommended for music majors; portfolio recommended for art majors.

High school preparation. College-preparatory program required. 15 units required. Required and recommended units include English 4, mathematics

3, social studies 3, science 3 (laboratory 3), foreign language 2 and academic electives 2. At least 2 years of history or government required; 2 years foreign language, music, dance, theater, art, or vocational education (1 year maximum) electives recommended; 1 year chemistry and 1 year biology required.

2011-2012 Annual costs. Tuition/fees: $8,865; $18,810 out-of-state. Required fees include book rental. Room/board: $8,051. Books/supplies: $696. Personal expenses: $1,506.

2011-2012 Financial aid. All financial aid based on need. 1,840 full-time freshmen applied for aid; 1,482 were judged to have need; 1,440 of these received aid. Average need met was 69%. Average scholarship/grant was $9,007; average loan $3,715. 44% of total undergraduate aid awarded as scholarships/grants, 56% as loans/jobs.

Application procedures. Admission: Priority date 12/1; deadline 5/1 (postmark date). $30 fee, may be waived for applicants with need. Admission notification on a rolling basis beginning on or about 9/15. Must reply by May 1 or within 2 week(s) if notified thereafter. **Financial aid:** Priority date 3/1, closing date 6/1. FAFSA required. Applicants notified on a rolling basis starting 3/15; must reply within 4 week(s) of notification.

Academics. Senior project required. **Special study options:** Accelerated study, combined bachelor's/graduate degree, cooperative education, cross-registration, distance learning, double major, honors, independent study, internships, student-designed major, study abroad, teacher certification program. **Credit/placement by examination:** AP, CLEP, SAT, ACT, institutional tests. 32 credit hours maximum toward bachelor's degree. Placement tests required for some students in reading, writing and/or math; determination based on test scores and GPA. **Support services:** Learning center, pre-admission summer program, reduced course load, remedial instruction, study skills assistance, tutoring, writing center.

Majors. Biology: General. **Business:** Accounting, business admin, management information systems, managerial economics. **Communications:** Media studies. **Computer sciences:** Computer science. **Education:** Early childhood, elementary, health, physical, science, special ed. **Engineering:** Civil, computer, electrical, industrial, manufacturing, mechanical. **English:** English lit, rhetoric/composition. **Foreign languages:** General. **Health services:** Audiology/speech pathology, nursing (RN). **History:** General. **Human services:** Social work. **Liberal arts:** Arts/sciences. **Math:** General. **Parks/recreation:** Exercise sciences. **Philosophy/religion:** Philosophy. **Physical sciences:** Chemistry, physics. **Protective services:** Criminal justice. **Psychology:** General. **Social sciences:** Anthropology, economics, geography, political science, sociology. **Visual/performing arts:** Art, dramatic, music, studio arts.

Most popular majors. Biology 8%, business/marketing 20%, education 11%, engineering/engineering technologies 8%, health sciences 12%, psychology 6%, social sciences 8%.

Computing on campus. 600 workstations in dormitories, library, computer center, student center. Dormitories wired for high-speed internet access and linked to campus network. Commuter students can connect to campus network. Online course registration, online library, helpline, student web hosting, wireless network available.

Student life. Freshman orientation: Mandatory, $150 fee. Preregistration for classes offered. Pre-entry advisement and course-registration program including orientation. Two-day overnight summer program. **Housing:** Coed dorms, special housing for disabled, apartments, fraternity/sorority housing, wellness housing available. $300 nonrefundable deposit, deadline 5/1. Focused-interest communities. **Activities:** Bands, campus ministries, choral groups, dance, drama, international student organizations, literary magazine, music ensembles, musical theater, opera, radio station, student government, student newspaper, symphony orchestra, More than 200 organizations and honor societies available.

Athletics. NCAA. **Intercollegiate:** Baseball M, basketball, cross-country, golf, soccer, softball W, tennis, track and field, volleyball W, wrestling M. **Intramural:** Badminton, basketball, bowling, cross-country, fencing, football (non-tackle), golf, racquetball, soccer, softball, table tennis, tennis, volleyball, water polo, weight lifting. **Team name:** Cougars.

Student services. Alcohol/substance abuse counseling, career counseling, services for economically disadvantaged, student employment services, financial aid counseling, health services, legal services, on-campus daycare, personal counseling, placement for graduates, veterans' counselor. **Physically disabled:** Services for visually, speech, hearing impaired.

Contact. E-mail: admissions@siue.edu
Phone: (618) 650-3705 Toll-free number: (800) 447-7483
Fax: (618) 650-5013
Todd Burrell, Director of Admissions, Southern Illinois University Edwardsville, Rendleman Hall, Rm 2120, Edwardsville, IL 62026-1600

St. Augustine College
Chicago, Illinois
www.staugustine.edu   CB code: 0697

- Private 4-year liberal arts college affiliated with Episcopal Church
- Commuter campus in very large city
- 1,691 undergraduates

General. Founded in 1980. Regionally accredited. **Degrees:** 8 bachelor's, 221 associate awarded. **Calendar:** Semester, limited summer session. **Full-time faculty:** 25 total. **Part-time faculty:** 141 total.

Basis for selection. Open admission. Must demonstrate ability to benefit through high school diploma, GED or Ability to Benefit testing. **Home schooled:** Placement test in English, math, and Spanish required.

2011-2012 Annual costs. Tuition/fees: $10,950. Books/supplies: $600.

Application procedures. Admission: No deadline. No application fee. Application must be submitted on paper. Admission notification on a rolling basis. **Financial aid:** No deadline. FAFSA, institutional form required. Applicants notified on a rolling basis.

Academics. Special study options: Cooperative education, double major, ESL, independent study, internships, liberal arts/career combination. **Credit/placement by examination:** AP, CLEP, IB, institutional tests. **Support services:** Learning center, pre-admission summer program, remedial instruction, tutoring.

Majors. Human services: Social work.

Computing on campus. 100 workstations in library, computer center. Online library available.

Student life. Freshman orientation: Mandatory. Preregistration for classes offered.

Student services. Adult student services, alcohol/substance abuse counseling, career counseling, services for economically disadvantaged, financial aid counseling, minority student services, on-campus daycare, personal counseling, placement for graduates.

Contact. Phone: (773) 878-8756 Fax: (773) 878-0937
Gloria Quiroz, Director of Admission, St. Augustine College, 1345 West Argyle, Chicago, IL 60640-3501

St. Francis Medical Center College of Nursing
Peoria, Illinois
www.sfmccon.edu   CB code: 1756

- Private two-year upper-division nursing college affiliated with Roman Catholic Church
- Commuter campus in small city
- 56% of applicants admitted
- Application essay required

General. Founded in 1905. Regionally accredited. Located at large medical center. National League of Nursing accredited. NCA accredited. Offers experience at Tazewell County, Fulton County, Peoria City/County Health Departments, Human Service Center and other community agencies. **Degrees:** 158 bachelor's awarded; master's, professional offered. **Location:** 180 miles from Chicago, 160 miles from St. Louis. **Calendar:** Semester, limited summer session. **Full-time faculty:** 34 total; 24% have terminal degrees, 100% women. **Part-time faculty:** 15 total; 93% women. **Class size:** 28% < 20, 42% 20-39, 22% 40-49, 8% 50-99.

Student profile. 354 degree-seeking undergraduates, 186 degree-seeking graduate students. 320 applied as first time-transfer students, 180 admitted, 172 enrolled. 100% entered as juniors. 95% transferred from two-year, 5% transferred from four-year institutions.

Women:	89%	International:	1%
African American:	6%	Part-time:	19%
Asian American:	1%	Live on campus:	20%
Hispanic American:	3%	25 or older:	46%

Basis for selection. High school transcript, college transcript, application essay required. Enrollment depends on satisfactory completion of 62 semester hours of a specified prenursing curriculum. Applications may be submitted after satisfactory completion of 30 semester hours of required prenursing courses. Must include 8 semester hours of physical/life sciences. 2.5 GPA required. Transfer accepted as juniors.

2012-2013 Annual costs. Tuition/fees (projected): $15,576. Room only: $3,000. Books/supplies: $1,626. Personal expenses: $4,212.

Financial aid. Need-based: 240 applied for aid; 202 were judged to have need; 202 of these received aid. Average need met was 54%. 38% of total undergraduate aid awarded as scholarships/grants, 62% as loans/jobs. **Non-need-based:** Awarded to 20 undergraduates. Scholarships awarded for academics, alumni affiliation. **Additional information:** OSF Saint Francis Medical Center Education student loan available to full-time students on a limited basis. Tuition waiver program for hospital employees available.

Application procedures. Admission: Deadline 9/1. $50 fee. Application must be submitted on paper. **Financial aid:** No deadline. Applicants notified on a rolling basis starting 5/15; must reply within 4 weeks of notification. FAFSA, institutional form required.

Academics. Special study options: Accelerated study, combined bachelor's/graduate degree, distance learning. **Credit/placement by examination:** AP, CLEP.

Majors. Health services: Nursing (RN).

Computing on campus. 49 workstations in library, computer center. Dormitories linked to campus network. Commuter students can connect to campus network. Online library, helpline, repair service, wireless network available.

Student life. Housing: Coed dorms, wellness housing available. **Activities:** Student government, Christian fellowship, student nurses' association, minority association.

Student services. Adult student services, services for economically disadvantaged, financial aid counseling, health services, personal counseling.

Contact. E-mail: janice.farquharson@osfhealthcare.org
Phone: (309) 655-2245 Fax: (309) 624-8973
Janice Farquharson, Director of Admissions and Recruitment, St. Francis Medical Center College of Nursing, 511 NE Greenleaf Street, Peoria, IL 61603-3783

St. John's College
Springfield, Illinois
www.stjohnscollegespringfield.edu

- Private two-year upper-division nursing college affiliated with Roman Catholic Church
- Commuter campus in small city
- Test scores required

General. Degrees: 31 bachelor's awarded. **Location:** 220 miles from Chicago, 100 miles from St. Louis. **Calendar:** Semester. **Full-time faculty:** 14 total. **Part-time faculty:** 6 total. **Class size:** 43% 20-39, 57% 50-99.

Student profile. 111 degree-seeking undergraduates. 7% transferred from two-year, 93% transferred from four-year institutions.

Basis for selection. High school transcript, college transcript, standardized test scores required. Transfer accepted as juniors.

2011-2012 Annual costs. Tuition/fees: $14,626. Books/supplies: $1,528. Personal expenses: $1,890.

Application procedures. Admission: Rolling admission. $60 fee.

Academics. Credit/placement by examination: AP, CLEP.

Majors. Health services: Nursing (RN).

Computing on campus. 23 workstations in library, computer center. Commuter students can connect to campus network. Online library, helpline, repair service, wireless network available.

Student services. Alcohol/substance abuse counseling, chaplain/spiritual director, financial aid counseling, health services, personal counseling.

Contact. E-mail: linda.quigley@stjohnscollegespringfield.edu
Phone: (217) 525-5628 Fax: (217) 757-6870
Linda Quigley, Admissions Officer, St. John's College, 729 East Carpenter Street, Springfield, IL 62702

Telshe Yeshiva-Chicago
Chicago, Illinois

CB code: 7009

◆ Private 4-year rabbinical college for men affiliated with Jewish faith
◆ Very large city

General. Accredited by AARTS. **Degrees:** 2 bachelor's awarded; master's offered. **Calendar:** Differs by program. **Full-time faculty:** 5 total. **Part-time faculty:** 1 total.

2011-2012 Annual costs. Comprehensive fee: $12,000.

Application procedures. Admission: No deadline. No application fee.

Academics. Credit/placement by examination: AP, CLEP.

Majors. Theology: Talmudic.

Contact. Phone: (773) 463-7738 Fax: (773) 463-2894
Director of Admissions, Telshe Yeshiva-Chicago, 3535 West Foster Avenue, Chicago, IL 60625

Trinity Christian College
Palos Heights, Illinois
www.trnty.edu

CB code: 1820

◆ Private 4-year liberal arts college affiliated with Reformed (unaffiliated) Church
◆ Residential campus in very large city
◆ 1,326 degree-seeking undergraduates: 18% part-time, 66% women, 10% African American, 2% Asian American, 8% Hispanic American, 2% international
◆ 85% of applicants admitted
◆ SAT or ACT (ACT writing optional), application essay, interview required
◆ 64% graduate within 6 years; 15% enter graduate study

General. Founded in 1959. Regionally accredited. **Degrees:** 295 bachelor's awarded. **Location:** 20 miles from downtown. **Calendar:** Semester, limited summer session. **Full-time faculty:** 89 total; 58% have terminal degrees, 15% minority, 46% women. **Part-time faculty:** 72 total; 15% have terminal degrees, 8% minority, 58% women. **Class size:** 58% < 20, 38% 20-39, 3% 40-49, 2% 50-99. **Special facilities:** Dutch heritage center archives.

Freshman class profile. 799 applied, 683 admitted, 235 enrolled.

Mid 50% test scores			
SAT critical reading:	480-610	Rank in top quarter:	25%
SAT math:	470-580	Rank in top tenth:	15%
ACT composite:	20-27	Return as sophomores:	80%
GPA 3.75 or higher:	31%	Out-of-state:	43%
GPA 3.50-3.74:	14%	Live on campus:	84%
GPA 3.0-3.49:	30%		
GPA 2.0-2.99:	25%		

Basis for selection. Minimum 2.25 GPA, Composite ACT 17, 830 SAT (exclusive of Writing) required. Students meeting only minimum scores for SAT and GPA are often admitted conditionally if they show exceptional ability to succeed. Statement of religious faith required. **Learning Disabled:** Documented diagnosis of disability is requested.

High school preparation. College-preparatory program recommended. 16 units required; 18 recommended. Required and recommended units include English 3-4, mathematics 3-4, social studies 2-3, history 2, science 2-3 and foreign language 2. One 3-year major in mathematics, science, or social studies, and 2 2-year minors in mathematics, science, social studies, or foreign language recommended.

2011-2012 Annual costs. Tuition/fees: $22,572. Room/board: $8,448. Books/supplies: $1,300. Personal expenses: $2,800.

2011-2012 Financial aid. Need-based: 231 full-time freshmen applied for aid; 195 were judged to have need; 195 of these received aid. Average need met was 27%. Average scholarship/grant was $5,087; average loan $4,626. 49% of total undergraduate aid awarded as scholarships/grants, 51% as loans/jobs. **Non-need-based:** Awarded to 1,335 full-time undergraduates, including 458 freshmen. Scholarships awarded for academics, alumni affiliation, art, athletics, leadership, minority status, music/drama, religious affiliation. **Additional information:** High school transcripts and ACT or SAT scores required for merit scholarships.

Application procedures. Admission: No deadline. $20 fee, may be waived for applicants with need. Admission notification on a rolling basis beginning on or about 9/1. Must reply by May 1 or within 2 week(s) if notified thereafter. **Financial aid:** Priority date 2/15, closing date 3/1. FAFSA, institutional form required. Applicants notified on a rolling basis starting 3/1; must reply by 5/1 or within 2 week(s) of notification.

Academics. Special study options: Double major, ESL, honors, independent study, internships, liberal arts/career combination, study abroad, teacher certification program, urban semester. **Credit/placement by examination:** AP, CLEP, IB, SAT, ACT, institutional tests. 30 credit hours maximum toward bachelor's degree. **Support services:** Learning center, pre-admission summer program, reduced course load, remedial instruction, study skills assistance, tutoring, writing center.

Honors college/program. Must have 28 ACT, be in top 10% of high school class, and have 3.5 high school GPA. 13-19 semester hours of unique courses. Approximately 15 freshmen admitted each year.

Majors. Biology: General. **Business:** General, accounting, communications. **Communications:** Communications/speech/rhetoric. **Computer sciences:** Computer science, information systems. **Education:** Art, biology, business, chemistry, elementary, English, history, mathematics, music, physical, Spanish, special ed. **English:** English lit. **Foreign languages:** Spanish. **Health services:** Nursing (RN). **History:** General. **Human services:** Social work. **Math:** General. **Parks/recreation:** Exercise sciences, health/fitness. **Philosophy/religion:** Philosophy. **Physical sciences:** Chemistry. **Protective services:** Criminal justice. **Psychology:** General. **Social sciences:** Political science, sociology. **Theology:** Theology. **Visual/performing arts:** Music, music performance, studio arts.

Most popular majors. Business/marketing 16%, education 40%, health sciences 12%, theological studies 7%.

Computing on campus. 140 workstations in dormitories, library, computer center. Dormitories wired for high-speed internet access and linked to campus network. Commuter students can connect to campus network. Helpline, wireless network available.

Student life. Freshman orientation: Mandatory, $220 fee. Preregistration for classes offered. Two-day program in early July and two-week program in late August. **Housing:** Guaranteed on-campus for freshmen. Coed dorms, apartments available. $75 fully refundable deposit, deadline 9/1. **Activities:** Bands, campus ministries, choral groups, dance, drama, music ensembles, musical theater, student government, student newspaper, religious drama club, theology club, pro-life, Bread for the World, Inter-Varsity Fellowship, Big Brother/Big Sister, Association for Public Justice, PACE literacy program in Cook County jail.

Athletics. NAIA, NCCAA. **Intercollegiate:** Baseball M, basketball, cross-country, soccer, softball W, track and field, volleyball W. **Intramural:** Basketball, racquetball, soccer, volleyball. **Team name:** Trolls.

Student services. Adult student services, alcohol/substance abuse counseling, chaplain/spiritual director, career counseling, student employment services, financial aid counseling, health services, minority student services, personal counseling, placement for graduates, veterans' counselor. **Physically disabled:** Services for visually, speech, hearing impaired.

Contact. E-mail: admissions@trnty.edu
Phone: (708) 239-4708 Toll-free number: (866) 874-6463 ext. 4708
Fax: (708) 239-4826
Jeremy Klyn, Director of Admissions, Trinity Christian College, 6601 West College Drive, Palos Heights, IL 60463

Trinity College of Nursing and Health Sciences
Rock Island, Illinois
www.trinitycollegeqc.edu

CB code: 2555

◆ Private 4-year health science and nursing college
◆ Commuter campus in large city
◆ 222 degree-seeking undergraduates: 51% part-time, 87% women, 5% African American, 3% Asian American, 6% Hispanic American
◆ 50% of applicants admitted

General. Affiliated with Trinity Medical Center, part of Iowa Health System. **Degrees:** 23 bachelor's, 50 associate awarded. **Calendar:** Semester, limited summer session. **Full-time faculty:** 15 total; 20% have terminal degrees, 93% women. **Part-time faculty:** 6 total; 100% women. **Class size:** 100% < 20. **Special facilities:** Learning laboratories with simulation mannequins, radiography and respiratory care learning laboratories.

Freshman class profile. 4 applied, 2 admitted, 2 enrolled.

Mid 50% test scores			
ACT composite:	18-24	GPA 3.0-3.49:	43%
GPA 3.50-3.74:	29%	GPA 2.0-2.99:	28%
		Out-of-state:	45%

Basis for selection. Quality of high school work and GPA, ACT score, previous college credit and GPA most important. Reuqirements vary by program. ACT and SAT scores are used for admission purposes only, not course placement. Interview requirement varies by program. **Home schooled:** Transcript of courses and grades required.

High school preparation. College-preparatory program recommended. Required units include English 4, mathematics 3, social studies 3, science 3 (laboratory 1).

2011-2012 Annual costs. Tuition/fees: $15,482. Students required to have a uniform and other health equipment.

2010-2011 Financial aid. All financial aid based on need. 46% of total undergraduate aid awarded as scholarships/grants, 54% as loans/jobs.

Application procedures. Admission: Priority date 10/31; no deadline. $50 fee, may be waived for applicants with need. Admission notification on a rolling basis beginning on or about 2/1. Students who have been accepted have 2 weeks from the receipt of their acceptance letter to reply and pay a $100 tuition deposit to hold their seat in the program. **Financial aid:** No deadline. FAFSA, institutional form required.

Academics. Special study options: Accelerated study, combined bachelor's/graduate degree, distance learning, dual enrollment of high school students, internships. 15 month accelerated BSN program for students with bachelors degree. **Credit/placement by examination:** AP, CLEP, institutional tests. 18 credit hours maximum toward associate degree, 18 toward bachelor's. **Support services:** Study skills assistance, tutoring.

Majors. Health services: Nursing (RN).

Computing on campus. 20 workstations in library, computer center. Commuter students can connect to campus network. Online library, helpline, wireless network available.

Student life. Freshman orientation: Mandatory, $10 fee. Preregistration for classes offered. **Activities:** Student government.

Student services. Alcohol/substance abuse counseling, chaplain/spiritual director, career counseling, financial aid counseling, health services, minority student services, on-campus daycare, personal counseling.

Contact. E-mail: perezlj@ihs.org
Phone: (309) 779-7812 Fax: (309) 779-7748
Joann Lay, Director of Student Services and External Relations, Trinity College of Nursing and Health Sciences, 2122 25th Avenue, Rock Island, IL 61201-5317

Trinity International University
Deerfield, Illinois **CB member**
www.tiu.edu **CB code: 1810**

- Private 4-year university and liberal arts college affiliated with Evangelical Free Church of America
- Residential campus in large town
- 986 degree-seeking undergraduates
- 98% of applicants admitted
- SAT or ACT (ACT writing optional), application essay required

General. Founded in 1897. Regionally accredited. Off-campus programs available through Christian College Consortium. **Degrees:** 188 bachelor's awarded; master's, doctoral offered. **Location:** 25 miles from Chicago. **Calendar:** Semester, limited summer session. **Full-time faculty:** 39 total. **Part-time faculty:** 37 total. **Class size:** 41% < 20, 39% 20-39, 16% 40-49, 5% 50-99. **Special facilities:** Seminary facilities.

Freshman class profile. 365 applied, 358 admitted, 158 enrolled.

Mid 50% test scores			
SAT critical reading:	390-530	GPA 3.0-3.49:	27%
SAT math:	450-570	GPA 2.0-2.99:	30%
ACT composite:	19-26	Rank in top quarter:	43%
GPA 3.75 or higher:	29%	Rank in top tenth:	37%
GPA 3.50-3.74:	14%	Out-of-state:	51%
		Live on campus:	93%

Basis for selection. School achievement record, test scores, recommendations, evidence of Christian commitment, essays most important. Interview recommended for borderline applicants. **Home schooled:** Transcript of courses and grades required.

High school preparation. College-preparatory program required. Required units include English 4, mathematics 2, social studies 2, history 2, science 2 (laboratory 1), foreign language 2 and visual/performing arts 2.

2011-2012 Annual costs. Tuition/fees: $24,610. Room/board: $8,260. Books/supplies: $1,080. Personal expenses: $1,130.

Financial aid. Non-need-based: Scholarships awarded for academics, alumni affiliation, athletics, minority status, music/drama, religious affiliation.

Application procedures. Admission: No deadline. $25 fee, may be waived for applicants with need. Admission notification on a rolling basis beginning on or about 9/1. **Financial aid:** Priority date 4/1; no closing date. FAFSA required. Applicants notified on a rolling basis starting 2/15; must reply within 4 week(s) of notification.

Academics. Special study options: Accelerated study, cooperative education, cross-registration, distance learning, double major, dual enrollment of high school students, exchange student, honors, independent study, internships, liberal arts/career combination, student-designed major, study abroad, teacher certification program, urban semester, Washington semester. REACH (for nontraditional students with previous college credit), graduate courses available to undergraduates with junior or senior standing. **Credit/placement by examination:** AP, CLEP, IB, SAT, ACT, institutional tests. Permission and approval by department chair required. May not be used to satisfy senior residency requirement. **Support services:** Learning center, remedial instruction, study skills assistance, tutoring, writing center.

Majors. Biology: General. **Business:** General, accounting, human resources, management science, marketing, nonprofit/public, organizational behavior, training/development. **Communications:** Communications/speech/rhetoric. **Education:** Biology, elementary, English, history, mathematics, music, physical, secondary. **English:** English lit. **Health services:** Athletic training, premedicine. **History:** General. **Liberal arts:** Humanities. **Math:** General. **Parks/recreation:** Health/fitness. **Philosophy/religion:** Philosophy. **Physical sciences:** Chemistry. **Psychology:** General. **Social sciences:** General. **Theology:** Bible, pastoral counseling, preministerial, religious ed, sacred music, theology, youth ministry. **Visual/performing arts:** Music, music pedagogy, music performance, music theory/composition, piano/keyboard, voice/opera.

Most popular majors. Business/marketing 22%, education 26%, health sciences 7%, liberal arts 6%, psychology 10%, theological studies 17%.

Computing on campus. 100 workstations in library, computer center, student center. Dormitories wired for high-speed internet access and linked to campus network. Commuter students can connect to campus network. Online course registration, online library, helpline, repair service, student web hosting, wireless network available.

Student life. Freshman orientation: Mandatory. Preregistration for classes offered. Orientation held the week before classes each fall and spring. Generally lasts entire week. **Policies:** Community expectations, general patterns of Christian lifestyle, policy on drug and alcohol abuse. Religious observance required. **Housing:** Guaranteed on-campus for freshmen. Single-sex dorms, special housing for disabled, apartments, wellness housing available. $50 partly refundable deposit, deadline 5/1. **Activities:** Bands, campus ministries, choral groups, dance, drama, music ensembles, musical theater, student government, student newspaper, symphony orchestra, Association of Believers for Black America, Global Christian Movement, Kappa Tau, Discipleship Cabinet, FAT Thursdays, Chapel Cabinet, Kids on Kampus, Wives Fellowship, Men's Ministry.

Athletics. NAIA, NCCAA. **Intercollegiate:** Baseball M, basketball, football (tackle) M, soccer, softball W, volleyball W. **Intramural:** Baseball M, basketball, bowling, football (non-tackle) M, racquetball, rugby M, soccer, softball, volleyball. **Team name:** Trojans.

Student services. Alcohol/substance abuse counseling, chaplain/spiritual director, career counseling, student employment services, financial aid counseling, health services, minority student services, on-campus daycare, personal counseling, placement for graduates. **Physically disabled:** Services for visually impaired.

Contact. E-mail: tcadmissions@tiu.edu
Phone: (847) 317-7000 Toll-free number: (800) 822-3225
Fax: (847) 317-8097
Aaron Mahl, Director of Admissions, Trinity International University, 2065 Half Day Road, Deerfield, IL 60015

University of Chicago
Chicago, Illinois
www.uchicago.edu

CB member
CB code: 1832

- Private 4-year university and liberal arts college
- Residential campus in very large city
- 5,377 degree-seeking undergraduates: 1% part-time, 48% women, 5% African American, 17% Asian American, 6% Hispanic American, 9% international
- 6,612 degree-seeking graduate students
- 16% of applicants admitted
- SAT or ACT (ACT writing optional), application essay required
- 92% graduate within 6 years

General. Founded in 1891. Regionally accredited. **Degrees:** 1,270 bachelor's awarded; master's, professional, doctoral offered. **ROTC:** Army, Air Force. **Location:** 7 miles from Chicago. **Calendar:** Quarter, extensive summer session. **Full-time faculty:** 1,135 total; 100% have terminal degrees, 20% minority, 29% women. **Part-time faculty:** 566 total; 64% have terminal degrees, 16% minority, 36% women. **Class size:** 74% < 20, 18% 20-39, 3% 40-49, 4% 50-99, 1% >100. **Special facilities:** Oriental institute, art museum, theater, modern art gallery, Argonne National Laboratory, library of sciences, Fermi National Accelerator Laboratory, film studies center, observatory.

Freshman class profile. 21,762 applied, 3,539 admitted, 1,411 enrolled.

Mid 50% test scores			
SAT critical reading:	700-790	Rank in top quarter:	99%
SAT math:	700-780	Rank in top tenth:	95%
SAT writing:	700-780	End year in good standing:	99%
ACT composite:	31-34	Return as sophomores:	99%
GPA 3.75 or higher:	87%	Out-of-state:	81%
GPA 3.50-3.74:	9%	Live on campus:	100%
GPA 3.0-3.49:	4%	International:	11%

Basis for selection. Secondary school record, recommendations, essay, talent/ability and character/personal qualities very important. Interview recommended.

High school preparation. Recommended units include English 4, mathematics 4, social studies 2, history 2, science 4 and foreign language 3.

2011-2012 Annual costs. Tuition/fees: $42,783. Room/board: $12,633.

2011-2012 Financial aid. Need-based: 827 full-time freshmen applied for aid; 625 were judged to have need; 625 of these received aid. Average need met was 100%. Average scholarship/grant was $36,454; average loan $3,052. 90% of total undergraduate aid awarded as scholarships/grants, 10% as loans/jobs. **Non-need-based:** Awarded to 635 full-time undergraduates, including 219 freshmen. Scholarships awarded for academics, leadership. **Additional information:** Odyssey Scholarship program eliminates or reduces indebtedness of needy full-time undergraduates from low to moderate income families. A freshman student whose parental income is less than $75,000 is not expected to borrow. A student whose parental income is between $75,000 & $90,000 is expected to borrow half of the sum a typical needy freshman student is expected to borrow.

Application procedures. Admission: Closing date 1/3 (postmark date). $75 fee, may be waived for applicants with need. Admission notification by 4/1. Must reply by 5/1. **Financial aid:** Priority date 11/1, closing date 2/1. FAFSA, CSS PROFILE required. Applicants notified by 4/16; must reply by 5/1.

Academics. Special study options: Accelerated study, combined bachelor's/graduate degree, cross-registration, double major, ESL, exchange student, honors, independent study, internships, student-designed major, study abroad, teacher certification program. **Credit/placement by examination:** AP, CLEP, IB, institutional tests. **Support services:** Learning center, preadmission summer program, study skills assistance, tutoring, writing center.

Majors. Area/ethnic studies: African, African-American, East Asian, German, Latin American, Near/Middle Eastern, Russian/Slavic, Slavic, South Asian. **Biology:** General, biochemistry. **Computer sciences:** General. **Conservation:** Environmental studies. **English:** English lit. **Foreign languages:** Ancient Greek, Arabic, Biblical, classics, comparative lit, East Asian, French, German, Hebrew, Italian, Latin, linguistics, Portuguese, Russian, Scandinavian, Slavic, South Asian, Spanish. **History:** General. **Human services:** Public policy. **Liberal arts:** Arts/sciences. **Math:** General, applied, statistics. **Philosophy/religion:** Judaic, philosophy, religion. **Physical sciences:** Chemistry, geophysics, physics. **Psychology:** General. **Social sciences:** Anthropology, economics, geography, international relations, political science, sociology. **Visual/performing arts:** General, art history/conservation, film/cinema/video, music.

Most popular majors. Biology 11%, foreign language 6%, mathematics 7%, physical sciences 7%, psychology 6%, social sciences 38%.

Computing on campus. 1,000 workstations in dormitories, library, computer center, student center. Dormitories wired for high-speed internet access and linked to campus network. Commuter students can connect to campus network. Online course registration, online library, helpline, repair service, student web hosting, wireless network available.

Student life. Freshman orientation: Mandatory, $536 fee. Preregistration for classes offered. Held 10 days before classes begin in the fall. **Housing:** Guaranteed on-campus for all undergraduates. Coed dorms, apartments, fraternity/sorority housing available. **Activities:** Bands, campus ministries, choral groups, dance, drama, film society, international student organizations, literary magazine, music ensembles, Model UN, musical theater, radio station, student government, student newspaper, symphony orchestra, over 400 organizations.

Athletics. NCAA. **Intercollegiate:** Baseball M, basketball, cross-country, diving, football (tackle) M, soccer, softball W, swimming, tennis, track and field, volleyball W, wrestling M. **Intramural:** Badminton, basketball, bowling, football (non-tackle), racquetball, soccer, softball, swimming, table tennis, tennis, track and field, volleyball. **Team name:** Maroons.

Student services. Adult student services, alcohol/substance abuse counseling, chaplain/spiritual director, career counseling, services for economically disadvantaged, student employment services, financial aid counseling, health services, minority student services, personal counseling, placement for graduates, veterans' counselor, women's services. **Physically disabled:** Services for visually, speech, hearing impaired.

Contact. E-mail: collegeadmissions@uchicago.edu
Phone: (773) 702-8650 Fax: (773) 702-4199
James Nondorf, Vice President, Dean of Admissions and Financial Aid, University of Chicago, 1101 East 58th Street, Chicago, IL 60637

University of Illinois at Chicago
Chicago, Illinois
www.uic.edu

CB member
CB code: 1851

- Public 4-year university
- Commuter campus in very large city
- 16,789 degree-seeking undergraduates: 8% part-time, 52% women, 8% African American, 21% Asian American, 22% Hispanic American, 1% international
- 10,354 degree-seeking graduate students
- 63% of applicants admitted
- SAT or ACT (ACT writing optional), application essay required
- 55% graduate within 6 years

General. Founded in 1946. Regionally accredited. Medical, dental, nursing and pharmacy colleges, and medical center within university complex. **Degrees:** 3,526 bachelor's awarded; master's, professional, doctoral offered. **ROTC:** Army, Naval, Air Force. **Location:** One mile from downtown. **Calendar:** Semester, limited summer session. **Full-time faculty:** 1,146 total; 75% have terminal degrees, 22% minority, 45% women. **Part-time faculty:** 444 total; 46% have terminal degrees, 17% minority, 53% women. **Class size:** 29% < 20, 45% 20-39, 7% 40-49, 10% 50-99, 10% >100. **Special facilities:** Jane Addams' Hull House museum, prairie preserve, health sciences center, software technologies research facility.

Freshman class profile. 14,564 applied, 9,151 admitted, 3,115 enrolled.

Mid 50% test scores			
SAT critical reading:	450-600	Rank in top quarter:	60%
SAT math:	500-650	Rank in top tenth:	28%
SAT writing:	480-610	Return as sophomores:	79%
ACT composite:	21-26	Out-of-state:	3%
GPA 3.75 or higher:	9%	Live on campus:	40%
GPA 3.50-3.74:	13%	International:	1%
GPA 3.0-3.49:	39%	Fraternities:	2%
GPA 2.0-2.99:	39%	Sororities:	2%

Basis for selection. Class rank, GPA, and test scores most important. High school course selection and personal statement strongly considered. Auditions required of music and theater majors. Portfolio required of art majors. **Home schooled:** Transcript of courses and grades required. **Learning Disabled:** Students may add learning disability information to personal essay.

High school preparation. College-preparatory program required. 15 units required. Required and recommended units include English 4, mathematics 3-4, social studies 3, science 3 and foreign language 2. Additional course requirements vary with college and program.

2011-2012 Annual costs. Tuition/fees: $12,656; $25,046 out-of-state. Health Insurance: $802; refundable fees: $6. Room/board: $10,194. Books/supplies: $1,400. Personal expenses: $2,176.

2010-2011 Financial aid. Need-based: 2,810 full-time freshmen applied for aid; 2,433 were judged to have need; 2,313 of these received aid. Average need met was 72%. Average scholarship/grant was $13,910; average loan $3,387. 63% of total undergraduate aid awarded as scholarships/grants, 37% as loans/jobs. **Non-need-based:** Awarded to 1,016 full-time undergraduates, including 231 freshmen. Scholarships awarded for academics, art, athletics, music/drama, ROTC.

Application procedures. Admission: Closing date 1/15 (postmark date). $50 fee, may be waived for applicants with need. Admission notification on a rolling basis beginning on or about 11/30. Must reply by May 1 or within 2 week(s) if notified thereafter. **Financial aid:** Priority date 3/1; no closing date. FAFSA required. Applicants notified on a rolling basis starting 3/15; must reply by 5/1.

Academics. Special study options: Accelerated study, combined bachelor's/graduate degree, cooperative education, cross-registration, distance learning, double major, dual enrollment of high school students, honors, independent study, internships, student-designed major, study abroad, teacher certification program. **Credit/placement by examination:** AP, CLEP, IB, institutional tests. 30 credit hours maximum toward bachelor's degree. **Support services:** Learning center, pre-admission summer program, remedial instruction, study skills assistance, tutoring, writing center.

Majors. Architecture: Architecture. **Area/ethnic studies:** African-American, German, Latin American. **Biology:** General, biochemistry, neuroscience. **Business:** Accounting, business admin, entrepreneurial studies, finance, management science, marketing. **Communications:** Communications/speech/rhetoric. **Computer sciences:** Computer science, information systems. **Education:** Art, biology, chemistry, elementary, English, French, German, history, mathematics, physics, Spanish. **Engineering:** Applied physics, biomedical, chemical, civil, computer, electrical, industrial, mechanical. **English:** English lit. **Foreign languages:** Classics, French, Italian, Polish, Russian, Spanish. **Health services:** Dietetics, medical records admin, nursing (RN), predental. **History:** General. **Liberal arts:** Arts/sciences. **Math:** General, statistics. **Parks/recreation:** Exercise sciences. **Philosophy/religion:** Philosophy. **Physical sciences:** Chemistry, geology, physics. **Protective services:** Criminal justice. **Psychology:** General. **Social sciences:** Anthropology, economics, political science, sociology, urban studies. **Visual/performing arts:** Art history/conservation, cinematography, dramatic, graphic design, industrial design, music, photography, studio arts.

Most popular majors. Biology 12%, business/marketing 17%, engineering/engineering technologies 10%, health sciences 6%, psychology 14%, social sciences 9%.

Computing on campus. 1,333 workstations in dormitories, library, computer center, student center. Dormitories wired for high-speed internet access and linked to campus network. Commuter students can connect to campus network. Online course registration, online library, helpline, student web hosting, wireless network available.

Student life. Freshman orientation: Mandatory, $149 fee. Preregistration for classes offered. Two-day, overnight offered from early June to mid-August. **Housing:** Coed dorms, special housing for disabled, apartments, wellness housing available. Presidential Award House, honors, entrepreneur, women in science and engineering floors available. **Activities:** Bands, campus ministries, choral groups, dance, drama, international student organizations, literary magazine, music ensembles, Model UN, radio station, student government, student newspaper, over 200 student groups available.

Athletics. NCAA. **Intercollegiate:** Baseball M, basketball, cheerleading, cross-country, diving, gymnastics, soccer M, softball W, swimming, tennis, track and field, volleyball W. **Intramural:** Badminton, basketball, bowling, cross-country, football (non-tackle), racquetball, soccer, softball, table tennis, tennis, volleyball. **Team name:** Flames.

Student services. Adult student services, alcohol/substance abuse counseling, career counseling, services for economically disadvantaged, student employment services, financial aid counseling, health services, legal services, minority student services, on-campus daycare, personal counseling, placement for graduates, veterans' counselor, women's services. **Physically disabled:** Services for visually, speech, hearing impaired.

Contact. E-mail: uicadmit@uic.edu
Phone: (312) 996-4350 Fax: (312) 413-7628
Thomas Glenn, Executive Director Admissions and Records, University of Illinois at Chicago, PO Box 5220, Chicago, IL 60680-5220

University of Illinois at Urbana-Champaign
Champaign, Illinois — CB member
www.illinois.edu — CB code: 1836

- Public 4-year university
- Residential campus in small city
- 31,350 degree-seeking undergraduates: 1% part-time, 45% women, 6% African American, 14% Asian American, 7% Hispanic American, 12% international
- 12,145 graduate students
- 68% of applicants admitted
- SAT or ACT with writing, application essay required
- 82% graduate within 6 years; 25% enter graduate study

General. Founded in 1867. Regionally accredited. **Degrees:** 7,667 bachelor's awarded; master's, professional, doctoral offered. **ROTC:** Army, Naval, Air Force. **Location:** 130 miles from Chicago, 125 miles from Indianapolis. **Calendar:** Semester, extensive summer session. **Full-time faculty:** 1,872 total; 92% have terminal degrees, 25% minority, 32% women. **Class size:** 34% < 20, 40% 20-39, 6% 40-49, 10% 50-99, 10% >100. **Special facilities:** Natural history museum, museum of world history and culture, performing and visual arts centers, 37 public libraries, institute of genomic biology, institute for advanced science and technology, computer science center, national center for supercomputing applications, arboretum, observatory, hiking trails, Japanese house and gardens, ice arena.

Freshman class profile. 28,751 applied, 19,434 admitted, 7,255 enrolled.

Mid 50% test scores			
SAT critical reading:	540-660	Return as sophomores:	94%
SAT math:	690-780	Out-of-state:	11%
SAT writing:	590-680	Live on campus:	99%
ACT composite:	26-31	International:	13%
Rank in top quarter:	90%	Fraternities:	21%
Rank in top tenth:	52%	Sororities:	21%

Basis for selection. High school course work, personal essay, class rank, SAT/ACT test scores most important. Audition required of dance, music, theater (performance) majors. Professional interest statement required of all applicants. **Home schooled:** Provide detailed information about home school environment/coursework; applicants should contact admissions office early in high school career with questions or concerns. **Learning Disabled:** Recommended that students address disability and any accommodations they receive in required personal statement section.

High school preparation. College-preparatory program required. 15.5 units required; 24 recommended. Required and recommended units include English 4, mathematics 3.5-4, social studies 2-4, science 2-4 (laboratory 2-4), foreign language 2-4 and academic electives 2-4. Specific subject requirements vary with college and program.

2011-2012 Annual costs. Tuition/fees: $13,838; $27,980 out-of-state. Health Insurance $438, refundable fees $138. International students assessed additional $750 per year. Room/board: $10,080. Books/supplies: $1,200. Personal expenses: $2,510.

2010-2011 Financial aid. Need-based: 4,894 full-time freshmen applied for aid; 3,496 were judged to have need; 3,279 of these received aid. Average need met was 69%. Average scholarship/grant was $12,743; average loan $4,047. 50% of total undergraduate aid awarded as scholarships/grants, 50% as loans/jobs. **Non-need-based:** Awarded to 4,775 full-time undergraduates, including 1,427 freshmen. Scholarships awarded for academics, alumni affiliation, art, athletics, leadership, minority status, music/drama, ROTC, state residency.

Application procedures. Admission: Priority date 11/1; deadline 1/2 (postmark date). $50 fee, may be waived for applicants with need. Admission notification by 2/17. Must reply by May 1 or within 2 week(s) if notified thereafter. **Financial aid:** Priority date 3/15; no closing date. FAFSA required. Applicants notified on a rolling basis starting 3/15; must reply by 5/1 or within 3 week(s) of notification.

Academics. Students generally declare a major upon enrollment. Students without a declared major may apply for the general curriculum option in the Division of General Studies. **Special study options:** Accelerated study, combined bachelor's/graduate degree, cooperative education, cross-registration, distance learning, double major, dual enrollment of high school students, ESL, exchange student, honors, independent study, internships, liberal arts/career combination, semester at sea, student-designed major, study abroad, teacher certification program, Washington semester. Honors programs, campus honors, Illinois Leadership & Entrepreneurial programs. **Credit/placement by examination:** AP, CLEP, IB, SAT, ACT, institutional tests. Unlimited credit hours may be counted toward a degree. **Support**

services: Learning center, reduced course load, study skills assistance, tutoring, writing center.

Majors. Architecture: Architecture, landscape, urban/community planning. **Area/ethnic studies:** East Asian, Latin American, Russian/Slavic, women's. **Biology:** General, biochemistry, biophysics, biotechnology, botany, cell/histology, cellular/molecular, entomology, microbiology, physiology, plant molecular. **Business:** General, accounting, accounting/business management, actuarial science, auditing, banking/financial services, business admin, entrepreneurial studies, finance, financial planning, hospitality admin, human resources, insurance, logistics, management information systems, management science, market research, marketing, operations, organizational behavior, purchasing, real estate, sales/distribution. **Communications:** Advertising, broadcast journalism, communications/speech/rhetoric, journalism, media studies, organizational. **Computer sciences:** General, computer science, programming, security. **Conservation:** General, environmental science, forest sciences, management/policy, urban forestry, wildlife/wilderness. **Education:** Agricultural, art, biology, chemistry, early childhood, early childhood special, elementary, English, foreign languages, French, German, history, kindergarten/preschool, Latin, mathematics, multi-level teacher, multiple handicapped, music, physical, physics, science, secondary, social science, social studies, Spanish, special ed. **Engineering:** General, aerospace, agricultural, applied physics, biomedical, ceramic, chemical, civil, computer, computer hardware, construction, electrical, engineering mechanics, environmental, geotechnical, industrial, manufacturing, materials, mechanical, metallurgical, nuclear, operations research, polymer, software, structural, transportation, water resource. **English:** English lit, rhetoric/composition, writing. **Foreign languages:** Classics, comparative lit, East Asian, French, German, Hebrew, Italian, linguistics, Portuguese, Russian, Spanish. **General:** Agronomy, animal husbandry, animal sciences, business, communications, economics, education services, food processing, food science, horticultural science, horticulture, international, mechanization, ornamental horticulture. **Health services:** Athletic training, audiology/hearing, audiology/speech pathology, community health, dietetics, environmental health, health services admin, preveterinary, vocational rehab counseling. **History:** General. **Liberal arts:** Arts/sciences, humanities. **Math:** General, computational, statistics. **Parks/recreation:** General, exercise sciences, sports admin. **Philosophy/religion:** Philosophy, religion. **Physical sciences:** Astronomy, atmospheric science, chemistry, geology, materials science, physics. **Psychology:** General. **Social sciences:** Anthropology, economics, geography, political science, sociology. **Visual/performing arts:** Acting, art history/conservation, crafts, dance, directing/producing, dramatic, film/cinema/video, graphic design, jazz, music, music history, music performance, music theory/composition, painting, photography, sculpture, studio arts, theater history, voice/opera. **Work/family studies:** Child development, consumer economics, family studies, human nutrition.

Most popular majors. Agriculture 6%, biology 7%, business/marketing 11%, communications/journalism 8%, engineering/engineering technologies 14%, psychology 7%, social sciences 11%.

Computing on campus. Dormitories wired for high-speed internet access and linked to campus network. Commuter students can connect to campus network. Online course registration, online library, helpline, repair service, student web hosting, wireless network available.

Student life. Freshman orientation: Mandatory. Preregistration for classes offered. One-day program, held end of May through July. **Policies:** Freshmen required to live on campus (or campus-approved housing) unless over 21 years, married, or living with parents. **Housing:** Guaranteed on-campus for freshmen. Coed dorms, single-sex dorms, special housing for disabled, apartments, cooperative housing, fraternity/sorority housing, wellness housing available. $150 fully refundable deposit, deadline 5/15. Living/learning communities available. **Activities:** Bands, campus ministries, choral groups, dance, drama, film society, international student organizations, literary magazine, music ensembles, Model UN, musical theater, opera, radio station, student government, student newspaper, symphony orchestra, TV station, more than 1,000 registered student organizations.

Athletics. NCAA. **Intercollegiate:** Baseball M, basketball, cheerleading, cross-country, diving W, football (tackle) M, golf, gymnastics, soccer W, softball W, swimming W, tennis, track and field, volleyball W, wrestling M. **Intramural:** Badminton, basketball, cross-country, diving, football (non-tackle), football (tackle) M, golf, racquetball, soccer, softball W, tennis, volleyball, wrestling M. **Team name:** Fighting Illini.

Student services. Alcohol/substance abuse counseling, career counseling, services for economically disadvantaged, student employment services, financial aid counseling, health services, legal services, minority student services, on-campus daycare, personal counseling, placement for graduates, veterans' counselor, women's services. **Physically disabled:** Services for visually, speech, hearing impaired.

Contact. E-mail: admissions@illinois.edu
Phone: (217) 333-0302 Fax: (217) 244-4614
Stacey Kostell, Director of Undergraduate Admissions, University of Illinois at Urbana-Champaign, 901 West Illinois, Urbana, IL 61801-3028

University of Illinois: Springfield
Springfield, Illinois
www.uis.edu

CB member
CB code: 0834

- Public 4-year university and liberal arts college
- Commuter campus in small city
- 3,012 degree-seeking undergraduates: 33% part-time, 52% women, 11% African American, 3% Asian American, 4% Hispanic American, 1% international
- 1,844 degree-seeking graduate students
- 60% of applicants admitted
- SAT or ACT (ACT writing optional) required
- 61% graduate within 6 years

General. Founded in 1969. Regionally accredited. Smallest campus of University of Illinois system. **Degrees:** 719 bachelor's awarded; master's, doctoral offered. **Location:** 95 miles from St. Louis, 200 miles from Chicago. **Calendar:** Semester, extensive summer session. **Full-time faculty:** 208 total; 18% minority, 44% women. **Part-time faculty:** 150 total; 9% minority, 47% women. **Class size:** 51% < 20, 46% 20-39, 3% 40-49, less than 1% 50-99. **Special facilities:** Observatory, studio theater.

Freshman class profile. 1,243 applied, 747 admitted, 241 enrolled.

Mid 50% test scores		Rank in top quarter:	46%
ACT composite:	20-26	Rank in top tenth:	15%
GPA 3.75 or higher:	32%	Return as sophomores:	75%
GPA 3.50-3.74:	14%	Out-of-state:	6%
GPA 3.0-3.49:	30%	Live on campus:	82%
GPA 2.0-2.99:	24%	International:	3%

Basis for selection. GPA, rank, record, completion of college-prepatory program, recommendations, admission test scores, and formal demonstration of competencies all fully considered. Personal or telephone interview may be required.

High school preparation. College-preparatory program required. Required units include English 4, mathematics 3, social studies 3, science 3 (laboratory 2) and foreign language 2. Fine arts can be substituted for foreign language.

2011-2012 Annual costs. Tuition/fees: $10,408; $19,558 out-of-state. Health Insurance: $568; refundable fees: $8. Room/board: $9,670.

2010-2011 Financial aid. Need-based: 280 full-time freshmen applied for aid; 223 were judged to have need; 222 of these received aid. Average need met was 72%. Average scholarship/grant was $9,840; average loan $3,152. 45% of total undergraduate aid awarded as scholarships/grants, 55% as loans/jobs. **Non-need-based:** Awarded to 466 full-time undergraduates, including 125 freshmen. Scholarships awarded for academics, alumni affiliation, art, athletics, job skills, leadership, minority status, music/drama, state residency.

Application procedures. Admission: Priority date 5/1; no deadline. $50 fee, may be waived for applicants with need. Admission notification on a rolling basis beginning on or about 9/15. It is requested that students reply as soon as possible after notification of admissions decision. **Financial aid:** Priority date 3/1, closing date 11/15. FAFSA required. Applicants notified on a rolling basis starting 1/1; must reply within 3 week(s) of notification.

Academics. Special study options: Distance learning, ESL, honors, independent study, internships, study abroad, teacher certification program. **Credit/placement by examination:** AP, CLEP, IB, ACT, institutional tests. 30 credit hours maximum toward bachelor's degree. **Support services:** Learning center, reduced course load, remedial instruction, study skills assistance, tutoring, writing center.

Majors. Biology: General. **Business:** Accounting, business admin, management information systems. **Communications:** General. **Computer sciences:** Computer science. **English:** English lit. **Health services:** Clinical lab science. **History:** General. **Human services:** Social work. **Liberal arts:** Arts/sciences. **Math:** General. **Philosophy/religion:** Philosophy. **Physical sciences:** Chemistry. **Protective services:** Criminal justice. **Psychology:** General. **Social sciences:** Economics, political science, sociology/anthropology. **Visual/performing arts:** Studio arts.

Most popular majors. Business/marketing 30%, communications/journalism 7%, computer/information sciences 8%, liberal arts 6%, psychology 9%, public administration/social services 6%, social sciences 6%.

Computing on campus. 500 workstations in dormitories, library, computer center, student center. Dormitories wired for high-speed internet access and linked to campus network. Commuter students can connect to campus

network. Online course registration, online library, helpline, student web hosting, wireless network available.

Student life. Freshman orientation: Mandatory. Preregistration for classes offered. **Housing:** Guaranteed on-campus for freshmen. Coed dorms, special housing for disabled, apartments, wellness housing available. $200 partly refundable deposit. Family housing available. **Activities:** Bands, campus ministries, choral groups, dance, drama, film society, international student organizations, literary magazine, music ensembles, Model UN, radio station, student government, student newspaper, Christian student fellowship, ACLU, Indian student organization, Habitat for Humanity, Living Word Bible Study, College Democrats, College Republicans, Queer Straight Alliance.

Athletics. NCAA. **Intercollegiate:** Baseball M, basketball, golf, soccer, softball W, tennis, volleyball W. **Intramural:** Badminton, basketball, football (non-tackle), racquetball, soccer, softball, squash, volleyball. **Team name:** Prairie Stars.

Student services. Alcohol/substance abuse counseling, career counseling, student employment services, financial aid counseling, health services, minority student services, on-campus daycare, personal counseling, veterans' counselor, women's services. **Physically disabled:** Services for visually, speech, hearing impaired.

Contact. E-mail: admissions@uis.edu
Phone: (217) 206-4847 Toll-free number: (800) 977-4847
Fax: (217) 206-6620
Lori Giordano, Associate Director of Admissions, University of Illinois: Springfield, One University Plaza, MS UHB 1080, Springfield, IL 62703

University of Phoenix: Chicago
Schaumburg, Illinois
www.phoenix.edu

- For-profit 4-year university
- Very large city
- 1,356 degree-seeking undergraduates

General. Regionally accredited. **Degrees:** 183 bachelor's awarded; master's offered. **Calendar:** Differs by program. **Full-time faculty:** 21 total. **Part-time faculty:** 239 total.

Basis for selection. Open admission.

2011-2012 Annual costs. Estimated costs as of August 2011: per-credit-hour charge, $420 to $450, depending upon level and course of study; electronic course materials fee, $95, if applicable. Book and material charges may vary by course and program. All fees are subject to change.

Application procedures. Admission: No deadline. No application fee. **Financial aid:** No deadline.

Academics. Credit/placement by examination: AP, CLEP.

Majors. Business: General, accounting, management science, marketing. **Computer sciences:** Information technology, webmaster. **Protective services:** Law enforcement admin.

Contact. Marc Booker, Director of Admission and Evaluation, University of Phoenix: Chicago, 1500 McConnor Parkway, Schaumburg, IL 60173

University of St. Francis
Joliet, Illinois
www.stfrancis.edu   CB code: 1130

- Private 4-year university and liberal arts college affiliated with Roman Catholic Church
- Commuter campus in small city
- 1,379 degree-seeking undergraduates: 3% part-time, 68% women, 7% African American, 2% Asian American, 14% Hispanic American, 1% international
- 827 degree-seeking graduate students
- 45% of applicants admitted
- SAT or ACT (ACT writing optional) required
- 63% graduate within 6 years; 27% enter graduate study

General. Founded in 1920. Regionally accredited. **Degrees:** 261 bachelor's awarded; master's, doctoral offered. **ROTC:** Army. **Location:** 35 miles from Chicago. **Calendar:** Semester, extensive summer session. **Full-time faculty:** 90 total; 70% have terminal degrees, 17% minority, 57% women. **Part-time faculty:** 158 total; 23% have terminal degrees, 11% minority, 52% women. **Class size:** 62% < 20, 37% 20-39, 1% 40-49. **Special facilities:** Performing arts center, greenhouse, health and wellness center operated by nursing faculty and students, arthouse for visual arts majors.

Freshman class profile. 1,482 applied, 662 admitted, 180 enrolled.

Mid 50% test scores			
SAT critical reading:	420-490	GPA 2.0-2.99:	29%
SAT math:	490-520	Rank in top quarter:	44%
SAT writing:	380-480	Rank in top tenth:	19%
ACT composite:	21-25	End year in good standing:	90%
GPA 3.75 or higher:	17%	Return as sophomores:	79%
GPA 3.50-3.74:	14%	Out-of-state:	9%
GPA 3.0-3.49:	40%	Live on campus:	59%
		International:	1%

Basis for selection. High school GPA and rank, test scores important. Essay and letters of recommendation required and interview recommended for students who do not meet admissions requirements.

High school preparation. College-preparatory program required. 17 units required. Required units include English 4, mathematics 3, social studies 2, science 2 (laboratory 1) and academic electives 3. 3 units required from 2 areas: foreign language, music/art, or computer science.

2011-2012 Annual costs. Tuition/fees: $25,932. Room/board: $8,462.

2011-2012 Financial aid. Need-based: 174 full-time freshmen applied for aid; 155 were judged to have need; 155 of these received aid. Average need met was 68%. Average scholarship/grant was $9,278; average loan $3,621. 76% of total undergraduate aid awarded as scholarships/grants, 24% as loans/jobs. **Non-need-based:** Awarded to 1,355 full-time undergraduates, including 185 freshmen. Scholarships awarded for academics, alumni affiliation, art, athletics, leadership, music/drama, religious affiliation, state residency.

Application procedures. Admission: Priority date 5/1; deadline 8/1 (receipt date). No application fee. Admission notification on a rolling basis beginning on or about 9/15. Must reply by 5/1. **Financial aid:** Priority date 3/15; no closing date. FAFSA, institutional form required. Applicants notified on a rolling basis starting 2/15.

Academics. Special study options: Combined bachelor's/graduate degree, cross-registration, distance learning, double major, dual enrollment of high school students, honors, independent study, internships, student-designed major, study abroad, teacher certification program, Washington semester. **Credit/placement by examination:** AP, CLEP, IB, SAT, ACT, institutional tests. 33 credit hours maximum toward bachelor's degree. **Support services:** Learning center, pre-admission summer program, reduced course load, remedial instruction, study skills assistance, tutoring, writing center.

Majors. Biology: General. **Business:** Accounting, actuarial science, business admin, finance, human resources, management science, marketing, organizational behavior. **Communications:** Advertising, broadcast journalism, media studies, public relations, radio/TV. **Computer sciences:** Computer science, information technology, webmaster. **Conservation:** Environmental science. **Education:** Art, elementary, English, mathematics, music, science, social studies, special ed. **English:** English lit. **Health services:** Clinical lab science, health care admin, medical radiologic technology/radiation therapy, nuclear medical technology, nursing (RN), predental, premedicine, prepharmacy, prephysical therapy, preveterinary, radiologic technology/medical imaging, recreational therapy. **History:** General. **Human services:** Social work. **Liberal arts:** Arts/sciences. **Math:** General. **Parks/recreation:** Facilities management. **Protective services:** Law enforcement admin. **Psychology:** General. **Social sciences:** Political science. **Theology:** Theology. **Visual/performing arts:** General, music, music performance.

Most popular majors. Biology 6%, business/marketing 11%, education 17%, health sciences 30%.

Computing on campus. 446 workstations in dormitories, library, computer center, student center. Dormitories wired for high-speed internet access and linked to campus network. Commuter students can connect to campus network. Online course registration, online library, helpline, wireless network available.

Student life. Freshman orientation: Mandatory, $120 fee. Preregistration for classes offered. **Policies:** Visitation between 9am and 2am. Marian Hall is alcohol-free. All halls close during major breaks (fall break, winter break, spring break) unless special permission received to remain in hall. **Housing:** Guaranteed on-campus for freshmen. Coed dorms, apartments, wellness housing available. $50 fully refundable deposit, deadline 5/1. **Activities:** Campus ministries, choral groups, drama, international student organizations, literary magazine, music ensembles, musical theater, opera, radio station, student government, student newspaper, symphony orchestra, TV station, ethnic affairs council, Fellowship of Christian Athletes, Council for Environmental

and Scientific Awareness, Council for Social Activism, mock trial, Pro-Life Group, social work club, Spectrum, student nurses organization, Unidos Vamos a Alcanzar.

Athletics. NAIA. **Intercollegiate:** Baseball M, basketball, cheerleading M, cross-country, football (tackle) M, golf, soccer, softball W, tennis, track and field, volleyball W. **Intramural:** Basketball, bowling, volleyball. **Team name:** Saints.

Student services. Adult student services, chaplain/spiritual director, career counseling, student employment services, financial aid counseling, health services, minority student services, personal counseling, placement for graduates. **Physically disabled:** Services for visually, speech, hearing impaired.

Contact. E-mail: admissions@stfrancis.edu
Phone: (815) 740-5037 Toll-free number: (800) 735-7500
Fax: (815) 740-3431
Julie Marlatt, Director Undergraduate Admissions, University of St. Francis, 500 Wilcox Street, Joliet, IL 60435

VanderCook College of Music
Chicago, Illinois
www.vandercook.edu   CB code: 1872

♦ Private 4-year music and teachers college
♦ Residential campus in very large city
♦ 134 degree-seeking undergraduates: 6% part-time, 51% women
♦ 53 degree-seeking graduate students
♦ Application essay, interview required
♦ 45% graduate within 6 years

General. Founded in 1909. Regionally accredited. Students have full access to student services at Illinois Institute of Technology. **Degrees:** 22 bachelor's awarded; master's offered. **Location:** Located in central Chicago, three miles south of downtown. **Calendar:** Semester. **Full-time faculty:** 10 total; 50% have terminal degrees, 30% minority, 60% women. **Part-time faculty:** 23 total; 17% have terminal degrees, 39% women. **Class size:** 69% < 20, 24% 20-39, 1% 40-49, 1% 50-99, 4% >100. **Special facilities:** MIDI/electronic music laboratory; archival collection of recordings, photographs, sheet music, and materials from early 20th century to present.

Freshman class profile. 21 enrolled.

Mid 50% test scores			
ACT composite:	19-26	Rank in top quarter:	44%
GPA 3.75 or higher:	14%	Rank in top tenth:	22%
GPA 3.50-3.74:	34%	Return as sophomores:	82%
GPA 3.0-3.49:	28%	Out-of-state:	14%
GPA 2.0-2.99:	24%	Live on campus:	67%

Basis for selection. Academic credentials, SAT or ACT scores and recommendations are weighed along with student's musical audition and interview. Audition required. **Home schooled:** Should obtain experience performing with a concert band or chorus. Minimum of three credits of music recommended.

High school preparation. College-preparatory program recommended. 15 units recommended. Recommended units include English 3, mathematics 2, social studies 3, science 2, foreign language 2 and academic electives 3. Art may be substituted for foreign language.

2011-2012 Annual costs. Tuition/fees: $23,190. Room/board: $10,464. Books/supplies: $1,900. Personal expenses: $2,310.

2010-2011 Financial aid. Need-based: 21 full-time freshmen applied for aid; 21 were judged to have need; 21 of these received aid. Average scholarship/grant was $6,566; average loan $3,514. 57% of total undergraduate aid awarded as scholarships/grants, 43% as loans/jobs. **Non-need-based:** Awarded to 81 full-time undergraduates, including 22 freshmen. Scholarships awarded for academics, music/drama. **Additional information:** Musical talent considered for partial tuition waiver.

Application procedures. Admission: Priority date 4/1; no deadline. $35 fee. Application must be submitted on paper. Admission notification on a rolling basis. Accepted candidates should submit non-refundable tuition deposit of $100 by May 1 as indication of intent to enroll. **Financial aid:** Priority date 4/1; no closing date. FAFSA required. Applicants notified on a rolling basis starting 5/1; must reply within 2 week(s) of notification.

Academics. Special study options: Teacher certification program. **Credit/placement by examination:** AP, CLEP, IB, SAT, ACT, institutional tests. 18 credit hours maximum toward bachelor's degree. **Support services:** Remedial instruction, tutoring.

Majors. Education: Music.

Computing on campus. 21 workstations in dormitories, library, computer center, student center. Dormitories wired for high-speed internet access and linked to campus network. Commuter students can connect to campus network. Wireless network available.

Student life. Freshman orientation: Mandatory. Preregistration for classes offered. **Housing:** Guaranteed on-campus for all undergraduates. Coed dorms, apartments, fraternity/sorority housing available. Apartments for single students over 23 available. **Activities:** Bands, choral groups, music ensembles, musical theater, radio station.

Student services. Career counseling, student employment services, health services, personal counseling, placement for graduates.

Contact. E-mail: admissions@vandercook.edu
Phone: (312) 225-6288 ext. 230 Fax: (312) 225-5211
Amy Lenting, Director of Admissions and Retention, VanderCook College of Music, 3140 South Federal Street, Chicago, IL 60616-3731

Western Illinois University
Macomb, Illinois
www.wiu.edu   CB code: 1900

♦ Public 4-year university
♦ Residential campus in large town
♦ 10,518 degree-seeking undergraduates: 9% part-time, 48% women, 14% African American, 1% Asian American, 6% Hispanic American, 1% international
♦ 1,936 degree-seeking graduate students
♦ 66% of applicants admitted
♦ SAT or ACT (ACT writing optional) required
♦ 53% graduate within 6 years

General. Founded in 1899. Regionally accredited. **Degrees:** 2,413 bachelor's awarded; master's, doctoral offered. **ROTC:** Army. **Location:** 83 miles from Rock Island, 78 miles from Peoria. **Calendar:** Semester, limited summer session. **Full-time faculty:** 666 total; 72% have terminal degrees, 16% minority, 45% women. **Part-time faculty:** 65 total; 25% have terminal degrees, 14% minority, 42% women. **Class size:** 43% < 20, 47% 20-39, 6% 40-49, 4% 50-99, less than 1% >100. **Special facilities:** Geology museum, life sciences station, 92-acre nature retreat, university farm.

Freshman class profile. 9,731 applied, 6,384 admitted, 1,955 enrolled.

Mid 50% test scores			
ACT composite:	18-23	Rank in top quarter:	26%
GPA 3.75 or higher:	10%	Rank in top tenth:	8%
GPA 3.50-3.74:	9%	End year in good standing:	84%
GPA 3.0-3.49:	26%	Return as sophomores:	71%
GPA 2.0-2.99:	55%	Out-of-state:	6%
		Live on campus:	89%

Basis for selection. Standardized test scores very important. Audition required for music majors. **Home schooled:** Transcript of courses and grades required.

High school preparation. College-preparatory program recommended. 15 units recommended. Recommended units include English 4, mathematics 3, social studies 3, science 3 and academic electives 2. 2 units of art, film, foreign language, music, speech, theater, journalism, religion, philosophy or vocational education also recommended.

2011-2012 Annual costs. Tuition/fees: $9,981; $13,805 out-of-state. Room/board: $8,460.

2011-2012 Financial aid. Need-based: 1,660 full-time freshmen applied for aid; 1,445 were judged to have need; 1,410 of these received aid. Average need met was 53%. Average scholarship/grant was $8,643; average loan $3,428. 52% of total undergraduate aid awarded as scholarships/grants, 48% as loans/jobs. **Non-need-based:** Awarded to 536 full-time undergraduates, including 107 freshmen. Scholarships awarded for academics, alumni affiliation, art, athletics, leadership, minority status, music/drama, ROTC.

Application procedures. Admission: Priority date 5/15; no deadline. $30 fee. Admission notification on a rolling basis. **Financial aid:** No deadline. FAFSA required. Applicants notified on a rolling basis starting 1/15.

Academics. Special study options: Combined bachelor's/graduate degree, distance learning, double major, dual enrollment of high school students, ESL, external degree, honors, independent study, internships, student-designed major, study abroad, teacher certification program, weekend college. **Credit/placement by examination:** AP, CLEP, IB. 30 credit hours maximum

toward bachelor's degree. **Support services:** Remedial instruction, study skills assistance, tutoring, writing center.

Honors college/program. 28 ACT or upper 10% of class and 24 ACT.

Majors. Area/ethnic studies: African-American, women's. **Biology:** General. **Business:** Accounting, business admin, construction management, finance, human resources, logistics, management information systems, managerial economics, marketing. **Communications:** Communications/speech/rhetoric, journalism, radio/TV. **Communications technology:** Graphic/printing. **Computer sciences:** General, networking. **Education:** Bilingual, educational technology, elementary, health, special ed. **Engineering:** Electrical. **English:** English lit. **Foreign languages:** French, Spanish. **Health services:** Athletic training, clinical lab science, communication disorders, health care admin, nursing (RN). **History:** General. **Human services:** Social work. **Liberal arts:** Arts/sciences. **Math:** General. **Parks/recreation:** Exercise sciences, facilities management. **Philosophy/religion:** Philosophy, religion. **Physical sciences:** Chemistry, forensic chemistry, geology, meteorology, physics. **Protective services:** Homeland security, law enforcement admin. **Psychology:** General. **Social sciences:** Economics, geography, political science, sociology. **Visual/performing arts:** Art, dramatic, music, music performance, musical theater, studio arts. **Work/family studies:** General.

Most popular majors. Agriculture 6%, biology 6%, business/marketing 12%, communications/journalism 6%, education 9%, liberal arts 12%, security/protective services 14%.

Computing on campus. 1,000 workstations in dormitories, library, computer center. Dormitories wired for high-speed internet access and linked to campus network. Commuter students can connect to campus network. Online course registration, online library, helpline, wireless network available.

Student life. Freshman orientation: Mandatory. Preregistration for classes offered. Held week prior to beginning of classes. **Housing:** Guaranteed on-campus for all undergraduates. Coed dorms, single-sex dorms, apartments, fraternity/sorority housing, wellness housing available. $100 partly refundable deposit. **Activities:** Bands, choral groups, dance, drama, music ensembles, musical theater, radio station, student government, student newspaper, symphony orchestra, TV station, 67 special-interest organizations, 5 service organizations, 14 religious organizations, 32 national honorary and professional fraternities.

Athletics. NCAA. **Intercollegiate:** Baseball M, basketball, cheerleading, cross-country, diving, football (tackle) M, golf, soccer, softball W, swimming, tennis, track and field, volleyball W. **Intramural:** Badminton, basketball, bowling, cross-country, football (non-tackle), football (tackle) M, golf, handball, lacrosse M, racquetball, rugby, skin diving, soccer, softball, swimming, table tennis, tennis, volleyball, water polo. **Team name:** Leathernecks.

Student services. Adult student services, alcohol/substance abuse counseling, career counseling, student employment services, financial aid counseling, health services, legal services, minority student services, on-campus daycare, personal counseling, placement for graduates, veterans' counselor, women's services. **Physically disabled:** Services for visually, speech, hearing impaired.

Contact. E-mail: wiuadm@wiu.edu
Phone: (309) 298-3157 Toll-free number: (877) 742-5948
Fax: (309) 298-3111
Andrew Borst, Director of Admissions, Western Illinois University, One University Circle, Macomb, IL 61455-1390

Westwood College: Chicago Loop
Chicago, Illinois
www.westwood.edu

- For-profit 4-year technical college
- Commuter campus in very large city

General. Regionally accredited. **Calendar:** Differs by program.

Annual costs/financial aid. Tuition/fees (2011-2012): $15,020. Books/supplies: $1,106.

Contact. Phone: (312) 739-0850
Director of Admissions, 17 North State Street, Third Floor, Chicago, IL 60602

Westwood College: DuPage
Woodridge, Illinois
www.westwood.edu   CB code: 5096

- For-profit 4-year technical college
- Commuter campus in large city
- 437 undergraduates
- Interview required

General. Regionally accredited; also accredited by ACICS. **Degrees:** 80 bachelor's, 11 associate awarded. **Location:** 20 miles from downtown Chicago. **Calendar:** Quarter. **Full-time faculty:** 6 total. **Part-time faculty:** 73 total.

Basis for selection. Successful completion of Accuplacer test required prior to admission; SAT/ACT scores may be used in lieu of Accuplacer. SAT or ACT recommended.

2011-2012 Annual costs. Tuition/fees: $15,020. Books/supplies: $1,106.

Application procedures. Admission: No deadline. $50 fee.

Academics. Special study options: Accelerated study, independent study. **Credit/placement by examination:** AP, CLEP, institutional tests.

Majors. Business: Business admin. **Computer sciences:** Security, webmaster. **Protective services:** Criminal justice. **Visual/performing arts:** Game design, interior design.

Student life. Activities: Student government.

Contact. Phone: (630) 434-8244 Toll-free number: (866) 721-7646
Fax: (630) 743-0667
Scott Kawall, Director of Admissions, Westwood College: DuPage, 7155 Janes Avenue, Woodridge, IL 60517

Westwood College: O'Hare Airport
Chicago, Illinois
www.westwood.edu

- For-profit 4-year technical and career college
- Commuter campus in very large city
- 655 undergraduates
- Application essay, interview required

General. Regionally accredited; also accredited by ACICS. **Degrees:** 137 bachelor's, 11 associate awarded. **Location:** Downtown. **Calendar:** Differs by program, extensive summer session. **Full-time faculty:** 16 total. **Part-time faculty:** 85 total. **Special facilities:** Graphic design finishing room, information systems security laboratory, interior design resource room, medical assisting laboratory, computer assisted drawing and design laboratory, game software design laboratory, animation and visual communication laboratory.

Basis for selection. Placement test and letter of intent required. Assessment given to all students; passing score required for admission to college programs.

2011-2012 Annual costs. Tuition/fees: $15,020. Books/supplies: $1,106. Personal expenses: $400.

Application procedures. Admission: No deadline. $50 fee. Application must be submitted on paper. **Financial aid:** Priority date 3/1, closing date 6/30. FAFSA, institutional form required.

Academics. Special study options: Accelerated study, cooperative education, distance learning, double major, independent study, internships, liberal arts/career combination, study abroad. **Credit/placement by examination:** AP, CLEP, institutional tests. **Support services:** Learning center, reduced course load, remedial instruction, study skills assistance, tutoring, writing center.

Majors. Business: Marketing. **Communications technology:** Animation/special effects. **Computer sciences:** Security. **Health services:** Facilities admin, office admin. **Human services:** General, community org/advocacy, public policy. **Protective services:** Correctional facilities, corrections, criminal justice, criminalistics, forensics, juvenile corrections, law enforcement admin, police science, security management, security services. **Social sciences:** Criminology. **Visual/performing arts:** Design, graphic design, interior design.

Computing on campus. Commuter students can connect to campus network. Online library, wireless network available.

Student life. Freshman orientation: Mandatory. Preregistration for classes offered. **Housing:** Wellness housing available. **Activities:** Student government, student newspaper.

Student services. Adult student services, alcohol/substance abuse counseling, career counseling, student employment services, financial aid counseling, minority student services, personal counseling, placement for graduates, veterans' counselor, women's services. **Physically disabled:** Services for visually, hearing impaired.

Contact. E-mail: skasem@westwood.edu
Phone: (773) 380-6800 Toll-free number: (877) 877-8857
Fax: (773) 714-0828
Shahed Kasem, Director of Admissions, Westwood College: O'Hare Airport, 8501 West Higgins Road, Chicago, IL 60631

Westwood College: River Oaks
Calumet City, Illinois
www.westwood.edu

- For-profit 4-year career college
- Commuter campus in very large city
- 523 undergraduates

General. Regionally accredited; also accredited by ACICS. **Degrees:** 52 bachelor's, 4 associate awarded. **Calendar:** Differs by program, limited summer session. **Full-time faculty:** 11 total. **Part-time faculty:** 65 total.

Basis for selection. Must pass institutional admissions test.

2011-2012 Annual costs. Tuition/fees: $15,020. Books/supplies: $1,106.

Application procedures. Admission: No deadline. $50 fee.

Academics. Credit/placement by examination: AP, CLEP.

Contact. Phone: (708) 832-1988
Gus Pyroulis, Director of Admissions, Westwood College: River Oaks, 80 River Oaks Center Drive, Suite D-49, Calumet City, IL 60409-5802

Wheaton College
Wheaton, Illinois
www.wheaton.edu
CB member
CB code: 1905

- Private 4-year liberal arts college affiliated with nondenominational tradition
- Residential campus in small city
- 2,410 degree-seeking undergraduates: 2% part-time, 50% women, 3% African American, 8% Asian American, 4% Hispanic American, 1% international
- 452 degree-seeking graduate students
- 65% of applicants admitted
- SAT or ACT with writing, application essay required
- 87% graduate within 6 years; 28% enter graduate study

General. Founded in 1860. Regionally accredited. **Degrees:** 612 bachelor's awarded; master's, professional, doctoral offered. **ROTC:** Army, Air Force. **Location:** 25 miles from Chicago. **Calendar:** Semester, limited summer session. **Full-time faculty:** 197 total; 98% have terminal degrees, 11% minority, 31% women. **Part-time faculty:** 75 total; 51% have terminal degrees, 9% minority, 48% women. **Class size:** 58% < 20, 29% 20-39, 7% 40-49, 4% 50-99, 1% >100.

Freshman class profile. 2,050 applied, 1,327 admitted, 596 enrolled.

Mid 50% test scores		GPA 2.0-2.99:	2%
SAT critical reading:	610-710	Rank in top quarter:	81%
SAT math:	610-690	Rank in top tenth:	50%
SAT writing:	600-700	Return as sophomores:	95%
ACT composite:	27-32	Out-of-state:	76%
GPA 3.75 or higher:	55%	Live on campus:	100%
GPA 3.50-3.74:	26%	International:	2%
GPA 3.0-3.49:	17%		

Basis for selection. Evidence of a vital Christian experience, moral character, personal integrity, social concern, academic ability, and desire for a liberal arts education as defined by the college are most important. Interview recommended. Audition required of music majors. **Home schooled:** Statement describing home school structure and mission required. Applicants advised to take the ACT to satisfy the "Ability to Benefit" requirements. **Learning Disabled:** Personal interview required at enrollment. Must contact Academic Support Coordinator to request services or equipment and provide documentation/diagnosis of disability.

High school preparation. College-preparatory program required. 18 units required. Required and recommended units include English 4, mathematics 4, social studies 4, science 4 and foreign language 3.

2011-2012 Annual costs. Tuition/fees: $28,960. Room/board: $8,220. Books/supplies: $800. Personal expenses: $2,000.

2010-2011 Financial aid. Need-based: 443 full-time freshmen applied for aid; 323 were judged to have need; 323 of these received aid. Average need met was 87%. Average scholarship/grant was $17,542; average loan $4,598. 74% of total undergraduate aid awarded as scholarships/grants, 26% as loans/jobs. **Non-need-based:** Awarded to 724 full-time undergraduates, including 207 freshmen. Scholarships awarded for academics, alumni affiliation, art, minority status, music/drama. **Additional information:** First $500 to $2,000 of need awarded as grant instead of loan.

Application procedures. Admission: Closing date 1/10 (receipt date). $50 fee, may be waived for applicants with need. Admission notification by 4/1. Must reply by May 1 or within 2 week(s) if notified thereafter. **Financial aid:** Priority date 2/15; no closing date. FAFSA, institutional form, CSS PROFILE required. Applicants notified on a rolling basis starting 3/10.

Academics. Special study options: Combined bachelor's/graduate degree, cross-registration, double major, exchange student, independent study, internships, liberal arts/career combination, student-designed major, study abroad, teacher certification program, urban semester, Washington semester. **Credit/placement by examination:** AP, CLEP, IB, SAT, ACT, institutional tests. 76 credit hours maximum toward bachelor's degree. **Support services:** Study skills assistance, tutoring, writing center.

Majors. Biology: General. **Business:** Managerial economics. **Communications:** Communications/speech/rhetoric. **Computer sciences:** Computer science. **Conservation:** Environmental studies. **Education:** Elementary, music, secondary, social studies. **Engineering:** General. **English:** English lit. **Foreign languages:** Classics, French, German, Spanish. **Health services:** Nursing (RN). **History:** General. **Math:** General. **Philosophy/religion:** Philosophy. **Physical sciences:** Chemistry, geology, physics. **Psychology:** General. **Social sciences:** Anthropology, archaeology, economics, international relations, political science, sociology. **Theology:** Bible, religious ed. **Visual/performing arts:** Art, music, music history, music performance, music theory/composition.

Most popular majors. Business/marketing 8%, communications/journalism 7%, English 9%, health sciences 8%, social sciences 15%, theological studies 10%, visual/performing arts 8%.

Computing on campus. 125 workstations in dormitories, library, computer center, student center. Dormitories wired for high-speed internet access and linked to campus network. Commuter students can connect to campus network. Online library, helpline, wireless network available.

Student life. Freshman orientation: Mandatory. Preregistration for classes offered. Five-day program during week before classes begin. Optional pre-orientation offered during the 2-weeks before orientation begins. **Policies:** All college and college-related functions are alcohol and tobacco free. Religious observance required. Freshmen not permitted cars on campus. **Housing:** Guaranteed on-campus for freshmen. Coed dorms, single-sex dorms, special housing for disabled, apartments, cooperative housing available. **Activities:** Bands, campus ministries, choral groups, dance, drama, film society, international student organizations, literary magazine, music ensembles, Model UN, musical theater, opera, radio station, student government, student newspaper, symphony orchestra, TV station, Christian Service Council, Gospel Choir, Honduras Project, International Justice Mission, Solidarity Cabinet, Justice Coalition, College Republicans, College Democrats, World Christian Fellowship.

Athletics. NCAA. **Intercollegiate:** Baseball M, basketball, cross-country, football (tackle) M, golf, soccer, softball W, swimming, tennis, track and field, volleyball W, water polo W, wrestling M. **Intramural:** Basketball, football (non-tackle) M, golf, soccer, softball M, volleyball. **Team name:** Thunder.

Student services. Chaplain/spiritual director, career counseling, student employment services, financial aid counseling, health services, minority student services, personal counseling, placement for graduates, veterans' counselor. **Physically disabled:** Services for visually, speech, hearing impaired.

Contact. E-mail: admissions@wheaton.edu
Phone: (630) 752-5006 Toll-free number: (800) 222-2419
Fax: (630) 752-5285
Shawn Leftwich, Director of Undergraduate Admissions, Wheaton
College, 501 College Avenue, Wheaton, IL 60187-5593

Indiana

Anderson University

Anderson, Indiana
www.anderson.edu

CB member
CB code: 1016

- Private 4-year liberal arts college affiliated with Church of God
- Residential campus in small city
- 2,025 degree-seeking undergraduates: 6% part-time, 58% women, 6% African American, 2% Hispanic American, 3% international
- 560 degree-seeking graduate students
- 56% of applicants admitted
- SAT or ACT with writing required
- 63% graduate within 6 years

General. Founded in 1917. Regionally accredited. **Degrees:** 377 bachelor's, 3 associate awarded; master's, doctoral offered. **Location:** 45 miles from Indianapolis. **Calendar:** Semester, limited summer session. **Full-time faculty:** 135 total; 70% have terminal degrees, 5% minority, 40% women. **Part-time faculty:** 118 total; less than 1% have terminal degrees, 10% minority, 49% women. **Class size:** 66% < 20, 29% 20-39, 3% 40-49, 1% 50-99, less than 1% >100. **Special facilities:** Religious art collection, museum of Bible and Near Eastern studies, glass studio, wellness center.

Freshman class profile. 3,079 applied, 1,736 admitted, 506 enrolled.

Mid 50% test scores			
SAT critical reading:	460-570	Rank in top quarter:	50%
SAT math:	480-590	Rank in top tenth:	23%
ACT composite:	22-26	End year in good standing:	87%
GPA 3.75 or higher:	28%	Return as sophomores:	79%
GPA 3.50-3.74:	15%	Out-of-state:	25%
GPA 3.0-3.49:	36%	Live on campus:	90%
GPA 2.0-2.99:	21%	International:	4%

Basis for selection. Rank in top half of class, test scores, reference important. School, church, and community activities also considered. Additional requirements for nursing, athletic training, and educational programs. Essay recommended. Interview required of academically weak applicants. Audition required of music majors. Portfolio recommended for art majors. **Home schooled:** Interview may be required.

High school preparation. College-preparatory program required. 17 units required; 30 recommended. Required and recommended units include English 4, mathematics 3-4, social studies 1-2, history 1-2, science 3-4 (laboratory 3-4), foreign language 2-3, computer science 1, visual/performing arts 1 and academic electives 5.

2011-2012 Annual costs. Tuition/fees: $24,610. Room/board: $8,560. Books/supplies: $1,050. Personal expenses: $1,650.

Financial aid. Non-need-based: Scholarships awarded for academics, alumni affiliation, art, leadership, minority status, music/drama, religious affiliation.

Application procedures. Admission: Priority date 1/15; deadline 7/1. $25 fee, may be waived for applicants with need, free for online applicants. Admission notification on a rolling basis beginning on or about 9/1. Must reply by May 1 or within 2 week(s) if notified thereafter. **Financial aid:** Priority date 3/1; no closing date. FAFSA required. Applicants notified on a rolling basis starting 3/1.

Academics. Special study options: Accelerated study, combined bachelor's/graduate degree, cross-registration, distance learning, double major, dual enrollment of high school students, honors, independent study, internships, student-designed major, study abroad, teacher certification program, urban semester. **Credit/placement by examination:** AP, CLEP, IB, SAT, ACT, institutional tests. 30 credit hours maximum toward bachelor's degree. **Support services:** Learning center, pre-admission summer program, reduced course load, tutoring.

Majors. Biology: General, biochemistry. **Business:** Accounting, business admin, entrepreneurial studies, finance, international, managerial economics, marketing, organizational behavior. **Communications:** Media studies. **Computer sciences:** Computer science, information systems. **Education:** General, art, biology, chemistry, drama/dance, elementary, English, French, mathematics, music, physical, physics, social studies, Spanish. **English:** English lit.

Foreign languages: French, Spanish. **Health services:** Athletic training, nursing (RN). **History:** General. **Human services:** Social work. **Math:** General. **Parks/recreation:** Exercise sciences. **Philosophy/religion:** Philosophy, religion. **Physical sciences:** General, chemistry, physics. **Protective services:** Criminal justice. **Psychology:** General. **Social sciences:** Political science, sociology. **Theology:** Bible, sacred music, theology, youth ministry. **Visual/performing arts:** Dance, design, dramatic, music, music management, music performance, studio arts, voice/opera. **Work/family studies:** Family systems.

Most popular majors. Business/marketing 23%, communications/journalism 7%, education 11%, health sciences 6%, visual/performing arts 7%.

Computing on campus. 338 workstations in dormitories, library, computer center, student center. Dormitories linked to campus network. Commuter students can connect to campus network. Online course registration, wireless network available.

Student life. Freshman orientation: Mandatory. Preregistration for classes offered. **Policies:** Religious observance required. **Housing:** Coed dorms, single-sex dorms, apartments, wellness housing available. $100 nonrefundable deposit, deadline 5/1. **Activities:** Bands, campus ministries, choral groups, dance, drama, international student organizations, literary magazine, music ensembles, Model UN, musical theater, opera, radio station, student government, student newspaper, symphony orchestra, multicultural student union, Religious Life Council, business club, women's clubs, men's clubs.

Athletics. NCAA. **Intercollegiate:** Baseball M, basketball, cross-country, football (tackle) M, golf, soccer, softball W, tennis, track and field, volleyball W. **Intramural:** Badminton, basketball, bowling, soccer, softball, tennis, volleyball. **Team name:** Ravens.

Student services. Adult student services, chaplain/spiritual director, career counseling, student employment services, financial aid counseling, health services, minority student services, personal counseling, placement for graduates, veterans' counselor. **Physically disabled:** Services for visually, speech impaired.

Contact. E-mail: info@anderson.edu
Phone: (765) 641-4080 Toll-free number: (800) 428-6414
Fax: (765) 641-4091
Joe Davis, Director of Admissions, Anderson University, 1100 East Fifth Street, Anderson, IN 46012-3495

Ball State University

Muncie, Indiana
www.bsu.edu

CB member
CB code: 1051

- Public 4-year university
- Residential campus in small city
- 17,143 degree-seeking undergraduates: 6% part-time, 56% women, 6% African American, 1% Asian American, 3% Hispanic American, 2% international
- 4,186 degree-seeking graduate students
- 68% of applicants admitted
- 57% graduate within 6 years; 26% enter graduate study

General. Founded in 1918. Regionally accredited. **Degrees:** 3,173 bachelor's, 446 associate awarded; master's, professional, doctoral offered. **ROTC:** Army. **Location:** 56 miles from Indianapolis. **Calendar:** Semester, extensive summer session. **Full-time faculty:** 938 total; 75% have terminal degrees, 10% minority, 45% women. **Part-time faculty:** 207 total; 30% have terminal degrees, 3% minority, 56% women. **Class size:** 33% < 20, 49% 20-39, 7% 40-49, 7% 50-99, 4% >100. **Special facilities:** Planetarium, nature preserves, wellness institute, art museum, media design center, glass center, student wellness and recreational facility.

Freshman class profile. 14,302 applied, 9,659 admitted, 3,844 enrolled.

Mid 50% test scores			
SAT critical reading:	480-580	Rank in top quarter:	48%
SAT math:	480-580	Rank in top tenth:	17%
SAT writing:	460-560	End year in good standing:	84%
ACT composite:	20-24	Return as sophomores:	79%
GPA 3.75 or higher:	21%	Out-of-state:	13%
GPA 3.50-3.74:	16%	Live on campus:	93%
GPA 3.0-3.49:	39%	Fraternities:	8%
GPA 2.0-2.99:	24%	Sororities:	9%

Basis for selection. High school curriculum, GPA, standardized test scores considered. Credentials of non-traditional students (age 23 or older) evaluated for admission on individual basis. Personal statement required of all non-traditional students. Audition required of music, dance and theater majors; portfolio recommended for art and architecture majors. **Home**

schooled: Statement describing home school structure and mission, transcript of courses and grades required. **Learning Disabled:** Students may self-disclose if they choose.

High school preparation. College-preparatory program required. Required and recommended units include English 4, mathematics 3-4, social studies 3, science 3 (laboratory 2) and foreign language 3. Social studies includes history.

2012-2013 Annual costs. Tuition/fees (projected): $8,980; $23,650 out-of-state. Room/board: $8,714. Books/supplies: $1,020. Personal expenses: $1,630.

2011-2012 Financial aid. **Need-based:** 3,498 full-time freshmen applied for aid; 2,694 were judged to have need; 2,689 of these received aid. Average need met was 50%. Average scholarship/grant was $6,401; average loan $3,507. 47% of total undergraduate aid awarded as scholarships/grants, 53% as loans/jobs. **Non-need-based:** Awarded to 5,990 full-time undergraduates, including 1,924 freshmen. Scholarships awarded for academics, athletics, leadership, minority status, music/drama, ROTC, state residency.

Application procedures. **Admission:** Priority date 3/1; deadline 8/15 (postmark date). $55 fee, may be waived for applicants with need. Admission notification on a rolling basis. Must reply by May 1 or within 2 week(s) if notified thereafter. **Financial aid:** Priority date 3/10; no closing date. FAFSA required. Applicants notified on a rolling basis starting 4/1.

Academics. All undergraduates must meet writing proficiency requirement. **Special study options:** Accelerated study, combined bachelor's/graduate degree, cooperative education, distance learning, double major, dual enrollment of high school students, ESL, external degree, honors, independent study, internships, liberal arts/career combination, student-designed major, study abroad, teacher certification program. **Credit/placement by examination:** AP, CLEP, IB, SAT, ACT, institutional tests. 15 credit hours maximum toward associate degree, 63 toward bachelor's. **Support services:** Learning center, pre-admission summer program, reduced course load, study skills assistance, tutoring, writing center.

Majors. **Architecture:** Architecture, environmental design, landscape, urban/community planning. **Area/ethnic studies:** Women's. **Biology:** General. **Business:** General, accounting, actuarial science, business admin, entrepreneurial studies, finance, human resources, management information systems, managerial economics, marketing, office management, operations. **Communications:** Journalism, radio/TV. **Computer sciences:** General. **Conservation:** General. **Education:** Business, elementary, health, kindergarten/preschool, multiple handicapped, physical, science, technology/industrial arts. **Engineering:** General. **English:** English lit, rhetoric/composition. **Foreign languages:** Classics, French, German, Japanese, Latin, Spanish. **Health services:** Audiology/speech pathology, clinical lab science, dietetics, medical radiologic technology/radiation therapy, nursing (RN), predental, premedicine, respiratory therapy technology. **History:** General. **Human services:** Social work. **Liberal arts:** Arts/sciences, library science. **Math:** General. **Philosophy/religion:** Philosophy, religion. **Physical sciences:** Chemistry, geology, physics. **Protective services:** Criminal justice. **Psychology:** General. **Social sciences:** General, anthropology, economics, geography, political science, sociology, urban studies. **Visual/performing arts:** Art, dance, dramatic, music. **Work/family studies:** General.

Most popular majors. Business/marketing 14%, communications/journalism 10%, education 14%, health sciences 9%, liberal arts 11%, visual/performing arts 7%.

Computing on campus. 888 workstations in dormitories, library, computer center, student center. Dormitories wired for high-speed internet access and linked to campus network. Commuter students can connect to campus network. Online course registration, online library, helpline, repair service, student web hosting, wireless network available.

Student life. **Freshman orientation:** Mandatory, $100 fee. Preregistration for classes offered. 2-day program held in June and July. Family members encouraged to attend. **Policies:** All students required to live in university housing unless they will be 21 years of age prior to beginning of term for which they are enrolling, have 24 or more semester hours, are married or are custodial parent of a dependent child, or are living with their parents in parents' primary residence within 60-mile radius of campus. **Housing:** Guaranteed on-campus for freshmen. Coed dorms, single-sex dorms, special housing for disabled, apartments, fraternity/sorority housing, wellness housing available. $125 nonrefundable deposit. Living/learning communities available. **Activities:** Bands, campus ministries, choral groups, dance, drama, film society, international student organizations, literary magazine, music ensembles, musical theater, opera, radio station, student government, student newspaper, symphony orchestra, TV station, more than 380 student organizations.

Athletics. NCAA. **Intercollegiate:** Baseball M, basketball, cheerleading, cross-country W, diving, field hockey W, football (tackle) M, golf, gymnastics W, soccer W, softball W, swimming, tennis, track and field W, volleyball.

Intramural: Badminton, basketball, bowling, football (non-tackle), golf, racquetball, soccer, softball, swimming, table tennis, tennis, track and field, volleyball. **Team name:** Cardinals.

Student services. Adult student services, alcohol/substance abuse counseling, career counseling, services for economically disadvantaged, student employment services, financial aid counseling, health services, legal services, minority student services, on-campus daycare, personal counseling, placement for graduates, veterans' counselor, women's services. **Physically disabled:** Services for visually, speech, hearing impaired.

Contact. E-mail: askus@bsu.edu
Phone: (765) 285-8300 Toll-free number: (800) 482-4278
Fax: (765) 285-1632
Chris Munchel, Director of Admissions and Orientation, Ball State University, Office of Admissions, Ball State University, Muncie, IN 47306-0855

Bethel College
Mishawaka, Indiana
www.BethelCollege.edu   CB code: 1079

- Private 4-year liberal arts college affiliated with Missionary Church
- Residential campus in small city
- 1,826 degree-seeking undergraduates: 19% part-time, 66% women, 12% African American, 1% Asian American, 4% Hispanic American, 2% international
- 189 degree-seeking graduate students
- 69% of applicants admitted
- SAT or ACT (ACT writing optional), application essay required
- 60% graduate within 6 years

General. Founded in 1947. Regionally accredited. **Degrees:** 385 bachelor's, 94 associate awarded; master's offered. **ROTC:** Army, Air Force. **Location:** 140 miles from Indianapolis, 90 miles from Chicago. **Calendar:** Semester, limited summer session. **Full-time faculty:** 84 total; 62% have terminal degrees, 8% minority, 44% women. **Part-time faculty:** 133 total; 12% have terminal degrees, 4% minority, 62% women. **Class size:** 70% < 20, 26% 20-39, 2% 40-49, 2% 50-99. **Special facilities:** Otis Bowen museum & archives, Missionary Church archives, environmental prairie.

Freshman class profile. 1,128 applied, 777 admitted, 279 enrolled.

Mid 50% test scores			
SAT critical reading:	440-570	GPA 2.0-2.99:	20%
SAT math:	440-580	Rank in top quarter:	48%
SAT writing:	440-560	Rank in top tenth:	24%
ACT composite:	19-26	Return as sophomores:	84%
GPA 3.75 or higher:	34%	Out-of-state:	29%
GPA 3.50-3.74:	16%	Live on campus:	89%
GPA 3.0-3.49:	30%	International:	2%

Basis for selection. School achievement record, test scores, character recommendations, personal statement important. Interview recommended for all applicants, required for some scholarship awards. Audition/portfolio required of art, music and theater majors for scholarship consideration. **Learning Disabled:** Provide documentation of assessment and accommodations suggested (IEP).

High school preparation. College-preparatory program recommended. 17 units recommended. Recommended units include English 4, mathematics 3, social studies 1, history 2, science 1 (laboratory 1), foreign language 2 and academic electives 3.

2012-2013 Annual costs. Tuition/fees (projected): $24,280. Room/board: $7,280. Books/supplies: $1,600. Personal expenses: $1,400.

2011-2012 Financial aid. **Need-based:** Average need met was 67%. Average scholarship/grant was $8,164; average loan $3,550. **Non-need-based:** Scholarships awarded for academics, alumni affiliation, art, athletics, job skills, leadership, minority status, music/drama, religious affiliation, ROTC.

Application procedures. **Admission:** Priority date 12/1; deadline 8/15 (postmark date). $25 fee, may be waived for applicants with need, free for online applicants. Admission notification on a rolling basis beginning on or about 10/1. Must reply by 5/1. **Financial aid:** Priority date 3/1, closing date 3/10. FAFSA, institutional form required. Applicants notified on a rolling basis starting 4/1.

Academics. **Special study options:** Accelerated study, cross-registration, distance learning, double major, dual enrollment of high school students, ESL, exchange student, honors, independent study, internships, liberal arts/

career combination, student-designed major, study abroad, teacher certification program, urban semester, Washington semester. Off-campus study options include: China, Dominican Republic, Pacific Rim (Australia, New Zealand, China), Russia. May term options have included Israel, Spain, Hawaii, England. **Credit/placement by examination:** AP, CLEP, IB, SAT, ACT, institutional tests. 20 credit hours maximum toward bachelor's degree. **Support services:** Learning center, reduced course load, remedial instruction, study skills assistance, tutoring, writing center.

Majors. Biology: General, cellular/molecular, environmental. **Business:** Accounting, business admin, human resources. **Communications:** Communications/speech/rhetoric. **Conservation:** General. **Education:** Art, biology, business, chemistry, early childhood, elementary, English, foreign languages, mathematics, middle, music, physical, physics, science, secondary, social studies. **Engineering:** General, engineering science. **English:** English lit. **Foreign languages:** Sign language interpretation, Spanish. **Health services:** Nursing (RN), prechiropractic, predental, premedicine, preoccupational therapy, preoptometry, prephysical therapy, preveterinary. **History:** General. **Liberal arts:** Arts/sciences, humanities. **Math:** General. **Parks/recreation:** Exercise sciences, facilities management, health/fitness, sports admin, sports studies. **Philosophy/religion:** General, Christian, philosophy, religion. **Physical sciences:** General, chemistry. **Protective services:** Law enforcement admin. **Psychology:** General. **Social sciences:** General, sociology. **Theology:** Bible, missionary, preministerial, sacred music, theology, youth ministry. **Visual/performing arts:** General, art, dramatic, graphic design, interior design, music, music performance, theater arts management.

Most popular majors. Business/marketing 35%, education 12%, health sciences 8%, liberal arts 13%.

Computing on campus. 160 workstations in dormitories, library, computer center, student center. Dormitories wired for high-speed internet access and linked to campus network. Commuter students can connect to campus network. Online library, helpline, repair service, wireless network available.

Student life. Freshman orientation: Mandatory. Preregistration for classes offered. 4.5-hour session begins the Saturday evening before start of classes. **Policies:** Chapel service 3 times per week; full-time traditional students required to attend specified number each semester; students agree to the community life covenant. Religious observance required. Freshmen not permitted cars on campus. **Housing:** Guaranteed on-campus for freshmen. Single-sex dorms, special housing for disabled, apartments available. $100 nonrefundable deposit, deadline 5/1. **Activities:** Bands, campus ministries, choral groups, drama, international student organizations, literary magazine, music ensembles, musical theater, opera, radio station, student government, student newspaper, symphony orchestra, Fellowship of Christian Athletes, service learning/community service, cross-cultural ministries, Agape Fellowship, ministerial association, Rotoract, Young Republicans, honors program, special interest clubs.

Athletics. NAIA, NCCAA. **Intercollegiate:** Baseball M, basketball, cheerleading, cross-country, golf, soccer, softball W, tennis, track and field, volleyball W. **Intramural:** Badminton, baseball M, basketball, football (non-tackle) M, soccer, softball, table tennis, tennis, volleyball. **Team name:** Pilots.

Student services. Adult student services, alcohol/substance abuse counseling, chaplain/spiritual director, career counseling, student employment services, financial aid counseling, health services, minority student services, personal counseling, placement for graduates. **Physically disabled:** Services for visually, hearing impaired.

Contact. E-mail: admissions@BethelCollege.edu
Phone: (574) 807-7600 Toll-free number: (800) 422-4101
Fax: (574) 807-7650
Randy Beachy, Assistant Vice President, Bethel College, 1001 Bethel Circle, Mishawaka, IN 46545-5591

Butler University

Indianapolis, Indiana   **CB member**
www.butler.edu   **CB code: 1073**

- Private 4-year university
- Residential campus in very large city
- 3,846 degree-seeking undergraduates: 2% part-time, 59% women, 4% African American, 3% Asian American, 3% Hispanic American, 2% international
- 737 degree-seeking graduate students
- 61% of applicants admitted
- SAT or ACT with writing, application essay required
- 73% graduate within 6 years; 23% enter graduate study

General. Founded in 1855. Regionally accredited. **Degrees:** 735 bachelor's, 3 associate awarded; master's, professional offered. **ROTC:** Army, Air Force. **Location:** 5 miles from downtown. **Calendar:** Semester, limited summer session. **Full-time faculty:** 336 total; 80% have terminal degrees, 11% minority, 46% women. **Part-time faculty:** 139 total; 13% have terminal degrees, 8% minority, 35% women. **Class size:** 54% < 20, 40% 20-39, 2% 40-49, 2% 50-99, 1% >100. **Special facilities:** Observatory, planetarium, herbarium, performing arts auditorium, canal, nature preserve.

Freshman class profile. 9,518 applied, 5,792 admitted, 927 enrolled.

Mid 50% test scores			
SAT critical reading:	530-620	Rank in top quarter:	81%
SAT math:	540-640	Rank in top tenth:	53%
SAT writing:	520-620	End year in good standing:	96%
ACT composite:	25-30	Return as sophomores:	87%
GPA 3.75 or higher:	56%	Out-of-state:	52%
GPA 3.50-3.74:	19%	Live on campus:	97%
GPA 3.0-3.49:	21%	International:	2%
GPA 2.0-2.99:	4%		

Basis for selection. Applicants reviewed based on overall academic preparation. 3.3 GPA and 1200 SAT/26 ACT required for applicants to pre-pharmacy or pre-physician assistant programs. Four years of math and lab science strongly encouraged for students interested in all STEM programs. Audition/interview required of all applicants to fine arts. **Home schooled:** Statement describing home school structure and mission, transcript of courses and grades, letter of recommendation (nonparent) required.

High school preparation. College-preparatory program required. 17 units required; 20 recommended. Required and recommended units include English 4, mathematics 3-4, social studies 2-4, history 2-4, science 3-4 (laboratory 3) and foreign language 2-4.

2011-2012 Annual costs. Tuition/fees: $31,948. Room/board: $10,600. Books/supplies: $1,000. Personal expenses: $1,550.

2011-2012 Financial aid. Need-based: 848 full-time freshmen applied for aid; 617 were judged to have need; 617 of these received aid. Average need met was 76%. Average scholarship/grant was $19,160; average loan $4,264. 66% of total undergraduate aid awarded as scholarships/grants, 34% as loans/jobs. **Non-need-based:** Scholarships awarded for academics, athletics, music/drama.

Application procedures. Admission: Closing date 2/1 (postmark date). $35 fee, may be waived for applicants with need, free for online applicants. Admission notification by 2/15. Must reply by May 1 or within 2 week(s) if notified thereafter. **Financial aid:** Priority date 3/1; no closing date. FAFSA required. Applicants notified on a rolling basis starting 3/15; must reply within 3 week(s) of notification.

Academics. Special study options: Combined bachelor's/graduate degree, cross-registration, double major, dual enrollment of high school students, exchange student, honors, independent study, internships, student-designed major, study abroad, teacher certification program, Washington semester. Dual-degree engineering program with Indiana University-Purdue, cooperative program in business. **Credit/placement by examination:** AP, CLEP, IB, SAT, ACT, institutional tests. **Support services:** Learning center, reduced course load, study skills assistance, tutoring, writing center.

Majors. Biology: General. **Business:** Accounting, actuarial science, finance, international, marketing. **Communications:** Communications/speech/rhetoric, digital media, journalism, persuasive communications, radio/TV. **Communications technology:** Recording arts. **Computer sciences:** General, information systems. **Education:** Early childhood, elementary, kindergarten/preschool, middle, music, secondary. **English:** Creative writing, English lit. **Foreign languages:** French, German, Latin, modern Greek, Spanish. **Health services:** Communication disorders, pharmaceutical sciences, physician assistant. **History:** General. **Liberal arts:** Arts/sciences. **Math:** General. **Philosophy/religion:** Philosophy, religion. **Physical sciences:** Chemistry, physics. **Protective services:** Criminal justice. **Psychology:** General. **Social sciences:** Anthropology, criminology, economics, international relations, political science, sociology, urban studies. **Visual/performing arts:** Arts management, dance, dramatic, music, music management, music pedagogy, music performance, music theory/composition, piano/keyboard, stringed instruments, voice/opera.

Most popular majors. Business/marketing 17%, communications/journalism 9%, education 12%, foreign language 7%, health sciences 9%, physical sciences 6%, social sciences 9%, visual/performing arts 10%.

Computing on campus. 430 workstations in dormitories, library, computer center, student center. Dormitories wired for high-speed internet access and linked to campus network. Commuter students can connect to campus network. Online course registration, online library, helpline, repair service, wireless network available.

Student life. Freshman orientation: Mandatory, $100 fee. Preregistration for classes offered. Three-day program held in August. Early registration for

Fall classes held March through June. **Housing:** Guaranteed on-campus for all undergraduates. Coed dorms, single-sex dorms, apartments, fraternity/sorority housing available. $100 fully refundable deposit, deadline 5/1. **Activities:** Bands, campus ministries, choral groups, dance, drama, literary magazine, music ensembles, Model UN, musical theater, opera, student government, student newspaper, symphony orchestra, TV station, volunteer center, black student union, Campus Crusade for Christ, YMCA, College Republicans, Mortar Board, academic honoraries, Alpha Phi Omega.

Athletics. NCAA. **Intercollegiate:** Baseball M, basketball, cross-country, football (tackle) M, golf, soccer, softball W, swimming W, tennis, track and field, volleyball W. **Intramural:** Badminton, baseball M, basketball, bowling, football (tackle) M, golf, soccer, softball, swimming, table tennis, tennis, track and field, volleyball, weight lifting. **Team name:** Bulldogs.

Student services. Alcohol/substance abuse counseling, career counseling, student employment services, financial aid counseling, health services, minority student services, personal counseling, placement for graduates. **Physically disabled:** Services for visually, speech impaired.

Contact. E-mail: admission@butler.edu
Phone: (317) 940-8100 Toll-free number: (888) 940-8100
Fax: (317) 940-8150
Scott Ham, Director of Admissions, Butler University, 4600 Sunset Avenue, Indianapolis, IN 46208

Calumet College of St. Joseph
Whiting, Indiana
www.ccsj.edu   CB code: 1776

▶ Private 4-year liberal arts college affiliated with Roman Catholic Church
▶ Commuter campus in small city
▶ 973 degree-seeking undergraduates: 48% part-time, 49% women
▶ 168 degree-seeking graduate students
▶ 38% of applicants admitted
▶ Application essay required

General. Founded in 1951. Regionally accredited. **Degrees:** 235 bachelor's, 15 associate awarded; master's offered. **Location:** 20 miles from Chicago. **Calendar:** Semester, limited summer session. **Full-time faculty:** 34 total; 65% have terminal degrees, 9% minority, 26% women. **Part-time faculty:** 16 total; 19% have terminal degrees, 19% minority, 62% women. **Class size:** 84% < 20, 15% 20-39, less than 1% 50-99.

Freshman class profile. 580 applied, 218 admitted, 118 enrolled.

GPA 3.75 or higher:	2%	GPA 2.0-2.99:	59%
GPA 3.50-3.74:	4%	Rank in top quarter:	25%
GPA 3.0-3.49:	10%	Rank in top tenth:	8%

Basis for selection. High school record most important. ACT/COMPASS Assessment Test, rank top half of class, 2.0 GPA required. COMPASS testing used for placement. Essay used to place students in English courses as part of placement exam. SAT or ACT recommended. Interview recommended. **Home schooled:** State high school equivalency certificate required.

High school preparation. 15 units recommended. Recommended units include English 4, mathematics 3, social studies 3, science 2 (laboratory 1) and foreign language 1.

2011-2012 Annual costs. Tuition/fees: $14,780. Books/supplies: $1,500. Personal expenses: $1,140.

2010-2011 Financial aid. Need-based: 165 full-time freshmen applied for aid; 151 were judged to have need; 111 of these received aid. Average need met was 62%. Average scholarship/grant was $7,890; average loan $1,606. 64% of total undergraduate aid awarded as scholarships/grants, 36% as loans/jobs. **Non-need-based:** Awarded to 326 full-time undergraduates, including 69 freshmen. Scholarships awarded for academics, alumni affiliation, athletics, religious affiliation. **Additional information:** Immediate computerized estimate of financial aid eligibility available to students applying in person.

Application procedures. Admission: No deadline. No application fee. Admission notification on a rolling basis. **Financial aid:** Priority date 3/1; no closing date. FAFSA required. Applicants notified on a rolling basis starting 4/30; must reply within 2 week(s) of notification.

Academics. Special study options: Accelerated study, cooperative education, double major, dual enrollment of high school students, ESL, honors, independent study, internships, liberal arts/career combination, student-designed major, teacher certification program, weekend college. **Credit/placement by examination:** AP, CLEP, SAT, ACT, institutional tests. 30

credit hours maximum toward associate degree, 60 toward bachelor's. **Support services:** Learning center, reduced course load, remedial instruction, study skills assistance, tutoring, writing center.

Majors. Business: General, accounting, business admin, organizational behavior. **Communications:** Communications/speech/rhetoric, media studies. **Computer sciences:** General. **Education:** General, elementary, science, secondary. **English:** English lit. **Health services:** Health care admin. **Liberal arts:** Arts/sciences. **Philosophy/religion:** Religion. **Protective services:** Police science. **Psychology:** General. **Social sciences:** General. **Visual/performing arts:** Studio arts.

Most popular majors. Business/marketing 23%, education 14%, legal studies 44%.

Computing on campus. 72 workstations in library, computer center. Online library, wireless network available.

Student life. Freshman orientation: Mandatory, $85 fee. Preregistration for classes offered. Held 1 week before classes begin, followed up by mentoring program. **Activities:** Pep band, campus ministries, choral groups, dance, drama, literary magazine, student government, student newspaper, Los Amigos, black student organization, criminal justice club, media and fine arts club, creative writing club, paralegal studies club, booster club, human services club, educators club.

Athletics. NAIA. **Intercollegiate:** Baseball M, basketball, bowling, cheerleading M, cross-country, golf, soccer, softball W, tennis, track and field, volleyball, wrestling M. **Team name:** Crimson Wave.

Student services. Adult student services, chaplain/spiritual director, career counseling, student employment services, financial aid counseling, on-campus daycare, personal counseling, placement for graduates, veterans' counselor.

Contact. E-mail: admissions@ccsj.edu
Phone: (219) 473-4215 Toll-free number: (877) 700-9100
Fax: (219) 473-4259
Mary Severa, Director of Enrollment Management, Calumet College of St. Joseph, 2400 New York Avenue, Whiting, IN 46394-2195

DePauw University
Greencastle, Indiana   **CB member**
www.depauw.edu   **CB code: 1166**

▶ Private 4-year music and liberal arts college affiliated with United Methodist Church
▶ Residential campus in small town
▶ 2,326 degree-seeking undergraduates: 55% women, 7% African American, 3% Asian American, 4% Hispanic American, 11% international
▶ 58% of applicants admitted
▶ SAT or ACT (ACT writing optional), application essay required
▶ 85% graduate within 6 years

General. Founded in 1837. Regionally accredited. **Degrees:** 525 bachelor's awarded. **ROTC:** Army, Air Force. **Location:** 45 miles from Indianapolis. **Calendar:** 4-1-4. **Full-time faculty:** 224 total; 94% have terminal degrees, 19% minority, 41% women. **Part-time faculty:** 51 total; 31% have terminal degrees, 14% minority, 49% women. **Class size:** 63% < 20, 37% 20-39. **Special facilities:** Nature park and arboretum, ethnographic museums, closed circuit tv studio facilities, music instructional technology studio, digital media laboratory, visual resources library with digital image collection, digital video studio, observatory, 2 theaters, 2 music concert halls, concert pipe organ.

Freshman class profile. 5,048 applied, 2,950 admitted, 584 enrolled.

Mid 50% test scores			
SAT critical reading:	530-660	GPA 2.0-2.99:	8%
SAT math:	570-680	Rank in top quarter:	81%
SAT writing:	540-650	Rank in top tenth:	50%
ACT composite:	24-29	Return as sophomores:	92%
GPA 3.75 or higher:	36%	Out-of-state:	58%
GPA 3.50-3.74:	24%	Live on campus:	100%
GPA 3.0-3.49:	32%	International:	10%

Basis for selection. Academic achievement and preparation, demonstrated verbal and quantitative skills, evidence of continuing commitment to learning most important. Interview strongly recommended. Audition required for School of Music candidates. **Home schooled:** Transcript of courses and grades, interview required.

High school preparation. College-preparatory program recommended. 32 units recommended. Recommended units include English 4, mathematics

4, social studies 4, science 4 (laboratory 2), foreign language 4 and academic electives 10.

2011-2012 Annual costs. Tuition/fees: $36,970. Incoming freshman students pay additional fee for mandatory purchase of laptop computer; costs range from $1,435 to $2,004. Room/board: $9,730. Books/supplies: $750. Personal expenses: $1,000.

Financial aid. Non-need-based: Scholarships awarded for academics, alumni affiliation, art, leadership, music/drama, state residency.

Application procedures. Admission: Closing date 2/1 (postmark date). $40 fee, may be waived for applicants with need, free for online applicants. Admission notification by 4/1. Must reply by May 1 or within 2 week(s) if notified thereafter. **Financial aid:** Priority date 2/15, closing date 3/1. FAFSA, institutional form required. Applicants notified on a rolling basis starting 3/15; must reply by 5/1.

Academics. Demonstrated competence in writing, quantitative reasoning, and oral communication required of all students. Seminar, thesis, project, or comprehensive examination in major also required. More than 700 students participate in off-campus winter term programs; 40% study off-campus. **Special study options:** Combined bachelor's/graduate degree, double major, dual enrollment of high school students, exchange student, honors, independent study, internships, student-designed major, study abroad, teacher certification program. **Credit/placement by examination:** AP, CLEP, IB, SAT, ACT, institutional tests. 32 credit hours maximum toward bachelor's degree. **Support services:** Learning center, study skills assistance, tutoring, writing center.

Majors. Area/ethnic studies: African-American, East Asian, women's. **Biology:** General, biochemistry. **Communications:** Media studies. **Computer sciences:** Computer science. **Conservation:** Environmental science. **Education:** Music. **English:** English lit, writing. **Foreign languages:** Ancient Greek, classics, French, German, Latin, Romance, Spanish. **Health services:** Athletic training. **History:** General. **Math:** General. **Parks/recreation:** Exercise sciences. **Philosophy/religion:** Philosophy, religion. **Physical sciences:** Chemistry, geology, physics. **Psychology:** General. **Social sciences:** Anthropology, economics, political science, sociology. **Visual/performing arts:** Art history/conservation, dramatic, film/cinema/video, music, music management, music performance, music theory/composition, studio arts.

Most popular majors. Biology 11%, communications/journalism 12%, English 11%, foreign language 6%, social sciences 19%, visual/performing arts 8%.

Computing on campus. PC or laptop required. 413 workstations in dormitories, library, computer center, student center. Dormitories wired for high-speed internet access and linked to campus network. Commuter students can connect to campus network. Online course registration, online library, helpline, repair service, student web hosting, wireless network available.

Student life. Freshman orientation: Mandatory. Preregistration for classes offered. Four-day program in August. **Housing:** Guaranteed on-campus for all undergraduates. Coed dorms, special housing for disabled, apartments, fraternity/sorority housing available. $400 nonrefundable deposit, deadline 5/1. **Activities:** Bands, campus ministries, choral groups, dance, drama, film society, international student organizations, literary magazine, music ensembles, musical theater, opera, radio station, student government, student newspaper, symphony orchestra, TV station, African American students association, union board, coalition for women's concerns, College Republicans, College Democrats, Habitat for Humanity, Christian fellowship, United DePauw, Latino concerns committee.

Athletics. NCAA. **Intercollegiate:** Baseball M, basketball, cheerleading, cross-country, diving, field hockey W, football (tackle) M, golf, soccer, softball W, swimming, tennis, track and field, volleyball W. **Intramural:** Badminton, basketball, bowling, football (non-tackle), golf, racquetball, soccer, softball, table tennis, tennis, volleyball. **Team name:** Tigers.

Student services. Alcohol/substance abuse counseling, chaplain/spiritual director, career counseling, student employment services, financial aid counseling, health services, minority student services, on-campus daycare, personal counseling, placement for graduates, women's services. **Physically disabled:** Services for visually, hearing impaired.

Contact. E-mail: admission@depauw.edu
Phone: (765) 658-4006 Toll-free number: (800) 447-2495
Fax: (765) 658-4007
Earl Macam, Director of Admission, DePauw University, 101 East Seminary Street, Greencastle, IN 46135-1611

Earlham College
Richmond, Indiana
www.earlham.edu

CB member
CB code: 1195

- Private 4-year liberal arts and seminary college affiliated with Society of Friends (Quaker)
- Residential campus in large town
- 1,047 degree-seeking undergraduates: 1% part-time, 56% women, 8% African American, 2% Asian American, 4% Hispanic American, 1% Native American, 17% international
- 112 degree-seeking graduate students
- 68% of applicants admitted
- Application essay required
- 67% graduate within 6 years

General. Founded in 1847. Regionally accredited; also accredited by ATS. **Degrees:** 223 bachelor's awarded; master's offered. **Location:** 70 miles from Indianapolis; 45 miles from Dayton, Ohio. **Calendar:** Semester. **Full-time faculty:** 93 total; 88% have terminal degrees, 18% minority, 48% women. **Part-time faculty:** 14 total; 100% have terminal degrees, 64% women. **Class size:** 82% < 20, 14% 20-39, 2% 40-49, 2% 50-99. **Special facilities:** Natural history museum, observatory, planetarium, herbarium, working farm, biological field stations.

Freshman class profile. 1,620 applied, 1,109 admitted, 234 enrolled.

Mid 50% test scores			
SAT critical reading:	490-660	GPA 2.0-2.99:	14%
SAT math:	510-620	Rank in top quarter:	53%
SAT writing:	490-630	Rank in top tenth:	25%
ACT composite:	24-30	End year in good standing:	84%
GPA 3.75 or higher:	26%	Return as sophomores:	86%
GPA 3.50-3.74:	23%	Out-of-state:	78%
GPA 3.0-3.49:	37%	Live on campus:	98%
		International:	17%

Basis for selection. Combination of GPA, quality of high school program, SAT/ACT, recommendations, essay, and extracurricular activities important. Interview preferred. **Home schooled:** Statement describing home school structure and mission, interview, letter of recommendation (nonparent) required. Portfolio or other evidence of learning, test scores, and essay.

High school preparation. College-preparatory program required. Required and recommended units include English 4, mathematics 3-4, social studies 4, history 2, science 3-4 (laboratory 2), foreign language 2-4 and visual/performing arts 1.

2011-2012 Annual costs. Tuition/fees: $38,284. Room/board: $7,570. Books/supplies: $1,200. Personal expenses: $1,000.

2011-2012 Financial aid. Need-based: 163 full-time freshmen applied for aid; 146 were judged to have need; 146 of these received aid. Average need met was 91%. Average scholarship/grant was $23,878; average loan $4,336. 82% of total undergraduate aid awarded as scholarships/grants, 18% as loans/jobs. **Non-need-based:** Awarded to 351 full-time undergraduates, including 78 freshmen. Scholarships awarded for academics, minority status, religious affiliation.

Application procedures. Admission: Closing date 2/15 (postmark date). No application fee. Admission notification by 3/15. Must reply by 5/1. **Financial aid:** Closing date 3/1. FAFSA required. Applicants notified on a rolling basis starting 3/1; must reply by 5/1 or within 3 week(s) of notification.

Academics. Special study options: Accelerated study, combined bachelor's/graduate degree, cross-registration, double major, dual enrollment of high school students, ESL, independent study, internships, New York semester, student-designed major, study abroad, urban semester. Teacher certification at Master's level only. **Credit/placement by examination:** AP, CLEP, IB, institutional tests. 18 credit hours maximum toward bachelor's degree. **Support services:** Learning center, pre-admission summer program, reduced course load, study skills assistance, tutoring, writing center.

Majors. Area/ethnic studies: African-American, Japanese, Latin American, women's. **Biology:** General, biochemistry, neuroscience. **Business:** Nonprofit/public. **Computer sciences:** General. **Conservation:** Environmental science, environmental studies. **English:** English lit. **Foreign languages:** Classics, comparative lit, French, German, Spanish. **Health services:** Premedicine. **History:** General. **Math:** General. **Philosophy/religion:** Philosophy, religion. **Physical sciences:** Chemistry, geology, physics. **Psychology:** General. **Social sciences:** Economics, political science, sociology. **Visual/performing arts:** Art, dramatic, music.

Most popular majors. Biology 17%, English 6%, foreign language 6%, interdisciplinary studies 18%, physical sciences 7%, social sciences 14%, visual/performing arts 6%.

Computing on campus. 164 workstations in library, computer center. Dormitories wired for high-speed internet access and linked to campus network. Commuter students can connect to campus network. Online course registration, online library, helpline, repair service, student web hosting, wireless network available.

Student life. Freshman orientation: Mandatory. Preregistration for classes offered. Five-day program held just prior to beginning of fall semester. **Policies:** Community and academic honor codes. **Housing:** Guaranteed on-campus for all undergraduates. Coed dorms, single-sex dorms, special housing for disabled, cooperative housing, wellness housing available. Friendship houses. **Activities:** Jazz band, campus ministries, choral groups, dance, drama, film society, international student organizations, literary magazine, music ensembles, Model UN, radio station, student government, student newspaper, symphony orchestra, Young Friends, Questing Catholics, Christian Fellowship, Jewish student union, Muslim student union, Bahai club, Amnesty International, Model UN, Coalition for Racial Justice, Fellowship of Christian Athletes.

Athletics. NCAA. **Intercollegiate:** Baseball M, basketball, cross-country, field hockey W, football (tackle) M, soccer, tennis, track and field, volleyball W. **Intramural:** Basketball, bowling, football (non-tackle) M, racquetball, soccer, triathlon. **Team name:** Quakers.

Student services. Chaplain/spiritual director, career counseling, student employment services, financial aid counseling, health services, minority student services, on-campus daycare, personal counseling, placement for graduates, women's services. **Physically disabled:** Services for visually, speech, hearing impaired.

Contact. E-mail: admission@earlham.edu
Phone: (765) 983-1600 Toll-free number: (800) 327-5426
Fax: (765) 983-1560
Nancy Sinex, Director of Admissions, Earlham College, 801 National Road West, Richmond, IN 47374-4095

Franklin College
Franklin, Indiana
www.franklincollege.edu

CB member
CB code: 1228

- Private 4-year liberal arts college affiliated with American Baptist Churches in the USA
- Residential campus in large town
- 1,051 degree-seeking undergraduates: 5% part-time, 48% women
- 60% of applicants admitted
- SAT or ACT with writing, application essay required

General. Founded in 1834. Regionally accredited. **Degrees:** 231 bachelor's awarded. **ROTC:** Army. **Location:** 20 miles from Indianapolis. **Calendar:** 4-1-4, limited summer session. **Full-time faculty:** 75 total; 77% have terminal degrees, 7% minority. **Part-time faculty:** 36 total; 19% have terminal degrees, 50% women. **Class size:** 79% < 20, 21% 20-39, less than 1% 40-49.

Freshman class profile. 1,926 applied, 1,147 admitted, 277 enrolled.

GPA 3.75 or higher:	25%	Rank in top tenth:	23%
GPA 3.50-3.74:	17%	Live on campus:	93%
GPA 3.0-3.49:	36%	Fraternities:	49%
GPA 2.0-2.99:	22%	Sororities:	54%
Rank in top quarter:	55%		

Basis for selection. Class rank, test scores, essay and counselor recommendations important. Extracurricular activities considered. Interview recommended for all. **Home schooled:** Transcript of courses and grades, interview, letter of recommendation (nonparent) required. Submit research paper(s), art work, community service projects, educational trip or programs, writing samples, other pertinent documents. Formal interview on campus required. **Learning Disabled:** Students with learning disabilities asked to schedule meeting with Director of Academic Support Services.

High school preparation. Required and recommended units include English 4, mathematics 4, social studies 3, science 2 and foreign language 2.

2011-2012 Annual costs. Tuition/fees: $25,865. Room/board: $7,650. Books/supplies: $1,000.

2010-2011 Financial aid. Need-based: 283 full-time freshmen applied for aid; 260 were judged to have need; 260 of these received aid. Average need met was 71%. Average scholarship/grant was $15,999; average loan $2,949. **Non-need-based:** Awarded to 231 full-time undergraduates, including 64 freshmen. Scholarships awarded for academics, alumni affiliation, art, leadership, minority status, religious affiliation, state residency.

Application procedures. Admission: Priority date 1/15; no deadline. $30 fee, may be waived for applicants with need. Admission notification on a rolling basis beginning on or about 9/1. **Financial aid:** Closing date 3/10. FAFSA, institutional form required. Applicants notified on a rolling basis starting 3/1; must reply by 5/1 or within 4 week(s) of notification.

Academics. Special study options: Combined bachelor's/graduate degree, cross-registration, double major, dual enrollment of high school students, exchange student, independent study, internships, semester at sea, study abroad, teacher certification program, United Nations semester, Washington semester. **Credit/placement by examination:** AP, CLEP, SAT, ACT, institutional tests. 30 credit hours maximum toward bachelor's degree. **Support services:** Learning center, remedial instruction, study skills assistance, tutoring, writing center.

Majors. Area/ethnic studies: American, Canadian. **Biology:** General. **Business:** General, accounting, finance, marketing. **Communications:** Broadcast journalism, journalism, persuasive communications. **Computer sciences:** General, computer science. **Education:** Biology, chemistry, elementary, English, French, history, mathematics, physical, Spanish. **English:** English lit. **Foreign languages:** French, Spanish. **Health services:** General, athletic training. **History:** General. **Math:** General. **Parks/recreation:** General. **Philosophy/religion:** Philosophy, religion. **Physical sciences:** Chemistry. **Psychology:** General. **Social sciences:** Criminology, economics, political science, sociology. **Visual/performing arts:** Dramatic, music.

Most popular majors. Biology 11%, business/marketing 11%, communications/journalism 12%, education 16%, foreign language 7%, psychology 7%, social sciences 14%.

Computing on campus. 250 workstations in dormitories, library, student center. Dormitories wired for high-speed internet access and linked to campus network. Commuter students can connect to campus network. Online course registration, online library, helpline, repair service, wireless network available.

Student life. Freshman orientation: Mandatory, $50 fee. Preregistration for classes offered. Session held 4 days prior to start of classes. **Policies:** All students must live on campus until senior year unless living with family. **Housing:** Guaranteed on-campus for all undergraduates. Coed dorms, single-sex dorms, special housing for disabled, fraternity/sorority housing, wellness housing available. $100 deposit, deadline 5/1. **Activities:** Bands, campus ministries, choral groups, dance, drama, literary magazine, music ensembles, musical theater, radio station, student government, student newspaper, student association for the support of multiculturalism, Habitat for Humanity, college mentors for kids, Fellowship of Christian Athletes, ODK Leadership, international club.

Athletics. NCAA. **Intercollegiate:** Baseball M, basketball, cheerleading M, cross-country, diving, football (tackle) M, golf, soccer, softball W, swimming, tennis, track and field, volleyball W. **Intramural:** Basketball, football (non-tackle), racquetball, softball, volleyball. **Team name:** Grizzlies.

Student services. Alcohol/substance abuse counseling, chaplain/spiritual director, career counseling, student employment services, financial aid counseling, health services, minority student services, personal counseling, placement for graduates, veterans' counselor, women's services.

Contact. E-mail: admissions@franklincollege.edu
Phone: (317) 738-8062 Toll-free number: (800) 852-0232
Fax: (317) 738-8274
Alan Hill, Vice President of Enrollment Management, Franklin College, 101 Branigin Boulevard, Franklin, IN 46131-2623

Goshen College
Goshen, Indiana
www.goshen.edu

CB code: 1251

- Private 4-year liberal arts college affiliated with Mennonite Church
- Residential campus in large town
- 826 degree-seeking undergraduates: 4% part-time, 57% women, 3% African American, 1% Asian American, 9% Hispanic American, 8% international
- 52 degree-seeking graduate students
- 60% of applicants admitted
- SAT or ACT (ACT writing optional), application essay required
- 72% graduate within 6 years; 10% enter graduate study

General. Founded in 1894. Regionally accredited. 1,150 acre environmental study facility located 30 miles from campus. **Degrees:** 236 bachelor's awarded; master's offered. **Location:** 25 miles from South Bend, 120 miles

from Chicago. **Calendar:** Semester, limited summer session. **Full-time faculty:** 68 total; 68% have terminal degrees, 6% minority, 52% women. **Part-time faculty:** 32 total; 3% have terminal degrees, 6% minority, 69% women. **Class size:** 62% < 20, 34% 20-39, 2% 40-49, 3% 50-99. **Special facilities:** Concert hall, X-ray precision laboratory, electron microscope, marine biology laboratory in Florida Keys, Mennonite historical library and archives, laboratory kindergarten and child care center, media production studio, nature preserve, student-run coffee shop.

Freshman class profile. 699 applied, 416 admitted, 320 enrolled.

Mid 50% test scores			
SAT critical reading:	500-580	GPA 2.0-2.99:	12%
SAT math:	490-580	Rank in top quarter:	54%
SAT writing:	470-570	Rank in top tenth:	30%
ACT composite:	22-27	End year in good standing:	90%
GPA 3.75 or higher:	37%	Return as sophomores:	79%
GPA 3.50-3.74:	19%	Out-of-state:	51%
GPA 3.0-3.49:	32%	Live on campus:	82%
		International:	10%

Basis for selection. GPA, ACT/SAT, class rank, recommendations, and high school curriculum important. Nursing and education programs require 2.5 college GPA for entrance and continuation. Interview recommended. **Home schooled:** Statement describing home school structure and mission, transcript of courses and grades required. **Learning Disabled:** Documentation of disability and special requirements dated within last 3 years required. Exit interview with high school special needs counselor, if working with one, required.

High school preparation. College-preparatory program recommended. 12 units required; 16 recommended. Required and recommended units include English 4, mathematics 2-3, social studies 2, history 2, science 2-3 and foreign language 2.

2011-2012 Annual costs. Tuition/fees: $25,700. Room/board: $8,650. Books/supplies: $890. Personal expenses: $1,100.

2011-2012 Financial aid. Need-based: Average need met was 83%. Average scholarship/grant was $17,839; average loan $3,572. 73% of total undergraduate aid awarded as scholarships/grants, 27% as loans/jobs. **Non-need-based:** Scholarships awarded for academics, art, athletics, leadership, minority status, music/drama.

Application procedures. Admission: Priority date 2/1; deadline 8/1 (postmark date). $25 fee, may be waived for applicants with need. Admission notification on a rolling basis beginning on or about 9/15. Must reply by May 1 or within 2 week(s) if notified thereafter. **Financial aid:** Priority date 2/1; no closing date. FAFSA required. Applicants notified on a rolling basis starting 3/1; must reply by 5/1 or within 2 week(s) of notification.

Academics. Practicum/internship and senior seminar required in all majors. International/Intercultural education through domestic or international study service term. Study abroad incorporates language study, academic and cultural learning and community service. Students live in homes of national host families. **Special study options:** Combined bachelor's/graduate degree, cross-registration, double major, dual enrollment of high school students, independent study, internships, liberal arts/career combination, student-designed major, study abroad, teacher certification program, urban semester, Washington semester. Adult degree completion program (one evening per week, concentrated study). **Credit/placement by examination:** AP, CLEP, IB, SAT, ACT, institutional tests. No limit on credit by examination. **Support services:** Learning center, pre-admission summer program, reduced course load, remedial instruction, study skills assistance, tutoring, writing center.

Majors. Biology: General, molecular. **Business:** Accounting, business admin. **Communications:** General, broadcast journalism, journalism, public relations. **Computer sciences:** Informatics. **Conservation:** Environmental science. **Education:** General, art, biology, business, chemistry, elementary, English, ESL, mathematics, music, physical, physics, science, secondary, social studies, Spanish, special ed. **English:** English lit, writing. **Foreign languages:** American Sign Language, sign language interpretation, Spanish. **Health services:** Nursing (RN). **History:** General. **Human services:** Social work. **Math:** General. **Parks/recreation:** Health/fitness. **Physical sciences:** Chemistry, physics. **Psychology:** General. **Social sciences:** Sociology. **Theology:** Youth ministry. **Visual/performing arts:** Art, dramatic, music.

Most popular majors. Biology 6%, business/marketing 17%, communications/journalism 6%, education 7%, health sciences 18%, visual/performing arts 10%.

Computing on campus. 130 workstations in dormitories, library, computer center, student center. Dormitories wired for high-speed internet access and linked to campus network. Commuter students can connect to campus network. Online course registration, online library, helpline, student web hosting, wireless network available.

Student life. Freshman orientation: Mandatory. Preregistration for classes offered. One-day sessions in June, plus 3 days prior to fall semester in August. **Policies:** No smoking, drinking alcoholic beverages, firearms or fireworks on-campus. **Housing:** Guaranteed on-campus for all undergraduates. Coed dorms, single-sex dorms, special housing for disabled, apartments, wellness housing available. $200 fully refundable deposit, deadline 5/1. **Activities:** Jazz band, campus ministries, choral groups, drama, international student organizations, music ensembles, musical theater, opera, radio station, student government, student newspaper, symphony orchestra, black student union, Latino student union, women's association, Catholic student association, eco-pax club, peace club, Fellowship of Christian Athletes, social work action association, nursing students association, business club.

Athletics. NAIA. **Intercollegiate:** Baseball M, basketball, cross-country, golf, soccer, softball W, tennis, track and field, volleyball W. **Intramural:** Badminton, basketball, racquetball, soccer, softball, table tennis, volleyball. **Team name:** Maple Leafs.

Student services. Adult student services, alcohol/substance abuse counseling, chaplain/spiritual director, career counseling, student employment services, financial aid counseling, health services, minority student services, on-campus daycare, personal counseling, placement for graduates, veterans' counselor, women's services. **Physically disabled:** Services for visually, speech, hearing impaired.

Contact. E-mail: admission@goshen.edu
Phone: (574) 535-7535 Toll-free number: (800) 348-7422
Fax: (574) 535-7609
Dan Koop Liechty, Director of Admissions, Goshen College, 1700 South Main Street, Goshen, IN 46526-4724

Grace College
Winona Lake, Indiana
www.grace.edu CB code: 1252

- Private 4-year liberal arts college affiliated with Brethren Church
- Residential campus in small town
- 1,155 degree-seeking undergraduates: 7% part-time, 56% women, 5% African American, 1% Asian American, 3% Hispanic American, 1% international
- 306 degree-seeking graduate students
- 95% of applicants admitted
- SAT or ACT (ACT writing recommended), application essay required
- 56% graduate within 6 years

General. Founded in 1948. Regionally accredited. **Degrees:** 307 bachelor's, 100 associate awarded; master's, doctoral offered. **Location:** 40 miles from Fort Wayne, 50 miles from South Bend. **Calendar:** Semester, limited summer session. **Full-time faculty:** 40 total; 70% have terminal degrees, 8% minority, 18% women. **Part-time faculty:** 65 total; 34% have terminal degrees, 2% minority, 26% women. **Class size:** 43% < 20, 43% 20-39, 9% 40-49, 4% 50-99, less than 1% >100. **Special facilities:** Creation science center, Winona history museum.

Freshman class profile. 1,821 applied, 1,731 admitted, 296 enrolled.

Mid 50% test scores			
SAT critical reading:	440-510	GPA 2.0-2.99:	21%
SAT math:	450-500	Rank in top quarter:	54%
ACT composite:	20-28	Rank in top tenth:	29%
GPA 3.75 or higher:	36%	Return as sophomores:	79%
GPA 3.50-3.74:	16%	Out-of-state:	43%
GPA 3.0-3.49:	27%	Live on campus:	95%
		International:	1%

Basis for selection. References, religious affiliation/commitment, high school class rank, test scores most important. Interview recommended for music and art majors. Audition recommended for music majors. Portfolio recommended for art majors. **Home schooled:** Transcript of courses and grades required.

High school preparation. College-preparatory program recommended. Required and recommended units include English 3-4, mathematics 2-4, social studies 2-3, history 2-3, science 2-3 (laboratory 2-3) and foreign language 2-4.

2011-2012 Annual costs. Tuition/fees: $22,546. Room/board: $7,214. Books/supplies: $1,200. Personal expenses: $1,000.

2010-2011 Financial aid. Non-need-based: Scholarships awarded for academics, art, athletics, leadership, minority status, music/drama, religious affiliation, state residency.

Application procedures. Admission: Priority date 12/1; deadline 8/1 (postmark date). $30 fee, may be waived for applicants with need, free for online applicants. Admission notification on a rolling basis beginning on or

about 9/15. Must reply by May 1 or within 2 week(s) if notified thereafter. **Financial aid:** Closing date 3/1. FAFSA required. Applicants notified on a rolling basis starting 3/1; must reply by 5/1.

Academics. Special study options: Accelerated study, cooperative education, cross-registration, distance learning, double major, dual enrollment of high school students, exchange student, honors, independent study, internships, liberal arts/career combination, study abroad, teacher certification program. **Credit/placement by examination:** AP, CLEP, IB, SAT, ACT, institutional tests. 30 credit hours maximum toward associate degree, 30 toward bachelor's. **Support services:** Learning center, reduced course load, remedial instruction, study skills assistance, tutoring, writing center.

Majors. Biology: General, environmental. **Business:** General, accounting, business admin, finance, financial planning, international, management information systems, marketing, nonprofit/public. **Communications:** Communications/speech/rhetoric, journalism, public relations. **Computer sciences:** Web page design. **Conservation:** Environmental science, environmental studies. **Education:** Art, business, elementary, English, French, mathematics, music, science, social studies, Spanish, special ed. **Engineering:** Biomedical, civil, mechanical. **English:** English lit. **Foreign languages:** General, French, Spanish. **History:** General. **Math:** General. **Parks/recreation:** Sports admin. **Physical sciences:** General. **Protective services:** Law enforcement admin. **Psychology:** General. **Social sciences:** Political science, sociology. **Theology:** Bible, missionary, youth ministry. **Visual/performing arts:** Art, dramatic, drawing, film/cinema/video, graphic design, illustration.

Most popular majors. Business/marketing 44%, education 14%, psychology 15%, visual/performing arts 6%.

Computing on campus. 160 workstations in dormitories, library, computer center, student center. Dormitories wired for high-speed internet access and linked to campus network. Commuter students can connect to campus network. Online course registration, helpline, wireless network available.

Student life. Freshman orientation: Mandatory. Preregistration for classes offered. Weekend program held at beginning of fall semester. **Policies:** Students are to refrain from use of alcoholic beverages, illegal drugs, tobacco, sexual misconduct, morally degrading media and literature, coarse or obscene language or any other conduct inconsistent with the goals and traditions of the college. Religious observance required. **Housing:** Guaranteed on-campus for all undergraduates. Single-sex dorms, apartments available. $200 nonrefundable deposit, deadline 5/1. **Activities:** Bands, campus ministries, choral groups, drama, international student organizations, literary magazine, music ensembles, musical theater, student government, student newspaper, 20 Christian clubs and organizations.

Athletics. NAIA, NCCAA. **Intercollegiate:** Baseball M, basketball, cross-country, golf M, soccer, softball W, tennis, track and field, volleyball W. **Intramural:** Badminton, basketball, football (non-tackle) M, soccer, table tennis, volleyball. **Team name:** Lancers.

Student services. Chaplain/spiritual director, career counseling, student employment services, financial aid counseling, health services, personal counseling, placement for graduates, veterans' counselor. **Physically disabled:** Services for visually impaired.

Contact. E-mail: admissions@grace.edu
Phone: (574) 372-5100 ext. 6008
Toll-free number: (800) 544-7223 ext. 6008 Fax: (574) 372-5120
Cynthia Sisson, Dean of Admissions, Grace College, 200 Seminary Drive, Winona Lake, IN 46590

Hanover College

Hanover, Indiana	**CB member**
www.hanover.edu	**CB code: 1290**

- Private 4-year liberal arts college affiliated with Presbyterian Church (USA)
- Residential campus in rural community
- 1,064 degree-seeking undergraduates: 55% women, 5% African American, 1% Asian American, 2% Hispanic American, 3% international
- 68% of applicants admitted
- SAT or ACT (ACT writing recommended), application essay required
- 71% graduate within 6 years; 27% enter graduate study

General. Founded in 1827. Regionally accredited. **Degrees:** 173 bachelor's awarded. **Location:** 45 miles from Louisville, KY; 70 miles from Cincinnati, OH. **Calendar:** 4-1-4. **Full-time faculty:** 94 total; 100% have terminal degrees, 7% minority, 36% women. **Part-time faculty:** 6 total; 67% have terminal degrees, 67% women. **Class size:** 78% < 20, 21% 20-39, less than 1% 40-49. **Special facilities:** Human cadaver lab, geology museum, observatory, national wildlife refuge.

Freshman class profile. 3,015 applied, 2,058 admitted, 321 enrolled.

Mid 50% test scores			
SAT critical reading:	510-620	GPA 2.0-2.99:	5%
SAT math:	510-610	Rank in top quarter:	66%
SAT writing:	470-570	Rank in top tenth:	31%
ACT composite:	22-28	End year in good standing:	92%
GPA 3.75 or higher:	37%	Return as sophomores:	80%
GPA 3.50-3.74:	23%	Out-of-state:	33%
GPA 3.0-3.49:	35%	Live on campus:	98%
		International:	4%

Basis for selection. GED not accepted. Selection of and performance in academic courses most important. Interview recommended. **Home schooled:** Transcript of courses and grades required.

High school preparation. College-preparatory program required. 18 units required; 26 recommended. Required and recommended units include English 4, mathematics 3-4, social studies 2-3, history 2-3, science 3-4 (laboratory 2-3), foreign language 2-4, visual/performing arts 1 and academic electives 2-3.

2011-2012 Annual costs. Tuition/fees: $28,850. Room/board: $8,650. Books/supplies: $900. Personal expenses: $900.

2010-2011 Financial aid. Need-based: 304 full-time freshmen applied for aid; 212 were judged to have need; 212 of these received aid. Average need met was 84%. Average scholarship/grant was $20,116; average loan $4,434. 77% of total undergraduate aid awarded as scholarships/grants, 23% as loans/jobs. **Non-need-based:** Awarded to 262 full-time undergraduates, including 60 freshmen. Scholarships awarded for academics, alumni affiliation, art, leadership, minority status, music/drama, religious affiliation, state residency. **Additional information:** Academic Honors Diploma Scholarship is a grant program committed to meeting 100% of Indiana student's demonstrated need. Available to Indiana students who graduate with an Academic Honors Diploma (AHD), have completed their application for admission by January 15, and file a complete and valid FAFSA by March 10.

Application procedures. Admission: Closing date 3/1 (postmark date). $40 fee, may be waived for applicants with need, free for online applicants. Admission notification on a rolling basis beginning on or about 9/1. Must reply by May 1 or within 2 week(s) if notified thereafter. **Financial aid:** Priority date 3/1; no closing date. FAFSA required. Applicants notified on a rolling basis starting 3/1; must reply by 5/1 or within 2 week(s) of notification.

Academics. Students take only one course in the 4-week spring term. **Special study options:** Double major, dual enrollment of high school students, independent study, internships, student-designed major, study abroad, teacher certification program, Washington semester. Philadelphia Center, Washington Center, Associated Colleges of the Midwest internships, Business Scholars Program. **Credit/placement by examination:** AP, CLEP, IB, institutional tests. **Support services:** Learning center, reduced course load, study skills assistance, tutoring, writing center.

Majors. Biology: General. **Communications:** Communications/speech/rhetoric. **Computer sciences:** General. **Conservation:** Environmental science. **Education:** Elementary. **English:** English lit. **Foreign languages:** Classics, French, German, Spanish. **History:** General. **Math:** General. **Parks/recreation:** Exercise sciences, health/fitness. **Philosophy/religion:** Philosophy. **Physical sciences:** Chemistry, geology, physics. **Psychology:** General. **Social sciences:** Anthropology, economics, political science, sociology. **Theology:** Theology. **Visual/performing arts:** Art history/conservation, dramatic, music, studio arts.

Most popular majors. Biology 10%, communications/journalism 6%, education 6%, English 9%, foreign language 7%, history 9%, parks/recreation 7%, physical sciences 6%, psychology 9%, social sciences 15%.

Computing on campus. 205 workstations in library, computer center, student center. Dormitories wired for high-speed internet access and linked to campus network. Commuter students can connect to campus network. Online course registration, online library, helpline, student web hosting, wireless network available.

Student life. Freshman orientation: Available. Preregistration for classes offered. Five 1-day orientation sessions in April, May, June, and August. Additional orientation starts 1 week before classes begin. **Housing:** Guaranteed on-campus for all undergraduates. Coed dorms, single-sex dorms, apartments, fraternity/sorority housing, wellness housing available. $250 fully refundable deposit, deadline 5/1. **Activities:** Bands, campus ministries, choral groups, dance, drama, film society, international student organizations, literary magazine, music ensembles, musical theater, radio station, student government, student newspaper, symphony orchestra, TV station, Campus Fellowship, political and social service organizations, academic clubs, Christian Life, Love Out Loud (GLBT group), Kaleidoscope.

Athletics. NCAA. **Intercollegiate:** Baseball M, basketball, cross-country, football (tackle) M, golf, lacrosse M, soccer, softball W, tennis, track and field, volleyball W. **Intramural:** Basketball, football (non-tackle) W, football

(tackle) M, racquetball, soccer, softball, volleyball. **Team name:** Panthers.

Student services. Alcohol/substance abuse counseling, chaplain/spiritual director, career counseling, student employment services, financial aid counseling, health services, minority student services, personal counseling, placement for graduates.

Contact. E-mail: admission@hanover.edu
Phone: (812) 866-7021 Toll-free number: (800) 213-2178
Fax: (812) 866-7098
Jon Riester, Dean of Admission and Financial Assistance, Hanover College, PO Box 108, Hanover, IN 47243-0108

Holy Cross College
Notre Dame, Indiana
www.hcc-nd.edu
CB member
CB code: 1309

- Private 4-year liberal arts college affiliated with Roman Catholic Church
- Residential campus in small city
- 446 degree-seeking undergraduates: 4% part-time, 35% women
- 83% of applicants admitted
- SAT or ACT (ACT writing recommended) required

General. Founded in 1966. Regionally accredited. **Degrees:** 61 bachelor's, 7 associate awarded. **ROTC:** Army, Air Force. **Location:** 140 miles from Indianapolis, 90 miles from Chicago. **Calendar:** Semester, limited summer session. **Full-time faculty:** 22 total; 50% have terminal degrees, 9% minority, 41% women. **Part-time faculty:** 26 total; 8% have terminal degrees, 54% women. **Class size:** 64% < 20, 35% 20-39, less than 1% 50-99.

Freshman class profile. 387 applied, 322 admitted, 122 enrolled.

GPA 3.75 or higher:	9%	GPA 2.0-2.99:	58%
GPA 3.50-3.74:	7%	Out-of-state:	50%
GPA 3.0-3.49:	24%	Live on campus:	79%

Basis for selection. Freshmen seeking admission submit an application, high school transcripts, ACT/SAT scores. The admission committee meets to review each candidate and make a determination regarding admission based on material submitted. Interview recommended. **Home schooled:** Statement describing home school structure and mission required.

High school preparation. College-preparatory program recommended. Required and recommended units include English 4, mathematics 3-4, social studies 2-4, science 2-4 and foreign language 2.

2012-2013 Annual costs. Tuition/fees (projected): $23,900. Room/board: $8,400. Books/supplies: $2,000. Personal expenses: $750.

2010-2011 Financial aid. Need-based: 72% of total undergraduate aid awarded as scholarships/grants, 28% as loans/jobs. **Non-need-based:** Scholarships awarded for academics, athletics, leadership.

Application procedures. Admission: Priority date 3/1; deadline 8/15. No application fee. Admission notification on a rolling basis beginning on or about 5/3. Must reply by May 1 or within 3 week(s) if notified thereafter. **Financial aid:** Priority date 3/1; no closing date. FAFSA required. Applicants notified on a rolling basis starting 5/1; must reply within 2 week(s) of notification.

Academics. Special study options: Cross-registration, double major, dual enrollment of high school students, ESL, honors, internships, liberal arts/career combination, study abroad, teacher certification program. Service learning. **Credit/placement by examination:** AP, CLEP, IB, SAT, ACT, institutional tests. 30 credit hours maximum toward associate degree, 30 toward bachelor's. **Support services:** Learning center, reduced course load, remedial instruction, study skills assistance, tutoring, writing center.

Majors. Business: General, business admin. **Communications:** Advertising, communications/speech/rhetoric, media studies, persuasive communications. **Education:** Elementary. **English:** English lit. **History:** General. **Liberal arts:** Arts/sciences. **Psychology:** General. **Theology:** Theology. **Visual/performing arts:** General.

Most popular majors. Business/marketing 34%, communications/journalism 11%, education 13%, liberal arts 11%, psychology 11%.

Computing on campus. 95 workstations in library, computer center, student center. Dormitories wired for high-speed internet access and linked to campus network. Commuter students can connect to campus network. Online course registration, online library, helpline, repair service, student web hosting, wireless network available.

Student life. Freshman orientation: Mandatory. Preregistration for classes offered. Held 3 days prior to start of fall classes. **Housing:** Single-sex dorms, special housing for disabled, apartments available. $200 partly refundable deposit, deadline 5/3. **Activities:** Bands, campus ministries, choral groups, drama, literary magazine, music ensembles, student government, student newspaper, mission team, Right to Life, multicultural organization.

Athletics. NAIA. **Intercollegiate:** Baseball M, basketball, cross-country, golf, soccer, track and field. **Intramural:** Basketball, football (non-tackle), table tennis, volleyball. **Team name:** Saints.

Student services. Alcohol/substance abuse counseling, chaplain/spiritual director, career counseling, student employment services, financial aid counseling, health services, personal counseling, placement for graduates.

Contact. E-mail: admissions@hcc-nd.edu
Phone: (574) 239-8400 Fax: (574) 239-8323
Marie Bensman, Dean of Enrollment Management, Holy Cross College, 54515 State Road 933 North, Notre Dame, IN 46556-0308

Huntington University
Huntington, Indiana
www.huntington.edu
CB code: 1304

- Private 4-year liberal arts college affiliated with United Brethren in Christ
- Residential campus in large town
- 1,122 degree-seeking undergraduates: 6% part-time, 57% women, 2% African American, 1% Asian American, 2% Hispanic American, 3% international
- 90 degree-seeking graduate students
- 88% of applicants admitted
- SAT or ACT with writing, application essay required
- 62% graduate within 6 years; 16% enter graduate study

General. Founded in 1897. Regionally accredited. **Degrees:** 238 bachelor's, 8 associate awarded; master's offered. **Location:** 20 miles from Fort Wayne. **Calendar:** 4-1-4, limited summer session. **Full-time faculty:** 59 total; 80% have terminal degrees, 3% minority, 39% women. **Part-time faculty:** 57 total; 18% have terminal degrees, 5% minority, 47% women. **Class size:** 69% < 20, 26% 20-39, 4% 40-49, 1% 50-99. **Special facilities:** Life sciences education consortium, simulated nursing lab, radio telescope, nature preserve, greenhouse, disc golf course.

Freshman class profile. 968 applied, 856 admitted, 248 enrolled.

Mid 50% test scores		GPA 2.0-2.99:	24%
SAT critical reading:	450-580	Rank in top quarter:	44%
SAT math:	460-570	Rank in top tenth:	22%
SAT writing:	440-560	Return as sophomores:	79%
ACT composite:	21-28	Out-of-state:	11%
GPA 3.75 or higher:	30%	Live on campus:	93%
GPA 3.50-3.74:	17%	International:	3%
GPA 3.0-3.49:	28%		

Basis for selection. Class rank in top half, satisfactory test scores, 2.3 GPA most important. Selected students with 860 SAT (exclusive of Writing), 2.0 GPA, or rank in top 50% of class may be admitted on a minimum load. Interview recommended. Audition required of music majors. Portfolio required for art scholarships. Essay required for presidential scholarships. Test required for journalism scholarships. **Learning Disabled:** Documentation of learning disability required in some cases where both GPA and standardized test results are below minimum requirement for admission.

High school preparation. College-preparatory program required. Required and recommended units include English 4, mathematics 2-3, social studies 2-3, history 2-3, science 2-3 (laboratory 1-2), foreign language 2, computer science 1, visual/performing arts 2 and academic electives 2.

2011-2012 Annual costs. Tuition/fees: $23,210. Room/board: $7,680. Books/supplies: $950. Personal expenses: $1,300.

2011-2012 Financial aid. Need-based: 226 full-time freshmen applied for aid; 207 were judged to have need; 207 of these received aid. Average need met was 71%. Average scholarship/grant was $11,825; average loan $3,657. 60% of total undergraduate aid awarded as scholarships/grants, 40% as loans/jobs. **Non-need-based:** Awarded to 393 full-time undergraduates, including 103 freshmen. Scholarships awarded for academics, alumni affiliation, art, athletics, leadership, minority status, music/drama, religious affiliation.

Application procedures. Admission: Priority date 3/1; deadline 8/1 (receipt date). $20 fee, may be waived for applicants with need. Admission notification on a rolling basis beginning on or about 10/1. Education majors

must apply separately to the Education Department before entering those major classes. Performance grants also require a separate application process for those majoring in music, theatre, art, and communication. **Financial aid:** Priority date 3/1; no closing date. FAFSA required. Applicants notified on a rolling basis starting 2/1; must reply by 5/1 or within 2 week(s) of notification.

Academics. **Special study options:** Accelerated study, cross-registration, distance learning, double major, dual enrollment of high school students, independent study, internships, semester at sea, study abroad, teacher certification program, urban semester, Washington semester. TESOL certificate. **Credit/placement by examination:** AP, CLEP, SAT, ACT, institutional tests. 38 credit hours maximum toward bachelor's degree. **Support services:** Learning center, pre-admission summer program, reduced course load, remedial instruction, study skills assistance, tutoring, writing center.

Majors. **Biology:** General. **Business:** General, accounting, accounting/finance, business admin, entrepreneurial studies, human resources, managerial economics, marketing, nonprofit/public, small business admin. **Communications:** Broadcast journalism, communications/speech/rhetoric, digital media, journalism, public relations, radio/TV. **Computer sciences:** General, computer science. **Education:** General, art, biology, business, chemistry, elementary, English, mathematics, music, physical, science, secondary, social studies, special ed. **English:** General lit, writing. **Health services:** Nursing (RN), premedicine. **History:** General. **Human services:** Social work. **Math:** General. **Parks/recreation:** General, exercise sciences, health/fitness, outdoor education, sports admin, sports studies. **Philosophy/religion:** Philosophy, religion. **Physical sciences:** Chemistry. **Psychology:** General. **Social sciences:** Political science, sociology. **Theology:** Bible, missionary, religious ed, sacred music, youth ministry. **Visual/performing arts:** Art, cinematography, dramatic, film/cinema/video, graphic design, music, music management, music performance, piano/keyboard, studio arts, theater design, voice/opera.

Most popular majors. Business/marketing 25%, communications/journalism 6%, communication technologies 7%, education 13%, psychology 6%, theological studies 16%, visual/performing arts 8%.

Computing on campus. 270 workstations in dormitories, library, computer center, student center. Dormitories wired for high-speed internet access and linked to campus network. Commuter students can connect to campus network. Online library, helpline, student web hosting, wireless network available.

Student life. **Freshman orientation:** Mandatory. Preregistration for classes offered. Three-day orientation held immediately before first semester. **Policies:** Chapel/convocation attendance required 2 out of 4 weekly programs. Use of alcohol, drugs, and tobacco prohibited. Religious observance required. **Housing:** Guaranteed on-campus for all undergraduates. Single-sex dorms, special housing for disabled, apartments available. $150 partly refundable deposit, deadline 8/15. **Activities:** Bands, campus ministries, choral groups, drama, film society, international student organizations, literary magazine, music ensembles, musical theater, radio station, student government, student newspaper, symphony orchestra, TV station, Acting on AIDS, Amnesty International, Global Vision, Habitat for Humanity, Mu Kappa, volunteer service center, psychology, social work student council, nursing student council.

Athletics. NAIA, NCCAA. **Intercollegiate:** Baseball M, basketball, bowling, cross-country, golf M, soccer, softball W, tennis, track and field, volleyball W. **Intramural:** Basketball, football (non-tackle), racquetball, soccer, softball, volleyball. **Team name:** Foresters.

Student services. Adult student services, alcohol/substance abuse counseling, chaplain/spiritual director, career counseling, student employment services, financial aid counseling, health services, minority student services, on-campus daycare, personal counseling, placement for graduates, women's services. **Physically disabled:** Services for visually, speech, hearing impaired.

Contact. E-mail: admissions@huntington.edu
Phone: (260) 359-4000 Toll-free number: (800) 642-6493
Fax: (260) 358-3699
Jeffrey Berggren, Senior Vice President for Enrollment Management & Marketing, Huntington University, 2303 College Avenue, Huntington, IN 46750-1237

Indiana Institute of Technology
Fort Wayne, Indiana
www.indianatech.edu

CB member
CB code: 1323

- Private 4-year business and engineering college
- Residential campus in large city
- 3,934 degree-seeking undergraduates: 32% part-time, 58% women
- 442 graduate students

- 65% of applicants admitted
- SAT or ACT (ACT writing optional) required

General. Founded in 1930. Regionally accredited. **Degrees:** 528 bachelor's, 181 associate awarded; master's, doctoral offered. **ROTC:** Army. **Location:** 125 miles from Indianapolis, 165 miles from Chicago. **Calendar:** Semester, limited summer session. **Full-time faculty:** 40 total; 12% minority, 25% women. **Part-time faculty:** 266 total. **Class size:** 83% < 20, 17% 20-39, less than 1% 40-49. **Special facilities:** Computer-aided design center, outdoor amphitheater, 200 seat on-campus movie theater, bowling alley, Leadership in Energy and Environmental Design (LEED).

Freshman class profile. 3,172 applied, 2,054 admitted, 405 enrolled.

Mid 50% test scores			
SAT critical reading:	400-510	GPA 3.0-3.49:	29%
SAT math:	430-540	GPA 2.0-2.99:	50%
SAT writing:	380-490	Rank in top quarter:	23%
ACT composite:	17-22	Rank in top tenth:	8%
GPA 3.75 or higher:	7%	Return as sophomores:	73%
GPA 3.50-3.74:	10%	Out-of-state:	29%
		International:	1%

Basis for selection. GPA and ACT/SAT most important; applicants are individually evaluated and given consideration based on other criteria. Minimum admissions requirements vary based upon program. Interviews and essays or personal statements recommended. **Home schooled:** For out-of-state students, require certification that homeschool organization is registered with that state.

High school preparation. College-preparatory program recommended. Required and recommended units include English 4, mathematics 3-4, social studies 3, science 3, foreign language 1 and academic electives 7. Engineering and computer science majors require 13.5 units including 4 English; 3.5 math; 2 physical science; 4 history, social studies, or language.

2012-2013 Annual costs. Tuition/fees: $24,370. Books are included in the cost of tuition. Room/board: $9,160. Personal expenses: $3,302.

Financial aid. **Non-need-based:** Scholarships awarded for academics, alumni affiliation, athletics, leadership, minority status, music/drama, state residency.

Application procedures. **Admission:** No deadline. $50 fee, may be waived for applicants with need, free for online applicants. Admission notification on a rolling basis beginning on or about 9/15. **Financial aid:** Closing date 3/10. FAFSA, institutional form required. Applicants notified on a rolling basis starting 2/2; must reply within 2 week(s) of notification.

Academics. TRIO program, Title III (Strengthening Institutions) Grant program. **Special study options:** Accelerated study, cross-registration, distance learning, double major, dual enrollment of high school students, external degree, independent study, internships, student-designed major. **Credit/placement by examination:** AP, CLEP, IB, SAT, ACT, institutional tests. 45 credit hours maximum toward associate degree, 90 toward bachelor's. **Support services:** Reduced course load, remedial instruction, study skills assistance, tutoring.

Majors. **Business:** Accounting, business admin, organizational leadership. **Communications:** Communications/speech/rhetoric. **Computer sciences:** Computer science, networking, security, webmaster. **Education:** Elementary, physical. **Engineering:** Biomedical, computer, electrical, environmental, industrial, mechanical, software. **Health services:** Recreational therapy. **Parks/recreation:** Facilities management, sports admin. **Protective services:** Criminalistics, law enforcement admin. **Psychology:** General. **Work/family studies:** Apparel marketing.

Most popular majors. Business/marketing 72%, engineering/engineering technologies 8%.

Computing on campus. 370 workstations in library, computer center. Dormitories wired for high-speed internet access and linked to campus network. Commuter students can connect to campus network. Online course registration, online library, helpline, repair service, student web hosting, wireless network available.

Student life. **Freshman orientation:** Mandatory. Preregistration for classes offered. One-day program held on campus that emphasizes new students familiarizing themselves with individuals and resources on campus, as well as promoting leadership building and opportunities. **Housing:** Guaranteed on-campus for freshmen. Coed dorms, special housing for disabled, apartments, fraternity/sorority housing, wellness housing available. $350 fully refundable deposit. **Activities:** Bands, campus ministries, choral groups, dance, student government, student newspaper, student board, black student association, Indiana Tech Gaming Society, Society for Women Engineers, American Society of Mechanical Engineers, Society for Human Resource Management, Society of Automotive Engineering, Collegiate Cyber Defense Team, Sport Recreation and Leisure Society.

Athletics. NAIA. **Intercollegiate:** Baseball M, basketball, bowling, cheerleading, cross-country, golf, lacrosse, soccer, softball W, tennis, track and field, volleyball W, wrestling M. **Intramural:** Basketball, bowling, football (non-tackle), soccer, volleyball. **Team name:** Warriors.

Student services. Adult student services, chaplain/spiritual director, career counseling, services for economically disadvantaged, student employment services, financial aid counseling, health services, placement for graduates. **Physically disabled:** Services for visually, speech, hearing impaired.

Contact. E-mail: admissions@indianatech.edu
Phone: (260) 422-5561 ext. 2205
Toll-free number: (800) 937-2448 ext. 2205 Fax: (260) 422-7696
Monica Chamberlain, Associate Vice President of Enrollment
Management, Indiana Institute of Technology, 1600 East Washington
Boulevard, Fort Wayne, IN 46803-1297

Indiana State University

Terre Haute, Indiana **CB member**
www.indstate.edu **CB code: 1322**

- Public 4-year university
- Residential campus in small city
- 9,349 degree-seeking undergraduates: 12% part-time, 53% women, 16% African American, 1% Asian American, 3% Hispanic American, 3% international
- 2,057 degree-seeking graduate students
- 51% of applicants admitted
- SAT or ACT with writing required
- 44% graduate within 6 years

General. Founded in 1865. Regionally accredited. **Degrees:** 1,318 bachelor's, 173 associate awarded; master's, doctoral offered. **ROTC:** Army, Air Force. **Location:** 70 miles from Indianapolis. **Calendar:** Semester, extensive summer session. **Full-time faculty:** 468 total; 74% have terminal degrees, 15% minority, 45% women. **Part-time faculty:** 193 total; 30% have terminal degrees, 7% minority, 53% women. **Class size:** 30% < 20, 51% 20-39, 10% 40-49, 8% 50-99, 2% >100. **Special facilities:** Observatory, museum, flight simulator.

Freshman class profile. 13,030 applied, 6,588 admitted, 2,521 enrolled.

Mid 50% test scores		Rank in top quarter:	29%
SAT critical reading:	400-510	Rank in top tenth:	9%
SAT math:	410-520	Return as sophomores:	58%
SAT writing:	390-490	Out-of-state:	12%
ACT composite:	17-22	Live on campus:	75%
GPA 3.75 or higher:	8%	International:	2%
GPA 3.50-3.74:	10%	Fraternities:	21%
GPA 3.0-3.49:	34%	Sororities:	12%
GPA 2.0-2.99:	48%		

Basis for selection. Students who rank in top 50% of high school class usually admitted. High school curriculum, GPA, test scores, class rank, type of high school, and interview all considered. Interview required of some scholarship applicants, recommended for applicants below 50th percentile of high school graduating class. Essay recommended. Audition required of music majors. Portfolio recommended for art majors.

High school preparation. College-preparatory program recommended. 40 units recommended. Recommended units include English 8, mathematics 8, social studies 4, history 2, science 6 (laboratory 6), foreign language 2 and academic electives 4. 3 or more units in career area recommended. 1 unit health & safety/physical education recommended.

2011-2012 Annual costs. Tuition/fees: $7,982; $17,206 out-of-state. Room/board: $7,990. Books/supplies: $1,170. Personal expenses: $1,670.

2010-2011 Financial aid. All financial aid based on need. 2,532 full-time freshmen applied for aid; 2,150 were judged to have need; 2,110 of these received aid. Average need met was 77%. Average scholarship/grant was $6,276; average loan $3,121. 59% of total undergraduate aid awarded as scholarships/grants, 41% as loans/jobs. **Additional information:** Financial aid application deadline March 1 for Indiana residents applying for state grant.

Application procedures. Admission: Priority date 7/1; deadline 8/15 (postmark date). $25 fee, may be waived for applicants with need. Admission notification on a rolling basis. Must reply by 5/1. **Financial aid:** Priority date 3/1; no closing date. FAFSA required. Applicants notified on a rolling basis starting 4/1.

Academics. Special study options: Accelerated study, cooperative education, distance learning, double major, dual enrollment of high school students,

ESL, honors, independent study, internships, semester at sea, study abroad, teacher certification program. **Credit/placement by examination:** AP, CLEP, SAT, ACT, institutional tests. 31 credit hours maximum toward bachelor's degree. **Support services:** Learning center, pre-admission summer program, study skills assistance, tutoring, writing center.

Majors. Architecture: Interior. **Area/ethnic studies:** African-American. **Biology:** General. **Business:** Accounting, business admin, finance, human resources, insurance, management information systems, marketing, office management. **Communications:** Communications/speech/rhetoric. **Computer sciences:** General, information technology. **Education:** Art, business, elementary, physical, science, social studies, special ed, trade/industrial. **English:** English lit. **Health services:** Athletic training, audiology/speech pathology, clinical lab science, community health services, nursing (RN). **History:** General. **Human services:** Social work. **Liberal arts:** Arts/sciences. **Math:** General. **Parks/recreation:** Facilities management. **Philosophy/religion:** Philosophy. **Physical sciences:** Chemistry, geology. **Psychology:** General. **Social sciences:** Anthropology, criminology, economics, geography, political science. **Visual/performing arts:** Art, dramatic, music, music performance, studio arts. **Work/family studies:** General, clothing/textiles, family studies, food/nutrition.

Most popular majors. Business/marketing 16%, education 14%, engineering/engineering technologies 8%, health sciences 13%, social sciences 14%.

Computing on campus. PC or laptop required. 329 workstations in library, computer center, student center. Dormitories wired for high-speed internet access and linked to campus network. Commuter students can connect to campus network. Online course registration, online library, helpline, repair service, student web hosting, wireless network available.

Student life. Freshman orientation: Mandatory. Preregistration for classes offered. Two-day program designed for students and parents. **Housing:** Guaranteed on-campus for freshmen. Coed dorms, single-sex dorms, special housing for disabled, apartments, fraternity/sorority housing, wellness housing available. Apartments for students with dependent children and special housing for freshmen. **Activities:** Bands, campus ministries, choral groups, dance, drama, film society, international student organizations, literary magazine, music ensembles, musical theater, radio station, student government, student newspaper, symphony orchestra, over 170 student organizations available.

Athletics. NCAA. **Intercollegiate:** Baseball M, basketball, cross-country, football (tackle) M, golf W, soccer W, softball W, track and field, volleyball W. **Intramural:** Badminton, basketball, football (non-tackle), handball, racquetball, soccer, softball, swimming, tennis, volleyball. **Team name:** Sycamores.

Student services. Adult student services, chaplain/spiritual director, career counseling, student employment services, financial aid counseling, health services, minority student services, on-campus daycare, personal counseling, placement for graduates, veterans' counselor, women's services. **Physically disabled:** Services for visually, speech, hearing impaired.

Contact. E-mail: admissions@indstate.edu
Phone: (812) 237-2121 Toll-free number: (800) 468-6478
Fax: (812) 237-8023
Richard Toomey, Director, Indiana State University, Office of
Admissions, Erickson 114, Terre Haute, IN 47809-9989

Indiana University Bloomington

Bloomington, Indiana **CB member**
www.iub.edu **CB code: 1324**

- Public 4-year university
- Residential campus in small city
- 32,041 degree-seeking undergraduates: 3% part-time, 51% women, 4% African American, 4% Asian American, 4% Hispanic American, 9% international
- 9,723 degree-seeking graduate students
- 72% of applicants admitted
- SAT or ACT with writing required
- 72% graduate within 6 years

General. Founded in 1820. Regionally accredited. **Degrees:** 7,243 bachelor's, 29 associate awarded; master's, professional, doctoral offered. **ROTC:** Army, Air Force. **Location:** 50 miles from Indianapolis. **Calendar:** Semester, extensive summer session. **Full-time faculty:** 1,944 total; 79% have terminal degrees, 18% minority, 39% women. **Part-time faculty:** 353 total; 26% have terminal degrees, 14% minority, 50% women. **Class size:** 34% < 20, 41% 20-39, 6% 40-49, 11% 50-99, 7% >100. **Special facilities:** Cyclotron, 2

observatories, museum of anthropology/history/folklore, rare book library, outdoor educational center, center for excellence in education, garden and nature center, arboretum, automated virtual environment.

Freshman class profile. 35,218 applied, 25,455 admitted, 7,424 enrolled.

Mid 50% test scores			
SAT critical reading:	510-630	GPA 3.0-3.49:	30%
SAT math:	540-650	GPA 2.0-2.99:	4%
SAT writing:	510-620	Rank in top quarter:	74%
ACT composite:	24-29	Rank in top tenth:	37%
GPA 3.75 or higher:	42%	Return as sophomores:	89%
GPA 3.50-3.74:	24%	Out-of-state:	32%

Basis for selection. Strength of student's college preparatory program, senior year program, grade trends, class rank (if provided), and SAT or ACT test scores important. SAT Subject Tests recommended. Campus visit encouraged. Audition required for majority of music majors. **Learning Disabled:** Current and comprehensive documentation of disability required to receive services.

High school preparation. College-preparatory program required. 17 units required. Required units include English 4, mathematics 3.5, social studies 3, science 3 (laboratory 2), foreign language 2, academic electives 1.5. Indiana residents must be on track to complete a Core 40 curriculum, a Core 40 Academic Honors curriculum, or the equivalent as a condition of being offered admission. Additional math credits recommended for students intending to pursue science degree. Additional world language credits recommended for all.

2011-2012 Annual costs. Tuition/fees: $9,524; $29,540 out-of-state. Room/board: $8,419. Books/supplies: $824. Personal expenses: $2,448.

2010-2011 Financial aid. **Need-based:** 4,918 full-time freshmen applied for aid; 3,371 were judged to have need; 3,213 of these received aid. Average need met was 89%. Average scholarship/grant was $10,712; average loan $3,177. 59% of total undergraduate aid awarded as scholarships/grants, 41% as loans/jobs. **Non-need-based:** Awarded to 9,303 full-time undergraduates, including 1,701 freshmen. Scholarships awarded for academics, art, athletics, leadership, minority status, music/drama, religious affiliation, ROTC. **Additional information:** Majority of institutional gift aid merit-based. Some need-based grants go to merit winners with financial need.

Application procedures. **Admission:** $55 fee, may be waived for applicants with need. Admission notification on a rolling basis. Must reply by May 1 or within 3 week(s) if notified thereafter. **Financial aid:** Priority date 3/10; no closing date. FAFSA required. Applicants notified on a rolling basis starting 4/1.

Academics. **Special study options:** Accelerated study, combined bachelor's/graduate degree, cooperative education, distance learning, double major, dual enrollment of high school students, ESL, external degree, honors, independent study, internships, liberal arts/career combination, semester at sea, student-designed major, study abroad, teacher certification program, United Nations semester, Washington semester. **Credit/placement by examination:** AP, CLEP, IB, SAT, ACT, institutional tests. **Support services:** Learning center, pre-admission summer program, reduced course load, remedial instruction, study skills assistance, tutoring, writing center.

Honors college/program. Top 5% of high school graduating class or 3.95 GPA and 1350-1380 SAT or 31 ACT required. Qualified students will receive application to Honors College Scholarship automatically. Completed applications reviewed by faculty panel. Honors College participants complete at least 3 approved honors courses during first 4 semesters on campus.

Majors. **Area/ethnic studies:** African-American, American, East Asian, South Asian, women's. **Biology:** General, bacteriology, biochemistry, biotechnology, microbiology, neuroscience. **Business:** General, accounting, business admin, finance, labor relations, labor studies. **Communications:** Communications/speech/rhetoric, digital media, journalism. **Communications technology:** Recording arts. **Computer sciences:** General, information technology. **Conservation:** General, environmental science. **Education:** General, art, biology, chemistry, early childhood, elementary, English, French, German, health, Latin, mathematics, multi-level teacher, music, physical, physics, science, secondary, social studies, Spanish, special ed, speech. **English:** English lit, writing. **Foreign languages:** General, African, ancient Greek, classics, comparative lit, East Asian, French, German, Germanic, Italian, Latin, linguistics, Portuguese, Slavic, Spanish. **Health services:** Athletic training, audiology/hearing, audiology/speech pathology, clinical lab science, community health, cytotechnology, dental hygiene, health care admin, medical radiologic technology/radiation therapy, medical records admin, medical records technology, nuclear medical technology, nursing (RN), occupational health, radiation protection, respiratory therapy technology, sonography. **History:** General. **Human services:** General, social work. **Liberal arts:** Arts/sciences. **Math:** General, statistics. **Parks/recreation:** General, exercise sciences, facilities management. **Philosophy/religion:** Judaic, philosophy, religion. **Physical sciences:** Astronomy, astrophysics,

chemistry, geology, physics. **Protective services:** Criminal justice. **Psychology:** General. **Social sciences:** General, anthropology, economics, geography, international relations, political science, sociology. **Visual/performing arts:** General, art, art history/conservation, ballet, commercial/advertising art, conducting, dance, dramatic, interior design, jazz, music, music performance, music theory/composition, piano/keyboard, studio arts, studio arts management, voice/opera. **Work/family studies:** Clothing/textiles.

Most popular majors. Biology 6%, business/marketing 20%, communications/journalism 10%, education 8%, parks/recreation 8%, public administration/social services 7%, social sciences 7%, visual/performing arts 6%.

Computing on campus. 2,262 workstations in dormitories, library, computer center, student center. Dormitories wired for high-speed internet access and linked to campus network. Commuter students can connect to campus network. Online course registration, online library, helpline, repair service, student web hosting, wireless network available.

Student life. **Freshman orientation:** Mandatory, $125 fee. Preregistration for classes offered. Two-day program held between June 14 and July 20. **Housing:** Guaranteed on-campus for freshmen. Coed dorms, single-sex dorms, special housing for disabled, apartments, cooperative housing, fraternity/sorority housing available. $300 deposit. Residential language houses, living/learning centers, wellness center, African-American living/learning center, honors college floors, first-year academic interest group housing available. **Activities:** Bands, campus ministries, choral groups, dance, drama, international student organizations, literary magazine, music ensembles, musical theater, opera, radio station, student government, student newspaper, symphony orchestra, TV station, College Democrats, College Republicans, Young Americans for Freedom, black student union, Latinos Unidos, Asian-American association, Alpha Phi Omega, volunteers student bureau, College Mentors for Kids, Golden Key.

Athletics. NCAA. **Intercollegiate:** Baseball M, basketball, cross-country, diving, field hockey W, football (tackle) M, golf, rowing (crew) W, soccer, softball W, swimming, tennis, track and field, volleyball W, water polo W, wrestling M. **Intramural:** Archery, badminton, basketball, bowling, cross-country, diving, equestrian, fencing, field hockey W, golf, gymnastics, handball, ice hockey M, lacrosse, racquetball, rifle, rowing (crew), rugby, sailing, skiing, skin diving, soccer, softball, squash, swimming, table tennis, tennis, track and field, volleyball, water polo, wrestling M. **Team name:** Hoosiers.

Student services. Adult student services, alcohol/substance abuse counseling, chaplain/spiritual director, career counseling, services for economically disadvantaged, student employment services, financial aid counseling, health services, legal services, minority student services, on-campus daycare, personal counseling, placement for graduates, veterans' counselor, women's services. **Physically disabled:** Services for visually, speech, hearing impaired.

Contact. E-mail: iuadmit@indiana.edu
Phone: (812) 855-0661 Fax: (812) 855-5102
Mary Ellen Anderson, Director of Undergraduate Admissions, Indiana University Bloomington, 300 North Jordan Avenue, Bloomington, IN 47405-1106

Indiana University East
Richmond, Indiana
www.iue.edu

CB code: 1194

- Public 4-year university and branch campus college
- Commuter campus in large town
- 2,813 degree-seeking undergraduates: 33% part-time, 67% women, 4% African American, 1% Asian American, 2% Hispanic American
- 58 degree-seeking graduate students
- 64% of applicants admitted
- SAT or ACT with writing required

General. Founded in 1971. Regionally accredited. **Degrees:** 327 bachelor's, 4 associate awarded; master's offered. **Location:** 70 miles from Indianapolis. **Calendar:** Semester, extensive summer session. **Full-time faculty:** 96 total; 57% have terminal degrees, 15% minority, 62% women. **Part-time faculty:** 162 total; 17% have terminal degrees, 4% minority, 59% women. **Class size:** 63% < 20, 32% 20-39, 4% 40-49, 2% 50-99.

Freshman class profile. 1,122 applied, 714 admitted, 411 enrolled.

Mid 50% test scores			
SAT critical reading:	410-510	GPA 3.0-3.49:	32%
SAT math:	410-510	GPA 2.0-2.99:	47%
SAT writing:	390-480	Rank in top quarter:	24%
ACT composite:	18-23	Rank in top tenth:	7%
GPA 3.75 or higher:	10%	Return as sophomores:	66%
GPA 3.50-3.74:	10%	Out-of-state:	13%

Basis for selection. Traditional students (3 years or less after high school graduation) required to take SAT or ACT for placement. May attend 1 semester while waiting to take test. Additional admission criteria for nursing program. Interview recommended. **Home schooled:** Must graduate from national accredited home school program or take GED.

High school preparation. College-preparatory program recommended. 14 units required. Required units include English 4, mathematics 3, social studies 3, science 3 (laboratory 3) and academic electives 4. Four units of academic electives include additional math, lab science, social science, computer science, foreign language, or other college-prep courses.

2011-2012 Annual costs. Tuition/fees: $6,280; $16,865 out-of-state. Books/supplies: $980. Personal expenses: $2,350.

2010-2011 Financial aid. Need-based: 359 full-time freshmen applied for aid; 308 were judged to have need; 300 of these received aid. Average need met was 97%. Average scholarship/grant was $6,076; average loan $2,779. 47% of total undergraduate aid awarded as scholarships/grants, 53% as loans/jobs. **Non-need-based:** Awarded to 148 full-time undergraduates, including 44 freshmen. Scholarships awarded for academics, alumni affiliation, leadership.

Application procedures. Admission: No deadline. $35 fee, may be waived for applicants with need. Admission notification on a rolling basis beginning on or about 9/1. **Financial aid:** Priority date 3/10; no closing date. FAFSA, institutional form required. Applicants notified on a rolling basis starting 5/1; must reply within 2 week(s) of notification.

Academics. Special study options: Cooperative education, cross-registration, distance learning, double major, dual enrollment of high school students, external degree, honors, independent study, internships, study abroad, teacher certification program, weekend college. State-wide technology program with Purdue University. **Credit/placement by examination:** AP, CLEP, SAT, ACT, institutional tests. **Support services:** Remedial instruction, study skills assistance, tutoring, writing center.

Majors. Biology: General, biotechnology. **Business:** General, accounting, business admin, management information systems, marketing. **Communications:** Communications/speech/rhetoric. **Computer sciences:** Information technology. **Education:** Elementary, secondary. **English:** English lit. **Health services:** Medical records admin, nursing (RN). **Human services:** Social work. **Liberal arts:** Humanities. **Protective services:** Criminal justice. **Psychology:** General. **Social sciences:** Political science, sociology. **Visual/performing arts:** Art.

Most popular majors. Business/marketing 34%, education 7%, health sciences 19%, liberal arts 9%, psychology 6%, public administration/social services 8%.

Computing on campus. 120 workstations in library, computer center. Helpline, wireless network available.

Student life. Freshman orientation: Mandatory, $50 fee. Preregistration for classes offered. **Activities:** Drama, literary magazine, student government, student newspaper, TV station.

Athletics. NAIA. **Intramural:** Basketball, cheerleading M, cross-country, golf, softball, tennis, track and field, volleyball. **Team name:** Pioneers.

Student services. Adult student services, career counseling, student employment services, financial aid counseling, health services, on-campus daycare, personal counseling, placement for graduates. **Physically disabled:** Services for visually, speech, hearing impaired.

Contact. E-mail: eaadmit@indiana.edu
Phone: (765) 973-8208 Toll-free number: (800) 959-3278
Fax: (765) 973-8288
Molly Vanderpool, Director of Admissions, Indiana University East, 2325 Chester Boulevard, Richmond, IN 47374-1289

Indiana University Kokomo
Kokomo, Indiana
www.iuk.edu
CB code: 1337

- Public 4-year university
- Commuter campus in large town
- 2,501 degree-seeking undergraduates: 30% part-time, 67% women, 4% African American, 1% Asian American, 3% Hispanic American
- 82 degree-seeking graduate students
- 70% of applicants admitted
- SAT or ACT with writing required

General. Founded in 1945. Regionally accredited. **Degrees:** 388 bachelor's, 53 associate awarded; master's offered. **ROTC:** Army. **Location:** 50 miles from Indianapolis. **Calendar:** Semester, limited summer session. **Full-time faculty:** 99 total; 62% have terminal degrees, 14% minority, 59% women. **Part-time faculty:** 88 total; 9% have terminal degrees, 7% minority, 59% women. **Class size:** 51% < 20, 38% 20-39, 9% 40-49, 2% 50-99, less than 1% >100. **Special facilities:** Observatory.

Freshman class profile. 932 applied, 653 admitted, 435 enrolled.

Mid 50% test scores			
SAT critical reading:	420-530	GPA 3.0-3.49:	30%
SAT math:	430-530	GPA 2.0-2.99:	45%
SAT writing:	400-510	Rank in top quarter:	28%
ACT composite:	18-23	Rank in top tenth:	5%
GPA 3.75 or higher:	8%	Return as sophomores:	64%
GPA 3.50-3.74:	14%	Out-of-state:	1%

Basis for selection. Test scores, class rank, course work important. In-state applicants should be in top half of graduating class (top third for out-of-state applicants).

High school preparation. College-preparatory program required. 20 units required. Required and recommended units include English 4, mathematics 3, social studies 3, science 3, foreign language 2 and academic electives 7. Academic electives include foreign language, additional mathematics, laboratory science, social science, computer science or other college preparatory courses.

2011-2012 Annual costs. Tuition/fees: $6,323; $16,430 out-of-state. Books/supplies: $902. Personal expenses: $4,346.

2010-2011 Financial aid. Need-based: 329 full-time freshmen applied for aid; 268 were judged to have need; 252 of these received aid. Average need met was 94%. Average scholarship/grant was $7,088; average loan $2,826. 49% of total undergraduate aid awarded as scholarships/grants, 51% as loans/jobs. **Non-need-based:** Awarded to 138 full-time undergraduates, including 18 freshmen. Scholarships awarded for academics.

Application procedures. Admission: Priority date 8/3; deadline 8/6. $35 fee, may be waived for applicants with need. Admission notification on a rolling basis. **Financial aid:** Priority date 3/10; no closing date. FAFSA, institutional form required. Applicants notified on a rolling basis starting 5/1; must reply within 4 week(s) of notification.

Academics. Special study options: Accelerated study, cross-registration, distance learning, double major, dual enrollment of high school students, external degree, honors, independent study, internships, liberal arts/career combination, study abroad, teacher certification program. **Credit/placement by examination:** AP, CLEP, SAT, ACT, institutional tests. **Support services:** Learning center, reduced course load, remedial instruction, tutoring, writing center.

Majors. Biology: General. **Business:** General, accounting, business admin, labor relations, labor studies, marketing. **Communications:** Communications/speech/rhetoric. **Computer sciences:** General, informatics. **Education:** Early childhood, elementary. **English:** English lit. **Health services:** General, medical radiologic technology/radiation therapy, medical records admin, nursing (RN), respiratory therapy technology. **Human services:** Social work. **Liberal arts:** Humanities. **Math:** General. **Physical sciences:** Chemistry. **Protective services:** Criminal justice. **Psychology:** General. **Social sciences:** General, sociology. **Visual/performing arts:** Art.

Most popular majors. Business/marketing 11%, education 10%, health sciences 45%, liberal arts 17%.

Computing on campus. 100 workstations in library, computer center, student center. Online course registration, helpline, wireless network available.

Student life. Freshman orientation: Available. Preregistration for classes offered. **Activities:** Choral groups, drama, music ensembles, student government, student newspaper.

Athletics. Intramural: Basketball M, soccer, softball, volleyball. **Team name:** Cougars.

Student services. Adult student services, career counseling, student employment services, financial aid counseling, minority student services, on-campus daycare, personal counseling, placement for graduates, veterans' counselor. **Physically disabled:** Services for visually, hearing impaired.

Contact. E-mail: iuadmis@iuk.edu
Phone: (765) 455-9217 Toll-free number: (888) 875-4485
Fax: (765) 455-9537
Tyana Lange, Director Enrollment Management, Indiana University Kokomo, Kelley Student Center, Room 230, Kokomo, IN 46904-9003

Indiana University Northwest
Gary, Indiana
www.iun.edu CB code: 1338

- Public 4-year university
- Commuter campus in small city
- 4,960 degree-seeking undergraduates: 34% part-time, 69% women, 23% African American, 2% Asian American, 15% Hispanic American
- 588 degree-seeking graduate students
- 76% of applicants admitted
- SAT or ACT with writing required

General. Founded in 1948. Regionally accredited. **Degrees:** 467 bachelor's, 124 associate awarded; master's offered. **ROTC:** Army. **Location:** 35 miles from Chicago. **Calendar:** Semester, limited summer session. **Full-time faculty:** 186 total; 68% have terminal degrees, 25% minority, 54% women. **Part-time faculty:** 215 total; 16% have terminal degrees, 20% minority, 63% women. **Class size:** 36% < 20, 52% 20-39, 5% 40-49, 7% 50-99, 1% >100.

Freshman class profile. 1,793 applied, 1,364 admitted, 907 enrolled.

Mid 50% test scores			
SAT critical reading:	390-500	GPA 3.0-3.49:	21%
SAT math:	390-500	GPA 2.0-2.99:	58%
SAT writing:	380-480	Rank in top quarter:	25%
ACT composite:	16-24	Rank in top tenth:	7%
GPA 3.75 or higher:	6%	Return as sophomores:	63%
GPA 3.50-3.74:	5%	Out-of-state:	1%

Basis for selection. School achievement record and test scores most important. Applicants should be in top half of class and have 2.0 GPA.

High school preparation. College-preparatory program required. 17 units required. Required and recommended units include English 4, mathematics 3, social studies 3, science 3 (laboratory 3), foreign language 2 and academic electives 4. The four academic electives are in some combination of additional mathematics, laboratory science, social science, computer science, and other courses of a college-preparatory nature.

2011-2012 Annual costs. Tuition/fees: $6,408; $16,929 out-of-state. Books/supplies: $1,386. Personal expenses: $4,114.

2010-2011 Financial aid. Need-based: 680 full-time freshmen applied for aid; 609 were judged to have need; 576 of these received aid. Average need met was 90%. Average scholarship/grant was $6,000; average loan $3,160. 41% of total undergraduate aid awarded as scholarships/grants, 59% as loans/jobs. **Non-need-based:** Awarded to 262 full-time undergraduates, including 49 freshmen. Scholarships awarded for academics, athletics.

Application procedures. Admission: Priority date 8/1; no deadline. $35 fee, may be waived for applicants with need. Admission notification on a rolling basis. **Financial aid:** Priority date 3/1; no closing date. FAFSA, institutional form required. Applicants notified on a rolling basis starting 5/1; must reply within 2 week(s) of notification.

Academics. Special study options: Accelerated study, cooperative education, distance learning, double major, dual enrollment of high school students, external degree, independent study, internships, liberal arts/career combination, student-designed major, study abroad, teacher certification program, Washington semester, weekend college. **Credit/placement by examination:** AP, CLEP, institutional tests. **Support services:** Learning center, pre-admission summer program, reduced course load, remedial instruction, tutoring, writing center.

Majors. Area/ethnic studies: African-American. **Biology:** General. **Business:** General, actuarial science, labor studies. **Communications:** Communications/speech/rhetoric. **Computer sciences:** General. **Education:** Elementary, English, mathematics, secondary, social studies, Spanish. **English:** English lit. **Foreign languages:** French, Spanish. **Health services:** Health services admin, medical records admin, nursing (RN), radiologic technology/medical imaging. **History:** General. **Human services:** General, social work. **Math:** General. **Philosophy/religion:** Philosophy. **Physical sciences:** Chemistry, geology. **Protective services:** Criminal justice. **Psychology:** General. **Social sciences:** Anthropology, economics, political science, sociology. **Visual/performing arts:** Art, dramatic.

Most popular majors. Business/marketing 15%, education 12%, health sciences 26%, liberal arts 14%, psychology 8%, security/protective services 13%.

Computing on campus. 170 workstations in library, computer center, student center. Commuter students can connect to campus network. Online course registration, helpline available.

Student life. Freshman orientation: Available. Preregistration for classes offered. **Activities:** Choral groups, dance, drama, international student organizations, literary magazine, musical theater, radio station, student government, student newspaper, Christian student fellowship, Young Republicans, Young Democrats, Women with a Challenge, student guide services, black student union.

Athletics. NAIA. **Intercollegiate:** Basketball, golf, volleyball W. **Intramural:** Baseball M, basketball M, bowling, cheerleading W, golf. **Team name:** Red Hawks.

Student services. Adult student services, career counseling, student employment services, financial aid counseling, health services, on-campus daycare, personal counseling, placement for graduates, veterans' counselor, women's services. **Physically disabled:** Services for visually impaired.

Contact. E-mail: admit@iun.edu
Phone: (219) 980-6991 Toll-free number: (800) 968-7486
Fax: (219) 981-4219
Linda Templeton, Director of Admissions, Indiana University Northwest, 3400 Broadway, Gary, IN 46408

Indiana University South Bend
South Bend, Indiana
www.iusb.edu CB code: 1339

- Public 4-year university
- Commuter campus in small city
- 6,189 degree-seeking undergraduates: 31% part-time, 61% women, 8% African American, 1% Asian American, 6% Hispanic American, 2% international
- 561 degree-seeking graduate students
- 71% of applicants admitted
- SAT or ACT required

General. Founded in 1922. Regionally accredited. Off-campus course offerings in Elkhart, Warsaw, Plymouth. **Degrees:** 625 bachelor's, 126 associate awarded; master's offered. **ROTC:** Army, Naval, Air Force. **Location:** 90 miles from Chicago. **Calendar:** Semester, limited summer session. **Full-time faculty:** 288 total; 62% have terminal degrees, 21% minority, 51% women. **Part-time faculty:** 254 total; 16% have terminal degrees, 11% minority, 53% women. **Class size:** 46% < 20, 47% 20-39, 4% 40-49, 3% 50-99, less than 1% >100.

Freshman class profile. 2,441 applied, 1,725 admitted, 986 enrolled.

Mid 50% test scores			
SAT critical reading:	420-530	GPA 3.0-3.49:	30%
SAT math:	430-530	GPA 2.0-2.99:	55%
SAT writing:	410-510	Rank in top quarter:	27%
ACT composite:	19-23	Rank in top tenth:	7%
GPA 3.75 or higher:	6%	Return as sophomores:	64%
GPA 3.50-3.74:	8%	Out-of-state:	3%
		International:	2%

Basis for selection. Rank in top half of class important. Core 40 completion with 2.0 or higher. Interview recommended for academically weak applicants or those with unusual circumstances. Audition required of music majors. Portfolios required for some art majors. **Home schooled:** Applicants to degree-seeking programs must meet institution's requirement for college-prep courses.

High school preparation. College-preparatory program required. 20 units required. Required and recommended units include English 4, mathematics 3, social studies 3, science 3 (laboratory 3), foreign language 2 and academic electives 7.

2011-2012 Annual costs. Tuition/fees: $6,507; $17,050 out-of-state. Room only: $6,672. Books/supplies: $1,386. Personal expenses: $2,348.

2010-2011 Financial aid. Need-based: 787 full-time freshmen applied for aid; 665 were judged to have need; 638 of these received aid. Average need met was 92%. Average scholarship/grant was $6,477; average loan $3,022. 48% of total undergraduate aid awarded as scholarships/grants, 52% as loans/jobs. **Non-need-based:** Awarded to 329 full-time undergraduates, including 23 freshmen. Scholarships awarded for academics, athletics.

Application procedures. Admission: Priority date 7/1; no deadline. $35 fee, may be waived for applicants with need. Admission notification on a rolling basis. **Financial aid:** Priority date 3/10; no closing date. FAFSA, institutional form required. Applicants notified on a rolling basis starting 5/1.

Academics. Most allied health programs must be completed at Indianapolis campus. **Special study options:** Accelerated study, cross-registration, distance learning, double major, ESL, external degree, honors, independent study, internships, liberal arts/career combination, study abroad, teacher certification program, weekend college. Electrical, mechanical engineering, computer technology with Purdue University on Indiana University South Bend campus; Northern Indiana Consortium for Education (part of 6 member institutions sharing library resources, faculty expertise, and academic strengths). **Credit/placement by examination:** AP, CLEP, IB, institutional tests. 90 credit hours maximum toward bachelor's degree. **Support services:** Learning center, pre-admission summer program, reduced course load, remedial instruction, tutoring, writing center.

Majors. **Area/ethnic studies:** Women's. **Biology:** General. **Business:** General, actuarial science, business admin, finance, labor studies, marketing. **Communications:** Media studies. **Computer sciences:** General, information technology. **Education:** Biology, chemistry, elementary, English, mathematics, music, physics, science, secondary, social studies, Spanish, special ed. **English:** English lit, rhetoric/composition, writing. **Foreign languages:** French, German, Spanish. **Health services:** Health care admin, health services admin, nursing (RN). **History:** General. **Human services:** General. **Math:** General, applied. **Philosophy/religion:** Philosophy. **Physical sciences:** Chemistry, physics. **Protective services:** Criminal justice. **Psychology:** General. **Social sciences:** Anthropology, economics, political science, sociology. **Visual/performing arts:** Art, dramatic, music, music performance, studio arts.

Most popular majors. Business/marketing 15%, communications/journalism 6%, education 12%, health sciences 17%, liberal arts 14%, security/protective services 6%, social sciences 6%.

Computing on campus. 790 workstations in library, computer center. Dormitories linked to campus network. Commuter students can connect to campus network. Online library, helpline, wireless network available.

Student life. **Freshman orientation:** Available, $35 fee. Preregistration for classes offered. Two and a half hour sessions held in May, June, July and August. **Housing:** Coed dorms, apartments available. **Activities:** Jazz band, choral groups, drama, film society, international student organizations, literary magazine, music ensembles, musical theater, opera, student government, student newspaper, symphony orchestra, student educational association, black student union, student council for exceptional children, Latino student union, Asian student union, women's student union, Habitat for Humanity, departmental clubs.

Athletics. NAIA. **Intercollegiate:** Basketball. **Intramural:** Badminton, basketball, bowling, football (tackle), racquetball, softball, table tennis, tennis, volleyball. **Team name:** Titans.

Student services. Adult student services, chaplain/spiritual director, career counseling, student employment services, on-campus daycare, personal counseling, placement for graduates, veterans' counselor. **Physically disabled:** Services for visually, speech, hearing impaired.

Contact. E-mail: admissions@iusb.edu
Phone: (574) 520-4839 Fax: (574) 520-4834
Michael Renfrow, Associate Director of Admissions, Indiana University South Bend, 1700 Mishawaka Avenue, South Bend, IN 46634-7111

Indiana University Southeast

New Albany, Indiana	CB member
www.ius.edu	CB code: 1314

- Public 4-year university
- Commuter campus in large town
- 6,066 degree-seeking undergraduates: 33% part-time, 58% women, 6% African American, 1% Asian American, 2% Hispanic American
- 640 degree-seeking graduate students
- 77% of applicants admitted
- SAT or ACT with writing required

General. Founded in 1941. Regionally accredited. **Degrees:** 729 bachelor's, 90 associate awarded; master's offered. **ROTC:** Army, Air Force. **Location:** 10 miles from Louisville. **Calendar:** Semester, limited summer session. **Full-time faculty:** 210 total; 70% have terminal degrees, 17% minority, 51% women. **Part-time faculty:** 277 total; 20% have terminal degrees, 7% minority, 54% women. **Class size:** 31% < 20, 65% 20-39, 2% 40-49, 1% 50-99. **Special facilities:** Cultural and community center.

Freshman class profile. 2,102 applied, 1,617 admitted, 981 enrolled.

Mid 50% test scores			
SAT critical reading:	420-530	GPA 3.0-3.49:	32%
SAT math:	420-520	GPA 2.0-2.99:	46%
SAT writing:	410-510	Rank in top quarter:	31%
ACT composite:	18-22	Rank in top tenth:	10%
GPA 3.75 or higher:	10%	Return as sophomores:	64%
GPA 3.50-3.74:	11%	Out-of-state:	22%

Basis for selection. Rank in top half of class for in-state applicants. Interview recommended.

High school preparation. College-preparatory program required. 20 units required. Required and recommended units include English 4, mathematics 3, social studies 3, science 3 (laboratory 3), foreign language 2 and academic electives 7.

2011-2012 Annual costs. Tuition/fees: $6,365; $16,466 out-of-state. Room/board: $5,890. Books/supplies: $1,100. Personal expenses: $2,060.

2010-2011 Financial aid. **Need-based:** 839 full-time freshmen applied for aid; 672 were judged to have need; 648 of these received aid. Average need met was 92%. Average scholarship/grant was $6,087; average loan $3,095. 47% of total undergraduate aid awarded as scholarships/grants, 53% as loans/jobs. **Non-need-based:** Awarded to 391 full-time undergraduates, including 53 freshmen. Scholarships awarded for academics, art, athletics, leadership, minority status, music/drama.

Application procedures. **Admission:** No deadline. $35 fee, may be waived for applicants with need. Admission notification on a rolling basis. **Financial aid:** Priority date 3/1; no closing date. FAFSA required. Applicants notified on a rolling basis starting 5/1; must reply within 3 week(s) of notification.

Academics. **Special study options:** Accelerated study, cross-registration, distance learning, double major, dual enrollment of high school students, external degree, honors, independent study, internships, student-designed major, study abroad, teacher certification program, weekend college. Member of Metroversity consortium of institutions of higher education in Louisville area. **Credit/placement by examination:** AP, CLEP, IB, institutional tests. **Support services:** Reduced course load, remedial instruction, study skills assistance, tutoring, writing center.

Majors. **Biology:** General. **Business:** General, accounting, accounting technology, labor relations. **Communications:** Communications/speech/rhetoric, journalism. **Computer sciences:** General, information technology. **Education:** General, biology, elementary, English, mathematics, science, secondary, social studies, special ed. **English:** English lit. **Foreign languages:** French, German, Spanish. **Health services:** Clinical lab science, nursing (RN). **History:** General. **Math:** General. **Philosophy/religion:** Philosophy. **Physical sciences:** Chemistry, physics. **Protective services:** Criminal justice. **Psychology:** General. **Social sciences:** Economics, geography, international relations, political science, sociology. **Visual/performing arts:** Art, music, studio arts.

Most popular majors. Business/marketing 21%, communications/journalism 6%, education 13%, health sciences 8%, liberal arts 20%, psychology 6%.

Computing on campus. 833 workstations in library, computer center, student center. Commuter students can connect to campus network. Online course registration, online library, helpline, student web hosting, wireless network available.

Student life. **Freshman orientation:** Mandatory, $50 fee. Preregistration for classes offered. One-day summer program. **Housing:** Apartments available. **Activities:** Concert band, choral groups, drama, literary magazine, music ensembles, student government, student newspaper, symphony orchestra, Christian fellowship, students for world peace, multicultural student union.

Athletics. NAIA. **Intercollegiate:** Baseball M, basketball, cross-country, tennis, volleyball W. **Intramural:** Basketball, bowling, softball, tennis, volleyball. **Team name:** Grenadier.

Student services. Adult student services, alcohol/substance abuse counseling, chaplain/spiritual director, career counseling, student employment services, financial aid counseling, minority student services, on-campus daycare, personal counseling, placement for graduates, veterans' counselor. **Physically disabled:** Services for visually, speech, hearing impaired.

Contact. E-mail: admissions@ius.edu
Phone: (812) 941-2212 Toll-free number: (800) 852-8835
Fax: (812) 941-2595
Anne Skuce, Assistant Vice Chancellor for Enrollment Management, Indiana University Southeast, 4201 Grant Line Road, New Albany, IN 47150-6405

Indiana University-Purdue University Fort Wayne

Fort Wayne, Indiana
www.ipfw.edu

CB member
CB code: 1336

- Public 4-year university and branch campus college
- Commuter campus in large city
- 11,655 degree-seeking undergraduates: 26% part-time, 54% women, 8% African American, 2% Asian American, 5% Hispanic American, 2% international
- 671 degree-seeking graduate students
- 91% of applicants admitted
- SAT or ACT (ACT writing optional) required

General. Founded in 1964. Regionally accredited. Degrees awarded through Indiana University or Purdue University, depending on course of study. **Degrees:** 1,144 bachelor's, 377 associate awarded; master's offered. **ROTC:** Army. **Location:** 110 miles from Indianapolis. **Calendar:** Semester, limited summer session. **Full-time faculty:** 430 total; 81% have terminal degrees, 15% minority, 43% women. **Part-time faculty:** 450 total; 13% have terminal degrees, 10% minority, 53% women. **Class size:** 50% < 20, 44% 20-39, 3% 40-49, 3% 50-99, less than 1% >100. **Special facilities:** Lake biological research station.

Freshman class profile. 2,779 applied, 2,530 admitted, 2,044 enrolled.

Mid 50% test scores			
SAT critical reading:	420-530	GPA 2.0-2.99:	42%
SAT math:	430-550	Rank in top quarter:	33%
SAT writing:	410-520	Rank in top tenth:	12%
ACT composite:	18-24	End year in good standing:	95%
GPA 3.75 or higher:	14%	Return as sophomores:	58%
GPA 3.50-3.74:	14%	Out-of-state:	4%
GPA 3.0-3.49:	29%	Live on campus:	23%
		International:	2%

Basis for selection. In-state applicants should rank in top half of high school class, out-of-state in top third. Test scores important. TOEFL or Michigan Test may be used to assess English proficiency. Audition required of music majors. Portfolio required of visual arts majors. **Home schooled:** Transcript of courses and grades required.

High school preparation. College-preparatory program required. 20 units required. Required units include English 4, mathematics 3, social studies 3, science 3, foreign language 2 and academic electives 5. Additional requirements vary by program.

2011-2012 Annual costs. Tuition/fees: $7,454; $17,903 out-of-state. Beginning freshmen pay a one-time first year programming fee of $100. Room only: $5,868. Books/supplies: $1,300. Personal expenses: $2,795.

2010-2011 Financial aid. **Need-based:** 1,919 full-time freshmen applied for aid; 1,651 were judged to have need; 1,565 of these received aid. Average need met was 45%. Average scholarship/grant was $5,934; average loan $3,094. 40% of total undergraduate aid awarded as scholarships/grants, 60% as loans/jobs. **Non-need-based:** Awarded to 1,632 full-time undergraduates, including 549 freshmen. Scholarships awarded for academics, alumni affiliation, art, athletics, leadership, minority status, music/drama, ROTC, state residency.

Application procedures. **Admission:** Closing date 8/1. $50 fee, may be waived for applicants with need. Admission notification on a rolling basis beginning on or about 11/1. **Financial aid:** Priority date 3/10; no closing date. FAFSA required. Applicants notified on a rolling basis starting 6/1; must reply within 3 week(s) of notification.

Academics. **Special study options:** Accelerated study, cooperative education, distance learning, double major, dual enrollment of high school students, ESL, exchange student, honors, independent study, internships, liberal arts/career combination, student-designed major, study abroad, teacher certification program, Washington semester, weekend college. **Credit/placement by examination:** AP, CLEP, IB, institutional tests. Hours of credit awarded by examination varies by program. **Support services:** Learning center, preadmission summer program, remedial instruction, study skills assistance, tutoring, writing center.

Majors. **Area/ethnic studies:** Women's. **Biology:** General. **Business:** General, accounting, business admin, finance, hospitality admin, hotel/motel admin, labor relations, managerial economics, marketing, operations. **Communications:** Communications/speech/rhetoric. **Computer sciences:** General, information technology. **Education:** Art, biology, chemistry, elementary, English, French, German, history, mathematics, music, physics, science, secondary, social studies, Spanish, speech. **Engineering:** Civil, computer, electrical, mechanical. **English:** British lit, English lit, technical writing, writing. **Foreign languages:** French, German, Spanish. **Health services:**

Audiology/speech pathology, clinical lab science, clinical lab technology, community health services, health care admin, health services admin, mental health services, music therapy, nursing (RN), predental, premedicine, preveterinary, substance abuse counseling. **History:** General. **Human services:** General, public policy. **Math:** General, computational, statistics. **Philosophy/religion:** Philosophy. **Physical sciences:** Chemistry, geology, physics. **Psychology:** General. **Social sciences:** Anthropology, economics, political science, sociology. **Visual/performing arts:** Art, commercial/advertising art, crafts, dramatic, drawing, graphic design, interior design, music, music performance, painting, photography, piano/keyboard, printmaking, sculpture, studio arts, voice/opera.

Most popular majors. Business/marketing 20%, education 11%, engineering/engineering technologies 7%, health sciences 10%, liberal arts 17%, public administration/social services 6%, visual/performing arts 6%.

Computing on campus. 642 workstations in dormitories, library, computer center, student center. Dormitories wired for high-speed internet access and linked to campus network. Commuter students can connect to campus network. Online course registration, online library, helpline, repair service, student web hosting, wireless network available.

Student life. **Freshman orientation:** Mandatory, $30 fee. Preregistration for classes offered. 8-hour program; 15 dates available between June and August; Freshmen Fest held 2 days in late August. **Housing:** Apartments available. $150 fully refundable deposit. **Activities:** Bands, campus ministries, choral groups, dance, drama, film society, international student organizations, literary magazine, music ensembles, musical theater, opera, student government, student newspaper, symphony orchestra, TV station, Black Collegian Caucus, Hispanos Unidos, InterVarsity Christian Fellowship, Campus Crusade for Christ, Bangladesh student association, College Republicans, University Democrats.

Athletics. NCAA. **Intercollegiate:** Baseball M, basketball, cross-country, golf, soccer, softball W, tennis, track and field W, volleyball. **Intramural:** Basketball, football (non-tackle), golf, softball W, table tennis, tennis, volleyball. **Team name:** Mastodons.

Student services. Adult student services, alcohol/substance abuse counseling, chaplain/spiritual director, career counseling, student employment services, financial aid counseling, health services, minority student services, personal counseling, placement for graduates, veterans' counselor, women's services. **Physically disabled:** Services for visually, speech, hearing impaired.

Contact. E-mail: ask@ipfw.edu
Phone: (260) 481-6812 Toll-free number: (800) 324-4739
Fax: (260) 481-6880
Carol Isaacs, Director of Admissions, Indiana University-Purdue University Fort Wayne, 2101 East Coliseum Boulevard, Fort Wayne, IN 46805-1499

Indiana University-Purdue University Indianapolis

Indianapolis, Indiana
www.iupui.edu

CB member
CB code: 1325

- Public 4-year university
- Commuter campus in very large city
- 21,235 degree-seeking undergraduates: 25% part-time, 57% women, 11% African American, 3% Asian American, 4% Hispanic American, 3% international
- 7,810 degree-seeking graduate students
- 69% of applicants admitted
- SAT or ACT with writing required
- 33% graduate within 6 years

General. Founded in 1969. Regionally accredited. **Degrees:** 3,404 bachelor's, 229 associate awarded; master's, professional, doctoral offered. **ROTC:** Army, Air Force. **Calendar:** Semester, extensive summer session. **Full-time faculty:** 2,182 total; 83% have terminal degrees, 22% minority, 40% women. **Part-time faculty:** 1,026 total; 26% have terminal degrees, 12% minority, 51% women. **Class size:** 38% < 20, 45% 20-39, 8% 40-49, 8% 50-99, 1% >100.

Freshman class profile. 10,164 applied, 7,048 admitted, 3,059 enrolled.

Mid 50% test scores			
SAT critical reading:	430-550	GPA 3.0-3.49:	39%
SAT math:	450-560	GPA 2.0-2.99:	30%
SAT writing:	420-530	Rank in top quarter:	44%
ACT composite:	19-25	Rank in top tenth:	15%
GPA 3.75 or higher:	17%	Return as sophomores:	82%
GPA 3.50-3.74:	14%	Out-of-state:	4%
		International:	3%

Basis for selection. Course curriculum, grades, trend in grades, and test scores are the factors used. Portfolio recommended for some art applicants.

High school preparation. College-preparatory program required. 17 units required. Required and recommended units include English 4, mathematics 3, social studies 3, science 3 (laboratory 3), foreign language 3 and academic electives 4. The units of academic electives can be a combination of additional mathematics, laboratory science, social science, computer science, foreign language, or other courses of college preparatory nature. Additional math and science units required for science, engineering and nursing programs. Courses that develop writing composition skills strongly recommended.

2011-2012 Annual costs. Tuition/fees: $8,243; $26,606 out-of-state. Room only: $3,774. Books/supplies: $672. Personal expenses: $3,520.

2010-2011 Financial aid. Need-based: 2,399 full-time freshmen applied for aid; 1,999 were judged to have need; 1,927 of these received aid. Average need met was 90%. Average scholarship/grant was $8,224; average loan $3,241. 45% of total undergraduate aid awarded as scholarships/grants, 55% as loans/jobs. **Non-need-based:** Awarded to 2,015 full-time undergraduates, including 314 freshmen. Scholarships awarded for academics, ROTC.

Application procedures. Admission: Closing date 5/1. $50 fee, may be waived for applicants with need. Admission notification on a rolling basis. Application deadlines for nursing and allied health programs range from October 15 to February 1. **Financial aid:** Priority date 3/10; no closing date. FAFSA required. Applicants notified on a rolling basis starting 4/1.

Academics. Special study options: Accelerated study, cooperative education, cross-registration, distance learning, double major, dual enrollment of high school students, ESL, exchange student, external degree, honors, independent study, internships, student-designed major, study abroad, teacher certification program, weekend college. **Credit/placement by examination:** AP, CLEP, IB, SAT, ACT, institutional tests. Policy varies by school. **Support services:** Learning center, reduced course load, remedial instruction, tutoring, writing center.

Majors. Area/ethnic studies: African-American. **Biology:** General, biotechnology. **Business:** General, accounting, finance, human resources, international, labor relations, labor studies, management information systems, market research, nonprofit/public, operations, tourism/travel. **Communications:** Advertising, communications/speech/rhetoric, digital media, journalism, public relations. **Computer sciences:** General, computer graphics, information systems, system admin, web page design, webmaster. **Conservation:** Environmental science. **Education:** Art, biology, chemistry, elementary, English, ESL, French, German, health occupations, mathematics, physical, physics, school counseling, secondary, social studies, Spanish, speech. **Engineering:** General, biomedical, computer, electrical, mechanical. **English:** English lit. **Foreign languages:** American Sign Language, French, German, sign language interpretation, Spanish. **Health services:** Clinical lab science, community health, cytotechnology, dental hygiene, health care admin, health services admin, medical informatics, medical radiologic technology/radiation therapy, medical records admin, nuclear medical technology, nursing (RN), predental, premedicine, prenursing, prepharmacy, preveterinary, radiation protection, radiologic technology/medical imaging, respiratory therapy assistant, respiratory therapy technology. **History:** General. **Human services:** General, social work. **Liberal arts:** Arts/sciences. **Math:** General. **Parks/recreation:** Exercise sciences. **Philosophy/religion:** Philosophy, religion. **Physical sciences:** Chemistry, geology, physics. **Protective services:** Criminal justice, forensics. **Psychology:** General. **Social sciences:** Anthropology, economics, geography, international relations, political science, sociology. **Visual/performing arts:** Art, art history/conservation, ceramics, design, interior design, music management, painting, photography, printmaking, sculpture, studio arts.

Most popular majors. Business/marketing 16%, education 9%, engineering/engineering technologies 10%, health sciences 14%, liberal arts 14%.

Computing on campus. 750 workstations in library, computer center, student center. Dormitories wired for high-speed internet access and linked to campus network. Commuter students can connect to campus network. Online course registration, helpline, repair service, wireless network available.

Student life. Freshman orientation: Mandatory, $110 fee. Preregistration for classes offered. **Policies:** Smoking policy, code of conduct. **Housing:** Coed dorms, apartments available. $100 deposit. **Activities:** Bands, campus ministries, choral groups, dance, drama, international student organizations, literary magazine, music ensembles, student government, student newspaper, black student union, international affairs club.

Athletics. NCAA. **Intercollegiate:** Basketball, cheerleading, cross-country, diving, golf, soccer, softball W, swimming, tennis, track and field, volleyball W. **Intramural:** Basketball, football (non-tackle), golf, ice hockey, racquetball, soccer, softball, tennis, track and field, volleyball. **Team name:** Jaguars.

Student services. Adult student services, chaplain/spiritual director, career counseling, student employment services, financial aid counseling,

health services, minority student services, on-campus daycare, personal counseling, placement for graduates, veterans' counselor, women's services. **Physically disabled:** Services for visually, speech, hearing impaired.

Contact. E-mail: apply@iupui.edu
Phone: (317) 274-4591 Fax: (317) 278-1862
Chris Foley, Director of Admissions, Indiana University-Purdue University Indianapolis, 420 University Boulevard, Suite CE 255, Campus Center, Indianapolis, IN 46202-5143

Indiana Wesleyan University
Marion, Indiana
www.indwes.edu   CB code: 1446

- Private 4-year university and liberal arts college affiliated with Wesleyan Church
- Residential campus in large town
- 3,028 degree-seeking undergraduates: 2% part-time, 63% women, 2% African American, 1% Asian American, 3% Hispanic American
- 99 degree-seeking graduate students
- 67% of applicants admitted
- SAT or ACT (ACT writing recommended), application essay required
- 70% graduate within 6 years

General. Founded in 1920. Regionally accredited. **Degrees:** 657 bachelor's, 6 associate awarded; master's offered. **ROTC:** Army. **Location:** 65 miles from Indianapolis, 57 miles from Fort Wayne. **Calendar:** Semester, extensive summer session. **Full-time faculty:** 179 total; 64% have terminal degrees, 8% minority, 41% women. **Part-time faculty:** 113 total; 3% have terminal degrees, 6% minority, 50% women. **Class size:** 61% < 20, 31% 20-39, 5% 40-49, 3% 50-99, less than 1% >100. **Special facilities:** 1920 gallery, adventure center.

Freshman class profile. 3,512 applied, 2,340 admitted, 753 enrolled.

Mid 50% test scores			
SAT critical reading:	470-590	GPA 2.0-2.99:	16%
SAT math:	470-580	Rank in top quarter:	57%
SAT writing:	460-570	Rank in top tenth:	26%
ACT composite:	21-27	End year in good standing:	91%
GPA 3.75 or higher:	43%	Return as sophomores:	75%
GPA 3.50-3.74:	20%	Out-of-state:	52%
GPA 3.0-3.49:	21%	Live on campus:	97%
		International:	1%

Basis for selection. 2.6 GPA and 880 SAT (Math and Critical Reading) or 18 ACT required to qualify for regular admission. Applicants who do not meet the requirements for regular admission may request special consideration. Audition recommended for music majors. Portfolio recommended for art majors. **Home schooled:** Transcript of courses and grades, letter of recommendation (nonparent) required. Transcript must have GPA on 4.0 scale. Recommendation from pastor required.

High school preparation. College-preparatory program recommended. 20 units recommended. Recommended units include English 4, mathematics 3, social studies 3, science 3, foreign language 2 and academic electives 5.

2011-2012 Annual costs. Tuition/fees: $21,956. Room/board: $7,148. Books/supplies: $1,266. Personal expenses: $1,456.

2010-2011 Financial aid. Need-based: 748 full-time freshmen applied for aid; 637 were judged to have need; 637 of these received aid. Average need met was 83%. Average scholarship/grant was $13,444; average loan $6,135. 65% of total undergraduate aid awarded as scholarships/grants, 35% as loans/jobs. **Non-need-based:** Awarded to 783 full-time undergraduates, including 192 freshmen. Scholarships awarded for academics, alumni affiliation, art, athletics, music/drama, ROTC.

Application procedures. Admission: Priority date 3/1; no deadline. $25 fee, may be waived for applicants with need. Admission notification on a rolling basis. **Financial aid:** Closing date 3/10. FAFSA required. Applicants notified on a rolling basis.

Academics. Special study options: Accelerated study, cross-registration, distance learning, double major, dual enrollment of high school students, honors, independent study, internships, liberal arts/career combination, New York semester, semester at sea, study abroad, teacher certification program, United Nations semester, urban semester, Washington semester. **Credit/placement by examination:** AP, CLEP, SAT, ACT, institutional tests. 18 credit hours maximum toward associate degree, 40 toward bachelor's. Credit through examination (CLEP/DANTES/Advance Placement) may only be awarded with official test scores from an official testing center and an Indiana Wesleyan University individual assessment. The maximum number of credits awarded shall be limited to a total of 40 semester hours for the baccalaureate

Housing: Guaranteed on-campus for freshmen. Coed dorms, special housing for disabled, apartments, wellness housing available. $250 fully refundable deposit, deadline 5/1. **Activities:** Bands, campus ministries, choral groups, dance, drama, international student organizations, literary magazine, music ensembles, Model UN, musical theater, opera, radio station, student government, student newspaper, symphony orchestra, political clubs, black student union, Hispanos Unidos, Habitat for Humanity, volunteer corps, intercollegiate ministries, Amnesty International, environmental club.

Athletics. NCAA. **Intercollegiate:** Baseball M, basketball, cross-country, equestrian W, football (tackle) M, golf, soccer, softball W, tennis, track and field, volleyball W, wrestling M. **Intramural:** Badminton, basketball, bowling, cross-country, golf, racquetball, soccer, softball, swimming, table tennis, tennis, track and field, volleyball, wrestling M. **Team name:** Spartans.

Student services. Chaplain/spiritual director, career counseling, student employment services, financial aid counseling, health services, minority student services, personal counseling, placement for graduates, veterans' counselor. **Physically disabled:** Services for visually, hearing impaired.

Contact. E-mail: admitinfo@manchester.edu
Phone: (260) 982-5055 Toll-free number: (800) 852-3648
Fax: (260) 982-5239
Adam Hohman, Director of Admissions, Manchester College, 604 East College Avenue, North Manchester, IN 46962-0365

Marian University
Indianapolis, Indiana
www.marian.edu

CB member
CB code: 1442

- Private 4-year liberal arts college affiliated with Roman Catholic Church
- Residential campus in very large city
- 2,040 degree-seeking undergraduates
- 54% of applicants admitted
- SAT or ACT with writing required

General. Founded in 1851. Regionally accredited. **Degrees:** 316 bachelor's, 59 associate awarded; master's offered. **ROTC:** Army. **Location:** 4 miles from downtown. **Calendar:** Semester, limited summer session. **Full-time faculty:** 91 total. **Part-time faculty:** 142 total. **Class size:** 62% < 20, 36% 20-39, less than 1% 40-49, less than 1% 50-99. **Special facilities:** Archives (materials on development of education in Archdiocese), 35 acre wetlands biology/ecology laboratory, Allison and Wheeler-Stokely mansions, Japanese tea house and garden, undergraduate seminary.

Freshman class profile. 2,193 applied, 1,184 admitted, 308 enrolled.

Mid 50% test scores			
SAT critical reading:	430-540	GPA 3.0-3.49:	32%
SAT math:	450-540	GPA 2.0-2.99:	29%
SAT writing:	410-530	Rank in top quarter:	47%
ACT composite:	19-25	Rank in top tenth:	14%
GPA 3.75 or higher:	23%	Out-of-state:	12%
GPA 3.50-3.74:	16%	Live on campus:	81%

Basis for selection. School achievement record, test scores, recommendations important. Interview recommended. Essay recommended for academically weak applicants.

High school preparation. College-preparatory program required. 20 units required. Required and recommended units include English 4, mathematics 2-3, social studies 1, history 1, science 2-3 (laboratory 2), foreign language 1-2 and academic electives 9.

2011-2012 Annual costs. Tuition/fees: $26,000. Room/board: $8,084. Books/supplies: $1,200. Personal expenses: $2,474.

Financial aid. Non-need-based: Scholarships awarded for academics, alumni affiliation, art, athletics, leadership, music/drama, religious affiliation.

Application procedures. Admission: Priority date 3/1; deadline 8/1 (receipt date). $35 fee, may be waived for applicants with need, free for online applicants. Admission notification on a rolling basis beginning on or about 9/1. Must reply by May 1 or within 2 week(s) if notified thereafter. **Financial aid:** Priority date 3/15; no closing date. FAFSA, institutional form required. Applicants notified on a rolling basis starting 3/15; must reply within 2 week(s) of notification.

Academics. Special study options: Accelerated study, cooperative education, cross-registration, distance learning, double major, dual enrollment of high school students, honors, independent study, internships, liberal arts/career combination, study abroad, teacher certification program. **Credit/placement by examination:** AP, CLEP, IB, SAT, ACT, institutional tests. 30 credit hours maximum toward associate degree, 60 toward bachelor's.

Support services: Learning center, reduced course load, remedial instruction, study skills assistance, tutoring, writing center.

Majors. Biology: General. **Business:** General, accounting, finance, management information systems, marketing. **Communications:** Communications/speech/rhetoric. **Education:** Elementary, music, physical. **English:** English lit. **Foreign languages:** French, Spanish. **Health services:** Nursing (RN). **History:** General. **Math:** General. **Parks/recreation:** Sports admin. **Philosophy/religion:** Philosophy. **Physical sciences:** Chemistry. **Psychology:** General. **Social sciences:** Economics, political science, sociology. **Theology:** Religious ed, theology. **Visual/performing arts:** Art, art history/conservation, commercial/advertising art, music.

Most popular majors. Business/marketing 39%, education 7%, health sciences 17%, parks/recreation 6%.

Computing on campus. 300 workstations in dormitories, library, computer center, student center. Dormitories wired for high-speed internet access and linked to campus network. Online course registration, online library, helpline, wireless network available.

Student life. Freshman orientation: Mandatory. Preregistration for classes offered. Held weekend prior to start of school. Community service project required. **Policies:** Drinking under the age of 21 on campus prohibited. **Housing:** Guaranteed on-campus for freshmen. Coed dorms, special housing for disabled, apartments, cooperative housing, wellness housing available. $125 fully refundable deposit, deadline 5/1. College-owned apartments for students 21 or older, voluntary spiritual living community, nonsmoking areas, suite-style rooms, singles available. **Activities:** Bands, campus ministries, choral groups, dance, drama, international student organizations, literary magazine, music ensembles, musical theater, student government, student newspaper, service organization, Campus America Life League, BACCHUS, Project Earth, community ministries, Union for Black Identity, Fellowship of Christian Athletes, Campus Crusade for Christ.

Athletics. NAIA. **Intercollegiate:** Baseball M, basketball, bowling, cheerleading, cross-country, football (tackle) M, golf, soccer, softball W, tennis, track and field, volleyball W. **Intramural:** Basketball, football (non-tackle), racquetball, softball W, volleyball W. **Team name:** Knights.

Student services. Adult student services, alcohol/substance abuse counseling, chaplain/spiritual director, career counseling, student employment services, financial aid counseling, health services, personal counseling, placement for graduates. **Physically disabled:** Services for visually, hearing impaired.

Contact. E-mail: admissions@marian.edu
Phone: (317) 955-6300 Toll-free number: (800) 772-7264
Fax: (317) 955-6401
Luann Brames, Director of Enrollment, Marian University, 3200 Cold Spring Road, Indianapolis, IN 46222-1997

Martin University
Indianapolis, Indiana
www.martin.edu

CB code: 1379

- Private 4-year university and liberal arts college
- Commuter campus in very large city
- 897 degree-seeking undergraduates: 63% part-time, 70% women
- 81 degree-seeking graduate students

General. Founded in 1977. Regionally accredited. **Degrees:** 58 bachelor's awarded; master's offered. **Calendar:** Semester, extensive summer session. **Full-time faculty:** 25 total. **Part-time faculty:** 15 total.

Basis for selection. Open admission.

2011-2012 Annual costs. Tuition/fees: $13,520. Books/supplies: $1,000. Personal expenses: $1,300.

Application procedures. Admission: Priority date 3/1; no deadline. $25 fee, may be waived for applicants with need. Application must be submitted on paper. Admission notification on a rolling basis. **Financial aid:** Priority date 5/1, closing date 6/30. FAFSA required. Applicants notified on a rolling basis starting 6/1; must reply within 2 week(s) of notification.

Academics. Special study options: Accelerated study, cross-registration, double major, internships, liberal arts/career combination, student-designed major. **Credit/placement by examination:** AP, CLEP. **Support services:** Learning center, remedial instruction, study skills assistance, tutoring.

Majors. Biology: General. **Business:** General, accounting, insurance. **Conservation:** Environmental science. **Education:** Early childhood. **Health services:** Substance abuse counseling. **Liberal arts:** Arts/sciences. **Philosophy/**

religion: Religion. **Physical sciences:** Chemistry. **Protective services:** Criminal justice. **Psychology:** General. **Social sciences:** Sociology.

Computing on campus. 14 workstations in computer center.

Student life. Freshman orientation: Available. Preregistration for classes offered. **Activities:** Choral groups, dance, drama, music ensembles, student government.

Student services. Adult student services, career counseling, student employment services, veterans' counselor.

Contact. E-mail: hglinsey@martin.edu
Phone: (317) 917-3308 Fax: (317) 543-4790
Hodari Glinsey, Director of Admissions, Martin University, 2171 Avondale Place, Indianapolis, IN 46218

Oakland City University
Oakland City, Indiana
www.oak.edu
CB code: 1585

▶ Private 4-year university and liberal arts college affiliated with Baptist General Conference
▶ Commuter campus in small town
▶ 929 degree-seeking undergraduates: 19% part-time, 49% women, 10% African American, 1% Asian American, 3% Hispanic American
▶ 173 degree-seeking graduate students
▶ 69% of applicants admitted
▶ SAT or ACT (ACT writing optional) required
▶ 62% graduate within 6 years

General. Founded in 1885. Regionally accredited. Branches in Bedford and at Branchville Training Center. Accelerated degrees offered at several off-campus sites (National Guard bases and civilian locations). **Degrees:** 196 bachelor's, 217 associate awarded; master's, professional, doctoral offered. **Location:** 30 miles from Evansville. **Calendar:** Semester, limited summer session. **Full-time faculty:** 65 total; 83% have terminal degrees, 3% minority, 57% women. **Part-time faculty:** 19 total; 26% have terminal degrees, 5% minority, 53% women. **Class size:** 81% < 20, 19% 20-39, less than 1% 40-49.

Freshman class profile. 225 applied, 155 admitted, 116 enrolled.

Mid 50% test scores			
SAT critical reading:	410-530	GPA 2.0-2.99:	27%
SAT math:	430-540	Rank in top quarter:	16%
SAT writing:	400-480	Rank in top tenth:	9%
ACT composite:	18-23	End year in good standing:	84%
GPA 3.75 or higher:	16%	Return as sophomores:	74%
GPA 3.50-3.74:	14%	Out-of-state:	10%
GPA 3.0-3.49:	31%	Live on campus:	60%

Basis for selection. 2.5 GPA or average mean score of 450 on GED required. SAT/ACT test scores most important; 1250 on SAT or 19 ACT required. Recommendations considered. Interview and essay recommended. **Home schooled:** Transcript of courses and grades required.

High school preparation. College-preparatory program recommended. 15 units recommended. Recommended units include English 4, mathematics 3, social studies 3, science 3 and foreign language 2.

2011-2012 Annual costs. Tuition/fees: $16,200. Room/board: $7,700. Books/supplies: $1,500. Personal expenses: $1,500.

2011-2012 Financial aid. Need-based: 87% of total undergraduate aid awarded as scholarships/grants, 13% as loans/jobs. **Non-need-based:** Scholarships awarded for academics, alumni affiliation, art, athletics, minority status, music/drama, religious affiliation.

Application procedures. Admission: Closing date 9/8 (receipt date). $35 fee, may be waived for applicants with need. Admission notification on a rolling basis. **Financial aid:** Closing date 3/1. FAFSA required. Applicants notified on a rolling basis starting 5/1.

Academics. Special study options: Accelerated study, combined bachelor's/graduate degree, cooperative education, distance learning, double major, dual enrollment of high school students, external degree, honors, independent study, internships, liberal arts/career combination, teacher certification program. Combined bachelor's/graduate degree: M.S. in Management. **Credit/placement by examination:** AP, CLEP, IB, SAT, ACT, institutional tests. 16 credit hours maximum toward associate degree, 32 toward bachelor's. **Support services:** Learning center, pre-admission summer program, reduced course load, remedial instruction, tutoring.

Majors. Biology: General. **Business:** General, accounting, business admin, human resources, management information systems, organizational behavior. **Education:** Art, biology, business, early childhood, elementary, English, health, history, mathematics, music, physical, reading, science, social science, social studies, special ed, voc/tech. **English:** English lit. **History:** General. **Liberal arts:** Arts/sciences, humanities. **Math:** Applied. **Parks/recreation:** Health/fitness. **Philosophy/religion:** Religion. **Protective services:** Criminal justice. **Psychology:** General. **Social sciences:** General, sociology. **Visual/performing arts:** Art, graphic design, industrial design, music, music performance.

Most popular majors. Business/marketing 53%, education 24%, liberal arts 6%.

Computing on campus. 120 workstations in library, computer center, student center. Dormitories wired for high-speed internet access and linked to campus network. Commuter students can connect to campus network. Online course registration, online library, helpline, wireless network available.

Student life. Freshman orientation: Mandatory, $75 fee. Preregistration for classes offered. One day immediately before each semester. **Housing:** Guaranteed on-campus for all undergraduates. Single-sex dorms, apartments, wellness housing available. $100 fully refundable deposit, deadline 7/22. **Activities:** Pep band, campus ministries, choral groups, drama, literary magazine, music ensembles, student government, student newspaper, mental health assistance group, Circle-K, Student Christian Association, Fellowship of Christian Athletes, Theologs, student education association.

Athletics. NCAA, NCCAA. **Intercollegiate:** Baseball M, basketball, cheerleading M, cross-country, golf, soccer, softball W, tennis, volleyball W. **Intramural:** Basketball, bowling, football (non-tackle), softball, table tennis, tennis, volleyball. **Team name:** Oaks.

Student services. Adult student services, chaplain/spiritual director, career counseling, services for economically disadvantaged, student employment services, financial aid counseling, health services, personal counseling, placement for graduates, veterans' counselor.

Contact. E-mail: ocuadmit@oak.edu
Phone: (812) 749-4781 ext. 222 Toll-free number: (800) 737-5125
Fax: (812) 749-1433
Kim Heldt, Director of Admissions, Oakland City University, 138 North Lucretia Street, Oakland City, IN 47660

Purdue University
West Lafayette, Indiana
www.purdue.edu
CB member
CB code: 1631

▶ Public 4-year university
▶ Residential campus in small city
▶ 30,603 degree-seeking undergraduates: 4% part-time, 43% women, 4% African American, 5% Asian American, 3% Hispanic American, 15% international
▶ 8,575 degree-seeking graduate students
▶ 68% of applicants admitted
▶ SAT or ACT with writing, application essay required
▶ 69% graduate within 6 years

General. Founded in 1869. Regionally accredited. **Degrees:** 6,848 bachelor's, 209 associate awarded; master's, professional, doctoral offered. **ROTC:** Army, Naval, Air Force. **Location:** 65 miles from Indianapolis. **Calendar:** Semester, limited summer session. **Full-time faculty:** 2,081 total; 98% have terminal degrees, 21% minority, 31% women. **Part-time faculty:** 273 total; 86% have terminal degrees, 6% minority, 52% women. **Class size:** 37% < 20, 40% 20-39, 6% 40-49, 10% 50-99, 7% >100. **Special facilities:** Linear accelerator, horticultural park, concert hall, 3 theaters, outdoor concert facility, 2 professional golf courses, on-campus airport, center for data perceptualization.

Freshman class profile. 29,513 applied, 20,163 admitted, 6,684 enrolled.

Mid 50% test scores			
SAT critical reading:	490-610	GPA 2.0-2.99:	4%
SAT math:	550-690	Rank in top quarter:	74%
SAT writing:	500-610	Rank in top tenth:	39%
ACT composite:	24-30	End year in good standing:	91%
GPA 3.75 or higher:	44%	Return as sophomores:	90%
GPA 3.50-3.74:	25%	Out-of-state:	35%
GPA 3.0-3.49:	27%	International:	20%

Basis for selection. Rigor of high school curriculum, standardized test scores, GPA and information provided by both applicant and high school

counselor considered. Interview required for veterinary medicine, veterinary technology and pharmacy applicants.

High school preparation. College-preparatory program recommended. Required and recommended units include English 4, mathematics 4, social studies 3, science 3 (laboratory 3), foreign language 2 and computer science 1.

2011-2012 Annual costs. Tuition/fees: $9,478; $27,646 out-of-state. Differential general service fees: Engineering undergraduate students pay an additional $1,300 per academic year. Management undergraduate students pay an additional $1,384 per academic year. School of Technology undergraduate students pay an additional $546 per academic year. Room/board: $9,510. Books/supplies: $1,050. Personal expenses: $1,690.

2011-2012 Financial aid. Need-based: 4,611 full-time freshmen applied for aid; 3,382 were judged to have need; 3,382 of these received aid. Average need met was 94%. Average scholarship/grant was $11,302; average loan $3,851. 44% of total undergraduate aid awarded as scholarships/grants, 56% as loans/jobs. **Non-need-based:** Awarded to 8,106 full-time undergraduates, including 2,136 freshmen. Scholarships awarded for academics, athletics, leadership, music/drama, ROTC, state residency. **Additional information:** Cooperative work for credit available in many programs. Purdue Promise replaces need based loans with institutional funds after and in conjunction with federal and state eligibility for high-need students.

Application procedures. Admission: Priority date 3/1; no deadline. $50 fee, may be waived for applicants with need. Admission notification on a rolling basis. November 15 deadline for veterinary technology program, preferential deadline for pre-pharmacy, health sciences and nursing, and scholarships. **Financial aid:** Priority date 3/1; no closing date. FAFSA required.

Academics. Minimal number of courses outside major allowed on pass/ fail basis, not to exceed 20% of total credit hours required. **Special study options:** Accelerated study, combined bachelor's/graduate degree, cooperative education, cross-registration, distance learning, double major, dual enrollment of high school students, exchange student, honors, independent study, internships, liberal arts/career combination, New York semester, study abroad, teacher certification program, weekend college. **Credit/placement by examination:** AP, CLEP, IB, SAT, ACT, institutional tests. **Support services:** Learning center, pre-admission summer program, reduced course load, remedial instruction, study skills assistance, tutoring, writing center.

Majors. Architecture: Landscape. **Area/ethnic studies:** African-American, Asian, French, German, Japanese, women's. **Biology:** General, biochemistry, Biochemistry/molecular biology, botany, cellular/molecular, entomology, microbiology, molecular, plant genetics, zoology. **Business:** Accounting, accounting/business management, accounting/finance, actuarial science, business admin, construction management, fashion, financial planning, hospitality admin, hospitality/recreation, hotel/motel admin, human resources, labor studies, management information systems, marketing, operations, organizational behavior, retailing, selling, telecom management, tourism/travel, training/development. **Communications:** Advertising, broadcast journalism, communications/speech/rhetoric, journalism, organizational, persuasive communications, public relations. **Computer sciences:** General, computer graphics, computer science, information systems, LAN/WAN management, networking, programming, systems analysis. **Conservation:** General, environmental science, fisheries, forestry, management/policy, wildlife/wilderness. **Education:** General, agricultural, art, biology, chemistry, developmentally delayed, early childhood, early childhood special, elementary, elementary special ed, family/consumer sciences, foreign languages, French, German, health, kindergarten/preschool, mathematics, multi-level teacher, physical, physics, secondary, social studies, Spanish, technology/industrial arts. **Engineering:** Aerospace, agricultural, biomedical, chemical, civil, computer, construction, electrical, industrial, materials, mechanical, nuclear, surveying. **English:** Creative writing, English lit, technical writing. **Foreign languages:** General, classics, East Asian, French, German, Italian, Japanese, Russian, Spanish. **General:** Agronomy, animal breeding, animal health, animal husbandry, animal nutrition, animal sciences, business, communications, crop production, dairy, economics, farm/ranch, food science, greenhouse operations, horticultural science, horticulture, international, landscaping, livestock, mechanization, nursery operations, ornamental horticulture, plant breeding, plant protection, plant sciences, production, products processing, range science, soil chem/physics, soil science, turf management. **Health services:** Athletic training, audiology/hearing, audiology/speech pathology, clinical lab science, dietetic technician, dietetics, nursing (RN), occupational health, predental, premedicine, speech pathology, veterinary technology/ assistant. **History:** General. **Human services:** Social work. **Liberal arts:** Arts/sciences, humanities. **Math:** General, applied, statistics. **Parks/recreation:** Exercise sciences, facilities management, health/fitness, sports studies. **Philosophy/religion:** Philosophy, religion. **Physical sciences:** Atmospheric science, chemistry, geology, meteorology, physics. **Protective services:** Law enforcement admin. **Psychology:** General. **Social sciences:** General, anthropology, political science, sociology. **Visual/performing arts:** General, acting, art, art history/conservation, design, dramatic, fashion design, film/cinema/video, interior design, music, photography, studio arts, theater arts management. **Work/family studies:** General, clothing/textiles, family studies, family/community services, food/nutrition.

Most popular majors. Agriculture 6%, business/marketing 13%, education 7%, engineering/engineering technologies 28%, family/consumer sciences 7%, health sciences 6%, social sciences 6%.

Computing on campus. 5,502 workstations in dormitories, library, computer center, student center. Dormitories wired for high-speed internet access and linked to campus network. Commuter students can connect to campus network. Online course registration, helpline, wireless network available.

Student life. Freshman orientation: Available, $320 fee. Preregistration for classes offered. Held the week before classes. **Policies:** Nondiscrimination, anti-harassment, anti-hazing policies; bill of students' rights. **Housing:** Coed dorms, single-sex dorms, special housing for disabled, apartments, cooperative housing, fraternity/sorority housing, wellness housing available. $100 nonrefundable deposit, deadline 5/1. **Activities:** Bands, campus ministries, choral groups, dance, drama, international student organizations, literary magazine, music ensembles, radio station, student government, student newspaper, symphony orchestra, TV station, over 850 organizations.

Athletics. NCAA. **Intercollegiate:** Baseball M, basketball, cross-country, diving, football (tackle) M, golf, soccer W, softball W, swimming, tennis, track and field, volleyball W, wrestling M. **Intramural:** Badminton, basketball, cross-country, football (non-tackle), golf, racquetball, soccer, softball, swimming, table tennis, tennis, track and field, volleyball. **Team name:** Boilermakers.

Student services. Adult student services, alcohol/substance abuse counseling, career counseling, services for economically disadvantaged, student employment services, financial aid counseling, health services, legal services, minority student services, on-campus daycare, personal counseling, placement for graduates, veterans' counselor, women's services. **Physically disabled:** Services for visually, speech, hearing impaired.

Contact. E-mail: admissions@purdue.edu
Phone: (765) 494-1776 Fax: (765) 494-0544
Pamela Horne, Dean of Admissions, Purdue University, 475 Stadium Mall Drive, West Lafayette, IN 47907-2050

Purdue University Calumet
Hammond, Indiana
www.calumet.purdue.edu

CB member
CB code: 1638

- Public 4-year university and branch campus college
- Commuter campus in small city
- 8,040 degree-seeking undergraduates: 31% part-time, 55% women, 17% African American, 2% Asian American, 17% Hispanic American, 6% international
- 956 degree-seeking graduate students
- 48% of applicants admitted
- SAT or ACT with writing required

General. Founded in 1943. Regionally accredited. Experiential learning curricular components required by all undergraduate students. **Degrees:** 1,007 bachelor's, 164 associate awarded; master's offered. **Location:** 20 miles from Chicago. **Calendar:** Semester, extensive summer session. **Full-time faculty:** 308 total; 67% have terminal degrees, 21% minority, 49% women. **Part-time faculty:** 296 total; 13% have terminal degrees, 19% minority, 51% women. **Class size:** 31% < 20, 60% 20-39, 5% 40-49, 4% 50-99, less than 1% >100.

Freshman class profile. 4,072 applied, 1,943 admitted, 961 enrolled.

Mid 50% test scores			
SAT critical reading:	430-530	Rank in top quarter:	33%
SAT math:	440-540	Rank in top tenth:	13%
SAT writing:	410-510	Return as sophomores:	69%
GPA 3.75 or higher:	12%	Out-of-state:	13%
GPA 3.50-3.74:	8%	Live on campus:	13%
GPA 3.0-3.49:	26%	International:	3%
GPA 2.0-2.99:	51%	Fraternities:	1%
		Sororities:	1%

Basis for selection. Class rank, grade average in subjects related to degree objectives, trends in achievement throughout high school, satisfactory high school subject matter requirements, strength of college preparatory program, and standardized test results most important. Graduation from high school with minimum of 15 units of credit required. **Home schooled:** Transcript of courses and grades required.

High school preparation. College-preparatory program recommended. 20 units required. Required and recommended units include English 4, mathematics 3, social studies 3, history 1, science 3 (laboratory 1-2) and foreign language 1-2. Course requirements vary according to program.

2011-2012 Annual costs. Tuition/fees: $6,789; $15,336 out-of-state. Room only: $5,040. Books/supplies: $1,125.

2010-2011 Financial aid. Need-based: 849 full-time freshmen applied for aid; 698 were judged to have need; 631 of these received aid. Average need met was 10%. Average scholarship/grant was $3,320; average loan $1,814. 39% of total undergraduate aid awarded as scholarships/grants, 61% as loans/jobs. **Non-need-based:** Awarded to 959 full-time undergraduates, including 231 freshmen. Scholarships awarded for academics, athletics, minority status, state residency.

Application procedures. Admission: No deadline. No application fee. Admission notification on a rolling basis. **Financial aid:** Priority date 3/10, closing date 6/30. FAFSA required. Applicants notified on a rolling basis starting 4/15; must reply within 2 week(s) of notification.

Academics. Special study options: Accelerated study, combined bachelor's/graduate degree, cooperative education, distance learning, double major, dual enrollment of high school students, ESL, honors, independent study, internships, study abroad, teacher certification program, weekend college. **Credit/placement by examination:** AP, CLEP, SAT, ACT, institutional tests. **Support services:** Learning center, reduced course load, remedial instruction, study skills assistance, tutoring, writing center.

Honors college/program. 3.5 GPA, 27 ACT/1200 SAT (exclusive of Writing) required. Must maintain 3.5 GPA. Additional factors include outstanding academic achievement, strength of academic program, demonstrated leadership, creativity, community involvement, essay, and letter(s) of recommendation.

Majors. Biology: General. **Business:** General, accounting, business admin, entrepreneurial studies, finance, human resources, retailing, small business admin. **Communications:** Broadcast journalism, communications/speech/rhetoric, journalism, public relations. **Computer sciences:** General, computer graphics, computer science, database management, information systems, networking, programming. **Education:** General, biology, chemistry, early childhood, elementary, English, French, multi-level teacher, physics, science, secondary, social science, social studies. **Engineering:** General, computer, electrical, engineering mechanics, mechanical, software. **English:** American lit, English lit, writing. **Foreign languages:** General, French, Spanish. **Health services:** Clinical lab science, nursing (RN), premedicine, preop/surgical nursing, prepharmacy, preveterinary. **History:** General. **Math:** General, applied. **Philosophy/religion:** Philosophy. **Physical sciences:** Chemistry, physics. **Protective services:** Law enforcement admin. **Psychology:** General. **Social sciences:** Political science, sociology.

Most popular majors. Business/marketing 26%, communications/journalism 8%, engineering/engineering technologies 13%, family/consumer sciences 6%, health sciences 11%, social sciences 12%.

Computing on campus. 1,500 workstations in library, computer center, student center. Dormitories wired for high-speed internet access and linked to campus network. Commuter students can connect to campus network. Online course registration, online library, helpline, wireless network available.

Student life. Freshman orientation: Mandatory. Preregistration for classes offered. **Housing:** Apartments, wellness housing available. **Activities:** Campus ministries, choral groups, dance, drama, international student organizations, literary magazine, student government, student newspaper, black student union, Los Latinos, Society of Professional Hispanic Engineers, InterVarsity Christian Fellowship, Muslim student association, New Life Ministries, National Society of Black Engineers, Indian students association, Korean student organization, social justice club.

Athletics. NAIA. **Intercollegiate:** Basketball, cheerleading. **Intramural:** Basketball, bowling, golf, racquetball, sailing, soccer, softball, table tennis, volleyball, weight lifting. **Team name:** Peregrines.

Student services. Adult student services, career counseling, student employment services, financial aid counseling, health services, on-campus daycare, personal counseling, placement for graduates, veterans' counselor. **Physically disabled:** Services for visually, speech, hearing impaired.

Contact. E-mail: adms@calumet.purdue.edu
Phone: (219) 989-2213 Toll-free number: (800) 447-76383 ext. 2213
Fax: (219) 989-2775
Dorothy Fink, Director of Admissions, Purdue University Calumet, 2200 169th Street, Hammond, IN 46323-2094

Purdue University North Central
Westville, Indiana   **CB member**
www.pnc.edu   **CB code: 1640**

- Public 4-year branch campus college
- Commuter campus in rural community

- 3,518 degree-seeking undergraduates: 27% part-time, 58% women, 5% African American, 1% Asian American, 7% Hispanic American, 1% Native American
- 76 degree-seeking graduate students
- 71% of applicants admitted

General. Founded in 1943. Regionally accredited. **Degrees:** 387 bachelor's, 196 associate awarded; master's offered. **Location:** 10 miles from Michigan City, 13 miles from Laporte. **Calendar:** Semester, limited summer session. **Full-time faculty:** 119 total; 61% have terminal degrees, 18% minority, 43% women. **Part-time faculty:** 163 total; 14% have terminal degrees, 10% minority, 58% women. **Class size:** 53% < 20, 43% 20-39, 1% 40-49, 2% 50-99, less than 1% >100.

Freshman class profile. 1,659 applied, 1,177 admitted, 627 enrolled.

Mid 50% test scores			
SAT critical reading:	430-540	GPA 3.0-3.49:	30%
SAT math:	440-540	GPA 2.0-2.99:	52%
SAT writing:	420-510	Rank in top quarter:	25%
ACT composite:	18-23	Rank in top tenth:	7%
GPA 3.75 or higher:	6%	Return as sophomores:	51%
GPA 3.50-3.74:	10%	Out-of-state:	2%

Basis for selection. Academic record and test scores important. SAT or ACT recommended. Interview recommended for academically weak applicants.

High school preparation. College-preparatory program recommended. 15 units recommended. Recommended units include English 4, mathematics 3, social studies 1, history 1, science 3 (laboratory 3) and foreign language 2.

2011-2012 Annual costs. Tuition/fees: $6,872; $16,360 out-of-state.

2010-2011 Financial aid. Need-based: 710 full-time freshmen applied for aid; 564 were judged to have need; 496 of these received aid. Average need met was 47%. Average scholarship/grant was $5,955; average loan $2,970. 60% of total undergraduate aid awarded as scholarships/grants, 40% as loans/jobs. **Non-need-based:** Awarded to 462 full-time undergraduates, including 145 freshmen. Scholarships awarded for academics, athletics, leadership.

Application procedures. Admission: Priority date 8/1; no deadline. No application fee. Admission notification on a rolling basis. **Financial aid:** Priority date 3/10, closing date 6/30. FAFSA required. Applicants notified on a rolling basis starting 4/1; must reply by 8/1 or within 2 week(s) of notification.

Academics. Special study options: Combined bachelor's/graduate degree, distance learning, double major, dual enrollment of high school students, honors, independent study, internships, study abroad, teacher certification program, weekend college. **Credit/placement by examination:** AP, CLEP, SAT, ACT, institutional tests. **Support services:** Learning center, reduced course load, remedial instruction, tutoring, writing center.

Majors. Biology: General. **Business:** Human resources, operations. **Communications:** Communications/speech/rhetoric. **Computer sciences:** Networking. **Education:** Early childhood, elementary. **Engineering:** Electrical, mechanical. **English:** English lit. **Health services:** Nursing (RN). **Human services:** Social work. **Liberal arts:** Arts/sciences.

Most popular majors. Business/marketing 30%, education 7%, engineering/engineering technologies 14%, interdisciplinary studies 6%, liberal arts 27%.

Computing on campus. 330 workstations in library, computer center. Commuter students can connect to campus network. Online course registration, online library, helpline, wireless network available.

Student life. Freshman orientation: Available. Preregistration for classes offered. **Activities:** Campus ministries, choral groups, drama, literary magazine, student government, student newspaper, Active Voices, Alpha Phi Alpha, Christian bible study, Rotaract club, TRIO service club.

Athletics. NAIA. **Intercollegiate:** Baseball M, basketball M, golf M, softball W, volleyball W. **Team name:** Panthers.

Student services. Career counseling, student employment services, financial aid counseling, on-campus daycare, personal counseling, placement for graduates. **Physically disabled:** Services for visually, hearing impaired.

Contact. E-mail: admissions@pnc.edu
Phone: (219) 785-5505 Toll-free number: (800) 782-1231
Fax: (219) 785-5653
Janice Whisler, Director Enrollment Outreach Recruitment, Purdue University North Central, 1401 South US Highway 421, Westville, IN 46391-9542

Rose-Hulman Institute of Technology

Terre Haute, Indiana
www.rose-hulman.edu

CB member
CB code: 1668

◆ Private 4-year engineering college
◆ Residential campus in small city
◆ 1,893 degree-seeking undergraduates: 21% women, 2% African American, 3% Asian American, 3% Hispanic American, 6% international
◆ 85 degree-seeking graduate students
◆ 62% of applicants admitted
◆ SAT or ACT (ACT writing optional) required
◆ 77% graduate within 6 years; 22% enter graduate study

General. Founded in 1874. Regionally accredited. **Degrees:** 427 bachelor's awarded; master's offered. **ROTC:** Army, Air Force. **Location:** 73 miles from Indianapolis. **Calendar:** Quarter, limited summer session. **Full-time faculty:** 163 total; 98% have terminal degrees, 13% minority, 21% women. **Part-time faculty:** 14 total; 100% have terminal degrees, 29% women. **Class size:** 37% < 20, 62% 20-39, less than 1% 40-49, less than 1% 50-99. **Special facilities:** Advanced learning center, observatory, center for technological research with industry.

Freshman class profile. 4,298 applied, 2,675 admitted, 506 enrolled.

Mid 50% test scores			
SAT critical reading:	550-670	Rank in top quarter:	93%
SAT math:	630-720	Rank in top tenth:	62%
SAT writing:	530-640	End year in good standing:	82%
ACT composite:	27-32	Return as sophomores:	92%
GPA 3.75 or higher:	69%	Out-of-state:	60%
GPA 3.50-3.74:	21%	Live on campus:	98%
GPA 3.0-3.49:	10%	International:	8%

Basis for selection. GED not accepted. Primary consideration given to school achievement record and subjects taken. Applicants must rank in top quarter of graduating class. Test scores also very important. Recommendations important. Extracurricular and leadership activities, alumni ties considered. Interviews, although not required, can be determining factor. **Home schooled:** Statement describing home school structure and mission, transcript of courses and grades, letter of recommendation (nonparent) required. Lab courses must have been taken at high school or community college.

High school preparation. College-preparatory program required. 16 units required. Required and recommended units include English 4, mathematics 4-5, social studies 2, science 2-3 (laboratory 2) and academic electives 4.

2011-2012 Annual costs. Tuition/fees: $40,447. Required fees for incoming freshman students only include mandatory purchase of laptop computer, which is a $2,500 expense. Room/board: $10,455. Books/supplies: $1,500. Personal expenses: $1,500.

2011-2012 Financial aid. Need-based: 411 full-time freshmen applied for aid; 361 were judged to have need; 361 of these received aid. Average need met was 86%. Average scholarship/grant was $24,271; average loan $4,313. 69% of total undergraduate aid awarded as scholarships/grants, 31% as loans/jobs. **Non-need-based:** Awarded to 590 full-time undergraduates, including 173 freshmen. Scholarships awarded for academics, minority status, ROTC.

Application procedures. Admission: Priority date 12/1; deadline 3/1 (postmark date). $40 fee, may be waived for applicants with need. Application must be submitted online. Admission notification on a rolling basis beginning on or about 10/15. Must reply by 5/1. **Financial aid:** Priority date 3/1; no closing date. FAFSA required. Applicants notified on a rolling basis starting 3/10; must reply by 5/1.

Academics. Area minor programs in science, engineering, humanities and social sciences. Additional certificate and interdisciplinary programs available in imaging systems, technical translation, semiconductor materials and devices, management studies, and optical communications. **Special study options:** Accelerated study, cooperative education, cross-registration, double major, independent study, internships, study abroad. **Credit/placement by examination:** AP, CLEP, IB, institutional tests. **Support services:** Learning center, reduced course load, study skills assistance, tutoring, writing center.

Majors. Biology: General, biochemistry. **Computer sciences:** Computer science. **Engineering:** Applied physics, biomedical, chemical, civil, computer, electrical, mechanical, software. **Math:** General. **Physical sciences:** Chemistry, physics. **Social sciences:** Economics.

Most popular majors. Computer/information sciences 6%, engineering/engineering technologies 84%.

Computing on campus. PC or laptop required. 14 workstations in library. Dormitories wired for high-speed internet access and linked to campus network. Commuter students can connect to campus network. Online course registration, online library, helpline, repair service, student web hosting, wireless network available.

Student life. Freshman orientation: Mandatory. Preregistration for classes offered. **Housing:** Guaranteed on-campus for freshmen. Coed dorms, single-sex dorms, apartments, fraternity/sorority housing available. $75 fully refundable deposit, deadline 6/7. Pets allowed in dorm rooms. **Activities:** Bands, campus ministries, choral groups, dance, drama, international student organizations, literary magazine, music ensembles, musical theater, radio station, student government, student newspaper, Inter-Varsity Christian Fellowship, Circle K, National Society of Black Engineers, student activities board, Society of Woman Engineers, Alpha Phi Omega service fraternity.

Athletics. NCAA. **Intercollegiate:** Baseball M, basketball, cross-country, diving, football (tackle) M, golf, rifle, soccer, softball W, swimming, tennis, track and field, volleyball W. **Intramural:** Basketball, bowling, cross-country, football (non-tackle), golf, racquetball, soccer, softball, swimming, table tennis, tennis, track and field, volleyball. **Team name:** Fightin' Engineers.

Student services. Alcohol/substance abuse counseling, career counseling, student employment services, financial aid counseling, health services, personal counseling, placement for graduates.

Contact. E-mail: admissions@rose-hulman.edu
Phone: (812) 877-8213 Toll-free number: (800) 248-7448
Fax: (812) 877-8941
Lisa Norton, Director of Admissions, Rose-Hulman Institute of Technology, Office of Admissions, Terre Haute, IN 47803-3999

Saint Joseph's College

Rensselaer, Indiana
www.saintjoe.edu

CB member
CB code: 1697

◆ Private 4-year liberal arts college affiliated with Roman Catholic Church
◆ Residential campus in small town
◆ 1,045 degree-seeking undergraduates: 4% part-time, 59% women, 10% African American, 1% Asian American, 5% Hispanic American, 1% Native American
◆ 10 degree-seeking graduate students
◆ 60% of applicants admitted
◆ SAT or ACT (ACT writing optional) required
◆ 57% graduate within 6 years; 29% enter graduate study

General. Founded in 1889. Regionally accredited. **Degrees:** 234 bachelor's awarded; master's offered. **Location:** 80 miles from Chicago, 90 miles from Indianapolis. **Calendar:** Semester, limited summer session. **Full-time faculty:** 57 total; 72% have terminal degrees, 4% minority, 40% women. **Part-time faculty:** 56 total; 12% have terminal degrees, 2% minority, 52% women. **Class size:** 81% < 20, 17% 20-39, less than 1% 40-49, 1% 50-99.

Freshman class profile. 1,799 applied, 1,081 admitted, 263 enrolled.

Mid 50% test scores			
		GPA 2.0-2.99:	44%
SAT critical reading:	410-520	Rank in top quarter:	36%
SAT math:	430-530	Rank in top tenth:	15%
ACT composite:	19-24	End year in good standing:	94%
GPA 3.75 or higher:	13%	Return as sophomores:	66%
GPA 3.50-3.74:	12%	Out-of-state:	27%
GPA 3.0-3.49:	31%	Live on campus:	92%

Basis for selection. For applicants with requirement deficiencies, admissions decision may be deferred until additional requirements (which may include an interview, recommendations, further course work, or an essay) are evaluated. Limited number of these applicants will be admitted under the Freshman Academic Support Program. **Home schooled:** Statement describing home school structure and mission, transcript of courses and grades required. **Learning Disabled:** After admission, documentation of learning disability must be submitted to Director of Counseling Services in order to receive academic accommodations.

High school preparation. College-preparatory program recommended. 15 units recommended. Recommended units include English 4, mathematics 3, social studies 3, science 3 (laboratory 2) and foreign language 2. 10 recommended units must be from English, foreign language, social studies, math, and natural science. 3 units distributed among social studies, history, and academic electives.

2011-2012 Annual costs. Tuition/fees: $26,330. Room/board: $7,980. Books/supplies: $900. Personal expenses: $740.

2010-2011 Financial aid. Need-based: 241 full-time freshmen applied for aid; 222 were judged to have need; 222 of these received aid. Average need met was 83%. Average scholarship/grant was $19,094; average loan $3,635. 70% of total undergraduate aid awarded as scholarships/grants, 30% as loans/jobs. **Non-need-based:** Awarded to 288 full-time undergraduates, including 67 freshmen. Scholarships awarded for academics, alumni affiliation, athletics, minority status, music/drama.

Application procedures. Admission: No deadline. $25 fee, may be waived for applicants with need, free for online applicants. Admission notification on a rolling basis beginning on or about 9/1. Must reply by May 1 or within 3 week(s) if notified thereafter. **Financial aid:** Priority date 3/1; no closing date. FAFSA required. Applicants notified on a rolling basis starting 3/1; must reply by 5/1 or within 2 week(s) of notification.

Academics. Core program is a sequence of 10 interdisciplinary courses and seeks to integrate Christian humanism with critical appraisal of human condition. **Special study options:** Accelerated study, cross-registration, double major, dual enrollment of high school students, honors, independent study, internships, liberal arts/career combination, student-designed major, study abroad, teacher certification program, Washington semester. **Credit/placement by examination:** AP, CLEP, institutional tests. **Support services:** Learning center, reduced course load, study skills assistance, tutoring, writing center.

Majors. Biology: General, biochemistry. **Business:** General, accounting, management information systems. **Communications:** Communications/speech/rhetoric, media studies. **Computer sciences:** General. **Education:** Elementary, secondary. **English:** Creative writing, English lit. **Health services:** Athletic training, clinical lab science, nursing (RN), predental, premedicine, preveterinary. **History:** General. **Math:** General. **Parks/recreation:** Health/fitness, sports admin. **Philosophy/religion:** Philosophy. **Physical sciences:** Chemistry. **Protective services:** Criminal justice. **Psychology:** General. **Social sciences:** Economics, international relations, political science, sociology. **Theology:** Pastoral counseling. **Visual/performing arts:** Directing/producing, music history, music management, studio arts.

Most popular majors. Biology 9%, business/marketing 13%, education 7%, health sciences 33%.

Computing on campus. 69 workstations in library, computer center, student center. Dormitories wired for high-speed internet access and linked to campus network. Online course registration, helpline, student web hosting, wireless network available.

Student life. Freshman orientation: Mandatory. Preregistration for classes offered. One-day optional early registrations in April, June and July; 4-day required orientation in August. **Housing:** Guaranteed on-campus for all undergraduates. Coed dorms, single-sex dorms, special housing for disabled, apartments, wellness housing available. $200 nonrefundable deposit, deadline 5/1. Special dormitories available for non-traditional full-time students. **Activities:** Bands, campus ministries, choral groups, dance, drama, literary magazine, music ensembles, Model UN, musical theater, radio station, student government, student newspaper, TV station, charitable society, Habitat for Humanity, Kairos Team, College Republicans, College Democrats, peer ministry, Right to Life, volunteer corps, diversity coalition, St. Thomas Aquinas Catholic Society, Knights of Columbus.

Athletics. NCAA. **Intercollegiate:** Baseball M, basketball, cross-country, football (tackle) M, golf, soccer, softball W, tennis, track and field, volleyball W. **Intramural:** Basketball, football (non-tackle), softball, volleyball. **Team name:** Pumas.

Student services. Chaplain/spiritual director, career counseling, financial aid counseling, health services, personal counseling, placement for graduates. **Physically disabled:** Services for visually impaired.

Contact. E-mail: admissions@saintjoe.edu
Phone: (219) 866-6170 Toll-free number: (800) 447-8781
Fax: (219) 866-6122
John Wadell, Assistant Vice President, Enrollment Management, Saint Joseph's College, Box 890, Rensselaer, IN 47978-0890

Saint Mary's College
Notre Dame, Indiana
www.saintmarys.edu

CB member
CB code: 1702

- Private 4-year liberal arts college for women affiliated with Roman Catholic Church
- Residential campus in small city
- 1,491 degree-seeking undergraduates: 100% women, 2% African American, 1% Asian American, 9% Hispanic American, 1% international
- 84% of applicants admitted

- SAT or ACT with writing, application essay required
- 79% graduate within 6 years; 28% enter graduate study

General. Founded in 1844. Regionally accredited. **Degrees:** 401 bachelor's awarded. **ROTC:** Army, Naval, Air Force. **Location:** 3 miles from South Bend, 90 miles from Chicago. **Calendar:** Semester, limited summer session. **Full-time faculty:** 119 total; 87% have terminal degrees, 8% minority, 65% women. **Part-time faculty:** 100 total; 40% have terminal degrees, 5% minority, 77% women. **Class size:** 63% < 20, 34% 20-39, less than 1% 40-49, 2% 50-99. **Special facilities:** Performing arts center, greenhouse, galleries.

Freshman class profile. 1,453 applied, 1,220 admitted, 393 enrolled.

Mid 50% test scores			
SAT critical reading:	510-620	GPA 2.0-2.99:	3%
SAT math:	510-610	Rank in top quarter:	69%
SAT writing:	520-620	Rank in top tenth:	31%
ACT composite:	22-27	End year in good standing:	98%
GPA 3.75 or higher:	49%	Return as sophomores:	86%
GPA 3.50-3.74:	22%	Out-of-state:	76%
GPA 3.0-3.49:	26%	Live on campus:	98%
		International:	2%

Basis for selection. School achievement record, high school transcript, GPA, test scores, activities important. Essay, class rank, school recommendations considered. Students must submit at least one writing component; ACT with Writing required if applicant is not also taking SAT (with mandatory Writing); ACT with Writing recommended even if applicant is also taking SAT. Interview recommended. Audition recommended for music majors. Portfolio recommended for art majors. **Home schooled:** Statement describing home school structure and mission, transcript of courses and grades required.

High school preparation. College-preparatory program recommended. 16 units required; 20 recommended. Required and recommended units include English 4, mathematics 3-4, history 2, science 2-4 (laboratory 2), foreign language 2-4 and academic electives 3. 3 additional units distributed among English, math, science, foreign language, and social studies required. 2 years of same foreign language required.

2011-2012 Annual costs. Tuition/fees: $32,000. Room/board: $9,800. Books/supplies: $1,200. Personal expenses: $1,000.

2011-2012 Financial aid. Need-based: 335 full-time freshmen applied for aid; 278 were judged to have need; 278 of these received aid. Average need met was 82%. Average scholarship/grant was $21,767; average loan $3,517. 70% of total undergraduate aid awarded as scholarships/grants, 30% as loans/jobs. **Non-need-based:** Awarded to 1,129 full-time undergraduates, including 326 freshmen. Scholarships awarded for academics, art, music/drama.

Application procedures. Admission: Priority date 2/15; no deadline. No application fee. Admission notification on a rolling basis beginning on or about 12/15. Must reply by May 1 or within 3 week(s) if notified thereafter. **Financial aid:** Closing date 3/1. FAFSA, CSS PROFILE required. Applicants notified on a rolling basis starting 12/15.

Academics. Department of Religious Studies coordinated with Department of Theology at University of Notre Dame. After first year, student can take courses in either department. **Special study options:** Accelerated study, combined bachelor's/graduate degree, cross-registration, distance learning, double major, ESL, exchange student, independent study, internships, liberal arts/career combination, student-designed major, study abroad, teacher certification program, Washington semester. Distance learning offered during summer terms. Campus in Rome, Italy and study abroad programs in Ireland, Spain, France, Argentina, Austria, Australia, South Africa, Uganda, South Korea, Greece, Honduras, Ecuador, China, and Nicaragua. Women's Studies in Europe. Summer European study tour. Academic and extra-curricular co-exchange with University of Notre Dame. Volunteer service opportunities in the U.S. and abroad. Semester Break in El Salvador Program. **Credit/placement by examination:** AP, CLEP, IB, institutional tests. 30 credit hours maximum toward bachelor's degree. **Support services:** Reduced course load, study skills assistance, tutoring, writing center.

Majors. Biology: General. **Business:** Accounting, business admin, management information systems. **Communications:** Communications/speech/rhetoric. **Education:** Elementary. **English:** British lit, creative writing. **Foreign languages:** French, Italian, Spanish. **Health services:** Communication disorders, nursing (RN). **History:** General. **Human services:** Social work. **Liberal arts:** Humanities. **Math:** General, applied, statistics. **Philosophy/religion:** Philosophy, religion. **Physical sciences:** Chemistry. **Psychology:** General. **Social sciences:** Economics, political science, sociology. **Visual/performing arts:** Art, dramatic, music, studio arts.

Most popular majors. Biology 8%, business/marketing 10%, communications/journalism 12%, education 9%, English 9%, health sciences 13%, psychology 6%, social sciences 9%.

Computing on campus. 291 workstations in dormitories, library, computer center, student center. Dormitories wired for high-speed internet access and linked to campus network. Commuter students can connect to campus network. Online course registration, online library, helpline, student web hosting, wireless network available.

Student life. Freshman orientation: Mandatory. Preregistration for classes offered. Held weekend prior to beginning of fall semester. Summer orientation sessions held for fall admits during June. **Policies:** Educational judicial system guaranteeing certain due process rights to all students involved in discipline situation; student judicial board provides opportunity for peer review system. **Housing:** Guaranteed on-campus for all undergraduates. Special housing for disabled, apartments available. $400 fully refundable deposit, deadline 5/1. **Activities:** Bands, campus ministries, choral groups, dance, drama, international student organizations, literary magazine, music ensembles, musical theater, opera, radio station, student government, student newspaper, TV station, neighborhood study help program, Community of International Lay Apostolate, Urban Plunge community program, Circle-K, World Hunger Coalition, Student Alliance for Women's Colleges, Right to Life, Women for the Environment, Sisters of Nefertiti, La Fuerza.

Athletics. NCAA. **Intercollegiate:** Basketball W, cross-country W, diving W, golf W, soccer W, softball W, swimming W, tennis W, volleyball W. **Intramural:** Soccer W, softball W, tennis W, volleyball W. **Team name:** Belles.

Student services. Chaplain/spiritual director, career counseling, student employment services, financial aid counseling, health services, minority student services, on-campus daycare, personal counseling, placement for graduates, women's services. **Physically disabled:** Services for visually, speech, hearing impaired.

Contact. E-mail: admission@saintmarys.edu
Phone: (574) 284-4587 Toll-free number: (800) 551-7621
Fax: (574) 284-4841
Kristin McAndrew, Director of Admission, Saint Mary's College, 122 Le Mans Hall, Notre Dame, IN 46556-5001

St. Mary-of-the-Woods College

St. Mary-of-the-Woods, Indiana	CB member
www.smwc.edu	CB code: 1704

- Private 4-year liberal arts college for women affiliated with Roman Catholic Church
- Commuter campus in rural community
- 1,101 degree-seeking undergraduates: 61% part-time, 95% women
- 208 degree-seeking graduate students
- SAT or ACT with writing, application essay required
- 55% graduate within 6 years; 33% enter graduate study

General. Founded in 1840. Regionally accredited. Traditional campus program open to women only. External degree (distance education) undergraduate programs and graduate programs open to men and women. **Degrees:** 153 bachelor's, 6 associate awarded; master's offered. **ROTC:** Army, Air Force. **Location:** 4 miles from Terre Haute, 70 miles from Indianapolis. **Calendar:** Semester, extensive summer session. **Full-time faculty:** 67 total; 54% have terminal degrees, 12% minority, 69% women. **Part-time faculty:** 103 total; 7% have terminal degrees, 2% minority, 81% women. **Class size:** 92% < 20, 8% 20-39. **Special facilities:** Equine indoor and outdoor arenas, wildlife habitat restoration areas.

Freshman class profile.

Mid 50% test scores		GPA 3.0-3.49:	23%
SAT critical reading:	420-550	GPA 2.0-2.99:	38%
SAT math:	430-520	End year in good standing:	92%
SAT writing:	420-530	Return as sophomores:	59%
ACT composite:	18-24	Out-of-state:	25%
GPA 3.75 or higher:	27%	Live on campus:	70%
GPA 3.50-3.74:	12%		

Basis for selection. School achievement record, test scores most important. Recommendations considered. Interview recommended. Audition required of music majors. Portfolio required of art and journalism majors. **Home schooled:** Letter of recommendation (nonparent) required. **Learning Disabled:** Meeting with Learning Resource Coordinator strongly recommended, IEP report required.

High school preparation. College-preparatory program recommended. 13 units required; 16 recommended. Required and recommended units include English 4, mathematics 3, social studies 3, science 3 (laboratory 3) and foreign language 2.

2011-2012 Annual costs. Tuition/fees: $27,622. Freshmen will enter with a 4-year locked in rate of $26,872. Tuition for undergraduates above freshmen is $24,940. Room/board: $9,334. Books/supplies: $1,500. Personal expenses: $1,000.

2010-2011 Financial aid. Need-based: 104 full-time freshmen applied for aid; 101 were judged to have need; 101 of these received aid. Average need met was 91%. Average scholarship/grant was $4,670; average loan $3,009. 58% of total undergraduate aid awarded as scholarships/grants, 42% as loans/jobs. **Non-need-based:** Awarded to 393 full-time undergraduates, including 121 freshmen. Scholarships awarded for academics, alumni affiliation, art, athletics, leadership, minority status, music/drama, state residency. **Additional information:** Portfolio or audition required of applicants who wish to be considered for Creative Arts Scholarship.

Application procedures. Admission: No deadline. $50 fee, may be waived for applicants with need, free for online applicants. Admission notification on a rolling basis beginning on or about 10/1. **Financial aid:** Priority date 3/1; no closing date. FAFSA required. Applicants notified on a rolling basis starting 12/1; must reply within 6 week(s) of notification.

Academics. Special study options: Accelerated study, cross-registration, distance learning, double major, external degree, honors, independent study, internships, student-designed major, study abroad, teacher certification program, weekend college. Two Undergraduate External Degree Programs: students throughout the country and abroad do course work on-line from home. Exchange program with Providence University in Taiwan. International Agreements with Regent's College, London, and others. **Credit/placement by examination:** AP, CLEP, IB, SAT, ACT, institutional tests. 30 credit hours maximum toward associate degree, 60 toward bachelor's. **Support services:** Learning center, reduced course load, study skills assistance, tutoring, writing center.

Honors college/program. SAT/ACT, GPA, teacher recommendations, and written essays considered; average of 12 first-year students selected each year. Students complete specially-designed Honors Program courses to fulfill general studies requirements.

Majors. Biology: General. **Business:** General, accounting, business admin, communications, human resources, marketing, nonprofit/public. **Communications:** Journalism, media studies. **Computer sciences:** General, web page design. **Education:** General, art, biology, early childhood, elementary, English, kindergarten/preschool, mathematics, music, science, secondary, social studies, special ed. **English:** Creative writing, English lit, technical writing. **General:** Animal husbandry, equestrian studies, equine science. **Health services:** Music therapy, predental, premedicine, prepharmacy, preveterinary. **Liberal arts:** Arts/sciences, humanities. **Math:** General. **Psychology:** General. **Social sciences:** General, criminology. **Theology:** Theology. **Visual/performing arts:** Art, design, dramatic, graphic design, music.

Most popular majors. Agriculture 7%, business/marketing 15%, education 27%, English 6%, psychology 10%, public administration/social services 6%, social sciences 6%.

Computing on campus. 65 workstations in dormitories, library, computer center, student center. Dormitories wired for high-speed internet access and linked to campus network. Commuter students can connect to campus network. Online library, helpline, wireless network available.

Student life. Freshman orientation: Mandatory, $100 fee. Preregistration for classes offered. Three-day program before classes start for traditional undergraduate; requires service component. **Policies:** All students in traditional on-campus program whose families do not live in a contiguous county must live on-campus all 4 years. **Housing:** Guaranteed on-campus for all undergraduates. Wellness housing available. **Activities:** Bands, campus ministries, choral groups, dance, drama, international student organizations, literary magazine, music ensembles, musical theater, student government, student newspaper, symphony orchestra, Habitat for Humanity, literacy volunteers, environmentalist activities, peace and justice committee, arts and issues committee, United Way, sustainability club.

Athletics. USCAA. **Intercollegiate:** Basketball W, cross-country W, equestrian W, golf W, soccer W, softball W. **Team name:** Pomeroys.

Student services. Adult student services, alcohol/substance abuse counseling, chaplain/spiritual director, career counseling, student employment services, financial aid counseling, health services, on-campus daycare, personal counseling, placement for graduates. **Physically disabled:** Services for visually, hearing impaired.

Contact. E-mail: smwcadms@smwc.edu
Phone: (812) 535-5106 Toll-free number: (800) 926-7692
Fax: (812) 535-5010
Beth Terrell, Assistant Vice President for Enrollment Management, St. Mary-of-the-Woods College, Rooney Library, SMWC, St. Mary of the Woods, IN 47876

Taylor University

Upland, Indiana
www.taylor.edu

CB member
CB code: 1802

- Private 4-year university and liberal arts college affiliated with interdenominational tradition
- Residential campus in small town
- 1,875 degree-seeking undergraduates: 3% part-time, 56% women, 2% African American, 2% Asian American, 2% Hispanic American, 4% international
- 105 degree-seeking graduate students
- 84% of applicants admitted
- SAT or ACT (ACT writing recommended), application essay required
- 80% graduate within 6 years; 20% enter graduate study

General. Founded in 1846. Regionally accredited. Christ-centered, covenant community committed to service. **Degrees:** 440 bachelor's, 4 associate awarded; master's offered. **Location:** 20 miles from Muncie, 70 miles from Indianapolis. **Calendar:** 4-1-4, limited summer session. **Full-time faculty:** 138 total; 79% have terminal degrees, 7% minority, 29% women. **Part-time faculty:** 113 total; 38% have terminal degrees, 3% minority, 38% women. **Class size:** 59% < 20, 34% 20-39, 4% 40-49, 3% 50-99, 1% >100. **Special facilities:** Photo-voltaic solar array, wind turbines, arboretum, environmental studies laboratory, NASA-approved clean room, particle accelerator, NASA project space research equipment, C.S. Lewis collection of original manuscripts.

Freshman class profile. 1,839 applied, 1,541 admitted, 464 enrolled.

Mid 50% test scores			
SAT critical reading:	510-650	GPA 2.0-2.99:	9%
SAT math:	500-640	Rank in top quarter:	67%
SAT writing:	490-620	Rank in top tenth:	38%
ACT composite:	23-29	End year in good standing:	92%
GPA 3.75 or higher:	55%	Return as sophomores:	85%
GPA 3.50-3.74:	12%	Out-of-state:	64%
GPA 3.0-3.49:	24%	Live on campus:	96%
		International:	4%

Basis for selection. High school transcript, test scores important. Recommend rank in top 25% of graduating class with 3.3 GPA and 1000 SAT (exclusive of Writing). Recommendations from applicant's pastor and counselor required. Cocurricular activities considered. Audition required of music majors. Portfolio recommended for art majors. Interviews required for some financial and academic programs. **Home schooled:** Letter of recommendation (nonparent) required.

High school preparation. College-preparatory program recommended. 15 units required. Required and recommended units include English 4, mathematics 3-4, social studies 2-3, science 3-4 (laboratory 3-4), foreign language 2, computer science 1, visual/performing arts 1 and academic electives 3.

2011-2012 Annual costs. Tuition/fees: $27,438. Room/board: $7,532. Books/supplies: $1,000. Personal expenses: $1,800.

2011-2012 Financial aid. Need-based: 373 full-time freshmen applied for aid; 307 were judged to have need; 307 of these received aid. Average need met was 72%. Average scholarship/grant was $14,518; average loan $4,387. 64% of total undergraduate aid awarded as scholarships/grants, 36% as loans/jobs. **Non-need-based:** Awarded to 662 full-time undergraduates, including 185 freshmen. Scholarships awarded for academics, alumni affiliation, art, athletics, leadership, minority status, music/drama, religious affiliation, state residency.

Application procedures. Admission: No deadline. $25 fee, may be waived for applicants with need, free for online applicants. Admission notification on a rolling basis beginning on or about 10/1. Must reply by May 1 or within 2 week(s) if notified thereafter. **Financial aid:** Closing date 3/10. FAFSA required. Applicants notified on a rolling basis starting 3/1; must reply by 5/1.

Academics. Special study options: Combined bachelor's/graduate degree, cooperative education, distance learning, double major, dual enrollment of high school students, exchange student, honors, independent study, internships, semester at sea, student-designed major, study abroad, teacher certification program, urban semester, Washington semester. **Credit/placement by examination:** AP, CLEP, IB, institutional tests. 30 credit hours maximum toward associate degree, 30 toward bachelor's. **Support services:** Learning center, remedial instruction, study skills assistance, tutoring, writing center.

Majors. Biology: General. **Business:** Accounting, business admin, finance, international, managerial economics, marketing. **Communications:** Communications/speech/rhetoric, media studies, persuasive communications. **Computer sciences:** General. **Conservation:** Environmental science. **Education:** General, art, elementary, English, French, mathematics, music, physical,

science, social studies, Spanish. **Engineering:** Applied physics, computer, environmental. **English:** English lit, technical writing. **Foreign languages:** French, Spanish. **History:** General. **Human services:** Social work. **Math:** General, applied. **Parks/recreation:** Exercise sciences, sports admin. **Philosophy/religion:** Philosophy. **Physical sciences:** Chemistry, geology, physics. **Psychology:** General. **Social sciences:** Economics, geography, international economic development, international relations, political science, sociology. **Theology:** Bible, religious ed. **Visual/performing arts:** Art, cinematography, dramatic, music.

Most popular majors. Biology 6%, business/marketing 13%, communications/journalism 8%, education 13%, English 8%, psychology 10%, social sciences 7%, theological studies 9%.

Computing on campus. 505 workstations in library, computer center. Dormitories wired for high-speed internet access and linked to campus network. Commuter students can connect to campus network. Online course registration, online library, helpline, repair service, student web hosting, wireless network available.

Student life. Freshman orientation: Available, $15 fee. Preregistration for classes offered. One-day session held twice in June. Welcome Weekend held Friday through Monday before start of fall classes. **Policies:** Students and faculty sign Life Together Covenant explaining expectations and responsibilities of living in Christian community where faith is integrated with academic progress. Religious observance required. **Housing:** Guaranteed on-campus for freshmen. Single-sex dorms, apartments, wellness housing available. $50 nonrefundable deposit, deadline 5/1. Some off-campus apartments available to upperclassmen with special permission. **Activities:** Bands, choral groups, drama, film society, international student organizations, literary magazine, music ensembles, musical theater, opera, radio station, student government, student newspaper, symphony orchestra, TV station, missions service program, multicultural society, missionary kids organizations, community service programs, global outreach, Fellow Christian Athletes, Carpenter's Hands Ministry, high school youth conference, Acting on AIDS.

Athletics. NAIA, NCCAA. **Intercollegiate:** Baseball M, basketball, cross-country, football (tackle) M, golf M, soccer, softball W, tennis, track and field, volleyball W. **Intramural:** Badminton, basketball, football (non-tackle), golf, racquetball, soccer, softball, table tennis, tennis, volleyball. **Team name:** Trojans.

Student services. Chaplain/spiritual director, career counseling, student employment services, financial aid counseling, health services, minority student services, personal counseling, placement for graduates. **Physically disabled:** Services for visually, speech, hearing impaired.

Contact. E-mail: admissions@tayloru.edu
Phone: (765) 998-5511 Toll-free number: (800) 882-3456
Fax: (765) 998-4925
Amy Barnett, Director of Admissions, Taylor University, 236 West Reade Avenue, Upland, IN 46989-1001

Trine University

Angola, Indiana
www.trine.edu

CB member
CB code: 1811

- Private 4-year university and engineering college
- Residential campus in small town
- 1,493 degree-seeking undergraduates: 3% part-time, 30% women, 4% African American, 1% Asian American, 2% Hispanic American, 1% Native American, 4% international
- 5 degree-seeking graduate students
- 72% of applicants admitted
- SAT or ACT (ACT writing optional) required
- 45% graduate within 6 years; 25% enter graduate study

General. Founded in 1884. Regionally accredited. **Degrees:** 244 bachelor's, 3 associate awarded; master's offered. **ROTC:** Air Force. **Location:** 40 miles from Fort Wayne; 80 miles from Toledo, Ohio. **Calendar:** Semester, limited summer session. **Full-time faculty:** 79 total; 61% have terminal degrees, 11% minority, 32% women. **Part-time faculty:** 58 total; 10% have terminal degrees, 2% minority, 47% women. **Class size:** 48% < 20, 52% 20-39, less than 1% 50-99. **Special facilities:** Educational media resource center, 18 hole championship golf course, student-operated radio station.

Freshman class profile. 2,867 applied, 2,052 admitted, 421 enrolled.

Mid 50% test scores			
SAT critical reading:	460-550	Rank in top quarter:	53%
SAT math:	500-620	Rank in top tenth:	23%
ACT composite:	20-23	End year in good standing:	90%
GPA 3.75 or higher:	29%	Return as sophomores:	73%
GPA 3.50-3.74:	17%	Out-of-state:	46%
GPA 3.0-3.49:	34%	Live on campus:	91%
GPA 2.0-2.99:	20%	Fraternities:	5%
		Sororities:	1%

Basis for selection. School achievement, class rank, test scores, school and community activities, and recommendations important. Interview and essay recommended. **Home schooled:** Statement describing home school structure and mission, transcript of courses and grades required. **Learning Disabled:** Must submit clinical evaluation of learning disability completed within 5 years prior to enrollment.

High school preparation. College-preparatory program required. 18 units required. Required units include English 4, mathematics 3, social studies 3, science 3 (laboratory 2) and academic electives 3. 3 1/2 years of math, physics, and chemistry required for engineering, math and computer science majors.

2011-2012 Annual costs. Tuition/fees: $26,730. New Engineering tuition: Freshmen only $28,600. Room/board: $8,800. Books/supplies: $1,600. Personal expenses: $3,000.

2011-2012 Financial aid. Need-based: 421 full-time freshmen applied for aid; 379 were judged to have need; 379 of these received aid. Average need met was 77%. Average scholarship/grant was $4,612; average loan $4,021. 62% of total undergraduate aid awarded as scholarships/grants, 38% as loans/jobs. **Non-need-based:** Awarded to 289 full-time undergraduates, including 77 freshmen. Scholarships awarded for academics, alumni affiliation, minority status, music/drama, ROTC.

Application procedures. Admission: Priority date 6/1; deadline 8/1. No application fee. Application must be submitted online. Admission notification by 8/1. Admission notification on a rolling basis. **Financial aid:** Priority date 3/1; no closing date. FAFSA required. Applicants notified on a rolling basis starting 3/15; must reply by 5/1 or within 2 week(s) of notification.

Academics. Special study options: Combined bachelor's/graduate degree, cooperative education, distance learning, double major, dual enrollment of high school students, ESL, honors, internships, study abroad, teacher certification program. **Credit/placement by examination:** AP, CLEP, IB, institutional tests. **Support services:** Learning center, reduced course load, remedial instruction, study skills assistance, tutoring, writing center.

Majors. Biology: General. **Business:** Accounting, business admin, entrepreneurial studies, finance, operations. **Communications:** Communications/speech/rhetoric. **Computer sciences:** Computer science, informatics. **Education:** Elementary, English, health, mathematics, middle, physical, science, social studies. **Engineering:** Chemical, civil, computer, electrical, mechanical. **Health services:** Premedicine. **Math:** General. **Parks/recreation:** Golf management, health/fitness, sports admin. **Physical sciences:** Chemistry. **Protective services:** Criminal justice, forensics. **Psychology:** General. **Social sciences:** General.

Most popular majors. Business/marketing 19%, education 9%, engineering/engineering technologies 40%, psychology 7%, security/protective services 10%.

Computing on campus. 600 workstations in dormitories, library, computer center, student center. Dormitories wired for high-speed internet access and linked to campus network. Commuter students can connect to campus network. Online library, helpline, wireless network available.

Student life. Freshman orientation: Mandatory. Preregistration for classes offered. Held 3 days at start of fall semester. **Housing:** Guaranteed on-campus for all undergraduates. Coed dorms, single-sex dorms, apartments available. $150 nonrefundable deposit, deadline 5/1. Honors housing; independent fraternity/sorority housing available. **Activities:** Bands, campus ministries, choral groups, dance, drama, international student organizations, music ensembles, radio station, student government, student newspaper, Circle K, Newman Fellowship, InterVarsity Christian Fellowship, Christian campus house, multicultural student association, Students Against Destructive Decisions, Habitat for Humanity, SPEAK (environmental/ecological concerns).

Athletics. NCAA. Intercollegiate: Baseball M, basketball, cross-country, football (tackle) M, golf, lacrosse, soccer, softball W, tennis, track and field, volleyball W, wrestling M. **Intramural:** Badminton, basketball, cheerleading, football (non-tackle) M, golf, handball, racquetball, softball, table tennis, volleyball. **Team name:** Thunder.

Student services. Alcohol/substance abuse counseling, chaplain/spiritual director, career counseling, student employment services, financial aid counseling, health services, personal counseling, placement for graduates, veterans' counselor.

Contact. E-mail: admit@trine.edu
Phone: (260) 665-4100 Toll-free number: (800) 347-4878
Fax: (260) 665-4578
Scott Goplin, Dean of Admission, Trine University, One University Avenue, Angola, IN 46703

University of Evansville
Evansville, Indiana — **CB member**
www.evansville.edu — **CB code: 1208**

- Private 4-year university and liberal arts college affiliated with United Methodist Church
- Residential campus in small city
- 2,554 degree-seeking undergraduates: 3% part-time, 61% women, 3% African American, 1% Asian American, 2% Hispanic American, 5% international
- 175 degree-seeking graduate students
- 83% of applicants admitted
- SAT or ACT with writing, application essay required
- 63% graduate within 6 years; 22% enter graduate study

General. Founded in 1854. Regionally accredited. **Degrees:** 522 bachelor's, 11 associate awarded; master's, professional offered. **ROTC:** Army. **Location:** 170 miles from Indianapolis and St. Louis. **Calendar:** Semester, limited summer session. **Full-time faculty:** 177 total; 85% have terminal degrees, 9% minority, 37% women. **Part-time faculty:** 53 total; 36% have terminal degrees, 47% women. **Class size:** 52% < 20, 40% 20-39, 7% 40-49, 2% 50-99.

Freshman class profile. 3,522 applied, 2,915 admitted, 622 enrolled.

Mid 50% test scores			
SAT critical reading:	510-620	Rank in top quarter:	72%
SAT math:	520-620	Rank in top tenth:	39%
SAT writing:	500-610	End year in good standing:	89%
ACT composite:	23-28	Return as sophomores:	83%
GPA 3.75 or higher:	57%	Out-of-state:	45%
GPA 3.50-3.74:	13%	Live on campus:	88%
GPA 3.0-3.49:	21%	International:	5%
GPA 2.0-2.99:	9%	Fraternities:	29%
		Sororities:	24%

Basis for selection. Weighted GPA calculated using academic courses only. Extracurricular activities important. Interview recommended. Audition required of music and theater majors. **Home schooled:** Letter of recommendation (nonparent) required. **Learning Disabled:** Students requesting accommodations must provide documentation of the disability and the significant impact of the disability on academic functioning.

High school preparation. College-preparatory program required. 11 units required; 15 recommended. Required and recommended units include English 4, mathematics 3-4, social studies 1, history 1, science 2-3 (laboratory 2) and foreign language 2. 1 or more physics, additional chemistry and math, 2 or more years of foreign language recommended for engineering programs. 1 chemistry required for nursing program.

2011-2012 Annual costs. Tuition/fees: $29,416. Room/board: $9,530.

2011-2012 Financial aid. Need-based: 558 full-time freshmen applied for aid; 498 were judged to have need; 498 of these received aid. Average need met was 86%. Average scholarship/grant was $22,693; average loan $3,879. 76% of total undergraduate aid awarded as scholarships/grants, 24% as loans/jobs. **Non-need-based:** Awarded to 2,209 full-time undergraduates, including 617 freshmen. Scholarships awarded for academics, alumni affiliation, art, athletics, minority status, music/drama, religious affiliation, ROTC.

Application procedures. Admission: Priority date 2/1; deadline 8/1 (postmark date). $35 fee, may be waived for applicants with need. Admission notification by 2/15. Must reply by May 1 or within 2 week(s) if notified thereafter. **Financial aid:** Priority date 3/10; no closing date. FAFSA required. Applicants notified on a rolling basis starting 3/25; must reply by 5/1.

Academics. Special study options: Accelerated study, cooperative education, double major, dual enrollment of high school students, ESL, external degree, honors, independent study, internships, semester at sea, student-designed major, study abroad, teacher certification program, Washington semester. British Campus at Harlaxton College, the Washington Center for Internships, and undergraduate research. **Credit/placement by examination:** AP, CLEP, IB, SAT, ACT, institutional tests. 6 credit hours maximum toward associate degree, 6 toward bachelor's. **Support services:** Pre-admission summer program, study skills assistance, tutoring, writing center.

Majors. Biology: General, biochemistry, neuroscience. **Business:** Accounting, business admin, finance, international, management information systems, managerial economics, marketing, organizational leadership. **Communications:** General, sports. **Computer sciences:** Computer science. **Conservation:** Environmental science, environmental studies. **Education:** General, art, biology, chemistry, drama/dance, elementary, English, French, German, mathematics, music, physical, physics, social studies, Spanish, special ed. **Engineering:** Civil, computer, electrical, mechanical. **English:** Creative writing, English lit, writing. **Foreign languages:** Classics, French, German, Spanish. **Health services:** Athletic training, clinical lab science, health care admin,

music therapy, nursing (RN), predental, premedicine, preoptometry, prepharmacy, preveterinary. **History:** General. **Liberal arts:** Arts/sciences. **Math:** General. **Parks/recreation:** Exercise sciences, sports admin. **Philosophy/religion:** Philosophy. **Physical sciences:** Chemistry, physics. **Protective services:** Criminal justice. **Psychology:** General. **Social sciences:** Archaeology, economics, international relations, political science, sociology. **Theology:** Bible, theology. **Visual/performing arts:** Art, art history/conservation, design, dramatic, music, music management, music performance, theater arts management.

Most popular majors. Business/marketing 17%, education 8%, engineering/engineering technologies 9%, health sciences 8%, parks/recreation 9%, social sciences 10%, visual/performing arts 9%.

Computing on campus. 385 workstations in dormitories, library, student center. Dormitories wired for high-speed internet access and linked to campus network. Commuter students can connect to campus network. Online course registration, online library, helpline, repair service, student web hosting, wireless network available.

Student life. Freshman orientation: Mandatory. Preregistration for classes offered. One session in summer includes testing, advising, and registration; 3 1/2 day program held prior to beginning of semester. **Housing:** Guaranteed on-campus for freshmen. Coed dorms, single-sex dorms, apartments, fraternity/sorority housing available. $100 nonrefundable deposit, deadline 5/1. **Activities:** Bands, campus ministries, choral groups, dance, drama, film society, international student organizations, literary magazine, music ensembles, musical theater, opera, radio station, student government, student newspaper, symphony orchestra, black student union, Hillel, Kappa Chi (service), Amnesty International, Habitat for Humanity, Circle K, College Democrats, UE College Republicans, Student Christian Fellowship, Asian culture club.

Athletics. NCAA. **Intercollegiate:** Baseball M, basketball, cross-country, diving, golf, soccer, softball W, swimming, tennis W, volleyball W. **Intramural:** Badminton, basketball, cross-country, diving, football (non-tackle), golf, racquetball, soccer, softball, swimming, tennis, volleyball. **Team name:** Purple Aces.

Student services. Adult student services, alcohol/substance abuse counseling, chaplain/spiritual director, career counseling, student employment services, financial aid counseling, health services, minority student services, personal counseling, placement for graduates, veterans' counselor. **Physically disabled:** Services for visually, speech, hearing impaired.

Contact. E-mail: admission@evansville.edu
Phone: (812) 488-2468 Toll-free number: (800) 423-8633 ext. 2468
Fax: (812) 488-4076
Don Vos, Dean of Admission, University of Evansville, 1800 Lincoln Avenue, Evansville, IN 47722

University of Indianapolis
Indianapolis, Indiana
www.uindy.edu

CB member
CB code: 1321

▶ Private 4-year university and liberal arts college affiliated with United Methodist Church
▶ Residential campus in very large city
▶ 4,138 degree-seeking undergraduates: 27% part-time, 68% women, 13% African American, 1% Asian American, 2% Hispanic American, 5% international
▶ 1,191 degree-seeking graduate students
▶ 79% of applicants admitted
▶ SAT or ACT (ACT writing optional) required
▶ 52% graduate within 6 years

General. Founded in 1902. Regionally accredited. **Degrees:** 730 bachelor's, 57 associate awarded; master's, professional, doctoral offered. **ROTC:** Army. **Location:** 5 miles from downtown. **Calendar:** Semester, limited summer session. **Full-time faculty:** 218 total; 76% have terminal degrees, 6% minority, 57% women. **Part-time faculty:** 275 total; 28% have terminal degrees, 6% minority, 53% women. **Class size:** 55% < 20, 42% 20-39, 2% 40-49, less than 1% 50-99. **Special facilities:** Observatory, fine arts center.

Freshman class profile. 5,396 applied, 4,245 admitted, 797 enrolled.

Mid 50% test scores			
SAT critical reading:	450-560	GPA 3.0-3.49:	34%
SAT math:	460-570	GPA 2.0-2.99:	20%
SAT writing:	440-550	Rank in top quarter:	56%
ACT composite:	19-25	Rank in top tenth:	27%
GPA 3.75 or higher:	27%	Return as sophomores:	74%
GPA 3.50-3.74:	19%	Out-of-state:	10%
		Live on campus:	79%

Basis for selection. Recommendations, GPA, SAT/ACT, class rank important. Involvement in extracurricular activities considered. Essay recommended. Interview recommended for borderline applicants. Audition required of music majors. Portfolio recommended for art majors. **Home schooled:** Transcript of courses and grades required. **Learning Disabled:** Students with learning disabilities may apply to the BUILD program through separate application process.

High school preparation. 18 units required; 20 recommended. Required and recommended units include English 4, mathematics 3, social studies 2, history 1, science 2-3 (laboratory 1-2), foreign language 2-3, computer science 1, visual/performing arts 2 and academic electives 3.

2011-2012 Annual costs. Tuition/fees: $23,010. Room/board: $8,730. Books/supplies: $1,044. Personal expenses: $1,582.

2010-2011 Financial aid. Need-based: 819 full-time freshmen applied for aid; 731 were judged to have need; 730 of these received aid. Average need met was 72%. Average scholarship/grant was $9,530; average loan $3,557. 32% of total undergraduate aid awarded as scholarships/grants, 68% as loans/jobs. **Non-need-based:** Awarded to 2,960 full-time undergraduates, including 894 freshmen. Scholarships awarded for academics, alumni affiliation, art, athletics, music/drama, religious affiliation, state residency.

Application procedures. Admission: Closing date 8/20. $25 fee, may be waived for applicants with need, free for online applicants. Admission notification on a rolling basis beginning on or about 9/1. Must reply by May 1 or within 2 week(s) if notified thereafter. **Financial aid:** Priority date 3/10; no closing date. FAFSA, institutional form required. Applicants notified on a rolling basis starting 3/1; must reply within 3 week(s) of notification.

Academics. Special study options: Accelerated study, combined bachelor's/graduate degree, cross-registration, double major, dual enrollment of high school students, ESL, honors, independent study, internships, liberal arts/career combination, student-designed major, study abroad, teacher certification program. Baccalaureate for University of Indianapolis Learning Disabled (BUILD), Wellness, Judaic-Christian Traditions, New Student Experience. **Credit/placement by examination:** AP, CLEP, IB, SAT, ACT, institutional tests. 3-8 hours awarded for International Baccalaureate based on scores. **Support services:** Learning center, pre-admission summer program, reduced course load, remedial instruction, study skills assistance, tutoring, writing center.

Honors college/program. Presidential Scholars, Dean's Scholars, or Lugar Scholars with Distinguished Admission invited to participate. Students make formal application to Honors College in second semester for full admission to the College.

Majors. Biology: General, cell/histology. **Business:** Accounting, business admin, international, management information systems, managerial economics, marketing, tourism/travel. **Communications:** Communications/speech/rhetoric. **Computer sciences:** General, computer science, information systems. **Conservation:** Environmental science. **Education:** General, art, biology, business, chemistry, elementary, English, foreign languages, French, history, mathematics, music, physical, physics, science, secondary, social studies, Spanish, speech. **English:** English lit. **Foreign languages:** French, German, Spanish. **Health services:** Art therapy, athletic training, clinical lab technology, nursing (RN), respiratory therapy technology. **History:** General. **Human services:** Social work. **Math:** General. **Parks/recreation:** Exercise sciences, sports admin. **Philosophy/religion:** Philosophy, religion. **Physical sciences:** Chemistry, geology, physics. **Protective services:** Law enforcement admin. **Psychology:** General. **Social sciences:** Anthropology, archaeology, economics, international relations, political science, sociology. **Visual/performing arts:** Art, commercial/advertising art, design, dramatic, music, music performance.

Most popular majors. Biology 6%, business/marketing 28%, education 12%, health sciences 16%, liberal arts 6%, psychology 9%.

Computing on campus. 222 workstations in dormitories, library, computer center, student center. Dormitories wired for high-speed internet access and linked to campus network. Commuter students can connect to campus network. Online library, helpline, wireless network available.

Student life. Freshman orientation: Mandatory, $40 fee. Preregistration for classes offered. Student attends one of 6 summer registration programs. **Housing:** Coed dorms, single-sex dorms, apartments, wellness housing available. $50 fully refundable deposit, deadline 5/1. **Activities:** Bands, campus ministries, choral groups, dance, drama, international student organizations, literary magazine, music ensembles, musical theater, opera, radio station, student government, student newspaper, TV station, Young Democrats, Young Republicans, Fellowship of Christian Athletes, Circle-K, social service, honorary societies.

Athletics. NCAA. **Intercollegiate:** Baseball M, basketball, cross-country, diving, football (tackle) M, golf, soccer, softball W, swimming, tennis, track

and field, volleyball W, wrestling M. **Intramural:** Basketball, football (non-tackle) M, soccer, softball, volleyball. **Team name:** Greyhounds.

Student services. Adult student services, chaplain/spiritual director, career counseling, student employment services, health services, personal counseling, placement for graduates, veterans' counselor. **Physically disabled:** Services for visually, speech, hearing impaired.

Contact. E-mail: admissions@uindy.edu
Phone: (317) 788-3216 Toll-free number: (800) 232-8634
Fax: (317) 788-3300
Ron Wilks, Director of Admissions, University of Indianapolis, 1400 East Hanna Avenue, Indianapolis, IN 46227-3697

University of Notre Dame
Notre Dame, Indiana
www.nd.edu

CB member
CB code: 1841

- Private 4-year university affiliated with Roman Catholic Church
- Residential campus in small city
- 8,444 degree-seeking undergraduates: 46% women, 3% African American, 6% Asian American, 9% Hispanic American, 3% international
- 3,346 degree-seeking graduate students
- 24% of applicants admitted
- SAT or ACT (ACT writing optional), application essay required
- 96% graduate within 6 years

General. Founded in 1842. Regionally accredited. Notre Dame Study Centers in Washington, DC; Dublin, Ireland; London, England; Rome, Italy; several other countries. **Degrees:** 2,078 bachelor's awarded; master's, professional, doctoral offered. **ROTC:** Army, Naval, Air Force. **Location:** 90 miles from Chicago. **Calendar:** Semester, extensive summer session. **Full-time faculty:** 980 total. **Part-time faculty:** 100 total. **Special facilities:** Germ-free research facility, radiation laboratory, nature preserve for biological research, wind-tunnel research facility, art museum.

Freshman class profile. 16,548 applied, 4,019 admitted, 2,020 enrolled.

Mid 50% test scores			
SAT critical reading:	660-750	Rank in top tenth:	89%
SAT math:	680-770	Return as sophomores:	97%
SAT writing:	650-740	Out-of-state:	92%
ACT composite:	32-34	Live on campus:	100%
Rank in top quarter:	97%	International:	3%

Basis for selection. GED not accepted. Demonstrated academic achievement and test scores most important. Essay, teacher recommendations, extracurricular activities, and personal statement also important. Three SAT Subject Tests required for home schooled students. Audition recommended for music majors. Portfolio recommended for art majors.

High school preparation. College-preparatory program required. 16 units required; 20 recommended. Required and recommended units include English 4, mathematics 3-4, history 2-4, science 2-4 (laboratory 2), foreign language 2-4 and academic electives 3. Pre-calculus or calculus, chemistry and physics recommended for architecture, engineering and science programs. Social studies requirement should include history.

2012-2013 Annual costs. Tuition/fees (projected): $42,971. Room/board: $11,394. Books/supplies: $950. Personal expenses: $1,200.

2010-2011 Financial aid. **Need-based:** 1,457 full-time freshmen applied for aid; 1,080 were judged to have need; 1,080 of these received aid. Average need met was 99%. Average scholarship/grant was $28,953; average loan $3,290. 82% of total undergraduate aid awarded as scholarships/grants, 18% as loans/jobs. **Non-need-based:** Awarded to 3,272 full-time undergraduates, including 876 freshmen. Scholarships awarded for athletics, ROTC.

Application procedures. Admission: Closing date 12/31 (postmark date). $65 fee, may be waived for applicants with need. Admission notification by 4/10. Must reply by 5/1. **Financial aid:** Closing date 2/15. FAFSA, CSS PROFILE required. Applicants notified by 4/1; must reply by 5/1.

Academics. Special study options: Cross-registration, double major, dual enrollment of high school students, exchange student, honors, independent study, internships, liberal arts/career combination, student-designed major, study abroad, teacher certification program, Washington semester. Teacher certification available only through cross-registration with St. Mary's College; triple majors, quadruple majors, triple degrees, double majors within dual degrees. **Credit/placement by examination:** AP, CLEP, IB, institutional tests. Students with HL score of 6 or 7 eligible to receive credit in anthropology, biology, chemistry, English, French, German, Greek, American history,

Latin, math, music, physics, psychology, and Spanish. **Support services:** Learning center, study skills assistance, tutoring, writing center.

Majors. Architecture: Architecture. **Area/ethnic studies:** African-American, American. **Biology:** General, biochemistry. **Business:** General, accounting, finance, management information systems, marketing. **Computer sciences:** General. **Conservation:** Environmental science. **Education:** Science. **Engineering:** Aerospace, chemical, civil, computer, electrical, environmental, mechanical. **English:** English lit. **Foreign languages:** Ancient Greek, Arabic, Chinese, classics, French, German, Italian, Japanese, Romance, Russian, Spanish. **Health services:** Premedicine. **History:** General. **Liberal arts:** Arts/sciences. **Math:** General. **Philosophy/religion:** Philosophy. **Physical sciences:** Chemistry, physics. **Psychology:** General. **Social sciences:** Anthropology, economics, political science, sociology. **Theology:** Theology. **Visual/performing arts:** Art history/conservation, design, dramatic, music, studio arts.

Most popular majors. Business/marketing 20%, engineering/engineering technologies 9%, foreign language 9%, health sciences 7%, social sciences 16%.

Computing on campus. 261 workstations in dormitories, library, computer center, student center, student center. Dormitories wired for high-speed internet access and linked to campus network. Commuter students can connect to campus network. Online course registration, online library, helpline, repair service, wireless network available.

Student life. Freshman orientation: Mandatory. Preregistration for classes offered. **Housing:** Guaranteed on-campus for freshmen. Single-sex dorms available. $50 deposit, deadline 5/1. Requests for ground level housing or housing suitable for a disabled student will be honored. **Activities:** Bands, campus ministries, choral groups, dance, drama, film society, literary magazine, music ensembles, musical theater, opera, radio station, student government, student newspaper, symphony orchestra, More than 260 clubs and organizations available.

Athletics. NCAA. **Intercollegiate:** Baseball M, basketball, cross-country, diving, fencing, football (tackle) M, golf, ice hockey M, lacrosse, rowing (crew) W, soccer, softball W, swimming, tennis, track and field, volleyball W. **Intramural:** Badminton, baseball M, basketball, bowling, cross-country, football (non-tackle), football (tackle) M, golf, ice hockey M, lacrosse, racquetball, soccer, softball, table tennis, tennis, volleyball, water polo. **Team name:** Fighting Irish.

Student services. Alcohol/substance abuse counseling, chaplain/spiritual director, career counseling, student employment services, health services, minority student services, personal counseling, placement for graduates, women's services. **Physically disabled:** Services for visually, hearing impaired.

Contact. E-mail: admissions@nd.edu
Phone: (574) 631-7505 Fax: (574) 631-8865
Donald Bishop, Assistant Vice President Undergraduate Enrollment, University of Notre Dame, 220 Main Building, Notre Dame, IN 46556

University of Phoenix: Indianapolis
Indianapolis, Indiana
www.phoenix.edu

- For-profit 4-year university and business college
- Commuter campus in very large city
- 579 degree-seeking undergraduates

General. Regionally accredited. **Degrees:** 44 bachelor's awarded; master's offered. **Calendar:** Differs by program. **Full-time faculty:** 10 total. **Part-time faculty:** 109 total.

Basis for selection. Open admission, but selective for some programs.

2011-2012 Annual costs. Estimated costs as of August 2011: per-credit-hour charge, $420 to $450, depending upon level and course of study; electronic course materials fee, $95, if applicable. Book and material charges may vary by course and program. All fees are subject to change.

Application procedures. Admission: No deadline. No application fee. **Financial aid:** No deadline.

Academics. Credit/placement by examination: AP, CLEP.

Majors. Business: Accounting, business admin, credit management, e-commerce, entrepreneurial studies, marketing, operations. **Computer sciences:** Networking, programming, security, systems analysis, web page design, webmaster. **Education:** General. **Health services:** Facilities admin, health care admin, long term care admin, medical records technology. **Human**

405

services: General. **Protective services:** Disaster management, law enforcement admin. **Psychology:** General.

Most popular majors. Business/marketing 85%, health sciences 7%.

Contact. Toll-free number: (866) 766-0766
Marc Booker, Director of Admission and Evaluation, University of Phoenix: Indianapolis, 7999 Knue Road, Indianapolis, IN 46250-1932

University of Southern Indiana
Evansville, Indiana
www.usi.edu   CB code: 1335

- Public 4-year university and liberal arts college
- Commuter campus in small city
- 9,697 degree-seeking undergraduates: 16% part-time, 59% women, 6% African American, 1% Asian American, 1% Hispanic American, 2% international
- 873 degree-seeking graduate students
- 72% of applicants admitted
- SAT or ACT (ACT writing recommended) required
- 35% graduate within 6 years

General. Founded in 1965. Regionally accredited. Credit courses offered at various off-campus sites in Evansville and surrounding areas. **Degrees:** 1,353 bachelor's, 76 associate awarded; master's, doctoral offered. **ROTC:** Army. **Location:** 150 miles from Indianapolis. **Calendar:** Semester, limited summer session. **Full-time faculty:** 339 total; 70% have terminal degrees, 6% minority, 52% women. **Part-time faculty:** 321 total; 22% have terminal degrees, 6% minority, 56% women. **Class size:** 36% < 20, 53% 20-39, 6% 40-49, 4% 50-99, 2% >100. **Special facilities:** Restored historic town managed by university.

Freshman class profile. 6,469 applied, 4,632 admitted, 2,025 enrolled.

Mid 50% test scores			
SAT critical reading:	440-540	Rank in top quarter:	23%
SAT math:	440-540	Rank in top tenth:	10%
SAT writing:	410-510	End year in good standing:	72%
ACT composite:	18-24	Return as sophomores:	65%
GPA 3.75 or higher:	13%	Out-of-state:	8%
GPA 3.50-3.74:	14%	Live on campus:	63%
GPA 3.0-3.49:	30%	International:	1%
GPA 2.0-2.99:	42%	Fraternities:	9%
		Sororities:	7%

Basis for selection. 2.0 GPA required for out-of-state applicants. 900 SAT (exclusive of Writing) required for applicants to health programs. Students accepted at 1 of 3 levels based on academic record and test scores. Placement test administered prior to registration. SAT/ACT used to place students at 1 of 3 levels within institution. **Home schooled:** Transcript of courses and grades required.

High school preparation. College-preparatory program recommended. 18 units recommended. Recommended units include English 4, mathematics 4, social studies 2, history 2, science 2, foreign language 2 and academic electives 2. 2 units computer and/or art recommended.

2011-2012 Annual costs. Tuition/fees: $5,992; $13,987 out-of-state. Room/board: $6,920. Books/supplies: $1,100. Personal expenses: $2,800.

2011-2012 Financial aid. **Need-based:** 1,941 full-time freshmen applied for aid; 1,383 were judged to have need; 1,371 of these received aid. Average need met was 78%. Average scholarship/grant was $6,357; average loan $3,317. 40% of total undergraduate aid awarded as scholarships/grants, 60% as loans/jobs. **Non-need-based:** Awarded to 1,548 full-time undergraduates, including 562 freshmen. Scholarships awarded for academics, art, athletics, leadership, music/drama, state residency.

Application procedures. **Admission:** Closing date 8/15 (receipt date). $35 fee, may be waived for applicants with need. Admission notification on a rolling basis beginning on or about 7/1. Applicants accepted through first week of classes, but encouraged to apply by August 15 for fall and January 1 for spring. **Financial aid:** Closing date 3/1. FAFSA, institutional form required. Applicants notified on a rolling basis starting 4/1.

Academics. **Special study options:** Combined bachelor's/graduate degree, cooperative education, distance learning, double major, dual enrollment of high school students, ESL, honors, independent study, internships, study abroad, teacher certification program. **Credit/placement by examination:** AP, CLEP, SAT, ACT, institutional tests. 46 credit hours maximum toward associate degree, 94 toward bachelor's. **Support services:** Learning center, reduced course load, remedial instruction, study skills assistance, tutoring, writing center.

Majors. **Biology:** General, biochemistry, biophysics. **Business:** General, accounting, business admin, entrepreneurial studies, finance, marketing, office management, operations. **Communications:** Advertising, journalism, media studies, radio/TV. **Computer sciences:** General, computer science. **Education:** Business, early childhood, elementary, physical. **Engineering:** General. **English:** English lit. **Foreign languages:** French, German, Spanish. **Health services:** Dental hygiene, health care admin, medical radiologic technology/radiation therapy, nursing (RN). **History:** General. **Human services:** Social work. **Liberal arts:** Arts/sciences. **Math:** General. **Parks/recreation:** Exercise sciences, sports admin. **Philosophy/religion:** Philosophy. **Physical sciences:** Chemistry, geology. **Protective services:** Criminal justice. **Psychology:** General. **Social sciences:** General, economics, international relations, political science, sociology. **Visual/performing arts:** Art, dramatic.

Most popular majors. Business/marketing 19%, communications/journalism 8%, education 9%, health sciences 23%, social sciences 7%.

Computing on campus. 306 workstations in dormitories, library, computer center, student center. Dormitories linked to campus network. Commuter students can connect to campus network. Online course registration, online library, helpline, wireless network available.

Student life. **Freshman orientation:** Mandatory, $65 fee. Preregistration for classes offered. Two-day program, includes parent participation. **Housing:** Coed dorms, special housing for disabled, apartments, cooperative housing, fraternity/sorority housing, wellness housing available. $200 partly refundable deposit, deadline 3/1. **Activities:** Bands, campus ministries, choral groups, dance, drama, international student organizations, literary magazine, Model UN, radio station, student government, student newspaper, black student union, Habitat for Humanity, Kappa Chi (Christian service fraternity), Baptist student ministry, Newman Catholic student organization, Collegiate Democrats, Collegiate Republicans.

Athletics. NCAA. **Intercollegiate:** Baseball M, basketball, cheerleading, cross-country, golf, soccer, softball W, tennis, track and field, volleyball W. **Intramural:** Badminton, basketball, bowling, cross-country, football (non-tackle), golf, soccer, softball, swimming, table tennis, tennis, volleyball. **Team name:** Screaming Eagles.

Student services. Adult student services, chaplain/spiritual director, career counseling, student employment services, financial aid counseling, health services, minority student services, on-campus daycare, personal counseling, placement for graduates, veterans' counselor. **Physically disabled:** Services for visually, speech, hearing impaired.

Contact. E-mail: enroll@usi.edu
Phone: (812) 464-1765 Toll-free number: (800) 467-1965
Fax: (812) 465-7154
Eric Otto, Director of Admission, University of Southern Indiana, 8600 University Boulevard, Evansville, IN 47712

University of St. Francis
Fort Wayne, Indiana
www.sf.edu   CB code: 1693

- Private 4-year university and liberal arts college affiliated with Roman Catholic Church
- Commuter campus in small city
- 1,898 degree-seeking undergraduates
- 330 graduate students
- 54% of applicants admitted
- SAT or ACT (ACT writing optional) required
- 61% graduate within 6 years

General. Founded in 1890. Regionally accredited. **Degrees:** 240 bachelor's, 153 associate awarded; master's offered. **ROTC:** Army. **Location:** 120 miles from Indianapolis, 150 miles from Chicago. **Calendar:** Semester, limited summer session. **Full-time faculty:** 128 total. **Part-time faculty:** 121 total. **Special facilities:** Planetarium, nature preserve, cadaver lab, nursing simulation lab.

Freshman class profile. 1,783 applied, 960 admitted, 375 enrolled.

Mid 50% test scores			
SAT critical reading:	430-530	GPA 3.0-3.49:	27%
SAT math:	430-540	GPA 2.0-2.99:	33%
SAT writing:	410-520	Rank in top quarter:	42%
ACT composite:	18-57	Rank in top tenth:	10%
GPA 3.75 or higher:	20%	Out-of-state:	13%
GPA 3.50-3.74:	20%	Live on campus:	58%

Basis for selection. School achievement record, rank in top half of class, and test scores most important. Additional requirements for health care

majors, education majors. Admission procedures may vary among schools within the university. Essay and portfolio recommended. Interview recommended for underprepared applicants. **Home schooled:** State high school equivalency certificate, letter of recommendation (nonparent) required. Bibliography of books read, extracurricular activities.

High school preparation. College-preparatory program recommended. 20 units required; 26 recommended. Required and recommended units include English 4, mathematics 2-3, social studies 2-3, history 1, science 2-3 and academic electives 1-4.

2012-2013 Annual costs. Tuition/fees (projected): $23,950. Room/board: $7,666. Books/supplies: $1,000. Personal expenses: $1,100.

2010-2011 Financial aid. Need-based: 342 full-time freshmen applied for aid; 316 were judged to have need; 316 of these received aid. Average need met was 77%. Average scholarship/grant was $15,417; average loan $3,273. 55% of total undergraduate aid awarded as scholarships/grants, 45% as loans/jobs. **Non-need-based:** Awarded to 335 full-time undergraduates, including 87 freshmen. Scholarships awarded for academics, alumni affiliation, art, athletics, music/drama.

Application procedures. Admission: Priority date 8/1; no deadline. $20 fee, may be waived for applicants with need, free for online applicants. Admission notification on a rolling basis beginning on or about 8/1. **Financial aid:** Priority date 3/10; no closing date. FAFSA required. Applicants notified on a rolling basis starting 3/1.

Academics. Special study options: Combined bachelor's/graduate degree, cross-registration, distance learning, double major, dual enrollment of high school students, exchange student, honors, independent study, internships, liberal arts/career combination, teacher certification program. **Credit/placement by examination:** AP, CLEP, SAT, ACT, institutional tests. 16 credit hours maximum toward associate degree, 32 toward bachelor's. **Support services:** Learning center, reduced course load, remedial instruction, study skills assistance, tutoring, writing center.

Majors. Area/ethnic studies: American. **Biology:** General. **Business:** Accounting, business admin. **Communications:** Communications/speech/ rhetoric, public relations. **Conservation:** General, environmental studies. **Education:** Art, business, chemistry, elementary, English, health, science, social studies, special ed. **English:** English lit. **Health services:** Clinical lab science, nursing (RN), physician assistant, predental, premedicine, prepharmacy. **History:** General. **Human services:** Social work. **Liberal arts:** Arts/ sciences. **Math:** General. **Philosophy/religion:** Philosophy. **Physical sciences:** Chemistry, forensic chemistry. **Psychology:** General. **Social sciences:** Political science, sociology. **Theology:** Theology. **Visual/performing arts:** Art, art history/conservation, commercial/advertising art, graphic design, music, studio arts.

Most popular majors. Business/marketing 9%, communication technologies 12%, education 8%, health sciences 30%, public administration/social services 6%, visual/performing arts 7%.

Computing on campus. PC or laptop required. 415 workstations in dormitories, library, computer center, student center. Dormitories wired for high-speed internet access and linked to campus network. Commuter students can connect to campus network. Online course registration, online library, helpline, repair service, wireless network available.

Student life. Freshman orientation: Mandatory, $50 fee. Preregistration for classes offered. Three-day program held weekend prior to beginning of classes. **Policies:** No alcohol allowed in residence halls, no smoking in campus buildings. Full-time students under 21 not living at home or with adult relatives must live in residence halls. **Housing:** Guaranteed on-campus for freshmen. Coed dorms, apartments available. $200 fully refundable deposit. **Activities:** Bands, campus ministries, choral groups, dance, drama, film society, music ensembles, student government, student newspaper, Educators in Action, student nursing association, peer ministers, Fellowship of Christian Athletes.

Athletics. NAIA. **Intercollegiate:** Baseball M, basketball, cheerleading, cross-country, football (tackle) M, golf, soccer, softball W, tennis, track and field, volleyball W. **Intramural:** Basketball, bowling, football (non-tackle), soccer, volleyball. **Team name:** Cougars.

Student services. Adult student services, chaplain/spiritual director, career counseling, student employment services, financial aid counseling, health services, personal counseling, placement for graduates. **Physically disabled:** Services for visually, hearing impaired.

Contact. E-mail: admiss@sf.edu
Phone: (260) 399-8000 ext. 6300 Toll-free number: (800) 729-4732
Fax: (260) 434-7590
JP Spagnolo, Director of Admissions, University of St. Francis, 2701 Spring Street, Fort Wayne, IN 46808

Valparaiso University

Valparaiso, Indiana
www.valpo.edu

CB member
CB code: 1874

- Private 4-year university affiliated with Lutheran Church
- Residential campus in large town
- 2,785 degree-seeking undergraduates: 4% part-time, 55% women, 5% African American, 2% Asian American, 6% Hispanic American, 4% international
- 1,105 degree-seeking graduate students
- 74% of applicants admitted
- SAT or ACT (ACT writing recommended), application essay required
- 71% graduate within 6 years; 28% enter graduate study

General. Founded in 1859. Regionally accredited. **Degrees:** 645 bachelor's, 4 associate awarded; master's, professional, doctoral offered. **ROTC:** Army, Air Force. **Location:** 55 miles from Chicago. **Calendar:** Semester, limited summer session. **Full-time faculty:** 263 total; 89% have terminal degrees, 8% minority, 40% women. **Part-time faculty:** 112 total; 34% have terminal degrees, 7% minority, 54% women. **Class size:** 52% < 20, 41% 20-39, 2% 40-49, 4% 50-99, less than 1% >100. **Special facilities:** Electron microscope, observatory, storm chasing equipment, weather station, Doppler Radar facility, planetarium, center for learning and information resources, virtual nursing learning center, scientific visualization laboratory.

Freshman class profile. 5,418 applied, 4,027 admitted, 698 enrolled.

Mid 50% test scores			
SAT critical reading:	490-610	Rank in top quarter:	64%
SAT math:	490-610	Rank in top tenth:	34%
SAT writing:	470-590	End year in good standing:	85%
ACT composite:	23-29	Return as sophomores:	81%
GPA 3.75 or higher:	43%	Out-of-state:	63%
GPA 3.50-3.74:	18%	Live on campus:	90%
GPA 3.0-3.49:	31%	International:	3%
GPA 2.0-2.99:	8%	Fraternities:	24%
		Sororities:	19%

Basis for selection. High school record most important. Test scores next in importance, followed by recommendations and activities. Nature of high school program considered. Interview recommended. Audition required of music majors. Portfolio recommended for art majors. **Home schooled:** Transcript of courses and grades required. Must specify primary educator and provide course description list or reading list. **Learning Disabled:** Student should submit suitable documentation to the Disability Support Services Office following admission into the University in order to determine eligibility of services.

High school preparation. College-preparatory program recommended. 16 units required; 19 recommended. Required and recommended units include English 4, mathematics 3-4, social studies 1, history 2, science 2-3 (laboratory 2-3), foreign language 2 and academic electives 3.

2011-2012 Annual costs. Tuition/fees: $31,040. Room/board: $8,756. Books/supplies: $1,200. Personal expenses: $890.

2010-2011 Financial aid. Need-based: 630 full-time freshmen applied for aid; 563 were judged to have need; 563 of these received aid. Average need met was 81%. Average scholarship/grant was $20,749; average loan $4,564. 70% of total undergraduate aid awarded as scholarships/grants, 30% as loans/jobs. **Non-need-based:** Awarded to 914 full-time undergraduates, including 229 freshmen. Scholarships awarded for academics, alumni affiliation, art, athletics, leadership, music/drama, religious affiliation, ROTC, state residency. **Additional information:** Financial assistance based on need, academic record, talent available through university.

Application procedures. Admission: Priority date 12/1; no deadline. No application fee. Admission notification on a rolling basis beginning on or about 10/1. Must reply by May 1 or within 4 week(s) if notified thereafter. **Financial aid:** Priority date 3/1; no closing date. FAFSA required. Applicants notified on a rolling basis starting 3/1; must reply by 5/1 or within 4 week(s) of notification.

Academics. Special study options: Accelerated study, combined bachelor's/graduate degree, cooperative education, cross-registration, distance learning, double major, ESL, exchange student, honors, independent study, internships, liberal arts/career combination, student-designed major, study abroad, teacher certification program, United Nations semester, urban semester, Washington semester. **Credit/placement by examination:** AP, CLEP, IB, institutional tests. **Support services:** Learning center, reduced course load, study skills assistance, tutoring, writing center.

Honors college/program. Approximately 80 students enroll per year in Christ College, the Honors College. Must demonstrate academic excellence

in high school, intellectual curiosity, and leadership skills. Program integrates history, literature, philosophy, religion, and art.

Majors. Area/ethnic studies: American, East Asian. **Biology:** General, biochemistry. **Business:** Accounting, actuarial science, finance, international, management science, marketing. **Communications:** Communications/speech/rhetoric, digital media. **Computer sciences:** Computer science. **Conservation:** Environmental science. **Education:** Art, biology, chemistry, drama/dance, elementary, English, foreign languages, French, geography, German, history, mathematics, middle, music, physical, physics, psychology, science, secondary, social science, Spanish. **Engineering:** Civil, computer, electrical, mechanical. **English:** Creative writing, English lit, technical writing. **Foreign languages:** Classics, French, German, Spanish. **Health services:** Health care admin, nursing (RN). **History:** General. **Human services:** Social work. **Liberal arts:** Humanities. **Math:** General. **Parks/recreation:** Exercise sciences, health/fitness, sports admin. **Philosophy/religion:** Philosophy. **Physical sciences:** Astronomy, atmospheric science, chemistry, geology, physics. **Psychology:** General. **Social sciences:** General, criminology, economics, geography, international economics, international relations, political science, sociology. **Theology:** Theology. **Visual/performing arts:** Art, dramatic, music, music performance, music theory/composition, piano/keyboard, voice/opera.

Most popular majors. Business/marketing 13%, engineering/engineering technologies 10%, health sciences 12%, social sciences 9%.

Computing on campus. 900 workstations in dormitories, library, computer center, student center. Dormitories wired for high-speed internet access and linked to campus network. Commuter students can connect to campus network. Online course registration, helpline, student web hosting, wireless network available.

Student life. Freshman orientation: Mandatory, $115 fee. Preregistration for classes offered. Overnight program held in June. **Policies:** Freshmen not permitted cars on campus. **Housing:** Guaranteed on-campus for all undergraduates. Coed dorms, single-sex dorms, apartments, fraternity/sorority housing, wellness housing available. $100 fully refundable deposit, deadline 5/1. **Activities:** Bands, campus ministries, choral groups, dance, drama, international student organizations, literary magazine, music ensembles, musical theater, radio station, student government, student newspaper, symphony orchestra, Alpha Phi Omega, Earthtones, InterVarsity Christian Fellowship, St. Teresa of Avila, black student organization, Asian American association, Latinos for Excellence, College Democrats, College Republicans.

Athletics. NCAA. **Intercollegiate:** Baseball M, basketball, bowling W, cross-country, diving, football (tackle) M, golf, soccer, softball W, swimming, tennis, track and field, volleyball W. **Intramural:** Badminton, basketball, bowling, football (non-tackle), golf, racquetball, soccer, softball, swimming, table tennis, tennis, volleyball. **Team name:** Crusaders.

Student services. Adult student services, alcohol/substance abuse counseling, chaplain/spiritual director, career counseling, student employment services, financial aid counseling, health services, legal services, minority student services, personal counseling, placement for graduates. **Physically disabled:** Services for visually impaired.

Contact. E-mail: undergrad.admission@valpo.edu
Phone: (219) 464-5011 Toll-free number: (888) 468-2576
Fax: (219) 464-6898
David Fevig, Dean of Undergraduate Admission, Valparaiso University, Kretzmann Hall, 1700 Chapel Drive, Valparaiso, IN 46383-6493

Wabash College
Crawfordsville, Indiana **CB member**
www.wabash.edu **CB code: 1895**

- Private 4-year liberal arts college for men
- Residential campus in large town
- 903 degree-seeking undergraduates: 5% African American, 2% Asian American, 5% Hispanic American, 1% Native American, 7% international
- 63% of applicants admitted
- SAT or ACT with writing, application essay required
- 75% graduate within 6 years; 32% enter graduate study

General. Founded in 1832. Regionally accredited. **Degrees:** 171 bachelor's awarded. **Location:** 45 miles from Indianapolis, 125 miles from Chicago. **Calendar:** Semester. **Full-time faculty:** 81 total; 100% have terminal degrees, 15% minority, 35% women. **Part-time faculty:** 8 total; 88% have terminal degrees, 38% women. **Class size:** 81% < 20, 17% 20-39, less than 1% 40-49, 1% 50-99, less than 1% >100. **Special facilities:** Two biology field stations, qualitative and quantitative skills center, electron microscope, parallel computer, nature preserve, archival center.

Freshman class profile. 1,456 applied, 916 admitted, 293 enrolled.

Mid 50% test scores			
SAT critical reading:	510-610	Rank in top quarter:	70%
SAT math:	540-650	Rank in top tenth:	37%
SAT writing:	490-590	End year in good standing:	92%
ACT composite:	22-27	Return as sophomores:	83%
GPA 3.75 or higher:	39%	Out-of-state:	30%
GPA 3.50-3.74:	26%	Live on campus:	100%
GPA 3.0-3.49:	29%	International:	9%
GPA 2.0-2.99:	6%	Fraternities:	51%

Basis for selection. Class rank, school achievement, recommendation, essay and test scores important. Interview recommended. Character and personal qualities considered. **Learning Disabled:** All students considered on an individual basis.

High school preparation. College-preparatory program required. Recommended units include English 4, mathematics 4, social studies 2, science 2 (laboratory 2), foreign language 2 and academic electives 3.

2011-2012 Annual costs. Tuition/fees: $32,450. Room/board: $8,500. Books/supplies: $750. Personal expenses: $1,500.

2011-2012 Financial aid. Need-based: 279 full-time freshmen applied for aid; 249 were judged to have need; 249 of these received aid. Average need met was 99%. Average scholarship/grant was $19,010; average loan $6,938. 69% of total undergraduate aid awarded as scholarships/grants, 31% as loans/jobs. **Non-need-based:** Awarded to 233 full-time undergraduates, including 68 freshmen. Scholarships awarded for academics, art, leadership, music/drama, state residency.

Application procedures. Admission: Priority date 12/1; no deadline. $40 fee, may be waived for applicants with need. Admission notification on a rolling basis beginning on or about 12/1. Must reply by May 1 or within 2 week(s) if notified thereafter. **Financial aid:** Priority date 2/15, closing date 3/1. FAFSA, CSS PROFILE required. Applicants notified by 3/31; must reply by 5/1 or within 2 week(s) of notification.

Academics. Special study options: Combined bachelor's/graduate degree, double major, independent study, internships, New York semester, semester at sea, study abroad, teacher certification program, United Nations semester, urban semester, Washington semester. Cooperative law program with Columbia University, international and domestic study program of Great Lakes Colleges Association, 3-2 engineering programs with Purdue University/Columbia University/Washington University. **Credit/placement by examination:** AP, CLEP, SAT, ACT, institutional tests. AP credit based on AP exam scores and with in-house exams and subsequent coursework. **Support services:** Learning center, pre-admission summer program, study skills assistance, tutoring, writing center.

Majors. Biology: General, biochemistry. **English:** English lit, rhetoric/composition. **Foreign languages:** Ancient Greek, classics, French, German, Latin, Spanish. **History:** General. **Liberal arts:** Arts/sciences. **Math:** General. **Philosophy/religion:** Philosophy, religion. **Physical sciences:** Chemistry, physics. **Psychology:** General. **Social sciences:** Economics, political science. **Visual/performing arts:** Art, dramatic, music.

Most popular majors. Biology 6%, communications/journalism 6%, English 9%, foreign language 8%, history 11%, mathematics 10%, philosophy/religious studies 14%, physical sciences 8%, psychology 7%, social sciences 16%.

Computing on campus. 360 workstations in dormitories, library, computer center, student center. Dormitories wired for high-speed internet access and linked to campus network. Commuter students can connect to campus network. Online library, helpline, repair service, student web hosting, wireless network available.

Student life. Freshman orientation: Mandatory. Preregistration for classes offered. Held 5 days leading up to start of classes. **Policies:** Gentleman's Rule enforced. **Housing:** Guaranteed on-campus for all undergraduates. Special housing for disabled, apartments, cooperative housing, fraternity/sorority housing, wellness housing available. $250 nonrefundable deposit, deadline 6/25. **Activities:** Bands, campus ministries, choral groups, dance, drama, film society, international student organizations, literary magazine, music ensembles, Model UN, musical theater, radio station, student government, student newspaper, symphony orchestra, political groups, Newman Center, Alpha Phi Omega, Fellowship of Christian Athletes, Muslim student association, Christian Fellowship, pre-law society, moot court competition, Sphinx club, Malcolm X Institute of Black Studies.

Athletics. NCAA. **Intercollegiate:** Baseball M, basketball M, cross-country M, diving M, football (tackle) M, golf M, soccer M, swimming M, tennis M, track and field M, wrestling M. **Intramural:** Badminton M, basketball M, bowling M, cross-country M, diving M, football (non-tackle) M, golf M, handball M, racquetball M, soccer M, softball M, swimming M,

table tennis M, tennis M, track and field M, volleyball M, wrestling M. **Team name:** Little Giants.

Student services. Alcohol/substance abuse counseling, chaplain/spiritual director, career counseling, student employment services, financial aid counseling, health services, minority student services, personal counseling, placement for graduates. **Physically disabled:** Services for visually, speech, hearing impaired.

Contact. E-mail: admissions@wabash.edu
Phone: (765) 361-6225 Toll-free number: (800) 345-5385
Fax: (765) 361-6437
Steven Klein, Dean of Admissions and Financial Aid, Wabash College,
PO Box 352, Crawfordsville, IN 47933

Iowa

Allen College
Waterloo, Iowa
www.allencollege.edu   CB code: 3610

- Private 4-year health science and nursing college
- Commuter campus in small city
- 348 degree-seeking undergraduates: 26% part-time, 92% women
- 138 degree-seeking graduate students
- 75% of applicants admitted
- SAT or ACT (ACT writing optional), application essay required

General. Regionally accredited. **Degrees:** 130 bachelor's, 16 associate awarded; master's, professional offered. **ROTC:** Army. **Calendar:** Semester, limited summer session. **Full-time faculty:** 30 total; 30% have terminal degrees, 3% minority, 97% women. **Part-time faculty:** 9 total; 100% women. **Class size:** 64% < 20, 29% 20-39, 5% 40-49, 2% 50-99.

Freshman class profile. 4 applied, 3 admitted, 2 enrolled.

GPA 3.75 or higher:	50%	Rank in top quarter:	100%
GPA 3.0-3.49:	50%	Rank in top tenth:	100%

Basis for selection. College and secondary school record, class rank, test scores important; recommendations, essay considered. Pre-requisite courses required prior to admission to BSN and health science degree programs.

High school preparation. 4 units required. Required units include English 4, mathematics 3, social studies 3, science 3 (laboratory 2).

2011-2012 Annual costs. Tuition/fees: $17,616. Room/board: $7,281. Books/supplies: $1,063. Personal expenses: $3,248.

2010-2011 Financial aid. Need-based: 5 full-time freshmen applied for aid; 5 were judged to have need; 5 of these received aid. Average need met was 32%. Average scholarship/grant was $12,010; average loan $3,500. 43% of total undergraduate aid awarded as scholarships/grants, 57% as loans/jobs. **Non-need-based:** Scholarships awarded for academics, leadership, minority status, ROTC.

Application procedures. Admission: Priority date 3/1; deadline 8/1 (receipt date). $50 fee, may be waived for applicants with need. Admission notification on a rolling basis. Must reply by May 1 or within 4 week(s) if notified thereafter. **Financial aid:** No deadline. FAFSA, institutional form required. Applicants notified on a rolling basis starting 6/1; must reply within 2 week(s) of notification.

Academics. Special study options: Accelerated study, combined bachelor's/graduate degree, cooperative education, distance learning, external degree, honors, independent study, internships, liberal arts/career combination. **Credit/placement by examination:** AP, CLEP, IB. **Support services:** Learning center, study skills assistance, tutoring.

Honors college/program. Honors program for service to the community.

Majors. Health services: Clinical lab science, nuclear medical technology, nursing (RN), sonography.

Computing on campus. 32 workstations in dormitories, library, computer center. Dormitories wired for high-speed internet access. Online library, helpline, wireless network available.

Student life. Freshman orientation: Mandatory. Preregistration for classes offered. Includes registration, assessment testing, and completion of mandatory health career training. **Housing:** Coed dorms, single-sex dorms, special housing for disabled, apartments, cooperative housing, wellness housing available. $200 nonrefundable deposit. On-campus suite housing available and dorm-style housing offered at cooperating institutions. **Activities:** Choral groups, student government.

Student services. Alcohol/substance abuse counseling, chaplain/spiritual director, career counseling, financial aid counseling, health services, minority student services, on-campus daycare, personal counseling, placement for graduates, women's services. **Physically disabled:** Services for visually, speech, hearing impaired.

Contact. E-mail: allencollegeadmissions@ihs.org
Phone: (319) 226-2000 Fax: (319) 226-2051
Michelle Koehn, Admissions Counselor, Allen College, 1825 Logan Avenue, Waterloo, IA 50703

Ashford University
Clinton, Iowa   CB member
www.ashford.edu   CB code: 6418

- For-profit 4-year university
- Commuter campus in large town
- 66,862 degree-seeking undergraduates
- 90% of applicants admitted
- 37% graduate within 6 years

General. Founded in 1918. Regionally accredited. Traditional campus in Clinton, as well as comprehensive online campus. **Degrees:** 8,839 bachelor's, 732 associate awarded; master's offered. **Location:** 35 miles from Davenport, 138 miles from Chicago. **Calendar:** Semester, extensive summer session.

Freshman class profile. 6,496 applied, 5,849 admitted, 2,946 enrolled.

Mid 50% test scores			
SAT critical reading:	400-510	SAT writing:	400-500
SAT math:	480-520	ACT composite:	18-22

Basis for selection. Applicants to on-campus program should meet 2 of the following: 2.0 GPA (GED equivalency accepted), rank in upper half of graduating class, 18 ACT/860 SAT (exclusive of Writing). Requirements for online programs may vary. Differing admission requirements for traditional and online campuses. Test scores may be considered for traditional campus in Clinton; not required of applicants to online programs. For applicants to Clinton campus, interviews required for teacher education majors, portfolios recommended for art majors.

High school preparation. College-preparatory program recommended. 20 units recommended. Recommended units include English 4, mathematics 3, social studies 2, history 3, science 3, foreign language 2 and academic electives 3.

2011-2012 Annual costs. Tuition/fees: $16,270. Room/board: $6,000. Books/supplies: $1,150.

Financial aid. Non-need-based: Scholarships awarded for academics, art, athletics, music/drama. **Additional information:** Work study only available to students at traditional campus in Clinton.

Application procedures. Admission: Closing date 8/1. No application fee. Admission notification on a rolling basis. Application deadline applies to on-campus admission only. **Financial aid:** Priority date 3/1; no closing date. FAFSA, institutional form required. Applicants notified on a rolling basis starting 2/15; must reply within 2 week(s) of notification.

Academics. Special study options: Combined bachelor's/graduate degree, distance learning, double major, dual enrollment of high school students, ESL, external degree, honors, independent study, internships, study abroad, teacher certification program. **Credit/placement by examination:** AP, CLEP, institutional tests. 30 credit hours maximum toward associate degree, 30 toward bachelor's. Awards credit for CLEP exams in accordance with the American Council on Education (ACE) designated passing score and recommended credit. **Support services:** Learning center, reduced course load, tutoring, writing center.

Majors. Biology: General. **Business:** Accounting, business admin, customer service, e-commerce, entrepreneurial studies, finance, human resources, international, logistics, management information systems, managerial economics, operations, organizational behavior, organizational leadership, project management, real estate. **Communications:** Communications/speech/rhetoric, journalism. **Computer sciences:** General, computer science. **Conservation:** Environmental science, environmental studies. **Education:** General, business, early childhood, educational technology, elementary, foundations, learning sciences, physical, secondary. **English:** English lit. **Foreign languages:** Applied linguistics. **Health services:** General, health care admin, holistic, medical records admin. **History:** General. **Human services:** General. **Liberal arts:** Arts/sciences, library science. **Parks/recreation:** Sports admin. **Protective services:** Criminal justice, law enforcement admin. **Psychology:** General. **Social sciences:** General, cultural anthropology, political science, sociology. **Visual/performing arts:** General, commercial/advertising art. **Work/family studies:** Aging, child development, family resources.

Most popular majors. Business/marketing 35%, education 8%, health sciences 8%, psychology 15%, social sciences 25%.

Computing on campus. PC or laptop required. 109 workstations in dormitories, library, computer center. Dormitories wired for high-speed internet access and linked to campus network. Online library, helpline, repair service, wireless network available.

Student life. Freshman orientation: Mandatory. Preregistration for classes offered. Two-day program held in summer prior to beginning of fall classes. **Housing:** Guaranteed on-campus for all undergraduates. Coed dorms available. $100 fully refundable deposit. **Activities:** Choral groups, dance, drama, music ensembles, student government, student newspaper, photography club, media production club.

Athletics. NAIA. **Intercollegiate:** Baseball M, basketball, cross-country, golf M, soccer, softball W, track and field, volleyball W. **Intramural:** Basketball, bowling, football (non-tackle), swimming, volleyball. **Team name:** Saints.

Student services. Career counseling, student employment services, financial aid counseling. **Physically disabled:** Services for visually, speech, hearing impaired.

Contact. E-mail: admissions@ashford.edu
Phone: (563) 242-4153 Toll-free number: (800) 242-4153
Fax: (563) 243-6102
Alice Parenti, Vice President of Admissions, Ashford University, 400 North Bluff Boulevard, Clinton, IA 52733-2967

Briar Cliff University
Sioux City, Iowa
www.briarcliff.edu

CB member
CB code: 6046

- Private 4-year university and liberal arts college affiliated with Roman Catholic Church
- Residential campus in small city
- 971 degree-seeking undergraduates: 12% part-time, 56% women, 7% African American, 2% Asian American, 9% Hispanic American, 1% Native American, 2% international
- 91 degree-seeking graduate students
- 54% of applicants admitted
- ACT (writing optional) required
- 45% graduate within 6 years; 25% enter graduate study

General. Founded in 1930. Regionally accredited. **Degrees:** 234 bachelor's awarded; master's offered. **ROTC:** Army. **Location:** 90 miles from Omaha, Nebraska, 80 miles from Sioux Falls, South Dakota. **Calendar:** Semester, limited summer session. **Full-time faculty:** 61 total; 74% have terminal degrees, 3% minority, 48% women. **Part-time faculty:** 45 total; 13% have terminal degrees, 2% minority, 47% women. **Class size:** 70% < 20, 25% 20-39, 3% 40-49, 2% 50-99. **Special facilities:** Prairie nature preserve, human anatomy/cadaver laboratory, integrated media lab, nursing simulation lab, entrepreneurship lab, music lab.

Freshman class profile. 2,379 applied, 1,293 admitted, 237 enrolled.

Mid 50% test scores			
SAT critical reading:	420-490	Rank in top quarter:	31%
SAT math:	430-530	Rank in top tenth:	1%
ACT composite:	18-23	End year in good standing:	77%
GPA 3.75 or higher:	19%	Return as sophomores:	69%
GPA 3.50-3.74:	12%	Out-of-state:	58%
GPA 3.0-3.49:	31%	Live on campus:	88%
GPA 2.0-2.99:	38%	International:	5%

Basis for selection. 2.0 GPA and 18 ACT required for full acceptance. Students not meeting requirement may be accepted conditionally or may appeal admission decision if not accepted. Interview and essay recommended. **Home schooled:** Transcript of high school work should be obtained from the school district where the student resides full time. **Learning Disabled:** Students should submit official documentation directly to Student Support Services office.

High school preparation. 16 units recommended. Recommended units include English 4, mathematics 3, social studies 3, science 3, foreign language 2 and academic electives 1.

2012-2013 Annual costs. Tuition/fees (projected): $25,642. Room/board: $7,542. Books/supplies: $1,100. Personal expenses: $2,066.

Financial aid. Non-need-based: Scholarships awarded for academics, alumni affiliation, art, athletics, leadership, music/drama, religious affiliation, state residency.

Application procedures. Admission: No deadline. $20 fee, may be waived for applicants with need. Admission notification on a rolling basis beginning on or about 6/1. **Financial aid:** Priority date 3/15; no closing date. FAFSA required. Applicants notified on a rolling basis starting 3/15; must reply by 5/1 or within 2 week(s) of notification.

Academics. Special study options: Accelerated study, cross-registration, distance learning, double major, honors, independent study, internships, liberal arts/career combination, student-designed major, study abroad, teacher certification program, urban semester, weekend college. Radiologic technology 1-2-1 program, medical technology 3-1 program. **Credit/placement by examination:** AP, CLEP, IB, ACT, institutional tests. 45 credit hours maximum toward bachelor's degree. Examinations must be taken before student enters last 30 hours of study. **Support services:** Learning center, pre-admission summer program, reduced course load, remedial instruction, study skills assistance, tutoring, writing center.

Majors. Biology: General. **Business:** Accounting, business admin, human resources, management information systems. **Communications:** Digital media, media studies. **Communications technology:** Graphics. **Computer sciences:** General, computer science. **Conservation:** Environmental science. **Education:** General, art, biology, chemistry, elementary, English, history, mathematics, music, physical, reading, science, secondary, social science. **English:** Creative writing, English lit, writing. **Foreign languages:** Spanish. **Health services:** Clinical lab science, medical radiologic technology/radiation therapy, nursing (RN). **History:** General. **Human services:** Social work. **Math:** General. **Parks/recreation:** Exercise sciences, health/fitness, sports admin. **Physical sciences:** Chemistry. **Protective services:** Law enforcement admin. **Psychology:** General. **Social sciences:** Political science, sociology. **Theology:** Theology. **Visual/performing arts:** Art, dramatic, film/cinema/video, graphic design, music.

Most popular majors. Biology 9%, business/marketing 30%, education 10%, health sciences 15%.

Computing on campus. 100 workstations in dormitories, library, computer center, student center. Dormitories wired for high-speed internet access and linked to campus network. Commuter students can connect to campus network. Online library, helpline, repair service, wireless network available.

Student life. Freshman orientation: Mandatory, $125 fee. Preregistration for classes offered. Offered on three seperate occasions the summer prior to fall semester. **Housing:** Guaranteed on-campus for freshmen. Coed dorms available. $150 fully refundable deposit. Pets allowed in dorm rooms. Quad suites available. **Activities:** Jazz band, campus ministries, choral groups, dance, drama, international student organizations, literary magazine, music ensembles, musical theater, opera, radio station, student government, student newspaper, Best Buddies, BCCares, Champions of Characters Council of Athletes, College Democrats, College Republicans, criminal justice club, departmental clubs, ethnic relations club, mentors in violence prevention.

Athletics. NAIA. **Intercollegiate:** Baseball M, basketball, cheerleading M, cross-country, football (tackle) M, golf, soccer, softball W, tennis, track and field, volleyball W, wrestling M. **Intramural:** Basketball, bowling, football (non-tackle) M, golf, soccer, softball, table tennis, tennis, volleyball. **Team name:** Chargers.

Student services. Alcohol/substance abuse counseling, chaplain/spiritual director, career counseling, services for economically disadvantaged, student employment services, financial aid counseling, health services, minority student services, personal counseling, placement for graduates. **Physically disabled:** Services for visually impaired.

Contact. E-mail: admissions@briarcliff.edu
Phone: (712) 279-5200 Toll-free number: (800) 662-3303 ext. 5200
Fax: (712) 279-1632
Brian Eben, Assistant Vice President for Enrollment Management, Briar Cliff University, 3303 Rebecca Street, Sioux City, IA 51104-2324

Buena Vista University
Storm Lake, Iowa
www.bvu.edu

CB code: 6047

- Private 4-year liberal arts college affiliated with Presbyterian Church (USA)
- Residential campus in large town
- 915 degree-seeking undergraduates: 1% part-time, 50% women, 4% African American, 2% Asian American, 6% Hispanic American, 4% international
- 61 degree-seeking graduate students
- 64% of applicants admitted

◗ SAT or ACT (ACT writing optional) required

◗ 55% graduate within 6 years; 22% enter graduate study

General. Founded in 1891. Regionally accredited. 15 branch sites throughout Iowa and online programs provide educational opportunities for nontraditional students. **Degrees:** 796 bachelor's awarded; master's offered. **ROTC:** Army. **Location:** 150 miles from Des Moines, 80 miles from Sioux City. **Calendar:** 4-1-4, limited summer session. **Full-time faculty:** 86 total; 73% have terminal degrees, 7% minority, 46% women. **Part-time faculty:** 22 total; 9% minority, 64% women. **Class size:** 70% < 20, 29% 20-39, less than 1% 40-49, less than 1% 50-99. **Special facilities:** Multimedia production facilities, underground buildings, information technology center, digitally-controlled acoustic music practice rooms.

Freshman class profile. 896 applied, 572 admitted, 203 enrolled.

Mid 50% test scores			
ACT composite:	20-25	Rank in top quarter:	42%
GPA 3.75 or higher:	33%	Rank in top tenth:	22%
GPA 3.50-3.74:	14%	Return as sophomores:	73%
GPA 3.0-3.49:	29%	Out-of-state:	25%
GPA 2.0-2.99:	24%	Live on campus:	98%

Basis for selection. High school GPA and curriculum, rank in class, standardized test scores, interview, school and community activities important. Essay recommended.

High school preparation. College-preparatory program recommended. 15 units recommended. Recommended units include English 4, mathematics 4, social studies 3, science 3 (laboratory 1).

2011-2012 Annual costs. Tuition/fees: $27,226. Room/board: $7,770. Books/supplies: $1,000. Personal expenses: $1,500.

Financial aid. **Non-need-based:** Scholarships awarded for academics, art, minority status, music/drama, religious affiliation. **Additional information:** Portfolio required of art scholarship applicants, audition required of music and drama scholarship applicants.

Application procedures. **Admission:** No deadline. No application fee. Admission notification on a rolling basis. **Financial aid:** Priority date 6/1; no closing date. FAFSA required. Applicants notified on a rolling basis starting 2/15.

Academics. Students must earn credit by attending the Academic and Cultural Events Series, featuring lectures by national and international leaders and performances by world-famous classical performing groups and artists. **Special study options:** Combined bachelor's/graduate degree, distance learning, double major, dual enrollment of high school students, ESL, external degree, honors, independent study, internships, student-designed major, study abroad, teacher certification program, Washington semester. Rollins Fellows (competitive international internships). **Credit/placement by examination:** AP, CLEP, IB, ACT, institutional tests. 20 credit hours maximum toward bachelor's degree. **Support services:** Learning center, reduced course load, remedial instruction, study skills assistance, tutoring, writing center.

Majors. **Biology:** General, biochemistry. **Business:** Accounting, banking/financial services, business admin, entrepreneurial studies, human resources, international, management information systems, managerial economics, marketing. **Communications:** Communications/speech/rhetoric, digital media, media studies, organizational. **Computer sciences:** Computer science. **Conservation:** Environmental science. **Education:** Art, biology, business, chemistry, computer, elementary, English, history, mathematics, music, physical, physics, psychology, reading, science, social science, Spanish, special ed, speech. **English:** English lit. **Foreign languages:** Spanish. **Health services:** Athletic training. **History:** General. **Human services:** General, social work. **Math:** General. **Parks/recreation:** Exercise sciences, sports admin. **Philosophy/religion:** Philosophy. **Physical sciences:** Chemistry, physics. **Protective services:** Criminal justice. **Psychology:** General. **Social sciences:** General, political science, sociology. **Visual/performing arts:** Art, commercial/advertising art, music, music performance, music technology, studio arts management, theater history.

Most popular majors. Business/marketing 34%, education 14%, interdisciplinary studies 18%, psychology 11%, security/protective services 6%.

Computing on campus. 400 workstations in dormitories, library, computer center, student center. Dormitories wired for high-speed internet access and linked to campus network. Commuter students can connect to campus network. Online course registration, online library, helpline, repair service, wireless network available.

Student life. **Freshman orientation:** Mandatory. Preregistration for classes offered. Two-day orientation offered during summer. **Housing:** Guaranteed on-campus housing for all undergraduates. Coed dorms, single-sex dorms, special housing for disabled, wellness housing available. $200 fully refundable deposit. **Activities:** Bands, campus ministries, choral groups, dance, drama, international student organizations, music ensembles, musical theater, radio station, student government, student newspaper, TV station, Circle-K, Students Concerned about Tomorrow's Environment, intervarsity multicultural club, Fellowship of Christian Athletes, College Democrats, College Republicans, Reshaping Our Campus Community.

Athletics. NCAA. **Intercollegiate:** Baseball M, basketball, cross-country, football (tackle) M, golf, soccer, softball W, tennis, track and field, volleyball W, wrestling M. **Intramural:** Basketball, football (non-tackle) M, racquetball, softball, table tennis, tennis, volleyball. **Team name:** Beavers.

Student services. Adult student services, alcohol/substance abuse counseling, chaplain/spiritual director, career counseling, student employment services, financial aid counseling, health services, minority student services, personal counseling, placement for graduates, veterans' counselor. **Physically disabled:** Services for visually, speech, hearing impaired.

Contact. E-mail: admissions@bvu.edu
Phone: (712) 749-2235 Toll-free number: (800) 383-9600
Fax: (712) 749-2037
Bridget Kurkowski, Director of Admissions, Buena Vista University, 610 West Fourth Street, Storm Lake, IA 50588

Central College
Pella, Iowa   **CB member**
www.central.edu   **CB code: 6087**

◗ Private 4-year liberal arts college affiliated with Reformed Church in America

◗ Residential campus in large town

◗ 1,493 degree-seeking undergraduates: 2% part-time, 53% women

◗ 73% of applicants admitted

◗ SAT or ACT (ACT writing optional) required

◗ 63% graduate within 6 years; 23% enter graduate study

General. Founded in 1853. Regionally accredited. International study centers in England, Mexico, the Netherlands, Wales, Spain, France and Austria. **Degrees:** 344 bachelor's awarded. **Location:** 40 miles from Des Moines. **Calendar:** Semester, limited summer session. **Full-time faculty:** 103 total; 87% have terminal degrees, 6% minority, 41% women. **Part-time faculty:** 26 total; 15% have terminal degrees, 4% minority, 54% women. **Class size:** 59% < 20, 40% 20-39, less than 1% 40-49. **Special facilities:** 79-acre field station, glassblowing studio, classrooms with lecture-capture technology.

Freshman class profile. 2,633 applied, 1,926 admitted, 412 enrolled.

Mid 50% test scores			
SAT critical reading:	430-560	GPA 2.0-2.99:	14%
SAT math:	460-610	Rank in top quarter:	53%
ACT composite:	21-26	Rank in top tenth:	20%
GPA 3.75 or higher:	32%	End year in good standing:	90%
GPA 3.50-3.74:	23%	Return as sophomores:	79%
GPA 3.0-3.49:	31%	Out-of-state:	20%
		Live on campus:	100%

Basis for selection. High school curriculum, GPA, class rank, test scores important. Recommendations, school and community activities, alumni affiliation also considered. Interview and essay recommended. Audition recommended for music and theater majors; required for scholarships. Portfolio recommended for art majors; required for scholarships. **Home schooled:** Transcript of courses and grades, state high school equivalency certificate required.

High school preparation. College-preparatory program recommended. 15 units recommended. Recommended units include English 4, mathematics 2, social studies 3, science 2 (laboratory 2) and foreign language 2.

2011-2012 Annual costs. Tuition/fees: $27,844. Room/board: $9,136. Books/supplies: $1,040. Personal expenses: $1,756.

2011-2012 Financial aid. **Need-based:** 392 full-time freshmen applied for aid; 356 were judged to have need; 356 of these received aid. Average need met was 79%. Average scholarship/grant was $19,981; average loan $2,706. 71% of total undergraduate aid awarded as scholarships/grants, 29% as loans/jobs. **Non-need-based:** Awarded to 1,493 full-time undergraduates, including 154 freshmen. Scholarships awarded for academics, alumni affiliation, art, minority status, music/drama, religious affiliation, state residency. **Additional information:** Funds are awarded to students who qualify as National Merit Finalists.

Application procedures. **Admission:** Closing date 8/15 (receipt date). $25 fee, may be waived for applicants with need, free for online applicants. Admission notification on a rolling basis beginning on or about 9/15. Must reply by May 1 or within 2 week(s) if notified thereafter. **Financial aid:**

Priority date 3/15; no closing date. FAFSA required. Applicants notified on a rolling basis starting 3/15; must reply by 5/1 or within 2 week(s) of notification.

Academics. All students take first-year seminar in which faculty members from all academic divisions provide interdisciplinary introduction to the liberal arts. **Special study options:** Combined bachelor's/graduate degree, cooperative education, distance learning, double major, dual enrollment of high school students, honors, independent study, internships, student-designed major, study abroad, teacher certification program, urban semester, Washington semester. Study abroad in 9 countries and programs in Chicago and Washington, DC. Dual degree programs in engineering, physical therapy/chiropractic and nursing. **Credit/placement by examination:** AP, CLEP, IB, ACT, institutional tests. **Support services:** Learning center, reduced course load, study skills assistance, tutoring, writing center.

Majors. Biology: General, biochemistry. **Business:** Accounting, actuarial science, business admin, international. **Communications:** Communications/speech/rhetoric. **Computer sciences:** General, information systems. **Conservation:** Environmental studies. **Education:** Elementary, music. **English:** English lit. **Foreign languages:** French, German, linguistics, Spanish. **Health services:** Athletic training. **History:** General. **Math:** General. **Parks/recreation:** Exercise sciences. **Philosophy/religion:** Philosophy, religion. **Physical sciences:** Chemistry, physics. **Psychology:** General. **Social sciences:** General, anthropology, economics, political science, sociology. **Visual/performing arts:** Art, dramatic, music.

Most popular majors. Biology 8%, business/marketing 17%, education 7%, foreign language 7%, parks/recreation 13%, social sciences 12%.

Computing on campus. 391 workstations in dormitories, library, computer center, student center. Dormitories wired for high-speed internet access and linked to campus network. Commuter students can connect to campus network. Online library, helpline, repair service, student web hosting, wireless network available.

Student life. Freshman orientation: Mandatory. Preregistration for classes offered. Choice of 1 of 4 days in late June to meet with academic advisor and register for classes. In-depth Welcome Week activities begin immediately prior to start of fall classes. **Housing:** Guaranteed on-campus for all undergraduates. Coed dorms, single-sex dorms, special housing for disabled, fraternity/sorority housing available. $200 fully refundable deposit, deadline 5/1. Housing in green LEED rated building available. **Activities:** Bands, campus ministries, choral groups, dance, drama, international student organizations, literary magazine, music ensembles, musical theater, student government, student newspaper, symphony orchestra, Central volunteer center, Students Concerned About the Environment, Coalition for a Multicultural Campus, Common Ground, Habitat for Humanity, campus activities board, Amnesty International.

Athletics. NCAA. **Intercollegiate:** Baseball M, basketball, cross-country, football (tackle) M, golf, soccer, softball W, tennis, track and field, volleyball W, wrestling M. **Intramural:** Basketball, racquetball, rugby, softball, volleyball. **Team name:** Dutch.

Student services. Alcohol/substance abuse counseling, chaplain/spiritual director, career counseling, services for economically disadvantaged, student employment services, financial aid counseling, health services, minority student services, personal counseling, placement for graduates, veterans' counselor. **Physically disabled:** Services for visually, speech, hearing impaired.

Contact. E-mail: admissions@central.edu
Phone: (641) 628-5286 Toll-free number: (877) 462-3687
Fax: (641) 628-5316
Chevy Freiburger, Director of Admission, Central College, 812 University Street, Pella, IA 50219-1999

Clarke University
Dubuque, Iowa
www.clarke.edu   CB code: 6099

- Private 4-year university and liberal arts college affiliated with Roman Catholic Church
- Residential campus in small city
- 971 degree-seeking undergraduates: 12% part-time, 68% women, 3% African American, 1% Asian American, 3% Hispanic American, 2% international
- 253 graduate students
- 74% of applicants admitted
- SAT or ACT (ACT writing optional) required
- 60% graduate within 6 years; 20% enter graduate study

General. Founded in 1843. Regionally accredited. **Degrees:** 218 bachelor's awarded; master's, professional offered. **ROTC:** Army. **Location:** 150 miles from Chicago. **Calendar:** Semester, limited summer session. **Full-time faculty:** 85 total; 62% have terminal degrees, 1% minority, 67% women. **Part-time faculty:** 64 total; 6% have terminal degrees, 3% minority, 58% women. **Class size:** 76% < 20, 22% 20-39, 1% 40-49, less than 1% 50-99. **Special facilities:** Planetarium, art and communications laboratory, writing center, art slide library, computerized mathematics laboratory, nursing laboratory, human gross anatomy laboratory with A.D.A.M. software.

Freshman class profile. 901 applied, 670 admitted, 163 enrolled.

Mid 50% test scores			
SAT critical reading:	460-490	GPA 2.0-2.99:	15%
SAT math:	460-560	Rank in top quarter:	48%
ACT composite:	21-25	Rank in top tenth:	18%
GPA 3.75 or higher:	26%	Return as sophomores:	80%
GPA 3.50-3.74:	26%	Out-of-state:	53%
GPA 3.0-3.49:	33%	Live on campus:	90%
		International:	2%

Basis for selection. High school record of primary importance. Particular attention paid to grades on college preparatory course work and test scores. Interview required of the academically weak. Auditions required of music and drama majors. Portfolio required of art majors.

High school preparation. College-preparatory program required. 21 units required. Required and recommended units include English 4, mathematics 3-4, social studies 3, science 3-4 (laboratory 2), foreign language 2 and academic electives 4. 4 college preparatory math and science, including 3 lab, required for physical therapy program.

2011-2012 Annual costs. Tuition/fees: $25,760. Room/board: $7,740. Books/supplies: $1,040. Personal expenses: $1,250.

2011-2012 Financial aid. Need-based: 159 full-time freshmen applied for aid; 148 were judged to have need; 148 of these received aid. Average need met was 76%. Average scholarship/grant was $19,029; average loan $3,482. 69% of total undergraduate aid awarded as scholarships/grants, 31% as loans/jobs. **Non-need-based:** Awarded to 992 full-time undergraduates, including 231 freshmen. Scholarships awarded for academics, alumni affiliation, art, athletics, leadership, music/drama, religious affiliation, state residency. **Additional information:** Reduced tuition for family members of BVMs.

Application procedures. Admission: No deadline. $25 fee, may be waived for applicants with need, free for online applicants. Admission notification on a rolling basis beginning on or about 1/15. Must reply by May 1 or within 3 week(s) if notified thereafter. **Financial aid:** Priority date 4/15; no closing date. Applicants notified on a rolling basis starting 3/12; must reply by 5/1 or within 2 week(s) of notification.

Academics. Special study options: Accelerated study, cooperative education, cross-registration, distance learning, double major, ESL, honors, independent study, internships, liberal arts/career combination, student-designed major, study abroad, teacher certification program. **Credit/placement by examination:** AP, CLEP, IB, SAT, ACT, institutional tests. 15 credit hours maximum toward associate degree, 30 toward bachelor's. Students applying for prior learning assessment (PLA) credit must be 24 years of age or older. Maximum of 30 credits granted for PLA, CLEP or DANTES within 5-year period. If more than 15 PLA credits are awarded based on portfolio evaluation, additional credit up to 30 hours must be matched by regular college credit. PLA does not count toward the 30 hour residency requirement and is awarded only after 5 hours in degree program are completed. Guidelines may vary by department. **Support services:** Learning center, reduced course load, remedial instruction, study skills assistance, tutoring, writing center.

Majors. Biology: General, biochemistry. **Business:** Accounting, business admin. **Communications:** General. **Computer sciences:** General. **Education:** Elementary, music, physical. **English:** English lit. **Foreign languages:** Spanish. **Health services:** Athletic training, nursing (RN), predental, premedicine, prepharmacy, preveterinary. **History:** General. **Human services:** Social work. **Math:** General. **Parks/recreation:** Sports admin. **Philosophy/religion:** Philosophy, religion. **Physical sciences:** Chemistry. **Psychology:** General. **Visual/performing arts:** Art history/conservation, dramatic, music, studio arts.

Most popular majors. Business/marketing 16%, communications/journalism 6%, education 15%, health sciences 25%, psychology 9%, public administration/social services 6%.

Computing on campus. 237 workstations in dormitories, library, computer center, student center. Dormitories wired for high-speed internet access and linked to campus network. Commuter students can connect to campus network. Online course registration, online library, helpline, wireless network available.

Student life. Freshman orientation: Available. Preregistration for classes offered. **Housing:** Guaranteed on-campus for freshmen. Coed dorms, single-sex dorms, apartments, wellness housing available. $100 fully refundable deposit, deadline 7/15. **Activities:** Jazz band, campus ministries, choral groups, drama, literary magazine, music ensembles, musical theater, radio station, student government, student newspaper, Amnesty International, peace and justice, peer ministry program, minority student organization, Walden Society.

Athletics. NAIA. **Intercollegiate:** Baseball M, basketball, bowling, cheerleading M, cross-country, golf, soccer, softball W, track and field, volleyball. **Intramural:** Basketball, bowling, football (non-tackle), softball, table tennis, tennis, volleyball. **Team name:** Crusaders.

Student services. Adult student services, alcohol/substance abuse counseling, chaplain/spiritual director, career counseling, student employment services, financial aid counseling, health services, minority student services, personal counseling. **Physically disabled:** Services for visually, hearing impaired.

Contact. E-mail: admissions@clarke.edu
Phone: (563) 588-6316 Toll-free number: (800) 383-2345
Fax: (563) 588-6789
Emily Kruse, Director of Admission, Clarke University, 1550 Clarke Drive, Dubuque, IA 52001-3198

Coe College
Cedar Rapids, Iowa **CB member**
www.coe.edu **CB code: 6101**

- Private 4-year nursing and liberal arts college affiliated with Presbyterian Church (USA)
- Residential campus in small city
- 1,325 degree-seeking undergraduates: 2% part-time, 55% women
- 9 graduate students
- 64% of applicants admitted
- SAT or ACT (ACT writing optional), application essay required
- 72% graduate within 6 years; 28% enter graduate study

General. Founded in 1851. Regionally accredited. **Degrees:** 269 bachelor's awarded; master's offered. **ROTC:** Army, Air Force. **Location:** 230 miles from Chicago, 300 miles from Minneapolis-St. Paul. **Calendar:** Semester, limited summer session. **Full-time faculty:** 89 total; 86% have terminal degrees, 8% minority, 39% women. **Part-time faculty:** 82 total; 27% have terminal degrees, 6% minority, 54% women. **Class size:** 68% < 20, 30% 20-39, less than 1% 40-49, 1% 50-99. **Special facilities:** Infrared spectrometer, analytical physiology units, music library, wilderness field station.

Freshman class profile. 2,405 applied, 1,547 admitted, 361 enrolled.

Mid 50% test scores			
SAT critical reading:	490-650	GPA 2.0-2.99:	8%
SAT math:	520-660	Rank in top quarter:	61%
SAT writing:	490-600	Rank in top tenth:	29%
ACT composite:	24-28	Return as sophomores:	80%
GPA 3.75 or higher:	43%	Out-of-state:	49%
GPA 3.50-3.74:	20%	Live on campus:	99%
GPA 3.0-3.49:	29%	International:	3%

Basis for selection. School achievement record and test scores most important. Recommendations and school activities also important. Interview and community activities considered. **Home schooled:** GED and portfolio required. **Learning Disabled:** Submission of disability assessment required.

High school preparation. College-preparatory program recommended. 18 units recommended. Recommended units include English 4, mathematics 3, social studies 3, science 3 (laboratory 1), foreign language 2 and academic electives 2.

2012-2013 Annual costs. Tuition/fees (projected): $34,220. Room/board: $7,700. Books/supplies: $1,000. Personal expenses: $1,600.

2011-2012 Financial aid. Need-based: 322 full-time freshmen applied for aid; 283 were judged to have need; 283 of these received aid. Average need met was 87%. Average scholarship/grant was $23,036; average loan $4,369. 76% of total undergraduate aid awarded as scholarships/grants, 24% as loans/jobs. **Non-need-based:** Awarded to 423 full-time undergraduates, including 106 freshmen. Scholarships awarded for academics, leadership, minority status, music/drama, ROTC.

Application procedures. Admission: Priority date 12/10; deadline 3/1 (postmark date). $30 fee, may be waived for applicants with need, free for online applicants. Admission notification on a rolling basis beginning on or about 10/1. Must reply by 5/1. **Financial aid:** Priority date 3/1; no closing date. FAFSA required. Applicants notified on a rolling basis starting 3/15; must reply by 5/1 or within 2 week(s) of notification.

Academics. Writing emphasis courses required. Semester practicum required for all students. **Special study options:** Accelerated study, combined bachelor's/graduate degree, cross-registration, double major, dual enrollment of high school students, ESL, exchange student, honors, independent study, internships, New York semester, student-designed major, study abroad, teacher certification program, urban semester, Washington semester. Oak Ridge science semester; research program at the Coe College wilderness field station- Minnesota Superior National Forest; tropical field research in Costa Rica; travel abroad to England, Hong Kong, India, Italy, Japan, Russia, Latin America, Czech Republic, Tanzania, Germany, Sweden, Spain, France, Korea, Thailand, Ireland. **Credit/placement by examination:** AP, CLEP, IB, SAT, ACT, institutional tests. **Support services:** Pre-admission summer program, reduced course load, study skills assistance, tutoring, writing center.

Majors. Area/ethnic studies: African-American, American, Asian, French, German, Spanish/Iberian. **Biology:** General, biochemistry, molecular. **Business:** Accounting, business admin. **Communications:** Communications/speech/rhetoric, public relations. **Computer sciences:** Computer science. **Conservation:** Environmental science. **Education:** General, art, elementary, middle, music, physical, science, secondary. **English:** Creative writing, English lit, rhetoric/composition. **Foreign languages:** Classics, French, German, Spanish. **Health services:** Athletic training, nursing (RN), predental, premedicine, preveterinary. **History:** General. **Math:** General. **Parks/recreation:** Health/fitness. **Philosophy/religion:** Philosophy, religion. **Physical sciences:** General, chemistry, physics. **Psychology:** General. **Social sciences:** Economics, political science, sociology. **Visual/performing arts:** Acting, art, ceramics, directing/producing, dramatic, music, music performance, music theory/composition, painting, photography, studio arts, theater design.

Most popular majors. Biology 11%, business/marketing 20%, education 12%, English 8%, health sciences 7%, physical sciences 6%, visual/performing arts 12%.

Computing on campus. Dormitories wired for high-speed internet access and linked to campus network. Commuter students can connect to campus network. Online course registration, online library, helpline, student web hosting, wireless network available.

Student life. Freshman orientation: Mandatory, $150 fee. Preregistration for classes offered. Four- or five-day program. **Policies:** Students must live on campus unless residing with relatives or granted off-campus permission by Department of Residence Life. **Housing:** Guaranteed on-campus for all undergraduates. Coed dorms, single-sex dorms, apartments, fraternity/sorority housing, wellness housing available. $200 nonrefundable deposit, deadline 5/1. **Activities:** Bands, campus ministries, choral groups, dance, drama, international student organizations, literary magazine, music ensembles, musical theater, radio station, student government, student newspaper, symphony orchestra, TV station, black self-education organization, Friends club, Egalitarians Supporting the Advancement of Women, Christian Fellowship, College Republicans, Habitat for Humanity, green club, College Democrats, Fellowship of Christian Athletes.

Athletics. NCAA. **Intercollegiate:** Baseball M, basketball, cheerleading M, cross-country, diving, football (tackle) M, golf, soccer, softball W, swimming, tennis, track and field, volleyball W, wrestling M. **Intramural:** Badminton, basketball, football (non-tackle) M, racquetball, soccer, softball, squash, table tennis, tennis, volleyball, wrestling M. **Team name:** Kohawks.

Student services. Adult student services, alcohol/substance abuse counseling, career counseling, student employment services, financial aid counseling, health services, minority student services, personal counseling, placement for graduates.

Contact. E-mail: admission@coe.edu
Phone: (319) 399-8500 Toll-free number: (877) 225-5263
Fax: (319) 399-8816
Julie Staker, Dean of Admission, Coe College, 1220 First Avenue NE, Cedar Rapids, IA 52402

Cornell College
Mount Vernon, Iowa **CB member**
www.cornellcollege.edu **CB code: 6119**

- Private 4-year liberal arts college affiliated with United Methodist Church
- Residential campus in small town
- 1,190 degree-seeking undergraduates: 1% part-time, 54% women, 5% African American, 4% Asian American, 8% Hispanic American, 1% Native American, 6% international
- 46% of applicants admitted

◆ SAT or ACT (ACT writing optional), application essay required
◆ 70% graduate within 6 years

General. Founded in 1853. Regionally accredited. **Degrees:** 251 bachelor's awarded. **Location:** 15 miles from Cedar Rapids, 20 miles from Iowa City. **Calendar:** Eight terms of 3 and 1/2 weeks, one course per term. Extensive summer session. **Full-time faculty:** 84 total; 95% have terminal degrees, 6% minority, 48% women. **Part-time faculty:** 6 total; 33% have terminal degrees, 17% minority, 83% women. **Class size:** 65% < 20, 35% 20-39. **Special facilities:** Geology museum, observatory, Chicago center, creative writing house.

Freshman class profile. 3,202 applied, 1,457 admitted, 339 enrolled.

Mid 50% test scores			
SAT critical reading:	540-680	GPA 2.0-2.99:	11%
SAT math:	540-680	Rank in top quarter:	58%
SAT writing:	520-660	Rank in top tenth:	31%
ACT composite:	23-29	End year in good standing:	98%
GPA 3.75 or higher:	40%	Return as sophomores:	79%
GPA 3.50-3.74:	20%	Out-of-state:	80%
GPA 3.0-3.49:	29%	Live on campus:	99%
		International:	7%

Basis for selection. Academic record, essay, co-curricular involvement, evidence of character, standardized test score, letters of reference, and recommended optional interview important. Primary consideration given to academic performance in college preparatory courses. Portfolio required for art scholarship applicants. Audition required for music and theater scholarship applicants. **Home schooled:** Transcript of courses and grades, interview, letter of recommendation (nonparent) required. Applicants asked to provide as many documents pertaining to their education as possible. **Learning Disabled:** Must have recent documentation of disability from official source if student requires special arrangements in academic setting.

High school preparation. College-preparatory program recommended. 15 units recommended. Recommended units include English 4, mathematics 3, social studies 3, science 3, foreign language 2 and academic electives 1. As many advanced, honors, and/or AP courses as possible recommended.

2011-2012 Annual costs. Tuition/fees: $32,920. Room/board: $7,730. Books/supplies: $720. Personal expenses: $540.

2010-2011 Financial aid. Need-based: 79% of total undergraduate aid awarded as scholarships/grants, 21% as loans/jobs. **Non-need-based:** Scholarships awarded for academics, art, leadership, minority status, music/drama, religious affiliation, state residency.

Application procedures. Admission: Priority date 12/1; deadline 2/1 (postmark date). $30 fee, may be waived for applicants with need, free for online applicants. Admission notification on a rolling basis beginning on or about 12/1. Must reply by May 1 or within 2 week(s) if notified thereafter. **Financial aid:** Closing date 3/1. FAFSA, institutional form required. Applicants notified on a rolling basis starting 3/1; must reply by 5/1 or within 2 week(s) of notification.

Academics. Special study options: Accelerated study, combined bachelor's/graduate degree, double major, ESL, exchange student, independent study, internships, liberal arts/career combination, semester at sea, student-designed major, study abroad, teacher certification program, urban semester, Washington semester. **Credit/placement by examination:** AP, CLEP, IB, institutional tests. **Support services:** Learning center, study skills assistance, tutoring, writing center.

Majors. Area/ethnic studies: German, Latin American, Russian/Slavic, women's. **Biology:** General, biochemistry, Biochemistry/molecular biology, ecology, molecular, molecular biochemistry. **Computer sciences:** Computer science. **Conservation:** Environmental studies. **Education:** General, art, biology, chemistry, elementary, English, foreign languages, French, German, history, mathematics, middle, multi-level teacher, music, physical, physics, science, secondary, social science, social studies, Spanish. **English:** Creative writing, English lit. **Foreign languages:** General, classics, French, German, Russian, Spanish. **Health services:** Prechiropractic, predental, premedicine, prenursing, preoptometry, prepharmacy, prephysical therapy, preveterinary. **History:** General. **Math:** General, mathematics/statistics, statistics. **Parks/recreation:** Exercise sciences, health/fitness. **Philosophy/religion:** Philosophy, religion. **Physical sciences:** Chemistry, geology, physics. **Psychology:** General. **Social sciences:** Anthropology, archaeology, economics, international relations, political science, sociology. **Visual/performing arts:** Art, art history/conservation, dramatic, music, music history, music performance, music theory/composition, stringed instruments, studio arts, theater design, voice/opera.

Most popular majors. Biology 10%, English 8%, foreign language 6%, psychology 8%, social sciences 18%, visual/performing arts 12%.

Computing on campus. 190 workstations in library, computer center, student center. Dormitories wired for high-speed internet access and linked to campus network. Commuter students can connect to campus network. Online course registration, online library, helpline, repair service, student web hosting, wireless network available.

Student life. Freshman orientation: Mandatory. Preregistration for classes offered. Five-day orientation held before fall classes begin. **Housing:** Guaranteed on-campus for freshmen. Coed dorms, single-sex dorms, apartments, wellness housing available. $300 nonrefundable deposit, deadline 5/1. Pets allowed in dorm rooms. First-year halls/floors available. **Activities:** Bands, campus ministries, choral groups, dance, drama, film society, international student organizations, literary magazine, music ensembles, musical theater, opera, radio station, student government, student newspaper, symphony orchestra, Alpha Phi Omega, alumni student association, Fellowship of Christian Athletes, Black awareness cultural organization, women's action group, Young Democrats, College Republicans, Habitat for Humanity, Organization for Latino Awareness, lunch buddies/youth mentoring.

Athletics. NCAA. **Intercollegiate:** Baseball M, basketball, cross-country, football (tackle) M, golf, soccer, softball W, tennis, track and field, volleyball W, wrestling M. **Intramural:** Badminton, basketball, bowling, football (non-tackle), racquetball, soccer, softball, table tennis, track and field, volleyball. **Team name:** Rams.

Student services. Adult student services, alcohol/substance abuse counseling, chaplain/spiritual director, career counseling, student employment services, financial aid counseling, health services, minority student services, personal counseling, placement for graduates, women's services.

Contact. E-mail: admissions@cornellcollege.edu
Phone: (319) 895-4215 Toll-free number: (800) 747-1112
Fax: (319) 895-4451
Jonathan Stroud, Vice President for Enrollment, Cornell College, 600 First Street SW, Mount Vernon, IA 52314-1098

Divine Word College
Epworth, Iowa
www.dwci.edu   CB code: 6174

◆ Private 4-year liberal arts and seminary college affiliated with Roman Catholic Church
◆ Residential campus in rural community
◆ 89 degree-seeking undergraduates
◆ 93% of applicants admitted
◆ Application essay, interview required

General. Founded in 1912. Regionally accredited. **Degrees:** 5 bachelor's, 1 associate awarded. **Location:** 15 miles from Dubuque. **Calendar:** Semester. **Full-time faculty:** 19 total. **Part-time faculty:** 6 total.

Freshman class profile. 14 applied, 13 admitted, 13 enrolled.

Basis for selection. Desire to pursue vocation to missionary priesthood or Brotherhood most important. SAT or ACT recommended. Minnesota Multiphasic Personality Inventory (MMPI) used for admission and counseling. **Home schooled:** Transcript of courses and grades, state high school equivalency certificate, interview, letter of recommendation (nonparent) required.

High school preparation. College-preparatory program recommended.

2011-2012 Annual costs. Tuition/fees: $11,785. Room/board: $3,150. Books/supplies: $500.

Application procedures. Admission: Closing date 7/15. $25 fee, may be waived for applicants with need. Admission notification on a rolling basis beginning on or about 1/1. **Financial aid:** Priority date 8/31; no closing date. Applicants notified on a rolling basis starting 8/1.

Academics. Special study options: Double major, dual enrollment of high school students, ESL, independent study. **Credit/placement by examination:** AP, CLEP, institutional tests. **Support services:** Reduced course load, remedial instruction, tutoring.

Majors. Philosophy/religion: Philosophy, religion.

Computing on campus. 26 workstations in computer center.

Student life. Freshman orientation: Mandatory. Preregistration for classes offered. **Policies:** All students live in dormitories on campus. Religious observance required. **Housing:** Single-sex dorms available. **Activities:** Campus ministries, choral groups, student government, Vietnamese student organization, Sudanese student organization, social justice committee, Right to Life committee.

Athletics. Intramural: Basketball M, soccer M, swimming M, table tennis M, tennis M, volleyball M.

Student services. Career counseling, health services, personal counseling.

Contact. E-mail: svdvocations@dwci.edu
Phone: (563) 876-3332 Toll-free number: (800) 553-3321
Fax: (563) 876-5515
Len Uhal, Vice President for Recruitment and Admissions, Divine Word College, 102 Jacoby Drive SW, Epworth, IA 52045

Dordt College
Sioux Center, Iowa
www.dordt.edu   **CB code: 6171**

- Private 4-year liberal arts college affiliated with Christian Reformed Church
- Residential campus in small town
- 1,340 degree-seeking undergraduates: 1% part-time, 47% women, 1% African American, 1% Asian American, 1% Hispanic American, 9% international
- 11 degree-seeking graduate students
- 80% of applicants admitted
- SAT or ACT (ACT writing optional) required
- 62% graduate within 6 years; 15% enter graduate study

General. Founded in 1955. Regionally accredited. **Degrees:** 265 bachelor's, 26 associate awarded; master's offered. **Location:** 45 miles from Sioux City; 55 miles from Sioux Falls, SD. **Calendar:** Semester. **Full-time faculty:** 79 total; 70% have terminal degrees, 4% minority, 23% women. **Part-time faculty:** 27 total; 11% have terminal degrees, 59% women. **Class size:** 62% < 20, 29% 20-39, 4% 40-49, 4% 50-99, less than 1% >100. **Special facilities:** Farm, biotechnology research facility, natural prairie plot.

Freshman class profile. 1,196 applied, 952 admitted, 373 enrolled.

Mid 50% test scores		GPA 2.0-2.99:	17%
SAT critical reading:	480-600	Rank in top quarter:	19%
SAT math:	510-630	Rank in top tenth:	16%
SAT writing:	460-590	End year in good standing:	78%
ACT composite:	21-27	Return as sophomores:	80%
GPA 3.75 or higher:	38%	Out-of-state:	65%
GPA 3.50-3.74:	21%	Live on campus:	90%
GPA 3.0-3.49:	24%	International:	7%

Basis for selection. School achievement record, high school GPA, test scores, religious affiliation or commitment important. Applicants with less than 2.25 GPA considered on individual basis, may be admitted provisionally. Interview recommended for academically borderline applicants. **Home schooled:** Transcript of courses and grades required. Must submit certified GPA. **Learning Disabled:** Copies of prior testing and interview with learning disabilities advisor required.

High school preparation. College-preparatory program required. 19 units required; 25 recommended. Required and recommended units include English 3-4, mathematics 2-3, social studies 1, history 2, science 2-4, foreign language 2-3 and academic electives 6. 10 units must be in social science, English, foreign language, natural science, or math. Math must include algebra, geometry.

2011-2012 Annual costs. Tuition/fees: $24,300. Room/board: $6,870. Books/supplies: $1,030. Personal expenses: $2,000.

2011-2012 Financial aid. Need-based: 322 full-time freshmen applied for aid; 276 were judged to have need; 276 of these received aid. Average need met was 88%. Average scholarship/grant was $13,458; average loan $5,410. 57% of total undergraduate aid awarded as scholarships/grants, 43% as loans/jobs. **Non-need-based:** Awarded to 346 full-time undergraduates, including 98 freshmen. Scholarships awarded for academics, alumni affiliation, art, athletics, job skills, leadership, music/drama, religious affiliation, state residency.

Application procedures. Admission: Closing date 7/31. $25 fee, may be waived for applicants with need. Admission notification on a rolling basis beginning on or about 10/1. Must reply by May 1 or within 1 week(s) if notified thereafter. **Financial aid:** Priority date 4/1; no closing date. FAFSA, institutional form required. Applicants notified on a rolling basis starting 3/1; must reply within 3 week(s) of notification.

Academics. Special study options: Combined bachelor's/graduate degree, double major, ESL, exchange student, honors, independent study, internships, liberal arts/career combination, student-designed major, study abroad, teacher certification program, urban semester, Washington semester. Iowa Legislative

Intern program; China, England, Costa Rica, Russia, Latin America, Netherlands, and Germany semesters; Los Angeles-Film Institute semester, Chicago Metro semester, American Studies semester. **Credit/placement by examination:** AP, CLEP, IB, SAT, ACT, institutional tests. Registrar makes determination on case-by-case basis. Some credit may be given for work experience. **Support services:** Learning center, reduced course load, remedial instruction, study skills assistance, tutoring.

Majors. Biology: General. **Business:** General, accounting, accounting/business management, information resources management, marketing. **Communications:** Broadcast journalism, communications/speech/rhetoric, digital media, journalism, media studies, public relations. **Communications technology:** General, graphics. **Computer sciences:** General, computer science, information systems, LAN/WAN management, system admin. **Conservation:** General, environmental studies. **Education:** General, art, biology, business, chemistry, drama/dance, elementary, English, foreign languages, health, history, mathematics, middle, music, physical, physics, reading, science, secondary, social science, social studies, Spanish, special ed, speech. **Engineering:** General, agricultural, biomedical, civil, computer, construction, electrical, mechanical. **English:** English lit, rhetoric/composition, writing. **Foreign languages:** Dutch/Flemish, Spanish. **General:** Agribusiness operations, animal sciences, business, plant sciences. **Health services:** Athletic training, clinical lab science, clinical lab technology, nursing (RN), predental, premedicine, prepharmacy, preveterinary. **History:** General. **Human services:** General, social work. **Liberal arts:** Arts/sciences. **Math:** General. **Parks/recreation:** General, exercise sciences, health/fitness, sports admin. **Philosophy/religion:** Philosophy, religion. **Physical sciences:** General, chemistry, physics. **Protective services:** Police science. **Psychology:** General. **Social sciences:** General, political science. **Theology:** Missionary, sacred music, theology, youth ministry. **Visual/performing arts:** Art, commercial/advertising art, design, dramatic, music, piano/keyboard, stringed instruments, voice/opera.

Computing on campus. 200 workstations in dormitories, library, computer center, student center. Dormitories wired for high-speed internet access and linked to campus network. Commuter students can connect to campus network. Online course registration, online library, helpline, wireless network available.

Student life. Freshman orientation: Mandatory. Preregistration for classes offered. Two-day program prior to beginning of classes. **Policies:** No smoking or alcohol allowed on-campus. Religious observance required. **Housing:** Guaranteed on-campus for all undergraduates. Single-sex dorms, special housing for disabled, apartments, wellness housing available. $200 deposit, deadline 6/1. **Activities:** Bands, campus ministries, choral groups, dance, drama, film society, international student organizations, literary magazine, music ensembles, musical theater, opera, radio station, student government, student newspaper, symphony orchestra, 50 clubs and student organizations available.

Athletics. NAIA. **Intercollegiate:** Baseball M, basketball, cross-country, football (tackle) M, golf, ice hockey M, soccer, softball W, track and field, volleyball W. **Intramural:** Badminton, basketball, bowling, cross-country, field hockey, golf, racquetball, soccer, softball, swimming, tennis, volleyball, weight lifting. **Team name:** Defenders.

Student services. Adult student services, alcohol/substance abuse counseling, chaplain/spiritual director, career counseling, student employment services, financial aid counseling, health services, minority student services, personal counseling, placement for graduates, veterans' counselor, women's services. **Physically disabled:** Services for visually, speech, hearing impaired.

Contact. E-mail: admission@dordt.edu
Phone: (712) 722-6080 Toll-free number: (800) 343-6738
Fax: (712) 722-6035
Quentin Van Essen, Executive Director of Admissions, Dordt College, 498 Fourth Avenue, NE, Sioux Center, IA 51250

Drake University
Des Moines, Iowa   **CB member**
www.drake.edu   **CB code: 6168**

- Private 4-year university
- Residential campus in large city
- 3,348 degree-seeking undergraduates: 5% part-time, 57% women, 3% African American, 3% Asian American, 3% Hispanic American, 7% international
- 1,902 degree-seeking graduate students
- 63% of applicants admitted
- SAT or ACT (ACT writing optional), application essay required
- 78% graduate within 6 years

General. Founded in 1881. Regionally accredited. **Degrees:** 338 bachelor's awarded; master's, professional, doctoral offered. **ROTC:** Army, Air Force. **Location:** 150 miles from Omaha, NE; 194 miles from Kansas City, MO. **Calendar:** Semester, extensive summer session. **Full-time faculty:** 283 total; 89% have terminal degrees, 13% minority, 46% women. **Part-time faculty:** 178 total; 4% minority, 49% women. **Class size:** 52% < 20, 31% 20-39, 11% 40-49, 4% 50-99, 2% >100. **Special facilities:** Observatory, greenhouse.

Freshman class profile. 6,093 applied, 3,849 admitted, 812 enrolled.

Mid 50% test scores		Rank in top quarter:	75%
SAT critical reading:	530-650	Rank in top tenth:	42%
SAT math:	580-680	Return as sophomores:	88%
ACT composite:	25-29	Out-of-state:	69%
GPA 3.75 or higher:	56%	Live on campus:	96%
GPA 3.50-3.74:	20%	International:	3%
GPA 3.0-3.49:	21%	Fraternities:	31%
GPA 2.0-2.99:	3%	Sororities:	30%

Basis for selection. High school academic record, test scores, extracurricular activities, counselor recommendation, and essay important. Comprehensive review completed and each item in student's file considered. Interview recommended for all, required for some. Audition required of music and theater majors. Portfolio recommended for art majors.

High school preparation. College-preparatory program recommended. 16 units recommended. Recommended units include English 4, mathematics 3, social studies 4, science 2 (laboratory 1) and foreign language 2.

2011-2012 Annual costs. Tuition/fees: $28,382. Room/board: $8,410. Books/supplies: $900. Personal expenses: $1,500.

2011-2012 Financial aid. Need-based: 715 full-time freshmen applied for aid; 566 were judged to have need; 566 of these received aid. Average need met was 76%. Average scholarship/grant was $14,940; average loan $3,330. 64% of total undergraduate aid awarded as scholarships/grants, 36% as loans/jobs. **Non-need-based:** Awarded to 1,433 full-time undergraduates, including 348 freshmen. Scholarships awarded for academics, alumni affiliation, art, athletics, music/drama, ROTC, state residency.

Application procedures. Admission: Priority date 3/1; no deadline. $25 fee, may be waived for applicants with need, free for online applicants. Admission notification on a rolling basis beginning on or about 10/15. **Financial aid:** No deadline. FAFSA required. Applicants notified on a rolling basis starting 3/1; must reply by 5/1 or within 3 week(s) of notification.

Academics. Peer support through academic departments and residence halls offered. **Special study options:** Accelerated study, combined bachelor's/graduate degree, cooperative education, distance learning, double major, dual enrollment of high school students, ESL, honors, independent study, internships, liberal arts/career combination, semester at sea, student-designed major, study abroad, teacher certification program, Washington semester. **Credit/placement by examination:** AP, CLEP, IB, institutional tests. 66 credit hours maximum toward bachelor's degree. **Support services:** Study skills assistance, tutoring, writing center.

Majors. Biology: General, biochemistry, cellular/molecular, neuroscience, pharmacology. **Business:** General, accounting, actuarial science, finance, international, management information systems, management science, managerial economics, marketing. **Communications:** Advertising, broadcast journalism, communications/speech/rhetoric, journalism, media studies, public relations, radio/TV. **Computer sciences:** General, computer science, information technology. **Conservation:** Environmental science, management/policy. **Education:** Curriculum, elementary, mathematics, music, secondary. **English:** English lit, rhetoric/composition, writing. **Health services:** Pharmaceutical sciences. **History:** General. **Math:** General. **Philosophy/religion:** Ethics, philosophy, religion. **Physical sciences:** Astronomy, chemistry, physics. **Psychology:** General. **Social sciences:** General, anthropology, economics, international relations, political science, sociology. **Visual/performing arts:** Acting, art history/conservation, commercial/advertising art, directing/producing, dramatic, drawing, music, music management, music performance, painting, printmaking, sculpture, theater design.

Most popular majors. Biology 6%, business/marketing 39%, communications/journalism 12%, education 9%, social sciences 10%.

Computing on campus. 4,900 workstations in dormitories, library, computer center, student center. Dormitories wired for high-speed internet access and linked to campus network. Commuter students can connect to campus network. Online course registration, online library, helpline, repair service, student web hosting, wireless network available.

Student life. Freshman orientation: Available, $90 fee. Preregistration for classes offered. Four 1-1/2 day sessions held in June; includes parents. **Policies:** Student leaders must maintain 2.0 GPA. Students must live on-campus first 2 years following high school. **Housing:** Guaranteed on-campus for freshmen. Coed dorms, apartments, fraternity/sorority housing available.

$250 nonrefundable deposit, deadline 5/1. **Activities:** Bands, campus ministries, choral groups, dance, drama, international student organizations, literary magazine, music ensembles, Model UN, musical theater, radio station, student government, student newspaper, symphony orchestra, coalition of Black students, Best Buddies, College Republicans, College Democrats, La Fuerza Latina, Alpha Phi Omega, South Asian student association, Rainbow Union, Drake Hillel.

Athletics. NCAA. **Intercollegiate:** Basketball, cheerleading, cross-country, football (tackle) M, golf, rowing (crew) W, soccer, softball W, tennis, track and field, volleyball W. **Intramural:** Badminton, basketball, football (non-tackle), football (tackle) M, golf, racquetball, soccer, swimming, tennis, volleyball. **Team name:** Bulldogs.

Student services. Career counseling, student employment services, financial aid counseling, health services, legal services, personal counseling, placement for graduates. **Physically disabled:** Services for visually, speech, hearing impaired.

Contact. E-mail: admission@drake.edu
Phone: (515) 271-3181 Toll-free number: (800) 443-7253
Fax: (515) 271-2831
Laura Linn, Director of Admission, Drake University, 2507 University Avenue, Des Moines, IA 50311-4505

Emmaus Bible College
Dubuque, Iowa
www.emmaus.edu   **CB code: 1215**

- Private 4-year Bible college affiliated with Brethren Church
- Residential campus in small city
- 242 degree-seeking undergraduates: 8% part-time, 57% women, 1% African American, 2% Asian American, 6% Hispanic American
- 78% of applicants admitted
- SAT or ACT (ACT writing optional), application essay required

General. Founded in 1942. Accredited by ABHE. **Degrees:** 35 bachelor's, 6 associate awarded. **Location:** 90 miles from Waterloo, 150 miles from Chicago. **Calendar:** Semester. **Full-time faculty:** 23 total; 35% have terminal degrees, 13% minority, 30% women. **Part-time faculty:** 14 total; 21% have terminal degrees, 29% women. **Class size:** 75% < 20, 14% 20-39, 4% 40-49, 7% 50-99.

Freshman class profile. 118 applied, 92 admitted, 60 enrolled.

Mid 50% test scores		GPA 3.50-3.74:	21%
SAT critical reading:	430-530	GPA 3.0-3.49:	32%
SAT math:	370-510	GPA 2.0-2.99:	14%
ACT composite:	18-26	Rank in top quarter:	48%
GPA 3.75 or higher:	26%	Rank in top tenth:	16%

Basis for selection. Recommendations and essay most important. GPA also important. Tests not required of students who have earned 24 college credits or have been out of high school at least two years. **Home schooled:** Transcript of courses and grades, letter of recommendation (nonparent) required.

2011-2012 Annual costs. Tuition/fees: $13,470. Room/board: $6,050. Books/supplies: $600. Personal expenses: $1,600.

Financial aid. Non-need-based: Scholarships awarded for academics, leadership, minority status, music/drama.

Application procedures. Admission: Priority date 7/9; no deadline. $25 fee, may be waived for applicants with need. Admission notification on a rolling basis. Must reply by May 1 or within 2 week(s) if notified thereafter. **Financial aid:** No deadline. FAFSA required. Applicants notified on a rolling basis starting 3/1; must reply within 2 week(s) of notification.

Academics. Special study options: Combined bachelor's/graduate degree, double major, dual enrollment of high school students, ESL, internships, teacher certification program. **Credit/placement by examination:** AP, CLEP, IB, institutional tests. 9 credit hours maximum toward associate degree, 18 toward bachelor's. **Support services:** Reduced course load, remedial instruction, study skills assistance, tutoring.

Majors. Business: Business admin. **Computer sciences:** General. **Education:** Elementary, music. **Psychology:** Counseling. **Theology:** Bible, missionary, theology, youth ministry. **Visual/performing arts:** Music.

Most popular majors. Computer/information sciences 10%, education 38%, theological studies 34%.

Computing on campus. 60 workstations in library, computer center, student center. Dormitories wired for high-speed internet access and linked to campus network. Online course registration, online library, wireless network available.

Student life. Freshman orientation: Mandatory. Preregistration for classes offered. Held 4 days immediately preceding first day of class. **Policies:** No smoking, alcohol consumption, dancing. Religious observance required. **Housing:** Guaranteed on-campus for all undergraduates. Single-sex dorms available. $170 nonrefundable deposit, deadline 7/9. **Activities:** Choral groups, drama, international student organizations, radio station, student government.

Athletics. NCCAA. **Intercollegiate:** Basketball, soccer M, volleyball W. **Intramural:** Badminton, basketball, cross-country, football (non-tackle), golf, racquetball, soccer, softball, table tennis, tennis, volleyball. **Team name:** Eagles.

Student services. Chaplain/spiritual director, career counseling, student employment services, financial aid counseling, health services, personal counseling, veterans' counselor.

Contact. E-mail: info@emmaus.edu
Phone: (563) 588-8000 ext. 1310 Fax: (563) 588-1216
Israel Chavez, Director of Admissions, Emmaus Bible College, 2570 Asbury Road, Dubuque, IA 52001

Faith Baptist Bible College and Theological Seminary
Ankeny, Iowa
www.faith.edu   CB code: 6214

♦ Private 4-year Bible and seminary college affiliated with General Association of Regular Baptist Churches
♦ Residential campus in large town
♦ 290 degree-seeking undergraduates: 6% part-time, 53% women, 1% African American, 2% Asian American, 1% Hispanic American, 1% Native American, 1% international
♦ 41 degree-seeking graduate students
♦ 75% of applicants admitted
♦ SAT or ACT (ACT writing optional), application essay required
♦ 44% graduate within 6 years

General. Founded in 1921. Regionally accredited; also accredited by ABHE. **Degrees:** 59 bachelor's, 29 associate awarded; master's offered. **Location:** 6 miles from Des Moines. **Calendar:** Semester, limited summer session. **Full-time faculty:** 19 total; 63% have terminal degrees, 5% minority, 10% women. **Part-time faculty:** 15 total; 33% have terminal degrees, 7% minority, 40% women. **Class size:** 63% < 20, 20% 20-39, 6% 40-49, 11% 50-99.

Freshman class profile. 147 applied, 110 admitted, 86 enrolled.

Mid 50% test scores			
SAT critical reading:	470-730	GPA 3.0-3.49:	22%
SAT math:	440-510	GPA 2.0-2.99:	17%
SAT writing:	460-650	Rank in top quarter:	45%
ACT composite:	19-25	Rank in top tenth:	13%
GPA 3.75 or higher:	33%	Return as sophomores:	80%
GPA 3.50-3.74:	26%	Out-of-state:	41%
		Live on campus:	88%

Basis for selection. Recommendations, church affiliation, character qualities important. Interview recommended for borderline applicants. **Home schooled:** Transcript of courses and grades required. **Learning Disabled:** Request for accommodation must be submitted.

High school preparation. College-preparatory program required. Recommended units include English 4, mathematics 4, social studies 3, history 4, science 3 (laboratory 3), foreign language 2 and computer science 4.

2011-2012 Annual costs. Tuition/fees: $14,478. Room/board: $5,812. Books/supplies: $1,014. Personal expenses: $1,734.

Financial aid. Non-need-based: Scholarships awarded for academics, leadership, music/drama.

Application procedures. Admission: Priority date 6/1; deadline 8/1 (postmark date). $25 fee, may be waived for applicants with need, free for online applicants. Admission notification on a rolling basis. **Financial aid:** Priority date 4/1; no closing date. FAFSA required. Applicants notified on a rolling basis starting 3/15.

Academics. Special study options: Double major, independent study, internships, liberal arts/career combination, study abroad, teacher certification program. **Credit/placement by examination:** AP, CLEP, institutional tests. 6 credit hours maximum toward associate degree, 12 toward bachelor's. **Support services:** Learning center, reduced course load, remedial instruction, study skills assistance, tutoring, writing center.

Majors. Business: Administrative services. **Education:** Elementary, English, middle, music, secondary. **Theology:** Bible, missionary, religious ed, sacred music, theology.

Most popular majors. Business/marketing 7%, education 39%, philosophy/religious studies 8%, theological studies 46%.

Computing on campus. 46 workstations in dormitories, library, computer center, student center. Dormitories wired for high-speed internet access and linked to campus network. Online library, repair service, wireless network available.

Student life. Freshman orientation: Mandatory. Preregistration for classes offered. Held weekend before classes start in fall. **Policies:** All single students under the age of 26 and not living at home must live in the residence halls. Religious observance required. **Housing:** Guaranteed on-campus for all undergraduates. Single-sex dorms, special housing for disabled, apartments available. $200 deposit, deadline 6/1. **Activities:** Bands, choral groups, drama, music ensembles, student government, student missionary fellowship, missionary kids fellowship, missions ambassadors, student association, Future Christian Teachers Association, ladies fellowship, Future Preacher's Association.

Athletics. NCCAA. **Intercollegiate:** Basketball, soccer, track and field, volleyball W. **Intramural:** Basketball, football (tackle), soccer, table tennis. **Team name:** Eagles.

Student services. Chaplain/spiritual director, career counseling, student employment services, financial aid counseling, health services, personal counseling, placement for graduates, veterans' counselor, women's services.

Contact. E-mail: admissions@faith.edu
Phone: (515) 964-0601 ext. 233 Toll-free number: (888) 324-8448
Fax: (515) 964-1638
Mark Davis, Director of Admissions, Faith Baptist Bible College and Theological Seminary, 1900 NW Fourth Street, Ankeny, IA 50023

Graceland University
Lamoni, Iowa
www.graceland.edu   CB code: 6249

♦ Private 4-year university and liberal arts college affiliated with Community of Christ
♦ Residential campus in rural community
♦ 1,364 degree-seeking undergraduates: 12% part-time, 57% women, 10% African American, 2% Hispanic American, 1% Native American, 9% international
♦ 776 degree-seeking graduate students
♦ 50% of applicants admitted
♦ SAT or ACT (ACT writing optional) required
♦ 50% graduate within 6 years; 26% enter graduate study

General. Founded in 1895. Regionally accredited. Additional campus in Independence, Missouri. Evening and weekend programs offered at Indian Hills Community College and North Central Missouri College. **Degrees:** 382 bachelor's awarded; master's, doctoral offered. **Location:** 75 miles from Des Moines, 110 miles from Kansas City. **Calendar:** 4-1-4, limited summer session. **Full-time faculty:** 81 total; 72% have terminal degrees, 11% minority, 57% women. **Part-time faculty:** 91 total; 44% have terminal degrees, 2% minority, 71% women. **Class size:** 64% < 20, 29% 20-39, 3% 40-49, 4% 50-99. **Special facilities:** International health center, Korean War study center, science center, nuclear magnetic resonance spectrometer, ultracentrifuge, -80 degrees freezer, free enterprise study center.

Freshman class profile. 1,512 applied, 762 admitted, 260 enrolled.

Mid 50% test scores			
SAT critical reading:	390-500	Rank in top quarter:	36%
SAT math:	400-540	Rank in top tenth:	18%
ACT composite:	18-24	End year in good standing:	65%
GPA 3.75 or higher:	19%	Return as sophomores:	67%
GPA 3.50-3.74:	17%	Out-of-state:	74%
GPA 3.0-3.49:	28%	Live on campus:	97%
GPA 2.0-2.99:	34%	International:	7%

Basis for selection. Rank in upper 50% of class, 2.5 GPA, 21 ACT or 960 SAT (exclusive of Writing) important. Applicants who do not meet admissions criteria may be considered and will be required to take developmental courses if accepted. Some applicants must test for Chance Program prior to being considered. Interview required of applicants who do not meet admissions requirements, recommended for others. Portfolio recommended of art majors. **Home schooled:** 2.5 GPA plus two of the following required: 21 ACT/960 SAT (exclusive of Writing); portfolio demonstrating the breadth and depth of learning by the applicant and sufficient preparation for college success; home school transcript prepared by the teachers/parents, an independent or supervising teacher, or an organization with whom the student is registered or affiliated.

High school preparation. College-preparatory program recommended. 16 units recommended. Recommended units include English 4, mathematics 4, social studies 4 and science 4.

2012-2013 Annual costs. Tuition/fees: $22,680. Room/board: $7,580. Books/supplies: $1,000. Personal expenses: $1,812.

2011-2012 Financial aid. **Need-based:** 234 full-time freshmen applied for aid; 207 were judged to have need; 204 of these received aid. Average need met was 82%. Average scholarship/grant was $18,147; average loan $4,251. 56% of total undergraduate aid awarded as scholarships/grants, 44% as loans/jobs. **Non-need-based:** Scholarships awarded for academics, alumni affiliation, art, athletics, job skills, leadership, music/drama, religious affiliation. **Additional information:** Founders Scholarship will supplement other gift aid until percentage of calculated need has been met.

Application procedures. **Admission:** No deadline. No application fee. Admission notification on a rolling basis. **Financial aid:** No deadline. FAFSA required. Applicants notified on a rolling basis starting 2/1; must reply within 2 week(s) of notification.

Academics. Distance Learning programs delivered to online cohorts and at multiple off-campus locations. Nursing program delivered through online study and on-campus residency sessions. **Special study options:** Accelerated study, combined bachelor's/graduate degree, distance learning, double major, dual enrollment of high school students, ESL, honors, independent study, internships, liberal arts/career combination, semester at sea, student-designed major, study abroad, teacher certification program. Accelerated nursing program available. **Credit/placement by examination:** AP, CLEP, IB, SAT, ACT, institutional tests. 30 credit hours maximum toward bachelor's degree. Credit by standardized examinations is awarded based on American Council on Education recommendations. **Support services:** Learning center, reduced course load, remedial instruction, study skills assistance, tutoring, writing center.

Majors. **Biology:** General. **Business:** Accounting, business admin. **Communications:** Communications/speech/rhetoric. **Communications technology:** Desktop publishing. **Computer sciences:** General, web page design. **Education:** Elementary. **English:** English lit. **Foreign languages:** Spanish. **General:** Business. **Health services:** Athletic training, nursing (RN). **History:** General. **Liberal arts:** Arts/sciences. **Math:** General. **Parks/recreation:** Health/fitness, sports admin. **Philosophy/religion:** Religion. **Physical sciences:** Chemistry. **Protective services:** Law enforcement admin. **Psychology:** General. **Social sciences:** Economics. **Visual/performing arts:** General, commercial/advertising art, music, studio arts. **Work/family studies:** Food/nutrition.

Most popular majors. Business/marketing 15%, education 29%, health sciences 25%, liberal arts 6%, visual/performing arts 6%.

Computing on campus. 106 workstations in dormitories, library, computer center, student center. Dormitories wired for high-speed internet access and linked to campus network. Commuter students can connect to campus network. Online library, helpline, student web hosting, wireless network available.

Student life. Freshman orientation: Mandatory. Preregistration for classes offered. Early 1-day orientation sessions in spring and summer. Additional 2-3 day orientation at beginning of semester. **Policies:** No tobacco, alcohol, or drug use on campus. Students required to live on campus through sophomore year unless married or living with relatives. **Housing:** Guaranteed on-campus for all undergraduates. Single-sex dorms, special housing for disabled, apartments available. $200 fully refundable deposit, deadline 5/1. **Activities:** Bands, campus ministries, choral groups, dance, drama, international student organizations, music ensembles, radio station, student government, student newspaper, symphony orchestra, religious clubs, environmental sustainability club, Outreach International, Students for Free Enterprise, Habitat for Humanity, Young Republicans, Young Democrats, black student union, New Latino Generation club, gay/straight alliance.

Athletics. NAIA. **Intercollegiate:** Baseball M, basketball, cheerleading, cross-country, football (tackle) M, golf, soccer, softball W, tennis, track and field, volleyball. **Intramural:** Badminton, baseball M, basketball, cross-country, football (non-tackle), golf, handball, racquetball, soccer, softball,

swimming, table tennis, tennis, track and field, volleyball. **Team name:** Yellowjackets.

Student services. Adult student services, alcohol/substance abuse counseling, chaplain/spiritual director, career counseling, services for economically disadvantaged, student employment services, financial aid counseling, health services, minority student services, personal counseling, placement for graduates, veterans' counselor. **Physically disabled:** Services for visually impaired.

Contact. E-mail: admissions@graceland.edu
Phone: (641) 784-5196 Toll-free number: (866) 472-2352
Fax: (641) 784-5480
Kevin Brown, Director of Admissions, Graceland University, One University Place, Lamoni, IA 50140

Grand View University
Des Moines, Iowa   **CB member**
www.grandview.edu   **CB code: 6251**

- Private 4-year university and liberal arts college affiliated with Evangelical Lutheran Church in America
- Residential campus in large city
- 2,163 degree-seeking undergraduates: 17% part-time, 60% women, 7% African American, 2% Asian American, 3% Hispanic American, 2% international
- 34 degree-seeking graduate students
- 93% of applicants admitted
- SAT or ACT (ACT writing recommended) required
- 41% graduate within 6 years

General. Founded in 1896. Regionally accredited. **Degrees:** 464 bachelor's, 2 associate awarded; master's offered. **ROTC:** Army, Air Force. **Location:** 200 miles from Kansas City, 250 miles from Minneapolis-St. Paul. **Calendar:** Semester, extensive summer session. **Full-time faculty:** 92 total; 61% have terminal degrees, 6% minority, 58% women. **Part-time faculty:** 146 total; 10% have terminal degrees, 4% minority, 60% women. **Class size:** 65% < 20, 34% 20-39, less than 1% 40-49, less than 1% 50-99.

Freshman class profile. 949 applied, 883 admitted, 358 enrolled.

Mid 50% test scores			
SAT critical reading:	380-450	GPA 2.0-2.99:	40%
SAT math:	420-490	Rank in top quarter:	29%
SAT writing:	350-450	Rank in top tenth:	11%
ACT composite:	19-23	Return as sophomores:	66%
GPA 3.75 or higher:	15%	Out-of-state:	23%
GPA 3.50-3.74:	13%	Live on campus:	86%
GPA 3.0-3.49:	32%	International:	1%

Basis for selection. Admissions based on individualized evaluation of applicant's secondary school record and SAT or ACT score. **Home schooled:** Transcript of courses and grades required.

High school preparation. College-preparatory program recommended. 15 units recommended. Recommended units include English 4, mathematics 3, social studies 3, science 3 and foreign language 2.

2011-2012 Annual costs. Tuition/fees: $21,088. Room/board: $7,316. Books/supplies: $900. Personal expenses: $2,150.

2011-2012 Financial aid. **Need-based:** 341 full-time freshmen applied for aid; 303 were judged to have need; 303 of these received aid. Average need met was 82%. Average scholarship/grant was $15,606; average loan $3,683. 55% of total undergraduate aid awarded as scholarships/grants, 45% as loans/jobs. **Non-need-based:** Awarded to 483 full-time undergraduates, including 271 freshmen. Scholarships awarded for academics, alumni affiliation, art, athletics, leadership, music/drama, religious affiliation.

Application procedures. **Admission:** Closing date 8/15 (receipt date). No application fee. Admission notification on a rolling basis beginning on or about 9/15. **Financial aid:** Priority date 3/1; no closing date. FAFSA required. Applicants notified on a rolling basis starting 3/1; must reply by 5/1 or within 4 week(s) of notification.

Academics. University emphasizes integration of liberal arts core with career-related majors. Internships are primary focus in many majors. **Special study options:** Accelerated study, combined bachelor's/graduate degree, cooperative education, cross-registration, distance learning, double major, dual enrollment of high school students, honors, independent study, internships, liberal arts/career combination, student-designed major, study abroad, teacher certification program, Washington semester, weekend college. **Credit/placement by examination:** AP, CLEP, IB, SAT, ACT, institutional

tests. 32 credit hours maximum toward bachelor's degree. ACT PEP credit accepted, DANTES accepted. **Support services:** Learning center, reduced course load, remedial instruction, study skills assistance, tutoring, writing center.

Majors. Biology: General, biochemistry. **Business:** General, accounting, entrepreneurial studies, finance, hospitality admin, human resources, marketing, real estate. **Communications:** Broadcast journalism, journalism, media studies, public relations, radio/TV. **Communications technology:** Graphics. **Computer sciences:** General, information technology, programming. **Education:** Elementary, secondary. **English:** English lit. **General:** Business. **Health services:** Nursing (RN), premedicine, prepharmacy. **History:** General. **Liberal arts:** Arts/sciences. **Math:** Applied. **Parks/recreation:** Health/fitness, sports admin. **Philosophy/religion:** Religion. **Protective services:** Criminal justice. **Psychology:** General. **Social sciences:** General, political science. **Visual/performing arts:** Dramatic, graphic design, music, studio arts.

Most popular majors. Business/marketing 21%, health sciences 17%, liberal arts 7%, psychology 7%, visual/performing arts 7%.

Computing on campus. 275 workstations in dormitories, library, computer center, student center. Dormitories wired for high-speed internet access and linked to campus network. Commuter students can connect to campus network. Online course registration, online library, helpline, student web hosting, wireless network available.

Student life. Freshman orientation: Mandatory. Preregistration for classes offered. Three-day program just before start of fall semester, includes low ropes course at nearby camp. **Housing:** Coed dorms, apartments available. $200 deposit. **Activities:** Campus ministries, choral groups, dance, drama, international student organizations, literary magazine, music ensembles, radio station, student government, student newspaper, TV station, Campus Crusade, campus fellowship, criminal justice club, diversity alliance, international relations council, Viking Volunteers.

Athletics. NAIA. **Intercollegiate:** Baseball M, basketball, bowling, cheerleading M, cross-country, football (tackle) M, golf, soccer, softball W, tennis, track and field, volleyball, wrestling M. **Intramural:** Badminton, basketball, football (non-tackle), soccer, softball, swimming, table tennis, track and field, volleyball. **Team name:** Vikings.

Student services. Adult student services, alcohol/substance abuse counseling, chaplain/spiritual director, career counseling, student employment services, financial aid counseling, health services, minority student services, personal counseling, placement for graduates, veterans' counselor. **Physically disabled:** Services for visually, speech, hearing impaired.

Contact. E-mail: admissions@GrandView.edu
Phone: (515) 263-2810 Toll-free number: (800) 444-6083
Fax: (515) 263-2974
Diane Johnson, Director of Admissions, Grand View University, 1200 Grandview Avenue, Des Moines, IA 50316-1599

Grinnell College
Grinnell, Iowa
www.grinnell.edu
CB member
CB code: 6252

- Private 4-year liberal arts college
- Residential campus in small town
- 1,639 degree-seeking undergraduates: 55% women, 5% African American, 6% Asian American, 8% Hispanic American, 12% international
- 51% of applicants admitted
- SAT or ACT (ACT writing optional), application essay required
- 88% graduate within 6 years

General. Founded in 1846. Regionally accredited. **Degrees:** 373 bachelor's awarded. **Location:** 55 miles from DesMoines. **Calendar:** Semester, limited summer session. **Full-time faculty:** 159 total; 98% have terminal degrees, 21% minority, 43% women. **Part-time faculty:** 47 total; 23% have terminal degrees, 13% minority, 60% women. **Class size:** 62% < 20, 37% 20-39, less than 1% 40-49, less than 1% 50-99. **Special facilities:** 365-acre environmental research area, observatory.

Freshman class profile. 2,613 applied, 1,330 admitted, 448 enrolled.

Mid 50% test scores			
SAT critical reading:	600-720	Rank in top tenth:	62%
SAT math:	610-710	Return as sophomores:	93%
ACT composite:	28-32	Out-of-state:	92%
Rank in top quarter:	88%	Live on campus:	100%
		International:	10%

Basis for selection. Scholastic ability plus extracurricular pursuits, accomplishments most important. Curiosity, motivation, persistence, social

and emotional maturity stressed. Interview recommended. **Home schooled:** Statement describing home school structure and mission, transcript of courses and grades, interview, letter of recommendation (nonparent) required. Copy of curriculum, writing sample required. SAT Subject Tests strongly recommended.

High school preparation. College-preparatory program recommended. 20 units recommended. Recommended units include English 4, mathematics 4, social studies 4, science 4 (laboratory 3) and foreign language 4.

2011-2012 Annual costs. Tuition/fees: $39,810. Room/board: $9,334. Books/supplies: $900. Personal expenses: $1,100.

2011-2012 Financial aid. Need-based: 380 full-time freshmen applied for aid; 335 were judged to have need; 335 of these received aid. Average need met was 100%. Average scholarship/grant was $32,249; average loan $3,273. 89% of total undergraduate aid awarded as scholarships/grants, 11% as loans/jobs. **Non-need-based:** Awarded to 319 full-time undergraduates, including 66 freshmen. Scholarships awarded for academics. **Additional information:** Need-blind admission policy, meets 100% of demonstrated institutional need for all domestic students, with loan cap programs. Students may apply financial aid to off-campus study programs.

Application procedures. Admission: Closing date 1/15 (postmark date). $30 fee, may be waived for applicants with need, free for online applicants. Admission notification by 4/1. Must reply by May 1 or within 2 week(s) if notified thereafter. **Financial aid:** Closing date 2/1. FAFSA, institutional form required. Applicants notified by 4/1; must reply by 5/1.

Academics. Internships available in public agencies, private organizations, and corporations. **Special study options:** Accelerated study, double major, independent study, internships, liberal arts/career combination, student-designed major, study abroad, teacher certification program, urban semester, Washington semester. Study abroad available in more than 30 countries. Other programs include study in Washington, 3-2 engineering, architecture, and law. **Credit/placement by examination:** AP, CLEP, IB, institutional tests. **Support services:** Learning center, reduced course load, study skills assistance, tutoring, writing center.

Majors. Area/ethnic studies: Women's. **Biology:** General, biochemistry. **Computer sciences:** Computer science. **English:** English lit. **Foreign languages:** Chinese, classics, French, German, Russian, Spanish. **History:** General. **Math:** General. **Philosophy/religion:** Philosophy, religion. **Physical sciences:** Chemistry, physics. **Psychology:** General. **Social sciences:** Anthropology, economics, political science, sociology. **Visual/performing arts:** Art, dramatic, music.

Most popular majors. Biology 11%, English 8%, foreign language 12%, history 8%, physical sciences 8%, psychology 7%, social sciences 27%, visual/performing arts 6%.

Computing on campus. 400 workstations in dormitories, library, computer center, student center. Dormitories wired for high-speed internet access and linked to campus network. Commuter students can connect to campus network. Online library, helpline, student web hosting, wireless network available.

Student life. Freshman orientation: Mandatory. Preregistration for classes offered. Held immediately prior to start of classes. **Policies:** All residence halls and college-owned off-campus houses are self-governing: residents decide how their individual hall will operate and share responsibility for budget, quiet hours, social policy, regulations. **Housing:** Guaranteed on-campus for all undergraduates. Coed dorms, special housing for disabled, cooperative housing, wellness housing available. $200 nonrefundable deposit, deadline 5/1. Pets allowed in dorm rooms. **Activities:** Bands, campus ministries, choral groups, dance, drama, film society, international student organizations, literary magazine, music ensembles, Model UN, musical theater, radio station, student government, student newspaper, symphony orchestra, Muslim student association, Chalutzim, Concerned Black Students, Asian and Asian American association, Babel Tower Language Academy, Campus Democrats, Feminist Action Coalition, Alternative Break, student organization of Latinas/os, social justice action group.

Athletics. NCAA. **Intercollegiate:** Baseball M, basketball, cross-country, diving, football (tackle) M, golf, soccer, softball W, swimming, tennis, track and field, volleyball W. **Intramural:** Badminton, basketball, football (non-tackle), racquetball, rowing (crew), soccer, softball, table tennis, tennis, volleyball. **Team name:** Pioneers.

Student services. Alcohol/substance abuse counseling, chaplain/spiritual director, career counseling, student employment services, financial aid counseling, health services, minority student services, personal counseling, placement for graduates, veterans' counselor. **Physically disabled:** Services for visually, speech, hearing impaired.

Contact. E-mail: askgrin@grinnell.edu
Phone: (641) 269-3600 Toll-free number: (800) 247-0113
Fax: (641) 269-4800
Doug Badger, Dean of Admissions, Grinnell College, 1103 Park Street, Grinnell, IA 50112-1690

Hamilton Technical College
Davenport, Iowa
www.hamiltontechcollege.com   CB code: 1588

- For-profit 3-year technical college
- Commuter campus in small city
- 174 degree-seeking undergraduates
- Interview required

General. Founded in 1969. Accredited by ACCSC. **Degrees:** 1 bachelor's, 1 associate awarded. **Location:** 190 miles from Des Moines, 175 miles from Chicago. **Calendar:** Semester, extensive summer session. **Full-time faculty:** 12 total.

Basis for selection. Open admission. Pseudoisochromatic Color Plates vision test required of all applicants.

2011-2012 Annual costs. Medical assistant and medical/insurance coding specialist programs tuition: $11,250; associate of science in electronic engineering technology: $29,700; bachelor of science in electronic engineering technology: $39,600; includes all costs for entire degree program.

Application procedures. Admission: No deadline. No application fee. Admission notification on a rolling basis. **Financial aid:** No deadline. FAFSA, institutional form required. Applicants notified on a rolling basis.

Academics. Credit/placement by examination: AP, CLEP. 35 credit hours maximum toward associate degree, 60 toward bachelor's. **Support services:** Tutoring.

Computing on campus. 125 workstations in library, computer center.

Student life. Freshman orientation: Mandatory. Preregistration for classes offered.

Student services. Career counseling, placement for graduates.

Contact. E-mail: servin@hamiltontechcollege.com
Phone: (563) 386-3570 Toll-free number: (866) 966-4825
Fax: (563) 386-6756
Scott Ervin, Admissions Director, Hamilton Technical College, 1011 East 53rd Street, Davenport, IA 52807

Iowa State University
Ames, Iowa   **CB member**
www.iastate.edu   **CB code: 6306**

- Public 4-year university
- Residential campus in small city
- 23,857 degree-seeking undergraduates: 4% part-time, 44% women, 3% African American, 3% Asian American, 4% Hispanic American, 7% international
- 4,900 degree-seeking graduate students
- 86% of applicants admitted
- SAT or ACT (ACT writing optional) required
- 68% graduate within 6 years; 22% enter graduate study

General. Founded in 1858. Regionally accredited. State's land-grant, doctoral/research university. **Degrees:** 4,937 bachelor's awarded; master's, professional, doctoral offered. **ROTC:** Army, Naval, Air Force. **Location:** 30 miles from Des Moines. **Calendar:** Semester, extensive summer session. **Full-time faculty:** 1,392 total; 94% have terminal degrees, 22% minority, 33% women. **Part-time faculty:** 275 total; 58% have terminal degrees, 12% minority, 54% women. **Class size:** 30% < 20, 40% 20-39, 9% 40-49, 13% 50-99, 8% >100. **Special facilities:** Observatory, nature preserve, research park, molecular biology building, computation center, center for designing foods, Department of Energy laboratory, virtual reality applications center, crop utilization center, transportation research and education center, sustainable environmental technologies center, gardens, field-oriented lakeside research facility.

Freshman class profile. 14,540 applied, 12,541 admitted, 5,048 enrolled.

Mid 50% test scores			
SAT critical reading:	480-630	Rank in top quarter:	55%
SAT math:	520-660	Rank in top tenth:	25%
ACT composite:	22-28	Return as sophomores:	88%
GPA 3.75 or higher:	35%	Out-of-state:	36%
GPA 3.50-3.74:	20%	Live on campus:	89%
GPA 3.0-3.49:	34%	International:	5%
GPA 2.0-2.99:	11%	Fraternities:	13%
		Sororities:	17%

Basis for selection. Admissions based on ACT, class rank, GPA and number of years of high school core courses completed. Students not meeting requirements may be considered on individual basis. Applicants not unconditionally admitted may be offered trial enrollment during summer term. **Home schooled:** Emphasis placed on standardized examinations.

High school preparation. College-preparatory program required. 12 units required; 19 recommended. Required and recommended units include English 4, mathematics 3-4, social studies 2-4, science 3-4 (laboratory 2-3) and foreign language 2-3. 2 years of foreign language required for Colleges of Liberal Arts & Sciences, and Engineering; 3 years of social studies required for College of Liberal Arts & Sciences.

2011-2012 Annual costs. Tuition/fees: $7,486; $19,358 out-of-state. Differential tuition for upper division business; upper division engineering majors. Room/board: $7,982. Books/supplies: $1,046. Personal expenses: $2,029.

2010-2011 Financial aid. Need-based: 3,732 full-time freshmen applied for aid; 2,566 were judged to have need; 2,527 of these received aid. Average need met was 83%. Average scholarship/grant was $7,975; average loan $3,408. 51% of total undergraduate aid awarded as scholarships/grants, 49% as loans/jobs. **Non-need-based:** Awarded to 12,064 full-time undergraduates, including 2,678 freshmen. Scholarships awarded for academics, alumni affiliation, art, athletics, leadership, minority status, music/drama, ROTC, state residency. **Additional information:** Short-term loan program available to meet unplanned needs. Financial counseling clinic provides budget and credit education assistance.

Application procedures. Admission: Closing date 7/1. $50 fee, may be waived for applicants with need. Admission notification on a rolling basis beginning on or about 7/1. Must reply by May 1 or within 2 week(s) if notified thereafter. **Financial aid:** Priority date 3/1; no closing date. FAFSA required. Applicants notified on a rolling basis starting 4/1; must reply by 5/1.

Academics. Classes offered over the Internet, by videotape, at distant locations through the state's fiber-optic communication network, and at off-campus locations taught face-to-face by the university's professors. **Special study options:** Accelerated study, combined bachelor's/graduate degree, cooperative education, cross-registration, distance learning, double major, dual enrollment of high school students, ESL, exchange student, external degree, honors, independent study, internships, liberal arts/career combination, student-designed major, study abroad, teacher certification program, Washington semester, weekend college. National Collegiate Honors Council Honors Semester. Combined bachelor's/graduate programs include: landscape architecture, agriculture and biosystems engineering, biochemistry and biophysics, electrical and computer engineering, civil and construction engineering, chemical engineering, food science and human nutrition, material science engineering, zoology and genetics. **Credit/placement by examination:** AP, CLEP, IB, SAT, ACT, institutional tests. No limit on number of hours of credit by examination that may be counted toward degree. **Support services:** Learning center, pre-admission summer program, reduced course load, remedial instruction, study skills assistance, tutoring, writing center.

Majors. Architecture: Architecture, landscape, urban/community planning. **Area/ethnic studies:** Women's. **Biology:** General, biochemistry, bioinformatics, biophysics, entomology, genetics, microbiology. **Business:** General, accounting, finance, hospitality admin, international, logistics, management information systems, managerial economics, marketing, operations, statistics. **Communications:** Advertising, communications/speech/rhetoric, journalism. **Computer sciences:** General. **Conservation:** Environmental science, environmental studies, forestry. **Education:** General, agricultural, early childhood, elementary, family/consumer sciences, health, kindergarten/preschool, music, technology/industrial arts, trade/industrial. **Engineering:** General, aerospace, agricultural, chemical, civil, computer, construction, electrical, industrial, materials, mechanical, software. **English:** English lit, rhetoric/composition, technical writing. **Foreign languages:** General, linguistics. **General:** Agribusiness operations, agronomy, animal sciences, dairy, education services, farm/ranch, horticulture, international, mechanization, plant protection, plant sciences. **Health services:** Dietetics, medical illustrating, premedicine, preveterinary. **History:** General. **Liberal arts:** Arts/sciences. **Math:** General, statistics. **Parks/recreation:** Exercise sciences. **Philosophy/religion:** Philosophy, religion. **Physical sciences:** Chemistry, geology, materials science, physics, planetary. **Psychology:** General. **Social sciences:** Anthropology, economics, international relations, political science, sociology. **Visual/performing arts:** General, art, commercial/advertising art, design, fashion design, graphic design, interior design, music. **Work/family studies:**

General, apparel marketing, clothing/textiles, family resources, family/community services, food/nutrition, housing, human nutrition, institutional food production, textile manufacture.

Most popular majors. Agriculture 9%, business/marketing 20%, engineering/engineering technologies 18%, visual/performing arts 7%.

Computing on campus. 2,450 workstations in dormitories, library, computer center, student center. Dormitories wired for high-speed internet access and linked to campus network. Commuter students can connect to campus network. Online course registration, online library, helpline, repair service, student web hosting, wireless network available.

Student life. Freshman orientation: Available. Preregistration for classes offered. Two-day, overnight program. **Housing:** Guaranteed on-campus for all undergraduates. Coed dorms, single-sex dorms, special housing for disabled, apartments, cooperative housing, fraternity/sorority housing, wellness housing available. $125 partly refundable deposit, deadline 5/1. Learning communities; non-smoking, non-alcohol, graduate/adult undergrad housing available. **Activities:** Bands, campus ministries, choral groups, dance, drama, film society, literary magazine, music ensembles, musical theater, opera, radio station, student government, student newspaper, symphony orchestra, TV station, more than 500 clubs and organizations.

Athletics. NCAA. **Intercollegiate:** Basketball, cross-country, football (tackle) M, golf, gymnastics W, soccer W, softball W, swimming W, tennis W, track and field, volleyball W, wrestling M. **Intramural:** Badminton, basketball, bowling, boxing M, cross-country, diving, golf, handball, ice hockey, racquetball, skiing, soccer, softball, squash, swimming, table tennis, tennis, volleyball, water polo, weight lifting, wrestling. **Team name:** Cyclones.

Student services. Adult student services, alcohol/substance abuse counseling, career counseling, student employment services, financial aid counseling, health services, legal services, minority student services, on-campus daycare, personal counseling, placement for graduates, veterans' counselor, women's services. **Physically disabled:** Services for visually, speech, hearing impaired.

Contact. E-mail: admissions@iastate.edu
Phone: (515) 294-5836 Toll-free number: (800) 262-3810
Fax: (515) 294-2592
Marc Harding, Director of Enrollment Services, Iowa State University, 100 Enrollment Services Center, Ames, IA 50011-2011

Iowa Wesleyan College
Mount Pleasant, Iowa
www.iwc.edu

CB member
CB code: 6308

▶ Private 4-year liberal arts college affiliated with United Methodist Church
▶ Residential campus in small town
▶ 740 degree-seeking undergraduates: 22% part-time, 57% women, 8% African American, 6% Hispanic American, 8% international
▶ 63% of applicants admitted
▶ SAT or ACT (ACT writing optional) required

General. Founded in 1842. Regionally accredited. **Degrees:** 177 bachelor's awarded. **Location:** 47 miles from Iowa City, 25 miles from Burlington. **Calendar:** Semester, limited summer session. **Full-time faculty:** 48 total; 60% have terminal degrees, 8% minority, 46% women. **Part-time faculty:** 59 total; 8% have terminal degrees, 54% women. **Class size:** 80% < 20, 19% 20-39, less than 1% 40-49. **Special facilities:** Public interest institute, Harlan-Lincoln house and museum.

Freshman class profile. 1,109 applied, 696 admitted, 113 enrolled.

Mid 50% test scores			
SAT critical reading:	440-520	GPA 3.0-3.49:	30%
SAT math:	460-520	GPA 2.0-2.99:	53%
SAT writing:	390-460	Return as sophomores:	42%
ACT composite:	18-22	Out-of-state:	78%
GPA 3.75 or higher:	10%	Live on campus:	91%
GPA 3.50-3.74:	6%	International:	5%
		Sororities:	8%

Basis for selection. Upper 50% class rank preferred. Automatic acceptance with 2.5 GPA and 19 ACT. Audition recommended for music majors. Portfolio recommended for art, creative programs majors. Essay recommended for applicants who do not meet regular admission requirements. **Home schooled:** Transcript of courses and grades required. GED or portfolio may be substituted for high school transcript requirement.

High school preparation. College-preparatory program recommended. 16 units recommended. Recommended units include English 4, mathematics 3, social studies 3, science 2 (laboratory 2) and academic electives 4.

2011-2012 Annual costs. Tuition/fees: $23,160. Room/board: $7,690. Books/supplies: $1,040. Personal expenses: $1,600.

2011-2012 Financial aid. Need-based: 112 full-time freshmen applied for aid; 112 were judged to have need; 112 of these received aid. 57% of total undergraduate aid awarded as scholarships/grants, 43% as loans/jobs. **Non-need-based:** Scholarships awarded for academics, alumni affiliation, art, music/drama.

Application procedures. Admission: Priority date 4/1; no deadline. $20 fee, may be waived for applicants with need, free for online applicants. Admission notification on a rolling basis beginning on or about 8/15. Must reply by May 1 or within 2 week(s) if notified thereafter. **Financial aid:** Priority date 4/1; no closing date. FAFSA required. Applicants notified on a rolling basis starting 1/1; must reply within 2 week(s) of notification.

Academics. Special study options: Combined bachelor's/graduate degree, cross-registration, distance learning, double major, dual enrollment of high school students, exchange student, independent study, internships, liberal arts/career combination, student-designed major, study abroad, teacher certification program, Washington semester. **Credit/placement by examination:** AP, CLEP, IB, institutional tests. 30 credit hours maximum toward bachelor's degree. **Support services:** Learning center, reduced course load, study skills assistance, tutoring, writing center.

Majors. Biology: General. **Business:** General, accounting, business admin. **Communications:** Communications/speech/rhetoric. **Computer sciences:** General, computer science, web page design. **Conservation:** Forestry. **Education:** General, art, biology, chemistry, early childhood, elementary, English, health, history, mathematics, middle, music, physical, physics, secondary, social studies. **Engineering:** General. **English:** English lit. **Health services:** Environmental health, nursing (RN), predental, premedicine, prepharmacy, prephysical therapy, preveterinary. **History:** General. **Math:** General. **Parks/recreation:** Exercise sciences, health/fitness. **Philosophy/religion:** Christian, philosophy, religion. **Physical sciences:** Chemistry. **Protective services:** Criminal justice. **Psychology:** General. **Social sciences:** Sociology. **Visual/performing arts:** Design, music, studio arts.

Most popular majors. Biology 9%, business/marketing 24%, education 20%, health sciences 14%, parks/recreation 10%, psychology 8%.

Computing on campus. 110 workstations in dormitories, library, computer center. Dormitories wired for high-speed internet access and linked to campus network. Commuter students can connect to campus network. Online library, repair service, wireless network available.

Student life. Freshman orientation: Mandatory. Preregistration for classes offered. Five-day program held week before classes begin. **Policies:** All full-time, unmarried students under the age of 22 who do not live with parents required to live in college residential facilities. Exemptions may be made for seniors, students with dependent children and veterans. **Housing:** Guaranteed on-campus for all undergraduates. Coed dorms, single-sex dorms, wellness housing available. $100 nonrefundable deposit, deadline 8/20. **Activities:** Bands, campus ministries, choral groups, international student organizations, literary magazine, music ensembles, radio station, student government, symphony orchestra, Black Awareness Organization, Fellowship of Christian Athletics, Bacchus, Unidad.

Athletics. NCAA. **Intercollegiate:** Baseball M, basketball, cross-country, football (tackle) M, golf, soccer, softball W, track and field, volleyball W. **Intramural:** Badminton, basketball, bowling, football (non-tackle), softball, table tennis, volleyball. **Team name:** Tigers.

Student services. Adult student services, alcohol/substance abuse counseling, chaplain/spiritual director, career counseling, student employment services, financial aid counseling, health services, personal counseling.

Contact. E-mail: admit@iwc.edu
Phone: (319) 385-6231 Toll-free number: (800) 582-2383 ext. 6231
Fax: (319) 385-6240
Mark Petty, Dean for Admissions, Iowa Wesleyan College, 601 North Main Street, Mount Pleasant, IA 52641-1398

Kaplan University: Cedar Falls
Cedar Falls, Iowa
www.kucampus.edu

▶ For-profit 4-year university and branch campus college
▶ Commuter campus in small city
▶ 413 degree-seeking undergraduates
▶ Application essay, interview required

General. Degrees: 88 bachelor's, 177 associate awarded. **Location:** 120 miles from Des Moines. **Calendar:** Differs by program, extensive summer

session. **Full-time faculty:** 14 total. **Part-time faculty:** 38 total. **Class size:** 64% < 20, 33% 20-39, 3% 40-49.

Basis for selection. Open admission, but selective for some programs. Entrance test required for most programs.

2011-2012 Annual costs. Estimated tuition and fees ranges for entire programs as of July 2011: certificate and diploma programs beginning with 5-week terms, $24,798-$25,085; certificate and diploma programs beginning with 10-week terms, $19,770-$23,676; associate degree programs beginning with 5-week terms, $32,586-$33,645; associate degree programs beginning with 10-week terms, $30,654-$35,763; bachelor's degree programs beginning with 5-week terms, $65,358; bachelor's degree programs beginning with 10-week terms, $66,417; does not include books and supplies, which vary by program. All costs subject to change at any time.

Financial aid. All financial aid based on need.

Application procedures. Admission: No deadline. $20 fee. Application must be submitted on paper. Admission notification on a rolling basis. **Financial aid:** No deadline. FAFSA, institutional form required. Applicants notified on a rolling basis.

Academics. Special study options: Cooperative education, distance learning. **Credit/placement by examination:** AP, CLEP, institutional tests. 32 credit hours maximum toward associate degree. **Support services:** Learning center, tutoring.

Majors. Business: Business admin.

Student life. Freshman orientation: Available, $20 fee. Preregistration for classes offered. **Activities:** Student government, student newspaper.

Student services. Student employment services, financial aid counseling, personal counseling, placement for graduates.

Contact. Phone: (319) 277-0220 Toll-free number: (800) 728-1220 Fax: (319) 243-2961
Jill Hansen, Director of Admissions, Kaplan University: Cedar Falls, 7009 Nordic Drive, Cedar Falls, IA 50613

Kaplan University: Davenport
Davenport, Iowa
www.kucampus.edu　　　　　**CB code: 5848**

▶ For-profit 4-year university
▶ Residential campus in large city

General. Founded in 1937. Regionally accredited. **Location:** 165 miles from Des Moines, 180 miles from Chicago. **Calendar:** Quarter.

Annual costs/financial aid. Estimated tuition and fees ranges for entire programs: certificate and diploma programs beginning with 5-week terms, $24,798-$25,085; certificate and diploma programs beginning with 10-week terms, $19,770-$23,676; associate degree programs beginning with 5-week terms, $32,586-$33,645; associate degree programs beginning with 10-week terms, $30,654-$35,763; bachelor's degree programs beginning with 5-week terms, $65,358; bachelor's degree programs beginning with 10-week terms, $66,417; does not include books and supplies, which vary by program. Need-based financial aid available to full-time and part-time students.

Contact. Phone: (563) 355-3500
Director of Admissions, 1801 East Kimberly Road, Suite 1, Davenport, IA 52807-2095

Kaplan University: Des Moines
Urbandale, Iowa
www.kucampus.edu　　　　　**CB code: 3388**

▶ For-profit 4-year university
▶ Commuter campus in large city
▶ 727 degree-seeking undergraduates
▶ Interview required

General. Regionally accredited. **Degrees:** 97 bachelor's, 318 associate awarded. **Location:** 4 miles from Des Moines. **Calendar:** Differs by program, extensive summer session. **Full-time faculty:** 13 total. **Part-time faculty:** 63 total.

Basis for selection. Open admission, but selective for some programs.

2011-2012 Annual costs. Estimated tuition and fees ranges for entire programs as of July 2011: certificate and diploma programs beginning with 5-week terms, $24,798-$25,085; certificate and diploma programs beginning with 10-week terms, $19,770-$23,676; associate degree programs beginning with 5-week terms, $32,586-$33,645; associate degree programs beginning with 10-week terms, $30,654-$35,763; bachelor's degree programs beginning with 5-week terms, $65,358; bachelor's degree programs beginning with 10-week terms, $66,417; does not include books and supplies, which vary by program. All costs subject to change at any time. Personal expenses: $1,500.

Financial aid. All financial aid based on need.

Application procedures. Admission: No deadline. $20 fee. Application must be submitted on paper. Admission notification on a rolling basis. **Financial aid:** Priority date 6/30; no closing date. FAFSA, institutional form required.

Academics. Special study options: Accelerated study, distance learning, independent study, internships, liberal arts/career combination. **Credit/placement by examination:** AP, CLEP, institutional tests. 32 credit hours maximum toward associate degree, 32 toward bachelor's. **Support services:** Learning center, remedial instruction, study skills assistance, tutoring.

Majors. Business: Accounting, business admin. **Computer sciences:** Information technology. **Protective services:** Law enforcement admin.

Computing on campus. 195 workstations in library, computer center. Commuter students can connect to campus network. Online library, repair service available.

Student life. Freshman orientation: Mandatory, $20 fee. Preregistration for classes offered. **Activities:** Student government, student newspaper.

Student services. Adult student services, career counseling, student employment services, financial aid counseling, placement for graduates.

Contact. Phone: (515) 727-2100 Toll-free number: (800) 383-0253 Fax: (515) 727-2115
Mark Bandy, Director of Admissions, Kaplan University: Des Moines, 4655 121st Street, Urbandale, IA 50323

Kaplan University: Mason City
Mason City, Iowa
www.ku-masoncity.edu　　　　　**CB code: 6289**

▶ For-profit 4-year branch campus college
▶ Commuter campus in large town
▶ 274 degree-seeking undergraduates
▶ Interview required

General. Regionally accredited. **Degrees:** 29 bachelor's, 110 associate awarded. **Location:** 127 miles from Des Moines. **Calendar:** Differs by program, extensive summer session. **Full-time faculty:** 6 total. **Part-time faculty:** 17 total. **Class size:** 92% < 20, 8% 20-39.

Basis for selection. Open admission. **Home schooled:** Transcript of courses and grades, state high school equivalency certificate required. GED required.

2011-2012 Annual costs. Personal expenses: $1,656.

Financial aid. Non-need-based: Scholarships awarded for academics.

Application procedures. Admission: No deadline. $20 fee. Application must be submitted on paper. Admission notification on a rolling basis. **Financial aid:** No deadline. FAFSA required. Applicants notified on a rolling basis.

Academics. Special study options: Accelerated study, combined bachelor's/graduate degree, distance learning, dual enrollment of high school students, independent study, internships, student-designed major, study abroad, teacher certification program. **Credit/placement by examination:** AP, CLEP. **Support services:** Learning center, study skills assistance, tutoring.

Majors. Business: Accounting, business admin. **Computer sciences:** Information technology.

Computing on campus. 140 workstations in library, computer center. Commuter students can connect to campus network. Online library, helpline, repair service, wireless network available.

Student life. Freshman orientation: Mandatory, $20 fee. Preregistration for classes offered. **Activities:** Student government.

Student services. Adult student services, student employment services, financial aid counseling, placement for graduates. **Physically disabled:** Services for hearing impaired.

Contact. E-mail: sturnbull@kaplan.edu
Phone: (641) 423-2530 Toll-free number: (800) 274-2530
Fax: (641) 423-7512
Sharon Turnbull, Director of Admissions, Kaplan University: Mason City, Plaza West 2570 Fourth Street, SW, Mason City, IA 50401

Loras College
Dubuque, Iowa
www.loras.edu   CB code: 6370

- Private 4-year liberal arts college affiliated with Roman Catholic Church
- Residential campus in small city
- 1,496 degree-seeking undergraduates: 2% part-time, 49% women
- 37 degree-seeking graduate students
- 76% of applicants admitted
- 58% graduate within 6 years

General. Founded in 1839. Regionally accredited. **Degrees:** 310 bachelor's awarded; master's offered. **ROTC:** Army. **Location:** 180 miles from Chicago. **Calendar:** Semester, extensive summer session. **Full-time faculty:** 110 total; 61% have terminal degrees, 4% minority, 41% women. **Part-time faculty:** 31 total; 10% have terminal degrees. **Class size:** 55% < 20, 44% 20-39, less than 1% 50-99. **Special facilities:** Planetarium, observatory, residential arts complex.

Freshman class profile. 1,540 applied, 1,174 admitted, 361 enrolled.

Mid 50% test scores			
ACT composite:	21-26	Rank in top quarter:	43%
GPA 3.75 or higher:	30%	Rank in top tenth:	21%
GPA 3.50-3.74:	19%	Return as sophomores:	79%
GPA 3.0-3.49:	30%	Out-of-state:	57%
GPA 2.0-2.99:	21%	Live on campus:	99%
		Sororities:	1%

Basis for selection. High school academic record and test scores most important. ACT recommended. Interview and essay recommended. **Learning Disabled:** All students applying for the enhanced learning disabilities program must have materials submitted by the required date. All files reviewed by learning disabilities program.

High school preparation. 16 units required. Required units include English 4, mathematics 3, social studies 3, history 3 and science 4.

2012-2013 Annual costs. Tuition/fees (projected): $28,167. Room/board: $7,825. Books/supplies: $1,144. Personal expenses: $624.

2011-2012 Financial aid. Need-based: 313 full-time freshmen applied for aid; 263 were judged to have need; 263 of these received aid. Average need met was 77%. Average scholarship/grant was $17,387; average loan $4,363. 78% of total undergraduate aid awarded as scholarships/grants, 22% as loans/jobs. **Non-need-based:** Awarded to 528 full-time undergraduates, including 126 freshmen. Scholarships awarded for academics, alumni affiliation, music/drama. **Additional information:** Audition or portfolio recommended for music and art financial aid applicants.

Application procedures. Admission: No deadline. $25 fee, may be waived for applicants with need. Admission notification on a rolling basis. Must reply by May 1 or within 2 week(s) if notified thereafter. **Financial aid:** Priority date 4/15; no closing date. FAFSA required. Applicants notified on a rolling basis starting 3/1; must reply within 2 week(s) of notification.

Academics. Special study options: Cooperative education, cross-registration, double major, dual enrollment of high school students, ESL, exchange student, honors, independent study, internships, student-designed major, study abroad, teacher certification program, urban semester, Washington semester. Graduate courses open to undegraduates if certain requirements are met. **Credit/placement by examination:** AP, CLEP, IB. **Support services:** Learning center, reduced course load, remedial instruction, study skills assistance, tutoring, writing center.

Majors. Biology: General, biochemistry. **Business:** General, accounting, business admin, finance, management information systems, marketing. **Communications:** Journalism, media studies, public relations. **Computer sciences:** Computer science. **Education:** General, art, early childhood, elementary, emotionally handicapped, mentally handicapped, multi-level teacher, physical, secondary, special ed. **Engineering:** Applied physics, electrical. **English:** Creative writing, English lit. **Foreign languages:** Spanish. **Health services:** Athletic training. **History:** General. **Human services:** Social work. **Liberal arts:** Arts/sciences. **Math:** General. **Parks/recreation:** Exercise

sciences. **Philosophy/religion:** Philosophy, religion. **Physical sciences:** General, chemistry. **Protective services:** Criminal justice. **Psychology:** General. **Social sciences:** Economics, international relations, political science, sociology. **Visual/performing arts:** General, music.

Most popular majors. Biology 7%, business/marketing 27%, communications/journalism 6%, education 13%, English 7%, psychology 6%, security/protective services 6%, social sciences 9%.

Computing on campus. PC or laptop required. 20 workstations in library, computer center, student center. Dormitories wired for high-speed internet access and linked to campus network. Commuter students can connect to campus network. Online course registration, online library, helpline, repair service, student web hosting, wireless network available.

Student life. Freshman orientation: Mandatory. Preregistration for classes offered. Held from early June through the start of fall term. **Housing:** Guaranteed on-campus for freshmen. Coed dorms, single-sex dorms, apartments, fraternity/sorority housing available. $100 fully refundable deposit. **Activities:** Bands, campus ministries, choral groups, dance, drama, international student organizations, music ensembles, musical theater, radio station, student government, student newspaper, TV station, peace and justice club, African/Hispanic/Asian/Native American club, Amnesty International, environmental action forum, Fellowship of Christian Athletes.

Athletics. NCAA. **Intercollegiate:** Baseball M, basketball, cross-country, diving, football M, golf, soccer, softball W, swimming, tennis W, track and field, volleyball W, wrestling M. **Intramural:** Badminton, baseball M, basketball, bowling, cheerleading, cross-country, diving, football (non-tackle), golf, handball, racquetball, soccer, softball, swimming, table tennis, tennis, track and field, volleyball, water polo, weight lifting, wrestling M. **Team name:** Duhawks.

Student services. Adult student services, alcohol/substance abuse counseling, chaplain/spiritual director, career counseling, student employment services, financial aid counseling, health services, minority student services, personal counseling, placement for graduates, veterans' counselor. **Physically disabled:** Services for visually, speech, hearing impaired.

Contact. E-mail: adms@loras.edu
Phone: (563) 588-7236 Toll-free number: (800) 245-6727
Fax: (563) 588-7119
Sharon Lyons, Director of Admissions, Loras College, 1450 Alta Vista Street, Dubuque, IA 52004-0178

Luther College
Decorah, Iowa   CB member
www.luther.edu   CB code: 6375

- Private 4-year liberal arts college affiliated with Evangelical Lutheran Church in America
- Residential campus in small town
- 2,411 degree-seeking undergraduates: 57% women, 1% African American, 2% Asian American, 3% Hispanic American, 5% international
- 71% of applicants admitted
- SAT or ACT (ACT writing optional), application essay required
- 74% graduate within 6 years; 20% enter graduate study

General. Founded in 1861. Regionally accredited. **Degrees:** 544 bachelor's awarded. **Location:** 70 miles from Rochester, MN; 50 miles from LaCrosse, WI. **Calendar:** 4-1-4, limited summer session. **Full-time faculty:** 178 total; 96% have terminal degrees, 6% minority, 44% women. **Part-time faculty:** 79 total; 40% have terminal degrees, 4% minority, 56% women. **Class size:** 54% < 20, 44% 20-39, 1% 40-49, 1% 50-99, less than 1% >100. **Special facilities:** Planetarium, Norwegian-American museum, extensive biology field study areas, cadaver laboratory, wind turbine.

Freshman class profile. 3,683 applied, 2,631 admitted, 627 enrolled.

Mid 50% test scores			
		GPA 2.0-2.99:	9%
SAT critical reading:	440-620	Rank in top quarter:	62%
SAT math:	510-640	Rank in top tenth:	31%
SAT writing:	460-620	End year in good standing:	95%
ACT composite:	24-29	Return as sophomores:	87%
GPA 3.75 or higher:	46%	Out-of-state:	69%
GPA 3.50-3.74:	22%	Live on campus:	99%
GPA 3.0-3.49:	23%	International:	6%

Basis for selection. Rigor of high school curriculum most important, followed by test scores and teacher recommendation(s). Applicants should rank in top half of high school class. Audition recommended for music scholarships. Portfolio recommended for art majors. Interview recommended for borderline students. **Home schooled:** If graduate of non-diploma-granting

organization, evidence of preparation for college required. Must provide at least 2 of the following: home school transcript listing all courses; detailed portfolio of high school work completed; bibliography of major books read, with brief essay on one of the selected works; additional reference letter completed by an educator assessing the applicant's academic preparation; scores from any AP exams and/or GED test results.

High school preparation. College-preparatory program recommended. 14 units recommended. Recommended units include English 4, mathematics 3, social studies 3, science 2 (laboratory 1) and foreign language 2.

2011-2012 Annual costs. Tuition/fees: $34,885. Room/board: $5,850. Books/supplies: $1,040. Personal expenses: $1,725.

2011-2012 Financial aid. Need-based: 542 full-time freshmen applied for aid; 462 were judged to have need; 462 of these received aid. Average need met was 89%. Average scholarship/grant was $21,497; average loan $4,863. 74% of total undergraduate aid awarded as scholarships/grants, 26% as loans/jobs. **Non-need-based:** Awarded to 522 full-time undergraduates, including 147 freshmen. Scholarships awarded for academics, alumni affiliation, art, minority status, music/drama.

Application procedures. Admission: No deadline. $25 fee, may be waived for applicants with need, free for online applicants. Admission notification on a rolling basis beginning on or about 9/1. Must reply by May 1 or within 4 week(s) if notified thereafter. **Financial aid:** Priority date 3/1; no closing date. FAFSA, institutional form required. Applicants notified on a rolling basis starting 3/15; must reply by 5/1 or within 4 week(s) of notification.

Academics. Special study options: Combined bachelor's/graduate degree, double major, dual enrollment of high school students, honors, independent study, internships, student-designed major, study abroad, teacher certification program, Washington semester. **Credit/placement by examination:** AP, CLEP, IB, institutional tests. No limit, but student must satisfy residency requirement. **Support services:** Learning center, reduced course load, remedial instruction, study skills assistance, tutoring, writing center.

Majors. Area/ethnic studies: African-American, Russian/Slavic, women's. **Biology:** General. **Business:** Accounting, business admin, management information systems. **Communications:** Communications/speech/rhetoric. **Computer sciences:** Computer science. **Conservation:** Environmental studies. **Education:** Elementary. **English:** English lit. **Foreign languages:** Biblical, classics, French, German, Scandinavian, Spanish. **Health services:** Athletic training, nursing (RN). **History:** General. **Human services:** Social work. **Math:** General, mathematics/statistics. **Parks/recreation:** Health/fitness. **Philosophy/religion:** Philosophy, religion. **Physical sciences:** Chemistry, physics. **Psychology:** General. **Social sciences:** Anthropology, economics, political science, sociology. **Visual/performing arts:** Art, dramatic, music.

Most popular majors. Biology 10%, business/marketing 13%, foreign language 6%, health sciences 6%, parks/recreation 6%, social sciences 12%, visual/performing arts 11%.

Computing on campus. 500 workstations in dormitories, library, computer center, student center. Dormitories wired for high-speed internet access and linked to campus network. Commuter students can connect to campus network. Online course registration, online library, helpline, student web hosting, wireless network available.

Student life. Freshman orientation: Mandatory. Preregistration for classes offered. Held prior to start of classes. **Housing:** Guaranteed on-campus for all undergraduates. Coed dorms, special housing for disabled, apartments, wellness housing available. Sustainability house, clusters, quiet floors, honors floor available. **Activities:** Bands, campus ministries, choral groups, dance, drama, international student organizations, literary magazine, music ensembles, Model UN, musical theater, radio station, student government, student newspaper, symphony orchestra, various religious and political clubs, black student union, Asian student association, Phi Beta Kappa, Amnesty International, Alpha Phi Omega.

Athletics. NCAA. **Intercollegiate:** Baseball M, basketball, cheerleading, cross-country, diving, football (tackle) M, golf, soccer, softball W, swimming, tennis, track and field, volleyball W, wrestling M. **Intramural:** Archery, badminton, basketball, football (non-tackle), handball, racquetball, soccer, softball, table tennis, tennis, track and field, volleyball. **Team name:** Norse.

Student services. Alcohol/substance abuse counseling, chaplain/spiritual director, career counseling, student employment services, financial aid counseling, health services, minority student services, personal counseling, placement for graduates. **Physically disabled:** Services for visually, hearing impaired.

Contact. E-mail: admissions@luther.edu
Phone: (563) 387-1287 Toll-free number: (800) 458-8437
Fax: (563) 387-2159
Scot Schaeffer, Vice President for Enrollment Management, Luther College, 700 College Drive, Decorah, IA 52101-1042

Maharishi University of Management
Fairfield, Iowa
www.mum.edu   CB code: 4497

- Private 4-year university and liberal arts college
- Residential campus in small town
- 347 degree-seeking undergraduates: 4% part-time, 50% women, 8% African American, 3% Asian American, 10% Hispanic American, 15% international
- 737 degree-seeking graduate students
- 41% of applicants admitted
- Application essay required
- 72% graduate within 6 years

General. Founded in 1971. Regionally accredited. **Degrees:** 56 bachelor's awarded; master's, doctoral offered. **Location:** 60 miles from Iowa City, 110 miles from Des Moines. **Calendar:** Semester. Modular block system: students study one subject per month, 10 subjects per year. Limited summer session. **Full-time faculty:** 67 total; 45% have terminal degrees, 13% minority, 33% women. **Part-time faculty:** 31 total; 36% have terminal degrees, 6% minority, 23% women. **Class size:** 73% < 20, 20% 20-39, 2% 40-49, 5% 50-99. **Special facilities:** Buildings for practice of transcendental meditation, organic greenhouses, college prep-school, indoor rock-climbing wall, basketball and tennis courts, weight training room, sustainable student center.

Freshman class profile. 107 applied, 44 admitted, 32 enrolled.

GPA 3.75 or higher:	5%	Rank in top tenth:	15%
GPA 3.50-3.74:	5%	Return as sophomores:	76%
GPA 3.0-3.49:	30%	Out-of-state:	80%
GPA 2.0-2.99:	60%	Live on campus:	76%
Rank in top quarter:	25%	International:	29%

Basis for selection. Academics, grades, academic test scores, recommendations, high school and college transcripts, advanced placement tests, extracurricular activities, work experience, interview with admissions officer, and essay important. Students encouraged to visit campus for 4-day weekend. **Home schooled:** Must supply detailed record of courses and objectives. Home school certification required.

High school preparation. College-preparatory program recommended. 15 units recommended. Recommended units include English 4, mathematics 3, social studies 3, science 3 and foreign language 2.

2012-2013 Annual costs. Tuition/fees (projected): $26,430. Room/board: $7,400. Books/supplies: $800. Personal expenses: $1,500.

2011-2012 Financial aid. Additional information: Students may earn scholarships through volunteer staff program.

Application procedures. Admission: Closing date 8/1. $25 fee. Application must be submitted online. **Financial aid:** Priority date 7/15, closing date 7/30. FAFSA required. Applicants notified on a rolling basis starting 3/1; must reply within 4 week(s) of notification.

Academics. Offers consciousness-based education through Transcendental Meditation technique. **Special study options:** Cooperative education, distance learning, double major, honors, independent study, internships, student-designed major, study abroad. **Credit/placement by examination:** AP, CLEP, IB, institutional tests. 12 credit hours maximum toward bachelor's degree. **Support services:** Study skills assistance.

Majors. Business: Business admin. **Communications:** Media studies. **Computer sciences:** Computer science. **Education:** Elementary, secondary. **English:** English lit. **Health services:** Premedicine. **Math:** General. **Visual/performing arts:** Studio arts.

Most popular majors. Architecture 29%, biology 11%, business/marketing 12%, natural resources/environmental science 25%.

Computing on campus. 400 workstations in library, computer center, student center. Dormitories wired for high-speed internet access and linked to campus network. Commuter students can connect to campus network. Online library, helpline available.

Student life. Freshman orientation: Mandatory. Preregistration for classes offered. One-day program held the first day of class. **Policies:** Daily practice of Transcendental Meditation program by all students, faculty, and staff. Smoking, alcohol and drugs not permitted on campus. Organic, vegetarian food served in dining halls. **Housing:** Guaranteed on-campus for all undergraduates. Single-sex dorms, special housing for disabled, apartments, wellness housing available. $100 nonrefundable deposit, deadline 7/15. Family housing, quiet dorms available. **Activities:** Choral groups, dance, drama,

international student organizations, music ensembles, radio station, student government, student newspaper, many clubs and activities available.

Athletics. Team name: Flyers.

Student services. Career counseling, financial aid counseling, health services, on-campus daycare, personal counseling, placement for graduates.

Contact. E-mail: admissions@mum.edu
Phone: (641) 472-1110 Toll-free number: (800) 369-6480
Fax: (641) 472-1179
Michelle Paton, U.S. Director of Admissions, Maharishi University of Management, Office of Admissions, Fairfield, IA 52557

Mercy College of Health Sciences
Des Moines, Iowa
www.mchs.edu
CB code: 2803

- Private 4-year health science college affiliated with Roman Catholic Church
- Commuter campus in large city
- 820 degree-seeking undergraduates: 47% part-time, 87% women, 4% African American, 2% Asian American, 3% Hispanic American
- 55% of applicants admitted

General. Regionally accredited. Clinical education components at a variety of local medical facilities and health care agencies including within the community. **Degrees:** 49 bachelor's, 183 associate awarded. **Location:** Downtown. **Calendar:** Semester, extensive summer session. **Full-time faculty:** 49 total; 18% have terminal degrees, 6% minority, 88% women. **Part-time faculty:** 31 total; 32% have terminal degrees, 10% minority, 64% women. **Class size:** 81% < 20, 15% 20-39, 1% 40-49, 3% 50-99. **Special facilities:** Science and health care laboratory facilities.

Freshman class profile. 414 applied, 227 admitted, 152 enrolled.

Basis for selection. First-time college student admissions based primarily on GPA or standardized test scores; high school completion student admissions based on standardized test scores. **Home schooled:** Transcript signed by student's academic evaluator documenting courses taken, credit earned in each course, and letter grade achieved; 2.25 GPA and 18 ACT required.

2011-2012 Annual costs. Tuition/fees: $13,900. Books/supplies: $1,400. Personal expenses: $4,800.

2010-2011 Financial aid. Need-based: 69 full-time freshmen applied for aid; 64 were judged to have need; 64 of these received aid. Average need met was 36%. Average scholarship/grant was $7,312; average loan $3,184. 56% of total undergraduate aid awarded as scholarships/grants, 44% as loans/jobs. **Non-need-based:** Awarded to 170 full-time undergraduates, including 42 freshmen. Scholarships awarded for academics, minority status.

Application procedures. Admission: Closing date 7/1 (receipt date). $30 fee, may be waived for applicants with need, free for online applicants. Admission notification on a rolling basis. **Financial aid:** Closing date 7/1. FAFSA required. Applicants notified on a rolling basis starting 3/1; must reply by 8/1 or within 3 week(s) of notification.

Academics. Special study options: Accelerated study, distance learning, double major, dual enrollment of high school students. Practicum experience in clinical settings. **Credit/placement by examination:** AP, CLEP. 24 credit hours maximum toward associate degree, 24 toward bachelor's. **Support services:** Study skills assistance, tutoring.

Majors. Health services: Health care admin, nursing (RN), premedicine.

Computing on campus. 61 workstations in library, computer center. Commuter students can connect to campus network. Online library, wireless network available.

Student life. Freshman orientation: Mandatory. Preregistration for classes offered. **Activities:** Campus ministries, student government, student newspaper, service learning opportunities.

Student services. Chaplain/spiritual director, student employment services, financial aid counseling, health services, personal counseling.

Contact. E-mail: admissions@mchs.edu
Phone: (515) 643-6715 Toll-free number: (800) 637-2994 ext. 6715
Fax: (515) 643-6702
Kara Donovan, Admissions Manager, Mercy College of Health Sciences, 921 Sixth Avenue, Des Moines, IA 50309-1200

Morningside College
Sioux City, Iowa
www.morningside.edu
CB code: 6415

- Private 4-year liberal arts college affiliated with United Methodist Church
- Residential campus in small city
- 1,278 degree-seeking undergraduates: 2% part-time, 53% women, 1% African American, 5% Hispanic American, 1% international
- 391 degree-seeking graduate students
- 60% of applicants admitted
- SAT or ACT (ACT writing optional) required
- 57% graduate within 6 years; 12% enter graduate study

General. Founded in 1894. Regionally accredited. All full-time students receive notebook computers. **Degrees:** 256 bachelor's awarded; master's offered. **ROTC:** Army. **Location:** 90 miles from Omaha, NE; 90 miles from Sioux Falls, SD. **Calendar:** Semester, limited summer session. **Full-time faculty:** 76 total; 71% have terminal degrees, 3% minority, 45% women. **Part-time faculty:** 108 total; less than 1% minority, 69% women. **Class size:** 48% < 20, 47% 20-39, 5% 40-49, less than 1% 50-99. **Special facilities:** Biology research station.

Freshman class profile. 2,978 applied, 1,792 admitted, 377 enrolled.

Mid 50% test scores		End year in good standing:	90%
ACT composite:	21-25	Return as sophomores:	75%
GPA 3.75 or higher:	31%	Out-of-state:	40%
GPA 3.50-3.74:	16%	Live on campus:	94%
GPA 3.0-3.49:	33%	International:	1%
GPA 2.0-2.99:	20%	Fraternities:	1%
Rank in top quarter:	45%	Sororities:	2%
Rank in top tenth:	19%		

Basis for selection. 20 ACT/1410 SAT and either rank in top half of class or 2.5 GPA required. Interview recommended. Audition or audition tape recommended for music majors and theater applicants. Portfolio recommended for art majors. **Home schooled:** Transcript of courses and grades required. Home School Credit Evaluation form may be submitted in place of transcript.

High school preparation. College-preparatory program recommended. 10 units recommended. Recommended units include English 3, mathematics 2, social studies 3 and science 2. 4 units math and science required of math or science majors.

2011-2012 Annual costs. Tuition/fees: $24,050. Room/board: $7,320.

Financial aid. Non-need-based: Scholarships awarded for academics, alumni affiliation, art, athletics, job skills, leadership, music/drama, religious affiliation, ROTC, state residency.

Application procedures. Admission: Priority date 8/15; no deadline. No application fee. Admission notification on a rolling basis. **Financial aid:** Priority date 3/1; no closing date. FAFSA required. Applicants notified on a rolling basis starting 3/31.

Academics. Special study options: Distance learning, double major, dual enrollment of high school students, honors, independent study, internships, liberal arts/career combination, student-designed major, study abroad, teacher certification program, United Nations semester, Washington semester. **Credit/placement by examination:** AP, CLEP, IB, SAT, ACT, institutional tests. 32 credit hours maximum toward bachelor's degree. Maximum 12 hours may be used for general studies core requirements. **Support services:** Learning center, reduced course load, remedial instruction, study skills assistance, tutoring, writing center.

Majors. Biology: General. **Business:** Business admin, communications. **Communications:** Advertising, media studies. **Computer sciences:** Programming. **Education:** Art, biology, chemistry, elementary, English, history, mathematics, music, physics, science, Spanish, special ed. **Engineering:** Applied physics. **English:** English lit. **Foreign languages:** Spanish. **Health services:** Clinical lab science, nursing (RN). **History:** General, American. **Math:** General. **Philosophy/religion:** Philosophy, religion. **Physical sciences:** Chemistry, physics. **Psychology:** General, counseling, industrial. **Social sciences:** International relations, political science. **Visual/performing arts:** Dramatic, graphic design, music, music performance, photography, studio arts.

Most popular majors. Biology 9%, business/marketing 23%, communications/journalism 6%, education 19%, psychology 8%, visual/performing arts 10%.

Computing on campus. PC or laptop required. Dormitories wired for high-speed internet access and linked to campus network. Commuter students

can connect to campus network. Online library, helpline, repair service, student web hosting, wireless network available.

Student life. Freshman orientation: Mandatory. Preregistration for classes offered. Held 4 days before school begins. **Housing:** Guaranteed on-campus for freshmen. Coed dorms, apartments, fraternity/sorority housing available. Apartments for adult non-traditional students available. **Activities:** Bands, campus ministries, choral groups, dance, drama, international student organizations, literary magazine, music ensembles, musical theater, radio station, student government, student newspaper, TV station, Civic Union, Project Hope, Fellowship of Christian Athletes, peace and justice club, mission trips, Crossed by Color, Spanish club.

Athletics. NAIA. **Intercollegiate:** Baseball M, basketball, cross-country, football (tackle) M, golf, soccer, softball W, swimming, tennis, track and field, volleyball W. **Intramural:** Basketball, bowling, football (non-tackle), golf, soccer, softball, swimming, tennis, track and field, volleyball. **Team name:** Mustangs.

Student services. Alcohol/substance abuse counseling, chaplain/spiritual director, career counseling, student employment services, financial aid counseling, health services, minority student services, personal counseling, placement for graduates, veterans' counselor. **Physically disabled:** Services for visually, speech, hearing impaired.

Contact. E-mail: mscadm@morningside.edu
Phone: (712) 274-5000 ext. 5511 Toll-free number: (800) 831-0806
Fax: (712) 274-5101
Stephanie Peters, Director of Admissions, Morningside College, 1501 Morningside Avenue, Sioux City, IA 51106

Mount Mercy University
Cedar Rapids, Iowa
www.mtmercy.edu
CB code: 6417

- Private 4-year liberal arts college affiliated with Roman Catholic Church
- Residential campus in small city
- 1,430 degree-seeking undergraduates: 38% part-time, 69% women, 3% African American, 1% Asian American, 3% Hispanic American, 3% international
- 275 degree-seeking graduate students
- 70% of applicants admitted
- SAT or ACT (ACT writing optional) required
- 60% graduate within 6 years; 17% enter graduate study

General. Founded in 1928. Regionally accredited. Available adult accelerated program with evening classes. **Degrees:** 387 bachelor's awarded; master's offered. **Location:** 220 miles from Chicago. **Calendar:** 4-1-4, limited summer session. **Full-time faculty:** 85 total; 62% have terminal degrees, 8% minority, 59% women. **Part-time faculty:** 66 total; 6% have terminal degrees, 6% minority, 56% women. **Class size:** 60% < 20, 36% 20-39, 2% 40-49, 2% 50-99. **Special facilities:** Campus buildings connected by tunnel system.

Freshman class profile. 529 applied, 370 admitted, 151 enrolled.

Mid 50% test scores		Rank in top tenth:	14%
ACT composite:	20-24	End year in good standing:	99%
GPA 3.75 or higher:	25%	Return as sophomores:	76%
GPA 3.50-3.74:	17%	Out-of-state:	6%
GPA 3.0-3.49:	45%	Live on campus:	93%
GPA 2.0-2.99:	13%	International:	5%
Rank in top quarter:	36%		

Basis for selection. 2.5 GPA, rank in top half of class, 20 ACT required. **Home schooled:** Transcript of courses and grades, letter of recommendation (nonparent) required. Submit records of studies or detailed account of subjects and materials.

High school preparation. College-preparatory program recommended. Recommended units include English 4, mathematics 3, social studies 3, history 3, science 3 (laboratory 1) and foreign language 2.

2011-2012 Annual costs. Tuition/fees: $24,360. Room/board: $7,470. Books/supplies: $1,200. Personal expenses: $2,026.

2011-2012 Financial aid. **Need-based:** Average need met was 74%. Average scholarship/grant was $15,433; average loan $3,427. 58% of total undergraduate aid awarded as scholarships/grants, 42% as loans/jobs. **Non-need-based:** Scholarships awarded for academics, alumni affiliation, art, athletics, leadership, music/drama, religious affiliation.

Application procedures. Admission: Closing date 8/15 (receipt date). No application fee. Admission notification on a rolling basis. Must reply by

May 1 or within 2 week(s) if notified thereafter. **Financial aid:** Priority date 3/1; no closing date. FAFSA required. Applicants notified on a rolling basis starting 3/15; must reply by 5/1 or within 3 week(s) of notification.

Academics. Special study options: Accelerated study, cross-registration, double major, dual enrollment of high school students, honors, independent study, internships, liberal arts/career combination, study abroad, teacher certification program. **Credit/placement by examination:** AP, CLEP, IB, ACT, institutional tests. 60 credit hours maximum toward bachelor's degree. **Support services:** Learning center, remedial instruction, study skills assistance, tutoring, writing center.

Majors. Biology: General. **Business:** General, accounting, business admin, finance, management information systems, marketing. **Communications:** Communications/speech/rhetoric, digital media, journalism, public relations. **Computer sciences:** General, computer science. **Conservation:** General. **Education:** Elementary, secondary. **English:** English lit, rhetoric/composition. **Health services:** Clinical lab science, health care admin, nursing (RN). **History:** General. **Human services:** Social work. **Math:** General. **Philosophy/religion:** Philosophy, religion. **Protective services:** Law enforcement admin. **Psychology:** General. **Social sciences:** International relations, political science, sociology. **Visual/performing arts:** Art, graphic design, music.

Most popular majors. Business/marketing 40%, education 9%, health sciences 26%, public administration/social services 10%.

Computing on campus. 135 workstations in dormitories, library, computer center. Dormitories wired for high-speed internet access and linked to campus network. Commuter students can connect to campus network. Online course registration, online library, helpline, wireless network available.

Student life. Freshman orientation: Available. Preregistration for classes offered. Three-day orientation held prior to start of fall term; 3 one-day orientation/registration sessions in the spring and summer. **Housing:** Guaranteed on-campus for freshmen. Coed dorms, apartments, wellness housing available. $200 nonrefundable deposit, deadline 8/15. **Activities:** Choral groups, drama, literary magazine, musical theater, student government, student newspaper, Best Buddies, biology club, Circle K International, criminal justice association, English club, green club, history club, honors student association.

Athletics. NAIA. **Intercollegiate:** Baseball M, basketball, bowling, cheerleading M, cross-country, golf, soccer, softball W, track and field, volleyball W. **Intramural:** Basketball, football (non-tackle) M, racquetball, soccer, softball, table tennis, tennis, volleyball. **Team name:** Mustangs.

Student services. Adult student services, alcohol/substance abuse counseling, chaplain/spiritual director, career counseling, student employment services, financial aid counseling, health services, personal counseling, placement for graduates, veterans' counselor. **Physically disabled:** Services for visually, speech, hearing impaired.

Contact. E-mail: admission@mtmercy.edu
Phone: (319) 368-6460 Toll-free number: (800) 248-4504
Fax: (319) 363-5270
Scott Baumler, Dean of Admissions, Mount Mercy University, 1330 Elmhurst Drive NE, Cedar Rapids, IA 52402-4797

Northwestern College
Orange City, Iowa
www.nwciowa.edu
CB code: 6490

- Private 4-year liberal arts college affiliated with Reformed Church in America
- Residential campus in small town
- 1,184 degree-seeking undergraduates: 2% part-time, 58% women, 1% African American, 1% Asian American, 4% Hispanic American, 3% international
- 75% of applicants admitted
- SAT or ACT (ACT writing optional) required
- 64% graduate within 6 years

General. Founded in 1882. Regionally accredited. **Degrees:** 241 bachelor's awarded. **Location:** 40 miles from Sioux City; 75 miles from Sioux Falls, South Dakota. **Calendar:** Semester, limited summer session. **Full-time faculty:** 85 total; 79% have terminal degrees, 5% minority, 38% women. **Part-time faculty:** 49 total; 4% have terminal degrees, 61% women. **Class size:** 66% < 20, 31% 20-39, 2% 40-49, less than 1% 50-99. **Special facilities:** Natural prairie restoration project.

Freshman class profile. 1,422 applied, 1,060 admitted, 324 enrolled.

Mid 50% test scores		Rank in top quarter:	52%
ACT composite:	21-27	Rank in top tenth:	24%
GPA 3.75 or higher:	37%	Return as sophomores:	76%
GPA 3.50-3.74:	24%	Out-of-state:	46%
GPA 3.0-3.49:	26%	Live on campus:	98%
GPA 2.0-2.99:	13%	International:	2%

Basis for selection. 2.0 GPA required. Rank in top half of class and test scores above 50th percentile most important. Recommendations also important. Interview and essay recommended. Audition recommended for theater, music majors. Portfolio recommended for art majors. **Home schooled:** Transcript of courses and grades required. **Learning Disabled:** Students provide documentation to Director of Academic Support upon admittance.

High school preparation. College-preparatory program recommended. 16 units recommended. Recommended units include English 4, mathematics 3, social studies 3, science 3 and foreign language 3.

2011-2012 Annual costs. Tuition/fees: $24,630. 1-4 credits, $520 per credit hour; 5-8 credits, $770 per credit hour; 9-11 credits, $1010 per credit hour. Room/board: $7,436. Books/supplies: $1,040. Personal expenses: $1,728.

2010-2011 Financial aid. **Need-based:** 67% of total undergraduate aid awarded as scholarships/grants, 33% as loans/jobs. **Non-need-based:** Scholarships awarded for academics, alumni affiliation, art, athletics, music/drama, religious affiliation, state residency.

Application procedures. **Admission:** Priority date 6/1; no deadline. $25 fee, may be waived for applicants with need, free for online applicants. Admission notification on a rolling basis beginning on or about 10/1. Must reply by May 1 or within 3 week(s) if notified thereafter. **Financial aid:** Priority date 4/1, closing date 6/30. FAFSA required. Applicants notified on a rolling basis starting 3/15; must reply within 3 week(s) of notification.

Academics. **Special study options:** Double major, ESL, honors, independent study, internships, liberal arts/career combination, student-designed major, study abroad, teacher certification program, Washington semester. American Studies Program (Washington, D.C.), AuSable Institute of Environmental Studies Program (Michigan), Los Angeles Film Studies Semester, Chicago Metropolitan Studies Program, China Studies Program (Xiaman), Middle East Studies Program (Cairo), Oxford Summer Program (Oxford), Russian Studies Program, Contemporary Music Center (Martha's Vineyard, MA), Latin American Studies Program (Costa Rica), Oxford Honours Programme (England), Trinity Christian College: Semester in Spain, Creation Care Study Program, Summer Institute of Journalism (Washington, D.C.), Semester in Romania, Semester in Oman. **Credit/placement by examination:** AP, CLEP, IB, SAT, ACT, institutional tests. 24 credit hours maximum toward bachelor's degree. **Support services:** Learning center, reduced course load, remedial instruction, study skills assistance, tutoring, writing center.

Majors. **Biology:** General, environmental. **Business:** Accounting, actuarial science, business admin, finance, human resources, managerial economics, marketing. **Communications:** Journalism, public relations. **Computer sciences:** General, computer science. **Conservation:** General. **Education:** General, elementary. **English:** Creative writing, English lit. **Foreign languages:** Spanish, translation. **General:** Business. **Health services:** Athletic training, clinical lab technology, nursing (RN). **History:** General. **Human services:** Social work. **Liberal arts:** Arts/sciences. **Math:** General. **Parks/recreation:** Exercise sciences, health/fitness, sports admin. **Philosophy/religion:** Philosophy, religion. **Physical sciences:** Chemistry. **Psychology:** General. **Social sciences:** Economics, political science, sociology. **Theology:** Religious ed, sacred music. **Visual/performing arts:** Art, dramatic, music.

Most popular majors. Biology 10%, business/marketing 18%, education 15%, English 6%, health sciences 10%, visual/performing arts 8%.

Computing on campus. 250 workstations in dormitories, library, computer center, student center. Dormitories wired for high-speed internet access and linked to campus network. Commuter students can connect to campus network. Online course registration, online library, helpline, repair service, wireless network available.

Student life. **Freshman orientation:** Available. Preregistration for classes offered. One-day orientation program in late May and mid-to-late August. **Policies:** Use of alcohol prohibited on campus. Resident living required for all students unless granted commuting status, married, or living with parents. Religious observance required. **Housing:** Guaranteed on-campus for all undergraduates. Single-sex dorms, special housing for disabled, apartments available. $100 fully refundable deposit, deadline 8/1. **Activities:** Bands, campus ministries, choral groups, dance, drama, international student organizations, literary magazine, music ensembles, student government, student newspaper, symphony orchestra, TV station, student activities council, Fellowship of Christian Athletes, College Republicans, Campus Democrats, Phi Beta Lambda, Sigma Tau, Spanish club, education club, business club.

Athletics. NAIA. **Intercollegiate:** Baseball M, basketball, cheerleading, cross-country, football (tackle) M, golf, soccer, softball W, tennis, track and field, volleyball W, wrestling M. **Intramural:** Badminton, basketball, bowling, football (non-tackle), golf, racquetball, soccer, softball, table tennis, tennis, volleyball. **Team name:** Red Raiders.

Student services. Alcohol/substance abuse counseling, chaplain/spiritual director, career counseling, student employment services, financial aid counseling, health services, personal counseling, placement for graduates, veterans' counselor. **Physically disabled:** Services for visually, speech, hearing impaired.

Contact. E-mail: admissions@nwciowa.edu
Phone: (712) 707-7130 Toll-free number: (800) 747-4757
Fax: (712) 707-7164
Kenton Pauls, Dean of Enrollment Management, Northwestern College, 101 Seventh Street SW, Orange City, IA 51041

Simpson College
Indianola, Iowa   **CB member**
www.simpson.edu   **CB code: 6650**

- Private 4-year liberal arts college affiliated with United Methodist Church
- Residential campus in large town
- 1,817 degree-seeking undergraduates: 23% part-time, 56% women
- 22 degree-seeking graduate students
- 85% of applicants admitted
- SAT or ACT (ACT writing optional) required
- 70% graduate within 6 years; 22% enter graduate study

General. Founded in 1860. Regionally accredited. **Degrees:** 402 bachelor's awarded; master's offered. **Location:** 12 miles from Des Moines. **Calendar:** 4-4-1. Extensive summer session. **Full-time faculty:** 91 total; 78% have terminal degrees, 2% minority, 47% women. **Part-time faculty:** 99 total; 30% have terminal degrees, 3% minority, 35% women. **Class size:** 73% < 20, 25% 20-39, less than 1% 40-49, 1% 50-99. **Special facilities:** Antebellum-era literature collection, cadaver laboratory, art galleries, education lab, Iowa history center, urban studies institute, vocational and integrative learning center, public policy center.

Freshman class profile. 1,343 applied, 1,145 admitted, 338 enrolled.

Mid 50% test scores		Out-of-state:	16%
ACT composite:	21-26	Live on campus:	98%
Rank in top quarter:	50%	International:	1%
Rank in top tenth:	23%	Fraternities:	27%
End year in good standing:	97%	Sororities:	30%
Return as sophomores:	77%		

Basis for selection. High school record, class rank, GPA, and ACT/SAT most important. Recommendations also considered. Campus visit/interview recommended. Audition strongly recommended for music, drama majors. Portfolio strongly recommended for art majors. **Home schooled:** Letter of recommendation (nonparent) required. Must submit transcript(s) with course content descriptions. **Learning Disabled:** Should submit documentation of disability to ensure adequate facilities and programming can be provided.

High school preparation. College-preparatory program recommended. 16 units recommended. Recommended units include English 4, mathematics 3, social studies 3, science 3 (laboratory 3) and foreign language 3. English units should include composition, literature; math units should include 2 algebra, 1 geometry; 4 units math strongly recommended of math or science majors. Foreign language units should be one language.

2011-2012 Annual costs. Tuition/fees: $28,123. Room/board: $7,963. Books/supplies: $900. Personal expenses: $1,300.

2011-2012 Financial aid. **Need-based:** 332 full-time freshmen applied for aid; 292 were judged to have need; 292 of these received aid. Average need met was 92%. Average scholarship/grant was $18,802; average loan $3,663. 70% of total undergraduate aid awarded as scholarships/grants, 30% as loans/jobs. **Non-need-based:** Awarded to 370 full-time undergraduates, including 91 freshmen. Scholarships awarded for academics, alumni affiliation, art, leadership, minority status, music/drama, religious affiliation, state residency. **Additional information:** Music and theater scholarships based on audition. Art scholarships based on portfolio.

Application procedures. **Admission:** Priority date 5/1; deadline 8/15. No application fee. Admission notification on a rolling basis beginning on or about 9/15. Must reply by May 1 or within 3 week(s) if notified thereafter. $200 enrollment deposit required; nonrefundable after May 1. **Financial aid:** Priority date 4/1; no closing date. FAFSA required. Applicants notified on

a rolling basis starting 3/15; must reply by 5/1 or within 3 week(s) of notification.

Academics. Tutoring services offered free of charge. **Special study options:** Accelerated study, combined bachelor's/graduate degree, double major, honors, independent study, internships, liberal arts/career combination, New York semester, student-designed major, study abroad, teacher certification program, Washington semester. 3-2 and 4-2 engineering program with Washington University in St. Louis, Iowa State University, and Institute of Technology, University of Minnesota, Minneapolis. 3 year-15 months nursing program with Allen College. **Credit/placement by examination:** AP, CLEP, IB, SAT, ACT, institutional tests. 24 credit hours maximum toward bachelor's degree. **Support services:** Learning center, pre-admission summer program, reduced course load, study skills assistance, tutoring, writing center.

Majors. Biology: General, biochemistry. **Business:** Accounting, business admin, international, marketing. **Computer sciences:** Computer science, information systems. **Conservation:** Environmental science. **Education:** General, elementary, music, physical. **Engineering:** Pre-engineering. **English:** English lit. **Foreign languages:** French, German, Spanish. **Health services:** Athletic training, predental, premedicine, prenursing, preoptometry, prepharmacy, prephysical therapy, preveterinary. **History:** General. **Liberal arts:** Arts/sciences. **Math:** General. **Parks/recreation:** Exercise sciences, sports admin. **Philosophy/religion:** Philosophy, religion. **Physical sciences:** Chemistry, physics. **Protective services:** Criminal justice, forensics. **Psychology:** General. **Social sciences:** Economics, international relations, political science, sociology. **Theology:** Preministerial. **Visual/performing arts:** Art, dramatic, graphic design, music, music performance, studio arts.

Most popular majors. Biology 6%, business/marketing 19%, education 14%, liberal arts 7%, social sciences 9%.

Computing on campus. 374 workstations in dormitories, library, computer center, student center. Dormitories wired for high-speed internet access and linked to campus network. Commuter students can connect to campus network. Online library, wireless network available.

Student life. Freshman orientation: Mandatory. Preregistration for classes offered. Four 1-day summer registration programs in June. Fall orientation held first week students are on campus. **Housing:** Guaranteed on-campus for all undergraduates. Coed dorms, apartments, fraternity/sorority housing, wellness housing available. Single sex rooms and floors in co-ed dorms; medical single rooms available. **Activities:** Bands, campus ministries, choral groups, drama, international student organizations, literary magazine, music ensembles, Model UN, musical theater, opera, radio station, student government, student newspaper, Religious Life Community, interfaith fellowship, Alpha Phi Omega service fraternity, College Democrats, College Republicans, Fellowship of Christian Athletes, Habitat for Humanity, Catholic Worker House, Center for Vocation and Integrative Learning.

Athletics. NCAA. **Intercollegiate:** Baseball M, basketball, cheerleading, cross-country, football (tackle) M, golf, soccer, softball W, swimming, tennis, track and field, volleyball W, wrestling M. **Intramural:** Badminton, basketball, football (non-tackle), golf, racquetball, soccer, softball, swimming, table tennis, tennis, volleyball, weight lifting. **Team name:** Storm.

Student services. Adult student services, alcohol/substance abuse counseling, chaplain/spiritual director, career counseling, services for economically disadvantaged, student employment services, financial aid counseling, health services, minority student services, personal counseling, women's services. **Physically disabled:** Services for visually, speech, hearing impaired.

Contact. E-mail: admiss@simpson.edu
Phone: (515) 961-1624 Toll-free number: (800) 362-2454 ext. 1624
Fax: (515) 961-1870
Deborah Tierney, Vice President for Enrollment, Simpson College, 701 North C Street, Indianola, IA 50125

St. Ambrose University
Davenport, Iowa
www.sau.edu   **CB code: 6617**

- Private 4-year university and liberal arts college affiliated with Roman Catholic Church
- Residential campus in small city
- 2,686 degree-seeking undergraduates: 12% part-time, 59% women, 3% African American, 1% Asian American, 6% Hispanic American, 1% international
- 806 degree-seeking graduate students
- 84% of applicants admitted
- SAT or ACT (ACT writing optional) required
- 62% graduate within 6 years

General. Founded in 1882. Regionally accredited. **Degrees:** 609 bachelor's awarded; master's, professional, doctoral offered. **Location:** 180 miles from Des Moines, 175 miles from Chicago. **Calendar:** Semester, extensive summer session. **Full-time faculty:** 211 total; 69% have terminal degrees, 8% minority, 49% women. **Part-time faculty:** 190 total; 10% have terminal degrees, 8% minority, 45% women. **Class size:** 66% < 20, 33% 20-39, less than 1% 40-49, less than 1% >100. **Special facilities:** Transmission electron microscope, cable television channel, observatory, national prairie garden, radio station.

Freshman class profile. 2,257 applied, 1,894 admitted, 551 enrolled.

Mid 50% test scores		Rank in top tenth:	19%
ACT composite:	20-25	End year in good standing:	76%
GPA 3.75 or higher:	21%	Return as sophomores:	78%
GPA 3.50-3.74:	13%	Out-of-state:	72%
GPA 3.0-3.49:	29%	Live on campus:	95%
GPA 2.0-2.99:	37%	International:	1%
Rank in top quarter:	37%		

Basis for selection. 2.5 GPA and 20 ACT/950 SAT (exclusive of Writing) or 18-19 ACT/870-950 SAT and rank in top half of class required. Interview recommended. Portfolio required for art majors. **Home schooled:** Students without high school diploma required to score 50 on GED with 18 ACT or 860 SAT (exclusive of Writing).

High school preparation. College-preparatory program recommended. 18 units recommended. Recommended units include English 4, mathematics 3, social studies 1, history 1, science 2 (laboratory 2), foreign language 1 and academic electives 4.

2012-2013 Annual costs. Tuition/fees: $25,970. Room/board: $9,195. Books/supplies: $1,200. Personal expenses: $1,200.

2011-2012 Financial aid. Need-based: 520 full-time freshmen applied for aid; 452 were judged to have need; 452 of these received aid. Average need met was 74%. Average scholarship/grant was $11,878; average loan $3,238. 55% of total undergraduate aid awarded as scholarships/grants, 45% as loans/jobs. **Non-need-based:** Awarded to 1,532 full-time undergraduates, including 389 freshmen. Scholarships awarded for academics, alumni affiliation, art, athletics, minority status, music/drama. **Additional information:** Iowa applicants must apply for financial aid by July 1. Audition required for music, drama scholarship applicants.

Application procedures. Admission: No deadline. $25 fee, may be waived for applicants with need, free for online applicants. Admission notification on a rolling basis beginning on or about 10/1. Must reply by May 1 or within 2 week(s) if notified thereafter. **Financial aid:** Priority date 3/15; no closing date. FAFSA required. Applicants notified on a rolling basis starting 2/1; must reply within 2 week(s) of notification.

Academics. Special study options: Accelerated study, combined bachelor's/graduate degree, cooperative education, distance learning, double major, independent study, internships, liberal arts/career combination, student-designed major, study abroad, teacher certification program. Service learning program in which students work as volunteers for community and earn 1-3 semester hours credit, license preparation for occupational therapy on campus, accounting majors volunteer to work on income tax forms for low income families on campus. **Credit/placement by examination:** AP, CLEP, IB, SAT, ACT, institutional tests. 60 credit hours maximum toward bachelor's degree. **Support services:** Learning center, pre-admission summer program, reduced course load, remedial instruction, study skills assistance, tutoring, writing center.

Majors. Biology: General, neuroscience. **Business:** General, accounting, business admin, finance, international, management science, marketing, organizational behavior. **Communications:** Advertising, broadcast journalism, communications/speech/rhetoric, journalism, media studies, public relations, radio/TV. **Computer sciences:** General, computer science, information systems, LAN/WAN management, security, systems analysis. **Education:** General, art, biology, business, chemistry, early childhood, elementary, English, foreign languages, French, German, health, history, mathematics, music, physical, physics, psychology, science, secondary, social science, Spanish. **Engineering:** Applied physics, industrial. **English:** English lit, rhetoric/composition. **Foreign languages:** French, German, Spanish. **Health services:** Nursing (RN). **History:** General. **Human services:** General. **Math:** General. **Parks/recreation:** Exercise sciences, health/fitness, sports admin. **Philosophy/religion:** Philosophy. **Physical sciences:** Chemistry, physics. **Protective services:** Criminal justice, criminalistics. **Psychology:** General, forensic. **Social sciences:** Economics, political science, sociology. **Visual/performing arts:** Commercial/advertising art, dramatic, graphic design, multimedia, music, studio arts, theater arts management.

Most popular majors. Business/marketing 28%, education 11%, health sciences 8%, parks/recreation 10%, psychology 13%.

Computing on campus. 190 workstations in library, computer center, student center. Dormitories wired for high-speed internet access and linked

to campus network. Commuter students can connect to campus network. Online course registration, online library, helpline, wireless network available.

Student life. Freshman orientation: Mandatory, $100 fee. Preregistration for classes offered. Held 2 days per month in April, June, August. **Policies:** All campus buildings smoke-free. **Housing:** Guaranteed on-campus for freshmen. Coed dorms, single-sex dorms, special housing for disabled, apartments, wellness housing available. $250 partly refundable deposit, deadline 5/1. Townhouses for seniors, houses for juniors and seniors available. **Activities:** Bands, campus ministries, choral groups, dance, drama, literary magazine, music ensembles, musical theater, opera, radio station, student government, student newspaper, symphony orchestra, TV station, Fellowship of Christian Athletes, Black student union, philosophy club, Young Republicans, Young Democrats, veterans club, art club, music club, psychology club, multicultural club.

Athletics. NAIA. **Intercollegiate:** Baseball M, basketball, bowling, cheerleading, cross-country, football (tackle) M, golf, soccer, softball W, tennis, track and field, volleyball. **Intramural:** Badminton, basketball, bowling, football (non-tackle), golf, handball, racquetball, softball, tennis, triathlon, volleyball. **Team name:** Fighting Bees.

Student services. Adult student services, alcohol/substance abuse counseling, career counseling, student employment services, financial aid counseling, health services, minority student services, on-campus daycare, personal counseling, placement for graduates, veterans' counselor, women's services. **Physically disabled:** Services for visually, speech, hearing impaired.

Contact. E-mail: admit@sau.edu
Phone: (563) 333-6300 Toll-free number: (800) 383-2627
Fax: (563) 333-6243
Meg Halligan, Director of Admissions, St. Ambrose University, 518 West Locust Street, Davenport, IA 52803-2898

University of Dubuque
Dubuque, Iowa
www.dbq.edu

CB member
CB code: 6869

- Private 4-year university and seminary college affiliated with Presbyterian Church (USA)
- Residential campus in small city
- 1,674 degree-seeking undergraduates: 9% part-time, 43% women
- 329 degree-seeking graduate students
- 80% of applicants admitted
- SAT or ACT (ACT writing optional), application essay required
- 41% graduate within 6 years; 7% enter graduate study

General. Founded in 1852. Regionally accredited. **Degrees:** 290 bachelor's awarded; master's, doctoral offered. **ROTC:** Army. **Location:** 180 miles from Chicago. **Calendar:** 4-1-4, limited summer session. **Full-time faculty:** 87 total; 56% have terminal degrees, 10% minority, 40% women. **Part-time faculty:** 79 total; 8% minority, 40% women. **Class size:** 59% < 20, 39% 20-39, 2% 40-49, less than 1% 50-99. **Special facilities:** Floating laboratory on Mississippi River, curriculum laboratory for teachers, aviation operations center, studio laboratory for animation program, wetland area management, science center.

Freshman class profile. 1,264 applied, 1,009 admitted, 405 enrolled.

Mid 50% test scores		Rank in top quarter:	25%
SAT critical reading:	400-490	Rank in top tenth:	8%
SAT math:	390-520	End year in good standing:	95%
ACT composite:	18-23	Return as sophomores:	72%
GPA 3.75 or higher:	10%	Out-of-state:	68%
GPA 3.50-3.74:	16%	Live on campus:	80%
GPA 3.0-3.49:	25%	Fraternities:	4%
GPA 2.0-2.99:	44%	Sororities:	3%

Basis for selection. 18 ACT, 860 SAT (exclusive of Writing), rank in top half of class most important. 2.0 GPA in college preparatory classes also considered. Rolling admission; must receive test scores before final enrollment. Recommendations required. **Learning Disabled:** Students must request assistance.

High school preparation. College-preparatory program recommended. 16 units required. Required and recommended units include English 4, mathematics 3, social studies 3, science 3, foreign language 2 and academic electives 3.

2011-2012 Annual costs. Tuition/fees: $22,590. Room/board: $7,360. Books/supplies: $950.

2011-2012 Financial aid. Need-based: 380 full-time freshmen applied for aid; 348 were judged to have need; 346 of these received aid. Average need met was 77%. Average scholarship/grant was $14,857; average loan $7,085. 61% of total undergraduate aid awarded as scholarships/grants, 39% as loans/jobs. **Non-need-based:** Awarded to 331 full-time undergraduates, including 134 freshmen. Scholarships awarded for academics, alumni affiliation, leadership, music/drama, religious affiliation, ROTC.

Application procedures. Admission: No deadline. $25 fee, may be waived for applicants with need. Admission notification on a rolling basis beginning on or about 9/1. Must reply by May 1 or within 4 week(s) if notified thereafter. **Financial aid:** Priority date 4/1; no closing date. FAFSA required. Applicants notified on a rolling basis starting 3/1; must reply within 3 week(s) of notification.

Academics. Special study options: Accelerated study, combined bachelor's/graduate degree, cooperative education, cross-registration, distance learning, double major, dual enrollment of high school students, honors, independent study, internships, liberal arts/career combination, student-designed major, study abroad, teacher certification program, urban semester. Undergraduate students may take graduate courses. Off-campus study: semester-away programs. **Credit/placement by examination:** AP, CLEP, IB, SAT, ACT, institutional tests. 24 credit hours maximum toward associate degree, 24 toward bachelor's. **Support services:** Learning center, reduced course load, remedial instruction, study skills assistance, tutoring, writing center.

Majors. Biology: General. **Business:** Accounting, business admin. **Communications:** General. **Computer sciences:** General, computer graphics, data processing. **Conservation:** Environmental science. **Education:** Biology, chemistry, elementary, English, environmental, health, mathematics, physical, science. **English:** English lit. **Health services:** Nursing (RN). **Liberal arts:** Arts/sciences. **Parks/recreation:** Health/fitness. **Philosophy/religion:** Philosophy, religion. **Protective services:** Criminal justice. **Psychology:** General. **Social sciences:** Sociology.

Most popular majors. Business/marketing 21%, computer/information sciences 12%, education 11%, health sciences 9%, trade and industry 15%.

Computing on campus. 200 workstations in dormitories, library, computer center, student center. Dormitories wired for high-speed internet access and linked to campus network. Commuter students can connect to campus network. Online course registration, online library, helpline, student web hosting, wireless network available.

Student life. Freshman orientation: Mandatory, $100 fee. Preregistration for classes offered. Held 4 days prior to beginning of class. **Policies:** Students required to live on-campus through junior year or until they reach 21 years of age unless living with parents within 50 miles of campus. **Housing:** Guaranteed on-campus for freshmen. Coed dorms, special housing for disabled, apartments, wellness housing available. $200 fully refundable deposit, deadline 6/1. Houses and townhouses available. **Activities:** Bands, campus ministries, choral groups, dance, drama, film society, international student organizations, literary magazine, music ensembles, student government, student newspaper, social service organizations, service fraternity, environmental group, student activities board, College Republicans, College Democrats.

Athletics. NCAA. **Intercollegiate:** Baseball M, basketball, cross-country, football (tackle) M, golf, soccer, softball W, tennis, track and field, volleyball W, wrestling M. **Intramural:** Archery, badminton, baseball M, basketball, bowling, cheerleading, football (non-tackle) M, golf, racquetball, soccer, softball, table tennis, tennis, volleyball. **Team name:** Spartans.

Student services. Alcohol/substance abuse counseling, chaplain/spiritual director, career counseling, student employment services, financial aid counseling, health services, minority student services, on-campus daycare, personal counseling, placement for graduates, veterans' counselor.

Contact. E-mail: admssns@dbq.edu
Phone: (563) 589-3200 Toll-free number: (800) 722-5583
Fax: (563) 589-3690
Jesse James, Dean of Admission, University of Dubuque, 2000 University Avenue, Dubuque, IA 52001-5099

University of Iowa
Iowa City, Iowa
www.uiowa.edu

CB member
CB code: 6681

- Public 4-year university
- Residential campus in small city
- 20,954 degree-seeking undergraduates: 9% part-time, 52% women, 3% African American, 3% Asian American, 5% Hispanic American, 8% international

- 8,246 graduate students
- 80% of applicants admitted
- SAT or ACT (ACT writing optional) required
- 71% graduate within 6 years

General. Founded in 1847. Regionally accredited. **Degrees:** 4,538 bachelor's awarded; master's, professional, doctoral offered. **ROTC:** Army, Air Force. **Location:** 20 miles from Cedar Rapids, 110 miles from Des Moines. **Calendar:** Semester, extensive summer session. **Full-time faculty:** 1,513 total; 97% have terminal degrees, 16% minority, 33% women. **Part-time faculty:** 100 total; 97% have terminal degrees, 15% minority, 29% women. **Class size:** 49% < 20, 35% 20-39, 4% 40-49, 8% 50-99, 4% >100. **Special facilities:** Hydraulics laboratory, riverside environmental research station, field campus, nature preserve, accelerator, observatory, natural history museum, driving simulator, native birds-of-prey rehabilitation and research project.

Freshman class profile. 18,939 applied, 15,105 admitted, 4,565 enrolled.

Mid 50% test scores			
SAT critical reading:	450-630	GPA 2.0-2.99:	5%
SAT math:	540-680	Rank in top quarter:	56%
ACT composite:	23-28	Rank in top tenth:	24%
GPA 3.75 or higher:	39%	Return as sophomores:	86%
GPA 3.50-3.74:	24%	Out-of-state:	49%
GPA 3.0-3.49:	32%	Live on campus:	94%
		International:	11%

Basis for selection. Regent Admission Index (RAI) computed based on ACT/SAT, class rank, GPA and number of high school core courses. Iowa residents must have 245 RAI; nonresidents must have 255 RAI. College of Engineering applicants must demonstrate success (As or Bs) in math and science courses; have 25 ACT with 25 ACT math or 1130 SAT (exclusive of Writing) with 620 SAT math; and have 265 RAI. Admission to BSN program requires satisfactory completion of pre-nursing courses. Audition required of music, dance majors. **Home schooled:** Transcript of courses and grades required. Personal essay describing home school experience strongly recommended and required in certain circumstances.

High school preparation. College-preparatory program required. 15 units required. Required and recommended units include English 4, mathematics 3-4, social studies 3, science 3 and foreign language 2-4. Math units must include 2 algebra, 1 geometry. Science units must include 2 of the following: biology, chemistry, and physics. Engineering majors require fourth unit of higher math, 1 chemistry and 1 physics, and only 2 units social studies.

2011-2012 Annual costs. Tuition/fees: $7,765; $25,099 out-of-state. Room/board: $8,750. Books/supplies: $1,090. Personal expenses: $2,625.

Financial aid. Non-need-based: Scholarships awarded for academics, alumni affiliation, art, athletics, leadership, music/drama, ROTC, state residency.

Application procedures. Admission: Closing date 4/1 (postmark date). $40 fee, may be waived for applicants with need. Admission notification on a rolling basis beginning on or about 9/15. Must reply by May 1 or within 2 week(s) if notified thereafter. **Financial aid:** No deadline. FAFSA, institutional form required. Applicants notified on a rolling basis starting 3/15; must reply by 5/1 or within 2 week(s) of notification.

Academics. Bachelor of liberal studies, bachelor of applied studies, bachelor in business administration may be earned with distance education course work. **Special study options:** Accelerated study, combined bachelor's/graduate degree, cooperative education, distance learning, double major, dual enrollment of high school students, ESL, exchange student, external degree, honors, independent study, internships, New York semester, semester at sea, student-designed major, study abroad, teacher certification program, Washington semester. **Credit/placement by examination:** AP, CLEP, IB, SAT, ACT, institutional tests. 30 credit hours maximum toward bachelor's degree. **Support services:** Learning center, pre-admission summer program, reduced course load, remedial instruction, study skills assistance, tutoring, writing center.

Majors. Area/ethnic studies: African, African-American, American, Asian, Latin American, Native American, Russian/Slavic, women's. **Biology:** General, biochemistry, botany, microbiology. **Business:** Accounting, actuarial science, business admin, finance, human resources, labor relations, management information systems, management science, managerial economics, marketing. **Communications:** Communications/speech/rhetoric, journalism, media studies. **Computer sciences:** General, computer science. **Conservation:** Environmental science, environmental studies. **Education:** Elementary, physical, science, secondary. **Engineering:** General, biomedical, chemical, civil, electrical, industrial, mechanical. **English:** English lit, rhetoric/composition. **Foreign languages:** Ancient Greek, Chinese, classics, comparative lit, French, German, Italian, Japanese, Latin, linguistics, Portuguese, Russian, Sanskrit, sign language interpretation, Spanish. **Health services:** Athletic training, audiology/hearing, audiology/speech pathology, clinical lab science,

international public health, music therapy, nuclear medical technology, nursing (RN), physician assistant, predental, premedicine, prenursing, prepharmacy, preveterinary, radiologic technology/medical imaging, recreational therapy. **History:** General. **Human services:** Social work. **Liberal arts:** Arts/sciences. **Math:** General, applied, statistics. **Parks/recreation:** General, exercise sciences, facilities management, sports admin. **Philosophy/religion:** Philosophy, religion. **Physical sciences:** Astronomy, chemistry, geology, physics. **Psychology:** General. **Social sciences:** General, anthropology, economics, geography, political science, sociology. **Visual/performing arts:** Art, art history/conservation, ceramics, cinematography, dance, dramatic, drawing, film/cinema/video, jazz, metal/jewelry, music, music management, music performance, music theory/composition, painting, photography, piano/keyboard, printmaking, sculpture, stringed instruments, studio arts, studio arts management, voice/opera.

Most popular majors. Business/marketing 18%, communications/journalism 8%, engineering/engineering technologies 6%, health sciences 8%, liberal arts 8%, psychology 7%, social sciences 9%.

Computing on campus. 1,200 workstations in dormitories, library, computer center, student center. Dormitories wired for high-speed internet access and linked to campus network. Commuter students can connect to campus network. Online course registration, online library, helpline, repair service, student web hosting, wireless network available.

Student life. Freshman orientation: Mandatory, $250 fee. Preregistration for classes offered. 1.5 day summer program. Concurrent parent/guardian program offered. **Policies:** Non-smoking campus. **Housing:** Coed dorms, special housing for disabled, apartments, fraternity/sorority housing, wellness housing available. $50 nonrefundable deposit. Honors, business, education, health sciences, writers, journalism, career leadership and service, quiet houses, major-specific, sustainability, law housing available. **Activities:** Bands, campus ministries, choral groups, dance, drama, film society, international student organizations, literary magazine, music ensembles, musical theater, opera, radio station, student government, student newspaper, symphony orchestra, TV station, College Republicans, University Democrats, Hispanic Society, black student union, Christian Fellowship, environmental coalition, gay/lesbian/bisexual/transgendered and allied union, honor societies, Habitat for Humanity, global health club.

Athletics. NCAA. **Intercollegiate:** Baseball M, basketball, cheerleading, cross-country, diving, field hockey W, football (tackle) M, golf, gymnastics, rowing (crew) W, soccer W, softball W, swimming, tennis, track and field, volleyball W, wrestling M. **Intramural:** Badminton, basketball, bowling, football (non-tackle), golf, racquetball, soccer, softball, swimming, table tennis, tennis, volleyball, wrestling. **Team name:** Hawkeyes.

Student services. Adult student services, alcohol/substance abuse counseling, career counseling, services for economically disadvantaged, student employment services, financial aid counseling, health services, legal services, minority student services, on-campus daycare, personal counseling, placement for graduates, veterans' counselor, women's services. **Physically disabled:** Services for visually, speech, hearing impaired.

Contact. E-mail: admissions@uiowa.edu
Phone: (319) 335-3847 Toll-free number: (800) 553-4692
Fax: (319) 335-1535
Michael Barron, Assistant Provost for Enrollment Management and Executive Director of Admissions, University of Iowa, 107 Calvin Hall, Iowa City, IA 52242-1396

University of Northern Iowa
Cedar Falls, Iowa   **CB member**
www.uni.edu   **CB code: 6307**

- Public 4-year university
- Residential campus in small city
- 11,255 degree-seeking undergraduates: 10% part-time, 56% women, 3% African American, 1% Asian American, 2% Hispanic American, 3% international
- 1,761 degree-seeking graduate students
- 77% of applicants admitted
- SAT or ACT (ACT writing optional) required
- 66% graduate within 6 years

General. Founded in 1876. Regionally accredited. **Degrees:** 2,198 bachelor's awarded; master's, doctoral offered. **ROTC:** Army. **Location:** 63 miles from Cedar Rapids. **Calendar:** Semester, limited summer session. **Full-time faculty:** 649 total; 74% have terminal degrees, 13% minority, 44% women. **Part-time faculty:** 183 total; 32% have terminal degrees, 8% minority, 56% women. **Class size:** 42% < 20, 46% 20-39, 6% 40-49, 5% 50-99, 2% >100. **Special facilities:** Performing arts center, center for energy and environmental

education, NASA teacher resource center, observatory, natural preserve, museum, wellness and recreation center.

Freshman class profile. 4,666 applied, 3,607 admitted, 1,937 enrolled.

Mid 50% test scores		Rank in top tenth:	18%
ACT composite:	21-26	Return as sophomores:	82%
GPA 3.75 or higher:	29%	Out-of-state:	7%
GPA 3.50-3.74:	22%	Live on campus:	92%
GPA 3.0-3.49:	35%	International:	2%
GPA 2.0-2.99:	14%	Fraternities:	2%
Rank in top quarter:	46%	Sororities:	4%

Basis for selection. High school GPA, rank in top half of class, completion of high school curriculum requirements most important. In the absence of class rank, standardized test scores may carry greater weight. Audition required of music majors. Interview may be recommended for borderline applicants who do not meet admission requirements. **Home schooled:** Statement describing home school structure and mission, transcript of courses and grades required.

High school preparation. College-preparatory program required. 15 units required. Required and recommended units include English 4, mathematics 3, social studies 3, science 3 (laboratory 1), foreign language 2 and academic electives 2. English units must include 1 composition. Math units must include algebra, geometry and advanced algebra. 2 electives required in subjects listed above and/or fine arts.

2011-2012 Annual costs. Tuition/fees: $7,350; $16,106 out-of-state. Differential tuition for upper division business majors. Room/board: $7,426. Books/supplies: $1,054. Personal expenses: $2,146.

2010-2011 Financial aid. **Need-based:** 1,755 full-time freshmen applied for aid; 1,231 were judged to have need; 1,230 of these received aid. Average need met was 70%. Average scholarship/grant was $4,715; average loan $3,345. 50% of total undergraduate aid awarded as scholarships/grants, 50% as loans/jobs. **Non-need-based:** Awarded to 4,390 full-time undergraduates, including 1,321 freshmen. Scholarships awarded for academics, alumni affiliation, art, athletics, leadership, minority status, music/drama, ROTC, state residency.

Application procedures. **Admission:** Closing date 8/15 (postmark date). $40 fee. Admission notification on a rolling basis beginning on or about 9/1. **Financial aid:** No deadline. FAFSA required. Applicants notified on a rolling basis starting 3/1.

Academics. Six graduate degree programs available via online delivery. Additional programs available to Iowa residents through blended delivery using the Iowa Communications Network (interactive video) and, on-campus instruction. The bachelor of liberal studies external undergraduate degree completion program available to both Iowa and non-resident students. **Special study options:** Accelerated study, combined bachelor's/graduate degree, cooperative education, distance learning, double major, dual enrollment of high school students, ESL, exchange student, external degree, honors, independent study, internships, liberal arts/career combination, student-designed major, study abroad, teacher certification program, Washington semester, weekend college. Combined bachelors/masters degree programs (BA/MA, BS/MS, BA/MS); undergraduate dual degree majors; Additional programs leading to combined bachelor's/graduate degree: biology, physics, and technology. **Credit/placement by examination:** AP, CLEP, IB, ACT, institutional tests. 32 credit hours maximum toward bachelor's degree. **Support services:** Learning center, pre-admission summer program, reduced course load, remedial instruction, study skills assistance, tutoring, writing center.

Majors. **Area/ethnic studies:** American, Latin American. **Biology:** General, biochemistry, bioinformatics, biomedical sciences, biotechnology, ecology, microbiology. **Business:** Accounting, business admin, construction management, finance, management information systems, marketing, real estate. **Communications:** Communications/speech/rhetoric, digital media, organizational, public relations. **Communications technology:** Graphics. **Computer sciences:** General, computer science, networking. **Conservation:** Environmental science. **Education:** Business, elementary, ESL, foreign languages, health, kindergarten/preschool, middle, music, physical, reading, science, social science, speech, technology/industrial arts. **Engineering:** Applied physics. **English:** English lit, rhetoric/composition. **Foreign languages:** General, French, German, Russian, Spanish. **Health services:** Athletic training, speech pathology. **History:** General. **Human services:** General, social work. **Liberal arts:** Arts/sciences, humanities. **Math:** General, applied. **Parks/recreation:** General, health/fitness. **Philosophy/religion:** Philosophy, religion. **Physical sciences:** Chemistry, geology, physics. **Psychology:** General. **Social sciences:** Anthropology, applied economics, criminology, econometrics, economics, geography, political science, sociology. **Visual/performing arts:** Acting, art, art history/conservation, dramatic, interior design, music, music performance, music theory/composition, studio arts, theater design. **Work/family studies:** Clothing/textiles, family/community services.

Most popular majors. Biology 6%, business/marketing 22%, communications/journalism 6%, education 18%, social sciences 7%.

Computing on campus. 2,500 workstations in dormitories, library, computer center, student center. Dormitories wired for high-speed internet access and linked to campus network. Online course registration, online library, helpline, student web hosting, wireless network available.

Student life. **Freshman orientation:** Available, $125 fee. Preregistration for classes offered. Nine 2-day sessions in summer and immediately preceding beginning of semesters. **Housing:** Guaranteed on-campus for all undergraduates. Coed dorms, single-sex dorms, special housing for disabled, apartments, wellness housing available. $200 partly refundable deposit. **Activities:** Bands, campus ministries, choral groups, dance, drama, international student organizations, literary magazine, music ensembles, Model UN, musical theater, opera, radio station, student government, student newspaper, symphony orchestra, Amnesty International, Asian American student union, black student union, Campus Crusade for Christ, Catholic student association, College Republicans, conservation club, Fellowship of Christian Athletes, Habitat for Humanity, Democrat club.

Athletics. NCAA. **Intercollegiate:** Basketball, cross-country, diving W, football (tackle) M, golf, soccer W, softball W, swimming W, tennis W, track and field, volleyball W, wrestling M. **Intramural:** Badminton, basketball, bowling, cheerleading, cross-country, football (non-tackle), football (tackle) M, golf, racquetball, soccer, softball, swimming, table tennis, tennis, track and field, volleyball, weight lifting, wrestling M. **Team name:** Panthers.

Student services. Adult student services, alcohol/substance abuse counseling, career counseling, services for economically disadvantaged, student employment services, financial aid counseling, health services, minority student services, on-campus daycare, personal counseling, placement for graduates, veterans' counselor. **Physically disabled:** Services for visually, speech, hearing impaired.

Contact. E-mail: admissions@uni.edu
Phone: (319) 273-2281 Toll-free number: (800) 772-2037
Fax: (319) 273-2885
Christie Kangas, Director of Admissions, University of Northern Iowa, 1227 West 27th Street, Cedar Falls, IA 50614-0018

University of Phoenix: Des Moines
West Des Moines, Iowa
www.phoenix.edu

▶ For-profit 4-year university
▶ Small city
▶ 33 degree-seeking undergraduates

General. Regionally accredited. **Degrees:** 11 bachelor's awarded; master's offered. **Calendar:** Differs by program. **Full-time faculty:** 3 total. **Part-time faculty:** 12 total.

Basis for selection. Open admission.

2011-2012 Annual costs. Estimated costs as of August 2011: per-credit-hour charge, $380 to $415, depending upon level and course of study; electronic course materials fee, $95, if applicable. Book and material charges may vary by course and program. All fees are subject to change.

Application procedures. **Admission:** No deadline. No application fee. **Financial aid:** No deadline.

Academics. **Credit/placement by examination:** AP, CLEP.

Majors. **Business:** Business admin, e-commerce, marketing. **Computer sciences:** Database management, programming, security, systems analysis, web page design. **Human services:** General.

Contact. Marc Booker, Director of Admission and Evaluation, University of Phoenix: Des Moines, 6600 Westown Parkway, West Des Moines, IA 50266-7724

Upper Iowa University
Fayette, Iowa
www.uiu.edu   CB code: 6885

▶ Private 4-year university and liberal arts college
▶ Commuter campus in rural community
▶ 4,976 degree-seeking undergraduates: 38% part-time, 60% women, 18% African American, 1% Asian American, 4% Hispanic American, 2% international
▶ 534 degree-seeking graduate students

♦ 60% of applicants admitted
♦ 45% graduate within 6 years; 37% enter graduate study

General. Founded in 1857. Regionally accredited. 17 U.S. education centers and online and independent study programs; education centers in Hong Kong and Malaysia. **Degrees:** 1,353 bachelor's, 81 associate awarded; master's offered. **Location:** 50 miles from Waterloo, 70 miles from Cedar Rapids. **Calendar:** Semester, limited summer session. **Full-time faculty:** 77 total; 70% have terminal degrees, 1% minority, 52% women. **Part-time faculty:** 431 total; 31% have terminal degrees, 10% minority, 48% women. **Class size:** 82% < 20, 17% 20-39, less than 1% 40-49, less than 1% 50-99. **Special facilities:** Electron microscope lab, greenhouse, television and media lab with computer animation suite.

Freshman class profile. 1,186 applied, 713 admitted, 164 enrolled.

Mid 50% test scores		Rank in top quarter:	31%
SAT critical reading:	420-460	Rank in top tenth:	10%
SAT math:	380-510	End year in good standing:	72%
ACT composite:	19-24	Return as sophomores:	56%
GPA 3.75 or higher:	18%	Out-of-state:	50%
GPA 3.50-3.74:	11%	Live on campus:	90%
GPA 3.0-3.49:	31%	International:	10%
GPA 2.0-2.99:	35%		

Basis for selection. 2.0 GPA, 18 ACT, 870 SAT (exclusive of Writing) important. SAT or ACT recommended. Interview recommended for academically weak applicants. Portfolio recommended for art majors. **Home schooled:** Letters of recommendation strongly encouraged. GED or proof of completed coursework required.

High school preparation. College-preparatory program recommended. 14 units recommended. Recommended units include English 4, mathematics 3, social studies 2, history 1, science 3 (laboratory 1).

2011-2012 Annual costs. Tuition/fees: $23,356. Room/board: $7,070. Books/supplies: $1,400. Personal expenses: $1,600.

2011-2012 Financial aid. **Need-based:** 204 full-time freshmen applied for aid; 174 were judged to have need; 174 of these received aid. Average need met was 55%. Average scholarship/grant was $12,200; average loan $3,000. 55% of total undergraduate aid awarded as scholarships/grants, 45% as loans/jobs. **Non-need-based:** Awarded to 1,130 full-time undergraduates, including 217 freshmen. Scholarships awarded for academics, alumni affiliation, athletics.

Application procedures. Admission: No deadline. $50 fee, may be waived for applicants with need. Admission notification on a rolling basis. **Financial aid:** Priority date 3/1; no closing date. FAFSA required. Applicants notified on a rolling basis starting 3/1; must reply within 9 week(s) of notification.

Academics. 2 consecutive 8-week terms equal one semester. **Special study options:** Accelerated study, distance learning, double major, dual enrollment of high school students, ESL, external degree, independent study, internships, liberal arts/career combination, student-designed major, study abroad, teacher certification program. **Credit/placement by examination:** AP, CLEP, IB, institutional tests. 30 credit hours maximum toward associate degree, 30 toward bachelor's. **Support services:** Learning center, remedial instruction, study skills assistance, tutoring, writing center.

Majors. **Area/ethnic studies:** American. **Biology:** General. **Business:** General, accounting, business admin, management information systems. **Communications:** Communications/speech/rhetoric. **Computer sciences:** Information technology. **Conservation:** General, environmental science, forestry, management/policy. **Education:** General, biology, chemistry, early childhood, elementary, health, history, kindergarten/preschool, middle, physical, reading, science, secondary, social science, social studies, special ed. **English:** English lit. **Health services:** Athletic training, facilities admin, health care admin, physical therapy assistant, predental, premedicine, prepharmacy, preveterinary. **Liberal arts:** Arts/sciences. **Math:** General. **Parks/recreation:** Facilities management, health/fitness. **Physical sciences:** Chemistry. **Protective services:** Criminal justice. **Psychology:** General. **Social sciences:** General, criminology, sociology. **Visual/performing arts:** Art, commercial/advertising art, studio arts, studio arts management.

Most popular majors. Business/marketing 40%, education 6%, psychology 10%, public administration/social services 18%, social sciences 14%.

Computing on campus. 600 workstations in dormitories, library, computer center, student center. Dormitories wired for high-speed internet access and linked to campus network. Commuter students can connect to campus network. Online course registration, online library, helpline, repair service, wireless network available.

Student life. Freshman orientation: Mandatory. Preregistration for classes offered. Held during summer, includes financial aid counseling. **Housing:** Guaranteed on-campus for all undergraduates. Coed dorms, single-sex dorms available. $250 partly refundable deposit. Suite-style housing available. **Activities:** Pep band, campus ministries, choral groups, international student organizations, radio station, student government, student newspaper, Peacocks for Progress, Black student union, diversity club.

Athletics. NCAA. **Intercollegiate:** Baseball M, basketball, cheerleading, football (tackle) M, golf, soccer, softball W, tennis, volleyball W, wrestling M. **Intramural:** Badminton, basketball, bowling, football (tackle), soccer M, softball, table tennis, volleyball. **Team name:** Peacocks.

Student services. Career counseling, student employment services, financial aid counseling, health services, personal counseling, placement for graduates.

Contact. E-mail: admission@uiu.edu
Phone: (563) 425-5281 Toll-free number: (800) 553-4150 ext. 2
Fax: (563) 425-5323
Jobyna Johnston, Vice President of Admissions and Financial Aid, Upper Iowa University, Parker Fox Hall, Fayette, IA 52142

Waldorf College
Forest City, Iowa
www.waldorf.edu

CB member
CB code: 6925

♦ Private 4-year liberal arts college affiliated with Evangelical Lutheran Church in America
♦ Residential campus in small town
♦ 787 degree-seeking undergraduates: 12% part-time, 38% women
♦ 57% of applicants admitted
♦ SAT or ACT (ACT writing optional) required
♦ 36% graduate within 6 years

General. Founded in 1903. Regionally accredited. **Degrees:** 124 bachelor's, 2 associate awarded. **Location:** 125 miles from Des Moines. **Calendar:** Semester, limited summer session. **Full-time faculty:** 41 total; 63% have terminal degrees, 39% women. **Part-time faculty:** 5 total; 20% have terminal degrees, 40% women. **Class size:** 64% < 20, 36% 20-39. **Special facilities:** Digital multimedia lab, exercise physiology laboratory with hydrostatic metabolic chamber, GeoWall, FM radio station, cable access TV station.

Freshman class profile. 1,546 applied, 877 admitted, 158 enrolled.

Mid 50% test scores		GPA 2.0-2.99:	48%
SAT critical reading:	360-530	Rank in top quarter:	20%
SAT math:	380-540	Rank in top tenth:	9%
ACT composite:	16-24	End year in good standing:	74%
GPA 3.75 or higher:	9%	Return as sophomores:	37%
GPA 3.50-3.74:	9%	Out-of-state:	84%
GPA 3.0-3.49:	33%	Live on campus:	94%

Basis for selection. School record and test scores most important, recommendations important, class rank and interview (when administered) considered. Interview recommended. Audition and portfolio recommended for music, theater majors. **Home schooled:** Transcript of courses and grades required. **Learning Disabled:** Interview during campus visit required.

High school preparation. College-preparatory program recommended. 16 units recommended. Recommended units include English 4, mathematics 3, social studies 4, science 3 and foreign language 2.

2011-2012 Annual costs. Tuition/fees: $18,876. Room/board: $6,370. Books/supplies: $1,040. Personal expenses: $1,728.

2010-2011 Financial aid. **Need-based:** 185 full-time freshmen applied for aid; 174 were judged to have need; 174 of these received aid. Average need met was 70%. Average scholarship/grant was $9,850; average loan $3,177. 56% of total undergraduate aid awarded as scholarships/grants, 44% as loans/jobs. **Non-need-based:** Awarded to 258 full-time undergraduates, including 111 freshmen. Scholarships awarded for academics, alumni affiliation, athletics, job skills, leadership, music/drama, religious affiliation, state residency.

Application procedures. Admission: No deadline. No application fee. Admission notification on a rolling basis beginning on or about 9/10. **Financial aid:** Priority date 3/1; no closing date. FAFSA, institutional form required. Applicants notified on a rolling basis starting 3/1; must reply within 2 week(s) of notification.

Academics. Internships required in all baccalaureate programs. **Special study options:** Accelerated study, combined bachelor's/graduate degree, distance learning, double major, dual enrollment of high school students, honors,

independent study, internships, student-designed major, study abroad, teacher certification program. **Credit/placement by examination:** AP, CLEP, IB, SAT, ACT, institutional tests. 8 credit hours maximum toward associate degree, 8 toward bachelor's. **Support services:** Learning center, reduced course load, remedial instruction, study skills assistance, tutoring, writing center.

Majors. Biology: General. **Business:** General, business admin, finance, marketing. **Communications:** Broadcast journalism, journalism, media studies, radio/TV. **Communications technology:** General. **Computer sciences:** General, information systems. **Education:** Drama/dance, elementary, English, history, middle, multi-level teacher, music, science, secondary, social studies. **English:** British lit, creative writing, English lit, writing. **History:** General. **Liberal arts:** Arts/sciences, humanities. **Parks/recreation:** Sports admin. **Protective services:** Fire services admin, law enforcement admin. **Psychology:** General. **Social sciences:** General, political science. **Visual/performing arts:** General, dramatic, music, music management, music performance, piano/keyboard, studio arts management, theater arts management, voice/opera. **Work/family studies:** Food/nutrition.

Most popular majors. Business/marketing 32%, communications/journalism 17%, education 15%, English 6%, health sciences 7%, history 6%, psychology 9%.

Computing on campus. PC or laptop required. Dormitories wired for high-speed internet access and linked to campus network. Commuter students can connect to campus network. Online library, helpline, repair service, wireless network available.

Student life. Freshman orientation: Mandatory. Preregistration for classes offered. Held 2 days prior to start of school. **Policies:** No alcohol or tobacco on campus. Three year residency requirement. **Housing:** Guaranteed on-campus for all undergraduates. Coed dorms, single-sex dorms, special housing for disabled, apartments, wellness housing available. $125 fully refundable deposit, deadline 9/10. Community service based housing available. **Activities:** Bands, campus ministries, choral groups, drama, film society, international student organizations, literary magazine, music ensembles, musical theater, radio station, student government, student newspaper, TV station, Fellowship of Christian Athletes, science club, student senate, global culture club, Amnesty International, awareness ambassadors, praise and worship groups, history club, Gay Straight Alliance, Campus Democrats/Republicans.

Athletics. NAIA. **Intercollegiate:** Baseball M, basketball, bowling, cheerleading M, cross-country, football (tackle) M, golf, ice hockey M, soccer, softball W, volleyball W, wrestling. **Intramural:** Badminton, basketball, football (non-tackle), racquetball, rugby W, skiing, soccer, softball, table tennis, tennis, volleyball, weight lifting. **Team name:** Warriors.

Student services. Alcohol/substance abuse counseling, chaplain/spiritual director, career counseling, student employment services, financial aid counseling, health services, personal counseling, placement for graduates. **Physically disabled:** Services for visually, hearing impaired.

Contact. E-mail: admissions@waldorf.edu
Phone: (641) 585-8112 Toll-free number: (800) 292-1903
Fax: (641) 585-8125
Scott Pitcher, Director of Admissions, Waldorf College, 106 South Sixth Street, Forest City, IA 50436-1713

Wartburg College
Waverly, Iowa
www.wartburg.edu

CB code: 6926

- Private 4-year liberal arts college affiliated with Evangelical Lutheran Church in America
- Residential campus in small town
- 1,757 degree-seeking undergraduates: 1% part-time, 53% women, 7% African American, 1% Asian American, 2% Hispanic American, 7% international
- 76% of applicants admitted
- SAT or ACT (ACT writing optional) required
- 61% graduate within 6 years; 25% enter graduate study

General. Founded in 1852. Regionally accredited. **Degrees:** 401 bachelor's awarded. **Location:** 15 miles from Waterloo-Cedar Falls. **Calendar:** 4-4-1. Limited summer session. **Full-time faculty:** 109 total; 74% have terminal degrees, 6% minority, 47% women. **Part-time faculty:** 62 total; 11% have terminal degrees, 6% minority, 56% women. **Class size:** 46% < 20, 49% 20-39, 3% 40-49, 1% 50-99, less than 1% >100. **Special facilities:** Planetarium/

observatory, prairie preserve, math simulation laboratory, institute for leadership education, music laboratory, science center, center for community engagement, sports and wellness center.

Freshman class profile. 2,346 applied, 1,784 admitted, 510 enrolled.

Mid 50% test scores		GPA 2.0-2.99:	17%
SAT critical reading:	400-540	Rank in top quarter:	58%
SAT math:	440-630	Rank in top tenth:	33%
SAT writing:	380-540	End year in good standing:	88%
ACT composite:	21-26	Out-of-state:	30%
GPA 3.75 or higher:	44%	Live on campus:	98%
GPA 3.50-3.74:	18%	International:	9%
GPA 3.0-3.49:	21%		

Basis for selection. Class rank, GPA, courses taken, test scores, recommendations important. Students with 18 ACT or below or who rank in lower half of high school class are reviewed by admission and scholarship committee for final decision. Interview recommended. Audition recommended for music majors. Portfolio recommended for art majors. **Learning Disabled:** Documentation of disability required.

High school preparation. College-preparatory program required. 15 units recommended. Recommended units include English 4, mathematics 3, social studies 2, science 3, foreign language 2 and computer science 1.

2012-2013 Annual costs. Tuition/fees: $32,740. Room/board: $8,315. Books/supplies: $1,100. Personal expenses: $700.

2010-2011 Financial aid. Need-based: 450 full-time freshmen applied for aid; 407 were judged to have need; 407 of these received aid. Average need met was 85%. Average scholarship/grant was $19,969; average loan $3,625. 75% of total undergraduate aid awarded as scholarships/grants, 25% as loans/jobs. **Non-need-based:** Awarded to 543 full-time undergraduates, including 151 freshmen. Scholarships awarded for academics, alumni affiliation, leadership, music/drama, religious affiliation.

Application procedures. Admission: Priority date 5/1; no deadline. No application fee. Admission notification on a rolling basis beginning on or about 9/1. **Financial aid:** Priority date 3/1; no closing date. FAFSA required. Applicants notified on a rolling basis starting 3/1; must reply within 2 week(s) of notification.

Academics. Special study options: Accelerated study, double major, dual enrollment of high school students, honors, independent study, internships, student-designed major, study abroad, teacher certification program, urban semester, Washington semester. Wartburg West urban academic internship experience in Denver, CO; Washington Center Academic Internship Program; cultural immersions in U.S. and around the world; Leadership Certificate Program; 3-2 engineering agreements; deferred admission program with the University of Iowa College of Dentistry, community-based learning courses and first-year seminars. **Credit/placement by examination:** AP, CLEP, SAT, ACT, institutional tests. **Support services:** Learning center, reduced course load, remedial instruction, study skills assistance, tutoring, writing center.

Majors. Biology: General, biochemistry. **Business:** Accounting, business admin, finance, international, marketing. **Communications:** Broadcast journalism, communications/speech/rhetoric, journalism, public relations. **Computer sciences:** General, information systems. **Education:** Art, elementary, history, music, physical. **Engineering:** Engineering science. **English:** English lit, rhetoric/composition, writing. **Foreign languages:** French, German, Spanish. **Health services:** Clinical lab science, music therapy. **History:** General. **Human services:** Social work. **Math:** General. **Parks/recreation:** Sports admin. **Philosophy/religion:** Philosophy, religion. **Physical sciences:** Chemistry, physics. **Psychology:** General. **Social sciences:** Economics, international relations, political science, sociology. **Theology:** Pastoral counseling, religious ed, sacred music. **Visual/performing arts:** Art, commercial/advertising art, dramatic, music, music performance, music theory/composition.

Most popular majors. Biology 14%, business/marketing 21%, communication technologies 15%, natural resources/environmental science 9%.

Computing on campus. 275 workstations in dormitories, library, computer center, student center. Dormitories wired for high-speed internet access and linked to campus network. Commuter students can connect to campus network. Online course registration, online library, helpline, wireless network available.

Student life. Freshman orientation: Mandatory, $160 fee. Preregistration for classes offered. Two-day program in summer; continues in fall for 1 week. **Housing:** Guaranteed on-campus for freshmen. Coed dorms, single-sex dorms, apartments available. $100 deposit, deadline 5/1. Suite-style housing available. **Activities:** Bands, campus ministries, choral groups, dance, drama, film society, international student organizations, literary magazine, music ensembles, musical theater, opera, radio station, student government, student newspaper, symphony orchestra, TV station, campus ministry board, Democrat club, Republican club, Habitat for Humanity, Students for Peace and

Justice, Fellowship of Christian Athletes, volunteer action center, EARTH, Mosaico Latino, Faith Alive.

Athletics. NCAA. **Intercollegiate:** Baseball M, basketball, cross-country, football (tackle) M, golf, soccer, softball W, tennis, track and field, volleyball W, wrestling M. **Intramural:** Basketball, bowling, football (non-tackle), racquetball, softball, tennis, volleyball. **Team name:** Knights.

Student services. Alcohol/substance abuse counseling, chaplain/spiritual director, career counseling, student employment services, financial aid counseling, health services, minority student services, personal counseling.

Contact. E-mail: admissions@wartburg.edu
Phone: (319) 352-8264 Toll-free number: (800) 772-2085
Fax: (319) 352-8579
Todd Coleman, Assistant Vice President for Admissions and Alumni/ Parent Programs, Wartburg College, 100 Wartburg Boulevard, PO Box 1003, Waverly, IA 50677-0903

William Penn University
Oskaloosa, Iowa
www.wmpenn.edu   CB code: 6943

- Private 4-year university and liberal arts college affiliated with Society of Friends (Quaker)
- Residential campus in large town
- 1,764 degree-seeking undergraduates
- 55% of applicants admitted
- SAT or ACT (ACT writing optional) required

General. Founded in 1873. Regionally accredited. Strong emphasis on leadership development. **Degrees:** 334 bachelor's, 47 associate awarded; master's offered. **Location:** 60 miles from Des Moines. **Calendar:** Continuous, limited summer session. **Full-time faculty:** 51 total. **Part-time faculty:** 94 total. **Class size:** 62% < 20, 32% 20-39, 1% 40-49, 5% 50-99. **Special facilities:** Applied technology laboratories, multipurpose activity center, professional-level theater, Middle Eastern art collection, prairie wildlife preserve.

Freshman class profile. 909 applied, 499 admitted, 277 enrolled.

Mid 50% test scores			
SAT critical reading:	350-450	**ACT composite:**	16-22
SAT math:	380-490	**Rank in top quarter:**	18%

Basis for selection. Class rank, test scores, high school GPA important. Extracurricular activities, alumni relationship, recommendation, personal essay considered. Interview and essay recommended for academically marginal applicants. Audition recommended for music grants. **Home schooled:** Transcript of courses and grades, state high school equivalency certificate required.

High school preparation. College-preparatory program recommended. 15 units required. Required and recommended units include English 4, mathematics 3, social studies 2, history 2, science 3 and academic electives 3.

2011-2012 Annual costs. Tuition/fees: $21,790. Room/board: $5,322. Books/supplies: $950. Personal expenses: $2,062.

Financial aid. Non-need-based: Scholarships awarded for academics, alumni affiliation, athletics, leadership, music/drama, religious affiliation.

Application procedures. Admission: No deadline. $20 fee, may be waived for applicants with need. Admission notification on a rolling basis beginning on or about 11/1. **Financial aid:** Priority date 4/15; no closing date. FAFSA required. Applicants notified on a rolling basis starting 1/1; must reply within 3 week(s) of notification.

Academics. College for Working Adults (CWA) degree program. Leadership core curriculum replaces general education requirements. **Special study options:** Accelerated study, distance learning, double major, dual enrollment of high school students, ESL, independent study, internships, liberal arts/ career combination, study abroad, teacher certification program. 3-2 engineering program with Iowa State University. **Credit/placement by examination:** AP, CLEP, IB, SAT, ACT. 16 credit hours maximum toward associate degree, 32 toward bachelor's. **Support services:** Learning center, reduced course load, remedial instruction, study skills assistance, tutoring, writing center.

Majors. Biology: General. **Business:** Accounting, business admin. **Communications:** General, broadcast journalism, communications/speech/rhetoric, digital media, public relations. **Computer sciences:** General, information technology. **Conservation:** Environmental studies. **Education:** Elementary, secondary. **Engineering:** Mechanical, software. **English:** English lit. **History:** General, American. **Math:** General, applied. **Parks/recreation:** Health/ fitness, sports admin. **Psychology:** General. **Social sciences:** Criminology, sociology, U.S. government. **Visual/performing arts:** Studio arts.

Most popular majors. Business/marketing 60%, education 10%, parks/ recreation 12%.

Computing on campus. 125 workstations in dormitories, library, computer center, student center. Dormitories wired for high-speed internet access and linked to campus network. Commuter students can connect to campus network. Online library, helpline, repair service, wireless network available.

Student life. Freshman orientation: Mandatory, $50 fee. Preregistration for classes offered. Held the weekend prior to start of Fall classes; freshmen retreat hosted by faculty the weekend following first week of classes. **Policies:** Student Code of Conduct identifies academic conduct, conduct toward society, general conduct, and conduct toward others. **Housing:** Guaranteed on-campus for freshmen. Coed dorms, single-sex dorms, special housing for disabled, apartments, wellness housing available. $100 partly refundable deposit, deadline 8/1. **Activities:** Bands, campus ministries, choral groups, dance, drama, literary magazine, music ensembles, musical theater, radio station, student government, student newspaper, literary magazine, Students for Minority Interests, international student club, Presidents Diplomats, strength and conditioning club, Greek Council, honor societies, computer club.

Athletics. NAIA. **Intercollegiate:** Baseball M, basketball, cheerleading M, cross-country, football (tackle) M, golf M, soccer, softball W, track and field, volleyball W, wrestling M. **Intramural:** Basketball, bowling, football (non-tackle) M, softball, table tennis, tennis, volleyball. **Team name:** Lady Statesmen, Statesmen.

Student services. Adult student services, alcohol/substance abuse counseling, chaplain/spiritual director, career counseling, services for economically disadvantaged, student employment services, financial aid counseling, minority student services, personal counseling, placement for graduates, veterans' counselor. **Physically disabled:** Services for visually, hearing impaired.

Contact. E-mail: admissions@wmpenn.edu
Phone: (641) 673-1012 Toll-free number: (800) 779-7366
Fax: (641) 673-2113
Kerra Strong, Director of Admissions, William Penn University, 201 Trueblood Avenue, Oskaloosa, IA 52577

Kansas

Baker University
Baldwin City, Kansas
www.bakeru.edu

CB member

CB code: 6031

- Private 4-year liberal arts and teachers college affiliated with United Methodist Church
- Residential campus in small town
- 834 degree-seeking undergraduates: 2% part-time, 48% women, 10% African American, 1% Asian American, 2% Hispanic American, 2% Native American, 1% international
- 92% of applicants admitted
- SAT or ACT (ACT writing optional) required
- 55% graduate within 6 years; 20% enter graduate study

General. Founded in 1858. Regionally accredited. Additional campus locations include Overland Park, Topeka, Wichita, and Lee's Summit in Missouri. **Degrees:** 157 bachelor's awarded. **ROTC:** Army, Air Force. **Location:** 15 miles from Lawrence, 35 miles from Kansas City, Missouri. **Calendar:** 4-1-4, limited summer session. **Full-time faculty:** 58 total; 76% have terminal degrees, 5% minority, 47% women. **Part-time faculty:** 27 total; 18% have terminal degrees, 7% minority, 37% women. **Class size:** 64% < 20, 30% 20-39, 6% 40-49, less than 1% 50-99. **Special facilities:** Wetlands, museum, bible collections.

Freshman class profile. 710 applied, 654 admitted, 200 enrolled.

Mid 50% test scores			
SAT critical reading:	450-560	Rank in top quarter:	45%
SAT math:	440-560	Rank in top tenth:	21%
ACT composite:	21-25	Return as sophomores:	77%
GPA 3.75 or higher:	28%	Out-of-state:	34%
GPA 3.50-3.74:	24%	International:	1%
GPA 3.0-3.49:	33%	Fraternities:	48%
GPA 2.0-2.99:	15%	Sororities:	57%

Basis for selection. Strong core curriculum during high school very important. GPA, class rank, course selection, ACT or SAT, and recommendation from high school core teacher or guidance counselor important. Involvement in school, community and church activities considered. Interview and essay recommended. Audition recommended for music and theater majors. Portfolio recommended for art majors. **Home schooled:** Interview, letter of recommendation (nonparent) required.

High school preparation. College-preparatory program recommended. 17 units recommended. Recommended units include English 4, mathematics 3, social studies 3, science 3 (laboratory 1) and foreign language 2. One fine arts and one computing course recommended.

2011-2012 Annual costs. Tuition/fees: $23,310. Room/board: $7,500. Books/supplies: $1,200. Personal expenses: $1,550.

2010-2011 Financial aid. Need-based: 176 full-time freshmen applied for aid; 154 were judged to have need; 154 of these received aid. Average need met was 81%. Average scholarship/grant was $10,631; average loan $4,500. 75% of total undergraduate aid awarded as scholarships/grants, 25% as loans/jobs. **Non-need-based:** Awarded to 913 full-time undergraduates, including 194 freshmen. Scholarships awarded for academics, alumni affiliation, art, athletics, music/drama, religious affiliation.

Application procedures. Admission: Priority date 3/1; no deadline. No application fee. Admission notification on a rolling basis beginning on or about 9/15. **Financial aid:** Priority date 3/1; no closing date. FAFSA, institutional form required. Applicants notified on a rolling basis starting 3/1; must reply by 5/1 or within 6 week(s) of notification.

Academics. Liberal arts core consisting of nine hours stressing critical thinking skills, strong writing ability, and application of these skills to various academic disciplines required. **Special study options:** Accelerated study, double major, honors, independent study, internships, liberal arts/career combination, student-designed major, study abroad, teacher certification program. **Credit/placement by examination:** AP, CLEP, IB, SAT, ACT. **Support services:** Learning center, reduced course load, study skills assistance, tutoring, writing center.

Majors. Biology: General. **Business:** General, accounting, international. **Communications:** Communications/speech/rhetoric, media studies. **Computer sciences:** Computer science. **Education:** Art, elementary, middle, music, secondary. **English:** English lit. **Foreign languages:** French, German, Spanish. **History:** General. **Math:** General. **Parks/recreation:** Exercise sciences, health/fitness, sports admin. **Philosophy/religion:** Philosophy, religion. **Physical sciences:** Chemistry, physics. **Psychology:** General. **Social sciences:** Economics, sociology. **Visual/performing arts:** Art history/conservation, dramatic, music, studio arts.

Most popular majors. Biology 7%, business/marketing 26%, education 19%, interdisciplinary studies 6%, parks/recreation 12%.

Computing on campus. 140 workstations in dormitories, library, computer center. Dormitories wired for high-speed internet access and linked to campus network. Online library, helpline, repair service, student web hosting, wireless network available.

Student life. Freshman orientation: Mandatory. Preregistration for classes offered. Five one-day programs held in June and July. **Policies:** Students required to live in campus or Greek housing unless granted permission to live off-campus. **Housing:** Guaranteed on-campus for freshmen. Coed dorms, single-sex dorms, special housing for disabled, apartments, fraternity/sorority housing available. $100 nonrefundable deposit. **Activities:** Bands, choral groups, dance, drama, international student organizations, literary magazine, music ensembles, radio station, student government, student newspaper, TV station, Fellowship of Christian Athletes, Parmentors, Baker Ambassadors, Earth We Are, Faith First, Students for globally-based Initiatives, Up 'til Dawn.

Athletics. NAIA. **Intercollegiate:** Baseball M, basketball, bowling W, cheerleading, cross-country, football (tackle) M, golf, soccer, softball W, tennis, track and field, volleyball W, wrestling M. **Intramural:** Basketball, football (non-tackle), softball, table tennis, volleyball. **Team name:** Wildcats.

Student services. Alcohol/substance abuse counseling, chaplain/spiritual director, career counseling, student employment services, financial aid counseling, health services, minority student services, personal counseling, placement for graduates, veterans' counselor, women's services. **Physically disabled:** Services for visually, hearing impaired.

Contact. E-mail: admission@bakeru.edu
Phone: (785) 594-8307 Toll-free number: (800) 873-4282
Fax: (785) 594-8353
Kevin Kropf, Director of Enrollment Management, Baker University, 618 Eighth Street, Baldwin City, KS 66006-0065

Barclay College
Haviland, Kansas
www.barclaycollege.edu

CB code: 6228

- Private 4-year Bible college affiliated with Society of Friends (Quaker)
- Residential campus in rural community
- 228 degree-seeking undergraduates: 8% part-time, 50% women
- 12 degree-seeking graduate students
- 100% of applicants admitted
- ACT (writing optional), application essay, interview required
- 41% graduate within 6 years; 20% enter graduate study

General. Founded in 1917. Accredited by ABHE. **Degrees:** 37 bachelor's, 4 associate awarded. **Location:** 100 miles from Wichita, 65 miles from Dodge City. **Calendar:** Semester, limited summer session. **Full-time faculty:** 15 total; 47% have terminal degrees, 7% minority, 13% women. **Part-time faculty:** 20 total; 10% have terminal degrees, 30% women. **Class size:** 81% < 20, 17% 20-39, 2% 50-99.

Freshman class profile. 52 applied, 52 admitted, 39 enrolled.

Mid 50% test scores			
		ACT composite:	17-25
SAT critical reading:	430-550	End year in good standing:	84%
SAT math:	390-530	Return as sophomores:	76%
SAT writing:	380-530	Out-of-state:	64%

Basis for selection. Personal references and commitment to Christian vocation important. Committee reviews file and conducts phone interview. Audition recommended for music majors.

2011-2012 Annual costs. Tuition/fees: $13,790. Room/board: $6,800. Books/supplies: $1,600. Personal expenses: $1,300.

2010-2011 Financial aid. Need-based: 40 full-time freshmen applied for aid; 40 were judged to have need; 40 of these received aid. Average scholarship/grant was $3,897; average loan $3,359. 63% of total undergraduate

aid awarded as scholarships/grants, 37% as loans/jobs. **Non-need-based:** Awarded to 397 full-time undergraduates, including 86 freshmen. Scholarships awarded for academics, alumni affiliation, leadership, music/drama, state residency.

Application procedures. Admission: Closing date 9/1. $25 fee, may be waived for applicants with need, free for online applicants. Admission notification on a rolling basis. **Financial aid:** Priority date 5/31, closing date 7/15. FAFSA, institutional form required. Applicants notified on a rolling basis starting 1/1; must reply within 4 week(s) of notification.

Academics. Each student has Bible major in addition to individually chosen major. Emphasis on practicums and internships. **Special study options:** Cooperative education, distance learning, double major, dual enrollment of high school students, independent study, internships, liberal arts/career combination, teacher certification program. Cooperative classes with Pratt Community College. **Credit/placement by examination:** AP, CLEP, IB, SAT, ACT, institutional tests. 15 credit hours maximum toward associate degree, 30 toward bachelor's. **Support services:** Learning center, remedial instruction, study skills assistance, tutoring, writing center.

Majors. Business: General, business admin. **Education:** Elementary. **Philosophy/religion:** Religion. **Psychology:** General. **Theology:** Bible, missionary, pastoral counseling, sacred music, theology, youth ministry.

Most popular majors. Business/marketing 16%, education 8%, psychology 30%, theological studies 46%.

Computing on campus. 25 workstations in dormitories, library, computer center. Dormitories wired for high-speed internet access and linked to campus network. Commuter students can connect to campus network. Online course registration, online library, repair service, wireless network available.

Student life. Freshman orientation: Mandatory. Preregistration for classes offered. **Policies:** Christian and social work required. Religious observance required. **Housing:** Guaranteed on-campus for freshmen. Single-sex dorms, wellness housing available. $50 deposit. **Activities:** Jazz band, choral groups, drama, music ensembles, student government.

Athletics. Intercollegiate: Basketball, cheerleading M, golf, soccer M, tennis, volleyball W. **Intramural:** Baseball, basketball, bowling, softball, volleyball. **Team name:** Bears.

Student services. Chaplain/spiritual director, career counseling, student employment services, financial aid counseling, health services, personal counseling, placement for graduates.

Contact. E-mail: admissions@barclaycollege.edu
Phone: (620) 862-5252 ext. 21 Toll-free number: (800) 862-0226
Fax: (620) 862-5242
Justin Kendall, Director of Admissions, Barclay College, 607 North Kingman, Haviland, KS 67059

Benedictine College
Atchison, Kansas
www.benedictine.edu

CB member
CB code: 6056

- Private 4-year liberal arts college affiliated with Roman Catholic Church
- Residential campus in large town
- 1,639 degree-seeking undergraduates: 1% part-time, 54% women, 4% African American, 1% Asian American, 8% Hispanic American, 1% Native American, 2% international
- 74 degree-seeking graduate students
- 59% of applicants admitted
- SAT or ACT (ACT writing optional) required
- 57% graduate within 6 years; 25% enter graduate study

General. Founded in 1858. Regionally accredited. **Degrees:** 311 bachelor's awarded; master's offered. **ROTC:** Army. **Location:** 45 miles from Kansas City, Missouri. **Calendar:** Semester, limited summer session. **Full-time faculty:** 92 total; 85% have terminal degrees, 9% minority, 30% women. **Part-time faculty:** 46 total; 37% have terminal degrees, 2% minority, 56% women. **Class size:** 63% < 20, 35% 20-39, 1% 40-49, less than 1% 50-99. **Special facilities:** Biological research area.

Freshman class profile. 3,538 applied, 2,081 admitted, 470 enrolled.

Mid 50% test scores			
ACT composite:	21-27	Rank in top tenth:	22%
GPA 3.75 or higher:	30%	End year in good standing:	89%
GPA 3.50-3.74:	20%	Return as sophomores:	78%
GPA 3.0-3.49:	26%	Out-of-state:	71%
GPA 2.0-2.99:	24%	Live on campus:	98%
Rank in top quarter:	40%	International:	1%

Basis for selection. Applicant must satisfy 2 of following requirements: GPA above 2.0, rank in top half of class, requisite ACT or SAT scores. Recommendations and interview considered. Interview recommended for academically weak applicants.

High school preparation. College-preparatory program recommended. Required and recommended units include English 4, mathematics 3-4, social studies 2, history 2, science 2-4 and foreign language 2-4.

2011-2012 Annual costs. Tuition/fees: $21,475. Room/board: $7,705. Books/supplies: $2,000. Personal expenses: $2,800.

2011-2012 Financial aid. Need-based: 424 full-time freshmen applied for aid; 363 were judged to have need; 363 of these received aid. Average need met was 77%. Average scholarship/grant was $14,917; average loan $4,245. 59% of total undergraduate aid awarded as scholarships/grants, 41% as loans/jobs. **Non-need-based:** Awarded to 708 full-time undergraduates, including 176 freshmen. Scholarships awarded for academics, alumni affiliation, art, athletics, job skills, leadership, minority status, music/drama, religious affiliation, ROTC.

Application procedures. Admission: No deadline. $25 fee, may be waived for applicants with need. Admission notification on a rolling basis. Must reply by May 1 or within 4 week(s) if notified thereafter. **Financial aid:** Priority date 3/15; no closing date. FAFSA required. Applicants notified on a rolling basis starting 2/1; must reply within 2 week(s) of notification.

Academics. Special study options: Combined bachelor's/graduate degree, cooperative education, double major, dual enrollment of high school students, ESL, exchange student, honors, independent study, internships, liberal arts/career combination, student-designed major, study abroad, teacher certification program. **Credit/placement by examination:** AP, CLEP, IB, ACT, institutional tests. 30 credit hours maximum toward associate degree, 30 toward bachelor's. **Support services:** Learning center, reduced course load, remedial instruction, study skills assistance, tutoring.

Majors. Biology: General, biochemistry. **Business:** Accounting, business admin, finance, international. **Communications:** Media studies. **Computer sciences:** Computer science. **Education:** Art, biology, chemistry, elementary, French, history, mathematics, music, physical, physics, secondary, Spanish, special ed. **Engineering:** General. **English:** English lit. **Foreign languages:** French, Spanish. **Health services:** Athletic training, nursing (RN). **History:** General. **Liberal arts:** Arts/sciences. **Math:** General. **Philosophy/religion:** Philosophy, religion. **Physical sciences:** Astronomy, chemistry, physics. **Psychology:** General. **Social sciences:** General, economics, political science, sociology. **Theology:** Youth ministry. **Visual/performing arts:** Art, dramatic, music, music management, theater arts management.

Most popular majors. Business/marketing 22%, education 16%, social sciences 8%, theological studies 16%.

Computing on campus. 85 workstations in dormitories, library, computer center. Dormitories wired for high-speed internet access and linked to campus network. Commuter students can connect to campus network. Online course registration, online library, helpline, repair service, wireless network available.

Student life. Freshman orientation: Mandatory. Preregistration for classes offered. Weekend program before classes commence. **Housing:** Guaranteed on-campus for freshmen. Single-sex dorms, special housing for disabled available. $100 fully refundable deposit. Off-campus college-owned housing available. **Activities:** Bands, campus ministries, choral groups, dance, drama, international student organizations, literary magazine, music ensembles, musical theater, student government, student newspaper, symphony orchestra, Ravens Respect Life, Young Democrats, Young Republicans, Knights of Columbus, hunger coalition, Fellowship of Catholic University Students, Students in Free Enterprise, Black Student Union.

Athletics. NAIA. Intercollegiate: Baseball M, basketball, cheerleading, cross-country, football (tackle) M, soccer, softball W, track and field, volleyball W, weight lifting M, wrestling M. **Intramural:** Baseball M, basketball, football (non-tackle) M, handball, racquetball, soccer, softball, table tennis, volleyball. **Team name:** Ravens.

Student services. Alcohol/substance abuse counseling, chaplain/spiritual director, career counseling, student employment services, financial aid counseling, health services, personal counseling, placement for graduates, veterans' counselor. **Physically disabled:** Services for visually, speech, hearing impaired.

Contact. E-mail: bcadmiss@benedictine.edu
Phone: (913) 360-7476 Toll-free number: (800) 467-5340
Fax: (913) 367-5462
Pete Helgesen, Dean of Enrollment Management, Benedictine College, 1020 North Second Street, Atchison, KS 66002-1499

Bethany College
Lindsborg, Kansas
www.bethanylb.edu　　　　　　　　　**CB code: 6034**

- Private 4-year liberal arts college affiliated with Evangelical Lutheran Church in America
- Residential campus in small town
- 581 degree-seeking undergraduates: 1% part-time, 46% women, 6% African American, 1% Asian American, 6% Hispanic American, 4% international
- 60% of applicants admitted
- SAT or ACT (ACT writing optional) required
- 37% graduate within 6 years

General. Founded in 1881. Regionally accredited. **Degrees:** 95 bachelor's awarded. **Location:** 15 miles from Salina, 60 miles from Wichita. **Calendar:** 4-1-4, limited summer session. **Full-time faculty:** 35 total; 80% have terminal degrees, 6% minority, 40% women. **Part-time faculty:** 35 total; 20% have terminal degrees, 49% women. **Class size:** 74% < 20, 24% 20-39, 1% 40-49.

Freshman class profile. 831 applied, 496 admitted, 156 enrolled.

Mid 50% test scores			
SAT critical reading:	450-530	GPA 3.0-3.49:	24%
SAT math:	450-540	GPA 2.0-2.99:	31%
SAT writing:	390-490	Rank in top quarter:	42%
ACT composite:	19-25	Rank in top tenth:	15%
GPA 3.75 or higher:	29%	Return as sophomores:	64%
GPA 3.50-3.74:	15%	Out-of-state:	50%
		Live on campus:	95%

Basis for selection. High school GPA, course selection, trends in grades, class rank, and standardized test scores very important. Interview, letters of recommendation, leadership, curriculum, and involvement considered. Interview and essay recommended for some. Audition required of music and theater majors. Portfolio required of art majors.

High school preparation. College-preparatory program recommended. Recommended units include English 4, mathematics 3, social studies 3, science 3 (laboratory 2) and foreign language 2.

2011-2012 Annual costs. Tuition/fees: $21,677. Room/board: $6,516. Books/supplies: $1,000. Personal expenses: $2,600.

Financial aid. Non-need-based: Scholarships awarded for academics, alumni affiliation, art, athletics, leadership, music/drama, religious affiliation. **Additional information:** State financial aid deadline March 15.

Application procedures. Admission: Priority date 2/1; no deadline. No application fee. Admission notification on a rolling basis. **Financial aid:** Priority date 3/15; no closing date. FAFSA required. Applicants notified on a rolling basis starting 2/1; must reply within 3 week(s) of notification.

Academics. Special study options: Accelerated study, combined bachelor's/graduate degree, cross-registration, double major, dual enrollment of high school students, exchange student, honors, independent study, internships, liberal arts/career combination, student-designed major, study abroad, teacher certification program, urban semester, Washington semester. Special education program with Associated Colleges of Central Kansas. **Credit/placement by examination:** AP, CLEP, IB. 32 credit hours maximum toward bachelor's degree. **Support services:** Learning center, reduced course load, remedial instruction, study skills assistance, tutoring, writing center.

Majors. Biology: General. **Business:** Accounting, business admin, finance, managerial economics, marketing, sales/distribution. **Communications:** Communications/speech/rhetoric. **Education:** General, art, biology, business, chemistry, elementary, English, health, history, mathematics, music, physical, secondary, social science. **English:** English lit, rhetoric/composition. **Health services:** Art therapy, athletic training. **History:** General. **Liberal arts:** Arts/sciences. **Math:** General. **Parks/recreation:** Facilities management, sports admin. **Philosophy/religion:** Christian. **Physical sciences:** Chemistry, physics. **Protective services:** Criminal justice, police science. **Psychology:** General. **Social sciences:** General, economics, sociology. **Visual/performing arts:** Art, graphic design, music, music performance.

Most popular majors. Biology 11%, business/marketing 20%, education 22%, parks/recreation 13%, public administration/social services 6%, security/protective services 6%, social sciences 9%.

Computing on campus. 50 workstations in library, computer center. Dormitories wired for high-speed internet access and linked to campus network. Commuter students can connect to campus network. Online library available.

Student life. Freshman orientation: Mandatory. Preregistration for classes offered. One week of activities prior to first day of classes; planned and organized by returning students. **Policies:** No alcohol allowed on campus. Full-time students required to live on campus until age 22 or special consideration given. **Housing:** Guaranteed on-campus for freshmen. Coed dorms, single-sex dorms, apartments, wellness housing available. $100 deposit, deadline 8/1. **Activities:** Bands, campus ministries, choral groups, dance, drama, international student organizations, music ensembles, musical theater, student government, student newspaper, symphony orchestra, SOAR, Blue Key, Gold Key, Alpha Omega, Bethany youth ministry program, Bread for the World, departmental organizations, honorary societies, Green Team.

Athletics. NAIA. **Intercollegiate:** Baseball M, basketball, cross-country, football (tackle) M, golf M, soccer, softball W, tennis, track and field, volleyball W, wrestling M. **Intramural:** Basketball, football (non-tackle), racquetball, soccer, softball, table tennis, volleyball, weight lifting. **Team name:** Swedes.

Student services. Alcohol/substance abuse counseling, chaplain/spiritual director, career counseling, student employment services, financial aid counseling, health services, minority student services, personal counseling, placement for graduates, veterans' counselor.

Contact. E-mail: admissions@bethanylb.edu
Phone: (785) 227-3380 ext. 8113 Toll-free number: (800) 826-2281
Fax: (785) 227-8993
Tricia Hawk, Dean of Admissions and Financial Aid, Bethany College, 335 East Swensson, Lindsborg, KS 67456-1897

Bethel College
North Newton, Kansas
www.bethelks.edu　　　　　　　　　**CB code: 6037**

- Private 4-year liberal arts college affiliated with Mennonite Church
- Residential campus in large town
- 523 degree-seeking undergraduates: 5% part-time, 51% women, 9% African American, 1% Asian American, 7% Hispanic American, 2% international
- 70% of applicants admitted
- SAT or ACT (ACT writing optional) required
- 52% graduate within 6 years

General. Founded in 1887. Regionally accredited. **Degrees:** 92 bachelor's awarded. **Location:** 25 miles from Wichita. **Calendar:** 4-1-4, limited summer session. **Full-time faculty:** 36 total; 58% have terminal degrees, 6% minority, 53% women. **Part-time faculty:** 23 total; 26% have terminal degrees, 4% minority, 56% women. **Class size:** 57% < 20, 37% 20-39, 2% 40-49, 3% 50-99, less than 1% >100. **Special facilities:** Natural history museum, 80-acre natural history field laboratory, institute for peace and conflict resolution, Mennonite library and archives, observatory, conservatory.

Freshman class profile. 469 applied, 327 admitted, 126 enrolled.

Mid 50% test scores			
SAT critical reading:	400-490	GPA 2.0-2.99:	16%
SAT math:	450-530	Rank in top quarter:	45%
SAT writing:	390-470	Rank in top tenth:	19%
ACT composite:	20-26	Return as sophomores:	77%
GPA 3.75 or higher:	33%	Out-of-state:	38%
GPA 3.50-3.74:	20%	Live on campus:	98%
GPA 3.0-3.49:	31%	International:	1%

Basis for selection. Automatic admission generally given to students with high school GPA of 2.5 and ACT score of at least 19 or SAT of at least 890 (exclusive of Writing). Essay recommended for academically weak applicants. Audition recommended for drama and music majors. Portfolio recommended for art majors. **Home schooled:** Evaluative transcript or GED score. ACT or SAT score is also required.

High school preparation. College-preparatory program recommended. 16 units recommended. Recommended units include English 4, mathematics 4, social studies 3, science 3 and foreign language 2.

2011-2012 Annual costs. Tuition/fees: $21,700. Room/board: $7,400. Books/supplies: $800. Personal expenses: $2,200.

2010-2011 Financial aid. Need-based: 124 full-time freshmen applied for aid; 114 were judged to have need; 114 of these received aid. Average need met was 100%. Average scholarship/grant was $6,060; average loan $6,633. 33% of total undergraduate aid awarded as scholarships/grants, 67% as loans/jobs. **Non-need-based:** Awarded to 648 full-time undergraduates, including 203 freshmen. Scholarships awarded for academics, alumni affiliation, art, athletics, minority status, music/drama, religious affiliation.

Application procedures. Admission: No deadline. $20 fee, may be waived for applicants with need. Admission notification on a rolling basis beginning on or about 9/1. **Financial aid:** Priority date 4/1; no closing date. FAFSA required. Applicants notified on a rolling basis starting 2/1; must reply within 2 week(s) of notification.

Academics. Curriculum founded on general education program in liberal arts and sciences. Distinctive elements include peace, justice and conflict studies, convocation, and cross-cultural learning requirements and senior capstone course focusing on basic issues of faith and life. **Special study options:** Cross-registration, double major, dual enrollment of high school students, independent study, internships, liberal arts/career combination, student-designed major, study abroad, teacher certification program, urban semester, Washington semester. **Credit/placement by examination:** AP, CLEP, IB, SAT, ACT, institutional tests. **Support services:** Learning center, study skills assistance, tutoring.

Majors. Biology: General. **Business:** General. **Communications:** Media studies. **Education:** Elementary. **English:** English lit. **Health services:** Athletic training, nursing (RN). **History:** General. **Human services:** Social work. **Math:** General. **Parks/recreation:** Health/fitness. **Philosophy/religion:** Religion. **Physical sciences:** Chemistry. **Psychology:** General. **Visual/performing arts:** Music, studio arts.

Most popular majors. Business/marketing 15%, education 8%, foreign language 6%, health sciences 16%, public administration/social services 7%, visual/performing arts 13%.

Computing on campus. 56 workstations in library, computer center. Dormitories wired for high-speed internet access and linked to campus network. Commuter students can connect to campus network. Helpline, repair service, student web hosting, wireless network available.

Student life. Freshman orientation: Mandatory. Preregistration for classes offered. Held the Wednesday through Monday before classes begin. **Policies:** Chapel services voluntary. 2 weekly convocations required and credited as part of general education. **Housing:** Guaranteed on-campus for all undergraduates. Coed dorms, special housing for disabled, apartments, wellness housing available. **Activities:** Bands, campus ministries, choral groups, drama, international student organizations, literary magazine, music ensembles, musical theater, opera, radio station, student government, student newspaper, symphony orchestra, TV station, Student Community Action Network for voluntary services, peace club, Bethel Christian Fellowship, service corps-disaster response, Fellowship of Christian Athletes, environmental action club, Catholic student organization.

Athletics. NAIA. **Intercollegiate:** Basketball, cross-country, football (tackle) M, golf, soccer, softball W, tennis, track and field, volleyball W. **Intramural:** Badminton, basketball, football (non-tackle), golf, racquetball, softball, table tennis, tennis, volleyball. **Team name:** Threshers.

Student services. Alcohol/substance abuse counseling, chaplain/spiritual director, career counseling, student employment services, financial aid counseling, health services, minority student services, personal counseling. **Physically disabled:** Services for visually, hearing impaired.

Contact. E-mail: admissions@bethelks.edu
Phone: (316) 284-5230 Toll-free number: (800) 522-1887 ext. 230
Fax: (316) 284-5870
Todd Moore, Vice President for Admissions, Bethel College, 300 E 27th Street, North Newton, KS 67117-8061

Central Christian College of Kansas
McPherson, Kansas
www.centralchristian.edu   **CB code: 6088**

- Private 4-year liberal arts college affiliated with Free Methodist Church of North America
- Residential campus in large town
- 391 degree-seeking undergraduates: 2% part-time, 42% women, 13% African American, 1% Asian American, 7% Hispanic American, 2% Native American, 2% international
- 42% of applicants admitted
- 33% graduate within 6 years; 18% enter graduate study

General. Founded in 1884. Regionally accredited. **Degrees:** 51 bachelor's, 15 associate awarded. **Location:** 55 miles from Wichita. **Calendar:** 4-1-4, limited summer session. **Full-time faculty:** 22 total; 18% have terminal degrees, 32% women. **Part-time faculty:** 34 total; 18% have terminal degrees, 6% minority, 35% women. **Class size:** 77% < 20, 19% 20-39, 2% 40-49, 2% 50-99, less than 1% >100.

Freshman class profile. 788 applied, 334 admitted, 109 enrolled.

GPA 3.75 or higher:	13%	End year in good standing:	78%
GPA 3.50-3.74:	13%	Return as sophomores:	58%
GPA 3.0-3.49:	27%	Out-of-state:	72%
GPA 2.0-2.99:	45%	Live on campus:	96%
Rank in top quarter:	21%	International:	3%
Rank in top tenth:	5%		

Basis for selection. Secondary school record, recommendations very important; test scores important. SAT or ACT recommended. Interview and essay recommended. **Home schooled:** Transcript of courses and grades, letter of recommendation (nonparent) required. **Learning Disabled:** Provide Individualized Education Program (IEP).

High school preparation. College-preparatory program recommended. 22 units required. Required units include English 4, mathematics 2, social studies 2, history 1, science 2 (laboratory 1). One computer technology course recommended.

2011-2012 Annual costs. Tuition/fees: $18,400. Room/board: $6,200. Books/supplies: $1,200. Personal expenses: $1,000.

2011-2012 Financial aid. Need-based: 100 full-time freshmen applied for aid; 90 were judged to have need; 90 of these received aid. Average need met was 70%. Average scholarship/grant was $4,940; average loan $3,962. 47% of total undergraduate aid awarded as scholarships/grants, 53% as loans/jobs. **Non-need-based:** Awarded to 305 full-time undergraduates, including 99 freshmen. Scholarships awarded for academics, alumni affiliation, athletics, leadership, music/drama, religious affiliation.

Application procedures. Admission: No deadline. $20 fee, may be waived for applicants with need, free for online applicants. Admission notification on a rolling basis. **Financial aid:** Priority date 3/1; no closing date. FAFSA required. Applicants notified on a rolling basis starting 3/1; must reply within 4 week(s) of notification.

Academics. Special study options: Accelerated study, cooperative education, cross-registration, distance learning, double major, dual enrollment of high school students, independent study, internships, liberal arts/career combination, student-designed major, teacher certification program, urban semester, Washington semester. **Credit/placement by examination:** AP, CLEP, IB, SAT, ACT, institutional tests. 30 credit hours maximum toward associate degree, 30 toward bachelor's. **Support services:** Learning center, reduced course load, remedial instruction, study skills assistance, tutoring.

Majors. Biology: General, exercise physiology. **Business:** Accounting, business admin, organizational behavior, small business admin. **Communications:** Communications/speech/rhetoric, media studies, organizational, persuasive communications. **Education:** Elementary, history, multi-level teacher, physical, secondary, social studies. **English:** English lit, rhetoric/composition. **History:** General. **Liberal arts:** Arts/sciences. **Math:** General. **Parks/recreation:** Exercise sciences, sports admin. **Philosophy/religion:** General. **Physical sciences:** Chemistry. **Psychology:** General. **Social sciences:** General. **Theology:** Pastoral counseling, sacred music, theology, youth ministry. **Visual/performing arts:** Music, music performance, piano/keyboard.

Most popular majors. Biology 7%, business/marketing 24%, liberal arts 15%, parks/recreation 16%, social sciences 7%, theological studies 15%.

Computing on campus. 40 workstations in dormitories, library, computer center, student center. Dormitories wired for high-speed internet access. Commuter students can connect to campus network. Online course registration, online library, helpline, repair service, wireless network available.

Student life. Freshman orientation: Mandatory, $30 fee. Preregistration for classes offered. Fall semester first seven weeks. Interterm and spring 1-2 days. **Policies:** Students must sign a life-style covenant. Alcohol, smoking, drugs not allowed on campus. **Housing:** Guaranteed on-campus for all undergraduates. Single-sex dorms, apartments, wellness housing available. $200 fully refundable deposit, deadline 8/1. Students 23 years of age or older can request to live off campus. **Activities:** Bands, campus ministries, choral groups, dance, drama, literary magazine, music ensembles, musical theater, radio station, student government, student newspaper, Christian service organization, Flying Tigers, performing arts club, PBL, student activities council.

Athletics. NAIA, NCCAA. **Intercollegiate:** Baseball M, basketball, cross-country, golf, soccer, softball W, tennis, volleyball W. **Intramural:** Badminton, basketball, football (non-tackle), soccer, softball, table tennis, tennis, volleyball. **Team name:** Tigers.

Student services. Adult student services, chaplain/spiritual director, career counseling, student employment services, financial aid counseling, health services, personal counseling, placement for graduates. **Physically disabled:** Services for visually, speech impaired.

Contact. E-mail: admissions@centralchristian.edu
Phone: (620) 241-0723 ext. 337
Toll-free number: (800) 835-0078 ext. 337 Fax: (620) 241-6032
Richard Wyatt, Director of Admissions, Central Christian College of
Kansas, 1200 South Main, McPherson, KS 67460-5740

Emporia State University
Emporia, Kansas
www.emporia.edu
CB code: 6335

- Public 4-year university
- Commuter campus in large town
- 3,709 degree-seeking undergraduates: 10% part-time, 60% women, 6% African American, 1% Asian American, 5% Hispanic American, 1% Native American, 7% international
- 1,807 degree-seeking graduate students
- 82% of applicants admitted
- SAT or ACT (ACT writing optional) required
- 44% graduate within 6 years

General. Founded in 1863. Regionally accredited. **Degrees:** 743 bachelor's awarded; master's, doctoral offered. **Location:** 50 miles from Topeka, 77 miles from Wichita. **Calendar:** Semester, extensive summer session. **Full-time faculty:** 254 total; 77% have terminal degrees, 11% minority, 48% women. **Part-time faculty:** 18 total; 17% have terminal degrees, 78% women. **Class size:** 49% < 20, 38% 20-39, 8% 40-49, 4% 50-99, less than 1% >100. **Special facilities:** Planetarium, natural history reserve, natural history museum, National Teachers Hall of Fame, Great Plains study center.

Freshman class profile. 1,488 applied, 1,224 admitted, 587 enrolled.

Mid 50% test scores			
SAT math:	430-500	Rank in top tenth:	12%
ACT composite:	19-24	End year in good standing:	82%
GPA 3.75 or higher:	22%	Return as sophomores:	69%
GPA 3.50-3.74:	17%	Out-of-state:	10%
GPA 3.0-3.49:	32%	Live on campus:	73%
GPA 2.0-2.99:	27%	International:	2%
Rank in top quarter:	31%	Fraternities:	22%
		Sororities:	21%

Basis for selection. Applicants must have one of following: minimum ACT score of 21, rank in top third of high school class, minimum 2.0 GPA in Kansas Core Curriculum for in-state students, or 2.5 GPA for out-of-state students. Limited number of students who do not meet qualifications may be admitted through 10% exceptions window. ACT scores must be received by end of first semester of study. **Home schooled:** State high school equivalency certificate required. GED must be submitted.

High school preparation. College-preparatory program recommended. Required units include English 4, mathematics 3, social studies 3, science 3 and academic electives 1. 1 computer technology recommended. These units required for students who do not have minimum ACT score of 21, or in top 1/3 of high school class.

2011-2012 Annual costs. Tuition/fees: $4,952; $15,332 out-of-state. Room/board: $6,380. Books/supplies: $900. Personal expenses: $2,500.

2010-2011 Financial aid. Need-based: 536 full-time freshmen applied for aid; 401 were judged to have need; 399 of these received aid. Average need met was 68%. Average scholarship/grant was $5,112; average loan $4,097. 45% of total undergraduate aid awarded as scholarships/grants, 55% as loans/jobs. **Non-need-based:** Awarded to 739 full-time undergraduates, including 200 freshmen. Scholarships awarded for academics, alumni affiliation, art, athletics, job skills, leadership, minority status, music/drama, religious affiliation, state residency. **Additional information:** Institution's own payment plan is available.

Application procedures. Admission: No deadline. $30 fee, may be waived for applicants with need. Admission notification on a rolling basis. Must reply by May 1 or within 2 week(s) if notified thereafter. **Financial aid:** Priority date 3/15; no closing date. FAFSA required. Applicants notified on a rolling basis starting 2/2; must reply within 2 week(s) of notification.

Academics. Special study options: Distance learning, double major, dual enrollment of high school students, honors, independent study, internships, student-designed major, study abroad, teacher certification program. Career development center and programs, continuing education courses, evening program, interdisciplinary or interdepartmental courses of study, learning assistance programs, pass-fail grading option, service members' opportunity college, summer sessions, tutorial program, trio programs. **Credit/placement by examination:** AP, CLEP, IB, ACT, institutional tests. 30 credit hours maximum toward bachelor's degree. **Support services:** Remedial instruction, writing center.

Majors. Biology: General, Biochemistry/molecular biology. **Business:** Accounting, business admin, human resources, marketing. **Communications:** Communications/speech/rhetoric. **Computer sciences:** General, information systems, security. **Education:** Elementary, health, music, secondary, speech. **English:** English lit. **Foreign languages:** General. **Health services:** Athletic training, nursing (RN), public health ed, vocational rehab counseling. **History:** General. **Liberal arts:** Arts/sciences. **Math:** General. **Parks/recreation:** General. **Physical sciences:** General, chemistry, geology, physics. **Psychology:** General. **Social sciences:** General, economics, political science, sociology. **Visual/performing arts:** Art, dramatic, music.

Most popular majors. Business/marketing 16%, education 27%, health sciences 9%, social sciences 11%, visual/performing arts 6%.

Computing on campus. 410 workstations in dormitories, library, computer center, student center. Dormitories wired for high-speed internet access and linked to campus network. Commuter students can connect to campus network. Online course registration, online library, helpline, student web hosting, wireless network available.

Student life. Freshman orientation: Available, $35 fee. Preregistration for classes offered. One-day program for students and parents; held during summer and prior to start of classes. **Housing:** Guaranteed on-campus for freshmen. Coed dorms, single-sex dorms, special housing for disabled, apartments, cooperative housing, fraternity/sorority housing, wellness housing available. $145 partly refundable deposit, deadline 7/1. **Activities:** Bands, campus ministries, choral groups, dance, drama, film society, international student organizations, literary magazine, music ensembles, musical theater, opera, student government, student newspaper, symphony orchestra, Black Student Union, Hispanic American leadership organization, Catholic Campus Community, Christian student center, Black women's network, Muslim student association, Fellowship of Christian Athletes, Arabic language club, East Asian club, Campus Crusade for Christ.

Athletics. NCAA. **Intercollegiate:** Baseball M, basketball, cheerleading, cross-country, football (tackle) M, soccer W, softball W, tennis, track and field, volleyball W. **Intramural:** Badminton, basketball, football (non-tackle), soccer, softball, table tennis, volleyball. **Team name:** Hornets.

Student services. Adult student services, alcohol/substance abuse counseling, career counseling, services for economically disadvantaged, student employment services, financial aid counseling, health services, legal services, minority student services, on-campus daycare, personal counseling, placement for graduates, veterans' counselor, women's services. **Physically disabled:** Services for visually, speech, hearing impaired.

Contact. E-mail: go2esu@emporia.edu
Phone: (620) 341-5465 Toll-free number: (877) 468-6378
Fax: (620) 341-5599
Laura Eddy, Director of Admissions, Emporia State University, 1200 Commercial, Campus Box 4034, Emporia, KS 66801-5087

Fort Hays State University
Hays, Kansas
www.fhsu.edu
CB member
CB code: 6218

- Public 4-year university
- Commuter campus in large town
- 11,158 undergraduates
- 1,644 graduate students
- SAT or ACT with writing required

General. Founded in 1902. Regionally accredited. **Degrees:** 1,909 bachelor's, 61 associate awarded; master's offered. **Location:** 170 miles from Wichita, 270 miles from Kansas City. **Calendar:** Semester, extensive summer session. **Full-time faculty:** 254 total. **Class size:** 50% < 20, 41% 20-39, 5% 40-49, 3% 50-99, less than 1% >100. **Special facilities:** Natural history museum.

Freshman class profile.

Out-of-state:	15%	Fraternities:	4%
Live on campus:	69%	Sororities:	3%

Basis for selection. One of the following required: 21 ACT, rank in top third of high school class, or 2.0 GPA on Kansas pre-college curriculum (2.5 GPA for out-of-state students). Audition recommended for music majors.

High school preparation. 14 units recommended. Recommended units include English 4, mathematics 3, social studies 2, history 1, science 3 and computer science 1.

2011-2012 Annual costs. Tuition/fees: $4,082; $12,358 out-of-state. Room/board: $6,837.

Financial aid. Non-need-based: Scholarships awarded for academics, art, athletics, leadership, minority status, music/drama.

Application procedures. Admission: No deadline. $30 fee. Admission notification on a rolling basis. **Financial aid:** Priority date 3/15; no closing date. FAFSA required. Applicants notified on a rolling basis starting 3/15; must reply within 2 week(s) of notification.

Academics. Special study options: Combined bachelor's/graduate degree, distance learning, double major, dual enrollment of high school students, ESL, exchange student, external degree, honors, independent study, internships, liberal arts/career combination, student-designed major, study abroad, teacher certification program, United Nations semester. **Credit/placement by examination:** AP, CLEP, ACT, institutional tests. **Support services:** Learning center, pre-admission summer program, reduced course load, remedial instruction, study skills assistance, tutoring, writing center.

Majors. Biology: General. **Business:** General, accounting, business admin, market research, marketing, office management. **Communications:** Communications/speech/rhetoric. **Computer sciences:** General. **Education:** Business, elementary, music, physical, technology/industrial arts, trade/industrial. **English:** English lit. **Foreign languages:** General. **General:** Business. **Health services:** Physical therapy assistant, sonography. **History:** General. **Human services:** Social work. **Math:** General. **Philosophy/religion:** Philosophy. **Physical sciences:** Chemistry, geology, physics. **Protective services:** Criminal justice. **Psychology:** General. **Social sciences:** Economics, political science, sociology. **Visual/performing arts:** Art, music.

Most popular majors. Business/marketing 11%, education 13%, health sciences 7%, liberal arts 46%.

Computing on campus. 1,400 workstations in dormitories, library, computer center, student center. Dormitories linked to campus network. Commuter students can connect to campus network. Online course registration, helpline, repair service, wireless network available.

Student life. Freshman orientation: Mandatory, $25 fee. Preregistration for classes offered. Three-day program before start of classes; includes skills training. **Housing:** Guaranteed on-campus for freshmen. Coed dorms, single-sex dorms, apartments, fraternity/sorority housing available. $35 nonrefundable deposit. **Activities:** Bands, campus ministries, choral groups, dance, drama, international student organizations, music ensembles, musical theater, radio station, student government, student newspaper, symphony orchestra, TV station, Campus Crusade for Christ, Disciples of the Catholic Campus Center, black student union, Hispanic American leadership organization, Young Republicans, Young Democrats.

Athletics. NCAA. **Intercollegiate:** Baseball M, basketball, cross-country, football (tackle) M, golf, gymnastics W, rodeo, soccer M, softball W, tennis, track and field, volleyball W, wrestling M. **Intramural:** Archery, badminton, baseball M, basketball, bowling, cross-country, diving, fencing, field hockey W, gymnastics W, racquetball, soccer, softball, swimming, table tennis, tennis, track and field, volleyball, water polo, wrestling M. **Team name:** Tigers.

Student services. Adult student services, career counseling, student employment services, financial aid counseling, health services, on-campus daycare, personal counseling, placement for graduates, veterans' counselor. **Physically disabled:** Services for visually, speech, hearing impaired.

Contact. E-mail: tigers@fhsu.edu
Phone: (785) 628-5666 Toll-free number: (800) 628-3478
Fax: (785) 432-0248
Tricia Cline, Director of Admissions, Fort Hays State University, 600 Park Street, Hays, KS 67601

Friends University
Wichita, Kansas
www.friends.edu   CB code: 6224

- Private 4-year university and liberal arts college affiliated with nondenominational tradition
- Commuter campus in large city
- 1,964 degree-seeking undergraduates: 20% part-time, 56% women, 10% African American, 2% Asian American, 4% Hispanic American, 2% Native American
- 774 degree-seeking graduate students
- 64% of applicants admitted
- SAT or ACT (ACT writing optional) required

General. Founded in 1898. Regionally accredited. **Degrees:** 584 bachelor's, 28 associate awarded; master's offered. **Location:** 1 mile from downtown. **Calendar:** Semester, limited summer session. **Full-time faculty:** 74 total;

66% have terminal degrees, 4% minority, 43% women. **Part-time faculty:** 555 total; 8% minority, 49% women. **Class size:** 81% < 20, 19% 20-39, less than 1% 40-49, less than 1% 50-99, less than 1% >100. **Special facilities:** Art center, observatory, Quaker collection.

Freshman class profile. 792 applied, 507 admitted, 237 enrolled.

Mid 50% test scores			
SAT critical reading:	400-520	GPA 2.0-2.99:	30%
SAT math:	470-580	Rank in top quarter:	35%
ACT composite:	19-25	Rank in top tenth:	11%
GPA 3.75 or higher:	23%	End year in good standing:	73%
GPA 3.50-3.74:	18%	Return as sophomores:	66%
GPA 3.0-3.49:	27%	Out-of-state:	21%
		Live on campus:	65%

Basis for selection. ACT score multiplied by GPA must equal 45 or above for admission. Those with a score of less than 45 but equal to 20 or above are admitted provisionally. SAT and SAT Subject Tests or ACT recommended. Audition required for music, dance, and theater programs. Portfolio required for art program. **Home schooled:** Transcript of courses and grades, interview, letter of recommendation (nonparent) required. Interview and letter of recommendation is required for early admit home schooled applicants.

High school preparation. College-preparatory program recommended. 19 units recommended. Recommended units include English 3, mathematics 3, social studies 2, history 2, science 1 (laboratory 1), foreign language 2 and computer science 1.

2011-2012 Annual costs. Tuition/fees: $21,030. Room/board: $5,966. Books/supplies: $1,200. Personal expenses: $1,762.

2010-2011 Financial aid. Need-based: 189 full-time freshmen applied for aid; 174 were judged to have need; 174 of these received aid. Average need met was 51%. Average scholarship/grant was $10,890; average loan $2,980. 44% of total undergraduate aid awarded as scholarships/grants, 56% as loans/jobs. **Non-need-based:** Awarded to 341 full-time undergraduates, including 61 freshmen. Scholarships awarded for academics, alumni affiliation, art, athletics, leadership, music/drama, religious affiliation. **Additional information:** Scholarships for clergy/family of clergy available.

Application procedures. Admission: No deadline. $35 fee, may be waived for applicants with need. Admission notification on a rolling basis. **Financial aid:** Priority date 3/15; no closing date. FAFSA, institutional form required. Applicants notified on a rolling basis starting 3/1; must reply within 3 week(s) of notification.

Academics. Special study options: Accelerated study, cooperative education, cross-registration, distance learning, double major, dual enrollment of high school students, exchange student, external degree, honors, internships, liberal arts/career combination, student-designed major, study abroad, teacher certification program, weekend college. Degree completion programs for working adults. **Credit/placement by examination:** AP, CLEP, IB, SAT, ACT, institutional tests. 60 credit hours maximum toward bachelor's degree. **Support services:** Reduced course load, remedial instruction, study skills assistance, tutoring, writing center.

Majors. Biology: General, environmental, wildlife. **Business:** Accounting, business admin, e-commerce, human resources, international, management information systems, management science, marketing, nonprofit/public. **Communications:** General. **Computer sciences:** General, information systems, programming. **Education:** Art, business, early childhood, elementary, English, history, mathematics, middle, music, physical, science, secondary, social science, Spanish, speech. **English:** English lit. **Foreign languages:** Spanish. **Health services:** Health care admin, radiologic technology/medical imaging. **History:** General. **Liberal arts:** Arts/sciences. **Math:** General. **Parks/recreation:** Health/fitness, sports admin. **Philosophy/religion:** General, Christian, religion. **Physical sciences:** Chemistry. **Protective services:** Criminal justice. **Psychology:** General. **Social sciences:** Political science, sociology. **Theology:** Youth ministry. **Visual/performing arts:** Art, ballet, dance, dramatic, music, music performance.

Most popular majors. Business/marketing 62%, education 6%.

Computing on campus. 360 workstations in dormitories, library, computer center. Dormitories wired for high-speed internet access and linked to campus network. Commuter students can connect to campus network. Online course registration, online library, helpline, wireless network available.

Student life. Freshman orientation: Mandatory. Preregistration for classes offered. Held in early August and early January. **Housing:** Coed dorms, apartments available. $100 nonrefundable deposit. **Activities:** Bands, campus ministries, choral groups, dance, drama, literary magazine, music ensembles, Model UN, musical theater, opera, student government, student newspaper, symphony orchestra, Acts of Faith, History/Political Science Club, The Group, Young Democrats, Student Government Association, Friends Enterprise Club.

Athletics. NAIA. **Intercollegiate:** Baseball M, basketball, cheerleading, cross-country, football (tackle) M, golf M, soccer, softball W, tennis, track and field, volleyball W. **Intramural:** Basketball, football (non-tackle), soccer, softball, table tennis, volleyball. **Team name:** Falcons.

Student services. Adult student services, alcohol/substance abuse counseling, chaplain/spiritual director, career counseling, student employment services, financial aid counseling, health services, personal counseling, placement for graduates, veterans' counselor. **Physically disabled:** Services for visually, speech, hearing impaired.

Contact. E-mail: learn@friends.edu
Phone: (316) 295-5100 Toll-free number: (800) 794-6945
Fax: (316) 295-5101
Erin Haneberg, Executive Director of Admissions, Friends University, 2100 West University Avenue, Wichita, KS 67213

Haskell Indian Nations University
Lawrence, Kansas
www.haskell.edu   CB code: 0919

- Public 4-year university
- Residential campus in small city
- 830 degree-seeking undergraduates
- 45% of applicants admitted
- SAT or ACT (ACT writing optional) required

General. Founded in 1884. Regionally accredited. Federally owned and operated college provides educational benefits to North American Indians who are under jurisdiction of Bureau of Indian Affairs. Students receive tuition, books, and some college housing. **Degrees:** 64 bachelor's, 95 associate awarded. **ROTC:** Air Force. **Location:** 38 miles from Kansas City, Missouri. **Calendar:** Semester, limited summer session. **Full-time faculty:** 39 total. **Part-time faculty:** 24 total. **Special facilities:** Wetlands south of campus.

Freshman class profile. 430 applied, 194 admitted, 149 enrolled.

Mid 50% test scores			
		ACT composite:	16-20
SAT critical reading:	390-450	**Out-of-state:**	90%
SAT math:	420-470	**Live on campus:**	90%

Basis for selection. For bachelor's programs, secondary school record, class rank important; recommendations, test scores considered. Associate degree programs are open admission. Students must be certified by Bureau of Indian Affairs as member of federally-recognized tribe or quarter degree descendant of tribal member. SAT/ACT scores not used in admission decisions for associate programs. **Learning Disabled:** Must provide IEP from high school and test scores not more than 2 years old.

2011-2012 Annual costs. Haskell does not charge tuition. On-campus students pay $430 (includes room/board and required fees) for academic year; off-campus students pay $220 (required fees) for academic year. Books/supplies: $220.

Financial aid. **Additional information:** Some personal expenses may be offset by Bureau of Indian Affairs grants. Most students qualify for only minimum Pell grant.

Application procedures. **Admission:** Closing date 6/30 (postmark date). $10 fee, may be waived for applicants with need. Admission notification on a rolling basis beginning on or about 3/10. **Financial aid:** Priority date 5/15; no closing date. FAFSA required. Applicants notified on a rolling basis starting 3/15; must reply within 9 week(s) of notification.

Academics. **Special study options:** Cooperative education, independent study, internships. **Credit/placement by examination:** AP, CLEP. 10 credit hours maximum toward associate degree. **Support services:** Learning center, reduced course load, remedial instruction, tutoring, writing center.

Majors. **Area/ethnic studies:** Native American. **Business:** Business admin. **Conservation:** General. **Education:** General, elementary.

Computing on campus. 45 workstations in dormitories, library, computer center, student center.

Student life. **Freshman orientation:** Mandatory. Preregistration for classes offered. 3 days preceding start of classes. **Housing:** Coed dorms, single-sex dorms available. $35 deposit. **Activities:** Choral groups, drama, student government, student newspaper, Native American clubs, Phi Beta Lambda (service organization), Baptist Student Union, LIGHT House (Lutheran organization), Catholic Center.

Athletics. NAIA. **Intercollegiate:** Basketball, cross-country, football (tackle) M, golf M, track and field, volleyball. **Intramural:** Basketball, bowling, racquetball, softball, volleyball, wrestling M. **Team name:** Indians.

Student services. Adult student services, alcohol/substance abuse counseling, career counseling, student employment services, financial aid counseling, health services, personal counseling, placement for graduates, veterans' counselor, women's services.

Contact. E-mail: pgrantorosco@haskell.edu
Phone: (785) 749-8454 Fax: (913) 749-8429
Patricia Grant Orosco, Director of Admissions and Records, Haskell Indian Nations University, 155 Indian Avenue #5031, Lawrence, KS 66046-4800

Kansas State University
Manhattan, Kansas   CB member
www.k-state.edu   CB code: 6334

- Public 4-year university
- Residential campus in small city
- 19,031 degree-seeking undergraduates: 10% part-time, 47% women, 4% African American, 1% Asian American, 5% Hispanic American, 5% international
- 3,885 degree-seeking graduate students
- 99% of applicants admitted
- 56% graduate within 6 years

General. Founded in 1863. Regionally accredited. Additional campus at Salina, Kansas. Off-campus site at Fort Riley army base. **Degrees:** 3,457 bachelor's, 65 associate awarded; master's, professional, doctoral offered. **ROTC:** Army, Air Force. **Location:** 120 miles from Kansas City, Missouri. **Calendar:** Semester, extensive summer session. **Full-time faculty:** 975 total; 84% have terminal degrees, 16% minority, 38% women. **Part-time faculty:** 179 total; 62% have terminal degrees, 7% minority, 52% women. **Class size:** 38% < 20, 39% 20-39, 9% 40-49, 8% 50-99, 6% >100. **Special facilities:** Prairie for biological research, laser laboratory, cancer research center, nuclear reactor, insect zoo.

Freshman class profile. 8,292 applied, 8,204 admitted, 3,644 enrolled.

Mid 50% test scores			
ACT composite:	21-27	**Rank in top tenth:**	20%
GPA 3.75 or higher:	32%	**Return as sophomores:**	82%
GPA 3.50-3.74:	21%	**Out-of-state:**	17%
GPA 3.0-3.49:	29%	**International:**	3%
GPA 2.0-2.99:	17%	**Fraternities:**	18%
Rank in top quarter:	45%	**Sororities:**	32%

Basis for selection. One of following required: minimum ACT score of 21, rank in top third of high school class, or minimum 2.0 GPA on Kansas pre-college curriculum (2.5 GPA for out-of-state students). ACT tests may be used to meet State of Kansas admissions requirements, but are not required. SAT or ACT recommended. Audition recommended for music and theater majors. Portfolio recommended for art and architecture majors.

High school preparation. College-preparatory program recommended. 14.5 units recommended. Recommended units include English 4, mathematics 3, social studies 2, history 1.5 and science 3. One unit of technology recommended.

2011-2012 Annual costs. Tuition/fees: $7,657; $19,123 out-of-state. Room/board: $7,198. Books/supplies: $1,100. Personal expenses: $3,674.

2010-2011 Financial aid. **Non-need-based:** Scholarships awarded for academics, alumni affiliation, art, athletics, leadership, music/drama, ROTC, state residency.

Application procedures. **Admission:** No deadline. $30 fee, may be waived for applicants with need. Admission notification on a rolling basis. **Financial aid:** Priority date 3/1; no closing date. FAFSA required. Applicants notified on a rolling basis starting 4/1; must reply within 2 week(s) of notification.

Academics. **Special study options:** Accelerated study, combined bachelor's/graduate degree, cooperative education, distance learning, double major, ESL, exchange student, honors, independent study, internships, study abroad, teacher certification program. **Credit/placement by examination:** AP, CLEP, IB, SAT, ACT. 10 credit hours maximum toward associate degree, 20 toward bachelor's. PEP, DANTES exams accepted for credit. **Support services:** Learning center, pre-admission summer program, reduced course load, remedial instruction, study skills assistance, tutoring, writing center.

Majors. **Area/ethnic studies:** General, women's. **Biology:** General, biochemistry, microbiology, wildlife. **Business:** General, accounting, business

admin, finance. **Communications:** Communications/speech/rhetoric, journalism. **Computer sciences:** General, information systems. **Conservation:** Environmental studies, management/policy. **Education:** Agricultural, art, elementary, family/consumer sciences, music, secondary. **Engineering:** Agricultural, architectural, chemical, civil, computer, electrical, industrial, mechanical. **English:** English lit. **Foreign languages:** General. **General:** Agronomy, animal sciences, business, communications, economics, food science, horticultural science, mechanization. **Health services:** Athletic training, communication disorders, dietetics, preveterinary. **History:** General. **Human services:** Social work. **Liberal arts:** Humanities. **Math:** General, statistics. **Parks/recreation:** Exercise sciences, facilities management. **Philosophy/religion:** Philosophy. **Physical sciences:** General, chemistry, geology, physics. **Psychology:** General. **Social sciences:** General, anthropology, economics, geography, political science, sociology. **Visual/performing arts:** Dramatic, interior design, music, music performance, studio arts. **Work/family studies:** General, child development, clothing/textiles, family studies, human nutrition.

Most popular majors. Agriculture 12%, business/marketing 16%, education 9%, engineering/engineering technologies 13%, family/consumer sciences 7%, social sciences 10%.

Computing on campus. 547 workstations in dormitories, library, computer center, student center. Dormitories wired for high-speed internet access and linked to campus network. Commuter students can connect to campus network. Online course registration, online library, helpline, repair service, wireless network available.

Student life. Freshman orientation: Available, $25 fee. Preregistration for classes offered. **Housing:** Coed dorms, single-sex dorms, apartments, cooperative housing, fraternity/sorority housing available. $30 nonrefundable deposit. **Activities:** Bands, campus ministries, choral groups, dance, drama, international student organizations, music ensembles, musical theater, radio station, student government, student newspaper, symphony orchestra, TV station, 340 religious, political, ethnic, and social service clubs and organizations available.

Athletics. NCAA. **Intercollegiate:** Baseball M, basketball, cross-country, equestrian W, football (tackle) M, golf, rowing (crew) W, tennis W, track and field, volleyball W. **Intramural:** Badminton, basketball, bowling, cross-country, golf, handball, soccer, softball, squash, swimming, table tennis, tennis, track and field, volleyball, water polo, wrestling M. **Team name:** Wildcats.

Student services. Adult student services, alcohol/substance abuse counseling, career counseling, student employment services, financial aid counseling, health services, legal services, minority student services, on-campus daycare, personal counseling, placement for graduates, veterans' counselor, women's services. **Physically disabled:** Services for visually, speech, hearing impaired.

Contact. E-mail: k-state@k-state.edu
Phone: (785) 532-6250 Toll-free number: (800) 432-8270
Fax: (785) 532-6393
Larry Moeder, Assistant Vice President for Student Financial Assistance and Admissions, Kansas State University, 119 Anderson Hall, Manhattan, KS 66506

Kansas Wesleyan University
Salina, Kansas
www.kwu.edu   CB code: 6337

▸ Private 4-year liberal arts college affiliated with United Methodist Church
▸ Residential campus in large town
▸ 851 degree-seeking undergraduates
▸ 59% of applicants admitted
▸ SAT or ACT (ACT writing optional) required

General. Founded in 1886. Regionally accredited. **Degrees:** 155 bachelor's, 1 associate awarded; master's offered. **Location:** 90 miles from Wichita, 180 miles from Kansas City. **Calendar:** Semester, limited summer session. **Full-time faculty:** 45 total. **Part-time faculty:** 25 total. **Class size:** 66% < 20, 26% 20-39, 6% 40-49, 1% 50-99, less than 1% >100. **Special facilities:** Observatory with 16-inch Cassegrain telescope.

Freshman class profile. 668 applied, 394 admitted, 166 enrolled.

Mid 50% test scores		ACT composite:	20-23
SAT critical reading:	430-490	Out-of-state:	32%
SAT math:	440-540	Live on campus:	67%

Basis for selection. Applicant must have ACT composite score of 18 or SAT combined score of 850 (exclusive of Writing) and high school GPA of 2.5 or rank in top half of class. Interview recommended for academically

weak applicants. Audition recommended for music majors. Portfolio recommended for art majors.

2011-2012 Annual costs. Tuition/fees: $21,400. Room/board: $7,200. Books/supplies: $800. Personal expenses: $500.

Financial aid. Non-need-based: Scholarships awarded for academics, alumni affiliation, art, athletics, music/drama, state residency. **Additional information:** Awards available for residence hall students: minimum $7,000 for 3.0 GPA plus ACT score of 22 or SAT of 950 (exclusive of Writing); minimum $8,000 for 3.5 GPA plus ACT score of 22 or SAT score of 1030 (exclusive of Writing); minimum $9,000 for 3.75 GPA plus ACT score of 25 or SAT score of 1140 (exclusive of Writing). Application deadline March 15.

Application procedures. Admission: No deadline. $20 fee. Admission notification on a rolling basis. **Financial aid:** Closing date 3/15. FAFSA required. Applicants notified on a rolling basis starting 1/1; must reply by 8/1 or within 3 week(s) of notification.

Academics. Special study options: Accelerated study, cross-registration, double major, ESL, independent study, internships, liberal arts/career combination, student-designed major, teacher certification program. **Credit/placement by examination:** AP, CLEP, institutional tests. 30 credit hours maximum toward bachelor's degree. **Support services:** Learning center, reduced course load, remedial instruction, tutoring, writing center.

Majors. Biology: General. **Business:** General, accounting. **Communications:** Communications/speech/rhetoric, public relations. **Computer sciences:** General, computer science. **Education:** Art, elementary, English, secondary. **English:** English lit, rhetoric/composition. **Foreign languages:** General, German, Spanish. **Health services:** Preop/surgical nursing. **History:** General. **Math:** General. **Parks/recreation:** Health/fitness. **Philosophy/religion:** Religion. **Physical sciences:** Chemistry, physics. **Protective services:** Criminal justice. **Psychology:** General. **Social sciences:** Sociology. **Theology:** Religious ed. **Visual/performing arts:** Dramatic, music performance, studio arts, studio arts management.

Most popular majors. Business/marketing 32%, education 9%, health sciences 9%, parks/recreation 7%, physical sciences 7%, social sciences 7%.

Computing on campus. 50 workstations in library, computer center. Dormitories wired for high-speed internet access and linked to campus network. Online library available.

Student life. Freshman orientation: Available. Preregistration for classes offered. **Housing:** Guaranteed on-campus for freshmen. Single-sex dorms, apartments available. $100 deposit. **Activities:** Jazz band, choral groups, dance, drama, literary magazine, music ensembles, musical theater, radio station, student government, student newspaper, Fellowship of Christian Athletes, Religious Life Committee.

Athletics. NAIA. **Intercollegiate:** Baseball M, basketball, cross-country, football (tackle) M, golf, soccer, softball W, tennis, track and field, volleyball W. **Intramural:** Basketball, softball, volleyball, weight lifting. **Team name:** Coyotes.

Student services. Adult student services, career counseling, student employment services, financial aid counseling, personal counseling, placement for graduates, veterans' counselor. **Physically disabled:** Services for visually impaired.

Contact. E-mail: admissions@kwu.edu
Phone: (785) 827-5541 ext. 1285 Toll-free number: (800) 874-1154
Fax: (785) 827-0927
April Evans, Director of Admissions, Kansas Wesleyan University, 100 East Claflin Avenue, Salina, KS 67401-6196

Manhattan Christian College
Manhattan, Kansas
www.mccks.edu   CB code: 6392

▸ Private 4-year Bible college affiliated with Christian Church
▸ Residential campus in large town
▸ 384 undergraduates
▸ SAT or ACT (ACT writing optional), application essay required

General. Founded in 1927. Regionally accredited; also accredited by ABHE. Students have access to Kansas State University library and facilities at student rates. **Degrees:** 64 bachelor's, 4 associate awarded. **ROTC:** Army, Air Force. **Location:** 130 miles west from Kansas City. **Calendar:** Semester, limited summer session. **Full-time faculty:** 10 total. **Part-time faculty:** 18 total.

Freshman class profile.

Out-of-state:	38%	Live on campus:	98%

Basis for selection. High school record, test scores, recommendations important. Character recommendations required. Interview recommended. Audition required for music majors.

High school preparation. Recommended units include English 4, mathematics 2 and science 2.

2011-2012 Annual costs. Tuition/fees: $12,400. Room/board: $7,056. Books/supplies: $1,150. Personal expenses: $1,067.

Financial aid. Non-need-based: Scholarships awarded for academics, leadership.

Application procedures. Admission: Priority date 4/1; deadline 7/1. $25 fee, may be waived for applicants with need. Admission notification on a rolling basis beginning on or about 10/15. **Financial aid:** Priority date 4/1; no closing date. FAFSA required. Applicants notified on a rolling basis starting 4/1; must reply within 2 week(s) of notification.

Academics. Special study options: Combined bachelor's/graduate degree, double major, dual enrollment of high school students, internships, liberal arts/career combination. Dual degree program with Kansas State University. **Credit/placement by examination:** AP, CLEP, institutional tests. 36 credit hours maximum toward bachelor's degree. **Support services:** Reduced course load, tutoring.

Majors. Business: Business admin. **Philosophy/religion:** Religion. **Theology:** Bible, missionary, pastoral counseling, religious ed, theology.

Computing on campus. 12 workstations in library, computer center.

Student life. Freshman orientation: Mandatory. Preregistration for classes offered. 3-day program held before start of classes. **Policies:** Religious observance required. **Housing:** Guaranteed on-campus for freshmen. Single-sex dorms, apartments available. $125 fully refundable deposit, deadline 6/1. **Activities:** Bands, choral groups, drama, music ensembles, student government, student newspaper.

Athletics. NCCAA. **Intercollegiate:** Basketball, soccer, volleyball W. **Intramural:** Softball M. **Team name:** Crusaders.

Student services. Career counseling, student employment services, health services, personal counseling, placement for graduates. **Physically disabled:** Services for speech impaired.

Contact. E-mail: admit@mccks.edu
Phone: (785) 539-3571 Toll-free number: (877) 246-4622
Fax: (785) 776-9251
Eric Ingmire, Director of Admissions, Manhattan Christian College, 1415 Anderson Avenue, Manhattan, KS 66502

McPherson College
McPherson, Kansas
www.mcpherson.edu **CB code: 6404**

- Private 4-year liberal arts college affiliated with Church of the Brethren
- Residential campus in large town
- 620 degree-seeking undergraduates
- 57% of applicants admitted
- SAT or ACT (ACT writing optional) required

General. Founded in 1887. Regionally accredited. **Degrees:** 157 bachelor's awarded. **Location:** 60 miles from Wichita. **Calendar:** 4-1-4, limited summer session. **Full-time faculty:** 34 total; 82% have terminal degrees, 12% minority, 32% women. **Part-time faculty:** 20 total; 30% have terminal degrees, 10% minority, 45% women. **Class size:** 70% < 20, 29% 20-39, less than 1% 40-49.

Freshman class profile. 736 applied, 420 admitted, 134 enrolled.

Mid 50% test scores			
SAT critical reading:	400-490	GPA 3.0-3.49:	34%
SAT math:	460-520	GPA 2.0-2.99:	30%
ACT composite:	18-24	Rank in top quarter:	38%
GPA 3.75 or higher:	19%	Rank in top tenth:	14%
GPA 3.50-3.74:	16%	Out-of-state:	52%
		Live on campus:	96%

Basis for selection. Satisfactory high school performance or completion of GED, corresponding standardized test scores, and appropriate personal qualities. Portfolio required for auto restoration program.

High school preparation. College-preparatory program recommended.

2011-2012 Annual costs. Tuition/fees: $20,600. Room/board: $7,558. Books/supplies: $1,300. Personal expenses: $2,580.

Financial aid. Non-need-based: Scholarships awarded for academics, alumni affiliation, art, athletics, music/drama, religious affiliation, state residency.

Application procedures. Admission: Priority date 3/1; no deadline. $25 fee, may be waived for applicants with need, free for online applicants. Admission notification on a rolling basis beginning on or about 6/1. Must reply by May 1 or within 4 week(s) if notified thereafter. **Financial aid:** Priority date 3/1; no closing date. FAFSA required. Applicants notified on a rolling basis starting 3/1; must reply within 3 week(s) of notification.

Academics. Special study options: Cross-registration, double major, dual enrollment of high school students, ESL, independent study, internships, liberal arts/career combination, student-designed major, study abroad, teacher certification program, urban semester. **Credit/placement by examination:** AP, CLEP, IB, institutional tests. **Support services:** Learning center, reduced course load, remedial instruction, study skills assistance, tutoring, writing center.

Majors. Biology: General. **Business:** Accounting, business admin, finance, international. **Communications:** Communications/speech/rhetoric. **Education:** General, art, biology, business, chemistry, computer, early childhood, elementary, English, foreign languages, history, mathematics, middle, music, physical, science, social studies, Spanish, special ed, speech, technology/industrial arts. **English:** English lit. **Foreign languages:** General, Spanish. **Health services:** Predental, premedicine, prepharmacy, preveterinary. **History:** General. **Liberal arts:** Arts/sciences. **Math:** General. **Parks/recreation:** Health/fitness. **Physical sciences:** Chemistry. **Psychology:** General. **Social sciences:** Sociology. **Visual/performing arts:** Art, dramatic, music, music performance.

Most popular majors. Biology 7%, business/marketing 27%, engineering/engineering technologies 21%, parks/recreation 8%, visual/performing arts 9%.

Computing on campus. 72 workstations in dormitories, library, computer center, student center. Dormitories wired for high-speed internet access and linked to campus network. Commuter students can connect to campus network. Online library, helpline, repair service, wireless network available.

Student life. Freshman orientation: Mandatory. Preregistration for classes offered. **Policies:** No alcohol permitted on campus. Unmarried students under 23 years old are required to live in residence halls. **Housing:** Guaranteed on-campus for freshmen. Coed dorms, single-sex dorms, special housing for disabled available. $150 fully refundable deposit, deadline 5/1. **Activities:** Bands, choral groups, dance, drama, music ensembles, musical theater, student government, student newspaper, 28 clubs and organizations available.

Athletics. NAIA. **Intercollegiate:** Baseball M, basketball, cheerleading, cross-country, football (tackle) M, softball W, tennis, track and field, volleyball W. **Intramural:** Badminton, basketball, football (non-tackle), football (tackle) M, handball, racquetball, soccer, softball, table tennis, volleyball. **Team name:** Bulldogs.

Student services. Adult student services, chaplain/spiritual director, career counseling, student employment services, financial aid counseling, health services, personal counseling, placement for graduates. **Physically disabled:** Services for hearing impaired.

Contact. E-mail: admiss@mcpherson.edu
Phone: (620) 242-0400 Toll-free number: (800) 695-7402
Fax: (620) 241-8443
Matt Pffannenstiel, Director of Student Recruitment, McPherson College, 1600 East Euclid Street, McPherson, KS 67460-1402

MidAmerica Nazarene University
Olathe, Kansas
www.mnu.edu **CB code: 6437**

- Private 4-year university and liberal arts college affiliated with Church of the Nazarene
- Residential campus in small city
- 1,169 degree-seeking undergraduates: 26% part-time, 52% women
- 471 graduate students
- 98% of applicants admitted
- SAT or ACT (ACT writing optional) required
- 44% graduate within 6 years

General. Founded in 1966. Regionally accredited. **Degrees:** 410 bachelor's, 10 associate awarded; master's offered. **ROTC:** Army, Air Force. **Location:** 19 miles from Kansas City. **Calendar:** Semester, limited summer session. **Full-time faculty:** 80 total. **Part-time faculty:** 135 total. **Class size:** 72% < 20, 25% 20-39, 1% 40-49, 2% 50-99.

Freshman class profile. 509 applied, 498 admitted, 167 enrolled.

Mid 50% test scores			
SAT math:	410-460	GPA 3.0-3.49:	19%
ACT composite:	19-25	GPA 2.0-2.99:	26%
GPA 3.75 or higher:	31%	Return as sophomores:	72%
GPA 3.50-3.74:	21%	Out-of-state:	54%
		Live on campus:	85%

Basis for selection. Secondary school record, class rank, test scores, and moral principles important. Nursing, elementary education, and secondary education programs have higher standards for admission. Interview recommended for music, nursing, elementary and secondary education programs. Audition recommended for music majors. **Home schooled:** Transcript of courses and grades, letter of recommendation (nonparent) required.

High school preparation. 15 units recommended. Recommended units include English 4, mathematics 3, social studies 3, science 3 and foreign language 1.

2012-2013 Annual costs. Tuition/fees (projected): $21,500. Room/board: $7,000. Books/supplies: $1,180. Personal expenses: $1,270.

Financial aid. **Non-need-based:** Scholarships awarded for academics, athletics, leadership, music/drama, religious affiliation, ROTC.

Application procedures. **Admission:** Priority date 3/1; deadline 8/1 (postmark date). $25 fee. Admission notification on a rolling basis. **Financial aid:** Priority date 3/1; no closing date. FAFSA required. Applicants notified on a rolling basis starting 1/30; must reply within 2 week(s) of notification.

Academics. Students may earn bachelor's degree through professional program division. **Special study options:** Accelerated study, cooperative education, cross-registration, distance learning, double major, dual enrollment of high school students, independent study, internships, student-designed major, study abroad, teacher certification program, Washington semester. **Credit/placement by examination:** AP, CLEP, IB, SAT, ACT, institutional tests. 34 credit hours maximum toward associate degree, 34 toward bachelor's. **Support services:** Learning center, reduced course load, remedial instruction, study skills assistance, tutoring.

Majors. **Biology:** General. **Business:** General, accounting, business admin, communications, human resources. **Communications:** Communications/speech/rhetoric, media studies, public relations. **Education:** Biology, business, elementary, English, foreign languages, health, mathematics, middle, music, physical, secondary, social studies, Spanish. **English:** English lit. **Foreign languages:** Spanish. **Health services:** Athletic training, nursing (RN). **History:** General. **Human services:** General. **Math:** General. **Parks/recreation:** Exercise sciences, sports admin. **Philosophy/religion:** Religion. **Physical sciences:** Chemistry, physics. **Protective services:** Law enforcement admin. **Psychology:** General. **Social sciences:** General, sociology, urban studies. **Theology:** Missionary, religious ed, sacred music, youth ministry. **Visual/performing arts:** General, music, music performance, voice/opera.

Most popular majors. Business/marketing 50%, education 7%, health sciences 26%, theological studies 6%.

Computing on campus. 90 workstations in dormitories, library, computer center. Dormitories wired for high-speed internet access and linked to campus network. Commuter students can connect to campus network. Online course registration, online library, helpline, wireless network available.

Student life. **Freshman orientation:** Mandatory, $700 fee. Preregistration for classes offered. **Policies:** Religious observance required. **Housing:** Guaranteed on-campus for freshmen. Single-sex dorms, special housing for disabled, apartments, wellness housing available. $100 deposit, deadline 8/21. **Activities:** Bands, campus ministries, choral groups, drama, international student organizations, literary magazine, music ensembles, musical theater, radio station, student government, student newspaper, symphony orchestra, TV station, Circle K, College Republicans, gospel station, Fellowship of Christian Athletes, multicultural student association, BYTE, Psych Incorporated, medical careers club, covenant groups.

Athletics. NAIA. **Intercollegiate:** Baseball M, basketball, cheerleading, football (tackle) M, soccer, softball W, volleyball W. **Intramural:** Basketball, bowling, football (non-tackle), golf, soccer, softball, table tennis, tennis, volleyball. **Team name:** Pioneers.

Student services. Adult student services, alcohol/substance abuse counseling, chaplain/spiritual director, financial aid counseling, health services, minority student services, personal counseling, veterans' counselor. **Physically disabled:** Services for visually, speech, hearing impaired.

Contact. E-mail: admissions@mnu.edu
Phone: (913) 971-3380 Toll-free number: (800) 800-8887
Fax: (913) 971-3481
Waren Rogers, Director of Admissions, MidAmerica Nazarene University, 2030 East College Way, Olathe, KS 66062-1899

Newman University
Wichita, Kansas
www.newmanu.edu   CB code: 6615

- Private 4-year university and liberal arts college affiliated with Roman Catholic Church
- Commuter campus in large city
- 1,299 degree-seeking undergraduates: 15% part-time, 67% women, 7% African American, 5% Asian American, 10% Hispanic American, 2% Native American, 5% international
- 417 degree-seeking graduate students
- 44% of applicants admitted
- SAT and SAT Subject Tests or ACT (ACT writing optional) required
- 31% graduate within 6 years; 25% enter graduate study

General. Founded in 1933. Regionally accredited. The university is a sponsored ministry of the Adorers of the Blood of Christ and is named after Blessed John Henry Cardinal Newman. **Degrees:** 218 bachelor's, 61 associate awarded; master's offered. **Location:** 160 miles from Oklahoma City, 180 miles from Kansas City. **Calendar:** Semester, limited summer session. **Full-time faculty:** 81 total; 59% have terminal degrees, 5% minority, 57% women. **Part-time faculty:** 183 total; 7% minority, 66% women. **Class size:** 66% < 20, 31% 20-39, 2% 40-49, 2% 50-99. **Special facilities:** Photography laboratory, cadaver laboratory.

Freshman class profile. 2,521 applied, 1,097 admitted, 170 enrolled.

Mid 50% test scores			
SAT critical reading:	450-550	GPA 2.0-2.99:	15%
SAT math:	510-640	Rank in top quarter:	54%
SAT writing:	400-570	Rank in top tenth:	24%
ACT composite:	21-27	End year in good standing:	95%
GPA 3.75 or higher:	42%	Return as sophomores:	71%
GPA 3.50-3.74:	21%	Out-of-state:	15%
GPA 3.0-3.49:	22%	Live on campus:	44%
		International:	3%

Basis for selection. Minimum GPA 2.0, minimum ACT composite score of 18, or SAT score of 1290 (including Writing). Caliber of high school curriculum important. Portfolio recommended for art majors. **Learning Disabled:** Applicants should submit medical evaluation and recommendation.

High school preparation. College-preparatory program recommended. Recommended units include English 4, mathematics 3, social studies 3 and science 3.

2011-2012 Annual costs. Tuition/fees: $21,666. Room/board: $6,790. Books/supplies: $988.

2010-2011 Financial aid. **Need-based:** 186 full-time freshmen applied for aid; 147 were judged to have need; 147 of these received aid. Average need met was 76%. Average scholarship/grant was $4,270; average loan $3,019. 39% of total undergraduate aid awarded as scholarships/grants, 61% as loans/jobs. **Non-need-based:** Awarded to 1,178 full-time undergraduates, including 227 freshmen. Scholarships awarded for academics, alumni affiliation, art, athletics, leadership, music/drama.

Application procedures. **Admission:** No deadline. $20 fee, may be waived for applicants with need, free for online applicants. Admission notification on a rolling basis. **Financial aid:** Priority date 3/1; no closing date. FAFSA required. Applicants notified on a rolling basis starting 2/1.

Academics. **Special study options:** Accelerated study, combined bachelor's/graduate degree, cooperative education, cross-registration, distance learning, double major, dual enrollment of high school students, honors, independent study, internships, liberal arts/career combination, student-designed major, study abroad, teacher certification program. **Credit/placement by examination:** AP, CLEP, IB, institutional tests. 30 credit hours maximum toward bachelor's degree. **Support services:** Learning center, remedial instruction, study skills assistance, tutoring, writing center.

Majors. **Biology:** General, biochemistry. **Business:** Accounting, business admin, management information systems. **Communications:** Media studies, sports. **Computer sciences:** Information systems. **Education:** General, early childhood special, elementary, middle, secondary. **English:** English lit. **Health services:** Nursing (RN), sonography. **History:** General. **Liberal arts:** Arts/sciences. **Math:** General. **Philosophy/religion:** Philosophy. **Physical sciences:** Chemistry, forensic chemistry. **Protective services:** Forensics, law

enforcement admin. **Psychology:** General, counseling. **Social sciences:** Sociology. **Theology:** Pastoral counseling, theology. **Visual/performing arts:** Art.

Most popular majors. Biology 14%, business/marketing 12%, education 21%, health sciences 22%, social sciences 7%.

Computing on campus. 90 workstations in dormitories, library, computer center, student center. Dormitories wired for high-speed internet access and linked to campus network. Commuter students can connect to campus network. Online library, helpline, repair service, wireless network available.

Student life. Freshman orientation: Mandatory, $150 fee. Preregistration for classes offered. Weekend prior to first day of class. **Policies:** Freshmen required to live in college housing for first 2 years if not living with parents. **Housing:** Guaranteed on-campus for freshmen. Coed dorms, apartments, wellness housing available. $125 fully refundable deposit. **Activities:** Pep band, campus ministries, choral groups, dance, drama, international student organizations, literary magazine, student government, student newspaper, Koinonia, Service Scholars, Newman Club, Peer Educators, Kansas Catholic College Student Convention, Peer Ministers.

Athletics. NCAA. **Intercollegiate:** Baseball M, basketball, cross-country, golf, soccer, softball W, tennis, volleyball W, wrestling M. **Intramural:** Baseball M, basketball, bowling, football (tackle), golf, soccer, softball W, table tennis, volleyball, weight lifting. **Team name:** Jets.

Student services. Adult student services, chaplain/spiritual director, career counseling, student employment services, financial aid counseling, personal counseling, placement for graduates, veterans' counselor. **Physically disabled:** Services for visually, speech, hearing impaired.

Contact. E-mail: admissions@newmanu.edu
Phone: (316) 942-4291 ext. 2144 Toll-free number: (877) 639-6268
Fax: (316) 942-4483
John Clayton, Dean of Admissions, Newman University, 3100 McCormick, Wichita, KS 67213-2097

Ottawa University
Ottawa, Kansas
www.ottawa.edu

CB member
CB code: 6547

- Private 4-year university and liberal arts college affiliated with American Baptist Churches in the USA
- Residential campus in large town
- 558 degree-seeking undergraduates
- Application essay required

General. Founded in 1865. Regionally accredited. Degree programs offered at additional campuses in Overland Park, KS; Phoenix, AZ; Milwaukee, WI; Jeffersonville, IN, and through Ottawa Online. **Degrees:** 82 bachelor's awarded. **Location:** 45 miles from Kansas City. **Calendar:** Semester, limited summer session. **Full-time faculty:** 25 total; 52% have terminal degrees, 16% minority, 48% women. **Part-time faculty:** 13 total. **Class size:** 76% < 20, 24% 20-39, less than 1% 40-49.

Freshman class profile.

Mid 50% test scores		GPA 3.0-3.49:	37%
SAT critical reading:	420-530	GPA 2.0-2.99:	25%
SAT math:	430-520	Rank in top quarter:	36%
SAT writing:	380-500	Rank in top tenth:	12%
ACT composite:	18-24	Out-of-state:	42%
GPA 3.75 or higher:	19%	Live on campus:	99%
GPA 3.50-3.74:	17%		

Basis for selection. Class ranking, cumulative GPA, standardized test scores, and personal essay are considered in the admissions decision. SAT or ACT recommended. Auditions recommended for music and drama majors. Portfolio recommended for art majors. **Home schooled:** Transcript of courses and grades required. Must take ACT or SAT. Require a sample of most recent written work/portfolio.

High school preparation. College-preparatory program recommended. Recommended units include English 4, mathematics 3, social studies 1, history 2, science 3 (laboratory 2) and foreign language 1.

2011-2012 Annual costs. Tuition/fees: $21,680. Room/board: $6,208. Books/supplies: $1,200. Personal expenses: $1,800.

Financial aid. Non-need-based: Scholarships awarded for academics, alumni affiliation, athletics, music/drama, religious affiliation.

Application procedures. Admission: Priority date 6/1; no deadline. $25 fee, may be waived for applicants with need. Admission notification on a rolling basis. **Financial aid:** Priority date 3/15; no closing date. FAFSA required. Applicants notified on a rolling basis starting 2/1; must reply within 4 week(s) of notification.

Academics. Special study options: Distance learning, double major, dual enrollment of high school students, independent study, internships, liberal arts/career combination, student-designed major, study abroad, teacher certification program. **Credit/placement by examination:** AP, CLEP, IB. **Support services:** Learning center, reduced course load, study skills assistance, tutoring.

Majors. Biology: General. **Business:** Accounting/business management, business admin. **Communications:** Communications/speech/rhetoric. **Computer sciences:** Information technology. **Education:** Elementary. **English:** English lit. **History:** General. **Math:** General. **Parks/recreation:** Health/fitness. **Philosophy/religion:** Religion. **Psychology:** General. **Social sciences:** Sociology. **Visual/performing arts:** Art, dramatic, music.

Most popular majors. Biology 6%, business/marketing 27%, communications/journalism 10%, education 11%, parks/recreation 22%.

Computing on campus. 59 workstations in library, computer center. Dormitories wired for high-speed internet access and linked to campus network. Commuter students can connect to campus network. Online course registration, online library, helpline, wireless network available.

Student life. Freshman orientation: Mandatory. Preregistration for classes offered. **Housing:** Guaranteed on-campus for freshmen. Coed dorms, single-sex dorms available. $150 fully refundable deposit. Pets allowed in dorm rooms. **Activities:** Jazz band, campus ministries, choral groups, dance, drama, music ensembles, radio station, student government, student newspaper, symphony orchestra, Christian Faith in Action, voluntary service organization, Whole Earth club, Fellowship of Christian Athletes, student activities force, Cognoscenti (literary group), Amnesty International.

Athletics. NAIA. **Intercollegiate:** Baseball M, basketball, cross-country, football (tackle) M, golf M, soccer, softball W, track and field, volleyball W. **Intramural:** Basketball, handball, racquetball, soccer, softball, track and field, volleyball. **Team name:** Braves.

Student services. Alcohol/substance abuse counseling, chaplain/spiritual director, career counseling, student employment services, financial aid counseling, health services, personal counseling, placement for graduates.

Contact. E-mail: admiss@ottawa.edu
Phone: (785) 242-5200 ext. 5421
Toll-free number: (800) 755-5200 ext. 5421 Fax: (785) 229-1008
Steed Bell, Manager of New Student Enrollment, Ottawa University, 1001 South Cedar Street, #17, Ottawa, KS 66067-3399

Pittsburg State University
Pittsburg, Kansas
www.pittstate.edu

CB code: 6336

- Public 4-year university and business college
- Residential campus in large town
- 5,930 degree-seeking undergraduates: 5% part-time, 47% women, 4% African American, 1% Asian American, 4% Hispanic American, 2% Native American, 4% international
- 1,117 degree-seeking graduate students
- 77% of applicants admitted
- ACT (writing optional) required
- 49% graduate within 6 years

General. Founded in 1903. Regionally accredited. Centers in Kansas City and Wichita. **Degrees:** 1,131 bachelor's, 34 associate awarded; master's offered. **ROTC:** Army. **Location:** 120 miles from Kansas City. **Calendar:** Semester, limited summer session. **Full-time faculty:** 316 total; 77% have terminal degrees, 10% minority, 42% women. **Part-time faculty:** 101 total; 23% have terminal degrees, 5% minority, 60% women. **Class size:** 46% < 20, 42% 20-39, 5% 40-49, 7% 50-99, less than 1% >100. **Special facilities:** Planetarium, observatory, field biology reserve, nature reach, herbarium, technology center, gorilla village, mammal collection, greenhouse, polymer research lab, broadcasting lab, cadaver lab, natural history reserve, Timmons Chapel.

Freshman class profile. 2,889 applied, 2,220 admitted, 1,161 enrolled.

Mid 50% test scores			
ACT composite:	19-24	Rank in top quarter:	37%
GPA 3.75 or higher:	23%	Rank in top tenth:	13%
GPA 3.50-3.74:	17%	Return as sophomores:	73%
GPA 3.0-3.49:	30%	Out-of-state:	29%
GPA 2.0-2.99:	29%	Live on campus:	65%
		International:	5%

Basis for selection. Academics, school record, class rank and test scores most important. **Home schooled:** GED, record of course content and completion required.

High school preparation. College-preparatory program recommended. 13 units recommended. Recommended units include English 4, mathematics 3, social studies 3 and science 3.

2011-2012 Annual costs. Tuition/fees: $5,162; $14,166 out-of-state. Room/board: $6,016. Books/supplies: $1,000. Personal expenses: $2,268.

Financial aid. Non-need-based: Scholarships awarded for academics, alumni affiliation, art, athletics, leadership, music/drama, ROTC.

Application procedures. Admission: No deadline. $30 fee, may be waived for applicants with need. Admission notification on a rolling basis. **Financial aid:** Priority date 3/1; no closing date. FAFSA, institutional form required. Applicants notified on a rolling basis; must reply within 2 week(s) of notification.

Academics. Special study options: Accelerated study, distance learning, double major, dual enrollment of high school students, honors, independent study, internships, student-designed major, study abroad, teacher certification program. **Credit/placement by examination:** AP, CLEP, IB, ACT, institutional tests. 24 credit hours maximum toward bachelor's degree. **Support services:** Learning center, tutoring, writing center.

Honors college/program. Separate application required. Criteria for selection include minimum 28 ACT score, minimum 3.5 GPA, recommendations, record of participation in academic and other extracurricular activities. 36 incoming freshmen are accepted each year.

Majors. Biology: General, biochemistry, cellular/molecular, plant molecular, plant physiology. **Business:** Accounting, business admin, construction management, fashion, finance, international, managerial economics, marketing. **Communications:** General, advertising, photojournalism, public relations, radio/TV. **Education:** Art, biology, chemistry, early childhood, elementary, English, family/consumer sciences, French, history, mathematics, music, physical, physics, psychology, Spanish, technology/industrial arts, voc/tech. **English:** Creative writing, English lit, technical writing. **Foreign languages:** French, Spanish. **Health services:** Clinical lab science, nursing (RN), predental, premedicine, prepharmacy, prephysical therapy, recreational therapy. **History:** General. **Human services:** Social work. **Math:** General. **Physical sciences:** Chemistry, environmental chemistry, physics, polymer chemistry. **Psychology:** General. **Social sciences:** Geography, political science, sociology. **Visual/performing arts:** Art, interior design, music, music performance, theater arts management. **Work/family studies:** General, child development.

Most popular majors. Biology 6%, business/marketing 15%, communications/journalism 7%, education 13%, engineering/engineering technologies 19%, health sciences 7%, psychology 6%.

Computing on campus. 927 workstations in library, computer center, student center. Dormitories wired for high-speed internet access and linked to campus network. Commuter students can connect to campus network. Online course registration, online library, repair service, student web hosting, wireless network available.

Student life. Freshman orientation: Mandatory, $30 fee. Preregistration for classes offered. Eight individual sessions are offered and last approximately eight hours each. **Housing:** Guaranteed on-campus for freshmen. Coed dorms, special housing for disabled, apartments, wellness housing available. $145 partly refundable deposit. **Activities:** Bands, campus ministries, choral groups, dance, drama, film society, international student organizations, literary magazine, music ensembles, musical theater, opera, radio station, student government, student newspaper, symphony orchestra, TV station, Over 150 clubs and organizations available.

Athletics. NCAA. **Intercollegiate:** Baseball M, basketball, cheerleading, cross-country, football (tackle) M, golf M, softball W, track and field, volleyball W. **Intramural:** Badminton, basketball, football (non-tackle), racquetball, soccer, softball, table tennis, tennis, volleyball. **Team name:** Gorillas.

Student services. Alcohol/substance abuse counseling, chaplain/spiritual director, career counseling, student employment services, financial aid counseling, health services, legal services, minority student services, personal counseling, placement for graduates, veterans' counselor. **Physically disabled:** Services for visually, speech, hearing impaired.

Contact. E-mail: psuadmit@pittstate.edu
Phone: (620) 235-4251 Toll-free number: (800) 854-7488
Fax: (620) 235-6003
Melinda Roelfs, Director of Admission, Pittsburg State University, 1701 South Broadway, Pittsburg, KS 66762

Southwestern College
Winfield, Kansas
www.sckans.edu   CB code: 6670

- Private 4-year liberal arts college affiliated with United Methodist Church
- Residential campus in large town
- 1,341 degree-seeking undergraduates: 57% part-time, 48% women, 10% African American, 1% Asian American, 7% Hispanic American, 1% Native American, 2% international
- 279 degree-seeking graduate students
- 87% of applicants admitted
- SAT or ACT (ACT writing optional), application essay required
- 57% graduate within 6 years

General. Founded in 1885. Regionally accredited. Laptop computers issued to all full-time students enrolled at main campus. **Degrees:** 647 bachelor's, 1 associate awarded; master's offered. **Location:** 40 miles from Wichita. **Calendar:** Semester, limited summer session. **Full-time faculty:** 48 total; 62% have terminal degrees, 6% minority, 44% women. **Part-time faculty:** 65 total; 9% have terminal degrees, 12% minority, 45% women. **Class size:** 82% < 20, 16% 20-39, 2% 50-99. **Special facilities:** Biological field station.

Freshman class profile. 378 applied, 330 admitted, 160 enrolled.

Mid 50% test scores			
SAT critical reading:	390-460	GPA 2.0-2.99:	17%
SAT math:	410-500	Rank in top quarter:	36%
SAT writing:	380-470	Rank in top tenth:	14%
ACT composite:	19-24	End year in good standing:	83%
GPA 3.75 or higher:	32%	Return as sophomores:	63%
GPA 3.50-3.74:	21%	Out-of-state:	50%
GPA 3.0-3.49:	30%	Live on campus:	99%
		International:	3%

Basis for selection. School achievement record, test scores, and personal essay statement most important. Portfolio required. Interview recommended for nursing majors. Audition required for music and drama majors.

High school preparation. College-preparatory program recommended. 13.5 units required. Required units include English 4, mathematics 3, social studies 0.5, history 2, science 2 (laboratory 1). Two units of foreign language, oral communications, computer science, or any combination of the three required.

2011-2012 Annual costs. Tuition/fees: $21,680. Room/board: $6,322. Books/supplies: $1,000. Personal expenses: $6,090.

2010-2011 Financial aid. Need-based: 160 full-time freshmen applied for aid; 142 were judged to have need; 142 of these received aid. Average need met was 73%. Average scholarship/grant was $13,936; average loan $4,297. 48% of total undergraduate aid awarded as scholarships/grants, 52% as loans/jobs. **Non-need-based:** Awarded to 168 full-time undergraduates, including 61 freshmen. Scholarships awarded for academics, athletics, leadership, minority status, music/drama.

Application procedures. Admission: Closing date 8/25 (receipt date). $25 fee, may be waived for applicants with need. Admission notification on a rolling basis beginning on or about 9/15. Must reply by May 1 or within 3 week(s) if notified thereafter. **Financial aid:** Priority date 4/1, closing date 8/15. FAFSA, institutional form required. Applicants notified on a rolling basis starting 2/1; must reply within 2 week(s) of notification.

Academics. Special study options: Accelerated study, distance learning, double major, honors, independent study, internships, student-designed major, teacher certification program, urban semester, Washington semester. **Credit/placement by examination:** AP, CLEP, ACT. 30 credit hours maximum toward bachelor's degree. **Support services:** Learning center, reduced course load, remedial instruction, study skills assistance, tutoring, writing center.

Majors. Biology: General, biochemistry, marine. **Business:** Accounting, business admin, communications, entrepreneurial studies, finance, management information systems, marketing. **Communications:** General, communications/speech/rhetoric, digital media, journalism, radio/TV. **Computer sciences:** Computer science. **Education:** Business, early childhood, elementary, English, mathematics, music, physical, speech. **English:** Creative writing, English lit, general lit. **Health services:** Athletic training, nursing (RN). **History:** General. **Liberal arts:** Arts/sciences. **Math:** General. **Parks/recreation:** Sports admin, sports studies. **Philosophy/religion:** General. **Physical**

sciences: Chemistry, physics. **Psychology:** General. **Visual/performing arts:** Digital arts, dramatic, film/cinema/video, game design, music, music performance, musical theater, theater design.

Most popular majors. Business/marketing 43%, computer/information sciences 11%, education 14%, security/protective services 11%.

Computing on campus. PC or laptop required. 18 workstations in library, computer center, student center. Dormitories wired for high-speed internet access and linked to campus network. Commuter students can connect to campus network. Online library, helpline, repair service, student web hosting, wireless network available.

Student life. Freshman orientation: Mandatory. Preregistration for classes offered. Three-day orientation held before upperclassmen arrive on campus. **Policies:** Drug and alcohol-free campus. **Housing:** Guaranteed on-campus for freshmen. Coed dorms, single-sex dorms, apartments available. $150 partly refundable deposit. **Activities:** Bands, campus ministries, choral groups, dance, drama, international student organizations, music ensembles, musical theater, radio station, student government, student newspaper, symphony orchestra, TV station, Campus Council on Ministries, Student Foundation, international club, Fellowship of Christian Athletes, Discipleship Southwestern, Leadership Southwestern, outreach teams, Nurses Christian Fellowship.

Athletics. NAIA. **Intercollegiate:** Basketball, cross-country, football (tackle) M, golf, soccer, softball W, tennis, track and field, volleyball W. **Intramural:** Badminton, basketball, softball, tennis, volleyball. **Team name:** Moundbuilders.

Student services. Adult student services, alcohol/substance abuse counseling, chaplain/spiritual director, career counseling, student employment services, financial aid counseling, health services, minority student services, personal counseling, placement for graduates. **Physically disabled:** Services for visually, hearing impaired.

Contact. E-mail: scadmit@sckans.edu
Phone: (620) 229-6236 Toll-free number: (800) 846-1543 ext. 6236
Fax: (620) 229-6344
Marla Sexson, Director of Admission, Southwestern College, 100 College Street, Winfield, KS 67156

Sterling College
Sterling, Kansas
www.sterling.edu
CB code: 6684

- Private 4-year liberal arts college affiliated with Presbyterian Church (USA)
- Residential campus in small town
- 639 degree-seeking undergraduates: 7% part-time, 46% women
- 51% of applicants admitted
- SAT or ACT (ACT writing optional), application essay required
- 47% graduate within 6 years

General. Founded in 1887. Regionally accredited. **Degrees:** 120 bachelor's awarded. **Location:** 20 miles from Hutchinson, 70 miles from Wichita. **Calendar:** 4-1-4, limited summer session. **Full-time faculty:** 39 total; 10% have terminal degrees, 5% minority, 49% women. **Part-time faculty:** 39 total; 44% have terminal degrees, 10% minority, 64% women. **Class size:** 78% < 20, 19% 20-39, 3% 40-49, less than 1% 50-99.

Freshman class profile. 806 applied, 415 admitted, 140 enrolled.

Mid 50% test scores			
SAT critical reading:	420-520	GPA 2.0-2.99:	36%
SAT math:	410-520	Rank in top quarter:	23%
SAT writing:	410-480	Rank in top tenth:	11%
ACT composite:	19-25	End year in good standing:	77%
GPA 3.75 or higher:	22%	Return as sophomores:	62%
GPA 3.50-3.74:	15%	Out-of-state:	51%
GPA 3.0-3.49:	25%	Live on campus:	96%
		International:	1%

Basis for selection. High school record, test scores, recommendations from school counselor and pastor important; commitment to Christian values and service also important. Interview recommended. Audition required of performing arts majors. Portfolio recommended for art majors. **Home schooled:** Transcript of courses and grades required. State certification of the home school or GED strongly recommended for athletic eligibility. **Learning Disabled:** Must provide official documentation with recommended accommodations.

High school preparation. College-preparatory program recommended. 18 units recommended. Recommended units include English 4, mathematics

---

3, social studies 1, history 2, science 3 (laboratory 2), foreign language 2, computer science 1 and academic electives 1. Physical education recommended.

2011-2012 Annual costs. Tuition/fees: $20,050. Room/board: $7,166. Books/supplies: $800. Personal expenses: $700.

2011-2012 Financial aid. Need-based: 32% of total undergraduate aid awarded as scholarships/grants, 68% as loans/jobs. **Non-need-based:** Scholarships awarded for academics, athletics.

Application procedures. Admission: Priority date 3/1; no deadline. $25 fee, may be waived for applicants with need, free for online applicants. Admission notification on a rolling basis beginning on or about 9/15. **Financial aid:** Priority date 3/15; no closing date. FAFSA required. Applicants notified on a rolling basis starting 2/1; must reply within 3 week(s) of notification.

Academics. Special study options: Distance learning, double major, dual enrollment of high school students, honors, independent study, internships, liberal arts/career combination, student-designed major, study abroad, teacher certification program, urban semester, Washington semester. **Credit/placement by examination:** AP, CLEP, IB, SAT, ACT, institutional tests. **Support services:** Learning center, reduced course load, remedial instruction, study skills assistance, tutoring, writing center.

Majors. Biology: General. **Business:** Business admin. **Communications:** Communications/speech/rhetoric. **Education:** Elementary, mathematics, music. **English:** English lit. **Health services:** Athletic training. **History:** General. **Math:** General. **Parks/recreation:** Health/fitness, sports admin. **Philosophy/religion:** General. **Physical sciences:** Chemistry. **Psychology:** General. **Theology:** Bible, missionary, religious ed, theology, urban ministry, youth ministry. **Visual/performing arts:** Art, dramatic, music.

Most popular majors. Biology 6%, business/marketing 22%, education 30%, parks/recreation 8%, theological studies 14%.

Computing on campus. 120 workstations in dormitories, library, computer center, student center. Dormitories wired for high-speed internet access and linked to campus network. Commuter students can connect to campus network. Online library, helpline, wireless network available.

Student life. Freshman orientation: Mandatory. Preregistration for classes offered. 3-day program prior to start of fall classes; includes service project. **Policies:** Prohibition of alcohol and tobacco products. All students under age 23 required to live in campus dormitories unless married or with dependents, living at home with parents, 5th-year senior, or by special circumstances. Religious observance required. **Housing:** Guaranteed on-campus for all undergraduates. Single-sex dorms, wellness housing available. $100 partly refundable deposit, deadline 8/1. **Activities:** Bands, campus ministries, choral groups, dance, drama, literary magazine, music ensembles, musical theater, radio station, student government, student newspaper, Future Science Professionals Association, Alpha Phi Omega, Fellowship of Christian Athletes, behavioral science club, Habitat for Humanity, Chi Beta Sigma, Pi Kappa Delta, Catholic student association.

Athletics. NAIA. **Intercollegiate:** Baseball M, basketball, cross-country, football (tackle) M, golf, soccer, softball W, track and field, volleyball W. **Intramural:** Basketball, football (non-tackle), softball, table tennis, volleyball. **Team name:** Warriors.

Student services. Chaplain/spiritual director, career counseling, student employment services, financial aid counseling, health services, personal counseling, veterans' counselor.

Contact. E-mail: admissions@sterling.edu
Phone: (620) 278-4275 Toll-free number: (800) 346-1017
Fax: (620) 278-4416
Dennis Dutton, Vice President for Enrollment Services, Sterling College, 125 West Cooper, Sterling, KS 67579

Tabor College
Hillsboro, Kansas
www.tabor.edu
CB code: 6815

- Private 4-year liberal arts college affiliated with Mennonite Brethren Church
- Residential campus in small town
- 709 degree-seeking undergraduates: 18% part-time, 48% women, 7% African American, 10% Hispanic American, 1% Native American, 2% international
- 13 degree-seeking graduate students
- 91% of applicants admitted

▶ SAT or ACT (ACT writing optional), application essay required
▶ 53% graduate within 6 years

General. Founded in 1908. Regionally accredited. Off-campus site in Wichita offers adult degree completion program and graduate studies. **Degrees:** 157 bachelor's, 1 associate awarded; master's offered. **Location:** 50 miles from Wichita. **Calendar:** 4-1-4, limited summer session. **Full-time faculty:** 29 total; 83% have terminal degrees, 7% minority, 38% women. **Part-time faculty:** 56 total; 12% have terminal degrees, 9% minority, 48% women. **Class size:** 49% < 20, 38% 20-39, 8% 40-49, 4% 50-99, less than 1% >100.

Freshman class profile. 407 applied, 371 admitted, 151 enrolled.

Mid 50% test scores		GPA 2.0-2.99:	34%
SAT critical reading:	400-470	Rank in top quarter:	38%
SAT math:	470-560	Rank in top tenth:	20%
ACT composite:	19-25	Return as sophomores:	70%
GPA 3.75 or higher:	26%	Out-of-state:	51%
GPA 3.50-3.74:	15%	Live on campus:	99%
GPA 3.0-3.49:	24%	International:	2%

Basis for selection. Life values and objectives, desire for Christian growth, and personal interviews important. Students must score a minimum of 18 on ACT and have ACT GPA (4.0 scale) product of 45 or above to be considered for admission. Audition recommended for music or drama. **Learning Disabled:** Must provide IEPs if special accommodations requested.

High school preparation. 17 units recommended. Recommended units include English 4, mathematics 3, social studies 2, history 2, science 3, foreign language 1 and academic electives 2.

2012-2013 Annual costs. Tuition/fees (projected): $21,740. Room/board: $8,120. Books/supplies: $1,000. Personal expenses: $3,100.

2010-2011 Financial aid. Need-based: 153 full-time freshmen applied for aid; 135 were judged to have need; 135 of these received aid. Average need met was 77%. Average scholarship/grant was $4,858; average loan $6,249. 30% of total undergraduate aid awarded as scholarships/grants, 70% as loans/jobs. **Non-need-based:** Awarded to 926 full-time undergraduates, including 257 freshmen. Scholarships awarded for academics, alumni affiliation, athletics, leadership, music/drama, religious affiliation.

Application procedures. Admission: No deadline. $30 fee, may be waived for applicants with need. Admission notification on a rolling basis beginning on or about 9/1. **Financial aid:** Priority date 3/1; no closing date. FAFSA required. Applicants notified on a rolling basis starting 2/15; must reply within 4 week(s) of notification.

Academics. Special study options: Accelerated study, combined bachelor's/graduate degree, cross-registration, distance learning, double major, dual enrollment of high school students, exchange student, independent study, internships, liberal arts/career combination, student-designed major, study abroad, teacher certification program, Washington semester. **Credit/placement by examination:** AP, CLEP, IB, SAT, ACT, institutional tests. 30 credit hours maximum toward bachelor's degree. **Support services:** Learning center, reduced course load, remedial instruction, study skills assistance, tutoring, writing center.

Majors. Biology: General, biochemistry. **Business:** Accounting/business management, administrative services, business admin, marketing, office management. **Communications:** Communications/speech/rhetoric, journalism, organizational, public relations. **Conservation:** Environmental studies. **Education:** General, biology, business, chemistry, developmentally delayed, elementary, emotionally handicapped, English, health, history, kindergarten/preschool, learning disabled, mathematics, mentally handicapped, middle, multi-level teacher, multiple handicapped, music, physical, science, secondary, social science, social studies, special ed. **English:** English lit. **Health services:** Athletic training, clinical lab technology, predental, premedicine, preop/surgical nursing, prepharmacy, preveterinary. **History:** General. **Liberal arts:** Humanities. **Math:** General. **Parks/recreation:** General, health/fitness, sports admin. **Philosophy/religion:** Philosophy, religion. **Physical sciences:** Chemistry. **Psychology:** General. **Social sciences:** General, sociology. **Theology:** Bible, theology, youth ministry. **Visual/performing arts:** Commercial/advertising art, music.

Most popular majors. Business/marketing 12%, education 14%, health sciences 15%, parks/recreation 7%, philosophy/religious studies 10%.

Computing on campus. 58 workstations in dormitories, library, computer center. Dormitories wired for high-speed internet access. Online library, wireless network available.

Student life. Freshman orientation: Mandatory. Preregistration for classes offered. 3-day program prior to fall semester; includes service day. **Policies:** Students required to live on campus until age 23. Religious observance required. **Housing:** Guaranteed on-campus for freshmen. Single-sex dorms, special housing for disabled available. $175 fully refundable deposit,

deadline 8/1. **Activities:** Bands, campus ministries, choral groups, drama, music ensembles, musical theater, student government, student newspaper, Science Club, Christian Ministries Council, Multicultural Student Union, Fellowship of Christian Athletes, CHUMS.

Athletics. NAIA. **Intercollegiate:** Baseball M, basketball, cheerleading, cross-country, football (tackle) M, soccer, softball W, tennis, track and field, volleyball W. **Intramural:** Basketball, football (non-tackle), racquetball, soccer, volleyball. **Team name:** Blue Jays.

Student services. Chaplain/spiritual director, career counseling, student employment services, financial aid counseling, minority student services, placement for graduates. **Physically disabled:** Services for visually, hearing impaired.

Contact. E-mail: admissions@tabor.edu
Phone: (620) 947-3121 ext. 1723 Toll-free number: (800) 822-6799
Fax: (620) 947-6276
Linda Cantwell, Vice President for Enrollment Management & Marketing, Tabor College, 400 South Jefferson, Hillsboro, KS 67063-7135

University of Kansas
Lawrence, Kansas
www.ku.edu

CB member
CB code: 6871

▶ Public 4-year university
▶ Commuter campus in small city
▶ 18,899 degree-seeking undergraduates: 10% part-time, 49% women
▶ 6,226 graduate students
▶ 93% of applicants admitted
▶ SAT or ACT (ACT writing optional) required
▶ 61% graduate within 6 years; 43% enter graduate study

General. Founded in 1866. Regionally accredited. **Degrees:** 3,818 bachelor's awarded; master's, professional, doctoral offered. **ROTC:** Army, Naval, Air Force. **Location:** 40 miles from Kansas City, 30 miles from Topeka. **Calendar:** Semester, extensive summer session. **Full-time faculty:** 1,076 total; 95% have terminal degrees, 17% minority, 36% women. **Part-time faculty:** 367 total; 45% have terminal degrees, 10% minority, 50% women. **Class size:** 42% < 20, 41% 20-39, 5% 40-49, 7% 50-99, 5% >100. **Special facilities:** 12 libraries including art and architecture, engineering, science, medicine, music, government documents and maps, rare books, manuscripts, and regional collections; art and natural history museums, space technology center, Institute for Life Span Studies, Performing Arts Center and Organ Recital Hall, Kansas Ecological Reserves, design lab, flight research lab, radar systems and remote sensing lab, film studio, Center for the Humanities, Multicultural Resource Center.

Freshman class profile. 10,035 applied, 9,306 admitted, 3,580 enrolled.

Mid 50% test scores		Rank in top quarter:	57%
ACT composite:	22-28	Rank in top tenth:	27%
GPA 3.75 or higher:	38%	Return as sophomores:	80%
GPA 3.50-3.74:	18%	Out-of-state:	28%
GPA 3.0-3.49:	27%	Live on campus:	58%
GPA 2.0-2.99:	17%	International:	2%

Basis for selection. Admission to College of Liberal Arts and Sciences requires one of following for in-state students: minimum ACT score of 21 or SAT score of 980 (exclusive of Writing), rank in top third of high school class, or completion of required college preparatory curriculum with 2.0 GPA. For out-of-state students: minimum test scores are 24 on ACT or 1090 on SAT (exclusive of Writing); minimum GPA 2.5 on college preparatory curriculum; rank in top third of high school class. Admission policies for other colleges within university may vary. Audition required for music performance, music education, music therapy, and dance. Essay and portfolio required for admission to Visual Art majors. **Home schooled:** Admission based on test scores.

High school preparation. College-preparatory program required. 13 units required; 16 recommended. Required and recommended units include English 4, mathematics 3-4, social studies 3, science 3 and foreign language 2. 1 science unit must be chemistry or physics. 4 units mathematics recommended for mathematics, engineering and architecture majors. Social studies units include history.

2011-2012 Annual costs. Tuition/fees: $9,222; $22,608 out-of-state. Room/board: $7,080. Books/supplies: $850. Personal expenses: $2,416.

2010-2011 Financial aid. Need-based: 2,486 full-time freshmen applied for aid; 1,695 were judged to have need; 1,637 of these received aid. Average need met was 60%. Average scholarship/grant was $5,692; average loan $3,185. 52% of total undergraduate aid awarded as scholarships/grants, 48%

as loans/jobs. **Non-need-based:** Awarded to 4,498 full-time undergraduates, including 1,421 freshmen. Scholarships awarded for academics, alumni affiliation, art, athletics, leadership, minority status, music/drama, ROTC, state residency.

Application procedures. Admission: Priority date 11/1; deadline 4/1 (receipt date). $30 fee. Admission notification on a rolling basis beginning on or about 9/1. Must reply by May 1 or within 2 week(s) if notified thereafter. **Financial aid:** Priority date 3/1; no closing date. FAFSA required. Applicants notified on a rolling basis starting 4/1; must reply within 2 week(s) of notification.

Academics. Special study options: Accelerated study, combined bachelor's/graduate degree, cooperative education, distance learning, double major, dual enrollment of high school students, ESL, honors, independent study, internships, liberal arts/career combination, study abroad, teacher certification program, Washington semester. **Credit/placement by examination:** AP, CLEP, IB, SAT, ACT, institutional tests. **Support services:** Learning center, remedial instruction, study skills assistance, tutoring, writing center.

Honors college/program. Students should have an ACT composite score of 30 or higher or an SAT combined verbal and math score of 1320 or higher, a rigorous college preparatory curriculum, an un-weighted GPA of 3.75 or higher, participation in activities that supplement academic work and/or demonstrate community involvement and a sense of social responsibility, and an essay that reveals intellectual curiosity and academic rigor. Admission is competitive.

Majors. Architecture: History/criticism. **Area/ethnic studies:** African, American, European, Latin American, Russian/Slavic, women's. **Biology:** General, biochemistry, microbiology, molecular. **Business:** General, accounting, business admin, finance, logistics, management information systems, marketing. **Communications:** Communications/speech/rhetoric, journalism. **Computer sciences:** General. **Conservation:** Environmental studies. **Education:** Art, early childhood, elementary, English, foreign languages, history, mathematics, middle, music, physical, science, secondary, social studies. **Engineering:** Aerospace, applied physics, architectural, chemical, civil, computer, electrical, mechanical, petroleum. **English:** English lit. **Foreign languages:** Classics, East Asian, French, Germanic, linguistics, Slavic, Spanish. **Health services:** Athletic training, communication disorders, community health services, music therapy. **History:** General. **Human services:** General, social work. **Liberal arts:** Arts/sciences, humanities. **Math:** General. **Parks/recreation:** Health/fitness. **Philosophy/religion:** Philosophy, religion. **Physical sciences:** Astronomy, atmospheric science, chemistry, geology, physics. **Psychology:** General, developmental. **Social sciences:** Anthropology, economics, geography, political science, sociology. **Visual/performing arts:** Art history/conservation, brass instruments, ceramics, dance, design, dramatic, fiber arts, film/cinema/video, graphic design, illustration, interior design, metal/jewelry, music, music performance, music theory/composition, musicology, painting, percussion instruments, piano/keyboard, printmaking, sculpture, stringed instruments, studio arts, theater design, voice/opera, woodwind instruments.

Most popular majors. Biology 6%, business/marketing 14%, communications/journalism 13%, engineering/engineering technologies 6%, social sciences 9%, visual/performing arts 8%.

Computing on campus. 1,500 workstations in dormitories, library, computer center, student center. Dormitories wired for high-speed internet access and linked to campus network. Commuter students can connect to campus network. Online course registration, online library, helpline, student web hosting, wireless network available.

Student life. Freshman orientation: Available. Preregistration for classes offered. One-day program throughout summer; several 2 day programs available. **Policies:** No alcohol or guns permitted on campus, no smoking in any buildings. Parking by permit only. **Housing:** Coed dorms, single-sex dorms, apartments, cooperative housing, fraternity/sorority housing, wellness housing available. Scholarship halls available to students with high scholastic achievement and financial need. **Activities:** Bands, choral groups, dance, drama, international student organizations, literary magazine, music ensembles, musical theater, opera, radio station, student government, student newspaper, symphony orchestra, TV station, over 600 student organizations and activities available.

Athletics. NCAA. **Intercollegiate:** Baseball M, basketball, cross-country, football (tackle) M, golf, rowing (crew) W, soccer W, softball W, swimming W, tennis W, track and field, volleyball W. **Intramural:** Basketball, bowling, football (non-tackle), golf, racquetball, soccer, softball, table tennis, tennis, volleyball. **Team name:** Jayhawks.

Student services. Adult student services, alcohol/substance abuse counseling, career counseling, services for economically disadvantaged, student employment services, financial aid counseling, health services, legal services, minority student services, on-campus daycare, personal counseling, placement for graduates, veterans' counselor, women's services. **Physically disabled:** Services for visually, speech, hearing impaired.

Contact. E-mail: adm@ku.edu
Phone: (785) 864-3911 Fax: (785) 864-5017
Lisa Pinamonti Kress, Director of Admissions, University of Kansas, 1502 Iowa Street, Lawrence, KS 66045-7576

University of Kansas Medical Center
Kansas City, Kansas
www.kumc.edu   CB code: 0414

- Public two-year upper-division university and health science college
- Commuter campus in very large city

General. Founded in 1905. Regionally accredited. **Degrees:** 227 bachelor's awarded; master's, professional, doctoral offered. **Location:** Downtown. **Calendar:** Semester, limited summer session.

Student profile. 449 degree-seeking undergraduates, 1,902 degree-seeking graduate students. 99 applied as first time-transfer students.

Women:	83%	International:	3%
African American:	4%	Part-time:	17%
Asian American:	4%	Out-of-state:	18%
Hispanic American:	5%	25 or older:	40%

Basis for selection. College transcript required. Admissions regulations, policies, and application closing dates vary by degree program. Transfer accepted as juniors, seniors.

2011-2012 Annual costs. Tuition/fees: $7,774; $19,777 out-of-state. Books/supplies: $1,800. Personal expenses: $5,226.

Financial aid. Need-based: 260 applied for aid; 208 were judged to have need; 208 of these received aid. Average need met was 52%. 40% of total undergraduate aid awarded as scholarships/grants, 60% as loans/jobs. **Non-need-based:** Awarded to 23 undergraduates. Scholarships awarded for academics, leadership, state residency.

Application procedures. Admission: $60 fee. Application must be submitted online. Admissions deadlines vary by academic school and program.

Academics. Assessment and reading skills screened. Assistance offered in reviewing APA-style papers. **Special study options:** Combined bachelor's/graduate degree, distance learning, ESL, honors, independent study, internships, study abroad. **Credit/placement by examination:** AP, CLEP.

Majors. Health services: Clinical lab science, cytotechnology, medical records admin, nursing (RN), respiratory therapy technology.

Computing on campus. 120 workstations in library, computer center, student center. Commuter students can connect to campus network. Online library, helpline, student web hosting, wireless network available.

Student life. Activities: Campus ministries, choral groups, international student organizations, student government, American Indian Health Student Association, Care 4 Kids, Christian Medical Fellowship, Chinese Student and Scholar's Association, community outreach program, Healthcare Professionals for Human Rights, Muslim student association, student governing council, Student World AIDS Group, Students for a National Healthcare Plan.

Athletics. Intramural: Basketball, racquetball, soccer, softball, volleyball.

Student services. Chaplain/spiritual director, career counseling, financial aid counseling, health services, legal services, personal counseling. **Physically disabled:** Services for visually, speech, hearing impaired.

Contact. E-mail: kumcregistrar@kumc.edu
Phone: (913) 588-7055 Fax: (913) 588-4697
University of Kansas Medical Center, Office of the Registrar, Mail Stop 4029, Kansas City, KS 66160-7116

University of Phoenix: Wichita
Wichita, Kansas
www.phoenix.edu

- For-profit 4-year university
- Large city
- 159 degree-seeking undergraduates

General. Regionally accredited. **Degrees:** 27 bachelor's awarded; master's offered. **Calendar:** Differs by program. **Full-time faculty:** 5 total. **Part-time faculty:** 47 total.

Basis for selection. Open admission, but selective for some programs.

2011-2012 Annual costs. Estimated costs as of August 2011: per-credit-hour charge, $380 to $415, depending upon level and course of study; electronic course materials fee, $95, if applicable. Book and material charges may vary by course and program. All fees are subject to change.

Application procedures. Admission: No deadline. No application fee. **Financial aid:** No deadline.

Academics. Credit/placement by examination: AP, CLEP.

Majors. Business: Accounting, business admin, marketing.

Contact. Marc Booker, Director of Admission and Evaluation, University of Phoenix: Wichita, 3020 North Cypress Drive, Suite 150, Wichita, KS 67226

University of St. Mary
Leavenworth, Kansas
www.stmary.edu   CB code: 6630

▸ Private 4-year university affiliated with Roman Catholic Church
▸ Residential campus in large town
▸ 710 degree-seeking undergraduates: 24% part-time, 64% women, 14% African American, 2% Asian American, 6% Hispanic American, 1% Native American, 1% international
▸ 227 degree-seeking graduate students
▸ 55% of applicants admitted
▸ SAT or ACT (ACT writing optional) required
▸ 42% graduate within 6 years

General. Founded in 1923. Regionally accredited. **Degrees:** 142 bachelor's awarded; master's offered. **ROTC:** Army, Air Force. **Location:** 26 miles from Kansas City. **Calendar:** Semester, limited summer session. **Full-time faculty:** 44 total; 64% have terminal degrees, 2% minority, 57% women. **Part-time faculty:** 74 total; 15% have terminal degrees, 5% minority, 64% women. **Class size:** 71% < 20, 24% 20-39, 5% 40-49. **Special facilities:** Sacred Scripture and History of the Catholic Church in Kansas collections in library.

Freshman class profile. 751 applied, 416 admitted, 109 enrolled.

Mid 50% test scores		Return as sophomores:	74%
SAT critical reading:	400-520	Out-of-state:	50%
SAT math:	420-540	Live on campus:	90%
ACT composite:	18-24	International:	1%
End year in good standing:	69%		

Basis for selection. 2.5 GPA, 18 ACT, 870 SAT (exclusive of Writing) required. Applicants below required GPA or ACT/SAT may be considered for admission. Portfolio recommended for fine and applied arts majors.

High school preparation. College-preparatory program recommended. 12 units required; 24 recommended. Required and recommended units include English 4, mathematics 2-4, social studies 2, history 2-4, science 2-4 (laboratory 2), foreign language 2 and academic electives 2. 1-2 computer programming recommended.

2011-2012 Annual costs. Tuition/fees: $20,770. Room/board: $6,600. Books/supplies: $1,200. Personal expenses: $2,060.

2010-2011 Financial aid. Need-based: 112 full-time freshmen applied for aid; 106 were judged to have need; 106 of these received aid. Average need met was 72%. Average scholarship/grant was $13,923; average loan $3,492. 57% of total undergraduate aid awarded as scholarships/grants, 43% as loans/jobs. **Non-need-based:** Awarded to 100 full-time undergraduates, including 18 freshmen. Scholarships awarded for academics, art, athletics, leadership, music/drama.

Application procedures. Admission: No deadline. $25 fee, may be waived for applicants with need. Admission notification on a rolling basis. Must reply by May 1 or within 4 week(s) if notified thereafter. **Financial aid:** Priority date 4/1; no closing date. FAFSA required. Applicants notified on a rolling basis starting 2/1; must reply within 2 week(s) of notification.

Academics. Special study options: Accelerated study, distance learning, double major, dual enrollment of high school students, exchange student, honors, independent study, internships, student-designed major, study abroad, teacher certification program. Degree completion programs. **Credit/placement by examination:** AP, CLEP, IB, SAT, ACT, institutional tests. 30 credit hours maximum toward bachelor's degree. **Support services:** Learning center, remedial instruction, study skills assistance, tutoring.

Majors. Biology: General. **Business:** General, accounting, business admin. **Computer sciences:** Information technology. **Education:** Elementary. **English:** English lit. **Health services:** Nursing (RN). **History:** General. **Liberal arts:** Arts/sciences. **Math:** General. **Parks/recreation:** Sports admin. **Physical sciences:** Chemistry. **Psychology:** General, community. **Social sciences:** Criminology, political science. **Theology:** Pastoral counseling, theology. **Visual/performing arts:** Art, dramatic. **Work/family studies:** Child development.

Most popular majors. Business/marketing 13%, education 9%, health sciences 36%, parks/recreation 6%, psychology 10%, social sciences 8%.

Computing on campus. 45 workstations in library, student center. Dormitories wired for high-speed internet access and linked to campus network. Commuter students can connect to campus network. Online course registration, helpline, repair service, wireless network available.

Student life. Freshman orientation: Mandatory. Preregistration for classes offered. Three-day program at beginning of fall semester. **Housing:** Guaranteed on-campus for freshmen. Coed dorms available. $100 nonrefundable deposit. **Activities:** Bands, campus ministries, choral groups, drama, international student organizations, literary magazine, music ensembles, musical theater, opera, student government, Bacchus, Aristotle Club, Amnesty International, Students in Free Enterprise, Young Democrats, Campus Republicans.

Athletics. NAIA. **Intercollegiate:** Baseball M, basketball, cheerleading, cross-country, football (tackle) M, soccer, softball W, track and field, volleyball W. **Intramural:** Basketball, bowling, racquetball, softball, table tennis, volleyball. **Team name:** Spires.

Student services. Adult student services, alcohol/substance abuse counseling, chaplain/spiritual director, career counseling, student employment services, financial aid counseling, health services, on-campus daycare, personal counseling, placement for graduates, veterans' counselor.

Contact. E-mail: admiss@stmary.edu
Phone: (913) 758-6118 Toll-free number: (800) 752-7043
Fax: (913) 758-6140
Ken Wuerzberger, Director of Admissions, University of St. Mary, 4100 South Fourth Street Trafficway, Leavenworth, KS 66048

Washburn University
Topeka, Kansas
www.washburn.edu   CB code: 6928

▸ Public 4-year university
▸ Commuter campus in small city
▸ 5,695 degree-seeking undergraduates: 28% part-time, 59% women
▸ 857 degree-seeking graduate students
▸ 41% graduate within 6 years

General. Founded in 1865. Regionally accredited. **Degrees:** 763 bachelor's, 106 associate awarded; master's, professional offered. **ROTC:** Army, Naval, Air Force. **Location:** 60 miles from Kansas City. **Calendar:** Semester, extensive summer session. **Full-time faculty:** 265 total; 87% have terminal degrees, 16% minority, 51% women. **Part-time faculty:** 293 total; 35% have terminal degrees, 10% minority, 57% women. **Class size:** 40% < 20, 51% 20-39, 5% 40-49, 4% 50-99. **Special facilities:** Concert hall, observatory, planetarium, 30-acre natural study and research area.

Freshman class profile. 1,817 applied, 1,817 admitted, 935 enrolled.

Mid 50% test scores		Rank in top tenth:	14%
ACT composite:	19-25	End year in good standing:	69%
GPA 3.75 or higher:	29%	Return as sophomores:	62%
GPA 3.50-3.74:	16%	Out-of-state:	6%
GPA 3.0-3.49:	30%	Live on campus:	37%
GPA 2.0-2.99:	24%	Fraternities:	6%
Rank in top quarter:	34%	Sororities:	11%

Basis for selection. Open admission, but selective for some programs. Special requirements for health science programs, nursing, school of business, and education. ACT or ASSET required of all students for placement purposes.

High school preparation. College-preparatory program recommended. Recommended units include English 4, mathematics 3, social studies 3, history 1, science 3, foreign language 2 and computer science 1.

2011-2012 Annual costs. Tuition/fees: $6,566; $14,756 out-of-state. Room/board: $6,059. Books/supplies: $1,000. Personal expenses: $2,538.

2011-2012 Financial aid. **Need-based:** 796 full-time freshmen applied for aid; 572 were judged to have need; 572 of these received aid. Average need met was 39%. Average scholarship/grant was $4,746; average loan $3,363. 42% of total undergraduate aid awarded as scholarships/grants, 58% as loans/jobs. **Non-need-based:** Awarded to 1,860 full-time undergraduates, including 523 freshmen. Scholarships awarded for academics, alumni affiliation, art, athletics, job skills, leadership, minority status, music/drama, religious affiliation, ROTC, state residency.

Application procedures. **Admission:** Closing date 8/1. $20 fee. Admission notification on a rolling basis beginning on or about 9/1. **Financial aid:** Priority date 2/15; no closing date. FAFSA required. Applicants notified on a rolling basis starting 4/1; must reply within 4 week(s) of notification.

Academics. **Special study options:** Cooperative education, cross-registration, distance learning, double major, dual enrollment of high school students, ESL, honors, independent study, internships, liberal arts/career combination, student-designed major, study abroad, teacher certification program. Transformational Experience. **Credit/placement by examination:** AP, CLEP, institutional tests. **Support services:** Learning center, remedial instruction, study skills assistance, tutoring, writing center.

Majors. **Biology:** General, biochemistry. **Business:** General, accounting, business admin, finance, managerial economics, marketing. **Communications:** Communications/speech/rhetoric, media studies. **Computer sciences:** General. **Education:** General, art, biology, chemistry, early childhood, elementary, English, French, German, history, mathematics, music, physical, secondary, Spanish. **English:** English lit. **Foreign languages:** French, German, Spanish. **Health services:** Athletic training, clinical lab science, nursing (RN), predental, premedicine, prepharmacy, preveterinary, sonography. **History:** General. **Human services:** General, social work. **Liberal arts:** Arts/sciences. **Math:** General. **Parks/recreation:** Exercise sciences, health/fitness, sports admin. **Philosophy/religion:** Philosophy, religion. **Physical sciences:** Chemistry, physics, theoretical physics. **Protective services:** Corrections, criminal justice, forensics, law enforcement admin, police science, security services. **Psychology:** General. **Social sciences:** Anthropology, economics, political science, sociology. **Visual/performing arts:** General, art, art history/conservation, dramatic, music, music performance, studio arts.

Most popular majors. Business/marketing 17%, communications/journalism 6%, education 8%, health sciences 28%, security/protective services 11%.

Computing on campus. 577 workstations in dormitories, library, computer center, student center. Dormitories wired for high-speed internet access and linked to campus network. Commuter students can connect to campus network. Online course registration, online library, helpline, student web hosting, wireless network available.

Student life. **Freshman orientation:** Available. Preregistration for classes offered. Full day session in summer; 3-day session prior to start of classes. **Housing:** Coed dorms, apartments, fraternity/sorority housing, wellness housing available. $200 partly refundable deposit. **Activities:** Bands, campus ministries, choral groups, dance, drama, film society, international student organizations, literary magazine, music ensembles, Model UN, musical theater, student government, student newspaper, symphony orchestra, TV station, College Republicans, College Democrats, Circle K, Hispanic American Leadership Organization, Black student union, Literacy Education Action Project, Community of Caring Club, Christian Challenge, campus ministry, Alternative Spring Break, Student Atheists of Washburn.

Athletics. NCAA. **Intercollegiate:** Baseball M, basketball, cheerleading, football (tackle) M, golf M, soccer W, softball W, tennis, volleyball W. **Intramural:** Badminton, basketball, football (non-tackle), golf, handball, soccer, softball, table tennis, tennis, volleyball. **Team name:** Ichabods.

Student services. Adult student services, alcohol/substance abuse counseling, career counseling, services for economically disadvantaged, student employment services, financial aid counseling, health services, minority student services, personal counseling, placement for graduates, veterans' counselor. **Physically disabled:** Services for visually, hearing impaired.

Contact. E-mail: admissions@washburn.edu
Phone: (785) 670-1030 Toll-free number: (877) 281-2637
Fax: (785) 670-1113
Susan Smith, Director, Washburn University, 1700 SW College Avenue, Morgan 114, Topeka, KS 66621

Wichita State University
Wichita, Kansas
www.wichita.edu   CB code: 6884

- Public 4-year university
- Commuter campus in large city

- 11,320 degree-seeking undergraduates: 27% part-time, 54% women, 7% African American, 6% Asian American, 7% Hispanic American, 1% Native American, 5% international
- 2,800 degree-seeking graduate students
- 94% of applicants admitted
- 43% graduate within 6 years

General. Founded in 1895. Regionally accredited. **Degrees:** 1,959 bachelor's, 32 associate awarded; master's, professional, doctoral offered. **Calendar:** Semester, extensive summer session. **Full-time faculty:** 445 total; 81% have terminal degrees, 18% minority, 42% women. **Part-time faculty:** 74 total; 38% have terminal degrees, 11% minority, 61% women. **Class size:** 43% < 20, 38% 20-39, 9% 40-49, 9% 50-99, 2% >100. **Special facilities:** Sculpture garden, wind tunnels, Marcusson pipe organ, flow-visualization water tunnel, National Aviation Research Institute, observatory, anthropology museum, rock climbing wall, bowling alley.

Freshman class profile. 3,304 applied, 3,102 admitted, 1,366 enrolled.

Mid 50% test scores			
SAT critical reading:	440-620	Rank in top tenth:	23%
SAT math:	480-630	End year in good standing:	73%
ACT composite:	21-26	Return as sophomores:	73%
GPA 3.75 or higher:	33%	Out-of-state:	6%
GPA 3.50-3.74:	16%	Live on campus:	36%
GPA 3.0-3.49:	31%	International:	3%
GPA 2.0-2.99:	18%	Fraternities:	12%
Rank in top quarter:	48%	Sororities:	12%

Basis for selection. In-state criteria: 21 ACT or greater or SAT score of 980 or greater, rank in top 1/3 of high school graduating class, or minimum 2.00 GPA in pre-college curriculum. Out-of-state criteria: 21 ACT or greater or SAT score of 980 or greater, rank in top 1/3 of high school graduating class, or minimum 2.5 GPA in pre-college curriculum. **Home schooled:** State high school equivalency certificate required. ACT required.

High school preparation. College-preparatory program recommended. 13 units required. Required units include English 4, mathematics 3, social studies 3 and science 3.

2011-2012 Annual costs. Tuition/fees: $6,191; $14,225 out-of-state. Room/board: $6,350. Books/supplies: $975. Personal expenses: $1,702.

2010-2011 Financial aid. **Need-based:** 1,063 full-time freshmen applied for aid; 477 were judged to have need; 471 of these received aid. Average need met was 47%. Average scholarship/grant was $4,681; average loan $3,135. 47% of total undergraduate aid awarded as scholarships/grants, 53% as loans/jobs. **Non-need-based:** Awarded to 3,015 full-time undergraduates, including 771 freshmen. Scholarships awarded for academics, alumni affiliation, art, athletics, leadership, music/drama.

Application procedures. **Admission:** No deadline. $30 fee. Admission notification on a rolling basis. **Financial aid:** Priority date 3/1; no closing date. FAFSA required. Applicants notified on a rolling basis starting 3/15; must reply within 2 week(s) of notification.

Academics. 24-hour study room with Internet access. All library databases and other software maintained for student use. **Special study options:** Accelerated study, cooperative education, cross-registration, distance learning, double major, dual enrollment of high school students, ESL, exchange student, honors, independent study, internships, liberal arts/career combination, study abroad, teacher certification program, Washington semester. **Credit/placement by examination:** AP, CLEP, IB, SAT, ACT, institutional tests. 30 credit hours maximum toward associate degree, 60 toward bachelor's. **Support services:** Learning center, pre-admission summer program, reduced course load, remedial instruction, study skills assistance, tutoring, writing center.

Honors college/program. Students with less than 24 credit hours must have a high school GPA of 3.7 or higher or an ACT composite score of 27. Students with 24 or more credit hours must have a college GPA of 3.5 or higher. Approximately 123 freshmen join the Honors Program each fall semester.

Majors. **Area/ethnic studies:** General, women's. **Biology:** General, biochemistry. **Business:** Accounting, business admin, entrepreneurial studies, finance, human resources, international, management information systems, marketing. **Communications:** Communications/speech/rhetoric. **Computer sciences:** General, computer science. **Education:** General, art, early childhood, elementary, ESL, music, physical, secondary. **Engineering:** General, aerospace, biomedical, computer, electrical, industrial, manufacturing, mechanical. **English:** English lit. **Foreign languages:** General, French, Latin, Spanish. **Health services:** Athletic training, clinical lab science, communication disorders, dental hygiene, health care admin. **History:** General. **Human services:** Social work. **Liberal arts:** Arts/sciences. **Math:** General. **Parks/recreation:** Exercise sciences, sports admin. **Philosophy/religion:** Philosophy. **Physical sciences:** Chemistry, geology, physics. **Protective services:**

Criminal justice, forensics. **Psychology:** General. **Social sciences:** Anthropology, economics, political science, sociology. **Visual/performing arts:** General, art, art history/conservation, dramatic, graphic design, music, music performance, music theory/composition, musical theater, studio arts, voice/opera.

Most popular majors. Business/marketing 23%, education 11%, engineering/engineering technologies 9%, health sciences 14%.

Computing on campus. 1,500 workstations in dormitories, library, computer center, student center. Dormitories wired for high-speed internet access and linked to campus network. Commuter students can connect to campus network. Online course registration, online library, helpline, wireless network available.

Student life. Freshman orientation: Mandatory. Preregistration for classes offered. Held prior to fall semester and spring semester. **Policies:** Freshmen are required to live on campus, however, exceptions are made for freshmen who are 21 or older, married, living with a parent, legal gaurdian, grandparent, aunt or uncle in the greater Sedgwick County area, are taking fewer than 9 credit hours, or living in official Greek housing. **Housing:** Guaranteed on-campus for freshmen. Coed dorms, special housing for disabled, apartments, fraternity/sorority housing available. $200 nonrefundable deposit, deadline 8/19. Special floors available for Fine Arts, Emory Lindquist Honors Program, Shocker Scholars, Health Professions students. **Activities:** Bands, campus ministries, choral groups, dance, drama, film society, international student organizations, literary magazine, music ensembles, Model UN, musical theater, opera, radio station, student government, student newspaper, symphony orchestra, TV station, Campus Crusade for Christ, College Republicans, Chinese Student Friendship Association, Black Student Union, Hispanic American Leadership Association, Students in Free Enterprise, Association of Hindu Students, Muslim Student Association, That Gay Group, Emory Lindquist Honor Society.

Athletics. NCAA. **Intercollegiate:** Baseball M, basketball, cheerleading, cross-country, golf, softball W, tennis, track and field, volleyball W. **Intramural:** Badminton, basketball, football (non-tackle), golf, racquetball, rowing (crew), soccer, softball, swimming, table tennis, tennis, volleyball. **Team name:** Shockers.

Student services. Adult student services, alcohol/substance abuse counseling, chaplain/spiritual director, career counseling, services for economically disadvantaged, student employment services, financial aid counseling, health services, minority student services, on-campus daycare, personal counseling, placement for graduates, veterans' counselor, women's services. **Physically disabled:** Services for visually, speech, hearing impaired.

Contact. E-mail: admissions@wichita.edu
Phone: (316) 978-3085 Toll-free number: (800) 362-2594
Fax: (316) 978-3174
Bobby Gandu, Director of Admissions, Wichita State University, 1845 Fairmount, Box 124, Wichita, KS 67260-0124

Kentucky

Alice Lloyd College
Pippa Passes, Kentucky
www.alc.edu   **CB code: 1098**

- Private 4-year liberal arts college
- Residential campus in rural community
- 593 degree-seeking undergraduates
- 33% of applicants admitted
- SAT or ACT (ACT writing optional) required

General. Founded in 1923. Regionally accredited. **Degrees:** 88 bachelor's awarded. **Location:** 150 miles from Lexington; 100 miles from Huntington, West Virginia. **Calendar:** Semester. **Full-time faculty:** 29 total. **Part-time faculty:** 11 total. **Class size:** 41% < 20, 54% 20-39, 5% 40-49. **Special facilities:** Appalachian history collection, photographic archives.

Freshman class profile. 2,250 applied, 743 admitted, 178 enrolled.

Mid 50% test scores			
SAT critical reading:	440-530	GPA 3.0-3.49:	33%
SAT math:	470-600	GPA 2.0-2.99:	23%
SAT writing:	420-560	Rank in top quarter:	58%
ACT composite:	20-22	Rank in top tenth:	21%
GPA 3.75 or higher:	21%	Out-of-state:	21%
GPA 3.50-3.74:	21%	Live on campus:	91%

Basis for selection. High school record and test scores important. Essay and interview recommended. **Home schooled:** Transcript of courses and grades, letter of recommendation (nonparent) required. Interview highly recommended.

High school preparation. 12 units required. Required units include English 4, mathematics 3, social studies 2 and science 3.

2011-2012 Annual costs. Tuition/fees: $9,500. Guaranteed tuition for students from 108-county central Appalachian service area in Kentucky, West Virginia, Virginia, Tennessee, and Ohio. Room/board: $4,650. Books/supplies: $950. Personal expenses: $1,300.

Financial aid. **Non-need-based:** Scholarships awarded for athletics, minority status, state residency. **Additional information:** All students receive financial aid through student work program. No student denied admission because of inability to pay. All full-time students required to work minimum of 10 hours per week.

Application procedures. **Admission:** Priority date 5/1; no deadline. No application fee. Admission notification on a rolling basis beginning on or about 9/1. **Financial aid:** Priority date 3/15; no closing date. FAFSA required. Applicants notified on a rolling basis starting 4/1; must reply within 6 week(s) of notification.

Academics. Scholarships for graduate work following graduation. **Special study options:** Double major, independent study, internships, liberal arts/career combination, student-designed major, study abroad, teacher certification program, Washington semester. **Credit/placement by examination:** AP, CLEP, IB, SAT, ACT, institutional tests. 30 credit hours maximum toward bachelor's degree. Limited number of hours of credit by examination may be counted toward degree, decided on individual basis. **Support services:** Reduced course load, remedial instruction, study skills assistance, tutoring, writing center.

Majors. **Biology:** General. **Business:** Business admin. **Education:** Biology, elementary, English, mathematics, middle, physical, science, secondary, social studies. **English:** English lit. **History:** General. **Parks/recreation:** General. **Social sciences:** General.

Most popular majors. Biology 26%, business/marketing 18%, education 23%, English 6%, history 10%, social sciences 11%.

Computing on campus. 80 workstations in library, computer center. Dormitories wired for high-speed internet access and linked to campus network. Online library, helpline, repair service, wireless network available.

Student life. Freshman orientation: Mandatory. Preregistration for classes offered. Held 3 days before start of first semester. **Policies:** Zero tolerance of on-campus alcohol and/or drug usage or possession. **Housing:** Guaranteed on-campus for all undergraduates. Single-sex dorms available. $50 deposit, deadline 5/15. **Activities:** Choral groups, drama, radio station, student government, student newspaper, Students for Christ, Baptist student union, cultural diversity club, children's outreach club, community service volunteers, Circle K.

Athletics. NAIA. **Intercollegiate:** Baseball M, basketball, cheerleading M, cross-country, softball W. **Intramural:** Basketball, bowling, football (non-tackle), golf, racquetball, soccer, softball, swimming, table tennis, tennis, volleyball, weight lifting. **Team name:** Eagles.

Student services. Alcohol/substance abuse counseling, career counseling, student employment services, financial aid counseling, health services, on-campus daycare, personal counseling, placement for graduates, veterans' counselor.

Contact. E-mail: admissions@alc.edu
Phone: (606) 368-6036 Toll-free number: (888) 280-4252
Fax: (606) 368-6215
Angela Phipps, Director of Admissions, Alice Lloyd College, 100 Purpose Road, Pippa Passes, KY 41844

Asbury University
Wilmore, Kentucky   **CB member**
www.asbury.edu   **CB code: 1019**

- Private 4-year university and liberal arts college affiliated with interdenominational tradition
- Residential campus in small town
- 1,333 degree-seeking undergraduates: 3% part-time, 61% women, 3% African American, 1% Asian American, 3% Hispanic American, 1% international
- 174 degree-seeking graduate students
- 63% of applicants admitted
- SAT or ACT (ACT writing optional), application essay required
- 70% graduate within 6 years

General. Founded in 1890. Regionally accredited. **Degrees:** 281 bachelor's, 2 associate awarded; master's offered. **ROTC:** Army, Air Force. **Location:** 20 miles from Lexington. **Calendar:** Semester, limited summer session. **Full-time faculty:** 86 total; 72% have terminal degrees, 4% minority, 28% women. **Part-time faculty:** 68 total; 29% have terminal degrees, 7% minority, 46% women. **Class size:** 62% < 20, 33% 20-39, 5% 40-49, less than 1% 50-99. **Special facilities:** TV and recording studios, film sets, news bureau, film sound stage, three back lots, black box theater, indoor riding arena, horse stables.

Freshman class profile. 1,427 applied, 899 admitted, 308 enrolled.

Mid 50% test scores			
SAT critical reading:	510-630	GPA 2.0-2.99:	13%
SAT math:	470-600	Rank in top quarter:	58%
ACT composite:	21-27	Rank in top tenth:	26%
GPA 3.75 or higher:	45%	Return as sophomores:	80%
GPA 3.50-3.74:	17%	Out-of-state:	60%
GPA 3.0-3.49:	25%	Live on campus:	96%
		International:	1%

Basis for selection. Careful consideration given to academic records, test scores, application essays, references, and ability to benefit. Probationary acceptance possible if GPA below 2.5. ACT required prior to admission to education department; both ACT and SAT required for presidential level scholarships. Interview recommended for music majors, academically weak applicants, scholarship applicants. Audition required for music majors. Portfolio recommended for art majors. **Home schooled:** Transcript of courses and grades, state high school equivalency certificate required.

High school preparation. College-preparatory program recommended. 15 units recommended. Recommended units include English 4, mathematics 3, social studies 1, history 1, science 2 (laboratory 2) and foreign language 2.

2011-2012 Annual costs. Tuition/fees: $24,229. Room/board: $5,634. Books/supplies: $815. Personal expenses: $1,240.

Financial aid. Non-need-based: Scholarships awarded for academics, alumni affiliation, art, athletics, leadership, minority status, music/drama, religious affiliation, ROTC.

Application procedures. Admission: Priority date 5/1; no deadline. $30 fee, may be waived for applicants with need, free for online applicants. Admission notification on a rolling basis. Confirmation of intention to enroll requires $200 pre-tuition deposit within 30 days of admission notification. **Financial aid:** Priority date 3/1; no closing date. Applicants notified on a rolling basis starting 1/31; must reply within 4 week(s) of notification.

Academics. **Special study options:** Double major, ESL, internships, study abroad, teacher certification program, urban semester, Washington semester. Exchange program with colleges in Christian College Consortium, 3-2 programs in engineering with the University of Kentucky. **Credit/placement by examination:** AP, CLEP, IB, SAT, ACT, institutional tests. **Support services:** Study skills assistance, tutoring, writing center.

Majors. **Biology:** General, biochemistry. **Business:** General, accounting, business admin. **Communications:** General, journalism. **Communications technology:** Radio/TV. **Education:** Art, elementary, middle, music, physical. **Engineering:** Pre-engineering. **English:** Creative writing, English lit. **Foreign languages:** Biblical, classics, French, Spanish. **General:** Equestrian studies. **Health services:** Prephysical therapy. **History:** General. **Human services:** Social work. **Math:** General, computational, financial. **Parks/recreation:** Facilities management, health/fitness, sports admin. **Philosophy/religion:** Philosophy. **Physical sciences:** Chemistry. **Psychology:** General. **Social sciences:** General, political science, sociology. **Theology:** Bible, missionary, religious ed, sacred music, youth ministry. **Visual/performing arts:** Dramatic, music, studio arts.

Most popular majors. Business/marketing 9%, communications/journalism 8%, communication technologies 11%, education 10%, English 6%, psychology 8%, theological studies 9%, visual/performing arts 6%.

Computing on campus. 200 workstations in dormitories, library, computer center, student center. Dormitories wired for high-speed internet access and linked to campus network. Commuter students can connect to campus network. Online course registration, online library, helpline, repair service, wireless network available.

Student life. **Freshman orientation:** Mandatory. Preregistration for classes offered. Held four days before start of classes. **Policies:** Christian values stressed. Religious observance required. **Housing:** Guaranteed on-campus for freshmen. Single-sex dorms, apartments available. **Activities:** Bands, campus ministries, choral groups, drama, literary magazine, music ensembles, musical theater, opera, radio station, student government, student newspaper, symphony orchestra, TV station, Christian service association, student fellowships, Impact, Asburians for Life, ministerial association, outdoors club.

Athletics. NAIA, NCCAA. **Intercollegiate:** Baseball M, basketball, cross-country, diving, golf, soccer, softball W, swimming, tennis, volleyball W. **Intramural:** Basketball, football (non-tackle), golf, racquetball, soccer, softball, volleyball. **Team name:** Eagles.

Student services. Adult student services, chaplain/spiritual director, career counseling, student employment services, financial aid counseling, health services, minority student services, personal counseling.

Contact. E-mail: admissions@asbury.edu
Phone: (859) 858-3511 ext. 2142 Toll-free number: (800) 888-1818
Fax: (859) 858-3921
Lisa Harper, Director of Admissions, Asbury University, One Macklem Drive, Wilmore, KY 40390-1198

Beckfield College
Florence, Kentucky
www.beckfield.edu
CB code: 3404

- For-profit 4-year business and health science college
- Commuter campus in large town
- 977 degree-seeking undergraduates
- Interview required

General. Accredited by ACICS. **Degrees:** 31 bachelor's, 196 associate awarded. **Location:** 10 miles from Cincinnati. **Calendar:** Quarter, extensive summer session. **Full-time faculty:** 14 total. **Part-time faculty:** 88 total. **Class size:** 100% < 20.

Freshman class profile. 101 enrolled.

Basis for selection. Open admission, but selective for some programs. Nursing program requires qualifying ACT/SAT scores. Certificate programs require an earned degree for admission. Personal training and medical massage therapy programs require qualifying ACT Compass scores. **Home schooled:** Transcript of courses and grades required. Accredited home study course will be considered for admission.

2011-2012 Annual costs. Tuition/fees: $14,481. Books and supplies expense includes $200 for a required Netbook. Books/supplies: $1,800. Personal expenses: $2,484.

Financial aid. All financial aid based on need. **Additional information:** Deadline for filing of financial aid forms is end of first week of classes.

Application procedures. **Admission:** No deadline. No application fee. **Financial aid:** FAFSA required. Applicants notified on a rolling basis.

Academics. **Special study options:** Combined bachelor's/graduate degree, independent study, internships. **Credit/placement by examination:** AP, CLEP, IB, institutional tests. **Support services:** Reduced course load, remedial instruction, study skills assistance, tutoring.

Majors. **Business:** Business admin. **Health services:** Nursing (RN). **Protective services:** Law enforcement admin.

Computing on campus. 90 workstations in library, computer center. Online library, wireless network available.

Student life. **Freshman orientation:** Mandatory. Preregistration for classes offered. Held for half day 3 days before beginning of quarter.

Student services. Alcohol/substance abuse counseling, career counseling, student employment services, financial aid counseling, personal counseling, placement for graduates, veterans' counselor.

Contact. Phone: (859) 371-9393 Fax: (859) 371-5096
Kathy Bender, Director of Admissions, Beckfield College, 16 Spiral Drive, Florence, KY 41042

Bellarmine University
Louisville, Kentucky
www.bellarmine.edu
CB member
CB code: 1056

- Private 4-year university and liberal arts college affiliated with Roman Catholic Church
- Commuter campus in very large city
- 2,391 degree-seeking undergraduates: 6% part-time, 64% women, 4% Asian American, 4% Hispanic American, 2% international
- 774 degree-seeking graduate students
- 52% of applicants admitted
- SAT or ACT (ACT writing optional), application essay required
- 69% graduate within 6 years; 24% enter graduate study

General. Founded in 1950. Regionally accredited. **Degrees:** 592 bachelor's awarded; master's, professional offered. **ROTC:** Army, Air Force. **Location:** 7 miles from downtown, 100 miles from Cincinnati. **Calendar:** Semester, extensive summer session. **Full-time faculty:** 150 total; 82% have terminal degrees, 10% minority, 53% women. **Part-time faculty:** 213 total; 29% have terminal degrees, 7% minority, 48% women. **Class size:** 55% < 20, 41% 20-39, 3% 40-49, 2% 50-99.

Freshman class profile. 6,955 applied, 3,604 admitted, 601 enrolled.

Mid 50% test scores			
SAT critical reading:	490-580	Rank in top tenth:	26%
SAT math:	490-600	End year in good standing:	94%
ACT composite:	22-27	Return as sophomores:	78%
GPA 3.75 or higher:	34%	Out-of-state:	38%
GPA 3.50-3.74:	23%	Live on campus:	77%
GPA 3.0-3.49:	33%	International:	2%
GPA 2.0-2.99:	10%	Fraternities:	1%
Rank in top quarter:	59%	Sororities:	1%

Basis for selection. Admissions based on 2.5 GPA, college preparatory curriculum, 21 ACT or 1000 SAT (exclusive of Writing), strong high school recommendation, submission of acceptable essay (if requested). Applicants not meeting requirements may be admitted on strength of each criterion. School activities also considered. Interview recommended. Audition required of music majors. Portfolio recommended for art majors. **Home schooled:** Transcript of courses and grades, letter of recommendation (nonparent) required.

High school preparation. College-preparatory program required. 20 units required; 26 recommended. Required and recommended units include English 4, mathematics 3-4, social studies 2-3, history 1-2, science 3-4 (laboratory 2), foreign language 2 and academic electives 5-7.

2011-2012 Annual costs. Tuition/fees: $32,140. Room/board: $9,560. Books/supplies: $836. Personal expenses: $4,060.

2011-2012 Financial aid. **Need-based:** 553 full-time freshmen applied for aid; 491 were judged to have need; 491 of these received aid. Average need met was 76%. Average scholarship/grant was $18,862; average loan $3,722. 76% of total undergraduate aid awarded as scholarships/grants, 24% as loans/jobs. **Non-need-based:** Awarded to 1,151 full-time undergraduates,

including 296 freshmen. Scholarships awarded for academics, alumni affiliation, art, athletics, leadership, minority status, music/drama, religious affiliation, ROTC, state residency.

Application procedures. Admission: Priority date 2/1; deadline 8/15 (postmark date). $25 fee, may be waived for applicants with need, free for online applicants. Admission notification on a rolling basis beginning on or about 9/1. Must reply by May 1 or within 3 week(s) if notified thereafter. **Financial aid:** Priority date 3/1; no closing date. FAFSA required. Applicants notified on a rolling basis starting 3/15.

Academics. Special study options: Accelerated study, combined bachelor's/graduate degree, cross-registration, double major, dual enrollment of high school students, honors, independent study, internships, liberal arts/career combination, semester at sea, student-designed major, study abroad, teacher certification program, Washington semester. **Credit/placement by examination:** AP, CLEP, IB, institutional tests. **Support services:** Learning center, reduced course load, study skills assistance, tutoring, writing center.

Majors. Biology: General, biochemistry. **Business:** Accounting, actuarial science, business admin, finance. **Communications:** Communications/speech/rhetoric. **Computer sciences:** General, systems analysis. **Conservation:** Environmental science, environmental studies. **Education:** Elementary, middle, special ed. **Engineering:** Computer. **English:** English lit. **Foreign languages:** Spanish. **Health services:** Clinical lab science, nursing (RN), respiratory therapy technology. **History:** General. **Liberal arts:** Arts/sciences. **Math:** General. **Parks/recreation:** Exercise sciences. **Philosophy/religion:** Philosophy. **Physical sciences:** Chemistry, physics. **Protective services:** Law enforcement admin. **Psychology:** General. **Social sciences:** Economics, political science, sociology. **Theology:** Theology. **Visual/performing arts:** Art, music, studio arts management.

Most popular majors. Business/marketing 14%, health sciences 27%, psychology 10%, social sciences 9%.

Computing on campus. 434 workstations in dormitories, library, computer center, student center. Dormitories wired for high-speed internet access and linked to campus network. Commuter students can connect to campus network. Online course registration, helpline, repair service, wireless network available.

Student life. Freshman orientation: Mandatory, $300 fee. Preregistration for classes offered. Off-campus 3-day session held in August before classes begin. **Housing:** Guaranteed on-campus for freshmen. Coed dorms, single-sex dorms, special housing for disabled, apartments, wellness housing available. $200 fully refundable deposit, deadline 5/1. Pets allowed in dorm rooms. Suites available to upperclassmen. **Activities:** Bands, campus ministries, choral groups, dance, drama, literary magazine, music ensembles, musical theater, opera, radio station, student government, student newspaper, symphony orchestra, Catholic students association, Fellowship of Christian Athletes, Hillel, Highland community ministries, Habitat for Humanity.

Athletics. NCAA. **Intercollegiate:** Baseball M, basketball, bowling, cross-country, field hockey W, golf, lacrosse M, soccer, softball W, tennis, track and field, volleyball W. **Intramural:** Basketball, cheerleading, football (non-tackle) M, golf, soccer, softball, swimming, tennis, volleyball. **Team name:** Knights.

Student services. Adult student services, chaplain/spiritual director, career counseling, student employment services, financial aid counseling, health services, personal counseling, placement for graduates. **Physically disabled:** Services for visually, hearing impaired.

Contact. E-mail: admissions@bellarmine.edu
Phone: (502) 272-8131 Toll-free number: (800) 274-4723 ext. 8131
Fax: (502) 272-8002
Timothy Sturgeon, Dean of Admissions, Bellarmine University, 2001 Newburg Road, Louisville, KY 40205

Berea College
Berea, Kentucky
www.berea.edu

CB member
CB code: 1060

♦ Private 4-year liberal arts college
♦ Residential campus in small town
♦ 1,613 degree-seeking undergraduates: 57% women, 15% African American, 1% Asian American, 3% Hispanic American, 7% international
♦ 12% of applicants admitted
♦ SAT or ACT (ACT writing optional), application essay, interview required
♦ 62% graduate within 6 years

General. Founded in 1855. Regionally accredited. Each student is provided with a laptop computer. Departmental computer labs offer access to specialized functions such as video editing and graphical production. **Degrees:** 272 bachelor's awarded. **Location:** 40 miles from Lexington, 100 miles from Louisville. **Calendar:** Semester, limited summer session. **Full-time faculty:** 124 total; 89% have terminal degrees, 13% minority, 46% women. **Part-time faculty:** 49 total; 43% have terminal degrees, 10% minority, 53% women. **Class size:** 67% < 20, 33% 20-39, less than 1% 40-49. **Special facilities:** Appalachian gallery, planetarium and observatory, geology museum, Ecovillage, child development laboratory, early technology lab, crafts program.

Freshman class profile. 4,707 applied, 586 admitted, 418 enrolled.

Mid 50% test scores			
SAT critical reading:	500-640	GPA 2.0-2.99:	19%
SAT math:	480-590	Rank in top quarter:	73%
SAT writing:	510-610	Rank in top tenth:	31%
ACT composite:	22-27	Return as sophomores:	79%
GPA 3.75 or higher:	32%	Out-of-state:	53%
GPA 3.50-3.74:	20%	Live on campus:	97%
GPA 3.0-3.49:	28%	International:	6%

Basis for selection. Admissions based on comprehensive review of application including academic credentials, recommendations, essay, financial eligibility, and interview. **Home schooled:** List of courses and titles of textbooks required if transcript is not available.

High school preparation. College-preparatory program recommended. 13 units recommended. Recommended units include English 4, mathematics 3, social studies 1, history 1, science 2 (laboratory 2) and foreign language 2.

2011-2012 Annual costs. Only those with financial need admitted. All students awarded 4-year tuition scholarship. Amount of scholarship varies depending on financial need and presence of any additional outside scholarships. Resources cover entire cost of tuition, which totals $21,300. Financial aid and scholarships available for meeting additional costs of room/board ($5,792) and fees ($910), depending on financial need. Every student is provided a personal notebook computer by the college.

2011-2012 Financial aid. All financial aid based on need. 418 full-time freshmen applied for aid; 418 were judged to have need; 418 of these received aid. Average need met was 94%. Average scholarship/grant was $27,117; average loan $1,476. 93% of total undergraduate aid awarded as scholarships/grants, 7% as loans/jobs.

Application procedures. Admission: Closing date 4/30. No application fee. Admission notification on a rolling basis beginning on or about 11/1. Must reply by 5/1. **Financial aid:** Priority date 2/1, closing date 5/1. FAFSA required. Applicants notified on a rolling basis starting 4/1.

Academics. Special study options: Combined bachelor's/graduate degree, double major, ESL, exchange student, honors, independent study, internships, student-designed major, study abroad, teacher certification program. 3-2 engineering program with Washington University (MO) and University of Kentucky. **Credit/placement by examination:** AP, CLEP, SAT, ACT, institutional tests. Unlimited number of credit hours may be counted toward degree. **Support services:** Learning center, remedial instruction, study skills assistance, tutoring, writing center.

Majors. Area/ethnic studies: African-American, Asian, women's. **Biology:** General, neuroanatomy. **Business:** General, accounting, finance, marketing. **Communications:** Media studies. **Computer sciences:** General. **Education:** General, art, elementary, family/consumer sciences, kindergarten/preschool, middle, music, secondary, technology/industrial arts. **English:** British lit, creative writing, English lit. **Foreign languages:** French, German, Latin, Spanish. **Health services:** Nursing (RN). **History:** General. **Math:** General, applied. **Parks/recreation:** Exercise sciences, health/fitness. **Philosophy/religion:** Philosophy, religion. **Physical sciences:** Chemistry, physics. **Psychology:** General. **Social sciences:** Economics, political science, sociology. **Visual/performing arts:** Art, art history/conservation, dramatic, music, music performance, studio arts, voice/opera. **Work/family studies:** General.

Most popular majors. Biology 8%, business/marketing 6%, communications/journalism 7%, education 9%, engineering/engineering technologies 6%, family/consumer sciences 7%, health sciences 6%, psychology 6%, visual/performing arts 10%.

Computing on campus. Dormitories wired for high-speed internet access and linked to campus network. Online course registration, online library, helpline, repair service, wireless network available.

Student life. Freshman orientation: Mandatory. Preregistration for classes offered. **Policies:** Freshmen not permitted cars on campus. **Housing:** Guaranteed on-campus for all undergraduates. Single-sex dorms, apartments available. Apartments for single parent students, Ecovillage. **Activities:** Bands, campus ministries, choral groups, dance, drama, international student

organizations, literary magazine, music ensembles, student government, student newspaper, religious organizations, People Who Care, Students for Appalachia, Habitat for Humanity, Cosmopolitan Club.

Athletics. NAIA. **Intercollegiate:** Baseball M, basketball, cross-country, diving, golf M, soccer, softball W, swimming, tennis, track and field, volleyball W. **Intramural:** Basketball, football (non-tackle), soccer, softball, volleyball. **Team name:** Mountaineers.

Student services. Adult student services, alcohol/substance abuse counseling, chaplain/spiritual director, career counseling, services for economically disadvantaged, student employment services, financial aid counseling, health services, minority student services, on-campus daycare, personal counseling, placement for graduates, veterans' counselor, women's services. **Physically disabled:** Services for visually, speech, hearing impaired.

Contact. E-mail: admissions@berea.edu
Phone: (859) 985-3500 Toll-free number: (800) 326-5948
Fax: (859) 985-3512
Luke Hodson, Director of Admissions Operations, Berea College, CPO 2220, Berea, KY 40404

Brescia University
Owensboro, Kentucky
www.brescia.edu   **CB code: 1071**

- Private 4-year university and liberal arts college affiliated with Roman Catholic Church
- Commuter campus in small city
- 689 degree-seeking undergraduates: 21% part-time, 67% women, 11% African American, 3% Hispanic American, 2% international
- 22 degree-seeking graduate students
- 48% of applicants admitted
- SAT or ACT (ACT writing optional), application essay required
- 45% graduate within 6 years

General. Founded in 1950. Regionally accredited. Weekend college for MBA students. Lay ministry formation program nationally accredited. Online associate and bachelor's degree completion programs available as well as online Master of Science in Management program. **Degrees:** 87 bachelor's, 1 associate awarded; master's offered. **Location:** 120 miles from Louisville; 120 miles from Nashville, TN. **Calendar:** Semester, limited summer session. **Full-time faculty:** 37 total; 73% have terminal degrees, 16% minority, 51% women. **Part-time faculty:** 28 total; 7% have terminal degrees, 54% women. **Class size:** 88% < 20, 11% 20-39, less than 1% 40-49. **Special facilities:** Observatory, greenhouse.

Freshman class profile. 2,437 applied, 1,167 admitted, 153 enrolled.

Mid 50% test scores		GPA 2.0-2.99:	31%
SAT math:	420-470	Return as sophomores:	61%
ACT composite:	19-24	Out-of-state:	20%
GPA 3.75 or higher:	17%	Live on campus:	83%
GPA 3.50-3.74:	17%	International:	3%
GPA 3.0-3.49:	35%		

Basis for selection. Students admitted based on GPA and ACT/SAT. **Home schooled:** Transcript of courses and grades required. **Learning Disabled:** Applicants should inform admission counselor of learning disability and arrange appointment with Student Support Services staff member if requesting assistance.

High school preparation. College-preparatory program required. 17 units recommended. Recommended units include English 4, mathematics 3, social studies 2, history 2, science 2, foreign language 2 and academic electives 2. 2 units in fine arts, 2 units in computer science also recommended.

2011-2012 Annual costs. Tuition/fees: $18,140. Room/board: $8,000. Books/supplies: $1,000. Personal expenses: $1,800.

Financial aid. Non-need-based: Scholarships awarded for academics, alumni affiliation, art, athletics, minority status, music/drama, religious affiliation, state residency.

Application procedures. Admission: No deadline. $25 fee, may be waived for applicants with need. Admission notification on a rolling basis beginning on or about 9/1. **Financial aid:** Priority date 8/1, closing date 8/23. FAFSA required. Applicants notified on a rolling basis starting 3/1; must reply within 3 week(s) of notification.

Academics. Special study options: Accelerated study, combined bachelor's/graduate degree, cross-registration, distance learning, double major, ESL, exchange student, honors, independent study, internships, liberal arts/

career combination, student-designed major, study abroad, teacher certification program, weekend college. **Credit/placement by examination:** AP, CLEP, IB, SAT, ACT, institutional tests. 18 credit hours maximum toward associate degree, 36 toward bachelor's. **Support services:** Pre-admission summer program, reduced course load, remedial instruction, study skills assistance, tutoring.

Majors. Biology: General. **Business:** General, accounting, business admin. **Computer sciences:** General. **Education:** Art, elementary, middle, secondary, social studies, Spanish, special ed. **English:** English lit. **Foreign languages:** Spanish. **Health services:** Audiology/speech pathology, clinical lab science, substance abuse counseling. **History:** General. **Human services:** Social work. **Math:** Applied. **Philosophy/religion:** Religion. **Physical sciences:** Chemistry. **Psychology:** General. **Social sciences:** Political science. **Theology:** Pastoral counseling, theology. **Visual/performing arts:** Art, dramatic, graphic design.

Most popular majors. Business/marketing 26%, education 7%, English 6%, health sciences 8%, mathematics 6%, public administration/social services 26%.

Computing on campus. 77 workstations in library, computer center. Dormitories wired for high-speed internet access and linked to campus network. Commuter students can connect to campus network. Online library, wireless network available.

Student life. Freshman orientation: Mandatory, $200 fee. Preregistration for classes offered. Saturday-Tuesday program held prior to start of classes. **Housing:** Guaranteed on-campus for freshmen. Coed dorms, single-sex dorms, special housing for disabled, apartments available. $100 fully refundable deposit, deadline 8/23. Shared apartment houses available. **Activities:** Pep band, campus ministries, choral groups, drama, international student organizations, student government, student newspaper, Fellowship of Christian Athletes, social work club, Council for Exceptional Children, Grave Robbers, St. Angela's Messengers, Alternative Spring Break, Right to Life, psychology club.

Athletics. NAIA. **Intercollegiate:** Baseball M, basketball, cross-country, golf, soccer, softball W, tennis, track and field, volleyball W. **Intramural:** Basketball, racquetball, table tennis, volleyball. **Team name:** Bearcats.

Student services. Adult student services, alcohol/substance abuse counseling, chaplain/spiritual director, career counseling, services for economically disadvantaged, student employment services, financial aid counseling, personal counseling, placement for graduates, veterans' counselor, women's services. **Physically disabled:** Services for visually, speech, hearing impaired.

Contact. E-mail: admissions@brescia.edu
Phone: (270) 686-4241 Toll-free number: (877) 273-7242
Fax: (270) 686-4314
Chris Houk, Vice President for Enrollment Management, Brescia University, 717 Frederica Street, Owensboro, KY 42301-3023

Campbellsville University
Campbellsville, Kentucky   **CB member**
www.campbellsville.edu   **CB code: 1097**

- Private 4-year university affiliated with Baptist faith
- Residential campus in large town
- 2,141 degree-seeking undergraduates: 12% part-time, 56% women, 13% African American, 1% Hispanic American, 6% international
- 541 degree-seeking graduate students
- 63% of applicants admitted
- SAT or ACT (ACT writing optional) required
- 42% graduate within 6 years

General. Founded in 1906. Regionally accredited. Affiliated with Kentucky Baptist Convention. **Degrees:** 281 bachelor's, 25 associate awarded; master's offered. **ROTC:** Army. **Location:** 80 miles from Louisville; 140 miles from Nashville, Tennessee. **Calendar:** Semester, extensive summer session. **Full-time faculty:** 141 total; 63% have terminal degrees, 8% minority, 51% women. **Part-time faculty:** 161 total; 6% minority, 65% women. **Class size:** 66% < 20, 33% 20-39, 1% 40-49, less than 1% 50-99. **Special facilities:** Educational and research woodland, American Civil War institute, fine arts center with computer-enhanced practice room with acoustical adjustment system.

Freshman class profile. 2,279 applied, 1,442 admitted, 521 enrolled.

Mid 50% test scores			
SAT critical reading:	430-550	GPA 3.0-3.49:	28%
SAT math:	410-580	GPA 2.0-2.99:	33%
SAT writing:	390-500	End year in good standing:	86%
ACT composite:	18-23	Return as sophomores:	65%
GPA 3.75 or higher:	20%	Out-of-state:	16%
GPA 3.50-3.74:	14%	Live on campus:	70%

Basis for selection. Achievement in strong high school program and satisfactory SAT/ACT most important. Special consideration for entry to basic skills program may be given to other highly motivated and potentially successful applicants. Interview and essay recommended. **Home schooled:** State high school equivalency certificate required.

High school preparation. College-preparatory program recommended. 21 units recommended. Recommended units include English 4, mathematics 3, social studies 2, history 2, science 3 (laboratory 1), foreign language 1 and academic electives 6. At least 2 units in the arts recommended for academic elective.

2011-2012 Annual costs. Tuition/fees: $20,740. Room/board: $6,980. Books/supplies: $1,000. Personal expenses: $2,700.

Financial aid. Non-need-based: Scholarships awarded for academics, art, athletics, leadership, minority status, music/drama, religious affiliation, ROTC, state residency. **Additional information:** Matching scholarships available for students whose church contributes $200 annually. Performance grants available to members of marching band.

Application procedures. Admission: Priority date 4/15; no deadline. $20 fee, may be waived for applicants with need, free for online applicants. Admission notification on a rolling basis beginning on or about 1/2. **Financial aid:** Priority date 4/1; no closing date. FAFSA required. Applicants notified on a rolling basis starting 5/15.

Academics. Special study options: Cooperative education, distance learning, double major, dual enrollment of high school students, ESL, exchange student, honors, independent study, internships, study abroad, teacher certification program, Washington semester. London semester. **Credit/placement by examination:** AP, CLEP, institutional tests. 32 credit hours maximum toward bachelor's degree. Institutional/departmental examinations given in some areas. **Support services:** Learning center, pre-admission summer program, reduced course load, remedial instruction, study skills assistance, tutoring, writing center.

Majors. Biology: General. **Business:** General, accounting, business admin, marketing, office management. **Communications:** Broadcast journalism, communications/speech/rhetoric, journalism, public relations. **Computer sciences:** General. **Education:** General, art, biology, chemistry, early childhood, elementary, English, ESL, health, history, mathematics, middle, music, physical, physics, reading, science, secondary, social science, social studies. **English:** English lit. **Health services:** Athletic training, predental, premedicine, prepharmacy, preveterinary. **History:** General. **Human services:** Social work. **Math:** General. **Parks/recreation:** General, exercise sciences, health/fitness. **Philosophy/religion:** Religion. **Physical sciences:** Chemistry, physics. **Protective services:** Law enforcement admin. **Psychology:** General. **Social sciences:** General, economics, political science, sociology. **Theology:** Bible, religious ed, sacred music. **Visual/performing arts:** Art, conducting, dramatic, music, music performance, music theory/composition, piano/keyboard, studio arts, voice/opera.

Most popular majors. Business/marketing 19%, communications/journalism 6%, education 24%, security/protective services 7%, theological studies 10%.

Computing on campus. 250 workstations in dormitories, library, computer center, student center. Dormitories wired for high-speed internet access and linked to campus network. Commuter students can connect to campus network. Online course registration, online library, repair service available.

Student life. Freshman orientation: Mandatory. Preregistration for classes offered. Held in June and July. **Policies:** Religious observance required. **Housing:** Guaranteed on-campus for all undergraduates. Single-sex dorms, apartments, wellness housing available. $100 deposit, deadline 7/1. **Activities:** Bands, campus ministries, choral groups, dance, drama, literary magazine, music ensembles, musical theater, opera, radio station, student government, student newspaper, symphony orchestra, TV station, Baptist student union, Young Republicans, Young Democrats, Student Foundation, Fellowship of Christian Athletes, student ambassadors, African American leadership league, world community club.

Athletics. NAIA. **Intercollegiate:** Baseball M, basketball, bowling, cheerleading, cross-country, football (tackle) M, golf, soccer, softball W, swimming, tennis, track and field, volleyball W, wrestling. **Intramural:** Basketball, racquetball, soccer, softball, swimming, table tennis, tennis, volleyball. **Team name:** Tigers.

Student services. Adult student services, alcohol/substance abuse counseling, chaplain/spiritual director, career counseling, student employment services, financial aid counseling, health services, personal counseling, placement for graduates, veterans' counselor.

Contact. E-mail: admissions@campbellsville.edu
Phone: (270) 789-5220 Toll-free number: (800) 264-6014
Fax: (270) 789-5071
David Walters, Vice President for Admissions, Campbellsville University, One University Drive, Campbellsville, KY 42718-2799

Centre College
Danville, Kentucky
www.centre.edu

CB member
CB code: 1109

- Private 4-year liberal arts college affiliated with Presbyterian Church (USA)
- Residential campus in large town
- 1,306 degree-seeking undergraduates: 53% women, 4% African American, 2% Asian American, 3% Hispanic American, 2% international
- 70% of applicants admitted
- SAT or ACT (ACT writing optional), application essay required
- 82% graduate within 6 years

General. Founded in 1819. Regionally accredited. **Degrees:** 269 bachelor's awarded. **ROTC:** Army, Air Force. **Location:** 35 miles from Lexington, 85 miles from Louisville. **Calendar:** 4-1-4. **Full-time faculty:** 109 total; 94% have terminal degrees, 13% minority, 39% women. **Part-time faculty:** 32 total; 56% have terminal degrees, 12% minority, 47% women. **Class size:** 53% < 20, 47% 20-39, less than 1% 40-49. **Special facilities:** Regional performing arts center, hot glass studio.

Freshman class profile. 2,413 applied, 1,700 admitted, 374 enrolled.

Mid 50% test scores			
SAT critical reading:	560-690	GPA 2.0-2.99:	9%
SAT math:	560-670	Rank in top quarter:	83%
SAT writing:	570-670	Rank in top tenth:	54%
ACT composite:	26-31	Return as sophomores:	91%
GPA 3.75 or higher:	49%	Out-of-state:	42%
GPA 3.50-3.74:	19%	Live on campus:	99%
GPA 3.0-3.49:	23%	International:	2%

Basis for selection. Achievement and quality of high school program most important. Recommendations, test scores, academic and nonacademic interests, experiences considered. Interview recommended.

High school preparation. College-preparatory program required. 13 units required; 20 recommended. Required and recommended units include English 4, mathematics 3-4, social studies 1-2, history 1-2, science 2-4 (laboratory 2-3), foreign language 2-4 and visual/performing arts 1.

2011-2012 Annual costs. Comprehensive fee: $42,500. Reduced comprehensive fee may be available if student is approved to live off-campus by dean of students. Books/supplies: $1,000. Personal expenses: $1,300.

2011-2012 Financial aid. Need-based: 321 full-time freshmen applied for aid; 262 were judged to have need; 262 of these received aid. Average need met was 88%. Average scholarship/grant was $24,248; average loan $3,366. 87% of total undergraduate aid awarded as scholarships/grants, 13% as loans/jobs. **Non-need-based:** Awarded to 440 full-time undergraduates, including 105 freshmen. Scholarships awarded for academics, alumni affiliation, music/drama, ROTC.

Application procedures. Admission: Closing date 2/1 (postmark date). $40 fee, may be waived for applicants with need, free for online applicants. Admission notification by 3/15. Must reply by May 1 or within 2 week(s) if notified thereafter. **Financial aid:** Closing date 3/1. FAFSA, institutional form required. Applicants notified by 4/1; must reply by 5/1 or within 2 week(s) of notification.

Academics. Unusual courses and off-campus study options offered during 3-week winter term. Long-term study abroad sites in England, France, Mexico, Japan, and Ireland. Winter-term international locations vary. **Special study options:** Double major, honors, independent study, internships, liberal arts/career combination, student-designed major, study abroad, teacher certification program, Washington semester. Science semester at Oak Ridge National Laboratories, Tennessee, and 5 other national science laboratories, 3-2 engineering program with Columbia University (NY), Washington University (MO), Vanderbilt University (TN), and University of Kentucky. **Credit/placement by examination:** AP, CLEP, IB, SAT, ACT, institutional tests. **Support services:** Study skills assistance, tutoring, writing center.

Majors. Biology: General, biochemistry, molecular. **Computer sciences:** Computer science. **Education:** Elementary. **English:** English lit. **Foreign languages:** Classics, French, German, Spanish. **History:** General. **Math:** General. **Philosophy/religion:** Philosophy, religion. **Physical sciences:** Chemical physics, chemistry, physics. **Psychology:** General. **Social sciences:** Anthropology, economics, international relations, political science, sociology. **Visual/performing arts:** Art, dramatic, music.

Most popular majors. Biology 10%, English 7%, foreign language 12%, history 12%, psychology 7%, social sciences 22%, visual/performing arts 8%.

Computing on campus. 170 workstations in dormitories, library, computer center, student center. Dormitories wired for high-speed internet access and linked to campus network. Commuter students can connect to campus network. Online course registration, helpline, repair service, student web hosting, wireless network available.

Student life. Freshman orientation: Mandatory. Preregistration for classes offered. Held at beginning of fall term. **Housing:** Guaranteed on-campus for all undergraduates. Coed dorms, single-sex dorms, special housing for disabled, apartments, fraternity/sorority housing, wellness housing available. **Activities:** Bands, campus ministries, choral groups, dance, drama, film society, international student organizations, literary magazine, music ensembles, student government, student newspaper, symphony orchestra, TV station, student activities council, volunteer services, diversity student union, Christian Fellowship, Campus Democrats and Republicans, ecumenical organization, peace organization, student environmental organization, Muslim student association.

Athletics. NCAA. **Intercollegiate:** Baseball M, basketball, cross-country, diving, field hockey W, football (tackle) M, golf, lacrosse M, soccer, softball W, swimming, tennis, track and field, volleyball W. **Intramural:** Badminton, basketball, bowling, cross-country, fencing, field hockey W, football (tackle), golf, racquetball, rugby M, soccer, softball, swimming, table tennis, tennis, track and field, volleyball, wrestling M. **Team name:** Colonels.

Student services. Alcohol/substance abuse counseling, chaplain/spiritual director, career counseling, student employment services, financial aid counseling, health services, minority student services, personal counseling, placement for graduates. **Physically disabled:** Services for visually, hearing impaired.

Contact. E-mail: admission@centre.edu
Phone: (859) 238-5350 Toll-free number: (800) 423-6236
Fax: (859) 238-5373
Bob Nesmith, Director of Admission, Centre College, 600 West Walnut Street, Danville, KY 40422-1394

Clear Creek Baptist Bible College
Pineville, Kentucky
www.ccbbc.edu   **CB code: 5975**

- Private 4-year Bible college affiliated with Southern Baptist Convention
- Residential campus in small town
- 153 degree-seeking undergraduates: 31% part-time, 24% women
- Application essay, interview required
- 37% graduate within 6 years

General. Founded in 1926. Regionally accredited; also accredited by ABHE. Adult family Bible college affiliated with Kentucky Baptist Convention that trains individuals for ministry in local church. Prefer students to be at least 21 years of age. **Degrees:** 26 bachelor's, 8 associate awarded. **Location:** 110 miles from Lexington; 76 miles from Knoxville, TN. **Calendar:** Semester, limited summer session. **Full-time faculty:** 6 total; 83% have terminal degrees. **Part-time faculty:** 23 total; 39% have terminal degrees, 26% women. **Class size:** 80% < 20, 20% 20-39. **Special facilities:** Family life center, hiking/walking trails, campus thrift store.

Freshman class profile. 23 applied, 17 admitted, 17 enrolled.

Return as sophomores:	81%	Live on campus:	82%
Out-of-state:	59%		

Basis for selection. Open admission, but selective for some programs. Recommendations by church required. **Home schooled:** Transcript of courses and grades required.

2011-2012 Annual costs. Tuition/fees: $5,570. Room/board: $3,750. Books/supplies: $1,500. Personal expenses: $1,600.

2010-2011 Financial aid. **Need-based:** 20 full-time freshmen applied for aid; 16 were judged to have need; 16 of these received aid. Average need met was 71%. Average scholarship/grant was $7,134. 96% of total undergraduate aid awarded as scholarships/grants, 4% as loans/jobs. **Non-need-based:**

Awarded to 42 full-time undergraduates, including 18 freshmen. Scholarships awarded for academics.

Application procedures. Admission: Priority date 7/15; deadline 8/2 (receipt date). $40 fee. Admission notification on a rolling basis. **Financial aid:** Priority date 6/30; no closing date. FAFSA, institutional form required. Applicants notified on a rolling basis.

Academics. Special study options: Cross-registration, distance learning, double major, dual enrollment of high school students, independent study. **Credit/placement by examination:** AP, CLEP, institutional tests. **Support services:** Reduced course load, remedial instruction, study skills assistance, tutoring.

Majors. Theology: Bible.

Computing on campus. 12 workstations in library, computer center. Dormitories wired for high-speed internet access and linked to campus network. Online course registration, online library, wireless network available.

Student life. Freshman orientation: Available. Preregistration for classes offered. Four-day program held week of registration. **Policies:** Dress code; no tobacco, alcohol, or drugs on campus. Religious observance required. **Housing:** Single-sex dorms, apartments, wellness housing available. $50 nonrefundable deposit, deadline 7/25. Cottages, family housing available. **Activities:** Campus ministries, choral groups, drama, music ensembles, radio station, student government, student newspaper, Women's Missionary Union, Brotherhood, Young Disciples, Acteens, Royal Ambassadors, Girls in Action, Mission Friends.

Athletics. Intramural: Basketball, football (non-tackle), softball, swimming, table tennis, tennis, volleyball.

Student services. Chaplain/spiritual director, career counseling, student employment services, financial aid counseling, health services, on-campus daycare, personal counseling, placement for graduates, veterans' counselor.

Contact. E-mail: ccbbc@ccbbc.edu
Phone: (606) 337-3196 Toll-free number: (866) 340-3196
Fax: (606) 337-2372
Billy Howell, Director of Admissions, Clear Creek Baptist Bible College, 300 Clear Creek Road, Pineville, KY 40977-9754

Eastern Kentucky University
Richmond, Kentucky   **CB member**
www.eku.edu   **CB code: 1200**

- Public 4-year university
- Residential campus in large town
- 13,385 degree-seeking undergraduates
- 66% of applicants admitted
- SAT or ACT (ACT writing optional) required

General. Founded in 1906. Regionally accredited. Courses offered at additional sites in Corbin, Danville, Manchester, Lancaster, London, Somerset and Barbourville. **Degrees:** 2,135 bachelor's, 215 associate awarded; master's, professional offered. **ROTC:** Army. **Location:** 28 miles from Lexington, 110 miles from Cincinnati. **Calendar:** Semester, extensive summer session. **Full-time faculty:** 680 total. **Part-time faculty:** 434 total. **Class size:** 48% < 20, 44% 20-39, 4% 40-49, 3% 50-99, 1% >100. **Special facilities:** Planetarium, nature preserves, law enforcement facilities, music library.

Freshman class profile. 9,461 applied, 6,272 admitted, 2,421 enrolled.

Mid 50% test scores			
SAT math:	440-550	Live on campus:	69%
ACT composite:	18-24	Fraternities:	13%
Out-of-state:	17%	Sororities:	8%

Basis for selection. Out-of-state applicants must rank in top half of graduating class or have 21 ACT or 890 SAT (exclusive of Writing). Resident applicants must have completed specified high school curriculum. Applicants without college preparatory courses subject to remediation. ACT only required for placement for in-state applicants. Interview recommended. Audition recommended for music majors. Portfolio recommended for art and graphic art majors. **Home schooled:** Transcript of courses and grades required.

High school preparation. 25 units required. Required units include English 4, mathematics 3, social studies 3, science 3 (laboratory 1), foreign language 2 and academic electives 7. Art, drama, music, and computer science also recommended.

2011-2012 Annual costs. Tuition/fees: $6,960; $19,056 out-of-state. Room/board: $6,868. Books/supplies: $1,000. Personal expenses: $1,500.

Financial aid. Non-need-based: Scholarships awarded for academics, alumni affiliation, art, athletics, job skills, leadership, minority status, music/drama, ROTC, state residency.

Application procedures. Admission: Closing date 8/1. $30 fee, may be waived for applicants with need. Admission notification on a rolling basis beginning on or about 8/1. **Financial aid:** Priority date 3/15; no closing date. FAFSA required. Applicants notified on a rolling basis starting 4/1.

Academics. Special study options: Cooperative education, distance learning, double major, ESL, honors, independent study, internships, liberal arts/career combination, student-designed major, study abroad, teacher certification program. **Credit/placement by examination:** AP, CLEP, SAT, ACT, institutional tests. 30 credit hours maximum toward associate degree, 65 toward bachelor's. **Support services:** Learning center, pre-admission summer program, reduced course load, remedial instruction, study skills assistance, tutoring, writing center.

Majors. Area/ethnic studies: Canadian. **Biology:** General, bacteriology, ecology. **Business:** General, accounting, business admin, fashion, finance, insurance, management information systems, managerial economics, marketing, office management. **Communications:** Broadcast journalism, communications/speech/rhetoric, journalism, public relations. **Computer sciences:** General, computer science. **Conservation:** Management/policy, wildlife/wilderness. **Education:** Art, biology, business, Deaf/hearing impaired, elementary, family/consumer sciences, geography, mathematics, middle, music, physical, science, Spanish, special ed, speech impaired, technology/industrial arts, trade/industrial. **Engineering:** Engineering science. **English:** English lit, rhetoric/composition. **Foreign languages:** General, French, German, sign language interpretation, Spanish. **General:** Ornamental horticulture, turf management. **Health services:** Clinical lab assistant, clinical lab science, clinical lab technology, EMT paramedic, health care admin, medical assistant, medical records admin, medical records technology, nursing (RN), predental, premedicine, preop/surgical nursing, prepharmacy. **History:** General. **Human services:** Social work. **Liberal arts:** Arts/sciences. **Math:** General, statistics. **Parks/recreation:** General, facilities management. **Philosophy/religion:** Philosophy. **Physical sciences:** Chemistry, geology, physics. **Protective services:** Corrections, fire safety technology, forensics, police science, security services. **Psychology:** General. **Social sciences:** Anthropology, economics, geography, political science, sociology. **Visual/performing arts:** Art, ceramics, dramatic, drawing, interior design, music, painting, printmaking, sculpture, studio arts. **Work/family studies:** Family studies, food/nutrition, housing.

Most popular majors. Business/marketing 14%, communications/journalism 6%, education 16%, health sciences 19%, security/protective services 15%, social sciences 6%.

Computing on campus. 250 workstations in dormitories, library, computer center, student center. Dormitories wired for high-speed internet access and linked to campus network. Commuter students can connect to campus network. Online course registration, online library, helpline, wireless network available.

Student life. Freshman orientation: Mandatory. Preregistration for classes offered. **Policies:** Students required to live on-campus until age 21 unless living with parent or guardian. **Housing:** Guaranteed on-campus for freshmen. Coed dorms, single-sex dorms, apartments, fraternity/sorority housing available. $100 fully refundable deposit. **Activities:** Bands, choral groups, dance, drama, literary magazine, music ensembles, musical theater, radio station, student government, student newspaper, symphony orchestra, 160 organizations available.

Athletics. NCAA. **Intercollegiate:** Baseball M, basketball, cheerleading, cross-country, football (tackle) M, golf, soccer W, softball W, swimming, tennis, track and field, volleyball W. **Intramural:** Basketball, football (tackle) M, golf, racquetball, softball, tennis, volleyball. **Team name:** Colonels.

Student services. Alcohol/substance abuse counseling, chaplain/spiritual director, career counseling, student employment services, financial aid counseling, health services, personal counseling, placement for graduates, veterans' counselor. **Physically disabled:** Services for visually, speech, hearing impaired.

Contact. E-mail: admissions@eku.edu
Phone: (859) 622-2106 Toll-free number: (800) 465-9191
Fax: (859) 622-8024
Brett Morris, Director of Admissions, Eastern Kentucky University, SSB CPO 54, 521 Lancaster Avenue, Richmond, KY 40475-3102

Georgetown College
Georgetown, Kentucky
www.georgetowncollege.edu   CB code: 1249

♦ Private 4-year liberal arts college affiliated with Baptist faith
♦ Residential campus in large town
♦ 1,233 degree-seeking undergraduates: 1% part-time, 55% women, 9% African American, 2% Hispanic American, 1% international
♦ 526 degree-seeking graduate students
♦ 89% of applicants admitted
♦ SAT or ACT (ACT writing optional) required
♦ 59% graduate within 6 years; 48% enter graduate study

General. Founded in 1829. Regionally accredited. **Degrees:** 235 bachelor's awarded; master's offered. **ROTC:** Army, Air Force. **Location:** 12 miles from Lexington, 60 miles from Louisville. **Calendar:** Semester, limited summer session. **Full-time faculty:** 116 total; 95% have terminal degrees, 5% minority, 47% women. **Part-time faculty:** 45 total; 18% have terminal degrees, 11% minority, 53% women. **Class size:** 71% < 20, 26% 20-39, 2% 40-49, 1% 50-99. **Special facilities:** Planetarium, Foucault pendulum, arboretum, fine arts building.

Freshman class profile. 2,125 applied, 1,895 admitted, 353 enrolled.

Mid 50% test scores			
SAT critical reading:	460-570	Rank in top quarter:	59%
SAT math:	450-550	Rank in top tenth:	24%
ACT composite:	21-27	Return as sophomores:	72%
GPA 3.75 or higher:	31%	Out-of-state:	21%
GPA 3.50-3.74:	23%	Live on campus:	98%
GPA 3.0-3.49:	29%	International:	1%
GPA 2.0-2.99:	17%	Fraternities:	30%
		Sororities:	36%

Basis for selection. School achievement record, test scores, and rank in top half of class most important. Interview recommended for academically weak or special needs applicants. Audition recommended for music and communication arts majors. Portfolio recommended for art majors. **Home schooled:** Transcript of courses and grades required. Essay required.

High school preparation. College-preparatory program recommended. 20 units recommended. Recommended units include English 4, mathematics 3, social studies 2, science 3 and foreign language 2.

2011-2012 Annual costs. Tuition/fees: $29,300. Undergraduates taking one course are charged $900/credit hour; for more than one course, the standard per-credit-hour charge of $1,210 applies. Students taking more than 18 hours in one semester will incur an extra $420/credit hour for all hours over 18. Room/board: $7,610.

2011-2012 Financial aid. Need-based: 326 full-time freshmen applied for aid; 298 were judged to have need; 298 of these received aid. Average need met was 82%. Average scholarship/grant was $21,635; average loan $3,427. 83% of total undergraduate aid awarded as scholarships/grants, 17% as loans/jobs. **Non-need-based:** Awarded to 545 full-time undergraduates, including 120 freshmen. Scholarships awarded for academics, alumni affiliation, art, athletics, leadership, minority status, music/drama, religious affiliation, ROTC, state residency.

Application procedures. Admission: Priority date 5/1; deadline 8/1 (postmark date). $30 fee, may be waived for applicants with need, free for online applicants. Admission notification on a rolling basis beginning on or about 10/1. Must reply by May 1 or within 4 week(s) if notified thereafter. **Financial aid:** Priority date 2/1, closing date 3/15. FAFSA required. Applicants notified on a rolling basis starting 3/1; must reply by 5/1.

Academics. Special study options: Accelerated study, cooperative education, distance learning, double major, dual enrollment of high school students, ESL, honors, independent study, internships, liberal arts/career combination, student-designed major, study abroad, teacher certification program. 3-2 programs in Nursing and in Engineering with the University of Kentucky. **Credit/placement by examination:** AP, CLEP, IB, SAT, ACT, institutional tests. **Support services:** Study skills assistance, tutoring, writing center.

Majors. Area/ethnic studies: American, European, German. **Biology:** General, ecology. **Business:** General, accounting. **Communications:** Media studies. **Computer sciences:** General. **Education:** Elementary, middle, music, secondary, special ed. **English:** English lit. **Foreign languages:** French, German, Spanish. **Health services:** Athletic training, predental, prenursing, prepharmacy, preveterinary. **History:** General. **Liberal arts:** Arts/sciences. **Math:** General. **Parks/recreation:** Exercise sciences, health/fitness. **Philosophy/religion:** Philosophy, religion. **Physical sciences:** Chemistry, physics. **Psychology:** General. **Social sciences:** Economics, political science, sociology. **Visual/performing arts:** Dramatic, music, studio arts.

Most popular majors. Biology 12%, business/marketing 10%, communications/journalism 7%, education 8%, history 6%, parks/recreation 11%, psychology 11%, social sciences 9%, visual/performing arts 6%.

Computing on campus. 115 workstations in library, computer center, student center. Dormitories wired for high-speed internet access and linked to campus network. Commuter students can connect to campus network. Online course registration, online library, helpline, repair service, wireless network available.

Student life. Freshman orientation: Mandatory. Preregistration for classes offered. Five-day orientation held prior to beginning of fall semester. **Policies:** Academic honor code enforced. **Housing:** Single-sex dorms, apartments, fraternity/sorority housing available. $200 fully refundable deposit, deadline 5/1. Minidorms of fewer than 80 students available; some apartments available for upperclassmen. **Activities:** Bands, campus ministries, choral groups, dance, drama, literary magazine, music ensembles, musical theater, radio station, student government, student newspaper, Baptist Student Union, Fellowship of Christian Athletes, Union of Black Leaders, Habitat for Humanity.

Athletics. NAIA. **Intercollegiate:** Baseball M, basketball, cheerleading M, cross-country, football (tackle) M, golf, soccer, softball W, tennis, track and field, volleyball W. **Intramural:** Basketball, equestrian, football (non-tackle), golf, racquetball, soccer, softball, table tennis, tennis, volleyball. **Team name:** Tigers.

Student services. Alcohol/substance abuse counseling, chaplain/spiritual director, career counseling, student employment services, financial aid counseling, health services, minority student services, personal counseling, placement for graduates.

Contact. E-mail: admissions@georgetowncollege.edu
Phone: (502) 863-8009 Toll-free number: (800) 788-9985
Fax: (502) 868-7733
Ann McCamy, Director of Admissions, Georgetown College, 400 East College Street, Georgetown, KY 40324

ITT Technical Institute: Louisville
Louisville, Kentucky
www.itt-tech.edu   **CB code: 2728**

- For-profit 4-year technical college
- Large city
- 993 undergraduates
- Interview required

General. Accredited by ACICS. **Degrees:** 58 bachelor's, 236 associate awarded. **Calendar:** Quarter, extensive summer session. **Full-time faculty:** 14 total. **Part-time faculty:** 98 total.

Basis for selection. Satisfactory scores from on-site tests in English and mathematics required.

2011-2012 Annual costs. Estimated costs as of June 2011: per-credit-hour charge, $493, depending upon level and course of study; academic fee, $200. Certain programs of study require purchase of tools, which could cost an additional $100 to $655. All costs are subject to change.

Application procedures. Admission: No deadline. No application fee. Admission notification on a rolling basis. **Financial aid:** No deadline. FAFSA, institutional form required. Applicants notified on a rolling basis.

Academics. Credit/placement by examination: AP, CLEP. **Support services:** Learning center, tutoring.

Majors. Business: Business admin, construction management, e-commerce. **Communications technology:** Animation/special effects. **Computer sciences:** Security. **Protective services:** Law enforcement admin.

Computing on campus. Online library available.

Student services. Career counseling, student employment services, placement for graduates.

Contact. Phone: (502) 327-7424
Steve Allen, Director of Recruitment, ITT Technical Institute: Louisville, 9500 Ormsby Station Road, Louisville, KY 40223

Kentucky Christian University
Grayson, Kentucky
www.kcu.edu   **CB code: 1377**

- Private 4-year Bible and liberal arts college affiliated with Church of Christ
- Residential campus in small town
- 548 degree-seeking undergraduates: 7% part-time, 45% women
- 36 degree-seeking graduate students
- 76% of applicants admitted
- SAT or ACT (ACT writing optional), application essay required

General. Founded in 1919. Regionally accredited. **Degrees:** 81 bachelor's awarded; master's offered. **ROTC:** Army. **Location:** 25 miles from Ashland, 100 miles from Lexington. **Calendar:** Semester, limited summer session. **Full-time faculty:** 36 total; 53% have terminal degrees, 64% women. **Part-time faculty:** 16 total; 12% have terminal degrees, 38% women. **Class size:** 78% < 20, 15% 20-39, 4% 40-49, 3% 50-99.

Freshman class profile. 357 applied, 271 admitted, 186 enrolled.

Out-of-state:	44%	**Live on campus:**	89%

Basis for selection. High school grades and rank in class, ACT or SAT test scores, personal references, and religious commitment considered. Interview recommended for academically weak. **Home schooled:** Transcript of courses and grades, letter of recommendation (nonparent) required. **Learning Disabled:** Students with special needs should contact the Vice President of Student Services or the Director of Campus Counseling to make arrangements for special accommodations.

High school preparation. College-preparatory program recommended.

2012-2013 Annual costs. Tuition/fees: $15,750. Room/board: $6,750. Books/supplies: $1,200. Personal expenses: $2,316.

2010-2011 Financial aid. Need-based: 182 full-time freshmen applied for aid; 169 were judged to have need; 169 of these received aid. Average need met was 70%. Average scholarship/grant was $5,490; average loan $3,628. **Non-need-based:** Scholarships awarded for academics, alumni affiliation, leadership, minority status, music/drama, religious affiliation.

Application procedures. Admission: No deadline. $30 fee. Admission notification on a rolling basis. **Financial aid:** Priority date 3/1; no closing date. FAFSA required. Applicants notified on a rolling basis starting 3/15; must reply within 2 week(s) of notification.

Academics. All students required to major in Bible as a second degree. **Special study options:** Distance learning, double major, dual enrollment of high school students, independent study, internships, liberal arts/career combination, study abroad, teacher certification program. **Credit/placement by examination:** AP, CLEP, IB, SAT, ACT. **Support services:** Learning center, reduced course load, remedial instruction, study skills assistance, tutoring, writing center.

Majors. Biology: General. **Business:** Business admin. **Education:** Elementary, English, mathematics, middle, social studies. **Health services:** Nursing (RN). **History:** General. **Human services:** Social work. **Liberal arts:** Humanities. **Psychology:** Counseling. **Theology:** Bible, pastoral counseling, sacred music. **Visual/performing arts:** Music management, music performance.

Most popular majors. Business/marketing 12%, education 24%, health sciences 14%, interdisciplinary studies 8%, liberal arts 6%, social sciences 10%, theological studies 23%.

Computing on campus. 50 workstations in library, computer center, student center. Dormitories wired for high-speed internet access and linked to campus network. Commuter students can connect to campus network. Online library, helpline, repair service, wireless network available.

Student life. Freshman orientation: Mandatory. Preregistration for classes offered. **Policies:** All students under 26 not living with parents must live in on-campus housing. Religious observance required. **Housing:** Guaranteed on-campus for all undergraduates. Single-sex dorms, special housing for disabled, apartments available. $100 nonrefundable deposit. **Activities:** Bands, campus ministries, choral groups, drama, international student organizations, music ensembles, student government, Global Mission Awareness, Pi Chi Delta, Collegiate Music Educators National Conference, Herodotus Society, Laos Protos, American Association of Christian Counselors, Students in Free Enterprise.

Athletics. NAIA, NCCAA. **Intercollegiate:** Basketball, cheerleading M, cross-country, football (tackle) M, soccer, volleyball W. **Intramural:** Basketball, football (non-tackle) M, soccer, softball, table tennis, volleyball. **Team name:** Knights.

Student services. Chaplain/spiritual director, career counseling, financial aid counseling, health services, minority student services, personal counseling, women's services. **Physically disabled:** Services for visually, hearing impaired.

Contact. E-mail: knights@kcu.edu
Phone: (606) 474-3266 Toll-free number: (800) 522-3181
Fax: (606) 474-3155
Sheree Greer, Director of Admissions, Kentucky Christian University, 100 Academic Parkway, Grayson, KY 41143-2205

Kentucky Mountain Bible College
Vancleve, Kentucky
www.kmbc.edu   CB code: 1384

- Private 4-year Bible college affiliated with Kentucky Mountain Holiness Association
- Residential campus in rural community
- 75 degree-seeking undergraduates
- ACT (writing optional), application essay required

General. Founded in 1931. Accredited by ABHE. **Degrees:** 11 bachelor's, 1 associate awarded. **Location:** 75 miles from Lexington. **Calendar:** Semester. **Part-time faculty:** 15 total. **Class size:** 84% < 20, 16% 20-39.

Freshman class profile.

GPA 3.75 or higher:	7%	Rank in top quarter:	11%
GPA 3.50-3.74:	29%	Rank in top tenth:	11%
GPA 3.0-3.49:	14%	Out-of-state:	30%
GPA 2.0-2.99:	50%	Live on campus:	100%

Basis for selection. All students must have C average or above and provide 2 recommendations. 15 ACT required. Provisional admission granted. Interview recommended.

High school preparation. 18 units required. Required and recommended units include English 4, mathematics 2, history 2 and science 2. A total of 10 units in English, math, science or language required out of 18 units.

2011-2012 Annual costs. Tuition/fees: $6,690. Room/board: $4,100. Books/supplies: $500. Personal expenses: $250.

Financial aid. **Non-need-based:** Scholarships awarded for academics, job skills, leadership, music/drama.

Application procedures. **Admission:** Priority date 6/1; no deadline. $25 fee, may be waived for applicants with need. Admission notification on a rolling basis. **Financial aid:** Priority date 4/1, closing date 6/30. FAFSA, institutional form required. Applicants notified on a rolling basis starting 3/15.

Academics. **Special study options:** Combined bachelor's/graduate degree, distance learning, dual enrollment of high school students, independent study, internships, teacher certification program. **Credit/placement by examination:** AP, CLEP, ACT, institutional tests. 20 credit hours maximum toward associate degree, 20 toward bachelor's. **Support services:** Reduced course load, remedial instruction, study skills assistance, tutoring.

Majors. **Communications:** Communications/speech/rhetoric. **Education:** Elementary. **Theology:** Missionary, religious ed, sacred music, theology.

Computing on campus. 12 workstations in library, computer center. Dormitories wired for high-speed internet access and linked to campus network. Commuter students can connect to campus network. Repair service, wireless network available.

Student life. Freshman orientation: Mandatory. Preregistration for classes offered. Two-day program held immediately before semester; includes Bible-knowledge testing. **Policies:** No pets, except fish and turtles, allowed in dorms. Religious observance required. **Housing:** Guaranteed on-campus for all undergraduates. Single-sex dorms, apartments, wellness housing available. Pets allowed in dorm rooms. **Activities:** Campus ministries, choral groups, drama, radio station, student government, student newspaper, missionary student involvement group, student council, class organizations.

Student services. Chaplain/spiritual director, financial aid counseling, health services, personal counseling.

Contact. E-mail: kmbc@kmbc.edu
Phone: (606) 693-5000 ext. 130
Toll-free number: (800) 879-5622 ext. 130 Fax: (888) 742-1124
David Lorimer, Chief Admissions Counselor, Kentucky Mountain Bible College, Box 10, Vancleve, KY 41385-0010

Kentucky State University
Frankfort, Kentucky   CB member
www.kysu.edu   CB code: 1368

- Public 4-year university
- Residential campus in large town
- 2,263 degree-seeking undergraduates: 13% part-time, 60% women, 58% African American, 1% Hispanic American
- 238 degree-seeking graduate students
- 30% of applicants admitted
- SAT or ACT (ACT writing optional) required

General. Founded in 1886. Regionally accredited. Land grant institution, 1890 Historically Black College/University. **Degrees:** 226 bachelor's, 58 associate awarded; master's offered. **ROTC:** Army, Air Force. **Location:** 50 miles from Louisville, 25 miles from Lexington. **Calendar:** Semester, limited summer session. **Full-time faculty:** 130 total; 63% have terminal degrees, 37% minority, 45% women. **Part-time faculty:** 47 total; 2% have terminal degrees, 32% minority, 38% women. **Class size:** 60% < 20, 40% 20-39, less than 1% 40-49, less than 1% >100. **Special facilities:** Center of excellence for the study of Kentucky African Americans.

Freshman class profile. 10,322 applied, 3,126 admitted, 558 enrolled.

Mid 50% test scores		GPA 3.0-3.49:	17%
SAT critical reading:	380-470	GPA 2.0-2.99:	58%
SAT math:	380-470	Return as sophomores:	50%
SAT writing:	360-450	Out-of-state:	64%
ACT composite:	16-20	Live on campus:	82%
GPA 3.75 or higher:	5%	International:	1%
GPA 3.50-3.74:	6%		

Basis for selection. Unconditional admission for graduates of accredited high schools who meet Pre-College Curriculum requirements and have 430 admission index. Interview recommended for nursing majors. Audition recommended for music majors. Portfolio recommended for art majors. Interview recommended and essay required of applicants to College of Leadership Studies. **Home schooled:** Transcript of courses and grades required. Notarized statement from the homeschool teacher detailing the content and duration of the student's homeschool curriculum required.

High school preparation. College-preparatory program recommended. 17 units required. Required units include English 4, mathematics 3, social studies 3, science 3, foreign language 2 and visual/performing arts 1. Physical Education 0.5, Health Education 0.5.

2011-2012 Annual costs. Tuition/fees: $6,532; $14,368 out-of-state. Room/board: $6,480. Books/supplies: $1,300. Personal expenses: $3,200.

2011-2012 Financial aid. **Need-based:** 506 full-time freshmen applied for aid; 501 were judged to have need; 496 of these received aid. Average need met was 45%. Average scholarship/grant was $7,150; average loan $3,404. 44% of total undergraduate aid awarded as scholarships/grants, 56% as loans/jobs. **Non-need-based:** Awarded to 54 full-time undergraduates, including 21 freshmen. Scholarships awarded for academics, alumni affiliation, art, athletics, minority status, music/drama, state residency.

Application procedures. **Admission:** No deadline. $30 fee, may be waived for applicants with need. Admission notification on a rolling basis. **Financial aid:** Priority date 4/15; no closing date. FAFSA required. Applicants notified on a rolling basis starting 3/15; must reply within 2 week(s) of notification.

Academics. **Special study options:** Combined bachelor's/graduate degree, cooperative education, distance learning, double major, dual enrollment of high school students, ESL, honors, independent study, internships, liberal arts/career combination, student-designed major, study abroad, teacher certification program. **Credit/placement by examination:** AP, CLEP, IB, SAT, ACT. **Support services:** Learning center, pre-admission summer program, reduced course load, remedial instruction, study skills assistance, tutoring, writing center.

Majors. **Area/ethnic studies:** African. **Biology:** General. **Business:** General. **Computer sciences:** General, information technology. **Education:** Elementary, physical. **English:** English lit. **Foreign languages:** Spanish. **Health services:** Nursing (RN). **Human services:** General, social work. **Liberal**

arts: Arts/sciences. **Math:** General. **Physical sciences:** Chemistry. **Protective services:** Criminal justice. **Psychology:** General. **Social sciences:** General, political science. **Visual/performing arts:** Music, studio arts. **Work/family studies:** Family studies.

Most popular majors. Business/marketing 12%, education 12%, liberal arts 16%, psychology 8%, public administration/social services 7%, security/protective services 10%.

Computing on campus. 450 workstations in dormitories, library, computer center, student center. Dormitories wired for high-speed internet access and linked to campus network. Commuter students can connect to campus network. Online course registration, online library, helpline, wireless network available.

Student life. Freshman orientation: Mandatory. Preregistration for classes offered. **Housing:** Guaranteed on-campus for freshmen. Coed dorms, single-sex dorms available. $250 nonrefundable deposit. **Activities:** Bands, campus ministries, choral groups, dance, international student organizations, music ensembles, musical theater, opera, student government, student newspaper, Phi Beta Sigma Fraternity, Inc., Zeta Phi Beta Sorority, Inc., Alpha Kappa Alpha Sorority, Inc., Sigma Gamma Rho Sorority, Inc., Iota Phi Theta Fraternity, Inc., Kappa Alpha Psi Fraternity, Inc., Baptist Student Union, Wesley Foundation, NAACP, Fellowship of Christian Athletes.

Athletics. NCAA. **Intercollegiate:** Baseball M, basketball, cheerleading M, cross-country, football (tackle) M, golf M, softball W, track and field, volleyball W. **Team name:** Thorobreds.

Student services. Adult student services, alcohol/substance abuse counseling, chaplain/spiritual director, career counseling, student employment services, financial aid counseling, health services, minority student services, personal counseling, placement for graduates, veterans' counselor, women's services. **Physically disabled:** Services for visually, hearing impaired.

Contact. E-mail: admissions@kysu.edu
Phone: (502) 597-6813 Toll-free number: (877) 367-5978
Fax: (502) 597-5814
Director of Admissions, Kentucky State University, 400 East Main Street, ASB 312, Frankfort, KY 40601

Kentucky Wesleyan College
Owensboro, Kentucky
www.kwc.edu

CB member
CB code: 1369

- Private 4-year liberal arts college affiliated with United Methodist Church
- Residential campus in small city
- 730 degree-seeking undergraduates: 4% part-time, 47% women, 10% African American, 2% Hispanic American, 1% Native American, 1% international
- 52% of applicants admitted
- SAT or ACT (ACT writing optional) required

General. Founded in 1858. Regionally accredited. **Degrees:** 156 bachelor's awarded. **ROTC:** Army. **Location:** 116 miles from Louisville; 120 miles from Nashville, TN. **Calendar:** Semester, extensive summer session. **Full-time faculty:** 44 total; 73% have terminal degrees, 7% minority, 32% women. **Part-time faculty:** 37 total; 38% have terminal degrees, 3% minority, 54% women. **Class size:** 78% < 20, 21% 20-39, less than 1% 40-49, less than 1% 50-99. **Special facilities:** Center for the sciences, center for the arts, fully computerized writing workshop, center for business studies.

Freshman class profile. 2,000 applied, 1,043 admitted, 188 enrolled.

Mid 50% test scores		GPA 2.0-2.99:	35%
SAT critical reading:	400-530	Rank in top quarter:	45%
SAT math:	460-540	Rank in top tenth:	21%
SAT writing:	390-470	Out-of-state:	30%
ACT composite:	19-25	Live on campus:	72%
GPA 3.75 or higher:	16%	Fraternities:	30%
GPA 3.50-3.74:	12%	Sororities:	14%
GPA 3.0-3.49:	37%		

Basis for selection. Secondary school record very important. Test scores, GPA, class rank, and school activities important. **Home schooled:** Transcript of courses and grades required.

High school preparation. College-preparatory program recommended. 13 units required. Required and recommended units include English 4, mathematics 3, social studies 3, science 3 and foreign language 2.

2011-2012 Annual costs. Tuition/fees: $19,390. Room/board: $6,920. Books/supplies: $1,400. Personal expenses: $1,000.

2011-2012 Financial aid. Need-based: Average need met was 69%. Average scholarship/grant was $13,836; average loan $3,666. 72% of total undergraduate aid awarded as scholarships/grants, 28% as loans/jobs. **Non-need-based:** Scholarships awarded for academics, alumni affiliation, art, athletics, leadership, music/drama, religious affiliation, state residency.

Application procedures. Admission: No deadline. No application fee. Admission notification on a rolling basis beginning on or about 9/1. **Financial aid:** Closing date 3/15. FAFSA required. Applicants notified on a rolling basis starting 2/15; must reply within 2 week(s) of notification.

Academics. Special study options: Accelerated study, combined bachelor's/graduate degree, distance learning, double major, independent study, internships, liberal arts/career combination, student-designed major, study abroad, teacher certification program, Washington semester. **Credit/placement by examination:** AP, CLEP, IB, SAT, ACT, institutional tests. 42 credit hours maximum toward bachelor's degree. International Baccalaureate Diploma credit will be awarded for advanced course scores of 6 or 7, with up to 10 hours of credit awarded. **Support services:** Learning center, reduced course load, remedial instruction, study skills assistance, tutoring, writing center.

Majors. Biology: General, zoology. **Business:** General, accounting, business admin, communications. **Communications:** Communications/speech/rhetoric. **Computer sciences:** General. **Education:** Art, biology, chemistry, elementary, English, mathematics, middle, physical, social studies, Spanish. **English:** English lit. **Foreign languages:** Spanish. **History:** General. **Math:** General. **Parks/recreation:** Sports admin. **Philosophy/religion:** Religion. **Physical sciences:** Chemistry, physics. **Protective services:** Criminal justice. **Psychology:** General. **Social sciences:** Political science, sociology. **Visual/performing arts:** Art, music management, music performance, studio arts.

Most popular majors. Biology 13%, business/marketing 22%, education 13%, physical sciences 6%, psychology 6%, security/protective services 8%.

Computing on campus. 125 workstations in dormitories, library, computer center, student center. Dormitories wired for high-speed internet access and linked to campus network. Commuter students can connect to campus network. Online course registration, online library, helpline, repair service, wireless network available.

Student life. Freshman orientation: Mandatory, $125 fee. Preregistration for classes offered. **Housing:** Guaranteed on-campus for freshmen. Coed dorms, single-sex dorms, special housing for disabled, apartments, fraternity/sorority housing, wellness housing available. $100 fully refundable deposit, deadline 8/20. **Activities:** Bands, campus ministries, choral groups, dance, drama, literary magazine, music ensembles, radio station, student government, student newspaper, student activities programming board, Baptist Student Union, United Methodist Student Fellowship, Brothers and Sisters in Christ, Criminal Justice Association, College Republicans, Young Democrats, Fellowship of Christian Athletes, psychology club.

Athletics. NCAA. **Intercollegiate:** Baseball M, basketball, cross-country, football (tackle) M, golf, soccer, softball W, tennis W, volleyball W. **Intramural:** Basketball, bowling, football (non-tackle), soccer, softball, table tennis, tennis, volleyball. **Team name:** Panthers.

Student services. Alcohol/substance abuse counseling, chaplain/spiritual director, career counseling, student employment services, financial aid counseling, health services, personal counseling, placement for graduates. **Physically disabled:** Services for visually impaired.

Contact. E-mail: admitme@kwc.edu
Phone: (270) 852-3120 Toll-free number: (800) 999-0592
Fax: (270) 852-3133
Lauren Lee, Director of Admissions, Kentucky Wesleyan College, 3000 Frederica Street, Owensboro, KY 42301

Lindsey Wilson College
Columbia, Kentucky
www.lindsey.edu

CB code: 1409

- Private 4-year liberal arts college affiliated with United Methodist Church
- Residential campus in small town
- 2,192 degree-seeking undergraduates
- 416 graduate students
- ACT required

General. Founded in 1903. Regionally accredited. **Degrees:** 349 bachelor's, 36 associate awarded; master's offered. **Location:** 100 miles from Louisville. **Calendar:** Semester, limited summer session. **Full-time faculty:** 99 total. **Part-time faculty:** 130 total.

Freshman class profile. 3,005 applied, 2,111 admitted, 544 enrolled.

Out-of-state:	5%	Live on campus:	69%

Basis for selection. Open admission, but selective for some programs. Special requirements for education, human services and nursing programs. Interview recommended. **Home schooled:** Transcript of courses and grades required.

High school preparation. College-preparatory program recommended.

2012-2013 Annual costs. Tuition/fees: $21,230. Room/board: $8,130. Books/supplies: $900. Personal expenses: $1,200.

Financial aid. All financial aid based on need.

Application procedures. Admission: Priority date 6/1; no deadline. No application fee. Admission notification on a rolling basis beginning on or about 1/1. **Financial aid:** Priority date 3/1; no closing date. FAFSA, institutional form required. Applicants notified on a rolling basis starting 5/1; must reply within 2 week(s) of notification.

Academics. Special study options: Double major, dual enrollment of high school students, honors, independent study, internships, student-designed major, study abroad, teacher certification program, Washington semester, weekend college. On-campus and extension evening program for associate degree in business management and computer science, weekend extension program in human services. **Credit/placement by examination:** AP, CLEP. 16 credit hours maximum toward associate degree, 32 toward bachelor's. **Support services:** Learning center, reduced course load, remedial instruction, study skills assistance, tutoring, writing center.

Majors. Area/ethnic studies: American. **Biology:** General. **Business:** Business admin. **Communications:** Communications/speech/rhetoric, journalism. **Education:** Art, biology, elementary, English, mathematics, middle, music, physical, secondary, social science. **English:** English lit. **History:** General. **Liberal arts:** Humanities. **Math:** General. **Parks/recreation:** Health/fitness. **Philosophy/religion:** Christian. **Protective services:** Criminal justice. **Psychology:** General. **Social sciences:** General. **Visual/performing arts:** Studio arts.

Most popular majors. Biology 6%, business/marketing 13%, communications/journalism 7%, education 7%, public administration/social services 47%.

Computing on campus. 100 workstations in library, computer center, student center. Dormitories wired for high-speed internet access and linked to campus network. Commuter students can connect to campus network. Online course registration, online library, wireless network available.

Student life. Freshman orientation: Mandatory. Preregistration for classes offered. **Policies:** All students not living with family must live in campus housing. **Housing:** Single-sex dorms, apartments, wellness housing available. $40 deposit. **Activities:** Bands, campus ministries, choral groups, dance, drama, international student organizations, literary magazine, music ensembles, student government, student newspaper, Bonner Scholars, Humanity Hands, student activities board, Student Ambassadors.

Athletics. NAIA. **Intercollegiate:** Baseball M, basketball, bowling, cross-country, football (tackle) M, golf, soccer, softball W, swimming, tennis, track and field, volleyball W, wrestling M. **Intramural:** Basketball, football (non-tackle), racquetball, soccer, softball, swimming, table tennis, tennis, volleyball. **Team name:** Blue Raiders.

Student services. Alcohol/substance abuse counseling, chaplain/spiritual director, career counseling, student employment services, financial aid counseling, health services, minority student services, personal counseling, placement for graduates, veterans' counselor, women's services. **Physically disabled:** Services for visually impaired.

Contact. E-mail: admissions@lindsey.edu
Phone: (270) 384-8100 Toll-free number: (800) 264-0138
Fax: (270) 384-8591
Charity Ferguson, Director of Admissions, Lindsey Wilson College, 210 Lindsey Wilson Street, Columbia, KY 42728

Mid-Continent University
Mayfield, Kentucky
www.midcontinent.edu   **CB code: 0254**

- Private 4-year Bible and liberal arts college affiliated with Southern Baptist Convention
- Commuter campus in large town

- 2,367 degree-seeking undergraduates: 17% part-time, 62% women, 15% African American, 2% Hispanic American, 1% international
- 103 degree-seeking graduate students
- 95% of applicants admitted
- SAT or ACT (ACT writing optional), application essay required

General. Founded in 1949. Regionally accredited. **Degrees:** 414 bachelor's, 216 associate awarded; master's offered. **Location:** 20 miles from Paducah, 125 miles from Nashville, TN. **Calendar:** Semester, limited summer session. **Full-time faculty:** 45 total; 47% have terminal degrees, 20% minority, 22% women. **Part-time faculty:** 154 total; 9% have terminal degrees, 4% minority, 45% women. **Class size:** 77% < 20, 23% 20-39, less than 1% 40-49.

Freshman class profile. 401 applied, 382 admitted, 282 enrolled.

Mid 50% test scores			
SAT critical reading:	380-480	GPA 3.0-3.49:	26%
SAT math:	440-500	GPA 2.0-2.99:	53%
SAT writing:	360-480	Rank in top quarter:	18%
ACT composite:	17-22	Rank in top tenth:	5%
GPA 3.75 or higher:	11%	Out-of-state:	12%
GPA 3.50-3.74:	6%	Live on campus:	13%
		International:	1%

Basis for selection. Secondary school record and standardized test scores most important. Entering students tested in mathematics and English. **Home schooled:** Statement describing home school structure and mission, transcript of courses and grades, letter of recommendation (nonparent) required.

High school preparation. College-preparatory program recommended. Required units include English 4, mathematics 2, social studies 2, science 2 (laboratory 2) and foreign language 1.

2011-2012 Annual costs. Tuition/fees: $13,350. Room/board: $6,800. Books/supplies: $1,400. Personal expenses: $1,500.

2010-2011 Financial aid. Need-based: 284 full-time freshmen applied for aid; 279 were judged to have need; 279 of these received aid. Average need met was 35%. Average scholarship/grant was $15,917; average loan $6,745. 49% of total undergraduate aid awarded as scholarships/grants, 51% as loans/jobs. **Non-need-based:** Awarded to 95 full-time undergraduates, including 24 freshmen. Scholarships awarded for academics.

Application procedures. Admission: Priority date 8/1; no deadline. $50 fee, may be waived for applicants with need. Admission notification on a rolling basis. **Financial aid:** Priority date 3/15, closing date 5/30. FAFSA, institutional form required. Applicants notified on a rolling basis starting 4/1; must reply within 2 week(s) of notification.

Academics. Accelerated bachelor programs in Business Management and Psychology & Counseling and accelerated master program in Human Resources Management available for adult learners. **Special study options:** Accelerated study, combined bachelor's/graduate degree, double major, dual enrollment of high school students, independent study, study abroad, teacher certification program. **Credit/placement by examination:** AP, CLEP, SAT, ACT, institutional tests. 30 credit hours maximum toward bachelor's degree. **Support services:** Remedial instruction, tutoring.

Majors. Business: Business admin, organizational behavior. **Education:** Elementary. **English:** English lit. **Math:** General. **Philosophy/religion:** Christian. **Psychology:** General, counseling. **Social sciences:** General. **Theology:** Bible, missionary, religious ed.

Most popular majors. Business/marketing 84%, psychology 8%.

Computing on campus. 43 workstations in library, computer center, student center. Dormitories wired for high-speed internet access. Online library, wireless network available.

Student life. Freshman orientation: Mandatory. Preregistration for classes offered. 2-3 day orientation process at beginning of academic year. **Policies:** Religious observance required. **Housing:** Single-sex dorms available. $200 fully refundable deposit, deadline 8/1. **Activities:** Student government, student newspaper, Baptist Student Union, Fellowship of Christian Athletes, psychology club, international student association.

Athletics. NAIA, NCCAA. **Intercollegiate:** Baseball M, basketball, soccer M, softball W, volleyball W. **Team name:** Cougars, Lady Cougars.

Student services. Chaplain/spiritual director, career counseling, financial aid counseling, personal counseling, veterans' counselor. **Physically disabled:** Services for visually, hearing impaired.

Contact. E-mail: admissions@midcontinent.edu
Phone: (270) 247-8521 Toll-free number: (866) 894-8878
Fax: (270) 247-3115
Karl Hatton, Associate Dean for Student Life/Admissions/Orientation, Mid-Continent University, 99 Powell Road East, Mayfield, KY 42066-9007

Midway College

Midway, Kentucky
www.midway.edu

CB member
CB code: 1467

- Private 4-year liberal arts college for women affiliated with Christian Church (Disciples of Christ)
- Commuter campus in small town
- 1,624 degree-seeking undergraduates
- 52% of applicants admitted
- SAT or ACT required

General. Founded in 1847. Regionally accredited. Men admitted to evening, weekend and online programs. **Degrees:** 205 bachelor's, 127 associate awarded; master's, professional offered. **ROTC:** Army, Air Force. **Location:** 12 miles from Lexington, 60 miles from Louisville. **Calendar:** Semester, limited summer session. **Full-time faculty:** 54 total. **Part-time faculty:** 76 total. **Class size:** 80% < 20, 19% 20-39, 1% 40-49. **Special facilities:** Equine science center, riding arena, campus farm.

Freshman class profile. 2,306 applied, 1,199 admitted, 240 enrolled.

Mid 50% test scores			
SAT critical reading:	430-530	GPA 3.0-3.49:	36%
SAT math:	420-520	GPA 2.0-2.99:	24%
SAT writing:	420-520	Rank in top quarter:	42%
ACT composite:	18-26	Rank in top tenth:	16%
GPA 3.75 or higher:	15%	Out-of-state:	9%
GPA 3.50-3.74:	23%	Live on campus:	45%

Basis for selection. High school record and test scores important. Essay and letters of recommendation encouraged. More competitive requirements established for certain programs such as biology, education, nursing. Interview required for majors in nursing; also required of academically weak. Essay recommended for students who are conditionally admitted.

High school preparation. 15 units required. Required and recommended units include English 4, mathematics 2, social studies 1, history 1 and science 2. Specific college-preparatory program required for some majors.

2011-2012 Annual costs. Tuition/fees: $19,800. Room/board: $7,280. Books/supplies: $1,200. Personal expenses: $1,000.

Financial aid. Non-need-based: Scholarships awarded for academics, alumni affiliation, art, athletics, leadership, minority status, religious affiliation. **Additional information:** Audition required of applicants for music scholarships. Portfolio required for art scholarships.

Application procedures. Admission: Priority date 4/1; no deadline. $10 fee, may be waived for applicants with need, free for online applicants. Admission notification on a rolling basis. Must reply by May 1 or within 4 week(s) if notified thereafter. **Financial aid:** Priority date 4/1, closing date 8/1. FAFSA, institutional form required. Applicants notified on a rolling basis; must reply within 4 week(s) of notification.

Academics. Special study options: Accelerated study, cooperative education, distance learning, double major, dual enrollment of high school students, independent study, internships, liberal arts/career combination, study abroad, teacher certification program. Evening programs in business, nursing, and teacher certification. **Credit/placement by examination:** AP, CLEP, IB, institutional tests. 12 credit hours maximum toward associate degree, 12 toward bachelor's. **Support services:** Learning center, reduced course load, remedial instruction, tutoring, writing center.

Majors. Biology: General. **Business:** General, human resources, organizational behavior. **Computer sciences:** General. **Conservation:** Environmental science. **Education:** Elementary, middle, multi-level teacher, secondary, special ed. **English:** English lit. **General:** Equestrian studies. **Health services:** Health care admin, nursing (RN), pharmaceutical sciences, predental, premedicine, preoptometry, prepharmacy. **Liberal arts:** Arts/sciences. **Math:** General. **Parks/recreation:** Sports admin. **Protective services:** Disaster management, homeland security, security services. **Psychology:** General.

Most popular majors. Agriculture 9%, business/marketing 52%, education 18%.

Computing on campus. 60 workstations in dormitories, library, computer center, student center. Dormitories wired for high-speed internet access and linked to campus network. Commuter students can connect to campus network. Online course registration, online library, helpline, wireless network available.

Student life. Freshman orientation: Mandatory. Preregistration for classes offered. 2-3 day orientation prior to start of term. **Policies:** All students under 21, unmarried, and not living at home required to live in campus housing. **Housing:** Guaranteed on-campus for all undergraduates. Special housing for disabled, wellness housing available. $100 nonrefundable deposit, deadline 5/1. **Activities:** Campus ministries, choral groups, international student organizations, student government, commuters committee, Fellowship of Christian Athletes, Disciples on Campus, Ruth Slack Roach Scholars.

Athletics. NAIA. **Intercollegiate:** Basketball W, cross-country W, equestrian W, soccer W, softball W, tennis W, track and field W, volleyball W. **Team name:** Eagles.

Student services. Adult student services, chaplain/spiritual director, career counseling, student employment services, financial aid counseling, health services, personal counseling, placement for graduates.

Contact. E-mail: admissions@midway.edu
Phone: (859) 846-5347 Toll-free number: (800) 755-0031
Fax: (859) 846-5787
Johnie Dean, Vice President and Dean of Admissions, Midway College, 512 East Stephens Street, Midway, KY 40347-1120

Morehead State University

Morehead, Kentucky
www.moreheadstate.edu

CB member
CB code: 1487

- Public 4-year university
- Residential campus in large town
- 6,854 degree-seeking undergraduates: 20% part-time, 61% women, 4% African American, 1% Hispanic American, 1% international
- 1,362 degree-seeking graduate students
- 86% of applicants admitted
- SAT or ACT (ACT writing optional) required

General. Founded in 1922. Regionally accredited. **Degrees:** 1,079 bachelor's, 165 associate awarded; master's offered. **ROTC:** Army. **Location:** 65 miles from Lexington; 70 miles from Huntington, WV. **Calendar:** Semester, extensive summer session. **Full-time faculty:** 374 total; 12% minority, 48% women. **Part-time faculty:** 88 total; 10% minority, 58% women. **Class size:** 59% < 20, 34% 20-39, 4% 40-49, 3% 50-99, less than 1% >100. **Special facilities:** Planetarium, agriculture complex, outdoor learning center at Cave Run, Kentucky folk art center, space science center, space tracking radio telescope, Center for Traditional Music.

Freshman class profile. 3,461 applied, 2,968 admitted, 1,372 enrolled.

Mid 50% test scores			
SAT critical reading:	430-550	Rank in top quarter:	48%
SAT math:	460-570	Rank in top tenth:	21%
ACT composite:	19-25	Out-of-state:	15%
GPA 3.75 or higher:	24%	Live on campus:	79%
GPA 3.50-3.74:	18%	International:	1%
GPA 3.0-3.49:	32%	Fraternities:	8%
GPA 2.0-2.99:	25%	Sororities:	8%

Basis for selection. Test scores and GPA used to calculate index to determine admission. Status and review of pre-college curriculum important. Interview recommended for applicants to specialized allied health programs. Audition recommended for music majors. Students not meeting academic requirements may request an interview and submit additional documentation in order to be admitted with conditions. **Home schooled:** Statement describing home school structure and mission, transcript of courses and grades required.

High school preparation. College-preparatory program required. 22 units required. Required and recommended units include English 4, mathematics 3, social studies 3, history 1, science 3 (laboratory 1), foreign language 2, computer science 1, visual/performing arts 1 and academic electives 7. 1 unit history and appreciation of fine arts required.

2011-2012 Annual costs. Tuition/fees: $6,942; $17,370 out-of-state. Room/board: $7,014. Books/supplies: $1,200. Personal expenses: $1,556.

2011-2012 Financial aid. Need-based: 1,259 full-time freshmen applied for aid; 1,058 were judged to have need; 1,054 of these received aid. Average need met was 71%. Average scholarship/grant was $5,005; average loan $3,139. 53% of total undergraduate aid awarded as scholarships/grants, 47% as loans/jobs. **Non-need-based:** Awarded to 3,570 full-time undergraduates, including 769 freshmen. Scholarships awarded for academics, alumni affiliation, art, athletics, leadership, minority status, music/drama, ROTC, state residency.

Application procedures. Admission: No deadline. $30 fee, may be waived for applicants with need. Admission notification on a rolling basis. **Financial aid:** Priority date 3/15; no closing date. FAFSA, institutional form required. Applicants notified on a rolling basis.

Academics. 2-year transfer programs in pre-chiropractic, pre-dentistry, pre-engineering, pre-forestry, pre-law, pre-medicine, pre-optometry, pre-pharmacy, pre-physical therapy, pre-veterinary medicine, and others offered. **Special study options:** Accelerated study, cooperative education, cross-registration, distance learning, double major, dual enrollment of high school students, exchange student, honors, independent study, internships, student-designed major, study abroad, teacher certification program, Washington semester, weekend college. **Credit/placement by examination:** AP, CLEP, IB, SAT, ACT, institutional tests. 16 credit hours maximum toward associate degree, 32 toward bachelor's. **Support services:** Learning center, pre-admission summer program, remedial instruction, study skills assistance, tutoring, writing center.

Majors. Biology: General. **Business:** Accounting, business admin, finance, management information systems, managerial economics, marketing, real estate. **Communications:** Communications/speech/rhetoric. **Computer sciences:** General. **Education:** Business, early childhood, elementary, health, middle, physical, special ed. **English:** Creative writing, English lit. **Foreign languages:** French, Spanish. **Health services:** Medical radiologic technology/radiation therapy, nursing (RN). **History:** General. **Human services:** Social work. **Math:** General. **Parks/recreation:** Exercise sciences. **Philosophy/religion:** Philosophy. **Physical sciences:** Chemistry, geology, physics. **Psychology:** General. **Social sciences:** General, geography, political science, sociology. **Visual/performing arts:** Dramatic, music, studio arts.

Most popular majors. Business/marketing 10%, education 14%, health sciences 7%, liberal arts 14%, public administration/social services 8%, social sciences 7%, visual/performing arts 6%.

Computing on campus. 2,100 workstations in library, computer center, student center. Dormitories wired for high-speed internet access and linked to campus network. Commuter students can connect to campus network. Online course registration, online library, helpline, repair service, student web hosting, wireless network available.

Student life. Freshman orientation: Mandatory. Preregistration for classes offered. Offered several times in June and July. **Housing:** Coed dorms, special housing for disabled, apartments, fraternity/sorority housing available. $100 fully refundable deposit. Limited housing available at agriculture complex for agriculture science students. Housing for handicapped students and private rooms available. **Activities:** Bands, choral groups, dance, drama, international student organizations, literary magazine, music ensembles, musical theater, opera, radio station, student government, student newspaper, symphony orchestra, TV station, six religious organizations, Young Democrats, Young Republicans, several service organizations.

Athletics. NCAA. **Intercollegiate:** Baseball M, basketball, cheerleading, cross-country, football (tackle) M, golf M, rifle, soccer W, softball W, tennis, track and field, volleyball W. **Intramural:** Archery, badminton, basketball, bowling, football (non-tackle) M, golf, racquetball, soccer, softball, swimming, table tennis, tennis, track and field, volleyball. **Team name:** Eagles.

Student services. Adult student services, alcohol/substance abuse counseling, career counseling, services for economically disadvantaged, student employment services, financial aid counseling, health services, minority student services, personal counseling, veterans' counselor. **Physically disabled:** Services for visually, speech, hearing impaired.

Contact. E-mail: admissions@moreheadstate.edu
Phone: (606) 783-2000 Toll-free number: (800) 585-6781
Fax: (606) 783-5038
Jeffrey Liles, Assistant Vice President of Enrollment Services, Morehead State University, 100 Admissions Center, Morehead, KY 40351

Murray State University
Murray, Kentucky

CB member
CB code: 1494

www.murraystate.edu

- Public 4-year university
- Residential campus in large town
- 7,618 degree-seeking undergraduates: 11% part-time, 58% women, 8% African American, 1% Asian American, 2% Hispanic American, 3% international
- 1,752 degree-seeking graduate students
- 83% of applicants admitted
- ACT (writing recommended) required
- 54% graduate within 6 years

General. Founded in 1922. Regionally accredited. **Degrees:** 1,552 bachelor's, 18 associate awarded; master's offered. **ROTC:** Army. **Location:** 115 miles from Nashville, TN. **Calendar:** Semester, limited summer session. **Full-time faculty:** 421 total; 82% have terminal degrees, 10% minority,

41% women. **Part-time faculty:** 161 total; 30% have terminal degrees, 4% minority, 59% women. **Class size:** 57% < 20, 35% 20-39, 5% 40-49, 3% 50-99, less than 1% >100. **Special facilities:** Biological research station, two farms, equine program, aquatic wildlife area of study, veterinary diagnostic research center, center of excellence for reservoir research, regional museum, state center of excellence for telecommunication systems management, archaeological research and excavation site.

Freshman class profile. 4,276 applied, 3,563 admitted, 1,536 enrolled.

GPA 3.75 or higher:	28%	Return as sophomores:	72%
GPA 3.50-3.74:	16%	Out-of-state:	36%
GPA 3.0-3.49:	29%	Live on campus:	74%
GPA 2.0-2.99:	25%	International:	2%
Rank in top quarter:	40%	Fraternities:	16%
Rank in top tenth:	16%	Sororities:	13%
End year in good standing:	93%		

Basis for selection. Selective admission to nursing, business and social work programs. Other students must rank in top half of class or have 3.0 GPA, 18 ACT and complete pre-college curriculum. Interview recommended for art, music, nursing majors. Auditions recommended for music majors. Portfolio recommended for art majors. **Home schooled:** Transcript of courses and grades required. Students may be asked to verify lab experience and provide GED if ACT score is less than average. **Learning Disabled:** Students should contact Office for Students with Learning Disabilities.

High school preparation. College-preparatory program required. 22 units required. Required and recommended units include English 4, mathematics 3-4, social studies 3, science 3-4 (laboratory 1), foreign language 2 and academic electives 5. 1 art appreciation required. Social sciences must include U.S. history and world civilization. 1 arts and 1 computer science recommended. Math must include 3 algebra I and above. Sciences must include biology and chemistry or physics.

2011-2012 Annual costs. Tuition/fees: $6,576; $17,892 out-of-state. Students from Illinois, Indiana, Missouri, Ohio and Tennessee receive a reduced non-resident rate on tuition. Room/board: $7,000. Books/supplies: $990. Personal expenses: $1,500.

2011-2012 Financial aid. Need-based: 1,080 full-time freshmen applied for aid; 1,004 were judged to have need; 1,004 of these received aid. Average need met was 74%. Average scholarship/grant was $5,124; average loan $3,060. 48% of total undergraduate aid awarded as scholarships/grants, 52% as loans/jobs. **Non-need-based:** Awarded to 3,099 full-time undergraduates, including 1,008 freshmen. Scholarships awarded for academics, alumni affiliation, art, athletics, job skills, leadership, minority status, music/drama, ROTC, state residency.

Application procedures. Admission: Closing date 8/1 (postmark date). $30 fee, may be waived for applicants with need. Admission notification on a rolling basis. **Financial aid:** Priority date 4/1; no closing date. FAFSA, institutional form required. Applicants notified on a rolling basis starting 3/15.

Academics. Special study options: Combined bachelor's/graduate degree, cooperative education, cross-registration, distance learning, double major, dual enrollment of high school students, ESL, exchange student, external degree, honors, independent study, internships, liberal arts/career combination, semester at sea, study abroad, teacher certification program, weekend college. Cooperative center for study in Britain, Kentucky Institute for International Studies, national and international student exchange, 84 partner institutional agreements with universities in Asia, Canada, South America, Middle East, England, Europe, and Central America. **Credit/placement by examination:** AP, CLEP, SAT, ACT, institutional tests. 96 credit hours maximum toward bachelor's degree. **Support services:** Learning center, pre-admission summer program, reduced course load, remedial instruction, study skills assistance, tutoring, writing center.

Honors college/program. Admission based on standardized test scores, GPA, evidence of creative and leadership abilities as displayed in extracurricular interests and activities, and faculty recommendation.

Majors. Biology: General. **Business:** General, accounting, business admin, finance, international, marketing. **Communications:** Advertising, journalism, organizational, public relations, radio/TV. **Communications technology:** Graphics. **Computer sciences:** Computer science, information systems, information technology. **Conservation:** Wildlife/wilderness. **Education:** Art, early childhood, elementary, health, middle, special ed. **Engineering:** Applied physics. **English:** Creative writing, English lit. **Foreign languages:** French, German, Japanese, Spanish. **Health services:** Athletic training, audiology/speech pathology, nursing (RN), veterinary technology/assistant. **History:** General. **Human services:** General, social work. **Liberal arts:** Arts/sciences. **Math:** General. **Parks/recreation:** Exercise sciences, health/fitness, outdoor education. **Philosophy/religion:** Philosophy. **Physical sciences:** Chemistry, physics. **Protective services:** Criminal justice. **Psychology:** General. **Social sciences:** Economics, international relations, political science, sociology. **Visual/performing arts:** Dramatic, music, studio arts. **Work/family studies:** Food/nutrition.

Most popular majors. Business/marketing 15%, communications/journalism 7%, education 15%, engineering/engineering technologies 8%, health sciences 13%, liberal arts 9%.

Computing on campus. 1,800 workstations in dormitories, library, computer center, student center. Dormitories wired for high-speed internet access and linked to campus network. Commuter students can connect to campus network. Online course registration, online library, helpline, repair service, student web hosting, wireless network available.

Student life. Freshman orientation: Available, $100 fee. Preregistration for classes offered. **Housing:** Guaranteed on-campus for freshmen. Coed dorms, single-sex dorms, special housing for disabled, apartments, fraternity/sorority housing, wellness housing available. $150 fully refundable deposit, deadline 3/1. **Activities:** Bands, campus ministries, choral groups, dance, drama, film society, international student organizations, literary magazine, music ensembles, musical theater, opera, radio station, student government, student newspaper, symphony orchestra, TV station, Rotaract, College Democrats, College Republicans, black student council, Newman center, Baptist campus ministry, Christ Ambassadors, Chinese Association, Indian students associations.

Athletics. NCAA. **Intercollegiate:** Baseball M, basketball, bowling M, cheerleading, cross-country, equestrian, football (tackle) M, golf, rifle, rodeo, soccer W, softball W, tennis, track and field W, volleyball W. **Intramural:** Basketball, football (non-tackle), golf, racquetball, soccer, softball, tennis, volleyball. **Team name:** Racers.

Student services. Adult student services, alcohol/substance abuse counseling, chaplain/spiritual director, career counseling, services for economically disadvantaged, student employment services, financial aid counseling, health services, legal services, minority student services, on-campus daycare, personal counseling, placement for graduates, veterans' counselor, women's services. **Physically disabled:** Services for visually, hearing impaired.

Contact. E-mail: admissions@murraystate.edu
Phone: (270) 809-2896 Toll-free number: (800) 272-4678
Fax: (270) 809-3780
Shawn Smee, Director Office of Recruitment, Murray State University, 102 Curris Center Murray State University, Murray, KY 42071

Northern Kentucky University
Highland Heights, Kentucky   **CB member**
www.nku.edu   **CB code: 1574**

- Public 4-year university
- Commuter campus in small town
- 12,499 degree-seeking undergraduates: 20% part-time, 55% women, 7% African American, 1% Asian American, 2% Hispanic American, 2% international
- 2,286 degree-seeking graduate students
- 48% of applicants admitted
- SAT or ACT (ACT writing optional) required
- 34% graduate within 6 years

General. Founded in 1968. Regionally accredited. **Degrees:** 1,974 bachelor's, 105 associate awarded; master's, professional, doctoral offered. **ROTC:** Army, Air Force. **Location:** 7 miles from Cincinnati. **Calendar:** Semester, extensive summer session. **Full-time faculty:** 547 total; 10% minority, 52% women. **Part-time faculty:** 471 total; 6% minority, 56% women. **Special facilities:** Planetarium, anthropology museum, biology museum, cadaver lab.

Freshman class profile. 4,704 applied, 2,271 admitted, 2,128 enrolled.

| Out-of-state: | 33% | Fraternities: | 13% |
| International: | 2% | Sororities: | 18% |

Basis for selection. Requirements vary by program. Students with 2 or more deficiencies may be required to submit essay, letters of recommendation, and activities portfolio. **Home schooled:** Transcript of courses and grades required.

High school preparation. College-preparatory program required. 22 units required. Required units include English 4, mathematics 3, social studies 3, science 3 (laboratory 1), foreign language 2, visual/performing arts 1 and academic electives 5. .5 health, .33 physical education.

2011-2012 Annual costs. Tuition/fees: $7,488; $14,976 out-of-state. Room/board: $6,620.

2010-2011 Financial aid. Need-based: 1,985 full-time freshmen applied for aid; 1,602 were judged to have need; 1,591 of these received aid. Average need met was 60%. Average scholarship/grant was $6,302; average loan

$3,102. 44% of total undergraduate aid awarded as scholarships/grants, 56% as loans/jobs. **Non-need-based:** Awarded to 4,091 full-time undergraduates, including 1,319 freshmen. Scholarships awarded for academics, alumni affiliation, art, athletics, leadership, music/drama, ROTC, state residency.

Application procedures. Admission: Priority date 5/1; deadline 8/1 (postmark date). $40 fee, may be waived for applicants with need. Admission notification on a rolling basis beginning on or about 9/15. Must reply by May 1 or within 2 week(s) if notified thereafter. High school students admitted part-time. **Financial aid:** Priority date 3/1; no closing date. FAFSA required. Applicants notified on a rolling basis starting 4/1.

Academics. Special study options: Accelerated study, cooperative education, cross-registration, distance learning, double major, dual enrollment of high school students, ESL, honors, independent study, internships, student-designed major, study abroad, teacher certification program. **Credit/placement by examination:** AP, CLEP, IB, SAT, ACT, institutional tests. 24 credit hours maximum toward associate degree, 45 toward bachelor's. Credit awarded for CLEP, military, vocational, and National Occupational Competency Testing Institute exams. **Support services:** Learning center, reduced course load, remedial instruction, study skills assistance, tutoring, writing center.

Majors. Biology: General. **Business:** General, accounting, business admin, construction management, entrepreneurial studies, finance, labor relations, management information systems, managerial economics, marketing, organizational behavior, training/development. **Communications:** Broadcast journalism, journalism, public relations, radio/TV. **Computer sciences:** General, information systems, information technology. **Conservation:** Environmental science. **Education:** Business, elementary, kindergarten/preschool, middle, physical, trade/industrial. **English:** English lit, rhetoric/composition. **Foreign languages:** French, German, Spanish. **Health services:** Athletic training, mental health services, nursing (RN), nursing practice. **History:** General. **Human services:** Social work. **Liberal arts:** Arts/sciences. **Math:** General, statistics. **Parks/recreation:** Sports admin. **Philosophy/religion:** Philosophy. **Physical sciences:** Chemistry, geology, physics. **Protective services:** Criminal justice, law enforcement admin. **Psychology:** General. **Social sciences:** General, anthropology, geography, international relations, political science, sociology. **Visual/performing arts:** Commercial/advertising art, dramatic, music, studio arts.

Most popular majors. Business/marketing 28%, communications/journalism 6%, education 9%, health sciences 10%, visual/performing arts 7%.

Computing on campus. 2,000 workstations in dormitories, library, computer center, student center. Dormitories wired for high-speed internet access and linked to campus network. Commuter students can connect to campus network. Online course registration, online library, helpline, repair service, student web hosting, wireless network available.

Student life. Freshman orientation: Mandatory, $45 fee. Preregistration for classes offered. Two-day summer program. **Policies:** Student organizations required to register annually and attend student organization orientation session annually. **Housing:** Coed dorms, special housing for disabled, apartments, wellness housing available. $200 nonrefundable deposit, deadline 5/1. **Activities:** Bands, campus ministries, choral groups, dance, drama, international student organizations, literary magazine, music ensembles, Model UN, musical theater, radio station, student government, student newspaper, TV station, Baptist student union, Newman Center, Schools for Schools, Up til Dawn, Black united students, Common Ground, College Republicans, Campus Democrats, Latino student union.

Athletics. NCAA. **Intercollegiate:** Baseball M, basketball, cheerleading, cross-country, golf, soccer, softball W, tennis, volleyball W. **Intramural:** Basketball, bowling, football (non-tackle), racquetball, soccer, softball, tennis, volleyball, water polo, weight lifting. **Team name:** Norse.

Student services. Adult student services, alcohol/substance abuse counseling, career counseling, services for economically disadvantaged, student employment services, financial aid counseling, health services, legal services, minority student services, on-campus daycare, personal counseling, placement for graduates. **Physically disabled:** Services for visually, speech, hearing impaired.

Contact. E-mail: admitnku@nku.edu
Phone: (859) 572-5220 Toll-free number: (800) 637-9948
Fax: (859) 572-6665
Melissa Gorbandt, Director of Admissions - Outreach, Northern Kentucky University, Administrative Center 401, Northern Kentucky University, Highland Heights, KY 41099

Spalding University
Louisville, Kentucky
www.spalding.edu

CB member
CB code: 1552

- Private 4-year university affiliated with Roman Catholic Church
- Commuter campus in very large city
- 1,313 degree-seeking undergraduates: 25% part-time, 74% women, 29% African American, 1% Asian American, 3% Hispanic American
- 1,061 graduate students
- SAT or ACT (ACT writing optional) required
- 45% graduate within 6 years

General. Founded in 1814. Regionally accredited. **Degrees:** 178 bachelor's, 3 associate awarded; master's, doctoral offered. **ROTC:** Army, Air Force. **Location:** One mile from downtown. **Calendar:** Differs by program, extensive summer session. **Full-time faculty:** 87 total; 75% have terminal degrees, 22% minority, 66% women. **Part-time faculty:** 84 total; 39% have terminal degrees, 44% minority, 64% women. **Class size:** 67% < 20, 32% 20-39, less than 1% 40-49, less than 1% 50-99. **Special facilities:** Historical collection of Edith Stein works, art gallery.

Freshman class profile.

GPA 3.75 or higher:	13%	GPA 2.0-2.99:	48%
GPA 3.50-3.74:	8%	Out-of-state:	1%
GPA 3.0-3.49:	29%	Live on campus:	3%

Basis for selection. Automatic admission for students with 2.5 GPA and 20 ACT or 950 SAT (exclusive of Writing). Applicants who do not meet the stated automatic admission criteria must submit personal statement. **Home schooled:** Transcript of courses and grades, state high school equivalency certificate required.

High school preparation. College-preparatory program recommended. 13 units recommended. Recommended units include English 4, mathematics 3, social studies 2, science 2 and foreign language 2.

2011-2012 Annual costs. Tuition/fees: $19,350. We are building a new residence hall that is targeted to open this fall. New meal plans will be offered as well. Room/board: $10,356. Books/supplies: $1,260. Personal expenses: $2,700.

Financial aid. **Non-need-based:** Scholarships awarded for academics, religious affiliation.

Application procedures. **Admission:** No deadline. $20 fee, may be waived for applicants with need, free for online applicants. Admission notification on a rolling basis. **Financial aid:** Priority date 3/1; no closing date. FAFSA required. Applicants notified on a rolling basis starting 3/31; must reply within 2 week(s) of notification.

Academics. **Special study options:** Accelerated study, combined bachelor's/graduate degree, cross-registration, distance learning, double major, dual enrollment of high school students, independent study, internships, study abroad, teacher certification program, weekend college. **Credit/placement by examination:** AP, CLEP, SAT, ACT, institutional tests. 32 credit hours maximum toward associate degree, 32 toward bachelor's. **Support services:** Learning center, reduced course load, remedial instruction, study skills assistance, tutoring, writing center.

Majors. **Business:** General, accounting. **Communications:** Communications/speech/rhetoric. **Education:** General, early childhood, elementary, middle, special ed. **English:** Creative writing. **Health services:** Nursing (RN). **Human services:** Social work. **Liberal arts:** Arts/sciences. **Psychology:** General. **Social sciences:** General.

Most popular majors. Business/marketing 23%, education 7%, health sciences 43%, psychology 8%, public administration/social services 6%.

Computing on campus. 250 workstations in dormitories, library, student center. Dormitories wired for high-speed internet access and linked to campus network. Commuter students can connect to campus network. Online course registration, online library, helpline, wireless network available.

Student life. **Freshman orientation:** Mandatory. Preregistration for classes offered. **Housing:** Guaranteed on-campus for freshmen. Coed dorms available. $125 partly refundable deposit. **Activities:** Campus ministries, international student organizations, student government, international club, Campus Crusade for Christ, Fellowship of Christian Athletes, multicultural student association, Advocates for Campus Accessibility.

Athletics. NCAA. **Intercollegiate:** Baseball M, basketball, bowling W, cross-country, golf, soccer, softball W, track and field, volleyball W. **Team name:** Golden Eagles.

Student services. Adult student services, alcohol/substance abuse counseling, chaplain/spiritual director, career counseling, services for economically disadvantaged, student employment services, financial aid counseling, minority student services, personal counseling. **Physically disabled:** Services for visually, speech, hearing impaired.

Contact. E-mail: admissions@spalding.edu
Phone: (502) 585-9911 ext. 2111
Toll-free number: (800) 896-8941 ext. 2111 Fax: (502) 992-2418
Christopher Hart, Dean of Enrollment Management, Spalding University, 845 S Third Street, Louisville, KY 40203

St. Catharine College
St. Catharine, Kentucky
www.sccky.edu

CB code: 1690

- Private 4-year health science and liberal arts college affiliated with Roman Catholic Church
- Commuter campus in small town
- 700 degree-seeking undergraduates

General. Founded in 1931. Regionally accredited. **Degrees:** 56 bachelor's, 64 associate awarded; master's offered. **Location:** 50 miles from Louisville and Lexington. **Calendar:** Semester, limited summer session. **Full-time faculty:** 48 total. **Part-time faculty:** 1 total.

Basis for selection. Open admission. Assessment tests in mathematics, English and reading administered upon admission for course placement or remediation.

2011-2012 Annual costs. Tuition/fees: $17,050. Higher tuition applies for health science program. Room/board: $8,200. Books/supplies: $700. Personal expenses: $1,200.

Financial aid. All financial aid based on need.

Application procedures. **Admission:** No deadline. $15 fee, may be waived for applicants with need. Application must be submitted on paper. Admission notification on a rolling basis. **Financial aid:** Priority date 3/15; no closing date. FAFSA, institutional form required. Applicants notified on a rolling basis.

Academics. **Special study options:** Distance learning, dual enrollment of high school students, independent study, internships, liberal arts/career combination, student-designed major, study abroad, teacher certification program, weekend college. **Credit/placement by examination:** AP, CLEP, institutional tests. 35 credit hours maximum toward associate degree, 35 toward bachelor's. **Support services:** Learning center, reduced course load, remedial instruction, study skills assistance, tutoring.

Majors. **Business:** Business admin. **Education:** Elementary, middle. **Health services:** Sonography. **Liberal arts:** Arts/sciences. **Psychology:** General.

Most popular majors. Business/marketing 31%, education 22%, liberal arts 22%, psychology 18%, social sciences 7%.

Computing on campus. 35 workstations in library, computer center. Dormitories wired for high-speed internet access. Online library, wireless network available.

Student life. **Freshman orientation:** Mandatory, $40 fee. Preregistration for classes offered. Three-day program held before start of classes. **Housing:** Single-sex dorms, special housing for disabled, wellness housing available. $25 nonrefundable deposit, deadline 8/15. **Activities:** Campus ministries, choral groups, drama, literary magazine, student government, student newspaper, Phi Theta Kappa, Students Above Traditional Age, student ambassadors, health occupations student association.

Athletics. NAIA. **Intercollegiate:** Baseball M, basketball, bowling, cross-country, golf, soccer, softball W, track and field, volleyball W. **Team name:** Patriots.

Student services. Chaplain/spiritual director, career counseling, student employment services, financial aid counseling, legal services, on-campus daycare, personal counseling, veterans' counselor.

Contact. E-mail: paulpresta@sccky.edu
Phone: (859) 336-5082 ext. 1259
Toll-free number: (800) 599-2000 ext. 1259 Fax: (859) 336-9381
Paul Presta, Director of Admissions, St. Catharine College, 2735 Bardstown Road, St. Catharine, KY 40061

Sullivan University
Louisville, Kentucky
www.sullivan.edu

CB code: 0811

- For-profit 4-year university
- Commuter campus in large city
- 4,611 degree-seeking undergraduates
- Interview required

General. Founded in 1962. Regionally accredited. **Degrees:** 476 bachelor's, 572 associate awarded; master's, professional, doctoral offered. **Location:** 110 miles from Indianapolis, 110 miles from Cincinnati. **Calendar:** Quarter, extensive summer session. **Full-time faculty:** 152 total. **Part-time faculty:** 119 total. **Special facilities:** University-operated fine dining restaurant.

Freshman class profile.

Out-of-state:	17%	Live on campus:	19%

Basis for selection. Test scores, interview, high school record important. Institutional exam required for placement if no ACT or SAT scores are available.

2011-2012 Annual costs. Tuition, fees and per-credit-hour charges vary by program. Tuition costs range from $16,980 to $18,360 per academic year. Room only: $5,355. Books/supplies: $1,800. Personal expenses: $1,200.

Financial aid. All financial aid based on need.

Application procedures. Admission: No deadline. $100 fee. Admission notification on a rolling basis. **Financial aid:** No deadline. FAFSA required. Applicants notified on a rolling basis starting 1/2.

Academics. Day classes meet Monday-Thursday; special program on Friday for additional help. Night/weekend classes meet Monday-Sunday. **Special study options:** Accelerated study, combined bachelor's/graduate degree, distance learning, double major, independent study, internships, weekend college. **Credit/placement by examination:** AP, CLEP, IB, SAT, ACT, institutional tests. **Support services:** Reduced course load, remedial instruction, study skills assistance, tutoring.

Majors. Business: Accounting, business admin, tourism promotion. **Computer sciences:** General, applications programming.

Computing on campus. 252 workstations in dormitories, library, computer center. Commuter students can connect to campus network. Online course registration, online library, helpline, wireless network available.

Student life. Freshman orientation: Mandatory. Preregistration for classes offered. 1- and 2-day sessions held at beginning of quarter. **Housing:** Coed dorms, wellness housing available. $95 nonrefundable deposit, deadline 9/30. Housing available for students under 21. **Activities:** Choral groups, international student organizations, student newspaper, student activities committee, travel club, culinary competition team, student paralegal association, International Association of Administrative Professionals, Rotarac.

Athletics. Intramural: Basketball, bowling, softball, volleyball.

Student services. Career counseling, student employment services, financial aid counseling, personal counseling, placement for graduates, veterans' counselor.

Contact. E-mail: admissions@sullivan.edu
Phone: (502) 456-6505 Toll-free number: (800) 844-1354
Fax: (502) 456-0040
Terri Thomas, Director of Admissions, Sullivan University, 3101 Bardstown Road, Louisville, KY 40205

Thomas More College
Crestview Hills, Kentucky
www.thomasmore.edu

CB member
CB code: 1876

- Private 4-year liberal arts college affiliated with Roman Catholic Church
- Commuter campus in small town
- 1,382 degree-seeking undergraduates: 6% part-time, 51% women, 6% African American, 1% Asian American, 2% Hispanic American, 1% international
- 140 degree-seeking graduate students
- 86% of applicants admitted
- SAT or ACT (ACT writing optional) required
- 53% graduate within 6 years; 55% enter graduate study

General. Founded in 1921. Regionally accredited. **Degrees:** 280 bachelor's, 101 associate awarded; master's offered. **ROTC:** Army, Air Force. **Location:** 8 miles from Cincinnati. **Calendar:** Semester, limited summer session. **Full-time faculty:** 72 total; 74% have terminal degrees, 7% minority, 49% women. **Part-time faculty:** 75 total; 24% have terminal degrees, 4% minority, 47% women. **Class size:** 78% < 20, 22% 20-39. **Special facilities:** Biology field station, observatory.

Freshman class profile. 891 applied, 770 admitted, 259 enrolled.

Mid 50% test scores		GPA 2.0-2.99:	29%
SAT critical reading:	450-560	Rank in top quarter:	35%
SAT math:	440-600	Rank in top tenth:	16%
ACT composite:	20-25	Return as sophomores:	68%
GPA 3.75 or higher:	24%	Out-of-state:	55%
GPA 3.50-3.74:	16%	Live on campus:	63%
GPA 3.0-3.49:	29%		

Basis for selection. Students must have C+ average or 2.5 GPA, 20 ACT English/480 SAT verbal, and 20 ACT/1010 SAT. Students not meeting these requirements may be conditionally admitted.

High school preparation. College-preparatory program required. 17 units required. Required units include English 4, mathematics 3, social studies 3, science 3, foreign language 2, computer science 1 and visual/performing arts 1.

2011-2012 Annual costs. Tuition/fees: $25,720. Tuition for incoming Freshmen only - Each class is tiered with guaranteed 3% increase per year as Full-time student. Room/board: $7,030. Books/supplies: $1,000. Personal expenses: $2,300.

Financial aid. Non-need-based: Scholarships awarded for academics, alumni affiliation, art, job skills, leadership, minority status, music/drama, religious affiliation, ROTC, state residency.

Application procedures. Admission: Closing date 8/1 (postmark date). $25 fee, may be waived for applicants with need, free for online applicants. Admission notification on a rolling basis beginning on or about 10/1. **Financial aid:** Priority date 3/15; no closing date. FAFSA required. Applicants notified on a rolling basis starting 10/1.

Academics. Special study options: Accelerated study, cooperative education, cross-registration, double major, dual enrollment of high school students, honors, independent study, internships, student-designed major, study abroad, teacher certification program. **Credit/placement by examination:** AP, CLEP, IB, SAT, ACT, institutional tests. 30 credit hours maximum toward associate degree, 60 toward bachelor's. **Support services:** Learning center, reduced course load, remedial instruction, study skills assistance, tutoring, writing center.

Majors. Biology: General. **Business:** Accounting, business admin. **Communications:** Communications/speech/rhetoric. **Computer sciences:** General. **Conservation:** Environmental science. **Education:** Art, business, elementary, middle, secondary. **English:** English lit. **Foreign languages:** Spanish. **Health services:** Clinical lab science, health care admin, nursing (RN). **History:** General. **Liberal arts:** Arts/sciences, humanities. **Math:** General. **Parks/recreation:** Sports admin. **Philosophy/religion:** Philosophy, religion. **Physical sciences:** Chemistry, physics. **Protective services:** Criminal justice, forensics. **Psychology:** General. **Social sciences:** Economics, political science, sociology. **Visual/performing arts:** Dramatic, studio arts.

Most popular majors. Business/marketing 50%, health sciences 12%, liberal arts 8%.

Computing on campus. 95 workstations in library, computer center, student center. Dormitories wired for high-speed internet access and linked to campus network. Commuter students can connect to campus network. Online library, helpline, student web hosting, wireless network available.

Student life. Freshman orientation: Mandatory, $125 fee. Preregistration for classes offered. Two-day program held at beginning of fall semester in August. **Housing:** Coed dorms, single-sex dorms, special housing for disabled available. $100 nonrefundable deposit, deadline 5/1. **Activities:** Pep band, campus ministries, choral groups, drama, international student organizations, literary magazine, student government, student activities board, residence hall government association, African American Society, Habitat for Humanity, business society, social issues commune, student government association, campus ministry, international student organization.

Athletics. NCAA. **Intercollegiate:** Baseball M, basketball, cross-country, football (tackle) M, golf, soccer, softball W, tennis, track and field M, volleyball W. **Intramural:** Basketball, football (non-tackle), soccer, softball, volleyball. **Team name:** Saints.

Student services. Adult student services, alcohol/substance abuse counseling, chaplain/spiritual director, career counseling, student employment services, financial aid counseling, health services, minority student services,

personal counseling, placement for graduates, veterans' counselor. **Physically disabled:** Services for visually, speech, hearing impaired.

Contact. E-mail: admissions@thomasmore.edu
Phone: (859) 344-3332 Toll-free number: (800) 825-4557
Fax: (859) 344-3444
Billy Sarge, Assistant Director of Admissions, Thomas More College, 333 Thomas More Parkway, Crestview Hills, KY 41017-3495

Transylvania University
Lexington, Kentucky
www.transy.edu

CB member
CB code: 1808

- Private 4-year liberal arts college affiliated with Christian Church (Disciples of Christ)
- Residential campus in large city
- 1,025 degree-seeking undergraduates: 1% part-time, 60% women, 4% African American, 1% Asian American, 1% Hispanic American, 1% international
- 85% of applicants admitted
- SAT or ACT (ACT writing optional), application essay required
- 70% graduate within 6 years; 38% enter graduate study

General. Founded in 1780. Regionally accredited. **Degrees:** 252 bachelor's awarded. **ROTC:** Army, Air Force. **Location:** 80 miles from Louisville; 80 miles from Cincinnati, Ohio. **Calendar:** 4-1-4. 4-4-1. Limited summer session. **Full-time faculty:** 88 total; 92% have terminal degrees, 6% minority, 41% women. **Part-time faculty:** 16 total; 19% have terminal degrees, 38% women. **Class size:** 74% < 20, 26% 20-39. **Special facilities:** Museum of early scientific apparatus, special library collections of early medical and scientific works and Kentucky books.

Freshman class profile. 1,267 applied, 1,075 admitted, 245 enrolled.

Mid 50% test scores			
SAT critical reading:	570-680	Rank in top tenth:	43%
SAT math:	540-660	End year in good standing:	94%
ACT composite:	24-30	Return as sophomores:	87%
GPA 3.75 or higher:	56%	Out-of-state:	20%
GPA 3.50-3.74:	18%	Live on campus:	95%
GPA 3.0-3.49:	18%	International:	1%
GPA 2.0-2.99:	8%	Fraternities:	55%
Rank in top quarter:	73%	Sororities:	60%

Basis for selection. Rigor of curriculum, GPA, and test scores most important. Recommendations, essay, extracurricular activities, excellence of character and high personal goals important. Interview recommended. Audition required for music scholarship applicants. Portfolio required for art scholarship applicants. **Learning Disabled:** Students should meet with coordinator of disability services.

High school preparation. College-preparatory program required. 16 units required; 23 recommended. Required and recommended units include English 4, mathematics 3-4, social studies 2, history 1, science 3-4 (laboratory 1-2), foreign language 2-4, visual/performing arts 1 and academic electives 1. Broad high school curriculum important to allow full participation in required liberal arts course work. Solid background in English highly recommended.

2011-2012 Annual costs. Tuition/fees: $28,250. Room/board: $8,450. Books/supplies: $1,000. Personal expenses: $1,350.

2011-2012 Financial aid. Need-based: 207 full-time freshmen applied for aid; 176 were judged to have need; 176 of these received aid. Average need met was 83%. Average scholarship/grant was $20,393; average loan $3,733. 75% of total undergraduate aid awarded as scholarships/grants, 25% as loans/jobs. **Non-need-based:** Awarded to 400 full-time undergraduates, including 94 freshmen. Scholarships awarded for academics, art, leadership, minority status, music/drama, religious affiliation, ROTC, state residency. **Additional information:** Auditions and portfolios required for music and art scholarships respectively. Essays required for other scholarship programs. Applications for William T. Young scholarships must be received by December 1.

Application procedures. Admission: Priority date 12/1; deadline 2/1 (postmark date). $30 fee, may be waived for applicants with need, free for online applicants. Admission notification by 3/15. Must reply by May 1 or within 2 week(s) if notified thereafter. **Financial aid:** Priority date 2/1; no closing date. FAFSA required. Applicants notified on a rolling basis starting 3/15; must reply by 5/1 or within 2 week(s) of notification.

Academics. Special study options: Combined bachelor's/graduate degree, double major, independent study, internships, liberal arts/career combination, student-designed major, study abroad, teacher certification program, Washington semester. **Credit/placement by examination:** AP, CLEP, IB, SAT, ACT, institutional tests. No limit to credit for AP or IB. **Support services:** Learning center, study skills assistance, tutoring, writing center.

Majors. Biology: General. **Business:** General, accounting. **Communications:** Communications/speech/rhetoric. **Computer sciences:** General. **Education:** Elementary, foundations, middle, music, physical. **English:** English lit. **Foreign languages:** Classics, French, German. **History:** General. **Liberal arts:** Arts/sciences. **Math:** General. **Parks/recreation:** Exercise sciences. **Philosophy/religion:** Philosophy, religion. **Physical sciences:** Chemistry, physics. **Psychology:** General. **Social sciences:** Anthropology, economics, political science, sociology, sociology/anthropology. **Visual/performing arts:** Art history/conservation, dramatic, music performance, music technology, studio arts.

Most popular majors. Biology 11%, business/marketing 12%, foreign language 11%, history 6%, philosophy/religious studies 7%, psychology 11%, social sciences 12%, visual/performing arts 7%.

Computing on campus. 200 workstations in dormitories, library, computer center, student center. Dormitories wired for high-speed internet access and linked to campus network. Commuter students can connect to campus network. Online course registration, online library, helpline, repair service, student web hosting, wireless network available.

Student life. Freshman orientation: Mandatory. Preregistration for classes offered. Session begins the weekend prior to August term (three-week term for new students only). **Housing:** Guaranteed on-campus for freshmen. Coed dorms, single-sex dorms, special housing for disabled, apartments, wellness housing available. $210 fully refundable deposit, deadline 8/1. Efficiency apartment option for upperclassmen; two units with facilities for disabled students available. **Activities:** Bands, campus ministries, choral groups, dance, drama, literary magazine, music ensembles, musical theater, opera, radio station, student government, student newspaper, diversity action council, College Democrats, College Republicans, Alternative Spring Break, Campus Crusade, student government association, student activities board, student alumni association, Environmental Rights and Responsibilities Alliance.

Athletics. NCAA. **Intercollegiate:** Baseball M, basketball, cross-country, diving, equestrian, field hockey W, golf, lacrosse, soccer, softball W, swimming, tennis, track and field, volleyball W. **Intramural:** Badminton, basketball, bowling, cross-country, football (non-tackle), football (tackle), golf, handball, racquetball, soccer, softball, swimming, table tennis, tennis, volleyball. **Team name:** Pioneers.

Student services. Alcohol/substance abuse counseling, chaplain/spiritual director, career counseling, student employment services, financial aid counseling, health services, minority student services, personal counseling, veterans' counselor. **Physically disabled:** Services for visually, hearing impaired.

Contact. E-mail: admissions@transy.edu
Phone: (859) 233-8242 Toll-free number: (800) 872-6798
Fax: (859) 281-3649
Brad Goan, Vice President for Enrollment and Dean of Admissions, Transylvania University, 300 North Broadway, Lexington, KY 40508-1797

Union College
Barbourville, Kentucky
www.unionky.edu

CB code: 1825

- Private 4-year liberal arts and teachers college affiliated with United Methodist Church
- Residential campus in small town
- 816 degree-seeking undergraduates: 6% part-time, 49% women, 9% African American, 2% Hispanic American, 4% international
- 406 degree-seeking graduate students
- 74% of applicants admitted
- SAT or ACT (ACT writing optional) required
- 32% graduate within 6 years

General. Founded in 1879. Regionally accredited. **Degrees:** 142 bachelor's awarded; master's offered. **ROTC:** Army. **Location:** 107 miles from Lexington; 107 miles from Knoxville, TN. **Calendar:** Semester, limited summer session. **Full-time faculty:** 62 total; 66% have terminal degrees, 8% minority, 42% women. **Part-time faculty:** 45 total; 31% have terminal degrees, 4% minority, 51% women. **Class size:** 74% < 20, 26% 20-39, less than 1% 40-49.

Freshman class profile. 1,117 applied, 822 admitted, 194 enrolled.

Mid 50% test scores			
SAT critical reading:	410-490	GPA 2.0-2.99:	29%
SAT math:	440-520	End year in good standing:	78%
ACT composite:	19-23	Return as sophomores:	56%
GPA 3.75 or higher:	18%	Out-of-state:	28%
GPA 3.50-3.74:	16%	Live on campus:	56%
GPA 3.0-3.49:	35%	International:	3%

Basis for selection. School achievement record, course work, class rank, SAT/ACT important. ACT preferred for all, required for teacher education program. Interview recommended. **Home schooled:** Statement describing home school structure and mission, transcript of courses and grades, state high school equivalency certificate, letter of recommendation (nonparent) required. Academic calender with attendance required. Submission of writing sample, summary of travel-related experience or work history may be requested. **Learning Disabled:** Students must provide documentation to coordinator of special program to receive necessary accommodations.

High school preparation. College-preparatory program recommended. Recommended units include English 4, mathematics 3, social studies 2, science 2 (laboratory 2) and foreign language 1.

2012-2013 Annual costs. Tuition/fees (projected): $20,800. Room/board: $6,650. Books/supplies: $1,470. Personal expenses: $1,680.

2011-2012 Financial aid. Need-based: 185 full-time freshmen applied for aid; 176 were judged to have need; 175 of these received aid. Average need met was 69%. Average scholarship/grant was $14,448; average loan $3,761. 72% of total undergraduate aid awarded as scholarships/grants, 28% as loans/jobs. **Non-need-based:** Awarded to 133 full-time undergraduates, including 40 freshmen. Scholarships awarded for academics, alumni affiliation, athletics, leadership, music/drama, religious affiliation, ROTC, state residency.

Application procedures. Admission: No deadline. $10 fee, may be waived for applicants with need. Admission notification on a rolling basis. **Financial aid:** Priority date 3/15; no closing date. FAFSA required. Applicants notified on a rolling basis starting 3/1; must reply within 2 week(s) of notification.

Academics. Special study options: Combined bachelor's/graduate degree, distance learning, double major, honors, independent study, internships, liberal arts/career combination, student-designed major, study abroad, teacher certification program. **Credit/placement by examination:** AP, CLEP, SAT, ACT, institutional tests. 30 credit hours maximum toward bachelor's degree. **Support services:** Learning center, remedial instruction, study skills assistance, tutoring, writing center.

Majors. Biology: General. **Business:** Accounting, business admin. **Communications:** Communications/speech/rhetoric. **Education:** Elementary, health, middle, physical, science, secondary, social studies, special ed. **English:** English lit. **History:** General. **Human services:** Social work. **Math:** General. **Parks/recreation:** Facilities management, sports admin. **Philosophy/religion:** Religion. **Physical sciences:** Chemistry. **Protective services:** Law enforcement admin. **Psychology:** General. **Social sciences:** Sociology. **Theology:** Religious ed.

Most popular majors. Business/marketing 26%, education 24%, parks/recreation 10%, psychology 14%, social sciences 6%.

Computing on campus. 230 workstations in dormitories, library, computer center, student center. Dormitories wired for high-speed internet access and linked to campus network. Commuter students can connect to campus network. Online course registration, online library, wireless network available.

Student life. Freshman orientation: Mandatory, $100 fee. Preregistration for classes offered. One-day sessions offered in May, June, and July. **Housing:** Guaranteed on-campus for freshmen. Single-sex dorms, apartments available. $100 fully refundable deposit. Private rooms occasionally available to upperclassmen. **Activities:** Pep band, choral groups, drama, literary magazine, student government, student newspaper, Fellowship of Christian Athletes, Appalachian wilderness club, Baptist student union, Methodist student organizations, Newman club, student ambassadors, science society, philosophy society.

Athletics. NAIA. **Intercollegiate:** Baseball M, basketball, bowling, cross-country, football (tackle) M, golf, soccer, softball W, swimming, tennis, track and field, volleyball W. **Intramural:** Basketball, football (non-tackle), soccer, softball, table tennis, tennis, volleyball. **Team name:** Bulldogs.

Student services. Alcohol/substance abuse counseling, chaplain/spiritual director, career counseling, services for economically disadvantaged, student employment services, financial aid counseling, health services, personal counseling, placement for graduates. **Physically disabled:** Services for visually, hearing impaired.

Contact. E-mail: enrollme@unionky.edu
Phone: (606) 546-1229 Toll-free number: (800) 489-8646
Fax: (606) 546-1667
Jerry Jackson, Dean of Enrollment Management, Union College, 310 College Street, Box 005, Barbourville, KY 40906

University of Kentucky
Lexington, Kentucky — CB member
www.uky.edu — CB code: 1837

- Public 4-year university
- Commuter campus in large city
- 19,709 degree-seeking undergraduates: 7% part-time, 49% women, 7% African American, 2% Asian American, 2% Hispanic American, 2% international
- 6,764 degree-seeking graduate students
- 68% of applicants admitted
- SAT or ACT (ACT writing optional) required
- 59% graduate within 6 years

General. Founded in 1865. Regionally accredited. **Degrees:** 3,712 bachelor's awarded; master's, professional, doctoral offered. **ROTC:** Army, Air Force. **Location:** 80 miles from Louisville, 90 miles from Cincinnati. **Calendar:** Semester, limited summer session. **Full-time faculty:** 1,375 total; 93% have terminal degrees, 18% minority, 36% women. **Part-time faculty:** 350 total; 58% have terminal degrees, 6% minority, 49% women. **Class size:** 32% < 20, 47% 20-39, 6% 40-49, 9% 50-99, 6% >100. **Special facilities:** Center for the arts, Van de Graaff accelerator, equine research center, center for the humanities.

Freshman class profile. 15,153 applied, 10,362 admitted, 4,139 enrolled.

Mid 50% test scores			
SAT critical reading:	490-610	Rank in top quarter:	62%
SAT math:	500-630	Rank in top tenth:	33%
SAT writing:	470-600	Return as sophomores:	82%
ACT composite:	23-28	Out-of-state:	25%
GPA 3.75 or higher:	33%	Live on campus:	92%
GPA 3.50-3.74:	21%	International:	1%
GPA 3.0-3.49:	30%	Fraternities:	14%
GPA 2.0-2.99:	16%	Sororities:	26%

Basis for selection. Test scores and GPA should indicate potential for academic success. Required course work and extracurricular activities also considered. Students out of high school 2 years or more with no college credit admitted on probationary basis. Audition required of music majors. **Home schooled:** List of textbooks, attendance record and 2 letters of recommendation from persons outside family required.

High school preparation. College-preparatory program required. 22 units required. Required and recommended units include English 4, mathematics 3-4, social studies 3, science 3-4, foreign language 2 and academic electives 5. 1 fine or performing arts, .5 health, .5 physical education required.

2011-2012 Annual costs. Tuition/fees: $9,128; $18,740 out-of-state. Room/board: $9,974. Books/supplies: $800. Personal expenses: $1,540.

Financial aid. Non-need-based: Scholarships awarded for academics, alumni affiliation, art, athletics, job skills, leadership, minority status, music/drama, ROTC, state residency.

Application procedures. Admission: Closing date 2/15 (postmark date). $50 fee, may be waived for applicants with need. Admission notification on a rolling basis beginning on or about 10/1. Reply by 5/1 preferred. **Financial aid:** Priority date 2/15; no closing date. FAFSA required. Applicants notified on a rolling basis starting 4/1; must reply within 3 week(s) of notification.

Academics. Special study options: Accelerated study, combined bachelor's/graduate degree, cooperative education, distance learning, double major, ESL, exchange student, honors, independent study, internships, study abroad, teacher certification program, weekend college. **Credit/placement by examination:** AP, CLEP, IB, SAT, ACT, institutional tests. Students who receive Advanced Placement credit for a course may apply this credit the same way credit earned by passing a course is applied. **Support services:** Learning center, reduced course load, remedial instruction, tutoring, writing center.

Majors. Architecture: Architecture, landscape. **Area/ethnic studies:** Latin American. **Biology:** General, biotechnology. **Business:** General, accounting, finance, hospitality admin, management science, managerial economics, marketing. **Communications:** Communications/speech/rhetoric, journalism, persuasive communications, radio/TV. **Computer sciences:** General. **Conservation:** General, forest sciences. **Education:** Art, early childhood, elementary, health, middle, music, physical, science, social studies, special ed, voc/tech.

Engineering: Agricultural, chemical, civil, computer, electrical, materials, mechanical, mining. **English:** English lit. **Foreign languages:** Classics, French, German, Japanese, linguistics, Russian, Spanish. **General:** Agronomy, animal sciences, economics, equine science, food science. **Health services:** Audiology/speech pathology, clinical lab science, health care admin, nursing (RN), physician assistant, prephysical therapy. **History:** General. **Human services:** Social work. **Math:** General, financial. **Philosophy/religion:** Philosophy. **Physical sciences:** Chemistry, geology, physics. **Psychology:** General. **Social sciences:** Anthropology, economics, geography, political science, sociology. **Visual/performing arts:** Art history/conservation, arts management, dramatic, interior design, music history, music performance, studio arts. **Work/family studies:** General, clothing/textiles, food/nutrition.

Most popular majors. Biology 7%, business/marketing 18%, communications/journalism 10%, education 9%, engineering/engineering technologies 8%, health sciences 6%, psychology 6%, social sciences 8%.

Computing on campus. 810 workstations in dormitories, library, computer center, student center. Dormitories wired for high-speed internet access and linked to campus network. Commuter students can connect to campus network. Online course registration, online library, helpline, wireless network available.

Student life. Freshman orientation: Mandatory, $40 fee. Preregistration for classes offered. $20 additional charge per guest. **Housing:** Coed dorms, single-sex dorms, special housing for disabled, apartments, cooperative housing, fraternity/sorority housing, wellness housing available. $50 deposit, deadline 6/1. **Activities:** Bands, campus ministries, choral groups, dance, drama, international student organizations, literary magazine, music ensembles, musical theater, opera, radio station, student government, student newspaper, symphony orchestra, more than 300 organizations available.

Athletics. NCAA. **Intercollegiate:** Baseball M, basketball, cross-country, diving, football (tackle) M, golf, gymnastics W, rifle, soccer, softball W, swimming, tennis, track and field, volleyball W. **Intramural:** Archery, badminton, basketball, bowling, cross-country, fencing, field hockey W, football (non-tackle), golf, handball, ice hockey M, lacrosse, racquetball, rugby M, skiing, soccer, softball, squash, swimming, table tennis, tennis, track and field, volleyball, wrestling M. **Team name:** Wildcats.

Student services. Adult student services, alcohol/substance abuse counseling, career counseling, student employment services, financial aid counseling, health services, minority student services, on-campus daycare, personal counseling, placement for graduates, veterans' counselor, women's services. **Physically disabled:** Services for visually, speech, hearing impaired.

Contact. E-mail: admisso@uky.edu
Phone: (859) 257-2000 Toll-free number: (800) 432-0967
Fax: (859) 257-3823
Don Witt, Assistant Provost for Enrollment Management, University of Kentucky, 100 W.D. Funkhouser Building, Lexington, KY 40506-0054

University of Louisville
Louisville, Kentucky
www.louisville.edu

CB member
CB code: 1838

- Public 4-year university
- Commuter campus in very large city
- 14,737 degree-seeking undergraduates: 18% part-time, 51% women, 12% African American, 3% Asian American, 3% Hispanic American, 1% international
- 5,356 degree-seeking graduate students
- 73% of applicants admitted
- SAT or ACT (ACT writing optional) required
- 51% graduate within 6 years

General. Founded in 1798. Regionally accredited. **Degrees:** 2,618 bachelor's, 19 associate awarded; master's, professional, doctoral offered. **ROTC:** Army, Air Force. **Location:** 3 miles from downtown, 92 miles from Cincinnati. **Calendar:** Semester, extensive summer session. **Full-time faculty:** 850 total; 86% have terminal degrees, 24% minority, 39% women. **Part-time faculty:** 430 total; 30% have terminal degrees, 12% minority, 58% women. **Class size:** 25% < 20, 54% 20-39, 8% 40-49, 7% 50-99, 5% >100. **Special facilities:** Planetarium, computer-aided engineering building with robotics laboratory, rapid prototype facility with Sinterstation 2000 system, photographic archives.

Freshman class profile. 7,892 applied, 5,738 admitted, 2,569 enrolled.

Mid 50% test scores			
SAT critical reading:	490-620	GPA 2.0-2.99:	19%
SAT math:	500-630	End year in good standing:	87%
ACT composite:	21-28	Return as sophomores:	78%
GPA 3.75 or higher:	37%	Out-of-state:	16%
GPA 3.50-3.74:	16%	International:	1%
GPA 3.0-3.49:	27%	Fraternities:	17%
		Sororities:	12%

Basis for selection. High school grades, curriculum, and test scores very important. Diagnostic testing/interview option for students lacking requirements. Partnership with local community college for those lacking required academic units. SAT/ACT score reports must be received by registration before first day of class. **Home schooled:** Transcript of courses and grades required.

High school preparation. College-preparatory program required. 22 units required. Required and recommended units include English 4, mathematics 3-4, social studies 3, science 3-4 (laboratory 1), foreign language 2-3, visual/performing arts 1 and academic electives 5. 1 physical education and health (.5 each). History requirement included in social studies, 5 electives must be rigorous.

2011-2012 Annual costs. Tuition/fees: $8,930; $21,650 out-of-state. All full-time undergraduate students, enrolled in at least 12 credit hours, or which at least 9 are on Belknap campus, will be required to purchase a declining balance meal plan in the amount of $175/semester. Room/board: $7,440. Books/supplies: $1,000. Personal expenses: $2,160.

Financial aid. Non-need-based: Scholarships awarded for academics, art, athletics, leadership, minority status, music/drama, ROTC, state residency.

Application procedures. Admission: Priority date 2/15; deadline 8/19 (receipt date). $40 fee, may be waived for applicants with need. Admission notification on a rolling basis. **Financial aid:** Priority date 2/15; no closing date. FAFSA required. Applicants notified on a rolling basis starting 4/1.

Academics. Special study options: Accelerated study, combined bachelor's/graduate degree, cooperative education, cross-registration, distance learning, double major, dual enrollment of high school students, ESL, exchange student, honors, independent study, internships, semester at sea, student-designed major, study abroad, teacher certification program. **Credit/placement by examination:** AP, CLEP, IB, SAT, ACT, institutional tests. 24 credit hours maximum toward bachelor's degree. **Support services:** Learning center, pre-admission summer program, reduced course load, remedial instruction, study skills assistance, tutoring, writing center.

Majors. Area/ethnic studies: African-American, women's. **Biology:** General. **Business:** Accounting, business admin, finance, management information systems, managerial economics, marketing. **Communications:** Communications/speech/rhetoric. **Education:** Elementary, foreign languages, music, trade/industrial. **Engineering:** General, biomedical, chemical, civil, computer, electrical, industrial, mechanical. **English:** English lit. **Foreign languages:** French, sign language interpretation, Spanish. **Health services:** Dental hygiene, music therapy, nursing (RN). **History:** General. **Liberal arts:** Arts/sciences, humanities. **Math:** General. **Parks/recreation:** Health/fitness, sports admin. **Philosophy/religion:** Philosophy. **Physical sciences:** Atmospheric science, chemistry, physics. **Protective services:** Law enforcement admin. **Psychology:** General. **Social sciences:** Anthropology, economics, geography, political science, sociology. **Visual/performing arts:** Art history/conservation, dramatic, music, studio arts.

Most popular majors. Business/marketing 18%, communications/journalism 7%, education 8%, engineering/engineering technologies 9%, health sciences 7%, parks/recreation 8%, psychology 8%, social sciences 7%.

Computing on campus. 400 workstations in dormitories, library, computer center, student center. Dormitories wired for high-speed internet access and linked to campus network. Commuter students can connect to campus network. Online course registration, online library, helpline, repair service, student web hosting, wireless network available.

Student life. Freshman orientation: Mandatory, $125 fee. Preregistration for classes offered. **Housing:** Coed dorms, special housing for disabled, apartments, fraternity/sorority housing available. $200 fully refundable deposit. Special residence hall floors with in-house computer facilities for honors students, coed suites available. **Activities:** Bands, campus ministries, choral groups, dance, drama, international student organizations, literary magazine, music ensembles, musical theater, opera, radio station, student government, student newspaper, symphony orchestra, Association of Black Students, Authentic, Baptist campus ministry, College Democrats, College Republicans, Commonground, debate society, L-Raisers, Rho Lambda Honor Society, Society of Hispanic Professional Engineers.

Athletics. NCAA. **Intercollegiate:** Baseball M, basketball, cross-country, diving, field hockey W, football (tackle) M, golf, soccer, softball W, swimming, tennis, track and field, volleyball W. **Intramural:** Badminton, basketball, bowling, cheerleading, football (non-tackle) M, golf, racquetball, soccer, swimming, table tennis, tennis, track and field, volleyball. **Team name:** Cardinals.

Student services. Alcohol/substance abuse counseling, chaplain/spiritual director, career counseling, student employment services, financial aid counseling, health services, legal services, minority student services, on-campus daycare, personal counseling, placement for graduates, women's services. **Physically disabled:** Services for visually, speech, hearing impaired.

Contact. E-mail: admitme@louisville.edu
Phone: (502) 852-6531 Toll-free number: (800) 334-8635 ext. 6531
Fax: (502) 852-4776
Jenny Sawyer, Director of Admissions, University of Louisville, 2211 South Brook Street, Louisville, KY 40292

University of Phoenix: Louisville
Louisville, Kentucky
www.phoenix.edu

- For-profit 4-year university
- Large city
- 227 degree-seeking undergraduates

General. Regionally accredited. **Degrees:** 20 bachelor's awarded; master's offered. **Calendar:** Differs by program. **Full-time faculty:** 7 total. **Part-time faculty:** 90 total.

Basis for selection. Open admission.

2011-2012 Annual costs. Estimated costs as of August 2011: per-credit-hour charge, $380 to $415, depending upon level and course of study; electronic course materials fee, $95, if applicable. Book and material charges may vary by course and program. All fees are subject to change.

Application procedures. Admission: No deadline. No application fee. **Financial aid:** No deadline.

Academics. Credit/placement by examination: AP, CLEP.

Majors. Business: Business admin, operations. **Computer sciences:** Information technology, web page design. **Health services:** Health services admin.

Contact. Marc Booker, Director of Admissions and Evaluation, University of Phoenix: Louisville, 10400 Linn Station Road, Louisville, KY 40223-3839

University of Pikeville
Pikeville, Kentucky
www.upike.edu   CB code: 1625

- Private 4-year liberal arts college affiliated with Presbyterian Church (USA)
- Residential campus in small town
- 1,203 degree-seeking undergraduates: 3% part-time, 49% women, 11% African American, 1% Hispanic American, 2% international
- 332 degree-seeking graduate students
- 38% graduate within 6 years; 25% enter graduate study

General. Founded in 1889. Regionally accredited. **Degrees:** 131 bachelor's, 20 associate awarded; master's, professional, doctoral offered. **ROTC:** Army. **Location:** 150 miles from Lexington, 140 miles from Charleston, WV. **Calendar:** Semester, limited summer session. **Full-time faculty:** 62 total; 56% have terminal degrees, 3% minority, 52% women. **Part-time faculty:** 43 total; 9% have terminal degrees, 46% women. **Class size:** 44% < 20, 49% 20-39, 6% 40-49, 1% 50-99.

Freshman class profile. 1,665 applied, 1,665 admitted, 484 enrolled.

Mid 50% test scores		Rank in top tenth:	15%
ACT composite:	17-22	End year in good standing:	60%
GPA 3.75 or higher:	18%	Return as sophomores:	50%
GPA 3.50-3.74:	17%	Out-of-state:	17%
GPA 3.0-3.49:	29%	Live on campus:	80%
GPA 2.0-2.99:	32%	International:	2%
Rank in top quarter:	38%		

Basis for selection. Open admission, but selective for some programs. 19 ACT required for nursing, 21 ACT required for education majors.

High school preparation. College-preparatory program recommended. 13 units recommended. Recommended units include English 4, mathematics 3, social studies 2, history 1 and science 3.

2012-2013 Annual costs. Tuition/fees: $17,050. Room/board: $6,700. Books/supplies: $2,500. Personal expenses: $2,500.

2011-2012 Financial aid. All financial aid based on need. 478 full-time freshmen applied for aid; 478 were judged to have need; 478 of these received aid. Average need met was 87%. Average scholarship/grant was $15,827; average loan $3,431. 65% of total undergraduate aid awarded as scholarships/grants, 35% as loans/jobs.

Application procedures. Admission: Priority date 2/15; deadline 8/15 (receipt date). No application fee. Admission notification on a rolling basis beginning on or about 9/15. **Financial aid:** Priority date 3/15; no closing date. FAFSA, institutional form required. Applicants notified on a rolling basis starting 2/1; must reply by 5/1 or within 2 week(s) of notification.

Academics. Special study options: Combined bachelor's/graduate degree, double major, dual enrollment of high school students, independent study, internships, liberal arts/career combination, student-designed major, study abroad, Washington semester. **Credit/placement by examination:** AP, CLEP, institutional tests. 15 credit hours maximum toward associate degree, 15 toward bachelor's. **Support services:** Reduced course load, remedial instruction, study skills assistance, tutoring, writing center.

Majors. Biology: General. **Business:** Business admin. **Communications:** Communications/speech/rhetoric. **Computer sciences:** General. **Education:** Elementary, middle. **English:** English lit. **History:** General. **Human services:** Social work. **Math:** General. **Philosophy/religion:** Religion. **Physical sciences:** Chemistry. **Protective services:** Criminal justice. **Psychology:** General. **Social sciences:** Sociology. **Visual/performing arts:** Art.

Most popular majors. Biology 9%, business/marketing 21%, communications/journalism 11%, education 9%, English 9%, history 7%, philosophy/religious studies 6%, psychology 9%.

Computing on campus. 162 workstations in library, computer center. Dormitories wired for high-speed internet access and linked to campus network. Commuter students can connect to campus network. Online course registration, online library, student web hosting, wireless network available.

Student life. Freshman orientation: Mandatory. Preregistration for classes offered. Held first 3 days before start of classes. **Policies:** No alcohol allowed on campus. **Housing:** Coed dorms, single-sex dorms available. $100 nonrefundable deposit, deadline 5/30. **Activities:** Pep band, campus ministries, dance, student government, student newspaper, academic team, Appalachian Association for Justice, Baptist student union, Blessed Unity of God, Fellowship of Christian Athletes, Lambda Sigma society, Phi Beta Lambda, Psi Chi, Sigma Tau Delta, Young Republicans.

Athletics. NAIA. **Intercollegiate:** Baseball M, basketball, bowling, cheerleading, cross-country, football (tackle) M, golf, lacrosse W, soccer, softball W, tennis, track and field, volleyball W. **Intramural:** Basketball, football (non-tackle), softball. **Team name:** Bears.

Student services. Chaplain/spiritual director, career counseling, student employment services, financial aid counseling, health services, personal counseling, veterans' counselor.

Contact. E-mail: admissions@Upike.edu
Phone: (606) 218-5251 Toll-free number: (866) 232-7700
Fax: (606) 218-5255
Gary Jusitce, Director of Admissions and Student Financial Services, University of Pikeville, 147 Sycamore Street, Pikeville, KY 41501-1194

University of the Cumberlands
Williamsburg, Kentucky   CB member
www.ucumberlands.edu   CB code: 1145

- Private 4-year university and liberal arts college affiliated with Baptist faith
- Residential campus in small town
- 1,420 degree-seeking undergraduates: 3% part-time, 50% women, 7% African American, 3% Hispanic American, 5% international
- 1,871 degree-seeking graduate students
- 70% of applicants admitted

- SAT or ACT (ACT writing optional) required
- 43% graduate within 6 years; 35% enter graduate study

General. Founded in 1889. Regionally accredited. **Degrees:** 254 bachelor's awarded; master's, doctoral offered. **ROTC:** Army. **Location:** 100 miles from Lexington; 65 miles from Knoxville, TN. **Calendar:** Semester, limited summer session. **Full-time faculty:** 107 total; 76% have terminal degrees, 8% minority, 44% women. **Part-time faculty:** 75 total; 65% have terminal degrees, 7% minority, 39% women. **Class size:** 60% < 20, 32% 20-39, 6% 40-49, 2% 50-99. **Special facilities:** Life science museum, conference center and inn.

Freshman class profile. 2,290 applied, 1,598 admitted, 402 enrolled.

Mid 50% test scores		Rank in top quarter:	43%
SAT critical reading:	420-510	Rank in top tenth:	18%
SAT math:	440-540	End year in good standing:	84%
ACT composite:	19-24	Return as sophomores:	62%
GPA 3.75 or higher:	29%	Out-of-state:	37%
GPA 3.50-3.74:	14%	Live on campus:	89%
GPA 3.0-3.49:	27%	International:	3%
GPA 2.0-2.99:	30%		

Basis for selection. School achievement and activities, test scores important. **Home schooled:** Transcript of courses and grades required. Must have GED or high school transcript.

High school preparation. College-preparatory program recommended. Required and recommended units include English 4, mathematics 3, social studies 1-2 and science 2-3.

2012-2013 Annual costs. Tuition/fees: $19,000. Room/board: $7,000. Books/supplies: $1,000. Personal expenses: $2,950.

2011-2012 Financial aid. Need-based: 383 full-time freshmen applied for aid; 356 were judged to have need; 356 of these received aid. Average need met was 76%. Average scholarship/grant was $14,445; average loan $3,470. 69% of total undergraduate aid awarded as scholarships/grants, 31% as loans/jobs. **Non-need-based:** Awarded to 431 full-time undergraduates, including 116 freshmen. Scholarships awarded for academics, athletics, job skills, leadership, music/drama.

Application procedures. Admission: Priority date 3/1; deadline 8/15 (receipt date). $30 fee, may be waived for applicants with need. Admission notification on a rolling basis beginning on or about 9/1. Must reply by May 1 or within 2 week(s) if notified thereafter. **Financial aid:** Priority date 2/15; no closing date. FAFSA required. Applicants notified on a rolling basis starting 3/1; must reply within 2 week(s) of notification.

Academics. Individualized or computerized tutoring assistance. **Special study options:** Accelerated study, distance learning, double major, honors, independent study, internships, liberal arts/career combination, student-designed major, study abroad, teacher certification program. **Credit/placement by examination:** AP, CLEP, IB, SAT, ACT, institutional tests. 30 credit hours maximum toward bachelor's degree. **Support services:** Learning center, reduced course load, remedial instruction, study skills assistance, tutoring, writing center.

Majors. Biology: General. **Business:** General, accounting, management information systems. **Communications:** Communications/speech/rhetoric, journalism. **Education:** Art, elementary, health, middle, music, physical, secondary, social studies, Spanish, special ed. **English:** English lit. **Foreign languages:** Spanish. **Health services:** Community health services. **History:** General. **Math:** General. **Parks/recreation:** Health/fitness, sports admin. **Physical sciences:** Chemistry, physics. **Protective services:** Criminal justice. **Psychology:** General. **Social sciences:** Political science. **Theology:** Religious ed. **Visual/performing arts:** Dramatic, music, studio arts.

Most popular majors. Biology 14%, business/marketing 28%, education 14%, health sciences 7%.

Computing on campus. 225 workstations in dormitories, library, computer center, student center. Dormitories wired for high-speed internet access and linked to campus network. Commuter students can connect to campus network. Online course registration, online library, helpline, wireless network available.

Student life. Freshman orientation: Mandatory. Preregistration for classes offered. One-day session in summer. **Policies:** All students required to complete 40-hour community service project. Religious observance required. **Housing:** Guaranteed on-campus for all undergraduates. Single-sex dorms available. $125 partly refundable deposit, deadline 8/15. **Activities:** Bands, campus ministries, choral groups, dance, drama, international student organizations, music ensembles, musical theater, radio station, student government, student newspaper, TV station, Baptist student union, Fellowship of Christian Athletes, Appalachian ministries, Mountain Outreach.

Athletics. NAIA. **Intercollegiate:** Archery, baseball M, basketball, cheerleading, cross-country, football (non-tackle) M, football (tackle) M, golf, soccer, softball W, swimming, tennis, track and field, volleyball W, wrestling. **Intramural:** Archery, badminton, basketball, football (non-tackle), golf, soccer, softball, table tennis, volleyball. **Team name:** Patriots.

Student services. Alcohol/substance abuse counseling, chaplain/spiritual director, career counseling, services for economically disadvantaged, student employment services, financial aid counseling, health services, personal counseling, placement for graduates, veterans' counselor, women's services. **Physically disabled:** Services for visually, speech, hearing impaired.

Contact. E-mail: admiss@ucumberlands.edu
Phone: (606) 539-4241 Toll-free number: (800) 343-1609
Fax: (606) 539-4303
Erica Harris, Director of Admissions, University of the Cumberlands, 6178 College Station Drive, Williamsburg, KY 40769

Western Kentucky University
Bowling Green, Kentucky **CB member**
www.wku.edu **CB code: 1901**

- Public 4-year university
- Residential campus in small city
- 16,482 degree-seeking undergraduates: 16% part-time, 58% women, 11% African American, 1% Asian American, 2% Hispanic American, 2% international
- 2,673 degree-seeking graduate students
- 92% of applicants admitted
- SAT or ACT (ACT writing optional) required
- 50% graduate within 6 years

General. Founded in 1906. Regionally accredited. Regional campus located in Glasgow offering general education, nursing, and elementary education programs. Upper division and graduate courses also offered at regional campuses in Owensboro and Fort Knox/Elizabethtown/Radcliff area. **Degrees:** 2,591 bachelor's, 215 associate awarded; master's, doctoral offered. **ROTC:** Army, Air Force. **Location:** 110 miles from Louisville; 65 miles from Nashville, TN. **Calendar:** Semester, limited summer session. **Full-time faculty:** 771 total; 70% have terminal degrees, 18% minority, 49% women. **Part-time faculty:** 429 total; 18% have terminal degrees, 7% minority, 52% women. **Class size:** 47% < 20, 42% 20-39, 6% 40-49, 4% 50-99, less than 1% >100. **Special facilities:** University farm, planetarium, observatory, Kentucky museum.

Freshman class profile. 8,017 applied, 7,355 admitted, 3,385 enrolled.

Mid 50% test scores		Rank in top quarter:	40%
SAT critical reading:	440-580	Rank in top tenth:	18%
SAT math:	430-590	Return as sophomores:	73%
ACT composite:	18-24	Out-of-state:	18%
GPA 3.75 or higher:	19%	Live on campus:	74%
GPA 3.50-3.74:	14%	International:	2%
GPA 3.0-3.49:	30%	Fraternities:	10%
GPA 2.0-2.99:	34%	Sororities:	12%

Basis for selection. GPA and recommendations most important.

High school preparation. College-preparatory program recommended. 22 units required. Required units include English 4, mathematics 3, social studies 3, science 3 (laboratory 1), foreign language 2, visual/performing arts .5. 0.5 credits required in health, physical education, history, performing arts.

2011-2012 Annual costs. Tuition/fees: $8,084; $20,016 out-of-state. Room/board: $6,600.

2010-2011 Financial aid. Need-based: 2,881 full-time freshmen applied for aid; 2,289 were judged to have need; 2,272 of these received aid. Average need met was 31%. Average scholarship/grant was $5,557; average loan $3,069. 54% of total undergraduate aid awarded as scholarships/grants, 46% as loans/jobs. **Non-need-based:** Awarded to 6,623 full-time undergraduates, including 2,250 freshmen. Scholarships awarded for academics, alumni affiliation, art, athletics, job skills, leadership, minority status, music/drama, religious affiliation, ROTC, state residency.

Application procedures. Admission: Closing date 8/1 (postmark date). $40 fee, may be waived for applicants with need. Admission notification on a rolling basis. **Financial aid:** Priority date 2/15; no closing date. FAFSA required. Applicants notified on a rolling basis starting 3/1.

Academics. Special study options: Cooperative education, distance learning, double major, dual enrollment of high school students, ESL, exchange student, external degree, honors, independent study, internships, New York

semester, semester at sea, student-designed major, study abroad, teacher certification program, urban semester. **Credit/placement by examination:** AP, CLEP, IB, SAT, ACT, institutional tests. Unlimited number of hours of credit by examination may be counted toward degree. **Support services:** Learning center, pre-admission summer program, reduced course load, remedial instruction, study skills assistance, tutoring, writing center.

Honors college/program. 27 ACT/1210 SAT, 3.8 unweighted GPA, or top 15% of graduating class required.

Majors. Architecture: Technology. **Area/ethnic studies:** Asian. **Biology:** General, biochemistry, biotechnology. **Business:** Accounting, business admin, entrepreneurial studies, finance, hospitality admin, international, management information systems, management science, managerial economics, marketing, organizational leadership. **Communications:** Advertising, broadcast journalism, communications/speech/rhetoric, journalism, media studies, organizational, photojournalism, public relations, radio/TV. **Computer sciences:** General, information technology. **Education:** Business, early childhood, elementary, family/consumer sciences, middle, multi-level teacher, physical, special ed, trade/industrial. **Engineering:** Civil, electrical, mechanical. **English:** English lit. **Foreign languages:** French, German, Spanish. **Health services:** Clinical lab science, communication disorders, community health, dental hygiene, environmental health, health care admin, nursing (RN). **History:** General. **Human services:** Social work. **Math:** General. **Parks/recreation:** Exercise sciences, facilities management, sports studies. **Philosophy/religion:** Religion. **Physical sciences:** General, chemistry, geology, meteorology, physics. **Psychology:** General. **Social sciences:** General, anthropology, econometrics, economics, geography, GIS/cartography, international relations, political science, sociology. **Visual/performing arts:** Art history/conservation, dance, dramatic, music performance, studio arts. **Work/family studies:** Clothing/textiles.

Most popular majors. Business/marketing 16%, communications/journalism 9%, education 12%, health sciences 8%, liberal arts 10%, social sciences 9%.

Computing on campus. 1,350 workstations in dormitories, library, computer center, student center. Dormitories wired for high-speed internet access and linked to campus network. Commuter students can connect to campus network. Online course registration, online library, helpline, repair service, student web hosting, wireless network available.

Student life. Freshman orientation: Mandatory, $45 fee. Preregistration for classes offered. One-day program; several dates available. **Housing:** Coed dorms, single-sex dorms, fraternity/sorority housing, wellness housing available. $150 partly refundable deposit, deadline 3/31. Special housing for Honors College Students and Gatton Academy Students. **Activities:** Bands, campus ministries, choral groups, dance, drama, film society, international student organizations, literary magazine, music ensembles, Model UN, musical theater, opera, radio station, student government, student newspaper, symphony orchestra, TV station, American Democracy Project, Amnesty International, Habitat for Humanity, College Republicans, College Democrats, Campus Crusade, Women in Transition, NAACP, black student alliance, Green Party.

Athletics. NCAA. **Intercollegiate:** Baseball M, basketball, cross-country, diving, football (tackle) M, golf, soccer W, softball W, swimming, tennis, track and field, volleyball W. **Intramural:** Badminton, basketball, football (non-tackle), football (tackle), golf, handball, racquetball, soccer, softball, table tennis, volleyball. **Team name:** Hilltoppers.

Student services. Adult student services, alcohol/substance abuse counseling, career counseling, services for economically disadvantaged, student employment services, financial aid counseling, health services, legal services, minority student services, personal counseling, placement for graduates, veterans' counselor, women's services. **Physically disabled:** Services for visually, speech, hearing impaired.

Contact. E-mail: admission@wku.edu
Phone: (270) 745-2551 Toll-free number: (800) 495-8463
Fax: (270) 745-6133
Scott Gordon, Director of Admission and Academic Services, Western Kentucky University, 1906 College Heights Boulevard, Bowling Green, KY 42101

Louisiana

Centenary College of Louisiana

Shreveport, Louisiana
www.centenary.edu

CB member
CB code: 6082

- Private 4-year liberal arts college affiliated with United Methodist Church
- Residential campus in small city
- 800 degree-seeking undergraduates: 1% part-time, 56% women, 13% African American, 2% Asian American, 5% Hispanic American, 3% international
- 85 degree-seeking graduate students
- 63% of applicants admitted
- SAT or ACT (ACT writing optional), application essay required
- 58% graduate within 6 years

General. Founded in 1825. Regionally accredited. **Degrees:** 156 bachelor's awarded; master's offered. **Location:** 325 miles from New Orleans, 189 miles from Dallas. **Calendar:** Semester, extensive summer session. **Full-time faculty:** 61 total; 95% have terminal degrees, 5% minority, 39% women. **Part-time faculty:** 41 total; 37% have terminal degrees, 10% minority, 44% women. **Class size:** 72% < 20, 27% 20-39, less than 1% 40-49. **Special facilities:** Amphitheater, playhouse, music library, archives, Jack London collection.

Freshman class profile. 1,245 applied, 785 admitted, 238 enrolled.

Mid 50% test scores			
SAT critical reading:	480-600	GPA 2.0-2.99:	18%
SAT math:	490-550	Rank in top quarter:	86%
ACT composite:	21-27	Rank in top tenth:	26%
GPA 3.75 or higher:	30%	Return as sophomores:	68%
GPA 3.50-3.74:	19%	Out-of-state:	36%
GPA 3.0-3.49:	33%	Live on campus:	77%
		International:	1%

Basis for selection. Academic achievement record, high school GPA, test scores, essay, letters of recommendation, interview recommended. Extracurricular activities and leadership ability considered. Audition required of music, theater, dance majors. Portfolio recommended for art majors. **Home schooled:** Transcript of courses and grades, interview, letter of recommendation (nonparent) required.

High school preparation. College-preparatory program recommended. 15 units recommended. Recommended units include English 4, mathematics 3, social studies 3, science 3 and foreign language 2.

2011-2012 Annual costs. Tuition/fees: $25,290. Room/board: $8,730. Books/supplies: $1,200. Personal expenses: $1,830.

Financial aid. **Non-need-based:** Scholarships awarded for academics, art, music/drama, state residency.

Application procedures. **Admission:** Priority date 2/15; deadline 8/1 (postmark date). $30 fee, may be waived for applicants with need. Admission notification by 9/1. Admission notification on a rolling basis. Must reply by May 1 or within 3 week(s) if notified thereafter. **Financial aid:** Priority date 2/15; no closing date. FAFSA required. Applicants notified on a rolling basis starting 2/15.

Academics. **Special study options:** Combined bachelor's/graduate degree, double major, exchange student, honors, independent study, internships, student-designed major, study abroad, Washington semester. Oak Ridge National Laboratory semester, 3-2 engineering program, 3-2 communication disorders program. **Credit/placement by examination:** AP, CLEP, IB, SAT, ACT, institutional tests. 40 credit hours maximum toward bachelor's degree. Credit awarded only when the student has not already attempted to earn credit in a college classroom at or below the level of the subject covered by the exam. **Support services:** Learning center, reduced course load, study skills assistance, tutoring, writing center.

Majors. **Biology:** General, biochemistry, biophysics, neuroscience. **Business:** Accounting, business admin, finance, managerial economics. **Communications:** Communications/speech/rhetoric, digital media, media studies. **English:** English lit. **Foreign languages:** French. **Health services:** Predental, premedicine, prepharmacy, preveterinary, speech pathology. **History:** General. **Liberal arts:** Arts/sciences. **Math:** General. **Parks/recreation:** Exercise sciences, health/fitness. **Philosophy/religion:** Philosophy, religion. **Physical sciences:** Chemistry, geology, physics. **Psychology:** General. **Social sciences:** Economics, political science, sociology. **Theology:** Sacred music. **Visual/performing arts:** General, art, cinematography, dramatic, music, music performance, music theory/composition, painting, piano/keyboard, sculpture, studio arts, theater design, voice/opera.

Most popular majors. Biology 14%, business/marketing 15%, communications/journalism 6%, parks/recreation 8%, physical sciences 7%, psychology 8%, social sciences 6%, visual/performing arts 16%.

Computing on campus. 250 workstations in dormitories, library, computer center. Dormitories linked to campus network. Commuter students can connect to campus network. Online course registration, student web hosting, wireless network available.

Student life. **Freshman orientation:** Mandatory, $100 fee. Preregistration for classes offered. Held 3 days prior to beginning of fall classes. **Policies:** Students participate on enrollment management committee, academic affairs committee, student/faculty discipline and other college-wide committees. All students 21 years of age or younger who are not local residents required to live in college housing. **Housing:** Guaranteed on-campus for all undergraduates. Coed dorms, single-sex dorms, fraternity/sorority housing available. $250 nonrefundable deposit, deadline 7/1. Living learning communities. **Activities:** Bands, campus ministries, choral groups, drama, film society, international student organizations, literary magazine, music ensembles, musical theater, opera, radio station, student government, student newspaper, symphony orchestra, church careers institute, United Methodist student movement, Baptist collegiate ministry, Canterbury House, Fellowship of Christian Athletes, student government association, Young Democrats, Young Republicans, Students for Diversity, tutoring service.

Athletics. NCAA. **Intercollegiate:** Baseball M, basketball, cross-country, golf, gymnastics W, soccer, softball W, swimming, tennis, volleyball W. **Intramural:** Archery, badminton, basketball, bowling, football (non-tackle), golf, lacrosse M, racquetball, rowing (crew), soccer, softball, table tennis, tennis, volleyball. **Team name:** Gents/Ladies.

Student services. Alcohol/substance abuse counseling, chaplain/spiritual director, career counseling, financial aid counseling, health services, personal counseling, veterans' counselor. **Physically disabled:** Services for visually impaired.

Contact. E-mail: admissions@centenary.edu
Phone: (318) 869-5131 Toll-free number: (800) 234-4448
Fax: (318) 869-5005
Mickey Quinlan, Director of Admission, Centenary College of Louisiana, Box 41188, Shreveport, LA 71134-1188

Dillard University

New Orleans, Louisiana
www.dillard.edu

CB member
CB code: 6164

- Private 4-year university and liberal arts college affiliated with United Church of Christ and United Methodist Church
- Residential campus in large city
- 1,249 degree-seeking undergraduates: 6% part-time, 72% women, 96% African American, 1% Hispanic American, 2% international
- 93% of applicants admitted
- SAT or ACT (ACT writing optional), application essay required

General. Founded in 1869. Regionally accredited. **Degrees:** 152 bachelor's awarded. **ROTC:** Army, Naval, Air Force. **Calendar:** Semester, limited summer session. **Full-time faculty:** 80 total; 69% have terminal degrees, 80% minority, 54% women. **Part-time faculty:** 51 total; 47% minority, 67% women. **Class size:** 60% < 20, 35% 20-39, 4% 40-49, 1% 50-99, less than 1% >100.

Freshman class profile. 2,643 applied, 2,456 admitted, 354 enrolled.

Rank in top quarter:	36%	Out-of-state:	39%
Rank in top tenth:	16%	International:	1%
Return as sophomores:	65%		

Basis for selection. Preference to applicants in top 25% of class with 2.5 GPA. Test scores, class rank, participation in extracurricular activities and community projects considered. Interview recommended. **Home schooled:** Recommended that student apply for state diploma.

High school preparation. 19 units required. Required and recommended units include English 4, mathematics 3, social studies 3, science 3, foreign language 2 and academic electives 6.

2011-2012 Annual costs. Tuition/fees: $14,250. Room/board: $9,478. Books/supplies: $1,200. Personal expenses: $1,819.

Financial aid. All financial aid based on need.

Application procedures. Admission: Priority date 12/1; deadline 7/1 (postmark date). $30 fee, may be waived for applicants with need. Admission notification on a rolling basis. Must reply by May 1 or within 2 week(s) if notified thereafter. **Financial aid:** Priority date 12/1, closing date 3/1. FAFSA, institutional form required. Applicants notified on a rolling basis starting 3/1; must reply by 5/1 or within 2 week(s) of notification.

Academics. Special study options: Combined bachelor's/graduate degree, double major, dual enrollment of high school students, exchange student, honors, independent study, internships, liberal arts/career combination, study abroad, teacher certification program. **Credit/placement by examination:** AP, CLEP, IB, SAT, ACT, institutional tests. 20 credit hours maximum toward bachelor's degree. **Support services:** Learning center, pre-admission summer program, reduced course load, remedial instruction, tutoring, writing center.

Majors. Area/ethnic studies: African. **Biology:** General. **Business:** Accounting, business admin, finance. **Communications:** Communications/speech/rhetoric. **Computer sciences:** Computer science. **Education:** Early childhood, early childhood special, elementary, secondary, special ed. **English:** English lit. **Foreign languages:** General. **Health services:** Nursing (RN), public health ed. **History:** General. **Math:** General. **Philosophy/religion:** Philosophy, religion. **Physical sciences:** Chemistry, physics. **Psychology:** General. **Social sciences:** Economics, political science, sociology, urban studies. **Visual/performing arts:** Art, dramatic, music, studio arts management.

Most popular majors. Biology 11%, business/marketing 21%, communications/journalism 8%, education 7%, health sciences 11%, psychology 10%, social sciences 16%, visual/performing arts 8%.

Computing on campus. 400 workstations in dormitories, library, computer center. Dormitories wired for high-speed internet access and linked to campus network. Commuter students can connect to campus network. Online library, helpline, repair service available.

Student life. Freshman orientation: Mandatory, $200 fee. Preregistration for classes offered. One-week program held the week before classes begin; includes advising and registration. **Housing:** Guaranteed on-campus for freshmen. Coed dorms, single-sex dorms, special housing for disabled, apartments, wellness housing available. $300 nonrefundable deposit, deadline 5/1. **Activities:** Jazz band, choral groups, dance, drama, music ensembles, musical theater, radio station, student government, student newspaper, service sororities and fraternities, honor societies, religious groups, NAACP, Santa Filomena, Young Republicans, Baptist student union.

Athletics. NAIA. **Intercollegiate:** Basketball, cross-country, track and field, volleyball W. **Intramural:** Basketball, football (non-tackle), football (tackle) M, softball, tennis, volleyball. **Team name:** Blue Devils.

Student services. Chaplain/spiritual director, career counseling, student employment services, financial aid counseling, health services, personal counseling, placement for graduates.

Contact. E-mail: admission@dillard.edu
Phone: (504) 816-4670 Toll-free number: (800) 216-6637
Fax: (504) 816-4895
Alecia Cyprian, Director of Admissions, Dillard University, 2601 Gentilly Boulevard, New Orleans, LA 70122-3097

Grambling State University
Grambling, Louisiana
www.gram.edu
CB code: 6250

- Public 4-year university
- Residential campus in small town
- 4,457 degree-seeking undergraduates: 7% part-time, 60% women, 87% African American, 1% Hispanic American, 8% international
- 726 degree-seeking graduate students
- 55% of applicants admitted
- SAT or ACT (ACT writing optional) required

General. Founded in 1901. Regionally accredited. **Degrees:** 695 bachelor's, 35 associate awarded; master's, doctoral offered. **ROTC:** Army, Air Force. **Location:** 35 miles from Monroe, 65 miles from Shreveport. **Calendar:** Semester, limited summer session. **Full-time faculty:** 229 total; 62% have terminal degrees, 81% minority, 49% women. **Part-time faculty:** 31 total; 74% minority, 68% women. **Class size:** 40% < 20, 45% 20-39, 8% 40-49, 7% 50-99, less than 1% >100.

Freshman class profile. 3,656 applied, 2,014 admitted, 760 enrolled.

Mid 50% test scores			
SAT critical reading:	370-450	GPA 2.0-2.99:	57%
SAT math:	390-480	Rank in top quarter:	12%
ACT composite:	16-20	Rank in top tenth:	4%
GPA 3.75 or higher:	4%	End year in good standing:	84%
GPA 3.50-3.74:	9%	Return as sophomores:	68%
GPA 3.0-3.49:	27%	Out-of-state:	46%
		International:	5%

Basis for selection. 2.0 GPA or 20 ACT and completion of 17.5 high school core units required for in-state applicants. Graduates of non-Louisiana high schools must complete the required units plus have either a 2.0 GPA and 20 ACT or have a 23 ACT. Neither group can require more than 1 developmental course. **Home schooled:** State high school equivalency certificate required.

High school preparation. College-preparatory program required. 17.5 units required. Required units include English 4, mathematics 3, history 3, science 3, foreign language 2, computer science .5 and visual/performing arts 1. One additional unit of advanced math (geometry or above) or advanced science required (biology II, chemistry II, physics, or above). Foreign language units must be of the same language.

2011-2012 Annual costs. Tuition/fees: $4,886; $12,099 out-of-state. Room/board: $9,416. Books/supplies: $1,600. Personal expenses: $3,934.

2011-2012 Financial aid. Need-based: 694 full-time freshmen applied for aid; 694 were judged to have need; 688 of these received aid. Average scholarship/grant was $5,693; average loan $3,450. 51% of total undergraduate aid awarded as scholarships/grants, 49% as loans/jobs. **Non-need-based:** Awarded to 505 full-time undergraduates, including 184 freshmen. Scholarships awarded for academics, alumni affiliation, art, athletics, job skills, leadership, minority status, music/drama, religious affiliation, ROTC, state residency.

Application procedures. Admission: Priority date 4/1; deadline 8/15 (receipt date). $20 fee, may be waived for applicants with need. Admission notification on a rolling basis. **Financial aid:** Priority date 4/1, closing date 6/1. FAFSA required. Applicants notified on a rolling basis starting 3/1; must reply within 2 week(s) of notification.

Academics. Special study options: Cooperative education, cross-registration, distance learning, double major, exchange student, honors, independent study, internships, study abroad, teacher certification program. **Credit/placement by examination:** AP, CLEP, SAT, ACT, institutional tests. 30 credit hours maximum toward associate degree, 30 toward bachelor's. **Support services:** Learning center, reduced course load, remedial instruction, study skills assistance, tutoring, writing center.

Honors college/program. 25 ACT/SAT equivalent and 3.5 GPA required.

Majors. Biology: General. **Business:** Accounting, business admin, hotel/motel admin, managerial economics, marketing. **Communications:** Media studies. **Computer sciences:** Computer science, information systems. **Education:** Art, biology, early childhood, elementary, English, French, mathematics, middle, music, physical, physics, social studies, special ed. **English:** English lit. **Foreign languages:** French, Spanish. **Health services:** Nursing (RN). **History:** General. **Human services:** Social work. **Math:** General. **Parks/recreation:** General. **Physical sciences:** Chemistry, physics. **Protective services:** Criminal justice. **Psychology:** General. **Social sciences:** Political science, sociology. **Visual/performing arts:** Art, dramatic, music performance.

Most popular majors. Biology 8%, business/marketing 23%, computer/information sciences 8%, education 7%, health sciences 10%, security/protective services 11%.

Computing on campus. 300 workstations in dormitories, library, computer center, student center. Dormitories wired for high-speed internet access and linked to campus network. Commuter students can connect to campus network. Online course registration, online library, helpline, wireless network available.

Student life. Freshman orientation: Mandatory. Preregistration for classes offered. **Housing:** Single-sex dorms, special housing for disabled, apartments, wellness housing available. $50 fully refundable deposit, deadline 7/15. **Activities:** Bands, campus ministries, choral groups, dance, drama, international student organizations, music ensembles, Model UN, opera, radio station, student government, student newspaper, symphony orchestra, TV station, Bayou Boyz social organization, Favrot student union, College Democrats, Ladies of Essence, NAACP, Bayou Girlz.

Athletics. NCAA. **Intercollegiate:** Baseball M, basketball, bowling W, cross-country, football (tackle) M, golf W, soccer W, softball W, tennis, track and field, volleyball W. **Intramural:** Badminton, baseball M, basketball,

bowling, cross-country, golf, gymnastics M, softball W, swimming, tennis, track and field, volleyball. **Team name:** Tigers.

Student services. Career counseling, student employment services, financial aid counseling, health services, personal counseling, placement for graduates, veterans' counselor. **Physically disabled:** Services for visually, speech, hearing impaired.

Contact. E-mail: admissions@gram.edu
Phone: (318) 274-6183 Toll-free number: (888) 863-3655
Fax: (318) 274-3292
Annie Moss, Director of Admissions and Recruitment, Grambling State University, 403 Main Street, GSU Box 4200, Grambling, LA 71245

Herzing University: Kenner
Kenner, Louisiana
www.herzing.edu
CB code: 3430

- For-profit 4-year branch campus and technical college
- Commuter campus in very large city
- 404 degree-seeking undergraduates
- Interview required

General. Regionally accredited. **Degrees:** 16 bachelor's, 97 associate awarded. **Location:** 10 miles from downtown New Orleans. **Calendar:** Semester, extensive summer session. **Full-time faculty:** 16 total. **Part-time faculty:** 13 total. **Class size:** 16% < 20, 84% 20-39.

Basis for selection. Wonderlic entrance test required.

2011-2012 Annual costs. Tuition/fees: $11,040.

Application procedures. Admission: No deadline. No application fee. **Financial aid:** No deadline.

Academics. Special study options: Combined bachelor's/graduate degree, distance learning, liberal arts/career combination, weekend college. **Credit/placement by examination:** AP, CLEP, IB, institutional tests. **Support services:** Learning center, reduced course load, study skills assistance, tutoring.

Majors. Business: Accounting, accounting/business management, business admin, entrepreneurial studies, human resources, international, marketing. **Computer sciences:** Networking. **Health services:** Health care admin. **Protective services:** Criminal justice, homeland security. **Visual/performing arts:** Graphic design.

Computing on campus. 115 workstations in library, computer center, student center. Online library, helpline, repair service available.

Student life. Freshman orientation: Mandatory. Preregistration for classes offered. **Activities:** Student government.

Student services. Career counseling, student employment services, financial aid counseling, placement for graduates. **Physically disabled:** Services for visually, hearing impaired.

Contact. E-mail: info@nor.herzing.edu
Phone: (504) 733-0074 Fax: (504) 733-0020
Chrissy Kalivitis, Director of Admissions, Herzing University: Kenner, 2500 Williams Boulevard, Kenner, LA 70062

ITT Technical Institute: St. Rose
St. Rose, Louisiana
www.itt-tech.edu
CB code: 2766

- For-profit 4-year technical college
- Commuter campus in small town
- 767 undergraduates
- Interview required

General. Accredited by ACICS. **Degrees:** 30 bachelor's, 196 associate awarded. **Calendar:** Quarter, extensive summer session. **Full-time faculty:** 11 total. **Part-time faculty:** 40 total.

Basis for selection. Satisfactory scores from on-site tests in English and math required.

2011-2012 Annual costs. Estimated costs as of June 2011: per-credit-hour charge, $493, depending upon level and course of study; academic fee,

$200. Certain programs of study require purchase of tools, which could cost an additional $100 to $500. All costs are subject to change.

Application procedures. Admission: No deadline. No application fee. Admission notification on a rolling basis. **Financial aid:** No deadline. FAFSA, institutional form required. Applicants notified on a rolling basis.

Academics. Credit/placement by examination: AP, CLEP. **Support services:** Learning center, tutoring.

Majors. Business: Business admin, construction management. **Communications technology:** Animation/special effects. **Computer sciences:** Programming, security. **Protective services:** Law enforcement admin.

Computing on campus. Online library available.

Student life. Freshman orientation: Available. Preregistration for classes offered.

Student services. Career counseling, student employment services, placement for graduates.

Contact. Phone: (504) 463-0338 Toll-free number: (866) 463-0338
Heidi Munoz, Director of Recruitment, ITT Technical Institute: St. Rose, 140 James Drive East, St. Rose, LA 70087

Louisiana College
Pineville, Louisiana
www.lacollege.edu
CB code: 6371

- Private 4-year liberal arts college affiliated with Southern Baptist Convention
- Residential campus in small city
- 1,145 degree-seeking undergraduates: 7% part-time, 49% women, 18% African American, 1% Asian American, 3% Hispanic American, 1% Native American, 1% international
- 404 degree-seeking graduate students
- 74% of applicants admitted
- SAT or ACT (ACT writing optional) required
- 46% graduate within 6 years

General. Founded in 1906. Regionally accredited. **Degrees:** 160 bachelor's, 13 associate awarded; master's offered. **ROTC:** Army. **Location:** 110 miles from Shreveport, 140 miles from Baton Rouge. **Calendar:** Semester, limited summer session. **Full-time faculty:** 81 total; 60% have terminal degrees, 12% minority, 49% women. **Part-time faculty:** 34 total; 18% have terminal degrees, 44% women. **Class size:** 72% < 20, 22% 20-39, 4% 40-49, 2% 50-99, less than 1% >100.

Freshman class profile. 820 applied, 606 admitted, 323 enrolled.

GPA 3.75 or higher:	29%	GPA 2.0-2.99:	31%
GPA 3.50-3.74:	13%	End year in good standing:	73%
GPA 3.0-3.49:	22%	Return as sophomores:	62%

Basis for selection. 20 ACT (930 SAT) and 2.0 GPA OR 17 ACT (810 SAT), 2.0 GPA and rank in upper 50% of graduating class required. Interview required of nursing, respiratory care majors. Portfolio recommended for art majors.

High school preparation. 17 units required. Required units include English 4, mathematics 3, social studies 3, science 3 (laboratory 2) and academic electives 4.

2012-2013 Annual costs. Tuition/fees (projected): $13,580. Room/board: $5,170. Books/supplies: $1,200. Personal expenses: $1,040.

2010-2011 Financial aid. Need-based: 318 full-time freshmen applied for aid; 318 were judged to have need; 234 of these received aid. Average need met was 44%. Average scholarship/grant was $4,578; average loan $3,076. 64% of total undergraduate aid awarded as scholarships/grants, 36% as loans/jobs. **Non-need-based:** Awarded to 663 full-time undergraduates, including 224 freshmen. Scholarships awarded for academics, art, leadership, music/drama, ROTC.

Application procedures. Admission: Closing date 8/15. $25 fee, may be waived for applicants with need. Admission notification on a rolling basis. Must reply by May 1 or within 2 week(s) if notified thereafter. **Financial aid:** Priority date 3/31; no closing date. FAFSA, institutional form required. Applicants notified on a rolling basis starting 3/1; must reply by 5/1 or within 2 week(s) of notification.

Academics. **Special study options:** Double major, dual enrollment of high school students, independent study, internships, liberal arts/career combination, student-designed major, study abroad, teacher certification program. **Credit/placement by examination:** AP, CLEP, institutional tests. 30 credit hours maximum toward bachelor's degree. **Support services:** Pre-admission summer program, reduced course load, remedial instruction, tutoring.

Majors. **Biology:** General. **Business:** General, accounting, business admin, finance, marketing. **Communications:** Communications/speech/rhetoric, journalism, media studies. **Computer sciences:** Webmaster. **Education:** General, art, business, elementary, English, foreign languages, French, health, mathematics, middle, music, physical, physically handicapped, science, secondary, social studies, Spanish. **English:** English lit. **Foreign languages:** General, French. **Health services:** Athletic training, clinical lab technology, nursing (RN), physical therapy assistant, predental, premedicine, prepharmacy, preveterinary. **History:** General. **Human services:** General, social work. **Math:** General. **Parks/recreation:** Health/fitness. **Philosophy/religion:** Religion. **Physical sciences:** Chemistry. **Protective services:** Law enforcement admin. **Psychology:** General. **Social sciences:** General, economics, political science, sociology. **Theology:** Religious ed, sacred music. **Visual/performing arts:** Commercial/advertising art, dramatic, music, music pedagogy, music performance, piano/keyboard, studio arts, voice/opera.

Most popular majors. Biology 9%, business/marketing 16%, education 13%, English 6%, health sciences 14%, physical sciences 11%, psychology 8%, security/protective services 6%, theological studies 9%.

Computing on campus. 242 workstations in library, computer center, student center. Dormitories linked to campus network.

Student life. **Freshman orientation:** Mandatory. Preregistration for classes offered. **Policies:** Religious observance required. **Housing:** Guaranteed on-campus for all undergraduates. Single-sex dorms, apartments, wellness housing available. $75 deposit, deadline 8/1. **Activities:** Bands, campus ministries, choral groups, drama, international student organizations, literary magazine, music ensembles, musical theater, opera, radio station, student government, student newspaper, Lamda Chi Beta, Delta Xi Omega, Sigma Theta, Kappa Tau Beta, Union Board, church vocation fellowship, Fellowship of Christian Athletes, Jacob's Society.

Athletics. NCAA, NCCAA. **Intercollegiate:** Baseball M, basketball, cheerleading, cross-country, football (tackle) M, golf M, soccer, softball W, tennis W. **Intramural:** Badminton, basketball, bowling, golf, softball, swimming, table tennis, tennis, volleyball. **Team name:** Wildcats.

Student services. Chaplain/spiritual director, career counseling, student employment services, financial aid counseling, health services, personal counseling, placement for graduates. **Physically disabled:** Services for visually impaired.

Contact. E-mail: admissions@lacollege.edu
Phone: (318) 487-7259 Toll-free number: (800) 487-1906
Fax: (318) 487-7550
Byron McGee, Director of Enrollment Management and Admissions, Louisiana College, LC Box 566, Pineville, LA 71359

Louisiana State University and Agricultural and Mechanical College

Baton Rouge, Louisiana

CB member
CB code: 6373

www.lsu.edu

- ◗ Public 4-year university and agricultural college
- ◗ Commuter campus in large city
- ◗ 23,372 degree-seeking undergraduates: 5% part-time, 51% women, 10% African American, 3% Asian American, 4% Hispanic American, 2% international
- ◗ 5,557 degree-seeking graduate students
- ◗ 80% of applicants admitted
- ◗ SAT or ACT (ACT writing optional) required
- ◗ 62% graduate within 6 years

General. Founded in 1860. Regionally accredited. **Degrees:** 4,440 bachelor's awarded; master's, professional, doctoral offered. **ROTC:** Army, Naval, Air Force. **Location:** 80 miles from New Orleans. **Calendar:** Semester, extensive summer session. **Full-time faculty:** 1,187 total; 89% have terminal degrees, 16% minority, 34% women. **Part-time faculty:** 179 total; 71% have terminal degrees, 6% minority, 38% women. **Class size:** 34% < 20, 40% 20-39, 7% 40-49, 10% 50-99, 9% >100. **Special facilities:** Mycological herbarium, lichenological herbarium, natural science museum, geoscience museum, rural life museum, Anglo-American art museum, Civil War center, biomedical research center, coastal ecology center, center for advanced microstructures and devices.

Freshman class profile. 14,818 applied, 11,789 admitted, 5,290 enrolled.

Mid 50% test scores			
SAT critical reading:	500-610	Rank in top quarter:	51%
SAT math:	530-630	Rank in top tenth:	24%
ACT composite:	23-28	End year in good standing:	87%
GPA 3.75 or higher:	26%	Return as sophomores:	84%
GPA 3.50-3.74:	21%	Out-of-state:	23%
GPA 3.0-3.49:	42%	Live on campus:	59%
GPA 2.0-2.99:	11%	International:	1%

Basis for selection. Criteria include number of academic units earned, GPA, ACT or SAT scores. Students must also meet minimum Board of Regents Master Plan requirements. Applicants not meeting course units and/or grades or test score requirements may be considered by admissions committee. Audition required for MDA majors. Portfolio required for Art and Landscape Architecture majors. **Home schooled:** Statement describing home school structure and mission, transcript of courses and grades, state high school equivalency certificate required. Students with ACT score below 26 will be reviewed by admission committee. **Learning Disabled:** Students with learning disabilities who do not meet regular admission requirements may appeal to admission committee and submit documentation explaining disability diagnosis.

High school preparation. College-preparatory program required. 19 units required. Required units include English 4, mathematics 4, social studies 3, history 1, science 4, foreign language 2 and visual/performing arts 1. Specific courses required in some subject areas.

2011-2012 Annual costs. Tuition/fees: $5,870; $18,878 out-of-state. Room/board: $8,220. Books/supplies: $1,500. Personal expenses: $1,840.

2010-2011 Financial aid. **Need-based:** 3,683 full-time freshmen applied for aid; 2,351 were judged to have need; 2,351 of these received aid. Average need met was 79%. Average scholarship/grant was $9,391; average loan $4,741. 61% of total undergraduate aid awarded as scholarships/grants, 39% as loans/jobs. **Non-need-based:** Awarded to 4,519 full-time undergraduates, including 1,634 freshmen. Scholarships awarded for academics, athletics, music/drama, ROTC.

Application procedures. **Admission:** Priority date 11/15; deadline 4/15 (receipt date). $40 fee. Application must be submitted online. Admission notification on a rolling basis. Recommend responding by May 1. **Financial aid:** Priority date 4/1; no closing date. FAFSA, institutional form required. Applicants notified on a rolling basis starting 12/15; must reply by 5/1 or within 3 week(s) of notification.

Academics. **Special study options:** Accelerated study, cooperative education, cross-registration, distance learning, double major, dual enrollment of high school students, ESL, exchange student, honors, independent study, internships, student-designed major, study abroad, teacher certification program. **Credit/placement by examination:** AP, CLEP, IB, SAT, ACT, institutional tests. 30 credit hours maximum toward bachelor's degree. **Support services:** Learning center, study skills assistance, tutoring, writing center.

Honors college/program. 30 ACT with 30 English, or 29 ACT with 31 English, or 1320 SAT (exclusive of Writing) with 660 Verbal. 3.5 GPA and essay required. ACT/SAT writing component required.

Majors. **Architecture:** Architecture, interior, landscape. **Biology:** General, biochemistry, microbiology. **Business:** Accounting, business admin, construction management, fashion, finance, international, management science, managerial economics, marketing. **Communications:** Communications/speech/rhetoric, media studies. **Computer sciences:** Computer science. **Conservation:** Environmental science, forest management, management/policy. **Education:** Adult/continuing, agricultural, business, early childhood, elementary, music, physical. **Engineering:** Biomedical, chemical, civil, computer, electrical, environmental, industrial, mechanical, petroleum. **English:** English lit. **Foreign languages:** French, Spanish. **General:** Animal sciences, business, plant sciences. **Health services:** Athletic training, audiology/speech pathology. **History:** General. **Liberal arts:** Arts/sciences. **Math:** General. **Parks/recreation:** Sports admin. **Philosophy/religion:** Philosophy. **Physical sciences:** Chemistry, geology, oceanography, physics. **Psychology:** General. **Social sciences:** Anthropology, economics, geography, political science, sociology. **Visual/performing arts:** Dramatic, music, music performance, studio arts. **Work/family studies:** General.

Most popular majors. Biology 7%, business/marketing 18%, communications/journalism 8%, education 10%, engineering/engineering technologies 9%, liberal arts 7%, social sciences 8%.

Computing on campus. 1,400 workstations in dormitories, library, student center. Dormitories wired for high-speed internet access and linked to campus network. Commuter students can connect to campus network. Online course registration, online library, helpline, student web hosting, wireless network available.

Student life. Freshman orientation: Mandatory, $116 fee. Preregistration for classes offered. Held in June, July, and August; Spring Invitational held in April. **Housing:** Coed dorms, single-sex dorms, special housing for disabled, apartments, fraternity/sorority housing available. $150 partly refundable deposit. **Activities:** Bands, campus ministries, choral groups, dance, drama, film society, international student organizations, literary magazine, music ensembles, musical theater, opera, radio station, student government, student newspaper, symphony orchestra, TV station, various organizations available.

Athletics. NCAA. **Intercollegiate:** Baseball M, basketball, cross-country, football (tackle) M, golf, gymnastics W, soccer W, softball W, swimming, tennis, track and field, volleyball W. **Intramural:** Badminton, basketball, football (non-tackle), golf, racquetball, soccer, softball, table tennis, tennis, volleyball. **Team name:** Tigers.

Student services. Adult student services, alcohol/substance abuse counseling, career counseling, student employment services, financial aid counseling, health services, minority student services, on-campus daycare, personal counseling, placement for graduates, veterans' counselor, women's services. **Physically disabled:** Services for visually, speech, hearing impaired.

Contact. E-mail: admissions@lsu.edu
Phone: (225) 578-1175 Fax: (225) 578-4433
David Kurpius, Associate Vice Chancellor, Enrollment Management, Louisiana State University and Agricultural and Mechanical College, 1146 Pleasant Hall, Baton Rouge, LA 70803-2750

Louisiana State University at Alexandria
Alexandria, Louisiana
www.lsua.edu   **CB code: 1632**

- Public 4-year university
- Commuter campus in small city
- 2,238 degree-seeking undergraduates
- ACT required

General. Founded in 1959. Regionally accredited. **Degrees:** 161 bachelor's, 142 associate awarded. **ROTC:** Army. **Location:** 10 miles from downtown. **Calendar:** Semester, extensive summer session. **Full-time faculty:** 95 total. **Part-time faculty:** 53 total. **Class size:** 42% < 20, 50% 20-39, 4% 40-49, 3% 50-99.

Basis for selection. Admissibility based on high school curriculum, GPA, class rank, ACT, and the need, if any, for developmental course work. Completion of Regents high school core curriculum required, along with one of the following: 2.0 GPA or rank in top 50% of class or 20 ACT. Students must also need no more than one developmental course by having one of the following: 18 ACT English or 19 ACT math. **Home schooled:** Applicants must submit transcript of high school level work with graduation date.

High school preparation. 17.5 units required. Required units include English 4, mathematics 3, social studies 3, science 3 and foreign language 2. 1 additional unit in math or science, .5 units in computer studies and 1 unit in fine arts survey required. Foreign language units must be in same language.

2011-2012 Annual costs. Tuition/fees: $4,334; $8,312 out-of-state. Room/board: $6,410. Books/supplies: $1,200. Personal expenses: $1,726.

Financial aid. Non-need-based: Scholarships awarded for academics, state residency.

Application procedures. Admission: Priority date 8/1; deadline 8/21 (postmark date). $20 fee. Admission notification on a rolling basis. **Financial aid:** Priority date 4/1; no closing date. FAFSA, institutional form required. Applicants notified on a rolling basis starting 4/20; must reply within 3 week(s) of notification.

Academics. Special study options: Distance learning, dual enrollment of high school students. **Credit/placement by examination:** AP, CLEP, institutional tests. Credit by examination limited to one-fourth number of hours required for degree. **Support services:** Learning center, pre-admission summer program, remedial instruction, study skills assistance, tutoring, writing center.

Majors. Biology: General. **Business:** Business admin. **Education:** General, elementary. **Health services:** Nursing (RN). **History:** General. **Liberal arts:** Arts/sciences. **Math:** General. **Protective services:** Criminal justice. **Psychology:** General.

Most popular majors. Education 24%, liberal arts 74%.

Computing on campus. 163 workstations in library, computer center, student center. Commuter students can connect to campus network.

Student life. Freshman orientation: Mandatory, $35 fee. Preregistration for classes offered. **Housing:** Apartments available. **Activities:** Choral groups, drama, literary magazine, student government, student newspaper, Baptist ministry, Catholic student organization, Apostolic student fellowship, Canterbury club, College Republicans, College Democrats, international student organization, nontraditional student organization, Identity, Circle K.

Athletics. Intramural: Basketball, cross-country, football (non-tackle) M, soccer, softball, tennis, volleyball. **Team name:** Generals.

Student services. Adult student services, chaplain/spiritual director, career counseling, student employment services, financial aid counseling, minority student services, on-campus daycare, personal counseling, placement for graduates, veterans' counselor.

Contact. E-mail: generalinfo@lsua.edu
Phone: (318) 473-6417 Toll-free number: (888) 473-6417
Fax: (318) 473-6418
Shelly Kieffer, Director of Admissions and Recruiting, Louisiana State University at Alexandria, 8100 Highway 71 South, Alexandria, LA 71302-9121

Louisiana State University Health Sciences Center
New Orleans, Louisiana
www.lsuhsc.edu   **CB code: 1192**

- Public two-year upper-division health science and nursing college
- Commuter campus in large city
- Test scores, application essay, interview required

General. Founded in 1931. Regionally accredited. **Degrees:** 277 bachelor's, 11 associate awarded; master's, professional, doctoral offered. **Articulation:** Agreement with University of New Orleans. **Location:** Downtown. **Calendar:** Continuous, limited summer session. **Full-time faculty:** 713 total. **Part-time faculty:** 134 total.

Student profile. 884 degree-seeking undergraduates, 1,898 graduate students.

African American:	11%	Out-of-state:	1%
Asian American:	6%	Live on campus:	20%
Hispanic American:	4%	25 or older:	28%
International:	2%		

Basis for selection. College transcript, application essay, interview, standardized test scores required. Application closing, notification, and response dates vary by program. Transfer accepted as sophomores, juniors, seniors.

2011-2012 Annual costs. Tuition/fees: $5,393; $9,075 out-of-state. Tuition and fees quoted are for Allied Health program. Nursing: $4,083 residents, $6,627 non-residents. Dental Hygiene: $4,027 residents, $6,183 non-residents. Dental Laboratory Technology: $3,692 residents, $5,817 non-residents. Allied Health Shreveport campus: $5,772 residents, $9,813 non-residents. Room only: $2,187. Books/supplies: $3,262.

Financial aid. Non-need-based: Scholarships awarded for academics.

Application procedures. Admission: $50 fee. **Financial aid:** FAFSA, institutional form required.

Academics. Special study options: Double major, honors, independent study, internships. **Credit/placement by examination:** AP, CLEP.

Majors. Health services: Cardiovascular technology, clinical lab science, dental hygiene, nursing (RN).

Computing on campus. 227 workstations in dormitories, library, computer center, student center. Dormitories wired for high-speed internet access and linked to campus network. Commuter students can connect to campus network. Online library, helpline, repair service, wireless network available.

Student life. Housing: Coed dorms, apartments available. **Activities:** Student government.

Student services. Alcohol/substance abuse counseling, career counseling, financial aid counseling, health services, personal counseling. **Physically disabled:** Services for visually, speech, hearing impaired.

Contact. Phone: (504) 568-4808
Louisiana State University Health Sciences Center, 433 Bolivar Street, New Orleans, LA 70112-2223

Louisiana State University in Shreveport
Shreveport, Louisiana
www.lsus.edu   CB code: 6355

- Public 4-year university and teachers college
- Commuter campus in large city
- 3,073 degree-seeking undergraduates: 26% part-time, 60% women, 23% African American, 2% Asian American, 4% Hispanic American, 1% Native American, 2% international
- 370 degree-seeking graduate students
- 48% of applicants admitted
- ACT (writing optional), application essay required

General. Founded in 1965. Regionally accredited. **Degrees:** 565 bachelor's awarded; master's offered. **ROTC:** Army. **Location:** 180 miles from Dallas. **Calendar:** Semester, extensive summer session. **Full-time faculty:** 129 total; 78% have terminal degrees, 14% minority, 42% women. **Part-time faculty:** 64 total; 5% minority, 45% women. **Class size:** 42% < 20, 40% 20-39, 8% 40-49, 10% 50-99, less than 1% >100. **Special facilities:** Life science museum, pioneer heritage center.

Freshman class profile. 888 applied, 430 admitted, 321 enrolled.

Mid 50% test scores		GPA 3.0-3.49:	35%
SAT critical reading:	430-510	GPA 2.0-2.99:	34%
SAT math:	460-550	End year in good standing:	78%
ACT composite:	20-24	Return as sophomores:	65%
GPA 3.75 or higher:	17%	Out-of-state:	9%
GPA 3.50-3.74:	14%	International:	2%

Basis for selection. Completion of Regents high school core curriculum of 17.5 course units and one of the following required: 2.0 GPA, high school rank in top 50% of class, or 20 ACT. For early admission, principal's recommendation, 29 ACT, 15 specific high school units, 3.0 GPA required. Regardless of age, students who have accumulated at least 12 term hours of non-developmental college credit may transfer if all transfer requirements met. **Home schooled:** GED required.

High school preparation. Recommended units include English 4, mathematics 3, social studies 3, science 3, foreign language 2, computer science 1 and visual/performing arts 1.

2011-2012 Annual costs. Tuition/fees: $4,674; $11,410 out-of-state. Books/supplies: $1,200. Personal expenses: $1,839.

Application procedures. Admission: Closing date 7/15 (receipt date). $10 fee. Admission notification on a rolling basis. **Financial aid:** No deadline. Applicants notified on a rolling basis.

Academics. Special study options: Combined bachelor's/graduate degree, cooperative education, distance learning, double major, dual enrollment of high school students, independent study, internships, student-designed major, study abroad, teacher certification program, Washington semester. Cooperative education program with Southern University at Shreveport. **Credit/placement by examination:** AP, CLEP, ACT, institutional tests. 62 credit hours maximum toward bachelor's degree. **Support services:** Learning center, remedial instruction, study skills assistance, tutoring, writing center.

Majors. Biology: General. **Business:** Accounting, banking/financial services, business admin, financial planning, managerial economics, marketing. **Communications:** Media studies. **Computer sciences:** Computer science. **Education:** Art, biology, chemistry, early childhood, elementary, English, mathematics, physics, science, social studies. **English:** English lit, rhetoric/composition. **History:** General. **Liberal arts:** Arts/sciences. **Math:** General. **Parks/recreation:** Health/fitness. **Physical sciences:** Chemistry, physics. **Protective services:** Criminal justice. **Psychology:** General. **Social sciences:** Political science, sociology. **Visual/performing arts:** General, digital arts, dramatic, graphic design.

Most popular majors. Biology 11%, business/marketing 29%, communications/journalism 6%, education 9%, liberal arts 18%, psychology 6%.

Computing on campus. 250 workstations in library, computer center, student center. Commuter students can connect to campus network. Online course registration, online library, helpline, student web hosting, wireless network available.

Student life. Freshman orientation: Mandatory. Preregistration for classes offered. **Housing:** Guaranteed on-campus for all undergraduates. Apartments available. Pets allowed in dorm rooms. **Activities:** Jazz band, dance, drama, literary magazine, radio station, student government, student newspaper, Baptist student union, College Republicans, government and law society, Catholic student union, Rotaract, foreign language club, psychology club, black student association.

Athletics. NAIA. **Intercollegiate:** Baseball M. **Intramural:** Badminton, basketball, football (non-tackle), golf, racquetball, soccer, softball, swimming, table tennis, tennis, track and field, volleyball. **Team name:** Pilots.

Student services. Career counseling, student employment services, financial aid counseling, minority student services, personal counseling, placement for graduates, veterans' counselor. **Physically disabled:** Services for visually, speech, hearing impaired.

Contact. E-mail: admissions@pilot.lsus.edu
Phone: (318) 797-5061 Toll-free number: (800) 229-5957
Fax: (318) 797-5286
Mickey Diez, Dean of Enrollment Services & Registrar, Louisiana State University in Shreveport, One University Place, Shreveport, LA 71115-2399

Louisiana Tech University
Ruston, Louisiana   CB member
www.latech.edu   CB code: 6372

- Public 4-year university
- Commuter campus in large town
- 7,502 degree-seeking undergraduates
- SAT or ACT (ACT writing optional) required

General. Founded in 1894. Regionally accredited. **Degrees:** 1,234 bachelor's, 91 associate awarded; master's, doctoral offered. **ROTC:** Army, Naval. **Location:** 70 miles from Shreveport, 30 miles from Monroe. **Calendar:** Quarter, extensive summer session. **Full-time faculty:** 417 total. **Part-time faculty:** 110 total. **Class size:** 37% < 20, 42% 20-39, 11% 40-49, 8% 50-99, 2% >100. **Special facilities:** Natural history museum, on-campus lab school, arboretum, planetarium, rehabilitation science and biomedical engineering center, micromanufacturing institute, water resource center.

Freshman class profile.

Out-of-state:	14%	Sororities:	17%
Fraternities:	9%		

Basis for selection. High school record, test scores most important. Special talents, school and community activities, recommendations considered. To be admitted, applicant must need no more than one remedial course. Admission deadline for scholarship consideration is January 2 for the following fall term. **Home schooled:** Applicants must have 2.5 GPA, 23 ACT/1060 SAT (exclusive of Writing).

High school preparation. Required units include English 4, mathematics 3, social studies 3, science 3, academic electives 4.5. 2 algebra required. Social studies must include 1 U.S. history. 4.5 units of electives from foreign language, sciences, math, social studies, speech, advanced fine arts, or computer literacy required. Prefer English courses that emphasize grammar, composition, and literature.

2011-2012 Annual costs. Tuition/fees: $5,868; $12,993 out-of-state. Room/board: $5,265. Books/supplies: $1,800. Personal expenses: $1,500.

Financial aid. Non-need-based: Scholarships awarded for academics, alumni affiliation, art, athletics, job skills, leadership, minority status, music/drama, state residency.

Application procedures. Admission: Priority date 8/1; no deadline. $20 fee, may be waived for applicants with need. Admission notification on a rolling basis beginning on or about 6/1. **Financial aid:** Priority date 4/15; no closing date. FAFSA, institutional form required. Applicants notified on a rolling basis starting 4/1; must reply within 3 week(s) of notification.

Academics. Special study options: Combined bachelor's/graduate degree, cooperative education, cross-registration, distance learning, double major, dual enrollment of high school students, ESL, honors, independent study, internships, liberal arts/career combination, study abroad, teacher certification program. Cooperative programs with Grambling State University. **Credit/placement by examination:** AP, CLEP, institutional tests. 30 credit hours maximum toward associate degree, 30 toward bachelor's. **Support services:** Remedial instruction, study skills assistance, tutoring.

Majors. Architecture: Architecture, interior. **Biology:** General. **Business:** Accounting, business admin, finance, human resources, management information systems, management science, managerial economics, marketing. **Communications:** Journalism. **Computer sciences:** Computer science. **Conservation:** General, forest resources, forestry. **Education:** Art, early childhood, elementary, French, music, physical, secondary, special ed, speech impaired. **Engineering:** Biomedical, chemical, civil, electrical, mechanical. **English:**

English lit, rhetoric/composition. **Foreign languages:** French, Spanish. **General:** Animal sciences, business. **Health services:** Audiology/speech pathology, clinical lab science, medical records admin. **History:** General. **Liberal arts:** Arts/sciences. **Math:** General. **Parks/recreation:** Health/fitness. **Physical sciences:** Chemistry, geology, physics. **Psychology:** General. **Social sciences:** Geography, political science, sociology. **Visual/performing arts:** Art, commercial/advertising art, music, music performance, photography. **Work/family studies:** Family studies.

Computing on campus. 1,800 workstations in dormitories, library, computer center. Dormitories linked to campus network.

Student life. Freshman orientation: Available, $55 fee. Preregistration for classes offered. Four sessions offered during summer. **Housing:** Guaranteed on-campus for freshmen. Single-sex dorms, special housing for disabled, apartments available. $50 deposit, deadline 7/15. **Activities:** Bands, choral groups, dance, drama, music ensembles, musical theater, radio station, student government, student newspaper, Wesley Foundation, Baptist student union, Union Board, College Republicans, Campus Crusade for Christ, international student association, NAACP, Circle K, Angel Flight.

Athletics. NCAA. **Intercollegiate:** Baseball M, basketball, bowling W, cross-country, football (tackle) M, golf M, soccer W, softball W, tennis W, track and field, volleyball W. **Intramural:** Badminton, basketball, bowling, golf M, racquetball, soccer, softball, tennis, volleyball. **Team name:** Bulldogs (M), Lady Techsters (W).

Student services. Chaplain/spiritual director, career counseling, student employment services, financial aid counseling, health services, legal services, minority student services, personal counseling, placement for graduates, veterans' counselor, women's services. **Physically disabled:** Services for speech impaired.

Contact. E-mail: bulldog@latech.edu
Phone: (318) 257-3036 Toll-free number: (800) 528-3241
Fax: (318) 257-2499
Jan Albritton, Director of Admissions, College of Basic and Career Studies, Louisiana Tech University, Box 3178, Ruston, LA 71272

Loyola University New Orleans
New Orleans, Louisiana

CB member

www.loyno.edu/

CB code: 6374

♦ Private 4-year university and liberal arts college affiliated with Roman Catholic Church
♦ Residential campus in large city
♦ 3,095 degree-seeking undergraduates: 6% part-time, 57% women, 15% African American, 4% Asian American, 13% Hispanic American, 1% Native American, 3% international
♦ 1,799 degree-seeking graduate students
♦ 65% of applicants admitted
♦ SAT or ACT (ACT writing optional), application essay required
♦ 57% graduate within 6 years

General. Founded in 1912. Regionally accredited. **Degrees:** 448 bachelor's awarded; master's, professional, doctoral offered. **ROTC:** Army, Naval, Air Force. **Location:** Uptown. **Calendar:** Semester, limited summer session. **Full-time faculty:** 306 total; 92% have terminal degrees, 15% minority, 44% women. **Part-time faculty:** 175 total; 58% have terminal degrees, 13% minority, 42% women. **Class size:** 51% < 20, 46% 20-39, 2% 40-49, 1% 50-99, less than 1% >100. **Special facilities:** Humanities lab with Perseus Project and TLG TV, 24-hour microcomputer labs, computer science lab, graphics lab, visual arts lab, communications lab, business computer lab, multimedia training center and studio, non-profit communications center, audio recording studio, editing studio, international education center, career development center, Jesuit social research institute.

Freshman class profile. 6,386 applied, 4,143 admitted, 871 enrolled.

Mid 50% test scores		Rank in top tenth:	23%
SAT critical reading:	590-630	End year in good standing:	85%
SAT math:	560-610	Return as sophomores:	77%
ACT composite:	23-29	Out-of-state:	58%
GPA 3.75 or higher:	43%	Live on campus:	81%
GPA 3.50-3.74:	16%	International:	2%
GPA 3.0-3.49:	32%	Fraternities:	15%
GPA 2.0-2.99:	9%	Sororities:	21%
Rank in top quarter:	50%		

Basis for selection. High school performance, test scores, counselor/teacher evaluation, personal essay, extracurricular activity, community involvement and work experience considered. Interview recommended. Audition required for music, theater arts and dance majors. Portfolio required for visual arts program applicants. **Home schooled:** Require proof of high school graduation or its equivalent.

High school preparation. College-preparatory program recommended. 17 units required; 22 recommended. Required and recommended units include English 4, mathematics 2-3, social studies 2, science 2-3 (laboratory 1) and foreign language 2.

2012-2013 Annual costs. Tuition/fees: $34,952. Room/board: $11,630.

2011-2012 Financial aid. Need-based: 720 full-time freshmen applied for aid; 624 were judged to have need; 624 of these received aid. Average need met was 73%. Average scholarship/grant was $21,914; average loan $3,405. 76% of total undergraduate aid awarded as scholarships/grants, 24% as loans/jobs. **Non-need-based:** Awarded to 1,179 full-time undergraduates, including 336 freshmen. Scholarships awarded for academics, alumni affiliation, art, leadership, ROTC.

Application procedures. Admission: Priority date 12/1; no deadline. $20 fee, may be waived for applicants with need, free for online applicants. Admission notification on a rolling basis beginning on or about 10/20. Must reply by May 1 or within 2 week(s) if notified thereafter. Students recommended by high school principals and considered ready for college work by the Committee on Admissions may be admitted immediately following completion of junior year of high school. Program intended to serve applicants of unusual promise who will benefit from beginning college careers a year early. **Financial aid:** Priority date 2/15, closing date 6/1. FAFSA required. Applicants notified on a rolling basis starting 3/1; must reply by 5/1 or within 2 week(s) of notification.

Academics. Jesuit tradition of contributing to the liberal education of the whole person emphasized. **Special study options:** Accelerated study, combined bachelor's/graduate degree, cross-registration, distance learning, double major, dual enrollment of high school students, ESL, exchange student, honors, independent study, internships, liberal arts/career combination, student-designed major, study abroad, teacher certification program, Washington semester. Advanced Placement credit, evening courses, interdisciplinary majors and minors, student-designed minors, internet-based program in nursing. **Credit/placement by examination:** AP, CLEP, IB, SAT, ACT, institutional tests. 30 credit hours maximum toward bachelor's degree. **Support services:** Learning center, pre-admission summer program, reduced course load, remedial instruction, study skills assistance, tutoring, writing center.

Majors. Biology: General. **Business:** Accounting, business admin, finance, international, managerial economics, marketing. **Communications:** Communications/speech/rhetoric. **Education:** Music. **English:** English lit. **Foreign languages:** General, ancient Greek, French, German, Spanish. **Health services:** Music therapy, nursing (RN), predental, premedicine, preveterinary. **History:** General. **Math:** General. **Philosophy/religion:** Christian, philosophy, religion. **Physical sciences:** Chemistry, physics. **Protective services:** Criminal justice, forensics. **Psychology:** General. **Social sciences:** General, criminology, economics, political science, sociology. **Visual/performing arts:** General, art, commercial/advertising art, dramatic, jazz, music, music management, music performance, music theory/composition, studio arts.

Most popular majors. Business/marketing 19%, communications/journalism 9%, English 6%, health sciences 6%, psychology 7%, social sciences 15%, visual/performing arts 22%.

Computing on campus. 525 workstations in dormitories, library, computer center, student center. Dormitories wired for high-speed internet access and linked to campus network. Commuter students can connect to campus network. Online course registration, online library, helpline, repair service, student web hosting, wireless network available.

Student life. Freshman orientation: Mandatory, $250 fee. Preregistration for classes offered. Orientation session plus 5-day transition program available. **Housing:** Guaranteed on-campus for freshmen. Coed dorms, special housing for disabled, apartments, wellness housing available. $100 nonrefundable deposit, deadline 5/1. Honors floors available. **Activities:** Bands, campus ministries, choral groups, dance, drama, film society, international student organizations, literary magazine, music ensembles, musical theater, opera, radio station, student government, student newspaper, symphony orchestra, black student union, community action program, international student association, Muslim student association, Asian student organization, university programming board, Big Brothers/Big Sisters, civic engagement society, student government association, community action program, diversity team, Students Advocating for Gender Equality, Queer Straight Alliance.

Athletics. NAIA. **Intercollegiate:** Baseball M, basketball, cross-country, tennis, track and field, volleyball W. **Intramural:** Basketball, football (non-tackle), racquetball, soccer, softball, volleyball, weight lifting. **Team name:** Wolfpack.

Student services. Adult student services, alcohol/substance abuse counseling, chaplain/spiritual director, career counseling, student employment

services, financial aid counseling, health services, minority student services, on-campus daycare, personal counseling, placement for graduates, women's services. **Physically disabled:** Services for visually, speech, hearing impaired.

Contact. E-mail: admit@loyno.edu
Phone: (504) 865-3240 Toll-free number: (800) 456-9652
Fax: (504) 865-3383
Salvadore Liberto, Vice President for Enrollment Management, Loyola University New Orleans, 6363 St. Charles Avenue, New Orleans, LA 70118-6195

McNeese State University
Lake Charles, Louisiana
www.mcneese.edu   **CB code: 6403**

- Public 4-year university
- Commuter campus in small city
- 7,123 degree-seeking undergraduates: 14% part-time, 61% women, 18% African American, 1% Asian American, 2% Hispanic American, 1% Native American, 4% international
- 794 degree-seeking graduate students
- 69% of applicants admitted
- SAT or ACT (ACT writing optional) required
- 35% graduate within 6 years

General. Founded in 1939. Regionally accredited. **Degrees:** 983 bachelor's, 172 associate awarded; master's offered. **Location:** 193 miles from New Orleans, 124 miles from Houston. **Calendar:** Semester, extensive summer session. **Full-time faculty:** 297 total; 66% have terminal degrees, 16% minority, 44% women. **Part-time faculty:** 137 total; 18% have terminal degrees, 10% minority, 66% women. **Class size:** 37% < 20, 43% 20-39, 12% 40-49, 7% 50-99, less than 1% >100. **Special facilities:** Environmental research center, vertebrate museum, farm, community health care clinic, meat processing plant, Southwest Louisiana Entrepreneurial and Economic Development Center.

Freshman class profile. 2,964 applied, 2,035 admitted, 1,386 enrolled.

Mid 50% test scores		Rank in top quarter:	43%
ACT composite:	19-24	Rank in top tenth:	18%
GPA 3.75 or higher:	22%	Return as sophomores:	68%
GPA 3.50-3.74:	18%	Out-of-state:	9%
GPA 3.0-3.49:	33%	International:	2%
GPA 2.0-2.99:	27%		

Basis for selection. Applicants must complete Louisiana Board of Regents high school core curriculum with 18 ACT English or 19 ACT math (450 SAT verbal or 460 math) and 2.5 GPA and meet one of the following: 2.0 core GPA of 2.0 or 20 ACT (940 SAT critical reading and math combined). Audition required of music majors. **Home schooled:** Transcript of courses and grades required. Letter from State Board of Education approving the home school program required. **Learning Disabled:** Applicants should register with Office of Services for Students with Disabilities.

High school preparation. College-preparatory program required. 19 units required. Required units include English 4, mathematics 4, social studies 1, history 3, science 4, foreign language 2 and visual/performing arts 1.

2011-2012 Annual costs. Tuition/fees: $4,353; $13,175 out-of-state. Room/board: $5,748. Books/supplies: $1,200. Personal expenses: $1,840.

Financial aid. Non-need-based: Scholarships awarded for academics, alumni affiliation, art, athletics, leadership, minority status, music/drama, state residency. **Additional information:** Books may be charged and paid in 2 installments during semester.

Application procedures. Admission: $20 fee. Admission notification on a rolling basis beginning on or about 11/1. **Financial aid:** Priority date 5/1; no closing date. FAFSA, institutional form required. Applicants notified on a rolling basis starting 4/15; must reply within 2 week(s) of notification.

Academics. Special study options: Accelerated study, cooperative education, distance learning, double major, dual enrollment of high school students, ESL, honors, independent study, internships, study abroad, teacher certification program. **Credit/placement by examination:** AP, CLEP, SAT, ACT, institutional tests. 24 credit hours maximum toward associate degree, 45 toward bachelor's. **Support services:** Learning center, remedial instruction, tutoring, writing center.

Honors college/program. Requirements include 27 ACT, 3.4 GPA, essay, interview, and 3 recommendations.

Majors. Biology: General. **Business:** Accounting, business admin, finance, marketing. **Communications:** Media studies. **Computer sciences:** Computer science. **Conservation:** Wildlife/wilderness. **Education:** Early childhood, elementary, physical, secondary. **Engineering:** General. **English:** English lit, rhetoric/composition. **Foreign languages:** General. **Health services:** Athletic training, clinical lab science, nursing (RN). **History:** General. **Liberal arts:** Arts/sciences. **Math:** General. **Parks/recreation:** Exercise sciences. **Physical sciences:** Chemistry. **Protective services:** Criminal justice. **Psychology:** General. **Social sciences:** Political science, sociology. **Visual/performing arts:** Art, dramatic, music performance. **Work/family studies:** General.

Most popular majors. Business/marketing 15%, education 11%, engineering/engineering technologies 8%, health sciences 17%, liberal arts 17%.

Computing on campus. 450 workstations in dormitories, library, computer center, student center. Dormitories wired for high-speed internet access and linked to campus network. Commuter students can connect to campus network. Online course registration, online library, helpline, student web hosting, wireless network available.

Student life. Freshman orientation: Mandatory, $50 fee. Preregistration for classes offered. Five conferences offered in summer. **Housing:** Coed dorms, apartments, fraternity/sorority housing available. $325 partly refundable deposit. **Activities:** Bands, campus ministries, choral groups, dance, drama, international student organizations, literary magazine, music ensembles, musical theater, opera, student government, student newspaper, symphony orchestra, 93 organizations available.

Athletics. NCAA. **Intercollegiate:** Baseball M, basketball, cheerleading, cross-country, football (tackle) M, golf, rodeo, soccer W, softball W, tennis W, track and field, volleyball W. **Intramural:** Badminton, basketball, bowling, football (non-tackle), golf, handball, racquetball, softball, swimming, table tennis, tennis, volleyball, water polo. **Team name:** Cowboys.

Student services. Adult student services, alcohol/substance abuse counseling, chaplain/spiritual director, career counseling, student employment services, financial aid counseling, health services, minority student services, personal counseling, placement for graduates, veterans' counselor. **Physically disabled:** Services for visually, speech, hearing impaired.

Contact. E-mail: info@mcneese.edu
Phone: (337) 475-5504 Toll-free number: (800) 622-3352 ext. 5504
Fax: (337) 475-5151
Kara Smith, Director of Admissions and Recruiting, McNeese State University, MSU Box 91740, Lake Charles, LA 70609-1740

New Orleans Baptist Theological Seminary: Leavell College
New Orleans, Louisiana
www.nobts.edu   **CB code: 5034**

- Private 4-year Bible and seminary college affiliated with Southern Baptist Convention
- Very large city
- 263 full-time, degree-seeking undergraduates
- Application essay, interview required

General. Regionally accredited. **Degrees:** 52 bachelor's, 41 associate awarded; master's, professional, doctoral offered. **Calendar:** Semester, limited summer session. **Full-time faculty:** 16 total. **Part-time faculty:** 132 total. **Special facilities:** Learning extension centers in Baton Rouge, Lake Charles, and Shreveport. Other centers in Mississippi, Alabama, Florida, and Georgia.

Basis for selection. Must be at least 18 years old and a Christian for at least one year.

2011-2012 Annual costs. Tuition/fees: $5,580. Tuition reported for Southern Baptist students. Non-Baptist students pay tuition at a slightly higher rate. Room only: $2,520. Books/supplies: $500.

Application procedures. Admission: No deadline. $25 fee, may be waived for applicants with need. Admission notification on a rolling basis. **Financial aid:** Closing date 4/30.

Academics. Credit/placement by examination: AP, CLEP. 30 credit hours maximum toward bachelor's degree.

Majors. Philosophy/religion: Christian. **Theology:** Bible, religious ed, sacred music.

Student life. Freshman orientation: Mandatory. Preregistration for classes offered. **Housing:** Single-sex dorms, apartments available.

Contact. E-mail: leavelladmission@nobts.edu
Phone: (504) 282-4455
Paul Gregoire, Registrar and Dean of Admissions, New Orleans Baptist
Theological Seminary: Leavell College, 3939 Gentilly Boulevard, New
Orleans, LA 70126-4858

Nicholls State University
Thibodaux, Louisiana
www.nicholls.edu   **CB code: 6221**

- Public 4-year university
- Commuter campus in large town
- 5,923 degree-seeking undergraduates: 18% part-time, 63% women, 19% African American, 1% Asian American, 2% Hispanic American, 2% Native American, 2% international
- 480 degree-seeking graduate students
- 84% of applicants admitted
- SAT or ACT with writing required
- 33% graduate within 6 years

General. Founded in 1948. Regionally accredited. **Degrees:** 959 bachelor's, 152 associate awarded; master's offered. **Location:** 60 miles from New Orleans, 75 miles from Baton Rouge. **Calendar:** Semester, extensive summer session. **Full-time faculty:** 254 total; 58% have terminal degrees, 13% minority, 54% women. **Part-time faculty:** 35 total; 26% have terminal degrees, 11% minority, 46% women. **Class size:** 40% < 20, 42% 20-39, 5% 40-49, 11% 50-99, 2% >100. **Special facilities:** Marine research facility, culinary institute, center for women and government, marine biology laboratory, center for study of dyslexia, center for economic education, small business development center, center for traditional boat building, economic council.

Freshman class profile. 2,174 applied, 1,830 admitted, 1,135 enrolled.

Mid 50% test scores			
SAT critical reading:	420-550	Rank in top tenth:	17%
SAT math:	470-610	End year in good standing:	76%
ACT composite:	20-24	Return as sophomores:	69%
GPA 3.75 or higher:	16%	Out-of-state:	4%
GPA 3.50-3.74:	16%	Live on campus:	46%
GPA 3.0-3.49:	35%	International:	3%
GPA 2.0-2.99:	32%	Fraternities:	14%
Rank in top quarter:	43%	Sororities:	12%

Basis for selection. Must meet the Board of Regents Core (TOPS Core) requirement, have a 2.0 GPA, and meet at least one of the following: 20 ACT or rank in the top half of graduating class.

High school preparation. College-preparatory program recommended. 17.5 units required. Required units include English 4, mathematics 3, social studies 1, history 2, science 3, foreign language 2, visual/performing arts 1, academic electives 1.5.

2011-2012 Annual costs. Tuition/fees: $4,737; $12,687 out-of-state. Room/board: $8,580. Books/supplies: $1,200. Personal expenses: $1,750.

Financial aid. **Non-need-based:** Scholarships awarded for academics, athletics, state residency.

Application procedures. **Admission:** Priority date 8/15; no deadline. $20 fee ($30 out-of-state). Admission notification on a rolling basis. **Financial aid:** Closing date 4/15. FAFSA, institutional form required. Applicants notified on a rolling basis; must reply within 2 week(s) of notification.

Academics. **Special study options:** Cooperative education, cross-registration, distance learning, double major, dual enrollment of high school students, exchange student, honors, independent study, internships, teacher certification program. **Credit/placement by examination:** AP, CLEP, ACT, institutional tests. 15 credit hours maximum toward associate degree, 30 toward bachelor's. **Support services:** Learning center, pre-admission summer program, reduced course load, remedial instruction, study skills assistance, tutoring, writing center.

Majors. Biology: General. **Business:** Accounting, business admin, finance, management information systems, marketing. **Communications:** Media studies. **Education:** Art, business, early childhood, elementary, English, mathematics, middle, music, physical, science, social studies. **English:** English lit. **Health services:** Audiology/speech pathology, dietetics, nursing (RN). **History:** General. **Math:** General. **Physical sciences:** Chemistry. **Psychology:** General. **Social sciences:** Political science, sociology. **Visual/performing arts:** Art, music. **Work/family studies:** General.

Most popular majors. Business/marketing 26%, education 9%, health sciences 17%, liberal arts 17%.

Computing on campus. 304 workstations in dormitories, library, computer center. Dormitories wired for high-speed internet access and linked to campus network. Commuter students can connect to campus network. Online course registration, online library, wireless network available.

Student life. Freshman orientation: Mandatory, $50 fee. Preregistration for classes offered. **Housing:** Guaranteed on-campus for all undergraduates. Coed dorms, apartments available. $250 partly refundable deposit, deadline 8/15. **Activities:** Bands, campus ministries, choral groups, dance, drama, film society, international student organizations, literary magazine, music ensembles, musical theater, radio station, student government, student newspaper, TV station, Baptist student union, Circle K, Young Democrats, Support for Older and Returning Students, Order of Athena, Young Republicans, UNITE, Newman club, Muslim student association.

Athletics. NCAA. **Intercollegiate:** Baseball M, basketball, cross-country, football (tackle) M, golf, soccer W, softball W, tennis, track and field W, volleyball W. **Intramural:** Basketball, football (non-tackle), softball, volleyball. **Team name:** Colonels.

Student services. Adult student services, alcohol/substance abuse counseling, chaplain/spiritual director, career counseling, services for economically disadvantaged, student employment services, financial aid counseling, health services, legal services, minority student services, personal counseling, placement for graduates, veterans' counselor, women's services. **Physically disabled:** Services for visually, speech, hearing impaired.

Contact. E-mail: nicholls@nicholls.edu
Phone: (985) 448-4507 Toll-free number: (877) 642-4655
Fax: (985) 448-4929
Becky Durocher, Director of Admissions, Nicholls State University, PO Box 2004-NSU, Thibodaux, LA 70310

Northwestern State University
Natchitoches, Louisiana
www.nsula.edu   **CB code: 6492**

- Public 4-year university
- Commuter campus in large town
- 7,410 degree-seeking undergraduates: 28% part-time, 69% women, 30% African American, 1% Asian American, 3% Hispanic American, 1% Native American, 1% international
- 1,056 degree-seeking graduate students
- 82% of applicants admitted
- SAT or ACT (ACT writing optional) required
- 40% graduate within 6 years; 18% enter graduate study

General. Founded in 1884. Regionally accredited. Additional campuses in Shreveport, Leesville, Alexandria, and off-campus sites. **Degrees:** 1,078 bachelor's, 702 associate awarded; master's offered. **ROTC:** Army, Air Force. **Location:** 75 miles from Shreveport, 57 miles from Alexandria. **Calendar:** Semester, extensive summer session. **Full-time faculty:** 278 total; 60% have terminal degrees, 9% minority, 56% women. **Part-time faculty:** 239 total; 23% have terminal degrees, 15% minority, 63% women. **Class size:** 44% < 20, 38% 20-39, 7% 40-49, 10% 50-99, 1% >100. **Special facilities:** Regional folklife center, Creole heritage center, southern studies institute, heritage resources laboratory, preservation technology and training center, aquaculture center.

Freshman class profile. 2,756 applied, 2,270 admitted, 1,222 enrolled.

Mid 50% test scores			
SAT critical reading:	430-570	Rank in top quarter:	40%
SAT math:	470-560	Rank in top tenth:	17%
ACT composite:	19-23	End year in good standing:	89%
GPA 3.75 or higher:	14%	Return as sophomores:	69%
GPA 3.50-3.74:	15%	Out-of-state:	10%
GPA 3.0-3.49:	37%	Live on campus:	57%
GPA 2.0-2.99:	33%	International:	1%

Basis for selection. In-state applicants must have required 19 unit college preparatory program, 2.35 GPA, need no more than one developmental class, and have one of the following: 20 ACT/940 SAT or 2.0 core GPA. Out-of-state and homeschooled students must have between 17-19 units of college preparatory program and meet the rest of the quailifications above or have 23 ACT/1050 SAT and need no more than one developmental course.

High school preparation. College-preparatory program required. 19 units required. Required units include English 4, mathematics 4, social studies 4, science 4, foreign language 2 and visual/performing arts 1.

2011-2012 Annual costs. Tuition/fees: $4,972; $13,542 out-of-state. Room/board: $7,349. Books/supplies: $1,200. Personal expenses: $1,839.

2010-2011 Financial aid. Need-based: 979 full-time freshmen applied for aid; 793 were judged to have need; 772 of these received aid. Average need met was 68%. Average scholarship/grant was $5,477; average loan $3,060. 53% of total undergraduate aid awarded as scholarships/grants, 47% as loans/jobs. **Non-need-based:** Awarded to 4,338 full-time undergraduates, including 423 freshmen. Scholarships awarded for academics, alumni affiliation, art, athletics, job skills, leadership, minority status, music/drama, religious affiliation, ROTC, state residency.

Application procedures. Admission: Closing date 7/6 (receipt date). $20 fee. Admission notification on a rolling basis. Applications may be submitted after fall deadline but consideration is not guaranteed. **Financial aid:** Priority date 5/1; no closing date. FAFSA, institutional form required. Applicants notified on a rolling basis starting 5/1; must reply within 4 week(s) of notification.

Academics. Special study options: Cooperative education, distance learning, double major, dual enrollment of high school students, exchange student, honors, independent study, internships, liberal arts/career combination, study abroad, teacher certification program. **Credit/placement by examination:** AP, CLEP, IB, SAT, ACT, institutional tests. 30 credit hours maximum toward associate degree, 60 toward bachelor's. Maximum semester hours of credit by examination may not exceed half the number of credits required for degree. **Support services:** Learning center, pre-admission summer program, reduced course load, remedial instruction, study skills assistance, tutoring, writing center.

Honors college/program. 19 units of Louisiana Regents' high school core curriculum or comparable curriculum, 27 ACT with no subscore below 20 or 1220 SAT with no subscore below 480, and 3.3 unweighted GPA in Regents' curriculum or comparable curriculum recommended.

Majors. Biology: General. **Business:** Accounting, business admin, hospitality admin. **Communications:** Communications/speech/rhetoric. **Computer sciences:** Information systems. **Education:** Business, early childhood, elementary, English, family/consumer sciences, mathematics, middle, music, physical, social studies, speech. **English:** English lit. **Health services:** Nursing (RN), radiologic technology/medical imaging, substance abuse counseling. **History:** General. **Human services:** Social work. **Liberal arts:** Arts/sciences. **Math:** General. **Parks/recreation:** Health/fitness. **Protective services:** Criminal justice. **Psychology:** General. **Visual/performing arts:** Dramatic, music performance, studio arts. **Work/family studies:** General.

Most popular majors. Business/marketing 12%, education 6%, health sciences 19%, liberal arts 17%, psychology 12%.

Computing on campus. Dormitories linked to campus network. Commuter students can connect to campus network. Online course registration, online library, helpline, student web hosting, wireless network available.

Student life. Freshman orientation: Available, $80 fee. Preregistration for classes offered. One- to 2-day program held 3 times during the summer; includes program for parents. **Housing:** Coed dorms, special housing for disabled, apartments, fraternity/sorority housing available. $175 partly refundable deposit, deadline 3/5. **Activities:** Bands, campus ministries, choral groups, dance, drama, international student organizations, literary magazine, music ensembles, musical theater, opera, radio station, student government, student newspaper, symphony orchestra, TV station, Baptist collegiate ministry, Catholic student organization, Fellowship of Christian Athletes, Wesley campus ministries, Purple Jackets, College Republicans, College Democrats, African-American Caucus, Native American culture association, student government association.

Athletics. NCAA. Intercollegiate: Baseball M, basketball, cross-country, football (tackle) M, soccer W, softball W, tennis W, track and field, volleyball W. **Intramural:** Badminton, basketball, bowling, football (non-tackle), golf, racquetball, soccer, softball, swimming, table tennis, tennis, volleyball, water polo. **Team name:** Demons.

Student services. Adult student services, alcohol/substance abuse counseling, chaplain/spiritual director, career counseling, services for economically disadvantaged, student employment services, financial aid counseling, health services, minority student services, personal counseling, placement for graduates, veterans' counselor. **Physically disabled:** Services for visually, speech, hearing impaired.

Contact. E-mail: applications@nsula.edu
Phone: (318) 357-4078 Toll-free number: (800) 767-8115
Fax: (318) 357-4660
Andrea Maley, Director of Admissions, Northwestern State University, South Hall, 444 Caspari Street, Natchitoches, LA 71497

Our Lady of Holy Cross College
New Orleans, Louisiana
www.olhcc.edu   CB code: 6002

- Private 4-year liberal arts college affiliated with Roman Catholic Church
- Commuter campus in very large city
- 936 degree-seeking undergraduates
- ACT required

General. Founded in 1916. Regionally accredited. Campus offerings available for senior citizens. **Degrees:** 142 bachelor's, 7 associate awarded; master's offered. **ROTC:** Army, Naval, Air Force. **Location:** 3 miles from downtown. **Calendar:** Semester, limited summer session. **Full-time faculty:** 47 total. **Part-time faculty:** 85 total. **Class size:** 51% < 20, 43% 20-39, 3% 40-49, 2% 50-99. **Special facilities:** Training and counseling center.

Basis for selection. 2.5 GPA and 20 ACT required. Applicants with less than 2.5 GPA and 17 ACT will be denied, and can appeal to be accepted conditionally. Students entering directly from high school required to submit ACT. English and math proficiency tests required.

High school preparation. 17.5 units recommended. Recommended units include English 4, mathematics 2, social studies 3, science 4 and foreign language 2. .5 unit of computer literacy recommended.

2011-2012 Annual costs. Tuition/fees: $11,210. Books/supplies: $1,200. Personal expenses: $1,819.

Financial aid. Non-need-based: Scholarships awarded for academics, state residency.

Application procedures. Admission: Priority date 12/1; no deadline. $25 fee. Admission notification on a rolling basis. **Financial aid:** Priority date 7/1; no closing date. FAFSA required. Applicants notified on a rolling basis starting 5/15; must reply within 4 week(s) of notification.

Academics. Special study options: Cross-registration, distance learning, dual enrollment of high school students, exchange student, independent study, internships, study abroad, teacher certification program. **Credit/placement by examination:** AP, CLEP, institutional tests. 60 credit hours maximum toward bachelor's degree. **Support services:** Learning center, pre-admission summer program, reduced course load, remedial instruction, tutoring.

Majors. Biology: General. **Business:** Accounting, business admin. **Education:** Business, elementary, English, mathematics, secondary, social studies, special ed. **English:** English lit. **Health services:** Medical radiologic technology/radiation therapy, respiratory therapy technology. **History:** General. **Liberal arts:** Arts/sciences. **Social sciences:** General.

Computing on campus. 68 workstations in library, computer center. Commuter students can connect to campus network. Online library, wireless network available.

Student life. Freshman orientation: Mandatory. Preregistration for classes offered. **Activities:** Campus ministries, choral groups, drama, international student organizations, literary magazine, student government, student newspaper, Rotaract Club, various honor societies.

Athletics. Intramural: Bowling, soccer M, softball, volleyball. **Team name:** Hurricanes.

Student services. Adult student services, chaplain/spiritual director, career counseling, student employment services, financial aid counseling, health services, personal counseling, placement for graduates, veterans' counselor.

Contact. E-mail: admissions@olhcc.edu
Phone: (504) 394-7744 ext. 175 Toll-free number: (800) 259-7744
Fax: (504) 394-1182
Katharine Gonzales, Vice President for Enrollment Services, Our Lady of Holy Cross College, 4123 Woodland Drive, New Orleans, LA 70131-7399

Our Lady of the Lake College
Baton Rouge, Louisiana
www.ololcollege.edu   CB code: 3928

- Private 4-year health science and nursing college affiliated with Roman Catholic Church
- Commuter campus in large city

- 1,620 degree-seeking undergraduates: 68% part-time, 86% women, 26% African American, 3% Asian American, 1% Hispanic American, 1% Native American
- 128 degree-seeking graduate students
- SAT or ACT (ACT writing optional) required
- 67% graduate within 6 years

General. Regionally accredited. **Degrees:** 98 bachelor's, 318 associate awarded; master's offered. **ROTC:** Army, Air Force. **Calendar:** Semester, extensive summer session. **Full-time faculty:** 80 total; 26% have terminal degrees, 84% women. **Part-time faculty:** 32 total; 69% have terminal degrees, 50% women. **Class size:** 52% < 20, 43% 20-39, 3% 40-49, 2% 50-99.

Freshman class profile. 100 enrolled.

GPA 3.75 or higher:	5%	GPA 2.0-2.99:	30%
GPA 3.50-3.74:	15%	Return as sophomores:	63%
GPA 3.0-3.49:	50%		

Basis for selection. High school record and test scores important. **Home schooled:** State high school equivalency certificate required.

High school preparation. College-preparatory program recommended. Required units include English 4, mathematics 3, social studies 3, science 3, foreign language 2, computer science .5 and academic electives 2.

2011-2012 Annual costs. Tuition/fees: $11,694. Books/supplies: $1,200. Personal expenses: $1,840.

Application procedures. Admission: Priority date 7/15; deadline 8/15 (receipt date). $35 fee, may be waived for applicants with need. Admission notification on a rolling basis. **Financial aid:** Priority date 3/1; no closing date. FAFSA required.

Academics. Special study options: Accelerated study, combined bachelor's/graduate degree. **Credit/placement by examination:** AP, CLEP, ACT, institutional tests. 15 credit hours maximum toward associate degree, 30 toward bachelor's. **Support services:** Learning center, reduced course load, study skills assistance, tutoring.

Majors. Biology: General, biomedical sciences. **Health services:** Clinical lab science, facilities admin, health care admin, health services admin, nursing (RN), premedicine. **Liberal arts:** Humanities. **Psychology:** General.

Most popular majors. Health sciences 92%.

Computing on campus. 150 workstations in library. Commuter students can connect to campus network. Online library, helpline, wireless network available.

Student life. Freshman orientation: Mandatory. Preregistration for classes offered. One-day program held the week before classes begin. **Policies:** Smoke-free campus. **Activities:** Campus ministries, student government, American College of Healthcare Executives, Beta Epsilon Fraternity of Radiologic Technology Students, Beta Sigma Mu, Christian student fellowship, clinical laboratory scientist association, cultural arts association, Epsilon Mu Theta, math and science association, Phi Theta Alpha.

Student services. Adult student services, chaplain/spiritual director, career counseling, financial aid counseling, personal counseling.

Contact. E-mail: admission@ololcollege.edu
Phone: (225) 768-1700 Toll-free number: (877) 242-3509
Fax: (225) 768-1726
Rebecca Cannon, Director of Admissions, Our Lady of the Lake College, 7434 Perkins Road, Baton Rouge, LA 70808

Southeastern Louisiana University
Hammond, Louisiana
www.selu.edu   **CB code: 6656**

- Public 4-year university
- Commuter campus in large town
- 12,527 degree-seeking undergraduates: 15% part-time, 61% women, 15% African American, 1% Asian American, 3% Hispanic American, 2% international
- 1,091 degree-seeking graduate students
- SAT or ACT (ACT writing optional) required
- 33% graduate within 6 years

General. Founded in 1925. Regionally accredited. **Degrees:** 1,932 bachelor's, 173 associate awarded; master's, doctoral offered. **Location:** 55 miles from New Orleans, 40 miles from Baton Rouge. **Calendar:** Semester, extensive summer session. **Special facilities:** Environmental research station, social science research center, maritime museum, contemporary art gallery, performing arts theatre.

Freshman class profile.

End year in good standing:	81%	International:	2%
Return as sophomores:	69%		

Basis for selection. In-state admissions based on 21 ACT, or rank in upper 25% of class, or 2.5 GPA, and have no more than 1 developmental course requirement. Out-of-state students must meet same criteria as in-state students, or score 23 ACT and have no more than 1 development course requirement, or meet all of following criteria: 21 ACT, rank in upper 25% of high school graduating class, 2.5 GPA. Audition recommended for music majors. **Home schooled:** Program must be state-approved; applicant must have 23 ACT with no more than 1 developmental course requirement. **Learning Disabled:** No special requirements or procedures.

High school preparation. College-preparatory program required. 17.5 units required. Required units include English 4, mathematics 3, social studies 3, science 3, foreign language 2, computer science .5 and visual/performing arts 1. 1 additional math or science unit required.

2011-2012 Annual costs. Tuition/fees: $4,634; $14,139 out-of-state. Room/board: $6,620. Books/supplies: $1,200. Personal expenses: $1,838.

2010-2011 Financial aid. Need-based: 2,210 full-time freshmen applied for aid; 1,412 were judged to have need; 1,401 of these received aid. Average scholarship/grant was $5,682; average loan $2,826. 60% of total undergraduate aid awarded as scholarships/grants, 40% as loans/jobs. **Non-need-based:** Awarded to 4,749 full-time undergraduates, including 1,327 freshmen. Scholarships awarded for academics, athletics, job skills, leadership, music/drama, state residency.

Application procedures. Admission: Priority date 7/15; deadline 8/1 (postmark date). $20 fee. Admission notification on a rolling basis. **Financial aid:** Priority date 5/1; no closing date. FAFSA, institutional form required. Applicants notified on a rolling basis starting 4/1; must reply within 2 week(s) of notification.

Academics. Special study options: Accelerated study, cross-registration, distance learning, double major, dual enrollment of high school students, ESL, honors, independent study, internships, study abroad, teacher certification program. **Credit/placement by examination:** AP, CLEP, ACT, institutional tests. 30 credit hours maximum toward bachelor's degree. Credit will not be given through CLEP in last 30 hours. **Support services:** Learning center, remedial instruction, study skills assistance, tutoring, writing center.

Majors. Biology: General. **Business:** Accounting, business admin, finance, logistics, marketing. **Communications:** Communications/speech/rhetoric. **Computer sciences:** Computer science. **Education:** Art, biology, chemistry, computer, early childhood, elementary, English, family/consumer sciences, mathematics, middle, music, physical, physics, social studies, Spanish, special ed, speech. **English:** English lit. **Foreign languages:** Spanish. **Health services:** Athletic training, audiology/speech pathology, nursing (RN), public health ed, radiologic technology/medical imaging. **History:** General. **Human services:** Social work. **Liberal arts:** Arts/sciences. **Math:** General. **Parks/recreation:** Sports admin. **Physical sciences:** Chemistry, physics. **Protective services:** Criminal justice. **Psychology:** General. **Social sciences:** Political science, sociology. **Visual/performing arts:** Art, music performance, studio arts management. **Work/family studies:** General.

Computing on campus. 1,300 workstations in library, computer center, student center. Dormitories wired for high-speed internet access and linked to campus network. Commuter students can connect to campus network. Online course registration, online library, helpline, repair service, student web hosting, wireless network available.

Student life. Freshman orientation: Mandatory, $100 fee. Preregistration for classes offered. Sessions held during summer or at beginning of first semester; students pay room and board for summer session. **Policies:** Freshmen and sophomores must live on-campus. **Housing:** Coed dorms, single-sex dorms, apartments, fraternity/sorority housing available. $150 non-refundable deposit, deadline 6/15. **Activities:** Bands, campus ministries, choral groups, dance, drama, film society, international student organizations, literary magazine, music ensembles, musical theater, opera, radio station, student government, student newspaper, symphony orchestra, TV station, gospel choir, Baptist collegiate ministries, student government association, international student organization, Wesley Foundation, campus activities board, black student union, Circle K International, Best Buddies, Campus Crusade for Christ.

Athletics. NCAA. **Intercollegiate:** Baseball M, basketball, cross-country, football (tackle) M, golf M, soccer W, softball W, tennis W, track and field,

volleyball W. **Intramural:** Badminton, basketball, football (non-tackle), racquetball, soccer, softball, volleyball, weight lifting. **Team name:** Lions, Lady Lions.

Student services. Adult student services, alcohol/substance abuse counseling, career counseling, services for economically disadvantaged, student employment services, financial aid counseling, health services, minority student services, personal counseling, placement for graduates, veterans' counselor. **Physically disabled:** Services for visually, speech, hearing impaired.

Contact. E-mail: admissions@selu.edu
Phone: (985) 549-5637 Toll-free number: (800) 222-7358
Fax: (985) 549-5882
Lori Fairburn, Director of Enrollment Services, Southeastern Louisiana University, SLU 10752, Hammond, LA 70402

Southern University and Agricultural and Mechanical College
Baton Rouge, Louisiana
www.subr.edu   CB code: 6663

- Public 4-year university
- Commuter campus in large city
- 5,845 undergraduates
- 1,214 graduate students
- SAT or ACT (ACT writing optional) required

General. Founded in 1880. Regionally accredited. **Degrees:** 826 bachelor's awarded; master's, doctoral offered. **ROTC:** Army, Naval, Air Force. **Location:** 80 miles from New Orleans. **Calendar:** Semester, extensive summer session. **Full-time faculty:** 331 total; 75% have terminal degrees, 29% minority, 45% women. **Part-time faculty:** 84 total. **Special facilities:** Experimental (laboratory) farm, outdoor learning resource center, Black Heritage Musem.

Freshman class profile.

GPA 3.75 or higher:	21%	Rank in top quarter:	10%
GPA 3.50-3.74:	14%	Rank in top tenth:	3%
GPA 3.0-3.49:	23%	Out-of-state:	21%
GPA 2.0-2.99:	29%	Live on campus:	70%

Basis for selection. Admissions based on 20 ACT/940 SAT or 2.0 GPA or rank in top 50% of class and require no more than 1 remedial course by having 18 ACT English or 19 math (450 SAT verbal or 460-470 SAT math). Auditions required for music program. **Home schooled:** Transcript of courses and grades required. 20 ACT or 940 SAT (exclusive of writing) required.

High school preparation. College-preparatory program required. 17.5 units required. Required units include English 4, mathematics 3, social studies 2, history 1, science 3 and foreign language 2. .5 computer literacy, 1 fine arts required, 1 advanced math or science.

2011-2012 Annual costs. Tuition/fees: $5,074; $11,612 out-of-state. Room/board: $5,258. Books/supplies: $1,200. Personal expenses: $1,726.

Financial aid. Non-need-based: Scholarships awarded for academics, athletics, ROTC, state residency.

Application procedures. Admission: Closing date 7/1 (postmark date). $20 fee. Admission notification on a rolling basis. Admission can be deferred for 2 semesters. High school students admitted early must be in good academic standing and have approval from their high school. **Financial aid:** Priority date 1/31, closing date 3/30. FAFSA required. Applicants notified on a rolling basis starting 5/1; must reply within 3 week(s) of notification.

Academics. Special study options: Combined bachelor's/graduate degree, cooperative education, cross-registration, distance learning, double major, dual enrollment of high school students, exchange student, honors, independent study, internships, study abroad, teacher certification program, weekend college. **Credit/placement by examination:** AP, CLEP, SAT, ACT, institutional tests. 30 credit hours maximum toward bachelor's degree. **Support services:** Learning center, pre-admission summer program, reduced course load, remedial instruction, study skills assistance, tutoring, writing center.

Honors college/program. Must have 23 ACT (1070 SAT, exclusive of Writing) and 3.0 GPA.

Majors. Architecture: Architecture. **Biology:** General. **Business:** Accounting, business admin, finance, managerial economics, marketing. **Communications:** Media studies. **Computer sciences:** Computer science. **Conservation:** Urban forestry. **Education:** Biology, chemistry, elementary, mathematics, middle, music, physics, secondary, special ed. **Engineering:** Civil, electrical, mechanical. **English:** English lit, rhetoric/composition. **General:**

Animal sciences. **Health services:** Audiology/speech pathology, nursing (RN), recreational therapy, vocational rehab counseling. **History:** General. **Human services:** Social work. **Math:** General. **Physical sciences:** Chemistry, physics. **Protective services:** Criminal justice. **Psychology:** General. **Social sciences:** Political science, sociology. **Visual/performing arts:** Dramatic, music performance, studio arts. **Work/family studies:** General.

Most popular majors. Security/protective services 6%.

Computing on campus. 1,625 workstations in dormitories, library, computer center, student center. Dormitories wired for high-speed internet access and linked to campus network. Commuter students can connect to campus network. Online course registration, online library, helpline, wireless network available.

Student life. Freshman orientation: Mandatory. Preregistration for classes offered. Two-day program held during registration. **Policies:** First-time, first-year students must obtain special permission to have car on campus. **Housing:** Guaranteed on-campus for freshmen. Single-sex dorms, special housing for disabled, apartments, wellness housing available. $50 fully refundable deposit, deadline 12/20. **Activities:** Bands, campus ministries, choral groups, dance, drama, international student organizations, literary magazine, music ensembles, musical theater, radio station, student government, student newspaper, TV station, Catholic student club, Committed to Christ student organization, Love Alive Christian Fellowship, Muslim student organization, Nation of Islam student organization, Sigma Omega Delta social service organization, College Democrats, College Republicans, Collegiate 100 Black Men.

Athletics. NCAA. **Intercollegiate:** Baseball M, basketball, bowling W, cross-country, football (tackle) M, soccer W, softball W, tennis W, track and field, volleyball W. **Intramural:** Football (non-tackle). **Team name:** Jaguars.

Student services. Career counseling, student employment services, financial aid counseling, health services, personal counseling, placement for graduates, veterans' counselor. **Physically disabled:** Services for visually, speech, hearing impaired.

Contact. E-mail: admit@subr.edu
Phone: (225) 771-2430 Toll-free number: (800) 256-1531
Fax: (225) 771-2500
Arthur Gillis, Registrar/Director of Admission, Southern University and Agricultural and Mechanical College, T.H. Harris Hall, Baton Rouge, LA 70813

Southern University at New Orleans
New Orleans, Louisiana
www.suno.edu   CB code: 1647

- Public 4-year university
- Commuter campus in large city
- 2,598 degree-seeking undergraduates
- ACT (writing optional) required

General. Founded in 1959. Regionally accredited. Part of Southern University System. **Degrees:** 274 bachelor's, 24 associate awarded; master's offered. **ROTC:** Army, Naval, Air Force. **Location:** Downtown. **Calendar:** Semester, limited summer session. **Full-time faculty:** 113 total. **Part-time faculty:** 34 total. **Class size:** 49% < 20, 47% 20-39, 3% 40-49, less than 1% 50-99, less than 1% >100.

Basis for selection. Applicants must complete Louisiana Board of Regents high school core curriculum (also TOPS core curriculum); require no more than 1 remedial course for immediate admission; and satisfy one of the following: 2.0 GPA or 20 ACT (950 SAT) or rank to top 50% of class. ACT required by state law for placement.

High school preparation. 16 units recommended. Recommended units include English 4, mathematics 3, social studies 3, science 3 (laboratory 2) and foreign language 1.

2011-2012 Annual costs. Tuition/fees: $3,938; $8,386 out-of-state. Room/board: $7,680. Books/supplies: $1,000.

Financial aid. All financial aid based on need.

Application procedures. Admission: No deadline. $20 fee ($15 out-of-state). Admission notification on a rolling basis. **Financial aid:** Closing date 4/15. FAFSA required. Applicants notified by 5/15; must reply within 1 week(s) of notification.

Academics. Special study options: Combined bachelor's/graduate degree, cooperative education, cross-registration, distance learning, double major, dual enrollment of high school students, internships, teacher certification

program, weekend college. **Credit/placement by examination:** AP, CLEP. 30 credit hours maximum toward bachelor's degree. **Support services:** Reduced course load, remedial instruction, study skills assistance, tutoring, writing center.

Majors. Biology: General. **Business:** Entrepreneurial studies, management information systems. **Education:** Early childhood, elementary. **English:** English lit. **Health services:** Medical records admin, substance abuse counseling. **Human services:** General, social work. **Physical sciences:** Physics. **Protective services:** Criminal justice. **Psychology:** General. **Social sciences:** Sociology. **Work/family studies:** Family studies.

Most popular majors. Biology 6%, business/marketing 21%, computer/information sciences 10%, liberal arts 17%, psychology 15%, public administration/social services 10%, security/protective services 13%.

Computing on campus. 60 workstations in library, computer center. Online library, helpline, wireless network available.

Student life. Freshman orientation: Available. Preregistration for classes offered. **Housing:** Wellness housing available. **Activities:** Student government.

Athletics. NAIA. **Intercollegiate:** Basketball, cross-country. **Team name:** Knights.

Student services. Chaplain/spiritual director, career counseling, student employment services, financial aid counseling, health services, personal counseling, placement for graduates. **Physically disabled:** Services for visually, speech, hearing impaired.

Contact. Phone: (504) 286-5000 ext. 5314 Fax: (504) 284-5481
Shawn Vinnett, Director of Recruitment, Admissions, & Retention, Southern University at New Orleans, 6801 Press Drive, New Orleans, LA 70126

Southwest University
Kenner, Louisiana
www.southwest.edu

- For-profit 4-year virtual university
- Very large city
- 575 degree-seeking undergraduates

General. Accredited by DETC. **Degrees:** 42 bachelor's awarded; master's offered. **Calendar:** Differs by program. **Full-time faculty:** 6 total. **Part-time faculty:** 41 total.

Basis for selection. Open admission.

2011-2012 Annual costs. Tuition/fees: $5,975.

Application procedures. Admission: No deadline. $75 fee. Admission notification on a rolling basis.

Academics. Special study options: Accelerated study, distance learning, double major, independent study. **Credit/placement by examination:** AP, CLEP.

Majors. Business: Business admin, management science. **Protective services:** Law enforcement admin.

Computing on campus. Online library available.

Student services. Adult student services, veterans' counselor.

Contact. E-mail: admissions@southwest.edu
Phone: (504) 468-2900 Toll-free number: (800) 433-5923
Fax: (504) 468-3213
Lydia Ocmand, Director of Admissions, Southwest University, 2200 Veterans Memorial Boulevard, Kenner, LA 70062-4005

St. Joseph Seminary College
St. Benedict, Louisiana
www.sjasc.edu   CB code: 6689

- Private 4-year seminary college for men affiliated with Roman Catholic Church
- Residential campus in rural community
- 78 degree-seeking undergraduates

- 5 graduate students
- 100% of applicants admitted
- SAT or ACT (ACT writing optional) required

General. Founded in 1891. Regionally accredited. Non-seminarian, non-degree-seeking students may attend part-time. **Degrees:** 16 bachelor's awarded. **Location:** 40 miles from New Orleans. **Calendar:** Semester. **Full-time faculty:** 9 total; 33% have terminal degrees, 44% women. **Part-time faculty:** 16 total; 44% have terminal degrees, 25% women. **Class size:** 69% < 20, 31% 20-39. **Special facilities:** 1,200 acres of forest, Romanesque abbey church.

Freshman class profile. 10 applied, 10 admitted, 10 enrolled.

Out-of-state:	20%	**Live on campus:**	100%

Basis for selection. Recommendation by diocesan bishop, academic standing, and test scores required. Interview, essay required by dioceses prior to application to college. **Home schooled:** State high school equivalency certificate required.

High school preparation. 10 units recommended. Recommended units include English 3, mathematics 2, history 1, science 2 and foreign language 2. Additional units in English, second foreign language, social science and math recommended.

2011-2012 Annual costs. Tuition/fees: $14,370. Room/board: $12,440. Books/supplies: $1,200. Personal expenses: $1,387.

Financial aid. Non-need-based: Scholarships awarded for academics, leadership.

Application procedures. Admission: No deadline. No application fee. Application must be submitted on paper. **Financial aid:** Priority date 3/15; no closing date. FAFSA required. Applicants notified on a rolling basis starting 7/1; must reply within 4 week(s) of notification.

Academics. Writing Center has extended hours to include evenings and weekends if needed by students. **Special study options:** ESL. **Credit/placement by examination:** AP, CLEP, IB, institutional tests. 24 credit hours maximum toward bachelor's degree. **Support services:** Remedial instruction, tutoring, writing center.

Majors. Liberal arts: Arts/sciences.

Computing on campus. 14 workstations in dormitories, library, computer center. Dormitories wired for high-speed internet access. Online library, repair service, wireless network available.

Student life. Freshman orientation: Mandatory. Preregistration for classes offered. **Policies:** Closed formation weekends. Religious observance required. **Housing:** Guaranteed on-campus for all undergraduates. **Activities:** Campus ministries, choral groups, student government.

Athletics. Intramural: Basketball M, football (non-tackle) M, softball M, tennis M, volleyball M. **Team name:** Ravens.

Student services. Chaplain/spiritual director, financial aid counseling, health services, personal counseling, veterans' counselor. **Physically disabled:** Services for visually, speech, hearing impaired.

Contact. E-mail: acdean@sjasc.edu
Phone: (985) 867-2273 Fax: (985) 327-1085
Registrar, St. Joseph Seminary College, 75376 River Road, St. Benedict, LA 70457-9990

Tulane University
New Orleans, Louisiana   CB member
www.tulane.edu   CB code: 6832

- Private 4-year university
- Residential campus in very large city
- 8,317 degree-seeking undergraduates: 23% part-time, 58% women, 8% African American, 4% Asian American, 4% Hispanic American, 3% international
- 5,021 degree-seeking graduate students
- 25% of applicants admitted
- SAT or ACT (ACT writing recommended), application essay required
- 70% graduate within 6 years

General. Founded in 1834. Regionally accredited. **Degrees:** 1,621 bachelor's, 41 associate awarded; master's, professional, doctoral offered. **ROTC:**

Army, Naval, Air Force. **Location:** 4 miles from downtown. **Calendar:** Semester, limited summer session. **Full-time faculty:** 630 total; 93% have terminal degrees, 21% minority, 37% women. **Part-time faculty:** 440 total; 44% have terminal degrees, 19% minority, 46% women. **Class size:** 68% < 20, 22% 20-39, 4% 40-49, 4% 50-99, 1% >100. **Special facilities:** Jazz archive, Louisiana collection of historical materials, Southeastern architecture archive, center for research on women, political economy institute, center for Latin American studies, middle American research institute, center for bioenvironmental research, performing arts center, Amistad research center.

Freshman class profile. 37,767 applied, 9,422 admitted, 1,642 enrolled.

Mid 50% test scores			
SAT critical reading:	620-710	GPA 2.0-2.99:	7%
SAT math:	620-700	Rank in top quarter:	86%
SAT writing:	640-720	Rank in top tenth:	59%
ACT composite:	29-32	Return as sophomores:	90%
GPA 3.75 or higher:	34%	Out-of-state:	86%
GPA 3.50-3.74:	24%	Live on campus:	98%
GPA 3.0-3.49:	35%	International:	2%

Basis for selection. High school achievement record most important, followed by test scores, recommendation, personal qualities; special consideration for children of alumni and minority applicants. Candidates should be in top third of graduating class with 3.5 GPA. Audition recommended for music majors. Portfolio recommended for architecture, art majors. **Home schooled:** Statement describing home school structure and mission, state high school equivalency certificate, letter of recommendation (nonparent) required. SAT Subject Tests required.

High school preparation. College-preparatory program recommended. Recommended units include English 4, mathematics 4, social studies 3, science 4 (laboratory 4), foreign language 3 and academic electives 3.

2011-2012 Annual costs. Tuition/fees: $43,434. Room/board: $10,850. Books/supplies: $1,200. Personal expenses: $1,000.

2010-2011 Financial aid. **Need-based:** 1,095 full-time freshmen applied for aid; 735 were judged to have need; 735 of these received aid. Average need met was 92%. Average scholarship/grant was $25,423; average loan $5,407. 77% of total undergraduate aid awarded as scholarships/grants, 23% as loans/jobs. **Non-need-based:** Awarded to 2,985 full-time undergraduates, including 826 freshmen. Scholarships awarded for academics, athletics, leadership, music/drama, ROTC, state residency. **Additional information:** Application deadline for merit scholarships December 1. Full time freshmen entering in the fall and showing parental adjusted gross income (AGI on the custodial parents' current year federal tax return) being equal to or less than $75,000 will be reviewed for Tulane's No Loan Assistance (NOLA) if the aid application (including both the FAFSA and CSS Profile) are submitted to be processed by 2/15. Tulane's NOLA scholarship will be added if gift aid plus Tulane's Institutional Methodology Expected Family Contribution (IM EFC) does not total at least the tuition, fee and transportation components of the student's standard Cost of Attendance (COA), in an amount to make up the difference; however, final determination of eligibility for Tulane's NOLA program will adhere to the same merit threshold established for need-based Tulane Scholarship.

Application procedures. **Admission:** Closing date 1/15 (postmark date). No application fee. Admission notification by 4/1. Admission notification on a rolling basis. Must reply by May 1 or within 2 week(s) if notified thereafter. **Financial aid:** Priority date 2/15; no closing date. FAFSA, CSS PROFILE required. Applicants notified on a rolling basis starting 3/18; must reply within 2 week(s) of notification.

Academics. **Special study options:** Accelerated study, combined bachelor's/graduate degree, cross-registration, distance learning, double major, ESL, exchange student, honors, independent study, internships, liberal arts/career combination, student-designed major, study abroad, teacher certification program, Washington semester. **Credit/placement by examination:** AP, CLEP, IB, institutional tests. **Support services:** Learning center, study skills assistance, tutoring, writing center.

Majors. **Architecture:** Architecture. **Area/ethnic studies:** African, American, Asian, German, Latin American, Russian/Slavic, women's. **Biology:** General, biochemistry, cell/histology, ecology, evolutionary, molecular, neuroscience. **Business:** General, accounting, business admin, finance, management information systems, marketing. **Communications:** Media studies. **Conservation:** Environmental science, environmental studies. **Engineering:** Applied physics, biomedical, chemical. **English:** English lit. **Foreign languages:** Classics, French, German, Italian, linguistics, modern Greek, Portuguese, Russian, Spanish. **History:** General. **Math:** General. **Philosophy/religion:** Judaic, philosophy. **Physical sciences:** Chemistry, geology, physics. **Protective services:** Homeland security. **Psychology:** General. **Social sciences:** Anthropology, economics, international economics, political science, sociology, urban studies. **Visual/performing arts:** Art, art history/conservation, dance, dramatic, multimedia, music, music performance, music theory/composition, musical theater, studio arts, theater history.

Most popular majors. Biology 8%, business/marketing 22%, psychology 6%, social sciences 18%.

Computing on campus. 556 workstations in dormitories, library, computer center, student center. Dormitories wired for high-speed internet access and linked to campus network. Commuter students can connect to campus network. Online course registration, online library, helpline, repair service, student web hosting, wireless network available.

Student life. **Freshman orientation:** Mandatory, $400 fee. Preregistration for classes offered. **Policies:** Alcohol, substance abuse and sexual harassment policies in place. Freshmen not permitted cars on campus. **Housing:** Guaranteed on-campus for freshmen. Coed dorms, single-sex dorms, special housing for disabled, apartments, fraternity/sorority housing, wellness housing available. $300 fully refundable deposit, deadline 5/1. Honors program residence hall, language floors, women in science, healthy lifestyle, engineering and technology, performing and creative arts, pre-med and pre-law special living floors, quiet-study floors, and international living floors available. **Activities:** Bands, campus ministries, choral groups, dance, drama, film society, international student organizations, literary magazine, music ensembles, musical theater, radio station, student government, student newspaper, symphony orchestra, TV station, Hillel, Episcopal center, Inter-Varsity Christian Fellowship, Catholic center, Baptist student union, African-American Congress, Latin American students association, Amnesty International.

Athletics. NCAA. **Intercollegiate:** Baseball M, basketball, cross-country, diving W, football (tackle) M, golf W, swimming W, tennis, track and field, volleyball W. **Intramural:** Badminton, basketball, football (tackle) M, racquetball, softball, squash, swimming, tennis, triathlon, volleyball, wrestling M. **Team name:** Green Wave.

Student services. Alcohol/substance abuse counseling, chaplain/spiritual director, career counseling, student employment services, financial aid counseling, health services, legal services, minority student services, personal counseling, placement for graduates, women's services. **Physically disabled:** Services for visually, speech, hearing impaired.

Contact. E-mail: undergrad.admission@tulane.edu
Phone: (504) 865-5731 Toll-free number: (800) 873-9283
Fax: (504) 862-8715
Earl Retif, Vice President for Enrollment Management and University Registrar, Tulane University, 6823 St. Charles Avenue, New Orleans, LA 70118-5680

University of Louisiana at Lafayette
Lafayette, Louisiana — **CB member**
www.louisiana.edu — **CB code: 6672**

- Public 4-year university
- Commuter campus in small city
- 14,796 degree-seeking undergraduates: 12% part-time, 56% women, 21% African American, 2% Asian American, 3% Hispanic American, 2% international
- 1,443 degree-seeking graduate students
- 66% of applicants admitted
- SAT or ACT (ACT writing optional) required
- 42% graduate within 6 years

General. Founded in 1898. Regionally accredited. **Degrees:** 2,279 bachelor's awarded; master's, doctoral offered. **ROTC:** Army. **Location:** 130 miles from New Orleans, 200 miles from Houston. **Calendar:** Semester, extensive summer session. **Full-time faculty:** 584 total; 73% have terminal degrees, 17% minority, 44% women. **Part-time faculty:** 159 total; 18% have terminal degrees, 9% minority, 60% women. **Class size:** 31% < 20, 50% 20-39, 11% 40-49, 6% 50-99, 2% >100. **Special facilities:** 2 nuclear accelerators, 2 electron microscopes, CAD/CAM laboratory, Acadiana folklore archives, confocal microscope, atomic force microscope, emersive technology center, on-campus restaurant and hotel, nursery school laboratory, television production studio, marine research facility.

Freshman class profile. 9,062 applied, 5,975 admitted, 2,966 enrolled.

Mid 50% test scores			
ACT composite:	20-24	End year in good standing:	83%
GPA 3.75 or higher:	15%	Return as sophomores:	74%
GPA 3.50-3.74:	16%	Out-of-state:	3%
GPA 3.0-3.49:	36%	Live on campus:	36%
GPA 2.0-2.99:	33%	International:	1%
Rank in top quarter:	42%	Fraternities:	11%
Rank in top tenth:	17%	Sororities:	11%

Basis for selection. Guaranteed admissions for students who complete Louisiana Board of Regents' high school core curriculum with 19 ACT math

(460 SAT math) or 18 ACT English (450 SAT verbal) and one of the following: 2.5 unweighted GPA, 23 ACT (1050 SAT math and verbal) with 2.0 GPA, or rank in top 25% of class with 2.0 GPA. Audition required of music majors. Portfolio required of art, architecture majors. Essays required for some applicants.

High school preparation. College-preparatory program required. Required units include English 4, mathematics 4, social studies 1, history 2, science 3, foreign language 2 and visual/performing arts 1. Suggested electives: .5 unit computer science, 1 unit fine arts, 1 unit speech.

2011-2012 Annual costs. Tuition/fees: $4,864; $13,486 out-of-state. Room/board: $5,080. Books/supplies: $1,200. Personal expenses: $1,818.

2010-2011 Financial aid. All financial aid based on need. 2,719 full-time freshmen applied for aid; 1,690 were judged to have need; 1,649 of these received aid. Average need met was 65%. Average scholarship/grant was $6,432; average loan $3,068. 58% of total undergraduate aid awarded as scholarships/grants, 42% as loans/jobs.

Application procedures. Admission: Priority date 7/20; no deadline. $25 fee. Admission notification on a rolling basis. Financial aid: Priority date 5/1; no closing date. FAFSA required. Applicants notified on a rolling basis starting 4/1; must reply within 2 week(s) of notification.

Academics. Special study options: Accelerated study, cooperative education, cross-registration, distance learning, double major, dual enrollment of high school students, exchange student, honors, independent study, internships, student-designed major, study abroad, teacher certification program. Credit/placement by examination: AP, CLEP, SAT, ACT, institutional tests. 30 credit hours maximum toward bachelor's degree. Support services: Learning center, reduced course load, remedial instruction, study skills assistance, tutoring, writing center.

Majors. Architecture: Architecture, interior. **Biology:** General, conservation, microbiology. **Business:** Accounting, business admin, fashion, finance, hospitality admin, insurance, management information systems, managerial economics, marketing. **Communications:** Communications/speech/rhetoric, media studies, public relations. **Computer sciences:** Computer science. **Conservation:** Land use planning, management/policy. **Education:** Agricultural, art, biology, business, chemistry, early childhood, early childhood special, elementary, English, family/consumer sciences, French, German, mathematics, middle, music, physical, physics, science, secondary, social studies, Spanish, special ed, speech, technology/industrial arts. **Engineering:** Chemical, civil, computer, electrical, mechanical, petroleum. **Foreign languages:** General. **Health services:** Athletic training, audiology/speech pathology, dental hygiene, dietetics, medical records admin, nursing (RN). **History:** General. **Math:** General. **Physical sciences:** Chemistry, geology, physics. **Protective services:** Criminal justice. **Psychology:** General. **Social sciences:** Anthropology, political science, sociology. **Visual/performing arts:** General, art, film/cinema/video, industrial design, music performance. **Work/family studies:** Family studies.

Most popular majors. Business/marketing 22%, education 11%, engineering/engineering technologies 9%, health sciences 10%, liberal arts 15%.

Computing on campus. 2,000 workstations in dormitories, library, computer center, student center. Commuter students can connect to campus network. Online course registration, online library, helpline, wireless network available.

Student life. Freshman orientation: Mandatory, $75 fee. Preregistration for classes offered. **Housing:** Single-sex dorms, apartments, fraternity/sorority housing available. $50 deposit, deadline 6/15. **Activities:** Bands, campus ministries, choral groups, dance, drama, international student organizations, literary magazine, music ensembles, musical theater, opera, radio station, student government, student newspaper, symphony orchestra, Young Republicans, Young Democrats, Omega Phi Alpha, Afro-American student groups.

Athletics. NCAA. **Intercollegiate:** Baseball M, basketball, cheerleading, cross-country, football (tackle) M, golf M, soccer W, softball W, tennis, track and field, volleyball W. **Intramural:** Basketball, football (non-tackle), racquetball, soccer, softball, tennis, volleyball, water polo. **Team name:** Ragin' Cajuns.

Student services. Adult student services, career counseling, student employment services, financial aid counseling, health services, minority student services, on-campus daycare, personal counseling, placement for graduates, veterans' counselor. **Physically disabled:** Services for visually, speech, hearing impaired.

Contact. E-mail: enroll@louisiana.edu
Phone: (337) 482-6553 Toll-free number: (800) 752-6553
Fax: (337) 482-1112
Leroy Broussard, Director of Admissions, University of Louisiana at Lafayette, Box 41210, Lafayette, LA 70504-1210

University of Louisiana at Monroe
Monroe, Louisiana
www.ulm.edu   CB code: 6482

- Public 4-year university
- Commuter campus in small city
- 7,235 degree-seeking undergraduates: 27% part-time, 64% women, 26% African American, 2% Asian American, 2% Hispanic American, 2% international
- 1,143 degree-seeking graduate students
- 80% of applicants admitted
- SAT or ACT (ACT writing optional) required

General. Founded in 1931. Regionally accredited. **Degrees:** 1,100 bachelor's, 69 associate awarded; master's, professional, doctoral offered. **ROTC:** Army. **Location:** 90 miles from Shreveport; 120 miles from Jackson, Mississippi. **Calendar:** Semester, limited summer session. **Full-time faculty:** 332 total; 12% minority, 51% women. **Part-time faculty:** 88 total; 12% minority, 61% women. **Class size:** 40% < 20, 44% 20-39, 6% 40-49, 8% 50-99, 1% >100. **Special facilities:** National Public Radio station, Louisiana state cancer tumor registry archives, regional small business development center, weather research center, museum of natural history, flight simulator.

Freshman class profile. 2,273 applied, 1,811 admitted, 1,149 enrolled.

Mid 50% test scores			
SAT critical reading:	420-540	GPA 2.0-2.99:	28%
SAT math:	440-570	End year in good standing:	92%
ACT composite:	19-24	Return as sophomores:	68%
GPA 3.75 or higher:	20%	Out-of-state:	2%
GPA 3.50-3.74:	16%	Live on campus:	54%
GPA 3.0-3.49:	35%	International:	2%

Basis for selection. Students who do not meet defined criteria evaluated on other evidence of academic promise for admittance by exception. Only limited number of students will be granted admittance by exception. **Home schooled:** Transcript of courses and grades required. Must submit official transcript of grades and official proof of graduation or original diploma to admissions office.

High school preparation. College-preparatory program required. 17.5 units required. Required units include English 4, mathematics 4, social studies 1, history 2, science 3, foreign language 2, computer science .5. 1 fine arts, 0.5 free enterprise, 0.5 civics required.

2011-2012 Annual costs. Tuition/fees: $5,101; $13,047 out-of-state. Room/board: $6,212. Books/supplies: $1,200. Personal expenses: $1,839.

Financial aid. Non-need-based: Scholarships awarded for academics, alumni affiliation, art, athletics, job skills, leadership, minority status, music/drama, religious affiliation, ROTC, state residency.

Application procedures. Admission: Priority date 4/1; no deadline. $20 fee, may be waived for applicants with need. Admission notification on a rolling basis. Financial aid: Priority date 4/1; no closing date. FAFSA required. Applicants notified on a rolling basis starting 6/1; must reply within 2 week(s) of notification.

Academics. Credit hours toward graduation may be earned through examination, military service, correspondence and extension courses taken through accredited extension divisions of other colleges and universities. **Special study options:** Accelerated study, combined bachelor's/graduate degree, cooperative education, distance learning, double major, dual enrollment of high school students, ESL, honors, independent study, internships, study abroad, teacher certification program. Evening college. **Credit/placement by examination:** AP, CLEP, SAT, ACT, institutional tests. 22 credit hours maximum toward associate degree, 43 toward bachelor's. Maximum of one-third of credits required for degree may be earned through examination, military experience, and correspondence courses. **Support services:** Learning center, reduced course load, remedial instruction, study skills assistance, tutoring, writing center.

Majors. Biology: General, toxicology. **Business:** Accounting, business admin, construction management, finance, insurance, management information systems, marketing. **Communications:** Communications/speech/rhetoric, media studies. **Computer sciences:** Computer science. **Education:** Biology, chemistry, elementary, English, mathematics, secondary, social studies. **English:** English lit. **Foreign languages:** General. **General:** Business. **Health services:** Audiology/speech pathology, clinical lab science, dental hygiene, nursing (RN), radiologic technology/medical imaging. **History:** General. **Human services:** Social work. **Math:** General. **Parks/recreation:** Exercise sciences. **Physical sciences:** Atmospheric science. **Protective services:** Criminal justice. **Psychology:** General. **Social sciences:** Political science, sociology. **Visual/performing arts:** Music performance, studio arts.

Most popular majors. Biology 8%, business/marketing 15%, education 6%, health sciences 18%, liberal arts 18%.

Computing on campus. Dormitories wired for high-speed internet access and linked to campus network. Commuter students can connect to campus network. Online course registration, online library, helpline, repair service, student web hosting, wireless network available.

Student life. Freshman orientation: Mandatory. Preregistration for classes offered. Five regular sessions plus one computer PREP session available. **Housing:** Coed dorms, single-sex dorms, apartments, fraternity/sorority housing, wellness housing available. $50 partly refundable deposit, deadline 7/1. **Activities:** Bands, campus ministries, choral groups, dance, drama, international student organizations, literary magazine, music ensembles, musical theater, opera, radio station, student government, student newspaper, symphony orchestra.

Athletics. NCAA. **Intercollegiate:** Baseball M, basketball, cheerleading, cross-country, football (tackle) M, golf, soccer W, softball W, swimming, track and field, volleyball W. **Intramural:** Basketball, cross-country, football (non-tackle), golf, racquetball, soccer, softball, swimming, tennis, track and field, volleyball, weight lifting. **Team name:** Warhawks.

Student services. Adult student services, alcohol/substance abuse counseling, chaplain/spiritual director, career counseling, student employment services, financial aid counseling, health services, on-campus daycare, personal counseling, placement for graduates, veterans' counselor. **Physically disabled:** Services for visually, speech, hearing impaired.

Contact. E-mail: self@ulm.edu
Phone: (318) 342-5430 Toll-free number: (800) 372-5127
Fax: (318) 342-1915
Jennifer Malone, Director of Admissions, University of Louisiana at Monroe, 700 University Avenue, Monroe, LA 71209-1160

University of New Orleans
New Orleans, Louisiana
www.uno.edu

CB member
CB code: 6379

- Public 4-year university
- Commuter campus in very large city
- 8,028 degree-seeking undergraduates: 24% part-time, 49% women, 16% African American, 7% Asian American, 8% Hispanic American, 1% Native American, 4% international
- 2,411 degree-seeking graduate students
- 56% of applicants admitted
- SAT or ACT (ACT writing optional) required
- 38% graduate within 6 years

General. Founded in 1956. Regionally accredited. **Degrees:** 1,435 bachelor's awarded; master's, doctoral offered. **ROTC:** Army, Naval, Air Force. **Calendar:** Semester, extensive summer session. **Full-time faculty:** 368 total; 70% have terminal degrees, 17% minority, 39% women. **Part-time faculty:** 182 total; 32% have terminal degrees, 19% minority, 42% women. **Class size:** 32% < 20, 45% 20-39, 8% 40-49, 10% 50-99, 4% >100.

Freshman class profile. 3,353 applied, 1,862 admitted, 1,105 enrolled.

Mid 50% test scores		Rank in top quarter:	30%
SAT critical reading:	480-590	Rank in top tenth:	12%
SAT math:	460-590	Return as sophomores:	67%
ACT composite:	19-24	Out-of-state:	4%
GPA 3.75 or higher:	8%	Live on campus:	21%
GPA 3.50-3.74:	13%	International:	2%
GPA 3.0-3.49:	32%	Fraternities:	3%
GPA 2.0-2.99:	47%	Sororities:	4%

Basis for selection. 2.0 GPA required. Graduates from state-approved high schools must complete academic core curriculum and require no remedial coursework. 19 ACT Math (460 SAT); 18 ACT English (450 SAT) and one of the following required to avoid remedial classes: 23 ACT (1060 SAT) or 2.5 core GPA. Non-refundable $30 late fee will be assessed for all applications received after priority date for total application cost of $80. Audition or interview required of music majors; fine arts studio majors may apply for bypass credit for 1000 level studio courses by submitting portfolio. **Home schooled:** Students who do not meet core curriculum must have 23 ACT (1060 SAT) and 2.5 core GPA or have 26 ACT (1170 SAT) and require no remedial course. SAT scores exclusive of Writing. **Learning Disabled:** Learning Disability Documentation Packet must be completed by appropriate professional and submitted to Office of Disability Services, along with copy of evaluation, including test scores.

High school preparation. College-preparatory program required. 17.5 units required. Required units include English 4, mathematics 3, social studies 1, history 2, science 3, foreign language 2, computer science .5 and visual/performing arts 1. 1 additional math or science required.

2011-2012 Annual costs. Tuition/fees: $5,257; $16,781 out-of-state. Room/board: $8,310. Books/supplies: $1,300. Personal expenses: $1,891.

2011-2012 Financial aid. Need-based: 978 full-time freshmen applied for aid; 830 were judged to have need; 805 of these received aid. Average need met was 57%. Average scholarship/grant was $6,164; average loan $3,390. 64% of total undergraduate aid awarded as scholarships/grants, 36% as loans/jobs. **Non-need-based:** Awarded to 1,613 full-time undergraduates, including 468 freshmen. Scholarships awarded for academics, athletics. **Additional information:** Students in good academic and financial standing eligible to participate in Extended Payment Plan option.

Application procedures. Admission: Priority date 7/1; no deadline. $40 fee. Application must be submitted online. Admission notification on a rolling basis beginning on or about 10/1. **Financial aid:** Priority date 3/15; no closing date. FAFSA required. Applicants notified on a rolling basis starting 4/20; must reply within 4 week(s) of notification.

Academics. Special study options: Cooperative education, cross-registration, distance learning, double major, dual enrollment of high school students, ESL, exchange student, honors, independent study, internships, student-designed major, study abroad, teacher certification program, Washington semester, weekend college. **Credit/placement by examination:** AP, CLEP, IB, SAT, ACT, institutional tests. 30 credit hours maximum toward bachelor's degree. **Support services:** Learning center, tutoring, writing center.

Majors. Area/ethnic studies: Women's. **Biology:** General. **Business:** Accounting, business admin, finance, hospitality admin, management information systems, managerial economics, marketing. **Communications:** Communications/speech/rhetoric. **Computer sciences:** Computer science. **Education:** Biology, chemistry, early childhood, earth science, elementary, English, foreign languages, mathematics, music, physical, social studies. **Engineering:** Civil, electrical, marine, mechanical. **English:** English lit. **Foreign languages:** French, Spanish. **History:** General. **Math:** General. **Parks/recreation:** Health/fitness. **Philosophy/religion:** Philosophy. **Physical sciences:** Chemistry, geology, geophysics, physics. **Psychology:** General. **Social sciences:** Anthropology, geography, political science, sociology, urban studies. **Visual/performing arts:** Art history/conservation, music, studio arts.

Most popular majors. Business/marketing 38%, communications/journalism 7%, engineering/engineering technologies 8%, liberal arts 9%, psychology 8%, social sciences 6%.

Computing on campus. Dormitories wired for high-speed internet access and linked to campus network. Commuter students can connect to campus network. Online course registration, online library, helpline, wireless network available.

Student life. Freshman orientation: Mandatory, $100 fee. Preregistration for classes offered. One and a half-day program; fee includes housing and meals. **Housing:** Coed dorms, special housing for disabled, apartments available. **Activities:** Bands, campus ministries, choral groups, dance, drama, film society, international student organizations, literary magazine, music ensembles, Model UN, musical theater, opera, radio station, student government, student newspaper, over 120 registered clubs and organizations available.

Athletics. NCAA. **Intercollegiate:** Baseball M, basketball, cross-country, golf, tennis, volleyball W. **Intramural:** Basketball, football (non-tackle), racquetball, soccer, softball, table tennis, tennis, volleyball. **Team name:** Privateers.

Student services. Adult student services, alcohol/substance abuse counseling, career counseling, student employment services, financial aid counseling, health services, legal services, minority student services, on-campus daycare, personal counseling, placement for graduates, veterans' counselor, women's services. **Physically disabled:** Services for visually, speech, hearing impaired.

Contact. E-mail: admissions@uno.edu
Phone: (504) 280-6595 Toll-free number: (800) 256-5866
Fax: (504) 280-5522
Andy Benoit, Director of Admissions Office, University of New Orleans, Administration Building, Room 103, New Orleans, LA 70148

University of Phoenix: Baton Rouge
Baton Rouge, Louisiana
www.phoenix.edu

- For-profit 4-year university
- Small city
- 595 degree-seeking undergraduates

General. Regionally accredited. **Calendar:** Differs by program. **Part-time faculty:** 4 total.

Basis for selection. Open admission, but selective for some programs.

Application procedures. Admission: No deadline. No application fee. Admission notification on a rolling basis.

Academics. Credit/placement by examination: AP, CLEP.

Contact. University of Phoenix: Baton Rouge, 2431 South Acadian Thruway, Baton Rouge, LA 70808-2300

University of Phoenix: Lafayette
Lafayette, Louisiana
www.phoenix.edu

- For-profit 4-year university
- Small city
- 274 degree-seeking undergraduates

General. Regionally accredited. **Calendar:** Differs by program. **Part-time faculty:** 2 total.

Basis for selection. Open admission, but selective for some programs.

Application procedures. Admission: No deadline. No application fee. Admission notification on a rolling basis.

Academics. Credit/placement by examination: AP, CLEP.

Majors. Business: Business admin.

Contact. University of Phoenix: Lafayette, 202 Rue Iberville, Lafayette, LA 70508-3295

University of Phoenix: Louisiana
Metairie, Louisiana
www.phoenix.edu

- For-profit 4-year university
- Large city
- 603 degree-seeking undergraduates

General. Regionally accredited. **Degrees:** 252 bachelor's awarded; master's offered. **Calendar:** Differs by program. **Full-time faculty:** 26 total. **Part-time faculty:** 282 total.

Basis for selection. Open admission, but selective for some programs.

2011-2012 Annual costs. Estimated costs as of August 2011: per-credit-hour charge, $380 to $415, depending upon level and course of study; electronic course materials fee, $95, if applicable. Book and material charges may vary by course and program. All fees are subject to change.

Application procedures. Admission: No deadline. No application fee. **Financial aid:** No deadline.

Academics. Credit/placement by examination: AP, CLEP.

Majors. Business: Business admin, human resources. **Communications:** General. **Computer sciences:** Information technology. **Health services:** Health care admin, nursing (RN). **Protective services:** Law enforcement admin.

Contact. Marc Booker, Director of Admission and Evaluation, University of Phoenix: Louisiana, One Galleria Boulevard, Suite 725, Metairie, LA 70001-2082

University of Phoenix: Shreveport
Bossier City, Louisiana
www.phoenix.edu

- For-profit 4-year university
- Small city
- 319 degree-seeking undergraduates

General. Regionally accredited. **Calendar:** Differs by program. **Part-time faculty:** 3 total.

Basis for selection. Open admission, but selective for some programs.

Application procedures. Admission: No deadline. No application fee. Admission notification on a rolling basis.

Academics. Credit/placement by examination: AP, CLEP.

Majors. Business: Business admin.

Contact. University of Phoenix: Shreveport, 350 Plaza Loop Drive, Bossier City, LA 71111-4390

Xavier University of Louisiana
New Orleans, Louisiana   CB member
www.xula.edu   CB code: 6975

- Private 4-year university affiliated with Roman Catholic Church
- Commuter campus in very large city
- 2,725 degree-seeking undergraduates: 3% part-time, 71% women, 79% African American, 9% Asian American, 2% Hispanic American, 2% international
- 649 degree-seeking graduate students
- 64% of applicants admitted
- SAT or ACT (ACT writing recommended) required
- 53% graduate within 6 years

General. Founded in 1915. Regionally accredited. **Degrees:** 301 bachelor's awarded; master's, professional offered. **ROTC:** Army, Naval, Air Force. **Location:** One mile from downtown. **Calendar:** Semester, limited summer session. **Full-time faculty:** 240 total; 85% have terminal degrees, 50% minority, 49% women. **Part-time faculty:** 27 total; 30% have terminal degrees, 52% minority, 52% women. **Class size:** 50% < 20, 43% 20-39, 2% 40-49, 4% 50-99, 1% >100.

Freshman class profile. 4,463 applied, 2,860 admitted, 786 enrolled.

Mid 50% test scores			
SAT critical reading:	430-540	Rank in top quarter:	55%
SAT math:	430-540	Rank in top tenth:	29%
SAT writing:	410-520	Return as sophomores:	69%
ACT composite:	19-24	Out-of-state:	51%
GPA 3.75 or higher:	28%	Live on campus:	69%
GPA 3.50-3.74:	14%	International:	1%
GPA 3.0-3.49:	27%		
GPA 2.0-2.99:	30%		

Basis for selection. High school record or GED scores, standardized test results, and recommendation from counselor important. Interview recommended for academically weak. Audition required for music majors. Portfolio required for art majors.

High school preparation. College-preparatory program recommended. 16 units required. Required and recommended units include English 4, mathematics 2-4, social studies 1, history 1, science 1-3, foreign language 1 and academic electives 8. Math must include 1 algebra.

2011-2012 Annual costs. Tuition/fees: $17,900. Room/board: $7,400. Books/supplies: $1,200.

2010-2011 Financial aid. Need-based: 761 full-time freshmen applied for aid; 697 were judged to have need; 696 of these received aid. Average need met was 11%. Average scholarship/grant was $5,974; average loan $3,693. 36% of total undergraduate aid awarded as scholarships/grants, 64% as loans/jobs. **Non-need-based:** Awarded to 1,837 full-time undergraduates, including 680 freshmen. Scholarships awarded for music/drama.

Application procedures. Admission: Priority date 3/1; deadline 7/1 (postmark date). $25 fee, may be waived for applicants with need. Admission notification on a rolling basis beginning on or about 10/15. Must reply by May 1 or within 2 week(s) if notified thereafter. **Financial aid:** Priority date 1/1; no closing date. FAFSA required. Applicants notified on a rolling basis starting 4/1; must reply within 2 week(s) of notification.

Academics. Special study options: Accelerated study, combined bachelor's/graduate degree, cooperative education, cross-registration, double major, dual enrollment of high school students, exchange student, honors, independent study, internships, study abroad, teacher certification program. **Credit/placement by examination:** AP, CLEP, SAT, ACT, institutional tests. 30 credit hours maximum toward bachelor's degree. **Support services:** Learning center, pre-admission summer program, reduced course load, remedial instruction, study skills assistance, tutoring, writing center.

Majors. **Biology:** General, biochemistry, microbiology. **Business:** Accounting, business admin, finance, management science, marketing. **Communications:** Media studies. **Computer sciences:** General, computer science. **Education:** General, art, biology, chemistry, early childhood, elementary, English, foreign languages, French, history, mathematics, multi-level teacher, music, physical, science, social studies, Spanish, special ed. **Engineering:** Computer. **English:** English lit. **Foreign languages:** French, Spanish. **Health services:** Premedicine, prepharmacy, speech pathology. **History:** General. **Math:** General, statistics. **Philosophy/religion:** Philosophy. **Physical sciences:** Chemistry, physics. **Psychology:** General. **Social sciences:** Political science, sociology. **Theology:** Theology. **Visual/performing arts:** Art, music, music performance, piano/keyboard, stringed instruments, voice/opera.

Most popular majors. Biology 35%, business/marketing 14%, physical sciences 19%, psychology 13%.

Computing on campus. 350 workstations in dormitories, library, computer center. Dormitories wired for high-speed internet access and linked to campus network. Commuter students can connect to campus network. Online course registration, online library, helpline available.

Student life. **Freshman orientation:** Mandatory, $150 fee. Preregistration for classes offered. One-week program. **Policies:** All recognized student organizations must perform 2 community service activities per semester. **Housing:** Coed dorms, single-sex dorms, special housing for disabled available. $100 nonrefundable deposit. **Activities:** Bands, campus ministries, choral groups, dance, drama, international student organizations, literary magazine, music ensembles, opera, student government, student newspaper, symphony orchestra, TV station, over 30 organizations.

Athletics. NAIA. **Intercollegiate:** Basketball, cross-country, tennis, volleyball W. **Intramural:** Basketball, cheerleading, football (non-tackle), softball, swimming, table tennis, tennis, track and field, volleyball. **Team name:** Gold Rush.

Student services. Adult student services, alcohol/substance abuse counseling, chaplain/spiritual director, career counseling, student employment services, financial aid counseling, health services, personal counseling, placement for graduates, veterans' counselor, women's services. **Physically disabled:** Services for visually, speech, hearing impaired.

Contact. E-mail: apply@xula.edu
Phone: (504) 520-7388 Toll-free number: (877) 928-4378
Fax: (504) 520-7941
Winston Brown, Dean of Admissions, Xavier University of Louisiana, 1 Drexel Drive, New Orleans, LA 70125-1098

Maine

Bates College

Lewiston, Maine	**CB member**
www.bates.edu	**CB code: 3076**

- Private 4-year liberal arts college
- Residential campus in small city
- 1,769 degree-seeking undergraduates: 53% women, 5% African American, 5% Asian American, 5% Hispanic American, 6% international
- 27% of applicants admitted
- Application essay required
- 92% graduate within 6 years

General. Founded in 1855. Regionally accredited. **Degrees:** 437 bachelor's awarded. **Location:** 35 miles from Portland. **Calendar:** 4-4-1 semester system. **Full-time faculty:** 165 total; 88% have terminal degrees, 16% minority, 49% women. **Part-time faculty:** 24 total; 50% have terminal degrees, 67% women. **Class size:** 67% < 20, 26% 20-39, 5% 40-49, 3% 50-99. **Special facilities:** Mountain seacoast conservation area, Edmund S. Muskie Archives, art museum, observatory.

Freshman class profile. 5,196 applied, 1,405 admitted, 502 enrolled.

Mid 50% test scores			
SAT critical reading:	630-710	**Rank in top tenth:**	58%
SAT math:	630-710	**Return as sophomores:**	93%
SAT writing:	640-720	**Out-of-state:**	89%
ACT composite:	29-31	**Live on campus:**	100%
Rank in top quarter:	88%	**International:**	6%

Basis for selection. GED not accepted. School achievement record with an emphasis on rigor of curriculum, recommendations, special talents, leadership, essays are all of equal importance. Submission of standardized test scores is optional for admission. Interviews are recommended. **Home schooled:** Statement describing home school structure and mission, letter of recommendation (nonparent) required. Interview encouraged but not required for all applicants, including home school students.

High school preparation. College-preparatory program required. 17 units required; 23 recommended. Required and recommended units include English 4, mathematics 3-4, social studies 3-4, science 3-4 (laboratory 2-3) and foreign language 2-4. History included in social studies requirement.

2011-2012 Annual costs. Comprehensive fee: $55,300. Books/supplies: $1,750.

2011-2012 Financial aid. All financial aid based on need. 297 full-time freshmen applied for aid; 251 were judged to have need; 235 of these received aid. Average need met was 100%. Average scholarship/grant was $36,908; average loan $3,102. 90% of total undergraduate aid awarded as scholarships/grants, 10% as loans/jobs. **Additional information:** Priority date for filing required financial aid forms for early decision students is 11/15.

Application procedures. **Admission:** Closing date 1/1 (postmark date). $60 fee, may be waived for applicants with need. Admission notification by 3/31. Must reply by 5/1. **Financial aid:** Closing date 2/15. FAFSA, CSS PROFILE required. Applicants notified by 4/1; must reply by 5/1.

Academics. **Special study options:** Accelerated study, combined bachelor's/graduate degree, double major, exchange student, honors, independent study, internships, liberal arts/career combination, semester at sea, student-designed major, study abroad, teacher certification program, urban semester, Washington semester. Marine studies program at Mystic Seaport, liberal arts-engineering dual degree program with 5 universities. **Credit/placement by examination:** AP, CLEP, IB, institutional tests. **Support services:** Reduced course load, study skills assistance, tutoring, writing center.

Majors. **Area/ethnic studies:** African-American, American, East Asian, women's. **Biology:** General, biochemistry, neuroscience. **Conservation:** Environmental studies. **Engineering:** General. **English:** English lit, rhetoric/composition. **Foreign languages:** Chinese, French, German, Japanese, Russian, Spanish. **History:** General. **Math:** General. **Philosophy/religion:** Philosophy, religion. **Physical sciences:** Chemistry, geology, physics. **Psychology:** General. **Social sciences:** Anthropology, economics, political science, sociology. **Visual/performing arts:** Art, dance, dramatic, music.

Most popular majors. Biology 11%, English 8%, foreign language 6%, history 7%, psychology 10%, social sciences 26%, visual/performing arts 9%.

Computing on campus. 175 workstations in library, computer center. Dormitories wired for high-speed internet access and linked to campus network. Commuter students can connect to campus network. Online course registration, online library, helpline, repair service, student web hosting, wireless network available.

Student life. **Freshman orientation:** Mandatory. Preregistration for classes offered. Held 5 days prior to start of classes. **Housing:** Guaranteed on-campus for all undergraduates. Coed dorms, single-sex dorms, wellness housing available. $300 nonrefundable deposit, deadline 5/1. **Activities:** Bands, campus ministries, choral groups, dance, drama, film society, international student organizations, literary magazine, music ensembles, Model UN, radio station, student government, student newspaper, symphony orchestra, Amandla!, Bates Christian Fellowship, Bates Democrats, Bates Hindu Awareness Group, College Republicans, Feminist Action Coalition, Hillel, Latinos Unidos, Mushahada Association, OUTFront.

Athletics. NCAA. **Intercollegiate:** Baseball M, basketball, cross-country, diving, field hockey W, football (tackle) M, golf, lacrosse, rowing (crew), skiing, soccer, softball W, squash, swimming, tennis, track and field, volleyball W. **Intramural:** Basketball, bowling, football (non-tackle), handball, ice hockey, lacrosse W, racquetball, soccer, softball, squash, table tennis, tennis, volleyball. **Team name:** Bobcats.

Student services. Alcohol/substance abuse counseling, chaplain/spiritual director, career counseling, student employment services, financial aid counseling, health services, minority student services, personal counseling, placement for graduates, women's services. **Physically disabled:** Services for visually, hearing impaired.

Contact. E-mail: admission@bates.edu
Phone: (207) 786-6000 Toll-free number: (855) 228-3755
Fax: (207) 786-6025
Leigh Weisenburger, Director of Admission, Bates College, 23 Campus Avenue, Lindholm House, Lewiston, ME 04240-9917

Bowdoin College

Brunswick, Maine	**CB member**
www.bowdoin.edu	**CB code: 3089**

- Private 4-year liberal arts college
- Residential campus in large town
- 1,772 degree-seeking undergraduates: 49% women, 5% African American, 7% Asian American, 12% Hispanic American, 4% international
- 16% of applicants admitted
- Application essay required
- 92% graduate within 6 years; 15% enter graduate study

General. Founded in 1794. Regionally accredited. **Degrees:** 443 bachelor's awarded. **Location:** 25 miles from Portland, 120 miles from Boston. **Calendar:** Semester. **Full-time faculty:** 182 total; 100% have terminal degrees, 16% minority, 49% women. **Part-time faculty:** 40 total; 90% have terminal degrees, 18% minority, 50% women. **Class size:** 68% < 20, 26% 20-39, 3% 40-49, 3% 50-99. **Special facilities:** Art museum, arctic museum, arctic studies center, coastal marine biology and ornithology research facility, scientific station, farm, center for learning and teaching, 2 theaters, visual arts center, hall of music, environmental studies center, outdoor leadership center, community service resource center, African-American center, women's resource center, educational research and development program, boathouse, electronic classroom, recital hall, nature trails, language media center, recording studio, crafts center, ceramic studio, photography darkroom.

Freshman class profile. 6,554 applied, 1,056 admitted, 484 enrolled.

Mid 50% test scores			
SAT critical reading:	670-750	**Rank in top tenth:**	83%
SAT math:	660-740	**Return as sophomores:**	97%
SAT writing:	670-760	**Out-of-state:**	89%
ACT composite:	30-33	**Live on campus:**	100%
Rank in top quarter:	97%	**International:**	5%

Basis for selection. GED not accepted. Academic record, level of challenge represented in the candidate's course work, counselor/teacher recommendations, interview, quality of application and essay, character and personal qualities, extracurricular activities, talents and abilities, and overall academic potential most important. Test considered, but not required. Motivation of candidate also considered. Interview recommended. Candidates with unusual talent in music, theater or visual arts encouraged to complete Arts Supplement when applying for admission. Audition recommended for

music majors. Portfolio recommended for art majors. **Home schooled:** Applicants applying from systems providing written evaluations rather than grades are required to submit either SAT or ACT-plus-SAT-Subject Test results. SAT Subject Tests should include Math Level 1 or Math Level 2 and one science. Personal interview strongly recommended.

High school preparation. College-preparatory program required. 20 units recommended. Recommended units include English 4, mathematics 4, social studies 4, science 4 (laboratory 3) and foreign language 4. Arts, music and computer science or computer literacy recommended.

2011-2012 Annual costs. Tuition/fees: $42,816. Room/board: $11,654. Books/supplies: $820. Personal expenses: $1,250.

2010-2011 Financial aid. Need-based: 298 full-time freshmen applied for aid; 238 were judged to have need; 238 of these received aid. Average need met was 100%. Average scholarship/grant was $37,640. 96% of total undergraduate aid awarded as scholarships/grants, 4% as loans/jobs. **Non-need-based:** Awarded to 91 full-time undergraduates, including 32 freshmen. Scholarships awarded for academics, leadership. **Additional information:** Regardless of financial circumstances, students admitted will receive money they need to attend. International students for regular admission must submit their financial aid applications by January 1st.

Application procedures. Admission: Closing date 1/1 (receipt date). $60 fee, may be waived for applicants with need. 04/05. Must reply by May 1 or within 1 week(s) if notified thereafter. **Financial aid:** Closing date 2/15. FAFSA, CSS PROFILE required. Applicants notified by 4/5; must reply by 5/1 or within 1 week(s) of notification.

Academics. Most students pursue independent scholarly research, working closely with a faculty advisor, through an independent study or honors project. About half of the student body studies abroad for one or 2 semesters, usually during the junior year. First-year seminars are limited to 16 first-year students and emphasize college-level reading and writing. Interdisciplinary and self-designed majors are available. **Special study options:** Accelerated study, combined bachelor's/graduate degree, double major, exchange student, independent study, liberal arts/career combination, student-designed major, study abroad, teacher certification program, Washington semester. 3-2 or 4-2 engineering degree programs with California Institute of Technology, Dartmouth College, Columbia University, or University of Maine at Orono; 3-3 legal studies program with Columbia University Law School, first-year seminars, summer research fellowships, service-learning courses, The Writing Project, Quantitative Reasoning Program, Legal Studies Advisory Group, Health Professions Advising, English for Multi-Lingual Speakers (EMS). **Credit/placement by examination:** AP, CLEP, IB, institutional tests. **Support services:** Learning center, reduced course load, study skills assistance, tutoring, writing center.

Majors. Area/ethnic studies: African, Asian, Latin American, Russian/Eastern European/Eurasian, women's. **Biology:** General, biochemistry, neuroscience. **Computer sciences:** Computer science. **Conservation:** Environmental studies. **English:** English lit. **Foreign languages:** Classics, French, German, Romance, Russian, Spanish. **History:** General. **Math:** General. **Philosophy/religion:** Philosophy, religion. **Physical sciences:** Chemical physics, chemistry, geochemistry, geology, geophysics, physics. **Psychology:** General. **Social sciences:** Anthropology, econometrics, economics, political science, sociology. **Visual/performing arts:** Art history/conservation, music, studio arts, theater history.

Most popular majors. Biology 17%, foreign language 9%, history 6%, natural resources/environmental science 7%, social sciences 28%, visual/performing arts 7%.

Computing on campus. 450 workstations in dormitories, library, computer center, student center. Dormitories wired for high-speed internet access and linked to campus network. Commuter students can connect to campus network. Online library, helpline, repair service, student web hosting, wireless network available.

Student life. Freshman orientation: Mandatory. Preregistration for classes offered. 4-5 day program at the end of August, just before the start of classes. Pre-orientation outing trips offered over 4 nights prior to formal orientation; separate charge depending on the trip. **Policies:** Honor code, social code, judicial authority, drug and alcohol policies, policies on sexual misconduct, smoking, illegal drugs, discrimination, information technology use, residential life. **Housing:** Guaranteed on-campus for freshmen. Coed dorms, special housing for disabled, apartments, wellness housing available. Three small college houses and 8 college system houses available. **Activities:** Bands, choral groups, dance, drama, film society, international student organizations, literary magazine, music ensembles, musical theater, radio station, student government, student newspaper, symphony orchestra, TV station, African-American Society, Asian student association, Latin American student organization, Hillel, Catholic Students Union, Christian Fellowship, community service council, Bowdoin Green Alliance, Democrats, Republicans.

Athletics. NCAA. **Intercollegiate:** Baseball M, basketball, cross-country, diving, field hockey W, football (tackle) M, golf, ice hockey, lacrosse, rugby W, sailing, skiing, soccer, softball W, squash, swimming, tennis, track and field, volleyball W. **Intramural:** Badminton, basketball, football (non-tackle), ice hockey, soccer, softball, tennis. **Team name:** Polar Bears.

Student services. Alcohol/substance abuse counseling, career counseling, student employment services, health services, minority student services, on-campus daycare, personal counseling, placement for graduates, women's services. **Physically disabled:** Services for visually, speech, hearing impaired.

Contact. E-mail: admissions@bowdoin.edu
Phone: (207) 725-3100 Fax: (207) 725-3101
Scott Meiklejohn, Dean of Admissions and Student Aid, Bowdoin College, 5000 College Station, Brunswick, ME 04011-8441

Colby College
Waterville, Maine
www.colby.edu

CB member
CB code: 3280

- Private 4-year liberal arts college
- Residential campus in large town
- 1,815 degree-seeking undergraduates: 53% women, 3% African American, 5% Asian American, 4% Hispanic American, 6% international
- 29% of applicants admitted
- Application essay required
- 91% graduate within 6 years; 32% enter graduate study

General. Founded in 1813. Regionally accredited. Off-campus facilities available for teaching and research in biology, ecology, geology. **Degrees:** 491 bachelor's awarded. **ROTC:** Army. **Location:** 180 miles from Boston, 75 miles from Portland. **Calendar:** 4-1-4. **Full-time faculty:** 163 total; 98% have terminal degrees, 15% minority, 44% women. **Part-time faculty:** 37 total; 76% have terminal degrees, 49% women. **Class size:** 68% < 20, 26% 20-39, 3% 40-49, 2% 50-99. **Special facilities:** Astronomical observatory, arboretum, research greenhouses, kettlehole research bog, professional blacksmith's forge, woodworking shop, crew rowing center, technical climbing wall, Nordic ski trails, two synthetic turf fields, community radio station, scanning and transmission electron microscopes, laser flash photolysis, 400 MHz NMR, x-ray diffractometer, spectrophotometers, chromatographs, GIS lab, microcalorimeters, piezometers (groundwater monitoring wells), biomass steam plant.

Freshman class profile. 5,186 applied, 1,527 admitted, 467 enrolled.

Mid 50% test scores			
SAT critical reading:	620-710	Rank in top tenth:	61%
SAT math:	630-710	End year in good standing:	97%
SAT writing:	610-710	Return as sophomores:	94%
ACT composite:	28-32	Out-of-state:	86%
Rank in top quarter:	90%	Live on campus:	100%
		International:	9%

Basis for selection. School record and personal qualities very important. Test scores, recommendations, potential contribution to college life, and essay important. Interview, social, economic, racial, and geographic diversity considered. SAT/ACT or three Subject Tests of the student's choice are required.

High school preparation. College-preparatory program recommended. 16 units recommended. Recommended units include English 4, mathematics 3, social studies 2, science 2 (laboratory 2), foreign language 3 and academic electives 2. Social studies units recommended could include history courses.

2011-2012 Annual costs. Comprehensive fee: $53,800. Books/supplies: $700. Personal expenses: $900.

2011-2012 Financial aid. Need-based: 295 full-time freshmen applied for aid; 180 were judged to have need; 180 of these received aid. Average need met was 100%. Average scholarship/grant was $39,882; average loan $1,675. 96% of total undergraduate aid awarded as scholarships/grants, 4% as loans/jobs. **Non-need-based:** Awarded to 60 full-time undergraduates, including 6 freshmen. Scholarships awarded for academics. **Additional information:** Institutional loans have been replaced with institutional grants.

Application procedures. Admission: Closing date 1/1 (postmark date). $65 fee, may be waived for applicants with need, free for online applicants. Admission notification by 4/1. Must reply by 5/1. **Financial aid:** Closing date 2/1. FAFSA, CSS PROFILE required. Applicants notified by 4/1; must reply by 5/1.

Academics. Special study options: Combined bachelor's/graduate degree, cross-registration, double major, dual enrollment of high school students, exchange student, honors, independent study, internships, semester at sea,

student-designed major, study abroad, teacher certification program, Washington semester. Numerous research, service learning, and internship opportunities through the Goldfarb Center for Public Affairs and Civic Engagement; summer research assistantships; course exchange programs with Bowdoin College, Bates College, Thomas College; stipends to enable student internships; coordinated 3-2 engineering program with Dartmouth; Idea Network of Biomedical Research Excellence (partnerships with Jackson Labs, Mt. Desert Island Biological Labs, and other colleges), exchange programs with Howard University and Pomona College, January Program term for focused studies, extensive study-abroad opportunities, Colby in Washington program. **Credit/placement by examination:** AP, CLEP, IB, institutional tests. 12 credit hours maximum toward bachelor's degree. When appropriate, distribution requirements, as well as certain requirements for the major, may be absolved by examination without course enrollment at the discretion of the department concerned. Matriculated students may earn credit by examination in 100- or 200-level courses to a maximum of 12 hours. Departmental examinations or external examinations approved by the department may be used, with credit given for the equivalent of at least C-level work. The cost of each examination is paid by the student. The college will exempt students from the language requirement for attaining before entrance a score of 64 in a SAT Subject Test in a foreign language or for attaining a score of 64 in Colby's placement test during first-year orientation; in either case, no academic credit will be granted. **Support services:** Pre-admission summer program, tutoring, writing center.

Majors. **Area/ethnic studies:** African-American, American, East Asian, Latin American, women's. **Biology:** General, biochemistry, cell/histology, computational, environmental, molecular, molecular biochemistry, neuroscience. **Computer sciences:** Computer science. **Conservation:** Environmental science, environmental studies. **English:** Creative writing, English lit. **Foreign languages:** Classics, French, German, Russian, Spanish. **History:** General. **Math:** General. **Philosophy/religion:** Philosophy, religion. **Physical sciences:** Chemistry, geology, physics. **Psychology:** General. **Social sciences:** Anthropology, econometrics, economics, international relations, political science, sociology. **Visual/performing arts:** Art, art history/conservation, dramatic, music, studio arts.

Most popular majors. Area/ethnic studies 6%, biology 11%, English 8%, history 6%, interdisciplinary studies 13%, physical sciences 7%, psychology 6%, social sciences 23%.

Computing on campus. 350 workstations in library, computer center, student center. Dormitories wired for high-speed internet access and linked to campus network. Commuter students can connect to campus network. Online course registration, online library, helpline, repair service, student web hosting, wireless network available.

Student life. **Freshman orientation:** Mandatory, $280 fee. Preregistration for classes offered. 4-day required outdoor component; 3-day on-campus component follows, both held the week before classes begin. **Policies:** Students participate in forming policies and governing social and community activities through student government and serving on official college committees up to and including the Board of Trustees. **Housing:** Guaranteed on-campus for all undergraduates. Coed dorms, wellness housing available. Senior apartments. **Activities:** Bands, campus ministries, choral groups, dance, drama, film society, international student organizations, literary magazine, music ensembles, Model UN, musical theater, radio station, student government, student newspaper, symphony orchestra, Approximately 100 student clubs and organizations.

Athletics. NCAA. **Intercollegiate:** Baseball M, basketball, cross-country, diving, field hockey W, football (tackle) M, golf, ice hockey, lacrosse, rowing (crew), skiing, soccer, softball W, squash, swimming, tennis, track and field, volleyball W. **Intramural:** Basketball, field hockey, football (non-tackle), soccer, softball. **Team name:** White Mules.

Student services. Alcohol/substance abuse counseling, chaplain/spiritual director, career counseling, student employment services, financial aid counseling, health services, minority student services, personal counseling, placement for graduates, women's services. **Physically disabled:** Services for visually, hearing impaired.

Contact. E-mail: admissions@colby.edu
Phone: (800) 723-3032 Toll-free number: (800) 723-3032
Fax: (207) 859-4828
Terry Cowdrey, Dean of Admissions and Financial Aid, Colby College, 4800 Mayflower Hill, Waterville, ME 04901-8848

College of the Atlantic
Bar Harbor, Maine
www.coa.edu   **CB code: 3305**

- Private 4-year liberal arts college
- Residential campus in small town

- 340 degree-seeking undergraduates: 3% part-time, 72% women, 1% African American, 1% Asian American, 2% Hispanic American, 17% international
- 9 degree-seeking graduate students
- 58% of applicants admitted
- Application essay required
- 71% graduate within 6 years; 15% enter graduate study

General. Founded in 1969. Regionally accredited. College of the Atlantic is an oceanside campus, built 40 years ago from several historic homes, with Acadia National Park as its back yard. **Degrees:** 82 bachelor's awarded; master's offered. **Location:** 300 miles from Boston, 50 miles from Bangor. **Calendar:** Trimester, limited summer session. **Full-time faculty:** 28 total; 86% have terminal degrees, 7% minority, 32% women. **Part-time faculty:** 13 total; 46% have terminal degrees, 46% women. **Class size:** 88% < 20, 12% 20-39. **Special facilities:** Natural history museum, herbarium, greenhouse, pier, research boats, two organic farms, island research stations, arboretum, solar powered ceramics studio, nature preserve.

Freshman class profile. 400 applied, 233 admitted, 76 enrolled.

Mid 50% test scores			
SAT critical reading:	610-700	GPA 2.0-2.99:	4%
SAT math:	570-660	Rank in top quarter:	72%
SAT writing:	570-670	Rank in top tenth:	24%
ACT composite:	29-30	End year in good standing:	95%
GPA 3.75 or higher:	41%	Return as sophomores:	86%
GPA 3.50-3.74:	30%	Out-of-state:	82%
GPA 3.0-3.49:	25%	Live on campus:	100%
		International:	20%

Basis for selection. Academic ability, motivation, intellectual enthusiasm, independence, creativity, commitment to ecological concerns and to philosophies of college as demonstrated by high school record, recommendations, and interview all considered important. **Home schooled:** Thorough outline of topics covered, books read, homework completed, the evaluation process used in assessing work and the progress made over the years required. Standardized test scores recommended. **Learning Disabled:** Meeting with academic dean recommended.

High school preparation. 15 units required; 19 recommended. Required and recommended units include English 4, mathematics 3-4, social studies 2, history 2, science 2-3 (laboratory 2), foreign language 2 and academic electives 1.

2011-2012 Annual costs. Tuition/fees: $36,063. Room/board: $8,820. Books/supplies: $600. Personal expenses: $630.

2011-2012 Financial aid. All financial aid based on need. 77 full-time freshmen applied for aid; 75 were judged to have need; 75 of these received aid. Average need met was 96%. Average scholarship/grant was $28,135; average loan $3,932. 84% of total undergraduate aid awarded as scholarships/grants, 16% as loans/jobs. **Additional information:** Low-cost classes available for local residents; some business courses covered by grant to the college.

Application procedures. **Admission:** Closing date 2/15 (postmark date). $50 fee, may be waived for applicants with need. Admission notification by 4/1. Must reply by May 1 or within 2 week(s) if notified thereafter. **Financial aid:** Closing date 2/15. FAFSA, institutional form required. Applicants notified by 4/1; must reply by 5/1.

Academics. Interdisciplinary, hands-on curriculum consists of problem-solving course work, strong mentorships, seminars, independent study, tutorials, specialized skill courses, supervised internships away from college. Each student chooses his or her own major; no two students follow same path. **Special study options:** Independent study, internships, semester at sea, student-designed major, study abroad, teacher certification program. Winter term program in Yucatan, Mexico and (less frequently) Guatemala. Study abroad in Vichy, France. Consortium agreement (Eco-League) with four other colleges for student exchanges: Alaska Pacific University, Green Mountain College, Northland College, Prescott College; academic partnerships with SALT Institute for Documentary Studies, National Outdoor Leadership School, and Sea Education Association. Residencies (one term on self-directed study) under direction of faculty members. Group study. Tutorials. **Credit/placement by examination:** AP, CLEP, IB. 30 credit hours maximum toward bachelor's degree. **Support services:** Reduced course load, remedial instruction, study skills assistance, tutoring, writing center.

Majors. **Architecture:** Landscape. **Area/ethnic studies:** General, gay/lesbian, Latin American/Caribbean, women's. **Biology:** General, animal behavior, animal physiology, aquatic, botany, conservation, ecology, embryology, entomology, environmental, evolutionary, genetics, marine, microbiology/immunology, mycology, wildlife, zoology. **Business:** Entrepreneurial studies, nonprofit/public. **Communications:** General. **Conservation:** General, environmental science, environmental studies, management/policy. **English:** Child lit, creative writing, English lit, general lit, writing. **Health services:**

Holistic, massage therapy. **History:** General, applied. **Human services:** Community org/advocacy, education policy, international policy, public policy. **Liberal arts:** Arts/sciences, humanities. **Parks/recreation:** Outdoor education. **Philosophy/religion:** General. **Psychology:** General, environmental. **Social sciences:** General, anthropology, applied economics, cultural anthropology, economics, international economic development, international economics, international relations, political economy, political science, research methodology, U.S. government. **Visual/performing arts:** General, art history/conservation, ceramics, cinematography, commercial/advertising art, crafts, design, digital arts, documentaries, drawing, film/cinema/video, graphic design, illustration, multimedia, music, music history, painting, photography, play/screenwriting, printmaking, sculpture, studio arts.

Computing on campus. 32 workstations in library, computer center. Dormitories wired for high-speed internet access and linked to campus network. Online course registration, online library, helpline, student web hosting, wireless network available.

Student life. Freshman orientation: Mandatory, $120 fee. Preregistration for classes offered. 4 days on campus with optional 6-day outdoor adventure trips available. **Housing:** Guaranteed on-campus for freshmen. Coed dorms, special housing for disabled, wellness housing available. $150 nonrefundable deposit, deadline 5/1. **Activities:** Bands, choral groups, dance, drama, international student organizations, literary magazine, music ensembles, radio station, student government, student newspaper, outdoor experience program, life-drawing club, poetry groups, student Democrats, international culture and issue group, circus group, GLBTQ group, sustainability committee, meditation group, bible study.

Athletics. Intramural: Badminton, basketball, cricket, ice hockey, sailing, soccer, softball, table tennis, volleyball, water polo. **Team name:** Black Flies.

Student services. Alcohol/substance abuse counseling, career counseling, student employment services, financial aid counseling, health services, minority student services, personal counseling, placement for graduates. **Physically disabled:** Services for visually, hearing impaired.

Contact. E-mail: inquiry@coa.edu
Phone: (207) 801-5641 Toll-free number: (800) 528-0025
Fax: (207) 288-4126
Sarah Baker, Dean of Admission, College of the Atlantic, 105 Eden Street, Bar Harbor, ME 04609

Husson University
Bangor, Maine
www.husson.edu

CB member
CB code: 3440

- Private 4-year business and health science college
- Commuter campus in large town
- 2,465 degree-seeking undergraduates: 19% part-time, 59% women, 4% African American, 1% Asian American, 1% Hispanic American, 1% international
- 557 degree-seeking graduate students
- 75% of applicants admitted
- SAT or ACT with writing, application essay required
- 38% graduate within 6 years

General. Founded in 1898. Regionally accredited. Small campus, easily accessible with surrounding woods for walks and cross country skiing. **Degrees:** 356 bachelor's, 26 associate awarded; master's, professional offered. **ROTC:** Army, Naval. **Location:** 125 miles from Portland. **Calendar:** Semester, extensive summer session. **Full-time faculty:** 108 total; 64% have terminal degrees, 6% minority, 48% women. **Part-time faculty:** 200 total; 28% have terminal degrees, 2% minority, 46% women. **Class size:** 56% < 20, 39% 20-39, 3% 40-49, 2% 50-99. **Special facilities:** Center for family business.

Freshman class profile. 1,560 applied, 1,172 admitted, 450 enrolled.

Mid 50% test scores				
SAT critical reading:	430-510	Rank in top quarter:		35%
SAT math:	420-530	Rank in top tenth:		15%
SAT writing:	420-520	Return as sophomores:		72%
ACT composite:	17-21	Out-of-state:		15%
GPA 3.75 or higher:	10%	Live on campus:		85%
GPA 3.50-3.74:	24%	Fraternities:		1%
GPA 3.0-3.49:	43%	Sororities:		1%
GPA 2.0-2.99:	22%			

Basis for selection. Class rank and school achievement record most important. Counselor recommendations considered. Test scores important for nursing applicants and occupational and physical therapy applicants. Test scores are used only for placement purposes for business and humanities school applicants. SAT recommended but not required for 2-year program and undeclared majors. Interview recommended. **Home schooled:** Transcript

of courses and grades, state high school equivalency certificate, letter of recommendation (nonparent) required. GED required for financial aid to be awarded. **Learning Disabled:** School must be apprised of special accommodation needs at time of payment of tuition deposit.

High school preparation. College-preparatory program recommended. Recommended units include English 4, mathematics 3, social studies 1, history 1, science 3 (laboratory 2).

2011-2012 Annual costs. Tuition/fees: $13,980. Room/board: $7,520. Books/supplies: $1,150. Personal expenses: $1,200.

2011-2012 Financial aid. Need-based: 446 full-time freshmen applied for aid; 401 were judged to have need; 396 of these received aid. Average need met was 61%. Average scholarship/grant was $9,477; average loan $3,283. 60% of total undergraduate aid awarded as scholarships/grants, 40% as loans/jobs. **Non-need-based:** Awarded to 132 full-time undergraduates, including 47 freshmen. Scholarships awarded for academics, leadership.

Application procedures. Admission: Priority date 3/1; deadline 8/15 (postmark date). $40 fee, may be waived for applicants with need. Admission notification on a rolling basis beginning on or about 12/1. Must reply by May 1 or within 2 week(s) if notified thereafter. **Financial aid:** Priority date 4/15; no closing date. FAFSA required. Applicants notified on a rolling basis starting 4/1; must reply by 5/1 or within 2 week(s) of notification.

Academics. Strong liberal arts core within business and health programs. **Special study options:** Combined bachelor's/graduate degree, cooperative education, double major, dual enrollment of high school students, independent study, internships, liberal arts/career combination, student-designed major, teacher certification program, weekend college. **Credit/placement by examination:** AP, CLEP, IB, SAT, institutional tests. 30 credit hours maximum toward bachelor's degree. **Support services:** Learning center, pre-admission summer program, reduced course load, remedial instruction, study skills assistance, tutoring, writing center.

Majors. Biology: General. **Business:** General, accounting, accounting/business management, banking/financial services, business admin, entrepreneurial studies, finance, hospitality admin, hospitality/recreation, hotel/motel admin, international, international marketing, management information systems, managerial economics, market research, marketing, public finance, sales/distribution, small business admin. **Computer sciences:** General. **Education:** Biology, elementary, English, physical, secondary. **English:** English lit. **Health services:** Nursing (RN), prepharmacy. **Liberal arts:** Arts/sciences. **Parks/recreation:** Facilities management, health/fitness, sports admin. **Physical sciences:** Chemistry. **Protective services:** Criminal justice, law enforcement admin. **Psychology:** General, clinical. **Social sciences:** Criminology.

Most popular majors. Business/marketing 37%, education 6%, health sciences 23%, psychology 11%.

Computing on campus. 116 workstations in library, computer center, student center. Dormitories wired for high-speed internet access and linked to campus network. Commuter students can connect to campus network. Online course registration, online library, helpline, student web hosting, wireless network available.

Student life. Freshman orientation: Mandatory, $75 fee. Preregistration for classes offered. Held during the summer and the weekend before classes start. **Housing:** Guaranteed on-campus for all undergraduates. Coed dorms, apartments, fraternity/sorority housing, wellness housing available. **Activities:** Pep band, campus ministries, choral groups, drama, international student organizations, literary magazine, musical theater, radio station, student government, student newspaper, Campus Crusade for Christ, Chi Alpha, political clubs.

Athletics. NCAA. **Intercollegiate:** Baseball M, basketball, cross-country W, field hockey W, football (tackle) M, golf M, lacrosse, soccer, softball W, swimming W, volleyball W. **Intramural:** Basketball, football (non-tackle) M, ice hockey, lacrosse, soccer, swimming W, tennis, volleyball. **Team name:** Eagles.

Student services. Adult student services, alcohol/substance abuse counseling, chaplain/spiritual director, career counseling, student employment services, financial aid counseling, health services, personal counseling, placement for graduates, veterans' counselor.

Contact. E-mail: admit@husson.edu
Phone: (207) 941-7100 Toll-free number: (800) 448-7766
Fax: (207) 941-7935
Carlena Bean, Director of Admissions, Husson University, One College Circle, Bangor, ME 04401-2999

Maine College of Art
Portland, Maine
www.meca.edu

CB member
CB code: 3701

- Private 4-year visual arts college
- Commuter campus in small city
- 355 degree-seeking undergraduates
- 95% of applicants admitted
- Application essay required

General. Founded in 1882. Regionally accredited. Personal studio space for all juniors and seniors. **Degrees:** 73 bachelor's awarded; master's offered. **Location:** 100 miles from Boston. **Calendar:** Semester. **Full-time faculty:** 17 total; 94% have terminal degrees, 12% minority, 53% women. **Part-time faculty:** 53 total; 66% have terminal degrees, 4% minority. **Class size:** 68% < 20, 28% 20-39, 3% 40-49. **Special facilities:** 2 art galleries, visual arts library.

Freshman class profile. 323 applied, 307 admitted, 101 enrolled.

GPA 3.75 or higher:	10%	Rank in top quarter:	31%
GPA 3.50-3.74:	12%	Rank in top tenth:	10%
GPA 3.0-3.49:	37%	Out-of-state:	68%
GPA 2.0-2.99:	41%		

Basis for selection. Decision based on interview and portfolio in conjunction with high school achievement record; essay, recommendations important, test scores considered. Interview recommended. Portfolio required. **Home schooled:** Transcript of courses and grades required. Show evidence through state's certification of completion of high school program or GED. **Learning Disabled:** Once admitted, submit proper documentation to student affairs director and request specific accommodations.

High school preparation. 27 units recommended. Recommended units include English 4, mathematics 3, social studies 4, history 4, science 3, foreign language 2 and academic electives 3. 4 units of art strongly recommended.

2011-2012 Annual costs. Tuition/fees: $29,395. Room/board: $10,330. Books/supplies: $2,200. Personal expenses: $675.

Financial aid. Non-need-based: Scholarships awarded for academics, art.

Application procedures. Admission: Priority date 2/1; no deadline. $40 fee, may be waived for applicants with need. Admission notification on a rolling basis beginning on or about 1/2. Students strongly encouraged to reply by May 1 or within 3 weeks if notified thereafter. **Financial aid:** Priority date 3/1; no closing date. FAFSA required. Applicants notified on a rolling basis starting 2/15; must reply within 2 week(s) of notification.

Academics. 1 to 2 year foundation program in drawing, color, digital imaging, and 2 and 3 dimensional design, followed by transitional year, and final 2 years in major. **Special study options:** Combined bachelor's/graduate degree, cross-registration, double major, exchange student, independent study, internships, liberal arts/career combination, study abroad, teacher certification program. Mobility program with 36 AICAD (Associated Independent Colleges of Art and Design) across the country and in Canada, cross-registration program with 4 other colleges and universities in the greater Portland area; special exchange program with Hanoi Fine Arts College, Vietnam; BFA credit available through Provincetown (MA) Fine Arts Work Center. **Credit/placement by examination:** AP, CLEP. **Support services:** Learning center, study skills assistance, tutoring, writing center.

Majors. Visual/performing arts: Art, ceramics, graphic design, illustration, metal/jewelry, painting, photography, printmaking, sculpture, studio arts.

Computing on campus. 86 workstations in library, computer center, student center. Dormitories wired for high-speed internet access and linked to campus network. Commuter students can connect to campus network. Online library, helpline, student web hosting, wireless network available.

Student life. Freshman orientation: Mandatory. Preregistration for classes offered. Held the week before the start of classes. **Housing:** Coed dorms, wellness housing available. $500 partly refundable deposit. **Activities:** Film society, student government, student senate, community action group, green (ecology) group, movie club, peer mentor scholarships.

Student services. Adult student services, alcohol/substance abuse counseling, career counseling, student employment services, financial aid counseling, minority student services, personal counseling.

Contact. E-mail: admissions@meca.edu
Phone: (207) 699-5026 Toll-free number: (800) 699-1509
Fax: (207) 699-5080
Shannon Cote, Director of Admissions, Maine College of Art, 522 Congress Street, Portland, ME 04101

Maine Maritime Academy
Castine, Maine
www.mainemaritime.edu

CB code: 3505

- Public 4-year maritime college
- Residential campus in rural community
- 950 degree-seeking undergraduates
- SAT or ACT with writing required

General. Founded in 1941. Regionally accredited. **Degrees:** 179 bachelor's, 5 associate awarded; master's offered. **ROTC:** Army, Naval. **Location:** 38 miles from Bangor. **Calendar:** Semester. **Full-time faculty:** 70 total; 33% have terminal degrees, 4% minority. **Part-time faculty:** 23 total. **Special facilities:** 500-foot training ship, 40-foot marine research vessel, 80-foot oceangoing tugboat and barge, two-masted arctic schooner, steam and diesel engine laboratories, power plant simulators, bridge simulator, planetarium, ocean classrooms.

Freshman class profile.

Out-of-state:	31%	Live on campus:	95%

Basis for selection. High school academic record followed by SAT/ACT test scores the most important. Interview, school and community activities, work ethic, and recommendations also considered. Interview and personal statement are highly recommended. **Home schooled:** Transcript of courses and grades, letter of recommendation (nonparent) required. ACT/SAT scores and possible evaluation of transcripts/course records by Maine Department of Education.

High school preparation. College-preparatory program required. Required and recommended units include English 4, mathematics 4, science 2-3 (laboratory 2) and foreign language 2. 1 unit computer literacy recommended.

2011-2012 Annual costs. Tuition/fees: $11,305; $15,605 out-of-district; $20,705 out-of-state. Room/board: $9,320. Books/supplies: $1,000. Personal expenses: $800.

Financial aid. Non-need-based: Scholarships awarded for academics, leadership, state residency.

Application procedures. Admission: Priority date 12/31; deadline 3/1 (receipt date). No application fee. Admission notification on a rolling basis beginning on or about 1/1. Must reply by 5/1. **Financial aid:** Closing date 4/15. FAFSA required. Applicants notified on a rolling basis starting 4/1; must reply within 4 week(s) of notification.

Academics. Special study options: Cooperative education, double major, internships, liberal arts/career combination, semester at sea, student-designed major, study abroad, teacher certification program. 2-month training cruise for USCG unlimited license majors. **Credit/placement by examination:** AP, CLEP, institutional tests. **Support services:** Study skills assistance, tutoring, writing center.

Majors. Biology: Marine. **Business:** General, business admin, entrepreneurial studies, international, logistics. **Engineering:** Marine, systems. **Physical sciences:** Oceanography.

Most popular majors. Biology 8%, business/marketing 8%, engineering/engineering technologies 64%, trade and industry 20%.

Computing on campus. PC or laptop required. 40 workstations in dormitories, library. Dormitories wired for high-speed internet access and linked to campus network. Commuter students can connect to campus network. Online library, helpline, repair service, wireless network available.

Student life. Freshman orientation: Mandatory. Preregistration for classes offered. 2.5 days available through 4 different sessions in August. **Policies:** Regimental lifestyle optional for the 2-year program and those majoring in power engineering, ocean studies, international business, and small vessel operations. Regiment is mandatory for United States Coast Guard unlimited license programs (marine transportation and marine engineering). No military obligation. Students required to live on-campus unless married, over age 23, or have completed 2 or more years of active military service or 6 semesters of study. **Housing:** Guaranteed on-campus for all undergraduates. Coed dorms, apartments, wellness housing available. $200 nonrefundable deposit, deadline 8/15. **Activities:** Bands, choral groups, drama, music ensembles, student government, student newspaper, Alpha Phi Omega, other service organizations.

Athletics. NCAA. **Intercollegiate:** Basketball, cross-country, football (tackle) M, golf M, lacrosse M, sailing, soccer, softball W, volleyball W. **Intramural:** Basketball, golf, handball, ice hockey M, racquetball, rifle,

rugby M, sailing, skiing, soccer, softball, squash, tennis, volleyball, water polo. **Team name:** Mariners.

Student services. Alcohol/substance abuse counseling, career counseling, student employment services, financial aid counseling, health services, personal counseling, placement for graduates, veterans' counselor, women's services.

Contact. E-mail: admissions@mma.edu
Phone: (207) 326-2206 Toll-free number: (800) 227-8465
Fax: (207) 326-2515
Jeffrey Wright, Director of Admissions, Maine Maritime Academy, Pleasant Street, Castine, ME 04420

New England School of Communications
Bangor, Maine
www.nescom.edu   **CB code: 3101**

- Private 4-year college of communications
- Residential campus in small city
- 528 degree-seeking undergraduates: 4% part-time, 25% women, 2% African American, 1% Asian American, 1% Hispanic American, 1% Native American
- 66% of applicants admitted
- Application essay, interview required

General. Accredited by ACCSC. **Degrees:** 70 bachelor's, 9 associate awarded. **ROTC:** Army. **Location:** 250 miles from Boston. **Calendar:** Semester, limited summer session. **Full-time faculty:** 24 total; 12% have terminal degrees, 12% women. **Part-time faculty:** 54 total; 13% have terminal degrees, 4% minority, 32% women. **Class size:** 65% < 20, 34% 20-39, 1% 50-99. **Special facilities:** Sound recording studio, digital photography lab, television studio, mobile production studio.

Freshman class profile. 280 applied, 186 admitted, 119 enrolled.

End year in good standing:	88%	Out-of-state:	31%
Return as sophomores:	65%	Live on campus:	71%

Basis for selection. Interview and placement test most important; high school record and essay also important. SAT or ACT recommended. Timed scholastic placement exam. **Home schooled:** Transcript of courses and grades, state high school equivalency certificate, interview, letter of recommendation (nonparent) required. Require GED score if home schooling is not through an accredited curriculum-based program. **Learning Disabled:** Students requiring additional placement test time must provide professional evaluation documentation requesting extra time prior to interview date.

High school preparation. College-preparatory program recommended. Recommended units include English 4, mathematics 2, social studies 1, history 2, science 2, foreign language 2, computer science 1 and visual/performing arts 1. Recommend additional computer, public speaking, creative arts coursework.

2011-2012 Annual costs. Tuition/fees: $12,145. Additional cost of $140 for FireWire hard drive. Room/board: $7,520. Books/supplies: $1,300. Personal expenses: $1,000.

2011-2012 Financial aid. Need-based: 106 full-time freshmen applied for aid; 106 were judged to have need; 87 of these received aid. Average scholarship/grant was $2,605; average loan $3,356. 41% of total undergraduate aid awarded as scholarships/grants, 59% as loans/jobs. **Non-need-based:** Awarded to 45 full-time undergraduates, including 20 freshmen. Scholarships awarded for academics, leadership.

Application procedures. Admission: Priority date 4/1; no deadline. $25 fee, may be waived for applicants with need. Admission notification on a rolling basis. **Financial aid:** Priority date 4/15; no closing date. FAFSA, institutional form required. Applicants notified on a rolling basis starting 2/1; must reply by 8/12.

Academics. Special study options: Cross-registration, double major, internships, liberal arts/career combination. **Credit/placement by examination:** AP, CLEP, institutional tests. 6 credit hours maximum toward associate degree, 15 toward bachelor's. **Support services:** Reduced course load, study skills assistance, tutoring, writing center.

Majors. Business: Marketing. **Communications:** Broadcast journalism, digital media, journalism, persuasive communications, public relations, radio/TV. **Communications technology:** General, photo/film/video, radio/TV, recording arts. **Computer sciences:** Web page design. **Visual/performing arts:** Theater design.

Computing on campus. 195 workstations in dormitories, library, computer center, student center. Dormitories wired for high-speed internet access and linked to campus network. Commuter students can connect to campus network. Online library, helpline, wireless network available.

Student life. Freshman orientation: Mandatory, $50 fee. Preregistration for classes offered. Summer orientation occurs for those students attending in the fall semester. **Housing:** Guaranteed on-campus for freshmen. Coed dorms, fraternity/sorority housing, wellness housing available. $50 nonrefundable deposit. **Activities:** Pep band, campus ministries, choral groups, drama, international student organizations, literary magazine, music ensembles, musical theater, radio station, student government, student newspaper, TV station, Campus Crusade for Christ, Habitat for Humanity.

Athletics. Intramural: Baseball, basketball, cheerleading, diving, field hockey, football (non-tackle), skiing, soccer, softball, swimming, table tennis, tennis, volleyball, water polo.

Student services. Alcohol/substance abuse counseling, chaplain/spiritual director, career counseling, student employment services, financial aid counseling, health services, personal counseling, placement for graduates, veterans' counselor.

Contact. E-mail: info@nescom.edu
Phone: (207) 941-7176 Toll-free number: (888) 877-1876 ext. 1093
Fax: (207) 947-3987
Louise Grant, Director of Admissions, New England School of Communications, One College Circle, Bangor, ME 04401

Saint Joseph's College of Maine
Standish, Maine   **CB member**
www.sjcme.edu   **CB code: 3755**

- Private 4-year liberal arts college affiliated with Roman Catholic Church
- Residential campus in small town
- 998 degree-seeking undergraduates
- SAT or ACT (ACT writing optional), application essay required

General. Founded in 1912. Regionally accredited. **Degrees:** 279 bachelor's, 5 associate awarded; master's offered. **ROTC:** Army. **Location:** 18 miles from Portland, 120 miles from Boston. **Calendar:** Semester, limited summer session. **Full-time faculty:** 67 total. **Part-time faculty:** 73 total. **Class size:** 60% < 20, 36% 20-39, 2% 40-49, 1% 50-99. **Special facilities:** Telescope, observatory.

Freshman class profile.

GPA 3.75 or higher:	17%	Rank in top quarter:	41%
GPA 3.50-3.74:	14%	Rank in top tenth:	14%
GPA 3.0-3.49:	29%	Out-of-state:	44%
GPA 2.0-2.99:	37%	Live on campus:	93%

Basis for selection. School record, class rank, test scores, recommendations, essays, extracurricular activities all considered. Interview optional, but recommended.

High school preparation. College-preparatory program recommended. 20 units recommended. Recommended units include English 4, mathematics 3, social studies 3, science 3, foreign language 1, visual/performing arts 1 and academic electives 5. Laboratory biology and laboratory chemistry required of nursing and science applicants. For any intended major, transcripts from candidates for admission should include 16 or more college-preparatory courses.

2011-2012 Annual costs. Tuition/fees: $28,700. Room/board: $11,000. Books/supplies: $1,100. Personal expenses: $1,200.

Financial aid. Non-need-based: Scholarships awarded for academics, alumni affiliation, leadership.

Application procedures. Admission: Priority date 3/1; no deadline. No application fee. Admission notification on a rolling basis beginning on or about 12/17. Must reply by May 1 or within 2 week(s) if notified thereafter. **Financial aid:** Priority date 3/1; no closing date. FAFSA, institutional form required. Applicants notified on a rolling basis starting 3/1; must reply within 3 week(s) of notification.

Academics. College belongs to Greater Portland Alliance, a 5-college consortium with cross registration. **Special study options:** Combined bachelor's/graduate degree, cooperative education, cross-registration, distance learning, double major, honors, independent study, internships, liberal arts/career combination, semester at sea, student-designed major, study abroad, teacher certification program, Washington semester. **Credit/placement by examination:** AP, CLEP, SAT, ACT, institutional tests. 30 credit hours

maximum toward bachelor's degree. **Support services:** Study skills assistance, tutoring, writing center.

Majors. Biology: General. **Business:** Accounting, business admin, finance, human resources, international, marketing. **Communications:** Digital media, journalism, public relations. **Conservation:** Environmental science, environmental studies. **Education:** Biology, elementary, English, history, mathematics, physical. **English:** English lit. **Health services:** Medical radiologic technology/radiation therapy, nursing (RN). **History:** General. **Math:** General. **Parks/recreation:** Exercise sciences, sports admin. **Philosophy/religion:** Philosophy. **Physical sciences:** Chemistry. **Protective services:** Criminal justice. **Psychology:** General. **Social sciences:** General, political science, sociology. **Theology:** Theology.

Most popular majors. Biology 6%, business/marketing 20%, communications/journalism 8%, education 13%, health sciences 21%, parks/recreation 6%, social sciences 6%.

Computing on campus. 102 workstations in library, computer center, student center. Dormitories wired for high-speed internet access and linked to campus network. Commuter students can connect to campus network. Helpline, repair service, wireless network available.

Student life. Freshman orientation: Available, $50 fee. Preregistration for classes offered. Two-day session in June or July. **Policies:** Mass available daily on campus. **Housing:** Guaranteed on-campus for all undergraduates. Coed dorms, single-sex dorms, wellness housing available. $100 deposit, deadline 5/1. **Activities:** Choral groups, dance, drama, literary magazine, radio station, student government, student newspaper, Habitat for Humanity, High Adventure, Superkids, business club, campus ministry, culture and heritage club, interhall council, student nurses association.

Athletics. NCAA. **Intercollegiate:** Baseball M, basketball, cross-country, field hockey W, golf M, lacrosse, soccer, softball W, swimming, track and field M, volleyball W. **Intramural:** Basketball, football (non-tackle), soccer, softball, swimming, volleyball. **Team name:** Monks.

Student services. Alcohol/substance abuse counseling, chaplain/spiritual director, career counseling, student employment services, financial aid counseling, health services, personal counseling, placement for graduates, veterans' counselor. **Physically disabled:** Services for visually, speech, hearing impaired.

Contact. E-mail: admission@sjcme.edu
Phone: (207) 893-7746 Toll-free number: (800) 338-7057
Fax: (207) 893-7862
Nikolas Ray, Dean of Admission, Saint Joseph's College of Maine, 278 Whites Bridge Road, Standish, ME 04084-5236

Thomas College
Waterville, Maine   CB member
www.thomas.edu   CB code: 3903

- Private 4-year business and liberal arts college
- Residential campus in large town
- 781 degree-seeking undergraduates: 12% part-time, 52% women, 4% African American, 1% Asian American, 1% Hispanic American, 1% Native American, 1% international
- 115 degree-seeking graduate students
- 93% of applicants admitted
- SAT or ACT (ACT writing optional), application essay required
- 46% graduate within 6 years

General. Founded in 1894. Regionally accredited. Evening division (undergraduate and graduate) on trimester system. **Degrees:** 128 bachelor's, 3 associate awarded; master's offered. **ROTC:** Army. **Location:** 75 miles from Portland. **Calendar:** Semester, limited summer session. **Full-time faculty:** 30 total; 57% have terminal degrees, 7% minority, 40% women. **Part-time faculty:** 43 total; 19% have terminal degrees, 2% minority, 49% women. **Class size:** 55% < 20, 45% 20-39.

Freshman class profile. 923 applied, 854 admitted, 225 enrolled.

Mid 50% test scores			
SAT critical reading:	370-490	Rank in top quarter:	30%
SAT math:	350-470	Rank in top tenth:	8%
SAT writing:	340-440	End year in good standing:	72%
ACT composite:	16-19	Return as sophomores:	60%
GPA 3.75 or higher:	5%	Out-of-state:	26%
GPA 3.50-3.74:	9%	Live on campus:	79%
GPA 3.0-3.49:	36%	International:	2%
GPA 2.0-2.99:	43%		

Basis for selection. Academic transcripts most important. Letters of recommendation, college essay, SAT, ACT and/or TOEFL Exam scores also important. Recommend minimum 2.0 overall GPA, rank in top half of class. Test scores required of bachelor's degree candidates, but not required of associate degree candidates. Interview recommended. **Home schooled:** Transcript of courses and grades, state high school equivalency certificate, letter of recommendation (nonparent) required.

High school preparation. College-preparatory program recommended. 16 units recommended. Recommended units include English 4, mathematics 3, social studies 2, history 2, science 3 and foreign language 2.

2011-2012 Annual costs. Tuition/fees: $22,770. Room/board: $9,170. Books/supplies: $800. Personal expenses: $1,000.

2011-2012 Financial aid. Need-based: 214 full-time freshmen applied for aid; 206 were judged to have need; 206 of these received aid. Average need met was 85%. Average scholarship/grant was $16,366; average loan $4,035. 74% of total undergraduate aid awarded as scholarships/grants, 26% as loans/jobs. **Non-need-based:** Awarded to 114 full-time undergraduates, including 64 freshmen. Scholarships awarded for academics, leadership, state residency.

Application procedures. Admission: No deadline. $50 fee, may be waived for applicants with need. Admission notification on a rolling basis beginning on or about 12/1. Must reply by May 1 or within 4 week(s) if notified thereafter. **Financial aid:** Priority date 2/15; no closing date. FAFSA required. Applicants notified on a rolling basis starting 3/15; must reply within 2 week(s) of notification.

Academics. Special study options: Accelerated study, combined bachelor's/graduate degree, cross-registration, double major, dual enrollment of high school students, independent study, internships, study abroad, teacher certification program, Washington semester. **Credit/placement by examination:** AP, CLEP. 15 credit hours maximum toward associate degree, 15 toward bachelor's. **Support services:** Learning center, reduced course load, study skills assistance, tutoring.

Majors. Business: Accounting, business admin, finance, hospitality admin, human resources, international, marketing. **Communications:** Persuasive communications. **Computer sciences:** General, computer science. **Education:** Early childhood, elementary. **Parks/recreation:** Sports admin. **Protective services:** Criminal justice, law enforcement admin. **Psychology:** General, forensic. **Social sciences:** U.S. government.

Most popular majors. Business/marketing 40%, communications/journalism 7%, education 7%, parks/recreation 9%, psychology 11%, security/protective services 15%.

Computing on campus. 203 workstations in dormitories, library, computer center, student center. Dormitories wired for high-speed internet access and linked to campus network. Commuter students can connect to campus network. Online course registration, online library, helpline, repair service, student web hosting, wireless network available.

Student life. Freshman orientation: Mandatory. Preregistration for classes offered. 3-day program held at the end of August; extended programs during fall semester. **Housing:** Guaranteed on-campus for freshmen. Coed dorms, wellness housing available. $200 nonrefundable deposit, deadline 5/1. **Activities:** Dance, drama, student government, student newspaper, Fellowship Group, Habitat for Humanity, Environmental Awareness Club, ASSIST (A Society of Students in Service Together), Student Veterans Organization.

Athletics. NCAA. **Intercollegiate:** Baseball M, basketball, cross-country, field hockey W, lacrosse, soccer, softball W, tennis. **Intramural:** Badminton, basketball, bowling, football (non-tackle), soccer, softball, table tennis, tennis, volleyball, weight lifting. **Team name:** Terriers.

Student services. Alcohol/substance abuse counseling, chaplain/spiritual director, career counseling, student employment services, financial aid counseling, health services, personal counseling, placement for graduates.

Contact. E-mail: admiss@thomas.edu
Phone: (207) 859-1101 Toll-free number: (800) 339-7001
Fax: (207) 859-1114
Wendy Martin, Dean for Undergraduate Admissions, Thomas College, 180 West River Road, Waterville, ME 04901

Unity College in Maine
Unity, Maine
www.unity.edu   CB code: 3925

- Private 4-year liberal arts college
- Residential campus in rural community

- 574 degree-seeking undergraduates: 1% part-time, 55% women, 1% African American, 1% Asian American, 2% Hispanic American, 2% Native American
- 61% of applicants admitted
- Application essay required
- 46% graduate within 6 years; 25% enter graduate study

General. Founded in 1965. Regionally accredited. **Degrees:** 110 bachelor's, 3 associate awarded. **Location:** 20 miles from Waterville. **Calendar:** Semester, limited summer session. **Full-time faculty:** 37 total; 89% have terminal degrees, 54% women. **Part-time faculty:** 31 total; 68% have terminal degrees, 45% women. **Class size:** 66% < 20, 34% 20-39. **Special facilities:** Wetlands research area, outdoor pottery kiln, outdoor classroom.

Freshman class profile. 737 applied, 453 admitted, 172 enrolled.

Mid 50% test scores			
SAT critical reading:	480-560	GPA 2.0-2.99:	32%
SAT math:	490-560	Rank in top quarter:	33%
SAT writing:	450-520	Rank in top tenth:	14%
ACT composite:	22-25	End year in good standing:	89%
GPA 3.75 or higher:	16%	Return as sophomores:	71%
GPA 3.50-3.74:	21%	Out-of-state:	79%
GPA 3.0-3.49:	31%	Live on campus:	98%

Basis for selection. High school transcripts, interviews, recommendations and essay most important. Test scores not required but highly recommended. SAT or ACT recommended. Interview is optional but recommended. **Home schooled:** Informative portfolio.

High school preparation. College-preparatory program recommended. 18 units recommended. Required and recommended units include English 4, mathematics 4, social studies 3, history 3, science 3 (laboratory 3) and foreign language 2.

2011-2012 Annual costs. Tuition/fees: $23,240. Room/board: $8,380. Books/supplies: $500. Personal expenses: $600.

2011-2012 Financial aid. **Need-based:** 115 full-time freshmen applied for aid; 105 were judged to have need; 105 of these received aid. Average need met was 69%. Average scholarship/grant was $12,643; average loan $4,583. 55% of total undergraduate aid awarded as scholarships/grants, 45% as loans/jobs. **Non-need-based:** Awarded to 87 full-time undergraduates, including 24 freshmen. Scholarships awarded for academics, leadership, minority status.

Application procedures. **Admission:** Priority date 12/15; deadline 2/15 (postmark date). $25 fee, may be waived for applicants with need. Admission notification by 3/15. Admission notification on a rolling basis. **Financial aid:** Priority date 3/1; no closing date. FAFSA required. Applicants notified on a rolling basis starting 3/10; must reply within 2 week(s) of notification.

Academics. **Special study options:** Accelerated study, double major, independent study, internships, semester at sea, study abroad, teacher certification program, Washington semester. **Credit/placement by examination:** AP, CLEP, IB, SAT, ACT, institutional tests. 15 credit hours maximum toward associate degree, 15 toward bachelor's. **Support services:** Learning center, reduced course load, study skills assistance, tutoring, writing center.

Majors. **Biology:** Ecology, environmental, marine, wildlife. **Conservation:** Environmental science, environmental studies, management/policy, wildlife/wilderness. **Education:** General. **General:** Aquaculture. **Health services:** Recreational therapy. **Liberal arts:** Arts/sciences. **Parks/recreation:** General, facilities management.

Most popular majors. Agriculture 7%, biology 26%, natural resources/environmental science 48%, parks/recreation 12%.

Computing on campus. 90 workstations in dormitories, library, computer center, student center. Dormitories wired for high-speed internet access and linked to campus network. Commuter students can connect to campus network. Online course registration, online library, helpline, wireless network available.

Student life. **Freshman orientation:** Mandatory, $100 fee. Preregistration for classes offered. 5-day outdoor wilderness-based program. **Policies:** Students are required to live on campus unless they are 21 years of age, married, live with their parents (within 50 miles of the campus), or have earned a minimum of 60 credits. **Housing:** Guaranteed on-campus for freshmen. Coed dorms, single-sex dorms, special housing for disabled, cooperative housing, wellness housing available. $100 nonrefundable deposit. Eco-cottage living. **Activities:** Drama, literary magazine, student government, Constructive Activists, search and rescue crew, trail crew; also groups devoted to environmental awareness, recycling, community service.

Athletics. USCAA. **Intercollegiate:** Basketball W, cross-country, soccer, volleyball W. **Intramural:** Basketball, football (non-tackle), soccer, softball, volleyball. **Team name:** Rams.

Student services. Alcohol/substance abuse counseling, chaplain/spiritual director, career counseling, student employment services, financial aid counseling, health services, personal counseling, placement for graduates, veterans' counselor. **Physically disabled:** Services for hearing impaired.

Contact. E-mail: admissions@unity.edu
Phone: (207) 948-3131 ext. 231 Toll-free number: (800) 624-1024
Fax: (207) 948-2928
Alisa Johnson, Dean of Enrollment Management, Unity College in Maine, P.O. 532, Unity, ME 04988-0532

University of Maine
Orono, Maine
www.umaine.edu

CB member
CB code: 3916

- Public 4-year university
- Residential campus in large town
- 8,271 degree-seeking undergraduates: 9% part-time, 48% women, 2% African American, 1% Asian American, 2% Hispanic American, 1% Native American, 2% international
- 1,676 degree-seeking graduate students
- 78% of applicants admitted
- SAT or ACT (ACT writing recommended), application essay required
- 60% graduate within 6 years

General. Founded in 1865. Regionally accredited. **Degrees:** 1,831 bachelor's awarded; master's, professional, doctoral offered. **ROTC:** Army, Naval. **Location:** 12 miles from Bangor. **Calendar:** Semester, extensive summer session. **Full-time faculty:** 555 total; 75% have terminal degrees, 7% minority, 34% women. **Part-time faculty:** 234 total; 35% have terminal degrees, 4% minority, 56% women. **Class size:** 53% < 20, 30% 20-39, 5% 40-49, 8% 50-99, 3% >100. **Special facilities:** Advanced manufacturing center, machine tool lab, laboratory for surface science and technology, planetarium, anthropology museum, woodland preserve, botanical garden, art museum, observatory, environmental research facility, performing arts hall, Canadian-American center, Franco-American center, digital media lab, farm museum, marine lab, aquatic production facility, climbing wall, center for undergraduate research, student innovation center.

Freshman class profile. 8,093 applied, 6,289 admitted, 1,750 enrolled.

Mid 50% test scores			
SAT critical reading:	480-590	GPA 2.0-2.99:	20%
SAT math:	490-600	Rank in top quarter:	51%
SAT writing:	470-580	Rank in top tenth:	21%
ACT composite:	21-26	Return as sophomores:	78%
GPA 3.75 or higher:	23%	Out-of-state:	23%
GPA 3.50-3.74:	9%	Live on campus:	89%
GPA 3.0-3.49:	47%	International:	2%

Basis for selection. Strong emphasis on grades earned, GPA, class rank (if available) and standardized test scores. Academic requirements for admission may vary by program. Interviews available. Audition required of music majors. Portfolio recommended for art majors. **Home schooled:** Statement describing home school structure and mission, transcript of courses and grades, state high school equivalency certificate, letter of recommendation (nonparent) required. GED requirement may be waived if thorough records submitted.

High school preparation. College-preparatory program required. 17 units required; 21 recommended. Required and recommended units include English 4, mathematics 3-4, social studies 2-3, history 1, science 2-4 (laboratory 2-3), foreign language 2 and academic electives 4. 1 unit physical education required of all College of Education candidates.

2011-2012 Annual costs. Tuition/fees: $10,588; $26,308 out-of-state. New England Regional Student Program tuition is $12,570. Room/board: $8,944. Books/supplies: $1,000.

2011-2012 Financial aid. **Need-based:** 1,585 full-time freshmen applied for aid; 1,322 were judged to have need; 1,310 of these received aid. Average need met was 83%. Average scholarship/grant was $8,161; average loan $3,737. 46% of total undergraduate aid awarded as scholarships/grants, 54% as loans/jobs. **Non-need-based:** Awarded to 580 full-time undergraduates, including 215 freshmen. Scholarships awarded for academics, alumni affiliation, art, athletics, job skills, leadership, minority status, music/drama, ROTC, state residency. **Additional information:** Financial aid is available for students entering in the spring.

Application procedures. Admission: Priority date 2/1; no deadline. $40 fee, may be waived for applicants with need. Admission notification on a rolling basis beginning on or about 2/1. Must reply by May 1 or within 2 week(s) if notified thereafter. **Financial aid:** Priority date 3/1, closing date 5/1. FAFSA required. Applicants notified on a rolling basis starting 3/15; must reply by 5/1 or within 2 week(s) of notification.

Academics. Special study options: Accelerated study, combined bachelor's/graduate degree, cooperative education, distance learning, double major, ESL, exchange student, honors, independent study, internships, liberal arts/career combination, semester at sea, study abroad, teacher certification program. **Credit/placement by examination:** AP, CLEP, IB, institutional tests. Duplicate credit may not be granted. Each department may develop or adopt examinations other than CLEP examinations for the purpose of granting credit for specific courses. **Support services:** Reduced course load, remedial instruction, study skills assistance, tutoring, writing center.

Honors college/program. Admission for first-time and transfer students based on test scores and high school record.

Majors. Area/ethnic studies: Women's. **Biology:** General, bacteriology, biochemistry, biomedical sciences, botany, cell/histology, ecology, entomology, marine, molecular, pathology, zoology. **Business:** General, accounting, business admin, finance, labor relations, management information systems, managerial economics. **Communications:** Communications/speech/rhetoric, journalism. **Computer sciences:** General. **Conservation:** General, environmental studies, forest management, forest resources, forestry, management/policy, wildlife/wilderness, wood science. **Education:** General, art, biology, chemistry, elementary, English, foreign languages, French, history, mathematics, music, physical, science, secondary, social studies, Spanish. **Engineering:** General, agricultural, applied physics, chemical, civil, computer, electrical, forest, mechanical, surveying, systems. **English:** English lit, rhetoric/composition. **Foreign languages:** General, French, German, Latin, Spanish. **General:** Animal sciences, business, economics, food science, greenhouse operations, horticultural science, landscaping, nursery operations, ornamental horticulture, plant sciences, soil science, sustainable agriculture, turf management. **Health services:** Audiology/speech pathology, clinical lab science, communication disorders, nursing (RN). **History:** General. **Human services:** General, social work. **Liberal arts:** Arts/sciences. **Math:** General. **Parks/recreation:** Facilities management. **Philosophy/religion:** Philosophy. **Physical sciences:** Chemistry, geology, oceanography, physics. **Psychology:** General. **Social sciences:** Anthropology, economics, international relations, political science, sociology. **Visual/performing arts:** Art history/conservation, dramatic, music, music performance, studio arts. **Work/family studies:** Family/community services, food/nutrition.

Most popular majors. Agriculture 6%, biology 6%, business/marketing 11%, education 10%, engineering/engineering technologies 16%, health sciences 7%, psychology 6%, social sciences 9%.

Computing on campus. 500 workstations in library, computer center, student center. Dormitories wired for high-speed internet access and linked to campus network. Commuter students can connect to campus network. Online course registration, online library, helpline, repair service, student web hosting, wireless network available.

Student life. Freshman orientation: Available. Preregistration for classes offered. 2-day events in June, parents invited; 4-day welcome program in fall; additional adventure orientations available. **Housing:** Guaranteed on-campus for freshmen. Coed dorms, special housing for disabled, apartments, fraternity/sorority housing, wellness housing available. Academic grouping wings, men-only sections, women-only sections available. **Activities:** Bands, campus ministries, choral groups, dance, drama, film society, international student organizations, literary magazine, music ensembles, musical theater, opera, radio station, student government, student newspaper, symphony orchestra, TV station, InterVarsity Christian Fellowship, Campus Crusade for Christ, Catholic Student Association, Hillel, Maine Christian Association, Muslim student organization, Newman Center.

Athletics. NCAA. Intercollegiate: Baseball M, basketball, cheerleading, cross-country, diving, field hockey W, football (tackle) M, ice hockey, soccer W, softball, swimming, track and field, volleyball W. **Intramural:** Badminton, basketball, cross-country, diving, field hockey W, football (non-tackle) M, golf, racquetball, skiing, soccer, softball, squash, swimming, table tennis, tennis, track and field, triathlon, volleyball, water polo. **Team name:** Black Bears.

Student services. Adult student services, alcohol/substance abuse counseling, chaplain/spiritual director, career counseling, services for economically disadvantaged, student employment services, financial aid counseling, health services, legal services, minority student services, on-campus daycare, personal counseling, placement for graduates, veterans' counselor, women's services. **Physically disabled:** Services for visually, speech, hearing impaired.

Contact. E-mail: um-admit@maine.edu
Phone: (207) 581-1561 Toll-free number: (877) 486-2364
Fax: (207) 581-1213
Sharon Oliver, Director of Admissions, University of Maine, 5713 Chadbourne Hall, Orono, ME 04469-5713

University of Maine at Augusta
Augusta, Maine
www.uma.edu

CB member
CB code: 3929

- Public 4-year university
- Commuter campus in large town
- 4,501 degree-seeking undergraduates: 61% part-time, 73% women, 1% African American, 1% Asian American, 1% Hispanic American, 2% Native American
- 31 degree-seeking graduate students

General. Founded in 1965. Regionally accredited. Additional centers in Rockland, Brunswick, Rumford, Saco, Ellsworth, South Paris, East Millinocket; additional campus in Bangor. **Degrees:** 336 bachelor's, 257 associate awarded. **ROTC:** Army, Naval, Air Force. **Location:** 2 miles from downtown, 65 miles from Portland. **Calendar:** Semester, extensive summer session. **Full-time faculty:** 104 total; 52% have terminal degrees, 58% women. **Part-time faculty:** 186 total; 1% minority, 54% women. **Class size:** 70% < 20, 27% 20-39, less than 1% 40-49, 3% 50-99. **Special facilities:** Holocaust and human rights center.

Freshman class profile. 948 applied, 907 admitted, 609 enrolled.

Return as sophomores: 54% **Out-of-state:** 26%

Basis for selection. Open admission, but selective for some programs. High school achievement record and test scores considered for admission to allied health and bachelor's degree programs. Talent/ability assessed for admission to music programs. TOEFL is requested of non-native English speakers. Interviews required of dental hygiene and medical laboratory technology majors. Audition required of music majors. **Home schooled:** Transcript of courses and grades required. Documentation of high school completion required.

High school preparation. College-preparatory program recommended. Recommended units include English 4, mathematics 2, social studies 2, history 2, science 2 (laboratory 2). Applicants to health science programs must have biology, chemistry, and Algebra II. Business administration and public administration applicants must have Algebra II and geometry.

2011-2012 Annual costs. Tuition/fees: $7,447; $16,687 out-of-state. New England Regional Student Program tuition is $9,750. Books/supplies: $1,040. Personal expenses: $1,800.

2011-2012 Financial aid. Need-based: 376 full-time freshmen applied for aid; 364 were judged to have need; 354 of these received aid. Average need met was 59%. Average scholarship/grant was $5,695; average loan $6,119. 45% of total undergraduate aid awarded as scholarships/grants, 55% as loans/jobs. **Non-need-based:** Awarded to 21 full-time undergraduates, including 2 freshmen. Scholarships awarded for academics, athletics, leadership, music/drama, state residency.

Application procedures. Admission: Priority date 6/15; deadline 8/1 (receipt date). $40 fee, may be waived for applicants with need. Admission notification on a rolling basis. Must reply by May 1 or within 2 week(s) if notified thereafter. **Financial aid:** Priority date 3/1; no closing date. FAFSA required. Applicants notified on a rolling basis starting 3/15; must reply within 2 week(s) of notification.

Academics. Special study options: Combined bachelor's/graduate degree, cross-registration, distance learning, double major, dual enrollment of high school students, honors, independent study, internships, liberal arts/career combination, student-designed major, study abroad. **Credit/placement by examination:** AP, CLEP, institutional tests. 45 credit hours maximum toward associate degree, 90 toward bachelor's. **Support services:** Reduced course load, remedial instruction, study skills assistance, tutoring.

Majors. Architecture: Technology. **Biology:** General. **Business:** Accounting, business admin, financial planning. **Computer sciences:** General. **English:** English lit. **Health services:** Dental hygiene, nursing (RN). **Human services:** General. **Liberal arts:** Library science. **Protective services:** Law enforcement admin. **Social sciences:** General. **Visual/performing arts:** Music, studio arts.

Most popular majors. Business/marketing 10%, computer/information sciences 6%, health sciences 42%, liberal arts 16%, library sciences 7%, security/protective services 7%.

Computing on campus. 415 workstations in library, computer center, student center. Commuter students can connect to campus network. Online course registration, online library, student web hosting, wireless network available.

Student life. Freshman orientation: Available. Preregistration for classes offered. One-day program held 1 week prior to start of each semester and mid-summer. **Activities:** Bands, drama, international student organizations, music ensembles, student government, student newspaper, Art and Architectural Student Association, Gay Lesbian Bisexual Transgender Friends and Associates, Honors English Program, English Society, Student Nursing Association, Pi Alpha Alpha, College Republicans, Mental Health and Human Services Club, Campus Crusade for Christ.

Athletics. USCAA. **Intercollegiate:** Basketball, bowling, cross-country, golf, soccer. **Intramural:** Basketball, racquetball, soccer. **Team name:** Moose.

Student services. Adult student services, alcohol/substance abuse counseling, career counseling, services for economically disadvantaged, financial aid counseling, personal counseling, veterans' counselor. **Physically disabled:** Services for visually, hearing impaired.

Contact. E-mail: umaadm@maine.edu
Phone: (207) 621-3465 Toll-free number: (877) 862-1234
Fax: (207) 621-3333
Jonathan Henry, Vice President of Enrollment Management and Director of Admissions, University of Maine at Augusta, 46 University Drive, Augusta, ME 04330

University of Maine at Farmington
Farmington, Maine
www.farmington.edu

CB member
CB code: 3506

- Public 4-year liberal arts and teachers college
- Residential campus in small town
- 2,198 degree-seeking undergraduates: 10% part-time, 65% women, 1% African American, 1% Asian American, 1% Hispanic American
- 40 degree-seeking graduate students
- 82% of applicants admitted
- Application essay required
- 58% graduate within 6 years

General. Founded in 1863. Regionally accredited. **Degrees:** 391 bachelor's awarded; master's offered. **Location:** 38 miles from Augusta, 80 miles from Portland. **Calendar:** Semester, extensive summer session. **Full-time faculty:** 124 total; 90% have terminal degrees, 6% minority, 55% women. **Part-time faculty:** 64 total; 44% have terminal degrees, 3% minority, 66% women. **Class size:** 68% < 20, 30% 20-39, less than 1% 40-49, 1% 50-99. **Special facilities:** Archaeology research center, campus-wide wireless laptop network, 24/7 computer center, on-site nursery school, day care center teaching labs, multi-media graphics lab, observatory.

Freshman class profile. 1,580 applied, 1,291 admitted, 483 enrolled.

Mid 50% test scores			
SAT critical reading:	440-570	Rank in top tenth:	11%
SAT math:	440-540	Return as sophomores:	74%
SAT writing:	460-570	Out-of-state:	18%
Rank in top quarter:	38%	Live on campus:	84%

Basis for selection. School achievement record and recommendation most important. School and community activities, interviews and personal essay also important. On-campus placement tests required for those with SAT scores below 490 Verbal, 450 Math. Interview recommended. 13-15 page writing sample required for Creative Writing BFA. **Home schooled:** Transcript of courses and grades, state high school equivalency certificate required. **Learning Disabled:** Students may submit disclosure of learning disability to learning center after admission.

High school preparation. College-preparatory program required. 19 units recommended. Required and recommended units include English 4, mathematics 3-4, social studies 2-3, science 2-3 (laboratory 2-3), foreign language 2-3 and academic electives 3. Algebra I and II and geometry required. Two years of same foreign language required. General college preparatory program required for all except those admitted to Liberal Studies Bridge.

2011-2012 Annual costs. Tuition/fees: $9,137; $18,225 out-of-state. New England Regional Student Program tuition and fees: $12,544. Room/board: $8,168. Books/supplies: $832. Personal expenses: $2,163.

2010-2011 Financial aid. Need-based: 538 full-time freshmen applied for aid; 468 were judged to have need; 463 of these received aid. Average

need met was 75%. Average scholarship/grant was $7,506; average loan $3,462. 46% of total undergraduate aid awarded as scholarships/grants, 54% as loans/jobs. **Non-need-based:** Awarded to 250 full-time undergraduates, including 69 freshmen. Scholarships awarded for academics, leadership, minority status, state residency. **Additional information:** Federal processor must receive FAFSA by 3/1.

Application procedures. Admission: No deadline. $40 fee, may be waived for applicants with need. Admission notification on a rolling basis beginning on or about 12/15. Must reply by May 1 or within 3 week(s) if notified thereafter. **Financial aid:** Priority date 3/1; no closing date. FAFSA required. Applicants notified on a rolling basis starting 3/15; must reply within 2 week(s) of notification.

Academics. Interdisciplinary first year seminar. **Special study options:** Accelerated study, cross-registration, distance learning, double major, dual enrollment of high school students, exchange student, honors, independent study, internships, liberal arts/career combination, semester at sea, student-designed major, study abroad, teacher certification program. **Credit/placement by examination:** AP, CLEP, IB, SAT, institutional tests. 16 credit hours maximum toward bachelor's degree. CLEP tests must have been taken prior to matriculation. **Support services:** Learning center, pre-admission summer program, reduced course load, remedial instruction, study skills assistance, tutoring, writing center.

Majors. Area/ethnic studies: Women's. **Biology:** General. **Business:** Managerial economics. **Computer sciences:** Computer science. **Conservation:** Environmental science, land use planning. **Education:** Biology, early childhood, early childhood special, elementary, English, health, kindergarten/preschool, mathematics, science, secondary, social science, special ed. **English:** Creative writing, English lit. **Health services:** Community health, public health ed. **History:** General. **Math:** General. **Physical sciences:** Geochemistry, geology. **Psychology:** General. **Social sciences:** Anthropology, geography, political science. **Visual/performing arts:** Art, dramatic, music, music management, studio arts management, theater arts management.

Most popular majors. Business/marketing 6%, education 51%, English 9%, psychology 15%, social sciences 9%.

Computing on campus. 180 workstations in library, computer center, student center. Dormitories wired for high-speed internet access and linked to campus network. Commuter students can connect to campus network. Online course registration, online library, helpline, wireless network available.

Student life. Freshman orientation: Available, $175 fee. Preregistration for classes offered. Held immmediately before classes; includes outdoor activities and community service. **Housing:** Guaranteed on-campus for freshmen. Coed dorms, single-sex dorms, special housing for disabled, wellness housing available. Housing for students maintaining certain GPA, medical single rooms, quiet floors, wellness community, independent living environment housing available. **Activities:** Concert band, choral groups, dance, drama, literary magazine, music ensembles, radio station, student government, student newspaper, symphony orchestra, Justice Uniting Students Together, student environmental and political awareness club, Amnesty International, Inter-Varsity Christian Fellowship, student alcohol educators, student admissions club, Alpha Phi Omega, literary guild, Newman Club, student-run entertainment board.

Athletics. NCAA. **Intercollegiate:** Baseball M, basketball, cross-country, field hockey W, golf, soccer, softball W, volleyball W. **Intramural:** Basketball, football (non-tackle), soccer, softball, swimming, tennis, volleyball. **Team name:** Beavers.

Student services. Alcohol/substance abuse counseling, career counseling, services for economically disadvantaged, student employment services, financial aid counseling, health services, on-campus daycare, personal counseling, placement for graduates, veterans' counselor, women's services. **Physically disabled:** Services for visually, hearing impaired.

Contact. E-mail: umfadmit@maine.edu
Phone: (207) 778-7050 Fax: (207) 778-8182
Jamie Marcus, Director of Admission, University of Maine at Farmington, 246 Main Street, Farmington, ME 04938

University of Maine at Fort Kent
Fort Kent, Maine
www.umfk.maine.edu

CB member
CB code: 3393

- Public 4-year university and branch campus college
- Commuter campus in small town
- 756 degree-seeking undergraduates: 26% part-time, 64% women, 2% African American, 1% Hispanic American, 1% Native American, 10% international

- 69% of applicants admitted
- Application essay required
- 34% graduate within 6 years

General. Founded in 1878. Regionally accredited. Bilingual Franco-American region. **Degrees:** 177 bachelor's, 18 associate awarded. **Location:** 200 miles from Bangor, 21 miles from Edmundston, Canada. **Calendar:** Semester, extensive summer session. **Full-time faculty:** 36 total; 92% have terminal degrees, 8% minority, 47% women. **Part-time faculty:** 39 total; 10% have terminal degrees, 62% women. **Class size:** 59% < 20, 38% 20-39, 3% 40-49. **Special facilities:** 16-acre biological park, Acadian Archives, interactive television site, Northern Maine Center for Rural Health Science, Center for Sustainable Rural Development.

Freshman class profile. 534 applied, 370 admitted, 166 enrolled.

Mid 50% test scores			
SAT critical reading:	400-510	Rank in top quarter:	8%
SAT math:	390-510	Rank in top tenth:	1%
SAT writing:	390-490	Return as sophomores:	59%
ACT composite:	17-25	Out-of-state:	95%
GPA 3.75 or higher:	8%	Live on campus:	57%
GPA 3.50-3.74:	13%	International:	13%
GPA 3.0-3.49:	45%	Fraternities:	1%
GPA 2.0-2.99:	29%	Sororities:	1%

Basis for selection. High school courses and achievement record most important. Recommendations considered. SAT, ACT scores, or on-campus placement exams required. SAT and SAT Subject Tests or ACT recommended. Interview recommended.

High school preparation. College-preparatory program recommended. 16 units required. Required and recommended units include English 4, mathematics 2, science 2 and foreign language 2. Biology and chemistry required for nursing and environmental studies.

2011-2012 Annual costs. Tuition/fees: $7,575; $17,535 out-of-state. New England Regional Student Program tuition is $9,900. Room/board: $7,400. Books/supplies: $1,000. Personal expenses: $1,000.

2010-2011 Financial aid. Need-based: 118 full-time freshmen applied for aid; 113 were judged to have need; 111 of these received aid. Average need met was 62%. Average scholarship/grant was $5,884; average loan $1,000. 84% of total undergraduate aid awarded as scholarships/grants, 16% as loans/jobs. **Non-need-based:** Awarded to 153 full-time undergraduates, including 54 freshmen. Scholarships awarded for academics, leadership.

Application procedures. Admission: No deadline. $40 fee, may be waived for applicants with need. Admission notification on a rolling basis. **Financial aid:** Priority date 3/1; no closing date. FAFSA, institutional form required. Applicants notified on a rolling basis starting 3/15.

Academics. Special study options: Accelerated study, cross-registration, distance learning, double major, honors, independent study, internships, liberal arts/career combination, student-designed major, study abroad, teacher certification program. **Credit/placement by examination:** AP, CLEP, IB, SAT, institutional tests. 30 credit hours maximum toward associate degree, 90 toward bachelor's. **Support services:** Learning center, pre-admission summer program, reduced course load, remedial instruction, tutoring, writing center.

Majors. Biology: General. **Business:** General, business admin, e-commerce, management information systems. **Computer sciences:** General, information technology. **Conservation:** Environmental science, management/policy. **Education:** General, business, elementary, English, multi-level teacher, music, science, secondary, social studies. **English:** American lit, British lit, English lit. **Foreign languages:** General, comparative lit, French. **Health services:** Nursing (RN). **Human services:** Social work. **Liberal arts:** Arts/sciences. **Psychology:** General. **Social sciences:** General.

Most popular majors. Biology 11%, business/marketing 11%, education 23%, health sciences 33%, social sciences 8%.

Computing on campus. 100 workstations in dormitories, library, computer center, student center. Dormitories wired for high-speed internet access and linked to campus network. Commuter students can connect to campus network. Online course registration, helpline, repair service, student web hosting, wireless network available.

Student life. Freshman orientation: Mandatory. Preregistration for classes offered. 3-day social and educational orientation; includes workshops. **Housing:** Coed dorms, special housing for disabled available. $100 fully refundable deposit, deadline 8/15. **Activities:** Campus ministries, choral groups, drama, international student organizations, literary magazine, music ensembles, musical theater, student government, student newspaper, Christian Fellowship, Newman Club.

Athletics. NAIA. **Intercollegiate:** Basketball, skiing, soccer, volleyball W. **Intramural:** Baseball, basketball, golf, ice hockey M, racquetball, skiing, soccer, softball, table tennis, tennis, volleyball, weight lifting. **Team name:** Bengals.

Student services. Adult student services, alcohol/substance abuse counseling, career counseling, services for economically disadvantaged, financial aid counseling, health services, personal counseling, placement for graduates, veterans' counselor. **Physically disabled:** Services for visually, speech, hearing impaired.

Contact. E-mail: umfkadm@maine.edu
Phone: (888) 879-8635 Toll-free number: (888) 879-8635
Fax: (207) 834-7609
Jill Cairns, Director of Admissions, University of Maine at Fort Kent, 23 University Drive, Fort Kent, ME 04743

University of Maine at Machias
Machias, Maine
www.umm.maine.edu

CB member
CB code: 3956

- Public 4-year university and liberal arts college
- Commuter campus in rural community
- 863 undergraduates
- 79% of applicants admitted
- SAT or ACT (ACT writing optional), application essay required

General. Founded in 1909. Regionally accredited. **Degrees:** 79 bachelor's, 3 associate awarded. **Location:** 85 miles from Bangor, 65 miles from Bar Harbor. **Calendar:** Semester, limited summer session. **Full-time faculty:** 31 total; 81% have terminal degrees, 3% minority, 32% women. **Part-time faculty:** 37 total; 40% have terminal degrees, 3% minority. **Class size:** 78% < 20, 22% 20-39. **Special facilities:** Institute for applied marine research and education, mariculture student research facility, greenhouse, GIS lab, early childhood center, field station, international park, sail loft.

Freshman class profile. 405 applied, 320 admitted, 138 enrolled.

Mid 50% test scores			
SAT critical reading:	410-530	ACT composite:	17-24
SAT math:	400-510	Out-of-state:	23%
SAT writing:	390-520	Live on campus:	76%

Basis for selection. Applicants should rank in top half of class and have a B average. Recommendations and test scores important. Essay and outstanding nonacademic achievement (extracurricular, community, military, life, or work) considered. SAT/ACT not required of applicants for associate of science degree. Test score for fall-term admission must be received before first day of classes. Interview recommended. **Home schooled:** Statement describing home school structure and mission, transcript of courses and grades required. Records of all completed coursework plus documentation verifying proficiency in coursework (such as examples of writing, math skills). Portfolio beneficial for some coursework. Standardized test scores required; campus visit with interview important. **Learning Disabled:** Students evaluated on results of required college preparatory work. Documentation of disability important if seeking assistance from Student Resource Center.

High school preparation. College-preparatory program required. 11 units required. Required and recommended units include English 4, mathematics 3, social studies 2, science 2 (laboratory 2), foreign language 2, computer science 1 and academic electives 3. Social studies may include history. Computer applications, fine arts also recommended.

2011-2012 Annual costs. Tuition/fees: $7,480; $19,300 out-of-state. New England Regional Student Program tuition is $9,990. Room/board: $7,648. Books/supplies: $800. Personal expenses: $1,600.

Financial aid. Non-need-based: Scholarships awarded for academics, alumni affiliation, art, athletics, job skills.

Application procedures. Admission: Closing date 8/15 (receipt date). $40 fee, may be waived for applicants with need. Admission notification on a rolling basis. Must reply by May 1 or within 2 week(s) if notified thereafter. **Financial aid:** Priority date 3/1; no closing date. FAFSA required. Applicants notified on a rolling basis starting 3/1.

Academics. Internships and/or cooperative education program available in business studies, recreation management, biology, environmental studies, and behavioral science. **Special study options:** Cooperative education, distance learning, double major, dual enrollment of high school students, independent study, internships, student-designed major, study abroad, teacher certification program. **Credit/placement by examination:** AP, CLEP, SAT, ACT, institutional tests. **Support services:** Learning center, reduced course load, remedial instruction, study skills assistance, tutoring, writing center.

Majors. Biology: General, ecology, marine. **Business:** General, accounting, business admin, hospitality admin, hospitality/recreation, marketing, office management, office/clerical, tourism promotion, tourism/travel. **Conservation:** General, environmental studies. **Education:** Elementary, secondary. **English:** English lit. **Health services:** Mental health services. **History:** General. **Liberal arts:** Arts/sciences. **Parks/recreation:** General, facilities management. **Psychology:** General. **Visual/performing arts:** General.

Most popular majors. Biology 22%, business/marketing 10%, education 10%, interdisciplinary studies 22%, liberal arts 6%, natural resources/environmental science 6%, parks/recreation 14%.

Computing on campus. 117 workstations in dormitories, library, computer center. Dormitories wired for high-speed internet access and linked to campus network. Commuter students can connect to campus network. Online course registration, online library, helpline, repair service, wireless network available.

Student life. Freshman orientation: Available. Preregistration for classes offered. Orientation in June, August, and January. **Policies:** Students over 21 may drink in their rooms. Firearms must be stored in safe in Resident Director's office. **Housing:** Guaranteed on-campus for all undergraduates. Coed dorms, wellness housing available. $100 nonrefundable deposit. Pets allowed in dorm rooms. **Activities:** Bands, choral groups, dance, drama, international student organizations, literary magazine, music ensembles, musical theater, radio station, student government, Newman Club, Students of Service.

Athletics. NAIA. **Intercollegiate:** Basketball, cross-country, soccer, volleyball W. **Intramural:** Basketball, cheerleading W, fencing, football (non-tackle), soccer, softball W, water polo. **Team name:** Clippers.

Student services. Career counseling, student employment services, financial aid counseling, health services, on-campus daycare, personal counseling, placement for graduates, veterans' counselor.

Contact. E-mail: ummadmissions@maine.edu
Phone: (207) 255-1318 Toll-free number: (888) 468-6866
Fax: (207) 255-1363
David Dollins, Director of Admissions, University of Maine at Machias, 116 O'Brien Avenue, Machias, ME 04654-1397

University of Maine at Presque Isle
Presque Isle, Maine — **CB member**
www.umpi.edu — **CB code: 3008**

- Public 4-year university
- Commuter campus in small town
- 1,027 degree-seeking undergraduates: 21% part-time, 59% women, 1% African American, 1% Hispanic American, 5% Native American, 11% international
- 82% of applicants admitted
- Application essay required
- 30% graduate within 6 years

General. Founded in 1903. Regionally accredited. **Degrees:** 230 bachelor's, 14 associate awarded. **Location:** 165 miles from Bangor. **Calendar:** Semester, limited summer session. **Full-time faculty:** 45 total. **Part-time faculty:** 58 total. **Class size:** 63% < 20, 37% 20-39. **Special facilities:** Climbing wall, kinesiology laboratory, museum of science.

Freshman class profile. 504 applied, 411 admitted, 199 enrolled.

Mid 50% test scores			
SAT critical reading:	390-530	Rank in top quarter:	23%
SAT math:	390-530	Rank in top tenth:	8%
GPA 3.75 or higher:	12%	Return as sophomores:	63%
GPA 3.50-3.74:	9%	Out-of-state:	4%
GPA 3.0-3.49:	38%	Live on campus:	18%
GPA 2.0-2.99:	40%	International:	4%

Basis for selection. Admissions based on secondary school record, class rank, recommendations, and essay. Interview recommended for academically borderline. Portfolio required of bachelor of fine arts applicants. **Home schooled:** Transcript of courses and grades, letter of recommendation (non-parent) required.

High school preparation. College-preparatory program recommended. 16 units required. Required units include English 4, mathematics 3, social studies 3, science 2 (laboratory 2), foreign language 2 and academic electives 2. Medical laboratory technology and nursing programs: 4 English, 1 biology w/lab, 1 chemistry w/lab, 2 math, 1 social studies, 6 electives, totaling 15.

2011-2012 Annual costs. Tuition/fees: $7,300; $17,260 out-of-state. New England Regional Student Program tuition is $9,900. Room/board: $7,172. Books/supplies: $900. Personal expenses: $1,100.

2011-2012 Financial aid. Need-based: 172 full-time freshmen applied for aid; 156 were judged to have need; 156 of these received aid. Average need met was 84%. Average scholarship/grant was $5,367; average loan $4,829. 56% of total undergraduate aid awarded as scholarships/grants, 44% as loans/jobs. **Non-need-based:** Awarded to 347 full-time undergraduates, including 127 freshmen. Scholarships awarded for academics, alumni affiliation, art, job skills, leadership, minority status, music/drama, state residency.

Application procedures. Admission: No deadline. $40 fee, may be waived for applicants with need. Admission notification on a rolling basis. **Financial aid:** Priority date 4/1; no closing date. FAFSA required. Applicants notified on a rolling basis starting 3/1; must reply within 2 week(s) of notification.

Academics. Special study options: Accelerated study, combined bachelor's/graduate degree, cross-registration, distance learning, double major, exchange student, honors, independent study, internships, semester at sea, student-designed major, study abroad, teacher certification program. **Credit/placement by examination:** AP, CLEP, IB, SAT, ACT, institutional tests. Scores of 3, 4, and 5 acceptable on AP tests; hours awarded decided on case-by-case basis. **Support services:** Learning center, reduced course load, remedial instruction, study skills assistance, tutoring, writing center.

Majors. Biology: General. **Business:** Business admin, communications. **Conservation:** Environmental studies. **Education:** General, art, elementary, physical, secondary. **English:** English lit. **Health services:** Athletic training. **History:** General. **Human services:** Social work. **Liberal arts:** Arts/sciences. **Math:** General. **Parks/recreation:** General. **Physical sciences:** Geology. **Protective services:** Criminal justice. **Psychology:** General. **Social sciences:** Political science, sociology. **Visual/performing arts:** Art, studio arts.

Most popular majors. Business/marketing 11%, education 30%, liberal arts 26%, public administration/social services 6%.

Computing on campus. 120 workstations in library, computer center. Dormitories wired for high-speed internet access and linked to campus network. Commuter students can connect to campus network. Helpline available.

Student life. Freshman orientation: Mandatory. Preregistration for classes offered. Held the Friday prior to opening. **Policies:** Campus smoking policy: allowed in gazebos only. **Housing:** Guaranteed on-campus for all undergraduates. Coed dorms, special housing for disabled, apartments, fraternity/sorority housing, wellness housing available. $100 deposit, deadline 8/1. **Activities:** Concert band, campus ministries, choral groups, dance, international student organizations, radio station, student government, student newspaper, Campus Crusade for Christ, Fellowship of Christian Athletes, Presque Isle Student Ministries, College Republicans, College Democrats, Kappa Delta Phi, Kappa Delta Phi NAS, Phi Eta Sigma National Honors Society, international students club.

Athletics. NCAA. **Intercollegiate:** Baseball M, basketball, cross-country, golf M, skiing, soccer, softball W, volleyball W. **Intramural:** Baseball, basketball, football (non-tackle), soccer, softball, tennis, volleyball. **Team name:** Owls.

Student services. Adult student services, alcohol/substance abuse counseling, chaplain/spiritual director, career counseling, student employment services, financial aid counseling, health services, on-campus daycare, personal counseling, placement for graduates, veterans' counselor. **Physically disabled:** Services for visually, speech, hearing impaired.

Contact. E-mail: admissions@umpi.edu
Phone: (207) 768-9532 Fax: (207) 768-9777
Erin Benson, Director of Admissions, University of Maine at Presque Isle, 181 Main Street, Presque Isle, ME 04769

University of New England
Biddeford, Maine — **CB member**
www.une.edu — **CB code: 3751**

- Private 4-year university
- Residential campus in small city
- 2,231 degree-seeking undergraduates: 3% part-time, 68% women, 1% African American, 2% Asian American, 1% Hispanic American, 1% international
- 2,756 degree-seeking graduate students
- 82% of applicants admitted
- SAT or ACT (ACT writing optional) required
- 57% graduate within 6 years

General. Founded in 1831. Regionally accredited. **Degrees:** 389 bachelor's, 88 associate awarded; master's, professional offered. **ROTC:** Army. **Location:** 15 miles from Portland. **Calendar:** Semester, limited summer session. **Full-time faculty:** 246 total; 79% have terminal degrees, 5% minority. **Part-time faculty:** 194 total; 14% have terminal degrees, 5% minority. **Class size:** 44% < 20, 43% 20-39, 2% 40-49, 8% 50-99, 2% >100. **Special facilities:** Maine Women Writers collection, osteopathic center, performance enhancement and evaluation center, marine science education and research center.

Freshman class profile. 3,717 applied, 3,034 admitted, 640 enrolled.

Mid 50% test scores			
SAT critical reading:	470-570	GPA 3.0-3.49:	37%
SAT math:	490-590	GPA 2.0-2.99:	28%
ACT composite:	21-26	Return as sophomores:	75%
GPA 3.75 or higher:	16%	Out-of-state:	69%
GPA 3.50-3.74:	19%	Live on campus:	93%
		International:	1%

Basis for selection. School achievement record most important. Test scores, school, community activities considered. Exposure to health careers recommended if seeking admission to health science majors. Rigor of curriculum considered. Essay recommended. Interview required for nursing program, recommended for all, strongly recommended for academically weaker students. **Home schooled:** Statement describing home school structure and mission, transcript of courses and grades required.

High school preparation. College-preparatory program recommended. 16 units required; 20 recommended. Required and recommended units include English 4, mathematics 3-4, social studies 1-2, history 1-2, science 2-3 (laboratory 2-3), foreign language 2 and academic electives 2-4.

2011-2012 Annual costs. Tuition/fees: $30,500. Room/board: $12,020. Books/supplies: $1,350. Personal expenses: $1,400.

Financial aid. Non-need-based: Scholarships awarded for academics, alumni affiliation, leadership.

Application procedures. Admission: Priority date 12/1; deadline 2/15 (postmark date). $40 fee, may be waived for applicants with need. Admission notification on a rolling basis beginning on or about 12/15. Must reply by May 1 or within 4 week(s) if notified thereafter. **Financial aid:** Priority date 5/1; no closing date. FAFSA required. Applicants notified on a rolling basis starting 2/1.

Academics. Special study options: Combined bachelor's/graduate degree, cooperative education, cross-registration, distance learning, double major, dual enrollment of high school students, honors, independent study, internships, liberal arts/career combination, student-designed major, study abroad, teacher certification program. **Credit/placement by examination:** AP, CLEP, IB, SAT, ACT, institutional tests. **Support services:** Learning center, reduced course load, remedial instruction, study skills assistance, tutoring, writing center.

Majors. Biology: General, biochemistry, marine. **Business:** Business admin. **Conservation:** Environmental science, environmental studies. **Education:** General, art, elementary, leadership. **English:** English lit. **General:** Aquaculture. **Health services:** Athletic training, dental hygiene, health services admin, nursing (RN), substance abuse counseling. **History:** General. **Liberal arts:** Arts/sciences. **Math:** General. **Parks/recreation:** Exercise sciences, sports admin. **Physical sciences:** Chemistry. **Psychology:** General, psychobiology, social. **Social sciences:** Political science, sociology.

Most popular majors. Biology 24%, health sciences 28%, parks/recreation 15%, psychology 11%.

Computing on campus. 170 workstations in dormitories, library, computer center, student center. Dormitories wired for high-speed internet access and linked to campus network. Commuter students can connect to campus network. Online course registration, online library, helpline, student web hosting, wireless network available.

Student life. Freshman orientation: Mandatory. Preregistration for classes offered. **Housing:** Guaranteed on-campus for freshmen. Coed dorms, single-sex dorms, wellness housing available. $200 partly refundable deposit, deadline 5/1. **Activities:** Literary magazine, student government, student newspaper, Earth's ECO, Rotoract, Marine Animal Stranding Helpline, Make A Wish, EMS, campus diversity club, Intervarsity Christian Fellowship, Cross Seekers, Habitat for Humanity, College Democrats.

Athletics. NCAA. **Intercollegiate:** Basketball, cross-country, field hockey W, golf M, lacrosse, soccer, softball W, swimming W, volleyball W. **Intramural:** Basketball, gymnastics, racquetball, soccer, softball, table tennis, volleyball W, water polo. **Team name:** Nor-easters.

Student services. Adult student services, alcohol/substance abuse counseling, chaplain/spiritual director, career counseling, student employment services, financial aid counseling, health services, minority student services, personal counseling, veterans' counselor.

Contact. E-mail: admissions@une.edu
Phone: (207) 283-0170 ext. 2297 Toll-free number: (800) 477-4863
Fax: (207) 602-5900
Robert Pecchia, Associate Dean of Admissions, University of New England, Hills Beach Road, Biddeford, ME 04005

University of Southern Maine
Portland, Maine
www.usm.maine.edu

CB member
CB code: 3691

- Public 4-year university and liberal arts college
- Commuter campus in small city
- 6,378 degree-seeking undergraduates
- 78% of applicants admitted
- SAT or ACT with writing, application essay required

General. Founded in 1878. Regionally accredited. **Degrees:** 1,317 bachelor's, 2 associate awarded; master's, professional, doctoral offered. **ROTC:** Army, Air Force. **Location:** 110 miles from Boston. **Calendar:** Semester, extensive summer session. **Full-time faculty:** 370 total; 85% have terminal degrees, 4% minority. **Part-time faculty:** 273 total; 24% have terminal degrees, 2% minority. **Class size:** 41% < 20, 49% 20-39, 7% 40-49, 2% 50-99, less than 1% >100. **Special facilities:** Planetarium, cartographic collection, Olympic-sized ice arena.

Freshman class profile. 4,351 applied, 3,394 admitted, 848 enrolled.

Mid 50% test scores			
SAT critical reading:	440-550	GPA 2.0-2.99:	47%
SAT math:	440-550	Rank in top quarter:	31%
SAT writing:	440-550	Rank in top tenth:	9%
ACT composite:	19-22	Out-of-state:	16%
GPA 3.75 or higher:	8%	Live on campus:	59%
GPA 3.50-3.74:	14%	Fraternities:	2%
GPA 3.0-3.49:	31%	Sororities:	2%

Basis for selection. Level and content of academic program with performance or achievement record, class rank, and standardized test scores most important. Counselor recommendation, essay, and experience outside classroom also important. Interview recommended for all. Audition required of music majors. **Home schooled:** Transcript of courses and grades, letter of recommendation (nonparent) required. SAT or ACT, annual assessment of courses, and GED required for financial aid purposes. **Learning Disabled:** Must be otherwise qualified for admission; may be asked to provide documentation.

High school preparation. 16 units required. Required and recommended units include English 4, mathematics 3-4, social studies 2-3, history 2-3, science 2-3 (laboratory 2-3) and foreign language 2-3. 3 lab sciences for science majors. Math, business and electrical engineering majors require 4 years of math.

2011-2012 Annual costs. Tuition/fees: $8,540; $20,900 out-of-state. New England Regional Student Program tuition is $11,400. Room/board: $9,287. Books/supplies: $1,232. Personal expenses: $2,000.

Financial aid. Non-need-based: Scholarships awarded for academics, music/drama.

Application procedures. Admission: Priority date 2/15; no deadline. $40 fee, may be waived for applicants with need. Admission notification on a rolling basis beginning on or about 1/1. Must reply by May 1 or within 2 week(s) if notified thereafter. **Financial aid:** Priority date 2/15; no closing date. FAFSA required. Applicants notified on a rolling basis starting 3/15; must reply by 5/1 or within 2 week(s) of notification.

Academics. Special study options: Accelerated study, combined bachelor's/graduate degree, cooperative education, cross-registration, distance learning, double major, ESL, exchange student, honors, independent study, internships, liberal arts/career combination, semester at sea, student-designed major, study abroad, teacher certification program, Washington semester, weekend college. Preengineering program with University of Maine at Orono, living/learning scholars program, Greater Portland Alliance; cross registration with University of New England, St. Joseph's (Maine), Southern Maine Technical College, and Maine College of Art. **Credit/placement by examination:** AP, CLEP, IB, SAT, ACT, institutional tests. No numerical limit. Students must meet all course requirements and 30 credit residency for BA/BS and 15 credit residency for AA/AS degrees. **Support services:** Learning center, reduced course load, remedial instruction, study skills assistance, tutoring, writing center.

Honors college/program. Honors application required. Several course options available. Interdisciplinary curriculum with small seminar classes.

Majors. **Area/ethnic studies:** Chicano/Hispanic-American/Latino, French, Russian/Slavic, women's. **Biology:** General, biotechnology. **Business:** General, accounting, accounting/finance, business admin, finance, management information systems, marketing, organizational behavior. **Communications:** Communications/speech/rhetoric, media studies. **Computer sciences:** General, applications programming, computer science, programming. **Conservation:** Environmental science, environmental studies. **Education:** Art, elementary, mathematics, music, technology/industrial arts, voc/tech. **Engineering:** Electrical, mechanical. **English:** English lit, writing. **Foreign languages:** General, classics, French, linguistics. **Health services:** Athletic training, environmental health, medical radiologic technology/radiation therapy, nursing (RN), pediatric nursing, predental, premedicine, preop/surgical nursing, preveterinary, psychiatric nursing, recreational therapy. **History:** General. **Human services:** Social work. **Liberal arts:** Arts/sciences, humanities. **Math:** General. **Parks/recreation:** General, exercise sciences. **Philosophy/religion:** Philosophy. **Physical sciences:** Chemistry, geology, physics. **Psychology:** General. **Social sciences:** General, anthropology, criminology, economics, geography, international relations, political science, sociology. **Visual/performing arts:** General, acting, art, art history/conservation, directing/producing, dramatic, drawing, jazz, music, music performance, painting, piano/keyboard, sculpture, stringed instruments, studio arts, studio arts management, theater arts management, voice/opera.

Most popular majors. Business/marketing 17%, communications/journalism 9%, health sciences 18%, psychology 7%, social sciences 16%.

Computing on campus. 219 workstations in dormitories, library, computer center, student center. Dormitories wired for high-speed internet access and linked to campus network. Commuter students can connect to campus network. Online course registration, helpline, repair service, wireless network available.

Student life. Freshman orientation: Mandatory. Preregistration for classes offered. Sessions in summer and fall. **Policies:** Smoking is not allowed within 50 feet of any dormitory. **Housing:** Coed dorms, special housing for disabled, apartments, fraternity/sorority housing, wellness housing available. $75 partly refundable deposit, deadline 5/1. **Activities:** Bands, choral groups, dance, drama, international student organizations, literary magazine, music ensembles, musical theater, opera, radio station, student government, student newspaper, symphony orchestra, TV station, American Indian student association, Environmental Coalition, College Republicans, Alliance of Sexual Diversity, Women's Forum, Bahai Association, ethnic student association.

Athletics. NCAA. **Intercollegiate:** Baseball M, basketball, cheerleading, cross-country, field hockey W, golf, ice hockey, lacrosse, soccer, softball W, tennis, track and field, volleyball W, wrestling M. **Intramural:** Basketball, cheerleading W, football (non-tackle), football (tackle) M, ice hockey, lacrosse, racquetball, rugby, sailing, skiing, soccer, softball, squash, table tennis, tennis, volleyball, weight lifting. **Team name:** Huskies.

Student services. Adult student services, alcohol/substance abuse counseling, chaplain/spiritual director, career counseling, services for economically disadvantaged, student employment services, financial aid counseling, health services, legal services, minority student services, on-campus daycare, personal counseling, placement for graduates, veterans' counselor, women's services. **Physically disabled:** Services for visually, speech, hearing impaired.

Contact. E-mail: usmadm@usm.maine.edu
Phone: (207) 780-5670 Toll-free number: (800) 800-4876 ext. 5670
Fax: (207) 780-5640
Susan Campbell, Dean of Undergraduate Admission, University of Southern Maine, PO Box 9300, Portland, ME 04104

Maryland

Bowie State University

Bowie, Maryland
www.bowiestate.edu

CB member
CB code: 5401

- Public 4-year university
- Commuter campus in small city
- 4,392 degree-seeking undergraduates: 17% part-time, 61% women, 91% African American, 2% Asian American, 2% Hispanic American
- 1,156 degree-seeking graduate students
- SAT or ACT (ACT writing optional) required
- 37% graduate within 6 years

General. Founded in 1865. Regionally accredited. Limited courses offered at off-site locations. **Degrees:** 683 bachelor's awarded; master's, doctoral offered. **ROTC:** Army, Air Force. **Location:** 25 miles from Baltimore, 20 miles from Washington, DC. **Calendar:** Semester, extensive summer session. **Full-time faculty:** 229 total; 93% have terminal degrees, 78% minority, 49% women. **Part-time faculty:** 184 total; 32% have terminal degrees, 74% minority, 50% women. **Class size:** 45% < 20, 50% 20-39, 5% 40-49, less than 1% 50-99. **Special facilities:** NASA operations and control center, art gallery, green house, super computer center (limited access).

Freshman class profile.

Mid 50% test scores			
SAT critical reading:	460-800	GPA 3.0-3.49:	24%
SAT math:	470-800	GPA 2.0-2.99:	60%
SAT writing:	430-800	Live on campus:	92%
GPA 3.75 or higher:	4%	Fraternities:	1%
GPA 3.50-3.74:	6%	Sororities:	3%

Basis for selection. School achievement record in college-preparatory curriculum, test scores, minimum GPA of 2.0, counselor/school recommendation important. Audition required for music program. Portfolio required for art program. Praxis I required for education program. **Home schooled:** Statement describing home school structure and mission required.

High school preparation. Required units include English 4, mathematics 3, social studies 1, history 2, science 3 and foreign language 2.

2011-2012 Annual costs. Tuition/fees: $6,347; $16,888 out-of-state. Room/board: $8,340. Books/supplies: $1,338. Personal expenses: $1,804.

2011-2012 Financial aid. Need-based: Average need met was 45%. Average scholarship/grant was $6,831; average loan $3,425. 47% of total undergraduate aid awarded as scholarships/grants, 53% as loans/jobs. **Non-need-based:** Scholarships awarded for academics, alumni affiliation, art, athletics, leadership, music/drama, ROTC, state residency.

Application procedures. Admission: No deadline. $40 fee, may be waived for applicants with need. Admission notification on a rolling basis. **Financial aid:** Closing date 3/1. FAFSA required. Applicants notified on a rolling basis starting 4/1; must reply within 2 week(s) of notification.

Academics. Special study options: Combined bachelor's/graduate degree, cooperative education, cross-registration, distance learning, double major, dual enrollment of high school students, exchange student, honors, independent study, internships, liberal arts/career combination, study abroad, teacher certification program. Dual degree programs in engineering and dentistry with cooperating universities. **Credit/placement by examination:** AP, CLEP, institutional tests. 60 credit hours maximum toward bachelor's degree. **Support services:** Learning center, pre-admission summer program, reduced course load, remedial instruction, tutoring, writing center.

Majors. Biology: General. **Business:** Business admin. **Communications technology:** Radio/TV. **Computer sciences:** Computer science. **Education:** Elementary, kindergarten/preschool, science. **English:** English lit. **Health services:** Nursing (RN). **History:** General. **Human services:** Social work. **Math:** General. **Psychology:** General. **Social sciences:** Sociology. **Visual/performing arts:** Art, dramatic. **Work/family studies:** Child development.

Most popular majors. Business/marketing 25%, communication technologies 13%, computer/information sciences 6%, English 12%, health sciences 7%, psychology 10%, public administration/social services 6%, social sciences 12%.

Computing on campus. 150 workstations in dormitories, library, computer center. Dormitories wired for high-speed internet access and linked to campus network. Commuter students can connect to campus network. Online course registration, online library, helpline, repair service, wireless network available.

Student life. Freshman orientation: Mandatory, $75 fee. Preregistration for classes offered. One-day session in the 2nd or 3rd week of August. **Policies:** Zero tolerance policy for illegal substance use and violence. Freshmen not permitted cars on campus. **Housing:** Coed dorms, single-sex dorms, apartments, wellness housing available. $150 fully refundable deposit, deadline 5/29. **Activities:** Bands, campus ministries, choral groups, dance, drama, international student organizations, music ensembles, musical theater, radio station, student government, student newspaper, TV station, NAACP, greater Washington urban league chapter, commuter senate.

Athletics. NCAA. **Intercollegiate:** Basketball, bowling W, cross-country, football (tackle) M, softball W, tennis W, track and field, volleyball W. **Intramural:** Basketball, football (non-tackle), golf, gymnastics, racquetball, soccer, softball, swimming, table tennis, tennis, volleyball, weight lifting. **Team name:** Bulldogs.

Student services. Adult student services, alcohol/substance abuse counseling, chaplain/spiritual director, career counseling, student employment services, financial aid counseling, health services, personal counseling, placement for graduates, veterans' counselor. **Physically disabled:** Services for visually, hearing impaired.

Contact. E-mail: dkiah@bowiestate.edu
Phone: (301) 860-3415 Fax: (301) 860-3438
Don Kiah, Assistant Vice President, Enrollment Management, Bowie State University, 14000 Jericho Park Road, Bowie, MD 20715

Capitol College

Laurel, Maryland
www.capitol-college.edu

CB code: 5101

- Private 4-year business and engineering college
- Commuter campus in large town
- 400 degree-seeking undergraduates
- 56% of applicants admitted
- SAT or ACT (ACT writing optional), application essay required

General. Founded in 1964. Regionally accredited. **Degrees:** 47 bachelor's awarded; master's offered. **ROTC:** Army. **Location:** 19 miles from Washington, DC, 22 miles from Baltimore. **Calendar:** Semester, limited summer session. **Full-time faculty:** 20 total. **Part-time faculty:** 60 total. **Special facilities:** Video lab, interactive computer classrooms, two engineering labs, telecommunications lab.

Freshman class profile. 344 applied, 193 admitted, 65 enrolled.

Basis for selection. Academic preparation, school record and test scores most important. Mathematics foundation necessary for successful completion of programs. Interview and essay recommended.

High school preparation. 20 units required. Required and recommended units include English 4, mathematics 3-4, social studies 2, history 2, science 1-3 (laboratory 1-2) and academic electives 2-3. Mathematic units include algebra I, geometry, algebra II/trigonometry. Calculus recommended for advanced standing.

2011-2012 Annual costs. Tuition/fees: $21,194. Room and board is based on a triple; institution no longer offers double rooms. Room only: $3,862. Books/supplies: $800. Personal expenses: $1,900.

Financial aid. Non-need-based: Scholarships awarded for academics, alumni affiliation, leadership, minority status.

Application procedures. Admission: Priority date 5/1; no deadline. $25 fee, may be waived for applicants with need, free for online applicants. Admission notification on a rolling basis beginning on or about 3/1. Must reply by May 1 or within 3 week(s) if notified thereafter. **Financial aid:** Priority date 2/1; no closing date. FAFSA, institutional form required. Applicants notified on a rolling basis starting 6/3; must reply by 5/1 or within 3 week(s) of notification.

Academics. Special study options: Combined bachelor's/graduate degree, cooperative education, distance learning, double major, independent study, liberal arts/career combination, weekend college. **Credit/placement by examination:** AP, CLEP, institutional tests. **Support services:** Learning center, pre-admission summer program, reduced course load, remedial instruction, tutoring.

Majors. Business: Business admin. **Computer sciences:** Computer science. **Engineering:** Computer, electrical, software.

Most popular majors. Business/marketing 12%, computer/information sciences 29%, engineering/engineering technologies 59%.

Computing on campus. 60 workstations in library, computer center. Dormitories wired for high-speed internet access and linked to campus network. Helpline, wireless network available.

Student life. Freshman orientation: Mandatory. Preregistration for classes offered. **Housing:** Coed dorms available. $200 deposit, deadline 5/1. **Activities:** Drama, literary magazine, radio station, student government, student newspaper, computer club, chess club, robotics club, music club, Society of Black Engineers, Society of Women Engineers.

Athletics. Intramural: Basketball M, boxing M, fencing M, golf M, soccer M, softball M, table tennis, tennis, track and field, volleyball, water polo.

Student services. Adult student services, career counseling, student employment services, personal counseling, placement for graduates, veterans' counselor.

Contact. E-mail: admissions@capitol-college.edu
Phone: (301) 369-2800 Toll-free number: (800) 950-1992
Fax: (301) 953-1442
George Walls, Director of Admissions, Capitol College, 11301 Springfield Road, Laurel, MD 20708

Coppin State University
Baltimore, Maryland **CB member**
www.coppin.edu **CB code: 5122**

- Public 4-year liberal arts college
- Commuter campus in very large city
- 3,208 degree-seeking undergraduates: 26% part-time, 76% women, 87% African American, 1% Asian American, 1% Hispanic American, 5% international
- 317 degree-seeking graduate students
- 35% of applicants admitted
- SAT or ACT (ACT writing optional) required

General. Founded in 1900. Regionally accredited. Manages Rosemont Elementary School; educational corridor between Coppin and selected elementary, middle, and high schools; mentorship program with elementary students. **Degrees:** 379 bachelor's awarded; master's offered. **ROTC:** Army. **Location:** 50 miles from Washington, DC. **Calendar:** Semester, extensive summer session. **Full-time faculty:** 162 total; 59% have terminal degrees, 56% women. **Part-time faculty:** 139 total; 20% have terminal degrees, 56% women.

Freshman class profile. 5,741 applied, 1,988 admitted, 528 enrolled.

Mid 50% test scores			
SAT critical reading:	400-470	GPA 3.0-3.49:	20%
SAT math:	400-460	GPA 2.0-2.99:	61%
GPA 3.75 or higher:	3%	Return as sophomores:	63%
GPA 3.50-3.74:	5%	Out-of-state:	16%
		International:	6%

Basis for selection. Minimum GPA of 2.5 and predictive index based on test scores and school achievement record. Essay recommended. Interview recommended for nursing majors. Portfolio recommended for art majors. **Home schooled:** Location must be certified by Maryland Department of Education.

High school preparation. 16 units required. Required units include English 4, mathematics 3, social studies 3, science 2 (laboratory 2) and foreign language 2. 2 years of advanced tech program courses can be substituted for foreign language requirement.

2011-2012 Annual costs. Tuition/fees: $5,491; $9,982 out-of-state. Room/board: $8,018. Books/supplies: $700. Personal expenses: $3,085.

Financial aid. Non-need-based: Scholarships awarded for academics, alumni affiliation, athletics, ROTC, state residency. **Additional information:** Funds allocated by State of Maryland for minority students enrolled for at least 6 credits who are Maryland residents and US citizens (Minority Grant).

Application procedures. Admission: Closing date 7/15. $35 fee, may be waived for applicants with need. Admission notification on a rolling basis beginning on or about 3/15. **Financial aid:** Priority date 3/1; no closing date. FAFSA required. Applicants notified on a rolling basis starting 4/15; must reply within 2 week(s) of notification.

Academics. Special study options: Accelerated study, combined bachelor's/graduate degree, cooperative education, distance learning, double major, dual enrollment of high school students, external degree, honors, independent study, internships, liberal arts/career combination, study abroad, teacher certification program, weekend college. 3-2 programs in engineering, pharmacy, dentistry, physical therapy. **Credit/placement by examination:** AP, CLEP, IB, SAT, institutional tests. 30 credit hours maximum toward bachelor's degree. **Support services:** Learning center, pre-admission summer program, remedial instruction, study skills assistance, tutoring, writing center.

Majors. Biology: General. **Business:** Management science. **Computer sciences:** Computer science. **Education:** Biology, chemistry, early childhood, elementary, mathematics, secondary, special ed. **English:** English lit. **Health services:** Medical records admin, nursing (RN). **History:** General. **Human services:** Social work. **Liberal arts:** Arts/sciences. **Math:** General. **Parks/recreation:** Sports admin. **Physical sciences:** Chemistry. **Protective services:** Criminal justice. **Psychology:** General. **Social sciences:** General, political science, sociology. **Visual/performing arts:** Art.

Computing on campus. 371 workstations in dormitories, library, computer center, student center. Dormitories wired for high-speed internet access and linked to campus network. Commuter students can connect to campus network. Online course registration, online library, helpline, repair service, student web hosting, wireless network available.

Student life. Freshman orientation: Mandatory. Preregistration for classes offered. **Housing:** Coed dorms, special housing for disabled, wellness housing available. $150 deposit. **Activities:** Campus ministries, choral groups, dance, drama, film society, international student organizations, music ensembles, radio station, student government, student newspaper, TV station, criminal justice club, gospel choir, history club, psychology club, Thurgood Marshall Club, social work association.

Athletics. NCAA. Intercollegiate: Baseball M, basketball, bowling W, cheerleading M, cross-country, golf W, softball W, tennis, track and field, volleyball W. **Intramural:** Basketball, football (non-tackle), softball, tennis, volleyball. **Team name:** Eagles.

Student services. Adult student services, alcohol/substance abuse counseling, career counseling, services for economically disadvantaged, student employment services, financial aid counseling, health services, minority student services, personal counseling, placement for graduates, veterans' counselor, women's services. **Physically disabled:** Services for visually, hearing impaired.

Contact. E-mail: admissions@coppin.edu
Phone: (410) 951-3600 Toll-free number: (800) 635-3674
Fax: (410) 523-7351
Michelle Gross, Director of Admissions, Coppin State University, 2500 West North Avenue, Baltimore, MD 21216

Frostburg State University
Frostburg, Maryland **CB member**
www.frostburg.edu **CB code: 5402**

- Public 4-year university and teachers college
- Residential campus in small town
- 4,617 degree-seeking undergraduates: 6% part-time, 49% women, 25% African American, 1% Asian American, 4% Hispanic American, 1% international
- 676 degree-seeking graduate students
- 55% of applicants admitted
- SAT or ACT (ACT writing optional) required
- 46% graduate within 6 years; 36% enter graduate study

General. Founded in 1898. Regionally accredited. Center in Hagerstown offers upper-division undergraduate and graduate courses. **Degrees:** 850 bachelor's awarded; master's offered. **Location:** 150 miles from Baltimore. **Calendar:** Semester, limited summer session. **Full-time faculty:** 247 total; 13% minority, 42% women. **Part-time faculty:** 122 total; 4% minority, 56% women. **Class size:** 50% < 20, 46% 20-39, 2% 40-49, 2% 50-99, less than 1% >100. **Special facilities:** Planetarium, arboretum, electron microscope, exploratorium.

Freshman class profile. 4,323 applied, 2,388 admitted, 828 enrolled.

Mid 50% test scores			
SAT critical reading:	440-540	GPA 2.0-2.99:	37%
SAT math:	440-540	Rank in top quarter:	29%
SAT writing:	420-520	Rank in top tenth:	11%
ACT composite:	17-21	Return as sophomores:	71%
GPA 3.75 or higher:	13%	Out-of-state:	7%
GPA 3.50-3.74:	14%	Live on campus:	77%
GPA 3.0-3.49:	36%	International:	1%

Basis for selection. High school record and SAT scores most important. Interview recommended. Audition required of music majors. Portfolio required of art majors.

High school preparation. 15 units required. Required units include English 4, mathematics 3, social studies 3, science 3 (laboratory 2) and foreign language 2.

2011-2012 Annual costs. Tuition/fees: $7,128; $17,020 out-of-state. Room/board: $7,648. Books/supplies: $750. Personal expenses: $900.

Financial aid. Non-need-based: Scholarships awarded for academics, leadership, minority status.

Application procedures. Admission: No deadline. $30 fee, may be waived for applicants with need. Admission notification on a rolling basis beginning on or about 11/1. Must reply by May 1 or within 4 week(s) if notified thereafter. **Financial aid:** Priority date 3/1; no closing date. FAFSA required. Applicants notified on a rolling basis starting 3/15; must reply within 3 week(s) of notification.

Academics. Special study options: Combined bachelor's/graduate degree, distance learning, double major, dual enrollment of high school students, honors, independent study, internships, study abroad, teacher certification program. International student exchange program, dual degree program, combined bachelor's program. **Credit/placement by examination:** AP, CLEP, IB, institutional tests. 30 credit hours maximum toward bachelor's degree. **Support services:** Learning center, reduced course load, remedial instruction, tutoring, writing center.

Majors. Architecture: Urban/community planning. **Biology:** General. **Business:** Accounting, business admin. **Communications:** Communications/ speech/rhetoric. **Computer sciences:** General, information systems, information technology. **Conservation:** General, environmental studies, fisheries, wildlife/wilderness. **Education:** Early childhood, elementary, English, mathematics, music, physical, social science. **Engineering:** General. **English:** English lit, rhetoric/composition. **Foreign languages:** General. **Health services:** Nursing (RN), predental, premedicine, prenursing, prepharmacy, preveterinary. **History:** General. **Human services:** Social work. **Liberal arts:** Arts/sciences. **Math:** General. **Parks/recreation:** General, exercise sciences, health/fitness, sports admin. **Philosophy/religion:** Philosophy. **Physical sciences:** Chemistry, physics. **Protective services:** Law enforcement admin, police science. **Psychology:** General. **Social sciences:** General, economics, geography, international relations, political science, sociology. **Visual/performing arts:** General, commercial/advertising art, dramatic, music, studio arts.

Most popular majors. Business/marketing 16%, education 11%, liberal arts 6%, parks/recreation 6%, psychology 9%, security/protective services 6%, social sciences 9%, visual/performing arts 7%.

Computing on campus. 668 workstations in dormitories, library, computer center, student center. Dormitories wired for high-speed internet access and linked to campus network. Commuter students can connect to campus network. Online course registration, online library, helpline, wireless network available.

Student life. Freshman orientation: Mandatory. Preregistration for classes offered. **Housing:** Coed dorms, single-sex dorms, special housing for disabled, wellness housing available. $100 deposit. **Activities:** Bands, campus ministries, choral groups, dance, drama, literary magazine, music ensembles, Model UN, radio station, student government, student newspaper, TV station, social, religious, political, and ethnic organizations.

Athletics. NCAA. **Intercollegiate:** Baseball M, basketball, cross-country, diving, field hockey W, football (tackle) M, lacrosse, soccer, softball W, swimming, tennis, track and field, volleyball W. **Intramural:** Basketball, field hockey, football (tackle), golf, lacrosse, racquetball, rugby M, soccer, softball, table tennis, tennis, volleyball, weight lifting, wrestling M. **Team name:** Bobcats.

Student services. Chaplain/spiritual director, career counseling, student employment services, health services, minority student services, on-campus daycare, personal counseling, placement for graduates, veterans' counselor. **Physically disabled:** Services for visually, speech, hearing impaired.

Contact. E-mail: fsuadmissions@frostburg.edu
Phone: (301) 687-4201 Fax: (301) 687-7074
Trish Gregory, Director of Admissions, Frostburg State University, 101 Braddock Road, Frostburg, MD 21532-1099

Goucher College

Baltimore, Maryland
www.goucher.edu

CB member
CB code: 5257

- Private 4-year liberal arts college
- Residential campus in small city
- 1,420 degree-seeking undergraduates: 2% part-time, 67% women, 10% African American, 4% Asian American, 6% Hispanic American, 1% Native American, 2% international
- 537 degree-seeking graduate students
- 73% of applicants admitted
- Application essay required
- 70% graduate within 6 years

General. Founded in 1885. Regionally accredited. Students are required to study abroad and are given a voucher of at least $1,200 to help offset travel expenses. **Degrees:** 331 bachelor's awarded; master's offered. **ROTC:** Army. **Location:** 8 miles from Baltimore. **Calendar:** Semester, limited summer session. **Full-time faculty:** 134 total; 16% minority, 62% women. **Part-time faculty:** 78 total; 9% minority, 64% women. **Class size:** 76% < 20, 22% 20-39, 2% 40-49, less than 1% 50-99.

Freshman class profile. 3,763 applied, 2,764 admitted, 367 enrolled.

Mid 50% test scores			
SAT critical reading:	510-660	GPA 2.0-2.99:	38%
SAT math:	500-610	Rank in top quarter:	55%
SAT writing:	510-640	Rank in top tenth:	28%
ACT composite:	22-28	Return as sophomores:	81%
GPA 3.75 or higher:	12%	Out-of-state:	77%
GPA 3.50-3.74:	8%	Live on campus:	97%
GPA 3.0-3.49:	42%	International:	2%

Basis for selection. Record in traditional college-preparatory program, secondary school record, and recommendations most important. Interview recommended. **Home schooled:** Statement describing home school structure and mission, transcript of courses and grades, state high school equivalency certificate, letter of recommendation (nonparent) required.

High school preparation. College-preparatory program required. 16 units required; 20 recommended. Required and recommended units include English 4, mathematics 3-4, social studies 3, science 2-3, foreign language 2-4 and academic electives 2.

2011-2012 Annual costs. Tuition/fees: $36,553. Room/board: $10,569. Books/supplies: $800. Personal expenses: $11,482.

2011-2012 Financial aid. Need-based: 291 full-time freshmen applied for aid; 237 were judged to have need; 237 of these received aid. Average need met was 74%. Average scholarship/grant was $23,604; average loan $3,193. 77% of total undergraduate aid awarded as scholarships/grants, 23% as loans/jobs. **Non-need-based:** Awarded to 331 full-time undergraduates, including 64 freshmen. Scholarships awarded for academics, art, leadership, music/drama.

Application procedures. Admission: Closing date 2/1 (postmark date). $55 fee, may be waived for applicants with need. Admission notification by 4/1. Must reply by 5/1. **Financial aid:** Closing date 2/1. FAFSA, CSS PROFILE required. Applicants notified by 4/1; Applicants notified on a rolling basis starting 3/1; must reply by 5/1 or within 2 week(s) of notification.

Academics. Special study options: Combined bachelor's/graduate degree, cross-registration, distance learning, double major, dual enrollment of high school students, independent study, internships, student-designed major, study abroad, teacher certification program, Washington semester. Community-Based Service, Service Learning. **Credit/placement by examination:** AP, CLEP, IB, SAT, ACT, institutional tests. 30 credit hours maximum toward bachelor's degree. **Support services:** Learning center, reduced course load, study skills assistance, tutoring, writing center.

Majors. Area/ethnic studies: American, women's. **Biology:** General, radiobiology. **Business:** Business admin. **Communications:** General. **Computer sciences:** Computer science. **Conservation:** Environmental studies. **Education:** General, special ed. **English:** English lit. **Foreign languages:** French, Russian, Spanish. **History:** General. **Math:** General. **Philosophy/religion:** Philosophy, religion. **Physical sciences:** Chemistry, physics. **Psychology:** General. **Social sciences:** Economics, international relations, political science, sociology, sociology/anthropology. **Visual/performing arts:** Art, dance, dramatic, music.

Most popular majors. Biology 7%, English 8%, foreign language 8%, psychology 14%, social sciences 16%, visual/performing arts 13%.

Computing on campus. 190 workstations in library, computer center, student center. Dormitories wired for high-speed internet access and linked to campus network. Commuter students can connect to campus network. Online course registration, online library, helpline, repair service, student web hosting, wireless network available.

Student life. Freshman orientation: Mandatory. Preregistration for classes offered. **Housing:** Guaranteed on-campus for freshmen. Coed dorms, single-sex dorms, special housing for disabled, apartments, wellness housing available. $100 nonrefundable deposit, deadline 5/1. **Activities:** Jazz band, campus ministries, choral groups, dance, drama, film society, international student organizations, literary magazine, music ensembles, Model UN, musical theater, opera, radio station, student government, student newspaper, symphony orchestra, TV station, African alliance, community action program, Prism, Hillel, Christian fellowship, Amnesty International, environmental organization, Jubilate Deo, Concern for International Children.

Athletics. NCAA. **Intercollegiate:** Basketball, cross-country, equestrian, field hockey W, lacrosse, soccer, swimming, tennis, track and field, volleyball W. **Intramural:** Football (tackle), soccer. **Team name:** Gophers.

Student services. Adult student services, alcohol/substance abuse counseling, chaplain/spiritual director, career counseling, services for economically disadvantaged, student employment services, financial aid counseling, health services, minority student services, personal counseling, placement for graduates, veterans' counselor, women's services. **Physically disabled:** Services for visually, hearing impaired.

Contact. E-mail: admissions@goucher.edu
Phone: (410) 337-6100 Toll-free number: (800) 468-2437
Fax: (410) 337-6354
Carlton Surbeck, Director of Admissions, Goucher College, 1021 Dulaney Valley Road, Baltimore, MD 21204-2753

Hood College
Frederick, Maryland   CB member
www.hood.edu   CB code: 5296

- Private 4-year liberal arts college
- Residential campus in small city
- 1,436 degree-seeking undergraduates: 7% part-time, 66% women, 12% African American, 3% Asian American, 7% Hispanic American, 2% international
- 823 degree-seeking graduate students
- 79% of applicants admitted
- SAT or ACT (ACT writing optional), application essay required
- 68% graduate within 6 years; 45% enter graduate study

General. Founded in 1893. Regionally accredited. **Degrees:** 334 bachelor's awarded; master's offered. **ROTC:** Army. **Location:** 52 miles from Baltimore, 52 miles from Washington, DC. **Calendar:** Semester, limited summer session. **Full-time faculty:** 88 total; 96% have terminal degrees, 17% minority, 57% women. **Part-time faculty:** 171 total; 41% have terminal degrees, 8% minority, 53% women. **Class size:** 64% < 20, 36% 20-39, less than 1% 40-49, less than 1% 50-99. **Special facilities:** Psychology and preschool laboratories, observatory.

Freshman class profile. 1,686 applied, 1,334 admitted, 311 enrolled.

Mid 50% test scores		GPA 2.0-2.99:	16%
SAT critical reading:	490-600	Rank in top quarter:	54%
SAT math:	480-600	Rank in top tenth:	24%
SAT writing:	470-590	End year in good standing:	84%
ACT composite:	20-22	Return as sophomores:	76%
GPA 3.75 or higher:	35%	Out-of-state:	31%
GPA 3.50-3.74:	17%	Live on campus:	84%
GPA 3.0-3.49:	32%	International:	2%

Basis for selection. High school record, class rank, test scores important. Recommendations, contributions to school, family and community, essay considered. Interview recommended. **Home schooled:** Interview, letter of recommendation (nonparent) required. Must interview and present bibliography of all reading materials used; two recommendations; partial portfolio of work.

High school preparation. College-preparatory program required. 17 units required. Required and recommended units include English 4, mathematics 3-4, social studies 1-2, history 3, science 3-4 (laboratory 2), foreign language 2-3 and academic electives 1-2.

2011-2012 Annual costs. Tuition/fees: $31,060. Room/board: $10,390. Books/supplies: $1,200. Personal expenses: $1,220.

2011-2012 Financial aid. Need-based: 269 full-time freshmen applied for aid; 257 were judged to have need; 257 of these received aid. Average need met was 82%. Average scholarship/grant was $24,457; average loan $3,151. 77% of total undergraduate aid awarded as scholarships/grants, 23% as loans/jobs. **Non-need-based:** Awarded to 317 full-time undergraduates, including 75 freshmen. Scholarships awarded for academics, alumni affiliation, minority status, music/drama, ROTC.

Application procedures. Admission: Priority date 2/15; deadline 8/1 (postmark date). $35 fee, may be waived for applicants with need, free for online applicants. Multiple Notification Dates 11/15, 12/15, 2/1, 3/1, rolling after 3/1 on space available. Must reply by May 1 or within 2 week(s) if notified thereafter. Early Action closing dates of 10/1, 11/1 and 12/1. Applications received after February 1 considered on a space available basis. **Financial aid:** Priority date 2/15; no closing date. FAFSA required. Applicants notified on a rolling basis starting 3/1; must reply by 5/1 or within 3 week(s) of notification.

Academics. Students in all fields may earn academic credits for internships. Opportunities available for students to earn degree in 3 years, 2 degrees in 4 years, or bachelor's and master's in 5 years. **Special study options:** Combined bachelor's/graduate degree, double major, dual enrollment of high school students, honors, independent study, internships, liberal arts/career combination, student-designed major, study abroad, teacher certification program, Washington semester. **Credit/placement by examination:** AP, CLEP, IB, SAT, institutional tests. 30 credit hours maximum toward bachelor's degree. **Support services:** Learning center, pre-admission summer program, reduced course load, remedial instruction, study skills assistance, tutoring.

Majors. Area/ethnic studies: Latin American, Near/Middle Eastern. **Biology:** General, biochemistry. **Business:** Business admin. **Communications:** General. **Computer sciences:** Computer science. **Conservation:** Environmental science. **Education:** Early childhood, special ed. **English:** English lit. **Foreign languages:** French, German, Spanish. **History:** General. **Human services:** Social work. **Math:** General. **Philosophy/religion:** Philosophy, religion. **Physical sciences:** Chemistry. **Psychology:** General. **Social sciences:** Economics, political science, sociology. **Visual/performing arts:** Art, music.

Most popular majors. Biology 8%, business/marketing 13%, communications/journalism 7%, education 9%, history 7%, psychology 12%, social sciences 7%.

Computing on campus. 252 workstations in dormitories, library, computer center, student center. Dormitories wired for high-speed internet access and linked to campus network. Commuter students can connect to campus network. Online course registration, online library, helpline, wireless network available.

Student life. Freshman orientation: Mandatory. Preregistration for classes offered. Choice of 3 programs held on weekends in June for preregistration with the final program 4 days prior to start of classes. **Policies:** Students responsible for governing themselves through honor code. **Housing:** Guaranteed on-campus for all undergraduates. Coed dorms, single-sex dorms, apartments available. $300 nonrefundable deposit, deadline 5/1. **Activities:** Jazz band, campus ministries, choral groups, dance, drama, film society, international student organizations, literary magazine, music ensembles, Model UN, musical theater, radio station, student government, student newspaper, Black student union, Circle K, La Union Latina, Best Buddies, Intervarsity Christian Fellowship, College Democrats, Jewish Student Union, College Republicans.

Athletics. NCAA. **Intercollegiate:** Basketball, cross-country, field hockey W, golf M, lacrosse, soccer, softball W, swimming, tennis, track and field, volleyball W. **Intramural:** Basketball, football (non-tackle) M, football (tackle) M, golf W, soccer, table tennis, volleyball W. **Team name:** Blazers.

Student services. Adult student services, alcohol/substance abuse counseling, chaplain/spiritual director, career counseling, student employment services, financial aid counseling, health services, minority student services, personal counseling, placement for graduates, veterans' counselor, women's services. **Physically disabled:** Services for speech, hearing impaired.

Contact. E-mail: admissions@hood.edu
Phone: (301) 696-3400 Toll-free number: (800) 922-1599
Fax: (301) 696-3819
David Adams, Director of Admissions, Hood College, 401 Rosemont Avenue, Frederick, MD 21701-8575

ITT Technical Institute: Owings Mills
Owings Mills, Maryland
www.itt-tech.edu

- For-profit 4-year business and technical college
- Large town
- 1,496 degree-seeking undergraduates

General. Accredited by ACICS. **Degrees:** 27 bachelor's, 324 associate awarded. **Calendar:** Quarter. **Full-time faculty:** 26 total. **Part-time faculty:** 55 total.

Basis for selection. Additional requirements for some programs.

2011-2012 Annual costs. Estimated costs as of June 2011: per-credit-hour charge, $493, depending upon level and course of study; academic fee, $200. Certain programs of study require purchase of tools, which could cost an additional $100 to $500. All costs are subject to change.

Academics. Credit/placement by examination: AP, CLEP.

Majors. Business: Construction management, e-commerce. **Computer sciences:** Security, system admin.

Contact. ITT Technical Institute: Owings Mills, 11301 Red Run Boulevard, Owings Mills, MD 21117

Johns Hopkins University

Baltimore, Maryland

www.jhu.edu

CB member

CB code: 5332

- Private 4-year university
- Residential campus in very large city
- 5,047 degree-seeking undergraduates: 47% women, 5% African American, 20% Asian American, 9% Hispanic American, 9% international
- 1,924 degree-seeking graduate students
- 18% of applicants admitted
- SAT or ACT with writing, application essay required
- 92% graduate within 6 years; 38% enter graduate study

General. Founded in 1876. Regionally accredited. Centers in Bologna and Florence, Italy, and Nanjing, China. **Degrees:** 1,550 bachelor's awarded; master's, professional, doctoral offered. **ROTC:** Army, Air Force. **Location:** 4 miles from downtown. **Calendar:** 4-1-4, limited summer session. **Full-time faculty:** 450 total. **Part-time faculty:** 75 total. **Special facilities:** Space telescope science institute.

Freshman class profile. 19,391 applied, 3,576 admitted, 1,279 enrolled.

Mid 50% test scores			
SAT critical reading:	640-740	Rank in top quarter:	98%
SAT math:	670-770	Rank in top tenth:	86%
SAT writing:	650-750	Return as sophomores:	96%
ACT composite:	30-33	Out-of-state:	90%
GPA 3.75 or higher:	56%	Live on campus:	99%
GPA 3.50-3.74:	28%	International:	9%
GPA 3.0-3.49:	15%	Fraternities:	22%
GPA 2.0-2.99:	1%	Sororities:	26%

Basis for selection. School achievement record most important, with emphasis on course grades related to applicant's major field of academic interest. Intellectual interests and accomplishments, recommendations, personal character, extracurricular activities significant. Test scores are also important. Students wishing to enroll in the biomedical engineering major (BME) must indicate BME as their first-choice major and are admitted specifically into BME major based on evaluation of credentials and space availability. SAT Subject Tests recommended. Early Decision applicants should have test scores in by November 1. Recommend 3 SAT Subject Tests. SAT Math Level 2 recommended for students applying to the school of engineering. Interview recommended. Audition required of applicants to dual-degree program with Peabody Institute. **Home schooled:** Statement describing home school structure and mission, transcript of courses and grades, letter of recommendation (nonparent) required. Secondary school report must include summary of program, complete transcript with course descriptions, bibliography of textbooks, description of evaluation methods, and actual grades or evaluations.

High school preparation. College-preparatory program recommended. Recommended units include English 4, mathematics 4, social studies 2, history 2, science 4 and foreign language 4. 4 combined units recommended for social studies and history.

2011-2012 Annual costs. Tuition/fees: $42,780. Room/board: $12,962.

2011-2012 Financial aid. Need-based: 618 full-time freshmen applied for aid; 618 were judged to have need; 618 of these received aid. Average need met was 99%. Average scholarship/grant was $34,052; average loan $3,345. 85% of total undergraduate aid awarded as scholarships/grants, 15% as loans/jobs. **Non-need-based:** Awarded to 285 full-time undergraduates, including 82 freshmen. Scholarships awarded for academics, athletics, leadership, ROTC, state residency. **Additional information:** Selected students

receive aid packages without loan expectation, grants to full need. Private merit aid does not reduce Hopkins grant.

Application procedures. Admission: Closing date 1/1 (postmark date). $70 fee, may be waived for applicants with need. Admission notification by 4/1. Must reply by May 1 or within 2 week(s) if notified thereafter. **Financial aid:** Closing date 3/1. FAFSA, CSS PROFILE required. Applicants notified by 4/1; must reply by 5/1 or within 2 week(s) of notification.

Academics. Special study options: Combined bachelor's/graduate degree, cross-registration, double major, independent study, internships, student-designed major, study abroad, Washington semester. Combined bachelor's/master's programs. **Credit/placement by examination:** AP, CLEP, IB, institutional tests. **Support services:** Pre-admission summer program, reduced course load, study skills assistance, tutoring, writing center.

Majors. Area/ethnic studies: African-American, East Asian, Latin American, Near/Middle Eastern. **Biology:** General, biophysics, cell/histology, molecular, neuroscience. **Computer sciences:** General. **Conservation:** Environmental studies. **Engineering:** General, biomedical, chemical, civil, computer, electrical, engineering mechanics, environmental, materials, mechanical. **English:** Creative writing, English lit. **Foreign languages:** Classics, French, German, Italian, Spanish. **History:** General, science/technology. **Human services:** Public policy. **Liberal arts:** Arts/sciences. **Math:** General, statistics. **Philosophy/religion:** Philosophy. **Physical sciences:** Astronomy, chemistry, geology, materials science, physics. **Psychology:** General. **Social sciences:** General, anthropology, archaeology, economics, geography, international relations, political science, sociology. **Visual/performing arts:** Art history/conservation, film/cinema/video.

Most popular majors. Biology 13%, engineering/engineering technologies 18%, health sciences 25%, social sciences 16%.

Computing on campus. 140 workstations in dormitories, library, computer center. Dormitories wired for high-speed internet access and linked to campus network. Commuter students can connect to campus network. Online course registration, online library, helpline, repair service, student web hosting, wireless network available.

Student life. Freshman orientation: Mandatory. Preregistration for classes offered. 5-day extensive program held in week prior to start of fall classes. **Policies:** Freshmen and sophomores required to live on campus unless they live with a parent or legal guardian within commuting distance. **Housing:** Guaranteed on-campus for freshmen. Coed dorms, single-sex dorms, special housing for disabled, apartments, fraternity/sorority housing, wellness housing available. $200 nonrefundable deposit, deadline 5/30. Substance-free and vacation housing floors available. Specific spaces accessible or modified for disabled students. **Activities:** Bands, campus ministries, choral groups, dance, drama, film society, international student organizations, literary magazine, music ensembles, musical theater, radio station, student government, student newspaper, symphony orchestra, Jewish Student Association, Catholic Community, Christian Fellowship, Black Student Union, Organizacion Latina Estudiantil, Chinese Student Association, emergency response organization, senior citizens community outreach program, College Democrats, College Republicans.

Athletics. NCAA. **Intercollegiate:** Baseball M, basketball, cross-country, fencing, field hockey W, football (tackle) M, lacrosse, soccer, swimming, tennis, track and field, volleyball W, water polo M, wrestling M. **Intramural:** Basketball, football (non-tackle), soccer, volleyball. **Team name:** Blue Jays.

Student services. Alcohol/substance abuse counseling, chaplain/spiritual director, career counseling, student employment services, financial aid counseling, health services, minority student services, personal counseling, placement for graduates. **Physically disabled:** Services for visually, speech, hearing impaired.

Contact. E-mail: gotojhu@jhu.edu
Phone: (410) 516-8171 Fax: (410) 516-6025
Dean of Undergraduate Admissions, Johns Hopkins University, 3400 North Charles Street, Mason Hall, Baltimore, MD 21218

Johns Hopkins University: Peabody Conservatory of Music

Baltimore, Maryland

www.peabody.jhu.edu

CB code: 5532

- Private 4-year music college
- Residential campus in very large city
- 329 degree-seeking undergraduates: 47% women, 2% African American, 12% Asian American, 3% Hispanic American, 1% Native American, 22% international
- 395 degree-seeking graduate students

- 42% of applicants admitted
- SAT or ACT, application essay required
- 71% graduate within 6 years

General. Founded in 1857. Regionally accredited. **Degrees:** 69 bachelor's awarded; master's, doctoral offered. **Location:** 36 miles from Washington, DC. **Calendar:** Semester. **Full-time faculty:** 76 total; 26% women. **Part-time faculty:** 84 total; 34% women. **Class size:** 91% < 20, 7% 20-39, less than 1% 40-49, 2% 50-99. **Special facilities:** Concert halls.

Freshman class profile. 767 applied, 322 admitted, 87 enrolled.

End year in good standing:	90%	Live on campus:	100%
Return as sophomores:	87%	International:	32%

Basis for selection. Audition most important; secondary school record, test scores also important. Interview recommended. Audition required. **Home schooled:** Statement describing home school structure and mission, state high school equivalency certificate required.

High school preparation. College-preparatory program recommended.

2011-2012 Annual costs. Tuition/fees: $38,125. Room/board: $12,200. Books/supplies: $750. Personal expenses: $1,400.

2010-2011 Financial aid. Need-based: 71 full-time freshmen applied for aid; 61 were judged to have need; 59 of these received aid. Average need met was 68%. Average scholarship/grant was $13,012; average loan $5,039. 56% of total undergraduate aid awarded as scholarships/grants, 44% as loans/jobs. **Non-need-based:** Awarded to 162 full-time undergraduates, including 34 freshmen. Scholarships awarded for academics, music/drama.

Application procedures. Admission: Priority date 12/1; deadline 4/1 (postmark date). $100 fee, may be waived for applicants with need. Admission notification by 4/1. Must reply by 5/1. Must apply by December 15 for guarantee of scholarship consideration. **Financial aid:** Closing date 2/1. FAFSA, institutional form required. Applicants notified by 4/1; must reply by 5/1.

Academics. Special study options: Cross-registration, double major, ESL, independent study, internships, study abroad, teacher certification program. **Credit/placement by examination:** AP, CLEP, IB, institutional tests. 8 credit hours maximum toward bachelor's degree. **Support services:** Remedial instruction, tutoring.

Majors. Communications technology: Recording arts. **Education:** Music. **Visual/performing arts:** Music performance, music theory/composition, piano/keyboard, voice/opera.

Most popular majors. Education 6%, visual/performing arts 94%.

Computing on campus. 28 workstations in dormitories, library, computer center. Dormitories wired for high-speed internet access and linked to campus network. Commuter students can connect to campus network. Online course registration, online library, helpline, repair service, wireless network available.

Student life. Freshman orientation: Available. Preregistration for classes offered. **Housing:** Guaranteed on-campus for freshmen. Coed dorms, single-sex dorms available. $250 partly refundable deposit, deadline 1/7. **Activities:** Bands, choral groups, music ensembles, opera, student government, symphony orchestra.

Student services. Alcohol/substance abuse counseling, career counseling, student employment services, financial aid counseling, health services, personal counseling, placement for graduates. **Physically disabled:** Services for visually, speech, hearing impaired.

Contact. E-mail: admissions@peabody.jhu.edu
Phone: (410) 234-4848 Toll-free number: (800) 368-2521
Fax: (410) 659-8102
David Lane, Director of Admissions, Johns Hopkins University: Peabody Conservatory of Music, One East Mount Vernon Place, Baltimore, MD 21202

Loyola University Maryland
Baltimore, Maryland
www.loyola.edu

CB member
CB code: 5370

- Private 4-year university affiliated with Roman Catholic Church
- Residential campus in very large city

- 3,835 degree-seeking undergraduates: 1% part-time, 61% women, 4% African American, 3% Asian American, 7% Hispanic American, 1% international
- 2,132 degree-seeking graduate students
- 63% of applicants admitted
- Application essay required
- 83% graduate within 6 years

General. Founded in 1852. Regionally accredited. **Degrees:** 880 bachelor's awarded; master's, professional, doctoral offered. **ROTC:** Army, Air Force. **Location:** 42 miles from Washington, DC, 101 miles from Philadelphia. **Calendar:** Semester, extensive summer session. **Full-time faculty:** 330 total; 83% have terminal degrees, 13% minority, 47% women. **Part-time faculty:** 201 total; 10% have terminal degrees, 10% minority, 48% women. **Class size:** 46% < 20, 53% 20-39, less than 1% 40-49, less than 1% 50-99. **Special facilities:** Fitness and aquatic center.

Freshman class profile. 12,066 applied, 7,651 admitted, 1,071 enrolled.

Mid 50% test scores		GPA 2.0-2.99:	7%
SAT critical reading:	540-640	Rank in top quarter:	70%
SAT math:	560-650	Rank in top tenth:	34%
ACT composite:	25-28	End year in good standing:	99%
GPA 3.75 or higher:	19%	Return as sophomores:	89%
GPA 3.50-3.74:	32%	Out-of-state:	85%
GPA 3.0-3.49:	42%	Live on campus:	98%

Basis for selection. All applicants are admitted on the condition that they satisfactorily complete their secondary school courses. **Home schooled:** Letter of recommendation (nonparent) required. SAT or ACT scores need to be submitted.

High school preparation. College-preparatory program required. 15 units required; 19 recommended. Required and recommended units include English 4, mathematics 3, social studies 2-3, history 2-3, science 3-4, foreign language 3-4, computer science 1 and visual/performing arts 1.

2011-2012 Annual costs. Tuition/fees: $41,035. Room/board: $11,450. Books/supplies: $1,180. Personal expenses: $1,000.

2010-2011 Financial aid. Need-based: 766 full-time freshmen applied for aid; 632 were judged to have need; 632 of these received aid. Average need met was 100%. Average scholarship/grant was $19,100; average loan $5,750. 81% of total undergraduate aid awarded as scholarships/grants, 19% as loans/jobs. **Non-need-based:** Awarded to 938 full-time undergraduates, including 242 freshmen. Scholarships awarded for academics, athletics, ROTC.

Application procedures. Admission: Priority date 11/1; deadline 1/15 (postmark date). $50 fee, may be waived for applicants with need. Admission notification by 3/15. Must reply by May 1 or within 3 week(s) if notified thereafter. **Financial aid:** Closing date 2/15. FAFSA, CSS PROFILE required. Applicants notified by 4/1; must reply by 5/1.

Academics. Service learning courses available. **Special study options:** Combined bachelor's/graduate degree, cross-registration, double major, exchange student, honors, independent study, internships, liberal arts/career combination, study abroad, teacher certification program. **Credit/placement by examination:** AP, CLEP, IB, institutional tests. **Support services:** Learning center, reduced course load, remedial instruction, study skills assistance, tutoring, writing center.

Majors. Biology: General. **Business:** General, accounting. **Communications:** Communications/speech/rhetoric. **Computer sciences:** General. **Education:** Elementary. **Engineering:** General, electrical. **English:** Creative writing, English lit. **Foreign languages:** Classics, French, German, Latin, Spanish. **Health services:** Speech pathology. **History:** General. **Math:** Applied. **Philosophy/religion:** Philosophy, religion. **Physical sciences:** Chemistry, physics. **Psychology:** General. **Social sciences:** Economics, political science, sociology. **Visual/performing arts:** Art.

Most popular majors. Business/marketing 36%, communications/journalism 11%, English 7%, health sciences 6%, psychology 6%, social sciences 11%.

Computing on campus. 775 workstations in dormitories, library, computer center, student center. Dormitories wired for high-speed internet access and linked to campus network. Commuter students can connect to campus network. Online course registration, online library, helpline, student web hosting, wireless network available.

Student life. Freshman orientation: Mandatory, $165 fee. Preregistration for classes offered. Must attend 1 of 4 programs offered in summer; parents invited to attend. **Policies:** Freshmen not permitted cars on campus. **Housing:** Guaranteed on-campus for freshmen. Coed dorms, cooperative housing, wellness housing available. $500 nonrefundable deposit, deadline 5/1. **Activities:**

Campus ministries, choral groups, dance, drama, film society, international student organizations, literary magazine, music ensembles, musical theater, radio station, student government, student newspaper, TV station, Black student association, College Republicans, Korean students association, Circle K, Amnesty International, Jewish students association, College Democrats, Evergreens for Life.

Athletics. NCAA. **Intercollegiate:** Basketball, cross-country, diving, golf M, lacrosse, rowing (crew), soccer, swimming, tennis, track and field W, volleyball W. **Intramural:** Baseball M, basketball, racquetball, soccer, softball, squash, tennis, track and field M, volleyball. **Team name:** Greyhounds.

Student services. Alcohol/substance abuse counseling, chaplain/spiritual director, career counseling, student employment services, financial aid counseling, health services, minority student services, personal counseling, placement for graduates, women's services. **Physically disabled:** Services for visually, speech, hearing impaired.

Contact. E-mail: admissions@loyola.edu
Phone: (410) 617-5012 Toll-free number: (800) 221-9107
Fax: (410) 617-2176
Elena Hicks, Director of Undergraduate Admission, Loyola University Maryland, 4501 North Charles Street, Baltimore, MD 21210-2699

Maryland Institute College of Art
Baltimore, Maryland
www.mica.edu

CB member
CB code: 5399

- Private 4-year visual arts college
- Residential campus in very large city
- 1,828 degree-seeking undergraduates: 1% part-time, 71% women, 5% African American, 10% Asian American, 5% Hispanic American, 6% international
- 303 degree-seeking graduate students
- 55% of applicants admitted
- SAT or ACT (ACT writing optional), application essay required
- 71% graduate within 6 years; 23% enter graduate study

General. Founded in 1826. Regionally accredited. **Degrees:** 366 bachelor's awarded; master's offered. **ROTC:** Army. **Location:** 180 miles from New York City, 50 miles from Washington, DC. **Calendar:** Semester, extensive summer session. **Full-time faculty:** 146 total; 82% have terminal degrees, 8% minority, 53% women. **Part-time faculty:** 223 total; 82% have terminal degrees, 8% minority, 54% women. **Class size:** 76% < 20, 24% 20-39, less than 1% 40-49, less than 1% 50-99. **Special facilities:** Nature library, slide library, graphics laboratory, independent studios, digital print studio, smart textile classroom, 3D fabrication studio, BBOX performance space.

Freshman class profile. 3,233 applied, 1,777 admitted, 496 enrolled.

Mid 50% test scores		Return as sophomores:	85%
SAT critical reading:	540-660	Out-of-state:	81%
SAT math:	500-620	Live on campus:	88%
SAT writing:	530-650	International:	8%
End year in good standing:	98%		

Basis for selection. Emphasis placed on artistic ability as demonstrated in portfolio, academic achievement, test scores, GPA, and level of coursework. Essays, recommendations, interview, and extra-curricular activities also considered. Interview recommended. Portfolio of 12-20 pieces of artwork required. **Learning Disabled:** Students with documented learning disabilities not required to submit SAT or ACT test scores.

High school preparation. College-preparatory program required. 24 units required. Required and recommended units include English 4, mathematics 2-3, social studies 4, history 3-4, science 2-3 (laboratory 1) and academic electives 6. 2 studio art required, 4 studio art recommended, 1 art history recommended.

2011-2012 Annual costs. Tuition/fees: $37,470. Room/board: $10,770. Books/supplies: $1,450. Personal expenses: $675.

Financial aid. **Non-need-based:** Scholarships awarded for academics, art.

Application procedures. Admission: Closing date 2/15 (receipt date). $60 fee, may be waived for applicants with need. Application must be submitted on paper. Admission notification by 3/12. Must reply by 5/1. **Financial aid:** Closing date 2/15. FAFSA, institutional form required. Applicants notified by 4/13; must reply by 5/1.

Academics. One-third of course work in liberal arts and two-thirds in studio art required for graduation. Minors available in academic subjects. Independent studio and study requirement sometimes met by job internships.

Foundation program required in the first year. **Special study options:** Accelerated study, combined bachelor's/graduate degree, cross-registration, distance learning, double major, dual enrollment of high school students, exchange student, independent study, internships, liberal arts/career combination, New York semester, student-designed major, study abroad, teacher certification program. Cooperative exchange programs with Johns Hopkins University, Goucher College, Peabody Conservatory of Music, University of Baltimore, Loyola College, Notre Dame College, University of Maryland Baltimore County, Morgan State University, Baltimore Hebrew Institute and Towson University; 5-year BFA/MAT. **Credit/placement by examination:** AP, CLEP, IB, institutional tests. 27 credit hours maximum toward bachelor's degree. **Support services:** Learning center, pre-admission summer program, reduced course load, remedial instruction, study skills assistance, tutoring, writing center.

Majors. Education: Art. **Visual/performing arts:** Art history/conservation, ceramics, drawing, fiber arts, graphic design, illustration, interior design, multimedia, painting, photography, printmaking, sculpture.

Most popular majors. Education 6%, visual/performing arts 94%.

Computing on campus. 600 workstations in dormitories, library, computer center, student center. Dormitories wired for high-speed internet access and linked to campus network. Commuter students can connect to campus network. Online library, helpline, student web hosting, wireless network available.

Student life. Freshman orientation: Mandatory, $150 fee. Preregistration for classes offered. **Housing:** Guaranteed on-campus for freshmen. Coed dorms, special housing for disabled, apartments available. $550 partly refundable deposit, deadline 5/1. **Activities:** Choral groups, dance, drama, film society, international student organizations, literary magazine, music ensembles, musical theater, radio station, student government, Prisoner Writing, Koinonia Christian Fellowship, Students of Sustainabillity, Asian Student Alliance, Black Student Union, Disciples on Campus, Korean Student Association, Mission in Christian Artists, Student Voice Association, Buddhism in Action.

Student services. Alcohol/substance abuse counseling, career counseling, student employment services, financial aid counseling, health services, minority student services, personal counseling, placement for graduates.

Contact. E-mail: admissions@mica.edu
Phone: (410) 225-2222 Fax: (410) 225-2337
Theresa Bedoya, Vice President and Dean of Admission and Financial Aid, Maryland Institute College of Art, 1300 Mount Royal Avenue, Baltimore, MD 21217-4134

McDaniel College
Westminster, Maryland
www.mcdaniel.edu

CB member
CB code: 5898

- Private 4-year liberal arts college
- Residential campus in large town
- 1,583 degree-seeking undergraduates: 1% part-time, 52% women, 10% African American, 4% Asian American, 5% Hispanic American, 1% Native American
- 1,390 degree-seeking graduate students
- 75% of applicants admitted
- SAT or ACT (ACT writing optional), application essay required
- 73% graduate within 6 years

General. Founded in 1867. Regionally accredited. **Degrees:** 398 bachelor's awarded; master's offered. **ROTC:** Army. **Location:** 30 miles from Baltimore, 60 miles from Washington, DC. **Calendar:** 4-1-4, limited summer session. **Full-time faculty:** 101 total; 99% have terminal degrees, 12% minority, 52% women. **Part-time faculty:** 255 total; 31% have terminal degrees, 6% minority, 54% women. **Class size:** 64% < 20, 35% 20-39, less than 1% 50-99. **Special facilities:** 9-hole golf course, film/video production laboratory, photography studio, audiology laboratory, human performance laboratory, graphics laboratory, physics observatory.

Freshman class profile. 2,754 applied, 2,074 admitted, 424 enrolled.

Mid 50% test scores		GPA 2.0-2.99:	18%
SAT critical reading:	480-610	Rank in top quarter:	54%
SAT math:	490-610	Rank in top tenth:	26%
ACT composite:	20-26	Return as sophomores:	79%
GPA 3.75 or higher:	31%	Out-of-state:	40%
GPA 3.50-3.74:	16%	Live on campus:	94%
GPA 3.0-3.49:	35%		

Basis for selection. Rigor of course work completed and academic performance test scores, writing skills, personal and academic accomplishments, recommendations by counselors and teachers, leadership and participation in non-academic activities. Academic recommendations required. Interview recommended. **Home schooled:** Statement describing home school structure and mission, transcript of courses and grades, letter of recommendation (nonparent) required. Must submit documentation used to satisfy your state graduation requirement.

High school preparation. College-preparatory program required. 16 units required; 19 recommended. Required and recommended units include English 4, mathematics 3-4, social studies 3, science 3-4 (laboratory 3) and foreign language 3-4.

2011-2012 Annual costs. Tuition/fees: $34,780. Room/board: $7,380. Books/supplies: $1,200. Personal expenses: $1,000.

2011-2012 Financial aid. Need-based: 369 full-time freshmen applied for aid; 320 were judged to have need; 319 of these received aid. Average need met was 83%. Average scholarship/grant was $25,851; average loan $4,415. 85% of total undergraduate aid awarded as scholarships/grants, 15% as loans/jobs. **Non-need-based:** Awarded to 515 full-time undergraduates, including 142 freshmen. Scholarships awarded for academics, ROTC, state residency.

Application procedures. Admission: Priority date 2/15; deadline 2/15 (postmark date). $50 fee, may be waived for applicants with need. Admission notification by 3/9. Must reply by May 1 or within 2 week(s) if notified thereafter. **Financial aid:** Priority date 3/1; no closing date. FAFSA, institutional form required. Applicants notified on a rolling basis starting 2/15; must reply by 5/1 or within 2 week(s) of notification.

Academics. January term offered as a two-credit period of concentrated study. May include travel, classroom study or independent study. **Special study options:** Accelerated study, distance learning, double major, dual enrollment of high school students, exchange student, honors, independent study, internships, New York semester, semester at sea, student-designed major, study abroad, teacher certification program, United Nations semester, Washington semester. **Credit/placement by examination:** AP, CLEP, IB, SAT, ACT, institutional tests. 32 credit hours maximum toward bachelor's degree. **Support services:** Learning center, reduced course load, remedial instruction, study skills assistance, tutoring, writing center.

Majors. Biology: General, biochemistry, environmental. **Business:** Business admin. **Communications:** Communications/speech/rhetoric. **Computer sciences:** General. **Conservation:** Environmental science. **English:** English lit. **Foreign languages:** French, German, Spanish. **History:** General. **Human services:** Social work. **Math:** General. **Parks/recreation:** Exercise sciences. **Philosophy/religion:** Philosophy, religion. **Physical sciences:** Chemistry, physics. **Psychology:** General. **Social sciences:** Economics, political science, sociology. **Visual/performing arts:** Art, art history/conservation, dramatic, music.

Most popular majors. Biology 7%, business/marketing 12%, communications/journalism 7%, history 7%, interdisciplinary studies 10%, parks/recreation 8%, psychology 13%, social sciences 16%, visual/performing arts 11%.

Computing on campus. 175 workstations in library, computer center. Dormitories wired for high-speed internet access and linked to campus network. Commuter students can connect to campus network. Online course registration, helpline, wireless network available.

Student life. Freshman orientation: Mandatory. Preregistration for classes offered. 5-day program. **Housing:** Guaranteed on-campus for freshmen. Coed dorms, single-sex dorms, apartments, fraternity/sorority housing, wellness housing available. Single-family homes available. **Activities:** Bands, campus ministries, choral groups, dance, drama, literary magazine, music ensembles, musical theater, radio station, student government, student newspaper, symphony orchestra, TV station, Jewish student union, Christian fellowship, Circle K, ecology club, Black student union, multicultural student association, German club, French club, Spanish club.

Athletics. NCAA. **Intercollegiate:** Baseball M, basketball, cross-country, field hockey W, football (tackle) M, golf, lacrosse, soccer, softball W, swimming, tennis, track and field, volleyball W, wrestling M. **Intramural:** Badminton, basketball, football (non-tackle) M, golf, soccer, softball, swimming, tennis, volleyball. **Team name:** The Green Terror.

Student services. Career counseling, student employment services, financial aid counseling, health services, minority student services, personal counseling. **Physically disabled:** Services for visually, hearing impaired.

Contact. E-mail: admissions@mcdaniel.edu
Phone: (410) 857-2230 Toll-free number: (800) 638-5005
Fax: (410) 857-2757
Florence Hines, Vice President for Enrollment Management and Dean of Admissions, McDaniel College, Two College Hill, Westminster, MD 21157-4390

Morgan State University
Baltimore, Maryland
www.morgan.edu

CB member
CB code: 5416

- Public 4-year university and liberal arts college
- Commuter campus in large city
- 6,672 degree-seeking undergraduates: 11% part-time, 57% women, 85% African American, 1% Asian American, 3% Hispanic American, 4% international
- 1,261 degree-seeking graduate students
- 56% of applicants admitted
- 32% graduate within 6 years

General. Founded in 1867. Regionally accredited. **Degrees:** 813 bachelor's awarded; master's, doctoral offered. **ROTC:** Army. **Location:** 45 miles from Washington, DC, 100 miles from Philadelphia. **Calendar:** Semester, limited summer session. **Full-time faculty:** 463 total; 68% have terminal degrees, 73% minority, 41% women. **Part-time faculty:** 180 total; 33% have terminal degrees, 81% minority, 43% women. **Special facilities:** Historical and government documents collections, special collections of African American history, super computer, engineering complex.

Freshman class profile. 5,592 applied, 3,134 admitted, 1,086 enrolled.

Mid 50% test scores			
SAT critical reading:	410-490	GPA 3.0-3.49:	22%
SAT math:	410-490	GPA 2.0-2.99:	68%
SAT writing:	400-480	Return as sophomores:	73%
ACT composite:	15-19	Out-of-state:	30%
GPA 3.75 or higher:	3%	Live on campus:	93%
GPA 3.50-3.74:	5%	International:	2%

Basis for selection. School achievement record and test scores most important. 820 SAT (exclusive of Writing) with 2.5 high school GPA or 900 SAT (exclusive of Writing) with 2.0 high school GPA, principal's recommendation, and parents' consent form (for minors) required. Interview and essay recommended. Audition recommended for music majors. **Home schooled:** State high school equivalency certificate required. State-recognized diploma. **Learning Disabled:** Students with learning disability must provide documentation and take untimed SAT with assistance from counseling center.

High school preparation. College-preparatory program recommended. 13 units recommended. Recommended units include English 4, mathematics 3, social studies 2, history 3, science 3 and foreign language 1. History can be substituted for social studies; computer science can be used in place of foreign language.

2011-2012 Annual costs. Tuition/fees: $6,896; $16,134 out-of-state. Room/board: $8,750. Books/supplies: $2,000. Personal expenses: $2,395.

Application procedures. Admission: Priority date 2/15; deadline 4/15. $35 fee, may be waived for applicants with need. Admission notification on a rolling basis beginning on or about 11/15. Must reply by May 1 or within 2 week(s) if notified thereafter. **Financial aid:** Priority date 4/1; no closing date. FAFSA required. Applicants notified on a rolling basis starting 6/1; must reply within 2 week(s) of notification.

Academics. Special study options: Cooperative education, cross-registration, distance learning, double major, dual enrollment of high school students, honors, independent study, internships, liberal arts/career combination, teacher certification program, weekend college, Fulbright Program. **Credit/placement by examination:** AP, CLEP, institutional tests. 46 credit hours maximum toward bachelor's degree. Proficiency tests in general education requirements. **Support services:** Learning center, pre-admission summer program, reduced course load, remedial instruction, study skills assistance, tutoring, writing center.

Majors. Architecture: Architecture, environmental design. **Area/ethnic studies:** African-American. **Biology:** General. **Business:** Accounting, business admin, finance, hospitality admin, marketing. **Computer sciences:** Computer science, information systems, networking. **Education:** Elementary, health, physical, science. **Engineering:** General, applied physics, civil, electrical, industrial. **English:** English lit, rhetoric/composition. **Health services:** Staff services technology. **History:** General. **Math:** General. **Physical sciences:** Chemistry, physics. **Psychology:** General. **Social sciences:** Economics, political science, sociology. **Visual/performing arts:** Dramatic, music, studio arts. **Work/family studies:** Food/nutrition.

Most popular majors. Biology 6%, business/marketing 20%, communications/journalism 10%, education 7%, engineering/engineering technologies 11%, health sciences 8%, psychology 6%, social sciences 8%.

Computing on campus. Dormitories wired for high-speed internet access and linked to campus network. Commuter students can connect to campus

network. Online course registration, online library, helpline, repair service, student web hosting, wireless network available.

Student life. Freshman orientation: Mandatory. Preregistration for classes offered. Held twice during summer for 5 days. **Housing:** Coed dorms, single-sex dorms, special housing for disabled, apartments, wellness housing available. $200 nonrefundable deposit, deadline 5/1. **Activities:** Bands, choral groups, dance, drama, film society, international student organizations, music ensembles, musical theater, radio station, student government, student newspaper, TV station, Council on Religious Life.

Athletics. NCAA. **Intercollegiate:** Basketball, bowling W, cheerleading M, cross-country, football (tackle) M, softball W, tennis, track and field, volleyball W. **Intramural:** Basketball, cross-country, handball, racquetball, rifle, soccer, softball, swimming, table tennis, tennis, track and field, volleyball. **Team name:** Bears.

Student services. Alcohol/substance abuse counseling, career counseling, student employment services, health services, on-campus daycare, personal counseling, placement for graduates, veterans' counselor. **Physically disabled:** Services for visually, speech, hearing impaired.

Contact. E-mail: admissions@morgan.edu
Phone: (443) 885-3000 Toll-free number: (800) 332-6674
Fax: (443) 885-8260
Shonda Gray, Director of Admissions/Recruitment, Morgan State University, 1700 East Cold Spring Lane, Baltimore, MD 21251

Mount St. Mary's University
Emmitsburg, Maryland
www.msmary.edu

CB member
CB code: 5421

▶ Private 4-year university and liberal arts college affiliated with Roman Catholic Church
▶ Residential campus in rural community
▶ 1,776 degree-seeking undergraduates: 5% part-time, 56% women, 10% African American, 2% Asian American, 9% Hispanic American, 1% international
▶ 511 degree-seeking graduate students
▶ 66% of applicants admitted
▶ SAT or ACT (ACT writing optional) required
▶ 76% graduate within 6 years; 32% enter graduate study

General. Founded in 1808. Regionally accredited. **Degrees:** 364 bachelor's awarded; master's offered. **ROTC:** Army. **Location:** 65 miles from Washington, DC, 50 miles from Baltimore. **Calendar:** Semester, limited summer session. **Full-time faculty:** 109 total; 92% have terminal degrees, 5% minority, 41% women. **Part-time faculty:** 72 total; 31% have terminal degrees, 3% minority, 46% women. **Class size:** 38% < 20, 60% 20-39, 1% 50-99. **Special facilities:** 300 acre recreation area.

Freshman class profile. 5,166 applied, 3,389 admitted, 572 enrolled.

Mid 50% test scores		GPA 2.0-2.99:	26%
SAT critical reading:	490-590	Rank in top quarter:	37%
SAT math:	490-580	Rank in top tenth:	14%
SAT writing:	470-590	End year in good standing:	92%
ACT composite:	19-23	Return as sophomores:	82%
GPA 3.75 or higher:	28%	Out-of-state:	46%
GPA 3.50-3.74:	16%	Live on campus:	95%
GPA 3.0-3.49:	30%	International:	1%

Basis for selection. High school record most important followed by standardized test scores, character, extracurricular activities. Interview and essay recommended. Auditions and/or portfolios are recommended for VPA majors, but not required. **Home schooled:** Letter of recommendation (nonparent) required. **Learning Disabled:** Current and valid documentation of disability, including functional limitations and the impact of disability on academic performance, is required.

High school preparation. College-preparatory program required. 16 units required. Required units include English 4, mathematics 3, social studies 3, science 3 (laboratory 2), foreign language 2 and academic electives 1.

2011-2012 Annual costs. Tuition/fees: $31,536. Room/board: $10,544. Books/supplies: $1,000. Personal expenses: $500.

2011-2012 Financial aid. Need-based: 510 full-time freshmen applied for aid; 428 were judged to have need; 428 of these received aid. Average need met was 78%. Average scholarship/grant was $18,376; average loan $4,256. 71% of total undergraduate aid awarded as scholarships/grants, 29% as loans/jobs. **Non-need-based:** Awarded to 789 full-time undergraduates,

including 258 freshmen. Scholarships awarded for academics, art, athletics, leadership, minority status, music/drama, ROTC.

Application procedures. Admission: No deadline. $35 fee, may be waived for applicants with need. Admission notification on a rolling basis beginning on or about 11/1. **Financial aid:** Closing date 3/1. FAFSA required. Applicants notified on a rolling basis starting 2/15; must reply by 5/1.

Academics. Liberal arts core curriculum integrated over 4 years includes: western civilization (clustered with literature and art courses), American experience, philosophy, theology, ethics, non-western cultures, mathematical science, foreign language, social science, written and oral communication. Undergraduate professional studies programs in business and criminal justice in an accelerated format offered off-campus; open to adult students only. **Special study options:** Accelerated study, combined bachelor's/graduate degree, cross-registration, double major, dual enrollment of high school students, honors, independent study, internships, liberal arts/career combination, student-designed major, study abroad, teacher certification program, Washington semester, weekend college. 3-2 with Johns Hopkins University (BS Biology, BS Nursing); 3-2 with Shenandoah Univ. in Nursing; 3-3 with Sacred Heart University (BS in Biology, Ph.D in Physical Therapy); 4-2 with Sacred Heart University (BS in Biology, MS in Occupational Therapy). **Credit/placement by examination:** AP, CLEP, IB, SAT, ACT, institutional tests. 30 credit hours maximum toward bachelor's degree. **Support services:** Learning center, reduced course load, remedial instruction, study skills assistance, tutoring, writing center.

Majors. Biology: General, biochemistry. **Business:** General, accounting, information resources management. **Communications:** Communications/speech/rhetoric. **Computer sciences:** General. **Conservation:** Environmental studies. **Education:** Elementary. **English:** English lit. **Foreign languages:** French, German, Spanish. **History:** General. **Math:** General. **Parks/recreation:** Sports admin. **Philosophy/religion:** Philosophy. **Physical sciences:** Chemistry. **Psychology:** General. **Social sciences:** Criminology, economics, international relations, political science, sociology. **Theology:** Theology. **Visual/performing arts:** General.

Most popular majors. Architecture 7%, biology 6%, business/marketing 25%, communications/journalism 7%, education 8%, social sciences 17%.

Computing on campus. 80 workstations in library, computer center, student center. Dormitories wired for high-speed internet access and linked to campus network. Commuter students can connect to campus network. Online course registration, online library, helpline, repair service, student web hosting, wireless network available.

Student life. Freshman orientation: Mandatory, $100 fee. Preregistration for classes offered. 3-day weekend in August and choice of 1 of 2 weekends in June for pre-registration. **Housing:** Guaranteed on-campus for all undergraduates. Coed dorms, special housing for disabled, apartments, wellness housing available. **Activities:** Bands, campus ministries, choral groups, dance, drama, international student organizations, literary magazine, music ensembles, musical theater, radio station, student government, student newspaper, TV station, College Democrats, College Republicans, Amnesty International, Circle K, Students for Life, Community Outreach Realizing Equality, Mount Mentors 4 Kids, Fellowship of Catholic University Students, Black Student Union, Hispanic Cultural Association.

Athletics. NCAA. **Intercollegiate:** Baseball M, basketball, cross-country, golf, lacrosse, soccer, softball W, swimming W, tennis, track and field. **Intramural:** Basketball, field hockey W, football (non-tackle) M, racquetball, skiing, soccer, softball, swimming, tennis, volleyball. **Team name:** Mountaineers.

Student services. Adult student services, alcohol/substance abuse counseling, chaplain/spiritual director, career counseling, student employment services, financial aid counseling, health services, minority student services, personal counseling, placement for graduates. **Physically disabled:** Services for visually, hearing impaired.

Contact. E-mail: admissions@msmary.edu
Phone: (301) 447-5214 Toll-free number: (800) 448-4347
Fax: (301) 447-5860
Michael Post, Dean of Admissions and Enrollment Management, Mount St. Mary's University, 16300 Old Emmitsburg Road, Emmitsburg, MD 21727

National Labor College
Silver Spring, Maryland
www.nlc.edu

CB code: 3930

▶ Private 4-year liberal arts and career college
▶ Commuter campus in small city

- 522 undergraduates
- Application essay required

General. Regionally accredited. **Degrees:** 85 bachelor's awarded. **Calendar:** Trimester, limited summer session. **Full-time faculty:** 9 total. **Part-time faculty:** 6 total. **Class size:** 100% 20-39. **Special facilities:** The George Meany Memorial Archives.

Basis for selection. Open admission. **Home schooled:** Transcript of courses and grades required.

2011-2012 Annual costs. $235 per-credit-hour for union members affiliated with the AFL-CIO. $285 per-credit-hour for union members not affiliated with the AFL-CIO. $235 per-credit-hour for members of Working America. $30 per-credit-hour for required fees.

Application procedures. **Admission:** No deadline. $65 fee. Admission notification on a rolling basis.

Academics. **Special study options:** Double major, independent study. **Credit/placement by examination:** AP, CLEP. **Support services:** Reduced course load, study skills assistance, tutoring, writing center.

Majors. **Business:** Labor studies. **Health services:** Occupational health.

Computing on campus. 30 workstations in computer center, student center. Dormitories wired for high-speed internet access. Commuter students can connect to campus network. Online course registration, online library, wireless network available.

Student life. **Freshman orientation:** Available. Preregistration for classes offered.

Student services. Financial aid counseling, personal counseling.

Contact. E-mail: admissions@nlc.edu
Phone: (888) 427-8500 Toll-free number: (888) 427-8500
Fax: (301) 628-0160
Carol Rodgers, Director of Admissions, National Labor College, 10000 New Hampshire Avenue, Silver Spring, MD 20903

Ner Israel Rabbinical College
Baltimore, Maryland
CB code: 0839

- Private 4-year rabbinical college for men affiliated with Jewish faith
- Very large city
- 604 degree-seeking undergraduates
- 87% of applicants admitted
- Interview required

General. Accredited by AARTS. **Degrees:** 31 bachelor's awarded; master's, professional, doctoral offered. **Calendar:** Semester, limited summer session. **Full-time faculty:** 18 total.

Freshman class profile. 60 applied, 52 admitted, 47 enrolled.

Basis for selection. Interview, character, religious affiliation most important. High school record and recommendations also important. **Home schooled:** Transcript of courses and grades, state high school equivalency certificate, interview, letter of recommendation (nonparent) required.

2011-2012 Annual costs. Tuition/fees: $9,400. Room/board: $6,600.

Application procedures. **Admission:** No deadline. $50 fee. Admission notification on a rolling basis. **Financial aid:** Closing date 3/1.

Academics. **Special study options:** Study abroad. **Credit/placement by examination:** AP, CLEP, institutional tests. 21 credit hours maximum toward bachelor's degree.

Majors. **Theology:** Talmudic.

Student life. **Policies:** Religious observance required.

Student services. **Physically disabled:** Services for visually, speech, hearing impaired.

Contact. Phone: (410) 484-7200
Rabbi Beryl Weisbord, Admissions Director, Ner Israel Rabbinical College, 400 Mount Wilson Lane, Baltimore, MD 21208

Notre Dame of Maryland University
Baltimore, Maryland
www.ndm.edu
CB member
CB code: 5114

- Private 4-year liberal arts college for women affiliated with Roman Catholic Church
- Residential campus in very large city
- 508 degree-seeking undergraduates: 6% part-time, 100% women, 35% African American, 7% Asian American, 6% Hispanic American, 1% Native American, 3% international
- 1,568 graduate students
- 55% of applicants admitted
- SAT or ACT (ACT writing recommended), application essay required
- 52% graduate within 6 years

General. Founded in 1873. Regionally accredited. Men admitted only to undergraduate and graduate weekend college programs. **Degrees:** 312 bachelor's awarded; master's, professional offered. **ROTC:** Army. **Location:** 5 miles from Baltimore, 37 miles from Washington, DC. **Calendar:** Semester, limited summer session. **Full-time faculty:** 104 total; 85% have terminal degrees, 16% minority, 71% women. **Part-time faculty:** 17 total; 71% have terminal degrees, 6% minority, 59% women. **Class size:** 78% < 20, 22% 20-39. **Special facilities:** Planetarium, photography laboratories.

Freshman class profile. 756 applied, 418 admitted, 137 enrolled.

Mid 50% test scores			
SAT critical reading:	450-590	GPA 2.0-2.99:	18%
SAT math:	450-570	Rank in top quarter:	46%
ACT composite:	19-26	Rank in top tenth:	15%
GPA 3.75 or higher:	29%	Return as sophomores:	71%
GPA 3.50-3.74:	21%	Out-of-state:	21%
GPA 3.0-3.49:	32%	Live on campus:	76%

Basis for selection. Careful evaluation of academic record, high school curriculum, test scores, recommendations, personal abilities/talents and goals, intellectual potential and eagerness to learn and be challenged. Students should take SAT by December of senior year. Interview and campus visit highly recommended. Portfolio recommended for art majors. **Home schooled:** Transcript or GED required. **Learning Disabled:** Students with learning disabilities should self-report during admissions process.

High school preparation. College-preparatory program required. 18 units required. Required units include English 4, mathematics 3, social studies 2, science 2 (laboratory 2), foreign language 3 and academic electives 4.

2011-2012 Annual costs. Tuition/fees: $29,700. Room/board: $9,900. Books/supplies: $1,200. Personal expenses: $1,000.

2010-2011 Financial aid. **Need-based:** 112 full-time freshmen applied for aid; 107 were judged to have need; 107 of these received aid. Average need met was 73%. Average scholarship/grant was $18,962; average loan $3,570. 58% of total undergraduate aid awarded as scholarships/grants, 42% as loans/jobs. **Non-need-based:** Awarded to 94 full-time undergraduates, including 28 freshmen. Scholarships awarded for academics, alumni affiliation, art, leadership, music/drama, ROTC. **Additional information:** Maximum consideration for financial aid if application received by February 15. Auditions and portfolios in areas of art, music and writing considered for scholarships.

Application procedures. **Admission:** Priority date 2/1; no deadline. $45 fee, may be waived for applicants with need, free for online applicants. Admission notification on a rolling basis beginning on or about 12/1. Must reply by May 1 or within 2 week(s) if notified thereafter. **Financial aid:** Priority date 2/15; no closing date. FAFSA required. Applicants notified on a rolling basis starting 3/15; must reply by 5/1 or within 2 week(s) of notification.

Academics. **Special study options:** Accelerated study, combined bachelor's/graduate degree, cross-registration, distance learning, double major, dual enrollment of high school students, ESL, honors, independent study, internships, liberal arts/career combination, student-designed major, study abroad, teacher certification program. 3-2 programs in engineering and nursing with Johns Hopkins University; academic consortium with seven local colleges and universities. **Credit/placement by examination:** AP, CLEP, IB, SAT, ACT, institutional tests. 30 credit hours maximum toward bachelor's degree. AP, CLEP and IB credits are posted upon admissions to college. Students should send testing information with their admissions application or prior to start of their first semester. **Support services:** Learning center, pre-admission summer program, reduced course load, study skills assistance, tutoring, writing center.

Majors. Biology: General. **Business:** General, finance, international, non-profit/public. **Communications:** Communications/speech/rhetoric. **Computer sciences:** General, computer science. **Education:** Early childhood, elementary, secondary, special ed. **Engineering:** General. **English:** English lit. **Foreign languages:** General, classics, French, Spanish. **Health services:** Medical radiologic technology/radiation therapy. **History:** General. **Human services:** Community org/advocacy. **Liberal arts:** Arts/sciences. **Math:** General. **Philosophy/religion:** Philosophy, religion. **Physical sciences:** Chemistry, physics. **Psychology:** General. **Social sciences:** Criminology, economics, international relations, political science. **Visual/performing arts:** Art, art history/conservation, photography, studio arts.

Most popular majors. Biology 7%, business/marketing 21%, communications/journalism 8%, education 14%, health sciences 7%, interdisciplinary studies 6%, liberal arts 11%.

Computing on campus. 80 workstations in dormitories, library, computer center, student center. Dormitories wired for high-speed internet access and linked to campus network. Commuter students can connect to campus network. Online course registration, online library, helpline, repair service, wireless network available.

Student life. Freshman orientation: Mandatory. Preregistration for classes offered. 2-day program in June; 4-day program prior to start of school in late August/early September. **Policies:** Must abide by honor code. **Housing:** Guaranteed on-campus for all undergraduates. Wellness housing available. $500 nonrefundable deposit, deadline 5/1. **Activities:** Campus ministries, choral groups, dance, drama, international student organizations, literary magazine, music ensembles, musical theater, radio station, student government, student newspaper, TV station, community service organization, Hispanic society, Black student organization, inter-organizational council, student environmental organization, international student organization, campus ministry student organization, student health educators.

Athletics. NCAA. **Intercollegiate:** Basketball W, field hockey W, lacrosse W, soccer W, softball W, swimming W, tennis W, volleyball W. **Team name:** Gators.

Student services. Adult student services, alcohol/substance abuse counseling, chaplain/spiritual director, career counseling, student employment services, financial aid counseling, health services, personal counseling, placement for graduates, veterans' counselor. **Physically disabled:** Services for visually, speech, hearing impaired.

Contact. E-mail: admiss@ndm.edu
Phone: (410) 532-5330 Toll-free number: (800) 435-0200
Fax: (410) 532-6287
Lucas Sifuentes, Director of Admissions, Notre Dame of Maryland University, 4701 North Charles Street, Baltimore, MD 21210

Salisbury University
Salisbury, Maryland
www.salisbury.edu

CB member
CB code: 5403

- Public 4-year university and liberal arts college
- Residential campus in large town
- 7,758 degree-seeking undergraduates: 6% part-time, 57% women, 11% African American, 2% Asian American, 4% Hispanic American, 1% international
- 638 degree-seeking graduate students
- 53% of applicants admitted
- Application essay required
- 67% graduate within 6 years; 24% enter graduate study

General. Founded in 1925. Regionally accredited. **Degrees:** 1,709 bachelor's awarded; master's offered. **ROTC:** Army, Air Force. **Location:** 110 miles from Baltimore and Washington, DC. **Calendar:** 4-1-4, extensive summer session. **Full-time faculty:** 390 total; 83% have terminal degrees, 13% minority, 46% women. **Part-time faculty:** 224 total; 15% have terminal degrees, 8% minority, 31% women. **Class size:** 32% < 20, 60% 20-39, 4% 40-49, 3% 50-99, less than 1% >100. **Special facilities:** Arboretum, galleries, history and culture research center, center for conflict resolution, small business development center, museum of wildfowl art.

Freshman class profile. 8,021 applied, 4,232 admitted, 1,248 enrolled.

Mid 50% test scores		Rank in top quarter:	59%
SAT critical reading:	530-600	Rank in top tenth:	25%
SAT math:	540-620	End year in good standing:	84%
SAT writing:	530-600	Return as sophomores:	83%
ACT composite:	22-26	Out-of-state:	22%
GPA 3.75 or higher:	41%	Live on campus:	88%
GPA 3.50-3.74:	31%	International:	1%
GPA 3.0-3.49:	21%	Sororities:	2%
GPA 2.0-2.99:	7%		

Basis for selection. Rigor of secondary school record, including level of courses, depth of subjects, GPA, most important. Activities, leadership roles, artistic or athletic talents, ability to contribute to a culturally diverse community also important. SAT and ACT not required for students who have been out of high school for more than 3 years or for whom TOEFL is required. Students earning a weighed grade point average of a 3.5 or higher on a 4.0 scale upon high school graduation may choose whether or not to submit SAT or ACT scores. Auditions are required for admission into the music program once admission to the University is granted.

High school preparation. College-preparatory program recommended. 15 units required; 21 recommended. Required and recommended units include English 4, mathematics 3-4, social studies 3, science 3-4 (laboratory 2-3), foreign language 2-3 and academic electives 3.

2011-2012 Annual costs. Tuition/fees: $7,332; $15,678 out-of-state. Room/board: $8,958. Books/supplies: $1,300. Personal expenses: $1,510.

2010-2011 Financial aid. Need-based: 1,073 full-time freshmen applied for aid; 658 were judged to have need; 656 of these received aid. Average need met was 57%. Average scholarship/grant was $5,858; average loan $3,160. 42% of total undergraduate aid awarded as scholarships/grants, 58% as loans/jobs. **Non-need-based:** Awarded to 690 full-time undergraduates, including 279 freshmen. Scholarships awarded for academics, alumni affiliation, art, leadership, music/drama, ROTC, state residency.

Application procedures. Admission: Closing date 1/15 (postmark date). $45 fee, may be waived for applicants with need. Application must be submitted online. Admission notification by 3/15. Must reply by 5/1. **Financial aid:** Priority date 3/1, closing date 5/31. FAFSA required. Applicants notified by 3/15; Applicants notified on a rolling basis starting 3/15; must reply by 5/1.

Academics. Special study options: Accelerated study, combined bachelor's/graduate degree, cooperative education, cross-registration, distance learning, double major, dual enrollment of high school students, ESL, exchange student, honors, independent study, internships, liberal arts/career combination, student-designed major, study abroad, teacher certification program, Washington semester. **Credit/placement by examination:** AP, CLEP, IB, institutional tests. 60 credit hours maximum toward bachelor's degree. **Support services:** Learning center, study skills assistance, tutoring, writing center.

Majors. Biology: General. **Business:** Accounting, business admin, finance, marketing. **Communications:** Communications/speech/rhetoric. **Computer sciences:** General, information systems. **Conservation:** Environmental science. **Education:** Early childhood, elementary, ESL, health, physical. **English:** English lit. **Foreign languages:** French, Spanish. **Health services:** Athletic training, clinical lab science, nursing (RN), respiratory therapy technology. **History:** General. **Human services:** Social work. **Math:** General. **Parks/recreation:** Exercise sciences. **Philosophy/religion:** Philosophy. **Physical sciences:** Chemistry, physics. **Psychology:** General. **Social sciences:** Economics, geography, political science, sociology. **Visual/performing arts:** Art, dramatic, music, studio arts.

Most popular majors. Biology 6%, business/marketing 17%, communications/journalism 8%, education 12%, health sciences 8%, psychology 7%, social sciences 6%.

Computing on campus. 390 workstations in library, computer center, student center. Dormitories wired for high-speed internet access and linked to campus network. Commuter students can connect to campus network. Online course registration, online library, helpline, repair service, student web hosting, wireless network available.

Student life. Freshman orientation: Available. Preregistration for classes offered. Orientation fee varies by program. **Policies:** Class attendance policies vary by instructor. Hazing and smoking is prohibited. **Housing:** Coed dorms, special housing for disabled, apartments, wellness housing available. $300 nonrefundable deposit, deadline 5/13. **Activities:** Bands, campus ministries, choral groups, dance, drama, film society, international student organizations, literary magazine, music ensembles, musical theater, radio station, student government, student newspaper, symphony orchestra, TV station, Campus Crusade for Christ, Fellowship of Christian Athletes, Catholic Campus Ministry, Baptist Student Ministries, Union of African-Americans, NAACP, African American Historical & Philosophical Society, Muslim student organization.

Athletics. NCAA. **Intercollegiate:** Baseball M, basketball, cross-country, field hockey W, football (tackle) M, lacrosse, soccer, softball W, swimming, tennis, track and field, volleyball W. **Intramural:** Basketball, football (nontackle), racquetball, soccer, softball, volleyball, water polo. **Team name:** Seagulls.

Student services. Alcohol/substance abuse counseling, career counseling, student employment services, financial aid counseling, health services, minority student services, personal counseling, veterans' counselor. **Physically disabled:** Services for visually, speech, hearing impaired.

Contact. E-mail: admissions@salisbury.edu
Phone: (410) 543-6161 Toll-free number: (888) 543-0148
Fax: (410) 546-6016
Aaron Basko, Director of Admissions, Salisbury University, 1200 Camden Avenue, Salisbury, MD 21801-6862

Sojourner-Douglass College
Baltimore, Maryland
www.sdc.edu   **CB code: 0504**

- Private 4-year liberal arts college
- Very large city

General. Founded in 1980. Regionally accredited. **Location:** Downtown. **Calendar:** Semester.

Annual costs/financial aid. Tuition/fees (2011-2012): $8,850. Books/supplies: $800. Personal expenses: $2,800. Need-based financial aid available to full-time and part-time students.

Contact. Phone: (410) 276-0306 ext. 248
Director of Admissions, 500 North Caroline Street, Baltimore, MD 21205

St. John's College
Annapolis, Maryland   **CB member**
www.stjohnscollege.edu   **CB code: 5598**

- Private 4-year liberal arts college
- Residential campus in large town
- 490 degree-seeking undergraduates: 43% women, 1% African American, 2% Asian American, 4% Hispanic American, 7% international
- 59 degree-seeking graduate students
- 78% of applicants admitted
- Application essay required
- 60% graduate within 6 years

General. Founded in 1784. Regionally accredited. Second campus in Santa Fe, New Mexico. Students may transfer between campuses. **Degrees:** 88 bachelor's awarded; master's offered. **Location:** 35 miles from Washington, DC, 30 miles from Baltimore. **Calendar:** Semester. **Full-time faculty:** 70 total; 81% have terminal degrees, 7% minority, 27% women. **Part-time faculty:** 5 total; 20% have terminal degrees. **Class size:** 93% < 20, 7% 20-39, less than 1% >100. **Special facilities:** Planetarium, boathouse, observatory.

Freshman class profile. 433 applied, 338 admitted, 150 enrolled.

Mid 50% test scores		Return as sophomores:	90%
SAT critical reading:	640-730	Out-of-state:	89%
SAT math:	570-680	Live on campus:	100%
Rank in top quarter:	51%	International:	4%
Rank in top tenth:	31%		

Basis for selection. One optional and 3 required essays most important. School achievement record and teacher recommendations important. 2-day campus visit and interview recommended. Standardized tests required for homeschooled and international students. **Home schooled:** Statement describing home school structure and mission, letter of recommendation (nonparent) required. Must submit results of PSAT, SAT, or ACT if high school diploma will not be earned.

High school preparation. College-preparatory program recommended. 5 units required. Required and recommended units include English 4, mathematics 3-4, social studies 2, history 2, science 3 (laboratory 3) and foreign language 2-4.

2012-2013 Annual costs. Tuition/fees (projected): $44,994. Room/board: $10,644. Books/supplies: $630. Personal expenses: $400.

2011-2012 Financial aid. All financial aid based on need. Average scholarship/grant was $30,805; average loan $4,047. 77% of total undergraduate aid awarded as scholarships/grants, 23% as loans/jobs.

Application procedures. Admission: Priority date 3/1; no deadline. No application fee. Admission notification on a rolling basis. Must reply by May 1 or within 2 week(s) if notified thereafter. Early application encouraged as class generally fills by first week in May. **Financial aid:** Priority date 2/15; no closing date. FAFSA, CSS PROFILE required. Applicants notified on a rolling basis starting 1/15; must reply by 5/1.

Academics. Credit/placement by examination: AP, CLEP. **Support services:** Tutoring, writing center.

Majors. Liberal arts: Arts/sciences.

Computing on campus. 20 workstations in library, computer center. Dormitories wired for high-speed internet access and linked to campus network. Commuter students can connect to campus network.

Student life. Freshman orientation: Mandatory. Preregistration for classes offered. 2-day program, after registration and prior to start of classes. **Policies:** Freshmen required to live in dormitories. **Housing:** Guaranteed on-campus for freshmen. Coed dorms, wellness housing available. **Activities:** Choral groups, dance, drama, film society, international student organizations, literary magazine, music ensembles, musical theater, student government, student newspaper, Political Forum, Project Politae, Pink Triangle Society, Christian Fellowship, Jewish Students Society, Student Committee on Instruction, Environmental Club, Amnesty International, Delegate Council.

Athletics. Intramural: Badminton, basketball, boxing M, fencing, football (non-tackle) M, handball, rowing (crew), sailing, soccer, softball, table tennis, tennis, track and field, volleyball.

Student services. Alcohol/substance abuse counseling, career counseling, student employment services, financial aid counseling, health services, personal counseling, placement for graduates, women's services.

Contact. E-mail: admissions@sjca.edu
Phone: (410) 626-2522 Toll-free number: (800) 727-9238
Fax: (410) 269-7916
Sarah Morse, Director of Admissions, St. John's College, PO Box 2800, Annapolis, MD 21404

St. Mary's College of Maryland
St. Mary's City, Maryland   **CB member**
www.smcm.edu   **CB code: 5601**

- Public 4-year liberal arts college
- Residential campus in small town
- 1,908 degree-seeking undergraduates: 2% part-time, 59% women, 8% African American, 3% Asian American, 4% Hispanic American, 2% international
- 30 degree-seeking graduate students
- 61% of applicants admitted
- SAT or ACT (ACT writing optional), application essay required
- 79% graduate within 6 years; 34% enter graduate study

General. Founded in 1840. Regionally accredited. **Degrees:** 410 bachelor's awarded; master's offered. **Location:** 70 miles from Washington, DC. **Calendar:** Semester, limited summer session. **Full-time faculty:** 136 total; 98% have terminal degrees, 12% minority, 46% women. **Part-time faculty:** 90 total; 40% have terminal degrees, 8% minority, 54% women. **Class size:** 66% < 20, 32% 20-39, 2% 40-49, less than 1% 50-99. **Special facilities:** Archaeological site of Historic St. Mary's City, electron microscope, marine research vessel, fresh and salt water research facilities, comprehensive neuroscience laboratory facilities.

Freshman class profile. 2,398 applied, 1,472 admitted, 446 enrolled.

Mid 50% test scores		GPA 3.0-3.49:	41%
SAT critical reading:	560-680	GPA 2.0-2.99:	21%
SAT math:	540-650	Return as sophomores:	87%
SAT writing:	550-670	Out-of-state:	17%
GPA 3.75 or higher:	19%	Live on campus:	96%
GPA 3.50-3.74:	18%	International:	2%

Basis for selection. High school record, SAT or ACT scores, recommendations by counselors/teachers, co-curricular resume, and essay most important. Interview recommended for admissions. **Home schooled:** Transcript of courses and grades, state high school equivalency certificate required. Personal statement.

High school preparation. College-preparatory program recommended. 20 units required; 24 recommended. Required and recommended units include English 4, mathematics 3-4, social studies 2, history 1-2, science 3 (laboratory 2) and foreign language 2-4.

2011-2012 Annual costs. Tuition/fees: $14,445; $26,522 out-of-state. Room/board: $10,900. Books/supplies: $1,000. Personal expenses: $1,500.

2010-2011 Financial aid. Need-based: 356 full-time freshmen applied for aid; 205 were judged to have need; 201 of these received aid. Average need met was 62%. Average scholarship/grant was $8,334; average loan

$3,172. 58% of total undergraduate aid awarded as scholarships/grants, 42% as loans/jobs. **Non-need-based:** Awarded to 879 full-time undergraduates, including 219 freshmen. Scholarships awarded for academics, alumni affiliation, leadership.

Application procedures. Admission: Closing date 1/1 (postmark date). $50 fee, may be waived for applicants with need. Admission notification by 4/1. Must reply by 5/1. **Financial aid:** Closing date 3/1. FAFSA required. Applicants notified by 4/1; must reply by 5/1.

Academics. Special study options: Double major, dual enrollment of high school students, exchange student, honors, independent study, internships, semester at sea, student-designed major, study abroad. International study programs in Argentina, Australia, China, Costa Rica, England, France, the Gambia, Germany, Japan, India, Italy, Thailand, and many other short-term study tours around the world. Opportunities for participating in colonial and archaeological research. **Credit/placement by examination:** AP, CLEP, IB, SAT, institutional tests. 45 credit hours maximum toward bachelor's degree. **Support services:** Reduced course load, study skills assistance, tutoring, writing center.

Majors. Area/ethnic studies: Asian. **Biology:** General, biochemistry. **Computer sciences:** General. **English:** English lit. **Foreign languages:** General. **History:** General. **Human services:** Public policy. **Liberal arts:** Humanities. **Math:** General. **Philosophy/religion:** Philosophy, religion. **Physical sciences:** Chemistry, physics. **Psychology:** General. **Social sciences:** Anthropology, economics, political science, sociology. **Visual/performing arts:** Art, dramatic, music.

Most popular majors. Biology 10%, English 11%, foreign language 6%, psychology 15%, social sciences 34%.

Computing on campus. 400 workstations in library, computer center, student center. Dormitories wired for high-speed internet access and linked to campus network. Commuter students can connect to campus network. Online course registration, online library, helpline, student web hosting, wireless network available.

Student life. Freshman orientation: Mandatory, $100 fee. Preregistration for classes offered. **Policies:** Membership in student organizations is available to all full-time, degree-seeking students. Elected student leaders must be in good standing with the institution in order to serve. **Housing:** Guaranteed on-campus for all undergraduates. Coed dorms, single-sex dorms, special housing for disabled, apartments, wellness housing available. $500 nonrefundable deposit, deadline 5/1. Pets allowed in dorm rooms. Townhouses and suites available for upper-class students. **Activities:** Jazz band, choral groups, dance, drama, film society, international student organizations, literary magazine, music ensembles, musical theater, radio station, student government, student newspaper, symphony orchestra, Black student union, College Republicans, College Democrats, Amnesty International, For Goodness Sake, Hillel, Habitat for Humanity, Student Environmental Action Coalition, Intervarsity Christian Fellowship, St. Mary's Triangle.

Athletics. NCAA. **Intercollegiate:** Baseball M, basketball, cross-country, field hockey W, lacrosse, sailing, soccer, swimming, tennis, volleyball W. **Intramural:** Badminton, basketball, cross-country, field hockey, football (non-tackle), soccer, volleyball, water polo. **Team name:** Seahawks.

Student services. Alcohol/substance abuse counseling, career counseling, student employment services, financial aid counseling, health services, minority student services, personal counseling, placement for graduates, veterans' counselor, women's services. **Physically disabled:** Services for visually, hearing impaired.

Contact. E-mail: admissions@smcm.edu
Phone: (240) 895-5000 Toll-free number: (800) 492-7181
Fax: (240) 895-5001
Richard Edgar, Director of Admissions, St. Mary's College of Maryland, 18952 East Fisher Road, St. Mary's City, MD 20686-3001

Stevenson University
Stevenson, Maryland
www.stevenson.edu
CB member
CB code: 5856

- Private 4-year university
- Residential campus in very large city
- 3,804 degree-seeking undergraduates: 16% part-time, 65% women, 26% African American, 3% Asian American, 3% Hispanic American
- 444 degree-seeking graduate students
- 58% of applicants admitted
- SAT or ACT (ACT writing optional), application essay required
- 62% graduate within 6 years

General. Founded in 1947. Regionally accredited. **Degrees:** 722 bachelor's awarded; master's offered. **ROTC:** Army, Air Force. **Location:** 8 miles from Baltimore. **Calendar:** Semester, extensive summer session. **Full-time faculty:** 117 total; 67% have terminal degrees, 14% minority, 53% women. **Part-time faculty:** 331 total. **Class size:** 62% < 20, 38% 20-39.

Freshman class profile. 5,794 applied, 3,369 admitted, 870 enrolled.

Mid 50% test scores			
SAT critical reading:	430-540	GPA 3.0-3.49:	36%
SAT math:	440-550	GPA 2.0-2.99:	28%
SAT writing:	430-530	Rank in top quarter:	43%
ACT composite:	17-22	Rank in top tenth:	3%
GPA 3.75 or higher:	22%	Return as sophomores:	75%
GPA 3.50-3.74:	13%	Out-of-state:	24%
		Live on campus:	83%

Basis for selection. High school record and test scores most important. Optional interview, recommendations, essay, extracurricular activities also important. Interviews are recommended but not required.

High school preparation. College-preparatory program recommended. 17 units required. Required and recommended units include English 4, mathematics 3, social studies 2, history 1, science 3 (laboratory 2), foreign language 2 and academic electives 4.

2011-2012 Annual costs. Tuition/fees: $23,636. Room and board fees includes laundry. Room/board: $11,278.

2010-2011 Financial aid. Need-based: 829 full-time freshmen applied for aid; 717 were judged to have need; 716 of these received aid. Average need met was 61%. Average scholarship/grant was $13,080; average loan $3,300. 64% of total undergraduate aid awarded as scholarships/grants, 36% as loans/jobs. **Non-need-based:** Awarded to 422 full-time undergraduates, including 150 freshmen. Scholarships awarded for academics, art, leadership, music/drama, ROTC. **Additional information:** Cooperative Education Program allows students to work in their field of study with area corporations.

Application procedures. Admission: Priority date 3/1; no deadline. $40 fee, may be waived for applicants with need, free for online applicants. Admission notification on a rolling basis beginning on or about 12/1. Must reply by May 1 or within 2 week(s) if notified thereafter. **Financial aid:** Priority date 2/15; no closing date. FAFSA required. Applicants notified on a rolling basis starting 3/15; must reply by 5/1 or within 2 week(s) of notification.

Academics. Advanced technology programs, forensic science program and forensic studies programs offered. Cooperative education program available to third- and fourth-year students. Career Architecture, a program for personal and professional development, is integrated into all programs. **Special study options:** Accelerated study, cooperative education, cross-registration, distance learning, double major, dual enrollment of high school students, honors, independent study, internships, liberal arts/career combination, student-designed major, study abroad, teacher certification program, Washington semester. **Credit/placement by examination:** AP, CLEP, IB, SAT, ACT, institutional tests. 15 credit hours maximum toward associate degree, 30 toward bachelor's. **Support services:** Learning center, pre-admission summer program, reduced course load, remedial instruction, study skills assistance, tutoring, writing center.

Majors. Biology: General, biotechnology. **Business:** Accounting, business admin, communications, fashion, management information systems. **Computer sciences:** Information systems, networking. **Education:** Elementary, kindergarten/preschool, middle. **English:** English lit. **Health services:** Clinical lab science, nursing (RN). **History:** Applied. **Math:** Applied. **Physical sciences:** Chemistry. **Protective services:** Law enforcement admin. **Psychology:** General. **Visual/performing arts:** Design, film/cinema/video. **Work/family studies:** Family/community services.

Most popular majors. Business/marketing 22%, computer/information sciences 9%, education 9%, health sciences 22%, psychology 6%, visual/performing arts 6%.

Computing on campus. 600 workstations in library, computer center, student center. Dormitories wired for high-speed internet access and linked to campus network. Commuter students can connect to campus network. Online course registration, online library, helpline, repair service, wireless network available.

Student life. Freshman orientation: Mandatory. Preregistration for classes offered. Full-day program, conducted by major, held during June. Freshmen also attend second orientation in August, prior to start of fall semester. **Housing:** Apartments, wellness housing available. Suite style housing (2 bedrooms, share bath); accomodations made for students with disabilities. **Activities:** Bands, campus ministries, choral groups, dance, drama, international student organizations, literary magazine, music ensembles, radio station, student government, student newspaper, symphony orchestra, TV station, Black Student Union, Service Corps, Campus Crusade for Christ,

Extreme Acts, Mustang Activities and Program Board, Accounting Association, Students Helping Students.

Athletics. NCAA. **Intercollegiate:** Basketball, cross-country, field hockey W, football (tackle) M, golf, ice hockey W, lacrosse, soccer, softball W, tennis, track and field, volleyball. **Intramural:** Badminton, basketball, fencing, football (non-tackle) M, sailing, skiing, soccer, table tennis, tennis, track and field, volleyball. **Team name:** Mustangs.

Student services. Adult student services, alcohol/substance abuse counseling, career counseling, student employment services, financial aid counseling, health services, minority student services, personal counseling, placement for graduates, veterans' counselor. **Physically disabled:** Services for visually, hearing impaired.

Contact. E-mail: admissions@stevenson.edu
Phone: (410) 486-7001 Toll-free number: (877) 468-6852
Fax: (443) 352-4440
Mark Hergan, Vice President for Enrollment Management, Stevenson University, 1525 Greenspring Valley Road, Stevenson, MD 21153-0641

Towson University
Towson, Maryland   **CB member**
www.towson.edu   **CB code: 5404**

- Public 4-year university
- Commuter campus in large city
- 17,138 degree-seeking undergraduates: 10% part-time, 60% women, 13% African American, 4% Asian American, 4% Hispanic American, 2% international
- 3,746 degree-seeking graduate students
- 54% of applicants admitted
- SAT or ACT with writing required
- 64% graduate within 6 years

General. Founded in 1866. Regionally accredited. **Degrees:** 3,948 bachelor's awarded; master's, professional, doctoral offered. **ROTC:** Army, Air Force. **Location:** 1.5 miles from Baltimore. **Calendar:** Semester, extensive summer session. **Full-time faculty:** 841 total; 75% have terminal degrees, 16% minority, 55% women. **Part-time faculty:** 830 total; 26% have terminal degrees, 13% minority, 54% women. **Class size:** 36% < 20, 59% 20-39, 4% 40-49, less than 1% 50-99, less than 1% >100. **Special facilities:** Planetarium, Asian art collection, concert hall, greenhouse, herbarium, observatory, animal museum.

Freshman class profile. 15,880 applied, 8,610 admitted, 2,543 enrolled.

Mid 50% test scores				
SAT critical reading:	490-580	GPA 2.0-2.99:		2%
SAT math:	500-590	Rank in top quarter:		58%
SAT writing:	500-590	Rank in top tenth:		22%
ACT composite:	21-25	Return as sophomores:		84%
GPA 3.75 or higher:	37%	Out-of-state:		28%
GPA 3.50-3.74:	24%	Live on campus:		86%
GPA 3.0-3.49:	37%	International:		1%

Basis for selection. High school record, test scores important; class rank, recommendations, essay considered. Interview and essay recommended. Audition required of music, dance majors. **Home schooled:** Writing samples, 3 letters of recommendation, course-work summary required.

High school preparation. 21 units required. Required units include English 4, mathematics 3, social studies 3, science 3 (laboratory 2), foreign language 2 and academic electives 6.

2011-2012 Annual costs. Tuition/fees: $7,906; $19,418 out-of-state. Room/board: $9,942. Books/supplies: $1,080. Personal expenses: $2,050.

2011-2012 Financial aid. **Need-based:** 2,158 full-time freshmen applied for aid; 1,466 were judged to have need; 1,349 of these received aid. Average need met was 60%. Average scholarship/grant was $8,744; average loan $3,154. 57% of total undergraduate aid awarded as scholarships/grants, 43% as loans/jobs. **Non-need-based:** Awarded to 3,330 full-time undergraduates, including 782 freshmen. Scholarships awarded for academics, alumni affiliation, art, athletics, music/drama, ROTC.

Application procedures. **Admission:** Priority date 12/1; deadline 2/15 (postmark date). $45 fee, may be waived for applicants with need. Admission notification on a rolling basis beginning on or about 10/15. Must reply by May 1 or within 2 week(s) if notified thereafter. **Financial aid:** Priority date 3/1, closing date 2/10. FAFSA required. Applicants notified on a rolling basis starting 3/21; must reply by 5/1 or within 2 week(s) of notification.

Academics. **Special study options:** Combined bachelor's/graduate degree, cooperative education, cross-registration, distance learning, double major, dual enrollment of high school students, ESL, exchange student, honors, independent study, internships, liberal arts/career combination, student-designed major, study abroad, teacher certification program. 3-2 engineering with University of Maryland, College Park. **Credit/placement by examination:** AP, CLEP, IB, SAT, ACT, institutional tests. 45 credit hours maximum toward bachelor's degree. Portfolio reviews, oral exams, demonstrations or written reports/papers considered for credit. **Support services:** Learning center, remedial instruction, study skills assistance, tutoring, writing center.

Honors college/program. Guaranteed admission with unweighted GPA of 3.60 on 4.00 scale and score of 1800 on SAT. If either criterion lacking, admission based on comprehensive review of course selection, HS curriculum, and skills.

Majors. **Area/ethnic studies:** American, women's. **Biology:** General, Biochemistry/molecular biology, ecology. **Business:** Accounting, business admin. **Communications:** Communications/speech/rhetoric, journalism, media studies. **Communications technology:** Radio/TV. **Computer sciences:** General, computer science, information technology. **Conservation:** Environmental studies. **Education:** Art, early childhood, elementary, music, physical, special ed. **English:** English lit. **Foreign languages:** General. **Health services:** Athletic training, audiology/speech pathology, health care admin, nursing (RN), substance abuse counseling. **History:** General. **Math:** General. **Parks/recreation:** Exercise sciences, sports admin. **Philosophy/religion:** Judaic, philosophy, religion. **Physical sciences:** Chemistry, geology, physics, planetary. **Protective services:** Forensics. **Psychology:** General. **Social sciences:** General, economics, geography, international relations, political science, sociology, urban studies. **Visual/performing arts:** Art, dance, dramatic, music, studio arts. **Work/family studies:** Family systems.

Most popular majors. Business/marketing 18%, communications/journalism 9%, education 12%, health sciences 10%, psychology 7%, social sciences 10%, visual/performing arts 6%.

Computing on campus. 1,200 workstations in dormitories, library, computer center, student center. Dormitories wired for high-speed internet access and linked to campus network. Commuter students can connect to campus network. Online course registration, online library, helpline, student web hosting, wireless network available.

Student life. **Freshman orientation:** Mandatory. Preregistration for classes offered. **Policies:** Students play active role in university governance. **Housing:** Guaranteed on-campus for freshmen. Coed dorms, special housing for disabled, apartments, wellness housing available. $350 nonrefundable deposit, deadline 5/1. Honors hall, alcohol free floors, academic emphasis floors, non-traditional age area, non-smoking floors, leadership floor, special quiet floors available. **Activities:** Bands, campus ministries, choral groups, dance, drama, international student organizations, literary magazine, music ensembles, musical theater, radio station, student government, student newspaper, symphony orchestra, TV station, Black student union, Jewish student association, Circle K, student ambassadors, Newman Club, Campus Crusades, Hillel, sisterhood.

Athletics. NCAA. **Intercollegiate:** Baseball M, basketball, cheerleading, cross-country, diving, field hockey W, football (tackle) M, golf M, gymnastics W, lacrosse, soccer, softball W, swimming, tennis, track and field, volleyball W. **Intramural:** Basketball, cross-country, football (non-tackle), lacrosse, racquetball, soccer, softball, tennis, triathlon, volleyball. **Team name:** Tigers.

Student services. Adult student services, alcohol/substance abuse counseling, chaplain/spiritual director, career counseling, student employment services, financial aid counseling, health services, minority student services, on-campus daycare, personal counseling, placement for graduates, veterans' counselor, women's services. **Physically disabled:** Services for visually, speech, hearing impaired.

Contact. E-mail: admissions@towson.edu
Phone: (410) 704-2113 Toll-free number: (888) 486-9766
Fax: (410) 704-3030
Brian Hazlett, Director of Undergraduate Admissions, Towson University, 8000 York Road, Towson, MD 21252-0001

United States Naval Academy
Annapolis, Maryland   **CB member**
www.usna.edu   **CB code: 5809**

- Public 4-year military college
- Residential campus in large town
- 4,576 degree-seeking undergraduates: 20% women, 6% African American, 5% Asian American, 12% Hispanic American, 1% international
- 7% of applicants admitted

◆ SAT or ACT (ACT writing optional), application essay, interview required

◆ 90% graduate within 6 years; 6% enter graduate study

General. Founded in 1845. Regionally accredited. **Degrees:** 1,017 bachelor's awarded. **Location:** 30 miles from Baltimore, 32 miles from Washington, DC. **Calendar:** Semester, limited summer session. **Full-time faculty:** 478 total; 70% have terminal degrees, 11% minority, 26% women. **Part-time faculty:** 50 total; 44% have terminal degrees, 8% minority, 54% women. **Class size:** 61% < 20, 39% 20-39, less than 1% 40-49. **Special facilities:** Observatory, planetarium, satellite EarthStation, oceanographic research vessel, weather station, tow tanks, propulsion laboratory, transsonic and hypersonic wind tunnels, museum.

Freshman class profile. 19,145 applied, 1,426 admitted, 1,229 enrolled.

Mid 50% test scores		End year in good standing:	98%
SAT critical reading:	560-680	Return as sophomores:	95%
SAT math:	600-700	Out-of-state:	93%
Rank in top quarter:	79%	Live on campus:	100%
Rank in top tenth:	52%	International:	1%

Basis for selection. Test scores, school achievement record, interview, recommendations of school officials, participation in sports, school, and community activities important. Rank in top 40% of class usually required. Successful candidate must be qualified medically, pass a candidate physical fitness assessment, and be nominated by an official source.

High school preparation. College-preparatory program recommended. Recommended units include English 4, mathematics 4, history 2, science 2 (laboratory 2) and foreign language 2. Familiarity with the use of personal computers, including the Windows operating system, word processing, spreadsheets, and the Internet required.

2012-2013 Annual costs. The Naval Academy does not charge tuition, room, board, or any other fees. Medical and dental care are provided by the United States government. Each midshipman receives monthly salary of about $970 to cover costs of books, supplies, uniforms, laundry, and equipment including a microcomputer and netbook.

Application procedures. Admission: Closing date 1/31 (receipt date). No application fee. Application must be submitted online. Admission notification on a rolling basis beginning on or about 9/1. Must reply by May 1 or within 2 week(s) if notified thereafter. Nomination essential prior to consideration for appointment. Nominating authorities include President, Vice President, Secretary of Navy, members of Congress, delegates to Congress, governors of United States Territories, and resident commissioner of Puerto Rico. Applicants for presidential appointments limited by law to sons and daughters of career military personnel, active or retired. Applicants encouraged to apply to the Academy and nominating authority by May one year prior to desired admission.

Academics. Military environment and organization under student leadership with military officer supervision. Professional training at US bases and with units of the United States Navy and United States Marine Corps during summer months. Graduates receive B.S. degree with a major in one of 23 disciplines, plus commission as Ensign in US Navy or Second Lieutenant in US Marine Corps. **Special study options:** Double major, exchange student, honors, independent study, study abroad. Qualified students have opportunities to begin work in second semester of senior year towards a Master's degree at local graduate schools. Selected midshipmen can also engage in research with thesis, or work towards honors in their majors. **Credit/placement by examination:** AP, CLEP, IB, SAT, ACT, institutional tests. Midshipmen take local examinations after admission for placement. AP Exam scores also used for validation of some courses. **Support services:** Learning center, remedial instruction, study skills assistance, tutoring, writing center.

Majors. Computer sciences: General, information technology. **Engineering:** General, aerospace, computer hardware, electrical, marine, mechanical, ocean, operations research, systems. **English:** English lit. **Foreign languages:** Arabic, Chinese. **History:** General. **Math:** General, applied. **Physical sciences:** General, chemistry, oceanography, physics. **Social sciences:** Econometrics, economics, political science.

Most popular majors. Engineering/engineering technologies 30%, English 6%, history 9%, physical sciences 17%, social sciences 30%.

Computing on campus. PC or laptop required. Dormitories wired for high-speed internet access and linked to campus network. Online course registration, online library, helpline, repair service, wireless network available.

Student life. Freshman orientation: Mandatory. Preregistration for classes offered. All freshmen (plebes) report in late June/early July for approximately 6 weeks of military indoctrination. **Policies:** The Naval Academy has an Honor Concept administered by the Brigade of Midshipmen. Freshmen

not permitted cars on campus. **Housing:** Guaranteed on-campus for all undergraduates. Coed dorms, wellness housing available. Midshipmen must live in the dormitory on campus all four years. **Activities:** Bands, choral groups, drama, film society, literary magazine, music ensembles, musical theater, radio station, student newspaper, Fellowship of Christian Athletes, Black Studies Club, Midshipmen Action Group, Officers' Christian Fellowship, Foreign Affairs Conference, Women's Professional Association.

Athletics. NCAA. **Intercollegiate:** Baseball M, basketball, cross-country, diving, football (tackle) M, golf M, gymnastics M, lacrosse, rifle, rowing (crew), sailing, soccer, squash M, swimming, tennis, track and field, volleyball W, water polo M, wrestling M. **Intramural:** Basketball, boxing, cross-country, football (non-tackle), golf, handball, judo, racquetball, sailing, soccer, softball, swimming, volleyball, weight lifting, wrestling. **Team name:** Midshipmen.

Student services. Alcohol/substance abuse counseling, chaplain/spiritual director, career counseling, health services, legal services, minority student services, personal counseling, placement for graduates, women's services.

Contact. E-mail: webmail@usna.edu
Phone: (410) 293-4361 Toll-free number: (888) 249-7707
Fax: (410) 293-1815
Dean of Admissions, United States Naval Academy, 117 Decatur Road, Annapolis, MD 21402-5018

University of Baltimore
Baltimore, Maryland   **CB member**
www.ubalt.edu   **CB code: 5810**

◆ Public 4-year university and liberal arts college
◆ Commuter campus in very large city

General. Founded in 1925. Regionally accredited. **Location:** Midtown Baltimore. **Calendar:** Semester.

Annual costs/financial aid. Tuition/fees (2011-2012): $7,494; $17,446 out-of-state. Books/supplies: $730. Need-based financial aid available to full-time and part-time students.

Contact. Phone: (410) 837-4777
Director of Freshman Admission, 1420 North Charles Street, Baltimore, MD 21201-5779

University of Maryland: Baltimore
Baltimore, Maryland
www.umaryland.edu   **CB code: 0527**

◆ Public two-year upper-division university and health science college
◆ Commuter campus in very large city
◆ 37% of applicants admitted

General. Founded in 1807. Regionally accredited. **Degrees:** 359 bachelor's awarded; master's, professional, doctoral offered. **Articulation:** Agreements with all Maryland community colleges. **Location:** Downtown. **Calendar:** 4-1-4, limited summer session. **Full-time faculty:** 411 total; 66% have terminal degrees, 24% minority, 61% women. **Part-time faculty:** 608 total; 46% have terminal degrees, 18% minority, 62% women. **Special facilities:** Dental, medical, pharmacy and nursing museums; law library, health sciences library, center for health policy and health services research, center for research on aging, center for vaccine development, biotechnology institute, center for health and homeland security.

Student profile. 723 degree-seeking undergraduates, 5,505 degree-seeking graduate students. 717 applied as first time-transfer students, 262 admitted, 196 enrolled.

Women:	84%	International:	3%
African American:	17%	Part-time:	30%
Asian American:	14%	Out-of-state:	6%
Hispanic American:	5%	25 or older:	64%

Basis for selection. College transcript required. Undergraduate deadlines range from February 1 to August 15 (nursing, dental hygiene, medical technology). Transfer accepted as juniors, seniors.

2011-2012 Annual costs. Tuition/fees: $8,966; $27,426 out-of-state. Books/supplies: $1,955. Personal expenses: $425.

Financial aid. Additional information: Maryland state deadline 3/1.

Application procedures. Admission: $50 fee. Admission process, fees, and dates differ among undergraduate programs (nursing, dental hygiene, medical technology). **Financial aid:** FAFSA required.

Academics. Special study options: Combined bachelor's/graduate degree, distance learning, double major. **Credit/placement by examination:** AP, CLEP, institutional tests. 30 credit hours maximum toward bachelor's degree.

Majors. Health services: Clinical lab science, dental hygiene, nursing (RN).

Computing on campus. 100 workstations in library, computer center, student center. Dormitories wired for high-speed internet access and linked to campus network. Commuter students can connect to campus network. Online library, helpline, wireless network available.

Student life. Housing: Apartments available. **Activities:** International student organizations, student government, Jewish student association, Muslim student and scholars association, United Students of African Descent, Project Jump Start.

Athletics. Intramural: Badminton, basketball, football (non-tackle), golf, racquetball, soccer, softball, squash, table tennis, volleyball.

Student services. Alcohol/substance abuse counseling, career counseling, services for economically disadvantaged, student employment services, financial aid counseling, health services, minority student services, on-campus daycare, personal counseling, placement for graduates, women's services. **Physically disabled:** Services for visually, speech, hearing impaired.

Contact. E-mail: gradinfo@umaryland.edu
Phone: (410) 706-7480 Fax: (410) 706-4053
Thomas Day, Director of Records and Registration, University of Maryland: Baltimore, 620 West Lexington Street, Baltimore, MD 21201

University of Maryland: Baltimore County
Baltimore, Maryland — **CB member**
www.umbc.edu — **CB code: 5835**

▸ Public 4-year university
▸ Residential campus in large city
▸ 10,429 degree-seeking undergraduates: 13% part-time, 45% women, 16% African American, 21% Asian American, 5% Hispanic American, 4% international
▸ 2,404 degree-seeking graduate students
▸ 61% of applicants admitted
▸ SAT or ACT (ACT writing optional), application essay required
▸ 57% graduate within 6 years

General. Founded in 1963. Regionally accredited. **Degrees:** 1,905 bachelor's awarded; master's, doctoral offered. **ROTC:** Army, Air Force. **Location:** 5 miles from Baltimore, 35 miles from Washington, DC. **Calendar:** 4-1-4, extensive summer session. **Full-time faculty:** 482 total; 86% have terminal degrees, 21% minority, 44% women. **Part-time faculty:** 258 total; 28% have terminal degrees, 20% minority, 40% women. **Class size:** 36% < 20, 42% 20-39, 9% 40-49, 9% 50-99, 4% >100. **Special facilities:** Research telescope, greenhouse, research spectrometers, nuclear magnetic resonance machines, electron microscope facility, imaging/digital art laboratory, healthcare informatics laboratory, two galleries - contemporary art and photography, conservation and environmental research area.

Freshman class profile. 8,099 applied, 4,925 admitted, 1,425 enrolled.

Mid 50% test scores			
SAT critical reading:	540-640	GPA 2.0-2.99:	13%
SAT math:	570-670	Rank in top quarter:	52%
SAT writing:	530-630	Rank in top tenth:	25%
ACT composite:	24-29	Return as sophomores:	85%
GPA 3.75 or higher:	40%	Out-of-state:	9%
GPA 3.50-3.74:	18%	Live on campus:	73%
GPA 3.0-3.49:	28%	International:	7%

Basis for selection. High school record, test scores important. Audition required for music, dance, theater majors. Portfolio required for visual arts majors.

High school preparation. College-preparatory program recommended. Required units include English 4, mathematics 4, science 3 and foreign language 2. Algebra I and II, and geometry required. History combined with Social Studies.

2011-2012 Annual costs. Tuition/fees: $9,467; $19,870 out-of-state. Room/board: $10,649. Books/supplies: $1,200. Personal expenses: $1,450.

2010-2011 Financial aid. Need-based: 1,083 full-time freshmen applied for aid; 773 were judged to have need; 663 of these received aid. Average need met was 61%. Average scholarship/grant was $8,145; average loan $3,415. 65% of total undergraduate aid awarded as scholarships/grants, 35% as loans/jobs. **Non-need-based:** Awarded to 1,640 full-time undergraduates, including 455 freshmen. Scholarships awarded for academics, alumni affiliation, art, athletics, music/drama.

Application procedures. Admission: Priority date 11/1; deadline 2/1 (postmark date). $50 fee, may be waived for applicants with need. Admission notification on a rolling basis beginning on or about 12/15. Must reply by May 1 or within 2 week(s) if notified thereafter. **Financial aid:** Priority date 2/14; no closing date. FAFSA required. Applicants notified on a rolling basis starting 3/26; must reply within 2 week(s) of notification.

Academics. Special study options: Accelerated study, combined bachelor's/graduate degree, cooperative education, cross-registration, double major, dual enrollment of high school students, ESL, honors, independent study, internships, liberal arts/career combination, semester at sea, student-designed major, study abroad, teacher certification program. **Credit/placement by examination:** AP, CLEP, IB, institutional tests. 60 credit hours maximum toward bachelor's degree. **Support services:** Learning center, study skills assistance, tutoring, writing center.

Honors college/program. Minimum 1300 SAT (exclusive of Writing) and 3.5 GPA required. Approximately 140 students accepted each year, with average SAT of 1300 (exclusive of Writing) and 3.81 GPA. Each semester 40-50 courses offered along with non-curricular activities.

Majors. Area/ethnic studies: African-American, American. **Biology:** General, Biochemistry/molecular biology, bioinformatics. **Communications:** Media studies. **Computer sciences:** General, computer science, information systems. **Conservation:** Environmental science, environmental studies. **Education:** Physics. **Engineering:** General, chemical, computer, mechanical. **English:** English lit. **Foreign languages:** General, linguistics. **Health services:** EMT paramedic. **History:** General. **Human services:** Social work. **Math:** General, statistics. **Philosophy/religion:** Philosophy. **Physical sciences:** Chemistry, physics. **Psychology:** General. **Social sciences:** Anthropology, economics, geography, political science, sociology. **Visual/performing arts:** General, acting, art, dance, dramatic, music, studio arts.

Most popular majors. Biology 14%, computer/information sciences 14%, engineering/engineering technologies 7%, psychology 12%, social sciences 17%, visual/performing arts 8%.

Computing on campus. 1,100 workstations in dormitories, library, computer center, student center. Dormitories wired for high-speed internet access and linked to campus network. Commuter students can connect to campus network. Online course registration, online library, helpline, repair service, student web hosting, wireless network available.

Student life. Freshman orientation: Mandatory, $125 fee. Preregistration for classes offered. Held June and July. Separate program for honors college students. **Housing:** Guaranteed on-campus for freshmen. Coed dorms, special housing for disabled, apartments available. $200 nonrefundable deposit, deadline 5/1. **Activities:** Pep band, campus ministries, choral groups, dance, drama, film society, international student organizations, literary magazine, music ensembles, musical theater, opera, radio station, student government, student newspaper, symphony orchestra, Black student union, Chinese student association, Jewish student association, Korean club, gay and lesbian organization, progressive action committee, Christian Fellowship, women's union.

Athletics. NCAA. **Intercollegiate:** Baseball M, basketball, cross-country, lacrosse, soccer, softball W, swimming, tennis, track and field, volleyball W. **Intramural:** Lacrosse, soccer, softball W, swimming, tennis, track and field, volleyball W. **Team name:** Retrievers.

Student services. Adult student services, alcohol/substance abuse counseling, chaplain/spiritual director, career counseling, services for economically disadvantaged, student employment services, financial aid counseling, health services, minority student services, on-campus daycare, personal counseling, placement for graduates, veterans' counselor, women's services. **Physically disabled:** Services for visually, hearing impaired.

Contact. E-mail: admissions@umbc.edu
Phone: (410) 455-2291 Toll-free number: (800) 862-2482
Fax: (410) 455-1094
Dale Bittinger, Director of Admissions, University of Maryland: Baltimore County, 1000 Hilltop Circle, Baltimore, MD 21250

University of Maryland: College Park
College Park, Maryland — **CB member**
www.maryland.edu — **CB code: 5814**

▸ Public 4-year university
▸ Commuter campus in large town

- 26,111 degree-seeking undergraduates: 6% part-time, 47% women, 12% African American, 15% Asian American, 8% Hispanic American, 3% international
- 10,153 degree-seeking graduate students
- 45% of applicants admitted
- SAT or ACT with writing, application essay required
- 82% graduate within 6 years

General. Founded in 1856. Regionally accredited. Research and internship opportunities at Smithsonian Institution, National Institutes for Health, NASA, US Capitol, White House, FBI, Department of Agriculture, other federal agencies. **Degrees:** 6,987 bachelor's awarded; master's, professional, doctoral offered. **ROTC:** Army, Naval, Air Force. **Location:** 30 miles from Baltimore, 3 miles from Washington, DC. **Calendar:** Semester, extensive summer session. **Full-time faculty:** 1,668 total; 92% have terminal degrees, 22% minority, 35% women. **Part-time faculty:** 660 total; 52% have terminal degrees, 10% minority, 40% women. **Class size:** 35% < 20, 42% 20-39, 7% 40-49, 10% 50-99, 7% >100. **Special facilities:** National Archives II, astronomy observatory, engineering wind tunnel, space systems lab, nuclear reactor, performing arts center, center for young children, agricultural biotechnology, superconductivity research, institute for systems research, fire and rescue institute.

Freshman class profile. 26,310 applied, 11,762 admitted, 3,992 enrolled.

Mid 50% test scores			
SAT critical reading:	580-680	Return as sophomores:	95%
SAT math:	610-720	Out-of-state:	33%
GPA 3.75 or higher:	73%	Live on campus:	93%
GPA 3.50-3.74:	14%	International:	3%
GPA 3.0-3.49:	11%	Fraternities:	9%
GPA 2.0-2.99:	1%	Sororities:	15%

Basis for selection. Academic record, rigor of the high school academic program, standardized admission test scores, class rank (if available), essay, extracurricular activities, counselor recommendation, and other letters of recommendation reviewed. Audition required of music majors. Drawing required of applicants to architecture program. **Home schooled:** Statement describing home school structure and mission, transcript of courses and grades required. Transcript should include description of course work, books used, method of evaluation and actual grades or evaluation. Letter of recommendation required and must be from academic professional.

High school preparation. College-preparatory program recommended. 16 units required. Required units include English 4, mathematics 4, social studies 3, science 3 (laboratory 2) and foreign language 2. Social studies units must include history.

2011-2012 Annual costs. Tuition/fees: $8,655; $26,026 out-of-state. Room/board: $9,942. Books/supplies: $1,076. Personal expenses: $2,268.

Financial aid. **Non-need-based:** Scholarships awarded for academics, art, athletics. **Additional information:** Prepaid tuition plans available through state. University of Maryland has created a financial assistance program called "Maryland Pathways." This three-tiered program reduces the debt component and increases the grant component of the student's financial aid package.

Application procedures. **Admission:** Priority date 11/1; deadline 1/20 (receipt date). $65 fee, may be waived for applicants with need. Application must be submitted online. Admission notification by 4/1. Must reply by 5/1. Housing deposit refundable in full if requested before 5/1. If it is not requested before 5/1, no refund will be given. Housing deposit is part of the $400 confirmation fee. **Financial aid:** Priority date 2/15; no closing date. FAFSA required. Applicants notified on a rolling basis starting 4/1; must reply by 5/1.

Academics. **Special study options:** Accelerated study, combined bachelor's/graduate degree, cooperative education, cross-registration, distance learning, double major, dual enrollment of high school students, ESL, exchange student, external degree, honors, independent study, internships, liberal arts/career combination, semester at sea, student-designed major, study abroad, teacher certification program. Living/learning programs. **Credit/placement by examination:** AP, CLEP, IB, SAT, ACT, institutional tests. 60 credit hours maximum toward bachelor's degree. **Support services:** Learning center, pre-admission summer program, reduced course load, remedial instruction, study skills assistance, tutoring, writing center.

Majors. **Architecture:** Architecture, landscape. **Area/ethnic studies:** African-American, American, Russian/Slavic, women's. **Biology:** General, biochemistry, ecology, microbiology. **Business:** General, accounting, finance, international, logistics, management science, marketing. **Communications:** Communications/speech/rhetoric, journalism. **Computer sciences:** General, information systems. **Conservation:** General, environmental science. **Education:** Art, elementary, English, foreign languages, health, kindergarten/preschool, mathematics, middle, music, physical, secondary, special ed. **Engineering:** Aerospace, agricultural, chemical, civil, computer, electrical, materials, mechanical. **English:** English lit. **Foreign languages:** Arabic, Chinese, classics, French, German, Iranian, Italian, Japanese, linguistics, Romance, Russian, Spanish. **General:** Animal sciences, economics, food science. **Health services:** Communication disorders, dietetics, nursing (RN), predental, preveterinary. **History:** General. **Math:** General. **Parks/recreation:** Exercise sciences. **Philosophy/religion:** Judaic, philosophy. **Physical sciences:** General, astronomy, chemistry, geology, physics. **Psychology:** General. **Social sciences:** Anthropology, criminology, economics, geography, political science, sociology. **Visual/performing arts:** Art history/conservation, dance, dramatic, music, music performance, studio arts. **Work/family studies:** Family/community services.

Most popular majors. Biology 9%, business/marketing 15%, communications/journalism 7%, engineering/engineering technologies 10%, social sciences 20%.

Computing on campus. 3,890 workstations in dormitories, library, computer center, student center. Dormitories wired for high-speed internet access and linked to campus network. Commuter students can connect to campus network. Online course registration, online library, helpline, repair service, student web hosting, wireless network available.

Student life. **Freshman orientation:** Mandatory, $160 fee. Preregistration for classes offered. 2-day program. **Housing:** Guaranteed on-campus for freshmen. Coed dorms, single-sex dorms, special housing for disabled, apartments, cooperative housing, fraternity/sorority housing, wellness housing available. **Activities:** Bands, campus ministries, choral groups, dance, drama, film society, international student organizations, literary magazine, music ensembles, Model UN, musical theater, opera, radio station, student government, student newspaper, symphony orchestra, TV station, Black student union, Asian American student union, Latino student union, Native American student union, Alpha Phi Omega, Habitat for Humanity.

Athletics. NCAA. **Intercollegiate:** Baseball M, basketball, cheerleading M, cross-country, field hockey W, football (tackle) M, golf, gymnastics W, lacrosse, soccer, softball W, swimming, tennis, track and field, volleyball W, water polo W, wrestling M. **Intramural:** Badminton, basketball, football (non-tackle), soccer, tennis, volleyball. **Team name:** Terrapins.

Student services. Adult student services, alcohol/substance abuse counseling, chaplain/spiritual director, career counseling, services for economically disadvantaged, student employment services, financial aid counseling, health services, legal services, minority student services, on-campus daycare, personal counseling, placement for graduates, veterans' counselor, women's services. **Physically disabled:** Services for visually, speech, hearing impaired.

Contact. E-mail: um-admit@uga.umd.edu
Phone: (301) 314-8385 Toll-free number: (800) 422-5867
Fax: (301) 314-9693
Barbara Gill, Director of Undergraduate Admissions, University of Maryland: College Park, College Park, MD 20742-5235

University of Maryland: Eastern Shore
Princess Anne, Maryland   **CB member**
www.umes.edu   **CB code: 5400**

- Public 4-year university
- Residential campus in rural community
- 3,765 degree-seeking undergraduates: 6% part-time, 57% women, 78% African American, 1% Asian American, 2% Hispanic American, 3% international
- 612 degree-seeking graduate students
- 50% of applicants admitted
- SAT or ACT (ACT writing optional), application essay required
- 31% graduate within 6 years

General. Founded in 1886. Regionally accredited. **Degrees:** 506 bachelor's awarded; master's, professional, doctoral offered. **Location:** 12 miles from Salisbury. **Calendar:** Semester, extensive summer session. **Full-time faculty:** 205 total; 70% have terminal degrees, 60% minority, 44% women. **Part-time faculty:** 149 total; 19% have terminal degrees, 39% minority, 50% women. **Class size:** 56% < 20, 39% 20-39, 2% 40-49, 3% 50-99, less than 1% >100. **Special facilities:** Arts and technology center, performing arts center, hydroponic greenhouse, education center.

Freshman class profile. 4,201 applied, 2,100 admitted, 790 enrolled.

Mid 50% test scores			
		GPA 3.0-3.49:	20%
SAT critical reading:	390-470	GPA 2.0-2.99:	69%
SAT math:	390-480	End year in good standing:	68%
SAT writing:	380-460	Return as sophomores:	68%
ACT composite:	16-19	Out-of-state:	19%
GPA 3.75 or higher:	5%	Live on campus:	89%
GPA 3.50-3.74:	6%	International:	1%

Basis for selection. School record, class rank, and test scores most important. Interview recommended for honors program and physical therapy applicants. Audition required for music majors. **Home schooled:** Transcript of courses and grades required. Must demonstrate compliance with state and local education regulations.

High school preparation. 20 units required. Required units include English 4, mathematics 3, social studies 3, science 2, foreign language 2 and academic electives 6.

2011-2012 Annual costs. Tuition/fees: $6,482; $14,263 out-of-state. Room/board: $7,758. Books/supplies: $1,800. Personal expenses: $1,800.

Financial aid. Non-need-based: Scholarships awarded for academics, alumni affiliation, art, athletics, leadership, music/drama, ROTC, state residency.

Application procedures. Admission: Priority date 3/1; deadline 7/15. $25 fee, may be waived for applicants with need. Admission notification by 9/14. Admission notification on a rolling basis. **Financial aid:** Priority date 3/1, closing date 4/1. FAFSA required. Applicants notified on a rolling basis starting 4/15.

Academics. The doctoral program in organizational leadership is a weekend program to meet scheduling needs of its students who are mostly full-time employees. The Library opens in the evenings. **Special study options:** Accelerated study, cooperative education, cross-registration, distance learning, double major, dual enrollment of high school students, exchange student, honors, independent study, internships, liberal arts/career combination, New York semester, study abroad, teacher certification program. **Credit/placement by examination:** AP, CLEP, IB, institutional tests. 60 credit hours maximum toward bachelor's degree. **Support services:** Learning center, preadmission summer program, reduced course load, remedial instruction, study skills assistance, tutoring, writing center.

Majors. Area/ethnic studies: African-American. **Biology:** General, ecology. **Business:** Accounting, business admin, hospitality admin, hotel/motel admin. **Computer sciences:** General. **Conservation:** Urban forestry. **Education:** Art, business, music, special ed, technology/industrial arts. **Engineering:** General. **English:** English lit. **General:** Business. **Health services:** Physician assistant. **History:** General. **Math:** General. **Parks/recreation:** Exercise sciences, golf management. **Physical sciences:** Chemistry. **Protective services:** Police science. **Psychology:** General. **Social sciences:** Sociology. **Visual/performing arts:** Commercial/advertising art. **Work/family studies:** General.

Most popular majors. Biology 6%, business/marketing 19%, English 8%, health sciences 13%, security/protective services 12%, social sciences 9%.

Computing on campus. 739 workstations in dormitories, library, computer center. Dormitories wired for high-speed internet access and linked to campus network. Commuter students can connect to campus network. Online library, helpline, wireless network available.

Student life. Freshman orientation: Mandatory, $100 fee. Preregistration for classes offered. 2 day program in the Fall. **Housing:** Coed dorms, single-sex dorms, apartments, wellness housing available. $300 partly refundable deposit, deadline 5/1. **Activities:** Bands, campus ministries, choral groups, dance, drama, international student organizations, music ensembles, radio station, student government, student newspaper, NAACP, Students for Progressive Action, Phenomenal Women, Rotaract club, College Democrats of America, Students in Free Enterprise, For Sisters Only, National Student Business League, Minorities In Agriculture, Natural Resources and Related Sciences.

Athletics. NCAA. **Intercollegiate:** Baseball M, basketball, bowling W, cheerleading M, cross-country, golf M, softball W, tennis, track and field, volleyball W. **Intramural:** Basketball, bowling, football (non-tackle) M, soccer, softball W, swimming, table tennis, volleyball. **Team name:** Hawks.

Student services. Adult student services, alcohol/substance abuse counseling, career counseling, student employment services, financial aid counseling, health services, on-campus daycare, personal counseling, placement for graduates, veterans' counselor. **Physically disabled:** Services for speech, hearing impaired.

Contact. E-mail: umesadmissions@umes.edu
Phone: (410) 651-6410 Fax: (410) 651-7922
Tyrone Young, Director of Admissions and Recruitment, University of Maryland: Eastern Shore, Student Development Center, Suite 1140, Princess Anne, MD 21853

University of Maryland: University College
Adelphi, Maryland
www.umuc.edu **CB code: 0551**

- Public 4-year university
- Commuter campus in large town
- 27,239 degree-seeking undergraduates: 79% part-time, 53% women, 33% African American, 4% Asian American, 8% Hispanic American, 1% Native American, 1% international
- 14,299 degree-seeking graduate students

General. Founded in 1947. Regionally accredited. Courses held at over 20 locations throughout Maryland, Virginia and Washington, DC. Associate degree programs available only to active military personnel. Courses offered at more than 100 locations in Europe and Asia. **Degrees:** 3,270 bachelor's, 285 associate awarded; master's, professional offered. **Location:** 9 miles from Washington, DC. **Calendar:** Semester, extensive summer session. **Full-time faculty:** 219 total; 84% have terminal degrees, 16% minority, 47% women. **Part-time faculty:** 2,183 total; 64% have terminal degrees, 25% minority, 42% women. **Class size:** 45% < 20, 54% 20-39, less than 1% 40-49.

Freshman class profile.

Out-of-state: 44%   International: 1%

Basis for selection. Open admission.

2011-2012 Annual costs. Tuition/fees: $6,246; $12,366 out-of-state. Books/supplies: $1,000. Personal expenses: $2,420.

2010-2011 Financial aid. Need-based: 118 full-time freshmen applied for aid; 114 were judged to have need; 106 of these received aid. Average need met was 29%. Average scholarship/grant was $4,262; average loan $3,095. 39% of total undergraduate aid awarded as scholarships/grants, 61% as loans/jobs. **Non-need-based:** Awarded to 322 full-time undergraduates, including 3 freshmen. Scholarships awarded for academics, leadership.

Application procedures. Admission: No deadline. $50 fee. **Financial aid:** Priority date 6/1; no closing date. FAFSA required. Applicants notified on a rolling basis starting 5/1; must reply within 2 week(s) of notification.

Academics. Degree programs offered primarily for adults attending part-time. No traditional freshman class. **Special study options:** Accelerated study, cooperative education, cross-registration, distance learning, double major, dual enrollment of high school students, external degree, independent study, internships, teacher certification program, weekend college. **Credit/placement by examination:** AP, CLEP, IB, institutional tests. 30 credit hours maximum toward associate degree, 60 toward bachelor's. **Support services:** Tutoring, writing center.

Majors. Area/ethnic studies: Asian. **Business:** Accounting, business admin, finance, human resources, international, marketing. **Communications:** Communications/speech/rhetoric. **Computer sciences:** General, information systems, security. **Conservation:** General. **English:** English lit. **History:** General. **Liberal arts:** Arts/sciences. **Protective services:** Criminal justice, fire services admin, forensics. **Psychology:** General. **Social sciences:** General, political science.

Most popular majors. Business/marketing 40%, computer/information sciences 20%, psychology 8%, security/protective services 6%.

Computing on campus. 280 workstations in library, computer center. Commuter students can connect to campus network. Online course registration, online library, helpline, wireless network available.

Student life. Freshman orientation: Available. Preregistration for classes offered.

Student services. Adult student services, career counseling, financial aid counseling, veterans' counselor. **Physically disabled:** Services for visually, speech, hearing impaired.

Contact. E-mail: enroll@umuc.edu
Phone: (301) 985-7000 Toll-free number: (800) 888-8682
Fax: (240) 684-2151
Jessica Sadaka, Director of Admissions, University of Maryland: University College, 1616 McCormick Drive, Largo, MD 20774

University of Phoenix: Maryland
Columbia, Maryland
www.phoenix.edu

- For-profit 4-year university
- Small city
- 680 degree-seeking undergraduates

General. Regionally accredited. **Degrees:** 133 bachelor's awarded; master's offered. **Calendar:** Differs by program. **Full-time faculty:** 12 total. **Part-time faculty:** 124 total.

Basis for selection. Open admission, but selective for some programs.

2011-2012 Annual costs. Estimated costs as of August 2011: per-credit-hour charge, $380 to $480, depending upon level and course of study; electronic course materials fee, $95, if applicable. Book and material charges may vary by course and program. All fees are subject to change.

Application procedures. Admission: No deadline. No application fee. **Financial aid:** No deadline.

Academics. Credit/placement by examination: AP, CLEP.

Majors. Business: Business admin. **Computer sciences:** Database management, information technology, systems analysis.

Contact. Marc Booker, Director of Admission and Evaluation, University of Phoenix: Maryland, 8830 Stanford Boulevard, Suite 100, Coumbia, MD 20145

Washington Adventist University
Takoma Park, Maryland
www.cuc.edu   CB code: 5890

- Private 4-year liberal arts college affiliated with Seventh-day Adventists
- Residential campus in large town
- 1,282 degree-seeking undergraduates: 17% part-time, 68% women, 60% African American, 7% Asian American, 10% Hispanic American
- 156 degree-seeking graduate students
- SAT or ACT (ACT writing optional) required

General. Founded in 1904. Regionally accredited. **Degrees:** 237 bachelor's, 5 associate awarded; master's offered. **Location:** 1 mile from Washington, DC. **Calendar:** Semester, limited summer session. **Full-time faculty:** 52 total; 46% have terminal degrees, 46% women. **Part-time faculty:** 82 total; 1% have terminal degrees, 38% women.

Basis for selection. High school GPA of 2.5, school achievement record, test scores very important; recommendations considered. Audition required of music majors. **Home schooled:** Transcript of courses and grades required. Recognized high school diploma or GED required. **Learning Disabled:** Students must provide written documentation of disabilities and submit written request for all needed services for review by the Disabilities Coordinator three months before registration. All forms may be obtained from Center for Learning Resources.

High school preparation. 18 units required; 29 recommended. Required and recommended units include English 4, mathematics 2-4, social studies 2, history 4, science 2-4 (laboratory 2), foreign language 2, computer science 1 and academic electives 4. One unit of computer science also recommended.

2011-2012 Annual costs. Tuition/fees: $20,180. Room/board: $7,600. Books/supplies: $1,100. Personal expenses: $1,100.

Financial aid. Non-need-based: Scholarships awarded for academics, alumni affiliation, athletics, religious affiliation.

Application procedures. Admission: Closing date 8/1 (postmark date). $25 fee, may be waived for applicants with need, free for online applicants. Admission notification on a rolling basis. Must reply by 8/15. **Financial aid:** Closing date 3/31. FAFSA required. Applicants notified on a rolling basis starting 5/31; must reply within 4 week(s) of notification.

Academics. Special study options: Accelerated study, combined bachelor's/graduate degree, cooperative education, cross-registration, distance learning, double major, dual enrollment of high school students, ESL, external degree, honors, independent study, internships, liberal arts/career combination, student-designed major, study abroad, teacher certification program, Washington semester. Co-Op Programs: Business, Biochemistry, Communications/Journalism, Computer Science, English. **Credit/placement by examination:** AP, CLEP, SAT, ACT, institutional tests. 12 credit hours maximum

toward associate degree, 24 toward bachelor's. CLEP business exams not accepted for traditional business majors. **Support services:** Learning center, reduced course load, remedial instruction, study skills assistance, tutoring, writing center.

Majors. Biology: General, biochemistry. **Business:** Accounting, business admin, marketing, organizational behavior. **Communications:** Broadcast journalism, communications/speech/rhetoric, journalism. **Computer sciences:** General, computer science, information systems. **Education:** General, elementary, English, mathematics, music, physical, science, secondary. **English:** English lit. **Health services:** Health care admin, nursing (RN), predental, premedicine, prepharmacy, preveterinary. **History:** General. **Liberal arts:** Arts/sciences. **Math:** General. **Parks/recreation:** Health/fitness, sports admin. **Philosophy/religion:** Religion. **Physical sciences:** Chemistry. **Psychology:** General, counseling. **Social sciences:** Political science. **Theology:** Religious ed, theology. **Visual/performing arts:** Music, music performance.

Most popular majors. Business/marketing 13%, education 10%, health sciences 49%, psychology 12%.

Computing on campus. Dormitories wired for high-speed internet access and linked to campus network. Commuter students can connect to campus network. Online library, wireless network available.

Student life. Freshman orientation: Mandatory, $150 fee. Preregistration for classes offered. **Policies:** Attendance required at weekly chapel service. Resident students required to attend dormitory worships. Religious observance required. **Housing:** Guaranteed on-campus for freshmen. Single-sex dorms, apartments available. $200 fully refundable deposit, deadline 8/15. **Activities:** Bands, campus ministries, choral groups, international student organizations, literary magazine, music ensembles, musical theater, radio station, student government, student newspaper, symphony orchestra, Humanitas, Loaves and Fishes, Shepherd's Hands (puppet ministry), Teach-a-Kid, Youth-to-Youth (drug prevention), student mission club.

Athletics. NCAA. **Intercollegiate:** Baseball M, basketball, cross-country, soccer, softball W, track and field. **Intramural:** Basketball M, soccer M, volleyball. **Team name:** Pioneers.

Student services. Adult student services, chaplain/spiritual director, career counseling, student employment services, financial aid counseling, health services, personal counseling, placement for graduates, veterans' counselor.

Contact. E-mail: admissions@cuc.edu
Phone: (301) 891-4080 Toll-free number: (800) 835-4212
Fax: (301) 891-4230
Elaine Oliver, Vice President of Enrollment Management, Washington Adventist University, 7600 Flower Avenue, Takoma Park, MD 20912

Washington Bible College
Lanham, Maryland
www.bible.edu   CB code: 5884

- Private 4-year Bible and seminary college affiliated with nondenominational tradition
- Commuter campus in large town
- 261 degree-seeking undergraduates
- 97% of applicants admitted
- SAT or ACT (ACT writing optional), application essay required

General. Founded in 1938. Regionally accredited; also accredited by ABHE. Main Campus in Lanham, MD. Branch sites in Annapolis, MD and in Springfield, VA. **Degrees:** 41 bachelor's, 1 associate awarded; master's offered. **Location:** 10 miles from Washington, DC. **Calendar:** Semester, limited summer session. **Full-time faculty:** 5 total. **Part-time faculty:** 27 total.

Freshman class profile. 35 applied, 34 admitted, 12 enrolled.

Basis for selection. Student's spiritual qualifications most important, followed by academic achievement, test scores, essay, recommendations. 2 references required. Interview recommended. Audition required of music majors. **Home schooled:** Transcript of courses and grades, interview, letter of recommendation (nonparent) required.

High school preparation. 15 units recommended. Recommended units include English 4, mathematics 2, social studies 2, science 2 and academic electives 5. Typing recommended.

2011-2012 Annual costs. Tuition/fees: $13,984. Room/board: $6,860. Books/supplies: $500. Personal expenses: $1,300.

Financial aid. Non-need-based: Scholarships awarded for academics, leadership, music/drama, state residency.

Application procedures. Admission: Priority date 5/1; deadline 8/1 (receipt date). $40 fee, may be waived for applicants with need. Admission notification on a rolling basis. Campus visit suggested. Deadline for housing deposit 30 days after acceptance. **Financial aid:** Closing date 3/1. FAFSA, institutional form required. Applicants notified on a rolling basis starting 7/1; must reply within 2 week(s) of notification.

Academics. All students major in Bible; other areas may be studied for concentrations. **Special study options:** Accelerated study, double major, ESL, independent study, internships, study abroad, teacher certification program. **Credit/placement by examination:** AP, CLEP, SAT, ACT, institutional tests. 15 credit hours maximum toward bachelor's degree. **Support services:** Reduced course load, tutoring, writing center.

Majors. Education: General, early childhood, elementary, multi-level teacher, music, physical, school counseling. **Psychology:** Counseling. **Theology:** Bible, missionary, pastoral counseling, preministerial, religious ed, sacred music, theology, youth ministry. **Visual/performing arts:** Music, music performance, piano/keyboard, voice/opera.

Computing on campus. 10 workstations in library, student center. Dormitories wired for high-speed internet access and linked to campus network. Commuter students can connect to campus network. Online library, helpline, wireless network available.

Student life. Freshman orientation: Mandatory. Preregistration for classes offered. 2-day spring and summer programs. **Policies:** Religious observance required. **Housing:** Guaranteed on-campus for freshmen. Single-sex dorms, apartments, wellness housing available. $100 nonrefundable deposit, deadline 6/1. **Activities:** Choral groups, drama, music ensembles, student government, student newspaper, Student Missions Fellowship, Fellowship of Christian Athletes.

Athletics. NCCAA. **Intercollegiate:** Basketball M, volleyball W. **Intramural:** Basketball, cheerleading, football (tackle) M, racquetball, soccer, table tennis, volleyball, weight lifting. **Team name:** Cougars.

Student services. Chaplain/spiritual director, career counseling, student employment services, financial aid counseling, health services, personal counseling, placement for graduates, veterans' counselor. **Physically disabled:** Services for visually, hearing impaired.

Contact. E-mail: iadmissions@bible.edu
Phone: (301) 552-1400 ext. 1280
Toll-free number: (877) 793-7227 ext. 1280 Fax: (301) 552-2775
Barbara Fox, Director of Admission, Washington Bible College, 6511 Princess Garden Parkway, Lanham, MD 20706-3599

Washington College	
Chestertown, Maryland	**CB member**
www.washcoll.edu	**CB code: 5888**

▶ Private 4-year liberal arts college

▶ Residential campus in small town

▶ 1,453 degree-seeking undergraduates: 58% women, 4% African American, 2% Asian American, 3% Hispanic American, 1% international

▶ 25 degree-seeking graduate students

▶ 57% of applicants admitted

▶ SAT or ACT (ACT writing optional), application essay required

▶ 76% graduate within 6 years

General. Founded in 1782. Regionally accredited. **Degrees:** 256 bachelor's awarded; master's offered. **Location:** 70 miles from Baltimore, 75 miles from Washington, DC. **Calendar:** Semester, limited summer session. **Full-time faculty:** 99 total; 91% have terminal degrees, 12% minority, 40% women. **Part-time faculty:** 67 total; 40% have terminal degrees, 12% minority, 46% women. **Class size:** 62% < 20, 34% 20-39, 2% 40-49, 2% 50-99. **Special facilities:** Center for the study of the American experience, center for environment and society.

Freshman class profile. 4,799 applied, 2,715 admitted, 399 enrolled.

Mid 50% test scores		GPA 2.0-2.99:	10%
SAT critical reading:	550-630	Rank in top quarter:	66%
SAT math:	540-610	Rank in top tenth:	32%
SAT writing:	520-620	Return as sophomores:	82%
ACT composite:	21-27	Out-of-state:	52%
GPA 3.75 or higher:	36%	Live on campus:	99%
GPA 3.50-3.74:	25%	Fraternities:	9%
GPA 3.0-3.49:	29%	Sororities:	24%

Basis for selection. High school program and grades, class rank, test scores, recommendations important, extracurricular activities considered. Interview recommended. **Home schooled:** Interview required.

High school preparation. College-preparatory program required. 16 units required; 20 recommended. Required and recommended units include English 4, mathematics 3-4, social studies 2-4, history 2, science 3-4 (laboratory 2-3) and foreign language 2-4.

2011-2012 Annual costs. Tuition/fees: $38,542. Room/board: $8,228. Books/supplies: $1,250. Personal expenses: $1,500.

2011-2012 Financial aid. Need-based: 319 full-time freshmen applied for aid; 265 were judged to have need; 265 of these received aid. Average need met was 92%. Average scholarship/grant was $24,526; average loan $2,726. 83% of total undergraduate aid awarded as scholarships/grants, 17% as loans/jobs. **Non-need-based:** Awarded to 469 full-time undergraduates, including 165 freshmen. Scholarships awarded for academics.

Application procedures. Admission: Priority date 2/15; no deadline. $50 fee, may be waived for applicants with need. Admission notification on a rolling basis beginning on or about 10/1. Must reply by May 1 or within 2 week(s) if notified thereafter. Applicants applying after February 15 may be wait-listed. **Financial aid:** Priority date 2/15; no closing date. FAFSA, institutional form required. Applicants notified on a rolling basis starting 2/1; must reply by 5/1.

Academics. Special study options: Combined bachelor's/graduate degree, cross-registration, double major, dual enrollment of high school students, exchange student, honors, independent study, internships, liberal arts/career combination, student-designed major, study abroad, teacher certification program, Washington semester. **Credit/placement by examination:** AP, CLEP, IB, institutional tests. **Support services:** Learning center, reduced course load, study skills assistance, tutoring, writing center.

Majors. Area/ethnic studies: American. **Biology:** General. **Business:** General. **Computer sciences:** Computer science. **Conservation:** Environmental studies. **Education:** General. **English:** English lit. **Foreign languages:** French, German, Spanish. **History:** General. **Liberal arts:** Arts/sciences, humanities. **Math:** General. **Philosophy/religion:** Philosophy. **Physical sciences:** Chemistry, physics. **Psychology:** General. **Social sciences:** Anthropology, economics, international relations, political science, sociology. **Visual/performing arts:** Art, dramatic, music.

Most popular majors. Biology 9%, business/marketing 20%, English 10%, natural resources/environmental science 6%, psychology 6%, social sciences 27%, visual/performing arts 7%.

Computing on campus. 100 workstations in dormitories, library, computer center, student center. Dormitories wired for high-speed internet access and linked to campus network. Commuter students can connect to campus network. Online course registration, online library, helpline, repair service, student web hosting, wireless network available.

Student life. Freshman orientation: Mandatory. Preregistration for classes offered. Thursday - Sunday before fall classes begin. **Housing:** Guaranteed on-campus for freshmen. Coed dorms, single-sex dorms, special housing for disabled, fraternity/sorority housing, wellness housing available. $200 nonrefundable deposit, deadline 6/1. **Activities:** Bands, campus ministries, choral groups, dance, drama, international student organizations, literary magazine, music ensembles, Model UN, radio station, student government, student newspaper, College Republicans, Christian Fellowship, Amnesty International, Hillel, Black Student Alliance, Cleopatra's Daughters, College Democrats, Best Buddies, Newman Club.

Athletics. NCAA. **Intercollegiate:** Baseball M, basketball, field hockey W, lacrosse, rowing (crew), sailing, soccer, softball W, swimming, tennis, volleyball W. **Intramural:** Basketball, fencing, golf M, ice hockey M, racquetball, rugby, sailing, soccer, softball, squash, tennis, volleyball. **Team name:** Shoremen/Shorewomen.

Student services. Adult student services, alcohol/substance abuse counseling, career counseling, student employment services, financial aid counseling, health services, minority student services, personal counseling, placement for graduates, veterans' counselor. **Physically disabled:** Services for hearing impaired.

Contact. E-mail: adm.off@washcoll.edu
Phone: (410) 778-7700 Toll-free number: (800) 442-1782
Fax: (410) 778-7287
Kevin Coveney, Vice President for Admissions, Washington College, 300 Washington Avenue, Chestertown, MD 21620-1197

Yeshiva College of the Nations Capital
Silver Spring, Maryland

- Private 4-year rabbinical college for men affiliated with Jewish faith
- Residential campus in small city
- 55 degree-seeking undergraduates

General. Accredited by AARTS. **Degrees:** 12 bachelor's awarded. **Calendar:** Differs by program. **Full-time faculty:** 5 total. **Part-time faculty:** 3 total.

Academics.   Credit/placement by examination: AP, CLEP.

Majors.   Philosophy/religion: Judaic. **Theology:** Talmudic.

Contact.   Phone: (301) 593-2534
David Hyatt, Academic Dean, Yeshiva College of the Nations Capital, 1216 Arcola Avenue, Silver Spring, MD 20902

Massachusetts

Advertising, broadcast journalism, journalism, media studies, public relations, radio/TV. **Computer sciences:** Computer science, information systems. **Education:** Early childhood, elementary, middle, secondary, special ed. **English:** English lit. **Health services:** Nursing (RN), predental, premedicine, preveterinary. **History:** General. **Liberal arts:** Arts/sciences. **Parks/recreation:** General, sports admin. **Physical sciences:** Chemistry. **Protective services:** Criminal justice, law enforcement admin, police science. **Psychology:** General. **Social sciences:** Criminology, economics, international relations, political science, sociology.

Most popular majors. Business/marketing 26%, health sciences 28%, interdisciplinary studies 7%, psychology 8%, security/protective services 12%, social sciences 9%.

Computing on campus. 100 workstations in dormitories, library, computer center, student center. Dormitories wired for high-speed internet access and linked to campus network. Commuter students can connect to campus network. Online course registration, online library, helpline, wireless network available.

Student life. Freshman orientation: Available. Preregistration for classes offered. Three-day program in early September prior to start of Fall term. **Housing:** Guaranteed on-campus for all undergraduates. Coed dorms, single-sex dorms, apartments, wellness housing available. $100 fully refundable deposit, deadline 8/1. **Activities:** Pep band, campus ministries, choral groups, dance, drama, international student organizations, literary magazine, musical theater, radio station, student government, student newspaper, Model Congress, minority student organizations, Partners, Best Buddies, Intervarsity Christian Fellowship, Young Professionals for International Cooperation, Students in Free Enterprise, student entrepreneur group.

Athletics. NCAA. **Intercollegiate:** Baseball M, basketball, cheerleading, cross-country, field hockey W, football (tackle) M, golf M, ice hockey M, lacrosse, soccer, softball W, tennis, track and field, volleyball W, wrestling M. **Intramural:** Basketball, football (non-tackle) M, skiing, soccer, softball, swimming, volleyball. **Team name:** Yellow Jackets.

Student services. Adult student services, alcohol/substance abuse counseling, chaplain/spiritual director, career counseling, services for economically disadvantaged, student employment services, financial aid counseling, health services, minority student services, personal counseling, placement for graduates, veterans' counselor, women's services. **Physically disabled:** Services for visually impaired.

Contact. E-mail: inquiry@aic.edu
Phone: (413) 205-3201 Toll-free number: (800) 242-3142
Fax: (413) 205-3051
Peter Miller, Vice President for Admission Services, American International College, 1000 State Street, Springfield, MA 01109

American International College
Springfield, Massachusetts — CB member
www.aic.edu — CB code: 3002

- Private 4-year liberal arts college
- Residential campus in small city
- 1,720 degree-seeking undergraduates: 9% part-time, 57% women, 25% African American, 2% Asian American, 10% Hispanic American, 1% Native American, 4% international
- 1,789 degree-seeking graduate students
- 75% of applicants admitted
- SAT or ACT (ACT writing recommended) required
- 37% graduate within 6 years

General. Founded in 1885. Regionally accredited. **Degrees:** 298 bachelor's, 1 associate awarded; master's, professional, doctoral offered. **ROTC:** Army, Air Force. **Location:** 90 miles from Boston; 27 miles from Hartford, Connecticut. **Calendar:** Semester, extensive summer session. **Full-time faculty:** 89 total; 47% have terminal degrees, 7% minority, 60% women. **Part-time faculty:** 234 total; 19% have terminal degrees, 5% minority, 55% women. **Class size:** 53% < 20, 42% 20-39, 1% 40-49, 2% 50-99, less than 1% >100. **Special facilities:** Cultural arts center, performing arts center, anatomical laboratory, communications media laboratory.

Freshman class profile. 1,540 applied, 1,155 admitted, 370 enrolled.

Mid 50% test scores			
SAT critical reading:	430-530	GPA 2.0-2.99:	46%
SAT math:	440-550	Rank in top quarter:	28%
SAT writing:	420-500	Rank in top tenth:	22%
ACT composite:	18-23	Return as sophomores:	64%
GPA 3.75 or higher:	4%	Out-of-state:	51%
GPA 3.50-3.74:	8%	Live on campus:	79%
GPA 3.0-3.49:	38%	International:	3%

Basis for selection. Must have satisfied school's graduation requirements except for one course in English and one course in Social Studies. Must have unqualified approval of school counselor or principal and must possess strong academic skills and maturity necessary for success in college. Essay or personal statement recommended. **Home schooled:** Statement describing home school structure and mission, transcript of courses and grades, interview, letter of recommendation (nonparent) required. **Learning Disabled:** Wechsler Adult Intelligence Scale, interview, diagnostic documentation recommended.

High school preparation. College-preparatory program recommended. 16 units required. Required and recommended units include English 4, mathematics 3-4, social studies 1-2, history 2, science 2-3 (laboratory 2), foreign language 1-2 and academic electives 4.

2011-2012 Annual costs. Tuition/fees: $27,902. Room/board: $11,314. Books/supplies: $1,200. Personal expenses: $1,000.

Financial aid. Non-need-based: Scholarships awarded for academics, alumni affiliation, athletics, leadership.

Application procedures. Admission: Priority date 7/1; no deadline. $25 fee, may be waived for applicants with need. Admission notification on a rolling basis beginning on or about 12/1. Must reply by May 1 or within 2 week(s) if notified thereafter. **Financial aid:** Priority date 5/1; no closing date. FAFSA required. Applicants notified on a rolling basis starting 3/15; must reply by 5/1 or within 2 week(s) of notification.

Academics. Special study options: Accelerated study, combined bachelor's/graduate degree, cross-registration, distance learning, double major, dual enrollment of high school students, ESL, honors, independent study, internships, liberal arts/career combination, study abroad, teacher certification program, Washington semester, weekend college. **Credit/placement by examination:** AP, CLEP, IB, institutional tests. 30 credit hours maximum toward bachelor's degree. **Support services:** Learning center, reduced course load, remedial instruction, study skills assistance, tutoring, writing center.

Majors. Area/ethnic studies: American. **Biology:** General, biochemistry. **Business:** General, accounting, business admin, finance, international, management science, managerial economics, marketing. **Communications:**

Amherst College
Amherst, Massachusetts — CB member
www.amherst.edu — CB code: 3003

- Private 4-year liberal arts college
- Residential campus in large town
- 1,791 degree-seeking undergraduates: 49% women, 12% African American, 11% Asian American, 11% Hispanic American, 10% international
- 13% of applicants admitted
- SAT and SAT Subject Tests or ACT (ACT writing recommended), application essay required
- 96% graduate within 6 years

General. Founded in 1821. Regionally accredited. **Degrees:** 483 bachelor's awarded. **ROTC:** Army, Air Force. **Location:** 90 miles from Boston, 150 miles from New York City. **Calendar:** Semester. **Full-time faculty:** 204 total; 99% have terminal degrees, 20% minority, 43% women. **Part-time faculty:** 36 total; 86% have terminal degrees, 3% minority, 33% women. **Class size:** 70% < 20, 25% 20-39, 3% 40-49, 2% 50-99, less than 1% >100. **Special facilities:** Recital hall, observatory, planetarium, center for Russian culture, Dickinson homestead, natural history museum, fine arts museum, center for community engagement.

Freshman class profile. 8,461 applied, 1,127 admitted, 461 enrolled.

Mid 50% test scores			
SAT critical reading:	660-760	Rank in top tenth:	84%
SAT math:	660-770	Return as sophomores:	97%
SAT writing:	670-770	Out-of-state:	89%
ACT composite:	30-34	Live on campus:	100%
Rank in top quarter:	97%	International:	8%

Basis for selection. Grades, test scores, essays, recommendations, independent work, quality of individual's secondary school program, and achievements outside of classroom important.

High school preparation. College-preparatory program recommended. Recommended units include English 4, mathematics 4, social studies 2, history 2, science 3 (laboratory 1) and foreign language 4.

2011-2012 Annual costs. Tuition/fees: $42,898. Room/board: $11,200. Books/supplies: $1,000. Personal expenses: $1,800.

2011-2012 Financial aid. All financial aid based on need. 298 full-time freshmen applied for aid; 270 were judged to have need; 270 of these received aid. Average need met was 100%. Average scholarship/grant was $41,853; average loan $2,540. 95% of total undergraduate aid awarded as scholarships/grants, 5% as loans/jobs.

Application procedures. **Admission:** Closing date 1/1 (postmark date). $60 fee, may be waived for applicants with need. Admission notification by 4/1. Must reply by 5/1. **Financial aid:** Priority date 2/15; no closing date. FAFSA, CSS PROFILE required.

Academics. First-year students must choose 1 seminar from range of 20 special topics, often interdisciplinary. No core curriculum, no distribution requirements. Students select major at end of sophomore year. **Special study options:** Cross-registration, double major, exchange student, honors, independent study, internships, student-designed major, study abroad, teacher certification program. Member of 5-college consortium. **Credit/placement by examination:** AP, CLEP, IB, institutional tests. **Support services:** Study skills assistance, tutoring, writing center.

Majors. **Area/ethnic studies:** African, African-American, American, Asian, European, Russian/Eastern European/Eurasian, Western European, women's. **Biology:** General, neuroscience. **Computer sciences:** Computer science. **English:** English lit. **Foreign languages:** Ancient Greek, classics, French, German, Latin, Russian, Spanish. **History:** General. **Math:** General. **Philosophy/religion:** Philosophy, religion. **Physical sciences:** Astronomy, chemistry, geology, physics. **Psychology:** General. **Social sciences:** Anthropology, economics, political science, sociology. **Visual/performing arts:** Dance, dramatic, music, studio arts.

Most popular majors. Area/ethnic studies 6%, English 11%, foreign language 7%, history 6%, physical sciences 6%, psychology 7%, social sciences 26%, visual/performing arts 7%.

Computing on campus. 230 workstations in library, computer center, student center. Dormitories wired for high-speed internet access and linked to campus network. Commuter students can connect to campus network. Helpline, repair service, wireless network available.

Student life. **Freshman orientation:** Mandatory. Preregistration for classes offered. Eight-day orientation with events planned by student groups and cultural organizations. **Housing:** Guaranteed on-campus for all undergraduates. Coed dorms, special housing for disabled, cooperative housing, wellness housing available. Language and other theme houses available including French/Spanish, Russian/German, Latino, African American, health and wellness house, and arts house. Men's and women's floors available to all students. **Activities:** Bands, campus ministries, choral groups, dance, drama, film society, international student organizations, literary magazine, music ensembles, Model UN, musical theater, opera, radio station, student government, student newspaper, symphony orchestra, Hillel, service organization, Christian association, Newman club, black student union, Asian student association, Cambodian family tutoring, LaCausa, Christian Fellowship, Korean American students association.

Athletics. NCAA. **Intercollegiate:** Baseball M, basketball, cross-country, diving, field hockey W, football (tackle) M, golf, ice hockey, lacrosse, soccer, softball W, squash, swimming, tennis, track and field, volleyball W. **Intramural:** Badminton, basketball, football (non-tackle), golf, ice hockey, soccer, softball, squash, table tennis, tennis, volleyball. **Team name:** Lord Jeffs.

Student services. Alcohol/substance abuse counseling, chaplain/spiritual director, career counseling, services for economically disadvantaged, student employment services, financial aid counseling, health services, minority student services, personal counseling, placement for graduates, women's services. **Physically disabled:** Services for visually, speech, hearing impaired.

Contact. E-mail: admission@amherst.edu
Phone: (413) 542-2328 Fax: (413) 542-2040
Katharine Fretwell, Director of Admission & Senior Associate Dean of Admission, Amherst College, PO Box 5000, Amherst, MA 01002-5000

Anna Maria College
Paxton, Massachusetts
www.annamaria.edu

CB member
CB code: 3005

- Private 4-year liberal arts college affiliated with Roman Catholic Church
- Residential campus in small town
- 997 degree-seeking undergraduates: 19% part-time, 50% women, 8% African American, 1% Asian American, 8% Hispanic American, 1% Native American
- 425 degree-seeking graduate students
- 60% of applicants admitted
- 49% graduate within 6 years

General. Founded in 1946. Regionally accredited. **Degrees:** 174 bachelor's, 16 associate awarded; master's offered. **ROTC:** Air Force. **Location:** 8 miles from Worcester, 40 miles from Boston. **Calendar:** Semester, limited summer session. **Special facilities:** Nature trails, arts building.

Freshman class profile. 2,394 applied, 1,445 admitted, 223 enrolled.

Mid 50% test scores			
SAT critical reading:	400-480	GPA 3.50-3.74:	6%
SAT math:	410-510	GPA 3.0-3.49:	26%
SAT writing:	400-480	GPA 2.0-2.99:	60%
ACT composite:	16-22	Return as sophomores:	61%
GPA 3.75 or higher:	5%	Out-of-state:	24%
		Live on campus:	83%

Basis for selection. High school record most important, followed by test scores, recommendations, school and community activities, interview. SAT or ACT recommended. Test scores optional for all students except for those majoring in paramedic science. Audition required of music majors; portfolio required of art majors, essays required of nursing and transfer students.

High school preparation. College-preparatory program recommended. 21 units required. Required units include English 4, mathematics 3, social studies 2, history 2, science 3 (laboratory 1), foreign language 2 and academic electives 4.

2011-2012 Annual costs. Tuition/fees: $29,860. Room/board: $10,804. Books/supplies: $1,000.

Financial aid. **Non-need-based:** Scholarships awarded for academics, alumni affiliation, music/drama, religious affiliation, state residency.

Application procedures. **Admission:** Priority date 3/1; no deadline. $40 fee, may be waived for applicants with need, free for online applicants. Admission notification on a rolling basis. **Financial aid:** Priority date 3/1; no closing date. FAFSA required. Applicants notified on a rolling basis starting 4/1; must reply within 4 week(s) of notification.

Academics. **Special study options:** Accelerated study, combined bachelor's/graduate degree, cooperative education, cross-registration, distance learning, double major, honors, independent study, internships, liberal arts/career combination, student-designed major, study abroad, teacher certification program, Washington semester. Member of 13-college Worcester Consortium. **Credit/placement by examination:** AP, CLEP, SAT, ACT, institutional tests. 30 credit hours maximum toward bachelor's degree. **Support services:** Learning center, reduced course load, remedial instruction, study skills assistance, tutoring, writing center.

Majors. **Biology:** General. **Business:** Business admin, management information systems. **Communications:** Media studies. **Computer sciences:** General. **Conservation:** Environmental science. **Education:** General, art, early childhood, elementary, English, history, kindergarten/preschool, middle, music, secondary. **English:** English lit. **Health services:** Art therapy, music therapy, nursing (RN). **History:** General. **Human services:** Public policy, social work. **Liberal arts:** Arts/sciences, humanities. **Philosophy/religion:** Philosophy. **Protective services:** Firefighting, forensics, law enforcement admin. **Psychology:** General. **Social sciences:** Political science, sociology. **Theology:** Theology. **Visual/performing arts:** Art, graphic design, music, music performance, piano/keyboard, studio arts management, voice/opera.

Most popular majors. Security/protective services 40%.

Computing on campus. 94 workstations in dormitories, library, computer center, student center. Dormitories wired for high-speed internet access and linked to campus network. Commuter students can connect to campus network. Online course registration, online library, helpline, wireless network available.

Student life. **Freshman orientation:** Mandatory. Preregistration for classes offered. **Housing:** Guaranteed on-campus for freshmen. Coed dorms, special housing for disabled, wellness housing available. $300 fully refundable deposit, deadline 5/1. **Activities:** Bands, campus ministries, choral

groups, dance, drama, music ensembles, musical theater, student government, student newspaper.

Athletics. NCAA. **Intercollegiate:** Baseball M, basketball, cross-country, field hockey W, football (tackle) M, golf, lacrosse, soccer, softball W, tennis, volleyball W. **Intramural:** Baseball, basketball, football (non-tackle), volleyball. **Team name:** Amcats.

Student services. Alcohol/substance abuse counseling, chaplain/spiritual director, career counseling, student employment services, financial aid counseling, health services, minority student services, personal counseling, placement for graduates. **Physically disabled:** Services for visually, speech, hearing impaired.

Contact. E-mail: admission@annamaria.edu
Phone: (508) 849-3360 Toll-free number: (800) 344-4586 ext. 360
Fax: (508) 849-3362
Meghan McDonough, Director of Admissions, Anna Maria College, 50 Sunset Lane, Box O, Paxton, MA 01612-1198

Art Institute of Boston at Lesley University
Boston, Massachusetts
www.aiboston.edu   **CB code: 3777**

▶ Private 4-year visual arts college
▶ Residential campus in very large city

General. Regionally accredited. **Location:** Downtown. **Calendar:** Semester.

Annual costs/financial aid. Tuition/fees (2011-2012): $28,750. Room/board: $13,250. Books/supplies: $1,575. Personal expenses: $1,580. Need-based financial aid available to full-time and part-time students.

Contact. Phone: (617) 585-6710
Director of Operations, 700 Beacon Street, Boston, MA 02215-2598

Assumption College
Worcester, Massachusetts   **CB member**
www.assumption.edu   **CB code: 3009**

▶ Private 4-year liberal arts college affiliated with Roman Catholic Church
▶ Residential campus in small city
▶ 2,083 degree-seeking undergraduates: 60% women, 3% African American, 2% Asian American, 6% Hispanic American, 1% international
▶ 448 degree-seeking graduate students
▶ 75% of applicants admitted
▶ Application essay required
▶ 67% graduate within 6 years; 23% enter graduate study

General. Founded in 1904. Regionally accredited. Students may register for courses at 11 area colleges. Volunteer programs available: comprehensive 2-week programs in Mexico and Puerto Rico, 1-week spring break programs in various locations. **Degrees:** 469 bachelor's awarded; master's offered. **ROTC:** Army, Air Force. **Location:** 45 miles from Boston. **Calendar:** Semester, limited summer session. **Full-time faculty:** 147 total; 91% have terminal degrees, 5% minority, 41% women. **Part-time faculty:** 75 total; 60% have terminal degrees, 9% minority, 53% women. **Class size:** 40% < 20, 59% 20-39, less than 1% 40-49, less than 1% 50-99. **Special facilities:** French institute (academic research center for study of Francophone questions).

Freshman class profile. 4,380 applied, 3,290 admitted, 607 enrolled.

Mid 50% test scores		GPA 2.0-2.99:	24%
SAT critical reading:	500-580	Rank in top quarter:	42%
SAT math:	500-600	Rank in top tenth:	21%
ACT composite:	23-27	End year in good standing:	92%
GPA 3.75 or higher:	15%	Return as sophomores:	86%
GPA 3.50-3.74:	16%	Out-of-state:	36%
GPA 3.0-3.49:	45%	Live on campus:	93%

Basis for selection. School achievement most important, followed by class rank in top 40%, extracurricular activities, interview, recommendations. **Home schooled:** Statement describing home school structure and mission, letter of recommendation (nonparent) required.

High school preparation. College-preparatory program required. 18 units required. Required units include English 4, mathematics 3, history 2, science 2, foreign language 2 and academic electives 5.

2012-2013 Annual costs. Tuition/fees: $34,070. Room/board: $10,590. Books/supplies: $1,000. Personal expenses: $1,000.

2011-2012 Financial aid. Need-based: 567 full-time freshmen applied for aid; 500 were judged to have need; 500 of these received aid. Average need met was 75%. Average scholarship/grant was $18,518; average loan $3,823. 70% of total undergraduate aid awarded as scholarships/grants, 30% as loans/jobs. **Non-need-based:** Awarded to 503 full-time undergraduates, including 175 freshmen. Scholarships awarded for academics, athletics.

Application procedures. Admission: Closing date 2/15 (postmark date). $50 fee, may be waived for applicants with need. Admission notification on a rolling basis beginning on or about 3/15. Must reply by May 1 or within 2 week(s) if notified thereafter. **Financial aid:** Closing date 2/15. FAFSA required. Applicants notified on a rolling basis starting 2/16; must reply by 5/1.

Academics. Special study options: Combined bachelor's/graduate degree, cross-registration, double major, honors, independent study, internships, New York semester, semester at sea, student-designed major, study abroad, teacher certification program, Washington semester. Worcester Consortium gerontology studies program; 3-2 engineering program (BA/BS) with Worcester Polytechnic Institute. **Credit/placement by examination:** AP, CLEP, IB, institutional tests. **Support services:** Learning center, study skills assistance, tutoring, writing center.

Majors. Area/ethnic studies: Latin American. **Biology:** General, biotechnology. **Business:** Accounting, business admin, international, marketing. **Communications:** Organizational. **Computer sciences:** General. **Conservation:** Environmental science. **English:** English lit. **Foreign languages:** General, classics, French, Italian, Spanish. **History:** General. **Math:** General. **Philosophy/religion:** Philosophy. **Physical sciences:** Chemistry. **Psychology:** General. **Social sciences:** Economics, political science, sociology. **Theology:** Theology. **Visual/performing arts:** General, graphic design, music.

Most popular majors. Business/marketing 29%, communications/journalism 9%, health sciences 9%, history 7%, psychology 9%, social sciences 12%.

Computing on campus. 335 workstations in dormitories, library, computer center, student center. Dormitories wired for high-speed internet access and linked to campus network. Commuter students can connect to campus network. Online course registration, online library, helpline, repair service, student web hosting, wireless network available.

Student life. Freshman orientation: Mandatory, $265 fee. Preregistration for classes offered. Two-day program held in June. **Policies:** Freshmen not permitted cars on campus. **Housing:** Guaranteed on-campus for all undergraduates. Coed dorms, single-sex dorms, special housing for disabled, wellness housing available. Freshman dorms, substance-free dorms, living/learning center available. **Activities:** Bands, campus ministries, choral groups, dance, drama, film society, literary magazine, music ensembles, musical theater, student government, student newspaper, TV station, ALANA network, College Democrats, College Republicans, student volunteer organization, students advocating change, student health network, service program, Omicron Delta Kappa leadership circle, retreat programs.

Athletics. NCAA. **Intercollegiate:** Baseball M, basketball, cross-country, field hockey W, football (tackle) M, golf M, ice hockey M, lacrosse, rowing (crew) W, soccer, softball W, swimming W, tennis, track and field, volleyball W. **Intramural:** Basketball, football (non-tackle), golf, ice hockey, racquetball, soccer, softball, tennis, volleyball. **Team name:** Greyhounds.

Student services. Alcohol/substance abuse counseling, chaplain/spiritual director, career counseling, student employment services, financial aid counseling, health services, minority student services, personal counseling, placement for graduates. **Physically disabled:** Services for visually, speech, hearing impaired.

Contact. E-mail: admiss@assumption.edu
Phone: (508) 767-7285 Toll-free number: (866) 477-7776
Fax: (508) 799-4412
Evan Lipp, Vice President for Enrollment Management, Assumption College, 500 Salisbury Street, Worcester, MA 01609-1296

Babson College
Babson Park, Massachusetts   **CB member**
www.babson.edu   **CB code: 3075**

▶ Private 4-year business college
▶ Residential campus in large town
▶ 2,007 degree-seeking undergraduates: 44% women, 4% African American, 12% Asian American, 10% Hispanic American, 27% international
▶ 1,356 degree-seeking graduate students
▶ 34% of applicants admitted

- SAT or ACT with writing, application essay required
- 90% graduate within 6 years

General. Founded in 1919. Regionally accredited. **Degrees:** 481 bachelor's awarded; master's offered. **ROTC:** Army, Air Force. **Location:** 14 miles from Boston. **Calendar:** Semester, extensive summer session. **Full-time faculty:** 163 total; 87% have terminal degrees, 16% minority, 34% women. **Part-time faculty:** 104 total; 38% have terminal degrees, 8% minority, 32% women. **Class size:** 20% < 20, 59% 20-39, 17% 40-49, 3% 50-99. **Special facilities:** Entrepreneurship center, woman's leadership center, social entrepreneurship institute, investment center.

Freshman class profile. 5,079 applied, 1,718 admitted, 487 enrolled.

Mid 50% test scores			
SAT critical reading:	580-680	Rank in top quarter:	77%
SAT math:	640-740	Rank in top tenth:	45%
SAT writing:	610-700	Return as sophomores:	94%
ACT composite:	27-31	Out-of-state:	81%
GPA 3.75 or higher:	30%	Live on campus:	100%
GPA 3.50-3.74:	30%	International:	28%
GPA 3.0-3.49:	36%	Fraternities:	17%
GPA 2.0-2.99:	4%	Sororities:	23%

Basis for selection. Academic performance and level of course work (college preparatory, honors, Advanced Placement) most important; followed by academic motivation, including interest in learning and willingness to challenge oneself; test scores; writing ability; involvement in cocurricular activities and/or work experience; leadership, creativity, enthusiasm. SAT Subject Tests recommended. **Home schooled:** Statement describing home school structure and mission, transcript of courses and grades, state high school equivalency certificate, letter of recommendation (nonparent) required. Applicants must provide information about completed courses, schooling, testing, and diploma requirements.

High school preparation. College-preparatory program required. 20 units required. Required and recommended units include English 4, mathematics 4, history 4, science 4 (laboratory 3) and foreign language 4. Pre-calculus strongly recommended.

2011-2012 Annual costs. Tuition/fees: $40,400. Room/board: $13,330. Books/supplies: $1,020. Personal expenses: $1,784.

2011-2012 Financial aid. All financial aid based on need. 249 full-time freshmen applied for aid; 205 were judged to have need; 205 of these received aid. Average need met was 94%. Average scholarship/grant was $27,325; average loan $3,073. 83% of total undergraduate aid awarded as scholarships/grants, 17% as loans/jobs.

Application procedures. Admission: Priority date 11/1; deadline 1/1 (postmark date). $75 fee, may be waived for applicants with need. Admission notification by 4/15. Must reply by 5/1. **Financial aid:** Closing date 2/15. FAFSA, CSS PROFILE required. Applicants notified by 4/15; must reply by 5/1.

Academics. Special study options: Accelerated study, combined bachelor's/graduate degree, cross-registration, exchange student, honors, independent study, internships, liberal arts/career combination, student-designed major, study abroad. **Credit/placement by examination:** AP, CLEP, IB, institutional tests. 63 credit hours maximum toward bachelor's degree. **Support services:** Reduced course load, study skills assistance, tutoring, writing center.

Majors. Business: General, accounting, accounting/business management, accounting/finance, auditing, business admin, communications, entrepreneurial studies, finance, international, international finance, international marketing, investments/securities, management information systems, management science, managerial economics, marketing, office management, operations, sales/distribution, small business admin, statistics. **Communications:** Advertising. **Computer sciences:** General, information systems.

Computing on campus. PC or laptop required. Dormitories wired for high-speed internet access and linked to campus network. Commuter students can connect to campus network. Online course registration, online library, helpline, repair service, wireless network available.

Student life. Freshman orientation: Mandatory. Preregistration for classes offered. Three-day program preceding start of classes. **Policies:** First-year students required to live on-campus. **Housing:** Guaranteed on-campus for all undergraduates. Coed dorms, special housing for disabled, apartments, fraternity/sorority housing, wellness housing available. $500 nonrefundable deposit, deadline 5/1. **Activities:** Jazz band, campus ministries, choral groups, dance, drama, international student organizations, literary magazine, music ensembles, musical theater, radio station, student government, student newspaper, 90 organizations available.

Athletics. NCAA. **Intercollegiate:** Baseball M, basketball, cross-country, diving, field hockey W, golf M, ice hockey M, lacrosse, skiing, soccer, softball W, swimming, tennis, track and field, volleyball W. **Intramural:** Basketball, football (non-tackle), ice hockey, racquetball, soccer, softball, squash, tennis, volleyball, water polo. **Team name:** Beavers.

Student services. Alcohol/substance abuse counseling, chaplain/spiritual director, career counseling, student employment services, financial aid counseling, health services, minority student services, personal counseling, placement for graduates, women's services. **Physically disabled:** Services for visually, speech, hearing impaired.

Contact. E-mail: ugradadmission@babson.edu
Phone: (781) 239-5522 Toll-free number: (800) 488-3696
Fax: (781) 239-4135
Grant Gosselin, Dean of Undergraduate Admission, Babson College, 231 Forest Street, Babson Park, MA 02457-0310

Bard College at Simon's Rock
Great Barrington, Massachusetts
www.simons-rock.edu CB code: 3795

- Private 4-year liberal arts college
- Residential campus in small town
- 346 degree-seeking undergraduates: 1% part-time, 66% women, 10% African American, 7% Asian American, 5% Hispanic American, 5% international
- 87% of applicants admitted
- Application essay, interview required

General. Founded in 1964. Regionally accredited. Provides students with the opportunity to begin college in a residential environment after completing the 10th or 11th grade. **Degrees:** 48 bachelor's, 106 associate awarded. **Location:** 135 miles from Boston, 132 miles from New York. **Calendar:** Semester. **Full-time faculty:** 45 total; 89% have terminal degrees, 16% minority, 42% women. **Part-time faculty:** 26 total; 54% have terminal degrees, 8% minority, 46% women. **Class size:** 97% < 20, 3% 20-39. **Special facilities:** Theaters, dance studio, 3-D design studio, wood/metal studio, sculpture terrace.

Freshman class profile. 290 applied, 253 admitted, 118 enrolled.

Mid 50% test scores			
		GPA 2.0-2.99:	19%
SAT critical reading:	670-740	Rank in top quarter:	84%
SAT math:	590-690	Rank in top tenth:	53%
SAT writing:	610-730	Return as sophomores:	81%
ACT composite:	21-31	Out-of-state:	86%
GPA 3.75 or higher:	34%	Live on campus:	93%
GPA 3.50-3.74:	12%	International:	5%
GPA 3.0-3.49:	34%		

Basis for selection. School achievement record, essays, recommendations (counselor and teacher), interview most important. Institutional testing used for math and foreign language placement. Students in home schooled or ungraded schooling should submit test scores if available. **Home schooled:** Statement describing home school structure and mission, transcript of courses and grades, interview required.

High school preparation. College-preparatory program recommended. Recommended units include English 2, mathematics 2, social studies 2, history 2, science 2 and foreign language 2. Applicants who have completed 10th or 11th grade should have 2 or 3 years college-preparatory curriculum respectively.

2011-2012 Annual costs. Tuition/fees: $43,000. Annual health services fee of $690. Student activity fee $150. Room/board: $11,960. Books/supplies: $1,000. Personal expenses: $640.

2011-2012 Financial aid. Need-based: 96 full-time freshmen applied for aid; 87 were judged to have need; 87 of these received aid. Average need met was 76%. Average scholarship/grant was $20,342; average loan $4,304. 69% of total undergraduate aid awarded as scholarships/grants, 31% as loans/jobs. **Non-need-based:** Awarded to 263 full-time undergraduates, including 84 freshmen. Scholarships awarded for academics, alumni affiliation, minority status.

Application procedures. Admission: Priority date 4/15; deadline 5/31 (postmark date). $50 fee, may be waived for applicants with need. Application must be submitted on paper. Admission notification on a rolling basis beginning on or about 12/1. Must reply by May 1 or within 2 week(s) if notified thereafter. **Financial aid:** Priority date 2/15; no closing date. FAFSA, CSS PROFILE required. Applicants notified on a rolling basis starting 3/15; must reply within 2 week(s) of notification.

Academics. Upper-class students may take tutorials, independent projects, and extended campus projects (internships or courses). Seniors must complete 8-credit, year-long senior thesis project. **Special study options:** Double major, external degree, independent study, internships, student-designed major, study abroad. Bard Globalization and International Affairs, 3/2 engineering program with Columbia University, articulation agreements with Lincoln College at Oxford University and the Centre for New Writing at the University of Manchester, articulation agreement with the International Center for Photography/Bard. **Credit/placement by examination:** AP, CLEP, institutional tests. 10 credit hours maximum toward associate degree, 10 toward bachelor's. **Support services:** Learning center, reduced course load, study skills assistance, tutoring, writing center.

Majors. Area/ethnic studies: African-American, American, Asian, Chinese, East Asian, European, French, German, Latin American, Russian/Slavic, Spanish/Iberian. **Biology:** General, ecology. **Computer sciences:** Computer science. **Conservation:** Environmental studies. **Engineering:** Pre-engineering. **English:** American lit, creative writing, English lit, general lit. **Foreign languages:** Classics, French, German, linguistics, Spanish. **Health services:** Premedicine. **History:** General, American. **Liberal arts:** Arts/sciences. **Math:** General, applied. **Philosophy/religion:** Ethics, philosophy. **Physical sciences:** Chemistry, physics. **Psychology:** General. **Social sciences:** Anthropology, geography, international relations, political science. **Visual/performing arts:** General, acting, art history/conservation, cinematography, dance, dramatic, film/cinema/video, multimedia, music, photography, play/screenwriting, sculpture, studio arts, theater design.

Most popular majors. Area/ethnic studies 8%, English 9%, interdisciplinary studies 8%, liberal arts 17%, social sciences 9%, visual/performing arts 24%.

Computing on campus. 72 workstations in dormitories, library, student center. Dormitories wired for high-speed internet access and linked to campus network. Commuter students can connect to campus network. Online library, helpline, repair service, student web hosting, wireless network available.

Student life. Freshman orientation: Mandatory, $575 fee. Preregistration for classes offered. One-week writing and thinking workshop held prior to start of semester in August. **Policies:** Dry campus. No smoking on campus or in buildings except in designated smoking areas. Freshmen not permitted cars on campus. **Housing:** Guaranteed on-campus for freshmen. Coed dorms, single-sex dorms available. **Activities:** Bands, choral groups, dance, drama, international student organizations, literary magazine, music ensembles, Model UN, musical theater, student government, student newspaper, black student union, community conservation and clean up, chemistry club, international students club, Latino/a students alliance, QueerSA, women's center.

Athletics. Intercollegiate: Basketball, soccer, swimming. **Intramural:** Archery, basketball, cross-country, racquetball, soccer, squash, swimming, tennis, water polo, weight lifting. **Team name:** Llamas.

Student services. Alcohol/substance abuse counseling, chaplain/spiritual director, career counseling, student employment services, financial aid counseling, health services, minority student services, personal counseling, placement for graduates, women's services. **Physically disabled:** Services for hearing impaired.

Contact. E-mail: admit@simons-rock.edu
Phone: (413) 528-7312 Toll-free number: (800) 235-7186
Fax: (413) 541-0081
Mary Davidson, Dean of the College, Bard College at Simon's Rock, Office of Admission, Great Barrington, MA 01230-1990

Bay Path College
Longmeadow, Massachusetts
www.baypath.edu   **CB code: 3078**

- Private 4-year liberal arts college for women
- Residential campus in large town
- 1,570 degree-seeking undergraduates: 20% part-time, 100% women, 11% African American, 2% Asian American, 14% Hispanic American
- 619 degree-seeking graduate students
- 59% of applicants admitted
- 65% graduate within 6 years

General. Founded in 1897. Regionally accredited. Member of 8-college consortium. **Degrees:** 355 bachelor's, 56 associate awarded; master's offered. **ROTC:** Army, Air Force. **Location:** 5 miles from Springfield; 23 miles from Hartford, Connecticut. **Calendar:** Semester, limited summer session. **Full-time faculty:** 48 total; 12% minority, 65% women. **Part-time faculty:** 188 total; 12% minority, 66% women. **Class size:** 74% < 20, 26% 20-39. **Special facilities:** Academic development center, occupational therapy laboratory, physicians assistant laboratory, business hall, career development center.

Freshman class profile. 993 applied, 583 admitted, 155 enrolled.

Mid 50% test scores			
SAT critical reading:	430-520	GPA 3.0-3.49:	41%
SAT math:	430-520	GPA 2.0-2.99:	33%
SAT writing:	430-530	Rank in top quarter:	36%
ACT composite:	20-23	Rank in top tenth:	1%
GPA 3.75 or higher:	15%	Return as sophomores:	76%
GPA 3.50-3.74:	10%	Out-of-state:	57%
		Live on campus:	80%

Basis for selection. High school transcript and performance, class rank, GPA, SAT or ACT, letters of recommendation, and essay. Interview and essay or personal statement recommended. **Home schooled:** Statement describing home school structure and mission, transcript of courses and grades, state high school equivalency certificate, letter of recommendation (nonparent) required.

High school preparation. College-preparatory program recommended. 15 units required; 20 recommended. Required and recommended units include English 4, mathematics 3-4, social studies 2, history 1-2, science 2-3 (laboratory 2) and foreign language 2.

2011-2012 Annual costs. Tuition/fees: $27,045. Room/board: $12,220.

2011-2012 Financial aid. Need-based: 141 full-time freshmen applied for aid; 136 were judged to have need; 136 of these received aid. Average need met was 78%. Average scholarship/grant was $19,068; average loan $5,330. 74% of total undergraduate aid awarded as scholarships/grants, 26% as loans/jobs. **Non-need-based:** Scholarships awarded for academics. **Additional information:** Opportunity Grant program for students whose family may be facing financial difficulties paying tuition resulting from economic conditions. Additional funding available in an endowment program to assist students who qualify.

Application procedures. Admission: Priority date 12/15; no deadline. $25 fee, may be waived for applicants with need, free for online applicants. Admission notification on a rolling basis beginning on or about 9/15. Must reply by May 1 or within 2 week(s) if notified thereafter. **Financial aid:** Priority date 3/1; no closing date. FAFSA required. Applicants notified on a rolling basis starting 3/1; must reply within 2 week(s) of notification.

Academics. Special study options: Accelerated study, combined bachelor's/graduate degree, cooperative education, cross-registration, distance learning, double major, ESL, exchange student, honors, independent study, internships, student-designed major, study abroad, teacher certification program, Washington semester, weekend college. **Credit/placement by examination:** AP, CLEP, IB, institutional tests. 12 credit hours maximum toward associate degree, 12 toward bachelor's. **Support services:** Learning center, study skills assistance, tutoring, writing center.

Majors. Biology: General, biotechnology. **Business:** Accounting, business admin, marketing. **Education:** Early childhood, elementary. **Liberal arts:** Arts/sciences. **Protective services:** Criminalistics, forensics. **Psychology:** General, developmental, forensic. **Visual/performing arts:** Interior design.

Most popular majors. Biology 6%, business/marketing 25%, education 6%, legal studies 6%, liberal arts 31%, psychology 16%, security/protective services 14%.

Computing on campus. 340 workstations in dormitories, library, computer center, student center. Dormitories wired for high-speed internet access and linked to campus network. Commuter students can connect to campus network. Online course registration, online library, helpline, wireless network available.

Student life. Freshman orientation: Mandatory. Preregistration for classes offered. Two-part program: 2-day program in July covers departmental meetings, placement testing, student registration and roommate requests; 3-day program at end of August covers advisor meetings, community service, and transition events. **Policies:** No smoking or alcohol in dormitories. **Housing:** Guaranteed on-campus for all undergraduates. $300 nonrefundable deposit, deadline 5/1. **Activities:** Choral groups, dance, drama, international student organizations, literary magazine, Model UN, musical theater, student government, student newspaper, interfaith council, Habitat for Humanity, women of culture, Alliance, Phi Beta Lambda.

Athletics. NCAA. **Intercollegiate:** Basketball W, cross-country W, field hockey W, soccer W, softball W, tennis W, volleyball W. **Team name:** Wildcats.

Student services. Adult student services, career counseling, student employment services, financial aid counseling, health services, minority student services, personal counseling, placement for graduates, women's services.

Contact. E-mail: admiss@baypath.edu
Phone: (413) 565-1000 ext. 1331
Toll-free number: (800) 782-7284 ext. 1331 Fax: (413) 565-1105
Stefanie Sanchez, Director of Traditional Admissions, Bay Path College, 588 Longmeadow Street, Longmeadow, MA 01106

Becker College
Worcester, Massachusetts
www.becker.edu

CB member
CB code: 3079

- Private 4-year liberal arts college
- Residential campus in small city
- 1,740 degree-seeking undergraduates: 20% part-time, 62% women, 8% African American, 1% Asian American, 8% Hispanic American, 1% Native American
- 72% of applicants admitted
- SAT or ACT with writing required

General. Founded in 1887. Regionally accredited. Additional campus in Leicester. Member of Colleges of the Worcester Consortium. **Degrees:** 225 bachelor's, 111 associate awarded. **ROTC:** Army. **Location:** 49 miles from Boston; 39 miles from Providence, Rhode Island. **Calendar:** Semester, limited summer session. **Full-time faculty:** 45 total; 64% have terminal degrees, 9% minority, 60% women. **Part-time faculty:** 132 total; 4% minority, 58% women. **Class size:** 51% < 20, 46% 20-39, 1% 40-49, 2% 50-99. **Special facilities:** Veterinary clinic, 96-acre off-campus stable for equine programs, Massachusetts Digital Games Institute.

Freshman class profile. 2,509 applied, 1,818 admitted, 416 enrolled.

Mid 50% test scores			
SAT critical reading:	400-520	GPA 3.0-3.49:	27%
SAT math:	410-540	GPA 2.0-2.99:	58%
SAT writing:	390-500	Rank in top quarter:	21%
ACT composite:	16-20	Rank in top tenth:	5%
GPA 3.75 or higher:	5%	Return as sophomores:	64%
GPA 3.50-3.74:	8%	Out-of-state:	42%
		Live on campus:	74%

Basis for selection. High school record, GPA, extracurricular activities important. Recommendations, interview considered. Additional prerequisites for nursing, veterinary technology, veterinary science programs. Essay recommended. **Home schooled:** Statement describing home school structure and mission, letter of recommendation (nonparent) required. Official transcript required from high school with which student is affiliated.

High school preparation. College-preparatory program required. 18 units recommended. Recommended units include English 4, mathematics 3, social studies 2, history 2, science 3 (laboratory 2) and foreign language 2. 1 chemistry with lab, 1 biology with lab required for nursing, veterinary technician, veterinary science, pre-vet programs.

2011-2012 Annual costs. Tuition/fees: $28,490. Room/board: $10,420. Books/supplies: $1,100. Personal expenses: $1,500.

Financial aid. **Non-need-based:** Scholarships awarded for academics.

Application procedures. **Admission:** Priority date 2/15; no deadline. $30 fee, may be waived for applicants with need. Admission notification on a rolling basis beginning on or about 11/15. Must reply by May 1 or within 4 week(s) if notified thereafter. **Financial aid:** Priority date 3/1; no closing date. FAFSA required. Applicants notified on a rolling basis starting 2/1; must reply within 2 week(s) of notification.

Academics. **Special study options:** Accelerated study, cross-registration, distance learning, double major, dual enrollment of high school students, honors, independent study, internships, liberal arts/career combination, semester at sea, study abroad, teacher certification program. **Credit/placement by examination:** AP, CLEP, IB, SAT, institutional tests. 30 credit hours maximum toward associate degree, 60 toward bachelor's. **Support services:** Learning center, reduced course load, remedial instruction, study skills assistance, tutoring, writing center.

Majors. **Biology:** General. **Business:** Business admin, hospitality admin, marketing, tourism/travel. **Computer sciences:** Networking. **Education:** Early childhood, elementary. **General:** Equestrian studies, equine science. **Health services:** Nursing (RN), preveterinary, veterinary technology/assistant. **Liberal arts:** Arts/sciences. **Parks/recreation:** Health/fitness, sports admin. **Protective services:** Criminal justice, forensics, law enforcement admin, police science. **Psychology:** General. **Visual/performing arts:** Game design, graphic design, interior design.

Most popular majors. Business/marketing 32%, communication technologies 8%, health sciences 15%, parks/recreation 8%, psychology 15%, visual/performing arts 10%.

Computing on campus. 155 workstations in dormitories, library, computer center. Dormitories wired for high-speed internet access and linked to campus network. Commuter students can connect to campus network. Online course registration, online library, helpline, wireless network available.

Student life. **Freshman orientation:** Mandatory. Preregistration for classes offered. **Housing:** Guaranteed on-campus for all undergraduates. Coed dorms, single-sex dorms, apartments available. $100 nonrefundable deposit, deadline 6/1. **Activities:** Pep band, choral groups, dance, drama, musical theater, student government, student newspaper, TV station, campus community service club, international club, animal health club, business club, commuter club, early childhood education club, outdoors club, travel club, nursing club.

Athletics. NCAA. **Intercollegiate:** Baseball M, basketball, equestrian, field hockey W, football (tackle) M, golf M, ice hockey M, lacrosse, soccer, softball W, tennis, volleyball W. **Intramural:** Basketball, soccer, table tennis, volleyball. **Team name:** Hawks.

Student services. Adult student services, alcohol/substance abuse counseling, career counseling, student employment services, financial aid counseling, health services, personal counseling, placement for graduates. **Physically disabled:** Services for visually, speech, hearing impaired.

Contact. E-mail: admissions@beckercollege.edu
Phone: (508) 373-9400 Toll-free number: (877) 523-2537
Fax: (508) 890-1500
Michael Perron, Director of Admissions, Becker College, 61 Sever Street, Worcester, MA 01609

Bentley University
Waltham, Massachusetts
www.bentley.edu

CB member
CB code: 3096

- Private 4-year university and business college
- Residential campus in small city
- 4,154 degree-seeking undergraduates: 3% part-time, 41% women, 3% African American, 7% Asian American, 7% Hispanic American, 12% international
- 1,334 degree-seeking graduate students
- 43% of applicants admitted
- SAT or ACT with writing, application essay required
- 89% graduate within 6 years; 21% enter graduate study

General. Founded in 1917. Regionally accredited. **Degrees:** 998 bachelor's awarded; master's, doctoral offered. **ROTC:** Army, Air Force. **Location:** 10 miles from Boston. **Calendar:** Semester, extensive summer session. **Full-time faculty:** 280 total; 82% have terminal degrees, 14% minority, 39% women. **Part-time faculty:** 178 total; 39% have terminal degrees, 9% minority, 39% women. **Class size:** 23% < 20, 77% 20-39, less than 1% 40-49. **Special facilities:** Accounting center, academic technology center, alliance for ethics and social responsibility, business ethics center, languages and international collaboration center, marketing technology center, quantitative analysis center, design and usability center, financial services center, media and culture labs and studio, trading room, service-learning center, international students and scholars center, multicultural center, spiritual life center, center for women in business.

Freshman class profile. 6,695 applied, 2,902 admitted, 911 enrolled.

Mid 50% test scores			
SAT critical reading:	540-640	End year in good standing:	98%
SAT math:	600-680	Return as sophomores:	94%
SAT writing:	550-650	Out-of-state:	59%
ACT composite:	25-29	Live on campus:	98%
Rank in top quarter:	82%	International:	14%
Rank in top tenth:	45%	Fraternities:	10%
		Sororities:	17%

Basis for selection. Decisions based on holistic review of applicant's file. School competitiveness, course leveling, performance throughout secondary school, standardized test scores, activities in and out of school, recommendation letters and any supplemental information reviewed. Interviews strongly recommended. **Home schooled:** Statement describing home school structure and mission, transcript of courses and grades, state high school equivalency certificate, letter of recommendation (nonparent) required. Interview strongly recommended.

High school preparation. College-preparatory program required. 19 units recommended. Recommended units include English 4, mathematics 4, social studies 3, science 3 (laboratory 3) and foreign language 3. Two additional units of English, math, science, or foreign language recommended. History is combined with social studies.

2011-2012 Annual costs. Tuition/fees: $38,328. Required fees include cost of laptop computer. Room/board: $12,520. Books/supplies: $1,100. Personal expenses: $1,150.

2010-2011 Financial aid. Need-based: 690 full-time freshmen applied for aid; 506 were judged to have need; 505 of these received aid. Average need met was 97%. Average scholarship/grant was $25,290; average loan $4,448. 76% of total undergraduate aid awarded as scholarships/grants, 24% as loans/jobs. **Non-need-based:** Awarded to 1,228 full-time undergraduates, including 335 freshmen. Scholarships awarded for academics, athletics, leadership, minority status.

Application procedures. Admission: $50 fee, may be waived for applicants with need. Admission notification by 4/1. **Financial aid:** Closing date 2/1. FAFSA required. CSS PROFILE required if applying for institutional grants. Deadlines for receipt of CSS Profile: Early Decision, 12/1; Early Action and Regular Decision, 2/1. Applicants notified by 3/25.

Academics. Special study options: Accelerated study, combined bachelor's/graduate degree, cross-registration, double major, honors, independent study, internships, liberal arts/career combination, New York semester, semester at sea, student-designed major, study abroad, United Nations semester, Washington semester. 5-year bachelor's/master's programs in business administration, accountancy, finance, marketing analytics, information technology, financial planning and taxation. **Credit/placement by examination:** AP, CLEP, IB, SAT, institutional tests. 30 credit hours maximum toward bachelor's degree. Full-time day students may not take language CLEP exam. **Support services:** Learning center, reduced course load, study skills assistance, tutoring, writing center.

Majors. Business: General, accounting, accounting/finance, business admin, communications, finance, managerial economics, marketing. **Communications:** Media studies. **Computer sciences:** General. **English:** English lit. **Human services:** Public policy. **Liberal arts:** Arts/sciences. **Math:** General. **Philosophy/religion:** Philosophy.

Most popular majors. Business/marketing 93%.

Computing on campus. PC or laptop required. 4,489 workstations in dormitories, library, computer center, student center. Dormitories wired for high-speed internet access and linked to campus network. Commuter students can connect to campus network. Online course registration, online library, helpline, repair service, student web hosting, wireless network available.

Student life. Freshman orientation: Available, $175 fee. Preregistration for classes offered. Three-day program usually held in summer. **Policies:** Academic honesty system, minimum GPA for student leaders. Freshmen not permitted cars on campus. **Housing:** Guaranteed on-campus for all undergraduates. Coed dorms, special housing for disabled, apartments, wellness housing available. Global living floors, women's leadership floor. **Activities:** Bands, campus ministries, choral groups, dance, drama, film society, international student organizations, literary magazine, music ensembles, Model UN, musical theater, radio station, student government, student newspaper, TV station, Black United Body, South Asian student association, La Cultura Latina, People Respecting Individuality and Diversity Through Education, Green Society, Muslim students' association, Circle K, Habitat For Humanity, Hillel, Christian Fellowship.

Athletics. NCAA. **Intercollegiate:** Baseball M, basketball, cross-country, diving, field hockey W, football (tackle) M, golf M, ice hockey M, lacrosse, soccer, softball W, swimming, tennis, track and field, volleyball W. **Intramural:** Basketball, football (non-tackle) M, soccer, softball, volleyball. **Team name:** Falcons.

Student services. Adult student services, alcohol/substance abuse counseling, chaplain/spiritual director, career counseling, services for economically disadvantaged, student employment services, financial aid counseling, health services, minority student services, personal counseling, placement for graduates, veterans' counselor, women's services. **Physically disabled:** Services for visually, speech, hearing impaired.

Contact. E-mail: ugadmission@bentley.edu
Phone: (781) 891-2244 Toll-free number: (800) 523-2354
Fax: (781) 891-3414
Erika Vardaro, Director of Admissions, Bentley University, 175 Forest Street, Waltham, MA 02452-4717

Berklee College of Music
Boston, Massachusetts
www.berklee.edu

CB member
CB code: 3107

- Private 4-year music college
- Commuter campus in very large city
- 3,668 degree-seeking undergraduates: 9% part-time, 31% women, 7% African American, 3% Asian American, 9% Hispanic American, 23% international
- 28% of applicants admitted

- Application essay, interview required
- 53% graduate within 6 years

General. Founded in 1945. Regionally accredited. **Degrees:** 668 bachelor's awarded. **Calendar:** Semester, extensive summer session. **Full-time faculty:** 243 total; 18% minority, 23% women. **Part-time faculty:** 334 total; 17% minority, 31% women. **Class size:** 90% < 20, 9% 20-39, less than 1% 40-49, less than 1% 50-99, less than 1% >100. **Special facilities:** Performance center, student-run music venue and coffee house, music technology facilities and practice spaces, synthesizer laboratories, recording studios, film scoring laboratories, technology labs, media center.

Freshman class profile. 4,956 applied, 1,388 admitted, 918 enrolled.

GPA 3.75 or higher:	29%	Return as sophomores:	83%
GPA 3.50-3.74:	30%	Out-of-state:	84%
GPA 3.0-3.49:	33%	Live on campus:	61%
GPA 2.0-2.99:	8%	International:	24%

Basis for selection. Musical training and experience, recommendations, academic record, test scores, extracurricular music activities, interview important. Auditions required. **Home schooled:** Statement describing home school structure and mission, state high school equivalency certificate required. **Learning Disabled:** Students with disabilities should contact Special Services Coordinator.

High school preparation. Recommended units include English 4, mathematics 1, history 1, science 1 (laboratory 1) and academic electives 6. Minimum 2 years recent formal musical study on principal instrument covering standard methods/materials and/or significant practical performance experience plus knowledge of written-music fundamentals normally required of all applicants.

2011-2012 Annual costs. Tuition/fees: $38,995. Required fees include comprehensive fee of $610 per semester and one-time charge of $2,985 for purchase of laptop computer (equipped with various software products), which all freshman students must purchase. Room/board: $16,620. Books/supplies: $470. Personal expenses: $2,378.

2011-2012 Financial aid. Need-based: 399 full-time freshmen applied for aid; 349 were judged to have need; 345 of these received aid. Average need met was 36%. Average scholarship/grant was $11,317; average loan $3,974. 65% of total undergraduate aid awarded as scholarships/grants, 35% as loans/jobs. **Non-need-based:** Awarded to 925 full-time undergraduates, including 310 freshmen. Scholarships awarded for academics, music/drama.

Application procedures. Admission: Priority date 11/1; deadline 1/15 (postmark date). $150 fee, may be waived for applicants with need. Application must be submitted online. Admission notification by 3/31. Must reply by 5/1. Applicants should submit completed application materials well in advance of deadline to ensure placement in desired entry class. **Financial aid:** Priority date 3/1, closing date 5/7. FAFSA required. Applicants notified on a rolling basis starting 1/31; must reply within 2 week(s) of notification

Academics. Bachelor's degree program includes 30 credits general education courses. Four-year professional diploma available (not including general education). **Special study options:** Cooperative education, cross-registration, distance learning, double major, dual enrollment of high school students, ESL, internships, student-designed major, study abroad, teacher certification program. ProArts Consortium with Boston Architectural Center, Boston Conservatory, Emerson College, Massachusetts College of Art, School of the Museum of Fine Arts. **Credit/placement by examination:** AP, CLEP, institutional tests. 60 credit hours maximum toward bachelor's degree. **Support services:** Learning center, pre-admission summer program, tutoring, writing center.

Majors. Health services: Music therapy. **Visual/performing arts:** Jazz, music, music management, music performance, music theory/composition, piano/keyboard, voice/opera.

Most popular majors. Communication technologies 17%, visual/performing arts 79%.

Computing on campus. PC or laptop required. 50 workstations in dormitories, library, computer center. Dormitories wired for high-speed internet access and linked to campus network. Online library, helpline, repair service, student web hosting, wireless network available.

Student life. Freshman orientation: Available. Preregistration for classes offered. Series of events before and during registration week. **Housing:** Coed dorms available. $300 nonrefundable deposit, deadline 5/1. Residence space limited. **Activities:** Bands, choral groups, dance, film society, international student organizations, literary magazine, music ensembles, musical theater, radio station, student government, student newspaper, symphony orchestra, black student union, Christian Fellowship, Berklee Cares, women musicians' network, Latinos association, GLBT Allies at Berklee, Korean student association, Amnesty International.

Athletics. Intramural: Basketball, football (non-tackle), ice hockey, soccer. **Team name:** IceCats.

Student services. Career counseling, student employment services, minority student services, personal counseling, veterans' counselor. **Physically disabled:** Services for visually impaired.

Contact. E-mail: admissions@berklee.edu
Phone: (617) 747-2221 Toll-free number: (800) 237-5533
Fax: (617) 747-2047
Damien Bracken, Director of Admissions/OSSE, Berklee College of Music, 1140 Boylston Street, Boston, MA 02215

Boston Architectural College
Boston, Massachusetts
www.the-bac.edu   **CB code: 1168**

- Private 6-year Architecture and design college
- Commuter campus in very large city
- 538 degree-seeking undergraduates: 1% part-time, 31% women, 6% African American, 7% Asian American, 13% Hispanic American
- 435 degree-seeking graduate students

General. Founded in 1889. Regionally accredited. Program offers practice-based learning with simultaneous employment in field and academic study. **Degrees:** 48 bachelor's awarded; master's offered. **Location:** Downtown. **Calendar:** Semester, limited summer session. **Full-time faculty:** 1 total; 100% have terminal degrees, 100% women. **Part-time faculty:** 364 total; 100% have terminal degrees, 16% minority, 50% women. **Class size:** 61% < 20, 16% 20-39, 6% 40-49, 14% 50-99, 3% >100. **Special facilities:** On-campus gallery featuring exhibits of architectural and interior design interest, CAD lab, photography studio.

Freshman class profile. 68 applied, 68 admitted, 29 enrolled.

GPA 3.75 or higher:	9%	Rank in top quarter:	23%
GPA 3.50-3.74:	9%	Rank in top tenth:	6%
GPA 3.0-3.49:	18%	Return as sophomores:	63%
GPA 2.0-2.99:	64%	Out-of-state:	63%

Basis for selection. Open admission, but selective for some programs. Creative exercise required. **Learning Disabled:** Students with learning disabilities are strongly encouraged to notify the Learning Resource Center of any special accommodations prior to matriculation.

High school preparation. College-preparatory program recommended. 16 units recommended. Recommended units include English 4, mathematics 3, social studies 2, history 2, science 3 and foreign language 2.

2011-2012 Annual costs. Tuition/fees: $16,826. Academic Only program tuition is $22,308 plus $50 required fee. Books/supplies: $1,528. Personal expenses: $4,332.

2010-2011 Financial aid. **Need-based:** Average need met was 17%. Average scholarship/grant was $3,476; average loan $3,691. 16% of total undergraduate aid awarded as scholarships/grants, 84% as loans/jobs. **Non-need-based:** Scholarships awarded for academics, art, leadership.

Application procedures. Admission: Priority date 2/15; deadline 8/15 (receipt date). $50 fee, may be waived for applicants with need. Admission notification on a rolling basis beginning on or about 1/25. Must reply by May 1 or within 2 week(s) if notified thereafter. **Financial aid:** Priority date 4/15; no closing date. FAFSA required. Applicants notified on a rolling basis starting 3/30; must reply within 2 week(s) of notification.

Academics. Bachelor of architecture or interior design awarded after 6-year program of concurrent work and academic curriculum. Students usually transfer into program during second or third years. **Special study options:** Combined bachelor's/graduate degree, cross-registration, distance learning, independent study, internships, liberal arts/career combination. Member Professional Arts Consortium. **Credit/placement by examination:** AP, CLEP, institutional tests. **Support services:** Learning center, study skills assistance, tutoring, writing center.

Majors. Architecture: Architecture, interior, landscape.

Computing on campus. 63 workstations in library, computer center. Commuter students can connect to campus network. Online library, helpline, wireless network available.

Student life. Freshman orientation: Mandatory. Preregistration for classes offered. Several dates; includes writing test. **Policies:** Code of conduct, alcohol and substance abuse policy, anti-hazing policy in effect. **Housing:**

Dormitory space, when available, at ProArts Consortium schools. **Activities:** International student organizations, student government.

Student services. Adult student services, career counseling, student employment services, financial aid counseling, minority student services, veterans' counselor. **Physically disabled:** Services for visually, speech, hearing impaired.

Contact. E-mail: admissions@the-bac.edu
Phone: (617) 585-0123 Toll-free number: (877) 585-0100
Fax: (617) 585-0121
Richard Moyer, Director of Admissions, Boston Architectural College, Boston Architectural College, Boston, MA 02115-2795

Boston Baptist College
Boston, Massachusetts
www.boston.edu/   **CB code: 4323**

- Private 4-year Bible college affiliated with Baptist faith
- Very large city

General. Regionally accredited. **Calendar:** Semester.

Annual costs/financial aid. Tuition/fees (2011-2012): $15,040. Room/board: $7,710. Books/supplies: $800. Need-based financial aid available to full-time and part-time students.

Contact. Phone: (617) 364-3510 ext. 217
Director of Admissions, 950 Metropolitan Avenue, Boston, MA 02136

Boston College
Chestnut Hill, Massachusetts   **CB member**
www.bc.edu   **CB code: 3083**

- Private 4-year university affiliated with Roman Catholic Church
- Residential campus in small city
- 9,088 degree-seeking undergraduates: 53% women, 4% African American, 9% Asian American, 10% Hispanic American, 4% international
- 4,819 graduate students
- 28% of applicants admitted
- SAT and SAT Subject Tests or ACT with writing, application essay required
- 91% graduate within 6 years; 27% enter graduate study

General. Founded in 1863. Regionally accredited. **Degrees:** 2,397 bachelor's awarded; master's, professional, doctoral offered. **ROTC:** Army, Naval, Air Force. **Location:** 6 miles from downtown Boston. **Calendar:** Semester, extensive summer session. **Full-time faculty:** 737 total; 98% have terminal degrees, 15% minority, 39% women. **Part-time faculty:** 634 total; 95% have terminal degrees, 27% minority, 62% women. **Class size:** 52% < 20, 33% 20-39, 9% 40-49, 4% 50-99, 3% >100. **Special facilities:** Observatory, theater, arts center, chemistry center, art museum, rare books and special collections library.

Freshman class profile. 32,974 applied, 9,227 admitted, 2,113 enrolled.

Mid 50% test scores			
SAT critical reading:	620-710	Rank in top quarter:	95%
SAT math:	640-730	Rank in top tenth:	82%
SAT writing:	630-720	Return as sophomores:	95%
ACT composite:	29-32	Out-of-state:	77%
		Live on campus:	99%

Basis for selection. Evidence of academic ability, intellectual curiosity, strength of character, motivation, creativity, energy, and promise for personal growth and development very important. Recommendations by counselors and teachers, required personal statement and extracurricular activities important. 2 SAT Subject Tests of student's choice required if SAT is submitted. Portfolio recommended for studio art majors. Students interested in music, theater, or dance encouraged to send examples of work via DVD or CD. **Learning Disabled:** May provide documentation of disability at option of applicant.

High school preparation. College-preparatory program recommended. 20 units recommended. Recommended units include English 4, mathematics 4, social studies 4, science 4 (laboratory 4) and foreign language 4. 4 combined social studies and history recommended. 2 laboratory science (including 1 chemistry) required of nursing applicants.

2011-2012 Annual costs. Tuition/fees: $42,204. Room/board: $12,875. Books/supplies: $900. Personal expenses: $1,000.

2010-2011 Financial aid. Need-based: 1,276 full-time freshmen applied for aid; 1,082 were judged to have need; 1,082 of these received aid. Average need met was 100%. Average scholarship/grant was $29,202; average loan $3,888. 79% of total undergraduate aid awarded as scholarships/grants, 21% as loans/jobs. **Non-need-based:** Awarded to 512 full-time undergraduates, including 91 freshmen. Scholarships awarded for academics, athletics, leadership, ROTC.

Application procedures. Admission: Closing date 1/1 (postmark date). $70 fee, may be waived for applicants with need. Admission notification by 4/15. Must reply by 5/1. **Financial aid:** Priority date 2/1; no closing date. FAFSA, CSS PROFILE required. Applicants notified on a rolling basis starting 4/1.

Academics. Special study options: Accelerated study, combined bachelor's/graduate degree, cross-registration, distance learning, double major, ESL, exchange student, honors, independent study, internships, liberal arts/career combination, student-designed major, study abroad, teacher certification program, Washington semester. Tufts Medical School early acceptance, 5th year masters program can be combined with bachelor's degree attainment in certain fields. **Credit/placement by examination:** AP, CLEP, IB. 24 credit hours maximum toward bachelor's degree. **Support services:** Learning center, pre-admission summer program, reduced course load, study skills assistance, tutoring, writing center.

Majors. Area/ethnic studies: Chicano/Hispanic-American/Latino. **Biology:** General, biochemistry. **Business:** Accounting, business admin, finance, human resources, management information systems, managerial economics, operations. **Communications:** Communications/speech/rhetoric. **Computer sciences:** General, computer science, information systems. **Education:** Early childhood, elementary, secondary. **English:** English lit. **Foreign languages:** Ancient Greek, classics, French, German, Italian, Latin, linguistics, Russian, Spanish. **Health services:** Nursing (RN). **History:** General. **Math:** General. **Philosophy/religion:** Philosophy. **Physical sciences:** Chemistry, geology, geophysics, physics. **Psychology:** General. **Social sciences:** Economics, political science, sociology. **Visual/performing arts:** Art history/conservation, dramatic, film/cinema/video, music, studio arts.

Most popular majors. Biology 6%, business/marketing 24%, communications/journalism 9%, English 7%, history 6%, psychology 9%, social sciences 17%.

Computing on campus. 1,000 workstations in library, computer center, student center. Dormitories wired for high-speed internet access and linked to campus network. Commuter students can connect to campus network. Online course registration, online library, helpline, repair service, student web hosting, wireless network available.

Student life. Freshman orientation: Mandatory, $420 fee. Preregistration for classes offered. Three-day, 2-night program; 4-6 scheduled options offered during summer. **Policies:** Alcohol prohibited for students under 21, smoking prohibited in all residence halls. Halogen lights, space heaters, egg crate style foam mattress pads, and candles prohibited in dorm rooms. Freshmen not permitted cars on campus. **Housing:** Guaranteed on-campus for freshmen. Coed dorms, single-sex dorms, special housing for disabled, apartments, wellness housing available. $250 partly refundable deposit, deadline 5/1. Honors house, multicultural floor, 24-hour quiet living floor, social justice floor available. Apartment-style housing and townhouse-style housing available for upperclassmen. **Activities:** Bands, campus ministries, choral groups, dance, drama, film society, international student organizations, literary magazine, music ensembles, musical theater, radio station, student government, student newspaper, symphony orchestra, TV station, 4Boston, Amnesty International, Appalachia volunteers, Asian caucus, black student forum, Buddhist club, Hillel, Ignatian Society, Puerto Rican association, Muslim students association.

Athletics. NCAA. **Intercollegiate:** Baseball M, basketball, cross-country, diving, fencing, field hockey W, football (tackle) M, golf, ice hockey, lacrosse W, rowing (crew) W, sailing, skiing, soccer, softball W, swimming, tennis, track and field, volleyball W. **Intramural:** Basketball, football (non-tackle), golf, ice hockey, racquetball, soccer, softball, squash, tennis, volleyball. **Team name:** Eagles.

Student services. Alcohol/substance abuse counseling, chaplain/spiritual director, career counseling, services for economically disadvantaged, student employment services, financial aid counseling, health services, minority student services, on-campus daycare, personal counseling, placement for graduates, veterans' counselor, women's services. **Physically disabled:** Services for visually, speech, hearing impaired.

Contact. Phone: (617) 552-3100 Toll-free number: (800) 360-2522 Fax: (617) 552-0798
John Mahoney, Director of Undergraduate Admission, Boston College, 140 Commonwealth Avenue, Devlin Hall 208, Chestnut Hill, MA 02467-3809

Boston Conservatory
Boston, Massachusetts
www.bostonconservatory.edu

CB member
CB code: 3084

- Private 4-year music and performing arts college
- Residential campus in very large city
- 519 degree-seeking undergraduates: 1% part-time, 60% women, 4% Asian American, 11% international
- 217 degree-seeking graduate students
- 36% of applicants admitted
- SAT or ACT (ACT writing optional), application essay required
- 58% graduate within 6 years

General. Founded in 1867. Regionally accredited. **Degrees:** 111 bachelor's awarded; master's offered. **Location:** Downtown. **Calendar:** Semester, limited summer session. **Full-time faculty:** 74 total. **Part-time faculty:** 115 total. **Class size:** 90% < 20, 8% 20-39, 1% 40-49, 1% 50-99, less than 1% >100. **Special facilities:** College operated theater.

Freshman class profile. 1,265 applied, 454 admitted, 147 enrolled.

Return as sophomores:	85%	Live on campus:	98%
Out-of-state:	94%	Sororities:	5%

Basis for selection. Audition carries most weight. Academic record and artistic background strongly considered. Test scores, recommendations, personal essay, school and community activities, interview important. Audition required. Interview required of music education, composition majors. **Home schooled:** Statement describing home school structure and mission, transcript of courses and grades, state high school equivalency certificate required.

High school preparation. College-preparatory program recommended.

2012-2013 Annual costs. Tuition/fees (projected): $37,270. Room/board: $16,890. Books/supplies: $750. Personal expenses: $3,254.

2011-2012 Financial aid. Need-based: 103 full-time freshmen applied for aid; 86 were judged to have need; 86 of these received aid. Average scholarship/grant was $11,538; average loan $4,301. 56% of total undergraduate aid awarded as scholarships/grants, 44% as loans/jobs. **Non-need-based:** Awarded to 145 full-time undergraduates, including 36 freshmen. Scholarships awarded for music/drama.

Application procedures. Admission: Closing date 12/1 (postmark date). $110 fee, may be waived for applicants with need. Application must be submitted online. Admission notification by 4/1. Must reply by May 1 or within 2 week(s) if notified thereafter. **Financial aid:** Priority date 3/1; no closing date. FAFSA required. Applicants notified on a rolling basis.

Academics. Special study options: Cross-registration, double major, ESL, independent study, teacher certification program. **Credit/placement by examination:** AP, CLEP, institutional tests. 75 credit hours maximum toward bachelor's degree. **Support services:** Pre-admission summer program, study skills assistance, tutoring, writing center.

Majors. Visual/performing arts: Dance, music performance, music theory/composition, piano/keyboard, voice/opera.

Computing on campus. 20 workstations in dormitories, library, student center. Dormitories linked to campus network. Online library, wireless network available.

Student life. Freshman orientation: Mandatory, $388 fee. Preregistration for classes offered. Held the week prior to registration; includes college life seminar, advising, parent luncheon, school tours, city-wide tours, placements, auditions. Fee for music education students is $117. **Housing:** Coed dorms, single-sex dorms available. $250 nonrefundable deposit, deadline 5/1. **Activities:** International student organizations, literary magazine, student government, student newspaper, African American artists' association, community services association, Christian Fellowship, environmental awareness group, peer support aides, Taiwan Chinese student association, gay and lesbian artists' association, Organizacion De Artistas Hispanos, Korean society.

Student services. Career counseling, health services, personal counseling.

Contact. E-mail: admissions@bostonconservatory.edu
Phone: (617) 912-9153 Fax: (617) 536-3176
Sipra Agrawal Kolar, Associate Director of Admissions, Boston Conservatory, 8 The Fenway, Boston, MA 02215

Boston University
Boston, Massachusetts
www.bu.edu

CB member
CB code: 3087

- Private 4-year university
- Residential campus in very large city
- 16,575 degree-seeking undergraduates: 3% part-time, 60% women, 3% African American, 14% Asian American, 9% Hispanic American, 12% international
- 13,684 degree-seeking graduate students
- 49% of applicants admitted
- SAT or ACT with writing, SAT Subject Tests, application essay required
- 85% graduate within 6 years; 26% enter graduate study

General. Founded in 1839. Regionally accredited. **Degrees:** 4,093 bachelor's awarded; master's, professional, doctoral offered. **ROTC:** Army, Naval, Air Force. **Location:** Downtown. **Calendar:** Semester, extensive summer session. **Full-time faculty:** 1,632 total; 26% have terminal degrees, 18% minority, 38% women. **Part-time faculty:** 998 total. **Class size:** 53% < 20, 32% 20-39, 6% 40-49, 6% 50-99, 4% >100. **Special facilities:** Biodiversity station in Ecuador, dedicated management library, planetarium, National Public Radio station, 20th century archives, professional theater/theater company, center for remote sensing, speech, language and hearing clinic, culinary center, communication multimedia lab.

Freshman class profile. 41,802 applied, 20,662 admitted, 4,023 enrolled.

Mid 50% test scores			
SAT critical reading:	570-670	Rank in top quarter:	86%
SAT math:	610-700	Rank in top tenth:	55%
SAT writing:	600-680	End year in good standing:	90%
ACT composite:	26-30	Return as sophomores:	92%
GPA 3.75 or higher:	26%	Out-of-state:	80%
GPA 3.50-3.74:	34%	Live on campus:	99%
GPA 3.0-3.49:	38%	International:	16%
GPA 2.0-2.99:	2%	Fraternities:	5%
		Sororities:	15%

Basis for selection. Evidence of strong academic performance in challenging college-prep curriculum most important. SAT Subject Tests in Chemistry and Math (level 2) required for accelerated medical and dental programs. Others required to submit 2 subject tests in subject areas of their choice. Subject Tests recommended for College of Fine Arts, College of General Studies and the Science and Engineering Program in Metropolitan College. Interview required for accelerated medical/dental programs, all nonperformance theater arts majors. Audition required for music, theater performance programs. Portfolio required of visual arts, stage management, theatrical design majors. Portfolio or audition required for College of Fine Arts. **Home schooled:** Students should contact Office of Admissions prior to application.

High school preparation. College-preparatory program required. 15 units required; 20 recommended. Required and recommended units include English 4, mathematics 3-4, social studies 3-4, science 3-4 (laboratory 3-4) and foreign language 2-4. Pre-calculus required. Social studies should include history.

2011-2012 Annual costs. Tuition/fees: $41,420. Room/board: $12,710. Books/supplies: $940. Personal expenses: $1,290.

2011-2012 Financial aid. Need-based: 2,010 full-time freshmen applied for aid; 1,666 were judged to have need; 1,662 of these received aid. Average need met was 89%. Average scholarship/grant was $23,061; average loan $6,870. 84% of total undergraduate aid awarded as scholarships/grants, 16% as loans/jobs. **Non-need-based:** Awarded to 6,454 full-time undergraduates, including 980 freshmen. Scholarships awarded for academics, alumni affiliation, art, athletics, leadership, music/drama, religious affiliation, ROTC, state residency. **Additional information:** Financial aid deadline for early decision applicants: 11/1; notification date: 2/15. Graduates of Boston's public high schools who complete their financial aid application and demonstrate need will be awarded financial aid packages that contain no loans and meet their full demonstrated need.

Application procedures. Admission: Closing date 1/1 (receipt date). $75 fee, may be waived for applicants with need. Admission notification by 4/15. Must reply by 5/1. Application deadline December 1 for accelerated medical and dental combined degree and trustee, Boston high school, Cardinal Medeiros Scholar programs. **Financial aid:** Closing date 2/15. FAFSA, CSS PROFILE required. Applicants notified on a rolling basis starting 3/15; must reply by 5/1 or within 2 week(s) of notification.

Academics. Special study options: Accelerated study, combined bachelor's/graduate degree, cooperative education, cross-registration, distance learning, double major, dual enrollment of high school students, ESL, honors, independent study, internships, liberal arts/career combination, semester at sea, student-designed major, study abroad, teacher certification program, Washington semester, weekend college. Extensive opportunities for study abroad as well as internships available in South and Central America, Europe, Africa, China, Pacific Rim, Russia. Field study in marine science at Woods Hole Institute, in environmental/ecological science in Ecuador, and at Photonics Center, combined bachelor's/master's degrees, 6-year physical therapy (BS/DPT) program, 5-year occupational therapy (BS/MS) program; 7-year accelerated MD, DMD programs. **Credit/placement by examination:** AP, CLEP, IB, SAT, ACT, institutional tests. 32 credit hours maximum toward bachelor's degree. Credits assigned vary by school and college. Scores higher than minimums may result in additional credit depending on department. **Support services:** Learning center, study skills assistance, tutoring, writing center.

Majors. Architecture: History/criticism. **Area/ethnic studies:** American, East Asian, Italian, Latin American, Russian/Slavic. **Biology:** General, biochemistry, ecology, marine, molecular, neuroscience. **Business:** Accounting, business admin, entrepreneurial studies, finance, hospitality admin, international, international finance, management information systems, market research, marketing, operations, organizational behavior. **Communications:** Advertising, broadcast journalism, communications/speech/rhetoric, journalism, public relations. **Computer sciences:** General. **Conservation:** General, environmental science, environmental studies, management/policy. **Education:** General, art, bilingual, chemistry, Deaf/hearing impaired, drama/dance, early childhood, elementary, English, mathematics, music, physical, science, social studies, special ed. **Engineering:** General, aerospace, biomedical, computer, electrical, mechanical. **English:** English lit. **Foreign languages:** General, ancient Greek, classics, French, German, Italian, Latin, linguistics, modern Greek, Russian, Spanish. **Health services:** Athletic training, communication disorders, dental lab technology. **History:** General. **Math:** General. **Parks/recreation:** Exercise sciences. **Philosophy/religion:** Philosophy, religion. **Physical sciences:** Astronomy, astrophysics, chemistry, geology, geophysics, physics, planetary. **Psychology:** General. **Social sciences:** Anthropology, archaeology, economics, geography, international relations, political science, sociology, urban studies. **Visual/performing arts:** General, acting, art history/conservation, cinematography, commercial/advertising art, directing/producing, drawing, music history, music performance, music theory/composition, painting, piano/keyboard, sculpture, theater design, theater history, voice/opera.

Most popular majors. Biology 6%, business/marketing 21%, communications/journalism 15%, engineering/engineering technologies 7%, health sciences 8%, psychology 6%, social sciences 17%.

Computing on campus. 750 workstations in dormitories, library, computer center, student center. Dormitories wired for high-speed internet access and linked to campus network. Commuter students can connect to campus network. Online course registration, online library, helpline, repair service, student web hosting, wireless network available.

Student life. Freshman orientation: Mandatory, $135 fee. Preregistration for classes offered. Summer program. **Policies:** Campus residents must abide by guest/visitor policy. **Housing:** Guaranteed on-campus for all undergraduates. Coed dorms, single-sex dorms, special housing for disabled, apartments, cooperative housing, wellness housing available. $650 nonrefundable deposit, deadline 5/1. Specialty halls/floors available for groups of students with common interest or academic major. **Activities:** Bands, campus ministries, choral groups, dance, drama, film society, international student organizations, literary magazine, music ensembles, Model UN, musical theater, opera, radio station, student government, student newspaper, symphony orchestra, TV station, 525 student organizations available.

Athletics. NCAA. **Intercollegiate:** Basketball, cross-country, diving, field hockey W, golf, ice hockey, lacrosse W, rowing (crew), soccer, softball W, swimming, tennis, track and field, wrestling M. **Intramural:** Basketball, football (non-tackle), ice hockey W, soccer, softball, swimming, tennis, volleyball, water polo. **Team name:** Terriers.

Student services. Adult student services, chaplain/spiritual director, career counseling, student employment services, financial aid counseling, health services, minority student services, personal counseling, placement for graduates, veterans' counselor. **Physically disabled:** Services for visually, speech, hearing impaired.

Contact. E-mail: admissions@bu.edu
Phone: (617) 353-2300 Fax: (617) 353-9695
Kelly Walter, Director, Office of Undergraduate Admissions, Boston University, 121 Bay State Road, Boston, MA 02215

Brandeis University
Waltham, Massachusetts
www.brandeis.edu

CB member
CB code: 3092

- Private 4-year university
- Residential campus in small city

♦ 3,493 degree-seeking undergraduates: 57% women, 4% African American, 13% Asian American, 6% Hispanic American, 12% international

♦ 2,249 degree-seeking graduate students

♦ 40% of applicants admitted

♦ SAT or ACT with writing, application essay required

♦ 91% graduate within 6 years

General. Founded in 1948. Regionally accredited. **Degrees:** 1,136 bachelor's awarded; master's, doctoral offered. **ROTC:** Army, Air Force. **Location:** 10 miles from Boston. **Calendar:** Semester, limited summer session. **Full-time faculty:** 364 total; 95% have terminal degrees, 13% minority, 41% women. **Part-time faculty:** 143 total; 67% have terminal degrees, 6% minority, 38% women. **Class size:** 61% < 20, 25% 20-39, 6% 40-49, 6% 50-99, 2% >100. **Special facilities:** Medical sciences research center, spatial orientation laboratory, center for complex systems, art museum, materials research science and engineering center.

Freshman class profile. 8,917 applied, 3,566 admitted, 858 enrolled.

Mid 50% test scores		GPA 2.0-2.99:	3%
SAT critical reading:	600-710	Rank in top quarter:	94%
SAT math:	630-740	Rank in top tenth:	64%
SAT writing:	630-720	Return as sophomores:	93%
ACT composite:	28-32	Out-of-state:	73%
GPA 3.75 or higher:	56%	Live on campus:	98%
GPA 3.50-3.74:	27%	International:	13%
GPA 3.0-3.49:	14%		

Basis for selection. Academic record, extracurricular activities, essay, recommendations and standardized tests considered. Interview recommended. **Home schooled:** Statement describing home school structure and mission, letter of recommendation (nonparent) required. Detailed description of curriculum; information regarding any affiliation with state or national home-schooling organization; secondary letter of recommendation from outside teacher if course work was taken beyond the home school or, when not available, from employer, coach, art instructor or other community leader; supplemental essay describing why student chose to be home-schooled; and graded paper required.

High school preparation. College-preparatory program required. 20 units recommended. Recommended units include English 4, mathematics 4, social studies 4, science 4 (laboratory 2) and foreign language 4.

2011-2012 Annual costs. Tuition/fees: $42,060. Room/board: $11,894. Books/supplies: $1,000. Personal expenses: $1,500.

2010-2011 Financial aid. All financial aid based on need. 508 full-time freshmen applied for aid; 418 were judged to have need; 409 of these received aid. Average need met was 84%. Average scholarship/grant was $29,160; average loan $3,808. 77% of total undergraduate aid awarded as scholarships/grants, 23% as loans/jobs.

Application procedures. Admission: Closing date 1/15 (receipt date). $55 fee, may be waived for applicants with need. Admission notification by 4/1. Must reply by May 1 or within 2 week(s) if notified thereafter. **Financial aid:** Closing date 2/1. CSS PROFILE required. Applicants notified by 4/1; must reply by 5/1.

Academics. Special study options: Combined bachelor's/graduate degree, cross-registration, double major, exchange student, independent study, internships, student-designed major, study abroad, teacher certification program, Washington semester. 5-year BA/MA programs in international economics and finance, computer science, computational linguistics, and Near Eastern and Judaic studies; early admission to Mt. Sinai Medical School and Tufts Medical School. **Credit/placement by examination:** AP, CLEP, IB, institutional tests. **Support services:** Reduced course load, remedial instruction, study skills assistance, tutoring, writing center.

Majors. Area/ethnic studies: African-American, American, East Asian, European, Italian, Latin American, Near/Middle Eastern, women's. **Biology:** General, biochemistry, biophysics, neuroscience. **Business:** General. **Computer sciences:** Computer science. **Conservation:** Environmental studies. **Education:** General. **English:** Creative writing, English lit. **Foreign languages:** Classics, comparative lit, French, German, Hebrew, linguistics, Russian, Spanish. **Health services:** Health care admin. **History:** General. **Math:** General. **Philosophy/religion:** Judaic, philosophy. **Physical sciences:** Chemistry, physics. **Psychology:** General. **Social sciences:** Anthropology, economics, political science, sociology, U.S. government. **Visual/performing arts:** Art history/conservation, dramatic, film/cinema/video, music, studio arts.

Most popular majors. Area/ethnic studies 6%, biology 10%, business/marketing 10%, computer/information sciences 6%, interdisciplinary studies 6%, public administration/social services 8%, social sciences 28%, visual/performing arts 6%.

Computing on campus. 104 workstations in library, computer center, student center. Dormitories wired for high-speed internet access and linked to campus network. Commuter students can connect to campus network. Online course registration, online library, helpline, repair service, student web hosting, wireless network available.

Student life. Freshman orientation: Mandatory, $200 fee. Preregistration for classes offered. Five-day program begins weekend before Labor Day weekend. **Policies:** Freshmen not permitted cars on campus. **Housing:** Guaranteed on-campus for freshmen. Coed dorms, single-sex dorms, apartments available. Thematic learning communities available. **Activities:** Bands, campus ministries, choral groups, dance, drama, film society, international student organizations, literary magazine, music ensembles, musical theater, radio station, student government, student newspaper, symphony orchestra, TV station, 246 recognized clubs and organizations.

Athletics. NCAA. **Intercollegiate:** Baseball M, basketball, cross-country, fencing, soccer, softball W, tennis, track and field, volleyball W. **Intramural:** Basketball, equestrian, football (non-tackle), soccer, softball, squash, tennis, volleyball, water polo. **Team name:** Judges.

Student services. Alcohol/substance abuse counseling, chaplain/spiritual director, career counseling, student employment services, financial aid counseling, health services, minority student services, on-campus daycare, personal counseling, placement for graduates, veterans' counselor, women's services. **Physically disabled:** Services for visually, speech, hearing impaired.

Contact. E-mail: admissions@brandeis.edu
Phone: (781) 736-3500 Toll-free number: (800) 622-0622
Fax: (781) 736-3536
Mark Spencer, Dean of Admissions, Brandeis University, Box 549110, Waltham, MA 02454-9110

Bridgewater State University
Bridgewater, Massachusetts   **CB member**
www.bridgew.edu   **CB code: 3517**

♦ Public 4-year university and teachers college

♦ Commuter campus in large town

♦ 9,422 degree-seeking undergraduates: 16% part-time, 59% women, 5% African American, 2% Asian American, 5% Hispanic American, 1% international

♦ 1,358 degree-seeking graduate students

♦ 65% of applicants admitted

♦ SAT or ACT (ACT writing recommended) required

♦ 51% graduate within 6 years

General. Founded in 1840. Regionally accredited. **Degrees:** 1,680 bachelor's awarded; master's offered. **ROTC:** Army, Air Force. **Location:** 30 miles from Boston; 35 miles from Providence, RI. **Calendar:** Semester, extensive summer session. **Full-time faculty:** 316 total; 87% have terminal degrees, 16% minority, 48% women. **Part-time faculty:** 417 total; 7% minority, 51% women. **Class size:** 38% < 20, 59% 20-39, 2% 40-49, less than 1% 50-99.

Freshman class profile. 7,039 applied, 4,549 admitted, 1,494 enrolled.

Mid 50% test scores		GPA 2.0-2.99:	42%
SAT critical reading:	460-550	Rank in top quarter:	33%
SAT math:	470-560	Rank in top tenth:	8%
ACT composite:	21-24	Return as sophomores:	81%
GPA 3.75 or higher:	11%	Out-of-state:	5%
GPA 3.50-3.74:	11%	Live on campus:	62%
GPA 3.0-3.49:	36%		

Basis for selection. High school achievement most important, including weighted high school GPA and completion of 16 college preparatory courses. Test scores, essay, extracurricular activities also important. Class rank, recommendations considered. Essay recommended. **Learning Disabled:** Exemption from admissions standardized testing upon documentation of diagnostic test results. Must complete 16 required academic courses with 3.0 GPA or present evidence of potential for academic success.

High school preparation. College-preparatory program required. 16 units required. Required units include English 4, mathematics 3, social studies 1, history 1, science 3 (laboratory 2), foreign language 2 and academic electives 2.

2011-2012 Annual costs. Tuition/fees: $7,552; $13,692 out-of-state. Room/board: $10,367. Books/supplies: $1,000. Personal expenses: $2,000.

2010-2011 Financial aid. Need-based: 1,354 full-time freshmen applied for aid; 1,005 were judged to have need; 996 of these received aid. Average

scholarship/grant was $4,608; average loan $3,200. 41% of total undergraduate aid awarded as scholarships/grants, 59% as loans/jobs. **Non-need-based:** Awarded to 1,272 full-time undergraduates, including 464 freshmen. Scholarships awarded for academics, minority status, state residency.

Application procedures. Admission: No deadline. $40 fee, may be waived for applicants with need. Admission notification on a rolling basis beginning on or about 12/15. **Financial aid:** Priority date 3/1; no closing date. FAFSA required. Applicants notified on a rolling basis starting 3/30.

Academics. Special study options: Accelerated study, combined bachelor's/graduate degree, cross-registration, distance learning, double major, dual enrollment of high school students, ESL, exchange student, honors, independent study, internships, study abroad, teacher certification program, Washington semester. **Credit/placement by examination:** AP, CLEP, IB, institutional tests. **Support services:** Learning center, pre-admission summer program, reduced course load, remedial instruction, study skills assistance, tutoring, writing center.

Majors. Architecture: Urban/community planning. **Biology:** General, biochemistry, biomedical sciences, cellular/molecular, environmental. **Business:** Accounting, business admin, finance, international, management information systems, marketing, transportation. **Communications:** Communications/speech/rhetoric. **Computer sciences:** Computer science. **Education:** Art, biology, drama/dance, early childhood, elementary, English, health, health occupations, kindergarten/preschool, music, physical, special ed. **English:** Creative writing, English lit. **Foreign languages:** Spanish. **Health services:** Athletic training, communication disorders, kinesiotherapy. **History:** General. **Human services:** Social work. **Math:** General. **Parks/recreation:** General, exercise sciences, sports admin. **Philosophy/religion:** Ethics, philosophy. **Physical sciences:** Chemistry, geochemistry, geology, physics. **Protective services:** Criminal justice. **Psychology:** General. **Social sciences:** Anthropology, archaeology, economics, geography, international relations, political science, sociology, U.S. government, urban studies. **Visual/performing arts:** Art history/conservation, crafts, dramatic, graphic design, music, photography, studio arts.

Most popular majors. Business/marketing 16%, communications/journalism 8%, education 18%, English 7%, psychology 11%, security/protective services 10%, social sciences 8%.

Computing on campus. PC or laptop required. 780 workstations in library, computer center, student center. Dormitories wired for high-speed internet access and linked to campus network. Commuter students can connect to campus network. Online course registration, online library, helpline, repair service, wireless network available.

Student life. Freshman orientation: Mandatory, $160 fee. Preregistration for classes offered. **Policies:** Freshmen not permitted cars on campus. **Housing:** Coed dorms, apartments, wellness housing available. $300 nonrefundable deposit, deadline 3/4. Quiet floor, nonsmoking floor available in residence hall. Housing available over breaks for athletes, student teachers, international students. **Activities:** Bands, campus ministries, choral groups, dance, drama, international student organizations, literary magazine, music ensembles, musical theater, radio station, student government, student newspaper, Christian Fellowship, College Democrats, Afro-American society, international club, La Sociedad Latina, Amnesty International, Big Brothers/Big Sisters, Habitat for Humanity.

Athletics. NCAA. **Intercollegiate:** Baseball M, basketball, cross-country, diving, field hockey W, football (tackle) M, lacrosse W, soccer, softball W, swimming, tennis, track and field, volleyball W, wrestling M. **Intramural:** Basketball, football (tackle) M, lacrosse M, soccer, softball, tennis, volleyball, water polo. **Team name:** Bears.

Student services. Adult student services, chaplain/spiritual director, career counseling, student employment services, financial aid counseling, health services, minority student services, on-campus daycare, personal counseling, placement for graduates, veterans' counselor, women's services. **Physically disabled:** Services for visually, speech, hearing impaired.

Contact. E-mail: admission@bridgew.edu
Phone: (508) 531-1237 Fax: (508) 531-1746
Gregg Meyer, Director of Admissions, Bridgewater State University, Gates House, Bridgewater, MA 02325

Cambridge College
Cambridge, Massachusetts
www.cambridgecollege.edu CB code: 3612

▸ Private 4-year liberal arts and teachers college
▸ Commuter campus in small city

▸ 1,002 degree-seeking undergraduates: 68% part-time, 75% women, 30% African American, 3% Asian American, 22% Hispanic American, 9% international
▸ 2,695 degree-seeking graduate students
▸ Application essay required

General. Regionally accredited. **Degrees:** 266 bachelor's awarded; master's, doctoral offered. **Calendar:** Trimester, extensive summer session. **Full-time faculty:** 19 total; 68% have terminal degrees, 26% minority, 47% women. **Part-time faculty:** 434 total; 59% have terminal degrees, 36% minority, 59% women. **Class size:** 80% < 20, 20% 20-39.

Freshman class profile.

Out-of-state:	10%	**International:**	31%

Basis for selection. Open admission.

2011-2012 Annual costs. Cost of 3-semester academic year tuition and fees: $13,240; for 2-semester, $10,950. Books/supplies: $750. Personal expenses: $900.

2011-2012 Financial aid. All financial aid based on need. 3 full-time freshmen applied for aid; 1 were judged to have need; 1 of these received aid. Average loan was $3,500. 24% of total undergraduate aid awarded as scholarships/grants, 76% as loans/jobs.

Application procedures. Admission: No deadline. $30 fee, may be waived for applicants with need. Admission notification on a rolling basis beginning on or about 9/1. **Financial aid:** Priority date 9/1; no closing date. FAFSA, institutional form required. Applicants notified on a rolling basis starting 6/1.

Academics. Special study options: Accelerated study, distance learning, double major, independent study, internships, weekend college. **Credit/placement by examination:** AP, CLEP. **Support services:** Learning center, reduced course load, remedial instruction, study skills assistance, tutoring, writing center.

Majors. Business: General. **Liberal arts:** Arts/sciences. **Psychology:** General, community.

Most popular majors. Business/marketing 29%, liberal arts 44%, psychology 27%.

Computing on campus. Commuter students can connect to campus network. Online course registration, online library, wireless network available.

Student life. Freshman orientation: Mandatory. Preregistration for classes offered. **Activities:** Student government.

Student services. Adult student services, career counseling, services for economically disadvantaged, financial aid counseling. **Physically disabled:** Services for visually, speech, hearing impaired.

Contact. E-mail: admit@cambridgecollege.edu
Phone: (888) 800-4723 Toll-free number: (800) 877-4723
Fax: (617) 349-3561
Denise Haile, Director of Admissions, Cambridge College, 1000 Massachusetts Avenue, Cambridge, MA 02138-5304

Clark University
Worcester, Massachusetts CB member
www.clarku.edu CB code: 3279

▸ Private 4-year university and liberal arts college
▸ Residential campus in small city
▸ 2,240 degree-seeking undergraduates: 1% part-time, 58% women, 4% African American, 5% Asian American, 6% Hispanic American, 9% international
▸ 1,096 degree-seeking graduate students
▸ 68% of applicants admitted
▸ Application essay required
▸ 80% graduate within 6 years; 50% enter graduate study

General. Founded in 1887. Regionally accredited. **Degrees:** 525 bachelor's awarded; master's, doctoral offered. **ROTC:** Army, Naval, Air Force. **Location:** 50 miles from Boston. **Calendar:** Semester, limited summer session. **Full-time faculty:** 197 total; 96% have terminal degrees, 20% minority, 46% women. **Part-time faculty:** 48 total; 2% minority, 46% women. **Class size:** 60% < 20, 31% 20-39, 4% 40-49, 4% 50-99, less than 1% >100. **Special facilities:** Robert Goddard exhibition, map library, rare book room, NMR

research facility, observatory, electronic music facility, arboretum, crafts studio, 2 theaters, environmental education laboratory, student-run recycling center, pulsed magnetic field laboratory, Holocaust studies center.

Freshman class profile. 4,127 applied, 2,803 admitted, 546 enrolled.

Mid 50% test scores			
SAT critical reading:	540-660	GPA 2.0-2.99:	12%
SAT math:	540-650	Rank in top quarter:	73%
SAT writing:	540-650	Rank in top tenth:	30%
ACT composite:	23-29	End year in good standing:	94%
GPA 3.75 or higher:	28%	Return as sophomores:	87%
GPA 3.50-3.74:	22%	Out-of-state:	63%
GPA 3.0-3.49:	38%	Live on campus:	97%
		International:	10%

Basis for selection. School achievement record and courses, recommendations, test scores most important. Special talents, accomplishments, motivation, and individual circumstances, including outside activities and jobs, also important. SAT is optional. Interview recommended. Portfolio recommended for art majors. **Learning Disabled:** Students should self-identify as soon as possible.

High school preparation. College-preparatory program required. 16 units recommended. Recommended units include English 4, mathematics 3, social studies 2, history 2, science 3 (laboratory 2) and foreign language 2.

2012-2013 Annual costs. Tuition/fees: $38,450. Room/board: $7,320. Books/supplies: $800. Personal expenses: $700.

2011-2012 Financial aid. Need-based: 419 full-time freshmen applied for aid; 322 were judged to have need; 320 of these received aid. Average need met was 95%. Average scholarship/grant was $24,810; average loan $3,605. 78% of total undergraduate aid awarded as scholarships/grants, 22% as loans/jobs. **Non-need-based:** Awarded to 1,169 full-time undergraduates, including 288 freshmen. Scholarships awarded for academics, leadership.

Application procedures. Admission: Closing date 1/15 (postmark date). $55 fee, may be waived for applicants with need. Admission notification by 4/1. Must reply by May 1 or within 2 week(s) if notified thereafter. **Financial aid:** Closing date 2/1. FAFSA, CSS PROFILE required. Applicants notified by 3/31; must reply by 5/1.

Academics. Interdisciplinary majors, special programs, and accelerated bachelor's/master's program with fifth-year tuition-free available. **Special study options:** Combined bachelor's/graduate degree, cross-registration, double major, ESL, independent study, internships, liberal arts/career combination, student-designed major, study abroad, teacher certification program, Washington semester. Courses at Bermuda Biological Station, May term at Clark European Center in Luxembourg, semester-long environmental science program at marine biological laboratory at Woods Hole Oceanographic Institute. 3-2 engineering programs with Columbia University, Worcester Polytechnic Institute, Washington University. **Credit/placement by examination:** AP, CLEP, IB, SAT, institutional tests. 16 credit hours maximum toward bachelor's degree. **Support services:** Reduced course load, study skills assistance, writing center.

Majors. Area/ethnic studies: Women's. **Biology:** General, biochemistry, bioinformatics, molecular. **Business:** General, business admin. **Communications:** Communications/speech/rhetoric. **Computer sciences:** General, computer science. **Conservation:** Environmental science, environmental studies. **English:** English lit. **Foreign languages:** General, classics, comparative lit, French, Spanish. **History:** General. **Human services:** General. **Liberal arts:** Arts/sciences. **Math:** General. **Philosophy/religion:** Philosophy. **Physical sciences:** Chemistry, physics. **Psychology:** General. **Social sciences:** Economics, geography, international relations, political science, sociology. **Visual/performing arts:** General, art, art history/conservation, dramatic, film/cinema/video, music, studio arts.

Most popular majors. Biology 7%, communications/journalism 7%, psychology 17%, social sciences 28%, visual/performing arts 8%.

Computing on campus. 110 workstations in dormitories, library, computer center, student center. Dormitories wired for high-speed internet access and linked to campus network. Commuter students can connect to campus network. Online course registration, online library, helpline, student web hosting, wireless network available.

Student life. Freshman orientation: Mandatory, $200 fee. Preregistration for classes offered. Program held during week prior to fall semester; includes course selection and registration. **Housing:** Guaranteed on-campus for freshmen. Coed dorms, single-sex dorms, special housing for disabled, apartments, wellness housing available. $100 nonrefundable deposit, deadline 5/1. Some university-owned off-campus housing available. Year-round house, quiet house, other special interest houses available. All residence halls non-smoking. **Activities:** Bands, campus ministries, choral groups, dance, drama, film society, international student organizations, literary magazine, music ensembles, Model UN, musical theater, radio station, student government,

student newspaper, symphony orchestra, TV station, 120 student clubs and organizations.

Athletics. NCAA. **Intercollegiate:** Baseball M, basketball, cross-country, diving, field hockey W, lacrosse M, rowing (crew), soccer, softball W, swimming, tennis, volleyball W. **Intramural:** Basketball, racquetball, soccer, softball, water polo. **Team name:** Cougars.

Student services. Adult student services, alcohol/substance abuse counseling, chaplain/spiritual director, career counseling, services for economically disadvantaged, student employment services, financial aid counseling, health services, minority student services, personal counseling, placement for graduates, women's services. **Physically disabled:** Services for visually, speech, hearing impaired.

Contact. E-mail: admissions@clarku.edu
Phone: (508) 793-7431 Toll-free number: (800) 462-5275
Fax: (508) 793-8821
Donald Honeman, Dean of Admissions, Clark University, 950 Main Street, Worcester, MA 01610-1477

College of the Holy Cross
Worcester, Massachusetts
www.holycross.edu

CB member
CB code: 3282

- Private 4-year liberal arts college affiliated with Roman Catholic Church
- Residential campus in small city
- 2,872 degree-seeking undergraduates: 53% women, 5% African American, 5% Asian American, 10% Hispanic American, 1% international
- 33% of applicants admitted
- Application essay required
- 91% graduate within 6 years; 26% enter graduate study

General. Founded in 1843. Regionally accredited. Campus is a registered arboretum. **Degrees:** 696 bachelor's awarded. **ROTC:** Army, Naval, Air Force. **Location:** 45 miles from Boston. **Calendar:** Semester. **Full-time faculty:** 258 total; 96% have terminal degrees, 12% minority, 45% women. **Part-time faculty:** 67 total; 66% have terminal degrees, 9% minority, 43% women. **Class size:** 53% < 20, 44% 20-39, 2% 40-49, 1% 50-99. **Special facilities:** Research-level scientific equipment, Nuclear Magnetic Resonance (NMR) equipment, scanning electron and confocal microscopes, greenhouse.

Freshman class profile. 7,353 applied, 2,435 admitted, 751 enrolled.

Mid 50% test scores			
SAT critical reading:	600-690	GPA 2.0-2.99:	1%
SAT math:	610-690	Rank in top quarter:	95%
SAT writing:	600-700	Rank in top tenth:	61%
ACT composite:	27-31	End year in good standing:	94%
GPA 3.75 or higher:	61%	Return as sophomores:	95%
GPA 3.50-3.74:	23%	Out-of-state:	61%
GPA 3.0-3.49:	15%	Live on campus:	100%
		International:	1%

Basis for selection. Candidates urged to complete the most challenging college-preparatory program available at their school. Evidence of superior achievement in analytical reading and writing are of particular importance. Advanced placement and honors courses recommended. Standardized test scores are optional. Students may submit scores if they believe the results present a fuller picture of their achievements and potential. Students who do not submit scores will not be at any disadvantage in admissions decisions. Personal interview optional but highly recommended. **Home schooled:** On-campus interview highly encouraged. Applicants should submit course work samples, personal statement, and college transcripts if applicable. If home-schooling associated with particular organization or program, submit description.

High school preparation. College-preparatory program recommended. 20 units recommended. Recommended units include English 4, mathematics 4, social studies 2, history 2, science 4 (laboratory 2) and foreign language 4.

2011-2012 Annual costs. Tuition/fees: $41,488. Room/board: $11,270. Books/supplies: $700. Personal expenses: $900.

2011-2012 Financial aid. Need-based: 552 full-time freshmen applied for aid; 467 were judged to have need; 456 of these received aid. Average need met was 100%. Average scholarship/grant was $30,530; average loan $5,006. 75% of total undergraduate aid awarded as scholarships/grants, 25% as loans/jobs. **Non-need-based:** Awarded to 108 full-time undergraduates, including 31 freshmen. Scholarships awarded for academics, athletics, music/drama. **Additional information:** Cost of tuition above amount of Pell Grant waived for Worcester residents whose families earn less than $50,000.

Application procedures. Admission: Closing date 1/15 (receipt date). $60 fee, may be waived for applicants with need. Application must be

submitted online. Admission notification by 4/1. Must reply by 5/1. **Financial aid:** Closing date 2/1. FAFSA required. CSS PROFILE required of all students applying for institutional aid. Applicants notified by 4/1; must reply by 5/1.

Academics. Students encouraged to participate in Oxford-style tutorials. 32 courses of 1 or more units required for graduation; 10-14 courses of 1 or more units required in major. **Special study options:** Accelerated study, cross-registration, double major, dual enrollment of high school students, exchange student, honors, independent study, internships, liberal arts/career combination, semester at sea, student-designed major, study abroad, teacher certification program, Washington semester. First-year living and learning academic enrichment program. **Credit/placement by examination:** AP, CLEP, IB, institutional tests. Language placement determined by departmental testing. **Support services:** Learning center, study skills assistance, tutoring, writing center.

Majors. Architecture: Architecture. **Area/ethnic studies:** Asian, German, Italian, Russian/Slavic. **Biology:** General. **Business:** Accounting. **Computer sciences:** General. **Conservation:** Environmental studies. **English:** English lit. **Foreign languages:** Chinese, classics, comparative lit, French, German, Italian, Russian, Spanish. **History:** General. **Math:** General. **Philosophy/religion:** Philosophy, religion. **Physical sciences:** Chemistry, physics. **Psychology:** General. **Social sciences:** Anthropology, economics, political science, sociology. **Visual/performing arts:** Art history/conservation, dramatic, music, studio arts.

Most popular majors. Biology 6%, English 11%, foreign language 9%, history 8%, psychology 11%, social sciences 33%.

Computing on campus. 485 workstations in dormitories, library, computer center, student center. Dormitories wired for high-speed internet access and linked to campus network. Commuter students can connect to campus network. Online library, helpline, repair service, student web hosting, wireless network available.

Student life. Freshman orientation: Available, $230 fee. Preregistration for classes offered. Two-day programs available in mid-June; 3-day orientation prior to fall registration. **Policies:** Responsible drinking policy for students 21 and older. Initiation hazing prohibited. Freshmen not permitted cars on campus. **Housing:** Guaranteed on-campus for all undergraduates. Coed dorms, special housing for disabled, apartments, wellness housing available. $500 nonrefundable deposit, deadline 5/1. **Activities:** Bands, campus ministries, choral groups, dance, drama, international student organizations, literary magazine, music ensembles, musical theater, radio station, student government, student newspaper, black student union, Purple Key society, student program for urban development, women's forum, Latin American student organization, Asian student society, Muslim student association, Appalachia service project, Habitat for Humanity, association of bisexuals/gays/lesbians.

Athletics. NCAA. **Intercollegiate:** Baseball M, basketball, cross-country, diving, field hockey W, football (tackle) M, golf, ice hockey, lacrosse, rowing (crew), soccer, softball W, swimming, tennis, track and field, volleyball W. **Intramural:** Basketball, football (non-tackle), soccer, softball, volleyball, water polo. **Team name:** Crusaders.

Student services. Alcohol/substance abuse counseling, chaplain/spiritual director, career counseling, student employment services, financial aid counseling, health services, minority student services, personal counseling, placement for graduates, women's services. **Physically disabled:** Services for visually, hearing impaired.

Contact. E-mail: admissions@holycross.edu
Phone: (508) 793-2443 Toll-free number: (800) 442-2421
Fax: (508) 793-3888
Ann McDermott, Director of Admissions, College of the Holy Cross, One College Street, Worcester, MA 01610-2395

Curry College
Milton, Massachusetts
www.curry.edu

CB member
CB code: 3285

- Private 4-year nursing and liberal arts college
- Residential campus in large town
- 2,622 degree-seeking undergraduates: 25% part-time, 61% women, 8% African American, 1% Asian American, 4% Hispanic American, 1% international
- 286 degree-seeking graduate students
- 72% of applicants admitted
- Application essay required
- 47% graduate within 6 years

General. Founded in 1879. Regionally accredited. **Degrees:** 609 bachelor's awarded; master's offered. **ROTC:** Army, Air Force. **Location:** Seven miles from downtown Boston. **Calendar:** Semester, limited summer session. **Full-time faculty:** 123 total; 66% women. **Part-time faculty:** 377 total; 64% women. **Class size:** 58% < 20, 42% 20-39, less than 1% 40-49. **Special facilities:** Communication center, television studio with full TV production services.

Freshman class profile. 5,063 applied, 3,636 admitted, 608 enrolled.

Mid 50% test scores			
SAT critical reading:	420-500	GPA 2.0-2.99:	67%
SAT math:	420-510	Rank in top quarter:	17%
SAT writing:	420-510	Rank in top tenth:	4%
ACT composite:	18-22	End year in good standing:	71%
GPA 3.75 or higher:	2%	Return as sophomores:	66%
GPA 3.50-3.74:	4%	Out-of-state:	36%
GPA 3.0-3.49:	22%	Live on campus:	86%

Basis for selection. High school record, recommendations, extracurricular activities most important. Test scores also important. Interviews strongly recommended. **Home schooled:** Statement describing home school structure and mission, transcript of courses and grades, state high school equivalency certificate required. **Learning Disabled:** Wechsler Adult Intelligence Scale required of learning disabled applicants and replaces SAT requirement. SAT or ACT still recommended.

High school preparation. College-preparatory program recommended. 16 units required. Required and recommended units include English 4, mathematics 3, social studies 2, history 2, science 2 (laboratory 1) and foreign language 2. 3 math through algebra II, 1 chemistry, and 1 biology required for nursing applicants.

2011-2012 Annual costs. Tuition/fees: $32,210. Room/board: $12,285. Books/supplies: $800. Personal expenses: $1,000.

2010-2011 Financial aid. Need-based: 438 full-time freshmen applied for aid; 437 were judged to have need; 437 of these received aid. Average need met was 58%. Average scholarship/grant was $12,315; average loan $3,432. 75% of total undergraduate aid awarded as scholarships/grants, 25% as loans/jobs. **Non-need-based:** Awarded to 112 full-time undergraduates, including 37 freshmen. Scholarships awarded for academics, leadership.

Application procedures. Admission: Priority date 4/1; no deadline. $50 fee, may be waived for applicants with need. Admission notification on a rolling basis beginning on or about 11/1. Must reply by May 1 or within 2 week(s) if notified thereafter. **Financial aid:** Priority date 3/1; no closing date. FAFSA required. Applicants notified on a rolling basis starting 3/1; must reply by 5/1 or within 2 week(s) of notification.

Academics. Special study options: Accelerated study, cross-registration, double major, honors, independent study, internships, liberal arts/career combination, New York semester, semester at sea, student-designed major, study abroad, teacher certification program. **Credit/placement by examination:** AP, CLEP, IB, institutional tests. 60 credit hours maximum toward bachelor's degree. **Support services:** Learning center, pre-admission summer program, reduced course load, remedial instruction, study skills assistance, tutoring, writing center.

Majors. Biology: General. **Business:** Business admin. **Communications:** General. **Computer sciences:** General. **Conservation:** Environmental science. **Education:** General, early childhood, elementary, special ed. **English:** English lit. **Health services:** Nursing (RN). **Liberal arts:** Arts/sciences. **Philosophy/religion:** Philosophy. **Protective services:** Criminal justice. **Psychology:** General. **Social sciences:** Sociology. **Visual/performing arts:** Graphic design, studio arts.

Most popular majors. Business/marketing 15%, communications/journalism 11%, health sciences 32%, psychology 8%, security/protective services 21%.

Computing on campus. 245 workstations in dormitories, library, computer center. Dormitories wired for high-speed internet access and linked to campus network. Commuter students can connect to campus network. Online library, helpline, student web hosting, wireless network available.

Student life. Freshman orientation: Available, $150 fee. Preregistration for classes offered. Four summer 2-day programs and 2-day August program available. **Policies:** Freshmen not permitted cars on campus. **Housing:** Coed dorms, single-sex dorms, special housing for disabled available. $300 partly refundable deposit, deadline 5/1. **Activities:** Campus ministries, choral groups, dance, drama, film society, international student organizations, literary magazine, musical theater, radio station, student government, student newspaper, TV station, student government association, campus activities board, community service organization, Hillel, One Curry, Newman club, multicultural student union, gay straight alliance, politics & history club.

Athletics. NCAA. **Intercollegiate:** Baseball M, basketball, cross-country W, football (tackle) M, ice hockey M, lacrosse, soccer, softball W, tennis, volleyball W. **Intramural:** Basketball, field hockey W, football (non-tackle), golf, skiing, soccer, softball, tennis, volleyball. **Team name:** Colonels.

Student services. Adult student services, alcohol/substance abuse counseling, chaplain/spiritual director, career counseling, student employment services, financial aid counseling, health services, minority student services, on-campus daycare, personal counseling, placement for graduates, veterans' counselor, women's services. **Physically disabled:** Services for visually, hearing impaired.

Contact. E-mail: curryadm@curry.edu
Phone: (617) 333-2210 Toll-free number: (800) 669-0686
Fax: (617) 333-2114
Jane Fidler, Dean of Admission, Curry College, 1071 Blue Hill Avenue, Milton, MA 02186-9984

Eastern Nazarene College
Quincy, Massachusetts
www.enc.edu

CB member
CB code: 3365

- Private 4-year liberal arts college affiliated with Church of the Nazarene
- Residential campus in small city
- 778 degree-seeking undergraduates: 1% part-time, 56% women, 15% African American, 4% Asian American, 11% Hispanic American, 1% international
- 174 degree-seeking graduate students
- 63% of applicants admitted
- SAT or ACT (ACT writing recommended) required

General. Founded in 1900. Regionally accredited. **Degrees:** 218 bachelor's, 32 associate awarded; master's offered. **ROTC:** Army, Air Force. **Location:** 2 miles from Boston. **Calendar:** Semester, limited summer session. **Full-time faculty:** 45 total; 82% have terminal degrees, 9% minority, 29% women. **Part-time faculty:** 103 total. **Class size:** 80% < 20, 16% 20-39, 1% 40-49, 3% 50-99, less than 1% >100. **Special facilities:** Arboretum; early childhood education center; center for history, law, and government; business center.

Freshman class profile. 989 applied, 620 admitted, 164 enrolled.

Mid 50% test scores			
SAT critical reading:	410-570	GPA 3.0-3.49:	37%
SAT math:	430-560	GPA 2.0-2.99:	34%
SAT writing:	420-560	Rank in top quarter:	32%
ACT composite:	20-28	Rank in top tenth:	13%
GPA 3.75 or higher:	10%	Out-of-state:	45%
GPA 3.50-3.74:	13%	Live on campus:	77%
		International:	3%

Basis for selection. Applicants should demonstrate academic achievement, extracurricular involvement, and community engagement. Accuplacer test may also be required. Audition required of students intending to major in music. **Home schooled:** Statement describing home school structure and mission, transcript of courses and grades, interview, letter of recommendation (nonparent) required.

High school preparation. College-preparatory program required. 15 units required. Required and recommended units include English 4, mathematics 2-4, social studies 1-2, history 1-2, science 2-4 (laboratory 2-4), foreign language 2-4, visual/performing arts 1-2 and academic electives 5.

2011-2012 Annual costs. Tuition/fees: $25,300. Room/board: $8,100. Books/supplies: $1,100.

Financial aid. Non-need-based: Scholarships awarded for academics, alumni affiliation, leadership, religious affiliation, ROTC. **Additional information:** Participant in Massachusetts University pre-payment plan.

Application procedures. Admission: Priority date 1/1; no deadline. No application fee. Application must be submitted online. Admission notification on a rolling basis. **Financial aid:** Priority date 3/1, closing date 8/1. FAFSA, institutional form required. Applicants notified on a rolling basis starting 3/14; must reply by 8/1 or within 2 week(s) of notification.

Academics. Special study options: Accelerated study, combined bachelor's/graduate degree, cross-registration, double major, dual enrollment of high school students, exchange student, honors, independent study, internships, liberal arts/career combination, semester at sea, study abroad, teacher certification program, urban semester, Washington semester. **Credit/placement by examination:** AP, CLEP, IB, SAT, ACT, institutional tests. **Support services:** Learning center, pre-admission summer program, remedial instruction, study skills assistance, tutoring, writing center.

Majors. Biology: General, biochemistry. **Business:** General, accounting, accounting/business management, accounting/finance, business admin, marketing. **Communications:** Journalism. **Conservation:** Environmental science, environmental studies. **Education:** General, biology, business, chemistry, early childhood, elementary, English, history, kindergarten/preschool, mathematics, middle, music, physical, physics, science, social studies, special ed. **Engineering:** General, applied physics, computer, electrical. **English:** Creative writing, English lit. **Health services:** Movement therapy, predental, premedicine, prenursing, prepharmacy, preveterinary. **History:** General. **Human services:** Social work. **Liberal arts:** Arts/sciences. **Math:** General. **Parks/recreation:** Health/fitness, sports admin. **Philosophy/religion:** Religion. **Physical sciences:** Chemistry, physics. **Protective services:** Criminal justice, forensics, law enforcement admin, police science. **Psychology:** General, clinical, counseling, developmental, social. **Theology:** Pastoral counseling, preministerial, sacred music, theology, youth ministry. **Visual/performing arts:** Dramatic, music, music history, music management, music pedagogy, music performance, music theory/composition, piano/keyboard, stringed instruments, theater arts management, voice/opera.

Most popular majors. Business/marketing 14%, communications/journalism 6%, education 9%, English 6%, liberal arts 11%, philosophy/religious studies 6%, psychology 16%, social sciences 6%.

Computing on campus. 98 workstations in library, computer center, student center. Dormitories wired for high-speed internet access and linked to campus network. Commuter students can connect to campus network. Online library, helpline, repair service, wireless network available.

Student life. Freshman orientation: Mandatory. Preregistration for classes offered. **Policies:** Students must abstain from use of illegal drugs, alcohol and tobacco, and are to avoid attendance at bars, clubs, or other activities or places of entertainment that promote themes of inappropriate sexuality, violence, profanity, pornography or activities demeaning to human life. Religious observance required. **Housing:** Guaranteed on-campus for all undergraduates. Coed dorms, single-sex dorms, special housing for disabled, apartments available. $300 nonrefundable deposit, deadline 8/25. **Activities:** Bands, campus ministries, choral groups, dance, drama, film society, literary magazine, music ensembles, musical theater, student government, student newspaper, symphony orchestra, ACTS/JUMP, Barnabas, Big Brother Big Sister, Causeway, Fellowship of Christian Athletes, Germantown Tutoring, Open Hand Open Heart, Refiner's Fire, Students for Social Justice, Women of Grace.

Athletics. NCAA. **Intercollegiate:** Baseball M, basketball, cross-country, soccer, softball W, tennis, volleyball W. **Intramural:** Basketball, field hockey W, football (non-tackle), lacrosse, skiing, soccer, volleyball. **Team name:** Lions.

Student services. Adult student services, alcohol/substance abuse counseling, chaplain/spiritual director, career counseling, services for economically disadvantaged, student employment services, financial aid counseling, health services, minority student services, personal counseling, placement for graduates, veterans' counselor, women's services. **Physically disabled:** Services for visually impaired.

Contact. E-mail: admissions@enc.edu
Phone: (617) 745-3711 Toll-free number: (800) 883-6288
Fax: (617) 745-3992
Andrew Wright, Director of Admissions, Eastern Nazarene College, 23 East Elm Avenue, Quincy, MA 02170

Elms College
Chicopee, Massachusetts
www.elms.edu

CB member
CB code: 3283

- Private 4-year liberal arts college affiliated with Roman Catholic Church
- Residential campus in small city
- 1,159 degree-seeking undergraduates
- SAT or ACT with writing, application essay required

General. Founded in 1928. Regionally accredited. **Degrees:** 240 bachelor's, 10 associate awarded; master's offered. **ROTC:** Army, Air Force. **Location:** 2 miles from Springfield; 30 miles from Hartford, Connecticut. **Calendar:** Semester, limited summer session. **Full-time faculty:** 66 total. **Part-time faculty:** 9 total. **Special facilities:** Rare book collection, Federal Depository, Irish cultural center, Polish center for discovery and learning.

Freshman class profile.

GPA 3.75 or higher:	10%	Rank in top quarter:	35%
GPA 3.50-3.74:	13%	Rank in top tenth:	10%
GPA 3.0-3.49:	36%	Out-of-state:	22%
GPA 2.0-2.99:	40%	Live on campus:	54%

Basis for selection. Students should rank in top half of high school class; 2.8 GPA, 1000 SAT (exclusive of Writing) recommended. Interview recommended. **Home schooled:** Transcript of courses and grades, letter of recommendation (nonparent) required.

High school preparation. College-preparatory program recommended. 15 units required; 22 recommended. Required and recommended units include English 4, mathematics 2-4, social studies 1-2, history 2, science 2-4 (laboratory 2) and foreign language 2-4. Algebra II, biology, chemistry required for nursing applicants.

2011-2012 Annual costs. Tuition/fees: $28,128. Room/board: $10,202. Books/supplies: $1,000. Personal expenses: $1,000.

Financial aid. Non-need-based: Scholarships awarded for academics, alumni affiliation, leadership, religious affiliation, state residency.

Application procedures. Admission: No deadline. $30 fee, may be waived for applicants with need. Admission notification on a rolling basis beginning on or about 12/15. Must reply by May 1 or within 2 week(s) if notified thereafter. **Financial aid:** Priority date 3/1; no closing date. FAFSA required. Applicants notified on a rolling basis starting 3/10; must reply by 5/1 or within 2 week(s) of notification.

Academics. Tutor training certified by College Reading and Learning Association. **Special study options:** Combined bachelor's/graduate degree, cross-registration, distance learning, double major, dual enrollment of high school students, ESL, exchange student, honors, independent study, internships, liberal arts/career combination, study abroad, teacher certification program, Washington semester, weekend college. **Credit/placement by examination:** AP, CLEP, IB, SAT, ACT, institutional tests. 12 credit hours maximum toward bachelor's degree. **Support services:** Learning center, reduced course load, study skills assistance, tutoring, writing center.

Majors. Area/ethnic studies: American, Spanish/Iberian. **Biology:** General. **Business:** Accounting, accounting/business management, business admin, international, marketing. **Communications:** Communications/speech/rhetoric. **Computer sciences:** General. **Education:** General, bilingual, Deaf/hearing impaired, early childhood, elementary, English, ESL, secondary, special ed. **English:** English lit. **Foreign languages:** Spanish. **Health services:** Audiology/hearing, audiology/speech pathology, communication disorders, facilities admin, health care admin, health services admin, nursing (RN), pediatric nursing, predental, premedicine, preop/surgical nursing, preveterinary, public health nursing, speech pathology, speech-language pathology assistant. **History:** General, American, European. **Human services:** Social work. **Liberal arts:** Arts/sciences. **Math:** General. **Parks/recreation:** Sports admin. **Philosophy/religion:** Religion. **Physical sciences:** Chemistry. **Psychology:** General. **Social sciences:** International relations, sociology. **Visual/performing arts:** Studio arts.

Computing on campus. 70 workstations in dormitories, library, computer center, student center. Dormitories wired for high-speed internet access and linked to campus network. Commuter students can connect to campus network. Helpline, wireless network available.

Student life. Freshman orientation: Mandatory. Preregistration for classes offered. One-day programs held in June and August. **Housing:** Guaranteed on-campus for all undergraduates. Coed dorms, wellness housing available. **Activities:** Campus ministries, choral groups, dance, drama, international student organizations, literary magazine, music ensembles, radio station, student government, student newspaper, student government association, social work club, international club, speech pathology and audiology club, Student Ambassadors organization, student nurse association, drama club.

Athletics. NCAA. **Intercollegiate:** Baseball M, basketball, cross-country, field hockey W, golf M, lacrosse W, soccer, softball W, swimming, volleyball. **Intramural:** Baseball M, basketball, cross-country, field hockey W, football (non-tackle), golf M, lacrosse W, soccer, softball W, swimming, volleyball. **Team name:** Blazers.

Student services. Adult student services, alcohol/substance abuse counseling, chaplain/spiritual director, career counseling, student employment services, financial aid counseling, health services, minority student services, personal counseling, placement for graduates. **Physically disabled:** Services for visually, speech, hearing impaired.

Contact. E-mail: admissions@elms.edu
Phone: (413) 592-3189 Toll-free number: (800) 255-3567
Fax: (413) 594-2781
Joseph Wagner, Director of Admission, Elms College, 291 Springfield Street, Chicopee, MA 01013-2839

Emerson College
Boston, Massachusetts
www.emerson.edu

CB member
CB code: 3367

- Private 4-year college of communication and the arts
- Residential campus in very large city
- 3,572 degree-seeking undergraduates: 1% part-time, 61% women, 3% African American, 4% Asian American, 10% Hispanic American, 4% international
- 841 degree-seeking graduate students
- 48% of applicants admitted
- SAT or ACT with writing, application essay required
- 81% graduate within 6 years; 9% enter graduate study

General. Founded in 1880. Regionally accredited. **Degrees:** 939 bachelor's awarded; master's, doctoral offered. **Calendar:** Semester, limited summer session. **Full-time faculty:** 185 total; 70% have terminal degrees, 21% minority, 43% women. **Part-time faculty:** 257 total; 34% have terminal degrees, 48% women. **Class size:** 62% < 20, 29% 20-39, 7% 40-49, 1% 50-99. **Special facilities:** 2 historic theaters, performance and production center, sound treated television studios, integrated digital newsroom, film production facilities and film screening room, clinics/programs to observe speech and hearing therapy, marketing research suite.

Freshman class profile. 7,432 applied, 3,600 admitted, 912 enrolled.

Mid 50% test scores			
SAT critical reading:	580-680	GPA 2.0-2.99:	2%
SAT math:	550-640	Rank in top quarter:	77%
SAT writing:	580-670	Rank in top tenth:	41%
ACT composite:	25-29	Return as sophomores:	89%
GPA 3.75 or higher:	40%	Out-of-state:	83%
GPA 3.50-3.74:	28%	Live on campus:	99%
GPA 3.0-3.49:	30%	International:	4%

Basis for selection. Secondary school record, recommendations, writing competency, and personal qualities as seen in extracurricular activities, community involvement, demonstrated leadership important. Performing arts applicants must submit theatrical resume and, depending upon the major, either audition/interview or submit portfolio/essay. Candidates for film program must submit either a 5-8 minute video (20MB) accompanied by statement describing their role in its production or 5-10 page script. **Home schooled:** State high school equivalency certificate required. Common Application Home School Supplement required.

High school preparation. College-preparatory program required. 16 units required; 20 recommended. Required and recommended units include English 4, mathematics 3, social studies 3, (laboratory 3), foreign language 3 and academic electives 4.

2011-2012 Annual costs. Tuition/fees: $32,658. Room/board: $13,422. Books/supplies: $976. Personal expenses: $1,431.

2010-2011 Financial aid. Need-based: 569 full-time freshmen applied for aid; 457 were judged to have need; 456 of these received aid. Average need met was 70%. Average scholarship/grant was $16,874; average loan $3,498. 60% of total undergraduate aid awarded as scholarships/grants, 40% as loans/jobs. **Non-need-based:** Awarded to 270 full-time undergraduates, including 110 freshmen. Scholarships awarded for academics, leadership, music/drama, state residency. **Additional information:** Massachusetts Loan Plan available for parents of dependent undergraduates.

Application procedures. Admission: Closing date 1/5 (postmark date). $65 fee, may be waived for applicants with need. Admission notification by 4/1. Must reply by May 1 or within 2 week(s) if notified thereafter. **Financial aid:** Priority date 3/1; no closing date. FAFSA, CSS PROFILE required. Must reply by 5/1 or within 3 week(s) of notification.

Academics. Special study options: Cross-registration, double major, honors, independent study, internships, liberal arts/career combination, student-designed major, study abroad, teacher certification program, Washington semester. Study and internship programs in Los Angeles and Washington, DC. Course cross-registration through the six-member Boston ProArts Consortium (Berklee College of Music, Boston Architectural Center, Boston Conservatory, Emerson, Massachusetts College of Art, School of the Museum of Fine Arts). **Credit/placement by examination:** AP, CLEP, IB, SAT, ACT, institutional tests. 32 credit hours maximum toward bachelor's degree. Math requirement waived with 550 SAT math or 24 ACT math. **Support services:** Learning center, reduced course load, study skills assistance, tutoring, writing center.

Majors. Business: Communications, marketing. **Communications:** Advertising, broadcast journalism, communications/speech/rhetoric, journalism, media studies, political, public relations, publishing. **Education:** Autistic,

Deaf/hearing impaired, drama/dance, speech, speech impaired. **English:** Creative writing, rhetoric/composition. **Health services:** Audiology/hearing, audiology/speech pathology, communication disorders, speech pathology. **Visual/performing arts:** General, acting, cinematography, directing/producing, dramatic, film/cinema/video, play/screenwriting, theater arts management, theater design.

Most popular majors. Business/marketing 14%, communications/journalism 32%, English 19%, visual/performing arts 29%.

Computing on campus. 480 workstations in dormitories, library, computer center, student center. Dormitories wired for high-speed internet access and linked to campus network. Commuter students can connect to campus network. Online course registration, online library, helpline, repair service, wireless network available.

Student life. Freshman orientation: Mandatory, $150 fee. Preregistration for classes offered. Multi-day event preceding first day of classes that includes computer workshops, library tours, advising, social activities, and field trips around Boston. **Housing:** Coed dorms, wellness housing available. $500 nonrefundable deposit, deadline 5/1. **Activities:** Campus ministries, choral groups, dance, drama, film society, international student organizations, literary magazine, music ensembles, Model UN, musical theater, radio station, student government, student newspaper, TV station, Hillel, Newman Club, Goodnews Fellowship, Islamic community, Alliance of Gays and Lesbians and Everyone, Latino student organization, international club, Earth Emerson, Asian Students for Intercultural Awareness, Amnesty International.

Athletics. NCAA. **Intercollegiate:** Baseball M, basketball, cross-country, golf, lacrosse, soccer, softball W, tennis, track and field, volleyball W. **Team name:** Lions.

Student services. Adult student services, chaplain/spiritual director, career counseling, student employment services, financial aid counseling, health services, minority student services, personal counseling, placement for graduates. **Physically disabled:** Services for visually, speech, hearing impaired.

Contact. E-mail: admission@emerson.edu
Phone: (617) 824-8600 Fax: (617) 824-8609
Christopher Wright, Senior Associate Director of Undergraduate Admission, Emerson College, 120 Boylston Street, Boston, MA 02116-4624

Emmanuel College
Boston, Massachusetts
www.emmanuel.edu

CB member
CB code: 3368

- Private 4-year liberal arts college affiliated with Roman Catholic Church
- Residential campus in very large city
- 2,029 degree-seeking undergraduates: 12% part-time, 73% women, 6% African American, 3% Asian American, 6% Hispanic American, 1% international
- 283 degree-seeking graduate students
- 56% of applicants admitted
- SAT or ACT (ACT writing optional), application essay required
- 63% graduate within 6 years

General. Founded in 1919. Regionally accredited. Many departments require internships. Through the Colleges of the Fenway consortium, students can cross-register at Simmons College, Wentworth Institute of Technology, Wheelock College, Massachusetts College of Art, Massachusetts College of Pharmacy and Health Sciences. **Degrees:** 479 bachelor's awarded; master's offered. **ROTC:** Army. **Calendar:** Semester, limited summer session. **Full-time faculty:** 98 total; 76% have terminal degrees, 19% minority, 62% women. **Part-time faculty:** 133 total; 38% have terminal degrees, 14% minority, 55% women. **Class size:** 49% < 20, 50% 20-39, less than 1% 40-49. **Special facilities:** Community leadership center, center for mission and spirituality, science center.

Freshman class profile. 6,640 applied, 3,701 admitted, 550 enrolled.

Mid 50% test scores			
SAT critical reading:	490-590	GPA 2.0-2.99:	17%
SAT math:	490-580	Rank in top quarter:	48%
SAT writing:	500-600	Rank in top tenth:	13%
ACT composite:	21-26	Return as sophomores:	82%
GPA 3.75 or higher:	31%	Out-of-state:	43%
GPA 3.50-3.74:	16%	Live on campus:	90%
GPA 3.0-3.49:	36%	International:	2%

Basis for selection. High school curriculum and record most important, followed by recommendations, test scores, essay, creativity, initiative. Interviews encouraged. **Home schooled:** Portfolio, on-campus interview recommended.

High school preparation. College-preparatory program required. 16 units required. Required units include English 4, mathematics 3, social studies 2, science 2 (laboratory 2) and foreign language 2.

2011-2012 Annual costs. Tuition/fees: $32,300. Room/board: $12,750. Books/supplies: $880. Personal expenses: $1,935.

2011-2012 Financial aid. Need-based: 486 full-time freshmen applied for aid; 439 were judged to have need; 439 of these received aid. Average need met was 84%. Average scholarship/grant was $7,999; average loan $3,704. 64% of total undergraduate aid awarded as scholarships/grants, 36% as loans/jobs. **Non-need-based:** Awarded to 1,699 full-time undergraduates, including 540 freshmen. Scholarships awarded for academics, alumni affiliation, leadership.

Application procedures. Admission: Priority date 12/1; deadline 3/1 (postmark date). $60 fee, may be waived for applicants with need, free for online applicants. Admission notification on a rolling basis beginning on or about 12/1. Must reply by May 1 or within 2 week(s) if notified thereafter. **Financial aid:** Priority date 2/15; no closing date. FAFSA, institutional form required. Applicants notified on a rolling basis starting 3/1.

Academics. One-semester Capstone Experience required; designed to provide an opportunity to integrate and present content and methodology acquired in the major. This course may take the form of a seminar, internship, research project or creative project. As part of the general requirements of the College, one course in a student's program must deal with some aspect of United States society and one course must deal with a society or culture outside North America. **Special study options:** Accelerated study, cross-registration, distance learning, double major, exchange student, honors, independent study, internships, liberal arts/career combination, semester at sea, student-designed major, study abroad, teacher certification program, Washington semester. **Credit/placement by examination:** AP, CLEP, IB, SAT, ACT, institutional tests. **Support services:** Learning center, pre-admission summer program, reduced course load, remedial instruction, study skills assistance, tutoring, writing center.

Honors college/program. Four-year academic and co-curricular program that combines rigorous, discussion-based course work with special complementary opportunities such as cultural activities, faculty-directed research projects, and service in the community.

Majors. Area/ethnic studies: American. **Biology:** General, biochemistry, biostatistics, neuroscience. **Business:** Business admin. **Communications:** Communications/speech/rhetoric. **Education:** Elementary, secondary. **English:** English lit. **Foreign languages:** Spanish. **Health services:** Art therapy. **History:** General. **Liberal arts:** Arts/sciences. **Math:** General. **Philosophy/religion:** General. **Physical sciences:** Chemistry, forensic chemistry. **Psychology:** General, counseling, developmental. **Social sciences:** Political science, sociology. **Visual/performing arts:** Graphic design, studio arts.

Most popular majors. Biology 6%, business/marketing 20%, communications/journalism 10%, English 6%, health sciences 7%, history 7%, interdisciplinary studies 8%, psychology 10%, social sciences 10%.

Computing on campus. 216 workstations in dormitories, library, computer center, student center. Dormitories wired for high-speed internet access and linked to campus network. Commuter students can connect to campus network. Online course registration, online library, helpline, student web hosting, wireless network available.

Student life. Freshman orientation: Mandatory, $100 fee. Preregistration for classes offered. Three 2-day orientations during summer; includes assessment of foundation skills, course selection, placement examinations, academic advising and educational sessions. **Policies:** No alcohol permitted on campus. Freshmen not permitted cars on campus. **Housing:** Guaranteed on-campus for all undergraduates. Coed dorms, special housing for disabled available. $200 nonrefundable deposit, deadline 5/1. **Activities:** Jazz band, campus ministries, choral groups, dance, drama, film society, international student organizations, literary magazine, music ensembles, Model UN, musical theater, radio station, student government, student newspaper, symphony orchestra, Association of Countries Cultures Events Nations and Traditions, Asian student association, black student union, Helping Unite Latinos to Lead and Achieve Success, College Democrats, College Republicans, social awareness club, students for environmental action, core ministry team.

Athletics. NCAA. **Intercollegiate:** Basketball, cross-country, golf M, lacrosse, soccer, softball W, tennis W, track and field, volleyball. **Intramural:** Badminton, basketball, bowling, football (non-tackle), racquetball, soccer, softball, tennis, volleyball. **Team name:** Saints.

Student services. Adult student services, alcohol/substance abuse counseling, chaplain/spiritual director, career counseling, student employment services, financial aid counseling, health services, minority student services, personal counseling, placement for graduates, veterans' counselor. **Physically disabled:** Services for visually, speech, hearing impaired.

Contact. E-mail: enroll@emmanuel.edu
Phone: (617) 735-9715 Fax: (617) 735-9801
Sandra Robbins, Dean of Enrollment, Emmanuel College, 400 The Fenway, Boston, MA 02115

Endicott College
Beverly, Massachusetts
www.endicott.edu

CB member
CB code: 3369

- Private 4-year liberal arts college
- Residential campus in large town
- 2,476 degree-seeking undergraduates: 7% part-time, 59% women, 2% African American, 1% Asian American, 3% Hispanic American, 2% international
- 695 degree-seeking graduate students
- 67% of applicants admitted
- SAT or ACT with writing, application essay required
- 67% graduate within 6 years; 18% enter graduate study

General. Founded in 1939. Regionally accredited. Three internships required of all traditional undergraduates. Single parent program available. **Degrees:** 459 bachelor's, 19 associate awarded; master's, professional offered. **ROTC:** Army. **Location:** 24 miles from Boston. **Calendar:** 4-1-4, limited summer session. **Full-time faculty:** 92 total; 63% have terminal degrees, 8% minority, 56% women. **Part-time faculty:** 245 total; 31% have terminal degrees, 3% minority, 51% women. **Class size:** 53% < 20, 47% 20-39, less than 1% 40-49. **Special facilities:** Student-run restaurant/classroom, archives museum, nature trails.

Freshman class profile. 3,477 applied, 2,328 admitted, 647 enrolled.

Mid 50% test scores			
SAT critical reading:	480-570	GPA 2.0-2.99:	39%
SAT math:	490-580	Rank in top quarter:	38%
SAT writing:	480-570	Rank in top tenth:	12%
ACT composite:	20-24	End year in good standing:	95%
GPA 3.75 or higher:	12%	Return as sophomores:	88%
GPA 3.50-3.74:	11%	Out-of-state:	55%
GPA 3.0-3.49:	37%	Live on campus:	94%
		International:	2%

Basis for selection. School achievement record and SAT/ACT most important. Class rank, essay, volunteer work, extracurricular activities, leadership also important. Teacher, counselor recommendations considered. Interview recommended. **Home schooled:** Verification that curriculum has been certified by local school system or state, or GED.

High school preparation. College-preparatory program recommended. 16 units recommended. Recommended units include English 4, mathematics 3, social studies 2, history 1, science 2 and academic electives 4. One chemistry with laboratory and algebra required for nursing and athletic training programs.

2011-2012 Annual costs. Tuition/fees: $27,230. Room/board: $12,760. Books/supplies: $1,018. Personal expenses: $1,034.

2011-2012 Financial aid. Need-based: 591 full-time freshmen applied for aid; 456 were judged to have need; 452 of these received aid. Average need met was 60%. Average scholarship/grant was $10,075; average loan $3,752. 71% of total undergraduate aid awarded as scholarships/grants, 29% as loans/jobs. **Non-need-based:** Awarded to 1,271 full-time undergraduates, including 396 freshmen. Scholarships awarded for academics, alumni affiliation, art, leadership, religious affiliation, ROTC, state residency.

Application procedures. Admission: Closing date 2/15 (postmark date). $50 fee, may be waived for applicants with need. Admission notification on a rolling basis beginning on or about 11/1. Must reply by May 1 or within 1 week(s) if notified thereafter. **Financial aid:** Priority date 3/15; no closing date. FAFSA, institutional form required. Applicants notified on a rolling basis starting 3/15; must reply within 2 week(s) of notification.

Academics. Three internships required of most traditional undergraduates. **Special study options:** Accelerated study, combined bachelor's/graduate degree, cross-registration, distance learning, dual enrollment of high school students, exchange student, honors, independent study, internships, liberal arts/career combination, student-designed major, study abroad, teacher certification program. **Credit/placement by examination:** AP, CLEP, IB, SAT, institutional tests. 32 credit hours maximum toward associate degree, 85

toward bachelor's. **Support services:** Learning center, study skills assistance, tutoring, writing center.

Majors. Biology: General, biotechnology, environmental. **Business:** Accounting, business admin, entrepreneurial studies, event planning, finance, hospitality admin, international, marketing. **Communications:** Digital media, media studies. **Computer sciences:** Computer science. **Conservation:** Environmental science. **Education:** Early childhood, elementary, physical. **English:** Creative writing, English lit, general lit. **Health services:** Athletic training, nursing (RN). **History:** General. **Liberal arts:** Arts/sciences. **Parks/recreation:** General, sports admin. **Protective services:** Criminal justice. **Psychology:** General. **Social sciences:** Political science. **Visual/performing arts:** Design, graphic design, interior design, photography, studio arts.

Most popular majors. Business/marketing 32%, communications/journalism 8%, education 7%, health sciences 9%, parks/recreation 10%, psychology 8%, visual/performing arts 11%.

Computing on campus. 158 workstations in library, computer center. Dormitories wired for high-speed internet access and linked to campus network. Commuter students can connect to campus network. Online course registration, online library, helpline, repair service, wireless network available.

Student life. Freshman orientation: Available. Preregistration for classes offered. Orientation sessions held in July and September; includes preparation for fall course assignment. **Policies:** Freshmen not permitted cars on campus. **Housing:** Guaranteed on-campus for freshmen. Coed dorms, single-sex dorms, special housing for disabled, apartments, wellness housing available. $500 deposit, deadline 5/1. Single-parent housing, ocean-front, academic, suites, converted mansions, modular housing available. **Activities:** Bands, campus ministries, choral groups, dance, drama, film society, international student organizations, literary magazine, music ensembles, Model UN, musical theater, student government, student newspaper, TV station, Coast-2-Coast (intercultural), ALANA, EC Alliance, Random Cards of Kindness, Rotaract service club.

Athletics. NCAA. **Intercollegiate:** Baseball M, basketball, cross-country, equestrian, field hockey W, football (tackle) M, golf M, lacrosse, rowing (crew), sailing, soccer, softball W, tennis, volleyball. **Intramural:** Basketball, football (non-tackle), lacrosse, racquetball, soccer, softball, volleyball. **Team name:** Gulls.

Student services. Alcohol/substance abuse counseling, chaplain/spiritual director, career counseling, financial aid counseling, health services, personal counseling, women's services. **Physically disabled:** Services for visually, speech, hearing impaired.

Contact. E-mail: admission@endicott.edu
Phone: (978) 921-1000 Toll-free number: (800) 325-1114
Fax: (978) 232-2520
Thomas Redman, Vice President for Admissions and Financial Aid, Endicott College, 376 Hale Street, Beverly, MA 01915-9985

Fitchburg State University
Fitchburg, Massachusetts
www.fitchburgstate.edu

CB member
CB code: 3518

- Public 4-year liberal arts and teachers college
- Residential campus in small city
- 3,958 degree-seeking undergraduates: 14% part-time, 54% women, 4% African American, 2% Asian American, 6% Hispanic American
- 955 degree-seeking graduate students
- 70% of applicants admitted
- SAT or ACT (ACT writing optional), application essay required
- 47% graduate within 6 years

General. Founded in 1894. Regionally accredited. **Degrees:** 697 bachelor's awarded; master's offered. **ROTC:** Army. **Location:** 50 miles from Boston, 25 miles from Worcester. **Calendar:** Semester, limited summer session. **Full-time faculty:** 184 total; 91% have terminal degrees, 11% minority, 46% women. **Part-time faculty:** 90 total; 30% have terminal degrees, 6% minority, 51% women. **Class size:** 35% < 20, 65% 20-39, less than 1% 40-49, less than 1% 50-99. **Special facilities:** Teacher education laboratory school, 120-acre conservation area.

Freshman class profile. 3,104 applied, 2,163 admitted, 698 enrolled.

Mid 50% test scores			
SAT critical reading:	450-560	GPA 3.0-3.49:	35%
SAT math:	450-560	GPA 2.0-2.99:	45%
SAT writing:	450-540	Return as sophomores:	73%
ACT composite:	19-23	Out-of-state:	9%
GPA 3.75 or higher:	11%	Live on campus:	70%
GPA 3.50-3.74:	9%	Fraternities:	2%
		Sororities:	3%

Basis for selection. Secondary school record, test scores, essay important. Recommendations considered. Interview recommended for nursing, undeclared major, computer science, business administration, communications/media majors. **Learning Disabled:** Students with professionally diagnosed learning disabilities exempt from standardized test requirements.

High school preparation. 16 units required. Required units include English 4, mathematics 3, social studies 1, history 1, science 3 (laboratory 2), foreign language 2 and academic electives 2. Additional units of math and science preferred for nursing, computer science, and business applicants.

2011-2012 Annual costs. Tuition/fees: $8,300; $14,380 out-of-state. Room/board: $8,256. Books/supplies: $800. Personal expenses: $1,500.

Financial aid. Non-need-based: Scholarships awarded for academics, alumni affiliation, leadership, ROTC, state residency.

Application procedures. Admission: Priority date 1/1; no deadline. $25 fee, may be waived for applicants with need. Admission notification on a rolling basis beginning on or about 12/1. Must reply by May 1 or within 2 week(s) if notified thereafter. **Financial aid:** Priority date 3/1; no closing date. FAFSA required. Applicants notified on a rolling basis starting 3/15.

Academics. Many major programs include internship, practicum, or clinical experience. All degree programs require completion of 48 credits in liberal arts and sciences. **Special study options:** Cross-registration, distance learning, double major, dual enrollment of high school students, honors, independent study, internships, liberal arts/career combination, student-designed major, study abroad, teacher certification program. **Credit/placement by examination:** AP, CLEP, institutional tests. 60 credit hours maximum toward bachelor's degree. **Support services:** Learning center, preadmission summer program, reduced course load, remedial instruction, study skills assistance, tutoring, writing center.

Honors college/program. Admissions based on high school preparation, test scores, and leadership potential. Students complete integrated sequence of courses over 4-year period and are expected to demonstrate leadership through extracurricular activities, volunteer positions, and service learning placements. 3.3 GPA required to continue in the program.

Majors. Architecture: Technology. **Biology:** General, biomedical sciences, biotechnology, environmental, exercise physiology, neurobiology/behavior. **Business:** Accounting, business admin, finance, international, management science, marketing. **Communications:** Communications/speech/rhetoric, digital media. **Computer sciences:** General, computer science. **Education:** General, biology, early childhood, elementary, English, geography, history, mathematics, middle, secondary, special ed, technology/industrial arts, trade/industrial. **English:** English lit, technical writing. **Health services:** Nursing (RN). **History:** General. **Liberal arts:** Arts/sciences. **Math:** General, applied. **Parks/recreation:** Exercise sciences, sports admin. **Protective services:** Criminal justice. **Psychology:** General, cognitive, developmental, industrial. **Social sciences:** Economics, geography, international economics, international relations, political science, sociology, U.S. government. **Visual/performing arts:** Cinematography, dramatic, graphic design, photography, theater design.

Most popular majors. Business/marketing 16%, education 9%, health sciences 7%, interdisciplinary studies 12%, security/protective services 6%, visual/performing arts 15%.

Computing on campus. PC or laptop required. 150 workstations in dormitories, library, computer center, student center. Dormitories wired for high-speed internet access and linked to campus network. Commuter students can connect to campus network. Online course registration, online library, helpline, repair service, wireless network available.

Student life. Freshman orientation: Mandatory. Preregistration for classes offered. Testing, academic advising, registration for classes are key components of the program. **Housing:** Coed dorms, special housing for disabled, apartments, wellness housing available. $150 nonrefundable deposit, deadline 5/1. Quiet halls available. **Activities:** Bands, choral groups, dance, drama, film society, literary magazine, Model UN, radio station, student government, student newspaper, student government association, Christian Fellowship, black student union, Habitat for Humanity, Latin American student organization, MASSPIRG, Asian cultural society, First Responders, Rotoract club.

Athletics. NCAA. **Intercollegiate:** Baseball M, basketball, cross-country, field hockey W, football (tackle) M, ice hockey M, lacrosse W, soccer, softball W, track and field. **Intramural:** Basketball, bowling, football (nontackle), handball, racquetball, soccer, softball, swimming, table tennis, volleyball, water polo. **Team name:** Falcons.

Student services. Alcohol/substance abuse counseling, career counseling, services for economically disadvantaged, student employment services, financial aid counseling, health services, minority student services, personal counseling. **Physically disabled:** Services for visually, speech, hearing impaired.

Contact. E-mail: admissions@fitchburgstate.edu
Phone: (978) 665-3144 Toll-free number: (800) 705-9692
Fax: (978) 665-4540
Kay Reynolds, Director of Admissions, Fitchburg State University, 160 Pearl Street, Fitchburg, MA 01420-2697

Framingham State University
Framingham, Massachusetts   **CB member**
www.framingham.edu   **CB code: 3519**

- Public 4-year liberal arts and teachers college
- Residential campus in small city
- 3,885 degree-seeking undergraduates: 10% part-time, 64% women, 7% African American, 2% Asian American, 7% Hispanic American, 1% international
- 931 degree-seeking graduate students
- 58% of applicants admitted
- SAT or ACT with writing required
- 52% graduate within 6 years

General. Founded in 1839. Regionally accredited. **Degrees:** 729 bachelor's awarded; master's offered. **Location:** 20 miles from Boston. **Calendar:** Semester, extensive summer session. **Full-time faculty:** 175 total; 85% have terminal degrees, 5% minority, 59% women. **Part-time faculty:** 119 total; 27% have terminal degrees, 3% minority, 44% women. **Class size:** 37% < 20, 61% 20-39, less than 1% 40-49, 1% 50-99. **Special facilities:** Global education center, social research center, learning center, economic research center, STEM pipeline center, food and nutrition institute, greenhouse, early childhood demonstration lab, education curriculum library, Mazmanian Gallery.

Freshman class profile. 4,909 applied, 2,861 admitted, 924 enrolled.

Mid 50% test scores			
SAT critical reading:	460-560	GPA 3.50-3.74:	11%
SAT math:	470-560	GPA 3.0-3.49:	36%
SAT writing:	460-550	GPA 2.0-2.99:	41%
ACT composite:	21-25	Return as sophomores:	74%
GPA 3.75 or higher:	12%	Out-of-state:	5%
		Live on campus:	83%

Basis for selection. Strength of high school curriculum, weighted GPA, class rank, test scores most important. Some attention given to organized and volunteer activities, special talents, and recommendations (when requested). Consideration given to students whose educational opportunities have been limited due to economic disadvantage. Admission standards policy of Massachusetts Department of Higher Education requires 16 college-preparatory courses with 3.0 recalculated GPA. Students with lower GPA may qualify based on sliding scale combining SAT scores with GPA. Portfolio required of studio art majors. Essay may be required for selected applicants. Interviews welcomed but not required. **Home schooled:** Students may be required to submit results of additional nationally normed tests, such as SAT Subject Tests. **Learning Disabled:** Students with diagnosed learning disability must submit individualized educational plan/504 plan along with all psychoeducational testing current within last 3 years.

High school preparation. College-preparatory program required. 16 units required; 21 recommended. Required and recommended units include English 4, mathematics 3-4, social studies 1, history 1-2, science 3-4 (laboratory 2-3), foreign language 2-4 and academic electives 2. Math must include algebra I, algebra II, and geometry. Additional unit of math strongly recommended for computer science, math, pre-engineering, and science majors. Additional units of biology, chemistry, physics recommended for science majors. Foreign language must be 2 units of same language. All units must be college-preparatory level.

2011-2012 Annual costs. Tuition/fees: $7,580; $13,660 out-of-state. Fees include mandatory laptop purchase by new students. New England Regional tuition rate $1,455. Room/board: $9,170. Books/supplies: $1,000. Personal expenses: $1,200.

Financial aid. Non-need-based: Scholarships awarded for academics.

Application procedures. Admission: Priority date 2/15; no deadline. $40 fee, may be waived for applicants with need. Admission notification on a rolling basis beginning on or about 1/15. Must reply by May 1 or within 2 week(s) if notified thereafter. Students should contact admissions office after priority date of 2/15 to determine if applications are still being accepted. Some majors and on-campus housing may be filled by priority date. Application fee waiver available to students who submit College Board fee waiver. **Financial aid:** Priority date 3/1; no closing date. FAFSA required. Applicants notified on a rolling basis starting 3/15; must reply by 5/1 or within 2 week(s) of notification.

Academics. E-tutoring available on-line. **Special study options:** Cross-registration, distance learning, double major, honors, independent study, internships, liberal arts/career combination, study abroad, teacher certification program, Washington semester. Pre-engineering program in conjunction with University of Massachusetts at Amherst, University of Massachusetts at Dartmouth, University of Massachusetts at Lowell. **Credit/placement by examination:** AP, CLEP, IB, institutional tests. 64 credit hours maximum toward bachelor's degree. **Support services:** Learning center, reduced course load, remedial instruction, study skills assistance, tutoring, writing center.

Majors. **Biology:** General. **Business:** General, knowledge management. **Computer sciences:** General. **Conservation:** Environmental studies. **Education:** Early childhood, elementary. **English:** English lit. **Foreign languages:** General. **General:** Food science. **Health services:** Nursing (RN). **History:** General. **Liberal arts:** Arts/sciences. **Math:** General. **Physical sciences:** Chemistry. **Psychology:** General. **Social sciences:** Economics, geography, political science, sociology. **Visual/performing arts:** Art. **Work/family studies:** General, clothing/textiles, food/nutrition.

Most popular majors. Business/marketing 16%, communication technologies 11%, education 6%, English 6%, family/consumer sciences 14%, psychology 7%, social sciences 13%.

Computing on campus. PC or laptop required. 232 workstations in dormitories, library, computer center, student center. Dormitories wired for high-speed internet access and linked to campus network. Online course registration, online library, helpline, repair service, wireless network available.

Student life. Freshman orientation: Mandatory. Preregistration for classes offered. Weekend session held during the summer; additional 1-day session in late August or early September. **Housing:** Coed dorms, single-sex dorms, wellness housing available. $150 nonrefundable deposit, deadline 5/1. **Activities:** Campus ministries, choral groups, dance, drama, international student organizations, literary magazine, musical theater, radio station, student government, student newspaper, active sociologists, black student union, Christian fellowship, Newman Association, 10% Alliance and Allies, Amnesty International, animal rights, global change initiative, Human Rights Action Awareness Committee, wildlife club, Amigos, Alternate Spring Break, Women's Empowerment.

Athletics. NCAA. **Intercollegiate:** Baseball M, basketball, cross-country, field hockey W, football (tackle) M, ice hockey M, lacrosse W, soccer, softball W, volleyball W. **Intramural:** Badminton, basketball, football (non-tackle), golf, soccer, volleyball, weight lifting. **Team name:** Rams.

Student services. Alcohol/substance abuse counseling, chaplain/spiritual director, career counseling, services for economically disadvantaged, student employment services, financial aid counseling, health services, minority student services, on-campus daycare, personal counseling, placement for graduates, veterans' counselor. **Physically disabled:** Services for visually, hearing impaired.

Contact. E-mail: admissions@framingham.edu
Phone: (508) 626-4500 Fax: (508) 626-4017
Jeremy Spencer, Dean of Undergraduate Admissions, Framingham State University, PO Box 9101, Framingham, MA 01701-9101

Franklin W. Olin College of Engineering
Needham, Massachusetts   **CB member**
www.olin.edu   **CB code: 2824**

- Private 4-year engineering college
- Residential campus in large town
- 326 degree-seeking undergraduates: 48% women, 1% African American, 16% Asian American, 2% Hispanic American, 6% international
- 16% of applicants admitted
- SAT or ACT (ACT writing optional), SAT Subject Tests, application essay, interview required
- 96% graduate within 6 years; 38% enter graduate study

General. Regionally accredited. All students receive Olin Scholarship, currently valued at one-half tuition. Additional need-based aid is available to cover other costs. **Degrees:** 89 bachelor's awarded. **Location:** 14 miles from Boston. **Calendar:** Semester. **Full-time faculty:** 35 total; 100% have terminal degrees, 26% minority, 40% women. **Part-time faculty:** 9 total; 67% have terminal degrees, 11% minority, 22% women. **Class size:** 47% < 20, 52% 20-39, 1% 40-49.

Freshman class profile. 768 applied, 126 admitted, 87 enrolled.

Mid 50% test scores		Rank in top quarter:	99%
SAT critical reading:	660-740	Rank in top tenth:	95%
SAT math:	700-780	Return as sophomores:	91%
SAT writing:	670-750	Out-of-state:	84%
ACT composite:	32-34	Live on campus:	99%
GPA 3.75 or higher:	100%	International:	1%

Basis for selection. Secondary school achievement, course rigor, test scores, personal character most important; creativity and entrepreneurial spirit also very important. Cultural, economic, geographic diversity encouraged. Candidates for admission selected from all applicants. Candidates required to attend 1 of 2 weekends on campus to participate in design project, individual interviews, and team exercises. Incoming class selected from this group. Financial support provided if needed. 2 SAT Subject Tests required: Math (Level 2 preferred, Level 1 accepted) and any science subject. **Home schooled:** Statement describing home school structure and mission, transcript of courses and grades, letter of recommendation (nonparent) required.

High school preparation. College-preparatory program recommended. Recommended units include English 4, mathematics 4, social studies 2, history 2, science 3 (laboratory 3) and foreign language 2. 1 calculus unit and 1 physics unit required.

2011-2012 Annual costs. Tuition/fees: $39,450. All admitted students receive a half-tuition scholarship; Additional need-based aid available to cover other costs. Room/board: $14,000. Books/supplies: $750.

2011-2012 Financial aid. **Need-based:** 59 full-time freshmen applied for aid; 50 were judged to have need; 50 of these received aid. Average need met was 100%. Average scholarship/grant was $18,592; average loan $3,155. 89% of total undergraduate aid awarded as scholarships/grants, 11% as loans/jobs. **Non-need-based:** Awarded to 326 full-time undergraduates, including 81 freshmen. Scholarships awarded for academics, leadership. **Additional information:** Financial aid forms not needed for one-half tuition scholarship which all students receive; FAFSA forms required for need-based aid considerations.

Application procedures. **Admission:** Closing date 1/1 (postmark date). $80 fee, may be waived for applicants with need. Application must be submitted online. Admission notification by 3/21. Must reply by 5/1. **Financial aid:** Closing date 2/15. FAFSA required. Applicants notified on a rolling basis starting 4/1; must reply by 5/1.

Academics. **Special study options:** Combined bachelor's/graduate degree, cross-registration, exchange student, independent study, internships, liberal arts/career combination, semester at sea, student-designed major, study abroad. **Credit/placement by examination:** AP, CLEP. **Support services:** Study skills assistance, tutoring, writing center.

Majors. **Engineering:** General, electrical, mechanical.

Computing on campus. PC or laptop required. Dormitories wired for high-speed internet access and linked to campus network. Commuter students can connect to campus network. Online course registration, online library, helpline, repair service, student web hosting, wireless network available.

Student life. Freshman orientation: Mandatory. Preregistration for classes offered. Held the 3 days before classes begin in late August. **Policies:** All students sign honor code that addresses personal and academic integrity. **Housing:** Guaranteed on-campus for all undergraduates. Coed dorms, special housing for disabled available. **Activities:** Jazz band, choral groups, dance, drama, international student organizations, music ensembles, musical theater, student government, student newspaper, symphony orchestra, Christian fellowship, volunteerism club, Korean club, martial arts club, Chinese club, Catholic association, art club, environmental club, women engineers, a cappella clubs.

Athletics. **Intramural:** Basketball, football (non-tackle), soccer, softball, volleyball.

Student services. Alcohol/substance abuse counseling, chaplain/spiritual director, career counseling, student employment services, financial aid counseling, health services, minority student services, personal counseling, placement for graduates, veterans' counselor, women's services. **Physically disabled:** Services for hearing impaired.

Contact. E-mail: info@olin.edu
Phone: (781) 292-2222 Fax: (781) 292-2210
Charles Nolan, Dean of Admission, Franklin W. Olin College of Engineering, Olin Way, Needham, MA 02492

Gordon College
Wenham, Massachusetts
www.gordon.edu

CB member
CB code: 3417

- Private 4-year liberal arts college affiliated with nondenominational tradition
- Residential campus in small town
- 1,543 degree-seeking undergraduates: 2% part-time, 60% women, 2% African American, 2% Asian American, 7% Hispanic American, 4% international
- 325 degree-seeking graduate students
- 40% of applicants admitted
- SAT or ACT with writing, interview required
- 74% graduate within 6 years

General. Founded in 1889. Regionally accredited. **Degrees:** 364 bachelor's awarded; master's offered. **ROTC:** Army. **Location:** 25 miles from Boston. **Calendar:** Semester, limited summer session. **Full-time faculty:** 98 total; 87% have terminal degrees, 10% minority, 34% women. **Part-time faculty:** 75 total. **Class size:** 69% < 20, 24% 20-39, 4% 40-49, 2% 50-99, 2% >100. **Special facilities:** Christian studies center, international office for Christians in the Visual Arts, electron microscope, gene sequencing machine, Shakespearean folios, center for balance/mobility/wellness, indoor and outdoor ropes course.

Freshman class profile. 4,315 applied, 1,713 admitted, 465 enrolled.

Mid 50% test scores				
SAT critical reading:	520-670	GPA 2.0-2.99:		10%
SAT math:	510-650	Rank in top quarter:		67%
SAT writing:	520-650	Rank in top tenth:		37%
ACT composite:	22-28	Return as sophomores:		82%
GPA 3.75 or higher:	36%	Out-of-state:		71%
GPA 3.50-3.74:	26%	Live on campus:		98%
GPA 3.0-3.49:	27%	International:		4%

Basis for selection. Course selection and grades, class rank, essay of Christian commitment, test scores, references, interiew, school and community activities considered. SAT Subject Tests not required but may be used for placement. Audition required of music majors. Portfolio required of visual art majors. **Home schooled:** Statement describing home school structure and mission, letter of recommendation (nonparent) required. Information regarding course of study, including description of curriculum and reading list required. **Learning Disabled:** Students with diagnosed learning disability may submit documentation with application, as well as any learning plans used through high school. Some requirements may be substituted with appropriate documentation.

High school preparation. College-preparatory program required. 18 units required; 22 recommended. Required and recommended units include English 4, mathematics 2-3, social studies 2, science 2-3 (laboratory 1), foreign language 2-4 and academic electives 5. Academic profile should include AP, honors, or accelerated courses.

2011-2012 Annual costs. Tuition/fees: $30,606. Room/board: $8,434. Books/supplies: $800. Personal expenses: $1,000.

2011-2012 Financial aid. Need-based: 419 full-time freshmen applied for aid; 365 were judged to have need; 364 of these received aid. Average need met was 68%. Average scholarship/grant was $15,923; average loan $3,602. 64% of total undergraduate aid awarded as scholarships/grants, 36% as loans/jobs. **Non-need-based:** Awarded to 423 full-time undergraduates, including 132 freshmen. Scholarships awarded for academics, alumni affiliation, art, leadership, minority status, music/drama, state residency.

Application procedures. Admission: Priority date 3/1; no deadline. $50 fee, may be waived for applicants with need. Admission notification on a rolling basis beginning on or about 9/15. Must reply by May 1 or within 2 week(s) if notified thereafter. **Financial aid:** Priority date 3/1; no closing date. Institutional form, CSS PROFILE required. Applicants notified on a rolling basis starting 2/15; must reply by 5/1 or within 2 week(s) of notification.

Academics. Integration of faith and learning emphasized within every academic discipline. **Special study options:** Combined bachelor's/graduate degree, cooperative education, cross-registration, double major, exchange student, honors, independent study, internships, liberal arts/career combination, student-designed major, study abroad, teacher certification program, urban semester, Washington semester. Gordon-in-France; Italian Semester in Orvieto, Italy; Oregon Extension; Outdoor Education Immersion Semester; LaVida Wilderness Expedition; Co-Op Programs: Arts, Business, Computer Science, Education, Engineering, Health Professions, Humanities, Natural Science, Social/Behavioral Science. **Credit/placement by examination:** AP, CLEP, IB, institutional tests. **Support services:** Learning center, reduced course load, remedial instruction, study skills assistance, tutoring, writing center.

Majors. Biology: General, exercise physiology. **Business:** Accounting, business admin, finance. **Communications:** Communications/speech/rhetoric. **Computer sciences:** Computer science. **Education:** Early childhood, elementary, middle, music, secondary, special ed. **Engineering:** Applied physics. **English:** English lit. **Foreign languages:** General, French, German, linguistics, Spanish. **History:** General. **Human services:** Social work. **Math:** General. **Parks/recreation:** General. **Philosophy/religion:** Christian, philosophy. **Physical sciences:** Chemistry, physics. **Psychology:** General. **Social sciences:** Economics, international relations, political science, sociology. **Theology:** Youth ministry. **Visual/performing arts:** Art, dramatic, music, music pedagogy, music performance.

Most popular majors. Biology 9%, business/marketing 10%, communications/journalism 10%, English 10%, foreign language 7%, history 7%, psychology 7%, public administration/social services 6%, social sciences 8%, visual/performing arts 11%.

Computing on campus. 115 workstations in dormitories, library, computer center, student center. Dormitories wired for high-speed internet access and linked to campus network. Commuter students can connect to campus network. Online course registration, online library, helpline, repair service, wireless network available.

Student life. Freshman orientation: Mandatory, $100 fee. Preregistration for classes offered. Five-day program held in the days prior to start of semester; includes program for parents during first two days. **Policies:** No alcohol or smoking allowed on campus or at college-sponsored events. Religious observance required. **Housing:** Guaranteed on-campus for all undergraduates. Coed dorms, single-sex dorms, special housing for disabled, apartments available. $250 nonrefundable deposit, deadline 5/1. **Activities:** Bands, campus ministries, choral groups, dance, drama, film society, international student organizations, literary magazine, music ensembles, Model UN, musical theater, opera, radio station, student government, student newspaper, symphony orchestra, society for new politics, advocates for cultural diversity, Christians for social action, fellowship group for children of missionaries, ministry to deaf persons, outreach service, short-term mission trips, Amnesty International, ALANA.

Athletics. NCAA. **Intercollegiate:** Baseball M, basketball, cross-country, field hockey W, golf, lacrosse, soccer, softball W, swimming, tennis, track and field, volleyball W. **Intramural:** Basketball, football (non-tackle), racquetball, soccer, softball, table tennis. **Team name:** Fighting Scots.

Student services. Alcohol/substance abuse counseling, chaplain/spiritual director, career counseling, student employment services, financial aid counseling, health services, minority student services, personal counseling, placement for graduates. **Physically disabled:** Services for visually, speech, hearing impaired.

Contact. E-mail: admissions@gordon.edu
Phone: (978) 867-4218 Toll-free number: (866) 464-6736
Fax: (978) 867-4682
June Bodoni, Executive Director of Admissions and Advancement Operations, Gordon College, 255 Grapevine Road, Wenham, MA 01984-0198

Hampshire College
Amherst, Massachusetts
www.hampshire.edu

CB member
CB code: 3447

- Private 4-year liberal arts college
- Residential campus in large town
- 1,475 degree-seeking undergraduates: 58% women, 3% African American, 2% Asian American, 9% Hispanic American, 5% international
- 71% of applicants admitted
- Application essay required
- 63% graduate within 6 years; 10% enter graduate study

General. Founded in 1965. Regionally accredited. All students work closely with faculty advisors to design individual academic programs and complete capstone project. **Degrees:** 308 bachelor's awarded. **ROTC:** Army. **Location:** 90 miles from Boston, 20 miles from Springfield. **Calendar:** 4-1-4. **Full-time faculty:** 98 total; 88% have terminal degrees, 20% minority, 56% women. **Part-time faculty:** 62 total; 61% have terminal degrees, 21% minority, 48% women. **Class size:** 68% < 20, 31% 20-39, less than 1% 40-49. **Special facilities:** Bioshelter (integrated greenhouse/aquaculture facility), farm center, electronic music production studio, extensive film and photography facilities, fabrication center, national Yiddish book center, picturebook art museum.

Freshman class profile. 2,517 applied, 1,797 admitted, 366 enrolled.

Mid 50% test scores			
SAT critical reading:	590-700	GPA 2.0-2.99:	22%
SAT math:	540-650	Rank in top quarter:	52%
SAT writing:	580-670	Rank in top tenth:	19%
ACT composite:	25-29	Return as sophomores:	78%
GPA 3.75 or higher:	20%	Out-of-state:	85%
GPA 3.50-3.74:	22%	Live on campus:	100%
GPA 3.0-3.49:	35%	International:	9%

Basis for selection. Criteria include desire to do rigorous independent work, school record, academic writing samples, recommendations, school and community activities. Interview recommended. **Home schooled:** Common Application's Home School Supplement required.

High school preparation. College-preparatory program required. 16 units required; 20 recommended. Required and recommended units include English 4, mathematics 3-4, history 3-4, science 3-4 (laboratory 2) and foreign language 3-4.

2011-2012 Annual costs. Tuition/fees: $42,880. Room/board: $11,180. Books/supplies: $700. Personal expenses: $700.

2011-2012 Financial aid. Need-based: 257 full-time freshmen applied for aid; 215 were judged to have need; 215 of these received aid. Average need met was 94%. Average scholarship/grant was $28,830; average loan $3,500. 82% of total undergraduate aid awarded as scholarships/grants, 18% as loans/jobs. **Non-need-based:** Awarded to 728 full-time undergraduates, including 137 freshmen. Scholarships awarded for academics, leadership.

Application procedures. Admission: Priority date 11/15; deadline 1/1 (receipt date). $60 fee, may be waived for applicants with need, free for online applicants. Admission notification by 4/1. Must reply by May 1 or within 2 week(s) if notified thereafter. **Financial aid:** Closing date 2/1. FAFSA, CSS PROFILE required. Applicants notified by 4/1; must reply by 5/1 or within 2 week(s) of notification.

Academics. All students pursue individualized program of study. Requirements for graduation not based on credit, but on completion of division one courses in all 5 schools, an independent concentration consisting of combination of courses, independent project work, year-long thesis. **Special study options:** Exchange student, independent study, internships, student-designed major, study abroad, teacher certification program. Member 5-college consortium; may take classes at other member institutions. **Credit/placement by examination:** AP, CLEP. **Support services:** Study skills assistance, writing center.

Majors. Architecture: Architecture. **Area/ethnic studies:** General, African, African-American, American, East Asian, European, gay/lesbian, Latin American, Native American, Near/Middle Eastern, South Asian, women's. **Biology:** General, animal behavior, neuroscience. **Business:** Entrepreneurial studies. **Communications:** Communications/speech/rhetoric. **Computer sciences:** Computer graphics, computer science. **Conservation:** Environmental studies. **Education:** General. **English:** Creative writing, English lit, general lit. **Foreign languages:** Linguistics. **Health services:** Public health ed. **History:** General. **Human services:** Public policy. **Math:** General. **Philosophy/religion:** Philosophy, religion. **Physical sciences:** Astronomy, chemistry, geology, physics. **Psychology:** General. **Social sciences:** Anthropology, economics, international economics, international relations, political science, sociology, urban studies. **Visual/performing arts:** Art history/conservation, dance, design, dramatic, film/cinema/video, music, studio arts.

Most popular majors. Area/ethnic studies 6%, English 13%, interdisciplinary studies 7%, social sciences 14%, visual/performing arts 26%.

Computing on campus. 215 workstations in library, computer center, student center. Dormitories wired for high-speed internet access and linked to campus network. Commuter students can connect to campus network. Online course registration, online library, helpline, repair service, student web hosting, wireless network available.

Student life. Freshman orientation: Mandatory, $200 fee. Preregistration for classes offered. Program held during week immediately before matriculation. **Housing:** Guaranteed on-campus for freshmen. Coed dorms, special housing for disabled, apartments, wellness housing available. $200 nonrefundable deposit, deadline 5/1. **Activities:** Jazz band, choral groups, dance, drama, film society, international student organizations, music ensembles, radio station, student government, student newspaper, Re-Radicalization of Hampshire College, Students for Justice in Palestine, Pan Asian student association, RAICES, Christian Fellowship, College Quakers, College Democrats, SISTERS, Union of Activists, Building Awareness Across Bars.

Athletics. USCAA. **Intercollegiate:** Basketball, cross-country, fencing, soccer. **Intramural:** Basketball.

Student services. Alcohol/substance abuse counseling, chaplain/spiritual director, career counseling, financial aid counseling, health services, minority student services, on-campus daycare, personal counseling, women's services. **Physically disabled:** Services for visually, speech, hearing impaired.

Contact. E-mail: admissions@hampshire.edu
Phone: (413) 559-5471 Toll-free number: (877) 937-4267
Fax: (413) 559-5631
Julie Richardson, Dean of Admissions, Hampshire College, 893 West Street, Amherst, MA 01002-9988

Harvard College
Cambridge, Massachusetts
www.college.harvard.edu

CB member
CB code: 3434

- Private 4-year university and liberal arts college
- Residential campus in small city
- 6,676 degree-seeking undergraduates: 50% women, 7% African American, 18% Asian American, 9% Hispanic American, 10% international
- 3,893 degree-seeking graduate students
- 6% of applicants admitted
- SAT or ACT with writing, SAT Subject Tests, application essay, interview required
- 97% graduate within 6 years

General. Founded in 1636. Regionally accredited. Harvard College is the undergraduate program within Harvard University, part of the faculty of arts and sciences, and offers programs in liberal arts. **Degrees:** 1,637 bachelor's awarded; master's, doctoral offered. **ROTC:** Army, Naval, Air Force. **Location:** 3 miles from Boston. **Calendar:** Semester, extensive summer session. **Full-time faculty:** 928 total; 85% have terminal degrees, 18% minority, 32% women. **Part-time faculty:** 185 total; 74% have terminal degrees, 9% minority, 48% women. **Class size:** 78% < 20, 12% 20-39, 2% 40-49, 5% 50-99, 3% >100. **Special facilities:** Museum of Scandinavian and Germanic art, experimental forest in New York state, center for study of Italian Renaissance in Florence, center for Byzantine studies (Washington, DC), Smithsonian astrophysical observatory.

Freshman class profile. 34,950 applied, 2,188 admitted, 1,661 enrolled.

Mid 50% test scores			
SAT critical reading:	690-790	GPA 3.0-3.49:	4%
SAT math:	700-800	Rank in top quarter:	100%
SAT writing:	690-790	Rank in top tenth:	95%
ACT composite:	31-35	Return as sophomores:	97%
GPA 3.75 or higher:	91%	Out-of-state:	86%
GPA 3.50-3.74:	5%	Live on campus:	100%
		International:	12%

Basis for selection. Secondary school record most important; character, creative ability in some discipline or activity, leadership, liveliness of mind, demonstrated stamina and ability to carry out demanding college program, and strong sense of social responsibility important. Any 2 SAT Subject Tests required. Interview with alumnus/alumna required of all applicants if possible; documentation of special talents encouraged.

High school preparation. College-preparatory program recommended. Recommended units include English 4, mathematics 4, social studies 3, history 2, science 4 and foreign language 4. Applicants encouraged to take rigorous courses and make the most of any opportunities for enrichment.

2011-2012 Annual costs. Tuition/fees: $39,849. Room/board: $12,801.

2010-2011 Financial aid. All financial aid based on need. 1,191 full-time freshmen applied for aid; 1,053 were judged to have need; 1,053 of these received aid. Average need met was 100%. Average scholarship/grant was $42,229. 93% of total undergraduate aid awarded as scholarships/grants, 7% as loans/jobs. **Additional information:** Institution meets full need of all admitted students. Aid includes no loans; home equity and retirement excluded from need analysis; families with incomes below $60,000 have zero parent contribution; $60,000 to $180,000 and standard assets have reduced parent expectations, on average 0-10% of income.

Application procedures. Admission: Closing date 1/1 (postmark date). $75 fee, may be waived for applicants with need. Admission notification by 4/1. Must reply by 5/1. **Financial aid:** Closing date 2/1. FAFSA, CSS PROFILE required. Applicants notified by 4/1; must reply by 5/1 or within 2 week(s) of notification.

Academics. Require 12 one-term courses for completion of major and 32 one-term courses for graduation. **Special study options:** Accelerated study, cross-registration, double major, exchange student, honors, independent study, internships, student-designed major, study abroad, teacher certification program. **Credit/placement by examination:** AP, CLEP, IB, institutional tests. SAT Subject Test policy varies depending on subject matter and score. Sophomore standing available on basis of 4 AP exams with qualifying scores,

or on basis of IB scores. Students with fewer than 4 AP qualifying scores eligible for placement in more challenging courses. **Support services:** Learning center, study skills assistance, tutoring, writing center.

Majors. Area/ethnic studies: African-American, East Asian, Near/Middle Eastern, women's. **Biology:** General, biochemistry, evolutionary, neurobiology/anatomy. **Computer sciences:** Computer science. **Conservation:** Environmental studies. **Engineering:** Engineering science. **English:** English lit. **Foreign languages:** Ancient Greek, classics, comparative lit, German, Latin, linguistics, Romance, Sanskrit, Slavic. **History:** General, science/technology. **Liberal arts:** Arts/sciences. **Math:** General, applied, statistics. **Philosophy/ religion:** Philosophy, religion. **Physical sciences:** Chemistry, geology, molecular physics, physics. **Psychology:** General. **Social sciences:** General, anthropology, economics, political science, sociology. **Visual/performing arts:** General, art history/conservation, music.

Most popular majors. Biology 13%, history 10%, mathematics 6%, physical sciences 6%, psychology 6%, social sciences 35%.

Computing on campus. 605 workstations in dormitories, library, computer center. Dormitories wired for high-speed internet access and linked to campus network. Commuter students can connect to campus network. Online course registration, online library, helpline, repair service, student web hosting, wireless network available.

Student life. Freshman orientation: Mandatory. Preregistration for classes offered. Week-long program in early September. **Housing:** Guaranteed on-campus for all undergraduates. Coed dorms, special housing for disabled, apartments, cooperative housing available. All freshmen live together. Other students and some faculty members reside in 13 on-campus houses, self-contained communities offering seminars and tutorials. **Activities:** Bands, campus ministries, choral groups, dance, drama, film society, international student organizations, literary magazine, music ensembles, Model UN, musical theater, opera, radio station, student government, student newspaper, symphony orchestra, TV station, over 320 official clubs available.

Athletics. NCAA. **Intercollegiate:** Baseball M, basketball, cross-country, diving, fencing, field hockey W, football (tackle) M, golf, ice hockey, lacrosse, rowing (crew), sailing, skiing, soccer, softball W, squash, swimming, tennis, track and field, volleyball, water polo, wrestling M. **Intramural:** Basketball, cross-country, fencing, football (non-tackle), ice hockey, rowing (crew), soccer, softball, squash, swimming, table tennis, tennis, volleyball. **Team name:** Crimson.

Student services. Alcohol/substance abuse counseling, chaplain/spiritual director, career counseling, services for economically disadvantaged, student employment services, financial aid counseling, health services, on-campus daycare, personal counseling, placement for graduates, women's services. **Physically disabled:** Services for visually, speech, hearing impaired.

Contact. E-mail: college@fas.harvard.edu
Phone: (617) 495-1551 Fax: (617) 495-8821
William Fitzsimmons, Dean of Admissions, Harvard College, 86 Brattle Street, Cambridge, MA 02138

Hellenic College/Holy Cross
Brookline, Massachusetts
www.hchc.edu

CB member
CB code: 3449

- Private 4-year liberal arts and seminary college affiliated with Eastern Orthodox Church
- Residential campus in large town
- 99 degree-seeking undergraduates: 38% women, 2% Hispanic American, 8% international
- 135 degree-seeking graduate students
- 81% of applicants admitted
- SAT or ACT (ACT writing optional), application essay, interview required

General. Founded in 1937. Regionally accredited. **Degrees:** 15 bachelor's awarded; master's offered. **Location:** 5 miles from downtown Boston. **Calendar:** Semester, limited summer session. **Full-time faculty:** 13 total; 85% have terminal degrees, 54% women. **Part-time faculty:** 23 total; 35% have terminal degrees, 35% women. **Class size:** 49% < 20, 51% 20-39.

Freshman class profile. 64 applied, 52 admitted, 38 enrolled.

Mid 50% test scores			
SAT critical reading:	400-700	GPA 3.50-3.74:	17%
SAT math:	390-750	GPA 3.0-3.49:	34%
SAT writing:	390-640	GPA 2.0-2.99:	38%
ACT composite:	20-23	Out-of-state:	90%
GPA 3.75 or higher:	11%	Live on campus:	95%

Basis for selection. High school achievement, GPA, 2 recommendations from instructors, test scores very important, school and community activities also important. For religious studies majors, 2 letters from clergy important if members of Orthodox Christian Church. **Home schooled:** Transcript of courses and grades, state high school equivalency certificate required.

High school preparation. 15 units required. Required units include English 4, mathematics 2, social studies 2, history 2, science 3 and foreign language 2.

2011-2012 Annual costs. Tuition/fees: $20,450. Room/board: $12,740. Books/supplies: $1,500. Personal expenses: $1,500.

2010-2011 Financial aid. All financial aid based on need. 39 full-time freshmen applied for aid; 39 were judged to have need; 39 of these received aid. Average need met was 60%. Average scholarship/grant was $15,300; average loan $4,500. 75% of total undergraduate aid awarded as scholarships/ grants, 25% as loans/jobs.

Application procedures. Admission: Priority date 5/1; deadline 8/15 (receipt date). $50 fee, may be waived for applicants with need. Admission notification on a rolling basis. Students who apply by December 1 eligible to have application fee waived and receive priority consideration for scholarships; early applications encouraged. **Financial aid:** Closing date 4/1. FAFSA, institutional form required. Applicants notified by 4/1; must reply within 2 week(s) of notification.

Academics. Special study options: Cross-registration, exchange student, honors, independent study, internships, liberal arts/career combination, study abroad. **Credit/placement by examination:** AP, CLEP, IB, institutional tests. Credit granted varies by degree program. **Support services:** Remedial instruction, tutoring.

Majors. Education: Elementary. **Liberal arts:** Arts/sciences. **Psychology:** General. **Theology:** Theology.

Computing on campus. Dormitories linked to campus network. Online library, helpline, repair service, wireless network available.

Student life. Freshman orientation: Mandatory. Preregistration for classes offered. **Policies:** Religious observance required for some students. **Housing:** Guaranteed on-campus for freshmen. Single-sex dorms, apartments available. $300 nonrefundable deposit. **Activities:** Campus ministries, choral groups, dance, music ensembles, student government, several Orthodox groups, prison ministry, missions group.

Athletics. Intramural: Basketball, soccer M, table tennis, tennis, volleyball.

Student services. Chaplain/spiritual director, career counseling, student employment services, financial aid counseling, personal counseling, placement for graduates.

Contact. E-mail: admissions@hchc.edu
Phone: (617) 850-1260 Toll-free number: (866) 424-2338
Fax: (617) 850-1460
Gregory Floor, Director of Admissions, Hellenic College/Holy Cross, 50 Goddard Avenue, Brookline, MA 02445

Lasell College
Newton, Massachusetts
www.lasell.edu

CB member
CB code: 3481

- Private 4-year business and liberal arts college
- Residential campus in small city
- 1,523 degree-seeking undergraduates: 1% part-time, 64% women, 7% African American, 3% Asian American, 8% Hispanic American, 2% international
- 216 graduate students
- 74% of applicants admitted
- SAT or ACT (ACT writing optional), application essay required
- 46% graduate within 6 years

General. Founded in 1851. Regionally accredited. **Degrees:** 271 bachelor's awarded; master's offered. **Location:** 8 miles from Boston. **Calendar:** Semester, limited summer session. **Full-time faculty:** 74 total; 69% have terminal degrees, 15% minority, 69% women. **Part-time faculty:** 138 total; 36% have terminal degrees, 4% minority, 56% women. **Class size:** 70% < 20, 30% 20-39. **Special facilities:** Community-based learning center, art and cultural center with historic clothing collection, center for research on aging and intergenerational studies, institute for values and public life, technology for learning center, child study centers.

Freshman class profile. 2,867 applied, 2,125 admitted, 375 enrolled.

Mid 50% test scores			
SAT critical reading:	440-530	GPA 3.0-3.49:	21%
SAT math:	450-540	GPA 2.0-2.99:	62%
SAT writing:	430-530	Return as sophomores:	64%
ACT composite:	19-22	Out-of-state:	53%
GPA 3.75 or higher:	6%	Live on campus:	88%
GPA 3.50-3.74:	9%	International:	3%

Basis for selection. GPA, curriculum, class rank, interview, recommendations, extracurricular activities, personal essay, and standardized test scores considered. Interview recommended. **Home schooled:** Transcript of courses and grades, letter of recommendation (nonparent) required.

High school preparation. College-preparatory program required. 15 units required; 21 recommended. Required and recommended units include English 4, mathematics 3-4, social studies 2-3, history 2-3, science 2-3 (laboratory 2) and foreign language 2.

2012-2013 Annual costs. Tuition/fees (projected): $29,000. Room/board: $12,300. Books/supplies: $1,000. Personal expenses: $2,000.

2010-2011 Financial aid. Need-based: 371 full-time freshmen applied for aid; 333 were judged to have need; 333 of these received aid. Average need met was 65%. Average scholarship/grant was $16,438; average loan $3,387. 64% of total undergraduate aid awarded as scholarships/grants, 36% as loans/jobs. **Non-need-based:** Awarded to 390 full-time undergraduates, including 392 freshmen. Scholarships awarded for academics, alumni affiliation.

Application procedures. Admission: Priority date 3/15; deadline 9/1 (postmark date). $40 fee, may be waived for applicants with need, free for online applicants. Admission notification on a rolling basis beginning on or about 12/1. Must reply by May 1 or within 2 week(s) if notified thereafter. Length of deferment after admission is limited to 1 year. **Financial aid:** Priority date 3/1; no closing date. FAFSA, institutional form required. Applicants notified on a rolling basis starting 2/15; must reply by 5/1 or within 2 week(s) of notification.

Academics. Free tutoring available in all academic subjects. **Special study options:** Double major, honors, independent study, internships, liberal arts/career combination, student-designed major, study abroad, teacher certification program, Washington semester. **Credit/placement by examination:** AP, CLEP, IB, SAT, ACT, institutional tests. **Support services:** Learning center, reduced course load, study skills assistance, tutoring.

Majors. Business: Accounting, accounting/business management, accounting/finance, apparel, business admin, entrepreneurial studies, event planning, fashion, finance, hospitality admin, international, management science, marketing. **Communications:** Advertising, digital media, journalism, media studies, public relations, radio/TV, sports. **Conservation:** Environmental studies. **Education:** Early childhood, elementary, English, history, mathematics, secondary. **English:** English lit. **Health services:** Athletic training. **History:** General. **Liberal arts:** Humanities. **Math:** Applied. **Parks/recreation:** Exercise sciences, sports admin. **Protective services:** Law enforcement admin. **Psychology:** General. **Social sciences:** General, sociology. **Visual/performing arts:** Fashion design, graphic design.

Most popular majors. Business/marketing 42%, communications/journalism 10%, health sciences 6%, parks/recreation 9%, visual/performing arts 10%.

Computing on campus. 175 workstations in dormitories, library, computer center, student center. Dormitories wired for high-speed internet access and linked to campus network. Commuter students can connect to campus network. Online course registration, online library, helpline, wireless network available.

Student life. Freshman orientation: Mandatory, $40 fee. Preregistration for classes offered. Two-day sessions held in June prior to Fall enrollment. **Policies:** Freshmen not permitted cars on campus. **Housing:** Guaranteed on-campus for all undergraduates. Coed dorms, single-sex dorms, wellness housing available. $200 nonrefundable deposit, deadline 5/1. Community service special interest housing available. **Activities:** Jazz band, campus ministries, choral groups, dance, drama, international student organizations, literary magazine, music ensembles, musical theater, radio station, student government, student newspaper, Amnesty International, Ninos de Veracruz, multicultural student union, students advocating for equality, fashion and service society, environment club, religious club.

Athletics. NCAA. **Intercollegiate:** Baseball M, basketball, cross-country, field hockey W, lacrosse, soccer, softball W, track and field, volleyball. **Intramural:** Basketball, football (non-tackle), soccer, softball, volleyball. **Team name:** Lasers.

Student services. Alcohol/substance abuse counseling, chaplain/spiritual director, career counseling, student employment services, financial aid counseling, health services, personal counseling, placement for graduates.

Contact. E-mail: info@lasell.edu
Phone: (617) 243-2225 Toll-free number: (888) 527-3554
Fax: (617) 243-2380
James Tweed, Dean of Undergraduate Admission, Lasell College, 1844 Commonwealth Avenue, Newton, MA 02466-2709

Lesley University
Cambridge, Massachusetts
www.lesley.edu

CB member
CB code: 3483

- Private 4-year liberal arts and teachers college
- Residential campus in very large city
- 1,469 degree-seeking undergraduates: 3% part-time, 76% women, 3% African American, 3% Asian American, 6% Hispanic American, 1% Native American, 2% international
- 3,684 degree-seeking graduate students
- 66% of applicants admitted
- SAT or ACT with writing, application essay required
- 47% graduate within 6 years

General. Founded in 1909. Regionally accredited. Lesley University includes 2 undergraduate colleges, Lesley College and The Art Institute of Boston. Main campus in Cambridge. **Degrees:** 367 bachelor's awarded; master's, doctoral offered. **Calendar:** Semester, limited summer session. **Full-time faculty:** 65 total; 86% have terminal degrees, 15% minority, 54% women. **Part-time faculty:** 173 total; 36% have terminal degrees, 56% women. **Class size:** 73% < 20, 27% 20-39, less than 1% 40-49. **Special facilities:** Teaching resources center, media production facility, fine arts studios.

Freshman class profile. 2,763 applied, 1,836 admitted, 367 enrolled.

Mid 50% test scores			
SAT critical reading:	480-590	GPA 2.0-2.99:	46%
SAT math:	460-570	Rank in top quarter:	45%
SAT writing:	480-580	Rank in top tenth:	12%
ACT composite:	21-25	Return as sophomores:	76%
GPA 3.75 or higher:	5%	Out-of-state:	50%
GPA 3.50-3.74:	12%	Live on campus:	88%
GPA 3.0-3.49:	35%	International:	2%

Basis for selection. Primary focus given to academic record, both grades and challenging courses. Test scores, recommendations, interview, community service, leadership experience also considered.

High school preparation. College-preparatory program required. 18 units required; 20 recommended. Required and recommended units include English 4, mathematics 3-4, social studies 1-2, history 1-2, science 3-4 (laboratory 2), foreign language 2 and academic electives 4. 2 units visual/performing arts recommended for some programs in art or expressive therapies.

2012-2013 Annual costs. Tuition/fees (projected): $31,450. Room/board: $13,650. Books/supplies: $700. Personal expenses: $1,580.

2011-2012 Financial aid. Need-based: 311 full-time freshmen applied for aid; 271 were judged to have need; 271 of these received aid. Average need met was 75%. Average scholarship/grant was $14,481; average loan $3,267. 77% of total undergraduate aid awarded as scholarships/grants, 23% as loans/jobs. **Non-need-based:** Scholarships awarded for academics, art, leadership, minority status, state residency.

Application procedures. Admission: Priority date 2/15; no deadline. $50 fee, may be waived for applicants with need, free for online applicants. Admission notification on a rolling basis beginning on or about 1/15. Must reply by May 1 or within 2 week(s) if notified thereafter. **Financial aid:** Priority date 2/15; no closing date. FAFSA required. Applicants notified on a rolling basis starting 2/1.

Academics. Students complete between 450 and 650 hours of significant internship experience that begins freshman year. **Special study options:** Accelerated study, combined bachelor's/graduate degree, cross-registration, distance learning, double major, dual enrollment of high school students, exchange student, honors, independent study, internships, liberal arts/career combination, New York semester, student-designed major, study abroad, teacher certification program, Washington semester. Studio courses. **Credit/placement by examination:** AP, CLEP, IB, SAT, ACT, institutional tests. 16 credit hours maximum toward bachelor's degree. **Support services:** Learning center, pre-admission summer program, reduced course load, study skills assistance, tutoring, writing center.

Majors. **Area/ethnic studies:** American. **Biology:** General. **Business:** Business admin. **Communications technology:** General. **Conservation:** Environmental studies. **Education:** General, art, early childhood, early childhood special, elementary, English, kindergarten/preschool, mathematics, middle, science, secondary, social studies, special ed. **English:** English lit. **Health services:** Art therapy. **Liberal arts:** Arts/sciences. **Math:** General. **Social sciences:** General. **Visual/performing arts:** Art, studio arts. **Work/family studies:** Child development, family studies.

Most popular majors. Business/marketing 6%, English 6%, family/consumer sciences 6%, liberal arts 21%, psychology 20%, visual/performing arts 20%.

Computing on campus. 195 workstations in dormitories, library, computer center, student center. Dormitories wired for high-speed internet access and linked to campus network. Commuter students can connect to campus network. Online course registration, online library, helpline, wireless network available.

Student life. Freshman orientation: Mandatory. Preregistration for classes offered. Begins 1 week prior to start of classes. **Housing:** Coed dorms, single-sex dorms, wellness housing available. $300 nonrefundable deposit, deadline 5/1. Victorian houses and suite-style residences available. **Activities:** Campus ministries, choral groups, dance, drama, international student organizations, literary magazine, musical theater, student government, student newspaper, women for social justice, Hillel, Third Wave women's group, Prism, Students for a Free Tibet, ALANA, Christian Fellowship.

Athletics. NCAA. **Intercollegiate:** Baseball M, basketball, cross-country, soccer, softball W, tennis, track and field M, volleyball. **Team name:** Lynx.

Student services. Adult student services, alcohol/substance abuse counseling, chaplain/spiritual director, career counseling, student employment services, financial aid counseling, health services, minority student services, personal counseling, placement for graduates. **Physically disabled:** Services for visually, speech, hearing impaired.

Contact. E-mail: lcadmissions@lesley.edu
Phone: (617) 349-8800 Toll-free number: (800) 999-1959 ext. 8800
Fax: (617) 349-8810
Deb Kocar, Director of Admissions, Lesley University, 29 Everett Street, Cambridge, MA 02140-2790

Massachusetts College of Art and Design
Boston, Massachusetts   **CB member**
www.massart.edu   **CB code: 3516**

▶ Public 4-year visual arts college
▶ Residential campus in very large city
▶ 1,853 degree-seeking undergraduates: 12% part-time, 67% women, 3% African American, 6% Asian American, 5% Hispanic American, 2% international
▶ 164 degree-seeking graduate students
▶ 64% of applicants admitted
▶ SAT or ACT with writing, application essay required
▶ 68% graduate within 6 years

General. Founded in 1873. Regionally accredited. **Degrees:** 339 bachelor's awarded; master's offered. **Calendar:** Semester, extensive summer session. **Full-time faculty:** 101 total. **Part-time faculty:** 180 total. **Class size:** 82% < 20, 18% 20-39. **Special facilities:** 7 art galleries, foundry, glass furnaces, ceramic kilns, video and film studios, performance and studio spaces, Polaroid 20X24 camera.

Freshman class profile. 1,418 applied, 913 admitted, 313 enrolled.

Mid 50% test scores			
SAT critical reading:	480-600	GPA 3.0-3.49:	43%
SAT math:	480-590	GPA 2.0-2.99:	14%
SAT writing:	490-590	Return as sophomores:	90%
ACT composite:	20-25	Out-of-state:	29%
GPA 3.75 or higher:	20%	Live on campus:	87%
GPA 3.50-3.74:	23%	International:	3%

Basis for selection. Emphasis on portfolio, academic record, essay, test scores, recommendations. 3.0 GPA recommended. For GPA between 2.0 and 2.9, SAT/ACT considered in combination with GPA on sliding scale. Applicants must meet Massachusetts public college admission standards. Portfolio of at least 15 pieces of artwork required. Work may also be submitted in digital or time-based formats. **Home schooled:** Students who earn high school diploma must provide course curriculum that includes evaluations/grades as well as SAT or ACT scores. Students who do not earn high school diploma must submit official GED exam scores. **Learning Disabled:** Testing

may be waived for applicants with professionally certified learning disabilities.

High school preparation. 17 units required. Required units include English 4, mathematics 3, social studies 2, science 3 (laboratory 2), foreign language 2 and academic electives 2. At least 2 additional academic units of computer science, humanities, or visual and performing arts required. Social Studies requirement must include 1 U.S. history course. Foreign language units must be in same language.

2011-2012 Annual costs. Tuition/fees: $9,700; $26,400 out-of-state. Tuition for New England resident students $16,600. Room/board: $12,150. Books/supplies: $2,100. Personal expenses: $1,350.

Financial aid. **Non-need-based:** Scholarships awarded for academics, art, leadership, state residency. **Additional information:** Tuition waiver available to Vietnam veterans.

Application procedures. Admission: Closing date 2/1. $50 fee, may be waived for applicants with need. Admission notification on a rolling basis. Must reply by May, 1 or within 3 week(s) if notified thereafter. **Financial aid:** Priority date 3/1; no closing date. FAFSA required. Applicants notified on a rolling basis starting 3/15; must reply within 3 week(s) of notification.

Academics. Three-year certificates available. **Special study options:** Cross-registration, distance learning, double major, exchange student, independent study, internships, liberal arts/career combination, student-designed major, study abroad. Member of American Independent Colleges of Art and Design (AICAD), College Academic Program Sharing (CAPS), Colleges of the Fenway, and Pro Arts Consortium. Exchange programs available in Holland, England, Germany, Ireland, Italy, France. Study abroad available in Spain, Greece, China, Mexico. **Credit/placement by examination:** AP, CLEP, IB, institutional tests. **Support services:** Pre-admission summer program, reduced course load, remedial instruction, study skills assistance, tutoring.

Majors. Education: Art. **Visual/performing arts:** Art history/conservation, ceramics, cinematography, design, fashion design, fiber arts, film/cinema/video, graphic design, industrial design, metal/jewelry, multimedia, painting, photography, printmaking, sculpture, studio arts.

Most popular majors. Education 8%, visual/performing arts 92%.

Computing on campus. 370 workstations in library, computer center. Dormitories wired for high-speed internet access and linked to campus network. Commuter students can connect to campus network. Online course registration, online library, helpline, wireless network available.

Student life. Freshman orientation: Mandatory. Preregistration for classes offered. **Housing:** Guaranteed on-campus for freshmen. Coed dorms available. $240 nonrefundable deposit, deadline 5/1. **Activities:** Dance, drama, film society, music ensembles, radio station, student government, student newspaper, TV station, minority student organization, gay/lesbian organization, student-run design firm, international student organization, nontraditional student organization.

Athletics. Intramural: Basketball, cross-country, field hockey, football (non-tackle), ice hockey, soccer, softball W, table tennis, tennis, volleyball.

Student services. Adult student services, career counseling, student employment services, health services, personal counseling, placement for graduates, veterans' counselor. **Physically disabled:** Services for visually, hearing impaired.

Contact. E-mail: admissions@massart.edu
Phone: (617) 879-7222 Fax: (617) 879-7250
Karen Townsend, Dean of Admissions, Massachusetts College of Art and Design, 621 Huntington Avenue, Boston, MA 02115-5882

Massachusetts College of Liberal Arts
North Adams, Massachusetts   **CB member**
www.mcla.edu   **CB code: 3521**

▶ Public 4-year liberal arts college
▶ Residential campus in large town
▶ 1,610 degree-seeking undergraduates: 10% part-time, 58% women, 8% African American, 1% Asian American, 6% Hispanic American
▶ 144 degree-seeking graduate students
▶ 67% of applicants admitted
▶ SAT or ACT (ACT writing optional), application essay required
▶ 52% graduate within 6 years

General. Founded in 1894. Regionally accredited. **Degrees:** 354 bachelor's awarded; master's offered. **Location:** 65 miles from Springfield, 130 miles from Boston. **Calendar:** Semester, limited summer session. **Class size:** 66% < 20, 33% 20-39, less than 1% 40-49.

Freshman class profile. 1,698 applied, 1,136 admitted, 308 enrolled.

Mid 50% test scores			
SAT critical reading:	470-560	GPA 2.0-2.99:	48%
SAT math:	460-550	Rank in top quarter:	41%
GPA 3.75 or higher:	11%	Rank in top tenth:	9%
GPA 3.50-3.74:	11%	Return as sophomores:	72%
GPA 3.0-3.49:	30%	Out-of-state:	25%
		Live on campus:	90%

Basis for selection. Secondary school record most important; test scores, essay also important; recommendations, extracurricular activities considered. Interview recommended. **Home schooled:** State high school equivalency certificate required. **Learning Disabled:** Massachusetts law prohibits requiring standardized test scores from students with documented learning disabilities.

High school preparation. College-preparatory program required. 16 units required. Required units include English 4, mathematics 3, science 3 (laboratory 2), foreign language 2 and academic electives 2.

2011-2012 Annual costs. Tuition/fees: $8,250; $17,195 out-of-state. Room/board: $8,658.

2011-2012 Financial aid. Need-based: 294 full-time freshmen applied for aid; 231 were judged to have need; 229 of these received aid. Average need met was 88%. Average scholarship/grant was $7,068; average loan $3,292. 41% of total undergraduate aid awarded as scholarships/grants, 59% as loans/jobs. **Non-need-based:** Awarded to 266 full-time undergraduates, including 99 freshmen. Scholarships awarded for academics, art, leadership, minority status, music/drama.

Application procedures. Admission: Priority date 3/1; no deadline. $35 fee, may be waived for applicants with need. Admission notification on a rolling basis beginning on or about 12/15. Must reply by May 1 or within 2 week(s) if notified thereafter. **Financial aid:** Priority date 3/1; no closing date. FAFSA, institutional form required. Applicants notified on a rolling basis starting 3/1; must reply by 5/1 or within 2 week(s) of notification.

Academics. Special study options: Accelerated study, combined bachelor's/graduate degree, cross-registration, distance learning, double major, dual enrollment of high school students, exchange student, honors, independent study, internships, liberal arts/career combination, semester at sea, student-designed major, study abroad, teacher certification program, Washington semester. **Credit/placement by examination:** AP, CLEP, IB, SAT, institutional tests. **Support services:** Learning center, pre-admission summer program, reduced course load, remedial instruction, study skills assistance, tutoring, writing center.

Majors. Biology: General, biotechnology. **Business:** Accounting, business admin, entrepreneurial studies, international, management information systems, marketing. **Communications:** General, broadcast journalism, journalism, persuasive communications. **Computer sciences:** General. **Conservation:** Environmental studies. **Education:** General. **English:** Creative writing, English lit, general lit, technical writing, writing. **Health services:** Athletic training, cytotechnology, premedicine, prephysical therapy. **History:** General. **Human services:** Public policy. **Liberal arts:** Arts/sciences. **Math:** General. **Philosophy/religion:** Philosophy. **Physical sciences:** Chemistry, physics. **Psychology:** General. **Social sciences:** Political science, sociology. **Visual/performing arts:** General, art, music, studio arts management, theater arts management.

Most popular majors. Biology 6%, business/marketing 20%, English 20%, interdisciplinary studies 10%, psychology 8%, social sciences 14%, visual/performing arts 8%.

Computing on campus. PC or laptop required. 140 workstations in dormitories, library, computer center, student center. Dormitories wired for high-speed internet access and linked to campus network. Commuter students can connect to campus network. Online course registration, helpline, wireless network available.

Student life. Freshman orientation: Mandatory, $75 fee. Preregistration for classes offered. **Policies:** Freshmen not permitted cars on campus. **Housing:** Guaranteed on-campus for all undergraduates. Coed dorms, special housing for disabled, wellness housing available. $100 nonrefundable deposit. **Activities:** Bands, choral groups, dance, drama, international student organizations, literary magazine, music ensembles, musical theater, radio station, student government, student newspaper, TV station, interfaith association, Campus Christian Fellowship, Jewish student organization, Newman club, gay and lesbian student society, multicultural society.

Athletics. NCAA. **Intercollegiate:** Baseball M, basketball, cross-country, golf M, soccer, softball W, tennis, volleyball W. **Intramural:** Basketball, bowling, equestrian, football (non-tackle), soccer, softball, swimming, tennis, volleyball, water polo M. **Team name:** Trailblazers.

Student services. Adult student services, alcohol/substance abuse counseling, career counseling, services for economically disadvantaged, student employment services, financial aid counseling, health services, minority student services, personal counseling, placement for graduates, veterans' counselor, women's services. **Physically disabled:** Services for visually, hearing impaired.

Contact. E-mail: admissions@mcla.edu
Phone: (413) 662-5410 Toll-free number: (800) 969-6252
Fax: (413) 662-5179
Steve King, Assistant Dean, Director of Admission and Student Records, Massachusetts College of Liberal Arts, 375 Church Street, North Adams, MA 01247

Massachusetts College of Pharmacy and Health Sciences

Boston, Massachusetts — CB member
www.mcphs.edu — CB code: 3512

- Private 4-year health science and pharmacy college
- Commuter campus in very large city
- 3,205 degree-seeking undergraduates: 4% part-time, 69% women, 5% African American, 27% Asian American, 3% Hispanic American, 5% international
- 2,086 degree-seeking graduate students
- 80% of applicants admitted
- SAT or ACT (ACT writing optional), application essay required
- 69% graduate within 6 years

General. Founded in 1823. Regionally accredited. Member of Fenway College Consortium, 14-college library consortium, Worcester Consortium, and Manchester Area College Consortium. Students have access to Harvard Medical School library. Accelerated PharmD program available at Worcester campus and Manchester campus; Physician Assistant program and Nursing also offered at Boston, Manchester, and Worcester campuses. **Degrees:** 390 bachelor's awarded; master's, professional, doctoral offered. **ROTC:** Army, Naval, Air Force. **Calendar:** Semester, limited summer session. **Full-time faculty:** 206 total; 85% have terminal degrees, 65% women. **Part-time faculty:** 4 total; 100% have terminal degrees, 75% women. **Class size:** 24% < 20, 47% 20-39, 9% 40-49, 9% 50-99, 11% >100. **Special facilities:** Pharmacy practice lab, dental hygiene clinic, patient assessment lab, nursing skills and technology lab.

Freshman class profile. 4,692 applied, 3,733 admitted, 818 enrolled.

Mid 50% test scores			
SAT critical reading:	460-550	GPA 3.0-3.49:	38%
SAT math:	500-590	GPA 2.0-2.99:	24%
SAT writing:	470-560	Return as sophomores:	83%
ACT composite:	21-24	Out-of-state:	43%
GPA 3.75 or higher:	20%	Live on campus:	78%
GPA 3.50-3.74:	18%	International:	8%

Basis for selection. School academic record most important, with emphasis on math and science courses. Student's interest, aptitude for pharmacy and allied health fields considered. **Home schooled:** Require documentation of curriculum and program of study; equivalency exam. **Learning Disabled:** Must submit documents to Academic Support Services.

High school preparation. College-preparatory program required. 16 units required. Required units include English 4, mathematics 3, social studies 1, history 1, science 2 (laboratory 2) and academic electives 5.

2011-2012 Annual costs. Tuition/fees: $26,460. Room/board: $12,850. Books/supplies: $890. Personal expenses: $2,222.

2010-2011 Financial aid. Need-based: 678 full-time freshmen applied for aid; 627 were judged to have need; 627 of these received aid. Average need met was 47%. Average scholarship/grant was $10,797; average loan $6,289. 59% of total undergraduate aid awarded as scholarships/grants, 41% as loans/jobs. **Non-need-based:** Awarded to 388 full-time undergraduates, including 114 freshmen. Scholarships awarded for academics.

Application procedures. Admission: Priority date 2/1; no deadline. No application fee. Admission notification on a rolling basis beginning on or about 2/15. Must reply by May 1 or within 2 week(s) if notified thereafter. **Financial aid:** Priority date 3/15; no closing date. FAFSA required. Applicants notified on a rolling basis.

through continuing education division only. **Special study options:** Accelerated study, combined bachelor's/graduate degree, cooperative education, cross-registration, double major, dual enrollment of high school students, ESL, honors, independent study, internships, liberal arts/career combination, student-designed major, study abroad, teacher certification program, Washington semester. 5-year combined BA/BS program. **Credit/placement by examination:** AP, CLEP, IB, institutional tests. **Support services:** Learning center, reduced course load, remedial instruction, study skills assistance, tutoring, writing center.

Majors. Biology: General, biochemistry. **Business:** Accounting, business admin, finance, international, marketing. **Communications:** Communications/speech/rhetoric. **Computer sciences:** Computer science, information technology. **Conservation:** Environmental studies. **Education:** Biology, chemistry, elementary, English, history, mathematics, middle, multi-level teacher, science, secondary, social studies. **Engineering:** General, civil, computer, electrical. **English:** English lit. **Foreign languages:** French, Romance, Spanish. **Health services:** Athletic training. **History:** General. **Liberal arts:** Arts/sciences. **Math:** General. **Philosophy/religion:** Philosophy, religion. **Physical sciences:** Chemistry, physics. **Protective services:** Law enforcement admin. **Psychology:** General. **Social sciences:** Economics, political science, sociology. **Visual/performing arts:** Studio arts.

Most popular majors. Biology 6%, business/marketing 32%, liberal arts 6%, psychology 7%, social sciences 11%.

Computing on campus. Dormitories wired for high-speed internet access and linked to campus network. Online course registration, online library, helpline, repair service, wireless network available.

Student life. Freshman orientation: Mandatory. Preregistration for classes offered. Two-day June sessions and 3-day August pre-class orientation. **Policies:** All residence halls are drug-free. **Housing:** Guaranteed on-campus for freshmen. Coed dorms, special housing for disabled, apartments, wellness housing available. Townhouses for upperclassmen. Applications accepted from groups of students for theme housing in townhouses. Austin Scholars residential program available to selected students. **Activities:** Bands, campus ministries, choral groups, dance, drama, film society, international student organizations, music ensembles, Model UN, musical theater, student government, student newspaper, TV station, Democrats club, Republicans club, ALANA (Asian, Latino, African, Native American Affairs), Best Buddies, justice & peace coalition, Friends coalition.

Athletics. NCAA. **Intercollegiate:** Baseball M, basketball, cross-country, field hockey W, football (tackle) M, golf W, ice hockey M, lacrosse, rowing (crew) W, soccer, softball W, tennis, track and field, volleyball W. **Intramural:** Basketball, football (non-tackle) M, ice hockey, soccer, softball, volleyball. **Team name:** Warriors.

Student services. Adult student services, alcohol/substance abuse counseling, chaplain/spiritual director, career counseling, student employment services, financial aid counseling, health services, minority student services, personal counseling, placement for graduates. **Physically disabled:** Services for visually, speech impaired.

Contact. E-mail: admission@merrimack.edu
Phone: (978) 837-5000 ext. 5100 Fax: (978) 837-5133
Mark Barrett, Dean of Admissions, Merrimack College, 315 Turnpike Street, North Andover, MA 01845

Montserrat College of Art
Beverly, Massachusetts

CB member
CB code: 9101

www.montserrat.edu

- Private 4-year visual arts college
- Residential campus in large town
- 390 degree-seeking undergraduates: 73% women, 2% African American, 4% Hispanic American, 1% international
- 79% of applicants admitted
- Application essay required
- 49% graduate within 6 years

General. Founded in 1970. Regionally accredited. **Degrees:** 62 bachelor's awarded. **Location:** 18 miles from Boston. **Calendar:** Semester, limited summer session. **Full-time faculty:** 19 total; 74% have terminal degrees, 5% minority, 47% women. **Part-time faculty:** 58 total; 74% have terminal degrees, 12% minority, 55% women. **Class size:** 87% < 20, 13% 20-39. **Special facilities:** Computer design laboratories, college-operated galleries, 2 student-operated galleries.

Freshman class profile. 404 applied, 320 admitted, 129 enrolled.

Mid 50% test scores			
SAT critical reading:	470-590	GPA 2.0-2.99:	46%
SAT math:	440-530	End year in good standing:	83%
GPA 3.75 or higher:	5%	Return as sophomores:	79%
GPA 3.50-3.74:	16%	Out-of-state:	58%
GPA 3.0-3.49:	26%	Live on campus:	95%

Basis for selection. Visual art portfolio most important. High school record, interview, artist statement, and letters of recommendation required of BFA applicants. If personal visit is impractical, portfolio in digital or slide form may be sent; follow-up telephone interview will be conducted. SAT or ACT required for applicants with GED. Interview recommended; portfolio required. **Home schooled:** Transcript of courses and grades, state high school equivalency certificate, letter of recommendation (nonparent) required. Must take SAT/ACT and successfully pass GED. **Learning Disabled:** Official documentation of disability and any previous accommodation plans required if accommodation requested.

High school preparation. College-preparatory program recommended. Recommended units include English 4, social studies 2, history 2 and visual/performing arts 2. Visual arts courses including drawing recommended.

2012-2013 Annual costs. Tuition/fees (projected): $26,600. Room only: $7,300. Books/supplies: $1,200. Personal expenses: $1,300.

2011-2012 Financial aid. Need-based: Average need met was 32%. Average scholarship/grant was $10,315; average loan $3,277. 60% of total undergraduate aid awarded as scholarships/grants, 40% as loans/jobs. **Non-need-based:** Scholarships awarded for academics, art.

Application procedures. Admission: Priority date 2/15; no deadline. $50 fee, may be waived for applicants with need. Admission notification on a rolling basis beginning on or about 12/15. Must reply by May 1 or within 3 week(s) if notified thereafter. **Financial aid:** Priority date 3/1; no closing date. FAFSA, institutional form required. Applicants notified on a rolling basis starting 3/1; must reply by 5/1 or within 2 week(s) of notification.

Academics. In addition to frequent class critiques, students' work is reviewed by faculty panel in semester-end evaluations. **Special study options:** Cross-registration, double major, dual enrollment of high school students, exchange student, independent study, internships, New York semester, student-designed major, study abroad, teacher certification program. Summer study abroad opportunities in Italy and Japan; winter study abroad opportunities in Africa and Puerto Rico; on-campus summer and winter session classes available. **Credit/placement by examination:** AP, CLEP, IB. **Support services:** Learning center, pre-admission summer program, reduced course load, remedial instruction, study skills assistance, tutoring, writing center.

Majors. Communications technology: Animation/special effects. **Visual/performing arts:** Art, crafts, design, drawing, graphic design, illustration, multimedia, painting, photography, printmaking, sculpture, studio arts.

Computing on campus. 158 workstations in dormitories, library, computer center, student center. Dormitories wired for high-speed internet access. Online library, helpline, wireless network available.

Student life. Freshman orientation: Mandatory, $100 fee. Preregistration for classes offered. **Policies:** Student Handbook policies enforced. Freshmen not permitted cars on campus. **Housing:** Coed dorms, single-sex dorms, wellness housing available. $275 nonrefundable deposit, deadline 5/1. **Activities:** Dance, drama, music ensembles, student government, student newspaper, Food Not Bombs, community service corp, Student Voice, Intervarsity, Big Table Talks.

Athletics. Intramural: Basketball, football (tackle).

Student services. Adult student services, alcohol/substance abuse counseling, career counseling, student employment services, financial aid counseling, health services, personal counseling, placement for graduates. **Physically disabled:** Services for visually, speech, hearing impaired.

Contact. E-mail: admissions@montserrat.edu
Phone: (978) 921-4242 ext. 1153
Toll-free number: (800) 836-0487 ext. 1153 Fax: (978) 921-4241
Jeffrey Newell, Director of Admissions, Montserrat College of Art, 23 Essex Street, Beverly, MA 01915

Mount Holyoke College
South Hadley, Massachusetts

CB member
CB code: 3529

www.mtholyoke.edu

- Private 4-year liberal arts college for women
- Residential campus in large town

- 2,317 degree-seeking undergraduates: 1% part-time, 100% women, 6% African American, 7% Asian American, 9% Hispanic American, 23% international
- 10 degree-seeking graduate students
- 51% of applicants admitted
- Application essay required
- 85% graduate within 6 years; 21.2% enter graduate study

General. Founded in 1837. Regionally accredited. Member of 5-college consortium with Amherst College, Hampshire College, Smith College, and University of Massachusetts at Amherst. Member of 12 College Exchange with Amherst College, Bowdoin, Connecticut College, Dartmouth College, O'Neill National Theatre Institute, Smith College, Trinity College, Vassar, Wellesley College, Wesleyan University, Wheaton College, Williams/Mystic Seaport Program in Maritime Studies. **Degrees:** 565 bachelor's awarded; master's offered. **ROTC:** Army, Air Force. **Location:** 10 miles from Springfield; 40 miles from Hartford, CT. **Calendar:** Semester. **Full-time faculty:** 231 total; 93% have terminal degrees, 22% minority, 55% women. **Part-time faculty:** 52 total; 73% have terminal degrees, 12% minority, 56% women. **Class size:** 67% < 20, 26% 20-39, 4% 40-49, 2% 50-99, less than 1% >100. **Special facilities:** Nuclear accelerator, nuclear magnetic resonance equipment, electron microscope, bronze-casting foundry, solar greenhouse, Japanese meditation garden and tea house, equestrian center, language learning center with satellite communication and interactive video, child study center, global initiatives center, greenhouse and botanical garden, leadership and liberal arts center, art museum, center for the environment, observatory, spiritual places.

Freshman class profile. 3,416 applied, 1,759 admitted, 605 enrolled.

Mid 50% test scores			
SAT critical reading:	610-720	GPA 2.0-2.99:	4%
SAT math:	590-700	Rank in top quarter:	88%
SAT writing:	620-710	Rank in top tenth:	57%
ACT composite:	27-31	Return as sophomores:	92%
GPA 3.75 or higher:	44%	Out-of-state:	82%
GPA 3.50-3.74:	26%	Live on campus:	100%
GPA 3.0-3.49:	26%	International:	21%

Basis for selection. Entrance determined by overall record. School record and evaluations most important; special talents, particular goals, and character considered. Personal interview on campus recommended if candidate lives within 200 miles of college, or with alumna admissions representative if applicant resides outside of area. **Home schooled:** Detailed outline of study and SAT Subject Tests or ACT required.

High school preparation. College-preparatory program recommended. Recommended units include English 4, mathematics 4, history 3, science 4 (laboratory 3), foreign language 4 and academic electives 1.

2011-2012 Annual costs. Tuition/fees: $41,456. Room/board: $12,140.

2011-2012 Financial aid. Need-based: 473 full-time freshmen applied for aid; 405 were judged to have need; 405 of these received aid. Average need met was 100%. Average scholarship/grant was $31,950; average loan $3,532. 82% of total undergraduate aid awarded as scholarships/grants, 18% as loans/jobs. **Non-need-based:** Awarded to 254 full-time undergraduates, including 83 freshmen. Scholarships awarded for academics, leadership.

Application procedures. Admission: Closing date 1/15 (postmark date). $60 fee, may be waived for applicants with need, free for online applicants. Admission notification by 4/1. Must reply by 5/1. **Financial aid:** Priority date 2/15, closing date 3/1. FAFSA, CSS PROFILE required. Applicants notified by 4/1; must reply by 5/1.

Academics. Honor system and self-scheduled examinations practiced. All students must complete minor. **Special study options:** Combined bachelor's/graduate degree, cross-registration, double major, ESL, exchange student, independent study, internships, liberal arts/career combination, student-designed major, study abroad, teacher certification program, Washington semester. Community-based learning courses and first-year seminars. **Credit/placement by examination:** AP, CLEP, IB, institutional tests. 32 credit hours maximum toward bachelor's degree. Credit will not satisfy any distribution or language requirement, but may satisfy some prerequisites. **Support services:** Reduced course load, study skills assistance, tutoring, writing center.

Majors. Architecture: Architecture. **Area/ethnic studies:** African-American, Asian, East Asian, European, German, Latin American/Caribbean, Near/Middle Eastern, Russian/Slavic, South Asian. **Biology:** General, biochemistry, neuroscience. **Computer sciences:** Computer science. **Conservation:** Environmental studies. **Education:** General. **English:** English lit. **Foreign languages:** Ancient Greek, classics, French, Italian, Latin, Romance, Spanish. **History:** General. **Math:** General, statistics. **Philosophy/religion:** Philosophy, religion. **Physical sciences:** Astronomy, chemistry, geology, physics. **Psychology:** General. **Social sciences:** Anthropology, economics,

geography, international relations, political science, sociology. **Visual/performing arts:** Art history/conservation, dance, dramatic, film/cinema/video, music, studio arts.

Most popular majors. Biology 10%, English 9%, foreign language 7%, psychology 8%, social sciences 27%, visual/performing arts 7%.

Computing on campus. 447 workstations in dormitories, library, computer center, student center. Dormitories wired for high-speed internet access and linked to campus network. Commuter students can connect to campus network. Online course registration, online library, helpline, repair service, student web hosting, wireless network available.

Student life. Freshman orientation: Available. Preregistration for classes offered. Program held week before start of classes. **Policies:** Smoke-free campus. **Housing:** Guaranteed on-campus for all undergraduates. Special housing for disabled, apartments available. Kosher/halal kitchen available; special accommodations by need. **Activities:** Jazz band, campus ministries, choral groups, dance, drama, film society, international student organizations, literary magazine, music ensembles, Model UN, radio station, student government, student newspaper, symphony orchestra, Amnesty International, American Civil Liberties Union, Multi-Faith Council, Jewish Student Union, Chinese Christian Fellowship, International Club, Bulgarian Club, Best Buddies, Creating Awareness and Unity for Social Equality (CAUSE), Environmental Action Coalition (EAC).

Athletics. NCAA. **Intercollegiate:** Basketball W, cross-country W, diving W, equestrian W, field hockey W, golf W, lacrosse W, rowing (crew) W, soccer W, squash W, swimming W, tennis W, track and field W, volleyball W. **Team name:** Lyons.

Student services. Adult student services, alcohol/substance abuse counseling, chaplain/spiritual director, career counseling, student employment services, financial aid counseling, health services, minority student services, personal counseling, placement for graduates, veterans' counselor, women's services. **Physically disabled:** Services for visually, speech, hearing impaired.

Contact. E-mail: admission@mtholyoke.edu
Phone: (413) 538-2023 Fax: (413) 538-2409
Diane Anci, Vice President for Enrollment and College Relations/Dean of Admissions, Mount Holyoke College, Newhall Center, South Hadley, MA 01075-1488

Mount Ida College
Newton, Massachusetts
www.mountida.edu

CB member
CB code: 3530

- Private 4-year business and liberal arts college
- Residential campus in small city
- 1,449 degree-seeking undergraduates: 6% part-time, 66% women, 15% African American, 2% Asian American, 8% Hispanic American, 4% international
- 20 degree-seeking graduate students
- 75% of applicants admitted
- SAT or ACT (ACT writing recommended) required
- 38% graduate within 6 years

General. Founded in 1899. Regionally accredited. **Degrees:** 216 bachelor's, 42 associate awarded; master's offered. **Location:** 8 miles from downtown Boston. **Calendar:** Semester, limited summer session. **Full-time faculty:** 66 total; 54% have terminal degrees, 8% minority, 61% women. **Part-time faculty:** 123 total; 31% have terminal degrees, 11% minority, 54% women. **Class size:** 53% < 20, 45% 20-39, 2% 40-49, less than 1% 50-99. **Special facilities:** Darkroom, blueprint making facility, veterinary kennel and operating facility, dental laboratory, design labs.

Freshman class profile. 1,730 applied, 1,297 admitted, 394 enrolled.

Mid 50% test scores			
SAT critical reading:	380-470	GPA 3.0-3.49:	19%
SAT math:	380-490	GPA 2.0-2.99:	56%
SAT writing:	370-480	Return as sophomores:	64%
ACT composite:	15-19	Out-of-state:	42%
GPA 3.75 or higher:	5%	Live on campus:	85%
GPA 3.50-3.74:	5%	International:	2%

Basis for selection. School record, GPA, recommendations, test scores, and essay most important. Essay or personal statement, campus visit strongly recommended. Interviews may be required.

High school preparation. College-preparatory program recommended. 14 units recommended. Recommended units include English 4, mathematics

3, social studies 2, science 3 (laboratory 3) and foreign language 2. 4 math and 2 physical science strongly recommended for science majors.

2011-2012 Annual costs. Tuition/fees: $25,915. Room/board: $12,500. Books/supplies: $1,000. Personal expenses: $1,200.

Application procedures. Admission: No deadline. $45 fee, may be waived for applicants with need, free for online applicants. Admission notification on a rolling basis beginning on or about 10/1. **Financial aid:** Priority date 4/15; no closing date. FAFSA, institutional form required. Applicants notified on a rolling basis starting 3/1; must reply within 3 week(s) of notification.

Academics. Professionally intensive courses of study coupled with liberal arts requirements. **Special study options:** Distance learning, double major, ESL, honors, independent study, internships, semester at sea, study abroad, teacher certification program. **Credit/placement by examination:** AP, CLEP, IB, institutional tests. **Support services:** Learning center, reduced course load, remedial instruction, study skills assistance, tutoring, writing center.

Majors. Area/ethnic studies: American. **Biology:** General. **Business:** Business admin, fashion, hospitality admin. **Communications technology:** Animation/special effects. **Education:** Early childhood. **English:** English lit. **General:** Equestrian studies. **Health services:** Veterinary technology/assistant. **Liberal arts:** Arts/sciences. **Parks/recreation:** Sports admin. **Protective services:** Criminal justice, forensics. **Psychology:** General. **Visual/performing arts:** Fashion design, graphic design, interior design.

Most popular majors. Business/marketing 30%, communication technologies 6%, health sciences 17%, security/protective services 11%, visual/performing arts 18%.

Computing on campus. 122 workstations in library, computer center. Dormitories wired for high-speed internet access and linked to campus network. Commuter students can connect to campus network. Online library, wireless network available.

Student life. Freshman orientation: Mandatory. Preregistration for classes offered. Held in July. Activities also held prior to first day of class in late August. **Policies:** Freshmen not permitted cars on campus. **Housing:** Guaranteed on-campus for freshmen. Coed dorms, single-sex dorms, special housing for disabled, wellness housing available. $300 partly refundable deposit. **Activities:** Choral groups, dance, drama, international student organizations, literary magazine, radio station, student government, student newspaper, black student achievement coalition, gay/lesbian and everyone else, student association for Latino and Spanish Americans, volunteers in action.

Athletics. NCAA. **Intercollegiate:** Basketball, cheerleading, cross-country, equestrian W, football (tackle) M, lacrosse, soccer, softball W, tennis W, volleyball. **Intramural:** Basketball, football (non-tackle), rugby, soccer. **Team name:** Mustangs.

Student services. Adult student services, alcohol/substance abuse counseling, chaplain/spiritual director, career counseling, services for economically disadvantaged, student employment services, financial aid counseling, health services, minority student services, personal counseling, placement for graduates.

Contact. E-mail: admissions@mountida.edu
Phone: (617) 928-4553 Fax: (617) 928-4507
Maureen Moriarty, Vice President for Enrollment Management and Marketing, Mount Ida College, 777 Dedham Street, Newton, MA 02459

New England Conservatory of Music
Boston, Massachusetts   **CB member**
www.necmusic.edu   **CB code: 3659**

- Private 4-year music college
- Commuter campus in very large city
- 396 degree-seeking undergraduates: 4% part-time, 44% women, 4% African American, 9% Asian American, 6% Hispanic American, 30% international
- 296 degree-seeking graduate students
- 30% of applicants admitted
- Application essay required
- 77% graduate within 6 years

General. Founded in 1867. Regionally accredited. In close proximity to Symphony Hall. Faculty includes members of Boston Symphony Orchestra. **Degrees:** 81 bachelor's awarded; master's, doctoral offered. **Location:** 2 miles from downtown. **Calendar:** Semester, limited summer session. **Full-time

faculty: 94 total; 23% have terminal degrees, 34% women. **Part-time faculty:** 140 total; 5% have terminal degrees, 72% women. **Class size:** 80% < 20, 20% 20-39, less than 1% 50-99. **Special facilities:** Listening library.

Freshman class profile. 1,092 applied, 331 admitted, 93 enrolled.

End year in good standing:	95%	**Live on campus:**	90%
Return as sophomores:	95%	**International:**	30%
Out-of-state:	87%		

Basis for selection. Audition most important, followed by recommendations, high school record, essay. Live or taped auditions required. **Home schooled:** Must provide curriculum overview.

2011-2012 Annual costs. Tuition/fees: $36,700. Room/board: $12,100. Books/supplies: $700. Personal expenses: $2,200.

2011-2012 Financial aid. Need-based: 71 full-time freshmen applied for aid; 58 were judged to have need; 57 of these received aid. Average need met was 56%. Average scholarship/grant was $15,647; average loan $4,215. 63% of total undergraduate aid awarded as scholarships/grants, 37% as loans/jobs. **Non-need-based:** Awarded to 188 full-time undergraduates, including 46 freshmen. Scholarships awarded for academics, music/drama.

Application procedures. Admission: Priority date 12/1; no deadline. $115 fee. Application must be submitted online. Admission notification on a rolling basis beginning on or about 4/1. Must reply by May 1 or within 2 week(s) if notified thereafter. **Financial aid:** Closing date 12/1. FAFSA, institutional form required. Applicants notified by 4/1; must reply by 5/1 or within 2 week(s) of notification.

Academics. Undergraduate diploma available in lieu of bachelor's degree (performance-oriented, with fewer academic requirements). Artist's diploma (professional degree) available for particularly gifted performers. Graduate diploma also available. **Special study options:** Cross-registration, dual enrollment of high school students, ESL, independent study, internships, study abroad. 5-year double degree program with Tufts University; 5-year AB/MM program with Harvard University. **Credit/placement by examination:** AP, CLEP, IB, institutional tests. 12 credit hours maximum toward bachelor's degree. **Support services:** Remedial instruction, tutoring, writing center.

Majors. Visual/performing arts: Brass instruments, jazz, music, music history, music performance, music theory/composition, musicology, percussion instruments, piano/keyboard, stringed instruments, voice/opera, woodwind instruments.

Computing on campus. 83 workstations in library, computer center, student center. Online library, helpline, wireless network available.

Student life. Freshman orientation: Mandatory. Preregistration for classes offered. Held 1 week before start of classes. **Policies:** Freshmen not permitted cars on campus. **Housing:** Guaranteed on-campus for freshmen. Coed dorms available. $525 fully refundable deposit, deadline 5/1. **Activities:** Bands, choral groups, music ensembles, opera, student government, student newspaper, symphony orchestra, Christian Fellowship, feminist and minority student organizations.

Athletics. Team name: Penguins.

Student services. Career counseling, student employment services, financial aid counseling, health services, personal counseling, placement for graduates. **Physically disabled:** Services for visually impaired.

Contact. E-mail: ADMStaff@necmusic.edu
Phone: (617) 585-1101 Fax: (617) 585-1115
Christina Daly, Director of Admissions, New England Conservatory of Music, 290 Huntington Avenue, Boston, MA 02115-5018

New England Institute of Art
Brookline, Massachusetts
www.artinstitutes.edu/boston   **CB code: 3636**

- For-profit 4-year visual arts and technical college
- Commuter campus in very large city
- 1,290 degree-seeking undergraduates
- Application essay, interview required

General. Regionally accredited. **Degrees:** 244 bachelor's, 68 associate awarded. **Calendar:** Semester, extensive summer session. **Full-time faculty:** 49 total. **Part-time faculty:** 110 total. **Class size:** 79% < 20, 19% 20-39, 2% 40-49. **Special facilities:** Audio production studios, drafting rooms, animation studio.

Basis for selection. Essay and interview most important, followed by secondary school record. Class rank, recommendations, test scores considered. Second interview required for audio programs. Portfolio required for Media Arts and Animation program.

2011-2012 Annual costs. Tuition/fees: $23,365. Books/supplies: $1,570. Personal expenses: $2,600.

Financial aid. Non-need-based: Scholarships awarded for academics.

Application procedures. Admission: No deadline. $150 fee. Admission notification on a rolling basis. **Financial aid:** Priority date 5/1; no closing date. FAFSA, institutional form required. Applicants notified on a rolling basis starting 3/1.

Academics. Special study options: Internships. **Credit/placement by examination:** AP, CLEP, institutional tests. **Support services:** Learning center, remedial instruction, study skills assistance, tutoring.

Majors. Business: Fashion. **Communications:** Digital media. **Communications technology:** Graphics, photo/film/video, recording arts. **Computer sciences:** Web page design. **Visual/performing arts:** Commercial/advertising art, fashion design, graphic design, illustration, multimedia.

Computing on campus. Dormitories wired for high-speed internet access. Student web hosting available.

Student life. Freshman orientation: Mandatory. Preregistration for classes offered. Half-day program held prior to start of semester. **Policies:** Student code of conduct. **Housing:** Coed dorms, apartments available. $400 nonrefundable deposit. **Activities:** Film society, literary magazine, radio station, student government.

Student services. Adult student services, alcohol/substance abuse counseling, career counseling, student employment services, financial aid counseling, personal counseling, placement for graduates.

Contact. E-mail: neiaadm@aii.edu
Phone: (617) 739-1700 Toll-free number: (800) 903-4425
Fax: (617) 582-4500
Mary Burne, Senior Director of Admissions, New England Institute of Art, 10 Brookline Place West, Brookline, MA 02445-7295

Newbury College

Brookline, Massachusetts
www.newbury.edu

CB member
CB code: 3639

- Private 4-year business and liberal arts college
- Residential campus in large city
- 1,011 degree-seeking undergraduates: 13% part-time, 58% women
- 61% of applicants admitted
- Application essay required

General. Founded in 1962. Regionally accredited. **Degrees:** 133 bachelor's, 13 associate awarded. **Location:** 3 miles from Boston. **Calendar:** Semester, limited summer session. **Full-time faculty:** 33 total; 12% minority, 42% women. **Part-time faculty:** 77 total; 17% minority, 58% women. **Class size:** 35% < 20, 65% 20-39. **Special facilities:** 7 culinary arts production kitchens, on-campus restaurant open to the public.

Freshman class profile. 4,718 applied, 2,867 admitted, 329 enrolled.

Mid 50% test scores			
SAT critical reading:	340-520	GPA 3.50-3.74:	5%
SAT math:	340-520	GPA 3.0-3.49:	14%
SAT writing:	330-530	GPA 2.0-2.99:	63%
GPA 3.75 or higher:	2%	Out-of-state:	34%
		Live on campus:	61%

Basis for selection. Holistic approach includes application, essay, high school transcript, extra-curricular activities and 2 letters of recommendation. Standardized test scores are optional. Students may submit scores if they believe the results present a fuller picture of their achievements and potential. Students who do not submit scores will not be at any disadvantage in admissions decisions. Interviews recommended. **Home schooled:** Statement describing home school structure and mission, transcript of courses and grades, interview required.

High school preparation. College-preparatory program recommended. Recommended units include English 3, mathematics 3, social studies 3, history 3, science 2, foreign language 2 and computer science 1.

2011-2012 Annual costs. Tuition/fees: $26,600. Room/board: $12,150. Books/supplies: $1,500. Personal expenses: $1,000.

2010-2011 Financial aid. All financial aid based on need. 320 full-time freshmen applied for aid; 310 were judged to have need; 310 of these received aid. Average scholarship/grant was $11,420; average loan $3,500. 86% of total undergraduate aid awarded as scholarships/grants, 14% as loans/jobs.

Application procedures. Admission: Priority date 3/1; no deadline. $25 fee, may be waived for applicants with need, free for online applicants. Admission notification on a rolling basis beginning on or about 10/1. Must reply by May 1 or within 4 week(s) if notified thereafter. **Financial aid:** Priority date 3/1, closing date 5/1. FAFSA required. Applicants notified on a rolling basis starting 3/1; must reply by 5/1 or within 2 week(s) of notification.

Academics. Academic enrichment program available for students entering who demonstrate need for academic support. **Special study options:** Distance learning, double major, honors, independent study, internships, liberal arts/career combination, student-designed major, study abroad, weekend college. **Credit/placement by examination:** AP, CLEP, IB, institutional tests. 30 credit hours maximum toward associate degree, 60 toward bachelor's. **Support services:** Learning center, reduced course load, remedial instruction, study skills assistance, tutoring.

Majors. Business: Accounting, business admin, fashion, hospitality admin, international, marketing. **Communications:** Communications/speech/rhetoric, journalism, media studies. **Computer sciences:** General, computer graphics, computer science. **Health services:** Health care admin. **Protective services:** Law enforcement admin. **Psychology:** General. **Visual/performing arts:** Graphic design, interior design.

Most popular majors. Business/marketing 11%, communications/journalism 9%, personal/culinary services 8%, psychology 8%.

Computing on campus. 105 workstations in dormitories, library, computer center, student center. Dormitories wired for high-speed internet access and linked to campus network. Commuter students can connect to campus network. Online course registration, online library, helpline, repair service, wireless network available.

Student life. Freshman orientation: Mandatory, $150 fee. Preregistration for classes offered. Information sessions and activities held a few days before each semester. **Policies:** Freshmen not permitted cars on campus. **Housing:** Guaranteed on-campus for freshmen. Coed dorms, single-sex dorms available. $250 nonrefundable deposit, deadline 5/1. Summer housing available. **Activities:** Choral groups, dance, drama, international student organizations, radio station, student government, TV station, international student organization, Habitat for Humanity, innkeepers club, business club, radio club, student programming board.

Athletics. NCAA. **Intercollegiate:** Baseball M, basketball, cross-country, golf, soccer, softball W, tennis, volleyball. **Intramural:** Lacrosse. **Team name:** Nighthawks.

Student services. Alcohol/substance abuse counseling, career counseling, student employment services, financial aid counseling, personal counseling, placement for graduates.

Contact. E-mail: admissions@newbury.edu
Phone: (617) 730-7007 Toll-free number: (800) 639-2879
Fax: (617) 731-9618
Joseph Chillo, Vice President for Enrollment Management, Newbury College, 129 Fisher Avenue, Brookline, MA 02445

Nichols College

Dudley, Massachusetts
www.nichols.edu

CB member
CB code: 3666

- Private 4-year business and liberal arts college
- Residential campus in rural community
- 1,298 degree-seeking undergraduates: 13% part-time, 40% women, 5% African American, 2% Asian American, 4% Hispanic American, 1% international
- 189 degree-seeking graduate students
- 78% of applicants admitted
- SAT or ACT (ACT writing recommended), application essay required
- 52% graduate within 6 years

General. Founded in 1815. Regionally accredited. One-credit Professional Development Seminar program required each year; coursework helps with resume writing, building a work portfolio and successful interviewing skills. **Degrees:** 266 bachelor's, 19 associate awarded; master's offered. **ROTC:** Army, Air Force. **Location:** 20 miles from Worcester, 50 miles from Boston. **Calendar:** Semester, limited summer session. **Full-time faculty:** 36 total; 61% have terminal degrees, 6% minority, 33% women. **Part-time faculty:**

General. Founded in 1927. Regionally accredited. College founded by Sisters of St. Joseph of Boston. **Degrees:** 218 bachelor's, 125 associate awarded; master's, professional offered. **ROTC:** Army. **Location:** 12 miles from Boston. **Calendar:** Semester, limited summer session. **Full-time faculty:** 71 total; 76% have terminal degrees, 6% minority, 78% women. **Part-time faculty:** 85 total; 36% have terminal degrees, 12% minority, 71% women. **Class size:** 53% < 20, 44% 20-39, 3% 40-49. **Special facilities:** Philatelic museum, fine arts center, 2 digital imaging studios, music laboratory with electronic keyboards and computers.

Freshman class profile. 2,015 applied, 1,532 admitted, 262 enrolled.

Mid 50% test scores		GPA 2.0-2.99:	58%
SAT critical reading:	410-510	Rank in top quarter:	23%
SAT math:	420-520	Rank in top tenth:	8%
SAT writing:	410-520	End year in good standing:	85%
ACT composite:	16-21	Return as sophomores:	82%
GPA 3.75 or higher:	6%	Out-of-state:	20%
GPA 3.50-3.74:	6%	Live on campus:	89%
GPA 3.0-3.49:	29%	International:	2%

Basis for selection. All credentials within student's file reviewed. At times, interview or additional grades requested or guidance counselors called. Interview highly recommended. **Home schooled:** Statement describing home school structure and mission, transcript of courses and grades, letter of recommendation (nonparent) required. **Learning Disabled:** Should apprise Director of Student Disabilities of disability status and document condition to receive appropriate accommodations.

High school preparation. College-preparatory program recommended. 16 units required. Required and recommended units include English 4, mathematics 3, social studies 2, science 2 (laboratory 1), foreign language 2-3 and academic electives 3. 4 math and 4 science recommended for nursing.

2011-2012 Annual costs. Tuition/fees: $31,785. Room/board: $12,800. Books/supplies: $1,000. Personal expenses: $1,520.

2011-2012 Financial aid. **Need-based:** 251 full-time freshmen applied for aid; 239 were judged to have need; 239 of these received aid. Average need met was 48%. Average scholarship/grant was $14,283; average loan $3,473. 66% of total undergraduate aid awarded as scholarships/grants, 34% as loans/jobs. **Non-need-based:** Awarded to 620 full-time undergraduates, including 189 freshmen. Scholarships awarded for academics, alumni affiliation, leadership, religious affiliation, ROTC. **Additional information:** Family tuition discount scholarship; offered during any semester in which 2 or more unmarried, dependent siblings attend full-time.

Application procedures. **Admission:** Priority date 2/15; deadline 6/1 (postmark date). $50 fee, may be waived for applicants with need. Admission notification on a rolling basis beginning on or about 12/20. Must reply by May 1 or within 2 week(s) if notified thereafter. Students encouraged to apply by January 1. **Financial aid:** Priority date 2/15; no closing date. FAFSA, institutional form required. Applicants notified on a rolling basis starting 3/15; must reply by 5/1 or within 2 week(s) of notification.

Academics. Online tutoring assistance, professional math and writing tutor, and academic skills workshops available. **Special study options:** Accelerated study, combined bachelor's/graduate degree, cross-registration, double major, dual enrollment of high school students, ESL, exchange student, honors, independent study, internships, student-designed major, study abroad, teacher certification program, Washington semester. **Credit/placement by examination:** AP, CLEP, IB, SAT, ACT, institutional tests. 24 credit hours maximum toward bachelor's degree. **Support services:** Learning center, reduced course load, remedial instruction, study skills assistance, tutoring, writing center.

Majors. Biology: General, biochemistry. **Business:** General. **Communications:** Communications/speech/rhetoric. **Education:** Mathematics. **English:** English lit. **Foreign languages:** Spanish. **Health services:** Nursing (RN). **History:** General. **Human services:** Social work. **Liberal arts:** Arts/sciences. **Parks/recreation:** Health/fitness. **Physical sciences:** Chemistry. **Psychology:** General. **Social sciences:** International relations, political science, sociology.

Most popular majors. Biology 8%, business/marketing 11%, communications/journalism 7%, health sciences 50%, social sciences 6%.

Computing on campus. 196 workstations in library, computer center. Dormitories wired for high-speed internet access and linked to campus network. Commuter students can connect to campus network. Online course registration, online library, helpline, wireless network available.

Student life. Freshman orientation: Mandatory, $195 fee. Preregistration for classes offered. Two-day summer session and 2-day fall session during opening weekend. **Policies:** Must complete series of effective decision-making courses in order to obtain guest privileges. All residences smoke-free. **Housing:** Guaranteed on-campus for all undergraduates. Coed dorms, single-sex dorms, special housing for disabled, wellness housing available. $450 nonrefundable deposit, deadline 5/1. Quiet floors available. **Activities:**

Campus ministries, choral groups, dance, drama, international student organizations, literary magazine, music ensembles, Model UN, musical theater, radio station, student government, Asian American organization, African American organization, Hispanic organization, Asian organization, Native American organization, student organization for Latino culture, campus activities board, student government association, student athletic advisory committee.

Athletics. NCAA. **Intercollegiate:** Basketball, diving, field hockey W, lacrosse, soccer, softball W, swimming, tennis, track and field, volleyball. **Intramural:** Basketball, soccer, softball. **Team name:** Regis Pride.

Student services. Adult student services, alcohol/substance abuse counseling, chaplain/spiritual director, career counseling, services for economically disadvantaged, student employment services, financial aid counseling, health services, minority student services, on-campus daycare, personal counseling, placement for graduates, veterans' counselor. **Physically disabled:** Services for visually, hearing impaired.

Contact. E-mail: admission@regiscollege.edu
Phone: (781) 768-7100 Toll-free number: (866) 438-7344
Fax: (781) 768-7071
Wanda Suriel, Director of Admission, Regis College, 235 Wellesley Street, Weston, MA 02493-1571

Salem State University
Salem, Massachusetts — CB member
www.salemstate.edu/ — CB code: 3522

- Public 4-year university
- Commuter campus in large town
- 7,136 degree-seeking undergraduates: 18% part-time, 61% women, 8% African American, 3% Asian American, 9% Hispanic American, 3% international
- 1,402 degree-seeking graduate students
- 67% of applicants admitted
- SAT or ACT (ACT writing optional) required
- 42% graduate within 6 years

General. Founded in 1854. Regionally accredited. **Degrees:** 1,330 bachelor's awarded; master's offered. **ROTC:** Army, Air Force. **Location:** 15 miles from Boston. **Calendar:** Semester, extensive summer session. **Full-time faculty:** 337 total; 54% women. **Part-time faculty:** 424 total; 60% women. **Class size:** 59% < 20, 39% 20-39, 1% 40-49, less than 1% 50-99. **Special facilities:** Media facility, center for creative and performing arts, observatories, glass blowing studio.

Freshman class profile. 4,760 applied, 3,193 admitted, 1,005 enrolled.

Mid 50% test scores		GPA 3.0-3.49:	34%
SAT critical reading:	450-550	GPA 2.0-2.99:	44%
SAT math:	450-540	Return as sophomores:	73%
GPA 3.75 or higher:	11%	Live on campus:	67%
GPA 3.50-3.74:	11%	International:	1%

Basis for selection. Students with 3.0 GPA and college prep curriculum admitted. Students with less than 3.0 GPA admitted with balancing SAT/ACT scores. Special consideration possible. Some majors require higher GPA. Recommendations considered. Portfolio required for art applicants. Audition required for music applicants. **Home schooled:** State high school equivalency certificate required.

High school preparation. College-preparatory program required. Required and recommended units include English 4, mathematics 3, social studies 2-3, history 2, science 3 (laboratory 2), foreign language 2, computer science 1 and visual/performing arts 1. Additional requirements for some programs.

2011-2012 Annual costs. Tuition/fees: $7,670; $13,810 out-of-state. Room/board: $10,010. Books/supplies: $900. Personal expenses: $1,938.

Financial aid. **Non-need-based:** Scholarships awarded for academics.

Application procedures. **Admission:** Priority date 3/1; deadline 4/15 (postmark date). $75 fee. Admission notification on a rolling basis beginning on or about 12/1. Must reply by May 1 or within 2 week(s) if notified thereafter. **Financial aid:** Priority date 3/1, closing date 9/1. FAFSA required. Applicants notified on a rolling basis starting 3/15; must reply within 2 week(s) of notification.

Academics. Reading lab available. **Special study options:** Accelerated study, combined bachelor's/graduate degree, cooperative education, cross-registration, distance learning, double major, dual enrollment of high school

students, ESL, honors, independent study, internships, semester at sea, student-designed major, study abroad, teacher certification program, Washington semester. **Credit/placement by examination:** AP, CLEP, SAT, institutional tests. **Support services:** Learning center, pre-admission summer program, reduced course load, remedial instruction, tutoring, writing center.

Majors. Biology: General, biochemistry, ecology, marine. **Business:** Accounting, accounting/finance, business admin, entrepreneurial studies, finance, hospitality admin, human resources, international, management information systems, managerial economics, marketing, tourism/travel. **Communications:** Advertising, communications/speech/rhetoric, journalism, media studies, public relations. **Computer sciences:** General. **Education:** General, early childhood, elementary, middle, physical, secondary, Spanish. **English:** Creative writing, English lit, technical writing, writing. **Foreign languages:** Comparative lit, Spanish, translation. **Health services:** Athletic training, clinical lab science, nuclear medical technology, nursing (RN). **History:** General, American, applied, European. **Human services:** Social work. **Liberal arts:** Arts/sciences. **Math:** General. **Parks/recreation:** General, exercise sciences, health/fitness, sports admin. **Physical sciences:** Chemistry, geology. **Protective services:** Fire services admin, law enforcement admin. **Psychology:** General. **Social sciences:** Economics, geography, GIS/cartography, political science, sociology. **Visual/performing arts:** Acting, art, art history/conservation, commercial/advertising art, dramatic, drawing, music, painting, photography, printmaking, sculpture, theater design, theater history.

Most popular majors. Business/marketing 24%, education 10%, health sciences 19%, psychology 6%, security/protective services 10%.

Computing on campus. PC or laptop required. 160 workstations in library, computer center, student center. Dormitories wired for high-speed internet access and linked to campus network. Commuter students can connect to campus network. Online course registration, online library, helpline, repair service, student web hosting, wireless network available.

Student life. Freshman orientation: Mandatory, $175 fee. Preregistration for classes offered. Sessions held prior to start of semester. **Housing:** Coed dorms, apartments, wellness housing available. $225 nonrefundable deposit, deadline 5/1. **Activities:** Bands, campus ministries, choral groups, dance, drama, international student organizations, literary magazine, music ensembles, musical theater, radio station, student government, student newspaper, Hispanic-American society, multicultural student association, Asian student association, community service group, campus educators on sexual assault, political science academy, student action resource team.

Athletics. NCAA. **Intercollegiate:** Baseball M, basketball, cross-country, field hockey W, golf M, ice hockey M, lacrosse M, soccer, softball W, tennis, track and field, volleyball W. **Intramural:** Baseball M, basketball, cheerleading W, football (non-tackle), ice hockey, softball W, volleyball. **Team name:** Vikings.

Student services. Adult student services, alcohol/substance abuse counseling, chaplain/spiritual director, career counseling, services for economically disadvantaged, student employment services, financial aid counseling, health services, legal services, minority student services, on-campus daycare, personal counseling, placement for graduates, veterans' counselor, women's services. **Physically disabled:** Services for visually, speech, hearing impaired.

Contact. E-mail: admissions@salemstate.edu
Phone: (978) 542-6200 Fax: (978) 542-6893
Mary Dunn, Assistant Dean of Undergraduate Admissions, Salem State University, 352 Lafayette Street, Salem, MA 01970-5353

School of the Museum of Fine Arts
Boston, Massachusetts
www.smfa.edu   **CB code: 3794**

- Private 4-year visual arts college
- Commuter campus in very large city
- 467 degree-seeking undergraduates: 7% part-time, 65% women, 3% African American, 4% Asian American, 10% Hispanic American, 8% international
- 171 degree-seeking graduate students
- 71% of applicants admitted
- Application essay required
- 56% graduate within 6 years

General. Founded in 1876. Part of the Museum of Fine Arts. **Degrees:** 136 bachelor's awarded; master's offered. **Location:** One mile from downtown. **Calendar:** Semester, limited summer session. **Full-time faculty:** 46 total; 74% have terminal degrees, 9% minority, 50% women. **Part-time faculty:** 105 total; 67% have terminal degrees, 4% minority, 57% women. **Class size:**

96% < 20, 4% 20-39. **Special facilities:** Gallery space, exhibiting opportunities, partnership with Tufts University.

Freshman class profile. 681 applied, 485 admitted, 91 enrolled.

End year in good standing:	90%	Live on campus:	55%
Return as sophomores:	75%	International:	11%
Out-of-state:	72%		

Basis for selection. Portfolio, previous schooling, level of applicant's interest, and quality and content of essays important. Test scores, volunteer work and work experience considered if submitted. Combined Degree program applicants must apply to Museum School and Tufts University simultaneously. Scores accepted on a rolling basis after February 1. Portfolio required. Interview available by appointment. **Home schooled:** Transcript of courses and grades required. Must have graduation date indicating successful completion of program; must be signed and dated by recognized record keeper, which may include outside testing agency, home school representative, or parent.

2011-2012 Annual costs. Tuition/fees: $36,930. Room only: $13,562. Books/supplies: $1,600. Personal expenses: $1,800.

2011-2012 Financial aid. Need-based: Average need met was 49%. Average scholarship/grant was $12,175; average loan $3,500. 64% of total undergraduate aid awarded as scholarships/grants, 36% as loans/jobs. **Non-need-based:** Scholarships awarded for art.

Application procedures. Admission: Priority date 2/1; no deadline. $65 fee, may be waived for applicants with need. Admission notification on a rolling basis beginning on or about 2/15. Must reply by May 1 or within 2 week(s) if notified thereafter. Students may apply early and request early notification of admission. **Financial aid:** Closing date 3/15. FAFSA, institutional form required. Applicants notified by 4/15; must reply by 5/1 or within 2 week(s) of notification.

Academics. Special study options: Combined bachelor's/graduate degree, cross-registration, double major, exchange student, independent study, internships, liberal arts/career combination, New York semester, student-designed major, study abroad, teacher certification program. 5-year Dual Degree BFA/BA with Tufts University; all studio art elective Studio Diploma (no academic requirements). Extensive exchange and cross-registration opportunities within Boston, the United States, and around the world. Studio programs are interdisciplinary and self-directed. **Credit/placement by examination:** AP, CLEP. **Support services:** Pre-admission summer program, study skills assistance, writing center.

Majors. Communications technology: Animation/special effects. **Visual/performing arts:** Art, ceramics, cinematography, drawing, illustration, metal/jewelry, multimedia, painting, photography, printmaking, sculpture, studio arts.

Computing on campus. 170 workstations in library, computer center, student center. Dormitories wired for high-speed internet access. Online course registration, helpline, wireless network available.

Student life. Freshman orientation: Mandatory, $125 fee. Preregistration for classes offered. Typically held during last week in August, right before beginning of semester. **Housing:** Coed dorms available. $450 nonrefundable deposit, deadline 5/1. Professional off-campus housing assistance available. **Activities:** Film society, international student organizations, student government, bike club, comics club, Creative Futures, SMFA in New Orleans, Maum Meditation, Queer Group of SMFA.

Student services. Adult student services, career counseling, student employment services, financial aid counseling, personal counseling, placement for graduates. **Physically disabled:** Services for hearing impaired.

Contact. E-mail: admissions@smfa.edu
Phone: (617) 369-3626 Toll-free number: (800) 643-6078
Fax: (617) 369-4264
Eric Thompson, Vice President for Enrollment, School of the Museum of Fine Arts, 230 The Fenway, Boston, MA 02115

Simmons College
Boston, Massachusetts   **CB member**
www.simmons.edu   **CB code: 3761**

- Private 4-year health science and liberal arts college for women
- Residential campus in very large city
- 1,762 degree-seeking undergraduates: 9% part-time, 100% women, 7% African American, 8% Asian American, 6% Hispanic American, 1% Native American, 3% international
- 2,865 degree-seeking graduate students

- 47% of applicants admitted
- SAT or ACT with writing, application essay required
- 69% graduate within 6 years

General. Founded in 1899. Regionally accredited. **Degrees:** 565 bachelor's awarded; master's, professional, doctoral offered. **Location:** 2 miles from downtown. **Calendar:** Semester, extensive summer session. **Class size:** 69% < 20, 22% 20-39, 4% 40-49, 5% 50-99, less than 1% >100. **Special facilities:** Art gallery, technology resource center.

Freshman class profile. 4,528 applied, 2,109 admitted, 344 enrolled.

Mid 50% test scores		GPA 2.0-2.99:	25%
SAT critical reading:	510-620	Rank in top quarter:	56%
SAT math:	510-610	Rank in top tenth:	22%
SAT writing:	520-620	End year in good standing:	95%
ACT composite:	22-27	Return as sophomores:	85%
GPA 3.75 or higher:	11%	Out-of-state:	41%
GPA 3.50-3.74:	18%	Live on campus:	93%
GPA 3.0-3.49:	46%	International:	2%

Basis for selection. School achievement record most important. Test scores, 2 recommendations, essay, interview (if available), personal qualities also important. Interests, accomplishments considered. **Home schooled:** Statement describing home school structure and mission, transcript of courses and grades, letter of recommendation (nonparent) required.

High school preparation. College-preparatory program required. Required and recommended units include English 4, mathematics 3-4, history 3, science 3 (laboratory 3), foreign language 3-4 and academic electives 3-4.

2011-2012 Annual costs. Tuition/fees: $33,356. Room/board: $12,906.

Application procedures. **Admission:** Priority date 12/1; deadline 2/1 (postmark date). $55 fee, may be waived for applicants with need, free for online applicants. Admission notification by 3/15. Must reply by 5/1.

Academics. **Special study options:** Combined bachelor's/graduate degree, cross-registration, double major, exchange student, honors, independent study, internships, liberal arts/career combination, semester at sea, student-designed major, study abroad, Washington semester. Exchange program with Mills College, Spelman College, Colleges of the Fenway, double degree programs with Massachusetts College of Pharmacy. **Credit/placement by examination:** AP, CLEP, IB, SAT, ACT, institutional tests. **Support services:** Learning center, reduced course load, study skills assistance, tutoring, writing center.

Majors. **Area/ethnic studies:** African, American, East Asian, women's. **Biology:** General, biochemistry, biostatistics. **Business:** Accounting, accounting/finance, business admin, finance, international, management information systems, marketing, sales/distribution. **Communications:** Advertising, communications/speech/rhetoric, public relations. **Computer sciences:** General, information technology, system admin. **Conservation:** Environmental science. **Education:** General, early childhood, elementary, ESL, secondary, special ed. **English:** American lit, British lit, English lit. **Foreign languages:** French, Spanish. **General:** Food science. **Health services:** Dietetics, medical informatics, nursing (RN), physical therapy, public health ed. **History:** General. **Human services:** Public policy. **Liberal arts:** Arts/sciences. **Math:** General. **Parks/recreation:** Exercise sciences. **Philosophy/religion:** Philosophy. **Physical sciences:** Chemistry, physics. **Psychology:** General, psychobiology. **Social sciences:** Economics, international relations, political science, sociology. **Visual/performing arts:** Art, commercial/advertising art, music, studio arts management. **Work/family studies:** Institutional food production, merchandising.

Most popular majors. Biology 6%, business/marketing 6%, communications/journalism 9%, health sciences 37%, psychology 9%, social sciences 9%.

Computing on campus. 570 workstations in dormitories, library, computer center, student center. Dormitories wired for high-speed internet access and linked to campus network. Commuter students can connect to campus network. Online course registration, online library, helpline, student web hosting, wireless network available.

Student life. **Freshman orientation:** Mandatory, $99 fee. Preregistration for classes offered. Optional program held in June; mandatory program held the day before classes begin. **Policies:** Residency requirement for first-year students, service animals allowed in dorm rooms. Freshmen not permitted cars on campus. **Housing:** Guaranteed on-campus for freshmen. Wellness housing available. $250 nonrefundable deposit, deadline 5/1. **Activities:** Campus ministries, choral groups, dance, film society, international student organizations, literary magazine, Model UN, radio station, student government, student newspaper, student government association, black student organization, organizacion Latino Americana, Hillel, Amnesty International, women's center, The Alliance, chemistry-physics liaison, dance company.

Athletics. NCAA. **Intercollegiate:** Basketball W, cross-country W, diving W, field hockey W, lacrosse W, rowing (crew) W, soccer W, softball W, swimming W, tennis W, volleyball W. **Intramural:** Basketball, soccer, volleyball. **Team name:** Sharks.

Student services. Adult student services, alcohol/substance abuse counseling, chaplain/spiritual director, career counseling, student employment services, financial aid counseling, health services, personal counseling, placement for graduates, women's services. **Physically disabled:** Services for visually, speech, hearing impaired.

Contact. E-mail: ugadm@simmons.edu
Phone: (617) 521-2051 Toll-free number: (800) 345-8468
Fax: (617) 521-3190
Catherine Capolupo, Assistant Vice President, Undergraduate Admission & Marketing, Simmons College, 300 The Fenway, Boston, MA 02115-5898

Smith College
Northampton, Massachusetts   CB member
www.smith.edu   CB code: 3762

- Private 4-year liberal arts college for women
- Residential campus in large town
- 2,627 degree-seeking undergraduates: 1% part-time, 100% women, 5% African American, 12% Asian American, 8% Hispanic American, 11% international
- 533 degree-seeking graduate students
- 45% of applicants admitted
- Application essay required
- 85% graduate within 6 years

General. Founded in 1871. Regionally accredited. **Degrees:** 696 bachelor's awarded; master's, doctoral offered. **ROTC:** Army, Air Force. **Location:** 35 miles from Hartford, Connecticut; 90 miles from Boston. **Calendar:** Semester. **Full-time faculty:** 273 total; 99% have terminal degrees, 16% minority, 55% women. **Part-time faculty:** 27 total; 85% have terminal degrees, 7% minority, 52% women. **Class size:** 66% < 20, 25% 20-39, 4% 40-49, 4% 50-99, less than 1% >100. **Special facilities:** Physiology and horticultural laboratories, printmaking studio, darkroom and sculpture (including bronze casting studio) facilities, dance, theater and television studios, electronic music studio, recital hall, digital design studio, animal care facilities, electron microscopes, on-campus elementary school, multimedia language lab, greenhouses, astronomy observatories.

Freshman class profile. 4,128 applied, 1,877 admitted, 694 enrolled.

Mid 50% test scores		GPA 2.0-2.99:	1%
SAT critical reading:	600-730	Rank in top quarter:	89%
SAT math:	600-710	Rank in top tenth:	60%
SAT writing:	620-720	Return as sophomores:	94%
ACT composite:	27-31	Out-of-state:	84%
GPA 3.75 or higher:	51%	Live on campus:	100%
GPA 3.50-3.74:	36%	International:	14%
GPA 3.0-3.49:	12%		

Basis for selection. Secondary school record, including GPA and difficulty of courses, recommendations most important. Class rank, essay, school and community activities and test scores also important. Interview strongly recommended, may be conducted off-campus by alumna. **Home schooled:** Statement describing home school structure and mission, transcript of courses and grades, letter of recommendation (nonparent) required. Submit portfolio and evaluation of coursework and sample of short research or analytical paper with evaluator's remarks.

High school preparation. College-preparatory program required. 16 units recommended. Recommended units include English 4, mathematics 3, history 2, science 3 (laboratory 3), foreign language 3 and academic electives 1. 3 units of 1 foreign language or 2 each of 2 languages recommended.

2011-2012 Annual costs. Tuition/fees: $40,070. Room/board: $13,390. Books/supplies: $800. Personal expenses: $1,256.

2011-2012 Financial aid. **Need-based:** 533 full-time freshmen applied for aid; 422 were judged to have need; 422 of these received aid. Average need met was 100%. Average scholarship/grant was $34,713; average loan $3,170. 80% of total undergraduate aid awarded as scholarships/grants, 20% as loans/jobs. **Non-need-based:** Awarded to 123 full-time undergraduates, including 34 freshmen. Scholarships awarded for academics, state residency. **Additional information:** Financial aid policy guarantees to meet full financial need, as calculated by college, of all admitted students who have met application deadlines.

Application procedures. Admission: Closing date 1/15 (postmark date). $60 fee, may be waived for applicants with need, free for online applicants. Notification by early April. Must reply by May 1 or within 2 week(s) if notified thereafter. **Financial aid:** Closing date 2/15. FAFSA, institutional form, CSS PROFILE required. Applicants notified by 4/1; must reply by 5/1.

Academics. Academic honor code; writing course required in first year. **Special study options:** Accelerated study, cross-registration, double major, exchange student, honors, independent study, internships, semester at sea, student-designed major, study abroad, teacher certification program, Washington semester. Member of Five College Consortium, program in engineering and technology, engineering science program within liberal arts curriculum leading to BS degree, post-baccalaureate certificate in American studies (available to international students). **Credit/placement by examination:** AP, CLEP, IB, institutional tests. 32 credit hours maximum toward bachelor's degree. **Support services:** Learning center, study skills assistance, tutoring, writing center.

Majors. Area/ethnic studies: African-American, American, Asian, Latin American, women's. **Biology:** General, biochemistry, neuroscience. **Computer sciences:** Computer science. **Education:** General. **Engineering:** General, biomedical, chemical, civil, computer, electrical, engineering mechanics, engineering science, environmental, mechanical. **English:** English lit. **Foreign languages:** Ancient Greek, classics, comparative lit, East Asian, French, German, Italian, Latin, Portuguese, Russian, Spanish. **History:** General. **Math:** General. **Philosophy/religion:** Philosophy, religion. **Physical sciences:** Astronomy, astrophysics, chemistry, geology, physics. **Psychology:** General. **Social sciences:** Anthropology, economics, political science, sociology. **Visual/performing arts:** Art, art history/conservation, dance, dramatic, film/cinema/video, studio arts.

Most popular majors. Area/ethnic studies 9%, biology 10%, English 6%, foreign language 12%, psychology 9%, social sciences 22%, visual/performing arts 9%.

Computing on campus. 532 workstations in dormitories, library, computer center, student center. Dormitories wired for high-speed internet access and linked to campus network. Commuter students can connect to campus network. Online course registration, online library, helpline, repair service, student web hosting, wireless network available.

Student life. Freshman orientation: Mandatory. Preregistration for classes offered. Program held 4-5 days prior to beginning of classes; includes parent day. **Policies:** Each residence self-governed within framework of college regulations. Residents determine house responsibilities. **Housing:** Guaranteed on-campus for all undergraduates. Cooperative housing, wellness housing available. $200 nonrefundable deposit, deadline 5/1. French-speaking house, senior house, nontraditional age house, apartment complexes for juniors and seniors, housing for students with children available. **Activities:** Bands, campus ministries, choral groups, dance, drama, international student organizations, literary magazine, music ensembles, Model UN, musical theater, radio station, student government, student newspaper, TV station, service organizations, women's resource center, black student alliance, Asian student association, Hillel, Newman Club, Christian council, international relations club, Latina organization, Native American organization.

Athletics. NCAA. **Intercollegiate:** Basketball W, cross-country W, diving W, equestrian W, field hockey W, lacrosse W, rowing (crew) W, skiing W, soccer W, softball W, squash W, swimming W, tennis W, track and field W, volleyball W. **Intramural:** Basketball W, soccer W. **Team name:** Pioneers.

Student services. Adult student services, alcohol/substance abuse counseling, chaplain/spiritual director, career counseling, services for economically disadvantaged, student employment services, financial aid counseling, health services, minority student services, on-campus daycare, personal counseling, placement for graduates, women's services. **Physically disabled:** Services for visually, speech, hearing impaired.

Contact. E-mail: admission@smith.edu
Phone: (413) 585-2500 Fax: (413) 585-2527
Debra Shaver, Director of Admission, Smith College, 7 College Lane, Northampton, MA 01063

Springfield College

Springfield, Massachusetts
www.springfieldcollege.edu

CB member
CB code: 3763

- Private 4-year health science and liberal arts college
- Residential campus in small city
- 3,255 full-time, degree-seeking undergraduates
- 68% of applicants admitted
- SAT or ACT with writing, application essay required

General. Founded in 1885. Regionally accredited. Adult weekend programs at 11 sites across the country. **Degrees:** 481 bachelor's awarded; master's, doctoral offered. **ROTC:** Army, Air Force. **Location:** 90 miles from Boston; 26 miles from Hartford, Connecticut. **Calendar:** Semester, limited summer session. **Full-time faculty:** 210 total; 40% have terminal degrees. **Part-time faculty:** 155 total. **Class size:** 46% < 20, 52% 20-39, less than 1% 40-49, less than 1% 50-99, less than 1% >100. **Special facilities:** 57-acre campground and outdoor adventure area.

Freshman class profile. 2,319 applied, 1,577 admitted, 583 enrolled.

Mid 50% test scores			
SAT critical reading:	450-560	Rank in top tenth:	13%
SAT math:	430-580	Out-of-state:	72%
Rank in top quarter:	38%	Live on campus:	98%

Basis for selection. School achievement record, essay, extracurricular activities, personal references, and test scores important. Portfolio required of art majors. **Home schooled:** Statement describing home school structure and mission, transcript of courses and grades, letter of recommendation (nonparent) required.

High school preparation. College-preparatory program required. 16 units required. Required and recommended units include English 4, mathematics 3, social studies 2, history 1, science 3 (laboratory 2) and foreign language 3. Emphasis on science for majors in allied health fields.

2011-2012 Annual costs. Tuition/fees: $30,660. Room/board: $10,830. Books/supplies: $900. Personal expenses: $1,200.

Financial aid. Additional information: Co-operative education program available to students after freshman year.

Application procedures. Admission: Priority date 3/1; deadline 4/1 (postmark date). $50 fee, may be waived for applicants with need. Admission notification on a rolling basis beginning on or about 12/1. Must reply by May 1 or within 2 week(s) if notified thereafter. Application closing date for athletic training, physical therapy majors 12/1; closing date for physician assistant and occupational therapy majors 1/15. **Financial aid:** Priority date 3/15; no closing date. FAFSA, institutional form required. Applicants notified on a rolling basis starting 3/15; must reply by 5/1 or within 2 week(s) of notification.

Academics. Emphasis on practical fieldwork experiences to supplement classroom learning. **Special study options:** Combined bachelor's/graduate degree, cooperative education, cross-registration, double major, ESL, independent study, internships, liberal arts/career combination, study abroad, teacher certification program, weekend college. **Credit/placement by examination:** AP, CLEP, IB, SAT, ACT, institutional tests. 30 credit hours maximum toward bachelor's degree. **Support services:** Learning center, reduced course load, study skills assistance, tutoring, writing center.

Majors. Biology: General. **Business:** Business admin. **Computer sciences:** General, computer graphics, information systems. **Conservation:** General, environmental studies. **Education:** Art, early childhood, elementary, health, physical, secondary, special ed. **English:** English lit. **Health services:** Art therapy, athletic training, clinical lab science, clinical lab technology, EMT paramedic, health care admin, medical records admin, physician assistant, predental, recreational therapy. **History:** General. **Human services:** Community org/advocacy. **Liberal arts:** Arts/sciences. **Math:** General. **Parks/recreation:** Exercise sciences, facilities management, health/fitness, sports admin. **Protective services:** Law enforcement admin. **Psychology:** General. **Social sciences:** Political science, sociology. **Visual/performing arts:** Art, dance.

Computing on campus. 235 workstations in dormitories, library, computer center, student center. Dormitories wired for high-speed internet access and linked to campus network. Commuter students can connect to campus network. Online course registration, helpline, wireless network available.

Student life. Freshman orientation: Mandatory, $125 fee. Preregistration for classes offered. Four-day program immediately preceding fall semester. **Housing:** Guaranteed on-campus for all undergraduates. Coed dorms, single-sex dorms, special housing for disabled, apartments, wellness housing available. **Activities:** Jazz band, campus ministries, choral groups, dance, drama, international student organizations, literary magazine, music ensembles, musical theater, radio station, student government, student newspaper, environmental club, Fellowship of Christian Athletes, Habitat for Humanity, Hillel, Newman community, outreach committee, student society for cultural diversity, Students Against Violence Everywhere.

Athletics. NCAA. **Intercollegiate:** Baseball M, basketball, cross-country, diving, field hockey W, football (tackle) M, golf, gymnastics, lacrosse, soccer, softball W, swimming, tennis, track and field, volleyball, wrestling M. **Intramural:** Basketball, bowling, field hockey, football (non-tackle), golf, handball, lacrosse, racquetball, soccer, softball, swimming, tennis, track and field, volleyball, wrestling M. **Team name:** Pride.

Student services. Adult student services, alcohol/substance abuse counseling, chaplain/spiritual director, career counseling, student employment services, financial aid counseling, health services, minority student services, on-campus daycare, personal counseling, placement for graduates, veterans' counselor, women's services. **Physically disabled:** Services for visually, speech, hearing impaired.

Contact. E-mail: admissions@springfieldcollege.edu
Phone: (413) 748-3136 Toll-free number: (800) 343-1257
Fax: (413) 748-3694
Richard Veres, Director of Admissions, Springfield College, 263 Alden Street, Springfield, MA 01109

Stonehill College
Easton, Massachusetts
www.stonehill.edu

CB member
CB code: 3770

- Private 4-year liberal arts college affiliated with Roman Catholic Church
- Residential campus in large town
- 2,463 degree-seeking undergraduates: 1% part-time, 61% women, 3% African American, 1% Asian American, 3% Hispanic American, 1% international
- 65% of applicants admitted
- Application essay required
- 81% graduate within 6 years; 37% enter graduate study

General. Founded in 1948. Regionally accredited. **Degrees:** 616 bachelor's awarded. **ROTC:** Army. **Location:** 19 miles from Boston, 25 miles from Providence. **Calendar:** Semester, limited summer session. **Full-time faculty:** 160 total; 86% have terminal degrees, 9% minority, 41% women. **Part-time faculty:** 107 total; 42% have terminal degrees, 4% minority, 48% women. **Class size:** 51% < 20, 47% 20-39, 1% 40-49, less than 1% 50-99, less than 1% >100. **Special facilities:** Observatory, shovel museum.

Freshman class profile. 7,200 applied, 4,693 admitted, 568 enrolled.

Mid 50% test scores			
SAT critical reading:	550-650	Rank in top quarter:	78%
SAT math:	560-640	Rank in top tenth:	42%
ACT composite:	25-29	End year in good standing:	91%
GPA 3.75 or higher:	16%	Return as sophomores:	88%
GPA 3.50-3.74:	26%	Out-of-state:	42%
GPA 3.0-3.49:	40%	Live on campus:	97%
GPA 2.0-2.99:	18%	International:	1%

Basis for selection. Competitive high school course profile, grades, weighted GPA, class rank, high school profile, counselor recommendation important. **Home schooled:** Statement describing home school structure and mission, transcript of courses and grades required. Common Application Home Schooled Supplement form required.

High school preparation. College-preparatory program required. 16 units required; 20 recommended. Required and recommended units include English 4, mathematics 3-4, history 3, science 1-3 (laboratory 1-2), foreign language 2-3 and academic electives 3. Foreign language units should be in same language. 3 combined units in history, political science, social science required. Math units should consist of algegra I, algebra II, and geometry. Additional units in science and math recommended for science applicants. Additional math units recommended for business applicants.

2011-2012 Annual costs. Tuition/fees: $33,920. Room/board: $12,860. Books/supplies: $586. Personal expenses: $634.

2011-2012 Financial aid. Need-based: 481 full-time freshmen applied for aid; 341 were judged to have need; 339 of these received aid. Average need met was 89%. Average scholarship/grant was $19,181; average loan $4,297. 78% of total undergraduate aid awarded as scholarships/grants, 22% as loans/jobs. **Non-need-based:** Awarded to 1,067 full-time undergraduates, including 261 freshmen. Scholarships awarded for academics, athletics, ROTC.

Application procedures. Admission: Closing date 1/15 (postmark date). $60 fee may be waived for applicants with need. Admission notification by 3/15. Admission notification on a rolling basis. Must reply by 5/1. **Financial aid:** Closing date 2/1. FAFSA, CSS PROFILE required. Applicants notified by 4/1; must reply by 5/1.

Academics. Special study options: Cross-registration, double major, dual enrollment of high school students, exchange student, honors, independent study, internships, liberal arts/career combination, New York semester, student-designed major, study abroad, teacher certification program, Washington semester. Full-semester international internship sites in Dublin,

Geneva, London, Madrid, and Paris; 3-2 computer engineering BA/BS program with University of Notre Dame, Indiana; Stonehill Undergraduate Research Experience (SURE) program. **Credit/placement by examination:** AP, CLEP, IB, SAT, ACT, institutional tests. **Support services:** Learning center, reduced course load, study skills assistance, tutoring, writing center.

Majors. Area/ethnic studies: General, American. **Biology:** General, biochemistry, neuroscience. **Business:** Accounting, business admin, finance, international, marketing. **Communications:** Communications/speech/rhetoric. **Computer sciences:** Computer science. **Conservation:** Environmental studies. **Education:** Early childhood, elementary. **English:** English lit. **Foreign languages:** General, French, Spanish. **Health services:** Health care admin. **History:** General. **Human services:** General. **Math:** General. **Philosophy/religion:** Christian, philosophy, religion. **Physical sciences:** Chemistry, physics. **Psychology:** General. **Social sciences:** Criminology, economics, international relations, political science, sociology. **Visual/performing arts:** General, art history/conservation, graphic design, studio arts.

Most popular majors. Biology 9%, business/marketing 21%, communications/journalism 7%, education 7%, psychology 12%, social sciences 15%.

Computing on campus. 370 workstations in library, computer center, student center. Dormitories wired for high-speed internet access and linked to campus network. Commuter students can connect to campus network. Online course registration, online library, helpline, repair service, student web hosting, wireless network available.

Student life. Freshman orientation: Mandatory. Preregistration for classes offered. Two-day program in June. **Housing:** Guaranteed on-campus for all undergraduates. Coed dorms, single-sex dorms, special housing for disabled, wellness housing available. $300 nonrefundable deposit, deadline 5/1. Special interest housing proposals considered for groups. **Activities:** Pep band, campus ministries, choral groups, dance, drama, film society, literary magazine, music ensembles, musical theater, radio station, student government, student newspaper, student government association, Asian American society, Diversity on Campus, Model UN, PRIDE, activism club, ACES, Habitat for Humanity, College Democrats, College Republicans, politics society.

Athletics. NCAA. **Intercollegiate:** Baseball M, basketball, cross-country, equestrian W, field hockey W, football (tackle) M, ice hockey M, lacrosse W, soccer, softball W, tennis, track and field, volleyball W. **Intramural:** Basketball, field hockey, football (non-tackle), soccer, softball, tennis, volleyball. **Team name:** Skyhawks.

Student services. Adult student services, alcohol/substance abuse counseling, chaplain/spiritual director, career counseling, services for economically disadvantaged, student employment services, financial aid counseling, health services, minority student services, on-campus daycare, personal counseling, placement for graduates, women's services. **Physically disabled:** Services for visually, speech, hearing impaired.

Contact. E-mail: admissions@stonehill.edu
Phone: (508) 565-1373 Fax: (508) 565-1545
Daniel Monahan, Dean of Admissions, Stonehill College, 320 Washington Street, Easton, MA 02357-0100

Suffolk University
Boston, Massachusetts
www.suffolk.edu

CB member
CB code: 3771

- Private 4-year university
- Commuter campus in very large city
- 5,682 degree-seeking undergraduates: 5% part-time, 56% women, 5% African American, 7% Asian American, 9% Hispanic American, 15% international
- 3,385 degree-seeking graduate students
- 79% of applicants admitted
- SAT or ACT with writing required
- 55% graduate within 6 years; 24% enter graduate study

General. Founded in 1906. Regionally accredited. Campus in Spain, branch campuses in Cape Cod and North Andover. **Degrees:** 1,351 bachelor's, 1 associate awarded; master's, professional, doctoral offered. **ROTC:** Army. **Location:** Downtown. **Calendar:** Semester, extensive summer session. **Full-time faculty:** 419 total; 92% have terminal degrees, 13% minority, 40% women. **Part-time faculty:** 544 total; 14% have terminal degrees, 12% minority, 45% women. **Class size:** 42% < 20, 56% 20-39, less than 1% 40-49, 1% 50-99. **Special facilities:** Poetry center, energy research lab, political research center, television studio, field station, river station.

Freshman class profile. 9,137 applied, 7,217 admitted, 1,239 enrolled.

Mid 50% test scores				
SAT critical reading:	450-570	GPA 2.0-2.99:		50%
SAT math:	460-570	Rank in top quarter:		36%
SAT writing:	460-570	Rank in top tenth:		13%
ACT composite:	21-25	End year in good standing:		92%
GPA 3.75 or higher:	8%	Return as sophomores:		75%
GPA 3.50-3.74:	9%	Out-of-state:		38%
GPA 3.0-3.49:	33%	Live on campus:		70%
		International:		15%

Basis for selection. High school record including courses taken, level of study, class rank, test scores, essay important. Counselor recommendation considered. Interview recommended. Portfolio required for BFA program applicants. **Home schooled:** Transcript of courses and grades, state high school equivalency certificate, letter of recommendation (nonparent) required. Admission interview highly recommended. Transcript/Record of courses and grades or written evaluation of work required.

High school preparation. College-preparatory program recommended. 17 units required; 23 recommended. Required and recommended units include English 4, mathematics 3-4, history 1-4, science 2-4 (laboratory 1), foreign language 2-3 and academic electives 4.

2011-2012 Annual costs. Tuition/fees: $29,894. Room/board: $14,624. Books/supplies: $1,200. Personal expenses: $2,200.

2011-2012 Financial aid. Need-based: 928 full-time freshmen applied for aid; 825 were judged to have need; 823 of these received aid. Average need met was 66%. Average scholarship/grant was $14,599; average loan $3,457. 70% of total undergraduate aid awarded as scholarships/grants, 30% as loans/jobs. **Non-need-based:** Awarded to 1,605 full-time undergraduates, including 327 freshmen. Scholarships awarded for academics, alumni affiliation. **Additional information:** Foreign students may apply for institutional employment awards.

Application procedures. Admission: Closing date 2/15 (postmark date). $50 fee, may be waived for applicants with need. Admission notification on a rolling basis beginning on or about 3/20. Must reply by May 1 or within 2 week(s) if notified thereafter. Strongly suggest housing deposit before March 15. Housing awarded on first-come first-served basis by date of the admission deposit. **Financial aid:** Closing date 2/15. FAFSA, institutional form required. Applicants notified on a rolling basis starting 2/5; must reply by 5/1 or within 2 week(s) of notification.

Academics. Special study options: Accelerated study, combined bachelor's/graduate degree, cooperative education, cross-registration, distance learning, double major, ESL, honors, independent study, internships, liberal arts/career combination, study abroad, Washington semester. **Credit/placement by examination:** AP, CLEP, IB, SAT, ACT, institutional tests. 30 credit hours maximum toward associate degree, 30 toward bachelor's. **Support services:** Learning center, pre-admission summer program, reduced course load, remedial instruction, study skills assistance, tutoring, writing center.

Honors college/program. Separate application required. Class rank, GPA, personal essay, interview, and quality of secondary school curriculum, including advanced placement, honors, and other types of accelerated courses, and any other relevant information considered. Applicants from the College of Arts and Sciences and Sawyer Business School will normally meet at least 2 of the following criteria: 3.7 GPA, class rank within upper 10% (if class rank is available), 1300 SAT (exclusive of Writing), or 29 ACT.

Majors. Area/ethnic studies: African-American, French, German, women's. **Biology:** General, biochemistry, biomedical sciences, biophysics, environmental, marine, radiobiology. **Business:** General, accounting, business admin, entrepreneurial studies, finance, international, management information systems, marketing, office technology. **Communications:** Advertising, broadcast journalism, communications/speech/rhetoric, journalism, media studies, organizational, political, public relations. **Communications technology:** General, animation/special effects, radio/TV. **Computer sciences:** General, computer science, information systems. **Conservation:** Environmental science. **Education:** General. **Engineering:** Computer, electrical, environmental. **English:** Creative writing, English lit. **Foreign languages:** General, French, German, Spanish. **History:** General, American, European. **Human services:** General, public policy. **Liberal arts:** Arts/sciences, humanities. **Math:** General. **Philosophy/religion:** Philosophy. **Physical sciences:** General, chemistry, physics. **Protective services:** Law enforcement admin. **Psychology:** General. **Social sciences:** General, criminology, economics, international economics, international relations, political science, sociology, U.S. government. **Visual/performing arts:** General, acting, art, art history/conservation, commercial/advertising art, dramatic, film/cinema/video, interior design, studio arts, studio arts management, theater history.

Most popular majors. Business/marketing 40%, communications/journalism 15%, psychology 7%, social sciences 16%.

Computing on campus. 539 workstations in dormitories, library, computer center, student center. Dormitories wired for high-speed internet access and linked to campus network. Commuter students can connect to campus network. Online course registration, online library, helpline, wireless network available.

Student life. Freshman orientation: Mandatory, $85 fee. Preregistration for classes offered. Three-day orientation held in June and August. **Housing:** Coed dorms, apartments available. $600 nonrefundable deposit, deadline 5/1. **Activities:** Campus ministries, choral groups, dance, drama, international student organizations, literary magazine, music ensembles, Model UN, musical theater, radio station, student government, student newspaper, TV station, Islamic cultural society, Newman club, Jewish society, finance committee, student government association, student judiciary review board, Jumpstart Inc., S.O.U.L.S., Best Buddies, Up 'Til Dawn.

Athletics. NCAA. **Intercollegiate:** Baseball M, basketball, cross-country, golf M, ice hockey M, soccer M, softball W, tennis, volleyball W. **Intramural:** Basketball, football (non-tackle), soccer W, table tennis, volleyball. **Team name:** Rams.

Student services. Adult student services, alcohol/substance abuse counseling, chaplain/spiritual director, career counseling, student employment services, financial aid counseling, health services, minority student services, personal counseling, placement for graduates, veterans' counselor, women's services. **Physically disabled:** Services for visually, speech, hearing impaired.

Contact. E-mail: admission@suffolk.edu
Phone: (617) 573-8460 Toll-free number: (800) 678-3365
Fax: (617) 557-1574
John Hamel, Director of Admissions, Suffolk University, 8 Ashburton Place, Boston, MA 02108

Tufts University
Medford, Massachusetts
www.tufts.edu

CB member
CB code: 3901

- Private 4-year university
- Residential campus in small city
- 5,136 degree-seeking undergraduates: 1% part-time, 51% women, 4% African American, 10% Asian American, 7% Hispanic American, 7% international
- 5,252 degree-seeking graduate students
- 22% of applicants admitted
- SAT and SAT Subject Tests or ACT with writing, application essay required
- 90% graduate within 6 years

General. Founded in 1852. Regionally accredited. **Degrees:** 1,463 bachelor's awarded; master's, professional, doctoral offered. **ROTC:** Army, Naval, Air Force. **Location:** 5 miles from Boston. **Calendar:** Semester, limited summer session. **Full-time faculty:** 687 total; 94% have terminal degrees, 18% minority, 40% women. **Part-time faculty:** 338 total; 60% have terminal degrees, 12% minority, 52% women. **Class size:** 69% < 20, 22% 20-39, 3% 40-49, 3% 50-99, 2% >100. **Special facilities:** Computer-aided design laboratory, arts center, theater in the round, engineering project design center.

Freshman class profile. 17,104 applied, 3,743 admitted, 1,317 enrolled.

Mid 50% test scores			
SAT critical reading:	680-740	Rank in top tenth:	89%
SAT math:	680-760	Return as sophomores:	96%
SAT writing:	680-760	Out-of-state:	81%
ACT composite:	30-33	Live on campus:	100%
Rank in top quarter:	99%	International:	7%

Basis for selection. School achievement record most important. School recommendations, test scores, character, personality, extracurricular participation, special talents also important. Geographical distribution, alumni relationship, minority status, socioeconomic status all considered. For applicants who submit SAT: 2 SAT Subject Tests required of liberal arts applicants; Math 1 or 2 and either physics or chemistry required of engineering applicants. Interview optional but recommended. **Home schooled:** Transcript of courses and grades required.

High school preparation. College-preparatory program required. Recommended units include English 4, mathematics 4, history 4, science 4 and foreign language 4. 4 math, 2 laboratory science recommended for engineering, math, and science majors.

2011-2012 Annual costs. Tuition/fees: $42,962. Room/board: $11,512. Books/supplies: $2,134.

Financial aid. All financial aid based on need. **Additional information:** Students from families with incomes less than $40,000 receive aid awards in which student loans are replaced by grants.

Application procedures. Admission: Closing date 1/1 (postmark date). $70 fee, may be waived for applicants with need. Admission notification by 4/1. Must reply by 5/1. **Financial aid:** Closing date 2/15. FAFSA, CSS PROFILE required. Applicants notified by 4/1; must reply by 5/1.

Academics. Special study options: Combined bachelor's/graduate degree, cross-registration, double major, exchange student, independent study, internships, liberal arts/career combination, semester at sea, student-designed major, study abroad, teacher certification program, Washington semester. Experimental college, semester exchange with Lincoln University and Swarthmore College, 3-2 programs with New England Conservatory of Music (BA/BM), School of the Museum of Fine Arts (BA/BFA) European Center in Talloires, France. **Credit/placement by examination:** AP, CLEP, IB, SAT, institutional tests. Limit 1 year of credit by acceleration. **Support services:** Learning center, study skills assistance, tutoring.

Majors. Area/ethnic studies: African, African-American, American, Asian, East Asian, European, Latin American, Near/Middle Eastern, Russian/Eastern European/Eurasian, Russian/Slavic, Western European, women's. **Biology:** General, ecology. **Computer sciences:** General, computer science, information systems, programming. **Conservation:** Environmental studies. **Education:** Early childhood. **Engineering:** General, applied physics, architectural, biomedical, chemical, civil, computer, electrical, engineering science, environmental, mechanical. **English:** American lit, British lit, English lit. **Foreign languages:** General, ancient Greek, Chinese, classics, comparative lit, French, German, Italian, Japanese, Latin, Russian, Spanish. **History:** General. **Liberal arts:** Arts/sciences. **Math:** General, applied. **Philosophy/religion:** Philosophy, religion. **Physical sciences:** Astronomy, chemistry, geology, physics. **Psychology:** General. **Social sciences:** Anthropology, archaeology, economics, international relations, political science, sociology. **Visual/performing arts:** Art history/conservation, music, music history, music theory/composition, musicology, studio arts, theater history.

Most popular majors. Engineering/engineering technologies 10%, foreign language 7%, psychology 6%, social sciences 31%, visual/performing arts 10%.

Computing on campus. 500 workstations in library, computer center. Dormitories wired for high-speed internet access and linked to campus network. Commuter students can connect to campus network. Online course registration, online library, helpline, repair service, student web hosting, wireless network available.

Student life. Freshman orientation: Mandatory. Preregistration for classes offered. Three-day program prior to beginning of fall semester. **Policies:** Freshmen not permitted cars on campus. **Housing:** Guaranteed on-campus for freshmen. Coed dorms, single-sex dorms, special housing for disabled, apartments, cooperative housing, fraternity/sorority housing, wellness housing available. Culture, special interest, language houses available. **Activities:** Bands, campus ministries, choral groups, dance, drama, film society, international student organizations, literary magazine, music ensembles, Model UN, musical theater, opera, radio station, student government, student newspaper, symphony orchestra, TV station, over 200 student organizations available.

Athletics. NCAA. **Intercollegiate:** Baseball M, basketball, cross-country, diving, fencing W, field hockey W, football (tackle) M, golf M, ice hockey M, lacrosse, rowing (crew), rugby, sailing, soccer, softball W, squash, swimming, tennis, track and field, volleyball W. **Intramural:** Basketball, fencing M, handball, racquetball, softball, squash, tennis, volleyball. **Team name:** Jumbos.

Student services. Adult student services, alcohol/substance abuse counseling, chaplain/spiritual director, career counseling, services for economically disadvantaged, student employment services, financial aid counseling, health services, legal services, minority student services, on-campus daycare, personal counseling, placement for graduates, women's services. **Physically disabled:** Services for visually, speech, hearing impaired.

Contact. E-mail: admissions.inquiry@ase.tufts.edu
Phone: (617) 627-3170 Fax: (617) 627-3860
Lee Coffin, Dean of Undergraduate Admissions and Enrollment Management, Tufts University, Bendetson Hall, Medford, MA 02155

University of Massachusetts Amherst
Amherst, Massachusetts
www.umass.edu

CB member
CB code: 3917

- Public 4-year university
- Residential campus in large town

- 21,265 degree-seeking undergraduates: 5% part-time, 49% women, 4% African American, 7% Asian American, 5% Hispanic American, 1% international
- 5,770 degree-seeking graduate students
- 66% of applicants admitted
- SAT or ACT (ACT writing recommended), application essay required
- 67% graduate within 6 years; 22% enter graduate study

General. Founded in 1863. Regionally accredited. **Degrees:** 5,391 bachelor's, 75 associate awarded; master's, professional, doctoral offered. **ROTC:** Army, Air Force. **Location:** 90 miles from Boston, 30 miles from Springfield. **Calendar:** Semester, limited summer session. **Full-time faculty:** 1,203 total; 93% have terminal degrees, 20% minority, 39% women. **Part-time faculty:** 142 total; 61% have terminal degrees, 9% minority, 54% women. **Class size:** 42% < 20, 35% 20-39, 5% 40-49, 9% 50-99, 9% >100. **Special facilities:** Observatory, botanical gardens, sports arena with ice rink, contemporary art museum, recreation center.

Freshman class profile. 32,564 applied, 21,373 admitted, 4,688 enrolled.

Mid 50% test scores			
SAT critical reading:	530-630	Rank in top quarter:	65%
SAT math:	560-650	Rank in top tenth:	25%
ACT composite:	24-28	Return as sophomores:	89%
GPA 3.75 or higher:	37%	Out-of-state:	26%
GPA 3.50-3.74:	29%	Live on campus:	100%
GPA 3.0-3.49:	32%	International:	2%
GPA 2.0-2.99:	2%	Fraternities:	5%
		Sororities:	6%

Basis for selection. High school grades most important, followed by test scores, extracurricular activities, essay and recommendations. Audition required of music and dance majors. Portfolio required of art and design majors. **Home schooled:** Detailed transcript required. **Learning Disabled:** Applicants must submit diagnostic data and/or individualized educational plan. Massachusetts residents with documented learning disabilities not required to submit standardized test scores for admissions consideration.

High school preparation. College-preparatory program required. 16 units required. Required units include English 4, mathematics 3, social studies 2, science 3 (laboratory 2), foreign language 2 and academic electives 2.

2011-2012 Annual costs. Tuition/fees: $12,797; $25,585 out-of-state. Room/board: $10,310. Books/supplies: $1,000. Personal expenses: $1,000.

2010-2011 Financial aid. Need-based: 4,045 full-time freshmen applied for aid; 2,803 were judged to have need; 2,724 of these received aid. Average need met was 82%. Average scholarship/grant was $9,245; average loan $3,503. 54% of total undergraduate aid awarded as scholarships/grants, 46% as loans/jobs. **Non-need-based:** Awarded to 2,268 full-time undergraduates, including 611 freshmen. Scholarships awarded for academics, art, athletics, music/drama, state residency.

Application procedures. Admission: Closing date 1/15 (postmark date). $70 fee, may be waived for applicants with need. Admission notification on a rolling basis beginning on or about 3/7. Must reply by 5/1. **Financial aid:** Priority date 3/1; no closing date. FAFSA required. Applicants notified on a rolling basis starting 4/1.

Academics. Students may take courses at Amherst, Hampshire, Mt. Holyoke and Smith Colleges at no extra charge. **Special study options:** Combined bachelor's/graduate degree, cooperative education, cross-registration, distance learning, double major, dual enrollment of high school students, ESL, exchange student, honors, independent study, internships, liberal arts/career combination, student-designed major, study abroad, teacher certification program, weekend college. **Credit/placement by examination:** AP, CLEP, IB, institutional tests. 30 credit hours maximum toward bachelor's degree. Credit awarded for International Baccalaureate scores of 4-7. **Support services:** Learning center, reduced course load, study skills assistance, tutoring, writing center.

Honors college/program. First-year students admitted by invitation, approximately 600 freshmen admitted. Interdisciplinary seminars, enriched honors courses, colloquia, independent study, service learning offered; honors thesis, project, or activity required.

Majors. Architecture: Environmental design, interior, landscape. **Area/ethnic studies:** African-American, Near/Middle Eastern, Russian/Slavic, women's. **Biology:** General, Biochemistry/molecular biology, exercise physiology, microbiology. **Business:** Accounting, business admin, finance, hospitality admin, marketing. **Communications:** General, journalism. **Computer sciences:** Computer science. **Conservation:** General, environmental science, forestry, wildlife/wilderness. **Engineering:** Chemical, civil, computer, electrical, industrial, mechanical. **English:** English lit. **Foreign languages:** Chinese, classics, comparative lit, French, Italian, Japanese, linguistics, Portuguese, Spanish. **General:** Animal sciences, economics, food science, plant

sciences. **Health services:** Communication disorders, nursing (RN), predental, premedicine, preveterinary. **History:** General. **Liberal arts:** Humanities. **Math:** General. **Parks/recreation:** Sports admin. **Philosophy/religion:** Judaic, philosophy. **Physical sciences:** Astronomy, chemistry, geology, physics. **Psychology:** General. **Social sciences:** Anthropology, economics, geography, political science, sociology. **Visual/performing arts:** Art history/conservation, dance, dramatic, music, music performance, studio arts.

Most popular majors. Biology 8%, business/marketing 17%, communications/journalism 7%, health sciences 6%, psychology 9%, social sciences 11%.

Computing on campus. 419 workstations in library, computer center. Dormitories wired for high-speed internet access and linked to campus network. Commuter students can connect to campus network. Online course registration, online library, helpline, repair service, student web hosting, wireless network available.

Student life. Freshman orientation: Mandatory. Preregistration for classes offered. Two-and-a-half-day sessions in June or July, make-up orientation at end of August, and 3-day session in September at beginning of school year. **Policies:** Students required to live on-campus through freshman year unless eligible for housing exemption (parents of dependent children, veterans, commuting students). **Housing:** Guaranteed on-campus for freshmen. Coed dorms, single-sex dorms, special housing for disabled, apartments, fraternity/sorority housing, wellness housing available. Special interest housing; residential academic programs for first-year students. Gradual penalty for cancellation of housing up to $300. **Activities:** Bands, campus ministries, choral groups, dance, drama, film society, international student organizations, literary magazine, music ensembles, Model UN, musical theater, opera, radio station, student government, student newspaper, symphony orchestra, TV station, over 300 student organizations.

Athletics. NCAA. **Intercollegiate:** Baseball M, basketball, cross-country, diving, field hockey W, football (tackle) M, ice hockey M, lacrosse, rowing (crew) W, soccer, softball W, swimming, tennis W, track and field. **Intramural:** Basketball, field hockey W, football (non-tackle), ice hockey M, racquetball, soccer, softball, tennis, volleyball. **Team name:** Minutemen, Minutewomen.

Student services. Adult student services, alcohol/substance abuse counseling, chaplain/spiritual director, career counseling, student employment services, financial aid counseling, health services, legal services, minority student services, on-campus daycare, personal counseling, placement for graduates, veterans' counselor, women's services. **Physically disabled:** Services for visually, speech, hearing impaired.

Contact. E-mail: mail@admissions.umass.edu
Phone: (413) 545-0222 Fax: (413) 545-4312
Kevin Kelly, Director of Admissions, University of Massachusetts Amherst, University Admissions Center, Amherst, MA 01003-9291

University of Massachusetts Boston
Boston, Massachusetts   **CB member**
www.umb.edu   **CB code: 3924**

- Public 4-year university
- Commuter campus in very large city
- 11,065 degree-seeking undergraduates: 27% part-time, 57% women, 16% African American, 12% Asian American, 11% Hispanic American, 6% international
- 3,155 degree-seeking graduate students
- 68% of applicants admitted
- SAT or ACT (ACT writing recommended), application essay required
- 40% graduate within 6 years

General. Founded in 1964. Regionally accredited. One of 5 campuses of the University of Massachusetts. **Degrees:** 1,941 bachelor's awarded; master's, professional, doctoral offered. **ROTC:** Army, Naval, Air Force. **Location:** 3 miles from downtown. **Calendar:** Semester, extensive summer session. **Full-time faculty:** 547 total; 98% have terminal degrees, 22% minority, 50% women. **Part-time faculty:** 541 total; 30% have terminal degrees, 10% minority, 59% women. **Class size:** 33% < 20, 59% 20-39, 2% 40-49, 4% 50-99, 2% >100. **Special facilities:** Tropical greenhouse, observatory, adaptive computer laboratory.

Freshman class profile. 6,454 applied, 4,417 admitted, 1,297 enrolled.

Mid 50% test scores			
SAT critical reading:	450-560	GPA 3.0-3.49:	36%
SAT math:	480-580	GPA 2.0-2.99:	40%
GPA 3.75 or higher:	12%	Return as sophomores:	75%
GPA 3.50-3.74:	12%	Out-of-state:	8%
		International:	13%

Basis for selection. School achievement record, range of test scores, GPA most important. Recommendations, essay also important. Extracurricular activities considered. Grades for college preparatory background should be B- or better. Interview recommended for nontraditional students.

High school preparation. College-preparatory program required. 16 units required. Required units include English 4, mathematics 3, social studies 1, history 1, science 3 (laboratory 2), foreign language 2 and academic electives 2.

2011-2012 Annual costs. Tuition/fees: $11,407; $24,927 out-of-state. Books/supplies: $800. Personal expenses: $1,240.

2010-2011 Financial aid. Need-based: 898 full-time freshmen applied for aid; 753 were judged to have need; 753 of these received aid. Average need met was 92%. Average scholarship/grant was $7,855; average loan $4,821. 49% of total undergraduate aid awarded as scholarships/grants, 51% as loans/jobs. **Non-need-based:** Awarded to 343 full-time undergraduates, including 121 freshmen. Scholarships awarded for academics, leadership. **Additional information:** Some Massachusetts state employees and Massachusetts Vietnam veterans eligible for tuition waiver. Some waivers available based on talent and academic excellence.

Application procedures. Admission: Priority date 3/1; deadline 4/1. $60 fee, may be waived for applicants with need. Admission notification on a rolling basis. Must reply by May 1 or within 3 week(s) if notified thereafter. **Financial aid:** Priority date 3/1; no closing date. FAFSA required. Applicants notified on a rolling basis starting 3/22.

Academics. Special study options: Combined bachelor's/graduate degree, cooperative education, cross-registration, distance learning, double major, dual enrollment of high school students, ESL, exchange student, honors, independent study, internships, liberal arts/career combination, student-designed major, study abroad, teacher certification program. 2-2 programs in engineering with area institutions. **Credit/placement by examination:** AP, CLEP, SAT, ACT, institutional tests. 90 credit hours maximum toward bachelor's degree. **Support services:** Learning center, pre-admission summer program, reduced course load, remedial instruction, study skills assistance, tutoring, writing center.

Majors. Area/ethnic studies: African-American, American, Asian, women's. **Biology:** General, biochemistry. **Business:** Business admin. **Computer sciences:** General, information technology. **Education:** Early childhood. **Engineering:** Applied physics. **English:** English lit. **Foreign languages:** Classics, French, Italian, Spanish. **Health services:** Nursing (RN). **History:** General. **Human services:** General, community org/advocacy. **Math:** General. **Parks/recreation:** Health/fitness. **Philosophy/religion:** Philosophy. **Physical sciences:** Chemistry, geology, physics. **Protective services:** Criminal justice. **Psychology:** General. **Social sciences:** General, anthropology, economics, political science, sociology. **Visual/performing arts:** Art, dramatic, music.

Most popular majors. Biology 6%, business/marketing 23%, English 6%, health sciences 17%, psychology 11%, security/protective services 6%, social sciences 12%.

Computing on campus. 350 workstations in library, computer center, student center. Commuter students can connect to campus network. Online course registration, online library, helpline, repair service, wireless network available.

Student life. Freshman orientation: Mandatory, $25 fee. Preregistration for classes offered. **Housing:** Housing referral services available. **Activities:** Bands, campus ministries, choral groups, dance, drama, film society, international student organizations, literary magazine, music ensembles, Model UN, radio station, student government, student newspaper, symphony orchestra.

Athletics. NCAA. **Intercollegiate:** Baseball M, basketball, cross-country, ice hockey M, lacrosse M, soccer, softball W, tennis, track and field, volleyball W. **Intramural:** Basketball, ice hockey M, racquetball, sailing, soccer, softball, squash, tennis, volleyball. **Team name:** Beacons.

Student services. Adult student services, alcohol/substance abuse counseling, chaplain/spiritual director, career counseling, student employment services, health services, legal services, minority student services, on-campus daycare, personal counseling, placement for graduates, veterans' counselor, women's services. **Physically disabled:** Services for visually, speech, hearing impaired.

Contact. E-mail: enrollment.info@umb.edu
Phone: (617) 287-6000 Fax: (617) 287-5999
John Drew, Director of Admissions, University of Massachusetts Boston, 100 Morrissey Boulevard, Boston, MA 02125-3393

University of Massachusetts Dartmouth
North Dartmouth, Massachusetts   **CB member**
www.umassd.edu   **CB code: 3786**

- Public 4-year university
- Residential campus in large town
- 7,372 degree-seeking undergraduates: 12% part-time, 48% women, 10% African American, 3% Asian American, 6% Hispanic American
- 1,514 degree-seeking graduate students
- 70% of applicants admitted
- SAT or ACT (ACT writing optional), application essay required
- 48% graduate within 6 years

General. Founded in 1895. Regionally accredited. **Degrees:** 1,328 bachelor's awarded; master's, professional, doctoral offered. **ROTC:** Army. **Location:** 60 miles from Boston; 30 miles from Providence, Rhode Island. **Calendar:** Semester, extensive summer session. **Full-time faculty:** 380 total; 84% have terminal degrees, 21% minority, 43% women. **Part-time faculty:** 256 total; 20% have terminal degrees, 8% minority, 51% women. **Class size:** 34% <20, 41% 20-39, 11% 40-49, 12% 50-99, 2% >100. **Special facilities:** Observatory, marine research vessel, coastal marine laboratory, full art studios, Jewish culture and Portuguese studies centers, Robert F. Kennedy assassination archive.

Freshman class profile. 8,164 applied, 5,711 admitted, 1,429 enrolled.

Mid 50% test scores			
SAT critical reading:	460-570	GPA 2.0-2.99:	40%
SAT math:	490-580	Rank in top quarter:	39%
SAT writing:	450-550	Rank in top tenth:	15%
ACT composite:	20-25	End year in good standing:	85%
GPA 3.75 or higher:	15%	Return as sophomores:	73%
GPA 3.50-3.74:	12%	Out-of-state:	4%
GPA 3.0-3.49:	33%	Live on campus:	78%

Basis for selection. High school record, test scores most important; class rank, essay, recommendations considered. 2.0 GPA required; 3.0 GPA recommended. Audition required for music majors; portfolio required for design majors. **Home schooled:** State high school equivalency certificate required. Must get certification or equivalency from local high school. **Learning Disabled:** SAT scores may be waived for Massachusetts students with documented disability.

High school preparation. College-preparatory program required. 16 units required. Required units include English 4, mathematics 3, social studies 1, history 1, science 3 (laboratory 2), foreign language 2 and academic electives 2. 1 U.S. history required. Programs in science, engineering and business require additional math. Science and engineering require physical science. 2 foreign language must be same language.

2011-2012 Annual costs. Tuition/fees: $11,135; $21,952 out-of-state. Room/board: $9,840. Books/supplies: $1,200. Personal expenses: $1,320.

Financial aid. Non-need-based: Scholarships awarded for academics, minority status, ROTC, state residency.

Application procedures. Admission: No deadline. $50 fee ($60 out-of-state), may be waived for applicants with need. Admission notification on a rolling basis beginning on or about 1/1. Must reply by May 1 or within 2 week(s) if notified thereafter. Competitive programs may be filled by March 1. Nursing closes by late January. Freshman applicants advised to apply before end of December and not later than March. **Financial aid:** Priority date 3/1; no closing date. FAFSA required. Applicants notified on a rolling basis starting 3/25; must reply within 3 week(s) of notification.

Academics. Alternative admissions program for academically disadvantaged Massachusetts residents; program offers special freshman curriculum and counseling support. **Special study options:** Combined bachelor's/graduate degree, cooperative education, cross-registration, distance learning, double major, dual enrollment of high school students, exchange student, honors, independent study, internships, semester at sea, student-designed major, study abroad, teacher certification program, Washington semester. **Credit/placement by examination:** AP, CLEP, IB, SAT, ACT, institutional tests. 30 credit hours maximum toward bachelor's degree. **Support services:** Learning center, reduced course load, remedial instruction, study skills assistance, tutoring, writing center.

Majors. Area/ethnic studies: Women's. **Biology:** General. **Business:** General, accounting, business admin, finance, human resources, management information systems, marketing, operations. **Computer sciences:** General. **Education:** Art. **Engineering:** Biomedical, civil, computer, electrical, mechanical, textile. **English:** English lit. **Foreign languages:** French, Portuguese, Spanish. **Health services:** Clinical lab science, health care admin, nursing (RN). **History:** General. **Liberal arts:** Arts/sciences. **Math:** General.

Philosophy/religion: Philosophy. **Physical sciences:** Chemistry, physics. **Psychology:** General. **Social sciences:** Criminology, economics, political science, sociology, sociology/anthropology. **Visual/performing arts:** General, art history/conservation, ceramics, commercial/advertising art, design, fiber arts, metal/jewelry, multimedia, music, painting, photography, sculpture, studio arts.

Most popular majors. Business/marketing 31%, engineering/engineering technologies 9%, health sciences 12%, psychology 8%, social sciences 10%, visual/performing arts 8%.

Computing on campus. 650 workstations in dormitories, library, computer center, student center. Dormitories wired for high-speed internet access and linked to campus network. Commuter students can connect to campus network. Helpline, repair service, wireless network available.

Student life. Freshman orientation: Mandatory, $200 fee. Preregistration for classes offered. Three-day, 2-night program in June and July. **Housing:** Coed dorms, special housing for disabled, apartments, wellness housing available. $200 nonrefundable deposit, deadline 5/1. Quiet, substance-free, smoke-free, program-dedicated suites, first year living learning communities available. **Activities:** Bands, choral groups, dance, drama, international student organizations, literary magazine, music ensembles, musical theater, radio station, student government, student newspaper, symphony orchestra, women's center, Portuguese center, Unity House, Indian student organization, Arab student organization, Luso-American student organization, Taiwanese student organization, MASSPIRG.

Athletics. NCAA. **Intercollegiate:** Baseball M, basketball, cheerleading M, cross-country, diving, equestrian W, field hockey W, football (tackle) M, golf M, ice hockey M, lacrosse, soccer, softball W, swimming, tennis, track and field, volleyball W. **Intramural:** Badminton, basketball, cross-country, football (non-tackle), sailing, soccer, softball, swimming, table tennis, tennis, volleyball. **Team name:** Corsairs.

Student services. Adult student services, alcohol/substance abuse counseling, chaplain/spiritual director, career counseling, student employment services, financial aid counseling, health services, minority student services, on-campus daycare, personal counseling, placement for graduates, veterans' counselor, women's services. **Physically disabled:** Services for visually, speech, hearing impaired.

Contact. E-mail: admissions@umassd.edu
Phone: (508) 999-8605 Fax: (508) 999-8755
Michael Lynch, Director of Admissions, University of Massachusetts Dartmouth, 285 Old Westport Road, North Dartmouth, MA 02747-2300

University of Massachusetts Lowell
Lowell, Massachusetts   **CB member**
www.uml.edu   **CB code: 3911**

- Public 4-year university
- Commuter campus in small city
- 11,025 degree-seeking undergraduates: 24% part-time, 39% women, 7% African American, 9% Asian American, 9% Hispanic American, 1% international
- 3,200 degree-seeking graduate students
- 65% of applicants admitted
- SAT or ACT (ACT writing optional), application essay required
- 50% graduate within 6 years

General. Founded in 1894. Regionally accredited. **Degrees:** 1,653 bachelor's, 25 associate awarded; master's, professional, doctoral offered. **ROTC:** Army, Air Force. **Location:** 40 miles from Boston, 45 miles from Worcester. **Calendar:** Semester, extensive summer session. **Full-time faculty:** 402 total; 86% have terminal degrees, 17% minority, 35% women. **Part-time faculty:** 312 total; 6% minority, 44% women. **Class size:** 49% <20, 36% 20-39, 10% 40-49, 3% 50-99, 2% >100. **Special facilities:** Tsongas industrial history center, teaching and research laboratories in sound recording technology, digital imaging, wellness resource room, boathouse.

Freshman class profile. 7,720 applied, 5,020 admitted, 1,433 enrolled.

Mid 50% test scores			
SAT critical reading:	480-590	GPA 2.0-2.99:	33%
SAT math:	520-620	Rank in top quarter:	43%
GPA 3.75 or higher:	19%	Rank in top tenth:	17%
GPA 3.50-3.74:	12%	Return as sophomores:	79%
GPA 3.0-3.49:	36%	Out-of-state:	11%
		Live on campus:	70%

Basis for selection. Admissions primarily based on academic assessment, which includes curriculum, performance as measured by grades and grade

trends, preparation for undergraduate major, and standardized testing. Recommendations, essay, and extracurricular activities considered. Audition required of music majors. **Home schooled:** Statement describing home school structure and mission, transcript of courses and grades, state high school equivalency certificate, letter of recommendation (nonparent) required. **Learning Disabled:** Students with a documented learning difference can have standardized testing requirement waived with appropriate testing documentation.

High school preparation. College-preparatory program recommended. 16 units required. Required and recommended units include English 4, mathematics 3-4, social studies 2, science 3-4 (laboratory 2), foreign language 2 and academic electives 2. 1 social studies unit must be U.S. History.

2011-2012 Annual costs. Tuition/fees: $11,297; $23,736 out-of-state. Room/board: $9,520. Books/supplies: $1,200. Personal expenses: $808.

2011-2012 Financial aid. Need-based: 1,279 full-time freshmen applied for aid; 984 were judged to have need; 984 of these received aid. Average need met was 93%. Average scholarship/grant was $8,377; average loan $5,870. 45% of total undergraduate aid awarded as scholarships/grants, 55% as loans/jobs. **Non-need-based:** Awarded to 850 full-time undergraduates, including 278 freshmen. Scholarships awarded for academics, alumni affiliation, art, athletics, job skills, leadership, minority status, music/drama, ROTC, state residency.

Application procedures. Admission: Priority date 12/1; deadline 2/15 (postmark date). $60 fee, may be waived for applicants with need. Admission notification on a rolling basis beginning on or about 1/12. Must reply by 5/1. Must reply within 2 weeks of notification of acceptance. **Financial aid:** Priority date 3/1; no closing date. FAFSA required. Applicants notified on a rolling basis starting 3/22.

Academics. Special focus on applied science and technology; coursework emphasizes context and implications of each discipline. Funded research initiatives available in nanotechnology, bioinformatics, advanced materials, photonics. **Special study options:** Accelerated study, combined bachelor's/graduate degree, cooperative education, cross-registration, distance learning, double major, dual enrollment of high school students, honors, independent study, internships, liberal arts/career combination, study abroad, teacher certification program. **Credit/placement by examination:** AP, CLEP, IB, SAT, ACT, institutional tests. 30 credit hours maximum toward associate degree, 30 toward bachelor's. **Support services:** Learning center, pre-admission summer program, reduced course load, study skills assistance, tutoring, writing center.

Majors. Area/ethnic studies: American. **Biology:** General. **Business:** Business admin, entrepreneurial studies. **Computer sciences:** Computer science, information systems. **Education:** Music. **Engineering:** Chemical, civil, electrical, mechanical, polymer. **English:** English lit. **Foreign languages:** General. **Health services:** Clinical lab science, community health services, nursing (RN). **History:** General. **Liberal arts:** Arts/sciences. **Math:** General, applied. **Philosophy/religion:** Philosophy. **Physical sciences:** Chemistry, physics. **Protective services:** Law enforcement admin. **Psychology:** General. **Social sciences:** Economics, political science, sociology. **Visual/performing arts:** General, art, graphic design, music, music management, music performance, studio arts.

Most popular majors. Business/marketing 20%, computer/information sciences 9%, engineering/engineering technologies 14%, health sciences 11%, liberal arts 7%, psychology 7%, security/protective services 12%.

Computing on campus. 3,125 workstations in dormitories, library, computer center, student center. Dormitories wired for high-speed internet access and linked to campus network. Commuter students can connect to campus network. Online course registration, online library, helpline, wireless network available.

Student life. Freshman orientation: Mandatory. Preregistration for classes offered. Two-day sessions available 12 times throughout summer; includes optional program for parents. **Housing:** Guaranteed on-campus for freshmen. Coed dorms, special housing for disabled, apartments, cooperative housing available. $300 fully refundable deposit, deadline 5/1. **Activities:** Bands, campus ministries, choral groups, dance, drama, international student organizations, literary magazine, music ensembles, Model UN, radio station, student government, student newspaper, Abundant Life Christian Fellowship, Chi Alpha, Latter-day Saints student association, Association of Students of African Origin, Cambodian student association, Latin American student association, community service organization, College Democrats, College Republicans.

Athletics. NCAA. **Intercollegiate:** Baseball M, basketball, cross-country, field hockey W, golf M, ice hockey M, rowing (crew) W, soccer, softball W, track and field, volleyball. **Intramural:** Badminton, basketball, football (non-tackle), handball, ice hockey, racquetball, skiing, soccer, softball, squash, swimming, table tennis, tennis, volleyball, weight lifting. **Team name:** River Hawks.

Student services. Adult student services, alcohol/substance abuse counseling, chaplain/spiritual director, career counseling, student employment services, financial aid counseling, health services, minority student services, personal counseling, placement for graduates, veterans' counselor. **Physically disabled:** Services for visually, speech, hearing impaired.

Contact. E-mail: admissions@uml.edu
Phone: (978) 934-3931 Fax: (978) 934-3086
Kerri Johnston, Associate Dean of Enrollment and Director of Undergraduate Admissions, University of Massachusetts Lowell, 883 Broadway Street, Room 110, Lowell, MA 01854-5104

University of Phoenix: Boston
Braintree, Massachusetts
www.phoenix.edu

- For-profit 4-year university
- Very large city
- 261 degree-seeking undergraduates

General. Regionally accredited. **Degrees:** 70 bachelor's awarded; master's offered. **Calendar:** Differs by program. **Full-time faculty:** 13 total. **Part-time faculty:** 114 total.

Basis for selection. Open admission, but selective for some programs.

2011-2012 Annual costs. Estimated costs as of August 2011: per-credit-hour charge, $380 to $520, depending upon level and course of study; electronic course materials fee, $95, if applicable. Book and material charges may vary by course and program. All fees are subject to change.

Application procedures. Admission: No deadline. No application fee. **Financial aid:** No deadline.

Academics. Credit/placement by examination: AP, CLEP.

Majors. Business: General, accounting, business admin, finance, marketing. **Computer sciences:** Information technology, web page design. **Engineering:** Software.

Contact. Toll-free number: (866) 766-0766
Marc Booker, Director of Admission and Evaluation, University of Phoenix: Boston, 19 Granite Street, Suite 300, Braintree, MA 02169-1744

Wellesley College
Wellesley, Massachusetts
www.wellesley.edu

	CB member
	CB code: 3957

- Private 4-year liberal arts college for women
- Residential campus in large town
- 2,372 degree-seeking undergraduates: 1% part-time, 100% women, 7% African American, 22% Asian American, 7% Hispanic American, 11% international
- 31% of applicants admitted
- SAT and SAT Subject Tests or ACT with writing, application essay required
- 92% graduate within 6 years

General. Founded in 1870. Regionally accredited. **Degrees:** 610 bachelor's awarded. **ROTC:** Army, Air Force. **Location:** 12 miles from Boston. **Calendar:** Semester, limited summer session. **Full-time faculty:** 289 total; 92% have terminal degrees, 25% minority, 55% women. **Part-time faculty:** 62 total; 71% have terminal degrees, 21% minority, 73% women. **Class size:** 63% < 20, 35% 20-39, less than 1% 40-49, less than 1% 50-99. **Special facilities:** Science center with X-ray diffractometer, nuclear magnetic resonance, spectrometers (NMR and microMRI), electron microscopes, argon and dye lasers, observatory with three telescopes (6-, 12-, and 24-inch), cultural center, greenhouses, botanic gardens, arboretum, media and technology center with linear editing room for video, digital-based video editing suite, plotter, film recorder, slide scanner.

Freshman class profile. 4,400 applied, 1,362 admitted, 574 enrolled.

Mid 50% test scores				
SAT critical reading:	650-740	Rank in top tenth:		78%
SAT math:	640-750	Return as sophomores:		95%
SAT writing:	660-750	Out-of-state:		86%
ACT composite:	29-32	Live on campus:		100%
Rank in top quarter:	93%	International:		12%

Basis for selection. Evidence in student's record, both in and out of the classroom, of ability to meet rigorous academic standards and willingness to engage in the community is important. Candidates should have taken full advantage of the opportunities available in high school. 2 SAT Subject Tests required if SAT is submitted; at least one quantitative Subject Test recommended. Interviews recommended; on- and off-campus interviews available. **Home schooled:** Statement describing home school structure and mission, transcript of courses and grades, letter of recommendation (nonparent) required. Applicants must meet homeschooling requirements of their state.

High school preparation. College-preparatory program recommended. Recommended units include English 4, mathematics 4, social studies 4, history 4, science 3 (laboratory 2) and foreign language 4.

2011-2012 Annual costs. Tuition/fees: $40,660. Room/board: $12,590. Books/supplies: $800. Personal expenses: $1,200.

2011-2012 Financial aid. All financial aid based on need. 397 full-time freshmen applied for aid; 322 were judged to have need; 322 of these received aid. Average need met was 100%. Average scholarship/grant was $36,306; average loan $2,491. 92% of total undergraduate aid awarded as scholarships/grants, 8% as loans/jobs. **Additional information:** No student will graduate with more than $12,825 in packaged student loans. Students from families with a calculated income between $60,000 and $100,000 will graduate with no more than $8,600 in packaged student loans. Students from families with the greatest need ($60,000 income or less) will graduate with $0 in packaged student loans; their packages will consist of scholarship and work-study money.

Application procedures. Admission: Closing date 1/15 (postmark date). $50 fee, may be waived for applicants with need, free for online applicants. Admission notification by 4/1. Must reply by 5/1. **Financial aid:** Priority date 1/15; no closing date. FAFSA, CSS PROFILE required.

Academics. **Special study options:** Cross-registration, double major, dual enrollment of high school students, exchange student, honors, independent study, internships, semester at sea, student-designed major, study abroad, teacher certification program, Washington semester. **Credit/placement by examination:** AP, CLEP, IB, institutional tests. 16 credit hours maximum toward bachelor's degree. Students may receive credit for score of 5 on most AP exams or a 5, 6, or 7 on most IB exams. **Support services:** Learning center, reduced course load, study skills assistance, tutoring, writing center.

Majors. **Architecture:** Architecture. **Area/ethnic studies:** African, African-American, American, Asian, East Asian, European, French, German, Latin American, Near/Middle Eastern, Russian/Eastern European/Eurasian, Russian/Slavic, South Asian, women's. **Biology:** General, biochemistry, neuroscience. **Computer sciences:** General, computer science. **Conservation:** Environmental studies. **Engineering:** General. **English:** English lit. **Foreign languages:** General, African, ancient Greek, Arabic, Chinese, classics, comparative lit, French, German, Italian, Japanese, Latin, linguistics, Russian, Spanish. **History:** General. **Math:** General. **Philosophy/religion:** Judaic, philosophy, religion. **Physical sciences:** Astronomy, astrophysics, chemistry, geology, physics. **Psychology:** General. **Social sciences:** Anthropology, archaeology, economics, international relations, political science, sociology. **Visual/performing arts:** Art history/conservation, dramatic, music, music history, studio arts.

Most popular majors. Area/ethnic studies 9%, biology 9%, English 7%, foreign language 9%, psychology 8%, social sciences 28%, visual/performing arts 8%.

Computing on campus. 481 workstations in dormitories, library, computer center, student center. Dormitories wired for high-speed internet access and linked to campus network. Commuter students can connect to campus network. Online course registration, online library, helpline, repair service, student web hosting, wireless network available.

Student life. **Freshman orientation:** Mandatory. Preregistration for classes offered. Held the week before classes begin. **Policies:** Honor Code in effect. **Housing:** Guaranteed on-campus for all undergraduates. Apartments, cooperative housing, wellness housing available. $300 nonrefundable deposit, deadline 5/1. Pets allowed in dorm rooms. French and Spanish language houses available. **Activities:** Jazz band, campus ministries, choral groups, dance, drama, film society, international student organizations, literary magazine, music ensembles, Model UN, radio station, student government, student newspaper, symphony orchestra, black student club, Latina student club, Asian student union, Hillel, Al-Muslimat, Intervarsity Christian Fellowship, political and legislative action organization, Best Buddies, Habitat for Humanity.

Athletics. NCAA. **Intercollegiate:** Basketball W, cross-country W, diving W, fencing W, field hockey W, golf W, lacrosse W, rowing (crew) W, soccer W, softball W, squash W, swimming W, tennis W, track and field W, volleyball W. **Intramural:** Basketball W, ice hockey W, racquetball W,

rowing (crew) W, rugby W, sailing W, soccer W, table tennis W. **Team name:** Wellesley Blue.

Student services. Adult student services, alcohol/substance abuse counseling, chaplain/spiritual director, career counseling, services for economically disadvantaged, student employment services, financial aid counseling, health services, minority student services, on-campus daycare, personal counseling, placement for graduates, women's services. **Physically disabled:** Services for visually, hearing impaired.

Contact. E-mail: admission@wellesley.edu
Phone: (781) 283-2270 Fax: (781) 283-3678
Jennifer Desjarlais, Dean of Admission and Financial Aid, Wellesley College, 106 Central Street, Wellesley, MA 02481

Wentworth Institute of Technology
Boston, Massachusetts **CB member**
www.wit.edu **CB code: 3958**

- Private 4-year engineering and technical college
- Residential campus in very large city
- 3,833 degree-seeking undergraduates: 10% part-time, 18% women, 5% African American, 6% Asian American, 4% Hispanic American, 4% international
- 133 degree-seeking graduate students
- 61% of applicants admitted
- SAT or ACT (ACT writing optional), application essay required
- 61% graduate within 6 years; 21% enter graduate study

General. Founded in 1904. Regionally accredited. Mandatory cooperative education program. Member of Colleges of the Fenway. **Degrees:** 673 bachelor's, 72 associate awarded; master's offered. **ROTC:** Army, Air Force. **Location:** 2 miles from downtown. **Calendar:** Semester, limited summer session. **Full-time faculty:** 142 total; 70% have terminal degrees, 14% minority, 23% women. **Part-time faculty:** 158 total; 8% minority, 32% women. **Class size:** 37% < 20, 60% 20-39, 1% 40-49, less than 1% 50-99, less than 1% >100.

Freshman class profile. 4,967 applied, 3,043 admitted, 974 enrolled.

Mid 50% test scores			
SAT critical reading:	460-570	GPA 2.0-2.99:	46%
SAT math:	520-610	Rank in top quarter:	41%
SAT writing:	450-560	Rank in top tenth:	14%
ACT composite:	21-26	End year in good standing:	86%
GPA 3.75 or higher:	6%	Return as sophomores:	79%
GPA 3.50-3.74:	11%	Out-of-state:	36%
GPA 3.0-3.49:	35%	Live on campus:	77%
		International:	6%

Basis for selection. School achievement record most important, followed by test scores. Teacher recommendations, personal statement, extracurricular activities also considered. **Home schooled:** Transcript of courses and grades, letter of recommendation (nonparent) required. Course content description may be requested.

High school preparation. College-preparatory program recommended. Required and recommended units include English 4, mathematics 3-4, science 2 (laboratory 1). 3 college-preparatory math, 1 physics recommended for many programs. Additional math required for some.

2011-2012 Annual costs. Tuition/fees: $24,000. Tuition includes cost of laptop computer. Room/board: $11,300. Books/supplies: $1,200. Personal expenses: $2,500.

2011-2012 Financial aid. **Need-based:** 748 full-time freshmen applied for aid; 695 were judged to have need; 695 of these received aid. Average scholarship/grant was $6,251; average loan $3,368. 57% of total undergraduate aid awarded as scholarships/grants, 43% as loans/jobs. **Non-need-based:** Awarded to 2,027 full-time undergraduates, including 716 freshmen. Scholarships awarded for academics, leadership, ROTC, state residency.

Application procedures. Admission: Priority date 5/1; no deadline. $50 fee, may be waived for applicants with need. Admission notification on a rolling basis beginning on or about 10/30. Must reply by May 1 or within 2 week(s) if notified thereafter. **Financial aid:** Priority date 3/1; no closing date. FAFSA required. Applicants notified on a rolling basis starting 3/15; must reply within 2 week(s) of notification.

Academics. Some bachelor's programs require 5 years. All bachelor's candidates required to complete 2 semesters full-time co-op. **Special study options:** Combined bachelor's/graduate degree, cooperative education, cross-registration, study abroad. Cross-registration with Simmons College, Emmanuel College, Wheelock College, Massachusetts College of Pharmacy and Health Sciences, Massachusetts College of Art (Colleges of the Fenway).

Credit/placement by examination: AP, CLEP, IB, institutional tests. 32 credit hours maximum toward associate degree, 64 toward bachelor's. Students may only receive maximum of one half of total credit requirement from credit by examination. **Support services:** Learning center, reduced course load, study skills assistance, tutoring, writing center.

Majors. Architecture: Architecture. **Business:** Business admin, construction management, operations, project management. **Computer sciences:** Computer science, networking. **Engineering:** General, biomedical, civil, computer, electrical, electromechanical, mechanical. **Math:** Applied. **Visual/performing arts:** Industrial design, interior design.

Most popular majors. Architecture 23%, business/marketing 26%, computer/information sciences 9%, engineering/engineering technologies 32%, visual/performing arts 9%.

Computing on campus. PC or laptop required. 300 workstations in dormitories, library, computer center. Dormitories wired for high-speed internet access and linked to campus network. Commuter students can connect to campus network. Online course registration, online library, helpline, repair service, student web hosting, wireless network available.

Student life. Freshman orientation: Mandatory. Preregistration for classes offered. Week-long session held week before classes begin. **Policies:** Alcohol permitted in certain residential halls if every resident of the room is 21 or older. Smoke-free campus. Freshmen not permitted cars on campus. **Housing:** Coed dorms available. $500 fully refundable deposit, deadline 5/1. Apartments available for upperclassmen. **Activities:** Dance, film society, international student organizations, radio station, student government, honor society, Society of Women Engineers, Student Association of Interior Design, National Society of Black Engineers, Society of Hispanic Professional Engineers, architecture club, American Society of Civil Engineers, Society of Manufacturing Engineers, Institute of Electrical & Electronic Engineers, Industrial Design Society of America.

Athletics. NCAA. **Intercollegiate:** Baseball M, basketball, golf M, ice hockey M, lacrosse M, rifle, soccer, softball W, tennis, volleyball. **Intramural:** Basketball, softball, volleyball. **Team name:** Leopards.

Student services. Alcohol/substance abuse counseling, career counseling, student employment services, financial aid counseling, health services, minority student services, personal counseling, placement for graduates, veterans' counselor, women's services. **Physically disabled:** Services for hearing impaired.

Contact. E-mail: admissions@wit.edu
Phone: (617) 989-4000 Toll-free number: (800) 556-0610
Fax: (617) 989-4010
Maureen Dischino, Director of Admissions, Wentworth Institute of Technology, 550 Huntington Avenue, Boston, MA 02115

Western New England University

Springfield, Massachusetts
www.wne.edu

CB member
CB code: 3962

- Private 4-year university
- Residential campus in small city
- 2,665 degree-seeking undergraduates: 7% part-time, 39% women, 5% African American, 3% Asian American, 6% Hispanic American, 1% international
- 1,023 degree-seeking graduate students
- 80% of applicants admitted
- SAT or ACT (ACT writing optional), application essay required
- 61% graduate within 6 years

General. Founded in 1919. Regionally accredited. **Degrees:** 611 bachelor's awarded; master's, professional, doctoral offered. **ROTC:** Army, Air Force. **Location:** 95 miles from Boston, 20 miles from Hartford. **Calendar:** Semester, limited summer session. **Full-time faculty:** 205 total; 89% have terminal degrees, 11% minority, 38% women. **Part-time faculty:** 132 total; 50% have terminal degrees, 6% minority, 35% women. **Class size:** 43% < 20, 57% 20-39.

Freshman class profile. 5,792 applied, 4,625 admitted, 756 enrolled.

Mid 50% test scores			
SAT critical reading:	470-570	**GPA 2.0-2.99:**	37%
SAT math:	490-600	**Rank in top quarter:**	41%
ACT composite:	22-26	**Rank in top tenth:**	15%
GPA 3.75 or higher:	23%	**Return as sophomores:**	73%
GPA 3.50-3.74:	13%	**Out-of-state:**	61%
GPA 3.0-3.49:	27%	**Live on campus:**	87%
		International:	1%

Basis for selection. School achievement record, test scores, recommendation most important. Interview, class rank, extracurricular activities also considered.

High school preparation. College-preparatory program required. 10 units required; 18 recommended. Required and recommended units include English 4, mathematics 2-4, social studies 1-2, history 1-2, science 1-2 (laboratory 1-2) and foreign language 1-2. 1 American history required. Additional science and math required for certain programs.

2011-2012 Annual costs. Tuition/fees: $30,844. Room/board: $11,732. Books/supplies: $1,100. Personal expenses: $1,400.

Financial aid. Non-need-based: Scholarships awarded for academics, music/drama, ROTC.

Application procedures. Admission: Priority date 2/15; no deadline. $40 fee, may be waived for applicants with need. Admission notification on a rolling basis beginning on or about 11/15. Must reply by May 1 or within 2 week(s) if notified thereafter. **Financial aid:** Closing date 4/15. FAFSA required. Applicants notified on a rolling basis starting 3/1; must reply by 5/1 or within 2 week(s) of notification.

Academics. Special study options: Accelerated study, combined bachelor's/graduate degree, cross-registration, distance learning, double major, dual enrollment of high school students, ESL, exchange student, honors, independent study, internships, liberal arts/career combination, student-designed major, study abroad, teacher certification program, Washington semester. 3+3 law program. Accelerated part-time degree completion. 3+2 programs for completion of MBA or MSA for a variety of majors. **Credit/placement by examination:** AP, CLEP, IB, SAT, ACT, institutional tests. **Support services:** Pre-admission summer program, reduced course load, study skills assistance, tutoring, writing center.

Majors. Biology: General, molecular. **Business:** General, accounting, business admin, finance, management information systems, marketing. **Communications:** Advertising, communications/speech/rhetoric, journalism, media studies, public relations. **Computer sciences:** Computer science, information systems. **Education:** Elementary, secondary. **Engineering:** Biomedical, civil, electrical, industrial, mechanical. **English:** Creative writing, English lit. **Health services:** Prepharmacy. **History:** General. **Human services:** Social work. **Liberal arts:** Arts/sciences. **Math:** General. **Parks/recreation:** Sports admin. **Philosophy/religion:** Philosophy. **Physical sciences:** Chemistry. **Protective services:** Criminal justice. **Psychology:** General. **Social sciences:** Economics, political science, sociology. **Visual/performing arts:** Arts management.

Most popular majors. Business/marketing 35%, engineering/engineering technologies 15%, parks/recreation 8%, psychology 10%, security/protective services 10%.

Computing on campus. 400 workstations in dormitories, library, computer center, student center. Dormitories wired for high-speed internet access and linked to campus network. Commuter students can connect to campus network. Online library, helpline, repair service, wireless network available.

Student life. Freshman orientation: Available. Preregistration for classes offered. Two-day program held over summer for students and parents. Parents assessed meals and materials fee. **Housing:** Guaranteed on-campus for freshmen. Coed dorms, special housing for disabled, apartments available. $400 nonrefundable deposit, deadline 5/1. **Activities:** Bands, campus ministries, choral groups, dance, drama, international student organizations, literary magazine, music ensembles, radio station, student government, student newspaper, United and Mutually Equal, Helping Hands Society.

Athletics. NCAA. **Intercollegiate:** Baseball M, basketball, bowling, cross-country, field hockey W, football (tackle) M, golf M, ice hockey M, lacrosse, soccer, softball W, swimming W, tennis, volleyball W, wrestling M. **Intramural:** Badminton, basketball, football (non-tackle), handball, soccer, softball, table tennis, volleyball, water polo. **Team name:** Golden Bears.

Student services. Adult student services, alcohol/substance abuse counseling, chaplain/spiritual director, career counseling, student employment services, financial aid counseling, health services, minority student services, personal counseling, veterans' counselor. **Physically disabled:** Services for visually, hearing impaired.

Contact. E-mail: learn@wne.edu
Phone: (413) 782-1321 Toll-free number: (800) 325-1122 ext. 1321
Fax: (413) 782-1777
Charles Pollock, Vice President for Enrollment Management, Western New England University, 1215 Wilbraham Road, Springfield, MA 01119-2684

Westfield State University

Westfield, Massachusetts
www.westfield.ma.edu

CB member
CB code: 3523

- Public 4-year university
- Residential campus in large town
- 5,254 degree-seeking undergraduates: 9% part-time, 53% women, 4% African American, 1% Asian American, 5% Hispanic American
- 544 degree-seeking graduate students
- 61% of applicants admitted
- SAT or ACT (ACT writing optional) required
- 58% graduate within 6 years

General. Founded in 1838. Regionally accredited. **Degrees:** 1,044 bachelor's awarded; master's offered. **ROTC:** Army, Air Force. **Location:** 10 miles from Springfield, 100 miles from Boston. **Calendar:** Semester, limited summer session. **Full-time faculty:** 221 total; 88% have terminal degrees, 14% minority, 47% women. **Part-time faculty:** 244 total; 27% have terminal degrees, 4% minority, 47% women. **Class size:** 41% < 20, 55% 20-39, 1% 40-49, 2% 50-99, less than 1% >100. **Special facilities:** Television production studio, radio studio, natural history museum/collections, GIS lab.

Freshman class profile. 5,192 applied, 3,178 admitted, 1,133 enrolled.

Mid 50% test scores			
SAT critical reading:	450-550	GPA 2.0-2.99:	43%
SAT math:	470-560	End year in good standing:	86%
ACT composite:	20-25	Return as sophomores:	80%
GPA 3.75 or higher:	10%	Out-of-state:	8%
GPA 3.50-3.74:	11%	Live on campus:	86%
GPA 3.0-3.49:	36%	International:	1%

Basis for selection. Rigor of secondary school record, academic grade point average, and standardized testing are the most important factors. Personal essay and recommendations may be considered if submitted. Extracurricular activities, community involvement, and family educational background may also be considered. SAT/ACT waived for students with documented learning disability. Interview required for learning disabled applicants at request of Director of Disability Services. Essay recommended. Audition required of music majors. Portfolio required of art majors. **Home schooled:** Requirements based on AACROA standards. **Learning Disabled:** SAT/ACT test score requirement waived for students with documented learning disability. Interview required for learning disabled applicants at the request of the Director of Disability Services.

High school preparation. College-preparatory program required. 16 units required. Required units include English 4, mathematics 3, social studies 1, history 1, science 3 (laboratory 2), foreign language 2 and academic electives 2.

2011-2012 Annual costs. Tuition/fees: $7,886; $13,966 out-of-state. Room/board: $8,946. Books/supplies: $1,035. Personal expenses: $1,200.

2010-2011 Financial aid. **Need-based:** 1,078 full-time freshmen applied for aid; 703 were judged to have need; 685 of these received aid. Average need met was 64%. Average scholarship/grant was $5,649; average loan $3,191. 40% of total undergraduate aid awarded as scholarships/grants, 60% as loans/jobs. **Non-need-based:** Awarded to 455 full-time undergraduates, including 183 freshmen.

Application procedures. **Admission:** Closing date 3/1 (postmark date). $50 fee, may be waived for applicants with need. Admission notification by 3/15. Admission notification on a rolling basis beginning on or about 1/15. Must reply by May 1 or within 2 week(s) if notified thereafter. **Financial aid:** Priority date 3/1; no closing date. FAFSA required. Applicants notified on a rolling basis starting 4/1.

Academics. **Special study options:** Cooperative education, cross-registration, distance learning, double major, dual enrollment of high school students, exchange student, honors, independent study, internships, semester at sea, student-designed major, study abroad, teacher certification program, Washington semester. **Credit/placement by examination:** AP, CLEP, institutional tests. 60 credit hours maximum toward bachelor's degree. Maximum of 3 credits awarded for AP tests in English. Students taking CLEP tests in English Composition with Essay or Freshman Composition must also submit writing portfolio; portfolio evaluated before credit can be awarded. Maximum of 3 credits awarded for composition. **Support services:** Learning center, pre-admission summer program, reduced course load, study skills assistance, tutoring, writing center.

Majors. **Architecture:** Urban/community planning. **Area/ethnic studies:** General. **Biology:** General. **Business:** General. **Communications:** Communications/speech/rhetoric. **Computer sciences:** Computer science, information systems. **Conservation:** Environmental science. **Education:** Elementary, kindergarten/preschool, special ed, technology/industrial arts. **English:** English lit. **Foreign languages:** Spanish. **Health services:** Athletic training, nursing (RN). **History:** General. **Human services:** Social work. **Liberal arts:** Arts/sciences. **Math:** General. **Parks/recreation:** Health/fitness. **Physical sciences:** General, chemistry. **Protective services:** Criminal justice. **Psychology:** General. **Social sciences:** Economics, political science, sociology. **Visual/performing arts:** Art, dramatic, music.

Most popular majors. Business/marketing 14%, communications/journalism 7%, education 10%, liberal arts 13%, psychology 7%, security/protective services 16%.

Computing on campus. 363 workstations in dormitories, library, computer center, student center. Dormitories wired for high-speed internet access and linked to campus network. Commuter students can connect to campus network. Online course registration, online library, helpline, student web hosting, wireless network available.

Student life. **Freshman orientation:** Available. Preregistration for classes offered. Several 2-day sessions held in June and August; includes mandatory testing, course selection. **Policies:** Freshmen not permitted cars on campus. **Housing:** Coed dorms, special housing for disabled, apartments available. $150 nonrefundable deposit, deadline 5/1. Living/learning (academic intensive), quiet living, honors housing. **Activities:** Bands, campus ministries, choral groups, dance, drama, international student organizations, literary magazine, music ensembles, Model UN, musical theater, opera, radio station, student government, student newspaper, symphony orchestra, TV station, third world group, public interest research group, Campus Crusade, Circle K, Habitat for Humanity, international relations club, Latino association for empowerment, gay straight alliance, peace and justice club, Republican club.

Athletics. NCAA. **Intercollegiate:** Baseball M, basketball, cheerleading, cross-country, diving W, field hockey W, football (tackle) M, golf, ice hockey M, lacrosse W, soccer, softball W, swimming W, track and field, volleyball W. **Intramural:** Basketball, cross-country, field hockey, football (non-tackle), golf, racquetball, soccer, softball, table tennis, volleyball, water polo, wrestling M. **Team name:** Owls.

Student services. Adult student services, alcohol/substance abuse counseling, career counseling, services for economically disadvantaged, student employment services, financial aid counseling, health services, minority student services, personal counseling, placement for graduates, veterans' counselor. **Physically disabled:** Services for visually, speech, hearing impaired.

Contact. E-mail: admissions@westfield.ma.edu
Phone: (413) 572-5218 Toll-free number: (800) 322-8401
Fax: (413) 572-0520
Kelly Hart, Director of Admission, Westfield State University, 577 Western Avenue, Westfield, MA 01086-1630

Wheaton College

Norton, Massachusetts
www.wheatoncollege.edu

CB member
CB code: 3963

- Private 4-year liberal arts college
- Residential campus in large town
- 1,622 degree-seeking undergraduates: 64% women, 5% African American, 2% Asian American, 7% Hispanic American, 8% international
- 60% of applicants admitted
- Application essay required
- 77% graduate within 6 years; 43% enter graduate study

General. Founded in 1834. Regionally accredited. **Degrees:** 428 bachelor's awarded. **ROTC:** Army. **Location:** 35 miles from Boston; 20 miles from Providence, Rhode Island. **Calendar:** Semester. **Full-time faculty:** 139 total; 88% have terminal degrees, 19% minority, 50% women. **Part-time faculty:** 27 total; 37% have terminal degrees, 22% minority, 59% women. **Class size:** 67% < 20, 27% 20-39, 5% 40-49, 1% 50-99. **Special facilities:** Observatory, language laboratory, early childhood lab school.

Freshman class profile. 3,448 applied, 2,075 admitted, 437 enrolled.

Mid 50% test scores			
SAT critical reading:	580-680	Rank in top quarter:	79%
SAT math:	580-660	Rank in top tenth:	42%
ACT composite:	26-30	End year in good standing:	86%
GPA 3.75 or higher:	31%	Return as sophomores:	86%
GPA 3.50-3.74:	20%	Out-of-state:	68%
GPA 3.0-3.49:	33%	Live on campus:	100%
GPA 2.0-2.99:	16%	International:	11%

Basis for selection. Academic achievement, writing ability, difficulty of high school curriculum and co-curricular achievement considered. Interviews

strongly recommended. **Home schooled:** Statement describing home school structure and mission, transcript of courses and grades required. **Learning Disabled:** Students who have diagnosed learning difference encouraged to submit supporting testing for review.

High school preparation. College-preparatory program recommended. 20 units recommended. Recommended units include English 4, mathematics 4, social studies 3, history 2, science 3 (laboratory 2) and foreign language 4. English should emphasize composition skills.

2012-2013 Annual costs. Tuition/fees: $43,774. Room/board: $11,160. Books/supplies: $940. Personal expenses: $760.

2011-2012 Financial aid. Need-based: 329 full-time freshmen applied for aid; 295 were judged to have need; 295 of these received aid. Average need met was 95%. Average scholarship/grant was $29,534; average loan $3,961. 83% of total undergraduate aid awarded as scholarships/grants, 17% as loans/jobs. **Non-need-based:** Awarded to 249 full-time undergraduates, including 74 freshmen. Scholarships awarded for academics.

Application procedures. Admission: Closing date 1/15 (postmark date). $55 fee, may be waived for applicants with need, free for online applicants. Admission notification by 4/1. Must reply by 5/1. **Financial aid:** Closing date 2/1. FAFSA, CSS PROFILE required. Applicants notified by 4/1; must reply by 5/1.

Academics. Special study options: Accelerated study, combined bachelor's/graduate degree, cross-registration, double major, dual enrollment of high school students, exchange student, honors, independent study, internships, liberal arts/career combination, student-designed major, study abroad, teacher certification program, Washington semester. BS in engineering with George Washington University and Dartmouth College; MA in Intergrated Marketing Communication Studies with Emerson College; MBA in management with University of Rochester; BFA in studio art with School of the Museum of Fine Arts; MA in religion with Andover- Newton Theological School; Doctor of Optometry with New England School of Optometry. **Credit/placement by examination:** AP, CLEP, IB, institutional tests. 8 credit hours maximum toward bachelor's degree. **Support services:** Learning center, pre-admission summer program, reduced course load, study skills assistance, tutoring, writing center.

Majors. Area/ethnic studies: American, Asian, French, Italian, Russian/Slavic, women's. **Biology:** General, biochemistry, bioinformatics, neuroscience. **Computer sciences:** Computer science. **Conservation:** Environmental science. **English:** English lit, writing. **Foreign languages:** Classics, French, German, Italian, Latin, modern Greek, Russian, Spanish. **History:** General. **Liberal arts:** Arts/sciences. **Math:** General. **Philosophy/religion:** Philosophy, religion. **Physical sciences:** Chemistry, physics. **Psychology:** General. **Social sciences:** Anthropology, economics, international relations, political science, sociology. **Visual/performing arts:** Art history/conservation, film/cinema/video, music, studio arts.

Most popular majors. Area/ethnic studies 8%, biology 7%, English 7%, psychology 19%, social sciences 27%, visual/performing arts 13%.

Computing on campus. 289 workstations in library, computer center, student center. Dormitories wired for high-speed internet access and linked to campus network. Commuter students can connect to campus network. Online course registration, online library, helpline, repair service, student web hosting, wireless network available.

Student life. Freshman orientation: Mandatory. Preregistration for classes offered. Three 2-day programs offered in June; includes class registration. Parents encouraged to attend. **Housing:** Guaranteed on-campus for all undergraduates. Coed dorms, single-sex dorms, special housing for disabled, wellness housing available. Quiet housing available. **Activities:** Bands, choral groups, dance, drama, film society, international student organizations, literary magazine, music ensembles, Model UN, musical theater, radio station, student government, student newspaper, symphony orchestra, Hillel, Christian Fellowship, Interfaith Alliance, student government association, Amnesty International, Habitat for Humanity, black student association, Latino student association, Asian American coalition.

Athletics. NCAA. **Intercollegiate:** Baseball M, basketball, cross-country, diving, field hockey W, lacrosse, soccer, softball W, swimming, synchronized swimming W, tennis, track and field, volleyball W. **Intramural:** Badminton, basketball, football (non-tackle), soccer, softball, tennis, volleyball. **Team name:** Lyons.

Student services. Alcohol/substance abuse counseling, career counseling, student employment services, financial aid counseling, health services, minority student services, personal counseling, placement for graduates, women's services. **Physically disabled:** Services for visually, hearing impaired.

Contact. E-mail: admission@wheatoncollege.edu
Phone: (508) 286-8251 Toll-free number: (800) 394-6003
Fax: (508) 286-8271
Gail Berson, Vice President for Enrollment and Dean of Admission and Student Aid, Wheaton College, 26 East Main Street, Norton, MA 02766

Wheelock College
Boston, Massachusetts
www.wheelock.edu
CB member
CB code: 3964

- Private 4-year liberal arts and teachers college
- Residential campus in very large city
- 871 degree-seeking undergraduates: 4% part-time, 90% women, 12% African American, 2% Asian American, 11% Hispanic American
- 366 degree-seeking graduate students
- 71% of applicants admitted
- SAT or ACT (ACT writing optional), application essay required
- 58% graduate within 6 years

General. Founded in 1888. Regionally accredited. Member of the Colleges of the Fenway. **Degrees:** 149 bachelor's awarded; master's offered. **Calendar:** Semester, limited summer session. **Full-time faculty:** 65 total; 89% have terminal degrees, 29% minority, 75% women. **Part-time faculty:** 102 total; 11% have terminal degrees, 13% minority, 79% women. **Class size:** 54% < 20, 46% 20-39.

Freshman class profile. 1,537 applied, 1,086 admitted, 233 enrolled.

Mid 50% test scores			
SAT critical reading:	440-540	GPA 2.0-2.99:	45%
SAT math:	430-520	Rank in top quarter:	36%
SAT writing:	450-550	Rank in top tenth:	7%
ACT composite:	17-22	Return as sophomores:	69%
GPA 3.75 or higher:	12%	Out-of-state:	37%
GPA 3.50-3.74:	12%	Live on campus:	91%
GPA 3.0-3.49:	31%	International:	1%

Basis for selection. School achievement record most important. Test scores, school and community activities considered. Interview recommended.

High school preparation. College-preparatory program recommended. 16 units required. Required units include English 4, mathematics 3, social studies 2, science 2 (laboratory 1). Child development courses considered.

2011-2012 Annual costs. Tuition/fees: $30,055. Room/board: $12,370. Books/supplies: $880. Personal expenses: $1,400.

2011-2012 Financial aid. Need-based: 216 full-time freshmen applied for aid; 195 were judged to have need; 195 of these received aid. Average need met was 63%. Average scholarship/grant was $17,440; average loan $3,433. 63% of total undergraduate aid awarded as scholarships/grants, 37% as loans/jobs. **Non-need-based:** Awarded to 185 full-time undergraduates, including 48 freshmen. Scholarships awarded for academics, leadership, state residency.

Application procedures. Admission: Priority date 3/1; no deadline. $15 fee, may be waived for applicants with need, free for online applicants. Admission notification on a rolling basis beginning on or about 1/10. Must reply by May 1 or within 2 week(s) if notified thereafter. **Financial aid:** Priority date 2/15; no closing date. FAFSA required. Applicants notified on a rolling basis starting 3/1.

Academics. Special study options: Combined bachelor's/graduate degree, cross-registration, double major, exchange student, honors, independent study, internships, liberal arts/career combination, study abroad, teacher certification program. **Credit/placement by examination:** AP, CLEP, institutional tests. 32 credit hours maximum toward bachelor's degree. **Support services:** Learning center, pre-admission summer program, reduced course load, study skills assistance, tutoring, writing center.

Majors. Area/ethnic studies: American. **Communications:** Media studies. **Education:** Early childhood, elementary, special ed. **Human services:** Social work, youth services. **Liberal arts:** Arts/sciences, humanities. **Math:** General. **Visual/performing arts:** General. **Work/family studies:** Child care management, child development, family studies.

Most popular majors. Education 25%, family/consumer sciences 41%, public administration/social services 17%, visual/performing arts 6%.

Computing on campus. 120 workstations in dormitories, library, computer center, student center. Dormitories wired for high-speed internet access and linked to campus network. Commuter students can connect to campus network. Online course registration, online library, helpline, repair service, wireless network available.

Student life. Freshman orientation: Mandatory, $200 fee. Preregistration for classes offered. Two-day program held in summer; students have choice of 2 sessions. **Housing:** Guaranteed on-campus for freshmen. Coed dorms, single-sex dorms, special housing for disabled, cooperative housing, wellness

housing available. $100 nonrefundable deposit, deadline 5/1. **Activities:** Choral groups, dance, drama, musical theater, student government, symphony orchestra, social work club, women's center, Boston Association for the Education of Young Children, child life council, sign language club, Bible study, juvenile justice and youth advocacy council.

Athletics. NCAA. **Intercollegiate:** Basketball, cross-country, field hockey W, lacrosse, soccer, softball W, tennis M. **Intramural:** Basketball, racquetball, soccer, softball, squash, volleyball. **Team name:** Wildcats.

Student services. Alcohol/substance abuse counseling, career counseling, student employment services, financial aid counseling, health services, minority student services, personal counseling, placement for graduates, women's services. **Physically disabled:** Services for visually, speech, hearing impaired.

Contact. E-mail: undergrad@wheelock.edu
Phone: (617) 879-2206 Toll-free number: (800) 734-5212
Fax: (617) 879-2449
Kristen Harrington, Senior Director of Undergraduate Admissions, Wheelock College, 200 The Riverway, Boston, MA 02215-4176

Williams College
Williamstown, Massachusetts **CB member**
www.williams.edu **CB code: 3965**

- Private 4-year liberal arts college
- Residential campus in small town
- 2,010 degree-seeking undergraduates: 51% women, 8% African American, 11% Asian American, 11% Hispanic American, 7% international
- 56 degree-seeking graduate students
- 17% of applicants admitted
- SAT or ACT with writing, SAT Subject Tests, application essay required
- 95% graduate within 6 years

General. Founded in 1793. Regionally accredited. **Degrees:** 528 bachelor's awarded; master's offered. **ROTC:** Air Force. **Location:** 35 miles from Albany, New York; 150 miles from Boston. **Calendar:** 4-1-4. **Full-time faculty:** 262 total; 96% have terminal degrees, 20% minority, 40% women. **Part-time faculty:** 58 total; 71% have terminal degrees, 10% minority, 55% women. **Class size:** 71% < 20, 22% 20-39, 4% 40-49, 3% 50-99, less than 1% >100. **Special facilities:** Performing arts center, experimental forest, environmental studies center, observatory, electron-scanning microscope, transmission microscopes, studio art center, nuclear magnetic resonance imager, college museum.

Freshman class profile. 7,030 applied, 1,215 admitted, 545 enrolled.

Mid 50% test scores		Rank in top tenth:	91%
SAT critical reading:	660-770	Return as sophomores:	97%
SAT math:	650-760	Out-of-state:	89%
ACT composite:	30-34	Live on campus:	100%
Rank in top quarter:	98%	International:	7%

Basis for selection. School achievement record, character and personal promise, test scores, essay important. College seeks diversity of social, economic, and geographic backgrounds. Leadership and accomplishment in extracurricular activities also considered. Two SAT Subject Tests required of all.

High school preparation. College-preparatory program required. Recommended units include English 4, mathematics 4, social studies 3, science 3 (laboratory 3) and foreign language 4. Writing skills stressed. Course work should be at highest level available.

2011-2012 Annual costs. Tuition/fees: $43,190. Room/board: $11,370. Books/supplies: $800. Personal expenses: $1,200.

2010-2011 Financial aid. All financial aid based on need. 354 full-time freshmen applied for aid; 291 were judged to have need; 291 of these received aid. Average need met was 100%. Average scholarship/grant was $38,561. 96% of total undergraduate aid awarded as scholarships/grants, 4% as loans/jobs.

Application procedures. Admission: Closing date 1/1 (postmark date). $65 fee, may be waived for applicants with need. Admission notification by 4/1. Must reply by May 1 or within 2 week(s) if notified thereafter. **Financial aid:** Closing date 2/1. FAFSA, CSS PROFILE required. Applicants notified by 4/1; must reply by 5/1.

Academics. Special study options: Combined bachelor's/graduate degree, cross-registration, double major, independent study, internships, student-designed major, study abroad. Summer science research program, Williams

in Oxford, Mystic maritime studies program, tutorials, 3-2 engineering program with Columbia University and Washington University. **Credit/placement by examination:** AP, CLEP, IB, institutional tests. **Support services:** Pre-admission summer program, study skills assistance, tutoring, writing center.

Majors. Area/ethnic studies: American, Asian, women's. **Biology:** General. **Computer sciences:** Computer science. **English:** English lit. **Foreign languages:** Chinese, classics, comparative lit, French, German, Japanese, Russian, Spanish. **History:** General. **Math:** General. **Philosophy/religion:** Philosophy, religion. **Physical sciences:** Astronomy, astrophysics, chemistry, geology, physics. **Psychology:** General. **Social sciences:** Anthropology, economics, political economy, political science, sociology. **Visual/performing arts:** Art history/conservation, dramatic, music, studio arts.

Most popular majors. Biology 7%, English 8%, foreign language 8%, history 9%, mathematics 7%, physical sciences 7%, psychology 10%, social sciences 25%, visual/performing arts 8%.

Computing on campus. 247 workstations in library, computer center, student center. Dormitories wired for high-speed internet access and linked to campus network. Commuter students can connect to campus network. Online course registration, online library, helpline, repair service, student web hosting, wireless network available.

Student life. Freshman orientation: Mandatory. Preregistration for classes offered. **Housing:** Guaranteed on-campus for all undergraduates. Coed dorms, cooperative housing available. $200 nonrefundable deposit, deadline 5/1. Quiet housing. **Activities:** Bands, campus ministries, choral groups, dance, drama, film society, international student organizations, literary magazine, music ensembles, radio station, student government, student newspaper, symphony orchestra, black student union, Purple Key, Asian Link, Hispanic students club, Korean club, minority coalition, nonviolent alternatives committee, women's club, Hillel, LGBTQ student organization.

Athletics. NCAA. **Intercollegiate:** Baseball M, basketball, cross-country, diving, field hockey W, football (tackle) M, golf, ice hockey, lacrosse, rowing (crew), skiing, soccer, softball W, squash, swimming, tennis, track and field, volleyball W, wrestling M. **Intramural:** Badminton, basketball, ice hockey M, soccer, softball, volleyball. **Team name:** Ephs.

Student services. Alcohol/substance abuse counseling, chaplain/spiritual director, career counseling, services for economically disadvantaged, student employment services, financial aid counseling, health services, minority student services, on-campus daycare, personal counseling, placement for graduates. **Physically disabled:** Services for visually, hearing impaired.

Contact. E-mail: admission@williams.edu
Phone: (413) 597-2211 Fax: (413) 597-4052
Richard Nesbitt, Director of Admissions, Williams College, 33 Stetson Court, Williamstown, MA 01267

Worcester Polytechnic Institute
Worcester, Massachusetts **CB member**
www.wpi.edu **CB code: 3969**

- Private 4-year university
- Residential campus in small city
- 3,746 degree-seeking undergraduates: 3% part-time, 31% women, 3% African American, 5% Asian American, 8% Hispanic American, 11% international
- 1,557 degree-seeking graduate students
- 57% of applicants admitted
- Application essay required
- 80% graduate within 6 years; 28% enter graduate study

General. Founded in 1865. Regionally accredited. Participation by most students in overseas or off-campus projects; over 30 project centers located throughout North America, Central America, Africa, Australia, Asia and Europe. **Degrees:** 707 bachelor's awarded; master's, doctoral offered. **ROTC:** Army, Naval, Air Force. **Location:** 35 miles from Boston. **Calendar:** Quarter, limited summer session. **Full-time faculty:** 288 total; 90% have terminal degrees, 15% minority, 24% women. **Part-time faculty:** 136 total; 47% have terminal degrees, 8% minority, 28% women. **Special facilities:** Centers for life sciences and bioengineering, biomaterials, bioprocessing, comparative neuroimaging, molecular sensors, nanoscience and technology, untethered healthcare, water research, computer-controlled machining, holographic studies and laser technology, wireless information network studies, fuel cell, industrial math and statistics, fire science laboratory, pavement research laboratory, atomic force microscopy laboratory.

Freshman class profile. 7,049 applied, 3,998 admitted, 1,005 enrolled.

Mid 50% test scores			
SAT critical reading:	560-670	Rank in top quarter:	93%
SAT math:	640-730	Rank in top tenth:	65%
SAT writing:	560-660	End year in good standing:	94%
ACT composite:	27-31	Return as sophomores:	95%
GPA 3.75 or higher:	70%	Out-of-state:	58%
GPA 3.50-3.74:	19%	Live on campus:	90%
GPA 3.0-3.49:	10%	International:	14%
GPA 2.0-2.99:	1%	Fraternities:	33%
		Sororities:	40%

Basis for selection. High school record including academic rigor most important. Extracurricular activities, recommendations, motivation, creativity, initiative important. In lieu of test scores, students may submit alternative documentation of potential for academic success. SAT/ACT or alternative materials that will better reflect the applicant's potential for success (Flex Path) required. Students who choose the Flex Path encouraged to submit examples of academic work or extracurricular projects that reflect a high level of organization, motivation, creativity and problem-solving ability. Interviews offered, but not required. **Home schooled:** Statement describing home school structure and mission, transcript of courses and grades, interview, letter of recommendation (nonparent) required. Submit as much relevant support material as possible and outside recommendations. Detailed course descriptions recommended.

High school preparation. College-preparatory program required. 10 units required. Required and recommended units include English 4, mathematics 4, social studies 2, history 1, science 2-4 (laboratory 2), foreign language 2 and computer science 1. Math requirement includes algebra, geometry, trigonometry and pre-calculus. Science should include physics, chemistry, or biology.

2012-2013 Annual costs. Tuition/fees (projected): $41,234. Room/board: $12,292. Books/supplies: $1,000. Personal expenses: $1,000.

2010-2011 Financial aid. Need-based: 802 full-time freshmen applied for aid; 687 were judged to have need; 687 of these received aid. Average need met was 71%. Average scholarship/grant was $19,474; average loan $2,850. 78% of total undergraduate aid awarded as scholarships/grants, 22% as loans/jobs. **Non-need-based:** Awarded to 1,592 full-time undergraduates, including 453 freshmen. Scholarships awarded for academics, leadership, minority status, ROTC.

Application procedures. Admission: Closing date 2/1 (postmark date). $60 fee, may be waived for applicants with need. Admission notification by 4/1. Must reply by May 1 or within 2 week(s) if notified thereafter. Second early action closing date January 1; notification date February 10. **Financial aid:** Priority date 2/1; no closing date. FAFSA, CSS PROFILE required.

Academics. Special study options: Accelerated study, combined bachelor's/graduate degree, cooperative education, cross-registration, distance learning, double major, ESL, honors, independent study, internships, liberal arts/career combination, New York semester, student-designed major, study abroad, teacher certification program, Washington semester. Completion of degree-required projects at off-campus locations (international and domestic) supervised by institution's faculty; students resides at site for 2 months after having prepared for the experience for 2 months while on campus. **Credit/placement by examination:** AP, CLEP, IB, institutional tests. **Support services:** Pre-admission summer program, reduced course load, study skills assistance, tutoring, writing center.

Majors. Biology: General, biochemistry, bioinformatics, biotechnology. **Business:** Actuarial science, business admin, management information systems, management science, operations. **Computer sciences:** Artificial intelligence, computer science, web page design. **Conservation:** Environmental studies. **Engineering:** Aerospace, applied physics, biomedical, chemical, civil, electrical, environmental, industrial, mechanical, systems. **English:** Technical writing. **Health services:** Predental, premedicine, preveterinary. **Liberal arts:** Humanities. **Math:** General, applied. **Physical sciences:** Chemistry, physics. **Social sciences:** General, economics. **Visual/performing arts:** Game design.

Most popular majors. Biology 10%, computer/information sciences 9%, engineering/engineering technologies 64%.

Computing on campus. 300 workstations in dormitories, library, computer center, student center. Dormitories wired for high-speed internet access and linked to campus network. Commuter students can connect to campus network. Online course registration, online library, helpline, repair service, student web hosting, wireless network available.

Student life. Freshman orientation: Available, $200 fee. Preregistration for classes offered. Program held in late August. **Policies:** Freshmen not permitted cars on campus. **Housing:** Guaranteed on-campus for freshmen. Coed dorms, special housing for disabled, apartments, fraternity/sorority housing, wellness housing available. Special interest housing available. **Activities:** Bands, campus ministries, choral groups, dance, drama, film society,

international student organizations, literary magazine, music ensembles, musical theater, radio station, student government, student newspaper, symphony orchestra, African American cultural society, volunteer tutoring group, Big Brother/Big Sister, World House, European student association, Asian society, Hispanic student association, women's awareness group, students for social awareness, Amnesty International.

Athletics. NCAA. **Intercollegiate:** Baseball M, basketball, cross-country, field hockey W, football (tackle) M, rowing (crew), soccer, softball W, swimming, track and field, volleyball W, wrestling M. **Intramural:** Basketball, bowling, cross-country, fencing, football (non-tackle) M, racquetball, soccer, softball, swimming, table tennis, volleyball, water polo M, wrestling M. **Team name:** Engineers.

Student services. Adult student services, alcohol/substance abuse counseling, chaplain/spiritual director, career counseling, student employment services, financial aid counseling, health services, minority student services, personal counseling, placement for graduates, veterans' counselor, women's services. **Physically disabled:** Services for visually, speech, hearing impaired.

Contact. E-mail: admissions@wpi.edu
Phone: (508) 831-5286 Fax: (508) 831-5875
Edward Connor, Dean of Admissions, Worcester Polytechnic Institute, 100 Institute Road, Worcester, MA 01609-2280

Worcester State University
Worcester, Massachusetts   **CB member**
www.worcester.edu   **CB code: 3524**

- Public 4-year liberal arts and teachers college
- Commuter campus in small city
- 4,775 degree-seeking undergraduates: 19% part-time, 59% women, 6% African American, 3% Asian American, 7% Hispanic American, 1% Native American, 1% international
- 616 degree-seeking graduate students
- 65% of applicants admitted
- SAT or ACT with writing required
- 47% graduate within 6 years

General. Founded in 1874. Regionally accredited. **Degrees:** 809 bachelor's awarded; master's offered. **ROTC:** Army, Naval, Air Force. **Location:** 45 miles from Boston; 65 miles from Hartford, Connecticut. **Calendar:** Semester, extensive summer session. **Full-time faculty:** 187 total; 78% have terminal degrees, 19% minority, 57% women. **Part-time faculty:** 233 total; 22% have terminal degrees, 10% minority, 55% women. **Class size:** 57% < 20, 43% 20-39, less than 1% 40-49, less than 1% 50-99. **Special facilities:** Photographic labs, multimedia classrooms with satellite connectivity, speech/language/hearing clinic.

Freshman class profile. 3,647 applied, 2,385 admitted, 796 enrolled.

Mid 50% test scores			
SAT critical reading:	450-540	GPA 3.0-3.49:	31%
SAT math:	470-560	GPA 2.0-2.99:	48%
SAT writing:	450-540	Return as sophomores:	80%
ACT composite:	19-24	Out-of-state:	5%
GPA 3.75 or higher:	11%	Live on campus:	61%
GPA 3.50-3.74:	10%	International:	1%

Basis for selection. Secondary school record most important; test scores important; extracurricular activities considered. Interview and personal essay recommended for academically weak. **Home schooled:** Student must submit documentation that home school plan meets district curriculum standards. **Learning Disabled:** SAT waiver available for students with learning disabilities with IEP plan.

High school preparation. College-preparatory program required. 16 units required. Required units include English 4, mathematics 3, social studies 1, history 1, science 3 (laboratory 2), foreign language 2 and academic electives 2. History unit must be US history.

2011-2012 Annual costs. Tuition/fees: $7,653; $13,733 out-of-state. Room/board: $10,400.

2010-2011 Financial aid. Need-based: 750 full-time freshmen applied for aid; 505 were judged to have need; 495 of these received aid. Average need met was 82%. Average scholarship/grant was $4,695; average loan $2,389. 59% of total undergraduate aid awarded as scholarships/grants, 41% as loans/jobs. **Non-need-based:** Awarded to 739 full-time undergraduates, including 260 freshmen. Scholarships awarded for academics, ROTC. **Additional information:** Veterans, Native Americans and those certified by Massachusetts Rehabilitation Commission and Massachusetts Commission for the Blind considered for tuition waivers while funds available. Tuition also

waived for needy Massachusetts residents and in-state National Guard members.

Application procedures. Admission: Priority date 2/1; deadline 5/1 (receipt date). $40 fee, may be waived for applicants with need. Admission notification on a rolling basis beginning on or about 12/1. Must reply by May 1 or within 4 week(s) if notified thereafter. **Financial aid:** Priority date 3/1, closing date 5/1. FAFSA required. Applicants notified on a rolling basis starting 3/1; must reply within 2 week(s) of notification.

Academics. Special study options: Accelerated study, combined bachelor's/graduate degree, cross-registration, distance learning, double major, ESL, exchange student, honors, independent study, internships, liberal arts/career combination, study abroad, teacher certification program, Washington semester. Foreign exchange student program. **Credit/placement by examination:** AP, CLEP, IB, institutional tests. 30 credit hours maximum toward bachelor's degree. **Support services:** Learning center, pre-admission summer program, reduced course load, remedial instruction, study skills assistance, tutoring, writing center.

Majors. Biology: General, biotechnology. **Business:** Business admin. **Communications:** Communications/speech/rhetoric, media studies. **Communications technology:** Radio/TV. **Computer sciences:** General. **Education:** Early childhood, elementary, health. **English:** English lit. **Foreign languages:** Spanish. **Health services:** Adult health nursing, communication disorders, community health services, nursing (RN). **History:** General. **Math:** General. **Physical sciences:** General, chemistry. **Protective services:** Criminal justice. **Psychology:** General. **Social sciences:** Economics, geography, sociology, urban studies. **Visual/performing arts:** General.

Most popular majors. Biology 6%, business/marketing 23%, communications/journalism 6%, education 6%, health sciences 16%, psychology 12%, security/protective services 7%.

Computing on campus. PC or laptop required. 500 workstations in dormitories, library, computer center, student center. Dormitories wired for high-speed internet access and linked to campus network. Commuter students can connect to campus network. Online course registration, online library, helpline, repair service, student web hosting, wireless network available.

Student life. Freshman orientation: Mandatory, $75 fee. Preregistration for classes offered. Four-hour parent orientation in Spring; 4-1/2 day session for students last week in August. **Housing:** Coed dorms, single-sex dorms, special housing for disabled available. $150 nonrefundable deposit, deadline 2/15. **Activities:** Bands, campus ministries, choral groups, dance, drama, music ensembles, radio station, student government, student newspaper, TV station, student events committee, Third World alliance, campus ambassadors, gay-straight alliance, surreal games and sci-fi, ski/snow board club.

Athletics. NCAA. Intercollegiate: Baseball M, basketball, cheerleading, cross-country, field hockey W, football (tackle) M, golf M, ice hockey M, lacrosse W, soccer, softball W, tennis W, track and field, volleyball. **Intramural:** Baseball M, basketball, cross-country, field hockey W, football (tackle) M, golf M, ice hockey M, lacrosse W, rowing (crew), soccer, softball W, tennis W, track and field, volleyball. **Team name:** Lancers.

Student services. Adult student services, alcohol/substance abuse counseling, chaplain/spiritual director, career counseling, services for economically disadvantaged, student employment services, financial aid counseling, health services, minority student services, personal counseling, placement for graduates, veterans' counselor, women's services. **Physically disabled:** Services for visually, speech, hearing impaired.

Contact. E-mail: admissions@worcester.edu
Phone: (508) 929-8040 Fax: (508) 929-8183
Beth Axelson, Director of Admissions, Worcester State University, Office of Undergraduate Admission, Worcester, MA 01602-2597

Zion Bible College
Haverhill, Massachusetts
www.zbc.edu   CB code: 3942

- Private 4-year Bible college affiliated with Assemblies of God
- Residential campus in small city
- 313 degree-seeking undergraduates: 16% part-time, 44% women, 9% African American, 2% Asian American, 11% Hispanic American, 4% international
- 78% of applicants admitted
- Application essay required
- 43% graduate within 6 years

General. Accredited by ABHE. **Degrees:** 39 bachelor's awarded. **Location:** 40 miles from Boston. **Calendar:** Semester, limited summer session. **Full-time faculty:** 10 total; 20% have terminal degrees, 10% women. **Part-time faculty:** 13 total; 15% have terminal degrees, 8% minority, 38% women. **Class size:** 66% < 20, 24% 20-39, 7% 40-49, 3% 50-99.

Freshman class profile. 101 applied, 79 admitted, 59 enrolled.

Mid 50% test scores			
SAT critical reading:	450-550	GPA 3.0-3.49:	35%
SAT math:	380-550	GPA 2.0-2.99:	39%
SAT writing:	410-530	Rank in top quarter:	12%
ACT composite:	17-22	Rank in top tenth:	4%
GPA 3.75 or higher:	12%	Out-of-state:	64%
GPA 3.50-3.74:	2%	Live on campus:	88%

Basis for selection. References weighed heavily in correlation with student's application material and personal statements. **Home schooled:** Transcript of courses and grades required. Applicants must produce diploma and transcript that verify graduation by the state department of education, local school district or accrediting association. Curriculum used and a copy of the student's state home school requirements must also be submitted. Students who cannot produce this must submit GED.

2011-2012 Annual costs. Tuition/fees: $9,980. Room/board: $7,400. Books/supplies: $1,800. Personal expenses: $1,500.

2010-2011 Financial aid. Need-based: 39 full-time freshmen applied for aid; 37 were judged to have need; 37 of these received aid. Average scholarship/grant was $1,982; average loan $1,702. 36% of total undergraduate aid awarded as scholarships/grants, 64% as loans/jobs. **Non-need-based:** Awarded to 92 full-time undergraduates, including 19 freshmen. Scholarships awarded for academics, leadership, minority status, music/drama, state residency.

Application procedures. Admission: No deadline. $35 fee, may be waived for applicants with need. Admission notification on a rolling basis. Letter of Intent with deposit (tuition and board) required one month after notification. High school transcript, immunization record, health certificate, 3 references (including pastoral recommendation) required. SAT/ACT required for placement only. **Financial aid:** Priority date 6/1; no closing date. FAFSA required. Applicants notified on a rolling basis; must reply within 4 week(s) of notification.

Academics. Special study options: Distance learning, independent study, internships, weekend college. **Credit/placement by examination:** AP, CLEP. **Support services:** Learning center, reduced course load, study skills assistance.

Majors. Theology: Bible.

Computing on campus. 12 workstations in computer center. Dormitories wired for high-speed internet access. Wireless network available.

Student life. Freshman orientation: Mandatory. Preregistration for classes offered. **Policies:** Nightly curfew of 10:30, except for Fridays (11:00 or midnight for seniors). Chapel attendance required Tuesday through Friday. No alcohol, drugs, or smoking permitted on or off-campus. Full-time students assigned to assist in an area church. Religious observance required. **Housing:** Guaranteed on-campus for all undergraduates. Single-sex dorms available. $100 fully refundable deposit. **Activities:** Campus ministries, choral groups, music ensembles, student government.

Student services. Chaplain/spiritual director, financial aid counseling.

Contact. E-mail: admissions@zbc.edu
Phone: (978) 478-3400 ext. 3431 Toll-free number: (800) 356-4014
Fax: (978) 478-3406
Rev. David Hodge, Director of Admissions and Records, Zion Bible College, 320 South Main Street, Haverhill, MA 01835

Michigan

Adrian College

| Adrian, Michigan | CB member |
| www.adrian.edu | CB code: 1001 |

- Private 4-year liberal arts college affiliated with United Methodist Church
- Residential campus in large town
- 1,657 degree-seeking undergraduates
- 64% of applicants admitted
- SAT or ACT (ACT writing optional) required

General. Founded in 1859. Regionally accredited. **Degrees:** 207 bachelor's awarded; master's offered. **ROTC:** Army. **Location:** 75 miles from Detroit, 30 miles from Toledo, OH. **Calendar:** Semester, limited summer session. **Full-time faculty:** 85 total. **Special facilities:** Arboretum, observatory and planetarium, solar greenhouse, Sojourner Truth Underground Railroad Center, WVAC radio and television studios, education curriculum center, human anatomy laboratory, writing laboratory.

Freshman class profile. 3,263 applied, 2,101 admitted, 460 enrolled.

Mid 50% test scores	
ACT composite:	20-25

Basis for selection. School achievement most important, followed by test scores. Applicants should rank in top half of high school class. School recommendations and extracurricular activities considered. ACT preferred.

High school preparation. College-preparatory program recommended. 15 units recommended. Recommended units include English 4, mathematics 3, social studies 1, history 1, science 2 (laboratory 1), foreign language 2 and academic electives 2.

2011-2012 Annual costs. Tuition/fees: $27,440. Room/board: $8,346. Books/supplies: $650.

Financial aid. Non-need-based: Scholarships awarded for academics, alumni affiliation, art, leadership, music/drama, religious affiliation, state residency.

Application procedures. Admission: Closing date 3/15 (receipt date). No application fee. Admission notification on a rolling basis beginning on or about 9/1. **Financial aid:** Priority date 3/1; no closing date. FAFSA required. Applicants notified on a rolling basis starting 3/15; must reply by 5/1 or within 2 week(s) of notification.

Academics. Special study options: Combined bachelor's/graduate degree, double major, dual enrollment of high school students, honors, independent study, internships, semester at sea, student-designed major, study abroad, teacher certification program, Washington semester. **Credit/placement by examination:** AP, CLEP, IB, institutional tests. 15 credit hours maximum toward associate degree, 30 toward bachelor's. **Support services:** Learning center, pre-admission summer program, reduced course load, remedial instruction, study skills assistance, tutoring, writing center.

Majors. Biology: General. **Business:** Accounting, business admin, international, marketing. **Communications:** Communications/speech/rhetoric. **Conservation:** Environmental science, environmental studies. **Education:** Art, biology, English, French, German, health, history, mathematics, music, physical, science, social studies, Spanish. **English:** English lit. **Foreign languages:** French, German, Japanese, Spanish. **Health services:** Athletic training, predental, premedicine, prepharmacy, preveterinary. **History:** General. **Human services:** Social work. **Math:** General. **Parks/recreation:** Exercise sciences. **Philosophy/religion:** Philosophy, religion. **Physical sciences:** Chemistry, geology, physics. **Protective services:** Law enforcement admin. **Psychology:** General. **Social sciences:** Economics, political science, sociology. **Theology:** Preministerial. **Visual/performing arts:** Art, arts management, dramatic, interior design, music, music performance, musical theater, studio arts, studio arts management.

Most popular majors. Biology 9%, business/marketing 27%, education 6%, parks/recreation 7%, social sciences 7%, visual/performing arts 8%.

Computing on campus. 180 workstations in library, computer center, student center. Dormitories wired for high-speed internet access and linked to campus network. Commuter students can connect to campus network. Online course registration, online library, helpline, student web hosting, wireless network available.

Student life. Freshman orientation: Mandatory, $350 fee. Preregistration for classes offered. Week-long program in August. Students take placement exams, take a first-year trip, and perform community service. **Policies:** All full-time students are required to live on campus for four years. Exemptions based on local residence, marital status, 5th year senior or part-time student may be made by application to the Housing Office. Health insurance mandatory for all students registered for 12 hours or more. All motor vehicles possessed or used on campus must be registered every academic year. **Housing:** Guaranteed on-campus for all undergraduates. Coed dorms, single-sex dorms, apartments, fraternity/sorority housing available. $100 deposit, deadline 7/1. **Activities:** Bands, campus ministries, choral groups, dance, drama, international student organizations, literary magazine, music ensembles, Model UN, musical theater, opera, radio station, student government, student newspaper, symphony orchestra, Adrian Latinos Moviendose Adelente, African-American Leaders Promoting Higher Achievement, Safe Place, Feminist Empowerment Movement, Green Action Club, Campus Crusade for Christ, Catholic Student Association, Circle K.

Athletics. NCAA. **Intercollegiate:** Baseball M, basketball, bowling W, cross-country, football (tackle) M, golf, ice hockey, lacrosse, soccer, softball W, tennis, track and field, volleyball W. **Intramural:** Basketball, football (non-tackle), lacrosse, racquetball, soccer, softball, tennis, volleyball. **Team name:** Bulldogs.

Student services. Adult student services, alcohol/substance abuse counseling, chaplain/spiritual director, career counseling, student employment services, financial aid counseling, health services, minority student services, personal counseling, placement for graduates. **Physically disabled:** Services for visually, speech, hearing impaired.

Contact. E-mail: admissions@adrian.edu
Phone: (517) 265-5161 ext. 4326 Toll-free number: (800) 877-2246
Fax: (517) 264-3878
Frank Hribar, Vice President of Enrollment, Adrian College, 110 South Madison Street, Adrian, MI 49221-2575

Albion College

| Albion, Michigan | CB member |
| www.albion.edu | CB code: 1007 |

- Private 4-year liberal arts college affiliated with United Methodist Church
- Residential campus in small town
- 1,495 degree-seeking undergraduates: 49% women, 4% African American, 2% Asian American, 3% Hispanic American, 4% international
- 92% of applicants admitted
- SAT or ACT (ACT writing optional), application essay required
- 74% graduate within 6 years; 43% enter graduate study

General. Founded in 1835. Regionally accredited. **Degrees:** 401 bachelor's awarded. **Location:** 55 miles from Lansing, 55 miles from Ann Arbor. **Calendar:** Semester, limited summer session. **Full-time faculty:** 101 total; 89% have terminal degrees, 12% minority, 44% women. **Part-time faculty:** 54 total; 46% have terminal degrees, 4% minority, 46% women. **Class size:** 63% < 20, 34% 20-39, 2% 40-49, less than 1% 50-99. **Special facilities:** Science complex, 144-acre nature center, observatory, equestrian center.

Freshman class profile. 1,637 applied, 1,499 admitted, 386 enrolled.

Mid 50% test scores			
SAT critical reading:	520-630	Rank in top quarter:	44%
SAT math:	570-670	Rank in top tenth:	16%
SAT writing:	510-600	Return as sophomores:	84%
ACT composite:	22-28	Out-of-state:	8%
GPA 3.75 or higher:	25%	Live on campus:	97%
GPA 3.50-3.74:	17%	International:	5%
GPA 3.0-3.49:	37%	Fraternities:	44%
GPA 2.0-2.99:	21%	Sororities:	38%

Basis for selection. Admission based on school achievement record, ACT/SAT test scores, recommendations from counselor or principal. Interview recommended. Audition recommended for music and theater majors. **Home schooled:** Transcript of courses and grades required.

High school preparation. College-preparatory program required. 17 units required. Required units include English 4, mathematics 3, social studies 2, history 1, science 3 (laboratory 2) and foreign language 2.

2011-2012 Annual costs. Tuition/fees: $32,662. Room/board: $9,260.

2011-2012 Financial aid. Need-based: 334 full-time freshmen applied for aid; 285 were judged to have need; 285 of these received aid. Average need met was 88%. Average scholarship/grant was $23,433; average loan $4,897. 82% of total undergraduate aid awarded as scholarships/grants, 18%

as loans/jobs. **Non-need-based:** Awarded to 1,373 full-time undergraduates, including 334 freshmen. Scholarships awarded for academics, alumni affiliation, art, leadership, music/drama.

Application procedures. Admission: Priority date 12/1; deadline 8/1 (receipt date). $40 fee, may be waived for applicants with need, free for online applicants. Admission notification on a rolling basis beginning on or about 10/1. Must reply by 5/1. **Financial aid:** Priority date 3/1; no closing date. FAFSA required. Applicants notified on a rolling basis starting 3/15.

Academics. Academic coaching, organization and college level study skills sessions are offered. Disability services is housed within Academic Skills Center providing ease of access to multiple support systems. **Special study options:** Combined bachelor's/graduate degree, double major, dual enrollment of high school students, honors, independent study, internships, liberal arts/career combination, New York semester, semester at sea, student-designed major, study abroad, teacher certification program, urban semester, Washington semester. Environmental institute, public service institute, liberal arts program in professional management. **Credit/placement by examination:** AP, CLEP, IB, institutional tests. 8 credit hours maximum toward bachelor's degree. **Support services:** Learning center, reduced course load, study skills assistance, tutoring, writing center.

Majors. Area/ethnic studies: American. **Biology:** General, biochemistry. **Business:** Business admin. **Communications:** Communications/speech/rhetoric. **Conservation:** Environmental science, environmental studies. **Education:** Art, biology, chemistry, English, foreign languages, French, German, history, mathematics, music, physics, psychology, science, social studies, Spanish. **English:** Creative writing, English lit. **Foreign languages:** French, German, Spanish. **Health services:** Athletic training. **History:** General. **Human services:** Public policy. **Liberal arts:** Arts/sciences. **Math:** General. **Parks/recreation:** Exercise sciences. **Philosophy/religion:** Philosophy, religion. **Physical sciences:** Chemistry, geology, physics. **Psychology:** General. **Social sciences:** Anthropology, economics, international relations, political science, sociology. **Visual/performing arts:** General, art, art history/conservation, dramatic, music, music performance, studio arts.

Most popular majors. Biology 11%, business/marketing 7%, communications/journalism 6%, English 7%, physical sciences 7%, psychology 10%, social sciences 19%.

Computing on campus. 410 workstations in dormitories, library, computer center, student center. Dormitories wired for high-speed internet access and linked to campus network. Commuter students can connect to campus network. Online course registration, online library, helpline, repair service, student web hosting, wireless network available.

Student life. Freshman orientation: Mandatory. Preregistration for classes offered. **Policies:** All students are required to reside and board within the College residential system. Exemptions are granted to students commuting from home (defined as those students who reside with their parents or legal guardians within 50 miles of the campus), married students, students with legal dependents, students age 23 or older (housing can be provided if desired), and United States veterans. **Housing:** Guaranteed on-campus for all undergraduates. Coed dorms, single-sex dorms, special housing for disabled, apartments, cooperative housing, fraternity/sorority housing available. Special interest and male/female annexes available. **Activities:** Bands, campus ministries, choral groups, dance, drama, international student organizations, literary magazine, music ensembles, Model UN, musical theater, radio station, student government, student newspaper, symphony orchestra, 110 campus organizations.

Athletics. NCAA. **Intercollegiate:** Baseball M, basketball, cross-country, diving, equestrian, football (tackle) M, golf, lacrosse, soccer, softball W, swimming, tennis, track and field, volleyball W. **Intramural:** Basketball, football (non-tackle), racquetball, rugby, soccer, softball, swimming, tennis, volleyball. **Team name:** Britons.

Student services. Alcohol/substance abuse counseling, chaplain/spiritual director, career counseling, services for economically disadvantaged, student employment services, financial aid counseling, health services, minority student services, personal counseling, placement for graduates, veterans' counselor, women's services. **Physically disabled:** Services for visually, speech, hearing impaired.

Contact. E-mail: admission@albion.edu
Phone: (517) 629-0321 Toll-free number: (800) 858-6770
Fax: (517) 629-0569
Mandy Dubiel, Director of Admissions, Albion College, 611 East Porter Street, Albion, MI 49224-1831

Alma College

Alma, Michigan
www.alma.edu

CB member
CB code: 1010

- Private 4-year liberal arts college affiliated with Presbyterian Church (USA)
- Residential campus in small town
- 1,390 degree-seeking undergraduates: 1% part-time, 58% women, 2% African American, 2% Asian American, 3% Hispanic American, 1% Native American
- 73% of applicants admitted
- SAT or ACT (ACT writing optional) required
- 67% graduate within 6 years

General. Founded in 1886. Regionally accredited. Scottish heritage honored through marching band clad in kilts, Scottish dance troupe, student pipers, tartan, Alma Highland Festival and Games. **Degrees:** 269 bachelor's awarded. **ROTC:** Army. **Location:** 50 miles from Lansing, 45 miles from Saginaw. **Calendar:** 4-4-1 semester system. Limited summer session. **Full-time faculty:** 88 total; 90% have terminal degrees, 10% minority, 38% women. **Part-time faculty:** 67 total; 31% have terminal degrees, 8% minority, 39% women. **Class size:** 62% < 20, 34% 20-39, 2% 40-49, 3% 50-99, less than 1% >100. **Special facilities:** Planetarium, performing arts center, climbing wall, ecological station, bike trail.

Freshman class profile. 1,893 applied, 1,379 admitted, 387 enrolled.

Mid 50% test scores			
SAT critical reading:	480-710	GPA 2.0-2.99:	14%
SAT math:	510-630	Rank in top quarter:	55%
SAT writing:	470-620	Rank in top tenth:	27%
ACT composite:	22-27	Return as sophomores:	85%
GPA 3.75 or higher:	35%	Out-of-state:	8%
GPA 3.50-3.74:	22%	Live on campus:	96%
GPA 3.0-3.49:	29%	Fraternities:	35%
		Sororities:	26%

Basis for selection. Applicant should be in top half of class, have 3.0 high school GPA or 22 ACT or 1030 SAT (exclusive of Writing). Co-curricular activities considered. Portfolio recommended for art majors. Interview recommended for all, strongly recommended for academically weak and those whose grades and test scores show discrepancies.

High school preparation. College-preparatory program required. 16 units required. Required and recommended units include English 4, mathematics 3, social studies 3, science 3 and foreign language 2.

2011-2012 Annual costs. Tuition/fees: $29,230. Room/board: $8,840. Books/supplies: $830. Personal expenses: $736.

2011-2012 Financial aid. Need-based: 377 full-time freshmen applied for aid; 322 were judged to have need; 322 of these received aid. Average need met was 86%. Average scholarship/grant was $20,735; average loan $3,301. 77% of total undergraduate aid awarded as scholarships/grants, 23% as loans/jobs. **Non-need-based:** Awarded to 384 full-time undergraduates, including 111 freshmen. Scholarships awarded for academics, alumni affiliation, art, minority status, music/drama, religious affiliation, state residency. **Additional information:** Auditions required for music, drama, dance scholarship candidates. Portfolios required for art scholarship candidates.

Application procedures. Admission: No deadline. $25 fee, may be waived for applicants with need, free for online applicants. Admission notification on a rolling basis beginning on or about 9/1. Must reply by May 1 or within 3 week(s) if notified thereafter. **Financial aid:** Priority date 3/1; no closing date. FAFSA required. Applicants notified on a rolling basis starting 3/1; must reply within 3 week(s) of notification.

Academics. One-month spring term provides special opportunities for study in United States or overseas. Students required to complete 2 spring terms. **Special study options:** Combined bachelor's/graduate degree, double major, dual enrollment of high school students, honors, independent study, internships, New York semester, student-designed major, study abroad, teacher certification program, urban semester, Washington semester. Pre-engineering 3-2 programs with University of Michigan, Michigan Technological University; pre-occupational therapy 3-2 program with Washington University (MO). **Credit/placement by examination:** AP, CLEP, IB, SAT, ACT, institutional tests. 32 credit hours maximum toward bachelor's degree. **Support services:** Pre-admission summer program, reduced course load, remedial instruction, study skills assistance, tutoring, writing center.

Majors. Biology: General, biochemistry. **Business:** Accounting, business admin. **Communications:** Media studies. **Conservation:** Environmental studies. **Education:** General, elementary, secondary. **English:** English lit. **Foreign languages:** French, German, Spanish. **Health services:** Health care

admin. **History:** General. **Math:** General. **Parks/recreation:** Exercise sciences, health/fitness. **Philosophy/religion:** Philosophy, religion. **Physical sciences:** Chemistry, physics. **Psychology:** General. **Social sciences:** Economics, political science, sociology/anthropology. **Visual/performing arts:** Dance, design, dramatic, music.

Most popular majors. Biology 14%, business/marketing 21%, health sciences 10%, history 7%, psychology 6%, social sciences 7%, visual/performing arts 10%.

Computing on campus. 260 workstations in dormitories, library, computer center, student center. Dormitories wired for high-speed internet access and linked to campus network. Commuter students can connect to campus network. Online course registration, online library, helpline, student web hosting, wireless network available.

Student life. **Freshman orientation:** Mandatory, $325 fee. Preregistration for classes offered. Last weekend of August prior to the start of the fall term. **Housing:** Guaranteed on-campus for all undergraduates. Coed dorms, apartments, fraternity/sorority housing available. $200 nonrefundable deposit, deadline 5/1. **Activities:** Bands, campus ministries, choral groups, dance, drama, international student organizations, literary magazine, music ensembles, Model UN, radio station, student government, student newspaper, symphony orchestra, College Republicans/College Democrats, Amnesty International, Big Brothers/Big Sisters, Catholic Student Organization, Habitat for Humanity.

Athletics. NCAA. **Intercollegiate:** Baseball M, basketball, bowling W, cross-country, diving, football (tackle) M, golf, lacrosse, soccer, softball W, swimming, tennis, track and field, volleyball W, wrestling M. **Intramural:** Basketball, soccer W, softball, volleyball. **Team name:** Scots.

Student services. Alcohol/substance abuse counseling, chaplain/spiritual director, career counseling, student employment services, financial aid counseling, health services, personal counseling. **Physically disabled:** Services for visually, hearing impaired.

Contact. E-mail: admissions@alma.edu
Phone: (989) 463-7139 Toll-free number: (800) 321-2562
Fax: (989) 463-7057
Bob Garcia, Director of Admissions, Alma College, 614 West Superior Street, Alma, MI 48801-1599

Andrews University
Berrien Springs, Michigan
www.andrews.edu   CB code: 1030

- Private 4-year university affiliated with Seventh-day Adventists
- Residential campus in small town
- 1,844 degree-seeking undergraduates: 7% part-time, 55% women, 25% African American, 9% Asian American, 16% Hispanic American, 13% international
- 1,585 degree-seeking graduate students
- 36% of applicants admitted
- SAT or ACT (ACT writing optional), application essay required
- 63% graduate within 6 years

General. Founded in 1874. Regionally accredited. **Degrees:** 367 bachelor's, 2 associate awarded; master's, doctoral offered. **Location:** 10 miles from St. Joseph-Benton Harbor, 25 miles from South Bend, Indiana. **Calendar:** Semester, limited summer session. **Full-time faculty:** 227 total; 74% have terminal degrees, 24% minority, 36% women. **Part-time faculty:** 63 total; 24% have terminal degrees, 33% minority, 46% women. **Class size:** 62% < 20, 28% 20-39, 3% 40-49, 6% 50-99, 1% >100. **Special facilities:** Natural history museum, archaeology museum, performing arts center, arboretum.

Freshman class profile. 2,487 applied, 897 admitted, 393 enrolled.

Mid 50% test scores			
SAT critical reading:	470-590	Rank in top quarter:	44%
SAT math:	440-590	Rank in top tenth:	23%
SAT writing:	470-570	Return as sophomores:	78%
ACT composite:	20-26	Out-of-state:	65%
GPA 3.75 or higher:	34%	Live on campus:	81%
GPA 3.50-3.74:	17%	International:	19%
GPA 3.0-3.49:	30%		
GPA 2.0-2.99:	19%		

Basis for selection. School achievement record, test scores, recommendations important. Interview recommended. Audition recommended for music majors. Portfolios recommended for architecture, art majors. **Home schooled:** Portfolio required. **Learning Disabled:** Must advise student services of learning disability prior to admission interview and testing.

High school preparation. College-preparatory program recommended. 13 units required; 15 recommended. Required and recommended units include English 3-4, mathematics 2-3, social studies 1, history 2, science 2 and academic electives 3. Additional 1 unit chemistry, 1 unit physics, 1 unit computer recommended.

2011-2012 Annual costs. Tuition/fees: $23,428. Room/board: $7,374. Books/supplies: $1,050. Personal expenses: $900.

2010-2011 Financial aid. **Need-based:** 275 full-time freshmen applied for aid; 229 were judged to have need; 229 of these received aid. Average need met was 85%. Average scholarship/grant was $6,709; average loan $3,399. 77% of total undergraduate aid awarded as scholarships/grants, 23% as loans/jobs. **Non-need-based:** Awarded to 1,669 full-time undergraduates, including 358 freshmen. Scholarships awarded for academics, alumni affiliation, job skills, leadership, music/drama, religious affiliation.

Application procedures. **Admission:** No deadline. $30 fee. Admission notification on a rolling basis beginning on or about 1/1. **Financial aid:** Priority date 3/31; no closing date. FAFSA, institutional form required. Applicants notified on a rolling basis starting 3/15.

Academics. **Special study options:** Accelerated study, combined bachelor's/graduate degree, cooperative education, distance learning, double major, dual enrollment of high school students, ESL, honors, internships, student-designed major, study abroad, teacher certification program. **Credit/placement by examination:** AP, CLEP, IB, institutional tests. 32 credit hours maximum toward associate degree, 32 toward bachelor's. DANTES (for nontraditional students). **Support services:** Learning center, pre-admission summer program, reduced course load, remedial instruction, study skills assistance, tutoring, writing center.

Majors. **Architecture:** Architecture. **Biology:** General, biochemistry, biophysics, botany, molecular, neuroscience, zoology. **Business:** Accounting, business admin, entrepreneurial studies, finance, managerial economics, nonprofit/public, training/development. **Communications:** Communications/speech/rhetoric, journalism, public relations. **Communications technology:** General. **Computer sciences:** General, information systems. **Conservation:** Environmental science. **Education:** Elementary, mathematics, secondary, social science, social studies. **Engineering:** General, electrical, industrial, mechanical. **English:** English lit. **Foreign languages:** French, Spanish. **General:** Animal sciences, business, horticulture. **Health services:** Audiology/speech pathology, clinical lab science, dietetics, nursing (RN). **History:** General. **Human services:** Social work. **Math:** General. **Philosophy/religion:** Religion. **Physical sciences:** Chemistry, physics. **Psychology:** General. **Social sciences:** General, anthropology, economics, international economic development, political science, sociology. **Theology:** Religious ed, sacred music, theology, youth ministry. **Visual/performing arts:** General, art, art history/conservation, ceramics, commercial/advertising art, design, graphic design, multimedia, music, music performance, painting, photography, printmaking, studio arts. **Work/family studies:** Family studies, food/nutrition.

Most popular majors. Business/marketing 11%, education 11%, engineering/engineering technologies 7%, social sciences 7%, trade and industry 8%, visual/performing arts 7%.

Computing on campus. 130 workstations in dormitories, library, computer center. Dormitories wired for high-speed internet access and linked to campus network. Commuter students can connect to campus network. Online course registration, online library, helpline, repair service, student web hosting, wireless network available.

Student life. **Freshman orientation:** Mandatory. Preregistration for classes offered. Held week before fall registration. **Policies:** Students expected to abide by ethical and moral standards of the university, which are mission-driven as published in official documents. Resident students required to live in dorm until age 22. Religious observance required. **Housing:** Guaranteed on-campus for all undergraduates. Single-sex dorms, apartments, wellness housing available. $200 deposit. **Activities:** Concert band, choral groups, drama, international student organizations, music ensembles, musical theater, radio station, student government, student newspaper, symphony orchestra, Christian Youth Action.

Athletics. **Intramural:** Badminton, basketball, field hockey, football (non-tackle), soccer, softball, triathlon, volleyball.

Student services. Chaplain/spiritual director, career counseling, student employment services, financial aid counseling, health services, on-campus daycare, personal counseling, placement for graduates, veterans' counselor. **Physically disabled:** Services for visually, speech, hearing impaired.

Contact. E-mail: enroll@andrews.edu
Phone: (800) 253-2874 Toll-free number: (800) 253-2874
Fax: (269) 471-3228
Stephen Payne, Vice President for Enrollment Management, Andrews University, 100 US Highway 31, Berrien Springs, MI 49104

Aquinas College
Grand Rapids, Michigan
www.aquinas.edu

CB code: 1018

- Private 4-year liberal arts college affiliated with Roman Catholic Church
- Residential campus in small city
- 2,086 degree-seeking undergraduates: 11% part-time, 64% women
- 213 degree-seeking graduate students
- 78% of applicants admitted
- SAT or ACT (ACT writing optional) required
- 52% graduate within 6 years; 17% enter graduate study

General. Founded in 1886. Regionally accredited. **Degrees:** 324 bachelor's, 2 associate awarded; master's offered. **ROTC:** Army. **Location:** 140 miles from Detroit, 180 miles from Chicago. **Calendar:** Semester, extensive summer session. **Full-time faculty:** 90 total; 77% have terminal degrees, 10% minority, 50% women. **Part-time faculty:** 161 total; 19% have terminal degrees, 7% minority, 44% women. **Class size:** 57% < 20, 40% 20-39, 2% 40-49, 1% 50-99. **Special facilities:** Greenhouse, astronomy tower, nature trails, community theater, center for sustainability.

Freshman class profile. 2,282 applied, 1,790 admitted, 376 enrolled.

Mid 50% test scores			
ACT composite:	21-27	Rank in top tenth:	20%
GPA 3.75 or higher:	31%	End year in good standing:	74%
GPA 3.50-3.74:	18%	Return as sophomores:	75%
GPA 3.0-3.49:	29%	Out-of-state:	10%
GPA 2.0-2.99:	22%	Live on campus:	86%
Rank in top quarter:	48%	International:	1%

Basis for selection. GED not accepted. 2.5 high school GPA in academic subjects. Test scores important. Interview required for applicants with above average test scores but less than 2.5 high school GPA in academic subjects and recommended for others. Audition recommended for music majors. Portfolio recommended for art majors. **Home schooled:** Transcript of courses and grades required. Greater emphasis placed upon results of ACT or SAT. Students may be required to complete Ability to Benefit test. **Learning Disabled:** Make appointment with Academic Achievement Center to express needed accommodations prior to enrollment.

High school preparation. College-preparatory program recommended. 15 units required. Required units include English 4, mathematics 4, social studies 4 and science 3.

2011-2012 Annual costs. Tuition/fees: $24,286. Room/board: $7,438. Books/supplies: $798. Personal expenses: $768.

2011-2012 Financial aid. Need-based: 361 full-time freshmen applied for aid; 322 were judged to have need; 322 of these received aid. Average need met was 86%. Average scholarship/grant was $18,118; average loan $3,314. 82% of total undergraduate aid awarded as scholarships/grants, 18% as loans/jobs. **Non-need-based:** Scholarships awarded for academics, alumni affiliation, art, athletics, leadership, music/drama.

Application procedures. Admission: Priority date 5/1; no deadline. No application fee. Admission notification on a rolling basis beginning on or about 8/1. **Financial aid:** Priority date 3/1; no closing date. FAFSA required. Applicants notified on a rolling basis starting 2/15; must reply within 2 week(s) of notification.

Academics. Special study options: Accelerated study, cooperative education, cross-registration, distance learning, double major, dual enrollment of high school students, exchange student, honors, independent study, internships, liberal arts/career combination, student-designed major, study abroad, teacher certification program, urban semester. **Credit/placement by examination:** AP, CLEP, institutional tests. 30 credit hours maximum toward bachelor's degree. **Support services:** Learning center, remedial instruction, study skills assistance, tutoring, writing center.

Majors. Biology: General. **Business:** Accounting, accounting/finance, business admin, communications, international, management information systems. **Communications:** General. **Computer sciences:** General. **Conservation:** Environmental science, environmental studies. **Education:** English, learning disabled, music, physical, science, social science, social studies, special ed. **English:** English lit. **Foreign languages:** French, German, Spanish. **Health services:** Athletic training. **History:** General. **Human services:** Community org/advocacy. **Liberal arts:** Arts/sciences, humanities. **Math:** General. **Parks/recreation:** General, health/fitness, sports admin. **Philosophy/religion:** Philosophy, religion. **Physical sciences:** Chemistry. **Psychology:** General. **Social sciences:** General, economics, geography, international relations, political science, sociology. **Theology:** Sacred music. **Visual/performing arts:** Art, art history/conservation, music performance, studio arts management, theater arts management.

Most popular majors. Biology 6%, business/marketing 15%, education 9%, psychology 7%, social sciences 11%, visual/performing arts 6%.

Computing on campus. 173 workstations in dormitories, library, computer center, student center. Dormitories wired for high-speed internet access and linked to campus network. Commuter students can connect to campus network. Online library, helpline, wireless network available.

Student life. Freshman orientation: Mandatory, $100 fee. Preregistration for classes offered. 3 days during week before fall classes begin. Includes start of common freshman class. **Policies:** Students serve on administrative and faculty committees. **Housing:** Guaranteed on-campus for freshmen. Coed dorms, apartments, wellness housing available. $100 deposit, deadline 8/15. **Activities:** Jazz band, campus ministries, choral groups, dance, drama, international student organizations, literary magazine, music ensembles, Model UN, radio station, student government, student newspaper, community action volunteers, social action commission, community senate, Bible Study, College Democrats, College Republicans, Catholic studies club, Habitat for Humanity.

Athletics. NAIA. **Intercollegiate:** Baseball M, basketball, bowling M, cross-country, golf, ice hockey M, lacrosse, soccer, softball W, tennis, track and field, volleyball W. **Intramural:** Basketball, fencing M, golf, ice hockey M, lacrosse, skiing, soccer, softball, tennis, volleyball. **Team name:** Saints.

Student services. Adult student services, alcohol/substance abuse counseling, chaplain/spiritual director, career counseling, services for economically disadvantaged, student employment services, financial aid counseling, health services, minority student services, personal counseling, placement for graduates, veterans' counselor, women's services. **Physically disabled:** Services for visually, speech, hearing impaired.

Contact. E-mail: admissions@aquinas.edu
Phone: (616) 632-2900 Toll-free number: (800) 678-9593
Fax: (616) 732-4469
Angela Schlosser-Bacon, Director of Admissions, Aquinas College, 1607 Robinson Road Southeast, Grand Rapids, MI 49506-1799

Art Institute of Michigan
Novi, Michigan
www.artinstitutes.edu/detroit

CB code: 5750

- For-profit 4-year branch campus and visual arts college
- Large city
- 880 undergraduates
- Application essay, interview required

General. Regionally accredited; also accredited by ACCSC. **Degrees:** 13 bachelor's, 72 associate awarded. **Calendar:** Quarter. **Full-time faculty:** 10 total. **Part-time faculty:** 59 total.

Basis for selection. Academic record and interview very important. SAT or ACT recommended. **Home schooled:** Transcript of courses and grades, state high school equivalency certificate required.

2011-2012 Annual costs. Tuition/fees: $21,735. Required fees vary by program.

Application procedures. Admission: Closing date 10/12 (receipt date). $50 fee, may be waived for applicants with need. Admission notification on a rolling basis. **Financial aid:** Closing date 10/12.

Academics. Credit/placement by examination: AP, CLEP, SAT, ACT.

Majors. Business: Apparel. **Communications technology:** Recording arts. **Computer sciences:** Computer graphics, web page design. **Visual/performing arts:** Commercial photography, graphic design, interior design.

Contact. Phone: (248) 675-3800 Toll-free number: (800) 479-0087
Fax: (248) 675-3830
Dave Molnar, Senior Director of Admissions, Art Institute of Michigan, 28125 Cabot Drive, Suite 120, Novi, MI 48377

Baker College of Allen Park
Allen Park, Michigan
www.baker.edu

CB code: 6588

- Private 4-year business and health science college
- Commuter campus in large city
- 3,954 degree-seeking undergraduates

General. Regionally accredited. **Degrees:** 96 bachelor's, 281 associate awarded. **Location:** 10 miles from Detroit. **Calendar:** Quarter, limited summer session. **Full-time faculty:** 2 total; 50% women. **Part-time faculty:** 86 total; 13% have terminal degrees, 60% women.

Basis for selection. Open admission, but selective for some programs. **Home schooled:** Transcript of courses and grades required.

2011-2012 Annual costs. Tuition/fees: $9,450. Books/supplies: $1,800.

Application procedures. Admission: No deadline. $20 fee, may be waived for applicants with need. Admission notification on a rolling basis.

Academics. Special study options: Combined bachelor's/graduate degree, cooperative education, distance learning, double major, dual enrollment of high school students, independent study, internships, teacher certification program. **Credit/placement by examination:** AP, CLEP. **Support services:** Learning center, remedial instruction, study skills assistance, tutoring.

Majors. Business: Human resources. **Computer sciences:** Information technology. **Education:** Elementary, middle, secondary.

Computing on campus. 208 workstations in library, computer center, student center. Online library, helpline, wireless network available.

Student life. Freshman orientation: Mandatory. Preregistration for classes offered.

Contact. Phone: (313) 425-3700
Steve Peterson, Vice President for Admissions, Baker College of Allen Park, 4500 Enterprise Drive, Allen Park, MI 48101

Baker College of Auburn Hills
Auburn Hills, Michigan
www.baker.edu   CB code: 1457

- Private 4-year business and technical college
- Commuter campus in small city
- 3,803 degree-seeking undergraduates

General. Founded in 1990. Regionally accredited. Part of multi-campus system specializing in career education. **Degrees:** 215 bachelor's, 327 associate awarded. **Location:** 30 miles from Detroit. **Calendar:** Quarter, limited summer session. **Full-time faculty:** 11 total; 18% have terminal degrees, 46% women. **Part-time faculty:** 144 total; 15% have terminal degrees, 55% women. **Class size:** 45% < 20, 55% 20-39.

Basis for selection. Open admission, but selective for some programs. Specific entrance requirements for allied health programs and bachelor of business leadership degree program. Interview recommended.

2011-2012 Annual costs. Tuition/fees: $9,450. Books/supplies: $1,000.

Financial aid. Non-need-based: Scholarships awarded for academics, alumni affiliation.

Application procedures. Admission: No deadline. $20 fee, may be waived for applicants with need. Admission notification on a rolling basis. **Financial aid:** Priority date 2/21, closing date 9/1. FAFSA, institutional form required. Applicants notified on a rolling basis starting 4/1.

Academics. 2+2 system allows students to begin required courses in major while completing associate degree. **Special study options:** Accelerated study, combined bachelor's/graduate degree, distance learning, double major, dual enrollment of high school students, independent study, internships, liberal arts/career combination, teacher certification program. **Credit/placement by examination:** AP, CLEP, IB, institutional tests. 48 credit hours maximum toward associate degree, 96 toward bachelor's. **Support services:** Learning center, reduced course load, remedial instruction, study skills assistance, tutoring, writing center.

Majors. Business: General, accounting, business admin, management science. **Education:** General, elementary, middle, multi-level teacher, secondary.

Computing on campus. 131 workstations in library, computer center, student center. Commuter students can connect to campus network. Helpline available.

Student life. Freshman orientation: Mandatory. Preregistration for classes offered. **Activities:** Accounting club, management club, interior design society, society of automotive engineers, marketing club.

Student services. Career counseling, student employment services, financial aid counseling, personal counseling, placement for graduates, veterans' counselor. **Physically disabled:** Services for visually, hearing impaired.

Contact. Phone: (248) 340-0600 Toll-free number: (888) 429-0410
Fax: (248) 340-0600
Nicole Chirco, Director of Admissions, Baker College of Auburn Hills, 1500 University Drive, Auburn Hills, MI 48326

Baker College of Cadillac
Cadillac, Michigan
www.baker.edu   CB code: 1381

- Private 4-year business and health science college
- Commuter campus in large town
- 1,639 undergraduates

General. Founded in 1911. Regionally accredited. Part of multicampus system specializing in career education. **Degrees:** 43 bachelor's, 199 associate awarded. **Location:** 90 miles from Grand Rapids, 45 miles from Traverse City. **Calendar:** Quarter, limited summer session. **Full-time faculty:** 4 total; 25% women. **Part-time faculty:** 101 total; 5% have terminal degrees, 52% women. **Class size:** 68% < 20, 31% 20-39, 1% 40-49. **Special facilities:** Mock operating room, massage therapy room.

Basis for selection. Open admission. Some allied health programs require health appraisal. Interview recommended.

2011-2012 Annual costs. Tuition/fees: $9,450. Books/supplies: $1,000.

Financial aid. Non-need-based: Scholarships awarded for academics.

Application procedures. Admission: No deadline. $20 fee, may be waived for applicants with need. Admission notification on a rolling basis beginning on or about 10/1. **Financial aid:** Priority date 2/21; no closing date. FAFSA, institutional form required. Applicants notified on a rolling basis starting 5/1.

Academics. Special study options: Accelerated study, combined bachelor's/graduate degree, cooperative education, distance learning, double major, dual enrollment of high school students, external degree, independent study, internships, liberal arts/career combination, weekend college. 2+2 bachelor's degree and bachelor of business leadership degree. **Credit/placement by examination:** AP, CLEP, IB, institutional tests. 48 credit hours maximum toward associate degree, 96 toward bachelor's. **Support services:** Learning center, reduced course load, remedial instruction, study skills assistance, tutoring, writing center.

Majors. Business: Accounting, business admin, human resources, office management. **Computer sciences:** Computer science.

Computing on campus. 154 workstations in library, computer center. Commuter students can connect to campus network. Online library, helpline, repair service available.

Student life. Freshman orientation: Mandatory. Preregistration for classes offered. **Activities:** Student activities group, professional student organizations.

Student services. Career counseling, student employment services, financial aid counseling, personal counseling, placement for graduates, veterans' counselor. **Physically disabled:** Services for visually, hearing impaired.

Contact. E-mail: mike.tisdale@baker.edu
Phone: (231) 876-3100 Toll-free number: (888) 313-3463
Fax: (231) 775-8505
Audrey Charmoli, Director of Admissions, Baker College of Cadillac, 9600 East 13th Street, Cadillac, MI 49601

Baker College of Clinton Township
Clinton Township, Michigan
www.baker.edu   CB code: 1386

- Private 4-year business and technical college
- Commuter campus in very large city
- 6,225 degree-seeking undergraduates

General. Founded in 1911. Regionally accredited. Part of multicampus system specializing in career education. **Degrees:** 262 bachelor's, 505 associate awarded. **Location:** 15 miles from Detroit. **Calendar:** Quarter, limited summer session. **Full-time faculty:** 17 total; 18% have terminal degrees,

76% women. **Part-time faculty:** 191 total; 11% have terminal degrees, 61% women. **Class size:** 25% < 20, 74% 20-39, less than 1% 40-49.

Basis for selection. Open admission, but selective for some programs. Physical exam may be required for some programs. Interview recommended. **Learning Disabled:** Students must complete special needs intake form signed by professional.

High school preparation. Recommended units include English 4, mathematics 4, social studies 2, science 3 and foreign language 4.

2011-2012 Annual costs. Tuition/fees: $9,450. Books/supplies: $1,800. Personal expenses: $2,000.

Financial aid. Non-need-based: Scholarships awarded for academics, minority status.

Application procedures. Admission: Priority date 9/1; no deadline. $20 fee, may be waived for applicants with need. Admission notification on a rolling basis. **Financial aid:** Priority date 2/21, closing date 9/1. FAFSA, institutional form required. Applicants notified on a rolling basis starting 4/1.

Academics. 2+2 system allows students to begin required courses in major while completing associate degree. **Special study options:** Accelerated study, combined bachelor's/graduate degree, cooperative education, distance learning, double major, dual enrollment of high school students, external degree, independent study, internships, teacher certification program. **Credit/placement by examination:** AP, CLEP, IB, institutional tests. 48 credit hours maximum toward associate degree, 96 toward bachelor's. **Support services:** Learning center, reduced course load, remedial instruction, study skills assistance, tutoring, writing center.

Majors. Business: Accounting, administrative services, business admin, human resources, management science, office management. **Computer sciences:** General, computer science. **Education:** Elementary, middle, multi-level teacher, secondary. **Health services:** Health care admin, nursing (RN), office admin.

Computing on campus. 120 workstations in library, computer center. Commuter students can connect to campus network. Helpline available.

Student life. Freshman orientation: Mandatory. Preregistration for classes offered.

Student services. Adult student services, career counseling, student employment services, financial aid counseling, personal counseling, placement for graduates, veterans' counselor. **Physically disabled:** Services for visually, hearing impaired.

Contact. E-mail: adm_mc@baker.edu
Phone: (586) 791-3000 Toll-free number: (888) 272-2842
Fax: (586) 791-6610
Annette Looser, Director of Admissions, Baker College of Clinton Township, 34950 Little Mack Avenue, Clinton Township, MI 48035

Baker College of Flint
Flint, Michigan
www.baker.edu   **CB code: 0806**

- Private 4-year business and technical college
- Commuter campus in large city
- 6,329 degree-seeking undergraduates

General. Founded in 1911. Regionally accredited. Corporate services division offers degree-granting programs on campus and/or at work site, coordinated with corporate training and professional development programs. Part of multicampus system specializing in career education. **Degrees:** 145 bachelor's, 579 associate awarded; master's offered. **Location:** 10 miles from downtown, 60 miles from Detroit. **Calendar:** Quarter, limited summer session. **Full-time faculty:** 40 total; 15% have terminal degrees, 58% women. **Part-time faculty:** 275 total; 12% have terminal degrees, 59% women. **Special facilities:** Polysommnography sleep lab, orthotic/prosthetic lab.

Freshman class profile.

Out-of-state:	2%	Live on campus:	5%

Basis for selection. Open admission, but selective for some programs. Health applicants must have health appraisal. Occupational therapy applicants must present minimum of 1 year biology, 1 year chemistry/physics, 2 years math including algebra or equivalent. All health programs require 2.0 GPA for entrance to professional classes. Class size may be limited. Trucking programs require drug screening prior to enrollment acceptance. Interview recommended.

2011-2012 Annual costs. Tuition/fees: $9,450. Additional fees vary with program. Room only: $2,800. Books/supplies: $1,800.

Financial aid. Non-need-based: Scholarships awarded for academics, minority status.

Application procedures. Admission: Priority date 9/1; no deadline. $20 fee, may be waived for applicants with need. Admission notification on a rolling basis. **Financial aid:** Priority date 2/21, closing date 9/1. FAFSA, institutional form required. Applicants notified on a rolling basis starting 4/1.

Academics. 2+2 system allows students to begin required courses in major while completing associate degree. Calendar based on 10-week quarters. **Special study options:** Accelerated study, combined bachelor's/graduate degree, cooperative education, distance learning, double major, dual enrollment of high school students, external degree, independent study, internships. **Credit/placement by examination:** AP, CLEP, IB, institutional tests. 48 credit hours maximum toward associate degree, 96 toward bachelor's. **Support services:** Learning center, reduced course load, remedial instruction, study skills assistance, tutoring, writing center.

Majors. Business: Accounting, business admin, management information systems, office management, operations. **Computer sciences:** General. **Education:** Elementary, middle, multi-level teacher, secondary. **Engineering:** Mechanical. **Health services:** Health care admin, medical records admin, nursing (RN). **Visual/performing arts:** Commercial/advertising art, interior design.

Most popular majors. Business/marketing 65%, health sciences 25%.

Computing on campus. 300 workstations in library, computer center. Commuter students can connect to campus network. Helpline available.

Student life. Freshman orientation: Mandatory. Preregistration for classes offered. **Housing:** Guaranteed on-campus for freshmen. Coed dorms, wellness housing available. $50 deposit, deadline 9/20. **Activities:** Literary magazine, National Association of Accountants, American Marketing Association, Interior Design Society, travel club, environmental club, physical therapy assistant club, medical assistants student organization, Health Information Management Association, graphic communications club, Society of Manufacturing Engineers student chapter.

Athletics. Intramural: Basketball, volleyball.

Student services. Career counseling, student employment services, on-campus daycare, personal counseling, placement for graduates, veterans' counselor. **Physically disabled:** Services for visually, hearing impaired.

Contact. E-mail: adm-fl@baker.edu
Phone: (810) 766-4000 Toll-free number: (800) 964-4299
Fax: (810) 766-4293
Jodi Cunez, Director of Admissions, Baker College of Flint, 1050 West Bristol Road, Flint, MI 48507

Baker College of Jackson
Jackson, Michigan
www.baker.edu   **CB code: 1887**

- Private 4-year business and technical college
- Commuter campus in small city
- 2,730 degree-seeking undergraduates

General. Founded in 1994. Regionally accredited. Part of multicampus system specializing in career education. **Degrees:** 82 bachelor's, 211 associate awarded. **Location:** 40 miles from Lansing, 40 miles from Ann Arbor. **Calendar:** Quarter, limited summer session. **Full-time faculty:** 5 total; 40% have terminal degrees, 60% women. **Part-time faculty:** 80 total; 11% have terminal degrees, 58% women.

Basis for selection. Open admission, but selective for some programs. Physical exam may be required for allied health programs. All health programs require specific GPA. Interview recommended.

2011-2012 Annual costs. Tuition/fees: $9,450. Books/supplies: $975.

Financial aid. Non-need-based: Scholarships awarded for academics, minority status.

Application procedures. Admission: No deadline. $20 fee, may be waived for applicants with need. Admission notification on a rolling basis. **Financial aid:** Priority date 2/21, closing date 9/1. FAFSA, institutional form required. Applicants notified on a rolling basis starting 4/1.

Academics. 2+2 system allows students to begin required courses in major while completing associate degree. **Special study options:** Accelerated study, combined bachelor's/graduate degree, cooperative education, distance learning, double major, dual enrollment of high school students, external degree, independent study, internships. **Credit/placement by examination:** AP, CLEP, IB, institutional tests. 48 credit hours maximum toward associate degree, 96 toward bachelor's. **Support services:** Learning center, reduced course load, remedial instruction, study skills assistance, tutoring, writing center.

Majors. Business: General, accounting. **Education:** Elementary, middle, multi-level teacher, secondary.

Computing on campus. 114 workstations in library, computer center. Commuter students can connect to campus network. Helpline available.

Student life. Freshman orientation: Mandatory. Preregistration for classes offered. **Activities:** Student government.

Student services. Career counseling, student employment services, personal counseling, placement for graduates, veterans' counselor. **Physically disabled:** Services for visually, hearing impaired.

Contact. E-mail: adm-jk@baker.edu
Phone: (517) 788-7800 Toll-free number: (888) 343-3683
Fax: (517) 789-7331
Kevin Pnacek, Vice President for Admissions, Baker College of Jackson, 2800 Springport Road, Jackson, MI 49202

Baker College of Muskegon
Muskegon, Michigan
www.baker.edu   CB code: 1527

- Private 4-year business and technical college
- Commuter campus in small city
- 4,994 degree-seeking undergraduates

General. Founded in 1888. Regionally accredited. Part of multicampus system specializing in career education. All associate degree programs include internship, co-op or clinical affiliation experience. **Degrees:** 193 bachelor's, 560 associate awarded. **Location:** 40 miles from Grand Rapids. **Calendar:** Quarter, limited summer session. **Full-time faculty:** 17 total; 6% have terminal degrees, 53% women. **Part-time faculty:** 160 total; 9% have terminal degrees, 55% women. **Class size:** 38% < 20, 57% 20-39, 3% 40-49, 2% 50-99. **Special facilities:** Restaurant run by culinary and food and beverage management students.

Basis for selection. Open admission, but selective for some programs. 2.75 GPA required for admission to occupational therapy assisting, physical therapist assisting, veterinary technician, surgical technology, teacher preparation. Class size may be limited in some programs. Physical examination, background check required for some programs. Interview recommended. **Home schooled:** Basic skills placement assessments in math, language arts, and reading part of orientation/registration process. **Learning Disabled:** Learning disability must be documented and presented to counseling staff before registering for classes.

2011-2012 Annual costs. Tuition/fees: $9,450. Room only: $2,925. Books/supplies: $1,800. Personal expenses: $2,000.

Financial aid. Non-need-based: Scholarships awarded for academics, minority status.

Application procedures. Admission: Priority date 9/1; no deadline. $20 fee, may be waived for applicants with need. Admission notification on a rolling basis. **Financial aid:** Priority date 2/21; no closing date. FAFSA, institutional form required. Applicants notified on a rolling basis starting 4/1.

Academics. 2+2 system allows students to begin required courses in major while completing associate degree. Maximum number of credits awarded for prior work and/or life experiences, 48 for associate and 144 for bachelor. **Special study options:** Accelerated study, combined bachelor's/graduate degree, cooperative education, distance learning, double major, dual enrollment of high school students, external degree, independent study, internships, liberal arts/career combination, teacher certification program. Accelerated bachelor of business administration offered in weekend delivery format. **Credit/placement by examination:** AP, CLEP, IB, institutional tests. 48 credit hours maximum toward associate degree, 144 toward bachelor's. **Support services:** Learning center, reduced course load, remedial instruction, study skills assistance, tutoring.

Majors. Business: Accounting, accounting/business management, administrative services, business admin, human resources, management science, marketing, office management, restaurant/food services. **Computer sciences:**

General, computer science, information systems, systems analysis. **Education:** Elementary, kindergarten/preschool, middle, multi-level teacher, secondary. **Health services:** Health care admin.

Computing on campus. 180 workstations in dormitories, library, computer center. Dormitories wired for high-speed internet access and linked to campus network. Commuter students can connect to campus network. Online course registration, online library, helpline, wireless network available.

Student life. Freshman orientation: Mandatory. Preregistration for classes offered. 3-4 hour session prior to start of quarter; includes COMPASS testing, registration, academic advising. **Policies:** No drug or alcohol use permitted anywhere on campus or in residence halls. **Housing:** Coed dorms, special housing for disabled, apartments, wellness housing available. $50 deposit, deadline 9/1. **Activities:** Student government, travel club, rehab club, residence hall association, culinary arts club, human resource management club.

Athletics. Intramural: Bowling.

Student services. Adult student services, career counseling, student employment services, financial aid counseling, personal counseling, placement for graduates, veterans' counselor. **Physically disabled:** Services for visually, hearing impaired.

Contact. E-mail: kathy.jacobson@baker.edu
Phone: (231) 777-5200 Toll-free number: (800) 937-0337
Fax: (231) 777-5201
Kathy Jacobson, Vice President and Director of Admissions, Baker College of Muskegon, 1903 Marquette Avenue, Muskegon, MI 49442

Baker College of Owosso
Owosso, Michigan
www.baker.edu   CB code: 5270

- Private 4-year business and technical college
- Commuter campus in large town
- 3,078 degree-seeking undergraduates

General. Founded in 1911. Regionally accredited. Part of multicampus system, with affiliated graduate school, specializing in career education. Master's degree available at Flint campus. **Degrees:** 82 bachelor's, 287 associate awarded. **Location:** 30 miles from Lansing, 300 miles from Flint. **Calendar:** Quarter, limited summer session. **Full-time faculty:** 8 total; 25% have terminal degrees, 50% women. **Part-time faculty:** 136 total; 14% have terminal degrees, 57% women. **Special facilities:** Diesel technology center.

Freshman class profile.

Out-of-state:	3%	**Live on campus:**	30%

Basis for selection. Open admission, but selective for some programs. Limited enrollment for medical programs.

2011-2012 Annual costs. Tuition/fees: $9,450. Room only: $2,800. Books/supplies: $1,800.

Financial aid. Non-need-based: Scholarships awarded for academics, minority status.

Application procedures. Admission: Priority date 9/1; no deadline. $20 fee, may be waived for applicants with need. Admission notification on a rolling basis. **Financial aid:** Priority date 2/21, closing date 9/1. FAFSA, institutional form required. Applicants notified on a rolling basis starting 4/1.

Academics. 2+2 system allows students to begin required courses in major while completing associate degree. **Special study options:** Accelerated study, combined bachelor's/graduate degree, cooperative education, distance learning, double major, dual enrollment of high school students, external degree, independent study, internships. **Credit/placement by examination:** AP, CLEP, IB, institutional tests. 48 credit hours maximum toward associate degree, 96 toward bachelor's. **Support services:** Learning center, reduced course load, remedial instruction, study skills assistance, tutoring, writing center.

Majors. Business: Accounting, administrative services, business admin, human resources, management information systems, marketing, office management. **Communications technology:** Graphics. **Computer sciences:** General, computer graphics, computer science. **Education:** Elementary, middle, multi-level teacher, secondary. **Health services:** Health care admin.

Computing on campus. 226 workstations in dormitories, library, computer center. Dormitories wired for high-speed internet access. Commuter students can connect to campus network. Online library, helpline available.

Student life. Freshman orientation: Mandatory. Preregistration for classes offered. **Housing:** Guaranteed on-campus for freshmen. Coed dorms, wellness housing available. $50 deposit. **Activities:** Student newspaper, accounting club, MLT club, interior design club, radiology club, graphics club.

Athletics. Intramural: Basketball, volleyball.

Student services. Adult student services, career counseling, services for economically disadvantaged, student employment services, financial aid counseling, on-campus daycare, personal counseling, placement for graduates, veterans' counselor. **Physically disabled:** Services for visually, speech, hearing impaired.

Contact. E-mail: michael.konopacke@baker.edu
Phone: (989) 729-3350 Toll-free number: (800) 879-3797
Fax: (989) 729-3359
Michael Konopacke, Vice President of Admissions, Baker College of Owosso, 1020 South Washington Street, Owosso, MI 48867

Baker College of Port Huron
Port Huron, Michigan
www.baker.edu   **CB code: 1413**

- Private 4-year business and technical college
- Commuter campus in large town
- 1,453 undergraduates

General. Founded in 1911. Regionally accredited. Part of multicampus system specializing in career education. **Degrees:** 69 bachelor's, 261 associate awarded; master's offered. **Location:** 60 miles from Detroit. **Calendar:** Quarter, limited summer session. **Full-time faculty:** 12 total; 17% have terminal degrees, 67% women. **Part-time faculty:** 114 total; 6% have terminal degrees, 56% women. **Class size:** 58% < 20, 37% 20-39, 1% 40-49, 4% 50-99. **Special facilities:** Dental hygiene clinic.

Basis for selection. Open admission, but selective for some programs. Specific entrance requirements for health and human services programs. Waiting list for Dental Hygiene. Interview recommended.

2011-2012 Annual costs. Tuition/fees: $9,450. Books/supplies: $1,800. Personal expenses: $2,000.

Financial aid. All financial aid based on need.

Application procedures. Admission: Priority date 9/1; no deadline. $20 fee, may be waived for applicants with need. Admission notification on a rolling basis. **Financial aid:** Priority date 2/21; no closing date. FAFSA, institutional form required. Applicants notified on a rolling basis starting 4/1.

Academics. 2+2 system allows students to begin required courses in major while completing associate degree. Accelerated BBA available. **Special study options:** Accelerated study, combined bachelor's/graduate degree, cooperative education, distance learning, double major, dual enrollment of high school students, external degree, independent study, internships, liberal arts/career combination. **Credit/placement by examination:** AP, CLEP, IB, institutional tests. 48 credit hours maximum toward associate degree, 96 toward bachelor's. **Support services:** Learning center, reduced course load, remedial instruction, study skills assistance, tutoring, writing center.

Majors. Business: General, accounting, administrative services, business admin, human resources, international, management information systems, marketing, office management. **Computer sciences:** General, computer science, information systems. **Health services:** Health care admin.

Computing on campus. 229 workstations in library, computer center. Commuter students can connect to campus network. Online course registration, helpline available.

Student life. Freshman orientation: Mandatory. Preregistration for classes offered. **Activities:** Dental hygiene society.

Student services. Adult student services, career counseling, student employment services, personal counseling, placement for graduates, veterans' counselor. **Physically disabled:** Services for visually, hearing impaired.

Contact. E-mail: daniel.kenny@baker.edu
Phone: (810) 985-7000 Toll-free number: (888) 262-2442
Fax: (810) 985-7066
Daniel Kenny, Vice President of Admissions, Baker College of Port Huron, 3403 Lapeer Road, Port Huron, MI 48060-2597

Calvin College
Grand Rapids, Michigan   **CB member**
www.calvin.edu   **CB code: 1095**

- Private 4-year liberal arts college affiliated with Christian Reformed Church
- Residential campus in large city
- 3,797 degree-seeking undergraduates: 2% part-time, 53% women, 3% African American, 4% Asian American, 3% Hispanic American, 9% international
- 66 degree-seeking graduate students
- 75% of applicants admitted
- SAT or ACT (ACT writing optional), application essay required
- 76% graduate within 6 years; 30% enter graduate study

General. Founded in 1876. Regionally accredited. **Degrees:** 869 bachelor's awarded; master's offered. **ROTC:** Army. **Location:** 150 miles from Detroit and Chicago. **Calendar:** 4-1-4, limited summer session. **Full-time faculty:** 312 total; 83% have terminal degrees, 10% minority, 35% women. **Part-time faculty:** 72 total; 25% have terminal degrees, 3% minority, 57% women. **Class size:** 44% < 20, 53% 20-39, 2% 40-49, 1% 50-99. **Special facilities:** Ecosystem preserve and interpretive center, electron microscope, rhetoric center, observatory.

Freshman class profile. 3,182 applied, 2,395 admitted, 961 enrolled.

Mid 50% test scores			
SAT critical reading:	500-650	Rank in top quarter:	53%
SAT math:	530-660	Rank in top tenth:	28%
ACT composite:	23-29	End year in good standing:	92%
GPA 3.75 or higher:	44%	Return as sophomores:	87%
GPA 3.50-3.74:	19%	Out-of-state:	44%
GPA 3.0-3.49:	27%	Live on campus:	97%
GPA 2.0-2.99:	9%	International:	10%

Basis for selection. Genuine interest in Christian goals of college and 2.5 GPA required. Recommendation, personal statement important. Minimum 20 ACT or 470 SAT Verbal and 470 SAT Math recommended. GED accepted only for those age 19 years or over. SAT Subject Tests recommended. **Home schooled:** Letter of recommendation (nonparent) required. Must provide some form of transcript with grades.

High school preparation. College-preparatory program recommended. 12 units required; 17 recommended. Required and recommended units include English 3-4, mathematics 3, social studies 2-3, science 2 (laboratory 1), foreign language 2 and academic electives 3. Math must include algebra and geometry.

2011-2012 Annual costs. Tuition/fees: $25,565. Room/board: $8,760. Books/supplies: $1,010. Personal expenses: $1,280.

2011-2012 Financial aid. Need-based: 851 full-time freshmen applied for aid; 660 were judged to have need; 658 of these received aid. Average need met was 77%. Average scholarship/grant was $13,577; average loan $4,661. 60% of total undergraduate aid awarded as scholarships/grants, 40% as loans/jobs. **Non-need-based:** Awarded to 1,421 full-time undergraduates, including 369 freshmen. Scholarships awarded for academics, alumni affiliation, art, leadership, minority status, music/drama, religious affiliation, state residency.

Application procedures. Admission: Closing date 8/15 (postmark date). $35 fee, may be waived for applicants with need. Admission notification on a rolling basis beginning on or about 11/1. Must reply by May 1 or within 4 week(s) if notified thereafter. **Financial aid:** Priority date 2/15; no closing date. FAFSA required. Applicants notified on a rolling basis starting 3/15.

Academics. Special study options: Accelerated study, combined bachelor's/graduate degree, double major, dual enrollment of high school students, honors, independent study, internships, student-designed major, study abroad, teacher certification program, urban semester, Washington semester. Overseas programs with Central College, January interim exchange with other colleges, academically-based service-learning. **Credit/placement by examination:** AP, CLEP, IB, institutional tests. **Support services:** Learning center, reduced course load, remedial instruction, study skills assistance, tutoring, writing center.

Majors. Area/ethnic studies: Asian. **Biology:** General, biochemistry, biotechnology. **Business:** Accounting, business admin, communications, management information systems. **Communications:** Communications/speech/rhetoric, digital media, media studies, organizational. **Computer sciences:** Computer science. **Conservation:** Environmental science. **Education:** Art, bilingual, biology, chemistry, early childhood, earth science, elementary, English, foreign languages, French, German, history, mathematics, middle, music, physical, physics, reading, science, secondary, social science, social

studies, Spanish, special ed. **Engineering:** General, chemical, civil, electrical, mechanical. **English:** English lit, general lit, rhetoric/composition, writing. **Foreign languages:** Ancient Greek, Biblical, Chinese, classics, Dutch/Flemish, French, German, Japanese, Latin, linguistics, modern Greek, Spanish. **Health services:** Athletic training, nursing (RN), predental, premedicine, prepharmacy, prephysical therapy, preveterinary, recreational therapy, speech pathology. **History:** General. **Human services:** General, social work. **Math:** General. **Parks/recreation:** General, exercise sciences, health/fitness. **Philosophy/religion:** Philosophy, religion. **Physical sciences:** Chemistry, geology, physics. **Psychology:** General. **Social sciences:** General, economics, geography, international economic development, international relations, political science, sociology. **Theology:** Bible, sacred music. **Visual/performing arts:** General, art, art history/conservation, cinematography, dramatic, film/cinema/video, music, music history, music performance, music theory/composition, studio arts.

Most popular majors. Biology 7%, business/marketing 13%, education 13%, engineering/engineering technologies 6%, foreign language 7%, health sciences 8%, psychology 6%, social sciences 8%.

Computing on campus. 900 workstations in dormitories, library, computer center. Dormitories wired for high-speed internet access and linked to campus network. Commuter students can connect to campus network. Online course registration, online library, helpline, student web hosting, wireless network available.

Student life. Freshman orientation: Mandatory, $225 fee. Preregistration for classes offered. 2-day program on-campus held in the summer. Numerous options for a week-long wilderness orientation are also available. **Policies:** Strong emphasis on student leadership and service. Religious observance strongly expected and encouraged. First- and second-year students (under 21) not living at home required to live in residence halls. **Housing:** Guaranteed on-campus for freshmen. Single-sex dorms, apartments available. $50 deposit, deadline 5/1. Project Neighborhood houses available. **Activities:** Bands, campus ministries, choral groups, dance, drama, film society, international student organizations, literary magazine, music ensembles, Model UN, musical theater, student government, student newspaper, symphony orchestra, Amnesty International, Asia Club, Calvin College Democrats, Calvin College Conservatives, Democracy Matters, Engineers´ Without Borders, Environmental Stewardship, Global Business Brigades, International Health and Development.

Athletics. NCAA. **Intercollegiate:** Baseball M, basketball, cross-country, diving, golf, lacrosse, soccer, softball W, swimming, tennis, track and field, volleyball W. **Intramural:** Badminton, basketball, football (non-tackle), golf, racquetball, soccer, softball, swimming, table tennis, tennis, track and field, volleyball, water polo. **Team name:** Knights.

Student services. Adult student services, alcohol/substance abuse counseling, chaplain/spiritual director, career counseling, student employment services, financial aid counseling, health services, minority student services, personal counseling, placement for graduates. **Physically disabled:** Services for visually, speech, hearing impaired.

Contact. E-mail: admissions@calvin.edu
Phone: (616) 526-6106 Toll-free number: (800) 688-0122
Fax: (616) 526-6777
Dale Kuiper, Director of Admissions, Calvin College, 3201 Burton Street Southeast, Grand Rapids, MI 49546

Central Michigan University
Mount Pleasant, Michigan   **CB member**
www.cmich.edu   **CB code: 1106**

- Public 4-year university
- Residential campus in large town
- 21,232 degree-seeking undergraduates: 11% part-time, 55% women, 6% African American, 1% Asian American, 2% Hispanic American, 1% Native American, 1% international
- 6,105 degree-seeking graduate students
- 68% of applicants admitted
- SAT or ACT (ACT writing recommended) required
- 54% graduate within 6 years; 20% enter graduate study

General. Founded in 1892. Regionally accredited. 60 off-campus locations in the United States and surrounding countries. **Degrees:** 3,717 bachelor's awarded; master's, professional, doctoral offered. **ROTC:** Army, Air Force. **Location:** 70 miles from Lansing. **Calendar:** Semester, limited summer session. **Full-time faculty:** 768 total; 80% have terminal degrees, 18% minority, 42% women. **Part-time faculty:** 369 total; 28% have terminal degrees, 9% minority, 52% women. **Class size:** 26% < 20, 48% 20-39, 13% 40-49,

10% 50-99, 3% >100. **Special facilities:** Center for clinical care and education, English language institute, center for applied research and rural studies, Michigan services for children and young adults who are deaf-blind, psychological training and consultation center, language learning center, biological station, conservation genetics lab, water research center, museum of cultural and natural history, historical library, 255-acre natural woodland.

Freshman class profile. 18,509 applied, 12,670 admitted, 3,838 enrolled.

Mid 50% test scores			
SAT critical reading:	450-570	Rank in top quarter:	40%
SAT math:	450-600	Rank in top tenth:	14%
ACT composite:	20-25	End year in good standing:	86%
GPA 3.75 or higher:	20%	Return as sophomores:	76%
GPA 3.50-3.74:	19%	Out-of-state:	5%
GPA 3.0-3.49:	40%	Live on campus:	96%
GPA 2.0-2.99:	21%	Fraternities:	3%
		Sororities:	4%

Basis for selection. School achievement record, test scores, and recommendations are important. ACT recommended. Transfer students with over 30 credits are not required to take the ACT. Interview and essay are recommended of some. Auditions may be required for music majors. **Learning Disabled:** Students are prompted to register with Student Disability Services following admission.

High school preparation. College-preparatory program recommended. 21 units recommended. Recommended units include English 4, mathematics 4, social studies 2, history 2, science 4 (laboratory 1), foreign language 2, computer science 1 and visual/performing arts 2.

2011-2012 Annual costs. Tuition/fees: $10,740; $23,670 out-of-state. Room/board: $8,212. Books/supplies: $1,000. Personal expenses: $1,050.

2010-2011 Financial aid. **Need-based:** 3,591 full-time freshmen applied for aid; 2,741 were judged to have need; 2,661 of these received aid. Average need met was 83%. Average scholarship/grant was $6,409; average loan $5,620. 37% of total undergraduate aid awarded as scholarships/grants, 63% as loans/jobs. **Non-need-based:** Awarded to 2,102 full-time undergraduates, including 724 freshmen. **Additional information:** Tuition waiver for Native American students qualifying under state program criteria.

Application procedures. Admission: Priority date 10/1; deadline 7/1 (receipt date). $35 fee, may be waived for applicants with need. Admission notification on a rolling basis. Must reply by 5/1. **Financial aid:** Priority date 3/1; no closing date. FAFSA required. Applicants notified on a rolling basis starting 4/1.

Academics. Special study options: Combined bachelor's/graduate degree, distance learning, double major, dual enrollment of high school students, ESL, honors, independent study, internships, semester at sea, student-designed major, study abroad, teacher certification program, Washington semester. Leadership Institute, Pre-professional studies, Recognition of Cultural Competency, First Year Experience, NcNair Scholars Program. **Credit/ placement by examination:** AP, CLEP, IB, ACT, institutional tests. 40 credit hours maximum toward bachelor's degree. Credit by examination may not be used to repeat any course previously taken. **Support services:** Learning center, pre-admission summer program, reduced course load, remedial instruction, study skills assistance, tutoring, writing center.

Honors college/program. Applicants must have 3.75 GPA or 3.6 GPA and 25 ACT.

Majors. Architecture: Interior. **Area/ethnic studies:** European, women's. **Biology:** General, biochemistry, biomedical sciences, neuroscience. **Business:** Accounting, actuarial science, business admin, entrepreneurial studies, fashion, finance, financial planning, hospitality admin, hotel/motel admin, human resources, international, logistics, management information systems, marketing, operations, purchasing, real estate, retail management. **Communications:** Advertising, communications/speech/rhetoric, journalism, organizational, photojournalism, public relations. **Computer sciences:** Computer science, information technology. **Conservation:** General, environmental science, environmental studies, land use planning. **Education:** Art, biology, business, chemistry, early childhood, earth science, elementary, emotionally handicapped, English, family/consumer sciences, French, geography, German, health, history, mathematics, mentally handicapped, music, physical, physics, science, social studies, Spanish, speech, technology/industrial arts. **Engineering:** Electrical, manufacturing, mechanical. **English:** Creative writing, English lit. **Foreign languages:** French, German, Spanish. **Health services:** Athletic training, clinical lab science, communication disorders, dietetics, health care admin, public health ed, recreational therapy. **History:** General. **Human services:** Community org/advocacy, social work. **Liberal arts:** Arts/sciences. **Math:** General, statistics. **Parks/recreation:** General, exercise sciences, facilities management, health/fitness, sports admin, sports studies. **Philosophy/religion:** Philosophy, religion. **Physical sciences:** Astronomy, chemistry, geology, meteorology, oceanography, physics. **Psychology:** General. **Social sciences:** General, anthropology, economics, geography, GIS/ cartography, international relations, political science, sociology. **Visual/performing arts:** Acting, art, dramatic, graphic design, music, music theory/

composition, musical theater, studio arts, theater design. **Work/family studies:** Child development, family systems, institutional food production.

Most popular majors. Business/marketing 24%, communications/journalism 7%, education 16%, health sciences 6%, parks/recreation 8%, social sciences 6%.

Computing on campus. 3,000 workstations in dormitories, library, computer center, student center. Dormitories wired for high-speed internet access and linked to campus network. Commuter students can connect to campus network. Online course registration, online library, helpline, repair service, student web hosting, wireless network available.

Student life. Freshman orientation: Mandatory, $175 fee. Preregistration for classes offered. One-day sessions; morning refreshments and lunch provided. **Housing:** Guaranteed on-campus for freshmen. Coed dorms, single-sex dorms, special housing for disabled, apartments, fraternity/sorority housing, wellness housing available. $800 partly refundable deposit, deadline 5/1. Residential Colleges (Business Administration, Education & Human Services, Health Professions, Science & Technology, School of Music). **Activities:** Bands, choral groups, dance, drama, film society, international student organizations, literary magazine, music ensembles, Model UN, musical theater, opera, radio station, student government, student newspaper, symphony orchestra, TV station, Asian cultural organization, Hispanic student organization, North American Indian student organization, organization for Black unity, gay/lesbian/bisexual club, College Republicans, University Democrats, Baha'i club, Campus Crusade for Christ, Fellowship of Christian Athletes.

Athletics. NCAA. **Intercollegiate:** Baseball M, basketball, cross-country, field hockey W, football (tackle) M, gymnastics W, soccer W, softball W, track and field, volleyball W, wrestling M. **Intramural:** Basketball, football (non-tackle), golf, racquetball, soccer, softball, table tennis, tennis, volleyball, wrestling M. **Team name:** Chippewas.

Student services. Alcohol/substance abuse counseling, career counseling, services for economically disadvantaged, student employment services, financial aid counseling, health services, minority student services, personal counseling, placement for graduates, veterans' counselor. **Physically disabled:** Services for visually, speech, hearing impaired.

Contact. E-mail: cmuadmit@cmich.edu
Phone: (989) 774-3076 Toll-free number: (888) 292-5366
Fax: (989) 774-7267
Betty Wagner, Director of Admissions, Central Michigan University, Admissions Office, Mount Pleasant, MI 48859

Cleary University
Howell, Michigan
www.cleary.edu   CB code: 1123

- Private 4-year university and business college
- Commuter campus in small city
- 511 degree-seeking undergraduates: 50% part-time, 60% women
- 93 degree-seeking graduate students

General. Founded in 1883. Regionally accredited. Campuses in Howell and Ann Arbor; extension sites throughout Southeastern Michigan. **Degrees:** 82 bachelor's, 69 associate awarded; master's offered. **Location:** 55 miles from Detroit, 27 miles from Ann Arbor. **Calendar:** Quarter, limited summer session. **Full-time faculty:** 5 total; 20% have terminal degrees, 20% minority, 80% women. **Part-time faculty:** 81 total; 17% have terminal degrees, 12% minority, 43% women. **Class size:** 98% < 20, 2% 20-39. **Special facilities:** Nature trails, disc golf course.

Freshman class profile. 33 applied, 19 admitted, 13 enrolled.

Basis for selection. Open admission, but selective for some programs. Traditional students must have minimum grade point average of 2.5 on a 4.0 scale and a minimum ACT score of 19. Nontraditional students (with 0-12 college credits) must be at least twenty years old, must have minimum grade point average of 2.0 on a 4.0 scale for high school and college (if applicable). Additional admissions requirements for Executive BBA program. Regular, special, guest, dual, provisional, transfer, and international admissions available. Applicants with below 2.0 GPA may be accepted if probable success in chosen program indicated.

High school preparation. 24 units recommended. Recommended units include English 4, mathematics 2, social studies 2, history 2, science 2 and academic electives 12.

2011-2012 Annual costs. Tuition/fees: $17,760. No charge for books. Tuition Guaranty program: student pays same tuition rate based on being continuously enrolled. Discount of up to 30% for veteran/military students

(depending on eligibility, honorable discharge, and entitlement of VA benefits). Personal expenses: $881.

2010-2011 Financial aid. All financial aid based on need. 46 full-time freshmen applied for aid; 46 were judged to have need; 46 of these received aid. Average need met was 39%. Average scholarship/grant was $1,150; average loan $1,253. 36% of total undergraduate aid awarded as scholarships/grants, 64% as loans/jobs. **Additional information:** Filing electronically preferred; paper applications available. Tuition guarantee based on continuous enrollment. Essay and recommendations required for scholarship consideration.

Application procedures. Admission: Closing date 8/15. $25 fee, may be waived for applicants with need. Admission notification on a rolling basis. **Financial aid:** No deadline. FAFSA required. Applicants notified on a rolling basis starting 4/1; must reply within 2 week(s) of notification.

Academics. Compressed academic calendar reduces time to degree completion. First-time college students can complete bachelor's degree in 3.5 years and adults with previous college experience can complete degree in just over 1 year. **Special study options:** Accelerated study, combined bachelor's/graduate degree, cooperative education, distance learning, double major, dual enrollment of high school students, independent study, internships. Academic minors (BBA only). **Credit/placement by examination:** AP, CLEP, institutional tests. 36 credit hours maximum toward bachelor's degree. **Support services:** Pre-admission summer program, reduced course load, remedial instruction, study skills assistance, tutoring.

Majors. Business: Accounting, business admin, communications, e-commerce, entrepreneurial studies, finance, financial planning, human resources, management information systems, marketing, sales/distribution. **Computer sciences:** Security.

Computing on campus. PC or laptop required. 50 workstations in computer center, student center. Commuter students can connect to campus network. Online library, helpline, wireless network available.

Student life. Freshman orientation: Mandatory. Preregistration for classes offered. **Activities:** Student newspaper, DECA, Rotaract, Automation Alley, Michigan Quality Council, Livingston Economic Club, Washtenaw Economic Club.

Athletics. Intramural: Basketball, cross-country, golf, volleyball. **Team name:** Cleary Cougars.

Student services. Adult student services, career counseling, student employment services, financial aid counseling, personal counseling, placement for graduates, veterans' counselor.

Contact. E-mail: admissions@cleary.edu
Phone: (517) 338-3330 Toll-free number: (888) 525-3279
Fax: (517) 338-3336
Carrie Bonofiglio, Director of Admissions, Cleary University, 3750 Cleary Drive, Howell, MI 48843

College for Creative Studies
Detroit, Michigan   CB member
www.collegeforcreativestudies.edu   CB code: 1035

- Private 4-year visual arts college
- Commuter campus in very large city
- 1,339 degree-seeking undergraduates: 17% part-time, 48% women, 8% African American, 4% Asian American, 5% Hispanic American, 1% Native American, 7% international
- 43 degree-seeking graduate students
- 42% of applicants admitted
- SAT or ACT with writing required
- 59% graduate within 6 years

General. Founded in 1926. Regionally accredited. **Degrees:** 252 bachelor's awarded; master's offered. **Calendar:** Semester, limited summer session. **Full-time faculty:** 48 total; 60% have terminal degrees, 19% minority, 27% women. **Part-time faculty:** 205 total; 13% minority, 44% women. **Special facilities:** Foundry, computer studios, wood shop, metal shop, glassblowing studio, ceramic studio, fiber studio, large capacity spray booth, rapid prototype equipment.

Freshman class profile. 1,458 applied, 610 admitted, 235 enrolled.

Mid 50% test scores		Out-of-state:	18%
ACT composite:	19-26	International:	3%

Basis for selection. Art portfolio, test scores, and high school record important. Minimum 2.5 high school GPA for applicants. ACT/SAT scores required. Art portfolio required for all applicants. **Home schooled:** Transcript of courses and grades required. Must have a ACT or SAT test score and may be required to submit a GED test score.

High school preparation. College-preparatory program recommended. 13 units recommended. Recommended units include English 4, mathematics 3, social studies 2, science 2 and foreign language 2. College-preparatory program recommended, art courses highly recommended.

2011-2012 Annual costs. Tuition/fees: $32,785. Room/board: $8,500. Books/supplies: $2,600. Personal expenses: $1,700.

Financial aid. Non-need-based: Scholarships awarded for academics, art.

Application procedures. Admission: Closing date 8/1 (postmark date). $35 fee, may be waived for applicants with need, free for online applicants. Admission notification on a rolling basis beginning on or about 9/15. Must reply by May 1 or within 3 week(s) if notified thereafter. **Financial aid:** Priority date 7/1; no closing date. FAFSA required. Applicants notified on a rolling basis starting 3/15; must reply within 3 week(s) of notification.

Academics. Special study options: Combined bachelor's/graduate degree, double major, dual enrollment of high school students, exchange student, independent study, internships, New York semester, study abroad, teacher certification program. Advanced students may petition for 1 semester in New York studio space. **Credit/placement by examination:** AP, CLEP, IB, institutional tests. 6 credit hours maximum toward bachelor's degree. **Support services:** Learning center, pre-admission summer program, reduced course load, remedial instruction, study skills assistance, tutoring, writing center.

Majors. Business: Transportation. **Communications:** Advertising, digital media. **Communications technology:** Animation/special effects. **Visual/performing arts:** Ceramics, cinematography, commercial photography, commercial/advertising art, crafts, design, drawing, fiber arts, film/cinema/video, game design, graphic design, illustration, industrial design, interior design, metal/jewelry, multimedia, painting, photography, printmaking, sculpture, studio arts.

Computing on campus. 400 workstations in dormitories, library, computer center, student center. Dormitories wired for high-speed internet access and linked to campus network. Commuter students can connect to campus network. Online course registration, online library, helpline, student web hosting, wireless network available.

Student life. Freshman orientation: Mandatory. Preregistration for classes offered. **Housing:** Coed dorms, apartments available. $200 fully refundable deposit, deadline 5/1. Furnished, college-owned apartments and dorm rooms available. **Activities:** Student government, Black artists researching trends, industrial design club, graphic design club.

Student services. Alcohol/substance abuse counseling, career counseling, student employment services, financial aid counseling, health services, minority student services, personal counseling, placement for graduates. **Physically disabled:** Services for hearing impaired.

Contact. E-mail: admissions@collegeforcreativestudies.edu
Phone: (313) 664-7425 Toll-free number: (800) 952-2787
Fax: (313) 872-2739
Lori Watson, Director of Admissions, College for Creative Studies, 201 East Kirby, Detroit, MI 48202-4034

Concordia University
Ann Arbor, Michigan
www.cuaa.edu   **CB code: 1094**

- Private 4-year liberal arts and teachers college affiliated with Lutheran Church - Missouri Synod
- Residential campus in small city
- 496 degree-seeking undergraduates: 4% part-time, 44% women
- 202 graduate students
- 56% of applicants admitted
- SAT or ACT (ACT writing optional) required
- 39% graduate within 6 years

General. Founded in 1962. Regionally accredited. **Degrees:** 84 bachelor's, 1 associate awarded; master's offered. **ROTC:** Army, Air Force. **Location:** 40 miles from Detroit. **Calendar:** Semester, limited summer session. **Full-time faculty:** 28 total; 36% have terminal degrees, 7% minority, 29% women. **Part-time faculty:** 96 total; 20% have terminal degrees, 53% women. **Class size:** 85% < 20, 14% 20-39, less than 1% 40-49. **Special facilities:** Earhart Manor (certified Michigan Historical Landmark).

Freshman class profile. 837 applied, 467 admitted, 168 enrolled.

Mid 50% test scores			
		ACT composite:	19-24
SAT critical reading:	480-580	Return as sophomores:	58%
SAT math:	450-580	Out-of-state:	28%
SAT writing:	480-580		

Basis for selection. School achievement record most important. Test scores and rank in top half of class also important. Interview and essay recommended. Audition recommended for music majors. Portfolio recommended for art majors. **Home schooled:** Letter of recommendation (nonparent) required. 300-500 word personal statement and resume or extracurricular activities sheet required. **Learning Disabled:** Require an explanation of the disability and written recommended accommodations from an appropriate professional.

High school preparation. 20 units recommended. Recommended units include English 4, mathematics 3, social studies 2, science 2 (laboratory 2), foreign language 2 and academic electives 5. Math should include two units of algebra and one unit of geometry.

2012-2013 Annual costs. Tuition/fees (projected): $22,464. Room/board: $8,298.

2010-2011 Financial aid. Need-based: 93 full-time freshmen applied for aid; 73 were judged to have need; 73 of these received aid. Average need met was 78%. Average scholarship/grant was $13,056; average loan $4,002. 62% of total undergraduate aid awarded as scholarships/grants, 38% as loans/jobs. **Non-need-based:** Awarded to 137 full-time undergraduates, including 45 freshmen. Scholarships awarded for academics, alumni affiliation, art, athletics, leadership, music/drama, religious affiliation.

Application procedures. Admission: Closing date 8/15. $25 fee, may be waived for applicants with need, free for online applicants. Admission notification on a rolling basis. **Financial aid:** Closing date 3/1. FAFSA required. Applicants notified on a rolling basis starting 3/1; must reply within 3 week(s) of notification.

Academics. Special study options: Accelerated study, cross-registration, distance learning, double major, dual enrollment of high school students, ESL, exchange student, independent study, internships, liberal arts/career combination, student-designed major, study abroad, teacher certification program, weekend college. Accelerated degree program for mature students. **Credit/placement by examination:** AP, CLEP, IB, institutional tests. 32 credit hours maximum toward associate degree, 32 toward bachelor's. **Support services:** Learning center, pre-admission summer program, reduced course load, remedial instruction, study skills assistance, tutoring, writing center.

Majors. Biology: General. **Business:** Business admin. **Communications:** General. **Education:** Art, biology, elementary, English, mathematics, multi-level teacher, music, physical, science, secondary, social studies. **English:** English lit. **Foreign languages:** Biblical. **Health services:** Premedicine, prepharmacy, prephysical therapy. **Math:** General. **Parks/recreation:** Exercise sciences, health/fitness. **Philosophy/religion:** Religion. **Protective services:** Law enforcement admin. **Psychology:** General. **Social sciences:** General. **Theology:** Preministerial. **Visual/performing arts:** Art, music. **Work/family studies:** Family studies.

Most popular majors. Business/marketing 26%, education 33%, family/consumer sciences 13%, psychology 6%, security/protective services 7%.

Computing on campus. 60 workstations in library, computer center, student center. Dormitories wired for high-speed internet access and linked to campus network. Commuter students can connect to campus network. Online library, helpline, repair service, student web hosting, wireless network available.

Student life. Freshman orientation: Mandatory, $125 fee. Preregistration for classes offered. 3-day program includes academic, social, and orientation events. **Policies:** Students must live on campus (or with parents/guardian) until attaining junior status or 21 years of age. **Housing:** Guaranteed on-campus for all undergraduates. Single-sex dorms, apartments, wellness housing available. $100 nonrefundable deposit, deadline 8/15. **Activities:** Bands, campus ministries, choral groups, dance, drama, literary magazine, music ensembles, musical theater, student government, student newspaper, several religious and community service groups.

Athletics. NAIA. **Intercollegiate:** Baseball M, basketball, bowling, cheerleading, cross-country, football (tackle) M, golf, soccer, softball W, track and field, volleyball W. **Intramural:** Badminton, basketball, football (nontackle), soccer, softball, table tennis, volleyball. **Team name:** Cardinals.

Student services. Adult student services, alcohol/substance abuse counseling, chaplain/spiritual director, career counseling, student employment services, financial aid counseling, health services, personal counseling, placement for graduates, women's services. **Physically disabled:** Services for visually, speech, hearing impaired.

groups, dance, drama, film society, international student organizations, literary magazine, music ensembles, Model UN, musical theater, opera, radio station, student government, student newspaper, symphony orchestra, TV station, over 140 student organizations.

Athletics. NCAA. **Intercollegiate:** Baseball M, basketball, cross-country, diving, football (tackle), golf, gymnastics W, rowing (crew) W, soccer W, softball W, swimming, tennis W, track and field, volleyball W, wrestling M. **Intramural:** Badminton, basketball, bowling, cross-country, football (non-tackle), golf, racquetball, soccer, softball, swimming, table tennis, tennis, track and field, volleyball, weight lifting. **Team name:** Eagles.

Student services. Adult student services, alcohol/substance abuse counseling, chaplain/spiritual director, career counseling, student employment services, financial aid counseling, health services, minority student services, on-campus daycare, personal counseling, placement for graduates, veterans' counselor, women's services. **Physically disabled:** Services for visually, speech, hearing impaired.

Contact. E-mail: admissions@emich.edu
Phone: (734) 487-3060 Toll-free number: (800) 468-6368
Fax: (734) 487-6559
Kathryn Orscheln, Director, Admissions, Eastern Michigan University, 400 Pierce Hall, Ypsilanti, MI 48197

Ferris State University
Big Rapids, Michigan   **CB member**
www.ferris.edu   **CB code: 1222**

- Public 4-year university
- Residential campus in large town
- 12,744 degree-seeking undergraduates: 28% part-time, 50% women, 7% African American, 1% Asian American, 3% Hispanic American, 1% Native American, 1% international
- 1,181 degree-seeking graduate students
- SAT or ACT (ACT writing optional) required
- 47% graduate within 6 years

General. Founded in 1884. Regionally accredited. **Degrees:** 2,254 bachelor's, 736 associate awarded; master's, professional offered. **ROTC:** Army. **Location:** 55 miles from Grand Rapids. **Calendar:** Semester, limited summer session. **Full-time faculty:** 483 total; 49% have terminal degrees, 11% minority, 38% women. **Part-time faculty:** 292 total; 19% have terminal degrees, 4% minority, 50% women. **Class size:** 36% < 20, 54% 20-39, 7% 40-49, 3% 50-99, less than 1% >100. **Special facilities:** Observatory, wildlife museum, Jim Crow museum, art walk, greenhouse.

Freshman class profile. 8,487 applied, 6,573 admitted, 2,556 enrolled.

Mid 50% test scores			
ACT composite:	19-24	GPA 2.0-2.99:	37%
GPA 3.75 or higher:	19%	Return as sophomores:	71%
GPA 3.50-3.74:	16%	Out-of-state:	5%
GPA 3.0-3.49:	28%	Live on campus:	77%
		International:	2%

Basis for selection. Open admission, but selective for some programs. School achievement record most important. General admission requirements: 2.5 GPA (509 GED) or 17 ACT/1210 SAT. ACT and SAT scores used for admissions purposes for marginal applicants. Specific program requirements vary. Interview recommended. Portfolio recommended of visual communication majors. **Home schooled:** Statement describing home school structure and mission, transcript of courses and grades required. Course descriptions and grading scale, official ACT or SAT. **Learning Disabled:** Students with learning disabilities should submit documentation from professional psychologist or social worker to Disabilities Services Office in the Educational and Career Services Counseling Center.

High school preparation. College-preparatory program recommended. 24 units recommended. Recommended units include English 4, mathematics 4, social studies 2, history 1, science 3 (laboratory 2), foreign language 2 and academic electives 3. 2 units in fine arts and 1 unit in computer literacy recommended.

2011-2012 Annual costs. Tuition/fees: $10,440; $15,660 out-of-state. Room/board: $9,344. Books/supplies: $1,020. Personal expenses: $780.

2011-2012 Financial aid. Need-based: 1,888 full-time freshmen applied for aid; 1,591 were judged to have need; 1,578 of these received aid. Average need met was 64%. Average scholarship/grant was $4,580; average loan $3,650. 45% of total undergraduate aid awarded as scholarships/grants, 55% as loans/jobs. **Non-need-based:** Awarded to 4,268 full-time undergraduates,

including 1,461 freshmen. Scholarships awarded for academics, alumni affiliation, art, athletics, leadership, minority status, music/drama, ROTC, state residency.

Application procedures. Admission: Closing date 8/1 (postmark date). $30 fee, may be waived for applicants with need, free for online applicants. Admission notification on a rolling basis beginning on or about 7/1. **Financial aid:** Priority date 2/1; no closing date. FAFSA required. Applicants notified on a rolling basis starting 3/15; must reply within 3 week(s) of notification.

Academics. Special study options: Accelerated study, combined bachelor's/graduate degree, cooperative education, distance learning, double major, dual enrollment of high school students, exchange student, external degree, honors, independent study, internships, liberal arts/career combination, student-designed major, study abroad, teacher certification program, weekend college. **Credit/placement by examination:** AP, CLEP, SAT, ACT, institutional tests. **Support services:** Learning center, remedial instruction, study skills assistance, tutoring, writing center.

Honors college/program. Minimum high school GPA of 3.4, minimum composite ACT of 24 or SAT of 1120 (Math & Reading only), must submit essay. 100-300 freshmen admitted annually, depending on space in Honors dorms.

Majors. Architecture: Interior. **Biology:** General, biochemistry, biotechnology, environmental. **Business:** Accounting, accounting technology, accounting/finance, business admin, construction management, finance, hospitality admin, hospitality/recreation, hotel/motel admin, human resources, marketing, operations, statistics. **Communications:** Advertising, communications/speech/rhetoric, public relations. **Communications technology:** Animation/special effects, radio/TV. **Computer sciences:** Information technology, networking. **Education:** Art, biology, business, chemistry, elementary, English, family/consumer sciences, geography, history, mathematics, sales/marketing, social science, social studies. **Engineering:** Construction, systems. **English:** Rhetoric/composition, writing. **Health services:** Clinical lab science, health care admin, nuclear medical technology, nursing (RN). **History:** General. **Human services:** Social work. **Math:** General, applied. **Parks/recreation:** Facilities management. **Physical sciences:** Chemistry. **Psychology:** General. **Social sciences:** Political science, sociology. **Visual/performing arts:** Art history/conservation, commercial/advertising art, design, drawing, fashion design, illustration, industrial design, interior design, metal/jewelry, music management, painting, photography, sculpture, studio arts. **Work/family studies:** Child care management.

Most popular majors. Business/marketing 26%, engineering/engineering technologies 12%, health sciences 15%, security/protective services 14%, visual/performing arts 10%.

Computing on campus. 1,195 workstations in dormitories, library, computer center, student center. Dormitories wired for high-speed internet access and linked to campus network. Commuter students can connect to campus network. Online course registration, online library, helpline, repair service, wireless network available.

Student life. Freshman orientation: Mandatory, $80 fee. Preregistration for classes offered. Held on 16 days in June & July. **Policies:** All students sign ethics statement during orientation. **Housing:** Guaranteed on-campus for all undergraduates. Coed dorms, special housing for disabled, apartments, wellness housing available. $200 fully refundable deposit. Honors, substance free. **Activities:** Bands, campus ministries, choral groups, dance, drama, film society, international student organizations, music ensembles, musical theater, radio station, student government, student newspaper, symphony orchestra, TV station, Alpha Omega Co-ed Christian Fraternity, Circle K, Diverse Sexuality and Gender Alliance, Lyrical Praise Gospel Choir, Habitat for Humanity, Indian students association, international student organization, National Organization for Women, Red Cross Student Chapter, Young Americans for Liberty.

Athletics. NCAA. **Intercollegiate:** Basketball, cheerleading, cross-country, football (tackle) M, golf, ice hockey M, soccer W, softball W, tennis, track and field, volleyball W. **Intramural:** Basketball, football (non-tackle), ice hockey, soccer, softball, table tennis, volleyball. **Team name:** Bulldogs.

Student services. Adult student services, alcohol/substance abuse counseling, chaplain/spiritual director, career counseling, services for economically disadvantaged, student employment services, financial aid counseling, health services, legal services, minority student services, on-campus daycare, personal counseling, placement for graduates, veterans' counselor. **Physically disabled:** Services for visually, speech, hearing impaired.

Contact. E-mail: admissions@ferris.edu
Phone: (231) 591-2100 Toll-free number: (800) 433-7747
Fax: (231) 591-3944
Kristen Salomonson, Dean of Enrollment Services, Ferris State University, 1201 South State Street, CSS 201, Big Rapids, MI 49307-2714

Finlandia University
Hancock, Michigan
www.finlandia.edu   **CB code: 1743**

- Private 4-year university and liberal arts college affiliated with Evangelical Lutheran Church in America
- Commuter campus in small town
- 585 degree-seeking undergraduates
- Application essay required

General. Founded in 1896. Regionally accredited. **Degrees:** 81 bachelor's, 27 associate awarded. **ROTC:** Army, Naval, Air Force. **Location:** 100 miles from Marquette, 220 miles from Green Bay, Wisconsin. **Calendar:** Semester, limited summer session. **Full-time faculty:** 32 total. **Part-time faculty:** 36 total. **Class size:** 69% < 20, 27% 20-39, 4% 40-49. **Special facilities:** Finnish-American historical archive.

Freshman class profile. 631 applied, 416 admitted, 137 enrolled.

GPA 3.75 or higher:	4%	**GPA 2.0-2.99:**	59%
GPA 3.50-3.74:	3%	**Out-of-state:**	19%
GPA 3.0-3.49:	33%	**Live on campus:**	28%

Basis for selection. Open admission, but selective for some programs. One unit of algebra and chemistry with grade of 3.0 and 2.5 cumulative GPA required for nursing. 1 unit of algebra and biology with grade of 3.0 and 3.0 cumulative GPA required for physical therapist assistant. GPA of 2.0 required of all other programs. If GPA below 2.0, special consideration given in determining admission. Student may obtain admission into academic warning program based on placement test results. Nursing applicants should apply by March 15, physical therapy assistant applicants by April 15. SAT or ACT recommended. **Home schooled:** Transcript of courses and grades required. Placement tests required. **Learning Disabled:** Evaluation results and/or IEP that specifically states the disability is required for eligibility for accommodations, but not for admission to the university.

High school preparation. College-preparatory program recommended. Recommended units include English 4, mathematics 2, science 2 (laboratory 2).

2011-2012 Annual costs. Tuition/fees: $19,898. Room/board: $6,700. Books/supplies: $1,300. Personal expenses: $100.

Financial aid. Non-need-based: Scholarships awarded for academics, leadership, religious affiliation, state residency. **Additional information:** Work/study program; up to $2,800 per year.

Application procedures. Admission: Closing date 8/19 (postmark date). No application fee. Admission notification on a rolling basis. **Financial aid:** Priority date 3/1; no closing date. FAFSA, institutional form required. Applicants notified on a rolling basis starting 3/1; must reply within 2 week(s) of notification.

Academics. Special study options: Double major, dual enrollment of high school students, ESL, exchange student, honors, independent study, internships, liberal arts/career combination, student-designed major, study abroad, teacher certification program. **Credit/placement by examination:** AP, CLEP, IB, SAT, ACT, institutional tests. 18 credit hours maximum toward associate degree, 30 toward bachelor's. **Support services:** Learning center, remedial instruction, study skills assistance, tutoring, writing center.

Majors. Business: Accounting, business admin, international, marketing. **Education:** Elementary. **English:** English lit. **Health services:** Nursing (RN). **Liberal arts:** Arts/sciences. **Psychology:** General. **Social sciences:** General. **Visual/performing arts:** Art, ceramics, commercial/advertising art, design, drawing, fashion design, fiber arts, graphic design, illustration, interior design, painting, studio arts.

Most popular majors. Business/marketing 19%, education 8%, health sciences 38%, liberal arts 8%, public administration/social services 8%, visual/performing arts 19%.

Computing on campus. 80 workstations in dormitories, library, computer center. Dormitories wired for high-speed internet access and linked to campus network. Online library, helpline, wireless network available.

Student life. Freshman orientation: Mandatory. Preregistration for classes offered. 3-day program includes testing, workshops, and special speakers. **Housing:** Guaranteed on-campus for all undergraduates. Coed dorms available. $100 nonrefundable deposit, deadline 8/29. **Activities:** Pep band, campus ministries, choral groups, dance, drama, music ensembles, musical theater, student government, student newspaper, servant leadership program, local agency volunteer programs.

Athletics. NCAA. **Intercollegiate:** Baseball M, basketball, cross-country, golf, ice hockey, soccer, softball W, tennis W, volleyball W. **Intramural:** Bowling, football (non-tackle), softball, swimming, table tennis, volleyball. **Team name:** Lions.

Student services. Chaplain/spiritual director, career counseling, services for economically disadvantaged, student employment services, financial aid counseling, personal counseling, placement for graduates, veterans' counselor.

Contact. E-mail: admissions@finlandia.edu
Phone: (906) 487-7274 Toll-free number: (877) 202-5491
Fax: (906) 487-7383
Kitti Loukus, Associate Director of Admissions, Finlandia University, 601 Quincy Street, Hancock, MI 49930-1882

Grace Bible College
Grand Rapids, Michigan
www.gbcol.edu   **CB code: 0809**

- Private 4-year Bible and liberal arts college affiliated with Grace Gospel Fellowship
- Residential campus in small city

General. Founded in 1945. Regionally accredited. **Location:** 50 miles from Kalamazoo. **Calendar:** Semester.

Annual costs/financial aid. Tuition/fees (2011-2012): $14,850. Room/board: $6,850. Books/supplies: $548. Personal expenses: $1,018. Need-based financial aid available to full-time and part-time students.

Contact. Phone: (616) 538-2330
Enrollment Director, 1011 Aldon Street SW, PO Box 910, Grand Rapids, MI 49509

Grand Valley State University
Allendale, Michigan
www.gvsu.edu   **CB member**   **CB code: 1258**

- Public 4-year university
- Residential campus in large town
- 21,124 degree-seeking undergraduates: 12% part-time, 58% women, 5% African American, 2% Asian American, 4% Hispanic American, 1% international
- 3,100 degree-seeking graduate students
- 83% of applicants admitted
- SAT or ACT (ACT writing recommended) required
- 61% graduate within 6 years; 17% enter graduate study

General. Founded in 1960. Regionally accredited. **Degrees:** 4,060 bachelor's awarded; master's, professional offered. **Location:** 12 miles from Grand Rapids. **Calendar:** Semester, extensive summer session. **Full-time faculty:** 1,066 total; 77% have terminal degrees, 16% minority, 47% women. **Part-time faculty:** 565 total; 7% have terminal degrees, 9% minority, 54% women. **Class size:** 26% < 20, 57% 20-39, 10% 40-49, 5% 50-99, 1% >100. **Special facilities:** Cross-country fitness trail, recital hall, two Great Lakes research vessels, water resources research institute, center for presidential studies.

Freshman class profile. 16,697 applied, 13,877 admitted, 3,865 enrolled.

Mid 50% test scores			
SAT critical reading:	470-600	GPA 2.0-2.99:	8%
SAT math:	510-620	Rank in top quarter:	51%
SAT writing:	530-580	Rank in top tenth:	20%
ACT composite:	21-26	End year in good standing:	87%
GPA 3.75 or higher:	29%	Return as sophomores:	82%
GPA 3.50-3.74:	24%	Out-of-state:	7%
GPA 3.0-3.49:	39%	Live on campus:	85%
		International:	1%

Basis for selection. Admission based on secondary school grades, courses, personal and academic data, ACT/SAT results.

High school preparation. College-preparatory program recommended. Required units include English 4, mathematics 3, social studies 3, science 3 (laboratory 1) and foreign language 2.

2011-2012 Annual costs. Tuition/fees: $9,716; $14,030 out-of-state. Room/board: $7,774. Books/supplies: $1,000. Personal expenses: $2,330.

2011-2012 Financial aid. Need-based: 3,461 full-time freshmen applied for aid; 2,582 were judged to have need; 2,560 of these received aid. Average

need met was 69%. Average scholarship/grant was $6,872; average loan $3,804. 48% of total undergraduate aid awarded as scholarships/grants, 52% as loans/jobs. **Non-need-based:** Awarded to 2,391 full-time undergraduates, including 677 freshmen. Scholarships awarded for academics, alumni affiliation, art, athletics, music/drama, state residency.

Application procedures. Admission: Closing date 5/1. $30 fee, may be waived for applicants with need. Admission notification on a rolling basis. Must reply by 5/1. Application closing date December 31 for scholarships. **Financial aid:** Priority date 3/1; no closing date. FAFSA required. Applicants notified on a rolling basis starting 3/1; must reply by 5/1 or within 4 week(s) of notification.

Academics. Special study options: Combined bachelor's/graduate degree, distance learning, double major, dual enrollment of high school students, ESL, honors, independent study, internships, student-designed major, study abroad, teacher certification program, Washington semester. Undergraduates may take graduate level classes as seniors; co-op programs in education, engineering, health professions. **Credit/placement by examination:** AP, CLEP, IB, SAT, ACT, institutional tests. 32 credit hours maximum toward bachelor's degree. **Support services:** Learning center, pre-admission summer program, remedial instruction, study skills assistance, tutoring, writing center.

Honors college/program. 3.5 GPA and 28 ACT required.

Majors. Architecture: Urban/community planning. **Area/ethnic studies:** Chinese, Russian/Slavic. **Biology:** General, biochemistry, cellular/molecular. **Business:** Accounting, business admin, finance, human resources, international, management science, managerial economics, marketing, tourism promotion, tourism/travel. **Communications:** Advertising, broadcast journalism, communications/speech/rhetoric, journalism, public relations. **Computer sciences:** General, computer science, information systems, programming. **Conservation:** Management/policy. **Education:** Music, physical, science, special ed. **Engineering:** Electrical, manufacturing, mechanical. **English:** Creative writing, English lit, technical writing. **Foreign languages:** Ancient Greek, classics, French, German, Latin, Spanish. **Health services:** Athletic training, clinical lab science, medical radiologic technology/radiation therapy, nursing (RN), occupational health, predental, premedicine, prepharmacy, preveterinary. **History:** General. **Human services:** General, social work. **Liberal arts:** Arts/sciences. **Math:** General, statistics. **Parks/recreation:** General, health/fitness. **Philosophy/religion:** Philosophy. **Physical sciences:** Chemistry, geochemistry, geology, physics. **Protective services:** Law enforcement admin, security services. **Psychology:** General, social. **Social sciences:** General, anthropology, economics, geography, international relations, political science, sociology. **Visual/performing arts:** Art, art history/conservation, ceramics, commercial/advertising art, dance, dramatic, film/cinema/video, metal/jewelry, music, painting, photography, printmaking, sculpture, studio arts.

Most popular majors. Biology 8%, business/marketing 19%, communication technologies 7%, health sciences 12%, psychology 9%, social sciences 7%, visual/performing arts 6%.

Computing on campus. 1,270 workstations in dormitories, library, computer center, student center. Dormitories wired for high-speed internet access and linked to campus network. Commuter students can connect to campus network. Online course registration, helpline, repair service, student web hosting, wireless network available.

Student life. Freshman orientation: Mandatory, $75 fee. Preregistration for classes offered. One day long and held for small groups on 50 possible dates through May, June, July, and August. Students register for classes for full year. **Housing:** Guaranteed on-campus for freshmen. Coed dorms, apartments, fraternity/sorority housing available. $150 fully refundable deposit, deadline 3/1. **Activities:** Bands, campus ministries, choral groups, dance, drama, international student organizations, literary magazine, music ensembles, musical theater, radio station, student government, student newspaper, symphony orchestra, TV station, 143 registered organizations.

Athletics. NCAA. **Intercollegiate:** Baseball M, basketball, cheerleading, cross-country, diving, football (tackle) M, golf, soccer W, softball W, swimming, tennis, track and field, volleyball W. **Intramural:** Archery, badminton, basketball, bowling, cross-country, diving, fencing, field hockey, football (tackle) M, golf, gymnastics, racquetball, rowing (crew), skiing, skin diving, soccer, softball, squash, swimming, table tennis, tennis, volleyball, wrestling M. **Team name:** Lakers.

Student services. Adult student services, alcohol/substance abuse counseling, chaplain/spiritual director, career counseling, services for economically disadvantaged, student employment services, financial aid counseling, health services, minority student services, on-campus daycare, personal counseling, placement for graduates, women's services. **Physically disabled:** Services for visually, speech, hearing impaired.

Contact. E-mail: go2gvsu@gvsu.edu
Phone: (616) 331-2025 Toll-free number: (800) 748-0246
Fax: (616) 331-2000
Jodi Chycinski, Director of Admissions, Grand Valley State University, 1 Campus Drive, Allendale, MI 49401-9403

Great Lakes Christian College
Lansing, Michigan
www.glcc.edu   **CB code: 7320**

- Private 4-year Bible college affiliated with Christian Churches/Churches of Christ
- Residential campus in small city
- 220 degree-seeking undergraduates
- SAT or ACT (ACT writing optional) required

General. Founded in 1949. Accredited by ABHE. **Degrees:** 25 bachelor's, 2 associate awarded. **Location:** 90 miles from Detroit, 65 miles from Grand Rapids. **Calendar:** Semester, limited summer session. **Full-time faculty:** 11 total. **Part-time faculty:** 15 total.

Basis for selection. Recommendations of character from applicant's minister and church leaders required. Students with GPA below 2.25 or ACT below 16 or SAT below 820 (exclusive of Writing) admitted on probation. **Home schooled:** Transcript of courses and grades, letter of recommendation (nonparent) required.

2011-2012 Annual costs. Tuition/fees: $12,840. Room/board: $8,200. Books/supplies: $1,000. Personal expenses: $1,800.

Financial aid. Non-need-based: Scholarships awarded for academics, alumni affiliation, music/drama.

Application procedures. Admission: Closing date 3/1 (receipt date). $30 fee, may be waived for applicants with need. Admission notification on a rolling basis. **Financial aid:** Closing date 8/1. FAFSA, institutional form required. Applicants notified on a rolling basis starting 5/1; must reply within 3 week(s) of notification.

Academics. Special study options: Combined bachelor's/graduate degree, cooperative education, double major, dual enrollment of high school students, internships. **Credit/placement by examination:** AP, CLEP. **Support services:** Remedial instruction, study skills assistance, tutoring.

Majors. History: General. **Theology:** Bible, religious ed, sacred music.

Computing on campus. 23 workstations in library, computer center, student center. Dormitories wired for high-speed internet access and linked to campus network. Commuter students can connect to campus network. Online library, helpline, repair service, wireless network available.

Student life. Freshman orientation: Mandatory. Preregistration for classes offered. **Policies:** Regular Christian service participation required of all graduates. Religious observance required. **Housing:** Single-sex dorms, apartments, wellness housing available. $200 fully refundable deposit, deadline 6/1. **Activities:** Campus ministries, choral groups, drama, music ensembles, musical theater, student government, student newspaper.

Athletics. NCCAA. **Intercollegiate:** Basketball M, soccer M. **Intramural:** Volleyball M. **Team name:** Crusaders.

Student services. Chaplain/spiritual director, financial aid counseling, personal counseling. **Physically disabled:** Services for visually, hearing impaired.

Contact. E-mail: admissions@glcc.edu
Phone: (517) 321-0242 ext. 221 Toll-free number: (800) 937-4522
Fax: (517) 321-5902
Lloyd Scharer, Vice President of Enrollment Management, Great Lakes Christian College, 6211 West Willow Highway, Lansing, MI 48917-1231

Griggs University
Berrien Springs, Michigan
www.griggs.edu

- Private 4-year virtual liberal arts college affiliated with Seventh-day Adventists
- Small town

General. Accredited by DETC. **Location:** 45 miles from Kalamazoo, Michigan. **Calendar:** Semester.

Annual costs/financial aid. Tuition/fees (2011-2012): $10,510.

Contact. Phone: (269) 471-6570
Undergraduate Enrollment Coordinator, 8903 U.S. Hwy 31, Berrien Springs, MI 49104-1900

Hillsdale College
Hillsdale, Michigan
www.hillsdale.edu

CB member
CB code: 1295

- Private 4-year liberal arts college
- Residential campus in large town
- 1,406 degree-seeking undergraduates: 52% women
- 42% of applicants admitted
- SAT or ACT (ACT writing optional), application essay required
- 77% graduate within 6 years; 43% enter graduate study

General. Founded in 1844. Regionally accredited. Core course requirements include Rhetoric and Great Books I and II, Western and American Heritage and a course on the US Constitution. Honor Code signature required of all students each year. **Degrees:** 268 bachelor's awarded. **Location:** 120 miles from Detroit, 75 miles from Ann Arbor. **Calendar:** Semester, limited summer session. **Full-time faculty:** 118 total. **Part-time faculty:** 45 total. **Class size:** 77% < 20, 22% 20-39, less than 1% 40-49, less than 1% 50-99. **Special facilities:** Arboretum, preschool, K-12 private academy, economics library, special collections library for first editions, 685-acre lake biological station, center for constitutional studies and citizenship, outdoor shooting facility.

Freshman class profile. 2,207 applied, 925 admitted, 393 enrolled.

Mid 50% test scores			
SAT critical reading:	620-750	Rank in top quarter:	82%
SAT math:	590-680	Rank in top tenth:	54%
SAT writing:	590-730	End year in good standing:	96%
ACT composite:	27-32	Return as sophomores:	98%
GPA 3.75 or higher:	68%	Out-of-state:	67%
GPA 3.50-3.74:	20%	Live on campus:	99%
GPA 3.0-3.49:	11%	Fraternities:	31%
GPA 2.0-2.99:	1%	Sororities:	38%

Basis for selection. Minimum 3.5 GPA, class rank in top quarter preferred. Test scores, recommendations, interview, personal essay important. SAT Subject Tests recommended. Portfolio recommended for art majors. Audition required for music scholarship applicants. **Home schooled:** Transcript of courses and grades required.

High school preparation. College-preparatory program recommended. 16 units recommended. Recommended units include English 4, mathematics 4, social studies 1, history 2, science 3 (laboratory 1) and foreign language 2.

2012-2013 Annual costs. Tuition/fees (projected): $21,920. Room/board: $8,560. Books/supplies: $1,000. Personal expenses: $1,000.

2011-2012 Financial aid. **Need-based:** Average need met was 60%. Average scholarship/grant was $2,200; average loan $5,100. 57% of total undergraduate aid awarded as scholarships/grants, 43% as loans/jobs. **Non-need-based:** Scholarships awarded for academics, alumni affiliation, art, athletics, leadership, music/drama, state residency. **Additional information:** Campus employment available.

Application procedures. **Admission:** Priority date 11/15; deadline 2/15 (postmark date). $35 fee. Admission notification on a rolling basis beginning on or about 12/1. Must reply by 5/1. **Financial aid:** Priority date 2/1, closing date 3/15. Institutional form required. CSS PROFILE required for returning students only. Applicants notified on a rolling basis starting 2/1; must reply by 5/1 or within 4 week(s) of notification.

Academics. Highly qualified students may study at Oxford University, England for semester or summer. Summer business program at Regents College, London, England as well as study abroad programs in France, Germany and Spain. **Special study options:** Accelerated study, double major, dual enrollment of high school students, honors, independent study, internships, study abroad, teacher certification program, Washington semester. **Credit/placement by examination:** AP, CLEP, IB, SAT, ACT, institutional tests. **Support services:** Reduced course load, study skills assistance, tutoring, writing center.

Majors. **Area/ethnic studies:** American, European. **Biology:** General, biochemistry. **Business:** General, accounting, business admin, finance, international marketing, marketing. **Communications:** Communications/speech/rhetoric, journalism. **Computer sciences:** Computer science. **Education:** General, early childhood, elementary, multi-level teacher, physical, secondary. **English:** English lit, rhetoric/composition. **Foreign languages:** Classics, comparative lit, French, German, Spanish. **Health services:** Predental, premedicine, prenursing, prepharmacy, preveterinary. **History:** General. **Liberal arts:** Arts/sciences. **Math:** General, computational. **Philosophy/religion:** Christian, philosophy, religion. **Physical sciences:** Chemistry, physics. **Psychology:** General. **Social sciences:** Economics, political science, sociology. **Theology:** Preministerial. **Visual/performing arts:** Art, dramatic, music.

Most popular majors. Biology 8%, business/marketing 15%, education 10%, English 11%, history 14%, social sciences 15%, visual/performing arts 7%.

Computing on campus. 220 workstations in dormitories, library, computer center, student center. Dormitories wired for high-speed internet access and linked to campus network. Commuter students can connect to campus network. Online library, helpline, repair service, wireless network available.

Student life. **Freshman orientation:** Mandatory. Preregistration for classes offered. 3-day program in the fall. **Housing:** Guaranteed on-campus for all undergraduates. Single-sex dorms, apartments, fraternity/sorority housing, wellness housing available. $300 nonrefundable deposit, deadline 5/1. **Activities:** Bands, campus ministries, choral groups, dance, drama, international student organizations, literary magazine, music ensembles, musical theater, student government, student newspaper, symphony orchestra, Catholic student council, Varsity H-Club, student federation, enterprising leaders, Intervarsity Christian Fellowship, Fellowship of Christian Athletes, College Republicans, Young Life, Praxis, Charis.

Athletics. NCAA. **Intercollegiate:** Baseball M, basketball, cheerleading, cross-country, diving W, equestrian W, football (tackle) M, softball W, swimming W, tennis W, track and field, volleyball W. **Intramural:** Basketball, bowling, football (non-tackle), racquetball, soccer, softball, swimming, table tennis, tennis, track and field, volleyball. **Team name:** Chargers.

Student services. Chaplain/spiritual director, career counseling, student employment services, financial aid counseling, health services, personal counseling, placement for graduates. **Physically disabled:** Services for visually impaired.

Contact. E-mail: admissions@hillsdale.edu
Phone: (517) 607-2327 Fax: (517) 607-2223
Jeffrey Lantis, Director of Admissions, Hillsdale College, 33 East College Street, Hillsdale, MI 49242

Hope College
Holland, Michigan
www.hope.edu

CB member
CB code: 1301

- Private 4-year liberal arts college affiliated with Reformed Church in America
- Residential campus in small city
- 3,168 degree-seeking undergraduates: 2% part-time, 62% women, 2% African American, 2% Asian American, 5% Hispanic American, 2% international
- 82% of applicants admitted
- SAT or ACT (ACT writing optional), application essay required
- 79% graduate within 6 years

General. Founded in 1862. Regionally accredited. **Degrees:** 729 bachelor's awarded. **ROTC:** Army. **Location:** 30 miles from Grand Rapids, 160 miles from Chicago. **Calendar:** Semester, limited summer session. **Full-time faculty:** 220 total; 79% have terminal degrees, 15% minority, 42% women. **Part-time faculty:** 96 total; 17% have terminal degrees, 56% women. **Class size:** 54% < 20, 43% 20-39, less than 1% 40-49, 2% 50-99. **Special facilities:** Museum, Pelletron particle accelerator, biological field station, electron microscopes, laser research, cadaver lab.

Freshman class profile. 3,575 applied, 2,940 admitted, 815 enrolled.

Mid 50% test scores			
SAT critical reading:	530-670	Rank in top quarter:	46%
SAT math:	530-650	Rank in top tenth:	26%
ACT composite:	24-29	End year in good standing:	97%
GPA 3.75 or higher:	56%	Return as sophomores:	89%
GPA 3.50-3.74:	19%	Out-of-state:	34%
GPA 3.0-3.49:	22%	Live on campus:	99%
GPA 2.0-2.99:	3%	International:	2%

Basis for selection. Strength of curriculum, achievement, test scores, perceived ability to succeed important. Interviews recommended. **Home schooled:** Transcript of courses and grades, letter of recommendation (nonparent) required. Paper of at least 3 pages from final 2 years of homeschooling, list of non-textbooks read in last 2 years of homeschooling, homeschooled certification statement. **Learning Disabled:** Students should consult the director of the academic support program to ensure available resources and personnel to accommodate the disability.

High school preparation. College-preparatory program recommended. 18 units recommended. Recommended units include English 4, mathematics 3, science 2 (laboratory 2), foreign language 2 and academic electives 5.

2011-2012 Annual costs. Tuition/fees: $27,010. Room/board: $8,260. Books/supplies: $820. Personal expenses: $1,230.

2011-2012 Financial aid. Need-based: 712 full-time freshmen applied for aid; 561 were judged to have need; 560 of these received aid. Average need met was 82%. Average scholarship/grant was $18,804; average loan $3,796. 75% of total undergraduate aid awarded as scholarships/grants, 25% as loans/jobs. **Non-need-based:** Awarded to 2,061 full-time undergraduates, including 638 freshmen. Scholarships awarded for academics, art, minority status, music/drama, religious affiliation.

Application procedures. Admission: Priority date 3/1; no deadline. $50 fee, may be waived for applicants with need. Admission notification on a rolling basis beginning on or about 11/24. Must reply by May 1 or within 2 week(s) if notified thereafter. **Financial aid:** Priority date 3/1; no closing date. FAFSA, institutional form required. Applicants notified on a rolling basis starting 3/15.

Academics. Extensive undergraduate scientific research opportunities available. All fine arts divisions nationally accredited. **Special study options:** Distance learning, double major, ESL, independent study, internships, New York semester, student-designed major, study abroad, teacher certification program, urban semester, Washington semester. Internships in Chicago, New York City, Washington DC, Philadelphia. **Credit/placement by examination:** AP, CLEP, IB, institutional tests. 32 credit hours maximum toward bachelor's degree. **Support services:** Reduced course load, study skills assistance, tutoring, writing center.

Majors. Area/ethnic studies: Japanese, women's. **Biology:** General. **Business:** Accounting, business admin, managerial economics. **Communications:** Communications/speech/rhetoric, journalism. **Computer sciences:** General. **Conservation:** Environmental science. **Education:** Art, biology, chemistry, drama/dance, emotionally handicapped, English, French, German, history, learning disabled, mathematics, music, physical, physics, science, social studies, Spanish. **Engineering:** General. **English:** English lit. **Foreign languages:** Classics, French, German, Spanish. **Health services:** Athletic training, nursing (RN). **History:** General. **Human services:** Social work. **Math:** General. **Parks/recreation:** Exercise sciences. **Philosophy/religion:** Philosophy, religion. **Physical sciences:** Chemistry, geology, physics. **Psychology:** General. **Social sciences:** Economics, political science, sociology. **Visual/performing arts:** Art history/conservation, dance, dramatic, jazz, music, music performance, music theory/composition, piano/keyboard, stringed instruments, studio arts, voice/opera.

Most popular majors. Business/marketing 12%, communications/journalism 7%, education 16%, parks/recreation 6%, physical sciences 6%, psychology 9%, social sciences 6%.

Computing on campus. 350 workstations in dormitories, library, computer center, student center. Dormitories wired for high-speed internet access and linked to campus network. Commuter students can connect to campus network. Online library, helpline, repair service, student web hosting, wireless network available.

Student life. Freshman orientation: Mandatory. Preregistration for classes offered. 3-day orientation for students and parents begins Friday before school starts. **Policies:** Visitors of opposite gender not allowed after midnight on weekdays and 2 a.m. on weekends. No alcohol allowed on campus. **Housing:** Guaranteed on-campus for all undergraduates. Coed dorms, single-sex dorms, special housing for disabled, apartments, fraternity/sorority housing, wellness housing available. $300 nonrefundable deposit, deadline 5/1. Cottages (houses on or near campus). **Activities:** Bands, campus ministries, choral groups, dance, drama, international student organizations, literary magazine, music ensembles, Model UN, radio station, student government, student newspaper, symphony orchestra, TV station, Fellowship of Christian Athletes, Inter-Varsity Christian Fellowship, Fellowship of Christian Students, College Republicans and Democrats, Higher Horizons, Black student union, Hispanic students organization, Catholic student union.

Athletics. NCAA. **Intercollegiate:** Baseball M, basketball, cheerleading, cross-country, diving, football (tackle) M, golf, soccer, softball W, swimming, tennis, track and field, volleyball W. **Intramural:** Badminton W, basketball, football (non-tackle), soccer, softball, tennis, volleyball, water polo. **Team name:** Flying Dutchmen, Flying Dutch.

Student services. Adult student services, alcohol/substance abuse counseling, chaplain/spiritual director, career counseling, student employment services, financial aid counseling, health services, minority student services, personal counseling, placement for graduates, women's services. **Physically disabled:** Services for visually, speech, hearing impaired.

Contact. E-mail: admissions@hope.edu
Phone: (616) 395-7850 Toll-free number: (800) 968-7850
Fax: (616) 395-7130
William Vanderbilt, Vice President for Admissions, Hope College, 69 East 10th Street, Holland, MI 49422-9000

International Academy of Design and Technology: Detroit
Troy, Michigan
www.iadt.edu

♦ For-profit 4-year visual arts and technical college
♦ Small city

General. Accredited by ACICS. **Calendar:** Semester.

Annual costs/financial aid. Books/supplies: $1,500.

Contact. Phone: (248) 457-2700
Director of Admissions, 1850 Research Drive, Troy, MI 48083

Kalamazoo College
Kalamazoo, Michigan
www.kzoo.edu
CB member
CB code: 1365

♦ Private 4-year liberal arts college
♦ Residential campus in small city
♦ 1,374 degree-seeking undergraduates: 1% part-time, 57% women, 4% African American, 4% Asian American, 7% Hispanic American, 1% Native American, 7% international
♦ 69% of applicants admitted
♦ SAT or ACT with writing, application essay required
♦ 83% graduate within 6 years

General. Founded in 1833. Regionally accredited. Study abroad centers in Kenya, Senegal, Egypt, India, Thailand, Chile, Japan, Australia, UK, Ecuador, Spain, France, Germany, Mexico, Costa Rica, and China. **Degrees:** 299 bachelor's awarded. **ROTC:** Army. **Location:** 140 miles from Detroit, 140 miles from Chicago. **Calendar:** Trimester. **Full-time faculty:** 96 total; 93% have terminal degrees, 21% minority, 54% women. **Part-time faculty:** 17 total; 65% have terminal degrees, 12% minority, 59% women. **Class size:** 61% < 20, 36% 20-39, 3% 40-49, less than 1% 50-99. **Special facilities:** 3 theaters, rare books collection, science center, 100 acre arboretum.

Freshman class profile. 2,225 applied, 1,531 admitted, 371 enrolled.

Mid 50% test scores		GPA 2.0-2.99:	6%
SAT critical reading:	560-680	Rank in top quarter:	83%
SAT math:	550-670	Rank in top tenth:	47%
SAT writing:	530-660	Return as sophomores:	90%
ACT composite:	25-30	Out-of-state:	34%
GPA 3.75 or higher:	37%	Live on campus:	100%
GPA 3.50-3.74:	27%	International:	4%
GPA 3.0-3.49:	30%		

Basis for selection. Curriculum, grades, essay, recommendations, and special accomplishments influence decision. Interview recommended. **Home schooled:** Statement describing home school structure and mission, transcript of courses and grades, interview, letter of recommendation (nonparent) required.

High school preparation. College-preparatory program required. 18 units required. Required and recommended units include English 4, mathematics 3-4, social studies 2, history 2, science 3-4 and foreign language 3-4.

2011-2012 Annual costs. Tuition/fees: $35,820. Room/board: $8,079. Books/supplies: $825. Personal expenses: $828.

2011-2012 Financial aid. Need-based: 279 full-time freshmen applied for aid; 228 were judged to have need; 228 of these received aid. Average need met was 87%. Average scholarship/grant was $20,021; average loan $4,471. 83% of total undergraduate aid awarded as scholarships/grants, 17% as loans/jobs. **Non-need-based:** Scholarships awarded for academics, alumni affiliation, art, leadership, minority status, music/drama. **Additional information:** Paid career development internship and senior project experiences available on campus.

Application procedures. Admission: Priority date 11/20; deadline 2/1 (postmark date). $40 fee, may be waived for applicants with need. Application must be submitted online. Admission notification by 4/1. Must reply by 5/1. **Financial aid:** Priority date 2/15; no closing date. FAFSA, institutional form required. CSS PROFILE required for Early Decision applicants requesting need-based financial aid. Applicants notified on a rolling basis starting 3/21; must reply by 5/1.

Academics. Most students participate in career internships and study abroad. College subsidizes most study abroad expenses. Students complete

a senior individualized project as part of graduation requirements. **Special study options:** Combined bachelor's/graduate degree, cross-registration, double major, dual enrollment of high school students, exchange student, independent study, internships, New York semester, student-designed major, study abroad, urban semester. **Credit/placement by examination:** AP, CLEP, IB, institutional tests. 18 credit hours maximum toward bachelor's degree. **Support services:** Learning center, reduced course load, study skills assistance, tutoring, writing center.

Majors. Biology: General. **Business:** General. **Computer sciences:** General. **English:** Creative writing, English lit. **Foreign languages:** Classics, French, German, Spanish. **Health services:** Predental, premedicine, preveterinary. **History:** General. **Math:** General. **Philosophy/religion:** Philosophy, religion. **Physical sciences:** Chemistry, physics. **Psychology:** General. **Social sciences:** Anthropology, economics, political science, sociology. **Visual/performing arts:** Art, art history/conservation, dramatic, music. **Work/family studies:** Family studies.

Most popular majors. Biology 12%, English 8%, foreign language 7%, physical sciences 11%, psychology 10%, social sciences 25%, visual/performing arts 7%.

Computing on campus. 130 workstations in library, computer center, student center. Dormitories wired for high-speed internet access and linked to campus network. Commuter students can connect to campus network. Online course registration, online library, helpline, student web hosting, wireless network available.

Student life. Freshman orientation: Mandatory. Preregistration for classes offered. Held on campus the week before fall classes begin. **Housing:** Guaranteed on-campus for all undergraduates. Coed dorms, wellness housing available. **Activities:** Bands, campus ministries, choral groups, dance, drama, international student organizations, literary magazine, music ensembles, Model UN, musical theater, radio station, student government, student newspaper, symphony orchestra, TV station, African American student organization, women's equity coalition, volunteer bureau, environmental organization, film society, Habitat for Humanity, Amnesty International, coalition on racial diversity.

Athletics. NCAA. **Intercollegiate:** Baseball M, basketball, cross-country, diving, football (tackle) M, golf, soccer, softball W, swimming, tennis, volleyball W. **Intramural:** Basketball, cheerleading W, golf, gymnastics W, racquetball, rugby, skiing, soccer, softball, squash, table tennis, tennis, volleyball, water polo. **Team name:** Hornets.

Student services. Alcohol/substance abuse counseling, chaplain/spiritual director, career counseling, student employment services, financial aid counseling, health services, minority student services, personal counseling, placement for graduates, women's services. **Physically disabled:** Services for visually, speech, hearing impaired.

Contact. E-mail: admission@kzoo.edu
Phone: (269) 337-7166 Toll-free number: (800) 253-3602
Fax: (269) 337-7390
Eric Staab, Dean of Admission, Kalamazoo College, 1200 Academy Street, Kalamazoo, MI 49006

Kettering University
Flint, Michigan
www.kettering.edu

CB member
CB code: 1246

- Private 4-year university and engineering college
- Residential campus in small city
- 1,684 degree-seeking undergraduates: 2% part-time, 19% women, 4% African American, 2% Asian American, 3% Hispanic American, 3% international
- 327 degree-seeking graduate students
- 62% of applicants admitted
- SAT or ACT (ACT writing optional) required
- 58% graduate within 6 years

General. Founded in 1919. Regionally accredited. Formerly GMI Engineering and Management Institute. **Degrees:** 329 bachelor's awarded; master's offered. **Location:** 70 miles from Detroit. **Calendar:** Semester, extensive summer session. **Full-time faculty:** 122 total; 90% have terminal degrees, 21% minority, 22% women. **Part-time faculty:** 32 total; 25% have terminal degrees, 12% minority, 34% women. **Class size:** 58% < 20, 37% 20-39, 4% 40-49, 2% 50-99. **Special facilities:** Computer-integrated manufacturing laboratory, GM-PACE e-design and e-manufacturing studio, acoustics laboratory, polymer optimization center, engine test center, SAE vehicle development laboratory, mechatronics laboratory, biomedical laboratories on campus

and at nearby medical center, Ford design simulation studio, crash study lab, fuel cell research center.

Freshman class profile. 1,770 applied, 1,098 admitted, 329 enrolled.

Mid 50% test scores			
SAT critical reading:	520-650	GPA 2.0-2.99:	16%
SAT math:	600-690	Rank in top quarter:	71%
ACT composite:	24-29	Rank in top tenth:	36%
GPA 3.75 or higher:	31%	Return as sophomores:	89%
GPA 3.50-3.74:	20%	Out-of-state:	23%
GPA 3.0-3.49:	33%	Live on campus:	100%
		International:	2%

Basis for selection. Strength of preparation, performance in school, test scores, nonscholastic activities and achievements most important. Accepted students encouraged to confirm enrollment plans early so co-op employment search process can begin. SAT Subject Tests (especially math level II, chemistry, and physics), while not required, helpful when presented. Interview recommended. **Home schooled:** Laboratory science experience very important and may need to be documented.

High school preparation. College-preparatory program required. 10.5 units required; 21 recommended. Required and recommended units include English 3-4, mathematics 3.5-4, social studies 2, history 2, science 2-3 (laboratory 2-3), foreign language 2 and computer science 1. At least 1 unit of either chemistry or physics with laboratory required. Both chemistry and physics strongly recommended. Algebra I and II, geometry and trigonometry required. Drafting or CAD recommended, especially for those considering engineering.

2011-2012 Annual costs. Tuition/fees: $30,018. Room/board: $6,560. Books/supplies: $1,200. Personal expenses: $2,955.

2011-2012 Financial aid. Need-based: 303 full-time freshmen applied for aid; 268 were judged to have need; 268 of these received aid. Average need met was 70%. Average scholarship/grant was $16,186; average loan $3,405. 64% of total undergraduate aid awarded as scholarships/grants, 36% as loans/jobs. **Non-need-based:** Awarded to 789 full-time undergraduates, including 118 freshmen. Scholarships awarded for academics, leadership, minority status.

Application procedures. Admission: No deadline. $35 fee, may be waived for applicants with need, free for online applicants. Admission notification on a rolling basis beginning on or about 10/15. Must reply by May 1 or within 3 week(s) if notified thereafter. Enrollment may be postponed 1 year after admission. **Financial aid:** No deadline. FAFSA required. Applicants notified on a rolling basis starting 1/31.

Academics. Special study options: Combined bachelor's/graduate degree, cooperative education, distance learning, double major, dual enrollment of high school students, independent study, study abroad. Paid professional co-op experience in industry required of all undergraduates. Co-op typically begins in first year. Each 24-week semester divided into 11 weeks of classes and 12 weeks of co-op. **Credit/placement by examination:** AP, CLEP, IB, institutional tests. **Support services:** Learning center, study skills assistance, tutoring.

Majors. Biology: Biochemistry. **Business:** Business admin. **Computer sciences:** Computer science. **Engineering:** Applied physics, chemical, computer, electrical, industrial, mechanical. **Math:** Applied. **Physical sciences:** Chemistry, physics.

Most popular majors. Engineering/engineering technologies 91%.

Computing on campus. 450 workstations in dormitories, library, computer center, student center. Dormitories wired for high-speed internet access and linked to campus network. Commuter students can connect to campus network. Online library, helpline, wireless network available.

Student life. Freshman orientation: Mandatory, $150 fee. Preregistration for classes offered. 4-day program; begins Thursday before start of classes. **Policies:** Grade requirement to be eligible to join or maintain active membership in Greek letter organizations. **Housing:** Guaranteed on-campus for freshmen. Coed dorms, apartments, fraternity/sorority housing, wellness housing available. $100 fully refundable deposit, deadline 6/1. **Activities:** Bands, campus ministries, choral groups, dance, drama, international student organizations, literary magazine, music ensembles, Model UN, radio station, student government, student newspaper, Christians in Action, Real Service, National Society of Black Engineers, Society of Hispanic Professional Engineers, Asian American Association, Black Unity Congress, Kettering Crusade for Christ, India Student Organization.

Athletics. Intramural: Basketball, bowling, football (non-tackle), racquetball, soccer, softball, squash, tennis, volleyball, water polo. **Team name:** Bulldogs.

Student services. Alcohol/substance abuse counseling, career counseling, student employment services, financial aid counseling, health services, minority student services, personal counseling, placement for graduates, women's services. **Physically disabled:** Services for visually, speech, hearing impaired.

Contact. E-mail: admissions@kettering.edu
Phone: (810) 762-7865 Toll-free number: (800) 955-4464 ext. 7865
Fax: (810) 762-9837
Karen Full, Director of Admissions, Kettering University, 1700 University Avenue, Flint, MI 48504-6214

Kuyper College
Grand Rapids, Michigan
www.kuyper.edu   CB code: 1672

- Private 4-year liberal arts college affiliated with Christian Reformed Church
- Residential campus in large city
- 310 degree-seeking undergraduates: 11% part-time, 54% women, 4% African American, 2% Asian American, 1% Hispanic American, 1% Native American, 4% international
- 2 graduate students
- 55% of applicants admitted
- SAT or ACT (ACT writing optional), application essay required

General. Founded in 1939. Regionally accredited; also accredited by ABHE. **Degrees:** 52 bachelor's, 5 associate awarded. **ROTC:** Army. **Location:** 7 miles from downtown, 180 miles from Chicago. **Calendar:** Semester. **Full-time faculty:** 13 total; 62% have terminal degrees, 15% minority, 54% women. **Part-time faculty:** 24 total; 12% have terminal degrees, 8% minority, 25% women. **Class size:** 72% < 20, 27% 20-39, 2% 50-99.

Freshman class profile. 277 applied, 152 admitted, 81 enrolled.

Mid 50% test scores		Rank in top quarter:	19%
ACT composite:	20-25	Rank in top tenth:	8%
GPA 3.75 or higher:	19%	Out-of-state:	15%
GPA 3.50-3.74:	19%	Live on campus:	26%
GPA 3.0-3.49:	26%	International:	2%
GPA 2.0-2.99:	36%		

Basis for selection. Secondary school record, test scores important. Applicants with 2.0-2.5 GPA evaluated individually and possibly admitted on conditional acceptance. Interview required for borderline applicants. **Home schooled:** Transcript of courses and grades required.

High school preparation. Recommended units include English 4, mathematics 3, social studies 3, science 3, foreign language 1 and academic electives 3.

2011-2012 Annual costs. Tuition/fees: $17,486. Room/board: $6,720. Books/supplies: $676. Personal expenses: $848.

2011-2012 Financial aid. **Need-based:** 43 full-time freshmen applied for aid; 38 were judged to have need; 38 of these received aid. Average need met was 69%. Average scholarship/grant was $9,229; average loan $4,266. 53% of total undergraduate aid awarded as scholarships/grants, 47% as loans/jobs. **Non-need-based:** Awarded to 24 full-time undergraduates, including 5 freshmen. Scholarships awarded for academics, leadership, minority status.

Application procedures. **Admission:** Priority date 8/15; no deadline. $30 fee, may be waived for applicants with need, free for online applicants. Admission notification on a rolling basis. **Financial aid:** Priority date 3/1; no closing date. FAFSA required. Applicants notified on a rolling basis starting 3/15; must reply within 2 week(s) of notification.

Academics. **Special study options:** Combined bachelor's/graduate degree, cooperative education, double major, dual enrollment of high school students, ESL, independent study, internships, study abroad, teacher certification program. **Credit/placement by examination:** AP, CLEP, SAT, ACT, institutional tests. **Support services:** Learning center, pre-admission summer program, reduced course load, remedial instruction, study skills assistance, tutoring, writing center.

Majors. **Business:** Accounting, business admin, international. **Communications:** Communications/speech/rhetoric, journalism, media studies, public relations. **Education:** Elementary, kindergarten/preschool, secondary. **Health services:** Prenursing. **Human services:** Social work. **Parks/recreation:** Exercise sciences. **Theology:** Bible, missionary, preministerial, religious ed, sacred music, youth ministry. **Visual/performing arts:** Dramatic.

Most popular majors. Education 6%, liberal arts 19%, public administration/social services 16%, theological studies 54%.

Computing on campus. 54 workstations in dormitories, library, computer center. Dormitories linked to campus network. Commuter students can connect to campus network. Online library, helpline, student web hosting, wireless network available.

Student life. **Freshman orientation:** Available. Preregistration for classes offered. Held first week of fall semester. **Policies:** Smoke-free campus, alcohol and drug-free campus, standards of conduct and housing policies in accordance with school's moral values. **Housing:** Guaranteed on-campus for freshmen. Coed dorms, special housing for disabled, apartments, wellness housing available. $100 nonrefundable deposit. **Activities:** Choral groups, drama, international student organizations, music ensembles, student government, Bible studies, Student Activities Committee, Spiritual Life Committee, Social Work organization, Intramurals Committee, Street Team.

Athletics. NCCAA. **Intercollegiate:** Basketball. **Intramural:** Baseball, basketball, field hockey, football (non-tackle), soccer, softball, table tennis, volleyball. **Team name:** Cougars.

Student services. Alcohol/substance abuse counseling, chaplain/spiritual director, career counseling, student employment services, financial aid counseling, health services, minority student services, personal counseling, placement for graduates, veterans' counselor. **Physically disabled:** Services for visually impaired.

Contact. E-mail: admissions@kuyper.edu
Phone: (616) 988-3621 Toll-free number: (800) 511-3749
Fax: (616) 988-3608
Ryan Struck-VanderHaak, Vice President for Enrollment, Kuyper College, 3333 East Beltline Avenue Northeast, Grand Rapids, MI 49525-9749

Lake Superior State University
Sault Ste. Marie, Michigan   CB member
www.lssu.edu   CB code: 1421

- Public 4-year university and engineering college
- Residential campus in large town
- 2,610 degree-seeking undergraduates: 14% part-time, 51% women, 1% African American, 1% Asian American, 2% Hispanic American, 8% Native American, 9% international
- 2 degree-seeking graduate students
- 91% of applicants admitted
- SAT or ACT (ACT writing optional) required
- 35% graduate within 6 years

General. Founded in 1946. Regionally accredited. **Degrees:** 423 bachelor's, 141 associate awarded; master's offered. **Location:** 180 miles from Marquette. **Calendar:** Semester, limited summer session. **Full-time faculty:** 115 total; 56% have terminal degrees, 9% minority, 44% women. **Part-time faculty:** 69 total; 9% have terminal degrees, 1% minority, 55% women. **Class size:** 47% < 20, 40% 20-39, 6% 40-49, 5% 50-99, 1% >100. **Special facilities:** Aquatic research laboratory with fish hatchery and toxicology lab, planetarium, natural science museum, 200-acre biology station, robotic engineering laboratory, indoor rifle range, indoor ice arena.

Freshman class profile. 1,613 applied, 1,471 admitted, 502 enrolled.

Mid 50% test scores		Return as sophomores:	70%
ACT composite:	20-24	Out-of-state:	2%
Rank in top quarter:	35%	Live on campus:	74%
Rank in top tenth:	14%	International:	5%

Basis for selection. Cumulative GPA, high school course curriculum, and ACT or SAT most important. ACT recommended. **Learning Disabled:** Students with learning disabilities referred to coordinator for Resource Center for Students with Disabilities.

High school preparation. College-preparatory program recommended. 18 units recommended. Recommended units include English 4, mathematics 4, social studies 2, history 1, science 3 (laboratory 3), foreign language 2, computer science 1 and visual/performing arts 1. Specific academic units required vary by college program.

2011-2012 Annual costs. Tuition/fees: $9,264; $13,896 out-of-state. Residents of Ontario pay in-state tuition. Room/board: $8,319. Books/supplies: $1,000. Personal expenses: $1,600.

2010-2011 Financial aid. **Need-based:** 450 full-time freshmen applied for aid; 389 were judged to have need; 389 of these received aid. Average need met was 85%. Average scholarship/grant was $6,310; average loan $5,437. 35% of total undergraduate aid awarded as scholarships/grants, 65% as loans/jobs. **Non-need-based:** Awarded to 1,179 full-time undergraduates,

including 370 freshmen. Scholarships awarded for academics, athletics, state residency.

Application procedures. Admission: Priority date 3/1; deadline 8/15 (receipt date). $35 fee, may be waived for applicants with need. Admission notification on a rolling basis beginning on or about 9/1. **Financial aid:** Priority date 3/1; no closing date. FAFSA required. Applicants notified on a rolling basis starting 10/1; must reply by 5/1 or within 3 week(s) of notification.

Academics. Free tutoring offered to students in all academic departments. **Special study options:** Accelerated study, combined bachelor's/graduate degree, cooperative education, distance learning, double major, dual enrollment of high school students, honors, independent study, internships, student-designed major, study abroad, teacher certification program. **Credit/placement by examination:** AP, CLEP, IB, SAT, ACT, institutional tests. **Support services:** Learning center, reduced course load, remedial instruction, study skills assistance, tutoring, writing center.

Majors. Biology: General. **Business:** General, accounting, business admin, entrepreneurial studies, finance, managerial economics, marketing. **Communications:** Communications/speech/rhetoric. **Computer sciences:** General. **Conservation:** General, environmental science, fisheries, management/policy, wildlife/wilderness. **Education:** Early childhood, elementary, multi-level teacher, secondary. **Engineering:** Computer, electrical, mechanical. **English:** Creative writing, English lit. **Foreign languages:** French, Spanish. **Health services:** Clinical lab science, nursing (RN), recreational therapy. **History:** General. **Liberal arts:** Arts/sciences. **Math:** General. **Parks/recreation:** Exercise sciences, facilities management. **Physical sciences:** Chemistry, forensic chemistry, geology. **Protective services:** Corrections, criminal justice, criminalistics, fire safety technology, firefighting, forensics, homeland security, law enforcement admin, security services. **Psychology:** General. **Social sciences:** General, political science, sociology. **Visual/performing arts:** Studio arts.

Most popular majors. Business/marketing 16%, education 10%, engineering/engineering technologies 8%, health sciences 17%, security/protective services 20%.

Computing on campus. 450 workstations in library, computer center, student center. Dormitories wired for high-speed internet access and linked to campus network. Commuter students can connect to campus network. Online course registration, online library, helpline, repair service, wireless network available.

Student life. Freshman orientation: Mandatory, $125 fee. Preregistration for classes offered. One-day program held during the summer; 5 dates available. **Housing:** Guaranteed on-campus for freshmen. Coed dorms, single-sex dorms, apartments, fraternity/sorority housing, wellness housing available. $300 partly refundable deposit, deadline 6/1. Honors housing, living learning communities. **Activities:** Pep band, campus ministries, choral groups, dance, drama, international student organizations, literary magazine, radio station, student government, student newspaper, Campus Crusade for Christ, Christian fellowship, Newman Center, Native American students' council, political science club, environmental awareness club, professional organizations, Gay Straight Alliance (GSA).

Athletics. NCAA. **Intercollegiate:** Basketball, cross-country, golf, ice hockey M, softball W, tennis, track and field, volleyball W. **Intramural:** Badminton, basketball, football (non-tackle), handball, ice hockey, racquetball, soccer, softball, tennis, track and field, volleyball, water polo. **Team name:** Lakers.

Student services. Adult student services, alcohol/substance abuse counseling, chaplain/spiritual director, career counseling, services for economically disadvantaged, student employment services, financial aid counseling, health services, minority student services, on-campus daycare, personal counseling, placement for graduates, veterans' counselor. **Physically disabled:** Services for visually, speech, hearing impaired.

Contact. E-mail: admissions@lssu.edu
Phone: (906) 635-2231 Toll-free number: (888) 800-5778
Fax: (906) 635-6696
Susan Camp, Director of Admissions, Lake Superior State University, 650 West Easterday Avenue, Sault Ste. Marie, MI 49783-1699

Lawrence Technological University
Southfield, Michigan
www.ltu.edu

CB member
CB code: 1399

- Private 4-year university
- Commuter campus in small city

- 1,962 degree-seeking undergraduates: 27% part-time, 25% women, 11% African American, 3% Asian American, 3% Hispanic American, 5% international
- 1,188 degree-seeking graduate students
- 51% of applicants admitted
- SAT or ACT (ACT writing optional), application essay required
- 39% graduate within 6 years; 32% enter graduate study

General. Founded in 1932. Regionally accredited. **Degrees:** 412 bachelor's, 17 associate awarded; master's, doctoral offered. **ROTC:** Air Force. **Location:** 20 miles from Detroit. **Calendar:** Semester, extensive summer session. **Full-time faculty:** 115 total; 78% have terminal degrees, 23% minority, 30% women. **Part-time faculty:** 308 total; 35% have terminal degrees, 14% minority, 30% women. **Class size:** 78% < 20, 22% 20-39, less than 1% 40-49, less than 1% 50-99. **Special facilities:** Frank Lloyd Wright-designed residence for academic study.

Freshman class profile. 1,712 applied, 873 admitted, 269 enrolled.

Mid 50% test scores		Rank in top tenth:	21%
ACT composite:	21-28	End year in good standing:	86%
GPA 3.75 or higher:	31%	Return as sophomores:	77%
GPA 3.50-3.74:	15%	Out-of-state:	7%
GPA 3.0-3.49:	31%	Live on campus:	51%
GPA 2.0-2.99:	21%	International:	4%
Rank in top quarter:	56%		

Basis for selection. Minimum 2.50 GPA required; Architecture/Transportation Design program requires 2.75. **Home schooled:** Transcript of courses and grades, letter of recommendation (nonparent) required.

High school preparation. College-preparatory program recommended. 12 units required; 16 recommended. Required and recommended units include English 4, mathematics 3-4, social studies 3, history 2, science 2-4 (laboratory 2).

2011-2012 Annual costs. Tuition/fees: $26,278. Room/board: $8,306. Books/supplies: $1,341. Personal expenses: $2,111.

2010-2011 Financial aid. Need-based: 251 full-time freshmen applied for aid; 210 were judged to have need; 205 of these received aid. Average need met was 70%. Average scholarship/grant was $13,429; average loan $6,190. 58% of total undergraduate aid awarded as scholarships/grants, 42% as loans/jobs. **Non-need-based:** Awarded to 907 full-time undergraduates, including 198 freshmen. Scholarships awarded for academics, alumni affiliation, art, job skills, leadership, minority status, ROTC, state residency. **Additional information:** March 1 state deadline for Michigan Competitive Scholarship and Michigan Tuition Grant.

Application procedures. Admission: No deadline. $30 fee, may be waived for applicants with need. Admission notification on a rolling basis. **Financial aid:** Priority date 4/1; no closing date. FAFSA required. Applicants notified on a rolling basis starting 3/1; must reply within 2 week(s) of notification.

Academics. Special study options: Combined bachelor's/graduate degree, cooperative education, cross-registration, distance learning, double major, dual enrollment of high school students, ESL, honors, independent study, internships, liberal arts/career combination, study abroad, weekend college. **Credit/placement by examination:** AP, CLEP, IB, institutional tests. **Support services:** Learning center, pre-admission summer program, reduced course load, remedial instruction, study skills assistance, tutoring, writing center.

Majors. Architecture: Architecture, environmental design, interior, technology. **Biology:** Biochemistry, molecular. **Business:** Business admin, construction management, international. **Communications:** Communications/speech/rhetoric. **Computer sciences:** Computer science, information technology. **Engineering:** Architectural, biomedical, civil, computer, electrical, industrial, mechanical, robotics. **English:** English lit. **Liberal arts:** Humanities. **Math:** General. **Physical sciences:** Chemistry, environmental chemistry, physics. **Psychology:** General. **Visual/performing arts:** Design, digital arts, illustration, industrial design.

Most popular majors. Architecture 34%, computer/information sciences 9%, engineering/engineering technologies 41%, visual/performing arts 6%.

Computing on campus. PC or laptop required. Dormitories wired for high-speed internet access and linked to campus network. Commuter students can connect to campus network. Online course registration, online library, helpline, repair service, student web hosting, wireless network available.

Student life. Freshman orientation: Mandatory. Preregistration for classes offered. Held in late June. **Policies:** Student Code of Conduct. **Housing:** Special housing for disabled, apartments, fraternity/sorority housing, wellness housing available. $200 fully refundable deposit, deadline 6/30.

Pets allowed in dorm rooms. **Activities:** Drama, literary magazine, music ensembles, student government, student newspaper, Campus Crusade for Christ, Athenaeum, Alpha Sigma Phi, Delta Phi, Epsilon, Delta tau Sigma, Black Student Union, computer gaming club, Chi Epsilon, Chi Omega Rho, artist's guild.

Athletics. NAIA. **Intercollegiate:** Bowling M, ice hockey M, soccer M, volleyball W. **Intramural:** Badminton, basketball, bowling, cricket M, football (non-tackle), golf, racquetball, skiing, soccer, softball, table tennis, tennis, volleyball. **Team name:** Blue Devils.

Student services. Alcohol/substance abuse counseling, career counseling, services for economically disadvantaged, student employment services, financial aid counseling, minority student services, personal counseling, placement for graduates, veterans' counselor. **Physically disabled:** Services for visually, speech, hearing impaired.

Contact. E-mail: admissions@ltu.edu
Phone: (248) 204-3160 Toll-free number: (800) 225-5588
Fax: (248) 204-2228
Jane Rohrback, Director of Admissions, Lawrence Technological University, 21000 West Ten Mile Road, Southfield, MI 48075-1058

Madonna University
Livonia, Michigan
www.madonna.edu
CB code: 1437

- Private 4-year university and liberal arts college affiliated with Roman Catholic Church
- Commuter campus in small city
- 2,967 degree-seeking undergraduates: 44% part-time, 74% women, 14% African American, 1% Asian American, 3% Hispanic American, 1% Native American, 4% international
- 1,253 graduate students
- 65% of applicants admitted
- SAT or ACT (ACT writing recommended), application essay required
- 43% graduate within 6 years

General. Founded in 1947. Regionally accredited. **Degrees:** 613 bachelor's, 26 associate awarded; master's, professional offered. **ROTC:** Army. **Location:** 18 miles from Detroit, 20 miles from Ann Arbor. **Calendar:** Semester, limited summer session. **Full-time faculty:** 125 total; 98% have terminal degrees, 10% minority, 64% women. **Part-time faculty:** 295 total; 97% have terminal degrees, 10% minority, 65% women. **Class size:** 71% < 20, 26% 20-39, 1% 40-49, 2% 50-99.

Freshman class profile. 834 applied, 544 admitted, 192 enrolled.

Mid 50% test scores			
SAT critical reading:	300-640	GPA 2.0-2.99:	26%
SAT math:	330-580	Rank in top quarter:	39%
SAT writing:	390-660	Rank in top tenth:	12%
ACT composite:	20-25	End year in good standing:	93%
GPA 3.75 or higher:	15%	Return as sophomores:	82%
GPA 3.50-3.74:	20%	Out-of-state:	2%
GPA 3.0-3.49:	37%	Live on campus:	34%
		International:	3%

Basis for selection. GPA and curriculum most important. Majors in sciences, allied health and nursing, and math require specific high school subjects. ACT test results important. Some majors require letters of recommendation. ACT preferred. Interview recommended.

High school preparation. College-preparatory program recommended. 19 units required. Required and recommended units include English 3-4, mathematics 2-4, social studies 3-4, history 4, science 3-4 (laboratory 1) and foreign language 2. 1 biology, 1 chemistry, 1 algebra required for nursing applicants; biology, 1 chemistry, 2 algebra recommended for medical and radiologic technology program applicants.

2011-2012 Annual costs. Tuition/fees: $14,700. Room/board: $7,430. Books/supplies: $1,080. Personal expenses: $1,124.

2010-2011 Financial aid. Need-based: 143 full-time freshmen applied for aid; 112 were judged to have need; 110 of these received aid. Average need met was 51%. Average scholarship/grant was $7,716; average loan $2,894. 36% of total undergraduate aid awarded as scholarships/grants, 64% as loans/jobs. **Non-need-based:** Awarded to 252 full-time undergraduates, including 61 freshmen. Scholarships awarded for academics, alumni affiliation, art, athletics, leadership, minority status, music/drama, religious affiliation, state residency.

Application procedures. Admission: Priority date 9/1; no deadline. $25 fee ($55 out-of-state), may be waived for applicants with need, free for online applicants. Admission notification on a rolling basis. **Financial aid:** Priority date 3/1; no closing date. FAFSA required. Applicants notified on a rolling basis starting 3/15; must reply by 9/1 or within 2 week(s) of notification.

Academics. Special study options: Accelerated study, combined bachelor's/graduate degree, cooperative education, cross-registration, distance learning, double major, dual enrollment of high school students, ESL, independent study, internships, liberal arts/career combination, student-designed major, study abroad, teacher certification program. **Credit/placement by examination:** AP, CLEP, IB, ACT, institutional tests. 30 credit hours maximum toward associate degree, 60 toward bachelor's. **Support services:** Learning center, pre-admission summer program, reduced course load, remedial instruction, study skills assistance, tutoring, writing center.

Majors. Biology: General, biochemistry. **Business:** Accounting, business admin, hospitality admin, human resources, international, management information systems, marketing. **Communications:** Journalism. **Computer sciences:** Computer science. **Conservation:** Environmental science. **Education:** Early childhood, elementary, English, mathematics, music, physical, science, social studies. **English:** English lit, technical writing. **Foreign languages:** American Sign Language, Spanish. **Health services:** Clinical lab science, health care admin, nursing (RN), palliative care nursing, predental, premedicine, prenursing, preveterinary. **History:** General. **Human services:** Social work. **Liberal arts:** Humanities. **Math:** General. **Parks/recreation:** Sports admin. **Philosophy/religion:** Philosophy, religion. **Physical sciences:** Chemistry, physics. **Protective services:** Criminal justice, firefighting, forensics. **Psychology:** General. **Social sciences:** Political science, sociology. **Theology:** Sacred music. **Visual/performing arts:** Art history/conservation, design, graphic design, music, music performance, music theory/composition, studio arts. **Work/family studies:** General, aging, child development, food/nutrition, merchandising.

Most popular majors. Business/marketing 18%, health sciences 23%, security/protective services 12%.

Computing on campus. 199 workstations in dormitories, library, computer center. Dormitories wired for high-speed internet access and linked to campus network. Commuter students can connect to campus network. Online course registration, online library, helpline, wireless network available.

Student life. Freshman orientation: Mandatory. Preregistration for classes offered. All day orientation held in June, July, and August. Half day orientation for adult and transfer students in December, January, May, June, July, August. Saturday half day orientations for first-year, adult, and transfer students held in August and December. **Policies:** Use of alcohol or drugs prohibited on campus; all buildings smoke-free; sexual assault, harassment policies in place. **Housing:** Single-sex dorms, wellness housing available. $75 nonrefundable deposit, deadline 9/1. **Activities:** Campus ministries, choral groups, international student organizations, music ensembles, Model UN, musical theater, radio station, student government, student newspaper, TV station, Gamma Sigma Sigma, Phi-Am Cultural Student Association, Red Cross club, social work association, sociology club, Students for Liberty, Student United Way.

Athletics. NAIA. **Intercollegiate:** Baseball M, basketball, cross-country, golf, soccer, softball W, volleyball W. **Intramural:** Volleyball. **Team name:** Crusaders.

Student services. Adult student services, alcohol/substance abuse counseling, chaplain/spiritual director, career counseling, services for economically disadvantaged, student employment services, financial aid counseling, health services, minority student services, personal counseling, placement for graduates, women's services. **Physically disabled:** Services for visually, speech, hearing impaired.

Contact. E-mail: admissions@madonna.edu
Phone: (734) 432-5339 Toll-free number: (800) 852-4951
Fax: (734) 432-5424
Michael Quattro, Director of Undergraduate Admission, Madonna University, 36600 Schoolcraft Road, Livonia, MI 48150-1176

Marygrove College
Detroit, Michigan
www.marygrove.edu
CB code: 1452

- Private 4-year liberal arts college affiliated with Roman Catholic Church
- Commuter campus in very large city
- 1,010 degree-seeking undergraduates
- 45% of applicants admitted
- Application essay required

General. Founded in 1905. Regionally accredited. **Degrees:** 105 bachelor's, 4 associate awarded; master's offered. **Location:** 6 miles from downtown.

Calendar: Semester, limited summer session. **Full-time faculty:** 58 total. **Part-time faculty:** 182 total.

Freshman class profile. 953 applied, 429 admitted, 99 enrolled.

Mid 50% test scores		Out-of-state:	2%
ACT composite:	14-19	Live on campus:	34%

Basis for selection. School achievement record and test scores most important. ACT recommended. Audition required of music, theater, dance majors. Portfolio required of art majors. Interview required of older applicants and academically weak applicants.

High school preparation. College-preparatory program recommended. 17 units recommended. Recommended units include English 4, mathematics 2, social studies 2, history 2, science 3 (laboratory 1), foreign language 2 and computer science 1.

2011-2012 Annual costs. Tuition/fees: $18,020. Room/board: $7,600. Books/supplies: $1,040. Personal expenses: $2,200.

Financial aid. All financial aid based on need.

Application procedures. Admission: Priority date 12/1; deadline 3/15 (postmark date). $25 fee, may be waived for applicants with need. Admission notification on a rolling basis. Must reply by 5/1. **Financial aid:** Priority date 3/15; no closing date. FAFSA, institutional form required. Applicants notified on a rolling basis starting 5/15; must reply within 2 week(s) of notification.

Academics. Special study options: Cooperative education, cross-registration, distance learning, double major, dual enrollment of high school students, honors, independent study, internships, student-designed major, study abroad, teacher certification program. **Credit/placement by examination:** AP, CLEP, ACT, institutional tests. 16 credit hours maximum toward associate degree, 32 toward bachelor's. Credit awarded for score of 3 or higher on AP exam. Credit hours awarded determined by faculty. **Support services:** Learning center, pre-admission summer program, reduced course load, remedial instruction, study skills assistance, tutoring, writing center.

Majors. Biology: General. **Business:** General, accounting, business admin, international. **Computer sciences:** General. **Conservation:** Environmental science. **Education:** General, early childhood, special ed. **English:** English lit. **Health services:** Art therapy. **History:** General. **Human services:** Social work. **Math:** General. **Philosophy/religion:** Religion. **Physical sciences:** Chemistry. **Psychology:** General. **Social sciences:** General, political science. **Visual/performing arts:** Art, dance, music performance, music theory/composition, studio arts.

Computing on campus. 50 workstations in dormitories, library, computer center, student center. Dormitories wired for high-speed internet access and linked to campus network. Commuter students can connect to campus network. Online course registration, online library, helpline, wireless network available.

Student life. Freshman orientation: Mandatory. Preregistration for classes offered. 2-day weekday program; students spend night in dorms. **Housing:** Coed dorms available. $250 fully refundable deposit, deadline 8/1. **Activities:** Campus ministries, choral groups, dance, international student organizations, music ensembles, student government, student newspaper, debate teams (political & philosophical), Black social worker club, Ensemble gospel choir, art club, diversity club, optimist club, criminal justice, math & science club, English Honors Society, Hype Squad.

Athletics. NAIA. **Intercollegiate:** Basketball, cross-country, golf, soccer, volleyball W. **Intramural:** Badminton, basketball, bowling, football (non-tackle), golf, soccer, softball, table tennis, track and field, volleyball. **Team name:** Mustangs.

Student services. Alcohol/substance abuse counseling, chaplain/spiritual director, career counseling, services for economically disadvantaged, student employment services, financial aid counseling, health services, on-campus daycare, personal counseling, placement for graduates, women's services.

Contact. E-mail: info@marygrove.edu
Phone: (313) 927-1240 Toll-free number: (866) 313-1927
Fax: (313) 927-1345
Edwina Tansil, Associate Director Undergraduate Admissions, Marygrove College, 8425 West McNichols Road, Detroit, MI 48221

Michigan Jewish Institute
West Bloomfield, Michigan
www.mji.edu   **CB code: 1505**

- Private 4-year business and liberal arts college affiliated with Jewish faith
- Commuter campus in very large city

General. Accredited by ACICS. **Calendar:** Semester.

Annual costs/financial aid. Tuition/fees (2011-2012): $10,500. Books/supplies: $1,215. Personal expenses: $1,060.

Contact. Phone: (248) 414-6900 ext. 105
Registrar, 6890 West Maple Road, West Bloomfield, MI 48322

Michigan State University
East Lansing, Michigan   **CB member**
www.msu.edu   **CB code: 1465**

- Public 4-year university
- Residential campus in small city
- 36,276 degree-seeking undergraduates: 9% part-time, 51% women, 7% African American, 4% Asian American, 3% Hispanic American, 9% international
- 10,128 degree-seeking graduate students
- 73% of applicants admitted
- SAT or ACT with writing, application essay required
- 77% graduate within 6 years; 7% enter graduate study

General. Founded in 1855. Regionally accredited. **Degrees:** 8,067 bachelor's awarded; master's, professional, doctoral offered. **ROTC:** Army, Air Force. **Location:** 3 miles from Lansing, 80 miles from Detroit. **Calendar:** Semester, extensive summer session. **Full-time faculty:** 2,540 total. **Part-time faculty:** 400 total. **Class size:** 24% < 20, 48% 20-39, 8% 40-49, 9% 50-99, 12% >100. **Special facilities:** Planetarium, observatory, botanical garden, center for environmental toxicology, superconducting cyclotron laboratory, pesticide research center, experimental farms, 2 museums, center for performing arts, 2 golf courses, agricultural and livestock pavilion, children's garden.

Freshman class profile. 28,416 applied, 20,728 admitted, 7,984 enrolled.

Mid 50% test scores		GPA 2.0-2.99:	5%
SAT critical reading:	440-600	Rank in top quarter:	68%
SAT math:	540-670	Rank in top tenth:	28%
SAT writing:	450-600	Return as sophomores:	91%
ACT composite:	23-28	Out-of-state:	13%
GPA 3.75 or higher:	37%	Live on campus:	93%
GPA 3.50-3.74:	32%	International:	13%
GPA 3.0-3.49:	26%		

Basis for selection. Freshman admission based upon academic performance in high school, strength and quality of curriculum, recent trends in academic performance, class rank, test scores, leadership, talents, conduct and diversity of experience. SAT and SAT Subject Tests or ACT recommended. Audition required of music majors. **Home schooled:** Submit grades, even if from parent. List or provide information on curriculum and be prepared to answer questions. Test scores have stronger emphasis; transcript required.

High school preparation. College-preparatory program required. Required units include English 4, mathematics 3, social studies 3, science 3 (laboratory 2) and foreign language 2.

2011-2012 Annual costs. Tuition/fees: $12,203; $31,148 out-of-state. Room/board: $8,154. Books/supplies: $996. Personal expenses: $1,282.

2011-2012 Financial aid. Need-based: 5,500 full-time freshmen applied for aid; 3,919 were judged to have need; 3,816 of these received aid. Average need met was 64%. Average scholarship/grant was $9,204; average loan $3,470. 59% of total undergraduate aid awarded as scholarships/grants, 41% as loans/jobs. **Non-need-based:** Awarded to 6,060 full-time undergraduates, including 2,020 freshmen. Scholarships awarded for academics, alumni affiliation, art, athletics, leadership, music/drama, ROTC, state residency.

Application procedures. Admission: Priority date 11/1; no deadline. $50 fee, may be waived for applicants with need. Admission notification on a rolling basis beginning on or about 10/15. **Financial aid:** No deadline. FAFSA required. Applicants notified on a rolling basis starting 3/15; must reply within 4 week(s) of notification.

Academics. Special study options: Accelerated study, combined bachelor's/graduate degree, cooperative education, distance learning, double major, dual enrollment of high school students, ESL, exchange student, honors, independent study, internships, liberal arts/career combination, student-designed major, study abroad, teacher certification program, weekend college. **Credit/placement by examination:** AP, CLEP, IB, SAT, ACT, institutional tests. 60 credit hours maximum toward bachelor's degree. **Support services:** Learning center, pre-admission summer program, reduced course load, remedial instruction, study skills assistance, tutoring, writing center.

library, helpline, repair service, student web hosting, wireless network available.

Student life. Freshman orientation: Mandatory, $75 fee. Preregistration for classes offered. 3-day sessions held throughout the summer prior to start of classes. **Housing:** Guaranteed on-campus for all undergraduates. Coed dorms, special housing for disabled, apartments, wellness housing available. $125 partly refundable deposit. **Activities:** Bands, campus ministries, choral groups, dance, drama, film society, international student organizations, literary magazine, music ensembles, Model UN, musical theater, radio station, student government, student newspaper, symphony orchestra, TV station, Room at the Inn Student Chapter, Catholic Campus Ministry, Presque Isle Zen Community, Amnesty International, Political Review, Native American Student Association, All Nations Club, International Dancers, Superior Edge citizen-leader program, Student Leader Fellowship Program.

Athletics. NCAA. **Intercollegiate:** Basketball, cheerleading, cross-country W, diving W, football (tackle) M, golf M, ice hockey M, skiing, soccer W, swimming W, track and field W, volleyball W. **Intramural:** Badminton, basketball, football (non-tackle), football (tackle), ice hockey, racquetball, soccer, table tennis, volleyball, water polo. **Team name:** Wildcats.

Student services. Adult student services, chaplain/spiritual director, career counseling, student employment services, financial aid counseling, health services, minority student services, personal counseling, placement for graduates, veterans' counselor. **Physically disabled:** Services for visually, speech, hearing impaired.

Contact. E-mail: admiss@nmu.edu
Phone: (906) 227-2650 Toll-free number: (800) 682-9797
Fax: (906) 227-1747
Gerri Daniels, Director of Admissions, Northern Michigan University, 1401 Presque Isle Avenue, Marquette, MI 49855

Northwood University: Michigan
Midland, Michigan
www.northwood.edu   CB code: 1568

- Private 4-year university and business college
- Residential campus in large town
- 1,627 degree-seeking undergraduates: 4% part-time, 37% women, 10% African American, 2% Hispanic American, 11% international
- 347 degree-seeking graduate students
- 68% of applicants admitted
- SAT or ACT (ACT writing optional), application essay required
- 53% graduate within 6 years

General. Founded in 1959. Regionally accredited. Specialty university offering only business degrees in professional management; 3 residential campuses in Michigan, Florida, and Texas; over 20 program centers across the United States; 6 international program centers; affiliation with the Margaret Chase Smith Congressional Library in Maine. **Degrees:** 533 bachelor's, 61 associate awarded; master's offered. **Location:** 125 miles from Detroit, 25 miles from Saginaw. **Calendar:** Semester, extensive summer session. **Full-time faculty:** 50 total; 32% have terminal degrees, 14% minority, 30% women. **Part-time faculty:** 51 total; 18% have terminal degrees, 2% minority, 41% women. **Class size:** 42% < 20, 48% 20-39, 9% 40-49, less than 1% >100. **Special facilities:** Creativity center, university-operated hotel.

Freshman class profile. 1,466 applied, 998 admitted, 321 enrolled.

Mid 50% test scores			
SAT critical reading:	400-540	Rank in top quarter:	30%
SAT math:	440-530	Rank in top tenth:	10%
SAT writing:	400-500	End year in good standing:	88%
ACT composite:	20-24	Return as sophomores:	78%
GPA 3.75 or higher:	17%	Out-of-state:	13%
GPA 3.50-3.74:	17%	Live on campus:	89%
GPA 3.0-3.49:	40%	International:	3%
GPA 2.0-2.99:	25%	Fraternities:	6%
		Sororities:	5%

Basis for selection. Minimum 2.0 GPA and strong interest in business or related field important. Test scores considered. Students with lower GPA possibly admitted on probation. Interview recommended. **Home schooled:** State high school equivalency certificate required.

High school preparation. College-preparatory program recommended. 17 units recommended. Recommended units include English 4, mathematics 3, social studies 3, science 3 (laboratory 2), foreign language 1 and computer science 1.

2011-2012 Annual costs. Tuition/fees: $20,140. Room/board: $8,350. Books/supplies: $1,182.

2011-2012 Financial aid. Need-based: 277 full-time freshmen applied for aid; 245 were judged to have need; 245 of these received aid. Average need met was 64%. Average scholarship/grant was $5,588; average loan $3,284. 61% of total undergraduate aid awarded as scholarships/grants, 39% as loans/jobs. **Non-need-based:** Awarded to 753 full-time undergraduates, including 171 freshmen. Scholarships awarded for academics, athletics, leadership, minority status, ROTC.

Application procedures. Admission: No deadline. $25 fee, may be waived for applicants with need, free for online applicants. Admission notification on a rolling basis beginning on or about 9/1. **Financial aid:** No deadline. FAFSA required. Applicants notified on a rolling basis starting 3/1.

Academics. Special study options: Accelerated study, combined bachelor's/graduate degree, distance learning, double major, dual enrollment of high school students, ESL, external degree, honors, independent study, internships, study abroad, weekend college. **Credit/placement by examination:** AP, CLEP, IB, SAT, ACT, institutional tests. 12 credit hours maximum toward bachelor's degree. **Support services:** Learning center, pre-admission summer program, reduced course load, remedial instruction, study skills assistance, tutoring.

Majors. Business: Accounting, business admin, entrepreneurial studies, fashion, finance, hotel/motel admin, international, management information systems, managerial economics, marketing, vehicle parts marketing. **Communications:** Advertising. **Computer sciences:** General. **Parks/recreation:** General.

Most popular majors. Business/marketing 88%, parks/recreation 10%.

Computing on campus. 215 workstations in dormitories, library, computer center. Dormitories wired for high-speed internet access and linked to campus network. Commuter students can connect to campus network. Online course registration, online library, helpline, student web hosting, wireless network available.

Student life. Freshman orientation: Mandatory, $125 fee. Preregistration for classes offered. Several sessions held in the summer. **Housing:** Guaranteed on-campus for freshmen. Single-sex dorms, special housing for disabled, apartments available. $100 fully refundable deposit, deadline 8/1. **Activities:** Campus ministries, choral groups, dance, drama, international student organizations, student government, student newspaper, Business Professionals of America, American Marketing Association, ambassador club, Rotaract, law club, International Business Association, Minority Business Women, American Advertising Federation, The Church Reloaded, diversity club.

Athletics. NCAA. **Intercollegiate:** Baseball M, basketball, cheerleading, cross-country, football (tackle) M, golf, soccer, softball W, tennis, track and field, volleyball W. **Intramural:** Badminton, basketball, field hockey, football (non-tackle) M, soccer, tennis, volleyball. **Team name:** Timberwolves.

Student services. Adult student services, alcohol/substance abuse counseling, career counseling, student employment services, financial aid counseling, health services, minority student services, personal counseling, placement for graduates, veterans' counselor. **Physically disabled:** Services for visually, speech, hearing impaired.

Contact. E-mail: miadmit@northwood.edu
Phone: (989) 837-4273 Toll-free number: (800) 457-7878
Fax: (989) 837-4490
Greg Stiffler, Director of Admissions, Northwood University: Michigan, 4000 Whiting Drive, Midland, MI 48640

Oakland University
Rochester, Michigan   CB member
www.oakland.edu   CB code: 1497

- Public 4-year university
- Commuter campus in small city
- 15,359 degree-seeking undergraduates: 24% part-time, 60% women, 9% African American, 4% Asian American, 2% Hispanic American, 1% international
- 3,371 degree-seeking graduate students
- 68% of applicants admitted
- 40% graduate within 6 years; 23% enter graduate study

General. Founded in 1957. Regionally accredited. **Degrees:** 2,580 bachelor's awarded; master's, professional, doctoral offered. **ROTC:** Air Force. **Location:** 30 miles from Detroit. **Calendar:** Semester, limited summer session. **Full-time faculty:** 534 total; 88% have terminal degrees, 22% minority, 46% women. **Class size:** 40% < 20, 41% 20-39, 7% 40-49, 9% 50-99, 2% >100. **Special facilities:** Music pavilion, theater, engineering and science

research laboratories, robotics laboratory, product development and manufacturing center, historic house.

Freshman class profile. 10,272 applied, 6,941 admitted, 2,361 enrolled.

Mid 50% test scores		End year in good standing:	82%
ACT composite:	19-25	Return as sophomores:	73%
GPA 3.75 or higher:	20%	Out-of-state:	1%
GPA 3.50-3.74:	15%	Live on campus:	39%
GPA 3.0-3.49:	35%	International:	1%
GPA 2.0-2.99:	30%	Fraternities:	2%
Rank in top quarter:	40%	Sororities:	3%
Rank in top tenth:	15%		

Basis for selection. Admission based on 2.5 GPA in academic subjects, school and community activities, recommendations. Applicants with minimum 2.0 GPA may be admitted to summer program. Engineering, business, education, nursing, and physical therapy programs require higher GPA. TOEFL required of all non-native speakers of English. SAT or ACT recommended. Except for home schooled students, ACT scores used only for placement and scholarship purposes. Audition required of music, theater, dance majors. **Home schooled:** ACT composite score of 20 or above.

High school preparation. College-preparatory program required. Required and recommended units include English 4, mathematics 4, social studies 3, science 3 and foreign language 2.

2011-2012 Annual costs. Tuition/fees: $9,938; $23,190 out-of-state. Room/board: $7,986. Books/supplies: $1,362. Personal expenses: $2,340.

Financial aid. Non-need-based: Scholarships awarded for academics, art, athletics, leadership, music/drama, state residency.

Application procedures. Admission: No deadline. No application fee. Admission notification on a rolling basis beginning on or about 9/15. **Financial aid:** Priority date 2/15; no closing date. FAFSA required. Applicants notified on a rolling basis starting 3/15.

Academics. Special study options: Accelerated study, cooperative education, cross-registration, distance learning, double major, dual enrollment of high school students, ESL, honors, independent study, internships, student-designed major, study abroad, teacher certification program. **Credit/placement by examination:** AP, CLEP, IB, ACT, institutional tests. 60 credit hours maximum toward bachelor's degree. **Support services:** Learning center, pre-admission summer program, reduced course load, remedial instruction, study skills assistance, tutoring, writing center.

Majors. Area/ethnic studies: East Asian, Latin American, women's. **Biology:** General, biochemistry, biophysics. **Business:** General, accounting, actuarial science, finance, human resources, management information systems, managerial economics, marketing, operations, training/development. **Communications:** Communications/speech/rhetoric, journalism. **Computer sciences:** General, information technology. **Conservation:** Environmental science. **Education:** Elementary, music. **Engineering:** Applied physics, computer, electrical, industrial, mechanical. **English:** English lit, writing. **Foreign languages:** General, French, German, Japanese, linguistics, Spanish. **Health services:** Clinical lab science, cytotechnology, environmental health, histologic technology, medical radiologic technology/radiation therapy, nuclear medical technology, nursing (RN), occupational health, radiologic technology/medical imaging. **History:** General. **Human services:** General, social work. **Liberal arts:** Arts/sciences. **Math:** General, statistics. **Philosophy/religion:** Philosophy. **Physical sciences:** Chemistry, physics. **Psychology:** General. **Social sciences:** Anthropology, economics, international relations, political science, sociology, sociology/anthropology. **Visual/performing arts:** Acting, art history/conservation, dance, dramatic, drawing, film/cinema/video, music, music performance, musical theater, painting, photography, piano/keyboard, studio arts, theater design, voice/opera.

Most popular majors. Business/marketing 18%, communications/journalism 7%, computer/information sciences 18%, health sciences 23%.

Computing on campus. Dormitories linked to campus network. Commuter students can connect to campus network. Online course registration, online library, helpline, student web hosting, wireless network available.

Student life. Freshman orientation: Mandatory. Preregistration for classes offered. Held on weekdays from end of June through mid-July. 1.5-day program requires overnight stay in residence halls. Condensed 1-day orientation available. **Housing:** Guaranteed on-campus for freshmen. Coed dorms, special housing for disabled, apartments, cooperative housing, fraternity/sorority housing, wellness housing available. Residence halls easily accessible to handicapped persons. **Activities:** Bands, campus ministries, choral groups, dance, drama, film society, international student organizations, literary magazine, music ensembles, musical theater, opera, radio station, student government, student newspaper, symphony orchestra, TV station, Association of black students, Indian students association, Asian American association, College Democrats, College Republicans, Inter Varsity Christian

Fellowship, Hillel, Muslim student association, Chinese friendship association, Gay/Straight Alliance.

Athletics. NCAA. **Intercollegiate:** Basketball, cross-country, diving, golf, soccer, softball W, swimming, tennis W, track and field, volleyball W. **Intramural:** Badminton, baseball, basketball, bowling, football (non-tackle), racquetball, soccer, softball, table tennis, volleyball. **Team name:** Golden Grizzlies.

Student services. Adult student services, alcohol/substance abuse counseling, chaplain/spiritual director, career counseling, services for economically disadvantaged, student employment services, financial aid counseling, health services, minority student services, on-campus daycare, personal counseling, placement for graduates, veterans' counselor. **Physically disabled:** Services for visually, speech, hearing impaired.

Contact. E-mail: ouinfo@oakland.edu
Phone: (248) 370-3360 Toll-free number: (800) 625-8648
Fax: (248) 370-4462
Eleanor Reynolds, Assistant Vice President Student Affairs Admissions, Oakland University, 101 North Foundation Hall, Rochester, MI 48309-4401

Olivet College
Olivet, Michigan
www.olivetcollege.edu

CB member
CB code: 1595

- Private 4-year liberal arts college affiliated with United Church of Christ
- Residential campus in rural community
- 1,042 degree-seeking undergraduates: 4% part-time, 47% women
- 47 degree-seeking graduate students
- 53% of applicants admitted
- ACT (writing recommended) required

General. Founded in 1844. Regionally accredited. **Degrees:** 157 bachelor's awarded; master's offered. **ROTC:** Air Force. **Location:** 30 miles from Lansing, 120 miles from Detroit. **Calendar:** Semester, limited summer session. **Full-time faculty:** 42 total; 55% have terminal degrees, 10% minority, 48% women. **Part-time faculty:** 59 total; 15% have terminal degrees, 12% minority, 54% women. **Class size:** 54% < 20, 44% 20-39, 1% 40-49, less than 1% 50-99, less than 1% >100. **Special facilities:** Observatory/planetarium, dynamic ecology laboratory, character education resource center, women's resource center, biological preserve.

Freshman class profile. 1,412 applied, 746 admitted, 267 enrolled.

Mid 50% test scores		Out-of-state:	2%
ACT composite:	17-21	Live on campus:	75%
Rank in top quarter:	38%	Fraternities:	40%
Rank in top tenth:	25%	Sororities:	60%

Basis for selection. GED not accepted. Minimum 2.6 GPA most important. Test scores, school achievement record, recommendations for those below 2.6 GPA important. Interview recommended. Portfolio recommended for art majors. **Home schooled:** Transcript of courses and grades required.

2011-2012 Annual costs. Tuition/fees: $21,092. Room/board: $7,000. Books/supplies: $900. Personal expenses: $1,000.

2011-2012 Financial aid. All financial aid based on need. 215 full-time freshmen applied for aid; 200 were judged to have need; 200 of these received aid. Average need met was 67%. Average scholarship/grant was $9,800; average loan $2,885. 57% of total undergraduate aid awarded as scholarships/grants, 43% as loans/jobs.

Application procedures. Admission: No deadline. $25 fee, may be waived for applicants with need, free for online applicants. Admission notification on a rolling basis beginning on or about 11/1. **Financial aid:** No deadline. FAFSA required. Applicants notified on a rolling basis starting 2/1; must reply within 3 week(s) of notification.

Academics. Olivet Plan degree program includes service learning experience, portfolio assessment measuring 6 essential competencies, senior experience, professional mentoring, and 3 1/2 week intensive learning term. **Special study options:** Combined bachelor's/graduate degree, cooperative education, double major, dual enrollment of high school students, honors, independent study, internships, liberal arts/career combination, student-designed major, teacher certification program. **Credit/placement by examination:** AP, CLEP, ACT, institutional tests. 9 credit hours maximum toward bachelor's degree. **Support services:** Learning center, pre-admission summer program, remedial instruction, study skills assistance, tutoring, writing center.

Majors. Biology: General, biochemistry. **Business:** Business admin, financial planning, insurance, managerial economics, marketing. **Communications:** Journalism, media studies. **Computer sciences:** Computer science. **Conservation:** Environmental science. **Education:** General, art, biology, chemistry, emotionally handicapped, English, health, mathematics, music, science, social studies. **English:** English lit. **History:** General. **Liberal arts:** Arts/sciences. **Math:** General. **Parks/recreation:** Health/fitness, sports admin. **Physical sciences:** Chemistry. **Protective services:** Criminal justice. **Psychology:** General. **Social sciences:** General, sociology. **Visual/performing arts:** Art, music.

Most popular majors. Biology 13%, business/marketing 17%, education 31%, psychology 6%, security/protective services 16%.

Computing on campus. 140 workstations in dormitories, library, computer center, student center. Dormitories wired for high-speed internet access and linked to campus network. Commuter students can connect to campus network. Online course registration, helpline, repair service, student web hosting, wireless network available.

Student life. Freshman orientation: Mandatory, $75 fee. Preregistration for classes offered. One full-day program required, 4 different days offered in June and July, two days usually offered in August. **Policies:** Alcohol Education for student clubs, organizations and Greek societies. Must be completed by all members of any organization that would like to host a registered party on campus. **Housing:** Guaranteed on-campus for all undergraduates. Coed dorms, single-sex dorms, apartments, fraternity/sorority housing, wellness housing available. **Activities:** Bands, choral groups, drama, international student organizations, literary magazine, music ensembles, musical theater, radio station, student government, student newspaper, symphony orchestra, Phi Kappa Delta, Psi Chi, Earth Bound, Black student union, NOW, Olivet gospel choir, Helping Hands, international club, Ladies of Excellence, Middle Ground, Olivet Chapter of NAACP, United Latino Club.

Athletics. NCAA. Intercollegiate: Baseball M, basketball, cheerleading, cross-country, diving, football (tackle) M, golf, lacrosse W, soccer, softball W, swimming, tennis W, track and field, volleyball W, wrestling M. **Intramural:** Basketball, football (non-tackle) M, weight lifting M. **Team name:** Comets.

Student services. Adult student services, alcohol/substance abuse counseling, chaplain/spiritual director, career counseling, services for economically disadvantaged, student employment services, financial aid counseling, health services, minority student services, personal counseling, placement for graduates, women's services.

Contact. E-mail: admissions@olivetcollege.edu
Phone: (269) 749-7635 Toll-free number: (800) 456-7189
Fax: (269) 749-6617
Melissa Casarez, Director of Admissions, Olivet College, 320 South Main Street, Olivet, MI 49076

Robert B. Miller College
Battle Creek, Michigan
www.millercollege.edu   CB code: 4801

▶ Private 4-year liberal arts college
▶ Commuter campus in small city
▶ 367 degree-seeking undergraduates: 80% part-time, 77% women

General. Regionally accredited. **Degrees:** 61 bachelor's awarded. **Calendar:** Semester. **Full-time faculty:** 7 total; 43% have terminal degrees, 43% women. **Part-time faculty:** 3 total; 100% women.

Basis for selection. Admission requirements vary by program.

2011-2012 Annual costs. Tuition/fees: $9,990.

2011-2012 Financial aid. Need-based: 45% of total undergraduate aid awarded as scholarships/grants, 55% as loans/jobs. **Non-need-based:** Scholarships awarded for academics, leadership.

Academics. Special study options: Distance learning, honors, independent study, internships, teacher certification program, weekend college. **Credit/placement by examination:** AP, CLEP. Prior work and/or life experiences credit has no maximum limit. **Support services:** Tutoring.

Majors. Business: Business admin, entrepreneurial studies. **Education:** Adult/continuing, elementary. **Health services:** Health care admin, long term care admin, nursing (RN). **Liberal arts:** Arts/sciences.

Most popular majors. Business/marketing 40%, education 24%, health sciences 16%, liberal arts 19%.

Computing on campus. Online library, wireless network available.

Student services. Adult student services, student employment services.

Contact. Phone: (269) 660-8021 ext. 2933
Chad Danielson, Director of Admissions, Robert B. Miller College, 450 North Avenue, Battle Creek, MI 49017

Rochester College
Rochester Hills, Michigan
www.rc.edu   CB code: 1516

▶ Private 4-year liberal arts college affiliated with Church of Christ
▶ Residential campus in small city
▶ 1,044 degree-seeking undergraduates
▶ 63% of applicants admitted
▶ ACT (writing optional), application essay required

General. Founded in 1959. Regionally accredited. **Degrees:** 252 bachelor's, 16 associate awarded; master's offered. **Location:** 25 miles from Detroit. **Calendar:** Semester, limited summer session. **Full-time faculty:** 36 total. **Part-time faculty:** 115 total. **Class size:** 86% < 20, 14% 20-39, less than 1% 40-49.

Freshman class profile. 628 applied, 396 admitted, 162 enrolled.

Mid 50% test scores			
SAT critical reading:	430-540	GPA 3.50-3.74:	15%
SAT math:	480-530	GPA 3.0-3.49:	26%
ACT composite:	18-23	GPA 2.0-2.99:	38%
GPA 3.75 or higher:	18%	Rank in top quarter:	28%
		Rank in top tenth:	14%

Basis for selection. ACT score and high school GPA most important. Recommendations and interview considered. **Home schooled:** Transcript of courses and grades required.

2011-2012 Annual costs. Tuition/fees: $19,122. Room/board: $6,214. Books/supplies: $600. Personal expenses: $750.

Financial aid. Non-need-based: Scholarships awarded for academics, alumni affiliation, athletics, leadership, music/drama, state residency.

Application procedures. Admission: No deadline. $35 fee. Admission notification on a rolling basis. **Financial aid:** Priority date 8/1; no closing date. FAFSA required. Applicants notified on a rolling basis starting 6/1; must reply within 2 week(s) of notification.

Academics. Special study options: Accelerated study, combined bachelor's/graduate degree, cross-registration, double major, dual enrollment of high school students, honors, independent study, internships, liberal arts/career combination, study abroad, teacher certification program, weekend college. **Credit/placement by examination:** AP, CLEP, IB, institutional tests. 32 credit hours maximum toward associate degree, 64 toward bachelor's. Credit awarded for successful completion of selected DANTES Subject Standardized Testing Program. **Support services:** Learning center, reduced course load, remedial instruction, study skills assistance, tutoring, writing center.

Majors. Business: Accounting, business admin, management information systems, marketing. **Communications:** Communications/speech/rhetoric. **Computer sciences:** General. **Education:** General, early childhood, elementary, English, history, mathematics, middle, music, science, secondary. **English:** English lit. **History:** General. **Human services:** Social work. **Philosophy/religion:** Religion. **Psychology:** General. **Theology:** Bible, theology. **Visual/performing arts:** Music, music performance.

Most popular majors. Business/marketing 35%, communications/journalism 6%, education 22%, psychology 20%.

Computing on campus. 34 workstations in dormitories, library, computer center. Dormitories wired for high-speed internet access and linked to campus network. Online library, helpline, student web hosting, wireless network available.

Student life. Freshman orientation: Mandatory, $100 fee. Preregistration for classes offered. **Housing:** Guaranteed on-campus for freshmen. Single-sex dorms, apartments available. $180 deposit, deadline 5/1. **Activities:** Bands, choral groups, drama, music ensembles, musical theater, opera, student government, student newspaper, service and mission organizations, social clubs, departmental organizations, honor societies.

Athletics. NCCAA. Intercollegiate: Baseball M, basketball, soccer, softball W, volleyball W. **Intramural:** Basketball, football (non-tackle), softball, volleyball. **Team name:** Warriors.

Student services. Adult student services, alcohol/substance abuse counseling, chaplain/spiritual director, career counseling, student employment

services, financial aid counseling, minority student services, personal counseling, placement for graduates, veterans' counselor. **Physically disabled:** Services for visually, speech, hearing impaired.

Contact. E-mail: admissions@rc.edu
Phone: (248) 218-2031 Toll-free number: (800) 521-6010
Fax: (248) 218-2035
Scott Samuels, Admissions Director, Rochester College, 800 West Avon Road, Rochester Hills, MI 48307

Sacred Heart Major Seminary
Detroit, Michigan
www.shms.edu   **CB code: 1686**

- Private 4-year seminary college affiliated with Roman Catholic Church
- Commuter campus in very large city
- 93 degree-seeking undergraduates: 41% part-time, 23% women, 4% African American, 5% Hispanic American, 1% Native American, 3% international
- 188 degree-seeking graduate students
- 100% of applicants admitted
- SAT or ACT (ACT writing optional), application essay, interview required

General. Founded in 1919. Regionally accredited. **Degrees:** 23 bachelor's, 4 associate awarded; master's offered. **Calendar:** Semester, limited summer session. **Full-time faculty:** 29 total; 79% have terminal degrees, 10% minority, 17% women. **Part-time faculty:** 46 total; 22% have terminal degrees, 2% minority, 46% women. **Class size:** 70% < 20, 30% 20-39.

Freshman class profile. 4 applied, 4 admitted, 3 enrolled.

Mid 50% test scores			
ACT composite:	21-26	GPA 3.0-3.49:	33%
GPA 3.75 or higher:	34%	Out-of-state:	67%
GPA 3.50-3.74:	33%	Live on campus:	100%

Basis for selection. Recommendations of parish pastor, high school principal, and college counselor vital. School, community, and church-related activities viewed as important formative experiences. Religious commitment very important. Interview required for priesthood candidates. **Home schooled:** Transcript of courses and grades, interview, letter of recommendation (nonparent) required. **Learning Disabled:** Once admitted, students should contact the Office of the Dean of Studies for accommodations.

High school preparation. College-preparatory program recommended. 13 units required. Required and recommended units include English 4, mathematics 3, social studies 3, science 1 (laboratory 1) and foreign language 2.

2011-2012 Annual costs. Tuition/fees: $16,027. Room/board: $8,681. Books/supplies: $1,452. Personal expenses: $36.

2010-2011 Financial aid. **Need-based:** 1 full-time freshmen applied for aid; 1 were judged to have need; 1 of these received aid. Average need met was 84%. Average scholarship/grant was $23,900; average loan $3,500. 85% of total undergraduate aid awarded as scholarships/grants, 15% as loans/jobs. **Non-need-based:** Scholarships awarded for academics, religious affiliation.

Application procedures. **Admission:** Closing date 8/15 (postmark date). $30 fee. Application must be submitted online. Admission notification by 8/22. **Financial aid:** No deadline. FAFSA, institutional form required. Applicants notified on a rolling basis; must reply within 2 week(s) of notification.

Academics. 30 to 40% of undergraduate course work taken at other consortium colleges. **Special study options:** Double major, dual enrollment of high school students, ESL, independent study. **Credit/placement by examination:** AP, CLEP, institutional tests. 6 credit hours maximum toward associate degree, 12 toward bachelor's. Must accumulate 15 hours at SHMS before credit is recorded. **Support services:** Learning center, reduced course load, study skills assistance, tutoring.

Majors. **Liberal arts:** Arts/sciences. **Philosophy/religion:** Philosophy.

Most popular majors. Liberal arts 48%, philosophy/religious studies 39%, theological studies 13%.

Computing on campus. 12 workstations in library, computer center. Online library available.

Student life. **Freshman orientation:** Mandatory. Preregistration for classes offered. 3 days for seminarians, 1 day for commuters at beginning of fall term. **Policies:** On-campus housing available and guaranteed to seminarians only. Religious observance required. **Housing:** On-campus housing available and guaranteed to seminarians only. **Activities:** Campus ministries, choral groups, music ensembles, student government, student newspaper.

Student services. Chaplain/spiritual director, financial aid counseling.

Contact. E-mail: IFM@shms.edu
Phone: (313) 883-8520 Fax: (313) 883-8530
Tamra Fromm, Director of Admissions and Enrollment Management, Sacred Heart Major Seminary, 2701 Chicago Boulevard, Detroit, MI 48206-1799

Saginaw Valley State University
University Center, Michigan
www.svsu.edu   **CB code: 1766**

- Public 4-year university
- Commuter campus in small city
- 8,862 degree-seeking undergraduates: 14% part-time, 57% women, 10% African American, 1% Asian American, 3% Hispanic American, 3% international
- 1,673 degree-seeking graduate students
- 80% of applicants admitted
- ACT (writing optional) required
- 38% graduate within 6 years

General. Founded in 1963. Regionally accredited. **Degrees:** 1,218 bachelor's awarded; master's offered. **Location:** 10 miles from Bay City and Saginaw. **Calendar:** Semester, limited summer session. **Full-time faculty:** 297 total; 73% have terminal degrees. **Part-time faculty:** 300 total. **Class size:** 30% < 20, 62% 20-39, 3% 40-49, 4% 50-99. **Special facilities:** Fine arts center, sculpture museum, observatory.

Freshman class profile. 6,811 applied, 5,442 admitted, 1,776 enrolled.

Mid 50% test scores			
ACT composite:	18-24	Rank in top quarter:	39%
GPA 3.75 or higher:	21%	Rank in top tenth:	18%
GPA 3.50-3.74:	14%	Return as sophomores:	70%
GPA 3.0-3.49:	29%	Out-of-state:	2%
GPA 2.0-2.99:	36%	Live on campus:	69%
		International:	3%

Basis for selection. Minimum high school GPA of 2.5 preferred. **Home schooled:** Interview required.

High school preparation. Required and recommended units include English 4, mathematics 3-4, social studies 3-4, science 2-4 and foreign language 2. One unit of communications recommended.

2011-2012 Annual costs. Tuition/fees: $8,085; $18,348 out-of-state. Room/board: $7,770. Books/supplies: $1,000. Personal expenses: $1,026.

Financial aid. **Non-need-based:** Scholarships awarded for academics, art, athletics, leadership, minority status, music/drama.

Application procedures. **Admission:** No deadline. $25 fee, may be waived for applicants with need. Admission notification on a rolling basis. **Financial aid:** Priority date 2/14; no closing date. FAFSA required. Applicants notified on a rolling basis starting 3/20; must reply within 10 week(s) of notification.

Academics. **Special study options:** Accelerated study, cooperative education, distance learning, double major, dual enrollment of high school students, ESL, honors, independent study, internships, student-designed major, study abroad, teacher certification program. **Credit/placement by examination:** AP, CLEP, IB, ACT, institutional tests. 62 credit hours maximum toward bachelor's degree. **Support services:** Learning center, reduced course load, remedial instruction, study skills assistance, tutoring, writing center.

Majors. **Biology:** General, biochemistry. **Business:** General, accounting, business admin, finance, international, managerial economics, marketing, operations. **Communications:** Communications/speech/rhetoric. **Computer sciences:** General, systems analysis. **Education:** Elementary, physical, special ed. **Engineering:** Electrical, mechanical. **English:** English lit. **Foreign languages:** French, Spanish. **Health services:** Athletic training, clinical lab science, nursing (RN). **History:** General. **Human services:** General, social work. **Math:** General, applied. **Parks/recreation:** Exercise sciences. **Physical sciences:** Chemical physics, chemistry, optics, physics. **Protective services:** Criminal justice. **Psychology:** General. **Social sciences:** Economics, political science, sociology. **Visual/performing arts:** Art, dramatic, graphic design, music, studio arts.

Most popular majors. Business/marketing 18%, education 17%, health sciences 14%, public administration/social services 7%.

Computing on campus. 1,100 workstations in library, computer center, student center. Dormitories linked to campus network. Commuter students can connect to campus network. Online course registration, online library, helpline, student web hosting, wireless network available.

Student life. Freshman orientation: Mandatory, $55 fee. Preregistration for classes offered. Day-long sessions before each semester include university placement testing, advising, and registration. **Housing:** Coed dorms, special housing for disabled, apartments, wellness housing available. $200 partly refundable deposit. **Activities:** Bands, campus ministries, choral groups, dance, drama, film society, international student organizations, literary magazine, music ensembles, musical theater, student government, student newspaper, over 110 student clubs and organizations.

Athletics. NCAA. **Intercollegiate:** Baseball M, basketball, bowling M, cheerleading, cross-country, football (tackle) M, golf M, soccer, softball W, tennis W, track and field, volleyball W. **Intramural:** Badminton, basketball, football (non-tackle), golf, lacrosse, racquetball, soccer, softball, squash, table tennis, tennis, volleyball. **Team name:** Cardinals.

Student services. Adult student services, alcohol/substance abuse counseling, career counseling, services for economically disadvantaged, student employment services, financial aid counseling, health services, legal services, minority student services, personal counseling, placement for graduates, veterans' counselor, women's services. **Physically disabled:** Services for visually, hearing impaired.

Contact. E-mail: admissions@svsu.edu
Phone: (989) 964-4200 Toll-free number: (800) 968-9500
Fax: (989) 790-0180
Jennifer Pahl, Director of Admissions, Saginaw Valley State University, 7400 Bay Road, University Center, MI 48710

Siena Heights University
Adrian, Michigan
www.sienaheights.edu

CB member
CB code: 1719

- Private 4-year university and liberal arts college affiliated with Roman Catholic Church
- Residential campus in large town
- 2,262 degree-seeking undergraduates: 46% part-time, 58% women, 12% African American, 2% Asian American, 5% Hispanic American, 1% international
- 308 degree-seeking graduate students
- 55% of applicants admitted
- SAT or ACT (ACT writing optional) required
- 42% graduate within 6 years; 53% enter graduate study

General. Founded in 1919. Regionally accredited. Degree completion programs offered in Ann Arbor, Battle Creek, Benton Harbor, Jackson, Lansing, Monroe, Port Huron and Southfield. Completely online programs are also available. **Degrees:** 931 bachelor's, 13 associate awarded; master's offered. **Location:** 30 miles from Toledo, Ohio; 60 miles from Detroit. **Calendar:** Semester, limited summer session. **Full-time faculty:** 66 total. **Part-time faculty:** 152 total.

Freshman class profile. 1,728 applied, 959 admitted, 302 enrolled.

Mid 50% test scores		GPA 3.0-3.49:	33%
SAT critical reading:	420-540	GPA 2.0-2.99:	39%
SAT math:	490-530	End year in good standing:	75%
ACT composite:	18-23	Return as sophomores:	66%
GPA 3.75 or higher:	15%	Out-of-state:	11%
GPA 3.50-3.74:	13%	Live on campus:	70%

Basis for selection. Admission for a first time freshmen is determined by high school grades and standardized test scores. Admission for a student transferring from another university is determined by post high school grades. **Home schooled:** Transcript of courses and grades required. Must complete GED for state or federal assistance.

High school preparation. College-preparatory program recommended. Recommended units include English 4, mathematics 3, social studies 3, history 3, science 3, foreign language 2, computer science 1 and visual/performing arts 1.

2011-2012 Annual costs. Tuition/fees: $20,554. Room/board: $7,890. Books/supplies: $1,000. Personal expenses: $788.

Financial aid. Non-need-based: Scholarships awarded for academics, alumni affiliation, art, athletics, music/drama, religious affiliation.

Application procedures. Admission: No deadline. $25 fee, may be waived for applicants with need. Application must be submitted online. Admission notification on a rolling basis. **Financial aid:** Priority date 3/15, closing date 8/15. FAFSA, institutional form, CSS PROFILE required. Applicants notified on a rolling basis starting 2/15.

Academics. Special study options: Combined bachelor's/graduate degree, cooperative education, distance learning, double major, dual enrollment of high school students, ESL, exchange student, external degree, internships, liberal arts/career combination, student-designed major, study abroad, teacher certification program, weekend college. **Credit/placement by examination:** AP, CLEP, ACT, institutional tests. 18 credit hours maximum toward associate degree, 36 toward bachelor's. **Support services:** Learning center, preadmission summer program, reduced course load, remedial instruction, study skills assistance, tutoring, writing center.

Majors. Area/ethnic studies: American. **Biology:** General. **Business:** General, accounting, hospitality/recreation. **Communications:** Communications/speech/rhetoric. **Computer sciences:** General. **Education:** Business, elementary, secondary. **English:** Creative writing, English lit. **Foreign languages:** Spanish. **Health services:** Nursing (RN), predental, premedicine, prenursing, prepharmacy. **History:** General. **Human services:** Social work. **Liberal arts:** Arts/sciences. **Math:** General. **Parks/recreation:** Sports admin. **Philosophy/religion:** Philosophy, religion. **Physical sciences:** Chemistry. **Protective services:** Criminal justice. **Psychology:** General. **Social sciences:** General. **Visual/performing arts:** Art, ceramics, commercial/advertising art, dramatic, drawing, metal/jewelry, music, painting, photography, sculpture, studio arts.

Computing on campus. 80 workstations in dormitories, library, computer center. Dormitories linked to campus network. Commuter students can connect to campus network. Online course registration, online library, helpline, repair service, wireless network available.

Student life. Freshman orientation: Mandatory. Preregistration for classes offered. **Housing:** Guaranteed on-campus for all undergraduates. Coed dorms, single-sex dorms, apartments available. $100 nonrefundable deposit. **Activities:** Bands, campus ministries, choral groups, dance, drama, film society, international student organizations, literary magazine, music ensembles, musical theater, student government, student newspaper, Siena Heights African American Knowledge Association, student programming association, Greek council, residence hall council.

Athletics. NAIA. **Intercollegiate:** Baseball M, basketball, bowling, cross-country, football (tackle) M, golf, lacrosse, soccer, softball W, track and field, volleyball. **Intramural:** Basketball, softball, volleyball. **Team name:** Saints.

Student services. Adult student services, alcohol/substance abuse counseling, chaplain/spiritual director, career counseling, student employment services, financial aid counseling, health services, minority student services, personal counseling, placement for graduates, veterans' counselor. **Physically disabled:** Services for visually, hearing impaired.

Contact. E-mail: admissions@sienaheights.edu
Phone: (517) 264-7180 Toll-free number: (800) 521-0009 ext. 7180
Fax: (517) 264-7745
Sara Johnson, Director of Admissions, Siena Heights University, 1247 East Siena Heights Drive, Adrian, MI 49221-1796

Spring Arbor University
Spring Arbor, Michigan
www.arbor.edu

CB code: 1732

- Private 4-year university and liberal arts college affiliated with Free Methodist Church of North America
- Residential campus in rural community
- 2,984 degree-seeking undergraduates: 28% part-time, 69% women
- 1,117 degree-seeking graduate students
- 70% of applicants admitted
- SAT or ACT (ACT writing optional) required
- 55% graduate within 6 years; 37% enter graduate study

General. Founded in 1873. Regionally accredited. Adult degree completion offered through the School of Graduate and Professional Studies. Nine degree completion programs available at 14 regional sites. **Degrees:** 721 bachelor's, 10 associate awarded; master's offered. **ROTC:** Army, Air Force. **Location:** 8 miles from Jackson, 40 miles from Lansing. **Calendar:** Semester, limited summer session. **Full-time faculty:** 83 total; 66% have terminal degrees, 10% minority, 35% women. **Part-time faculty:** 60 total; 12% have terminal degrees, 3% minority, 65% women. **Class size:** 67% < 20, 30% 20-39, 2% 40-49, 1% 50-99. **Special facilities:** Trading center.

Freshman class profile. 2,849 applied, 1,985 admitted, 404 enrolled.

Mid 50% test scores			
SAT critical reading:	460-610	GPA 2.0-2.99:	22%
SAT math:	480-580	Rank in top quarter:	41%
SAT writing:	460-590	Rank in top tenth:	20%
ACT composite:	20-26	End year in good standing:	90%
GPA 3.75 or higher:	31%	Return as sophomores:	73%
GPA 3.50-3.74:	16%	Out-of-state:	16%
GPA 3.0-3.49:	30%	Live on campus:	91%
		International:	1%

Basis for selection. An ACT composite score of 20 or an SAT of 930 and a High School GPA of 2.60 GPA are recommended. Applicants whose scores are below these recommendations may be admitted conditionally. ACT recommended. Interview is recommended for borderline applicants. **Home schooled:** Letter of recommendation from the parent/teacher and a 2-3 page paper regarding applicant's home school experience.

High school preparation. College-preparatory program required. 14 units required. Required and recommended units include English 4, mathematics 3, history 3, science 3 (laboratory 3), foreign language 2 and computer science 1.

2011-2012 Annual costs. Tuition/fees: $21,520. Room/board: $7,570. Books/supplies: $800. Personal expenses: $880.

2011-2012 Financial aid. Need-based: 385 full-time freshmen applied for aid; 355 were judged to have need; 355 of these received aid. Average need met was 85%. Average scholarship/grant was $13,134; average loan $4,472. 61% of total undergraduate aid awarded as scholarships/grants, 39% as loans/jobs. **Non-need-based:** Scholarships awarded for academics, art, athletics, minority status, music/drama, religious affiliation.

Application procedures. Admission: Priority date 2/15; deadline 8/1 (receipt date). $30 fee, may be waived for applicants with need, free for online applicants. Admission notification on a rolling basis beginning on or about 9/1. **Financial aid:** Priority date 3/1; no closing date. FAFSA required. Applicants notified on a rolling basis starting 3/1; must reply within 2 week(s) of notification.

Academics. Special study options: Accelerated study, combined bachelor's/graduate degree, cross-registration, distance learning, double major, dual enrollment of high school students, ESL, honors, independent study, internships, student-designed major, study abroad, teacher certification program, Washington semester, weekend college. Environmental study semester offered at AuSable Trails Institute in northern Michigan; cross-cultural program with several destinations. **Credit/placement by examination:** AP, CLEP, IB, SAT, ACT, institutional tests. 10 credit hours maximum toward associate degree, 60 toward bachelor's. No more than 1/3 of credits for a major can be earned through credit by examination. **Support services:** Learning center, pre-admission summer program, reduced course load, remedial instruction, study skills assistance, tutoring, writing center.

Majors. Biology: General, biochemistry. **Business:** Accounting, actuarial science, business admin, finance, management information systems, managerial economics, operations. **Communications:** General, advertising, broadcast journalism, communications/speech/rhetoric, public relations. **Computer sciences:** Computer science. **Education:** Art, biology, chemistry, early childhood, elementary, English, history, mathematics, music, physical, secondary, social science, social studies, Spanish, special ed. **English:** Creative writing, English lit, rhetoric/composition. **Foreign languages:** Spanish. **Health services:** Health care admin, nursing (RN). **History:** General. **Human services:** Social work. **Math:** General. **Parks/recreation:** General, health/fitness. **Philosophy/religion:** Christian, philosophy, religion. **Physical sciences:** Chemistry, theoretical physics. **Protective services:** Law enforcement admin. **Psychology:** General. **Social sciences:** General, political economy, sociology, urban studies. **Theology:** Bible, missionary, pastoral counseling, sacred music, theology, youth ministry. **Visual/performing arts:** Art, design, dramatic, film/cinema/video, graphic design, music, music performance. **Work/family studies:** Family studies.

Most popular majors. Business/marketing 32%, family/consumer sciences 15%, health sciences 13%, public administration/social services 9%.

Computing on campus. 362 workstations in dormitories, library, computer center, student center. Dormitories wired for high-speed internet access and linked to campus network. Commuter students can connect to campus network. Online course registration, helpline, repair service, student web hosting, wireless network available.

Student life. Freshman orientation: Mandatory. Preregistration for classes offered. Three-day session held at the beginning of September each year. Parents are encouraged to attend the first day. **Policies:** Emphasis is placed on an active commitment to Jesus Christ and His teachings. Chapel attendance is required twice a week. Religious observance required. **Housing:** Guaranteed on-campus for freshmen. Single-sex dorms, special housing for disabled, apartments, wellness housing available. $200 fully refundable deposit, deadline 5/1. Community homes on campus. **Activities:** Bands,

campus ministries, choral groups, drama, film society, international student organizations, literary magazine, music ensembles, Model UN, musical theater, radio station, student government, student newspaper, symphony orchestra, Inter-faith shelter ministries, Habitat for Humanity, Band of Brothers, Circle of Sisters, Bandfire, Heartside Homeless, Wellspring, multicultural organization.

Athletics. NAIA, NCCAA. **Intercollegiate:** Baseball M, basketball, cross-country, golf M, soccer, softball W, tennis, track and field, volleyball W. **Intramural:** Basketball, field hockey M, football (non-tackle) M, golf M, soccer, softball, table tennis, tennis, volleyball. **Team name:** Cougars.

Student services. Adult student services, chaplain/spiritual director, career counseling, student employment services, financial aid counseling, health services, minority student services, personal counseling, placement for graduates. **Physically disabled:** Services for visually, speech, hearing impaired.

Contact. E-mail: admissions@arbor.edu
Phone: (517) 750-6468 Toll-free number: (800) 968-0011
Fax: (517) 750-6620
Randy Comfort, Executive Director of Admissions, Spring Arbor University, 106 East Main Street, Spring Arbor, MI 49283-9799

University of Detroit Mercy
Detroit, Michigan
www.udmercy.edu

CB member
CB code: 1835

- Private 4-year university affiliated with Roman Catholic Church
- Commuter campus in very large city
- 2,899 degree-seeking undergraduates: 20% part-time, 65% women, 15% African American, 4% Asian American, 3% Hispanic American, 5% international
- 2,347 degree-seeking graduate students
- 63% of applicants admitted
- SAT or ACT (ACT writing optional) required

General. Founded in 1991. Regionally accredited. **Degrees:** 722 bachelor's awarded; master's, professional, doctoral offered. **Calendar:** Semester, extensive summer session. **Full-time faculty:** 312 total. **Part-time faculty:** 342 total. **Class size:** 61% < 20, 35% 20-39, 3% 40-49, 2% 50-99.

Freshman class profile. 3,421 applied, 2,149 admitted, 562 enrolled.

Mid 50% test scores			
SAT critical reading:	460-600	Rank in top quarter:	63%
SAT math:	500-630	Rank in top tenth:	31%
SAT writing:	430-640	Out-of-state:	4%
ACT composite:	22-27	Live on campus:	45%
		International:	3%

Basis for selection. High school GPA in college-preparatory work, test scores, counselor's recommendation considered. Interview required for University College applicants, recommended for all others.

High school preparation. College-preparatory program required. 16 units required. Required and recommended units include English 4, mathematics 3-4, social studies 2, history 2, science 2-3 (laboratory 1) and academic electives 4. Units in speech, foreign language, music, art recommended.

2011-2012 Annual costs. Tuition/fees: $32,500. Engineering and architecture students pay slightly higher tuition; $34,020. Room/board: $9,290. Books/supplies: $1,568. Personal expenses: $3,167.

Financial aid. Non-need-based: Scholarships awarded for academics, alumni affiliation, athletics, leadership, minority status, music/drama, religious affiliation.

Application procedures. Admission: Closing date 7/1. $25 fee, may be waived for applicants with need, free for online applicants. Admission notification on a rolling basis beginning on or about 9/1. Must reply by May 1 or within 3 week(s) if notified thereafter. **Financial aid:** Priority date 3/1; no closing date. FAFSA required. Applicants notified on a rolling basis starting 3/1; must reply within 3 week(s) of notification.

Academics. Special study options: Accelerated study, combined bachelor's/graduate degree, cooperative education, distance learning, double major, dual enrollment of high school students, ESL, honors, independent study, internships, liberal arts/career combination, study abroad, teacher certification program, Washington semester, weekend college. Bachelor's degree completion program for registered nurses, 5-year program leading to master's degree in architecture, combination bachelor's/master's in 5 years for some programs, 7 yr Bachelor's Biology and DDS degree combination. **Credit/placement by examination:** AP, CLEP. 30 credit hours maximum toward bachelor's

degree. **Support services:** Learning center, reduced course load, remedial instruction, study skills assistance, tutoring, writing center.

Majors. Architecture: Architecture. **Biology:** General, biochemistry. **Business:** Accounting, business admin. **Communications:** Communications/speech/rhetoric. **Computer sciences:** General, computer science. **Education:** General, biology, chemistry, elementary, emotionally handicapped, history, mathematics, middle, reading, science, secondary, social science, social studies, special ed. **Engineering:** General, architectural, civil, computer, electrical, manufacturing, mechanical, software. **English:** Creative writing, English lit, rhetoric/composition. **Health services:** Dental hygiene, health care admin, nursing (RN), predental, premedicine, substance abuse counseling. **History:** General. **Human services:** Social work. **Liberal arts:** Arts/sciences. **Math:** General, applied. **Philosophy/religion:** Philosophy, religion. **Physical sciences:** Chemistry. **Protective services:** Criminal justice, law enforcement admin, police science. **Psychology:** General, developmental, industrial. **Social sciences:** Economics, political science, sociology. **Visual/performing arts:** Dramatic.

Most popular majors. Biology 8%, business/marketing 12%, engineering/engineering technologies 13%, health sciences 36%.

Computing on campus. Dormitories linked to campus network.

Student life. Freshman orientation: Available, $200 fee. Preregistration for classes offered. **Housing:** Coed dorms available. $100 deposit. **Activities:** Pep band, campus ministries, drama, international student organizations, literary magazine, radio station, student government, student newspaper.

Athletics. NCAA. **Intercollegiate:** Basketball, cheerleading, cross-country, fencing, golf, lacrosse, soccer, softball W, tennis W, track and field. **Intramural:** Baseball M, basketball, racquetball, soccer M, softball, table tennis, tennis, volleyball. **Team name:** Detroit Titans.

Student services. Adult student services, alcohol/substance abuse counseling, chaplain/spiritual director, career counseling, student employment services, financial aid counseling, health services, personal counseling, placement for graduates.

Contact. E-mail: admissions@udmercy.edu
Phone: (313) 993-1245 Toll-free number: (800) 635-5020
Fax: (313) 993-3326
Denise Williams, Vice President for Enrollment Management and Student Life, University of Detroit Mercy, 4001 West McNichols Road, Detroit, MI 48221-3038

University of Michigan
Ann Arbor, Michigan **CB member**
www.umich.edu **CB code: 1839**

▶ Public 4-year university
▶ Residential campus in small city
▶ 27,226 degree-seeking undergraduates: 3% part-time, 49% women, 4% African American, 12% Asian American, 4% Hispanic American, 6% international
▶ 15,039 degree-seeking graduate students
▶ 41% of applicants admitted
▶ SAT or ACT with writing, application essay required
▶ 90% graduate within 6 years

General. Founded in 1817. Regionally accredited. Over 150 first-year seminars and several thousand undergraduate research opportunities. **Degrees:** 6,553 bachelor's awarded; master's, professional, doctoral offered. **ROTC:** Army, Naval, Air Force. **Location:** 40 miles from Detroit. **Calendar:** Trimester, limited summer session. **Full-time faculty:** 2,547 total; 91% have terminal degrees, 25% minority, 38% women. **Part-time faculty:** 592 total; 74% have terminal degrees, 14% minority, 49% women. **Class size:** 46% < 20, 34% 20-39, 3% 40-49, 10% 50-99, 8% >100. **Special facilities:** Botanical garden, biological station in northern Michigan, arboretum, planetarium, laboratories, observatory, field station in the greater Yellowstone ecosystem, exhibit museum, art museum, herbarium, galleries.

Freshman class profile. 39,584 applied, 16,073 admitted, 6,236 enrolled.

Mid 50% test scores		GPA 2.0-2.99:	1%
SAT critical reading:	600-700	End year in good standing:	96%
SAT math:	650-750	Out-of-state:	38%
SAT writing:	620-720	Live on campus:	98%
ACT composite:	28-32	International:	4%
GPA 3.75 or higher:	69%	Fraternities:	14%
GPA 3.50-3.74:	24%	Sororities:	24%
GPA 3.0-3.49:	6%		

Basis for selection. Admissions based on school achievement record, including quality of school and courses elected, and test scores. Talents and extracurricular activities considered. Audition required for music majors; portfolio required for art majors. **Home schooled:** Students and their parents strongly urged to call Office of Undergraduate Admissions with questions regarding admission process or required materials.

High school preparation. College-preparatory program recommended. 16 units required; 20 recommended. Required and recommended units include English 4, mathematics 3-4, social studies 3-4, history 3-4, science 3-4 (laboratory 1), foreign language 2-4, computer science 1, visual/performing arts 2 and academic electives 1. Recommend AP, IB, honors, enriched, accelerated courses. Two units of foreign language required for College of LSA.

2011-2012 Annual costs. Tuition/fees: $12,634; $37,782 out-of-state. Room/board: $10,258. Books/supplies: $1,048. Personal expenses: $2,054.

2010-2011 Financial aid. Need-based: 3,971 full-time freshmen applied for aid; 3,020 were judged to have need; 3,020 of these received aid. Average need met was 90%. Average scholarship/grant was $11,656; average loan $7,312. 61% of total undergraduate aid awarded as scholarships/grants, 39% as loans/jobs. **Non-need-based:** Awarded to 16,143 full-time undergraduates, including 5,220 freshmen. Scholarships awarded for academics, alumni affiliation, art, athletics, leadership, music/drama, religious affiliation, ROTC, state residency.

Application procedures. Admission: Priority date 11/1; deadline 2/1 (postmark date). $65 fee, may be waived for applicants with need. Admission notification on a rolling basis. Must reply by 5/1. Students should apply early in the fall of senior year. Applications may be considered after 2/1 for School of Art and Design, School of Music, Theatre and Dance, School of Natural Resources and Environment, and School of Nursing programs on space availability basis. **Financial aid:** Priority date 4/30, closing date 5/31. FAFSA, CSS PROFILE required. Applicants notified on a rolling basis starting 3/15.

Academics. Small-scale, interdisciplinary instruction programs in residence halls; freshman and sophomore seminars, undergraduate research, study abroad opportunities. Numerous interdisciplinary undergraduate programs between Engineering, LSA, Business, and other schools/colleges. **Special study options:** Accelerated study, combined bachelor's/graduate degree, cooperative education, cross-registration, distance learning, double major, ESL, exchange student, external degree, honors, independent study, internships, liberal arts/career combination, semester at sea, student-designed major, study abroad, teacher certification program, Washington semester, weekend college. Numerous graduate/professional programs in Engineering and Business (some offered on-line or through blended coursework); customized programs for Engineering professionals; dual and combined baccalaureate degree options in the College of Engineering; dual degree options in the Ross School of Business, College of Literature, Science and Arts, School of Kinesiology, and School of Music, Theatre and Dance. **Credit/placement by examination:** AP, CLEP, IB, institutional tests. 60 credit hours maximum toward bachelor's degree. Policies on credit by examination vary by exam. **Support services:** Learning center, reduced course load, study skills assistance, tutoring, writing center.

Honors college/program. Roughly 500 members of each incoming freshman class admitted; grades, test scores, recommendations, essay used in decision process. Students must elect Honors courses, maintain a minimum course load and GPA, and pursue an Honors major.

Majors. Architecture: Architecture. **Area/ethnic studies:** African-American, American, Asian, Chicano/Hispanic-American/Latino, Latin American/Caribbean, Near/Middle Eastern, Russian/Slavic, women's. **Biology:** General, biochemistry, biophysics, cellular/molecular, ecology/evolutionary, microbiology, neuroscience. **Business:** Business admin, organizational behavior. **Communications:** Communications/speech/rhetoric. **Computer sciences:** General, informatics. **Conservation:** Environmental studies. **Education:** Elementary, music, physical, secondary. **Engineering:** General, aerospace, applied physics, biomedical, chemical, civil, computer, electrical, engineering science, geological, industrial, marine, materials, mechanical, nuclear. **English:** Creative writing, English lit. **Foreign languages:** Ancient Greek, Arabic, classics, comparative lit, French, German, Hebrew, Italian, Latin, linguistics, modern Greek, Polish, Russian, Spanish. **Health services:** Athletic training, dental hygiene, nursing (RN), pharmaceutical sciences. **History:** General. **Human services:** Public policy. **Liberal arts:** Humanities. **Math:** General, statistics. **Parks/recreation:** Exercise sciences, sports admin. **Philosophy/religion:** Judaic, philosophy, religion. **Physical sciences:** Astronomy, atmospheric science, chemistry, geology, oceanography, physics. **Psychology:** General. **Social sciences:** General, anthropology, economics, political science, sociology. **Visual/performing arts:** Art, art history/conservation, ceramics, dance, dramatic, drawing, fiber arts, film/cinema/video, graphic design, illustration, industrial design, jazz, metal/jewelry, music, music history, music performance, music technology, music theory/composition, musical theater, printmaking, sculpture, theater design, woodwind instruments.

Most popular majors. Biology 8%, engineering/engineering technologies 15%, psychology 11%, social sciences 17%, visual/performing arts 6%.

Computing on campus. 1,609 workstations in dormitories, library, computer center, student center. Dormitories wired for high-speed internet access and linked to campus network. Commuter students can connect to campus network. Online course registration, online library, helpline, repair service, student web hosting, wireless network available.

Student life. Freshman orientation: Mandatory, $290 fee. Preregistration for classes offered. Students must attend one of numerous 3-day programs offered throughout the summer. **Policies:** "Expect Respect" is a campus-wide campaign aimed at creating a unified community and educating students on what it means to respect others. The campaign seeks to help campus become more of a place where students can succeed academically and socially in a safe and inclusive environment. Smoke-free campus. **Housing:** Guaranteed on-campus for freshmen. Coed dorms, single-sex dorms, special housing for disabled, apartments, cooperative housing, fraternity/sorority housing, wellness housing available. Living-learning communities available. **Activities:** Bands, campus ministries, choral groups, dance, drama, film society, international student organizations, literary magazine, music ensembles, Model UN, musical theater, opera, radio station, student government, student newspaper, symphony orchestra, TV station, 1,228 student organizations.

Athletics. NCAA. **Intercollegiate:** Baseball M, basketball, cross-country, diving, field hockey W, football (tackle) M, golf, gymnastics, ice hockey M, lacrosse M, rowing (crew) W, soccer, softball W, swimming, tennis, track and field, volleyball W, water polo W, wrestling M. **Intramural:** Badminton, basketball, bowling, cross-country, diving, football (non-tackle), golf, racquetball, swimming, table tennis, track and field, volleyball, wrestling. **Team name:** Wolverines.

Student services. Adult student services, alcohol/substance abuse counseling, chaplain/spiritual director, career counseling, student employment services, financial aid counseling, health services, legal services, minority student services, on-campus daycare, personal counseling, placement for graduates, veterans' counselor, women's services. **Physically disabled:** Services for visually, speech, hearing impaired.

Contact. Phone: (734) 764-7433 Fax: (734) 936-0740
Theodore Spencer, Associate Vice Provost and Executive Director, Undergraduate Admissions, University of Michigan, 1220 Student Activities Building, Ann Arbor, MI 48109-1316

University of Michigan: Dearborn

Dearborn, Michigan **CB member**
www.umd.umich.edu **CB code: 1861**

- Public 4-year university
- Commuter campus in small city
- 6,960 degree-seeking undergraduates: 31% part-time, 52% women, 11% African American, 6% Asian American, 5% Hispanic American, 1% international
- 1,417 degree-seeking graduate students
- 59% of applicants admitted
- SAT or ACT (ACT writing optional) required
- 52% graduate within 6 years

General. Founded in 1959. Regionally accredited. **Degrees:** 1,137 bachelor's awarded; master's, doctoral offered. **ROTC:** Army, Naval, Air Force. **Location:** 10 miles from Detroit. **Calendar:** Semester, limited summer session. **Full-time faculty:** 312 total; 86% have terminal degrees, 33% minority, 39% women. **Part-time faculty:** 227 total; 32% have terminal degrees, 12% minority, 40% women. **Class size:** 27% < 20, 53% 20-39, 14% 40-49, 5% 50-99, less than 1% >100. **Special facilities:** Environmental study area, extensive rotating art collection, engineering CAD-CAM robotics laboratory, Armenian research center.

Freshman class profile. 4,684 applied, 2,769 admitted, 954 enrolled.

Mid 50% test scores			
SAT critical reading:	510-620	Rank in top quarter:	59%
SAT math:	610-720	Rank in top tenth:	26%
ACT composite:	21-26	Return as sophomores:	82%
GPA 3.75 or higher:	33%	Out-of-state:	1%
GPA 3.50-3.74:	20%	International:	1%
GPA 3.0-3.49:	32%	Fraternities:	2%
GPA 2.0-2.99:	15%	Sororities:	2%

Basis for selection. Minimum 3.0 GPA with 500 SAT verbal and math or 22 ACT preferred; class rank considered. Interview recommended for applicants with less than 3.0 GPA or 20 ACT or 1000 SAT (exclusive of Writing). Essay recommended for all.

High school preparation. 15 units required; 20 recommended. Required and recommended units include English 4, mathematics 4, social studies 4, history 4, science 2 (laboratory 1) and foreign language 2. 1 unit information technology and 1 unit fine and performing arts recommended.

2011-2012 Annual costs. Tuition/fees: $10,470; $22,448 out-of-state. Books/supplies: $960. Personal expenses: $1,465.

2010-2011 Financial aid. Need-based: 760 full-time freshmen applied for aid; 554 were judged to have need; 553 of these received aid. Average need met was 80%. Average scholarship/grant was $5,611; average loan $3,345. 45% of total undergraduate aid awarded as scholarships/grants, 55% as loans/jobs. Non-need-based: Awarded to 1,563 full-time undergraduates, including 470 freshmen. Scholarships awarded for academics, alumni affiliation, athletics, leadership, minority status, ROTC, state residency.

Application procedures. Admission: Priority date 5/1; no deadline. $30 fee, may be waived for applicants with need. Admission notification on a rolling basis beginning on or about 9/1. Must reply by May 1 or within 4 week(s) if notified thereafter. **Financial aid:** Priority date 2/15; no closing date. FAFSA required. Applicants notified on a rolling basis starting 3/1; must reply within 3 week(s) of notification.

Academics. Special study options: Cooperative education, cross-registration, distance learning, double major, dual enrollment of high school students, ESL, honors, independent study, internships, liberal arts/career combination, student-designed major, study abroad, teacher certification program, Washington semester. Professional development courses in education, engineering, liberal arts, and management. **Credit/placement by examination:** AP, CLEP, institutional tests. 30 credit hours maximum toward bachelor's degree. **Support services:** Learning center, pre-admission summer program, tutoring, writing center.

Majors. Area/ethnic studies: American. **Biology:** General, bacteriology, biochemistry, ecology. **Business:** Business admin, management science. **Communications:** Communications/speech/rhetoric. **Computer sciences:** General, programming. **Conservation:** General, environmental studies. **Education:** General, art, business, chemistry, early childhood, foreign languages, mathematics, science, secondary, social studies. **Engineering:** General, computer, electrical, manufacturing, mechanical. **English:** English lit. **Foreign languages:** French, Spanish. **Health services:** Health care admin. **History:** General. **Human services:** General. **Liberal arts:** Arts/sciences. **Math:** General. **Philosophy/religion:** Philosophy. **Physical sciences:** Chemistry, physics. **Psychology:** General. **Social sciences:** Anthropology, economics, political science, sociology. **Visual/performing arts:** Music, painting.

Most popular majors. Biology 7%, business/marketing 21%, education 14%, engineering/engineering technologies 11%, psychology 9%, social sciences 9%.

Computing on campus. 962 workstations in library, computer center, student center. Commuter students can connect to campus network. Online course registration, helpline, wireless network available.

Student life. Freshman orientation: Mandatory, $50 fee. Preregistration for classes offered. **Activities:** Campus ministries, choral groups, drama, film society, literary magazine, radio station, student government, student newspaper, TV station, Arab student union, African American association, campus engineers, Asian American association, student activities board, professional accounting society, Muslim student association.

Athletics. NAIA. **Intercollegiate:** Basketball, softball W, volleyball W. **Intramural:** Basketball, volleyball. **Team name:** Wolves.

Student services. Adult student services, alcohol/substance abuse counseling, career counseling, services for economically disadvantaged, student employment services, financial aid counseling, health services, on-campus daycare, personal counseling, placement for graduates, veterans' counselor, women's services. **Physically disabled:** Services for visually, speech, hearing impaired.

Contact. E-mail: admissions@umd.umich.edu
Phone: (313) 436-9156 Fax: (313) 436-9167
Deb Peffer, Director of Admissions and Orientation, University of Michigan: Dearborn, 4901 Evergreen Road, 1145 UC, Dearborn, MI 48128-1491

University of Michigan: Flint

Flint, Michigan **CB member**
www.umflint.edu **CB code: 1853**

- Public 4-year university and branch campus college
- Commuter campus in small city

- 6,720 degree-seeking undergraduates: 33% part-time, 61% women, 13% African American, 1% Asian American, 4% Hispanic American, 1% Native American, 3% international
- 1,272 degree-seeking graduate students
- 71% of applicants admitted
- SAT or ACT (ACT writing optional) required
- 37% graduate within 6 years

General. Founded in 1956. Regionally accredited. Institution shares many resources of entire University of Michigan system. **Degrees:** 918 bachelor's awarded; master's, professional offered. **ROTC:** Army. **Location:** 60 miles from Detroit. **Calendar:** Semester, limited summer session. **Full-time faculty:** 278 total; 70% have terminal degrees, 23% minority, 51% women. **Part-time faculty:** 252 total; 22% have terminal degrees, 15% minority, 60% women. **Class size:** 39% < 20, 49% 20-39, 7% 40-49, 4% 50-99, less than 1% >100.

Freshman class profile. 3,164 applied, 2,232 admitted, 686 enrolled.

Mid 50% test scores			
SAT critical reading:	480-660	Rank in top quarter:	47%
SAT math:	600-640	Rank in top tenth:	17%
SAT writing:	490-620	End year in good standing:	79%
ACT composite:	20-25	Return as sophomores:	70%
GPA 3.75 or higher:	22%	Out-of-state:	1%
GPA 3.50-3.74:	19%	Live on campus:	19%
GPA 3.0-3.49:	32%	International:	8%
GPA 2.0-2.99:	27%	Fraternities:	10%
		Sororities:	7%

Basis for selection. GPA of 2.7 or higher and test scores equaling national average recommended. Essay and interview recommended. Audition required for art and music majors. **Home schooled:** Transcript of courses and grades required.

High school preparation. College-preparatory program recommended. 16 units recommended. Recommended units include English 4, mathematics 4, history 3, science 3 and foreign language 3.

2011-2012 Annual costs. Tuition/fees: $9,184; $17,536 out-of-state. Room/board: $7,287. Books/supplies: $1,000. Personal expenses: $1,160.

2010-2011 Financial aid. Need-based: 638 full-time freshmen applied for aid; 501 were judged to have need; 477 of these received aid. Average need met was 73%. Average scholarship/grant was $5,595; average loan $3,287. 33% of total undergraduate aid awarded as scholarships/grants, 67% as loans/jobs. **Non-need-based:** Awarded to 810 full-time undergraduates, including 227 freshmen. Scholarships awarded for academics, art, leadership, music/drama. **Additional information:** SAT/ACT scores must be submitted for scholarship consideration.

Application procedures. Admission: No deadline. $30 fee, may be waived for applicants with need. Admission notification on a rolling basis. **Financial aid:** Priority date 3/1; no closing date. FAFSA, institutional form required. Applicants notified on a rolling basis starting 3/15.

Academics. Special study options: Accelerated study, combined bachelor's/graduate degree, cooperative education, distance learning, double major, dual enrollment of high school students, ESL, honors, independent study, internships, student-designed major, study abroad, teacher certification program. **Credit/placement by examination:** AP, CLEP, SAT, ACT, institutional tests. 9 credit hours maximum toward bachelor's degree. Maximum of 3 courses may be passed by examination in Arts & Sciences, School of Education and Human Services, School of Management and Nursing. **Support services:** Learning center, reduced course load, remedial instruction, study skills assistance, tutoring, writing center.

Majors. Area/ethnic studies: African-American. **Biology:** General, biochemistry, Biochemistry/molecular biology, biomedical sciences, ecology, molecular, wildlife. **Business:** Accounting, actuarial science, business admin, finance, international, marketing. **Communications:** General, media studies. **Computer sciences:** General, computer science, information systems. **Conservation:** Environmental science. **Education:** General, art, early childhood, elementary, English, French, history, mathematics, music, secondary, social studies, Spanish. **Engineering:** Applied physics, computer, engineering science, environmental, mechanical. **English:** English lit, rhetoric/composition, writing. **Foreign languages:** French, linguistics, Spanish. **Health services:** Clinical lab science, environmental health, facilities admin, health care admin, medical radiologic technology/radiation therapy, nursing (RN), predental, premedicine, prenursing, prepharmacy, prephysical therapy, preveterinary, public health ed. **History:** General. **Human services:** General, social work. **Liberal arts:** Arts/sciences. **Math:** General. **Philosophy/religion:** Ethics, philosophy. **Physical sciences:** Chemistry, physics. **Protective services:** Law enforcement admin. **Psychology:** General, applied. **Social sciences:** General, anthropology, economics, political science, sociology. **Visual/performing arts:** General, design, dramatic, music, music performance, studio arts, theater design.

Most popular majors. Business/marketing 19%, communications/journalism 6%, education 10%, health sciences 27%, psychology 6%.

Computing on campus. 227 workstations in library, computer center, student center. Dormitories wired for high-speed internet access and linked to campus network. Commuter students can connect to campus network. Online course registration, online library, helpline, repair service, student web hosting, wireless network available.

Student life. Freshman orientation: Mandatory, $80 fee. Preregistration for classes offered. One-day program for students and parents before start of fall semester. **Housing:** Coed dorms available. $100 nonrefundable deposit, deadline 2/1. **Activities:** Bands, choral groups, dance, drama, literary magazine, music ensembles, musical theater, student government, student newspaper, College Democrats, College Republicans, College Libertarians, Intervarsity Christian Fellowship, Muslim student association, Students Moving the UCEN Forward, Voices for Women on Campus, chess club, Music, Art and Culture Revival Organization.

Athletics. Intramural: Basketball, golf, soccer, table tennis, volleyball.

Student services. Adult student services, alcohol/substance abuse counseling, career counseling, services for economically disadvantaged, student employment services, financial aid counseling, health services, minority student services, on-campus daycare, personal counseling, veterans' counselor, women's services. **Physically disabled:** Services for visually, speech, hearing impaired.

Contact. E-mail: admissions@umflint.edu
Phone: (810) 762-3300 Fax: (810) 762-3272
Jon Davidson, Admissions Director, University of Michigan: Flint, 303 East Kearsley Street, Flint, MI 48502-1950

University of Phoenix: Metro Detroit
Troy, Michigan
www.phoenix.edu

- For-profit 4-year university
- Very large city
- 1,649 degree-seeking undergraduates

General. Regionally accredited. **Degrees:** 378 bachelor's awarded; master's offered. **Calendar:** Differs by program. **Full-time faculty:** 25 total. **Part-time faculty:** 427 total.

Basis for selection. Open admission.

2011-2012 Annual costs. Estimated costs as of August 2011: per-credit-hour charge, $465 to $480, depending upon level and course of study; electronic course materials fee, $75, if applicable. Book and material charges may vary by course and program. All fees are subject to change.

Application procedures. Admission: No deadline. No application fee. **Financial aid:** No deadline.

Academics. Credit/placement by examination: AP, CLEP.

Majors. Business: Accounting, business admin, human resources. **Conservation:** Environmental science. **Health services:** Health services admin. **Protective services:** Law enforcement admin.

Contact. Marc Booker, Director of Admission and Evaluation, University of Phoenix: Metro Detroit, 5480 Corporoate Drive, Suite 240, Troy, MI 48098-2623

University of Phoenix: West Michigan
Grand Rapids, Michigan
www.phoenix.edu

- For-profit 4-year university and business college
- Small city
- 750 degree-seeking undergraduates

General. Regionally accredited. **Degrees:** 74 bachelor's awarded; master's offered. **Calendar:** Differs by program. **Full-time faculty:** 15 total. **Part-time faculty:** 178 total.

Basis for selection. Open admission.

2011-2012 Annual costs. Estimated costs as of August 2011: per-credit-hour charge, $435 to $480, depending upon level and course of study; electronic course materials fee, $95, if applicable. Book and material charges may vary by course and program. All fees are subject to change.

Application procedures. Admission: No deadline. No application fee. **Financial aid:** No deadline.

Academics. Credit/placement by examination: AP, CLEP.

Majors. Business: Accounting, business admin. **Health services:** Health care admin, nursing practice. **Protective services:** Law enforcement admin.

Contact. Marc Booker, Director of Admission and Evaluation, University of Phoenix: West Michigan, 318 River Ridge Drive NW, Grand Rapids, MI 49544-1683

Walsh College of Accountancy and Business Administration
Troy, Michigan
www.walshcollege.edu   CB code: 0372

- Private two-year upper-division business college
- Commuter campus in large city

General. Founded in 1922. Regionally accredited. **Location:** 17 miles from Detroit. **Calendar:** Semester.

Annual costs/financial aid. Tuition/fees (2011-2012): $10,300. Books/supplies: $1,000. Need-based financial aid available to full-time and part-time students.

Contact. Phone: (248) 823-1610
Director of Admissions and Academic Advising, PO Box 7006, Troy, MI 48007-7006

Wayne State University
Detroit, Michigan   **CB member**
www.wayne.edu   **CB code: 1898**

- Public 4-year university
- Commuter campus in very large city
- 19,558 degree-seeking undergraduates: 35% part-time, 57% women
- 9,899 degree-seeking graduate students
- 76% of applicants admitted
- SAT or ACT (ACT writing optional) required

General. Founded in 1868. Regionally accredited. 4 extension center locations, 2 university centers and an advanced technology center at Southeastern Michigan community colleges. **Degrees:** 2,642 bachelor's awarded; master's, professional, doctoral offered. **ROTC:** Army, Naval, Air Force. **Location:** 3 miles from downtown. **Calendar:** Semester, extensive summer session. **Full-time faculty:** 1,033 total; 26% minority, 42% women. **Part-time faculty:** 875 total; 24% minority, 51% women. **Class size:** 46% < 20, 41% 20-39, 4% 40-49, 7% 50-99, 3% >100. **Special facilities:** 3 theaters, planetarium.

Freshman class profile. 9,468 applied, 7,150 admitted, 2,466 enrolled.

GPA 3.75 or higher:	17%	Out-of-state:	2%
GPA 3.50-3.74:	14%	Live on campus:	33%
GPA 3.0-3.49:	31%	Fraternities:	3%
GPA 2.0-2.99:	38%	Sororities:	3%

Basis for selection. First-year students with a 2.75 grade-point average or a 2.00-2.74 grade-point average with an ACT composite of 21 or an SAT total of 990 are admissible. Transfer students need to have at least 12 transferable credits of previous college work and a minimum 2.0 cumulative grade-point average from all higher education institutions attended. Audition required for music or dance applicants.

High school preparation. College-preparatory program recommended. 19 units recommended. Recommended units include English 4, mathematics 4, history 3, science 3, foreign language 2, computer science 1 and visual/performing arts 2.

2011-2012 Annual costs. Tuition/fees: $9,809; $20,921 out-of-state. Room/board: $7,940. Books/supplies: $1,100. Personal expenses: $2,880.

2010-2011 Financial aid. Need-based: 2,188 full-time freshmen applied for aid; 1,930 were judged to have need; 1,926 of these received aid. Average

need met was 71%. Average scholarship/grant was $7,363; average loan $3,648. 32% of total undergraduate aid awarded as scholarships/grants, 68% as loans/jobs. **Non-need-based:** Awarded to 5,239 full-time undergraduates, including 1,121 freshmen. Scholarships awarded for academics, art, athletics, leadership, music/drama. **Additional information:** Need-based institutional grants cover tuition and fees with grants and EFC (no loans).

Application procedures. Admission: Priority date 8/1; no deadline. $30 fee, may be waived for applicants with need. Admission notification on a rolling basis. **Financial aid:** Priority date 2/15, closing date 4/30. FAFSA required. Applicants notified by 3/1; Applicants notified on a rolling basis starting 3/1; must reply within 2 week(s) of notification.

Academics. Special study options: Accelerated study, combined bachelor's/graduate degree, cooperative education, cross-registration, distance learning, double major, dual enrollment of high school students, ESL, exchange student, honors, independent study, internships, liberal arts/career combination, study abroad, teacher certification program, weekend college. Off-campus courses for credit, city-wide adult education program, international exchange student programs. **Credit/placement by examination:** AP, CLEP, IB, institutional tests. 32 credit hours maximum toward bachelor's degree. **Support services:** Learning center, reduced course load, remedial instruction, study skills assistance, tutoring, writing center.

Honors college/program. Selected incoming freshmen are invited into the program each year through Scholars Day and are awarded at least $2,000 a year in a tuition scholarship for four years if they attend the event.

Majors. Area/ethnic studies: African-American, American, East Asian, Russian/Eastern European/Eurasian. **Biology:** General. **Business:** Accounting, finance, international, labor studies, management information systems, marketing, organizational behavior. **Communications:** Communications/speech/rhetoric, journalism, public relations, radio/TV. **Computer sciences:** General, information systems. **Conservation:** Environmental science. **Education:** Art, elementary, English, health, mathematics, physical, science, social studies, special ed, speech impaired, voc/tech. **Engineering:** Biomedical, chemical, civil, electrical, industrial, mechanical. **English:** English lit. **Foreign languages:** General, classics, German, linguistics, Slavic. **Health services:** Clinical lab science, communication disorders, dietetics, medical radiologic technology/radiation therapy, pathology assistant. **History:** General. **Human services:** General, social work. **Math:** General. **Philosophy/religion:** Philosophy. **Physical sciences:** Astronomy, chemistry, geology, physics. **Protective services:** Criminal justice. **Psychology:** General. **Social sciences:** Anthropology, economics, political science, sociology, urban studies. **Visual/performing arts:** Art, art history/conservation, cinematography, dance, dramatic, film/cinema/video, music. **Work/family studies:** Apparel marketing, food/nutrition.

Most popular majors. Biology 7%, business/marketing 17%, education 9%, engineering/engineering technologies 6%, health sciences 8%, psychology 10%, social sciences 7%, visual/performing arts 7%.

Computing on campus. 1,020 workstations in library. Dormitories wired for high-speed internet access and linked to campus network. Commuter students can connect to campus network. Online course registration, online library, helpline, repair service, wireless network available.

Student life. Freshman orientation: Mandatory, $100 fee. Preregistration for classes offered. Held at the Welcome Center several times a year. **Housing:** Coed dorms, special housing for disabled, apartments available. $100 nonrefundable deposit. **Activities:** Bands, campus ministries, choral groups, dance, drama, film society, international student organizations, literary magazine, music ensembles, musical theater, opera, radio station, student government, student newspaper, symphony orchestra, TV station, Indian student association, Albanian American student association, cultural diversity council, Slavic club, Campus Crusade for Christ, College Democrats, cancer awareness association, Habitat for Humanity, UNICEF, university mentors.

Athletics. NCAA. **Intercollegiate:** Baseball M, basketball, cheerleading, cross-country, diving, fencing, football (tackle) M, golf M, ice hockey W, softball W, swimming, tennis, volleyball W. **Intramural:** Badminton, basketball, bowling, football (non-tackle), racquetball, soccer, softball, table tennis, tennis, volleyball, weight lifting. **Team name:** Warriors.

Student services. Adult student services, alcohol/substance abuse counseling, chaplain/spiritual director, career counseling, services for economically disadvantaged, student employment services, financial aid counseling, health services, legal services, minority student services, on-campus daycare, personal counseling, placement for graduates, veterans' counselor, women's services. **Physically disabled:** Services for visually, speech, hearing impaired.

Contact. E-mail: admissions@wayne.edu
Phone: (313) 577-3577 Toll-free number: (877) 978-4636
Fax: (313) 577-7536
Judy Tatum, Senior Director of Undergraduate Admissions, Wayne State University, P.O. Box 02759, Detroit, MI 48202-0759

Western Michigan University
Kalamazoo, Michigan
www.wmich.edu

CB member
CB code: 1902

- Public 4-year university
- Residential campus in small city
- 19,700 degree-seeking undergraduates: 14% part-time, 49% women, 10% African American, 1% Asian American, 4% Hispanic American, 3% international
- 4,515 degree-seeking graduate students
- 83% of applicants admitted
- SAT or ACT (ACT writing optional) required
- 52% graduate within 6 years

General. Founded in 1903. Regionally accredited. **Degrees:** 3,835 bachelor's awarded; master's, professional, doctoral offered. **ROTC:** Army. **Location:** 140 miles from Detroit, 140 miles from Chicago. **Calendar:** Semester, extensive summer session. **Full-time faculty:** 915 total; 80% have terminal degrees, 17% minority, 41% women. **Part-time faculty:** 522 total; 55% women. **Class size:** 36% < 20, 44% 20-39, 9% 40-49, 7% 50-99, 4% >100. **Special facilities:** Van de Graaff particle accelerator, pilot plant for manufacturing and printing of paper and fiber recovery, aviation flight simulators, business technology park.

Freshman class profile. 14,413 applied, 11,986 admitted, 3,166 enrolled.

Mid 50% test scores		End year in good standing:	78%
ACT composite:	20-25	Return as sophomores:	74%
GPA 3.75 or higher:	19%	Out-of-state:	10%
GPA 3.50-3.74:	13%	Live on campus:	87%
GPA 3.0-3.49:	37%	International:	2%
GPA 2.0-2.99:	31%	Fraternities:	4%
Rank in top quarter:	32%	Sororities:	8%
Rank in top tenth:	11%		

Basis for selection. School achievement record, test scores most important. Trend of grades and number of solid high school academic subjects completed considered; students not meeting college-preparatory program requirements may be admitted conditionally if they meet other admission requirements. Audition required for dance, music, and theater applicants. Portfolio required for some art applicants. **Home schooled:** Transcript of courses and grades required. Applicants should present a transcript of course work and an ACT/SAT score. Must meet the same admission criteria as all other applicants; however, emphasis is placed on test scores. **Learning Disabled:** Students with learning disabilities do not have special requirements or procedures, all students are considered for admissions with the same criteria.

High school preparation. College-preparatory program recommended. 11 units recommended. Recommended units include English 4, mathematics 3, social studies 2 and science 2. 2 units recommended in foreign language if going into an arts or science major.

2011-2012 Annual costs. Tuition/fees: $9,606; $22,338 out-of-state. Room/board: $8,249.

2010-2011 Financial aid. Need-based: 3,221 full-time freshmen applied for aid; 2,620 were judged to have need; 2,620 of these received aid. Average need met was 84%. Average scholarship/grant was $5,775; average loan $3,352. 41% of total undergraduate aid awarded as scholarships/grants, 59% as loans/jobs. **Non-need-based:** Awarded to 6,942 full-time undergraduates, including 1,703 freshmen. Scholarships awarded for academics, alumni affiliation, art, athletics, minority status, music/drama, ROTC, state residency.

Application procedures. Admission: No deadline. $35 fee, may be waived for applicants with need. Admission notification on a rolling basis beginning on or about 7/1. **Financial aid:** Priority date 3/1; no closing date. FAFSA required. Applicants notified on a rolling basis starting 3/15.

Academics. Special study options: Accelerated study, combined bachelor's/graduate degree, cooperative education, cross-registration, distance learning, double major, dual enrollment of high school students, ESL, honors, independent study, internships, student-designed major, study abroad, teacher certification program, Washington semester. **Credit/placement by examination:** AP, CLEP, IB, SAT, ACT, institutional tests. Maximum semester hours of credit by examination which may be counted toward degree varies by department. Credit by examination may not be used to satisfy minimum residency requirement of 30 semester hours. **Support services:** Learning center, pre-admission summer program, reduced course load, remedial instruction, study skills assistance, tutoring, writing center.

Honors college/program. High school GPA of 3.6 or better on a 4-point scale, ACT composite score of 26 or better required for admission. Approximately 250 freshmen admitted each year. The honors college uses

course clusters as a way to begin focusing on academic themes. Some cluster themes include: Medical Career Foundations; Business Environment; The World and Its People; and Science and Technology for engineering majors.

Majors. Architecture: Urban/community planning. **Area/ethnic studies:** African-American, women's. **Biology:** General, biochemistry, biomedical sciences. **Business:** General, accounting, e-commerce, finance, financial planning, information resources management, logistics, managerial economics, marketing, travel services. **Communications:** Advertising, communications/speech/rhetoric, journalism, organizational. **Computer sciences:** General, computer science. **Conservation:** Environmental studies. **Education:** Art, biology, business, chemistry, early childhood, earth science, elementary, emotionally handicapped, English, family/consumer sciences, French, geography, German, health, history, Latin, mathematics, mentally handicapped, music, physical, physics, sales/marketing, social science, social studies, Spanish, technology/industrial arts, trade/industrial, voc/tech. **Engineering:** Aerospace, chemical, civil, computer, electrical, industrial, manufacturing, mechanical, paper, structural. **English:** Creative writing, English lit, writing. **Foreign languages:** French, German, Latin, Spanish. **Health services:** Athletic training, audiology/speech pathology, music therapy, nursing (RN), occupational therapy. **History:** General, applied. **Human services:** Social work. **Math:** General, applied, statistics. **Parks/recreation:** General, exercise sciences. **Philosophy/religion:** Philosophy, professional ethics, religion. **Physical sciences:** Chemistry, geochemistry, geology, geophysics, hydrology, physics. **Protective services:** Criminal justice. **Psychology:** General, behavior analysis, social. **Social sciences:** Anthropology, economics, geography, GIS/cartography, political science, sociology, U.S. government. **Visual/performing arts:** Acting, art, art history/conservation, dance, graphic design, interior design, jazz, music, music performance, music theory/composition, piano/keyboard, studio arts, theater design, theater history, voice/opera. **Work/family studies:** Child development, clothing/textiles, family systems, institutional food production.

Most popular majors. Business/marketing 22%, communications/journalism 6%, education 11%, engineering/engineering technologies 7%, health sciences 8%.

Computing on campus. 2,244 workstations in library, computer center, student center. Dormitories wired for high-speed internet access and linked to campus network. Commuter students can connect to campus network. Online course registration, online library, helpline, repair service, student web hosting, wireless network available.

Student life. Freshman orientation: Mandatory, $195 fee. Preregistration for classes offered. 2-day program in June; includes session for parents. **Housing:** Guaranteed on-campus for freshmen. Coed dorms, single-sex dorms, special housing for disabled, apartments, fraternity/sorority housing, wellness housing available. Aviation house, business, education, engineering and applied sciences houses, fine arts house, health and human services house, honors community, second year experience, science scholars, transfer student communities, Magellan house. **Activities:** Bands, campus ministries, choral groups, dance, drama, film society, international student organizations, literary magazine, music ensembles, musical theater, opera, radio station, student government, student newspaper, symphony orchestra, Asian Pacific Islander Network, Association of Chinese Scholars & Students, Dominican student organization, Campus Crusade for Christ, Christian Challenge Collegiate, Black and Christian International Conservatives, OUTreach, Peace Hope and Development in Sudan.

Athletics. NCAA. **Intercollegiate:** Baseball M, basketball, cross-country W, football (tackle) M, golf W, gymnastics W, ice hockey M, soccer, softball W, tennis, track and field W, volleyball W. **Intramural:** Badminton, basketball, football (non-tackle), golf, ice hockey, racquetball, soccer, softball, tennis, volleyball. **Team name:** Broncos.

Student services. Adult student services, alcohol/substance abuse counseling, chaplain/spiritual director, career counseling, student employment services, financial aid counseling, health services, minority student services, on-campus daycare, personal counseling, placement for graduates, veterans' counselor, women's services. **Physically disabled:** Services for visually, speech, hearing impaired.

Contact. E-mail: ask-wmu@wmich.edu
Phone: (269) 387-2000 Fax: (269) 387-2096
Penny Bundy, Director of Admissions, Western Michigan University, 1903 West Michigan Avenue, Kalamazoo, MI 49008-5211

Yeshiva Beth Yehuda-Yeshiva Gedolah of Greater Detroit
Oak Park, Michigan

CB code: 7010

- Private 5-year rabbinical college for men affiliated with Jewish faith
- Residential campus in large town
- Interview required

General. Accredited by AARTS. **Degrees:** 4 bachelor's awarded; master's offered. **Calendar:** Semester. **Full-time faculty:** 6 total. **Part-time faculty:** 8 total.

Basis for selection. GED not accepted. Qualifications include independent comprehension of basic Talmudic text and completion of 150 folios of Talmud with commentary of Rashi, completion of Pentateuch and substantial parts of Prophets and Hagiography, ability to read and write classical Hebrew, working knowledge of Aramaic language of Talmud, and Yiddish.

2011-2012 Annual costs. Tuition/fees: $6,100. Room/board: $4,000. Books/supplies: $500. Personal expenses: $500.

Application procedures. Admission: No deadline. No application fee. **Financial aid:** Closing date 8/1. Applicants notified on a rolling basis.

Academics. Special study options: Independent study. **Credit/placement by examination:** AP, CLEP. **Support services:** Tutoring.

Majors. Theology: Talmudic.

Student life. Housing: Guaranteed on-campus for all undergraduates.

Student services. Adult student services, career counseling, health services, on-campus daycare, personal counseling, placement for graduates.

Contact. Phone: (248) 968-3360 Fax: (248) 968-8613
Yeshiva Beth Yehuda-Yeshiva Gedolah of Greater Detroit, 24600
Greenfield Road, Oak Park, MI 48237

Minnesota

Argosy University: Twin Cities
Eagan, Minnesota
www.argosy.edu/twincities   CB code: 6427

▶ For-profit 4-year university
▶ Very large city
▶ 1,430 degree-seeking undergraduates

General. **Degrees:** 34 bachelor's, 330 associate awarded; master's, professional, doctoral offered. **Calendar:** Differs by program. **Full-time faculty:** 52 total. **Part-time faculty:** 157 total.

Basis for selection. Open admission.

2011-2012 Annual costs. Tuition/fees: $17,962.

Application procedures. **Admission:** Closing date 9/14. $50 fee. **Financial aid:** No deadline.

Academics. **Credit/placement by examination:** AP, CLEP.

Majors. **Business:** Business admin. **Health services:** Clinical lab science. **Liberal arts:** Arts/sciences. **Protective services:** Police science. **Psychology:** General.

Contact. E-mail: autcadmissions@argosy.edu
Phone: (651) 846-3300
Janet Zimprich, Senior Director of Admissions, Argosy University: Twin Cities, 1515 Central Parkway, Eagan, MN 55121

Art Institutes International Minnesota
Minneapolis, Minnesota
www.artinstitutes.edu/minneapolis   CB code: 2332

▶ For-profit 4-year culinary school and visual arts college
▶ Commuter campus in large city
▶ 1,804 degree-seeking undergraduates
▶ Application essay, interview required

General. Accredited by ACICS. **Degrees:** 231 bachelor's, 81 associate awarded. **Calendar:** Quarter, extensive summer session. **Full-time faculty:** 69 total. **Part-time faculty:** 63 total. **Special facilities:** Student-run dining lab.

Basis for selection. Open admission. School tour required prior to admission. **Home schooled:** Transcript of courses and grades, interview required. **Learning Disabled:** Notify Dean of Student Affairs.

2011-2012 Annual costs. Books/supplies: $1,649. Personal expenses: $2,880.

Financial aid. **Non-need-based:** Scholarships awarded for academics.

Application procedures. **Admission:** No deadline. $50 fee. Admission notification on a rolling basis. **Financial aid:** FAFSA required.

Academics. **Special study options:** Cooperative education, distance learning, honors, independent study, internships, study abroad, weekend college. **Credit/placement by examination:** AP, CLEP, institutional tests. **Support services:** Learning center, reduced course load, remedial instruction, study skills assistance, tutoring.

Majors. **Business:** Customer service, fashion, hospitality admin, hospitality/recreation, hotel/motel admin, marketing, merchandising, resort management, restaurant/food services, retailing, selling. **Communications:** Advertising, digital media, photojournalism. **Communications technology:** Animation/special effects, graphics, photo/film/video, recording arts. **Computer sciences:** Computer graphics, web page design, webmaster. **Visual/performing arts:** Cinematography, commercial photography, commercial/advertising art, design, film/cinema/video, graphic design, interior design, multimedia, photography, studio arts management.

Most popular majors. Business/marketing 9%, communications/journalism 10%, computer/information sciences 21%, personal/culinary services 7%, visual/performing arts 51%.

Computing on campus. 320 workstations in dormitories, library, computer center, student center. Dormitories wired for high-speed internet access and linked to campus network. Online library, student web hosting, wireless network available.

Student life. **Freshman orientation:** Mandatory. Preregistration for classes offered. **Housing:** Apartments, wellness housing available. $250 deposit. **Activities:** Campus ministries, film society, student government, student newspaper.

Student services. Alcohol/substance abuse counseling, career counseling, student employment services, financial aid counseling, personal counseling, placement for graduates, veterans' counselor. **Physically disabled:** Services for hearing impaired.

Contact. E-mail: aimadm@aii.edu
Phone: (612) 332-3361 Toll-free number: (800) 777-3643
Fax: (612) 332-3934
Mary Strand, Senior Director of Admissions, Art Institutes International Minnesota, 15 South Ninth Street, Minneapolis, MN 55402

Augsburg College
Minneapolis, Minnesota   CB member
www.augsburg.edu   CB code: 6014

▶ Private 4-year liberal arts college affiliated with Evangelical Lutheran Church in America
▶ Residential campus in large city

General. Founded in 1869. Regionally accredited. **Location:** 5 miles from downtown. **Calendar:** Continuous.

Annual costs/financial aid. Tuition/fees (2011-2012): $30,418. Room/board: $8,072. Books/supplies: $1,000. Personal expenses: $1,670. Need-based financial aid available to full-time and part-time students.

Contact. Phone: (612) 330-1001
Director of Admissions, 2211 Riverside Avenue, Minneapolis, MN 55454

Bemidji State University
Bemidji, Minnesota
www.bemidjistate.edu   CB code: 6676

▶ Public 4-year university
▶ Residential campus in large town
▶ 4,572 degree-seeking undergraduates: 19% part-time, 53% women, 1% African American, 1% Asian American, 2% Hispanic American, 3% Native American, 3% international
▶ 262 degree-seeking graduate students
▶ 90% of applicants admitted
▶ SAT or ACT (ACT writing optional) required
▶ 50% graduate within 6 years

General. Founded in 1919. Regionally accredited. Arrowhead University Center located on Minnesota's Mesabi Iron Range offers several degree programs. **Degrees:** 849 bachelor's, 53 associate awarded; master's offered. **Location:** 150 miles from Duluth, 230 miles from Minneapolis-St. Paul. **Calendar:** Semester, extensive summer session. **Full-time faculty:** 161 total; 77% have terminal degrees, 11% minority, 44% women. **Part-time faculty:** 110 total; 7% have terminal degrees, 4% minority, 59% women. **Class size:** 42% < 20, 46% 20-39, 5% 40-49, 5% 50-99, 2% >100. **Special facilities:** Freshwater aquatics laboratory, research center, forest and nature preserve.

Freshman class profile. 2,085 applied, 1,886 admitted, 822 enrolled.

Mid 50% test scores			
ACT composite:	19-24	Rank in top quarter:	24%
GPA 3.75 or higher:	10%	Rank in top tenth:	7%
GPA 3.50-3.74:	15%	Return as sophomores:	68%
GPA 3.0-3.49:	40%	Out-of-state:	9%
GPA 2.0-2.99:	33%	Live on campus:	84%
		International:	2%

Basis for selection. Rank in top half of class or test scores above 50th percentile preferred. ACT scores considered for applicants in bottom half of class. Composite score of 21 or higher preferred. Interview recommended. Audition recommended for music applicants; portfolio recommended for art

applicants. **Learning Disabled:** Students encouraged to identify themselves to Office of Disabilities to be apprised of services available.

High school preparation. College-preparatory program recommended. 16 units required. Required units include English 4, mathematics 3, social studies 3, science 3, foreign language 2 and academic electives 1. 1 unit of art, music, world culture required.

2011-2012 Annual costs. Tuition/fees: $7,855; $7,855 out-of-state. Room/board: $6,690. Books/supplies: $840. Personal expenses: $1,350.

2010-2011 Financial aid. Need-based: 756 full-time freshmen applied for aid; 561 were judged to have need; 556 of these received aid. Average need met was 68%. Average scholarship/grant was $5,524; average loan $3,385. 46% of total undergraduate aid awarded as scholarships/grants, 54% as loans/jobs. **Non-need-based:** Awarded to 2,602 full-time undergraduates, including 622 freshmen. Scholarships awarded for academics, alumni affiliation, art, athletics, job skills, leadership, minority status, music/drama, ROTC.

Application procedures. Admission: Priority date 2/1; no deadline. $20 fee, may be waived for applicants with need. Admission notification on a rolling basis. **Financial aid:** Priority date 4/15; no closing date. FAFSA, institutional form required. Applicants notified on a rolling basis starting 3/24.

Academics. Special study options: Combined bachelor's/graduate degree, cross-registration, distance learning, double major, dual enrollment of high school students, ESL, honors, independent study, internships, study abroad, teacher certification program. Exchange program with other Minnesota state universities, Euro-spring semester, Sino-summer semester. **Credit/placement by examination:** AP, CLEP, IB, ACT, institutional tests. Department defined number of hours of credit by examination may be counted towards degree. **Support services:** Learning center, reduced course load, remedial instruction, study skills assistance, tutoring, writing center.

Majors. Area/ethnic studies: Native American. **Biology:** General, aquatic. **Business:** Accounting, business admin, management information systems. **Communications:** Digital media, media studies. **Computer sciences:** General, computer science. **Conservation:** Environmental studies. **Education:** General, elementary, kindergarten/preschool, voc/tech. **Engineering:** Industrial. **English:** English lit. **Foreign languages:** German, Spanish. **Health services:** Clinical lab science, community health services. **History:** General. **Human services:** Social work. **Liberal arts:** Humanities. **Math:** General. **Parks/recreation:** Exercise sciences, sports admin. **Philosophy/religion:** Philosophy. **Physical sciences:** Chemistry, physics. **Protective services:** Criminal justice. **Psychology:** General. **Social sciences:** General, economics, geography, political science, sociology. **Visual/performing arts:** Art, commercial/advertising art, dramatic, music.

Most popular majors. Business/marketing 17%, education 20%, health sciences 9%, psychology 7%, security/protective services 6%, visual/performing arts 6%.

Computing on campus. 1,600 workstations in dormitories, library, computer center, student center. Dormitories wired for high-speed internet access and linked to campus network. Commuter students can connect to campus network. Online course registration, online library, helpline, repair service, student web hosting, wireless network available.

Student life. Freshman orientation: Available, $25 fee. Preregistration for classes offered. One-day orientation for students and parents. Student orientation program is also scheduled the weekend prior to first day of class. **Policies:** Zero tolerance for discrimination, racism, sexual violence, illegal activities including drug use. **Housing:** Coed dorms, special housing for disabled available. $150 partly refundable deposit, deadline 8/1. Single parents hall (includes child care facilities), quiet floors, hall/dorm for students older than average age available. **Activities:** Pep band, campus ministries, choral groups, dance, drama, film society, international student organizations, Model UN, musical theater, opera, radio station, student government, student newspaper, symphony orchestra, TV station, Newman Center, Lutheran center, Young Republicans, Young Democrats, social service organization, veterans club, Council of Indian Students, Black Student Coalition.

Athletics. NCAA. **Intercollegiate:** Baseball M, basketball, cross-country, football (tackle) M, golf, ice hockey, soccer W, softball W, tennis W, track and field W, volleyball W. **Intramural:** Badminton, baseball, basketball, field hockey, football (non-tackle), golf, ice hockey, racquetball, skiing, soccer, softball, table tennis, tennis, triathlon, volleyball, weight lifting M, wrestling M. **Team name:** Beavers.

Student services. Adult student services, alcohol/substance abuse counseling, chaplain/spiritual director, career counseling, services for economically disadvantaged, student employment services, financial aid counseling, health services, minority student services, on-campus daycare, personal counseling, placement for graduates, veterans' counselor, women's services. **Physically disabled:** Services for visually, speech, hearing impaired.

Contact. E-mail: admissions@bemidjistate.edu
Phone: (218) 755-2040 Toll-free number: (877) 236-4354
Fax: (218) 755-2390
Lincoln Morris, Director of Admissions, Bemidji State University, 102 Deputy Hall #13, Bemidji, MN 56601-2699

Bethany Lutheran College
Mankato, Minnesota
www.blc.edu   CB code: 6035

- Private 4-year liberal arts college affiliated with Evangelical Lutheran Synod
- Residential campus in large town
- 586 degree-seeking undergraduates: 2% part-time, 55% women, 2% African American, 1% Asian American, 3% Hispanic American, 1% international
- 84% of applicants admitted
- SAT or ACT (ACT writing optional), application essay required
- 42% graduate within 6 years; 25% enter graduate study

General. Founded in 1927. Regionally accredited. **Degrees:** 105 bachelor's awarded. **ROTC:** Army. **Location:** 80 miles from Minneapolis-St. Paul. **Calendar:** Semester. **Full-time faculty:** 38 total; 47% have terminal degrees, 3% minority, 21% women. **Part-time faculty:** 27 total; 15% have terminal degrees, 44% women. **Class size:** 72% < 20, 26% 20-39, 2% 40-49, less than 1% 50-99.

Freshman class profile. 452 applied, 381 admitted, 162 enrolled.

Mid 50% test scores		Rank in top tenth:	14%
ACT composite:	21-27	End year in good standing:	95%
GPA 3.75 or higher:	31%	Return as sophomores:	71%
GPA 3.50-3.74:	18%	Out-of-state:	31%
GPA 3.0-3.49:	31%	Live on campus:	91%
GPA 2.0-2.99:	20%	International:	1%
Rank in top quarter:	38%		

Basis for selection. College-prep GPA, overall GPA, test scores most important. **Learning Disabled:** Students with learning disabilities must meet with head of tutorial program.

High school preparation. College-preparatory program recommended. Recommended units include English 4, mathematics 3, social studies 3, history 3, science 3 (laboratory 1) and foreign language 2.

2011-2012 Annual costs. Tuition/fees: $22,280. Room/board: $7,000. Books/supplies: $900. Personal expenses: $2,000.

2010-2011 Financial aid. Need-based: 156 full-time freshmen applied for aid; 140 were judged to have need; 140 of these received aid. Average need met was 80%. Average scholarship/grant was $13,560; average loan $4,234. 66% of total undergraduate aid awarded as scholarships/grants, 34% as loans/jobs. **Non-need-based:** Awarded to 124 full-time undergraduates, including 34 freshmen. Scholarships awarded for academics, art, music/drama.

Application procedures. Admission: Closing date 7/1 (postmark date). No application fee. Admission notification on a rolling basis beginning on or about 9/15. Early admission only through the Post Secondary Options Program by the State of Minnesota. **Financial aid:** Priority date 4/15; no closing date. FAFSA, institutional form required. Applicants notified on a rolling basis starting 3/1; must reply within 4 week(s) of notification.

Academics. Special study options: Combined bachelor's/graduate degree, cross-registration, double major, dual enrollment of high school students, independent study, internships, student-designed major, study abroad, teacher certification program. **Credit/placement by examination:** AP, CLEP, IB, SAT, ACT, institutional tests. **Support services:** Reduced course load, remedial instruction, tutoring, writing center.

Majors. Biology: General, exercise physiology. **Business:** Business admin. **Communications:** Communications/speech/rhetoric. **Education:** Elementary. **English:** English lit. **History:** General. **Liberal arts:** Arts/sciences. **Math:** General. **Philosophy/religion:** Religion. **Physical sciences:** General, chemistry. **Psychology:** General. **Social sciences:** General, sociology. **Visual/performing arts:** Digital arts, dramatic, music, studio arts.

Most popular majors. Biology 13%, business/marketing 14%, communications/journalism 14%, education 7%, English 7%, psychology 10%, social sciences 7%, visual/performing arts 18%.

Computing on campus. 100 workstations in dormitories, library, computer center, student center. Dormitories wired for high-speed internet access

and linked to campus network. Commuter students can connect to campus network. Helpline, repair service, student web hosting, wireless network available.

Student life. Freshman orientation: Mandatory. Preregistration for classes offered. Orientation held weekly for 50 minutes during the first semester for first year, first time students. **Policies:** Freshmen and sophomores not living with family required to live on campus. **Housing:** Guaranteed on-campus for all undergraduates. Single-sex dorms, apartments, wellness housing available. **Activities:** Bands, choral groups, dance, drama, literary magazine, music ensembles, musical theater, student government, student newspaper, TV station, spiritual life committee, Lutherans for Life, student senate, Lambda Pi Eta, scholastic leadership society.

Athletics. NCAA. **Intercollegiate:** Baseball M, basketball, cross-country, golf, soccer, softball W, tennis, volleyball W. **Intramural:** Baseball M, basketball, football (non-tackle), soccer, softball, table tennis, tennis, volleyball. **Team name:** Vikings.

Student services. Chaplain/spiritual director, career counseling, financial aid counseling, health services, minority student services, personal counseling.

Contact. E-mail: admissions@blc.edu
Phone: (507) 344-7331 Toll-free number: (800) 944-3066
Fax: (507) 344-7376
Don Westphal, Dean of Admissions, Bethany Lutheran College, 700 Luther Drive, Mankato, MN 56001-4490

Bethel University
Saint Paul, Minnesota
www.bethel.edu

CB member
CB code: 6038

♦ Private 4-year university and liberal arts college affiliated with Baptist General Conference
♦ Residential campus in large city
♦ 3,396 degree-seeking undergraduates: 19% part-time, 62% women, 5% African American, 2% Asian American, 2% Hispanic American
♦ 1,872 degree-seeking graduate students
♦ 82% of applicants admitted
♦ SAT or ACT (ACT writing optional), application essay required
♦ 73% graduate within 6 years; 27% enter graduate study

General. Founded in 1871. Regionally accredited. **Degrees:** 811 bachelor's, 40 associate awarded; master's, professional, doctoral offered. **ROTC:** Army, Air Force. **Location:** 10 miles from Minneapolis-St. Paul. **Calendar:** Continuous, limited summer session. **Full-time faculty:** 185 total; 80% have terminal degrees, 4% minority, 44% women. **Part-time faculty:** 123 total; 28% have terminal degrees, 2% minority, 60% women. **Class size:** 46% < 20, 46% 20-39, 5% 40-49, 3% 50-99, 1% >100.

Freshman class profile. 2,314 applied, 1,905 admitted, 677 enrolled.

Mid 50% test scores		GPA 2.0-2.99:	15%
SAT critical reading:	500-670	Rank in top quarter:	57%
SAT math:	520-640	Rank in top tenth:	28%
ACT composite:	22-28	End year in good standing:	90%
GPA 3.75 or higher:	36%	Return as sophomores:	85%
GPA 3.50-3.74:	23%	Out-of-state:	25%
GPA 3.0-3.49:	26%	Live on campus:	96%

Basis for selection. Students must show academic ability based on standardized test scores and high school process toward graduation, must have high school diploma or GED, and have personal and character fit with the mission of BU.

High school preparation. College-preparatory program required. 14 units required. Required and recommended units include English 4, mathematics 3, social studies 4, history 2, science 3 (laboratory 2), foreign language 2, computer science 1 and visual/performing arts 1.

2011-2012 Annual costs. Tuition/fees: $29,460. Housing rate frozen as long as student continues to reside in campus housing. Room/board: $8,530. Books/supplies: $1,060. Personal expenses: $1,640.

2010-2011 Financial aid. Need-based: 509 full-time freshmen applied for aid; 448 were judged to have need; 448 of these received aid. Average need met was 78%. Average scholarship/grant was $17,239; average loan $3,904. 64% of total undergraduate aid awarded as scholarships/grants, 36% as loans/jobs. **Non-need-based:** Awarded to 731 full-time undergraduates, including 159 freshmen. Scholarships awarded for academics, alumni affiliation, art, leadership, music/drama, state residency.

Application procedures. Admission: Priority date 12/1; no deadline. No application fee. Admission notification on a rolling basis beginning on or about 10/1. **Financial aid:** Priority date 4/15; no closing date. FAFSA, institutional form required. Applicants notified on a rolling basis starting 2/1.

Academics. Tutoring labs offered in science, math, business, exercise science and general education, course support provided for Christianity & Western Culture; one on one tutoring available for any course if the student has been approved by their instructor. Multilingual support services provided (writing and speaking). Academic support counselors meet with students on a variety of study skill topics. **Special study options:** Combined bachelor's/ graduate degree, distance learning, double major, dual enrollment of high school students, exchange student, honors, independent study, internships, New York semester, semester at sea, student-designed major, study abroad, teacher certification program, urban semester, Washington semester. Dual degree program for engineering science with the University of Minnesota or other schools on individual basis. **Credit/placement by examination:** AP, CLEP, IB, institutional tests. 30 credit hours maximum toward associate degree, 30 toward bachelor's. **Support services:** Learning center, study skills assistance, tutoring, writing center.

Majors. Biology: General. **Business:** Accounting/finance, business admin, human resources, organizational behavior. **Communications:** Communications/speech/rhetoric, journalism, media studies. **Computer sciences:** General. **Conservation:** Environmental science, environmental studies. **Education:** General, art, biology, business, chemistry, early childhood, elementary, English, ESL, French, health, kindergarten/preschool, mathematics, middle, music, physical, physics, secondary, social studies, Spanish. **Engineering:** Engineering science. **English:** English lit. **Foreign languages:** French, linguistics, Spanish. **Health services:** Athletic training, nursing (RN). **History:** General. **Human services:** Social work. **Math:** General. **Parks/recreation:** Exercise sciences, health/fitness. **Philosophy/religion:** Philosophy. **Physical sciences:** Chemistry, physics. **Psychology:** General. **Social sciences:** General, economics, international relations, political science. **Theology:** Bible, sacred music, youth ministry. **Visual/performing arts:** Art, dramatic, music, music performance, studio arts.

Most popular majors. Business/marketing 17%, communications/journalism 8%, education 13%, health sciences 14%, psychology 8%.

Computing on campus. 420 workstations in dormitories, library, computer center, student center. Dormitories wired for high-speed internet access and linked to campus network. Commuter students can connect to campus network. Online course registration, online library, helpline, repair service, student web hosting, wireless network available.

Student life. Freshman orientation: Mandatory. Preregistration for classes offered. 2 days prior to the start of classes. **Policies:** High moral standards stressed. Use of tobacco and alcohol prohibited. Freshmen not permitted cars on campus. **Housing:** Guaranteed on-campus for freshmen. Coed dorms, special housing for disabled, apartments available. $150 fully refundable deposit. **Activities:** Bands, campus ministries, choral groups, dance, drama, film society, international student organizations, literary magazine, music ensembles, musical theater, radio station, student government, student newspaper, symphony orchestra, United Cultures of Bethel, College Republicans, College Democrats, Habitat for Humanity, dormitory discipleship programs, Mu Kappa (for students from missionary homes), Twin Cities Outreach.

Athletics. NCAA. **Intercollegiate:** Baseball M, basketball, cross-country, football (tackle) M, golf, ice hockey, soccer, softball W, tennis, track and field, volleyball W. **Intramural:** Badminton, basketball, football (non-tackle) M, ice hockey, softball, volleyball. **Team name:** Royals.

Student services. Adult student services, alcohol/substance abuse counseling, chaplain/spiritual director, career counseling, student employment services, financial aid counseling, health services, minority student services, on-campus daycare, personal counseling, placement for graduates, veterans' counselor, women's services. **Physically disabled:** Services for visually, speech, hearing impaired.

Contact. E-mail: buadmissions-cas@bethel.edu
Phone: (651) 638-6242 Toll-free number: (800) 255-8706 ext. 6242
Fax: (651) 635-1490
Jay Fedje, Director of Admissions, Bethel University, 3900 Bethel Dr., Saint Paul, MN 55112

Brown College: Brooklyn Center
Brooklyn Center, Minnesota
www.browncollege.edu

♦ For-profit 3-year branch campus college
♦ Very large city

General. Regionally accredited. **Calendar:** Quarter.

Contact. Phone: (763) 279-2549
Director of Admissions, 6860 Shingle Creek Parkway, Brooklyn Center, MN 55430

Brown College: Mendota Heights
Mendota Heights, Minnesota
www.browncollege.edu   **CB code: 1210**

- For-profit 4-year business and liberal arts college
- Commuter campus in small city

General. Founded in 1946. Regionally accredited. **Location:** 14 miles from Minneapolis-St. Paul. **Calendar:** Quarter.

Annual costs/financial aid. Books/supplies: $3,000. Personal expenses: $1,600.

Contact. Phone: (651) 905-3400
Vice President Admissions and Marketing, 1440 Northland Drive, Mendota Heights, MN 55120

Capella University
Minneapolis, Minnesota
www.capella.edu   **CB code: 3829**

- For-profit 4-year virtual university
- Commuter campus in very large city
- 7,476 degree-seeking undergraduates
- 28,888 graduate students

General. Regionally accredited. **Degrees:** 651 bachelor's awarded; master's, professional, doctoral offered. **Calendar:** Quarter, extensive summer session.

Basis for selection. Open admission, but selective for some programs. Applicants must be at least 24 years of age unless in military or unless they enter with 90 college level credits from previous institution. Bachelor's programs are completion programs for students who have associate degree or at least 90 quarter credits of undergraduate coursework completed. Requirements vary by degree.

2011-2012 Annual costs. Tuition/fees: $14,625.

Application procedures. **Admission:** No deadline. $50 fee. Admission notification on a rolling basis.

Academics. **Special study options:** Accelerated study, combined bachelor's/graduate degree, distance learning, double major, internships. **Credit/placement by examination:** AP, CLEP, IB. **Support services:** Learning center, tutoring, writing center.

Majors. **Business:** Accounting, finance, human resources, marketing. **Computer sciences:** Computer graphics, information technology, LAN/WAN management, security, web page design. **Health services:** Medical informatics, nursing (RN).

Most popular majors. Business/marketing 62%, computer/information sciences 32%.

Computing on campus. PC or laptop required.

Student life. **Freshman orientation:** Available. Preregistration for classes offered. Online seminar that provides students with knowledge, skills, and advice needed to be successful in Capella's online environment.

Student services. Adult student services, career counseling, financial aid counseling. **Physically disabled:** Services for visually, hearing impaired.

Contact. E-mail: info@capella.edu
Phone: (888) 227-2736
Capella University, 225 South Sixth Street, Capella Tower, Minneapolis, MN 55402

Carleton College
Northfield, Minnesota
www.carleton.edu   **CB member**
                                    CB code: 6081

- Private 4-year liberal arts college
- Residential campus in large town

- 2,000 degree-seeking undergraduates: 52% women, 4% African American, 7% Asian American, 6% Hispanic American, 8% international
- 31% of applicants admitted
- SAT or ACT with writing, application essay required
- 93% graduate within 6 years

General. Founded in 1866. Regionally accredited. Sustainability initiatives include green roofs, eco-building class, eco house built by students, 2 wind turbines. **Degrees:** 484 bachelor's awarded. **Location:** 35 miles from Minneapolis-St. Paul. **Calendar:** Trimester. **Full-time faculty:** 220 total; 97% have terminal degrees, 22% minority, 47% women. **Part-time faculty:** 23 total; 74% have terminal degrees, 9% minority, 30% women. **Class size:** 65% < 20, 33% 20-39, 1% 40-49, 1% 50-99. **Special facilities:** 880 acre arboretum, 35 acre virgin prairie, greenhouse, observatory, scanning and transmission electron microscope, refractor and reflector telescopes, nuclear magnet resonance spectrometer, center for creativity.

Freshman class profile. 4,988 applied, 1,546 admitted, 519 enrolled.

Mid 50% test scores			
SAT critical reading:	660-750	Rank in top tenth:	78%
SAT math:	660-760	Return as sophomores:	96%
SAT writing:	660-750	Out-of-state:	79%
ACT composite:	29-33	Live on campus:	100%
Rank in top quarter:	98%	International:	10%

Basis for selection. School achievement record and recommendations most important. Test scores, extracurricular school and community activities also important. SAT Subject Tests recommended. Interview recommended. **Learning Disabled:** Untimed standardized tests and GED accepted.

High school preparation. College-preparatory program recommended. Recommended units include English 4, mathematics 3, social studies 3, science 3 (laboratory 1) and foreign language 3. 3 units distributed between history and social sciences recommended.

2011-2012 Annual costs. Tuition/fees: $42,942. Room/board: $11,238. Books/supplies: $730. Personal expenses: $727.

2011-2012 Financial aid. All financial aid based on need. 401 full-time freshmen applied for aid; 287 were judged to have need; 287 of these received aid. Average need met was 100%. Average scholarship/grant was $30,503; average loan $4,377. 81% of total undergraduate aid awarded as scholarships/grants, 19% as loans/jobs. **Additional information:** Full financial need of all admitted applicants met through combination of work, loans, grants.

Application procedures. **Admission:** Closing date 1/15 (postmark date). $30 fee, may be waived for applicants with need, free for online applicants. Admission notification by 4/15. Must reply by May 1 or within 2 week(s) if notified thereafter. **Financial aid:** Closing date 2/15. FAFSA, CSS PROFILE required. Applicants notified by 4/1; must reply within 2 week(s) of notification.

Academics. **Special study options:** Accelerated study, cross-registration, double major, dual enrollment of high school students, independent study, internships, student-designed major, study abroad, teacher certification program, urban semester. **Credit/placement by examination:** AP, CLEP, IB, institutional tests. 36 credit hours maximum toward bachelor's degree. **Support services:** Learning center, tutoring, writing center.

Majors. **Area/ethnic studies:** African, African-American, American, Asian, Latin American, Russian/Slavic, women's. **Biology:** General. **Computer sciences:** Computer science. **English:** English lit. **Foreign languages:** Ancient Greek, classics, French, German, Hebrew, Latin, linguistics, Romance, Russian, Spanish. **History:** General. **Math:** General. **Philosophy/religion:** Philosophy, religion. **Physical sciences:** Chemistry, geology, physics. **Psychology:** General. **Social sciences:** Anthropology, economics, international relations, political science, sociology. **Visual/performing arts:** Art history/conservation, music, studio arts.

Most popular majors. Biology 9%, English 6%, history 6%, physical sciences 14%, psychology 6%, social sciences 23%, visual/performing arts 10%.

Computing on campus. 388 workstations in library, computer center, student center. Dormitories wired for high-speed internet access and linked to campus network. Online course registration, online library, helpline, repair service, student web hosting, wireless network available.

Student life. **Freshman orientation:** Mandatory. Preregistration for classes offered. 4 days prior to start of fall classes. **Policies:** Freshmen not permitted cars on campus. **Housing:** Guaranteed on-campus for all undergraduates. Coed dorms, special housing for disabled, apartments, wellness housing available. College-owned houses within 2 blocks of campus, some coeducational, with varying board options; several for special interest groups available. **Activities:** Bands, campus ministries, choral groups, dance, drama,

film society, international student organizations, literary magazine, music ensembles, Model UN, musical theater, radio station, student government, student newspaper, symphony orchestra, 132 registered student organizations.

Athletics. NCAA. **Intercollegiate:** Baseball M, basketball, cross-country, diving, football (tackle) M, golf, soccer, softball W, swimming, tennis, track and field, volleyball W, wrestling M. **Intramural:** Basketball, ice hockey, racquetball, soccer, softball, table tennis, tennis, triathlon, volleyball. **Team name:** Knights.

Student services. Alcohol/substance abuse counseling, chaplain/spiritual director, career counseling, student employment services, financial aid counseling, health services, minority student services, personal counseling, placement for graduates, women's services. **Physically disabled:** Services for visually, hearing impaired.

Contact. E-mail: admissions@carleton.edu
Phone: (507) 222-4190 Toll-free number: (800) 995-2275
Fax: (507) 222-4526
Paul Thiboutot, Vice President and Dean of Admissions and Financial Aid, Carleton College, 100 South College Street, Northfield, MN 55057

College of St. Benedict
St. Joseph, Minnesota   **CB member**
www.csbsju.edu   **CB code: 6104**

- Private 4-year liberal arts college for women affiliated with Roman Catholic Church
- Residential campus in small town
- 2,086 degree-seeking undergraduates: 2% part-time, 100% women, 1% African American, 5% Asian American, 3% Hispanic American, 1% Native American, 6% international
- 73% of applicants admitted
- SAT or ACT (ACT writing optional), application essay required
- 81% graduate within 6 years; 22% enter graduate study

General. Founded in 1887. Regionally accredited. CSB located six miles from St. John's University; students enrolled on both campuses have access to classes, activities and events held by the two institutions. **Degrees:** 479 bachelor's awarded. **ROTC:** Army. **Location:** 10 miles from St. Cloud, 70 miles from Minneapolis-St. Paul. **Calendar:** Semester, limited summer session. **Full-time faculty:** 170 total; 84% have terminal degrees, 10% minority, 51% women. **Part-time faculty:** 28 total; 29% have terminal degrees, 4% minority, 43% women. **Class size:** 55% < 20, 44% 20-39, less than 1% 40-49, less than 1% 50-99. **Special facilities:** Labyrinth, performing arts center, observatory, ecumenical center, hill museum and manuscript library, liturgical press, nature preserve, arboretum, natural history museum, pottery studio, kiln at St. John's University.

Freshman class profile. 1,972 applied, 1,444 admitted, 525 enrolled.

Mid 50% test scores			
SAT critical reading:	510-640	GPA 2.0-2.99:	1%
SAT math:	510-650	Rank in top quarter:	79%
SAT writing:	520-650	Rank in top tenth:	44%
ACT composite:	23-28	End year in good standing:	98%
GPA 3.75 or higher:	56%	Return as sophomores:	89%
GPA 3.50-3.74:	22%	Out-of-state:	17%
GPA 3.0-3.49:	21%	Live on campus:	100%
		International:	5%

Basis for selection. Course selection, scholastic achievement, GPA, test scores and essay are most important. Extracurricular involvement and recommendations are also important. Interview recommended for conditionally accepted/academically weak applicants. **Home schooled:** Applicants are not required to have a high school diploma but are required to provide appropriate documentation of college preparatory curriculum.

High school preparation. College-preparatory program required. 15 units required. Required and recommended units include English 4, mathematics 3, social studies 2, science 2 (laboratory 2), foreign language 2 and academic electives 4.

2011-2012 Annual costs. Tuition/fees: $34,308. Room/board: $8,956. Books/supplies: $1,000. Personal expenses: $1,300.

2011-2012 Financial aid. **Need-based:** 438 full-time freshmen applied for aid; 381 were judged to have need; 381 of these received aid. Average need met was 89%. Average scholarship/grant was $22,209; average loan $4,147. 63% of total undergraduate aid awarded as scholarships/grants, 37% as loans/jobs. **Non-need-based:** Awarded to 1,750 full-time undergraduates, including 459 freshmen. Scholarships awarded for academics, art, leadership, music/drama, ROTC. **Additional information:** Scholarship letters will be

mailed on a rolling basis approximately two weeks from the time the admission acceptance letter is sent.

Application procedures. **Admission:** Priority date 11/15; no deadline. No application fee. A non-refundable enrollment deposit of $300 is due May 1. **Financial aid:** Priority date 3/15; no closing date. FAFSA, institutional form required. Applicants notified on a rolling basis starting 3/15; must reply by 5/1.

Academics. **Special study options:** Combined bachelor's/graduate degree, cross-registration, double major, dual enrollment of high school students, ESL, honors, independent study, internships, student-designed major, study abroad, teacher certification program. 3-2 program in engineering with University of Minnesota, 3-1 program in dentistry with University of Minnesota, cross registration with St. Cloud State University. **Credit/placement by examination:** AP, CLEP, IB, SAT, ACT, institutional tests. **Support services:** Reduced course load, study skills assistance, tutoring, writing center.

Majors. **Area/ethnic studies:** Women's. **Biology:** General, biochemistry. **Business:** Accounting, business admin. **Computer sciences:** Computer science. **Conservation:** Environmental studies. **Education:** General, elementary. **English:** English lit, rhetoric/composition. **Foreign languages:** Classics, French, German, Spanish. **Health services:** Dietetics, nursing (RN), predental, premedicine, prepharmacy, preveterinary. **History:** General. **Liberal arts:** Arts/sciences, humanities. **Math:** General. **Philosophy/religion:** Philosophy. **Physical sciences:** Chemistry, physics. **Psychology:** General. **Social sciences:** General, economics, political science, sociology. **Theology:** Theology. **Visual/performing arts:** Art, dramatic, music.

Most popular majors. Biology 10%, business/marketing 12%, education 6%, English 16%, foreign language 7%, health sciences 8%, interdisciplinary studies 10%, psychology 11%.

Computing on campus. 940 workstations in dormitories, library, computer center, student center. Dormitories wired for high-speed internet access and linked to campus network. Commuter students can connect to campus network. Online course registration, online library, helpline, repair service, student web hosting, wireless network available.

Student life. **Freshman orientation:** Mandatory. Preregistration for classes offered. Fall orientation begins the evening of move-in day and concludes with convocation the first day of classes. **Policies:** There is a 4 year residency requirement. **Housing:** Guaranteed on-campus for freshmen. Special housing for disabled, apartments, wellness housing available. **Activities:** Bands, campus ministries, choral groups, dance, drama, international student organizations, literary magazine, music ensembles, Model UN, musical theater, opera, radio station, student government, student newspaper, symphony orchestra, Volunteers in Service to Others, College Republicans, College Democrats, Joint Events Council, Asia Club, Student Coalition for Global Solidarity, Students in Free Enterprise, Magis, Cultural Fusion Club, Outdoor Leadership Center.

Athletics. NCAA. **Intercollegiate:** Basketball W, cross-country W, diving W, golf W, ice hockey W, soccer W, softball W, swimming W, tennis W, track and field W, volleyball W. **Intramural:** Badminton W, basketball W, racquetball W, soccer W, softball W, table tennis W, tennis W, volleyball W. **Team name:** Blazers.

Student services. Alcohol/substance abuse counseling, chaplain/spiritual director, career counseling, financial aid counseling, health services, minority student services, personal counseling, placement for graduates, women's services. **Physically disabled:** Services for hearing impaired.

Contact. E-mail: admissions@csbsju.edu
Phone: (320) 363-5055 Toll-free number: (800) 544-1489
Fax: (320) 363-5650
Calvin Mosley, Vice President for Admission and Financial Aid, College of St. Benedict, College of St Benedict/St John's University, Collegeville, MN 56321-7155

College of St. Scholastica
Duluth, Minnesota   **CB member**
www.css.edu   **CB code: 6107**

- Private 4-year liberal arts college affiliated with Roman Catholic Church
- Residential campus in small city
- 2,838 degree-seeking undergraduates: 12% part-time, 68% women, 2% African American, 1% Asian American, 2% Hispanic American, 2% Native American, 4% international
- 1,132 degree-seeking graduate students
- 81% of applicants admitted

♦ SAT or ACT (ACT writing optional) required
♦ 65% graduate within 6 years; 39% enter graduate study

General. Founded in 1912. Regionally accredited. **Degrees:** 743 bachelor's awarded; master's, professional offered. **ROTC:** Air Force. **Location:** 2 miles from downtown, 150 miles from Minneapolis-St. Paul. **Calendar:** Semester, limited summer session. **Full-time faculty:** 171 total; 54% have terminal degrees, 10% minority, 61% women. **Part-time faculty:** 204 total. **Class size:** 51% < 20, 43% 20-39, 2% 40-49, 3% 50-99, less than 1% >100. **Special facilities:** Wellness center with climbing wall.

Freshman class profile. 1,806 applied, 1,466 admitted, 486 enrolled.

Mid 50% test scores			
SAT critical reading:	450-630	Rank in top quarter:	50%
SAT math:	470-580	Rank in top tenth:	18%
SAT writing:	440-600	End year in good standing:	97%
ACT composite:	21-26	Return as sophomores:	77%
GPA 3.75 or higher:	33%	Out-of-state:	14%
GPA 3.50-3.74:	23%	Live on campus:	88%
GPA 3.0-3.49:	30%	International:	5%
GPA 2.0-2.99:	13%		

Basis for selection. School achievement record and test scores most important. Interview recommended.

High school preparation. College-preparatory program required. Recommended units include English 4, mathematics 2, social studies 3, history 3, science 3 and foreign language 3.

2011-2012 Annual costs. Tuition/fees: $29,506. Room/board: $7,716. Books/supplies: $1,100. Personal expenses: $1,074.

2011-2012 Financial aid. Need-based: 450 full-time freshmen applied for aid; 406 were judged to have need; 405 of these received aid. Average need met was 72%. Average scholarship/grant was $7,135; average loan $3,789. 57% of total undergraduate aid awarded as scholarships/grants, 43% as loans/jobs. **Non-need-based:** Awarded to 1,766 full-time undergraduates, including 414 freshmen. Scholarships awarded for academics, alumni affiliation, minority status, music/drama, religious affiliation, ROTC, state residency.

Application procedures. Admission: No deadline. No application fee. Admission notification on a rolling basis beginning on or about 9/1. Must reply by May 1 or within 2 week(s) if notified thereafter. **Financial aid:** Priority date 3/1; no closing date. FAFSA required. Applicants notified on a rolling basis starting 3/1; must reply by 5/1 or within 2 week(s) of notification.

Academics. Special study options: Accelerated study, combined bachelor's/graduate degree, cross-registration, distance learning, double major, dual enrollment of high school students, external degree, honors, independent study, internships, liberal arts/career combination, student-designed major, study abroad, teacher certification program, Washington semester. **Credit/placement by examination:** AP, CLEP, IB, ACT, institutional tests. 96 credit hours maximum toward bachelor's degree. All external credit meeting score expectations will be accepted; last 32 semester hours must be completed in residence. **Support services:** Pre-admission summer program, reduced course load, study skills assistance, tutoring, writing center.

Honors college/program. Should meet 2 of the following: top 15% of high school class, 26 ACT or 1100 (exclusive of Writing) SAT, GPA of 3.5; others may apply by contacting the honors director. Students must complete 20 honors credits, at least 8 of which are upper division level credits.

Majors. Biology: General, biochemistry, exercise physiology. **Business:** Accounting, business admin, finance, marketing, organizational behavior. **Communications:** Advertising, communications/speech/rhetoric, journalism. **Computer sciences:** General. **Education:** Elementary, multi-level teacher, Native American, school librarian, social science. **English:** English lit. **Foreign languages:** Spanish. **Health services:** Medical records admin, nursing (RN). **History:** General. **Human services:** Social work. **Liberal arts:** Humanities. **Math:** General. **Philosophy/religion:** Christian, religion. **Physical sciences:** Chemistry. **Psychology:** General. **Social sciences:** General, applied economics. **Visual/performing arts:** Art, music performance.

Most popular majors. Biology 9%, business/marketing 30%, health sciences 34%, public administration/social services 6%.

Computing on campus. 394 workstations in dormitories, library, computer center, student center. Dormitories wired for high-speed internet access and linked to campus network. Commuter students can connect to campus network. Online course registration, online library, helpline, student web hosting, wireless network available.

Student life. Freshman orientation: Mandatory. Preregistration for classes offered. **Housing:** Guaranteed on-campus for freshmen. Coed dorms, special housing for disabled, apartments, wellness housing available. $150 fully refundable deposit. Pets allowed in dorm rooms. Quiet or study wing; housing for students with dependent children. **Activities:** Bands, campus ministries, choral groups, dance, drama, international student organizations, literary magazine, music ensembles, student government, student newspaper, TV station, Circle-K, InterVarsity Christian Fellowship, Indigenous Students' Association, Benedictine Friends, Volunteers Involved Through Action, Amnesty International, Kaleidoscope Multicultural Club, Habitat for Humanity, United for Africa, Earth Action.

Athletics. NCAA. **Intercollegiate:** Baseball M, basketball, cross-country, football (tackle) M, ice hockey, skiing, soccer, softball W, tennis, track and field, volleyball W. **Intramural:** Badminton, basketball, bowling, football (non-tackle), softball, tennis, volleyball. **Team name:** Saints.

Student services. Adult student services, alcohol/substance abuse counseling, chaplain/spiritual director, career counseling, student employment services, financial aid counseling, health services, minority student services, personal counseling, placement for graduates, veterans' counselor, women's services. **Physically disabled:** Services for visually, hearing impaired.

Contact. E-mail: admissions@css.edu
Phone: (218) 723-6046 Toll-free number: (800) 249-6412
Fax: (218) 723-5991
Eric Berg, Vice President for Enrollment Management, College of St. Scholastica, 1200 Kenwood Avenue, Duluth, MN 55811-4199

College of Visual Arts
Saint Paul, Minnesota
www.cva.edu   CB code: 6147

♦ Private 4-year visual arts college
♦ Commuter campus in large city
♦ 201 degree-seeking undergraduates: 74% women
♦ 76% of applicants admitted
♦ SAT or ACT (ACT writing optional), application essay required
♦ 45% graduate within 6 years

General. Founded in 1924. Regionally accredited. **Degrees:** 42 bachelor's awarded. **Calendar:** Semester, limited summer session. **Full-time faculty:** 9 total; 22% have terminal degrees, 56% women. **Part-time faculty:** 42 total; 12% have terminal degrees, 2% minority, 55% women. **Class size:** 92% < 20, 8% 20-39. **Special facilities:** Exhibition gallery, traditional black and white, color, digital, and alternative photographic methods photography facilities, sculpture studio, printmaking studio, drawing studio, painting studio and 5 digital labs.

Freshman class profile. 153 applied, 117 admitted, 63 enrolled.

End year in good standing:	88%	Out-of-state:	11%
Return as sophomores:	71%		

Basis for selection. Statement of interest, ACT of SAT score, secondary and post-secondary transcripts, and portfolio. Students with 30+ college credits are not required to submit ACT or SAT scores. **Home schooled:** Transcript of courses and grades, letter of recommendation (nonparent) required. Course and textbook list required. **Learning Disabled:** Documentation of disabilities required.

High school preparation. Recommended units include English 4, mathematics 4, social studies 4, science 4 and visual/performing arts 2. Progression of classes in art preferred.

2011-2012 Annual costs. Tuition/fees: $24,810. Books/supplies: $2,595.

Financial aid. Non-need-based: Scholarships awarded for academics, art.

Application procedures. Admission: Priority date 3/1; deadline 8/1 (postmark date). $40 fee, may be waived for applicants with need. Admission notification on a rolling basis. **Financial aid:** Priority date 3/1; no closing date. FAFSA, institutional form required. Applicants notified on a rolling basis starting 2/15; must reply within 2 week(s) of notification.

Academics. Special study options: Honors, independent study, internships, study abroad. **Credit/placement by examination:** AP, CLEP, SAT, ACT. **Support services:** Learning center, study skills assistance, tutoring, writing center.

Majors. Visual/performing arts: Drawing, fashion design, graphic design, illustration, painting, photography, printmaking, sculpture, studio arts.

Computing on campus. 50 workstations in library, computer center. Online library, helpline, wireless network available.

Student life. Freshman orientation: Mandatory. Preregistration for classes offered. **Housing:** Housing coordinator and roommate matching services available. **Activities:** Student government.

Student services. Alcohol/substance abuse counseling, career counseling, services for economically disadvantaged, student employment services, financial aid counseling, minority student services, personal counseling, placement for graduates.

Contact. E-mail: admissions@cva.edu
Phone: (651) 757-4040 Toll-free number: (800) 224-1536
Fax: (651) 757-4010
Elyan Paz, Director of Admissions, College of Visual Arts, 344 Summit Avenue, Saint Paul, MN 55102-2199

Concordia College: Moorhead

Moorhead, Minnesota — CB member
www.ConcordiaCollege.edu — CB code: 6113

- Private 4-year business and liberal arts college affiliated with Evangelical Lutheran Church in America
- Residential campus in small city
- 2,667 degree-seeking undergraduates: 1% part-time, 62% women, 2% African American, 2% Asian American, 1% Hispanic American, 3% international
- 26 degree-seeking graduate students
- 95% of applicants admitted
- SAT or ACT (ACT writing optional) required
- 69% graduate within 6 years; 23% enter graduate study

General. Founded in 1891. Regionally accredited. **Degrees:** 605 bachelor's awarded; master's offered. **ROTC:** Army, Air Force. **Location:** 234 miles from Minneapolis-St. Paul, 1 mile from Fargo, North Dakota. **Calendar:** Semester, limited summer session. **Full-time faculty:** 181 total; 83% have terminal degrees, 6% minority, 46% women. **Part-time faculty:** 76 total; 30% have terminal degrees, 4% minority, 53% women. **Class size:** 44% < 20, 51% 20-39, 3% 40-49, 2% 50-99. **Special facilities:** Observatory, 2MeV hypervelocity dust particle accelerator, language villages, television production studio, field biology research facility, nursing lab, laser facility.

Freshman class profile. 2,150 applied, 2,033 admitted, 722 enrolled.

Mid 50% test scores			
SAT critical reading:	530-650	Rank in top quarter:	65%
SAT math:	530-650	Rank in top tenth:	37%
ACT composite:	22-28	Return as sophomores:	85%
GPA 3.75 or higher:	45%	Out-of-state:	27%
GPA 3.50-3.74:	21%	Live on campus:	97%
GPA 3.0-3.49:	26%	International:	2%
GPA 2.0-2.99:	8%		

Basis for selection. Academic record (types of courses and grades) most important, followed by test scores and recommendations. Interview recommended. **Home schooled:** Transcript of courses and grades, letter of recommendation (nonparent) required.

High school preparation. College-preparatory program recommended. Recommended units include English 4, mathematics 3, social studies 3, science 3, foreign language 2, computer science 1 and visual/performing arts 1.

2011-2012 Annual costs. Tuition/fees: $29,360. Room/board: $6,790. Books/supplies: $900. Personal expenses: $1,170.

2010-2011 Financial aid. Need-based: 625 full-time freshmen applied for aid; 534 were judged to have need; 533 of these received aid. Average need met was 92%. Average scholarship/grant was $17,626; average loan $6,012. 65% of total undergraduate aid awarded as scholarships/grants, 35% as loans/jobs. **Non-need-based:** Awarded to 857 full-time undergraduates, including 206 freshmen. Scholarships awarded for academics, art, leadership, minority status, music/drama.

Application procedures. Admission: No deadline. $20 fee, may be waived for applicants with need, free for online applicants. Admission notification on a rolling basis beginning on or about 6/15. **Financial aid:** No deadline. FAFSA required. Applicants notified on a rolling basis starting 3/15.

Academics. Special study options: Cooperative education, double major, exchange student, honors, independent study, internships, liberal arts/career combination, study abroad, teacher certification program, urban semester, Washington semester. University of Dar es Salaam, Lutheran College Consortium for Tanzania; a wide variety of global education opportunities including exploration seminars, summer field studies, semester and year long programs, May seminars, summer school abroad, summer research abroad, music ensemble tours, global cooperative education, and student teacher placements.

Credit/placement by examination: AP, CLEP, IB, institutional tests. 20 credit hours maximum toward bachelor's degree. **Support services:** Learning center, reduced course load, study skills assistance, tutoring, writing center.

Majors. Area/ethnic studies: Scandinavian. **Biology:** General. **Business:** Accounting, business admin, international, management information systems. **Communications:** General. **Computer sciences:** General. **Conservation:** Environmental studies. **Education:** Art, biology, business, chemistry, elementary, foreign languages, French, German, health, Latin, mathematics, music, physical, physics, social studies, Spanish. **English:** English lit. **Foreign languages:** Chinese, classics, French, German, Latin, Spanish. **Health services:** Nursing (RN). **History:** General. **Human services:** Social work. **Liberal arts:** Humanities. **Math:** General. **Parks/recreation:** Health/fitness. **Philosophy/religion:** Philosophy, religion. **Physical sciences:** Chemistry, physics. **Psychology:** General. **Social sciences:** General, political science, sociology. **Visual/performing arts:** Art, dramatic, music, music performance, music theory/composition.

Most popular majors. Biology 9%, business/marketing 11%, communications/journalism 9%, education 13%, foreign language 7%, psychology 6%, social sciences 9%, visual/performing arts 7%.

Computing on campus. 570 workstations in dormitories, library, computer center, student center. Dormitories wired for high-speed internet access and linked to campus network. Commuter students can connect to campus network. Online course registration, online library, helpline, repair service, student web hosting, wireless network available.

Student life. Freshman orientation: Mandatory. Preregistration for classes offered. 4-day program prior to the beginning of Fall semester classes. **Housing:** Guaranteed on-campus for freshmen. Coed dorms, single-sex dorms, apartments, wellness housing available. $200 fully refundable deposit, deadline 8/1. Students studying Spanish, French or German have an opportunity to live with native speakers in campus apartments. **Activities:** Bands, campus ministries, choral groups, dance, drama, international student organizations, literary magazine, music ensembles, musical theater, radio station, student government, student newspaper, symphony orchestra, TV station, over 100 clubs and organizations.

Athletics. NCAA. **Intercollegiate:** Baseball M, basketball, cross-country, diving W, football (tackle) M, golf, ice hockey, soccer, softball W, swimming W, tennis, track and field, volleyball W, wrestling M. **Intramural:** Basketball, bowling, football (non-tackle) M, swimming, volleyball. **Team name:** Cobbers.

Student services. Alcohol/substance abuse counseling, chaplain/spiritual director, career counseling, student employment services, financial aid counseling, health services, minority student services, on-campus daycare, personal counseling, placement for graduates. **Physically disabled:** Services for visually, speech, hearing impaired.

Contact. E-mail: admissions@cord.edu
Phone: (218) 299-3004 Toll-free number: (800) 699-9897
Fax: (218) 299-4720
Scott Ellingson, Admissions Director, Concordia College: Moorhead, 901 Eighth Street South, Moorhead, MN 56562

Concordia University St. Paul

Saint Paul, Minnesota — CB member
www.csp.edu — CB code: 6114

- Private 4-year university affiliated with Lutheran Church - Missouri Synod
- Residential campus in large city
- 1,376 degree-seeking undergraduates: 30% part-time, 59% women, 12% African American, 6% Asian American, 4% Hispanic American
- 1,108 degree-seeking graduate students
- 56% of applicants admitted
- SAT or ACT (ACT writing optional) required
- 46% graduate within 6 years

General. Founded in 1893. Regionally accredited. **Degrees:** 405 bachelor's, 3 associate awarded; master's offered. **ROTC:** Army, Naval, Air Force. **Location:** 2 miles from downtown Minneapolis and St. Paul. **Calendar:** Semester, limited summer session. **Full-time faculty:** 80 total; 66% have terminal degrees, 9% minority, 48% women. **Part-time faculty:** 248 total; 31% have terminal degrees, 6% minority, 52% women. **Class size:** 74% < 20, 25% 20-39, less than 1% 40-49.

Freshman class profile. 1,062 applied, 600 admitted, 197 enrolled.

Mid 50% test scores		Rank in top quarter:	31%
ACT composite:	18-24	Rank in top tenth:	13%
GPA 3.75 or higher:	16%	End year in good standing:	73%
GPA 3.50-3.74:	16%	Return as sophomores:	67%
GPA 3.0-3.49:	26%	Out-of-state:	19%
GPA 2.0-2.99:	41%	Live on campus:	79%

Basis for selection. School record, test scores, recommendations important. ACT preferred. Interview recommended.

High school preparation. 15 units required; 16 recommended. Required and recommended units include English 4, mathematics 2, social studies 1, history 1, science 2 (laboratory 2) and foreign language 1. 2 units of fine arts, 1 unit of health/physical education.

2012-2013 Annual costs. Tuition/fees: $29,700. Room/board: $7,750. Books/supplies: $1,400. Personal expenses: $1,032.

2011-2012 Financial aid. Need-based: 195 full-time freshmen applied for aid; 175 were judged to have need; 175 of these received aid. Average need met was 75%. Average scholarship/grant was $19,547; average loan $3,457. 59% of total undergraduate aid awarded as scholarships/grants, 41% as loans/jobs. **Non-need-based:** Awarded to 214 full-time undergraduates, including 45 freshmen. Scholarships awarded for academics, art, athletics, minority status, music/drama, religious affiliation. **Additional information:** Church districts and local congregations are major sources of aid for church-vocation students.

Application procedures. Admission: Priority date 5/1; deadline 8/1 (receipt date). $30 fee, may be waived for applicants with need. Admission notification on a rolling basis. **Financial aid:** Priority date 5/1; no closing date. FAFSA, institutional form required. Applicants notified on a rolling basis starting 3/1.

Academics. Offers a variety of non-traditional undergraduate degree completion programs designed for working adults in both face-to-face and distance education formats. Approximately 33% of the undergraduates fall into this non-traditional category. **Special study options:** Accelerated study, cross-registration, distance learning, double major, dual enrollment of high school students, exchange student, honors, independent study, internships, student-designed major, study abroad, teacher certification program. **Credit/placement by examination:** AP, CLEP, IB, ACT, institutional tests. **Support services:** Learning center, reduced course load, remedial instruction, study skills assistance, tutoring, writing center.

Majors. Biology: General. **Business:** Accounting, business admin, finance, human resources, marketing, sales/distribution. **Communications:** Media studies. **Education:** Art, bilingual, biology, chemistry, early childhood, elementary, English, ESL, health, history, kindergarten/preschool, mathematics, middle, music, physical, science, secondary, social studies. **English:** Creative writing, English lit, general lit, technical writing. **Health services:** Athletic training, respiratory therapy technology. **History:** General. **Math:** General. **Parks/recreation:** Exercise sciences, health/fitness, sports studies. **Protective services:** Criminal justice. **Psychology:** General. **Social sciences:** Sociology. **Theology:** Missionary, religious ed, sacred music, theology. **Visual/performing arts:** Art, design, dramatic, graphic design, music, studio arts. **Work/family studies:** Child development, family studies.

Most popular majors. Business/marketing 53%, education 10%.

Computing on campus. 6 workstations in dormitories, library, computer center, student center. Dormitories wired for high-speed internet access and linked to campus network. Commuter students can connect to campus network. Online library, helpline, repair service, wireless network available.

Student life. Freshman orientation: Mandatory. Preregistration for classes offered. 3-day program prior to start of fall semester provides information about student life, support services, social programs, employment opportunities, and technology training. **Housing:** Guaranteed on-campus for freshmen. Coed dorms, single-sex dorms, special housing for disabled, apartments, wellness housing available. $125 deposit. **Activities:** Bands, campus ministries, choral groups, dance, drama, music ensembles, musical theater, student government, student newspaper, TV station, Fellowship of Christian Athletes, Southeast Asian student association, United Minds of Joint Action, student senate, mission society.

Athletics. NCAA. **Intercollegiate:** Baseball M, basketball, cross-country, football (tackle) M, golf, soccer W, softball W, track and field, volleyball W. **Intramural:** Basketball, cheerleading, racquetball, softball, volleyball. **Team name:** Golden Bears.

Student services. Adult student services, alcohol/substance abuse counseling, chaplain/spiritual director, career counseling, services for economically disadvantaged, student employment services, financial aid counseling,

health services, minority student services, on-campus daycare, personal counseling, placement for graduates, veterans' counselor. **Physically disabled:** Services for visually, speech, hearing impaired.

Contact. E-mail: admission@csp.edu
Phone: (651) 641-8230 Toll-free number: (800) 333-4705
Fax: (651) 603-6320
Kristin Schoon, Director of Undergraduate Admission, Concordia University St. Paul, 275 Syndicate Street North, St. Paul, MN 55104-5494

Crossroads College
Rochester, Minnesota
www.crossroadscollege.edu   **CB code: 6412**

- Private 4-year Bible college affiliated with Christian Church
- Residential campus in small city
- 160 degree-seeking undergraduates
- SAT or ACT (ACT writing recommended), application essay required

General. Founded in 1913. Accredited by ABHE. Offers degree completion program with evening and online courses available. **Degrees:** 33 bachelor's, 6 associate awarded. **Location:** 85 miles from Minneapolis-St. Paul. **Calendar:** Semester, limited summer session. **Full-time faculty:** 9 total. **Part-time faculty:** 14 total. **Class size:** 79% < 20, 16% 20-39, 2% 40-49, 4% 50-99. **Special facilities:** Nature trails, pond.

Freshman class profile.

Rank in top quarter:	58%	Live on campus:	86%
Out-of-state:	28%		

Basis for selection. High school rank, experience, aptitude for Christian ministry, character references, and personal statement of goals considered. High school GPA, rank and ACT/SAT scores determine number of credit hours a student may take during first semester if accepted. Interview recommended. **Learning Disabled:** Provide Vice President of Student Development with verification of learning disability.

2011-2012 Annual costs. Tuition/fees: $15,280. Room only: $4,070. Books/supplies: $800. Personal expenses: $1,500.

Financial aid. Non-need-based: Scholarships awarded for academics, leadership, music/drama, religious affiliation.

Application procedures. Admission: Closing date 8/15 (receipt date). $30 fee. Admission notification on a rolling basis. **Financial aid:** Priority date 4/1; no closing date. FAFSA, institutional form required. Applicants notified on a rolling basis starting 2/1; must reply within 4 week(s) of notification.

Academics. Minors in religious music, counseling psychology, biblical and classical languages, missions, youth ministries. **Special study options:** Accelerated study, distance learning, double major, independent study, internships, liberal arts/career combination, student-designed major. **Credit/placement by examination:** AP, CLEP, SAT, ACT, institutional tests. 30 credit hours maximum toward bachelor's degree. **Support services:** Reduced course load, remedial instruction, study skills assistance, tutoring, writing center.

Majors. Business: Business admin, nonprofit/public. **Psychology:** Counseling. **Theology:** Missionary, religious ed, sacred music, theology, youth ministry. **Visual/performing arts:** Music.

Computing on campus. 17 workstations in library, computer center, student center. Dormitories wired for high-speed internet access. Online course registration, repair service, wireless network available.

Student life. Freshman orientation: Mandatory. Preregistration for classes offered. 2-day session with some placement testing in August; one-day session in January. **Policies:** Attendance required at weekly Chapel and Spiritual Formation Group meetings; Field Service participation required. Religious observance required. **Housing:** Guaranteed on-campus for freshmen. Single-sex dorms, special housing for disabled, apartments, wellness housing available. **Activities:** Choral groups, drama, music ensembles, student government, student newspaper, Christians outdoors, ambassadors group, international students fellowship.

Athletics. Intercollegiate: Basketball, golf M, soccer M, volleyball W. **Intramural:** Bowling, golf, ice hockey, racquetball, skiing, soccer W, swimming, table tennis, tennis, volleyball. **Team name:** Knights.

Student services. Adult student services, chaplain/spiritual director, career counseling, student employment services, financial aid counseling, personal counseling, placement for graduates, veterans' counselor.

Contact. E-mail: admissions@crossroads.edu
Phone: (507) 288-4563 ext. 313 Toll-free number: (800) 456-7651
Fax: (507) 288-9046
Chris Williams, Director of Admissions, Crossroads College, 920
Mayowood Road, SW, Rochester, MN 55902

Crown College
St. Bonifacius, Minnesota
www.crown.edu   **CB code: 6639**

◆ Private 4-year liberal arts college affiliated with Christian and Missionary Alliance
◆ Residential campus in small town
◆ 991 degree-seeking undergraduates
◆ 245 graduate students
◆ 78% of applicants admitted
◆ SAT or ACT (ACT writing optional), application essay required

General. Founded in 1916. Regionally accredited. **Degrees:** 226 bachelor's,
14 associate awarded; master's offered. **ROTC:** Army. **Location:** 25 miles
from Minneapolis-St. Paul. **Calendar:** Semester, limited summer session.
Full-time faculty: 31 total; 48% have terminal degrees, 3% minority, 26%
women. **Part-time faculty:** 82 total; 50% women. **Class size:** 68% < 20,
25% 20-39, 5% 40-49, 3% 50-99. **Special facilities:** Nursing lab with SIM
man and other mannequins, 18-hole disc golf course.

Freshman class profile. 453 applied, 352 admitted, 158 enrolled.

Mid 50% test scores			
SAT critical reading:	510-600	GPA 3.0-3.49:	37%
SAT math:	480-600	GPA 2.0-2.99:	16%
SAT writing:	530-620	Rank in top quarter:	38%
ACT composite:	21-25	Rank in top tenth:	13%
GPA 3.75 or higher:	26%	Return as sophomores:	63%
GPA 3.50-3.74:	20%	Out-of-state:	33%
		Live on campus:	94%

Basis for selection. Applicants must profess personal faith in Jesus Christ.
Academic records and test scores important. **Learning Disabled:** Applicant
should meet with director of academic support.

High school preparation. College-preparatory program recommended.
Recommended units include English 4, mathematics 3, social studies 3,
science 3 and foreign language 2.

2012-2013 Annual costs. Tuition/fees: $22,100. Room/board: $7,480.
Books/supplies: $1,140. Personal expenses: $2,500.

Financial aid. Non-need-based: Scholarships awarded for academics,
alumni affiliation, leadership, minority status, music/drama, religious affiliation.

Application procedures. Admission: Closing date 8/18 (postmark date).
$20 fee, may be waived for applicants with need. Admission notification on
a rolling basis. Within 30 days of acceptance notification. **Financial aid:**
Priority date 4/1, closing date 8/1. FAFSA required. Applicants notified on
a rolling basis starting 4/1; must reply within 3 week(s) of notification.

Academics. Special study options: Accelerated study, distance learning,
double major, dual enrollment of high school students, ESL, exchange student,
honors, independent study, internships, liberal arts/career combination, study
abroad, teacher certification program, urban semester, weekend college. 2-
2 with non-accredited Bible colleges. **Credit/placement by examination:**
AP, CLEP, IB, SAT, ACT. 30 credit hours maximum toward associate degree,
30 toward bachelor's. **Support services:** Learning center, reduced course
load, remedial instruction, study skills assistance, tutoring, writing center.

Majors. Biology: General. **Business:** General, business admin, entrepreneurial studies, operations. **Communications:** General, advertising, digital
media, persuasive communications. **Education:** Early childhood, elementary,
English, ESL, music, physical, science, secondary, social studies. **English:**
English lit. **Foreign languages:** Linguistics. **History:** General. **Liberal arts:**
Arts/sciences. **Parks/recreation:** Sports admin. **Psychology:** General, counseling. **Social sciences:** Urban studies. **Theology:** Bible, missionary, pastoral
counseling, religious ed, theology, youth ministry. **Visual/performing arts:**
Music, music performance.

Most popular majors. Business/marketing 7%, communications/journal-
ism 8%, education 20%, health sciences 16%, psychology 7%, theological
studies 30%.

Computing on campus. 105 workstations in library, computer center.
Dormitories wired for high-speed internet access and linked to campus network. Commuter students can connect to campus network. Online library,
helpline, repair service, wireless network available.

Student life. Freshman orientation: Mandatory. Preregistration for
classes offered. 2-day orientation program at the beginning of the spring
semester, 4 days prior to fall semester. **Policies:** Must abide by Crown College
Covenant. Religious observance required. **Housing:** Guaranteed on-campus
for all undergraduates. Single-sex dorms, special housing for disabled, apartments, wellness housing available. $150 fully refundable deposit. **Activities:**
Bands, campus ministries, choral groups, dance, drama, film society, international student organizations, literary magazine, music ensembles, musical
theater, radio station, student government, student newspaper, Hmong student
fellowship, Hispanic/Spanish club, multi-cultural committee, African-
American club, Team Managers' club, Student Family Association, outdoor
adventure club, The Session (skiing & snowboarding), Students in Free
Enterprise, College Conservatives.

Athletics. NCAA. **Intercollegiate:** Baseball M, basketball, cross-country,
football (tackle) M, golf, soccer, softball W, volleyball W. **Intramural:**
Basketball, soccer, softball, volleyball. **Team name:** Storm.

Student services. Adult student services, chaplain/spiritual director,
career counseling, student employment services, financial aid counseling,
health services, personal counseling. **Physically disabled:** Services for visually, hearing impaired.

Contact. E-mail: admissions@crown.edu
Phone: (952) 446-4142 Toll-free number: (800) 682-7696
Fax: (952) 446-4149
Jim Hunter, Director of Admissions, Crown College, 8700 College View
Drive, St. Bonifacius, MN 55375-9001

Globe University: Minneapolis
Minneapolis, Minnesota
www.globeuniversity.edu

◆ For-profit 4-year university and career college
◆ Large city
◆ 347 degree-seeking undergraduates

General. Regionally accredited; also accredited by ACICS. **Degrees:** 6
bachelor's, 10 associate awarded; master's, doctoral offered. **Calendar:** Quarter. **Full-time faculty:** 9 total. **Part-time faculty:** 22 total.

Basis for selection. Open admission.

Application procedures. Admission: No deadline. $50 fee. **Financial
aid:** No deadline.

Academics. Credit/placement by examination: AP, CLEP.

Majors. Business: Business admin. **Health services:** Health care admin.
Protective services: Police science.

Contact. Toll-free number: (877) 455-3697 Fax: (612) 455-3001
Adam Schefers, Director of Admissions, Globe University: Minneapolis,
80 South 8th Street, Minneapolis, MN 55402

Globe University: Woodbury
Woodbury, Minnesota
www.globeuniversity.edu   **CB code: 2296**

◆ For-profit 4-year business and health science college
◆ Commuter campus in small city
◆ 1,435 degree-seeking undergraduates
◆ Interview required

General. Accredited by ACICS. **Degrees:** 81 bachelor's, 168 associate
awarded; master's offered. **Location:** 8 miles from Minneapolis-St. Paul.
Calendar: Quarter, extensive summer session. **Full-time faculty:** 24 total.
Part-time faculty: 43 total. **Class size:** 87% < 20, 13% 20-39. **Special
facilities:** Music business labs, medical assisting labs, health fitness labs,
research vet tech facility with full AVMA accreditation.

Basis for selection. Open admission. **Learning Disabled:** Interview with
Dean of Students.

2011-2012 Annual costs. Tuition/fees: $19,575. Books/supplies: $1,620.
Personal expenses: $2,628.

Application procedures. Admission: No deadline. $50 fee. Admission
notification on a rolling basis. **Financial aid:** No deadline. FAFSA, institutional form required. Applicants notified on a rolling basis starting 5/1.

Academics. Special study options: Distance learning, honors, independent study, internships, liberal arts/career combination. **Credit/placement by examination:** AP, CLEP, institutional tests. **Support services:** Learning center, reduced course load, remedial instruction, study skills assistance, tutoring, writing center.

Majors. Business: Accounting, business admin. **Computer sciences:** General, information technology, LAN/WAN management, security, system admin, web page design. **Engineering:** Software. **General:** Animal sciences. **Health services:** Office admin. **Parks/recreation:** Exercise sciences.

Computing on campus. 173 workstations in library, computer center, student center. Commuter students can connect to campus network. Online course registration, online library, helpline, repair service, wireless network available.

Student life. Freshman orientation: Mandatory. Preregistration for classes offered. Day and evening sessions available the week prior to classes starting. **Activities:** Student government, student newspaper, Vet Tech club, Medical Assisting club, paralegal club, accounting club, business/professional club.

Student services. Career counseling, services for economically disadvantaged, student employment services, financial aid counseling, placement for graduates. **Physically disabled:** Services for visually, speech, hearing impaired.

Contact. E-mail: admissions@globeuniversity.edu
Phone: (651) 730-5100 Toll-free number: (800) 231-0660
Fax: (651) 730-5151
Jessica McCabe, Director of Admissions, Globe University: Woodbury, 8089 Globe Drive, Woodbury, MN 55125

Gustavus Adolphus College
St. Peter, Minnesota
www.gustavus.edu

CB member
CB code: 6253

- Private 4-year liberal arts college affiliated with Evangelical Lutheran Church in America
- Residential campus in small town
- 2,442 degree-seeking undergraduates: 56% women, 3% African American, 5% Asian American, 3% Hispanic American, 2% international
- 64% of applicants admitted
- Application essay required
- 82% graduate within 6 years

General. Founded in 1862. Regionally accredited. **Degrees:** 588 bachelor's awarded. **ROTC:** Army. **Location:** 65 miles from Minneapolis-St. Paul, 10 miles from Mankato. **Calendar:** 4-1-4, limited summer session. **Full-time faculty:** 201 total; 89% have terminal degrees, 14% minority, 47% women. **Part-time faculty:** 68 total; 43% have terminal degrees, 2% minority, 50% women. **Class size:** 54% < 20, 39% 20-39, 6% 40-49, 2% 50-99. **Special facilities:** Arboretum with walking and skiing paths, theme gardens, native woods and prairies, art museum, interpretive center.

Freshman class profile. 4,818 applied, 3,088 admitted, 727 enrolled.

Mid 50% test scores			
SAT critical reading:	580-680	Rank in top quarter:	69%
SAT math:	570-670	Rank in top tenth:	35%
SAT writing:	580-680	Return as sophomores:	93%
ACT composite:	25-30	Out-of-state:	19%
GPA 3.75 or higher:	47%	Live on campus:	100%
GPA 3.50-3.74:	23%	International:	2%
GPA 3.0-3.49:	26%		
GPA 2.0-2.99:	4%		

Basis for selection. School achievement record, test scores, recommendations, interview, essay or personal statement, school and community activities most important. Special consideration given to children of alumni and minority applicants. **Home schooled:** Statement describing home school structure and mission, interview, letter of recommendation (nonparent) required.

High school preparation. College-preparatory program recommended. 17 units required; 22 recommended. Required and recommended units include English 4, mathematics 3-4, social studies 2, history 2, science 2-3 (laboratory 2-3), foreign language 2-3 and academic electives 2.

2011-2012 Annual costs. Tuition/fees: $35,897. Room/board: $8,700. Books/supplies: $900. Personal expenses: $610.

2010-2011 Financial aid. Need-based: 632 full-time freshmen applied for aid; 567 were judged to have need; 561 of these received aid. Average need met was 93%. Average scholarship/grant was $27,256; average loan

$4,129. 82% of total undergraduate aid awarded as scholarships/grants, 18% as loans/jobs. **Non-need-based:** Awarded to 830 full-time undergraduates, including 247 freshmen. Scholarships awarded for academics, alumni affiliation, art, music/drama, ROTC.

Application procedures. Admission: Closing date 4/1. No application fee. Admission notification by 4/15. Admission notification on a rolling basis beginning on or about 11/20. Must reply by May 1 or within 2 week(s) if notified thereafter. **Financial aid:** Priority date 3/15, closing date 5/1. FAFSA required. CSS PROFILE required of students applying for need-based assistance. Applicants notified on a rolling basis starting 3/15; must reply by 5/1 or within 2 week(s) of notification.

Academics. Special study options: Cooperative education, cross-registration, double major, dual enrollment of high school students, exchange student, honors, independent study, internships, liberal arts/career combination, student-designed major, study abroad, teacher certification program, Washington semester. **Credit/placement by examination:** AP, CLEP, IB, institutional tests. **Support services:** Reduced course load, study skills assistance, tutoring, writing center.

Majors. Area/ethnic studies: Japanese, Russian/Slavic, Scandinavian, women's. **Biology:** General, biochemistry. **Business:** General, accounting, international. **Communications:** Communications/speech/rhetoric. **Computer sciences:** General, computer science. **Conservation:** Environmental studies. **Education:** General, elementary, secondary. **English:** English lit. **Foreign languages:** Classics, French, German, Japanese, Russian, Scandinavian, Spanish. **Health services:** Athletic training, nursing (RN), predental, premedicine, preveterinary. **History:** General. **Math:** General. **Parks/recreation:** Health/fitness. **Philosophy/religion:** Philosophy, religion. **Physical sciences:** Chemistry, geology, physics. **Protective services:** Criminal justice. **Psychology:** General. **Social sciences:** Anthropology, economics, geography, political science, sociology. **Theology:** Sacred music. **Visual/performing arts:** Art, art history/conservation, dance, dramatic, music, music performance.

Most popular majors. Biology 13%, business/marketing 12%, communication technologies 6%, education 7%, parks/recreation 7%, physical sciences 6%, psychology 7%, social sciences 13%.

Computing on campus. 440 workstations in dormitories, library, computer center, student center. Dormitories wired for high-speed internet access and linked to campus network. Commuter students can connect to campus network. Online course registration, online library, helpline, repair service, student web hosting, wireless network available.

Student life. Freshman orientation: Mandatory, $100 fee. Preregistration for classes offered. On-campus registration and pre-orientation sessions take place in June for students and families. Orientation program begins for first-year students four days prior to the beginning of classes. **Housing:** Guaranteed on-campus for all undergraduates. Coed dorms, special housing for disabled, apartments, wellness housing available. $300 nonrefundable deposit, deadline 5/1. **Activities:** Bands, campus ministries, choral groups, dance, drama, international student organizations, literary magazine, music ensembles, musical theater, radio station, student government, student newspaper, symphony orchestra, over 100 religious, political, ethnic, and social service organizations.

Athletics. NCAA. **Intercollegiate:** Baseball M, basketball, cross-country, diving, football (tackle) M, golf, gymnastics W, ice hockey, skiing, soccer, softball W, swimming, tennis, track and field, volleyball W. **Intramural:** Badminton, basketball, football (non-tackle) M, golf, handball, ice hockey, lacrosse M, racquetball, rugby, skiing, soccer, softball, swimming, table tennis, tennis, volleyball. **Team name:** Gusties.

Student services. Alcohol/substance abuse counseling, chaplain/spiritual director, career counseling, student employment services, financial aid counseling, health services, minority student services, personal counseling, placement for graduates, women's services. **Physically disabled:** Services for visually, hearing impaired.

Contact. E-mail: admission@gustavus.edu
Phone: (507) 933-7676 Toll-free number: (800) 487-8288
Fax: (507) 933-7474
Tom Crady, Vice-President for Enrollment Management, Gustavus Adolphus College, 800 West College Avenue, St. Peter, MN 56082

Hamline University
St. Paul, Minnesota
www.hamline.edu

CB member
CB code: 6265

- Private 4-year university and liberal arts college affiliated with United Methodist Church
- Residential campus in very large city

- 1,907 degree-seeking undergraduates: 2% part-time, 56% women, 7% African American, 6% Asian American, 5% Hispanic American, 1% Native American, 3% international
- 2,341 degree-seeking graduate students
- 71% of applicants admitted
- SAT or ACT (ACT writing recommended), application essay required
- 68% graduate within 6 years; 31% enter graduate study

General. Founded in 1854. Regionally accredited. **Degrees:** 446 bachelor's awarded; master's, professional, doctoral offered. **ROTC:** Army, Air Force. **Location:** 5 miles from downtown St. Paul, 5 miles from downtown Minneapolis. **Calendar:** 4-1-4, extensive summer session. **Full-time faculty:** 193 total; 78% have terminal degrees, 11% minority, 56% women. **Part-time faculty:** 292 total; 27% have terminal degrees, 9% minority, 54% women. **Class size:** 61% < 20, 31% 20-39, 4% 40-49, 3% 50-99. **Special facilities:** Art museum, theater, concert hall, athletics complex including fitness center with new equipment.

Freshman class profile. 2,982 applied, 2,131 admitted, 515 enrolled.

Mid 50% test scores			
SAT critical reading:	480-620	GPA 2.0-2.99:	18%
SAT math:	480-610	Rank in top quarter:	51%
SAT writing:	480-610	Rank in top tenth:	22%
ACT composite:	21-27	End year in good standing:	80%
GPA 3.75 or higher:	31%	Return as sophomores:	80%
GPA 3.50-3.74:	21%	Out-of-state:	24%
GPA 3.0-3.49:	30%	Live on campus:	87%
		International:	2%

Basis for selection. High school GPA, class rank, and selection of college-preparatory courses of primary importance. Test scores, extracurricular activities, recommendations of teacher and guidance counselor also emphasized. ACT writing exam preferred but not required. Interviews recommended. **Home schooled:** Transcript of courses and grades, letter of recommendation (nonparent) required.

High school preparation. College-preparatory program recommended. 20 units recommended. Recommended units include English 4, mathematics 3, social studies 4, science 3 (laboratory 3), foreign language 2 and academic electives 4.

2012-2013 Annual costs. Tuition/fees: $33,588. Room/board: $8,700.

2010-2011 Financial aid. Need-based: 408 full-time freshmen applied for aid; 369 were judged to have need; 369 of these received aid. Average need met was 84%. Average scholarship/grant was $20,547; average loan $4,037. 74% of total undergraduate aid awarded as scholarships/grants, 26% as loans/jobs. **Non-need-based:** Awarded to 387 full-time undergraduates, including 80 freshmen. Scholarships awarded for academics, alumni affiliation, art, leadership, minority status, music/drama, religious affiliation.

Application procedures. Admission: Priority date 2/1; no deadline. No application fee. Admission notification on a rolling basis beginning on or about 10/1. Must reply by May 1 or within 2 week(s) if notified thereafter. **Financial aid:** Priority date 3/15; no closing date. FAFSA required. Applicants notified on a rolling basis starting 3/15; must reply by 5/1 or within 2 week(s) of notification.

Academics. Intensive fall semester course for conditionally admitted students. **Special study options:** Combined bachelor's/graduate degree, cross-registration, double major, dual enrollment of high school students, ESL, exchange student, honors, independent study, internships, student-designed major, study abroad, teacher certification program, urban semester, Washington semester. **Credit/placement by examination:** AP, CLEP, IB, institutional tests. 64 credit hours maximum toward bachelor's degree. **Support services:** Learning center, pre-admission summer program, reduced course load, study skills assistance, tutoring, writing center.

Majors. Area/ethnic studies: East Asian, Latin American, women's. **Biology:** General, biochemistry. **Business:** Accounting, business admin, finance, international, marketing. **Communications:** Communications/speech/rhetoric. **Conservation:** Environmental studies. **Education:** General, ESL, multilevel teacher. **English:** Creative writing, English lit. **Foreign languages:** German, Spanish. **Health services:** Predental, premedicine, prepharmacy, preveterinary. **History:** General. **Math:** General. **Parks/recreation:** Sports admin. **Philosophy/religion:** Philosophy, religion. **Physical sciences:** Chemistry, physics. **Protective services:** Criminal justice, forensics. **Psychology:** General. **Social sciences:** Anthropology, economics, political science, sociology. **Visual/performing arts:** Art history/conservation, dramatic, music, music performance, studio arts.

Most popular majors. Business/marketing 15%, communications/journalism 6%, English 7%, legal studies 6%, psychology 12%, security/protective services 6%, social sciences 21%.

Computing on campus. 300 workstations in dormitories, library, computer center, student center. Dormitories wired for high-speed internet access and linked to campus network. Commuter students can connect to campus network. Online course registration, online library, helpline, repair service, student web hosting, wireless network available.

Student life. Freshman orientation: Mandatory. Preregistration for classes offered. Fall orientation begins in September, the weekend before classes start, and lasts three days. Previews of orientation are held in June and July. **Housing:** Guaranteed on-campus for freshmen. Coed dorms, apartments, fraternity/sorority housing, wellness housing available. $100 nonrefundable deposit, deadline 5/1. PRIDE Black student alliance house, Spanish language house, Spectrum GLBT and allies house, graduate international student house, Amity scholar house, Hmong student house. **Activities:** Bands, choral groups, dance, drama, international student organizations, literary magazine, music ensembles, Model UN, musical theater, radio station, student government, student newspaper, symphony orchestra, Asian Pacific American Coalition, College Democrats, College Republicans, Habitat for Humanity, Hamline African Student Association, Hmong Student Association, Inter-Varsity Christian Fellowship, Minnesota Public Interest Research Group, PRIDE Black Student Alliance, Spectrum (awareness of LGBT issues).

Athletics. NCAA. **Intercollegiate:** Baseball M, basketball, cross-country, diving, football (tackle) M, gymnastics W, ice hockey, soccer, softball W, swimming, tennis, track and field, volleyball W. **Intramural:** Basketball, football (non-tackle), soccer, volleyball. **Team name:** Pipers.

Student services. Chaplain/spiritual director, career counseling, student employment services, financial aid counseling, health services, minority student services, personal counseling, placement for graduates, women's services. **Physically disabled:** Services for visually, speech, hearing impaired.

Contact. E-mail: admission@hamline.edu
Phone: (651) 523-2207 Toll-free number: (800) 753-9753
Fax: (651) 523-2458
Milyon Trulove, Director of Admission, Hamline University, 1536 Hewitt Avenue, St. Paul, MN 55104-1284

Macalester College
St. Paul, Minnesota | CB member
www.macalester.edu | CB code: 6390

- Private 4-year liberal arts college affiliated with Presbyterian Church (USA)
- Residential campus in very large city
- 1,988 degree-seeking undergraduates: 1% part-time, 59% women, 3% African American, 6% Asian American, 6% Hispanic American, 1% Native American, 12% international
- 35% of applicants admitted
- SAT or ACT (ACT writing optional), application essay required
- 87% graduate within 6 years

General. Founded in 1874. Regionally accredited. **Degrees:** 462 bachelor's awarded. **ROTC:** Army, Naval, Air Force. **Location:** 5 miles from Minneapolis and St. Paul. **Calendar:** Semester. **Full-time faculty:** 170 total; 94% have terminal degrees, 17% minority, 49% women. **Part-time faculty:** 63 total; 62% have terminal degrees, 14% minority, 59% women. **Class size:** 70% < 20, 28% 20-39, 1% 40-49, less than 1% 50-99. **Special facilities:** Observatory with DT-M 16 inch F/8 cassegrain telescope, 250-acre nature preserve, nuclear accelerator, computer modeling facilities, laser spectroscopy laboratory, x-ray diffractometer and a nuclear magnetic spectrometer, fully-equipped animal operant chamber, international research center, econometrics lab, ethnographic lab, geographic information systems (GIS) lab.

Freshman class profile. 6,111 applied, 2,137 admitted, 478 enrolled.

Mid 50% test scores			
SAT critical reading:	650-740	Rank in top tenth:	70%
SAT math:	630-710	Return as sophomores:	94%
SAT writing:	640-730	Out-of-state:	81%
ACT composite:	28-32	Live on campus:	100%
Rank in top quarter:	94%	International:	14%

Basis for selection. Test scores and curriculum most important. Leadership potential and extracurricular involvements also important, with special attention given to service to others. Students whose native language is not English must also submit results of the Test of English as a Foreign Language (TOEFL). SAT Critical Reading is not required of these students. Interview recommended. **Home schooled:** Transcript of courses and grades, letter of recommendation (nonparent) required.

High school preparation. College-preparatory program recommended. Recommended units include English 4, mathematics 3, social studies 3,

science 3 (laboratory 3) and foreign language 3. Honors, AP, or IB level courses recommended.

2012-2013 Annual costs. Tuition/fees: $43,693. Room/board: $9,726. Books/supplies: $1,010. Personal expenses: $888.

2011-2012 Financial aid. Need-based: 380 full-time freshmen applied for aid; 331 were judged to have need; 331 of these received aid. Average need met was 100%. Average scholarship/grant was $32,124; average loan $3,236. 81% of total undergraduate aid awarded as scholarships/grants, 19% as loans/jobs. **Non-need-based:** Awarded to 151 full-time undergraduates, including 49 freshmen. Scholarships awarded for academics, minority status. **Additional information:** College constructs a financial aid package that meets full need for all admitted students.

Application procedures. Admission: Closing date 1/15 (postmark date). $40 fee, may be waived for applicants with need. Admission notification by 3/30. Must reply by 5/1. **Financial aid:** Priority date 2/8, closing date 3/1. FAFSA, CSS PROFILE required. Applicants notified by 4/1; must reply by 5/1.

Academics. Special study options: Cross-registration, double major, honors, independent study, internships, New York semester, student-designed major, study abroad, urban semester, Washington semester. BA/Master's in Architecture with Washington University, St. Louis, Missouri, BA/BS in Engineering with Washington University, St. Louis or the University of Minnesota. **Credit/placement by examination:** AP, CLEP, IB, institutional tests. **Support services:** Learning center, remedial instruction, study skills assistance, tutoring, writing center.

Majors. Area/ethnic studies: Asian, Latin American, women's. **Biology:** General, neuroscience. **Communications:** Media studies. **Computer sciences:** General. **Conservation:** Environmental studies. **Education:** General. **English:** English lit. **Foreign languages:** Chinese, classics, French, German, Japanese, linguistics, Russian, Spanish. **History:** General. **Math:** General. **Philosophy/religion:** Philosophy, religion. **Physical sciences:** Chemistry, geology, physics. **Psychology:** General. **Social sciences:** Anthropology, economics, geography, political science, sociology. **Visual/performing arts:** Art, dramatic, music.

Most popular majors. Biology 6%, foreign language 10%, interdisciplinary studies 8%, physical sciences 6%, psychology 6%, social sciences 27%.

Computing on campus. 486 workstations in dormitories, library, computer center, student center. Dormitories wired for high-speed internet access and linked to campus network. Commuter students can connect to campus network. Online course registration, online library, helpline, repair service, student web hosting, wireless network available.

Student life. Freshman orientation: Mandatory. Preregistration for classes offered. 5 days prior to classes in September. **Policies:** 2-year residency requirement for first-year students. **Housing:** Guaranteed on-campus for freshmen. Coed dorms, apartments available. $300 nonrefundable deposit, deadline 5/1. 6 language houses (French, German, Russian, Spanish, Japanese, Chinese), EcoHous (green living), Jewish cultural house, vegetarian co-op housing, single-sex floors within coed dorms available. **Activities:** Bands, campus ministries, choral groups, dance, drama, international student organizations, literary magazine, music ensembles, Model UN, radio station, student government, student newspaper, symphony orchestra, conservation & renewable energy society, Voices of Tamani, Asian student alliance, Habitat for Humanity, Amnesty International, council for religious understanding, multifaith council, Christian fellowship, Afrika.

Athletics. NCAA. **Intercollegiate:** Baseball M, basketball, cross-country, diving, football (tackle) M, golf, soccer, softball W, swimming, tennis, track and field, volleyball W, water polo W. **Intramural:** Basketball, racquetball, soccer, softball, table tennis, volleyball. **Team name:** Fighting Scots.

Student services. Alcohol/substance abuse counseling, chaplain/spiritual director, career counseling, student employment services, financial aid counseling, health services, minority student services, personal counseling, placement for graduates. **Physically disabled:** Services for visually, speech, hearing impaired.

Contact. E-mail: admissions@macalester.edu
Phone: (651) 696-6357 Toll-free number: (800) 231-7974
Fax: (651) 696-6724
Lorne Robinson, Dean of Admissions and Financial Aid, Macalester College, 1600 Grand Avenue, St. Paul, MN 55105-1899

Martin Luther College
New Ulm, Minnesota
www.mlc-wels.edu   CB code: 6435

♦ Private 4-year college of theology and education affiliated with Wisconsin Evangelical Lutheran Synod
♦ Residential campus in large town

♦ 711 degree-seeking undergraduates: 5% part-time, 52% women, 1% Hispanic American, 1% international
♦ 47 degree-seeking graduate students
♦ 95% of applicants admitted
♦ ACT with writing required
♦ 73% graduate within 6 years

General. Founded in 1995. Regionally accredited. Offers programs of study in early childhood education and staff ministry. **Degrees:** 165 bachelor's awarded; master's offered. **Location:** 90 miles from Minneapolis-St. Paul. **Calendar:** Semester, limited summer session. **Full-time faculty:** 49 total; 51% have terminal degrees, 14% women. **Part-time faculty:** 24 total; 29% have terminal degrees, 46% women. **Class size:** 41% < 20, 56% 20-39, less than 1% 40-49, 2% 50-99.

Freshman class profile. 223 applied, 212 admitted, 172 enrolled.

Mid 50% test scores			
ACT composite:	22-28	Rank in top quarter:	43%
GPA 3.75 or higher:	42%	Rank in top tenth:	18%
GPA 3.50-3.74:	23%	Return as sophomores:	84%
GPA 3.0-3.49:	21%	Out-of-state:	86%
GPA 2.0-2.99:	14%	Live on campus:	97%
		International:	1%

Basis for selection. Primarily pastor's letter of recommendation, high school transcript, and test scores required. Rating provided by student's high school considered.

High school preparation. College-preparatory program required. 14 units required. Required and recommended units include English 4, mathematics 3, social studies 2, science 3 (laboratory 2), foreign language 2 and academic electives 2. 5 units in foreign language required for pastoral program.

2011-2012 Annual costs. Tuition/fees: $11,320. Room/board: $4,395. Books/supplies: $800. Personal expenses: $2,000.

2010-2011 Financial aid. Need-based: 143 full-time freshmen applied for aid; 124 were judged to have need; 124 of these received aid. Average need met was 71%. Average scholarship/grant was $7,164; average loan $3,457. 61% of total undergraduate aid awarded as scholarships/grants, 39% as loans/jobs. **Non-need-based:** Awarded to 118 full-time undergraduates, including 27 freshmen. Scholarships awarded for academics, leadership, music/drama.

Application procedures. Admission: Closing date 5/1 (postmark date). No application fee. Admission notification on a rolling basis beginning on or about 9/15. Must reply by May 1 or within 2 week(s) if notified thereafter. **Financial aid:** Closing date 4/15. FAFSA, institutional form required. Applicants notified on a rolling basis starting 4/1.

Academics. Special study options: Distance learning, double major, teacher certification program. **Credit/placement by examination:** AP, CLEP, ACT, institutional tests. **Support services:** Learning center, reduced course load, remedial instruction, study skills assistance, tutoring.

Majors. Education: Early childhood, elementary, English, mathematics, multi-level teacher, science. **Theology:** Preministerial.

Most popular majors. Education 65%, theological studies 35%.

Computing on campus. 129 workstations in dormitories, library, computer center. Dormitories linked to campus network. Helpline, repair service available.

Student life. Freshman orientation: Mandatory, $20 fee. Preregistration for classes offered. **Policies:** Religious observance required. **Housing:** Guaranteed on-campus for freshmen. Single-sex dorms available. $135 partly refundable deposit, deadline 5/15. **Activities:** Bands, campus ministries, choral groups, dance, drama, music ensembles, musical theater, student government, symphony orchestra.

Athletics. NAIA, NCAA. **Intercollegiate:** Baseball M, basketball, cross-country, football (tackle) M, golf M, soccer, softball W, tennis, track and field, volleyball W. **Intramural:** Badminton, basketball, bowling, football (tackle) M, soccer, softball, tennis, volleyball. **Team name:** Knights.

Student services. Chaplain/spiritual director, student employment services, financial aid counseling, health services, personal counseling.

Contact. E-mail: mlcadmit@mlc-wels.edu
Phone: (507) 354-8221 Toll-free number: (877) 652-1995
Fax: (507) 354-8225
Ronald Brutlag, Director of Admissions, Martin Luther College, 1995 Luther Court, New Ulm, MN 56073-3965

Metropolitan State University
St. Paul, Minnesota
www.metrostate.edu   CB code: 1245

- Public 4-year university
- Commuter campus in very large city
- 6,960 degree-seeking undergraduates: 62% part-time, 57% women, 15% African American, 10% Asian American, 5% Hispanic American, 1% international
- 736 degree-seeking graduate students

General. Founded in 1971. Regionally accredited. **Degrees:** 1,752 bachelor's awarded; master's, doctoral offered. **Calendar:** Semester, extensive summer session.

Basis for selection. School achievement record and test scores most important. ACT or SAT at or above national median or high school rank in upper half of class. Interview and essays only used as part of the appeals process if admission was denied.

High school preparation. 16 units required. Required units include English 4, mathematics 3, social studies 3, science 3 (laboratory 1) and academic electives 3. 3 years of electives from language, world culture, or arts.

2011-2012 Annual costs. Tuition/fees: $6,341; $12,612 out-of-state.

Financial aid. Non-need-based: Scholarships awarded for academics, leadership, minority status, state residency.

Application procedures. Admission: Closing date 6/15. $20 fee, may be waived for applicants with need. Admission notification on a rolling basis. **Financial aid:** Priority date 5/1; no closing date. FAFSA required. Applicants notified on a rolling basis starting 5/1; must reply within 2 week(s) of notification.

Academics. Special study options: Cross-registration, distance learning, double major, dual enrollment of high school students, external degree, independent study, internships, liberal arts/career combination, student-designed major, teacher certification program, weekend college. **Credit/placement by examination:** AP, CLEP, IB, institutional tests. 90 credit hours maximum toward bachelor's degree. **Support services:** Learning center, reduced course load, remedial instruction, study skills assistance, tutoring, writing center.

Majors. Area/ethnic studies: General, women's. **Biology:** General. **Business:** Accounting, business admin, finance, hospitality admin, human resources, information resources management, international, management information systems, marketing, operations, sales/distribution. **Communications:** Advertising, communications/speech/rhetoric, public relations. **Computer sciences:** Computer science, information systems, security. **Education:** Biology, elementary, English, kindergarten/preschool, mathematics, social studies. **English:** English lit, technical writing, writing. **Health services:** Dental hygiene, nursing (RN), substance abuse counseling. **History:** General. **Human services:** Social work. **Liberal arts:** Arts/sciences. **Math:** Applied. **Philosophy/religion:** Philosophy. **Protective services:** Criminal justice, police science. **Psychology:** General, developmental. **Social sciences:** General, economics. **Visual/performing arts:** Dramatic, play/screenwriting.

Most popular majors. Security/protective services 9%.

Computing on campus. 550 workstations in library, computer center. Commuter students can connect to campus network. Online course registration, online library, helpline, wireless network available.

Student life. Freshman orientation: Mandatory, $10 fee. Preregistration for classes offered. Orientation sessions of 3-1/2 hours are held several times each semester. **Policies:** Annual registration required of all student organizations. **Activities:** Drama, international student organizations, literary magazine, student government, student newspaper, Asian student organization, Lavender Bridge, African-American student association, graduate student advisory committee, Voice of Indian Council for Educational Success, social work student association, psychology club, Muslim student association, Urban Teachers Student Program Organization.

Student services. Adult student services, career counseling, minority student services, personal counseling, veterans' counselor, women's services. **Physically disabled:** Services for visually, speech, hearing impaired.

Contact. E-mail: admission.metro@metrostate.edu
Phone: (651) 793-1300 Fax: (651) 793-1310
Crystal Comer, Admissions Director, Metropolitan State University, 700 East Seventh Street, St. Paul, MN 55106-5000

Minneapolis College of Art and Design
Minneapolis, Minnesota   CB member
www.mcad.edu   CB code: 6411

- Private 4-year visual arts college
- Residential campus in very large city
- 594 degree-seeking undergraduates: 4% part-time, 61% women
- 73 degree-seeking graduate students
- 64% of applicants admitted
- SAT or ACT (ACT writing optional), application essay required

General. Founded in 1886. Regionally accredited. **Degrees:** 136 bachelor's awarded; master's offered. **Location:** Within the city of Minneapolis. **Calendar:** Semester, limited summer session. **Full-time faculty:** 43 total; 100% have terminal degrees, 35% women. **Part-time faculty:** 85 total; 85% have terminal degrees, 47% women. **Class size:** 84% < 20, 16% 20-39. **Special facilities:** Art and design galleries, personal on-campus studio space, 3-D furniture/sculpture studios, animation studios, drawing studios, film studios, print/paper/book studios, painting studios, photo studios, on-campus professional design studio, extensive on-campus printing services, art and design focused library, ample computer labs.

Freshman class profile. 406 applied, 258 admitted, 84 enrolled.

Mid 50% test scores			
SAT critical reading:	500-680	GPA 3.50-3.74:	24%
SAT math:	430-600	GPA 3.0-3.49:	36%
SAT writing:	470-640	GPA 2.0-2.99:	21%
ACT composite:	21-27	Out-of-state:	58%
GPA 3.75 or higher:	18%	Live on campus:	81%

Basis for selection. Bachelor of Fine Arts applicants are required to submit a portfolio of visual art work. For all BFA and Bachelor of Science students, academic record and test scores reviewed. Level of interest and motivation determined through personal statement of interest, letter of recommendation, and essay requirement. Tests not required for transfer applicants who have completed 12 or more satisfactory credits (C or better) at the college level. Interview recommended. Personal statement, essay required on specific topic for all BS applications. **Home schooled:** Transcript of courses and grades required. **Learning Disabled:** It is recommended that students disclose any learning disabilities for appropriate accommodations to be prepared.

High school preparation. College-preparatory program recommended. Recommended units include English 4, social studies 4, history 4 and visual/performing arts 6.

2012-2013 Annual costs. Tuition/fees: $31,650. New undergraduate students only: required laptop computer purchase $1,400. Room only: $4,540. Books/supplies: $2,724. Personal expenses: $1,000.

Financial aid. Non-need-based: Scholarships awarded for academics, alumni affiliation, art.

Application procedures. Admission: Priority date 2/15; deadline 5/1 (receipt date). $50 fee, may be waived for applicants with need. Application must be submitted online. Admission notification on a rolling basis. Must reply by May 1 or within 2 week(s) if notified thereafter. **Financial aid:** Priority date 3/1, closing date 6/1. FAFSA required. Applicants notified on a rolling basis starting 2/15; must reply by 5/1 or within 2 week(s) of notification.

Academics. Special study options: Combined bachelor's/graduate degree, cooperative education, cross-registration, distance learning, exchange student, independent study, internships, New York semester, study abroad. **Credit/placement by examination:** AP, CLEP, IB. **Support services:** Learning center, reduced course load, study skills assistance, tutoring, writing center.

Majors. Communications: Advertising, public relations. **Communications technology:** Animation/special effects. **Visual/performing arts:** Drawing, graphic design, illustration, painting, photography, printmaking, sculpture, studio arts.

Computing on campus. PC or laptop required. 160 workstations in library, computer center, student center. Dormitories wired for high-speed internet access and linked to campus network. Commuter students can connect to campus network. Online library, helpline, repair service, student web hosting, wireless network available.

Student life. Freshman orientation: Mandatory. Preregistration for classes offered. Held 3 days prior to first day of fall semester classes; includes 1 day for parent/guardian orientation. **Policies:** Freshmen not permitted cars on campus. **Housing:** Guaranteed on-campus for freshmen. Coed dorms, apartments available. $175 fully refundable deposit, deadline 5/1. **Activities:**

Dance, drama, film society, international student organizations, music ensembles, musical theater, student government, animation club, anime club, bike club, Comic Heads, film club, musicians club, design club, green club, OH NO HOMO, recess club.

Student services. Alcohol/substance abuse counseling, career counseling, student employment services, financial aid counseling, personal counseling, placement for graduates.

Contact. E-mail: admissions@mcad.edu
Phone: (612) 874-3760 Toll-free number: (800) 874-6223 ext. 1
Fax: (612) 874-3701
Melissa Huybrecht, Director, Admissions, Minneapolis College of Art and Design, 2501 Stevens Avenue, Minneapolis, MN 55404

Minnesota School of Business: Blaine
Blaine, Minnesota
www.msbcollege.edu

- For-profit 4-year branch campus and business college
- Very large city
- 758 degree-seeking undergraduates

General. Regionally accredited; also accredited by ACICS. **Degrees:** 53 bachelor's, 145 associate awarded. **Calendar:** Quarter, extensive summer session. **Full-time faculty:** 15 total. **Part-time faculty:** 50 total.

Basis for selection. Open admission, but selective for some programs.

2011-2012 Annual costs. Tuition/fees: $19,575.

Application procedures. Admission: No deadline. $50 fee. **Financial aid:** No deadline.

Academics. Credit/placement by examination: AP, CLEP.

Majors. Business: Accounting, business admin. **Computer sciences:** Information technology.

Student life. Activities: Student newspaper.

Contact. E-mail: kswanson@msbcollege.edu
Toll-free number: (877) 655-7676
Janea Okoye, Director of Admissions, Minnesota School of Business: Blaine, 3680 Pheasant Ridge Dr. NE, Blaine, MN 55449

Minnesota School of Business: Elk River
Elk River, Minnesota
www.msbcollege.edu

- For-profit 4-year university and career college
- Large town
- 452 degree-seeking undergraduates

General. Regionally accredited; also accredited by ACICS. **Degrees:** 4 bachelor's, 41 associate awarded. **Calendar:** Quarter. **Full-time faculty:** 10 total. **Part-time faculty:** 23 total.

Basis for selection. Open admission.

Application procedures. Admission: $50 fee.

Academics. Credit/placement by examination: AP, CLEP.

Majors. Business: Business admin. **Health services:** Health care admin. **Protective services:** Police science.

Contact. Tim Elliott, Director of Admissions, Minnesota School of Business: Elk River, 11500 193rd Avenue NW, Elk River, MN 55330

Minnesota School of Business: Lakeville
Lakeville, Minnesota
www.msbcollege.edu

- For-profit 4-year career college
- Small city
- 272 degree-seeking undergraduates

General. Regionally accredited; also accredited by ACICS. **Degrees:** 4 bachelor's, 19 associate awarded. **Calendar:** Quarter. **Full-time faculty:** 9 total. **Part-time faculty:** 26 total.

Basis for selection. Open admission.

Application procedures. Admission: $50 fee.

Academics. Credit/placement by examination: AP, CLEP.

Majors. Business: Business admin. **Health services:** Health care admin. **Protective services:** Police science.

Contact. Brian Saintey, Director of Admissions, Minnesota School of Business: Lakeville, 17685 Juniper Path, Lakeville, MN 55044

Minnesota School of Business: Moorhead
Moorhead, Minnesota
www.msbcollege.edu

- For-profit 4-year university and career college
- Large town
- 283 degree-seeking undergraduates

General. Regionally accredited; also accredited by ACICS. **Degrees:** 14 bachelor's, 85 associate awarded. **Calendar:** Quarter. **Full-time faculty:** 7 total. **Part-time faculty:** 29 total.

Basis for selection. Open admission.

Application procedures. Admission: $50 fee.

Academics. Credit/placement by examination: AP, CLEP.

Majors. Business: Business admin. **Protective services:** Police science.

Contact. Angelique Goulet, Director of Admissions, Minnesota School of Business: Moorhead, 2777 34th Street South, Moorhead, MN 56560

Minnesota School of Business: Plymouth
Plymouth, Minnesota
www.msbcollege.edu

- For-profit 4-year business and technical college
- Commuter campus in small city
- 423 degree-seeking undergraduates

General. Accredited by ACICS. **Degrees:** 38 bachelor's, 96 associate awarded. **Calendar:** Quarter. **Full-time faculty:** 8 total. **Part-time faculty:** 29 total.

Basis for selection. Admissions based on results of Accuplacer entrance exam; testing required in math and reading skills. Students must meet the testing requirement for the specific program to which they are applying.

2011-2012 Annual costs. Tuition/fees: $19,575.

Application procedures. Admission: No deadline. $50 fee. **Financial aid:** No deadline.

Academics. Special study options: Distance learning, independent study, internships, liberal arts/career combination. **Credit/placement by examination:** AP, CLEP.

Majors. Business: Accounting, business admin. **Computer sciences:** Information technology. **Health services:** Health care admin.

Contact. Phone: (866) 476-2121 Fax: (736) 476-1000
Charles Andria, Director of Admissions, Minnesota School of Business: Plymouth, 1455 County Road 101 North, Plymouth, MN 55447

Minnesota School of Business: Richfield
Richfield, Minnesota
www.msbcollege.edu

- For-profit 4-year business and technical college
- Commuter campus in very large city

- 1,636 degree-seeking undergraduates
- Interview required

General. Accredited by ACICS. **Degrees:** 169 bachelor's, 183 associate awarded; master's offered. **Calendar:** Quarter, extensive summer session. **Full-time faculty:** 30 total. **Part-time faculty:** 212 total. **Class size:** 97% < 20, 3% 20-39.

Basis for selection. Open admission, but selective for some programs. Standardized test scores most important. Special requirements for students seeking admission to Cosmetology Business and Transportation Business associate degree programs, and Media Business and Nursing bachelor's degree programs. Applicants for the nursing program must register minimum scores on the assessment and ACCUPLACER exams. Application fee for nursing program is $100. Interviews important. **Learning Disabled:** Students with learning disabilities are allowed 90 minutes for exams while all other students are allowed 60 minutes.

2011-2012 Annual costs. Tuition/fees: $19,575. Books/supplies: $1,500. Personal expenses: $2,178.

Application procedures. Admission: No deadline. $50 fee. Application must be submitted online. Admission notification on a rolling basis. **Financial aid:** No deadline. FAFSA, institutional form required. Applicants notified on a rolling basis starting 7/1; must reply within 2 week(s) of notification.

Academics. Special study options: Combined bachelor's/graduate degree, distance learning, liberal arts/career combination. **Credit/placement by examination:** AP, CLEP. **Support services:** Study skills assistance, tutoring, writing center.

Majors. Business: Accounting, business admin. **Computer sciences:** Information technology. **Health services:** Nursing (RN).

Most popular majors. Business/marketing 60%, computer/information sciences 10%, health sciences 24%, legal studies 6%.

Computing on campus. 12 workstations in library, computer center. Online library, helpline, wireless network available.

Student life. Freshman orientation: Mandatory. Preregistration for classes offered.

Student services. Career counseling, student employment services, financial aid counseling, placement for graduates.

Contact. E-mail: pmurray@msbcollege.edu
Phone: (612) 861-2000 Toll-free number: (800) 752-4223
Fax: (612) 861-5548
Chad Peterson, Director of Admissions, Minnesota School of Business: Richfield, 1401 West 76 Street, Suite 500, Richfield, MN 55423

Minnesota School of Business: Rochester
Rochester, Minnesota
www.msbcollege.edu

- For-profit 4-year career college
- Commuter campus in small city
- 468 degree-seeking undergraduates

General. Accredited by ACICS. **Degrees:** 53 bachelor's, 134 associate awarded. **Calendar:** Quarter. **Full-time faculty:** 12 total. **Part-time faculty:** 31 total.

Basis for selection. Admissions based on results of Accuplacer entrance exam.

2011-2012 Annual costs. Tuition/fees: $19,575. Books/supplies: $1,200.

Application procedures. Admission: No deadline. $50 fee. Application must be submitted online. Admission notification on a rolling basis. **Financial aid:** No deadline.

Academics. Special study options: Distance learning. **Credit/placement by examination:** AP, CLEP. **Support services:** Learning center, remedial instruction, study skills assistance, tutoring, writing center.

Majors. Business: Accounting, business admin.

Computing on campus. 14 workstations in library, student center. Online library, helpline, wireless network available.

Contact. Phone: (507) 536-9500
Angie Helm, Director of Admissions, Minnesota School of Business: Rochester, 2521 Pennington Drive NW, Rochester, MN 55901

Minnesota School of Business: Shakopee
Shakopee, Minnesota
www.msbcollege.edu

- For-profit 4-year business and technical college
- Commuter campus in large town
- 307 degree-seeking undergraduates
- Interview required

General. Accredited by ACICS. **Degrees:** 33 bachelor's, 88 associate awarded; master's offered. **Calendar:** Quarter. **Full-time faculty:** 13 total. **Part-time faculty:** 15 total. **Class size:** 97% < 20, 3% 20-39.

Basis for selection. Interview with admissions and SAT, ACT, or entrance exam (Accuplacer) important.

2011-2012 Annual costs. Tuition/fees: $19,575.

Financial aid. Non-need-based: Scholarships awarded for academics.

Application procedures. Admission: No deadline. $50 fee. Admission notification on a rolling basis. **Financial aid:** No deadline. FAFSA, institutional form required. Applicants notified on a rolling basis.

Academics. Special study options: Combined bachelor's/graduate degree, distance learning, liberal arts/career combination. **Credit/placement by examination:** AP, CLEP, SAT, ACT, institutional tests. 75 credit hours maximum toward associate degree, 75 toward bachelor's. **Support services:** Learning center, remedial instruction, study skills assistance, tutoring, writing center.

Majors. Business: Business admin.

Computing on campus. 50 workstations in computer center. Online course registration, online library, helpline, wireless network available.

Student life. Freshman orientation: Mandatory. Preregistration for classes offered.

Contact. Phone: (866) 776-1200
Gretchen Seifert, Director of Admissions, Minnesota School of Business: Shakopee, 1200 Shakopee Town Square, Shakopee, MN 55379

Minnesota School of Business: St. Cloud
Waite Park, Minnesota
www.msbcollege.edu

- For-profit 4-year virtual university
- Commuter campus in small city
- 671 degree-seeking undergraduates

General. Accredited by ACICS. **Degrees:** 61 bachelor's, 200 associate awarded; master's offered. **Calendar:** Quarter, extensive summer session. **Full-time faculty:** 18 total. **Part-time faculty:** 39 total.

Basis for selection. Applicants to all diploma, associate, and bachelor degree programs must achieve minimum scores on the Accuplacer test administered at the college: 35 (reading comprehension), 35 (sentence skills), 21 (arithmetic). **Home schooled:** State high school equivalency certificate required.

2011-2012 Annual costs. Tuition/fees: $19,575.

Application procedures. Admission: No deadline. $50 fee. Application must be submitted online. Admission notification on a rolling basis. **Financial aid:** No deadline.

Academics. Special study options: Combined bachelor's/graduate degree, distance learning, internships. **Credit/placement by examination:** AP, CLEP. **Support services:** Remedial instruction, study skills assistance, tutoring, writing center.

Majors. Business: Accounting, business admin. **Computer sciences:** Information technology. **Health services:** Health care admin.

Computing on campus. Online course registration, helpline, wireless network available.

Contact. E-mail: info@msbcollege.edu
Phone: (866) 403-3333
Kim Plombon, Director of Admissions, Minnesota School of Business: St. Cloud, 1201 Second Street South, Waite Park, MN 55387

Minnesota State University Mankato
Mankato, Minnesota CB member
www.mnsu.edu CB code: 6677

- Public 4-year university
- Residential campus in large town
- 12,799 degree-seeking undergraduates: 9% part-time, 51% women
- 1,954 graduate students
- 89% of applicants admitted
- SAT or ACT (ACT writing optional) required
- 50% graduate within 6 years

General. Founded in 1867. Regionally accredited. **Degrees:** 2,359 bachelor's, 49 associate awarded; master's, professional offered. **ROTC:** Army. **Location:** 85 miles from Minneapolis-St. Paul. **Calendar:** Semester, extensive summer session. **Full-time faculty:** 499 total; 82% have terminal degrees, 9% minority, 45% women. **Part-time faculty:** 262 total; 8% have terminal degrees, 2% minority, 60% women. **Class size:** 33% < 20, 49% 20-39, 7% 40-49, 8% 50-99, 3% >100. **Special facilities:** 2 observatories, ropes course, rock climbing wall.

Freshman class profile. 6,411 applied, 5,706 admitted, 2,568 enrolled.

Mid 50% test scores			
ACT composite:	20-24	Return as sophomores:	77%
Rank in top quarter:	27%	Out-of-state:	14%
Rank in top tenth:	7%	Live on campus:	85%

Basis for selection. Students must rank in top 50 percent of high school class or score 21 or better on the ACT. College preparatory courses also reviewed. ACT used only when admission cannot be achieved using high school rank and college preparatory courses. Essays and/or recommendations used only for contract/admission review by faculty committees. **Home schooled:** Must submit standardized test results in lieu of rank/record.

High school preparation. College-preparatory program required. 16 units required. Required units include English 4, mathematics 3, social studies 2, history 1, science 3 (laboratory 3) and foreign language 2. One year world culture course or arts course.

2011-2012 Annual costs. Tuition/fees: $7,148; $14,270 out-of-state. Room/board: $6,340. Books/supplies: $820. Personal expenses: $2,600.

Financial aid. Non-need-based: Scholarships awarded for academics, art, athletics, leadership, minority status, music/drama.

Application procedures. Admission: Closing date 8/15. $20 fee, may be waived for applicants with need. Admission notification on a rolling basis. **Financial aid:** Priority date 3/15; no closing date. FAFSA required. Applicants notified on a rolling basis starting 3/30; must reply within 2 week(s) of notification.

Academics. Special study options: Combined bachelor's/graduate degree, cross-registration, distance learning, double major, dual enrollment of high school students, ESL, exchange student, external degree, honors, independent study, internships, semester at sea, student-designed major, study abroad, teacher certification program. **Credit/placement by examination:** AP, CLEP, IB, institutional tests. **Support services:** Learning center, reduced course load, remedial instruction, study skills assistance, tutoring, writing center.

Majors. Architecture: Urban/community planning. **Area/ethnic studies:** French, German, Scandinavian, women's. **Biology:** General, anatomy, bacteriology, biochemistry, biotechnology, botany, ecology, genetics, toxicology, zoology. **Business:** General, accounting, banking/financial services, business admin, finance, financial planning, human resources, international, management information systems, management science, operations. **Communications:** Communications/speech/rhetoric, journalism, media studies, public relations. **Computer sciences:** General, computer science. **Conservation:** General, environmental studies. **Education:** General, art, biology, business, chemistry, computer, curriculum, drama/dance, early childhood, elementary, English, family/consumer sciences, foreign languages, French, German, health, health occupations, history, mathematics, middle, music, physical, physics, science, secondary, social science, social studies, Spanish, speech, technology/industrial arts, voc/tech. **Engineering:** General, civil, computer,

electrical, mechanical. **English:** Creative writing, English lit, rhetoric/composition, technical writing. **Foreign languages:** French, German, Spanish. **General:** Food science, plant sciences. **Health services:** Athletic training, communication disorders, cytotechnology, dental hygiene, health care admin, nursing (RN), predental, premedicine, preop/surgical nursing, prepharmacy, preveterinary, public health ed, recreational therapy. **History:** General. **Human services:** General, social work. **Math:** General. **Parks/recreation:** General, exercise sciences, facilities management, health/fitness, sports admin. **Philosophy/religion:** Philosophy. **Physical sciences:** Astronomy, chemistry, physics. **Protective services:** Corrections, law enforcement admin, police science. **Psychology:** General. **Social sciences:** Anthropology, economics, geography, international relations, political science, sociology, urban studies. **Visual/performing arts:** General, art, art history/conservation, ceramics, commercial/advertising art, dramatic, drawing, fiber arts, music, music management, music performance, painting, sculpture, studio arts, theater design. **Work/family studies:** General, clothing/textiles, family studies, family/community services, food/nutrition, housing.

Computing on campus. 900 workstations in dormitories, library, computer center, student center. Dormitories wired for high-speed internet access and linked to campus network. Commuter students can connect to campus network. Online course registration, online library, helpline, repair service, student web hosting, wireless network available.

Student life. Freshman orientation: Mandatory, $65 fee. Preregistration for classes offered. Includes overnight stay. **Housing:** Coed dorms, special housing for disabled available. $250 partly refundable deposit. **Activities:** Bands, campus ministries, choral groups, dance, drama, international student organizations, music ensembles, musical theater, radio station, student government, student newspaper, symphony orchestra, Hmong student association, American Indian student association, Chicano Latino AM student association, Fellowship of Christian Athletes, InterVarsity, MSU Pagan Organization.

Athletics. NCAA. **Intercollegiate:** Baseball M, basketball, cheerleading, cross-country, diving, football (tackle) M, golf, ice hockey, soccer W, softball W, swimming W, tennis W, track and field, volleyball W, wrestling M. **Intramural:** Archery, basketball, bowling, football (non-tackle), golf, ice hockey, racquetball, rugby, soccer, softball, swimming, tennis, track and field, triathlon, volleyball, wrestling M. **Team name:** Mavericks.

Student services. Adult student services, alcohol/substance abuse counseling, chaplain/spiritual director, career counseling, services for economically disadvantaged, student employment services, financial aid counseling, health services, legal services, minority student services, on-campus daycare, personal counseling, placement for graduates, veterans' counselor, women's services. **Physically disabled:** Services for visually, speech, hearing impaired.

Contact. E-mail: admissions@mnsu.edu
Phone: (507) 389-1822 Toll-free number: (800) 722-0544
Fax: (507) 389-1511
Brian Jones, Director of Admissions, Minnesota State University Mankato, 122 Taylor Center, Mankato, MN 56001

Minnesota State University Moorhead
Moorhead, Minnesota
www.mnstate.edu CB code: 6678

- Public 4-year university
- Residential campus in small city
- 6,388 degree-seeking undergraduates: 14% part-time, 58% women, 2% African American, 1% Asian American, 1% Hispanic American, 1% Native American, 6% international
- 409 degree-seeking graduate students
- 63% of applicants admitted
- SAT or ACT (ACT writing optional) required

General. Founded in 1885. Regionally accredited. **Degrees:** 1,287 bachelor's, 11 associate awarded; master's, doctoral offered. **ROTC:** Army, Air Force. **Location:** 240 miles from Minneapolis-St. Paul. **Calendar:** Semester, limited summer session. **Special facilities:** On-campus planetarium, 300-acre regional science center.

Freshman class profile. 4,174 applied, 2,622 admitted, 1,121 enrolled.

Mid 50% test scores			
SAT critical reading:	520-560	Rank in top tenth:	9%
SAT math:	490-560	Return as sophomores:	67%
ACT composite:	20-24	Out-of-state:	38%
Rank in top quarter:	26%	Live on campus:	84%
		International:	4%

Basis for selection. Applicants must rank in top half of class or have minimum ACT composite score of 21 or equivalent scores on SAT or PSAT/NMSQT. Some applicants not meeting requirements will be admitted to

transitional college program. Applicants must also fulfill minimum requirements of secondary course work. **Learning Disabled:** Contact Office of Disability Services to make sure appropriate accommodations can be provided.

High school preparation. College-preparatory program required. 16 units required. Required units include English 4, mathematics 3, social studies 3, science 3 (laboratory 1) and foreign language 2. One unit fine arts, .5 computer science recommended.

2011-2012 Annual costs. Tuition/fees: $7,378; $7,378 out-of-state. Room/board: $6,726.

2010-2011 Financial aid. Non-need-based: Scholarships awarded for academics, art, athletics, leadership, music/drama, state residency.

Application procedures. Admission: Closing date 8/1 (postmark date). $20 fee. Admission notification on a rolling basis beginning on or about 10/1. **Financial aid:** Priority date 2/15; no closing date. FAFSA required. Applicants notified on a rolling basis starting 6/1; must reply within 2 week(s) of notification.

Academics. Special study options: Cross-registration, distance learning, double major, dual enrollment of high school students, exchange student, external degree, honors, independent study, internships, student-designed major, study abroad, teacher certification program. **Credit/placement by examination:** AP, CLEP, ACT, institutional tests. 12 credit hours maximum toward bachelor's degree. **Support services:** Pre-admission summer program, reduced course load, remedial instruction, study skills assistance, tutoring, writing center.

Majors. Area/ethnic studies: General, East Asian, women's. **Biology:** General, Biochemistry/molecular biology. **Business:** Accounting, business admin, construction management, finance, operations. **Communications:** Media studies. **Computer sciences:** General, computer science, information technology. **Conservation:** Environmental studies. **Education:** Art, biology, chemistry, elementary, English, health, kindergarten/preschool, mathematics, music, physical, physics, science, social studies, Spanish, special ed. **English:** English lit. **Foreign languages:** Spanish. **Health services:** Athletic training, audiology/speech pathology, clinical lab science, community health services, health care admin, nurse practitioner. **History:** General. **Human services:** Social work. **Math:** General. **Parks/recreation:** Exercise sciences. **Philosophy/religion:** Philosophy. **Physical sciences:** Chemistry, physics. **Protective services:** Criminal justice. **Psychology:** General. **Social sciences:** Anthropology, economics, political science, sociology. **Visual/performing arts:** Art, commercial/advertising art, dramatic, film/cinema/video, music, music performance, music theory/composition.

Most popular majors. Biology 6%, business/marketing 18%, communications/journalism 7%, education 15%, health sciences 12%, visual/performing arts 10%.

Computing on campus. 791 workstations in dormitories, library, computer center. Dormitories linked to campus network. Commuter students can connect to campus network. Online course registration, online library, helpline, repair service, student web hosting, wireless network available.

Student life. Freshman orientation: Available. Preregistration for classes offered. **Housing:** Coed dorms, single-sex dorms, special housing for disabled, apartments, fraternity/sorority housing available. $250 partly refundable deposit, deadline 3/15. Students participating in Living Learning Communities program take at least three of their fall semester classes together as well as live together on the same residence hall floor. **Activities:** Bands, campus ministries, choral groups, dance, drama, film society, international student organizations, literary magazine, music ensembles, Model UN, musical theater, radio station, student government, student newspaper, symphony orchestra, TV station, over 130 student clubs.

Athletics. NCAA. **Intercollegiate:** Basketball, cross-country, diving W, football (tackle) M, golf W, soccer W, softball W, swimming W, tennis W, track and field, volleyball W, wrestling M. **Intramural:** Badminton, basketball, bowling, football (tackle) M, ice hockey M, racquetball, soccer, softball, tennis, triathlon, volleyball. **Team name:** Dragons.

Student services. Adult student services, alcohol/substance abuse counseling, career counseling, student employment services, financial aid counseling, health services, minority student services, on-campus daycare, personal counseling, placement for graduates, veterans' counselor, women's services. **Physically disabled:** Services for visually, speech, hearing impaired.

Contact. E-mail: dragon@mnstate.edu
Phone: (218) 477-2161 Toll-free number: (800) 593-7246
Fax: (218) 477-4374
Jeremy Johnson, Director of Admissions, Minnesota State University Moorhead, Owens Hall, Moorhead, MN 56563

National American University: Bloomington
Bloomington, Minnesota
www.national.edu   CB code: 5358

▸ For-profit 4-year business and nursing college
▸ Commuter campus in very large city

General. Founded in 1974. Regionally accredited. **Calendar:** Quarter.

Annual costs/financial aid. Books/supplies: $1,000. Need-based financial aid available to full-time and part-time students.

Contact. Phone: (952) 356-3600
Director of Admissions, 7801 Metro Parkway Suite 200, Bloomington, MN 55425

National American University: Roseville
Roseville, Minnesota
www.national.edu

▸ For-profit 4-year university and branch campus college
▸ Very large city

General. Regionally accredited. **Calendar:** Quarter.

Annual costs/financial aid. Tuition/fees (2011-2012): $15,585.

Contact. Director of Admissions, 1550 West Highway 36, Roseville, MN 55431

North Central University
Minneapolis, Minnesota
www.northcentral.edu   CB code: 0051

▸ Private 4-year university and Bible college affiliated with Assemblies of God
▸ Residential campus in large city
▸ 1,188 degree-seeking undergraduates
▸ 68% of applicants admitted
▸ SAT or ACT (ACT writing optional), application essay required

General. Founded in 1930. Regionally accredited. **Degrees:** 187 bachelor's, 5 associate awarded. **ROTC:** Army, Air Force. **Calendar:** Semester, limited summer session. **Full-time faculty:** 45 total. **Part-time faculty:** 79 total. **Class size:** 49% < 20, 37% 20-39, 10% 40-49, 2% 50-99, 1% >100. **Special facilities:** Private recording studio on-campus, center for youth and leadership, children's literature library.

Freshman class profile. 743 applied, 502 admitted, 262 enrolled.

Mid 50% test scores			
SAT critical reading:	470-560	GPA 3.0-3.49:	34%
SAT math:	460-600	GPA 2.0-2.99:	34%
ACT composite:	19-24	Rank in top quarter:	31%
GPA 3.75 or higher:	14%	Rank in top tenth:	14%
GPA 3.50-3.74:	17%	Out-of-state:	61%
		Live on campus:	93%

Basis for selection. School achievement record, essay character recommendation, and pastor's recommendation are most important. Conditional admission available for students not in good standing at previous institution. Applicants with GPA below 2.2 or ACT scores below 18 may be provisionally admitted. The writing portions of the ACT and SAT are not required and not taken into consideration for admission or scholarship. **Home schooled:** Statement describing home school structure and mission, transcript of courses and grades required. Must meet their state's requirements for graduation.

High school preparation. 9 units recommended. Recommended units include English 3, mathematics 1, social studies 2, history 1, science 1 and foreign language 1.

2011-2012 Annual costs. Tuition/fees: $17,440. Room/board: $5,410. Books/supplies: $900.

Financial aid. Non-need-based: Scholarships awarded for academics, leadership, music/drama.

Application procedures. Admission: Priority date 1/15; deadline 6/1 (postmark date). $25 fee, may be waived for applicants with need. Admission notification on a rolling basis. **Financial aid:** No deadline. FAFSA required.

Applicants notified on a rolling basis starting 3/1; must reply within 2 week(s) of notification.

Academics. Special study options: Combined bachelor's/graduate degree, double major, dual enrollment of high school students, exchange student, independent study, internships, liberal arts/career combination, student-designed major, study abroad, teacher certification program, weekend college. **Credit/placement by examination:** AP, CLEP, SAT, ACT. **Support services:** Learning center, pre-admission summer program, reduced course load, remedial instruction, study skills assistance, tutoring, writing center.

Majors. Business: Business admin. **Communications:** Journalism, media studies. **Education:** Elementary, ESL, secondary. **English:** English lit. **Foreign languages:** American Sign Language, sign language interpretation. **Health services:** Substance abuse counseling. **Human services:** Social work. **Parks/recreation:** Sports admin. **Philosophy/religion:** Christian, religion. **Psychology:** General. **Social sciences:** Urban studies. **Theology:** Bible, missionary, pastoral counseling, religious ed, sacred music, theology, youth ministry. **Visual/performing arts:** Dramatic, music, music management, music performance.

Most popular majors. Business/marketing 9%, education 9%, family/consumer sciences 6%, interdisciplinary studies 25%, psychology 10%, theological studies 23%, visual/performing arts 9%.

Computing on campus. 120 workstations in dormitories, library, computer center, student center. Dormitories wired for high-speed internet access and linked to campus network. Commuter students can connect to campus network. Online course registration, online library, helpline, wireless network available.

Student life. Freshman orientation: Mandatory, $115 fee. Preregistration for classes offered. 4-5 optional dates in the summer months. **Policies:** North Central requires all members of the community to refrain from any form of sexual immorality. Students must refrain from the possession, use or distribution of non-medical drugs, alcoholic beverages, and tobacco in any form. Religious observance required. **Housing:** Guaranteed on-campus for freshmen. Single-sex dorms, special housing for disabled, apartments, wellness housing available. $200 partly refundable deposit, deadline 6/1. **Activities:** Bands, campus ministries, choral groups, dance, drama, literary magazine, music ensembles, musical theater, student government, student newspaper, leadership development committee, student committee, the Northern Light, SIFE, Alpha Kai, deaf culture fellowship, student senate, student missions fellowship, student activities committee.

Athletics. NCAA, NCCAA. **Intercollegiate:** Baseball M, basketball, cross-country, golf M, soccer, softball W, track and field, volleyball W. **Intramural:** Basketball M, football (non-tackle). **Team name:** Rams.

Student services. Chaplain/spiritual director, career counseling, student employment services, financial aid counseling, health services, personal counseling, placement for graduates, women's services. **Physically disabled:** Services for visually, speech, hearing impaired.

Contact. E-mail: admissions@northcentral.edu
Phone: (612) 343-4460 Toll-free number: (800) 289-6222
Fax: (612) 343-4146
Troy Pearson, Executive Director of Admissions and Enrollment, North Central University, 910 Elliot Avenue, Minneapolis, MN 55404

Northwestern College
Saint Paul, Minnesota
www.nwc.edu   CB code: 6489

▶ Private 4-year liberal arts college affiliated with nondenominational tradition

▶ Residential campus in very large city

▶ 1,698 degree-seeking undergraduates: 3% part-time, 59% women

▶ 116 degree-seeking graduate students

▶ 75% of applicants admitted

▶ SAT or ACT (ACT writing optional), application essay required

▶ 62% graduate within 6 years; 8% enter graduate study

General. Founded in 1902. Regionally accredited. Northwestern is situated on a lake shore location, with access to canoeing, swimming, and nature walks. **Degrees:** 455 bachelor's, 3 associate awarded; master's offered. **ROTC:** Army, Air Force. **Location:** 9 miles from Minneapolis-St. Paul. **Calendar:** Semester, limited summer session. **Full-time faculty:** 94 total; 77% have terminal degrees, 8% minority, 35% women. **Part-time faculty:** 58 total; 36% have terminal degrees, 7% minority, 52% women. **Class size:** 57% < 20, 36% 20-39, 4% 40-49, 3% 50-99, less than 1% >100.

Freshman class profile. 1,289 applied, 969 admitted, 467 enrolled.

Mid 50% test scores			
SAT critical reading:	510-660	GPA 2.0-2.99:	19%
SAT math:	490-610	Rank in top quarter:	51%
ACT composite:	21-27	Rank in top tenth:	21%
GPA 3.75 or higher:	36%	End year in good standing:	87%
GPA 3.50-3.74:	22%	Return as sophomores:	76%
GPA 3.0-3.49:	23%	Out-of-state:	27%
		Live on campus:	96%

Basis for selection. Evidence that student will benefit from the education and contribute to the community is important. School record, recommendations, test scores, essay, character, and religious affiliation very important. ACT recommended. Audition required for music students. Portfolio recommended for art students. Interview recommended for borderline students. **Learning Disabled:** Students should contact the DOSS office at 651-286-7446 or email dpgolias@nwc.edu to review specific needs for disability services.

High school preparation. College-preparatory program recommended. 16 units recommended. Recommended units include English 4, mathematics 3, social studies 3, science 3, foreign language 2 and academic electives 1.

2011-2012 Annual costs. Tuition/fees: $25,700. Room/board: $8,000. Books/supplies: $610. Personal expenses: $1,600.

2010-2011 Financial aid. Need-based: 445 full-time freshmen applied for aid; 383 were judged to have need; 383 of these received aid. Average need met was 71%. Average scholarship/grant was $15,959; average loan $3,741. 64% of total undergraduate aid awarded as scholarships/grants, 36% as loans/jobs. **Non-need-based:** Awarded to 460 full-time undergraduates, including 124 freshmen. Scholarships awarded for academics, alumni affiliation, leadership, music/drama. **Additional information:** Students enrolled at least half-time in the FOCUS or Distance Education degree programs may apply for financial aid from the same Federal and state sources as traditional undergraduates. However, their expense budgets and aid are less due to lower tuition.

Application procedures. Admission: Priority date 5/1; deadline 8/1 (receipt date). No application fee. Admission notification on a rolling basis beginning on or about 10/1. **Financial aid:** Priority date 3/1, closing date 8/1. FAFSA, institutional form required. Applicants notified on a rolling basis starting 3/1; must reply within 2 week(s) of notification.

Academics. Core curriculum built around a biblical worldview theme thoroughly integrates general education and biblical studies (64-68 credits). Transfer students meet core curriculum requirements on a proportional basis. **Special study options:** Combined bachelor's/graduate degree, distance learning, double major, exchange student, honors, independent study, internships, liberal arts/career combination, student-designed major, study abroad, teacher certification program, Washington semester. **Credit/placement by examination:** AP, CLEP, IB, SAT, ACT, institutional tests. 32 credit hours maximum toward associate degree, 32 toward bachelor's. **Support services:** Learning center, reduced course load, remedial instruction, study skills assistance, tutoring.

Majors. Biology: General, biochemistry. **Business:** Accounting, business admin, finance, international, management information systems, marketing. **Communications:** Communications/speech/rhetoric, journalism, public relations, radio/TV. **Communications technology:** Animation/special effects. **Education:** Art, early childhood, elementary, English, ESL, mathematics, music, physical, social studies. **Engineering:** General. **English:** English lit, technical writing. **Foreign languages:** Spanish. **History:** General. **Math:** General. **Parks/recreation:** Exercise sciences, health/fitness. **Protective services:** Criminal justice. **Psychology:** General. **Social sciences:** Urban studies. **Theology:** Bible, missionary, preministerial, youth ministry. **Visual/performing arts:** Dramatic, graphic design, music, music performance, music theory/composition, piano/keyboard, stringed instruments, studio arts, voice/opera. **Work/family studies:** Family studies.

Most popular majors. Business/marketing 20%, education 12%, psychology 11%, theological studies 17%, visual/performing arts 7%.

Computing on campus. PC or laptop required. 100 workstations in dormitories, library, computer center, student center. Dormitories wired for high-speed internet access and linked to campus network. Commuter students can connect to campus network. Online course registration, online library, helpline, student web hosting, wireless network available.

Student life. Freshman orientation: Mandatory. Preregistration for classes offered. 6 one-day events during late spring and summer. General orientation: 4 days prior to start of classes. Multicultural orientation: 4 days prior to general orientation. **Policies:** Religious observance required. Freshmen not permitted cars on campus. **Housing:** Guaranteed on-campus for freshmen. Single-sex dorms, special housing for disabled, apartments, wellness housing available. $200 fully refundable deposit, deadline 5/1. Some special housing accommodations for disabilities available. **Activities:** Bands, campus ministries, choral groups, drama, literary magazine, music ensembles,

musical theater, opera, radio station, student government, student newspaper, symphony orchestra, TV station, Student Missions Fellowship, The Gathering, Transfer Student Organization, Guardian Angels, Mu Kappa, Intercultural Unity Organization, Young Republicans.

Athletics. NCAA, NCCAA. **Intercollegiate:** Baseball M, basketball, cross-country, football (tackle) M, golf M, soccer, softball W, tennis, track and field, volleyball W. **Intramural:** Basketball, football (non-tackle), softball, table tennis, tennis, volleyball. **Team name:** Eagles.

Student services. Adult student services, chaplain/spiritual director, career counseling, student employment services, financial aid counseling, health services, minority student services, personal counseling, placement for graduates, veterans' counselor. **Physically disabled:** Services for visually impaired.

Contact. E-mail: admissions@nwc.edu
Phone: (651) 631-5111 Toll-free number: (800) 827-6827
Fax: (651) 631-5680
Kenneth Faffler, Director of Admissions, Northwestern College, 3003 Snelling Avenue North, Saint Paul, MN 55113-1598

Northwestern Health Sciences University
Bloomington, Minnesota
www.nwhealth.edu   CB code: 6516

- Private two-year upper-division university and health science college
- Very large city

General. Regionally accredited. **Degrees:** 53 bachelor's awarded; master's, professional offered. **Calendar:** Trimester, limited summer session. **Full-time faculty:** 63 total. **Part-time faculty:** 63 total.

Student profile. 74 degree-seeking undergraduates, 731 graduate students.

2011-2012 Annual costs. Books/supplies: $972. Personal expenses: $2,400.

Application procedures. Admission: $50 fee.

Academics. Credit/placement by examination: AP, CLEP.

Computing on campus. Wireless network available.

Contact. E-mail: admit@nwhealth.edu
Phone: (952) 888-4777 ext. 409
Bill Kuehl, Director of Admissions, Northwestern Health Sciences University, 2501 West 84th Street, Bloomington, MN 55431

Oak Hills Christian College
Bemidji, Minnesota
www.oakhills.edu   CB code: 7247

- Private 4-year Bible college affiliated with interdenominational tradition
- Residential campus in large town
- 124 degree-seeking undergraduates: 15% part-time, 54% women, 2% African American, 1% Hispanic American, 3% Native American, 1% international
- 59% of applicants admitted
- ACT (writing optional), application essay required
- 35% graduate within 6 years

General. Founded in 1946. Accredited by ABHE. **Degrees:** 21 bachelor's, 5 associate awarded. **Location:** 4 miles from Bemidji, 230 miles from Minneapolis-St. Paul. **Calendar:** Semester. **Full-time faculty:** 4 total; 75% have terminal degrees, 25% women. **Part-time faculty:** 12 total; 33% have terminal degrees, 17% women. **Class size:** 60% < 20, 29% 20-39, 9% 40-49, 3% 50-99. **Special facilities:** Center for Indian ministries resource center.

Freshman class profile. 59 applied, 35 admitted, 31 enrolled.

Mid 50% test scores		Rank in top quarter:	28%
ACT composite:	19-25	Rank in top tenth:	9%
GPA 3.75 or higher:	14%	Return as sophomores:	60%
GPA 3.50-3.74:	17%	Out-of-state:	4%
GPA 3.0-3.49:	20%	Live on campus:	80%
GPA 2.0-2.99:	45%		

Basis for selection. Applicants must have high school GPA of 2.0 or above and/or ACT score of 18 or above to be eligible for consideration.

Applicants not meeting minimum requirements considered on individual basis. SAT/ACT scores must be received at latest 4 weeks after first day of classes. Not required if student has 24 college credits past high school or if 2 years out of high school. An essay or personal statement may generate an interview. **Home schooled:** Transcript of courses and grades, letter of recommendation (nonparent) required. Proof of graduation from high school. **Learning Disabled:** All special education or diagnostic (IEP) records required. Interview may be requested.

2012-2013 Annual costs. Tuition/fees: $14,670. Room/board: $5,340.

2010-2011 Financial aid. Need-based: 33 full-time freshmen applied for aid; 32 were judged to have need; 32 of these received aid. Average need met was 60%. Average scholarship/grant was $8,108; average loan $3,261. 72% of total undergraduate aid awarded as scholarships/grants, 28% as loans/jobs. **Non-need-based:** Awarded to 6 full-time undergraduates, including 1 freshmen. Scholarships awarded for academics, alumni affiliation.

Application procedures. Admission: No deadline. $25 fee, may be waived for applicants with need. Admission notification on a rolling basis beginning on or about 9/1. Early Admission of high school students is allowed if they are PSEO students. **Financial aid:** No deadline. FAFSA, institutional form required. Applicants notified on a rolling basis starting 3/1.

Academics. Special study options: Combined bachelor's/graduate degree, double major, dual enrollment of high school students, independent study, internships, study abroad. **Credit/placement by examination:** AP, CLEP, ACT, institutional tests. **Support services:** Reduced course load, remedial instruction, study skills assistance, tutoring, writing center.

Majors. Psychology: General. **Theology:** Bible, missionary, sacred music, youth ministry.

Most popular majors. Liberal arts 24%, theological studies 76%.

Computing on campus. 8 workstations in computer center. Dormitories wired for high-speed internet access and linked to campus network. Online course registration, wireless network available.

Student life. Freshman orientation: Mandatory. Preregistration for classes offered. Held first weekend prior to start of fall classes. **Policies:** Mandatory chapel, no alcohol, illegal drugs, gambling, or smoking on campus. Religious observance required. **Housing:** Guaranteed on-campus for freshmen. Single-sex dorms, apartments, wellness housing available. $100 nonrefundable deposit. Apartments for students with dependent children available. **Activities:** Campus ministries, choral groups, music ensembles, student government, married students group, students older than average group, women's group, engaged couples group, many outreach programs, single student cell groups.

Athletics. Intercollegiate: Basketball M, volleyball W. **Intramural:** Basketball, football (non-tackle), golf, soccer, softball, table tennis, volleyball. **Team name:** Wolfpack.

Student services. Adult student services, chaplain/spiritual director, career counseling, student employment services, financial aid counseling, health services, placement for graduates. **Physically disabled:** Services for visually, speech, hearing impaired.

Contact. E-mail: admissions@oakhills.edu
Phone: (218) 751-8671 ext. 1285
Toll-free number: (866) 307-6422 ext. 1285 Fax: (218) 444-1311
John Engquist, Director of Admissions, Oak Hills Christian College, 1600 Oak Hills Road SW, Bemidji, MN 56601-8826

Rasmussen College: Blaine
Blaine, Minnesota
www.rasmussen.edu

- For-profit 4-year branch campus and career college
- Small city

General. Regionally accredited. **Calendar:** Quarter.

Freshman class profile. 446 enrolled.

Basis for selection. Open admission, but selective for some programs.

Application procedures. Admission: No deadline. $40 fee.

Academics. Credit/placement by examination: AP, CLEP.

Majors. Business: Accounting, human resources. **Computer sciences:** Computer science, IT project management. **Health services:** Nursing (RN).

Protective services: Corrections, homeland security, investigation and interviewing.

Contact. Toll-free number: (888) 549-6755
Susan Hammerstrom, Director of Admissions, Rasmussen College: Blaine, 3629 95th Avenue NE, Blaine, MN 55014

Rasmussen College: Lake Elmo/Woodbury
Lake Elmo, Minnesota
www.rasmussen.edu

▶ For-profit 4-year technical college
▶ Commuter campus in small city
▶ 735 degree-seeking undergraduates

General. Regionally accredited. **Degrees:** 20 bachelor's, 124 associate awarded. **Calendar:** Quarter. **Full-time faculty:** 11 total. **Part-time faculty:** 20 total.

Basis for selection. Open admission, but selective for some programs.

2011-2012 Annual costs. Tuition/fees: $17,775. Full-time tuition varies according to program of study. Examples of per-credit-hour charges include Early Childhood Education ($310), Medical Lab Technician, Surgical Technician, Practical Nursing ($395), Professional Nursing, Information Systems Mgmt, Multimedia Technician ($395). Personal expenses: $2,214.

Application procedures. Admission: No deadline. $40 fee. **Financial aid:** No deadline.

Academics. Credit/placement by examination: AP, CLEP.

Majors. Business: Business admin.

Contact. Phone: (651) 259-6600 Fax: (651) 259-6601
Susan Hammerstrom, Director of Admissions, Rasmussen College: Lake Elmo/Woodbury, 8565 Eagle Point Circle, Lake Elmo, MN 55042-8637

Rasmussen College: Moorhead
Moorhead, Minnesota
www.rasmussen.edu

▶ For-profit 4-year branch campus and career college
▶ Small city

General. Degrees: 3 bachelor's, 122 associate awarded. **Calendar:** Quarter.

Freshman class profile. 525 enrolled.

Basis for selection. Open admission, but selective for some programs.

Application procedures. Admission: No deadline. $40 fee.

Academics. Credit/placement by examination: AP, CLEP.

Majors. Business: Accounting, business admin, human resources. **Computer sciences:** General, IT project management. **Protective services:** Corrections, criminalistics, homeland security, investigation and interviewing. **Visual/performing arts:** Digital arts, game design.

Contact. Phone: (218) 304-6200 Fax: (218) 304-6201
Susan Hammerstrom, Director of Admissions, Rasmussen College: Moorhead, 1250 29th Avenue South, Moorhead, MN 56560

Saint Cloud State University
St. Cloud, Minnesota
www.stcloudstate.edu   **CB code: 6679**

▶ Public 4-year university
▶ Commuter campus in small city
▶ 13,030 degree-seeking undergraduates: 16% part-time, 50% women, 5% African American, 3% Asian American, 3% Hispanic American, 6% international
▶ 1,515 degree-seeking graduate students
▶ 90% of applicants admitted

▶ SAT or ACT (ACT writing optional) required
▶ 48% graduate within 6 years

General. Founded in 1869. Regionally accredited. **Degrees:** 2,516 bachelor's, 118 associate awarded; master's, professional offered. **ROTC:** Army. **Location:** 80 miles from Minneapolis-St. Paul. **Calendar:** Semester, limited summer session. **Full-time faculty:** 557 total; 84% have terminal degrees, 21% minority, 45% women. **Part-time faculty:** 315 total; 15% have terminal degrees, 8% minority, 54% women. **Class size:** 34% < 20, 53% 20-39, 8% 40-49, 3% 50-99, 2% >100. **Special facilities:** Planetarium, greenhouse, nature preserve, observatory, GIS cartographic center, aviation facilities, weather labs, National Hockey Center, AVID editing equipment.

Freshman class profile. 5,256 applied, 4,726 admitted, 1,902 enrolled.

Mid 50% test scores			
ACT composite:	19-24	Rank in top quarter:	22%
GPA 3.75 or higher:	11%	Rank in top tenth:	7%
GPA 3.50-3.74:	13%	Return as sophomores:	69%
GPA 3.0-3.49:	35%	Out-of-state:	12%
GPA 2.0-2.99:	40%	Live on campus:	72%
		International:	4%

Basis for selection. Each application individually reviewed and evaluated using a combination of high school rank, GPA, curriculum, test scores, and other indicators of academic performance and potential.

High school preparation. College-preparatory program recommended. 16 units required. Required units include English 4, mathematics 3, social studies 2, history 1, science 3 (laboratory 1), foreign language 2 and visual/performing arts 1.

2011-2012 Annual costs. Tuition/fees: $7,129; $14,425 out-of-state. Room/board: $6,662. Books/supplies: $1,200. Personal expenses: $3,096.

Financial aid. Non-need-based: Scholarships awarded for academics, art, athletics, leadership, music/drama.

Application procedures. Admission: Priority date 12/15; deadline 8/1 (receipt date). $20 fee, may be waived for applicants with need. Admission notification on a rolling basis beginning on or about 9/15. Early application recommended for those who want to live on-campus. **Financial aid:** No deadline. FAFSA, institutional form required. Applicants notified on a rolling basis starting 6/15.

Academics. Special study options: Accelerated study, cooperative education, cross-registration, distance learning, double major, dual enrollment of high school students, ESL, honors, independent study, internships, student-designed major, study abroad, teacher certification program, weekend college. **Credit/placement by examination:** AP, CLEP, IB, ACT, institutional tests. 32 credit hours maximum toward bachelor's degree. **Support services:** Learning center, pre-admission summer program, remedial instruction, study skills assistance, tutoring, writing center.

Majors. Area/ethnic studies: Latin American, women's. **Biology:** General, aquatic, biochemistry, biotechnology, cellular/anatomical, ecology, marine. **Business:** General, accounting, business admin, entrepreneurial studies, finance, human resources, insurance, international, management information systems, marketing, real estate, tourism/travel. **Communications:** Advertising, broadcast journalism, communications/speech/rhetoric, journalism, media studies, public relations, radio/TV. **Computer sciences:** General, computer science, networking, security. **Conservation:** Environmental science, environmental studies. **Education:** Art, biology, chemistry, drama/dance, driver/safety, early childhood, educational technology, elementary, English, foreign languages, French, German, health, history, kindergarten/preschool, mathematics, multi-level teacher, music, physical, physics, psychology, reading, science, secondary, social science, social studies, Spanish, special ed, speech, technology/industrial arts, voc/tech. **Engineering:** Computer, electrical, manufacturing, mechanical. **English:** American lit, creative writing, English lit, rhetoric/composition, writing. **Foreign languages:** French, German, linguistics, Spanish. **Health services:** Audiology/speech pathology, clinical lab science, communication disorders, community health services, medical radiologic technology/radiation therapy, nuclear medical technology, nursing (RN), predental, premedicine, prepharmacy, preveterinary, public health ed, recreational therapy, substance abuse counseling. **History:** General. **Human services:** General, social work. **Liberal arts:** Arts/sciences, library science. **Math:** General, statistics. **Parks/recreation:** General, health/fitness. **Philosophy/religion:** Philosophy. **Physical sciences:** General, atmospheric science, chemistry, geology, hydrology, meteorology, physics, planetary. **Protective services:** Criminal justice. **Psychology:** General, community. **Social sciences:** General, anthropology, econometrics, economics, geography, international relations, political science, sociology, urban studies. **Visual/performing arts:** Acting, art, art history/conservation, ceramics, dramatic, drawing, film/cinema/video, jazz, music, music history, music performance, painting, piano/keyboard, printmaking, sculpture, stringed instruments, studio arts, voice/opera.

Most popular majors. Business/marketing 28%, communications/journalism 8%, education 12%, psychology 7%, social sciences 7%.

Computing on campus. 1,489 workstations in dormitories, library, computer center, student center. Dormitories wired for high-speed internet access and linked to campus network. Commuter students can connect to campus network. Online course registration, online library, helpline, repair service, student web hosting, wireless network available.

Student life. Freshman orientation: Mandatory. Preregistration for classes offered. Includes assistance with fall term registration. **Housing:** Coed dorms, single-sex dorms, special housing for disabled, apartments available. $250 partly refundable deposit, deadline 5/1. **Activities:** Bands, campus ministries, choral groups, dance, drama, film society, international student organizations, literary magazine, music ensembles, Model UN, musical theater, opera, radio station, student government, student newspaper, symphony orchestra, TV station, more than 240 clubs and departmental organizations.

Athletics. NCAA. **Intercollegiate:** Baseball M, basketball, cross-country, diving, football (tackle) M, golf, ice hockey, skiing W, soccer W, softball W, swimming, tennis, track and field, volleyball W, wrestling M. **Intramural:** Badminton, basketball, football (non-tackle), golf, ice hockey, racquetball, soccer, softball, tennis, volleyball, water polo. **Team name:** Huskies.

Student services. Adult student services, alcohol/substance abuse counseling, career counseling, student employment services, financial aid counseling, health services, legal services, minority student services, on-campus daycare, personal counseling, placement for graduates, veterans' counselor, women's services. **Physically disabled:** Services for visually, speech, hearing impaired.

Contact. E-mail: scsu4u@stcloudstate.edu
Phone: (320) 308-2244 Toll-free number: (877) 654-7278
Fax: (320) 308-2243
Richard Shearer, Director of Admissions, Saint Cloud State University, 720 Fourth Avenue South, AS 115, St. Cloud, MN 56301

Southwest Minnesota State University
Marshall, Minnesota
www.smsu.edu   CB code: 6703

- Public 4-year university and liberal arts college
- Residential campus in large town
- 2,450 degree-seeking undergraduates: 19% part-time, 57% women, 4% African American, 2% Asian American, 2% Hispanic American, 1% Native American, 4% international
- 428 degree-seeking graduate students
- 80% of applicants admitted
- SAT or ACT (ACT writing optional) required
- 40% graduate within 6 years

General. Founded in 1963. Regionally accredited. **Degrees:** 535 bachelor's, 2 associate awarded; master's offered. **Location:** 150 miles from Minneapolis-St. Paul. **Calendar:** Semester, limited summer session. **Full-time faculty:** 118 total; 83% have terminal degrees, 12% minority, 48% women. **Part-time faculty:** 62 total; 18% have terminal degrees, 2% minority, 60% women. **Class size:** 39% < 20, 48% 20-39, 9% 40-49, 3% 50-99, less than 1% >100. **Special facilities:** Natural history museum, anthropology museum, planetarium, wildlife area.

Freshman class profile. 1,455 applied, 1,167 admitted, 408 enrolled.

Mid 50% test scores		Rank in top tenth:	9%
ACT composite:	19-24	End year in good standing:	94%
GPA 3.75 or higher:	14%	Return as sophomores:	70%
GPA 3.50-3.74:	16%	Out-of-state:	23%
GPA 3.0-3.49:	37%	Live on campus:	86%
GPA 2.0-2.99:	29%	International:	2%
Rank in top quarter:	27%		

Basis for selection. Class rank in top half of class or SAT combined score of 970 (exclusive of Writing) or ACT composite score of 21. Provisional admission may be granted to students who rank in top two-thirds of class or have ACT composite score of 19 or SAT combined score of 890. GED students must submit ACT. ACT recommended. PSAT/NMSQT may be submitted in place of SAT or ACT. Interview recommended for academically weak students; audition recommended for music students. **Home schooled:** Transcript of courses and grades required.

High school preparation. College-preparatory program required. 16 units required. Required units include English 4, mathematics 3, social studies 3, history 1, science 3 and foreign language 2. Social studies units must include American history and geography.

2011-2012 Annual costs. Tuition/fees: $7,739; $7,739 out-of-state. Room/board: $6,944. Books/supplies: $1,200. Personal expenses: $1,578.

2011-2012 Financial aid. Need-based: Average need met was 51%. Average scholarship/grant was $5,558; average loan $3,324. 45% of total undergraduate aid awarded as scholarships/grants, 55% as loans/jobs. **Non-need-based:** Scholarships awarded for academics, alumni affiliation, art, athletics, leadership, minority status, music/drama, state residency.

Application procedures. Admission: Priority date 8/15; deadline 9/1 (receipt date). $20 fee. Admission notification on a rolling basis. **Financial aid:** Priority date 3/1; no closing date. FAFSA, institutional form required. Applicants notified on a rolling basis starting 6/1.

Academics. Special study options: Accelerated study, combined bachelor's/graduate degree, cooperative education, cross-registration, distance learning, double major, dual enrollment of high school students, ESL, external degree, honors, independent study, internships, student-designed major, study abroad, teacher certification program. 2+2 bachelor's programs with Ridgewater College, St. Cloud Technical College, Minnesota West, South Central (Mankato) and Riverland College. Visiting Exchange Student Program. **Credit/placement by examination:** AP, CLEP, ACT, institutional tests. 10 credit hours maximum toward associate degree, 20 toward bachelor's. **Support services:** Learning center, reduced course load, remedial instruction, study skills assistance, tutoring, writing center.

Majors. Biology: General, cell/histology, ecology. **Business:** Accounting, business admin, finance, hospitality admin, marketing, nonprofit/public, restaurant/food services. **Communications:** Broadcast journalism, communications/speech/rhetoric, public relations, radio/TV. **Computer sciences:** General, information technology. **Conservation:** Environmental science. **Education:** Art, biology, chemistry, drama/dance, early childhood, elementary, health, mathematics, music, physical, science, speech. **English:** Creative writing, English lit, rhetoric/composition. **Foreign languages:** Spanish. **General:** Agribusiness operations, food science, soil science. **History:** General. **Human services:** General, social work. **Liberal arts:** Arts/sciences. **Math:** General. **Parks/recreation:** Exercise sciences, health/fitness. **Philosophy/religion:** Philosophy. **Physical sciences:** Chemistry. **Protective services:** Criminal justice, fire services admin, law enforcement admin. **Psychology:** General. **Social sciences:** Political science, sociology. **Visual/performing arts:** Art, dramatic, music, music management.

Most popular majors. Business/marketing 39%, education 16%, parks/recreation 8%.

Computing on campus. 300 workstations in dormitories, library, computer center, student center. Dormitories wired for high-speed internet access and linked to campus network. Commuter students can connect to campus network. Online course registration, online library, helpline, repair service, student web hosting, wireless network available.

Student life. Freshman orientation: Available, $135 fee. Preregistration for classes offered. **Housing:** Coed dorms, single-sex dorms, special housing for disabled, apartments available. $100 fully refundable deposit. **Activities:** Bands, campus ministries, choral groups, dance, drama, film society, international student organizations, literary magazine, music ensembles, musical theater, radio station, student government, student newspaper, symphony orchestra, TV station, Black Student Union, Inter-Varsity Christian Fellowship, Lutheran Student Commission, student activities committee, Republican Speakers Club, Young DFL, non-traditional students organization.

Athletics. NAIA. **Intercollegiate:** Baseball M, basketball, football (tackle) M, golf W, soccer W, softball W, tennis W, volleyball W, wrestling M. **Intramural:** Basketball, ice hockey M, racquetball, skiing, softball, tennis, track and field, volleyball, wrestling M. **Team name:** Mustangs.

Student services. Adult student services, alcohol/substance abuse counseling, chaplain/spiritual director, career counseling, student employment services, financial aid counseling, health services, minority student services, on-campus daycare, personal counseling, placement for graduates, veterans' counselor, women's services. **Physically disabled:** Services for visually, speech, hearing impaired.

Contact. E-mail: andrew.hlubek@smsu.edu
Phone: (507) 537-6286 Toll-free number: (800) 642-0684
Fax: (507) 537-7154
Andrew Hlubek, Director of Admissions, Southwest Minnesota State University, 1501 State Street, Marshall, MN 56258-1598

St. Catherine University
Saint Paul, Minnesota
www.stkate.edu   CB member   CB code: 6105

- Private 4-year health science and liberal arts college for women affiliated with Roman Catholic Church
- Commuter campus in large city

- 3,734 degree-seeking undergraduates: 34% part-time, 97% women, 11% African American, 11% Asian American, 4% Hispanic American, 1% Native American, 1% international
- 1,355 degree-seeking graduate students
- 52% of applicants admitted
- SAT or ACT (ACT writing optional) required
- 66% graduate within 6 years

General. Founded in 1905. Regionally accredited. St. Catherine University is organized into 4 schools: Humanities, Art & Science; Health; Business & Leadership; and Professional Studies. **Degrees:** 522 bachelor's, 212 associate awarded; master's, professional offered. **ROTC:** Army, Air Force. **Location:** 6 miles from downtown St. Paul and downtown Minneapolis. **Calendar:** 4-1-4, extensive summer session. **Full-time faculty:** 292 total; 82% have terminal degrees, 10% minority, 81% women. **Part-time faculty:** 166 total; 31% have terminal degrees, 7% minority, 75% women. **Class size:** 59% < 20, 38% 20-39, 2% 40-49, 2% 50-99. **Special facilities:** Center for women's research, observatory, art gallery.

Freshman class profile. 2,808 applied, 1,451 admitted, 370 enrolled.

Mid 50% test scores		Rank in top quarter:	63%
ACT composite:	22-26	Rank in top tenth:	26%
GPA 3.75 or higher:	40%	Return as sophomores:	84%
GPA 3.50-3.74:	22%	Out-of-state:	15%
GPA 3.0-3.49:	28%	Live on campus:	78%
GPA 2.0-2.99:	10%	International:	1%

Basis for selection. School achievement record with rank in top half of class and test scores important. Extracurricular and community involvement also considered. Recommendations important. Interview recommended for all applicants, required for marginal students. Audition recommended for music students; portfolio recommended for art students. Essay recommended for marginal students.

High school preparation. College-preparatory program recommended. 15 units recommended. Recommended units include English 4, mathematics 3, social studies 2, science 2 and foreign language 4.

2011-2012 Annual costs. Tuition/fees: $29,780. Room/board: $8,002. Books/supplies: $1,000. Personal expenses: $3,250.

2011-2012 Financial aid. **Need-based:** Average need met was 90%. Average scholarship/grant was $12,100; average loan $3,900. 61% of total undergraduate aid awarded as scholarships/grants, 39% as loans/jobs. **Non-need-based:** Scholarships awarded for academics, alumni affiliation, leadership, state residency. **Additional information:** Audition required for music scholarships.

Application procedures. **Admission:** No deadline. No application fee. Admission notification on a rolling basis. Must reply by May 1 or within 2 week(s) if notified thereafter. Students must be accepted by 2/1 to be eligible to compete in merit scholarship competition. **Financial aid:** Priority date 4/15; no closing date. FAFSA, institutional form required. Applicants notified on a rolling basis starting 3/30; must reply within 2 week(s) of notification.

Academics. **Special study options:** Combined bachelor's/graduate degree, cross-registration, double major, dual enrollment of high school students, exchange student, honors, independent study, internships, student-designed major, study abroad, teacher certification program, urban semester, Washington semester, weekend college. Cooperative program in fashion merchandising with Fashion Institute of Technology in New York City and Fashion Institute of Design in Los Angeles, academic year of study in New York City, exchange program with other Carondolet Colleges, internship program includes over 500 sites in Twin Cities area. **Credit/placement by examination:** AP, CLEP, IB, institutional tests. 32 credit hours maximum toward bachelor's degree. **Support services:** Learning center, reduced course load, remedial instruction, study skills assistance, tutoring, writing center.

Majors. **Area/ethnic studies:** Women's. **Biology:** General, biochemistry. **Business:** Accounting, business admin, fashion, international, management information systems, sales/distribution. **Communications:** Communications/ speech/rhetoric. **Computer sciences:** General, information systems. **Education:** General, art, business, early childhood, elementary, English, family/ consumer sciences, foreign languages, mathematics, middle, music, physical, secondary. **English:** English lit, rhetoric/composition. **Foreign languages:** American Sign Language, French, sign language interpretation, Spanish. **Health services:** Dietetics, medical records admin, nursing (RN), predental, premedicine, prepharmacy, preveterinary, respiratory therapy technology. **History:** General. **Human services:** Social work. **Math:** General. **Parks/ recreation:** Exercise sciences. **Philosophy/religion:** Philosophy. **Physical sciences:** Chemistry, physics. **Psychology:** General. **Social sciences:** General, economics, international relations, political science, sociology. **Theology:** Theology. **Visual/performing arts:** Art history/conservation, dramatic, fashion design, music, music performance, studio arts. **Work/family studies:** General, food/nutrition.

Most popular majors. Business/marketing 14%, communications/journalism 6%, education 8%, health sciences 30%, public administration/social services 8%, social sciences 7%.

Computing on campus. 350 workstations in dormitories, library, computer center, student center. Dormitories wired for high-speed internet access and linked to campus network. Commuter students can connect to campus network. Online course registration, online library, helpline, wireless network available.

Student life. **Freshman orientation:** Mandatory. Preregistration for classes offered. **Housing:** Guaranteed on-campus for freshmen. Apartments available. $100 nonrefundable deposit. Apartments for student-parents available. **Activities:** Campus ministries, choral groups, dance, drama, international student organizations, literary magazine, music ensembles, musical theater, radio station, student government, student newspaper, Volunteers in Action, League of Women Voters, Minnesota Public Interest Research Group, Women of Color, clubs for majors, women's issues groups.

Athletics. NCAA. **Intercollegiate:** Basketball W, cross-country W, diving W, golf W, ice hockey W, soccer W, softball W, swimming W, tennis W, track and field W, volleyball W. **Intramural:** Basketball W, cheerleading W, football (non-tackle) W, golf W, lacrosse W, racquetball W, soccer W, softball W, tennis W, volleyball W. **Team name:** Wildcats.

Student services. Adult student services, chaplain/spiritual director, career counseling, student employment services, financial aid counseling, health services, minority student services, on-campus daycare, personal counseling, placement for graduates, women's services. **Physically disabled:** Services for visually, speech, hearing impaired.

Contact. E-mail: admissions@stkate.edu
Phone: (651) 690-8850 Toll-free number: (800) 945-4599
Fax: (651) 690-8868
Marlene Mohs, Associate Dean of Admissions, St. Catherine University, 2004 Randolph Avenue #F-02, St. Paul, MN 55105

St. John's University
Collegeville, Minnesota
www.csbsju.edu/

CB member
CB code: 6624

- Private 4-year university and liberal arts college for men affiliated with Roman Catholic Church
- Residential campus in rural community
- 1,890 degree-seeking undergraduates: 2% part-time, 3% African American, 3% Asian American, 3% Hispanic American, 1% Native American, 7% international
- 126 graduate students
- 74% of applicants admitted
- SAT or ACT (ACT writing optional), application essay required
- 80% graduate within 6 years; 20% enter graduate study

General. Founded in 1857. Regionally accredited. SJU located six miles from the College of Saint Benedict; students enrolled on both campuses have access to classes, activities held by the two institutions. **Degrees:** 450 bachelor's awarded; master's offered. **ROTC:** Army. **Location:** 70 miles from Minneapolis-St. Paul, 15 miles from St. Cloud. **Calendar:** Semester, limited summer session. **Full-time faculty:** 154 total; 84% have terminal degrees, 10% minority, 51% women. **Part-time faculty:** 26 total; 31% have terminal degrees, 46% women. **Class size:** 55% < 20, 44% 20-39, less than 1% 40-49, less than 1% 50-99. **Special facilities:** Observatory, ecumenical center, museum and manuscript library, arboretum, natural history museum, pottery studio and kiln, greenhouse, nature preserve and herbarium, labyrinth and performing arts center at College of St. Benedict.

Freshman class profile. 1,647 applied, 1,225 admitted, 494 enrolled.

Mid 50% test scores		GPA 2.0-2.99:	8%
SAT critical reading:	450-670	Rank in top quarter:	56%
SAT math:	490-640	Rank in top tenth:	23%
SAT writing:	470-620	End year in good standing:	92%
ACT composite:	22-29	Return as sophomores:	91%
GPA 3.75 or higher:	32%	Out-of-state:	18%
GPA 3.50-3.74:	20%	Live on campus:	100%
GPA 3.0-3.49:	40%	International:	6%

Basis for selection. Course selection, scholastic achievement, GPA, test scores and essay are most important. Extracurricular involvement and recommendations are also important. Interview recommended for conditionally accepted/academically weak students. **Home schooled:** Applicants are not required to have a high school diploma, but are required to provide appropriate documentation of college preparatory curriculum.

High school preparation. College-preparatory program required. 15 units required. Required and recommended units include English 4, mathematics 3, social studies 2, science 2 (laboratory 2), foreign language 2 and academic electives 4.

2011-2012 Annual costs. Tuition/fees: $33,606. Room/board: $8,344. Books/supplies: $1,000. Personal expenses: $1,300.

2011-2012 Financial aid. Need-based: 392 full-time freshmen applied for aid; 338 were judged to have need; 338 of these received aid. Average need met was 91%. Average scholarship/grant was $22,384; average loan $3,959. 64% of total undergraduate aid awarded as scholarships/grants, 36% as loans/jobs. **Non-need-based:** Awarded to 1,611 full-time undergraduates, including 449 freshmen. Scholarships awarded for academics, art, leadership, music/drama, ROTC. **Additional information:** Scholarship letters will be mailed on rolling basis approximately 2 weeks from the time admission acceptance letter is sent.

Application procedures. Admission: Priority date 11/15; no deadline. No application fee. A non-refundable enrollment deposit of $300 is due by May 1. **Financial aid:** Priority date 3/15; no closing date. FAFSA, institutional form required. Applicants notified on a rolling basis starting 3/15; must reply by 5/1.

Academics. Special study options: Combined bachelor's/graduate degree, cross-registration, double major, dual enrollment of high school students, ESL, exchange student, honors, independent study, internships, student-designed major, study abroad, teacher certification program. 3-2 program in engineering with University of Minnesota, 3-1 program in dentistry with University of Minnesota, cross registration with St. Cloud State University. **Credit/placement by examination:** AP, CLEP, IB, SAT, ACT, institutional tests. **Support services:** Reduced course load, study skills assistance, tutoring, writing center.

Majors. Area/ethnic studies: Women's. **Biology:** General, biochemistry. **Business:** Accounting, business admin. **Computer sciences:** Computer science. **Conservation:** Environmental science. **Education:** General, elementary. **English:** English lit, rhetoric/composition. **Foreign languages:** Classics, French, German, Spanish. **Health services:** Dietetics, nursing (RN), predental, premedicine, prepharmacy, preveterinary. **History:** General. **Liberal arts:** Arts/sciences, humanities. **Math:** General. **Philosophy/religion:** Philosophy. **Physical sciences:** Chemistry, physics. **Psychology:** General. **Social sciences:** General, economics, political science, sociology. **Theology:** Preministerial, theology. **Visual/performing arts:** Art, dramatic, music.

Most popular majors. Biology 11%, business/marketing 28%, English 8%, psychology 6%, social sciences 16%.

Computing on campus. 940 workstations in dormitories, library, computer center, student center. Dormitories wired for high-speed internet access and linked to campus network. Commuter students can connect to campus network. Online course registration, online library, helpline, repair service, student web hosting, wireless network available.

Student life. Freshman orientation: Mandatory. Preregistration for classes offered. Fall orientation begins the evening of move-in day and concludes with convocation the first day of classes. **Policies:** Four year residency requirement. **Housing:** Guaranteed on-campus for freshmen. Special housing for disabled, apartments available. **Activities:** Bands, campus ministries, choral groups, dance, drama, international student organizations, literary magazine, music ensembles, Model UN, musical theater, opera, radio station, student government, student newspaper, symphony orchestra, Volunteers in Service to Others, College Republicans, College Democrats, joints events council, Asia club, Student Coalition for Global Solidarity, Students in Free Enterprise, Magis, cultural fusion club, outdoor leadership center.

Athletics. NCAA. **Intercollegiate:** Baseball M, basketball M, cross-country M, diving M, football (tackle) M, golf M, ice hockey M, soccer M, swimming M, tennis M, track and field M, wrestling M. **Intramural:** Basketball M, football (tackle) M, ice hockey M, racquetball M, soccer M, softball M, table tennis M, tennis M, volleyball M, water polo M. **Team name:** Johnnies.

Student services. Alcohol/substance abuse counseling, chaplain/spiritual director, career counseling, financial aid counseling, health services, minority student services, personal counseling, placement for graduates. **Physically disabled:** Services for hearing impaired.

Contact. E-mail: admissions@csbsju.edu
Phone: (320) 363-5055 Toll-free number: (800) 544-1489
Fax: (320) 363-5650
Calvin Mosley, Vice President for Admission and Financial Aid, St. John's University, College of St Benedict/St John's University, Collegeville, MN 56321-7155

St. Mary's University of Minnesota
Winona, Minnesota   **CB member**
www.smumn.edu   **CB code: 6632**

- Private 4-year university affiliated with Roman Catholic Church
- Residential campus in large town
- 2,010 degree-seeking undergraduates: 29% part-time, 54% women, 6% African American, 2% Asian American, 4% Hispanic American, 2% international
- 3,357 degree-seeking graduate students
- 72% of applicants admitted
- SAT or ACT (ACT writing optional), application essay required
- 62% graduate within 6 years; 14% enter graduate study

General. Founded in 1912. Regionally accredited. **Degrees:** 495 bachelor's awarded; master's, professional, doctoral offered. **ROTC:** Army. **Location:** 110 miles from Minneapolis-St. Paul, 45 miles from Rochester. **Calendar:** Trimester, limited summer session. **Full-time faculty:** 105 total; 84% have terminal degrees, 5% minority, 38% women. **Part-time faculty:** 473 total; 38% have terminal degrees, 7% minority, 54% women. **Class size:** 62% < 20, 38% 20-39. **Special facilities:** Golf course, running, skiing and hiking trails, challenge ropes course, over 100 acres of forest with trails and creek.

Freshman class profile. 1,708 applied, 1,228 admitted, 373 enrolled.

Mid 50% test scores			
SAT critical reading:	430-560	Rank in top quarter:	42%
SAT math:	440-560	Rank in top tenth:	20%
ACT composite:	20-25	End year in good standing:	91%
GPA 3.75 or higher:	23%	Return as sophomores:	77%
GPA 3.50-3.74:	16%	Out-of-state:	43%
GPA 3.0-3.49:	31%	Live on campus:	99%
GPA 2.0-2.99:	29%	International:	2%

Basis for selection. Minimum 2.5 GPA, upper half of class, 50th percentile on standardized tests, essay, college prep coursework required. Recommendations, interview, school and community activities considered. Interview recommended for academically marginal students. **Home schooled:** Statement describing home school structure and mission, transcript of courses and grades required.

High school preparation. College-preparatory program required. 18 units required. Required and recommended units include English 4, mathematics 3, social studies 2, science 3 (laboratory 2), foreign language 2 and academic electives 6.

2012-2013 Annual costs. Tuition/fees: $28,320. Room/board: $7,440. Books/supplies: $1,300. Personal expenses: $820.

2011-2012 Financial aid. Need-based: 338 full-time freshmen applied for aid; 304 were judged to have need; 304 of these received aid. Average need met was 80%. Average scholarship/grant was $16,799; average loan $4,176. 61% of total undergraduate aid awarded as scholarships/grants, 39% as loans/jobs. **Non-need-based:** Awarded to 264 full-time undergraduates, including 95 freshmen. Scholarships awarded for academics, alumni affiliation, art, leadership, minority status, music/drama.

Application procedures. Admission: Priority date 4/1; deadline 5/1 (postmark date). $25 fee, may be waived for applicants with need, free for online applicants. Admission notification by 5/1. Admission notification on a rolling basis. Must reply by May 1 or within 2 week(s) if notified thereafter. **Financial aid:** Priority date 3/15; no closing date. FAFSA required. Applicants notified on a rolling basis starting 2/1; must reply within 3 week(s) of notification.

Academics. Special study options: Cooperative education, cross-registration, double major, dual enrollment of high school students, ESL, honors, independent study, internships, student-designed major, study abroad, teacher certification program, urban semester, Washington semester. **Credit/placement by examination:** AP, CLEP, IB, SAT, ACT, institutional tests. 15 credit hours maximum toward bachelor's degree. **Support services:** Learning center, reduced course load, remedial instruction, study skills assistance, tutoring, writing center.

Majors. Biology: General, biochemistry, environmental. **Business:** General, accounting, entrepreneurial studies, human resources, international, marketing, sales/distribution. **Communications:** Journalism, persuasive communications. **Communications technology:** Desktop publishing. **Computer sciences:** Information systems. **Education:** Biology, chemistry, elementary, English, French, mathematics, music, physics, social science, Spanish. **Engineering:** Applied physics. **English:** General lit. **Foreign languages:** Spanish. **Health services:** Clinical lab science, cytogenetics, cytotechnology, nuclear medical technology, nursing (RN), prephysical therapy. **History:** General.

Math: General. **Philosophy/religion:** Christian, philosophy. **Physical sciences:** Chemistry. **Protective services:** Corrections, law enforcement admin, police science, security management. **Psychology:** General. **Social sciences:** General, sociology. **Theology:** Lay ministry, religious ed, sacred music, theology. **Visual/performing arts:** Dramatic, graphic design, music, music performance, studio arts.

Most popular majors. Business/marketing 50%, security/protective services 7%.

Computing on campus. 365 workstations in dormitories, library, computer center, student center. Dormitories wired for high-speed internet access and linked to campus network. Commuter students can connect to campus network. Online course registration, online library, helpline, student web hosting, wireless network available.

Student life. Freshman orientation: Mandatory. Preregistration for classes offered. Held during summer prior to fall enrollment. **Housing:** Guaranteed on-campus for all undergraduates. Coed dorms, single-sex dorms, special housing for disabled, apartments available. **Activities:** Bands, campus ministries, choral groups, dance, drama, international student organizations, literary magazine, music ensembles, musical theater, radio station, student government, student newspaper, Big and Little Pals, College Democrats, College Republicans, Serving Others United in Love, Intercultural Awareness Association, liturgical ministers, BUDDIES, Habitat for Humanity, Colleges Against Cancer.

Athletics. NCAA. **Intercollegiate:** Baseball M, basketball, cross-country, diving, golf, ice hockey, soccer, softball W, swimming, tennis, track and field, volleyball W. **Intramural:** Basketball, football (non-tackle), handball, ice hockey, soccer, softball, volleyball. **Team name:** Cardinals.

Student services. Alcohol/substance abuse counseling, chaplain/spiritual director, career counseling, financial aid counseling, health services, personal counseling. **Physically disabled:** Services for visually, hearing impaired.

Contact. E-mail: admission@smumn.edu
Phone: (507) 457-1700 Toll-free number: (800) 635-5987
Fax: (507) 457-1722
Brandi DeFries, Director of Admission, St. Mary's University of Minnesota, 700 Terrace Heights #2, Winona, MN 55987-1399

St. Olaf College
Northfield, Minnesota

CB member
CB code: 6638

www.stolaf.edu

- Private 4-year liberal arts college affiliated with Evangelical Lutheran Church in America
- Residential campus in large town
- 3,128 degree-seeking undergraduates: 1% part-time, 56% women, 2% African American, 5% Asian American, 3% Hispanic American, 4% international
- 53% of applicants admitted
- SAT or ACT (ACT writing optional), application essay required
- 85% graduate within 6 years; 29% enter graduate study

General. Founded in 1874. Regionally accredited. **Degrees:** 703 bachelor's awarded. **Location:** 35 miles from Minneapolis-St. Paul. **Calendar:** 4-1-4, limited summer session. **Full-time faculty:** 218 total; 94% have terminal degrees, 13% minority, 44% women. **Part-time faculty:** 115 total; 52% have terminal degrees, 6% minority, 54% women. **Class size:** 58% < 20, 37% 20-39, 2% 40-49, 4% 50-99, less than 1% >100. **Special facilities:** 325 acres of restored native tallgrass prairie, wetlands, and woodlands, student-run organic farm.

Freshman class profile. 4,181 applied, 2,214 admitted, 739 enrolled.

Mid 50% test scores			
SAT critical reading:	590-720	Rank in top quarter:	86%
SAT math:	600-710	Rank in top tenth:	60%
SAT writing:	580-710	End year in good standing:	95%
ACT composite:	27-32	Return as sophomores:	94%
GPA 3.75 or higher:	53%	Out-of-state:	51%
GPA 3.50-3.74:	19%	Live on campus:	99%
GPA 3.0-3.49:	21%	International:	6%
GPA 2.0-2.99:	7%		

Basis for selection. Academic achievement most important, with academic aptitude and personal qualifications, as well as leadership and significant involvement in school and community, strongly considered. Interview recommended. Audition required for music students. **Home schooled:** Transcript of courses and grades, interview, letter of recommendation (nonparent) required. **Learning Disabled:** Personal interview recommended. Untimed standardized tests accepted.

High school preparation. College-preparatory program required. 20 units recommended. Recommended units include English 4, mathematics 4, social studies 4, science 4 (laboratory 2) and foreign language 4.

2011-2012 Annual costs. Tuition/fees: $38,150. Room/board: $8,800. Books/supplies: $1,000. Personal expenses: $900.

2011-2012 Financial aid. Need-based: 677 full-time freshmen applied for aid; 475 were judged to have need; 475 of these received aid. Average need met was 100%. Average scholarship/grant was $26,577; average loan $3,821. 81% of total undergraduate aid awarded as scholarships/grants, 19% as loans/jobs. **Non-need-based:** Awarded to 1,646 full-time undergraduates, including 449 freshmen. Scholarships awarded for academics, art, leadership, music/drama. **Additional information:** Limited number of music lesson fee waivers available for music majors, awarded on audition basis only.

Application procedures. Admission: Closing date 1/15 (postmark date). $40 fee, may be waived for applicants with need, free for online applicants. Admission notification by 3/15. Must reply by 5/1. **Financial aid:** Priority date 2/1, closing date 3/1. FAFSA required. CSS PROFILE due February 1. Applicants notified by 3/22; must reply by 5/1 or within 2 week(s) of notification.

Academics. Students may propose self-designed integrative majors. **Special study options:** Cross-registration, double major, dual enrollment of high school students, independent study, internships, student-designed major, study abroad, teacher certification program, urban semester, Washington semester. **Credit/placement by examination:** AP, CLEP, IB, SAT, ACT, institutional tests. Maximum of six St. Olaf-equivalent credits (one course = one credit) awarded from among all pre-college (PSEO/CIS/AP/IB) credits presented by matriculating first-year students. St. Olaf does not offer credit for any other exams. **Support services:** Learning center, pre-admission summer program, reduced course load, study skills assistance, tutoring, writing center.

Majors. Area/ethnic studies: General, American, Asian, Latin American, Russian/Slavic, women's. **Biology:** General. **Computer sciences:** Computer science. **Conservation:** Environmental studies. **Education:** Music, social studies. **English:** English lit. **Foreign languages:** Ancient Greek, classics, French, German, Latin, Norwegian, Russian, Spanish. **Health services:** Nursing (RN). **History:** General. **Human services:** Social work. **Liberal arts:** Arts/sciences. **Math:** General. **Parks/recreation:** Exercise sciences. **Philosophy/religion:** Philosophy, religion. **Physical sciences:** Chemistry, physics. **Psychology:** General. **Social sciences:** Economics, political science, sociology. **Theology:** Sacred music. **Visual/performing arts:** Art, art history/conservation, dance, dramatic, music, music performance, music theory/composition.

Most popular majors. Area/ethnic studies 6%, biology 12%, English 6%, mathematics 8%, physical sciences 8%, social sciences 16%, visual/performing arts 10%.

Computing on campus. 902 workstations in dormitories, library, computer center, student center. Dormitories wired for high-speed internet access and linked to campus network. Commuter students can connect to campus network. Online course registration, online library, helpline, student web hosting, wireless network available.

Student life. Freshman orientation: Mandatory. Preregistration for classes offered. Held 5 days before start of fall classes. **Policies:** Alcohol not permitted on campus. **Housing:** Guaranteed on-campus for all undergraduates. Coed dorms, special housing for disabled available. Honor houses, language houses, quiet houses, first-year only dorms. **Activities:** Bands, campus ministries, choral groups, dance, drama, film society, international student organizations, literary magazine, music ensembles, Model UN, musical theater, opera, radio station, student government, student newspaper, symphony orchestra, TV station, 205 registered student organizations.

Athletics. NCAA. **Intercollegiate:** Baseball M, basketball, cross-country, diving, football (tackle) M, golf, ice hockey, skiing, soccer, softball W, swimming, tennis, track and field, volleyball W, wrestling M. **Intramural:** Basketball, bowling, football (non-tackle), golf, soccer, softball, swimming, table tennis, triathlon, volleyball, wrestling. **Team name:** Oles.

Student services. Alcohol/substance abuse counseling, chaplain/spiritual director, career counseling, services for economically disadvantaged, student employment services, financial aid counseling, health services, minority student services, personal counseling. **Physically disabled:** Services for visually, hearing impaired.

Contact. E-mail: admissions@stolaf.edu
Phone: (507) 786-3025 Toll-free number: (800) 800-3025
Fax: (507) 786-3832
Derek Gueldenzoph, Dean of Admissions, St. Olaf College, 1520 St. Olaf Avenue, Northfield, MN 55057

University of Minnesota: Crookston
Crookston, Minnesota
www1.crk.umn.edu   CB code: 6893

♦ Public 4-year branch campus college
♦ Commuter campus in small town
♦ 1,600 degree-seeking undergraduates: 21% part-time, 48% women, 5% African American, 2% Asian American, 2% Hispanic American, 1% Native American, 9% international
♦ 74% of applicants admitted
♦ SAT or ACT (ACT writing optional) required
♦ 37% graduate within 6 years

General. Founded in 1965. Regionally accredited. **Degrees:** 297 bachelor's, 2 associate awarded. **ROTC:** Air Force. **Location:** 25 miles from Grand Forks, North Dakota; 70 miles from Fargo, North Dakota; 170 miles from Winnipeg, Canada. **Calendar:** Semester, limited summer session. **Full-time faculty:** 61 total; 44% have terminal degrees, 12% minority, 46% women. **Part-time faculty:** 55 total; 40% have terminal degrees, 6% minority, 46% women. **Class size:** 49% < 20, 40% 20-39, 5% 40-49, 5% 50-99. **Special facilities:** 85-acre Red River Valley Natural History Area containing prairie, marshes, and forests; visualization and informatics lab; telescope.

Freshman class profile. 862 applied, 636 admitted, 268 enrolled.

GPA 3.75 or higher:	14%	Out-of-state:	27%
GPA 3.50-3.74:	13%	Live on campus:	80%
GPA 3.0-3.49:	38%	International:	7%
GPA 2.0-2.99:	34%	Fraternities:	5%
Rank in top quarter:	25%	Sororities:	1%
Rank in top tenth:	10%		

Basis for selection. High school class rank and ACT test scores most important. ACT recommended. **Learning Disabled:** Students encouraged to contact Disability Services early in the admissions process to insure availability of appropriate services.

High school preparation. College-preparatory program recommended. 13 units required. Required and recommended units include English 4, mathematics 3, social studies 3, science 3 (laboratory 2) and foreign language 2.

2011-2012 Annual costs. Tuition/fees: $11,096; $11,096 out-of-state. Room/board: $6,764. Books/supplies: $1,000. Personal expenses: $1,000.

2011-2012 Financial aid. Need-based: 233 full-time freshmen applied for aid; 198 were judged to have need; 198 of these received aid. Average need met was 79%. Average scholarship/grant was $8,683; average loan $4,280. 48% of total undergraduate aid awarded as scholarships/grants, 52% as loans/jobs. **Non-need-based:** Scholarships awarded for academics, alumni affiliation, athletics, leadership, minority status, music/drama, ROTC, state residency. **Additional information:** Under the University of Minnesota Promise Scholarship (U Promise), eligible new Minnesota resident undergraduates with a family income of up to $100,000 will be guaranteed a U Promise Scholarship. Eligible new freshman and transfer students enrolling for the first time will receive a guaranteed, multi-year, U Promise Scholarship. Eligible new freshmen will receive a guaranteed need-based scholarship, ranging from $500 to $3,500 each year, for four years. Eligible new transfer students will receive a guaranteed, need-based scholarship, ranging from $500 to $1,500 each year, for two years.

Application procedures. Admission: Priority date 2/1; no deadline. $30 fee, may be waived for applicants with need. Admission notification on a rolling basis beginning on or about 9/1. **Financial aid:** Priority date 2/15; no closing date. FAFSA required. Applicants notified on a rolling basis starting 3/15.

Academics. Special study options: Cross-registration, distance learning, double major, dual enrollment of high school students, ESL, honors, independent study, internships, student-designed major, study abroad, teacher certification program. **Credit/placement by examination:** AP, CLEP, IB, ACT, institutional tests. Proficiency examinations are administered by appropriate academic department, require no fee, and yield no credit or grade but may fulfill prerequisites for advanced courses or satisfy requirements. Special Examinations for Credit have fee of $50 per credit. Credits earned by examination do not count as residence credits. Exams given at discretion of appropriate academic department. **Support services:** Learning center, reduced course load, remedial instruction, study skills assistance, tutoring, writing center.

Majors. Biology: General. **Business:** Accounting, business admin, entrepreneurial studies, hospitality admin, hotel/motel admin, management information systems, marketing, operations, resort management, restaurant/food services. **Communications:** General. **Conservation:** General, enforcement, management/policy, urban forestry, water/wetlands/marine. **Education:**

Agricultural, early childhood, environmental, kindergarten/preschool, technology/industrial arts. **Engineering:** Software. **General:** Agribusiness operations, agronomy, animal sciences, business technology, crop production, equine science, farm/ranch, greenhouse operations, horticultural science, landscaping, mechanization, plant sciences, power machinery, sustainable agriculture, turf management. **Health services:** Health care admin, preveterinary. **Math:** General. **Parks/recreation:** Facilities management, sports admin. **Protective services:** Corrections, law enforcement admin. **Psychology:** Community, industrial.

Most popular majors. Agriculture 26%, business/marketing 33%, health sciences 6%, interdisciplinary studies 6%, natural resources/environmental science 16%.

Computing on campus. PC or laptop required. 50 workstations in library. Dormitories wired for high-speed internet access and linked to campus network. Commuter students can connect to campus network. Online course registration, online library, helpline, repair service, student web hosting, wireless network available.

Student life. Freshman orientation: Mandatory, $75 fee. Preregistration for classes offered. The new student orientation program for the fall term begins three days before the first day of class; for the spring term begins the weekend before the first day of class. **Housing:** Coed dorms, special housing for disabled, apartments available. $100 nonrefundable deposit, deadline 9/1. **Activities:** Pep band, campus ministries, choral groups, drama, international student organizations, musical theater, student government, multicultural club, UMC Ambassadors, Students in Free Enterprise, Wildlife Society Chapter, Collegiate FFA, flying club, Habitat for Humanity, Rodeo Association, Student Athletic Advisory Committee.

Athletics. NCAA. **Intercollegiate:** Baseball M, basketball, equestrian W, football (tackle) M, golf, soccer W, softball W, tennis W, volleyball W. **Intramural:** Basketball, football (non-tackle), golf, racquetball, soccer, softball, table tennis, tennis, volleyball. **Team name:** Golden Eagles.

Student services. Adult student services, alcohol/substance abuse counseling, chaplain/spiritual director, career counseling, student employment services, financial aid counseling, health services, minority student services, on-campus daycare, personal counseling, placement for graduates, veterans' counselor, women's services. **Physically disabled:** Services for visually, hearing impaired.

Contact. E-mail: umcinfo@umn.edu
Phone: (218) 281-8569 Toll-free number: (800) 862-6466
Fax: (218) 281-8575 ext. 369
Amber Schultz, Director of Admissions, University of Minnesota: Crookston, 2900 University Avenue, Crookston, MN 56716-5001

University of Minnesota: Duluth
Duluth, Minnesota
www.d.umn.edu   CB code: 6873

♦ Public 4-year university
♦ Residential campus in small city
♦ 9,782 degree-seeking undergraduates: 4% part-time, 46% women, 2% African American, 3% Asian American, 1% Hispanic American, 1% Native American, 2% international
♦ 1,120 degree-seeking graduate students
♦ 76% of applicants admitted
♦ SAT or ACT with writing required
♦ 53% graduate within 6 years

General. Founded in 1947. Regionally accredited. All buildings at UMD are connected by a unique skyway and concourse system. **Degrees:** 1,943 bachelor's awarded; master's, professional offered. **ROTC:** Air Force. **Location:** 160 miles from Minneapolis-St. Paul. **Calendar:** Semester, extensive summer session. **Full-time faculty:** 440 total; 74% have terminal degrees, 15% minority, 44% women. **Part-time faculty:** 142 total; 31% have terminal degrees, 8% minority, 55% women. **Class size:** 42% < 20, 41% 20-39, 5% 40-49, 7% 50-99, 5% >100. **Special facilities:** Planetarium, visual imaging laboratory, Tweed Museum of Art, Glensheen Historic Congdon Estate, nature center, multi-cultural center.

Freshman class profile. 7,456 applied, 5,694 admitted, 2,101 enrolled.

Mid 50% test scores		Rank in top quarter:	43%
SAT critical reading:	450-580	Rank in top tenth:	16%
SAT math:	480-610	End year in good standing:	78%
SAT writing:	470-590	Return as sophomores:	77%
ACT composite:	22-26	Out-of-state:	12%
GPA 3.75 or higher:	22%	Live on campus:	20%
GPA 3.50-3.74:	22%	International:	1%
GPA 3.0-3.49:	42%	Fraternities:	1%
GPA 2.0-2.99:	14%	Sororities:	1%

641

Basis for selection. 65th percentile of high school class or above typically admitted. Test scores are required. Students ranking between the 40th and 64th percentile are selectively admitted based on test scores and academic preparation. Essays or personal statements considered in an admissions decision appeals process. Audition required for music students. **Learning Disabled:** Students must meet our general admission policy.

High school preparation. College-preparatory program required. 15 units required. Required and recommended units include English 4, mathematics 3, social studies 1, history 1, science 3, foreign language 2, computer science 1 and visual/performing arts 1. One year of physical and biological science required; mathematics sequence includes algebra, geometry, and higher algebra. Visual and performing arts courses and computer skills courses strongly recommended.

2011-2012 Annual costs. Tuition/fees: $12,380; $14,380 out-of-state. Room/board: $6,614. Books/supplies: $1,100. Personal expenses: $1,600.

2010-2011 Financial aid. Non-need-based: Scholarships awarded for academics, athletics, ROTC.

Application procedures. Admission: Priority date 12/15; deadline 8/1 (receipt date). $35 fee. Admission notification on a rolling basis beginning on or about 9/17. Must reply by May 1 or within 4 week(s) if notified thereafter. Applications accepted on a space available basis after 2/1. **Financial aid:** Priority date 3/1; no closing date. FAFSA required. Applicants notified on a rolling basis starting 3/1; must reply within 2 week(s) of notification.

Academics. Special study options: Accelerated study, cross-registration, distance learning, double major, dual enrollment of high school students, ESL, exchange student, honors, independent study, internships, liberal arts/career combination, study abroad, teacher certification program, weekend college. **Credit/placement by examination:** AP, CLEP, IB, ACT, institutional tests. **Support services:** Learning center, reduced course load, remedial instruction, study skills assistance, tutoring, writing center.

Majors. Area/ethnic studies: German, Native American, women's. **Biology:** General, biochemistry, Biochemistry/molecular biology, biomedical sciences, cell/histology, cellular/molecular, molecular. **Business:** Accounting, actuarial science, business admin, finance, human resources, management information systems, marketing. **Communications:** General. **Computer sciences:** General, computer science, information systems. **Conservation:** Environmental science, environmental studies. **Education:** Art, biology, chemistry, early childhood, elementary, English, French, German, health, mathematics, middle, music, physical, physics, science, secondary, social studies, Spanish. **Engineering:** Applied physics, chemical, civil, computer, electrical, industrial, mechanical. **English:** English lit, writing. **Foreign languages:** German, Spanish. **Health services:** Athletic training, communication disorders, health care admin. **History:** General. **Math:** General, statistics. **Parks/recreation:** General, exercise sciences, health/fitness, outdoor education. **Philosophy/religion:** Philosophy. **Physical sciences:** Chemistry, geology, physics. **Psychology:** General. **Social sciences:** Anthropology, criminology, economics, geography, political science, sociology, urban studies. **Visual/performing arts:** Acting, art, art history/conservation, digital arts, dramatic, graphic design, jazz, music, music pedagogy, music performance, music theory/composition, musical theater, studio arts, theater design. **Work/family studies:** Child development.

Most popular majors. Biology 9%, business/marketing 21%, education 11%, engineering/engineering technologies 6%, psychology 7%, social sciences 11%, visual/performing arts 6%.

Computing on campus. 465 workstations in library, computer center. Dormitories wired for high-speed internet access and linked to campus network. Commuter students can connect to campus network. Online course registration, online library, helpline, repair service, student web hosting, wireless network available.

Student life. Freshman orientation: Mandatory, $80 fee. Preregistration for classes offered. Academic advisement and registration (orientation) is held from March 1st to August 30. **Policies:** Smoke and alcohol free campus. **Housing:** Single-sex dorms, special housing for disabled, wellness housing available. $200 partly refundable deposit, deadline 5/1. Housing facilities are fully accessible to persons with physical disabilities. All facilities are smoke free. **Activities:** Bands, campus ministries, choral groups, dance, drama, film society, international student organizations, literary magazine, music ensembles, Model UN, musical theater, opera, radio station, student government, student newspaper, symphony orchestra, Intervarsity Christian Fellowship, Minnesota Public Interest Research Group, Anishinabe club, Black student association, Queer and Allied Students Union, Hispanic organization, Southeast Asian association, Students Engaged in Rewarding Volunteer Experiences.

Athletics. NCAA. **Intercollegiate:** Baseball M, basketball, cross-country, football (tackle) M, ice hockey, soccer W, softball W, tennis W, track and field, volleyball W. **Intramural:** Badminton, basketball, bowling, football (non-tackle), golf, ice hockey, sailing, skiing, soccer, softball, table tennis, tennis, track and field, volleyball, water polo. **Team name:** Bulldogs.

Student services. Adult student services, chaplain/spiritual director, career counseling, student employment services, financial aid counseling, health services, minority student services, on-campus daycare, personal counseling, placement for graduates, veterans' counselor, women's services. **Physically disabled:** Services for visually, speech, hearing impaired.

Contact. E-mail: umdadmis@d.umn.edu
Phone: (218) 726-7171 Toll-free number: (800) 232-1339
Fax: (218) 726-7040
Beth Esselstrom, Director of Admissions, University of Minnesota: Duluth, 25 Solon Campus Center, Duluth, MN 55812-3000

University of Minnesota: Morris
Morris, Minnesota
www.morris.umn.edu — CB code: 6890

- Public 4-year university and liberal arts college
- Residential campus in small town
- 1,822 degree-seeking undergraduates: 4% part-time, 55% women, 2% African American, 3% Asian American, 2% Hispanic American, 7% Native American, 8% international
- 62% of applicants admitted
- SAT or ACT with writing required
- 60% graduate within 6 years

General. Founded in 1959. Regionally accredited. **Degrees:** 280 bachelor's awarded. **Location:** 150 miles from Minneapolis-St. Paul; 100 miles from Fargo, North Dakota. **Calendar:** Semester, limited summer session. **Full-time faculty:** 113 total; 78% have terminal degrees, 8% minority, 46% women. **Part-time faculty:** 37 total; 19% have terminal degrees, 5% minority, 46% women. **Class size:** 57% < 20, 34% 20-39, 3% 40-49, 5% 50-99, less than 1% >100. **Special facilities:** Tropical conservatory, prairie gate press, historical center, experiment station, USDA soil laboratory, center for small towns, observatory.

Freshman class profile. 2,355 applied, 1,462 admitted, 465 enrolled.

Mid 50% test scores			
SAT critical reading:	510-650	Rank in top quarter:	61%
SAT math:	510-650	Rank in top tenth:	29%
SAT writing:	490-630	Return as sophomores:	83%
ACT composite:	23-28	Out-of-state:	11%
		International:	2%

Basis for selection. Admission based on four primary factors: high school performance, ACT/SAT scores, extra-curricular involvement/leadership experience/honors. Interview recommended. Audition required for music students receiving scholarships. **Home schooled:** Submit portfolio of works studied.

High school preparation. College-preparatory program required. 15 units required. Required units include English 4, mathematics 3, social studies 2, history 1, science 3 and foreign language 2. Science units must include 1 biological science and 1 physical science.

2011-2012 Annual costs. Tuition/fees: $12,091; $12,091 out-of-state. Room/board: $7,120. Books/supplies: $1,000. Personal expenses: $1,600.

2011-2012 Financial aid. Need-based: 429 full-time freshmen applied for aid; 325 were judged to have need; 322 of these received aid. Average need met was 83%. Average scholarship/grant was $8,994; average loan $7,451. 58% of total undergraduate aid awarded as scholarships/grants, 42% as loans/jobs. **Non-need-based:** Awarded to 692 full-time undergraduates, including 207 freshmen. Scholarships awarded for academics. **Additional information:** Land-grant program waiving tuition for Native Americans.

Application procedures. Admission: Priority date 12/15; deadline 3/15 (postmark date). $35 fee, may be waived for applicants with need. Admission notification on a rolling basis beginning on or about 9/16. Must reply by May 1 or within 2 week(s) if notified thereafter. **Financial aid:** No deadline. FAFSA required. Applicants notified on a rolling basis starting 4/1.

Academics. Academic opportunities that allow students to assist faculty in research or teaching endeavors and receive a stipend or expense allowances include: The Undergraduate Research Opportunities Program, The Morris Academic Partnership, The Minority Mentorship Program, The Morris Administrative Internship, and The Student Internship Program. **Special study options:** Combined bachelor's/graduate degree, cross-registration, distance learning, double major, dual enrollment of high school students, ESL, exchange student, honors, independent study, internships, New York semester, semester at sea, student-designed major, study abroad, teacher certification

program, United Nations semester, urban semester, Washington semester. **Credit/placement by examination:** AP, CLEP, IB, SAT, ACT, institutional tests. No limit for credit by exam, but the credit awarded does not count as resident credit; must have 30 resident credits. **Support services:** Learning center, pre-admission summer program, reduced course load, study skills assistance, tutoring, writing center.

Majors. Area/ethnic studies: European, Latin American, Native American, women's. **Biology:** General. **Business:** Management science. **Communications:** Communications/speech/rhetoric. **Computer sciences:** Computer science. **Conservation:** Environmental studies. **Education:** Elementary. **English:** English lit. **Foreign languages:** French, German, Spanish. **History:** General. **Human services:** Social work. **Liberal arts:** Humanities. **Math:** General, statistics. **Philosophy/religion:** Philosophy. **Physical sciences:** Chemistry, geology, physics. **Psychology:** General. **Social sciences:** Anthropology, economics, political science, sociology. **Visual/performing arts:** Art history/conservation, dramatic, music, music performance, studio arts.

Most popular majors. Biology 9%, business/marketing 8%, education 6%, English 8%, physical sciences 11%, psychology 12%, social sciences 10%, visual/performing arts 8%.

Computing on campus. 220 workstations in dormitories, library, computer center, student center. Dormitories wired for high-speed internet access and linked to campus network. Commuter students can connect to campus network. Online course registration, online library, helpline, repair service, wireless network available.

Student life. Freshman orientation: Mandatory. Preregistration for classes offered. Held 4 days prior to fall semester. **Housing:** Guaranteed on-campus for all undergraduates. Coed dorms, special housing for disabled, apartments available. $50 nonrefundable deposit, deadline 8/1. **Activities:** Bands, campus ministries, choral groups, dance, drama, international student organizations, literary magazine, music ensembles, musical theater, radio station, student government, student newspaper, symphony orchestra, Amnesty International, Big Friend/Little Friend, Campus Aglow Outreach, E-Quality, Habitat for Humanity, Intervarsity Christian Fellowship, Minnesota Public Interest Research Group, Morris Campus Student Association, Positive Spirituality, Women of Color Association.

Athletics. NCAA. **Intercollegiate:** Baseball M, basketball, cross-country, diving W, football (tackle) M, golf, soccer, softball W, swimming W, tennis, track and field, volleyball W. **Intramural:** Baseball, basketball, bowling, field hockey, football (non-tackle), ice hockey, softball, triathlon, volleyball. **Team name:** Cougars.

Student services. Alcohol/substance abuse counseling, career counseling, student employment services, financial aid counseling, health services, minority student services, personal counseling, placement for graduates, veterans' counselor, women's services. **Physically disabled:** Services for visually, speech, hearing impaired.

Contact. E-mail: admissions@morris.umn.edu
Phone: (320) 589-6035 Toll-free number: (888) 866-3382
Fax: (320) 589-1673
Bryan Herrmann, Director of Admission, University of Minnesota: Morris, 600 East 4th Street, Morris, MN 56267

University of Minnesota: Rochester
Rochester, Minnesota
www.r.umn.edu   CB code: 5877

- Public 4-year university and health science college
- Commuter campus in small city
- 253 degree-seeking undergraduates: 70% women, 7% African American, 6% Asian American, 3% Hispanic American, 1% Native American
- SAT or ACT with writing, application essay required

General. Regionally accredited. **Location:** 90 miles from Minneapolis-St Paul. **Calendar:** Semester, limited summer session. **Full-time faculty:** 29 total; 72% have terminal degrees, 28% minority, 48% women. **Part-time faculty:** 11 total; 54% women. **Class size:** 37% < 20, 43% 20-39, 17% 40-49, 3% 50-99.

Freshman class profile. 136 enrolled.

Mid 50% test scores			
ACT composite:	22-27	Rank in top quarter:	63%
GPA 3.75 or higher:	33%	Rank in top tenth:	21%
GPA 3.50-3.74:	28%	End year in good standing:	90%
GPA 3.0-3.49:	33%	Return as sophomores:	74%
GPA 2.0-2.99:	6%	Out-of-state:	19%
		Live on campus:	88%

Basis for selection. Academic record, GPA, and test scores very important. **Home schooled:** No additional requirements.

High school preparation. College-preparatory program required. Required and recommended units include English 4, mathematics 3-4, social studies 3, history 1, science 3-4 (laboratory 2-3), foreign language 2 and visual/performing arts 1.

2012-2013 Annual costs. Tuition/fees (projected): $13,412; $13,412 out-of-state. A mandatory laptop fee of $400 is included in the required fees above. Room/board: $7,728. Books/supplies: $1,000. Personal expenses: $2,000.

Financial aid. Non-need-based: Scholarships awarded for academics, leadership, state residency.

Application procedures. Admission: Priority date 12/15; no deadline. $35 fee, may be waived for applicants with need. Admission notification on a rolling basis beginning on or about 12/16. Must reply by May 1 or within 2 week(s) if notified thereafter. **Financial aid:** Priority date 3/1; no closing date. FAFSA required. Applicants notified on a rolling basis starting 3/30.

Academics. Special study options: Distance learning, exchange student, independent study, internships, study abroad. **Credit/placement by examination:** AP, CLEP, IB, institutional tests. **Support services:** Learning center, study skills assistance, tutoring, writing center.

Computing on campus. PC or laptop required. 12 workstations in library. Commuter students can connect to campus network. Online course registration, online library, repair service, wireless network available.

Student life. Freshman orientation: Mandatory. Preregistration for classes offered. **Housing:** Apartments available. $100 nonrefundable deposit, deadline 5/1. **Activities:** Dance, music ensembles, student government, Helping Us Give Service, Active Minds, Chi Alpha, CRU - Rochester, intercultural club, Greek, Exploratory Committee, Navigators, optimist club, Student Advocates for Public Health, pre-professional club.

Athletics. Intramural: Basketball, football (non-tackle), soccer, softball, tennis, volleyball. **Team name:** Raptors.

Student services. Adult student services, alcohol/substance abuse counseling, career counseling, student employment services, financial aid counseling, health services, legal services, personal counseling, veterans' counselor. **Physically disabled:** Services for visually, hearing impaired.

Contact. E-mail: applyumr@umn.edu
Phone: (507) 258-8687 Toll-free number: (877) 280-4699
Jade Grabau, Director of Admissions, University of Minnesota: Rochester, 111 South Broadway, Rochester, MN 55904

University of Minnesota: Twin Cities
Minneapolis, Minnesota   CB member
www.umn.edu   CB code: 6874

- Public 4-year university
- Residential campus in very large city
- 30,610 degree-seeking undergraduates: 8% part-time, 51% women, 4% African American, 8% Asian American, 3% Hispanic American, 8% international
- 17,187 degree-seeking graduate students
- 47% of applicants admitted
- SAT or ACT with writing required
- 70% graduate within 6 years

General. Founded in 1851. Regionally accredited. Campuses in Minneapolis and St. Paul. **Degrees:** 7,031 bachelor's awarded; master's, professional, doctoral offered. **ROTC:** Army, Naval, Air Force. **Calendar:** Semester, extensive summer session. **Full-time faculty:** 1,851 total; 79% have terminal degrees, 17% minority, 40% women. **Part-time faculty:** 849 total; 46% have terminal degrees, 7% minority, 44% women. **Class size:** 41% < 20, 34% 20-39, 6% 40-49, 11% 50-99, 8% >100. **Special facilities:** West bank arts quarter, natural history museum, showboat, rehabilitation museum, arboretum, concert hall.

Freshman class profile. 39,720 applied, 18,505 admitted, 5,368 enrolled.

Mid 50% test scores			
SAT critical reading:	540-690	Rank in top quarter:	84%
SAT math:	610-740	Rank in top tenth:	45%
SAT writing:	550-670	Out-of-state:	33%
ACT composite:	25-30	Live on campus:	85%
		International:	6%

Basis for selection. Successful completion of a college preparatory curriculum, high school rank percentile, grade point average, ACT or SAT scores, and strength of curriculum very important. Writing tests required. Results considered as secondary admission factor.

High school preparation. College-preparatory program required. 17 units required; 20 recommended. Required and recommended units include English 4, mathematics 3-4, social studies 3, history 1, science 3-4 (laboratory 1), foreign language 2 and visual/performing arts 1. Management, biological sciences, and technology applicants require a fourth year of mathematics and 3 years of science including 1 year each of biological science, chemistry, and physics.

2011-2012 Annual costs. Tuition/fees: $13,022; $18,022 out-of-state. Room/board: $7,932.

2011-2012 Financial aid. All financial aid based on need. 4,361 full-time freshmen applied for aid; 2,904 were judged to have need; 2,879 of these received aid. Average need met was 77%. Average scholarship/grant was $8,798; average loan $4,577. 46% of total undergraduate aid awarded as scholarships/grants, 54% as loans/jobs.

Application procedures. Admission: Priority date 12/15; no deadline. $45 fee, may be waived for applicants with need. Admission notification on a rolling basis. Must reply by May 1 or within 2 week(s) if notified thereafter. **Financial aid:** Priority date 3/1; no closing date. FAFSA, institutional form required. Applicants notified on a rolling basis starting 2/15.

Academics. Four year graduation guarantee offered. **Special study options:** Accelerated study, combined bachelor's/graduate degree, cooperative education, cross-registration, distance learning, double major, dual enrollment of high school students, ESL, exchange student, external degree, honors, independent study, internships, liberal arts/career combination, student-designed major, study abroad, teacher certification program. Qualified undergraduates may take graduate-level classes. **Credit/placement by examination:** AP, CLEP, IB, SAT, ACT, institutional tests. **Support services:** Learning center, pre-admission summer program, reduced course load, remedial instruction, study skills assistance, tutoring, writing center.

Majors. Architecture: Architecture, environmental design, landscape. **Area/ethnic studies:** African, African-American, American, Chicano/Hispanic-American/Latino, East Asian, European, Latin American, Native American, Near/Middle Eastern, Russian/Slavic, South Asian, women's. **Biology:** General, bacteriology, biochemistry, biometrics, biostatistics, botany, cell/histology, ecology, entomology, neuroscience, physiology, plant pathology, zoology. **Business:** General, accounting, actuarial science, business admin, fashion, finance, hospitality/recreation, human resources, insurance, international, labor relations, management information systems, marketing, nonprofit/public, operations, real estate, retailing, sales/distribution. **Communications:** Journalism. **Computer sciences:** Computer science, networking. **Conservation:** General, environmental studies, fisheries, forest management, forest sciences, forestry, management/policy, wildlife/wilderness, wood science. **Education:** General, agricultural, art, bilingual, biology, business, early childhood, elementary, English, ESL, family/consumer sciences, kindergarten/preschool, music, physical, sales/marketing, science, social studies, technology/industrial arts, trade/industrial, voc/tech. **Engineering:** Aerospace, agricultural, biomedical, chemical, civil, computer, electrical, geological, marine, materials, mechanical, metallurgical, mining. **English:** English lit, rhetoric/composition. **Foreign languages:** General, ancient Greek, Arabic, Chinese, classics, comparative lit, French, German, Hebrew, Italian, Japanese, Latin, linguistics, Russian, Scandinavian, South Asian, Spanish. **General:** Agribusiness operations, agronomy, animal husbandry, animal sciences, business, crop production, economics, food science, horticultural science, plant protection, plant sciences, soil science. **Health services:** Audiology/speech pathology, clinical lab science, communication disorders, dental hygiene, dietetics, music therapy, predental, premedicine, respiratory therapy technology. **History:** General. **Human services:** Community org/advocacy, social work. **Liberal arts:** Arts/sciences, humanities, library science. **Math:** General, statistics. **Parks/recreation:** General, exercise sciences, facilities management, sports admin. **Philosophy/religion:** Judaic, philosophy, religion. **Physical sciences:** General, astronomy, astrophysics, chemistry, geology, geophysics, materials science, organic chemistry, physics. **Psychology:** General, developmental. **Social sciences:** Anthropology, applied economics, criminology, econometrics, economics, geography, international relations, political science, sociology, urban studies. **Theology:** Theology. **Visual/performing arts:** Art, art history/conservation, commercial/advertising art, dance, design, dramatic, fashion design, film/cinema/video, graphic design, interior design, music, music history, studio arts. **Work/family studies:** General, child care management, clothing/textiles, family systems, food/nutrition, housing.

Most popular majors. Biology 9%, business/marketing 8%, engineering/engineering technologies 11%, psychology 7%, social sciences 13%.

Computing on campus. Dormitories wired for high-speed internet access and linked to campus network. Commuter students can connect to campus network. Online course registration, online library, helpline, repair service, student web hosting, wireless network available.

Student life. Freshman orientation: Mandatory. Preregistration for classes offered. **Housing:** Guaranteed on-campus for freshmen. Coed dorms, special housing for disabled, apartments, cooperative housing, fraternity/sorority housing, wellness housing available. $250 fully refundable deposit, deadline 5/1. Honors housing available. 24 living and learning communities. **Activities:** Bands, choral groups, dance, drama, film society, international student organizations, literary magazine, music ensembles, musical theater, opera, radio station, student government, student newspaper, symphony orchestra, TV station, 600 student-run organizations.

Athletics. NCAA. **Intercollegiate:** Baseball, basketball, cheerleading, cross-country, diving, football (tackle), golf, gymnastics, ice hockey, rowing (crew) W, soccer W, softball W, swimming, tennis, track and field, volleyball W, wrestling M. **Intramural:** Badminton, baseball, basketball, bowling, fencing, football (tackle) M, golf, gymnastics, handball, ice hockey, judo, lacrosse, racquetball, rugby, sailing, skiing, soccer, softball, squash, swimming, synchronized swimming, tennis, volleyball, water polo, wrestling M. **Team name:** Golden Gophers.

Student services. Adult student services, alcohol/substance abuse counseling, chaplain/spiritual director, career counseling, services for economically disadvantaged, student employment services, financial aid counseling, health services, legal services, minority student services, on-campus daycare, personal counseling, placement for graduates, veterans' counselor, women's services. **Physically disabled:** Services for visually, speech, hearing impaired.

Contact. Phone: (612) 625-2008 Toll-free number: (800) 752-1000 Fax: (612) 626-1693
Wayne Sigler, Director of Admissions, University of Minnesota: Twin Cities, 240 Williamson Hall, Minneapolis, MN 55455-0213

University of Phoenix: Minneapolis-St. Paul
Saint Louis Park, Minnesota
www.phoenix.edu

- For-profit 4-year university
- Commuter campus in large city
- 235 degree-seeking undergraduates

General. Regionally accredited. **Degrees:** 42 bachelor's awarded; master's offered. **Calendar:** Differs by program. **Full-time faculty:** 7 total. **Part-time faculty:** 65 total.

Basis for selection. Open admission.

2011-2012 Annual costs. Estimated costs as of August 2011: per-credit-hour charge, $465 to $480, depending upon level and course of study; electronic course materials fee, $95, if applicable. Book and material charges may vary by course and program. All fees are subject to change.

Application procedures. Admission: No deadline. No application fee. **Financial aid:** No deadline.

Academics. Credit/placement by examination: AP, CLEP.

Majors. Business: Accounting, business admin, credit management, e-commerce, entrepreneurial studies, marketing, operations. **Computer sciences:** General, networking, programming, security, systems analysis, web page design. **Health services:** Facilities admin, nursing (RN). **Human services:** General. **Protective services:** Law enforcement admin, security management. **Psychology:** General.

Most popular majors. Business/marketing 74%, health sciences 17%.

Contact. Toll-free number: (866) 766-0766
Marc Booker, Director of Admission and Evaluation, University of Phoenix: Minneapolis-St. Paul, 435 Ford Road, Suite 1000, Saint Louis Park, MN 55426-4915

University of St. Thomas
St. Paul, Minnesota
www.stthomas.edu

CB member
CB code: 6110

- Private 4-year university and liberal arts college affiliated with Roman Catholic Church
- Residential campus in very large city

- 6,101 degree-seeking undergraduates: 3% part-time, 47% women, 3% African American, 5% Asian American, 4% Hispanic American, 2% international
- 4,127 degree-seeking graduate students
- 84% of applicants admitted
- SAT or ACT (ACT writing optional), application essay required
- 74% graduate within 6 years

General. Founded in 1885. Regionally accredited. **Degrees:** 1,289 bachelor's awarded; master's, professional, doctoral offered. **ROTC:** Army, Naval, Air Force. **Location:** St. Paul campus is 5 miles from downtown St. Paul and Minneapolis; Minneapolis campus is downtown. **Calendar:** 4-1-4, limited summer session. **Full-time faculty:** 427 total. **Part-time faculty:** 465 total. **Class size:** 40% < 20, 56% 20-39, 1% 40-49, 3% 50-99. **Special facilities:** American Museum of Asmat Art.

Freshman class profile. 5,250 applied, 4,435 admitted, 1,324 enrolled.

Mid 50% test scores		GPA 2.0-2.99:	9%
SAT critical reading:	500-620	Rank in top quarter:	56%
SAT math:	530-640	Rank in top tenth:	27%
ACT composite:	23-28	Return as sophomores:	88%
GPA 3.75 or higher:	38%	Out-of-state:	17%
GPA 3.50-3.74:	22%	Live on campus:	93%
GPA 3.0-3.49:	31%	International:	2%

Basis for selection. Admissions decision by formula using combination of high school rank and standardized test scores, including consideration of the contributions the student has made to their school, community or church. Interview recommended. **Home schooled:** Submit course descriptions.

High school preparation. College-preparatory program recommended. Required and recommended units include English 4, mathematics 3-4, social studies 2, science 2 and foreign language 4. Some departments may require 3 units social studies (includes 1 geography), 1 US history, 1 unit visual or performing arts.

2011-2012 Annual costs. Tuition/fees: $32,073. Room/board: $8,924. Books/supplies: $1,520. Personal expenses: $2,641.

2011-2012 Financial aid. Need-based: 1,041 full-time freshmen applied for aid; 778 were judged to have need; 778 of these received aid. Average need met was 84%. Average scholarship/grant was $16,467; average loan $7,222. 65% of total undergraduate aid awarded as scholarships/grants, 35% as loans/jobs. **Non-need-based:** Awarded to 1,040 full-time undergraduates, including 336 freshmen. Scholarships awarded for academics, music/drama, ROTC.

Application procedures. Admission: No deadline. No application fee. Admission notification on a rolling basis beginning on or about 10/1. Applications accepted until class is full; reviewed starting 10/1. **Financial aid:** Priority date 4/1; no closing date. FAFSA required. Applicants notified on a rolling basis starting 3/1; must reply within 3 week(s) of notification.

Academics. Special study options: Cross-registration, double major, ESL, exchange student, honors, independent study, internships, semester at sea, student-designed major, study abroad, teacher certification program, urban semester, Washington semester. Renaissance Program in which students major in a liberal arts area, take career-oriented classes as a minor, and after graduation can take additional undergraduate business courses free of charge. **Credit/placement by examination:** AP, CLEP, IB, SAT, ACT, institutional tests. Typically credit by exam can be used for only 1/8 of a student's courses. CLEP credit awarded if student scores at 50th percentile or above for those examinations that have been approved by the department in which the subject is usually taught. **Support services:** Learning center, reduced course load, study skills assistance, tutoring, writing center.

Majors. Area/ethnic studies: Women's. **Biology:** General, biochemistry, neuroscience. **Business:** Accounting, actuarial science, business admin, entrepreneurial studies, finance, human resources, international, marketing, operations, real estate. **Communications:** General. **Computer sciences:** Computer science, information systems, information technology, security. **Conservation:** Environmental science, environmental studies. **Education:** Chemistry, elementary, English, French, German, health, mathematics, middle, multi-level teacher, music, physical, physics, science, social studies, Spanish. **Engineering:** General, electrical, mechanical. **English:** Creative writing, English lit. **Foreign languages:** Classics, comparative lit, French, German, Latin, Spanish. **Health services:** Predental, prephysical therapy, preveterinary, public health ed. **History:** General. **Human services:** Social work. **Liberal arts:** Arts/sciences. **Math:** General, statistics. **Philosophy/religion:** Philosophy, religion. **Physical sciences:** Chemistry, geology, physics. **Psychology:** General. **Social sciences:** General, criminology, econometrics, economics, geography, international economics, international relations, political science, sociology. **Theology:** Preministerial. **Visual/performing arts:** Art history/conservation, music, music performance.

Most popular majors. Business/marketing 43%, philosophy/religious studies 6%, psychology 6%, social sciences 7%.

Computing on campus. 4,280 workstations in dormitories, library, computer center, student center. Dormitories wired for high-speed internet access and linked to campus network. Commuter students can connect to campus network. Online course registration, online library, helpline, student web hosting, wireless network available.

Student life. Freshman orientation: Mandatory. Preregistration for classes offered. One day orientation for students and parents during the summer; students and parents can stay overnight in the dorms. Separate programs for students and parents. **Housing:** Single-sex dorms, apartments, wellness housing available. $200 fully refundable deposit, deadline 5/1. Chemical-free lifestyle, women in science house, first year experience houses, Catholic women's and Catholic men's communities. **Activities:** Bands, campus ministries, choral groups, dance, drama, international student organizations, literary magazine, music ensembles, Model UN, radio station, student government, student newspaper, TV station, Globally Minded Student Association, Volunteers in Action, Student Coalition for Social Justice, African Nations Students Association, Fellowship of Christian Athletes, St. Paul's Outreach student organization, theology club, Black Empowerment Student Alliance.

Athletics. NCAA. **Intercollegiate:** Baseball M, basketball, cross-country, football (tackle) M, golf, ice hockey, soccer, softball W, swimming, tennis, track and field, volleyball W. **Intramural:** Basketball, football (non-tackle), racquetball, soccer, softball, tennis, volleyball. **Team name:** Tommies.

Student services. Adult student services, alcohol/substance abuse counseling, chaplain/spiritual director, career counseling, student employment services, financial aid counseling, health services, minority student services, on-campus daycare, personal counseling, veterans' counselor, women's services. **Physically disabled:** Services for visually, speech, hearing impaired.

Contact. E-mail: admissions@stthomas.edu
Phone: (651) 962-6150 Toll-free number: (800) 328-6819 ext. 26150
Fax: (651) 962-6160
Marla Friederichs, Associate Vice President for Enrollment Management, University of St. Thomas, 2115 Summit Avenue, 32F, St. Paul, MN 55105

Walden University
Minneapolis, Minnesota
www.waldenu.edu   **CB code: 6755**

- For-profit 4-year virtual university
- Large city
- 8,559 degree-seeking undergraduates: 90% part-time, 75% women, 38% African American, 1% Asian American, 5% Hispanic American, 1% Native American, 8% international
- 40,099 degree-seeking graduate students
- Application essay required

General. Walden University is a fully online institution accredited by the Higher Learning Commission's North Central Association offering programs in a variety of disciplines and degree levels, from undergraduate to doctorate. **Degrees:** 657 bachelor's awarded; master's, doctoral offered. **Calendar:** Continuous, extensive summer session. **Full-time faculty:** 231 total; 94% have terminal degrees. **Part-time faculty:** 2,304 total; 86% have terminal degrees.

Basis for selection. Open admission, but selective for some programs. Must meet one of the following criteria: at least 24 years of age, between the ages of 21-23 with at least 12 transferable college credit hours, at least 90 college credit hours completed, or an active member of the military or a veteran with documentation of service.

2011-2012 Annual costs. Tuition/fees: $12,810.

2010-2011 Financial aid. All financial aid based on need. 23% of total undergraduate aid awarded as scholarships/grants, 77% as loans/jobs.

Application procedures. Admission: No deadline. $50 fee, may be waived for applicants with need. Application must be submitted online. Admission notification on a rolling basis. Offer remains in effect for 12 months. **Financial aid:** No deadline. FAFSA required. Applicants notified on a rolling basis.

Academics. Special study options: Combined bachelor's/graduate degree, distance learning, internships, student-designed major, study abroad, teacher certification program. **Credit/placement by examination:** AP, CLEP, IB. 30 credit hours maximum toward bachelor's degree. **Support services:** Remedial instruction, tutoring, writing center.

Majors. Business: Accounting, business admin. **Communications:** General. **Computer sciences:** General, information systems. **Education:** General, curriculum. **Health services:** Health care admin, nursing (RN). **Human services:** General. **Protective services:** Law enforcement admin. **Psychology:** General, forensic. **Work/family studies:** Family studies.

Most popular majors. Business/marketing 37%, family/consumer sciences 9%, health sciences 17%, psychology 28%.

Computing on campus. PC or laptop required. Commuter students can connect to campus network. Online course registration, online library, helpline available.

Student life. Freshman orientation: Available. Preregistration for classes offered.

Student services. Career counseling, financial aid counseling, personal counseling, veterans' counselor. **Physically disabled:** Services for visually, speech, hearing impaired.

Contact. E-mail: admissions@waldenu.edu
Phone: (800) 925-3368 Toll-free number: (800) 925-3368
Devon Loetz, Director of Admissions, Walden University, 650 South Exeter Street, 8th Floor, Baltimore, MD 21202

Winona State University
Winona, Minnesota
www.winona.edu   **CB code; 6680**

- Public 4-year university
- Residential campus in large town
- 8,232 degree-seeking undergraduates: 8% part-time, 60% women, 2% African American, 2% Asian American, 2% Hispanic American, 2% international
- 375 degree-seeking graduate students
- 69% of applicants admitted
- SAT or ACT (ACT writing optional) required
- 55% graduate within 6 years

General. Founded in 1858. Regionally accredited. **Degrees:** 1,513 bachelor's, 24 associate awarded; master's, doctoral offered. **ROTC:** Army. **Location:** 90 miles from Minneapolis-St. Paul. **Calendar:** Semester, extensive summer session. **Full-time faculty:** 293 total; 67% have terminal degrees, 12% minority. **Part-time faculty:** 263 total; 15% have terminal degrees, 5% minority. **Class size:** 28% < 20, 58% 20-39, 6% 40-49, 7% 50-99, 1% >100.

Freshman class profile. 6,528 applied, 4,506 admitted, 1,874 enrolled.

Mid 50% test scores			
SAT critical reading:	420-570	Rank in top quarter:	33%
SAT math:	420-570	Rank in top tenth:	10%
ACT composite:	21-25	Return as sophomores:	78%
GPA 3.75 or higher:	17%	Out-of-state:	36%
GPA 3.50-3.74:	19%	Live on campus:	93%
GPA 3.0-3.49:	40%	International:	2%
GPA 2.0-2.99:	24%		

Basis for selection. 16 units of college prep high school courses and rank in top 2/3 of class and SAT combined score of 1000 (exclusive of Writing) or ACT composite score of 21 required or top half of class with and ACT 18 or higher for regular admission. Interview required for academically marginal students.

High school preparation. College-preparatory program required. 16 units required. Required units include English 4, mathematics 3, social studies 2, history 1, science 3 (laboratory 3), foreign language 2 and academic electives 1. One English unit may be speech.

2011-2012 Annual costs. Tuition/fees: $8,586; $13,917 out-of-state. Fees include mandatory laptop lease for full-time students. Room/board: $7,540. Books/supplies: $1,200. Personal expenses: $1,740.

2010-2011 Financial aid. Need-based: 1,161 full-time freshmen applied for aid; 837 were judged to have need; 814 of these received aid. Average need met was 37%. Average scholarship/grant was $5,109; average loan $3,249. 41% of total undergraduate aid awarded as scholarships/grants, 59% as loans/jobs. **Non-need-based:** Awarded to 4,309 full-time undergraduates, including 1,718 freshmen. Scholarships awarded for academics, alumni affiliation, art, athletics, leadership, minority status, music/drama, ROTC, state residency.

Application procedures. Admission: Priority date 3/1; no deadline. $20 fee, may be waived for applicants with need. Admission notification on a rolling basis beginning on or about 8/15. **Financial aid:** No deadline. FAFSA required. Applicants notified on a rolling basis starting 5/1; must reply within 3 week(s) of notification.

Academics. Special study options: Accelerated study, cross-registration, distance learning, double major, dual enrollment of high school students, ESL, external degree, independent study, internships, student-designed major, study abroad, teacher certification program. **Credit/placement by examination:** AP, CLEP, IB, institutional tests. **Support services:** Learning center, reduced course load, study skills assistance, tutoring, writing center.

Majors. Biology: General, cell/histology, molecular. **Business:** General, accounting, administrative services, business admin, finance, human resources, management information systems, management science, managerial economics, market research, office/clerical, operations. **Communications:** Advertising, broadcast journalism, communications/speech/rhetoric, journalism, media studies, photojournalism, public relations. **Communications technology:** General. **Computer sciences:** General, applications programming, computer science, information technology, programming. **Conservation:** General, environmental studies. **Education:** General, art, bilingual, biology, business, chemistry, curriculum, drama/dance, early childhood, elementary, emotionally handicapped, English, foreign languages, French, German, health, health occupations, history, learning disabled, mathematics, mentally handicapped, middle, multi-level teacher, multiple handicapped, music, physical, physically handicapped, physics, reading, science, secondary, social science, social studies, Spanish, special ed, speech. **Engineering:** Materials, polymer. **English:** English lit, rhetoric/composition, writing. **Foreign languages:** General, French, German, Spanish. **Health services:** Athletic training, clinical lab technology, cytotechnology, health care admin, nursing (RN), predental, premedicine, preop/surgical nursing, prepharmacy, preveterinary, public health ed, recreational therapy. **History:** General. **Human services:** General, social work. **Liberal arts:** Arts/sciences. **Math:** General, applied, statistics. **Parks/recreation:** General, exercise sciences, facilities management, health/fitness, sports admin. **Physical sciences:** Chemistry, geology, materials science, physics, planetary, polymer chemistry. **Protective services:** Corrections, criminal justice, law enforcement admin, police science, security services. **Psychology:** General. **Social sciences:** General, economics, political science, sociology, urban studies. **Visual/performing arts:** General, art, commercial/advertising art, design, dramatic, music, music management, music performance, studio arts.

Most popular majors. Biology 6%, business/marketing 23%, education 18%, health sciences 12%.

Computing on campus. PC or laptop required. 100 workstations in dormitories, library, computer center, student center. Dormitories wired for high-speed internet access and linked to campus network. Commuter students can connect to campus network. Online course registration, online library, helpline, repair service, student web hosting, wireless network available.

Student life. Freshman orientation: Available, $25 fee. Preregistration for classes offered. **Housing:** Guaranteed on-campus for freshmen. Coed dorms, single-sex dorms, special housing for disabled, apartments available. $175 partly refundable deposit, deadline 3/1. Residence hall with classrooms and faculty offices available. **Activities:** Bands, choral groups, dance, drama, film society, international student organizations, literary magazine, music ensembles, Model UN, musical theater, radio station, student government, student newspaper, symphony orchestra, TV station, over 130 organizations.

Athletics. NCAA. **Intercollegiate:** Baseball M, basketball, cross-country, football (tackle) M, golf, gymnastics W, soccer W, softball W, tennis W, track and field W, volleyball W. **Intramural:** Archery, badminton, baseball M, basketball, bowling, cross-country, diving, equestrian, fencing, field hockey, golf, gymnastics W, handball, ice hockey, racquetball, rifle, rugby, skiing, soccer, softball, swimming, table tennis, tennis, track and field, volleyball, wrestling M. **Team name:** Warriors.

Student services. Adult student services, alcohol/substance abuse counseling, chaplain/spiritual director, career counseling, services for economically disadvantaged, student employment services, financial aid counseling, health services, legal services, minority student services, on-campus daycare, personal counseling, placement for graduates, veterans' counselor, women's services. **Physically disabled:** Services for visually, speech, hearing impaired.

Contact. E-mail: admissions@winona.edu
Phone: (507) 457-5100 Toll-free number: (800) 342-5978
Fax: (507) 457-5620
Carl Stange, Director of Admissions, Winona State University, Office of Admissions, Winona, MN 55987

Mississippi

Alcorn State University
Alcorn State, Mississippi
www.alcorn.edu
CB member
CB code: 1008

- Public 4-year university and agricultural college
- Residential campus in rural community
- 3,296 degree-seeking undergraduates: 11% part-time, 66% women, 93% African American, 1% Hispanic American, 1% international
- 722 degree-seeking graduate students
- 36% of applicants admitted
- SAT or ACT (ACT writing optional) required
- 33% graduate within 6 years; 45% enter graduate study

General. Founded in 1871. Regionally accredited. School of Nursing and Master of Business Administration program located in Natchez. **Degrees:** 369 bachelor's, 31 associate awarded; master's offered. **ROTC:** Army. **Location:** 40 miles from Natchez, 45 miles from Vicksburg. **Calendar:** Semester, limited summer session. **Full-time faculty:** 164 total; 64% have terminal degrees, 80% minority, 45% women. **Part-time faculty:** 35 total; 57% have terminal degrees, 86% minority, 54% women. **Special facilities:** Nature trails, lakes.

Freshman class profile. 4,535 applied, 1,652 admitted, 687 enrolled.

Mid 50% test scores			
SAT critical reading:	390-470	GPA 2.0-2.99:	49%
SAT math:	400-520	Return as sophomores:	67%
GPA 3.75 or higher:	6%	Out-of-state:	23%
GPA 3.50-3.74:	10%	Live on campus:	85%
GPA 3.0-3.49:	29%	International:	1%

Basis for selection. Test scores, school achievement record important; specific academic units considered. Test score requirements depend upon high school GPA. Audition required for music majors. Interview required for students not meeting regular admission criteria. **Home schooled:** Statement describing home school structure and mission, transcript of courses and grades required.

High school preparation. College-preparatory program required. 15.5 units required; 19.5 recommended. Required and recommended units include English 4, mathematics 3-4, social studies 3-4, science 3-4 (laboratory 2), foreign language 1, computer science .5, visual/performing arts 1 and academic electives 1. One advanced elective must be in foreign language or world geography.

2011-2012 Annual costs. Tuition/fees: $5,256; $12,912 out-of-state. Room/board: $7,036. Books/supplies: $1,466. Personal expenses: $2,442.

2011-2012 Financial aid. **Need-based:** 567 full-time freshmen applied for aid; 546 were judged to have need; 546 of these received aid. Average need met was 49%. Average scholarship/grant was $5,642; average loan $3,414. 58% of total undergraduate aid awarded as scholarships/grants, 42% as loans/jobs. **Non-need-based:** Awarded to 1,060 full-time undergraduates, including 346 freshmen. Scholarships awarded for academics, athletics, leadership, ROTC.

Application procedures. **Admission:** No deadline. No application fee. Application must be submitted online. Admission notification on a rolling basis. **Financial aid:** Priority date 4/1; no closing date. FAFSA, institutional form required. Applicants notified on a rolling basis starting 4/1; must reply within 4 week(s) of notification.

Academics. Math center available to students. On-line tutoring is available 24/7. **Special study options:** Accelerated study, cooperative education, distance learning, double major, dual enrollment of high school students, honors, independent study, internships, liberal arts/career combination, study abroad, teacher certification program. **Credit/placement by examination:** AP, CLEP, SAT, ACT, institutional tests. 15 credit hours maximum toward associate degree, 30 toward bachelor's. Student must earn 12 hours at Alcorn State University before credit by examination may be recorded on the student's transcript. **Support services:** Pre-admission summer program, reduced course load, remedial instruction, tutoring, writing center.

Majors. Biology: General. **Business:** Accounting, business admin. **Communications:** Media studies. **Computer sciences:** General, LAN/WAN management. **Education:** Elementary. **English:** English lit. **General:** Business, economics. **Health services:** Nursing (RN). **History:** General. **Liberal arts:** Arts/sciences. **Math:** General. **Parks/recreation:** General. **Physical sciences:** Chemistry. **Protective services:** Criminal justice. **Psychology:** General. **Social sciences:** Political science, sociology. **Visual/performing arts:** Music performance. **Work/family studies:** Child development, food/nutrition.

Most popular majors. Biology 16%, business/marketing 10%, family/consumer sciences 7%, health sciences 12%, liberal arts 14%, social sciences 6%.

Computing on campus. 500 workstations in dormitories, library, computer center, student center. Dormitories wired for high-speed internet access and linked to campus network. Commuter students can connect to campus network. Online course registration, online library, helpline, repair service, wireless network available.

Student life. **Freshman orientation:** Mandatory. Preregistration for classes offered. Entrance and placement exams given. **Housing:** Guaranteed on-campus for all undergraduates. Single-sex dorms available. $75 fully refundable deposit. **Activities:** Bands, choral groups, dance, drama, music ensembles, radio station, student government, student newspaper, TV station, Wesley Foundation, NAACP, YWCA, PHA Masonic Order, ASU Heritage Committee.

Athletics. NCAA. **Intercollegiate:** Baseball M, basketball, cross-country, football (tackle) M, golf, soccer W, softball W, tennis, track and field, volleyball W. **Intramural:** Basketball. **Team name:** Braves.

Student services. Alcohol/substance abuse counseling, chaplain/spiritual director, career counseling, student employment services, financial aid counseling, health services, on-campus daycare, personal counseling, placement for graduates, veterans' counselor.

Contact. E-mail: ebarnes@alcorn.edu
Phone: (601) 877-6147 Toll-free number: (800) 222-6790
Fax: (601) 877-6347
Emanuel Barnes, Director of Admissions and Recruiting, Alcorn State University, 1000 ASU Drive #300, Alcorn State, MS 39096-7500

Belhaven University
Jackson, Mississippi
www.belhaven.edu
CB code: 1055

- Private 4-year liberal arts college affiliated with Presbyterian Church (USA)
- Commuter campus in large city
- 2,406 degree-seeking undergraduates: 5% part-time, 66% women
- 755 degree-seeking graduate students
- 52% of applicants admitted
- SAT or ACT (ACT writing optional), application essay required
- 48% graduate within 6 years; 24% enter graduate study

General. Founded in 1883. Regionally accredited. Christian liberal arts college. **Degrees:** 455 bachelor's, 25 associate awarded; master's offered. **ROTC:** Army, Air Force. **Location:** 188 miles from New Orleans, 200 miles from Memphis, Tennessee. **Calendar:** Semester, extensive summer session. **Full-time faculty:** 60 total; 35% women. **Part-time faculty:** 71 total; 51% women. **Class size:** 70% < 20, 22% 20-39, 8% 40-49. **Special facilities:** Museum, heritage room.

Freshman class profile. 1,356 applied, 711 admitted, 167 enrolled.

Mid 50% test scores			
SAT critical reading:	470-660	GPA 2.0-2.99:	22%
SAT math:	460-580	Rank in top quarter:	29%
ACT composite:	20-25	Rank in top tenth:	14%
GPA 3.75 or higher:	29%	End year in good standing:	85%
GPA 3.50-3.74:	10%	Return as sophomores:	67%
GPA 3.0-3.49:	39%	Out-of-state:	70%
		Live on campus:	92%

Basis for selection. Test scores, school record, recommendations, and character important. Interview recommended for art, dance, music, and theater majors; portfolio recommended for art majors. Audition required for dance, music, and theater majors.

High school preparation. 16 units required. Required and recommended units include English 4, mathematics 2, social studies 1, science 1, computer science 1 and academic electives 8.

2012-2013 Annual costs. Tuition/fees (projected): $19,200. Room/board: $6,890. Books/supplies: $1,400.

2010-2011 Financial aid. Need-based: 164 full-time freshmen applied for aid; 143 were judged to have need; 143 of these received aid. Average need met was 65%. Average scholarship/grant was $11,750; average loan $3,036. 47% of total undergraduate aid awarded as scholarships/grants, 53% as loans/jobs. **Non-need-based:** Awarded to 247 full-time undergraduates, including 79 freshmen. Scholarships awarded for academics, alumni affiliation, art, athletics, job skills, leadership, music/drama.

Application procedures. Admission: No deadline. $25 fee, may be waived for applicants with need. Admission notification on a rolling basis. Accepted applicants must reply within 30 days. **Financial aid:** Priority date 1/31; no closing date. FAFSA required. Applicants notified on a rolling basis starting 2/1.

Academics. Special study options: Accelerated study, combined bachelor's/graduate degree, distance learning, double major, dual enrollment of high school students, ESL, honors, independent study, internships, student-designed major, study abroad, teacher certification program, weekend college. **Credit/placement by examination:** AP, CLEP, IB, SAT, ACT, institutional tests. 30 credit hours maximum toward bachelor's degree. **Support services:** Learning center, reduced course load, remedial instruction, study skills assistance, tutoring, writing center.

Majors. Biology: General. **Business:** Accounting, business admin. **Communications:** Communications/speech/rhetoric. **Computer sciences:** General, computer science. **Education:** Elementary. **English:** Creative writing, English lit. **Health services:** Health care admin. **History:** General. **Liberal arts:** Humanities. **Math:** General. **Parks/recreation:** Exercise sciences, sports admin. **Philosophy/religion:** Philosophy. **Physical sciences:** Chemistry. **Psychology:** General. **Social sciences:** General, political science. **Theology:** Bible. **Visual/performing arts:** Art, dance, dramatic, music, studio arts management.

Most popular majors. Business/marketing 19%, education 6%, parks/recreation 13%, psychology 6%, visual/performing arts 25%.

Computing on campus. 40 workstations in library, computer center. Dormitories wired for high-speed internet access and linked to campus network. Commuter students can connect to campus network. Online course registration, online library, wireless network available.

Student life. Freshman orientation: Mandatory. Preregistration for classes offered. Held 5 days before fall classes begin. **Policies:** Religious observance required. **Housing:** Guaranteed on-campus for all undergraduates. Single-sex dorms, wellness housing available. $100 fully refundable deposit, deadline 6/1. **Activities:** Bands, campus ministries, choral groups, dance, drama, international student organizations, literary magazine, music ensembles, student government, student newspaper, Baptist Student Union, College Republicans, Fellowship of Christian Athletes, Praise & Worship Fellowship, Reformed University Fellowship, Student Missions Fellowship.

Athletics. NAIA. **Intercollegiate:** Baseball M, basketball, cross-country, football (tackle) M, golf, soccer, softball W, tennis, volleyball W. **Intramural:** Basketball, football (non-tackle), soccer W, softball, volleyball, weight lifting W. **Team name:** Blazers.

Student services. Adult student services, chaplain/spiritual director, career counseling, student employment services, financial aid counseling, health services, personal counseling.

Contact. E-mail: admission@belhaven.edu
Phone: (601) 968-5940 Toll-free number: (800) 960-5940
Fax: (601) 968-8946
Suzanne Sullivan, Director of Admission, Belhaven University, 1500 Peachtree Street, Jackson, MS 39202

Blue Mountain College
Blue Mountain, Mississippi
www.bmc.edu   **CB code: 1066**

- Private 4-year liberal arts college affiliated with Southern Baptist Convention
- Commuter campus in rural community
- 538 degree-seeking undergraduates: 7% part-time, 59% women, 13% African American, 1% Hispanic American, 1% international
- 13 degree-seeking graduate students
- 50% of applicants admitted
- SAT or ACT (ACT writing optional) required
- 50% graduate within 6 years; 33% enter graduate study

General. Founded in 1873. Regionally accredited. **Degrees:** 102 bachelor's awarded; master's offered. **Location:** 69 miles from Memphis, TN. **Calendar:** Semester, limited summer session. **Full-time faculty:** 31 total; 84% have terminal degrees, 48% women. **Part-time faculty:** 12 total; 33% have terminal degrees, 75% women. **Class size:** 64% < 20, 32% 20-39, 3% 40-49, 2% 50-99.

Freshman class profile. 329 applied, 163 admitted, 88 enrolled.

Mid 50% test scores		Rank in top tenth:	20%
ACT composite:	18-23	End year in good standing:	87%
GPA 3.75 or higher:	25%	Return as sophomores:	68%
GPA 3.50-3.74:	14%	Out-of-state:	33%
GPA 3.0-3.49:	32%	Live on campus:	90%
GPA 2.0-2.99:	28%	International:	1%
Rank in top quarter:	38%		

Basis for selection. High school record, test scores, and individual motivation considered.

High school preparation. College-preparatory program recommended. 15 units recommended. Recommended units include English 4, mathematics 3, social studies 1, history 2, science 3 (laboratory 2) and foreign language 2.

2011-2012 Annual costs. Tuition/fees: $9,130. Room/board: $3,900. Books/supplies: $1,000. Personal expenses: $1,000.

Financial aid. Non-need-based: Scholarships awarded for academics, alumni affiliation, art, athletics, leadership, music/drama, religious affiliation, state residency.

Application procedures. Admission: No deadline. $10 fee, may be waived for applicants with need, free for online applicants. Admission notification on a rolling basis beginning on or about 10/1. **Financial aid:** Priority date 3/1, closing date 7/31. FAFSA, institutional form required. Applicants notified on a rolling basis starting 4/1; must reply within 4 week(s) of notification.

Academics. Special study options: Accelerated study, combined bachelor's/graduate degree, double major, dual enrollment of high school students, honors, internships, teacher certification program. **Credit/placement by examination:** AP, CLEP, IB, SAT, ACT, institutional tests. 30 credit hours maximum toward bachelor's degree. **Support services:** Learning center, reduced course load, remedial instruction.

Majors. Biology: General. **Business:** Business admin. **Education:** Biology, elementary, English, mathematics, music, physical, social science, Spanish. **English:** English lit. **Foreign languages:** Spanish. **Health services:** Clinical lab science. **History:** General. **Math:** General. **Parks/recreation:** Health/fitness. **Psychology:** General. **Social sciences:** General. **Theology:** Bible, sacred music. **Visual/performing arts:** General, music.

Most popular majors. Biology 7%, business/marketing 6%, education 44%, psychology 15%, social sciences 8%, theological studies 10%.

Computing on campus. 41 workstations in dormitories, library. Online library, wireless network available.

Student life. Freshman orientation: Mandatory, $50 fee. Preregistration for classes offered. Held the week prior to the opening of the fall semester; designed to provide opportunities for learning methods that support college success. **Policies:** Smoking and alcoholic beverages forbidden. Chapel attendance is required of all full-time students. Unmarried full-time students under the age of 21 are required to live on campus unless they are independent students, are living at home with parents or immediate family and commuting to school. **Housing:** Single-sex dorms, wellness housing available. $50 fully refundable deposit. **Activities:** Choral groups, drama, literary magazine, music ensembles, musical theater, student government, Alpha Psi Omega, Baptist student union, Cap and Gown Honor Society, Mississippi Association of Educators student chapter, psychology club, Society of Mathematicians and Scientists, Vivace club, Ministerial Association, Koinonia, social societies.

Athletics. NAIA. **Intercollegiate:** Baseball M, basketball, cross-country, golf, softball W. **Intramural:** Basketball, football (non-tackle) M, soccer M, softball, swimming, table tennis, tennis W, track and field, volleyball. **Team name:** Toppers.

Student services. Health services, placement for graduates. **Physically disabled:** Services for visually, hearing impaired.

Contact. E-mail: admissions@bmc.edu
Phone: (662) 685-4771 ext. 166 Toll-free number: (800) 235-0136
Fax: (662) 685-4776
Maria Teel, Director of Admissions, Blue Mountain College, 201 West Main Street, PO Box 160, Blue Mountain, MS 38610-0160

Delta State University
Cleveland, Mississippi
CB member
www.deltastate.edu
CB code: 1163

- Public 4-year university
- Commuter campus in large town
- 2,880 degree-seeking undergraduates: 19% part-time, 62% women, 39% African American, 1% Asian American, 1% Hispanic American, 2% international
- 1,744 degree-seeking graduate students
- 58% of applicants admitted
- ACT (writing optional) required
- 32% graduate within 6 years

General. Founded in 1924. Regionally accredited. **Degrees:** 559 bachelor's awarded; master's, doctoral offered. **ROTC:** Army. **Location:** 40 miles from Greenville, 110 miles from Memphis, Tennessee. **Calendar:** Semester, extensive summer session. **Full-time faculty:** 183 total; 66% have terminal degrees, 16% minority, 50% women. **Part-time faculty:** 76 total; 37% have terminal degrees, 12% minority, 74% women. **Class size:** 65% < 20, 31% 20-39, 3% 40-49, 2% 50-99. **Special facilities:** Planetarium, airport, archives & museum.

Freshman class profile. 720 applied, 418 admitted, 333 enrolled.

Mid 50% test scores			
SAT critical reading:	430-540	Rank in top quarter:	36%
SAT math:	460-540	Rank in top tenth:	13%
ACT composite:	18-23	Return as sophomores:	61%
GPA 3.75 or higher:	17%	Out-of-state:	16%
GPA 3.50-3.74:	19%	Live on campus:	81%
GPA 3.0-3.49:	32%	International:	2%
GPA 2.0-2.99:	30%	Fraternities:	21%
		Sororities:	24%

Basis for selection. Combination of college preparatory curriculum, test scores, class rank. Mississippi residents must take ACT for admission. Interview required for art, music majors. Audition recommended for music majors; portfolio recommended for art majors.

High school preparation. College-preparatory program required. 15.5 units required. Required units include English 4, mathematics 3, social studies 3, science 3 (laboratory 2), computer science .5 and academic electives 2.

2011-2012 Annual costs. Tuition/fees: $5,288; $13,688 out-of-state. Room/board: $6,025. Books/supplies: $900.

2010-2011 Financial aid. Need-based: 330 full-time freshmen applied for aid; 266 were judged to have need; 263 of these received aid. Average scholarship/grant was $5,346. 61% of total undergraduate aid awarded as scholarships/grants, 39% as loans/jobs. **Non-need-based:** Awarded to 288 full-time undergraduates, including 77 freshmen. Scholarships awarded for academics, alumni affiliation, art, athletics, leadership, music/drama, state residency.

Application procedures. Admission: Priority date 8/1; no deadline. $25 fee. Admission notification on a rolling basis. **Financial aid:** Priority date 3/1; no closing date. FAFSA, institutional form required. Applicants notified on a rolling basis starting 5/1.

Academics. Special study options: Distance learning, double major, dual enrollment of high school students, honors, independent study, internships, student-designed major, teacher certification program. **Credit/placement by examination:** AP, CLEP, SAT, ACT, institutional tests. 30 credit hours maximum toward bachelor's degree. **Support services:** Learning center, pre-admission summer program, remedial instruction, study skills assistance, tutoring, writing center.

Majors. Biology: General. **Business:** General, accounting, business admin, finance, hospitality admin, insurance, management information systems, marketing. **Communications:** Journalism. **Education:** Elementary, English, mathematics, music, physical, social science. **English:** English lit. **Foreign languages:** General. **Health services:** Athletic training, audiology/speech pathology, nursing (RN). **History:** General. **Human services:** Social work. **Math:** General. **Physical sciences:** Chemistry. **Protective services:** Criminal justice. **Psychology:** General. **Social sciences:** General, political science. **Visual/performing arts:** General, music. **Work/family studies:** General.

Most popular majors. Biology 6%, business/marketing 22%, education 20%, family/consumer sciences 6%, health sciences 13%.

Computing on campus. 293 workstations in dormitories, library, computer center, student center. Dormitories wired for high-speed internet access and linked to campus network. Commuter students can connect to campus network. Online course registration, online library, helpline, repair service, student web hosting, wireless network available.

Student life. Freshman orientation: Available, $35 fee. Preregistration for classes offered. Provides opportunity for academic advisement. **Housing:** Guaranteed on-campus for all undergraduates. Single-sex dorms, apartments, fraternity/sorority housing available. $50 fully refundable deposit, deadline 8/1. **Activities:** Bands, campus ministries, choral groups, dance, drama, international student organizations, literary magazine, music ensembles, musical theater, opera, student government, student newspaper, several religious, ethnic, social, political organizations available on campus.

Athletics. NCAA. **Intercollegiate:** Baseball M, basketball, cross-country W, diving, football (tackle) M, golf M, soccer, softball W, swimming, tennis. **Intramural:** Badminton, basketball, bowling, cross-country, diving, football (non-tackle), golf, racquetball, rifle, soccer, softball, swimming, table tennis, tennis, triathlon, volleyball. **Team name:** Statesmen; Lady Statesmen.

Student services. Alcohol/substance abuse counseling, career counseling, student employment services, financial aid counseling, health services, on-campus daycare, personal counseling, placement for graduates. **Physically disabled:** Services for speech, hearing impaired.

Contact. E-mail: admissions@deltastate.edu
Phone: (662) 846-4655 Toll-free number: (800) 468-6378
Fax: (662) 846-4684
Deborah Heslep, Dean of Enrollment Management, Delta State University, 117 Kent Wyatt Hall, Cleveland, MS 38733

Jackson State University
Jackson, Mississippi
CB member
www.jsums.edu
CB code: 1341

- Public 4-year university
- Commuter campus in large city
- 6,844 degree-seeking undergraduates: 14% part-time, 62% women, 93% African American, 2% international
- 2,059 degree-seeking graduate students
- 74% of applicants admitted
- SAT or ACT required
- 40% graduate within 6 years

General. Founded in 1877. Regionally accredited. **Degrees:** 1,033 bachelor's awarded; master's, doctoral offered. **ROTC:** Army, Air Force. **Location:** 210 miles from Memphis, TN, 190 miles from New Orleans. **Calendar:** Semester, extensive summer session. **Full-time faculty:** 378 total; 80% have terminal degrees, 81% minority, 46% women. **Part-time faculty:** 139 total; 48% have terminal degrees, 83% minority, 54% women. **Class size:** 40% < 20, 50% 20-39, 7% 40-49, 2% 50-99. **Special facilities:** National research center, science observatory, academic research and computing center, medical mall campus, e-Center.

Freshman class profile. 7,265 applied, 5,409 admitted, 1,002 enrolled.

Mid 50% test scores			
ACT composite:	17-20	End year in good standing:	63%
GPA 3.75 or higher:	5%	Return as sophomores:	78%
GPA 3.50-3.74:	9%	Out-of-state:	34%
GPA 3.0-3.49:	28%	Live on campus:	65%
GPA 2.0-2.99:	52%	International:	1%

Basis for selection. Test scores and high school transcript important. Audition recommended for music majors.

High school preparation. College-preparatory program required. 15.5 units required. Required units include English 4, mathematics 3, social studies 3, science 3, computer science .5 and academic electives 2.

2011-2012 Annual costs. Tuition/fees: $5,504; $13,494 out-of-state. Room/board: $6,494. Books/supplies: $800. Personal expenses: $2,250.

Financial aid. All financial aid based on need.

Application procedures. Admission: Closing date 8/1. No application fee. Admission notification on a rolling basis beginning on or about 1/1. **Financial aid:** Priority date 4/1, closing date 5/1. FAFSA required. Applicants notified on a rolling basis starting 5/1.

Academics. Special study options: Distance learning, double major, dual enrollment of high school students, ESL, honors, independent study, internships, study abroad, teacher certification program, weekend college. **Credit/placement by examination:** AP, CLEP, SAT, ACT. 30 credit hours maximum toward bachelor's degree. **Support services:** Learning center, pre-admission summer program, reduced course load, remedial instruction, study skills assistance, tutoring, writing center.

Majors. Biology: General. **Business:** Accounting, business admin, entrepreneurial studies, finance, managerial economics, marketing. **Communications:** Media studies. **Computer sciences:** General. **Education:** Educational technology, elementary, music, physical, social science, special ed. **Engineering:** Civil, computer, electrical. **English:** English lit, rhetoric/composition. **Foreign languages:** General. **Health services:** Communication disorders, health care admin, predental. **History:** General. **Human services:** Social work. **Math:** General. **Physical sciences:** Atmospheric science, chemistry, geology, physics. **Protective services:** Criminal justice. **Psychology:** General. **Social sciences:** General, political science, sociology, urban studies. **Visual/performing arts:** General, music performance.

Most popular majors. Biology 9%, business/marketing 20%, education 14%, interdisciplinary studies 12%, security/protective services 6%.

Computing on campus. 1,119 workstations in library, computer center, student center. Dormitories wired for high-speed internet access and linked to campus network. Commuter students can connect to campus network. Online course registration, online library, helpline, repair service, wireless network available.

Student life. Freshman orientation: Mandatory. Preregistration for classes offered. **Housing:** Single-sex dorms available. **Activities:** Bands, campus ministries, choral groups, dance, drama, film society, international student organizations, literary magazine, music ensembles, opera, radio station, student government, student newspaper, symphony orchestra, TV station, Pierre Toussaint Catholic Student Union, Baptist Student Union, Church of God in Christ club, NAACP, Alpha Phi Omega,.

Athletics. NCAA. **Intercollegiate:** Baseball M, basketball, bowling, cross-country, football (tackle) M, golf, rifle, soccer W, softball W, tennis, track and field, volleyball W. **Intramural:** Basketball, rifle, swimming, tennis, volleyball. **Team name:** JSU Tigers.

Student services. Adult student services, career counseling, student employment services, financial aid counseling, health services, on-campus daycare, personal counseling, placement for graduates, veterans' counselor, women's services. **Physically disabled:** Services for visually, speech, hearing impaired.

Contact. E-mail: admappl@jsums.edu
Phone: (601) 979-2100 Toll-free number: (800) 848-6817
Fax: (601) 979-3445
Stephanie Chatman, Director of Undergraduate Admissions, Jackson State University, 1400 John R. Lynch Street, Jackson, MS 39217

Millsaps College
Jackson, Mississippi
www.millsaps.edu

CB member
CB code: 1471

- Private 4-year business and liberal arts college affiliated with United Methodist Church
- Residential campus in large city
- 893 degree-seeking undergraduates: 1% part-time, 49% women, 9% African American, 5% Asian American, 3% Hispanic American, 1% Native American, 3% international
- 73 degree-seeking graduate students
- 61% of applicants admitted
- SAT or ACT (ACT writing optional), application essay required
- 66% graduate within 6 years; 52% enter graduate study

General. Founded in 1890. Regionally accredited. 4,000-acre biocultural reserve and learning center in the state of Yucatan, Mexico, for anthropology and archaeology and courses in various other disciplines. **Degrees:** 235 bachelor's awarded; master's offered. **ROTC:** Army, Air Force. **Location:** 190 miles from New Orleans, 210 miles from Memphis, Tennessee. **Calendar:** Semester, limited summer session. **Full-time faculty:** 97 total; 94% have terminal degrees, 14% minority, 44% women. **Part-time faculty:** 21 total; 14% have terminal degrees, 71% women. **Class size:** 76% < 20, 23% 20-39, less than 1% 40-49, less than 1% >100. **Special facilities:** Molecular biology/functional genomics research laboratory, fluorescence microscopy suite and imaging facility, GIS workstation, microsurgical lab for animal surgeries, hydrogeologic monitoring station, computational modeling laboratory, sorbent and environmental laboratory.

Freshman class profile. 1,779 applied, 1,077 admitted, 224 enrolled.

Mid 50% test scores			
SAT critical reading:	510-650	GPA 2.0-2.99:	12%
SAT math:	540-650	Return as sophomores:	88%
ACT composite:	23-29	Out-of-state:	58%
GPA 3.75 or higher:	43%	Live on campus:	98%
GPA 3.50-3.74:	14%	International:	2%
GPA 3.0-3.49:	31%	Fraternities:	53%
		Sororities:	66%

Basis for selection. Test scores, GPA in academic courses, recommendations, essays, and school and community activities are important. Advanced credit is awarded for A-Levels, International Baccalaureate, and some other systems. Students interested in fine and performing arts scholarships are required to submit a portfolio and/or audition for scholarships. **Home schooled:** Statement describing home school structure and mission, transcript of courses and grades, letter of recommendation (nonparent) required. **Learning Disabled:** No special admission requirements; students requesting accommodations are recommended to submit appropriate documentation to the Director of Disability Services prior to first semester.

High school preparation. 14 units required; 20 recommended. Required and recommended units include English 4, mathematics 3-4, social studies 2, history 2, science 3-4 (laboratory 2), foreign language 1-2 and academic electives 1-2.

2011-2012 Annual costs. Tuition/fees: $29,482. Room/board: $10,312. Books/supplies: $1,100. Personal expenses: $1,100.

2011-2012 Financial aid. Need-based: 192 full-time freshmen applied for aid; 142 were judged to have need; 142 of these received aid. Average need met was 83%. Average scholarship/grant was $21,359; average loan $3,516. 79% of total undergraduate aid awarded as scholarships/grants, 21% as loans/jobs. **Non-need-based:** Awarded to 438 full-time undergraduates, including 102 freshmen. Scholarships awarded for academics, art, leadership, music/drama, religious affiliation.

Application procedures. Admission: Closing date 2/1 (postmark date). No application fee. Admission notification on a rolling basis beginning on or about 10/15. Must reply by May 1 or within 2 week(s) if notified thereafter. Early action notification two weeks after application is complete. **Financial aid:** Priority date 3/1; no closing date. FAFSA required. Applicants notified on a rolling basis starting 3/15; must reply by 5/1 or within 2 week(s) of notification.

Academics. Special study options: Accelerated study, combined bachelor's/graduate degree, double major, honors, independent study, internships, liberal arts/career combination, New York semester, semester at sea, student-designed major, study abroad, teacher certification program, United Nations semester, urban semester, Washington semester. Faith and work service-learning opportunities; undergraduate field research opportunities in the Pacific Northwest, Yellowstone, Mexico, and Europe; multi-disciplinary study, including socio-cultural anthropology in Yucatan Peninsula; study abroad programs in Albania, Cambodia, China, Costa Rica, England, France, Germany, Ghana, Greece, Israel, Italy, Japan, Scotland, Mexico (Yucatan), Tanzania and Viet Nam; direct exchange programs in Albania, Japan, Ireland and Liechtenstein; pre-professional programs in dentistry, engineering, law, medicine, ministry, and social work; dual degree programs in engineering, applied science or nursing through Auburn University, Columbia University, Vanderbilt University, Washington University, and University of Mississippi Medical Health Center. Ford Teaching Fellows research and internships for students interested in college teaching; Weiner pre-medical fellows program for summer research. **Credit/placement by examination:** AP, CLEP, IB, SAT, ACT, institutional tests. 28 credit hours maximum toward bachelor's degree. Limited to two courses in any discipline and seven courses overall. **Support services:** Pre-admission summer program, reduced course load, study skills assistance, tutoring, writing center.

Majors. Area/ethnic studies: European, Latin American. **Biology:** General, biochemistry. **Business:** Accounting, business admin. **Communications:** Communications/speech/rhetoric. **Computer sciences:** General, computer science. **Education:** Elementary. **English:** English lit. **Foreign languages:** Classics, French, Spanish. **History:** General. **Human services:** General. **Math:** General, applied. **Philosophy/religion:** Philosophy, religion. **Physical sciences:** Chemistry, geology, physics. **Psychology:** General. **Social sciences:** Economics, political science, sociology/anthropology. **Visual/performing arts:** Art history/conservation, music, studio arts.

Most popular majors. Biology 15%, business/marketing 21%, English 6%, physical sciences 8%, psychology 6%, social sciences 14%, visual/performing arts 6%.

Computing on campus. 150 workstations in dormitories, library, computer center, student center. Dormitories wired for high-speed internet access and linked to campus network. Commuter students can connect to campus network. Online course registration, online library, helpline, student web hosting, wireless network available.

Student life. Freshman orientation: Mandatory. Preregistration for classes offered. 8 days of educational and social activities held 4 days prior to classes and 12-week Foundations course held once weekly. **Policies:** Students required to live on campus through sophomore year. Students with family in the area may be exempted. **Housing:** Guaranteed on-campus for freshmen. Coed dorms, single-sex dorms, special housing for disabled, fraternity/sorority housing available. Community service theme housing available. **Activities:** Campus ministries, choral groups, dance, drama, international

student organizations, literary magazine, music ensembles, Model UN, musical theater, student government, student newspaper, Circle K, Christian Fellowship, Black student association, Habitat for Humanity, Catholic student association, Fellowship of Christian Athletes, College Republicans, Young Democrats, Multicultural Affairs Diversity Group, E.A.R.T.H. (environmental service club), Jewish cultural organization.

Athletics. NCAA. **Intercollegiate:** Baseball M, basketball, cross-country, football (tackle) M, golf, lacrosse, soccer, softball W, tennis, track and field, volleyball W. **Intramural:** Basketball, bowling, football (non-tackle), golf, handball, racquetball, soccer, softball, table tennis, tennis, volleyball. **Team name:** Millsaps Majors, Lady Majors.

Student services. Adult student services, alcohol/substance abuse counseling, chaplain/spiritual director, career counseling, student employment services, financial aid counseling, health services, minority student services, personal counseling, placement for graduates.

Contact. E-mail: admissions@millsaps.edu
Phone: (601) 974-1050 Toll-free number: (800) 352-1050
Fax: (601) 974-1059
Michael Thorp, Dean of Enrollment Management, Millsaps College, 1701 North State Street, Jackson, MS 39210-0001

Mississippi College
Clinton, Mississippi
www.mc.edu   **CB code: 1477**

- Private 4-year university affiliated with Southern Baptist Convention
- Residential campus in large town
- 3,180 degree-seeking undergraduates: 12% part-time, 60% women, 24% African American, 1% Asian American, 1% Hispanic American, 1% Native American, 3% international
- 1,973 degree-seeking graduate students
- 45% of applicants admitted
- SAT or ACT (ACT writing optional) required
- 53% graduate within 6 years; 27% enter graduate study

General. Founded in 1826. Regionally accredited. **Degrees:** 656 bachelor's awarded; master's, professional, doctoral offered. **ROTC:** Army, Air Force. **Location:** 10 miles from Jackson. **Calendar:** Semester, limited summer session. **Full-time faculty:** 194 total; 79% have terminal degrees, 3% minority, 47% women. **Part-time faculty:** 263 total; 52% have terminal degrees, 8% minority, 48% women. **Class size:** 57% < 20, 36% 20-39, 6% 40-49, 1% 50-99. **Special facilities:** Baptist healthplex, Choctaw trails.

Freshman class profile. 1,821 applied, 816 admitted, 516 enrolled.

Mid 50% test scores		Rank in top quarter:	54%
SAT critical reading:	480-630	Rank in top tenth:	31%
SAT math:	490-590	End year in good standing:	88%
ACT composite:	21-27	Return as sophomores:	75%
GPA 3.75 or higher:	37%	Out-of-state:	43%
GPA 3.50-3.74:	18%	Live on campus:	95%
GPA 3.0-3.49:	27%	International:	3%
GPA 2.0-2.99:	17%		

Basis for selection. ACT/SAT scores most important, followed by high school record. Recommendations considered in marginal cases. For placement purposes, provisional admission if ACT score is less than 18. Admission and advising affects course load and course selection. Audition recommended for music majors; portfolio recommended for art majors. **Home schooled:** Transcript of courses and grades required.

High school preparation. College-preparatory program recommended. 22 units recommended. Recommended units include English 4, mathematics 4, social studies 2, history 2, science 4 (laboratory 2), foreign language 1, computer science .5, visual/performing arts 1, academic electives 3.5. 2 units of advanced electives recommended.

2012-2013 Annual costs. Tuition/fees (projected): $14,430. Room/board: $6,950. Books/supplies: $1,100. Personal expenses: $1,863.

2011-2012 Financial aid. Need-based: 417 full-time freshmen applied for aid; 203 were judged to have need; 203 of these received aid. Average need met was 35%. Average scholarship/grant was $2,993; average loan $1,783. 50% of total undergraduate aid awarded as scholarships/grants, 50% as loans/jobs. **Non-need-based:** Awarded to 2,362 full-time undergraduates, including 466 freshmen. Scholarships awarded for academics, alumni affiliation, art, leadership, music/drama, religious affiliation. **Additional information:** Student reply date for institutional scholarships: May 1.

Application procedures. Admission: Priority date 5/1; no deadline. No application fee. Admission notification on a rolling basis. Either SAT or ACT may be substituted for TOEFL scores for foreign students. **Financial aid:** Priority date 3/1; no closing date. FAFSA required. Applicants notified on a rolling basis starting 3/1; must reply by 5/1.

Academics. Special study options: Accelerated study, combined bachelor's/graduate degree, distance learning, double major, dual enrollment of high school students, ESL, honors, independent study, internships, study abroad, teacher certification program. **Credit/placement by examination:** AP, CLEP, IB, institutional tests. 30 credit hours maximum toward bachelor's degree. **Support services:** Reduced course load, remedial instruction, study skills assistance, tutoring, writing center.

Majors. Biology: General, biochemistry, biomedical sciences. **Business:** Accounting, business admin, finance, marketing. **Communications:** Communications/speech/rhetoric, media studies, public relations. **Computer sciences:** General, computer science. **Education:** Art, biology, business, chemistry, elementary, English, mathematics, music, physical, social studies, special ed. **Engineering:** Applied physics. **English:** English lit, general lit, writing. **Foreign languages:** French, Spanish, translation. **Health services:** Nursing (RN). **History:** General. **Human services:** Social work. **Math:** General. **Parks/recreation:** Exercise sciences, sports admin. **Philosophy/religion:** Christian. **Physical sciences:** Chemical physics, chemistry, physics. **Protective services:** Homeland security, law enforcement admin. **Psychology:** General. **Social sciences:** Political science, sociology. **Theology:** Sacred music. **Visual/performing arts:** Graphic design, interior design, music, music performance, music theory/composition, piano/keyboard, studio arts, voice/opera.

Most popular majors. Biology 11%, business/marketing 25%, education 13%, health sciences 10%, parks/recreation 11%.

Computing on campus. 350 workstations in dormitories, library, computer center, student center. Dormitories wired for high-speed internet access and linked to campus network. Commuter students can connect to campus network. Online course registration, helpline, student web hosting, wireless network available.

Student life. Freshman orientation: Mandatory, $100 fee. Preregistration for classes offered. Held on a Thursday, Friday, and Saturday in July. **Policies:** No alcohol allowed, no smoking on campus. **Housing:** Single-sex dorms, special housing for disabled, apartments, wellness housing available. $100 nonrefundable deposit, deadline 7/15. **Activities:** Bands, campus ministries, choral groups, dance, drama, international student organizations, literary magazine, music ensembles, musical theater, opera, radio station, student government, student newspaper, Baptist Student Union, Civitan, Circle-K, Rotoract, Young Democrats, Young Republicans, Black Student Association, 5 women's social/service clubs, Reformed University Fellowship, Habitat for Humanity.

Athletics. NCAA. **Intercollegiate:** Baseball M, basketball, cross-country, football (tackle) M, golf, soccer, softball W, tennis, track and field, volleyball W. **Intramural:** Badminton, basketball, field hockey, football (non-tackle), soccer, softball, table tennis, tennis, volleyball. **Team name:** Choctaws.

Student services. Adult student services, chaplain/spiritual director, career counseling, student employment services, financial aid counseling, health services, personal counseling, placement for graduates, veterans' counselor. **Physically disabled:** Services for visually, speech, hearing impaired.

Contact. E-mail: enrollment-services@mc.edu
Phone: (601) 925-3800 Toll-free number: (800) 738-1236
Fax: (601) 925-3950
Kyle Brantley, Director of Admissions, Mississippi College, PO Box 4026, Clinton, MS 39058-0001

Mississippi State University
Mississippi State, Mississippi   **CB member**
www.msstate.edu   **CB code: 1480**

- Public 4-year university and agricultural college
- Residential campus in large town
- 15,393 degree-seeking undergraduates: 7% part-time, 48% women
- 3,745 degree-seeking graduate students
- 68% of applicants admitted
- SAT or ACT (ACT writing optional) required
- 58% graduate within 6 years

General. Founded in 1878. Regionally accredited. Branch campus located in Meridian; extension offices in all 82 counties; branch experiment stations and research units in 15 locations. **Degrees:** 2,759 bachelor's awarded; master's, professional, doctoral offered. **ROTC:** Army, Air Force. **Location:** 125

miles from Jackson, 23 miles from Columbus. **Calendar:** Semester, extensive summer session. **Full-time faculty:** 833 total; 78% have terminal degrees, 15% minority, 36% women. **Part-time faculty:** 130 total; 42% have terminal degrees, 8% minority, 59% women. **Class size:** 36% < 20, 41% 20-39, 9% 40-49, 10% 50-99, 4% >100. **Special facilities:** Clock museum, historic costume and textiles collection, archaeology museum, Mississippi entomological museum, arboretum, music museum, observatory, advanced vehicular systems center, computational sciences center, computer security research center, computational simulation and design center, geosystems research institute, high performance computing collaboratory, high voltage laboratory, industrial assessment center, industrial outreach service, clean energy technology institute, digital biology institute, neurocognitive science and technology institute, microsystems prototyping laboratory, Mississippi transportation research center, flight research laboratory, forensics training center, sustainable energy research center.

Freshman class profile. 9,864 applied, 6,684 admitted, 2,898 enrolled.

Mid 50% test scores			
SAT critical reading:	480-600	Rank in top tenth:	28%
SAT math:	490-630	End year in good standing:	94%
ACT composite:	20-27	Return as sophomores:	83%
GPA 3.75 or higher:	27%	Out-of-state:	31%
GPA 3.50-3.74:	15%	Live on campus:	96%
GPA 3.0-3.49:	28%	International:	1%
GPA 2.0-2.99:	29%	Fraternities:	30%
Rank in top quarter:	28%	Sororities:	33%

Basis for selection. Admission based on standardized test scores, GPA, class rank. Students with academic deficiencies may be admitted after additional review. Requirements may vary by department; student should contact department to ensure that requirements are met. Successful completion of summer developmental program results in admission for fall term with mandatory participation in academic support program freshmen year. Audition/portfolio are required for specific majors or departments. Interview recommended for architecture, professional golf management, and veterinary medicine students. **Home schooled:** Transcript of courses and grades required.

High school preparation. College-preparatory program recommended. 16 units required; 21 recommended. Required and recommended units include English 4, mathematics 3-4, social studies 1-2, history 2, science 3-4 (laboratory 2), foreign language 1, computer science .5 and academic electives 2. One of the two academic electives must be a foreign language or world geography. Additional unit recommended.

2011-2012 Annual costs. Tuition/fees: $5,808; $14,670 out-of-state. Room/board: $8,162. Books/supplies: $1,200. Personal expenses: $2,760.

2010-2011 Financial aid. Need-based: 2,158 full-time freshmen applied for aid; 1,778 were judged to have need; 1,756 of these received aid. Average need met was 66%. Average scholarship/grant was $6,103; average loan $3,398. 38% of total undergraduate aid awarded as scholarships/grants, 62% as loans/jobs. **Non-need-based:** Awarded to 3,584 full-time undergraduates, including 1,021 freshmen. Scholarships awarded for academics, alumni affiliation, art, athletics, job skills, leadership, minority status, music/drama, ROTC, state residency.

Application procedures. Admission: No deadline. $40 fee, may be waived for applicants with need. Admission notification on a rolling basis beginning on or about 9/1. **Financial aid:** Priority date 4/1; no closing date. FAFSA required. Applicants notified on a rolling basis starting 12/1; must reply by 5/1.

Academics. Special study options: Combined bachelor's/graduate degree, cooperative education, distance learning, double major, dual enrollment of high school students, ESL, exchange student, honors, independent study, internships, liberal arts/career combination, semester at sea, student-designed major, study abroad, teacher certification program, weekend college. **Credit/placement by examination:** AP, CLEP, IB, SAT, ACT, institutional tests. Maximum of 25 percent of any curriculum may be earned by examination which includes correspondence and military. **Support services:** Learning center, pre-admission summer program, reduced course load, remedial instruction, study skills assistance, tutoring, writing center.

Honors college/program. ACT composite score of 30 or above (SAT 1230, exclusive of Writing) and a 3.8 high school core GPA. 469 freshmen admitted into the Honor College Program.

Majors. Architecture: Architecture, interior, landscape. **Biology:** General, bacteriology, biochemistry. **Business:** Accounting, business admin, construction management, finance, insurance, management information systems, managerial economics, marketing, real estate. **Communications:** Communications/speech/rhetoric. **Computer sciences:** General. **Conservation:** Forestry, wildlife/wilderness. **Education:** Agricultural, business, elementary, music, physical, secondary, special ed, voc/tech. **Engineering:** Aerospace, biomedical, chemical, civil, computer, electrical, industrial, mechanical. **English:** English lit. **Foreign languages:** General. **General:** Agribusiness operations, agronomy, animal sciences, economics, food science, horticultural science,

landscaping, poultry. **Health services:** Clinical lab science. **History:** General. **Human services:** Social work. **Liberal arts:** Arts/sciences. **Math:** General. **Philosophy/religion:** Philosophy. **Physical sciences:** Chemistry, geology, physics. **Psychology:** General, educational. **Social sciences:** Anthropology, economics, political science, sociology. **Visual/performing arts:** General, music. **Work/family studies:** General.

Most popular majors. Business/marketing 23%, education 17%, engineering/engineering technologies 14%, interdisciplinary studies 6%, psychology 6%.

Computing on campus. 1,000 workstations in dormitories, library, computer center, student center. Dormitories wired for high-speed internet access and linked to campus network. Commuter students can connect to campus network. Online course registration, online library, helpline, repair service, student web hosting, wireless network available.

Student life. Freshman orientation: Available, $30 fee. Preregistration for classes offered. 2-day program held in the fall; includes class registration fee & information book upon arrival. Additional fee for parents. **Policies:** Freshmen are required to live in residence hall and purchase a meal plan. **Housing:** Guaranteed on-campus for freshmen. Single-sex dorms, special housing for disabled, apartments, fraternity/sorority housing available. $60 nonrefundable deposit. Co-residential housing available. Residence halls are ADA accessible. Family housing is also available for qualifying students. **Activities:** Bands, campus ministries, choral groups, dance, drama, international student organizations, literary magazine, music ensembles, Model UN, musical theater, radio station, student government, student newspaper, symphony orchestra, TV station, more than 300 organizations on campus.

Athletics. NCAA. **Intercollegiate:** Baseball M, basketball, cross-country, football (tackle) M, golf, soccer W, softball W, tennis, track and field, volleyball W. **Intramural:** Badminton, basketball, bowling, cross-country, football (non-tackle), golf, racquetball, rifle, soccer, softball, swimming, table tennis, tennis, volleyball, water polo, weight lifting. **Team name:** Bulldogs.

Student services. Alcohol/substance abuse counseling, chaplain/spiritual director, career counseling, services for economically disadvantaged, student employment services, financial aid counseling, health services, minority student services, on-campus daycare, personal counseling, veterans' counselor. **Physically disabled:** Services for visually, speech, hearing impaired.

Contact. E-mail: admit@msstate.edu
Phone: (662) 325-2224 Fax: (662) 325-1678
Phil Bonfanti, Director of Admissions and Scholarships, Mississippi State University, Box 6334, Mississippi State, MS 39762

Mississippi University for Women
Columbus, Mississippi
www.muw.edu   CB code: 1481

- Public 4-year university and liberal arts college
- Commuter campus in large town
- 2,292 degree-seeking undergraduates
- 44% of applicants admitted

General. Founded in 1884. Regionally accredited. **Degrees:** 460 bachelor's, 54 associate awarded; master's offered. **ROTC:** Army, Air Force. **Location:** 120 miles from Birmingham, Alabama, 160 miles from Memphis, Tennessee. **Calendar:** Semester, limited summer session. **Full-time faculty:** 136 total. **Part-time faculty:** 66 total. **Class size:** 60% < 20, 33% 20-39, 4% 40-49, 2% 50-99, 2% >100. **Special facilities:** Environmental education center.

Freshman class profile. 1,360 applied, 598 admitted, 179 enrolled.

Mid 50% test scores			
SAT critical reading:	410-530	GPA 2.0-2.99:	30%
SAT math:	450-620	Rank in top quarter:	61%
ACT composite:	18-24	Rank in top tenth:	30%
GPA 3.75 or higher:	23%	Out-of-state:	10%
GPA 3.50-3.74:	18%	Live on campus:	66%
GPA 3.0-3.49:	29%	Fraternities:	42%
		Sororities:	43%

Basis for selection. Test scores, high school GPA, academic achievement considered in that order. SAT or ACT recommended. Students with a 3.2 GPA or higher not required to provide test scores. Interview required for students who are taking a placement test. **Home schooled:** Portfolio of work and/or transcript is required. Placement test may be required.

High school preparation. College-preparatory program recommended. 16 units required; 20 recommended. Required and recommended units include English 4, mathematics 3-4, social studies 3, science 3-4 (laboratory 2), foreign language 1, computer science .5 and academic electives 2. One elective of foreign language or world geography required; other elective must

be in foreign language, world geography, 4th year mathematics, or 4th year laboratory science.

2011-2012 Annual costs. Tuition/fees: $4,876; $13,287 out-of-state. Room/board: $5,748. Books/supplies: $800. Personal expenses: $1,200.

Financial aid. Non-need-based: Scholarships awarded for academics, alumni affiliation, leadership, minority status, music/drama, ROTC, state residency.

Application procedures. Admission: No deadline. No application fee. Admission notification on a rolling basis. **Financial aid:** Priority date 3/1; no closing date. FAFSA required. Applicants notified on a rolling basis starting 3/15; must reply within 2 week(s) of notification.

Academics. Special study options: Cross-registration, distance learning, double major, dual enrollment of high school students, honors, independent study, internships, study abroad, teacher certification program, weekend college. **Credit/placement by examination:** AP, CLEP, SAT, ACT, institutional tests. 60 credit hours maximum toward bachelor's degree. **Support services:** Learning center, pre-admission summer program, remedial instruction, tutoring.

Majors. Biology: General, bacteriology. **Business:** Accounting, business admin. **Communications:** Communications/speech/rhetoric. **Education:** Art, elementary, music. **English:** English lit. **Foreign languages:** Spanish. **Health services:** Music therapy, nursing (RN), speech pathology. **History:** General. **Liberal arts:** Arts/sciences. **Math:** General. **Parks/recreation:** Health/fitness. **Physical sciences:** General, chemistry. **Psychology:** General. **Social sciences:** General, political science. **Visual/performing arts:** General, music. **Work/family studies:** Family systems.

Most popular majors. Business/marketing 9%, education 15%, health sciences 33%.

Computing on campus. 500 workstations in dormitories, library, computer center. Dormitories wired for high-speed internet access and linked to campus network. Commuter students can connect to campus network. Online course registration, online library, helpline, student web hosting available.

Student life. Freshman orientation: Available, $60 fee. Preregistration for classes offered. **Housing:** Guaranteed on-campus for all undergraduates. Single-sex dorms, apartments, wellness housing available. $100 partly refundable deposit. **Activities:** Jazz band, choral groups, drama, international student organizations, literary magazine, music ensembles, radio station, student government, student newspaper, Methodist, Presbyterian, Episcopal, Baptist, Catholic, Student Interfaith Association, Black student organizations, College Republicans, Young Democrats.

Athletics. Intramural: Badminton, basketball, football (non-tackle), golf, racquetball, soccer, softball, table tennis, tennis, volleyball.

Student services. Adult student services, alcohol/substance abuse counseling, career counseling, student employment services, financial aid counseling, health services, on-campus daycare, personal counseling, placement for graduates, veterans' counselor. **Physically disabled:** Services for visually, speech, hearing impaired.

Contact. E-mail: admissions@muw.edu
Phone: (662) 329-7106 Toll-free number: (877) 462-8439
Fax: (662) 241-7481
Cassie Derden, Director of Admissions, Mississippi University for Women, 1100 College St. MUW-1613, Columbus, MS 39701

Mississippi Valley State University
Itta Bena, Mississippi
www.mvsu.edu

CB member
CB code: 1482

- Public 4-year university and liberal arts college
- Commuter campus in small town
- 2,033 degree-seeking undergraduates: 16% part-time, 61% women, 91% African American, 1% Hispanic American
- 362 degree-seeking graduate students
- SAT or ACT (ACT writing optional) required

General. Founded in 1946. Regionally accredited. **Degrees:** 305 bachelor's awarded; master's offered. **ROTC:** Army. **Location:** 100 miles from Jackson, 130 miles from Memphis, Tennessee. **Calendar:** Semester, extensive summer session. **Full-time faculty:** 130 total; 62% have terminal degrees, 31% minority, 48% women. **Part-time faculty:** 28 total; 46% have terminal degrees, 11% minority, 57% women. **Class size:** 69% < 20, 28% 20-39, 2% 40-49, 2% 50-99, less than 1% >100.

Freshman class profile.

Mid 50% test scores		GPA 2.0-2.99:	49%
ACT composite:	15-19	End year in good standing:	80%
GPA 3.75 or higher:	2%	Return as sophomores:	62%
GPA 3.50-3.74:	4%	Out-of-state:	31%
GPA 3.0-3.49:	28%	Live on campus:	75%

Basis for selection. High school curriculum and test scores very important. Audition required for music education majors. Interview required of some students, but recommended for all students.

High school preparation. 16 units required; 18 recommended. Required and recommended units include English 4, mathematics 3, social studies 3, science 3 (laboratory 2), foreign language 1 and academic electives 2. Mathematics requirement includes algebra I and II and geometry. Social sciences must include US government and US history. Sciences must be chosen from introductory and advanced biology, physics, and chemistry. Advanced science or mathematics may be substituted for a foreign language.

2011-2012 Annual costs. Tuition/fees: $5,232; $13,080 out-of-state. Room/board: $6,200.

Financial aid. Non-need-based: Scholarships awarded for academics, athletics, minority status, ROTC.

Application procedures. Admission: Priority date 8/1; deadline 8/17 (receipt date). No application fee. Admission notification on a rolling basis. **Financial aid:** Priority date 3/1, closing date 5/1. FAFSA, institutional form required. Applicants notified on a rolling basis starting 4/1; must reply within 2 week(s) of notification.

Academics. Special study options: Cooperative education, double major, dual enrollment of high school students, honors, independent study, internships, teacher certification program. **Credit/placement by examination:** AP, CLEP, ACT. 30 credit hours maximum toward bachelor's degree. **Support services:** Learning center, pre-admission summer program, reduced course load, remedial instruction, study skills assistance, tutoring, writing center.

Majors. Biology: General. **Business:** Accounting, business admin, office management. **Communications:** Communications/speech/rhetoric. **Computer sciences:** General. **Education:** Biology, early childhood, elementary, English, mathematics, music, physical, social science. **English:** English lit, rhetoric/composition. **Health services:** Environmental health. **History:** General. **Human services:** General, social work. **Math:** General. **Physical sciences:** Chemistry. **Protective services:** Criminal justice. **Social sciences:** Political science, sociology. **Visual/performing arts:** Music, music management, studio arts.

Most popular majors. Biology 6%, business/marketing 23%, education 29%, public administration/social services 19%, security/protective services 10%.

Computing on campus. 600 workstations in dormitories, library, computer center. Dormitories wired for high-speed internet access and linked to campus network. Commuter students can connect to campus network. Online course registration, online library, wireless network available.

Student life. Freshman orientation: Mandatory, $100 fee. Preregistration for classes offered. Three-day event held in late July. **Housing:** Single-sex dorms, apartments available. $50 nonrefundable deposit, deadline 7/31. **Activities:** Bands, choral groups, dance, drama, music ensembles, radio station, student government, student newspaper, TV station, numerous honor societies, political, social, religious organizations, prelaw club.

Athletics. NCAA. **Intercollegiate:** Baseball M, basketball, bowling, cross-country, football (tackle) M, golf, soccer W, softball W, tennis, track and field, volleyball W. **Intramural:** Baseball M, basketball, bowling, cross-country, softball W, swimming, tennis, volleyball. **Team name:** Delta Devils (M), Devilettes (W).

Student services. Adult student services, career counseling, student employment services, financial aid counseling, health services, on-campus daycare, personal counseling, placement for graduates, veterans' counselor.

Contact. E-mail: jawill@mvsu.edu
Phone: (662) 254-3347 Fax: (662) 254-3759
Jerald Adley, Director of Admissions and Recruitment, Mississippi Valley State University, 14000 Highway 82 West, Itta Bena, MS 38941-1400

Rust College
Holly Springs, Mississippi
www.rustcollege.edu **CB code: 1669**

◆ Private 4-year liberal arts and teachers college affiliated with United Methodist Church
◆ Residential campus in small town
◆ 922 degree-seeking undergraduates: 12% part-time, 63% women, 93% African American, 5% international
◆ 46% of applicants admitted
◆ ACT (writing optional) required

General. Founded in 1866. Regionally accredited. **Degrees:** 123 bachelor's, 16 associate awarded. **Location:** 35 miles from Memphis, TN. **Calendar:** Semester, limited summer session. **Full-time faculty:** 48 total; 56% have terminal degrees, 83% minority, 44% women. **Part-time faculty:** 2 total; 100% minority, 50% women. **Class size:** 54% < 20, 44% 20-39, 2% 40-49. **Special facilities:** Library for ministers and ministerial students, Inuit and African art collections, international artifacts' collection.

Freshman class profile. 3,983 applied, 1,817 admitted, 264 enrolled.

Mid 50% test scores		GPA 3.0-3.49:	20%
ACT composite:	14-21	GPA 2.0-2.99:	72%
GPA 3.75 or higher:	2%	Return as sophomores:	53%
GPA 3.50-3.74:	5%	International:	5%

Basis for selection. Recommendations most important; GPA and test scores important. Special requirements for teacher education program. **Home schooled:** State high school equivalency certificate, letter of recommendation (nonparent) required.

High school preparation. College-preparatory program recommended. 19 units required. Required units include English 4, mathematics 3, social studies 3, science 3 and academic electives 6.

2011-2012 Annual costs. Tuition/fees: $8,100. Room/board: $3,700.

2011-2012 Financial aid. Need-based: 238 full-time freshmen applied for aid; 235 were judged to have need; 235 of these received aid. Average need met was 81%. Average scholarship/grant was $5,744; average loan $3,220. 56% of total undergraduate aid awarded as scholarships/grants, 44% as loans/jobs. **Non-need-based:** Awarded to 256 full-time undergraduates, including 114 freshmen. Scholarships awarded for academics, leadership, music/drama, religious affiliation, state residency.

Application procedures. Admission: Priority date 5/5; no deadline. $10 fee, may be waived for applicants with need. Admission notification on a rolling basis. Must reply by May 1 or within 2 week(s) if notified thereafter. **Financial aid:** Priority date 3/15, closing date 6/30. FAFSA, institutional form required. Applicants notified on a rolling basis starting 4/1; must reply within 2 week(s) of notification.

Academics. Special study options: Accelerated study, combined bachelor's/graduate degree, distance learning, double major, dual enrollment of high school students, honors, independent study, internships, liberal arts/career combination, study abroad, teacher certification program. **Credit/placement by examination:** AP, CLEP, SAT, ACT, institutional tests. 12 credit hours maximum toward associate degree, 12 toward bachelor's. **Support services:** Learning center, pre-admission summer program, reduced course load, remedial instruction, study skills assistance, tutoring, writing center.

Majors. Biology: General. **Business:** Business admin. **Communications:** Broadcast journalism, journalism. **Computer sciences:** Computer science. **Education:** Biology, business, elementary, English, mathematics, social science. **English:** English lit. **Human services:** Social work. **Math:** General. **Physical sciences:** Chemistry. **Social sciences:** General, political science, sociology. **Visual/performing arts:** Music. **Work/family studies:** Child care management.

Most popular majors. Biology 22%, business/marketing 15%, communications/journalism 13%, computer/information sciences 7%, English 7%, family/consumer sciences 9%, public administration/social services 8%, social sciences 11%.

Computing on campus. 220 workstations in dormitories, library, computer center. Dormitories wired for high-speed internet access and linked to campus network. Commuter students can connect to campus network. Online library, helpline, wireless network available.

Student life. Freshman orientation: Mandatory. Preregistration for classes offered. Orientation and assessment program begins 1 week prior to registration. **Housing:** Guaranteed on-campus for freshmen. Single-sex dorms available. $50 fully refundable deposit. Housing for single parents available.

Activities: Bands, campus ministries, choral groups, drama, international student organizations, music ensembles, radio station, student government, student newspaper, TV station, Methodist Student Movement, Baptist Student Union, Catholic Student Association, pre-law club, NAACP, social work club, Sunday School.

Athletics. NCAA. **Intercollegiate:** Baseball M, basketball, cheerleading, cross-country, softball W, tennis, track and field, volleyball. **Intramural:** Basketball, football (non-tackle), swimming, volleyball. **Team name:** Bearcats.

Student services. Adult student services, chaplain/spiritual director, career counseling, financial aid counseling, health services, on-campus daycare, personal counseling, placement for graduates, veterans' counselor.

Contact. E-mail: jb_mcdonald@rustcollege.edu
Phone: (662) 252-8000 ext. 4059
Toll-free number: (888) 886-8492 ext. 4059 Fax: (662) 252-8895
Johnny McDonald, Director of Enrollment Services, Rust College, 150 Rust Avenue, Holly Springs, MS 38635-2328

Southeastern Baptist College
Laurel, Mississippi
www.southeasternbaptist.edu **CB code: 1781**

◆ Private 4-year Bible and business college affiliated with Baptist faith
◆ Commuter campus in large town
◆ 65 degree-seeking undergraduates: 34% African American, 2% Hispanic American

General. Founded in 1949. Accredited by ABHE. **Degrees:** 4 bachelor's, 24 associate awarded. **Location:** 90 miles from Jackson. **Calendar:** Semester, limited summer session. **Full-time faculty:** 4 total. **Part-time faculty:** 9 total. **Special facilities:** Game room, physical fitness room.

Freshman class profile. 12 applied, 12 admitted, 12 enrolled.

Basis for selection. Open admission. Secondary school record, recommendations important. Interview, essay recommended for all students. Audition recommended for religious music majors.

High school preparation. In place of high school diploma or GED, 17 high school units including 2 natural/biological sciences, 1 English, 1 mathematics, 2 social sciences accepted.

2011-2012 Annual costs. Tuition/fees: $6,100. Room only: $800. Books/supplies: $300. Personal expenses: $350.

Application procedures. Admission: Priority date 6/1; deadline 8/1 (receipt date). $25 fee. Application must be submitted on paper. Admission notification on a rolling basis beginning on or about 1/1. Students may attend classes for two weeks without enrollment. They must be enrolled the third week to attend classes. **Financial aid:** Priority date 7/1; no closing date. Institutional form required. Applicants notified on a rolling basis starting 7/15; must reply within 4 week(s) of notification.

Academics. Special study options: Distance learning, double major. **Credit/placement by examination:** AP, CLEP. **Support services:** Learning center, remedial instruction, tutoring.

Majors. Philosophy/religion: Religion. **Theology:** Bible, theology.

Computing on campus. 17 workstations in dormitories, library, computer center. Dormitories wired for high-speed internet access and linked to campus network. Commuter students can connect to campus network. Helpline, wireless network available.

Student life. Freshman orientation: Mandatory, $200 fee. Preregistration for classes offered. Offered as class taken during first semester. **Policies:** Student handbook for important policies. Religious observance required. **Housing:** Guaranteed on-campus for all undergraduates. Single-sex dorms, apartments available. $75 fully refundable deposit, deadline 8/1. **Activities:** Choral groups, music ensembles, student government, Association of Baptist Students, Ministerial Alliance.

Athletics. Intramural: Badminton, basketball, bowling, handball, softball, table tennis, tennis, volleyball.

Student services. Student employment services, financial aid counseling, personal counseling, placement for graduates, veterans' counselor.

Contact. E-mail: admissions@southeasternbaptist.edu
Phone: (601) 426-6346 Fax: (601) 426-6347
Ronnie Kitchens, Director of Admissions, Southeastern Baptist College,
4229 Highway 15 North, Laurel, MS 39440

Tougaloo College
Tougaloo, Mississippi
www.tougaloo.edu

CB member
CB code: 1807

- Private 4-year liberal arts college affiliated with United Christian Mission Society and United Church of Christ
- Residential campus in large city
- 942 degree-seeking undergraduates
- 35% of applicants admitted
- SAT or ACT (ACT writing optional) required

General. Founded in 1869. Regionally accredited. Cooperative program with Brown University provides exchange of financial resources and students. Exchange opportunities available between New York and Boston universities in pre-med and other areas. **Degrees:** 158 bachelor's, 5 associate awarded. **ROTC:** Army, Naval. **Calendar:** Semester, limited summer session. **Full-time faculty:** 76 total. **Part-time faculty:** 22 total. **Class size:** 65% < 20, 34% 20-39, less than 1% 40-49, less than 1% 50-99. **Special facilities:** Civil rights documents and prints, East and West African art and artifacts.

Freshman class profile. 3,075 applied, 1,076 admitted, 204 enrolled.

Mid 50% test scores			
		ACT composite:	15-20
SAT critical reading:	320-490	Out-of-state:	20%
SAT math:	300-500	Live on campus:	90%

Basis for selection. Transcript, test scores important. Minimum 3.0 GPA and ACT composite score of 18 required of applicants in junior year of high school. Audition required for music majors. Portfolio recommended for art majors.

High school preparation. College-preparatory program recommended. 16 units required. Required and recommended units include English 3, mathematics 2, social studies 2, science 2, foreign language 2 and academic electives 9.

2011-2012 Annual costs. Tuition/fees: $10,210. Room/board: $6,572. Books/supplies: $500. Personal expenses: $800.

Financial aid. **Non-need-based:** Scholarships awarded for academics, athletics, ROTC.

Application procedures. **Admission:** Priority date 4/15; no deadline. $25 fee, may be waived for applicants with need. Admission notification on a rolling basis. **Financial aid:** Priority date 4/15; no closing date. FAFSA, institutional form required. Applicants notified on a rolling basis starting 5/1; must reply within 2 week(s) of notification.

Academics. **Special study options:** Accelerated study, cooperative education, cross-registration, double major, dual enrollment of high school students, exchange student, honors, independent study, internships, liberal arts/career combination, New York semester, student-designed major, study abroad, teacher certification program, Washington semester. 3-2 program in pre-engineering and physical sciences with Brown University, Georgia Institute of Technology, University of Mississippi, University of Wisconsin Madison, Tuskegee Institute, Washington University St. Louis, Howard University, University of Memphis, Florida A&M. **Credit/placement by examination:** AP, CLEP, IB, SAT, ACT, institutional tests. 12 credit hours maximum toward bachelor's degree. **Support services:** Learning center, pre-admission summer program, reduced course load, remedial instruction, study skills assistance, tutoring, writing center.

Majors. **Biology:** General. **Communications:** Media studies. **Education:** Elementary, health, kindergarten/preschool, secondary, special ed. **English:** English lit. **History:** General. **Liberal arts:** Arts/sciences. **Math:** General. **Physical sciences:** Chemistry, physics. **Psychology:** General. **Social sciences:** Economics, political science, sociology. **Visual/performing arts:** Art, music.

Most popular majors. Biology 17%, communications/journalism 6%, English 6%, psychology 13%, social sciences 33%.

Computing on campus. 4 workstations in dormitories, library, computer center, student center. Dormitories linked to campus network. Commuter students can connect to campus network. Helpline, repair service available.

Student life. Freshman orientation: Mandatory. Preregistration for classes offered. **Policies:** Smoke-free campus, zero tolerance for drugs and alcohol. **Housing:** Single-sex dorms, wellness housing available. $50 nonrefundable deposit. **Activities:** Jazz band, choral groups, dance, drama, music ensembles, radio station, student government, student newspaper, Baptist student union, biology club, Afro-American studies group, College Republicans, foreign students club, French club, pre-health club, prelaw club, honor societies, human services clubs.

Athletics. NAIA. **Intercollegiate:** Baseball M, basketball, cross-country, golf, tennis. **Intramural:** Badminton, baseball M, basketball, cheerleading, cross-country M, football (non-tackle) M, golf, soccer M, softball, tennis, volleyball. **Team name:** Bulldogs.

Student services. Adult student services, chaplain/spiritual director, career counseling, student employment services, financial aid counseling, health services, personal counseling, placement for graduates, veterans' counselor.

Contact. E-mail: info@tougaloo.edu
Phone: (601) 977-7765 Toll-free number: (888) 424-2566
Fax: (601) 977-4501
Junoesque Jacobs, Director of Admissions, Tougaloo College, 500 West County Line Road, Tougaloo, MS 39174

University of Mississippi
University, Mississippi
www.olemiss.edu

CB member
CB code: 1840

- Public 4-year university
- Residential campus in large town
- 15,111 degree-seeking undergraduates: 7% part-time, 55% women, 17% African American, 1% Asian American, 2% Hispanic American, 1% international
- 2,722 degree-seeking graduate students
- 79% of applicants admitted

General. Founded in 1844. Regionally accredited. **Degrees:** 2,866 bachelor's awarded; master's, professional, doctoral offered. **ROTC:** Army, Naval, Air Force. **Location:** 75 miles from Memphis, Tennessee. **Calendar:** Semester, extensive summer session. **Full-time faculty:** 779 total; 82% have terminal degrees, 18% minority, 42% women. **Part-time faculty:** 143 total; 54% have terminal degrees, 10% minority, 59% women. **Class size:** 47% < 20, 33% 20-39, 6% 40-49, 11% 50-99, 3% >100. **Special facilities:** Accredited teaching museum, William Faulkner home and grounds, Southern culture center, National Center for Physical Acoustics, 2 super computers, National Center for the Development of Natural Products, National School Food Service Management Institute, water and wetland resources center.

Freshman class profile. 13,321 applied, 10,524 admitted, 3,569 enrolled.

Mid 50% test scores			
		GPA 2.0-2.99:	25%
SAT critical reading:	460-590	Rank in top quarter:	47%
SAT math:	470-590	Rank in top tenth:	25%
ACT composite:	20-27	Out-of-state:	48%
GPA 3.75 or higher:	29%	International:	1%
GPA 3.50-3.74:	15%	Fraternities:	47%
GPA 3.0-3.49:	31%	Sororities:	52%

Basis for selection. School achievement record and test scores important. SAT or ACT may be required for students with core GPA of under 3.2. Essay required for Croft Institute for International Studies, honors college; audition required for music, theater majors. Portfolio recommended for art majors. **Home schooled:** Transcript of courses and grades required. **Learning Disabled:** Report and document disabilities to student disabilities office.

High school preparation. College-preparatory program required. 15 units required. Required and recommended units include English 4, mathematics 3-4, social studies 1-2, history 2, science 3-4 (laboratory 2), foreign language 1-2, computer science .5 and academic electives 1. Mathematics units must include algebra and 2 higher courses. Social sciences units must include U.S. history and U.S. government. Academic electives must include 1 year world geography and fourth year math or science.

2011-2012 Annual costs. Tuition/fees: $5,792; $14,797 out-of-state. Room/board: $6,550.

2010-2011 Financial aid. **Need-based:** 2,272 full-time freshmen applied for aid; 1,589 were judged to have need; 1,536 of these received aid. Average need met was 77%. Average scholarship/grant was $8,056; average loan $3,582. 55% of total undergraduate aid awarded as scholarships/grants, 45% as loans/jobs. **Non-need-based:** Awarded to 3,173 full-time undergraduates, including 1,024 freshmen. Scholarships awarded for academics, alumni affiliation, art, athletics, leadership, minority status, music/drama, ROTC, state residency.

Application procedures. Admission: Priority date 4/1; deadline 7/20 (postmark date). $30 fee ($50 out-of-state), may be waived for applicants with need. Admission notification on a rolling basis beginning on or about 9/15. Online out-of-state application fee: $50. **Financial aid:** Priority date 3/1; no closing date. FAFSA required. Applicants notified on a rolling basis starting 4/1; must reply within 4 week(s) of notification.

Academics. Special study options: Accelerated study, combined bachelor's/graduate degree, cooperative education, distance learning, double major, dual enrollment of high school students, ESL, exchange student, honors, independent study, internships, study abroad, teacher certification program. **Credit/placement by examination:** AP, CLEP, IB, institutional tests. 63 credit hours maximum toward bachelor's degree. Student must earn 12 hours in residence before any credit-by-examination hours are recorded on transcript. **Support services:** Learning center, pre-admission summer program, reduced course load, remedial instruction, study skills assistance, tutoring, writing center.

Honors college/program. Requires test scores, transcript, essays, and recommendations. 120 students admitted each fall. Unique courses which meet general education requirements taught by senior/master faculty. Senior thesis required.

Majors. Area/ethnic studies: African-American. **Biology:** General. **Business:** Accounting, business admin, finance, hospitality admin, insurance, management information systems, managerial economics, marketing, real estate. **Communications:** Journalism. **Computer sciences:** General. **Education:** Elementary, English, foreign languages, mathematics, science, social studies, special ed. **Engineering:** General, chemical, civil, electrical, geological, mechanical. **English:** English lit. **Foreign languages:** Chinese, classics, French, German, linguistics, Spanish. **Health services:** Audiology/speech pathology, clinical lab science, dietetics, pharmaceutical sciences. **History:** General. **Human services:** Public policy, social work. **Liberal arts:** Arts/sciences. **Math:** General. **Parks/recreation:** Exercise sciences, facilities management. **Philosophy/religion:** Philosophy. **Physical sciences:** Chemistry, geology, physics. **Protective services:** Forensics, law enforcement admin. **Psychology:** General. **Social sciences:** Anthropology, economics, international relations, political science, sociology. **Visual/performing arts:** General, art history/conservation, dramatic, music.

Most popular majors. Business/marketing 26%, education 11%, engineering/engineering technologies 6%, health sciences 9%.

Computing on campus. 638 workstations in dormitories, library, computer center. Dormitories wired for high-speed internet access and linked to campus network. Commuter students can connect to campus network. Online course registration, online library, helpline, repair service, student web hosting, wireless network available.

Student life. Freshman orientation: Mandatory. Preregistration for classes offered. 2 days in June, additional session immediately before beginning of term. **Housing:** Guaranteed on-campus for freshmen. Single-sex dorms, apartments, fraternity/sorority housing, wellness housing available. $75 nonrefundable deposit. Intensive study floors available to honors and other students. Special interest, graduate/older students, substance-free, environmental interest housing available. **Activities:** Bands, campus ministries, choral groups, dance, drama, international student organizations, music ensembles, musical theater, opera, radio station, student government, student newspaper, symphony orchestra, TV station, Wesley Foundation, Baptist student union, Black student union, Students for Environmental Awareness, Mortar Board, Habitat for Humanity, Students Envisioning Equality through Diversity.

Athletics. NCAA. **Intercollegiate:** Baseball M, basketball, cheerleading, cross-country, fencing, football (tackle) M, golf, lacrosse M, racquetball M, rifle W, rugby M, skiing M, soccer, softball W, tennis, track and field, volleyball W. **Intramural:** Badminton, basketball, bowling, football (tackle), golf, handball, rifle, soccer, softball, swimming, table tennis, tennis, track and field, volleyball, water polo. **Team name:** Rebels.

Student services. Adult student services, alcohol/substance abuse counseling, chaplain/spiritual director, career counseling, student employment services, financial aid counseling, health services, legal services, minority student services, personal counseling, placement for graduates, veterans' counselor, women's services. **Physically disabled:** Services for visually, speech, hearing impaired.

Contact. E-mail: admissions@olemiss.edu
Phone: (662) 915-7226 Toll-free number: (800) 653-6477
Fax: (662) 915-5869
Charlotte Fant, Director of Admissions and Registrar, University of Mississippi, 145 Martindale, University, MS 38677-1848

University of Mississippi Medical Center
Jackson, Mississippi
www.umc.edu   **CB code: 0358**

● Public two-year upper-division health science college
● Commuter campus in large city

General. Founded in 1955. Regionally accredited. **Degrees:** 242 bachelor's awarded; master's, professional, doctoral offered. **Location:** 200 miles from Memphis, Tennessee. **Calendar:** Semester, limited summer session. **Full-time faculty:** 786 total. **Part-time faculty:** 149 total.

Student profile. 608 degree-seeking undergraduates, 1,731 graduate students.

Women:	86%	**Live on campus:**	3%
Part-time:	40%	**25 or older:**	80%
Out-of-state:	1%		

Basis for selection. College transcript required. Competitive admission to health science programs based on grades, recommendations, test scores, interviews. Transfer accepted as juniors.

2011-2012 Annual costs. Tuition/fees: $5,792; $14,797 out-of-state. Books/supplies: $1,596.

Application procedures. Admission: Deadline 2/11. $25 fee. Application must be submitted online. Admission notification 4/11. Must reply by 5/11. Application closing dates and reply dates vary by program. **Financial aid:** FAFSA, institutional form required.

Academics. Includes schools of medicine, nursing, health-related professions, and dentistry, graduate programs in medical and clinical health sciences, and 623-bed teaching hospital. Certificate programs in emergency medical technology and radiologic technology and clinical nuclear medicine offered. **Special study options:** Combined bachelor's/graduate degree, liberal arts/career combination. **Credit/placement by examination:** AP, CLEP. **Support services:** Pre-admission summer program, study skills assistance, tutoring.

Majors. Health services: Clinical lab science, cytotechnology, dental hygiene, medical records admin.

Computing on campus. 75 workstations in library, computer center. Online library available.

Student life. Housing: Single-sex dorms, apartments available. **Activities:** Student government, student newspaper, University Christian Fellowship, Catholic Student Organization.

Athletics. Intramural: Baseball, basketball, football (tackle) M, golf, soccer, softball, table tennis.

Student services. Alcohol/substance abuse counseling, chaplain/spiritual director, career counseling, financial aid counseling, health services, minority student services, personal counseling. **Physically disabled:** Services for speech, hearing impaired.

Contact. Phone: (601) 984-1080
Barbara Westerfield, Registrar, University of Mississippi Medical Center, 2500 North State Street, Jackson, MS 39216

University of Phoenix: Jackson
Florwood, Mississippi
www.phoenix.edu

● For-profit 4-year university
● Small town

General. Calendar: Differs by program.

Basis for selection. Open admission.

Academics. Credit/placement by examination: AP, CLEP.

Majors. Protective services: Law enforcement admin.

Contact. University of Phoenix: Jackson, 120 Stone Creek Boulevard, Florwood, MS 39232

University of Southern Mississippi
Hattiesburg, Mississippi
www.usm.edu

CB member
CB code: 1479

- Public 4-year university
- Commuter campus in small city
- 13,618 degree-seeking undergraduates: 17% part-time, 62% women, 31% African American, 1% Asian American, 3% Hispanic American, 1% international
- 2,986 degree-seeking graduate students
- 63% of applicants admitted
- SAT or ACT (ACT writing optional) required
- 47% graduate within 6 years

General. Founded in 1910. Regionally accredited. Dual campus with main campus in Hattiesburg and nonresidential, nontraditional campus in Long Beach; other sites along Mississippi Gulf Coast. **Degrees:** 2,361 bachelor's awarded; master's, doctoral offered. **ROTC:** Army, Air Force. **Location:** 85 miles from Jackson, 110 miles from New Orleans. **Calendar:** Semester, extensive summer session. **Full-time faculty:** 671 total; 73% have terminal degrees, 14% minority, 48% women. **Part-time faculty:** 171 total; 33% have terminal degrees, 9% minority, 53% women. **Class size:** 41% < 20, 40% 20-39, 8% 40-49, 7% 50-99, 4% >100. **Special facilities:** Marine education center, aquarium.

Freshman class profile. 6,426 applied, 4,060 admitted, 1,727 enrolled.

Mid 50% test scores		Rank in top quarter:	44%
SAT critical reading:	470-570	Rank in top tenth:	18%
SAT math:	470-570	Return as sophomores:	72%
ACT composite:	19-25	Out-of-state:	28%
GPA 3.75 or higher:	19%	Live on campus:	43%
GPA 3.50-3.74:	12%	International:	1%
GPA 3.0-3.49:	30%	Fraternities:	22%
GPA 2.0-2.99:	38%	Sororities:	22%

Basis for selection. Test scores, GPA, class rank important. Applicants who don't meet criteria may be required to participate in screening process that includes testing.

High school preparation. College-preparatory program required. 15.5 units required. Required units include English 4, mathematics 3, social studies 3, science 3, computer science 2, visual/performing arts .5.

2011-2012 Annual costs. Tuition/fees: $5,834; $13,789 out-of-state. Room/board: $6,555. Books/supplies: $1,400. Personal expenses: $3,314.

2010-2011 Financial aid. Need-based: 1,453 full-time freshmen applied for aid; 1,218 were judged to have need; 1,182 of these received aid. Average need met was 78%. Average scholarship/grant was $4,438; average loan $3,465. 54% of total undergraduate aid awarded as scholarships/grants, 46% as loans/jobs. **Non-need-based:** Awarded to 3,835 full-time undergraduates, including 855 freshmen.

Application procedures. Admission: No deadline. $35 fee, may be waived for applicants with need. Admission notification on a rolling basis beginning on or about 9/1. **Financial aid:** Priority date 3/15; no closing date. FAFSA, institutional form required.

Academics. Special study options: Double major, dual enrollment of high school students, ESL, exchange student, honors, independent study, internships, study abroad, teacher certification program. **Credit/placement by examination:** AP, CLEP, SAT, ACT, institutional tests. **Support services:** Learning center, pre-admission summer program, reduced course load, remedial instruction, study skills assistance, tutoring, writing center.

Honors college/program. Requires an ACT score of 26 or equivalent GPA requirement, and essay.

Majors. Architecture: Interior. **Area/ethnic studies:** American. **Biology:** General, marine. **Business:** Accounting, business admin, finance, hotel/motel admin, human resources, international, management information systems, managerial economics, marketing, tourism/travel. **Communications:** Advertising, communications/speech/rhetoric, journalism, radio/TV. **Computer sciences:** General, data processing. **Education:** Business, Deaf/hearing impaired, elementary, music, physical, special ed. **English:** English lit. **Foreign languages:** General. **Health services:** Athletic training, audiology/speech pathology, clinical lab science, dietetics, nursing (RN). **Human services:** Social work. **Liberal arts:** Library science. **Math:** General. **Parks/recreation:** General, sports admin. **Philosophy/religion:** Philosophy, religion. **Physical sciences:** Chemistry, geology, oceanography, physics. **Protective services:** Criminal justice, forensics. **Psychology:** General. **Social sciences:** Anthropology, geography, international relations, political science, sociology. **Visual/performing arts:** General, dance, dramatic, music, music management. **Work/family studies:** Clothing/textiles, family systems.

Most popular majors. Business/marketing 22%, education 13%, health sciences 14%.

Computing on campus. Dormitories wired for high-speed internet access and linked to campus network. Commuter students can connect to campus network. Online course registration, online library, helpline, student web hosting, wireless network available.

Student life. Freshman orientation: Available. Preregistration for classes offered. **Policies:** Freshmen who reside in area may live at home. All freshmen who request campus housing required to live in freshman dormitories. **Housing:** Single-sex dorms, special housing for disabled, apartments, fraternity/sorority housing available. $75 nonrefundable deposit, deadline 2/1. Honors. **Activities:** Bands, campus ministries, choral groups, dance, drama, film society, international student organizations, literary magazine, music ensembles, musical theater, opera, radio station, student government, student newspaper, symphony orchestra, Honor societies, service and religious Organizations, Young Republicans, Young Democrats.

Athletics. NCAA. **Intercollegiate:** Baseball M, basketball, cross-country, football (tackle) M, golf, rugby M, soccer W, softball W, tennis, track and field, volleyball W. **Intramural:** Badminton, basketball, bowling, golf, racquetball, soccer, softball, squash, swimming, table tennis, tennis, track and field, volleyball. **Team name:** Golden Eagles.

Student services. Adult student services, career counseling, student employment services, health services, minority student services, on-campus daycare, personal counseling, placement for graduates, veterans' counselor, women's services. **Physically disabled:** Services for visually, speech, hearing impaired.

Contact. E-mail: admissions@usm.edu
Phone: (601) 266-5000 Fax: (601) 266-5148
Amanda King, Admissions Operations, University of Southern Mississippi, 118 College Drive #5166, Hattiesburg, MS 39406-0001

William Carey University
Hattiesburg, Mississippi
www.wmcarey.edu

CB code: 1907

- Private 4-year university and liberal arts college affiliated with Baptist faith
- Commuter campus in small city

General. Founded in 1906. Regionally accredited. **Location:** 110 miles from New Orleans. **Calendar:** Trimester.

Annual costs/financial aid. Tuition/fees (2011-2012): $10,350. Room/board: $4,125. Books/supplies: $2,850. Personal expenses: $1,350. Need-based financial aid available to full-time and part-time students.

Contact. Phone: (601) 318-6103
Dean of Enrollment Management & Records, 498 Tuscan Avenue, Hattiesburg, MS 39401

Missouri

Avila University
Kansas City, Missouri
www.avila.edu
CB code: 6109

◆ Private 4-year university and liberal arts college affiliated with Roman Catholic Church

◆ Commuter campus in very large city

◆ 1,174 degree-seeking undergraduates: 19% part-time, 65% women, 18% African American, 1% Asian American, 7% Hispanic American, 1% Native American, 4% international

◆ 582 degree-seeking graduate students

◆ 53% of applicants admitted

◆ SAT or ACT (ACT writing optional) required

◆ 42% graduate within 6 years

General. Founded in 1916. Regionally accredited. **Degrees:** 238 bachelor's awarded; master's offered. **ROTC:** Army. **Calendar:** Semester, extensive summer session. **Full-time faculty:** 63 total; 73% have terminal degrees, 6% minority, 56% women. **Part-time faculty:** 137 total; 29% have terminal degrees, 6% minority, 62% women. **Class size:** 71% < 20, 27% 20-39, less than 1% 40-49, 1% 50-99. **Special facilities:** Radiological laboratory, campus media production facilities, nursing learning resource center, photography lab, Santa Fe Trail walking path.

Freshman class profile. 1,170 applied, 619 admitted, 138 enrolled.

Mid 50% test scores			
SAT critical reading:	380-620	Rank in top quarter:	38%
SAT math:	460-500	Rank in top tenth:	13%
ACT composite:	20-25	End year in good standing:	87%
GPA 3.75 or higher:	21%	Return as sophomores:	65%
GPA 3.50-3.74:	17%	Out-of-state:	32%
GPA 3.0-3.49:	30%	Live on campus:	76%
GPA 2.0-2.99:	32%	International:	4%

Basis for selection. Unconditional acceptance for applicants with minimum GPA of 2.5 and ACT composite of 20 or higher. Others may be considered. ACT subscores used for math and English placement. Audition recommended for drama, music students. **Home schooled:** SAT or ACT and home school transcripts required. GED may be requested.

High school preparation. 17 units required. Required and recommended units include English 4, mathematics 3, social studies 3, science 3 (laboratory 1), foreign language 3 and visual/performing arts 1.

2012-2013 Annual costs. Tuition/fees (projected): $24,050. Room/board: $6,850.

2011-2012 Financial aid. **Need-based:** Average need met was 70%. Average scholarship/grant was $16,214; average loan $3,598. 55% of total undergraduate aid awarded as scholarships/grants, 45% as loans/jobs. **Non-need-based:** Scholarships awarded for academics, alumni affiliation, art, athletics, music/drama, religious affiliation. **Additional information:** Financial aid adjusted based on need for increases in tuition.

Application procedures. **Admission:** No deadline. $25 fee, may be waived for applicants with need, free for online applicants. Admission notification on a rolling basis. **Financial aid:** Priority date 4/1; no closing date. FAFSA, institutional form required. Applicants notified on a rolling basis starting 2/1; must reply within 2 week(s) of notification.

Academics. Outcome-based core curriculum; interdisciplinary course work at junior level required; unique senior experience bridges transition from college to community. **Special study options:** Accelerated study, combined bachelor's/graduate degree, cooperative education, cross-registration, distance learning, double major, dual enrollment of high school students, ESL, exchange student, independent study, internships, liberal arts/career combination, study abroad, teacher certification program, Washington semester, weekend college. **Credit/placement by examination:** AP, CLEP, IB, SAT, ACT, institutional tests. 32 credit hours maximum toward bachelor's degree. **Support services:** Learning center, reduced course load, remedial instruction, study skills assistance, tutoring, writing center.

Majors. **Biology:** General. **Business:** General, accounting, business admin, entrepreneurial studies, finance, human resources, international, management information systems, sales/distribution. **Communications:** Communications/speech/rhetoric, public relations. **Computer sciences:** General. **Education:** General, elementary, learning disabled, middle. **English:** English lit. **Health services:** Facilities admin, medical radiologic technology/radiation therapy, nursing (RN), premedicine. **History:** General. **Human services:** Social work. **Math:** General. **Parks/recreation:** Exercise sciences. **Philosophy/religion:** Religion. **Physical sciences:** Chemistry. **Psychology:** General. **Social sciences:** Political science, sociology. **Visual/performing arts:** Art, dramatic, music performance.

Most popular majors. Business/marketing 12%, education 7%, health sciences 33%, psychology 11%, visual/performing arts 7%.

Computing on campus. 156 workstations in dormitories, library, computer center, student center. Dormitories wired for high-speed internet access and linked to campus network. Commuter students can connect to campus network. Online course registration, online library, helpline, wireless network available.

Student life. **Freshman orientation:** Mandatory. Preregistration for classes offered. Held 3 days prior to first day of classes; programs available for freshmen-adult transfer students and friends/family of new students. **Policies:** First-time, first-year students not living at home with parents/guardians required to live on campus through sophomore year. **Housing:** Guaranteed on-campus for freshmen. Coed dorms, apartments, wellness housing available. Single-sex floors available. **Activities:** Campus ministries, choral groups, dance, drama, international student organizations, literary magazine, musical theater, student government, student newspaper, student nurses association, psychology club, Black Student Union, premedical club, English club, education club, Association of Radiological Science, social work association, National Association of Masters in Psychology, Society of Life Scientists.

Athletics. NAIA. **Intercollegiate:** Baseball M, basketball, cheerleading M, cross-country, football (tackle) M, golf, soccer, softball W, volleyball W. **Intramural:** Basketball, table tennis, volleyball. **Team name:** Eagles.

Student services. Adult student services, alcohol/substance abuse counseling, chaplain/spiritual director, career counseling, student employment services, financial aid counseling, health services, on-campus daycare, personal counseling, placement for graduates, veterans' counselor, women's services. **Physically disabled:** Services for visually, speech, hearing impaired.

Contact. E-mail: admission@avila.edu
Phone: (816) 501-2400 Toll-free number: (800) 462-8452
Fax: (816) 501-2453
Brandon Johnson, Director of Undergraduate Admission, Avila University, 11901 Wornall Road, Kansas City, MO 64145-1007

Baptist Bible College
Springfield, Missouri
www.gobbc.edu
CB code: 0991

◆ Private 4-year Bible and seminary college affiliated with Baptist faith

◆ Residential campus in small city

◆ 343 full-time, degree-seeking undergraduates

◆ 89 graduate students

General. Founded in 1950. Candidate for regional accreditation; also accredited by ABHE. **Degrees:** 62 bachelor's, 7 associate awarded; master's offered. **Location:** 180 miles from Kansas City, 225 miles from St. Louis. **Calendar:** Semester, limited summer session. **Full-time faculty:** 25 total. **Part-time faculty:** 10 total.

Basis for selection. Open admission. Baptist pastor's recommendation required.

2011-2012 Annual costs. Tuition/fees: $6,500. Room/board: $5,400. Books/supplies: $840.

Application procedures. **Admission:** Priority date 8/1; no deadline. $40 fee. Admission notification on a rolling basis. **Financial aid:** Closing date 5/1. FAFSA, institutional form required. Applicants notified on a rolling basis; must reply within 2 week(s) of notification.

Academics. **Special study options:** Distance learning. **Credit/placement by examination:** AP, CLEP. **Support services:** Learning center, reduced course load, study skills assistance, tutoring.

Majors. **Business:** Administrative services. **Education:** Elementary, music. **Philosophy/religion:** Religion. **Theology:** Missionary, pastoral counseling, religious ed, sacred music, theology. **Visual/performing arts:** Music.

Computing on campus. 70 workstations in library, computer center, student center. Dormitories wired for high-speed internet access and linked

to campus network. Online library, helpline, repair service, wireless network available.

Student life. Freshman orientation: Mandatory. Preregistration for classes offered. **Policies:** Religious observance required. **Housing:** Guaranteed on-campus for freshmen. Single-sex dorms, apartments available. **Activities:** Concert band, choral groups, music ensembles, radio station, student government.

Athletics. NCCAA. **Intercollegiate:** Basketball, volleyball W. **Intramural:** Basketball, volleyball. **Team name:** Patriots.

Student services. Chaplain/spiritual director, financial aid counseling, health services, on-campus daycare, personal counseling, veterans' counselor.

Contact. E-mail: rherrin@gobbc.edu
Phone: (417) 268-6013 Toll-free number: (800) 228-5754 ext. 6601
Fax: (417) 268-6694
Reuben Herrin, Director of Recruiting, Baptist Bible College, 628 East Kearney Street, Springfield, MO 65803

Calvary Bible College and Theological Seminary
Kansas City, Missouri
www.calvary.edu
CB code: 6331

- Private 4-year Bible and seminary college affiliated with nondenominational tradition
- Residential campus in large city
- 265 degree-seeking undergraduates: 35% part-time, 48% women
- 54 graduate students
- 83% of applicants admitted
- SAT or ACT (ACT writing optional) required
- 49% graduate within 6 years

General. Founded in 1932. Regionally accredited; also accredited by ABHE. **Degrees:** 48 bachelor's, 10 associate awarded; master's offered. **ROTC:** Army. **Location:** 20 miles from downtown Kansas City. **Calendar:** Semester, limited summer session. **Full-time faculty:** 21 total. **Part-time faculty:** 19 total.

Freshman class profile. 52 applied, 43 admitted, 33 enrolled.

Mid 50% test scores		Return as sophomores:	70%
ACT composite:	18-22	Out-of-state:	70%

Basis for selection. Christian character stressed along with academic preparation. Pastor's and personal reference forms required. School achievement record and test scores considered. Applicants are required to submit a written Personal Testimony/Confirmation and Statement of Faith. Audition required for music students. **Home schooled:** Transcripts are required in compliance with state's home-school policies. **Learning Disabled:** Students should contact the Director of Admissions.

2012-2013 Annual costs. Tuition/fees (projected): $10,116. Room/board: $4,800. Books/supplies: $532. Personal expenses: $1,200.

Financial aid. Non-need-based: Scholarships awarded for academics, alumni affiliation, job skills, music/drama, religious affiliation, ROTC.

Application procedures. Admission: Closing date 7/15 (receipt date). $25 fee. Admission notification on a rolling basis. **Financial aid:** Priority date 3/1, closing date 4/1. FAFSA, institutional form required. Applicants notified on a rolling basis starting 5/1.

Academics. Each student carries major in Bible and theology and second major in a professional area. These majors prepare students for vocational and/or volunteer involvement in Christian ministry. **Special study options:** Cooperative education, distance learning, double major, dual enrollment of high school students, ESL, independent study, internships, student-designed major, teacher certification program. **Credit/placement by examination:** AP, CLEP, IB, institutional tests. **Support services:** Learning center, reduced course load, remedial instruction, study skills assistance, tutoring.

Majors. Business: Business admin, marketing, organizational leadership. **Computer sciences:** Computer science. **Education:** Elementary, music, secondary. **English:** Creative writing, English lit. **History:** General. **Math/ Science. Protective services:** Law enforcement admin. **Social sciences:** Political science, urban studies. **Theology:** Bible, pastoral counseling, youth ministry. **Visual/performing arts:** Art, art history/conservation, cinematography, dramatic, graphic design, music performance, photography.

Most popular majors. Business/marketing 10%, education 8%, interdisciplinary studies 17%, theological studies 58%.

Computing on campus. 21 workstations in library, student center. Dormitories wired for high-speed internet access. Online course registration, online library, repair service, wireless network available.

Student life. Freshman orientation: Mandatory, $60 fee. Preregistration for classes offered. **Policies:** Weekly Christian ministry, chapel and church attendance required. Single students required to live in college housing unless living with parents or at least 23 years of age. Religious observance required. **Housing:** Guaranteed on-campus for all undergraduates. Single-sex dorms, apartments available. $50 fully refundable deposit, deadline 8/15. Duplexes for married students available. **Activities:** Pep band, campus ministries, choral groups, drama, music ensembles, musical theater, radio station, student government, Missionary Prayer Fellowship, short-term missions.

Athletics. NCCAA. **Intercollegiate:** Basketball, soccer M, volleyball W. **Team name:** Warriors.

Student services. Adult student services, alcohol/substance abuse counseling, chaplain/spiritual director, student employment services, financial aid counseling, health services, personal counseling, veterans' counselor, women's services.

Contact. E-mail: admissions@calvary.edu
Phone: (816) 326-3960 Toll-free number: (800) 326-3960
Fax: (816) 331-4474
Robert Crank, Director of Admissions, Calvary Bible College and Theological Seminary, 15800 Calvary Road, Kansas City, MO 64147-1341

Central Bible College
Springfield, Missouri
www.cbcag.edu
CB code: 6085

- Private 4-year Bible college affiliated with Assemblies of God
- Residential campus in small city
- 640 undergraduates
- SAT or ACT (ACT writing optional), application essay required

General. Founded in 1922. Accredited by ABHE. **Degrees:** 95 bachelor's, 23 associate awarded. **ROTC:** Army, Air Force. **Location:** 210 miles from St. Louis, 174 miles from Kansas City. **Calendar:** Semester, extensive summer session. **Full-time faculty:** 28 total. **Part-time faculty:** 53 total. **Special facilities:** Observatory, Pentecostal library.

Basis for selection. Special consideration given to members of Assemblies of God and others committed to Christian principles, and applicants who rank in top half of graduating class who meet entrance requirements. Interview recommended for all students; audition recommended for music students. **Home schooled:** Transcript of courses and grades required.

High school preparation. Strong background in English, math, and science recommended. Computer literacy course recommended.

2011-2012 Annual costs. Tuition/fees: $12,050. Room/board: $5,392. Books/supplies: $550.

Application procedures. Admission: Priority date 8/15; no deadline. $25 fee, may be waived for applicants with need. Admission notification on a rolling basis. **Financial aid:** Priority date 5/1; no closing date. FAFSA required. Applicants notified on a rolling basis starting 5/15; must reply within 3 week(s) of notification.

Academics. Special study options: Accelerated study, cooperative education, cross-registration, double major, independent study, internships. **Credit/ placement by examination:** AP, CLEP, SAT, ACT, institutional tests. 24 credit hours maximum toward bachelor's degree. **Support services:** Reduced course load, remedial instruction, tutoring.

Majors. Theology: Bible, missionary, pastoral counseling, religious ed, sacred music, theology, youth ministry.

Computing on campus. 20 workstations in library, computer center.

Student life. Freshman orientation: Mandatory. Preregistration for classes offered. Held within week prior to start of both fall and spring classes. **Policies:** Practices which are known to be morally wrong by Biblical teaching are not acceptable for members of the college community. Religious observance required. **Housing:** Guaranteed on-campus for freshmen. Single-sex dorms, apartments, wellness housing available. **Activities:** Jazz band, choral groups, drama, music ensembles, radio station, student government, student

newspaper, Campus Missions Fellowship, Delta Chi, FOCAL, student government association, student ministries, multicultural club.

Athletics. NCCAA. **Intercollegiate:** Basketball, soccer M, volleyball W. **Intramural:** Basketball, softball. **Team name:** Spartans.

Student services. Student employment services, financial aid counseling, health services, personal counseling, placement for graduates, veterans' counselor. **Physically disabled:** Services for hearing impaired.

Contact. E-mail: info@cbcag.edu
Phone: (417) 833-2551 ext. 1290 Toll-free number: (800) 831-4222
Fax: (417) 833-5141
Lisa Dreckman, Team Lead, Central Bible College, 3000 North Grant Avenue, Springfield, MO 65803-1069

Central Christian College of the Bible
Moberly, Missouri
www.cccb.edu   **CB code: 6145**

▶ Private 4-year Bible college affiliated with Christian Church
▶ Residential campus in large town

General. Founded in 1957. Accredited by ABHE. **Location:** 35 miles from Columbia. **Calendar:** Semester.

Annual costs/financial aid. Tuition/fees (2011-2012): $13,200. Full-time students receive full scholarship for tuition only. Room/board: $4,200. Books/supplies: $375. Personal expenses: $1,858. Need-based financial aid available to full-time and part-time students.

Contact. Phone: (888) 263-3900
Director of Admission, 911 East Urbandale Drive, Moberly, MO 65270-1997

Central Methodist University
Fayette, Missouri
www.centralmethodist.edu   **CB code: 6089**

▶ Private 4-year university and liberal arts college affiliated with United Methodist Church
▶ Residential campus in small town
▶ 1,172 degree-seeking undergraduates: 6% part-time, 50% women, 6% African American, 1% Asian American, 2% Hispanic American, 1% Native American, 3% international
▶ 201 degree-seeking graduate students
▶ 54% of applicants admitted
▶ SAT or ACT (ACT writing optional) required
▶ 43% graduate within 6 years

General. Founded in 1854. Regionally accredited. **Degrees:** 190 bachelor's, 2 associate awarded; master's offered. **ROTC:** Army, Air Force. **Location:** 25 miles from Columbia, 150 miles from St. Louis. **Calendar:** Semester, limited summer session. **Full-time faculty:** 61 total. **Part-time faculty:** 53 total. **Class size:** 63% < 20, 29% 20-39, 5% 40-49, 3% 50-99. **Special facilities:** Observatory and laboratory, natural history museum, music conservatory.

Freshman class profile. 1,461 applied, 795 admitted, 281 enrolled.

Mid 50% test scores				
SAT critical reading:	410-480	GPA 2.0-2.99:		16%
SAT math:	410-500	Rank in top quarter:		38%
SAT writing:	400-500	Rank in top tenth:		13%
ACT composite:	20-24	End year in good standing:		90%
GPA 3.75 or higher:	54%	Return as sophomores:		62%
GPA 3.50-3.74:	2%	Out-of-state:		10%
GPA 3.0-3.49:	28%	Live on campus:		96%
		International:		3%

Basis for selection. Full acceptance requires 2.5 GPA and 21 ACT or equivalent SAT. Students transferring with more than 15 hours of college credit are not required to submit scores. Interview required for nursing applicants; audition recommended for drama, music students.

High school preparation. College-preparatory program recommended. 24 units recommended. Recommended units include English 4, mathematics 3, social studies 3, science 3 and foreign language 2. 2 humanities recommended.

2011-2012 Annual costs. Tuition/fees: $20,130. Room/board: $6,480. Books/supplies: $1,000. Personal expenses: $2,250.

2011-2012 Financial aid. Need-based: 270 full-time freshmen applied for aid; 225 were judged to have need; 225 of these received aid. Average need met was 90%. Average scholarship/grant was $4,500; average loan $5,244. 36% of total undergraduate aid awarded as scholarships/grants, 64% as loans/jobs. **Non-need-based:** Awarded to 1,203 full-time undergraduates, including 306 freshmen. Scholarships awarded for academics, alumni affiliation, athletics, leadership, music/drama, religious affiliation, ROTC.

Application procedures. Admission: Closing date 8/1. $20 fee, may be waived for applicants with need, free for online applicants. Admission notification on a rolling basis beginning on or about 10/1. Must reply by May 1 or within 4 week(s) if notified thereafter. **Financial aid:** Priority date 3/15; no closing date. FAFSA required. Applicants notified on a rolling basis starting 1/30; must reply within 2 week(s) of notification.

Academics. Special study options: Accelerated study, combined bachelor's/graduate degree, distance learning, double major, dual enrollment of high school students, honors, independent study, internships, liberal arts/career combination, student-designed major, study abroad, teacher certification program. 3-year bachelor's degree, 2-week January travel program. **Credit/placement by examination:** AP, CLEP, IB, ACT. 32 credit hours maximum toward associate degree, 32 toward bachelor's. **Support services:** Learning center, study skills assistance, tutoring.

Majors. Biology: General, marine. **Business:** General, accounting, banking/financial services, business admin, entrepreneurial studies, international, management science, marketing. **Communications:** Communications/speech/rhetoric. **Computer sciences:** Computer science. **Conservation:** Environmental science. **Education:** Biology, chemistry, early childhood, elementary, foreign languages, middle, music, physical, physics, science, secondary, social science, special ed. **English:** English lit. **Foreign languages:** Spanish. **Health services:** Athletic training, nursing (RN). **History:** General. **Math:** General. **Parks/recreation:** Facilities management. **Philosophy/religion:** Philosophy, religion. **Physical sciences:** Chemistry, physics. **Protective services:** Law enforcement admin. **Psychology:** General. **Social sciences:** Political science, sociology. **Visual/performing arts:** Dramatic, music, music performance. **Work/family studies:** Child development.

Most popular majors. Business/marketing 27%, education 21%, health sciences 15%.

Computing on campus. 300 workstations in dormitories, library, computer center, student center. Dormitories wired for high-speed internet access and linked to campus network. Commuter students can connect to campus network. Online library, helpline, repair service; wireless network available.

Student life. Freshman orientation: Mandatory. Preregistration for classes offered. **Housing:** Guaranteed on-campus for freshmen. Coed dorms, single-sex dorms, apartments, fraternity/sorority housing available. $100 fully refundable deposit. **Activities:** Bands, campus ministries, choral groups, dance, drama, international student organizations, literary magazine, music ensembles, musical theater, radio station, student government, student newspaper, various religious, service, business, music organizations.

Athletics. NAIA. **Intercollegiate:** Baseball M, basketball, cheerleading M, cross-country, football (tackle) M, golf, soccer, softball W, track and field, volleyball W. **Intramural:** Basketball, football (non-tackle), racquetball, soccer, softball, tennis, track and field, volleyball. **Team name:** Eagles.

Student services. Alcohol/substance abuse counseling, chaplain/spiritual director, career counseling, student employment services, financial aid counseling, health services, personal counseling, placement for graduates.

Contact. E-mail: admissions@centralmethodist.edu
Phone: (660) 248-6251 Toll-free number: (877) 268-1854
Fax: (660) 248-1872
Lawrence Anderson, Director of Admissions, Central Methodist University, 411 Central Methodist Square, Fayette, MO 65248-1198

Chamberlain College of Nursing: St. Louis
St Louis, Missouri
www.chamberlain.edu   **CB code: 3139**

▶ For-profit 4-year nursing college affiliated with United Church of Christ
▶ Commuter campus in very large city
▶ 7,952 degree-seeking undergraduates
▶ SAT or ACT with writing, application essay required

General. Founded in 1889. Regionally accredited. In addition to the St. Louis campus, there is a second campus in Columbus, OH. Affiliated with

Fontbonne College; general education requirements offered on both campuses. **Degrees:** 2,284 bachelor's awarded; master's offered. **Calendar:** Semester, limited summer session. **Full-time faculty:** 47 total. **Part-time faculty:** 199 total. **Special facilities:** Hospital, archives.

Basis for selection. High school GPA of 2.5, rank in top third of class, ACT scores, personal statement important. Interview and reference may be considered.

High school preparation. Required units include English 4, mathematics 3 and science 3.

2011-2012 Annual costs. Tuition/fees: $15,600. Books/supplies: $1,400. Personal expenses: $3,718.

Financial aid. Non-need-based: Scholarships awarded for academics.

Application procedures. Admission: No deadline. $95 fee, may be waived for applicants with need. Admission notification on a rolling basis. **Financial aid:** No deadline. FAFSA, institutional form required. Applicants notified on a rolling basis starting 4/1; must reply within 2 week(s) of notification.

Academics. Special study options: Accelerated study, cross-registration. **Credit/placement by examination:** AP, CLEP, institutional tests. 30 credit hours maximum toward bachelor's degree. **Support services:** Learning center, reduced course load, remedial instruction, tutoring.

Majors. Health services: Nursing (RN).

Computing on campus. 20 workstations in computer center.

Student life. Freshman orientation: Mandatory. Preregistration for classes offered. **Housing:** Single-sex dorms available. $50 deposit. **Activities:** Choral groups, student government, National Student Nurse Association.

Student services. Health services, on-campus daycare, personal counseling.

Contact. Phone: (314) 768-7528 Toll-free number: (800) 942-3410 Fax: (314) 768-5673
Chamberlain College of Nursing: St. Louis, St. Louis, MO 63139

College of the Ozarks
Point Lookout, Missouri
www.cofo.edu   CB code: 6713

▸ Private 4-year liberal arts college affiliated with interdenominational tradition
▸ Residential campus in small town
▸ 1,371 degree-seeking undergraduates: 1% part-time, 57% women, 1% African American, 1% Asian American, 2% Hispanic American, 1% Native American, 1% international
▸ 9% of applicants admitted
▸ SAT or ACT (ACT writing optional), interview required
▸ 62% graduate within 6 years; 15% enter graduate study

General. Founded in 1906. Regionally accredited. Entire cost of education met by students participation in Work Education Program, private and institutional scholarships, and federal/state student need-based grants. **Degrees:** 320 bachelor's awarded. **ROTC:** Army. **Location:** 2 miles from Branson, 45 miles from Springfield. **Calendar:** Semester. **Full-time faculty:** 87 total; 56% have terminal degrees, 3% minority, 40% women. **Part-time faculty:** 48 total; 21% have terminal degrees, 2% minority, 44% women. **Class size:** 57% < 20, 40% 20-39, 1% 40-49, 2% 50-99. **Special facilities:** Greenhouses, college-operated hotel, observatory, nature preserve, regional history museum.

Freshman class profile. 3,299 applied, 295 admitted, 282 enrolled.

Mid 50% test scores		GPA 2.0-2.99:	8%
SAT critical reading:	580-630	Rank in top quarter:	50%
SAT math:	530-560	Rank in top tenth:	17%
SAT writing:	540-570	End year in good standing:	84%
ACT composite:	21-24	Return as sophomores:	86%
GPA 3.75 or higher:	41%	Out-of-state:	22%
GPA 3.50-3.74:	26%	Live on campus:	86%
GPA 3.0-3.49:	25%	International:	1%

Basis for selection. High school record, financial need, test scores, class rank, recommendations, activities and interview important. Academic interest and growth, development of intellectual skills considered. ACT preferred. Audition recommended for music students; portfolio recommended for art

students. **Home schooled:** Pass grades are not acceptable. Candidates must present a transcript with a letter or percentage grade.

High school preparation. College-preparatory program recommended. 24 units recommended. Required and recommended units include English 4, mathematics 3, social studies 3, history 3, science 2 (laboratory 1) and foreign language 2. Public speaking, visual and performing arts recommended.

2011-2012 Annual costs. Tuition/fees: $18,030. Room/board: $5,500. Books/supplies: $800. Personal expenses: $430.

2010-2011 Financial aid. Need-based: 329 full-time freshmen applied for aid; 323 were judged to have need; 323 of these received aid. Average need met was 81%. Average scholarship/grant was $12,353. 82% of total undergraduate aid awarded as scholarships/grants, 18% as loans/jobs. **Non-need-based:** Awarded to 294 full-time undergraduates, including 54 freshmen. Scholarships awarded for academics, art, athletics, leadership, music/drama, ROTC, state residency. **Additional information:** Guarantees to meet all costs for full-time students through its endowment, mandatory student work education program, student aid grants, gifts and other sources.

Application procedures. Admission: Priority date 2/15; no deadline. No application fee. Admission notification on a rolling basis beginning on or about 3/1. Must reply by May 1 or within 2 week(s) if notified thereafter. Acceptance fee due within two weeks of admission offer. **Financial aid:** Priority date 2/15; no closing date. FAFSA required. Applicants notified on a rolling basis starting 7/1.

Academics. Curriculum offers liberal arts foundation with intensive concentration in special areas. **Special study options:** Combined bachelor's/ graduate degree, double major, dual enrollment of high school students, independent study, internships, student-designed major, teacher certification program. 3-2 engineering program, interdisciplinary programs, paraprofessional counseling certificate, pre-professional programs, dietetics program. **Credit/placement by examination:** AP, CLEP, IB, ACT, institutional tests. 15 credit hours maximum toward bachelor's degree. Five "credits by exam" classes unless specific approval by academic dean. **Support services:** Learning center, reduced course load, remedial instruction, study skills assistance, tutoring, writing center.

Majors. Biology: General. **Business:** Accounting, business admin, hospitality admin, international, managerial economics, marketing, restaurant/food services. **Communications:** Broadcast journalism, communications/speech/ rhetoric, journalism, public relations. **Communications technology:** Printing management, radio/TV. **Computer sciences:** Computer science, information technology. **Conservation:** Wildlife/wilderness. **Education:** Agricultural, art, biology, chemistry, early childhood, elementary, English, history, mathematics, music, physical, science, secondary, social studies. **English:** English lit. **Foreign languages:** Spanish. **General:** Agronomy, animal sciences, business, horticultural science. **Health services:** Dietetics, nursing (RN). **History:** General. **Human services:** Social work. **Math:** General. **Parks/recreation:** Facilities management, health/fitness. **Philosophy/religion:** General. **Physical sciences:** Chemistry. **Protective services:** Corrections, police science. **Psychology:** General. **Social sciences:** Sociology. **Theology:** Sacred music. **Visual/performing arts:** Art, dramatic, music, studio arts, theater design. **Work/family studies:** General, child development, food/nutrition.

Most popular majors. Agriculture 6%, business/marketing 17%, education 15%, health sciences 10%.

Computing on campus. 160 workstations in dormitories, library, computer center. Dormitories wired for high-speed internet access and linked to campus network. Commuter students can connect to campus network. Online course registration, online library, helpline, wireless network available.

Student life. Freshman orientation: Mandatory. Preregistration for classes offered. 8-day program held the week before classes begin. **Policies:** Convocations and chapel attendance required for some students. All full-time students must live in residence halls unless married, or living with parents. Religious observance required. **Housing:** Guaranteed on-campus for all undergraduates. Single-sex dorms, wellness housing available. $100 fully refundable deposit. **Activities:** Bands, campus ministries, choral groups, drama, film society, international student organizations, music ensembles, musical theater, radio station, student government, student newspaper, Baptist Student Union, fire department, InterVarsity Christian Fellowship, Wilderness Activities Club, Aggie club, Business Undergraduate Society, Bonner Organization, College Republicans, College Democrats.

Athletics. NAIA. **Intercollegiate:** Baseball M, basketball, volleyball W. **Intramural:** Baseball M, basketball, football (non-tackle) M, racquetball, softball, tennis, volleyball. **Team name:** Bobcats.

Student services. Chaplain/spiritual director, career counseling, student employment services, financial aid counseling, health services, on-campus daycare, personal counseling, placement for graduates, veterans' counselor. **Physically disabled:** Services for visually, hearing impaired.

Contact. E-mail: admiss4@cofo.edu
Phone: (417) 690-2636 Toll-free number: (800) 222-0525
Fax: (417) 690-2635
Marci Linson, Dean of Admissions, College of the Ozarks, PO Box 17,
Point Lookout, MO 65726-0017

Columbia College
Columbia, Missouri
www.ccis.edu   **CB code: 6095**

- Private 4-year liberal arts college affiliated with Christian Church (Disciples of Christ)
- Commuter campus in small city
- 930 degree-seeking undergraduates: 18% part-time, 59% women
- 240 degree-seeking graduate students
- 49% of applicants admitted
- SAT or ACT (ACT writing optional) required
- 48% graduate within 6 years; 26% enter graduate study

General. Founded in 1851. Regionally accredited. Programs for adult students offered on main campus and 35 locations in United States and Cuba. Classes for nursing students available through video conferencing. **Degrees:** 141 bachelor's, 12 associate awarded; master's offered. **ROTC:** Army, Naval, Air Force. **Location:** 120 miles from Kansas City, 120 miles from St. Louis. **Calendar:** Semester, extensive summer session. **Full-time faculty:** 69 total; 83% have terminal degrees, 7% minority, 48% women. **Part-time faculty:** 50 total; 6% have terminal degrees, 44% women. **Class size:** 81% < 20, 18% 20-39, less than 1% 40-49.

Freshman class profile. 731 applied, 360 admitted, 124 enrolled.

Mid 50% test scores			
SAT critical reading:	430-550	Rank in top quarter:	28%
SAT math:	460-530	Rank in top tenth:	19%
ACT composite:	20-26	End year in good standing:	87%
GPA 3.75 or higher:	29%	Return as sophomores:	65%
GPA 3.50-3.74:	19%	Out-of-state:	10%
GPA 3.0-3.49:	35%	Live on campus:	73%
GPA 2.0-2.99:	16%		

Basis for selection. School achievement, class rank, test scores most important. **Home schooled:** Statement describing home school structure and mission, transcript of courses and grades required. ACT/SAT required; no GED requirement.

High school preparation. College-preparatory program recommended. 14 units recommended. Recommended units include English 4, mathematics 3, social studies 2, science 3 and foreign language 2.

2011-2012 Annual costs. Tuition/fees: $16,532. Room/board: $6,254. Books/supplies: $880. Personal expenses: $5,556.

2010-2011 Financial aid. Need-based: 120 full-time freshmen applied for aid; 108 were judged to have need; 107 of these received aid. Average need met was 59%. Average scholarship/grant was $4,939; average loan $3,132. 51% of total undergraduate aid awarded as scholarships/grants, 49% as loans/jobs. **Non-need-based:** Awarded to 352 full-time undergraduates, including 84 freshmen. Scholarships awarded for academics, alumni affiliation, art, athletics, job skills, leadership, music/drama, religious affiliation, ROTC, state residency.

Application procedures. Admission: Closing date 8/15 (postmark date). $35 fee, may be waived for applicants with need. Admission notification on a rolling basis beginning on or about 8/15. **Financial aid:** Priority date 3/1; no closing date. FAFSA required. Applicants notified on a rolling basis starting 3/1.

Academics. Evening degree program available based on 8-week ongoing terms. **Special study options:** Combined bachelor's/graduate degree, cross-registration, distance learning, double major, dual enrollment of high school students, ESL, honors, independent study, internships, student-designed major, study abroad, teacher certification program. **Credit/placement by examination:** AP, CLEP, IB, SAT, ACT, institutional tests. 45 credit hours maximum toward associate degree, 60 toward bachelor's. **Support services:** Tutoring, writing center.

Honors college/program. Must demonstrate academic achievement with two of the following: 3.5 GPA; 78th percentile on ACT or equivalent SAT; 78th percentile on GED. Fifty-one freshmen admitted.

Majors. Area/ethnic studies: American. **Biology:** General. **Business:** General, accounting, business admin, finance, human resources, international, management information systems, marketing. **Communications:** Communications/speech/rhetoric, persuasive communications. **Computer sciences:**

General, computer science. **Conservation:** Environmental science. **English:** English lit. **History:** General. **Math:** General. **Parks/recreation:** Sports admin. **Philosophy/religion:** Philosophy. **Physical sciences:** Chemistry. **Protective services:** Forensics, law enforcement admin. **Psychology:** General. **Social sciences:** Political science, sociology. **Visual/performing arts:** Art, ceramics, graphic design, painting, photography, printmaking.

Most popular majors. Business/marketing 38%, psychology 12%, public administration/social services 6%, security/protective services 10%, visual/performing arts 12%.

Computing on campus. 121 workstations in dormitories, library, computer center, student center. Dormitories wired for high-speed internet access and linked to campus network. Commuter students can connect to campus network. Online course registration, online library, helpline, repair service, wireless network available.

Student life. Freshman orientation: Available. Preregistration for classes offered. Held weekend before classes start. **Policies:** Alcohol and illegal drugs forbidden on campus. Students with less than 52 credit hours must live on campus. **Housing:** Guaranteed on-campus for freshmen. Coed dorms, single-sex dorms, special housing for disabled, apartments available. **Activities:** Campus ministries, choral groups, dance, drama, international student organizations, literary magazine, music ensembles, Model UN, musical theater, student government, International Club, Columbia College Democrats, Columbia College Chi Alpha Christian Fellowship, Human Service Organization, Peace Club, Crossfire Campus Ministry, Model United Nations, Environmentally Conscious Organization, Committed and Serving Together, Columbia College Student Veterans.

Athletics. NAIA. **Intercollegiate:** Basketball, soccer M, softball W, volleyball W. **Intramural:** Basketball, football (non-tackle), soccer, softball, volleyball. **Team name:** Cougars.

Student services. Alcohol/substance abuse counseling, career counseling, services for economically disadvantaged, student employment services, financial aid counseling, health services, minority student services, personal counseling, placement for graduates, veterans' counselor. **Physically disabled:** Services for visually, speech, hearing impaired.

Contact. E-mail: admissions@ccis.edu
Phone: (573) 875-7352 Toll-free number: (800) 231-2391 ext. 7352
Fax: (573) 875-7506
Samantha White, Director, Admissions, Columbia College, 1001 Rogers Street, Columbia, MO 65216

Conception Seminary College
Conception, Missouri
www.conception.edu   **CB code: 6112**

- Private 4-year seminary college for men affiliated with Roman Catholic Church
- Residential campus in rural community
- 102 degree-seeking undergraduates
- 93% of applicants admitted
- ACT (writing optional), application essay required

General. Founded in 1883. Regionally accredited. Operated by Benedictine Monks of Conception Abbey, for both independent seminary students and candidates affiliated with sponsoring diocese. Women may enroll on part-time basis. **Degrees:** 31 bachelor's awarded. **Location:** 100 miles from Kansas City, 45 miles from St. Joseph. **Calendar:** Semester. **Full-time faculty:** 10 total. **Part-time faculty:** 18 total. **Special facilities:** Abbey Basilica of the Immaculate Conception.

Freshman class profile. 15 applied, 14 admitted, 14 enrolled.

Mid 50% test scores			
ACT composite:	21-28	Live on campus:	100%

Basis for selection. ACT composite scores tend to count more heavily than high school grades. Class rank considered. Applicants must be sponsored. Interview recommended. **Home schooled:** State high school equivalency certificate required. ACT score of 24 or better.

High school preparation. College-preparatory program recommended.

2011-2012 Annual costs. Tuition/fees: $17,060. Room/board: $10,126. Books/supplies: $650. Personal expenses: $850.

Financial aid. Non-need-based: Scholarships awarded for academics.

Application procedures. Admission: Priority date 6/1; deadline 7/31 (receipt date). No application fee. Admission notification on a rolling basis

beginning on or about 2/1. Foreign applications require written certification of financial, ecclesiastical sponsorship. **Financial aid:** No deadline. FAFSA required. Applicants notified on a rolling basis starting 8/1; must reply by 8/20.

Academics. Curriculum combines liberal arts and pre-theology training to accommodate varying degrees of vocational commitment. **Special study options:** ESL, independent study. **Credit/placement by examination:** AP, CLEP, ACT, institutional tests. 12 credit hours maximum toward bachelor's degree. **Support services:** Learning center, reduced course load, remedial instruction, study skills assistance, tutoring.

Majors. **Philosophy/religion:** Philosophy.

Computing on campus. 15 workstations in dormitories, library, computer center. Dormitories wired for high-speed internet access and linked to campus network. Online library, helpline, repair service, wireless network available.

Student life. Freshman orientation: Mandatory. Preregistration for classes offered. **Policies:** Religious observance required. **Housing:** Guaranteed on-campus for all undergraduates. Wellness housing available. $50 fully refundable deposit. **Activities:** Choral groups, drama, music ensembles, musical theater, student government, student newspaper, apostolic work, mission club, social concerns, community council, Inner-Life.

Athletics. Intercollegiate: Basketball M, soccer M, volleyball M. **Intramural:** Basketball M, football (non-tackle) M, racquetball M, soccer M, softball M, table tennis M, tennis M, track and field M, volleyball M, weight lifting M. **Team name:** Blue Knights.

Student services. Adult student services, alcohol/substance abuse counseling, chaplain/spiritual director, career counseling, financial aid counseling, health services, personal counseling.

Contact. E-mail: vocations@conception.edu
Phone: (660) 944-2886 Fax: (660) 944-2829
Br. Etienne Huard, Director of Admissions, Conception Seminary College, Box 502, Conception, MO 64433-0502

Cox College
Springfield, Missouri
www.coxcollege.edu   **CB code: 3932**

▸ Private 4-year health science and nursing college
▸ Commuter campus in small city

General. Regionally accredited. **Calendar:** Semester.

Annual costs/financial aid. Tuition/fees (2011-2012): $11,644. Books/supplies: $1,200.

Contact. Phone: (417) 269-3068
Director of Admission, 1423 North Jefferson Avenue, Springfield, MO 65802

Culver-Stockton College
Canton, Missouri   **CB member**
www.culver.edu   **CB code: 6123**

▸ Private 4-year liberal arts college affiliated with Christian Church (Disciples of Christ)
▸ Residential campus in small town
▸ 732 degree-seeking undergraduates: 4% part-time, 52% women, 10% African American, 3% Hispanic American, 1% Native American, 2% international
▸ 61% of applicants admitted
▸ SAT or ACT (ACT writing optional) required
▸ 41% graduate within 6 years; 17% enter graduate study

General. Founded in 1853. Regionally accredited. Blends traditional coursework and experiential opportunities. **Degrees:** 163 bachelor's awarded. **Location:** 130 miles from St. Louis, 20 miles from Quincy, Illinois. **Calendar:** Semester, limited summer session. **Full-time faculty:** 49 total; 74% have terminal degrees, 4% minority. **Part-time faculty:** 28 total; 14% have terminal degrees, 7% minority. **Class size:** 70% < 20, 28% 20-39, 1% 40-49. **Special facilities:** Phage genomics research facility with DNA sequencer, astronomy observation deck, biological research station, fine arts multi-media editing suite and recording studio, mock trial courtroom with legal research library.

Freshman class profile. 1,448 applied, 880 admitted, 198 enrolled.

Mid 50% test scores			
SAT critical reading:	390-510	Rank in top tenth:	8%
SAT math:	400-570	End year in good standing:	94%
ACT composite:	18-24	Return as sophomores:	65%
GPA 3.75 or higher:	13%	Out-of-state:	44%
GPA 3.50-3.74:	17%	Live on campus:	90%
GPA 3.0-3.49:	27%	International:	2%
GPA 2.0-2.99:	42%	Fraternities:	38%
Rank in top quarter:	26%	Sororities:	40%

Basis for selection. Secondary school record and test scores most important; recommendations, application essay and alumni relation considered. Students out of High School for over 5 year are not required to submit ACT or SAT. **Home schooled:** Transcript of courses and grades, state high school equivalency certificate required. **Learning Disabled:** Must request accommodations and submit appropriate documentation.

High school preparation. College-preparatory program recommended. 15 units recommended. Recommended units include English 4, mathematics 2, social studies 3, history 3, science 4 and foreign language 1.

2012-2013 Annual costs. Tuition/fees (projected): $22,550. Room/board: $7,600. Books/supplies: $1,000. Personal expenses: $340.

2011-2012 Financial aid. Need-based: 191 full-time freshmen applied for aid; 184 were judged to have need; 184 of these received aid. Average need met was 74%. Average scholarship/grant was $16,403; average loan $3,532. 66% of total undergraduate aid awarded as scholarships/grants, 34% as loans/jobs. **Non-need-based:** Awarded to 193 full-time undergraduates, including 32 freshmen. Scholarships awarded for academics, alumni affiliation, art, athletics, leadership, music/drama, religious affiliation.

Application procedures. Admission: Priority date 5/1; deadline 8/15 (receipt date). No application fee. Admission notification on a rolling basis beginning on or about 9/15. **Financial aid:** Priority date 3/1, closing date 6/1. FAFSA required. Applicants notified on a rolling basis starting 2/15; must reply within 2 week(s) of notification.

Academics. Special study options: Combined bachelor's/graduate degree, distance learning, double major, dual enrollment of high school students, honors, independent study, internships, liberal arts/career combination, semester at sea, student-designed major, study abroad, teacher certification program, Washington semester. **Credit/placement by examination:** AP, CLEP, IB, SAT, ACT, institutional tests. 90 credit hours maximum toward bachelor's degree. **Support services:** Learning center, reduced course load, remedial instruction, study skills assistance, tutoring, writing center.

Majors. Biology: General, biochemistry. **Business:** Accounting, business admin, finance. **Communications:** Communications/speech/rhetoric, media studies. **Education:** General, art, elementary, music, physical, speech. **English:** English lit. **Health services:** Athletic training, nursing (RN). **History:** General. **Liberal arts:** Arts/sciences. **Math:** General. **Parks/recreation:** Sports admin. **Philosophy/religion:** Religion. **Protective services:** Law enforcement admin. **Psychology:** General. **Social sciences:** Political science. **Visual/performing arts:** Art, dramatic, graphic design, music, musical theater, studio arts management.

Most popular majors. Biology 6%, business/marketing 23%, education 13%, health sciences 12%, parks/recreation 8%, visual/performing arts 8%.

Computing on campus. 75 workstations in dormitories, library, computer center, student center. Dormitories wired for high-speed internet access and linked to campus network. Commuter students can connect to campus network. Online course registration, online library, helpline, repair service, student web hosting, wireless network available.

Student life. Freshman orientation: Mandatory, $200 fee. Preregistration for classes offered. Held 3 days prior to beginning of fall semester. **Policies:** All students under age 21 are required to live on campus unless living with parents or married. Students have voting representation on faculty committees. **Housing:** Guaranteed on-campus for all undergraduates. Coed dorms, fraternity/sorority housing, wellness housing available. **Activities:** Bands, campus ministries, choral groups, dance, drama, international student organizations, literary magazine, music ensembles, Model UN, musical theater, radio station, student government, student newspaper, Disciples on Campus, Christians in Action, Men of Character, Black Student Union, International & Domestic Events Awareness Society, psychology club, Athletic Trainers Organization, Up 'Til Dawn, pre-law club.

Athletics. NAIA. **Intercollegiate:** Baseball M, basketball, cheerleading, cross-country, football (tackle) M, golf, soccer, softball W, track and field, volleyball W. **Intramural:** Basketball, bowling, football (non-tackle), golf, handball, racquetball, softball, volleyball. **Team name:** Wildcats.

Student services. Adult student services, alcohol/substance abuse counseling, chaplain/spiritual director, career counseling, student employment

services, financial aid counseling, health services, personal counseling, placement for graduates, veterans' counselor.

Contact. E-mail: enrollment@culver.edu
Phone: (573) 288-6331 Toll-free number: (800) 537-1883
Fax: (573) 288-6618
Misty McBee, Director of Admission, Culver-Stockton College, One College Hill, Canton, MO 63435-1299

DeVry University: Kansas City
Kansas City, Missouri
www.devry.edu   **CB code: 6092**

- For-profit 4-year university
- Commuter campus in large city
- 922 degree-seeking undergraduates
- Interview required

General. Founded in 1931. Regionally accredited. Additional locations: Kansas City Downtown, St. Louis West. **Degrees:** 154 bachelor's, 58 associate awarded; master's offered. **Location:** 15 miles from downtown. **Calendar:** Semester, extensive summer session. **Full-time faculty:** 25 total. **Part-time faculty:** 51 total.

Basis for selection. Applicants must have high school diploma or equivalent degree from accredited postsecondary institution and be at least 17 years of age on the first day of classes. New students may enter at beginning of any semester. CPT also accepted.

High school preparation. Required units include mathematics 1. Math unit must be algebra or higher.

2011-2012 Annual costs. Tuition/fees: $15,294. Books/supplies: $1,310. Personal expenses: $3,574.

Financial aid. All financial aid based on need.

Application procedures. Admission: No deadline. $50 fee, may be waived for applicants with need. Admission notification on a rolling basis. **Financial aid:** No deadline. FAFSA required. Applicants notified on a rolling basis.

Academics. Special study options: Accelerated study, distance learning, weekend college. **Credit/placement by examination:** AP, CLEP, institutional tests. **Support services:** Learning center, remedial instruction, tutoring.

Majors. Business: Business admin. **Computer sciences:** Networking, systems analysis, web page design.

Most popular majors. Business/marketing 41%, computer/information sciences 47%, engineering/engineering technologies 11%.

Computing on campus. 1,300 workstations in library, computer center. Online course registration, online library, helpline available.

Student life. Freshman orientation: Mandatory. Preregistration for classes offered. **Activities:** Association of Information Technology Professionals, Campus Crusade for Christ, Institute for Electrical & Electronics Engineers, Phi Beta Lambda, Tau Alpha Pi, professional certification club, drama club, Gamma Beta Phi.

Athletics. Intramural: Volleyball.

Student services. Career counseling, student employment services, financial aid counseling, placement for graduates, veterans' counselor. **Physically disabled:** Services for visually, hearing impaired.

Contact. E-mail: ssmeed@kc.devry.edu
Phone: (816) 941-2810 Toll-free number: (800) 821-3766
Fax: (816) 941-0896
Shane Smeed, Director of Admissions, DeVry University: Kansas City, 11224 Holmes Street, Kansas City, MO 64131-3626

Drury University
Springfield, Missouri
www.drury.edu   **CB code: 6169**

- Private 4-year university and liberal arts college affiliated with United Church of Christ
- Residential campus in large city

- 1,610 degree-seeking undergraduates: 2% part-time, 54% women, 3% African American, 3% Asian American, 2% Hispanic American, 1% Native American, 7% international
- 397 degree-seeking graduate students
- 73% of applicants admitted
- SAT or ACT (ACT writing optional) required
- 64% graduate within 6 years; 39% enter graduate study

General. Founded in 1873. Regionally accredited. **Degrees:** 338 bachelor's awarded; master's offered. **ROTC:** Army. **Location:** 220 miles from St. Louis, 170 miles from Kansas City. **Calendar:** Semester, limited summer session. **Full-time faculty:** 136 total; 96% have terminal degrees, 9% minority, 42% women. **Part-time faculty:** 45 total; 13% have terminal degrees, 53% women. **Class size:** 61% < 20, 38% 20-39, less than 1% 40-49, less than 1% 50-99. **Special facilities:** Science center, greenhouse, astronomical observation station, electronic music lab, Chalfant pipe organ, television and radio studios, outdoor student-built classroom, philosopher's table.

Freshman class profile. 1,554 applied, 1,134 admitted, 352 enrolled.

Mid 50% test scores		Return as sophomores:	93%
ACT composite:	23-29	Out-of-state:	19%
GPA 3.75 or higher:	63%	Live on campus:	79%
GPA 3.50-3.74:	16%	International:	7%
GPA 3.0-3.49:	16%	Fraternities:	33%
GPA 2.0-2.99:	5%	Sororities:	27%

Basis for selection. School achievement record, test scores, reference from high school counselor, essay important. Interview recommended for all. Audition recommended for music, theater students; portfolio recommended for architecture, art students. **Learning Disabled:** Encouraged to self-disclose early and seek resources and support of Disability Support Services office. Must present documentation outlining disability to receive accommodations. Documentation should be no more than 3 years old.

High school preparation. College-preparatory program recommended. 12 units required. Required and recommended units include English 4, mathematics 3-4, social studies 3, science 3 and foreign language 2.

2011-2012 Annual costs. Tuition/fees: $21,043. Room/board: $7,000. Books/supplies: $1,500. Personal expenses: $1,500.

2010-2011 Financial aid. Need-based: 333 full-time freshmen applied for aid; 298 were judged to have need; 298 of these received aid. Average need met was 80%. Average scholarship/grant was $5,970; average loan $4,500. 44% of total undergraduate aid awarded as scholarships/grants, 56% as loans/jobs. **Non-need-based:** Awarded to 1,551 full-time undergraduates, including 301 freshmen. Scholarships awarded for academics, alumni affiliation, art, athletics, job skills, leadership, minority status, music/drama, religious affiliation.

Application procedures. Admission: Priority date 1/15; deadline 8/1 (postmark date). $25 fee, may be waived for applicants with need. Admission notification on a rolling basis beginning on or about 10/1. Must reply by May 1 or within 3 week(s) if notified thereafter. Application fee waived if applicant visits campus. **Financial aid:** Priority date 2/15, closing date 3/1. FAFSA, institutional form required. Applicants notified on a rolling basis starting 3/30; must reply within 2 week(s) of notification.

Academics. General education curriculum leads to minor in global studies for each student. **Special study options:** Accelerated study, combined bachelor's/graduate degree, cooperative education, distance learning, double major, dual enrollment of high school students, ESL, honors, independent study, internships, liberal arts/career combination, student-designed major, study abroad, teacher certification program, Washington semester. Living-learning communities, leadership/community service communities, Drury Center in Greece. **Credit/placement by examination:** AP, CLEP, IB, institutional tests. **Support services:** Pre-admission summer program, reduced course load, remedial instruction, study skills assistance, tutoring, writing center.

Majors. Architecture: Architecture. **Biology:** General, exercise physiology. **Business:** Accounting, business admin, customer service, finance, management information systems, marketing. **Communications:** Advertising, communications/speech/rhetoric, public relations. **Computer sciences:** General, computer science. **Conservation:** Environmental science, environmental studies, management/policy. **Education:** General, elementary, music, physical, secondary, technology/industrial arts. **Engineering:** Applied physics. **English:** English lit, writing. **Foreign languages:** French, German, Spanish. **Health services:** EMT paramedic, medical radiologic technology/radiation therapy, music therapy, nursing (RN), predental, premedicine, prenursing, prepharmacy, prephysical therapy, preveterinary. **History:** General. **Liberal arts:** Arts/sciences. **Math:** General. **Parks/recreation:** Exercise sciences. **Philosophy/religion:** Philosophy, religion. **Physical sciences:** Chemistry, physics. **Psychology:** General. **Social sciences:** Criminology, economics, international relations, political science, sociology, U.S. government. **Visual/**

performing arts: Art history/conservation, dramatic, music, studio arts, studio arts management.

Most popular majors. Biology 10%, business/marketing 15%, communications/journalism 6%, education 11%, psychology 14%, security/protective services 10%, social sciences 6%, visual/performing arts 6%.

Computing on campus. 389 workstations in dormitories, library, computer center, student center. Dormitories wired for high-speed internet access and linked to campus network. Commuter students can connect to campus network. Online course registration, online library, helpline, repair service, student web hosting, wireless network available.

Student life. Freshman orientation: Mandatory, $145 fee. Preregistration for classes offered. 4-day program; includes parent session. **Housing:** Guaranteed on-campus for freshmen. Coed dorms, special housing for disabled, apartments, fraternity/sorority housing available. $200 fully refundable deposit, deadline 6/1. Living-learning, honors housing, leadership/service communities available. **Activities:** Bands, campus ministries, choral groups, dance, drama, film society, international student organizations, literary magazine, music ensembles, musical theater, opera, radio station, student government, student newspaper, symphony orchestra, TV station, Authentic Ministries, Think Green, College Republicans, College Democrats, Mortar Board, Habitat for Humanity Chapter, Students in Free Enterprise, Drury Volunteer Corps, student teacher association, Disciples on Campus, Amnesty International.

Athletics. NCAA. **Intercollegiate:** Baseball M, basketball, cheerleading M, cross-country, diving, golf, soccer, softball W, swimming, tennis, track and field, volleyball W. **Intramural:** Basketball, football (non-tackle), racquetball, rugby M, soccer, softball W, volleyball. **Team name:** Panthers.

Student services. Adult student services, alcohol/substance abuse counseling, chaplain/spiritual director, career counseling, services for economically disadvantaged, student employment services, financial aid counseling, health services, minority student services, personal counseling, placement for graduates, veterans' counselor, women's services. **Physically disabled:** Services for visually, speech, hearing impaired.

Contact. E-mail: druryad@drury.edu
Phone: (417) 873-7205 Toll-free number: (800) 922-2274
Fax: (417) 866-3873
Dawn Hiles, Dean of Admission, Drury University, 900 North Benton Avenue, Springfield, MO 65802-3712

Evangel University
Springfield, Missouri
www.evangel.edu CB code: 6198

- Private 4-year liberal arts college affiliated with Assemblies of God
- Residential campus in small city
- 1,729 degree-seeking undergraduates: 56% women
- 271 degree-seeking graduate students
- 70% of applicants admitted
- SAT or ACT with writing required
- 53% graduate within 6 years

General. Founded in 1955. Regionally accredited. **Degrees:** 380 bachelor's, 12 associate awarded; master's offered. **ROTC:** Army. **Location:** 170 miles from Kansas City, 212 miles from St. Louis. **Calendar:** Semester, limited summer session. **Full-time faculty:** 81 total; 69% have terminal degrees, 4% minority, 33% women. **Part-time faculty:** 41 total; 20% have terminal degrees, 5% minority, 49% women. **Class size:** 63% < 20, 26% 20-39, 6% 40-49, 5% 50-99, less than 1% >100.

Freshman class profile. 1,237 applied, 861 admitted, 409 enrolled.

Mid 50% test scores			
SAT critical reading:	450-580	Rank in top quarter:	44%
SAT math:	440-570	Rank in top tenth:	21%
SAT writing:	420-550	Out-of-state:	48%
ACT composite:	19-26	Live on campus:	93%

Basis for selection. Minimum 2.0 high school GPA, acceptance of college's moral and religious standards, acceptable ACT or SAT scores, rank in top half of graduating class. Statement of Christian faith required. Audition required for music, sport students. Essay and portfolio recommended. **Home schooled:** Letter of recommendation (nonparent) required. Admissions based upon ACT/SAT scores and letters of recommendation.

High school preparation. Recommended units include English 3, mathematics 1, social studies 2, science 1 (laboratory 1).

2011-2012 Annual costs. Tuition/fees: $17,900. Room/board: $6,310.

Financial aid. All financial aid based on need.

Application procedures. Admission: No deadline. $25 fee, may be waived for applicants with need. Admission notification on a rolling basis. **Financial aid:** Priority date 3/1; no closing date. FAFSA required. Applicants notified on a rolling basis starting 3/15; must reply within 3 week(s) of notification.

Academics. Special study options: Accelerated study, double major, independent study, internships, study abroad, teacher certification program, Washington semester, weekend college. **Credit/placement by examination:** AP, CLEP, IB, SAT, ACT, institutional tests. 30 credit hours maximum toward associate degree, 30 toward bachelor's. **Support services:** Learning center, reduced course load, remedial instruction, study skills assistance, tutoring, writing center.

Majors. Biology: General. **Business:** General, accounting, business admin, marketing. **Communications:** Broadcast journalism, communications/speech/rhetoric, journalism. **Communications technology:** General. **Computer sciences:** General. **Education:** Art, business, early childhood, elementary, English, foreign languages, mathematics, middle, music, physical, science, secondary, social studies, special ed. **English:** English lit, rhetoric/composition. **Foreign languages:** Spanish. **Health services:** Clinical lab technology, predental, premedicine, preveterinary. **History:** General. **Human services:** Social work. **Math:** General. **Parks/recreation:** General. **Physical sciences:** Chemistry. **Protective services:** Criminal justice. **Psychology:** General. **Social sciences:** General, criminology, political science, sociology. **Theology:** Bible, missionary, sacred music. **Visual/performing arts:** Dramatic, music, music performance, studio arts.

Most popular majors. Business/marketing 26%, communications/journalism 11%, education 13%, philosophy/religious studies 7%, public administration/social services 8%.

Computing on campus. 407 workstations in dormitories, library, computer center, student center. Dormitories wired for high-speed internet access and linked to campus network. Online library, helpline, wireless network available.

Student life. Freshman orientation: Mandatory, $50 fee. Preregistration for classes offered. **Policies:** Religious observance required. **Housing:** Guaranteed on-campus for freshmen. Coed dorms, single-sex dorms, apartments available. **Activities:** Bands, campus ministries, choral groups, drama, international student organizations, music ensembles, musical theater, opera, radio station, student government, student newspaper, symphony orchestra, TV station, honor fraternities, student ministries.

Athletics. NAIA. **Intercollegiate:** Baseball M, basketball, cross-country, football (tackle) M, golf, softball W, tennis, track and field, volleyball W. **Intramural:** Basketball, football (non-tackle), soccer, softball, volleyball W. **Team name:** Crusaders.

Student services. Chaplain/spiritual director, career counseling, student employment services, financial aid counseling, health services, personal counseling, placement for graduates, veterans' counselor. **Physically disabled:** Services for visually, hearing impaired.

Contact. E-mail: admission@evangel.edu
Phone: (417) 865-2811 ext. 7205 Toll-free number: (800) 382-6435
Fax: (417) 865-9599
Jeff Burnett, Director of Admissions, Evangel University, 1111 North Glenstone, Springfield, MO 65802

Fontbonne University
St. Louis, Missouri CB member
www.fontbonne.edu CB code: 6216

- Private 4-year university and liberal arts college affiliated with Roman Catholic Church
- Commuter campus in large city
- 1,443 degree-seeking undergraduates: 25% part-time, 68% women, 20% African American, 1% Asian American, 1% Hispanic American, 5% international
- 764 degree-seeking graduate students
- 63% of applicants admitted
- SAT or ACT (ACT writing recommended) required

General. Founded in 1923. Regionally accredited. **Degrees:** 437 bachelor's awarded; master's offered. **ROTC:** Army, Air Force. **Location:** 1 mile from downtown. **Calendar:** Semester, limited summer session. **Full-time faculty:**

81 total. **Part-time faculty:** 198 total. **Class size:** 85% < 20, 15% 20-39. **Special facilities:** Theater, speech, language, and hearing clinic, academic resource and ADA accommodations center.

Freshman class profile. 632 applied, 400 admitted, 125 enrolled.

Mid 50% test scores		Live on campus:	56%
ACT composite:	20-24	International:	18%
Out-of-state:	24%		

Basis for selection. High school GPA, class rank, test scores considered. Recommendations may be requested. Essay and interview recommended. Audition required for theater students; portfolio required for art students.

High school preparation. College-preparatory program required. 16 units required. Required units include English 4, mathematics 3, social studies 3, science 3 (laboratory 1), visual/performing arts 1 and academic electives 2. Core electives 3 units. Must include foreign language and 1 unit visual or performing arts.

2011-2012 Annual costs. Tuition/fees: $21,220. Room/board: $7,916. Books/supplies: $650. Personal expenses: $640.

Financial aid. Non-need-based: Scholarships awarded for academics, alumni affiliation, art, leadership, minority status, music/drama, religious affiliation, state residency.

Application procedures. Admission: Priority date 12/15; no deadline. $25 fee, may be waived for applicants with need. Admission notification on a rolling basis. Must reply by May 1 or within 3 week(s) if notified thereafter. **Financial aid:** Closing date 4/1. FAFSA, institutional form required. Applicants notified on a rolling basis starting 2/1; must reply within 2 week(s) of notification.

Academics. Special study options: Accelerated study, combined bachelor's/graduate degree, cooperative education, cross-registration, distance learning, double major, dual enrollment of high school students, ESL, exchange student, honors, independent study, internships, liberal arts/career combination, semester at sea, student-designed major, study abroad, teacher certification program, weekend college. 3-2 program in social work or engineering with Washington University. **Credit/placement by examination:** AP, CLEP, IB, institutional tests. 30 credit hours maximum toward bachelor's degree. Fontbonne will accept undergraduate credit by exam for non-standardized examinations given by accredited institutions. Course number, title, and credit hours must appear on official transcript. Determination as to fulfillment of certain course requirements will be reviewed and considered by department chairperson. **Support services:** Learning center, reduced course load, remedial instruction, study skills assistance, tutoring, writing center.

Majors. Biology: General. **Business:** Business admin, organizational behavior. **Communications:** Advertising, communications/speech/rhetoric. **Computer sciences:** General. **Education:** Deaf/hearing impaired, early childhood, elementary, family/consumer sciences, middle, special ed. **English:** English lit. **Health services:** Dietetics, speech pathology. **History:** General. **Human services:** Social work. **Liberal arts:** Arts/sciences. **Math:** General. **Parks/recreation:** Sports admin. **Psychology:** General. **Social sciences:** Sociology. **Visual/performing arts:** Art, dramatic, studio arts. **Work/family studies:** Clothing/textiles.

Computing on campus. 344 workstations in dormitories, library, computer center. Dormitories wired for high-speed internet access and linked to campus network. Commuter students can connect to campus network. Online course registration, online library, helpline, repair service, wireless network available.

Student life. Freshman orientation: Mandatory, $75 fee. Preregistration for classes offered. Held during week prior to classes, includes community service. **Housing:** Coed dorms, special housing for disabled, apartments, wellness housing available. $150 fully refundable deposit. Apartment style residence halls available. **Activities:** Campus ministries, choral groups, dance, drama, international student organizations, literary magazine, music ensembles, musical theater, radio station, student government, student newspaper, College Republicans, College Democrats, Fontbonne in Service and Humility, Straights and Gays for Equality, Students for the Enhancement of Black Awareness.

Athletics. NCAA. Intercollegiate: Baseball M, basketball, bowling, cross-country, field hockey W, golf, lacrosse, soccer, softball W, tennis, track and field, volleyball. **Intramural:** Badminton, basketball, bowling, football (non-tackle), soccer, softball, table tennis, tennis, volleyball. **Team name:** Griffins.

Student services. Adult student services, alcohol/substance abuse counseling, chaplain/spiritual director, career counseling, student employment services, financial aid counseling, health services, minority student services, personal counseling, placement for graduates. **Physically disabled:** Services for speech, hearing impaired.

Contact. E-mail: fbyou@fontbonne.edu
Phone: (314) 889-1400 Toll-free number: (800) 205-5862
Fax: (314) 889-1451
Vice President for Enrollment Management, Fontbonne University, 6800 Wydown Boulevard, St. Louis, MO 63105

Global University
Springfield, Missouri
www.globaluniversity.edu   CB code: 4916

- Private 4-year Bible and seminary college affiliated with Assemblies of God
- Commuter campus in small city
- 679 full-time, degree-seeking undergraduates
- 370 graduate students

General. Founded in 1948. Accredited by DETC. All course work completed via distance education. **Degrees:** 274 bachelor's, 5 associate awarded; master's offered. **Location:** 200 miles from St. Louis, 170 miles from Kansas City. **Calendar:** Differs by program, extensive summer session. **Full-time faculty:** 55 total. **Part-time faculty:** 450 total.

Basis for selection. Open admission.

2011-2012 Annual costs. Tuition/fees: $3,750. Books/supplies: $650.

Application procedures. Admission: No deadline. $40 fee. Admission notification on a rolling basis. Global University allows for rolling applications year round.

Academics. Special study options: Distance learning, external degree, independent study. **Credit/placement by examination:** AP, CLEP. 16 credit hours maximum toward associate degree, 32 toward bachelor's. **Support services:** Study skills assistance.

Majors. Theology: Bible, missionary, religious ed, theology.

Computing on campus. Online library available.

Student services. Chaplain/spiritual director.

Contact. E-mail: info@globaluniversity.edu
Phone: (417) 862-9533 Toll-free number: (800) 443-1083
Fax: (417) 865-7167
C. Kroh, Registrar and Associate Dean of Student Services, Global University, 1211 South Glenstone Avenue, Springfield, MO 65804

Goldfarb School of Nursing at Barnes-Jewish College
St. Louis, Missouri
www.barnesjewishcollege.edu   CB code: 6329

- Private two-year upper-division nursing college
- Commuter campus in very large city
- 65% of applicants admitted

General. Regionally accredited. Affiliated with Barnes-Jewish Hospital and Washington University Medical Center. **Degrees:** 300 bachelor's awarded; master's, doctoral offered. **Location:** Downtown. **Calendar:** Trimester, extensive summer session. **Full-time faculty:** 38 total; 47% have terminal degrees, 18% minority, 92% women. **Part-time faculty:** 14 total; 29% have terminal degrees, 21% minority, 79% women. **Class size:** 49% < 20, 21% 20-39, 14% 40-49, 16% 50-99.

Student profile. 580 degree-seeking undergraduates, 171 degree-seeking graduate students. 502 applied as first time-transfer students, 325 admitted, 201 enrolled. 90% transferred from two-year, 10% transferred from four-year institutions.

Women:	89%	Part-time:	16%
African American:	7%	Out-of-state:	19%
Asian American:	2%	25 or older:	87%
Hispanic American:	2%		

Basis for selection. Open admission. College transcript required. Transfer accepted as juniors, seniors.

2012-2013 Annual costs. Tuition/fees (projected): $24,990. Books/supplies: $1,600.

Financial aid. Non-need-based: Scholarships awarded for academics, leadership, minority status.

Application procedures. Admission: Rolling admission. $50 fee. Application must be submitted on paper. **Financial aid:** No deadline. Applicants notified on a rolling basis. FAFSA required.

Academics. Special study options: Accelerated study, combined bachelor's/graduate degree. **Credit/placement by examination:** AP, CLEP, IB, institutional tests. **Support services:** Tutoring, writing center.

Majors. Health services: Nursing (RN).

Computing on campus. 60 workstations in library, computer center. Commuter students can connect to campus network. Online library, helpline, wireless network available.

Student life. Activities: Student newspaper.

Student services. Career counseling, financial aid counseling, personal counseling.

Contact. E-mail: bjcon-admissions@bjc.org
Phone: (314) 454-7057 Toll-free number: (800) 832-9009
Fax: (314) 362-9250
Michael Ward, Associate Dean for Student Programs, Goldfarb School of Nursing at Barnes-Jewish College, 4483 Duncan Avenue, St. Louis, MO 63110-1091

Grantham University
Kansas City, Missouri
www.grantham.edu   CB code: 2244

- For-profit 4-year virtual university
- Large city
- 7,715 degree-seeking undergraduates

General. Founded in 1951. Accredited by DETC. Degree programs are 100 percent online. **Degrees:** 730 bachelor's, 524 associate awarded; master's offered. **Calendar:** Differs by program, extensive summer session. **Full-time faculty:** 14 total. **Part-time faculty:** 283 total.

Basis for selection. Open admission. High school diploma, GED, or equivalent required. Basic computer skills and use of computer with Windows, Internet access, e-mail account, printer also required. **Home schooled:** Requirements for home schooled student high school graduation vary by state, or state institution granting high school accreditation. Will accept any documentation certifying high school graduation if it is approved by issuing state or the military.

High school preparation. College-preparatory program recommended.

2011-2012 Annual costs. Tuition/fees: $8,050. Tuition includes required textbooks, software and domestic shipping.

Financial aid. Additional information: DANTES and some employer reimbursement programs available. Financial aid application must be submitted 30 days before classes begin; classes begin the first Wednesday of each month.

Application procedures. Admission: No deadline. $30 fee. Admission notification on a rolling basis. **Financial aid:** No deadline.

Academics. Special study options: Accelerated study, distance learning, independent study. **Credit/placement by examination:** AP, CLEP, IB. 45 credit hours maximum toward associate degree, 90 toward bachelor's. **Support services:** Learning center, tutoring, writing center.

Majors. Business: Accounting, business admin, information resources management. **Computer sciences:** Computer science, networking. **Protective services:** Law enforcement admin.

Most popular majors. Business/marketing 39%, computer/information sciences 10%, engineering/engineering technologies 13%, interdisciplinary studies 27%, security/protective services 10%.

Computing on campus. PC or laptop required. Online course registration, online library available.

Student life. Freshman orientation: Mandatory. Preregistration for classes offered.

Athletics. Team name: Fighting Eagles.

Student services. Adult student services, financial aid counseling, veterans' counselor.

Contact. E-mail: admissions@grantham.edu
Phone: (800) 955-2527 Toll-free number: (800) 955-2527
Fax: (816) 595-5757
Gretchen Lammle, Director of Enrollment - Admissions, Grantham University, 7200 NW 86th Street, Kansas City, MO 64153

Hannibal-LaGrange University
Hannibal, Missouri
www.hlg.edu   CB code: 6266

- Private 4-year university and liberal arts college affiliated with Southern Baptist Convention
- Residential campus in large town
- 1,063 degree-seeking undergraduates
- 60% of applicants admitted
- SAT or ACT (ACT writing optional), interview required

General. Founded in 1858. Regionally accredited. Christian environment. **Degrees:** 231 bachelor's, 36 associate awarded; master's offered. **Location:** 100 miles from St. Louis. **Calendar:** Semester, limited summer session. **Full-time faculty:** 60 total. **Part-time faculty:** 86 total. **Class size:** 75% < 20, 24% 20-39, 1% 40-49. **Special facilities:** Nature trail, fine arts theater, mission center.

Freshman class profile. 682 applied, 409 admitted, 159 enrolled.

Out-of-state:	33%	Live on campus:	88%

Basis for selection. Most applicants admitted. Test scores important. 20 or above ACT composite required. Applicants with 16-19 ACT composite admitted provisionally. ACT administered on campus on registration day. Applications without English composition 1 and college algebra must submit ACT scores and take mathematics placement exam. Interviews required for performance and honor students. **Home schooled:** Transcript of courses and grades required. ACT score required. **Learning Disabled:** Must provide appropriate ADA documentation.

High school preparation. College-preparatory program recommended. Recommended units include English 4, mathematics 3, history 3, science 2 (laboratory 1).

2011-2012 Annual costs. Tuition/fees: $16,890. Room/board: $6,200. Books/supplies: $800. Personal expenses: $2,061.

Financial aid. Non-need-based: Scholarships awarded for academics, art, athletics, music/drama, religious affiliation. **Additional information:** Work-study opportunities vary according to on- and off-campus needs.

Application procedures. Admission: Closing date 8/26. $25 fee. Admission notification on a rolling basis beginning on or about 9/1. **Financial aid:** No deadline. FAFSA, institutional form required. Applicants notified on a rolling basis; must reply by 8/31.

Academics. Special study options: Accelerated study, distance learning, double major, dual enrollment of high school students, ESL, honors, independent study, internships, student-designed major, study abroad, teacher certification program. **Credit/placement by examination:** AP, CLEP, SAT, ACT, institutional tests. 16 credit hours maximum toward associate degree, 30 toward bachelor's. No more than 8 credit hours in one discipline. **Support services:** Remedial instruction, study skills assistance, tutoring.

Honors college/program. Minimum ACT-27, essay. Additional 21 hours plus research project required, must maintain requirements for eligibility each semester. Approximately 9 freshmen enter the program each year.

Majors. Biology: General. **Business:** General, accounting, business admin, finance, marketing, organizational behavior. **Communications:** Communications/speech/rhetoric. **Computer sciences:** General. **Education:** General, art, business, early childhood, elementary, English, mathematics, music, physical, science, secondary, social studies. **English:** English lit. **Health services:** Nursing (RN). **History:** General. **Liberal arts:** Arts/sciences. **Math:** General. **Parks/recreation:** Facilities management. **Protective services:** Law enforcement admin. **Psychology:** General. **Social sciences:** Sociology. **Theology:** Bible, religious ed, sacred music. **Visual/performing arts:** Art, dramatic, music performance.

Most popular majors. Business/marketing 23%, education 27%, health sciences 10%, security/protective services 9%.

Computing on campus. 91 workstations in library, computer center, student center. Dormitories linked to campus network. Commuter students

can connect to campus network. Online library, repair service, wireless network available.

Student life. Freshman orientation: Mandatory, $65 fee. Preregistration for classes offered. Conducted 4 days before classes begin. **Policies:** Students under 21 years of age at beginning of enrollment required to live in residence housing unless living with approved relative. Religious observance required. **Housing:** Single-sex dorms, special housing for disabled, apartments, wellness housing available. $100 fully refundable deposit, deadline 8/26. **Activities:** Jazz band, campus ministries, choral groups, drama, international student organizations, music ensembles, student government, student newspaper, Democratic club, Fellowship of Christian Athletes, Phi Beta Delta (men's service), Phi Beta Lambda, Gatekeepers (mentoring), Students for Life, Natures Investigation Circulus, Missouri State Teachers Association, Republican club, art club, science club.

Athletics. NAIA, NCCAA. **Intercollegiate:** Baseball M, basketball, cross-country, golf, soccer, softball W, track and field, volleyball, wrestling M. **Intramural:** Badminton, basketball, racquetball, table tennis, volleyball. **Team name:** Trojans.

Student services. Adult student services, career counseling, student employment services, health services. **Physically disabled:** Services for visually, hearing impaired.

Contact. E-mail: admissio@hlg.edu
Phone: (573) 629-3264 Toll-free number: (800) 454-1119
Fax: (573) 221-6594
Ray Carty, Vice President of Enrollment Management, Hannibal-LaGrange University, 2800 Palmyra Road, Hannibal, MO 63401

Harris-Stowe State University
St. Louis, Missouri
www.hssu.edu   CB code: 6269

- Public 4-year university
- Commuter campus in large city
- 1,552 degree-seeking undergraduates: 26% part-time, 65% women, 85% African American

General. Founded in 1857. Regionally accredited. **Degrees:** 141 bachelor's awarded. **ROTC:** Army, Air Force. **Location:** Midtown. **Calendar:** Semester, limited summer session. **Full-time faculty:** 43 total; 72% have terminal degrees, 63% minority, 49% women. **Part-time faculty:** 149 total; 20% have terminal degrees, 73% minority, 58% women. **Class size:** 86% < 20, 14% 20-39. **Special facilities:** Jazz institute.

Freshman class profile.

Mid 50% test scores		Rank in top tenth:	2%
ACT composite:	15-18	End year in good standing:	49%
GPA 3.0-3.49:	8%	Return as sophomores:	43%
GPA 2.0-2.99:	62%	Out-of-state:	12%
Rank in top quarter:	14%	Live on campus:	49%

Basis for selection. Open admission. First-time freshmen with below a 2.0 GPA are required to complete summer enrichment program for admission. Institutional placement test required of applicants with scores below 18 on any section of the ACT or below 440 on any section of the SAT. Full-time, first-year freshmen are encouraged to meet the Missouri high school core curriculum requirements. **Learning Disabled:** Submit documentation of disability for review by Director of the Center for Retention and Student Success.

High school preparation. College-preparatory program recommended. Required and recommended units include English 4, mathematics 3, social studies 3, science 3 (laboratory 1), foreign language 2, visual/performing arts 1 and academic electives 7. 1 visual/performing arts and 1 practical art required. Finance, health and physical education also required. Social studies must include American government.

2011-2012 Annual costs. Tuition/fees: $5,586; $10,597 out-of-state. Room/board: $8,700. Books/supplies: $500. Personal expenses: $2,000.

2011-2012 Financial aid. Need-based: 301 full-time freshmen applied for aid; 298 were judged to have need; 298 of these received aid. Average need met was 84%. Average scholarship/grant was $6,000; average loan $2,389. 59% of total undergraduate aid awarded as scholarships/grants, 41% as loans/jobs. **Non-need-based:** Awarded to 148 full-time undergraduates, including 109 freshmen. Scholarships awarded for academics, alumni affiliation, art, athletics, leadership, music/drama, state residency.

Application procedures. Admission: Priority date 12/1; deadline 7/29 (receipt date). $15 fee. Admission notification on a rolling basis. **Financial aid:** Closing date 4/1. FAFSA, institutional form required. Applicants notified

on a rolling basis starting 4/1; must reply within 3 week(s) of notification.

Academics. Special study options: Accelerated study, cooperative education, ESL, internships, student-designed major, teacher certification program. **Credit/placement by examination:** AP, CLEP, institutional tests. **Support services:** Learning center, pre-admission summer program, reduced course load, remedial instruction, study skills assistance, tutoring, writing center.

Majors. Biology: General. **Business:** Accounting, business admin, hospitality admin. **Computer sciences:** Information systems. **Education:** Early childhood, elementary, middle, secondary. **Health services:** Health care admin. **Math:** General. **Protective services:** Criminal justice.

Most popular majors. Business/marketing 44%, computer/information sciences 6%, education 24%, security/protective services 11%.

Computing on campus. 205 workstations in dormitories, library, computer center, student center. Dormitories wired for high-speed internet access and linked to campus network. Commuter students can connect to campus network. Wireless network available.

Student life. Freshman orientation: Mandatory. Preregistration for classes offered. Program directed by counseling staff during semester. **Housing:** Guaranteed on-campus for freshmen. Coed dorms available. $500 fully refundable deposit. **Activities:** Choral groups, dance, drama, international student organizations, literary magazine, music ensembles, student government, student newspaper, African American Studies Society, multicultural council, 100 Strong, Organization for Cultural Progress, Student Ambassadors.

Athletics. NAIA. **Intercollegiate:** Baseball M, basketball, cheerleading, soccer, softball W, volleyball W. **Intramural:** Basketball, volleyball. **Team name:** Hornets.

Student services. Career counseling, student employment services, financial aid counseling, health services, personal counseling, placement for graduates, veterans' counselor.

Contact. E-mail: admissions@hssu.edu
Phone: (314) 340-3300 Fax: (314) 340-3555
Meghan Sprung, Director of Recruitment and Retention, Harris-Stowe State University, 3026 Laclede Avenue, St. Louis, MO 63103-2199

Hickey College
St. Louis, Missouri
www.hickeycollege.edu   CB code: 2308

- For-profit 4-year business and technical college
- Commuter campus in very large city
- 461 degree-seeking undergraduates

General. Founded in 1933. Accredited by ACICS. **Degrees:** 32 bachelor's, 180 associate awarded. **Location:** 15 miles from downtown. **Calendar:** Semester. **Full-time faculty:** 19 total. **Part-time faculty:** 22 total.

Basis for selection. Open admission, but selective for some programs. Selective enrollment for paralegal and veterinary technician programs.

2011-2012 Annual costs. Tuition/fees: $13,470. Room only: $5,740. Books/supplies: $1,000.

Application procedures. Admission: No deadline. $50 fee. Admission notification on a rolling basis. **Financial aid:** No deadline. FAFSA required. Applicants notified on a rolling basis.

Academics. Credit/placement by examination: AP, CLEP.

Majors. Business: Management science.

Computing on campus. 134 workstations in library, computer center.

Student life. Freshman orientation: Mandatory. Preregistration for classes offered. **Housing:** Apartments available.

Student services. Student employment services, placement for graduates.

Contact. E-mail: admin@hickeycollege.edu
Phone: (314) 434-2212 Toll-free number: (800) 777-1544
Fax: (314) 434-1974
Bill Lewis, Director of Admissions, Hickey College, 940 West Port Plaza, St. Louis, MO 63146

ITT Technical Institute: Arnold
Arnold, Missouri
www.itt-tech.edu   CB code: 2691

- For-profit 4-year technical college
- Commuter campus in large town
- 848 degree-seeking undergraduates
- Interview required

General. Accredited by ACICS. **Degrees:** 98 bachelor's, 187 associate awarded. **Calendar:** Quarter, extensive summer session. **Full-time faculty:** 13 total. **Part-time faculty:** 71 total.

Basis for selection. Satisfactory scores from on-site tests in English and mathematics required.

2011-2012 Annual costs. Estimated costs as of June 2011: per-credit-hour charge, $493, depending upon level and course of study; academic fee, $200. Certain programs of study require purchase of tools, which could cost an additional $100 to $500. All costs are subject to change.

Application procedures. Admission: No deadline. No application fee. Admission notification on a rolling basis. **Financial aid:** No deadline. FAFSA, institutional form required. Applicants notified on a rolling basis.

Academics. Credit/placement by examination: AP, CLEP. **Support services:** Learning center, tutoring.

Majors. Business: Business admin, construction management, e-commerce, project management. **Communications technology:** Animation/special effects. **Computer sciences:** Applications programming, IT project management, programming, security. **Protective services:** Law enforcement admin. **Visual/performing arts:** Game design.

Computing on campus. Online library available.

Student life. Freshman orientation: Available. Preregistration for classes offered.

Student services. Career counseling, student employment services, placement for graduates.

Contact. Phone: (636) 464-6600 Toll-free number: (888) 488-1082 Fax: (636) 464-6611
James Rowe, Director of Recruitment, ITT Technical Institute: Arnold, 1930 Meyer Drury Drive, Arnold, MO 63010

ITT Technical Institute: Earth City
Earth City, Missouri
www.itt-tech.edu   CB code: 1216

- For-profit 4-year technical college
- Commuter campus in large city
- 1,081 degree-seeking undergraduates
- Interview required

General. Founded in 1936. Accredited by ACICS. **Degrees:** 93 bachelor's, 231 associate awarded. **Location:** 15 miles from St. Louis. **Calendar:** Quarter, extensive summer session. **Full-time faculty:** 20 total. **Part-time faculty:** 60 total.

Basis for selection. Satisfactory scores from on-site tests in English and mathematics required.

2011-2012 Annual costs. Estimated costs as of June 2011: per-credit-hour charge, $493, depending upon level and course of study; academic fee, $200. Certain programs of study require purchase of tools, which could cost an additional $100 to $655. All costs are subject to change.

Application procedures. Admission: No deadline. , may be waived for applicants with need. No application fee. Admission notification on a rolling basis. **Financial aid:** No deadline. FAFSA, institutional form required. Applicants notified on a rolling basis.

Academics. Credit/placement by examination: AP, CLEP. **Support services:** Learning center, tutoring.

Majors. Business: Business admin, construction management, e-commerce, project management. **Communications technology:** Animation/special effects. **Computer sciences:** Applications programming, IT project management, programming, security. **Protective services:** Law enforcement admin.

Computing on campus. Online library available.

Student life. Freshman orientation: Available. Preregistration for classes offered.

Student services. Career counseling, student employment services, placement for graduates.

Contact. Phone: (314) 298-7800 Toll-free number: (800) 235-5488 Fax: (314) 298-0559
Arlen Freeman, Director of Recruitment, ITT Technical Institute: Earth City, 3640 Corporate Trail Drive, Earth City, MO 63045

Kansas City Art Institute
Kansas City, Missouri
www.kcai.edu   CB code: 6330

- Private 4-year visual arts college
- Residential campus in large city
- 777 degree-seeking undergraduates
- 67% of applicants admitted
- SAT or ACT (ACT writing optional), application essay required

General. Founded in 1885. Regionally accredited. One of oldest art and design colleges in the country. **Degrees:** 142 bachelor's awarded. **Location:** 250 miles from St. Louis, 500 miles from Denver. **Calendar:** Semester, limited summer session. **Full-time faculty:** 46 total. **Part-time faculty:** 55 total. **Class size:** 83% < 20, 17% 20-39. **Special facilities:** Gallery for contemporary artists.

Freshman class profile. 650 applied, 433 admitted, 196 enrolled.

Mid 50% test scores			
SAT critical reading:	500-640	GPA 3.0-3.49:	36%
SAT math:	440-570	GPA 2.0-2.99:	32%
SAT writing:	420-640	Rank in top quarter:	34%
ACT composite:	20-26	Rank in top tenth:	2%
GPA 3.75 or higher:	18%	Out-of-state:	64%
GPA 3.50-3.74:	14%	Live on campus:	90%

Basis for selection. High school or GED academic record, 2 letters of recommendation, ACT, SAT or TOEFL scores and a statement of purpose are all used to determine admissions decisions. Portfolio of minimum of 15 pieces of artwork is required/evaluated for admission decisions. **Home schooled:** State high school equivalency certificate required. **Learning Disabled:** Disclosure of special needs recommended but not required.

High school preparation. College-preparatory program recommended. 20 units recommended. Recommended units include English 4, mathematics 3, social studies 3, science 3, visual/performing arts 4 and academic electives 3.

2011-2012 Annual costs. Tuition/fees: $30,762. Room/board: $9,372. Books/supplies: $1,500. Personal expenses: $2,000.

2011-2012 Financial aid. Need-based: Average need met was 69%. Average scholarship/grant was $20,600; average loan $4,021. 71% of total undergraduate aid awarded as scholarships/grants, 29% as loans/jobs. **Non-need-based:** Scholarships awarded for academics, art.

Application procedures. Admission: Priority date 2/1; deadline 8/1 (postmark date). $35 fee, may be waived for applicants with need. Admission notification on a rolling basis beginning on or about 9/1. Must reply by May 1 or within 2 week(s) if notified thereafter. **Financial aid:** Priority date 3/15, closing date 4/1. FAFSA required. Applicants notified on a rolling basis starting 4/1; must reply within 2 week(s) of notification.

Academics. Special study options: Double major, ESL, exchange student, independent study, internships, New York semester, study abroad. **Credit/placement by examination:** AP, CLEP, IB. 15 credit hours maximum toward bachelor's degree. **Support services:** Learning center, reduced course load, remedial instruction, study skills assistance, tutoring, writing center.

Majors. English: Creative writing. **Visual/performing arts:** Art history/conservation, ceramics, cinematography, design, digital arts, drawing, fiber arts, game design, graphic design, illustration, painting, photography, printmaking, sculpture.

Computing on campus. 50 workstations in dormitories, library, computer center. Dormitories wired for high-speed internet access and linked to campus network. Commuter students can connect to campus network. Online course registration, online library, helpline, wireless network available.

Student life. Freshman orientation: Mandatory. Preregistration for classes offered. 3-day program held prior to start of academic year. **Housing:** Guaranteed on-campus for freshmen. Coed dorms, apartments, wellness housing available. $225 nonrefundable deposit, deadline 6/1. **Activities:** Film society, international student organizations, literary magazine, student government, Xenos Society, Black Artist's Culture and Community.

Student services. Adult student services, alcohol/substance abuse counseling, career counseling, student employment services, financial aid counseling, minority student services, personal counseling, veterans' counselor. **Physically disabled:** Services for visually, speech, hearing impaired.

Contact. E-mail: admiss@kcai.edu
Phone: (816) 474-5224 Toll-free number: (800) 522-5224
Fax: (816) 802-3309
Kansas City Art Institute, 4415 Warwick Boulevard, Kansas City, MO 64111

Lincoln University
Jefferson City, Missouri
www.lincolnu.edu   **CB code: 6366**

- Public 4-year university and liberal arts college
- Commuter campus in large town
- 2,686 degree-seeking undergraduates: 19% part-time, 60% women, 49% African American, 1% Asian American, 2% Hispanic American, 2% international
- 172 degree-seeking graduate students

General. Founded in 1866. Regionally accredited. 1890 land-grant institution. Historically Black College and University (HBCU). **Degrees:** 317 bachelor's, 85 associate awarded; master's offered. **ROTC:** Army, Naval, Air Force. **Location:** 132 miles from St. Louis, 157 miles from Kansas City. **Calendar:** Semester, limited summer session. **Full-time faculty:** 146 total; 32% minority, 47% women. **Part-time faculty:** 98 total; 5% minority, 56% women. **Class size:** 49% < 20, 46% 20-39, 4% 40-49, less than 1% 50-99. **Special facilities:** Ethnic studies center and archives, 3 research farms, agriculture and extension information center, native plants outdoor laboratory.

Freshman class profile.

Mid 50% test scores			
SAT critical reading:	340-470	Rank in top quarter:	13%
SAT math:	340-450	Rank in top tenth:	4%
ACT composite:	14-19	End year in good standing:	58%
GPA 3.75 or higher:	4%	Return as sophomores:	48%
GPA 3.50-3.74:	9%	Out-of-state:	26%
GPA 3.0-3.49:	13%	Live on campus:	65%
GPA 2.0-2.99:	52%	International:	2%

Basis for selection. Open admission, but selective for some programs and for out-of-state students. ACT or SAT scores required, but used for placement purposes only. Special requirements for nursing and education programs. Audition required for sacred music and music education students. **Home schooled:** Transcript of courses and grades required. Must submit a transcript with the parent's notarized signature, demonstrating completion of the Missouri Minimum Core Curriculum or its equivalency, as determined by the University. **Learning Disabled:** Comprehensive documentation of disability by qualified professional must be on file to request accommodations.

High school preparation. College-preparatory program recommended. 18 units required; 20 recommended. Required and recommended units include English 4, mathematics 3, social studies 3, science 3 (laboratory 1), foreign language 2, visual/performing arts 1 and academic electives 3. Social studies courses should include 1 unit of U.S. history and at least 1 semester of government.

2011-2012 Annual costs. Tuition/fees: $6,478; $11,965 out-of-state. Full-time students must pay $247.50 per semester for health insurance if proof of other coverage is not provided. Enrollment in the student health insurance program is required for international students. Lab and/or course fees are charged, depending on program. Room/board: $5,271. Books/supplies: $1,000. Personal expenses: $3,051.

2011-2012 Financial aid. Need-based: 587 full-time freshmen applied for aid; 565 were judged to have need; 565 of these received aid. Average need met was 59%. Average scholarship/grant was $5,316; average loan $3,446. 59% of total undergraduate aid awarded as scholarships/grants, 41% as loans/jobs. **Non-need-based:** Awarded to 129 full-time undergraduates, including 32 freshmen. Scholarships awarded for academics, art, athletics, job skills, leadership, minority status, music/drama, ROTC, state residency.

Application procedures. Admission: Closing date 7/15 (postmark date). $20 fee, may be waived for applicants with need. Admission notification on a rolling basis. **Financial aid:** Priority date 3/1; no closing date. FAFSA, institutional form required. Applicants notified on a rolling basis starting 3/15; must reply within 2 week(s) of notification.

Academics. Special study options: Accelerated study, cross-registration, distance learning, double major, dual enrollment of high school students, exchange student, honors, independent study, internships, study abroad, teacher certification program. Senior citizen program. **Credit/placement by examination:** AP, CLEP, SAT, ACT, institutional tests. 15 credit hours maximum toward associate degree, 20 toward bachelor's. Total number of alternative credit hours cannot exceed 30. Students may receive credit only for courses numbered 100-299. Each examination may be taken only once. Students must be currently enrolled during the semester in which he/she elects to take the exam. **Support services:** Learning center, pre-admission summer program, reduced course load, remedial instruction, study skills assistance, tutoring, writing center.

Majors. Biology: General. **Business:** Accounting, business admin, marketing. **Communications:** Journalism. **Computer sciences:** Information systems. **Conservation:** Environmental science. **Education:** Art, biology, business, chemistry, elementary, English, mathematics, middle, music, physical, physics, social science, special ed. **English:** English lit. **Foreign languages:** Spanish. **General:** Business. **Health services:** Clinical lab science, nursing (RN). **History:** General. **Human services:** General, social work. **Liberal arts:** Arts/sciences. **Math:** General. **Physical sciences:** Chemistry, physics. **Protective services:** Law enforcement admin. **Psychology:** General. **Social sciences:** Political science, sociology. **Theology:** Sacred music. **Visual/performing arts:** Studio arts. **Work/family studies:** Food/nutrition.

Most popular majors. Business/marketing 24%, education 13%, health sciences 7%, liberal arts 9%, psychology 6%, security/protective services 9%.

Computing on campus. 315 workstations in dormitories, library, computer center, student center. Dormitories wired for high-speed internet access and linked to campus network. Online library, helpline, wireless network available.

Student life. Freshman orientation: Mandatory, $50 fee. Preregistration for classes offered. Summer and Winter orientations are 1.5 day programs. Other sessions throughout the year. **Policies:** Unmarried students under 21, whose primary domicile is beyond a 60-mile radius of the University, are required to live in residence halls for four consecutive semesters. Armed Forces veterans and any student who has established a local primary domicile one year prior to entering the University are exempt. **Housing:** Guaranteed on-campus for freshmen. Coed dorms, single-sex dorms, wellness housing available. $125 fully refundable deposit, deadline 7/1. Honors housing available. **Activities:** Bands, campus ministries, choral groups, dance, drama, international student organizations, literary magazine, music ensembles, radio station, student government, student newspaper, TV station, Baptist Student Center, Wesley Foundation.

Athletics. NCAA. **Intercollegiate:** Baseball M, basketball, cheerleading M, cross-country W, football (tackle) M, golf, softball W, tennis W, track and field. **Intramural:** Basketball, bowling, volleyball, weight lifting. **Team name:** Blue Tigers.

Student services. Career counseling, services for economically disadvantaged, financial aid counseling, health services, personal counseling, veterans' counselor. **Physically disabled:** Services for visually, speech, hearing impaired.

Contact. E-mail: enroll@lincolnu.edu
Phone: (573) 681-5599 Toll-free number: (800) 521-5052
Fax: (573) 681-5889
Roxanne Seidner, Director of Admissions, Lincoln University, 820 Chestnut Street, B7 Young Hall, Jefferson City, MO 65102-0029

Lindenwood University
St. Charles, Missouri
www.lindenwood.edu/   **CB code: 6367**

- Private 4-year university and liberal arts college affiliated with Presbyterian Church (USA)
- Residential campus in large city
- 7,374 degree-seeking undergraduates: 5% part-time, 55% women, 16% African American, 1% Asian American, 1% Native American, 10% international
- 3,607 degree-seeking graduate students
- 53% of applicants admitted
- SAT or ACT (ACT writing optional), application essay required
- 45% graduate within 6 years

General. Founded in 1827. Regionally accredited. **Degrees:** 1,312 bachelor's awarded; master's, doctoral offered. **ROTC:** Army. **Location:** 20 miles from St. Louis. **Calendar:** 4-1-4, limited summer session. **Full-time faculty:** 240 total; 78% have terminal degrees, 8% minority, 39% women. **Part-time faculty:** 496 total; 34% have terminal degrees, 11% minority, 44% women. **Class size:** 64% < 20, 36% 20-39, less than 1% 40-49, less than 1% 50-99. **Special facilities:** Greenhouse, wetland program facility, success center, natural history, professional theater, archeological sites.

Freshman class profile. 3,335 applied, 1,780 admitted, 1,027 enrolled.

Mid 50% test scores		Rank in top quarter:	38%
SAT critical reading:	440-550	Rank in top tenth:	12%
SAT math:	470-570	Return as sophomores:	71%
SAT writing:	340-520	Out-of-state:	33%
ACT composite:	20-24	Live on campus:	79%
GPA 3.75 or higher:	20%	International:	11%
GPA 3.50-3.74:	13%	Fraternities:	1%
GPA 3.0-3.49:	34%	Sororities:	1%
GPA 2.0-2.99:	31%		

Basis for selection. Class rank, school record, high school GPA very important. **Home schooled:** Transcript of courses and grades required.

High school preparation. College-preparatory program recommended. 16 units recommended. Recommended units include English 4, mathematics 3, social studies 3, history 3, science 3 (laboratory 1), foreign language 2 and visual/performing arts 1.

2011-2012 Annual costs. Tuition/fees: $14,360. Room/board: $7,000. Books/supplies: $3,000. Personal expenses: $9,000.

2011-2012 Financial aid. Need-based: 762 full-time freshmen applied for aid; 670 were judged to have need; 670 of these received aid. Average need met was 90%. Average scholarship/grant was $7,113; average loan $3,294. 59% of total undergraduate aid awarded as scholarships/grants, 41% as loans/jobs. **Non-need-based:** Awarded to 6,692 full-time undergraduates, including 688 freshmen. Scholarships awarded for academics, alumni affiliation, art, athletics, job skills, music/drama, ROTC.

Application procedures. Admission: No deadline. $30 fee, may be waived for applicants with need. Admission notification on a rolling basis. **Financial aid:** Priority date 4/1; no closing date. FAFSA required. Applicants notified on a rolling basis.

Academics. Special study options: Accelerated study, combined bachelor's/graduate degree, distance learning, double major, dual enrollment of high school students, ESL, external degree, honors, independent study, internships, student-designed major, study abroad, teacher certification program. **Credit/placement by examination:** AP, CLEP, IB, institutional tests. **Support services:** Learning center, reduced course load, remedial instruction, study skills assistance, tutoring, writing center.

Majors. Area/ethnic studies: American. **Biology:** General, environmental. **Business:** General, accounting, business admin, communications, entrepreneurial studies, finance, hospitality admin, human resources, international, management information systems, marketing, nonprofit/public, retailing. **Communications:** Advertising, communications/speech/rhetoric, digital media, journalism, media studies, organizational. **Computer sciences:** General, computer science, information technology. **Conservation:** Environmental science. **Education:** Art, biology, business, chemistry, early childhood, early childhood special, elementary, French, history, middle, physical, science, social studies, Spanish, technology/industrial arts, trade/industrial. **English:** Creative writing, English lit. **Foreign languages:** French, Spanish. **Health services:** Athletic training, health care admin. **History:** General. **Human services:** General, social work. **Math:** General. **Parks/recreation:** General, exercise sciences, sports admin. **Philosophy/religion:** Christian, philosophy, religion. **Physical sciences:** Chemistry. **Protective services:** Criminal justice, fire services admin. **Psychology:** General. **Social sciences:** Anthropology, criminology, economics, international relations, political science, sociology. **Theology:** Pastoral counseling, youth ministry. **Visual/performing arts:** General, acting, art, art history/conservation, dance, directing/producing, dramatic, fashion design, multimedia, music, music management, music performance, music theory/composition, musical theater, studio arts, studio arts management, theater arts management, theater design.

Most popular majors. Business/marketing 42%, communications/journalism 6%, education 13%, security/protective services 8%, visual/performing arts 6%.

Computing on campus. 198 workstations in library, computer center, student center. Dormitories wired for high-speed internet access and linked to campus network. Commuter students can connect to campus network. Online course registration, online library, helpline, wireless network available.

Student life. Freshman orientation: Mandatory. Preregistration for classes offered. Held 5 days before the beginning of fall semester. **Policies:** Zero tolerance of illegal substances. **Housing:** Single-sex dorms, special housing for disabled, apartments, fraternity/sorority housing available. $300 nonrefundable deposit. **Activities:** Bands, campus ministries, choral groups, dance, drama, film society, international student organizations, literary magazine, music ensembles, musical theater, radio station, student government, student newspaper, symphony orchestra, TV station, Campus Crusade for Christ, Intercultural club, American Humanics, Circle K, Reform Campus Fellowship, Lewis & Clark Historical Society, Eastern Debating Society, Christian Life Group, Fellowship of Christian Athletes.

Athletics. NCAA. **Intercollegiate:** Baseball M, basketball, cross-country, diving, field hockey W, football (tackle) M, golf, ice hockey, lacrosse, soccer, softball W, swimming, tennis, track and field, water polo, wrestling M. **Intramural:** Basketball, football (non-tackle), soccer, volleyball, water polo. **Team name:** Lions.

Student services. Adult student services, chaplain/spiritual director, career counseling, student employment services, financial aid counseling, health services, personal counseling, placement for graduates, veterans' counselor. **Physically disabled:** Services for visually, hearing impaired.

Contact. E-mail: admissions@lindenwood.edu
Phone: (636) 949-4949 Fax: (636) 949-4989
Joe Parisi, Dean of Undergraduate Day Admissions, Lindenwood University, 209 South Kingshighway, St. Charles, MO 63301

Maryville University of Saint Louis
St. Louis, Missouri
www.maryville.edu
CB member
CB code: 6399

- Private 4-year university
- Commuter campus in very large city
- 2,948 degree-seeking undergraduates: 41% part-time, 74% women, 9% African American, 1% Asian American, 2% Hispanic American, 2% international
- 776 degree-seeking graduate students
- 67% of applicants admitted
- SAT or ACT (ACT writing optional) required
- 66% graduate within 6 years; 9% enter graduate study

General. Founded in 1872. Regionally accredited. **Degrees:** 579 bachelor's awarded; master's, doctoral offered. **ROTC:** Army. **Location:** 20 miles from downtown. **Calendar:** Semester, limited summer session. **Full-time faculty:** 107 total; 85% have terminal degrees, 15% minority, 60% women. **Part-time faculty:** 314 total; 35% have terminal degrees, 4% minority, 65% women. **Class size:** 67% < 20, 33% 20-39, less than 1% 50-99. **Special facilities:** Observatory, walking trails, coffeehouse, teaching laboratory, clinical laboratories, communications laboratory, multi-media classrooms.

Freshman class profile. 1,234 applied, 832 admitted, 354 enrolled.

Mid 50% test scores		Rank in top quarter:	57%
ACT composite:	23-27	Rank in top tenth:	23%
GPA 3.75 or higher:	44%	Return as sophomores:	82%
GPA 3.50-3.74:	20%	Out-of-state:	36%
GPA 3.0-3.49:	27%	Live on campus:	72%
GPA 2.0-2.99:	9%	International:	3%

Basis for selection. School record most important. Recommendations and extracurricular activities considered. ACT or SAT very important. Interview and 20 hours observation in clinical setting required for physical therapy students. Audition required for music therapy students; portfolio required for art education, graphic design, interior design, and studio art majors. **Home schooled:** Increased weight placed on ACT or SAT scores.

High school preparation. College-preparatory program recommended. 22 units required. Required and recommended units include English 4, mathematics 3, social studies 2, science 2, foreign language 3 and academic electives 8. Applicants for actuarial science, art, education, interior design, clinical laboratory science, nursing, occupational therapy, and physical therapy must meet other specific requirements.

2011-2012 Annual costs. Tuition/fees: $22,882. Room/board: $8,892. Books/supplies: $1,600. Personal expenses: $2,542.

Financial aid. Non-need-based: Scholarships awarded for academics, art, athletics, leadership, minority status, ROTC, state residency.

Application procedures. Admission: Priority date 12/15; deadline 8/15. $30 fee, may be waived for applicants with need, free for online applicants. Admission notification on a rolling basis. Must reply by May 1 or within 4 week(s) if notified thereafter. **Financial aid:** Priority date 3/1; no closing date. FAFSA required. Applicants notified on a rolling basis starting 2/15; must reply by 5/1 or within 2 week(s) of notification.

Academics. Special study options: Accelerated study, combined bachelor's/graduate degree, cooperative education, cross-registration, distance learning, double major, dual enrollment of high school students, honors, independent study, internships, liberal arts/career combination, semester at sea, student-designed major, study abroad, teacher certification program, Washington semester, weekend college. **Credit/placement by examination:** AP, CLEP, IB, SAT, ACT, institutional tests. 30 credit hours maximum toward bachelor's degree. **Support services:** Learning center, reduced course load, study skills assistance, tutoring, writing center.

Majors. Biology: General, biochemistry, biomedical sciences. **Business:** General, accounting, actuarial science, business admin, e-commerce, management information systems, marketing. **Communications:** Media studies. **Computer sciences:** Computer science. **Conservation:** Environmental science, environmental studies. **Education:** Art, early childhood, elementary, middle, science. **English:** English lit. **Health services:** Clinical lab science, music therapy, nursing (RN), predental, vocational rehab counseling. **History:** General. **Liberal arts:** Arts/sciences. **Math:** General, applied. **Parks/recreation:** Sports admin. **Philosophy/religion:** Philosophy. **Physical sciences:** Chemistry, forensic chemistry. **Psychology:** General, industrial, social. **Social sciences:** Criminology, sociology. **Visual/performing arts:** Graphic design, interior design, studio arts.

Most popular majors. Business/marketing 26%, health sciences 38%, psychology 9%, visual/performing arts 8%.

Computing on campus. 450 workstations in dormitories, library, computer center, student center. Dormitories wired for high-speed internet access and linked to campus network. Commuter students can connect to campus network. Online course registration, online library, helpline, student web hosting, wireless network available.

Student life. Freshman orientation: Available. Preregistration for classes offered. 3-day program prior to start of classes. **Housing:** Guaranteed on-campus for all undergraduates. Coed dorms, apartments, wellness housing available. $150 partly refundable deposit, deadline 5/1. **Activities:** Bands, campus ministries, choral groups, dance, drama, literary magazine, music ensembles, student government, student newspaper, symphony orchestra, Association of Black Collegians, multicultural club, community service club, Baptist Student Union, Fellowship of Christian Athletes, Lutheran Student Fellowship, Muslim student association, Jewish Student Union, Physical Therapy Club, Saints Nation.

Athletics. NCAA. **Intercollegiate:** Basketball, cross-country, golf, soccer, softball W, tennis, track and field, volleyball W, wrestling M. **Intramural:** Basketball, bowling, cheerleading, football (non-tackle), soccer, softball, volleyball. **Team name:** Saints.

Student services. Adult student services, alcohol/substance abuse counseling, chaplain/spiritual director, career counseling, student employment services, financial aid counseling, health services, minority student services, personal counseling, placement for graduates, veterans' counselor. **Physically disabled:** Services for visually, speech, hearing impaired.

Contact. E-mail: admissions@maryville.edu
Phone: (314) 529-9350 Toll-free number: (800) 627-9855 ext. 9350
Fax: (314) 529-9927
Shani Lenore-Jenkins, Assistant Vice President of Enrollment, Maryville University of Saint Louis, 650 Maryville University Drive, St. Louis, MO 63141-7299

Midwest University
Wentzville, Missouri
www.midwest.edu

‣ Private two-year upper-division university and seminary college
‣ Large town

General. Regionally accredited. **Calendar:** Semester.

Annual costs/financial aid. Tuition/fees (2011-2012): $7,610. Room: $3,024. Books/supplies: $450.

Contact. Phone: (636) 327-4645
Registrar and Director of Admissions, 851 Parr Road, Wentzville, MO 63385

Missouri Baptist University
St. Louis, Missouri
www.mobap.edu   CB code: 2258

‣ Private 4-year university and liberal arts college affiliated with Baptist faith
‣ Commuter campus in very large city
‣ 1,691 degree-seeking undergraduates: 17% part-time, 58% women, 9% African American, 1% Asian American, 3% Hispanic American, 1% Native American, 2% international
‣ 1,289 degree-seeking graduate students
‣ 58% of applicants admitted
‣ 37% graduate within 6 years

General. Founded in 1963. Regionally accredited. **Degrees:** 374 bachelor's, 3 associate awarded; master's, doctoral offered. **ROTC:** Army. **Location:** 20 miles from downtown. **Calendar:** Semester, limited summer session. **Full-time faculty:** 75 total. **Part-time faculty:** 225 total. **Special facilities:** Coffee house.

Freshman class profile. 740 applied, 432 admitted, 235 enrolled.

Mid 50% test scores			
SAT critical reading:	370-460	ACT composite:	19-24
SAT math:	420-490	Return as sophomores:	66%
		International:	1%

Basis for selection. Minimum 2.0 high school GPA. Minimum score of 20 is required for ACT and/or a minimum score of 950 (exclusive of Writing) on SAT. Final class rank must be in the upper 50 percent of graduating class. Applicants with high school GPA below 2.0 may be admitted on a probational status. An ACT or SAT test score is not required if the high school graduation date is more than two years from the date of matriculation. Interview and/or essay required for academically weak students; audition required for music majors. **Learning Disabled:** Must self-identify to the Special Needs Access Office, provide current written documentation of disability from qualified professional or agency, and request accommodations. Documentation must meet institutional criteria, indicate substantial limitation, and be completed 6 weeks prior to start of class.

High school preparation. 24 units required. Required units include English 4, mathematics 3, social studies 3, science 3 (laboratory 1), visual/performing arts 1 and academic electives 7. 1 practical arts, 1 physical education, .5 health education, .5 personal finance required.

2011-2012 Annual costs. Tuition/fees: $19,510. Room/board: $8,490. Books/supplies: $2,000. Personal expenses: $1,659.

Financial aid. Non-need-based: Scholarships awarded for academics, alumni affiliation, athletics, leadership, music/drama, religious affiliation.

Application procedures. Admission: No deadline. $30 fee, may be waived for applicants with need, free for online applicants. Admission notification on a rolling basis. **Financial aid:** Priority date 4/1; no closing date. FAFSA, institutional form required. Applicants notified on a rolling basis starting 4/15; must reply within 2 week(s) of notification.

Academics. Special study options: Accelerated study, combined bachelor's/graduate degree, cooperative education, cross-registration, distance learning, double major, dual enrollment of high school students, independent study, internships, liberal arts/career combination, student-designed major, study abroad, teacher certification program, urban semester, Washington semester. **Credit/placement by examination:** AP, CLEP, institutional tests. 45 credit hours maximum toward bachelor's degree. No single source may account for more than 30 of the 45 credit-hour maximum. **Support services:** Learning center, reduced course load, remedial instruction, study skills assistance, tutoring, writing center.

Majors. Biology: General, biochemistry, biotechnology. **Business:** Accounting, business admin, marketing, operations. **Communications:** Media studies, public relations, radio/TV. **Computer sciences:** Information technology. **Education:** General, business, drama/dance, early childhood, elementary, health, middle, music, physical, science, secondary. **English:** English lit. **Health services:** Health care admin. **History:** General. **Human services:** Community org/advocacy. **Liberal arts:** Arts/sciences. **Math:** General. **Parks/recreation:** Exercise sciences, sports admin. **Philosophy/religion:** Christian. **Physical sciences:** Chemistry. **Protective services:** Criminal justice. **Psychology:** General. **Social sciences:** General. **Theology:** Sacred music. **Visual/performing arts:** Music, music management, music performance, musical theater. **Work/family studies:** Child development.

Computing on campus. 60 workstations in dormitories, library, computer center, student center. Dormitories wired for high-speed internet access and linked to campus network. Commuter students can connect to campus network. Online library, helpline, wireless network available.

Student life. Freshman orientation: Mandatory. Preregistration for classes offered. **Policies:** Religious observance required. **Housing:** Single-sex dorms, apartments, wellness housing available. $250 deposit, deadline 6/1. **Activities:** Bands, campus ministries, choral groups, drama, international student organizations, literary magazine, music ensembles, musical theater, opera, radio station, student government, student newspaper, Baptist Student Union, Fellowship of Christian Athletes, Student Mission, state teachers association, Ministerial Alliance, science club, computer club, College Music Educators National Conference, Students in Free Enterprise.

Athletics. NAIA. **Intercollegiate:** Baseball M, basketball, bowling, cheerleading, cross-country, golf, lacrosse W, soccer, softball W, tennis W, track and field, volleyball, wrestling M. **Intramural:** Basketball, softball, volleyball. **Team name:** Spartans.

Student services. Adult student services, chaplain/spiritual director, career counseling, student employment services, financial aid counseling, personal counseling, placement for graduates, veterans' counselor. **Physically disabled:** Services for visually, hearing impaired.

Contact. E-mail: admissions@mobap.edu
Phone: (314) 392-2290 Toll-free number: (877) 434-1115
Fax: (314) 392-2292
Aaron Black, Director of Admissions, Missouri Baptist University, One College Park Drive, St. Louis, MO 63141-8660

Missouri Southern State University
Joplin, Missouri
www.mssu.edu   CB code: 6322

- Public 4-year university and liberal arts college
- Commuter campus in large town
- 5,140 degree-seeking undergraduates: 22% part-time, 58% women
- 46 degree-seeking graduate students
- 97% of applicants admitted
- SAT or ACT (ACT writing optional), SAT Subject Tests required

General. Founded in 1937. Regionally accredited. Extension courses offered in Lamar, Monett, Nevada (evening only), limited weekend courses. Television and online courses offered. **Degrees:** 860 bachelor's, 175 associate awarded; master's offered. **Location:** 138 miles from Kansas City, 126 miles from Tulsa, Oklahoma. **Calendar:** Semester, extensive summer session. **Full-time faculty:** 206 total. **Part-time faculty:** 100 total. **Class size:** 48% < 20, 50% 20-39, 2% 40-49, less than 1% 50-99. **Special facilities:** Biology pond, crime lab, child development center, small business development center, indoor "livefire" firearms range, performing arts center, greenhouse, law library, cyber coffee shop.

Freshman class profile. 1,691 applied, 1,640 admitted, 771 enrolled.

Mid 50% test scores		Rank in top quarter:	24%
ACT composite:	18-24	Rank in top tenth:	12%
GPA 3.75 or higher:	20%	Out-of-state:	14%
GPA 3.50-3.74:	15%	Live on campus:	47%
GPA 3.0-3.49:	25%	Fraternities:	1%
GPA 2.0-2.99:	36%	Sororities:	1%

Basis for selection. Minimum 18 ACT or rank in upper 50% of class. ACT recommended. International students must score in 75th percentile on Michigan Test for English as foreign language. **Home schooled:** Transcript of courses and grades required. Transcript with GPA; final transcript with date of graduation needed prior to enrollment; ACT composite score of 21 or GPA of 2.25. Must meet high school core requirements. **Learning Disabled:** Submission of documentation is not the same as the request for services. Request for services and/or accommodations must be initiated by the student after admission.

High school preparation. College-preparatory program recommended. 16 units required. Required and recommended units include English 4, mathematics 3, science 2 (laboratory 1), visual/performing arts 1 and academic electives 3.

2011-2012 Annual costs. Tuition/fees: $5,386; $10,276 out-of-state. Room/board: $5,976. Books/supplies: $800. Personal expenses: $1,350.

Financial aid. Non-need-based: Scholarships awarded for academics, alumni affiliation, art, athletics, minority status, music/drama, religious affiliation, state residency.

Application procedures. Admission: Priority date 8/1; no deadline. $25 fee, may be waived for applicants with need. Admission notification on a rolling basis beginning on or about 9/1. **Financial aid:** Closing date 4/1. FAFSA required. Applicants notified on a rolling basis starting 3/1; must reply by 5/1.

Academics. Special study options: Accelerated study, combined bachelor's/graduate degree, cooperative education, distance learning, double major, dual enrollment of high school students, ESL, exchange student, honors, independent study, internships, liberal arts/career combination, study abroad, teacher certification program, weekend college. **Credit/placement by examination:** AP, CLEP, IB, SAT, ACT, institutional tests. **Support services:** Learning center, reduced course load, remedial instruction, study skills assistance, tutoring, writing center.

Honors college/program. Entrance by invitation. Approximately 30 students admitted each year. Application closing date March 1. Require 28 ACT or 3.5 GPA.

Majors. Biology: General, bacteriology, biochemistry, biotechnology, conservation, ecology, genetics, marine. **Business:** General, accounting, finance, financial planning, international, management science, marketing, operations. **Communications:** Communications/speech/rhetoric, media studies. **Computer sciences:** General, computer science, information systems, programming. **Conservation:** General, management/policy. **Education:** General, art, biology, business, chemistry, early childhood, elementary, English, ESL, foreign languages, French, German, health, history, mathematics, middle, multi-level teacher, music, physical, physics, reading, science, secondary, social science, Spanish, special ed, speech, technology/industrial arts. **Engineering:** Industrial. **English:** Creative writing, English lit, technical writing. **Foreign languages:** French, German, Spanish. **Health services:** Environmental health, nursing (RN), predental, premedicine, prepharmacy, preveterinary. **History:** General. **Math:** General, computational. **Parks/recreation:** Health/fitness. **Physical sciences:** Chemistry, physics. **Protective services:** Forensics, law enforcement admin. **Psychology:** General. **Social sciences:** General, international relations, political science, sociology. **Visual/performing arts:** Dramatic, music, studio arts.

Most popular majors. Business/marketing 23%, education 16%, English 12%, health sciences 10%, security/protective services 10%.

Computing on campus. 522 workstations in library, computer center, student center. Dormitories wired for high-speed internet access and linked to campus network. Commuter students can connect to campus network. Online library, helpline, repair service, student web hosting, wireless network available.

Student life. Freshman orientation: Mandatory, $50 fee. Preregistration for classes offered. One-day introduction to campus and enrollment process during summer, plus 8-week course. **Policies:** Freshmen must live in residence halls if space is available, unless married, residing with relatives, or excused by the Coordinator of Student Housing. **Housing:** Guaranteed on-campus for freshmen. Coed dorms, single-sex dorms, apartments available. **Activities:** Bands, campus ministries, choral groups, dance, drama, film society, international student organizations, literary magazine, music ensembles, Model UN, musical theater, opera, radio station, student government, student newspaper, symphony orchestra, TV station, over 90 clubs and organizations available.

Athletics. NCAA. **Intercollegiate:** Baseball M, basketball, cheerleading, cross-country, football (tackle) M, golf M, soccer W, softball W, tennis W, track and field, volleyball W. **Intramural:** Basketball, football (non-tackle), golf, racquetball, soccer, softball, table tennis, tennis, volleyball. **Team name:** Lions, Lady Lions.

Student services. Adult student services, alcohol/substance abuse counseling, career counseling, services for economically disadvantaged, student employment services, financial aid counseling, health services, on-campus daycare, personal counseling, placement for graduates, veterans' counselor. **Physically disabled:** Services for visually, speech, hearing impaired.

Contact. E-mail: admissions@mssu.edu
Phone: (417) 625-9378 Toll-free number: (866) 818-6778
Fax: (417) 659-4429
Derek Skaggs, Director of Enrollment Services, Missouri Southern State University, 3950 East Newman Road, Joplin, MO 64801-1595

Missouri State University
Springfield, Missouri
www.missouristate.edu   CB code: 6665

- Public 4-year university
- Residential campus in small city
- 15,263 degree-seeking undergraduates: 12% part-time, 55% women, 4% African American, 1% Asian American, 3% Hispanic American, 1% Native American, 4% international
- 2,608 degree-seeking graduate students
- 83% of applicants admitted
- SAT or ACT (ACT writing optional) required

General. Founded in 1906. Regionally accredited. **Degrees:** 3,131 bachelor's awarded; master's, professional offered. **ROTC:** Army. **Location:** 180 miles from Kansas City. **Calendar:** Semester, extensive summer session. **Full-time faculty:** 699 total; 79% have terminal degrees, 12% minority, 46% women. **Part-time faculty:** 332 total; 22% have terminal degrees, 4% minority, 55% women. **Class size:** 28% < 20, 48% 20-39, 9% 50-99, 3% >100. **Special facilities:** Observatory, 125-acre agriculture research and demonstration center, summer tent theater, archaeological research center, social research center, agriculture research center.

Freshman class profile. 7,072 applied, 5,876 admitted, 2,599 enrolled.

Mid 50% test scores		Rank in top quarter:	50%
SAT critical reading:	510-630	Rank in top tenth:	23%
SAT math:	460-600	Return as sophomores:	75%
ACT composite:	21-26	Out-of-state:	9%
GPA 3.75 or higher:	40%	Live on campus:	70%
GPA 3.50-3.74:	19%	International:	1%
GPA 3.0-3.49:	28%	Fraternities:	23%
GPA 2.0-2.99:	13%	Sororities:	22%

Basis for selection. Applicant must have 108 or higher on selection index (sum of high school class rank percentile and test score percentile).

High school preparation. College-preparatory program required. 24 units required. Required and recommended units include English 4, mathematics 3, social studies 2, history 1, science 3 (laboratory 1), foreign language 2, visual/performing arts 1 and academic electives 3. 7 additional electives required.

2011-2012 Annual costs. Tuition/fees: $6,598; $12,418 out-of-state. Room/board: $6,582. Books/supplies: $900. Personal expenses: $3,500.

2011-2012 Financial aid. Need-based: 2,298 full-time freshmen applied for aid; 1,657 were judged to have need; 1,630 of these received aid. Average need met was 56%. Average scholarship/grant was $5,027; average loan $2,999. 43% of total undergraduate aid awarded as scholarships/grants, 57% as loans/jobs. **Non-need-based:** Awarded to 2,423 full-time undergraduates, including 698 freshmen. Scholarships awarded for academics, alumni affiliation, art, athletics, job skills, leadership, minority status, music/drama, ROTC, state residency. **Additional information:** Extensive scholarship program offered to freshmen and transfer students. Out-of-state fee stipends available. Student employment service available to assist students in securing employment on campus and in community.

Application procedures. Admission: Priority date 3/1; deadline 7/20 (postmark date). $35 fee, may be waived for applicants with need. Admission notification on a rolling basis beginning on or about 7/1. **Financial aid:** Priority date 3/31; no closing date. FAFSA required. Applicants notified on a rolling basis starting 3/31; must reply within 4 week(s) of notification.

Academics. Special study options: Accelerated study, combined bachelor's/graduate degree, cooperative education, distance learning, double major, dual enrollment of high school students, ESL, exchange student, honors, independent study, internships, liberal arts/career combination, student-designed major, study abroad, teacher certification program. **Credit/placement by examination:** AP, CLEP, IB, SAT, ACT, institutional tests. **Support services:** Learning center, pre-admission summer program, study skills assistance, tutoring, writing center.

Honors college/program. Minimum 27 ACT or 1220 (exclusive of Writing) SAT, rank in top 10th percentile of high school class or graduated high school with a 3.9 cumulative GPA. Approximately 250 to 300 freshmen enroll each year. Program includes freshman honors seminar, honors general education courses, departmental honors courses, senior project, senior honors seminar.

Majors. Architecture: Urban/community planning. **Biology:** General, cellular/molecular. **Business:** General, accounting, business admin, construction management, entrepreneurial studies, finance, hospitality admin, insurance, logistics, management information systems, marketing. **Communications:** Communications/speech/rhetoric, journalism, media studies, organizational, political, public relations, radio/TV. **Computer sciences:** Computer science. **Conservation:** Wildlife/wilderness. **Education:** Agricultural, art, biology, business, chemistry, early childhood, elementary, English, family/consumer sciences, French, German, history, Latin, mathematics, middle, music, physical, physics, science, Spanish, special ed, technology/industrial arts. **English:** English lit, technical writing. **Foreign languages:** French, German, Latin, Spanish. **General:** Agribusiness operations, agronomy, animal sciences, horticultural science. **Health services:** Athletic training, audiology/speech pathology, clinical lab science, dietetics, nursing (RN), predental, premedicine, prepharmacy, preveterinary, radiologic technology/medical imaging, respiratory therapy technology. **History:** General. **Human services:** General, social work. **Liberal arts:** Humanities. **Math:** General. **Parks/recreation:** General, exercise sciences. **Philosophy/religion:** Philosophy, religion. **Physical sciences:** Chemistry, geology, physics. **Psychology:** General. **Social sciences:** Anthropology, criminology, economics, geography, political science, sociology. **Visual/performing arts:** General, art, art history/conservation,

dance, design, dramatic, multimedia, music, music performance. **Work/family studies:** Clothing/textiles, facilities/event planning, family studies, housing.

Most popular majors. Business/marketing 33%, education 14%, social sciences 8%.

Computing on campus. 2,000 workstations in dormitories, library, computer center, student center. Dormitories wired for high-speed internet access and linked to campus network. Commuter students can connect to campus network. Online library, helpline, student web hosting, wireless network available.

Student life. Freshman orientation: Mandatory, $40 fee. Preregistration for classes offered. 2-day program held during summer. **Housing:** Guaranteed on-campus for freshmen. Coed dorms, special housing for disabled, apartments, fraternity/sorority housing available. $100 fully refundable deposit, deadline 7/1. **Activities:** Bands, campus ministries, choral groups, dance, drama, film society, international student organizations, Model UN, radio station, student government, student newspaper, symphony orchestra, nearly 300 student organizations available.

Athletics. NCAA. **Intercollegiate:** Baseball M, basketball, cross-country, field hockey W, football (tackle) M, golf, soccer, softball W, swimming, track and field, volleyball W. **Intramural:** Basketball, bowling, football (non-tackle), golf, racquetball, soccer, softball, table tennis, tennis, track and field, volleyball, weight lifting, wrestling. **Team name:** Bears.

Student services. Adult student services, alcohol/substance abuse counseling, chaplain/spiritual director, career counseling, services for economically disadvantaged, student employment services, financial aid counseling, health services, legal services, minority student services, on-campus daycare, personal counseling, placement for graduates, veterans' counselor. **Physically disabled:** Services for visually, speech, hearing impaired.

Contact. E-mail: info@missouristate.edu
Phone: (417) 836-5517 Toll-free number: (800) 492-7900
Fax: (417) 836-5137
Andrew Wright, Director of Admissions, Missouri State University, 901 South National Avenue, Springfield, MO 65897

Missouri Technical School
St. Charles, Missouri
www.motech.edu   CB code: 2383

▶ For-profit 4-year engineering and technical college
▶ Commuter campus in very large city

General. Founded in 1932. Accredited by ACCSCT. **Location:** 20 miles from downtown. **Calendar:** Semester.

Annual costs/financial aid. Approximate cost of entire associate degree program: $40,000; bachelor's: $80,000. Varies by program major. Books/supplies: $800. Need-based financial aid available to full-time and part-time students.

Contact. Director of Admissions, 1690 Country Club Plaza Drive, St. Charles, MO 63303

Missouri University of Science and Technology
Rolla, Missouri   CB member
www.mst.edu   CB code: 6876

▶ Public 4-year university
▶ Residential campus in large town
▶ 5,604 degree-seeking undergraduates: 8% part-time, 23% women, 5% African American, 2% Asian American, 2% Hispanic American, 1% Native American, 5% international
▶ 1,838 degree-seeking graduate students
▶ 90% of applicants admitted
▶ SAT or ACT (ACT writing optional) required
▶ 67% graduate within 6 years

General. Founded in 1870. Regionally accredited. **Degrees:** 997 bachelor's awarded; master's, doctoral offered. **ROTC:** Army, Air Force. **Location:** 100 miles from St. Louis, 100 miles from Springfield. **Calendar:** Semester, extensive summer session. **Full-time faculty:** 362 total; 88% have terminal degrees, 31% minority, 23% women. **Part-time faculty:** 93 total; 44% have terminal degrees, 11% minority, 32% women. **Class size:** 40% < 20, 36%

20-39, 11% 40-49, 10% 50-99, 3% >100. **Special facilities:** Computerized manufacturing system, nuclear reactor, observatory, experimental mine, rocks, minerals, and gemstones museum, centers for environmental research, virtual reality laboratory; student design team center, wind tunnel, hot glass shop.

Freshman class profile. 2,779 applied, 2,495 admitted, 1,096 enrolled.

Mid 50% test scores		Out-of-state:	21%
SAT critical reading:	560-690	Live on campus:	96%
SAT math:	590-710	International:	1%
ACT composite:	25-31	Fraternities:	24%
Return as sophomores:	83%	Sororities:	3%

Basis for selection. Admission based on secondary school record, class rank, and standardized test scores. Recommendations considered. ACT or SAT score percentage, plus high school class rank percentile should equal 120 (minimum). Exceptions may be made on individual basis. ACT recommended. Campus visit and personal statement encouraged. **Home schooled:** Transcript of courses and grades required. Must submit a standardized test score. **Learning Disabled:** Should submit voluntary declaration of disability to receive accommodation.

High school preparation. College-preparatory program required. 17 units required. Required units include English 4, mathematics 4, social studies 3, science 3 (laboratory 1), foreign language 2 and visual/performing arts 1. Foreign language units must be in same language.

2011-2012 Annual costs. Tuition/fees: $9,084; $21,879 out-of-state. Room/board: $8,520. Books/supplies: $948. Personal expenses: $3,286.

2010-2011 Financial aid. Need-based: 1,109 full-time freshmen applied for aid; 789 were judged to have need; 789 of these received aid. Average need met was 61%. Average scholarship/grant was $7,218; average loan $3,390. 45% of total undergraduate aid awarded as scholarships/grants, 55% as loans/jobs. **Non-need-based:** Awarded to 3,773 full-time undergraduates, including 904 freshmen. Scholarships awarded for academics, alumni affiliation, athletics, job skills, leadership, minority status, music/drama, religious affiliation, ROTC, state residency.

Application procedures. Admission: Priority date 12/1; deadline 7/1 (postmark date). $45 fee, may be waived for applicants with need. Admission notification on a rolling basis beginning on or about 10/1. Must reply by May 1 or within 3 week(s) if notified thereafter. **Financial aid:** Priority date 3/1; no closing date. FAFSA required. Applicants notified on a rolling basis; must reply within 3 week(s) of notification.

Academics. Special study options: Accelerated study, combined bachelor's/graduate degree, cooperative education, distance learning, double major, dual enrollment of high school students, ESL, honors, independent study, internships, liberal arts/career combination, student-designed major, study abroad, teacher certification program. **Credit/placement by examination:** AP, CLEP, IB, institutional tests. **Support services:** Learning center, preadmission summer program, reduced course load, study skills assistance, tutoring, writing center.

Majors. Biology: General, biochemistry, biophysics. **Business:** General, business admin, management information systems. **Computer sciences:** General, computer science, information systems, information technology. **Engineering:** Aerospace, architectural, ceramic, chemical, civil, computer, electrical, engineering mechanics, environmental, geological, mechanical, metallurgical, mining, nuclear, petroleum, polymer. **English:** English lit, technical writing. **Health services:** Predental, premedicine. **History:** General. **Math:** Applied. **Philosophy/religion:** Philosophy. **Physical sciences:** Chemistry, geochemistry, geology, geophysics, physics. **Psychology:** General. **Social sciences:** Economics.

Most popular majors. Computer/information sciences 8%, engineering/engineering technologies 74%.

Computing on campus. PC or laptop required. 812 workstations in dormitories, library, computer center. Dormitories wired for high-speed internet access and linked to campus network. Commuter students can connect to campus network. Online course registration, online library, helpline, repair service, student web hosting, wireless network available.

Student life. Freshman orientation: Mandatory, $135 fee. Preregistration for classes offered. **Housing:** Guaranteed on-campus for freshmen. Coed dorms, special housing for disabled, apartments, cooperative housing, fraternity/sorority housing, wellness housing available. $200 partly refundable deposit, deadline 6/1. Residential college available. **Activities:** Bands, campus ministries, choral groups, dance, drama, international student organizations, literary magazine, music ensembles, musical theater, radio station, student government, student newspaper, symphony orchestra, over 200 student groups available.

Athletics. NCAA. **Intercollegiate:** Baseball M, basketball, cheerleading, cross-country, football (tackle) M, soccer, softball W, swimming M, track and field, volleyball W. **Intramural:** Badminton, basketball, bowling, cross-country, football (non-tackle), golf, racquetball, soccer, softball, swimming, table tennis, tennis, track and field, volleyball, weight lifting. **Team name:** Miners.

Student services. Adult student services, alcohol/substance abuse counseling, career counseling, student employment services, financial aid counseling, health services, legal services, minority student services, personal counseling, placement for graduates, women's services. **Physically disabled:** Services for visually, speech, hearing impaired.

Contact. E-mail: admissions@mst.edu
Phone: (573) 341-4164 Toll-free number: (800) 522-0938
Fax: (573) 341-4082
Rance Larsen, Director of Admissions, Missouri University of Science and Technology, 106 Parker Hall, Rolla, MO 65409-1060

Missouri Valley College
Marshall, Missouri
www.moval.edu　　　　　　　　　　　**CB code: 6413**

▶ Private 4-year liberal arts college affiliated with Presbyterian Church (USA)
▶ Residential campus in large town
▶ 1,430 degree-seeking undergraduates
▶ 9 graduate students
▶ SAT or ACT (ACT writing optional) required

General. Founded in 1889. Regionally accredited. **Degrees:** 185 bachelor's awarded; master's offered. **ROTC:** Army. **Location:** 75 miles from Kansas City, 65 miles from Columbia. **Calendar:** Semester, limited summer session. **Full-time faculty:** 70 total. **Part-time faculty:** 50 total. **Class size:** 45% < 20, 54% 20-39, less than 1% 40-49, less than 1% 50-99.

Freshman class profile.

Rank in top quarter:	19%	Live on campus:	90%
Rank in top tenth:	6%	Fraternities:	25%
Out-of-state:	25%	Sororities:	25%

Basis for selection. Interview, recommendations, high school record, test scores important; extracurricular activities, personal attributes also important; class rank considered. Essay recommended for academically weak students. Audition recommended for drama majors; portfolio recommended for art majors. **Home schooled:** Transcript of courses and grades required. GED in addition to acceptable ACT/SAT score is sufficient.

High school preparation. College-preparatory program recommended. Recommended units include English 4, mathematics 3, social studies 1, history 3, science 3 and foreign language 1.

2012-2013 Annual costs. Tuition/fees (projected): $17,900. Room/board: $7,300. Books/supplies: $1,300. Personal expenses: $2,900.

Financial aid. Non-need-based: Scholarships awarded for academics, state residency.

Application procedures. Admission: Priority date 3/1; no deadline. $15 fee, may be waived for applicants with need. Admission notification on a rolling basis. Must reply by May 1 or within 4 week(s) if notified thereafter. **Financial aid:** Priority date 3/1; no closing date. FAFSA required. Applicants notified on a rolling basis starting 2/1; must reply within 6 week(s) of notification.

Academics. Special study options: Combined bachelor's/graduate degree, double major, dual enrollment of high school students, ESL, external degree, independent study, internships, liberal arts/career combination, student-designed major, study abroad, teacher certification program. **Credit/placement by examination:** AP, CLEP, SAT, ACT, institutional tests. 30 credit hours maximum toward bachelor's degree. **Support services:** Learning center, reduced course load, remedial instruction, study skills assistance, tutoring, writing center.

Majors. Biology: General. **Business:** Accounting, business admin. **Communications:** Media studies. **Computer sciences:** General. **Education:** Elementary, multiple handicapped, physical, secondary, social studies, special ed. **English:** English lit. **Health services:** Athletic training, nursing (RN), substance abuse counseling. **History:** General. **Human services:** General. **Liberal arts:** Arts/sciences. **Math:** General. **Parks/recreation:** Exercise sciences, facilities management. **Philosophy/religion:** Philosophy, religion. **Protective services:** Law enforcement admin. **Psychology:** General. **Social sciences:** Economics, political science, sociology. **Visual/performing arts:** Art, dance, dramatic, music.

Computing on campus. 172 workstations in library, computer center, student center. Dormitories wired for high-speed internet access and linked to campus network. Commuter students can connect to campus network. Online library, helpline, repair service, wireless network available.

Student life. Freshman orientation: Mandatory. Preregistration for classes offered. Early Registration Days held in summer. **Housing:** Guaranteed on-campus for all undergraduates. Single-sex dorms, apartments, fraternity/sorority housing available. **Activities:** Bands, campus ministries, choral groups, dance, drama, film society, international student organizations, literary magazine, music ensembles, musical theater, radio station, student government, student newspaper, symphony orchestra, TV station, American Humanics, Minority Student Union, Fellowship of Christian Athletes, Student Council for Exceptional Children.

Athletics. NAIA. **Intercollegiate:** Baseball M, basketball, cheerleading, cross-country, football (tackle) M, golf, rodeo, soccer, softball W, tennis, track and field, volleyball, wrestling. **Intramural:** Badminton, baseball M, basketball, bowling, cross-country, football (non-tackle), soccer, softball, table tennis, track and field, volleyball, weight lifting. **Team name:** Vikings.

Student services. Alcohol/substance abuse counseling, chaplain/spiritual director, career counseling, student employment services, financial aid counseling, health services, personal counseling, placement for graduates, veterans' counselor.

Contact. E-mail: admissions@moval.edu
Phone: (660) 831-4114 Fax: (660) 831-4233
Tennille Langdon, Director of Admissions, Missouri Valley College, 500 East College Street, Marshall, MO 65340

Missouri Western State University
St. Joseph, Missouri
www.missouriwestern.edu CB code: 6625

▸ Public 4-year business and liberal arts college
▸ Commuter campus in small city
▸ 6,259 undergraduates
▸ SAT or ACT (ACT writing optional) required

General. Founded in 1915. Regionally accredited. **Degrees:** 658 bachelor's, 48 associate awarded; master's offered. **ROTC:** Army. **Location:** 48 miles from Kansas City. **Calendar:** Semester, extensive summer session. **Full-time faculty:** 195 total. **Part-time faculty:** 190 total. **Class size:** 40% < 20, 53% 20-39, 3% 40-49, 4% 50-99, less than 1% >100. **Special facilities:** Biology nature study area, planetarium.

Freshman class profile.

Out-of-state:	6%	Live on campus:	46%

Basis for selection. Open admission, but selective for some programs. School record, test scores, interview, recommendations important for education, nursing, mathematics, computer science, social work applicants. Special talents important for music, art applicants. High school units mandated by state law may vary by program. Interview required for education, nursing, social work programs. Portfolio recommended for art majors, audition recommended for music majors.

High school preparation. College-preparatory program required. 16 units required. Required and recommended units include English 4, mathematics 3, social studies 3, science 2 (laboratory 1), foreign language 2, visual/performing arts 1 and academic electives 3.

2011-2012 Annual costs. Tuition/fees: $6,041; $11,139 out-of-state. Room/board: $6,796. Books/supplies: $800. Personal expenses: $3,200.

Financial aid. Non-need-based: Scholarships awarded for academics, alumni affiliation, art, athletics, job skills, leadership, minority status, music/drama, state residency.

Application procedures. Admission: Priority date 3/1; deadline 5/1. $15 fee, may be waived for applicants with need. Admission notification on a rolling basis. **Financial aid:** Priority date 3/1; no closing date. FAFSA, institutional form required. Applicants notified on a rolling basis starting 4/5; must reply within 3 week(s) of notification.

Academics. Special study options: Combined bachelor's/graduate degree, distance learning, double major, dual enrollment of high school students, honors, internships, liberal arts/career combination, teacher certification program, weekend college. **Credit/placement by examination:** AP, CLEP, institutional tests. 30 credit hours maximum toward associate degree, 30 toward bachelor's. **Support services:** Learning center, pre-admission summer

---

program, reduced course load, remedial instruction, study skills assistance, tutoring, writing center.

Majors. Biology: General, biochemistry. **Business:** Accounting, business admin, finance, marketing. **Communications:** Communications/speech/rhetoric. **Computer sciences:** General, information systems. **Education:** Art, elementary, English, French, middle, music, Spanish. **English:** English lit, rhetoric/composition. **Foreign languages:** French, Spanish. **Health services:** Clinical lab technology, nursing (RN). **History:** General. **Human services:** Social work. **Liberal arts:** Arts/sciences. **Math:** General. **Parks/recreation:** Facilities management, health/fitness. **Physical sciences:** Chemistry. **Protective services:** Criminal justice. **Psychology:** General. **Social sciences:** Economics, political science. **Visual/performing arts:** Art, graphic design, music.

Computing on campus. 300 workstations in dormitories, library, computer center, student center. Dormitories linked to campus network. Commuter students can connect to campus network. Online course registration available.

Student life. Freshman orientation: Available, $60 fee. Preregistration for classes offered. **Housing:** Coed dorms, apartments, fraternity/sorority housing available. $100 deposit. **Activities:** Bands, choral groups, dance, drama, music ensembles, musical theater, student government, student newspaper, symphony orchestra, over 70 organizations.

Athletics. NCAA. **Intercollegiate:** Baseball M, basketball, football (tackle) M, golf, soccer W, softball W, tennis W, volleyball W, wrestling M. **Intramural:** Archery, badminton, baseball M, basketball, bowling, golf, handball, racquetball, rugby M, soccer M, softball, table tennis, tennis, volleyball. **Team name:** Griffons.

Student services. Adult student services, alcohol/substance abuse counseling, career counseling, student employment services, financial aid counseling, health services, minority student services, on-campus daycare, personal counseling, placement for graduates, veterans' counselor.

Contact. E-mail: admissions@missouriwestern.edu
Phone: (816) 271-4200 Toll-free number: (800) 662-7041
Fax: (816) 271-5833
Howard McCauley, Director of Admissions, Missouri Western State University, 4525 Downs Drive, St. Joseph, MO 64507

National American University: Kansas City
Independence, Missouri
www.national.edu CB code: 5357

▸ For-profit 4-year university
▸ Commuter campus in large city
▸ 868 degree-seeking undergraduates
▸ Interview required

General. Founded in 1941. Regionally accredited. **Degrees:** 7 bachelor's, 52 associate awarded; master's offered. **Location:** 8 miles from downtown. **Calendar:** Quarter, extensive summer session. **Full-time faculty:** 2 total. **Part-time faculty:** 29 total.

Basis for selection. Open admission. Open enrollment policy, but students have to test out of entry-level English/math in order to be enrolled in algebra and English comp I.

2011-2012 Annual costs. Tuition/fees: $14,205.

Financial aid. All financial aid based on need.

Application procedures. Admission: No deadline. No application fee. Admission notification on a rolling basis. **Financial aid:** No deadline. FAFSA, institutional form required. Applicants notified on a rolling basis starting 6/4.

Academics. Special study options: Accelerated study, distance learning, double major, independent study, internships, liberal arts/career combination. **Credit/placement by examination:** AP, CLEP, institutional tests. **Support services:** Learning center, study skills assistance, tutoring.

Majors. Business: Accounting, business admin, management information systems, marketing. **Computer sciences:** Information systems. **Health services:** Nursing (RN).

Computing on campus. 50 workstations in computer center. Online library available.

Student life. Freshman orientation: Mandatory. Preregistration for classes offered. **Activities:** Student government, student newspaper.

Athletics. Team name: Mavericks.

Student services. Adult student services, career counseling, student employment services, financial aid counseling, placement for graduates.

Contact. Phone: (866) 628-1288 Fax: (816) 412-7705
Sharon Anderson, Director of Admissions, National American University: Kansas City, 3620 Arrowhead Avenue, Independence, MO 64057

National American University: Lee's Summit
Lees Summit, Missouri
www.national.edu

▶ For-profit 3-year branch campus college
▶ Small city
▶ 246 degree-seeking undergraduates

General. Regionally accredited. **Calendar:** Quarter. **Full-time faculty:** 15 total. **Part-time faculty:** 10 total.

Basis for selection. Open admission.

2011-2012 Annual costs. Tuition/fees: $14,205.

Academics. Credit/placement by examination: AP, CLEP.

Majors. BACHELOR'S. Business: Accounting, business admin, organizational leadership. **Computer sciences:** Information technology. **Health services:** Health care admin, nursing (RN). **ASSOCIATE. Health services:** Medical assistant, pharmacy assistant.

Contact. E-mail: lsadmissions@national.edu
Phone: (816) 600-3900
Joey Landara, Director of Admissions, National American University: Lee's Summit, 401 NW Murray Road, Lee's Summit, MO 64081

Northwest Missouri State University
Maryville, Missouri
www.nwmissouri.edu   CB code: 6488

▶ Public 4-year university
▶ Residential campus in large town
▶ 5,891 degree-seeking undergraduates: 6% part-time, 56% women, 6% African American, 1% Asian American, 3% Hispanic American, 2% international
▶ 791 degree-seeking graduate students
▶ 86% of applicants admitted
▶ SAT or ACT (ACT writing optional) required
▶ 50% graduate within 6 years; 27% enter graduate study

General. Founded in 1905. Regionally accredited. **Degrees:** 1,027 bachelor's, 63 associate awarded; master's offered. **ROTC:** Army. **Location:** 100 miles from Kansas City. **Calendar:** Trimester, extensive summer session. **Full-time faculty:** 263 total; 65% have terminal degrees, 7% minority, 47% women. **Part-time faculty:** 82 total; 10% have terminal degrees, 6% minority, 67% women. **Class size:** 39% < 20, 47% 20-39, 5% 40-49, 9% 50-99, less than 1% >100. **Special facilities:** Arboretum, lake-front outdoor education recreation area, laboratory school, dairy operation, swine herd, horticulture complex, experimental farmland, center for innovation and entrepreneurship (incubator), studio/black box experimental theater, alternative energy learning center, observatory, online museum, science museum, agriculture museum, computing museum, museum of broadcasting.

Freshman class profile. 4,607 applied, 3,959 admitted, 1,595 enrolled.

Mid 50% test scores			
SAT critical reading:	470-620	Rank in top quarter:	39%
SAT math:	480-580	Rank in top tenth:	13%
ACT composite:	20-25	End year in good standing:	68%
GPA 3.75 or higher:	22%	Return as sophomores:	69%
GPA 3.50-3.74:	18%	Out-of-state:	25%
GPA 3.0-3.49:	36%	Live on campus:	93%
GPA 2.0-2.99:	24%	Fraternities:	24%
		Sororities:	22%

Basis for selection. School achievement record and test scores most important. Index based on class rank and national test. Audition recommended for dramatic arts and music students; portfolio recommended for art students. **Home schooled:** Transcript of courses and grades, state high school equivalency certificate required.

High school preparation. College-preparatory program required. 24 units required. Required and recommended units include English 4, mathematics 3-4, social studies 3, science 3 (laboratory 1), foreign language 2, visual/performing arts 1 and academic electives 3. One fine arts required. Foreign language and additional math and science highly recommended.

2011-2012 Annual costs. Tuition/fees: $7,434; $13,297 out-of-state. Room/board: $8,272. Books/supplies: $500. Personal expenses: $1,500.

2010-2011 Financial aid. Need-based: 1,346 full-time freshmen applied for aid; 1,012 were judged to have need; 1,010 of these received aid. Average need met was 76%. Average scholarship/grant was $5,693; average loan $3,309. 47% of total undergraduate aid awarded as scholarships/grants, 53% as loans/jobs. **Non-need-based:** Awarded to 1,809 full-time undergraduates, including 768 freshmen. Scholarships awarded for academics, alumni affiliation, art, athletics, job skills, leadership, minority status, music/drama, ROTC, state residency.

Application procedures. Admission: No deadline. $25 fee, may be waived for applicants with need, free for online applicants. Admission notification on a rolling basis beginning on or about 9/1. **Financial aid:** Priority date 4/1; no closing date. FAFSA required. Applicants notified on a rolling basis starting 3/15; must reply within 4 week(s) of notification.

Academics. Special study options: Cooperative education, cross-registration, distance learning, double major, dual enrollment of high school students, ESL, exchange student, honors, independent study, internships, liberal arts/career combination, study abroad, teacher certification program, Washington semester. **Credit/placement by examination:** AP, CLEP, IB, SAT, ACT, institutional tests. **Support services:** Learning center, reduced course load, remedial instruction, study skills assistance, tutoring, writing center.

Majors. Biology: General, marine. **Business:** Accounting, administrative services, business admin, finance, international, management information systems, managerial economics, marketing. **Communications:** Advertising, communications/speech/rhetoric, journalism, organizational, public relations, radio/TV. **Computer sciences:** General, web page design. **Conservation:** Wildlife/wilderness. **Education:** Agricultural, art, biology, business, chemistry, curriculum, elementary, English, family/consumer sciences, mathematics, middle, multiple handicapped, music, physical, physics, science, social science, Spanish. **English:** English lit. **Foreign languages:** Spanish. **General:** Agribusiness operations, agronomy, animal sciences, economics, horticultural science. **Health services:** Clinical lab science, dietetics, nursing (RN), preveterinary. **History:** General. **Human services:** General. **Liberal arts:** Humanities. **Math:** General, statistics. **Parks/recreation:** Facilities management. **Philosophy/religion:** Philosophy. **Physical sciences:** Chemistry, geology, physics. **Psychology:** General, industrial, psychobiology, social. **Social sciences:** Economics, geography, GIS/cartography, political science, sociology. **Visual/performing arts:** Acting, dramatic, music, studio arts, theater design. **Work/family studies:** Apparel marketing, family studies, institutional food production.

Most popular majors. Agriculture 7%, business/marketing 30%, communications/journalism 7%, education 19%, psychology 10%.

Computing on campus. 6,650 workstations in dormitories, library, computer center, student center. Dormitories wired for high-speed internet access and linked to campus network. Commuter students can connect to campus network. Online course registration, online library, helpline, repair service, student web hosting, wireless network available.

Student life. Freshman orientation: Mandatory, $100 fee. Preregistration for classes offered. One-day program in June plus 4-day program held before classes begin in August. **Policies:** Alcohol- and smoke-free campus. **Housing:** Guaranteed on-campus for freshmen. Coed dorms, special housing for disabled, apartments, fraternity/sorority housing available. $150 nonrefundable deposit. **Activities:** Bands, choral groups, dance, drama, film society, international student organizations, literary magazine, music ensembles, musical theater, radio station, student government, student newspaper, symphony orchestra, TV station, More than 180 student organizations available.

Athletics. NCAA. **Intercollegiate:** Baseball M, basketball, cheerleading, cross-country, football (tackle) M, golf W, soccer W, softball W, tennis, track and field, volleyball W. **Intramural:** Badminton, basketball, cross-country, football (non-tackle), golf, racquetball, skiing, softball W, swimming, table tennis, tennis, track and field, volleyball. **Team name:** Bearcats.

Student services. Alcohol/substance abuse counseling, chaplain/spiritual director, career counseling, services for economically disadvantaged, student employment services, financial aid counseling, health services, minority student services, personal counseling, placement for graduates. **Physically disabled:** Services for visually, speech, hearing impaired.

Contact. E-mail: admissions@nwmissouri.edu
Phone: (660) 562-1148 Toll-free number: (800) 633-1175
Fax: (660) 562-1821
Tamera Grow, Associate Director, Admissions, Northwest Missouri State University, 800 University Drive, Maryville, MO 64468-6001

Ozark Christian College
Joplin, Missouri
www.occ.edu   CB code: 6542

- Private 4-year Bible college affiliated with nondenominational tradition
- Residential campus in large town

General. Founded in 1942. Accredited by ABHE. **Location:** 70 miles from Springfield, 100 miles from Tulsa, Oklahoma. **Calendar:** Semester.

Annual costs/financial aid. Tuition/fees (2011-2012): $9,500. Room/board: $4,290. Books/supplies: $600. Personal expenses: $1,400. Need-based financial aid available to full-time and part-time students.

Contact. Phone: (417) 624-2518
Director of Admissions, 1111 North Main Street, Joplin, MO 64801

Park University
Parkville, Missouri   CB member
www.park.edu   CB code: 6574

- Private 4-year university
- Commuter campus in small town
- 1,619 degree-seeking undergraduates: 28% part-time, 56% women, 9% African American, 1% Asian American, 4% Hispanic American, 1% Native American, 18% international
- 763 degree-seeking graduate students
- 76% of applicants admitted
- 39% graduate within 6 years

General. Founded in 1875. Regionally accredited. MetroPark School for adult education in Kansas City offers bachelor's degree. School for Extended Learning (SEL) offers degree programs in 21 states. **Degrees:** 2,347 bachelor's, 84 associate awarded; master's offered. **ROTC:** Army. **Location:** 12 miles from downtown Kansas City. **Calendar:** Semester, extensive summer session. **Full-time faculty:** 82 total; 66% have terminal degrees, 4% minority, 38% women. **Part-time faculty:** 86 total. **Class size:** 82% < 20, 17% 20-39, less than 1% 40-49. **Special facilities:** 700 acres of woodland.

Freshman class profile. 552 applied, 417 admitted, 180 enrolled.

Mid 50% test scores		Rank in top quarter:	53%
ACT composite:	19-25	Rank in top tenth:	31%
GPA 3.75 or higher:	28%	Return as sophomores:	67%
GPA 3.50-3.74:	14%	Out-of-state:	18%
GPA 3.0-3.49:	26%	Live on campus:	88%
GPA 2.0-2.99:	29%	International:	18%

Basis for selection. Based on 6th semester transcript with 3.0 or higher GPA, or qualifying for Missouri's A-Plus program, or meet two of following three criteria: 2.0 GPA; ACT composite score of 20 or SAT of 940 (exclusive of Writing); top 50% of class. Admission may also be granted with total GED score of 2500, with no area less than 450, and ACT composite score of 20 or SAT of 940 (exclusive of Writing). Students not meeting criteria may be considered on individual basis. Students with 3.0 GPA not required to submit SAT/ACT for admission; however, institutional placement test must be substituted. Entering freshmen with GPA of 2.0 to 3.0 must either be in top half of graduating class or submit satisfactory SAT/ACT scores. Interview recommended for academically weak students; audition recommended for music and theater students; portfolio recommended for art students.

High school preparation. 19 units recommended. Recommended units include English 3, mathematics 2, social studies 3, history 1, science 2 (laboratory 1), foreign language 2 and academic electives 6.

2011-2012 Annual costs. Tuition/fees: $9,950. Room/board: $7,045. Books/supplies: $1,800. Personal expenses: $2,450.

Financial aid. Non-need-based: Scholarships awarded for academics, alumni affiliation, art, athletics, job skills, leadership, minority status, music/drama, religious affiliation, ROTC.

Application procedures. Admission: Priority date 4/15; deadline 8/1. $25 fee, may be waived for applicants with need. Admission notification on a rolling basis. **Financial aid:** Priority date 4/1, closing date 8/1. FAFSA, institutional form required. Applicants notified on a rolling basis starting 4/1.

Academics. Special study options: Accelerated study, cross-registration, distance learning, double major, dual enrollment of high school students, ESL, honors, independent study, internships, student-designed major, study abroad, teacher certification program, Washington semester, weekend college.

Credit/placement by examination: AP, CLEP, ACT, institutional tests. **Support services:** Learning center, reduced course load, remedial instruction, study skills assistance, tutoring, writing center.

Majors. Biology: General. **Business:** Accounting, accounting/business management, business admin, logistics, management information systems, managerial economics, marketing. **Communications:** Communications/speech/rhetoric. **Computer sciences:** General, computer science. **Education:** Early childhood, elementary. **English:** English lit. **Foreign languages:** Spanish. **Health services:** Athletic training. **History:** General. **Human services:** General, social work. **Liberal arts:** Arts/sciences. **Math:** General. **Physical sciences:** Chemistry. **Protective services:** Fire services admin, law enforcement admin. **Psychology:** General. **Social sciences:** Economics, geography, political science, sociology. **Visual/performing arts:** Dramatic, graphic design, interior design, music, studio arts. **Work/family studies:** Child development.

Most popular majors. Biology 8%, business/marketing 21%, communications/journalism 8%, education 17%, public administration/social services 7%, security/protective services 9%, visual/performing arts 12%.

Computing on campus. 300 workstations in dormitories, library, computer center, student center. Dormitories linked to campus network. Commuter students can connect to campus network. Online course registration available.

Student life. Freshman orientation: Mandatory. Preregistration for classes offered. **Housing:** Guaranteed on-campus for freshmen. Coed dorms, apartments available. $100 deposit. **Activities:** Choral groups, drama, literary magazine, radio station, student government, student newspaper, symphony orchestra, service organizations, Christian Fellowship, World Student Union, Brothers and Sisters United, accounting society, Latin American student organization, marketing club, honors club, non-traditional student organization.

Athletics. NAIA. **Intercollegiate:** Baseball M, basketball, cross-country, golf W, soccer, softball W, track and field, volleyball. **Intramural:** Basketball, soccer, softball, volleyball. **Team name:** Pirates.

Student services. Career counseling, student employment services, financial aid counseling, health services, on-campus daycare, personal counseling, placement for graduates, veterans' counselor. **Physically disabled:** Services for visually, speech, hearing impaired.

Contact. E-mail: admissions@park.edu
Phone: (816) 584-6215 Toll-free number: (800) 745-7275
Fax: (816) 741-4462
Cathy Colapietro, Executive Director of Admissions and Student Financial Services, Park University, 8700 NW River Park Drive, Parkville, MO 64152

Research College of Nursing
Kansas City, Missouri
www.researchcollege.edu   CB code: 6612

- For-profit 4-year nursing college
- Residential campus in very large city
- 262 degree-seeking undergraduates: 92% women, 7% African American, 2% Asian American, 4% Hispanic American
- 109 degree-seeking graduate students
- SAT or ACT (ACT writing optional) required

General. Founded in 1905. Regionally accredited. Natural science, social science, and liberal arts courses taken at Rockhurst University. Students have access to facilities, organizations, sports and activities on both campuses. Bachelor of Science in Nursing is awarded jointly by Research College of Nursing and Rockhurst University. **Degrees:** 140 bachelor's awarded; master's offered. **ROTC:** Army. **Location:** 5 miles from downtown Kansas City, Missouri. **Calendar:** Semester, limited summer session. **Full-time faculty:** 35 total; 26% have terminal degrees, 6% minority, 97% women. **Part-time faculty:** 2 total; 100% women. **Class size:** 100% 50-99. **Special facilities:** Medical library, 532-bed research medical center.

Freshman class profile.

Out-of-state:	25%	Live on campus:	77%

Basis for selection. Academic record, high school GPA, rank in top half of class, counselor's recommendation, test scores very important. ACT score of 20 required. Interview, high school activities considered. Interview recommended for all; strongly recommended for applicants with ACT scores below 20.

High school preparation. College-preparatory program recommended. 18 units recommended. Recommended units include English 4, mathematics 3, social studies 3, science 4 and foreign language 2. Visual or performing arts also recommended. Mathematics should include algebra II, science should include chemistry.

2011-2012 Annual costs. Tuition/fees: $28,510. Room/board: $7,890. Books/supplies: $720. Personal expenses: $915.

Financial aid. Non-need-based: Scholarships awarded for academics, alumni affiliation, leadership. **Additional information:** Financial aid handled by Rockhurst University for freshmen and sophomores.

Application procedures. Admission: Priority date 3/1; no deadline. $20 fee, may be waived for applicants with need, free for online applicants. Admission notification on a rolling basis beginning on or about 10/1. Must reply by May 1 or within 4 week(s) if notified thereafter. **Financial aid:** Priority date 3/15; no closing date. FAFSA, institutional form required. Applicants notified on a rolling basis starting 3/15.

Academics. Students admitted into nursing program in freshman year guaranteed place in upper-division nursing courses if academic requirements maintained. **Special study options:** Accelerated study, cross-registration, double major, dual enrollment of high school students, exchange student, honors, independent study, study abroad. **Credit/placement by examination:** AP, CLEP, IB, ACT, institutional tests. 32 credit hours maximum toward bachelor's degree. **Support services:** Learning center, reduced course load, tutoring.

Majors. Health services: Nursing (RN).

Computing on campus. 300 workstations in dormitories, library, computer center. Dormitories wired for high-speed internet access and linked to campus network. Commuter students can connect to campus network. Online course registration, helpline, wireless network available.

Student life. Freshman orientation: Mandatory, $50 fee. Preregistration for classes offered. **Housing:** Guaranteed on-campus for freshmen. Coed dorms, single-sex dorms, apartments, fraternity/sorority housing available. $200 fully refundable deposit. Freshman nursing students not living at home must live on Rockhurst College campus. All other undergraduates may choose to live on Research College campus or at Rockhurst College. **Activities:** Campus ministries, choral groups, drama, music ensembles, musical theater, radio station, student government, student newspaper, Alpha Phi Omega, Black Student Union, Young Republicans, Young Democrats, Missouri Student Nurses Association, National Student Nurses Association, Rockhurst Organization of Collegiate Women.

Athletics. NCAA. **Intercollegiate:** Baseball M, basketball, cross-country, golf, soccer, softball W, tennis, volleyball W. **Intramural:** Basketball, lacrosse, racquetball, rugby, table tennis, volleyball.

Student services. Chaplain/spiritual director, career counseling, student employment services, financial aid counseling, health services, on-campus daycare, personal counseling, placement for graduates, veterans' counselor.

Contact. Phone: (816) 995-2812 Toll-free number: (866) 855-0296 Fax: (816) 995-2813
Lane Ramey, Director of Freshmen Admission, Research College of Nursing, 2525 East Meyer Boulevard, Kansas City, MO 64132-1199

Rockhurst University
Kansas City, Missouri   **CB member**
www.rockhurst.edu   **CB code: 6611**

- Private 4-year business and liberal arts college affiliated with Roman Catholic Church
- Residential campus in very large city
- 1,509 degree-seeking undergraduates: 9% part-time, 62% women, 6% African American, 3% Asian American, 7% Hispanic American, 1% Native American, 1% international
- 656 degree-seeking graduate students
- 76% of applicants admitted
- SAT or ACT (ACT writing optional) required
- 74% graduate within 6 years

General. Founded in 1910. Regionally accredited. Students graduate with community service transcript in addition to academic transcript. **Degrees:** 430 bachelor's awarded; master's, professional offered. **ROTC:** Army. **Location:** 5 miles from downtown. **Calendar:** Semester, limited summer session. **Full-time faculty:** 129 total; 88% have terminal degrees, 12% minority, 52% women. **Part-time faculty:** 96 total; 28% have terminal degrees, 7% minority,

56% women. **Class size:** 36% < 20, 57% 20-39, 2% 40-49, 4% 50-99, less than 1% >100.

Freshman class profile. 2,113 applied, 1,609 admitted, 326 enrolled.

GPA 3.75 or higher:	44%	Rank in top tenth:	22%
GPA 3.50-3.74:	20%	Return as sophomores:	82%
GPA 3.0-3.49:	24%	Out-of-state:	32%
GPA 2.0-2.99:	12%	Live on campus:	85%
Rank in top quarter:	54%	International:	1%

Basis for selection. High school GPA, class rank, test scores, recommendations most important; school and community activities considered. Interviews recommended for all students. Essay or personal statement may be required or requested. **Home schooled:** Transcript of courses and grades, state high school equivalency certificate required. GED requested dependent on quality of grades presented on transcript.

High school preparation. College-preparatory program recommended. 16 units recommended. Recommended units include English 4, mathematics 3, social studies 3, history 2, science 3 (laboratory 3), foreign language 2 and academic electives 4.

2011-2012 Annual costs. Tuition/fees: $28,510. Room/board: $7,820. Books/supplies: $1,400. Personal expenses: $1,625.

Financial aid. Non-need-based: Scholarships awarded for academics, alumni affiliation, athletics, leadership, music/drama. **Additional information:** Auditions, portfolios required for some scholarships.

Application procedures. Admission: No deadline. $25 fee, may be waived for applicants with need, free for online applicants. Admission notification on a rolling basis beginning on or about 9/1. Must reply by May 1 or within 2 week(s) if notified thereafter. **Financial aid:** Priority date 3/1; no closing date. FAFSA required. Applicants notified on a rolling basis starting 3/1; must reply within 4 week(s) of notification.

Academics. Core curriculum based on 7 "modes of inquiry," different ways people approach reality to seek truth including artistic, literary, historical, scientific-causal, scientific-relational, philosophical, and theological. **Special study options:** Accelerated study, combined bachelor's/graduate degree, cooperative education, cross-registration, double major, dual enrollment of high school students, exchange student, honors, independent study, internships, liberal arts/career combination, New York semester, semester at sea, study abroad, teacher certification program, Washington semester. **Credit/placement by examination:** AP, CLEP, IB, SAT, ACT, institutional tests. 32 credit hours maximum toward bachelor's degree. **Support services:** Learning center, study skills assistance, tutoring, writing center.

Majors. Biology: General, biochemistry. **Business:** Business admin, communications, nonprofit/public. **Communications:** Communications/speech/rhetoric. **Education:** Elementary, secondary. **English:** English lit. **Foreign languages:** French, Spanish. **Health services:** Clinical lab science, nursing (RN), speech pathology. **History:** General. **Human services:** Community org/advocacy. **Math:** General. **Parks/recreation:** Exercise sciences. **Philosophy/religion:** Philosophy, religion. **Physical sciences:** Chemistry, physics. **Protective services:** Law enforcement admin. **Psychology:** General. **Social sciences:** General, economics, political science.

Most popular majors. Biology 10%, business/marketing 17%, health sciences 28%, parks/recreation 6%, psychology 12%, social sciences 6%.

Computing on campus. 227 workstations in dormitories, library, computer center, student center. Dormitories wired for high-speed internet access and linked to campus network. Commuter students can connect to campus network. Online course registration, online library, helpline, student web hosting, wireless network available.

Student life. Freshman orientation: Mandatory, $150 fee. Preregistration for classes offered. Programs held 4 days before fall semester begins. Includes participation in community service projects. **Policies:** Full-time unmarried freshmen and sophomores must live on campus if not living with family. **Housing:** Coed dorms, single-sex dorms, special housing for disabled, apartments, fraternity/sorority housing, wellness housing available. $200 nonrefundable deposit. **Activities:** Campus ministries, choral groups, dance, drama, international student organizations, literary magazine, student government, student newspaper, Alpha Phi Omega, Black Student Union, Multicultural Affairs Office, American Humanics, Student Senate, Delta Sigma Pi Business Fraternity, Student Activities Board, Student Organization of Latinos, theatre troupe.

Athletics. NCAA. **Intercollegiate:** Baseball M, basketball, golf, soccer, softball W, tennis, volleyball W. **Intramural:** Badminton, basketball, cross-country, field hockey, football (tackle), golf, handball M, racquetball, soccer, softball, tennis, volleyball, weight lifting M, wrestling M. **Team name:** Hawks.

Student services. Alcohol/substance abuse counseling, chaplain/spiritual director, career counseling, student employment services, financial aid counseling, health services, personal counseling, placement for graduates, veterans' counselor. **Physically disabled:** Services for visually, speech, hearing impaired.

Contact. E-mail: admission@rockhurst.edu
Phone: (816) 501-4100 Toll-free number: (800) 842-6776
Fax: (816) 501-4241
Lane Ramey, Director of Freshman Admissions, Rockhurst University, 1100 Rockhurst Road, Kansas City, MO 64110-2561

Saint Louis University
Saint Louis, Missouri
CB member
www.slu.edu
CB code: 6629

- Private 4-year university affiliated with Roman Catholic Church
- Residential campus in very large city
- 8,447 degree-seeking undergraduates: 10% part-time, 59% women, 7% African American, 7% Asian American, 4% Hispanic American, 8% international
- 5,309 degree-seeking graduate students
- 61% of applicants admitted
- SAT or ACT (ACT writing optional), application essay required
- 71% graduate within 6 years; 37% enter graduate study

General. Founded in 1818. Regionally accredited. Institution maintains campus in Madrid, Spain. **Degrees:** 1,631 bachelor's awarded; master's, professional, doctoral offered. **ROTC:** Army, Air Force. **Location:** Midtown. **Calendar:** Semester, extensive summer session. **Full-time faculty:** 742 total; 91% have terminal degrees, 12% minority, 44% women. **Part-time faculty:** 544 total; 18% have terminal degrees, 8% minority, 56% women. **Class size:** 54% < 20, 35% 20-39, 6% 40-49, 4% 50-99, 2% >100. **Special facilities:** Vatican manuscripts microfilm library, art museums, LEED certified research facility, arena, sculpture dog park, biological station, entrepreneurial studies center, earthquake research center, performing arts center, supersonic wind tunnel, water tunnel, shock tube, and fabrication labs, flight simulators, airport, sculpture/ceramics studio, physiology and gait research labs, demonstration clinics for counseling and family therapy, child development, speech and hearing, psychology, dental, occupational and physical therapy, organic gardening and food service.

Freshman class profile. 13,389 applied, 8,202 admitted, 1,707 enrolled.

Mid 50% test scores			
SAT critical reading:	530-660	Rank in top tenth:	40%
SAT math:	550-670	End year in good standing:	98%
ACT composite:	25-30	Return as sophomores:	86%
GPA 3.75 or higher:	55%	Out-of-state:	67%
GPA 3.50-3.74:	19%	Live on campus:	91%
GPA 3.0-3.49:	18%	International:	4%
GPA 2.0-2.99:	8%	Fraternities:	26%
Rank in top quarter:	70%	Sororities:	32%

Basis for selection. Secondary school record, standardized test scores important; recommendations, essay, extracurricular activities, character/personal qualities, volunteer work considered. Academic performance is most important for international applicants. However, for non-native English speakers, 525 on TOEFL or equivalent required for all full-time enrollment. Interviews with admission counselors recommended. Audition recommended for music majors; portfolio recommended for art majors. **Home schooled:** Strongly recommended to present 5 academic courses each semester for all four years. Should include 4 years of English, 4 years of mathematics (Algebra I & II, and Geometry), 3 years each of foreign language, natural science, social science and academic electives. **Learning Disabled:** Students with learning disabilities are responsible for contacting Disabilities Services.

High school preparation. College-preparatory program recommended. 20 units required. Required units include English 4, mathematics 4, social studies 3, science 3, foreign language 3 and academic electives 3.

2011-2012 Annual costs. Tuition/fees: $33,986. Room/board: $9,432.

2010-2011 Financial aid. **Need-based:** 1,326 full-time freshmen applied for aid; 1,132 were judged to have need; 1,132 of these received aid. Average need met was 70%. Average scholarship/grant was $19,442; average loan $3,723. 78% of total undergraduate aid awarded as scholarships/grants, 22% as loans/jobs. **Non-need-based:** Awarded to 2,385 full-time undergraduates, including 528 freshmen. Scholarships awarded for academics, art, athletics, leadership, music/drama, religious affiliation, ROTC. **Additional information:** Martin Luther King Jr. scholarship applications have a priority date of February 1, 2012. Emergency Scholarship Fund established to assist students and families with special circumstances, especially job loss. Institutional loan

program available to assist some students who do not have other financing options.

Application procedures. **Admission:** Closing date 12/1 (receipt date). $25 fee, may be waived for applicants with need, free for online applicants. Admission notification by 8/1. Admission notification on a rolling basis beginning on or about 9/15. Must reply by May 1 or within 2 week(s) if notified thereafter. **Financial aid:** Priority date 3/1; no closing date. FAFSA required. Applicants notified on a rolling basis starting 3/1; must reply by 5/1 or within 4 week(s) of notification.

Academics. **Special study options:** Accelerated study, combined bachelor's/graduate degree, cooperative education, cross-registration, distance learning, double major, dual enrollment of high school students, ESL, exchange student, honors, independent study, internships, liberal arts/career combination, student-designed major, study abroad, teacher certification program. **Credit/placement by examination:** AP, CLEP, IB, SAT, ACT, institutional tests. 30 credit hours maximum toward bachelor's degree. **Support services:** Pre-admission summer program, reduced course load, study skills assistance, tutoring, writing center.

Honors college/program. Admission Requirements: 30 ACT or 1330 SAT (exclusive of Writing) and 3.8 unweighted GPA. Approximately 225-250 freshman admitted each year. Academic offerings: honors core classes, honors opportunities in major, senior honors thesis.

Majors. **Area/ethnic studies:** African-American, American, Latin American, women's. **Biology:** General, biochemistry. **Business:** Accounting, business admin, finance, hospitality admin, international, knowledge management, management information systems, managerial economics, marketing, organizational behavior. **Communications:** Communications/speech/rhetoric. **Computer sciences:** General. **Conservation:** Environmental science. **Education:** General, elementary, middle, special ed. **Engineering:** General, aerospace, applied physics, biomedical, civil, computer, electrical, mechanical. **English:** English lit. **Foreign languages:** French, German, Italian, Russian, Spanish. **Health services:** Athletic training, audiology/speech pathology, clinical lab science, cytotechnology, health services admin, medical radiologic technology/radiation therapy, medical records admin, MRI technology, nuclear medical technology, nursing (RN), occupational therapy. **History:** General. **Human services:** Social work. **Liberal arts:** Arts/sciences, humanities. **Math:** General. **Parks/recreation:** Exercise sciences. **Philosophy/religion:** Philosophy. **Physical sciences:** Atmospheric science, chemistry, geology, geophysics, physics. **Protective services:** Corrections, law enforcement admin, security services. **Psychology:** General. **Social sciences:** Anthropology, international relations, political science, sociology, urban studies. **Theology:** Theology. **Visual/performing arts:** Art history/conservation, dramatic, music, studio arts. **Work/family studies:** Food/nutrition.

Most popular majors. Biology 6%, business/marketing 24%, health sciences 20%, psychology 6%, social sciences 6%.

Computing on campus. 581 workstations in dormitories, library, computer center, student center. Dormitories wired for high-speed internet access and linked to campus network. Commuter students can connect to campus network. Online course registration, online library, helpline, student web hosting, wireless network available.

Student life. **Freshman orientation:** Mandatory, $200 fee. Preregistration for classes offered. Two-day program scheduled 7 times in the summer before fall enrollment. Consists of campus tour, individual and group visits to a class or an academic department, and admissions and financial aid counseling. **Housing:** Guaranteed on-campus for freshmen. Coed dorms, single-sex dorms, special housing for disabled, apartments, fraternity/sorority housing available. $250 partly refundable deposit, deadline 5/1. Learning community houses, honors houses, special interest houses available. **Activities:** Bands, campus ministries, choral groups, dance, drama, international student organizations, literary magazine, music ensembles, Model UN, musical theater, radio station, student government, student newspaper, TV station, Black student alliance, Muslim student association, College Democrats, College Republicans, student activities board, Relay for Life, Hindu student council, interfaith ministries.

Athletics. NCAA. **Intercollegiate:** Baseball M, basketball, cross-country, diving, field hockey W, soccer, softball W, swimming, tennis, track and field, volleyball W. **Intramural:** Badminton, basketball, bowling, football (non-tackle), golf, handball, racquetball, soccer, softball, squash, swimming, table tennis, tennis, triathlon, volleyball. **Team name:** Billikens.

Student services. Adult student services, alcohol/substance abuse counseling, chaplain/spiritual director, career counseling, services for economically disadvantaged, student employment services, financial aid counseling, health services, minority student services, personal counseling, placement for graduates, veterans' counselor, women's services. **Physically disabled:** Services for visually, speech, hearing impaired.

Contact. E-mail: admitme@slu.edu
Phone: (314) 977-2500 Toll-free number: (800) 758-3678
Fax: (314) 977-7136
Jean Gilman, Dean of Undergraduate Admission, Saint Louis University,
221 North Grand Boulevard, St. Louis, MO 63103

Southeast Missouri State University
Cape Girardeau, Missouri   **CB member**
www.semo.edu   **CB code: 6655**

◗ Public 4-year university
◗ Commuter campus in large town
◗ 9,407 degree-seeking undergraduates: 15% part-time, 58% women, 9% African American, 1% Asian American, 1% Hispanic American, 5% international
◗ 954 degree-seeking graduate students
◗ 97% of applicants admitted
◗ SAT or ACT (ACT writing optional) required
◗ 46% graduate within 6 years

General. Founded in 1873. Regionally accredited. **Degrees:** 1,470 bachelor's, 6 associate awarded; master's offered. **ROTC:** Air Force. **Location:** 120 miles from St. Louis. **Calendar:** Semester, extensive summer session. **Full-time faculty:** 397 total; 73% have terminal degrees, 14% minority, 47% women. **Part-time faculty:** 185 total; 20% have terminal degrees, 5% minority, 57% women. **Class size:** 36% < 20, 58% 20-39, 3% 40-49, 2% 50-99, less than 1% >100. **Special facilities:** Demonstration farm, NASA educator resource center, mobile teaching and learning center, mobile health center, museum of archeology, history, and fine art.

Freshman class profile. 4,161 applied, 4,050 admitted, 1,904 enrolled.

Mid 50% test scores		Rank in top tenth:	18%
SAT critical reading:	440-590	End year in good standing:	77%
SAT math:	450-600	Return as sophomores:	71%
ACT composite:	20-25	Out-of-state:	14%
GPA 3.75 or higher:	27%	Live on campus:	66%
GPA 3.50-3.74:	16%	International:	4%
GPA 3.0-3.49:	31%	Fraternities:	17%
GPA 2.0-2.99:	25%	Sororities:	12%
Rank in top quarter:	42%		

Basis for selection. Standard test scores, academic GPA, rigor of secondary school records very important. Non-traditional students may take the ASSET exam. ACT preferred; SAT accepted. BFA in Performing Arts program requires audition or presentation of a portfolio for formal admittance.

High school preparation. College-preparatory program required. 17 units required. Required units include English 4, mathematics 3, social studies 2, history 1, science 3 (laboratory 1), visual/performing arts 1 and academic electives 3. Of social studies requirements, .5 units must be in U.S. government.

2011-2012 Annual costs. Tuition/fees: $6,555; $11,595 out-of-state. Room/board: $7,715. Books/supplies: $464. Personal expenses: $2,314.

2010-2011 Financial aid. Need-based: 1,533 full-time freshmen applied for aid; 1,194 were judged to have need; 1,183 of these received aid. Average need met was 65%. Average scholarship/grant was $6,111; average loan $3,045. 50% of total undergraduate aid awarded as scholarships/grants, 50% as loans/jobs. **Non-need-based:** Awarded to 1,567 full-time undergraduates, including 550 freshmen. Scholarships awarded for academics, alumni affiliation, art, athletics, job skills, leadership, minority status, music/drama, ROTC, state residency.

Application procedures. Admission: Priority date 12/15; deadline 6/1 (postmark date). $30 fee, may be waived for applicants with need. Admission notification on a rolling basis beginning on or about 9/1. Must reply by 5/1. **Financial aid:** Priority date 3/1; no closing date. FAFSA required. Applicants notified on a rolling basis starting 4/1; must reply within 3 week(s) of notification.

Academics. Special study options: Accelerated study, distance learning, double major, dual enrollment of high school students, ESL, honors, independent study, internships, liberal arts/career combination, student-designed major, study abroad, teacher certification program. **Credit/placement by examination:** AP, CLEP, IB, SAT, ACT, institutional tests. 30 credit hours maximum toward associate degree, 30 toward bachelor's. College credit earned by examination may be counted toward University Studies, major, minor or elective requirements. A maximum of 30 semester hours of combined credit from AP, CLEP, DANTES, DE, CPS, and IB options may be counted toward a single degree. **Support services:** Learning center, pre-admission summer program, reduced course load, remedial instruction, study skills assistance, tutoring, writing center.

Majors. Biology: General. **Business:** Accounting, business admin, finance, international, marketing, office management. **Communications:** Communications/speech/rhetoric, organizational. **Computer sciences:** General, security. **Conservation:** Environmental science. **Education:** Agricultural, art, business, early childhood, elementary, English, family/consumer sciences, foreign languages, mathematics, middle, music, physical, science, social studies, special ed, speech, technology/industrial arts. **Engineering:** Applied physics. **English:** English lit. **Foreign languages:** French, German, Spanish. **General:** Agribusiness operations, animal sciences, horticultural science, plant sciences. **Health services:** Athletic training, clinical lab science, communication disorders, nursing (RN). **History:** General. **Human services:** Social work. **Math:** General. **Parks/recreation:** General, health/fitness, sports admin. **Philosophy/religion:** Philosophy. **Physical sciences:** Chemistry, physics. **Protective services:** Corrections. **Psychology:** General. **Social sciences:** Anthropology, economics, political science. **Visual/performing arts:** General, art, dramatic, music. **Work/family studies:** General.

Most popular majors. Business/marketing 14%, communications/journalism 7%, education 16%, engineering/engineering technologies 6%, health sciences 7%, liberal arts 12%.

Computing on campus. 1,749 workstations in dormitories, library, student center. Dormitories wired for high-speed internet access and linked to campus network. Online course registration, online library, helpline, wireless network available.

Student life. Freshman orientation: Mandatory, $65 fee. Preregistration for classes offered. One-day program offered many times throughout the semester. **Housing:** Coed dorms, special housing for disabled, apartments, fraternity/sorority housing, wellness housing available. $150 partly refundable deposit. Apartments for students with dependents available. **Activities:** Bands, campus ministries, choral groups, dance, drama, film society, international student organizations, literary magazine, music ensembles, Model UN, musical theater, opera, radio station, student government, student newspaper, symphony orchestra, TV station, Baptist Student Union, Lutheran Student Fellowship, Association of Black Collegians, College Republicans, College Democrats, Students in Action, Indian Subcontinent Student Association, Catholic Campus Ministries, Chinese Students & Scholars Association.

Athletics. NCAA. **Intercollegiate:** Baseball M, basketball, cheerleading, cross-country, football (tackle) M, gymnastics W, soccer W, softball W, tennis W, track and field, volleyball W. **Intramural:** Badminton, basketball, bowling, football (non-tackle), golf, racquetball, soccer, softball, swimming, table tennis, tennis, volleyball, wrestling. **Team name:** Redhawks.

Student services. Adult student services, alcohol/substance abuse counseling, chaplain/spiritual director, career counseling, services for economically disadvantaged, student employment services, financial aid counseling, health services, minority student services, on-campus daycare, personal counseling, placement for graduates, veterans' counselor. **Physically disabled:** Services for visually, speech, hearing impaired.

Contact. E-mail: admissions@semo.edu
Phone: (573) 651-2590 Fax: (573) 651-5936
Deborah Below, Assistant Vice President for Enrollment Management & Director of Admissions, Southeast Missouri State University, One University Plaza, Cape Girardeau, MO 63701

Southwest Baptist University
Bolivar, Missouri
www.sbuniv.edu   **CB code: 6664**

◗ Private 4-year university affiliated with Southern Baptist Convention
◗ Residential campus in small town
◗ 2,584 degree-seeking undergraduates: 24% part-time, 64% women, 5% African American, 1% Asian American, 2% Hispanic American, 1% Native American, 1% international
◗ 536 degree-seeking graduate students
◗ 73% of applicants admitted

General. Founded in 1878. Regionally accredited. **Degrees:** 373 bachelor's, 175 associate awarded; master's, professional offered. **ROTC:** Army. **Location:** 25 miles from Springfield, 120 miles from Kansas City. **Calendar:** Semester, extensive summer session. **Full-time faculty:** 112 total; 70% have terminal degrees. **Part-time faculty:** 150 total. **Class size:** 67% < 20, 26% 20-39, 4% 40-49, 3% 50-99, less than 1% >100.

Freshman class profile. 1,687 applied, 1,239 admitted, 444 enrolled.

GPA 3.75 or higher:	36%	Rank in top tenth:	20%
GPA 3.50-3.74:	16%	Out-of-state:	25%
GPA 3.0-3.49:	22%	Live on campus:	91%
GPA 2.0-2.99:	19%	International:	1%
Rank in top quarter:	41%		

Basis for selection. Must meet 2 of 3 qualifiers: 2.50 GPA, 21 ACT or 990 SAT score (exclusive of Writing), top 50% high school class rank. Interview required for conditionally admitted applicants, recommended for all. Audition recommended for music, speech, and theater students.

High school preparation. College-preparatory program recommended. 13 units recommended. Recommended units include English 4, mathematics 3, social studies 2, science 2 and academic electives 2. 2 additional units of foreign language or computer science or 2 units of English, math, social studies or natural sciences recommended.

2011-2012 Annual costs. Tuition/fees: $18,200. Room/board: $6,050. Books/supplies: $1,500. Personal expenses: $2,000.

2011-2012 Financial aid. Need-based: 379 full-time freshmen applied for aid; 333 were judged to have need; 333 of these received aid. Average need met was 79%. Average scholarship/grant was $5,215; average loan $3,819. 80% of total undergraduate aid awarded as scholarships/grants, 20% as loans/jobs. **Non-need-based:** Awarded to 1,715 full-time undergraduates, including 458 freshmen. Scholarships awarded for academics, alumni affiliation, art, athletics, minority status, music/drama, religious affiliation.

Application procedures. Admission: No deadline. $30 fee, may be waived for applicants with need. Admission notification on a rolling basis. **Financial aid:** Priority date 3/15; no closing date. FAFSA required. Applicants notified on a rolling basis starting 3/1; must reply within 2 week(s) of notification.

Academics. Special study options: Accelerated study, cross-registration, distance learning, double major, dual enrollment of high school students, exchange student, honors, independent study, internships, liberal arts/career combination, study abroad, teacher certification program, Washington semester. **Credit/placement by examination:** AP, CLEP, IB, SAT, ACT, institutional tests. 16 credit hours maximum toward associate degree, 32 toward bachelor's. **Support services:** Learning center, reduced course load, remedial instruction, study skills assistance, tutoring, writing center.

Majors. Biology: General. **Business:** Accounting, business admin, customer service, finance, international, marketing, office management. **Communications:** Communications/speech/rhetoric. **Computer sciences:** General, computer science. **Education:** Art, biology, chemistry, elementary, English, health, middle, music, physical, science, social science. **English:** English lit. **Foreign languages:** Spanish. **Health services:** Athletic training, clinical lab science, nursing (RN). **History:** General. **Math:** General. **Parks/recreation:** General, health/fitness, sports admin. **Philosophy/religion:** Religion. **Physical sciences:** Chemistry. **Protective services:** Law enforcement admin. **Psychology:** General. **Social sciences:** Political science, sociology. **Theology:** Bible, missionary, religious ed, sacred music, theology. **Visual/performing arts:** Art, commercial/advertising art, dramatic, music.

Most popular majors. Business/marketing 13%, education 20%, health sciences 17%, psychology 10%, theological studies 9%.

Computing on campus. 242 workstations in dormitories, library, computer center, student center. Dormitories linked to campus network. Commuter students can connect to campus network. Online library, helpline, wireless network available.

Student life. Freshman orientation: Available. Preregistration for classes offered. 3-days prior to start of the fall semester. **Policies:** Religious observance required. **Housing:** Guaranteed on-campus for freshmen. Single-sex dorms, apartments, wellness housing available. **Activities:** Bands, campus ministries, choral groups, drama, music ensembles, musical theater, opera, student government, student newspaper, symphony orchestra, University Missions, Habitat for Humanity, Christian Service organization, Theatrical Evangelism and Mission, Students in Free Enterprise, Discipleship-Now teams.

Athletics. NCAA. **Intercollegiate:** Baseball M, basketball, cheerleading, cross-country, football (tackle) M, golf M, soccer W, softball W, tennis, track and field, volleyball W. **Intramural:** Basketball, football (non-tackle), racquetball, soccer, softball, volleyball. **Team name:** Bearcats.

Student services. Chaplain/spiritual director, career counseling, student employment services, financial aid counseling, health services, personal counseling, placement for graduates.

Contact. E-mail: dcrowder@sbuniv.edu
Phone: (417) 328-1810 Toll-free number: (800) 526-5859
Fax: (417) 328-1808
Darren Crowder, Director of Admissions, Southwest Baptist University, 1600 University Avenue, Bolivar, MO 65613-2597

St. Louis Christian College
Florissant, Missouri
www.slcconline.edu   CB code: 0334

- Private 4-year Bible college affiliated with Christian Church
- Residential campus in small city
- 263 degree-seeking undergraduates: 17% part-time, 43% women, 33% African American, 3% Hispanic American, 1% Native American, 2% international
- 33% of applicants admitted
- SAT or ACT (ACT writing optional), application essay required

General. Founded in 1956. Candidate for regional accreditation; also accredited by ABHE. Students highly involved in service and field education. **Degrees:** 46 bachelor's, 27 associate awarded. **Location:** 15 miles from downtown. **Calendar:** Semester, limited summer session. **Full-time faculty:** 12 total; 17% have terminal degrees, 17% women. **Part-time faculty:** 24 total; 25% have terminal degrees, 38% women.

Freshman class profile. 145 applied, 48 admitted, 25 enrolled.

Mid 50% test scores			
SAT critical reading:	360-670	GPA 2.0-2.99:	46%
SAT math:	450-600	Rank in top quarter:	17%
SAT writing:	200-570	Rank in top tenth:	6%
ACT composite:	17-21	End year in good standing:	78%
GPA 3.75 or higher:	13%	Return as sophomores:	57%
GPA 3.50-3.74:	15%	Out-of-state:	48%
GPA 3.0-3.49:	21%	Live on campus:	96%

Basis for selection. ACT score, high school class rank, and GPA very important. English and math placement based on ACT subscores or COMPASS tests. **Home schooled:** Transcript of courses and grades required. ACT required, GED recommended.

High school preparation. Recommended units include English 4, mathematics 3, social studies 3, science 3, foreign language 2 and academic electives 4.

2011-2012 Annual costs. Tuition/fees: $15,700. Full tuition scholarships for eligible students. Room/board: $9,000. Books/supplies: $800. Personal expenses: $600.

2010-2011 Financial aid. Need-based: 52 full-time freshmen applied for aid; 51 were judged to have need; 51 of these received aid. Average need met was 76%. Average scholarship/grant was $15,903; average loan $2,770. 82% of total undergraduate aid awarded as scholarships/grants, 18% as loans/jobs. **Non-need-based:** Awarded to 41 full-time undergraduates, including 5 freshmen.

Application procedures. Admission: Closing date 8/7 (receipt date). No application fee. Admission notification by 8/10. Admission notification on a rolling basis beginning on or about 9/1. **Financial aid:** Closing date 8/1. FAFSA required. Applicants notified on a rolling basis starting 7/20; must reply within 2 week(s) of notification.

Academics. Preparation for ministries in preaching, education, youth work, mission fields, music, worship and pre-seminary education. **Special study options:** Cross-registration, internships. **Credit/placement by examination:** AP, CLEP, ACT, institutional tests. 30 credit hours maximum toward associate degree, 30 toward bachelor's. **Support services:** Learning center, remedial instruction, study skills assistance, tutoring, writing center.

Majors. Education: General. **Theology:** Bible, missionary, religious ed, sacred music, theology.

Computing on campus. 13 workstations in library, computer center. Dormitories wired for high-speed internet access and linked to campus network.

Student life. Freshman orientation: Mandatory, $250 fee. Preregistration for classes offered. Held weekend before first day of class. **Policies:** Students involved in evangelistic activities of area churches. Religious observance required. **Housing:** Guaranteed on-campus for all undergraduates. Single-sex dorms, apartments available. $250 nonrefundable deposit, deadline 8/12. **Activities:** Campus ministries, choral groups, drama, music ensembles, student government, missions interest group.

Athletics. NCCAA. **Intercollegiate:** Baseball M, basketball, cross-country W, volleyball W. **Intramural:** Baseball M, basketball, cross-country, softball, tennis, volleyball. **Team name:** Soldiers.

Student services. Adult student services, chaplain/spiritual director, career counseling, student employment services, financial aid counseling,

personal counseling, veterans' counselor. **Physically disabled:** Services for visually, hearing impaired.

Contact. E-mail: admissions@slcconline.edu
Phone: (314) 837-6777 ext. 8110 Toll-free number: (800) 877-7522
Fax: (314) 837-8291
Carrie Chapman, Director of Admissions, St. Louis Christian College, 1360 Grandview Drive, Florissant, MO 63033

St. Luke's College
Kansas City, Missouri
www.saintlukescollege.edu　　　　　**CB code: 7127**

- Private two-year upper-division nursing college affiliated with Episcopal Church
- Commuter campus in large city
- 19% of applicants admitted
- Application essay, interview required

General. Founded in 1903. Regionally accredited. **Degrees:** 62 bachelor's awarded. **Calendar:** Semester, limited summer session. **Full-time faculty:** 14 total; 29% have terminal degrees, 100% women. **Class size:** 33% < 20, 44% 20-39, 6% 40-49, 17% 50-99. **Special facilities:** Hospital simulation center, learning exchange center with teleconferencing capability.

Student profile. 129 degree-seeking undergraduates. 355 applied as first time-transfer students, 68 admitted, 48 enrolled. 100% entered as juniors.

Women:	90%	Part-time:	16%
African American:	8%	25 or older:	46%
Hispanic American:	2%		

Basis for selection. High school transcript, college transcript, application essay, interview required. Recommendations required. Health care-related work and community service considered. Transfer accepted as juniors.

2012-2013 Annual costs. Tuition/fees (projected): $13,620. Final semester graduation fee of $262. Books/supplies: $1,300.

Financial aid. Need-based: 104 applied for aid; 98 were judged to have need; 98 of these received aid. Average need met was 65%. 31% of total undergraduate aid awarded as scholarships/grants, 69% as loans/jobs. **Non-need-based:** Awarded to 15 undergraduates.

Application procedures. Admission: Deadline 1/15. $35 fee. Application must be submitted on paper. Admission notification 3/1. **Financial aid:** No deadline. Applicants notified on a rolling basis; must reply within 3 weeks of notification.

Academics. Special study options: Combined bachelor's/graduate degree, study abroad. **Credit/placement by examination:** AP, CLEP. 15 credit hours maximum toward bachelor's degree. Exams must not be older than 10 years Only CLEP and AP exams accepted.

Majors. Health services: Nursing (RN).

Computing on campus. 30 workstations in library, computer center. Helpline, wireless network available.

Student life. Activities: Student government.

Student services. Career counseling, financial aid counseling, health services, personal counseling.

Contact. E-mail: slc-admissions@saint-lukes.org
Phone: (816) 932-2367 Fax: (816) 932-9064
St. Luke's College, 8320 Ward Parkway, Suite 300, Kansas City, MO 64114

Stephens College
Columbia, Missouri
www.stephens.edu　　　　　**CB member**
　　　　　CB code: 6683

- Private 4-year liberal arts and career college for women
- Residential campus in small city
- 730 degree-seeking undergraduates: 18% part-time, 97% women, 13% African American, 3% Hispanic American, 1% Native American
- 244 degree-seeking graduate students
- 58% of applicants admitted
- SAT or ACT (ACT writing optional), application essay required
- 43% graduate within 6 years

General. Founded in 1833. Regionally accredited. **Degrees:** 203 bachelor's awarded; master's offered. **ROTC:** Army, Naval, Air Force. **Location:** 120 miles from St. Louis and Kansas City. **Calendar:** Semester, limited summer session. **Full-time faculty:** 55 total; 46% have terminal degrees, 2% minority, 76% women. **Part-time faculty:** 42 total; 21% have terminal degrees, 2% minority, 48% women. **Class size:** 73% < 20, 25% 20-39, less than 1% 40-49, less than 1% 50-99. **Special facilities:** Professional theater, private elementary lab school and child study center; horse stables, historical costume collection.

Freshman class profile. 718 applied, 414 admitted, 162 enrolled.

Mid 50% test scores			
SAT critical reading:	470-580	GPA 2.0-2.99:	25%
SAT math:	410-570	Rank in top quarter:	42%
SAT writing:	470-570	Rank in top tenth:	20%
ACT composite:	19-25	End year in good standing:	91%
GPA 3.75 or higher:	22%	Return as sophomores:	65%
GPA 3.50-3.74:	17%	Out-of-state:	48%
GPA 3.0-3.49:	36%	Live on campus:	100%

Basis for selection. Admissions decisions are result of holistic review of application file including GPA, test scores, essay, resume, recommendations and student interaction with admissions office. Interview recommended for all students. Audition mandatory for dance, recommended for theater and musical theater students. **Home schooled:** Statement describing home school structure and mission, transcript of courses and grades, letter of recommendation (nonparent) required. Require short narrative by primary instructor describing secondary-level education. Examples of student's work may be provided as supplemental information. Narrative may be considered in lieu of transcript when transcript not available. Campus visit for individual meeting with admissions counselor encouraged.

High school preparation. College-preparatory program recommended. 12 units recommended. Recommended units include English 4, mathematics 3, social studies 1, science 2 and foreign language 2.

2011-2012 Annual costs. Tuition/fees: $26,420. Room/board: $8,680. Books/supplies: $1,400. Personal expenses: $1,400.

2010-2011 Financial aid. Need-based: 168 full-time freshmen applied for aid; 147 were judged to have need; 147 of these received aid. Average need met was 83%. Average scholarship/grant was $7,870; average loan $3,319. 59% of total undergraduate aid awarded as scholarships/grants, 41% as loans/jobs. **Non-need-based:** Awarded to 705 full-time undergraduates, including 137 freshmen. Scholarships awarded for academics, alumni affiliation, athletics, leadership, music/drama, state residency.

Application procedures. Admission: Priority date 1/1; no deadline. $25 fee, may be waived for applicants with need, free for online applicants. Admission notification on a rolling basis beginning on or about 1/1. Must reply by May 1 or within 2 week(s) if notified thereafter. **Financial aid:** Priority date 3/15; no closing date. FAFSA required. Applicants notified on a rolling basis starting 3/1.

Academics. Academic Resource Center offers one-on-one and group sessions in many course subjects, as well as time management, study skills and writing. **Special study options:** Accelerated study, combined bachelor's/graduate degree, cross-registration, distance learning, double major, dual enrollment of high school students, external degree, honors, independent study, internships, liberal arts/career combination, semester at sea, student-designed major, study abroad, teacher certification program. **Credit/placement by examination:** AP, CLEP, IB, SAT, ACT. 15 credit hours maximum toward associate degree, 30 toward bachelor's. **Support services:** Learning center, pre-admission summer program, study skills assistance, tutoring, writing center.

Honors college/program. Stephens College Honors House Plan is a living/learning community within the college. Members are selected for invitation based on application materials and credentials. Limited number of positions available; only new incoming freshman are selected for invitation.

Majors. Biology: General. **Business:** General, accounting, business admin, fashion, marketing. **Communications:** Advertising, broadcast journalism, communications/speech/rhetoric, journalism, media studies, public relations. **Education:** General, early childhood, elementary. **English:** Creative writing, English lit. **General:** Equine science. **Health services:** Medical records admin. **Liberal arts:** Arts/sciences. **Psychology:** General. **Visual/performing arts:** General, commercial/advertising art, dance, dramatic, fashion design, film/cinema/video, graphic design, interior design. **Work/family studies:** Clothing/textiles, family studies.

Most popular majors. Business/marketing 26%, education 7%, health sciences 14%, visual/performing arts 28%.

Computing on campus. 107 workstations in dormitories, library, computer center. Dormitories wired for high-speed internet access and linked to campus network. Commuter students can connect to campus network. Online library, helpline, repair service, student web hosting, wireless network available.

Student life. Freshman orientation: Mandatory. Preregistration for classes offered. Typically held third week of August, one week prior to start of classes. Registration held mid-June on campus with academic adviser. **Policies:** Undergraduate students are required to live on campus in college-sanctioned housing. **Housing:** Guaranteed on-campus for all undergraduates. Special housing for disabled, apartments available. $200 partly refundable deposit, deadline 5/1. Pets allowed in dorm rooms. Freshman academic residence hall, designated housing for students who bring pets, available. **Activities:** Campus ministries, choral groups, dance, drama, film society, literary magazine, music ensembles, musical theater, radio station, student government, student newspaper, TV station, Judicial Board; College Democrats; Martin Luther King Student Union; Minority Sistas; Champions of Character; Stephens College Ambassadors; Students in Free Enterprise; and Christian Outreach Fellowship.

Athletics. NAIA. **Intercollegiate:** Basketball W, cross-country W, golf W, softball W, tennis W, volleyball W. **Intramural:** Equestrian W. **Team name:** Stars.

Student services. Adult student services, career counseling, student employment services, financial aid counseling, health services, minority student services, personal counseling, placement for graduates, women's services.

Contact. E-mail: apply@stephens.edu
Phone: (573) 876-7207 Toll-free number: (800) 876-7207
Fax: (573) 876-7237
Chris Collier, Vice President of Enrollment Management, Stephens College, 1200 East Broadway, Columbia, MO 65215

Truman State University
Kirksville, Missouri

CB member

www.truman.edu

CB code: 6483

- Public 4-year university and liberal arts college
- Residential campus in large town
- 5,550 degree-seeking undergraduates: 2% part-time, 59% women, 4% African American, 2% Asian American, 3% Hispanic American, 1% Native American, 5% international
- 265 degree-seeking graduate students
- 75% of applicants admitted
- SAT or ACT (ACT writing optional), application essay required
- 69% graduate within 6 years; 70% enter graduate study

General. Founded in 1867. Regionally accredited. Member of the Council of Public Liberal Arts Colleges. **Degrees:** 1,170 bachelor's awarded; master's offered. **ROTC:** Army. **Location:** 85 miles from Columbia,195 miles from St. Louis. **Calendar:** Semester, extensive summer session. **Full-time faculty:** 318 total; 83% have terminal degrees, 9% minority, 40% women. **Part-time faculty:** 52 total; 50% have terminal degrees, 4% minority, 56% women. **Class size:** 30% < 20, 60% 20-39, 5% 40-49, 4% 50-99, less than 1% >100. **Special facilities:** Movement analysis lab, motor learning/biomechanics lab, observatory, greenhouse, local history museum, 400-acre farm, speech and hearing clinic, biofeedback laboratory, IR and NMR instrumentation, independent learning center for nursing, radio station, television studio, publications technology lab, 24-hour art studio space, Apple/Mac labs, language learning lab, strength and conditioning center, large format printer, human anatomy laboratory, medical resource library, ROTC classrooms and training facilities, SMART Board classrooms and lecture capture technology.

Freshman class profile. 4,569 applied, 3,428 admitted, 1,378 enrolled.

Mid 50% test scores			
SAT critical reading:	550-620	Rank in top tenth:	49%
SAT math:	560-640	End year in good standing:	88%
ACT composite:	25-30	Return as sophomores:	86%
GPA 3.75 or higher:	63%	Out-of-state:	17%
GPA 3.50-3.74:	19%	Live on campus:	98%
GPA 3.0-3.49:	17%	International:	3%
GPA 2.0-2.99:	1%	Fraternities:	21%
Rank in top quarter:	82%	Sororities:	16%

Basis for selection. High school performance (class rank, GPA, college preparatory curriculum), test scores, and essay are most important; special ability, talent and achievement are considered. Portfolio recommended for fine arts students. Audition required for music students. Additional nursing-specific application required for all students interested in pursuing a Nursing

degree. **Learning Disabled:** Students are welcome to provide additional documentation of their learning disability to Office of Disability Services.

High school preparation. College-preparatory program recommended. 21 units required; 22 recommended. Required and recommended units include English 4, mathematics 3-4, social studies 2, history 1, science 3 (laboratory 2), foreign language 2, visual/performing arts 1 and academic electives 5. 1 practical arts, 1 physical education, .5 health education, .5 personal finance required.

2011-2012 Annual costs. Tuition/fees: $7,012; $12,556 out-of-state. Special course fees may be assessed for courses in business, health sciences, education, art, music, theatre and the sciences. Room/board: $7,254. Books/supplies: $1,000. Personal expenses: $2,500.

2010-2011 Financial aid. Need-based: 1,156 full-time freshmen applied for aid; 767 were judged to have need; 766 of these received aid. Average need met was 87.4%. Average scholarship/grant was $6,972; average loan $3,364. 57% of total undergraduate aid awarded as scholarships/grants, 43% as loans/jobs. **Non-need-based:** Awarded to 4,241 full-time undergraduates, including 1,313 freshmen. Scholarships awarded for academics, alumni affiliation, art, athletics, leadership, minority status, music/drama, ROTC, state residency.

Application procedures. Admission: Priority date 12/1; no deadline. No application fee. Admission notification on a rolling basis beginning on or about 9/15. Must reply by May 1 or within 3 week(s) if notified thereafter. Housing deposit not refundable after May 1. **Financial aid:** Priority date 4/1; no closing date. FAFSA, institutional form required. Applicants notified on a rolling basis starting 3/1.

Academics. Special study options: Combined bachelor's/graduate degree, double major, dual enrollment of high school students, honors, independent study, internships, semester at sea, student-designed major, study abroad, teacher certification program. **Credit/placement by examination:** AP, CLEP, IB, institutional tests. Some majors require a grade for courses, in which case examination is not an option. Not every CLEP exam accepted for credit. Credit by exam does not count towards GPA. **Support services:** Learning center, study skills assistance, tutoring, writing center.

Majors. Biology: General. **Business:** Accounting, business admin. **Communications:** Communications/speech/rhetoric. **Computer sciences:** Computer science. **English:** Creative writing, English lit. **Foreign languages:** Classics, French, German, linguistics, Romance, Russian, Spanish. **Health services:** Athletic training, communication disorders, nursing (RN). **History:** General. **Math:** General. **Parks/recreation:** Exercise sciences, health/fitness. **Philosophy/religion:** General. **Physical sciences:** Chemistry, physics. **Protective services:** Criminal justice. **Psychology:** General. **Social sciences:** Economics, political science, sociology. **Visual/performing arts:** Art, art history/conservation, dramatic, music, music performance.

Most popular majors. Biology 10%, business/marketing 15%, English 10%, health sciences 6%, parks/recreation 10%, psychology 9%, social sciences 6%, visual/performing arts 7%.

Computing on campus. 748 workstations in dormitories, library, computer center, student center. Dormitories wired for high-speed internet access and linked to campus network. Commuter students can connect to campus network. Online course registration, online library, helpline, student web hosting, wireless network available.

Student life. Freshman orientation: Mandatory, $305 fee. Preregistration for classes offered. Sessions held during June and August, with additional "Truman Week" program a few days before fall semester begins. **Policies:** Dry campus. First-time freshmen are required to live on campus. **Housing:** Guaranteed on-campus for freshmen. Coed dorms, special housing for disabled, apartments, fraternity/sorority housing available. $150 partly refundable deposit, deadline 5/1. Pets allowed in dorm rooms. Spanish and French language, pre-med, volunteerism, first-year community housing available. **Activities:** Bands, campus ministries, choral groups, dance, drama, film society, international student organizations, literary magazine, music ensembles, Model UN, musical theater, opera, radio station, student government, student newspaper, symphony orchestra, TV station, Alpha Phi Omega, Association of Black Collegians, College Republicans, Campus Christian Fellowship, Blue Key, Cardinal Key, College Democrats, Baptist Student Union, Newman Center, Hispanic American Leadership Organization (HALO).

Athletics. NCAA. **Intercollegiate:** Baseball M, basketball, cross-country, football (tackle) M, golf W, soccer, softball W, swimming, tennis, track and field, volleyball W, wrestling M. **Intramural:** Badminton, basketball, bowling, football (non-tackle), racquetball, soccer, softball, swimming, table tennis, tennis, track and field, triathlon, volleyball, weight lifting. **Team name:** Bulldogs.

Student services. Alcohol/substance abuse counseling, career counseling, services for economically disadvantaged, student employment services, financial aid counseling, health services, minority student services, personal counseling, placement for graduates, veterans' counselor, women's services. **Physically disabled:** Services for visually, speech, hearing impaired.

Contact. E-mail: admissions@truman.edu
Phone: (660) 785-4114 Toll-free number: (800) 892-7792
Fax: (660) 785-7456
Melody Chambers, Director of Admission, Truman State University, 100
East Normal Avenue, Kirksville, MO 63501

University of Central Missouri
Warrensburg, Missouri
www.ucmo.edu   **CB code: 6090**

- Public 4-year university
- Commuter campus in large town
- 8,885 degree-seeking undergraduates: 11% part-time, 54% women, 8% African American, 2% Hispanic American, 3% international
- 1,819 degree-seeking graduate students
- 80% of applicants admitted
- SAT or ACT (ACT writing optional) required
- 50% graduate within 6 years

General. Founded in 1871. Regionally accredited. **Degrees:** 1,712 bachelor's awarded; master's offered. **ROTC:** Army, Air Force. **Location:** 50 miles from Kansas City. **Calendar:** Semester, extensive summer session. **Full-time faculty:** 446 total; 68% have terminal degrees, 13% minority, 45% women. **Part-time faculty:** 160 total. **Class size:** 44% < 20, 48% 20-39, 5% 40-49, 3% 50-99, less than 1% >100. **Special facilities:** Airport, 260-acre farm, children's literature collection, musical instruments collection, child development lab, advanced technology library.

Freshman class profile. 4,410 applied, 3,523 admitted, 1,689 enrolled.

Mid 50% test scores		Rank in top tenth:	11%
ACT composite:	19-24	End year in good standing:	72%
GPA 3.75 or higher:	22%	Out-of-state:	7%
GPA 3.50-3.74:	15%	Live on campus:	86%
GPA 3.0-3.49:	29%	International:	2%
GPA 2.0-2.99:	33%	Fraternities:	10%
Rank in top quarter:	33%	Sororities:	13%

Basis for selection. Applicant must be in top two-thirds of high school class, complete 16-unit core curriculum and have minimum ACT score of 20. Essay required for some programs; audition recommended for music students. **Home schooled:** Transcript of courses and grades required. Recommend ACT, GED, or equivalent.

High school preparation. College-preparatory program required. 16 units required. Required and recommended units include English 4, mathematics 3, social studies 3, science 2 (laboratory 1), foreign language 2 and academic electives 3. 1 fine/performing arts required.

2011-2012 Annual costs. Tuition/fees: $6,945; $13,500 out-of-state. Room/board: $7,094. Books/supplies: $600. Personal expenses: $1,000.

2010-2011 Financial aid. **Need-based:** 1,408 full-time freshmen applied for aid; 852 were judged to have need; 852 of these received aid. Average need met was 87%. Average scholarship/grant was $3,940; average loan $3,292. 54% of total undergraduate aid awarded as scholarships/grants, 46% as loans/jobs. **Non-need-based:** Awarded to 4,199 full-time undergraduates, including 1,249 freshmen. Scholarships awarded for academics, alumni affiliation, art, athletics, leadership, minority status, music/drama, ROTC, state residency.

Application procedures. **Admission:** Priority date 6/1; no deadline. $30 fee, may be waived for applicants with need. Admission notification on a rolling basis beginning on or about 8/18. Deferred admission is allowed for one semester. **Financial aid:** Priority date 3/1; no closing date. FAFSA required. Applicants notified on a rolling basis starting 3/1; must reply within 2 week(s) of notification.

Academics. Online services and resources include library, technical support, writing center and bookstore. Extensive international exchange program. **Special study options:** Combined bachelor's/graduate degree, cooperative education, cross-registration, distance learning, double major, dual enrollment of high school students, ESL, honors, internships, liberal arts/career combination, student-designed major, study abroad, teacher certification program, weekend college. Engineering program with University of Missouri (Columbia, Rolla) and University of Indiana, Missouri University of Science & Technology at Rolla. **Credit/placement by examination:** AP, CLEP, IB, SAT, ACT, institutional tests. 15 credit hours maximum toward associate degree, 30 toward bachelor's. **Support services:** Learning center, remedial instruction, study skills assistance, tutoring, writing center.

Honors college/program. Minimum ACT score of 25; 319 freshmen admitted; requires 48 credit hours.

Majors. **Biology:** General. **Business:** Accounting, actuarial science, business admin, finance, hotel/motel admin, human resources, management information systems, marketing, office management, tourism promotion. **Communications:** Broadcast journalism, communications/speech/rhetoric, journalism, public relations. **Communications technology:** Graphic/printing. **Computer sciences:** General, data processing. **Education:** Agricultural, art, biology, business, chemistry, elementary, English, family/consumer sciences, foreign languages, French, German, mathematics, middle, music, physical, physics, science, secondary, social studies, Spanish, special ed, speech, technology/industrial arts. **English:** English lit, rhetoric/composition. **Foreign languages:** French, German, Spanish. **General:** Business, economics. **Health services:** Nursing (RN), public health nursing, speech pathology. **History:** General. **Human services:** Social work. **Math:** General. **Parks/recreation:** General, facilities management. **Physical sciences:** Chemistry, geology, physics, planetary. **Protective services:** Law enforcement admin. **Psychology:** General. **Social sciences:** Economics, geography, political science, sociology. **Visual/performing arts:** Art, commercial/advertising art, dramatic, interior design, music, photography, studio arts. **Work/family studies:** General, child development, clothing/textiles, family studies.

Most popular majors. Business/marketing 17%, education 21%, engineering/engineering technologies 8%, health sciences 8%, security/protective services 8%, visual/performing arts 7%.

Computing on campus. 2,826 workstations in dormitories, library, computer center, student center. Dormitories wired for high-speed internet access and linked to campus network. Commuter students can connect to campus network. Online course registration, online library, helpline, student web hosting, wireless network available.

Student life. **Freshman orientation:** Mandatory. Preregistration for classes offered. 8 one-day sessions in early summer. **Policies:** First year freshmen required to live on campus. **Housing:** Guaranteed on-campus for all undergraduates. Coed dorms, single-sex dorms, apartments, fraternity/ sorority housing, wellness housing available. $100 nonrefundable deposit, deadline 6/1. Honors hall, economy suites available. **Activities:** Bands, campus ministries, choral groups, dance, drama, film society, international student organizations, literary magazine, music ensembles, musical theater, opera, radio station, student government, student newspaper, symphony orchestra, TV station, Association of Black Collegiates, nontraditional student association, student ambassadors, College Republicans, College Democrats, United Students for Equal Access, Student Government Association.

Athletics. NCAA. **Intercollegiate:** Baseball M, basketball, bowling W, cross-country, football (tackle) M, golf M, soccer W, softball W, track and field, volleyball W, wrestling M. **Intramural:** Archery M, badminton M, basketball, bowling, cross-country, diving, football (tackle), golf, racquetball, rifle, rugby M, soccer, softball, swimming, table tennis, tennis, track and field, volleyball, water polo, weight lifting M, wrestling M. **Team name:** Mules (M), Jennies (W).

Student services. Adult student services, alcohol/substance abuse counseling, chaplain/spiritual director, career counseling, student employment services, financial aid counseling, health services, minority student services, on-campus daycare, personal counseling, placement for graduates, veterans' counselor, women's services. **Physically disabled:** Services for visually, speech, hearing impaired.

Contact. E-mail: admit@ucmovmb.ucmo.edu
Phone: (660) 543-4290 Toll-free number: (877) 729-8266
Fax: (660) 543-8517
Ann Nordyke, Chief Admissions Officer, University of Central Missouri, WDE 1400, Warrensburg, MO 64093

University of Missouri: Columbia
Columbia, Missouri   **CB member**
www.missouri.edu   **CB code: 6875**

- Public 4-year university
- Residential campus in small city
- 25,687 degree-seeking undergraduates: 5% part-time, 52% women, 8% African American, 2% Asian American, 3% Hispanic American, 2% international
- 7,289 degree-seeking graduate students
- 82% of applicants admitted
- SAT or ACT (ACT writing optional) required
- 69% graduate within 6 years

General. Founded in 1839. Regionally accredited. **Degrees:** 5,087 bachelor's awarded; master's, professional, doctoral offered. **ROTC:** Army, Naval, Air Force. **Location:** 125 miles from Kansas City, 125 miles from St. Louis. **Calendar:** Semester, limited summer session. **Full-time faculty:** 1,326 total;

92% have terminal degrees, 18% minority, 37% women. **Part-time faculty:** 112 total; 89% have terminal degrees, 12% minority, 43% women. **Class size:** 45% < 20, 37% 20-39, 3% 40-49, 8% 50-99, 7% >100. **Special facilities:** Observatory, research nuclear reactor, freedom of information center, engineering experiment station, center for research in social behavior, equine center, research farms, child development laboratory, black culture center, state historical society, botanical garden, art and archaeology museum.

Freshman class profile. 18,103 applied, 14,924 admitted, 6,138 enrolled.

Mid 50% test scores			
SAT critical reading:	530-650	Rank in top tenth:	25%
SAT math:	520-650	Return as sophomores:	85%
ACT composite:	23-28	Out-of-state:	30%
Rank in top quarter:	56%	Live on campus:	87%
		International:	1%

Basis for selection. Admission based on required core courses and combination of high school rank and test scores. Individual programs may have additional requirements. Trial summer admission open to Missouri residents. Students must complete math and English with C or better to continue enrollment on probation in fall. ACT recommended. ACT preferred. **Learning Disabled:** Must submit current (within 5 years) official documentation of disability.

High school preparation. College-preparatory program required. 17 units required. Required units include English 4, mathematics 4, social studies 3, science 3 (laboratory 1) and foreign language 2. 1 fine arts required. Math must include algebra I or higher.

2011-2012 Annual costs. Tuition/fees: $8,989; $21,784 out-of-state. Room/board: $8,643. Books/supplies: $1,086. Personal expenses: $1,578.

2010-2011 Financial aid. Need-based: 4,698 full-time freshmen applied for aid; 3,238 were judged to have need; 3,134 of these received aid. Average need met was 84%. Average scholarship/grant was $7,922; average loan $3,600. 48% of total undergraduate aid awarded as scholarships/grants, 52% as loans/jobs. **Non-need-based:** Awarded to 5,307 full-time undergraduates, including 1,621 freshmen. Scholarships awarded for academics, alumni affiliation, art, athletics, leadership, minority status, music/drama, ROTC, state residency. **Additional information:** Scholarship available for international students based on success during 1st semester.

Application procedures. Admission: Priority date 5/1; no deadline. $50 fee, may be waived for applicants with need. Admission notification on a rolling basis beginning on or about 9/1. Must reply by May 1 or within 4 week(s) if notified thereafter. **Financial aid:** Priority date 3/1; no closing date. FAFSA required. Applicants notified on a rolling basis starting 4/1; must reply within 4 week(s) of notification.

Academics. Special study options: Accelerated study, combined bachelor's/graduate degree, cooperative education, cross-registration, distance learning, double major, dual enrollment of high school students, ESL, exchange student, external degree, honors, independent study, internships, New York semester, student-designed major, study abroad, teacher certification program, Washington semester. **Credit/placement by examination:** AP, CLEP, IB, ACT, institutional tests. Credit by examination policy varies by school/college. **Support services:** Learning center, pre-admission summer program, reduced course load, study skills assistance, tutoring, writing center.

Honors college/program. 29 ACT or 1280 SAT and top 10% of high school graduating class required. If school does not rank, core GPA of 3.71 necessary. Core GPA includes all English courses, all math courses Algebra I and higher, all science, social studies, and foreign language courses.

Majors. Area/ethnic studies: African-American, East Asian, European, Latin American, South Asian, women's. **Biology:** General, biochemistry, conservation, microbiology. **Business:** General, accounting, banking/financial services, business admin, hotel/motel admin, international, marketing, real estate, restaurant/food services, travel services. **Communications:** Advertising, broadcast journalism, communications/speech/rhetoric, journalism, photojournalism, radio/TV. **Computer sciences:** General, computer science, information technology. **Conservation:** Fisheries, forestry, wildlife/wilderness. **Education:** General, agricultural, art, biology, business, chemistry, early childhood, elementary, English, foreign languages, mathematics, middle, multiple handicapped, music, physics, science, secondary, social studies, Spanish, voc/tech. **Engineering:** Agricultural, biomedical, chemical, civil, computer, electrical, industrial, mechanical. **English:** English lit. **Foreign languages:** Classics, East Asian, French, German, linguistics, Russian, South Asian, Spanish. **General:** Animal sciences, business, communications, economics, food science, plant sciences, soil science. **Health services:** Audiology/speech pathology, dietetics, health services admin, medical radiologic technology/radiation therapy, nuclear medical technology, nursing (RN), premedicine, prepharmacy, preveterinary, radiologic technology/medical imaging, respiratory therapy technology, sonography. **History:** General. **Human services:** Social work. **Math:** General, statistics. **Parks/recreation:** General, exercise sciences. **Philosophy/religion:** Philosophy, religion. **Physical sciences:** Atmospheric science, chemistry, geology, physics. **Psychology:** General. **Social sciences:** Anthropology, archaeology, economics, geography,

political science, sociology. **Visual/performing arts:** Art, dramatic, music. **Work/family studies:** Clothing/textiles, family resources, family studies, food/nutrition, housing, human nutrition.

Most popular majors. Biology 6%, business/marketing 18%, communications/journalism 13%, engineering/engineering technologies 7%, health sciences 9%, social sciences 7%.

Computing on campus. 1,200 workstations in dormitories, library, computer center, student center. Dormitories wired for high-speed internet access and linked to campus network. Commuter students can connect to campus network. Online course registration, online library, helpline, repair service, student web hosting, wireless network available.

Student life. Freshman orientation: Available. Preregistration for classes offered. 2-day sessions during summer. **Policies:** Alcohol-free and smoke-free campus buildings, residence halls. **Housing:** Guaranteed on-campus for freshmen. Coed dorms, single-sex dorms, apartments, fraternity/sorority housing, wellness housing available. $300 partly refundable deposit, deadline 4/1. Specialized living/learning communities and freshman interest groups in residence halls available. **Activities:** Bands, campus ministries, choral groups, dance, drama, film society, international student organizations, literary magazine, music ensembles, Model UN, musical theater, opera, radio station, student government, student newspaper, symphony orchestra, TV station, Over 600 organizations available.

Athletics. NCAA. **Intercollegiate:** Baseball M, basketball, cross-country, diving, football (tackle) M, golf, gymnastics W, soccer W, softball W, swimming, tennis W, track and field, volleyball W, wrestling M. **Intramural:** Basketball, football (non-tackle), golf, soccer, softball, volleyball. **Team name:** Tigers.

Student services. Alcohol/substance abuse counseling, chaplain/spiritual director, career counseling, services for economically disadvantaged, student employment services, financial aid counseling, health services, legal services, minority student services, on-campus daycare, personal counseling, placement for graduates, veterans' counselor, women's services. **Physically disabled:** Services for visually, speech, hearing impaired.

Contact. E-mail: mu4u@missouri.edu
Phone: (573) 882-7786 Toll-free number: (800) 225-6075
Fax: (573) 882-7887
Barbara Rupp, Director of Admissions, University of Missouri: Columbia, 230 Jesse Hall, Columbia, MO 65211

University of Missouri: Kansas City
Kansas City, Missouri
www.umkc.edu

CB member
CB code: 6872

- Public 4-year university
- Residential campus in large city
- 8,459 degree-seeking undergraduates: 20% part-time, 57% women, 16% African American, 6% Asian American, 5% Hispanic American, 3% international
- 5,098 degree-seeking graduate students
- 69% of applicants admitted
- SAT or ACT (ACT writing optional) required
- 43% graduate within 6 years

General. Founded in 1929. Regionally accredited. **Degrees:** 1,523 bachelor's awarded; master's, professional, doctoral offered. **ROTC:** Army. **Location:** 500 miles from Chicago, 250 miles from St. Louis. **Calendar:** Semester, extensive summer session. **Full-time faculty:** 742 total; 86% have terminal degrees, 23% minority, 45% women. **Part-time faculty:** 443 total; 48% have terminal degrees, 10% minority, 49% women. **Class size:** 55% < 20, 34% 20-39, 4% 40-49, 6% 50-99, 2% >100. **Special facilities:** Observatory, science and technology library, music conservatory, miniature toy museum.

Freshman class profile. 4,442 applied, 3,078 admitted, 1,174 enrolled.

Mid 50% test scores			
SAT critical reading:	500-660	Rank in top tenth:	28%
SAT math:	480-700	End year in good standing:	77%
ACT composite:	20-27	Return as sophomores:	74%
GPA 3.75 or higher:	26%	Out-of-state:	22%
GPA 3.50-3.74:	14%	Live on campus:	59%
GPA 3.0-3.49:	28%	International:	4%
GPA 2.0-2.99:	31%	Fraternities:	10%
Rank in top quarter:	52%	Sororities:	11%

Basis for selection. Admission based on class rank, test scores, and high school course requirements. Admission is very selective to combined arts and sciences/medical; highly selective to pharmacy program; and selective to

Conservatory of Music. Interview required for six-year medicine applicants; audition required for Conservatory of Music and Dance applicants. **Home schooled:** Transcript of courses and grades required. ACT or SAT score required.

High school preparation. College-preparatory program required. 17 units required. Required units include English 4, mathematics 4, social studies 3, science 3 (laboratory 1), foreign language 2 and visual/performing arts 1.

2011-2012 Annual costs. Tuition/fees: $9,029; $21,197 out-of-state. Room/board: $8,965. Books/supplies: $1,180. Personal expenses: $4,900.

2011-2012 Financial aid. Need-based: 973 full-time freshmen applied for aid; 835 were judged to have need; 823 of these received aid. Average need met was 50%. Average scholarship/grant was $7,219; average loan $6,193. 39% of total undergraduate aid awarded as scholarships/grants, 61% as loans/jobs. **Non-need-based:** Awarded to 977 full-time undergraduates, including 201 freshmen. Scholarships awarded for academics, alumni affiliation, art, athletics, leadership, minority status, music/drama, state residency.

Application procedures. Admission: Priority date 4/1; no deadline. $45 fee, may be waived for applicants with need. Admission notification on a rolling basis. Architecture, six-year medicine, conservatory and pharmacy programs have separate application deadlines and specific admissions requirements. **Financial aid:** Priority date 3/1; no closing date. FAFSA required. Applicants notified on a rolling basis starting 4/15; must reply within 2 week(s) of notification.

Academics. Special study options: Accelerated study, combined bachelor's/graduate degree, cooperative education, distance learning, double major, dual enrollment of high school students, ESL, honors, independent study, internships, liberal arts/career combination, student-designed major, study abroad, teacher certification program. **Credit/placement by examination:** AP, CLEP, IB, ACT, institutional tests. 30 credit hours maximum toward bachelor's degree. **Support services:** Learning center, reduced course load, study skills assistance, tutoring, writing center.

Majors. Architecture: Architecture, urban/community planning. **Area/ethnic studies:** American. **Biology:** General. **Business:** General, accounting, accounting/business management, accounting/finance, business admin, entrepreneurial studies, finance, market research. **Communications:** Communications/speech/rhetoric. **Computer sciences:** Computer science, information technology. **Conservation:** Environmental science, environmental studies. **Education:** General, art, bilingual, biology, chemistry, early childhood, elementary, English, foreign languages, French, geography, German, history, kindergarten/preschool, middle, music, physics, science, secondary, social science, social studies, Spanish. **Engineering:** Civil, electrical, mechanical. **English:** English lit. **Foreign languages:** French, German, Spanish. **Health services:** Clinical lab science, dental hygiene, ethics, music therapy, nursing (RN), pharmaceutical sciences, predental, premedicine, prenursing, prepharmacy. **History:** General. **Liberal arts:** Arts/sciences. **Math:** General, statistics. **Philosophy/religion:** Philosophy. **Physical sciences:** Chemistry, geology, physics. **Protective services:** Criminal justice, law enforcement admin, police science. **Psychology:** General. **Social sciences:** Criminology, economics, geography, political science, sociology, urban studies. **Visual/performing arts:** Art, art history/conservation, dance, dramatic, music, music performance, music theory/composition, piano/keyboard, stringed instruments, studio arts, voice/opera.

Most popular majors. Business/marketing 14%, communications/journalism 8%, education 8%, health sciences 13%, liberal arts 12%, physical sciences 6%, psychology 6%.

Computing on campus. 680 workstations in dormitories, library, computer center, student center. Dormitories wired for high-speed internet access and linked to campus network. Commuter students can connect to campus network. Online course registration, online library, helpline, wireless network available.

Student life. Freshman orientation: Mandatory, $40 fee. Preregistration for classes offered. Several day-long orientations offered in spring and summer. **Housing:** Coed dorms, apartments, fraternity/sorority housing, wellness housing available. $300 partly refundable deposit. University owned houses available. **Activities:** Bands, campus ministries, choral groups, dance, drama, international student organizations, literary magazine, music ensembles, musical theater, opera, radio station, student government, student newspaper, symphony orchestra, over 300 religious, political, ethnic, and social service organizations.

Athletics. NCAA. **Intercollegiate:** Basketball, cheerleading, cross-country, golf, soccer, softball W, tennis, track and field, volleyball W. **Intramural:** Badminton, basketball, football (tackle), handball, racquetball, soccer, softball, tennis, volleyball. **Team name:** Kangaroos.

Student services. Adult student services, alcohol/substance abuse counseling, career counseling, student employment services, financial aid counseling, health services, minority student services, on-campus daycare, personal counseling, placement for graduates, veterans' counselor, women's services. **Physically disabled:** Services for visually, speech, hearing impaired.

Contact. E-mail: admit@umkc.edu
Phone: (816) 235-1111 Toll-free number: (800) 775-8652
Fax: (816) 235-5544
Doretta Kidd, Acting Director of Admissions, University of Missouri: Kansas City, 5100 Rockhill Road, AC120, Kansas City, MO 64110-2499

University of Missouri: St. Louis
St. Louis, Missouri   **CB member**
www.umsl.edu   **CB code: 6889**

‣ Public 4-year university
‣ Commuter campus in very large city
‣ 9,032 degree-seeking undergraduates: 35% part-time, 58% women, 21% African American, 3% Asian American, 2% Hispanic American, 4% international
‣ 3,531 degree-seeking graduate students
‣ 69% of applicants admitted
‣ SAT or ACT (ACT writing optional) required
‣ 43% graduate within 6 years; 21% enter graduate study

General. Founded in 1963. Regionally accredited. **Degrees:** 2,092 bachelor's awarded; master's, professional, doctoral offered. **ROTC:** Army, Air Force. **Location:** 7 miles from downtown. **Calendar:** Semester, extensive summer session. **Full-time faculty:** 467 total; 77% have terminal degrees, 20% minority, 52% women. **Part-time faculty:** 422 total; 24% have terminal degrees, 15% minority, 60% women. **Class size:** 45% < 20, 38% 20-39, 8% 40-49, 7% 50-99, 2% >100. **Special facilities:** Mercantile library, observatory, 3 art galleries, performing arts center.

Freshman class profile. 1,769 applied, 1,222 admitted, 504 enrolled.

Mid 50% test scores		Rank in top tenth:	33%
SAT math:	460-610	End year in good standing:	81%
ACT composite:	21-26	Out-of-state:	19%
Rank in top quarter:	61%	International:	9%

Basis for selection. Class rank, test scores and high school course requirements most important. Audition required for music majors; not required for admission but for the purpose of placement with instrument. **Home schooled:** ACT scores are key factor in determining admission. Students should strive for score of 24 or higher.

High school preparation. College-preparatory program required. 17 units required. Required units include English 4, mathematics 4, social studies 3, science 3 (laboratory 1) and foreign language 2. 1 fine art required.

2011-2012 Annual costs. Tuition/fees: $9,038; $21,206 out-of-state. Room/board: $8,444.

2011-2012 Financial aid. Non-need-based: Scholarships awarded for academics, alumni affiliation, art, athletics, minority status, music/drama, ROTC, state residency.

Application procedures. Admission: Closing date 8/20. $35 fee, may be waived for applicants with need. Admission notification on a rolling basis beginning on or about 10/1. **Financial aid:** Priority date 4/1; no closing date. FAFSA required. Applicants notified on a rolling basis starting 4/1; must reply within 2 week(s) of notification.

Academics. Special study options: Accelerated study, combined bachelor's/graduate degree, cooperative education, cross-registration, distance learning, double major, dual enrollment of high school students, ESL, exchange student, honors, independent study, internships, liberal arts/career combination, semester at sea, student-designed major, study abroad, teacher certification program. Engineering UMSL/WU, 2+3 B.S./M.A. Program in Economics, 2+3 B.A./B.S.-Ed and M.A. Program in History, 2+3 B.A./M.A. Program in Philosophy, 2+3 B.A./M.A. Program in Political Science, 2+3 B.A. in Psychology and M.S. in Gerontology Program, 2+3 B.A./M.A. Program in Sociology, Art and Art History 3+4 Program for School of Architecture at Washington University, Biology 3+4 Program for UMSL College of Optometry, Physics and Astronomy 3+4 Program for UMSL College of Optometry, Biology 3+3 Program for Logan Chiropractic College. **Credit/placement by examination:** AP, CLEP, IB, SAT, ACT, institutional tests. 30 credit hours maximum toward bachelor's degree. **Support services:** Learning center, pre-admission summer program, study skills assistance, tutoring, writing center.

Honors college/program. Selection based on scores, class rank, extracurricular activities, test scores, 2 recommendations, essay, interview with Dean.

Approximately 50 freshmen admitted each fall. Academic program includes honors classes.

Majors. Biology: General, biochemistry. **Business:** General, accounting, business admin, finance, international, logistics, management information systems, marketing, operations, organizational behavior. **Communications:** Communications/speech/rhetoric, media studies. **Computer sciences:** General, computer science. **Education:** General, early childhood, elementary, music, physical, secondary, special ed. **Engineering:** Civil, electrical, mechanical. **English:** English lit. **Foreign languages:** French, German, Spanish. **Health services:** Nursing (RN). **History:** General. **Human services:** General, social work. **Liberal arts:** Arts/sciences. **Math:** General, applied. **Philosophy/religion:** Philosophy. **Physical sciences:** Chemistry, physics. **Psychology:** General. **Social sciences:** Anthropology, criminology, economics, political science, sociology. **Visual/performing arts:** Art history/conservation, dramatic, music, music history, studio arts.

Most popular majors. Business/marketing 28%, communications/journalism 6%, education 12%, health sciences 10%, psychology 7%, social sciences 11%.

Computing on campus. 1,300 workstations in dormitories, library, computer center, student center. Dormitories wired for high-speed internet access and linked to campus network. Commuter students can connect to campus network. Online course registration, online library, helpline, student web hosting, wireless network available.

Student life. Freshman orientation: Mandatory. Preregistration for classes offered. One day program held several times throughout summer. Spring orientation session offered in January. **Housing:** Guaranteed on-campus for all undergraduates. Coed dorms, special housing for disabled, apartments, fraternity/sorority housing, wellness housing available. $200 partly refundable deposit, deadline 7/1. Optometry housing available. **Activities:** Bands, campus ministries, choral groups, dance, drama, film society, international student organizations, literary magazine, music ensembles, Model UN, musical theater, opera, radio station, student government, student newspaper, TV station, Associated Black Collegians, Spanish club, Alpha Phi Omega, Amnesty International, Pan-Hellenic Council, College Republicans, Catholic Students at Newman Center, Campus Crusade for Christ, Sigma Gamma Rho.

Athletics. NCAA. **Intercollegiate:** Baseball M, basketball, golf, soccer, softball W, tennis, volleyball W. **Intramural:** Football (tackle). **Team name:** Tritons.

Student services. Adult student services, alcohol/substance abuse counseling, chaplain/spiritual director, career counseling, services for economically disadvantaged, student employment services, financial aid counseling, health services, minority student services, on-campus daycare, personal counseling, placement for graduates, veterans' counselor, women's services. **Physically disabled:** Services for visually, speech, hearing impaired.

Contact. E-mail: admissions@umsl.edu
Phone: (314) 516-5451 Toll-free number: (888) 462-8675
Fax: (314) 516-5310
Alan Byrd, Director of Admissions, University of Missouri: St. Louis, One University Boulevard, St. Louis, MO 63121-4400

University of Phoenix: Kansas City
Kansas City, Missouri
www.phoenix.edu

- For-profit 4-year university
- Large city
- 766 degree-seeking undergraduates

General. Regionally accredited. **Degrees:** 95 bachelor's awarded; master's offered. **Calendar:** Differs by program. **Full-time faculty:** 13 total. **Part-time faculty:** 121 total.

Basis for selection. Open admission.

2011-2012 Annual costs. Estimated costs as of August 2011: per-credit-hour charge, $405 to $480, depending upon level and course of study; electronic course materials fee, $95, if applicable. Book and material charges may vary by course and program. All fees are subject to change.

Application procedures. Admission: No deadline. No application fee. **Financial aid:** No deadline.

Academics. Credit/placement by examination: AP, CLEP.

Majors. Business: Business admin, human resources, marketing. **Computer sciences:** General, information technology, web page design. **Health services:** Facilities admin, long term care admin, medical records technology. **Human services:** General. **Protective services:** Law enforcement admin. **Psychology:** General.

Contact. Marc Booker, Director of Admission and Evaluation, University of Phoenix: Kansas City, 901 East 104th Street, Suite 200, Kansas City, MO 64131-3459

University of Phoenix: Springfield
Springfield, Missouri
www.phoenix.edu

- For-profit 4-year university
- Small city
- 143 degree-seeking undergraduates

General. Regionally accredited. **Degrees:** 13 bachelor's awarded; master's offered. **Calendar:** Differs by program. **Full-time faculty:** 8 total. **Part-time faculty:** 65 total.

Basis for selection. Open admission.

2011-2012 Annual costs. Estimated costs as of August 2011: per-credit-hour charge, $380 to $415, depending upon level and course of study; electronic course materials fee, $95, if applicable. Book and material charges may vary by course and program. All fees are subject to change.

Application procedures. Admission: No deadline. No application fee. **Financial aid:** No deadline.

Academics. Credit/placement by examination: AP, CLEP.

Majors. Business: Business admin, marketing. **Computer sciences:** Information technology. **Health services:** Health care admin. **Protective services:** Law enforcement admin. **Psychology:** General.

Contact. Marc Booker, Director of Admission and Evaluation, University of Phoenix: Springfield, 1343 East Kingsley Street, Springfield, MO 65804-7216

University of Phoenix: St. Louis
St. Louis, Missouri
www.phoenix.edu

- For-profit 4-year university
- Large city
- 727 degree-seeking undergraduates

General. Regionally accredited. **Degrees:** 65 bachelor's awarded; master's offered. **Calendar:** Differs by program. **Full-time faculty:** 10 total. **Part-time faculty:** 117 total.

Basis for selection. Open admission.

2011-2012 Annual costs. Estimated costs as of August 2011: per-credit-hour charge, $405 to $480, depending upon level and course of study; electronic course materials fee, $95, if applicable. Book and material charges may vary by course and program. All fees are subject to change.

Application procedures. Admission: No deadline. No application fee. **Financial aid:** No deadline.

Academics. Credit/placement by examination: AP, CLEP.

Majors. Business: Business admin. **Computer sciences:** Information technology. **Conservation:** Environmental science. **Education:** General. **Health services:** Health care admin. **Human services:** General. **Protective services:** Law enforcement admin. **Psychology:** General.

Contact. Marc Booker, Director of Admission and Evaluation, University of Phoenix: St. Louis, 13801 Riverport Drive, Suite 102, St. Louis, MO 63043-4828

Washington University in St. Louis
Saint Louis, Missouri
www.wustl.edu

CB member
CB code: 6929

- Private 4-year university
- Residential campus in large city
- 6,658 degree-seeking undergraduates: 5% part-time, 50% women, 6% African American, 15% Asian American, 5% Hispanic American, 7% international
- 6,458 degree-seeking graduate students
- 17% of applicants admitted
- SAT or ACT (ACT writing optional), application essay required
- 93% graduate within 6 years

General. Founded in 1853. Regionally accredited. **Degrees:** 1,539 bachelor's awarded; master's, professional, doctoral offered. **ROTC:** Army, Air Force. **Location:** 7 miles from downtown St. Louis. **Calendar:** Semester, extensive summer session. **Full-time faculty:** 932 total; 98% have terminal degrees, 37% women. **Part-time faculty:** 157 total; 32% women. **Class size:** 68% < 20, 17% 20-39, 5% 40-49, 7% 50-99, 3% >100. **Special facilities:** Research center, 59-acre medical campus, observatory, plant growth facility, international writer's center, planetarium, business/economics experimental laboratory, laboratory science building, outdoor research center, theater.

Freshman class profile. 28,823 applied, 4,763 admitted, 1,488 enrolled.

Mid 50% test scores		Out-of-state:	93%
SAT critical reading:	690-760	Live on campus:	99%
SAT math:	710-780	International:	6%
ACT composite:	32-34	Fraternities:	25%
Return as sophomores:	97%	Sororities:	25%

Basis for selection. Rigor of high school curriculum and academic performance, GPA, test scores, extracurricular activities, essay, recommendations very important. Counselor and teacher recommendations required of all applicants. Portfolios required for art students; strongly encouraged for architecture students. **Home schooled:** Letter of recommendation (nonparent) required. Recommendation should be from someone in the community who can give information on the student's background.

High school preparation. College-preparatory program recommended. 20 units recommended. Recommended units include English 4, mathematics 4, social studies 4, history 4, science 4 (laboratory 4) and foreign language 2.

2012-2013 Annual costs. Tuition/fees: $43,705. Room/board: $13,580. Books/supplies: $1,110. Personal expenses: $1,950.

2011-2012 Financial aid. **Need-based:** 978 full-time freshmen applied for aid; 575 were judged to have need; 556 of these received aid. Average need met was 100%. Average scholarship/grant was $31,747; average loan $5,311. 86% of total undergraduate aid awarded as scholarships/grants, 14% as loans/jobs. **Non-need-based:** Awarded to 1,087 full-time undergraduates, including 332 freshmen. Scholarships awarded for academics, ROTC. **Additional information:** Offers program that seeks to eliminate need-based loans as part of its undergraduate financial assistance awards to students from low-to-middle income families.

Application procedures. **Admission:** Closing date 1/15. $55 fee, may be waived for applicants with need. Admission notification by 4/1. Must reply by 5/1. **Financial aid:** Closing date 2/1. FAFSA, CSS PROFILE required. Applicants notified by 4/1; must reply by 5/1.

Academics. **Special study options:** Accelerated study, combined bachelor's/graduate degree, cooperative education, cross-registration, double major, dual enrollment of high school students, ESL, exchange student, independent study, internships, liberal arts/career combination, student-designed major, study abroad, teacher certification program, Washington semester. University Scholars Program gives selected students the opportunity to be admitted to undergraduate study and the School of Medicine at the same time. **Credit/placement by examination:** AP, CLEP, IB, institutional tests. **Support services:** Learning center, pre-admission summer program, reduced course load, study skills assistance, tutoring, writing center.

Majors. Architecture: Architecture, technology. **Area/ethnic studies:** African-American, American, Asian, East Asian, European, German, Latin American, Near/Middle Eastern, women's. **Biology:** General, biochemistry, biophysics, ecology, environmental, neuroscience. **Business:** General, accounting, business admin, entrepreneurial studies, finance, human resources, international, international finance, managerial economics, marketing. **Communications:** Advertising, journalism. **Computer sciences:** General, computer science, data processing, information systems. **Conservation:** Environmental studies. **Education:** General, art, biology, chemistry, drama/dance, elementary, English, French, German, history, mathematics, middle,

physics, science, secondary, social science, social studies, Spanish. **Engineering:** Biomedical, chemical, computer, electrical, mechanical, systems. **English:** American lit, British lit, English lit, general lit. **Foreign languages:** General, ancient Greek, Arabic, Chinese, classics, comparative lit, French, German, Germanic, Hebrew, Iranian, Italian, Japanese, Latin, linguistics, Romance, Spanish. **Health services:** Health care admin, predental, premedicine, prepharmacy, preveterinary. **History:** General. **Liberal arts:** Arts/sciences, humanities. **Math:** General, applied, statistics. **Philosophy/religion:** Islamic, Judaic, philosophy, religion. **Physical sciences:** Chemistry, geology, physics, planetary. **Psychology:** General, industrial. **Social sciences:** General, anthropology, archaeology, economics, international relations, political science, urban studies. **Visual/performing arts:** General, art, art history/conservation, ceramics, commercial/advertising art, dance, design, dramatic, drawing, fashion design, film/cinema/video, graphic design, illustration, music, music history, music theory/composition, painting, photography, printmaking, sculpture, studio arts, theater history, voice/opera.

Most popular majors. Biology 9%, business/marketing 11%, engineering/engineering technologies 14%, psychology 9%, social sciences 16%, visual/performing arts 7%.

Computing on campus. 2,500 workstations in dormitories, library, computer center, student center. Dormitories wired for high-speed internet access and linked to campus network. Commuter students can connect to campus network. Online course registration, online library, helpline, repair service, student web hosting, wireless network available.

Student life. Freshman orientation: Mandatory. Preregistration for classes offered. **Housing:** Guaranteed on-campus for freshmen. Coed dorms, apartments, cooperative housing, fraternity/sorority housing, wellness housing available. $250 deposit, deadline 5/1. Special interest suites, upper-class housing, single-sex floors in coed buildings, on-campus housing for transfer students, small-group housing available. **Activities:** Bands, campus ministries, choral groups, dance, drama, film society, international student organizations, literary magazine, music ensembles, Model UN, musical theater, opera, radio station, student government, student newspaper, symphony orchestra, TV station, approximately 300 social clubs and organizations available.

Athletics. NCAA. **Intercollegiate:** Baseball M, basketball, cross-country, diving, football (tackle) M, golf W, soccer, softball W, swimming, tennis, track and field, volleyball W. **Intramural:** Badminton, basketball, bowling, cross-country, football (non-tackle), golf, racquetball, soccer, softball, swimming, table tennis, tennis, track and field, volleyball, water polo. **Team name:** Bears.

Student services. Adult student services, alcohol/substance abuse counseling, chaplain/spiritual director, career counseling, services for economically disadvantaged, student employment services, financial aid counseling, health services, minority student services, on-campus daycare, personal counseling, placement for graduates, veterans' counselor, women's services. **Physically disabled:** Services for visually, speech, hearing impaired.

Contact. E-mail: admissions@wustl.edu
Phone: (314) 935-6000 Toll-free number: (800) 638-0700
Fax: (314) 935-4290
Julie Shimabukuro, Director of Admissions, Washington University in St. Louis, Campus Box 1089, One Brookings Drive, St. Louis, MO 63130-4899

Webster University
St. Louis, Missouri
www.webster.edu

CB member
CB code: 6933

- Private 4-year university
- Commuter campus in very large city
- 2,963 degree-seeking undergraduates: 19% part-time, 57% women, 10% African American, 2% Asian American, 4% Hispanic American, 1% international
- 2,193 degree-seeking graduate students
- 58% of applicants admitted
- SAT or ACT (ACT writing recommended), application essay required
- 61% graduate within 6 years; 13% enter graduate study

General. Founded in 1915. Regionally accredited. Additional programs offered at five St. Louis area campuses. Undergraduate degrees offered at extended campus locations in Missouri, California, South Carolina, Florida, and international campuses in Vienna; Leiden, The Netherlands; Geneva, Switzerland; Cha-am, Thailand; London. **Degrees:** 837 bachelor's awarded; master's, doctoral offered. **ROTC:** Army, Air Force. **Location:** 6 miles from St. Louis. **Calendar:** Semester, limited summer session. **Full-time faculty:** 181 total; 82% have terminal degrees, 9% minority, 45% women. **Part-time faculty:** 723 total; 14% have terminal degrees. **Class size:** 90% < 20, 10%

20-39. **Special facilities:** Repertory theater, opera theater, community music school.

Freshman class profile. 1,738 applied, 1,014 admitted, 480 enrolled.

GPA 3.75 or higher:	34%	End year in good standing:	97%
GPA 3.50-3.74:	20%	Return as sophomores:	80%
GPA 3.0-3.49:	27%	Out-of-state:	39%
GPA 2.0-2.99:	19%	Live on campus:	63%
Rank in top quarter:	50%	International:	1%
Rank in top tenth:	21%		

Basis for selection. School achievement record, test scores important. Rank in top half of class recommended. Recommendations, essay, resume of activities considered. Interview recommended for all students. Audition required for dance, music, music theater, and theater students; portfolio required for art and film students. **Home schooled:** Transcript of courses and grades, letter of recommendation (nonparent) required. ACT or SAT scores,.

High school preparation. College-preparatory program recommended. 21 units recommended. Recommended units include English 4, mathematics 3, social studies 3, science 3 (laboratory 2), foreign language 2, visual/performing arts 1 and academic electives 3.

2011-2012 Annual costs. Tuition/fees: $22,340. Tuition is $25,940 for theatre conservatory students. Room/board: $9,680. Books/supplies: $1,300. Personal expenses: $1,500.

2011-2012 Financial aid. Need-based: 428 full-time freshmen applied for aid; 358 were judged to have need; 358 of these received aid. Average scholarship/grant was $10,253; average loan $3,692. 66% of total undergraduate aid awarded as scholarships/grants, 34% as loans/jobs. **Non-need-based:** Awarded to 552 full-time undergraduates, including 145 freshmen. Scholarships awarded for academics, art, leadership, music/drama, state residency.

Application procedures. Admission: Priority date 3/1; deadline 6/1. $35 fee, may be waived for applicants with need. Admission notification on a rolling basis beginning on or about 9/1. Must reply by May 1 or within 4 week(s) if notified thereafter. **Financial aid:** Priority date 4/1; no closing date. FAFSA, institutional form required. Applicants notified on a rolling basis starting 2/1; must reply within 2 week(s) of notification.

Academics. Professional Actors Equity theater company in residence for theater program. Internships and practicums available in most areas. **Special study options:** Combined bachelor's/graduate degree, cross-registration, distance learning, double major, dual enrollment of high school students, ESL, exchange student, independent study, internships, liberal arts/career combination, student-designed major, study abroad, teacher certification program. Certificate programs and combination bachelor's/master's degree in many subject areas, student leadership development program, individualized majors. **Credit/placement by examination:** AP, CLEP, IB. 64 credit hours maximum toward bachelor's degree. **Support services:** Learning center, reduced course load, remedial instruction, study skills assistance, tutoring, writing center.

Majors. Area/ethnic studies: American, European. **Biology:** General. **Business:** General, accounting, accounting/finance, business admin, finance, marketing. **Communications:** Advertising, broadcast journalism, communications/speech/rhetoric, digital media, journalism, public relations. **Computer sciences:** Computer science. **Education:** General, music. **English:** English lit. **Foreign languages:** General, French, German, Spanish. **Health services:** Nursing (RN). **History:** General. **Liberal arts:** Humanities. **Math:** General. **Philosophy/religion:** Ethics, philosophy, religion. **Psychology:** General. **Social sciences:** General, anthropology, economics, international relations, political science, sociology. **Visual/performing arts:** Acting, art, cinematography, dance, directing/producing, dramatic, film/cinema/video, jazz, music, music performance, music theory/composition, musical theater, photography.

Most popular majors. Business/marketing 36%, communications/journalism 12%, psychology 7%, social sciences 10%, visual/performing arts 12%.

Computing on campus. 450 workstations in dormitories, library, computer center, student center. Dormitories wired for high-speed internet access and linked to campus network. Commuter students can connect to campus network. Online course registration, online library, helpline, student web hosting, wireless network available.

Student life. Freshman orientation: Mandatory. Preregistration for classes offered. Held the 4 days before classes begin; includes events for both students and parents, including check-in and move-in, orientation group meetings, panel discussions and evening excursions. **Housing:** Guaranteed on-campus for freshmen. Coed dorms, special housing for disabled, apartments available. $175 partly refundable deposit, deadline 4/1. **Activities:** Jazz band, campus ministries, choral groups, dance, drama, film society, international student organizations, literary magazine, music ensembles, musical theater, opera, radio station, student government, student newspaper, symphony orchestra, TV station, African student association, Amnesty International, Campus Crusade for Christ, Catholic student union, Chinese student association, College Democrats, Habitat for Humanity, Japanese student association, Latin American student association, Sustainability Initiative, Webster LGBTQ Alliance.

Athletics. NCAA. **Intercollegiate:** Baseball M, basketball, cross-country, golf M, soccer, softball W, tennis, track and field, volleyball W. **Intramural:** Basketball, bowling, football (non-tackle), volleyball. **Team name:** Gorloks.

Student services. Alcohol/substance abuse counseling, chaplain/spiritual director, career counseling, student employment services, financial aid counseling, health services, minority student services, personal counseling, placement for graduates, veterans' counselor, women's services. **Physically disabled:** Services for visually, speech, hearing impaired.

Contact. E-mail: admit@webster.edu
Phone: (314) 968-6991 Toll-free number: (800) 753-6765
Fax: (314) 968-7115
Anne Edmunds, Associate Vice President Enrollment Management and Student Affairs, Webster University, 470 East Lockwood Avenue, St. Louis, MO 63119-3194

Westminster College
Fulton, Missouri
www.westminster-mo.edu

CB member
CB code: 6937

- Private 4-year liberal arts college affiliated with Presbyterian Church (USA)
- Residential campus in large town
- 1,076 degree-seeking undergraduates: 44% women, 7% African American, 2% Asian American, 3% Hispanic American, 3% Native American, 15% international
- 71% of applicants admitted
- SAT or ACT (ACT writing optional) required
- 67% graduate within 6 years; 33% enter graduate study

General. Founded in 1851. Regionally accredited. **Degrees:** 194 bachelor's awarded. **ROTC:** Army, Air Force. **Location:** 100 miles from St. Louis, 24 miles from Jefferson City. **Calendar:** Semester, limited summer session. **Full-time faculty:** 64 total; 86% have terminal degrees, 6% minority, 42% women. **Part-time faculty:** 29 total; 28% have terminal degrees, 3% minority, 48% women. **Class size:** 62% < 20, 38% 20-39. **Special facilities:** Churchill museum and library.

Freshman class profile. 1,387 applied, 978 admitted, 254 enrolled.

Mid 50% test scores			
SAT critical reading:	420-610	Rank in top quarter:	50%
SAT math:	460-600	Rank in top tenth:	22%
SAT writing:	410-570	Return as sophomores:	75%
ACT composite:	22-27	Out-of-state:	26%
GPA 3.75 or higher:	28%	Live on campus:	97%
GPA 3.50-3.74:	21%	International:	19%
GPA 3.0-3.49:	33%	Fraternities:	54%
GPA 2.0-2.99:	18%	Sororities:	31%

Basis for selection. High school achievement (including class rank, involvement, ACT scores, curriculum, GPA) and recommendations most important. Interview recommended for borderline students. **Learning Disabled:** Learning Disabilities Program applicants must have completed application credentials and personal interview prior to April 1, including untimed SAT/ACT results.

High school preparation. College-preparatory program recommended. 16 units required. Required and recommended units include English 4, mathematics 3, social studies 2, science 2 (laboratory 2), foreign language 2 and academic electives 2. Pre-med and pre-dental students should have at least 3 lab science, 1 advanced math.

2011-2012 Annual costs. Tuition/fees: $20,570. Room/board: $7,990. Books/supplies: $1,100. Personal expenses: $2,480.

2011-2012 Financial aid. Need-based: 193 full-time freshmen applied for aid; 151 were judged to have need; 151 of these received aid. Average need met was 85%. Average scholarship/grant was $15,979; average loan $3,245. 82% of total undergraduate aid awarded as scholarships/grants, 18% as loans/jobs. **Non-need-based:** Awarded to 382 full-time undergraduates, including 101 freshmen. Scholarships awarded for academics, alumni affiliation, leadership, minority status, music/drama, religious affiliation, ROTC.

Application procedures. Admission: Priority date 2/1; no deadline. No application fee. Admission notification on a rolling basis beginning on or about 10/1. Must reply by May 1 or within 3 week(s) if notified thereafter.

Financial aid: Priority date 2/15; no closing date. FAFSA required. Applicants notified on a rolling basis starting 3/1; must reply within 3 week(s) of notification.

Academics. Honors Program offers top students special courses that provide enriching academic experiences, as well as professional and leadership development activities. First-year seminar fosters communication, critical thinking and study skills. **Special study options:** Combined bachelor's/graduate degree, cooperative education, cross-registration, distance learning, double major, dual enrollment of high school students, ESL, exchange student, honors, independent study, internships, liberal arts/career combination, New York semester, semester at sea, student-designed major, study abroad, teacher certification program, urban semester, Washington semester. **Credit/placement by examination:** AP, CLEP, IB, institutional tests. 30 credit hours maximum toward bachelor's degree. **Support services:** Learning center, reduced course load, remedial instruction, study skills assistance, tutoring, writing center.

Majors. Biology: General, biochemistry. **Business:** Accounting, business admin, management information systems. **Communications:** Advertising, journalism, media studies. **Computer sciences:** General. **Conservation:** Environmental science, environmental studies. **Education:** Elementary, middle, physical, secondary. **English:** English lit. **Foreign languages:** French, Spanish. **History:** General. **Math:** General. **Parks/recreation:** Exercise sciences, sports admin. **Philosophy/religion:** Philosophy, religion. **Physical sciences:** Chemistry, physics. **Psychology:** General. **Social sciences:** Anthropology, economics, international relations, political science, sociology.

Most popular majors. Biology 13%, business/marketing 25%, education 11%, interdisciplinary studies 6%, psychology 7%, social sciences 11%.

Computing on campus. 200 workstations in library, computer center. Dormitories wired for high-speed internet access and linked to campus network. Commuter students can connect to campus network. Online course registration, online library, helpline, student web hosting, wireless network available.

Student life. Freshman orientation: Mandatory. Preregistration for classes offered. Held three days before classes start. **Housing:** Guaranteed on-campus for freshmen. Coed dorms, single-sex dorms, apartments, fraternity/sorority housing available. **Activities:** Bands, campus ministries, choral groups, international student organizations, literary magazine, music ensembles, Model UN, student government, student newspaper, Young Democrats, Young Republicans, Big Brother-Big Sister program, Environmentally Concerned Students, Chapel Leadership Council, Habitat For Humanity, Fellowship of Christian Students.

Athletics. NCAA. **Intercollegiate:** Baseball M, basketball, cheerleading M, cross-country, football (tackle) M, golf, soccer, softball W, tennis, track and field, volleyball W. **Intramural:** Basketball, football (non-tackle), soccer, softball, volleyball. **Team name:** Blue Jays.

Student services. Alcohol/substance abuse counseling, chaplain/spiritual director, career counseling, student employment services, financial aid counseling, health services, minority student services, personal counseling, placement for graduates, veterans' counselor, women's services. **Physically disabled:** Services for visually, speech, hearing impaired.

Contact. E-mail: admissions@westminster-mo.edu
Phone: (573) 592-5251 Toll-free number: (800) 475-3361
Fax: (573) 592-5255
George Wolf, Vice President and Dean of Enrollment Services, Westminster College, 501 Westminster Avenue, Fulton, MO 65251-1299

William Jewell College
Liberty, Missouri
www.jewell.edu

CB member
CB code: 6941

- Private 4-year liberal arts college
- Residential campus in large town
- 1,060 degree-seeking undergraduates: 5% part-time, 59% women, 4% African American, 2% Asian American, 4% Hispanic American, 1% Native American, 3% international
- 54% of applicants admitted
- SAT or ACT (ACT writing recommended), application essay required
- 63% graduate within 6 years; 27% enter graduate study

General. Founded in 1849. Regionally accredited. Campus in Harlaxton, England. **Degrees:** 244 bachelor's awarded. **ROTC:** Army. **Location:** 14 miles from downtown Kansas City. **Calendar:** Semester, limited summer session. **Full-time faculty:** 67 total; 78% have terminal degrees, 3% minority, 52% women. **Part-time faculty:** 80 total; 19% have terminal degrees, 8% minority, 58% women. **Class size:** 70% < 20, 28% 20-39, 2% 50-99. **Special**

facilities: Observatory, flow cytometer, high and low-ropes course, outdoor environmental learning lab, Quimby pipe organ.

Freshman class profile. 3,333 applied, 1,803 admitted, 270 enrolled.

Mid 50% test scores			
SAT critical reading:	490-640	Rank in top tenth:	25%
SAT math:	520-620	End year in good standing:	86%
ACT composite:	23-28	Return as sophomores:	75%
GPA 3.75 or higher:	49%	Out-of-state:	36%
GPA 3.50-3.74:	20%	Live on campus:	91%
GPA 3.0-3.49:	26%	International:	2%
GPA 2.0-2.99:	5%	Fraternities:	36%
Rank in top quarter:	59%	Sororities:	40%

Basis for selection. Admissions based on secondary school record. Class rank, standardized test scores, and essay also important. Audition or portfolio required for scholarship seeking music, theater, or art students.

High school preparation. College-preparatory program required. 15 units required; 19 recommended. Required and recommended units include English 4, mathematics 3-4, social studies 3, science 3 (laboratory 1), foreign language 2-3 and academic electives 2.

2011-2012 Annual costs. Tuition/fees: $29,600. Room/board: $7,560. Books/supplies: $1,100. Personal expenses: $2,520.

Financial aid. Non-need-based: Scholarships awarded for academics, alumni affiliation, athletics, music/drama, ROTC.

Application procedures. Admission: Priority date 12/1; deadline 8/15 (postmark date). $25 fee, may be waived for applicants with need, free for online applicants. Admission notification on a rolling basis beginning on or about 9/15. Must reply by May 1 or within 2 week(s) if notified thereafter. **Financial aid:** Priority date 3/1; no closing date. FAFSA required. Applicants notified on a rolling basis starting 2/15; must reply within 1.5 week(s) of notification.

Academics. Interdisciplinary core curriculum required. **Special study options:** Accelerated study, combined bachelor's/graduate degree, double major, dual enrollment of high school students, honors, independent study, internships, liberal arts/career combination, semester at sea, student-designed major, study abroad, teacher certification program, Washington semester. Pryor Leadership Studies. **Credit/placement by examination:** AP, CLEP, IB, SAT, ACT, institutional tests. No limit to credit by examination, but student must complete a minimum of 30 hours in residence. **Support services:** Study skills assistance, tutoring, writing center.

Honors college/program. Oxbridge Honors Program allows students to study their major subject using tutorial mode of instruction used at Oxford University and Cambridge University (England). Minimum 3.8 GPA, ACT score of 28 required for admission.

Majors. Biology: General, biochemistry, molecular. **Business:** Accounting, business admin, international, managerial economics, nonprofit/public. **Communications:** Communications/speech/rhetoric, organizational. **Education:** Art, biology, chemistry, drama/dance, elementary, English, foreign languages, French, mathematics, music, physical, physics, secondary, social studies, Spanish, speech. **English:** English lit, rhetoric/composition. **Foreign languages:** French, Spanish. **Health services:** Nursing (RN). **History:** General. **Liberal arts:** Arts/sciences. **Math:** General. **Parks/recreation:** General. **Philosophy/religion:** Philosophy, religion. **Physical sciences:** Chemistry, physics. **Psychology:** General. **Social sciences:** International relations, political science. **Theology:** Sacred music. **Visual/performing arts:** Art, dramatic, music, music history, music performance, music theory/composition.

Most popular majors. Business/marketing 21%, education 10%, health sciences 22%, psychology 7%.

Computing on campus. 253 workstations in library, computer center, student center. Dormitories wired for high-speed internet access and linked to campus network. Commuter students can connect to campus network. Online course registration, online library, helpline, student web hosting, wireless network available.

Student life. Freshman orientation: Mandatory. Preregistration for classes offered. 4-day program prior to the first day of classes. **Housing:** Guaranteed on-campus for all undergraduates. Coed dorms, single-sex dorms, special housing for disabled, fraternity/sorority housing, wellness housing available. $300 fully refundable deposit, deadline 5/1. **Activities:** Bands, campus ministries, choral groups, dance, drama, music ensembles, Model UN, musical theater, opera, radio station, student government, student newspaper, symphony orchestra, Young Democrats, College Republicans, Progressive Students for America, Amnesty International, UNITY, Rotaract, Fellowship of Christian Athletes, Black Student Association.

Athletics. NCAA. **Intercollegiate:** Baseball M, basketball, cheerleading, cross-country, football (tackle) M, golf, soccer, softball W, swimming, tennis,

track and field, volleyball W. **Intramural:** Basketball, football (non-tackle), golf, racquetball, soccer, softball, tennis, volleyball. **Team name:** Cardinals.

Student services. Alcohol/substance abuse counseling, chaplain/spiritual director, career counseling, student employment services, financial aid counseling, health services, minority student services, personal counseling, placement for graduates. **Physically disabled:** Services for visually, speech, hearing impaired.

Contact. E-mail: admission@william.jewell.edu
Phone: (816) 415-7511 Toll-free number: (888) 253-9355
Fax: (816) 415-5040
Clint Chapman, Dean of Admission, William Jewell College, 500 College Hill, Liberty, MO 64068

William Woods University
Fulton, Missouri
www.williamwoods.edu   **CB code: 6944**

- Private 4-year university and teachers college affiliated with Christian Church (Disciples of Christ)
- Residential campus in large town
- 1,019 degree-seeking undergraduates: 15% part-time, 73% women, 4% African American, 1% Asian American, 1% Hispanic American
- 953 degree-seeking graduate students
- 80% of applicants admitted
- SAT or ACT (ACT writing recommended) required
- 50% graduate within 6 years

General. Founded in 1870. Regionally accredited. Students may enroll in courses offered at 4 other mid-Missouri colleges and universities. **Degrees:** 226 bachelor's, 17 associate awarded; master's, doctoral offered. **ROTC:** Army, Naval, Air Force. **Location:** 100 miles from St. Louis, 30 miles from Columbia. **Calendar:** Semester, limited summer session. **Full-time faculty:** 60 total; 57% have terminal degrees, 10% minority, 50% women. **Part-time faculty:** 274 total; 26% have terminal degrees, 8% minority, 36% women. **Class size:** 75% < 20, 24% 20-39, less than 1% 40-49, less than 1% 50-99. **Special facilities:** Equestrian studies facilities, observatory, broadcasting laboratory, computer laboratories, model courtroom, ASL interpreting laboratories.

Freshman class profile. 753 applied, 602 admitted, 189 enrolled.

Mid 50% test scores			
SAT critical reading:	470-610	Rank in top quarter:	40%
SAT math:	480-590	Rank in top tenth:	17%
SAT writing:	450-580	Return as sophomores:	74%
ACT composite:	20-24	Out-of-state:	40%
GPA 3.75 or higher:	26%	Live on campus:	75%
GPA 3.50-3.74:	21%	Fraternities:	43%
GPA 3.0-3.49:	28%	Sororities:	46%
GPA 2.0-2.99:	25%		

Basis for selection. Secondary school record, class rank, test scores most important; extracurricular activities, 2 academic references also important; interview considered. Interview recommended for all students. Audition required for performing arts students; portfolio required for visual arts students. **Home schooled:** Letter of recommendation (nonparent) required. GED required; ACT/SAT must be submitted. Minimum ACT of 19/minimum SAT of 860. Must submit two letters of recommendation.

High school preparation. College-preparatory program recommended. 16 units required; 20 recommended. Required and recommended units include English 4, mathematics 3, social studies 2, history 3, science 3 (laboratory 3) and foreign language 2.

2011-2012 Annual costs. Tuition/fees: $19,050. Room/board: $7,550. Books/supplies: $1,200. Personal expenses: $3,000.

Financial aid. Non-need-based: Scholarships awarded for academics, alumni affiliation, art, athletics, leadership, music/drama, religious affiliation.

Application procedures. Admission: Priority date 3/1; no deadline. $25 fee, may be waived for applicants with need, free for online applicants. Admission notification on a rolling basis. Must reply by May 1 or within 2 week(s) if notified thereafter. **Financial aid:** Priority date 3/1; no closing date. FAFSA, institutional form required. Applicants notified on a rolling basis starting 3/15; must reply within 2 week(s) of notification.

Academics. ASL interpreting available. **Special study options:** Accelerated study, combined bachelor's/graduate degree, cross-registration, double major, dual enrollment of high school students, ESL, honors, independent study, internships, liberal arts/career combination, New York semester,

student-designed major, study abroad, teacher certification program, Washington semester. Hollywood semester, qualified students may complete bachelor's degree in 3 years through Century Scholars program, 5-year MBA. **Credit/placement by examination:** AP, CLEP, IB, SAT, ACT, institutional tests. 30 credit hours maximum toward bachelor's degree. **Support services:** Pre-admission summer program, reduced course load, remedial instruction, study skills assistance, tutoring, writing center.

Majors. Biology: General. **Business:** Accounting, business admin, international, management information systems, managerial economics. **Communications:** Advertising, broadcast journalism, communications/speech/rhetoric, journalism, public relations. **Computer sciences:** General. **Education:** General, art, elementary, English, mathematics, middle, physical, science, secondary, social science, special ed. **English:** English lit, writing. **Foreign languages:** American Sign Language, Spanish. **General:** Equestrian studies. **Health services:** Athletic training. **History:** General. **Human services:** Social work. **Math:** General. **Parks/recreation:** Sports admin. **Physical sciences:** General. **Psychology:** General. **Social sciences:** Political science. **Visual/performing arts:** Art, design, dramatic, graphic design, studio arts.

Most popular majors. Agriculture 22%, business/marketing 33%, education 12%, legal studies 6%.

Computing on campus. 75 workstations in dormitories, library, computer center, student center. Dormitories wired for high-speed internet access and linked to campus network. Online course registration, online library, helpline, repair service, wireless network available.

Student life. Freshman orientation: Mandatory. Preregistration for classes offered. 7 days prior to start of fall term. **Policies:** All residence halls non-smoking. Students under 23 must reside on campus unless married or living with parent or guardian; lottery offered in spring to students who wish to move off campus the following fall semester. **Housing:** Guaranteed on-campus for freshmen. Coed dorms, single-sex dorms, special housing for disabled, apartments, fraternity/sorority housing, wellness housing available. $250 partly refundable deposit, deadline 8/15. Senior housing, single rooms, independent housing, learning communities, upper-class halls and apartments available. **Activities:** Campus ministries, choral groups, dance, drama, international student organizations, literary magazine, musical theater, radio station, student government, student newspaper, Big Brothers/Big Sisters, campus activities board, Association of Christian Ecumenical Students, community action network, Jesters, Students for Social Work, departmental clubs.

Athletics. NAIA. **Intercollegiate:** Baseball M, basketball, cross-country, golf, soccer, softball W, track and field, volleyball. **Intramural:** Badminton, baseball M, basketball, equestrian, football (non-tackle), softball, table tennis, tennis, volleyball, weight lifting. **Team name:** Owls.

Student services. Adult student services, alcohol/substance abuse counseling, chaplain/spiritual director, career counseling, financial aid counseling, health services, personal counseling. **Physically disabled:** Services for visually, speech, hearing impaired.

Contact. E-mail: admissions@williamwoods.edu
Phone: (573) 592-4221 Toll-free number: (800) 995-3159
Fax: (573) 592-1146
Sarah Munns, Dean of Admissions, William Woods University, One University Avenue, Fulton, MO 65251-2388

Montana

Carroll College
Helena, Montana
www.carroll.edu

CB member
CB code: 4041

▶ Private 4-year liberal arts college affiliated with Roman Catholic Church
▶ Residential campus in large town
▶ 1,381 degree-seeking undergraduates: 4% part-time, 58% women, 1% African American, 1% Asian American, 3% Hispanic American, 2% Native American, 1% international
▶ 72% of applicants admitted
▶ SAT or ACT (ACT writing recommended) required
▶ 59% graduate within 6 years

General. Founded in 1909. Regionally accredited. **Degrees:** 284 bachelor's, 1 associate awarded. **ROTC:** Army. **Location:** 90 miles from Great Falls, 240 miles from Billings. **Calendar:** Semester, limited summer session. **Full-time faculty:** 85 total; 2% minority, 59% women. **Part-time faculty:** 58 total; 59% women. **Class size:** 63% < 20, 32% 20-39, 3% 40-49, 1% 50-99, less than 1% >100. **Special facilities:** Observatory, seismograph station, engineering lab, nursing lab including SimMan and SimBaby.

Freshman class profile. 1,588 applied, 1,141 admitted, 345 enrolled.

Mid 50% test scores		GPA 2.0-2.99:	14%
SAT critical reading:	500-600	Rank in top quarter:	57%
SAT math:	500-610	Rank in top tenth:	26%
SAT writing:	490-600	Return as sophomores:	78%
GPA 3.75 or higher:	32%	Out-of-state:	57%
GPA 3.50-3.74:	20%	Live on campus:	96%
GPA 3.0-3.49:	34%	International:	1%

Basis for selection. School achievement record, test scores, recommendations most important. SAT and SAT Subject Tests required of home schooled and nonaccredited high school graduates. Personal statement required. Interview recommended for academically weak students.

High school preparation. College-preparatory program recommended. Recommended units include English 4, mathematics 3, social studies 2, history 2, science 2 (laboratory 1), computer science 1, visual/performing arts 1 and academic electives 2. 1 technology recommended.

2011-2012 Annual costs. Tuition/fees: $25,198. Room/board: $7,750. Books/supplies: $800. Personal expenses: $1,600.

2010-2011 Financial aid. Need-based: 293 full-time freshmen applied for aid; 249 were judged to have need; 249 of these received aid. Average need met was 85%. Average scholarship/grant was $16,298; average loan $3,337. 68% of total undergraduate aid awarded as scholarships/grants, 32% as loans/jobs. **Non-need-based:** Awarded to 738 full-time undergraduates, including 199 freshmen. Scholarships awarded for academics, art, athletics, leadership, minority status, music/drama, religious affiliation, ROTC.

Application procedures. Admission: Priority date 2/15; deadline 5/1 (receipt date). $35 fee, may be waived for applicants with need, free for online applicants. Admission notification on a rolling basis beginning on or about 12/1. Must reply by May 1 or within 3 week(s) if notified thereafter. Housing deposit fully refundable prior to May 1; partially refundable prior to June 1. **Financial aid:** Priority date 3/1; no closing date. FAFSA required. Applicants notified on a rolling basis starting 3/1; must reply by 5/1 or within 2 week(s) of notification.

Academics. Special study options: Cooperative education, double major, dual enrollment of high school students, honors, independent study, internships, liberal arts/career combination, student-designed major, study abroad, teacher certification program. 3-2 engineering program with Notre Dame, Columbia University, USC, Gonzaga University, Montana State University-Bozeman, Montana Tech Butte. **Credit/placement by examination:** AP, CLEP, IB, SAT, ACT, institutional tests. 9 credit hours maximum toward associate degree, 18 toward bachelor's. **Support services:** Learning center, pre-admission summer program, reduced course load, study skills assistance, tutoring, writing center.

Majors. Biology: General. **Business:** Accounting, business admin. **Communications:** Communications/speech/rhetoric, public relations. **Computer**

sciences: Computer science. **Conservation:** Environmental studies. **Education:** Biology, chemistry, elementary, English, ESL, history, mathematics, physical, social science, social studies, Spanish, speech. **Engineering:** Civil. **English:** English lit, writing. **Foreign languages:** Classics, French, Spanish. **Health services:** Community health services, nursing (RN). **History:** General. **Human services:** General. **Math:** General, applied. **Parks/recreation:** Sports admin. **Philosophy/religion:** Ethics, philosophy. **Physical sciences:** Chemistry. **Psychology:** General. **Social sciences:** International relations, political science, sociology. **Theology:** Theology. **Visual/performing arts:** General.

Most popular majors. Biology 11%, business/marketing 16%, communications/journalism 7%, education 9%, health sciences 14%, parks/recreation 7%, psychology 7%, social sciences 6%.

Computing on campus. 85 workstations in dormitories, library, computer center, student center. Dormitories wired for high-speed internet access and linked to campus network. Commuter students can connect to campus network. Online course registration, helpline, wireless network available.

Student life. Freshman orientation: Mandatory, $100 fee. Preregistration for classes offered. Four-day program. Fee includes cost of meals, entertainment, and various activities. **Policies:** Freshmen and sophomores required to live on campus. **Housing:** Guaranteed on-campus for freshmen. Coed dorms, special housing for disabled, apartments available. $200 partly refundable deposit, deadline 5/1. **Activities:** Bands, campus ministries, choral groups, dance, drama, film society, international student organizations, literary magazine, music ensembles, musical theater, radio station, student government, student newspaper, TV station, College Democrats, Circle K, cultural exchange club, Into the Streets service organization, peer mentors, social work club, sociology club, student community outreach experience, Young Republicans.

Athletics. NAIA. **Intercollegiate:** Basketball, cross-country, football (tackle) M, golf, soccer W, swimming, volleyball W. **Intramural:** Badminton, basketball, bowling, cross-country, golf, handball, racquetball, skiing, soccer, softball, swimming, table tennis, volleyball, water polo. **Team name:** Saints.

Student services. Adult student services, alcohol/substance abuse counseling, chaplain/spiritual director, career counseling, student employment services, financial aid counseling, health services, personal counseling, placement for graduates, veterans' counselor.

Contact. E-mail: admission@carroll.edu
Phone: (406) 447-4384 Toll-free number: (800) 992-3648
Fax: (406) 447-4533
Cynthia Thornquist, Director of Admissions and Enrollment, Carroll College, 1601 North Benton Avenue, Helena, MT 59625

Montana State University
Bozeman, Montana
www.montana.edu

CB member
CB code: 4488

▶ Public 4-year university
▶ Residential campus in large town
▶ 12,054 degree-seeking undergraduates: 18% part-time, 46% women, 1% African American, 1% Asian American, 3% Hispanic American, 2% Native American, 3% international
▶ 1,638 degree-seeking graduate students
▶ 60% of applicants admitted
▶ SAT or ACT with writing required
▶ 47% graduate within 6 years

General. Founded in 1893. Regionally accredited. **Degrees:** 1,809 bachelor's, 9 associate awarded; master's, doctoral offered. **ROTC:** Army, Air Force. **Location:** 139 miles from Billings. **Calendar:** Semester, limited summer session. **Full-time faculty:** 569 total; 75% have terminal degrees, 6% minority, 37% women. **Part-time faculty:** 311 total; 23% have terminal degrees, 7% minority, 57% women. **Class size:** 42% < 20, 30% 20-39, 13% 40-49, 9% 50-99, 6% >100. **Special facilities:** Space science engineering lab, movement science/human performance lab, Center for Biofilm Engineering, architecture fabrication laboratory, music technology monster studios, sub-zero science and engineering research facility, simulation labs (nursing), imaging and chemical analysis laboratory, plant growth center, Montana microfabrication facility (nanotechnology), multimedia language resource center, spectrum lab, Montana PBS, Museum of the Rockies.

Freshman class profile. 9,871 applied, 5,938 admitted, 2,669 enrolled.

Mid 50% test scores		Rank in top quarter:	43%
SAT critical reading:	490-620	Rank in top tenth:	20%
SAT math:	500-630	End year in good standing:	42%
SAT writing:	470-600	Return as sophomores:	74%
ACT composite:	21-27	Out-of-state:	39%
GPA 3.75 or higher:	26%	Live on campus:	75%
GPA 3.50-3.74:	16%	International:	2%
GPA 3.0-3.49:	30%	Fraternities:	4%
GPA 2.0-2.99:	26%	Sororities:	3%

Basis for selection. Interviews recommended. Students may use SAT/ACT math scores for placement or take departmental exam. Students with 27 ACT English or 640 SAT verbal can waive freshman composition. **Home schooled:** GED required.

High school preparation. College-preparatory program required. 14 units required. Required units include English 4, mathematics 3, social studies 3, science 2 (laboratory 2). 4 math recommended for science majors. Substitutions for foreign language requirement possible. 2 foreign language, preferably 2 computer science, visual and performing arts, or approved vocational education units.

2011-2012 Annual costs. Tuition/fees: $6,472; $19,109 out-of-state. International/foreign students pay an additional one-time administrative fee. Room/board: $7,840. Books/supplies: $1,150. Personal expenses: $1,130.

2010-2011 Financial aid. Need-based: 1,530 full-time freshmen applied for aid; 1,086 were judged to have need; 1,069 of these received aid. Average need met was 77%. Average scholarship/grant was $5,456; average loan $3,977. 40% of total undergraduate aid awarded as scholarships/grants, 60% as loans/jobs. **Non-need-based:** Awarded to 529 full-time undergraduates, including 103 freshmen. Scholarships awarded for academics, alumni affiliation, art, athletics, job skills, leadership, minority status, music/drama, ROTC, state residency. **Additional information:** Tuition waiver for honorably discharged veterans, children of members of the United States armed forces who, at the time of entry into service, had legal residence in Montana and who were killed in action or who died as a result of injury, disease, or other disability incurred while in the service.

Application procedures. Admission: No deadline. $30 fee. Admission notification on a rolling basis. **Financial aid:** Priority date 3/1; no closing date. FAFSA required. Applicants notified on a rolling basis starting 4/1; must reply within 3 week(s) of notification.

Academics. Special study options: Combined bachelor's/graduate degree, cooperative education, cross-registration, distance learning, double major, dual enrollment of high school students, ESL, exchange student, honors, independent study, internships, student-designed major, study abroad, teacher certification program. Combined bachelor's/master's programs in environmental design/architecture and construction engineering technology/construction engineering management. **Credit/placement by examination:** AP, CLEP, IB, SAT, ACT, institutional tests. No more than 30 semester credits earned by correspondence, extension, or continuing education counted toward bachelor's degree. **Support services:** Learning center, remedial instruction, study skills assistance, tutoring, writing center.

Majors. Architecture: Environmental design. **Biology:** General, bacteriology, biotechnology. **Business:** General. **Computer sciences:** Computer science. **Conservation:** General, management/policy. **Education:** Agricultural, elementary, music, secondary, technology/industrial arts. **Engineering:** Chemical, civil, computer, electrical, mechanical. **English:** English lit. **Foreign languages:** General. **General:** Animal sciences, business, horticultural science, plant sciences, range science. **Health services:** Nursing (RN). **History:** General. **Math:** General. **Parks/recreation:** Sports admin. **Philosophy/religion:** Philosophy. **Physical sciences:** Chemistry, physics, planetary. **Psychology:** General. **Social sciences:** Anthropology, economics, political science, sociology. **Visual/performing arts:** Art, cinematography, music. **Work/family studies:** General.

Most popular majors. Biology 7%, business/marketing 10%, education 7%, engineering/engineering technologies 16%, family/consumer sciences 7%, health sciences 9%, visual/performing arts 8%.

Computing on campus. 1,200 workstations in dormitories, library, computer center. Dormitories wired for high-speed internet access and linked to campus network. Commuter students can connect to campus network. Online course registration, helpline, wireless network available.

Student life. Freshman orientation: Mandatory, $65 fee. Preregistration for classes offered. **Housing:** Guaranteed on-campus for freshmen. Coed dorms, single-sex dorms, special housing for disabled, apartments, fraternity/sorority housing, wellness housing available. $200 nonrefundable deposit. Wellness, non-smoking, older student floors available; housing for disabled students is limited. **Activities:** Bands, campus ministries, choral groups, dance, drama, film society, international student organizations, literary magazine, music ensembles, Model UN, musical theater, opera, radio station, student government, student newspaper, symphony orchestra, TV station.

Athletics. NCAA. **Intercollegiate:** Basketball, cheerleading, cross-country, football (tackle) M, golf W, rodeo, skiing, tennis, track and field, volleyball W. **Intramural:** Archery, badminton, basketball, bowling, cross-country, golf, gymnastics, handball, racquetball, rodeo, skiing, soccer, softball, swimming, table tennis, tennis, track and field, volleyball, water polo, weight lifting, wrestling M. **Team name:** Bobcats.

Student services. Adult student services, alcohol/substance abuse counseling, chaplain/spiritual director, career counseling, student employment services, financial aid counseling, health services, legal services, minority student services, on-campus daycare, personal counseling, placement for graduates, veterans' counselor, women's services. **Physically disabled:** Services for visually, speech, hearing impaired.

Contact. E-mail: admissions@montana.edu
Phone: (406) 994-2452 Toll-free number: (888) 678-2287
Fax: (406) 994-1923
Ronda Russell, Director of Admissions, Montana State University, PO Box 172190, Bozeman, MT 59717-2190

Montana State University: Billings

Billings, Montana   CB member
www.msubillings.edu   CB code: 4298

- Public 4-year university and technical college
- Commuter campus in small city
- 4,578 degree-seeking undergraduates: 26% part-time, 60% women, 1% African American, 1% Asian American, 4% Hispanic American, 7% Native American, 2% international
- 477 degree-seeking graduate students
- 99% of applicants admitted
- SAT or ACT (ACT writing recommended) required
- 36% graduate within 6 years; 15% enter graduate study

General. Founded in 1927. Regionally accredited. Montana State University Billings Downtown located in downtown Billings. **Degrees:** 533 bachelor's, 252 associate awarded; master's offered. **ROTC:** Army. **Location:** 224 miles from Helena, 560 miles from Denver. **Calendar:** Semester, limited summer session. **Full-time faculty:** 150 total; 64% have terminal degrees, 5% minority, 40% women. **Part-time faculty:** 192 total; 5% minority, 59% women. **Class size:** 51% < 20, 41% 20-39, 5% 40-49, 3% 50-99, less than 1% >100. **Special facilities:** Biological station, center for business enterprise, Montana Center for Disabilities, special education learning center, center for gerontological studies, small business institute, urban institute, public radio, center for applied economic research.

Freshman class profile. 1,523 applied, 1,515 admitted, 890 enrolled.

Mid 50% test scores		Rank in top quarter:	25%
SAT critical reading:	450-580	Rank in top tenth:	7%
SAT math:	440-560	End year in good standing:	65%
ACT composite:	19-24	Return as sophomores:	56%
GPA 3.75 or higher:	12%	Out-of-state:	7%
GPA 3.50-3.74:	12%	Live on campus:	41%
GPA 3.0-3.49:	36%	International:	3%
GPA 2.0-2.99:	37%		

Basis for selection. Applicants must meet one of the following: 2.5 GPA, 22 ACT/1030 SAT (exclusive of Writing), or rank in upper half of graduating class. **Home schooled:** Applicants may be admitted based on GED, ACT, or COMPASS scores.

High school preparation. College-preparatory program required. 14 units required. Required units include English 4, mathematics 3, social studies 3, science 2 (laboratory 2). 2 years foreign language, computer science, visual and performing arts, or vocational education also recommended.

2011-2012 Annual costs. Tuition/fees: $5,470; $15,850 out-of-state. Room/board: $5,960. Books/supplies: $1,200. Personal expenses: $3,400.

2010-2011 Financial aid. Need-based: 713 full-time freshmen applied for aid; 587 were judged to have need; 569 of these received aid. Average need met was 66%. Average scholarship/grant was $4,615; average loan $2,855. 49% of total undergraduate aid awarded as scholarships/grants, 51% as loans/jobs. **Non-need-based:** Awarded to 208 full-time undergraduates, including 47 freshmen. Scholarships awarded for academics, alumni affiliation, art, athletics, job skills, leadership, minority status, music/drama, state residency. **Additional information:** Veterans and honors fee waivers offered.

Application procedures. Admission: Priority date 7/1; no deadline. $30 fee. Admission notification on a rolling basis. **Financial aid:** Priority date 3/1; no closing date. FAFSA required. Applicants notified on a rolling basis starting 4/1; must reply within 3 week(s) of notification.

Academics. Full degree programs and many courses designed for working professionals. **Special study options:** Accelerated study, cooperative education, cross-registration, distance learning, double major, dual enrollment of high school students, ESL, external degree, honors, independent study, internships, liberal arts/career combination, study abroad, teacher certification program, weekend college. Evening College, with extensive online programs and courses. College of Technology offers training and retraining for employment by combining academics and vocational opportunities. **Credit/placement by examination:** AP, CLEP, SAT, ACT, institutional tests. **Support services:** Learning center, reduced course load, remedial instruction, study skills assistance, tutoring, writing center.

Majors. Biology: General, microbiology. **Business:** General. **Communications:** Communications/speech/rhetoric, media studies, public relations. **Conservation:** Environmental studies. **Education:** General, art, biology, chemistry, curriculum, elementary, English, foreign languages, health, history, mathematics, music, physical, physics, science, secondary, social science, social studies, Spanish, special ed. **English:** English lit. **Foreign languages:** Spanish. **Health services:** Athletic training, health care admin, vocational rehab counseling. **History:** General. **Liberal arts:** Arts/sciences. **Math:** General. **Parks/recreation:** Health/fitness, sports admin. **Physical sciences:** Chemistry. **Protective services:** Criminal justice. **Psychology:** General. **Social sciences:** Political science, sociology. **Visual/performing arts:** Art, dramatic, music, music performance.

Most popular majors. Business/marketing 24%, communications/journalism 7%, education 25%, liberal arts 9%, psychology 7%.

Computing on campus. 1,700 workstations in dormitories, library, computer center, student center. Dormitories wired for high-speed internet access and linked to campus network. Commuter students can connect to campus network. Online course registration, online library, helpline, student web hosting, wireless network available.

Student life. Freshman orientation: Mandatory, $75 fee. Preregistration for classes offered. Two-day orientation sessions held throughout summer. **Housing:** Coed dorms, single-sex dorms, special housing for disabled, apartments, wellness housing available. $100 fully refundable deposit. **Activities:** Bands, campus ministries, choral groups, drama, international student organizations, literary magazine, music ensembles, musical theater, radio station, student government, student newspaper, more than 50 student groups available.

Athletics. NCAA. **Intercollegiate:** Baseball M, basketball, cheerleading, cross-country, golf, soccer, softball W, tennis, track and field, volleyball W. **Intramural:** Archery, basketball, cross-country, golf, racquetball, skiing, softball, swimming, table tennis, tennis, volleyball. **Team name:** Yellowjackets.

Student services. Adult student services, alcohol/substance abuse counseling, chaplain/spiritual director, career counseling, services for economically disadvantaged, student employment services, financial aid counseling, health services, legal services, minority student services, on-campus daycare, personal counseling, placement for graduates, veterans' counselor. **Physically disabled:** Services for visually, speech, hearing impaired.

Contact. E-mail: cjohannes@msubillings.edu
Phone: (406) 657-2158 Toll-free number: (800) 656-6782
Fax: (406) 657-2051
Shelly Andersen, Director of Admissions, Montana State University: Billings, 1500 University Drive, Billings, MT 59101-0298

Montana State University: Northern
Havre, Montana
www.msun.edu   CB code: 4538

- Public 4-year university
- Residential campus in large town
- 1,198 degree-seeking undergraduates: 23% part-time, 50% women, 1% African American, 1% Asian American, 2% Hispanic American, 13% Native American, 1% international
- 55 degree-seeking graduate students
- 64% of applicants admitted
- SAT or ACT (ACT writing recommended) required

General. Founded in 1929. Regionally accredited. Extended campuses in Great Falls and Lewistown. **Degrees:** 142 bachelor's, 131 associate awarded; master's offered. **Location:** 115 miles from Great Falls. **Calendar:** Semester,

extensive summer session. **Full-time faculty:** 62 total; 36% have terminal degrees, 2% minority, 34% women. **Part-time faculty:** 34 total; 6% minority, 50% women. **Class size:** 70% < 20, 27% 20-39, 1% 40-49, 1% 50-99.

Freshman class profile. 378 applied, 242 admitted, 228 enrolled.

Mid 50% test scores			
SAT critical reading:	460-540	GPA 2.0-2.99:	50%
SAT math:	430-530	Rank in top quarter:	14%
SAT writing:	400-510	Rank in top tenth:	4%
ACT composite:	17-21	Return as sophomores:	58%
GPA 3.75 or higher:	6%	Out-of-state:	91%
GPA 3.50-3.74:	11%	Live on campus:	32%
GPA 3.0-3.49:	23%	International:	1%

Basis for selection. Bachelor degree-seeking admission requirements ONLY: 2.5 GPA or upper half of class, in conjunction with college preparatory program. Writing and math proficiency as scored on basis of ACT and/or writing assessment.

High school preparation. College-preparatory program recommended. 14 units required. Required units include English 4, mathematics 3, social studies 3, science 2 (laboratory 2) and academic electives 2.

2011-2012 Annual costs. Tuition/fees: $4,643; $15,820 out-of-state. Room/board: $6,461.

2010-2011 Financial aid. Need-based: 214 full-time freshmen applied for aid; 187 were judged to have need; 186 of these received aid. Average need met was 62%. Average scholarship/grant was $4,973; average loan $3,477. 51% of total undergraduate aid awarded as scholarships/grants, 49% as loans/jobs. **Non-need-based:** Awarded to 13 full-time undergraduates, including 9 freshmen. Scholarships awarded for academics, athletics.

Application procedures. Admission: No deadline. $30 fee, may be waived for applicants with need. Admission notification on a rolling basis. **Financial aid:** Priority date 4/15; no closing date. FAFSA, institutional form required. Applicants notified on a rolling basis starting 5/1; must reply within 4 week(s) of notification.

Academics. Special study options: Combined bachelor's/graduate degree, cooperative education, distance learning, double major, dual enrollment of high school students, independent study, internships, liberal arts/career combination, study abroad, teacher certification program. **Credit/placement by examination:** AP, CLEP, IB, SAT, ACT, institutional tests. **Support services:** Learning center, pre-admission summer program, reduced course load, remedial instruction, study skills assistance, tutoring.

Majors. Biology: General. **Business:** Business admin. **Computer sciences:** Information systems. **Education:** Elementary, mathematics, physical, science, secondary, social science, technology/industrial arts. **English:** English lit. **Foreign languages:** French. **General:** Agribusiness operations. **Health services:** Nursing (RN). **Human services:** Community org/advocacy. **Math:** General. **Visual/performing arts:** Studio arts.

Most popular majors. Business/marketing 8%, education 29%, engineering/engineering technologies 7%, health sciences 14%, trade and industry 25%.

Computing on campus. 250 workstations in dormitories, library, computer center, student center. Dormitories wired for high-speed internet access and linked to campus network. Commuter students can connect to campus network. Online course registration, online library, helpline, repair service, wireless network available.

Student life. Freshman orientation: Mandatory, $40 fee. Preregistration for classes offered. **Housing:** Guaranteed on-campus for all undergraduates. Coed dorms, single-sex dorms, apartments available. $75 fully refundable deposit, deadline 9/1. Limited housing available for nontraditional students. **Activities:** Pep band, radio station, student government, student newspaper, Inter-Christian fellowship, Sweetgrass Society, community involvement association, Mental Mafia, residence hall association, SkillsUSA, student education association.

Athletics. NAIA. **Intercollegiate:** Basketball, football (tackle) M, golf W, rodeo, volleyball W, wrestling M. **Intramural:** Badminton, basketball, bowling, cheerleading, football (non-tackle), racquetball, rodeo, soccer, softball, table tennis, tennis, volleyball. **Team name:** Lights, Skylights.

Student services. Adult student services, alcohol/substance abuse counseling, career counseling, services for economically disadvantaged, student employment services, financial aid counseling, health services, minority student services, personal counseling, placement for graduates, veterans' counselor. **Physically disabled:** Services for visually, speech, hearing impaired.

Contact. E-mail: admissions@msun.edu
Phone: (406) 265-3704 Toll-free number: (800) 662-6132 ext. 3704
Fax: (406) 265-3792
Lexy Fisher, Director of Admissions, Montana State University: Northern, Box 7751, Havre, MT 59501

Montana Tech of the University of Montana
Butte, Montana
www.mtech.edu   **CB code: 4487**

- Public 4-year engineering and technical college
- Commuter campus in large town
- 2,406 degree-seeking undergraduates: 9% part-time, 38% women, 1% African American, 1% Asian American, 2% Hispanic American, 2% Native American, 8% international
- 140 degree-seeking graduate students
- 89% of applicants admitted
- SAT or ACT (ACT writing recommended) required
- 51% graduate within 6 years; 14% enter graduate study

General. Founded in 1893. Regionally accredited. **Degrees:** 314 bachelor's, 93 associate awarded; master's offered. **Location:** 82 miles from Bozeman, 65 miles from Helena. **Calendar:** Semester, extensive summer session. **Full-time faculty:** 133 total; 59% have terminal degrees, 10% minority, 35% women. **Part-time faculty:** 79 total; 5% minority, 42% women. **Class size:** 61% < 20, 25% 20-39, 4% 40-49, 9% 50-99, less than 1% >100. **Special facilities:** Mineral museum, earthquake studies office.

Freshman class profile. 858 applied, 763 admitted, 475 enrolled.

Mid 50% test scores			
SAT critical reading:	480-590	GPA 3.0-3.49:	33%
SAT math:	500-630	GPA 2.0-2.99:	18%
SAT writing:	450-580	Rank in top quarter:	47%
ACT composite:	22-27	Rank in top tenth:	22%
GPA 3.75 or higher:	29%	Out-of-state:	15%
GPA 3.50-3.74:	19%	Live on campus:	41%
		International:	2%

Basis for selection. Rank in top half of graduating class, or graduate with minimum cumulative GPA of 2.5, or achieve minimum composite score on ACT of 22, or minimum total score on SAT of 1540; meet math and English standards, and complete preparatory requirements. **Home schooled:** Students can satisfy the requirement of high school graduation by obtaining a high school equivalency diploma based on the GED. examination, or satisfactory performance on either the ACT or COMPASS examinations. Home schooled students must also submit a transcript summarizing their academic history.

High school preparation. College-preparatory program required. Required and recommended units include English 4, mathematics 3-4, social studies 3, science 2 (laboratory 1). Combined 3 years of foreign language, visual and performing arts, computer science, or vocational education required.

2012-2013 Annual costs. Tuition/fees (projected): $6,175; $17,269 out-of-state. Room/board: $7,266. Books/supplies: $900. Personal expenses: $1,658.

Financial aid. Non-need-based: Scholarships awarded for academics, alumni affiliation, athletics, job skills, leadership, minority status, religious affiliation, ROTC, state residency.

Application procedures. Admission: No deadline. $30 fee. Admission notification on a rolling basis. **Financial aid:** Priority date 3/1; no closing date. FAFSA, institutional form required. Applicants notified on a rolling basis starting 3/15; must reply within 2 week(s) of notification.

Academics. Online, real time tutoring is available 24 hours a day, 7 days a week. **Special study options:** Combined bachelor's/graduate degree, cooperative education, cross-registration, distance learning, double major, dual enrollment of high school students, external degree, honors, independent study, internships, teacher certification program. 3-2 liberal arts-engineering program with Carroll College, dual enrollment agreement with Flathead Valley Community College, collaborative programs with UM Helena (BAS Business, BS BIT, BAS General Studies), UM Western (Elementary Education Certification and Secondary Education Certification in Biological Sciences, General Sciences, and Mathematical Sciences), and UM-COT (AAS Surgical Technology). **Credit/placement by examination:** AP, CLEP, IB, SAT, ACT, institutional tests. 10 credit hours maximum toward associate degree, 30 toward bachelor's. **Support services:** Learning center, pre-admission summer program, reduced course load, remedial instruction, study skills assistance, tutoring.

Majors. Biology: General. **Business:** General. **Computer sciences:** Computer science, networking. **Engineering:** General, electrical, environmental, geological, metallurgical, mining, petroleum, software. **English:** Technical writing. **Health services:** Medical informatics, nursing (RN), occupational health. **Liberal arts:** Arts/sciences. **Math:** General. **Physical sciences:** General, chemistry.

Most popular majors. Business/marketing 19%, engineering/engineering technologies 61%, health sciences 9%.

Computing on campus. 541 workstations in dormitories, library, computer center, student center. Dormitories wired for high-speed internet access and linked to campus network. Commuter students can connect to campus network. Online course registration, online library, helpline, wireless network available.

Student life. Freshman orientation: Mandatory. Preregistration for classes offered. Held several days before semester start. **Housing:** Guaranteed on-campus for freshmen. Coed dorms, special housing for disabled, apartments available. $100 fully refundable deposit. **Activities:** Pep band, campus ministries, international student organizations, radio station, student government, student newspaper, Baptist student union, Circle-K, American Indian Science and Engineering Society, Society of Women Engineers, Montana Tech Catholic Campus Ministry.

Athletics. NAIA. **Intercollegiate:** Basketball, football (tackle) M, golf, volleyball W. **Intramural:** Basketball, football (non-tackle), racquetball, softball, volleyball. **Team name:** Orediggers.

Student services. Adult student services, alcohol/substance abuse counseling, career counseling, services for economically disadvantaged, student employment services, financial aid counseling, health services, minority student services, personal counseling, placement for graduates, veterans' counselor, women's services. **Physically disabled:** Services for visually, speech, hearing impaired.

Contact. E-mail: enrollment@mtech.edu
Phone: (406) 496-4256 Toll-free number: (800) 445-8324
Fax: (406) 496-4710
Stephanie Crowe, Assistant Director of Admissions and Recruiting, Montana Tech of the University of Montana, 1300 West Park Street, Butte, MT 59701-8997

Rocky Mountain College
Billings, Montana
www.rocky.edu   **CB code: 4660**

- Private 4-year liberal arts college affiliated with Presbyterian Church (USA)
- Residential campus in small city
- 936 degree-seeking undergraduates: 1% part-time, 52% women, 1% African American, 1% Asian American, 4% Hispanic American, 2% Native American, 5% international
- 77 degree-seeking graduate students
- 58% of applicants admitted
- SAT or ACT (ACT writing optional) required
- 49% graduate within 6 years; 14% enter graduate study

General. Founded in 1878. Regionally accredited. **Degrees:** 163 bachelor's, 1 associate awarded; master's offered. **ROTC:** Army. **Calendar:** Semester, limited summer session. **Full-time faculty:** 63 total; 71% have terminal degrees, 43% women. **Part-time faculty:** 57 total; 19% have terminal degrees, 2% minority, 53% women. **Class size:** 67% < 20, 30% 20-39, 2% 40-49, less than 1% 50-99. **Special facilities:** Outdoor recreation center, flight school, equestrian facilities, geology library, rock climbing wall.

Freshman class profile. 1,327 applied, 766 admitted, 228 enrolled.

Mid 50% test scores			
SAT critical reading:	470-550	GPA 3.0-3.49:	34%
SAT math:	470-570	GPA 2.0-2.99:	16%
ACT composite:	21-25	Return as sophomores:	66%
GPA 3.75 or higher:	29%	Out-of-state:	58%
GPA 3.50-3.74:	21%	Live on campus:	82%
		International:	5%

Basis for selection. 2.5 GPA, ACT 21 or combined critical reading/math SAT of 1000 meets requirement for regular admission. Test scores accepted on a rolling basis. Essay recommended for all students. Interview recommended for students not meeting regular admission requirements. Audition recommended for music, theater students. Portfolio recommended for art students. **Home schooled:** Applicants must either have GED or pass ACT based on college entrance standards.

High school preparation. College-preparatory program recommended. 19 units required. Required units include English 4, mathematics 4, social studies 3, history 2, science 3 and academic electives 3.

2012-2013 Annual costs. Tuition/fees (projected): $22,892. Room/board: $7,122. Books/supplies: $1,300. Personal expenses: $750.

2011-2012 Financial aid. Need-based: 200 full-time freshmen applied for aid; 174 were judged to have need; 174 of these received aid. Average need met was 76%. Average scholarship/grant was $13,750; average loan $3,441. 64% of total undergraduate aid awarded as scholarships/grants, 36% as loans/jobs. **Non-need-based:** Awarded to 361 full-time undergraduates, including 68 freshmen. Scholarships awarded for academics, athletics.

Application procedures. Admission: No deadline. $35 fee, may be waived for applicants with need. Admission notification on a rolling basis. **Financial aid:** Priority date 3/1; no closing date. FAFSA required. Applicants notified on a rolling basis starting 2/15; must reply within 4 week(s) of notification.

Academics. Special study options: Accelerated study, combined bachelor's/graduate degree, distance learning, double major, dual enrollment of high school students, ESL, honors, independent study, internships, student-designed major, study abroad, teacher certification program. **Credit/placement by examination:** AP, CLEP, IB, SAT, ACT, institutional tests. 15 credit hours maximum toward associate degree, 31 toward bachelor's. **Support services:** Learning center, reduced course load, remedial instruction, study skills assistance, tutoring, writing center.

Majors. Biology: General. **Business:** Accounting/business management, business admin. **Communications:** Communications/speech/rhetoric. **Computer sciences:** Computer science. **Conservation:** Environmental science, environmental studies, management/policy. **Education:** General, art, biology, drama/dance, elementary, English, history, mathematics, middle, multi-level teacher, music, physical, secondary, social studies. **English:** Creative writing, English lit. **General:** Business, equestrian studies. **Health services:** Athletic training. **History:** General. **Math:** General. **Parks/recreation:** Exercise sciences, health/fitness, sports admin. **Physical sciences:** Chemistry, geology. **Psychology:** General. **Social sciences:** Sociology. **Visual/performing arts:** Art, dramatic, music performance, theater design.

Most popular majors. Biology 12%, business/marketing 17%, education 9%, parks/recreation 9%, psychology 6%, trade and industry 11%, visual/performing arts 6%.

Computing on campus. 129 workstations in dormitories, library, computer center, student center. Dormitories wired for high-speed internet access and linked to campus network. Commuter students can connect to campus network. Online course registration, online library, helpline, student web hosting, wireless network available.

Student life. Freshman orientation: Mandatory. Preregistration for classes offered. Held during the 4 days before classes start; includes mountain getaway trip. **Housing:** Guaranteed on-campus for freshmen. Coed dorms, special housing for disabled, apartments available. Suites available. **Activities:** Bands, campus ministries, choral groups, drama, international student organizations, music ensembles, musical theater, student government, symphony orchestra, Pi Kappa Delta-National Honorary Forensics Fraternity, Alpha Eta Rho National Aviation Fraternity Ambassador's Club, American Indian cultural association, American Indian science and engineering society, investing club, Intervarsity Christian Fellowship, geology club, equestrian club, ski club, Newman Club.

Athletics. NAIA. **Intercollegiate:** Basketball, cheerleading M, cross-country, equestrian, football (tackle) M, golf, skiing, soccer, track and field, volleyball W. **Intramural:** Basketball, football (tackle) M, golf, handball, racquetball, skiing, soccer, softball, swimming, table tennis, tennis, volleyball. **Team name:** Battlin' Bears.

Student services. Adult student services, alcohol/substance abuse counseling, chaplain/spiritual director, career counseling, student employment services, financial aid counseling, health services, on-campus daycare, personal counseling, placement for graduates. **Physically disabled:** Services for visually, speech, hearing impaired.

Contact. E-mail: admissions@rocky.edu
Phone: (406) 657-1026 Toll-free number: (800) 877-6259
Fax: (406) 657-1189
Kelly Edwards, Director of Admissions, Rocky Mountain College, 1511 Poly Drive, Billings, MT 59102-1796

Salish Kootenai College
Pablo, Montana
www.skc.edu

CB code: 0898

- Private 4-year liberal arts college
- Commuter campus in rural community

General. Founded in 1977. Regionally accredited. **Location:** 55 miles from Missoula, 65 miles from Kalispell. **Calendar:** Quarter.

Annual costs/financial aid. Books/supplies: $1,050. Personal expenses: $2,000. Need-based financial aid available to full-time and part-time students.

Contact. Phone: (406) 275-4866
Admissions, PO Box 70, Pablo, MT 59855

University of Great Falls
Great Falls, Montana
www.ugf.edu

CB code: 4058

- Private 4-year university and liberal arts college affiliated with Roman Catholic Church
- Residential campus in small city
- 1,003 degree-seeking undergraduates: 33% part-time, 66% women, 2% African American, 2% Asian American, 4% Hispanic American, 3% Native American
- 70 degree-seeking graduate students
- 27% of applicants admitted
- SAT or ACT (ACT writing optional), application essay required

General. Founded in 1932. Regionally accredited. **Degrees:** 182 bachelor's awarded; master's offered. **Location:** 600 miles from Seattle, 370 miles from Spokane, Washington. **Calendar:** Semester, limited summer session. **Full-time faculty:** 42 total; 81% have terminal degrees, 2% minority, 36% women. **Part-time faculty:** 72 total; 15% have terminal degrees, 4% minority, 56% women. **Class size:** 71% < 20, 28% 20-39, less than 1% 40-49. **Special facilities:** Herbarium.

Freshman class profile. 723 applied, 198 admitted, 187 enrolled.

Mid 50% test scores			
SAT critical reading:	430-540	GPA 3.50-3.74:	21%
SAT math:	430-560	GPA 3.0-3.49:	33%
SAT writing:	430-530	GPA 2.0-2.99:	28%
ACT composite:	19-24	Return as sophomores:	52%
GPA 3.75 or higher:	17%	Out-of-state:	38%
		Live on campus:	72%

Basis for selection. High school record and character most important. ACT/SAT scores may be considered when making scholarship decisions. SAT Subject Tests recommended. Interview recommended. **Home schooled:** Transcript of courses and grades required. Applicants should submit SAT/ACT test scores, bibliography of school literature and essay describing and evaluating preparation for university-level work.

High school preparation. Required and recommended units include mathematics 3, social studies 1-2, history 3, science 3 (laboratory 1) and academic electives 5.

2011-2012 Annual costs. Tuition/fees: $19,580. Room/board: $6,712. Books/supplies: $1,000. Personal expenses: $750.

2011-2012 Financial aid. Need-based: 155 full-time freshmen applied for aid; 141 were judged to have need; 140 of these received aid. Average need met was 72%. Average scholarship/grant was $10,616; average loan $3,203. 50% of total undergraduate aid awarded as scholarships/grants, 50% as loans/jobs. **Non-need-based:** Awarded to 135 full-time undergraduates, including 34 freshmen. Scholarships awarded for academics, alumni affiliation, art, athletics, music/drama, religious affiliation, state residency.

Application procedures. Admission: Priority date 5/5; deadline 9/1 (postmark date). $35 fee, may be waived for applicants with need. Admission notification on a rolling basis beginning on or about 10/1. Must reply by May 1 or within 2 week(s) if notified thereafter. Admission granted with 6th semester transcripts. **Financial aid:** Priority date 3/1; no closing date. FAFSA required. Applicants notified on a rolling basis starting 3/1; must reply within 3 week(s) of notification.

Academics. Trio Title IV Student Support Services program available to eligible students. **Special study options:** Combined bachelor's/graduate degree, cooperative education, distance learning, double major, dual enrollment of high school students, exchange student, honors, independent study,

internships, liberal arts/career combination, study abroad, teacher certification program, weekend college. **Credit/placement by examination:** AP, CLEP, IB, SAT, ACT, institutional tests. 30 credit hours maximum toward associate degree, 30 toward bachelor's. **Support services:** Learning center, pre-admission summer program, reduced course load, remedial instruction, study skills assistance, tutoring, writing center.

Majors. Biology: General, botany. **Business:** Accounting, accounting/business management, business admin. **Computer sciences:** General, applications programming, computer graphics, computer science, data processing, LAN/WAN management, networking, programming, security, system admin, systems analysis. **Education:** Art, biology, chemistry, early childhood, elementary, English, gifted/talented, health, history, kindergarten/preschool, mathematics, middle, physical, psychology, reading, science, secondary, social science, social studies, special ed. **English:** English lit. **Health services:** Predental, premedicine, preveterinary, substance abuse counseling. **History:** General. **Math:** General. **Parks/recreation:** Health/fitness. **Philosophy/religion:** Religion. **Physical sciences:** Chemistry. **Protective services:** Corrections, criminal justice, forensics, juvenile corrections, police science. **Psychology:** General. **Social sciences:** General, political science, sociology. **Visual/performing arts:** Art.

Most popular majors. Biology 6%, business/marketing 11%, education 25%, health sciences 18%, legal studies 6%, psychology 9%, public administration/social services 8%, security/protective services 10%.

Computing on campus. 120 workstations in dormitories, library, computer center, student center. Dormitories wired for high-speed internet access and linked to campus network. Commuter students can connect to campus network. Online course registration, online library, helpline, repair service, student web hosting, wireless network available.

Student life. Freshman orientation: Mandatory, $75 fee. Preregistration for classes offered. Programs held 3 days prior to fall and spring semesters; includes float trip down Missouri River. **Policies:** No drugs, alcohol, firearms or weapons allowed on campus. **Housing:** Guaranteed on-campus for freshmen. Coed dorms, apartments, wellness housing available. $150 fully refundable deposit, deadline 8/15. **Activities:** Bands, campus ministries, choral groups, dance, drama, film society, international student organizations, music ensembles, musical theater, student government, student newspaper, symphony orchestra, United Tribes Club, Americorps, drama club, art club, Students In Free Enterprise, international law and justice club, medical science club, student Montana education association, paralegal club.

Athletics. NAIA. **Intercollegiate:** Basketball, cross-country, golf, soccer W, softball W, volleyball W, wrestling M. **Intramural:** Baseball, basketball, bowling, cheerleading, football (non-tackle), softball, tennis, volleyball. **Team name:** Argonauts.

Student services. Adult student services, alcohol/substance abuse counseling, chaplain/spiritual director, career counseling, services for economically disadvantaged, student employment services, financial aid counseling, health services, minority student services, on-campus daycare, personal counseling, placement for graduates, veterans' counselor, women's services. **Physically disabled:** Services for visually, hearing impaired.

Contact. E-mail: enroll@ugf.edu
Phone: (406) 791-5200 Toll-free number: (800) 856-9544
Fax: (406) 791-5209
April Clutter, Assistant Director of Admissions, University of Great Falls, 1301 20th Street South, Great Falls, MT 59405

University of Montana
Missoula, Montana

www.umt.edu

CB member

CB code: 4489

- Public 4-year university and liberal arts college
- Residential campus in small city
- 13,237 degree-seeking undergraduates
- 94% of applicants admitted
- SAT or ACT (ACT writing recommended) required

General. Founded in 1893. Regionally accredited. Two-year technical college provides technical training, education and postsecondary academic preparation through general associate programs. **Degrees:** 2,017 bachelor's, 289 associate awarded; master's, professional, doctoral offered. **ROTC:** Army. **Location:** 210 miles from Spokane, Washington. **Calendar:** Semester, extensive summer session. **Full-time faculty:** 604 total. **Part-time faculty:** 297 total. **Class size:** 45% < 20, 36% 20-39, 6% 40-49, 8% 50-99, 5% >100. **Special facilities:** Broadcast media center (public radio and TV) and performing arts building, 3 art galleries, wildlife biology museum, 29,000-acre experimental forest, biological research station, geology field camp, biological, biomedical, kinesiology, physiology, and forestry-related research

centers and labs, environmental studies laboratory, primate colony, forensics lab, clinical psychology center, practical ethics center, Fort Missoula field research center.

Freshman class profile. 5,609 applied, 5,272 admitted, 2,162 enrolled.

Mid 50% test scores			
SAT critical reading:	490-600	Out-of-state:	27%
SAT math:	490-590	Live on campus:	69%
SAT writing:	470-580	Fraternities:	6%
ACT composite:	21-26	Sororities:	5%

Basis for selection. Must meet one of the following: 2.5 GPA, 22 ACT, 1540 SAT, or rank in top half of graduating class. TOEFL or Michigan Test and statement of intent and personal contribution required for international students. SAT/ACT not required for nontraditional students or international students.

High school preparation. College-preparatory program required. Required and recommended units include English 4, mathematics 3, social studies 3, history 1-2, science 2 (laboratory 2), foreign language 2 and academic electives 2. Computer science, visual and performing arts, and/or vocational education recommended.

2011-2012 Annual costs. Tuition/fees: $5,722; $20,099 out-of-state. Out-of-State tuition Includes mandatory annual $72 nonresident building fee. Room/board: $7,060. Books/supplies: $950. Personal expenses: $4,400.

Financial aid. Non-need-based: Scholarships awarded for academics, alumni affiliation, athletics, leadership, music/drama, ROTC, state residency.

Application procedures. Admission: Priority date 3/1; no deadline. $30 fee. Admission notification on a rolling basis beginning on or about 9/15. **Financial aid:** Priority date 2/15; no closing date. FAFSA, institutional form required. Applicants notified on a rolling basis starting 4/1; must reply by 8/1 or within 4 week(s) of notification.

Academics. Special study options: Combined bachelor's/graduate degree, cooperative education, cross-registration, distance learning, double major, ESL, exchange student, honors, independent study, internships, study abroad, teacher certification program. English language institute, combined programs with other institutions for bachelor in nursing and master in public administration with Montana State University-Bozeman. **Credit/placement by examination:** AP, CLEP, institutional tests. 10 credit hours maximum toward associate degree. Credit hours awarded determined by academic department. **Support services:** Learning center, pre-admission summer program, reduced course load, remedial instruction, study skills assistance, tutoring, writing center.

Majors. Architecture: Urban/community planning. **Area/ethnic studies:** Asian, Native American, women's. **Biology:** General, bacteriology, botany, cellular/molecular, zoology. **Business:** General, business admin, finance, international, management information systems, marketing. **Communications:** Broadcast journalism, communications/speech/rhetoric, journalism. **Computer sciences:** Computer science. **Conservation:** General, forestry, wildlife/wilderness. **Education:** General, art, biology, business, elementary, English, mathematics, music, physical, secondary. **English:** English lit, rhetoric/composition. **Foreign languages:** Classics, French, German, Japanese, Latin, Russian, Spanish. **Health services:** Athletic training, clinical lab science. **History:** General. **Human services:** Social work. **Liberal arts:** Arts/sciences. **Math:** General. **Parks/recreation:** Exercise sciences, facilities management, health/fitness. **Philosophy/religion:** Philosophy. **Physical sciences:** Chemistry, geology, physics. **Psychology:** General. **Social sciences:** Anthropology, criminology, economics, geography, GIS/cartography, international relations, political science, sociology. **Visual/performing arts:** General, art, art history/conservation, dance, dramatic, music, music performance, music theory/composition.

Computing on campus. 1,800 workstations in dormitories, library, computer center, student center. Dormitories wired for high-speed internet access and linked to campus network. Commuter students can connect to campus network. Online course registration, online library, helpline, repair service, wireless network available.

Student life. Freshman orientation: Mandatory, $60 fee. Preregistration for classes offered. Three-day summer session which includes parent track. **Housing:** Guaranteed on-campus for freshmen. Coed dorms, single-sex dorms, special housing for disabled, apartments, fraternity/sorority housing available. $120 deposit, deadline 3/1. Honors floors, international floors, quiet floors, activity dorms, personal development housing available. **Activities:** Bands, choral groups, dance, drama, literary magazine, music ensembles, musical theater, opera, radio station, student government, student newspaper, symphony orchestra, TV station, Associated Students of University of Montana, University of Montana Advocates, Mortar Board, Spurs, Circle-K, forestry student association, honors student association, Kyi-Yo (Native American organization), environmental action club, American Indian Business Leaders.

Athletics. NCAA. **Intercollegiate:** Basketball, cheerleading, cross-country, football (tackle) M, golf W, rodeo, soccer W, tennis, track and field, volleyball W. **Intramural:** Badminton, baseball M, basketball, football (tackle), golf, handball, racquetball, soccer, softball, swimming, table tennis, tennis, track and field, triathlon, volleyball. **Team name:** Grizzlies.

Student services. Adult student services, alcohol/substance abuse counseling, chaplain/spiritual director, career counseling, services for economically disadvantaged, student employment services, financial aid counseling, health services, legal services, minority student services, on-campus daycare, personal counseling, placement for graduates, veterans' counselor, women's services. **Physically disabled:** Services for visually, speech, hearing impaired.

Contact. E-mail: admiss@umontana.edu
Phone: (406) 243-6266 Toll-free number: (800) 462-8636
Fax: (406) 243-5711
Jed Liston, Assistant Vice President for Enrollment Services, University of Montana, Lommasson Center 103, Missoula, MT 59812

University of Montana: Western
Dillon, Montana   **CB member**
www.umwestern.edu   **CB code: 4945**

▶ Public 4-year liberal arts and teachers college
▶ Residential campus in small town
▶ 1,366 degree-seeking undergraduates: 13% part-time, 57% women, 1% African American, 2% Hispanic American, 2% Native American
▶ 33% graduate within 6 years; 16% enter graduate study

General. Founded in 1893. Regionally accredited. **Degrees:** 176 bachelor's, 26 associate awarded. **Location:** 65 miles from Butte, 145 miles from Idaho Falls. **Calendar:** Semester, limited summer session. **Full-time faculty:** 69 total; 75% have terminal degrees, 1% minority, 51% women. **Part-time faculty:** 22 total; 41% have terminal degrees, 41% women. **Class size:** 68% < 20, 32% 20-39. **Special facilities:** Outdoor education center, wildlife exhibit, office simulation center, public gallery, affiliation with La Cense Montana Ranch, Montana Center for Horsemanship.

Freshman class profile. 522 applied, 393 admitted, 264 enrolled.

Mid 50% test scores			
SAT critical reading:	400-560	GPA 2.0-2.99:	40%
SAT math:	420-550	Rank in top quarter:	23%
ACT composite:	17-22	Rank in top tenth:	5%
GPA 3.75 or higher:	10%	End year in good standing:	89%
GPA 3.50-3.74:	12%	Return as sophomores:	70%
GPA 3.0-3.49:	33%	Out-of-state:	27%
		Live on campus:	99%

Basis for selection. Open admission, but selective for some programs. **Home schooled:** State high school equivalency certificate required.

High school preparation. College-preparatory program required. 14 units recommended. Recommended units include English 4, mathematics 3, social studies 3, science 2 (laboratory 2) and academic electives 2. Vocational education, computer education, foreign language, visual or performing arts recommended.

2011-2012 Annual costs. Tuition/fees: $3,945; $13,706 out-of-state. Room/board: $5,834. Books/supplies: $750. Personal expenses: $2,000.

2010-2011 Financial aid. **Need-based:** 219 full-time freshmen applied for aid; 172 were judged to have need; 172 of these received aid. Average need met was 15%. Average scholarship/grant was $2,695; average loan $2,956. 43% of total undergraduate aid awarded as scholarships/grants, 57% as loans/jobs. **Non-need-based:** Awarded to 277 full-time undergraduates, including 109 freshmen. Scholarships awarded for academics, alumni affiliation, art, athletics, leadership, minority status, state residency. **Additional information:** Tuition and/or fee waivers for veterans, Native Americans, senior citizens, and dependents of Montana University System employees.

Application procedures. **Admission:** Priority date 7/1; no deadline. $30 fee. Admission notification on a rolling basis. **Financial aid:** Priority date 3/1; no closing date. FAFSA, institutional form required. Applicants notified on a rolling basis starting 4/1; must reply within 4 week(s) of notification.

Academics. Montana Western offers block scheduling. Students take one class at a time for three and a half weeks (18 days) before moving on to their next course; there is a four day "Block Break" between classes. Classes are three hours daily, Monday through Friday. Most courses are four credits. **Special study options:** Cooperative education, distance learning, double major, dual enrollment of high school students, honors, independent study, internships, liberal arts/career combination, study abroad, teacher certification program. **Credit/placement by examination:** AP, CLEP, IB, institutional tests. 30 credit hours maximum toward associate degree, 30 toward bachelor's.

Support services: Learning center, reduced course load, remedial instruction, study skills assistance, tutoring.

Majors. **Biology:** General, cellular/molecular, wildlife. **Business:** General, business admin, office management, small business admin, tourism/travel. **Communications:** Communications/speech/rhetoric. **Computer sciences:** Networking. **Conservation:** General, environmental science, wildlife/wilderness. **Education:** General, art, biology, business, chemistry, early childhood, elementary, English, health, history, mathematics, multi-level teacher, music, physical, school librarian, science, secondary, social studies, technology/industrial arts. **English:** Creative writing, English lit. **General:** Equestrian studies. **History:** General. **Liberal arts:** Arts/sciences. **Math:** General, applied. **Physical sciences:** Chemistry, geology. **Psychology:** General. **Social sciences:** General, anthropology, political science, sociology. **Visual/performing arts:** General, art, dramatic, illustration, music, studio arts.

Most popular majors. Business/marketing 28%, education 47%, liberal arts 19%.

Computing on campus. 140 workstations in dormitories, library, computer center. Dormitories wired for high-speed internet access and linked to campus network. Commuter students can connect to campus network. Online course registration, wireless network available.

Student life. **Freshman orientation:** Mandatory, $70 fee. Preregistration for classes offered. **Policies:** Tabacco free campus. **Housing:** Guaranteed on-campus for freshmen. Coed dorms, single-sex dorms, special housing for disabled, apartments, wellness housing available. $200 fully refundable deposit. Students with fewer than 30 credits not living with family required to live in dormitory. Transfer students under 21 with fewer than 30 credits not living with parents required to live on campus. **Activities:** Campus ministries, choral groups, dance, drama, music ensembles, musical theater, radio station, student newspaper, student government, admissions ambassadors, Chi Alpha-Christian fellowship, outdoor club, Polynesian club, rodeo club, IT club, academic clubs, baptist ministries, catholic campus ministry, humans in performance.

Athletics. NAIA. **Intercollegiate:** Basketball, equestrian, football (tackle) M, rodeo, volleyball W. **Intramural:** Basketball, football (non-tackle), racquetball, soccer, volleyball. **Team name:** Bulldogs.

Student services. Alcohol/substance abuse counseling, career counseling, services for economically disadvantaged, student employment services, financial aid counseling, health services, on-campus daycare, personal counseling, veterans' counselor. **Physically disabled:** Services for visually, speech, hearing impaired.

Contact. E-mail: admissions@umwestern.edu
Phone: (406) 683-7331 Toll-free number: (877) 683-7331
Fax: (406) 683-7493
Catherine Redhead, Director of Enrollment Services, University of Montana: Western, 710 South Atlantic Street, Dillon, MT 59725

Nebraska

Bellevue University
Bellevue, Nebraska
www.bellevue.edu

CB code: 6053

- Private 4-year university and business college
- Commuter campus in large city
- 6,312 degree-seeking undergraduates: 24% part-time, 49% women, 13% African American, 2% Asian American, 7% Hispanic American, 1% Native American, 2% international
- 3,476 degree-seeking graduate students

General. Founded in 1965. Regionally accredited. Satellite operations throughout a five-state area in the Midwest. Focus on adult learners, nontraditional students and customized programs for organizations and corporations. **Degrees:** 2,228 bachelor's awarded; master's, doctoral offered. **ROTC:** Army, Air Force. **Calendar:** Semester, extensive summer session. **Full-time faculty:** 89 total; 51% have terminal degrees, 14% minority, 40% women. **Part-time faculty:** 322 total; 36% women. **Class size:** 65% < 20, 35% 20-39.

Basis for selection. Open admission, but selective for some programs. Students dismissed from another institution for academic or disciplinary reasons will be accepted for admission after 1 year has lapsed since dismissal from that institution. Admission to Professional Studies program requires roughly 60 transfer credit hours from accredited institution. **Home schooled:** Students should submit official verification of completion.

High school preparation. Recommended units include English 3, mathematics 3, social studies 3, history 3, science 3 (laboratory 1), foreign language 3 and academic electives 3.

2011-2012 Annual costs. Tuition/fees: $7,950. Prices vary depending on program. Books/supplies: $1,500. Personal expenses: $1,845.

2010-2011 Financial aid. Need-based: Average scholarship/grant was $2,743; average loan $3,054. 13% of total undergraduate aid awarded as scholarships/grants, 87% as loans/jobs. **Non-need-based:** Scholarships awarded for academics, athletics, leadership.

Application procedures. Admission: No deadline. $50 fee, may be waived for applicants with need. Admission notification on a rolling basis. **Financial aid:** Priority date 4/15; no closing date. FAFSA, institutional form required. Applicants notified on a rolling basis starting 4/15; must reply within 2 week(s) of notification.

Academics. Special study options: Accelerated study, cross-registration, distance learning, double major, dual enrollment of high school students, ESL, independent study, internships, liberal arts/career combination, study abroad, weekend college. **Credit/placement by examination:** AP, CLEP, IB, institutional tests. Offer 12 computer proficiency exams, each worth 1 credit. Maximum of 12 credits allowed. **Support services:** Learning center, remedial instruction, study skills assistance, tutoring, writing center.

Majors. Biology: General. **Business:** General, accounting, business admin, customer service, fashion, human resources, management information systems, selling. **Communications:** General, organizational. **Computer sciences:** General, information technology, programming, system admin, webmaster. **Education:** General, early childhood, physical. **English:** English lit. **Foreign languages:** Spanish. **Health services:** Long term care admin. **History:** General. **Human services:** General, public policy. **Liberal arts:** Arts/sciences. **Math:** General. **Military:** "intel, generally", strategic intel. **Parks/recreation:** Sports admin. **Philosophy/religion:** Philosophy. **Protective services:** Correctional facilities, intelligence analysis. **Psychology:** General. **Social sciences:** General, geography, international relations, political science, sociology. **Visual/performing arts:** Art, design, graphic design. **Work/family studies:** Child care management.

Most popular majors. Business/marketing 57%, computer/information sciences 10%, health sciences 13%, social sciences 15%.

Computing on campus. 434 workstations in library, computer center. Commuter students can connect to campus network. Online course registration, online library, helpline, wireless network available.

Student life. Freshman orientation: Available. Preregistration for classes offered. 2-day programs held the beginning week of fall, winter and spring

semesters. **Policies:** No alcohol at any student events. Any event must be coordinated through the Student Activities Office. **Activities:** Student government, Alpha Chi, Campus Crusade for Christ, anime club, Delta Epsilon Chi, economics club, institute of management accountants, multicultural student organization, student advisory council, toastmasters, chapter of Student Veterans Association, sports management club, marketing club, Pi Gamma Mu.

Athletics. NAIA. **Intercollegiate:** Baseball M, basketball M, golf, soccer, softball W, volleyball W. **Team name:** Bruins.

Student services. Career counseling, student employment services, financial aid counseling, personal counseling, placement for graduates, veterans' counselor. **Physically disabled:** Services for visually, speech, hearing impaired.

Contact. E-mail: info@bellevue.edu
Phone: (402) 293-2000 Toll-free number: (800) 756-7920
Fax: (402) 557-7230
Nick Baker, Director, Undergraduate Admissions, Bellevue University, 1000 Galvin Road South, Bellevue, NE 68005-3098

BryanLGH College of Health Sciences
Lincoln, Nebraska
www.bryanlghcollege.edu

CB code: 6058

- Private 4-year health science college affiliated with United Methodist Church
- Commuter campus in large city
- 586 degree-seeking undergraduates
- SAT or ACT (ACT writing optional), application essay, interview required

General. Regionally accredited. **Degrees:** 81 bachelor's, 11 associate awarded; master's offered. **ROTC:** Army, Naval. **Calendar:** Semester, limited summer session. **Full-time faculty:** 30 total. **Part-time faculty:** 36 total. **Class size:** 66% < 20, 22% 20-39, 6% 40-49, 5% 50-99. **Special facilities:** 8 patient simulators, 2 human plastiates, affiliation with BryanLGH Medical Center and William Jennings Bryan home and museum.

Freshman class profile.

GPA 3.75 or higher:	54%	Rank in top quarter:	53%
GPA 3.50-3.74:	33%	Rank in top tenth:	17%
GPA 3.0-3.49:	10%	Out-of-state:	23%
GPA 2.0-2.99:	3%		

Basis for selection. Applicants are reviewed by a faculty admissions committee. Students scoring above a certain rubric level are admitted. **Home schooled:** Transcript of courses and grades required.

High school preparation. College-preparatory program recommended. 24 units recommended. Recommended units include English 4, mathematics 4, social studies 4, science 4 (laboratory 3), foreign language 4 and computer science 1.

2011-2012 Annual costs. Tuition/fees: $13,470. Books/supplies: $1,200. Personal expenses: $900.

Financial aid. Non-need-based: Scholarships awarded for academics, leadership.

Application procedures. Admission: Closing date 2/1 (postmark date). $40 fee, may be waived for applicants with need. Application must be submitted on paper. Admission notification on a rolling basis beginning on or about 3/1. Must reply by May 1 or within 4 week(s) if notified thereafter. **Financial aid:** Closing date 5/1. FAFSA, institutional form required. Applicants notified on a rolling basis starting 5/1; must reply within 3 week(s) of notification.

Academics. Special study options: Combined bachelor's/graduate degree, independent study. **Credit/placement by examination:** AP, CLEP, institutional tests. 3 credit hours maximum toward associate degree, 6 toward bachelor's. **Support services:** Learning center, pre-admission summer program, remedial instruction, study skills assistance, tutoring.

Majors. Health services: Cardiovascular technology, nursing (RN), sonography.

Computing on campus. 30 workstations in library, student center. Commuter students can connect to campus network. Online library, helpline, wireless network available.

Student life. Freshman orientation: Mandatory. Preregistration for classes offered. Held on-campus the Thursday and Friday before classes

begin each term. **Activities:** Student government, Red Cross, Caring with Christ, Action for Students, student nurses association, health promotion organization.

Student services. Alcohol/substance abuse counseling, chaplain/spiritual director, financial aid counseling, health services, personal counseling.

Contact. E-mail: admissions@bryanlghcollege.edu
Phone: (402) 481-8697 Toll-free number: (800) 742-7844 ext. 18697
Fax: (402) 481-8621
Deb Border, Dean of Students, BryanLGH College of Health Sciences, 5035 Everett Street, Lincoln, NE 68506

Chadron State College
Chadron, Nebraska
www.csc.edu
CB code: 6466

- Public 4-year business and liberal arts college
- Residential campus in small town
- 2,120 degree-seeking undergraduates

General. Founded in 1911. Regionally accredited. Limited distance education classes and programs offered online and at Scottsbluff, Alliance, Sidney, and throughout western Nebraska and eastern Wyoming. **Degrees:** 350 bachelor's awarded; master's offered. **ROTC:** Army. **Location:** 100 miles from Scottsbluff. **Calendar:** Semester, limited summer session. **Full-time faculty:** 90 total. **Part-time faculty:** 60 total. **Class size:** 65% < 20, 30% 20-39, 4% 40-49, less than 1% 50-99. **Special facilities:** Planetarium, herbarium, geological museum, high plains heritage center.

Freshman class profile.

GPA 3.75 or higher:	20%	Rank in top quarter:	26%
GPA 3.50-3.74:	11%	Rank in top tenth:	11%
GPA 3.0-3.49:	22%	Out-of-state:	29%
GPA 2.0-2.99:	28%	Live on campus:	90%

Basis for selection. Open admission, but selective for some programs. Test scores must be submitted for placement, but no minimum score required. Audition recommended for music program.

High school preparation. 12 units recommended. Recommended units include English 4, mathematics 3, social studies 3, science 2 (laboratory 2). Units in visual or performing arts, computer literacy, or foreign language recommended.

2011-2012 Annual costs. Tuition/fees: $5,331; $9,388 out-of-state. Room/board: $5,050. Books/supplies: $1,200. Personal expenses: $1,680.

Financial aid. Non-need-based: Scholarships awarded for academics, alumni affiliation, art, athletics, leadership, minority status, music/drama, state residency.

Application procedures. Admission: No deadline. Admission notification on a rolling basis. **Financial aid:** Priority date 6/1; no closing date. FAFSA, institutional form required. Applicants notified on a rolling basis starting 4/1; must reply within 2 week(s) of notification.

Academics. Special study options: Accelerated study, combined bachelor's/graduate degree, cooperative education, distance learning, double major, dual enrollment of high school students, honors, independent study, internships, student-designed major, study abroad, teacher certification program. **Credit/placement by examination:** AP, CLEP, SAT, ACT, institutional tests. 65 credit hours maximum toward bachelor's degree. **Support services:** Learning center, pre-admission summer program, reduced course load, remedial instruction, study skills assistance, tutoring, writing center.

Majors. Biology: General. **Business:** Accounting, business admin, finance, management information systems, management science, office management. **Computer sciences:** Information systems. **Education:** Art, biology, business, chemistry, drama/dance, elementary, English, family/consumer sciences, history, mathematics, middle, music, physical, physics, science, secondary, social science, Spanish, technology/industrial arts, trade/industrial. **English:** English lit, rhetoric/composition. **Foreign languages:** Spanish. **General:** Range science. **History:** General. **Human services:** Social work. **Liberal arts:** Arts/sciences, library science. **Math:** General. **Parks/recreation:** General. **Physical sciences:** Chemistry. **Psychology:** General. **Social sciences:** General, sociology. **Visual/performing arts:** Art, dramatic, music. **Work/family studies:** General.

Most popular majors. Biology 11%, business/marketing 20%, education 27%.

Computing on campus. 120 workstations in dormitories, library, computer center, student center. Dormitories wired for high-speed internet access

and linked to campus network. Commuter students can connect to campus network. Online course registration, online library, helpline, wireless network available.

Student life. Freshman orientation: Available, $100 fee. Preregistration for classes offered. Four or five 2-day weekend orientations held prior to start of fall term. **Housing:** Guaranteed on-campus for freshmen. Coed dorms, single-sex dorms, special housing for disabled, apartments, wellness housing available. $100 deposit, deadline 6/1. **Activities:** Bands, choral groups, dance, drama, international student organizations, music ensembles, musical theater, student government, student newspaper, Circle K, student education association, multicultural club, Intervarsity Christian Fellowship, White Buffalo Club.

Athletics. NCAA. **Intercollegiate:** Basketball, football (tackle) M, golf W, track and field, volleyball W, wrestling M. **Intramural:** Archery, badminton, basketball, bowling, golf, racquetball, rugby M, softball, track and field, volleyball, wrestling M. **Team name:** Eagles.

Student services. Adult student services, alcohol/substance abuse counseling, career counseling, services for economically disadvantaged, student employment services, financial aid counseling, health services, on-campus daycare, personal counseling, placement for graduates, veterans' counselor. **Physically disabled:** Services for visually, speech, hearing impaired.

Contact. E-mail: inquire@csc.edu
Phone: (308) 432-6263 Toll-free number: (800) 242-3766
Fax: (308) 432-6229
Tena Cook, Director of Admissions, Chadron State College, 1000 Main Street, Chadron, NE 69337

Clarkson College
Omaha, Nebraska
www.clarksoncollege.edu
CB code: 2250

- Private 4-year health science college affiliated with Episcopal Church
- Commuter campus in large city
- 1,114 undergraduates
- Application essay required

General. Founded in 1888. Regionally accredited. **Degrees:** 126 bachelor's, 59 associate awarded; master's offered. **ROTC:** Army, Air Force. **Location:** 50 miles from Lincoln. **Calendar:** Semester, extensive summer session. **Full-time faculty:** 45 total. **Part-time faculty:** 55 total. **Class size:** 66% < 20, 30% 20-39, less than 1% 40-49, 3% 50-99. **Special facilities:** Health care clinical facilities for professional education (more than 180 clinical sites), fully energized radiologic technology lab.

Freshman class profile.

Mid 50% test scores		Out-of-state:	79%
ACT composite:	20-24		

Basis for selection. Open admission, but selective for some programs. GPA, class rank, test scores, essay important. **Home schooled:** Must take GED and submit ACT scores. Essay required. Transcript or portfolio recommended.

High school preparation. 9 units required. Required and recommended units include English 3-4, mathematics 2-4, social studies 2-3, history 2, science 2-4 (laboratory 1-2) and foreign language 2.

2011-2012 Annual costs. Tuition/fees: $13,905. Room/board: $6,700. Books/supplies: $1,380. Personal expenses: $2,700.

Financial aid. Non-need-based: Scholarships awarded for academics, alumni affiliation, minority status, religious affiliation.

Application procedures. Admission: No deadline. $35 fee. Application must be submitted on paper. Admission notification on a rolling basis. Must reply by May 1 or within 4 week(s) if notified thereafter. Application deadlines may vary by program. Students should check with admissions office for program deadlines. **Financial aid:** Priority date 4/1; no closing date. FAFSA, institutional form required. Applicants notified on a rolling basis starting 4/13; must reply within 3 week(s) of notification.

Academics. Special study options: Accelerated study, combined bachelor's/graduate degree, cooperative education, cross-registration, distance learning, double major, dual enrollment of high school students, external degree, independent study, internships, study abroad. **Credit/placement by examination:** AP, CLEP, institutional tests. 40 credit hours maximum toward associate degree, 88 toward bachelor's. Unlimited number of hours of credit by examination may be counted toward degree if residency requirement of

40 hours is met. **Support services:** Learning center, reduced course load, study skills assistance, tutoring, writing center.

Majors. Business: General, business admin. **Health services:** Health care admin, medical radiologic technology/radiation therapy, nursing (RN), preop/surgical nursing, radiologic technology/medical imaging.

Computing on campus. 60 workstations in dormitories, library, computer center. Dormitories wired for high-speed internet access. Commuter students can connect to campus network. Online library, helpline, repair service available.

Student life. Freshman orientation: Mandatory. Preregistration for classes offered. One-day program held on Friday before classes begin. **Housing:** Guaranteed on-campus for freshmen. Coed dorms, apartments available. $250 deposit, deadline 6/30. Board plan not available, kitchens located in each apartment. **Activities:** Student government, student newspaper, Christian Fellowship, Red Cross, National Student Nurses Association, Fellows club, Ambassador club, student leadership council.

Athletics. Intercollegiate: Skiing M.

Student services. Adult student services, alcohol/substance abuse counseling, career counseling, student employment services, financial aid counseling, health services, minority student services, on-campus daycare, personal counseling, placement for graduates. **Physically disabled:** Services for visually, hearing impaired.

Contact. E-mail: admiss@clarksoncollege.edu
Phone: (402) 552-3041 Toll-free number: (800) 647-5500
Fax: (402) 552-6057
Denise Work, Director of Admission, Clarkson College, 101 South 42nd Street, Omaha, NE 68131-2739

College of Saint Mary
Omaha, Nebraska
www.csm.edu   CB code: 6106

- Private 4-year university and liberal arts college for women affiliated with Roman Catholic Church
- Commuter campus in large city
- 770 degree-seeking undergraduates: 14% part-time, 100% women
- 243 degree-seeking graduate students
- 47% of applicants admitted
- SAT or ACT (ACT writing optional) required
- 41% graduate within 6 years

General. Founded in 1923. Regionally accredited. Weekend accelerated master's in teaching program, extensive integrated service learning. **Degrees:** 106 bachelor's, 74 associate awarded; master's, doctoral offered. **ROTC:** Army, Air Force. **Location:** 10 miles from downtown. **Calendar:** Semester, limited summer session. **Full-time faculty:** 61 total; 66% have terminal degrees, 10% minority, 75% women. **Part-time faculty:** 108 total; 18% have terminal degrees, 5% minority, 79% women. **Class size:** 74% < 20, 25% 20-39, less than 1% 40-49, less than 1% 50-99. **Special facilities:** Nursing labs, on-site child development center, green house, cadaver lab, digital piano lab, residence hall for single mothers and their children.

Freshman class profile. 401 applied, 187 admitted, 88 enrolled.

Mid 50% test scores		Rank in top quarter:	36%
ACT composite:	19-24	Rank in top tenth:	13%
GPA 3.75 or higher:	22%	End year in good standing:	72%
GPA 3.50-3.74:	20%	Return as sophomores:	60%
GPA 3.0-3.49:	36%	Out-of-state:	20%
GPA 2.0-2.99:	22%	Live on campus:	83%

Basis for selection. Test scores, secondary school record, class rank important factors. Recommendations also considered. Nursing program requires a specific minimum score on the TEAS test (Test of Essential Academic Skills).

High school preparation. College-preparatory program recommended. Required and recommended units include English 4, mathematics 2-3, social studies 2 and science 2-3. Chemistry and biology required of nursing, occupational therapy, and pre-professional studies students.

2011-2012 Annual costs. Tuition/fees: $24,830. Room/board: $6,700. Books/supplies: $1,250. Personal expenses: $1,740.

2011-2012 Financial aid. Need-based: Average need met was 78%. Average scholarship/grant was $17,382; average loan $4,163. 51% of total undergraduate aid awarded as scholarships/grants, 49% as loans/jobs. **Non-need-based:** Scholarships awarded for academics, athletics, music/drama.

Application procedures. Admission: No deadline. $30 fee, may be waived for applicants with need. Admission notification on a rolling basis. **Financial aid:** Priority date 3/1; no closing date. FAFSA required. Applicants notified on a rolling basis starting 3/1; must reply within 2 week(s) of notification.

Academics. Special study options: Accelerated study, combined bachelor's/graduate degree, cooperative education, distance learning, double major, dual enrollment of high school students, exchange student, honors, independent study, internships, liberal arts/career combination, student-designed major, study abroad, teacher certification program, weekend college. **Credit/placement by examination:** AP, CLEP, IB, SAT, ACT, institutional tests. 15 credit hours maximum toward associate degree, 15 toward bachelor's. 10 percent of program may be earned through credit by examination. **Support services:** Learning center, reduced course load, remedial instruction, study skills assistance, tutoring, writing center.

Majors. Biology: General. **Business:** Business admin. **Education:** Biology, chemistry, early childhood, earth science, elementary, English, mathematics, middle, science, secondary, social science, Spanish, special ed. **English:** English lit. **Health services:** Nursing (RN), predental, premedicine, preoccupational therapy, prepharmacy, preveterinary. **Liberal arts:** Arts/sciences. **Math:** General. **Physical sciences:** Chemistry. **Psychology:** General. **Theology:** Theology. **Visual/performing arts:** Studio arts.

Most popular majors. Business/marketing 16%, education 9%, health sciences 58%, liberal arts 6%.

Computing on campus. 90 workstations in dormitories, library, computer center, student center. Dormitories wired for high-speed internet access and linked to campus network. Commuter students can connect to campus network. Online course registration, online library, helpline, wireless network available.

Student life. Freshman orientation: Mandatory. Preregistration for classes offered. One-day program offered several times during late spring and summer. **Policies:** Student Senate and Multicultural Association of Students members must have an overall 2.5 GPA to be eligible. **Housing:** Guaranteed on-campus for freshmen. $125 partly refundable deposit. Residence hall for single mothers with children available. **Activities:** Campus ministries, choral groups, drama, international student organizations, student government, Do Unto Others Board, residence hall council, Golden S (service club), campus activities board, Student Education Association of Nebraska, business student association, Multicultural Association of Students, student nurse association, green team, math/science club.

Athletics. NAIA. **Intercollegiate:** Basketball W, cross-country W, golf W, soccer W, softball W, swimming W, volleyball W. **Intramural:** Basketball W, bowling W, volleyball W. **Team name:** Flames.

Student services. Adult student services, alcohol/substance abuse counseling, chaplain/spiritual director, career counseling, services for economically disadvantaged, student employment services, financial aid counseling, health services, minority student services, on-campus daycare, personal counseling, placement for graduates, veterans' counselor, women's services. **Physically disabled:** Services for visually, speech, hearing impaired.

Contact. E-mail: enroll@csm.edu
Phone: (402) 399-2355 Toll-free number: (800) 926-5534 ext. 2355
Fax: (402) 399-2412
Rachel Richardson, Team Leader, High School Admissions, College of Saint Mary, 7000 Mercy Road, Omaha, NE 68106

Concordia University
Seward, Nebraska
www.cune.edu   CB code: 6116

- Private 4-year university affiliated with Lutheran Church - Missouri Synod
- Residential campus in small town
- 1,211 degree-seeking undergraduates: 5% part-time, 51% women, 3% African American, 2% Hispanic American, 1% international
- 644 degree-seeking graduate students
- 69% of applicants admitted
- SAT or ACT (ACT writing optional) required
- 55% graduate within 6 years; 29% enter graduate study

General. Founded in 1894. Regionally accredited. **Degrees:** 246 bachelor's awarded; master's offered. **ROTC:** Army, Air Force. **Location:** 25 miles from Lincoln, 75 miles from Omaha. **Calendar:** Semester, limited summer session. **Full-time faculty:** 58 total; 71% have terminal degrees, 3% minority, 29% women. **Part-time faculty:** 119 total; 28% have terminal degrees, less than 1% minority, 60% women. **Class size:** 62% < 20, 34% 20-39, 3% 40-49, less than 1% 50-99. **Special facilities:** Rock and mineral museum, observatory, arboretum.

Freshman class profile. 1,397 applied, 959 admitted, 315 enrolled.

Mid 50% test scores			
SAT critical reading:	480-590	GPA 2.0-2.99:	14%
SAT math:	490-610	Rank in top quarter:	48%
ACT composite:	21-27	Rank in top tenth:	20%
GPA 3.75 or higher:	45%	Return as sophomores:	81%
GPA 3.50-3.74:	18%	Out-of-state:	56%
GPA 3.0-3.49:	23%	Live on campus:	98%

Basis for selection. High school GPA and SAT/ACT scores important in admissions decisions. Audition required for drama, music, and speech programs; portfolio required for art program. **Home schooled:** Statement describing home school structure and mission, transcript of courses and grades, state high school equivalency certificate required.

High school preparation. College-preparatory program recommended. 16 units recommended. Recommended units include English 4, mathematics 3, social studies 3, science 2, foreign language 1 and academic electives 3. One unit each in music, art, and physical education recommended.

2012-2013 Annual costs. Tuition/fees: $23,800. Room/board: $6,440. Books/supplies: $900. Personal expenses: $1,300.

2011-2012 Financial aid. Non-need-based: Scholarships awarded for academics, alumni affiliation, art, athletics, leadership, music/drama, religious affiliation.

Application procedures. Admission: Priority date 7/1; deadline 8/1 (receipt date). No application fee. Admission notification on a rolling basis beginning on or about 9/1. Must reply within 30 days of receipt of acceptance letter or request extension. **Financial aid:** Priority date 3/1; no closing date. FAFSA required. Applicants notified on a rolling basis starting 3/1; must reply within 4 week(s) of notification.

Academics. Special study options: Accelerated study, distance learning, double major, dual enrollment of high school students, ESL, exchange student, independent study, internships, study abroad, teacher certification program. Undergraduate students may take graduate level classes. **Credit/placement by examination:** AP, CLEP, IB, SAT, ACT. **Support services:** Learning center, reduced course load, study skills assistance, tutoring, writing center.

Majors. Biology: General. **Business:** General, accounting, business admin, communications, management information systems, marketing. **Communications:** General, journalism. **Computer sciences:** Computer science. **Conservation:** Environmental science, environmental studies. **Education:** General, art, biology, business, chemistry, computer, early childhood, elementary, elementary special ed, English, ESL, geography, health, history, junior high special ed, mathematics, middle, multi-level teacher, music, physical, physics, science, secondary, social studies, Spanish, speech. **English:** English lit, rhetoric/composition. **Foreign languages:** Spanish. **General:** Business. **Health services:** Community health, prechiropractic, predental, premedicine, prenursing, preoccupational therapy, preoptometry, prepharmacy, prephysical therapy, preveterinary. **History:** General. **Math:** General. **Parks/recreation:** Exercise sciences, health/fitness, sports admin, sports studies. **Physical sciences:** General, chemistry. **Psychology:** General. **Social sciences:** Geography. **Theology:** Preministerial, religious ed, sacred music, theology, youth ministry. **Visual/performing arts:** General, art, dramatic, graphic design, music, piano/keyboard, studio arts, studio arts management, voice/opera.

Most popular majors. Business/marketing 21%, education 32%, psychology 6%, visual/performing arts 8%.

Computing on campus. 220 workstations in dormitories, library, computer center, student center. Dormitories wired for high-speed internet access and linked to campus network. Commuter students can connect to campus network. Online course registration, online library, helpline, student web hosting, wireless network available.

Student life. Freshman orientation: Mandatory. Preregistration for classes offered. 3 days before classes start. Includes community service events and community building. **Policies:** University responsibly maintains Christian standards of conduct among its students, faculty and staff. **Housing:** Guaranteed on-campus for all undergraduates. Single-sex dorms, special housing for disabled, apartments, wellness housing available. $200 fully refundable deposit, deadline 8/24. **Activities:** Bands, campus ministries, choral groups, dance, drama, international student organizations, literary magazine, music ensembles, musical theater, student government, student newspaper, symphony orchestra, Circle K, Ongoing Ambassadors for Christ, multicultural awareness club, Peers and Leaders Serving, Habitat for Humanity, Leaders in Physical Health Education, Mission Minded Students, Students in Free Enterprise, Students with Families Association.

Athletics. NAIA. **Intercollegiate:** Baseball M, basketball, cheerleading M, cross-country, football (tackle) M, golf, soccer, softball W, tennis, track and field, volleyball W, wrestling M. **Intramural:** Basketball, bowling, football (non-tackle), racquetball, soccer, softball, table tennis, tennis, track and field, volleyball. **Team name:** Bulldogs.

Student services. Adult student services, alcohol/substance abuse counseling, chaplain/spiritual director, career counseling, student employment services, financial aid counseling, health services, personal counseling, placement for graduates. **Physically disabled:** Services for visually, speech, hearing impaired.

Contact. E-mail: admiss@cune.edu
Phone: (800) 535-5494 Toll-free number: (800) 535-5494
Fax: (402) 643-4073
Aaron Roberts, Director of Undergraduate Recruitment, Concordia University, 800 North Columbia Avenue, Seward, NE 68434-1556

Creative Center
Omaha, Nebraska
www.creativecenter.edu

- For-profit 4-year visual arts and career college
- Commuter campus in large city
- 119 degree-seeking undergraduates: 2% part-time, 63% women
- 86% of applicants admitted
- Application essay, interview required

General. Accredited by ACCSC. **Degrees:** 26 bachelor's, 38 associate awarded. **Calendar:** Semester, limited summer session. **Full-time faculty:** 3 total; 33% women. **Part-time faculty:** 16 total; 44% women. **Class size:** 64% 20-39, 36% 50-99.

Freshman class profile. 88 applied, 76 admitted, 45 enrolled.

Basis for selection. Students must provide a letter of recommendation, letter of intent, high school transcript and portfolio to be reviewed and approved. Portfolio required.

2011-2012 Annual costs. Tuition/fees: $23,600. Tuition/fees may vary by program.

Financial aid. Non-need-based: Scholarships awarded for academics, art.

Application procedures. Admission: No deadline. $100 fee. Application must be submitted on paper. Admission notification on a rolling basis. **Financial aid:** Closing date 7/12. FAFSA required. Applicants notified on a rolling basis starting 1/1.

Academics. Credit/placement by examination: AP, CLEP. **Support services:** Reduced course load, study skills assistance, tutoring.

Majors. Visual/performing arts: Graphic design.

Computing on campus. PC or laptop required. 8 workstations in library. Online library, helpline, student web hosting, wireless network available.

Student life. Freshman orientation: Mandatory. Preregistration for classes offered. Orientation held throughout first week of class.

Student services. Career counseling, financial aid counseling, placement for graduates.

Contact. E-mail: admissions@creativecenter.edu
Phone: (402) 898-1000 ext. 216
Toll-free number: (888) 898-1789 ext. 216 Fax: (402) 898-1301
Richard Caldwell, Director of Admissions, Creative Center, 10850 Emmet Street, Omaha, NE 68164

Creative University
Omaha, Nebraska
www.creighton.edu

CB member
CB code: 6121

- Private 4-year university affiliated with Roman Catholic Church
- Residential campus in very large city

♦ 4,153 degree-seeking undergraduates: 6% part-time, 60% women, 3% African American, 10% Asian American, 6% Hispanic American, 1% Native American, 2% international

♦ 3,577 degree-seeking graduate students

♦ 78% of applicants admitted

♦ SAT or ACT (ACT writing optional), application essay required

♦ 77% graduate within 6 years

General. Founded in 1878. Regionally accredited. **Degrees:** 935 bachelor's, 1 associate awarded; master's, professional, doctoral offered. **ROTC:** Army, Air Force. **Location:** 167 miles from Kansas City, 290 miles from Minneapolis. **Calendar:** Semester, extensive summer session. **Full-time faculty:** 523 total; 90% have terminal degrees, 13% minority, 40% women. **Part-time faculty:** 249 total; 23% have terminal degrees, 7% minority, 53% women. **Class size:** 47% < 20, 45% 20-39, 4% 40-49, 4% 50-99, less than 1% >100. **Special facilities:** Largest solar array in the state of Nebraska used for prototype testing of solar cells.

Freshman class profile. 5,104 applied, 3,971 admitted, 978 enrolled.

Mid 50% test scores		Rank in top quarter:	75%
SAT critical reading:	520-640	Rank in top tenth:	44%
SAT math:	550-660	End year in good standing:	97%
SAT writing:	510-600	Return as sophomores:	88%
ACT composite:	24-30	Out-of-state:	77%
GPA 3.75 or higher:	59%	Live on campus:	95%
GPA 3.50-3.74:	19%	International:	1%
GPA 3.0-3.49:	17%	Fraternities:	32%
GPA 2.0-2.99:	5%	Sororities:	40%

Basis for selection. School record, high school GPA, test scores, and application essay important. Class rank considered. **Home schooled:** Statement describing home school structure and mission, transcript of courses and grades, letter of recommendation (nonparent) required. Description of curriculum and texts used.

High school preparation. College-preparatory program recommended. 16 units required; 21 recommended. Required and recommended units include English 4, mathematics 3-4, social studies 2-3, history 1, science 2-3, foreign language 2-3 and academic electives 3.

2011-2012 Annual costs. Tuition/fees: $31,894. Room/board: $9,238. Books/supplies: $1,200. Personal expenses: $1,400.

2011-2012 Financial aid. Need-based: 790 full-time freshmen applied for aid; 628 were judged to have need; 628 of these received aid. Average need met was 91%. Average scholarship/grant was $21,157; average loan $5,022. 74% of total undergraduate aid awarded as scholarships/grants, 26% as loans/jobs. **Non-need-based:** Awarded to 3,076 full-time undergraduates, including 856 freshmen. Scholarships awarded for academics, alumni affiliation, art, athletics, leadership, minority status, music/drama, ROTC.

Application procedures. Admission: Priority date 12/1; deadline 2/15 (postmark date). $40 fee, may be waived for applicants with need, free for online applicants. Admission notification on a rolling basis beginning on or about 12/15. Must reply by May 1 or within 2 week(s) if notified thereafter. **Financial aid:** Priority date 3/1; no closing date. FAFSA required. Applicants notified on a rolling basis starting 3/15; must reply by 5/1 or within 4 week(s) of notification.

Academics. Students are given admissions preference into all of university's professional schools. Core curriculum required (61 semester hours from 5 areas: cultures, ideas and civilizations; theology, philosophy and ethics; natural science; social and behavioral sciences; skills). **Special study options:** Accelerated study, combined bachelor's/graduate degree, cross-registration, distance learning, double major, dual enrollment of high school students, ESL, exchange student, honors, independent study, internships, liberal arts/career combination, semester at sea, study abroad, teacher certification program, Washington semester. 2-3 program in engineering with University of Detroit Mercy, 3-3 Law Program within Creighton University, study abroad opportunities at 110 partner institutions in 40 countries. **Credit/placement by examination:** AP, CLEP, IB, SAT, ACT, institutional tests. CLEP Subject Examinations must be taken with essay where applicable. **Support services:** Learning center, reduced course load, remedial instruction, study skills assistance, tutoring, writing center.

Honors college/program. The College of Arts and Sciences offers an Honors Program with a special curricula. Admission is by invitation only. Seven percent of the students entering the College of Arts & Sciences were admitted to the Honors Program.

Majors. Area/ethnic studies: American, Native American. **Biology:** General. **Business:** Accounting, business admin, communications, e-commerce, entrepreneurial studies, finance, international, management information systems, marketing. **Communications:** Communications/speech/rhetoric, journalism, organizational. **Computer sciences:** Computer science, information

technology, web page design. **Conservation:** Environmental science. **Education:** Chemistry, elementary, Latin, secondary. **English:** American lit, British lit, creative writing, English lit, writing. **Foreign languages:** Ancient Greek, classics, French, German, Latin, Spanish. **Health services:** EMT paramedic, health care admin, nursing (RN). **History:** General. **Human services:** Social work. **Math:** General, applied. **Parks/recreation:** Exercise sciences. **Philosophy/religion:** Philosophy. **Physical sciences:** Atmospheric science, chemistry, physics. **Psychology:** General. **Social sciences:** Anthropology, economics, international relations, medical anthropology, political science, sociology. **Theology:** Theology. **Visual/performing arts:** Art, dance, dramatic, graphic design, music, music performance, musical theater, studio arts.

Most popular majors. Biology 11%, business/marketing 11%, communications/journalism 6%, health sciences 15%, interdisciplinary studies 6%, philosophy/religious studies 6%, psychology 6%, social sciences 7%, theological studies 6%.

Computing on campus. 550 workstations in dormitories, library, computer center, student center. Dormitories wired for high-speed internet access and linked to campus network. Commuter students can connect to campus network. Online course registration, online library, helpline, repair service, student web hosting, wireless network available.

Student life. Freshman orientation: Mandatory, $60 fee. Preregistration for classes offered. Held first week of fall semester. **Housing:** Guaranteed on-campus for freshmen. Coed dorms, single-sex dorms, special housing for disabled, apartments available. $100 fully refundable deposit, deadline 5/1. Honors Program, Freshman Leadership Program. **Activities:** Bands, campus ministries, choral groups, dance, drama, international student organizations, literary magazine, music ensembles, Model UN, musical theater, student government, student newspaper, symphony orchestra, TV station, World Hunger Awareness Group, Afro-American Students Association, International Relations Club, Women's Resource Center, Community Service Center, Christian Life Community, Young Democrats, Young Republicans.

Athletics. NCAA. **Intercollegiate:** Baseball M, basketball, cross-country, golf, rowing (crew) W, soccer, softball W, tennis, volleyball W. **Intramural:** Basketball, football (non-tackle), racquetball, soccer, softball, tennis, volleyball. **Team name:** Bluejays.

Student services. Adult student services, alcohol/substance abuse counseling, chaplain/spiritual director, career counseling, services for economically disadvantaged, student employment services, financial aid counseling, health services, minority student services, on-campus daycare, personal counseling, placement for graduates, veterans' counselor, women's services. **Physically disabled:** Services for visually, speech, hearing impaired.

Contact. E-mail: admissions@creighton.edu
Phone: (402) 280-2703 Toll-free number: (800) 282-5835
Fax: (402) 280-2685
Sarah Richardson, Director of Admissions and Scholarships, Creighton University, 2500 California Plaza, Omaha, NE 68178-0001

Doane College
Crete, Nebraska
www.doane.edu

CB member
CB code: 6165

♦ Private 4-year liberal arts college affiliated with United Church of Christ

♦ Residential campus in small town

♦ 1,060 degree-seeking undergraduates: 52% women, 3% African American, 1% Asian American, 5% Hispanic American, 1% international

♦ 78% of applicants admitted

♦ SAT or ACT (ACT writing optional) required

♦ 62% graduate within 6 years; 15% enter graduate study

General. Founded in 1872. Regionally accredited. Campuses also in Lincoln and Grand Island. **Degrees:** 173 bachelor's awarded; master's offered. **ROTC:** Army, Air Force. **Location:** 25 miles from Lincoln, 75 miles from Omaha. **Calendar:** 4-1-4, limited summer session. **Full-time faculty:** 75 total; 79% have terminal degrees, 3% minority, 48% women. **Part-time faculty:** 52 total; 48% have terminal degrees, 8% minority, 54% women. **Class size:** 78% < 20, 22% 20-39. **Special facilities:** Arboretum, open-air theater, observatory, all-American rose test garden, ropes challenge course, fitness trail.

Freshman class profile. 1,462 applied, 1,144 admitted, 291 enrolled.

Mid 50% test scores		Rank in top tenth:	15%
ACT composite:	20-26	End year in good standing:	96%
GPA 3.75 or higher:	32%	Return as sophomores:	74%
GPA 3.50-3.74:	23%	Out-of-state:	16%
GPA 3.0-3.49:	30%	Live on campus:	97%
GPA 2.0-2.99:	15%	International:	1%
Rank in top quarter:	47%		

Basis for selection. Academic and personal record, recommendations, test scores important. Class rank considered. Interview required for academically marginal students; audition required for drama, music programs and forensics; portfolio required for art program.

High school preparation. College-preparatory program recommended. 13 units recommended. Recommended units include English 4, mathematics 3, social studies 3 and science 3.

2011-2012 Annual costs. Tuition/fees: $23,590. Room/board: $6,650. Books/supplies: $900.

2011-2012 Financial aid. Need-based: 282 full-time freshmen applied for aid; 243 were judged to have need; 243 of these received aid. Average need met was 91.5%. Average scholarship/grant was $15,281; average loan $3,883. 57% of total undergraduate aid awarded as scholarships/grants, 43% as loans/jobs. **Non-need-based:** Awarded to 460 full-time undergraduates, including 98 freshmen. Scholarships awarded for academics, art, athletics, music/drama, religious affiliation.

Application procedures. Admission: No deadline. No application fee. Admission notification on a rolling basis beginning on or about 9/15. Must reply by May 1 or within 4 week(s) if notified thereafter. **Financial aid:** Priority date 3/1; no closing date. FAFSA required. Applicants notified on a rolling basis starting 3/15; must reply within 2 week(s) of notification.

Academics. Midwest Institute for International Students prepares students to meet English language requirement for admission to Doane and other American colleges. **Special study options:** Combined bachelor's/graduate degree, double major, ESL, honors, independent study, internships, student-designed major, study abroad, teacher certification program. 3-2 programs in engineering with Washington University, Columbia University, 3-2 program in environmental and forestry studies with Duke University. **Credit/placement by examination:** AP, CLEP, IB, SAT, ACT, institutional tests. 36 credit hours maximum toward bachelor's degree. International students who successfully complete Midwest Institute ESL program may be admitted without TOEFL scores. **Support services:** Learning center, reduced course load, remedial instruction, study skills assistance, tutoring, writing center.

Majors. Biology: General, biochemistry. **Business:** Accounting, business admin, human resources. **Communications:** Journalism, organizational. **Computer sciences:** General, computer science, information systems. **Conservation:** Environmental studies. **Education:** Elementary, ESL, physical, special ed. **English:** English lit. **Foreign languages:** French, German, Spanish. **History:** General. **Human services:** General. **Liberal arts:** Arts/sciences. **Math:** General. **Philosophy/religion:** Philosophy, religion. **Physical sciences:** Chemistry, physics. **Psychology:** General. **Social sciences:** General, economics, international relations, political science, sociology. **Visual/performing arts:** Art, dramatic, graphic design, music.

Most popular majors. Biology 9%, business/marketing 13%, education 26%, psychology 6%, social sciences 9%, visual/performing arts 13%.

Computing on campus. 400 workstations in dormitories, library, computer center, student center. Dormitories wired for high-speed internet access and linked to campus network. Commuter students can connect to campus network. Online course registration, online library, helpline, student web hosting, wireless network available.

Student life. Freshman orientation: Available. Preregistration for classes offered. **Policies:** Unmarried students under 22 not living with parents expected to live on campus. **Housing:** Guaranteed on-campus for freshmen. Coed dorms, single-sex dorms available. $200 fully refundable deposit. **Activities:** Bands, campus ministries, choral groups, dance, drama, film society, literary magazine, music ensembles, musical theater, radio station, student government, student newspaper, TV station, student education association, Doane speakers, Club Internationale, Fellowship of Christian Athletes, American Minority Student Alliance, College Republicans, Young Democrats.

Athletics. NAIA. **Intercollegiate:** Baseball M, basketball, bowling, cheerleading M, cross-country, football (tackle) M, golf, soccer, softball W, tennis, track and field, volleyball W. **Intramural:** Basketball, cheerleading W, football (tackle) M, golf, softball, swimming, tennis, volleyball. **Team name:** Tigers.

Student services. Adult student services, chaplain/spiritual director, career counseling, student employment services, financial aid counseling, health services, personal counseling, placement for graduates, veterans' counselor.

Contact. E-mail: admissions@doane.edu
Phone: (402) 826-8222 Toll-free number: (800) 333-6263
Fax: (402) 826-8600
Joal Weyand, Vice President for Admission, Doane College, 1014 Boswell Avenue, Crete, NE 68333

Grace University
Omaha, Nebraska
www.graceuniversity.edu   **CB code: 6248**

- Private 4-year university and Bible college affiliated with interdenominational tradition
- Residential campus in very large city
- 379 degree-seeking undergraduates
- 58% of applicants admitted
- ACT (writing optional), application essay required

General. Founded in 1943. Regionally accredited; also accredited by ABHE. **Degrees:** 89 bachelor's, 4 associate awarded; master's offered. **ROTC:** Air Force. **Calendar:** Semester, limited summer session. **Full-time faculty:** 28 total. **Part-time faculty:** 41 total.

Freshman class profile. 233 applied, 134 admitted, 74 enrolled.

Mid 50% test scores	ACT composite:	19-26

Basis for selection. School achievement record, religious affiliation/commitment, test scores, and student profile important. Conditional admission for students who have not taken SAT/ACT. Audition required for music programs. **Home schooled:** Transcript of courses and grades required. ACT score of 20 or GED required.

High school preparation. College-preparatory program recommended. Teacher education program requires 4 language arts, 2 mathematics, 2 sciences, 2 social sciences.

2011-2012 Annual costs. Tuition/fees: $16,316. Room/board: $6,062. Books/supplies: $400.

Financial aid. Non-need-based: Scholarships awarded for academics, alumni affiliation, leadership, minority status, music/drama.

Application procedures. Admission: Priority date 3/1; no deadline. $35 fee, may be waived for applicants with need. Admission notification on a rolling basis. **Financial aid:** Priority date 3/1, closing date 4/1. FAFSA, institutional form required. Applicants notified on a rolling basis starting 3/1; must reply within 3 week(s) of notification.

Academics. Special study options: Accelerated study, combined bachelor's/graduate degree, cooperative education, distance learning, double major, dual enrollment of high school students, independent study, internships, liberal arts/career combination, student-designed major, study abroad, teacher certification program, urban semester. **Credit/placement by examination:** AP, CLEP, ACT. 15 credit hours maximum toward bachelor's degree. **Support services:** Learning center, reduced course load, study skills assistance, tutoring, writing center.

Majors. Business: Management science. **Communications technology:** General. **Computer sciences:** General. **Education:** Business, elementary, English, ESL, history, mathematics, middle, music, secondary, social science. **Health services:** Nursing (RN). **Liberal arts:** Humanities. **Psychology:** General. **Theology:** Bible, missionary, religious ed, sacred music, theology. **Visual/performing arts:** Music, music performance, music theory/composition, piano/keyboard, voice/opera.

Computing on campus. 43 workstations in dormitories, library, computer center. Dormitories wired for high-speed internet access and linked to campus network. Commuter students can connect to campus network. Online library, helpline, wireless network available.

Student life. Freshman orientation: Mandatory. Preregistration for classes offered. **Policies:** All on campus housing is alcohol/drug/smoke-free. Religious observance required. **Housing:** Guaranteed on-campus for freshmen. Single-sex dorms, apartments, wellness housing available. $200 partly refundable deposit. **Activities:** Concert band, campus ministries, choral groups, drama, music ensembles, student government.

Athletics. NCCAA. **Intercollegiate:** Basketball, soccer M, volleyball W. **Intramural:** Basketball M, volleyball W. **Team name:** Royals.

Student services. Adult student services, chaplain/spiritual director, career counseling, student employment services, financial aid counseling, health services, personal counseling, placement for graduates.

Contact. E-mail: admissions@graceuniversity.edu
Phone: (402) 449-2831 Toll-free number: (800) 383-1422
Fax: (402) 449-2999
Tara Koth, Manager of Undergraduate Admissions, Grace University, 1311 South Ninth Street, Omaha, NE 68108-3629

Hastings College
Hastings, Nebraska
www.hastings.edu
CB code: 6270

- Private 4-year liberal arts college affiliated with Presbyterian Church (USA)
- Residential campus in large town
- 1,204 degree-seeking undergraduates
- 70% of applicants admitted
- SAT or ACT (ACT writing optional) required

General. Founded in 1882. Regionally accredited. Vocation and Values program asks the campus community to explore how faith intersects with vocation. **Degrees:** 217 bachelor's awarded; master's offered. **Location:** 90 miles from Lincoln, 150 miles from Omaha. **Calendar:** 4-1-4, limited summer session. **Full-time faculty:** 86 total. **Part-time faculty:** 42 total. **Special facilities:** Glass blowing studio, observatory, music studios, communications center.

Freshman class profile. 1,481 applied, 1,036 admitted, 321 enrolled.

Mid 50% test scores			
SAT critical reading:	460-570	Rank in top quarter:	40%
SAT math:	460-550	Rank in top tenth:	16%
ACT composite:	20-26	Out-of-state:	31%
GPA 3.75 or higher:	24%	Live on campus:	90%
GPA 3.50-3.74:	14%	Fraternities:	28%
GPA 3.0-3.49:	38%	Sororities:	38%
		GPA 2.0-2.99:	24%

Basis for selection. Academic achievement record most important; counselor recommendations, test scores, class ranking also important. Placement interview strongly recommended for all applicants; interview required for allied health program; audition required for forensics, music, theater programs; portfolio required for art program. **Home schooled:** ACT or SAT scores, satisfactory completion of high school graduation equivalency required. **Learning Disabled:** Interview recommended.

High school preparation. Required and recommended units include English 3-4, mathematics 3-4, social studies 4, history 4, science 3-4 (laboratory 3-4) and foreign language 2.

2011-2012 Annual costs. Tuition/fees: $23,734. Room/board: $6,780. Books/supplies: $830. Personal expenses: $1,800.

Financial aid. Non-need-based: Scholarships awarded for academics, alumni affiliation, art, athletics, leadership, music/drama.

Application procedures. Admission: No deadline. $20 fee, may be waived for applicants with need, free for online applicants. Admission notification on a rolling basis beginning on or about 10/15. **Financial aid:** Closing date 5/1. FAFSA, institutional form required. Applicants notified on a rolling basis starting 2/15; must reply within 2 week(s) of notification.

Academics. College offers 4-year liberal arts program of required courses in arts and humanities, math and science, communications, and other areas. **Special study options:** Combined bachelor's/graduate degree, double major, exchange student, independent study, internships, student-designed major, study abroad, teacher certification program, urban semester. 3-2 engineering programs with Columbia University, Georgia Institute of Technology, and Washington University, Missouri; International exchange program with colleges in England, Holland, Germany and Ireland; BA-BSN program with Creighton University. **Credit/placement by examination:** AP, CLEP, IB. 20 credit hours maximum toward bachelor's degree. All credit by examinations subject to approval of department. **Support services:** Learning center, reduced course load, study skills assistance, tutoring, writing center.

Majors. Biology: General. **Business:** Accounting, business admin, human resources, marketing. **Communications:** Advertising, broadcast journalism, communications/speech/rhetoric, journalism, media studies, public relations, radio/TV. **Communications technology:** General. **Computer sciences:** General, computer science. **Education:** General, art, biology, business, chemistry, drama/dance, early childhood, elementary, English, foreign languages, history, mathematics, music, physical, physics, science, secondary, social science, social studies, special ed, speech. **English:** Creative writing, English lit, rhetoric/composition. **Foreign languages:** General, German, Spanish. **Health services:** Health care admin, predental, premedicine, preveterinary. **History:** General. **Human services:** General. **Liberal arts:** Arts/sciences. **Math:** General. **Parks/recreation:** Exercise sciences, facilities management, health/fitness, sports admin. **Philosophy/religion:** Philosophy, religion. **Physical sciences:** Chemistry, physics. **Protective services:** Corrections. **Psychology:** General. **Social sciences:** Economics, international relations, political science, sociology. **Visual/performing arts:** Art, art history/conservation, dramatic, music, music history, music pedagogy, music performance, piano/keyboard, stringed instruments, voice/opera.

Most popular majors. Biology 6%, business/marketing 16%, communications/journalism 6%, education 15%, psychology 12%, social sciences 9%, visual/performing arts 15%.

Computing on campus. 181 workstations in library, computer center, student center. Dormitories wired for high-speed internet access and linked to campus network. Commuter students can connect to campus network. Online library, repair service, wireless network available.

Student life. Freshman orientation: Mandatory. Preregistration for classes offered. Weekend-long program, prior to the first day of class. Includes community service project. **Policies:** Alcohol not permitted on campus except in apartments for students of legal age; smoking forbidden in campus buildings. **Housing:** Guaranteed on-campus for all undergraduates. Coed dorms, single-sex dorms, apartments, wellness housing available. $200 fully refundable deposit, deadline 8/1. Honors housing, campus houses, apartments available to upperclass students. **Activities:** Bands, choral groups, drama, literary magazine, music ensembles, musical theater, radio station, student government, student newspaper, symphony orchestra, TV station, Fellowship of Christian Athletes, student health advisory council, religious programs committee, Religion in Life Committee, Multicultural Student Union, Peer HIV Education Organization, College Democrats, College Republicans, Habitat for Humanity, gay/straight alliance.

Athletics. NAIA. **Intercollegiate:** Baseball M, basketball, cheerleading M, cross-country, football (tackle) M, golf, soccer, softball W, tennis, track and field, volleyball W, wrestling M. **Intramural:** Basketball, bowling, football (non-tackle), racquetball, softball, table tennis, volleyball. **Team name:** Broncos.

Student services. Adult student services, chaplain/spiritual director, career counseling, student employment services, financial aid counseling, health services, minority student services, personal counseling, placement for graduates. **Physically disabled:** Services for hearing impaired.

Contact. E-mail: mmolliconi@hastings.edu
Phone: (402) 461-7403 Toll-free number: (800) 532-7642
Fax: (402) 461-7490
Traci Boeve, Director of Admissions, Hastings College, 710 North Turner Avenue, Hastings, NE 68901-7621

Herzing University: Omaha School of Massage Therapy and Healthcare
Omaha, Nebraska
www.osmhc.com

- For-profit 4-year health science college
- Very large city
- 179 degree-seeking undergraduates

General. Regionally accredited. **Degrees:** 8 associate awarded. **Calendar:** Semester. **Full-time faculty:** 4 total. **Part-time faculty:** 15 total.

Basis for selection. Secondary school record very important, test scores recommended.

2011-2012 Annual costs. Tuition/fees: $9,720. Tuition is charged at a flat rate for Full-time Students (12 credits per semester or more). Tuition and per-credit-hour charge quoted are for Therapeutic Massage. All other programs: tuition $11,040; per-credit-hour charge $460; additional $300 per credit over 15 credits per semester. Books and supplies included in tuition. Personal expenses: $2,665.

Academics. Credit/placement by examination: AP, CLEP.

Majors. Business: Business admin. **Protective services:** Criminal justice. **Visual/performing arts:** Graphic design.

Contact. E-mail: info@osmhc.com
Angie Armstrong, Director of Admissions, Herzing University: Omaha School of Massage Therapy and Healthcare, 9748 Park Drive, Omaha, NE 68127

ITT Technical Institute: Omaha
Omaha, Nebraska
www.itt-tech.edu
CB code: 2740

- For-profit 4-year technical college
- Commuter campus in large city

- 732 undergraduates
- Interview required

General. Accredited by ACICS. **Degrees:** 23 bachelor's, 141 associate awarded. **Calendar:** Quarter, extensive summer session. **Full-time faculty:** 14 total. **Part-time faculty:** 61 total.

Basis for selection. Satisfactory scores from on-site tests in English and mathematics required.

2011-2012 Annual costs. Estimated costs as of July 2011: per-credit-hour charge, $493, depending upon level and course of study; academic fee, $200. Certain programs of study require purchase of tools, which could cost an additional $100 to $655. All costs are subject to change.

Application procedures. Admission: No deadline. No application fee. Admission notification on a rolling basis. **Financial aid:** No deadline. FAFSA, institutional form required. Applicants notified on a rolling basis.

Academics. Credit/placement by examination: AP, CLEP. **Support services:** Learning center, tutoring.

Majors. Business: Accounting/business management, business admin, construction management. **Communications technology:** Animation/special effects. **Computer sciences:** Networking, security.

Computing on campus. Online library available.

Student life. Freshman orientation: Available. Preregistration for classes offered.

Student services. Career counseling, student employment services, placement for graduates.

Contact. Phone: (402) 331-2900 Toll-free number: (800) 677-9260 Jacqueline Hawthorne, Director of Recruitment, ITT Technical Institute: Omaha, 9814 M Street, Omaha, NE 68127

Midland University
Fremont, Nebraska
www.mlc.edu   CB code: 6406

- Private 4-year liberal arts college affiliated with Evangelical Lutheran Church in America
- Residential campus in large town

General. Founded in 1883. Regionally accredited. **Location:** 35 miles from Omaha, 52 miles from Lincoln. **Calendar:** 4-1-4.

Annual costs/financial aid. Tuition/fees (2011-2012): $24,710. Room/board: $6,105. Books/supplies: $1,050. Personal expenses: $2,345. Need-based financial aid available to full-time and part-time students.

Contact. Phone: (402) 941-6501
Director of Admissions, 900 North Clarkson, Fremont, NE 68025

Nebraska Christian College
Papillion, Nebraska
www.nechristian.edu   CB code: 1332

- Private 4-year Bible college affiliated with Christian Churches and Churches of Christ
- Residential campus in large town
- 131 full-time, degree-seeking undergraduates
- SAT or ACT (ACT writing optional), application essay required

General. Founded in 1944. Accredited by ABHE. **Degrees:** 24 bachelor's, 10 associate awarded. **Location:** 10 miles from Omaha. **Calendar:** Semester, limited summer session. **Full-time faculty:** 11 total; 64% have terminal degrees. **Part-time faculty:** 7 total. **Class size:** 60% < 20, 27% 20-39, 7% 40-49, 7% 50-99.

Freshman class profile.

Out-of-state:	45%	Live on campus:	90%

Basis for selection. Christian commitment and references very important; high school transcript or GED required. Standardized test scores required. Transcript of any previous college work required. ACT recommended.

2011-2012 Annual costs. Tuition/fees: $11,200. Room/board: $5,800. Books/supplies: $600. Personal expenses: $1,900.

Financial aid. Non-need-based: Scholarships awarded for academics, leadership, religious affiliation.

Application procedures. Admission: Closing date 8/1 (postmark date). $25 fee, may be waived for applicants with need. Application must be submitted online. Admission notification on a rolling basis. Must reply by May 1 or within 4 week(s) if notified thereafter. **Financial aid:** Priority date 6/1; no closing date. FAFSA, institutional form required. Applicants notified on a rolling basis starting 5/5.

Academics. Special study options: Combined bachelor's/graduate degree, cooperative education, double major, dual enrollment of high school students, independent study, internships, teacher certification program. **Credit/placement by examination:** AP, CLEP, ACT. **Support services:** Learning center, reduced course load, remedial instruction, study skills assistance, tutoring, writing center.

Majors. Theology: Bible, missionary, religious ed, sacred music, theology.

Computing on campus. 15 workstations in library, computer center. Dormitories wired for high-speed internet access and linked to campus network. Online course registration, wireless network available.

Student life. Freshman orientation: Mandatory. Preregistration for classes offered. **Policies:** Religious observance required. **Housing:** Guaranteed on-campus for freshmen. Single-sex dorms, special housing for disabled, apartments, wellness housing available. **Activities:** Bands, campus ministries, choral groups, drama, literary magazine, music ensembles, student government.

Athletics. NCCAA. **Intercollegiate:** Basketball M, volleyball W. **Intramural:** Basketball, football (non-tackle), soccer, volleyball. **Team name:** Parsons.

Student services. Adult student services, alcohol/substance abuse counseling, chaplain/spiritual director, career counseling, student employment services, financial aid counseling, health services, minority student services, personal counseling, placement for graduates.

Contact. E-mail: admissions@nechristian.edu
Phone: (402) 935-9400 Fax: (402) 935-9500
Brian Taylor, Director of Admissions, Nebraska Christian College, 12550 South 114th Street, Papillion, NE 68046

Nebraska Methodist College of Nursing and Allied Health
Omaha, Nebraska
www.methodistcollege.edu   CB code: 6510

- Private 4-year health science and nursing college affiliated with United Methodist Church
- Commuter campus in large city
- 684 degree-seeking undergraduates
- 34% of applicants admitted
- SAT or ACT (ACT writing optional) required

General. Founded in 1891. Regionally accredited. **Degrees:** 129 bachelor's, 61 associate awarded; master's offered. **ROTC:** Army. **Location:** 120 miles from Des Moines, Iowa, 180 miles from Kansas City, Missouri. **Calendar:** Semester, limited summer session. **Full-time faculty:** 48 total; 44% have terminal degrees. **Part-time faculty:** 13 total; 31% have terminal degrees. **Class size:** 53% < 20, 40% 20-39, 4% 40-49, 2% 50-99. **Special facilities:** Human cadaver lab, human simulation labs, center for health partnerships.

Freshman class profile. 152 applied, 52 admitted, 34 enrolled.

Mid 50% test scores		Rank in top quarter:	50%
ACT composite:	20-23	Rank in top tenth:	20%
GPA 3.75 or higher:	55%	Out-of-state:	16%
GPA 3.50-3.74:	40%	Live on campus:	55%
GPA 2.0-2.99:	5%		

Basis for selection. School achievement, test scores most important. Written personal statement important. Recommendations, school and community activities considered. Deadlines vary by program. ACT or SAT is required of all current high school graduates and of students making application within two years of high school graduation. **Home schooled:** Educational transcript required. ACT or SAT required for all applicants within two years of home school completion. Students with home school completion of more than two

years and no results of ACT or SAT are required to show success in a minimum of 12 college credit hours.

High school preparation. College-preparatory program recommended. 10 units required. Required units include English 4, mathematics 2, social studies 2, history 1, science 4 (laboratory 2). Chemistry, biology, algebra, anatomy and physiology recommended. A background in physics is strongly recommended for applicants for radiologic technology, sonography, and physical therapist assistant.

2011-2012 Annual costs. Tuition/fees: $15,000. NMC has apartment style housing (with kitchens). No meal plans are available. Room only: $6,050. Books/supplies: $1,366. Personal expenses: $1,476.

2010-2011 Financial aid. Need-based: 39 full-time freshmen applied for aid; 32 were judged to have need; 32 of these received aid. Average need met was 62%. Average scholarship/grant was $7,684; average loan $4,712. 34% of total undergraduate aid awarded as scholarships/grants, 66% as loans/jobs. **Non-need-based:** Awarded to 61 full-time undergraduates, including 8 freshmen. Scholarships awarded for academics, leadership, religious affiliation, ROTC.

Application procedures. Admission: No deadline. $25 fee, may be waived for applicants with need. Application must be submitted online. Admission notification on a rolling basis. Required within two weeks of acceptance. Application deadlines vary by program. **Financial aid:** Priority date 4/1; no closing date. FAFSA, institutional form required. Applicants notified on a rolling basis starting 3/1; must reply within 3 week(s) of notification.

Academics. Peer tutoring available for most courses; supplemental instruction available for science and professional courses. **Special study options:** Accelerated study, combined bachelor's/graduate degree, distance learning, independent study, internships. **Credit/placement by examination:** AP, CLEP, institutional tests. 9 credit hours maximum toward associate degree, 9 toward bachelor's. Credit by examination considered on an individual basis. **Support services:** Learning center, reduced course load, remedial instruction, study skills assistance, tutoring, writing center.

Majors. Health services: Cardiovascular technology, nursing (RN), physical therapy assistant, public health ed, radiologic technology/medical imaging, respiratory therapy technology, sonography, surgical technology.

Computing on campus. 55 workstations in library, computer center, student center. Dormitories linked to campus network. Online course registration, online library, helpline available.

Student life. Freshman orientation: Mandatory. Preregistration for classes offered. 2-days held in August, one-day transfer orientation for allied health students held in May. **Housing:** Guaranteed on-campus for all undergraduates. Coed dorms, apartments, wellness housing available. $150 nonrefundable deposit, deadline 5/1. **Activities:** Campus ministries, student government, student nurse association (state and national), allied health student association, College Ambassadors, minority student organization, Pathfinders, residence hall council.

Student services. Adult student services, alcohol/substance abuse counseling, chaplain/spiritual director, career counseling, student employment services, financial aid counseling, health services, minority student services, personal counseling, placement for graduates, veterans' counselor.

Contact. E-mail: admissions@methodistcollege.edu
Phone: (402) 354-7200 Toll-free number: (800) 335-5510
Fax: (402) 354-7020
Sara Hanson, Director of Enrollment Services, Nebraska Methodist College of Nursing and Allied Health, 720 North 87th Street, Omaha, NE 68114

Nebraska Wesleyan University
Lincoln, Nebraska
www.nebrwesleyan.edu   CB code: 6470

- Private 4-year liberal arts college affiliated with United Methodist Church
- Residential campus in small city
- 1,750 degree-seeking undergraduates: 11% part-time, 60% women, 2% African American, 2% Asian American, 3% Hispanic American, 1% Native American
- 287 degree-seeking graduate students
- 82% of applicants admitted
- SAT or ACT (ACT writing optional) required
- 65% graduate within 6 years

General. Founded in 1887. Regionally accredited. Non-traditional programs on accelerated semesters. **Degrees:** 431 bachelor's awarded; master's offered. **ROTC:** Army, Air Force. **Location:** 55 miles from Omaha, 200 miles from Kansas City, Missouri. **Calendar:** Semester, limited summer session. **Full-time faculty:** 115 total; 90% have terminal degrees, 2% minority, 51% women. **Part-time faculty:** 58 total; 33% have terminal degrees, 9% minority, 60% women. **Class size:** 63% < 20, 34% 20-39, less than 1% 40-49, 2% 50-99, less than 1% >100. **Special facilities:** Planetarium, laboratory theater, greenhouse, herbarium, nuclear magnetic resonance laboratory, sleep laboratory, art gallery.

Freshman class profile. 1,459 applied, 1,196 admitted, 360 enrolled.

Mid 50% test scores		Rank in top tenth:	26%
ACT composite:	23-28	End year in good standing:	95%
GPA 3.75 or higher:	52%	Return as sophomores:	82%
GPA 3.50-3.74:	21%	Out-of-state:	12%
GPA 3.0-3.49:	18%	Live on campus:	90%
GPA 2.0-2.99:	9%	Fraternities:	28%
Rank in top quarter:	59%	Sororities:	26%

Basis for selection. Students who rank in the top half of their graduating class or achieve an ACT composite score of 20 or an SAT combined score of 950 (exclusive of Writing) are invited to apply for admission. Campus visit recommended for all students; audition required for drama, music scholarships; portfolio required for art scholarships. **Home schooled:** Transcript of courses and grades required. GED scores.

High school preparation. College-preparatory program recommended. Recommended units include English 4, mathematics 3, social studies 3, science 3 and foreign language 2.

2011-2012 Annual costs. Tuition/fees: $24,656. Room/board: $6,672. Books/supplies: $1,400. Personal expenses: $3,000.

2011-2012 Financial aid. Need-based: 357 full-time freshmen applied for aid; 271 were judged to have need; 271 of these received aid. Average need met was 73%. Average scholarship/grant was $13,453; average loan $4,023. 68% of total undergraduate aid awarded as scholarships/grants, 32% as loans/jobs. **Non-need-based:** Awarded to 471 full-time undergraduates, including 125 freshmen. Scholarships awarded for academics, alumni affiliation, art, minority status, music/drama.

Application procedures. Admission: Closing date 8/15 (postmark date). $20 fee, may be waived for applicants with need, free for online applicants. Admission notification on a rolling basis beginning on or about 1/15. Must reply by May 1 or within 4 week(s) if notified thereafter. **Financial aid:** No deadline. FAFSA required. Applicants notified on a rolling basis starting 2/1; must reply within 3 week(s) of notification.

Academics. Special study options: Combined bachelor's/graduate degree, double major, dual enrollment of high school students, exchange student, independent study, internships, liberal arts/career combination, semester at sea, study abroad, teacher certification program, United Nations semester, urban semester, Washington semester. 3-2 engineering with Washington University or Columbia University; Capitol Hill Internship Program; Chicago Center for Urban Life and Culture; summer research fellowships in the natural sciences; faculty led international study tours. **Credit/placement by examination:** AP, CLEP, IB, institutional tests. Unlimited number of hours of credit by examination may be counted toward degree. **Support services:** Reduced course load, study skills assistance, tutoring, writing center.

Majors. Biology: General, biochemistry, Biochemistry/molecular biology. **Business:** Accounting, business admin, international. **Communications:** Communications/speech/rhetoric, political. **Computer sciences:** Computer science, information technology. **Education:** Elementary, English, middle, music, physical, science, social science, special ed. **English:** English lit. **Foreign languages:** French, German, Spanish. **Health services:** Athletic training, nursing (RN). **History:** General. **Human services:** Social work. **Math:** General. **Parks/recreation:** Exercise sciences, health/fitness, sports admin. **Philosophy/religion:** Philosophy, religion. **Physical sciences:** Chemistry, physics. **Psychology:** General, industrial. **Social sciences:** Economics, political science, sociology. **Visual/performing arts:** Art, dramatic, music, music performance, studio arts.

Most popular majors. Biology 10%, business/marketing 18%, communications/journalism 8%, education 6%, health sciences 12%, parks/recreation 9%, psychology 8%, visual/performing arts 7%.

Computing on campus. 360 workstations in dormitories, library, computer center, student center. Dormitories wired for high-speed internet access and linked to campus network. Commuter students can connect to campus network. Online course registration, online library, helpline, repair service, student web hosting, wireless network available.

Student life. Freshman orientation: Mandatory. Preregistration for classes offered. One-day registration sessions in June; 4-day orientation program before fall classes begin. **Housing:** Guaranteed on-campus for all undergraduates. Coed dorms, single-sex dorms, special housing for disabled, apartments, fraternity/sorority housing available. $100 nonrefundable deposit, deadline 7/1. Residence hall suites and townhomes. **Activities:** Bands, campus ministries, choral groups, drama, international student organizations, literary magazine, music ensembles, musical theater, opera, student government, student newspaper, Student Fellowship, Fellowship of Christian Athletes, Meeting of Students Addressing Intercultural Concerns, College Republicans, Young Democrats, Nebraskans for Peace, International Relations Organization, Circle K, Environmental Action, Global Service Learning.

Athletics. NAIA, NCAA. **Intercollegiate:** Baseball M, basketball, cross-country, football (tackle) M, golf, soccer, softball W, tennis, track and field, volleyball W. **Intramural:** Basketball, bowling, football (non-tackle), racquetball, soccer, softball, tennis, volleyball, water polo. **Team name:** Prairie Wolves.

Student services. Adult student services, chaplain/spiritual director, career counseling, student employment services, financial aid counseling, health services, minority student services, personal counseling, placement for graduates, women's services. **Physically disabled:** Services for visually, speech, hearing impaired.

Contact. E-mail: admissions@nebrwesleyan.edu
Phone: (402) 465-2218 Toll-free number: (800) 541-3818
Fax: (402) 465-2177
David Duzik, Director of Admissions, Nebraska Wesleyan University, 5000 St. Paul Avenue, Lincoln, NE 68504

Peru State College
Peru, Nebraska
www.peru.edu
CB code: 6468

- Public 4-year liberal arts and teachers college
- Commuter campus in rural community
- 1,474 degree-seeking undergraduates: 22% part-time, 57% women, 5% African American, 1% Asian American, 4% Hispanic American, 1% Native American
- 283 degree-seeking graduate students
- 49% of applicants admitted
- SAT or ACT required

General. Founded in 1867. Regionally accredited. Elementary school teacher certification courses offered at Offutt Air Force Base. Online graduate degrees in education and organizational management offered. **Degrees:** 391 bachelor's awarded; master's offered. **Location:** 64 miles from Omaha, 67 miles from Lincoln. **Calendar:** Semester, limited summer session. **Full-time faculty:** 47 total; 74% have terminal degrees, 8% minority, 45% women. **Part-time faculty:** 62 total; 52% women.

Freshman class profile. 869 applied, 422 admitted, 187 enrolled.

GPA 3.75 or higher:	12%	GPA 2.0-2.99:	41%
GPA 3.50-3.74:	12%	Rank in top quarter:	13%
GPA 3.0-3.49:	27%	Live on campus:	96%

Basis for selection. Test scores very important. **Home schooled:** Transcript of courses and grades required.

High school preparation. College-preparatory program recommended. 16 units recommended. Recommended units include English 4, mathematics 2, social studies 3, science 2 and foreign language 1.

2011-2012 Annual costs. Tuition/fees: $5,371; $5,371 out-of-state. Room/board: $5,820.

Financial aid. All financial aid based on need.

Application procedures. Admission: Priority date 12/1; no deadline. No application fee. Admission notification on a rolling basis beginning on or about 9/1. **Financial aid:** Priority date 3/1; no closing date. FAFSA, institutional form required. Applicants notified on a rolling basis starting 3/1; must reply within 2 week(s) of notification.

Academics. Special study options: Cooperative education, cross-registration, distance learning, double major, dual enrollment of high school students, honors, independent study, internships, liberal arts/career combination, study abroad, teacher certification program. **Credit/placement by examination:** AP, CLEP, IB. 30 credit hours maximum toward bachelor's degree. **Support services:** Learning center, reduced course load, remedial instruction, study skills assistance, tutoring.

Majors. Biology: General, biochemistry. **Business:** Accounting, management information systems, management science, marketing. **Engineering:** Pre-engineering. **English:** English lit. **Health services:** Predental, premedicine, prenursing, preoptometry, prepharmacy, prephysical therapy, preveterinary. **Liberal arts:** Arts/sciences. **Math:** General. **Physical sciences:** Chemistry. **Psychology:** General. **Social sciences:** General. **Visual/performing arts:** Graphic design, music performance, studio arts.

Most popular majors. Business/marketing 40%, education 38%, psychology 6%, security/protective services 8%.

Computing on campus. 140 workstations in dormitories, library, computer center, student center. Dormitories wired for high-speed internet access and linked to campus network. Commuter students can connect to campus network. Online course registration, helpline, wireless network available.

Student life. Freshman orientation: Mandatory. Preregistration for classes offered. One-day sessions held in April, May, June, July, August. **Policies:** Drug/alcohol free and zero tolerance policy, smoke-free residential living. **Housing:** Guaranteed on-campus for freshmen. Coed dorms, single-sex dorms, special housing for disabled, apartments, wellness housing available. $100 fully refundable deposit. **Activities:** Bands, campus ministries, choral groups, dance, drama, film society, international student organizations, music ensembles, musical theater, student government, student newspaper, TV station, pilot club, Fellowship of Christian Athletes, multicultural club, Phi Beta Lambda, student senate, black student union, Riverside Ministries, CRU, student athlete advisory council.

Athletics. NAIA. **Intercollegiate:** Baseball M, basketball, cheerleading M, cross-country W, football (tackle) M, golf W, softball W, volleyball W. **Intramural:** Basketball, football (non-tackle), softball, volleyball. **Team name:** Bobcats.

Student services. Adult student services, alcohol/substance abuse counseling, chaplain/spiritual director, career counseling, services for economically disadvantaged, student employment services, financial aid counseling, health services, on-campus daycare, personal counseling, placement for graduates, veterans' counselor. **Physically disabled:** Services for visually, speech, hearing impaired.

Contact. E-mail: admissions@peru.edu
Phone: (402) 872-2221 Toll-free number: (800) 742-4412
Fax: (402) 872-2296
Micki Willis, Vice President for Enrollment Management and Student Affairs, Peru State College, P.O. Box 10, Peru, NE 68421-0010

Union College
Lincoln, Nebraska
www.ucollege.edu
CB code: 6865

- Private 4-year liberal arts college affiliated with Seventh-day Adventists
- Residential campus in large city
- 722 degree-seeking undergraduates: 8% part-time, 59% women, 6% African American, 3% Asian American, 13% Hispanic American, 6% international
- 76 degree-seeking graduate students
- 53% of applicants admitted
- SAT or ACT (ACT writing optional) required
- 55% graduate within 6 years

General. Founded in 1889. Regionally accredited. **Degrees:** 164 bachelor's, 16 associate awarded; master's offered. **Location:** 50 miles from Omaha. **Calendar:** Semester, limited summer session. **Full-time faculty:** 58 total; 43% have terminal degrees, 7% minority, 45% women. **Part-time faculty:** 59 total; 12% have terminal degrees, 7% minority, 66% women. **Class size:** 67% < 20, 27% 20-39, 3% 40-49, 3% 50-99. **Special facilities:** Arboretum.

Freshman class profile. 1,002 applied, 534 admitted, 160 enrolled.

Mid 50% test scores			
		GPA 3.0-3.49:	32%
SAT critical reading:	460-550	GPA 2.0-2.99:	28%
SAT math:	430-580	Rank in top quarter:	30%
SAT writing:	440-590	Rank in top tenth:	8%
ACT composite:	19-25	Return as sophomores:	70%
GPA 3.75 or higher:	23%	Out-of-state:	85%
GPA 3.50-3.74:	14%	Live on campus:	93%

Basis for selection. Test scores, GPA very important. Interview recommended for all students; audition recommended for music program; portfolio recommended for art program.

High school preparation. College-preparatory program recommended. Recommended units include English 4, mathematics 2, social studies 2,

science 2 (laboratory 2) and computer science 1. 2 algebra, 1 geometry, trigonometry recommended for mathematics and science-related programs. Physics and chemistry recommended for nursing, biology, chemistry, physics, engineering, medical technology, premedicine, and predental programs.

2011-2012 Annual costs. Tuition/fees: $18,780. Room/board: $6,020. Books/supplies: $1,000. Personal expenses: $1,200.

Financial aid. Non-need-based: Scholarships awarded for academics. **Additional information:** Special institutional grants offered to all freshmen and sophomores demonstrating exceptional financial need.

Application procedures. Admission: Priority date 3/1; deadline 8/1. No application fee. Admission notification on a rolling basis beginning on or about 10/1. Must reply by May 1 or within 2 week(s) if notified thereafter. **Financial aid:** Closing date 4/1. FAFSA required. Applicants notified on a rolling basis starting 4/15; must reply by 5/1 or within 3 week(s) of notification.

Academics. Special study options: Double major, dual enrollment of high school students, ESL, honors, independent study, internships, student-designed major, study abroad, teacher certification program. **Credit/placement by examination:** AP, CLEP, IB, SAT, ACT, institutional tests. **Support services:** Learning center, reduced course load, remedial instruction, study skills assistance, tutoring, writing center.

Majors. Biology: General, biochemistry. **Business:** Accounting, business admin, finance, international, international finance, organizational behavior. **Communications:** Communications/speech/rhetoric, journalism, public relations. **Computer sciences:** General, computer science, programming. **Education:** General, art, biology, business, chemistry, computer, elementary, English, ESL, history, mathematics, music, physical, physics, science, secondary, social science, technology/industrial arts. **English:** Creative writing, English lit. **Foreign languages:** General, German. **Health services:** General, clinical lab science, nursing (RN). **History:** General. **Human services:** Social work. **Math:** General. **Parks/recreation:** Exercise sciences, health/fitness, sports admin. **Philosophy/religion:** Religion. **Physical sciences:** Chemistry, physics. **Psychology:** General. **Social sciences:** General. **Theology:** Pastoral counseling, religious ed, theology. **Visual/performing arts:** General, commercial/advertising art, graphic design, music, music pedagogy, music performance, studio arts.

Most popular majors. Business/marketing 11%, education 13%, health sciences 37%, psychology 6%, theological studies 7%.

Computing on campus. 85 workstations in dormitories, library, computer center, student center. Dormitories wired for high-speed internet access and linked to campus network. Commuter students can connect to campus network. Online course registration, online library, helpline, student web hosting, wireless network available.

Student life. Freshman orientation: Mandatory. Preregistration for classes offered. **Policies:** Religious observance required. **Housing:** Guaranteed on-campus for all undergraduates. Single-sex dorms, apartments available. $105 fully refundable deposit. **Activities:** Bands, campus ministries, choral groups, drama, international student organizations, literary magazine, music ensembles, student government, student newspaper, symphony orchestra, Collegiate Adventists for Better Living, Union for Christ, Union for Kids.

Athletics. Intercollegiate: Basketball, soccer. **Intramural:** Badminton, basketball, bowling, football (non-tackle), golf, gymnastics, racquetball, soccer, softball, tennis, volleyball. **Team name:** Warriors.

Student services. Chaplain/spiritual director, career counseling, student employment services, financial aid counseling, health services, minority student services, personal counseling, placement for graduates. **Physically disabled:** Services for visually, speech, hearing impaired.

Contact. E-mail: ucenroll@ucollege.edu
Phone: (402) 486-2504 Toll-free number: (800) 228-4600
Fax: (402) 486-2895
Jennifer Enos, Admissions Assistant Director, Union College, 3800 South 48th Street, Lincoln, NE 68506-4300

University of Nebraska - Kearney
Kearney, Nebraska
www.unk.edu   **CB code: 6467**

- Public 4-year university
- Residential campus in large town
- 5,220 degree-seeking undergraduates: 9% part-time, 55% women, 1% African American, 1% Asian American, 7% Hispanic American, 6% international

- 1,152 degree-seeking graduate students
- 86% of applicants admitted
- SAT or ACT (ACT writing optional) required
- 52% graduate within 6 years

General. Founded in 1903. Regionally accredited. **Degrees:** 865 bachelor's awarded; master's offered. **ROTC:** Army. **Location:** 180 miles from Omaha. **Calendar:** Semester, extensive summer session. **Full-time faculty:** 310 total; 76% have terminal degrees, 8% minority, 48% women. **Part-time faculty:** 112 total; 16% have terminal degrees, 4% minority, 51% women. **Class size:** 41% < 20, 47% 20-39, 6% 40-49, 5% 50-99, less than 1% >100. **Special facilities:** Nebraska state art collection, state arboretum, planetarium.

Freshman class profile. 2,615 applied, 2,258 admitted, 1,074 enrolled.

Mid 50% test scores			
SAT critical reading:	440-570	Rank in top quarter:	45%
SAT math:	450-570	Rank in top tenth:	16%
ACT composite:	20-25	Out-of-state:	8%
GPA 3.75 or higher:	32%	Live on campus:	88%
GPA 3.50-3.74:	20%	International:	7%
GPA 3.0-3.49:	27%	Fraternities:	18%
GPA 2.0-2.99:	20%	Sororities:	18%

Basis for selection. Test scores, school achievement record most important. Applicants who show promise of academic success, but do not meet admission requirements, may be admitted on conditional basis.

High school preparation. 16 units required. Required units include English 4, mathematics 3, social studies 3, science 3 (laboratory 1), foreign language 2 and academic electives 1.

2011-2012 Annual costs. Tuition/fees: $6,199; $11,501 out-of-state. Room/board: $7,558. Books/supplies: $988. Personal expenses: $2,650.

2011-2012 Financial aid. Need-based: 853 full-time freshmen applied for aid; 692 were judged to have need; 692 of these received aid. Average need met was 77%. Average scholarship/grant was $6,239; average loan $3,353. 52% of total undergraduate aid awarded as scholarships/grants, 48% as loans/jobs. **Non-need-based:** Awarded to 1,186 full-time undergraduates, including 499 freshmen. Scholarships awarded for academics, alumni affiliation, art, athletics, leadership, minority status, music/drama, ROTC, state residency.

Application procedures. Admission: Priority date 8/1; no deadline. $45 fee, may be waived for applicants with need. Admission notification on a rolling basis beginning on or about 10/1. **Financial aid:** Priority date 4/1; no closing date. FAFSA, institutional form required. Applicants notified on a rolling basis starting 3/15; must reply within 2 week(s) of notification.

Academics. Special study options: Cooperative education, distance learning, double major, dual enrollment of high school students, ESL, exchange student, honors, independent study, internships, study abroad, teacher certification program. International student exchange program with Sapporo University and Kansai Gaidai, Japan; Nebraska semester abroad. **Credit/placement by examination:** AP, CLEP, SAT, ACT, institutional tests. 45 credit hours maximum toward bachelor's degree. **Support services:** Learning center, study skills assistance, tutoring, writing center.

Majors. Biology: General. **Business:** Business admin, office management, office/clerical, operations, tourism/travel. **Communications:** Advertising, broadcast journalism, communications/speech/rhetoric, journalism. **Computer sciences:** General, information systems. **Education:** General, art, biology, business, chemistry, early childhood, elementary, English, ESL, family/consumer sciences, foreign languages, French, German, health, history, learning disabled, mathematics, mentally handicapped, middle, multiple handicapped, music, physical, physically handicapped, physics, science, secondary, social science, Spanish, special ed, speech, speech impaired, technology/industrial arts, trade/industrial. **English:** English lit, rhetoric/composition. **Foreign languages:** French, German, Spanish, translation. **General:** Business. **Health services:** Medical radiologic technology/radiation therapy, respiratory therapy technology, speech pathology. **History:** General. **Human services:** Social work. **Liberal arts:** Arts/sciences. **Math:** General. **Parks/recreation:** Facilities management, sports admin. **Philosophy/religion:** Philosophy. **Physical sciences:** Chemistry, physics. **Protective services:** Criminal justice, police science. **Psychology:** General. **Social sciences:** General, economics, geography, international relations, political science, sociology. **Visual/performing arts:** General, art, art history/conservation, commercial/advertising art, dramatic, music, music performance, studio arts. **Work/family studies:** General, business, clothing/textiles, family studies, housing.

Most popular majors. Business/marketing 24%, education 20%, parks/recreation 6%.

Computing on campus. 411 workstations in dormitories, library, computer center, student center. Dormitories wired for high-speed internet access and linked to campus network. Commuter students can connect to campus

network. Online course registration, helpline, repair service, wireless network available.

Student life. Freshman orientation: Available. Preregistration for classes offered. **Housing:** Guaranteed on-campus for freshmen. Coed dorms, single-sex dorms, apartments, fraternity/sorority housing available. $50 nonrefundable deposit. **Activities:** Bands, campus ministries, choral groups, dance, drama, international student organizations, music ensembles, Model UN, musical theater, radio station, student government, student newspaper, symphony orchestra, TV station, Young Republicans, Young Democrats, Alpha Phi Omega, Fellowship of Christian Athletes, People of Color.

Athletics. NCAA. **Intercollegiate:** Baseball M, basketball, cross-country, diving W, football (tackle) M, golf, softball W, swimming W, tennis, track and field, volleyball W, wrestling M. **Intramural:** Archery, badminton, basketball, bowling, cross-country, diving, football (non-tackle), golf, racquetball, soccer, softball, swimming, table tennis, tennis, track and field, volleyball, water polo, wrestling M. **Team name:** Lopers.

Student services. Alcohol/substance abuse counseling, career counseling, student employment services, financial aid counseling, health services, minority student services, on-campus daycare, personal counseling, placement for graduates, veterans' counselor, women's services. **Physically disabled:** Services for visually, hearing impaired.

Contact. E-mail: admissionsug@unk.edu
Phone: (308) 865-8526 Toll-free number: (800) 532-7639
Fax: (308) 865-8987
Dusty Newton, Director of Admissions, University of Nebraska - Kearney, 905 West 25th, Kearney, NE 68849

University of Nebraska - Lincoln
Lincoln, Nebraska   **CB member**
www.unl.edu   **CB code: 6877**

- Public 4-year university
- Residential campus in large city
- 19,345 degree-seeking undergraduates: 7% part-time, 46% women, 2% African American, 2% Asian American, 4% Hispanic American, 4% international
- 4,460 degree-seeking graduate students
- 59% of applicants admitted
- SAT or ACT (ACT writing optional) required
- 67% graduate within 6 years

General. Founded in 1869. Regionally accredited. Nebraska's only land-grant university. Research opportunities impacting state's economic development available to students. **Degrees:** 3,621 bachelor's, 6 associate awarded; master's, professional, doctoral offered. **ROTC:** Army, Naval, Air Force. **Location:** 50 miles from Omaha. **Calendar:** Semester, extensive summer session. **Full-time faculty:** 1,045 total; 97% have terminal degrees, 20% minority, 30% women. **Part-time faculty:** 15 total; 100% have terminal degrees, 7% minority, 27% women. **Class size:** 38% < 20, 42% 20-39, 6% 40-49, 8% 50-99, 7% >100. **Special facilities:** Art museum, state museum, planetarium, observatory, center for performing arts, arboretum, center for Great Plains studies, center for biomaterials and genetic research, international quilt study center and museum, diocles laser/extreme light lab, midwest roadside safety facility.

Freshman class profile. 10,022 applied, 5,943 admitted, 4,094 enrolled.

Mid 50% test scores			
SAT critical reading:	510-660	Return as sophomores:	84%
SAT math:	520-670	Out-of-state:	18%
ACT composite:	22-28	International:	2%
Rank in top quarter:	53%	Fraternities:	22%
Rank in top tenth:	26%	Sororities:	29%

Basis for selection. Students must meet minimum requirements of 20 ACT composite score, SAT combined score of 950 (exclusive of Writing) or rank in top half of class. Audition required for music, dance, and theater programs. **Home schooled:** Statement describing home school structure and mission, transcript of courses and grades required. Primary teacher/administrator must provide a copy of letter confirming registration with Nebraska State Department of Education, a curriculum synopsis of the courses which parallel the University of Nebraska-Lincoln's 16 core course requirement, textbook information listed by course (including titles and authors). For courses in foreign language; must include description of how they learned the verbal component of the language. Administrator should also provide a detailed description of how the applicant fulfilled the natural science laboratory requirement.

High school preparation. College-preparatory program required. 16 units required. Required and recommended units include English 4, mathematics 4, social studies 3, history 1, science 3 (laboratory 1) and foreign language 2. Mathematics must include algebra I and II, geometry, and 1 higher level math. 2 units of foreign language must be in same language. At least 1 social studies should be U.S. and/or world history and 1 additional unit should be history, American government, and/or geography. College of Engineering and Technology requires 1 pre-calculus/trigonometry, 1 physics and 1 chemistry. Architecture requires 0.5 trigonometry or pre-calculus for pre-architecture.

2011-2012 Annual costs. Tuition/fees: $7,563; $19,848 out-of-state. Room/board: $8,647. Books/supplies: $1,020. Personal expenses: $3,422.

2010-2011 Financial aid. Need-based: 3,006 full-time freshmen applied for aid; 2,196 were judged to have need; 2,056 of these received aid. Average need met was 86%. Average scholarship/grant was $8,111; average loan $3,259. 53% of total undergraduate aid awarded as scholarships/grants, 47% as loans/jobs. **Non-need-based:** Awarded to 4,638 full-time undergraduates, including 1,356 freshmen. Scholarships awarded for academics, alumni affiliation, art, athletics, leadership, minority status, music/drama, state residency.

Application procedures. Admission: Priority date 1/15; deadline 5/1 (postmark date). $45 fee, may be waived for applicants with need. Admission notification on a rolling basis beginning on or about 9/1. Must reply by 5/1. **Financial aid:** Priority date 4/15; no closing date. FAFSA required. Applicants notified on a rolling basis starting 4/1.

Academics. Special study options: Accelerated study, combined bachelor's/graduate degree, cooperative education, cross-registration, distance learning, double major, dual enrollment of high school students, ESL, exchange student, honors, independent study, internships, liberal arts/career combination, New York semester, semester at sea, student-designed major, study abroad, teacher certification program, United Nations semester, urban semester, Washington semester. **Credit/placement by examination:** AP, CLEP, IB, SAT, ACT, institutional tests. Individual colleges have different policies. **Support services:** Learning center, pre-admission summer program, reduced course load, remedial instruction, study skills assistance, tutoring, writing center.

Honors college/program. Formal application required. Acceptance based on evaluation of the student's potential by the faculty committee.

Majors. Architecture: Architecture, interior, landscape. **Area/ethnic studies:** Latin American, Western European, women's. **Biology:** General, biochemistry, botany, entomology. **Business:** Accounting, actuarial science, banking/financial services, business admin, finance, hospitality admin, insurance, international, investments/securities, management science, managerial economics, marketing. **Communications:** Advertising, broadcast journalism, communications/speech/rhetoric. **Computer sciences:** General. **Conservation:** General, environmental studies, management/policy. **Education:** Agricultural, art, biology, business, chemistry, computer, Deaf/hearing impaired, elementary, English, foreign languages, French, German, health, mathematics, multi-level teacher, music, physical, physics, science, social science, Spanish, trade/industrial. **Engineering:** General, agricultural, architectural, biological, chemical, civil, computer, construction, electrical, industrial, mechanical. **English:** English lit. **Foreign languages:** Ancient Greek, classics, French, German, Latin, Russian, Spanish. **General:** Agronomy, animal sciences, business, communications, economics, food science, horticultural science, landscaping, mechanization, products processing, range science, soil science, turf management. **Health services:** Predental, premedicine, prepharmacy, preveterinary, speech pathology, veterinary technology/assistant. **History:** General. **Liberal arts:** Arts/sciences. **Math:** General. **Parks/recreation:** Health/fitness. **Philosophy/religion:** Philosophy. **Physical sciences:** Atmospheric science, chemistry, geology, physics. **Protective services:** Forensics. **Psychology:** General. **Social sciences:** Anthropology, economics, geography, international relations, political science, sociology. **Visual/performing arts:** Art history/conservation, dance, dramatic, film/cinema/video, music, studio arts. **Work/family studies:** Clothing/textiles, family studies, food/nutrition, merchandising.

Most popular majors. Agriculture 7%, business/marketing 21%, communications/journalism 7%, education 8%, engineering/engineering technologies 11%, family/consumer sciences 9%, social sciences 6%.

Computing on campus. 600 workstations in dormitories, library, computer center, student center. Dormitories wired for high-speed internet access and linked to campus network. Commuter students can connect to campus network. Online course registration, online library, helpline, repair service, student web hosting, wireless network available.

Student life. Freshman orientation: Mandatory. Preregistration for classes offered. Day-long program conducted from mid-June to mid-July. **Policies:** No smoking allowed in University buildings. No alcohol or firearms on campus. Freshmen required to live on campus if not living with parents or close relatives. **Housing:** Guaranteed on-campus for freshmen. Coed dorms, single-sex dorms, special housing for disabled, apartments, cooperative housing, fraternity/sorority housing available. $400 partly refundable deposit,

deadline 5/1. Special interest floors available. **Activities:** Bands, campus ministries, choral groups, dance, drama, film society, international student organizations, literary magazine, music ensembles, musical theater, opera, radio station, student government, student newspaper, symphony orchestra, TV station, University of Nebraska Inter-Tribal Exchange, Mexican-American Student Association, College Republicans, Young Democrats, Nebraskans for Peace, Campus Red Cross, Circle K, Ecology Now, Amnesty International.

Athletics. NCAA. **Intercollegiate:** Baseball M, basketball, bowling W, cross-country, diving W, football (tackle) M, golf, gymnastics, rifle W, soccer W, softball W, swimming W, tennis, track and field, volleyball W, wrestling M. **Intramural:** Basketball, cross-country, football (non-tackle), golf, rifle, soccer, softball, track and field, volleyball, weight lifting. **Team name:** Huskers.

Student services. Adult student services, alcohol/substance abuse counseling, chaplain/spiritual director, career counseling, services for economically disadvantaged, student employment services, financial aid counseling, health services, legal services, minority student services, on-campus daycare, personal counseling, placement for graduates, veterans' counselor, women's services. **Physically disabled:** Services for visually, speech, hearing impaired.

Contact. E-mail: admissions@unl.edu
Phone: (402) 472-2023 Toll-free number: (800) 742-8800
Fax: (402) 472-0670
Alan Cerveny, Dean of Admissions, University of Nebraska - Lincoln, 1410 Q Street, Lincoln, NE 68588-0417

University of Nebraska - Omaha

Omaha, Nebraska   **CB member**
www.unomaha.edu   **CB code: 6420**

- Public 4-year university
- Commuter campus in large city
- 11,717 degree-seeking undergraduates: 21% part-time, 52% women, 6% African American, 2% Asian American, 6% Hispanic American, 1% Native American, 3% international
- 2,580 degree-seeking graduate students
- 76% of applicants admitted
- SAT or ACT (ACT writing optional) required
- 43% graduate within 6 years

General. Founded in 1908. Regionally accredited. Cooperative classes at Offutt Strategic Air Command. Cooperative programs with UNMC medical center. **Degrees:** 1,997 bachelor's awarded; master's, doctoral offered. **ROTC:** Army, Air Force. **Location:** 160 miles from Kansas City, Missouri. **Calendar:** Semester, limited summer session. **Full-time faculty:** 478 total; 85% have terminal degrees, 19% minority, 43% women. **Part-time faculty:** 461 total; 23% have terminal degrees, 11% minority, 49% women. **Class size:** 31% < 20, 47% 20-39, 10% 40-49, 10% 50-99, 2% >100. **Special facilities:** Outdoor venture center, climbing wall, nature preserve, planetarium, Nebraska Book Arts Center.

Freshman class profile. 4,635 applied, 3,503 admitted, 1,785 enrolled.

Mid 50% test scores		Rank in top tenth:	14%
ACT composite:	20-25	Return as sophomores:	73%
GPA 3.75 or higher:	28%	Out-of-state:	8%
GPA 3.50-3.74:	15%	Live on campus:	31%
GPA 3.0-3.49:	28%	International:	2%
GPA 2.0-2.99:	28%	Fraternities:	5%
Rank in top quarter:	38%	Sororities:	4%

Basis for selection. School achievement record, test scores important. Must have ACT score of 20, comparable SAT score or class rank in upper half of graduating class. Admitted for special talent consideration on case by case basis. Open admission for non-degree applicants and non-traditional adult freshman applicants. Audition required for music program. **Home schooled:** Applicants must submit official GED scores verifying successful completion of the GED. An ACT composite score of 25+ may be substituted in lieu of the GED score.

High school preparation. College-preparatory program required. 16 units required. Required units include English 4, mathematics 3, social studies 1, history 2, science 3 (laboratory 1), foreign language 2 and academic electives 1. Specific course requirements for programs in business administration, human resources and family services for College of Engineering and Technology.

2011-2012 Annual costs. Tuition/fees: $7,027; $18,119 out-of-state. Room/board: $8,858. Books/supplies: $950. Personal expenses: $2,200.

2010-2011 Financial aid. Need-based: Average scholarship/grant was $2,163; average loan $2,705. 53% of total undergraduate aid awarded as scholarships/grants, 47% as loans/jobs. **Non-need-based:** Scholarships awarded for academics, alumni affiliation, art, athletics, leadership, minority status, music/drama, ROTC, state residency.

Application procedures. Admission: Closing date 8/1 (postmark date). $45 fee. Admission notification on a rolling basis. **Financial aid:** Priority date 3/1; no closing date. FAFSA required. Applicants notified on a rolling basis starting 4/15; must reply within 2 week(s) of notification.

Academics. Associate degree program available on Omaha campus through University of Nebraska-Lincoln in construction, drafting and design technology, electronic technology, fire control and safety technology, fire protection, manufacturing technology. On-line courses in aviation studies also available. **Special study options:** Combined bachelor's/graduate degree, cooperative education, cross-registration, distance learning, double major, dual enrollment of high school students, ESL, exchange student, honors, independent study, internships, student-designed major, study abroad, teacher certification program. **Credit/placement by examination:** AP, CLEP, ACT, institutional tests. 30 credit hours maximum toward bachelor's degree. CLEP exams in American History and Western Civilization must be accompanied by essay. **Support services:** Reduced course load, study skills assistance, tutoring, writing center.

Majors. Area/ethnic studies: African-American, Latin American, women's. **Biology:** General, bioinformatics, biotechnology. **Business:** General, accounting, banking/financial services, business admin, finance, investments/securities, management information systems, managerial economics, marketing, real estate, small business admin. **Communications:** Broadcast journalism, communications/speech/rhetoric, journalism. **Computer sciences:** Computer science. **Conservation:** Environmental studies. **Education:** Elementary, music, physical, secondary, special ed, speech impaired. **Engineering:** Applied physics, architectural, chemical, civil, computer, electrical. **English:** Creative writing, English lit, rhetoric/composition. **Foreign languages:** French, German, Spanish. **Health services:** Community health services, health care admin, premedicine. **History:** General. **Human services:** General, social work. **Liberal arts:** Library science. **Math:** General. **Parks/recreation:** General, exercise sciences. **Philosophy/religion:** Philosophy, religion. **Physical sciences:** Chemistry, geology, physics. **Protective services:** Criminal justice. **Psychology:** General. **Social sciences:** Geography, political science, sociology, urban studies. **Visual/performing arts:** Art, art history/conservation, dramatic, music, music performance, music theory/composition, piano/keyboard, stringed instruments, studio arts, voice/opera. **Work/family studies:** General, communication, family resources.

Most popular majors. Biology 7%, business/marketing 25%, communications/journalism 7%, education 12%, security/protective services 7%.

Computing on campus. 2,415 workstations in dormitories, library, computer center, student center. Dormitories wired for high-speed internet access and linked to campus network. Commuter students can connect to campus network. Online course registration, online library, helpline, student web hosting, wireless network available.

Student life. Freshman orientation: Mandatory. Preregistration for classes offered. Held every week April 15 thru August 1st. **Housing:** Coed dorms available. $260 partly refundable deposit. **Activities:** Bands, campus ministries, choral groups, dance, drama, film society, international student organizations, literary magazine, music ensembles, musical theater, opera, radio station, student government, student newspaper, symphony orchestra, TV station, American multi-cultural students, chapter summary Bible study, Campus Crusade for Christ, honor societies, Greek letter organizations.

Athletics. NCAA. **Intercollegiate:** Baseball M, basketball, golf, ice hockey M, soccer, softball W, swimming W, tennis, volleyball W. **Intramural:** Basketball, bowling, field hockey, football (non-tackle), golf, racquetball, soccer, softball, volleyball. **Team name:** Mavericks.

Student services. Adult student services, alcohol/substance abuse counseling, chaplain/spiritual director, career counseling, services for economically disadvantaged, student employment services, financial aid counseling, health services, minority student services, on-campus daycare, personal counseling, placement for graduates, veterans' counselor, women's services. **Physically disabled:** Services for visually, speech, hearing impaired.

Contact. E-mail: unoadm@mail.unomaha.edu
Phone: (402) 554-2393 Toll-free number: (800) 858-8648
Fax: (402) 554-3472
Jolene Adams, Director of Admissions, University of Nebraska - Omaha, 6001 Dodge Street, Omaha, NE 68182-0005

University of Nebraska Medical Center
Omaha, Nebraska
www.unmc.edu   CB code: 6896

- Public two-year upper-division health science college
- Commuter campus in very large city
- 25% of applicants admitted

General. Founded in 1869. Regionally accredited. **Degrees:** 359 bachelor's awarded; master's, professional, doctoral offered. **ROTC:** Army, Air Force. **Calendar:** Semester, limited summer session. **Full-time faculty:** 1,023 total; 87% have terminal degrees, 21% minority, 41% women. **Part-time faculty:** 209 total; 85% have terminal degrees, 8% minority, 52% women.

Student profile. 991 degree-seeking undergraduates, 2,093 degree-seeking graduate students. 5,281 applied as first time-transfer students, 1,334 admitted, 1,162 enrolled. 16% entered as juniors, 12% entered as seniors. 15% transferred from two-year, 85% transferred from four-year institutions.

Women:	88%	Native American:	1%
African American:	1%	International:	1%
Asian American:	2%	Part-time:	10%
Hispanic American:	3%		

Basis for selection. College transcript required. Admissions requirements, application procedures, and closing dates vary by program. Health professions program applicants must have completed prerequisite courses at another institution. Transfer accepted as sophomores, juniors, seniors.

2011-2012 Annual costs. Tuition/fees: $6,659; $18,944 out-of-state. Tuition varies by program. Books/supplies: $900. Personal expenses: $1,500.

Application procedures. Admission: $45 fee, may be waived for applicants with need. Application must be submitted online. **Financial aid:** No deadline. Applicants notified on a rolling basis starting 5/1; must reply within 2 weeks of notification. FAFSA, institutional form required.

Academics. Special study options: Accelerated study, combined bachelor's/graduate degree, distance learning, honors. **Credit/placement by examination:** AP, CLEP, IB, institutional tests. 24 credit hours maximum toward bachelor's degree.

Majors. Health services: Clinical lab science, dental hygiene, medical radiologic technology/radiation therapy, nuclear medical technology, nursing (RN), radiologic technology/medical imaging, sonography.

Computing on campus. 108 workstations in library, computer center, student center. Commuter students can connect to campus network. Online library, helpline, repair service, wireless network available.

Student life. Housing: Apartments available. **Activities:** Student government, committee on minority concerns, American Academy of Physician Assistants, Religious Life Council, Christian Fellowship, student association for rural health, student services council, student professional organizations.

Student services. Alcohol/substance abuse counseling, career counseling, services for economically disadvantaged, financial aid counseling, health services, minority student services, on-campus daycare, personal counseling, veterans' counselor. **Physically disabled:** Services for hearing impaired.

Contact. E-mail: tsing@unmc.edu
Phone: (402) 559-6468 Toll-free number: (800) 626-8431 ext. 96468
Fax: (402) 559-6796
University of Nebraska Medical Center, 984230 Nebraska Medical Center, Omaha, NE 68198-4230

University of Phoenix: Omaha
Omaha, Nebraska
www.phoenix.edu

- For-profit 4-year university
- Large city
- 62 degree-seeking undergraduates

General. Regionally accredited. **Degrees:** 8 bachelor's awarded; master's offered. **Calendar:** Differs by program. **Full-time faculty:** 5 total. **Part-time faculty:** 15 total.

Basis for selection. Open admission, but selective for some programs.

2011-2012 Annual costs. Estimated costs as of August 2011: per-credit-hour charge, $380 to $415, depending upon level and course of study; electronic course materials fee, $95, if applicable. Book and material charges may vary by course and program. All fees are subject to change.

Application procedures. Admission: No deadline. No application fee. **Financial aid:** No deadline.

Academics. Credit/placement by examination: AP, CLEP.

Majors. Business: Accounting, business admin, finance, human resources, international, marketing, operations.

Contact. Marc Booker, Director of Admission and Evaluation, University of Phoenix: Omaha, 13321 California Street, Suite 200, Omaha, NE 68154-5258

Wayne State College
Wayne, Nebraska
www.wsc.edu   CB code: 6469

- Public 4-year liberal arts and teachers college
- Residential campus in small town
- 2,983 degree-seeking undergraduates: 9% part-time, 56% women, 3% African American, 5% Hispanic American, 1% Native American
- 438 degree-seeking graduate students
- 47% graduate within 6 years

General. Founded in 1909. Regionally accredited. Campus is state arboretum. **Degrees:** 541 bachelor's awarded; master's offered. **ROTC:** Army. **Location:** 45 miles from Sioux City, Iowa. **Calendar:** Semester, extensive summer session. **Full-time faculty:** 122 total; 83% have terminal degrees, 5% minority, 45% women. **Part-time faculty:** 93 total; 13% have terminal degrees, 2% minority, 63% women. **Class size:** 44% < 20, 50% 20-39, 5% 40-49, 2% 50-99. **Special facilities:** Planetarium, outdoor amphitheater.

Freshman class profile.

Mid 50% test scores			
ACT composite:	18-24	Rank in top quarter:	32%
GPA 3.75 or higher:	23%	Rank in top tenth:	11%
GPA 3.50-3.74:	20%	Return as sophomores:	68%
GPA 3.0-3.49:	28%	Out-of-state:	12%
GPA 2.0-2.99:	26%	Live on campus:	96%

Basis for selection. Open admission.

High school preparation. College-preparatory program recommended. 18 units recommended. Recommended units include English 4, mathematics 3, social studies 3, science 2, foreign language 2, computer science 2 and visual/performing arts 2.

2011-2012 Annual costs. Tuition/fees: $5,318; $9,375 out-of-state. Additional Special Rates apply for residents of qualifying states. Room/board: $5,740. Books/supplies: $1,100. Personal expenses: $981.

2011-2012 Financial aid. Need-based: 608 full-time freshmen applied for aid; 459 were judged to have need; 448 of these received aid. Average need met was 57%. Average scholarship/grant was $4,111; average loan $3,188. 44% of total undergraduate aid awarded as scholarships/grants, 56% as loans/jobs. **Non-need-based:** Awarded to 1,392 full-time undergraduates, including 423 freshmen. Scholarships awarded for academics, art, athletics, leadership, minority status, music/drama, religious affiliation, state residency.

Application procedures. Admission: Priority date 12/1; deadline 8/20. No application fee. Admission notification on a rolling basis beginning on or about 9/15. **Financial aid:** Priority date 4/1; no closing date. FAFSA required. Applicants notified on a rolling basis starting 3/1; must reply within 4 week(s) of notification.

Academics. Special study options: Cooperative education, distance learning, double major, dual enrollment of high school students, honors, independent study, internships, student-designed major, study abroad, teacher certification program. Learning Communities, First-Year Experience. **Credit/placement by examination:** AP, CLEP, institutional tests. **Support services:** Learning center, reduced course load, study skills assistance, tutoring, writing center.

Majors. Biology: General. **Business:** Business admin. **Communications:** Communications/speech/rhetoric, journalism, media studies. **Computer sciences:** General, information systems. **Education:** Art, biology, business, chemistry, drama/dance, early childhood, elementary, English, family/consumer sciences, foreign languages, geography, history, mathematics, middle, music, physical, psychology, social science, special ed, speech, technology/

industrial arts. **English:** English lit. **Foreign languages:** General, Spanish. **Health services:** Athletic training. **History:** General. **Math:** General. **Parks/recreation:** Health/fitness, physical fitness technician, sports admin. **Physical sciences:** Chemistry. **Protective services:** Criminal justice. **Psychology:** General, counseling. **Social sciences:** General, geography, political science, sociology. **Visual/performing arts:** Art, dramatic, graphic design, music. **Work/family studies:** General, child care service, food/nutrition.

Most popular majors. Business/marketing 19%, education 30%, psychology 7%.

Computing on campus. 280 workstations in library, computer center, student center. Dormitories wired for high-speed internet access and linked to campus network. Commuter students can connect to campus network. Online course registration, helpline, wireless network available.

Student life. Freshman orientation: Available, $75 fee. Preregistration for classes offered. **Housing:** Guaranteed on-campus for freshmen. Coed dorms, wellness housing available. $50 fully refundable deposit. **Activities:** Bands, campus ministries, choral groups, dance, drama, international student organizations, literary magazine, music ensembles, musical theater, radio station, student government, student newspaper, TV station.

Athletics. NCAA. **Intercollegiate:** Baseball M, basketball, cross-country, football (tackle) M, golf, soccer W, softball W, track and field, volleyball W. **Intramural:** Archery, badminton, basketball, bowling, football (non-tackle), golf, handball, racquetball, softball, swimming, table tennis, tennis, track and field, volleyball, weight lifting M, wrestling M. **Team name:** Wildcats.

Student services. Alcohol/substance abuse counseling, chaplain/spiritual director, career counseling, services for economically disadvantaged, student employment services, financial aid counseling, health services, minority student services, personal counseling, placement for graduates, veterans' counselor. **Physically disabled:** Services for visually, speech, hearing impaired.

Contact. E-mail: admit1@wsc.edu
Phone: (402) 375-7234 Toll-free number: (800) 228-9972
Fax: (402) 375-7204
Kevin Halle, Director of Admissions, Wayne State College, 1111 Main Street, Wayne, NE 68787

York College
York, Nebraska
www.york.edu   CB code: 6984

- Private 4-year liberal arts and teachers college affiliated with Church of Christ
- Residential campus in small town
- 510 degree-seeking undergraduates
- SAT or ACT (ACT writing optional) required

General. Founded in 1956. Regionally accredited. **Degrees:** 65 bachelor's, 4 associate awarded. **ROTC:** Army, Naval, Air Force. **Location:** 50 miles from Lincoln. **Calendar:** Semester, limited summer session. **Full-time faculty:** 23 total. **Part-time faculty:** 18 total. **Class size:** 85% < 20, 13% 20-39, 2% 40-49, less than 1% 50-99. **Special facilities:** 35,000 sq. ft. indoor sports practice facility, historic prayer chapel.

Freshman class profile.

Mid 50% test scores			
SAT critical reading:	440-540	GPA 2.0-2.99:	36%
SAT math:	420-560	Rank in top quarter:	24%
ACT composite:	18-24	Rank in top tenth:	11%
GPA 3.75 or higher:	21%	Out-of-state:	66%
GPA 3.50-3.74:	10%	Live on campus:	95%
GPA 3.0-3.49:	30%	Fraternities:	66%
		Sororities:	76%

Basis for selection. ACT/SAT test scores, high school GPA, class rank very important. Essay recommended but not required. **Home schooled:** Transcript of courses and grades required. **Learning Disabled:** Submission of high school IEP is recommended for students who self-identify learning disabilities.

High school preparation. College-preparatory program recommended. 15 units required; 21 recommended. Required and recommended units include English 3-4, mathematics 2-4, social studies 1-4, history 1-4, science 2-4 and foreign language 3.

2011-2012 Annual costs. Tuition/fees: $15,300. Room/board: $5,850. Books/supplies: $1,500. Personal expenses: $2,400.

Financial aid. Non-need-based: Scholarships awarded for academics, alumni affiliation, athletics, leadership, music/drama.

Application procedures. Admission: Priority date 3/31; deadline 8/31 (receipt date). $20 fee, may be waived for applicants with need. Admission notification on a rolling basis. Must reply by 9/1. **Financial aid:** Priority date 4/1; no closing date. FAFSA required. Applicants notified on a rolling basis starting 3/1; must reply within 4 week(s) of notification.

Academics. Special study options: Accelerated study, double major, dual enrollment of high school students, independent study, internships, student-designed major, teacher certification program. **Credit/placement by examination:** AP, CLEP, IB, SAT, ACT, institutional tests. 12 credit hours maximum toward associate degree, 32 toward bachelor's. **Support services:** Reduced course load, remedial instruction, study skills assistance, tutoring.

Majors. Biology: General. **Business:** Accounting, business admin, finance, human resources. **Communications:** Communications/speech/rhetoric. **Education:** General, art, biology, business, drama/dance, elementary, English, history, mathematics, middle, multi-level teacher, music, physical, reading, secondary, social science, special ed, speech. **English:** English lit. **History:** General. **Math:** General. **Philosophy/religion:** Religion. **Protective services:** Law enforcement admin. **Psychology:** General. **Social sciences:** Criminology. **Theology:** Bible, religious ed. **Visual/performing arts:** Voice/opera.

Most popular majors. Biology 7%, business/marketing 26%, education 30%, liberal arts 11%, psychology 9%.

Computing on campus. 57 workstations in dormitories, library, computer center. Dormitories wired for high-speed internet access and linked to campus network. Online library, helpline, wireless network available.

Student life. Freshman orientation: Mandatory. Preregistration for classes offered. **Policies:** Students expected to conform to Christian norms. Alcohol and tobacco prohibited. Unmarried, full-time students under 21 required to live on campus or with relatives or staff off campus. **Housing:** Guaranteed on-campus for all undergraduates. Single-sex dorms, apartments, wellness housing available. $100 fully refundable deposit, deadline 8/31. **Activities:** Campus ministries, choral groups, drama, music ensembles, musical theater, student government, student newspaper, service clubs, Chi Rho, spiritual life committee.

Athletics. NAIA. **Intercollegiate:** Baseball M, basketball, soccer, softball W, volleyball W, wrestling M. **Intramural:** Basketball, football (non-tackle), soccer, softball, table tennis, volleyball. **Team name:** Panthers.

Student services. Adult student services, chaplain/spiritual director, career counseling, student employment services, financial aid counseling, personal counseling, placement for graduates, veterans' counselor.

Contact. E-mail: enroll@york.edu
Phone: (402) 363-5627 Toll-free number: (800) 950-9675
Fax: (402) 363-5623
Willie Sanchez, Director of Admissions, York College, 1125 East 8th Street, York, NE 68467

Nevada

Art Institute of Las Vegas
Henderson, Nevada
www.artinstitutes.edu/lasvegas/   CB code: 3832

- For-profit 3-year culinary school and visual arts college
- Commuter campus in very large city
- 1,196 degree-seeking undergraduates
- Application essay, interview required

General. Regionally accredited; also accredited by ACICS, ACCSC. **Degrees:** 139 bachelor's, 50 associate awarded. **Location:** 10 miles from Las Vegas. **Calendar:** Quarter, extensive summer session. **Full-time faculty:** 35 total. **Part-time faculty:** 57 total. **Class size:** 77% < 20, 19% 20-39, 2% 40-49, 2% 50-99. **Special facilities:** Sound-mixing studio, control room, isolation chamber, student-run restaurant, print and service bureaus, photography lab, supply store, learning resource center.

Freshman class profile.

GPA 3.75 or higher:	2%	GPA 2.0-2.99:	60%
GPA 3.50-3.74:	4%	Out-of-state:	7%
GPA 3.0-3.49:	17%	Live on campus:	12%

Basis for selection. Open admission, but selective for some programs. Minimum GPA of 2.5 required for game art & design and 2.0 for audio production applicants. Face-to-face or phone interview, an original essay of at least 150 words required. Personal portfolio may be required, depending upon the desired academic curriculum. Official transcripts for high school, GED, and/or college, ACCUPLACER test or satisfactory SAT or ACT scores required of all applicants. **Home schooled:** Institution must be recognized by state or national department of education. **Learning Disabled:** Accommodations to qualified students with disabilities available through the Student Affairs office.

2011-2012 Annual costs. Tuition/fees: $22,001.

Financial aid. Non-need-based: Scholarships awarded for academics, state residency.

Application procedures. Admission: No deadline. $50 fee. Application must be submitted on paper. Admission notification on a rolling basis. **Financial aid:** No deadline. Applicants notified on a rolling basis.

Academics. Special study options: Distance learning, honors, independent study, internships, liberal arts/career combination, study abroad. **Credit/placement by examination:** AP, CLEP, IB, institutional tests. 28 credit hours maximum toward associate degree, 48 toward bachelor's. **Support services:** Learning center, pre-admission summer program, reduced course load, remedial instruction, study skills assistance, tutoring, writing center.

Majors. Communications technology: Animation/special effects, recording arts. **Computer sciences:** Computer graphics. **Visual/performing arts:** General, cinematography, design, fashion design, game design, graphic design, interior design, multimedia, photography.

Most popular majors. Visual/performing arts 30%.

Computing on campus. 221 workstations in library, computer center. Commuter students can connect to campus network. Online course registration, online library, student web hosting, wireless network available.

Student life. Freshman orientation: Mandatory. Preregistration for classes offered. **Policies:** Resident Advisor (RA) available to on-campus students, apartment information and roommate referrals available to off-campus students. **Housing:** Apartments, wellness housing available. $150 partly refundable deposit. **Activities:** Film society.

Student services. Adult student services, alcohol/substance abuse counseling, career counseling, services for economically disadvantaged, student employment services, financial aid counseling, personal counseling, placement for graduates. **Physically disabled:** Services for visually, speech, hearing impaired.

Contact. Phone: (702) 369-9944
Laurie Perdue, Director of Admissions, Art Institute of Las Vegas, 2350 Corporate Circle, Henderson, NV 89074-7737

Great Basin College
Elko, Nevada
www.gbcnv.edu   CB code: 4293

- Public 4-year community and teachers college
- Commuter campus in large town
- 2,662 degree-seeking undergraduates: 64% part-time, 66% women, 3% African American, 1% Asian American, 13% Hispanic American, 3% Native American

General. Founded in 1967. Regionally accredited. **Degrees:** 55 bachelor's, 249 associate awarded. **Location:** 280 miles from Reno, 220 miles from Salt Lake City. **Calendar:** Semester, limited summer session. **Full-time faculty:** 67 total. **Part-time faculty:** 97 total.

Freshman class profile. 439 applied, 439 admitted, 439 enrolled.

Return as sophomores:	53%	Live on campus:	15%
Out-of-state:	10%		

Basis for selection. Open admission, but selective for some programs. Placement test required for some English and math courses. Nursing applicants selected on basis of point system. Points given for courses completed, grades, current work experience in health field, certifications, letters of recommendation, and scores obtained on required entrance exam which measures math and reading comprehension skills. **Home schooled:** State high school equivalency certificate required.

2011-2012 Annual costs. Tuition/fees: $2,513; $9,008 out-of-state. Room only: $2,299. Books/supplies: $1,450. Personal expenses: $1,500.

Application procedures. Admission: No deadline. $10 fee. Application must be submitted online. Admission notification on a rolling basis. **Financial aid:** Priority date 6/1; no closing date. FAFSA required. Applicants notified on a rolling basis starting 7/1.

Academics. Special study options: Cooperative education, distance learning, dual enrollment of high school students, ESL, independent study, internships, liberal arts/career combination, teacher certification program. **Credit/placement by examination:** AP, CLEP, institutional tests. 15 credit hours maximum toward associate degree, 30 toward bachelor's. **Support services:** Learning center, reduced course load, remedial instruction, study skills assistance, tutoring, writing center.

Majors. Business: Business admin. **Computer sciences:** LAN/WAN management. **Conservation:** General. **Education:** Agricultural, biology, business, elementary, English, history, mathematics, science, secondary, social science, trade/industrial. **Engineering:** Surveying. **Health services:** Nursing (RN). **Social sciences:** General.

Most popular majors. Business/marketing 40%, education 31%, social sciences 15%.

Computing on campus. 200 workstations in dormitories, library, computer center, student center. Dormitories wired for high-speed internet access and linked to campus network. Commuter students can connect to campus network. Online course registration, online library, helpline, wireless network available.

Student life. Freshman orientation: Mandatory, $42 fee. Preregistration for classes offered. One day program, held Saturday before school starts. Must compete assignment and receive passing grade. **Housing:** Coed dorms, apartments, wellness housing available. $250 partly refundable deposit. **Activities:** Drama, musical theater, student government, vocational clubs, nursing club, rodeo, intramural sports, student ambassadors.

Athletics. Intramural: Rodeo.

Student services. Adult student services, career counseling, services for economically disadvantaged, student employment services, financial aid counseling, minority student services, on-campus daycare, personal counseling, placement for graduates, veterans' counselor. **Physically disabled:** Services for visually, speech, hearing impaired.

Contact. E-mail: admissions@gbcnv.edu
Phone: (775) 753-2311 Fax: (775) 738-8771
Janice King, Director of Admissions, Great Basin College, 1500 College Parkway, Elko, NV 89801

International Academy of Design and Technology: Henderson
Henderson, Nevada
www.iadtvegas.com
CB code: 5971

- For-profit 3-year visual arts and technical college
- Very large city

General. Accredited by ACICS. **Location:** 10 miles from Las Vegas. **Calendar:** Quarter.

Annual costs/financial aid. Tuition/fees (2011-2012): $18,425. Tuition quoted is for three terms based on $405 per-credit-hour and 45 credits. Costs of books and supplies vary from $4,800 to $9,600 for entire program depending on course of study. Additional fees may apply.

Contact. Phone: (702) 990-0150
Director of Admissions, 2495 Village View Drive, Henderson, NV 89074

ITT Technical Institute: Henderson
Henderson, Nevada
www.itt-tech.edu
CB code: 2710

- For-profit 4-year technical college
- Commuter campus in small city
- 907 degree-seeking undergraduates
- Interview required

General. Accredited by ACICS. **Degrees:** 58 bachelor's, 213 associate awarded. **Calendar:** Quarter, extensive summer session. **Full-time faculty:** 18 total. **Part-time faculty:** 48 total.

Basis for selection. Satisfactory scores from on-site tests in English and mathematics required.

2011-2012 Annual costs. Estimated costs as of July 2011: per-credit-hour charge, $493, depending upon level and course of study; quarterly academic fee, $100. Certain programs of study require purchase of tools, which could cost an additional $100 to $655. All costs are subject to change.

Application procedures. Admission: No deadline. No application fee. Admission notification on a rolling basis. **Financial aid:** FAFSA, institutional form required. Applicants notified on a rolling basis.

Academics. Credit/placement by examination: AP, CLEP. **Support services:** Learning center, tutoring.

Majors. Business: Business admin, construction management. **Communications technology:** Animation/special effects. **Computer sciences:** Security. **Protective services:** Law enforcement admin.

Computing on campus. Online library available.

Student life. Freshman orientation: Available. Preregistration for classes offered.

Student services. Career counseling, student employment services, placement for graduates.

Contact. Phone: (702) 558-5404 Toll-free number: (800) 488-8459
Fax: (702) 558-5412
Anne Buzak, Director of Recruitment, ITT Technical Institute: Henderson, 168 North Gibson Road, Henderson, NV 89014

Morrison University
Reno, Nevada
www.morrisonuniversity.com
CB code: 2114

- For-profit 4-year university and business college
- Commuter campus in small city
- 124 degree-seeking undergraduates
- Interview required

General. Founded in 1902. Accredited by ACICS. **Degrees:** 20 bachelor's, 35 associate awarded; master's offered. **Location:** Half mile from downtown. **Calendar:** Quarter, extensive summer session. **Full-time faculty:** 1 total. **Part-time faculty:** 35 total. **Class size:** 71% < 20, 29% 20-39.

Basis for selection. Open admission.

2011-2012 Annual costs. Tuition/fees: $11,225. Tuition and fees quoted are average annual cost of bachelor's program. Program costs: Accounting $44,900 (bachelor), $23,580 (associate). Computer Science $23,580 (associate). Information System $47,060 (bachelor). Management $44,900 (bachelor), $22,500 (associate). Books/supplies: $800.

Application procedures. Admission: No deadline. $20 fee, may be waived for applicants with need. Application must be submitted on paper. Admission notification on a rolling basis. **Financial aid:** No deadline. FAFSA required. Applicants notified on a rolling basis starting 7/1.

Academics. Special study options: Accelerated study, combined bachelor's/graduate degree, weekend college. **Credit/placement by examination:** AP, CLEP, IB. 8 credit hours maximum toward associate degree, 20 toward bachelor's. A student enrolled in and attending a course may earn credit in that course by advanced standing examination up to the end of the add/drop period. **Support services:** Learning center, reduced course load, remedial instruction, study skills assistance, tutoring, writing center.

Majors. Business: Accounting, business admin.

Computing on campus. 62 workstations in library, computer center. Online library, wireless network available.

Student life. Freshman orientation: Available. Preregistration for classes offered. **Policies:** Dress code, appropriate conduct policy, zero tolerance for in-school alcohol and drug use. **Activities:** Student government, student newspaper.

Student services. Adult student services, alcohol/substance abuse counseling, career counseling, student employment services, financial aid counseling, personal counseling, placement for graduates, veterans' counselor.

Contact. E-mail: jdecker@morrison.anthem.edu
Phone: (775) 335-3900 Toll-free number: (866) 502-2627
Fax: (775) 850-0711
Joyce Decker, Director of Admissions, Morrison University, 10315 Professional Circle, #201, Reno, NV 89521

Nevada State College
Henderson, Nevada
www.nsc.nevada.edu
CB code: 4572

- Public 4-year liberal arts and teachers college
- Commuter campus in large city
- 2,836 degree-seeking undergraduates
- 66% of applicants admitted

General. Regionally accredited. Satellite campus in downtown Henderson. Offers dual enrollment programs with state community colleges. **Degrees:** 260 bachelor's awarded. **Location:** 15 miles from Las Vegas. **Calendar:** Semester, limited summer session. **Full-time faculty:** 41 total. **Part-time faculty:** 48 total. **Class size:** 25% < 20, 71% 20-39, 4% 40-49. **Special facilities:** Smart classrooms, seismograph, weather center, anatomy and physiology cadaver laboratories.

Freshman class profile. 1,401 applied, 925 admitted, 333 enrolled.

GPA 3.75 or higher:	4%	Rank in top quarter:	30%
GPA 3.50-3.74:	7%	Rank in top tenth:	8%
GPA 3.0-3.49:	27%	Out-of-state:	3%
GPA 2.0-2.99:	61%		

Basis for selection. Admission based on academic record. National college entrance tests, ACT/SAT, will be used as benchmarks for placement in English and mathematics courses. **Home schooled:** SAT/ACT required.

High school preparation. 12 units required. Required units include English 4, mathematics 3, social studies 3, science 2 (laboratory 1).

2011-2012 Annual costs. Tuition/fees: $4,205; $14,250 out-of-state. Books/supplies: $1,000. Personal expenses: $1,800.

Application procedures. Admission: Closing date 8/1. $30 fee, may be waived for applicants with need. Admission notification on a rolling basis. **Financial aid:** Priority date 3/1; no closing date. FAFSA, institutional form required. Applicants notified on a rolling basis starting 5/1.

Academics. Special study options: Accelerated study, combined bachelor's/graduate degree, distance learning, double major, dual enrollment of

high school students, independent study, internships, liberal arts/career combination, student-designed major, teacher certification program. **Credit/placement by examination:** AP, CLEP, SAT, ACT, institutional tests. 30 credit hours maximum toward bachelor's degree. **Support services:** Learning center, remedial instruction, study skills assistance, tutoring, writing center.

Majors. Biology: General. **Business:** Business admin, management science. **Communications technology:** Animation/special effects. **Conservation:** Environmental science. **Education:** Biology, Deaf/hearing impaired, elementary, elementary special ed, English, environmental, history, mathematics. **English:** English lit. **Health services:** Nursing (RN), speech pathology. **History:** General. **Math:** General. **Protective services:** Law enforcement admin. **Psychology:** General. **Social sciences:** Economics.

Most popular majors. Business/marketing 11%, education 25%, health sciences 44%, psychology 10%.

Computing on campus. 136 workstations in library, computer center, student center. Commuter students can connect to campus network. Online course registration, online library, helpline, student web hosting, wireless network available.

Student life. Freshman orientation: Mandatory. Preregistration for classes offered. One-day program held prior to start of Spring and Fall terms for freshman and transfer students. A separate program for parents and family members offered concurrently to student orientation. **Activities:** Choral groups, international student organizations, student government, student newspaper, Alpha Phi Omega/Venture Crew, Young Democrats, Asian Pacific Islander Coalition, Black Student Organization, American Sign Language Club.

Athletics. Team name: Scorpions.

Student services. Financial aid counseling, minority student services. **Physically disabled:** Services for visually, speech, hearing impaired.

Contact. E-mail: admissions@nsc.nevada.edu
Phone: (702) 992-2130 Fax: (702) 992-2110
Adelfa Sullivan, Associate Registrar, Nevada State College, 1125 Nevada State Drive, Henderson, NV 89002

Roseman University of Health Sciences
Henderson, Nevada
www.roseman.edu

▶ Private two-year upper-division university
▶ Commuter campus in very large city
▶ 58% of applicants admitted
▶ Test scores, application essay, interview required

General. Candidate for regional accreditation. **Degrees:** 54 bachelor's awarded; master's, professional offered. **Articulation:** Agreements with College of Southern Nevada, American River College, Cosumnes River College, Gavilan College, Grossmont College, Hartnell College, and Sacramento City College. **Location:** 9 miles from Las Vegas. **Calendar:** Continuous. **Full-time faculty:** 76 total; 100% have terminal degrees, 26% minority, 54% women. **Part-time faculty:** 75 total; 81% have terminal degrees, 28% minority, 63% women. **Class size:** 71% < 20, 20% 20-39, 9% 50-99.

Student profile. 258 degree-seeking undergraduates, 829 degree-seeking graduate students. 211 applied as first time-transfer students, 122 admitted, 95 enrolled. 52% transferred from two-year, 48% transferred from four-year institutions.

Women:	77%	Native American:	1%
African American:	6%	International:	2%
Asian American:	39%	Out-of-state:	74%
Hispanic American:	5%	25 or older:	67%

Basis for selection. College transcript, application essay, interview, standardized test scores required. Must complete specified courses. Transfer accepted as juniors.

2012-2013 Annual costs. Tuition/fees: $32,510. Tuition and fees reported cover the first 12 months of study within an 18 month expedited BSN program. Books/supplies: $1,800. Personal expenses: $2,900.

Financial aid. Need-based: 260 applied for aid; 260 were judged to have need; 260 of these received aid. Average need met was 75%. 11% of total undergraduate aid awarded as scholarships/grants, 89% as loans/jobs. **Non-need-based:** Awarded to 18 undergraduates. Scholarships awarded for academics, leadership.

Application procedures. Admission: Rolling admission. Application must be submitted on paper. **Financial aid:** Applicants notified on a rolling basis starting 7/1; must reply within 2 weeks of notification. FAFSA, institutional form required.

Academics. Special study options: Accelerated study. **Credit/placement by examination:** AP, CLEP.

Majors. Health services: Nursing (RN).

Computing on campus. PC or laptop required. 28 workstations in library. Commuter students can connect to campus network. Online library, helpline, repair service, wireless network available.

Student life. Activities: Student government.

Student services. Financial aid counseling, placement for graduates. **Physically disabled:** Services for visually, hearing impaired.

Contact. E-mail: bsnadmission@roseman.edu
Phone: (702) 968-2075 Fax: (702) 968-5279
Roseman University of Health Sciences, 11 Sunset Way, Henderson, NV 89014-2333

Sierra Nevada College
Incline Village, Nevada
www.sierranevada.edu   CB code: 4757

▶ Private 4-year liberal arts college
▶ Residential campus in small town
▶ 527 degree-seeking undergraduates: 3% part-time, 43% women, 1% African American, 1% Asian American, 3% Hispanic American, 2% Native American, 1% international
▶ 402 degree-seeking graduate students
▶ 58% of applicants admitted
▶ SAT or ACT (ACT writing optional), application essay required
▶ 37% graduate within 6 years

General. Founded in 1969. Regionally accredited. **Degrees:** 73 bachelor's awarded; master's offered. **Location:** 35 miles from Reno. **Calendar:** Semester, limited summer session. **Full-time faculty:** 28 total; 39% have terminal degrees, 11% minority, 50% women. **Part-time faculty:** 100 total; 56% have terminal degrees, 2% minority, 72% women. **Class size:** 80% < 20, 16% 20-39, 3% 40-49, less than 1% 50-99. **Special facilities:** Entertainment technology lab, LEED Center for Environmental Sciences, fine arts studio, student-managed demonstration garden.

Freshman class profile. 559 applied, 327 admitted, 100 enrolled.

Mid 50% test scores		GPA 2.0-2.99:	50%
SAT critical reading:	420-560	Rank in top quarter:	23%
SAT math:	450-540	Rank in top tenth:	9%
SAT writing:	440-540	End year in good standing:	90%
ACT composite:	19-23	Return as sophomores:	62%
GPA 3.75 or higher:	11%	Out-of-state:	90%
GPA 3.50-3.74:	7%	Live on campus:	90%
GPA 3.0-3.49:	30%		

Basis for selection. Standard admission requirements include a 2.6 cumulative GPA, 400 on each section of SAT (exclusive of Writing), or 19 ACT composite. Other factors, including leadership qualities, extracurricular activities, community involvement, and volunteer work, considered when evaluating application not meeting standard requirements. Interview not required. Campus visit and general meeting with an Admissions Counselor highly encouraged. **Home schooled:** Letter of recommendation (nonparent) required. Considered on a case by case basis. Must submit any documentation available regarding curriculum, as well as SAT or ACT scores and a letter of recommendation. **Learning Disabled:** Students may be admitted provisionally; academic support, tutoring, and other resources provided.

High school preparation. College-preparatory program recommended. Recommended units include English 4, mathematics 3, social studies 2, history 2, science 2 (laboratory 2) and foreign language 2.

2011-2012 Annual costs. Tuition/fees: $25,370. Room/board: $10,530. Books/supplies: $727. Personal expenses: $2,958.

2010-2011 Financial aid. Need-based: 70 full-time freshmen applied for aid; 63 were judged to have need; 63 of these received aid. Average need met was 55%. Average scholarship/grant was $12,299; average loan $4,750. 47% of total undergraduate aid awarded as scholarships/grants, 53% as loans/jobs. **Non-need-based:** Awarded to 356 full-time undergraduates, including 76 freshmen. Scholarships awarded for academics, alumni affiliation, art,

athletics. **Additional information:** SNC provides students with an institutional need based grant based on the remaining need after being awarded all scholarships and Federal Student Aid. First time Freshmen are awarded 50% of remaining need and 45% to continuing students.

Application procedures. Admission: Priority date 2/15; deadline 8/26 (receipt date). No application fee. Admission notification on a rolling basis. Must reply by May 1 or within 3 week(s) if notified thereafter. **Financial aid:** Priority date 1/1; no closing date. FAFSA required. Applicants notified on a rolling basis starting 4/1; must reply by 5/1 or within 4 week(s) of notification.

Academics. Special study options: Accelerated study, combined bachelor's/graduate degree, double major, dual enrollment of high school students, ESL, exchange student, honors, independent study, internships, liberal arts/career combination, student-designed major, study abroad, teacher certification program. Tuition exchange. **Credit/placement by examination:** AP, CLEP, IB, SAT, ACT, institutional tests. 30 credit hours maximum toward bachelor's degree. **Support services:** Reduced course load, remedial instruction, study skills assistance, tutoring, writing center.

Majors. Biology: General, ecology. **Business:** General, accounting, business admin, entrepreneurial studies, finance, managerial economics, marketing, nonprofit/public, resort management. **Communications:** Photojournalism. **Conservation:** Environmental science, management/policy. **English:** English lit. **Health services:** Premedicine, prenursing, prepharmacy. **Liberal arts:** Arts/sciences, humanities. **Parks/recreation:** Outdoor education. **Psychology:** General. **Social sciences:** Economics. **Visual/performing arts:** General, ceramics, drawing, painting, printmaking, sculpture, studio arts.

Most popular majors. Biology 8%, business/marketing 42%, liberal arts 13%, psychology 11%, visual/performing arts 8%.

Computing on campus. PC or laptop required. 30 workstations in dormitories, library, computer center, student center. Dormitories wired for high-speed internet access and linked to campus network. Commuter students can connect to campus network. Online library, helpline, repair service, wireless network available.

Student life. Freshman orientation: Mandatory. Preregistration for classes offered. **Housing:** Guaranteed on-campus for freshmen. Coed dorms, wellness housing available. $200 nonrefundable deposit, deadline 8/22. **Activities:** Jazz band, choral groups, dance, drama, film society, international student organizations, literary magazine, music ensembles, musical theater, student government, student newspaper, First Generation club, rock climbing club, clay club, gallery club, A Tribe of Many Nations club, sustainability club, pride club, golf club, skate club.

Athletics. Intercollegiate: Skiing. **Intramural:** Skiing, soccer, volleyball. **Team name:** Eagles.

Student services. Adult student services, career counseling, student employment services, financial aid counseling, health services, personal counseling, placement for graduates, veterans' counselor.

Contact. E-mail: admissions@sierranevada.edu
Phone: (775) 831-1314 Toll-free number: (866) 412-4636
Fax: (775) 831-6223
Amye Cole, Director of Admissions, Sierra Nevada College, 999 Tahoe Boulevard, Incline Village, NV 89451-4269

University of Nevada: Las Vegas
Las Vegas, Nevada
www.unlv.edu   CB code: 4861

- Public 4-year university
- Commuter campus in very large city
- 21,645 degree-seeking undergraduates: 26% part-time, 55% women, 8% African American, 16% Asian American, 19% Hispanic American, 1% Native American, 4% international
- 4,410 degree-seeking graduate students
- 82% of applicants admitted
- 40% graduate within 6 years

General. Founded in 1957. Regionally accredited. Credit courses available at Nellis Air Force Base. International campus in Singapore. **Degrees:** 3,771 bachelor's awarded; master's, professional, doctoral offered. **ROTC:** Army, Air Force. **Location:** 268 miles from Los Angeles, 290 miles from Phoenix. **Calendar:** Semester, extensive summer session. **Full-time faculty:** 780 total; 88% have terminal degrees, 23% minority, 36% women. **Part-time faculty:** 479 total. **Class size:** 28% < 20, 43% 20-39, 12% 40-49, 13% 50-99, 5% >100. **Special facilities:** National supercomputing center for energy and environment, natural history museum, arboretum, theaters, concert hall, international gaming institute, professional practice school for teachers, student recreation and wellness center.

Freshman class profile. 5,801 applied, 4,746 admitted, 2,870 enrolled.

Mid 50% test scores			
SAT critical reading:	440-560	Rank in top quarter:	48%
SAT math:	450-570	Rank in top tenth:	21%
ACT composite:	19-24	Return as sophomores:	76%
GPA 3.75 or higher:	12%	Out-of-state:	14%
GPA 3.50-3.74:	17%	Live on campus:	21%
GPA 3.0-3.49:	42%	International:	2%
GPA 2.0-2.99:	28%	Fraternities:	8%
		Sororities:	6%

Basis for selection. Require 3.0 GPA in core courses. ACT/SAT can waive GPA requirements, but all students must have core coursework. Recommendations, personal essay and test scores considered for students applying through Alternate Criteria program. SAT or ACT recommended. SAT/ACT required for students appealing admission through alternate criteria and for placement into English/math courses. Audition recommended for music, theater arts programs; portfolio recommended for art program. **Home schooled:** Transcript of courses and grades, letter of recommendation (non-parent) required. Personal statement, two letters of recommendation, ACT/SAT test scores required.

High school preparation. College-preparatory program required. 13 units required. Required units include English 4, mathematics 3, social studies 3, science 3 (laboratory 2). Algebra or higher level math required.

2011-2012 Annual costs. Tuition/fees: $6,304; $19,899 out-of-state. Room/board: $10,946. Books/supplies: $1,200. Personal expenses: $2,286.

2011-2012 Financial aid. Need-based: 2,188 full-time freshmen applied for aid; 1,839 were judged to have need; 1,829 of these received aid. Average need met was 60%. Average scholarship/grant was $5,012; average loan $3,234. 45% of total undergraduate aid awarded as scholarships/grants, 55% as loans/jobs. **Non-need-based:** Awarded to 4,772 full-time undergraduates, including 1,466 freshmen. Scholarships awarded for academics, alumni affiliation, athletics, music/drama. **Additional information:** Tuition reduction for state residents through consortium programs and for out-of-state students graduating from high schools in designated counties bordering Nevada, for military dependents residing in-state, and for dependents of children of alumni not residing in-state.

Application procedures. Admission: Priority date 2/1; deadline 7/1. $60 fee. Admission notification on a rolling basis beginning on or about 9/30. **Financial aid:** Priority date 2/1; no closing date. FAFSA required. Applicants notified on a rolling basis starting 3/20; must reply within 6 week(s) of notification.

Academics. Special study options: Accelerated study, combined bachelor's/graduate degree, cooperative education, cross-registration, distance learning, double major, dual enrollment of high school students, ESL, exchange student, honors, independent study, internships, student-designed major, study abroad, teacher certification program. 2+2 culinary arts program with College of Southern Nevada. **Credit/placement by examination:** AP, CLEP, IB, SAT, ACT, institutional tests. 30 credit hours maximum toward bachelor's degree. **Support services:** Learning center, pre-admission summer program, remedial instruction, study skills assistance, tutoring, writing center.

Honors college/program. Honors College applicants must complete the honors application, letters of recommendation, test scores, personal statements, and essay response.

Majors. Architecture: Architecture, interior, landscape, urban/community planning. **Area/ethnic studies:** Asian, Latin American, women's. **Biology:** General. **Business:** Accounting, finance, hospitality admin, human resources, international marketing, management information systems, managerial economics, marketing, real estate. **Communications:** Communications/speech/rhetoric. **Computer sciences:** Computer science. **Conservation:** General, environmental studies, management/policy. **Education:** Adult/continuing, computer, early childhood, elementary, health, physical, secondary, special ed. **Engineering:** Civil, computer, electrical, mechanical, software. **English:** English lit. **Foreign languages:** French, German, Spanish. **Health services:** Athletic training, clinical lab science, health care admin, medical radiologic technology/radiation therapy, nuclear medical technology, nursing (RN), physics/radiologic health. **History:** General. **Human services:** Social work. **Liberal arts:** Arts/sciences. **Math:** General, applied. **Parks/recreation:** General, exercise sciences, health/fitness. **Philosophy/religion:** Philosophy. **Physical sciences:** Chemistry, geology, physics. **Psychology:** General. **Social sciences:** Anthropology, political science, sociology. **Visual/performing arts:** Art, dance, dramatic, film/cinema/video, jazz, music, studio arts.

Most popular majors. Business/marketing 32%, education 7%, psychology 8%, social sciences 7%, visual/performing arts 6%.

Computing on campus. 1,550 workstations in dormitories, library, computer center, student center. Dormitories wired for high-speed internet access and linked to campus network. Commuter students can connect to campus network. Online course registration, online library, helpline, wireless network available.

Student life. Freshman orientation: Mandatory, $120 fee. Preregistration for classes offered. **Housing:** Guaranteed on-campus for freshmen. Coed dorms, special housing for disabled, wellness housing available. **Activities:** Bands, campus ministries, choral groups, dance, drama, film society, international student organizations, literary magazine, music ensembles, musical theater, opera, radio station, student government, student newspaper, symphony orchestra, TV station, Young Democrats/Republicans, Rebel Christian Fellowship, Hillel, ethnic student council, student organization of Latinos, black student association, Latter-day Saints student organization, Hawaii club, Circle K.

Athletics. NCAA. **Intercollegiate:** Baseball M, basketball, cheerleading, cross-country W, diving, football (tackle) M, golf, soccer, softball W, swimming, tennis, track and field W, volleyball W. **Intramural:** Badminton, basketball, bowling, cross-country, football (non-tackle), golf, racquetball, soccer, softball, swimming, table tennis, tennis, track and field, volleyball. **Team name:** Rebels.

Student services. Adult student services, alcohol/substance abuse counseling, career counseling, services for economically disadvantaged, student employment services, financial aid counseling, health services, legal services, minority student services, on-campus daycare, personal counseling, placement for graduates, veterans' counselor, women's services. **Physically disabled:** Services for visually, speech, hearing impaired.

Contact. E-mail: admissions@unlv.edu
Phone: (702) 774-8658 Fax: (702) 774-8008
Luke Schultheis, Executive Director of Admissions and Recruitment, University of Nevada: Las Vegas, 4505 Maryland Parkway, Box 451021, Las Vegas, NV 89154-1021

University of Nevada: Reno

Reno, Nevada	
www.unr.edu	**CB member**
	CB code: 4844

- Public 4-year university
- Commuter campus in small city
- 14,415 degree-seeking undergraduates: 17% part-time, 53% women, 3% African American, 6% Asian American, 13% Hispanic American, 1% Native American, 1% international
- 2,934 degree-seeking graduate students
- 86% of applicants admitted
- 53% graduate within 6 years

General. Founded in 1874. Regionally accredited. **Degrees:** 2,409 bachelor's awarded; master's, professional, doctoral offered. **ROTC:** Army. **Location:** 225 miles from San Francisco, 35 miles from Lake Tahoe. **Calendar:** Semester, extensive summer session. **Full-time faculty:** 546 total; 88% have terminal degrees, 17% minority, 38% women. **Part-time faculty:** 20 total; 95% have terminal degrees, 10% minority, 50% women. **Class size:** 42% < 20, 38% 20-39, 5% 40-49, 9% 50-99, 6% >100. **Special facilities:** Mineral museum, planetarium, arboretum, disability resource center, ethnic student resource center, internship center.

Freshman class profile. 7,182 applied, 6,191 admitted, 2,880 enrolled.

Mid 50% test scores		GPA 2.0-2.99:	21%
SAT critical reading:	470-580	Rank in top quarter:	49%
SAT math:	470-590	Rank in top tenth:	19%
SAT writing:	450-560	End year in good standing:	81%
ACT composite:	20-26	Return as sophomores:	78%
GPA 3.75 or higher:	16%	Out-of-state:	29%
GPA 3.50-3.74:	18%	Live on campus:	58%
GPA 3.0-3.49:	45%	International:	1%

Basis for selection. GED not accepted. Secondary school record most important, with 3.0 GPA in academic core of English, math, social sciences and natural sciences. Students who do not meet Board of Regents admission requirements may appeal for special admission. If student does not meet GPA requirement, 1040 SAT or 22 ACT may be used in place of GPA requirement. All students applying for scholarships must submit test scores. Interview recommended for nursing program; audition recommended for music program; portfolio recommended for fine arts program. **Home schooled:** Home schooled students who do not meet Board of Regents admission requirements may appeal for special admission.

High school preparation. College-preparatory program required. 13 units required. Required units include English 4, mathematics 3, social studies 3, science 3 (laboratory 2).

2011-2012 Annual costs. Tuition/fees: $6,176; $19,771 out-of-state. Room/board: $10,868. Books/supplies: $1,300. Personal expenses: $2,661.

2010-2011 Financial aid. Need-based: 2,088 full-time freshmen applied for aid; 1,466 were judged to have need; 1,398 of these received aid. Average need met was 62%. Average scholarship/grant was $6,323; average loan $3,270. 51% of total undergraduate aid awarded as scholarships/grants, 49% as loans/jobs. **Non-need-based:** Awarded to 7,165 full-time undergraduates, including 2,164 freshmen. Scholarships awarded for academics, alumni affiliation, art, athletics, leadership, music/drama, ROTC, state residency. **Additional information:** Reduced out-of-state tuition available for participants in WUE program.

Application procedures. Admission: Priority date 3/1; no deadline. $60 fee, may be waived for applicants with need. Admission notification on a rolling basis. **Financial aid:** Priority date 3/1; no closing date. FAFSA required. Applicants notified on a rolling basis starting 4/1; must reply within 2 week(s) of notification.

Academics. Special study options: Distance learning, double major, dual enrollment of high school students, ESL, honors, independent study, internships, study abroad, teacher certification program. **Credit/placement by examination:** AP, CLEP, IB, SAT, ACT, institutional tests. 60 credit hours maximum toward bachelor's degree. **Support services:** Learning center, preadmission summer program, reduced course load, remedial instruction, study skills assistance, tutoring, writing center.

Majors. Area/ethnic studies: Women's. **Biology:** General, biochemistry, biotechnology. **Business:** General, accounting, business admin, entrepreneurial studies, finance, international, managerial economics, marketing. **Communications:** Communications/speech/rhetoric, journalism. **Computer sciences:** General, computer science. **Conservation:** General, environmental science, forest management, forestry, management/policy, wildlife/wilderness. **Education:** Music, special ed. **Engineering:** Applied physics, chemical, civil, computer, electrical, environmental, geological, mechanical, metallurgical, mining, water resource. **English:** English lit. **Foreign languages:** French, Spanish. **Health services:** Nursing (RN), preveterinary, speech pathology. **History:** General. **Human services:** Social work. **Math:** General. **Philosophy/religion:** Philosophy. **Physical sciences:** Atmospheric science, chemistry, geology, geophysics, physics. **Psychology:** General. **Social sciences:** Anthropology, criminology, geography, international relations, political science, sociology. **Visual/performing arts:** Art, art history/conservation, dramatic, music, music performance. **Work/family studies:** Child development, family studies.

Most popular majors. Biology 7%, business/marketing 15%, communications/journalism 6%, education 8%, engineering/engineering technologies 8%, health sciences 9%, liberal arts 6%, social sciences 13%.

Computing on campus. Dormitories wired for high-speed internet access and linked to campus network. Commuter students can connect to campus network. Online course registration, online library, helpline, repair service, student web hosting, wireless network available.

Student life. Freshman orientation: Mandatory, $110 fee. Preregistration for classes offered. Sessions held before each semester. Family members welcome. **Housing:** Coed dorms, single-sex dorms, special housing for disabled, apartments, wellness housing available. $325 partly refundable deposit. Special interest floors (fitness, arts and culture, stereo limitation, alcohol prohibition, honors) available. **Activities:** Bands, choral groups, dance, drama, film society, international student organizations, literary magazine, music ensembles, Model UN, musical theater, radio station, student government, student newspaper, symphony orchestra, Intervarsity Christian Fellowship, black student union, American Indian organization, Asian American Alliance, Chinese students association, Young Republicans, Young Democrats, Hillel, MEXA.

Athletics. NCAA. **Intercollegiate:** Baseball M, basketball, cross-country W, diving W, football (tackle) M, golf, rifle, soccer W, softball W, swimming W, tennis, track and field W, volleyball W. **Intramural:** Badminton, basketball, bowling, football (non-tackle), golf, racquetball, soccer, softball, swimming, table tennis, tennis, track and field, volleyball, water polo, weight lifting. **Team name:** Wolf Pack.

Student services. Adult student services, alcohol/substance abuse counseling, career counseling, services for economically disadvantaged, student employment services, financial aid counseling, health services, legal services, minority student services, on-campus daycare, personal counseling, placement for graduates, veterans' counselor, women's services. **Physically disabled:** Services for visually, speech, hearing impaired.

Contact. E-mail: asknevada@unr.edu
Phone: (775) 784-4700 Toll-free number: (866) 263-8232
Fax: (775) 784-4283
Steve Maples, Director of Admissions, University of Nevada: Reno, Mail
Stop 120, Reno, NV 89557

University of Phoenix: Las Vegas
Las Vegas, Nevada
www.phoenix.edu

- For-profit 4-year university
- Very large city
- 2,199 degree-seeking undergraduates

General. Regionally accredited. **Degrees:** 442 bachelor's awarded; master's offered. **Calendar:** Differs by program. **Full-time faculty:** 49 total. **Part-time faculty:** 354 total.

Basis for selection. Open admission, but selective for some programs.

2011-2012 Annual costs. Estimated costs as of August 2011: per-credit-hour charge, $420 to $450, depending upon level and course of study; electronic course materials fee, $95, if applicable. Book and material charges may vary by course and program. All fees are subject to change.

Application procedures. Admission: No deadline. No application fee. **Financial aid:** No deadline.

Academics. Credit/placement by examination: AP, CLEP.

Majors. Business: Accounting, business admin, finance. **Computer sciences:** Information technology. **Health services:** Health care admin. **History:** General. **Protective services:** Law enforcement admin. **Psychology:** General.

Contact. Marc Booker, Director of Admission and Evaluation, University of Phoenix: Las Vegas, 7455 West Washington Avenue, Las Vegas, NV 89128-4340

University of Phoenix: Northern Nevada
Reno, Nevada
www.phoenix.edu

- For-profit 4-year university
- Small city
- 367 degree-seeking undergraduates

General. Regionally accredited. **Degrees:** 70 bachelor's awarded; master's offered. **Calendar:** Differs by program. **Full-time faculty:** 16 total. **Part-time faculty:** 115 total.

Basis for selection. Open admission, but selective for some programs.

2011-2012 Annual costs. Estimated costs as of August 2011: per-credit-hour charge, $420 to $450, depending upon level and course of study; electronic course materials fee, $95, if applicable. Book and material charges may vary by course and program. All fees are subject to change.

Application procedures. Admission: No deadline. No application fee. **Financial aid:** No deadline.

Academics. Credit/placement by examination: AP, CLEP.

Majors. Business: Accounting, marketing. **Education:** General. **Health services:** Health care admin. **Protective services:** Law enforcement admin. **Psychology:** General.

Contact. Marc Booker, Director of Admission and Evaluation, University of Phoenix: Northern Nevada, 10345 Professional Circle, Suite 200, Reno, NV 89521-5862

New Hampshire

Chester College of New England
Chester, New Hampshire
www.chestercollege.edu

CB member
CB code: 3977

- Private 4-year visual arts and liberal arts college
- Residential campus in rural community
- 175 degree-seeking undergraduates
- SAT or ACT (ACT writing optional), application essay required

General. Founded in 1965. Regionally accredited. **Degrees:** 35 bachelor's awarded. **Location:** 10 miles from Manchester, 50 miles from Boston. **Calendar:** Semester, limited summer session. **Full-time faculty:** 13 total. **Part-time faculty:** 28 total. **Class size:** 98% < 20, 2% 20-39.

Freshman class profile.

GPA 3.50-3.74:	11%	Out-of-state:	49%
GPA 3.0-3.49:	33%	Live on campus:	67%
GPA 2.0-2.99:	53%		

Basis for selection. Admission criteria includes academic performance, SAT/ACT, personal essay, and art or writing portfolio (or both). Interviews encouraged. **Home schooled:** Statement describing home school structure and mission, interview, letter of recommendation (nonparent) required. Students may be required to complete an essay under examination conditions.

High school preparation. Recommended units include English 4, mathematics 3, social studies 2, history 2, science 3 and foreign language 1.

2011-2012 Annual costs. Tuition/fees: $19,730. Room/board: $8,900. Books/supplies: $700. Personal expenses: $1,320.

Financial aid. **Non-need-based:** Scholarships awarded for academics, art, state residency.

Application procedures. **Admission:** Closing date 2/1. $45 fee, may be waived for applicants with need. Admission notification on a rolling basis beginning on or about 1/15. Must reply by May 1 or within 2 week(s) if notified thereafter. **Financial aid:** Priority date 3/15; no closing date. FAFSA required. Applicants notified on a rolling basis starting 12/1; must reply within 2 week(s) of notification.

Academics. **Special study options:** Cross-registration, double major, independent study, internships, liberal arts/career combination, student-designed major, study abroad. **Credit/placement by examination:** AP, CLEP. 60 credit hours maximum toward bachelor's degree. **Support services:** Reduced course load, remedial instruction, study skills assistance, tutoring.

Majors. **Communications:** Digital media, media studies. **Computer sciences:** Web page design. **English:** Creative writing. **Visual/performing arts:** Art, graphic design, photography, studio arts.

Most popular majors. English 31%, interdisciplinary studies 7%, visual/performing arts 62%.

Computing on campus. 60 workstations in library, computer center, student center. Dormitories wired for high-speed internet access. Online library, wireless network available.

Student life. **Freshman orientation:** Mandatory. Preregistration for classes offered. Three-day orientation. **Housing:** Guaranteed on-campus for all undergraduates. Coed dorms available. $300 nonrefundable deposit, deadline 8/15. Pets allowed in dorm rooms. **Activities:** Drama, literary magazine, student government, campus activities board, service organization, gay-straight alliance.

Student services. Alcohol/substance abuse counseling, career counseling, financial aid counseling, personal counseling.

Contact. E-mail: admissions@chestercollege.edu
Phone: (603) 887-7400 Toll-free number: (800) 974-6372
Fax: (603) 887-1777
Michael Hayes, Director of Admission, Chester College of New England, 40 Chester Street, Chester, NH 03036

Colby-Sawyer College
New London, New Hampshire
www.colby-sawyer.edu

CB member
CB code: 3281

- Private 4-year liberal arts college
- Residential campus in small town
- 1,281 degree-seeking undergraduates: 1% part-time, 69% women
- 84% of applicants admitted
- Application essay required

General. Founded in 1837. Regionally accredited. **Degrees:** 204 bachelor's, 4 associate awarded. **ROTC:** Army, Air Force. **Location:** 30 miles from Hanover, 35 miles from Concord. **Calendar:** Semester. **Full-time faculty:** 71 total; 83% have terminal degrees, 14% minority, 51% women. **Part-time faculty:** 53 total; 24% minority, 66% women. **Class size:** 54% < 20, 45% 20-39, 1% 40-49. **Special facilities:** Fine arts center, laboratory school (pre-school, K-3), library learning center, conservatory and greenhouse, science center, weather station.

Freshman class profile. 3,425 applied, 2,891 admitted, 444 enrolled.

Out-of-state:	73%	Live on campus:	99%

Basis for selection. High school transcript most important. Recommendations, school and community activities, essay also considered. Test scores considered if submitted. Interviews highly recommended. Portfolio recommended for art program.

High school preparation. College-preparatory program required. 15 units required. Required units include English 4, mathematics 3, social studies 3, science 3 (laboratory 3) and foreign language 2. Nursing applicants strongly encouraged to have 3 years of college-preparatory lab sciences, including biology and chemistry.

2011-2012 Annual costs. Tuition/fees: $34,110. Room/board: $11,700. Books/supplies: $750. Personal expenses: $1,000.

2010-2011 Financial aid. **Need-based:** 301 full-time freshmen applied for aid; 301 were judged to have need; 301 of these received aid. Average need met was 61%. Average scholarship/grant was $13,107; average loan $3,056. 67% of total undergraduate aid awarded as scholarships/grants, 33% as loans/jobs. **Non-need-based:** Awarded to 1,827 full-time undergraduates, including 648 freshmen. Scholarships awarded for academics, alumni affiliation, art, leadership, minority status, music/drama.

Application procedures. **Admission:** No deadline. $45 fee, may be waived for applicants with need, free for online applicants. Admission notification on a rolling basis beginning on or about 12/15. **Financial aid:** Priority date 2/15, closing date 3/1. FAFSA required. Applicants notified on a rolling basis starting 2/1; must reply by 5/1 or within 2 week(s) of notification.

Academics. Liberal arts and experiential education integrated. Internships or senior research projects required in all major programs. **Special study options:** Combined bachelor's/graduate degree, double major, exchange student, honors, independent study, internships, semester at sea, study abroad, teacher certification program, Washington semester. **Credit/placement by examination:** AP, CLEP, IB, institutional tests. 15 credit hours maximum toward associate degree, 15 toward bachelor's. **Support services:** Learning center, reduced course load, study skills assistance, tutoring.

Majors. **Biology:** General. **Business:** Business admin. **Communications:** Media studies. **Conservation:** Environmental science, environmental studies. **Education:** General, art, early childhood, English, social studies. **English:** Creative writing, English lit. **Health services:** Athletic training, health care admin, nursing (RN), public health ed. **History:** General. **Parks/recreation:** Exercise sciences, sports admin. **Philosophy/religion:** General, philosophy. **Psychology:** General, developmental. **Social sciences:** Sociology. **Visual/performing arts:** Art, graphic design, studio arts.

Most popular majors. Business/marketing 18%, communications/journalism 7%, health sciences 17%, natural resources/environmental science 6%, parks/recreation 15%, psychology 12%, social sciences 6%, visual/performing arts 8%.

Computing on campus. 150 workstations in library, computer center. Dormitories wired for high-speed internet access and linked to campus network. Commuter students can connect to campus network. Online course registration, online library, helpline, wireless network available.

Student life. **Freshman orientation:** Mandatory. Preregistration for classes offered. Two days immediately preceding beginning of fall semester. **Housing:** Guaranteed on-campus for all undergraduates. Coed dorms, single-sex dorms, special housing for disabled, wellness housing available. $500 deposit, deadline 5/1. **Activities:** Choral groups, dance, drama, international student organizations, literary magazine, Model UN, musical theater, radio

station, student government, student newspaper, community service club, Safe Zones, cross cultural club, Christian Fellowship, Coalition for Peace and Justice, Student Democrats.

Athletics. NCAA. Intercollegiate: Baseball M, basketball, cross-country, diving, equestrian, field hockey W, lacrosse W, skiing, soccer, swimming, tennis, track and field, volleyball W. **Intramural:** Basketball, football (non-tackle), golf, soccer, volleyball. **Team name:** Chargers.

Student services. Alcohol/substance abuse counseling, career counseling, student employment services, financial aid counseling, health services, personal counseling. **Physically disabled:** Services for visually, hearing impaired.

Contact. E-mail: admissions@colby-sawyer.edu
Phone: (603) 526-3700 Toll-free number: (800) 272-1015
Fax: (603) 526-3452
Tracey Perkins, Director of Admission Counseling, Colby-Sawyer College, 541 Main Street, New London, NH 03257-7835

College of St. Mary Magdalen
Warner, New Hampshire
www.magdalen.edu   **CB code: 3562**

♦ Private 4-year liberal arts college affiliated with Roman Catholic Church
♦ Residential campus in small town
♦ 56 degree-seeking undergraduates: 48% women
♦ 96% of applicants admitted
♦ SAT or ACT (ACT writing recommended), application essay required

General. Regionally accredited. **Degrees:** 15 bachelor's, 5 associate awarded. **Location:** 20 miles from Concord. **Calendar:** Semester, limited summer session. **Full-time faculty:** 4 total. **Part-time faculty:** 6 total. **Special facilities:** Observatory.

Freshman class profile. 24 applied, 23 admitted, 14 enrolled.

End year in good standing:	91%	Out-of-state:	93%
Return as sophomores:	91%	Live on campus:	100%

Basis for selection. Academic GPA, high school record very important. College prep courses recommended. **Home schooled:** Transcript of courses and grades, letter of recommendation (nonparent) required.

High school preparation. College-preparatory program recommended. 24 units recommended. Recommended units include English 4, mathematics 4, social studies 3, history 2, science 3, foreign language 2 and academic electives 6.

2012-2013 Annual costs. Tuition/fees (projected): $19,000. Room/board: $7,500. Books/supplies: $600. Personal expenses: $400.

2010-2011 Financial aid. All financial aid based on need. 10 full-time freshmen applied for aid; 10 were judged to have need; 10 of these received aid. Average need met was 45%. Average scholarship/grant was $4,289; average loan $1,750. 41% of total undergraduate aid awarded as scholarships/grants, 59% as loans/jobs.

Application procedures. Admission: Priority date 12/31; deadline 5/1 (postmark date). $35 fee, may be waived for applicants with need, free for online applicants. Admission notification on a rolling basis. Must reply by May 1 or within 2 week(s) if notified thereafter. **Financial aid:** Priority date 3/15, closing date 6/30. Institutional form required. Applicants notified on a rolling basis starting 3/15; must reply by 7/1 or within 4 week(s) of notification.

Academics. Special study options: Honors, internships, study abroad. **Credit/placement by examination:** AP, CLEP. **Support services:** Study skills assistance, tutoring.

Majors. Liberal arts: Arts/sciences.

Computing on campus. Online library, wireless network available.

Student life. Freshman orientation: Mandatory. Preregistration for classes offered. Two-day program in early September just prior to beginning of fall semester. **Policies:** Professional dress code for class. Curfews in dormitories. Religious observance required. **Housing:** Guaranteed on-campus for all undergraduates. Single-sex dorms, wellness housing available. $500 nonrefundable deposit, deadline 4/1. **Activities:** Campus ministries, choral groups, drama, music ensembles, student government, campus service organization, college choir, French club, pro-life club, polyphony choir.

Athletics. Intramural: Basketball, fencing M, football (non-tackle) M, soccer, volleyball.

Student services. Chaplain/spiritual director, career counseling, student employment services, financial aid counseling.

Contact. E-mail: admissions@magdalen.edu
Phone: (603) 456-2656 ext. 114 Toll-free number: (877) 498-1723
Fax: (603) 456-2660
Tim Van Damm, Vice President of Advancement and Admissions, College of St. Mary Magdalen, 511 Kearsarge Mountain Road, Warner, NH 03278

Daniel Webster College
Nashua, New Hampshire   **CB member**
www.dwc.edu   **CB code: 3648**

♦ For-profit 4-year business and engineering college
♦ Residential campus in small city
♦ 641 degree-seeking undergraduates: 10% part-time, 21% women
♦ 50 degree-seeking graduate students
♦ 65% of applicants admitted
♦ SAT or ACT (ACT writing optional) required
♦ 46% graduate within 6 years; 5% enter graduate study

General. Founded in 1965. Regionally accredited. STEM institution: (Science, Technology, Engineering & Management), AT-CTI (Air Traffic Collegiate Training Initiative). **Degrees:** 212 bachelor's, 18 associate awarded; master's offered. **ROTC:** Army, Air Force. **Location:** 18 miles from Manchester, 47 miles from Boston. **Calendar:** Semester, limited summer session. **Full-time faculty:** 31 total; 45% have terminal degrees, 16% minority, 26% women. **Part-time faculty:** 52 total; 12% have terminal degrees, 2% minority, 35% women. **Class size:** 75% < 20, 20% 20-39, 5% 50-99. **Special facilities:** On campus flight center, aircraft, air-traffic-control simulation system, wind tunnel, robotic arm.

Freshman class profile. 652 applied, 421 admitted, 128 enrolled.

End year in good standing:	66%	Out-of-state:	64%
Return as sophomores:	63%	Live on campus:	68%

Basis for selection. High school transcript and test scores most important. Extracurricular activities considered. Interview highly recommended. **Home schooled:** Statement describing home school structure and mission, transcript of courses and grades, state high school equivalency certificate, interview, letter of recommendation (nonparent) required. Must submit portfolio outline of high school work.

High school preparation. College-preparatory program recommended. 16 units required. Required and recommended units include English 4, mathematics 3-4, social studies 2, history 2, science 3 (laboratory 2), foreign language 2 and computer science 1.

2011-2012 Annual costs. Tuition/fees: $14,645. Room/board: $10,290. Books/supplies: $1,200. Personal expenses: $1,500.

2011-2012 Financial aid. Need-based: Average need met was 44%. Average scholarship/grant was $4,912; average loan $3,378. 36% of total undergraduate aid awarded as scholarships/grants, 64% as loans/jobs. **Non-need-based:** Scholarships awarded for academics.

Application procedures. Admission: No deadline. No application fee. Admission notification on a rolling basis. Must reply by May 1 or within 2 week(s) if notified thereafter. **Financial aid:** Priority date 3/1; no closing date. FAFSA, institutional form required. Applicants notified on a rolling basis starting 3/15; must reply within 2 week(s) of notification.

Academics. Special study options: Accelerated study, combined bachelor's/graduate degree, distance learning, double major, dual enrollment of high school students, independent study, internships, liberal arts/career combination, semester at sea, study abroad. **Credit/placement by examination:** AP, CLEP, IB, institutional tests. 30 credit hours maximum toward associate degree, 30 toward bachelor's. **Support services:** Learning center, reduced course load, remedial instruction, study skills assistance, tutoring, writing center.

Majors. Business: General, business admin, management information systems, marketing. **Computer sciences:** General, artificial intelligence, computer science, information systems, LAN/WAN management. **Engineering:** Aerospace, mechanical. **Parks/recreation:** Sports admin. **Protective services:** Homeland security. **Psychology:** General. **Visual/performing arts:** Game design.

Most popular majors. Business/marketing 28%, engineering/engineering technologies 6%, parks/recreation 7%, trade and industry 46%.

Computing on campus. 182 workstations in library, computer center, student center. Dormitories wired for high-speed internet access and linked to campus network. Online library, helpline, repair service, student web hosting, wireless network available.

Student life. Freshman orientation: Mandatory. Preregistration for classes offered. Two-day program. **Policies:** Zero tolerance for drugs policy. **Housing:** Guaranteed on-campus for all undergraduates. Coed dorms, single-sex dorms, apartments available. Townhouses and suites for 4 to 7 students available. **Activities:** Jazz band, campus ministries, music ensembles, student government, Campus Crusade for Christ, gay-straight alliance, intercultural club.

Athletics. NCAA. **Intercollegiate:** Baseball M, basketball, cross-country, field hockey W, golf, lacrosse, soccer, softball W, volleyball. **Intramural:** Basketball, football (non-tackle), ice hockey M, soccer, volleyball. **Team name:** Eagles.

Student services. Adult student services, alcohol/substance abuse counseling, career counseling, student employment services, financial aid counseling, health services, personal counseling, placement for graduates, veterans' counselor.

Contact. E-mail: admissions@dwc.edu
Phone: (603) 577-6600 Toll-free number: (800) 325-6876 ext. 3
Fax: (603) 577-6001
Martin Nilsson, Director of Admissions, Daniel Webster College, 20 University Drive, Nashua, NH 03063

Dartmouth College
Hanover, New Hampshire **CB member**
www.dartmouth.edu **CB code: 3351**

- Private 4-year university and liberal arts college
- Residential campus in large town
- 4,106 degree-seeking undergraduates: 49% women, 8% African American, 14% Asian American, 9% Hispanic American, 3% Native American, 7% international
- 1,879 degree-seeking graduate students
- 10% of applicants admitted
- SAT or ACT with writing, SAT Subject Tests, application essay required
- 95% graduate within 6 years

General. Founded in 1769. Regionally accredited. **Degrees:** 1,076 bachelor's awarded; master's, professional, doctoral offered. **ROTC:** Army. **Location:** 130 miles from Boston. **Calendar:** Quarter, extensive summer session. **Full-time faculty:** 492 total. **Part-time faculty:** 155 total. **Special facilities:** Observatory; centers for humanities, social sciences, physical science, performing arts, ethics, life science, computation.

Freshman class profile. 22,385 applied, 2,270 admitted, 1,113 enrolled.

Mid 50% test scores			
SAT critical reading:	670-780	Rank in top tenth:	90%
SAT math:	680-780	Return as sophomores:	98%
SAT writing:	680-790	Out-of-state:	97%
ACT composite:	30-34	Live on campus:	100%
Rank in top quarter:	99%	International:	6%

Basis for selection. Evidence of intellectual capability, motivation, and personal integrity of primary importance. Talent, accomplishment, and involvement in nonacademic areas also evaluated. 2 SAT Subject Tests of student's choice required. Interview optional.

High school preparation. College-preparatory program recommended. Recommended units include English 4, mathematics 4, social studies 3, history 3 and science 3. Strongest academic program available to applicant recommended.

2011-2012 Annual costs. Tuition/fees: $42,996. Room/board: $12,369. Books/supplies: $1,730. Personal expenses: $1,381.

2010-2011 Financial aid. All financial aid based on need. Average need met was 100%. Average scholarship/grant was $36,994; average loan $3,114. 89% of total undergraduate aid awarded as scholarships/grants, 11% as loans/jobs.

Application procedures. Admission: Closing date 1/1 (postmark date). $75 fee, may be waived for applicants with need. Admission notification by 4/10. Must reply by 5/1. **Financial aid:** Closing date 2/1. FAFSA, CSS PROFILE required. Applicants notified by 4/10; must reply by 5/1.

Academics. Undergraduate research encouraged. **Special study options:** Combined bachelor's/graduate degree, double major, exchange student, honors, independent study, internships, semester at sea, student-designed major, study abroad, teacher certification program, Washington semester. Williams Mystic Seaport Maritime Studies program, study at Eugene O'Neill National Theater Institute, Twelve College Exchange, University of California-San Diego exchange program, McGill University exchange program, exchange programs with over 50 foreign universities, special academic programs in Washington, DC and Tucson, AZ. **Credit/placement by examination:** AP, CLEP, IB, SAT, ACT, institutional tests. **Support services:** Learning center, study skills assistance, tutoring, writing center.

Majors. Area/ethnic studies: African, African-American, Asian, Caribbean, Chicano/Hispanic-American/Latino, German, Latin American, Native American, Near/Middle Eastern, Russian/Slavic, Spanish/Iberian, women's. **Biology:** General, biochemistry, Biochemistry/molecular biology, cell/histology, ecology, evolutionary, genetics, molecular, neuroscience. **Computer sciences:** Computer science. **Conservation:** General, environmental studies. **Engineering:** Applied physics, biomedical, engineering science. **English:** English lit. **Foreign languages:** Arabic, Chinese, classics, comparative lit, French, German, Hebrew, Italian, Japanese, linguistics, Russian, South Asian, Spanish. **History:** General. **Math:** General. **Philosophy/religion:** Philosophy, religion. **Physical sciences:** Astronomy, chemistry, geology, physics. **Psychology:** General. **Social sciences:** Anthropology, economics, geography, political science, sociology. **Visual/performing arts:** Art history/conservation, dramatic, film/cinema/video, music, studio arts.

Most popular majors. Area/ethnic studies 7%, biology 10%, engineering/engineering technologies 7%, English 6%, history 7%, psychology 6%, social sciences 33%.

Computing on campus. PC or laptop required. Dormitories wired for high-speed internet access and linked to campus network. Commuter students can connect to campus network. Online course registration, online library, helpline, repair service, student web hosting, wireless network available.

Student life. Freshman orientation: Mandatory. Preregistration for classes offered. Held week before fall classes begin; freshmen trips led by outing club. **Housing:** Guaranteed on-campus for freshmen. Coed dorms, apartments, cooperative housing, fraternity/sorority housing, wellness housing available. Academic affinity housing, faculty-in-residence programs, special interest housing available. **Activities:** Bands, campus ministries, choral groups, dance, drama, film society, international student organizations, literary magazine, music ensembles, Model UN, musical theater, opera, radio station, student government, student newspaper, symphony orchestra, TV station, community and service programs, religious groups, and political and ethnic organizations available.

Athletics. NCAA. **Intercollegiate:** Baseball M, basketball, cross-country, diving, equestrian, field hockey W, football (tackle) M, golf, ice hockey, lacrosse, rowing (crew), sailing, skiing, soccer, softball W, squash, swimming, tennis, track and field, volleyball W. **Intramural:** Baseball M, basketball, bowling, cross-country, football (non-tackle), golf, handball, ice hockey, lacrosse, racquetball, skiing, soccer, softball, squash, swimming, table tennis, tennis, track and field, volleyball, water polo, wrestling M. **Team name:** Big Green.

Student services. Alcohol/substance abuse counseling, chaplain/spiritual director, career counseling, student employment services, financial aid counseling, health services, minority student services, on-campus daycare, personal counseling, placement for graduates, women's services. **Physically disabled:** Services for visually, speech, hearing impaired.

Contact. E-mail: admissions.office@dartmouth.edu
Phone: (603) 646-2875 Fax: (603) 646-1216
Maria Laskaris, Dean of Admissions and Financial Aid, Dartmouth College, 6016 McNutt Hall, Hanover, NH 03755

Franklin Pierce University
Rindge, New Hampshire **CB member**
www.franklinpierce.edu **CB code: 3395**

- Private 4-year university and liberal arts college
- Residential campus in small town
- 1,749 full-time, degree-seeking undergraduates
- 92% of applicants admitted
- SAT or ACT with writing, application essay required

General. Founded in 1962. Regionally accredited. **Degrees:** 390 bachelor's, 23 associate awarded; master's, professional, doctoral offered. **ROTC:** Army,

Air Force. **Location:** 20 miles from Keene, 60 miles from Boston. **Calendar:** Semester, limited summer session. **Full-time faculty:** 98 total; 74% have terminal degrees, 8% minority, 48% women. **Part-time faculty:** 216 total; 23% have terminal degrees, 2% minority, 52% women. **Class size:** 73% < 20, 25% 20-39, less than 1% 40-49, 2% 50-99. **Special facilities:** Glass blowing studio, ceramic studio, graphic design workshop, costume design, archaeological dig site, television studio, media production studios, wood-pellet heating systems.

Freshman class profile. 2,823 applied, 2,604 admitted, 366 enrolled.

GPA 3.75 or higher:	4%	Rank in top quarter:	37%
GPA 3.50-3.74:	6%	Rank in top tenth:	8%
GPA 3.0-3.49:	22%	Out-of-state:	82%
GPA 2.0-2.99:	62%	Live on campus:	94%

Basis for selection. School achievement record and difficulty of course work important. Community service, leadership and school involvement also primary considerations. Test scores used primarily for placement. Interview and campus visit recommended for all. **Home schooled:** Letter of recommendation (nonparent) required. **Learning Disabled:** Students with disabilities invited to contact Center for Academic Excellence.

High school preparation. College-preparatory program recommended. 16 units required. Required and recommended units include English 4, mathematics 3, social studies 3, history 3, science 3 (laboratory 2), foreign language 1, computer science 3, visual/performing arts 3 and academic electives 3.

2011-2012 Annual costs. Tuition/fees: $29,450. Room/board: $10,620. Books/supplies: $1,000.

Financial aid. Non-need-based: Scholarships awarded for academics, alumni affiliation, art, athletics, leadership.

Application procedures. Admission: No deadline. $40 fee. Admission notification on a rolling basis beginning on or about 10/1. Must reply by May 1 or within 2 week(s) if notified thereafter. **Financial aid:** Closing date 3/1. FAFSA, institutional form required. Applicants notified on a rolling basis starting 3/1; must reply within 2 week(s) of notification.

Academics. Special study options: Accelerated study, combined bachelor's/graduate degree, distance learning, double major, dual enrollment of high school students, ESL, exchange student, honors, independent study, internships, liberal arts/career combination, student-designed major, study abroad, teacher certification program, Washington semester. Semester abroad locations include Costa Rica, The Camino, Athens, Lyon, China; The Sundance Film Festival 2 Week Course Intensive; Coastal Ecology Intensives. **Credit/placement by examination:** AP, CLEP, IB, SAT, ACT, institutional tests. 12 credit hours maximum toward associate degree, 30 toward bachelor's. **Support services:** Learning center, reduced course load, remedial instruction, study skills assistance, tutoring, writing center.

Majors. Area/ethnic studies: American. **Biology:** General. **Business:** Accounting/finance, business admin, management information systems, management science, marketing. **Communications:** Media studies. **Computer sciences:** Information technology. **Conservation:** Environmental science. **Education:** General, elementary, secondary. **English:** English lit. **Health services:** Nursing (RN). **History:** General. **Human services:** Social work. **Liberal arts:** Arts/sciences. **Math:** General. **Parks/recreation:** Facilities management. **Protective services:** Criminal justice. **Psychology:** General. **Social sciences:** Anthropology, political science. **Visual/performing arts:** General, commercial/advertising art, dance, dramatic, graphic design, music, studio arts, studio arts management, theater arts management, theater design.

Most popular majors. Business/marketing 26%, communications/journalism 7%, security/protective services 9%, visual/performing arts 7%.

Computing on campus. 117 workstations in dormitories, library, computer center. Dormitories wired for high-speed internet access and linked to campus network. Commuter students can connect to campus network. Online library, helpline, repair service, wireless network available.

Student life. Freshman orientation: Mandatory. Preregistration for classes offered. Held immediately before start of semester and lasts several days into semester. **Housing:** Guaranteed on-campus for all undergraduates. Coed dorms, special housing for disabled, apartments, wellness housing available. $250 nonrefundable deposit, deadline 7/15. **Activities:** Bands, campus ministries, choral groups, dance, drama, film society, international student organizations, literary magazine, music ensembles, radio station, student government, student newspaper, TV station, ALANA, Agape Christian club, black student alliance, College Democrats, College Republicans, gay/straight alliance, Jewish students alliance, Students for a Better Tomorrow, Students for a Sensible Drug Policy.

Athletics. NCAA. **Intercollegiate:** Baseball M, basketball, cross-country, field hockey W, golf M, ice hockey, lacrosse, rowing (crew), soccer, softball W, tennis, track and field, volleyball W. **Intramural:** Baseball M, basketball,

cross-country, field hockey W, sailing, skiing, soccer, softball, table tennis, tennis, volleyball. **Team name:** Ravens.

Student services. Alcohol/substance abuse counseling, chaplain/spiritual director, career counseling, student employment services, financial aid counseling, health services, minority student services, personal counseling, placement for graduates, women's services.

Contact. E-mail: admissions@franklinpierce.edu
Phone: (603) 899-4050 Toll-free number: (800) 437-0048
Fax: (603) 899-4394
Linda Quimby, Director of Admissions, College at Rindge, Franklin Pierce University, 40 University Drive, Rindge, NH 03461-0060

Granite State College
Concord, New Hampshire
www.granite.edu   **CB code: 0458**

▸ Public 4-year liberal arts college
▸ Commuter campus in large town
▸ 1,557 degree-seeking undergraduates: 48% part-time, 70% women, 1% African American, 1% Asian American, 2% Hispanic American
▸ 52 degree-seeking graduate students
▸ 56% graduate within 6 years

General. Founded in 1972. Regionally accredited. **Degrees:** 327 bachelor's, 94 associate awarded; master's offered. **ROTC:** Army, Air Force. **Calendar:** Trimester, extensive summer session. **Full-time faculty:** 1 total; 100% have terminal degrees, 100% women. **Part-time faculty:** 168 total; 39% have terminal degrees, 1% minority, 70% women. **Class size:** 98% < 20, 2% 20-39.

Freshman class profile. 187 applied, 187 admitted, 83 enrolled.

Return as sophomores:	78%	Out-of-state:	4%

Basis for selection. Open admission, but selective for some programs. Accuplacer tests used for placement. **Home schooled:** State high school equivalency certificate required.

2011-2012 Annual costs. Tuition/fees: $8,460; $8,760 out-of-state.

Financial aid. All financial aid based on need.

Application procedures. Admission: No deadline. No application fee. Admission notification on a rolling basis. **Financial aid:** No deadline. FAFSA, institutional form required. Applicants notified on a rolling basis starting 4/15.

Academics. Special study options: Accelerated study, cross-registration, distance learning, double major, dual enrollment of high school students, independent study, internships, liberal arts/career combination, student-designed major, teacher certification program. **Credit/placement by examination:** AP, CLEP, institutional tests. 32 credit hours maximum toward associate degree, 64 toward bachelor's. Exams must support degree program. **Support services:** Learning center, reduced course load, remedial instruction, study skills assistance, tutoring, writing center.

Majors. Business: Management science. **Education:** Early childhood, elementary, elementary special ed, English, ESL, middle, reading, secondary, social studies. **Health services:** Health care admin. **Liberal arts:** Arts/sciences. **Protective services:** Criminal justice, law enforcement admin. **Psychology:** General.

Most popular majors. Business/marketing 20%, education 7%, interdisciplinary studies 35%, liberal arts 32%.

Computing on campus. 150 workstations in computer center, student center. Commuter students can connect to campus network. Online course registration, online library, helpline, wireless network available.

Student life. Freshman orientation: Available. Preregistration for classes offered. **Activities:** Alumni Learner Association, Green Team.

Student services. Adult student services, career counseling, financial aid counseling, veterans' counselor. **Physically disabled:** Services for visually, speech, hearing impaired.

Contact. E-mail: ruth.nawn@granite.edu
Phone: (603) 228-3000 ext. 339
Toll-free number: (888) 228-3000 ext. 339 Fax: (603) 513-1386
Ruth Nawn, Associate Director of Admissions, Granite State College, 8 Old Suncook Road, Concord, NH 03301-7317

Hesser College
Manchester, New Hampshire
www.hesser.edu   CB code: 3452

- For-profit 4-year business and junior college
- Residential campus in small city
- 4,148 undergraduates
- Application essay, interview required

General. Founded in 1900. Regionally accredited. Courses also available at centers in Nashua, Salem, Portsmouth, and Concord. **Degrees:** 215 bachelor's, 680 associate awarded. **Location:** 50 miles from Boston. **Calendar:** Semester, limited summer session. **Full-time faculty:** 21 total. **Part-time faculty:** 90 total. **Class size:** 68% < 20, 32% 20-39.

Freshman class profile.

Out-of-state:	25%	Live on campus:	18%

Basis for selection. Open admission, but selective for some programs. Selective requirements for physical therapist and graphic design programs. Portfolio recommended for fashion design, interior design and graphic design programs. **Learning Disabled:** Must meet with director of center for teaching, learning and assessment.

2011-2012 Annual costs. Estimated tuition and fees ranges for entire programs as of July 2011: diploma programs, $22,702 -$30,609; associate degree programs, $46,870 -$70,371; bachelor's degree programs, $93,950 - $93,450. Includes on-campus room and board, as well as books, fees, and supplies. All costs subject to change at any time. Books/supplies: $1,200. Personal expenses: $450.

Financial aid. All financial aid based on need. **Additional information:** Two private loans available to assist students in paying their balance; Tree Loan, SLM Loan.

Application procedures. Admission: No deadline. $20 fee, may be waived for applicants with need. Admission notification on a rolling basis. **Financial aid:** Priority date 5/1; no closing date. FAFSA, institutional form required. Applicants notified on a rolling basis starting 3/1; must reply within 3 week(s) of notification.

Academics. Special study options: Accelerated study, independent study, internships. **Credit/placement by examination:** AP, CLEP, IB, institutional tests. Max of 50% of total program credits awarded via CLEP, DSST, and AP exams. Max of 25% of total program credits awarded via institutional exams. **Support services:** Learning center, reduced course load, remedial instruction, tutoring, writing center.

Majors. Business: Accounting, business admin. **Protective services:** Law enforcement admin.

Computing on campus. 20 workstations in library, computer center. Dormitories wired for high-speed internet access. Helpline, repair service available.

Student life. Freshman orientation: Mandatory. Preregistration for classes offered. **Housing:** Guaranteed on-campus for freshmen. Single-sex dorms, wellness housing available. $125 deposit. **Activities:** Choral groups, radio station, student government, TV station, special interest organizations relating to accounting, business, travel, and retailing, community service club.

Athletics. NJCAA. **Intercollegiate:** Baseball M, basketball, soccer, softball W, volleyball. **Intramural:** Basketball, cheerleading W, football (non-tackle), soccer, volleyball. **Team name:** Blue Devils.

Student services. Alcohol/substance abuse counseling, career counseling, student employment services, financial aid counseling, health services, personal counseling, placement for graduates, veterans' counselor.

Contact. E-mail: admissions@hesser.edu
Phone: (603) 668-6660 ext. 2110
Toll-free number: (800) 526-9231 ext. 2110 Fax: (603) 666-4722
Keith Scheib, Assistant Director of Admissions, Hesser College, 3 Sundial Avenue, Manchester, NH 03103

Keene State College
Keene, New Hampshire   CB member
www.keene.edu   CB code: 3472

- Public 4-year liberal arts and teachers college
- Residential campus in large town

- 4,947 degree-seeking undergraduates: 3% part-time, 57% women, 1% African American, 1% Asian American, 3% Hispanic American
- 105 degree-seeking graduate students
- 75% of applicants admitted
- SAT or ACT (ACT writing recommended), application essay required
- 57% graduate within 6 years

General. Founded in 1909. Regionally accredited. **Degrees:** 1,133 bachelor's, 29 associate awarded; master's offered. **ROTC:** Air Force. **Location:** 52 miles from Concord, 85 miles from Boston. **Calendar:** Semester, extensive summer session. **Full-time faculty:** 206 total; 88% have terminal degrees, 8% minority, 48% women. **Part-time faculty:** 258 total; 55% women. **Class size:** 51% < 20, 43% 20-39, 4% 40-49, 2% 50-99. **Special facilities:** Arboretum and gardens, center for Holocaust studies, child development center, community research center, curriculum materials library, small business institute, college-owned camp, 400-acre preserve, theater complex.

Freshman class profile. 6,887 applied, 5,152 admitted, 1,262 enrolled.

Mid 50% test scores			
SAT critical reading:	450-550	GPA 3.0-3.49:	38%
SAT math:	450-550	GPA 2.0-2.99:	45%
SAT writing:	450-550	Rank in top quarter:	23%
ACT composite:	19-23	Rank in top tenth:	6%
GPA 3.75 or higher:	6%	Return as sophomores:	79%
GPA 3.50-3.74:	11%	Out-of-state:	58%
		Live on campus:	95%

Basis for selection. High school record, including challenging courses, most important. SAT/ACT scores do not hold nearly as much weight as high school performance. Audition required for music education and music performance programs; portfolio required for art program. **Home schooled:** Statement describing home school structure and mission required. **Learning Disabled:** Documented proof of disability required for some services.

High school preparation. College-preparatory program recommended. 14 units required. Required units include English 4, mathematics 3, social studies 2, science 3 and academic electives 2.

2011-2012 Annual costs. Tuition/fees: $11,800; $19,260 out-of-state. New England Regional Student Program tuition is 175% of in-state tuition. Per term tuition for winter/summer is $4,560 (in-state); $5,040 (out-of-state). Room/board: $8,810. Books/supplies: $900. Personal expenses: $750.

2010-2011 Financial aid. Need-based: 1,099 full-time freshmen applied for aid; 843 were judged to have need; 818 of these received aid. Average need met was 67%. Average scholarship/grant was $7,058; average loan $3,893. 46% of total undergraduate aid awarded as scholarships/grants, 54% as loans/jobs. **Non-need-based:** Awarded to 949 full-time undergraduates, including 204 freshmen. Scholarships awarded for academics, alumni affiliation, art, music/drama.

Application procedures. Admission: Closing date 4/1 (receipt date). $50 fee, may be waived for applicants with need. Admission notification on a rolling basis. Must reply by 5/1. **Financial aid:** Closing date 3/1. FAFSA required. Applicants notified on a rolling basis; must reply within 4 week(s) of notification.

Academics. Special study options: Combined bachelor's/graduate degree, cooperative education, double major, ESL, exchange student, honors, independent study, internships, liberal arts/career combination, student-designed major, study abroad, teacher certification program. **Credit/placement by examination:** AP, CLEP. 60 credit hours maximum toward bachelor's degree. **Support services:** Learning center, pre-admission summer program, reduced course load, study skills assistance, tutoring, writing center.

Majors. Architecture: Architecture. **Area/ethnic studies:** American, women's. **Biology:** General. **Business:** Business admin. **Communications:** Communications/speech/rhetoric, journalism. **Computer sciences:** General. **Conservation:** Environmental studies. **Education:** Biology, chemistry, computer, drama/dance, early childhood, elementary, English, French, history, mathematics, music, physical, science, secondary, social studies, Spanish, technology/industrial arts. **English:** English lit. **Foreign languages:** French, Spanish. **Health services:** General, athletic training, dietetics, nursing (RN), substance abuse counseling. **History:** General, American, European. **Math:** General. **Parks/recreation:** Exercise sciences, health/fitness. **Physical sciences:** General, chemistry, geology. **Psychology:** General, clinical, developmental, experimental, social. **Social sciences:** General, economics, geography, political science, sociology. **Visual/performing arts:** Acting, cinematography, commercial/advertising art, dance, directing/producing, film/cinema/video, music history, music performance, music theory/composition, studio arts, theater design, theater history.

Most popular majors. Business/marketing 7%, communications/journalism 10%, education 16%, engineering/engineering technologies 8%, psychology 12%, social sciences 12%, visual/performing arts 8%.

Computing on campus. 600 workstations in dormitories, library, computer center, student center. Dormitories wired for high-speed internet access and linked to campus network. Commuter students can connect to campus network. Online course registration, online library, helpline, repair service, student web hosting, wireless network available.

Student life. Freshman orientation: Mandatory. Preregistration for classes offered. **Policies:** Freshmen not permitted cars on campus. **Housing:** Coed dorms, single-sex dorms, apartments, fraternity/sorority housing, wellness housing available. $300 nonrefundable deposit, deadline 5/1. **Activities:** Bands, campus ministries, choral groups, dance, drama, film society, international student organizations, literary magazine, music ensembles, musical theater, radio station, student government, student newspaper, TV station, Big Brothers/Big Sisters, campus ecology, Christian Impact, Circle K, feminist collective, Habitat for Humanity, Interfaith Voices, pride club, Republican club, Newman student organization.

Athletics. NCAA. **Intercollegiate:** Baseball M, basketball, cheerleading M, cross-country, diving, field hockey W, lacrosse, soccer, softball W, swimming, track and field, volleyball W. **Intramural:** Badminton, basketball, bowling, cross-country, football (non-tackle), racquetball, soccer, softball, tennis, track and field, volleyball, water polo. **Team name:** Owls.

Student services. Adult student services, alcohol/substance abuse counseling, chaplain/spiritual director, career counseling, student employment services, financial aid counseling, health services, minority student services, on-campus daycare, personal counseling, placement for graduates, veterans' counselor, women's services. **Physically disabled:** Services for visually, speech, hearing impaired.

Contact. E-mail: kscadmissions@keene.edu
Phone: (603) 358-2276 Toll-free number: (800) 572-1909
Fax: (603) 358-2767
Margaret Richmond, Director of Admissions, Keene State College, 229 Main Street, Keene, NH 03435-2604

New England College
Henniker, New Hampshire
www.nec.edu
CB code: 3657

- Private 4-year liberal arts and teachers college
- Residential campus in small town
- 947 degree-seeking undergraduates: 5% part-time, 47% women, 5% African American, 2% Asian American, 4% Hispanic American, 7% international
- 707 degree-seeking graduate students
- 77% of applicants admitted
- Application essay required
- 39% graduate within 6 years; 22% enter graduate study

General. Founded in 1946. Regionally accredited. Cross-registration with other 4-year institutions available through New Hampshire College and University Council. **Degrees:** 171 bachelor's, 1 associate awarded; master's, professional offered. **ROTC:** Army, Air Force. **Location:** 18 miles from Concord. **Calendar:** Semester, limited summer session. **Full-time faculty:** 64 total; 69% have terminal degrees, 3% minority, 39% women. **Part-time faculty:** 100 total; 26% have terminal degrees, 5% minority, 49% women. **Class size:** 77% < 20, 22% 20-39, less than 1% 40-49. **Special facilities:** Center for Educational Innovation.

Freshman class profile. 1,985 applied, 1,523 admitted, 265 enrolled.

Mid 50% test scores			
SAT critical reading:	400-530	Rank in top quarter:	12%
SAT math:	400-540	Rank in top tenth:	3%
SAT writing:	400-520	End year in good standing:	59%
ACT composite:	18-23	Return as sophomores:	58%
GPA 3.75 or higher:	4%	Out-of-state:	66%
GPA 3.50-3.74:	8%	Live on campus:	90%
GPA 3.0-3.49:	21%	International:	7%
GPA 2.0-2.99:	52%	Fraternities:	5%
		Sororities:	4%

Basis for selection. School achievement record most important, followed by recommendations, essay or personal statement, evidence of leadership and extracurricular activities. Interview recommended for all; portfolio recommended for art program. **Home schooled:** Transcript of courses and grades, state high school equivalency certificate, letter of recommendation (nonparent) required.

High school preparation. College-preparatory program recommended. 12 units required. Required and recommended units include English 4, mathematics 2-3, social studies 2-3, science 2-3 (laboratory 1-2) and foreign language 2.

2011-2012 Annual costs. Tuition/fees: $30,400. Room/board: $11,954. Books/supplies: $1,000. Personal expenses: $1,500.

2011-2012 Financial aid. Need-based: 234 full-time freshmen applied for aid; 225 were judged to have need; 223 of these received aid. Average need met was 74%. Average scholarship/grant was $18,592; average loan $4,986. 76% of total undergraduate aid awarded as scholarships/grants, 24% as loans/jobs. **Non-need-based:** Awarded to 234 full-time undergraduates, including 60 freshmen. Scholarships awarded for academics, alumni affiliation, art, job skills, leadership, music/drama, state residency. **Additional information:** Significant scholarship programs for veterans including non-Post 911 eligible veterans.

Application procedures. Admission: No deadline. $30 fee, may be waived for applicants with need. Admission notification on a rolling basis beginning on or about 11/1. Must reply by May 1 or within 2 week(s) if notified thereafter. **Financial aid:** Priority date 4/1; no closing date. FAFSA required. Applicants notified on a rolling basis starting 1/12; must reply within 2 week(s) of notification.

Academics. Special study options: Accelerated study, combined bachelor's/graduate degree, cross-registration, distance learning, double major, dual enrollment of high school students, ESL, exchange student, external degree, honors, independent study, internships, liberal arts/career combination, semester at sea, student-designed major, study abroad, teacher certification program, Washington semester. Exchange programs with Regent's College, London; American University of Paris; 18 colleges in Quebec, Canada; University of the Sunshine Coast, Australia. Students keep all financial aid when abroad. **Credit/placement by examination:** AP, CLEP, IB, institutional tests. 21 credit hours maximum toward associate degree, 21 toward bachelor's. **Support services:** Learning center, reduced course load, remedial instruction, study skills assistance, tutoring, writing center.

Majors. Biology: General. **Business:** Accounting, business admin, entrepreneurial studies, finance, human resources, management information systems, marketing. **Communications:** Advertising, communications/speech/rhetoric, public relations. **Computer sciences:** General. **Conservation:** General, environmental science. **Education:** Art, biology, elementary, English, learning disabled, mathematics, physical, science, secondary, social science, social studies, special ed. **Engineering:** Civil. **English:** Creative writing, English lit. **Foreign languages:** Comparative lit. **Health services:** Health care admin, premedicine. **History:** General. **Liberal arts:** Arts/sciences. **Math:** General. **Parks/recreation:** General, exercise sciences, facilities management, sports admin. **Philosophy/religion:** Philosophy. **Protective services:** Criminal justice. **Psychology:** General, clinical, developmental. **Social sciences:** Political science, sociology. **Visual/performing arts:** Art, art history/conservation, dramatic, photography.

Most popular majors. Business/marketing 18%, education 10%, health sciences 6%, parks/recreation 20%, psychology 7%, security/protective services 7%, social sciences 6%, visual/performing arts 6%.

Computing on campus. 250 workstations in library, computer center, student center. Dormitories wired for high-speed internet access and linked to campus network. Commuter students can connect to campus network. Online course registration, online library, helpline, wireless network available.

Student life. Freshman orientation: Available. Preregistration for classes offered. Held 3 days prior to first day of classes and 3 mid-summer options. **Housing:** Guaranteed on-campus for all undergraduates. Coed dorms, apartments, fraternity/sorority housing, wellness housing available. $100 nonrefundable deposit, deadline 9/12. Quiet study options, special interest housing available. **Activities:** Dance, drama, international student organizations, literary magazine, radio station, student government, student newspaper, Hillel, Servcorps, environmental action committee, Womyn's Network, international diplomacy council, Adventure Bound, TEACH.

Athletics. NCAA. **Intercollegiate:** Baseball M, basketball, cross-country, field hockey W, ice hockey, lacrosse, soccer, softball W. **Intramural:** Baseball M, basketball, ice hockey, soccer, softball, table tennis, tennis, volleyball. **Team name:** Pilgrims.

Student services. Adult student services, alcohol/substance abuse counseling, career counseling, student employment services, financial aid counseling, health services, personal counseling, placement for graduates, veterans' counselor.

Contact. E-mail: admission@nec.edu
Phone: (603) 428-2223 Toll-free number: (800) 521-7642
Fax: (603) 428-3155
Diane Raymond, Dean of Admissions, New England College, 103 Bridge Street, Henniker, NH 03242

Plymouth State University
Plymouth, New Hampshire
www.plymouth.edu

CB member
CB code: 3690

- Public 4-year university and teachers college
- Residential campus in small town
- 4,315 degree-seeking undergraduates: 4% part-time, 48% women, 1% African American, 1% Asian American, 2% Hispanic American, 1% international
- 1,022 degree-seeking graduate students
- 74% of applicants admitted
- SAT or ACT with writing, application essay required
- 59% graduate within 6 years

General. Founded in 1871. Regionally accredited. **Degrees:** 845 bachelor's awarded; master's, doctoral offered. **ROTC:** Army, Air Force. **Location:** 60 miles from Manchester, 115 miles from Boston. **Calendar:** Semester, limited summer session. **Full-time faculty:** 187 total; 88% have terminal degrees, 8% minority, 46% women. **Part-time faculty:** 231 total; 21% have terminal degrees, less than 1% minority, 52% women. **Class size:** 48% < 20, 49% 20-39, 2% 40-49, 2% 50-99, less than 1% >100. **Special facilities:** Planetarium, cultural arts center, child development and family center, geographic information systems lab, meteorology institute, center for the environment, climbing wall, ropes course, ice arena.

Freshman class profile. 5,279 applied, 3,898 admitted, 1,018 enrolled.

Mid 50% test scores			
SAT critical reading:	440-530	GPA 2.0-2.99:	54%
SAT math:	440-530	Rank in top quarter:	18%
ACT composite:	18-21	Rank in top tenth:	5%
GPA 3.75 or higher:	4%	Return as sophomores:	74%
GPA 3.50-3.74:	5%	Out-of-state:	50%
GPA 3.0-3.49:	36%	Live on campus:	95%

Basis for selection. School achievement record (most important) followed by test scores, recommendations, essay and extracurricular activities. Audition required for music, theater, and dance programs. Portfolio required for art program. **Home schooled:** Transcript of any work attempted in secondary school, GED or homeschool diploma, outline of homeschool curriculum required.

High school preparation. College-preparatory program required. 13 units required; 18 recommended. Required and recommended units include English 4, mathematics 3, social studies 2-3, history 1-2, science 2-3 (laboratory 1) and foreign language 2.

2011-2012 Annual costs. Tuition/fees: $11,518; $18,978 out-of-state. New England Regional Student Program tuition is 175% of in-state tuition. Room/board: $9,290.

2010-2011 Financial aid. Need-based: 958 full-time freshmen applied for aid; 678 were judged to have need; 673 of these received aid. Average need met was 62%. Average scholarship/grant was $7,552; average loan $3,411. 42% of total undergraduate aid awarded as scholarships/grants, 58% as loans/jobs. **Non-need-based:** Awarded to 1,116 full-time undergraduates, including 388 freshmen. Scholarships awarded for academics, alumni affiliation, art, leadership, music/drama.

Application procedures. Admission: Closing date 4/1 (postmark date). $50 fee, may be waived for applicants with need. Admission notification on a rolling basis beginning on or about 10/1. Must reply by May 1 or within 2 week(s) if notified thereafter. Common Application used. **Financial aid:** Priority date 3/1; no closing date. FAFSA required. Applicants notified on a rolling basis starting 3/1.

Academics. Special study options: Cross-registration, distance learning, double major, dual enrollment of high school students, ESL, exchange student, external degree, honors, independent study, internships, semester at sea, student-designed major, study abroad, teacher certification program, Washington semester. **Credit/placement by examination:** AP, CLEP, institutional tests. 30 credit hours maximum toward bachelor's degree. **Support services:** Study skills assistance, tutoring, writing center.

Majors. Architecture: Urban/community planning. **Biology:** General, biotechnology, environmental. **Business:** General, accounting, business admin, finance, marketing, tourism/travel. **Communications:** Communications/speech/rhetoric. **Computer sciences:** Computer science, information technology. **Conservation:** Environmental studies. **Education:** Art, early childhood, elementary, health, mathematics, music, social studies. **English:** English lit. **Foreign languages:** French, Spanish. **Health services:** Athletic training, nursing (RN), public health ed. **History:** General. **Human services:** General, social work. **Liberal arts:** Humanities. **Math:** General. **Parks/recreation:**

Health/fitness, sports admin. **Philosophy/religion:** Philosophy. **Physical sciences:** Atmospheric science, chemistry. **Protective services:** Criminal justice. **Psychology:** General. **Social sciences:** General, anthropology, geography, political science, sociology. **Visual/performing arts:** Art, art history/conservation, dramatic, graphic design, music, studio arts.

Most popular majors. Business/marketing 27%, education 15%, parks/recreation 7%, security/protective services 6%, visual/performing arts 8%.

Computing on campus. 500 workstations in dormitories, library, computer center, student center. Dormitories wired for high-speed internet access and linked to campus network. Commuter students can connect to campus network. Online course registration, online library, helpline, repair service, student web hosting, wireless network available.

Student life. Freshman orientation: Mandatory. Preregistration for classes offered. Five sessions in June, one in September. **Housing:** Guaranteed on-campus for all undergraduates. Coed dorms, apartments, wellness housing available. $90 fully refundable deposit, deadline 5/1. Music/theater/dance housing, honors housing, special interest housing, community service, non-traditional, and quiet study/academic housing available. **Activities:** Bands, campus ministries, choral groups, dance, drama, film society, international student organizations, music ensembles, Model UN, musical theater, radio station, student government, student newspaper, Chi Alpha Christian Fellowship, multicultural student organization, Nicaragua club, volunteer club, social work club, health and wellness club, peer educators, Alternative Spring Break.

Athletics. NCAA. **Intercollegiate:** Baseball M, basketball, cheerleading M, diving W, field hockey W, football (tackle) M, ice hockey, lacrosse, skiing, soccer, softball W, swimming W, tennis W, volleyball W, wrestling M. **Intramural:** Basketball, soccer, softball, volleyball. **Team name:** Panthers.

Student services. Adult student services, alcohol/substance abuse counseling, chaplain/spiritual director, career counseling, student employment services, financial aid counseling, health services, on-campus daycare, personal counseling, placement for graduates, veterans' counselor, women's services. **Physically disabled:** Services for visually, hearing impaired.

Contact. E-mail: plymouthadmit@plymouth.edu
Phone: (603) 535-2237 Toll-free number: (800) 842-6900
Fax: (603) 535-2714
Eugene Fahey, Senior Associate Director of Admission, Plymouth State University, 17 High Street MSC 52, Plymouth, NH 03264-1595

Rivier College
Nashua, New Hampshire
www.rivier.edu

CB member
CB code: 3728

- Private 4-year nursing and liberal arts college affiliated with Roman Catholic Church
- Commuter campus in small city
- 1,370 degree-seeking undergraduates: 33% part-time, 85% women, 2% African American, 2% Asian American, 5% Hispanic American, 1% Native American
- 738 degree-seeking graduate students
- 81% of applicants admitted
- SAT or ACT with writing, application essay required
- 54% graduate within 6 years

General. Founded in 1933. Regionally accredited. Founded by the Sisters of the Presentation of Mary Convent. **Degrees:** 287 bachelor's, 139 associate awarded; master's, doctoral offered. **ROTC:** Army, Naval, Air Force. **Location:** 19 miles from Manchester, 45 miles from Boston. **Calendar:** Semester, limited summer session. **Full-time faculty:** 71 total; 72% have terminal degrees, 62% women. **Part-time faculty:** 122 total; 21% have terminal degrees, 72% women. **Class size:** 59% < 20, 38% 20-39, 1% 40-49, 2% 50-99. **Special facilities:** Center for finance and economics, early childhood center/laboratory school, biology research lab.

Freshman class profile. 680 applied, 548 admitted, 201 enrolled.

Mid 50% test scores			
SAT critical reading:	410-510	GPA 3.0-3.49:	59%
SAT math:	410-510	GPA 2.0-2.99:	28%
SAT writing:	420-520	Rank in top quarter:	27%
ACT composite:	17-21	Rank in top tenth:	6%
GPA 3.75 or higher:	3%	Return as sophomores:	78%
GPA 3.50-3.74:	9%	Out-of-state:	53%
		Live on campus:	65%

Basis for selection. High school academic record (course selection, course level, grades), test scores, extracurricular activities, application essay, and

letters of recommendation considered. Interview recommended for all; portfolio required for art programs. **Home schooled:** Transcript of courses and grades, interview required. Portfolio.

High school preparation. College-preparatory program recommended. 16 units recommended. Recommended units include English 4, mathematics 3, social studies 2, history 1, science 1 (laboratory 1), foreign language 2 and academic electives 3. Nursing program applicants must have completed chemistry, biology or anatomy and physiology as well as algebra in addition to a second higher math (geometry, precalc, calculus, algebra II).

2011-2012 Annual costs. Tuition/fees: $26,010. Room/board: $10,398. Books/supplies: $1,200. Personal expenses: $1,600.

Financial aid. Non-need-based: Scholarships awarded for academics, alumni affiliation.

Application procedures. Admission: Priority date 3/1; no deadline. $25 fee, may be waived for applicants with need, free for online applicants. Admission notification on a rolling basis beginning on or about 11/1. Must reply by May 1 or within 4 week(s) if notified thereafter. **Financial aid:** Priority date 3/1; no closing date. FAFSA required. Applicants notified on a rolling basis starting 3/1; must reply by 5/1 or within 2 week(s) of notification.

Academics. Special study options: Combined bachelor's/graduate degree, cross-registration, distance learning, double major, dual enrollment of high school students, honors, independent study, internships, liberal arts/career combination, study abroad, teacher certification program. **Credit/placement by examination:** AP, CLEP, IB, institutional tests. 12 credit hours maximum toward associate degree, 12 toward bachelor's. **Support services:** Learning center, reduced course load, study skills assistance, tutoring, writing center.

Majors. Biology: General. **Business:** Business admin, management information systems, marketing. **Communications:** Communications/speech/rhetoric. **Education:** General, biology, early childhood, elementary, English, foreign languages, history, mathematics, science, secondary, social science, social studies, Spanish. **English:** English lit. **Foreign languages:** Spanish. **Health services:** Nursing (RN), predental, premedicine, preop/surgical nursing, preveterinary. **History:** General. **Liberal arts:** Arts/sciences. **Math:** General. **Psychology:** General. **Social sciences:** General, political science, sociology. **Visual/performing arts:** Design, photography, studio arts.

Most popular majors. Business/marketing 15%, education 14%, health sciences 33%, psychology 7%, social sciences 11%.

Computing on campus. 150 workstations in dormitories, library, computer center, student center. Dormitories linked to campus network. Commuter students can connect to campus network. Online course registration, online library, helpline, repair service, wireless network available.

Student life. Freshman orientation: Mandatory, $100 fee. Preregistration for classes offered. Two-day on-campus program in June; parallel program for parents. **Housing:** Guaranteed on-campus for all undergraduates. Coed dorms, special housing for disabled, wellness housing available. $100 fully refundable deposit, deadline 5/1. **Activities:** Campus ministries, choral groups, dance, drama, international student organizations, literary magazine, Model UN, musical theater, student government, student newspaper, symphony orchestra, environmental activists, Amnesty International, Chinese student association, America Reads, Americorps, Habitat for Humanity.

Athletics. NCAA. **Intercollegiate:** Baseball M, basketball, cross-country, field hockey W, lacrosse, soccer, softball W, volleyball. **Intramural:** Basketball, football (non-tackle), softball, volleyball. **Team name:** Raiders.

Student services. Adult student services, alcohol/substance abuse counseling, chaplain/spiritual director, career counseling, student employment services, financial aid counseling, health services, minority student services, on-campus daycare, personal counseling, placement for graduates, veterans' counselor.

Contact. E-mail: rivadmit@rivier.edu
Phone: (603) 897-8507 Toll-free number: (800) 447-4843
Fax: (603) 891-1799
David Boisvert, Vice President for Enrollment Management, Rivier College, 420 South Main Street, Nashua, NH 03060-5086

Saint Anselm College
Manchester, New Hampshire
www.anselm.edu

CB member
CB code: 3748

- Private 4-year nursing and liberal arts college affiliated with Roman Catholic Church
- Residential campus in small city

- 1,873 degree-seeking undergraduates: 1% part-time, 58% women, 2% African American, 1% Asian American, 3% Hispanic American
- 71% of applicants admitted
- Application essay required
- 73% graduate within 6 years

General. Founded in 1889. Regionally accredited. Founded by Order of St. Benedict. **Degrees:** 449 bachelor's awarded. **ROTC:** Army. **Location:** 50 miles from Boston. **Calendar:** Semester, limited summer session. **Full-time faculty:** 142 total; 91% have terminal degrees, 9% minority, 51% women. **Part-time faculty:** 63 total; 25% have terminal degrees, 5% minority, 60% women. **Class size:** 58% < 20, 38% 20-39, less than 1% 40-49, 2% 50-99, 1% >100. **Special facilities:** Observatory, New Hampshire Institute of Politics, art center, ice arena, humanities and performing arts center, Abbey Church.

Freshman class profile. 4,134 applied, 2,953 admitted, 550 enrolled.

Mid 50% test scores			
SAT critical reading:	500-600	GPA 3.0-3.49:	43%
SAT math:	510-610	GPA 2.0-2.99:	29%
SAT writing:	510-600	Return as sophomores:	85%
ACT composite:	24-27	Out-of-state:	78%
GPA 3.75 or higher:	8%	Live on campus:	97%
GPA 3.50-3.74:	20%	International:	1%

Basis for selection. School achievement record and character most important, followed by test scores, 2 recommendations, essay. SAT/ACT required for applicants to nursing; optional for all others. Interview recommended. **Home schooled:** Statement describing home school structure and mission, interview, letter of recommendation (nonparent) required.

High school preparation. College-preparatory program required. 16 units required. Required and recommended units include English 4, mathematics 3-4, social studies 2-4, science 3-4 (laboratory 2) and foreign language 2-4.

2011-2012 Annual costs. Tuition/fees: $32,365. Room/board: $11,930.

2011-2012 Financial aid. Need-based: 511 full-time freshmen applied for aid; 435 were judged to have need; 434 of these received aid. Average need met was 80%. Average scholarship/grant was $19,410; average loan $4,565. 70% of total undergraduate aid awarded as scholarships/grants, 30% as loans/jobs. **Non-need-based:** Awarded to 525 full-time undergraduates, including 184 freshmen. Scholarships awarded for academics, alumni affiliation, art, athletics, leadership, music/drama.

Application procedures. Admission: Closing date 2/15 (postmark date). $55 fee, may be waived for applicants with need. Admission notification on a rolling basis beginning on or about 12/1. Must reply by 5/1. **Financial aid:** Closing date 3/15. FAFSA, CSS PROFILE required. Applicants notified on a rolling basis starting 3/1; must reply by 5/1 or within 2 week(s) of notification.

Academics. 4-semester humanities program required of all students. Special studies minors in addition to major concentrations available in fine arts (visual arts, theater, music), international studies, communications, computational physical science, human relations and work, French, Spanish, German, Latin, Greek, Russian area studies, Latin American studies, Asian studies, Catholic studies, medieval studies, neuroscience, public policy studies, web design, sports studies, gender studies, forensics, environmental studies, campaign management. **Special study options:** Cross-registration, dual enrollment of high school students, exchange student, honors, independent study, internships, liberal arts/career combination, semester at sea, study abroad, teacher certification program, Washington semester. **Credit/placement by examination:** AP, CLEP, IB, institutional tests. 30 credit hours maximum toward bachelor's degree. **Support services:** Learning center, reduced course load, study skills assistance, tutoring, writing center.

Majors. Biology: General, biochemistry. **Business:** General, accounting, finance, managerial economics. **Communications:** Media studies. **Computer sciences:** Computer science. **Conservation:** Environmental science. **Engineering:** General, applied physics. **English:** English lit. **Foreign languages:** Classics, French, Spanish. **Health services:** Nursing (RN), predental, premedicine. **History:** General. **Liberal arts:** Arts/sciences. **Math:** General. **Philosophy/religion:** Philosophy. **Physical sciences:** Chemistry, physics. **Protective services:** Criminal justice. **Psychology:** General. **Social sciences:** Economics, international relations, political science, sociology. **Theology:** Theology. **Visual/performing arts:** Art.

Most popular majors. Business/marketing 23%, English 6%, health sciences 14%, history 6%, psychology 8%, social sciences 23%.

Computing on campus. 400 workstations in dormitories, library, computer center, student center. Dormitories wired for high-speed internet access and linked to campus network. Commuter students can connect to campus

network. Online course registration, online library, helpline, repair service, wireless network available.

Student life. Freshman orientation: Available, $25 fee. Preregistration for classes offered. Held 3 days prior to fall semester. **Housing:** Guaranteed on-campus for all undergraduates. Coed dorms, single-sex dorms, apartments, wellness housing available. $200 nonrefundable deposit, deadline 5/1. Substance-free housing. **Activities:** Jazz band, campus ministries, choral groups, dance, drama, film society, international student organizations, literary magazine, music ensembles, Model UN, student government, student newspaper, Muslim student associations, black student alliance, Knights of Columbus, College Republicans, College Democrats, rugby club, Oxford Companions, volunteers center, music society, Radio Flyers.

Athletics. NCAA. **Intercollegiate:** Baseball M, basketball, cross-country, field hockey W, football (tackle) M, golf, ice hockey, lacrosse, skiing, soccer, softball W, tennis, volleyball W. **Intramural:** Basketball, football (non-tackle), handball, ice hockey, racquetball, skiing, soccer, softball, table tennis, tennis, volleyball. **Team name:** Hawks.

Student services. Alcohol/substance abuse counseling, chaplain/spiritual director, career counseling, student employment services, financial aid counseling, health services, minority student services, personal counseling, placement for graduates, veterans' counselor.

Contact. E-mail: admission@anselm.edu
Phone: (603) 641-7500 Toll-free number: (888) 426-7356
Fax: (603) 641-7550
Nancy Griffin, Dean of Admission, Saint Anselm College, 100 Saint Anselm Drive, Manchester, NH 03102-1310

Southern New Hampshire University
Manchester, New Hampshire
www.snhu.edu

CB member
CB code: 3649

- Private 4-year university and culinary school
- Residential campus in small city
- 6,906 degree-seeking undergraduates: 38% part-time, 59% women, 1% African American, 1% Asian American, 1% Hispanic American, 2% international
- 4,084 degree-seeking graduate students
- 84% of applicants admitted
- Application essay required
- 58% graduate within 6 years

General. Founded in 1932. Regionally accredited. Graduate programs and continuing education centers in Manchester, Nashua, Salem, New Hampshire seacoast, Brunswick (Maine) and online. **Degrees:** 1,208 bachelor's, 199 associate awarded; master's, doctoral offered. **ROTC:** Army. **Location:** 55 miles from Boston. **Calendar:** Continuous, extensive summer session. **Full-time faculty:** 115 total; 55% have terminal degrees, 9% minority, 45% women. **Part-time faculty:** 618 total; 34% have terminal degrees, 5% minority, 47% women. **Class size:** 63% < 20, 37% 20-39, less than 1% 40-49. **Special facilities:** Culinary institute, financial studies center, advertising agency, audiovisual studio, psychology observation lab, career development center, iMAC graphics lab.

Freshman class profile. 4,164 applied, 3,483 admitted, 812 enrolled.

Mid 50% test scores			
SAT critical reading:	430-530	Rank in top quarter:	25%
SAT math:	450-550	Rank in top tenth:	6%
SAT writing:	430-540	Return as sophomores:	71%
GPA 3.75 or higher:	6%	Out-of-state:	66%
GPA 3.50-3.74:	15%	Live on campus:	81%
GPA 3.0-3.49:	32%	International:	3%
GPA 2.0-2.99:	46%	Fraternities:	2%
		Sororities:	3%

Basis for selection. High school academic record weighed most heavily, including courses and course levels, grades, and class rank (if applicable). SAT/ACT, extracurricular activities, work experience, recommendations, and essay also considered. SAT or ACT recommended. Test scores and interview required for 3-year bachelor's program. For all other programs, SAT/ACT not required for admission but considered in awarding of merit-based financial aid. Interview recommended. Creative writing majors must submit samples of original writing.

High school preparation. College-preparatory program required. 12 units required. Required and recommended units include English 4, mathematics 3, social studies 2-3, science 2-3 (laboratory 1).

2011-2012 Annual costs. Tuition/fees: $27,240. Room/board: $10,584. Books/supplies: $1,000. Personal expenses: $1,000.

2010-2011 Financial aid. Need-based: 728 full-time freshmen applied for aid; 653 were judged to have need; 651 of these received aid. Average need met was 75%. Average scholarship/grant was $16,208; average loan $3,958. **Non-need-based:** Awarded to 752 full-time undergraduates, including 317 freshmen. Scholarships awarded for academics, alumni affiliation, athletics, job skills, leadership, state residency.

Application procedures. Admission: Priority date 3/15; no deadline. $40 fee, may be waived for applicants with need. Admission notification on a rolling basis beginning on or about 11/15. Must reply by May 1 or within 4 week(s) if notified thereafter. **Financial aid:** Priority date 3/1; no closing date. FAFSA required. Applicants notified on a rolling basis starting 3/15; must reply within 3 week(s) of notification.

Academics. Special study options: Accelerated study, combined bachelor's/graduate degree, cooperative education, cross-registration, distance learning, double major, dual enrollment of high school students, ESL, honors, independent study, internships, semester at sea, student-designed major, study abroad, teacher certification program, United Nations semester, Washington semester, weekend college. Three-year honors program in business administration. **Credit/placement by examination:** AP, CLEP, IB. 15 credit hours maximum toward associate degree, 15 toward bachelor's. **Support services:** Learning center, pre-admission summer program, reduced course load, remedial instruction, study skills assistance, tutoring.

Majors. Business: Accounting, accounting/finance, business admin, hospitality admin, international, marketing, operations, retailing, tourism/travel. **Communications:** Advertising. **Computer sciences:** General, information technology. **Conservation:** Environmental studies. **Education:** General, business, early childhood, elementary, English, mathematics, music, science, social studies. **English:** Creative writing, English lit. **History:** General. **Human services:** General. **Math:** General. **Parks/recreation:** Sports admin. **Psychology:** General. **Social sciences:** General, economics, political science. **Visual/performing arts:** Graphic design. **Work/family studies:** Child development.

Most popular majors. Business/marketing 65%, psychology 11%.

Computing on campus. PC or laptop required. 674 workstations in library, computer center. Dormitories wired for high-speed internet access and linked to campus network. Commuter students can connect to campus network. Online course registration, online library, helpline, repair service, wireless network available.

Student life. Freshman orientation: Mandatory, $100 fee. Preregistration for classes offered. Five 1-day sessions held in June; 3-day program held at opening of fall term. **Housing:** Coed dorms, special housing for disabled, apartments, wellness housing available. $200 partly refundable deposit, deadline 5/1. Women's floor, wellness housing available. **Activities:** Bands, campus ministries, choral groups, dance, drama, international student organizations, literary magazine, Model UN, musical theater, radio station, student government, student newspaper, TV station.

Athletics. NCAA. **Intercollegiate:** Baseball M, basketball, cheerleading, cross-country, golf M, ice hockey M, lacrosse, soccer, softball W, tennis, volleyball W. **Intramural:** Badminton, basketball, football (tackle), racquetball, skiing, soccer, softball, table tennis, tennis, volleyball W. **Team name:** Penmen.

Student services. Adult student services, alcohol/substance abuse counseling, chaplain/spiritual director, career counseling, student employment services, financial aid counseling, health services, personal counseling, placement for graduates, veterans' counselor. **Physically disabled:** Services for visually, speech, hearing impaired.

Contact. E-mail: admission@snhu.edu
Phone: (603) 645-9611 Toll-free number: (800) 642-4968
Fax: (603) 645-9693
Steve Soba, Director of Admission, Southern New Hampshire University, 2500 North River Road, Manchester, NH 03106-1045

Thomas More College of Liberal Arts
Merrimack, New Hampshire
www.thomasmorecollege.edu

CB code: 3892

- Private 4-year liberal arts college affiliated with Roman Catholic Church
- Residential campus in large town
- 73 degree-seeking undergraduates
- SAT or ACT (ACT writing optional), application essay required

General. Founded in 1978. Regionally accredited. **Degrees:** 22 bachelor's awarded. **Location:** 45 miles from Boston. **Calendar:** Semester. **Full-time faculty:** 8 total. **Part-time faculty:** 3 total. **Class size:** 80% < 20, 10% 20-39, 10% 50-99.

Basis for selection. Evidence of student's desire to learn important. Complete application includes essay, 2 academic letters of recommendation, high school transcript, and SAT/ACT. Interviews and/or visits strongly recommended.

High school preparation. 17 units required. Required units include English 4, mathematics 3, social studies 2, history 2, science 2 (laboratory 2) and foreign language 2. Recommended languages: Latin, French, German, Greek. Recommended electives: music, art.

2011-2012 Annual costs. Tuition/fees: $16,100. Room/board: $9,100. Books/supplies: $350. Personal expenses: $150.

Financial aid. Non-need-based: Scholarships awarded for academics.

Application procedures. Admission: No deadline. No application fee. Financial aid: Priority date 5/1; no closing date. FAFSA required. Applicants notified on a rolling basis starting 5/15; must reply within 2 week(s) of notification.

Academics. Each student, regardless of major, takes 6-hour humanities course every semester throughout 4 years: philosophy, literature, politics, history, theology taught by faculty from various disciplines. **Special study options:** Independent study, internships, liberal arts/career combination, study abroad. Sophomore semester in Rome, Italy. **Credit/placement by examination:** AP, CLEP. **Support services:** Tutoring, writing center.

Majors. Liberal arts: Arts/sciences.

Computing on campus. 7 workstations in library.

Student life. Freshman orientation: Mandatory. Preregistration for classes offered. **Housing:** Guaranteed on-campus for all undergraduates. Single-sex dorms available. Pets allowed in dorm rooms. **Activities:** Campus ministries, choral groups, dance, drama, literary magazine, music ensembles, student government.

Athletics. Intramural: Basketball, football (non-tackle), racquetball, skiing, soccer, swimming, table tennis, tennis, volleyball M, weight lifting.

Student services. Chaplain/spiritual director, career counseling, financial aid counseling, personal counseling.

Contact. E-mail: admissions@thomasmorecollege.edu
Phone: (800) 880-8308 ext. 14 Toll-free number: (800) 880-8308 ext. 14
Fax: (603) 880-9280
Mark Schwerdt, Director of Admissions, Thomas More College of Liberal Arts, Six Manchester Street, Merrimack, NH 03054-4818

University of New Hampshire
Durham, New Hampshire
www.unh.edu

CB member
CB code: 3918

- Public 4-year university
- Residential campus in small town
- 12,339 degree-seeking undergraduates: 2% part-time, 55% women, 1% African American, 2% Asian American, 2% Hispanic American, 1% international
- 2,257 degree-seeking graduate students
- 74% of applicants admitted
- SAT or ACT with writing, application essay required
- 77% graduate within 6 years; 36% enter graduate study

General. Founded in 1866. Regionally accredited. **Degrees:** 2,671 bachelor's, 130 associate awarded; master's, doctoral offered. **ROTC:** Army, Air Force. **Location:** 50 miles from Boston; 50 miles from Portland, ME. **Calendar:** Semester, extensive summer session. **Full-time faculty:** 621 total; 86% have terminal degrees, 10% minority, 38% women. **Part-time faculty:** 406 total; 24% have terminal degrees, 3% minority, 58% women. **Class size:** 42% < 20, 35% 20-39, 8% 40-49, 8% 50-99, 7% >100. **Special facilities:** Journalism laboratory, optical observatory, marine research laboratory, experiential learning center, child development center, agricultural and equine facilities, electron microscope, sawmill, nature preserve, radio station, research centers, survey center, TV station.

Freshman class profile. 17,344 applied, 12,863 admitted, 2,949 enrolled.

Mid 50% test scores		End year in good standing:	93%
SAT critical reading:	500-590	Return as sophomores:	87%
SAT math:	510-620	Out-of-state:	46%
SAT writing:	500-600	Live on campus:	94%
ACT composite:	23-27	International:	1%
Rank in top quarter:	58%	Fraternities:	6%
Rank in top tenth:	20%	Sororities:	6%

Basis for selection. School achievement record most important, followed by course selection, class rank, recommendations, test scores. Co-curricular activities, character/leadership considered. SAT Subject Tests can satisfy foreign language requirement for students in BA program. Audition required for music programs. **Home schooled:** Supporting documents include GED scores, transcripts, education plans, syllabi, homeschool association information.

High school preparation. College-preparatory program required. 15 units required; 19 recommended. Required and recommended units include English 4, mathematics 3-4, social studies 3, science 3-4 (laboratory 2-3), foreign language 2-3 and visual/performing arts 1. Additional requirements determined by intended major.

2011-2012 Annual costs. Tuition/fees: $15,250; $28,570 out-of-state. Room/board: $10,252. Books/supplies: $1,200. Personal expenses: $1,998.

2010-2011 Financial aid. Need-based: 2,368 full-time freshmen applied for aid; 1,909 were judged to have need; 1,878 of these received aid. Average need met was 82%. Average scholarship/grant was $4,885; average loan $2,645. 51% of total undergraduate aid awarded as scholarships/grants, 49% as loans/jobs. **Non-need-based:** Awarded to 2,507 full-time undergraduates, including 565 freshmen. Scholarships awarded for academics, art, athletics, leadership, music/drama, religious affiliation, ROTC.

Application procedures. Admission: Closing date 2/1 (postmark date). $50 fee ($65 out-of-state), may be waived for applicants with need. Admission notification by 4/15. Admission notification on a rolling basis. Must reply by 5/1. **Financial aid:** Closing date 3/1. FAFSA required. Applicants notified on a rolling basis starting 3/1; must reply by 5/1.

Academics. All students must complete a set of writing intensive courses, including freshman composition and three additional courses, one of which must be in the student's major and one of which must be an upper-level course. **Special study options:** Accelerated study, combined bachelor's/graduate degree, cooperative education, cross-registration, distance learning, double major, ESL, exchange student, honors, independent study, internships, semester at sea, student-designed major, study abroad, teacher certification program, United Nations semester, Washington semester. Undergraduate research opportunities, international undergraduate research opportunities program, service learning, capstone experiences, experiential learning. **Credit/placement by examination:** AP, CLEP, IB, institutional tests. 32 credit hours maximum toward associate degree, 64 toward bachelor's. **Support services:** Learning center, reduced course load, study skills assistance, tutoring, writing center.

Majors. Architecture: Urban/community planning. **Area/ethnic studies:** European, French, women's. **Biology:** General, Biochemistry/molecular biology, biomedical sciences, botany, entomology, genetics, neurobiology/behavior, zoology. **Business:** General, business admin, hospitality admin. **Communications:** Communications/speech/rhetoric. **Computer sciences:** General, information technology. **Conservation:** General, economics, environmental science, forest technology, forestry, wildlife/wilderness. **Education:** Mathematics. **Engineering:** Chemical, civil, computer, electrical, environmental, mechanical. **English:** English lit. **Foreign languages:** Ancient Greek, classics, French, German, Latin, linguistics, Russian, Spanish. **General:** Animal sciences, dairy, equestrian studies, horticultural science, sustainable agriculture. **Health services:** Athletic training, health care admin, nursing (RN), recreational therapy. **History:** General. **Human services:** Social work. **Liberal arts:** Humanities. **Math:** General. **Parks/recreation:** Exercise sciences, facilities management. **Philosophy/religion:** Philosophy. **Physical sciences:** Chemistry, geology, hydrology, materials science, physics. **Psychology:** General. **Social sciences:** Anthropology, criminology, economics, geography, political science, sociology. **Visual/performing arts:** Art, dramatic, music, studio arts. **Work/family studies:** Family studies.

Most popular majors. Biology 6%, business/marketing 16%, engineering/engineering technologies 7%, English 6%, health sciences 10%, psychology 7%, social sciences 15%.

Computing on campus. 448 workstations in library, computer center, student center. Dormitories wired for high-speed internet access and linked to campus network. Commuter students can connect to campus network. Online course registration, online library, helpline, repair service, student web hosting, wireless network available.

Student life. Freshman orientation: Mandatory. Preregistration for classes offered. Two-day program held in June with additional session in fall. Minority student orientation also offered. **Policies:** Freshmen not permitted cars on campus. **Housing:** Guaranteed on-campus for freshmen. Coed dorms, special housing for disabled, apartments, fraternity/sorority housing, wellness housing available. $200 partly refundable deposit, deadline 5/1. **Activities:** Bands, campus ministries, choral groups, dance, drama, film society, international student organizations, literary magazine, music ensembles, Model UN, musical theater, radio station, student government, student newspaper, symphony orchestra, TV station, diversity support coalition, black student union, Indian student association, United Asian Coalition, Chinese

students and scholars association, Intervarsity Christian Fellowship, Young Life, Catholic student organization, College Democrats, College Republicans.

Athletics. NCAA. **Intercollegiate:** Basketball, cross-country, diving W, field hockey W, football (tackle) M, gymnastics W, ice hockey, lacrosse W, skiing, soccer, swimming W, track and field, volleyball W. **Intramural:** Basketball, field hockey W, football (non-tackle), ice hockey, racquetball, soccer, softball, swimming, table tennis, tennis, volleyball, water polo. **Team name:** Wildcats.

Student services. Adult student services, alcohol/substance abuse counseling, chaplain/spiritual director, career counseling, services for economically disadvantaged, student employment services, financial aid counseling, health services, legal services, minority student services, on-campus daycare, personal counseling, placement for graduates, veterans' counselor, women's services. **Physically disabled:** Services for visually, speech, hearing impaired.

Contact. E-mail: admissions@unh.edu
Phone: (603) 862-1360 Fax: (603) 862-0077
Robert McGann, Director of Admissions, University of New Hampshire, 3 Garrison Avenue, Durham, NH 03824

University of New Hampshire at Manchester
Manchester, New Hampshire   **CB member**
www.manchester.unh.edu   **CB code: 2094**

▸ Public 4-year university and liberal arts college
▸ Commuter campus in small city
▸ 846 degree-seeking undergraduates: 22% part-time, 52% women, 1% African American, 2% Asian American, 3% Hispanic American
▸ 48% of applicants admitted
▸ SAT or ACT (ACT writing optional), application essay required

General. Founded in 1985. Regionally accredited. **Degrees:** 157 bachelor's, 34 associate awarded; master's offered. **ROTC:** Army, Air Force. **Location:** 35 miles from Concord, 55 miles from Boston. **Calendar:** Semester, limited summer session. **Full-time faculty:** 36 total. **Part-time faculty:** 104 total.

Freshman class profile. 207 applied, 99 admitted, 99 enrolled.

Mid 50% test scores			
		SAT writing:	450-550
SAT critical reading:	460-580	**Out-of-state:**	1%
SAT math:	460-570		

Basis for selection. Achievement in high school college preparatory program most important. SAT scores should be consistent with achievement. Recommendation, essay, interview very helpful for students of moderate achievement or in nontraditional cases. Interview necessary for college transition program. **Home schooled:** Transcript of courses and grades, state high school equivalency certificate, letter of recommendation (nonparent) required. GED, syllabus of curriculum encouraged; diploma from homeschool association requested if available. **Learning Disabled:** To be eligible for services, students must provide documentation of disability as determined by licensed physician and/or certified psychologist who is skilled in the diagnosis of disabilities. Documentation must be current (generally within 3 years).

High school preparation. College-preparatory program recommended. Required and recommended units include English 4, mathematics 3-4, social studies 3, science 3-4 (laboratory 1) and foreign language 2-3.

2011-2012 Annual costs. Tuition/fees: $12,640; $25,960 out-of-state. New England Regional Student Program tuition is 175% of in-state tuition. Books/supplies: $700. Personal expenses: $2,020.

Financial aid. Non-need-based: Scholarships awarded for academics, state residency.

Application procedures. Admission: Priority date 4/1; deadline 6/15 (postmark date). $45 fee ($60 out-of-state), may be waived for applicants with need. Admission notification on a rolling basis. Must reply by May 1 or within 3 week(s) if notified thereafter. **Financial aid:** Closing date 3/1. FAFSA required. Applicants notified on a rolling basis starting 4/1; must reply within 2 week(s) of notification.

Academics. Special study options: Combined bachelor's/graduate degree, cross-registration, double major, ESL, exchange student, external degree, independent study, internships, semester at sea, student-designed major, study abroad, teacher certification program, Washington semester. **Credit/placement by examination:** AP, CLEP, IB, institutional tests. 48 credit hours maximum toward associate degree, 64 toward bachelor's. **Support services:** Learning center, pre-admission summer program, reduced course load, remedial instruction, study skills assistance, tutoring, writing center.

Majors. Biology: General. **Business:** Business admin. **Communications:** Communications/speech/rhetoric. **Computer sciences:** General. **English:** English lit. **Foreign languages:** Sign language interpretation. **History:** General. **Liberal arts:** Arts/sciences, humanities. **Psychology:** General. **Social sciences:** Political science.

Computing on campus. 64 workstations in library, computer center. Commuter students can connect to campus network. Online library, helpline, wireless network available.

Student life. Freshman orientation: Mandatory, $30 fee. Preregistration for classes offered. 3.5-hour day or evening session held in June. **Housing:** Dormitories at New Hampshire Institute of Art available. **Activities:** Choral groups, dance, drama, musical theater, student government.

Athletics. Team name: Wildcats.

Student services. Career counseling, financial aid counseling, veterans' counselor. **Physically disabled:** Services for visually, speech, hearing impaired.

Contact. E-mail: unhm.admissions@unh.edu
Phone: (603) 641-4150 Fax: (603) 641-4342
Miho Bean, Associate Director of Admissions, University of New Hampshire at Manchester, 400 Commercial Street, Manchester, NH 03101-1113

New Jersey

Berkeley College
Woodland Park, New Jersey
www.berkeleycollege.edu

CB member
CB code: 2061

- For-profit 4-year business and career college
- Commuter campus in large town
- 3,363 degree-seeking undergraduates

General. Founded in 1931. Regionally accredited. Additional campuses in Paramus, Newark, and Woodbridge. **Degrees:** 314 bachelor's, 193 associate awarded. **Location:** 20 miles from New York City. **Calendar:** Quarter, extensive summer session. **Full-time faculty:** 78 total. **Part-time faculty:** 150 total. **Class size:** 36% < 20, 64% 20-39, less than 1% 40-49.

Basis for selection. Class rank, high school record, interview most important. Passing grade on school entrance/placement exam required. Interviews strongly recommended.

2011-2012 Annual costs. Tuition/fees: $21,750. Books/supplies: $1,360. Personal expenses: $3,000.

Financial aid. Non-need-based: Scholarships awarded for academics, alumni affiliation. **Additional information:** Alumni scholarship examination given in November and December. Full and partial scholarships awarded.

Application procedures. Admission: No deadline. $50 fee. Admission notification on a rolling basis. Admitted applicants must reply within 2 weeks of notification. **Financial aid:** No deadline. FAFSA required. Applicants notified on a rolling basis starting 3/1; must reply within 6 week(s) of notification.

Academics. Special study options: Accelerated study, distance learning, honors, internships, New York semester, study abroad. **Credit/placement by examination:** AP, CLEP, SAT, ACT, institutional tests. **Support services:** Learning center, pre-admission summer program, remedial instruction, study skills assistance, tutoring, writing center.

Majors. Business: Accounting, business admin, entrepreneurial studies, fashion, financial planning, human resources, international, marketing, nonprofit/public. **Health services:** Health care admin. **Protective services:** Law enforcement admin.

Computing on campus. 358 workstations in library, computer center, student center. Dormitories linked to campus network. Commuter students can connect to campus network. Online library, helpline, wireless network available.

Student life. Freshman orientation: Mandatory. Preregistration for classes offered. **Housing:** Coed dorms available. $400 deposit. **Activities:** Choral groups, drama, literary magazine, student government, Phi Beta Lambda, paralegal club, interior design club, athletic club, fashion and marketing club, Phi Theta Kappa.

Athletics. Team name: Bulldogs.

Student services. Adult student services, career counseling, student employment services, financial aid counseling, personal counseling, placement for graduates, veterans' counselor.

Contact. E-mail: info@berkeleycollege.edu
Phone: (973) 278-5400 ext. 1210 Toll-free number: (800) 446-5400
Fax: (973) 278-9141
David Bertone, Director for High School Admissions, Berkeley College, 44 Rifle Camp Road, Woodland Park, NJ 07424-0440

Beth Medrash Govoha
Lakewood, New Jersey

CB code: 2166

- Private 4-year rabbinical college for men affiliated with Jewish faith
- Residential campus in small city
- 2,676 degree-seeking undergraduates
- Interview required

General. Founded in 1943. Accredited by AARTS. Talmudical college. **Degrees:** 530 bachelor's awarded; master's offered. **Calendar:** Semester. **Full-time faculty:** 130 total. **Part-time faculty:** 20 total.

Basis for selection. Interviews required.

2011-2012 Annual costs. Tuition/fees: $16,316. Room/board: $4,172. Books/supplies: $450.

Application procedures. Admission: Closing date 8/15. $125 fee, may be waived for applicants with need. **Financial aid:** No deadline.

Academics. Credit/placement by examination: AP, CLEP.

Majors. Theology: Talmudic.

Student life. Housing: Apartments available.

Student services. Financial aid counseling, placement for graduates.

Contact. Phone: (732) 367-1060 Fax: (732) 370-6559
Rabbi Abraham Feuer, Director of Admissions, Beth Medrash Govoha, 617 Sixth Street, Lakewood, NJ 08701

Bloomfield College
Bloomfield, New Jersey
www.bloomfield.edu

CB member
CB code: 2044

- Private 4-year nursing and liberal arts college affiliated with Presbyterian Church (USA)
- Commuter campus in large town
- 2,123 degree-seeking undergraduates: 13% part-time, 64% women, 52% African American, 3% Asian American, 18% Hispanic American, 2% international
- 15 degree-seeking graduate students
- 50% of applicants admitted
- SAT or ACT (ACT writing optional), application essay required
- 30% graduate within 6 years; 14% enter graduate study

General. Founded in 1868. Regionally accredited. **Degrees:** 269 bachelor's awarded; master's offered. **ROTC:** Army. **Location:** 7 miles from Newark, 15 miles from New York City. **Calendar:** Semester, limited summer session. **Full-time faculty:** 70 total; 73% have terminal degrees, 24% minority, 59% women. **Part-time faculty:** 169 total; 13% have terminal degrees, 34% minority, 48% women. **Class size:** 75% < 20, 24% 20-39, less than 1% 40-49, less than 1% 50-99. **Special facilities:** Technology and multimedia center, performing arts center, art gallery.

Freshman class profile. 3,673 applied, 1,854 admitted, 392 enrolled.

Mid 50% test scores		Rank in top quarter:	32%
SAT critical reading:	380-470	Rank in top tenth:	9%
SAT math:	390-470	End year in good standing:	63%
GPA 3.75 or higher:	1%	Return as sophomores:	66%
GPA 3.50-3.74:	5%	Out-of-state:	6%
GPA 3.0-3.49:	21%	Live on campus:	43%
GPA 2.0-2.99:	68%		

Basis for selection. Acceptance for regular admission requires 900 SAT (exclusive of Writing) and 2.8 GPA. Interviews strongly recommended. Essays must be self-recommendations or reflections on previous educational experiences. Recently graded term paper can be substituted for essay. **Home schooled:** Statement describing home school structure and mission, transcript of courses and grades, state high school equivalency certificate, interview, letter of recommendation (nonparent) required. Applicants must submit SAT scores and official transcript with information about organization that performed accreditation/conversion. **Learning Disabled:** Students should ask for special accommodations for SAT testing.

High school preparation. College-preparatory program recommended. 14 units required.

2011-2012 Annual costs. Tuition/fees: $23,700. Room/board: $10,600. Books/supplies: $1,000. Personal expenses: $1,800.

2011-2012 Financial aid. Need-based: 378 full-time freshmen applied for aid; 370 were judged to have need; 370 of these received aid. Average need met was 53%. Average scholarship/grant was $15,864; average loan $3,333. 75% of total undergraduate aid awarded as scholarships/grants, 25%

as loans/jobs. **Non-need-based:** Scholarships awarded for academics, alumni affiliation, athletics, leadership.

Application procedures. Admission: Priority date 3/14; deadline 8/1 (postmark date). $40 fee, may be waived for applicants with need. Admission notification on a rolling basis beginning on or about 10/1. Must reply by May 1 or within 2 week(s) if notified thereafter. **Financial aid:** Priority date 3/15, closing date 6/1. FAFSA required. Applicants notified on a rolling basis starting 1/1; must reply within 2 week(s) of notification.

Academics. Organized into 7 divisions: Business and Computer Information Systems, Creative Arts and Technology, Humanities, Natural Science and Mathematics, Nursing, and Social and Behavioral Sciences, and Education. **Special study options:** Accelerated study, distance learning, double major, dual enrollment of high school students, ESL, honors, independent study, internships, liberal arts/career combination, student-designed major, study abroad, teacher certification program. Four-year clinical laboratory science program and allied health technologies major offered in conjunction with University of Medicine and Dentistry of New Jersey; joint BS/MS in computer information systems program offered with NJIT; special programs offered by the Institute for Technology and Professional Studies. **Credit/placement by examination:** AP, CLEP, SAT, ACT, institutional tests. 16 credit hours maximum toward bachelor's degree. Maximum of 16 course units may be earned through combination of CLEP examinations, portfolio assessment, and nursing assessment. **Support services:** Learning center, pre-admission summer program, remedial instruction, study skills assistance, tutoring, writing center.

Majors. Biology: General. **Business:** Accounting, business admin, e-commerce. **Computer sciences:** General, networking. **Education:** General. **English:** English lit. **Health services:** Nursing (RN). **History:** General. **Math:** General, applied. **Philosophy/religion:** Philosophy, religion. **Physical sciences:** Chemistry. **Psychology:** General. **Social sciences:** Political science, sociology. **Visual/performing arts:** General.

Most popular majors. Business/marketing 16%, education 7%, health sciences 12%, psychology 12%, social sciences 15%, visual/performing arts 23%.

Computing on campus. 100 workstations in dormitories, library, computer center, student center. Dormitories wired for high-speed internet access and linked to campus network. Commuter students can connect to campus network. Online library, helpline, student web hosting, wireless network available.

Student life. Freshman orientation: Mandatory. Preregistration for classes offered. Multi-day sessions offered prior to beginning of fall semester. **Policies:** Statement of Shared Values adopted, addressing student conduct and standards for behavior. **Housing:** Coed dorms available. $100 fully refundable deposit, deadline 5/1. Housing also provided at University Centre off-campus hotel in Newark. **Activities:** Campus ministries, dance, drama, international student organizations, radio station, student government, African Student Association, Association of Latin American students, Team Infinite, Modern Era Japanese Club, Gay/Non-Gay Alliance, Green Hearts Environmental Movement, Men's Empowerment Network, Black Student Union, Christian Fellowship, National Association of Black Accountants.

Athletics. NCAA. **Intercollegiate:** Baseball M, basketball, cross-country, soccer, softball W, tennis M, volleyball W. **Intramural:** Basketball, volleyball M. **Team name:** Deacons.

Student services. Adult student services, alcohol/substance abuse counseling, chaplain/spiritual director, career counseling, student employment services, financial aid counseling, health services, personal counseling, placement for graduates. **Physically disabled:** Services for visually, speech, hearing impaired.

Contact. E-mail: admission@bloomfield.edu
Phone: (973) 748-9000 ext. 230 Toll-free number: (800) 848-4555
Fax: (973) 748-0916
Nicole Cibelli, Director of Admissions, Bloomfield College, One Park Place, Bloomfield, NJ 07003

Caldwell College
Caldwell, New Jersey
www.caldwell.edu

CB member
CB code: 2072

♦ Private 4-year liberal arts college affiliated with Roman Catholic Church
♦ Commuter campus in large town
♦ 1,630 degree-seeking undergraduates: 23% part-time, 67% women, 16% African American, 2% Asian American, 14% Hispanic American, 5% international
♦ 599 degree-seeking graduate students

♦ 84% of applicants admitted
♦ SAT or ACT with writing, application essay required
♦ 48% graduate within 6 years

General. Founded in 1939. Regionally accredited. **Degrees:** 338 bachelor's awarded; master's, doctoral offered. **ROTC:** Army. **Location:** 20 miles from New York City. **Calendar:** Semester, limited summer session. **Full-time faculty:** 81 total. **Part-time faculty:** 135 total. **Class size:** 65% < 20, 34% 20-39, less than 1% 40-49.

Freshman class profile. 1,260 applied, 1,057 admitted, 302 enrolled.

Mid 50% test scores			
SAT critical reading:	410-510	GPA 2.0-2.99:	39%
SAT math:	400-510	Rank in top quarter:	35%
SAT writing:	410-520	Rank in top tenth:	8%
ACT composite:	17-23	Return as sophomores:	76%
GPA 3.75 or higher:	15%	Out-of-state:	10%
GPA 3.50-3.74:	16%	Live on campus:	58%
GPA 3.0-3.49:	29%	International:	5%

Basis for selection. School achievement record, test scores, interview, extracurricular activities very important. Counselor's recommendation, volunteer work important. Essay, interview recommended for all, audition required for music programs, portfolio required for art programs. **Home schooled:** Statement describing home school structure and mission required.

High school preparation. College-preparatory program required. 16 units required. Required units include English 4, mathematics 2, history 1, science 2 (laboratory 1), foreign language 2 and academic electives 5.

2011-2012 Annual costs. Tuition/fees: $26,890. Room/board: $10,500. Books/supplies: $1,200. Personal expenses: $1,000.

2011-2012 Financial aid. Need-based: 265 full-time freshmen applied for aid; 252 were judged to have need; 250 of these received aid. Average need met was 73%. Average scholarship/grant was $20,287; average loan $3,121. 74% of total undergraduate aid awarded as scholarships/grants, 26% as loans/jobs. **Non-need-based:** Awarded to 328 full-time undergraduates, including 50 freshmen. Scholarships awarded for academics, alumni affiliation, art, athletics, leadership, music/drama, religious affiliation.

Application procedures. Admission: Priority date 12/1; no deadline. $40 fee, may be waived for applicants with need. Admission notification on a rolling basis beginning on or about 12/31. Must reply by May 1 or within 2 week(s) if notified thereafter. **Financial aid:** Priority date 4/1; no closing date. FAFSA, institutional form required. Applicants notified on a rolling basis starting 3/1; must reply within 4 week(s) of notification.

Academics. Special study options: Accelerated study, combined bachelor's/graduate degree, cooperative education, distance learning, double major, dual enrollment of high school students, ESL, exchange student, external degree, honors, independent study, internships, liberal arts/career combination, student-designed major, study abroad, teacher certification program, Washington semester, weekend college. **Credit/placement by examination:** AP, CLEP, IB, SAT, ACT, institutional tests. 30 credit hours maximum toward bachelor's degree. Credit by exam only available during first year (30 credits) of matriculation. Credit toward major dependent on departmental approval. Prior Learning Assessment (PLA) for adult students who must attend PLA workshop. **Support services:** Learning center, pre-admission summer program, reduced course load, remedial instruction, study skills assistance, tutoring, writing center.

Majors. Biology: General. **Business:** Accounting, business admin, international, marketing. **Communications:** Communications/speech/rhetoric. **Computer sciences:** General, information technology. **Education:** Elementary, secondary. **English:** English lit. **Foreign languages:** Spanish. **Health services:** Clinical lab science, nursing (RN). **History:** General. **Math:** General. **Physical sciences:** Chemistry. **Protective services:** Criminal justice. **Psychology:** General. **Social sciences:** General, economics, political science, sociology. **Theology:** Theology. **Visual/performing arts:** Art, graphic design, music, studio arts.

Most popular majors. Biology 6%, business/marketing 22%, education 10%, English 7%, psychology 19%, security/protective services 9%, social sciences 12%.

Computing on campus. 284 workstations in dormitories, library, computer center, student center. Dormitories wired for high-speed internet access and linked to campus network. Online course registration, online library, helpline, wireless network available.

Student life. Freshman orientation: Mandatory, $200 fee. Preregistration for classes offered. Two-day overnight program held in June; 3-day program prior to start of fall semester includes move in day and a day dedicated to community service. **Housing:** Guaranteed on-campus for freshmen. Coed dorms, wellness housing available. $200 nonrefundable deposit, deadline 5/1.

Activities: Bands, campus ministries, choral groups, dance, drama, international student organizations, literary magazine, music ensembles, musical theater, student government, student newspaper, Caribbean student association, international student organization, international business club, Italian club, French club, Spanish club.

Athletics. NCAA. **Intercollegiate:** Baseball M, basketball, cross-country W, soccer, softball W, tennis, track and field W, volleyball W. **Intramural:** Basketball, cricket M, football (non-tackle), soccer, softball W, volleyball. **Team name:** Cougars.

Student services. Adult student services, alcohol/substance abuse counseling, chaplain/spiritual director, career counseling, services for economically disadvantaged, student employment services, financial aid counseling, health services, minority student services, personal counseling, placement for graduates, veterans' counselor, women's services. **Physically disabled:** Services for visually, hearing impaired.

Contact. E-mail: admissions@caldwell.edu
Phone: (973) 618-3500 Toll-free number: (888) 864-9516
Fax: (973) 618-3600
Stephen Quinn, Executive Director of Undergraduate Admissions, Caldwell College, 120 Bloomfield Avenue, Caldwell, NJ 07006-6195

Centenary College
Hackettstown, New Jersey
www.centenarycollege.edu

CB member
CB code: 2080

- Private 4-year liberal arts college affiliated with United Methodist Church
- Residential campus in large town
- 1,915 degree-seeking undergraduates: 6% part-time, 62% women
- 71 degree-seeking graduate students
- 88% of applicants admitted
- SAT or ACT, application essay required
- 50% graduate within 6 years

General. Founded in 1867. Regionally accredited. **Degrees:** 453 bachelor's, 55 associate awarded; master's offered. **Location:** 55 miles from New York City. **Calendar:** Semester, limited summer session. **Full-time faculty:** 75 total; 53% have terminal degrees, 7% minority, 56% women. **Part-time faculty:** 147 total; 45% women. **Class size:** 65% < 20, 35% 20-39. **Special facilities:** Equestrian center.

Freshman class profile. 1,060 applied, 930 admitted, 292 enrolled.

Mid 50% test scores			
SAT critical reading:	410-500	Rank in top quarter:	28%
SAT math:	410-500	Rank in top tenth:	11%
ACT composite:	16-21	Return as sophomores:	76%
GPA 3.75 or higher:	2%	Out-of-state:	26%
GPA 3.50-3.74:	3%	Live on campus:	81%
GPA 3.0-3.49:	22%	International:	1%
GPA 2.0-2.99:	70%	Fraternities:	1%
		Sororities:	1%

Basis for selection. School achievement record, standardized test scores most important. Interview, recommendations, community activities also strongly considered. Interviews required for academically marginal students with special needs; recommended for others. Portfolio required for art and design, graphic arts majors. **Home schooled:** State high school equivalency certificate required. **Learning Disabled:** Interview with Director of Services, documentation of psycho-education evaluation and IEP required for supportive services programs.

High school preparation. College-preparatory program recommended. 16 units required; 20 recommended. Required and recommended units include English 4, mathematics 3-4, social studies 2, science 2-4 (laboratory 1-2) and foreign language 2. Major-related courses on high school level recommended.

2011-2012 Annual costs. Tuition/fees: $28,890. Additional fees required for equine majors and for comprehensive learning support program. Room/board: $9,720. Books/supplies: $1,400. Personal expenses: $1,200.

2010-2011 Financial aid. Need-based: 266 full-time freshmen applied for aid; 238 were judged to have need; 238 of these received aid. Average need met was 73%. Average scholarship/grant was $19,087; average loan $3,903. 66% of total undergraduate aid awarded as scholarships/grants, 34% as loans/jobs. **Non-need-based:** Awarded to 382 full-time undergraduates, including 74 freshmen. Scholarships awarded for academics, alumni affiliation, art, leadership, minority status, music/drama, religious affiliation, state residency.

Application procedures. Admission: Priority date 3/1; no deadline. $30 fee, may be waived for applicants with need, free for online applicants.

Admission notification on a rolling basis beginning on or about 12/15. Must reply by May 1 or within 4 week(s) if notified thereafter. **Financial aid:** Priority date 4/1, closing date 6/1. FAFSA required. Applicants notified on a rolling basis starting 3/1.

Academics. Core curriculum required. Educational program balances career and liberal arts. **Special study options:** Accelerated study, combined bachelor's/graduate degree, cross-registration, distance learning, double major, dual enrollment of high school students, ESL, exchange student, honors, independent study, internships, liberal arts/career combination, student-designed major, study abroad, teacher certification program, weekend college. **Credit/placement by examination:** AP, CLEP, IB. 15 credit hours maximum toward associate degree, 30 toward bachelor's. **Support services:** Learning center, pre-admission summer program, reduced course load, remedial instruction, study skills assistance, tutoring, writing center.

Majors. Biology: General. **Business:** Accounting, business admin. **Communications:** Communications/speech/rhetoric. **Computer sciences:** General. **Education:** General. **English:** English lit. **General:** Equestrian studies. **History:** General. **Math:** General. **Protective services:** Criminal justice. **Psychology:** General. **Social sciences:** Political science, sociology. **Visual/performing arts:** Commercial/advertising art, dramatic, fashion design.

Most popular majors. Agriculture 7%, business/marketing 42%, English 7%, liberal arts 6%, psychology 7%, social sciences 9%, visual/performing arts 10%.

Computing on campus. PC or laptop required. 750 workstations in dormitories, library, computer center. Dormitories wired for high-speed internet access and linked to campus network. Commuter students can connect to campus network. Online course registration, online library, helpline, repair service, wireless network available.

Student life. Freshman orientation: Mandatory. Preregistration for classes offered. Three-day orientation prior to start of classes. **Housing:** Coed dorms available. $150 deposit, deadline 5/1. **Activities:** Campus ministries, dance, drama, film society, international student organizations, literary magazine, Model UN, musical theater, radio station, student government, student newspaper, TV station, art guild, student activities committee, service groups, fashion group, academic clubs, professional and honor societies, special interest clubs, Students in Free Enterprise.

Athletics. NCAA. **Intercollegiate:** Baseball M, basketball, cross-country, equestrian, golf, lacrosse, soccer, softball W, volleyball W, wrestling M. **Intramural:** Basketball M, equestrian M. **Team name:** Cyclones.

Student services. Adult student services, alcohol/substance abuse counseling, chaplain/spiritual director, career counseling, services for economically disadvantaged, student employment services, financial aid counseling, health services, minority student services, personal counseling, placement for graduates, women's services.

Contact. E-mail: admissions@centenarycollege.edu
Phone: (908) 852-1400 ext. 2217 Toll-free number: (800) 236-8679
Fax: (908) 852-3454
Dianne Finnan, Vice President for Enrollment Management and Strategic Branding, Centenary College, 400 Jefferson Street, Hackettstown, NJ 07840-9989

The College of New Jersey
Ewing, New Jersey
www.tcnj.edu

CB member
CB code: 2519

- Public 4-year liberal arts college
- Residential campus in large town
- 6,445 degree-seeking undergraduates: 2% part-time, 56% women, 6% African American, 7% Asian American, 10% Hispanic American
- 516 degree-seeking graduate students
- 46% of applicants admitted
- SAT or ACT (ACT writing optional), application essay required
- 87% graduate within 6 years; 28% enter graduate study

General. Founded in 1855. Regionally accredited. **Degrees:** 1,479 bachelor's awarded; master's offered. **ROTC:** Army, Air Force. **Location:** 35 miles from Philadelphia. **Calendar:** Semester, limited summer session. **Full-time faculty:** 351 total; 87% have terminal degrees, 22% minority, 50% women. **Part-time faculty:** 443 total; 25% have terminal degrees, 10% minority, 55% women. **Class size:** 37% < 20, 59% 20-39, 4% 40-49, less than 1% 50-99. **Special facilities:** Concert hall, electron microscopy lab, nuclear magnetic resonance lab, optical spectroscopy lab, observatory, planetarium, greenhouse.

Freshman class profile. 10,150 applied, 4,710 admitted, 1,371 enrolled.

Mid 50% test scores			
SAT critical reading:	550-650	Rank in top tenth:	56%
SAT math:	580-680	Return as sophomores:	95%
SAT writing:	560-660	Out-of-state:	7%
Rank in top quarter:	89%	Live on campus:	91%
		International:	1%

Basis for selection. Standardized test scores, high school rank and choice of curriculum very important. Extracurricular service, activities and community involvement considered. Audition required for music; portfolio required for art. **Home schooled:** Statement describing home school structure and mission, transcript of courses and grades, state high school equivalency certificate, letter of recommendation (nonparent) required.

High school preparation. College-preparatory program recommended. 18 units required; 20 recommended. Required and recommended units include English 4, mathematics 3, social studies 2-3, science 3 (laboratory 2-3) and foreign language 2-3.

2011-2012 Annual costs. Tuition/fees: $13,887; $23,696 out-of-state. Room/board: $10,677. Books/supplies: $1,000. Personal expenses: $1,500.

2010-2011 Financial aid. Need-based: 1,227 full-time freshmen applied for aid; 786 were judged to have need; 774 of these received aid. Average need met was 44%. Average scholarship/grant was $10,883; average loan $3,458. 41% of total undergraduate aid awarded as scholarships/grants, 59% as loans/jobs. **Non-need-based:** Awarded to 2,152 full-time undergraduates, including 836 freshmen. Scholarships awarded for academics, art, music/drama. **Additional information:** Merit scholarships available to New Jersey high school graduates based on academic distinction. Limited number of scholarships available to out-of-state students who demonstrate exceptional academic achievement in high school and on SAT. The EOF Promise Award meets the direct cost of attendance freshman and sophomore years, with merit scholarship awards available in junior and senior years.

Application procedures. Admission: Priority date 11/15; deadline 1/15 (postmark date). $75 fee, may be waived for applicants with need. Admission notification on a rolling basis beginning on or about 1/15. Must reply by 5/1. **Financial aid:** Priority date 3/1, closing date 10/1. FAFSA required. Applicants notified on a rolling basis starting 6/1; must reply within 2 week(s) of notification.

Academics. Special study options: Accelerated study, combined bachelor's/graduate degree, double major, dual enrollment of high school students, exchange student, honors, independent study, internships, liberal arts/career combination, semester at sea, student-designed major, study abroad, teacher certification program, Washington semester. Mentored Undergraduate Summer Experience (MUSE). **Credit/placement by examination:** AP, CLEP, IB, SAT, institutional tests. 30 credit hours maximum toward bachelor's degree. **Support services:** Learning center, pre-admission summer program, reduced course load, remedial instruction, study skills assistance, tutoring, writing center.

Majors. Area/ethnic studies: Women's. **Biology:** General. **Business:** Accounting, business admin. **Communications:** General. **Computer sciences:** General. **Education:** Art, biology, chemistry, Deaf/hearing impaired, early childhood, elementary, English, history, kindergarten/preschool, mathematics, music, physical, physics, social studies, Spanish, special ed, technology/industrial arts. **Engineering:** Biomedical, civil, computer, electrical, engineering science, mechanical. **English:** English lit. **Foreign languages:** Spanish. **Health services:** Nursing (RN). **History:** General. **Math:** General. **Philosophy/religion:** Philosophy. **Physical sciences:** Chemistry, physics. **Protective services:** Law enforcement admin. **Psychology:** General. **Social sciences:** Economics, international relations, political science, sociology. **Visual/performing arts:** General, art, commercial/advertising art, multimedia, music, studio arts.

Most popular majors. Biology 7%, business/marketing 19%, education 27%, English 6%, psychology 7%, social sciences 6%.

Computing on campus. 631 workstations in dormitories, library, computer center, student center. Dormitories wired for high-speed internet access and linked to campus network. Commuter students can connect to campus network. Online course registration, online library, helpline, repair service, student web hosting, wireless network available.

Student life. Freshman orientation: Mandatory, $165 fee. Preregistration for classes offered. Four-part program including June advisement week, summer readings, welcome week, college seminar. **Policies:** Freshmen not permitted cars on campus. **Housing:** Guaranteed on-campus for freshmen. Coed dorms, single-sex dorms, special housing for disabled, apartments, wellness housing available. $150 nonrefundable deposit, deadline 5/1. Pets allowed in dorm rooms. Housing for transfer students available. **Activities:** Bands, campus ministries, choral groups, dance, drama, international student organizations, literary magazine, music ensembles, Model UN, musical theater, opera, radio station, student government, student newspaper, symphony orchestra, TV station, black student union, Amnesty International, Circle K,

EOF Alliance, PRISM, UNBOUND, Hillel, activist coalition, women in learning & leadership.

Athletics. NCAA. **Intercollegiate:** Baseball M, basketball, cross-country, diving, field hockey W, football (tackle) M, lacrosse W, soccer, softball W, swimming, tennis, track and field, wrestling M. **Intramural:** Basketball, bowling, football (non-tackle), ice hockey, rugby, skiing, soccer, softball, tennis, volleyball, water polo. **Team name:** Lions.

Student services. Alcohol/substance abuse counseling, chaplain/spiritual director, career counseling, services for economically disadvantaged, student employment services, financial aid counseling, health services, minority student services, personal counseling, placement for graduates, veterans' counselor, women's services. **Physically disabled:** Services for visually, speech, hearing impaired.

Contact. E-mail: tcnjinfo@tcnj.edu
Phone: (609) 771-2131 Fax: (609) 637-5174
Grecia Montero, Director of Admissions, The College of New Jersey, 2000 Pennington Road Box 7718, Ewing, NJ 08628-0718

College of St. Elizabeth

Morristown, New Jersey
www.cse.edu

CB member
CB code: 2090

- Private 4-year liberal arts college for women affiliated with Roman Catholic Church
- Residential campus in large town
- 1,122 degree-seeking undergraduates: 47% part-time, 91% women, 22% African American, 5% Asian American, 16% Hispanic American, 4% international
- 690 degree-seeking graduate students
- 53% of applicants admitted
- SAT or ACT (ACT writing optional), application essay required
- 58% graduate within 6 years

General. Founded in 1899. Regionally accredited. Men admitted to adult undergraduate programs and master's programs. **Degrees:** 233 bachelor's awarded; master's, doctoral offered. **Location:** 40 miles from New York City. **Calendar:** Semester, limited summer session. **Full-time faculty:** 72 total; 83% have terminal degrees, 4% minority, 68% women. **Part-time faculty:** 150 total; 17% have terminal degrees, 6% minority, 64% women. **Class size:** 85% < 20, 14% 20-39, less than 1% 40-49, less than 1% >100. **Special facilities:** Library of rare books and manuscripts, Greek theater, Shakespeare garden, Holocaust education resource center, center for Catholic women's history, center for theological and spiritual development.

Freshman class profile. 1,486 applied, 782 admitted, 180 enrolled.

Mid 50% test scores			
SAT critical reading:	360-470	Rank in top tenth:	11%
SAT math:	370-470	Return as sophomores:	64%
SAT writing:	380-470	Out-of-state:	4%
Rank in top quarter:	27%	Live on campus:	86%
		International:	2%

Basis for selection. School achievement record and recommendations most important, followed by test scores, class rank; interview recommended. **Home schooled:** Letter of recommendation (nonparent) required. Applicants processed on individual basis. Must provide approved curriculum guide.

High school preparation. College-preparatory program required. 16 units required; 23 recommended. Required and recommended units include English 3-4, mathematics 2-3, history 1-3, science 1-2 (laboratory 1-2), foreign language 2 and academic electives 7.

2011-2012 Annual costs. Tuition/fees: $28,145. Room/board: $11,560.

2010-2011 Financial aid. Need-based: 115 full-time freshmen applied for aid; 115 were judged to have need; 115 of these received aid. Average need met was 80%. Average scholarship/grant was $21,022; average loan $3,701. 74% of total undergraduate aid awarded as scholarships/grants, 26% as loans/jobs. **Non-need-based:** Awarded to 612 full-time undergraduates, including 124 freshmen. Scholarships awarded for academics, alumni affiliation, art, leadership, state residency.

Application procedures. Admission: Priority date 3/1; deadline 8/15 (receipt date). $35 fee, may be waived for applicants with need. Admission notification on a rolling basis beginning on or about 11/15. Must reply by May 1 or within 2 week(s) if notified thereafter. **Financial aid:** Closing date 10/1. FAFSA required. Applicants notified on a rolling basis starting 11/15; must reply by 5/1 or within 2 week(s) of notification.

Academics. Students with 60 undergraduate credits may take accelerated program in business or communication on Saturdays and complete bachelor's degree in 2 years. **Special study options:** Accelerated study, combined bachelor's/graduate degree, cross-registration, distance learning, double major, dual enrollment of high school students, ESL, exchange student, honors, independent study, internships, liberal arts/career combination, student-designed major, study abroad, teacher certification program, United Nations semester, weekend college. Accelerated co-ed baccalaureate program with majors in business, communication, nursing and psychology for adults over age 23 with classes evenings and on Saturdays. **Credit/placement by examination:** AP, CLEP, IB, institutional tests. 30 credit hours maximum toward bachelor's degree. Credit for prior work and/or life experience offered via portfolio. **Support services:** Learning center, pre-admission summer program, reduced course load, remedial instruction, study skills assistance, tutoring.

Majors. Area/ethnic studies: American, women's. **Biology:** General, biochemistry. **Business:** Business admin. **Communications:** Communications/speech/rhetoric. **Computer sciences:** Computer science. **Education:** Multi-level teacher. **English:** English lit. **Foreign languages:** Spanish. **Health services:** Clinical lab science, dietetics, nursing (RN). **History:** General. **Math:** General. **Philosophy/religion:** Philosophy. **Physical sciences:** Chemistry. **Psychology:** General. **Social sciences:** Economics, sociology. **Theology:** Theology. **Visual/performing arts:** Art, music.

Most popular majors. Biology 7%, business/marketing 12%, education 9%, health sciences 31%, interdisciplinary studies 15%, psychology 7%.

Computing on campus. 127 workstations in dormitories, library, computer center. Dormitories wired for high-speed internet access and linked to campus network. Commuter students can connect to campus network. Helpline, wireless network available.

Student life. Freshman orientation: Mandatory, $200 fee. Preregistration for classes offered. Comprehensive program held before start of classes for Women's College students. **Housing:** Guaranteed on-campus for all undergraduates. Wellness housing available. $200 deposit. **Activities:** Campus ministries, choral groups, drama, literary magazine, music ensembles, student government, student newspaper, volunteer services center, international/intercultural club, Latin Roots, Students Take Action Committee, foreign language club, American Chemical Society Affiliates, psychology club, sociology club.

Athletics. NCAA. **Intercollegiate:** Basketball W, equestrian W, soccer W, softball W, swimming W, tennis W, volleyball W. **Intramural:** Volleyball W. **Team name:** Eagles.

Student services. Adult student services, alcohol/substance abuse counseling, chaplain/spiritual director, career counseling, services for economically disadvantaged, student employment services, financial aid counseling, health services, minority student services, personal counseling, placement for graduates, women's services. **Physically disabled:** Services for visually, speech, hearing impaired.

Contact. E-mail: apply@cse.edu
Phone: (973) 290-4700 Toll-free number: (800) 210-7900
Fax: (973) 290-4710
Donna Tatarka, Dean of Admission, College of St. Elizabeth, 2 Convent Road, Morristown, NJ 07960-6989

DeVry University: North Brunswick
North Brunswick, New Jersey
www.devry.edu | **CB code: 2203**

- For-profit 4-year university
- Commuter campus in small city
- Interview required

General. Founded in 1996. Regionally accredited. Additional location in Paramus. **Degrees:** 170 bachelor's, 118 associate awarded. **Location:** 30 miles from New York City. **Calendar:** Semester, extensive summer session. **Full-time faculty:** 38 total. **Part-time faculty:** 115 total.

Basis for selection. Applicants must have high school diploma or equivalent, degree from an accredited postsecondary institution, or submit acceptable test scores and be at least 17 years of age on the first day of classes. New students may enter at beginning of any semester. SAT or ACT recommended. CPT also accepted.

High school preparation. Required units include mathematics 1. Math unit must be algebra or higher.

2011-2012 Annual costs. Tuition/fees: $15,294. Books/supplies: $1,300. Personal expenses: $3,152.

Financial aid. All financial aid based on need.

Application procedures. Admission: No deadline. $50 fee. Admission notification on a rolling basis. **Financial aid:** No deadline. FAFSA required. Applicants notified on a rolling basis.

Academics. Special study options: Accelerated study, cooperative education, distance learning, weekend college. **Credit/placement by examination:** AP, CLEP, institutional tests. **Support services:** Learning center, remedial instruction, tutoring.

Majors. Business: Business admin. **Computer sciences:** Networking, systems analysis.

Most popular majors. Business/marketing 37%, computer/information sciences 46%, engineering/engineering technologies 16%.

Computing on campus. 575 workstations in library, computer center. Online course registration, online library, helpline available.

Student life. Freshman orientation: Mandatory. Preregistration for classes offered. **Activities:** Student government, Phi Theta Kappa, Golden Key, Institution of Electrical and Electronics Engineers, cultural exchange club, chess club, art club, Crusade for Christ.

Student services. Career counseling, student employment services, financial aid counseling, on-campus daycare, placement for graduates, veterans' counselor. **Physically disabled:** Services for visually, hearing impaired.

Contact. E-mail: admissions@devry.edu
Phone: (732) 435-4850 Toll-free number: (800) 333-3879
Fax: (732) 435-4850
Gerald Wargo, Director of Admissions, DeVry University: North Brunswick, 630 US Highway One, North Brunswick, NJ 08902-3362

Drew University
Madison, New Jersey | **CB member**
www.drew.edu | **CB code: 2193**

- Private 4-year university and liberal arts college affiliated with United Methodist Church
- Residential campus in large town
- 1,676 degree-seeking undergraduates: 1% part-time, 60% women, 9% African American, 5% Asian American, 14% Hispanic American, 2% international
- 883 degree-seeking graduate students
- 84% of applicants admitted
- 71% graduate within 6 years; 25% enter graduate study

General. Founded in 1867. Regionally accredited. Easily accessible to NYC via NJ transit train. **Degrees:** 350 bachelor's awarded; master's, professional, doctoral offered. **Location:** 30 miles from New York City. **Calendar:** Semester, limited summer session. **Full-time faculty:** 169 total; 98% have terminal degrees, 20% minority, 53% women. **Part-time faculty:** 124 total; 12% minority, 48% women. **Class size:** 72% < 20, 22% 20-39, 4% 40-49, 2% 50-99. **Special facilities:** 80-acre forest preserve, arboretum, photography gallery, observatory, research greenhouse, laser holography laboratory, center for the arts, music hall.

Freshman class profile. 4,195 applied, 3,527 admitted, 454 enrolled.

Mid 50% test scores		GPA 2.0-2.99:	18%
SAT critical reading:	500-630	Rank in top quarter:	71%
SAT math:	500-610	Rank in top tenth:	38%
SAT writing:	500-610	Return as sophomores:	79%
ACT composite:	21-28	Out-of-state:	36%
GPA 3.75 or higher:	27%	Live on campus:	86%
GPA 3.50-3.74:	18%	International:	4%
GPA 3.0-3.49:	37%		

Basis for selection. School achievement record most important; test scores also important. Interview recommended. **Home schooled:** Statement describing home school structure and mission, transcript of courses and grades required.

High school preparation. College-preparatory program recommended. Recommended units include English 4, mathematics 3, social studies 2, history 2, science 2, foreign language 2 and academic electives 3.

2011-2012 Annual costs. Tuition/fees: $41,304. Room/board: $11,150. Books/supplies: $1,128. Personal expenses: $2,180.

2010-2011 Financial aid. Need-based: 410 full-time freshmen applied for aid; 357 were judged to have need; 357 of these received aid. Average need met was 76%. Average scholarship/grant was $27,201; average loan $3,691. 85% of total undergraduate aid awarded as scholarships/grants, 15% as loans/jobs. **Non-need-based:** Awarded to 662 full-time undergraduates, including 140 freshmen. Scholarships awarded for academics, art, minority status, music/drama.

Application procedures. Admission: Closing date 2/15 (postmark date). $50 fee, may be waived for applicants with need. Admission notification on a rolling basis beginning on or about 11/15. Must reply by 5/1. **Financial aid:** Closing date 2/15. FAFSA required. Must reply by 5/1.

Academics. RISE program enables students to conduct scientific research with retired scientists. **Special study options:** Accelerated study, combined bachelor's/graduate degree, cross-registration, double major, honors, independent study, internships, New York semester, student-designed major, study abroad, teacher certification program, United Nations semester, Washington semester. Seven year dual degree (BA/MD) program with UMDNJ - New Jersey Medical School. Five year dual degree (BA/BS or B Eng) programs in engineering and technologies with Columbia University, Stevens Institute of Technology, and Washington University. Five year dual degree (BA/Master of Forestry or Master of Environmental Management) program with Duke University. **Credit/placement by examination:** AP, CLEP, IB, institutional tests. 32 credit hours maximum toward bachelor's degree. **Support services:** Learning center, pre-admission summer program, reduced course load, study skills assistance, tutoring, writing center.

Majors. Area/ethnic studies: African, gay/lesbian, women's. **Biology:** General, Biochemistry/molecular biology, neuroscience. **Business:** Business admin, managerial economics. **Computer sciences:** Computer science. **Conservation:** Environmental studies. **English:** English lit. **Foreign languages:** Chinese, classics, French, German, Spanish. **History:** General. **Math:** General. **Philosophy/religion:** Philosophy, religion. **Physical sciences:** Chemistry, physics. **Psychology:** General. **Social sciences:** Anthropology, economics, political science, sociology. **Visual/performing arts:** Art, art history/conservation, dramatic, music.

Most popular majors. Biology 11%, English 8%, foreign language 8%, psychology 7%, social sciences 29%, visual/performing arts 14%.

Computing on campus. PC or laptop required. Dormitories wired for high-speed internet access and linked to campus network. Commuter students can connect to campus network. Online course registration, online library, helpline, repair service, wireless network available.

Student life. Freshman orientation: Mandatory, $250 fee. Preregistration for classes offered. Held the week before start of fall semester. **Policies:** Freshmen not permitted cars on campus. **Housing:** Guaranteed on-campus for all undergraduates. Coed dorms, special housing for disabled, apartments, wellness housing available. $250 nonrefundable deposit, deadline 6/1. **Activities:** Campus ministries, choral groups, dance, drama, film society, literary magazine, music ensembles, Model UN, radio station, student government, student newspaper, symphony orchestra, Amnesty International, Hispanic student organization, College Democrats, College Republicans, Pan-African student organization, Inter-Varsity Christian Fellowship, Jewish student organization/Hillel, environmental action league, Students Against Violence Everywhere, The Alliance.

Athletics. NCAA. **Intercollegiate:** Baseball M, basketball, cross-country, equestrian, fencing, field hockey W, lacrosse, soccer, softball W, swimming, tennis. **Intramural:** Basketball, football (non-tackle), racquetball, soccer, softball, squash, table tennis, volleyball. **Team name:** Rangers.

Student services. Adult student services, alcohol/substance abuse counseling, chaplain/spiritual director, career counseling, services for economically disadvantaged, student employment services, financial aid counseling, health services, minority student services, on-campus daycare, personal counseling, placement for graduates, women's services. **Physically disabled:** Services for visually, hearing impaired.

Contact. E-mail: cadm@drew.edu
Phone: (973) 408-3739 Fax: (973) 408-3068
Renee Volak, Vice President for Enrollment Management, Drew University, 36 Madison Avenue, Madison, NJ 07940-4063

Fairleigh Dickinson University: College at Florham
Madison, New Jersey
www.fdu.edu   CB code: 2262

◗ Private 4-year university
◗ Residential campus in large town

◗ 2,349 degree-seeking undergraduates: 5% part-time, 56% women, 11% African American, 4% Asian American, 11% Hispanic American, 1% Native American, 1% international
◗ 674 degree-seeking graduate students
◗ 66% of applicants admitted
◗ SAT or ACT (ACT writing optional) required
◗ 55% graduate within 6 years

General. Regionally accredited. Additional campus locations: Wroxton College, England and Vancouver, Canada. **Degrees:** 458 bachelor's awarded; master's offered. **ROTC:** Army, Air Force. **Location:** 27 miles from New York City. **Calendar:** Semester, extensive summer session. **Full-time faculty:** 131 total; 74% have terminal degrees, 18% minority, 42% women. **Part-time faculty:** 263 total; 12% minority, 43% women. **Class size:** 55% < 20, 44% 20-39, less than 1% 40-49, less than 1% 50-99, less than 1% >100. **Special facilities:** ITV multimedia classrooms, web-iab, regional center for college students with learning disabilities.

Freshman class profile. 4,332 applied, 2,851 admitted, 588 enrolled.

Mid 50% test scores			
SAT critical reading:	450-560	Rank in top quarter:	40%
SAT math:	460-570	Rank in top tenth:	15%
SAT writing:	450-560	Return as sophomores:	72%
GPA 3.75 or higher:	16%	Out-of-state:	23%
GPA 3.50-3.74:	14%	Live on campus:	83%
GPA 3.0-3.49:	32%	Fraternities:	10%
GPA 2.0-2.99:	38%	Sororities:	10%

Basis for selection. GPA and test scores most important. **Learning Disabled:** Separate application along with admissions application.

High school preparation. College-preparatory program required. 14 units required; 16 recommended. Required and recommended units include English 4, mathematics 3, history 2, science 2-3 (laboratory 2) and academic electives 3-4.

2011-2012 Annual costs. Tuition/fees: $35,437. Room/board: $11,662.

Application procedures. Admission: Priority date 1/15; no deadline. $40 fee, may be waived for applicants with need, free for online applicants. Admission notification on a rolling basis beginning on or about 11/28. Must reply by May 1 or within 2 week(s) if notified thereafter. **Financial aid:** Priority date 2/15; no closing date. FAFSA required. Applicants notified on a rolling basis starting 2/1; must reply by 5/1 or within 4 week(s) of notification.

Academics. Special study options: Accelerated study, combined bachelor's/graduate degree, cooperative education, cross-registration, distance learning, double major, external degree, honors, independent study, internships, liberal arts/career combination, student-designed major, study abroad, teacher certification program, Washington semester, weekend college. **Credit/placement by examination:** AP, CLEP, SAT, institutional tests. 30 credit hours maximum toward bachelor's degree. **Support services:** Learning center, pre-admission summer program, reduced course load, remedial instruction, study skills assistance, tutoring, writing center.

Majors. Biology: General, biochemistry. **Business:** Accounting, business admin, entrepreneurial studies, hospitality admin, managerial economics, marketing. **Communications:** Communications/speech/rhetoric. **Computer sciences:** General. **English:** Creative writing, English lit. **Foreign languages:** French, Spanish. **Health services:** Clinical lab science, medical radiologic technology/radiation therapy, nursing (RN), respiratory therapy technology. **History:** General. **Liberal arts:** Humanities. **Math:** General. **Philosophy/religion:** Philosophy. **Physical sciences:** Chemistry. **Psychology:** General. **Social sciences:** Criminology, economics, political science, sociology. **Visual/performing arts:** General, cinematography, dramatic.

Most popular majors. Business/marketing 34%, communications/journalism 8%, English 6%, liberal arts 6%, psychology 15%, social sciences 7%, visual/performing arts 10%.

Computing on campus. 150 workstations in library, computer center. Dormitories wired for high-speed internet access and linked to campus network. Commuter students can connect to campus network. Online library, helpline, wireless network available.

Student life. Freshman orientation: Mandatory. Preregistration for classes offered. **Policies:** Freshmen not permitted cars on campus. **Housing:** Guaranteed on-campus for freshmen. Coed dorms, special housing for disabled available. $350 nonrefundable deposit, deadline 5/1. **Activities:** Pep band, campus ministries, choral groups, dance, drama, film society, international student organizations, literary magazine, radio station, student government, student newspaper, Green club, Florham Programming Committee, Association of Black Collegians, Latin American student organization, Hillel, New Social Engine, Straight and Gay Alliance, Student Volunteer Association, Musician's Guild, animal rights club.

Athletics. NCAA. **Intercollegiate:** Baseball M, basketball, cross-country, field hockey W, football (tackle) M, golf, lacrosse, soccer, softball W, swimming, tennis, volleyball W. **Intramural:** Basketball, football (tackle), soccer, softball, volleyball, weight lifting. **Team name:** Devils.

Student services. Adult student services, alcohol/substance abuse counseling, chaplain/spiritual director, career counseling, services for economically disadvantaged, student employment services, financial aid counseling, health services, minority student services, personal counseling, placement for graduates, veterans' counselor, women's services. **Physically disabled:** Services for visually, speech, hearing impaired.

Contact. E-mail: globaleducation@fdu.edu
Phone: (800) 338-8803 Toll-free number: (800) 338-8803
Fax: (973) 443-8088
Jonathan Wexler, Vice President of Enrollment Management, Fairleigh Dickinson University: College at Florham, 285 Madison Avenue, Madison, NJ 07940

Fairleigh Dickinson University: Metropolitan Campus

Teaneck, New Jersey
www.fdu.edu   CB code: 2263

‣ Private 4-year university
‣ Commuter campus in large town
‣ 4,045 degree-seeking undergraduates: 32% part-time, 58% women, 14% African American, 6% Asian American, 33% Hispanic American, 7% international
‣ 2,466 degree-seeking graduate students
‣ 62% of applicants admitted
‣ SAT or ACT (ACT writing optional) required
‣ 41% graduate within 6 years

General. Founded in 1942. Regionally accredited. Additional campus at Wroxton College, England and Vancouver Canada. **Degrees:** 828 bachelor's, 64 associate awarded; master's, professional, doctoral offered. **ROTC:** Army, Air Force. **Location:** 13 miles from New York City. **Calendar:** Semester, extensive summer session. **Full-time faculty:** 191 total; 76% have terminal degrees, 20% minority, 44% women. **Part-time faculty:** 580 total; 23% minority, 46% women. **Class size:** 67% < 20, 30% 20-39, 2% 40-49, 2% 50-99, less than 1% >100. **Special facilities:** ITV multimedia classrooms, photonics lab, regional center for college students with learning disabilities, psychological services center, marine biology lab, cyber crime lab.

Freshman class profile. 6,466 applied, 4,038 admitted, 716 enrolled.

Mid 50% test scores			
SAT critical reading:	440-530	GPA 2.0-2.99:	34%
SAT math:	460-560	Rank in top quarter:	42%
SAT writing:	440-540	Rank in top tenth:	17%
GPA 3.75 or higher:	16%	Return as sophomores:	72%
GPA 3.50-3.74:	19%	Out-of-state:	14%
GPA 3.0-3.49:	31%	Live on campus:	40%
		International:	8%

Basis for selection. Standardized test scores and GPA most important. **Learning Disabled:** Regional center for college students with learning disabilities requires additional application.

High school preparation. College-preparatory program required. 14 units required; 18 recommended. Required and recommended units include English 4, mathematics 3, history 2, science 2-3 (laboratory 2), foreign language 2 and academic electives 3-4.

2011-2012 Annual costs. Tuition/fees: $32,973. Room/board: $12,046.

Application procedures. Admission: Priority date 3/15; no deadline. $40 fee, may be waived for applicants with need, free for online applicants. Admission notification on a rolling basis beginning on or about 11/28. Must reply by May 1 or within 2 week(s) if notified thereafter. **Financial aid:** Priority date 2/15; no closing date. Applicants notified on a rolling basis starting 3/1; must reply by 5/1 or within 2 week(s) of notification.

Academics. Core curriculum consists of 4 interdisciplinary courses. **Special study options:** Accelerated study, combined bachelor's/graduate degree, cooperative education, cross-registration, distance learning, double major, ESL, exchange student, honors, independent study, internships, liberal arts/career combination, student-designed major, study abroad, teacher certification program, Washington semester, weekend college. **Credit/placement by examination:** AP, CLEP, institutional tests. 30 credit hours maximum toward bachelor's degree. **Support services:** Learning center, pre-admission summer

program, reduced course load, remedial instruction, study skills assistance, tutoring, writing center.

Majors. Biology: General, biochemistry, marine. **Business:** Accounting, business admin, entrepreneurial studies, finance, hospitality admin, managerial economics, marketing, nonprofit/public. **Communications:** Organizational. **Computer sciences:** Computer science, information technology. **Conservation:** Environmental science. **Engineering:** Electrical. **English:** English lit. **Foreign languages:** French, Spanish. **Health services:** Clinical lab science, medical records admin, nursing (RN), radiologic technology/medical imaging. **History:** General. **Liberal arts:** Humanities. **Math:** General. **Philosophy/religion:** Philosophy. **Physical sciences:** Chemistry, physics. **Protective services:** Law enforcement admin. **Psychology:** General. **Social sciences:** Economics, international relations, political science, sociology. **Visual/performing arts:** General.

Most popular majors. Business/marketing 8%, health sciences 13%, liberal arts 51%, psychology 6%.

Computing on campus. 225 workstations in library, computer center. Dormitories wired for high-speed internet access and linked to campus network. Commuter students can connect to campus network. Online library, helpline, wireless network available.

Student life. Freshman orientation: Mandatory. Preregistration for classes offered. **Housing:** Coed dorms, single-sex dorms available. $350 nonrefundable deposit, deadline 5/1. LIFE house, honor's house, global scholar's hall. **Activities:** Campus ministries, choral groups, dance, drama, film society, international student organizations, literary magazine, music ensembles, musical theater, radio station, student government, student newspaper, over 70 organizations.

Athletics. NCAA. **Intercollegiate:** Baseball M, basketball, bowling W, cross-country, fencing W, golf, soccer, softball W, tennis, track and field, volleyball W. **Intramural:** Badminton, basketball, football (non-tackle), soccer, table tennis, volleyball. **Team name:** Knights.

Student services. Adult student services, alcohol/substance abuse counseling, chaplain/spiritual director, career counseling, services for economically disadvantaged, student employment services, financial aid counseling, health services, minority student services, personal counseling, placement for graduates, veterans' counselor, women's services. **Physically disabled:** Services for visually, speech, hearing impaired.

Contact. E-mail: globaleducation@fdu.edu
Phone: (201) 692-2553 Toll-free number: (800) 338-8803
Fax: (201) 692-7319
Jonathan Wexler, Associate Vice President for Admissions and Financial Aid, Fairleigh Dickinson University: Metropolitan Campus, 1000 River Road, H-DH3-10, Teaneck, NJ 07666-1996

Felician College

Lodi, New Jersey
www.felician.edu   CB code: 2321

‣ Private 4-year liberal arts college affiliated with Roman Catholic Church
‣ Commuter campus in large town
‣ 1,918 degree-seeking undergraduates: 19% part-time, 74% women
‣ 368 degree-seeking graduate students
‣ 81% of applicants admitted
‣ SAT or ACT (ACT writing optional) required

General. Founded in 1942. Regionally accredited. Additional campus in Rutherford. All programs spread through both campuses. **Degrees:** 351 bachelor's, 15 associate awarded; master's offered. **ROTC:** Army, Air Force. **Location:** 12 miles from New York City. **Calendar:** Semester, limited summer session. **Full-time faculty:** 113 total; 62% women. **Part-time faculty:** 115 total; 58% women. **Class size:** 76% < 20, 23% 20-39, less than 1% 40-49, less than 1% 50-99, less than 1% >100. **Special facilities:** Nursing skills laboratory, performance and theater facilities.

Freshman class profile. 2,116 applied, 1,723 admitted, 344 enrolled.

GPA 3.75 or higher:	12%	Rank in top quarter:	25%
GPA 3.50-3.74:	9%	Rank in top tenth:	8%
GPA 3.0-3.49:	32%	Out-of-state:	9%
GPA 2.0-2.99:	43%		

Basis for selection. School achievement record, test scores most important. Interview, school and community activities, recommendations of high school counselor considered. Interview recommended for all; portfolio recommended for art programs.

High school preparation. College-preparatory program recommended. 19 units recommended. Recommended units include English 4, mathematics 3, social studies 3, science 3 and academic electives 6. Biology, chemistry, algebra required for nursing and medical laboratory technology applicants.

2011-2012 Annual costs. Tuition/fees: $27,925. Room/board: $10,750. Books/supplies: $1,200. Personal expenses: $1,890.

2010-2011 Financial aid. Need-based: 68% of total undergraduate aid awarded as scholarships/grants, 32% as loans/jobs. **Non-need-based:** Scholarships awarded for academics, alumni affiliation, athletics, religious affiliation.

Application procedures. Admission: No deadline. $30 fee, may be waived for applicants with need. Admission notification on a rolling basis beginning on or about 11/15. Must reply by May 1 or within 2 week(s) if notified thereafter. **Financial aid:** Priority date 6/1; no closing date. FAFSA required. Applicants notified on a rolling basis starting 4/1; must reply within 2 week(s) of notification.

Academics. Post-baccalaureate certification available in elementary and secondary education. **Special study options:** Accelerated study, combined bachelor's/graduate degree, cooperative education, cross-registration, distance learning, double major, dual enrollment of high school students, ESL, honors, independent study, internships, liberal arts/career combination, student-designed major, study abroad, teacher certification program. **Credit/placement by examination:** AP, CLEP, IB, institutional tests. 15 credit hours maximum toward associate degree, 30 toward bachelor's. **Support services:** Learning center, tutoring, writing center.

Majors. Biology: General, toxicology. **Business:** Accounting, business admin, international, marketing. **Communications:** Broadcast journalism, communications/speech/rhetoric, digital media, journalism. **Computer sciences:** General, computer science. **Education:** Early childhood, early childhood special, elementary, mathematics, multi-level teacher, secondary. **English:** English lit. **Health services:** Cytotechnology, nuclear medical technology, nursing (RN), respiratory therapy technology. **History:** General. **Liberal arts:** Humanities. **Math:** General. **Philosophy/religion:** Philosophy, religion. **Protective services:** Law enforcement admin. **Psychology:** General. **Social sciences:** General, political science, sociology. **Visual/performing arts:** Art, music, studio arts.

Most popular majors. Business/marketing 31%, education 17%, health sciences 27%.

Computing on campus. 140 workstations in dormitories, library, computer center. Dormitories wired for high-speed internet access and linked to campus network. Commuter students can connect to campus network. Online library, repair service, wireless network available.

Student life. Freshman orientation: Mandatory. Preregistration for classes offered. 3 summer programs available. **Policies:** No drugs or alcohol on campus. **Housing:** Guaranteed on-campus for freshmen. Coed dorms, single-sex dorms, special housing for disabled available. $200 nonrefundable deposit. **Activities:** Campus ministries, choral groups, international student organizations, literary magazine, radio station, student government, Angelicum club, history club, RCIA, Kappa Sigma Xi, aspiring authors, Students in Free Enterprise, Kappa Gamma Pi.

Athletics. NAIA, NCAA. **Intercollegiate:** Baseball M, basketball, cross-country, golf M, soccer, softball W, track and field, volleyball W. **Intramural:** Basketball M, bowling. **Team name:** Golden Falcons.

Student services. Chaplain/spiritual director, career counseling, financial aid counseling, health services.

Contact. E-mail: admissions@felician.edu
Phone: (201) 559-6131 Fax: (201) 559-6188
Alexander Scott, Dean of Undergraduate Admissions, Felician College, 262 South Main Street, Lodi, NJ 07644-2198

Georgian Court University

Lakewood, New Jersey   **CB member**
www.georgian.edu   **CB code: 2274**

- Private 4-year university and liberal arts college for women affiliated with Roman Catholic Church
- Residential campus in large town
- 1,572 degree-seeking undergraduates: 12% part-time, 94% women, 14% African American, 2% Asian American, 10% Hispanic American
- 619 degree-seeking graduate students
- 66% of applicants admitted

- SAT or ACT (ACT writing optional) required
- 52% graduate within 6 years

General. Founded in 1908. Regionally accredited. Evening and graduate divisions coeducational. **Degrees:** 391 bachelor's awarded; master's offered. **Location:** 60 miles from New York City and Philadelphia. **Calendar:** Semester, limited summer session. **Full-time faculty:** 105 total; 92% have terminal degrees, 15% minority, 64% women. **Part-time faculty:** 167 total; 21% have terminal degrees, 10% minority, 70% women. **Class size:** 76% < 20, 24% 20-39. **Special facilities:** Arboretum, Gould estate and gardens, NASA Education Resource Center.

Freshman class profile. 1,134 applied, 743 admitted, 244 enrolled.

GPA 3.75 or higher:	17%	Rank in top tenth:	9%
GPA 3.50-3.74:	24%	Return as sophomores:	65%
GPA 3.0-3.49:	30%	Out-of-state:	8%
GPA 2.0-2.99:	28%	Live on campus:	57%
Rank in top quarter:	29%		

Basis for selection. Completed high school program reviewed for rigor of courses and grades received. Students should be completing program of 16 academic units with grades of 2.5 or higher. Students not meeting criteria referred to faculty committee for review. **Home schooled:** Statement describing home school structure and mission required.

High school preparation. College-preparatory program recommended. 16 units required. Required units include English 4, mathematics 2, history 1, (laboratory 1), foreign language 2 and academic electives 6.

2011-2012 Annual costs. Tuition/fees: $27,984. Room/board: $10,250. Books/supplies: $1,350. Personal expenses: $1,200.

2011-2012 Financial aid. Need-based: 239 full-time freshmen applied for aid; 227 were judged to have need; 227 of these received aid. Average need met was 85%. Average scholarship/grant was $19,617; average loan $5,536. 63% of total undergraduate aid awarded as scholarships/grants, 37% as loans/jobs. **Non-need-based:** Awarded to 161 full-time undergraduates, including 31 freshmen. Scholarships awarded for academics, alumni affiliation, art, athletics, leadership, music/drama, religious affiliation, state residency.

Application procedures. Admission: Closing date 8/1 (receipt date). $40 fee, may be waived for applicants with need. Admission notification on a rolling basis beginning on or about 10/1. Must reply by May 1 or within 2 week(s) if notified thereafter. **Financial aid:** Priority date 4/15, closing date 8/20. FAFSA, institutional form required. Applicants notified on a rolling basis starting 2/1; must reply within 2 week(s) of notification.

Academics. Special study options: Accelerated study, combined bachelor's/graduate degree, distance learning, double major, dual enrollment of high school students, ESL, honors, independent study, internships, liberal arts/career combination, study abroad, teacher certification program. **Credit/placement by examination:** AP, CLEP, institutional tests. 30 credit hours maximum toward bachelor's degree. **Support services:** Learning center, reduced course load, remedial instruction, study skills assistance, tutoring.

Majors. Biology: General, biochemistry. **Business:** Accounting, business admin, hospitality admin. **Communications:** Communications/speech/rhetoric. **Education:** Elementary. **English:** English lit. **Foreign languages:** Spanish. **Health services:** Clinical lab science, nursing (RN). **History:** General. **Human services:** Social work. **Liberal arts:** Humanities. **Math:** General. **Parks/recreation:** Exercise sciences. **Philosophy/religion:** Religion. **Physical sciences:** Chemistry. **Protective services:** Criminal justice. **Psychology:** General. **Social sciences:** Sociology. **Visual/performing arts:** Art, dance, music.

Most popular majors. Business/marketing 11%, education 25%, English 9%, psychology 25%.

Computing on campus. 257 workstations in dormitories, library, computer center. Dormitories wired for high-speed internet access and linked to campus network. Commuter students can connect to campus network. Online course registration, online library, helpline, wireless network available.

Student life. Freshman orientation: Mandatory, $160 fee. Preregistration for classes offered. Held the week before classes begin. **Housing:** Guaranteed on-campus for all undergraduates. Wellness housing available. $250 deposit, deadline 5/1. **Activities:** Bands, campus ministries, choral groups, dance, international student organizations, literary magazine, music ensembles, Model UN, student government, student newspaper, council for exceptional children, Sisters United, Re-Entry women's club, Alliance Francaise, Amnesty International, black student union, LASO, living/learning communities.

Athletics. NCAA. **Intercollegiate:** Basketball W, cross-country W, lacrosse W, soccer W, softball W, tennis W, track and field W, volleyball W. **Team name:** Lions.

Student services. Chaplain/spiritual director, career counseling, financial aid counseling, health services, personal counseling. **Physically disabled:** Services for visually, speech, hearing impaired.

Contact. E-mail: admissions@georgian.edu
Phone: (732) 987-2200 ext. 2700
Toll-free number: (800) 458-8422 ext. 2760 Fax: (732) 987-2000
Maria Colon, Assistant Director of Admissions, Georgian Court University, 900 Lakewood Avenue, Lakewood, NJ 08701-2697

Kean University
Union, New Jersey
www.kean.edu

CB member
CB code: 2517

- Public 4-year university and liberal arts college
- Commuter campus in small city
- 13,152 degree-seeking undergraduates: 21% part-time, 60% women, 19% African American, 6% Asian American, 23% Hispanic American, 1% international
- 1,961 degree-seeking graduate students
- 70% of applicants admitted
- SAT or ACT (ACT writing optional), application essay required
- 49% graduate within 6 years

General. Founded in 1855. Regionally accredited. **Degrees:** 2,519 bachelor's awarded; master's, doctoral offered. **ROTC:** Army, Air Force. **Location:** 12 miles from New York City. **Calendar:** Semester, limited summer session. **Full-time faculty:** 339 total; 91% have terminal degrees, 29% minority, 49% women. **Part-time faculty:** 1,122 total; 16% minority, 53% women. **Class size:** 34% < 20, 65% 20-39, less than 1% 40-49, less than 1% 50-99. **Special facilities:** Holocaust resource center, ethnic studies center, center for science/technology/mathematics, museum, Human Rights Institute.

Freshman class profile. 6,085 applied, 4,283 admitted, 1,837 enrolled.

Mid 50% test scores			
SAT critical reading:	400-500	Rank in top quarter:	27%
SAT math:	420-520	Rank in top tenth:	7%
GPA 3.75 or higher:	7%	Return as sophomores:	80%
GPA 3.50-3.74:	13%	Out-of-state:	3%
GPA 3.0-3.49:	36%	Live on campus:	39%
GPA 2.0-2.99:	44%	International:	2%

Basis for selection. 2.9 GPA, test scores, counselor recommendations important. Consideration given to military service, work, personal life experiences. Non-US-educated applicants evaluated based on academic record in home country. If needed, applicants advised of specific additional requirements.

High school preparation. College-preparatory program recommended. 16 units required. Required and recommended units include English 4, mathematics 3, social studies 2, history 2, science 2 (laboratory 2), foreign language 2 and academic electives 5.

2011-2012 Annual costs. Tuition/fees: $10,200; $16,012 out-of-state. Room/board: $13,528.

2011-2012 Financial aid. **Need-based:** 1,561 full-time freshmen applied for aid; 1,329 were judged to have need; 1,191 of these received aid. Average need met was 46%. Average scholarship/grant was $7,697; average loan $3,428. 51% of total undergraduate aid awarded as scholarships/grants, 49% as loans/jobs. **Non-need-based:** Awarded to 879 full-time undergraduates, including 173 freshmen. Scholarships awarded for academics, alumni affiliation, art, leadership, music/drama.

Application procedures. **Admission:** Closing date 5/31 (postmark date). $75 fee, may be waived for applicants with need. Admission notification on a rolling basis beginning on or about 11/15. Must reply by May 1 or within 2 week(s) if notified thereafter. **Financial aid:** Priority date 3/15; no closing date. FAFSA required. Applicants notified on a rolling basis starting 3/15; must reply by 5/1.

Academics. **Special study options:** Accelerated study, combined bachelor's/graduate degree, cooperative education, cross-registration, distance learning, double major, dual enrollment of high school students, ESL, honors, independent study, internships, liberal arts/career combination, semester at sea, study abroad, teacher certification program, Washington semester, weekend college. 2-year bachelor's degree program for RNs, Foreign Transfer Programs, TraveLearn. **Credit/placement by examination:** AP, CLEP, IB, SAT, institutional tests. **Support services:** Learning center, pre-admission summer program, reduced course load, remedial instruction, study skills assistance, tutoring, writing center.

Majors. **Area/ethnic studies:** Asian. **Biology:** General. **Business:** Accounting, business admin, finance, marketing. **Communications:** Communications/speech/rhetoric. **Communications technology:** Printing management. **Computer sciences:** General, networking. **Education:** Elementary, kindergarten/preschool, music, physical, special ed. **English:** English lit. **Foreign languages:** Spanish. **Health services:** Athletic training, clinical lab science, medical records admin. **History:** General. **Human services:** General. **Math:** General. **Parks/recreation:** Facilities management. **Philosophy/religion:** General. **Physical sciences:** Chemistry, geology. **Protective services:** Law enforcement admin. **Psychology:** General. **Social sciences:** Economics, political science, sociology. **Visual/performing arts:** Acting, art, art history/conservation, design, dramatic, film/cinema/video, industrial design, interior design, music, studio arts, theater design.

Most popular majors. Business/marketing 22%, education 19%, psychology 12%, social sciences 6%, visual/performing arts 6%.

Computing on campus. 1,700 workstations in dormitories, library, computer center, student center. Dormitories wired for high-speed internet access and linked to campus network. Commuter students can connect to campus network. Online course registration, online library, student web hosting, wireless network available.

Student life. **Freshman orientation:** Mandatory, $50 fee. Preregistration for classes offered. One-day program held prior to start of each semester. **Policies:** Student Leadership Criteria, Student Group Recognition Policy, Code of Conduct, FERPA. **Housing:** Coed dorms, special housing for disabled, apartments available. $125 nonrefundable deposit, deadline 5/1. Freshmen housing, floor for women-only housing available. **Activities:** Bands, campus ministries, choral groups, dance, drama, music ensembles, musical theater, opera, radio station, student government, student newspaper, symphony orchestra, TV station, African student association, Asian culture club, Latin American student association, Jewish culture club, Muslim student association, Campus Crusade for Christ, Circle K International, FOCUS, Marine Conservation in Action, Student Action Team for Sustainability.

Athletics. NCAA. **Intercollegiate:** Baseball M, basketball, field hockey W, football (tackle) M, lacrosse, soccer, softball W, tennis W, volleyball. **Intramural:** Basketball, football (non-tackle), soccer, softball, tennis, volleyball, weight lifting. **Team name:** Cougars.

Student services. Adult student services, alcohol/substance abuse counseling, chaplain/spiritual director, career counseling, services for economically disadvantaged, student employment services, financial aid counseling, health services, minority student services, on-campus daycare, personal counseling, placement for graduates, veterans' counselor, women's services. **Physically disabled:** Services for visually, speech, hearing impaired.

Contact. E-mail: admitme@kean.edu
Phone: (908) 737-7100 Fax: (908) 737-7105
Valerie Winslow, Director of Admissions, Kean University, 1000 Morris Avenue, Union, NJ 07083-0411

Monmouth University
West Long Branch, New Jersey
www.monmouth.edu

CB member
CB code: 2416

- Private 4-year university
- Residential campus in small town
- 4,652 degree-seeking undergraduates: 6% part-time, 58% women, 4% African American, 2% Asian American, 7% Hispanic American, 1% international
- 1,743 degree-seeking graduate students
- 63% of applicants admitted
- SAT or ACT with writing required
- 66% graduate within 6 years

General. Founded in 1933. Regionally accredited. **Degrees:** 986 bachelor's, 2 associate awarded; master's, professional offered. **ROTC:** Army, Air Force. **Location:** 50 miles from New York City, 75 miles from Philadelphia. **Calendar:** Semester, extensive summer session. **Full-time faculty:** 259 total; 83% have terminal degrees, 15% minority, 54% women. **Part-time faculty:** 344 total; 24% have terminal degrees, 6% minority, 54% women. **Class size:** 42% < 20, 57% 20-39, less than 1% 40-49. **Special facilities:** Multimedia communications center with TV and radio station, sculpture garden, ice house-gallery, multipurpose activity center with 4,100 seat arena, fitness center, 6 lane indoor track.

Freshman class profile. 6,491 applied, 4,110 admitted, 944 enrolled.

Mid 50% test scores		GPA 2.0-2.99:	14%
SAT critical reading:	480-560	Rank in top quarter:	55%
SAT math:	500-580	Rank in top tenth:	20%
SAT writing:	500-580	End year in good standing:	98%
ACT composite:	22-25	Return as sophomores:	80%
GPA 3.75 or higher:	21%	Out-of-state:	17%
GPA 3.50-3.74:	21%	Live on campus:	85%
GPA 3.0-3.49:	44%	International:	1%

Basis for selection. School record, GPA, test scores important followed by recommendations and essay. Resume of activities including community involvement and leadership positions encouraged. Audition recommended for music programs; portfolio recommended for art programs. Interview recommended for Music and Theatre Arts Department. **Home schooled:** Transcript of courses and grades required. All students who submit portfolio of coursework in lieu of transcript must also complete institution's curriculum chart for homeschooled students. State certificate required only when required by state where home schooled. Letter of recommendation optional.

High school preparation. College-preparatory program recommended. 16 units required; 20 recommended. Required and recommended units include English 4, mathematics 3, social studies 2, history 2, science 2 (laboratory 1), foreign language 2 and academic electives 5.

2011-2012 Annual costs. Tuition/fees: $28,000. Room/board: $10,459. Books/supplies: $1,200. Personal expenses: $1,996.

2011-2012 Financial aid. Need-based: 845 full-time freshmen applied for aid; 701 were judged to have need; 700 of these received aid. Average need met was 69%. Average scholarship/grant was $11,114; average loan $3,787. 54% of total undergraduate aid awarded as scholarships/grants, 46% as loans/jobs. **Non-need-based:** Awarded to 4,318 full-time undergraduates, including 955 freshmen. Scholarships awarded for academics, alumni affiliation, art, athletics, leadership.

Application procedures. Admission: Priority date 12/1; deadline 3/1 (postmark date). $50 fee, may be waived for applicants with need. Admission notification by 4/1. Must reply by 5/1. All deposits non-refundable after May 1. **Financial aid:** Priority date 2/15; no closing date. FAFSA required. Applicants notified on a rolling basis starting 3/1; must reply within 2 week(s) of notification.

Academics. Special study options: Accelerated study, combined bachelor's/graduate degree, cooperative education, cross-registration, double major, dual enrollment of high school students, honors, independent study, internships, liberal arts/career combination, student-designed major, study abroad, teacher certification program, Washington semester. **Credit/placement by examination:** AP, CLEP, IB, SAT, ACT, institutional tests. AP credit awarded only for institutional course equivalents. **Support services:** Learning center, reduced course load, remedial instruction, study skills assistance, tutoring, writing center.

Honors college/program. 1800 SAT (with no section score less than 540) and 3.5 GPA required.

Majors. Biology: General, environmental. **Business:** Business admin, international. **Communications:** Communications/speech/rhetoric. **Computer sciences:** General. **Education:** General, special ed. **Engineering:** Software. **English:** English lit. **Foreign languages:** General. **Health services:** Clinical lab science, nursing (RN). **History:** General. **Human services:** Social work. **Math:** General. **Parks/recreation:** Health/fitness. **Physical sciences:** Chemistry. **Protective services:** Criminal justice. **Psychology:** General. **Social sciences:** Anthropology, political science, sociology. **Visual/performing arts:** Art, dramatic, graphic design, music, studio arts.

Most popular majors. Business/marketing 33%, communications/journalism 14%, education 13%, psychology 6%, security/protective services 6%, visual/performing arts 7%.

Computing on campus. 600 workstations in dormitories, library, computer center, student center. Dormitories wired for high-speed internet access and linked to campus network. Commuter students can connect to campus network. Online library, helpline, student web hosting, wireless network available.

Student life. Freshman orientation: Mandatory, $200 fee. Preregistration for classes offered. Two-day orientation held in July. **Policies:** Must complete at least 12 credit hours to associate with a fraternity or sorority. Students must have 2.2 GPA and be registered full-time. Transfer students taking 12 or more credits may also associate. **Housing:** Guaranteed on-campus for freshmen. Coed dorms, apartments available. $150 deposit, deadline 5/1. Honors residence available. **Activities:** Bands, choral groups, dance, drama, international student organizations, literary magazine, music ensembles, musical theater, radio station, student government, student newspaper, TV station, Hillel, Christian Ambassadors, Catholic center, African-American

student union, Latin American club, Circle K, Rotaract Club, alternative lifestyles clubs.

Athletics. NCAA. **Intercollegiate:** Baseball M, basketball, bowling W, cross-country, field hockey W, football (tackle) M, golf, lacrosse W, sailing, soccer, softball W, tennis, track and field. **Intramural:** Badminton, basketball, football (non-tackle), soccer, softball, tennis, volleyball. **Team name:** Hawks.

Student services. Adult student services, alcohol/substance abuse counseling, chaplain/spiritual director, career counseling, services for economically disadvantaged, student employment services, financial aid counseling, health services, legal services, personal counseling, placement for graduates, veterans' counselor, women's services. **Physically disabled:** Services for visually, speech, hearing impaired.

Contact. E-mail: admission@monmouth.edu
Phone: (732) 571-3456 Toll-free number: (800) 543-9671
Fax: (732) 263-5166
Victoria Bobik, Director of Undergraduate Admission, Monmouth University, 400 Cedar Avenue, West Long Branch, NJ 07764-1898

Montclair State University
Montclair, New Jersey
www.montclair.edu

CB member
CB code: 2520

- Public 4-year university
- Residential campus in large town
- 14,243 degree-seeking undergraduates: 14% part-time, 60% women, 9% African American, 5% Asian American, 22% Hispanic American, 2% international
- 3,068 degree-seeking graduate students
- 57% of applicants admitted
- SAT or ACT (ACT writing recommended) required
- 62% graduate within 6 years; 31% enter graduate study

General. Founded in 1908. Regionally accredited. **Degrees:** 2,851 bachelor's awarded; master's, doctoral offered. **ROTC:** Army, Naval, Air Force. **Location:** 14 miles from New York City. **Calendar:** Semester, limited summer session. **Full-time faculty:** 569 total; 92% have terminal degrees, 27% minority, 49% women. **Part-time faculty:** 1,019 total; 6% have terminal degrees, 12% minority, 56% women. **Special facilities:** 2 ice skating rinks, Yogi Berra museum.

Freshman class profile. 12,584 applied, 7,130 admitted, 2,356 enrolled.

Mid 50% test scores		Rank in top quarter:	39%
SAT critical reading:	440-530	Rank in top tenth:	12%
SAT math:	460-550	End year in good standing:	94%
SAT writing:	450-540	Return as sophomores:	82%
GPA 3.75 or higher:	7%	Out-of-state:	4%
GPA 3.50-3.74:	14%	Live on campus:	62%
GPA 3.0-3.49:	53%	International:	1%
GPA 2.0-2.99:	26%		

Basis for selection. School achievement record most important. Extracurricular activities, test scores, community activities also important. Consideration given to disadvantaged applicants. Interview required for art, music, music therapy, speech, theater, and dance programs; audition required for dance, music, speech, theater programs; portfolio required for art programs. **Home schooled:** Statement describing home school structure and mission, transcript of courses and grades required.

High school preparation. College-preparatory program required. 16 units required. Required units include English 4, mathematics 3, social studies 2, science 2 (laboratory 2), foreign language 2 and academic electives 3. 4 math (including trigonometry) required of computer science majors. Algebra II required for business administration majors. 3 additional units in English, social studies, science, math, or foreign language required.

2011-2012 Annual costs. Tuition/fees: $10,646; $19,394 out-of-state. Room/board: $11,262. Books/supplies: $1,300. Personal expenses: $1,500.

2010-2011 Financial aid. Need-based: 1,675 full-time freshmen applied for aid; 1,363 were judged to have need; 1,273 of these received aid. Average need met was 67%. Average scholarship/grant was $9,302; average loan $3,444. 57% of total undergraduate aid awarded as scholarships/grants, 43% as loans/jobs. **Non-need-based:** Awarded to 1,365 full-time undergraduates, including 322 freshmen. Scholarships awarded for academics, alumni affiliation, art, leadership, minority status, music/drama, ROTC, state residency.

Application procedures. Admission: Closing date 3/1 (postmark date). $65 fee, may be waived for applicants with need. Admission notification on

a rolling basis beginning on or about 10/1. Must reply by 5/1. Immediate decision process available to seniors at some local high schools. **Financial aid:** Priority date 3/1; no closing date. FAFSA required. Applicants notified on a rolling basis starting 4/1; must reply within 2 week(s) of notification.

Academics. Special study options: Combined bachelor's/graduate degree, cooperative education, double major, ESL, honors, independent study, internships, study abroad, teacher certification program, Washington semester. Joint admission with UMDNJ. **Credit/placement by examination:** AP, CLEP, IB, institutional tests. 24 credit hours maximum toward bachelor's degree. **Support services:** Learning center, pre-admission summer program, reduced course load, remedial instruction, tutoring, writing center.

Honors college/program. Two of the following required: rank in top 10% of high school class; 600 SAT verbal or math; 1200 SAT (exclusive of Writing); unusual ability in creative arts or exceptional leadership or other extraordinary accomplishment.

Majors. Area/ethnic studies: Women's. **Biology:** General, biochemistry, molecular, toxicology. **Business:** Business admin, hospitality admin. **Communications:** Broadcast journalism, organizational, radio/TV. **Communications technology:** Animation/special effects. **Computer sciences:** General, computer science, information technology. **Education:** Business, drama/dance, health, physical, technology/industrial arts. **English:** English lit. **Foreign languages:** Classics, French, German, Italian, Latin, linguistics, Spanish. **Health services:** Athletic training, music therapy. **History:** General. **Liberal arts:** Arts/sciences, humanities. **Math:** General. **Parks/recreation:** Exercise sciences, facilities management. **Philosophy/religion:** Philosophy, religion. **Physical sciences:** Chemistry, geology, physics. **Psychology:** General. **Social sciences:** Anthropology, applied economics, economics, geography, political science, sociology. **Visual/performing arts:** Art, cinematography, dance, dramatic, fashion design, graphic design, illustration, industrial design, music, music performance. **Work/family studies:** General, food/nutrition.

Most popular majors. Biology 7%, business/marketing 16%, English 6%, family/consumer sciences 16%, psychology 8%, social sciences 6%, visual/performing arts 12%.

Computing on campus. 700 workstations in dormitories, library, computer center, student center. Dormitories wired for high-speed internet access and linked to campus network. Commuter students can connect to campus network. Online course registration, online library, helpline, repair service, wireless network available.

Student life. Freshman orientation: Mandatory, $175 fee. Preregistration for classes offered. **Housing:** Coed dorms, single-sex dorms, special housing for disabled, apartments available. $300 nonrefundable deposit, deadline 5/1. Pets allowed in dorm rooms. **Activities:** Bands, campus ministries, choral groups, dance, drama, international student organizations, literary magazine, music ensembles, musical theater, opera, radio station, student government, student newspaper, symphony orchestra, TV station, Newman center, college life union board, recreation board, organization for students of African unity, Latin American student organization, LEAD.

Athletics. NCAA. **Intercollegiate:** Baseball M, basketball, diving, field hockey W, football (tackle) M, lacrosse, soccer, softball W, swimming, track and field, volleyball W. **Intramural:** Badminton, basketball, bowling, football (tackle) M, golf, racquetball, softball, tennis, volleyball, water polo. **Team name:** Red Hawks.

Student services. Adult student services, alcohol/substance abuse counseling, chaplain/spiritual director, career counseling, services for economically disadvantaged, student employment services, financial aid counseling, health services, on-campus daycare, personal counseling, placement for graduates, veterans' counselor, women's services. **Physically disabled:** Services for visually, speech, hearing impaired.

Contact. E-mail: undergraduate.admissions@mail.montclair.edu
Phone: (973) 655-4444 Toll-free number: (800) 331-9205
Fax: (973) 655-7700
Lisa Kasper, Director of Admissions, Montclair State University, One Normal Avenue, Montclair, NJ 07042

New Jersey City University
Jersey City, New Jersey
www.njcu.edu

CB member
CB code: 2516

- Public 4-year university
- Commuter campus in small city
- 6,582 degree-seeking undergraduates: 26% part-time, 60% women, 20% African American, 8% Asian American, 37% Hispanic American, 1% international
- 1,048 degree-seeking graduate students

- 43% of applicants admitted
- Application essay required
- 38% graduate within 6 years

General. Founded in 1927. Regionally accredited. **Degrees:** 1,368 bachelor's awarded; master's offered. **Location:** 5 miles from New York City. **Calendar:** Semester, extensive summer session. **Full-time faculty:** 243 total; 87% have terminal degrees, 33% minority, 52% women. **Part-time faculty:** 451 total; 24% minority, 43% women. **Class size:** 54% < 20, 44% 20-39, less than 1% 40-49, 2% 50-99. **Special facilities:** Laboratory school for multihandicapped children, computer technology center, cooperative education, media studies center.

Freshman class profile. 4,399 applied, 1,893 admitted, 728 enrolled.

Mid 50% test scores			
SAT critical reading:	390-480	Rank in top tenth:	11%
SAT math:	420-500	Return as sophomores:	70%
Rank in top quarter:	41%	Out-of-state:	1%
		International:	1%

Basis for selection. High school courses, grades, class rank, and test scores most important, followed by essay or personal statement. Special program for educationally disadvantaged applicants available with above criteria. Interview recommended for all; audition required for music programs; portfolio recommended for art programs.

High school preparation. College-preparatory program recommended. 16 units required; 21 recommended. Required and recommended units include English 4, mathematics 4, social studies 4, science 4 (laboratory 2-3) and foreign language 2.

2011-2012 Annual costs. Tuition/fees: $10,129; $18,003 out-of-state. Room/board: $9,738. Books/supplies: $2,130. Personal expenses: $2,758.

2010-2011 Financial aid. Need-based: 639 full-time freshmen applied for aid; 596 were judged to have need; 573 of these received aid. Average need met was 57%. Average scholarship/grant was $8,685; average loan $10,055. 42% of total undergraduate aid awarded as scholarships/grants, 58% as loans/jobs. **Non-need-based:** Awarded to 400 full-time undergraduates, including 67 freshmen.

Application procedures. Admission: Closing date 4/1. $50 fee, may be waived for applicants with need. Admission notification on a rolling basis beginning on or about 1/1. Must reply by May 1 or within 3 week(s) if notified thereafter. **Financial aid:** Priority date 4/15; no closing date. FAFSA required.

Academics. Cooperative education placement offered in all majors. Professional diploma in school psychology offered. **Special study options:** Cooperative education, cross-registration, distance learning, double major, dual enrollment of high school students, ESL, honors, independent study, internships, liberal arts/career combination, study abroad, teacher certification program, Washington semester, weekend college. **Credit/placement by examination:** AP, CLEP, IB, institutional tests. 30 credit hours maximum toward bachelor's degree. **Support services:** Learning center, pre-admission summer program, reduced course load, remedial instruction, tutoring, writing center.

Majors. Area/ethnic studies: Women's. **Biology:** General. **Business:** Business admin. **Communications:** Communications/speech/rhetoric. **Computer sciences:** General. **Education:** Early childhood, elementary, reading, special ed. **English:** English lit. **Foreign languages:** Spanish. **Health services:** Clinical lab science, nursing (RN). **History:** General. **Math:** General. **Philosophy/religion:** Philosophy. **Physical sciences:** Chemistry, geology, physics. **Protective services:** Firefighting, security services. **Psychology:** General. **Social sciences:** Economics, political science, sociology. **Visual/performing arts:** Art, music, studio arts.

Most popular majors. Business/marketing 26%, health sciences 14%, psychology 9%, security/protective services 13%, social sciences 8%.

Computing on campus. 704 workstations in dormitories, library, computer center, student center. Dormitories wired for high-speed internet access and linked to campus network. Commuter students can connect to campus network. Online course registration, online library, helpline, wireless network available.

Student life. Freshman orientation: Mandatory. Preregistration for classes offered. **Housing:** Coed dorms, apartments available. $150 deposit, deadline 8/13. **Activities:** Bands, campus ministries, choral groups, dance, drama, film society, international student organizations, literary magazine, music ensembles, musical theater, opera, radio station, student government, student newspaper, symphony orchestra, Campus Christian fellowship, black freedom society, Latin power association, Africanan journal.

Athletics. NCAA. **Intercollegiate:** Baseball M, basketball, bowling W, cross-country, soccer, softball W, track and field W, volleyball. **Intramural:** Basketball, bowling, racquetball, soccer, softball, swimming, table tennis, volleyball, weight lifting. **Team name:** Gothic Knights.

Student services. Chaplain/spiritual director, career counseling, student employment services, financial aid counseling, health services, on-campus daycare, personal counseling, placement for graduates, veterans' counselor, women's services. **Physically disabled:** Services for visually, speech, hearing impaired.

Contact. E-mail: admissions@njcu.edu
Phone: (201) 200-3234 Toll-free number: (888) 441-6528
Jose Balda, Director of Admissions, New Jersey City University, 2039 Kennedy Boulevard, Jersey City, NJ 07305-1597

New Jersey Institute of Technology

Newark, New Jersey **CB member**
www.njit.edu **CB code: 2513**

- Public 4-year university
- Residential campus in large city
- 6,005 degree-seeking undergraduates: 14% part-time, 21% women, 10% African American, 21% Asian American, 21% Hispanic American, 4% international
- 2,824 degree-seeking graduate students
- 69% of applicants admitted
- SAT or ACT (ACT writing optional) required
- 53% graduate within 6 years; 75% enter graduate study

General. Founded in 1881. Regionally accredited. **Degrees:** 997 bachelor's awarded; master's, doctoral offered. **ROTC:** Army, Air Force. **Location:** 10 miles from New York City. **Calendar:** Semester, extensive summer session. **Full-time faculty:** 403 total; 25% minority, 18% women. **Part-time faculty:** 245 total; 25% minority, 25% women. **Class size:** 36% < 20, 56% 20-39, 5% 40-49, 3% 50-99, less than 1% >100. **Special facilities:** Computer chip manufacturing laboratory, multi-lifecycle engineering center, numerous government and industry-sponsored research laboratories, hazardous waste management research center, factory floor manufacturing center, observatory.

Freshman class profile. 4,068 applied, 2,787 admitted, 1,605 enrolled.

Mid 50% test scores		Return as sophomores:	82%
SAT critical reading:	470-580	Out-of-state:	5%
SAT math:	540-650	Live on campus:	47%
SAT writing:	460-580	International:	3%
Rank in top quarter:	55%	Fraternities:	8%
Rank in top tenth:	29%	Sororities:	5%

Basis for selection. Class rank, test scores, secondary school record including grades and curriculum most important. Grades in math and science very important, especially for engineering, engineering science and computer science applicants. Essay and interview required for honors college; interview and portfolio required for architecture programs. Interview required for conditional admission, educational opportunity program.

High school preparation. College-preparatory program required. 16 units required. Required and recommended units include English 4, mathematics 4, social studies 1, history 1, science 2 (laboratory 2), foreign language 2 and academic electives 3. 3 math required of management majors and science, technology and society majors. One lab science required for management majors.

2011-2012 Annual costs. Tuition/fees: $13,974; $25,334 out-of-state. Room/board: $11,292. Books/supplies: $1,900. Personal expenses: $1,400.

2010-2011 Financial aid. Need-based: 703 full-time freshmen applied for aid; 603 were judged to have need; 603 of these received aid. Average need met was 66%. Average scholarship/grant was $12,541; average loan $3,345. 76% of total undergraduate aid awarded as scholarships/grants, 24% as loans/jobs. **Non-need-based:** Awarded to 1,500 full-time undergraduates, including 402 freshmen. Scholarships awarded for academics, alumni affiliation, athletics, leadership, minority status, music/drama, religious affiliation, ROTC, state residency. **Additional information:** Extensive co-op program for all majors.

Application procedures. Admission: Closing date 3/1 (receipt date). $70 fee, may be waived for applicants with need. Admission notification on a rolling basis beginning on or about 11/15. Must reply by May 1 or within 2 week(s) if notified thereafter. **Financial aid:** Priority date 3/15; no closing date. FAFSA required. Applicants notified on a rolling basis starting 1/1; must reply by 5/1.

Academics. Numerous research opportunities available. **Special study options:** Accelerated study, combined bachelor's/graduate degree, cooperative education, cross-registration, distance learning, double major, ESL, honors, independent study, internships, study abroad, teacher certification program, weekend college. Environmental Scholars Program, Career Advancement Plan, University Research Experience. **Credit/placement by**

examination: AP, CLEP, SAT, institutional tests. **Support services:** Learning center, pre-admission summer program, reduced course load, remedial instruction, study skills assistance, tutoring.

Honors college/program. 1250 SAT required.

Majors. Architecture: Architecture. **Biology:** General, biochemistry, bioinformatics, biophysics. **Business:** Business admin, international. **Communications technology:** Animation/special effects. **Computer sciences:** General, computer science, information systems, information technology. **Conservation:** Environmental science. **Engineering:** Biomedical, chemical, civil, computer, electrical, engineering science, environmental, geological, industrial, manufacturing, mechanical. **English:** Technical writing. **History:** General. **Math:** General, applied. **Physical sciences:** Chemistry, physics. **Visual/performing arts:** Art, interior design.

Most popular majors. Architecture 13%, business/marketing 10%, computer/information sciences 16%, engineering/engineering technologies 52%.

Computing on campus. PC or laptop required. 1,500 workstations in dormitories, library, computer center, student center. Dormitories wired for high-speed internet access and linked to campus network. Commuter students can connect to campus network. Online course registration, online library, helpline, repair service, student web hosting, wireless network available.

Student life. Freshman orientation: Mandatory. Preregistration for classes offered. **Housing:** Guaranteed on-campus for freshmen. Coed dorms available. $50 nonrefundable deposit, deadline 6/2. **Activities:** Bands, dance, drama, international student organizations, literary magazine, musical theater, radio station, student government, student newspaper, Arab student association, black student engineers association, Caribbean student association, Chinese student association, Hispanic students in technology association, Intervarsity Christian Federation, Polish student association, Islamic student association, women engineers club.

Athletics. NCAA. **Intercollegiate:** Baseball M, basketball, cheerleading, cross-country, fencing, soccer, swimming, tennis, volleyball. **Intramural:** Badminton, basketball, bowling, cricket, fencing, racquetball, soccer, swimming, table tennis, tennis, track and field, volleyball, weight lifting. **Team name:** Highlanders.

Student services. Adult student services, alcohol/substance abuse counseling, career counseling, services for economically disadvantaged, student employment services, financial aid counseling, health services, minority student services, on-campus daycare, personal counseling, placement for graduates, veterans' counselor, women's services. **Physically disabled:** Services for visually, speech, hearing impaired.

Contact. E-mail: admissions@njit.edu
Phone: (973) 596-3300 Toll-free number: (800) 925-6548
Fax: (973) 596-3461
Stephen Eck, Director of Admissions, New Jersey Institute of Technology, University Heights, Newark, NJ 07102

Princeton University

Princeton, New Jersey **CB member**
www.princeton.edu **CB code: 2672**

- Private 4-year university
- Residential campus in large town
- 5,160 degree-seeking undergraduates: 49% women, 7% African American, 18% Asian American, 8% Hispanic American, 11% international
- 2,584 degree-seeking graduate students
- 8% of applicants admitted
- SAT or ACT with writing, SAT Subject Tests, application essay required
- 96% graduate within 6 years

General. Founded in 1746. Regionally accredited. **Degrees:** 1,219 bachelor's awarded; master's, doctoral offered. **ROTC:** Army, Air Force. **Location:** 50 miles from New York City, 45 miles from Philadelphia. **Calendar:** Semester. **Full-time faculty:** 859 total; 11% have terminal degrees, 19% minority, 29% women. **Part-time faculty:** 223 total; 10% have terminal degrees, 25% minority, 44% women. **Class size:** 71% < 20, 16% 20-39, 3% 40-49, 6% 50-99, 5% >100. **Special facilities:** Center for innovation in engineering education, center for African American studies, center for the arts, center for human values, plasma physics laboratory, observatory, center for energy and the environment.

Freshman class profile. 27,189 applied, 2,300 admitted, 1,300 enrolled.

Mid 50% test scores		GPA 3.0-3.49:	5%
SAT critical reading:	700-790	**Rank in top quarter:**	99%
SAT math:	710-800	**Rank in top tenth:**	93%
SAT writing:	700-790	**Return as sophomores:**	98%
ACT composite:	31-34	**Out-of-state:**	83%
GPA 3.75 or higher:	85%	**Live on campus:**	100%
GPA 3.50-3.74:	10%	**International:**	11%

Basis for selection. School achievement record and recommendations of guidance counselor and 2 teachers very important. SAT or ACT with Writing required along with 2 SAT Subject Test scores. Recommend prospective Engineering students take two SAT Subject Tests - math 1 or math 2 and either physics or chemistry. Interview recommended when possible. Submission of supplementary materials for the visual and performing arts considered. **Home schooled:** Statement describing home school structure and mission required.

High school preparation. College-preparatory program recommended. 21 units recommended. Recommended units include English 4, mathematics 4, social studies 2, history 2, science 4 (laboratory 2), foreign language 4 and visual/performing arts 1. 1 physics or chemistry (preferably both) and 4 math encouraged for prospective engineering majors.

2011-2012 Annual costs. Tuition/fees: $37,000. Room/board: $12,069. Books/supplies: $1,200. Personal expenses: $2,295.

2010-2011 Financial aid. All financial aid based on need. 909 full-time freshmen applied for aid; 774 were judged to have need; 774 of these received aid. Average need met was 100%. Average scholarship/grant was $35,330. 98% of total undergraduate aid awarded as scholarships/grants, 2% as loans/jobs. **Additional information:** All aid need-based; all aid grant money (no loans); institution meets full demonstrated need.

Application procedures. Admission: Closing date 1/1 (postmark date). $65 fee, may be waived for applicants with need. Admission notification by 3/29. Must reply by 5/1. **Financial aid:** Priority date 2/1; no closing date. FAFSA, institutional form required. Must reply by 5/1.

Academics. Independent project in junior year and senior thesis required for graduation. **Special study options:** Cross-registration, exchange student, independent study, student-designed major, study abroad, teacher certification program. **Credit/placement by examination:** AP, CLEP, IB, SAT, ACT, institutional tests. **Support services:** Learning center, pre-admission summer program, study skills assistance, tutoring, writing center.

Majors. Architecture: Architecture. **Area/ethnic studies:** East Asian, Near/Middle Eastern. **Biology:** Ecology/evolutionary, molecular. **Engineering:** Chemical, civil, computer, electrical, mechanical, operations research. **English:** English lit. **Foreign languages:** Classics, comparative lit, French, German, Italian, Portuguese, Slavic, Spanish. **History:** General. **Human services:** General. **Math:** General. **Philosophy/religion:** Philosophy, religion. **Physical sciences:** Astrophysics, chemistry, geology, physics. **Psychology:** General. **Social sciences:** Anthropology, economics, political science, sociology. **Visual/performing arts:** Art history/conservation, music.

Most popular majors. Biology 10%, engineering/engineering technologies 17%, English 6%, history 7%, physical sciences 6%, public administration/social services 7%, social sciences 25%.

Computing on campus. 650 workstations in dormitories, library, computer center, student center. Dormitories wired for high-speed internet access and linked to campus network. Commuter students can connect to campus network. Online course registration, online library, helpline, repair service, student web hosting, wireless network available.

Student life. Freshman orientation: Mandatory. Preregistration for classes offered. Three-day orientation. Optional 1-week trip with Outdoor Action or Student Volunteer Council. **Policies:** Freshmen not permitted cars on campus. **Housing:** Guaranteed on-campus for all undergraduates. Coed dorms, special housing for disabled, apartments available. Residential colleges for freshmen and sophomores. Kosher dining facilities available. **Activities:** Bands, campus ministries, choral groups, dance, drama, film society, international student organizations, literary magazine, music ensembles, Model UN, musical theater, opera, radio station, student government, student newspaper, symphony orchestra, over 300 student organizations available.

Athletics. NCAA. **Intercollegiate:** Baseball M, basketball, cross-country, diving, fencing, field hockey W, football (tackle) M, golf, ice hockey, lacrosse, rowing (crew), soccer, softball W, squash, swimming, tennis, track and field, volleyball, water polo, wrestling M. **Intramural:** Badminton, basketball, bowling, football (non-tackle), golf, ice hockey, judo, racquetball, soccer, softball, tennis, water polo. **Team name:** Tigers.

Student services. Alcohol/substance abuse counseling, chaplain/spiritual director, career counseling, student employment services, financial aid counseling, health services, minority student services, personal counseling, placement for graduates, women's services. **Physically disabled:** Services for visually, speech, hearing impaired.

Contact. E-mail: uaoffice@princeton.edu
Phone: (609) 258-3060 Fax: (609) 258-6743
Janet Rapelye, Dean of Admission, Princeton University, Box 430, Princeton, NJ 08542-0430

Rabbi Jacob Joseph School
Edison, New Jersey

- Private 4-year rabbinical college
- Large town
- 76 degree-seeking undergraduates

General. Accredited by AARTS. **Calendar:** Semester. **Full-time faculty:** 4 total. **Part-time faculty:** 2 total.

Basis for selection. Admission requirements will vary by program.

2011-2012 Annual costs. Tuition/fees: $10,900.

Academics. Credit/placement by examination: AP, CLEP.

Majors. Theology: Talmudic.

Contact. Phone: (732) 985-6533
Rabbi Jacob Joseph School, One Plainfield Avenue, Edison, NJ 08817

Rabbinical College of America
Morristown, New Jersey

CB code: 1546

- Private 4-year rabbinical college for men affiliated with Jewish faith
- Residential campus in large town
- 263 degree-seeking undergraduates

General. Founded in 1956. Accredited by AARTS. Affiliate of world-wide Lubavitch movement. **Degrees:** 44 bachelor's awarded. **Location:** One mile from downtown, 35 miles from New York City. **Calendar:** Semester, extensive summer session. **Full-time faculty:** 15 total. **Part-time faculty:** 1 total.

Basis for selection. Applicants must demonstrate interest, ability, and perseverance necessary for successful completion of required courses. Recommendation required, preferably from local rabbi. Interview recommended.

2011-2012 Annual costs. Tuition/fees: $10,200. Room/board: $6,800.

Application procedures. Admission: Closing date 9/1. $150 fee. Admission notification on a rolling basis. **Financial aid:** Priority date 10/20; no closing date. Applicants notified on a rolling basis starting 10/31.

Academics. New Direction program for young Jewish men with little or no Jewish education. Program ranges from basics of Judaism to Talmud and Chassidic philosophy. **Special study options:** Internships. **Credit/placement by examination:** AP, CLEP. **Support services:** Pre-admission summer program, remedial instruction.

Majors. Philosophy/religion: Judaic, religion.

Student life. Policies: Religious observance required. **Housing:** Guaranteed on-campus for all undergraduates. Apartments available. **Activities:** Student newspaper, community activities.

Student services. Personal counseling.

Contact. Phone: (973) 267-9404 Fax: (973) 267-5208
Israel Teitelbaum, Registrar, Rabbinical College of America, 226 Sussex Avenue, CN 1996, Morristown, NJ 07962-1996

Ramapo College of New Jersey
Mahwah, New Jersey
www.ramapo.edu

CB member
CB code: 2884

- Public 4-year liberal arts college
- Residential campus in large town
- 5,472 degree-seeking undergraduates: 8% part-time, 58% women, 5% African American, 5% Asian American, 11% Hispanic American, 1% international
- 187 degree-seeking graduate students

- 50% of applicants admitted
- SAT, application essay required
- 72% graduate within 6 years

General. Founded in 1969. Regionally accredited. **Degrees:** 1,325 bachelor's awarded; master's offered. **ROTC:** Air Force. **Location:** 35 miles from New York City. **Calendar:** Semester, extensive summer session. **Full-time faculty:** 223 total; 98% have terminal degrees, 26% minority, 50% women. **Part-time faculty:** 258 total; 12% minority, 53% women. **Class size:** 36% < 20, 62% 20-39, 2% 40-49, less than 1% 50-99. **Special facilities:** International telecommunications center, electron microscope, Holocaust center, performing arts center, international and intercultural education office, environmental studies/sustainability education center, greenhouse center, astronomical observatory, global financial markets trading laboratory, spirituality center.

Freshman class profile. 5,091 applied, 2,561 admitted, 895 enrolled.

Mid 50% test scores		GPA 2.0-2.99:	16%
SAT critical reading:	530-610	Rank in top quarter:	58%
SAT math:	560-640	Rank in top tenth:	27%
SAT writing:	530-610	Return as sophomores:	86%
GPA 3.75 or higher:	24%	Out-of-state:	3%
GPA 3.50-3.74:	18%	Live on campus:	85%
GPA 3.0-3.49:	42%	International:	1%

Basis for selection. School achievement record, test scores most important. Applicants should rank in top 25% of high school class. SAT Reading and ACT Reading/English may be used for academic advising. Certain majors have additional entrance requirements.

High school preparation. College-preparatory program required. 18 units required. Required units include English 4, mathematics 3, social studies 3, science 3 (laboratory 2), foreign language 2 and academic electives 3. Math must consist of algebra I, geometry, and algebra II.

2011-2012 Annual costs. Tuition/fees: $12,758; $20,945 out-of-state. Room/board: $12,000. Books/supplies: $1,200. Personal expenses: $2,350.

2010-2011 Financial aid. Need-based: 757 full-time freshmen applied for aid; 539 were judged to have need; 513 of these received aid. Average need met was 68%. Average scholarship/grant was $14,016; average loan $3,284. 51% of total undergraduate aid awarded as scholarships/grants, 49% as loans/jobs. **Non-need-based:** Awarded to 1,137 full-time undergraduates, including 244 freshmen. Scholarships awarded for academics, state residency.

Application procedures. Admission: Closing date 3/1. $60 fee, may be waived for applicants with need. Admission notification on a rolling basis beginning on or about 11/15. Must reply by 5/1. **Financial aid:** Priority date 3/1; no closing date. FAFSA required. Applicants notified on a rolling basis starting 4/1; must reply by 5/1 or within 2 week(s) of notification.

Academics. Thematic learning communities available. **Special study options:** Accelerated study, combined bachelor's/graduate degree, cooperative education, cross-registration, distance learning, double major, dual enrollment of high school students, exchange student, external degree, honors, independent study, internships, liberal arts/career combination, student-designed major, study abroad, teacher certification program. **Credit/placement by examination:** AP, CLEP, IB, SAT. 65 credit hours maximum toward bachelor's degree. **Support services:** Learning center, pre-admission summer program, reduced course load, remedial instruction, study skills assistance, tutoring, writing center.

Majors. Area/ethnic studies: African-American, American. **Biology:** General, biochemistry, bioinformatics. **Business:** Accounting, business admin, international. **Communications:** Communications/speech/rhetoric. **Computer sciences:** General, information systems. **Conservation:** Environmental science, environmental studies. **Foreign languages:** Comparative lit, Spanish. **Health services:** Clinical lab science. **History:** General. **Human services:** Social work. **Liberal arts:** Arts/sciences, humanities. **Math:** General. **Physical sciences:** Chemistry, physics. **Psychology:** General. **Social sciences:** Economics, political science, sociology. **Visual/performing arts:** General, art, dramatic, multimedia, music.

Most popular majors. Biology 8%, business/marketing 23%, communications/journalism 9%, health sciences 7%, psychology 15%, visual/performing arts 6%.

Computing on campus. 1,058 workstations in dormitories, library, computer center, student center. Dormitories wired for high-speed internet access and linked to campus network. Commuter students can connect to campus network. Online course registration, online library, helpline, repair service, student web hosting, wireless network available.

Student life. Freshman orientation: Mandatory, $130 fee. Preregistration for classes offered. Several sessions held throughout summer. **Policies:** Smoking prohibited in all physical buildings on campus. Smokers must stand 25 feet away from buildings. Freshmen not permitted cars on campus. **Housing:** Guaranteed on-campus for freshmen. Coed dorms, special housing for disabled, apartments, cooperative housing available. $200 partly refundable deposit, deadline 5/1. **Activities:** Campus ministries, choral groups, dance, drama, international student organizations, literary magazine, music ensembles, Model UN, musical theater, radio station, student government, student newspaper, TV station, United Asian Americans, Haitian Organization for Progress, College Democrats, College Republicans, Hillel, Intervarsity Christian Fellowship, Muslim student association, Community Builders Coalition, culture club.

Athletics. NCAA. **Intercollegiate:** Baseball M, basketball, cross-country, lacrosse W, track and field, volleyball. **Intramural:** Basketball, bowling, football (non-tackle) M, soccer, softball, volleyball. **Team name:** Roadrunners.

Student services. Adult student services, alcohol/substance abuse counseling, chaplain/spiritual director, career counseling, services for economically disadvantaged, student employment services, financial aid counseling, health services, minority student services, personal counseling, placement for graduates, veterans' counselor, women's services. **Physically disabled:** Services for visually, speech, hearing impaired.

Contact. E-mail: admissions@ramapo.edu
Phone: (201) 684-7300 Toll-free number: (800) 972-6276
Fax: (201) 684-7964
Peter Rice, Director of Admissions, Ramapo College of New Jersey, 505 Ramapo Valley Road, Mahwah, NJ 07430-1680

Richard Stockton College of New Jersey
Galloway, New Jersey   **CB member**
www.stockton.edu   **CB code: 2889**

- Public 4-year liberal arts college
- Residential campus in large town
- 7,159 degree-seeking undergraduates: 8% part-time, 58% women, 7% African American, 5% Asian American, 8% Hispanic American
- 717 degree-seeking graduate students
- 58% of applicants admitted
- SAT or ACT (ACT writing optional), application essay required
- 66% graduate within 6 years; 29% enter graduate study

General. Founded in 1969. Regionally accredited. 7-acre marine science field station located off-campus. **Degrees:** 1,863 bachelor's awarded; master's, professional offered. **Location:** 12 miles from Atlantic City, 50 miles from Philadelphia. **Calendar:** Semester, extensive summer session. **Full-time faculty:** 282 total; 94% have terminal degrees, 24% minority, 50% women. **Part-time faculty:** 319 total; 36% have terminal degrees, 12% minority, 53% women. **Class size:** 25% < 20, 71% 20-39, 2% 40-49, 1% 50-99, less than 1% >100. **Special facilities:** Nature path, arboretum, forestry nursery, ecologic succession plots and study preserve, child care center, interdisciplinary natural sciences laboratory, observatory, Holocaust center, geothermal plant, ITV classroom, performing arts theater, hospital located on college grounds, solar carport, learning lab of hotel, conference center and resort management.

Freshman class profile. 5,673 applied, 3,293 admitted, 973 enrolled.

Mid 50% test scores		Rank in top tenth:	23%
SAT critical reading:	470-570	End year in good standing:	88%
SAT math:	490-600	Return as sophomores:	84%
SAT writing:	470-560	Out-of-state:	1%
ACT composite:	19-23	Live on campus:	73%
Rank in top quarter:	56%		

Basis for selection. Secondary school record, class rank, test scores most important; essay, recommendations, extracurricular activities also important; interview, work experience considered. **Home schooled:** Statement describing home school structure and mission, transcript of courses and grades required.

High school preparation. College-preparatory program recommended. 16 units required; 18 recommended. Required and recommended units include English 4, mathematics 3, social studies 2, science 2 (laboratory 2), foreign language 2 and academic electives 5.

2011-2012 Annual costs. Tuition/fees: $11,963; $18,169 out-of-state. Room/board: $10,477. Books/supplies: $1,400. Personal expenses: $2,035.

2011-2012 Financial aid. Need-based: 903 full-time freshmen applied for aid; 760 were judged to have need; 731 of these received aid. Average need met was 69%. Average scholarship/grant was $9,318; average loan $3,487. 40% of total undergraduate aid awarded as scholarships/grants, 60%

as loans/jobs. **Non-need-based:** Awarded to 1,712 full-time undergraduates, including 303 freshmen. Scholarships awarded for academics, art, leadership, minority status, music/drama, state residency. **Additional information:** Institutional grants provided for majority of neediest incoming students.

Application procedures. Admission: Priority date 2/1; deadline 6/1 (postmark date). $50 fee, may be waived for applicants with need. Admission notification on a rolling basis beginning on or about 10/1. Must reply by May 1 or within 2 week(s) if notified thereafter. **Financial aid:** Priority date 3/1; no closing date. FAFSA required. Applicants notified on a rolling basis starting 4/1; must reply within 2 week(s) of notification.

Academics. Special study options: Accelerated study, combined bachelor's/graduate degree, cross-registration, distance learning, dual enrollment of high school students, honors, independent study, internships, liberal arts/career combination, semester at sea, student-designed major, study abroad, teacher certification program, Washington semester. Dual degree bachelor's program in engineering with Rutgers University and New Jersey Institute of Technology, preceptorial advising, opportunities for specialized research, extensive Washington internship available. Accelerated Health Professions Program. **Credit/placement by examination:** AP, CLEP, IB, SAT, ACT, institutional tests. 32 credit hours maximum toward bachelor's degree. **Support services:** Learning center, pre-admission summer program, reduced course load, remedial instruction, study skills assistance, tutoring, writing center.

Majors. Biology: General, biochemistry, marine. **Business:** Business admin, hospitality admin. **Communications:** Communications/speech/rhetoric. **Computer sciences:** Information systems. **Conservation:** Environmental studies. **Education:** Multi-level teacher. **English:** English lit. **Foreign languages:** General. **Health services:** Audiology/speech pathology, nursing (RN). **History:** General. **Human services:** Social work. **Liberal arts:** Arts/sciences. **Math:** General. **Physical sciences:** Chemistry, geology, physics. **Psychology:** General. **Social sciences:** Criminology, economics, political science, sociology. **Visual/performing arts:** General, studio arts.

Most popular majors. Biology 11%, business/marketing 20%, education 12%, health sciences 8%, psychology 11%, social sciences 14%.

Computing on campus. 930 workstations in dormitories, library, computer center, student center. Dormitories wired for high-speed internet access and linked to campus network. Commuter students can connect to campus network. Online course registration, online library, helpline, student web hosting, wireless network available.

Student life. Freshman orientation: Mandatory, $100 fee. Preregistration for classes offered. **Housing:** Guaranteed on-campus for freshmen. Coed dorms, special housing for disabled, apartments, wellness housing available. $150 partly refundable deposit, deadline 5/1. Academic units, Living/Learning Communities include themes of Diversity, Global Citizenship, Sustainability and Wellness. **Activities:** Concert band, campus ministries, choral groups, dance, drama, international student organizations, literary magazine, music ensembles, radio station, student government, student newspaper, TV station, Books Without Borders, unified black students society, Christian Fellowship, Jewish student union, Circle K International, Amnesty International, action volunteers for the environment, Water Watch, CHANGE, campus religious council.

Athletics. NCAA. **Intercollegiate:** Baseball M, basketball, cheerleading, cross-country, field hockey W, lacrosse M, rowing (crew) W, soccer, softball W, tennis W, track and field, volleyball W. **Intramural:** Basketball, football (non-tackle), soccer, softball, table tennis, volleyball. **Team name:** Ospreys.

Student services. Adult student services, alcohol/substance abuse counseling, chaplain/spiritual director, career counseling, services for economically disadvantaged, student employment services, financial aid counseling, health services, on-campus daycare, personal counseling, placement for graduates, veterans' counselor, women's services. **Physically disabled:** Services for visually, speech, hearing impaired.

Contact. E-mail: admissions@stockton.edu
Phone: (609) 652-4261 Toll-free number: (866) 772-2885
Fax: (609) 748-5541
John Iacovelli, Dean of Enrollment Management, Richard Stockton College of New Jersey, 101 Vera King Farris Drive, Galloway, NJ 08205

Rider University
Lawrenceville, New Jersey
www.rider.edu

CB member
CB code: 2758

- Private 4-year university
- Residential campus in small town

- 4,504 degree-seeking undergraduates: 13% part-time, 59% women, 10% African American, 4% Asian American, 9% Hispanic American, 2% international
- 806 degree-seeking graduate students
- 73% of applicants admitted
- SAT or ACT with writing, application essay required
- 63% graduate within 6 years; 23% enter graduate study

General. Founded in 1865. Regionally accredited. Westminster College of the Arts, located in Lawrenceville and Princeton campuses. **Degrees:** 1,106 bachelor's, 15 associate awarded; master's offered. **ROTC:** Army. **Location:** 5 miles from Princeton, 3 miles from Trenton. **Calendar:** Semester, extensive summer session. **Full-time faculty:** 248 total; 96% have terminal degrees, 14% minority, 43% women. **Part-time faculty:** 364 total; 47% have terminal degrees, 21% minority, 50% women. **Class size:** 49% < 20, 46% 20-39, 4% 40-49, less than 1% 50-99. **Special facilities:** Holocaust/genocide center, teaching and learning center, art gallery.

Freshman class profile. 7,947 applied, 5,827 admitted, 941 enrolled.

Mid 50% test scores			
SAT critical reading:	460-570	GPA 2.0-2.99:	26%
SAT math:	480-580	Rank in top quarter:	43%
SAT writing:	460-570	Rank in top tenth:	15%
ACT composite:	19-24	Return as sophomores:	83%
GPA 3.75 or higher:	17%	Out-of-state:	24%
GPA 3.50-3.74:	19%	Live on campus:	88%
GPA 3.0-3.49:	38%	International:	2%

Basis for selection. High school curriculum most important, followed by GPA, test scores, essay, and recommendations. Extracurricular activities, interview considered. Deadline for SAT/ACT for Early Action applicants 11/15. Interview recommended for all; audition required for music program with Westminster College of the Arts. **Home schooled:** Information about syllabi, reading lists, and/or course descriptions recommended.

High school preparation. College-preparatory program required. 16 units required. Required and recommended units include English 4, mathematics 3-4, social studies 2, history 2, science 4 (laboratory 4) and foreign language 2. Algebra I and II and geometry required for business administration, science, math majors.

2011-2012 Annual costs. Tuition/fees: $31,930. Room/board: $11,810. Books/supplies: $1,500. Personal expenses: $875.

2011-2012 Financial aid. Need-based: 834 full-time freshmen applied for aid; 735 were judged to have need; 735 of these received aid. Average need met was 72%. Average scholarship/grant was $17,310; average loan $3,495. 57% of total undergraduate aid awarded as scholarships/grants, 43% as loans/jobs. **Non-need-based:** Awarded to 1,413 full-time undergraduates, including 332 freshmen. Scholarships awarded for academics, alumni affiliation, athletics, leadership, minority status, music/drama.

Application procedures. Admission: Priority date 1/18; no deadline. $50 fee, may be waived for applicants with need. Admission notification on a rolling basis beginning on or about 12/15. Must reply by May 1 or within 4 week(s) if notified thereafter. Notification of admission decision sent within 3-4 weeks of receiving application. **Financial aid:** Priority date 3/1; no closing date. FAFSA required. Applicants notified on a rolling basis starting 2/20.

Academics. Special study options: Cooperative education, cross-registration, distance learning, double major, honors, independent study, internships, liberal arts/career combination, study abroad, teacher certification program, weekend college. **Credit/placement by examination:** AP, CLEP, IB, SAT, ACT, institutional tests. Policy varies by major. 30 hours of credit by general examination may be counted toward degree. No limit for subject examinations. Not acceptable for last 30 credits of degree program. 4-8 AP courses (24 credits) required for sophomore standing. **Support services:** Learning center, reduced course load, remedial instruction, study skills assistance, tutoring, writing center.

Majors. Area/ethnic studies: American. **Biology:** General, biochemistry. **Business:** Accounting, administrative services, business admin, entrepreneurial studies, finance, human resources, international, management science, managerial economics, marketing, office management, organizational behavior. **Communications:** Advertising, journalism. **Computer sciences:** General. **Conservation:** Environmental science. **Education:** Business, elementary, music, sales/marketing, science, secondary. **English:** English lit, rhetoric/composition. **Foreign languages:** French, German, Russian, Spanish. **History:** General. **Liberal arts:** Arts/sciences. **Math:** General. **Philosophy/religion:** Philosophy. **Physical sciences:** Chemistry, geology, oceanography, physics. **Psychology:** General. **Social sciences:** Economics, international relations, political science, sociology. **Theology:** Sacred music. **Visual/performing arts:** Art, music, music theory/composition, musical theater, piano/keyboard, studio arts, studio arts management, voice/opera.

Most popular majors. Business/marketing 34%, education 16%, English 14%, liberal arts 6%, psychology 8%, visual/performing arts 8%.

Computing on campus. 300 workstations in library, computer center, student center. Dormitories wired for high-speed internet access and linked to campus network. Commuter students can connect to campus network. Online course registration, online library, helpline, student web hosting, wireless network available.

Student life. Freshman orientation: Mandatory, $250 fee. Preregistration for classes offered. Two-day program for new students and family members. **Housing:** Guaranteed on-campus for freshmen. Coed dorms, single-sex dorms, special housing for disabled, apartments, fraternity/sorority housing, wellness housing available. $500 nonrefundable deposit, deadline 5/1. **Activities:** Bands, campus ministries, choral groups, dance, drama, film society, international student organizations, literary magazine, music ensembles, Model UN, musical theater, opera, radio station, student government, student newspaper, TV station, student entertainment council, residence hall association, finance board, Asian student organization, interfraternity council, hunger and homelessness awareness, College Republicans, Latin American student organization.

Athletics. NCAA. **Intercollegiate:** Baseball M, basketball, cheerleading, cross-country, diving, field hockey W, golf M, soccer, softball W, swimming, tennis, track and field, volleyball W, wrestling M. **Intramural:** Basketball, football (non-tackle), ice hockey M, lacrosse, soccer, softball, track and field, volleyball. **Team name:** Broncs.

Student services. Adult student services, alcohol/substance abuse counseling, chaplain/spiritual director, career counseling, services for economically disadvantaged, student employment services, financial aid counseling, health services, minority student services, personal counseling, placement for graduates, veterans' counselor, women's services. **Physically disabled:** Services for visually, speech, hearing impaired.

Contact. E-mail: admissions@rider.edu
Phone: (609) 896-5042 Toll-free number: (800) 257-9026
Fax: (609) 895-6645
William Larrousse, Director of Undergraduate Admissions, Rider University, 2083 Lawrenceville Road, Lawrenceville, NJ 08648-3099

Rowan University
Glassboro, New Jersey
www.rowan.edu

CB member
CB code: 2515

- Public 4-year university
- Residential campus in large town
- 10,159 degree-seeking undergraduates: 12% part-time, 51% women, 8% African American, 4% Asian American, 9% Hispanic American, 1% Native American, 1% international
- 1,105 degree-seeking graduate students
- 58% of applicants admitted
- SAT or ACT (ACT writing optional) required
- 67% graduate within 6 years

General. Founded in 1923. Regionally accredited. **Degrees:** 2,198 bachelor's awarded; master's, doctoral offered. **ROTC:** Army. **Location:** 20 miles from Philadelphia. **Calendar:** Semester, extensive summer session. **Full-time faculty:** 389 total; 90% have terminal degrees, 24% minority, 47% women. **Part-time faculty:** 660 total; 15% have terminal degrees, 12% minority, 49% women. **Class size:** 39% < 20, 60% 20-39, less than 1% 40-49, less than 1% 50-99, less than 1% >100. **Special facilities:** Observatory, early childhood demonstration center, greenhouse for biological studies, concert hall, CAVE automated virtual environment, planetarium.

Freshman class profile. 7,285 applied, 4,239 admitted, 1,584 enrolled.

Mid 50% test scores		Rank in top quarter:	53%
SAT critical reading:	510-600	Rank in top tenth:	21%
SAT math:	520-570	Return as sophomores:	86%
SAT writing:	500-590	Out-of-state:	3%
GPA 3.75 or higher:	34%	Live on campus:	81%
GPA 3.50-3.74:	19%	Fraternities:	5%
GPA 3.0-3.49:	32%	Sororities:	4%
GPA 2.0-2.99:	15%		

Basis for selection. School achievement record and test scores most important, followed by recommendations. Audition required for music, theater programs; portfolio interview required for art program. **Home schooled:** Transcript of courses and grades required.

High school preparation. College-preparatory program required. 16 units required; 18 recommended. Required and recommended units include English

4, mathematics 3-4, social studies 2, science 2-3 and foreign language 2. Engineering applicants should have 3 units of laboratory science including physics and chemistry, and 4 units of college preparatory math including precalculus. Calculus strongly recommended.

2011-2012 Annual costs. Tuition/fees: $12,018; $19,598 out-of-state. Room/board: $10,652. Books/supplies: $1,500. Personal expenses: $1,450.

2010-2011 Financial aid. Need-based: 1,348 full-time freshmen applied for aid; 995 were judged to have need; 929 of these received aid. Average need met was 82%. Average scholarship/grant was $9,817; average loan $3,261. 38% of total undergraduate aid awarded as scholarships/grants, 62% as loans/jobs. **Non-need-based:** Awarded to 1,380 full-time undergraduates, including 398 freshmen. Scholarships awarded for academics, art, music/drama.

Application procedures. Admission: Closing date 3/1 (receipt date). $65 fee, may be waived for applicants with need. Admission notification on a rolling basis beginning on or about 10/15. Must reply by 5/1. **Financial aid:** Priority date 3/1; no closing date. FAFSA required. Applicants notified on a rolling basis starting 3/16.

Academics. Camden campus offers general education courses and major programs in elementary education, business administration, law/justice, and sociology. **Special study options:** Accelerated study, combined bachelor's/graduate degree, cooperative education, cross-registration, distance learning, double major, dual enrollment of high school students, ESL, honors, independent study, internships, study abroad, teacher certification program, weekend college. **Credit/placement by examination:** AP, CLEP, IB, SAT, ACT. 30 credit hours maximum toward bachelor's degree. **Support services:** Pre-admission summer program, remedial instruction, study skills assistance, tutoring, writing center.

Majors. Biology: General, biochemistry. **Business:** Accounting, business admin, entrepreneurial studies, finance, human resources, management information systems, management science, marketing. **Communications:** Advertising, journalism, public relations. **Computer sciences:** Computer science. **Conservation:** Environmental studies. **Education:** General, art, early childhood, elementary, music, secondary, special ed. **Engineering:** Chemical, civil, electrical, mechanical. **English:** English lit, writing. **Foreign languages:** Spanish. **Health services:** Athletic training. **History:** General. **Liberal arts:** Arts/sciences. **Math:** General. **Parks/recreation:** Health/fitness, sports admin. **Philosophy/religion:** General. **Physical sciences:** Chemistry, physics. **Protective services:** Criminal justice. **Psychology:** General, developmental. **Social sciences:** Economics, geography, political science, sociology. **Visual/performing arts:** Art, dance, dramatic, film/cinema/video, jazz, music, music performance, music theory/composition, studio arts.

Most popular majors. Business/marketing 8%, communications/journalism 11%, education 19%, psychology 6%, security/protective services 6%, social sciences 6%.

Computing on campus. 1,200 workstations in dormitories, library, computer center. Dormitories wired for high-speed internet access and linked to campus network. Commuter students can connect to campus network. Online course registration, online library, helpline, repair service, wireless network available.

Student life. Freshman orientation: Available. Preregistration for classes offered. Overnight program for freshmen and their families during summer. **Policies:** Freshmen not permitted cars on campus. **Housing:** Guaranteed on-campus for freshmen. Coed dorms, special housing for disabled, apartments, wellness housing available. $200 nonrefundable deposit, deadline 5/1. Townhouses. **Activities:** Bands, campus ministries, choral groups, dance, drama, film society, music ensembles, opera, radio station, student government, student newspaper, symphony orchestra, TV station, over 100 clubs and student organizations available.

Athletics. NCAA. **Intercollegiate:** Baseball M, basketball, cross-country, diving, field hockey W, football (tackle) M, lacrosse W, soccer, softball W, swimming, track and field, volleyball W. **Intramural:** Basketball, bowling, golf, handball, racquetball, soccer, softball, table tennis, tennis, volleyball. **Team name:** Profs.

Student services. Adult student services, alcohol/substance abuse counseling, chaplain/spiritual director, career counseling, student employment services, financial aid counseling, health services, legal services, minority student services, on-campus daycare, personal counseling, placement for graduates, veterans' counselor, women's services. **Physically disabled:** Services for visually, speech, hearing impaired.

Contact. E-mail: admissions@rowan.edu
Phone: (856) 256-4200 Toll-free number: (877) 787-6926
Fax: (856) 256-4430
Albert Betts, Director of Admissions, Rowan University, Savitz Hall, 201 Mullica Hill Road, Glassboro, NJ 08028

Four-Year Colleges

Rutgers, The State University of New Jersey: Camden Regional Campus

Camden, New Jersey — CB member
www.rutgers.edu — CB code: 2742

- Public 4-year university
- Commuter campus in small city
- 4,606 degree-seeking undergraduates: 18% part-time, 55% women, 18% African American, 8% Asian American, 10% Hispanic American, 1% international
- 1,738 degree-seeking graduate students
- 54% of applicants admitted
- SAT or ACT with writing required
- 61% graduate within 6 years

General. Founded in 1927. Regionally accredited. Undergraduate schools: Camden College of Arts and Sciences, University College-Camden, School of Business-Camden. Graduate degrees available at School of Business. Graduate schools: Graduate School-Camden, School of Law-Camden. **Degrees:** 1,005 bachelor's awarded; master's, professional offered. **ROTC:** Army, Air Force. **Location:** One mile from Philadelphia. **Calendar:** Semester, extensive summer session. **Full-time faculty:** 281 total; 99% have terminal degrees, 17% minority, 40% women. **Part-time faculty:** 241 total; 99% have terminal degrees, 11% minority, 36% women. **Class size:** 38% < 20, 48% 20-39, 6% 40-49, 6% 50-99, 2% >100. **Special facilities:** Fine arts center.

Freshman class profile. 5,791 applied, 3,115 admitted, 536 enrolled.

Mid 50% test scores		
SAT critical reading:	480-580	
SAT math:	490-600	
SAT writing:	490-570	
Rank in top quarter:	48%	

Rank in top tenth:	19%
Return as sophomores:	83%
Out-of-state:	7%
Live on campus:	45%

Basis for selection. School achievement record (including grades, rank, strength of program, honors) and test scores most important. Extracurricular activities, talent, disadvantaged status considered. SAT Subject Tests required for applicants who will not have diploma from accredited high school by entrance date. May also be required of GED holders. **Home schooled:** SAT Subject Tests required for applicants who will not have diploma from accredited high school by entrance date.

High school preparation. College-preparatory program required. 16 units required. Required units include English 4, mathematics 3, science 2, foreign language 2 and academic electives 5.

2011-2012 Annual costs. Tuition/fees: $12,615; $25,277 out-of-state. School of Business tuition and fees are slightly higher. Room/board: $10,726. Books/supplies: $1,431. Personal expenses: $1,631.

2011-2012 Financial aid. **Need-based:** 449 full-time freshmen applied for aid; 388 were judged to have need; 388 of these received aid. Average need met was 56%. Average scholarship/grant was $10,612; average loan $3,326. 64% of total undergraduate aid awarded as scholarships/grants, 36% as loans/jobs. **Non-need-based:** Awarded to 534 full-time undergraduates, including 157 freshmen. Scholarships awarded for academics, alumni affiliation, art, athletics, leadership, minority status, music/drama.

Application procedures. **Admission:** Closing date 12/1. $65 fee, may be waived for applicants with need. Application must be submitted online. Admission notification on a rolling basis beginning on or about 2/28. Must reply by May 1 or within 2 week(s) if notified thereafter. May apply to up to 3 Rutgers colleges with 1 application. Students applying by December 1 notified by February 28. **Financial aid:** Priority date 3/15; no closing date. FAFSA required. Applicants notified on a rolling basis starting 3/1; must reply within 2 week(s) of notification.

Academics. **Special study options:** Accelerated study, combined bachelor's/graduate degree, cooperative education, cross-registration, distance learning, double major, dual enrollment of high school students, ESL, exchange student, honors, independent study, internships, liberal arts/career combination, student-designed major, study abroad, teacher certification program, weekend college. Cooperative baccalaureate program in Engineering with School of Engineering (New Brunswick Campus); Interdisciplinary program in African-American studies, general science. Cooperative baccalaureate in medical technology with approved hospital. BA/MA in Childhood Studies; English, History, Liberal Studies or Psychology; BA/MS in Biology, Chemistry or Mathematics (with the Graduate School-Camden). BA in Economics or Political Science/Master of Public Administration (with the Graduate School-Camden); BS/Master of Business and Science (MBS). **Credit/placement by examination:** AP, CLEP, IB, institutional tests. No more than 8 credits given for elementary or intermediate levels of any foreign language. Graduating seniors may take no more than one examination in their final term. **Support services:** Learning center, pre-admission summer program,

reduced course load, remedial instruction, study skills assistance, tutoring, writing center.

Majors. **Area/ethnic studies:** African-American. **Biology:** General, biomedical sciences. **Business:** Accounting, business admin, finance, hospitality admin, marketing. **Computer sciences:** Computer science. **Engineering:** Biomedical, ceramic, chemical, civil, electrical, engineering science, mechanical. **English:** English lit. **Foreign languages:** French, German, Spanish. **Health services:** Nursing (RN), predental, premedicine. **History:** General. **Human services:** Social work. **Liberal arts:** Arts/sciences. **Math:** General. **Philosophy/religion:** Philosophy. **Physical sciences:** Chemistry, physics. **Protective services:** Criminal justice. **Psychology:** General. **Social sciences:** Economics, political science, sociology, urban studies. **Visual/performing arts:** Art, dramatic, music.

Most popular majors. Biology 6%, business/marketing 23%, psychology 14%, security/protective services 7%, social sciences 13%.

Computing on campus. 187 workstations in dormitories, library, computer center, student center. Dormitories linked to campus network. Commuter students can connect to campus network. Online course registration, helpline, repair service, wireless network available.

Student life. **Freshman orientation:** Available. Preregistration for classes offered. **Housing:** Coed dorms, special housing for disabled, apartments available. $200 nonrefundable deposit. **Activities:** Drama, international student organizations, literary magazine, radio station, student government, student newspaper, accounting society, forensics society, political science association, black student union, Latin American students organization, physics society, Jewish student union, marketing association, psychology club.

Athletics. NCAA. **Intercollegiate:** Baseball M, basketball, cross-country, golf M, rowing (crew) W, soccer, softball W, tennis M, track and field, volleyball W. **Intramural:** Badminton, basketball, football (tackle) M, handball, racquetball, soccer, softball, squash, volleyball. **Team name:** Scarlet Raptors.

Student services. Career counseling, student employment services, health services, on-campus daycare, personal counseling, placement for graduates, veterans' counselor. **Physically disabled:** Services for visually, speech, hearing impaired.

Contact. E-mail: admissions@ugadm.rutgers.edu
Phone: (856) 225-6104 Fax: (856) 225-6498
Deborah Bowles, Director of Admissions, Rutgers, The State University of New Jersey: Camden Regional Campus, 406 Penn Street, Camden, NJ 08102

Rutgers, The State University of New Jersey: New Brunswick/Piscataway Campus

Piscataway, New Jersey — CB member
www.rutgers.edu — CB code: 2765

- Public 4-year university
- Residential campus in large town
- 30,926 degree-seeking undergraduates: 4% part-time, 48% women, 8% African American, 25% Asian American, 11% Hispanic American, 2% international
- 7,995 degree-seeking graduate students
- 61% of applicants admitted
- SAT or ACT with writing required
- 77% graduate within 6 years

General. Founded in 1969. Regionally accredited. Undergraduate schools include: School of Environmental and Biological Sciences, School of Arts and Sciences, School of Engineering, School of the Arts, School of Planning and Public Policy, College of Nursing, School of Pharmacy, School of Business-New Brunswick, School of Communication and Information. **Degrees:** 6,171 bachelor's awarded; master's, professional, doctoral offered. **ROTC:** Army, Air Force. **Location:** 33 miles from New York City. **Calendar:** Semester, extensive summer session. **Full-time faculty:** 1,736 total; 99% have terminal degrees, 18% minority, 38% women. **Part-time faculty:** 1,009 total; 99% have terminal degrees, 10% minority, 51% women. **Class size:** 41% < 20, 32% 20-39, 8% 40-49, 11% 50-99, 9% >100. **Special facilities:** Geology museum, ecological preserve, 2 theaters, center for urban policy research, institute for health, health care policy and aging research, journalism resources institute, laboratory for computer science research, center for math, science and computer education.

Freshman class profile. 28,602 applied, 17,487 admitted, 6,075 enrolled.

Mid 50% test scores			
SAT critical reading:	520-630	Rank in top tenth:	37%
SAT math:	560-680	Return as sophomores:	91%
SAT writing:	530-640	Out-of-state:	11%
Rank in top quarter:	72%	Live on campus:	91%
		International:	3%

Basis for selection. School achievement record (including grades, rank, strength of program, honors, AP) and test scores most important. Extracurricular activities, leadership talent, minority, disadvantaged status considered. State residents with educationally and economically disadvantaged backgrounds given consideration through state Educational Opportunity Fund program. SAT Subject Tests required of applicants who, by expected date of entrance, will not have diploma from accredited high school. May also be required of GED holders. Interview, audition, portfolio review required for School of the Arts. **Home schooled:** SAT Subject Tests required of graduates from non-accredited high schools.

High school preparation. College-preparatory program required. 16 units required. Required units include English 4, mathematics 3, science 2, foreign language 2 and academic electives 5.

2011-2012 Annual costs. Tuition/fees: $12,754; $25,416 out-of-state. Tuition and fees may vary by program. Room/board: $11,262. Books/supplies: $1,431. Personal expenses: $1,631.

2011-2012 Financial aid. **Need-based:** 4,723 full-time freshmen applied for aid; 3,839 were judged to have need; 3,839 of these received aid. Average need met was 52%. Average scholarship/grant was $10,721; average loan $3,361. 63% of total undergraduate aid awarded as scholarships/grants, 37% as loans/jobs. **Non-need-based:** Awarded to 4,611 full-time undergraduates, including 1,388 freshmen. Scholarships awarded for academics, alumni affiliation, art, athletics, leadership, minority status, music/drama, state residency.

Application procedures. Admission: Closing date 12/1. $65 fee, may be waived for applicants with need. Application must be submitted online. Admission notification on a rolling basis. Must reply by May 1 or within 2 week(s) if notified thereafter. May apply to up to 3 Rutgers colleges with 1 application. Applications received by December 1 will be answered by February 28. **Financial aid:** Priority date 3/15; no closing date. FAFSA required. Applicants notified on a rolling basis starting 3/1; must reply within 2 week(s) of notification.

Academics. Special study options: Accelerated study, combined bachelor's/graduate degree, cooperative education, cross-registration, distance learning, double major, dual enrollment of high school students, ESL, exchange student, honors, independent study, internships, liberal arts/career combination, student-designed major, study abroad, teacher certification program, Washington semester, weekend college. 5-year BA or BS/MPA program in Rutgers Business School; BS in Business Discipline/MBA; BA or BS in Science Discipline/MBA; 8-year Bachelor/Medical Dual Degree program with UMDNJ-Robert Wood Johnson Medical School; 5-year BS/BS in Bioenvironmental Engineering with the School of Engineering; 5-year accelerated baccalaureate-MBA with RU Business School; Bureau of Engineering Research, supported by the University, industry, state and federal government, provides research opportunities for students and faculty; continuing professional education; Exchange program between School of Engineering and the City University of London for qualified students majoring in civil, electrical, or mechanical engineering; 5-year BA/BS degree program in liberal arts and engineering; 5-year BA or BS/M.Ed. with the Graduate School of Education; interdepartmental programs and certificate programs are available; BA/Master of Communication and Information Studies (with SCI); BA/MLER with School of Management and Labor Relations; Baccalaureate/MCRP, MPH or MPP with EJB School of Planning and Public Policy; Baccalaureate in Business major/Master of Human Resources Management with School of Management and Labor Relations (SMLR); BS/Master of Business and Science (MBS). **Credit/placement by examination:** AP, CLEP, IB, institutional tests. 30 credit hours maximum toward bachelor's degree. **Support services:** Learning center, pre-admission summer program, reduced course load, remedial instruction, study skills assistance, tutoring, writing center.

Majors. Architecture: Environmental design, urban/community planning. **Area/ethnic studies:** African, African-American, American, Caribbean, Chicano/Hispanic-American/Latino, East Asian, Latin American, Near/Middle Eastern, Russian/Eastern European/Eurasian, Russian/Slavic, women's. **Biology:** General, bacteriology, biochemistry, biometrics, biotechnology, cell/histology, genetics, marine, molecular. **Business:** Accounting, business admin, finance, labor relations, management information systems, management science, marketing. **Communications:** Communications/speech/rhetoric, journalism. **Computer sciences:** Computer science. **Conservation:** General, environmental studies, management/policy. **Engineering:** Biomedical, ceramic, chemical, civil, electrical, engineering science, environmental, mechanical. **English:** English lit. **Foreign languages:** Chinese, classics, comparative lit, French, German, Italian, linguistics, Portuguese, Russian, Spanish. **General:** Animal sciences, food science, plant sciences. **Health services:**

Clinical lab technology, nursing (RN), physician assistant, predental, premedicine. **History:** General. **Human services:** Social work. **Math:** General, statistics. **Parks/recreation:** Exercise sciences. **Philosophy/religion:** Judaic, philosophy, religion. **Physical sciences:** Atmospheric science, chemistry, geology, physics. **Protective services:** Law enforcement admin. **Psychology:** General. **Social sciences:** Anthropology, economics, geography, political science, sociology, urban studies. **Visual/performing arts:** Art, art history/conservation, dance, dramatic, music.

Most popular majors. Biology 10%, business/marketing 8%, communications/journalism 10%, engineering/engineering technologies 8%, psychology 10%, social sciences 15%.

Computing on campus. 1,450 workstations in dormitories, library, computer center, student center. Dormitories linked to campus network. Commuter students can connect to campus network. Helpline, repair service available.

Student life. Freshman orientation: Available. Preregistration for classes offered. **Housing:** Guaranteed on-campus for freshmen. Coed dorms, single-sex dorms, special housing for disabled, apartments, cooperative housing, fraternity/sorority housing available. $100 deposit, deadline 6/15. **Activities:** Bands, campus ministries, choral groups, dance, drama, film society, international student organizations, literary magazine, music ensembles, musical theater, opera, radio station, student government, student newspaper, symphony orchestra, TV station, 400 organizations available.

Athletics. NCAA. **Intercollegiate:** Baseball M, basketball, cross-country, diving W, fencing M, field hockey W, football (tackle) M, golf, gymnastics W, lacrosse, rowing (crew), soccer, softball W, swimming W, tennis W, track and field, volleyball W, wrestling M. **Intramural:** Badminton, basketball, bowling, cross-country, golf, racquetball, soccer, softball, squash, swimming W, table tennis, tennis, track and field, volleyball, water polo, wrestling M. **Team name:** Scarlet Knights.

Student services. Adult student services, career counseling, student employment services, health services, on-campus daycare, personal counseling, placement for graduates, veterans' counselor. **Physically disabled:** Services for visually, speech, hearing impaired.

Contact. E-mail: admissions@ugadm.rutgers.edu
Phone: (732) 932-4636 Fax: (732) 445-0237
Diane Harris, Director of Undergraduate Admissions, Rutgers, The State University of New Jersey: New Brunswick/Piscataway Campus, 65 Davidson Road, Room 202, Piscataway, NJ 08854-8097

Rutgers, The State University of New Jersey: Newark Regional Campus
Newark, New Jersey
www.rutgers.edu   CB code: 2753

- Public 4-year university
- Commuter campus in large city
- 7,022 degree-seeking undergraduates: 14% part-time, 53% women, 18% African American, 23% Asian American, 22% Hispanic American, 2% international
- 4,169 degree-seeking graduate students
- 54% of applicants admitted
- SAT or ACT with writing required
- 68% graduate within 6 years

General. Founded in 1930. Regionally accredited. **Degrees:** 1,475 bachelor's awarded; master's, professional, doctoral offered. **ROTC:** Army, Air Force. **Location:** 10 miles from New York City. **Calendar:** Semester, extensive summer session. **Full-time faculty:** 496 total; 99% have terminal degrees, 21% minority, 39% women. **Part-time faculty:** 292 total; 99% have terminal degrees, 12% minority, 48% women. **Class size:** 32% < 20, 40% 20-39, 13% 40-49, 11% 50-99, 4% >100. **Special facilities:** Biology learning center, jazz institute, animal behavior institute, center for molecular and behavioral neuroscience, center for negotiation and conflict resolution.

Freshman class profile. 11,352 applied, 6,135 admitted, 986 enrolled.

Mid 50% test scores			
SAT critical reading:	460-560	Rank in top tenth:	26%
SAT math:	500-610	Return as sophomores:	83%
SAT writing:	480-570	Out-of-state:	64%
Rank in top quarter:	53%	Live on campus:	42%
		International:	3%

Basis for selection. School achievement record and test scores most important. Extracurricular activities, leadership talent, minority, disadvantaged status considered. State residents with educational and economically

disadvantaged backgrounds given consideration through state Educational Opportunity Fund program. SAT Subject Tests required of applicants who, by expected date of entrance, will not have diploma from accredited high school. May also be required of GED holders.

High school preparation. College-preparatory program required. 16 units required. Required units include English 4, mathematics 3, science 2, foreign language 2 and academic electives 5.

2011-2012 Annual costs. Tuition/fees: $12,294; $24,956 out-of-state. Room/board: $12,013. Books/supplies: $1,431. Personal expenses: $1,631.

2011-2012 Financial aid. Need-based: 752 full-time freshmen applied for aid; 680 were judged to have need; 680 of these received aid. Average need met was 58%. Average scholarship/grant was $10,865; average loan $3,334. 65% of total undergraduate aid awarded as scholarships/grants, 35% as loans/jobs. **Non-need-based:** Awarded to 529 full-time undergraduates, including 124 freshmen. Scholarships awarded for academics, alumni affiliation, art, athletics, leadership, minority status, music/drama, religious affiliation.

Application procedures. Admission: Closing date 12/1. $65 fee, may be waived for applicants with need. Application must be submitted online. Admission notification on a rolling basis beginning on or about 2/28. Must reply by May 1 or within 2 week(s) if notified thereafter. May apply to up to 3 Rutgers colleges with 1 application. Applications completed by December 1 will be answered by February 28. **Financial aid:** Priority date 3/15; no closing date. FAFSA required. Applicants notified on a rolling basis starting 3/1; must reply within 2 week(s) of notification.

Academics. Special study options: Accelerated study, combined bachelor's/graduate degree, cooperative education, cross-registration, distance learning, double major, dual enrollment of high school students, ESL, exchange student, honors, independent study, internships, liberal arts/career combination, student-designed major, study abroad, teacher certification program, Washington semester, weekend college. 5-year baccalaureate-MBA with RU Business School; BS in Business Discipline/MBA; BA or BS in Science Discipline/MBA; Baccalaureate/MA in Criminal Justice with the School of Criminal Justice; Baccalaureate/MPA with the School of Public Affairs and Administration; Cooperative baccalaureate program with the School of Engineering (New Brunswick campus); Cooperative baccalaureate in medical technology with affiliated hospitals; interdisciplinary program in archaeology, international affairs, legal studies, women's studies; continuing professional education; Baccalaureate in Business Major/Master of Human Resource Management (with School of Management and Labor Relations in New Brunswick); Baccalaureate-Master's dual degree programs with the School of Criminal Justice and Rutgers Business School; BA or BS in Biology/MS in Biology; BA in Chemistry/MS in Chemistry; BA in Economics/MA in Economics; BS in Environmental Sciences/MS in Environmental Geology; BS in Environmental Sciences/MS in Environmental Sciences; BA in Political Science, Sociology or Anthropology/MS in Global Affairs; BA in History/MA in History, Sociology or Anthropology/MA in Jazz History and Research; BA in Political Science/MA in Political Science; BS in Computer Science or Information Science/Master of Information Technology; BS in Accounting/Master of Accountancy (Governmental Accounting or Financial Accounting); BS in Accounting/MBA in Professional Accounting; BS in Finance/Master of Quantitative Finance; The College of Nursing offers a program on the New Brunswick Campus. Students are admitted in the fall semester only; BS in Nursing/MS in Nursing. **Credit/placement by examination:** AP, CLEP, IB, institutional tests. 24 credit hours maximum toward bachelor's degree. **Support services:** Learning center, pre-admission summer program, reduced course load, remedial instruction, study skills assistance, tutoring, writing center.

Honors college/program. By invitation.

Majors. Area/ethnic studies: African, African-American, American, Caribbean, Chicano/Hispanic-American/Latino, women's. **Biology:** General, botany, zoology. **Business:** Accounting, business admin, finance, marketing. **Communications:** Journalism. **Computer sciences:** Computer science, information systems. **Conservation:** General. **Engineering:** Biomedical, ceramic, chemical, civil, electrical, mechanical. **English:** English lit. **Foreign languages:** French, Spanish. **Health services:** Clinical lab science, clinical lab technology, nursing (RN), predental, premedicine. **History:** General. **Human services:** Social work. **Math:** General, applied. **Philosophy/religion:** Philosophy. **Physical sciences:** Chemistry, geology, physics. **Protective services:** Criminal justice. **Psychology:** General. **Social sciences:** Anthropology, economics, political science, sociology. **Visual/performing arts:** Art, dramatic, music.

Most popular majors. Biology 8%, business/marketing 36%, health sciences 11%, psychology 10%, security/protective services 14%, social sciences 8%.

Computing on campus. 450 workstations in dormitories, library, computer center. Dormitories linked to campus network. Commuter students can connect to campus network. Helpline, repair service available.

Student life. Freshman orientation: Available. Preregistration for classes offered. **Housing:** Coed dorms, special housing for disabled, apartments, fraternity/sorority housing available. $100 deposit. **Activities:** Choral groups, drama, international student organizations, radio station, student government, student newspaper, black organization of students, Puerto Rican and Latin American student organizations, political organizations, religious organizations, service organizations.

Athletics. NCAA. **Intercollegiate:** Baseball M, basketball, soccer, softball W, tennis, volleyball. **Intramural:** Basketball, racquetball, soccer, tennis, volleyball. **Team name:** Scarlet Raiders.

Student services. Career counseling, student employment services, health services, personal counseling, placement for graduates, veterans' counselor. **Physically disabled:** Services for visually, speech, hearing impaired.

Contact. E-mail: newarkadmissions@ugadm.rutgers.edu
Phone: (973) 353-5205 Fax: (973) 353-1440
Jason Hand, Director of Admissions at Newark, Rutgers, The State University of New Jersey: Newark Regional Campus, 249 University Avenue, Newark, NJ 07102-1896

Saint Peter's College
Jersey City, New Jersey
www.spc.edu

CB member
CB code: 2806

- Private 4-year liberal arts college affiliated with Roman Catholic Church
- Commuter campus in small city
- 2,254 degree-seeking undergraduates: 11% part-time, 59% women, 28% African American, 11% Asian American, 26% Hispanic American, 1% Native American, 3% international
- 613 degree-seeking graduate students
- 67% of applicants admitted
- SAT or ACT (ACT writing optional), application essay required
- 51% graduate within 6 years

General. Founded in 1872. Regionally accredited. Extensive evening program on main campus, at branch locations at Englewood Cliffs and South Amboy for adult learners, and other locations throughout metropolitan area. **Degrees:** 412 bachelor's, 26 associate awarded; master's, professional offered. **ROTC:** Army, Air Force. **Location:** 3 miles from New York City. **Calendar:** Semester, extensive summer session. **Full-time faculty:** 117 total; 80% have terminal degrees, 11% minority, 48% women. **Part-time faculty:** 166 total; 42% have terminal degrees, 37% women. **Class size:** 60% < 20, 40% 20-39.

Freshman class profile. 2,779 applied, 1,861 admitted, 421 enrolled.

Mid 50% test scores			
SAT critical reading:	410-520	GPA 3.0-3.49:	36%
SAT math:	420-530	GPA 2.0-2.99:	29%
SAT writing:	420-510	Return as sophomores:	74%
ACT composite:	17-21	Out-of-state:	15%
GPA 3.75 or higher:	17%	Live on campus:	50%
GPA 3.50-3.74:	17%	International:	3%

Basis for selection. Admissions decision based on (in rank order) school achievement record, test scores, essay, letters of recommendation, class activities. SAT required of international students who apply for scholarship. Interview recommended.

High school preparation. 16 units required; 19 recommended. Required and recommended units include English 4, mathematics 3-4, history 2-3, science 2-3 (laboratory 1), foreign language 2 and academic electives 3.

2011-2012 Annual costs. Tuition/fees: $29,800. Room/board: $12,240. Books/supplies: $800. Personal expenses: $600.

Financial aid. Non-need-based: Scholarships awarded for academics, athletics. **Additional information:** Cooperative education internships available in all majors, with average salaries exceeding $5,200.

Application procedures. Admission: Priority date 4/1; no deadline. No application fee. Admission notification on a rolling basis beginning on or about 11/1. **Financial aid:** Priority date 3/15; no closing date. FAFSA required. Applicants notified on a rolling basis starting 2/15; must reply by 5/1 or within 2 week(s) of notification.

Academics. Joint Pre-Med/MD program with UMDNJ, joint Pre-Law/Law and Occupational Therapy program with Seton Hall University, joint Pharmacy and Physical Therapy program with Rutgers University, joint Engineering Program with New Jersey Institute of Technology. **Special study options:** Combined bachelor's/graduate degree, cooperative education, distance learning, double major, dual enrollment of high school students, ESL,

exchange student, honors, independent study, internships, student-designed major, study abroad, teacher certification program, Washington semester, weekend college. Joint degree in clinical laboratory sciences with University of Medicine and Dentistry of New Jersey. **Credit/placement by examination:** AP, CLEP, IB, institutional tests. 30 credit hours maximum toward bachelor's degree. **Support services:** Learning center, pre-admission summer program, reduced course load, remedial instruction, study skills assistance, tutoring, writing center.

Majors. Area/ethnic studies: American. **Biology:** General, biochemistry, toxicology. **Business:** Accounting, banking/financial services, business admin, finance, international, management information systems, managerial economics. **Communications:** Communications/speech/rhetoric. **Computer sciences:** General, computer science, information systems, programming. **Education:** Elementary. **English:** English lit. **Foreign languages:** General, classics, Spanish. **Health services:** Clinical lab science, cytotechnology, nursing (RN). **History:** General. **Human services:** Public policy. **Math:** General. **Philosophy/religion:** Philosophy, religion. **Physical sciences:** Chemistry, physics. **Psychology:** General. **Social sciences:** General, economics, political science, sociology, urban studies. **Visual/performing arts:** Studio arts.

Most popular majors. Biology 9%, business/marketing 27%, education 7%, health sciences 11%, psychology 7%, security/protective services 11%, social sciences 9%.

Computing on campus. 225 workstations in dormitories, library, computer center, student center. Dormitories wired for high-speed internet access and linked to campus network. Commuter students can connect to campus network. Online library, helpline, student web hosting, wireless network available.

Student life. Freshman orientation: Mandatory, $200 fee. Preregistration for classes offered. Three-day sessions held throughout July. Program features academic advising, social activities, and introduction to community service. **Housing:** Guaranteed on-campus for all undergraduates. Coed dorms, special housing for disabled, apartments available. $250 partly refundable deposit, deadline 5/1. **Activities:** Campus ministries, choral groups, drama, international student organizations, literary magazine, radio station, student government, student newspaper, Alpha Phi Omega, Emmaus Spiritual Retreats, Circle K, Young Republicans, Hispanic culture club, Irish American club, Asian American student union, Black Action Committee, Indo-Pak culture club.

Athletics. NCAA. **Intercollegiate:** Baseball M, basketball, bowling, cheerleading, cross-country, diving, golf M, soccer, softball W, swimming, tennis, track and field, volleyball W. **Intramural:** Baseball M, basketball, bowling, racquetball, soccer, softball, swimming, table tennis, tennis, volleyball, water polo. **Team name:** Peacocks/Peahens.

Student services. Adult student services, alcohol/substance abuse counseling, chaplain/spiritual director, career counseling, services for economically disadvantaged, student employment services, financial aid counseling, health services, minority student services, personal counseling, placement for graduates, veterans' counselor. **Physically disabled:** Services for visually, speech, hearing impaired.

Contact. E-mail: admissions@spc.edu
Phone: (201) 761-7100 Toll-free number: (888) 772-9933
Fax: (201) 761-7105
Joe Giglio, Executive Director of Admission and Enrollment Marketing, Saint Peter's College, 2641 Kennedy Boulevard, Jersey City, NJ 07306

Seton Hall University
South Orange, New Jersey

CB member
www.shu.edu
CB code: 2811

- Private 4-year university affiliated with Roman Catholic Church
- Residential campus in large town
- 4,903 degree-seeking undergraduates: 6% part-time, 59% women, 14% African American, 8% Asian American, 14% Hispanic American, 2% international
- 4,209 degree-seeking graduate students
- 85% of applicants admitted
- SAT or ACT with writing, application essay required
- 66% graduate within 6 years

General. Founded in 1856. Regionally accredited. Immaculate Conception Seminary and School of Theology located on campus. Off-campus sites for nursing and education. **Degrees:** 993 bachelor's awarded; master's, professional, doctoral offered. **ROTC:** Army. **Location:** 14 miles from New York City. **Calendar:** Semester, extensive summer session. **Full-time faculty:** 456 total; 88% have terminal degrees, 17% minority, 49% women. **Part-time faculty:** 484 total; 16% minority, 50% women. **Class size:** 51% < 20, 44% 20-39, 2% 40-49, 2% 50-99, less than 1% >100. **Special facilities:** Computer graphics and communications laboratories, educational media center, nursing demonstration room, art center, music laboratories, special collections center.

Freshman class profile. 6,436 applied, 5,474 admitted, 993 enrolled.

Mid 50% test scores			
SAT critical reading:	470-580	GPA 2.0-2.99:	21%
SAT math:	490-590	Rank in top quarter:	56%
SAT writing:	490-600	Rank in top tenth:	26%
ACT composite:	21-26	Return as sophomores:	81%
GPA 3.75 or higher:	26%	Out-of-state:	28%
GPA 3.50-3.74:	19%	Live on campus:	73%
GPA 3.0-3.49:	34%	International:	2%

Basis for selection. School achievement record, test scores, recommendations, essay most important. Extracurricular activities, volunteer work, work experience important. Class rank, interview, talent/ability, character/personal qualities considered. Interview strongly recommended. Audition required for music majors. **Home schooled:** Statement describing home school structure and mission, transcript of courses and grades, state high school equivalency certificate, letter of recommendation (nonparent) required. Required to meet home state requirements and must submit supporting documentation. Students must submit transcript or portfolio of academic work completed.

High school preparation. College-preparatory program required. 16 units required. Required units include English 4, mathematics 3, social studies 2, science 1 (laboratory 1), foreign language 2 and academic electives 4. Nursing majors must have additional 2 units in science (biology and chemistry).

2011-2012 Annual costs. Tuition/fees: $33,490. Required fees include lease of laptop computer. Room/board: $12,412.

Financial aid. Non-need-based: Scholarships awarded for academics, alumni affiliation, athletics, minority status, ROTC, state residency.

Application procedures. Admission: Priority date 3/1; no deadline. $55 fee, may be waived for applicants with need. Admission notification on a rolling basis beginning on or about 12/1. Must reply by May 1 or within 4 week(s) if notified thereafter. **Financial aid:** Priority date 3/1; no closing date. FAFSA required. Applicants notified on a rolling basis starting 3/1; must reply by 5/1 or within 4 week(s) of notification.

Academics. Special study options: Accelerated study, combined bachelor's/graduate degree, cooperative education, cross-registration, distance learning, double major, dual enrollment of high school students, ESL, honors, independent study, internships, liberal arts/career combination, study abroad, teacher certification program, Washington semester. **Credit/placement by examination:** AP, CLEP, IB, SAT, institutional tests. 30 credit hours maximum toward bachelor's degree. **Support services:** Learning center, pre-admission summer program, reduced course load, remedial instruction, study skills assistance, tutoring, writing center.

Majors. Area/ethnic studies: African-American, Asian, Latin American. **Biology:** General, biochemistry. **Business:** Accounting, business admin, finance, information resources management, labor relations, management information systems, managerial economics, marketing. **Communications:** Communications/speech/rhetoric, journalism, public relations, radio/TV. **Computer sciences:** General. **Conservation:** Environmental studies. **Education:** Elementary, secondary, special ed. **English:** Creative writing, English lit. **Foreign languages:** General, classics, French, Italian, Spanish. **Health services:** Nursing (RN). **History:** General. **Human services:** Social work. **Liberal arts:** Arts/sciences, humanities. **Math:** General. **Parks/recreation:** Sports admin. **Philosophy/religion:** Philosophy, religion. **Physical sciences:** Chemistry, physics. **Protective services:** Criminal justice. **Psychology:** General. **Social sciences:** Anthropology, economics, international relations, political science, sociology. **Theology:** Religious ed, theology. **Visual/performing arts:** General, art history/conservation, commercial/advertising art, dramatic, music, music performance.

Most popular majors. Biology 7%, business/marketing 20%, communications/journalism 7%, education 7%, health sciences 12%, liberal arts 7%, social sciences 11%.

Computing on campus. PC or laptop required. 5,000 workstations in dormitories, library, computer center, student center. Dormitories wired for high-speed internet access and linked to campus network. Commuter students can connect to campus network. Online course registration, online library, helpline, repair service, student web hosting, wireless network available.

Student life. Freshman orientation: Mandatory, $300 fee. Preregistration for classes offered. Two-day program held at various times in June. **Policies:** 1.8 GPA housing requirement. Freshmen not permitted cars on campus. **Housing:** Coed dorms, special housing for disabled, apartments, wellness housing available. $250 partly refundable deposit, deadline 5/1. **Activities:**

Pep band, campus ministries, choral groups, dance, drama, international student organizations, literary magazine, Model UN, radio station, student government, student newspaper, TV station, Adelante, black student union, Buddhists for Peace, Jewish student union, Lusophone student association, SHU STAND, Kraut und Lederhosen, College Republicans, College Democrats, Students for Individual Liberty.

Athletics. NCAA. **Intercollegiate:** Baseball M, basketball, cross-country, golf, soccer, softball W, swimming, tennis W, volleyball W. **Intramural:** Basketball, football (non-tackle), racquetball, soccer, softball, tennis, volleyball. **Team name:** Pirates.

Student services. Alcohol/substance abuse counseling, chaplain/spiritual director, career counseling, services for economically disadvantaged, student employment services, financial aid counseling, health services, minority student services, personal counseling, placement for graduates. **Physically disabled:** Services for visually, speech, hearing impaired.

Contact. E-mail: thehall@shu.edu
Phone: (973) 313-6146 Toll-free number: (800) 843-4255
Fax: (973) 275-2040
Wendy Lin-Cook, Assistant Vice President for Admissions, Seton Hall University, 400 South Orange Avenue, South Orange, NJ 07079-2680

Somerset Christian College
Zarephath, New Jersey
www.somerset.edu   CB code: 3933

▶ Private 4-year Bible and liberal arts college affiliated with Pillar of Fire International
▶ Commuter campus in small town
▶ 275 degree-seeking undergraduates
▶ SAT or ACT (ACT writing optional), application essay required

General. Candidate for regional accreditation; also accredited by ABHE. **Degrees:** 55 bachelor's, 3 associate awarded. **Location:** 45 miles from New York City and Philadelphia. **Calendar:** Semester, limited summer session. **Full-time faculty:** 5 total. **Part-time faculty:** 30 total. **Class size:** 48% < 20, 52% 20-39. **Special facilities:** Instructional resource center, Delaware-Raritan Canal nature trail.

Basis for selection. Recommendations most important. High school record, standardized test scores, essay also important. **Home schooled:** Interview, letter of recommendation (nonparent) required. Transcript of study including subjects, grades and GPA required. Students must send proof of graduation date or GED scores. **Learning Disabled:** Students must have documented diagnosis and portfolio of prior school collaboration in accommodating students' learning disabilities.

High school preparation. 15 units required. Required units include English 4, mathematics 1, social studies 3, science 2, foreign language 2 and academic electives 3.

2011-2012 Annual costs. Tuition/fees: $15,225. Books/supplies: $1,200. Personal expenses: $1,120.

Financial aid. All financial aid based on need.

Application procedures. **Admission:** Closing date 8/30 (postmark date). $35 fee, may be waived for applicants with need. Application must be submitted online. Admission notification on a rolling basis. **Financial aid:** No deadline. FAFSA required. Applicants notified on a rolling basis starting 1/31.

Academics. **Special study options:** Distance learning, dual enrollment of high school students, independent study, internships. **Credit/placement by examination:** AP, CLEP, IB, institutional tests. **Support services:** Learning center, reduced course load, remedial instruction, study skills assistance, tutoring, writing center.

Majors. **Philosophy/religion:** Christian. **Theology:** Bible.

Computing on campus. 30 workstations in library, computer center. Online course registration, online library, wireless network available.

Student life. **Freshman orientation:** Mandatory. Preregistration for classes offered. **Policies:** Religious observance required. **Activities:** Student government, student newspaper.

Student services. Chaplain/spiritual director, career counseling, financial aid counseling.

Contact. E-mail: info@somerset.edu
Phone: (732) 356-1595 Toll-free number: (800) 234-9305
Fax: (732) 356-4846
Kobie Morgan, Director of Admissions, Somerset Christian College, 10 College Way, Zarephath, NJ 08890

Stevens Institute of Technology
Hoboken, New Jersey   CB member
www.stevens.edu   CB code: 2819

▶ Private 4-year university and engineering college
▶ Residential campus in small city
▶ 2,427 degree-seeking undergraduates: 25% women, 3% African American, 10% Asian American, 9% Hispanic American, 7% international
▶ 2,647 degree-seeking graduate students
▶ 42% of applicants admitted
▶ SAT or ACT (ACT writing optional), application essay, interview required
▶ 79% graduate within 6 years; 27% enter graduate study

General. Founded in 1870. Regionally accredited. Approximately 90% of all students participate in internships, externships, cooperative education and research. **Degrees:** 485 bachelor's awarded; master's, doctoral offered. **ROTC:** Army, Air Force. **Location:** One mile from New York City. **Calendar:** Semester, extensive summer session. **Full-time faculty:** 235 total. **Part-time faculty:** 171 total. **Class size:** 46% < 20, 40% 20-39, 5% 40-49, 6% 50-99, 3% >100. **Special facilities:** Laboratory for coastal, ocean and naval engineering, environmental laboratory, design and manufacturing institute, advanced telecommunications institute, geoenvironmental laboratory, optical communications lab, quantum cascade laser, center for mass spectrometry, center for microchemical systems, computer visualization laboratory.

Freshman class profile. 3,600 applied, 1,500 admitted, 559 enrolled.

Mid 50% test scores			
SAT critical reading:	560-660	Rank in top quarter:	88%
SAT math:	630-720	Rank in top tenth:	56%
SAT writing:	560-660	Return as sophomores:	92%
ACT composite:	26-30	Out-of-state:	36%
GPA 3.75 or higher:	59%	Live on campus:	91%
GPA 3.50-3.74:	22%	International:	2%
GPA 3.0-3.49:	18%	Fraternities:	27%
GPA 2.0-2.99:	1%	Sororities:	26%

Basis for selection. GED not accepted. Admissions committee meets to review applicant's file once official transcript and standardized test scores are received and the interview requirement completed. Other information submitted considered as well. SAT Subject Tests required for accelerated premed, predentistry, or prelaw programs and recommended for all others. Students who live outside 250-mile radius and are unable to visit campus may schedule phone interview. Additional interview with departmental committee required of applicants to accelerated premed, predentistry, and prelaw programs. **Home schooled:** Letter of recommendation (nonparent) required.

High school preparation. College-preparatory program required. 16 units required. Required and recommended units include English 4, mathematics 4, social studies 2, history 2, science 3-4 (laboratory 3-4), foreign language 2 and academic electives 4. Business, engineering, computer science, and applied science programs require 2 algebra, 1 geometry, 1 pre-calculus or calculus, 1 chemistry, 1 physics, 1 biology.

2011-2012 Annual costs. Tuition/fees: $42,376. Room/board: $12,900. Books/supplies: $950. Personal expenses: $900.

2010-2011 Financial aid. **Non-need-based:** Scholarships awarded for academics, leadership, music/drama, ROTC.

Application procedures. **Admission:** Closing date 2/1 (postmark date). $55 fee, may be waived for applicants with need, free for online applicants. Admission notification by 4/1. Must reply by May 1 or within 2 week(s) if notified thereafter. **Financial aid:** Priority date 2/15; no closing date. FAFSA required. Applicants notified on a rolling basis starting 3/30; must reply by 5/1 or within 2 week(s) of notification.

Academics. **Special study options:** Accelerated study, combined bachelor's/graduate degree, cooperative education, cross-registration, distance learning, double major, dual enrollment of high school students, honors, independent study, internships, study abroad. 4-year bachelor's/master's programs in all engineering and science disciplines. **Credit/placement by examination:** AP, CLEP, IB. **Support services:** Pre-admission summer program, reduced course load, remedial instruction, study skills assistance, tutoring, writing center.

Majors. Biology: Biochemistry, bioinformatics. **Business:** Business admin, management information systems. **Computer sciences:** General, networking, security. **Engineering:** General, applied physics, biomedical, chemical, civil, computer, electrical, environmental, mechanical. **English:** English lit. **History:** General. **Liberal arts:** Arts/sciences. **Math:** Applied. **Philosophy/religion:** Philosophy. **Physical sciences:** Chemistry, materials science, physics.

Most popular majors. Business/marketing 12%, computer/information sciences 6%, engineering/engineering technologies 71%.

Computing on campus. PC or laptop required. 500 workstations in dormitories, library, computer center, student center. Dormitories wired for high-speed internet access and linked to campus network. Commuter students can connect to campus network. Online course registration, online library, helpline, repair service, student web hosting, wireless network available.

Student life. Freshman orientation: Mandatory, $550 fee. Preregistration for classes offered. 3-day program. **Policies:** Honor system observed. Freshmen not living at home must live on campus. **Housing:** Guaranteed on-campus for all undergraduates. Coed dorms, single-sex dorms, apartments, fraternity/sorority housing, wellness housing available. $350 nonrefundable deposit, deadline 6/15. **Activities:** Bands, campus ministries, choral groups, dance, drama, film society, international student organizations, literary magazine, music ensembles, musical theater, radio station, student government, student newspaper, TV station, over 70 organizations.

Athletics. NCAA. **Intercollegiate:** Baseball M, basketball, cheerleading M, cross-country, equestrian W, fencing, field hockey W, golf M, lacrosse, soccer, softball W, swimming, tennis, track and field, volleyball, wrestling M. **Intramural:** Archery, badminton, basketball, bowling, cricket, football (non-tackle), lacrosse M, racquetball, soccer, softball, squash, tennis, volleyball. **Team name:** Ducks.

Student services. Alcohol/substance abuse counseling, chaplain/spiritual director, career counseling, services for economically disadvantaged, student employment services, financial aid counseling, health services, minority student services, personal counseling, placement for graduates, veterans' counselor, women's services. **Physically disabled:** Services for visually, speech, hearing impaired.

Contact. E-mail: admissions@stevens.edu
Phone: (201) 216-5194 Toll-free number: (800) 458-5323
Fax: (201) 216-8348
Daniel Gallagher, Dean of University Admissions, Stevens Institute of Technology, 1 Castle Point on Hudson, Hoboken, NJ 07030-5991

Talmudical Academy of New Jersey
Adelphia, New Jersey

CB code: 0686

- Private 4-year rabbinical college for men affiliated with Jewish faith
- Large town
- 60 degree-seeking undergraduates

General. Founded in 1967. Accredited by AARTS. Ordination available. **Degrees:** 6 bachelor's awarded. **Calendar:** Semester. **Full-time faculty:** 4 total. **Part-time faculty:** 1 total.

Basis for selection. Personal interview most important.

2011-2012 Annual costs. Tuition/fees: $10,750.

Application procedures. Admission: No deadline. No application fee. Admission notification on a rolling basis. **Financial aid:** No deadline. Applicants notified on a rolling basis.

Academics. Credit/placement by examination: AP, CLEP.

Majors. Theology: Talmudic.

Student life. Activities: Choral groups, TV station.

Contact. Phone: (732) 431-1600
Rabbi Yeruchim Shain, Registrar and Admissions Director, Talmudical Academy of New Jersey, Route 524, PO Box 7, Adelphia, NJ 07710

Thomas Edison State College
Trenton, New Jersey
www.tesc.edu

CB member
CB code: 0682

- Public 4-year liberal arts college
- Small city

- 19,140 degree-seeking undergraduates: 100% part-time, 41% women, 17% African American, 3% Asian American, 10% Hispanic American, 1% Native American, 1% international
- 1,111 degree-seeking graduate students

General. Founded in 1972. Regionally accredited. **Degrees:** 2,200 bachelor's, 525 associate awarded; master's offered. **Location:** 45 miles from Philadelphia, 76 miles from New York City. **Calendar:** Differs by program.

Basis for selection. Open admission, but selective for some programs. Applicants should be at least 21 years old. Certain programs in health professions limited to persons holding appropriate certification. Admission to bachelor's degree nursing program limited to registered nurses (RNs) currently licensed in the USA. Admission to Master of Arts in Educational Leadership degree limited to person with valid Teacher's Certificate. Applicants under the age of 21 may be accepted on case-by-case basis, or if they are member of a special population such as a corporate partner or member of U.S. military. Admission to Accelerated 2nd Degree BSN program limited to applicants who already have a non-nursing bachelor's degree.

2011-2012 Annual costs. Tuition/fees: $5,176; $7,621 out-of-state.

2010-2011 Financial aid. All financial aid based on need. 19% of total undergraduate aid awarded as scholarships/grants, 81% as loans/jobs. **Additional information:** Financial aid applications should be received two months before each new term begins.

Application procedures. Admission: No deadline. $75 fee. Admission notification on a rolling basis. **Financial aid:** No deadline. FAFSA, institutional form required. Applicants notified on a rolling basis starting 3/1.

Academics. Provides flexibility to complete degree, including credit by examination, assessment of experiential learning, guided study, online courses, e-pack courses and credit for licenses and certificates, corporate and military training. Contracts with subject matter experts to act as mentors to academic units of college. **Special study options:** Accelerated study, combined bachelor's/graduate degree, distance learning, dual enrollment of high school students, external degree, independent study, student-designed major. Bachelor of Science in Health Sciences program offered in partnership with University of Medicine and Dentistry of New Jersey School of Health-Related Professions. The 121-credit program is designed for those employed in the allied health field and requires students to possess professional certifications and licensures. **Credit/placement by examination:** AP, CLEP. 60 credit hours maximum toward associate degree, 120 toward bachelor's.

Majors. Biology: General. **Business:** Accounting, business admin, entrepreneurial studies, finance, hospitality admin, human resources, international, labor relations, marketing, operations, real estate. **Communications:** Communications/speech/rhetoric, journalism. **Computer sciences:** Computer science. **Conservation:** Environmental science, environmental studies. **English:** English lit. **Foreign languages:** General. **Health services:** Clinical lab science, dental hygiene, facilities admin, medical radiologic technology/radiation therapy, nuclear medical technology, nursing (RN), public health ed, radiation protection, respiratory therapy technology, veterinary technology/assistant. **History:** General. **Human services:** General, community org/advocacy. **Liberal arts:** Arts/sciences, humanities. **Math:** General. **Philosophy/religion:** Philosophy, religion. **Protective services:** Criminal justice, fire safety technology, law enforcement admin. **Psychology:** General. **Social sciences:** General, anthropology, economics, political science, sociology. **Visual/performing arts:** Art, dramatic, music, photography. **Work/family studies:** Child care management.

Most popular majors. Business/marketing 15%, engineering/engineering technologies 13%, health sciences 11%, interdisciplinary studies 7%, liberal arts 22%, psychology 6%, social sciences 6%.

Computing on campus. Commuter students can connect to campus network. Online course registration, online library, wireless network available.

Student life. Activities: Student newspaper.

Student services. Adult student services, financial aid counseling, veterans' counselor. **Physically disabled:** Services for visually, hearing impaired.

Contact. E-mail: admissions@tesc.edu
Phone: (888) 442-8372 Toll-free number: (888) 442-8372
Fax: (609) 984-8447
David Hoftiezer, Director, Admissions, Thomas Edison State College, 101 West State Street, Trenton, NJ 08608-1176

University of Medicine and Dentistry of New Jersey: School of Health Related Professions
Newark, New Jersey
www.shrp.umdnj.edu

CB code: 0598

- Public two-year upper-division health science college
- Commuter campus in large city

General. Founded in 1976. Regionally accredited. Courses offered through video conferencing in Newark, Scotch Plains, and Stratford. Possible opportunity to cross-enroll in courses offered by other schools within UMDNJ. **Degrees:** 168 bachelor's awarded; master's, professional, doctoral offered. **Location:** 15 miles from New York City. **Calendar:** Semester, limited summer session. **Full-time faculty:** 144 total. **Part-time faculty:** 289 total.

Student profile. 568 degree-seeking undergraduates.

Basis for selection. Open admission. College transcript required. Admission requirements vary per program; transfer applicants evaluated by faculty and associate dean. Minimum GPA and interview most important; health-related experience and letters of recommendation also important. Qualified minority, disabled and disadvantaged students encouraged to apply. Application procedures and closing dates vary per program. Transfer accepted as sophomores, juniors, seniors.

2011-2012 Annual costs. Undergraduate tuition and required fees: in-state, $11,484; out-of-state, $17,226. Costs may vary by program. Books/supplies: $1,000.

Application procedures. Admission: Rolling admission. $75 fee. **Financial aid:** FAFSA, institutional form required.

Academics. Special study options: Accelerated study, combined bachelor's/graduate degree, cross-registration, distance learning, double major, dual enrollment of high school students, independent study, internships, liberal arts/career combination, student-designed major. **Credit/placement by examination:** AP, CLEP, IB, institutional tests.

Majors. Health services: Clinical lab science, cytotechnology, dental hygiene, medical radiologic technology/radiation therapy, nuclear medical technology, respiratory therapy technology, sonography.

Computing on campus. PC or laptop required. Commuter students can connect to campus network. Online course registration, online library, helpline, repair service, wireless network available.

Student life. Housing: Coed dorms available. **Activities:** Student professional organizations.

Student services. Career counseling, services for economically disadvantaged, health services, personal counseling.

Contact. E-mail: shrpadm@umdnj.edu
Phone: (973) 972-5454 Fax: (973) 972-7463
Diane Hanrahan, Manager of Admissions, University of Medicine and Dentistry of New Jersey: School of Health Related Professions, 65 Bergen Street, Newark, NJ 07101-1709

University of Medicine and Dentistry of New Jersey: School of Nursing
Newark, New Jersey
www.sn.umdnj.edu

CB code: 0769

- Public 4-year nursing college
- Commuter campus in large city
- 590 degree-seeking undergraduates
- Application essay required

General. Founded in 1992. Regionally accredited. **Degrees:** 229 bachelor's awarded; master's, professional, doctoral offered. **Location:** 10 miles from New York City. **Calendar:** Semester, extensive summer session. **Full-time faculty:** 67 total. **Part-time faculty:** 5 total.

Basis for selection. Each program has established criteria for admissions. Minimum GPA and interview most important. Nursing and health related experiences and letters of recommendation also important. Qualified minority, handicapped, and disadvantaged students encouraged to apply.

High school preparation. Specific high school course requirements vary by program.

2011-2012 Annual costs. Tuition/fees: $16,192; $20,902 out-of-state. Costs vary by program; costs cited are for BSN program.

Application procedures. Admission: Closing date 7/1 (postmark date). $50 fee. Application must be submitted online. Admission notification on a rolling basis. Closing date varies for each program. **Financial aid:** Priority date 3/1; no closing date. Applicants notified on a rolling basis.

Academics. Special study options: Accelerated study, combined bachelor's/graduate degree. **Credit/placement by examination:** AP, CLEP. **Support services:** Reduced course load, tutoring.

Computing on campus. PC or laptop required. Commuter students can connect to campus network. Online library, helpline, repair service, wireless network available.

Student life. Freshman orientation: Mandatory. Preregistration for classes offered. **Housing:** Coed dorms available. **Activities:** Student government, student newspaper, student professional organizations by nursing specialty.

Student services. Health services, personal counseling. **Physically disabled:** Services for visually, hearing impaired.

Contact. E-mail: snadmissions@umdnj.edu
Phone: (973) 972-5336 Fax: (973) 972-7453
Diane Hanrahan, Admissions Manager, University of Medicine and Dentistry of New Jersey: School of Nursing, 65 Bergen Street, Room 149, Newark, NJ 07101-1709

University of Phoenix: Jersey City
Jersey City, New Jersey
www.phoenix.edu

- For-profit 4-year university
- Small city
- 578 degree-seeking undergraduates

General. Regionally accredited. **Degrees:** 48 bachelor's awarded. **Calendar:** Differs by program. **Full-time faculty:** 23 total. **Part-time faculty:** 91 total.

Basis for selection. Open admission, but selective for some programs.

2011-2012 Annual costs. Estimated costs as of August 2011: per-credit-hour charge, $380 to $520, depending upon level and course of study; electronic course materials fee, $95, if applicable. Book and material charges may vary by course and program. All fees are subject to change.

Academics. Credit/placement by examination: AP, CLEP.

Majors. Business: General, accounting, human resources. **Computer sciences:** Security.

Contact. Marc Booker, Director of Admission and Evaluation, University of Phoenix: Jersey City, 100 Town Square Place, Jersey City, NJ 07310

William Paterson University of New Jersey
Wayne, New Jersey

CB member

www.wpunj.edu

CB code: 2518

- Public 4-year university and liberal arts college
- Commuter campus in large town
- 9,921 degree-seeking undergraduates: 16% part-time, 55% women, 14% African American, 7% Asian American, 22% Hispanic American, 1% international
- 821 degree-seeking graduate students
- 71% of applicants admitted
- SAT or ACT (ACT writing optional) required
- 47% graduate within 6 years

General. Founded in 1855. Regionally accredited. **Degrees:** 1,616 bachelor's awarded; master's, professional offered. **ROTC:** Air Force. **Location:** 20 miles from New York City. **Calendar:** Semester, limited summer session. **Full-time faculty:** 389 total; 92% have terminal degrees, 33% minority, 51% women. **Part-time faculty:** 745 total. **Class size:** 46% < 20, 52% 20-39, 1% 40-49, less than 1% 50-99, less than 1% >100. **Special facilities:** Global financial center, science complex.

Freshman class profile. 10,059 applied, 7,111 admitted, 1,397 enrolled.

Mid 50% test scores			Return as sophomores:	76%
SAT critical reading:	440-550		Out-of-state:	2%
SAT math:	460-550		Live on campus:	49%
Rank in top quarter:	31%		International:	1%
Rank in top tenth:	11%			

Basis for selection. School record and test score most important; recommendations also important; class rank and essay considered. Audition required for music programs; portfolio required for art programs. Essays recommended. **Home schooled:** Transcript of courses and grades, state high school equivalency certificate required.

High school preparation. College-preparatory program required. 16 units required. Required units include English 4, mathematics 3, social studies 2, science 2 (laboratory 2) and academic electives 5. 5 additional college preparatory courses (advanced math, literature, foreign language, social science) also required.

2011-2012 Annual costs. Tuition/fees: $11,464; $18,628 out-of-state. Room/board: $9,880. Books/supplies: $1,300. Personal expenses: $2,300.

2011-2012 Financial aid. Need-based: 1,294 full-time freshmen applied for aid; 1,051 were judged to have need; 1,025 of these received aid. Average scholarship/grant was $8,827; average loan $3,432. 54% of total undergraduate aid awarded as scholarships/grants, 46% as loans/jobs. **Non-need-based:** Awarded to 1,385 full-time undergraduates, including 422 freshmen. Scholarships awarded for academics, alumni affiliation, music/drama.

Application procedures. Admission: Priority date 4/1; deadline 5/1 (postmark date). $50 fee, may be waived for applicants with need. Admission notification on a rolling basis beginning on or about 10/1. Must reply by May 1 or within 2 week(s) if notified thereafter. **Financial aid:** Priority date 4/1; no closing date. FAFSA required. Applicants notified on a rolling basis starting 3/15.

Academics. Honors programs available in biopsychology, humanities, cognitive science, life science and environmental ethics, music, nursing, performing, literary arts and University Core Curriculum. **Special study options:** Accelerated study, combined bachelor's/graduate degree, cross-registration, distance learning, double major, dual enrollment of high school students, ESL, exchange student, honors, independent study, internships, liberal arts/career combination, study abroad, teacher certification program, Washington semester. Cluster courses (program that provides opportunities for students and faculty to study and learn together in courses grouped in interdisciplinary clusters of three). **Credit/placement by examination:** AP, CLEP, SAT, ACT, institutional tests. 90 credit hours maximum toward bachelor's degree. **Support services:** Learning center, pre-admission summer program, reduced course load, remedial instruction, study skills assistance, tutoring, writing center.

Honors college/program. Generally, students accepted with 1200 SAT (math and reading) and solid B+ or above high school average. About 100 first-year students admitted each year.

Majors. Area/ethnic studies: African, African-American, Caribbean, French, Latin American, women's. **Biology:** General, biotechnology. **Business:** Accounting, business admin, finance, international finance, managerial economics. **Communications:** Communications/speech/rhetoric. **Computer sciences:** General, computer science. **Conservation:** General, environmental science. **Education:** General, art, early childhood, elementary, health, kindergarten/preschool, mathematics, music, physical, special ed. **English:** English lit. **Foreign languages:** French, Spanish. **Health services:** Nursing (RN), public health nursing, speech pathology. **History:** General. **Liberal arts:** Arts/sciences. **Math:** General. **Parks/recreation:** Exercise sciences. **Philosophy/religion:** Philosophy. **Physical sciences:** Chemistry. **Psychology:** General. **Social sciences:** Anthropology, economics, geography, political science, sociology. **Visual/performing arts:** Art, jazz, music, music management, music performance.

Most popular majors. Business/marketing 21%, communications/journalism 9%, education 13%, English 8%, health sciences 7%, psychology 10%, social sciences 12%.

Computing on campus. 700 workstations in dormitories, library, computer center. Dormitories wired for high-speed internet access and linked to campus network. Commuter students can connect to campus network. Online course registration, online library, helpline, student web hosting, wireless network available.

Student life. Freshman orientation: Mandatory, $75 fee. Preregistration for classes offered. Two-day program held twice in early summer. Freshmen and parents invited to stay overnight for nominal fee. **Policies:** Freshmen not permitted cars on campus. **Housing:** Guaranteed on-campus for all undergraduates. Coed dorms, special housing for disabled, apartments, wellness housing available. $150 nonrefundable deposit, deadline 6/1. Hall reserved for students 21-and-older, apartment-style housing, women's floor, academic

interest housing available. **Activities:** Bands, campus ministries, choral groups, dance, drama, film society, international student organizations, literary magazine, music ensembles, Model UN, radio station, student government, student newspaper, TV station, black student association, Christian Fellowship club, Jewish student association, Feminist Collective, organization of Latin American students, United Asian Americans, coalition of lesbians/gays/friends.

Athletics. NCAA. **Intercollegiate:** Baseball M, basketball, field hockey W, football (tackle) M, soccer, softball W, swimming, tennis, volleyball W. **Intramural:** Basketball, field hockey W, soccer W, softball, volleyball. **Team name:** Pioneers.

Student services. Adult student services, alcohol/substance abuse counseling, chaplain/spiritual director, career counseling, services for economically disadvantaged, student employment services, financial aid counseling, health services, legal services, minority student services, on-campus daycare, personal counseling, placement for graduates, veterans' counselor, women's services. **Physically disabled:** Services for visually, speech, hearing impaired.

Contact. E-mail: admissions@wpunj.edu
Phone: (973) 720-2125 Toll-free number: (877) 978-3923
Fax: (973) 720-2910
Colleen Fuller, Director of Admissions, William Paterson University of New Jersey, 300 Pompton Road, Wayne, NJ 07470

New Mexico

Eastern New Mexico University
Portales, New Mexico
www.enmu.edu
CB code: 4299

- Public 4-year university
- Residential campus in large town
- 3,882 degree-seeking undergraduates: 29% part-time, 57% women, 5% African American, 1% Asian American, 33% Hispanic American, 2% Native American, 3% international
- 829 degree-seeking graduate students
- 63% of applicants admitted
- SAT or ACT (ACT writing optional) required
- 54% graduate within 6 years

General. Founded in 1927. Regionally accredited. **Degrees:** 583 bachelor's, 5 associate awarded; master's offered. **Location:** 225 miles from Albuquerque,105 miles from Lubbock, Texas. **Calendar:** Semester, extensive summer session. **Full-time faculty:** 146 total; 80% have terminal degrees, 16% minority, 45% women. **Part-time faculty:** 193 total; 13% have terminal degrees, 24% minority, 46% women. **Class size:** 73% < 20, 26% 20-39, 1% 40-49, less than 1% 50-99. **Special facilities:** Roosevelt County museum, natural history museum, mineral museum, anthropology museum, scanning and transmission electron microscopes, anthropological dig site at Blackwater Draw, TV and radio broadcasting center.

Freshman class profile. 2,176 applied, 1,368 admitted, 690 enrolled.

Mid 50% test scores			
SAT critical reading:	410-550	Rank in top quarter:	35%
SAT math:	420-550	Rank in top tenth:	13%
ACT composite:	17-23	Return as sophomores:	52%
GPA 3.75 or higher:	18%	Out-of-state:	19%
GPA 3.50-3.74:	14%	Live on campus:	73%
GPA 3.0-3.49:	34%	International:	2%

(GPA 2.0-2.99: 33%)

Basis for selection. Admission based on either a national test score or a cumulative, unweighted grade point average. **Home schooled:** Transcript of courses and grades required. Recommend all in-state home-schooled students earn a GED no more than one semester before enrolling at ENMU.

High school preparation. College-preparatory program recommended. 12 units recommended. Recommended units include English 4, mathematics 4, social studies 2 and science 2.

2011-2012 Annual costs. Tuition/fees: $4,147; $9,658 out-of-state. Room/board: $5,830. Books/supplies: $1,000. Personal expenses: $2,350.

2011-2012 Financial aid. **Need-based:** 396 full-time freshmen applied for aid; 396 were judged to have need; 396 of these received aid. Average need met was 42%. Average scholarship/grant was $4,648; average loan $3,689. 57% of total undergraduate aid awarded as scholarships/grants, 43% as loans/jobs. **Non-need-based:** Awarded to 1,339 full-time undergraduates, including 543 freshmen. Scholarships awarded for academics, alumni affiliation, art, athletics, leadership, music/drama, state residency.

Application procedures. **Admission:** Priority date 8/15; no deadline. No application fee. Admission notification on a rolling basis. Housing deposit refundable if requested before August 1st. **Financial aid:** No deadline. FAFSA required. Applicants notified on a rolling basis starting 5/1.

Academics. **Special study options:** Accelerated study, combined bachelor's/graduate degree, distance learning, double major, dual enrollment of high school students, ESL, independent study, internships, student-designed major, teacher certification program. **Credit/placement by examination:** AP, CLEP, ACT, institutional tests. 32 credit hours maximum toward associate degree, 50 toward bachelor's. **Support services:** Learning center, pre-admission summer program, remedial instruction, tutoring, writing center.

Majors. **Biology:** General, biochemistry. **Business:** Accounting, business admin, finance, human resources, management information systems, managerial economics, marketing. **Communications:** Communications/speech/rhetoric. **Computer sciences:** General. **Conservation:** Environmental science, wildlife/wilderness. **Education:** Agricultural, business, early childhood, elementary, music, physical, sales/marketing, special ed, trade/industrial. **English:** English lit. **Foreign languages:** Spanish. **General:** Business, dairy.

Health services: Audiology/speech pathology, clinical lab science, nursing (RN). **History:** General. **Human services:** Social work. **Liberal arts:** Arts/sciences. **Math:** General. **Parks/recreation:** Health/fitness. **Philosophy/religion:** Religion. **Physical sciences:** Chemistry, geology. **Protective services:** Criminal justice, forensics. **Psychology:** General. **Social sciences:** General, anthropology, political science, sociology. **Visual/performing arts:** Art, cinematography, dramatic, music. **Work/family studies:** General.

Most popular majors. Education 19%, foreign language 14%, health sciences 8%, liberal arts 17%.

Computing on campus. 491 workstations in dormitories, library, computer center, student center. Dormitories wired for high-speed internet access and linked to campus network. Commuter students can connect to campus network. Online library, helpline, repair service, wireless network available.

Student life. **Freshman orientation:** Mandatory. Preregistration for classes offered. Incoming freshman are encouraged to take part in Dawg Days the week before the fall semester starts. **Policies:** All housing options are alcohol/drug/smoke-free facilities. All freshman are required to have on-campus housing and a meal plan for the first year unless already living within the immediate commuting area. **Housing:** Guaranteed on-campus for freshmen. Coed dorms, single-sex dorms, special housing for disabled, apartments, fraternity/sorority housing available. $150 nonrefundable deposit, deadline 8/1. **Activities:** Bands, campus ministries, choral groups, dance, drama, film society, international student organizations, literary magazine, music ensembles, musical theater, radio station, student government, student newspaper, TV station, Paradigm (religious), Association to Help Our Race Advance, N.A.T.I.V.E. club, Muslim students association, College Republicans, ENMU Society of Political Scholars, Student Association for Voters Empowerment, Gay-Straight Alliance of ENMU, Voices of Inclusive and Committed Education Students (VOICES).

Athletics. NCAA. **Intercollegiate:** Baseball M, basketball, cross-country, football (tackle) M, rodeo, soccer, softball W, track and field, volleyball W. **Intramural:** Badminton, basketball, cross-country, football (non-tackle), golf, racquetball, soccer, softball, tennis, volleyball. **Team name:** Greyhounds.

Student services. Adult student services, alcohol/substance abuse counseling, career counseling, student employment services, financial aid counseling, health services, minority student services, on-campus daycare, personal counseling, placement for graduates, veterans' counselor. **Physically disabled:** Services for visually, speech, hearing impaired.

Contact. E-mail: enrollment.services@enmu.edu
Phone: (575) 562-2178 Toll-free number: (800) 367-3668
Fax: (575) 562-2118
Cody Spitz, Director of Enrollment Services, Eastern New Mexico University, 1500 South Avenue K, Portales, NM 88130

Institute of American Indian Arts
Santa Fe, New Mexico
www.iaia.edu
CB code: 0180

- Public 4-year visual arts and liberal arts college
- Residential campus in small city
- 326 undergraduates
- Application essay required

General. Founded in 1962. Regionally accredited. Dedicated to providing education in fine arts and cultural studies to American Indians and Alaska Natives. **Degrees:** 25 bachelor's, 10 associate awarded. **Location:** 60 miles from Albuquerque. **Calendar:** Semester, limited summer session. **Full-time faculty:** 25 total. **Part-time faculty:** 25 total. **Special facilities:** Native American contemporary arts museum.

Basis for selection. Admissions decisions are based on completion of high school or GED, college test scores from ACT, SAT, Accuplacer, Compass or Asset. SAT or ACT recommended. Personal statement of educational intention required.

2011-2012 Annual costs. Tuition/fees: $3,870; $3,870 out-of-state. Room/board: $5,936. Books/supplies: $2,500. Personal expenses: $2,400.

Financial aid. **Non-need-based:** Scholarships awarded for academics, art. **Additional information:** For American Indian and Alaskan natives, financial aid available through Tribe or Native Corporation in which student is enrolled.

Application procedures. **Admission:** Closing date 8/4. $25 fee. Admission notification on a rolling basis beginning on or about 5/1. Must reply by May 1 or within 1 week(s) if notified thereafter. **Financial aid:** Priority date 3/15; no closing date. FAFSA, institutional form required. Applicants notified on a rolling basis starting 5/1.

Academics. Most courses emphasize American Indian perspective. **Special study options:** Cross-registration, double major, exchange student, independent study, internships. **Credit/placement by examination:** AP, CLEP, SAT, ACT, institutional tests. **Support services:** Learning center, remedial instruction, study skills assistance, tutoring.

Majors. English: Creative writing. **Visual/performing arts:** Studio arts.

Computing on campus. 3 workstations in dormitories, library, computer center. Dormitories linked to campus network.

Student life. Freshman orientation: Mandatory. Preregistration for classes offered. Conducted each semester one week before registration. **Housing:** Guaranteed on-campus for freshmen. Coed dorms available. $150 deposit. **Activities:** Literary magazine, student government, student newspaper, TV station, student senate, Pow-Wow club, traditional dance club, museum club, photography club, theater club, campus cleanup club.

Athletics. Intramural: Basketball M, skiing, softball, swimming, table tennis, tennis, volleyball.

Student services. Alcohol/substance abuse counseling, career counseling, student employment services, financial aid counseling, personal counseling, placement for graduates.

Contact. E-mail: admissions@iaia.edu
Phone: (505) 424-2334 Toll-free number: (800) 804-6422
Fax: (505) 424-4500
Undrell Person, Associate Director of Admissions, Institute of American Indian Arts, 83 Avan Nu Po Road, Santa Fe, NM 87508-1300

ITT Technical Institute: Albuquerque
Albuquerque, New Mexico
www.itt-tech.edu   **CB code: 2690**

- For-profit 4-year technical college
- Commuter campus in large city
- 934 undergraduates
- Interview required

General. Accredited by ACICS. **Degrees:** 88 bachelor's, 188 associate awarded. **Calendar:** Quarter, extensive summer session. **Full-time faculty:** 22 total. **Part-time faculty:** 71 total.

Basis for selection. Satisfactory scores from on-site tests in English and mathematics required.

2011-2012 Annual costs. Estimated costs as of June 2011: per-credit-hour charge, $529, depending upon level and course of study; academic fee, $200. Certain programs of study require purchase of tools, which could cost an additional $100 to $500. All costs are subject to change.

Application procedures. Admission: No deadline. No application fee. Admission notification on a rolling basis. **Financial aid:** No deadline. FAFSA, institutional form required. Applicants notified on a rolling basis.

Academics. Credit/placement by examination: AP, CLEP. **Support services:** Learning center, tutoring.

Majors. Business: Business admin, construction management, e-commerce. **Communications technology:** Animation/special effects. **Computer sciences:** Security. **Protective services:** Law enforcement admin.

Computing on campus. Online library available.

Student life. Freshman orientation: Available. Preregistration for classes offered.

Student services. Career counseling, student employment services, placement for graduates.

Contact. Phone: (505) 828-1114 Toll-free number: (800) 636-1114
Fax: (505) 828-1849
John Crooks, Director of Recruitment, ITT Technical Institute: Albuquerque, 5100 Masthead Street NE, Albuquerque, NM 87109

National American University: Rio Rancho
Rio Rancho, New Mexico
www.national.edu   **CB code: 5360**

- For-profit 4-year business college
- Large city

General. Founded in 1941. Regionally accredited. **Calendar:** Quarter.

Annual costs/financial aid. Books/supplies: $1,200.

Contact. Phone: (505) 348-3750
Director of Admissions, 4775 Indian School Road NE, Suite 200, Albuquerque, NM 87110

New Mexico Highlands University
Las Vegas, New Mexico   **CB member**
www.nmhu.edu   **CB code: 4532**

- Public 4-year university
- Commuter campus in large town
- 2,255 degree-seeking undergraduates: 27% part-time, 59% women, 7% African American, 56% Hispanic American, 7% Native American, 7% international
- 1,140 degree-seeking graduate students

General. Founded in 1893. Regionally accredited. **Degrees:** 356 bachelor's, 1 associate awarded; master's offered. **Location:** 68 miles from Santa Fe, 120 miles from Albuquerque. **Calendar:** Semester, limited summer session. **Full-time faculty:** 143 total; 76% have terminal degrees, 38% minority, 46% women. **Part-time faculty:** 155 total; 4% have terminal degrees, 41% minority, 59% women. **Class size:** 70% < 20, 26% 20-39, 2% 40-49, 2% 50-99, less than 1% >100.

Freshman class profile. 1,981 applied, 1,981 admitted, 419 enrolled.

Mid 50% test scores		Rank in top quarter:	10%
ACT composite:	16-21	Rank in top tenth:	4%
GPA 3.75 or higher:	8%	Return as sophomores:	48%
GPA 3.50-3.74:	10%	International:	8%
GPA 3.0-3.49:	27%	Fraternities:	1%
GPA 2.0-2.99:	52%	Sororities:	1%

Basis for selection. Open admission. **Home schooled:** Transcript of courses and grades, state high school equivalency certificate required.

2011-2012 Annual costs. Tuition/fees: $2,967; $4,667 out-of-state. Room/board: $6,213.

2010-2011 Financial aid. Need-based: 91% of total undergraduate aid awarded as scholarships/grants, 9% as loans/jobs. **Non-need-based:** Scholarships awarded for academics, athletics, leadership, minority status, music/drama, state residency. **Additional information:** Work study funds available on no-need basis to state residents.

Application procedures. Admission: No deadline. $15 fee, may be waived for applicants with need. Admission notification on a rolling basis. **Financial aid:** Priority date 3/1, closing date 5/1. FAFSA, institutional form required. Applicants notified on a rolling basis starting 5/15; must reply within 2 week(s) of notification.

Academics. Special study options: Combined bachelor's/graduate degree, cooperative education, distance learning, double major, dual enrollment of high school students, honors, independent study, internships, liberal arts/career combination, teacher certification program. **Credit/placement by examination:** AP, CLEP. As approved by appropriate department. **Support services:** Learning center, remedial instruction, study skills assistance, tutoring, writing center.

Majors. Biology: General. **Business:** Accounting, business admin, finance, international, management information systems, marketing. **Communications:** Media studies. **Computer sciences:** Computer science. **Conservation:** Forest management. **Education:** Art, biology, early childhood, elementary, mathematics, music, science, secondary, special ed. **English:** English lit. **Foreign languages:** Spanish. **Health services:** Nursing (RN). **History:** General. **Human services:** Social work. **Math:** General. **Parks/recreation:** Health/fitness, sports admin. **Physical sciences:** Chemistry, forensic chemistry, geology. **Protective services:** Criminal justice, forensics. **Psychology:** General. **Social sciences:** Anthropology, criminology, political science, sociology. **Visual/performing arts:** Art, music, music performance, studio arts.

Most popular majors. Business/marketing 22%, education 25%, health sciences 26%, social sciences 7%, visual/performing arts 8%.

Computing on campus. 250 workstations in dormitories, library, computer center, student center. Dormitories wired for high-speed internet access and linked to campus network. Commuter students can connect to campus network. Online library, helpline, repair service, wireless network available.

Student life. Freshman orientation: Mandatory, $50 fee. Preregistration for classes offered. **Housing:** Guaranteed on-campus for freshmen. Coed

dorms, single-sex dorms, apartments available. $100 partly refundable deposit, deadline 4/9. **Activities:** Bands, campus ministries, choral groups, dance, drama, international student organizations, literary magazine, music ensembles, musical theater, radio station, student government, TV station, social work club, several ethnic and religious groups.

Athletics. NAIA, NCAA. **Intercollegiate:** Baseball M, basketball, cross-country, football (tackle) M, rodeo, soccer W, softball W, track and field W, volleyball W, wrestling M. **Intramural:** Baseball M, basketball, golf, handball, racquetball, rifle, rugby, skiing, softball, swimming, table tennis, tennis, track and field. **Team name:** Cowboys, Cowgirls.

Student services. Adult student services, career counseling, services for economically disadvantaged, student employment services, financial aid counseling, health services, on-campus daycare, personal counseling. **Physically disabled:** Services for visually, speech, hearing impaired.

Contact. E-mail: mdbassett@nmhu.edu
Phone: (505) 454-3434 Toll-free number: (877) 850-9064
Fax: (505) 454-3552
John Coca, Director of Admissions, New Mexico Highlands University, Box 9000, Las Vegas, NM 87701

New Mexico Institute of Mining and Technology
Socorro, New Mexico   **CB member**
www.nmt.edu   **CB code: 4533**

- Public 4-year engineering and liberal arts college
- Residential campus in small town
- 1,303 degree-seeking undergraduates: 5% part-time, 27% women, 2% African American, 3% Asian American, 25% Hispanic American, 3% Native American, 1% international
- 405 degree-seeking graduate students
- 70% of applicants admitted
- SAT or ACT (ACT writing optional) required
- 48% graduate within 6 years

General. Founded in 1889. Regionally accredited. Student employment opportunities in research facilities and in faculty research. **Degrees:** 203 bachelor's, 2 associate awarded; master's, doctoral offered. **Location:** 75 miles from Albuquerque. **Calendar:** Semester, limited summer session. **Full-time faculty:** 123 total; 97% have terminal degrees, 20% minority, 20% women. **Part-time faculty:** 55 total; 18% minority, 46% women. **Class size:** 58% < 20, 31% 20-39, 5% 40-49, 5% 50-99, less than 1% >100. **Special facilities:** Experimental mine, mineral museum, laboratory for atmospheric physics and chemistry, energetic materials research, seismic research network, scanning electron microscope, scanning transmission electron microscope, transmission electron microscope, New Mexico Bureau of Geology, observatory.

Freshman class profile. 612 applied, 431 admitted, 324 enrolled.

Mid 50% test scores			
SAT critical reading:	540-660	GPA 2.0-2.99:	9%
SAT math:	570-680	Rank in top quarter:	67%
ACT composite:	23-28	Rank in top tenth:	40%
GPA 3.75 or higher:	46%	Return as sophomores:	71%
GPA 3.50-3.74:	20%	Out-of-state:	20%
GPA 3.0-3.49:	25%	Live on campus:	89%

Basis for selection. Test scores and high school GPA most important. Minimum 2.5 GPA required. Minimum 21 ACT or 970 SAT (exclusive of Writing) required. ACT recommended. Interview and recommendations considered if GPA and test scores are borderline or if other issues need to be addressed. **Home schooled:** Transcript of courses and grades required. Must supply documentation of courses completed.

High school preparation. College-preparatory program recommended. 15 units required; 18 recommended. Required and recommended units include English 4, mathematics 3-4, social studies 2-3, history 1, science 2-4 (laboratory 2-3), foreign language 2 and academic electives 3. High school courses in pre-calculus and calculus are strongly recommended.

2011-2012 Annual costs. Tuition/fees: $5,301; $15,753 out-of-state. Room/board: $6,108. Books/supplies: $1,050. Personal expenses: $1,592.

Financial aid. Non-need-based: Scholarships awarded for academics, alumni affiliation, minority status, state residency. **Additional information:** Campus research projects offer student employment based on abilities, interest, and merit.

Application procedures. Admission: Priority date 3/1; deadline 8/1. $15 fee, may be waived for applicants with need. Admission notification on a rolling basis beginning on or about 3/1. Must reply by May 1 or within 2 week(s) if notified thereafter. **Financial aid:** Priority date 6/1; no closing date. FAFSA, institutional form required. Applicants notified on a rolling basis starting 4/1; must reply within 2 week(s) of notification.

Academics. Special study options: Accelerated study, cooperative education, distance learning, double major, dual enrollment of high school students, exchange student, independent study, internships, student-designed major, teacher certification program. **Credit/placement by examination:** AP, CLEP, SAT, ACT, institutional tests. No limit to number of credits. Must have permission of instructor. **Support services:** Pre-admission summer program, reduced course load, study skills assistance, tutoring, writing center.

Majors. Biology: General, biochemistry. **Business:** Business admin. **Computer sciences:** General, computer science, information technology. **Conservation:** General, environmental studies. **Engineering:** General, chemical, civil, electrical, environmental, materials, mechanical, metallurgical, mining, petroleum. **English:** Technical writing. **Math:** General, applied. **Physical sciences:** Astrophysics, atmospheric physics, chemistry, geology, geophysics, physics. **Psychology:** General.

Most popular majors. Biology 8%, computer/information sciences 7%, engineering/engineering technologies 59%, physical sciences 12%.

Computing on campus. 225 workstations in dormitories, library, computer center, student center. Dormitories wired for high-speed internet access and linked to campus network. Commuter students can connect to campus network. Helpline, student web hosting, wireless network available.

Student life. Freshman orientation: Available, $40 fee. Preregistration for classes offered. 2-day event held weekend before classes start. **Policies:** Students living on-campus must purchase meal plan. **Housing:** Coed dorms, single-sex dorms, apartments, wellness housing available. $100 partly refundable deposit, deadline 6/1. **Activities:** Bands, choral groups, dance, drama, film society, international student organizations, music ensembles, musical theater, radio station, student government, student newspaper.

Athletics. Intramural: Badminton, basketball, fencing, golf, racquetball, rifle, rugby, soccer, softball, tennis, volleyball.

Student services. Adult student services, career counseling, student employment services, health services, on-campus daycare, personal counseling, placement for graduates. **Physically disabled:** Services for visually, hearing impaired.

Contact. E-mail: admission@admin.nmt.edu
Phone: (575) 835-5424 Toll-free number: (800) 428-8324
Fax: (575) 835-5989
Mike Kloeppel, Director of Admission, New Mexico Institute of Mining and Technology, 801 Leroy Place, Socorro, NM 87801

New Mexico State University
Las Cruces, New Mexico
www.nmsu.edu   **CB code: 4531**

- Public 4-year university
- Commuter campus in small city
- 13,605 degree-seeking undergraduates: 18% part-time, 53% women, 3% African American, 1% Asian American, 49% Hispanic American, 3% Native American, 3% international
- 3,488 degree-seeking graduate students
- 80% of applicants admitted
- SAT or ACT with writing required
- 47% graduate within 6 years

General. Founded in 1888. Regionally accredited. **Degrees:** 2,387 bachelor's, 10 associate awarded; master's, doctoral offered. **ROTC:** Army, Air Force. **Location:** 42 miles from El Paso, Texas. **Calendar:** Semester, extensive summer session. **Full-time faculty:** 669 total; 82% have terminal degrees, 25% minority, 41% women. **Part-time faculty:** 301 total; 26% have terminal degrees, 18% minority, 58% women. **Class size:** 44% < 20, 34% 20-39, 9% 40-49, 8% 50-99, 3% >100. **Special facilities:** Observatory, horse farm, rodeo grounds, electron microscope, CRAY supercomputer, sports medicine training clinic, Fabian Garcia farm.

Freshman class profile. 7,321 applied, 5,867 admitted, 2,163 enrolled.

Mid 50% test scores			
SAT critical reading:	410-530	GPA 2.0-2.99:	24%
SAT math:	430-540	Rank in top quarter:	47%
SAT writing:	390-520	Rank in top tenth:	21%
ACT composite:	18-24	End year in good standing:	80%
GPA 3.75 or higher:	25%	Return as sophomores:	71%
GPA 3.50-3.74:	16%	Out-of-state:	25%
GPA 3.0-3.49:	35%	Live on campus:	52%
		International:	3%

Basis for selection. School achievement record, test scores most important.

High school preparation. 10 units required. Required units include English 4, mathematics 3, science 2 (laboratory 2) and foreign language 1. English must include at least 2 composition, 1 of which must be at junior or senior level. Math must be algebra I, algebra II, geometry, trigonometry or advanced math. Will accept 1 foreign language or 1 fine arts.

2011-2012 Annual costs. Tuition/fees: $5,827; $18,268 out-of-state. Room/board: $6,620. Books/supplies: $1,032. Personal expenses: $2,212.

Financial aid. Non-need-based: Scholarships awarded for academics, alumni affiliation, athletics, leadership, minority status, state residency.

Application procedures. Admission: No deadline. $20 fee. Admission notification on a rolling basis. **Financial aid:** Priority date 3/1; no closing date. FAFSA, institutional form required. Applicants notified on a rolling basis starting 3/1.

Academics. Special study options: Accelerated study, cooperative education, cross-registration, distance learning, double major, exchange student, honors, independent study, internships, student-designed major, study abroad, teacher certification program, weekend college. **Credit/placement by examination:** AP, CLEP, institutional tests. **Support services:** Learning center, reduced course load, study skills assistance, tutoring, writing center.

Majors. Area/ethnic studies: Women's. **Biology:** General, bacteriology, biochemistry, ecology, genetics, plant pathology. **Business:** General, accounting, business admin, finance, hospitality admin, international, marketing, real estate. **Communications:** Journalism. **Computer sciences:** General, information systems, information technology. **Conservation:** Environmental science, wildlife/wilderness. **Education:** General, agricultural, early childhood, elementary, family/consumer sciences, music, physical, secondary, speech impaired. **Engineering:** Aerospace, applied physics, chemical, civil, electrical, industrial, mechanical. **English:** English lit. **Foreign languages:** General. **General:** Agribusiness operations, agronomy, animal sciences, horticultural science, range science, soil science, turf management. **Health services:** Athletic training, environmental health, nursing (RN), public health ed. **History:** General. **Human services:** Community org/advocacy, social work. **Math:** General. **Parks/recreation:** Facilities management. **Philosophy/religion:** Philosophy. **Physical sciences:** Chemistry, geology, physics. **Protective services:** Criminal justice. **Psychology:** General. **Social sciences:** Anthropology, economics, geography, political science, sociology. **Visual/performing arts:** General, cinematography, dance, dramatic, music performance, studio arts. **Work/family studies:** Clothing/textiles, family studies, food/nutrition.

Most popular majors. Business/marketing 19%, education 10%, engineering/engineering technologies 10%, health sciences 7%, liberal arts 7%, social sciences 6%.

Computing on campus. 743 workstations in dormitories, library, computer center, student center. Dormitories wired for high-speed internet access and linked to campus network. Commuter students can connect to campus network. Online course registration, online library, helpline, repair service, student web hosting, wireless network available.

Student life. Freshman orientation: Available, $40 fee. Preregistration for classes offered. **Housing:** Coed dorms, single-sex dorms, special housing for disabled, apartments, fraternity/sorority housing, wellness housing available. $100 deposit, deadline 7/1. Upper division dorms available. **Activities:** Bands, campus ministries, choral groups, dance, drama, literary magazine, music ensembles, musical theater, opera, radio station, student government, student newspaper, symphony orchestra, TV station, Baptist student union, Catholic center, Young Democrats, College Republicans, Black Allied Student Association, Movimiento Estudiantil Chicano de Azatlan, Native American organization.

Athletics. NCAA. **Intercollegiate:** Baseball M, basketball, cross-country, equestrian, football (tackle) M, golf, softball W, swimming W, tennis, track and field W, volleyball W. **Intramural:** Archery, badminton, basketball, cheerleading, football (non-tackle), football (tackle), golf, racquetball, soccer, softball, tennis, volleyball, water polo, weight lifting, wrestling M. **Team name:** Aggies.

Student services. Adult student services, alcohol/substance abuse counseling, career counseling, student employment services, health services, personal counseling, placement for graduates, veterans' counselor. **Physically disabled:** Services for visually, speech, hearing impaired.

Contact. E-mail: admissions@nmsu.edu
Phone: (575) 646-3121 Toll-free number: (800) 662-6678
Fax: (575) 646-6330
Valerie Pickett, Director of Admissions, New Mexico State University, Box 30001, MSC 3A, Las Cruces, NM 88003-8001

Santa Fe University of Art and Design
Santa Fe, New Mexico   **CB member**
www.santafeuniversity.edu   **CB code: 4676**

- For-profit 4-year visual arts college
- Residential campus in small city

General. Founded in 1947. Regionally accredited. **Location:** 60 miles from Albuquerque. **Calendar:** Semester.

Annual costs/financial aid. Tuition/fees (2011-2012): $29,296. Room/board: $8,338. Books/supplies: $1,180. Personal expenses: $1,380. Need-based financial aid available to full-time and part-time students.

Contact. Phone: (505) 473-6133
Executive Director of Admissions, 1600 Saint Michael's Drive, Santa Fe, NM 87505-7634

Southwest University of Visual Arts
Albuquerque, New Mexico
www.suva.edu   **CB code: 3039**

- For-profit 4-year visual arts college
- Commuter campus in very large city
- 268 degree-seeking undergraduates
- 93% of applicants admitted
- Application essay, interview required

General. Degrees: 27 bachelor's awarded. **ROTC:** Army. **Calendar:** Semester, extensive summer session. **Full-time faculty:** 18 total. **Part-time faculty:** 22 total.

Freshman class profile. 30 applied, 28 admitted, 24 enrolled.

Basis for selection. High school transcripts (GED accepted), ACT or SAT scores, essay, interview, personal statement form, and art work for illustration, animation, fine arts and graphic design programs. Applications accepted based on an evaluation of strengths, academic preparedness and communication skills. SAT or ACT recommended. **Home schooled:** Transcript of courses and grades required.

High school preparation. College-preparatory program recommended.

2011-2012 Annual costs. Tuition/fees: $18,360. Books/supplies: $1,250. Personal expenses: $3,204.

Financial aid. Non-need-based: Scholarships awarded for academics.

Application procedures. Admission: No deadline. $25 fee. Admission notification on a rolling basis. **Financial aid:** FAFSA required.

Academics. Special study options: Double major, independent study, internships, liberal arts/career combination. **Credit/placement by examination:** AP, CLEP, IB, SAT, ACT, institutional tests. **Support services:** Learning center, reduced course load, remedial instruction, study skills assistance, tutoring, writing center.

Majors. Architecture: Landscape. **Business:** Marketing. **Communications:** Advertising. **Communications technology:** Animation/special effects. **Visual/performing arts:** Graphic design, illustration, interior design, photography, studio arts.

Computing on campus. 50 workstations in library, computer center, student center. Online course registration, online library, student web hosting, wireless network available.

Student life. Freshman orientation: Mandatory, $100 fee. Preregistration for classes offered.

Student services. Adult student services, career counseling, student employment services, financial aid counseling, personal counseling, placement for graduates, veterans' counselor.

Contact. E-mail: inquire@suva.edu
Phone: (505) 254-7575 Toll-free number: (800) 825-8753
Fax: (505) 254-4754
Cindy Whitaker, Director of Admissions, Southwest University of Visual Arts, 5000 Marble Avenue NE, Albuquerque, NM 87119

St. John's College
Santa Fe, New Mexico
www.sjcsf.edu

CB member
CB code: 4737

- Private 4-year liberal arts college
- Residential campus in small city
- 365 degree-seeking undergraduates: 1% part-time, 41% women, 1% African American, 3% Asian American, 9% Hispanic American, 1% Native American, 12% international
- 83 degree-seeking graduate students
- 86% of applicants admitted
- Application essay required
- 54% graduate within 6 years; 11% enter graduate study

General. Founded in 1964. Regionally accredited. Second campus in Annapolis, MD, where students may transfer during their 4 years. **Degrees:** 92 bachelor's awarded; master's offered. **Location:** 60 miles from Albuquerque. **Calendar:** Semester, limited summer session. **Full-time faculty:** 63 total; 78% have terminal degrees, 5% minority, 25% women. **Class size:** 95% < 20, 5% 20-39. **Special facilities:** Search and rescue, Ptolemy stone, forest with hiking trails.

Freshman class profile. 263 applied, 227 admitted, 102 enrolled.

Mid 50% test scores		End year in good standing:	95%
SAT critical reading:	600-710	Return as sophomores:	69%
SAT math:	560-700	Out-of-state:	96%
ACT composite:	26-31	Live on campus:	98%
Rank in top quarter:	61%	International:	17%
Rank in top tenth:	32%		

Basis for selection. Three essays describing educational and personal background and goals are most important along with 2 letters of reference from teachers; secondary school reference from guidance counselor or other school official is requested. High school achievement record considered. SAT or ACT required of early admission, homeschooled, and international applicants; optional for others. Interview and overnight campus visit are strongly encouraged, as are interviews off-campus when offered by admissions officers. **Home schooled:** Statement describing home school structure and mission, transcript of courses and grades, letter of recommendation (nonparent) required.

High school preparation. College-preparatory program recommended. 5 units required; 20 recommended. Required and recommended units include English 4, mathematics 3-4, history 2, science 3 (laboratory 3) and foreign language 2-4. Math includes 2 algebra, 1 geometry required; precalculus or trigonometry recommended.

2011-2012 Annual costs. Tuition/fees: $43,656. Room/board: $10,334. Books/supplies: $630. Personal expenses: $516.

2010-2011 Financial aid. All financial aid based on need. 99 full-time freshmen applied for aid; 98 were judged to have need; 98 of these received aid. Average need met was 93%. Average scholarship/grant was $28,798; average loan $4,850. 83% of total undergraduate aid awarded as scholarships/grants, 17% as loans/jobs. **Additional information:** Families receive individual attention in determining need. Independent students must submit parental data. Financial aid information also required of noncustodial parent in cases of separation or divorce. Aid is awarded on a first-come, first-served basis until institutional money is exhausted. Apply by February 15; after April 1 aid is difficult to obtain.

Application procedures. **Admission:** Priority date 3/1; no deadline. No application fee. Admission notification on a rolling basis. Must reply by May 1 or within 2 week(s) if notified thereafter. Early application is for students wanting early notification of financial aid awards. **Financial aid:** Priority date 2/15; no closing date. FAFSA, CSS PROFILE required. Applicants notified on a rolling basis starting 12/1; must reply by 5/1 or within 3 week(s) of notification.

Academics. **Special study options:** Accelerated study, internships. **Credit/placement by examination:** AP, CLEP. **Support services:** Tutoring, writing center.

Majors. **Liberal arts:** Arts/sciences.

Computing on campus. 20 workstations in library, computer center. Dormitories wired for high-speed internet access and linked to campus network. Commuter students can connect to campus network. Helpline, wireless network available.

Student life. **Freshman orientation:** Mandatory. Preregistration for classes offered. Four-day program held twice a year. Includes on-campus service day, student activities fair, numerous community meals, and formal welcoming ceremony. **Housing:** Guaranteed on-campus for freshmen. Coed dorms, single-sex dorms, special housing for disabled, apartments, wellness housing available. **Activities:** Dance, drama, international student organizations, literary magazine, music ensembles, musical theater, student government, student newspaper, Amnesty International, Project Politae, Santa Fe Students for a Sustainable Future, gay/straight alliance, Student Polity, foreign relations study group.

Athletics. **Intramural:** Badminton, basketball, boxing, fencing, football (non-tackle), handball, racquetball, skiing, soccer, softball, squash, table tennis, tennis, volleyball.

Student services. Alcohol/substance abuse counseling, career counseling, student employment services, financial aid counseling, health services, personal counseling, placement for graduates, women's services.

Contact. E-mail: admissions@sjcsf.edu
Phone: (505) 984-6060 Toll-free number: (800) 331-5232
Fax: (505) 984-6162
Lawrence Clendenin, Director of Admissions, St. John's College, 1160 Camino Cruz Blanca, Santa Fe, NM 87505

University of New Mexico
Albuquerque, New Mexico
www.unm.edu

CB member
CB code: 4845

- Public 4-year university
- Commuter campus in very large city
- 20,935 degree-seeking undergraduates
- 64% of applicants admitted
- SAT or ACT (ACT writing recommended) required
- 45% graduate within 6 years

General. Founded in 1889. Regionally accredited. Campus in Rio Rancho; branch campuses in Valencia County, Los Alamos, Gallup, and Taos. **Degrees:** 3,350 bachelor's awarded; master's, professional, doctoral offered. **ROTC:** Army, Naval, Air Force. **Location:** 2 miles from downtown. **Calendar:** Semester, limited summer session. **Full-time faculty:** 949 total; 82% have terminal degrees, 24% minority, 46% women. **Part-time faculty:** 478 total; 30% have terminal degrees, 21% minority, 52% women. **Class size:** 39% < 20, 40% 20-39, 5% 40-49, 10% 50-99, 4% >100. **Special facilities:** 5 museums, observatory, meteoritics institute, arboretum, teaching hospital, research facilities in ceramics, optoelectronics, space nuclear power, high power devices and systems, institute of lithography, Latin American institute.

Freshman class profile. 11,410 applied, 7,288 admitted, 3,341 enrolled.

Mid 50% test scores		GPA 3.50-3.74:	16%
SAT critical reading:	470-600	GPA 3.0-3.49:	29%
SAT math:	470-590	GPA 2.0-2.99:	31%
ACT composite:	19-25	Return as sophomores:	74%
GPA 3.75 or higher:	24%	Out-of-state:	12%

Basis for selection. School achievement record (2.4 GPA required in college-preparatory units) most important. Test scores important. Essays, recommendations considered. Essay is considered in student appeal process. **Home schooled:** Applicants must either pass GED, submit SAT Subject Test scores, or have 2.4 GPA and complete 15 college prep academic units. **Learning Disabled:** Student who is not admissible according to numerical admissions and self-discloses disability can be admitted after being approved by Special Admissions Committee.

High school preparation. College-preparatory program required. 15 units required. Required units include English 4, mathematics 3, social studies 1, history 1, science 3 (laboratory 1) and foreign language 2. Foreign language requirements must be in same language. 1 science must be laboratory in biology, chemistry or physics. Math must be algebra I, geometry, algebra II, trigonometry or higher. 1 English must be 11th or 12th grade composition.

2011-2012 Annual costs. Tuition/fees: $5,809; $19,999 out-of-state. Room/board: $8,068. Books/supplies: $944. Personal expenses: $3,044.

2011-2012 Financial aid. **Non-need-based:** Scholarships awarded for academics, alumni affiliation, art, athletics, job skills, leadership, minority status, music/drama, religious affiliation, ROTC, state residency.

Application procedures. **Admission:** Priority date 6/15; no deadline. $20 fee, may be waived for applicants with need. Admission notification on a rolling basis. **Financial aid:** Priority date 3/1; no closing date. FAFSA required. Applicants notified on a rolling basis starting 3/31.

Academics. **Special study options:** Accelerated study, combined bachelor's/graduate degree, cooperative education, distance learning, double major, dual enrollment of high school students, ESL, exchange student, honors,

independent study, internships, semester at sea, student-designed major, study abroad, teacher certification program, Washington semester, weekend college. **Credit/placement by examination:** AP, CLEP, IB, SAT, ACT, institutional tests. **Support services:** Learning center, reduced course load, remedial instruction, study skills assistance, tutoring.

Majors. Architecture: Architecture, environmental design. **Area/ethnic studies:** African-American, American, Asian, European, Latin American, Native American, women's. **Biology:** General, biochemistry. **Business:** Business admin. **Communications:** Communications/speech/rhetoric, journalism, media studies. **Computer sciences:** General. **Conservation:** Environmental science. **Education:** Art, early childhood, elementary, health, music, physical, secondary, special ed, technology/industrial arts. **Engineering:** Chemical, civil, computer, electrical, engineering science, mechanical, nuclear. **English:** Rhetoric/composition. **Foreign languages:** General, classics, comparative lit, French, German, linguistics, Portuguese, sign language interpretation, Spanish. **Health services:** Audiology/speech pathology, clinical lab technology, dental hygiene, EMT paramedic, medical radiologic technology/radiation therapy, nursing (RN). **History:** General. **Human services:** Community org/advocacy. **Liberal arts:** Arts/sciences, humanities. **Math:** General, statistics. **Philosophy/religion:** Philosophy, religion. **Physical sciences:** Astrophysics, chemistry, geology, physics. **Protective services:** Corrections. **Psychology:** General. **Social sciences:** Anthropology, economics, geography, political science, sociology. **Visual/performing arts:** Art, art history/conservation, dance, dramatic, film/cinema/video, music performance, theater design. **Work/family studies:** General, family studies, food/nutrition.

Most popular majors. Biology 8%, business/marketing 15%, education 11%, health sciences 8%, psychology 9%, social sciences 10%, visual/performing arts 6%.

Computing on campus. 766 workstations in dormitories, library, computer center, student center. Dormitories wired for high-speed internet access and linked to campus network. Commuter students can connect to campus network. Online course registration, online library, helpline, student web hosting, wireless network available.

Student life. Freshman orientation: Mandatory, $125 fee. Preregistration for classes offered. Two-day sessions held June-August. **Housing:** Coed dorms, special housing for disabled, apartments, fraternity/sorority housing, wellness housing available. $200 deposit. Senior housing, academic floors, scholar's wing, global learning center, freshman living learning community, outdoors/wellness, major based units available. **Activities:** Bands, campus ministries, choral groups, dance, drama, film society, international student organizations, literary magazine, music ensembles, Model UN, musical theater, opera, radio station, student government, student newspaper, symphony orchestra, TV station, World Student Alliance, Residence Hall Association, Best Buddies NM, Baha'i Student Association, Raza Graduate Student Association, Nourish International, American Indian Business Association.

Athletics. NCAA. **Intercollegiate:** Baseball M, basketball, cross-country, diving W, football (tackle) M, golf, skiing, soccer, softball W, swimming W, tennis, track and field, volleyball W. **Intramural:** Archery, badminton, basketball, fencing, football (non-tackle), football (tackle) M, golf, racquetball, skiing, soccer, softball, swimming, tennis, triathlon, volleyball, water polo. **Team name:** Lobos.

Student services. Adult student services, alcohol/substance abuse counseling, career counseling, services for economically disadvantaged, student employment services, financial aid counseling, health services, legal services, minority student services, on-campus daycare, personal counseling, placement for graduates, veterans' counselor, women's services. **Physically disabled:** Services for visually, speech, hearing impaired.

Contact. E-mail: apply@unm.edu
Phone: (505) 277-8900 Toll-free number: (800) 225-5866
Fax: (505) 277-6686
Matthew Hulett, Director of Admissions and Recruiting Services, University of New Mexico, Office of Admissions, Albuquerque, NM 87196-4895

University of Phoenix: New Mexico
Albuquerque, New Mexico
www.phoenix.edu

- For-profit 4-year university
- Commuter campus in very large city
- 3,520 degree-seeking undergraduates

General. Regionally accredited. **Degrees:** 701 bachelor's awarded; master's offered. **Calendar:** Differs by program. **Full-time faculty:** 29 total. **Part-time faculty:** 367 total.

Basis for selection. Open admission.

2011-2012 Annual costs. Estimated costs as of August 2011: per-credit-hour charge, $380 to $415, depending upon level and course of study; electronic course materials fee, $95, if applicable. Book and material charges may vary by course and program. All fees are subject to change.

Application procedures. Admission: No deadline. No application fee. **Financial aid:** No deadline.

Academics. Credit/placement by examination: AP, CLEP.

Majors. Business: Accounting, business admin, e-commerce, management information systems, marketing. **Computer sciences:** General, database management, networking, programming, webmaster. **Education:** Elementary. **Health services:** Medical records technology, mental health counseling, nursing (RN). **Protective services:** Law enforcement admin, security management.

Most popular majors. Business/marketing 55%, computer/information sciences 7%, education 7%, public administration/social services 16%.

Contact. Toll-free number: (866) 766-0766
Marc Booker, Director of Admission and Evaluation, University of Phoenix: New Mexico, 5700 Pasadena NE, Albuquerque, NM 87113-8711

University of the Southwest
Hobbs, New Mexico   CB member
www.usw.edu   CB code: 4116

- Private 4-year liberal arts and teachers college
- Commuter campus in large town
- 333 degree-seeking undergraduates: 13% part-time, 46% women
- 453 degree-seeking graduate students
- 49% graduate within 6 years

General. Founded in 1956. Regionally accredited. **Degrees:** 55 bachelor's awarded; master's offered. **Location:** 110 miles from Lubbock, Texas. **Calendar:** Semester, limited summer session. **Full-time faculty:** 14 total; 64% have terminal degrees, 21% minority, 50% women. **Part-time faculty:** 29 total; 34% have terminal degrees, 3% minority, 52% women. **Class size:** 86% < 20, 14% 20-39.

Freshman class profile. 196 applied, 94 admitted, 67 enrolled.

Mid 50% test scores			
SAT critical reading:	350-450	Rank in top quarter:	37%
SAT math:	400-410	Rank in top tenth:	14%
ACT composite:	16-21	End year in good standing:	66%
GPA 3.75 or higher:	9%	Return as sophomores:	45%
GPA 3.50-3.74:	15%	Out-of-state:	55%
GPA 3.0-3.49:	54%	Live on campus:	75%
GPA 2.0-2.99:	22%	International:	3%

Basis for selection. Open admission, but selective for some programs. Applicants must meet 2 of 3 criteria: ACT 19 or SAT 910 (exclusive of Writing), 2.0 GPA; top half of graduating class. **Home schooled:** Statement describing home school structure and mission, transcript of courses and grades, state high school equivalency certificate required. **Learning Disabled:** Students with special needs are required to submit diagnostic test results in which special need was evaluated during last 3 years, Individual Education Plan (IEP), and other supporting documentation.

2012-2013 Annual costs. Tuition/fees: $14,305. Room/board: $6,640. Books/supplies: $1,200. Personal expenses: $1,000.

2011-2012 Financial aid. Need-based: 66 full-time freshmen applied for aid; 56 were judged to have need; 56 of these received aid. Average need met was 70%. Average scholarship/grant was $4,813; average loan $2,660. 62% of total undergraduate aid awarded as scholarships/grants, 38% as loans/jobs. **Non-need-based:** Awarded to 286 full-time undergraduates, including 59 freshmen. Scholarships awarded for academics, athletics, leadership.

Application procedures. Admission: No deadline. $25 fee, may be waived for applicants with need. Admission notification on a rolling basis beginning on or about 7/1. **Financial aid:** Priority date 4/1, closing date 6/1. FAFSA required. Applicants notified on a rolling basis starting 4/1; must reply within 2 week(s) of notification.

Academics. 6 hours religious studies, 3 hours economics (free enterprise) is required of all students. **Special study options:** Combined bachelor's/graduate degree, distance learning, double major, dual enrollment of high school students, internships, teacher certification program. Online program for criminal justice degree. **Credit/placement by examination:** AP, CLEP, IB, institutional tests. 30 credit hours maximum toward bachelor's degree.

Support services: Reduced course load, remedial instruction, study skills assistance, tutoring.

Majors. **Biology:** General. **Business:** Accounting, business admin, management information systems, marketing. **Education:** General, bilingual, elementary, English, mathematics, multi-level teacher, physical, science, secondary, social science, special ed. **English:** English lit. **History:** General. **Liberal arts:** Arts/sciences, humanities. **Parks/recreation:** Health/fitness, sports admin. **Protective services:** Criminal justice. **Psychology:** General. **Social sciences:** General. **Theology:** Pastoral counseling.

Most popular majors. Biology 15%, business/marketing 28%, education 26%, liberal arts 6%, psychology 17%.

Computing on campus. 35 workstations in library, computer center. Dormitories wired for high-speed internet access. Online course registration, online library, helpline, wireless network available.

Student life. Freshman orientation: Mandatory. Preregistration for classes offered. One day orientation, usually on Saturday, held 1 week prior to beginning of fall semester. **Housing:** Guaranteed on-campus for freshmen. Single-sex dorms, apartments, wellness housing available. $300 fully refundable deposit. **Activities:** Campus ministries, literary magazine, student government, debate club, teaching club, Students in Free Enterprise, Alpha Phi Omega, Sigma Tau Delta, USW Alumni Association.

Athletics. NAIA. **Intercollegiate:** Baseball M, basketball M, cross-country, golf, soccer, softball W, tennis, track and field. **Intramural:** Badminton, basketball, football (tackle) M, soccer, table tennis, volleyball. **Team name:** Mustangs.

Student services. Alcohol/substance abuse counseling, chaplain/spiritual director, financial aid counseling, personal counseling.

Contact. E-mail: admissions@usw.edu
Phone: (575) 392-6563 Toll-free number: (800) 530-4400
Fax: (575) 392-6006
Ashley Taylor, Admissions Coordinator, University of the Southwest, 6610 North Lovington Highway, #506, Hobbs, NM 88240

Western New Mexico University
Silver City, New Mexico
www.wnmu.edu

CB member
CB code: 4535

♦ Public 4-year university
♦ Commuter campus in large town

General. Founded in 1893. Regionally accredited. **Location:** 155 miles from El Paso, Texas, 193 miles from Tucson, Arizona. **Calendar:** Semester.

Annual costs/financial aid. Tuition/fees (2011-2012): $4,054; $13,438 out-of-state. Room/board: $6,094. Books/supplies: $810. Personal expenses: $2,060. Need-based financial aid available to full-time and part-time students.

Contact. Phone: (505) 538-6106
Director of Admissions, Castorena 106, Silver City, NM 88062

New York

Adelphi University
Garden City, New York
www.adelphi.edu

CB member
CB code: 2003

- Private 4-year university
- Commuter campus in large town
- 5,006 degree-seeking undergraduates: 11% part-time, 69% women, 11% African American, 6% Asian American, 10% Hispanic American, 3% international
- 2,852 degree-seeking graduate students
- 69% of applicants admitted
- Application essay required
- 66% graduate within 6 years; 31% enter graduate study

General. Founded in 1896. Regionally accredited. Program for students with learning disabilities. **Degrees:** 1,141 bachelor's, 23 associate awarded; master's, professional, doctoral offered. **ROTC:** Army, Air Force. **Location:** 20 miles from New York City. **Calendar:** Semester, limited summer session. **Full-time faculty:** 316 total; 82% have terminal degrees, 19% minority, 52% women. **Part-time faculty:** 659 total; 20% minority, 66% women. **Class size:** 49% < 20, 47% 20-39, 2% 40-49, 2% 50-99. **Special facilities:** Speech and hearing center, science library, observatory, arboretum, Center for Health Innovation.

Freshman class profile. 8,278 applied, 5,730 admitted, 988 enrolled.

Mid 50% test scores			
SAT critical reading:	480-580	GPA 2.0-2.99:	18%
SAT math:	500-600	Rank in top quarter:	54%
SAT writing:	500-600	Rank in top tenth:	22%
ACT composite:	21-26	End year in good standing:	92%
GPA 3.75 or higher:	23%	Return as sophomores:	81%
GPA 3.50-3.74:	25%	Out-of-state:	12%
GPA 3.0-3.49:	33%	Live on campus:	43%
		International:	3%

Basis for selection. 3.0 cumulative GPA, and combined critical reading, math and writing SAT score of 1500 or higher very important. Rank in top third of class, school and community activities, references also important. SAT/ACT scores accepted on rolling basis. SAT recommended for General Studies entrants, not required for adult academic programs in University College. Applicants to dance, drama, music, or art require audition and portfolio review, education majors must have 2.75 minimum GPA. **Home schooled:** State high school equivalency certificate required. GED required if applicant not receiving diploma from accredited high school or academy. **Learning Disabled:** Fee-based learning disability program where students receive academic and counseling support, requires admission: interview required, SAT recommended, WAIS-III, WJ-III required.

High school preparation. College-preparatory program recommended. 16 units recommended. Recommended units include English 4, mathematics 3, science 3 and foreign language 2. 4 additional units recommended in either social studies, history, English, mathematics, science or foreign language.

2011-2012 Annual costs. Tuition/fees: $28,460. Room/board: $11,420. Books/supplies: $1,400. Personal expenses: $1,200.

2011-2012 Financial aid. Need-based: 863 full-time freshmen applied for aid; 750 were judged to have need; 735 of these received aid. Average need met was 29%. Average scholarship/grant was $7,631; average loan $4,270. 69% of total undergraduate aid awarded as scholarships/grants, 31% as loans/jobs. **Non-need-based:** Awarded to 2,893 full-time undergraduates, including 695 freshmen. Scholarships awarded for academics, alumni affiliation, art, athletics, leadership, minority status, music/drama, religious affiliation.

Application procedures. Admission: No deadline. $40 fee, may be waived for applicants with need. Admission notification on a rolling basis beginning on or about 10/1. **Financial aid:** Priority date 3/1; no closing date. FAFSA required. Applicants notified on a rolling basis starting 3/1.

Academics. Special study options: Accelerated study, combined bachelor's/graduate degree, cross-registration, distance learning, double major, dual enrollment of high school students, ESL, honors, independent study, internships, liberal arts/career combination, student-designed major, study abroad,

teacher certification program, Washington semester, weekend college. Learning Disabilities program combining matriculation with support services; University College for adults 21 and over; 1-year intensive General Studies program for freshmen with HS records/SAT scores that do not meet school standards. Students who successfully complete this program invited to enroll in other school programs in their sophomore year. **Credit/placement by examination:** AP, CLEP, IB. 30 credit hours maximum toward bachelor's degree. **Support services:** Learning center, pre-admission summer program, reduced course load, study skills assistance, tutoring, writing center.

Honors college/program. SAT, 3.5 GPA, evidence of academic or creative writing and interview required. 60-90 freshmen admitted.

Majors. Area/ethnic studies: Latin American. **Biology:** General, biochemistry. **Business:** Accounting, business admin, finance, marketing. **Communications:** Journalism, media studies. **Computer sciences:** General, information systems. **Conservation:** Environmental studies. **Education:** Art, health, physical. **English:** English lit. **Foreign languages:** French, Spanish. **Health services:** Audiology/speech pathology, nursing (RN). **History:** General. **Human services:** Social work. **Liberal arts:** Arts/sciences, humanities. **Math:** General. **Parks/recreation:** Health/fitness, sports admin. **Philosophy/religion:** Philosophy. **Physical sciences:** Chemistry, physics. **Protective services:** Criminal justice, disaster management. **Psychology:** General. **Social sciences:** General, anthropology, economics, political science, sociology. **Visual/performing arts:** Art history/conservation, dance, dramatic, music.

Most popular majors. Business/marketing 13%, health sciences 23%, psychology 8%, social sciences 12%.

Computing on campus. 680 workstations in dormitories, library, computer center, student center. Dormitories wired for high-speed internet access and linked to campus network. Commuter students can connect to campus network. Online course registration, online library, helpline, repair service, student web hosting, wireless network available.

Student life. Freshman orientation: Mandatory, $275 fee. Preregistration for classes offered. 3-day orientation held on Garden City campus. **Housing:** Coed dorms, special housing for disabled available. $300 nonrefundable deposit, deadline 5/1. Special housing available for students in Honors College, Performing Arts, and Excel Mentoring Program. **Activities:** Bands, campus ministries, choral groups, dance, drama, film society, international student organizations, literary magazine, music ensembles, Model UN, musical theater, opera, radio station, student government, student newspaper, symphony orchestra, Approximately 80 activities are offered.

Athletics. NCAA. **Intercollegiate:** Baseball M, basketball, bowling W, cross-country, field hockey W, golf M, lacrosse, soccer, softball W, swimming, tennis, track and field, volleyball W. **Intramural:** Badminton, basketball, cheerleading W, football (non-tackle), soccer, volleyball, water polo, weight lifting M. **Team name:** Panthers.

Student services. Adult student services, alcohol/substance abuse counseling, chaplain/spiritual director, career counseling, student employment services, financial aid counseling, health services, minority student services, on-campus daycare, personal counseling, placement for graduates, veterans' counselor. **Physically disabled:** Services for visually, speech, hearing impaired.

Contact. E-mail: admissions@adelphi.edu
Phone: (516) 877-3050 Toll-free number: (800) 233-5744
Fax: (516) 877-3039
Christine Murphy, Director of Admissions, Adelphi University, One South Avenue, Levermore 110, Garden City, NY 11530-0701

Albany College of Pharmacy and Health Sciences
Albany, New York
www.acphs.edu

CB code: 2013

- Private 4-year health science and pharmacy college
- Residential campus in small city
- 1,077 degree-seeking undergraduates: 2% part-time, 58% women, 4% African American, 16% Asian American, 3% Hispanic American, 6% international
- 562 degree-seeking graduate students
- 64% of applicants admitted
- SAT or ACT with writing, application essay required
- 64% graduate within 6 years

General. Founded in 1881. Regionally accredited. **Degrees:** 33 bachelor's awarded; master's, professional offered. **ROTC:** Army, Naval, Air Force. **Location:** 200 miles from New York City. **Calendar:** Semester, limited

summer session. **Full-time faculty:** 110 total; 84% have terminal degrees, 14% minority, 46% women. **Part-time faculty:** 38 total; 53% have terminal degrees, 10% minority, 76% women. **Class size:** 39% < 20, 36% 20-39, 11% 50-99, 15% >100. **Special facilities:** Turn-of-the-century antique pharmacy.

Freshman class profile. 1,437 applied, 921 admitted, 213 enrolled.

Mid 50% test scores			
SAT critical reading:	530-620	GPA 2.0-2.99:	5%
SAT math:	560-650	Rank in top quarter:	92%
SAT writing:	510-600	Rank in top tenth:	53%
ACT composite:	24-27	Return as sophomores:	82%
GPA 3.75 or higher:	26%	Out-of-state:	19%
GPA 3.50-3.74:	47%	Live on campus:	84%
GPA 3.0-3.49:	22%	International:	2%

Basis for selection. High school record, test scores, essay, letters of recommendation, New York State Regents Examinations considered. Special emphasis on science and mathematics grades.

High school preparation. College-preparatory program recommended. 21 units required; 22 recommended. Required and recommended units include English 4, mathematics 3-4, science 4 (laboratory 4) and academic electives 6. Chemistry, pre-calculus or calculus.

2011-2012 Annual costs. Tuition/fees: $26,930. Room/board: $9,560. Books/supplies: $1,000. Personal expenses: $800.

2011-2012 Financial aid. **Need-based:** 202 full-time freshmen applied for aid; 166 were judged to have need; 163 of these received aid. Average need met was 54%. Average scholarship/grant was $11,767; average loan $3,679. 45% of total undergraduate aid awarded as scholarships/grants, 55% as loans/jobs. **Non-need-based:** Scholarships awarded for academics.

Application procedures. **Admission:** Priority date 2/1; no deadline. $75 fee, may be waived for applicants with need. Admission notification on a rolling basis beginning on or about 3/1. **Financial aid:** Priority date 2/1, closing date 5/1. FAFSA required. CSS PROFILE priority date 11/15, filing deadline 12/15. Applicants notified by 3/25; must reply within 2 week(s) of notification.

Academics. **Special study options:** Combined bachelor's/graduate degree, cross-registration, internships. **Credit/placement by examination:** AP, CLEP. **Support services:** Study skills assistance, tutoring, writing center.

Majors. **Health services:** Clinical lab science, cytotechnology, pharmaceutical sciences.

Computing on campus. PC or laptop required. 30 workstations in library. Dormitories wired for high-speed internet access and linked to campus network. Commuter students can connect to campus network. Online course registration, online library, helpline, repair service, wireless network available.

Student life. **Freshman orientation:** Mandatory, $250 fee. Preregistration for classes offered. Usually held over first weekend prior to class start. **Policies:** College observes honor code. Residency required in first 2 years of study except for students living within 30-mile radius of campus. **Housing:** Guaranteed on-campus for freshmen. Coed dorms, apartments available. $250 nonrefundable deposit, deadline 6/1. **Activities:** Dance, international student organizations, literary magazine, student government, student newspaper, Academy of Student Pharmacists, Student Society of Health Systems Pharmacists, Rho Chi, Phi Lambda Sigma.

Athletics. **Intercollegiate:** Basketball, cross-country, soccer. **Intramural:** Basketball, volleyball. **Team name:** Panthers.

Student services. Alcohol/substance abuse counseling, career counseling, student employment services, financial aid counseling, health services, personal counseling, placement for graduates.

Contact. E-mail: admissions@acphs.edu
Phone: (518) 694-7221 Toll-free number: (888) 203-8010
Fax: (518) 694-7322
Matthew Stever, Director of Admissions, Albany College of Pharmacy and Health Sciences, 106 New Scotland Avenue, Albany, NY 12208-3492

Alfred University
Alfred, New York
www.alfred.edu

CB member
CB code: 2005

- Private 4-year university
- Residential campus in rural community

- 1,918 degree-seeking undergraduates: 1% part-time, 49% women, 7% African American, 1% Asian American, 6% Hispanic American, 2% international
- 424 degree-seeking graduate students
- 72% of applicants admitted
- SAT or ACT (ACT writing optional), application essay required
- 60% graduate within 6 years

General. Founded in 1836. Regionally accredited. **Degrees:** 389 bachelor's awarded; master's, doctoral offered. **ROTC:** Army. **Location:** 75 miles from Rochester, 65 miles from Elmira. **Calendar:** Semester, limited summer session. **Full-time faculty:** 161 total; 7% minority, 43% women. **Part-time faculty:** 40 total; 2% minority, 62% women. **Class size:** 64% < 20, 31% 20-39, 2% 40-49, 2% 50-99, less than 1% >100. **Special facilities:** Observatory, memorial carillon, art galleries, ceramics museum and library, equestrian center.

Freshman class profile. 3,025 applied, 2,187 admitted, 559 enrolled.

Mid 50% test scores			
SAT critical reading:	480-580	GPA 2.0-2.99:	40%
SAT math:	500-600	Rank in top quarter:	43%
SAT writing:	460-570	Rank in top tenth:	17%
ACT composite:	21-26	Return as sophomores:	76%
GPA 3.75 or higher:	12%	Out-of-state:	20%
GPA 3.50-3.74:	15%	Live on campus:	97%
GPA 3.0-3.49:	32%	International:	2%

Basis for selection. Rigor of high school curriculum, grades, class rank, standardized ACT or SAT test results, extracurricular involvement, letters of recommendation, and character are all factors. International students required to submit TOEFL or IELTS results if they do not take the SAT or ACT. Interview recommended. Portfolio required for students seeking admission to the School of Art and Design. **Home schooled:** Advise students to document courses taken and provide reading list. SAT or ACT mandatory and relied on heavily.

High school preparation. College-preparatory program required. 16 units required. Required units include English 4, mathematics 2, social studies 2, science 2 (laboratory 2). College of Business: 3-4 units of social studies and history; 3-4 units of college prep math. College of Liberal Arts & Sciences: 3-4 units of social studies and history; 2-3 units of college prep math. School of Art & Design: 3-4 units of social studies and history. Inamori School of Engineering: 4 units of college prep math; 3 units of lab science.

2012-2013 Annual costs. Tuition/fees: $27,794. Room/board: $11,498. Books/supplies: $1,050.

2010-2011 Financial aid. **Need-based:** 493 full-time freshmen applied for aid; 441 were judged to have need; 441 of these received aid. Average need met was 87%. Average scholarship/grant was $19,031; average loan $5,034. 73% of total undergraduate aid awarded as scholarships/grants, 27% as loans/jobs. **Non-need-based:** Awarded to 916 full-time undergraduates, including 264 freshmen. Scholarships awarded for academics, art, leadership, music/drama.

Application procedures. **Admission:** Priority date 2/1; deadline 8/1 (postmark date). $50 fee, may be waived for applicants with need. Admission notification on a rolling basis beginning on or about 11/15. Must reply by May 1 or within 2 week(s) if notified thereafter. **Financial aid:** Closing date 3/15. FAFSA, institutional form required. Applicants notified on a rolling basis starting 2/15; must reply by 5/1 or within 2 week(s) of notification.

Academics. Credit hours needed for graduation vary from 120-138 depending on major. Physical education requirement for all students. Additional graduation requirements vary by college/school. Preadmission summer program is required for students enrolling at AU through Opportunity Programs (EOP or HEOP). **Special study options:** Combined bachelor's/graduate degree, cooperative education, cross-registration, double major, ESL, exchange student, honors, independent study, internships, liberal arts/career combination, New York semester, semester at sea, student-designed major, study abroad, teacher certification program, United Nations semester, Washington semester. **Credit/placement by examination:** AP, CLEP, IB, SAT, institutional tests. 75 credit hours maximum toward bachelor's degree. Credits awarded from AP, IB, CLEP or from any other standardized exam program are considered to be transfer credits. They count toward the 75 credit hour limit on total transfer credit, and they do not affect the AU GPA. **Support services:** Reduced course load, study skills assistance, tutoring, writing center.

Majors. **Biology:** General. **Business:** Accounting, business admin, finance, marketing. **Communications:** Communications/speech/rhetoric. **Conservation:** Environmental studies. **Education:** Art, biology, business, chemistry, elementary, English, French, mathematics, middle, physics, social studies, Spanish. **Engineering:** Biomedical, ceramic, materials, mechanical. **English:** English lit. **Foreign languages:** Spanish. **Health services:** Athletic training, predental, premedicine, preveterinary. **History:** General. **Liberal arts:** Arts/

sciences. **Math:** General. **Philosophy/religion:** Philosophy. **Physical sciences:** Chemistry, geology, materials science, physics. **Protective services:** Criminal justice. **Psychology:** General. **Social sciences:** Economics, political science, sociology. **Visual/performing arts:** Ceramics, dramatic, studio arts.

Most popular majors. Business/marketing 14%, engineering/engineering technologies 18%, psychology 9%, visual/performing arts 30%.

Computing on campus. 450 workstations in dormitories, library, computer center, student center. Dormitories wired for high-speed internet access and linked to campus network. Commuter students can connect to campus network. Online course registration, online library, helpline, student web hosting, wireless network available.

Student life. Freshman orientation: Mandatory. Preregistration for classes offered. Starts the Thursday before classes begin in the fall. **Policies:** Students must abide by Code of Honor. Policies against hazing and sexual harassment. All students required to live in residence halls 6 semesters. Students in poor academic standing required to live on campus. Exceptions granted for married students, students 23 and older, students living with parents/legal guardian and commuting from home, students with dependents, and veterans. **Housing:** Guaranteed on-campus for freshmen. Coed dorms, apartments, wellness housing available. $300 nonrefundable deposit, deadline 5/1. Experiential living available. **Activities:** Bands, choral groups, dance, drama, film society, international student organizations, literary magazine, music ensembles, musical theater, radio station, student government, student newspaper, symphony orchestra, TV station, Hillel, Brothers and Sisters in Christ, Spectrum, Student Volunteers for Community Action, Alpha Phi Omega, Habitat for Humanity, Students Acting for Equality, Umoja, Omicron Delta Kappa, Poder Latino.

Athletics. NCAA. **Intercollegiate:** Basketball, cross-country, diving, equestrian, football (tackle) M, lacrosse, skiing, soccer, softball W, swimming, tennis, track and field, volleyball W. **Intramural:** Basketball, football (non-tackle), lacrosse M, racquetball, skiing, soccer, softball, squash, tennis, volleyball. **Team name:** Saxons.

Student services. Alcohol/substance abuse counseling, chaplain/spiritual director, career counseling, services for economically disadvantaged, student employment services, financial aid counseling, health services, minority student services, personal counseling, placement for graduates, women's services. **Physically disabled:** Services for visually, speech, hearing impaired.

Contact. E-mail: admissions@alfred.edu
Phone: (607) 871-2115 Toll-free number: (800) 541-9229
Fax: (607) 871-2198
Corry Unis, Director of Admissions, Alfred University, Alumni Hall, Alfred, NY 14802-1205

Bard College

Annandale-on-Hudson, New York   **CB member**
www.bard.edu   **CB code: 2037**

- Private 4-year liberal arts college affiliated with Episcopal Church
- Residential campus in small town
- 1,940 degree-seeking undergraduates: 3% part-time, 58% women, 3% African American, 3% Asian American, 2% Hispanic American, 13% international
- 320 degree-seeking graduate students
- 35% of applicants admitted
- Application essay required
- 77% graduate within 6 years

General. Founded in 1860. Regionally accredited. **Degrees:** 420 bachelor's awarded; master's, doctoral offered. **Location:** 90 miles from New York City, 50 miles from Albany. **Calendar:** Semester. **Full-time faculty:** 153 total; 95% have terminal degrees, 13% minority, 42% women. **Part-time faculty:** 104 total; 85% have terminal degrees, 15% minority, 51% women. **Class size:** 77% < 20, 22% 20-39, less than 1% 40-49, less than 1% 50-99. **Special facilities:** Ecology field station contiguous to Hudson River Estuary Preserves, curatorial studies and art center, museum of late 20th-century art, archaeological field school, economics institute, center for studies in decorative arts, design and culture; performing arts center, science center.

Freshman class profile. 5,670 applied, 1,960 admitted, 486 enrolled.

Mid 50% test scores		End year in good standing:	90%
SAT critical reading:	680-740	Return as sophomores:	88%
SAT math:	650-680	Out-of-state:	70%
Rank in top quarter:	95%	Live on campus:	99%
Rank in top tenth:	62%	International:	13%

Basis for selection. School transcripts and achievement record, rigor of high school program, essays, academic recommendations, talents and dedication to activities, love of learning, and personal ambition important. Campus tour and information session recommended. Tape or CD, brief musical autobiography, and audition required of conservatory applicants. **Home schooled:** Statement describing home school structure and mission, transcript of courses and grades required.

High school preparation. College-preparatory program required. 24 units recommended. Recommended units include English 4, mathematics 4, social studies 4, history 4, science 4 (laboratory 3) and foreign language 4.

2011-2012 Annual costs. Tuition/fees: $43,306. Room/board: $12,286. Books/supplies: $950. Personal expenses: $800.

2011-2012 Financial aid. Need-based: 342 full-time freshmen applied for aid; 310 were judged to have need; 310 of these received aid. Average need met was 87%. Average scholarship/grant was $29,842; average loan $5,515. 85% of total undergraduate aid awarded as scholarships/grants, 15% as loans/jobs. **Non-need-based:** Awarded to 43 full-time undergraduates, including 10 freshmen. Scholarships awarded for academics. **Additional information:** Excellence and Equal Cost Program for students who graduate in top 10 of public high school class lowers fees to levels equivalent to those at home state university or college.

Application procedures. Admission: Closing date 1/1 (receipt date). $50 fee, may be waived for applicants with need. Application must be submitted on paper. Admission notification on a rolling basis beginning on or about 4/1. Must reply by May 1 or within 2 week(s) if notified thereafter. Applicants may be admitted through early action, regular procedure, or Immediate Decision Plan, which gives next-day decision after day-long program and individual interview. Sessions scheduled in early fall. **Financial aid:** Priority date 2/1, closing date 2/15. FAFSA, CSS PROFILE required. Applicants notified by 4/1; must reply by 5/1.

Academics. Strong tradition of independent study and tutorial work with faculty member. Writing-intensive, multidisciplinary programs. Extensive programs in languages, human rights and globalization and international affairs. Unique collaboration with The Rockefeller University. **Special study options:** Combined bachelor's/graduate degree, cross-registration, double major, dual enrollment of high school students, ESL, independent study, internships, New York semester, student-designed major, study abroad, Washington semester. Intensive language studies in Italy, Germany, France, Mexico, Russia, China, program in International Education (Central and Eastern Europe and Southern Africa). **Credit/placement by examination:** AP, CLEP, IB. **Support services:** Learning center, reduced course load, remedial instruction, study skills assistance, tutoring, writing center.

Majors. Area/ethnic studies: African, American, Asian, French, German, Italian, Latin American, Near/Middle Eastern, Russian/Slavic, Spanish/Iberian. **Biology:** General, neuroscience. **Computer sciences:** Computer science. **Conservation:** Environmental studies. **English:** American lit, British lit, creative writing, English lit. **Foreign languages:** General, ancient Greek, Arabic, Chinese, comparative lit, French, German, Hebrew, Italian, Japanese, Latin, Russian, Sanskrit, Spanish, translation. **Health services:** Premedicine. **History:** General, American, Asian, European. **Liberal arts:** Arts/sciences. **Math:** General. **Philosophy/religion:** Judaic, philosophy, religion. **Physical sciences:** Chemistry, physics. **Psychology:** General. **Social sciences:** General, anthropology, archaeology, economics, political science, sociology. **Visual/performing arts:** General, acting, art history/conservation, cinematography, conducting, dance, directing/producing, dramatic, film/cinema/video, jazz, multimedia, music, music history, music performance, music theory/composition, photography, piano/keyboard, play/screenwriting, stringed instruments, studio arts, theater history, voice/opera.

Most popular majors. Area/ethnic studies 6%, English 12%, foreign language 6%, social sciences 15%, visual/performing arts 35%.

Computing on campus. 425 workstations in library, computer center, student center. Dormitories wired for high-speed internet access and linked to campus network. Commuter students can connect to campus network. Online course registration, online library, helpline, student web hosting, wireless network available.

Student life. Freshman orientation: Mandatory, $570 fee. Preregistration for classes offered. 3-week writing-intensive Language and Thinking program held on campus in August immediately prior to fall semester. **Policies:** All students members of the student government association, a democratic forum that allocates funds, takes action on campus issues, and provides student representation on administrative and faculty committees. **Housing:** Guaranteed on-campus for freshmen. Coed dorms, single-sex dorms, cooperative housing, wellness housing available. Pets allowed in dorm rooms. Suites available. **Activities:** Bands, campus ministries, choral groups, dance, drama, film society, international student organizations, literary magazine, music ensembles, Model UN, musical theater, opera, radio station, student government, student newspaper, symphony orchestra, 150 clubs and organizations available.

Athletics. NCAA. **Intercollegiate:** Baseball M, basketball, cross-country, lacrosse, soccer, squash M, swimming, tennis, track and field, volleyball. **Intramural:** Badminton, basketball, bowling, golf, softball, squash, table tennis, tennis, volleyball. **Team name:** Raptors.

Student services. Adult student services, alcohol/substance abuse counseling, chaplain/spiritual director, career counseling, services for economically disadvantaged, student employment services, financial aid counseling, health services, minority student services, personal counseling, placement for graduates, women's services. **Physically disabled:** Services for visually, hearing impaired.

Contact. E-mail: admissions@bard.edu
Phone: (845) 758-7472 Fax: (845) 758-5208
Mary Backlund, Director of Admission, Bard College, 30 Campus Road, Annandale-on-Hudson, NY 12504-5000

Barnard College
New York, New York
www.barnard.edu

CB member
CB code: 2038

- Private 4-year liberal arts college for women
- Residential campus in very large city
- 2,445 degree-seeking undergraduates: 2% part-time, 100% women, 5% African American, 17% Asian American, 9% Hispanic American, 6% international
- 25% of applicants admitted
- SAT and SAT Subject Tests or ACT with writing, application essay required
- 95% graduate within 6 years; 19% enter graduate study

General. Founded in 1889. Regionally accredited. Cross-registration and shared facilities with Columbia University. Students receive Columbia University degrees. **Degrees:** 593 bachelor's awarded. **ROTC:** Air Force. **Calendar:** Semester. **Full-time faculty:** 207 total; 89% have terminal degrees, 16% minority, 61% women. **Part-time faculty:** 129 total; 52% have terminal degrees, 5% minority, 77% women. **Class size:** 73% < 20, 15% 20-39, 3% 40-49, 7% 50-99, 1% >100. **Special facilities:** Black box theater, center for toddler development, center for research on women, architecture and dance studios, access to 3,600-acre nature preserve in upstate New York, greenhouse, access to geological observatory.

Freshman class profile. 5,153 applied, 1,282 admitted, 612 enrolled.

Mid 50% test scores			
SAT critical reading:	630-730	GPA 2.0-2.99:	1%
SAT math:	620-710	Rank in top quarter:	99%
SAT writing:	650-750	Rank in top tenth:	81%
ACT composite:	28-32	Return as sophomores:	94%
GPA 3.75 or higher:	63%	Out-of-state:	69%
GPA 3.50-3.74:	26%	Live on campus:	98%
GPA 3.0-3.49:	10%	International:	7%

Basis for selection. High school record most important. Depth and difficulty of high school program considered. Test scores, recommendations, involvement in school and community activities, special talents, skills considered. Interview recommended. **Home schooled:** Statement describing home school structure and mission, transcript of courses and grades, letter of recommendation (nonparent) required.

High school preparation. College-preparatory program recommended. 16 units recommended. Recommended units include English 4, mathematics 3, science 3 (laboratory 2) and foreign language 3.

2011-2012 Annual costs. Tuition/fees: $42,184. Room/board: $13,382. Books/supplies: $1,146. Personal expenses: $1,366.

2011-2012 Financial aid. All financial aid based on need. 349 full-time freshmen applied for aid; 275 were judged to have need; 275 of these received aid. Average need met was 100%. Average scholarship/grant was $38,135; average loan $3,394. 87% of total undergraduate aid awarded as scholarships/grants, 13% as loans/jobs.

Application procedures. Admission: Closing date 1/1 (postmark date). $55 fee, may be waived for applicants with need. Admission notification by 4/1. Must reply by May 1 or within 2 week(s) if notified thereafter. **Financial aid:** Closing date 2/1. FAFSA required. CSS Profile required for returning students, except those who had a parent contribution less than $2,000 in the prior academic year. Returning international students also not required to complete the CSS Profile. Applicants notified by 3/31; must reply by 5/1.

Academics. Interdisciplinary first-year seminar; coursework in global cultures, which may also fulfill other degree requirements. **Special study**

options: Accelerated study, combined bachelor's/graduate degree, cross-registration, double major, dual enrollment of high school students, exchange student, honors, independent study, internships, liberal arts/career combination, student-designed major, study abroad, teacher certification program. Independent scholars program, BA/BS in engineering and applied science. **Credit/placement by examination:** AP, CLEP, IB, institutional tests. **Support services:** Pre-admission summer program, tutoring, writing center.

Majors. Architecture: Architecture, history/criticism. **Area/ethnic studies:** African, American, Asian, European, French, German, Latin American, Near/Middle Eastern, Russian/Slavic, Slavic, Spanish/Iberian, women's. **Biology:** General, biochemistry, biophysics, environmental, neuroscience. **Computer sciences:** General, computer science. **Conservation:** Environmental science, environmental studies. **Engineering:** Applied physics. **English:** English lit. **Foreign languages:** Ancient Greek, classics, comparative lit, French, German, Italian, Latin, linguistics, modern Greek, Russian, Spanish. **History:** General. **Math:** General, applied, statistics. **Philosophy/religion:** Philosophy, religion. **Physical sciences:** Astronomy, astrophysics, chemistry, physics. **Psychology:** General. **Social sciences:** Anthropology, economics, geography, political science, sociology, urban studies. **Visual/performing arts:** General, art history/conservation, dance, dramatic, film/cinema/video, music.

Most popular majors. Area/ethnic studies 9%, biology 8%, English 12%, history 7%, psychology 11%, social sciences 27%, visual/performing arts 11%.

Computing on campus. 164 workstations in dormitories, library, computer center, student center. Dormitories wired for high-speed internet access and linked to campus network. Commuter students can connect to campus network. Online course registration, online library, helpline, repair service, wireless network available.

Student life. Freshman orientation: Mandatory. Preregistration for classes offered. Week-long program that begins August 27. **Housing:** Guaranteed on-campus for all undergraduates. Special housing for disabled, apartments available. $400 nonrefundable deposit, deadline 6/15. Coed dorms offered through Columbia University. **Activities:** Bands, campus ministries, choral groups, dance, drama, film society, literary magazine, music ensembles, musical theater, opera, radio station, student government, student newspaper, symphony orchestra, TV station, united students of color council, multicultural international student association, late night theater, Athena pre-law society, network of pre-medical students of color, women in politics, Barnard Earth club, feminist thought, smart women lead, V-Day.

Athletics. NCAA. **Intercollegiate:** Archery W, basketball W, cross-country W, diving W, fencing W, field hockey W, golf W, lacrosse W, rowing (crew) W, soccer W, softball W, swimming W, tennis W, track and field W, volleyball W. **Intramural:** Archery W, badminton W, basketball W, bowling W, cross-country W, fencing W, racquetball W, sailing W, soccer W, softball W, swimming W, tennis W, volleyball W. **Team name:** Lions.

Student services. Alcohol/substance abuse counseling, career counseling, student employment services, financial aid counseling, health services, personal counseling, placement for graduates, women's services. **Physically disabled:** Services for visually, speech, hearing impaired.

Contact. E-mail: admissions@barnard.edu
Phone: (212) 854-2014 Fax: (212) 854-6220
Carolyn Middleton, Dean of Admissions, Barnard College, 3009 Broadway, New York, NY 10027-6598

Beis Medrash Heichal Dovid
Far Rockaway, New York

- Private 4-year rabbinical college for men affiliated with Jewish faith
- Residential campus in large city
- 118 degree-seeking undergraduates

General. Accredited by AARTS. **Degrees:** 10 bachelor's awarded; doctoral offered. **Calendar:** Semester. **Full-time faculty:** 4 total. **Part-time faculty:** 4 total.

Basis for selection. Religious faith most important criteria. **Home schooled:** Transcript of courses and grades, state high school equivalency certificate, interview, letter of recommendation (nonparent) required.

2011-2012 Annual costs. Tuition/fees: $6,900. Room/board: $4,500.

Application procedures. Admission: No deadline. $100 fee. Admission notification on a rolling basis.

Academics. Credit/placement by examination: AP, CLEP.

Majors. Theology: Talmudic.

Contact. Phone: (718) 868-2300 ext. 360 Fax: (718) 406-8359
Aaron Steinberg, Admin. Assist., Beis Medrash Heichal Dovid, 211 Beach
17th Street, Far Rockaway, NY 11691

Berkeley College
White Plains, New York
www.berkeleycollege.edu   CB code: 2064

- For-profit 4-year business college
- Commuter campus in small city
- 736 degree-seeking undergraduates

General. Founded in 1945. Regionally accredited. **Degrees:** 21 bachelor's,
17 associate awarded. **Location:** 28 miles from New York City. **Calendar:**
Quarter, extensive summer session. **Full-time faculty:** 27 total. **Part-time
faculty:** 38 total. **Special facilities:** Access to Manhattanville College facilities.

Basis for selection. Class rank, high school record, interview most important. Passing grade on school entrance examination required. SAT/ACT considered if submitted. Interviews strongly recommended.

2011-2012 Annual costs. Tuition/fees: $21,750. Room only: $8,400.
Books/supplies: $1,360. Personal expenses: $3,000.

Financial aid. Non-need-based: Scholarships awarded for academics,
alumni affiliation. **Additional information:** Alumni scholarship examination
given in November and December. Full and partial scholarships awarded.

Application procedures. Admission: No deadline. $50 fee. Admission
notification on a rolling basis. Admitted applicants must reply within 2 weeks
of notification. **Financial aid:** No deadline. FAFSA required. Applicants
notified on a rolling basis starting 3/1; must reply within 6 week(s) of notification.

Academics. Special study options: Accelerated study, distance learning,
ESL, honors, internships, New York semester, study abroad. **Credit/place-
ment by examination:** AP, CLEP, SAT, ACT, institutional tests. **Support
services:** Learning center, remedial instruction, study skills assistance,
tutoring, writing center.

Majors. Business: Accounting, business admin, fashion, financial planning,
international, management information systems, marketing. **Health services:**
Health care admin. **Protective services:** Law enforcement admin.

Most popular majors. Business/marketing 94%, security/protective services 6%.

Computing on campus. 150 workstations in library, computer center.
Dormitories linked to campus network. Commuter students can connect to
campus network. Online library, helpline, wireless network available.

Student life. Freshman orientation: Mandatory. Preregistration for
classes offered. **Housing:** Coed dorms available. $400 fully refundable
deposit. **Activities:** Student government, accounting club, Berkeley club, Phi
Beta Lambda, Phi Theta Kappa, international club, fashion club, paralegal
club.

Athletics. Intramural: Basketball, cheerleading, soccer. **Team name:**
Knights.

Student services. Adult student services, career counseling, student
employment services, financial aid counseling, personal counseling, placement for graduates.

Contact. E-mail: info@berkeleycollege.edu
Phone: (914) 694-1122 Toll-free number: (800) 446-5400
Fax: (914) 328-9469
Linda Pinsky, AVP Enrollment, NY, Berkeley College, 99 Church Street,
White Plains, NY 10601

Berkeley College of New York City
New York, New York
www.berkeleycollege.edu   CB code: 0954

- For-profit 4-year business college
- Commuter campus in very large city
- 4,589 degree-seeking undergraduates

General. Founded in 1936. Regionally accredited. Extension center located
in Lower Manhattan (Financial District) and a branch campus located in
Westchester County (White Plains). **Degrees:** 468 bachelor's, 148 associate
awarded. **Location:** Midtown Manhattan. **Calendar:** Quarter, extensive summer session. **Full-time faculty:** 101 total. **Part-time faculty:** 181 total. **Class
size:** 11% < 20, 89% 20-39.

Basis for selection. High school record and interview most important.
Institutional entrance tests required of all applicants. SAT or ACT accepted
in lieu of institutional entrance exam.

2011-2012 Annual costs. Tuition/fees: $21,750. Books/supplies: $1,360.
Personal expenses: $3,000.

Financial aid. Non-need-based: Scholarships awarded for academics,
alumni affiliation. **Additional information:** Alumni scholarship examination
given in November and December. Full and partial scholarships awarded.

Application procedures. Admission: No deadline. $50 fee. Admission
notification on a rolling basis. Admitted applicants must reply within 2 weeks
of notification. **Financial aid:** No deadline. FAFSA required. Applicants
notified on a rolling basis starting 3/1; must reply within 6 week(s) of notification.

Academics. Special study options: Accelerated study, distance learning,
ESL, honors, internships, study abroad. **Credit/placement by examination:**
AP, CLEP, SAT, ACT, institutional tests. **Support services:** Learning center,
remedial instruction, study skills assistance, tutoring, writing center.

Majors. Business: Accounting, business admin, fashion, financial planning,
international, management information systems, marketing. **Health services:**
Health care admin. **Protective services:** Law enforcement admin.

Computing on campus. 200 workstations in library, computer center.
Commuter students can connect to campus network. Online library, helpline,
wireless network available.

Student life. Freshman orientation: Mandatory. Preregistration for
classes offered. **Housing:** $400 deposit. **Activities:** Student government,
international club, multicultural club, fashion club, accounting club, paralegal
club, student government.

Athletics. Intramural: Basketball, cheerleading, soccer. **Team name:**
Knights.

Student services. Adult student services, alcohol/substance abuse counseling, career counseling, student employment services, financial aid counseling, personal counseling, placement for graduates.

Contact. E-mail: info@berkeleycollege.edu
Phone: (212) 986-4343 Toll-free number: (800) 446-5400
Fax: (212) 818-1079
AVP, Enrollment NY, Berkeley College of New York City, 3 East 43rd
Street, New York, NY 10017

Beth Hamedrash Shaarei Yosher Institute
Brooklyn, New York
                                           CB code: 0731

- Private 5-year rabbinical college for men affiliated with Jewish faith
- Very large city

General. Founded in 1962. Accredited by AARTS. First Talmudic degree
and ordination available. **Calendar:** Semester.

Basis for selection. Test scores most important. High school record considered.

2011-2012 Annual costs. Personal expenses: $1,600.

Application procedures. Admission: No deadline.

Academics. Credit/placement by examination: AP, CLEP.

Majors. Philosophy/religion: Judaic.

Contact. Phone: (718) 854-2290
Director of Student Financial Aid, Beth Hamedrash Shaarei Yosher
Institute, 4102-10 16th Avenue, Brooklyn, NY 11204

Beth Hatalmud Rabbinical College
Brooklyn, New York

CB code: 7317

- Private 4-year rabbinical college for men affiliated with Jewish faith
- Very large city

General. Founded in 1950. Accredited by AARTS. Ordination and First Rabbinic degree available. **Calendar:** Semester.

Basis for selection. Institutional examination.

2011-2012 Annual costs. Tuition/fees: $6,700.

Application procedures. Admission: Closing date 9/1. Admission notification on a rolling basis.

Academics. Credit/placement by examination: AP, CLEP.

Majors. Philosophy/religion: Judaic.

Student life. Policies: Religious observance required.

Contact. Phone: (718) 259-2525
Director of Admissions, Beth Hatalmud Rabbinical College, 2127 82nd Street, Brooklyn, NY 11214

Boricua College
New York, New York
www.boricuacollege.edu

CB code: 2901

- Private 4-year liberal arts college
- Commuter campus in very large city
- 1,209 degree-seeking undergraduates
- 86 graduate students
- Application essay, interview required

General. Founded in 1974. Regionally accredited. Boricua College has four centers: one each in Manhattan and the Bronx, and two in Brooklyn. **Degrees:** 121 bachelor's, 157 associate awarded; master's offered. **Calendar:** Semester, limited summer session. **Full-time faculty:** 63 total; 33% have terminal degrees, 51% women. **Part-time faculty:** 58 total; 22% women. **Class size:** 100% 20-39.

Basis for selection. Entrance examination, academic records, interview by the faculty, 2 letters of recommendation. Institutional tests required for admissions and placement. Final interview and approval by the faculty is required. **Home schooled:** Transcript of courses and grades, interview, letter of recommendation (nonparent) required. **Learning Disabled:** Evaluation is done based on individual needs of the candidate.

2011-2012 Annual costs. Tuition/fees: $9,525. Books/supplies: $400. Personal expenses: $3,625.

Application procedures. Admission: No deadline. $25 fee, may be waived for applicants with need. Admission notification on a rolling basis. **Financial aid:** Priority date 4/30; no closing date. FAFSA required. Applicants notified on a rolling basis; must reply within 3 week(s) of notification.

Academics. Academic load consists of 5 courses per semester: 3 applied studies courses (individualized instruction, colloquium, experiential), 1 theoretical, and 1 cultural class. Academic support services are available at different hours upon request. **Special study options:** Accelerated study, independent study, internships, liberal arts/career combination, teacher certification program. **Credit/placement by examination:** AP, CLEP, institutional tests. 30 credit hours maximum toward bachelor's degree. **Support services:** Reduced course load, tutoring.

Majors. Area/ethnic studies: Latin American. **Business:** Business admin. **Education:** Elementary. **Liberal arts:** Arts/sciences.

Computing on campus. 180 workstations in library, computer center, student center. Online library, helpline, wireless network available.

Student life. Freshman orientation: Mandatory. Preregistration for classes offered. Based on appointments. **Policies:** Student regulations include a sexual harassment policy. **Activities:** Choral groups, dance, drama, opera, student government, student newspaper.

Athletics. Intramural: Basketball, volleyball.

Student services. Adult student services, career counseling, student employment services, personal counseling, placement for graduates.

Contact. E-mail: acruz@boricuacollege.edu
Phone: (347) 964-8000 ext. 360 Fax: (212) 694-1015
Miriam Pfeffer, Director of Admissions, Boricua College, 3755 Broadway, New York, NY 10032

Briarcliffe College
Bethpage, New York
www.briarcliffe.edu

CB code: 3108

- For-profit 4-year business and technical college
- Commuter campus in large town
- 1,986 degree-seeking undergraduates

General. Founded in 1966. Regionally accredited. **Degrees:** 195 bachelor's, 268 associate awarded. **Location:** 20 miles from New York City. **Calendar:** Semester, extensive summer session. **Full-time faculty:** 26 total. **Part-time faculty:** 172 total.

Basis for selection. School achievement record important, recommendations suggested. Interviews recommended. **Home schooled:** Not accepted.

High school preparation. Recommended units include English 4, mathematics 2, social studies 4 and science 1.

2011-2012 Annual costs. Tuition/fees: $18,592.

Financial aid. Non-need-based: Scholarships awarded for academics, alumni affiliation.

Application procedures. Admission: No deadline. $35 fee. Admission notification on a rolling basis. **Financial aid:** No deadline. FAFSA, institutional form required. Applicants notified on a rolling basis.

Academics. Special study options: Distance learning, independent study, internships. **Credit/placement by examination:** AP, CLEP, SAT, ACT, institutional tests. **Support services:** Learning center, reduced course load, remedial instruction, study skills assistance, tutoring.

Majors. Business: Accounting, business admin, marketing. **Computer sciences:** Information technology, networking, programming. **Visual/performing arts:** General.

Computing on campus. 400 workstations in library, computer center. Commuter students can connect to campus network. Online library available.

Student life. Freshman orientation: Mandatory. Preregistration for classes offered. **Housing:** Coed dorms available. **Activities:** Student government.

Athletics. USCAA. **Intercollegiate:** Baseball M, bowling, lacrosse M, soccer M, softball W. **Team name:** Bulldogs.

Student services. Financial aid counseling, placement for graduates.

Contact. E-mail: info@bcl.edu
Phone: (516) 918-3600 Fax: (516) 470-6020
Richard Kleinman, Director of Admissions, Briarcliffe College, 1055 Stewart Avenue, Bethpage, NY 11714

Canisius College
Buffalo, New York
www.canisius.edu

CB member
CB code: 2073

- Private 4-year liberal arts and teachers college affiliated with Roman Catholic Church
- Residential campus in large city
- 3,079 degree-seeking undergraduates; 2% part-time, 52% women, 5% African American, 2% Asian American, 2% Hispanic American, 4% international
- 1,739 degree-seeking graduate students
- 75% of applicants admitted
- SAT or ACT (ACT writing optional) required
- 67% graduate within 6 years

General. Founded in 1870. Regionally accredited. Campus connected by underground tunnel system, rapid transit stations near campus. **Degrees:** 937

bachelor's, 8 associate awarded; master's offered. **ROTC:** Army. **Calendar:** Semester, limited summer session. **Full-time faculty:** 233 total; 95% have terminal degrees, 9% minority, 40% women. **Part-time faculty:** 313 total; 22% have terminal degrees, 6% minority, 51% women. **Class size:** 48% < 20, 48% 20-39, 3% 40-49, less than 1% 50-99. **Special facilities:** Mini-planetarium, seismograph station, rare book room, digital media lab, human performance lab, animal care unit.

Freshman class profile. 4,348 applied, 3,258 admitted, 814 enrolled.

Mid 50% test scores			
SAT critical reading:	500-600	Rank in top quarter:	57%
SAT math:	510-610	Rank in top tenth:	27%
ACT composite:	23-28	Return as sophomores:	84%
GPA 3.75 or higher:	31%	Out-of-state:	8%
GPA 3.50-3.74:	28%	Live on campus:	74%
GPA 3.0-3.49:	30%	International:	5%
GPA 2.0-2.99:	11%	Fraternities:	1%
		Sororities:	1%

Basis for selection. Primary emphasis placed on strength of academic record, achievement, class rank and SAT/ACT scores. Essays, recommendations important. Extracurricular activities, alumni affiliation factors. Interview and essay recommended.

High school preparation. College-preparatory program required. 16 units required; 26 recommended. Required and recommended units include English 4, mathematics 3-4, social studies 4, science 3-4 (laboratory 2), foreign language 2-4 and academic electives 4.

2011-2012 Annual costs. Tuition/fees: $30,657. Room/board: $11,360. Books/supplies: $700. Personal expenses: $700.

2011-2012 Financial aid. Need-based: 729 full-time freshmen applied for aid; 686 were judged to have need; 686 of these received aid. Average need met was 87%. Average scholarship/grant was $22,685; average loan $3,323. 77% of total undergraduate aid awarded as scholarships/grants, 23% as loans/jobs. **Non-need-based:** Awarded to 1,140 full-time undergraduates, including 270 freshmen. Scholarships awarded for academics, alumni affiliation, art, athletics, job skills, music/drama, religious affiliation, ROTC.

Application procedures. Admission: Priority date 3/1; deadline 5/1. $40 fee, may be waived for applicants with need, free for online applicants. Admission notification on a rolling basis beginning on or about 12/15. Must reply by 5/1. **Financial aid:** Priority date 2/15; no closing date. FAFSA required. Applicants notified on a rolling basis starting 3/1; must reply within 2 week(s) of notification.

Academics. Pre-professional programs include pre-engineering, prelaw, premedical, predentistry, preveterinary medicine, prepharmacy. **Special study options:** Combined bachelor's/graduate degree, cooperative education, cross-registration, distance learning, double major, dual enrollment of high school students, ESL, exchange student, honors, independent study, internships, study abroad, teacher certification program. Early assurance for medical and dental school with SUNY Buffalo Medical and Dental Schools (New York state residents only), and the Upstate Medical School at Syracuse; 7-year joint degree programs with SUNY Buffalo Dental School, the Ohio College of Podiatric Medicine, the New York College of Podiatric Medicine and SUNY State College of Optometry in NYC; AS/BS with Fashion Institute of Technology; 3+2 Dual Degree Physics-Engineering Programs: B.S. in Physics from Canisius and B.S. in Mechanical Engineering from Pennsylvania State University at Erie; B.S. in Physics from Canisius and B.S. in Electrical Engineering from University at Buffalo (SUNY); B.S. in Physics from Canisius and B.S. in Industrial Engineering from University at Buffalo (SUNY); B.S. in Physics from Canisius and B.S. in Mechanical Engineering from University at Buffalo (SUNY). **Credit/placement by examination:** AP, CLEP, IB, SAT, ACT, institutional tests. 30 credit hours maximum toward bachelor's degree. **Support services:** Learning center, pre-admission summer program, reduced course load, remedial instruction, study skills assistance, tutoring, writing center.

Majors. Area/ethnic studies: European. **Biology:** General, animal behavior, biochemistry, bioinformatics, zoology. **Business:** Accounting, accounting technology, entrepreneurial studies, finance, international, management information systems, management science, managerial economics, marketing. **Communications:** Communications/speech/rhetoric, digital media, journalism. **Computer sciences:** Computer science. **Conservation:** Environmental science, environmental studies. **Education:** Early childhood, early childhood special, elementary, elementary special ed, physical, secondary. **Engineering:** Pre-engineering. **English:** Creative writing, English lit. **Foreign languages:** Classics, French, Germanic, Spanish. **Health services:** General, athletic training, clinical lab science. **History:** General. **Liberal arts:** Arts/sciences, humanities. **Math:** General. **Parks/recreation:** Sports admin. **Philosophy/religion:** Philosophy, religion. **Physical sciences:** Chemistry, physics. **Protective services:** Criminal justice. **Psychology:** General. **Social sciences:** General, anthropology, economics, international relations, political science, sociology, urban studies. **Visual/performing arts:** Art history/conservation, music.

Most popular majors. Biology 7%, business/marketing 26%, communications/journalism 11%, education 13%, psychology 11%, social sciences 10%.

Computing on campus. 700 workstations in dormitories, library, computer center, student center. Dormitories wired for high-speed internet access and linked to campus network. Commuter students can connect to campus network. Online course registration, online library, helpline, repair service, student web hosting, wireless network available.

Student life. Freshman orientation: Mandatory, $200 fee. Preregistration for classes offered. Includes advisement, registration as necessary, introduction to student services. **Housing:** Coed dorms, special housing for disabled, apartments, wellness housing available. $200 fully refundable deposit, deadline 5/1. Science and honors housing, townhouses. **Activities:** Bands, campus ministries, choral groups, dance, drama, film society, international student organizations, literary magazine, music ensembles, Model UN, musical theater, radio station, student government, student newspaper, TV station, political science association, ethnic and social service organizations, international affairs society, social justice club, Circle K, Global Horizons, German club, Italian club, Little Theater.

Athletics. NCAA. **Intercollegiate:** Baseball M, basketball, cross-country, golf M, ice hockey M, lacrosse, soccer, softball W, swimming, synchronized swimming W, volleyball W. **Intramural:** Basketball, golf M, handball, soccer, volleyball. **Team name:** Golden Griffins.

Student services. Adult student services, alcohol/substance abuse counseling, chaplain/spiritual director, career counseling, services for economically disadvantaged, student employment services, financial aid counseling, health services, minority student services, personal counseling, placement for graduates, veterans' counselor. **Physically disabled:** Services for visually, speech, hearing impaired.

Contact. E-mail: admissions@canisius.edu
Phone: (716) 888-2200 Toll-free number: (800) 843-1517
Fax: (716) 888-3230
Donna Shaffner, Dean of Admissions, Canisius College, 2001 Main Street, Buffalo, NY 14208-1098

Cazenovia College
Cazenovia, New York
www.cazenovia.edu   **CB code: 2078**

- Private 4-year liberal arts college
- Residential campus in small town
- 1,025 degree-seeking undergraduates: 12% part-time, 75% women, 8% African American, 1% Asian American, 4% Hispanic American, 3% Native American
- 70% of applicants admitted
- 49% graduate within 6 years; 34% enter graduate study

General. Founded in 1824. Regionally accredited. **Degrees:** 246 bachelor's, 2 associate awarded. **ROTC:** Army, Air Force. **Location:** 20 miles from Syracuse. **Calendar:** Semester, limited summer session. **Full-time faculty:** 54 total; 76% have terminal degrees, 2% minority, 63% women. **Part-time faculty:** 74 total; 30% have terminal degrees, 5% minority, 68% women. **Special facilities:** 160-acre farm and equine center, art and design facility and gallery.

Freshman class profile. 2,293 applied, 1,616 admitted, 271 enrolled.

Mid 50% test scores			
SAT critical reading:	440-550	GPA 2.0-2.99:	27%
SAT math:	430-550	Rank in top quarter:	40%
ACT composite:	19-25	Rank in top tenth:	13%
GPA 3.75 or higher:	22%	Return as sophomores:	57%
GPA 3.50-3.74:	18%	Out-of-state:	16%
GPA 3.0-3.49:	33%	Live on campus:	99%

Basis for selection. Rigor of secondary school record very important; interview, recommendations, school activities important. SAT or ACT recommended. Portfolio recommended for art, graphic and interior design, photography programs.

High school preparation. College-preparatory program recommended. 16 units recommended. Recommended units include English 4, mathematics 2, social studies 4 and science 2. Art courses recommended for art and design majors.

2011-2012 Annual costs. Tuition/fees: $26,736. Room/board: $10,970. Books/supplies: $1,000. Personal expenses: $100.

Financial aid. Non-need-based: Scholarships awarded for academics.

Application procedures. Admission: Priority date 3/1; no deadline. $30 fee, may be waived for applicants with need, free for online applicants. Admission notification on a rolling basis beginning on or about 11/1. Must reply by May 1 or within 2 week(s) if notified thereafter. **Financial aid:** Priority date 3/1; no closing date. FAFSA required. Applicants notified on a rolling basis starting 3/1; must reply by 5/1 or within 2 week(s) of notification.

Academics. Special study options: Combined bachelor's/graduate degree, double major, exchange student, honors, independent study, internships, liberal arts/career combination, student-designed major, study abroad, teacher certification program, Washington semester. **Credit/placement by examination:** AP, CLEP, IB, institutional tests. **Support services:** Learning center, pre-admission summer program, reduced course load, remedial instruction, study skills assistance, tutoring, writing center.

Majors. Business: Accounting, business admin, fashion. **Communications:** Communications/speech/rhetoric. **Conservation:** Environmental studies. **Education:** Early childhood, special ed. **English:** English lit. **General:** Equine science. **Liberal arts:** Arts/sciences. **Parks/recreation:** Sports admin. **Protective services:** Criminal justice. **Psychology:** General. **Social sciences:** General. **Visual/performing arts:** Design, fashion design, interior design, photography, studio arts.

Most popular majors. Business/marketing 33%, public administration/social services 8%, visual/performing arts 31%.

Computing on campus. 400 workstations in dormitories, library, computer center. Dormitories wired for high-speed internet access and linked to campus network. Commuter students can connect to campus network. Online library, helpline, wireless network available.

Student life. Freshman orientation: Mandatory. Preregistration for classes offered. **Housing:** Guaranteed on-campus for freshmen. Coed dorms, single-sex dorms, special housing for disabled, apartments, wellness housing available. $200 nonrefundable deposit, deadline 5/1. Single room suites available. **Activities:** Pep band, campus ministries, choral groups, dance, drama, film society, musical theater, radio station, student government, student newspaper, human services club, overseas travel club, Young Democrats, Young Republicans, Cazventures outdoor club, Certified Peer Educators, You Are Not Alone-LGBT, Student Organization of Ethnic Diversity.

Athletics. NCAA. Intercollegiate: Baseball M, basketball, cheerleading, cross-country, equestrian, golf M, lacrosse, rowing (crew), soccer, softball W, volleyball W. **Intramural:** Basketball, bowling, equestrian, football (non-tackle), ice hockey M, rowing (crew), skiing, soccer, softball, swimming, volleyball, weight lifting. **Team name:** Wildcats.

Student services. Alcohol/substance abuse counseling, chaplain/spiritual director, career counseling, services for economically disadvantaged, student employment services, financial aid counseling, health services, personal counseling, placement for graduates. **Physically disabled:** Services for visually, speech, hearing impaired.

Contact. E-mail: admission@cazenovia.edu
Phone: (315) 655-7208 Toll-free number: (800) 654-3210
Fax: (315) 655-4860
Robert Croot, Vice President for Enrollment Management and Dean for Admissions and Financial Aid, Cazenovia College, 3 Sullivan Street, Cazenovia, NY 13035

Central Yeshiva Tomchei Tmimim-Lubavitch
Brooklyn, New York

CB code: 0549

- Private 4-year rabbinical college for men affiliated with Jewish faith
- Very large city

General. Accredited by AARTS. **Degrees:** 146 bachelor's awarded; master's offered. **Calendar:** Differs by program.

2011-2012 Annual costs. Tuition/fees: $5,700. Room/board: $2,300.

Application procedures. Admission: No deadline.

Academics. Credit/placement by examination: AP, CLEP.

Majors. Philosophy/religion: Judaic. **Theology:** Talmudic.

Contact. E-mail: uofiop@juno.com
Phone: (718) 859-7600
Central Yeshiva Tomchei Tmimim-Lubavitch, 841-853 Ocean Parkway, Brooklyn, NY 11230

City University of New York: Baruch College
New York, New York CB member
www.baruch.cuny.edu CB code: 2034

- Public 4-year business and liberal arts college
- Commuter campus in very large city
- 13,938 degree-seeking undergraduates: 24% part-time, 51% women, 10% African American, 34% Asian American, 14% Hispanic American, 12% international
- 3,775 degree-seeking graduate students
- 22% of applicants admitted
- SAT or ACT (ACT writing optional) required
- 63% graduate within 6 years

General. Founded in 1919. Regionally accredited. **Degrees:** 2,731 bachelor's awarded; master's offered. **ROTC:** Army. **Location:** Located in New York City. **Calendar:** Semester, extensive summer session. **Full-time faculty:** 473 total; 93% have terminal degrees, 28% minority, 38% women. **Part-time faculty:** 570 total; 60% have terminal degrees, 28% minority, 39% women. **Class size:** 21% < 20, 60% 20-39, 5% 40-49, 10% 50-99, 5% >100. **Special facilities:** Performing arts center, black box theater, gallery, various theaters and recital halls.

Freshman class profile. 19,283 applied, 4,325 admitted, 1,311 enrolled.

Mid 50% test scores			
SAT critical reading:	500-600	Rank in top tenth:	37%
SAT math:	580-680	End year in good standing:	87%
GPA 3.75 or higher:	15%	Return as sophomores:	89%
GPA 3.50-3.74:	15%	Out-of-state:	5%
GPA 3.0-3.49:	33%	Live on campus:	8%
GPA 2.0-2.99:	33%	International:	6%
Rank in top quarter:	63%	Fraternities:	1%
		Sororities:	1%

Basis for selection. Average high school GPA is 82-92 and average SAT score (out of 1600) is 1140-1280. Applicants must apply through the City University of New York (CUNY) Application, exclusively online. Students who did not score a minimum of 480 on the verbal and math SAT are required to take a skills assessment test. Essays are optional but recommended. **Home schooled:** 1200 SAT required. **Learning Disabled:** No special requirements; recommended that students call Disability Service Office to discuss available services.

High school preparation. 16 units required. Required and recommended units include English 4, mathematics 3-4, social studies 4, science 2 (laboratory 2), foreign language 2 and academic electives 1.

2011-2012 Annual costs. Tuition/fees: $5,610; $14,280 out-of-state. Books/supplies: $1,248. Personal expenses: $1,780.

Financial aid. Non-need-based: Scholarships awarded for academics, state residency.

Application procedures. Admission: $65 fee, may be waived for applicants with need. Application must be submitted online. Admission notification on a rolling basis beginning on or about 2/1. Must reply by May 1 or within 2 week(s) if notified thereafter. All CUNY schools operate on a rolling admission basis; therefore colleges and programs may close before the deadline date. **Financial aid:** Priority date 3/15, closing date 4/30. FAFSA required. Applicants notified on a rolling basis starting 4/1; must reply by 6/1 or within 6 week(s) of notification.

Academics. 120 credit hours required for BA/BS degrees, 124 for BBA. Optional humanities seminar examining 2 or more disciplines in arts and sciences; joint business/liberal arts and science majors; programs in arts administration, management of musical enterprise, real estate, and metropolitan development. **Special study options:** Accelerated study, combined bachelor's/graduate degree, cross-registration, double major, dual enrollment of high school students, ESL, exchange student, honors, independent study, internships, liberal arts/career combination, student-designed major, study abroad. **Credit/placement by examination:** AP, CLEP, IB, SAT, institutional tests. 21 credit hours maximum toward bachelor's degree. No more than 21 credits through AP and/or college courses taken in high school. **Support services:** Learning center, pre-admission summer program, reduced course load, study skills assistance, tutoring, writing center.

Honors college/program. Applicants must have high standardized test scores (1300+ on the SAT, exclusive of Writing) and high school averages (90+). Leadership potential and community involvement sought. Applicants must supply teacher recommendations and essay.

Majors. Architecture: Urban/community planning. **Biology:** General. **Business:** General, accounting, actuarial science, business admin, communications, finance, human resources, labor relations, management information

systems, managerial economics, marketing, operations, real estate, sales/distribution, statistics. **Communications:** Advertising, communications/speech/rhetoric, journalism. **Computer sciences:** General, computer science, information systems. **Engineering:** Operations research. **English:** American lit, British lit, creative writing, English lit. **Foreign languages:** Comparative lit, Hebrew, Spanish. **History:** General. **Human services:** General. **Liberal arts:** Arts/sciences. **Math:** General, statistics. **Philosophy/religion:** Philosophy, religion. **Psychology:** General. **Social sciences:** Economics, political science, sociology. **Visual/performing arts:** Design, music, music management, studio arts management.

Most popular majors. Business/marketing 72%, communications/journalism 7%, social sciences 6%.

Computing on campus. 1,300 workstations in library, computer center, student center. Online course registration, online library, helpline, wireless network available.

Student life. Freshman orientation: Mandatory. Preregistration for classes offered. Half day-long, on-campus session offered on multiple days. **Housing:** Coed dorms available. **Activities:** Campus ministries, choral groups, dance, drama, film society, literary magazine, music ensembles, Model UN, musical theater, radio station, student government, student newspaper, Hillel, National Association of Black Accountants, Golden Key, International Honor Society, Asian student association, Muslim student association, United International Student Body, Pre-Law Society, Caribbean student association.

Athletics. NCAA. **Intercollegiate:** Baseball M, basketball, cheerleading, cross-country, diving W, soccer M, softball W, swimming, tennis, volleyball. **Intramural:** Badminton, basketball, cross-country, racquetball, swimming, table tennis, volleyball. **Team name:** Bearcats.

Student services. Adult student services, alcohol/substance abuse counseling, chaplain/spiritual director, career counseling, student employment services, financial aid counseling, health services, legal services, personal counseling, placement for graduates, veterans' counselor. **Physically disabled:** Services for visually, speech, hearing impaired.

Contact. E-mail: admissions@baruch.cuny.edu
Phone: (646) 312-1400 Fax: (646) 312-1363
Marisa Delacruz, Director, Undergraduate Admissions, City University of New York: Baruch College, One Bernard Baruch Way, Box H-0720, New York, NY 10010-5585

City University of New York: Brooklyn College
Brooklyn, New York
www.brooklyn.cuny.edu   CB code: 2046

- Public 4-year liberal arts college
- Commuter campus in very large city
- 12,162 degree-seeking undergraduates: 24% part-time, 58% women, 24% African American, 17% Asian American, 12% Hispanic American, 4% international
- 3,220 degree-seeking graduate students
- 28% of applicants admitted
- SAT or ACT (ACT writing optional) required
- 48% graduate within 6 years

General. Founded in 1930. Regionally accredited. **Degrees:** 2,409 bachelor's awarded; master's offered. **Location:** 10 miles from Manhattan. **Calendar:** Semester, extensive summer session. **Full-time faculty:** 535 total; 91% have terminal degrees, 23% minority, 44% women. **Part-time faculty:** 793 total; 57% have terminal degrees, 22% minority, 51% women. **Class size:** 37% <20, 58% 20-39, 3% 40-49, 2% 50-99, less than 1% >100. **Special facilities:** Astronomical observatory, greenhouse, applied sciences institute, institute for the humanities, infant study center, Brooklyn Center for the Performing Arts, particle accelerator.

Freshman class profile. 19,152 applied, 5,408 admitted, 1,153 enrolled.

Mid 50% test scores			
SAT critical reading:	490-590	Rank in top quarter:	52%
SAT math:	520-620	Rank in top tenth:	19%
GPA 3.75 or higher:	8%	Return as sophomores:	82%
GPA 3.50-3.74:	22%	Out-of-state:	2%
GPA 3.0-3.49:	60%	International:	3%
GPA 2.0-2.99:	10%	Fraternities:	1%
		Sororities:	1%

Basis for selection. Students accepted based on SAT scores and academic average. Essay required for BA/MD, CHC and Scholars, interview recommended for scholars program. Audition required for music conservatory, theater programs; portfolio required for fine arts program.

High school preparation. College-preparatory program recommended. 21 units recommended. Recommended units include English 4, mathematics 3, social studies 4, science 3, foreign language 3 and academic electives 4.

2012-2013 Annual costs. Tuition/fees (projected): $5,884; $15,004 out-of-state. Books/supplies: $1,179. Personal expenses: $1,733.

2010-2011 Financial aid. Need-based: 1,002 full-time freshmen applied for aid; 895 were judged to have need; 835 of these received aid. Average need met was 99%. Average scholarship/grant was $3,350; average loan $3,200. 58% of total undergraduate aid awarded as scholarships/grants, 42% as loans/jobs. **Non-need-based:** Awarded to 3,345 full-time undergraduates, including 536 freshmen. Scholarships awarded for academics, art, leadership, music/drama, state residency.

Application procedures. Admission: Priority date 2/1; no deadline. $65 fee. Admission notification on a rolling basis beginning on or about 2/1. Must reply by May 1 or within 3 week(s) if notified thereafter. All CUNY schools operate on a rolling admission basis; therefore colleges and programs may close before the deadline date. **Financial aid:** Priority date 4/11; no closing date. FAFSA required. Applicants notified on a rolling basis starting 5/11.

Academics. Special study options: Accelerated study, combined bachelor's/graduate degree, distance learning, double major, dual enrollment of high school students, ESL, honors, independent study, internships, student-designed major, study abroad, teacher certification program, Washington semester, weekend college. **Credit/placement by examination:** AP, CLEP, IB, SAT, ACT, institutional tests. 35 credit hours maximum toward bachelor's degree. **Support services:** Learning center, pre-admission summer program, reduced course load, study skills assistance, tutoring, writing center.

Honors college/program. Through its six participating programs, the Honors Academy offers interdisciplinary seminars, honors sections of Core curriculum classes, senior thesis colloquia, individual academic and professional advisement, closely monitored internships, small class sizes, and a collaborative community of well-matched students. The programs of the Honors Academy are: Coordinated B.A.-M.D., Engineering Honors, Mellon Mays Undergraduate Fellowship, Minority Access to Research Careers (MARC), Scholars at Brooklyn College, and William E. Macaulay Honors College.

Majors. Area/ethnic studies: African-American, American, Caribbean, Chicano/Hispanic-American/Latino, Latin American, women's. **Biology:** General. **Business:** Accounting, business admin. **Communications:** Broadcast journalism, communications/speech/rhetoric, journalism, radio/TV. **Communications technology:** Radio/TV. **Computer sciences:** General, information systems, web page design. **Conservation:** Environmental studies. **Education:** Bilingual, biology, chemistry, early childhood, earth science, elementary, English, French, kindergarten/preschool, mathematics, music, physical, physics, social studies, Spanish, special ed. **English:** Creative writing, English lit, rhetoric/composition. **Foreign languages:** Classics, comparative lit, French, Italian, linguistics, Russian, Spanish. **Health services:** Audiology/speech pathology, speech pathology. **History:** General. **Liberal arts:** Arts/sciences. **Math:** General, computational. **Parks/recreation:** Exercise sciences, health/fitness. **Philosophy/religion:** Judaic, philosophy, religion. **Physical sciences:** Chemistry, geology, physics. **Psychology:** General. **Social sciences:** Anthropology, economics, political science, sociology. **Visual/performing arts:** Art, art history/conservation, cinematography, dramatic, music, music performance, music theory/composition, studio arts. **Work/family studies:** Food/nutrition.

Most popular majors. Business/marketing 34%, education 12%, health sciences 7%, psychology 12%, social sciences 6%.

Computing on campus. 2,000 workstations in library, computer center, student center. Online library, wireless network available.

Student life. Freshman orientation: Available. Preregistration for classes offered. **Activities:** Dance, drama, film society, international student organizations, literary magazine, music ensembles, musical theater, radio station, student government, student newspaper, symphony orchestra, TV station, Hillel, Newman Club, student Christian association, Alpha Phi Omega, Christian fellowship, Islamic society, Caribbean student union, accounting society, lesbian/gay/bisexual/transgender alliance.

Athletics. NCAA. **Intercollegiate:** Basketball, cross-country, soccer M, softball W, swimming, tennis, volleyball. **Intramural:** Badminton, basketball, soccer, tennis, volleyball. **Team name:** Bulldogs.

Student services. Adult student services, alcohol/substance abuse counseling, career counseling, services for economically disadvantaged, student employment services, financial aid counseling, health services, on-campus daycare, personal counseling, placement for graduates, veterans' counselor, women's services. **Physically disabled:** Services for visually, speech, hearing impaired.

Contact. E-mail: adminqry@brooklyn.cuny.edu
Phone: (718) 951-5001 Fax: (718) 951-4506
Penelope Terry, Director of Undergraduate Admissions, City University of New York: Brooklyn College, 2900 Bedford Avenue, Brooklyn, NY 11210

City University of New York: City College
New York, New York
CB member
www.ccny.cuny.edu
CB code: 2083

- Public 4-year university
- Commuter campus in very large city
- 12,642 degree-seeking undergraduates: 23% part-time, 52% women, 22% African American, 20% Asian American, 31% Hispanic American, 9% international
- 2,828 degree-seeking graduate students
- 32% of applicants admitted
- SAT required
- 39% graduate within 6 years

General. Founded in 1847. Regionally accredited. **Degrees:** 1,918 bachelor's awarded; master's, doctoral offered. **Calendar:** Semester, extensive summer session. **Full-time faculty:** 531 total; 78% have terminal degrees, 30% minority, 38% women. **Part-time faculty:** 959 total; 15% have terminal degrees, 38% minority, 45% women. **Class size:** 41% < 20, 57% 20-39, 2% 40-49, less than 1% 50-99, less than 1% >100. **Special facilities:** Planetarium, weather station, ultra-fast laser spectroscopy laboratory, microwave laboratory, computer-aided design facilities, slide library, darkroom facilities, sonic music arts facility, structural biology center.

Freshman class profile. 23,250 applied, 7,540 admitted, 1,519 enrolled.

Mid 50% test scores		GPA 2.0-2.99:	32%
SAT critical reading:	440-570	Return as sophomores:	85%
SAT math:	510-620	Out-of-state:	1%
GPA 3.75 or higher:	12%	Live on campus:	2%
GPA 3.50-3.74:	19%	International:	8%
GPA 3.0-3.49:	29%		

Basis for selection. Academic average and number of academic units achieved in high school, SAT, or GED score of 325 or better important. Units recommended for admission must be acquired before graduation from any CUNY senior college. SAT Critical Reading of 480 or ACT English score of 20 exempts a student from the reading and writing assessment test; SAT Math of 510 or ACT Math score of 21 exempts student from math assessment test. Interview required for biomedical education, audition required for music program; portfolio required for electronic design and multimedia. **Home schooled:** Applicants must obtain GED or diploma through regionally accredited program.

High school preparation. 19 units required. Required units include English 4, mathematics 3, social studies 4, science 2 (laboratory 2), foreign language 3 and academic electives 1.

2011-2012 Annual costs. Tuition/fees: $5,459; $14,129 out-of-state. Room only: $11,660. Books/supplies: $1,070.

2010-2011 Financial aid. Need-based: 1,113 full-time freshmen applied for aid; 1,072 were judged to have need; 1,020 of these received aid. Average need met was 82%. Average scholarship/grant was $7,566; average loan $1,920. 71% of total undergraduate aid awarded as scholarships/grants, 29% as loans/jobs. **Non-need-based:** Awarded to 1,769 full-time undergraduates, including 822 freshmen. Scholarships awarded for academics, alumni affiliation, art, leadership, music/drama, state residency.

Application procedures. Admission: Closing date 1/15 (postmark date). $65 fee. Admission notification on a rolling basis beginning on or about 3/1. All CUNY schools operate on a rolling admission basis; therefore colleges and programs may close before the deadline date. **Financial aid:** Priority date 3/15; no closing date. FAFSA required. Applicants notified on a rolling basis starting 4/1.

Academics. Special study options: Accelerated study, combined bachelor's/graduate degree, cooperative education, cross-registration, distance learning, double major, dual enrollment of high school students, ESL, honors, independent study, internships, study abroad, teacher certification program. Center for Worker Education, doctoral degrees through CUNY Graduate Center except for Engineering. **Credit/placement by examination:** AP, CLEP, IB, institutional tests. 32 credit hours maximum toward bachelor's degree. **Support services:** Learning center, pre-admission summer program, reduced course load, study skills assistance, tutoring, writing center.

Honors college/program. Admits only new first-year students, who must apply by special application. Application deadline November 1 for early admission, December 15 for regular admission. For the class admitted fall 2005 (Class of 2009), the average high school GPA was 93.7 (on a scale of 100) and the average SAT was 1371 (exclusive of Writing). Students are expected to achieve an overall 3.3 GPA by the end of their first year and a 3.5 GPA by the end of their second year, which must be maintained until graduation in four years.

Majors. Architecture: Architecture. **Area/ethnic studies:** African-American, Asian, Caribbean, Latin American. **Biology:** General, biochemistry. **Business:** General. **Communications:** Advertising, communications/speech/rhetoric, journalism, public relations. **Computer sciences:** Computer science. **Education:** Art, bilingual, biology, chemistry, early childhood, elementary, English, foreign languages, French, history, mathematics, music, physics, science, secondary, social studies, Spanish. **Engineering:** Biomedical, chemical, civil, computer, electrical, mechanical. **English:** English lit. **Foreign languages:** General, comparative lit, French, Spanish. **Health services:** Physician assistant, premedicine, prepharmacy, preveterinary. **History:** General. **Math:** General. **Philosophy/religion:** Judaic, philosophy. **Physical sciences:** Chemistry, geology, physics, planetary. **Psychology:** General. **Social sciences:** Anthropology, economics, international relations, political science, sociology. **Visual/performing arts:** General, art, art history/conservation, cinematography, commercial/advertising art, dramatic, film/cinema/video, graphic design, jazz, music, music performance, music theory/composition, studio arts.

Most popular majors. Biology 8%, communications/journalism 8%, engineering/engineering technologies 13%, English 6%, liberal arts 8%, psychology 15%, social sciences 13%, visual/performing arts 11%.

Computing on campus. 2,500 workstations in library, computer center, student center. Dormitories wired for high-speed internet access and linked to campus network. Commuter students can connect to campus network. Online course registration, online library, helpline, repair service, wireless network available.

Student life. Freshman orientation: Mandatory. Preregistration for classes offered. Full-day program, including registration, held in spring and summer. **Housing:** Apartments available. $400 nonrefundable deposit. **Activities:** Jazz band, choral groups, dance, drama, film society, international student organizations, literary magazine, music ensembles, Model UN, musical theater, radio station, student government, student newspaper, TV station, numerous religious, political, ethnic, and social service organizations.

Athletics. NCAA. **Intercollegiate:** Baseball M, basketball, cross-country, fencing, lacrosse M, soccer, tennis, track and field, volleyball. **Intramural:** Badminton M, basketball, fencing, soccer M, softball W, swimming, tennis, track and field, volleyball. **Team name:** Beavers.

Student services. Alcohol/substance abuse counseling, chaplain/spiritual director, career counseling, services for economically disadvantaged, student employment services, financial aid counseling, health services, minority student services, on-campus daycare, personal counseling, placement for graduates, veterans' counselor, women's services. **Physically disabled:** Services for visually, speech, hearing impaired.

Contact. E-mail: admissions@ccny.cuny.edu
Phone: (212) 650-6977 Fax: (212) 650-6417
Joseph Fatozzi, Director of Admissions, City University of New York: City College, 160 Convent Avenue, A100, New York, NY 10031

City University of New York: College of Staten Island
Staten Island, New York
CB member
www.csi.cuny.edu
CB code: 2778

- Public 4-year liberal arts college
- Commuter campus in very large city
- 12,806 degree-seeking undergraduates: 25% part-time, 57% women, 8% African American, 9% Asian American, 14% Hispanic American, 3% international
- 946 degree-seeking graduate students
- SAT or ACT (ACT writing optional) required
- 48% graduate within 6 years

General. Founded in 1955. Regionally accredited. **Degrees:** 1,270 bachelor's, 649 associate awarded; master's, professional, doctoral offered. **Location:** 10 miles from downtown Manhattan. **Calendar:** Semester, extensive summer session. **Full-time faculty:** 337 total; 85% have terminal degrees, 22% minority, 47% women. **Part-time faculty:** 919 total; 38% have terminal degrees, 18% minority, 49% women. **Class size:** 21% < 20, 55% 20-39,

18% 40-49, 5% 50-99, less than 1% >100. **Special facilities:** Astrophysical observatory, archives and special collections, artificial intelligence laboratory, center for developmental neuroscience and developmental disabilities, center for engineered polymeric materials, center for environmental science, nuclear magnetic resonance spectrometer, CUNY High Performance Computational Facility.

Freshman class profile.

Mid 50% test scores		GPA 3.0-3.49:	32%
SAT critical reading:	430-540	GPA 2.0-2.99:	47%
SAT math:	460-560	Return as sophomores:	83%
SAT writing:	430-530	Out-of-state:	1%
GPA 3.75 or higher:	3%	International:	2%
GPA 3.50-3.74:	14%		

Basis for selection. Open admission for associates degree programs. Specific admission criteria for baccalaureate programs based primarily on high school average (college academic average), SAT Critical Reading, SAT Math and in some cases academic units. **Home schooled:** State high school equivalency certificate required.

High school preparation. College-preparatory program required. 15 units required; 16 recommended. Required and recommended units include English 4, mathematics 2-3, social studies 4, science 2-3, foreign language 2-3, visual/performing arts .5.

2011-2012 Annual costs. Tuition/fees: $5,558; $14,228 out-of-state. Books/supplies: $1,146. Personal expenses: $1,744.

2010-2011 Financial aid. All financial aid based on need. 1,878 full-time freshmen applied for aid; 1,426 were judged to have need; 1,362 of these received aid. Average need met was 60%. Average scholarship/grant was $6,643; average loan $2,959. 81% of total undergraduate aid awarded as scholarships/grants, 19% as loans/jobs.

Application procedures. Admission: Priority date 2/1; no deadline. $65 fee, may be waived for applicants with need. Application must be submitted online. Admission notification on a rolling basis beginning on or about 2/1. Must reply by May 1 or within 4 week(s) if notified thereafter. All CUNY schools operate on a rolling admission basis; therefore colleges and programs may close after the priority deadline. **Financial aid:** Priority date 3/30; no closing date. FAFSA required. Applicants notified on a rolling basis starting 6/1.

Academics. Baccalaureate for Unique and Interdisciplinary Studies available, CUNY's individualized, university-wide BA/BS degree, where students formulate proposals for unique areas of concentration, then collaborate with CUNY faculty members to design their degrees. **Special study options:** Distance learning, double major, ESL, honors, independent study, internships, New York semester, study abroad, teacher certification program, Washington semester. Cross-registration at any CUNY. **Credit/placement by examination:** AP, CLEP, IB, SAT, ACT, institutional tests. 30 credit hours maximum toward associate degree, 30 toward bachelor's. **Support services:** Learning center, pre-admission summer program, remedial instruction, study skills assistance, tutoring.

Honors college/program. Admission open to prospective first-semester freshmen only. Minimum 1200 SAT (exclusive of Writing) and 90 high school average. 40 seats available. High school transcript, SAT or ACT score, essay, and letters of recommendation required. Personal interview may be requested. Accepted students receive free tuition, lap top, and access to funds to support enrichment opportunities, including study abroad, unpaid internships.

Majors. Area/ethnic studies: African-American, American, Italian, women's. **Biology:** General, biochemistry. **Business:** General, accounting. **Communications:** Communications/speech/rhetoric. **Computer sciences:** Computer science, information systems. **Education:** Biology, chemistry, English, history, mathematics, Spanish. **Engineering:** General. **English:** English lit. **Foreign languages:** Italian, Spanish. **Health services:** Clinical lab science, nursing (RN). **History:** General. **Human services:** Social work. **Liberal arts:** Arts/sciences. **Math:** General. **Philosophy/religion:** Philosophy. **Physical sciences:** Chemistry, physics. **Psychology:** General. **Social sciences:** Economics, international relations, political science. **Visual/performing arts:** Cinematography, dramatic, film/cinema/video, music, photography.

Most popular majors. Business/marketing 24%, communications/journalism 6%, English 8%, liberal arts 11%, psychology 12%, social sciences 17%.

Computing on campus. 1,254 workstations in library, computer center, student center. Commuter students can connect to campus network. Online course registration, online library, helpline, student web hosting, wireless network available.

Student life. Freshman orientation: Mandatory. Preregistration for classes offered. Scheduled at beginning of each semester, after or during time periods devoted to testing, advisement, and registration. Students with less than 6 credits are required to complete the orientation requirement during the first semester prior to completing 12 credits. **Activities:** Jazz band, campus ministries, choral groups, dance, drama, film society, international student organizations, literary magazine, music ensembles, radio station, student government, student newspaper, Muslim student association, Israel club, Chi Alpha Christian club, Hillel, armed forces club, Love Thy Neighbor, government and law society, Hunger Action Leaders of Tomorrow, Caribbean student association, Jewish awareness movement.

Athletics. NCAA. **Intercollegiate:** Baseball M, basketball, cross-country, diving, soccer, softball W, swimming, tennis, volleyball W. **Intramural:** Basketball, cricket, handball, racquetball, tennis, volleyball. **Team name:** Dolphins.

Student services. Adult student services, alcohol/substance abuse counseling, chaplain/spiritual director, career counseling, services for economically disadvantaged, student employment services, financial aid counseling, health services, minority student services, on-campus daycare, personal counseling, placement for graduates, veterans' counselor, women's services. **Physically disabled:** Services for visually, speech, hearing impaired.

Contact. E-mail: admissions@csi.cuny.edu
Phone: (718) 982-2010 Fax: (718) 982-2500
Emmanuel Esperance, Director of Recruitment & Admissions, City University of New York: College of Staten Island, 2800 Victory Boulevard 2A-104, Staten Island, NY 10314

City University of New York: CUNY Online
New York, New York
www.online.sps.cuny.edu/

- Public 4-year virtual university
- Commuter campus in very large city
- 1,003 degree-seeking undergraduates
- 379 graduate students
- Application essay required

General. Regionally accredited. CUNY Online offers fully asynchronous online bachelor's degree programs for students who have at least 30 earned credits, an MS in Business Management and Leadership, or a graduate certificate program in Immigration Law Studies. **Degrees:** 112 bachelor's awarded; master's offered. **Calendar:** Semester, limited summer session. **Part-time faculty:** 134 total; 78% have terminal degrees, 19% minority, 53% women. **Class size:** 62% < 20, 38% 20-39.

Basis for selection. Open admission, but selective for some programs. Accept only transfer applicants with at least 30 credits earned. **Home schooled:** State high school equivalency certificate required.

2011-2012 Annual costs. Tuition/fees: $5,510; $5,510 out-of-state. Books/supplies: $1,016.

2011-2012 Financial aid. Need-based: 28% of total undergraduate aid awarded as scholarships/grants, 72% as loans/jobs.

Application procedures. Admission: $70 fee, may be waived for applicants with need. Application must be submitted online. Admission notification on a rolling basis beginning on or about 2/1. All CUNY schools operate on a rolling admission basis; therefore colleges and programs may close before the deadline date. **Financial aid:** Closing date 8/1.

Academics. Special study options: Distance learning. **Credit/placement by examination:** AP, CLEP, IB. 45 credit hours maximum toward bachelor's degree. **Support services:** Study skills assistance, tutoring.

Majors. Business: General. **Communications:** Communications/speech/rhetoric.

Most popular majors. Business/marketing 10%, liberal arts 90%.

Computing on campus. PC or laptop required. Commuter students can connect to campus network. Helpline, student web hosting available.

Student services. Adult student services, financial aid counseling, veterans' counselor. **Physically disabled:** Services for visually, speech, hearing impaired.

Contact. E-mail: onlineba@mail.cuny.edu
Otilia Abraham, Coordinator of Admissions, City University of New York: CUNY Online, 101 West 31st Street, 9th Floor, New York, NY 10001-3507

City University of New York: Hunter College
New York, New York — CB member
www.hunter.cuny.edu/ — CB code: 2301

▶ Public 4-year liberal arts college
▶ Commuter campus in very large city
▶ 15,417 degree-seeking undergraduates: 25% part-time, 66% women, 11% African American, 24% Asian American, 18% Hispanic American, 7% international
▶ 5,847 degree-seeking graduate students
▶ 27% of applicants admitted
▶ SAT or ACT required
▶ 45% graduate within 6 years

General. Founded in 1870. Regionally accredited. **Degrees:** 2,634 bachelor's awarded; master's offered. **Calendar:** Semester, limited summer session. **Full-time faculty:** 693 total; 83% have terminal degrees, 20% minority, 49% women. **Part-time faculty:** 1,180 total; 21% have terminal degrees, 21% minority, 61% women. **Class size:** 42% < 20, 50% 20-39, 3% 40-49, 4% 50-99, less than 1% >100. **Special facilities:** Mathematics learning center, on-campus elementary and secondary schools.

Freshman class profile. 30,529 applied, 8,315 admitted, 2,177 enrolled.

Mid 50% test scores		GPA 3.0-3.49:	39%
SAT critical reading:	500-600	GPA 2.0-2.99:	26%
SAT math:	540-640	Return as sophomores:	85%
GPA 3.75 or higher:	15%	Out-of-state:	4%
GPA 3.50-3.74:	16%	International:	6%

Basis for selection. Requirements vary by program. Indexing formula using weighted averages, high school academic units, and SAT scores for admission to some programs. SAT or ACT not required, but recommended, of first-time freshmen who graduated high school more than a year preceding admission.

High school preparation. 16 units recommended. Required and recommended units include English 2-4, mathematics 2-3, social studies 4, science 1-2 (laboratory 1), foreign language 2 and academic electives 1. 1 fine art or performing art recommended.

2012-2013 Annual costs. Tuition/fees (projected): $5,529; $14,199 out-of-state. Room only: $4,810. Books/supplies: $1,179. Personal expenses: $4,823.

2010-2011 Financial aid. **Need-based:** 1,510 full-time freshmen applied for aid; 1,154 were judged to have need; 1,131 of these received aid. Average need met was 77%. Average scholarship/grant was $5,639; average loan $2,884. 55% of total undergraduate aid awarded as scholarships/grants, 45% as loans/jobs. **Non-need-based:** Awarded to 3,325 full-time undergraduates, including 1,169 freshmen. Scholarships awarded for academics.

Application procedures. **Admission:** $65 fee, may be waived for applicants with need. Admission notification on a rolling basis beginning on or about 2/1. All CUNY schools operate on a rolling admission basis; therefore colleges and programs may close before the deadline date. **Financial aid:** Priority date 5/1; no closing date. FAFSA required. Applicants notified on a rolling basis starting 5/15.

Academics. **Special study options:** Accelerated study, combined bachelor's/graduate degree, cross-registration, distance learning, double major, dual enrollment of high school students, exchange student, honors, independent study, internships, liberal arts/career combination, student-designed major, study abroad, teacher certification program. BA/MA/MS programs in anthropology, biology/EOPS, economics, English, history, math, music, physics, social research (MS). **Credit/placement by examination:** AP, CLEP, IB, institutional tests. 30 credit hours maximum toward bachelor's degree. **Support services:** Learning center, reduced course load, remedial instruction, study skills assistance, tutoring, writing center.

Majors. **Area/ethnic studies:** African-American, Latin American, Near/Middle Eastern, women's. **Biology:** General, bioinformatics, biophysics, biotechnology, pharmacology. **Business:** Accounting. **Communications:** Media studies. **Computer sciences:** General. **Education:** General, art, biology, chemistry, drama/dance, early childhood, elementary, English, foreign languages, French, geography, German, health, history, Latin, mathematics, music, physical, physics, secondary, social studies, Spanish. **English:** British lit, creative writing, English lit. **Foreign languages:** General, ancient Greek, Chinese, classics, comparative lit, French, German, Hebrew, Italian, Latin, Romance, Russian, Spanish. **Health services:** Adult health nursing, clinical lab science, clinical lab technology, maternal/child health nursing, nurse practitioner, nursing (RN), pediatric nursing, psychiatric nursing, public health nursing, speech pathology. **History:** General. **Liberal arts:** Humanities. **Math:** General, statistics. **Philosophy/religion:** Judaic, philosophy, religion. **Physical sciences:** Chemistry, physics. **Psychology:** General. **Social sciences:** Anthropology, archaeology, economics, geography, international relations, political science, sociology, urban studies. **Visual/performing arts:** Art history/conservation, cinematography, dance, dramatic, film/cinema/video, music, music performance, music theory/composition, studio arts. **Work/family studies:** Food/nutrition.

Most popular majors. Communications/journalism 8%, English 13%, health sciences 7%, psychology 16%, social sciences 20%, visual/performing arts 9%.

Computing on campus. 1,280 workstations in dormitories, library, computer center, student center. Commuter students can connect to campus network. Online course registration, online library, helpline, repair service, student web hosting, wireless network available.

Student life. **Freshman orientation:** Available. Preregistration for classes offered. **Housing:** Coed dorms, wellness housing available. **Activities:** Bands, choral groups, dance, drama, film society, literary magazine, music ensembles, musical theater, radio station, student government, student newspaper, symphony orchestra, TV station, over 100 political, ethnic, social, and religious organizations.

Athletics. NCAA. **Intercollegiate:** Basketball, cross-country, fencing, football (non-tackle) W, soccer M, softball W, swimming W, tennis, track and field, volleyball, wrestling M. **Intramural:** Basketball, bowling, football (non-tackle), racquetball, swimming, table tennis, tennis, volleyball. **Team name:** Hawks.

Student services. Adult student services, alcohol/substance abuse counseling, chaplain/spiritual director, career counseling, services for economically disadvantaged, student employment services, financial aid counseling, health services, legal services, minority student services, on-campus daycare, personal counseling, placement for graduates, veterans' counselor, women's services. **Physically disabled:** Services for visually, speech, hearing impaired.

Contact. E-mail: admissions@hunter.cuny.edu
Phone: (212) 772-4490
William Zlata, Director of Admissions, City University of New York: Hunter College, 695 Park Avenue, New York, NY 10065

City University of New York: John Jay College of Criminal Justice
New York, New York — CB member
www.jjay.cuny.edu/ — CB code: 2115

▶ Public 4-year College of criminal justice and public safety.
▶ Commuter campus in very large city
▶ 12,437 degree-seeking undergraduates: 20% part-time, 56% women, 22% African American, 10% Asian American, 40% Hispanic American, 3% international
▶ 1,767 degree-seeking graduate students
▶ 43% of applicants admitted
▶ SAT or ACT with writing required
▶ 38% graduate within 6 years; 14% enter graduate study

General. Founded in 1964. Regionally accredited. **Degrees:** 2,171 bachelor's, 255 associate awarded; master's offered. **Calendar:** Semester, limited summer session. **Class size:** 34% < 20, 63% 20-39, 3% 40-49, less than 1% 50-99, less than 1% >100. **Special facilities:** Security laboratory, fire science laboratory, explosion-proof toxicology research laboratory.

Freshman class profile. 13,858 applied, 5,985 admitted, 1,766 enrolled.

Mid 50% test scores		GPA 2.0-2.99:	68%
SAT critical reading:	410-500	End year in good standing:	76%
SAT math:	420-520	Return as sophomores:	78%
GPA 3.75 or higher:	2%	Out-of-state:	3%
GPA 3.50-3.74:	5%	International:	3%
GPA 3.0-3.49:	18%		

Basis for selection. Admission to baccalaureate degree program requires minimum SAT score from 960 to 1020 and minimum high school average of 80. A minimum of 14 academic units with a total of 4 units in English and mathematics with at least 1 unit in each discipline. **Home schooled:** State high school equivalency certificate required. Applicants must have diploma issued by local registered high school, and minimum combined verbal and math SAT of 1100.

High school preparation. College-preparatory program required. 14 units required; 19 recommended. Required and recommended units include English

4, mathematics 3-4, social studies 2-4, (laboratory 2-3), foreign language 2-3 and visual/performing arts 1. One unit in fine arts required/recommended.

2011-2012 Annual costs. Tuition/fees: $5,459; $14,129 out-of-state. Books/supplies: $1,146. Personal expenses: $4,724.

2011-2012 Financial aid. Need-based: Average need met was 85%. Average scholarship/grant was $3,175; average loan $3,500. 76% of total undergraduate aid awarded as scholarships/grants, 24% as loans/jobs. **Non-need-based:** Scholarships awarded for academics, leadership, minority status, state residency.

Application procedures. Admission: Priority date 2/1; deadline 5/31 (postmark date). $65 fee. Application must be submitted online. Admission notification on a rolling basis beginning on or about 1/15. Admission to John Jay on space-available basis. Centralized application processing allows students to apply to 6 academic programs within CUNY system at same time. **Financial aid:** Priority date 4/30; no closing date. FAFSA required. Applicants notified on a rolling basis starting 4/1; must reply within 2 week(s) of notification.

Academics. Degree requirements and curriculum combine professional education with the liberal arts. The Baccalaureate for Unique and Interdisciplinary Studies (CUNY BA), is CUNY's individualized, university-wide BA/BS degree, where students formulate proposals for unique areas of concentration, then collaborate with CUNY faculty members to design their degrees. **Special study options:** Combined bachelor's/graduate degree, cooperative education, cross-registration, distance learning, dual enrollment of high school students, ESL, exchange student, honors, independent study, internships, liberal arts/career combination, student-designed major, study abroad, weekend college. **Credit/placement by examination:** AP, CLEP, IB, SAT, ACT, institutional tests. 30 credit hours maximum toward associate degree, 30 toward bachelor's. **Support services:** Learning center, pre-admission summer program, reduced course load, remedial instruction, tutoring, writing center.

Honors college/program. Based on high school average and ACT or SAT score with rank in top 10 percent of the freshmen cohort. Classes taught seminar style and the concept of justice is the foundational theme of the interdisciplinary curriculum.

Majors. Computer sciences: General. **English:** English lit. **History:** General. **Human services:** General. **Protective services:** Fire services admin, firefighting, forensics, law enforcement admin. **Psychology:** General, forensic. **Social sciences:** Criminology, economics, political science.

Most popular majors. Psychology 20%, security/protective services 52%, social sciences 16%.

Computing on campus. 1,850 workstations in library, computer center. Commuter students can connect to campus network. Online course registration, helpline available.

Student life. Freshman orientation: Available. Preregistration for classes offered. **Policies:** Students represented on college committees. **Activities:** Choral groups, dance, drama, musical theater, radio station, student government, student newspaper, law society, Irish club, Students Against War and Racism, Haitian club, Christian Seekers Fellowship, Jewish students society, Newman club, Betances Society, Black student society, ethnic organizations.

Athletics. NCAA. **Intercollegiate:** Baseball M, basketball, cross-country, diving W, rifle, soccer M, softball W, swimming W, tennis, volleyball. **Intramural:** Basketball, rifle, soccer M, swimming. **Team name:** Bloodhounds.

Student services. Career counseling, services for economically disadvantaged, student employment services, financial aid counseling, health services, minority student services, on-campus daycare, personal counseling, placement for graduates, veterans' counselor, women's services. **Physically disabled:** Services for visually, speech, hearing impaired.

Contact. E-mail: admiss@jjay.cuny.edu
Phone: (212) 237-8865 Fax: (212) 237-8777
Sandra Palleja, Director of Admissions, City University of New York: John Jay College of Criminal Justice, 445 West 59th Street, New York, NY 10019

City University of New York: Lehman College
Bronx, New York   CB member
www.lehman.edu   CB code: 2312

- Public 4-year liberal arts college
- Commuter campus in very large city

- 8,948 degree-seeking undergraduates: 36% part-time, 69% women, 31% African American, 5% Asian American, 50% Hispanic American, 4% international
- 2,231 degree-seeking graduate students
- 20% of applicants admitted
- SAT or ACT (ACT writing optional) required
- 40% graduate within 6 years

General. Founded in 1931. Regionally accredited. **Degrees:** 1,310 bachelor's awarded; master's offered. **ROTC:** Army. **Location:** 8 miles from Manhattan. **Calendar:** Semester, limited summer session. **Full-time faculty:** 384 total; 73% have terminal degrees, 29% minority, 52% women. **Part-time faculty:** 516 total; 17% have terminal degrees, 40% minority, 54% women. **Class size:** 43% < 20, 56% 20-39, less than 1% 40-49, less than 1% 50-99, less than 1% >100. **Special facilities:** 2,500-seat performing arts center.

Freshman class profile. 15,348 applied, 3,124 admitted, 644 enrolled.

Mid 50% test scores			
SAT critical reading:	420-510	End year in good standing:	73%
SAT math:	440-530	Return as sophomores:	79%
SAT writing:	420-510	Out-of-state:	1%
		International:	6%

Basis for selection. High school record, GPA, and college preparatory courses most important. Tests are used to exempt students from placement tests. **Home schooled:** State high school equivalency certificate required.

High school preparation. 16 units required. Required units include English 4, mathematics 3, social studies 4, science 2 (laboratory 1), foreign language 2 and visual/performing arts 1.

2011-2012 Annual costs. Tuition/fees: $5,508; $14,178 out-of-state. Books/supplies: $1,146. Personal expenses: $2,764.

Financial aid. All financial aid based on need.

Application procedures. Admission: $65 fee. Admission notification on a rolling basis beginning on or about 2/1. All CUNY schools operate on a rolling admission basis; therefore colleges and programs may close before the deadline date. **Financial aid:** No deadline. FAFSA required. Applicants notified on a rolling basis starting 3/1.

Academics. Special study options: Accelerated study, cooperative education, cross-registration, distance learning, double major, dual enrollment of high school students, ESL, honors, independent study, internships, student-designed major, study abroad, teacher certification program. **Credit/placement by examination:** AP, CLEP, IB, institutional tests. 30 credit hours maximum toward bachelor's degree. **Support services:** Learning center, pre-admission summer program, reduced course load, remedial instruction, study skills assistance, tutoring, writing center.

Honors college/program. Criteria for selection include high school academic record, SAT/ACT scores, essay, 2 letters of recommendation and interview.

Majors. Area/ethnic studies: African-American, Latin American. **Biology:** General. **Business:** Accounting, business admin. **Communications:** Communications/speech/rhetoric. **Computer sciences:** General, information systems. **Education:** Health, mathematics, physical. **English:** English lit, rhetoric/composition. **Foreign languages:** Comparative lit, French, Italian, linguistics, Spanish. **Health services:** Audiology/speech pathology, facilities admin, nursing (RN). **History:** General. **Human services:** Social work. **Liberal arts:** Arts/sciences. **Math:** General. **Philosophy/religion:** Philosophy. **Physical sciences:** Chemistry, geology, physics. **Psychology:** General. **Social sciences:** Anthropology, economics, geography, political science, sociology. **Visual/performing arts:** Art history/conservation, commercial/advertising art, music performance. **Work/family studies:** Food/nutrition.

Most popular majors. Business/marketing 17%, education 23%, health sciences 21%, public administration/social services 8%, social sciences 9%.

Computing on campus. 88 workstations in library, computer center, student center. Commuter students can connect to campus network. Online library, helpline, repair service, student web hosting, wireless network available.

Student life. Freshman orientation: Mandatory. Preregistration for classes offered. **Activities:** Bands, choral groups, dance, drama, film society, literary magazine, music ensembles, musical theater, opera, radio station, student government, student newspaper, symphony orchestra, TV station, various religious, political, ethnic, and social service organizations.

Athletics. NCAA. **Intercollegiate:** Baseball M, basketball, cross-country, diving, softball W, swimming, tennis, track and field, volleyball. **Intramural:** Badminton, basketball, racquetball, soccer, softball, swimming, table tennis, tennis, volleyball. **Team name:** Lightning.

Student services. Adult student services, chaplain/spiritual director, career counseling, services for economically disadvantaged, student employment services, financial aid counseling, health services, on-campus daycare, personal counseling, placement for graduates, veterans' counselor, women's services. **Physically disabled:** Services for visually, speech, hearing impaired.

Contact. E-mail: enroll@lehman.cuny.edu
Phone: (718) 960-8713 Toll-free number: (877) 534-6261
Fax: (718) 960-8712
Laurie Austin, Director of Admissions, City University of New York: Lehman College, 250 Bedford Park Boulevard West, Bronx, NY 10468

City University of New York: Medgar Evers College

Brooklyn, New York	**CB member**
www.mec.cuny.edu	**CB code: 2460**

- Public 4-year liberal arts college
- Commuter campus in very large city
- 6,582 degree-seeking undergraduates: 31% part-time, 74% women, 85% African American, 2% Asian American, 9% Hispanic American, 1% international

General. Founded in 1969. Regionally accredited. **Degrees:** 478 bachelor's, 449 associate awarded. **Calendar:** Semester, extensive summer session. **Full-time faculty:** 186 total; 58% have terminal degrees, 83% minority, 46% women. **Part-time faculty:** 332 total; 89% minority, 43% women. **Class size:** 23% < 20, 73% 20-39, 4% 40-49, less than 1% 50-99.

Freshman class profile. 8,042 applied, 8,042 admitted, 1,201 enrolled.

Mid 50% test scores		GPA 2.0-2.99:	62%
SAT critical reading:	350-430	End year in good standing:	47%
SAT math:	340-440	Return as sophomores:	62%
SAT writing:	340-430	Out-of-state:	1%
GPA 3.50-3.74:	1%	International:	1%
GPA 3.0-3.49:	3%		

Basis for selection. Open admission, but selective for some programs. Special requirements for nursing and baccalaureate programs with school record, class rank, and test scores considered. Discretionary policy admits 25 students each semester without high school diplomas. Must be 21 years old, legal residents of New York City.

High school preparation. 17 units recommended. Recommended units include English 4, mathematics 3, social studies 4, science 2, foreign language 2 and academic electives 2.

2011-2012 Annual costs. Tuition/fees: $5,432; $14,102 out-of-state. Books/supplies: $1,146. Personal expenses: $2,764.

Financial aid. Non-need-based: Scholarships awarded for academics, leadership.

Application procedures. Admission: $65 fee, may be waived for applicants with need. Admission notification on a rolling basis beginning on or about 2/1. All CUNY schools operate on a rolling admission basis; therefore colleges and programs may close before the deadline date. **Financial aid:** Priority date 1/2, closing date 6/1. FAFSA required. Applicants notified on a rolling basis; must reply within 3 week(s) of notification.

Academics. Special study options: Cross-registration, distance learning, ESL, honors, independent study, internships, liberal arts/career combination, student-designed major, study abroad, teacher certification program. 2-year bachelor's program in nursing for RNs. **Credit/placement by examination:** AP, CLEP, IB, institutional tests. 15 credit hours maximum toward associate degree, 30 toward bachelor's. **Support services:** Learning center, remedial instruction, tutoring, writing center.

Majors. Biology: General. **Business:** General, accounting, business admin. **Computer sciences:** Information systems. **Conservation:** Environmental studies. **Education:** Elementary, special ed. **English:** English lit. **Health services:** Nursing (RN). **Human services:** General. **Liberal arts:** Arts/sciences. **Math:** General. **Psychology:** General.

Most popular majors. Biology 9%, business/marketing 45%, health sciences 9%, liberal arts 7%, psychology 12%, public administration/social services 7%.

Computing on campus. 200 workstations in library, computer center. Commuter students can connect to campus network. Online course registration, online library, wireless network available.

Student life. Freshman orientation: Available. Preregistration for classes offered. **Activities:** Jazz band, choral groups, dance, drama, literary magazine, radio station, student government, student newspaper, TV station, numerous religious, political, ethnic, and social service clubs.

Athletics. NCAA. **Intercollegiate:** Basketball, cross-country, soccer, softball W, track and field, volleyball. **Intramural:** Basketball, bowling, cheerleading W, soccer M, swimming, track and field W. **Team name:** Cougar.

Student services. Career counseling, student employment services, financial aid counseling, health services, on-campus daycare, personal counseling, placement for graduates, veterans' counselor, women's services. **Physically disabled:** Services for visually, speech, hearing impaired.

Contact. E-mail: enroll@mec.cuny.edu
Phone: (718) 270-6024 Fax: (718) 270-6411
Julie Augustine, Director of Admissions, City University of New York: Medgar Evers College, 1665 Bedford Avenue, Brooklyn, NY 11225-2201

City University of New York: New York City College of Technology

Brooklyn, New York	**CB member**
www.citytech.cuny.edu	**CB code: 2550**

- Public 4-year technical college
- Commuter campus in very large city
- 15,230 degree-seeking undergraduates: 35% part-time, 46% women, 36% African American, 16% Asian American, 28% Hispanic American, 5% international

General. Founded in 1946. Regionally accredited. Largest public college of technology in New York state. **Degrees:** 811 bachelor's, 1,220 associate awarded. **Calendar:** Semester, extensive summer session. **Full-time faculty:** 422 total; 63% have terminal degrees, 36% minority, 48% women. **Part-time faculty:** 789 total; 20% have terminal degrees, 43% minority, 41% women. **Class size:** 28% < 20, 65% 20-39, 7% 40-49. **Special facilities:** Ophthalmic dispensing and dental clinics, laboratory kitchens and dining room, immigration clinic, theater.

Freshman class profile. 16,848 applied, 14,696 admitted, 3,127 enrolled.

Return as sophomores:	74%	International:	4%
Out-of-state:	1%		

Basis for selection. Open admission, but selective for some programs.

High school preparation. College-preparatory program recommended. 15 units required; 18 recommended. Required and recommended units include English 4, mathematics 3-4, social studies 3-4, science 2-3 (laboratory 2-3), foreign language 2 and visual/performing arts 1.

2012-2013 Annual costs. Tuition/fees (projected): $5,469; $14,139 out-of-state. Books/supplies: $1,179. Personal expenses: $2,838.

2010-2011 Financial aid. Need-based: 2,437 full-time freshmen applied for aid; 2,227 were judged to have need; 2,179 of these received aid. Average need met was 64%. Average scholarship/grant was $7,889; average loan $2,898. 90% of total undergraduate aid awarded as scholarships/grants, 10% as loans/jobs. **Non-need-based:** Awarded to 682 full-time undergraduates, including 485 freshmen. Scholarships awarded for state residency. **Additional information:** Foreign students applying for aid must have resided in New York for at least 1 year.

Application procedures. Admission: Priority date 2/1; deadline 2/1 (postmark date). $65 fee, may be waived for applicants with need. Admission notification on a rolling basis beginning on or about 2/1. All CUNY schools operate on a rolling admission basis; therefore colleges and programs may close before the deadline date. **Financial aid:** Priority date 3/31; no closing date. FAFSA required.

Academics. Students in health science programs work under supervision with patients in clinical settings. Industry standard facilities used in hospitality management program. **Special study options:** Distance learning, dual enrollment of high school students, ESL, honors, independent study, internships, student-designed major, study abroad, teacher certification program, weekend college. Bridge programs to higher education or careers in engineering technology, alternate format program for those out of high school 5 years with or without diploma. **Credit/placement by examination:** AP, CLEP, IB, institutional tests. Students can earn credit by successfully completing examinations offered for certain courses. Eligibility and the nature, content and grading of each exam are determined by the departmental faculty and must be approved by the provost. **Support services:** Learning center, pre-admission

summer program, remedial instruction, study skills assistance, tutoring, writing center.

Majors. Architecture: Technology. **Business:** Hospitality admin. **Computer sciences:** Information systems, web page design. **Education:** Technology/industrial arts. **Health services:** Facilities admin, medical radiologic technology/radiation therapy, nursing (RN). **Liberal arts:** Arts/sciences. **Math:** Applied. **Visual/performing arts:** Commercial/advertising art, design, industrial design, theater design. **Work/family studies:** Facilities/event planning.

Most popular majors. Architecture 12%, business/marketing 13%, computer/information sciences 14%, engineering/engineering technologies 9%, health sciences 15%, legal studies 6%, public administration/social services 10%, visual/performing arts 14%.

Computing on campus. 340 workstations in library, computer center, student center. Commuter students can connect to campus network. Online course registration, online library, helpline, student web hosting, wireless network available.

Student life. Freshman orientation: Available. Preregistration for classes offered. Held the week before classes begin. **Housing:** Some housing available at nearby university. **Activities:** International student organizations, musical theater, student government, student newspaper, full range of student clubs.

Athletics. Intramural: Basketball, boxing, handball, soccer, table tennis, volleyball, weight lifting. **Team name:** Yellow Jackets.

Student services. Adult student services, career counseling, services for economically disadvantaged, student employment services, financial aid counseling, health services, minority student services, on-campus daycare, personal counseling, veterans' counselor. **Physically disabled:** Services for visually, speech, hearing impaired.

Contact. E-mail: admissions@citytech.cuny.edu
Phone: (718) 260-5500 Fax: (718) 260-5504
Alexis Chaconis, Director of Admissions, City University of New York: New York City College of Technology, 300 Jay Street Namm G17, Brooklyn, NY 11201

City University of New York: Queens College
Flushing, New York
www.qc.cuny.edu
CB code: 2750

- Public 4-year liberal arts and teachers college
- Commuter campus in very large city
- 15,449 degree-seeking undergraduates: 27% part-time, 57% women, 8% African American, 23% Asian American, 17% Hispanic American, 5% international
- 4,077 degree-seeking graduate students
- 31% of applicants admitted
- SAT or ACT (ACT writing optional) required
- 51% graduate within 6 years; 57% enter graduate study

General. Founded in 1937. Regionally accredited. **Degrees:** 2,952 bachelor's awarded; master's offered. **ROTC:** Army, Naval. **Location:** 17 miles from Manhattan. **Calendar:** Semester, extensive summer session. **Full-time faculty:** 606 total; 89% have terminal degrees, 21% minority, 44% women. **Part-time faculty:** 858 total; 29% have terminal degrees, 23% minority, 51% women. **Class size:** 32% < 20, 52% 20-39, 6% 40-49, 8% 50-99, 2% >100. **Special facilities:** Louis Armstrong archives, center for the performing arts, center for Byzantine and Modern Greek studies, neuroscience research center, museum, auditorium.

Freshman class profile. 18,722 applied, 5,746 admitted, 1,444 enrolled.

Mid 50% test scores			
SAT critical reading:	500-590	**End year in good standing:**	90%
SAT math:	540-630	**Return as sophomores:**	87%
SAT writing:	500-540	**Out-of-state:**	1%
GPA 3.75 or higher:	41%	**Live on campus:**	1%
GPA 3.50-3.74:	16%	**International:**	4%
GPA 3.0-3.49:	32%	**Fraternities:**	1%
GPA 2.0-2.99:	11%	**Sororities:**	1%

Basis for selection. Factors include high school grades, strength of academic program, and test scores. Successful candidates will have chosen well-rounded program of study and attained at least B+ average. SAT scores on Critical Reading and Mathematics are considered. SAT Subject Tests recommended. SAT and SAT Subject Test required of scholarship and honors college applicants. Essay and interview required for scholarship, honors

program; audition recommended for music, performance; portfolio recommended for bachelor of fine arts. Other criteria considered for appeals. **Home schooled:** Transcript of courses and grades, state high school equivalency certificate required. Students must submit a letter from the superintendent of their school district confirming that all high school graduation requirements of the district have been met through home schooling. If students cannot obtain the letter from the high school district, they must obtain a General Equivalency Development Diploma (GED). **Learning Disabled:** Untimed SAT/ACT accepted.

High school preparation. College-preparatory program required. 16 units required; 17 recommended. Required and recommended units include English 4, mathematics 3, social studies 4, science 2-3 (laboratory 2-3) and foreign language 3.

2012-2013 Annual costs. Tuition/fees (projected): $5,607; $11,517 out-of-state. Room/board: $11,840. Books/supplies: $1,179. Personal expenses: $4,823.

2011-2012 Financial aid. Need-based: 1,355 full-time freshmen applied for aid; 1,229 were judged to have need; 1,229 of these received aid. Average need met was 95%. Average scholarship/grant was $4,800; average loan $2,800. 78% of total undergraduate aid awarded as scholarships/grants, 22% as loans/jobs. **Non-need-based:** Scholarships awarded for academics, athletics, minority status, music/drama, ROTC, state residency.

Application procedures. Admission: $65 fee, may be waived for applicants with need. Application must be submitted online. Admission notification on a rolling basis beginning on or about 2/1. Must reply by May 1 or within 4 week(s) if notified thereafter. Admitted applicants must reply by May 1 for some programs, within 4 weeks after notification for others. All CUNY schools operate on a rolling admission basis; therefore colleges and programs may close before the deadline date. **Financial aid:** Priority date 2/15; no closing date. FAFSA, institutional form required. Applicants notified on a rolling basis starting 5/1; must reply within 3 week(s) of notification.

Academics. Required core liberal arts curriculum includes courses in the humanities, physical and biological sciences, scientific methodology and quantitative reasoning, social sciences, and pre-industrial/non-western civilization. The BA/MA Degree is offered in Chemistry and Biochemistry, Computer Science, Music, Philosophy, and Physics. **Special study options:** Accelerated study, combined bachelor's/graduate degree, cooperative education, cross-registration, distance learning, double major, dual enrollment of high school students, ESL, exchange student, honors, independent study, internships, liberal arts/career combination, student-designed major, study abroad, teacher certification program, weekend college. **Credit/placement by examination:** AP, CLEP, IB, SAT, ACT, institutional tests. 24 credit hours maximum toward bachelor's degree. **Support services:** Learning center, pre-admission summer program, study skills assistance, tutoring, writing center.

Honors college/program. 40 students, average SAT of 1300 (exclusive of Writing) or higher, high school average 95 or higher, required to submit SAT Subject Test scores, interview required.

Majors. Area/ethnic studies: African, American, East Asian, Latin American, women's. **Biology:** General. **Business:** Accounting, actuarial science, finance, international, labor studies. **Communications:** Media studies. **Computer sciences:** Computer science. **Conservation:** Environmental science, environmental studies. **Education:** Art, early childhood, elementary, ESL, family/consumer sciences, music, physical, social studies. **English:** English lit. **Foreign languages:** Ancient Greek, Chinese, comparative lit, French, German, Hebrew, Italian, Latin, linguistics, Russian, Spanish. **Health services:** Communication disorders. **History:** General. **Liberal arts:** Arts/sciences. **Math:** General. **Parks/recreation:** Exercise sciences. **Philosophy/religion:** Judaic, philosophy, religion. **Physical sciences:** Chemistry, geology, physics. **Psychology:** General. **Social sciences:** General, anthropology, economics, political science, sociology, urban studies. **Visual/performing arts:** Art history/conservation, dramatic, film/cinema/video, graphic design, music performance, studio arts. **Work/family studies:** General.

Most popular majors. Business/marketing 19%, education 6%, English 7%, psychology 14%, social sciences 24%.

Computing on campus. 2,500 workstations in dormitories, library, computer center, student center. Commuter students can connect to campus network. Online course registration, online library, helpline, repair service, student web hosting, wireless network available.

Student life. Freshman orientation: Mandatory. Preregistration for classes offered. 10 sessions available during June, July and August for freshmen and their families. **Policies:** Students found guilty of any form of academic dishonesty, such as plagiarism or cheating on an examination, are subject to discipline, including suspension or dismissal from the college. **Housing:** Coed dorms, apartments, wellness housing available. $400 partly refundable deposit, deadline 6/1. Dormitories available on a first-come, first-served basis. Disabled and international students do not have separate accommodations. **Activities:** Bands, campus ministries, choral groups, dance,

drama, film society, international student organizations, literary magazine, music ensembles, Model UN, musical theater, radio station, student government, student newspaper, symphony orchestra, TV station, Catholic, Protestant, Hindu, Jewish, Greek Orthodox, Muslim, African American, Asian, Bangladeshi, Guyanese, Haitian, Hispanic, Italian, Irish, lesbian, and gay student organizations; honor societies; various clubs; political student associations.

Athletics. NCAA. **Intercollegiate:** Baseball M, basketball, cross-country, diving, fencing W, lacrosse W, soccer, softball W, swimming, tennis, track and field, volleyball W. **Intramural:** Basketball, cross-country, football (nontackle), soccer, softball, table tennis, tennis, track and field, volleyball. **Team name:** Knights.

Student services. Adult student services, alcohol/substance abuse counseling, chaplain/spiritual director, career counseling, services for economically disadvantaged, student employment services, financial aid counseling, health services, minority student services, on-campus daycare, personal counseling, placement for graduates, veterans' counselor, women's services. **Physically disabled:** Services for visually, speech, hearing impaired.

Contact. E-mail: vincent.angrisani@qc.cuny.edu
Phone: (718) 997-5600 Fax: (718) 997-5617
Vincent Angrisani, Executive Director of Admissions and Enrollment Management, City University of New York: Queens College, 6530 Kissena Boulevard, Jefferson 117, Flushing, NY 11367-1597

City University of New York: York College
Jamaica, New York   CB member
www.york.cuny.edu   CB code: 2992

- Public 4-year liberal arts college
- Commuter campus in very large city
- 7,422 degree-seeking undergraduates: 31% part-time, 66% women, 38% African American, 16% Asian American, 19% Hispanic American, 1% Native American
- 32 graduate students
- SAT or ACT (ACT writing optional) required

General. Founded in 1966. Regionally accredited. **Degrees:** 916 bachelor's awarded; master's offered. **ROTC:** Army. **Location:** 14 miles from midtown Manhattan. **Calendar:** Semester, limited summer session. **Full-time faculty:** 220 total. **Class size:** 19% < 20, 33% 20-39, 8% 40-49, 17% 50-99, 23% >100. **Special facilities:** Theater, cardio-pneumo-simulator, flight simulator.

Freshman class profile.

Mid 50% test scores		End year in good standing:	83%
SAT critical reading:	370-470	Return as sophomores:	77%
SAT math:	390-490	Out-of-state:	1%

Basis for selection. 75 average with 12 high school academic units basic admission requirement; allowance made for higher average or test scores. Units recommended for admission must be acquired before graduation from any CUNY senior college. Admission requirements for CUNY senior colleges will be automatically satisfied with completion of our core requirement. Interview required for occupational therapy, nursing, physician assistant, and social work or for appeal.

High school preparation. College-preparatory program required. 12 units required; 14 recommended.

2011-2012 Annual costs. Tuition/fees: $5,496; $14,166 out-of-state. Books/supplies: $1,016. Personal expenses: $4,526.

2011-2012 Financial aid. **Need-based:** 932 full-time freshmen applied for aid; 745 were judged to have need; 688 of these received aid. Average need met was 6%. Average loan was $1,439. 80% of total undergraduate aid awarded as scholarships/grants, 20% as loans/jobs. **Non-need-based:** Awarded to 52 full-time undergraduates, including 11 freshmen. Scholarships awarded for leadership.

Application procedures. **Admission:** $65 fee. Admission notification on a rolling basis beginning on or about 5/1. Must reply by May 1 or within 2 week(s) if notified thereafter. All CUNY schools operate on a rolling admission basis; therefore colleges and programs may close before the deadline date. Centralized application processing allows students to apply to 6 schools within CUNY system at same time. **Financial aid:** Priority date 5/1, closing date 6/30. FAFSA required. Applicants notified on a rolling basis starting 2/15; must reply within 4 week(s) of notification.

Academics. **Special study options:** Accelerated study, combined bachelor's/graduate degree, cooperative education, cross-registration, distance

learning, double major, dual enrollment of high school students, ESL, honors, independent study, internships, liberal arts/career combination, study abroad, teacher certification program. Co-op programs in business, computer science, health professions. **Credit/placement by examination:** AP, CLEP, IB, SAT, ACT, institutional tests. 16 credit hours maximum toward bachelor's degree. Students with SAT/ACT scores exempt from CUNY skills assessment tests. **Support services:** Learning center, pre-admission summer program, remedial instruction, study skills assistance, tutoring, writing center.

Majors. **Area/ethnic studies:** African-American. **Biology:** General, biotechnology, pharmacology. **Business:** Accounting, business admin, management information systems, marketing. **Communications:** Communications/speech/rhetoric, journalism. **Communications technology:** General. **Computer sciences:** General, computer science. **Education:** Health, physical. **English:** English lit. **Foreign languages:** French, Spanish. **Health services:** Clinical lab science, clinical lab technology, environmental health, movement therapy, nursing (RN), physician assistant, public health ed. **History:** General. **Human services:** Social work, youth services. **Liberal arts:** Arts/sciences. **Math:** General. **Philosophy/religion:** Philosophy. **Physical sciences:** Chemistry, geology, physics. **Psychology:** General. **Social sciences:** General, anthropology, economics, political science, sociology. **Visual/performing arts:** Art history/conservation, dramatic, music, studio arts.

Most popular majors. Business/marketing 32%, health sciences 17%, psychology 17%, social sciences 9%.

Computing on campus. 300 workstations in library, computer center. Commuter students can connect to campus network. Online library, helpline, repair service, wireless network available.

Student life. **Freshman orientation:** Available. Preregistration for classes offered. **Housing:** Independently owned and operated dorm style housing available. **Activities:** Bands, choral groups, dance, drama, international student organizations, musical theater, student government, student newspaper, 48 organizations.

Athletics. NCAA. **Intercollegiate:** Basketball, cheerleading, cross-country, soccer, softball W, swimming, tennis, track and field, volleyball, weight lifting. **Intramural:** Badminton, basketball, soccer M, softball W, swimming, table tennis, tennis, track and field, volleyball, weight lifting. **Team name:** Cardinals.

Student services. Adult student services, chaplain/spiritual director, career counseling, student employment services, financial aid counseling, health services, on-campus daycare, personal counseling, placement for graduates, veterans' counselor, women's services. **Physically disabled:** Services for visually, speech, hearing impaired.

Contact. E-mail: admissions@york.cuny.edu
Phone: (718) 262-2165 Fax: (718) 262-2601
Laura Bruno, Associate Director of Admissions, City University of New York: York College, 94-20 Guy R. Brewer Boulevard, Jamaica, NY 11451-9989

Clarkson University
Potsdam, New York   CB member
www.clarkson.edu   CB code: 2084

- Private 4-year university
- Residential campus in small town
- 2,975 degree-seeking undergraduates: 28% women, 3% African American, 3% Asian American, 4% Hispanic American, 3% international
- 504 degree-seeking graduate students
- 77% of applicants admitted
- SAT or ACT (ACT writing optional), application essay required
- 75% graduate within 6 years; 19% enter graduate study

General. Founded in 1896. Regionally accredited. **Degrees:** 603 bachelor's awarded; master's, professional, doctoral offered. **ROTC:** Army, Air Force. **Location:** 85 miles from Ottawa, Canada, 69 miles from Olympic Village in Lake Placid. **Calendar:** Semester, extensive summer session. **Full-time faculty:** 214 total; 88% have terminal degrees, 22% minority, 26% women. **Part-time faculty:** 56 total; 25% have terminal degrees, 9% minority, 32% women. **Class size:** 49% < 20, 29% 20-39, 6% 40-49, 13% 50-99, 3% >100. **Special facilities:** Design prototyping and testing facilities for SPEED Team competitions (Student Projects for Engineering Experience and Design), Institute for a Sustainable Environment, Center for Sustainable Energy Systems, Center for Air Resources Engineering and Science, Center for Advanced Materials Processing, Beacon Institute for Rivers and Estuaries, Center for Rehabilitation Engineering, Science, and Technology, Shipley Center for Innovation, wind turbine test site, wind tunnel facility, greenhouse, observatory, nature preserve with hiking/cross-country ski trails, machine and electrical fabrication shops, welding shop.

Freshman class profile. 4,686 applied, 3,630 admitted, 851 enrolled.

Mid 50% test scores		GPA 2.0-2.99:	12%
SAT critical reading:	500-610	Rank in top quarter:	69%
SAT math:	560-650	Rank in top tenth:	35%
SAT writing:	480-590	End year in good standing:	80%
ACT composite:	23-28	Return as sophomores:	87%
GPA 3.75 or higher:	32%	Out-of-state:	25%
GPA 3.50-3.74:	30%	Live on campus:	98%
GPA 3.0-3.49:	26%	International:	3%

Basis for selection. Secondary school transcripts, test scores, recommendations, school and community involvement all given strong consideration. SAT Subject Tests recommended. Interview recommended. **Home schooled:** Transcript of courses and grades required. **Learning Disabled:** Documented information on disabilities is necessary.

High school preparation. College-preparatory program recommended. 16 units required. Required and recommended units include English 4, mathematics 3-4 and science 1-4. Engineering and science majors require an additional 1 credit in math and 3-4 credits in science (including chemistry and physics).

2011-2012 Annual costs. Tuition/fees: $36,780. Room/board: $12,050. Books/supplies: $1,100. Personal expenses: $1,000.

2011-2012 Financial aid. Need-based: 786 full-time freshmen applied for aid; 742 were judged to have need; 742 of these received aid. Average need met was 90%. Average scholarship/grant was $27,401; average loan $3,615. 78% of total undergraduate aid awarded as scholarships/grants, 22% as loans/jobs. **Non-need-based:** Awarded to 703 full-time undergraduates, including 195 freshmen. Scholarships awarded for academics, alumni affiliation, leadership, minority status, ROTC.

Application procedures. Admission: Closing date 1/15 (postmark date). $50 fee, may be waived for applicants with need, free for online applicants. Admission notification on a rolling basis beginning on or about 2/1. Must reply by May 1 or within 2 week(s) if notified thereafter. Candidates encouraged to submit completed applications between October 1 and March 1 of their final year in high school. **Financial aid:** Priority date 2/15, closing date 3/1. FAFSA required. Applicants notified on a rolling basis starting 3/19; must reply by 5/1 or within 2 week(s) of notification.

Academics. All students must fulfill the learning outcomes of the Clarkson Common Experience; a BS degree may be earned in 3 years by motivated, high achieving high school students; all students in the School of Business programs must complete a study-aboard experience; all business students experience a unique introduction to entrepreneurship through working with the Shipley Center for Innovation, the Clarkson Entrepreneurs Organization (CEO) and the Clarkson Center for Global Competitiveness; all students in the Coulter School of Engineering may participate in team-based activities that use the SPEED Laboratory. **Special study options:** Accelerated study, combined bachelor's/graduate degree, cooperative education, cross-registration, distance learning, double major, dual enrollment of high school students, ESL, honors, independent study, liberal arts/career combination, semester at sea, student-designed major, study abroad, Washington semester. Women In Science and Engineering (WISE) living/learning community; interdisciplinary degree programs that combine Engineering and Business, Business and Liberal Arts, Liberal Arts and Communication, and Environmental Science and Policy. **Credit/placement by examination:** AP, CLEP, IB, institutional tests. 30 credit hours maximum toward bachelor's degree. Credit may be awarded by examinations specially prepared or approved by the Clarkson departments involved or by transfer of college courses taken elsewhere. AP credit may be counted toward graduation requirements but it will not be used in computing a student's GPA. **Support services:** Learning center, pre-admission summer program, reduced course load, study skills assistance, tutoring, writing center.

Majors. Area/ethnic studies: American. **Biology:** General, environmental toxicology, molecular biochemistry. **Business:** Accounting/finance, business admin, entrepreneurial studies, logistics, management information systems. **Communications:** Communications/speech/rhetoric, digital media. **Computer sciences:** Computer science. **Conservation:** Environmental science. **Engineering:** General, aerospace, chemical, civil, computer, electrical, environmental, mechanical, software. **History:** General. **Liberal arts:** Arts/sciences, humanities. **Math:** General, applied. **Physical sciences:** Chemistry, physics. **Psychology:** General. **Social sciences:** General, political science, sociology.

Most popular majors. Biology 10%, business/marketing 15%, engineering/engineering technologies 57%.

Computing on campus. 350 workstations in library, computer center. Dormitories wired for high-speed internet access and linked to campus network. Commuter students can connect to campus network. Online course registration, online library, helpline, repair service, student web hosting, wireless network available.

Student life. Freshman orientation: Available. Preregistration for classes offered. **Housing:** Guaranteed on-campus for freshmen. Coed dorms, single-sex dorms, special housing for disabled, apartments, fraternity/sorority housing, wellness housing available. **Activities:** Bands, choral groups, drama, international student organizations, literary magazine, musical theater, radio station, student government, student newspaper, symphony orchestra, TV station, Alpha Phi Omega, America Indian science and engineering society, Circle K, College Republicans, Hillel Club, Intervarsity Christian Fellowship, Muslim students association, National Society of Black Engineers, Newman club, Society of Hispanic Professional Engineers, Young Democrats.

Athletics. NCAA. **Intercollegiate:** Baseball M, basketball, cross-country, diving, golf M, ice hockey, lacrosse, skiing, soccer, swimming, volleyball W. **Intramural:** Basketball, football (non-tackle), ice hockey, soccer, softball, volleyball. **Team name:** Golden Knights.

Student services. Alcohol/substance abuse counseling, career counseling, services for economically disadvantaged, student employment services, financial aid counseling, health services, legal services, minority student services, personal counseling, placement for graduates, veterans' counselor, women's services. **Physically disabled:** Services for visually, speech, hearing impaired.

Contact. E-mail: admission@clarkson.edu
Phone: (315) 268-6480 Toll-free number: (800) 527-6577
Fax: (315) 268-7647
Brian Grant, Dean of Admissions, Clarkson University, Holcroft House, Potsdam, NY 13699

Colgate University
Hamilton, New York   **CB member**
www.colgate.edu   **CB code: 2086**

- Private 4-year university and liberal arts college
- Residential campus in small town
- 2,927 degree-seeking undergraduates: 53% women, 5% African American, 3% Asian American, 8% Hispanic American, 7% international
- 9 degree-seeking graduate students
- 29% of applicants admitted
- SAT or ACT (ACT writing optional), application essay required
- 92% graduate within 6 years

General. Founded in 1819. Regionally accredited. **Degrees:** 698 bachelor's awarded; master's offered. **ROTC:** Army. **Location:** 38 miles from Syracuse, 25 miles from Utica. **Calendar:** Semester. **Full-time faculty:** 289 total; 98% have terminal degrees, 20% minority, 44% women. **Part-time faculty:** 54 total; 65% have terminal degrees, 11% minority, 56% women. **Class size:** 64% < 20, 34% 20-39, less than 1% 40-49, 1% 50-99, less than 1% >100. **Special facilities:** Visualization laboratory, anthropology museum, center for learning, teaching, and research, life sciences complex, geology/fossil collection, observatory, electron microscopes, laser lab, weather lab, geographic information system, center for outreach volunteerism and education.

Freshman class profile. 7,835 applied, 2,305 admitted, 764 enrolled.

Mid 50% test scores		GPA 2.0-2.99:	4%
SAT critical reading:	620-720	Rank in top quarter:	90%
SAT math:	640-720	Rank in top tenth:	67%
SAT writing:	620-730	Return as sophomores:	95%
ACT composite:	30-32	Out-of-state:	73%
GPA 3.75 or higher:	41%	Live on campus:	100%
GPA 3.50-3.74:	29%	International:	7%
GPA 3.0-3.49:	26%		

Basis for selection. School achievement record of primary importance. Teacher/counselor recommendations, test scores, and major talent or personal accomplishment considered. Disadvantaged, nontraditional, and minority applicants given special consideration. Colgate supplement required. **Home schooled:** Statement describing home school structure and mission, transcript of courses and grades, letter of recommendation (nonparent) required. **Learning Disabled:** Optional self-disclosure of disabilities in admissions process.

High school preparation. College-preparatory program recommended. 16 units required; 20 recommended. Required and recommended units include English 4, mathematics 3-4, social studies 3-4, science 3-4 (laboratory 2-4) and foreign language 3-4. Foreign language units should be in 1 language.

2011-2012 Annual costs. Tuition/fees: $42,920. Room/board: $10,650.

2011-2012 Financial aid. Need-based: 322 full-time freshmen applied for aid; 266 were judged to have need; 266 of these received aid. Average need met was 100%. Average scholarship/grant was $36,664; average loan $1,640. 90% of total undergraduate aid awarded as scholarships/grants, 10%

as loans/jobs. **Non-need-based:** Awarded to 190 full-time undergraduates, including 46 freshmen. Scholarships awarded for athletics.

Application procedures. Admission: Closing date 1/15 (postmark date). $60 fee, may be waived for applicants with need. Admission notification by 4/1. Must reply by May 1 or within 2 week(s) if notified thereafter. **Financial aid:** Closing date 1/15. CSS PROFILE required. Applicants notified by 3/25; must reply by 5/1 or within 2 week(s) of notification.

Academics. Special study options: Combined bachelor's/graduate degree, cross-registration, double major, honors, independent study, internships, liberal arts/career combination, semester at sea, student-designed major, study abroad, teacher certification program, urban semester, Washington semester. 3-4 architecture program with Washington University (MO), 3-2 program in engineering with Columbia University, Rensselaer Polytechnic Institute, and Washington University (MO); Early Assurance Medical School program with Washington University (MO) and University of Rochester; extended study program allows students to further academic work with a 3-5 week off-campus experience during the winter or summer breaks. Recent trips have included South Africa, Ireland, Mexico, and China. **Credit/placement by examination:** AP, CLEP, IB, institutional tests. **Support services:** Learning center, pre-admission summer program, reduced course load, study skills assistance, tutoring, writing center.

Majors. Area/ethnic studies: African, African-American, Asian, Latin American, Native American, Russian/Slavic, women's. **Biology:** General, biochemistry, molecular, neuroscience. **Computer sciences:** General, computer science. **Conservation:** General, environmental studies. **Education:** General. **English:** English lit. **Foreign languages:** Classics, French, German, Japanese, Latin, modern Greek, Russian, Spanish. **Health services:** Predental, premedicine, preveterinary. **History:** General. **Liberal arts:** Arts/sciences. **Math:** General. **Philosophy/religion:** Philosophy, religion. **Physical sciences:** Astronomy, astrophysics, chemistry, geology, physics. **Psychology:** General. **Social sciences:** General, anthropology, economics, geography, international economic development, international relations, political science, sociology. **Visual/performing arts:** Art, art history/conservation, dramatic, music, studio arts.

Most popular majors. Biology 10%, English 11%, foreign language 7%, history 6%, philosophy/religious studies 7%, social sciences 33%..

Computing on campus. 848 workstations in dormitories, library, computer center, student center. Dormitories wired for high-speed internet access and linked to campus network. Commuter students can connect to campus network. Online course registration, online library, helpline, repair service, student web hosting, wireless network available.

Student life. Freshman orientation: Mandatory. Preregistration for classes offered. 4-day program held 4 days before first day of classes. **Policies:** All students required to read, sign, and abide by Academic Honor Code. **Housing:** Guaranteed on-campus for all undergraduates. Coed dorms, special housing for disabled, apartments, cooperative housing, fraternity/sorority housing, wellness housing available. $500 nonrefundable deposit, deadline 5/1. Accommodations for students with special needs, townhouses for small groups of students available. **Activities:** Bands, campus ministries, choral groups, dance, drama, film society, international student organizations, literary magazine, music ensembles, Model UN, musical theater, radio station, student government, student newspaper, symphony orchestra, TV station, African student union, Asian awareness coalition, Brothers, Caribbean student association, aviation club, Christian fellowship, debate society, ballet company, Global Citizens for Peace, Colgate Dischords.

Athletics. NCAA. **Intercollegiate:** Basketball, cheerleading, cross-country, diving, field hockey W, football (tackle) M, golf M, ice hockey, lacrosse, rowing (crew), soccer, softball W, swimming, tennis, track and field, volleyball W. **Intramural:** Basketball, bowling, football (non-tackle), golf, ice hockey, racquetball, rifle, soccer, softball, squash, table tennis, tennis, volleyball. **Team name:** Raiders.

Student services. Alcohol/substance abuse counseling, chaplain/spiritual director, career counseling, services for economically disadvantaged, student employment services, financial aid counseling, health services, minority student services, personal counseling, placement for graduates, women's services. **Physically disabled:** Services for visually, hearing impaired.

Contact. E-mail: admission@colgate.edu
Phone: (315) 228-7401 Fax: (315) 228-7544
Gary Ross, Dean of Admission, Colgate University, 13 Oak Drive, Hamilton, NY 13346-1383

College of Mount St. Vincent
Riverdale, New York
www.mountsaintvincent.edu

CB member
CB code: 2088

- Private 4-year liberal arts college affiliated with Roman Catholic Church
- Residential campus in very large city

- 1,628 degree-seeking undergraduates: 14% part-time, 73% women, 15% African American, 3% Asian American, 32% Hispanic American, 1% international
- 145 degree-seeking graduate students
- 67% of applicants admitted
- SAT or ACT (ACT writing recommended), application essay required
- 56% graduate within 6 years

General. Founded in 1847. Regionally accredited. Dual certification in elementary and special education and secondary and special education. 5-year program for master of science in education. **Degrees:** 299 bachelor's awarded; master's offered. **ROTC:** Air Force. **Location:** 12 miles from midtown Manhattan. **Calendar:** Semester, limited summer session. **Full-time faculty:** 76 total; 90% have terminal degrees, 9% minority, 63% women. **Part-time faculty:** 137 total; 42% minority, 65% women. **Class size:** 56% < 20, 42% 20-39, 2% 40-49, less than 1% 50-99. **Special facilities:** NMR spectrometer, computer graphics and animation center, computer classrooms, forensic science equipment.

Freshman class profile. 3,184 applied, 2,120 admitted, 438 enrolled.

Mid 50% test scores			
SAT critical reading:	420-510	GPA 3.50-3.74:	12%
SAT math:	420-510	GPA 3.0-3.49:	26%
SAT writing:	410-510	GPA 2.0-2.99:	54%
ACT composite:	20-24	Return as sophomores:	74%
GPA 3.75 or higher:	4%	Out-of-state:	13%
		Live on campus:	59%

Basis for selection. School achievement record (3.0 high school GPA) most important, test scores and recommendations important, school and community activities considered. Interview recommended. **Home schooled:** Transcript of courses and grades required. **Learning Disabled:** Must submit IEP or other certification to receive service.

High school preparation. College-preparatory program required. 16 units required; 20 recommended. Required and recommended units include English 4, mathematics 3-4, social studies 3-4, science 2-3 (laboratory 2-3), foreign language 2-3 and academic electives 2-3. 3 math for nursing, science, and math majors; 3 science with lab for nursing and science majors.

2011-2012 Annual costs. Tuition/fees: $27,810. Room/board: $10,800. Books/supplies: $900. Personal expenses: $900.

Financial aid. Non-need-based: Scholarships awarded for academics, alumni affiliation, leadership.

Application procedures. Admission: Priority date 11/1; no deadline. $35 fee, may be waived for applicants with need, free for online applicants. Admission notification on a rolling basis beginning on or about 12/1. Must reply by May 1 or within 3 week(s) if notified thereafter. **Financial aid:** Priority date 3/1; no closing date. FAFSA required. Applicants notified on a rolling basis starting 3/1; must reply by 5/1 or within 3 week(s) of notification.

Academics. Special study options: Combined bachelor's/graduate degree, double major, honors, independent study, internships, study abroad, teacher certification program. 3-2 occupational therapy program with Columbia University, 3-2 physical therapy with New York Medical College. **Credit/placement by examination:** AP, CLEP, IB, SAT, ACT, institutional tests. 18 credit hours maximum toward bachelor's degree. **Support services:** Learning center, pre-admission summer program, reduced course load, remedial instruction, study skills assistance, tutoring, writing center.

Majors. Biology: General, biochemistry. **Business:** General, business admin. **Communications:** Communications/speech/rhetoric. **English:** English lit. **Foreign languages:** General, French, Spanish. **Health services:** Nursing (RN), preop/surgical nursing. **History:** General. **Liberal arts:** Arts/sciences. **Math:** General. **Philosophy/religion:** Philosophy, religion. **Physical sciences:** Chemistry. **Psychology:** General. **Social sciences:** Economics, sociology.

Most popular majors. Business/marketing 15%, communications/journalism 9%, health sciences 34%, liberal arts 13%, psychology 9%, social sciences 7%.

Computing on campus. 323 workstations in library, computer center. Dormitories wired for high-speed internet access and linked to campus network. Commuter students can connect to campus network. Online course registration, online library, helpline, repair service, wireless network available.

Student life. Freshman orientation: Mandatory, $125 fee. Preregistration for classes offered. 2 days with overnight for all freshmen; parent participation overnight optional. **Housing:** Guaranteed on-campus for all undergraduates. Coed dorms, special housing for disabled available. $200 fully refundable deposit, deadline 5/1. **Activities:** Campus ministries, choral groups, dance, drama, international student organizations, literary magazine, radio station,

student government, student newspaper, TV station, Culturally Aware Students of Today, Latino club, student nurses association, Circle-K, Student Action for Viable Earth, black student union, pep club, communications club.

Athletics. NCAA. **Intercollegiate:** Baseball M, basketball, cross-country, lacrosse, soccer, softball W, swimming, tennis, track and field W, volleyball. **Team name:** Dolphins.

Student services. Adult student services, chaplain/spiritual director, career counseling, student employment services, financial aid counseling, health services, personal counseling, placement for graduates. **Physically disabled:** Services for visually, hearing impaired.

Contact. E-mail: admissions.office@mountsaintvincent.edu
Phone: (718) 405-3267 Toll-free number: (800) 665-2678
Fax: (718) 549-7945
Roland Pinzon, Director of Admission, College of Mount St. Vincent, 6301 Riverdale Avenue, Riverdale, NY 10471-1093

College of New Rochelle
New Rochelle, New York
www.cnr.edu

CB member
CB code: 2089

- Private 4-year nursing and liberal arts college for women affiliated with Roman Catholic Church
- Residential campus in small city
- 814 degree-seeking undergraduates: 30% part-time, 92% women, 34% African American, 7% Asian American, 19% Hispanic American, 1% international
- 833 degree-seeking graduate students
- SAT or ACT (ACT writing optional) required
- 41% graduate within 6 years

General. Founded in 1904. Regionally accredited. Independent institution in Roman Catholic tradition. Coeducational school of nursing and graduate school. **Degrees:** 202 bachelor's awarded; master's offered. **ROTC:** Army, Naval. **Location:** 14 miles from New York City. **Calendar:** Semester, limited summer session. **Full-time faculty:** 83 total. **Part-time faculty:** 131 total. **Class size:** 73% < 20, 27% 20-39, less than 1% 50-99. **Special facilities:** 2 learning skills centers (including 1 for nursing), electron microscope, institute for entrepreneurial studies, computer graphics laboratory, model classroom, rare book collections of James Joyce, Thomas More, Ursuline Order.

Freshman class profile.

GPA 3.75 or higher:	4%	Rank in top tenth:	17%
GPA 3.50-3.74:	36%	Return as sophomores:	75%
GPA 3.0-3.49:	57%	Out-of-state:	16%
GPA 2.0-2.99:	3%	Live on campus:	93%
Rank in top quarter:	62%	International:	1%

Basis for selection. Admissions based on secondary school record. Class rank and standardized test scores also important. Essay, interview recommended; portfolio required for art program.

High school preparation. 16 units required. Required and recommended units include English 4, mathematics 3, social studies 3, science 3 (laboratory 2) and foreign language 2. Biology, chemistry, 3 math required for nursing and physical therapy.

2011-2012 Annual costs. Tuition/fees: $29,100. A laptop is provided free of charge to all incoming freshman in the School of Arts and Sciences and School of Nursing. Room/board: $10,600. Books/supplies: $600. Personal expenses: $1,000.

Financial aid. Non-need-based: Scholarships awarded for academics, art, leadership.

Application procedures. Admission: No deadline. $35 fee, may be waived for applicants with need. Admission notification on a rolling basis beginning on or about 11/1. Must reply by May 1 or within 3 week(s) if notified thereafter. **Financial aid:** Priority date 3/1; no closing date. FAFSA, institutional form required. Applicants notified on a rolling basis starting 1/1; must reply within 2 week(s) of notification.

Academics. Laptop computers given to all undergraduate students. **Special study options:** Accelerated study, combined bachelor's/graduate degree, cooperative education, cross-registration, double major, exchange student, honors, independent study, internships, liberal arts/career combination, study abroad, teacher certification program, United Nations semester, Washington semester. Preprofessional programs in law, medicine, health. **Credit/placement by examination:** AP, CLEP, institutional tests. 15 credit hours maximum toward bachelor's degree. **Support services:** Learning center, reduced

course load, remedial instruction, study skills assistance, tutoring, writing center.

Majors. Area/ethnic studies: American, women's. **Biology:** General. **Business:** General. **Communications:** Broadcast journalism, media studies. **Conservation:** Environmental studies. **Education:** General, art, elementary, special ed. **English:** English lit. **Foreign languages:** Classics, French, Latin, Spanish. **Health services:** Art therapy, nursing (RN). **History:** General. **Human services:** Social work. **Math:** General. **Philosophy/religion:** Philosophy, religion. **Physical sciences:** Chemistry. **Psychology:** General. **Social sciences:** Economics, political science, sociology. **Visual/performing arts:** Art history/conservation, studio arts.

Most popular majors. Health sciences 67%, psychology 9%.

Computing on campus. 223 workstations in dormitories, library, computer center. Dormitories wired for high-speed internet access and linked to campus network. Commuter students can connect to campus network. Online course registration, online library, helpline, wireless network available.

Student life. Freshman orientation: Available. Preregistration for classes offered. **Housing:** Guaranteed on-campus for all undergraduates. Wellness housing available. $100 deposit. **Activities:** Campus ministries, choral groups, dance, drama, film society, literary magazine, musical theater, student government, student newspaper, community services, Latin American Women Society, Black Student Union, CNR Drama, nurses gospel choir.

Athletics. NCAA. **Intercollegiate:** Basketball W, cross-country W, softball W, swimming W, tennis W, volleyball W. **Team name:** Blue Angels.

Student services. Adult student services, alcohol/substance abuse counseling, chaplain/spiritual director, career counseling, services for economically disadvantaged, student employment services, financial aid counseling, health services, personal counseling, placement for graduates, women's services. **Physically disabled:** Services for visually, speech, hearing impaired.

Contact. E-mail: admission@cnr.edu
Phone: (914) 654-5452 Toll-free number: (800) 933-5923
Fax: (914) 654-5464
Ellen Lockamy, Director of Admissions, College of New Rochelle, 29 Castle Place, New Rochelle, NY 10805-2339

College of Saint Rose
Albany, New York
www.strose.edu

CB member
CB code: 2091

- Private 4-year liberal arts and teachers college
- Residential campus in small city
- 2,890 degree-seeking undergraduates: 5% part-time, 68% women, 6% African American, 2% Asian American, 5% Hispanic American, 1% international
- 1,898 degree-seeking graduate students
- 61% of applicants admitted
- SAT or ACT (ACT writing optional) required
- 63% graduate within 6 years; 55% enter graduate study

General. Founded in 1920. Regionally accredited. **Degrees:** 666 bachelor's awarded; master's offered. **ROTC:** Army, Naval, Air Force. **Location:** 140 miles from New York City. **Calendar:** Semester, limited summer session. **Full-time faculty:** 213 total; 90% have terminal degrees, 13% minority, 57% women. **Part-time faculty:** 241 total; 82% have terminal degrees, 5% minority, 54% women. **Class size:** 71% < 20, 28% 20-39, less than 1% 40-49, less than 1% 50-99. **Special facilities:** Center for communications and interactive media, center for art and design, performance hall, personal studio spaces, center for technology and teaching.

Freshman class profile. 5,200 applied, 3,175 admitted, 595 enrolled.

Mid 50% test scores			
SAT critical reading:	470-570	Rank in top quarter:	44%
SAT math:	470-570	Rank in top tenth:	17%
ACT composite:	20-25	End year in good standing:	87%
GPA 3.75 or higher:	25%	Return as sophomores:	78%
GPA 3.50-3.74:	25%	Out-of-state:	14%
GPA 3.0-3.49:	31%	Live on campus:	83%
GPA 2.0-2.99:	19%	International:	1%

Basis for selection. High school transcript and SAT/ACT scores most important. Strongly consider extracurricular activities, overall academic rigor of high school work (Honors, AP, University in the High School courses). Rolling deadline to receive test scores. Interview, essay recommended. Portfolio review required for potential art majors, audition required for music majors. **Home schooled:** State high school equivalency certificate required.

High school preparation. College-preparatory program required. Required and recommended units include English 4, mathematics 3-4, social studies 4, history 4, science 3-4 (laboratory 2), foreign language 3-4, computer science 2 and visual/performing arts 2.

2011-2012 Annual costs. Tuition/fees: $25,464. Room/board: $10,534. Books/supplies: $1,200. Personal expenses: $1,500.

2010-2011 Financial aid. Need-based: Average need met was 46%. Average scholarship/grant was $9,835. 72% of total undergraduate aid awarded as scholarships/grants, 28% as loans/jobs. **Non-need-based:** Scholarships awarded for academics, alumni affiliation, art, athletics, leadership, minority status.

Application procedures. Admission: Priority date 12/1; no deadline. $40 fee, may be waived for applicants with need, free for online applicants. Admission notification on a rolling basis beginning on or about 10/1. **Financial aid:** Priority date 3/1; no closing date. FAFSA required. Applicants notified on a rolling basis starting 2/15; must reply by 5/1 or within 2 week(s) of notification.

Academics. Academic Support services for students with documented disabilities. **Special study options:** Accelerated study, combined bachelor's/graduate degree, cross-registration, distance learning, double major, exchange student, independent study, internships, liberal arts/career combination, student-designed major, study abroad, teacher certification program. **Credit/placement by examination:** AP, CLEP, IB, institutional tests. 15 credit hours maximum toward bachelor's degree. **Support services:** Learning center, pre-admission summer program, reduced course load, remedial instruction, study skills assistance, tutoring, writing center.

Majors. Area/ethnic studies: American, women's. **Biology:** General, biochemistry, bioinformatics, cell/histology. **Business:** Accounting, business admin. **Communications:** Communications/speech/rhetoric, media studies. **Communications technology:** Radio/TV. **Computer sciences:** General. **Education:** Art, biology, chemistry, earth science, elementary, English, kindergarten/preschool, mathematics, music, social studies, Spanish, special ed, trade/industrial. **English:** English lit. **Foreign languages:** Spanish. **Health services:** Audiology/speech pathology, clinical lab science. **History:** General. **Human services:** Social work. **Liberal arts:** Arts/sciences, humanities. **Math:** General. **Philosophy/religion:** Philosophy, religion. **Physical sciences:** Chemistry, geochemistry. **Protective services:** Forensics, law enforcement admin. **Psychology:** General, forensic. **Social sciences:** Political science, sociology. **Visual/performing arts:** Commercial/advertising art, music, music performance, studio arts.

Most popular majors. Business/marketing 14%, education 43%, psychology 6%, visual/performing arts 8%.

Computing on campus. 575 workstations in dormitories, library, computer center, student center. Dormitories wired for high-speed internet access and linked to campus network. Commuter students can connect to campus network. Online course registration, online library, helpline, student web hosting, wireless network available.

Student life. Freshman orientation: Mandatory, $265 fee. Preregistration for classes offered. Two-part orientation: 2-day overnight summer program and week-long program that begins 2 days prior to start of fall classes. **Policies:** Sanctions for plagiarism, cheating, academic misconduct, or any other submission of another's work as one's own. Use of alcohol by underage students prohibited, with limits on amounts students 21 and over can possess. Use of drugs prohibited. Sexual violence not tolerated. No smoking on college-owned or leased property or in any college-owned vehicle. Freshmen not permitted cars on campus. **Housing:** Coed dorms, single-sex dorms, special housing for disabled, apartments available. $150 nonrefundable deposit, deadline 5/1. **Activities:** Bands, campus ministries, choral groups, dance, drama, international student organizations, literary magazine, music ensembles, musical theater, radio station, student government, student newspaper, symphony orchestra, TV station, Brothers and Sisters in Christ, ALANA Steppers, Best Buddies, Big Brothers, Big Sisters, Habitat for Humanity, Amnesty International, social work organization, Spectrum (Alana Student Union).

Athletics. NCAA. **Intercollegiate:** Baseball M, basketball, cross-country, golf M, lacrosse M, soccer, softball W, swimming, tennis W, track and field, volleyball W. **Intramural:** Basketball, football (non-tackle) M, soccer, softball, volleyball. **Team name:** Golden Knights.

Student services. Adult student services, alcohol/substance abuse counseling, chaplain/spiritual director, career counseling, services for economically disadvantaged, student employment services, financial aid counseling, health services, legal services, minority student services, personal counseling, placement for graduates. **Physically disabled:** Services for visually, speech, hearing impaired.

Contact. E-mail: admit@strose.edu
Phone: (518) 454-5111 Toll-free number: (800) 637-8556
Fax: (518) 454-2013
Mary Grondahl, Associate Vice President for Enrollment Planning and Undergraduate Admissions, College of Saint Rose, 432 Western Avenue, Albany, NY 12203

Columbia University
New York, New York
www.columbia.edu

CB member
CB code: 2116

- Private 4-year university
- Residential campus in very large city
- 6,027 degree-seeking undergraduates: 47% women, 12% African American, 18% Asian American, 14% Hispanic American, 2% Native American, 11% international
- 7% of applicants admitted
- SAT or ACT with writing, SAT Subject Tests, application essay required
- 96% graduate within 6 years

General. Founded in 1754. Regionally accredited. **Degrees:** 1,378 bachelor's awarded; master's, professional, doctoral offered. **ROTC:** Army, Naval, Air Force. **Calendar:** Semester, extensive summer session. **Special facilities:** Art and architecture galleries, cinemas, theaters, geological observatory, interactive graphics laboratory, telecommunications research center, plasma laboratory, materials laboratory, astronomical observatory.

Freshman class profile. 34,810 applied, 2,418 admitted, 1,391 enrolled.

Mid 50% test scores			
SAT critical reading:	700-780	Return as sophomores:	99%
SAT math:	700-790	Out-of-state:	75%
SAT writing:	700-790	Live on campus:	99%
ACT composite:	32-35	International:	12%

Basis for selection. School achievement record most important. Test scores, recommendations, essay, extracurricular activities also important. TOEFL or IELTS exam required of all non-native speakers. Interview recommended for all; audition required for Julliard program. **Home schooled:** 2 additional SAT Subject Tests.

High school preparation. College-preparatory program required. Recommended units include English 4, mathematics 4, history 4, science 4 (laboratory 4), foreign language 4 and academic electives 4.

2011-2012 Annual costs. Tuition/fees: $45,290. Room/board: $11,020. Books/supplies: $2,807.

Financial aid. All financial aid based on need. **Additional information:** We have eliminated student loans for those receiving Columbia need-based aid and replaced them with additional University grants, and significantly reduced the parent contribution for families making less than $100,000 per year.

Application procedures. Admission: Closing date 1/1 (postmark date). $80 fee, may be waived for applicants with need. Admission notification by 4/1. Must reply by 5/1. **Financial aid:** Closing date 3/1. FAFSA, CSS PROFILE required. Applicants notified by 4/1; must reply by 5/1.

Academics. Special study options: Accelerated study, combined bachelor's/graduate degree, cooperative education, cross-registration, double major, dual enrollment of high school students, ESL, exchange student, independent study, internships, liberal arts/career combination, student-designed major, study abroad, teacher certification program. Combined 3-2 program with engineering with over 100 liberal arts colleges around the country. **Credit/placement by examination:** AP, CLEP, IB, institutional tests. 16 credit hours maximum toward bachelor's degree. **Support services:** Pre-admission summer program, study skills assistance, tutoring, writing center.

Majors. Architecture: Architecture. **Area/ethnic studies:** African, African-American, American, Asian, Asian-American, Chicano/Hispanic-American/Latino, Chinese, East Asian, European, French, German, Italian, Japanese, Korean, Latin American, Near/Middle Eastern, Polish, regional, Russian/Eastern European/Eurasian, Russian/Slavic, Slavic, Spanish/Iberian, women's. **Biology:** General, biochemistry, biophysics, ecology, environmental, evolutionary, neuroscience. **Computer sciences:** Computer science. **Conservation:** General, environmental science. **Education:** General. **Engineering:** Biomedical, chemical, civil, computer, electrical, engineering mechanics, environmental, geological, materials, mechanical, metallurgical, mining, operations research. **English:** American lit, British lit, creative writing, English lit. **Foreign languages:** Ancient Greek, Biblical, Chinese, classics, comparative lit, East Asian, French, German, Germanic, Italian, Japanese, Korean, Latin, linguistics, modern Greek, Russian, Slavic, Spanish.

History: General. **Math:** General, applied, statistics. **Philosophy/religion:** Philosophy, religion. **Physical sciences:** Astronomy, astrophysics, chemical physics, chemistry, geochemistry, geology, geophysics, materials science, physics, planetary. **Psychology:** General. **Social sciences:** Anthropology, archaeology, economics, political science, sociology, urban studies. **Visual/performing arts:** General, art history/conservation, dance, dramatic, film/cinema/video, jazz, music, studio arts, theater history.

Most popular majors. Biology 8%, engineering/engineering technologies 18%, English 6%, history 7%, social sciences 25%.

Computing on campus. 150 workstations in dormitories, library, computer center, student center. Dormitories wired for high-speed internet access and linked to campus network. Commuter students can connect to campus network. Online course registration, online library, helpline, student web hosting, wireless network available.

Student life. Freshman orientation: Mandatory, $511 fee. Preregistration for classes offered. A one-week program offering academic advising sessions, cultural events, parents orientation sessions, and more. Students may also choose to participate in pre-orientation programs like the Columbia Outdoor Orientation Program, International Student Orientation Program or the Columbia Urban Experience. **Housing:** Guaranteed on-campus for all undergraduates. Coed dorms, special housing for disabled, fraternity/sorority housing available. Special interest (group) housing available. **Activities:** Bands, campus ministries, choral groups, dance, drama, film society, international student organizations, literary magazine, music ensembles, Model UN, musical theater, opera, radio station, student government, student newspaper, symphony orchestra, TV station, African-American, Hispanic, Native American, Asian-American, Gay/Lesbian student organizations, community service groups, religious groups of all denominations.

Athletics. NCAA. **Intercollegiate:** Archery W, baseball M, basketball, cross-country, diving, fencing, field hockey W, football (tackle) M, golf, lacrosse W, rowing (crew), soccer, softball W, squash, swimming, tennis, track and field, volleyball W, wrestling M. **Intramural:** Basketball, football (non-tackle), racquetball, soccer, softball, tennis, volleyball. **Team name:** Lions.

Student services. Alcohol/substance abuse counseling, chaplain/spiritual director, career counseling, services for economically disadvantaged, student employment services, financial aid counseling, health services, minority student services, personal counseling, placement for graduates, women's services. **Physically disabled:** Services for visually, speech, hearing impaired.

Contact. E-mail: ugrad-ask@columbia.edu
Phone: (212) 854-2522 Fax: (212) 854-1209
Jessica Marinaccio, Dean of Undergraduate Admissions, Columbia University, 1130 Amsterdam Avenue, New York, NY 10027

Columbia University: School of General Studies
New York, New York
www.gs.columbia.edu   CB code: 2095

- Private 4-year university and liberal arts college
- Residential campus in very large city
- 1,444 degree-seeking undergraduates: 37% part-time, 45% women, 5% African American, 6% Asian American, 8% Hispanic American, 1% Native American, 15% international
- 35% of applicants admitted
- SAT or ACT (ACT writing optional), application essay required

General. Founded in 1947. Regionally accredited. Liberal arts division of university for nontraditional students whose undergraduate study has been interrupted or postponed for at least one year. Postbaccalaureate Premedical Program offered to students who have completed little or none of the required coursework for application to medical school. **Degrees:** 308 bachelor's awarded. **ROTC:** Army, Naval, Air Force. **Calendar:** Semester, extensive summer session. **Special facilities:** Earth Institute, observatory.

Freshman class profile. 321 applied, 113 admitted, 55 enrolled.

Out-of-state:	69%	Fraternities:	1%
Live on campus:	82%	Sororities:	1%
International:	20%		

Basis for selection. Maturity and varied backgrounds of students considered. Aptitude and motivation important together with academic performance and test scores. Spring semester deadlines are October 1 for Early Action applicants and November 1 for Regular Decision applicants. Interview requested when needed. **Home schooled:** State high school equivalency certificate required. **Learning Disabled:** Registration with the Office of Disability Services recommended.

2011-2012 Annual costs. Tuition/fees: $43,728. First-year students also pay a one-time transcript fee of $95. Room/board: $10,125.

2011-2012 Financial aid. All financial aid based on need. 46% of total undergraduate aid awarded as scholarships/grants, 54% as loans/jobs.

Application procedures. Admission: Priority date 3/1; deadline 6/1 (postmark date). $75 fee. Admission notification by 7/15. Admission notification on a rolling basis. Admissions attempts to make decisions within four to six weeks of receiving a completed application. The School of General Studies begins releasing admissions decisions in March for the summer and fall terms and in October for the spring term. Applicants for the spring term notified of admission decision on a rolling basis through December 15. **Financial aid:** Closing date 6/1. FAFSA, institutional form required. Applicants notified on a rolling basis; must reply within 3 week(s) of notification.

Academics. Special study options: Accelerated study, combined bachelor's/graduate degree, cross-registration, double major, dual enrollment of high school students, exchange student, honors, independent study, internships, student-designed major, study abroad, teacher certification program. Dual degree program with Jewish Theological Seminary, List College; Dual BA program with Sciences Po. **Credit/placement by examination:** AP, CLEP, SAT, ACT, institutional tests. 30 credit hours maximum toward bachelor's degree. **Support services:** Learning center, pre-admission summer program, reduced course load, remedial instruction, study skills assistance, tutoring, writing center.

Majors. Architecture: Architecture, history/criticism. **Area/ethnic studies:** African, African-American, American, Asian, Caribbean, Chicano/Hispanic-American/Latino, East Asian, French, German, Italian, Latin American, Near/Middle Eastern, Polish, Russian/Eastern European/Eurasian, Russian/Slavic, South Asian, Ukraine, women's. **Biology:** General, biochemistry, biophysics, evolutionary. **Computer sciences:** General, computer science. **Conservation:** General, environmental science, environmental studies. **Education:** Elementary, secondary. **English:** British lit, creative writing, English lit. **Foreign languages:** Classics, comparative lit, French, German, Italian, Portuguese, Russian, Spanish. **Health services:** Premedicine. **History:** General. **Math:** General, applied, mathematics/statistics, statistics. **Philosophy/religion:** Philosophy, religion. **Physical sciences:** Astronomy, astrophysics, chemistry, geochemistry, geology, geophysics, oceanography, physics. **Psychology:** General. **Social sciences:** Economics, political science, sociology, urban studies. **Visual/performing arts:** General, art history/conservation, dance, dramatic, film/cinema/video, music, music performance, musicology, painting, sculpture, voice/opera.

Most popular majors. Area/ethnic studies 13%, English 11%, history 7%, social sciences 35%.

Computing on campus. 347 workstations in dormitories, library, computer center, student center. Dormitories wired for high-speed internet access and linked to campus network. Commuter students can connect to campus network. Online course registration, online library, helpline, repair service, student web hosting, wireless network available.

Student life. Freshman orientation: Mandatory, $135 fee. Preregistration for classes offered. Generally held 1 week before classes start. Academic planning session (held prior to beginning of semester) required of all new students. **Housing:** Coed dorms, apartments, cooperative housing, fraternity/sorority housing available. Limited on-campus housing available. Off-campus housing registry provides listings of Columbia-affiliated apartments. **Activities:** Bands, campus ministries, choral groups, dance, drama, film society, international student organizations, literary magazine, music ensembles, Model UN, musical theater, opera, radio station, student government, student newspaper, TV station, many religious, political, and ethnic organizations.

Athletics. NCAA. **Intercollegiate:** Archery W, baseball M, basketball, cross-country, diving, fencing, field hockey W, football (tackle) M, golf, lacrosse W, rowing (crew), soccer, softball W, swimming, tennis, track and field, volleyball W, wrestling M. **Intramural:** Baseball M, basketball, boxing, cricket M, diving, fencing, lacrosse, racquetball, skiing, soccer, softball, squash, swimming, tennis, volleyball. **Team name:** Lions.

Student services. Adult student services, alcohol/substance abuse counseling, chaplain/spiritual director, career counseling, services for economically disadvantaged, student employment services, financial aid counseling, health services, minority student services, personal counseling, placement for graduates, veterans' counselor, women's services. **Physically disabled:** Services for visually impaired.

Contact. E-mail: gsdegree@columbia.edu
Phone: (212) 854-2772 Toll-free number: (800) 895-1169
Fax: (212) 854-6316
Curtis Rodgers, Dean of Enrollment Management, Columbia University: School of General Studies, 408 Lewisohn Hall, Mail Code 4101, New York, NY 10027

Concordia College
Bronxville, New York
www.concordia-ny.edu

CB member
CB code: 2096

- Private 4-year liberal arts college affiliated with Lutheran Church - Missouri Synod
- Residential campus in small town
- 820 degree-seeking undergraduates
- 6 degree-seeking graduate students
- 70% of applicants admitted
- SAT or ACT (ACT writing recommended), application essay required

General. Founded in 1881. Regionally accredited. **Degrees:** 161 bachelor's, 2 associate awarded; master's offered. **Location:** 14 miles from New York City. **Calendar:** Semester, limited summer session. **Full-time faculty:** 33 total; 67% have terminal degrees, 18% minority, 46% women. **Part-time faculty:** 44 total; 18% minority, 41% women. **Class size:** 62% < 20, 37% 20-39, 1% 40-49. **Special facilities:** Music laboratory, distance learning classroom, media and digital production center, art gallery and studio, nursing labs.

Freshman class profile. 870 applied, 605 admitted, 135 enrolled.

Mid 50% test scores			
SAT critical reading:	410-490	GPA 3.0-3.49:	23%
SAT math:	410-500	GPA 2.0-2.99:	56%
SAT writing:	410-480	Rank in top quarter:	21%
ACT composite:	18-21	Rank in top tenth:	4%
GPA 3.75 or higher:	7%	Out-of-state:	11%
GPA 3.50-3.74:	11%	Live on campus:	62%

Basis for selection. Test scores, school achievement record, interview important; community and church involvement considered. Interview required for some, recommended for others. **Home schooled:** Statement describing home school structure and mission, transcript of courses and grades, state high school equivalency certificate, interview, letter of recommendation (nonparent) required. Show explanation of all course work studied and grades obtained. **Learning Disabled:** Students required to meet with learning specialist and submit most recent psychological assessment.

High school preparation. 15 units recommended. Recommended units include English 4, mathematics 3, social studies 2, science 2 (laboratory 2) and foreign language 2.

2012-2013 Annual costs. Tuition/fees (projected): $27,450. Room/board: $9,750. Books/supplies: $1,000. Personal expenses: $950.

Financial aid. Non-need-based: Scholarships awarded for academics, athletics, leadership, music/drama, religious affiliation.

Application procedures. Admission: Priority date 3/15; no deadline. $50 fee, may be waived for applicants with need. Admission notification on a rolling basis beginning on or about 12/1. Must reply by May 1 or within 4 week(s) if notified thereafter. Student must interview with Admission Counselor and have approved plan of study for senior year completion. **Financial aid:** Priority date 4/1; no closing date. FAFSA required. Applicants notified on a rolling basis starting 2/15; must reply by 5/1 or within 3 week(s) of notification.

Academics. Special study options: Accelerated study, combined bachelor's/graduate degree, cooperative education, double major, ESL, exchange student, honors, independent study, internships, liberal arts/career combination, student-designed major, study abroad, teacher certification program. **Credit/placement by examination:** AP, CLEP, IB, institutional tests. 30 credit hours maximum toward associate degree, 30 toward bachelor's. **Support services:** Reduced course load, remedial instruction, study skills assistance, tutoring, writing center.

Majors. Biology: General, ecology. **Business:** General, accounting, business admin, finance, international. **Education:** General, elementary. **English:** English lit. **Foreign languages:** Comparative lit. **Health services:** Nursing (RN), premedicine. **History:** General. **Human services:** Social work. **Liberal arts:** Arts/sciences. **Math:** General. **Philosophy/religion:** Religion. **Physical sciences:** Geology. **Psychology:** General. **Social sciences:** General. **Theology:** Religious ed, sacred music. **Visual/performing arts:** Art, arts management, design, music.

Computing on campus. 30 workstations in library, computer center. Dormitories wired for high-speed internet access and linked to campus network. Commuter students can connect to campus network. Online course registration, online library, helpline, repair service, wireless network available.

Student life. Freshman orientation: Mandatory. Preregistration for classes offered. Held at beginning of semester with adviser. **Policies:**

Freshmen not permitted cars on campus. **Housing:** Guaranteed on-campus for all undergraduates. Single-sex dorms available. $300 nonrefundable deposit, deadline 5/1. **Activities:** Jazz band, campus ministries, choral groups, drama, international student organizations, music ensembles, musical theater, student government, student newspaper, Christian service organizations, Afro-Latino American club, social work club, Prayer Partners, environmental club, In His Name, Lutheran Women League, Rotaract club.

Athletics. NCAA. Intercollegiate: Baseball M, basketball, cross-country, golf M, soccer, softball W, tennis, volleyball W. **Intramural:** Basketball, football (non-tackle), softball W, squash, tennis, volleyball. **Team name:** Clippers.

Student services. Adult student services, alcohol/substance abuse counseling, chaplain/spiritual director, career counseling, student employment services, financial aid counseling, health services, minority student services, personal counseling, placement for graduates.

Contact. E-mail: admission@concordia-ny.edu
Phone: (914) 337-9300 ext. 2155 Toll-free number: (800) 937-2655
Fax: (914) 395-4636
Robert Piurowski, Director of Admission, Concordia College, 171 White Plains Road, Bronxville, NY 10708-1923

Cooper Union for the Advancement of Science and Art
New York, New York
www.cooper.edu

CB member
CB code: 2097

- Private 4-year visual arts and engineering college
- Commuter campus in very large city
- 887 degree-seeking undergraduates: 37% women, 6% African American, 18% Asian American, 9% Hispanic American, 1% Native American, 15% international
- 61 degree-seeking graduate students
- 8% of applicants admitted
- SAT or ACT (ACT writing optional), application essay required
- 86% graduate within 6 years; 60% enter graduate study

General. Founded in 1859. Regionally accredited. Full-tuition scholarship school of architecture, art, and engineering. All enrolled students receive a scholarship that covers the total cost of tuition. **Degrees:** 208 bachelor's awarded; master's offered. **Calendar:** Semester, limited summer session. **Full-time faculty:** 52 total; 90% have terminal degrees, 12% minority, 27% women. **Part-time faculty:** 177 total; 37% have terminal degrees, 11% minority, 25% women. **Class size:** 74% < 20, 25% 20-39, less than 1% 50-99, 1% >100. **Special facilities:** Special labs in: biomechanics, materials, soils, hydraulics, design systems, computers, circuits, signal processing, acoustics and audio engineering, combustion research and demonstration, robotic theater studio, rapid prototyping, energy reclamation and innovation, materials and micro/nano engineering, mechatronics, thermal/fluid/engines, tissue engineering.

Freshman class profile. 3,415 applied, 264 admitted, 198 enrolled.

Mid 50% test scores			
SAT critical reading:	610-720	GPA 2.0-2.99:	14%
SAT math:	650-780	Rank in top quarter:	98%
SAT writing:	620-730	Rank in top tenth:	93%
ACT composite:	29-33	End year in good standing:	96%
GPA 3.75 or higher:	40%	Return as sophomores:	96%
GPA 3.50-3.74:	15%	Out-of-state:	40%
GPA 3.0-3.49:	31%	Live on campus:	80%
		International:	9%

Basis for selection. Engineering applicants reviewed on high school record and courses selected, essays, SAT, and required SAT Subject Test scores. Art and architecture applicants selected on basis of home test, high school record and program, SAT. All international students must apply by using an address within the United States. 2 SAT Subject Tests required for engineering applicants: 1 math and 1 chemistry or 1 math and 1 physics. Portfolios required for art applicants. All art and architecture applicants must complete a home test. **Home schooled:** Statement describing home school structure and mission, transcript of courses and grades, letter of recommendation (nonparent) required. Must present proof of high school graduation certification (national) or equivalent.

High school preparation. College-preparatory program recommended. 16 units required; 18 recommended. Required and recommended units include English 4, mathematics 1-4, social studies 1-4, history 1, science 1-4 (laboratory 3), foreign language 2 and academic electives 8. 1 science required for architecture and art. 4 science and 4 math required for engineering including physics, chemistry, and precalculus; calculus preferred. 1 math required for

art, 3 math for architecture including trigonometry and precalculus. 18 total units recommended for engineering.

2011-2012 Annual costs. Tuition/fees: $39,150. All students receive a full-tuition scholarship (covering tuition only) for the duration of their enrollment. Room only: $9,700. Books/supplies: $1,600. Personal expenses: $1,575.

2010-2011 Financial aid. Need-based: 121 full-time freshmen applied for aid; 62 were judged to have need; 62 of these received aid. Average need met was 93%. Average scholarship/grant was $38,775; average loan $2,841. 61% of total undergraduate aid awarded as scholarships/grants, 39% as loans/jobs. **Non-need-based:** Awarded to 891 full-time undergraduates, including 214 freshmen. Scholarships awarded for academics. **Additional information:** All students receive full-tuition scholarships. Students able to document need receive financial aid package that may include combination of grants, loans, work-study, internships. Late financial aid applications processed on rolling basis.

Application procedures. Admission: Priority date 12/1; deadline 1/1 (postmark date). $65 fee, may be waived for applicants with need. Admission notification by 4/1. Must reply by May 1 or within 4 week(s) if notified thereafter. Regular application closing date for architecture January 6, for fine arts January 9, for engineering February 1. **Financial aid:** Priority date 4/15, closing date 6/1. FAFSA, CSS PROFILE required. Applicants notified on a rolling basis starting 6/1; must reply by 6/30 or within 2 week(s) of notification.

Academics. Engineering tutorials and engineering mentor program available. All freshman engineering majors required to prove or acquire computer literacy. 128 credit hours required for graduation in art program, 135 in engineering, and 160 in architecture. Students may take classes in all 3 schools. Art students encouraged to take courses throughout 7 disciplines. Architecture students take 5 years of design culminating in thesis year. Engineering students encouraged to take coursework in other majors. **Special study options:** Combined bachelor's/graduate degree, cross-registration, exchange student, independent study, internships, student-designed major, study abroad. Research opportunities. Students may take up to 1 year off between studies to pursue related experiences. **Credit/placement by examination:** AP, CLEP, institutional tests. Varies depending upon school and department. **Support services:** Tutoring, writing center.

Majors. Architecture: Architecture. **Engineering:** General, chemical, civil, electrical, mechanical. **Visual/performing arts:** Graphic design, studio arts.

Most popular majors. Architecture 11%, engineering/engineering technologies 58%, visual/performing arts 31%.

Computing on campus. 650 workstations in dormitories, library, computer center. Dormitories wired for high-speed internet access and linked to campus network. Commuter students can connect to campus network. Online library, helpline, repair service, student web hosting, wireless network available.

Student life. Freshman orientation: Available, $100 fee. Preregistration for classes offered. 2.5 days, part of which is spent off-campus. **Policies:** Residence hall primarily used by first-year students. Most if not all first-year students offered housing in the residence hall. **Housing:** Coed dorms, wellness housing available. $500 fully refundable deposit, deadline 6/1. **Activities:** Bands, choral groups, dance, drama, film society, literary magazine, music ensembles, musical theater, student government, student newspaper, symphony orchestra, 90 registered clubs available.

Athletics. Intercollegiate: Basketball, cross-country, equestrian W, lacrosse M, soccer M, tennis, volleyball. **Intramural:** Badminton, baseball M, basketball, bowling, cross-country, fencing, golf, judo, soccer, softball, table tennis, tennis, volleyball. **Team name:** Hawks.

Student services. Alcohol/substance abuse counseling, career counseling, student employment services, financial aid counseling, minority student services, personal counseling, placement for graduates, veterans' counselor. **Physically disabled:** Services for visually, hearing impaired.

Contact. E-mail: admissions@cooper.edu
Phone: (212) 353-4120 Fax: (212) 353-4342
Mitchell Lipton, Dean of Admissions and Records/Registrar, Cooper Union for the Advancement of Science and Art, 30 Cooper Square, Suite 300, New York, NY 10003-7183

Cornell University
Ithaca, New York
www.cornell.edu

CB member
CB code: 2098

- Private 4-year university
- Residential campus in large town

- 14,108 degree-seeking undergraduates: 50% women, 6% African American, 16% Asian American, 9% Hispanic American, 9% international
- 6,898 degree-seeking graduate students
- 18% of applicants admitted
- SAT or ACT with writing, application essay required
- 93% graduate within 6 years

General. Founded in 1865. Regionally accredited. 7 undergraduate colleges: Agriculture And Life Sciences; Architecture, Art, and Planning; Arts and Sciences; Engineering; Hotel Administration; Human Ecology; Industrial and Labor Relations. 6 graduate/professional colleges. **Degrees:** 3,542 bachelor's awarded; master's, professional, doctoral offered. **ROTC:** Army, Naval, Air Force. **Location:** 60 miles from Syracuse. **Calendar:** Semester, extensive summer session. **Full-time faculty:** 1,646 total; 93% have terminal degrees, 17% minority, 32% women. **Part-time faculty:** 181 total; 77% have terminal degrees, 7% minority, 32% women. **Class size:** 57% < 20, 20% 20-39, 5% 40-49, 12% 50-99, 6% >100. **Special facilities:** Art museum, Africana studies/research center, arboretum, particle accelerator, biotechnology institute, supercomputer, national research centers, center for performing arts, optical observatory, marine laboratory, woods sanctuary, ornithology laboratory, vertebrates museum.

Freshman class profile. 36,387 applied, 6,538 admitted, 3,307 enrolled.

Mid 50% test scores			
SAT critical reading:	630-730	Rank in top tenth:	89%
SAT math:	670-770	Return as sophomores:	97%
ACT composite:	29-33	Out-of-state:	66%
Rank in top quarter:	98%	Live on campus:	100%
		International:	10%

Basis for selection. School achievement record (difficulty of courses, grades earned), test scores, preparation and background for specific programs especially important. Essays, recommendations considered. Subject Test requirements depend upon college/school. Please consult admissions office. Interview required for architecture, hotel administration programs; portfolio required for design programs. **Home schooled:** Well-documented coursework required.

High school preparation. College-preparatory program recommended. 16 units required. Required and recommended units include English 4, mathematics 3, social studies 3, history 3, science 3 (laboratory 3) and foreign language 3.

2011-2012 Annual costs. Tuition/fees: $41,541. Tuition amounts listed are for Endowed/Private colleges only: Architecture, Art & Planning; Arts & Sciences; Engineering; Hotel Administration. Contract/State college tuition differs and varies by residency. Room/board: $13,154. Books/supplies: $800. Personal expenses: $1,630.

2011-2012 Financial aid. All financial aid based on need. 1,993 full-time freshmen applied for aid; 1,703 were judged to have need; 1,703 of these received aid. Average need met was 100%. Average scholarship/grant was $36,443; average loan $2,775. 87% of total undergraduate aid awarded as scholarships/grants, 13% as loans/jobs. **Additional information:** No parental contribution for students from families with incomes below $60,000 and assets below $100,000; need-based student loans capped at $7,500 annually whose families have annual incomes above $120,000; parental contribution reduced for selected students who have financial need and whose families have annual incomes above $60,000.

Application procedures. Admission: Closing date 1/2 (postmark date). $75 fee, may be waived for applicants with need. Early April. Must reply by May 1 or within 2 week(s) if notified thereafter. **Financial aid:** Closing date 1/2. FAFSA, institutional form, CSS PROFILE required. Applicants notified by 4/1; must reply by 5/1.

Academics. Cornell/Hughes Scholars program for independent research in neurobiology, physiology, genetics and development, and biochemistry (molecular and cell biology), Cornell in Rome program for studies in architecture and fine arts, undergraduate research opportunities in traditional majors as well as in many interdisciplinary fields including American Indian studies, cognitive studies, agriculture, food and society, FALCON language programs. **Special study options:** Accelerated study, cooperative education, cross-registration, distance learning, double major, ESL, exchange student, honors, independent study, internships, liberal arts/career combination, New York semester, semester at sea, student-designed major, study abroad, teacher certification program, urban semester, Washington semester. **Credit/placement by examination:** AP, CLEP, IB, institutional tests. Policy varies by college and program. **Support services:** Learning center, pre-admission summer program, reduced course load, study skills assistance, tutoring, writing center.

Majors. Architecture: Architecture, environmental design, history/criticism, landscape, urban/community planning. **Area/ethnic studies:** African-American, American, Asian, gay/lesbian, German, Near/Middle Eastern. **Biology:** General, biometrics, ecology, entomology. **Business:** Hotel/motel

admin, labor relations. **Communications:** Communications/speech/rhetoric. **Computer sciences:** General, computer science, information technology. **Conservation:** General. **Education:** Agricultural. **Engineering:** General, agricultural, applied physics, chemical, civil, electrical, environmental, materials, mechanical, operations research. **English:** English lit. **Foreign languages:** Classics, comparative lit, French, German, Italian, linguistics, Spanish. **General:** Agribusiness operations, animal sciences, business, economics, food science, international, plant sciences, viticulture. **History:** General. **Human services:** Public policy. **Liberal arts:** Arts/sciences. **Math:** General, statistics. **Philosophy/religion:** Philosophy, religion. **Physical sciences:** Astronomy, atmospheric science, chemistry, geology, physics. **Psychology:** General. **Social sciences:** Anthropology, archaeology, economics, political science, sociology. **Visual/performing arts:** Art history/conservation, dance, dramatic, fiber arts, film/cinema/video, music, studio arts. **Work/family studies:** Family studies.

Most popular majors. Agriculture 13%, biology 12%, business/marketing 14%, engineering/engineering technologies 18%, social sciences 11%.

Computing on campus. 2,650 workstations in dormitories, library, computer center, student center. Dormitories wired for high-speed internet access and linked to campus network. Commuter students can connect to campus network. Online course registration, online library, helpline, repair service, student web hosting, wireless network available.

Student life. Freshman orientation: Mandatory. Preregistration for classes offered. Six days and nights immediately prior to start of classes in August. Over 500 upper-level student Orientation Volunteers participate. All seven undergraduate colleges/schools provide orientations that include academic advising, information sessions, and a number of other programs. **Housing:** Guaranteed on-campus for freshmen. Coed dorms, single-sex dorms, special housing for disabled, apartments, cooperative housing, fraternity/sorority housing available. **Activities:** Bands, campus ministries, choral groups, dance, drama, film society, international student organizations, literary magazine, music ensembles, Model UN, musical theater, radio station, student government, student newspaper, symphony orchestra, TV station, Hillel, Campus Crusade for Christ, La Asociacion Latina, various African, Native American, Caribbean, Vietnamese, international, and lesbian/gay/bisexual groups, debate club.

Athletics. NCAA. **Intercollegiate:** Baseball M, basketball, cross-country, diving, equestrian W, fencing W, field hockey W, football (tackle) M, golf M, gymnastics W, ice hockey, lacrosse, rowing (crew), soccer, softball W, squash, swimming, tennis, track and field, volleyball W, wrestling M. **Intramural:** Badminton, basketball, bowling, football (non-tackle), golf, ice hockey, soccer, softball, squash, table tennis, tennis, volleyball. **Team name:** Big Red.

Student services. Alcohol/substance abuse counseling, chaplain/spiritual director, career counseling, student employment services, financial aid counseling, health services, minority student services, on-campus daycare, personal counseling, placement for graduates, veterans' counselor, women's services. **Physically disabled:** Services for visually, speech, hearing impaired.

Contact. E-mail: admissions@cornell.edu
Phone: (607) 255-5241 Fax: (607) 255-0659
Jason Locke, Director of Undergraduate Admissions, Cornell University, 410 Thurston Avenue, Ithaca, NY 14850-2488

Culinary Institute of America

Hyde Park, New York   **CB member**
www.ciachef.edu   **CB code: 3301**

- Private 4-year culinary school
- Residential campus in large town
- 2,736 degree-seeking undergraduates: 46% women
- 81% of applicants admitted
- Application essay required
- 38% graduate within 6 years

General. Founded in 1946. Regionally accredited. **Degrees:** 318 bachelor's, 1,058 associate awarded. **Location:** 80 miles from New York City. **Calendar:** Semester. **Full-time faculty:** 155 total; 9% minority, 24% women. **Part-time faculty:** 29 total; 7% minority, 55% women. **Special facilities:** 41 teaching kitchens and bakeshops, 5 restaurants, theaters.

Freshman class profile. 940 applied, 758 admitted, 463 enrolled.

Mid 50% test scores			
SAT critical reading:	470-570	GPA 2.0-2.99:	27%
SAT math:	460-580	Rank in top quarter:	38%
ACT composite:	20-25	Rank in top tenth:	14%
GPA 3.75 or higher:	15%	Return as sophomores:	91%
GPA 3.50-3.74:	21%	Out-of-state:	80%
GPA 3.0-3.49:	36%	International:	5%

Basis for selection. School achievement record, 6 months work experience (particularly in hands-on food preparation). SAT/ACT not used for admissions, but if tests taken recommended that students submit scores. **Home schooled:** District issued diploma, GED, or SAT/ACT.

High school preparation. Recommended units include English 4, mathematics 3, social studies 2, history 2 and science 2.

2011-2012 Annual costs. Tuition/fees: $26,180. Room/board: $8,820. Books/supplies: $2,000. Personal expenses: $3,100.

2010-2011 Financial aid. Need-based: 583 full-time freshmen applied for aid; 571 were judged to have need; 571 of these received aid. Average need met was 48%. Average scholarship/grant was $9,225; average loan $3,671. 70% of total undergraduate aid awarded as scholarships/grants, 30% as loans/jobs. **Non-need-based:** Awarded to 1,344 full-time undergraduates, including 83 freshmen. Scholarships awarded for academics, alumni affiliation, job skills, leadership, minority status.

Application procedures. Admission: No deadline. $50 fee, may be waived for applicants with need. Admission notification on a rolling basis. **Financial aid:** No deadline. FAFSA required. Applicants notified on a rolling basis; must reply by 5/1 or within 4 week(s) of notification.

Academics. Curriculum devoted exclusively to culinary arts and baking and pastry arts education. Freshmen may enroll in one of 4 enrollment seasons throughout the year. All students complete 18-week paid externship program. Two-thirds of class time involves hands-on cooking, baking, table service, and dining room operations management in kitchens, bakeshops, and 5 student-staffed public restaurants. **Special study options:** Cross-registration, internships. **Credit/placement by examination:** AP, CLEP, SAT, ACT, institutional tests. **Support services:** Learning center, reduced course load, remedial instruction, study skills assistance, tutoring, writing center.

Majors. Business: Restaurant/food services.

Computing on campus. 218 workstations in dormitories, library, computer center, student center. Dormitories wired for high-speed internet access and linked to campus network. Commuter students can connect to campus network. Online library, helpline, repair service, wireless network available.

Student life. Freshman orientation: Mandatory. Preregistration for classes offered. **Housing:** Guaranteed on-campus for freshmen. Coed dorms, special housing for disabled, wellness housing available. Hearing impaired student housing available. **Activities:** International student organizations, literary magazine, student government, student newspaper, Alliance, Eta Sigma Delta Honor Society, Baking and Pastry Arts Society, Black Culinarian Society, Chefs Supporting Agriculture, Culinary Christian Fellowship, Ice Carving Society, Global Culinary Society, Garden Society, Oye Me.

Athletics. Intercollegiate: Basketball, cross-country, soccer, tennis. **Intramural:** Basketball, football (non-tackle), soccer, softball, volleyball. **Team name:** Flames.

Student services. Alcohol/substance abuse counseling, chaplain/spiritual director, career counseling, student employment services, financial aid counseling, health services, personal counseling, placement for graduates, veterans' counselor. **Physically disabled:** Services for visually, speech, hearing impaired.

Contact. E-mail: admissions@culinary.edu
Phone: (845) 452-9430 Toll-free number: (800) 285-4627
Fax: (845) 451-1068
Rachel Birchwood, Director of Admissions, Culinary Institute of America, 1946 Campus Drive, Hyde Park, NY 12538-1499

Daemen College

Amherst, New York   **CB member**
www.daemen.edu   **CB code: 2762**

- Private 4-year liberal arts college
- Residential campus in small city
- 1,872 degree-seeking undergraduates: 12% part-time, 72% women, 10% African American, 2% Asian American, 4% Hispanic American, 3% international
- 831 degree-seeking graduate students
- 59% of applicants admitted
- Application essay required
- 44% graduate within 6 years

General. Founded in 1947. Regionally accredited. Comprehensive college with baccalaureate and graduate programs including two clinical doctorate

programs. **Degrees:** 332 bachelor's awarded; master's, professional, doctoral offered. **ROTC:** Army. **Location:** 9 miles from downtown Buffalo. **Calendar:** Semester, limited summer session. **Full-time faculty:** 120 total; 73% have terminal degrees, 7% minority, 60% women. **Part-time faculty:** 159 total. **Class size:** 57% < 20, 36% 20-39, 5% 40-49, 2% 50-99. **Special facilities:** Natural and health science research center, Center for Sustainable Communities and Civic Engagement, Thomas Reynolds Center for Special Education and After-School Programs, Research and Information Commons.

Freshman class profile. 2,372 applied, 1,405 admitted, 435 enrolled.

Mid 50% test scores			
SAT critical reading:	450-560	Rank in top quarter:	51%
SAT math:	460-570	Rank in top tenth:	15%
SAT writing:	440-550	End year in good standing:	86%
ACT composite:	21-25	Return as sophomores:	81%
GPA 3.75 or higher:	23%	Out-of-state:	1%
GPA 3.50-3.74:	48%	Live on campus:	60%
GPA 3.0-3.49:	28%	International:	2%
GPA 2.0-2.99:	1%	Fraternities:	1%

Basis for selection. Emphasis on rigor of high school academic program and test scores with secondary consideration given to school activities and recommendations. Work experience also considered for entry into physician assistant program. 30 credit hour transfer limit on International Baccalaureate coursework. SAT or ACT recommended. Applicants who have been out of high school for more than 2 years not required to submit SAT or ACT scores. Submission of tests are optional for all. If opting out of tests, must provide high school transcript, grades and rigor of courses, class rank, writing sample, teacher/counselor recommendation, and extracurricular activities. Essay and interview required for physician assistant program; portfolio required for art program. High school counselor completes recommendation section of the application. **Home schooled:** State high school equivalency certificate required. Applicants should provide evidence of equivalency of high school education by GED or attestation of equivalency by superintendent of schools in student's public school district of residence. This documentation needed for financial aid eligibility. **Learning Disabled:** Bring to the attention of Admission Office need for special accommodations and submit current medical evidence of disability and limitations that require accommodations. Feasibility determined by nature and cost of accommodation, availability of funding, and whether accommodation will impact fundamental nature of course or program, among other factors.

High school preparation. College-preparatory program recommended. 16 units recommended. Recommended units include English 4, mathematics 4, social studies 4, science 4 (laboratory 1). All science and allied health programs require 3 math and 3 science units. Business program requires 3 math. Foreign language programs require 3 foreign language units.

2011-2012 Annual costs. Tuition/fees: $22,310. Room/board: $10,300. Books/supplies: $800. Personal expenses: $800.

Financial aid. Non-need-based: Scholarships awarded for academics, art, athletics, leadership.

Application procedures. Admission: No deadline. $25 fee, may be waived for applicants with need, free for online applicants. Admission notification on a rolling basis beginning on or about 10/15. Must reply by May 1 or within 2 week(s) if notified thereafter. **Financial aid:** Priority date 2/15; no closing date. FAFSA required. Applicants notified on a rolling basis starting 2/1; must reply within 2 week(s) of notification.

Academics. All professional programs require internships or field placements. There is a general service-learning graduation requirement for all students. **Special study options:** Accelerated study, combined bachelor's/graduate degree, cross-registration, distance learning, double major, dual enrollment of high school students, exchange student, honors, independent study, internships, liberal arts/career combination, student-designed major, study abroad, teacher certification program, Washington semester, weekend college. Post-RN BS program in nursing and the 1-2-1 nursing program with RN and BS degree. Dual degree (BS/MS) in Physician Assistant Studies and Accounting/Professional Accountancy. **Credit/placement by examination:** AP, CLEP, IB, SAT, ACT, institutional tests. Veterans may receive credit for military educational experiences. Freshmen with transfer credits must take 9 credits in writing intensive courses, 3 credits in service learning, and 3 credits in quantitative literacy. **Support services:** Learning center, pre-admission summer program, remedial instruction, study skills assistance, tutoring, writing center.

Majors. Biology: General, biochemistry. **Business:** Accounting, business admin. **Education:** Art, early childhood, elementary, special ed. **English:** English lit. **Foreign languages:** French, Spanish. **Health services:** General, nursing (RN). **History:** General. **Human services:** Social work. **Math:** General. **Philosophy/religion:** Religion. **Psychology:** General. **Social sciences:** General, political science, U.S. government. **Visual/performing arts:** Art, graphic design, printmaking, studio arts, studio arts management.

Most popular majors. Business/marketing 14%, education 13%, health sciences 32%, interdisciplinary studies 20%, psychology 6%, visual/performing arts 6%.

Computing on campus. 156 workstations in library, computer center. Dormitories wired for high-speed internet access and linked to campus network. Commuter students can connect to campus network. Online course registration, online library, helpline, repair service, wireless network available.

Student life. Freshman orientation: Mandatory, $105 fee. Preregistration for classes offered. Two sessions (2 days each) offered in July for incoming freshmen. One day in mid-August for new transfer students. **Housing:** Guaranteed on-campus for freshmen. Coed dorms, wellness housing available. $200 fully refundable deposit, deadline 5/1. Coed apartment-style residence halls; some apartments are handicapped accessible. **Activities:** Choral groups, dance, drama, literary magazine, student government, student newspaper, multicultural association, Students without Borders, environmental club, Voices of Zion, American Red Cross club, Brother to Brother, Sister to Sister, Chinese culture club.

Athletics. NAIA. **Intercollegiate:** Basketball, cross-country, golf M, soccer, track and field, volleyball W. **Intramural:** Basketball, softball. **Team name:** Wildcats.

Student services. Alcohol/substance abuse counseling, chaplain/spiritual director, career counseling, financial aid counseling, personal counseling, veterans' counselor. **Physically disabled:** Services for hearing impaired.

Contact. E-mail: admissions@daemen.edu
Phone: (716) 839-8225 Toll-free number: (800) 462-7652
Fax: (716) 839-8229
Frank Williams, Dean of Admissions, Daemen College, 4380 Main Street, Amherst, NY 14226-3592

Davis College
Johnson City, New York
www.davisny.edu
CB code: 2233

- Private 4-year Bible college affiliated with nondenominational tradition
- Residential campus in large town
- 252 degree-seeking undergraduates
- 50% of applicants admitted
- SAT or ACT (ACT writing optional), application essay required

General. Regionally accredited; also accredited by ABHE. **Degrees:** 40 bachelor's, 7 associate awarded. **Location:** 2 miles from Binghamton. **Calendar:** Semester, limited summer session. **Full-time faculty:** 6 total. **Part-time faculty:** 17 total.

Freshman class profile. 105 applied, 53 admitted, 35 enrolled.

Mid 50% test scores			
SAT critical reading:	400-560	SAT writing:	400-520
SAT math:	390-500	ACT composite:	20-26

Basis for selection. Pastor recommendation and high school record most important. Must give evidence of personal knowledge of the Lord Jesus Christ as Savior. Applicant lifestyle consistency with biblical principles is important. **Home schooled:** Must submit evidence of completion of high school requirements such as a high school transcript, home school transcript or GED.

2012-2013 Annual costs. Tuition/fees (projected): $12,890. Room/board: $6,000.

Financial aid. Non-need-based: Scholarships awarded for academics, alumni affiliation.

Application procedures. Admission: No deadline. $45 fee. Admission notification on a rolling basis. Dual credit opportunities for high school juniors and seniors through on-campus and online courses. Possible for high school students to complete all freshman requirements prior to high school graduation. **Financial aid:** No deadline. FAFSA, institutional form required. Applicants notified on a rolling basis.

Academics. Special study options: Distance learning, dual enrollment of high school students, independent study, internships, student-designed major. **Credit/placement by examination:** AP, CLEP, SAT, ACT, institutional tests. **Support services:** Reduced course load, remedial instruction, study skills assistance, tutoring.

Majors. Theology: Religious ed.

Computing on campus. 1 workstations in library. Dormitories linked to campus network. Commuter students can connect to campus network. Wireless network available.

Student life. Freshman orientation: Mandatory. Preregistration for classes offered. **Policies:** Religious observance required. **Housing:** Guaranteed on-campus for freshmen. Single-sex dorms, apartments available. $150 partly refundable deposit. **Activities:** Campus ministries, choral groups, drama, international student organizations, music ensembles, student government.

Athletics. NCCAA. **Intercollegiate:** Basketball, soccer. **Intramural:** Soccer, volleyball. **Team name:** Falcons.

Student services. Chaplain/spiritual director, financial aid counseling, health services, personal counseling.

Contact. E-mail: admissions@davisny.edu
Phone: (607) 729-1581 ext. 406
Toll-free number: (800) 331-4137 ext. 406 Fax: (607) 798-7754
Rick Cramer, Admissions Director, Davis College, 400 Riverside Drive, Johnson City, NY 13790

DeVry College of New York: Midtown Campus
New York, New York
www.devry.edu   **CB code: 4276**

- For-profit 4-year business and technical college
- Commuter campus in very large city
- 1,279 degree-seeking undergraduates
- Interview required

General. Regionally accredited. Additional locations: Manhattan, Queens. **Degrees:** 138 bachelor's, 24 associate awarded; master's offered. **Calendar:** Semester, extensive summer session. **Full-time faculty:** 37 total. **Part-time faculty:** 56 total.

Basis for selection. Applicants must have high school diploma or equivalent, or degree from an accredited postsecondary institution. Must demonstrate proficiency in basic college-level skills through test scores and/or institutionally administered placement examinations, and be at least 17 years of age on the first day of classes. New students may enter at beginning of any semester. SAT/ACT considered but not required for admission. If applicant chooses not to submit either, must take institution-administered admissions test.

High school preparation. College-preparatory program recommended.

2011-2012 Annual costs. Tuition/fees: $15,294. Books/supplies: $1,310. Personal expenses: $3,574.

Financial aid. All financial aid based on need.

Application procedures. Admission: No deadline. $50 fee. Admission notification on a rolling basis. **Financial aid:** No deadline. Applicants notified on a rolling basis.

Academics. Special study options: Accelerated study, distance learning. **Credit/placement by examination:** AP, CLEP, institutional tests. **Support services:** Learning center, remedial instruction, tutoring.

Majors. Business: Business admin. **Computer sciences:** Networking, systems analysis.

Most popular majors. Business/marketing 53%, computer/information sciences 29%, engineering/engineering technologies 18%.

Computing on campus. 394 workstations in library, computer center. Online course registration, online library, helpline available.

Student life. Freshman orientation: Mandatory. Preregistration for classes offered. **Activities:** Muslim student association, martial arts club.

Student services. Career counseling, student employment services, financial aid counseling, placement for graduates, veterans' counselor. **Physically disabled:** Services for visually, hearing impaired.

Contact. Phone: (718) 472-2728 Toll-free number: (866) 338-7941
Newton Myvett, Director of Admissions, DeVry College of New York: Midtown Campus, 180 Madison Avenue, Suite 900, New York, NY 10016

Dominican College of Blauvelt
Orangeburg, New York   **CB member**
www.dc.edu   **CB code: 2190**

- Private 4-year health science and liberal arts college
- Residential campus in small town
- 1,609 degree-seeking undergraduates: 14% part-time, 67% women, 14% African American, 8% Asian American, 17% Hispanic American
- 415 degree-seeking graduate students
- 71% of applicants admitted
- SAT or ACT with writing required
- 40% graduate within 6 years

General. Founded in 1952. Regionally accredited. Private non-affiliated institution, Catholic in origin and Dominican in tradition. **Degrees:** 350 bachelor's, 12 associate awarded; master's, professional offered. **Location:** 17 miles from midtown Manhattan. **Calendar:** Continuous, limited summer session. **Full-time faculty:** 73 total; 56% have terminal degrees, 11% minority, 68% women. **Part-time faculty:** 160 total; 19% have terminal degrees, 13% minority, 63% women. **Class size:** 62% < 20, 37% 20-39, 1% 50-99.

Freshman class profile. 1,594 applied, 1,126 admitted, 352 enrolled.

Mid 50% test scores			
SAT critical reading:	400-490	GPA 3.0-3.49:	32%
SAT math:	390-490	GPA 2.0-2.99:	55%
SAT writing:	390-490	End year in good standing:	89%
ACT composite:	18-21	Return as sophomores:	66%
GPA 3.75 or higher:	3%	Out-of-state:	26%
GPA 3.50-3.74:	8%	Live on campus:	74%
		International:	1%

Basis for selection. Admissions based on secondary school records and standardized test scores. Interviews and written essays required in some cases. Meeting with admissions counselor not always required for admission but always desirable. Some applicants may be asked to meet with member of admissions staff. **Learning Disabled:** Students with current professional documentation of disabilities will be provided with reasonable accommodations to assure access to and full participation in mainstream of educational process.

High school preparation. College-preparatory program recommended. 16 units required; 18 recommended. Required and recommended units include English 4, mathematics 3, social studies 3-4, science 3 (laboratory 1), foreign language 1-2 and academic electives 2.

2011-2012 Annual costs. Tuition/fees: $22,940. Room/board: $10,980. Books/supplies: $1,800.

2011-2012 Financial aid. Need-based: 334 full-time freshmen applied for aid; 330 were judged to have need; 330 of these received aid. Average need met was 72%. Average scholarship/grant was $15,826; average loan $3,396. 51% of total undergraduate aid awarded as scholarships/grants, 49% as loans/jobs. **Non-need-based:** Awarded to 279 full-time undergraduates, including 88 freshmen. Scholarships awarded for academics, athletics. **Additional information:** Individual financial aid counseling available.

Application procedures. Admission: No deadline. $35 fee, may be waived for applicants with need. Admission notification on a rolling basis. **Financial aid:** Priority date 2/15; no closing date. FAFSA required. Applicants notified on a rolling basis starting 2/1; must reply within 2 week(s) of notification.

Academics. Special study options: Accelerated study, combined bachelor's/graduate degree, cooperative education, distance learning, dual enrollment of high school students, honors, independent study, internships, study abroad, teacher certification program, weekend college. Accelerated Bachelor of Science in Nursing for college graduates. **Credit/placement by examination:** AP, CLEP, IB, SAT, ACT, institutional tests. 30 credit hours maximum toward associate degree, 60 toward bachelor's. **Support services:** Learning center, remedial instruction, study skills assistance, tutoring, writing center.

Majors. Biology: General. **Business:** Accounting, business admin, finance, human resources, international, management information systems, marketing. **Communications:** Media studies. **Computer sciences:** General. **Education:** General, biology, elementary, English, mathematics, multiple handicapped, secondary, social science, special ed. **English:** English lit. **Foreign languages:** Spanish. **Health services:** Athletic training, nursing (RN). **History:** General. **Human services:** Social work. **Liberal arts:** Humanities. **Math:** General. **Psychology:** General. **Social sciences:** General, criminology, economics.

Most popular majors. Business/marketing 20%, education 7%, English 6%, health sciences 34%, social sciences 14%.

Computing on campus. 140 workstations in dormitories, library, computer center. Dormitories wired for high-speed internet access and linked to campus network. Commuter students can connect to campus network. Online library, repair service, wireless network available.

Student life. Freshman orientation: Mandatory. Preregistration for classes offered. Held end of August, early September. **Policies:** Alcohol-free campus. **Housing:** Guaranteed on-campus for all undergraduates. Coed dorms, wellness housing available. $250 fully refundable deposit. Suites with multiple bedrooms, a bathroom and kitchen available for upperclass students. **Activities:** Campus ministries, choral groups, dance, drama, literary magazine, Model UN, musical theater, radio station, student government, student newspaper, Dominicans Uniting Latinos for Cultural Education, Helping Hands, Bridges International Service Project, Campus Compact for Community Service and Civic Engagement, Students Against the Abuse of Women, United Nations Committee.

Athletics. NAIA, NCAA. **Intercollegiate:** Baseball M, basketball, cross-country W, golf M, lacrosse, soccer, softball W, track and field W, volleyball W. **Intramural:** Basketball, football (non-tackle), handball, rowing (crew), softball, volleyball. **Team name:** Chargers.

Student services. Alcohol/substance abuse counseling, chaplain/spiritual director, career counseling, student employment services, financial aid counseling, health services, personal counseling, placement for graduates. **Physically disabled:** Services for visually, hearing impaired.

Contact. E-mail: admissions@dc.edu
Phone: (845) 848-7901 Toll-free number: (866) 432-4636
Fax: (845) 365-3150
Joyce Elbe, Director of Admissions, Dominican College of Blauvelt, 470 Western Highway, Orangeburg, NY 10962-1210

Dowling College
Oakdale, New York
www.dowling.edu

CB member
CB code: 2011

- Private 4-year business and liberal arts college
- Commuter campus in large town
- 2,297 degree-seeking undergraduates: 17% part-time, 54% women, 9% African American, 1% Asian American, 9% Hispanic American, 4% international
- 1,533 degree-seeking graduate students
- 79% of applicants admitted
- Application essay required
- 36% graduate within 6 years

General. Founded in 1955. Regionally accredited. School of Aviation situated at Brookhaven Airport. **Degrees:** 511 bachelor's awarded; master's, doctoral offered. **ROTC:** Army, Air Force. **Location:** 50 miles from New York City. **Calendar:** Semester, extensive summer session. **Full-time faculty:** 115 total; 96% have terminal degrees, 10% minority, 37% women. **Part-time faculty:** 316 total; 27% have terminal degrees, 5% minority, 46% women. **Class size:** 64% < 20, 36% 20-39, less than 1% 40-49. **Special facilities:** FRASCA flight simulators; virtual airport; athletic complex; Center for Estuarine, Environmental and Coastal Oceans Monitoring.

Freshman class profile. 2,495 applied, 1,962 admitted, 358 enrolled.

Return as sophomores:	65%	Live on campus:	34%
Out-of-state:	4%	International:	6%

Basis for selection. Program of study, recent achievement, academic rank, school record, standardized test scores, counselor's recommendation considered. SAT or ACT recommended. Letter of recommendation required.

High school preparation. College-preparatory program recommended. 16 units required. Required units include English 4, mathematics 3, social studies 4, science 2, foreign language 2 and academic electives 1. 4 additional units recommended.

2011-2012 Annual costs. Tuition/fees: $25,908. Room/board: $10,830.

2010-2011 Financial aid. Need-based: 367 full-time freshmen applied for aid; 360 were judged to have need; 360 of these received aid. Average need met was 95%. Average scholarship/grant was $3,185; average loan $3,185. 89% of total undergraduate aid awarded as scholarships/grants, 11% as loans/jobs. **Non-need-based:** Awarded to 1,383 full-time undergraduates, including 306 freshmen. Scholarships awarded for academics, alumni affiliation, athletics.

Application procedures. Admission: No deadline. $35 fee, may be waived for applicants with need. Admission notification on a rolling basis beginning on or about 10/1. **Financial aid:** Priority date 2/15; no closing date. FAFSA required. Applicants notified on a rolling basis starting 3/15.

Academics. Optional winter and summer terms. **Special study options:** Accelerated study, combined bachelor's/graduate degree, cooperative education, distance learning, double major, ESL, honors, independent study, internships, liberal arts/career combination, student-designed major, study abroad, teacher certification program, weekend college. Federal Aviation Administration cooperative program, Higher Education Opportunity Program (HEOP). **Credit/placement by examination:** AP, CLEP, IB, SAT, ACT, institutional tests. 30 credit hours maximum toward bachelor's degree. **Support services:** Learning center, pre-admission summer program, reduced course load, remedial instruction, study skills assistance, tutoring, writing center.

Majors. Biology: General. **Business:** Accounting, business admin, finance. **Computer sciences:** Computer science. **Education:** General, art, biology, business, chemistry, early childhood, elementary, English, foreign languages, mathematics, middle, multi-level teacher, music, physical, science, social science, social studies, Spanish, special ed. **English:** English lit. **History:** General. **Liberal arts:** Arts/sciences, humanities. **Math:** General, applied. **Parks/recreation:** Sports admin. **Philosophy/religion:** Philosophy. **Physical sciences:** Chemistry. **Psychology:** General. **Social sciences:** General, anthropology, economics, political science, sociology. **Visual/performing arts:** General, dramatic, graphic design, music.

Most popular majors. Business/marketing 29%, education 20%, liberal arts 8%, psychology 7%, social sciences 9%, trade and industry 6%.

Computing on campus. 317 workstations in library, computer center. Dormitories wired for high-speed internet access and linked to campus network. Commuter students can connect to campus network. Online course registration, online library, helpline, wireless network available.

Student life. Freshman orientation: Available. Preregistration for classes offered. Approximately 1 full day. **Housing:** Coed dorms available. $200 nonrefundable deposit. **Activities:** Jazz band, campus ministries, choral groups, dance, drama, international student organizations, literary magazine, music ensembles, musical theater, radio station, student government, student newspaper, symphony orchestra, 41 clubs and organizations related to academics, honor societies in business, education, economics, and psychology, Circle-K, computer science, scholarship society.

Athletics. NCAA. **Intercollegiate:** Baseball M, basketball, cross-country, golf M, lacrosse, rowing (crew) W, soccer, softball W, tennis, volleyball W. **Intramural:** Basketball, football (non-tackle), handball, soccer, softball, volleyball. **Team name:** Golden Lions.

Student services. Adult student services, alcohol/substance abuse counseling, chaplain/spiritual director, career counseling, services for economically disadvantaged, student employment services, financial aid counseling, health services, minority student services, personal counseling, placement for graduates, veterans' counselor. **Physically disabled:** Services for visually, speech, hearing impaired.

Contact. E-mail: admissions@dowling.edu
Phone: (631) 244-3030 Toll-free number: (800) 369-5464
Fax: (631) 244-1059
Ronnie Macdonald, Vice-President for Enrollment and Student Services, Dowling College, 150 Idle Hour Boulevard, Oakdale, NY 11769-1999

D'Youville College
Buffalo, New York
www.dyc.edu

CB member
CB code: 2197

- Private 4-year health science and liberal arts college
- Commuter campus in large city
- 1,940 degree-seeking undergraduates: 15% part-time, 74% women, 10% African American, 2% Asian American, 4% Hispanic American, 1% Native American, 7% international
- 1,039 degree-seeking graduate students
- 84% of applicants admitted
- SAT or ACT (ACT writing optional) required
- 52% graduate within 6 years

General. Founded in 1908. Regionally accredited. **Degrees:** 334 bachelor's awarded; master's, professional, doctoral offered. **ROTC:** Army. **Location:** 1 mile from downtown. **Calendar:** Semester, extensive summer session. **Full-time faculty:** 178 total; 73% have terminal degrees, 11% minority, 61% women. **Part-time faculty:** 120 total; 18% have terminal degrees, 6% minority, 59% women. **Class size:** 67% < 20, 25% 20-39, 4% 40-49, 4% 50-99. **Special facilities:** Equipment for blind and visually impaired including

computer system with speech synthesizer, Braille printer, Versabraille and print enhancer, professional theater, gross anatomy lab.

Freshman class profile. 1,029 applied, 864 admitted, 228 enrolled.

Mid 50% test scores		Rank in top tenth:	21%
SAT critical reading:	470-560	Return as sophomores:	71%
SAT math:	490-590	Out-of-state:	5%
SAT writing:	450-550	Live on campus:	42%
ACT composite:	21-25	International:	1%
Rank in top quarter:	52%		

Basis for selection. High school GPA, class rank, test scores, type of high school program important. Interview, essay, letters of recommendation optional. 3 recommendations required for physician's assistant program. Interview required for physician's assistant and chiropractic programs. **Home schooled:** Transcript of courses and grades, state high school equivalency certificate, letter of recommendation (nonparent) required.

High school preparation. College-preparatory program recommended. 16 units recommended. Recommended units include English 4, mathematics 3, social studies 3, science 3 and foreign language 3. Biology and chemistry required for nursing, occupational therapy, physical therapy, dietetics, chiropractic and physician's assistant programs. 3 units of math required for accounting.

2011-2012 Annual costs. Tuition/fees: $21,760. Room/board: $10,000. Books/supplies: $1,200. Personal expenses: $800.

2011-2012 Financial aid. Need-based: Average need met was 75%. Average scholarship/grant was $14,438; average loan $3,740. 49% of total undergraduate aid awarded as scholarships/grants, 51% as loans/jobs. **Non-need-based:** Scholarships awarded for academics, leadership, religious affiliation, ROTC.

Application procedures. Admission: No deadline. $25 fee, may be waived for applicants with need, free for online applicants. Admission notification on a rolling basis. Must reply by May 1 or within 2 week(s) if notified thereafter. **Financial aid:** Priority date 3/1; no closing date. FAFSA required. Applicants notified on a rolling basis starting 4/1; must reply within 2 week(s) of notification.

Academics. Special study options: Accelerated study, combined bachelor's/graduate degree, cross-registration, distance learning, double major, dual enrollment of high school students, exchange student, independent study, internships, liberal arts/career combination, study abroad, teacher certification program, weekend college. Career Discovery Program for undecided students; teacher certification at the graduate level only. **Credit/placement by examination:** AP, CLEP, IB, institutional tests. 15 credit hours maximum toward bachelor's degree. Life experience may be granted credit through local Challenge Examinations. Prior to entering D'Youville, up to 15 credits may be earned via standardized examinations; additional 15 credits may be earned via standardized examinations after enrolling. **Support services:** Learning center, pre-admission summer program, reduced course load, remedial instruction, study skills assistance, tutoring, writing center.

Majors. Biology: General. **Business:** General, accounting, business admin. **Computer sciences:** Information technology. **English:** Creative writing, English lit, technical writing. **Health services:** Health care admin, nursing (RN), physician assistant, predental, premedicine, preop/surgical nursing, prepharmacy, preveterinary. **History:** General. **Math:** General. **Philosophy/religion:** Philosophy. **Physical sciences:** Chemistry. **Psychology:** General. **Social sciences:** Sociology.

Most popular majors. Business/marketing 13%, health sciences 62%, interdisciplinary studies 8%.

Computing on campus. 100 workstations in dormitories, library, computer center, student center. Dormitories wired for high-speed internet access and linked to campus network. Commuter students can connect to campus network. Online library, helpline, repair service, student web hosting, wireless network available.

Student life. Freshman orientation: Mandatory, $60 fee. Preregistration for classes offered. Programs vary for traditional, transfer, and graduate students. **Housing:** Guaranteed on-campus for freshmen. Coed dorms, special housing for disabled, apartments, wellness housing available. $100 fully refundable deposit. Quiet floors for upper level students. **Activities:** Campus ministries, choral groups, drama, international student organizations, literary magazine, Model UN, student government, student newspaper, black student union, Latin American club, Lambda Sigma, writers club, student nurses association, Asian student union.

Athletics. NCAA. **Intercollegiate:** Baseball M, basketball, cross-country, golf, rowing (crew) W, soccer, softball W, tennis, volleyball. **Intramural:** Basketball, cheerleading W, table tennis, volleyball. **Team name:** Spartans.

Student services. Adult student services, alcohol/substance abuse counseling, chaplain/spiritual director, career counseling, services for economically disadvantaged, student employment services, financial aid counseling, health services, minority student services, personal counseling, placement for graduates, veterans' counselor. **Physically disabled:** Services for visually, speech, hearing impaired.

Contact. E-mail: admissions@dyc.edu
Phone: (716) 829-7600 Toll-free number: (800) 777-3921
Fax: (716) 829-7900
Steve Smith, Director of Admissions, D'Youville College, 320 Porter Avenue, Buffalo, NY 14201-1084

Eastman School of Music of the University of Rochester
Rochester, New York
www.esm.rochester.edu   **CB code: 2224**

- Private 4-year music and performing arts college
- Residential campus in small city
- 516 degree-seeking undergraduates: 47% women
- 418 degree-seeking graduate students
- 31% of applicants admitted
- Application essay, interview required

General. Founded in 1921. Regionally accredited. Professional school within University of Rochester. Eastman students may take non-music classes, earn BA or BS degree, pursue minors, and attend events and activities at University of Rochester's River Campus. **Degrees:** 137 bachelor's awarded; master's, doctoral offered. **ROTC:** Naval. **Location:** 357 miles from New York City, 80 miles from Niagara Falls. **Calendar:** Semester, limited summer session. **Full-time faculty:** 96 total. **Part-time faculty:** 46 total. **Class size:** 89% < 20, 9% 20-39, 1% 40-49, less than 1% 50-99. **Special facilities:** 5 performance halls including 2,000 plus-seat theater and three recital halls, computers for synthesis and analysis of music, complete analog and digital recording studios, music library containing over 700,000 items, over 135 practice rooms.

Freshman class profile. 1,018 applied, 314 admitted, 144 enrolled.

Out-of-state:	75%	Fraternities:	7%
Live on campus:	99%	Sororities:	11%

Basis for selection. Proficiency in major area most important, in addition to academic record, test scores, interview, recommendations. Composition majors submit portfolio of scores. Some areas (jazz, composition, voice, piano, flute, clarinet, violin, cello) prescreened in advance of live audition. Candidates encouraged to audition at Eastman in the spring on designated audition dates, but auditions are held at regional sites in January, and auditions by recording are also possible in most areas. SAT and SAT Subject Tests or ACT recommended. Candidates who come to Eastman for a live audition are also given a music theory test. Some programs also require an aural skills test. Audition required for all; research/term paper required for theory majors; portfolio required for composition majors. Interview recommended for all, required for composition, music education, music theory majors. **Home schooled:** Statement describing home school structure and mission, transcript of courses and grades, letter of recommendation (nonparent) required. SAT or ACT scores, along with detailed documentation of texts, coursework, experiential learning, and transcripts of any college coursework. Taking college credit classes also encouraged. **Learning Disabled:** To facilitate a smooth audition day experience, Admissions Office requests advance notice of any special considerations.

High school preparation. 16 units required. Required units include English 4.

2011-2012 Annual costs. Tuition/fees: $42,291. Room/board: $12,330. Books/supplies: $650. Personal expenses: $1,500.

Financial aid. Non-need-based: Scholarships awarded for academics, alumni affiliation, job skills, leadership, minority status, music/drama, state residency.

Application procedures. Admission: Priority date 11/1; deadline 12/1 (receipt date). $125 fee, may be waived for applicants with need. Application must be submitted online. Admission notification by 4/15. Admission notification on a rolling basis beginning on or about 3/15. Must reply by May 1 or within 2 week(s) if notified thereafter. Admission review occurs following candidate's audition/interview. Regional auditions in United States typically occur in January, auditions at Eastman School of Music take place in February; typically, admission review and decisions follow final audition date in Rochester. Separate (additional) application required for dual degree program with University of Rochester's College of Arts, Sciences and Engineering.

Financial aid: Closing date 2/28. FAFSA, institutional form, CSS PROFILE required. Applicants notified on a rolling basis starting 3/15; must reply by 5/1 or within 2 week(s) of notification.

Academics. Certificate programs in arts leadership, college and/or community music teaching, world music available to matriculated students; diploma programs in orchestral studies, ethnomusicology and sacred music also available. **Special study options:** Double major, dual enrollment of high school students, ESL, independent study, internships, student-designed major, study abroad, teacher certification program. **Credit/placement by examination:** AP, CLEP, institutional tests. **Support services:** Pre-admission summer program, remedial instruction, study skills assistance, tutoring, writing center.

Majors. Education: Music. **Visual/performing arts:** Jazz, music, music performance, music theory/composition, piano/keyboard, voice/opera.

Most popular majors. Education 16%, visual/performing arts 84%.

Computing on campus. 50 workstations in dormitories, library, computer center, student center. Dormitories wired for high-speed internet access and linked to campus network. Commuter students can connect to campus network. Online course registration, online library, helpline, repair service, student web hosting, wireless network available.

Student life. Freshman orientation: Mandatory, $215 fee. Preregistration for classes offered. Includes mandatory placement testing. **Policies:** Undergraduates required to live in college housing for first 3 years unless released by Assistant Dean of Residential Life. **Housing:** Guaranteed on-campus for freshmen. Coed dorms, single-sex dorms, special housing for disabled, fraternity/sorority housing, wellness housing available. **Activities:** Bands, campus ministries, choral groups, dance, drama, international student organizations, literary magazine, music ensembles, opera, radio station, student government, student newspaper, symphony orchestra, international students association, Catholic Newman community, intervarsity Christian fellowship, Hillel, Mu Phi Epsilon, Sigma Alpha Iota, student association, graduate student association, musical organizations.

Student services. Adult student services, alcohol/substance abuse counseling, chaplain/spiritual director, career counseling, student employment services, financial aid counseling, health services, personal counseling, placement for graduates, women's services. **Physically disabled:** Services for visually, speech impaired.

Contact. E-mail: admissions@esm.rochester.edu
Phone: (585) 274-1060 Toll-free number: (800) 388-9695
Fax: (585) 232-8601
Matthew Ardizzone, Director of Admissions, Eastman School of Music of the University of Rochester, 26 Gibbs Street, Rochester, NY 14604-2599

Elmira College
Elmira, New York
www.elmira.edu
CB member
CB code: 2226

- Private 4-year liberal arts college
- Residential campus in large town
- 1,302 degree-seeking undergraduates: 17% part-time, 73% women
- 228 degree-seeking graduate students
- 75% of applicants admitted
- SAT or ACT (ACT writing optional), application essay required
- 58% graduate within 6 years; 62% enter graduate study

General. Founded in 1855. Regionally accredited. **Degrees:** 307 bachelor's, 5 associate awarded; master's optional. **ROTC:** Army, Air Force. **Location:** 106 miles from Rochester, 90 miles from Syracuse, 50 miles from Binghamton. **Calendar:** 4-4-1. Limited summer session. **Full-time faculty:** 92 total; 5% minority, 54% women. **Part-time faculty:** 129 total; 2% minority, 56% women. **Class size:** 83% < 20, 16% 20-39, less than 1% 40-49. **Special facilities:** Center for Mark Twain Studies.

Freshman class profile. 2,424 applied, 1,829 admitted, 349 enrolled.

Mid 50% test scores			
SAT critical reading:	490-600	GPA 2.0-2.99:	24%
SAT math:	480-590	Rank in top quarter:	56%
ACT composite:	24-27	Rank in top tenth:	35%
GPA 3.75 or higher:	31%	End year in good standing:	91%
GPA 3.50-3.74:	14%	Return as sophomores:	71%
GPA 3.0-3.49:	31%	Out-of-state:	43%
		Live on campus:	96%

Basis for selection. GED not accepted. School academic record primary. Test scores, recommendations, essay, character and extracurricular activities important. Interview is highly recommended. **Home schooled:** Statement describing home school structure and mission, transcript of courses and grades, interview, letter of recommendation (nonparent) required.

High school preparation. College-preparatory program recommended. 16 units required. Required and recommended units include English 4, mathematics 3, social studies 3, history 1, science 3 (laboratory 2), foreign language 2 and academic electives 2. 1 additional unit of foreign language recommended for foreign language, education, and international business majors.

2011-2012 Annual costs. Tuition/fees: $36,950. Room/board: $11,500. Books/supplies: $600. Personal expenses: $550.

2011-2012 Financial aid. Need-based: 289 full-time freshmen applied for aid; 272 were judged to have need; 272 of these received aid. Average need met was 80%. Average scholarship/grant was $25,933; average loan $3,218. 78% of total undergraduate aid awarded as scholarships/grants, 22% as loans/jobs. **Non-need-based:** Scholarships awarded for academics, leadership, ROTC, state residency. **Additional information:** Sibling Scholarship program provides 50% discounts on second immediate family member's room and board, regardless of need.

Application procedures. Admission: Priority date 2/1; deadline 3/15 (postmark date). $50 fee, may be waived for applicants with need. Admission notification on a rolling basis beginning on or about 10/1. Must reply by May 1 or within 2 week(s) if notified thereafter. **Financial aid:** Priority date 2/1; no closing date. FAFSA required. Applicants notified on a rolling basis starting 2/1; must reply by 5/1 or within 2 week(s) of notification.

Academics. Mandatory writing program for all freshmen. 7.5 credit internship/community service, often done during 6 week spring term, required of all students. International study emphasized. **Special study options:** Accelerated study, combined bachelor's/graduate degree, double major, ESL, independent study, internships, liberal arts/career combination, student-designed major, study abroad, teacher certification program. **Credit/placement by examination:** AP, CLEP, IB, SAT, institutional tests. 30 credit hours maximum toward bachelor's degree. **Support services:** Reduced course load, study skills assistance, tutoring, writing center.

Majors. Area/ethnic studies: American. **Biology:** General, biochemistry. **Business:** Accounting, business admin, international, managerial economics, marketing. **Conservation:** Environmental studies. **Education:** Art, biology, chemistry, elementary, English, foreign languages, French, history, mathematics, middle, multi-level teacher, science, secondary, social science, social studies, Spanish, speech, speech impaired. **English:** British lit, English lit. **Foreign languages:** General, classics, French, Spanish. **Health services:** Clinical lab science, nursing (RN), predental, premedicine, preveterinary, speech pathology. **History:** General. **Human services:** General. **Math:** General. **Philosophy/religion:** Philosophy, religion. **Physical sciences:** Chemistry. **Protective services:** Criminal justice. **Psychology:** General. **Social sciences:** General, anthropology, economics, international relations, political science, sociology. **Visual/performing arts:** Art, dramatic, music.

Most popular majors. Biology 9%, business/marketing 12%, education 16%, health sciences 11%, psychology 6%.

Computing on campus. 173 workstations in library, computer center. Dormitories wired for high-speed internet access and linked to campus network. Commuter students can connect to campus network. Online library, helpline, wireless network available.

Student life. Freshman orientation: Mandatory, $425 fee. Preregistration for classes offered. 2-day summer registration program for course registration, assessments, and get-acquainted activities. 4-day orientation program in the fall. **Housing:** Guaranteed on-campus for all undergraduates. Coed dorms, single-sex dorms, special housing for disabled, apartments, wellness housing available. Quiet floors. All undergraduates required to live in college housing unless living with family or over the age of 25. **Activities:** Concert band, campus ministries, choral groups, dance, drama, international student organizations, literary magazine, music ensembles, Model UN, musical theater, radio station, student government, student newspaper, More than 100 student interest groups including Christian Fellowship, Hillel, international student club, ski club, College Democrats, College Republicans, equestrian club, sports medicine club, Circle-K.

Athletics. NCAA. **Intercollegiate:** Basketball, cheerleading M, equestrian, field hockey W, golf, ice hockey, lacrosse, soccer, softball W, tennis, volleyball. **Intramural:** Badminton, basketball, bowling, equestrian, football (nontackle), handball, ice hockey, lacrosse M, racquetball, skiing, soccer, softball, squash, swimming, table tennis, volleyball. **Team name:** Soaring Eagles.

Student services. Alcohol/substance abuse counseling, chaplain/spiritual director, career counseling, student employment services, financial aid counseling, health services, personal counseling, placement for graduates, veterans' counselor, women's services. **Physically disabled:** Services for visually, speech, hearing impaired.

Contact. E-mail: admissions@elmira.edu
Phone: (607) 735-1724 Toll-free number: (800) 935-6472
Fax: (607) 735-1718
Brett Moore, Director of Admissions, Elmira College, One Park Place, Elmira, NY 14901

Eugene Lang College The New School for Liberal Arts
New York, New York
www.newschool.edu/lang/
CB member
CB code: 2521

- Private 4-year liberal arts college
- Commuter campus in very large city
- 1,472 degree-seeking undergraduates: 6% part-time, 67% women, 5% African American, 6% Asian American, 11% Hispanic American, 6% international
- 77% of applicants admitted
- Application essay required
- 48% graduate within 6 years

General. Founded in 1978. Regionally accredited. Students design academic programs with advisers. Students can select courses within The New School and Cooper Union. **Degrees:** 327 bachelor's awarded. **Location:** Located in Manhattan. **Calendar:** Semester, limited summer session. **Full-time faculty:** 70 total; 69% have terminal degrees, 20% minority, 54% women. **Part-time faculty:** 78 total; 1% have terminal degrees, 13% minority, 50% women. **Class size:** 89% < 20, 10% 20-39, less than 1% 40-49, less than 1% 50-99. **Special facilities:** Photography labs, screening rooms, art galleries, art and sound space, environment and design center, center for art and politics.

Freshman class profile. 1,515 applied, 1,167 admitted, 265 enrolled.

Mid 50% test scores			
SAT critical reading:	540-660	GPA 2.0-2.99:	12%
SAT math:	490-610	Rank in top quarter:	57%
SAT writing:	540-660	Rank in top tenth:	29%
ACT composite:	24-28	Return as sophomores:	73%
GPA 3.75 or higher:	21%	Out-of-state:	78%
GPA 3.50-3.74:	19%	Live on campus:	78%
GPA 3.0-3.49:	47%	International:	4%

Basis for selection. Success in college preparatory studies most important supplemented by writing ability, intellectual curiosity, interview. Extracurricular/community activities, evidence of special talents, recommendations important. Telephone interviews available to students who cannot travel to New York. Students have option of submitting graded academic paper in place of SAT/ACT scores, but if they opt to not, they are required to submit their SAT/ACT scores. Audition required for Jazz, BA/BFA; portfolio required for Art, BA/BFA.

High school preparation. College-preparatory program recommended. Recommended units include English 4, mathematics 4, social studies 4, history 4, science 4, foreign language 4 and academic electives 4.

2011-2012 Annual costs. Tuition/fees: $37,810. Room/board: $15,260. Books/supplies: $920. Personal expenses: $1,550.

2011-2012 Financial aid. Need-based: 141 full-time freshmen applied for aid; 128 were judged to have need; 124 of these received aid. Average need met was 62%. Average scholarship/grant was $23,787; average loan $6,070. 71% of total undergraduate aid awarded as scholarships/grants, 29% as loans/jobs. **Non-need-based:** Awarded to 96 full-time undergraduates, including 48 freshmen. Scholarships awarded for academics.

Application procedures. Admission: Closing date 1/6. $50 fee, may be waived for applicants with need. Admission notification by 4/1. Admission notification on a rolling basis. Must reply by May 1 or within 3 week(s) if notified thereafter. **Financial aid:** Priority date 3/1; no closing date. FAFSA required. Applicants notified on a rolling basis starting 4/1; must reply within 4 week(s) of notification.

Academics. Students map out individual program of study within 5 broad areas of concentration. Seminars rather than lecture classes. **Special study options:** Accelerated study, cross-registration, distance learning, double major, dual enrollment of high school students, exchange student, independent study, internships, liberal arts/career combination, student-designed major, study abroad, urban semester. Five-year combined BA/BFA. **Credit/placement by examination:** AP, CLEP, IB. **Support services:** Tutoring, writing center.

Majors. Education: General. **Foreign languages:** General, comparative lit. **History:** General. **Liberal arts:** Arts/sciences. **Philosophy/religion:** Judaic,

philosophy, religion. **Psychology:** General. **Social sciences:** General, economics, urban studies. **Visual/performing arts:** General.

Most popular majors. English 21%, history 6%, liberal arts 17%, psychology 8%, social sciences 18%, visual/performing arts 18%.

Computing on campus. Dormitories wired for high-speed internet access and linked to campus network. Commuter students can connect to campus network. Online course registration, online library, helpline, student web hosting, wireless network available.

Student life. Freshman orientation: Mandatory. Preregistration for classes offered. One week before classes begin. **Housing:** Guaranteed on-campus for all undergraduates. Coed dorms, special housing for disabled, apartments, wellness housing available. $250 nonrefundable deposit, deadline 7/1. **Activities:** Jazz band, choral groups, dance, drama, international student organizations, literary magazine, music ensembles, opera, radio station, student government, student newspaper, symphony orchestra, Sustainable Design Review, New School Styling Club, Roots & Shoots, Radical student union, Global Health student organization, international club, PHOTOfeast, the Theatre Collective, Jewish student union, New School Remnant Christian Fellowship.

Student services. Career counseling, student employment services, financial aid counseling, health services, minority student services, personal counseling.

Contact. E-mail: lang@newschool.edu
Phone: (212) 229-5665 Toll-free number: (877) 528-3321
Fax: (212) 229-5355
Karen Williams, Director of Admissions, Eugene Lang College The New School for Liberal Arts, 72 Fifth Avenue, New York, NY 10011

Excelsior College
Albany, New York
www.excelsior.edu
CB code: 0759

- Private 4-year virtual liberal arts college
- Commuter campus in small city
- 32,093 degree-seeking undergraduates

General. Founded in 1970. Regionally accredited. Nearly 30 percent of students are active duty or reserve military. **Degrees:** 2,677 bachelor's, 2,699 associate awarded; master's offered. **Calendar:** Differs by program, extensive summer session. **Full-time faculty:** 30 total. **Part-time faculty:** 500 total. **Class size:** 89% < 20, 11% 20-39.

Basis for selection. Open admission, but selective for some programs. Admission to associate degree nursing program limited to students with specified health care backgrounds. Admission to bachelor's degree and RN-to-MS in nursing degree programs require candidates to have current RN license. **Home schooled:** State high school equivalency certificate required.

2011-2012 Annual costs. Students charged $975 enrollment fee and $355 per credit hour. Because of nontraditional pricing, school does not charge set tuition based on 15 credit hours per semester.

Financial aid. All financial aid based on need. **Additional information:** Excelsior College is Title IV eligible for its degree programs, except for associate degree in nursing; approved for all veterans' education benefit programs.

Application procedures. Admission: No deadline. $80 fee. Admission notification on a rolling basis. **Financial aid:** Priority date 7/1; no closing date. FAFSA, institutional form required. Applicants notified on a rolling basis starting 8/1; must reply within 2 week(s) of notification.

Academics. Portfolio assessment option may be available in subject areas where proficiency or performance examinations unavailable. Online library provided in collaboration with Sheridan Libraries at Johns Hopkins University. **Special study options:** Combined bachelor's/graduate degree, distance learning, dual enrollment of high school students, external degree, independent study. Master of Arts in Liberal Studies students may design their thesis around career and/or personal interests. **Credit/placement by examination:** AP, CLEP, IB. Some degrees may be earned entirely by examination. **Support services:** Reduced course load, study skills assistance, tutoring, writing center.

Majors. Biology: General. **Business:** General, accounting, business admin, finance, hospitality admin, human resources, insurance, international, management information systems, marketing, operations. **Communications:** Communications/speech/rhetoric. **Computer sciences:** General, information systems, information technology. **English:** British lit. **Foreign languages:**

General. **Health services:** Health care admin, nursing (RN). **History:** General. **Liberal arts:** Arts/sciences. **Math:** General. **Philosophy/religion:** Philosophy. **Physical sciences:** Chemistry, geology, optics, physics. **Protective services:** Correctional facilities, homeland security, law enforcement admin, police science. **Psychology:** General. **Social sciences:** Economics, geography, political science, sociology. **Visual/performing arts:** Music.

Most popular majors. Business/marketing 9%, health sciences 6%, liberal arts 71%.

Computing on campus. PC or laptop required. Commuter students can connect to campus network. Online course registration, online library, helpline available.

Student life. Freshman orientation: Available. Preregistration for classes offered. Orientation conducted online for incoming students at all levels. **Activities:** Student newspaper.

Student services. Adult student services, career counseling, financial aid counseling, veterans' counselor.

Contact. E-mail: admissions@excelsior.edu
Phone: (518) 464-8500 Toll-free number: (888) 647-2388
Fax: (518) 464-8833
Roberto Figueroa, Director of Admissions, Excelsior College, 7 Columbia Circle, Albany, NY 12203-5159

Fashion Institute of Technology
New York, New York
www.fitnyc.edu
CB member
CB code: 2257

- Public 4-year visual arts and business college
- Commuter campus in very large city
- 8,014 degree-seeking undergraduates: 12% part-time, 85% women, 8% African American, 17% Asian American, 11% Hispanic American
- 191 degree-seeking graduate students
- 43% of applicants admitted
- Application essay required

General. Founded in 1944. Regionally accredited. SUNY institution. Specialized 2-year and 4-year programs provide professional preparation for fashion and design industries. **Degrees:** 1,396 bachelor's, 2,029 associate awarded; master's offered. **Calendar:** Semester, extensive summer session. **Full-time faculty:** 253 total; 53% women. **Part-time faculty:** 754 total; 53% women. **Class size:** 37% < 20, 63% 20-39. **Special facilities:** Textile and costume collection, fragrance laboratory, computer-aided design, textile, knitting, communications facility.

Freshman class profile. 4,417 applied, 1,916 admitted, 1,141 enrolled.

Basis for selection. Rank in class, portfolio, essay, community service, work experience, awards and honors considered. Portfolio required for art and design.

High school preparation. College-preparatory program recommended.

2011-2012 Annual costs. Tuition/fees: $4,469; $12,417 out-of-state. Room/board: $12,307. Books/supplies: $1,750. Personal expenses: $1,500.

Financial aid. All financial aid based on need.

Application procedures. Admission: Priority date 1/1; deadline 2/1. $50 fee, may be waived for applicants with need. Application must be submitted online. Admission notification by 4/1. Must reply by May 1 or within 3 week(s) if notified thereafter. **Financial aid:** Priority date 2/1; no closing date. FAFSA, institutional form required. Applicants notified on a rolling basis starting 4/15; must reply within 2 week(s) of notification.

Academics. Special study options: Distance learning, ESL, exchange student, honors, internships, study abroad. One-year programs, evening/weekend programs. **Credit/placement by examination:** AP, CLEP, IB, SAT, ACT, institutional tests. **Support services:** Learning center, remedial instruction, study skills assistance, tutoring, writing center.

Majors. Business: Fashion, international marketing, market research, special products marketing. **Communications:** Advertising. **Communications technology:** Animation/special effects. **Visual/performing arts:** Commercial photography, commercial/advertising art, fashion design, graphic design, illustration, industrial design, interior design, studio arts, studio arts management. **Work/family studies:** Clothing/textiles, textile manufacture.

Most popular majors. Business/marketing 36%, communications/journalism 15%, visual/performing arts 42%.

Computing on campus. 1,500 workstations in dormitories, library, computer center, student center. Dormitories wired for high-speed internet access and linked to campus network. Commuter students can connect to campus network. Online course registration, helpline, repair service, student web hosting, wireless network available.

Student life. Freshman orientation: Mandatory. Preregistration for classes offered. **Policies:** All clubs required to do community service. Student Government is part of the SUNY Student Assembly. **Housing:** Coed dorms, single-sex dorms, special housing for disabled, apartments, wellness housing available. **Activities:** Campus ministries, choral groups, drama, international student organizations, literary magazine, musical theater, radio station, student government, student newspaper, TV station, more than 70 groups and organizations available.

Athletics. NJCAA. **Intercollegiate:** Cheerleading M, cross-country, soccer W, swimming, table tennis, tennis W, track and field, volleyball W. **Team name:** Tigers.

Student services. Adult student services, alcohol/substance abuse counseling, chaplain/spiritual director, career counseling, services for economically disadvantaged, student employment services, financial aid counseling, health services, personal counseling, placement for graduates. **Physically disabled:** Services for visually, speech, hearing impaired.

Contact. E-mail: fitinfo@fitnyc.edu
Phone: (212) 217-3760 Fax: (212) 217-3761
Laura Arbogast, Director of Admissions and Strategic Recruitment, Fashion Institute of Technology, Seventh Avenue at 27th Street, New York, NY 10001-5992

Five Towns College
Dix Hills, New York
www.ftc.edu
CB code: 3142

- For-profit 4-year liberal arts and performing arts college
- Commuter campus in large town
- 987 degree-seeking undergraduates: 3% part-time, 34% women
- 48 degree-seeking graduate students
- 61% of applicants admitted
- SAT or ACT with writing, application essay required

General. Founded in 1972. Regionally accredited. **Degrees:** 160 bachelor's, 9 associate awarded; master's offered. **Location:** 40 miles from New York City. **Calendar:** Semester, limited summer session. **Full-time faculty:** 34 total. **Part-time faculty:** 179 total. **Class size:** 41% < 20, 50% 20-39, 6% 40-49, 2% 50-99. **Special facilities:** 72-channel recording studios with ProTools and surround sound, Korg MIDI technology studio with G-5 iMacs, AVID system, professional film/video arts studio with HD filming equipment and editing labs, theater technology labs.

Freshman class profile. 634 applied, 388 admitted, 232 enrolled.

Mid 50% test scores			
SAT critical reading:	400-510	GPA 3.0-3.49:	24%
SAT math:	380-500	GPA 2.0-2.99:	62%
SAT writing:	400-490	Rank in top quarter:	40%
ACT composite:	17-21	Rank in top tenth:	15%
GPA 3.75 or higher:	2%	End year in good standing:	85%
GPA 3.50-3.74:	4%	Out-of-state:	9%
		Live on campus:	20%

Basis for selection. Minimum 2.5 GPA required. Applicants for music and theater programs must pass audition and demonstrate competency in their field of study. SAT/ACT recommended but not required for transfer students. Audition required for music, theater, musical theater programs. Entrance exams and interviews required for some. **Home schooled:** Statement describing home school structure and mission, transcript of courses and grades, state high school equivalency certificate, interview, letter of recommendation (nonparent) required. **Learning Disabled:** Provide recent copy of individualized educational program and psychological report or 504 Plan.

High school preparation. 18 units recommended. Recommended units include English 4, mathematics 3, social studies 4, science 3 and foreign language 2. Music harmony and other applied music classes recommended for music students.

2011-2012 Annual costs. Tuition/fees: $19,570. Room/board: $12,960. Books/supplies: $1,000. Personal expenses: $3,200.

Financial aid. Non-need-based: Scholarships awarded for academics, music/drama.

Application procedures. Admission: No deadline. $35 fee, may be waived for applicants with need. Application must be submitted on paper.

Admission notification on a rolling basis beginning on or about 1/1. **Financial aid:** Priority date 3/31; no closing date. FAFSA, institutional form required. Applicants notified on a rolling basis; must reply within 4 week(s) of notification.

Academics. Number of credit hours required for students in major field of study varies by program. **Special study options:** Distance learning, independent study, internships, liberal arts/career combination, teacher certification program. **Credit/placement by examination:** AP, CLEP, institutional tests. **Support services:** Learning center, pre-admission summer program, reduced course load, tutoring.

Majors. Business: Business admin. **Communications:** Broadcast journalism, journalism, media studies, radio/TV. **Communications technology:** Recording arts. **Education:** Elementary, music. **Visual/performing arts:** Acting, cinematography, dramatic, film/cinema/video, jazz, music, music performance, music theory/composition, piano/keyboard, stringed instruments, voice/opera.

Most popular majors. Business/marketing 45%, education 15%, visual/performing arts 36%.

Computing on campus. 84 workstations in library, computer center, student center. Dormitories wired for high-speed internet access and linked to campus network. Commuter students can connect to campus network. Helpline, wireless network available.

Student life. Freshman orientation: Mandatory. Preregistration for classes offered. **Policies:** Freshmen not permitted cars on campus. **Housing:** Coed dorms, wellness housing available. $250 fully refundable deposit. **Activities:** Bands, choral groups, drama, music ensembles, musical theater, radio station, student government, student newspaper, symphony orchestra.

Student services. Alcohol/substance abuse counseling, career counseling, services for economically disadvantaged, student employment services, financial aid counseling, personal counseling.

Contact. E-mail: admissions@ftc.edu
Phone: (631) 656-2110 Fax: (631) 656-2172
Jerry Cohen, Dean of Enrollment, Five Towns College, 305 North Service Road, Dix Hills, NY 11746-6055

Fordham University
Bronx, New York
www.fordham.edu

CB member
CB code: 2259

- Private 4-year university affiliated with Roman Catholic Church
- Residential campus in very large city
- 8,328 degree-seeking undergraduates: 6% part-time, 53% women, 5% African American, 8% Asian American, 14% Hispanic American, 4% international
- 6,424 degree-seeking graduate students
- 42% of applicants admitted
- SAT or ACT (ACT writing optional), application essay required
- 81% graduate within 6 years

General. Founded in 1841. Regionally accredited. Rose Hill campus in Bronx, Lincoln Center campus in Manhattan. **Degrees:** 1,830 bachelor's awarded; master's, professional, doctoral offered. **ROTC:** Army, Naval, Air Force. **Calendar:** Semester, extensive summer session. **Full-time faculty:** 667 total; 96% have terminal degrees, 16% minority, 40% women. **Part-time faculty:** 736 total; 46% have terminal degrees, 13% minority, 47% women. **Class size:** 49% < 20, 48% 20-39, 1% 40-49, less than 1% 50-99, less than 1% >100. **Special facilities:** Calder environmental center, museum of Greek, Roman and Etruscan art.

Freshman class profile. 31,792 applied, 13,478 admitted, 1,986 enrolled.

Mid 50% test scores			
SAT critical reading:	570-670	GPA 3.0-3.49:	36%
SAT math:	580-670	GPA 2.0-2.99:	6%
SAT writing:	570-680	Rank in top quarter:	78%
ACT composite:	25-30	Rank in top tenth:	42%
GPA 3.75 or higher:	31%	Out-of-state:	60%
GPA 3.50-3.74:	27%	Live on campus:	74%
		International:	6%

Basis for selection. School achievement record most important, followed by test scores, class rank, extracurricular activities, recommendations, and essay. Personal characteristics, special talents, relationships to Fordham University also considered. SAT Subject Tests recommended. Audition required for dance and theater programs. **Home schooled:** Statement describing home school structure and mission, transcript of courses and grades required.

High school preparation. College-preparatory program required. 22 units required; 25 recommended. Required and recommended units include English 4, mathematics 3-4, social studies 2, history 2, science 3-4, foreign language 2-3 and academic electives 6.

2011-2012 Annual costs. Tuition/fees: $39,967. Room/board: $14,926.

2010-2011 Financial aid. Need-based: 1,693 full-time freshmen applied for aid; 1,250 were judged to have need; 1,248 of these received aid. Average need met was 78%. Average scholarship/grant was $19,234; average loan $4,907. 69% of total undergraduate aid awarded as scholarships/grants, 31% as loans/jobs. **Non-need-based:** Awarded to 3,769 full-time undergraduates, including 1,016 freshmen. Scholarships awarded for academics, athletics, ROTC.

Application procedures. Admission: Closing date 1/15 (postmark date). $70 fee, may be waived for applicants with need. Admission notification by 4/1. Must reply by 5/1. **Financial aid:** Closing date 2/1. FAFSA, CSS PROFILE required. Applicants notified by 4/1; must reply by 5/1 or within 2 week(s) of notification.

Academics. Special study options: Combined bachelor's/graduate degree, distance learning, double major, ESL, exchange student, honors, independent study, internships, student-designed major, study abroad, teacher certification program. Globe program in International Business. **Credit/placement by examination:** AP, CLEP, IB, institutional tests. Credit for CLEP examination only offered for School of Continuing and Professional Studies. **Support services:** Pre-admission summer program, tutoring, writing center.

Majors. Area/ethnic studies: African, African-American, American, Latin American, Near/Middle Eastern, Russian/Slavic, women's. **Biology:** General. **Business:** General, accounting, business admin, finance, international, management information systems, managerial economics, market research. **Communications:** General. **Computer sciences:** General. **Conservation:** Environmental science. **English:** English lit. **Foreign languages:** Ancient Greek, classics, comparative lit, French, German, Italian, Latin, modern Greek, Russian, Spanish. **Health services:** Predental, premedicine, prepharmacy, preveterinary. **History:** General. **Human services:** Social work. **Math:** General. **Philosophy/religion:** Philosophy, religion. **Physical sciences:** Chemistry, physics. **Psychology:** General. **Social sciences:** Anthropology, economics, political science, sociology, urban studies. **Visual/performing arts:** Art, art history/conservation, dance, dramatic, film/cinema/video, music, photography, studio arts, theater design.

Most popular majors. Business/marketing 29%, communications/journalism 13%, English 6%, psychology 7%, social sciences 19%.

Computing on campus. 900 workstations in dormitories, library, computer center. Dormitories wired for high-speed internet access and linked to campus network. Commuter students can connect to campus network. Online course registration, online library, helpline, repair service, wireless network available.

Student life. Freshman orientation: Mandatory, $325 fee. Preregistration for classes offered. Comprehensive academic and social orientation held 3 days prior to start of classes. **Housing:** Guaranteed on-campus for all undergraduates. Coed dorms, apartments, wellness housing available. $200 partly refundable deposit, deadline 5/1. Residential colleges. **Activities:** Bands, campus ministries, choral groups, dance, drama, film society, international student organizations, literary magazine, music ensembles, musical theater, radio station, student government, student newspaper, symphony orchestra, TV station, Ambassadors student tour guides, United student government, Mimes and Mummers, global outreach, Hip Hop coalition, Yoga and Mindfulness club, speech and debate, Molimo.

Athletics. NCAA. **Intercollegiate:** Baseball M, basketball, cross-country, diving, football (tackle) M, golf M, rowing (crew) W, soccer, softball W, squash M, swimming, tennis, track and field, volleyball W, water polo M. **Intramural:** Basketball, football (non-tackle), football (tackle), golf W, handball, racquetball, soccer, softball, swimming, tennis, triathlon, volleyball. **Team name:** Rams.

Student services. Adult student services, alcohol/substance abuse counseling, chaplain/spiritual director, career counseling, services for economically disadvantaged, student employment services, financial aid counseling, health services, minority student services, personal counseling, placement for graduates, veterans' counselor. **Physically disabled:** Services for visually, hearing impaired.

Contact. E-mail: enroll@fordham.edu
Phone: (718) 817-4000 Toll-free number: (800) 367-3426
Fax: (718) 367-9404
John Buckley, Associate Vice President of Enrollment, Fordham University, Office of Undergraduate Admission, Fordham University, Bronx, NY 10458-9993

Globe Institute of Technology
New York, New York
www.globe.edu

CB code: 3333

- For-profit 4-year university and business college
- Commuter campus in very large city
- 640 degree-seeking undergraduates

General. Regionally accredited. **Degrees:** 27 bachelor's, 79 associate awarded. **Calendar:** Trimester, extensive summer session. **Full-time faculty:** 12 total. **Part-time faculty:** 42 total. **Class size:** 55% < 20, 40% 20-39, 5% 40-49.

Basis for selection. Open admission, but selective for some programs. Special requirements for video game development program. Interviews strongly recommended. **Home schooled:** Transcript of courses and grades required. **Learning Disabled:** Student should meet with school psychologist to discuss needs.

2011-2012 Annual costs. Tuition/fees: $11,088. Books/supplies: $800. Personal expenses: $2,861.

Financial aid. **Non-need-based:** Scholarships awarded for academics, athletics.

Application procedures. **Admission:** No deadline. $50 fee, may be waived for applicants with need. Admission notification on a rolling basis. Housing deposit required 30 days before first day of the semester. **Financial aid:** No deadline. FAFSA, institutional form required. Applicants notified on a rolling basis.

Academics. **Special study options:** Combined bachelor's/graduate degree, distance learning, ESL, independent study, internships, liberal arts/career combination, weekend college. Video Game Development program admits only students in top 15% of graduating class and students with combined SAT score greater than 1950. **Credit/placement by examination:** AP, CLEP, institutional tests. 30 credit hours maximum toward associate degree, 60 toward bachelor's. **Support services:** Learning center, pre-admission summer program, reduced course load, remedial instruction, study skills assistance, tutoring, writing center.

Majors. **Business:** General, accounting, accounting technology, accounting/business management, accounting/finance, banking/financial services, business admin, customer service, finance, hospitality admin, hotel/motel admin, management information systems, nonprofit/public, office management, operations, resort management, restaurant/food services, small business admin, tourism/travel. **Computer sciences:** General, applications programming, artificial intelligence, computer graphics, computer science, database management, information technology, LAN/WAN management, networking, programming, security, system admin, systems analysis, vendor certification, web page design, webmaster. **Health services:** Facilities admin, health care admin, office admin.

Most popular majors. Business/marketing 60%, computer/information sciences 20%, health sciences 10%, legal studies 10%.

Computing on campus. 200 workstations in library, computer center, student center. Dormitories wired for high-speed internet access. Commuter students can connect to campus network. Online library, wireless network available.

Student life. **Freshman orientation:** Mandatory. Preregistration for classes offered. **Housing:** Apartments available. **Activities:** Choral groups, dance, student government, Women's Empowerment Group, Poetry Club, Caribbean Club.

Athletics. NJCAA. **Intercollegiate:** Baseball M, basketball, football (tackle) M, soccer, volleyball W. **Team name:** Knights.

Student services. Adult student services, career counseling, services for economically disadvantaged, student employment services, financial aid counseling, minority student services, placement for graduates, women's services.

Contact. E-mail: admissions@globe.edu
Phone: (212) 349-4330 Toll-free number: (877) 394-5623
Fax: (212) 302-9242
Michael Scalice, Admissions Director, Globe Institute of Technology, 500 Seventh Avenue, 2nd Floor, New York, NY 10018

Hamilton College
Clinton, New York
www.hamilton.edu

CB member
CB code: 2286

- Private 4-year liberal arts college
- Residential campus in rural community
- 1,843 degree-seeking undergraduates: 53% women, 4% African American, 6% Asian American, 6% Hispanic American, 5% international
- 27% of applicants admitted
- SAT and SAT Subject Tests or ACT (ACT writing optional), application essay required
- 89% graduate within 6 years; 17% enter graduate study

General. Founded in 1812. Regionally accredited. **Degrees:** 500 bachelor's awarded. **ROTC:** Army, Air Force. **Location:** 10 miles from Utica, 50 miles from Syracuse. **Calendar:** Semester. **Full-time faculty:** 183 total; 94% have terminal degrees, 18% minority, 42% women. **Part-time faculty:** 36 total; 44% have terminal degrees, 11% minority, 53% women. **Class size:** 74% < 20, 22% 20-39, 3% 40-49, less than 1% 50-99. **Special facilities:** Community garden, electron microscope, food coop, nature preserve, observatory, outdoor leadership center.

Freshman class profile. 5,265 applied, 1,441 admitted, 481 enrolled.

Mid 50% test scores			
SAT critical reading:	650-740	Rank in top tenth:	74%
SAT math:	660-730	Return as sophomores:	94%
SAT writing:	650-730	Out-of-state:	68%
ACT composite:	28-32	Live on campus:	100%
Rank in top quarter:	93%	International:	4%

Basis for selection. School achievement record, rank in high school class, school and community activities, application essay, recommendations important. Test scores and interview also considered. Some preference given to children of alumni. Special consideration given to students from minority groups, disadvantaged backgrounds, and certain geographic regions. There are a variety of ways to meet the standardized test requirement. They include: the SAT; OR the ACT; OR three exams, which must include a quantitative test, a verbal or writing test, and a third test of the student's choice. Acceptable quantitative tests: SAT Math, SAT Subject Tests in Math, Chemistry, or Physics; AP Computer Science, Chemistry, Economics, Math, or Physics; IB Chemistry, Computing Studies, Economics, Math, Physics, or Physical and Chemical Systems. Acceptable verbal/writing tests: SAT Critical Reading; SAT Writing; ACT Writing; AP English Language and Composition; IB Language (A1, A2, or B English); TOEFL exam (for International students ONLY). Interview strongly recommended for all; audition CD, videotape, or DVD recommended for music applicants; audition DVD recommended for theater and dance applicants; artist's statement and portfolio recommended for studio art applicants. **Home schooled:** Statement describing home school structure and mission required.

High school preparation. College-preparatory program recommended. 16 units recommended. Recommended units include English 4, mathematics 3, social studies 3, science 3 and foreign language 3.

2011-2012 Annual costs. Tuition/fees: $42,640. Room/board: $10,830. Books/supplies: $1,300. Personal expenses: $1,000.

2011-2012 Financial aid. All financial aid based on need. 257 full-time freshmen applied for aid; 227 were judged to have need; 227 of these received aid. Average need met was 100%. Average scholarship/grant was $33,695; average loan $3,056. 88% of total undergraduate aid awarded as scholarships/grants, 12% as loans/jobs.

Application procedures. **Admission:** Closing date 1/1 (postmark date). $60 fee, may be waived for applicants with need. Admission notification by 4/1. Must reply by 5/1. **Financial aid:** Closing date 2/8. FAFSA, institutional form, CSS PROFILE required. Applicants notified by 4/1; must reply by 5/1.

Academics. Sophomores may attain guaranteed early admission to a participating New York State medical school. Students may attain assurance of admission to Union Graduate College's Master of Arts in Teaching Program. May participate in Williams College Mystic Seaport Program. Students must complete senior program or project in their concentration. **Special study options:** Accelerated study, combined bachelor's/graduate degree, cross-registration, double major, ESL, independent study, internships, New York semester, student-designed major, study abroad, Washington semester. 3-2 program in engineering with Columbia University, Rensselaer Polytechnic Institute, Washington University (St. Louis); 3-3 program in law at Columbia University; New England Center for Children Cooperative Learning Program. **Credit/placement by examination:** AP, CLEP, IB, institutional tests. **Support services:** Learning center, pre-admission summer program, reduced course load, study skills assistance, tutoring, writing center.

Majors. Area/ethnic studies: African-American, American, Asian, German, Russian/Slavic, women's. **Biology:** General, biochemistry, neuroscience. **Communications:** General. **Computer sciences:** General. **Conservation:** Environmental studies. **English:** Creative writing, English lit. **Foreign languages:** General, Chinese, classics, comparative lit, French, Hispanic and Latin American. **History:** General. **Human services:** Public policy. **Math:** General. **Philosophy/religion:** Philosophy, religion. **Physical sciences:** Chemical physics, chemistry, geology, physics. **Psychology:** General. **Social sciences:** Anthropology, archaeology, economics, international relations, political science, sociology. **Visual/performing arts:** Art history/conservation, dance, dramatic, music, studio arts.

Most popular majors. Biology 8%, English 6%, foreign language 11%, mathematics 6%, psychology 6%, social sciences 28%, visual/performing arts 7%.

Computing on campus. 840 workstations in library, computer center, student center. Dormitories wired for high-speed internet access and linked to campus network. Commuter students can connect to campus network. Online course registration, online library, helpline, repair service, student web hosting, wireless network available.

Student life. Freshman orientation: Mandatory. Preregistration for classes offered. One week prior to start of classes. Pre-orientation programs include Urban Service Experience and Adirondack Adventure programs. **Policies:** Honor code covers all examinations, papers, research, and use of library. Statement of Community promotes engagement in dialogue to create mutual understanding and expanded knowledge. Freshmen not permitted cars on campus. **Housing:** Guaranteed on-campus for all undergraduates. Coed dorms, special housing for disabled, apartments, cooperative housing, wellness housing available. Special interest housing available including language houses and international house, quiet areas. **Activities:** Bands, campus ministries, choral groups, dance, drama, film society, international student organizations, literary magazine, music ensembles, Model UN, musical theater, radio station, student government, student newspaper, symphony orchestra, Christian fellowship, Newman council, Hillel, Muslim students association, black and Latino student union, Amnesty International, South Asian students association, Womyn's center, environmental action group.

Athletics. NCAA. **Intercollegiate:** Baseball M, basketball, cross-country, diving, field hockey W, football (tackle) M, golf M, ice hockey, lacrosse, rowing (crew), soccer, softball W, squash, swimming, tennis, track and field, volleyball W. **Intramural:** Badminton, basketball, football (non-tackle), golf, ice hockey, racquetball, skiing, soccer, softball, squash, tennis, volleyball, water polo. **Team name:** Continentals.

Student services. Adult student services, alcohol/substance abuse counseling, chaplain/spiritual director, career counseling, student employment services, financial aid counseling, health services, minority student services, on-campus daycare, personal counseling, placement for graduates, women's services. **Physically disabled:** Services for visually, speech, hearing impaired.

Contact. E-mail: admission@hamilton.edu
Phone: (315) 859-4421 Toll-free number: (800) 843-2655
Fax: (315) 859-4457
Monica Inzer, Vice President and Dean of Admission and Financial Aid, Hamilton College, 198 College Hill Road, Clinton, NY 13323-1293

Hartwick College
Oneonta, New York
www.hartwick.edu

CB member
CB code: 2288

- Private 4-year liberal arts college
- Residential campus in large town
- 1,560 degree-seeking undergraduates: 3% part-time, 59% women, 5% African American, 2% Asian American, 6% Hispanic American, 2% international
- 77% of applicants admitted
- 55% graduate within 6 years; 9% enter graduate study

General. Founded in 1797. Regionally accredited. Additional campus for recreation, research, student residences. **Degrees:** 314 bachelor's awarded. **Location:** 68 miles from Binghamton, 75 miles from Albany. **Calendar:** 4-1-4, limited summer session. **Full-time faculty:** 105 total; 75% have terminal degrees, 6% minority, 42% women. **Part-time faculty:** 94 total; 15% have terminal degrees, 11% minority, 63% women. **Class size:** 62% < 20, 35% 20-39, 2% 40-49, less than 1% 50-99. **Special facilities:** Environmental field station, museum, Native American artifact and library collections, tissue culture laboratory, electron microscope, 16-inch telescope and observatory, nuclear magnetic resonance spectrometer, fine and performing arts center.

Freshman class profile. 4,897 applied, 3,774 admitted, 489 enrolled.

Mid 50% test scores			
SAT critical reading:	510-610	Rank in top quarter:	54%
SAT math:	510-610	Rank in top tenth:	22%
SAT writing:	490-590	Return as sophomores:	77%
ACT composite:	23-27	Out-of-state:	26%
GPA 3.75 or higher:	6%	Live on campus:	99%
GPA 3.50-3.74:	30%	International:	2%
GPA 3.0-3.49:	35%	Fraternities:	3%
GPA 2.0-2.99:	29%	Sororities:	5%

Basis for selection. School achievement record, class rank, personal qualities, extracurricular activities, and recommendations considered. Test scores optional except for students applying to nursing program. SAT/ACT score submission not required for admission except for nursing majors and home-schooled candidates. Audition required for music program; portfolio recommended for art program. **Home schooled:** Transcript of courses and grades, letter of recommendation (nonparent) required. Must meet all stated application requirements and submit SAT or ACT test score. At least 3 SAT Subject Tests strongly recommended. Transcripts should be submitted with course description and/or syllabi.

High school preparation. College-preparatory program recommended. 19 units recommended. Recommended units include English 4, mathematics 3, social studies 2, history 2, science 3 (laboratory 2) and foreign language 3.

2011-2012 Annual costs. Tuition/fees: $36,440. Reported mandatory fees include $400 matriculation fee for new students. Room/board: $9,625. Books/supplies: $1,100. Personal expenses: $400.

Financial aid. Non-need-based: Scholarships awarded for academics, alumni affiliation, art, athletics, music/drama.

Application procedures. Admission: No deadline. Admission notification on a rolling basis beginning on or about 10/1. Must reply by May 1 or within 2 week(s) if notified thereafter. **Financial aid:** Priority date 2/15; no closing date. FAFSA required. Applicants notified on a rolling basis starting 1/15; must reply by 5/1 or within 2 week(s) of notification.

Academics. Curriculum includes first-year seminar, core requirements and contemporary issues seminar. Senior thesis required. **Special study options:** Accelerated study, combined bachelor's/graduate degree, cross-registration, double major, exchange student, honors, independent study, internships, semester at sea, student-designed major, study abroad, teacher certification program, urban semester, Washington semester. Off-campus January term changes yearly but has included programs in England, France, Ghana, Madagascar, South Africa; Philadelphia Urban Semester; Boston Semester; Outward Bound, NOLS programs; cooperative program in law with Albany Law School; 3-2 engineering with Clarkson University, Columbia University; 3-year accelerated bachelor's degree. **Credit/placement by examination:** AP, CLEP, IB, institutional tests. **Support services:** Pre-admission summer program, reduced course load, study skills assistance, tutoring, writing center.

Majors. Biology: General, biochemistry. **Business:** Accounting, business admin. **Computer sciences:** General, information systems. **Education:** Music. **English:** English lit. **Foreign languages:** French, German, Spanish. **Health services:** Clinical lab science, nursing (RN). **History:** General. **Liberal arts:** Arts/sciences. **Math:** General. **Philosophy/religion:** Philosophy, religion. **Physical sciences:** Chemistry, geology, physics. **Psychology:** General. **Social sciences:** Anthropology, economics, political science, sociology. **Visual/performing arts:** Art, art history/conservation, dramatic, music.

Most popular majors. Biology 7%, business/marketing 19%, English 8%, health sciences 11%, psychology 6%, social sciences 19%, visual/performing arts 11%.

Computing on campus. 56 workstations in library, computer center. Dormitories wired for high-speed internet access and linked to campus network. Commuter students can connect to campus network. Online course registration, online library, helpline, repair service, student web hosting, wireless network available.

Student life. Freshman orientation: Mandatory. Preregistration for classes offered. Summer registration/parent orientation and 4-day pre-semester in-residence program. **Housing:** Guaranteed on-campus for freshmen. Coed dorms, single-sex dorms, special housing for disabled, apartments, fraternity/sorority housing available. Housing at environmental campus available. **Activities:** Bands, campus ministries, choral groups, dance, drama, literary magazine, music ensembles, musical theater, radio station, student government, student newspaper, 66 academic and social organizations available.

Athletics. NCAA. **Intercollegiate:** Basketball, cheerleading M, cross-country, diving, equestrian W, field hockey W, football (tackle) M, lacrosse, soccer, swimming, tennis, volleyball W, water polo W. **Intramural:** Basketball, football (non-tackle), racquetball, soccer, volleyball. **Team name:** Hawks.

Student services. Alcohol/substance abuse counseling, career counseling, financial aid counseling, health services, personal counseling, placement for graduates. **Physically disabled:** Services for visually impaired.

Contact. E-mail: admissions@hartwick.edu
Phone: (607) 431-4150 Toll-free number: (888) 427-8942
Fax: (607) 431-4154
David Conway, VP Enrollment Management & Marketing, Hartwick College, Box 4022, Oneonta, NY 13820-4022

Hilbert College
Hamburg, New York
www.hilbert.edu   **CB code: 2334**

- Private 4-year liberal arts college affiliated with Roman Catholic Church
- Commuter campus in small city
- 1,051 degree-seeking undergraduates: 13% part-time, 58% women, 10% African American, 3% Hispanic American, 1% Native American
- 28 degree-seeking graduate students
- 69% of applicants admitted
- 43% graduate within 6 years

General. Founded in 1957. Regionally accredited. Affiliated with Franciscan Sisters of St. Joseph. Legal assistant program approved by American Bar Association. New for Fall 2012, accelerated BS degree programs offered in the evening: Organization Development; Conflict Studies and Dispute Resolution. Must have 50-60 credits transfered in to be eligible for these new accelerated degree completion programs. **Degrees:** 161 bachelor's, 23 associate awarded; master's offered. **ROTC:** Army. **Location:** 10 miles from Buffalo. **Calendar:** Semester, limited summer session. **Full-time faculty:** 46 total; 46% have terminal degrees, 4% minority, 50% women. **Part-time faculty:** 80 total; 19% have terminal degrees, 1% minority, 38% women. **Class size:** 74% < 20, 25% 20-39, less than 1% 40-49, less than 1% 50-99. **Special facilities:** Comprehensive law library.

Freshman class profile. 1,124 applied, 777 admitted, 227 enrolled.

Mid 50% test scores			
SAT critical reading:	390-500	GPA 2.0-2.99:	1%
SAT math:	410-510	Rank in top quarter:	19%
ACT composite:	18-23	Rank in top tenth:	4%
GPA 3.75 or higher:	4%	End year in good standing:	68%
GPA 3.50-3.74:	24%	Return as sophomores:	68%
GPA 3.0-3.49:	71%	Out-of-state:	4%
		Live on campus:	44%

Basis for selection. School achievement record and course selection important. Candidates must meet minimum academic criteria including high school GPA. SAT or ACT recommended. Essay, interview recommended. **Home schooled:** Transcript of courses and grades, state high school equivalency certificate required. **Learning Disabled:** Separate statement directly to academic services required.

High school preparation. College-preparatory program recommended. 16 units required; 21 recommended. Required and recommended units include English 4, mathematics 3-4, social studies 3-4, science 2-3 (laboratory 1-2) and foreign language 1-2.

2011-2012 Annual costs. Tuition/fees: $18,900. Room/board: $7,910. Books/supplies: $750. Personal expenses: $800.

2011-2012 Financial aid. Need-based: 215 full-time freshmen applied for aid; 198 were judged to have need; 198 of these received aid. Average need met was 68%. Average scholarship/grant was $10,155; average loan $3,754. 56% of total undergraduate aid awarded as scholarships/grants, 44% as loans/jobs. **Non-need-based:** Awarded to 108 full-time undergraduates, including 26 freshmen. Scholarships awarded for academics, alumni affiliation, leadership, minority status, state residency.

Application procedures. Admission: Priority date 6/30; deadline 8/15 (receipt date). $20 fee, may be waived for applicants with need. Admission notification by 8/15. Admission notification on a rolling basis beginning on or about 10/1. **Financial aid:** Priority date 3/1; no closing date. FAFSA required. Applicants notified on a rolling basis starting 3/1; must reply within 2 week(s) of notification.

Academics. Special study options: Combined bachelor's/graduate degree, cooperative education, cross-registration, distance learning, dual enrollment of high school students, honors, independent study, internships, liberal arts/career combination, study abroad, Washington semester. Member of Western New York consortium. **Credit/placement by examination:** AP, CLEP, IB, SAT, institutional tests. 18 credit hours maximum toward associate degree, 32 toward bachelor's. **Support services:** Learning center, pre-admission summer

program, reduced course load, remedial instruction, study skills assistance, tutoring, writing center.

Majors. Business: Accounting, business admin. **Communications:** Digital media. **Communications technology:** Photo/film/video. **English:** English lit. **Liberal arts:** Arts/sciences. **Protective services:** Criminal justice, forensics, police science. **Psychology:** General. **Social sciences:** Political science.

Most popular majors. Business/marketing 44%, communications/journalism 7%, legal studies 20%, security/protective services 46%.

Computing on campus. 146 workstations in dormitories, library, computer center, student center. Dormitories wired for high-speed internet access. Commuter students can connect to campus network. Online course registration, online library, helpline, wireless network available.

Student life. Freshman orientation: Mandatory, $25 fee. Preregistration for classes offered. 1-day programs held in June, July or August. **Housing:** Coed dorms, apartments available. $50 nonrefundable deposit, deadline 8/1. **Activities:** Campus ministries, choral groups, drama, literary magazine, student government, student newspaper, SADD, Human Service Association, Psychology Club, Great Expectations, Criminal Justice Club, Students in Free Enterprise, Common Grounds, Economic Crime Investigation Club.

Athletics. NCAA. **Intercollegiate:** Baseball M, basketball, cross-country, golf, lacrosse M, soccer, softball W, volleyball. **Intramural:** Basketball, football (non-tackle), soccer, softball, table tennis, volleyball. **Team name:** Hawks.

Student services. Adult student services, alcohol/substance abuse counseling, chaplain/spiritual director, career counseling, student employment services, financial aid counseling, health services, minority student services, personal counseling, placement for graduates, veterans' counselor. **Physically disabled:** Services for visually, hearing impaired.

Contact. E-mail: admissions@hilbert.edu
Phone: (716) 649-7900 ext. 211 Toll-free number: (800) 649-8003
Fax: (716) 649-1152
Timothy Lee, Director of Admissions, Hilbert College, 5200 South Park Avenue, Hamburg, NY 14075-1597

Hobart and William Smith Colleges
Geneva, New York
www.hws.edu   **CB member**
                                                        CB code: 2294

- Private 4-year liberal arts college
- Residential campus in large town
- 2,212 degree-seeking undergraduates: 56% women, 5% African American, 3% Asian American, 5% Hispanic American, 1% Native American, 4% international
- 8 degree-seeking graduate students
- 60% of applicants admitted
- Application essay required
- 75% graduate within 6 years

General. Founded in 1822. Regionally accredited. Hobart and William Smith are coordinate colleges. All classes coeducational with one faculty, one President, one Board of Trustees, and one campus, but with separate deans, student governments, and athletic departments. **Degrees:** 502 bachelor's awarded; master's offered. **Location:** 50 miles from Syracuse, 40 miles from Rochester. **Calendar:** Semester. **Full-time faculty:** 191 total; 97% have terminal degrees, 16% minority, 43% women. **Part-time faculty:** 23 total; 83% have terminal degrees, 13% minority, 56% women. **Class size:** 66% < 20, 33% 20-39, 1% 40-49. **Special facilities:** 70-foot research vessel, 100-acre nature preserve, Finger Lakes Institute, Center for Teaching and Learning.

Freshman class profile. 4,454 applied, 2,656 admitted, 683 enrolled.

Mid 50% test scores			
SAT critical reading:	560-650	GPA 2.0-2.99:	21%
SAT math:	570-650	Rank in top quarter:	72%
ACT composite:	26-29	Rank in top tenth:	35%
GPA 3.75 or higher:	30%	Return as sophomores:	87%
GPA 3.50-3.74:	18%	Out-of-state:	59%
GPA 3.0-3.49:	30%	Live on campus:	99%
		International:	4%

Basis for selection. High school record, school and community activities, recommendations, interview and talents all considered as part of the admissions decision. Economically and educationally disadvantaged NY state residents may apply through the Higher Education Opportunity Program. Standardized tests only required for those applying for the Trustee or Blackwell scholarships, those who come from a high school without a traditionally

graded transcript, or those for whom English is not a first language (TOEFL exam is acceptable for non-native English speakers). Interview strongly encouraged for all and required for trustee scholar applicants. Candidates for arts scholars program must submit portfolio. **Home schooled:** Students without a traditional, graded transcript must submit standardized test scores.

High school preparation. College-preparatory program required. 18 units required. Required and recommended units include English 4, mathematics 3, social studies 2-3, science 3 (laboratory 2), foreign language 2-3 and academic electives 2-4. Mathematics must include algebra, geometry, and trigonometry sequence.

2011-2012 Annual costs. Tuition/fees: $42,915. Room/board: $10,852. Books/supplies: $1,300. Personal expenses: $600.

2010-2011 Financial aid. Need-based: 449 full-time freshmen applied for aid; 368 were judged to have need; 364 of these received aid. Average need met was 79%. Average scholarship/grant was $25,868; average loan $3,444. 79% of total undergraduate aid awarded as scholarships/grants, 21% as loans/jobs. **Non-need-based:** Awarded to 567 full-time undergraduates, including 175 freshmen. Scholarships awarded for academics, art, leadership, music/drama.

Application procedures. Admission: Closing date 2/1 (postmark date). $45 fee, may be waived for applicants with need, free for online applicants. Admission notification by 4/1. Must reply by 5/1. **Financial aid:** Closing date 2/15. FAFSA, CSS PROFILE required. Applicants notified by 4/1; must reply by 5/1 or within 2 week(s) of notification.

Academics. All students must complete a major and a minor or a second major, 1 of which must be interdisciplinary. **Special study options:** Combined bachelor's/graduate degree, double major, ESL, honors, independent study, internships, liberal arts/career combination, student-designed major, study abroad, teacher certification program, Washington semester. **Credit/placement by examination:** AP, CLEP, IB, institutional tests. Credit by examination counted toward degree limited to equivalent of 7 courses. **Support services:** Learning center, pre-admission summer program, reduced course load, remedial instruction, study skills assistance, tutoring, writing center.

Majors. Architecture: Architecture. **Area/ethnic studies:** African, African-American, American, Asian, Chicano/Hispanic-American/Latino, European, gay/lesbian, Latin American, Russian/Slavic, women's. **Biology:** General, biochemistry. **Communications:** Media studies. **Computer sciences:** General, computer science. **Conservation:** Environmental studies. **English:** English lit. **Foreign languages:** Chinese, classics, comparative lit, French, Japanese, Latin, Russian, Spanish. **Health services:** Predental, premedicine, preveterinary. **History:** General. **Human services:** Public policy. **Math:** General. **Philosophy/religion:** Philosophy, religion. **Physical sciences:** Chemistry, geology, physics. **Psychology:** General. **Social sciences:** Anthropology, economics, international relations, political science, sociology, urban studies. **Visual/performing arts:** Art history/conservation, dance, dramatic, music, studio arts.

Most popular majors. Area/ethnic studies 9%, biology 6%, communications/journalism 7%, liberal arts 6%, natural resources/environmental science 7%, psychology 8%, social sciences 22%, visual/performing arts 6%.

Computing on campus. 150 workstations in dormitories, library, computer center, student center. Dormitories wired for high-speed internet access and linked to campus network. Commuter students can connect to campus network. Online course registration, online library, helpline, repair service, student web hosting, wireless network available.

Student life. Freshman orientation: Mandatory. Preregistration for classes offered. 3-day program in late August with optional pre-orientation adventure program. **Housing:** Guaranteed on-campus for all undergraduates. Coed dorms, single-sex dorms, special housing for disabled, apartments, cooperative housing, fraternity/sorority housing, wellness housing available. **Activities:** Bands, campus ministries, choral groups, dance, drama, film society, international student organizations, literary magazine, music ensembles, musical theater, radio station, student government, student newspaper, symphony orchestra, international students club, black student union, PRIDE Alliance, Hillel, Geneva Heroes (service), College Republicans, College Democrats, Caribbean student association, Latin American organization.

Athletics. NCAA. **Intercollegiate:** Basketball, cross-country, diving W, field hockey W, football (tackle) M, golf, ice hockey M, lacrosse, rowing (crew), sailing, soccer, squash, swimming W, tennis. **Intramural:** Badminton, basketball, bowling, cross-country, football (non-tackle), golf, ice hockey, lacrosse, racquetball, skiing, soccer, softball, squash, swimming, table tennis, tennis, track and field, volleyball, water polo. **Team name:** Statesmen (Hobart); Herons (William Smith).

Student services. Alcohol/substance abuse counseling, chaplain/spiritual director, career counseling, services for economically disadvantaged, student employment services, financial aid counseling, health services, minority student services, personal counseling, placement for graduates, veterans' counselor, women's services. **Physically disabled:** Services for visually, speech, hearing impaired.

Contact. E-mail: admissions@hws.edu
Phone: (315) 781-3622 Toll-free number: (800) 852-2256
Fax: (315) 781-3914
John Young, Director of Admissions, Hobart and William Smith Colleges, 629 South Main Street, Geneva, NY 14456

Hofstra University
Hempstead, New York
www.hofstra.edu

CB member
CB code: 2295

- Private 4-year university
- Residential campus in large city
- 7,059 degree-seeking undergraduates: 6% part-time, 53% women, 9% African American, 6% Asian American, 11% Hispanic American, 2% international
- 4,063 degree-seeking graduate students
- 59% of applicants admitted
- Application essay required
- 58% graduate within 6 years; 27% enter graduate study

General. Founded in 1935. Regionally accredited. 100% wireless campus. **Degrees:** 1,855 bachelor's awarded; master's, professional, doctoral offered. **ROTC:** Army. **Location:** 25 miles from New York City. **Calendar:** 4-1-4, extensive summer session. **Full-time faculty:** 525 total; 92% have terminal degrees, 19% minority, 42% women. **Part-time faculty:** 589 total; 42% have terminal degrees, 15% minority, 45% women. **Class size:** 51% < 20, 42% 20-39, 3% 40-49, 4% 50-99, less than 1% >100. **Special facilities:** Financial trading room, multi-media converged newsroom, comprehensive media production facility, digital language lab, technology, science and engineering labs, rooftop observatory, 6 theaters including black box teaching theater, cultural center, museum, arboretum, bird sanctuary.

Freshman class profile. 21,376 applied, 12,576 admitted, 1,675 enrolled.

Mid 50% test scores			
SAT critical reading:	530-620	Rank in top quarter:	56%
SAT math:	550-630	Rank in top tenth:	25%
ACT composite:	23-27	End year in good standing:	90%
GPA 3.75 or higher:	33%	Return as sophomores:	80%
GPA 3.50-3.74:	18%	Out-of-state:	43%
GPA 3.0-3.49:	31%	Live on campus:	72%
GPA 2.0-2.99:	18%	International:	2%

Basis for selection. Holistic review of each applicant. Secondary school record, standardized test scores, personal essay, letters of recommendation most important. SAT Subject Tests recommended. No deadline (rolling) for SAT or ACT test scores. Standardized tests not required for admission to New Opportunities at Hofstra (NOAH), School of University Studies, Program for Academic Learning Skills (PALS), or for international applicants (TOEFL is required). Interview required for NOAH (Hofstra HEOP program), School for University Studies and Program for Academic Learning Skills applicants. Audition recommended for music, theater programs; portfolio recommended for fine arts program. **Home schooled:** Statement describing home school structure and mission, transcript of courses and grades, state high school equivalency certificate required. Must provide at least 2 recommendations, including 1 from primary instructor or person who has primary responsibility for assessing applicant's academic performance. School required to certify completion of secondary school for all enrolled students prior to graduation. **Learning Disabled:** Students may apply to the Program for Academic Learning Skills. Application includes copy of psychological testing, WAISR.

High school preparation. College-preparatory program required. 16 units required. Required and recommended units include English 4, mathematics 3-4, social studies 3-4, science 3-4 (laboratory 1-2) and foreign language 2-3. Social studies includes history; 4 math, 1 chemistry, and 1 physics required for engineering.

2011-2012 Annual costs. Tuition/fees: $34,150. Room/board: $11,940. Books/supplies: $1,000. Personal expenses: $1,500.

2010-2011 Financial aid. Need-based: 1,234 full-time freshmen applied for aid; 1,010 were judged to have need; 1,001 of these received aid. Average need met was 64%. Average scholarship/grant was $15,570; average loan $3,452. 54% of total undergraduate aid awarded as scholarships/grants, 46% as loans/jobs. **Non-need-based:** Awarded to 1,782 full-time undergraduates, including 429 freshmen. Scholarships awarded for academics, alumni affiliation, art, athletics, leadership, music/drama, ROTC, state residency.

Application procedures. Admission: No deadline. $70 fee, may be waived for applicants with need. Admission notification on a rolling basis beginning on or about 2/1. Must reply by May 1 or within 2 week(s) if notified thereafter. Notification of Early Action I begins December 15, notification for Early Action II begins January 15. **Financial aid:** Priority date 2/15; no closing date. FAFSA required. Applicants notified on a rolling basis starting 3/1; must reply by 5/1 or within 2 week(s) of notification.

Academics. Special study options: Accelerated study, combined bachelor's/graduate degree, cross-registration, distance learning, double major, dual enrollment of high school students, ESL, external degree, honors, independent study, internships, liberal arts/career combination, student-designed major, study abroad, teacher certification program, Washington semester. **Credit/placement by examination:** AP, CLEP, IB, institutional tests. 30 credit hours maximum toward bachelor's degree. **Support services:** Learning center, pre-admission summer program, reduced course load, study skills assistance, tutoring, writing center.

Honors college/program. Typically only the top 10% of admits offered invitation. During first year, students enroll in small multidisciplinary courses. After first year, students choose from wide range of honors-level courses in all academic areas of study.

Majors. Area/ethnic studies: African, American, Asian, Caribbean, Chicano/Hispanic-American/Latino, Latin American, women's. **Biology:** General, biochemistry. **Business:** General, accounting, business admin, entrepreneurial studies, finance, international, labor studies, logistics, management information systems, managerial economics, marketing. **Communications:** Communications/speech/rhetoric, journalism, media studies, public relations, radio/TV. **Computer sciences:** Computer science. **Conservation:** Environmental studies. **Education:** Art, biology, business, chemistry, early childhood, elementary, English, foreign languages, French, German, health, mathematics, multi-level teacher, music, physical, physics, science, secondary, social studies, Spanish. **Engineering:** Biomedical, civil, computer, electrical, engineering science, environmental, industrial, manufacturing, mechanical. **English:** British lit, creative writing, English lit. **Foreign languages:** Chinese, classics, comparative lit, French, German, Hebrew, Italian, Latin, linguistics, Russian, Spanish. **Health services:** Athletic training, audiology/speech pathology, community health, physician assistant, predental, premedicine, preveterinary. **History:** General. **Liberal arts:** Arts/sciences. **Math:** General, applied. **Philosophy/religion:** Judaic, philosophy, religion. **Physical sciences:** Chemistry, geology, physics. **Protective services:** Forensics. **Psychology:** General. **Social sciences:** Anthropology, criminology, econometrics, economics, geography, political science, sociology. **Visual/performing arts:** Acting, art history/conservation, ceramics, dance, directing/producing, dramatic, jazz, metal/jewelry, music, music history, music management, music performance, music theory/composition, painting, photography, studio arts.

Most popular majors. Business/marketing 30%, communications/journalism 16%, education 8%, psychology 8%, social sciences 8%.

Computing on campus. 1,628 workstations in dormitories, library, computer center. Dormitories wired for high-speed internet access and linked to campus network. Commuter students can connect to campus network. Online course registration, online library, helpline, repair service, student web hosting, wireless network available.

Student life. Freshman orientation: Mandatory, $250 fee. Preregistration for classes offered. Several orientation programs. Summer orientation is a 3-day/2-night program in which new students live on campus and begin preparation for the fall semester. The program extends into the entire first year beginning with the full array of programs five days prior to the start of classes and then throughout the year with programs and events designed to acclimate students to student life. **Housing:** Guaranteed on-campus for all undergraduates. Coed dorms, special housing for disabled, apartments, wellness housing available. $300 nonrefundable deposit, deadline 5/1. Honors housing, living-learning community, quiet floors, women's floors. **Activities:** Bands, campus ministries, choral groups, dance, drama, film society, international student organizations, literary magazine, music ensembles, Model UN, musical theater, opera, radio station, student government, student newspaper, symphony orchestra, TV station, African Caribbean society, black student union, College Republicans, Entertainment Unlimited, Hillel, Hofstra Organization of Latin Americans, Hofstra Pride Network, Muslim student association, Progressive students union, Women of Action.

Athletics. NCAA. **Intercollegiate:** Baseball M, basketball, cross-country, field hockey W, golf, lacrosse, soccer, softball W, tennis, volleyball W, wrestling M. **Intramural:** Badminton, basketball, football (non-tackle), soccer, softball, table tennis, tennis, volleyball. **Team name:** Pride.

Student services. Adult student services, alcohol/substance abuse counseling, chaplain/spiritual director, career counseling, student employment services, financial aid counseling, health services, minority student services, on-campus daycare, personal counseling, placement for graduates, veterans' counselor. **Physically disabled:** Services for visually, speech, hearing impaired.

Contact. E-mail: admission@hofstra.edu
Phone: (516) 463-6700 Toll-free number: (800) 463-7872
Fax: (516) 463-5100
Sunil Samuel, Director of Admission, Hofstra University, Admissions Center, 100 Hofstra University, Hempstead, NY 11549

Holy Trinity Orthodox Seminary
Jordanville, New York
www.hts.edu   CB code: 2298

- Private 5-year seminary college for men affiliated with Russian Orthodox Church
- Residential campus in rural community
- 13 degree-seeking undergraduates
- 100% of applicants admitted
- Application essay required

General. Founded in 1948. Regionally accredited. **Degrees:** 7 bachelor's awarded. **Location:** 20 miles from Utica. **Calendar:** Semester, limited summer session. **Full-time faculty:** 14 total; 14% have terminal degrees, 7% women. **Part-time faculty:** 6 total. **Class size:** 100% < 20. **Special facilities:** Museum of Russian history, archives, icon painting studio.

Freshman class profile. 7 applied, 7 admitted, 7 enrolled.

Out-of-state: 50%   **Live on campus:**   100%

Basis for selection. Orthodoxy/Orthodox baptism, entrance exam required. Recommendation from spiritual father or parish priest necessary. **Home schooled:** Transcript of courses and grades, letter of recommendation (nonparent) required.

High school preparation. College-preparatory program required.

2012-2013 Annual costs. Tuition/fees: $3,000. Room/board: $2,500. Books/supplies: $200.

Financial aid. Additional information: Work-study program can reasonably pay for room and board over course of academic year.

Application procedures. Admission: Closing date 5/1 (postmark date). No application fee.

Academics. Special study options: Distance learning, ESL. **Credit/placement by examination:** AP, CLEP, institutional tests. **Support services:** Remedial instruction, tutoring.

Majors. Theology: Theology.

Computing on campus. 8 workstations in dormitories, library. Dormitories wired for high-speed internet access.

Student life. Freshman orientation: Mandatory. Preregistration for classes offered. **Policies:** Closed campus. Religious observance required. **Housing:** Guaranteed on-campus for all undergraduates. Wellness housing available. **Activities:** Choral groups, student newspaper.

Student services. Chaplain/spiritual director.

Contact. E-mail: info@hts.edu
Phone: (315) 858-0945 Fax: (315) 858-0945
V. Rev. Luke Murianka, Rector, Holy Trinity Orthodox Seminary, Box 36, Jordanville, NY 13361

Houghton College
Houghton, New York   CB member
www.houghton.edu   CB code: 2299

- Private 4-year liberal arts college affiliated with Wesleyan Church
- Residential campus in rural community
- 1,213 degree-seeking undergraduates: 2% part-time, 65% women, 3% African American, 1% Asian American, 2% Hispanic American, 1% Native American, 5% international
- 19 degree-seeking graduate students
- 72% of applicants admitted
- SAT or ACT (ACT writing optional), application essay required
- 69% graduate within 6 years; 37% enter graduate study

General. Founded in 1883. Regionally accredited. Study abroad programs in the Balkans, Tanzania, and Australia. School of Music accredited by National Association of Schools of Music. **Degrees:** 346 bachelor's, 6 associate awarded; master's offered. **ROTC:** Army. **Location:** 60 miles from Buffalo, 70 miles from Rochester. **Calendar:** Semester, limited summer session. **Full-time faculty:** 82 total; 84% have terminal degrees, 2% minority, 29% women. **Part-time faculty:** 53 total; 36% have terminal degrees, 9% minority, 49% women. **Class size:** 67% < 20, 28% 20-39, 4% 40-49, 1% 50-99. **Special facilities:** Equestrian center with indoor riding ring, ropes/initiatives course, downhill and cross-country skiing facilities, media arts computer lab, hiking and biking trails.

Freshman class profile. 1,085 applied, 777 admitted, 266 enrolled.

Mid 50% test scores		GPA 2.0-2.99:	8%
SAT critical reading:	530-630	Rank in top quarter:	68%
SAT math:	500-630	Rank in top tenth:	37%
SAT writing:	500-610	End year in good standing:	91%
ACT composite:	22-27	Return as sophomores:	86%
GPA 3.75 or higher:	42%	Out-of-state:	44%
GPA 3.50-3.74:	30%	Live on campus:	97%
GPA 3.0-3.49:	20%	International:	4%

Basis for selection. Student's high school transcript, standardized test scores of the utmost importance. Application essays, Christian character recommendation, other intangibles also considered. Interview recommended for all applicants. Audition and separate application required for entrance into the School of Music. **Learning Disabled:** Students must provide an IEP to receive services.

High school preparation. College-preparatory program recommended. 16 units recommended. Recommended units include English 4, mathematics 3, social studies 1, history 2, science 2 (laboratory 2) and foreign language 2.

2011-2012 Annual costs. Tuition/fees: $26,094. Room/board: $7,550. Books/supplies: $900. Personal expenses: $2,250.

2011-2012 Financial aid. **Need-based:** 249 full-time freshmen applied for aid; 231 were judged to have need; 231 of these received aid. Average need met was 79%. Average scholarship/grant was $17,199; average loan $4,223. 64% of total undergraduate aid awarded as scholarships/grants, 36% as loans/jobs. **Non-need-based:** Awarded to 291 full-time undergraduates, including 70 freshmen. Scholarships awarded for academics, art, athletics, music/drama, ROTC, state residency.

Application procedures. **Admission:** No deadline. $40 fee, may be waived for applicants with need. Admission notification on a rolling basis. Must reply by May 1 or within 4 week(s) if notified thereafter. **Financial aid:** Priority date 3/1; no closing date. FAFSA required. Applicants notified on a rolling basis starting 3/15; must reply by 5/1 or within 4 week(s) of notification.

Academics. **Special study options:** Combined bachelor's/graduate degree, cross-registration, distance learning, double major, exchange student, honors, independent study, internships, liberal arts/career combination, study abroad, teacher certification program, urban semester, Washington semester. **Credit/placement by examination:** AP, CLEP, IB, SAT, ACT, institutional tests. 16 credit hours maximum toward associate degree, 32 toward bachelor's. **Support services:** Learning center, reduced course load, study skills assistance, tutoring, writing center.

Honors college/program. Admission to the First-Year Honors Program requires separate application, academic reference, writing sample, and interview.

Majors. **Area/ethnic studies:** Regional. **Biology:** General, biochemistry, environmental. **Business:** General, business admin. **Communications:** Communications/speech/rhetoric, digital media, public relations. **Computer sciences:** Computer science, information technology. **Education:** General, art, biology, chemistry, elementary, English, ESL, foreign languages, history, mathematics, music, physical, physics, secondary, social studies, Spanish. **Engineering:** Applied physics. **English:** English lit. **Foreign languages:** Spanish. **General:** Equestrian studies. **Health services:** Predental, premedicine, prepharmacy, preveterinary. **History:** General. **Liberal arts:** Humanities. **Math:** General. **Parks/recreation:** General. **Philosophy/religion:** Philosophy, religion. **Physical sciences:** Chemistry, physics. **Psychology:** General. **Social sciences:** Political science, sociology. **Theology:** Bible, preministerial. **Visual/performing arts:** Art, brass instruments, music, music performance, music theory/composition, percussion instruments, piano/keyboard, stringed instruments, studio arts, voice/opera, woodwind instruments.

Most popular majors. Biology 7%, business/marketing 24%, communications/journalism 7%, education 15%, psychology 7%, visual/performing arts 8%.

Computing on campus. 30 workstations in library, student center. Dormitories wired for high-speed internet access and linked to campus network.

Commuter students can connect to campus network. Online library, helpline, repair service, wireless network available.

Student life. **Freshman orientation:** Mandatory. Preregistration for classes offered. **Policies:** Drinking of alcoholic beverages and smoking on or off campus is prohibited. The only pets allowed in dorm rooms are fish in tanks of 25 gallons and under. Religious observance required. **Housing:** Guaranteed on-campus for freshmen. Single-sex dorms, special housing for disabled, apartments, wellness housing available. $300 nonrefundable deposit, deadline 5/1. Pets allowed in dorm rooms. **Activities:** Bands, campus ministries, choral groups, drama, international student organizations, literary magazine, music ensembles, musical theater, opera, student government, student newspaper, symphony orchestra, Allegany County Outreach, Global Christian Fellowship, Habitat for Humanity, Youth for Christ, Fellowship of Christian Athletes, Intercultural Student Organization.

Athletics. NAIA. **Intercollegiate:** Baseball M, basketball, cross-country, field hockey W, soccer, softball W, track and field, volleyball W. **Intramural:** Basketball, equestrian, football (non-tackle) M, racquetball, soccer, table tennis, volleyball, water polo. **Team name:** Highlanders.

Student services. Chaplain/spiritual director, career counseling, student employment services, financial aid counseling, health services, personal counseling, placement for graduates. **Physically disabled:** Services for visually impaired.

Contact. E-mail: admission@houghton.edu
Phone: (585) 567-9353 Toll-free number: (800) 777-2556
Fax: (585) 567-9522
Matthew Reitnour, Director of Admission, Houghton College, 1 Willard Avenue/PO Box 128, Houghton, NY 14744-0128

Iona College
New Rochelle, New York **CB member**
www.iona.edu **CB code: 2324**

‣ Private 4-year business and liberal arts college affiliated with Roman Catholic Church
‣ Residential campus in small city
‣ 3,163 degree-seeking undergraduates: 2% part-time, 57% women, 6% African American, 2% Asian American, 16% Hispanic American, 2% international
‣ 864 degree-seeking graduate students
‣ 72% of applicants admitted
‣ SAT or ACT (ACT writing optional), application essay required
‣ 57% graduate within 6 years; 32% enter graduate study

General. Founded in 1940. Regionally accredited. Independent institution in Roman Catholic, Christian Brothers tradition. **Degrees:** 743 bachelor's awarded; master's offered. **ROTC:** Army, Air Force. **Location:** 20 miles from New York City. **Calendar:** Semester, extensive summer session. **Full-time faculty:** 179 total; 92% have terminal degrees, 14% minority, 36% women. **Part-time faculty:** 201 total; 11% minority, 39% women. **Class size:** 41% < 20, 54% 20-39, 5% 40-49. **Special facilities:** Extensive Irish and rare books collection, Thomas Paine archives.

Freshman class profile. 7,884 applied, 5,697 admitted, 812 enrolled.

Mid 50% test scores		GPA 2.0-2.99:	51%
SAT critical reading:	440-540	Rank in top quarter:	34%
SAT math:	450-540	Rank in top tenth:	10%
ACT composite:	19-24	Return as sophomores:	84%
GPA 3.75 or higher:	12%	Out-of-state:	25%
GPA 3.50-3.74:	9%	Live on campus:	64%
GPA 3.0-3.49:	26%	International:	2%

Basis for selection. High school curriculum and GPA most important, followed by test scores, recommendations, interview, extracurricular activities, essays, grade trends. Interviews recommended. **Home schooled:** Transcript of courses and grades, interview, letter of recommendation (nonparent) required.

High school preparation. College-preparatory program recommended. 16 units required; 20 recommended. Required and recommended units include English 4, mathematics 3-4, social studies 2, history 1-2, science 3 (laboratory 2), foreign language 2 and academic electives 1-3.

2012-2013 Annual costs. Tuition/fees (projected): $31,490. Room/board: $12,488. Books/supplies: $1,500. Personal expenses: $1,250.

2011-2012 Financial aid. **Need-based:** 801 full-time freshmen applied for aid; 679 were judged to have need; 677 of these received aid. Average need met was 26%. Average scholarship/grant was $5,860; average loan

$2,914. 68% of total undergraduate aid awarded as scholarships/grants, 32% as loans/jobs. **Non-need-based:** Awarded to 3,102 full-time undergraduates, including 834 freshmen. Scholarships awarded for academics, alumni affiliation, athletics, ROTC.

Application procedures. Admission: Closing date 2/15 (postmark date). $50 fee, may be waived for applicants with need. Admission notification by 3/20. Must reply by 5/1. **Financial aid:** Closing date 4/15. FAFSA required. Applicants notified on a rolling basis starting 3/1; must reply within 2 week(s) of notification.

Academics. Special study options: Combined bachelor's/graduate degree, distance learning, double major, honors, independent study, internships, liberal arts/career combination, study abroad, teacher certification program, weekend college. **Credit/placement by examination:** AP, CLEP, IB, SAT, ACT. 60 credit hours maximum toward bachelor's degree. **Support services:** Learning center, reduced course load, study skills assistance, tutoring, writing center.

Majors. Biology: General, biochemistry, environmental. **Business:** Accounting, business admin, finance, international, management information systems, marketing. **Communications:** Advertising, communications/speech/rhetoric, journalism, media studies, public relations, radio/TV. **Computer sciences:** Computer science, networking, web page design. **Education:** Biology, elementary, English, French, mathematics, secondary, social studies, Spanish. **English:** English lit. **Foreign languages:** French, Italian, Spanish. **Health services:** Audiology/speech pathology. **History:** General. **Human services:** Social work. **Liberal arts:** Arts/sciences. **Math:** General, applied. **Philosophy/religion:** Philosophy, religion. **Physical sciences:** Chemistry, physics. **Protective services:** Law enforcement admin. **Psychology:** General. **Social sciences:** Economics, political science, sociology.

Most popular majors. Business/marketing 38%, communications/journalism 17%, education 10%, health sciences 7%, psychology 8%, security/protective services 7%.

Computing on campus. 612 workstations in dormitories, library, computer center, student center. Dormitories wired for high-speed internet access and linked to campus network. Commuter students can connect to campus network. Online course registration, online library, helpline, wireless network available.

Student life. Freshman orientation: Mandatory. Preregistration for classes offered. Overnight summer program in June and July; 1-day welcome program. **Policies:** Freshmen not permitted cars on campus. **Housing:** Coed dorms, special housing for disabled, apartments, wellness housing available. $400 nonrefundable deposit, deadline 5/1. Living-learning communities. **Activities:** Pep band, campus ministries, choral groups, dance, drama, film society, international student organizations, literary magazine, music ensembles, Model UN, musical theater, radio station, student government, student newspaper, TV station, Gaelic Society, Council of Multicultural Leaders, Italian club, Students of Caribbean Ancestry, Hispanic Organization for Latin Awareness, Amnesty International, Democrats, Republicans, Hellenic Society, Asian student association, Students for American Awareness, Black Student Union, Gaels Activity Board, Gay Straight Alliance, Tara Knights Society, Edmund Rice Society.

Athletics. NCAA. **Intercollegiate:** Baseball M, basketball, cross-country, diving, golf M, lacrosse W, rowing (crew), soccer, softball W, swimming, track and field, volleyball W, water polo. **Intramural:** Basketball, football (non-tackle), soccer, table tennis, volleyball. **Team name:** Gaels.

Student services. Adult student services, alcohol/substance abuse counseling, chaplain/spiritual director, career counseling, services for economically disadvantaged, student employment services, financial aid counseling, health services, minority student services, personal counseling, placement for graduates, veterans' counselor, women's services. **Physically disabled:** Services for visually, speech, hearing impaired.

Contact. E-mail: icad@iona.edu
Phone: (914) 633-2502 Toll-free number: (800) 231-4662
Fax: (914) 633-2182
Kevin Cavanagh, Assistant VP for College Admissions, Iona College, 715 North Avenue, New Rochelle, NY 10801-1890

Ithaca College
Ithaca, New York
www.ithaca.edu
CB member
CB code: 2325

- Private 4-year health science and liberal arts college
- Residential campus in large town

- 6,228 degree-seeking undergraduates: 1% part-time, 57% women, 4% African American, 3% Asian American, 6% Hispanic American, 2% international
- 481 degree-seeking graduate students
- 68% of applicants admitted
- SAT or ACT with writing, application essay required
- 74% graduate within 6 years; 35% enter graduate study

General. Founded in 1892. Regionally accredited. **Degrees:** 1,581 bachelor's awarded; master's, professional offered. **ROTC:** Army, Air Force. **Location:** 250 miles from New York City, 60 miles from Syracuse. **Calendar:** Semester, extensive summer session. **Full-time faculty:** 478 total; 94% have terminal degrees, 10% minority, 46% women. **Part-time faculty:** 223 total; 67% have terminal degrees, 8% minority, 54% women. **Class size:** 53% < 20, 39% 20-39, 3% 40-49, 4% 50-99, 1% >100. **Special facilities:** Digital audio/video labs, photography labs, cinematography postproduction studio, film animation lab, lighting studio, physical therapy and occupational therapy clinics, speech and hearing clinic, exercise science labs, greenhouse, tissue culture laboratory, simulated trading room, recording and electroacoustic music studio, observatory.

Freshman class profile. 13,436 applied, 9,163 admitted, 1,625 enrolled.

Mid 50% test scores		End year in good standing:	83%
SAT critical reading:	520-620	Return as sophomores:	83%
SAT math:	520-630	Out-of-state:	57%
SAT writing:	530-630	Live on campus:	99%
Rank in top quarter:	68%	International:	2%
Rank in top tenth:	31%		

Basis for selection. School achievement record, test scores most important. School and community activities, accomplishments, special talents, interview also important. Audition required for music, theater arts programs; portfolio recommended for BFA program. **Home schooled:** Transcript of courses and grades, letter of recommendation (nonparent) required. Applicants encouraged to provide in-depth information regarding academic preparation.

High school preparation. College-preparatory program required. 16 units required; 19 recommended. Required and recommended units include English 4, mathematics 3-4, social studies 3-4, science 3-4, foreign language 2-3 and academic electives 1.

2011-2012 Annual costs. Tuition/fees: $35,278. Room/board: $12,854. Books/supplies: $1,340. Personal expenses: $1,680.

2011-2012 Financial aid. Need-based: 1,410 full-time freshmen applied for aid; 1,169 were judged to have need; 1,168 of these received aid. Average need met was 91%. Average scholarship/grant was $20,542; average loan $5,396. 71% of total undergraduate aid awarded as scholarships/grants, 29% as loans/jobs. **Non-need-based:** Awarded to 2,103 full-time undergraduates, including 583 freshmen. Scholarships awarded for academics, alumni affiliation, leadership, minority status, music/drama, ROTC.

Application procedures. Admission: Closing date 2/1. $60 fee, may be waived for applicants with need. Application must be submitted online. Admission notification by 4/15. Admission notification on a rolling basis beginning on or about 11/15. Must reply by May 1 or within 2 week(s) if notified thereafter. **Financial aid:** Priority date 2/1; no closing date. FAFSA, CSS PROFILE required. Applicants notified on a rolling basis starting 2/15; must reply by 5/1.

Academics. Over 100 degree programs and 70 minors available. **Special study options:** Accelerated study, combined bachelor's/graduate degree, cross-registration, distance learning, double major, dual enrollment of high school students, honors, independent study, internships, liberal arts/career combination, student-designed major, study abroad, teacher certification program. London Center (England), Los Angeles program, Washington semester, study opportunities in over 50 countries. **Credit/placement by examination:** AP, CLEP, IB, SAT, institutional tests. 36 credit hours maximum toward bachelor's degree. Maximum of 6 credits count toward General Education distribution requirements. **Support services:** Learning center, study skills assistance, tutoring, writing center.

Majors. Biology: General, biochemistry. **Business:** General, accounting, business admin, finance, international, managerial economics, market research, marketing. **Communications:** Broadcast journalism, communications/speech/rhetoric, digital media, journalism, media studies, organizational, persuasive communications, radio/TV, sports. **Communications technology:** Recording arts. **Computer sciences:** General, computer science, information systems, information technology, programming. **Conservation:** Environmental science, environmental studies. **Education:** Art, biology, chemistry, Deaf/hearing impaired, English, foreign languages, French, German, health, history, mathematics, multi-level teacher, music, physical, physics, science, secondary, social studies, Spanish, speech impaired. **English:**

Creative writing, English lit, rhetoric/composition, writing. **Foreign languages:** General, French, German, Italian, Spanish. **Health services:** Athletic training, community health, facilities admin, health services admin, occupational therapy assistant, predental, premedicine, preveterinary, public health ed, recreational therapy, speech pathology. **History:** General. **Liberal arts:** Arts/sciences. **Math:** General. **Parks/recreation:** Exercise sciences, health/fitness, sports admin, sports studies. **Philosophy/religion:** Philosophy. **Physical sciences:** Chemistry, physics. **Psychology:** General, industrial. **Social sciences:** General, anthropology, applied economics, econometrics, economics, political science, sociology. **Visual/performing arts:** General, acting, art, art history/conservation, cinematography, dance, documentaries, dramatic, film/cinema/video, jazz, music, music performance, music theory/composition, photography, studio arts, studio arts management, theater arts management, theater design.

Most popular majors. Business/marketing 12%, communications/journalism 19%, English 6%, health sciences 14%, parks/recreation 6%, social sciences 6%, visual/performing arts 17%.

Computing on campus. 640 workstations in library, computer center. Dormitories wired for high-speed internet access and linked to campus network. Commuter students can connect to campus network. Online course registration, online library, helpline, repair service, student web hosting, wireless network available.

Student life. Freshman orientation: Available, $265 fee. Preregistration for classes offered. 2.5 days in summer and 4 days before school highlighted by placement tests and registration. Separate parent orientation program offered in summer. **Housing:** Guaranteed on-campus for all undergraduates. Coed dorms, single-sex dorms, special housing for disabled, apartments, fraternity/sorority housing available. **Activities:** Bands, campus ministries, choral groups, dance, drama, film society, international student organizations, literary magazine, music ensembles, musical theater, opera, radio station, student government, student newspaper, symphony orchestra, TV station, Catholic, Buddhist, Protestant communities, Hillel, Spectrum, students for justice in Palestine, student alliance for Israel, IC human rights, IC Republicans, IC environmental society, African-Latino society, Habitat for Humanity.

Athletics. NCAA. **Intercollegiate:** Baseball M, basketball, cross-country, diving, field hockey W, football (tackle) M, golf W, gymnastics W, lacrosse, rowing (crew), soccer, softball W, swimming, tennis, track and field, volleyball W, wrestling M. **Intramural:** Basketball, bowling, football (non-tackle) M, soccer, softball, table tennis, tennis, volleyball, weight lifting. **Team name:** Bombers.

Student services. Adult student services, alcohol/substance abuse counseling, chaplain/spiritual director, career counseling, student employment services, financial aid counseling, health services, minority student services, personal counseling, placement for graduates, veterans' counselor. **Physically disabled:** Services for visually, speech, hearing impaired.

Contact. E-mail: admission@ithaca.edu
Phone: (607) 274-3124 Toll-free number: (800) 429-4274
Fax: (607) 274-1900
Gerard Turbide, Director of Admission, Ithaca College, 953 Danby Road, Ithaca, NY 14850-7002

Jewish Theological Seminary of America
New York, New York
www.jtsa.edu   CB code: 2339

- Private 4-year rabbinical and seminary college affiliated with Jewish faith
- Residential campus in very large city
- 168 degree-seeking undergraduates: 54% women
- 52% of applicants admitted
- SAT or ACT with writing, application essay required

General. Founded in 1886. Regionally accredited. **Degrees:** 38 bachelor's awarded; master's, doctoral offered. **ROTC:** Army, Naval, Air Force. **Calendar:** Semester, extensive summer session. **Full-time faculty:** 47 total. **Part-time faculty:** 70 total. **Special facilities:** Jewish museum containing over 27,000 objects (paintings, sculptures, works on paper, artifacts, etc.), library containing largest collection of Hebraica and Judaica outside of Israel.

Freshman class profile. 130 applied, 68 admitted, 43 enrolled.

Mid 50% test scores		GPA 3.75 or higher:	64%
SAT critical reading:	650-740	GPA 3.50-3.74:	22%
SAT math:	600-720	GPA 3.0-3.49:	14%
SAT writing:	630-730	Out-of-state:	82%
ACT composite:	29-33	International:	5%

Basis for selection. GED not accepted. School achievement record, interest in Jewish studies, test scores, recommendations important; leadership

potential considered. Interview recommended for residents in the New York area (within 100 mile radius).

High school preparation. Recommended units include English 4, mathematics 4, social studies 1, history 3, science 4, foreign language 4 and academic electives 4. Additional courses in Judaic studies, when available.

2011-2012 Annual costs. Tuition/fees: $16,740. Costs quoted paid to school only; separate costs assessed for dual-degree enrollment at Columbia University/Barnard College. Room only: $9,660. Books/supplies: $500. Personal expenses: $1,500.

Financial aid. Non-need-based: Scholarships awarded for academics, alumni affiliation, leadership.

Application procedures. Admission: Closing date 2/15 (postmark date). $65 fee, may be waived for applicants with need. Application must be submitted on paper. Admission notification by 4/1. Must reply by 5/1. Application deadline January 1 for double degree program with Barnard College, February 15 for joint program with Columbia University. **Financial aid:** Priority date 2/1, closing date 3/1. FAFSA, institutional form, CSS PROFILE required. Applicants notified on a rolling basis starting 4/1; must reply within 4 week(s) of notification.

Academics. Special study options: Cross-registration, distance learning, double major, exchange student, honors, independent study, liberal arts/career combination, student-designed major, study abroad. BA/MA program with The Graduate School or William Davidson School of Jewish Education. **Credit/placement by examination:** AP, CLEP, institutional tests. 6 credit hours maximum toward bachelor's degree. **Support services:** Pre-admission summer program, remedial instruction, tutoring, writing center.

Majors. Foreign languages: General. **Philosophy/religion:** Judaic. **Theology:** Sacred music. **Visual/performing arts:** Music performance, music theory/composition.

Computing on campus. 50 workstations in dormitories, library, computer center. Dormitories wired for high-speed internet access and linked to campus network. Commuter students can connect to campus network. Online course registration, online library, helpline, wireless network available.

Student life. Freshman orientation: Mandatory. Preregistration for classes offered. **Policies:** Student life centers around supportive Jewish community. Undergraduates enrolled in joint degree programs with Barnard and Columbia participate in their extracurricular activities. **Housing:** Coed dorms, special housing for disabled available. **Activities:** Concert band, choral groups, dance, musical theater, student government, student newspaper, community service organization.

Athletics. Intramural: Basketball, bowling, field hockey W, lacrosse M, softball, volleyball.

Student services. Career counseling, student employment services, health services, personal counseling, placement for graduates.

Contact. E-mail: lcadmissions@jtsa.edu
Phone: (212) 678-8832 Fax: (212) 280-6022
Melissa Present, Director of Admissions, Jewish Theological Seminary of America, 3080 Broadway, New York, NY 10027

Juilliard School
New York, New York
www.juilliard.edu   CB code: 2340

- Private 4-year music and performing arts college
- Commuter campus in very large city
- 522 degree-seeking undergraduates: 45% women
- 325 degree-seeking graduate students
- 6% of applicants admitted
- Application essay, interview required
- 93% graduate within 6 years

General. Founded in 1905. Regionally accredited. **Degrees:** 101 bachelor's awarded; master's, doctoral offered. **Calendar:** Semester. **Full-time faculty:** 124 total; 14% minority, 38% women. **Part-time faculty:** 183 total; 18% minority, 29% women. **Class size:** 90% < 20, 9% 20-39, less than 1% 40-49, less than 1% >100. **Special facilities:** Media center, over 100 practice rooms with over 200 pianos, scenery and costume shops, 15 2-story rehearsal studios, 5 theaters, 2 recital halls.

Freshman class profile. 2,566 applied, 153 admitted, 101 enrolled.

Out-of-state:	84%	International:	23%
Live on campus:	100%		

Basis for selection. Quality of performance at audition most important. Foreign students given English proficiency examination at time of audition or may present TOEFL. Audition required. **Home schooled:** Transcript of courses and grades, letter of recommendation (nonparent) required.

High school preparation. Extensive previous study in major field of dance, drama, or music required.

2011-2012 Annual costs. Tuition/fees: $33,630. Room/board: $12,770. Books/supplies: $711. Personal expenses: $3,563.

2011-2012 Financial aid. Need-based: 98 full-time freshmen applied for aid; 86 were judged to have need; 86 of these received aid. Average need met was 76%. Average scholarship/grant was $24,200; average loan $3,530. 75% of total undergraduate aid awarded as scholarships/grants, 25% as loans/jobs. **Non-need-based:** Awarded to 29 full-time undergraduates, including 5 freshmen. Scholarships awarded for music/drama.

Application procedures. Admission: Closing date 12/1. $100 fee, may be waived for applicants with need. Admission notification by 4/1. Must reply by May 1 or within 2 week(s) if notified thereafter. Music auditions held in March. Drama auditions in January and February. Dance auditions in February and March. Application closing date December 1; notification by April 1 or one month after audition. **Financial aid:** Closing date 3/1. FAFSA, institutional form required. Applicants notified by 4/1; must reply by 5/1.

Academics. 3-year diploma program available in performing arts. **Special study options:** Accelerated study, cross-registration. **Credit/placement by examination:** AP, CLEP, institutional tests. **Support services:** Tutoring.

Majors. Visual/performing arts: Dance, dramatic, jazz, music performance, music theory/composition, piano/keyboard, stringed instruments.

Computing on campus. 65 workstations in dormitories, library, computer center. Dormitories wired for high-speed internet access. Online library, wireless network available.

Student life. Freshman orientation: Mandatory, $200 fee. Preregistration for classes offered. For all new students, begins 10 days before first day of classes. **Housing:** Guaranteed on-campus for freshmen. Coed dorms available. $150 nonrefundable deposit, deadline 5/15. **Activities:** Student government, student newspaper, ArtREACH, Korea Campus Crusade for Christ, Christian Fellowship, Amnesty Juilliard.

Student services. Alcohol/substance abuse counseling, career counseling, student employment services, financial aid counseling, health services, minority student services, personal counseling, placement for graduates.

Contact. E-mail: admissions@juilliard.edu
Phone: (212) 799-5000 ext. 223 Fax: (212) 769-6420
Lee Cioppa, Associate Director for Admissions, Juilliard School, 60 Lincoln Center Plaza, New York, NY 10023-6588

Kehilath Yakov Rabbinical Seminary
Brooklyn, New York

CB code: 0619

- Private 4-year rabbinical college for men affiliated with Jewish faith
- Very large city
- 110 degree-seeking undergraduates

General. Accredited by AARTS. **Degrees:** 17 bachelor's awarded. **Calendar:** Differs by program. **Full-time faculty:** 3 total. **Part-time faculty:** 14 total.

2011-2012 Annual costs. Tuition/fees: $6,350. Room/board: $2,350.

Application procedures. Admission: No deadline.

Academics. Credit/placement by examination: AP, CLEP.

Majors. Philosophy/religion: Judaic. **Theology:** Talmudic.

Contact. Phone: (718) 963-3940 Fax: (718) 387-8586
Kehilath Yakov Rabbinical Seminary, 206 Wilson Street, Brooklyn, NY 11211

Keuka College
Keuka Park, New York
www.keuka.edu

CB member
CB code: 2350

- Private 4-year liberal arts college affiliated with American Baptist Churches in the USA
- Residential campus in rural community
- 1,702 degree-seeking undergraduates: 28% part-time, 75% women, 7% African American, 2% Asian American, 1% Native American
- 217 degree-seeking graduate students
- 77% of applicants admitted
- Application essay required
- 52% graduate within 6 years; 42% enter graduate study

General. Founded in 1890. Regionally accredited. **Degrees:** 322 bachelor's awarded; master's offered. **Location:** 50 miles from Rochester, 60 miles from Syracuse. **Calendar:** 4-1-4, limited summer session. **Full-time faculty:** 79 total; 82% have terminal degrees, 1% minority, 57% women. **Part-time faculty:** 106 total; 24% have terminal degrees, 11% minority, 56% women. **Class size:** 54% < 20, 45% 20-39, 1% 40-49. **Special facilities:** Lakefront for boating, sailing and science projects and research.

Freshman class profile. 840 applied, 646 admitted, 265 enrolled.

Mid 50% test scores			
SAT critical reading:	420-520	GPA 2.0-2.99:	27%
SAT math:	420-520	Rank in top quarter:	34%
SAT writing:	410-500	Rank in top tenth:	13%
ACT composite:	16-23	End year in good standing:	88%
GPA 3.75 or higher:	9%	Return as sophomores:	71%
GPA 3.50-3.74:	20%	Out-of-state:	6%
GPA 3.0-3.49:	43%	Live on campus:	97%

Basis for selection. Overall GPA, extracurricular activities, community service, leadership experience, letter of recommendation, quality of essay, SAT/ACT scores considered by committee. Interview recommended for all, required for some.

High school preparation. College-preparatory program recommended. 18 units recommended. Recommended units include English 4, mathematics 3, social studies 3, history 2, science 3 (laboratory 2) and foreign language 3.

2011-2012 Annual costs. Tuition/fees: $25,110. Room/board: $9,880. Books/supplies: $1,000. Personal expenses: $1,000.

2011-2012 Financial aid. Need-based: 265 full-time freshmen applied for aid; 256 were judged to have need; 256 of these received aid. Average need met was 70%. Average scholarship/grant was $16,752; average loan $4,225. 57% of total undergraduate aid awarded as scholarships/grants, 43% as loans/jobs. **Non-need-based:** Scholarships awarded for academics, alumni affiliation, leadership, minority status, religious affiliation.

Application procedures. Admission: No deadline. $50 fee, may be waived for applicants with need. Admission notification on a rolling basis beginning on or about 9/1. **Financial aid:** Priority date 3/15; no closing date. FAFSA required. Applicants notified on a rolling basis starting 3/1; must reply by 5/1 or within 2 week(s) of notification.

Academics. All students must complete 1 field period or internship each year, every 30 credit hours (experiential education). Field Period enables students to spend 4 weeks a year participating in an internship or international travel, or undertaking an independent project. **Special study options:** Accelerated study, combined bachelor's/graduate degree, cooperative education, cross-registration, double major, dual enrollment of high school students, independent study, internships, student-designed major, study abroad, teacher certification program. Albany semester; 3-1 in clinical science with New York Chiropractic College. **Credit/placement by examination:** AP, CLEP, SAT, ACT, institutional tests. 12 credit hours maximum toward bachelor's degree. **Support services:** Learning center, reduced course load, remedial instruction, study skills assistance, tutoring, writing center.

Majors. Biology: General, biochemistry. **Business:** Accounting, business admin, marketing. **Communications:** Communications/speech/rhetoric. **Conservation:** Environmental science. **Education:** Biology, early childhood, English, mathematics, secondary, social studies, special ed. **English:** English lit. **Foreign languages:** American Sign Language, sign language interpretation. **Health services:** Clinical lab science, nursing (RN). **History:** General. **Human services:** Social work. **Liberal arts:** Arts/sciences. **Math:** General. **Protective services:** Law enforcement admin. **Psychology:** General. **Social sciences:** General, criminology, sociology. **Visual/performing arts:** Art.

Most popular majors. Business/marketing 25%, education 23%, health sciences 28%, security/protective services 17%.

Computing on campus. 140 workstations in dormitories, library, computer center. Dormitories wired for high-speed internet access and linked to campus network. Helpline, repair service, wireless network available.

Student life. Freshman orientation: Mandatory, $150 fee. Preregistration for classes offered. 2-session summer program. **Policies:** No smoking allowed in any campus building, including residence halls. **Housing:** Guaranteed on-campus for all undergraduates. Coed dorms, single-sex dorms, special housing for disabled, apartments, cooperative housing, wellness housing available. $150 deposit. Leadership and management housing. **Activities:** Bands, campus ministries, choral groups, dance, drama, film society, international student organizations, literary magazine, musical theater, radio station, student government, student newspaper, social work club, Keuka Leaders club, Keuka Circle (community service), Newman Club, minority support group, political action coalition, Student Nurse Association.

Athletics. NCAA. **Intercollegiate:** Baseball M, basketball, cross-country, golf, lacrosse, soccer, softball W, synchronized swimming W, tennis, volleyball W. **Intramural:** Basketball, football (non-tackle), soccer, softball, volleyball. **Team name:** Storm.

Student services. Adult student services, alcohol/substance abuse counseling, chaplain/spiritual director, career counseling, student employment services, financial aid counseling, health services, minority student services, personal counseling, placement for graduates, women's services. **Physically disabled:** Services for visually, speech, hearing impaired.

Contact. E-mail: admissions@mail.keuka.edu
Phone: (315) 279-5254 Toll-free number: (800) 335-3852
Fax: (315) 279-5386
Jack Farrell, Director of Admissions, Keuka College, 141 Central Avenue, Keuka Park, NY 14478-0098

The King's College
New York, New York
www.tkc.edu   CB code: 2871

- Private 4-year liberal arts college affiliated with nondenominational tradition
- Residential campus in very large city
- 461 degree-seeking undergraduates: 2% part-time, 58% women, 3% African American, 2% Asian American, 6% Hispanic American, 1% Native American, 2% international
- 67% of applicants admitted
- SAT or ACT (ACT writing optional), interview required
- 51% graduate within 6 years

General. Regionally accredited. **Degrees:** 37 bachelor's awarded. **ROTC:** Army. **Calendar:** Semester, limited summer session. **Full-time faculty:** 24 total; 79% have terminal degrees, 4% minority, 12% women. **Part-time faculty:** 19 total; 68% have terminal degrees, 5% minority, 47% women. **Class size:** 48% < 20, 36% 20-39, 9% 40-49, 4% 50-99, 2% >100.

Freshman class profile. 3,388 applied, 2,255 admitted, 162 enrolled.

Mid 50% test scores			
SAT critical reading:	580-670	Rank in top quarter:	52%
SAT math:	520-610	Rank in top tenth:	24%
SAT writing:	570-650	End year in good standing:	85%
ACT composite:	24-28	Return as sophomores:	68%
GPA 3.75 or higher:	48%	Out-of-state:	94%
GPA 3.50-3.74:	21%	Live on campus:	94%
GPA 3.0-3.49:	17%	International:	1%
GPA 2.0-2.99:	13%		

Basis for selection. Admissions based on academic preparedness and leadership qualities, primarily assessed through transcript, SAT or ACT scores, and entrance interview. **Home schooled:** Transcript should include all information regarding state requirements for high school graduation. SAT and ACT scores especially important to determine student's ability to succeed academically. Personal interview required during which student can elaborate on courses they have studied and activities they have participated in outside the home. **Learning Disabled:** Documentation required of any learning disabilities that will require special accommodation.

High school preparation. Required and recommended units include English 4, mathematics 3-4, social studies 2, history 2, science 3-4, foreign language 1-2 and academic electives 2.

2011-2012 Annual costs. Tuition/fees: $29,240. Room only: $11,050.

2010-2011 Financial aid. Need-based: 129 full-time freshmen applied for aid; 121 were judged to have need; 121 of these received aid. Average need met was 68%. Average scholarship/grant was $22,293; average loan

$3,301. 76% of total undergraduate aid awarded as scholarships/grants, 24% as loans/jobs. **Non-need-based:** Awarded to 131 full-time undergraduates, including 101 freshmen. Scholarships awarded for academics.

Application procedures. Admission: Priority date 11/15; no deadline. $30 fee, may be waived for applicants with need. Admission notification on a rolling basis beginning on or about 9/15. Must reply by May 1 or within 4 week(s) if notified thereafter. **Financial aid:** No deadline. FAFSA required. Applicants notified on a rolling basis starting 2/15.

Academics. Bibically-based curriculum with a common core in politics, philosophy, and economics. **Special study options:** Distance learning, dual enrollment of high school students, independent study, internships. **Credit/placement by examination:** AP, CLEP, IB, SAT, ACT, institutional tests. **Support services:** Learning center, tutoring.

Majors. Business: Business admin. **Liberal arts:** Humanities.

Most popular majors. Business/marketing 22%, liberal arts 78%.

Computing on campus. PC or laptop required. 10 workstations in library. Dormitories wired for high-speed internet access and linked to campus network. Commuter students can connect to campus network. Wireless network available.

Student life. Freshman orientation: Mandatory. Preregistration for classes offered. Held two days prior to first day of class. **Policies:** No alcoholic beverages/drug usage permitted on campus or in housing. **Housing:** Guaranteed on-campus for freshmen. Single-sex dorms, special housing for disabled, apartments available. $600 nonrefundable deposit, deadline 6/30. **Activities:** Campus ministries, choral groups, dance, drama, literary magazine, music ensembles, student government, student newspaper.

Athletics. Team name: The Lions.

Student services. Chaplain/spiritual director, career counseling, student employment services, financial aid counseling.

Contact. E-mail: admissions@tkc.edu
Phone: (212) 659-3610 Toll-free number: (888) 969-7200 ext. 3610
Fax: (212) 659-3611
Brian Parker, Vice President of Admissions, The King's College, 350 Fifth Avenue, Lower Lobby, New York, NY 10118

Le Moyne College
Syracuse, New York   CB member
www.lemoyne.edu   CB code: 2366

- Private 4-year liberal arts college affiliated with Roman Catholic Church
- Residential campus in small city
- 2,640 degree-seeking undergraduates: 9% part-time, 60% women, 5% African American, 2% Asian American, 5% Hispanic American, 1% Native American
- 564 degree-seeking graduate students
- 62% of applicants admitted
- SAT or ACT (ACT writing optional), application essay required
- 72% graduate within 6 years; 40% enter graduate study

General. Founded in 1946. Regionally accredited. **Degrees:** 587 bachelor's awarded; master's offered. **ROTC:** Army, Air Force. **Location:** 2 miles from downtown. **Calendar:** Semester, extensive summer session. **Full-time faculty:** 155 total; 96% have terminal degrees, 16% minority, 44% women. **Part-time faculty:** 211 total; 30% have terminal degrees, 6% minority, 52% women. **Class size:** 48% < 20, 49% 20-39, 1% 40-49, 2% 50-99. **Special facilities:** Performing arts center, art gallery.

Freshman class profile. 5,772 applied, 3,559 admitted, 639 enrolled.

Mid 50% test scores			
SAT critical reading:	480-590	Rank in top quarter:	53%
SAT math:	500-610	Rank in top tenth:	22%
ACT composite:	21-26	End year in good standing:	94%
GPA 3.75 or higher:	23%	Return as sophomores:	83%
GPA 3.50-3.74:	22%	Out-of-state:	9%
GPA 3.0-3.49:	35%	Live on campus:	85%
GPA 2.0-2.99:	20%	International:	1%

Basis for selection. High school courses and performance most important; class rank, test scores, recommendations, essay, interview, extracurricular activities also important. Students from underrepresented populations encouraged. February 1 priority date by which SAT scores must be received for fall term admission. Interview recommended. **Home schooled:** Statement describing home school structure and mission, transcript of courses and

grades, interview, letter of recommendation (nonparent) required. **Learning Disabled:** Interview strongly recommended.

High school preparation. College-preparatory program recommended. 17 units required. Required and recommended units include English 4, mathematics 3-4, social studies 4, science 3-4 (laboratory 3) and foreign language 3. 4 math required for science and math majors.

2012-2013 Annual costs. Tuition/fees: $29,460. Room/board: $11,320. Books/supplies: $1,300. Personal expenses: $900.

2010-2011 Financial aid. Need-based: 583 full-time freshmen applied for aid; 529 were judged to have need; 529 of these received aid. Average need met was 75%. Average scholarship/grant was $17,158; average loan $3,792. 63% of total undergraduate aid awarded as scholarships/grants, 37% as loans/jobs. **Non-need-based:** Awarded to 567 full-time undergraduates, including 146 freshmen. Scholarships awarded for academics, alumni affiliation, athletics, leadership, minority status, ROTC. **Additional information:** Parent loan program at low interest, monthly payment plans and alternative loans for students.

Application procedures. Admission: Priority date 2/1; no deadline. $35 fee, may be waived for applicants with need, free for online applicants. Admission notification on a rolling basis beginning on or about 12/1. Must reply by May 1 or within 4 week(s) if notified thereafter. **Financial aid:** Priority date 2/1; no closing date. FAFSA, institutional form required. Must reply by 5/1 or within 2 week(s) of notification.

Academics. Academic accommodations and services for students with documented disabilities. **Special study options:** Accelerated study, combined bachelor's/graduate degree, double major, dual enrollment of high school students, honors, independent study, internships, liberal arts/career combination, semester at sea, study abroad, teacher certification program, Washington semester. Certificate of Advanced Studies in Educational Leadership and Certificate of Advanced Studies in Nursing. **Credit/placement by examination:** AP, CLEP, IB. **Support services:** Learning center, remedial instruction, study skills assistance, tutoring, writing center.

Majors. Biology: General, biochemistry, ecology. **Business:** Accounting, business admin, finance, management information systems, marketing, operations. **Communications:** General. **Computer sciences:** General. **Conservation:** Environmental studies. **Engineering:** Pre-engineering. **English:** English lit. **Foreign languages:** French, Spanish. **Health services:** Nursing (RN), predental, premedicine, preoptometry, prepharmacy, preveterinary. **History:** General. **Math:** General. **Philosophy/religion:** Philosophy, religion. **Physical sciences:** Chemistry, physics. **Psychology:** General. **Social sciences:** Criminology, economics, political science, sociology. **Visual/performing arts:** Dramatic.

Most popular majors. Biology 13%, business/marketing 25%, communications/journalism 7%, English 7%, psychology 17%, social sciences 11%.

Computing on campus. 330 workstations in dormitories, library, computer center, student center. Dormitories wired for high-speed internet access and linked to campus network. Commuter students can connect to campus network. Online course registration, online library, helpline, repair service, student web hosting, wireless network available.

Student life. Freshman orientation: Mandatory, $200 fee. Preregistration for classes offered. Four one-day summer welcome sessions and one four-day fall arrival session prior to the beginning of classes. **Housing:** Guaranteed on-campus for all undergraduates. Coed dorms, single-sex dorms, special housing for disabled, apartments available. Living/Learning communities available. **Activities:** Bands, campus ministries, choral groups, dance, drama, film society, international student organizations, literary magazine, music ensembles, Model UN, musical theater, radio station, student government, student newspaper, TV station, International Club, Amnesty International, Habitat for Humanity, Democrats Club, Republican Club, Gaelic Society, El Progreso, Pride in Our Work Ethnicity and Race, Muslim Student Association, Asian Students in Alliance.

Athletics. NCAA. **Intercollegiate:** Baseball M, basketball, cross-country, diving, golf, lacrosse, soccer, softball W, swimming, tennis, volleyball W. **Intramural:** Basketball, football (non-tackle) M, racquetball, soccer, softball, volleyball. **Team name:** Dolphins.

Student services. Adult student services, alcohol/substance abuse counseling, chaplain/spiritual director, career counseling, student employment services, financial aid counseling, health services, minority student services, personal counseling, placement for graduates, veterans' counselor. **Physically disabled:** Services for visually, speech, hearing impaired.

Contact. E-mail: admission@lemoyne.edu
Phone: (315) 445-4300 Toll-free number: (800) 333-4733
Fax: (315) 445-4711
Dennis Nicholson, Dean of Admission, Le Moyne College, 1419 Salt Springs Road, Syracuse, NY 13214-1301

Lebanese American University
Chouran-Beirut 1102 2801, Lebanon **CB member**
www.lau.edu.lb **CB code: 2595**

- Private 4-year university
- Commuter campus in very large city
- 7,463 degree-seeking undergraduates: 7% part-time, 48% women
- 773 degree-seeking graduate students
- 76% of applicants admitted
- SAT required
- 78% graduate within 6 years; 14% enter graduate study

General. Campuses in Beirut and Byblos. **Degrees:** 1,294 bachelor's, 34 associate awarded; master's, professional offered. **Calendar:** Semester, limited summer session. **Full-time faculty:** 270 total; 74% have terminal degrees, 43% women. **Part-time faculty:** 441 total; 22% have terminal degrees, 53% women. **Class size:** 36% < 20, 48% 20-39, 15% 40-49, less than 1% 50-99.

Freshman class profile. 3,617 applied, 2,754 admitted, 1,684 enrolled.

Mid 50% test scores			
SAT critical reading:	380-470	GPA 2.0-2.99:	62%
SAT math:	500-630	Rank in top quarter:	27%
SAT writing:	410-500	Rank in top tenth:	9%
GPA 3.75 or higher:	2%	End year in good standing:	86%
GPA 3.50-3.74:	6%	Return as sophomores:	92%
GPA 3.0-3.49:	28%	Out-of-state:	22%
		Live on campus:	4%

Basis for selection. Reigor of secondary school, academic GPA and test scores most important. Class rank, recommendations, and other factors considered. **Learning Disabled:** Students with learning disabilities should submit a medical report explaining their case; so university can decide if accommodations can be provided. Students should meet all general admissions requirements.

2011-2012 Annual costs. Books/supplies: $399. Personal expenses: $7,735.

2010-2011 Financial aid. Need-based: Average scholarship/grant was $2,514; average loan $1,864. 27% of total undergraduate aid awarded as scholarships/grants, 73% as loans/jobs. **Non-need-based:** Scholarships awarded for academics, athletics, leadership, music/drama, religious affiliation.

Application procedures. Admission: Closing date 7/31. $50 fee. Admission notification on a rolling basis beginning on or about 4/1. **Financial aid:** Priority date 2/28, closing date 7/31. Institutional form required. Applicants notified on a rolling basis starting 3/15.

Academics. Special study options: Cross-registration, internships, study abroad, teacher certification program. **Credit/placement by examination:** AP, CLEP, SAT, institutional tests. **Support services:** Learning center, tutoring, writing center.

Majors. Architecture: Architecture, interior. **Biology:** General. **Business:** Business admin, hospitality admin. **Communications:** General, journalism, radio/TV. **Computer sciences:** Computer science. **Education:** General, ESL. **Engineering:** Civil, computer, electrical, industrial, mechanical. **English:** English lit. **Health services:** Nursing practice, pharmaceutical sciences. **History:** General. **Human services:** Social work. **Math:** General. **Philosophy/religion:** Philosophy. **Physical sciences:** Chemistry. **Psychology:** General. **Social sciences:** Economics, international relations, political science. **Visual/performing arts:** Graphic design, interior design, studio arts.

Most popular majors. Business/marketing 62%, engineering/engineering technologies 6%, health sciences 7%.

Computing on campus. 825 workstations in dormitories, library, computer center. Dormitories linked to campus network. Online course registration, online library, wireless network available.

Student life. Freshman orientation: Available. Preregistration for classes offered. Provides chance to connect with faculty, staff, and other students, who will help integrate new students into university life, and introduce them to the many services, offices, and opportunities available. **Policies:** Freshmen not permitted cars on campus. **Housing:** Single-sex dorms, special housing for disabled, apartments available. $200 nonrefundable deposit. **Activities:** Bands, choral groups, dance, film society, international student organizations, Model UN, student government, student newspaper.

Athletics. Intercollegiate: Badminton, basketball, rugby M, soccer, swimming, table tennis, tennis, volleyball. **Intramural:** Basketball, skiing, soccer, swimming, table tennis, tennis, track and field, volleyball.

Student services. Career counseling, student employment services, health services, placement for graduates.

Contact. E-mail: admissions@lau.edu.lb
Phone: (961) 954-7254 ext. 2191 Fax: (961) 954-6560
Michel Najjar, Director of Admissions, Lebanese American University, PO Box 36/S-12, Byblos, LB

LIM College
New York, New York
www.limcollege.edu

CB member
CB code: 2380

- For-profit 4-year college of fashion business
- Commuter campus in very large city
- 1,538 degree-seeking undergraduates
- 73% of applicants admitted
- SAT or ACT (ACT writing optional), application essay, interview required

General. Founded in 1939. Regionally accredited. **Degrees:** 310 bachelor's, 22 associate awarded; master's offered. **Location:** Located in midtown Manhattan. **Calendar:** Semester, limited summer session. **Full-time faculty:** 26 total. **Part-time faculty:** 159 total. **Class size:** 66% < 20, 34% 20-39.

Freshman class profile. 1,280 applied, 933 admitted, 331 enrolled.

Mid 50% test scores			
SAT critical reading:	430-530	GPA 3.0-3.49:	29%
SAT math:	430-510	GPA 2.0-2.99:	52%
SAT writing:	430-510	Rank in top quarter:	17%
ACT composite:	19-24	Rank in top tenth:	3%
GPA 3.75 or higher:	11%	Out-of-state:	58%
GPA 3.50-3.74:	5%	Live on campus:	66%

Basis for selection. Interview, high school transcript, SAT/ACT scores, letters of recommendation, and college transcripts all considered. **Home schooled:** Transcript of courses and grades, state high school equivalency certificate, interview, letter of recommendation (nonparent) required.

High school preparation. College-preparatory program recommended.

2011-2012 Annual costs. Tuition/fees: $22,225. Room/board: $20,350. Books/supplies: $1,100. Personal expenses: $2,000.

Financial aid. All financial aid based on need.

Application procedures. Admission: No deadline. $40 fee, may be waived for applicants with need. Admission notification on a rolling basis beginning on or about 12/15. **Financial aid:** Priority date 4/1; no closing date. FAFSA, institutional form required. Applicants notified on a rolling basis starting 2/15; must reply within 2 week(s) of notification.

Academics. Associate degree program distributed among liberal arts, business, and professional courses, including 2 work projects of 3 credits and 5 weeks each. Bachelor's degree programs distributed among liberal arts, business, and professional courses with a semester-long, 13-credit cooperative work project. Freshmen and sophomores participate in 3-credit, 5-week work project. Seniors participate in 16-week full-semester co-op. Curriculum also includes weekly field trips into fashion industry and guest lecturer series featuring fashion professionals. **Special study options:** Combined bachelor's/graduate degree, cooperative education, internships, study abroad. 3-credit trip to Europe in winter/summer. **Credit/placement by examination:** AP, CLEP, SAT, ACT, institutional tests. **Support services:** Learning center, pre-admission summer program, reduced course load, remedial instruction, study skills assistance, tutoring, writing center.

Majors. Business: Business admin, fashion, management science, marketing. **Work/family studies:** Apparel marketing.

Most popular majors. Business/marketing 40%, family/consumer sciences 51%, visual/performing arts 9%.

Computing on campus. 270 workstations in library, computer center, student center. Dormitories wired for high-speed internet access. Commuter students can connect to campus network. Online library, helpline available.

Student life. Freshman orientation: Mandatory. Preregistration for classes offered. **Housing:** Coed dorms available. $700 partly refundable deposit. Affiliated with local YW-YMHA and Educational Housing Inc. in which traditional residence life experience available. **Activities:** Student government.

Student services. Alcohol/substance abuse counseling, career counseling, student employment services, financial aid counseling, personal counseling, placement for graduates.

Contact. E-mail: admissions@limcollege.edu
Phone: (212) 752-1530 ext. 289 Toll-free number: (800) 677-1323
Fax: (212) 750-3432
Kristina Ortiz, Director of Admissions, LIM College, 12 East 53rd Street, New York, NY 10022

Long Island University: Brooklyn Campus
Brooklyn, New York
www.liu.edu

CB member
CB code: 2369

- Private 4-year university and liberal arts college
- Commuter campus in very large city
- 5,117 degree-seeking undergraduates: 14% part-time, 72% women, 35% African American, 15% Asian American, 12% Hispanic American, 1% international
- 3,417 degree-seeking graduate students
- 84% of applicants admitted

General. Founded in 1926. Regionally accredited. **Degrees:** 590 bachelor's, 18 associate awarded; master's, professional, doctoral offered. **Calendar:** Semester, extensive summer session. **Full-time faculty:** 307 total; 34% minority, 53% women. **Part-time faculty:** 482 total; 38% minority, 58% women. **Class size:** 55% < 20, 39% 20-39, 4% 40-49, less than 1% 50-99, 1% >100.

Freshman class profile. 4,268 applied, 3,578 admitted, 1,031 enrolled.

Mid 50% test scores			
SAT critical reading:	380-490	GPA 2.0-2.99:	47%
SAT math:	390-530	Rank in top quarter:	33%
SAT writing:	390-500	Rank in top tenth:	12%
ACT composite:	16-23	End year in good standing:	72%
GPA 3.75 or higher:	9%	Return as sophomores:	64%
GPA 3.50-3.74:	10%	Out-of-state:	22%
GPA 3.0-3.49:	20%	Live on campus:	28%
		International:	1%

Basis for selection. Rigor of secondary school record, class rank, academic GPA, recommendations, test scores, essay considered. ACT or SAT required for admission to computer science, molecular biology, nursing, pharmacy, pre-athletic training, pre-occupational therapy, and pre-physician assistant majors. Interview, audition, and/or personal statement may be required for particular programs.

High school preparation. College-preparatory program required. 15 units recommended. Recommended units include English 4, mathematics 3, social studies 1, history 2, science 3 (laboratory 3) and foreign language 2. Academic electives include any electives from fields of foreign languages, social studies, mathematics or natural science. Other electives include 3 credits of any studies except physical education and military science that lead to graduation from accredited high school.

2011-2012 Annual costs. Tuition/fees: $29,730. Room/board: $11,300.

Financial aid. Non-need-based: Scholarships awarded for academics, alumni affiliation, art, athletics, leadership, music/drama.

Application procedures. Admission: Priority date 3/1; deadline 9/1. $40 fee, may be waived for applicants with need. Admission notification on a rolling basis beginning on or about 11/1. Must reply by 5/1. Some programs have February 1 application deadline. **Financial aid:** Priority date 3/15, closing date 5/1. FAFSA required. Applicants notified on a rolling basis starting 2/16; must reply within 4 week(s) of notification.

Academics. Special study options: Accelerated study, combined bachelor's/graduate degree, cooperative education, cross-registration, distance learning, double major, ESL, honors, independent study, internships, student-designed major, study abroad, teacher certification program. **Credit/placement by examination:** AP, CLEP, IB, SAT, ACT, institutional tests. 48 credit hours maximum toward associate degree, 96 toward bachelor's. **Support services:** Learning center, pre-admission summer program, reduced course load, remedial instruction, study skills assistance, tutoring, writing center.

Majors. Biology: General, biochemistry, molecular. **Business:** Accounting, business admin, finance, sales/distribution. **Communications:** Communications/speech/rhetoric, journalism. **Computer sciences:** General. **Education:** Art, biology, chemistry, elementary, English, mathematics, music, physical, secondary, Spanish, speech impaired. **English:** English lit, rhetoric/composition. **Foreign languages:** General. **Health services:** Audiology/speech pathology, clinical lab science, cytotechnology, nuclear medical technology,

nursing (RN), physician assistant, respiratory therapy assistant. **History:** General. **Human services:** Social work. **Liberal arts:** Arts/sciences, humanities. **Math:** General. **Parks/recreation:** Exercise sciences. **Philosophy/religion:** Philosophy. **Physical sciences:** Chemistry. **Psychology:** General. **Social sciences:** General, economics, political science, sociology. **Visual/performing arts:** General, commercial/advertising art, dance, jazz, music performance, studio arts.

Most popular majors. Biology 11%, business/marketing 12%, health sciences 47%.

Computing on campus. 300 workstations in dormitories, library, computer center, student center. Dormitories wired for high-speed internet access and linked to campus network. Commuter students can connect to campus network. Online course registration, online library, helpline, repair service, wireless network available.

Student life. Freshman orientation: Available, $55 fee. Preregistration for classes offered. **Policies:** Freshmen not permitted cars on campus. **Housing:** Guaranteed on-campus for freshmen. Coed dorms, special housing for disabled available. $150 fully refundable deposit. **Activities:** Bands, campus ministries, choral groups, dance, drama, literary magazine, music ensembles, Model UN, musical theater, radio station, student government, student newspaper, TV station, American Pharmacists Association, Hillel Jewish students organization, student activities board, Society of Health Systems Pharmacists.

Athletics. NCAA. **Intercollegiate:** Baseball M, basketball, bowling W, cross-country, golf, lacrosse W, soccer, softball W, tennis W, track and field, volleyball W. **Team name:** Blackbirds.

Student services. Chaplain/spiritual director, career counseling, student employment services, financial aid counseling, health services, personal counseling, placement for graduates. **Physically disabled:** Services for visually, speech, hearing impaired.

Contact. E-mail: admissions@brooklyn.liu.edu
Phone: (718) 488-1011 Toll-free number: (800) 548-7526
Fax: (718) 797-2399
Richard Sunday, Senior Associate Dean of Admissions, Long Island University: Brooklyn Campus, 1 University Plaza, Brooklyn, NY 11201-8423

Long Island University: C. W. Post Campus
Brookville, New York   **CB member**
www.liu.edu   **CB code: 2070**

- Private 4-year university and liberal arts college
- Commuter campus in small town
- 4,468 degree-seeking undergraduates: 11% part-time, 60% women, 11% African American, 3% Asian American, 10% Hispanic American, 9% international
- 2,810 degree-seeking graduate students
- 81% of applicants admitted
- SAT or ACT (ACT writing optional), application essay required
- 43% graduate within 6 years

General. Founded in 1954. Regionally accredited. **Degrees:** 864 bachelor's, 1 associate awarded; master's, doctoral offered. **ROTC:** Army. **Location:** 25 miles from New York City. **Calendar:** Semester, extensive summer session. **Full-time faculty:** 301 total; 16% minority, 48% women. **Part-time faculty:** 521 total; 11% minority, 50% women. **Class size:** 60% < 20, 34% 20-39, 5% 40-49, less than 1% 50-99, less than 1% >100. **Special facilities:** Tilles center for the performing arts.

Freshman class profile. 7,372 applied, 5,948 admitted, 942 enrolled.

Mid 50% test scores		GPA 2.0-2.99:	41%
SAT critical reading:	440-530	Rank in top quarter:	26%
SAT math:	440-550	Rank in top tenth:	9%
SAT writing:	430-540	End year in good standing:	84%
ACT composite:	19-24	Return as sophomores:	68%
GPA 3.75 or higher:	11%	Out-of-state:	11%
GPA 3.50-3.74:	16%	Live on campus:	59%
GPA 3.0-3.49:	30%	International:	11%

Basis for selection. Rigor of secondary school record, class rank, GPA, recommendations, test scores, essay considered. Audition required for dance, music, and theater programs; interview recommended for communication arts, dance, and theater/film programs; portfolio required for art programs.

High school preparation. College-preparatory program recommended. 22 units recommended. Recommended units include English 4, mathematics

---

3, social studies 4, history 4, science 3 (laboratory 1), foreign language 2 and visual/performing arts 1.

2011-2012 Annual costs. Tuition/fees: $31,646. Room/board: $11,840. Books/supplies: $675.

Financial aid. Non-need-based: Scholarships awarded for academics, alumni affiliation, art, athletics, leadership, music/drama.

Application procedures. Admission: Priority date 3/1; no deadline. $40 fee, may be waived for applicants with need. Admission notification on a rolling basis beginning on or about 11/1. Must reply by May 1 or within 2 week(s) if notified thereafter. **Financial aid:** Priority date 3/1; no closing date. FAFSA required. Applicants notified on a rolling basis starting 3/15; must reply by 5/1 or within 2 week(s) of notification.

Academics. Special study options: Accelerated study, combined bachelor's/graduate degree, cooperative education, cross-registration, double major, ESL, honors, independent study, internships, liberal arts/career combination, student-designed major, study abroad, teacher certification program, weekend college. **Credit/placement by examination:** AP, CLEP, IB, SAT, ACT, institutional tests. **Support services:** Learning center, reduced course load, remedial instruction, study skills assistance, tutoring, writing center.

Majors. Area/ethnic studies: American. **Biology:** General, cell/histology. **Business:** Accounting, business admin, finance. **Communications:** Advertising, journalism, public relations. **Communications technology:** Radio/TV. **Computer sciences:** Computer science, information systems, information technology. **Conservation:** Environmental science. **Education:** Art, biology, chemistry, elementary, English, foreign languages, French, health, kindergarten/preschool, mathematics, music, physical, social studies, Spanish. **English:** English lit. **Foreign languages:** General, French, Italian, Spanish. **Health services:** Art therapy, audiology/speech pathology, clinical lab science, cytotechnology, facilities admin, medical radiologic technology/radiation therapy, medical records admin, nursing (RN), prepharmacy. **History:** General. **Human services:** General, social work. **Liberal arts:** Arts/sciences. **Math:** General, applied. **Philosophy/religion:** Philosophy. **Physical sciences:** Chemistry, geology, physics. **Protective services:** Forensics, law enforcement admin. **Psychology:** General. **Social sciences:** Economics, geography, international relations, political science, sociology. **Visual/performing arts:** Art history/conservation, cinematography, commercial/advertising art, dance, digital arts, dramatic, multimedia, music performance, photography, studio arts, studio arts management.

Most popular majors. Business/marketing 19%, education 23%, health sciences 13%, psychology 7%, security/protective services 6%, social sciences 6%, visual/performing arts 8%.

Computing on campus. 500 workstations in dormitories, library, computer center, student center. Dormitories wired for high-speed internet access and linked to campus network. Commuter students can connect to campus network. Online course registration, online library, helpline, wireless network available.

Student life. Freshman orientation: Mandatory, $175 fee. Preregistration for classes offered. 2-day sessions for freshmen held in July and August prior to start of fall classes. **Housing:** Guaranteed on-campus for freshmen. Coed dorms, single-sex dorms available. $300 fully refundable deposit, deadline 5/1. 24-hour intensified study housing available. **Activities:** Bands, choral groups, dance, drama, film society, literary magazine, music ensembles, musical theater, radio station, student government, student newspaper, TV station, association for campus programming, African People's Organization, resident student association, Newman club.

Athletics. NCAA. **Intercollegiate:** Baseball M, basketball, cross-country, field hockey W, football (tackle) M, lacrosse, soccer, softball W, swimming W, tennis W, volleyball W. **Team name:** Pioneers.

Student services. Adult student services, alcohol/substance abuse counseling, chaplain/spiritual director, career counseling, student employment services, financial aid counseling, health services, personal counseling, placement for graduates, veterans' counselor. **Physically disabled:** Services for visually, speech, hearing impaired.

Contact. E-mail: enroll@cwpost.liu.edu
Phone: (516) 299-2900 Toll-free number: (800) 548-7526
Fax: (516) 299-2137
Joanne Graziano, Admissions Director, Long Island University: C. W. Post Campus, 720 Northern Boulevard, Brookville, NY 11548-1300

Machzikei Hadath Rabbinical College
Brooklyn, New York

                                          CB code: 0726

- Private 5-year rabbinical and seminary college for men affiliated with Jewish faith
- Commuter campus in very large city

- 142 degree-seeking undergraduates
- Interview required

General. Founded in 1956. Accredited by AARTS. First Talmudic degree and ordination available. **Degrees:** 14 bachelor's awarded. **Calendar:** Semester. **Full-time faculty:** 8 total. **Part-time faculty:** 3 total.

Basis for selection. Interview most important. Essay recommended.

2011-2012 Annual costs. Tuition/fees: $8,050.

Application procedures. Admission: Priority date 6/1; deadline 7/1. $150 fee, may be waived for applicants with need. Admission notification on a rolling basis. **Financial aid:** No deadline. Applicants notified on a rolling basis.

Academics. Special study options: Independent study, study abroad. **Credit/placement by examination:** AP, CLEP. **Support services:** Pre-admission summer program, remedial instruction.

Majors. Theology: Talmudic.

Student life. Policies: Religious observance required.

Contact. Phone: (718) 854-8777 ext. 23 Fax: (718) 851-1265 Rabbi A.M. Leizerowitz, Director of Admissions, Machzikei Hadath Rabbinical College, 5407 16th Avenue, Brooklyn, NY 11204

Manhattan College
Riverdale, New York
www.manhattan.edu

CB member
CB code: 2395

- Private 4-year engineering and liberal arts college affiliated with Roman Catholic Church
- Residential campus in very large city
- 3,237 degree-seeking undergraduates: 7% part-time, 45% women, 3% African American, 4% Asian American, 15% Hispanic American, 3% international
- 420 degree-seeking graduate students
- 69% of applicants admitted
- SAT or ACT with writing required
- 72% graduate within 6 years; 18% enter graduate study

General. Founded in 1853. Regionally accredited. Independent institution in the Roman Catholic tradition sponsored by De La Salle Christian Brothers. **Degrees:** 654 bachelor's awarded; master's offered. **ROTC:** Army, Air Force. **Location:** 10 miles from midtown Manhattan. **Calendar:** Semester, extensive summer session. **Full-time faculty:** 206 total; 95% have terminal degrees, 14% minority, 38% women. **Part-time faculty:** 196 total; 33% have terminal degrees, 13% minority, 37% women. **Class size:** 48% < 20, 52% 20-39, less than 1% 40-49, less than 1% 50-99. **Special facilities:** Holocaust, Genocide and Interfaith education center, plant morphogenesis laboratory.

Freshman class profile. 6,253 applied, 4,335 admitted, 803 enrolled.

Mid 50% test scores			
SAT critical reading:	500-630	Rank in top tenth:	14%
SAT math:	520-660	End year in good standing:	90%
ACT composite:	22-28	Return as sophomores:	82%
GPA 3.75 or higher:	18%	Out-of-state:	29%
GPA 3.50-3.74:	13%	Live on campus:	84%
GPA 3.0-3.49:	45%	International:	3%
GPA 2.0-2.99:	24%	Fraternities:	1%
Rank in top quarter:	48%	Sororities:	1%

Basis for selection. School achievement record and test scores most important. Essay, recommendations, and extracurricular activities also reviewed. Interview recommended. **Home schooled:** State high school equivalency certificate, letter of recommendation (nonparent) required.

High school preparation. College-preparatory program required. 16 units required; 17 recommended. Required and recommended units include English 4, mathematics 3-4, social studies 3, science 2-3, foreign language 2-3 and academic electives 2. 4 mathematics, 4 science (including precalculus, chemistry, and physics) recommended of engineering majors and most science majors.

2011-2012 Annual costs. Tuition/fees: $30,000. Room/board: $11,420. Books/supplies: $1,200. Personal expenses: $1,200.

2011-2012 Financial aid. All financial aid based on need. 696 full-time freshmen applied for aid; 612 were judged to have need; 612 of these received aid. Average need met was 69%. Average scholarship/grant was $16,015; average loan $3,415. 62% of total undergraduate aid awarded as scholarships/grants, 38% as loans/jobs.

Application procedures. Admission: Priority date 2/15; no deadline. $60 fee, may be waived for applicants with need. Application must be submitted on paper. Admission notification on a rolling basis beginning on or about 12/1. Must reply by May 1 or within 2 week(s) if notified thereafter. **Financial aid:** Priority date 3/1, closing date 4/15. FAFSA required. Applicants notified on a rolling basis starting 2/15; must reply by 5/1.

Academics. Special study options: Accelerated study, combined bachelor's/graduate degree, cooperative education, cross-registration, distance learning, double major, ESL, exchange student, honors, independent study, internships, liberal arts/career combination, student-designed major, study abroad, teacher certification program, Washington semester. **Credit/placement by examination:** AP, CLEP, IB, institutional tests. 30 credit hours maximum toward bachelor's degree. **Support services:** Reduced course load, remedial instruction, study skills assistance, tutoring, writing center.

Majors. Biology: General, biochemistry. **Business:** General, accounting, finance, international, labor relations, management information systems, managerial economics, statistics. **Communications:** Broadcast journalism, communications/speech/rhetoric, journalism. **Computer sciences:** General, computer science, information systems. **Education:** General, biology, chemistry, computer, early childhood, elementary, English, foreign languages, French, health, history, mathematics, middle, physical, physics, science, secondary, social science, social studies, Spanish, special ed. **Engineering:** Chemical, civil, computer, electrical, mechanical. **English:** Writing. **Foreign languages:** French, Spanish. **Health services:** Nuclear medical technology, predental, premedicine, preveterinary. **History:** General. **Math:** General. **Philosophy/religion:** Philosophy, religion. **Physical sciences:** Chemistry, physics. **Psychology:** General. **Social sciences:** Economics, sociology.

Most popular majors. Business/marketing 22%, communications/journalism 6%, education 16%, engineering/engineering technologies 24%, psychology 7%, social sciences 7%.

Computing on campus. 350 workstations in library, computer center, student center. Dormitories wired for high-speed internet access and linked to campus network. Commuter students can connect to campus network. Online course registration, online library, helpline, repair service, student web hosting, wireless network available.

Student life. Freshman orientation: Mandatory, $165 fee. Preregistration for classes offered. **Housing:** Guaranteed on-campus for all undergraduates. Coed dorms, special housing for disabled, apartments available. $400 nonrefundable deposit, deadline 5/1. Learning/living community for freshmen. **Activities:** Bands, campus ministries, choral groups, dance, drama, international student organizations, literary magazine, music ensembles, Model UN, musical theater, radio station, student government, student newspaper, symphony orchestra, TV station, association for black culture, Christ in Your Life, Gaelic society, international student association, Just Peace, LaSallian Collegians, Italian club, French club, society of Hispanic engineers, College Republicans.

Athletics. NCAA. **Intercollegiate:** Baseball M, basketball, cheerleading, cross-country, golf M, lacrosse, rowing (crew), soccer, softball W, swimming W, tennis, track and field, volleyball W. **Intramural:** Basketball, cross-country, football (tackle), golf M, ice hockey, soccer, softball, track and field, volleyball. **Team name:** Jaspers.

Student services. Alcohol/substance abuse counseling, chaplain/spiritual director, career counseling, student employment services, financial aid counseling, health services, personal counseling, placement for graduates, veterans' counselor. **Physically disabled:** Services for visually, hearing impaired.

Contact. E-mail: admit@manhattan.edu
Phone: (718) 862-7200 Toll-free number: (800) 622-9235
Fax: (718) 862-8019
William Bisset, Vice President for Enrollment Management, Manhattan College, 4513 Manhattan College Parkway, Riverdale, NY 10471

Manhattan School of Music
New York, New York
www.msmnyc.edu

CB code: 2396

- Private 4-year music college
- Residential campus in very large city
- 406 degree-seeking undergraduates
- 553 graduate students
- 41% of applicants admitted
- Application essay required

General. Founded in 1917. Regionally accredited. Extensive performance opportunities on campus and off. **Degrees:** 99 bachelor's awarded; master's, doctoral offered. **Calendar:** Semester. **Full-time faculty:** 98 total; 24% have terminal degrees, 1% minority, 44% women. **Part-time faculty:** 153 total; 20% have terminal degrees, 6% minority, 31% women. **Class size:** 83% < 20, 13% 20-39, 2% 50-99, 2% >100. **Special facilities:** 850-seat concert hall, recital halls, state-of-the-art-performance spaces, distance learning center, electronic music studios, recording studio, performance library.

Freshman class profile. 866 applied, 351 admitted, 100 enrolled.

GPA 3.75 or higher:	46%	GPA 2.0-2.99:	3%
GPA 3.50-3.74:	24%	Out-of-state:	74%
GPA 3.0-3.49:	27%	Live on campus:	83%

Basis for selection. Audition, availability of space in specific performance area, and academic record most important. Audition required. **Home schooled:** Statement describing home school structure and mission, transcript of courses and grades, letter of recommendation (nonparent) required. GED accepted, but if no GED, SAT or ACT required.

High school preparation. College-preparatory program recommended. Recommended units include English 4, mathematics 3, social studies 4, history 4, science 3 and foreign language 4. Extensive music training required.

2011-2012 Annual costs. Tuition/fees: $34,105. Room/board: $11,516. Books/supplies: $1,000. Personal expenses: $3,000.

2010-2011 Financial aid. Need-based: 52 full-time freshmen applied for aid; 39 were judged to have need; 37 of these received aid. Average need met was 51%. Average scholarship/grant was $19,681; average loan $3,647. 59% of total undergraduate aid awarded as scholarships/grants, 41% as loans/jobs. **Non-need-based:** Awarded to 35 full-time undergraduates, including 9 freshmen. Scholarships awarded for academics, alumni affiliation, leadership, music/drama.

Application procedures. Admission: Closing date 12/1 (receipt date). $100 fee, may be waived for applicants with need. Application must be submitted online. Admission notification by 4/1. Must reply by May 1 or within 2 week(s) if notified thereafter. **Financial aid:** Closing date 3/1. FAFSA, institutional form, CSS PROFILE required. Applicants notified by 4/1; must reply by 5/1 or within 2 week(s) of notification.

Academics. Special study options: Cross-registration, ESL, exchange student, independent study, study abroad. **Credit/placement by examination:** AP, CLEP, institutional tests. 60 credit hours maximum toward bachelor's degree. **Support services:** Reduced course load, remedial instruction, tutoring.

Majors. Visual/performing arts: Music performance, music theory/composition.

Computing on campus. 20 workstations in library, computer center. Dormitories wired for high-speed internet access and linked to campus network. Online library, helpline, wireless network available.

Student life. Freshman orientation: Mandatory. Preregistration for classes offered. 1-2 weeks before classes start. Placement exams, orchestra and opera auditions held. **Policies:** Undergraduates required to live in residence hall for first 2 years. Alcohol allowed only for those over 21 and only in designated areas. No smoking in the building. **Housing:** Guaranteed on-campus for freshmen. Coed dorms available. $500 nonrefundable deposit, deadline 6/15. Housing guaranteed only to students who submit documents and pay deposit by set deadline. **Activities:** Bands, choral groups, international student organizations, music ensembles, musical theater, opera, student government, student newspaper, symphony orchestra, Pan-African student union, international student organization, resident community council, student council, GLBT student group, chess club, soccer club.

Student services. Alcohol/substance abuse counseling, career counseling, student employment services, financial aid counseling, personal counseling. **Physically disabled:** Services for visually impaired.

Contact. E-mail: admission@msmnyc.edu
Phone: (917) 493-4436 Fax: (212) 749-3025
Amy Anderson, Associate Dean for Enrollment Management, Manhattan School of Music, 120 Claremont Avenue, New York, NY 10027-4698

Manhattanville College
Purchase, New York
www.manhattanville.edu

CB member
CB code: 2397

- Private 4-year liberal arts and teachers college
- Residential campus in small town

- 1,736 degree-seeking undergraduates: 5% part-time, 64% women
- 1,060 graduate students
- 60% of applicants admitted
- Application essay required
- 56% graduate within 6 years

General. Founded in 1841. Regionally accredited. Strong relationship with United Nations. **Degrees:** 387 bachelor's awarded; master's, doctoral offered. **Location:** 25 miles from New York City. **Calendar:** Semester, extensive summer session. **Full-time faculty:** 102 total; 96% have terminal degrees, 12% minority, 49% women. **Part-time faculty:** 238 total; 11% minority, 49% women. **Class size:** 73% < 20, 25% 20-39, 2% 40-49. **Special facilities:** Photography laboratory, observatory, environmental biology laboratory, TV production studio, blackbox theater.

Freshman class profile. 4,772 applied, 2,863 admitted, 534 enrolled.

GPA 3.75 or higher:	9%	Rank in top tenth:	22%
GPA 3.50-3.74:	12%	Return as sophomores:	69%
GPA 3.0-3.49:	36%	Out-of-state:	45%
GPA 2.0-2.99:	43%	Live on campus:	85%
Rank in top quarter:	47%	International:	7%

Basis for selection. School achievement record, recommendations, test scores or samples of academic work most important. Essay, school and community activities. Interview strongly recommended. SAT or ACT recommended. Portfolio required for fine arts program; audition recommended for dance, music and theater programs.

High school preparation. 16 units required. Required units include English 4, mathematics 3, social studies 2, science 2 and academic electives 5.

2011-2012 Annual costs. Tuition/fees: $35,370. Room/board: $14,340. Books/supplies: $2,983. Personal expenses: $1,550.

Financial aid. Non-need-based: Scholarships awarded for academics, alumni affiliation, art, leadership, music/drama. **Additional information:** Upper level students may earn additional money and academic credit through internship program.

Application procedures. Admission: Closing date 3/1 (postmark date). $75 fee, may be waived for applicants with need. Admission notification on a rolling basis beginning on or about 1/2. Must reply by May 1 or within 2 week(s) if notified thereafter. **Financial aid:** Closing date 3/1. FAFSA required. Applicants notified on a rolling basis starting 2/1; must reply by 5/1 or within 2 week(s) of notification.

Academics. Students must complete portfolio before graduation, which is individualized academic plan and profile. **Special study options:** Accelerated study, combined bachelor's/graduate degree, cross-registration, double major, dual enrollment of high school students, ESL, exchange student, external degree, honors, independent study, internships, liberal arts/career combination, student-designed major, study abroad, teacher certification program, weekend college. Study abroad programs in Oxford, Paris, Tokyo, Osaka, Madrid, Seville, Florence, Rome, Berlin, Galway and the world capitals program in Jerusalem, Santiago, Brussels, Buenos Aires, Prague, Moscow, and South Africa. **Credit/placement by examination:** AP, CLEP, IB, institutional tests. Up to 90 credits allowed: up to 30 AP credits, up to 18 IB credits, no CLEP limit. **Support services:** Learning center, reduced course load, remedial instruction, study skills assistance, tutoring, writing center.

Majors. Area/ethnic studies: American, Asian, French. **Biology:** General, biochemistry, neuroscience. **Business:** Business admin, finance. **Communications:** Communications/speech/rhetoric. **Computer sciences:** General. **Education:** General. **English:** English lit. **Foreign languages:** Romance. **History:** General. **Liberal arts:** Arts/sciences. **Math:** General. **Philosophy/religion:** Philosophy, religion. **Physical sciences:** Chemistry, physics. **Psychology:** General. **Social sciences:** Economics, political science, sociology. **Visual/performing arts:** Art history/conservation, dance, dramatic, music.

Most popular majors. Business/marketing 24%, communications/journalism 10%, English 9%, psychology 11%, social sciences 11%, visual/performing arts 15%.

Computing on campus. 270 workstations in dormitories, library, computer center, student center. Dormitories wired for high-speed internet access and linked to campus network. Commuter students can connect to campus network. Online course registration, online library, helpline, repair service, student web hosting, wireless network available.

Student life. Freshman orientation: Mandatory. Preregistration for classes offered. **Housing:** Coed dorms, wellness housing available. $385 deposit, deadline 5/1. **Activities:** Bands, campus ministries, choral groups, dance, drama, film society, international student organizations, literary magazine, music ensembles, Model UN, musical theater, opera, radio station, student government, student newspaper, symphony orchestra, TV station,

language and culture clubs, students organized against racism, women's resource center, gay/straight coalition, political science association, multicultural advisory board, black student union.

Athletics. NCAA. **Intercollegiate:** Baseball M, basketball, cheerleading M, field hockey W, golf M, ice hockey, lacrosse, soccer, softball W, tennis. **Intramural:** Basketball. **Team name:** Valiants.

Student services. Adult student services, alcohol/substance abuse counseling, chaplain/spiritual director, career counseling, services for economically disadvantaged, student employment services, financial aid counseling, health services, minority student services, personal counseling, placement for graduates, women's services. **Physically disabled:** Services for visually, speech, hearing impaired.

Contact. E-mail: admissions@mville.edu
Phone: (914) 323-5464 Toll-free number: (800) 328-4553
Fax: (914) 694-1732
Kevin O'Sullivan, Director of Admissions, Manhattanville College, 2900 Purchase Street, Purchase, NY 10577

Mannes College The New School for Music
New York, New York
www.mannes.edu CB code: 2398

- Private 4-year music college
- Commuter campus in very large city
- 200 degree-seeking undergraduates: 10% part-time, 51% women, 2% African American, 11% Asian American, 4% Hispanic American, 39% international
- 176 degree-seeking graduate students
- 35% of applicants admitted
- 72% graduate within 6 years

General. Founded in 1916. Regionally accredited. Division of The New School. **Degrees:** 25 bachelor's awarded; master's offered. **Location:** Located in Manhattan. **Calendar:** Semester, limited summer session. **Full-time faculty:** 18 total; 33% have terminal degrees, 11% minority, 44% women. **Part-time faculty:** 145 total; 13% minority, 42% women. **Class size:** 97% < 20, 2% 20-39, less than 1% 50-99. **Special facilities:** 2 concert halls.

Freshman class profile. 505 applied, 179 admitted, 56 enrolled.

GPA 3.75 or higher:	28%	Return as sophomores:	84%
GPA 3.50-3.74:	20%	Out-of-state:	35%
GPA 3.0-3.49:	40%	Live on campus:	27%
GPA 2.0-2.99:	12%	International:	42%

Basis for selection. In order of importance: specific talent for major as evidenced by audition in major instrument or evaluation of previous accomplishment for composers and theory majors, general musicianship skills (ear, theory, etc.), academic record. Institutionally designed entrance examination, including major audition. Written examinations in music theory, dictation, ear training, and English usage. Audition required, essay recommended. Placement exams and interviews required for all Bachelor of Music, Bachelor of Science, Undergraduate Diploma, and Master of Music applicants. If applicant does not complete all sessions, application incomplete and will not be considered for acceptance. Tapes may be submitted for advisory opinion.

2011-2012 Annual costs. Tuition/fees: $36,780. Room/board: $15,260. Books/supplies: $2,050. Personal expenses: $1,550.

Financial aid. Non-need-based: Scholarships awarded for music/drama. **Additional information:** Closing date for scholarship applications 2 weeks prior to audition date.

Application procedures. Admission: $100 fee. Admission notification by 4/1. Admission notification on a rolling basis. Must reply by May 1 or within 4 week(s) if notified thereafter. **Financial aid:** Priority date 3/1; no closing date. Applicants notified on a rolling basis; must reply within 4 week(s) of notification.

Academics. Special study options: Double major, ESL, independent study, internships. **Credit/placement by examination:** AP, CLEP, institutional tests. **Support services:** Remedial instruction, tutoring, writing center.

Majors. Visual/performing arts: Conducting, music performance, music theory/composition, piano/keyboard, stringed instruments, studio arts, voice/opera.

Computing on campus. Dormitories wired for high-speed internet access and linked to campus network. Commuter students can connect to campus

---

network. Online course registration, helpline, student web hosting, wireless network available.

Student life. Freshman orientation: Mandatory. Preregistration for classes offered. **Housing:** Guaranteed on-campus for all undergraduates. Coed dorms, special housing for disabled, apartments, wellness housing available. $250 nonrefundable deposit, deadline 7/1. **Activities:** Jazz band, choral groups, dance, drama, international student organizations, literary magazine, music ensembles, opera, radio station, student government, student newspaper, symphony orchestra, Sustainable Design Review, New School Styling Club, Roots & Shoots, Radical student union, Global Health student organization, international club, PHOTOfeast, the Theatre Collective, Jewish student union, New School Remnant Christian Fellowship.

Student services. Career counseling, student employment services, financial aid counseling, health services, minority student services, personal counseling.

Contact. E-mail: mannesadmissions@newschool.edu
Phone: (212) 580-0210 ext. 4862 Toll-free number: (800) 292-3040
Fax: (212) 580-1738
Georgia Schmitt, Director of Admissions, Mannes College The New School for Music, 150 West 85th Street, New York, NY 10024

Marist College
Poughkeepsie, New York
www.marist.edu/
CB member
CB code: 2400

- Private 4-year liberal arts college
- Residential campus in small city
- 5,019 degree-seeking undergraduates: 7% part-time, 59% women, 3% African American, 1% Asian American, 5% Hispanic American, 1% international
- 849 degree-seeking graduate students
- 34% of applicants admitted
- Application essay required
- 80% graduate within 6 years

General. Founded in 1929. Regionally accredited. **Degrees:** 1,119 bachelor's awarded; master's offered. **ROTC:** Army. **Location:** 75 miles from New York City, 75 miles from Albany. **Calendar:** Semester, limited summer session. **Full-time faculty:** 223 total; 77% have terminal degrees, 13% minority, 47% women. **Part-time faculty:** 388 total; 26% have terminal degrees, 6% minority, 50% women. **Class size:** 57% < 20, 43% 20-39, less than 1% 40-49. **Special facilities:** Bureau of Economic Research, Laboratory for Environmental Studies, Management Studies Center, Institute for Public Opinion, arboretum, online journalism laboratory.

Freshman class profile. 11,399 applied, 3,845 admitted, 1,174 enrolled.

Mid 50% test scores			
SAT critical reading:	540-630	Rank in top quarter:	70%
SAT math:	560-640	Rank in top tenth:	32%
SAT writing:	550-640	Return as sophomores:	92%
ACT composite:	24-28	Out-of-state:	52%
GPA 3.75 or higher:	22%	Live on campus:	92%
GPA 3.50-3.74:	20%	International:	1%
GPA 3.0-3.49:	40%	Fraternities:	1%
GPA 2.0-2.99:	17%	Sororities:	1%

Basis for selection. Secondary school achievement record, rank in top third of class primary consideration. Test scores, recommendations, activities, personal and leadership qualities also important. Campus visits and information sessions with admission counselors strongly recommended. **Home schooled:** Transcript of courses and grades, letter of recommendation (nonparent) required.

High school preparation. College-preparatory program required. 17 units required. Required and recommended units include English 4, mathematics 3-4, social studies 2, history 1, science 3-4 (laboratory 2-3), foreign language 2 and academic electives 2.

2011-2012 Annual costs. Tuition/fees: $28,800. Room/board: $12,100. Books/supplies: $1,700. Personal expenses: $835.

2011-2012 Financial aid. Need-based: 1,035 full-time freshmen applied for aid; 770 were judged to have need; 769 of these received aid. Average scholarship/grant was $15,033; average loan $3,543. 37% of total undergraduate aid awarded as scholarships/grants, 63% as loans/jobs. **Non-need-based:** Awarded to 3,752 full-time undergraduates, including 1,155 freshmen. Scholarships awarded for academics, athletics, music/drama, ROTC, state residency.

Application procedures. Admission: Closing date 2/1 (postmark date). $50 fee, may be waived for applicants with need. Admission notification by 3/30. Must reply by 5/1. **Financial aid:** Priority date 2/15, closing date 5/1. FAFSA, institutional form required. Applicants notified on a rolling basis starting 4/1; must reply by 5/1 or within 2 week(s) of notification.

Academics. Paralegal certificates offered. Substantial internship opportunities for all majors. Students participate in community service program. **Special study options:** Accelerated study, combined bachelor's/graduate degree, cooperative education, cross-registration, distance learning, double major, dual enrollment of high school students, ESL, honors, independent study, internships, liberal arts/career combination, semester at sea, study abroad, teacher certification program, United Nations semester, Washington semester, weekend college. Undergraduates may take graduate classes. Cooperative education in arts, business, computer science, education, humanities, natural science, social/behavioral science, technologies. **Credit/placement by examination:** AP, CLEP, IB, SAT, ACT, institutional tests. ACT-PEP accepted on individual basis. **Support services:** Learning center, reduced course load, study skills assistance, tutoring, writing center.

Majors. Area/ethnic studies: American. **Biology:** General, biochemistry, biomedical sciences. **Business:** Accounting, business admin, fashion, finance, human resources, international, marketing. **Communications:** Advertising, journalism, media studies, public relations, radio/TV, sports. **Computer sciences:** Computer science, information systems, information technology, programming. **Conservation:** Environmental science. **Education:** Biology, chemistry, English, French, mathematics, social studies, Spanish, special ed. **English:** English lit, writing. **Foreign languages:** French, Spanish. **Health services:** Athletic training, clinical lab science. **History:** General. **Human services:** Social work. **Math:** General, applied, computational. **Philosophy/religion:** Philosophy. **Physical sciences:** Chemistry. **Protective services:** Law enforcement admin. **Psychology:** General. **Social sciences:** Economics, political science. **Visual/performing arts:** Art, art history/conservation, fashion design, game design, studio arts.

Most popular majors. Business/marketing 25%, communications/journalism 16%, psychology 13%, visual/performing arts 12%.

Computing on campus. 646 workstations in dormitories, library, computer center, student center. Dormitories wired for high-speed internet access and linked to campus network. Commuter students can connect to campus network. Online course registration, online library, helpline, repair service, student web hosting, wireless network available.

Student life. Freshman orientation: Mandatory, $90 fee. Preregistration for classes offered. 1-day orientation in June. **Housing:** Guaranteed on-campus for freshmen. Coed dorms, special housing for disabled, apartments, wellness housing available. $500 nonrefundable deposit, deadline 5/1. Garden apartments, townhouses, suites available. **Activities:** Bands, campus ministries, choral groups, dance, drama, film society, literary magazine, music ensembles, musical theater, radio station, student government, student newspaper, TV station, black student union, Asian Alliance, Circle K, ARCO, community service programs, Habitat for Humanity, political science club, council on theatre arts, social action clubs.

Athletics. NCAA. **Intercollegiate:** Baseball M, basketball, cross-country, diving, football (tackle) M, lacrosse, rowing (crew), soccer, softball W, swimming, tennis, track and field, volleyball W, water polo W. **Intramural:** Basketball, soccer, softball, volleyball. **Team name:** Red Foxes.

Student services. Adult student services, alcohol/substance abuse counseling, chaplain/spiritual director, career counseling, student employment services, financial aid counseling, health services, personal counseling, placement for graduates, veterans' counselor. **Physically disabled:** Services for visually, hearing impaired.

Contact. E-mail: admission@marist.edu
Phone: (845) 575-3226 Toll-free number: (800) 436-5483
Fax: (845) 575-3215
Kent Rinehart, Dean of Undergraduate Admissions, Marist College, 3399 North Road, Poughkeepsie, NY 12601-1387

Marymount Manhattan College
New York, New York   CB member
www.mmm.edu   CB code: 2405

- Private 4-year liberal arts college
- Residential campus in very large city
- 1,901 degree-seeking undergraduates: 11% part-time, 76% women, 6% African American, 4% Asian American, 15% Hispanic American, 1% Native American, 4% international
- 79% of applicants admitted
- SAT or ACT (ACT writing optional), application essay required
- 40% graduate within 6 years

General. Founded in 1936. Regionally accredited. **Degrees:** 369 bachelor's, 14 associate awarded. **Calendar:** Semester, limited summer session. **Full-time faculty:** 104 total; 89% have terminal degrees, 14% minority, 61% women. **Part-time faculty:** 214 total; 55% have terminal degrees, 11% minority, 51% women. **Class size:** 69% < 20, 31% 20-39, less than 1% 40-49. **Special facilities:** Communications and learning center, communication arts multimedia suite, center for science education.

Freshman class profile. 3,664 applied, 2,892 admitted, 439 enrolled.

Mid 50% test scores			
SAT critical reading:	480-590	GPA 3.0-3.49:	43%
SAT math:	460-560	GPA 2.0-2.99:	30%
SAT writing:	480-590	End year in good standing:	67%
ACT composite:	21-26	Return as sophomores:	67%
GPA 3.75 or higher:	8%	Out-of-state:	62%
GPA 3.50-3.74:	18%	Live on campus:	75%
		International:	5%

Basis for selection. High school GPA of 3.0 and SAT verbal and math scores of 450 each recommended. Letters of recommendation from teachers and administrators, extracurricular and community activities important. Rolling deadline for SAT/ACT score receipt. Interview recommended for all; audition required for acting, dance, and theater programs; portfolio recommended for art program. **Home schooled:** Transcript of courses and grades required. Must submit official high school transcripts if high school attended before withdrawing. **Learning Disabled:** Interview and Wechsler Delta Adult Intelligence Scale test required.

High school preparation. College-preparatory program recommended. 17 units required. Required and recommended units include English 4, mathematics 3, social studies 3, science 3 (laboratory 2), foreign language 2 and academic electives 4.

2011-2012 Annual costs. Tuition/fees: $24,708. $2,100 annual charge for food card that students can draw against for meals. Room only: $11,930. Books/supplies: $1,000. Personal expenses: $4,300.

2010-2011 Financial aid. Need-based: 396 full-time freshmen applied for aid; 343 were judged to have need; 339 of these received aid. Average need met was 54%. Average scholarship/grant was $11,693; average loan $4,201. 61% of total undergraduate aid awarded as scholarships/grants, 39% as loans/jobs. **Non-need-based:** Awarded to 471 full-time undergraduates, including 82 freshmen. Scholarships awarded for academics, art, leadership, state residency. **Additional information:** Limited international scholarships for top applicants.

Application procedures. Admission: Priority date 3/15; no deadline. $60 fee, may be waived for applicants with need. Admission notification on a rolling basis beginning on or about 9/1. Must reply by May 1 or within 3 week(s) if notified thereafter. **Financial aid:** Priority date 3/15; no closing date. FAFSA required. Applicants notified on a rolling basis starting 3/15; must reply by 5/1 or within 2 week(s) of notification.

Academics. Special study options: Accelerated study, distance learning, double major, dual enrollment of high school students, exchange student, independent study, internships, liberal arts/career combination, study abroad. 5-year bachelor's/master's program in computer science with Polytechnic University, programs with Laboratory Institute of Merchandising, New York School of Interior Design, Deutsches Haus at New York University, China Institute, New York Institute of Finance, American Institute of Banking, Hunter College of CUNY, Martha Graham School of Dance, HEOP. **Credit/placement by examination:** AP, CLEP, IB, SAT, institutional tests. 30 credit hours maximum toward bachelor's degree. Maximum of 12 credits for language proficiency. SAT Subject used for placement if submitted. **Support services:** Learning center, reduced course load, remedial instruction, study skills assistance, tutoring.

Majors. Biology: General. **Business:** Accounting, business admin. **Communications:** Communications/speech/rhetoric. **English:** English lit. **Health services:** Audiology/speech pathology. **History:** General. **Philosophy/religion:** Philosophy, religion. **Psychology:** General. **Social sciences:** International relations, political science, sociology. **Visual/performing arts:** Acting, art, art history/conservation, dance, dramatic, graphic design, photography, studio arts.

Most popular majors. Business/marketing 9%, communications/journalism 25%, social sciences 9%, visual/performing arts 40%.

Computing on campus. 215 workstations in library, computer center, student center. Dormitories wired for high-speed internet access and linked to campus network. Commuter students can connect to campus network. Wireless network available.

Student life. Freshman orientation: Mandatory. Preregistration for classes offered. 3 days of introductions, information, activities, and social engagements. **Housing:** Coed dorms available. $500 nonrefundable deposit, deadline 5/1. **Activities:** Campus ministries, choral groups, dance, drama, international student organizations, literary magazine, music ensembles, musical theater, radio station, student government, student newspaper, ethnic, religious, political, women's, environmental, and cultural groups, student professional organizations, and honor societies.

Student services. Alcohol/substance abuse counseling, chaplain/spiritual director, career counseling, student employment services, financial aid counseling, health services, personal counseling, placement for graduates. **Physically disabled:** Services for speech, hearing impaired.

Contact. E-mail: admissions@mmm.edu
Phone: (212) 517-0430 Toll-free number: (800) 627-9668
Fax: (212) 517-0448
Jim Rogers, Dean of Admission, Marymount Manhattan College, 221 East 71st Street, New York, NY 10021-4597

Medaille College
Buffalo, New York
www.medaille.edu
CB code: 2422

- Private 4-year liberal arts college
- Commuter campus in large city
- 1,793 degree-seeking undergraduates: 7% part-time, 64% women, 16% African American, 3% Asian American, 5% Hispanic American, 1% Native American
- 876 degree-seeking graduate students
- 68% of applicants admitted
- SAT or ACT with writing, application essay required

General. Founded in 1875. Regionally accredited. **Degrees:** 316 bachelor's, 83 associate awarded; master's offered. **ROTC:** Army. **Location:** 3 miles from downtown. **Calendar:** Semester, limited summer session. **Full-time faculty:** 86 total; 70% have terminal degrees, 10% minority, 49% women. **Part-time faculty:** 198 total. **Class size:** 62% < 20, 36% 20-39, less than 1% 40-49, 1% 50-99.

Freshman class profile. 1,438 applied, 984 admitted, 375 enrolled.

Mid 50% test scores			
		ACT composite:	17-22
SAT critical reading:	390-490	**Out-of-state:**	3%
SAT math:	400-500	**Live on campus:**	40%

Basis for selection. Motivation and maturity, as well as academic record and test scores, considered. SAT recommended. Interview strongly recommended.

High school preparation. College-preparatory program recommended. 12 units required; 20 recommended. Required and recommended units include English 4, mathematics 2-3, social studies 4, history 2, science 2-3 (laboratory 2) and foreign language 2. 3 math, 3 science recommended for veterinary technology.

2011-2012 Annual costs. Tuition/fees: $21,598. Room/board: $10,244. Books/supplies: $1,100. Personal expenses: $3,100.

2010-2011 Financial aid. **Need-based:** 369 full-time freshmen applied for aid; 345 were judged to have need; 345 of these received aid. Average scholarship/grant was $13,603; average loan $3,824. 56% of total undergraduate aid awarded as scholarships/grants, 44% as loans/jobs. **Non-need-based:** Awarded to 52 full-time undergraduates, including 352 freshmen. Scholarships awarded for academics, leadership.

Application procedures. Admission: Priority date 8/1; no deadline. $25 fee, may be waived for applicants with need, free for online applicants. Admission notification on a rolling basis beginning on or about 10/1. Must reply by May 1 or within 4 week(s) if notified thereafter. **Financial aid:** Priority date 3/1; no closing date. FAFSA required. Applicants notified on a rolling basis starting 3/1; must reply within 2 week(s) of notification.

Academics. All pre-professional programs require participation in at least 1 internship. Branch campuses in Amherst and Rochester. **Special study options:** Accelerated study, combined bachelor's/graduate degree, cross-registration, distance learning, double major, honors, independent study, internships, liberal arts/career combination, student-designed major, teacher certification program, weekend college. Module system for full-time evening students and for full-time weekend students. **Credit/placement by examination:** AP, CLEP, IB, SAT. 30 credit hours maximum toward associate degree, 60 toward bachelor's. **Support services:** Learning center, reduced course load, remedial instruction, study skills assistance, tutoring.

Majors. Biology: General. **Business:** General, accounting, business admin, management information systems. **Communications:** Media studies. **Computer sciences:** General. **Education:** General, biology, elementary, English, mathematics, middle, secondary, social studies. **English:** English lit. **Health services:** Medical records admin, veterinary technology/assistant. **Liberal arts:** Arts/sciences. **Math:** General. **Parks/recreation:** Sports admin. **Protective services:** Homeland security, police science. **Psychology:** General. **Visual/performing arts:** General. **Work/family studies:** Child care management.

Most popular majors. Business/marketing 41%, communications/journalism 8%, education 11%, health sciences 7%, parks/recreation 7%, psychology 10%, security/protective services 9%.

Computing on campus. 120 workstations in dormitories, library, computer center, student center. Dormitories wired for high-speed internet access and linked to campus network. Commuter students can connect to campus network. Online library, wireless network available.

Student life. Freshman orientation: Mandatory. Preregistration for classes offered. **Housing:** Coed dorms, single-sex dorms, apartments, wellness housing available. $100 deposit, deadline 9/1. **Activities:** Drama, film society, literary magazine, musical theater, radio station, student government, student newspaper, TV station, African American student union, child and youth services club, student volunteer center, multicultural association, SADD, international student society, resident student council.

Athletics. NCAA. **Intercollegiate:** Baseball M, basketball, bowling W, cross-country, golf, lacrosse, soccer, softball W, volleyball. **Team name:** Mavericks.

Student services. Adult student services, career counseling, student employment services, financial aid counseling, health services, personal counseling, placement for graduates, veterans' counselor. **Physically disabled:** Services for visually, speech, hearing impaired.

Contact. E-mail: admissionsug@medaille.edu
Phone: (716) 880-2200 Toll-free number: (800) 292-1582
Fax: (716) 880-2007
Greg Florczak, Director of Undergraduate Admissions, Medaille College, 18 Agassiz Circle, Buffalo, NY 14214

Medaille College: Amherst
Williamsville, New York
www.medaille.edu

- Private 4-year liberal arts college
- Commuter campus in small town
- 264 degree-seeking undergraduates
- SAT or ACT with writing, application essay required

General. Branch campus of Medaille College. Financial aid data for this institution calculated on a system-wide basis and includes figures for all three Medaille campuses. The combined financial aid totals are reported under the main Medaille campus. **Degrees:** 68 bachelor's, 23 associate awarded; master's offered. **Calendar:** Semester. **Full-time faculty:** 3 total. **Part-time faculty:** 26 total.

Basis for selection. Motivation and maturity, as well as academic record and test scores, considered. SAT recommended.

High school preparation. College-preparatory program recommended. 12 units required; 20 recommended. Required and recommended units include English 4, mathematics 2-3, social studies 4, history 2, science 2-3 (laboratory 2) and foreign language 2.

2011-2012 Annual costs. Tuition/fees: $21,598. Books/supplies: $1,100. Personal expenses: $3,100.

Financial aid. Non-need-based: Scholarships awarded for academics, leadership.

Application procedures. Admission: No deadline. $25 fee, may be waived for applicants with need, free for online applicants. Admission notification on a rolling basis. Must reply by May 1 or within 4 week(s) if notified thereafter. **Financial aid:** No deadline.

Academics. Special study options: Accelerated study, combined bachelor's/graduate degree, teacher certification program, weekend college. **Credit/placement by examination:** AP, CLEP, IB, SAT. 30 credit hours maximum toward associate degree, 60 toward bachelor's. **Support services:** Learning center, study skills assistance, tutoring.

Majors. Business: General, business admin, management information systems.

Computing on campus. Dormitories wired for high-speed internet access. Commuter students can connect to campus network. Online library, helpline, wireless network available.

Student life. Freshman orientation: Mandatory. Preregistration for classes offered. **Activities:** Student newspaper.

Athletics. Team name: Mavericks.

Student services. Adult student services, career counseling, student employment services, financial aid counseling, health services, personal counseling, placement for graduates, veterans' counselor. **Physically disabled:** Services for visually, speech, hearing impaired.

Contact. E-mail: sageadmissions@medaille.edu
Phone: (716) 631-1061 Toll-free number: (888) 252-2235
Greg Florczak, Registrar, Medaille College: Amherst, 30 Wilson Road, Williamsville, NY 14221

Medaille College: Rochester
Rochester, New York
www.medaille.edu

- Private 4-year liberal arts college
- Commuter campus in small city
- 81 degree-seeking undergraduates

General. Branch campus of Medaille College. Financial aid data for this institution calculated on a system-wide basis and includes figures for all three Medaille campuses. The combined financial aid totals are reported under the main Medaille campus. **Degrees:** 20 bachelor's, 9 associate awarded; master's offered. **Calendar:** Semester. **Full-time faculty:** 3 total; 67% women. **Part-time faculty:** 26 total; 62% women.

Basis for selection. Motivation and maturity, as well as academic record and test scores considered.

High school preparation. 12 units required; 20 recommended. Required and recommended units include English 4, mathematics 2-3, social studies 4, history 2, science 2-3 (laboratory 2) and foreign language 2.

2011-2012 Annual costs. Tuition/fees: $21,598. Books/supplies: $1,100. Personal expenses: $3,100.

Application procedures. Admission: No deadline. $25 fee, may be waived for applicants with need, free for online applicants. Admission notification on a rolling basis.

Academics. Special study options: Accelerated study, combined bachelor's/graduate degree. **Credit/placement by examination:** AP, CLEP.

Majors. Business: General, business admin, management information systems.

Computing on campus. Online library, wireless network available.

Student life. Activities: Student newspaper.

Athletics. Team name: Mavericks.

Student services. Career counseling, financial aid counseling. **Physically disabled:** Services for visually, speech, hearing impaired.

Contact. E-mail: sageadmissions@medaille.edu
Phone: (585) 272-0030
Kathleen Lazar, Registrar, Medaille College: Rochester, 1880 South Winton Road, Rochester, NY 14618

Mercy College
Dobbs Ferry, New York
www.mercy.edu   CB code: 2409

- Private 4-year liberal arts college
- Commuter campus in large town
- 6,792 degree-seeking undergraduates: 20% part-time, 68% women, 29% African American, 3% Asian American, 34% Hispanic American, 1% international

---

- 3,295 degree-seeking graduate students
- 64% of applicants admitted

General. Founded in 1950. Regionally accredited. Main campus in Dobbs Ferry plus additional campus locations in Bronx, Manhattan, White Plains, and Yorktown Heights. **Degrees:** 1,074 bachelor's, 82 associate awarded; master's, professional offered. **ROTC:** Army, Air Force. **Location:** 22 miles from New York City. **Calendar:** Semester, extensive summer session. **Full-time faculty:** 198 total; 70% have terminal degrees, 20% minority, 56% women. **Part-time faculty:** 849 total; 20% minority, 54% women. **Class size:** 56% < 20, 44% 20-39, less than 1% 40-49, less than 1% 50-99. **Special facilities:** Music and recording studios, biological research labs, Roy Disney digital arts studio.

Freshman class profile. 6,647 applied, 4,286 admitted, 1,192 enrolled.

GPA 3.75 or higher:	4%	GPA 2.0-2.99:	64%
GPA 3.50-3.74:	6%	Return as sophomores:	68%
GPA 3.0-3.49:	20%	Out-of-state:	9%

Basis for selection. SAT/ACT optional. SAT or ACT, SAT Subject Tests recommended. Additional interview with program director required for nursing, occupational therapy, physical therapy, social work, veterinary technology, computer arts programs. **Home schooled:** State high school equivalency certificate required.

High school preparation. College-preparatory program recommended. 21 units required. Required units include English 4, mathematics 4, social studies 2, history 2, science 3 (laboratory 1), foreign language 3 and academic electives 3.

2011-2012 Annual costs. Tuition/fees: $17,360. Room/board: $11,610. Books/supplies: $1,384. Personal expenses: $1,656.

2010-2011 Financial aid. Need-based: 1,047 full-time freshmen applied for aid; 1,007 were judged to have need; 978 of these received aid. Average need met was 59%. Average scholarship/grant was $11,200; average loan $3,189. 66% of total undergraduate aid awarded as scholarships/grants, 34% as loans/jobs. **Non-need-based:** Awarded to 1,828 full-time undergraduates, including 664 freshmen. Scholarships awarded for academics, athletics.

Application procedures. Admission: No deadline. $40 fee, may be waived for applicants with need. Admission notification on a rolling basis beginning on or about 12/1. Must reply by May 1 or within 3 week(s) if notified thereafter. **Financial aid:** Priority date 2/15; no closing date. FAFSA required. Applicants notified on a rolling basis starting 2/20; must reply within 2 week(s) of notification.

Academics. Some graduate programs on trimester and quarter schedule. Programs leading to provisional state certification offered in education. **Special study options:** Accelerated study, combined bachelor's/graduate degree, cooperative education, distance learning, double major, dual enrollment of high school students, honors, independent study, internships, study abroad, teacher certification program, weekend college. Program for college students with learning disabilities. **Credit/placement by examination:** AP, CLEP, SAT, ACT, institutional tests. 30 credit hours maximum toward associate degree, 30 toward bachelor's. **Support services:** Learning center, pre-admission summer program, reduced course load, remedial instruction, study skills assistance, tutoring, writing center.

Honors college/program. Minimum 90 or above high school average required. Approximately 65 freshmen admitted. Students take honors English, speech and math freshmen year and additional four academic honors courses for total of 24 credits.

Majors. Biology: General. **Business:** Accounting, accounting/business management, business admin. **Communications:** Media studies. **Computer sciences:** General, information systems, security. **English:** English lit. **Foreign languages:** Spanish. **General:** Animal sciences. **Health services:** Audiology/speech pathology, clinical lab science. **History:** General. **Human services:** Social work. **Liberal arts:** Arts/sciences. **Math:** General. **Protective services:** Law enforcement admin. **Psychology:** General. **Social sciences:** General, political science, sociology. **Visual/performing arts:** Commercial/advertising art.

Most popular majors. Business/marketing 17%, health sciences 21%, psychology 10%, social sciences 32%.

Computing on campus. 708 workstations in dormitories, library, computer center, student center. Dormitories wired for high-speed internet access and linked to campus network. Commuter students can connect to campus network. Online course registration, online library, helpline, repair service, wireless network available.

Student life. Freshman orientation: Available. Preregistration for classes offered. Policies: Student services geared to commuter population with mid-day activities and programs. Housing: Coed dorms available. $300 nonrefundable deposit, deadline 5/1. Activities: Campus ministries, dance, Model UN, student government, student newspaper, Reporter's Impact, Military Veterans club, Green club, Dance Off Society Showstoppers, chess club, Latin American student association, Mercy College Models, Veterinary Technology club, Italian club, Accounting Society, Creative Minds poetry club.

Athletics. NCAA. Intercollegiate: Baseball M, basketball, cross-country W, lacrosse, soccer, softball W, tennis M, track and field, volleyball W. Intramural: Baseball M, basketball, softball. Team name: Mavericks.

Student services. Adult student services, alcohol/substance abuse counseling, career counseling, services for economically disadvantaged, student employment services, financial aid counseling, health services, minority student services, on-campus daycare, personal counseling, placement for graduates, veterans' counselor. Physically disabled: Services for visually, speech, hearing impaired.

Contact. E-mail: admissions@mercy.edu
Phone: (877) 637-2946 Toll-free number: (877) 637-2946
Fax: (914) 674-7608
Deirdre Whitman, Vice President for Enrollment Management, Mercy College, 555 Broadway, Dobbs Ferry, NY 10522

Mesivta Torah Vodaath Seminary
Brooklyn, New York
CB code: 0636

- Private 5-year rabbinical college for men affiliated with Jewish faith
- Very large city
- 116 degree-seeking undergraduates

General. Founded in 1918. Accredited by AARTS. First Talmudic degree and ordination available. Degrees: 17 bachelor's awarded. ROTC: Naval, Air Force. Calendar: Semester.

Basis for selection. Religious affiliation or commitment very important. Test scores, interview, school and community activities, recommendations, alumni relation important. School achievement record considered. Interview recommended.

2011-2012 Annual costs. Tuition/fees: $7,500. Room/board: $4,500.

Application procedures. Admission: No deadline. $200 fee.

Academics. Special study options: Independent study. Credit/placement by examination: AP, CLEP, institutional tests. Support services: Tutoring.

Majors. Theology: Talmudic.

Student life. Activities: Dance.

Student services. Career counseling, personal counseling, placement for graduates.

Contact. Phone: (718) 941-8000
Aaron Braun, Director of Admissions, Mesivta Torah Vodaath Seminary, 425 East Ninth Street, Brooklyn, NY 11218

Metropolitan College of New York
New York, New York
CB member
www.metropolitan.edu
CB code: 4802

- Private 4-year business and liberal arts college
- Commuter campus in very large city
- 825 degree-seeking undergraduates: 61% African American, 2% Asian American, 22% Hispanic American, 1% Native American, 3% international
- 326 graduate students
- Interview required

General. Founded in 1964. Regionally accredited. Degrees: 121 bachelor's, 66 associate awarded; master's offered. Location: Downtown Manhattan. Calendar: Semester, extensive summer session.

Basis for selection. Academic record, test scores, previous volunteer experience, school and community activities, motivation and communication skills as demonstrated in interviews considered. Combined SAT score of

1050 (exclusive of Writing) or higher can be substituted for institution-administered Test of Adult Basic Education or ACCUPLACER required for admission.

2011-2012 Annual costs. Tuition/fees: $16,750. Tuition reported is for undergraduate business program; costs for other programs may vary.

Financial aid. Additional information: Limited merit scholarships.

Application procedures. Financial aid: No deadline.

Academics. Class work integrated with field work. Class learning applied, documented and assessed in internship or employment setting. Special study options: Accelerated study, distance learning, internships, liberal arts/career combination, study abroad, teacher certification program, weekend college. Credit/placement by examination: AP, CLEP, IB. 32 credit hours maximum toward bachelor's degree. Support services: Learning center, remedial instruction, tutoring.

Majors. Business: General, business admin. Human services: Community org/advocacy, social work. Social sciences: General, sociology, urban studies.

Computing on campus. 130 workstations in library, computer center. Wireless network available.

Student life. Freshman orientation: Mandatory. Preregistration for classes offered. Activities: Student newspaper, honor societies, networking club, dance committee.

Student services. Adult student services, career counseling, student employment services, financial aid counseling, personal counseling, placement for graduates, veterans' counselor. Physically disabled: Services for visually, hearing impaired.

Contact. E-mail: admissions@mcny.edu
Phone: (212) 343-1234 ext. 5001 Toll-free number: (800) 338-4465
Fax: (212) 343-8470
Steven Lenhart, Dean of Enrollment Services, Metropolitan College of New York, 431 Canal Street, New York, NY 10013-1919

Mirrer Yeshiva Central Institute
Brooklyn, New York
CB code: 0661

- Private 4-year rabbinical college for men affiliated with Jewish faith
- Very large city
- 204 degree-seeking undergraduates

General. Accredited by AARTS. Degrees: 28 bachelor's awarded; master's, doctoral offered. Calendar: Differs by program. Full-time faculty: 16 total.

2011-2012 Annual costs. Tuition/fees: $4,700. Room/board: $4,000.

Application procedures. Admission: No deadline.

Academics. Credit/placement by examination: AP, CLEP.

Majors. Theology: Talmudic.

Contact. Phone: (718) 645-0536
Rabbi Pincus Hecht, Admissions Director, Mirrer Yeshiva Central Institute, 1795 Ocean Parkway, Brooklyn, NY 11223

Molloy College
Rockville Centre, New York
CB member
www.molloy.edu
CB code: 2415

- Private 4-year liberal arts college affiliated with Roman Catholic Church
- Commuter campus in large town
- 3,351 degree-seeking undergraduates: 21% part-time, 76% women, 14% African American, 7% Asian American, 12% Hispanic American
- 1,020 degree-seeking graduate students
- 63% of applicants admitted
- SAT or ACT with writing, application essay required
- 63% graduate within 6 years

General. Founded in 1955. Regionally accredited. Independent institution in Dominican tradition. Degrees: 509 bachelor's, 34 associate awarded; master's offered. ROTC: Army, Naval. Location: 20 miles from New York City.

Calendar: 4-1-4, limited summer session. **Full-time faculty:** 178 total; 67% have terminal degrees, 15% minority, 74% women. **Part-time faculty:** 475 total; 21% have terminal degrees, 16% minority, 65% women. **Class size:** 63% < 20, 36% 20-39, 1% 40-49. **Special facilities:** Weather station at Jones Beach, international business center.

Freshman class profile. 2,049 applied, 1,299 admitted, 403 enrolled.

Mid 50% test scores			
SAT critical reading:	470-570	GPA 3.0-3.49:	44%
SAT math:	490-590	GPA 2.0-2.99:	5%
SAT writing:	460-570	Rank in top quarter:	61%
ACT composite:	22-28	Rank in top tenth:	35%
GPA 3.75 or higher:	18%	Return as sophomores:	88%
GPA 3.50-3.74:	33%	Live on campus:	2%

Basis for selection. Secondary school achievement with particular attention to grade 11 performance most important. Test scores also important. Recommendations, school and community activities, interview considered. Audition required for music program; portfolio required for art program. **Home schooled:** State high school equivalency certificate required. **Learning Disabled:** Applicants reviewed by separate committee.

High school preparation. College-preparatory program required. 21 units required. Required and recommended units include English 4, mathematics 3-4, social studies 4, science 3-4, foreign language 3 and academic electives 4. Science, math, and nursing majors must have 1 biology, 1 chemistry, and 3 math.

2011-2012 Annual costs. Tuition/fees: $23,300. Room/board: $12,880.

2010-2011 Financial aid. Need-based: 388 full-time freshmen applied for aid; 325 were judged to have need; 325 of these received aid. Average need met was 61%. Average scholarship/grant was $12,273; average loan $3,711. 45% of total undergraduate aid awarded as scholarships/grants, 55% as loans/jobs. **Non-need-based:** Awarded to 375 full-time undergraduates, including 118 freshmen. Scholarships awarded for academics, alumni affiliation, art, athletics, leadership, music/drama, religious affiliation.

Application procedures. Admission: No deadline. $30 fee, may be waived for applicants with need. Admission notification on a rolling basis beginning on or about 10/15. Must reply by May 1 or within 2 week(s) if notified thereafter. **Financial aid:** Priority date 4/15, closing date 5/1. FAFSA required. Applicants notified by 2/1; Applicants notified on a rolling basis starting 2/1; must reply within 5 week(s) of notification.

Academics. Special study options: Combined bachelor's/graduate degree, double major, ESL, honors, independent study, internships, liberal arts/career combination, student-designed major, study abroad, teacher certification program. **Credit/placement by examination:** AP, CLEP, IB, institutional tests. 15 credit hours maximum toward associate degree, 30 toward bachelor's. **Support services:** Learning center, pre-admission summer program, reduced course load, remedial instruction, study skills assistance, tutoring, writing center.

Majors. Biology: General, ecology. **Business:** Accounting, business admin. **Communications:** Communications/speech/rhetoric. **Computer sciences:** Computer science, information systems. **Education:** General, art, biology, elementary, English, history, mathematics, music, secondary, social studies, Spanish, special ed. **English:** English lit. **Foreign languages:** Spanish. **Health services:** Audiology/speech pathology, health services admin, music therapy, nursing (RN), speech pathology. **History:** General. **Human services:** Social work. **Liberal arts:** Arts/sciences. **Math:** General. **Philosophy/religion:** Philosophy. **Protective services:** Law enforcement admin. **Psychology:** General. **Social sciences:** Political science, sociology. **Visual/performing arts:** General, art, music, music performance.

Most popular majors. Business/marketing 7%, education 15%, health sciences 50%.

Computing on campus. 420 workstations in library, computer center, student center. Commuter students can connect to campus network. Online course registration, online library, helpline, wireless network available.

Student life. Freshman orientation: Mandatory. Preregistration for classes offered. **Housing:** Coed dorms available. $500 nonrefundable deposit. **Activities:** Jazz band, campus ministries, choral groups, dance, drama, literary magazine, music ensembles, student government, student newspaper, African American and Caribbean organization, Gaelic society, Out for Acceptance, social work club, Union Hispana de Molloy, Youth for Christ, HOPE Team.

Athletics. NCAA. **Intercollegiate:** Baseball M, basketball, cross-country, equestrian, lacrosse, soccer, softball W, tennis W, volleyball W. **Team name:** Lions.

Student services. Adult student services, alcohol/substance abuse counseling, chaplain/spiritual director, career counseling, services for economically disadvantaged, student employment services, financial aid counseling,

health services, personal counseling, veterans' counselor. **Physically disabled:** Services for visually, hearing impaired.

Contact. E-mail: admissions@molloy.edu
Phone: (516) 678-5000 ext. 6240 Toll-free number: (888) 466-5569
Fax: (516) 256-2247
Marguerite Lane, Director of Admissions, Molloy College, PO Box 5002, Rockville Centre, NY 11570

Monroe College
Bronx, New York
www.monroecollege.edu   CB code: 2463

- For-profit 4-year business and health science college
- Commuter campus in very large city
- 6,034 degree-seeking undergraduates: 24% part-time, 68% women
- 374 degree-seeking graduate students
- 55% of applicants admitted
- Application essay, interview required

General. Founded in 1933. Regionally accredited. Branch campus in New Rochelle offers all programs, courses, and services available at main campus. **Degrees:** 1,042 bachelor's, 1,412 associate awarded; master's offered. **ROTC:** Army. **Calendar:** Semester, extensive summer session. **Full-time faculty:** 114 total. **Part-time faculty:** 315 total. **Class size:** 44% < 20, 55% 20-39, less than 1% 50-99.

Freshman class profile. 3,696 applied, 2,044 admitted, 1,169 enrolled.

End year in good standing:	72%	Out-of-state:	1%
Return as sophomores:	84%	Live on campus:	25%

Basis for selection. Interview, school achievement record, test scores required. Modified open admissions for students who pass admissions test.

2011-2012 Annual costs. Tuition/fees: $12,440. Room/board: $8,430. Books/supplies: $1,000. Personal expenses: $5,990.

Financial aid. All financial aid based on need.

Application procedures. Admission: No deadline. $35 fee. Admission notification on a rolling basis. **Financial aid:** Closing date 6/30. FAFSA required. Applicants notified on a rolling basis starting 7/1.

Academics. Special study options: Cooperative education, distance learning, dual enrollment of high school students, honors, internships, liberal arts/career combination, study abroad, weekend college. **Credit/placement by examination:** AP, CLEP, IB, institutional tests. 30 credit hours maximum toward associate degree, 30 toward bachelor's. **Support services:** Learning center, pre-admission summer program, remedial instruction, study skills assistance, tutoring, writing center.

Majors. Business: Accounting, business admin, hospitality admin. **Computer sciences:** General. **Health services:** Health services admin. **Protective services:** Law enforcement admin.

Most popular majors. Business/marketing 32%, computer/information sciences 11%, health sciences 38%, security/protective services 19%.

Computing on campus. 800 workstations in dormitories, library, computer center. Dormitories wired for high-speed internet access and linked to campus network. Commuter students can connect to campus network. Online course registration, online library, helpline, wireless network available.

Student life. Freshman orientation: Mandatory. Preregistration for classes offered. **Housing:** Coed dorms available. $100 deposit. Assistance for foreign students in securing local housing. Student apartments available near New Rochelle campus. On-campus housing at New Rochelle campus. **Activities:** Dance, international student organizations, Students in Free Enterprise, NABA.

Athletics. NJCAA. **Intercollegiate:** Baseball M, basketball, soccer M, volleyball W. **Intramural:** Basketball, softball W. **Team name:** Mustangs.

Student services. Adult student services, career counseling, student employment services, financial aid counseling, personal counseling, placement for graduates, veterans' counselor. **Physically disabled:** Services for visually, speech, hearing impaired.

Contact. E-mail: cwright@monroecollege.edu
Phone: (718) 933-6700 Toll-free number: (800) 556-6676
Fax: (718) 364-3552
Cecil Wright, Director of Admissions, Monroe College, 2501 Jerome Avenue, Bronx, NY 10468

Mount Saint Mary College
Newburgh, New York   **CB member**
www.msmc.edu   **CB code: 2423**

- Private 4-year liberal arts college affiliated with Roman Catholic Church
- Residential campus in large town
- 2,319 degree-seeking undergraduates: 17% part-time, 73% women, 7% African American, 2% Asian American, 12% Hispanic American, 1% Native American
- 344 degree-seeking graduate students
- 81% of applicants admitted
- SAT or ACT required
- 55% graduate within 6 years; 36% enter graduate study

General. Founded in 1954. Regionally accredited. Independent institution in Judeo-Christian tradition, founded by Dominican Sisters of Newburgh. **Degrees:** 428 bachelor's awarded; master's offered. **Location:** 58 miles from New York City. **Calendar:** Semester, limited summer session. **Full-time faculty:** 87 total; 86% have terminal degrees, 7% minority, 59% women. **Part-time faculty:** 189 total; 20% have terminal degrees, 10% minority, 55% women. **Class size:** 47% < 20, 49% 20-39, 3% 40-49, less than 1% 50-99. **Special facilities:** Elementary school on campus.

Freshman class profile. 3,347 applied, 2,711 admitted, 454 enrolled.

Mid 50% test scores		GPA 2.0-2.99:	25%
SAT critical reading:	450-540	Rank in top quarter:	30%
SAT math:	460-560	Rank in top tenth:	9%
SAT writing:	450-540	End year in good standing:	80%
ACT composite:	19-24	Return as sophomores:	68%
GPA 3.75 or higher:	12%	Out-of-state:	19%
GPA 3.50-3.74:	16%	Live on campus:	85%
GPA 3.0-3.49:	46%		

Basis for selection. Admissions decisions based on total admission score which weighs high school average, class rank, and test scores as well as teacher/counselor recommendations. Interviews are by invitation only after completed application is received. Personal essay required for transfer students. **Home schooled:** State high school equivalency certificate, interview required. Need SAT or ACT. **Learning Disabled:** Must include IEP with application. Must meet with Director of Counseling and Coordinator of Services for Persons with Disabilities.

High school preparation. College-preparatory program recommended. Recommended units include English 4, mathematics 3, social studies 4, science 3, foreign language 3, academic electives 3.5.

2011-2012 Annual costs. Tuition/fees: $24,410. Room/board: $12,320. Books/supplies: $1,100. Personal expenses: $1,000.

2011-2012 Financial aid. Need-based: 415 full-time freshmen applied for aid; 360 were judged to have need; 359 of these received aid. Average need met was 60%. Average scholarship/grant was $12,987; average loan $3,209. 56% of total undergraduate aid awarded as scholarships/grants, 44% as loans/jobs. **Non-need-based:** Awarded to 373 full-time undergraduates, including 112 freshmen. Scholarships awarded for academics, alumni affiliation, leadership, ROTC, state residency.

Application procedures. Admission: Closing date 8/15 (postmark date). $45 fee, may be waived for applicants with need, free for online applicants. Admission notification on a rolling basis beginning on or about 9/15. Must reply by May 1 or within 2 week(s) if notified thereafter. **Financial aid:** Priority date 2/15, closing date 3/1. FAFSA required. Applicants notified on a rolling basis starting 3/1; must reply by 5/1.

Academics. Special study options: Accelerated study, combined bachelor's/graduate degree, cooperative education, cross-registration, distance learning, double major, dual enrollment of high school students, exchange student, honors, independent study, internships, liberal arts/career combination, student-designed major, study abroad, teacher certification program. **Credit/placement by examination:** AP, CLEP, IB, SAT, ACT, institutional tests. 45 credit hours maximum toward bachelor's degree. **Support services:** Learning center, pre-admission summer program, reduced course load, remedial instruction, study skills assistance, tutoring, writing center.

Majors. Biology: General. **Business:** Accounting, business admin. **Communications:** Media studies, public relations. **Computer sciences:** Information technology. **Education:** Early childhood, multi-level teacher, secondary. **English:** English lit. **Foreign languages:** Spanish. **Health services:** Clinical lab science, nursing (RN). **History:** General. **Math:** General. **Physical sciences:** Chemistry. **Psychology:** General. **Social sciences:** General, sociology.

Most popular majors. Business/marketing 16%, English 7%, health sciences 19%, history 10%, mathematics 6%, psychology 10%, social sciences 8%.

Computing on campus. 576 workstations in dormitories, library, computer center, student center. Dormitories wired for high-speed internet access and linked to campus network. Commuter students can connect to campus network. Online course registration, online library, helpline, repair service, wireless network available.

Student life. Freshman orientation: Mandatory. Preregistration for classes offered. Two sessions held in July. **Policies:** Freshmen not permitted cars on campus. **Housing:** Guaranteed on-campus for all undergraduates. Coed dorms, single-sex dorms, special housing for disabled available. $450 nonrefundable deposit, deadline 5/1. **Activities:** Concert band, campus ministries, choral groups, dance, drama, film society, literary magazine, music ensembles, musical theater, radio station, student government, student newspaper, black student union, Habitat for Humanity, Big Brothers/Big Sisters, Christian fellowship, Latin student union.

Athletics. NCAA. **Intercollegiate:** Baseball M, basketball, cross-country, lacrosse, soccer, softball W, swimming, tennis, track and field, volleyball W. **Intramural:** Basketball, bowling, football (non-tackle) M, golf, soccer, softball, swimming, table tennis, volleyball. **Team name:** Knights.

Student services. Adult student services, alcohol/substance abuse counseling, chaplain/spiritual director, career counseling, services for economically disadvantaged, student employment services, financial aid counseling, health services, personal counseling. **Physically disabled:** Services for visually impaired.

Contact. E-mail: admissions@msmc.edu
Phone: (845) 569-3488 Toll-free number: (888) 937-6762
Fax: (845) 562-6762
Michelle Taylor, Director of Admissions, Mount Saint Mary College, 330 Powell Avenue, Newburgh, NY 12550

Nazareth College
Rochester, New York   **CB member**
www.naz.edu   **CB code: 2511**

- Private 4-year liberal arts college
- Residential campus in large city
- 2,122 degree-seeking undergraduates: 6% part-time, 76% women, 4% African American, 2% Asian American, 4% Hispanic American, 1% international
- 885 degree-seeking graduate students
- 70% of applicants admitted
- Application essay required
- 72% graduate within 6 years

General. Founded in 1924. Regionally accredited. **Degrees:** 510 bachelor's awarded; master's, professional offered. **ROTC:** Army, Air Force. **Location:** 7 miles from downtown. **Calendar:** Semester, extensive summer session. **Full-time faculty:** 163 total; 93% have terminal degrees, 14% minority, 63% women. **Part-time faculty:** 266 total; 25% have terminal degrees, 9% minority, 73% women. **Class size:** 61% < 20, 39% 20-39, less than 1% 40-49. **Special facilities:** Arts center, psychology research facility, speech clinic, physical therapy clinic, center for service learning, center for interfaith studies and dialogue.

Freshman class profile. 2,976 applied, 2,081 admitted, 439 enrolled.

Mid 50% test scores		GPA 2.0-2.99:	1%
SAT critical reading:	520-630	Rank in top quarter:	57%
SAT math:	540-620	Rank in top tenth:	29%
ACT composite:	23-27	Return as sophomores:	82%
GPA 3.75 or higher:	15%	Out-of-state:	8%
GPA 3.50-3.74:	42%	Live on campus:	89%
GPA 3.0-3.49:	42%	International:	2%

Basis for selection. School achievement record, strength of high school academic program, class rank, recommendations, extracurricular activities most important. Standardized test optional. Interview recommended for all; audition required for music and theater arts programs; portfolio required for art programs.

High school preparation. College-preparatory program required. 15 units required; 20 recommended. Required and recommended units include English 4, mathematics 3-4, social studies 3-4, science 3-4 (laboratory 2) and foreign language 3-4.

2011-2012 Annual costs. Tuition/fees: $28,332. Room/board: $11,144.

2011-2012 Financial aid. Need-based: Average need met was 75%. Average scholarship/grant was $14,428; average loan $3,526. 62% of total undergraduate aid awarded as scholarships/grants, 38% as loans/jobs. **Non-need-based:** Scholarships awarded for academics, alumni affiliation, art, leadership, minority status, music/drama, ROTC.

Application procedures. Admission: Priority date 12/15; deadline 2/15 (postmark date). $45 fee, may be waived for applicants with need, free for online applicants. Admission notification on a rolling basis beginning on or about 3/1. Must reply by May 1 or within 4 week(s) if notified thereafter. **Financial aid:** Priority date 2/15; no closing date. FAFSA required. CSS PROFILE required of early decision applicants only. Applicants notified on a rolling basis starting 2/1; must reply by 5/1.

Academics. Special study options: Combined bachelor's/graduate degree, cross-registration, distance learning, double major, exchange student, honors, independent study, internships, study abroad, teacher certification program, Washington semester. 2-2 bachelor's degree completion program for registered nurses and Monroe Community College graduates. **Credit/placement by examination:** AP, CLEP, IB, SAT, ACT. 30 credit hours maximum toward bachelor's degree. **Support services:** Reduced course load, remedial instruction, study skills assistance, tutoring, writing center.

Majors. Area/ethnic studies: American. **Biology:** General, biochemistry. **Business:** General, accounting, international, marketing. **Communications:** Communications/speech/rhetoric. **Computer sciences:** Information systems. **Conservation:** Environmental science. **Education:** Art, biology, business, chemistry, elementary, English, foreign languages, history, mathematics, music, secondary, special ed, speech, speech impaired. **English:** English lit. **Foreign languages:** French, German, Italian, Spanish. **Health services:** Communication disorders, music therapy, nursing (RN), speech pathology. **History:** General. **Human services:** Social work. **Math:** General. **Philosophy/religion:** Philosophy, religion. **Physical sciences:** Chemistry. **Psychology:** General. **Social sciences:** General, anthropology, economics, political science, sociology. **Visual/performing arts:** Art, art history/conservation, dramatic, graphic design, music, music history, music management, music performance, music theory/composition, musical theater, studio arts.

Most popular majors. Business/marketing 14%, education 18%, health sciences 11%, history 6%, psychology 9%, social sciences 9%, visual/performing arts 8%.

Computing on campus. 240 workstations in dormitories, library, computer center. Dormitories wired for high-speed internet access and linked to campus network. Commuter students can connect to campus network. Online course registration, online library, helpline, wireless network available.

Student life. Freshman orientation: Mandatory, $100 fee. Preregistration for classes offered. Orientation charge included in first-year fees. 3-day weekend program includes community service. **Policies:** First- and second-year students are required to live on campus, unless living with family. **Housing:** Guaranteed on-campus for all undergraduates. Coed dorms, special housing for disabled, apartments, wellness housing available. $100 nonrefundable deposit, deadline 5/1. Foreign language houses, special interest housing available. **Activities:** Bands, campus ministries, choral groups, dance, drama, international student organizations, literary magazine, music ensembles, musical theater, opera, radio station, student government, student newspaper, symphony orchestra, Amnesty International, Inter-Ethnic Nazareth Coalition, Center for Spirituality Council, Go Green!, undergraduate association, Rotaract, Students for Political Action and Awareness, French club, German club, Italian club.

Athletics. NCAA. **Intercollegiate:** Basketball, cross-country, diving, equestrian, field hockey W, golf, lacrosse, soccer, softball W, swimming, tennis, track and field, volleyball. **Intramural:** Basketball, racquetball, soccer, softball, swimming, tennis, volleyball. **Team name:** Golden Flyers.

Student services. Adult student services, alcohol/substance abuse counseling, chaplain/spiritual director, career counseling, services for economically disadvantaged, student employment services, financial aid counseling, health services, minority student services, on-campus daycare, personal counseling, placement for graduates, women's services. **Physically disabled:** Services for visually, speech, hearing impaired.

Contact. E-mail: admissions@naz.edu
Phone: (585) 389-2860 Toll-free number: (800) 462-3944
Fax: (585) 389-2826
Thomas DaRin, Vice President for Enrollment Management, Nazareth College, 4245 East Avenue, Rochester, NY 14618-3790

New York Institute of Technology
Old Westbury, New York
www.nyit.edu
CB code: 2561

- Private 4-year university and health science college
- Commuter campus in large town

- 4,741 degree-seeking undergraduates: 15% part-time, 38% women, 9% African American, 14% Asian American, 12% Hispanic American, 11% international
- 3,206 degree-seeking graduate students
- 69% of applicants admitted
- SAT or ACT (ACT writing recommended), application essay required
- 47% graduate within 6 years

General. Founded in 1955. Regionally accredited. Multiple sites, including campuses on Long Island, Manhattan, online, and at sites throughout the world. **Degrees:** 1,148 bachelor's, 24 associate awarded; master's, professional offered. **ROTC:** Army, Air Force. **Location:** 15 miles from New York City. **Calendar:** Semester, extensive summer session. **Full-time faculty:** 273 total; 37% women. **Part-time faculty:** 987 total; 40% women. **Class size:** 64% < 20, 33% 20-39, 1% 40-49, 2% 50-99. **Special facilities:** Center for urban/suburban studies, center for neighborhood revitalization, Parkinson's disease treatment center, center for labor and industrial relations, center for energy, environment and economics, center for teaching and learning with technology, culinary arts center, center for entrepreneurial and small business services, center for business information technologies, motion graphics laboratory.

Freshman class profile. 5,529 applied, 3,804 admitted, 841 enrolled.

Mid 50% test scores			
SAT critical reading:	480-580	Rank in top quarter:	48%
SAT math:	540-630	Rank in top tenth:	19%
ACT composite:	23-28	Return as sophomores:	70%
GPA 3.75 or higher:	18%	Out-of-state:	11%
GPA 3.50-3.74:	28%	Live on campus:	24%
GPA 3.0-3.49:	44%	International:	10%
GPA 2.0-2.99:	10%	Fraternities:	2%
		Sororities:	1%

Basis for selection. 2 letters of recommendation required for 4-year nursing, occupational therapy, physical therapy, physician assistant and all education programs. Proof of 100 hours of volunteer or work experience required for physical therapy, physician assistant, occupational therapy programs. SAT important, minimum scores vary with program. Interview required for occupational therapy, physician assistant, physical therapy, BS/doctor of osteopathic medicine, and BS/Juris Doctor program applicants. Portfolio required for fine arts program. **Home schooled:** State high school equivalency certificate required.

High school preparation. 17 units required. Required and recommended units include English 4, mathematics 3, social studies 3-4, science 3 (laboratory 1) and academic electives 7. Freshmen in selected majors required to prove or acquire computer literacy.

2011-2012 Annual costs. Tuition/fees: $27,290. Room and board charges apply to Old Westbury campus; board charges vary at other campuses. Tuition/fee costs reported are for nontechnology majors, vary for other programs. Room only: $11,304. Books/supplies: $1,600. Personal expenses: $2,946.

2010-2011 Financial aid. Need-based: 1,037 full-time freshmen applied for aid; 951 were judged to have need; 939 of these received aid. Average scholarship/grant was $5,129; average loan $3,512. 59% of total undergraduate aid awarded as scholarships/grants, 41% as loans/jobs. **Non-need-based:** Awarded to 3,097 full-time undergraduates, including 1,045 freshmen. Scholarships awarded for academics, athletics.

Application procedures. Admission: Closing date 3/1. $50 fee, may be waived for applicants with need. Admission notification on a rolling basis beginning on or about 1/1. Must reply by 5/1. Application closing date for nursing, occupational therapy, physical therapy and physician assistant programs February 1. Notification to applicants to these programs sent March 1. Applicants to these programs must reply by May 1 or within 30 days if notified thereafter. No deferred admission to these programs. **Financial aid:** Priority date 3/1; no closing date. FAFSA required. Applicants notified on a rolling basis starting 3/15; must reply by 5/1 or within 2 week(s) of notification.

Academics. School focuses on career-oriented professional education, applications-oriented research and service in public interest. **Special study options:** Accelerated study, combined bachelor's/graduate degree, cooperative education, cross-registration, distance learning, double major, dual enrollment of high school students, ESL, honors, independent study, internships, liberal arts/career combination, study abroad, teacher certification program, weekend college. Combined bachelor's/professional degree program in life sciences/osteopathic medicine, architectural technology/energy management, architectural technology/MBA, mechanical engineering/energy management, life sciences/physical therapy, life sciences/occupational therapy, behavioral sciences/law at Touro College Law Center. **Credit/placement by examination:** AP, CLEP, IB, institutional tests. 30 credit hours maximum toward associate degree, 60 toward bachelor's. **Support services:** Learning center, pre-admission summer program, reduced course load, remedial instruction, study skills assistance, tutoring, writing center.

Majors. Architecture: Architecture, technology. **Biology:** General. **Business:** Accounting, business admin, finance, hotel/motel admin, human resources, management information systems, marketing, tourism/travel. **Communications:** Advertising, broadcast journalism, communications/speech/rhetoric, radio/TV. **Computer sciences:** General, computer graphics, computer science, networking. **Engineering:** Biomedical, computer, electrical, mechanical. **English:** English lit. **Health services:** Nursing (RN), physician assistant, premedicine. **Physical sciences:** Chemistry. **Protective services:** Law enforcement admin. **Psychology:** General. **Social sciences:** Political science, sociology. **Visual/performing arts:** Commercial/advertising art, interior design, studio arts.

Most popular majors. Architecture 12%, biology 9%, business/marketing 17%, communications/journalism 12%, computer/information sciences 7%, engineering/engineering technologies 13%, interdisciplinary studies 9%, visual/performing arts 6%.

Computing on campus. PC or laptop required. 1,210 workstations in dormitories, library, computer center, student center. Dormitories wired for high-speed internet access and linked to campus network. Commuter students can connect to campus network. Online course registration, online library, helpline, student web hosting, wireless network available.

Student life. Freshman orientation: Available. Preregistration for classes offered. One day at end of August. **Housing:** Guaranteed on-campus for all undergraduates. Coed dorms, special housing for disabled, apartments available. $300 nonrefundable deposit. Central Islip campus fully residential, special housing for graduate, architecture students. Off-campus housing available for Manhattan campus. **Activities:** Choral groups, dance, drama, film society, literary magazine, musical theater, radio station, student government, student newspaper, TV station, American Institute of Architecture Students, biomedical society, National Society of Black Engineers, Newman Club, Christian fellowship, Jewish student union, African people's organization, Community Connection, South Asian student association, Chinese student association.

Athletics. NCAA. **Intercollegiate:** Baseball M, basketball, cross-country, lacrosse M, soccer, softball W, volleyball W. **Intramural:** Basketball, soccer, volleyball W. **Team name:** Bears.

Student services. Adult student services, alcohol/substance abuse counseling, chaplain/spiritual director, career counseling, student employment services, financial aid counseling, health services, personal counseling, placement for graduates, veterans' counselor. **Physically disabled:** Services for hearing impaired.

Contact. E-mail: admissions@nyit.edu
Phone: (516) 686-7520 Toll-free number: (800) 345-6948
Fax: (516) 686-7613
Jacquelyn Nealon, Vice President for Enrollment, New York Institute of Technology, Box 8000, Old Westbury, NY 11568

New York School of Interior Design
New York, New York
www.nysid.edu   CB code: 0333

- Private 4-year visual arts college
- Commuter campus in very large city
- 482 degree-seeking undergraduates: 66% part-time, 89% women, 4% African American, 11% Asian American, 11% Hispanic American, 7% international
- 149 degree-seeking graduate students
- 32% of applicants admitted
- Application essay required
- 34% graduate within 6 years

General. Founded in 1916. The college is devoted exclusively to interior design education. **Degrees:** 51 bachelor's, 65 associate awarded; master's offered. **Location:** Located in Manhattan. **Calendar:** Semester, extensive summer session. **Full-time faculty:** 8 total; 88% have terminal degrees, 50% women. **Part-time faculty:** 101 total; 58% have terminal degrees, 46% women. **Class size:** 91% < 20, 9% 50-99. **Special facilities:** Three galleries for architecture and interior design exhibits, lighting laboratory.

Freshman class profile. 188 applied, 60 admitted, 18 enrolled.

Mid 50% test scores			
SAT critical reading:	370-510	Rank in top quarter:	14%
SAT math:	400-490	Rank in top tenth:	14%
SAT writing:	380-490	End year in good standing:	95%
ACT composite:	17-19	Return as sophomores:	93%
GPA 3.50-3.74:	7%	Out-of-state:	36%
GPA 3.0-3.49:	47%	Live on campus:	53%
GPA 2.0-2.99:	46%	International:	18%

Basis for selection. High school transcripts, 2 letters of recommendation, essay, and portfolio in art/design. Portfolio required, interview optional. **Home schooled:** State high school equivalency certificate required.

High school preparation. 16 units recommended. Recommended units include English 4, mathematics 2, social studies 2, history 2, science 2 and foreign language 2. Studio art or drafting is recommended.

2012-2013 Annual costs. Tuition/fees (projected): $27,894. Books/supplies: $1,000. Personal expenses: $900.

2011-2012 Financial aid. Need-based: Average need met was 46%. Average scholarship/grant was $7,402; average loan $2,625. 36% of total undergraduate aid awarded as scholarships/grants, 64% as loans/jobs.

Application procedures. Admission: Priority date 2/1; no deadline. $60 fee, may be waived for applicants with need. Admission notification on a rolling basis beginning on or about 4/1. Must reply by May 1 or within 4 week(s) if notified thereafter. **Financial aid:** Priority date 5/1; no closing date. FAFSA required. Applicants notified on a rolling basis starting 4/1; must reply within 2 week(s) of notification.

Academics. Special study options: Independent study, internships, study abroad, weekend college. **Credit/placement by examination:** AP, CLEP, IB, institutional tests. 17 credit hours maximum toward associate degree, 41 toward bachelor's. **Support services:** Study skills assistance, tutoring, writing center.

Majors. Visual/performing arts: Interior design.

Computing on campus. 125 workstations in library, computer center. Dormitories wired for high-speed internet access and linked to campus network. Commuter students can connect to campus network. Online course registration, helpline, wireless network available.

Student life. Freshman orientation: Available. Preregistration for classes offered. General orientation is held the week before classes begin. **Housing:** Coed dorms available. $500 nonrefundable deposit. **Activities:** Student chapter of American Society of Interior Designers, student council.

Student services. Adult student services, career counseling, student employment services, financial aid counseling, personal counseling, placement for graduates.

Contact. E-mail: admissions@nysid.edu
Phone: (212) 472-1500 ext. 204
Toll-free number: (800) 336-9743 ext. 204 Fax: (212) 472-1867
David Sprouls, Director of Admissions, New York School of Interior Design, 170 East 70th Street, New York, NY 10021-5110

New York University
New York, New York   CB member
www.nyu.edu   CB code: 2562

- Private 4-year university
- Residential campus in very large city
- 21,820 degree-seeking undergraduates: 5% part-time, 60% women, 4% African American, 20% Asian American, 9% Hispanic American, 10% international
- 21,175 degree-seeking graduate students
- 32% of applicants admitted
- SAT or ACT with writing, application essay required
- 86% graduate within 6 years

General. Founded in 1831. Regionally accredited. Degrees offered by campuses in New York City, Abu Dhabi, and (soon) Shanghai. NYU's School of Continuing and Professional Studies is available for adult degree and noncredit programs. **Degrees:** 6,431 bachelor's, 302 associate awarded; master's, professional, doctoral offered. **ROTC:** Army, Air Force. **Calendar:** Semester, extensive summer session. **Full-time faculty:** 2,399 total; 93% have terminal degrees, 41% women. **Part-time faculty:** 2,945 total; 58% have terminal degrees, 48% women. **Class size:** 63% < 20, 24% 20-39, 3% 40-49, 6% 50-99, 3% >100. **Special facilities:** Special academic facilities for arts, business, culture, education, international relations, language, law, media, music, public service, research, and social policy.

Freshman class profile. 40,910 applied, 13,208 admitted, 4,861 enrolled.

Mid 50% test scores			
SAT critical reading:	630-720	Rank in top quarter:	91%
SAT math:	630-740	Rank in top tenth:	62%
SAT writing:	640-730	Return as sophomores:	92%
ACT composite:	29-32	Out-of-state:	73%
GPA 3.75 or higher:	31%	Live on campus:	88%
GPA 3.50-3.74:	37%	International:	12%
GPA 3.0-3.49:	30%	Fraternities:	2%
GPA 2.0-2.99:	2%	Sororities:	2%

Basis for selection. School achievement record most important. Standardized test scores, activities, essay, recommendations also important. Audition and/or submission of creative materials required for applicants to either Tisch School of the Arts or art and music programs within the School of Education. Applicants encouraged to submit scores that best demonstrate ability and mastery, chosen from the following options: SAT; or ACT (with Writing Test); or 3 SAT Subject Test scores (one in literature or the humanities, one in math or science, and one non-language test of the student's choice); or 3 AP exam scores (one in literature or the humanities, one in math or science, and one non-language of the student's choice); or the International Baccalaureate Diploma; or 3 IB higher-level exam scores (if not an IB Diploma candidate). Applicants may instead elect to submit results from a nationally accredited exam considered locally to signify the completion of secondary education and is administered independently of the student's school. Applicants to the Stern School of Business who choose to submit SAT Subject Tests or AP Exam scores must provide a score from a mathematics exam. Students who can demonstrate evidence of an extraordinary accomplishment outside of normal classroom or scholastic activity, such as a major publication in a national or international journal, a published book, a film or other outstanding visual or performing artistic accomplishment, a scientific or other remarkable discovery, winning a national competition, or the equivalent can substitute that accomplishment for one SAT Subject Test or one AP Exam if approved by the admissions office. Audition required for dance, drama, and music programs; portfolio required for art, theater design, photography, cinema studies, film, television, radio, and dramatic writing programs. Portfolios may include writing, photography, film or other creative work. **Home schooled:** Transcript of courses and grades, letter of recommendation (nonparent) required. Applicants must submit official score reports from either the SAT (including the Writing section), or the ACT with the ACT Writing Test, and at least two SAT Subject Test scores or two Advanced Placement test scores. Students must either be able to provide a home school diploma or certificate of completion that is considered the equivalent of a high school diploma in the applicant's home state, or they must be willing, if admitted, to apply for a New York State equivalency diploma upon the completion of twenty-four college credits.

High school preparation. College-preparatory program required. Required and recommended units include English 4, mathematics 3-4, history 4, science 3-4 and foreign language 2-4.

2011-2012 Annual costs. Tuition/fees: $41,606. Room/board: $15,181.

Financial aid. Non-need-based: Scholarships awarded for academics.

Application procedures. Admission: Closing date 1/1 (postmark date). $70 fee, may be waived for applicants with need. Application must be submitted online. Admission notification by 4/1. Must reply by 5/1. **Financial aid:** Closing date 2/15. FAFSA required. Applicants notified on a rolling basis starting 4/1; must reply by 5/1.

Academics. Special study options: Accelerated study, combined bachelor's/graduate degree, cooperative education, cross-registration, distance learning, double major, honors, independent study, internships, liberal arts/career combination, student-designed major, study abroad, teacher certification program, Washington semester. NYU offers an exchange program with several historically black colleges including Spelman College, Morehouse College, and Xavier University of Louisiana. **Credit/placement by examination:** AP, CLEP, IB. 32 credit hours maximum toward bachelor's degree. 8 to 32 hours of credit may be awarded for International Baccalaureate. **Support services:** Learning center, pre-admission summer program, reduced course load, study skills assistance, tutoring, writing center.

Majors. Architecture: Urban/community planning. **Area/ethnic studies:** African-American, East Asian, European, Latin American, Near/Middle Eastern. **Biology:** General, biochemistry, neuroscience. **Business:** General, accounting, finance, hotel/motel admin, international, labor relations, managerial economics, real estate, restaurant/food services. **Communications:** Communications/speech/rhetoric, journalism, radio/TV. **Communications technology:** Radio/TV. **Computer sciences:** General, computer science. **Education:** Art, business, elementary, ESL, kindergarten/preschool, mathematics, music, social studies, special ed, speech impaired. **Engineering:** Operations research. **English:** British lit, English lit, rhetoric/composition. **Foreign languages:** General, classics, comparative lit, French, German, Hebrew, Italian, linguistics, Russian, Spanish. **Health services:** Audiology/speech pathology, dental hygiene, nursing (RN). **History:** General. **Human services:** General, community org/advocacy, social work. **Liberal arts:** Arts/

sciences, humanities. **Math:** General. **Parks/recreation:** Facilities management. **Philosophy/religion:** Philosophy, religion. **Physical sciences:** Chemistry, physics. **Psychology:** General. **Social sciences:** General, anthropology, economics, international relations, political science, sociology, urban studies. **Visual/performing arts:** Cinematography, commercial/advertising art, dance, dramatic, music, music performance, musical theater, photography, studio arts. **Work/family studies:** Food/nutrition.

Most popular majors. Business/marketing 19%, communications/journalism 9%, health sciences 6%, liberal arts 7%, social sciences 15%, visual/performing arts 19%.

Computing on campus. Dormitories wired for high-speed internet access and linked to campus network. Commuter students can connect to campus network. Online course registration, online library, helpline, repair service, student web hosting, wireless network available.

Student life. Freshman orientation: Available. Preregistration for classes offered. Each undergraduate college handles its own orientation. Charges and program vary by school. **Housing:** Guaranteed on-campus for all undergraduates. Coed dorms, special housing for disabled, apartments, fraternity/sorority housing, wellness housing available. $500 nonrefundable deposit, deadline 5/1. First-year residential experience program for new students, substance free communities, sophomore residential experience, learning communities, mixed sex housing. **Activities:** Bands, campus ministries, choral groups, dance, drama, film society, international student organizations, literary magazine, music ensembles, Model UN, musical theater, opera, radio station, student government, student newspaper, symphony orchestra, TV station, Over 400 clubs and organizations available.

Athletics. NCAA. **Intercollegiate:** Basketball, cross-country, diving, fencing, golf, soccer, swimming, tennis, track and field, volleyball, wrestling M. **Intramural:** Basketball, bowling, cross-country, football (non-tackle), soccer, volleyball, weight lifting. **Team name:** Violets.

Student services. Adult student services, alcohol/substance abuse counseling, chaplain/spiritual director, career counseling, services for economically disadvantaged, student employment services, financial aid counseling, health services, minority student services, personal counseling, placement for graduates, women's services. **Physically disabled:** Services for visually, speech, hearing impaired.

Contact. E-mail: admissions@nyu.edu
Phone: (212) 998-4500 Fax: (212) 995-4902
Shawn Abbott, Assistant Vice President of Admissions, New York University, 665 Broadway, 11th floor, New York, NY 10012-2339

Niagara University
Niagara University, New York   **CB member**
www.niagara.edu   **CB code: 2558**

- Private 4-year university affiliated with Roman Catholic Church
- Residential campus in small city
- 3,246 degree-seeking undergraduates: 11% part-time, 62% women, 4% African American, 1% Asian American, 3% Hispanic American, 1% Native American, 18% international
- 824 degree-seeking graduate students
- 76% of applicants admitted
- SAT or ACT (ACT writing optional) required
- 65% graduate within 6 years; 41% enter graduate study

General. Founded in 1856. Regionally accredited. Independent institution in the Vincentian tradition. **Degrees:** 632 bachelor's, 4 associate awarded; master's, doctoral offered. **ROTC:** Army. **Location:** 20 miles from Buffalo; 90 miles from Toronto, Canada. **Calendar:** Semester, extensive summer session. **Full-time faculty:** 158 total; 95% have terminal degrees, 15% minority, 39% women. **Part-time faculty:** 206 total; 10% minority, 51% women. **Class size:** 46% < 20, 51% 20-39, 3% 40-49, less than 1% 50-99. **Special facilities:** Art museum, ice arena.

Freshman class profile. 3,241 applied, 2,456 admitted, 631 enrolled.

Mid 50% test scores			
SAT critical reading:	470-590	Rank in top quarter:	41%
SAT math:	470-580	Rank in top tenth:	13%
ACT composite:	21-25	End year in good standing:	91%
GPA 3.75 or higher:	10%	Return as sophomores:	81%
GPA 3.50-3.74:	22%	Out-of-state:	10%
GPA 3.0-3.49:	38%	Live on campus:	78%
GPA 2.0-2.99:	29%	International:	3%

Basis for selection. School achievement record, class rank, test scores most important. School recommendation also important. Character, personality, and extracurricular activities considered. Alumni relationship also considered. Interview, essay recommended for all; audition recommended for theater program. **Home schooled:** Transcript of courses and grades required. Letter from district superintendent or local district official confirming that the student has received an education "substantially equivalent" to instruction given to students graduating from the public high school in that district.

High school preparation. College-preparatory program recommended. 16 units required. Required units include English 4, mathematics 2, social studies 2, science 2, foreign language 2 and academic electives 4. 3 science (biology, chemistry mandatory, physics recommended) for math, science, nursing applicants. 2 foreign language required of all except business applicants. 3 math required for math, biology, business, biochemistry, chemistry, computer and information sciences, natural sciences, and nursing applicants. 3 social studies required for prospective social studies majors.

2011-2012 Annual costs. Tuition/fees: $26,400. Room/board: $11,000. Books/supplies: $900. Personal expenses: $750.

2011-2012 Financial aid. Need-based: 573 full-time freshmen applied for aid; 530 were judged to have need; 530 of these received aid. Average need met was 85%. Average scholarship/grant was $19,409; average loan $4,253. 67% of total undergraduate aid awarded as scholarships/grants, 33% as loans/jobs. **Non-need-based:** Awarded to 2,168 full-time undergraduates, including 532 freshmen. Scholarships awarded for academics, athletics, music/drama, ROTC. **Additional information:** Opportunity program available for academically and economically disadvantaged students.

Application procedures. Admission: Closing date 8/1 (receipt date). $30 fee, may be waived for applicants with need. Admission notification on a rolling basis. Must reply by May 1 or within 4 week(s) if notified thereafter. **Financial aid:** Priority date 2/15; no closing date. FAFSA required. Applicants notified on a rolling basis starting 3/1; must reply within 3 week(s) of notification.

Academics. Academic exploration program for students undecided about their choice of major. **Special study options:** Accelerated study, combined bachelor's/graduate degree, cooperative education, cross-registration, double major, dual enrollment of high school students, ESL, exchange student, honors, independent study, internships, liberal arts/career combination, New York semester, study abroad, teacher certification program, Washington semester. **Credit/placement by examination:** AP, CLEP, institutional tests. 15 credit hours maximum toward associate degree, 15 toward bachelor's. **Support services:** Learning center, pre-admission summer program, reduced course load, remedial instruction, study skills assistance, tutoring, writing center.

Majors. Biology: General, biochemistry. **Business:** Accounting, finance, hospitality admin, hotel/motel admin, human resources, international, logistics, managerial economics, marketing, restaurant/food services, tourism/travel, training/development. **Communications:** Communications/speech/rhetoric. **Computer sciences:** General, computer science, information systems. **Education:** General, biology, business, chemistry, early childhood, elementary, English, French, mathematics, secondary, social studies, Spanish, special ed. **English:** English lit. **Foreign languages:** French, Spanish. **Health services:** Nursing (RN), predental, premedicine, preveterinary. **History:** General. **Human services:** Social work. **Liberal arts:** Arts/sciences. **Math:** General. **Philosophy/religion:** Philosophy, religion. **Physical sciences:** Chemistry. **Protective services:** Criminal justice. **Psychology:** General. **Social sciences:** General, criminology, political science, sociology. **Visual/performing arts:** Dramatic.

Most popular majors. Business/marketing 24%, education 16%, security/protective services 8%, social sciences 7%.

Computing on campus. 150 workstations in dormitories, library, computer center, student center. Dormitories wired for high-speed internet access and linked to campus network. Commuter students can connect to campus network. Online course registration, online library, helpline, repair service, wireless network available.

Student life. Freshman orientation: Mandatory. Preregistration for classes offered. **Policies:** Freshmen not within reasonable commuting distance required to live on campus for 2 years. **Housing:** Guaranteed on-campus for all undergraduates. Coed dorms, apartments, wellness housing available. $100 nonrefundable deposit, deadline 5/1. **Activities:** Bands, campus ministries, choral groups, dance, drama, international student organizations, musical theater, radio station, student government, student newspaper, TV station, ethnic awareness society, Knights of Columbus, community action program, Muscular Dystrophy Association, foreign student council, St. Vincent de Paul Society, Black student union.

Athletics. NCAA. **Intercollegiate:** Baseball M, basketball, cross-country, diving, golf, ice hockey, lacrosse, soccer, softball W, swimming, tennis,

volleyball W. **Intramural:** Baseball M, basketball, bowling, golf, racquetball, skiing, softball, volleyball W, water polo. **Team name:** Purple Eagles.

Student services. Adult student services, alcohol/substance abuse counseling, chaplain/spiritual director, career counseling, services for economically disadvantaged, student employment services, financial aid counseling, health services, minority student services, personal counseling, placement for graduates, veterans' counselor.

Contact. E-mail: admissions@niagara.edu
Phone: (716) 286-8700 Fax: (716) 286-8733
Harry Gong, Director of Admissions, Niagara University, Niagara University, NY 14109

Nyack College
Nyack, New York
www.nyack.edu   **CB code: 2560**

- Private 4-year liberal arts college affiliated with Christian and Missionary Alliance
- Residential campus in large town
- 2,021 degree-seeking undergraduates: 13% part-time, 59% women, 34% African American, 9% Asian American, 26% Hispanic American, 4% international
- 1,199 degree-seeking graduate students
- Application essay required
- 36% graduate within 6 years

General. Founded in 1882. Regionally accredited. Additional campus in Lower Manhattan. **Degrees:** 484 bachelor's, 21 associate awarded; master's, professional offered. **Location:** 25 miles from New York City. **Calendar:** Continuous, limited summer session. **Full-time faculty:** 109 total; 72% have terminal degrees, 45% minority, 46% women. **Part-time faculty:** 196 total; 17% have terminal degrees, 46% minority, 46% women.

Freshman class profile. 303 enrolled.

Mid 50% test scores			
SAT critical reading:	390-510	GPA 2.0-2.99:	43%
SAT math:	390-510	Rank in top quarter:	26%
ACT composite:	17-23	Rank in top tenth:	8%
GPA 3.75 or higher:	6%	Return as sophomores:	66%
GPA 3.50-3.74:	12%	Out-of-state:	38%
GPA 3.0-3.49:	24%	International:	2%

Basis for selection. Applicants must have a Christian commitment and sign an agreement to abide by community life standards. Academic record, class rank, and test scores are the most important considerations. A Pastor's recommendation is required for students applying to the traditional undergraduate program. Interview recommended for those with unsatisfactory recommendations or academic concerns; audition required for music program. **Home schooled:** Ability-to-Benefit test (Accuplacer) required. **Learning Disabled:** Students should inform their admissions counselors.

High school preparation. 15 units recommended. Recommended units include English 4, mathematics 3, social studies 3, science 3 and foreign language 2.

2012-2013 Annual costs. Tuition/fees: $22,500. Room/board: $8,400. Books/supplies: $750. Personal expenses: $2,416.

2010-2011 Financial aid. Need-based: 302 full-time freshmen applied for aid; 289 were judged to have need; 289 of these received aid. Average need met was 67%. Average scholarship/grant was $14,562; average loan $3,522. 57% of total undergraduate aid awarded as scholarships/grants, 43% as loans/jobs. **Non-need-based:** Awarded to 275 full-time undergraduates, including 44 freshmen. Scholarships awarded for academics, alumni affiliation, athletics, leadership, music/drama, religious affiliation, state residency.

Application procedures. Admission: No deadline. $25 fee, may be waived for applicants with need. Admission notification on a rolling basis beginning on or about 9/1. **Financial aid:** No deadline. FAFSA required. Applicants notified on a rolling basis starting 3/1; must reply within 4 week(s) of notification.

Academics. Adult degree completion program offers accelerated study option for adult students, with classes held throughout the New York metropolitan and lower Hudson Valley regions and Washington, DC. **Special study options:** Combined bachelor's/graduate degree, distance learning, double major, ESL, honors, independent study, internships, liberal arts/career combination, study abroad, teacher certification program, Washington semester. Adult degree-completion program. **Credit/placement by examination:** AP, CLEP, SAT, institutional tests. 60 credit hours maximum toward bachelor's

degree. **Support services:** Learning center, pre-admission summer program, reduced course load, remedial instruction, study skills assistance, tutoring, writing center.

Majors. Business: Accounting, business admin. **Communications:** General. **Computer sciences:** Computer science. **Education:** Early childhood, elementary, English, ESL, mathematics, multi-level teacher, music, social studies. **English:** English lit. **Health services:** Nursing (RN). **History:** General. **Human services:** Social work. **Math:** General. **Philosophy/religion:** Philosophy, religion. **Protective services:** Criminal justice. **Psychology:** General. **Social sciences:** Sociology. **Theology:** Bible, missionary, preministerial, religious ed, sacred music, youth ministry. **Visual/performing arts:** Music, music performance, music theory/composition, piano/keyboard, voice/opera.

Most popular majors. Business/marketing 53%, education 7%, psychology 6%, theological studies 11%.

Computing on campus. 130 workstations in dormitories, library, computer center, student center. Dormitories wired for high-speed internet access and linked to campus network. Commuter students can connect to campus network. Online course registration, helpline, wireless network available.

Student life. Freshman orientation: Mandatory, $100 fee. Preregistration for classes offered. Usually 4 days (Rockland Campus), held the weekend prior to start of classes. **Policies:** Alcohol, tobacco, and narcotic drug use and possession prohibited on and off campus. Religious observance required. **Housing:** Guaranteed on-campus for all undergraduates. Single-sex dorms, special housing for disabled, apartments available. $150 fully refundable deposit. **Activities:** Concert band, campus ministries, choral groups, dance, drama, literary magazine, music ensembles, opera, radio station, student government, student newspaper, Asian student fellowship, Kingdom Praise dance team, social justice club, Hands of Compassion, Haiti solidarity committee, Servant Leaders, social work organization, More than Conquerors gospel choir.

Athletics. NCAA, NCCAA. **Intercollegiate:** Baseball M, basketball, cheerleading, cross-country, golf M, soccer, softball W, volleyball W. **Team name:** Warriors.

Student services. Adult student services, alcohol/substance abuse counseling, chaplain/spiritual director, career counseling, services for economically disadvantaged, student employment services, financial aid counseling, health services, personal counseling, placement for graduates, veterans' counselor. **Physically disabled:** Services for visually, speech impaired.

Contact. E-mail: admissions@nyack.edu
Phone: (845) 675-4401 Toll-free number: (800) 336-9225
Fax: (845) 358-3047
Dinesh Mahtani, Director of Undergraduate Admissions, Nyack College, 1 South Boulevard, Nyack, NY 10960-3698

Ohr Somayach Tanenbaum Education Center
Monsey, New York
www.os.edu   CB code: 3357

- Private 4-year rabbinical college for men affiliated with Jewish faith
- Residential campus in large town
- 50 degree-seeking undergraduates
- 13 graduate students
- Interview required

General. Founded in 1979. Accredited by AARTS. First and Second Talmudic degrees offered. **Degrees:** 10 bachelor's awarded; master's offered. **Location:** Half a mile from Spring Valley, 33 miles from New York City. **Calendar:** Semester, extensive summer session. **Full-time faculty:** 3 total. **Part-time faculty:** 2 total; 100% have terminal degrees.

Basis for selection. Potential for scholastic and character achievement evaluated through personal interview, recommendations, departmental examinations, and prior religious and secular studies. Essay recommended.

2011-2012 Annual costs. Tuition/fees: $7,000. Room/board: $7,000. Books/supplies: $300. Personal expenses: $725.

Application procedures. Admission: No deadline. $75 fee, may be waived for applicants with need. Admission notification on a rolling basis. **Financial aid:** No deadline. Applicants notified on a rolling basis starting 7/1; must reply within 4 week(s) of notification.

Academics. Special study options: Accelerated study, cross-registration, independent study, study abroad, teacher certification program. **Credit/placement by examination:** AP, CLEP, institutional tests. **Support services:** Pre-admission summer program, reduced course load, tutoring.

Majors. Philosophy/religion: Judaic. **Theology:** Talmudic.

Computing on campus. 3 workstations in computer center. Repair service available.

Student life. Policies: Religious observance required. **Housing:** Apartments available. $100 deposit. Students above age 30 must arrange own housing off campus. Assistance provided in locating housing. **Activities:** Singing group, community volunteers.

Athletics. Intramural: Baseball M, basketball M, skiing M, swimming M.

Student services. Career counseling, student employment services, personal counseling, placement for graduates.

Contact. E-mail: ohr@os.edu
Phone: (845) 425-1370 Fax: (845) 425-8865
Avrohom Braun, Dean of Students, Ohr Somayach Tanenbaum Education Center, 244 Route 306, Monsey, NY 10952

Pace University
New York, New York   CB member
www.pace.edu   CB code: 2635

- Private 4-year university
- Residential campus in very large city
- 7,620 degree-seeking undergraduates: 10% part-time, 59% women, 12% African American, 10% Asian American, 16% Hispanic American, 5% international
- 4,515 degree-seeking graduate students
- 84% of applicants admitted
- SAT or ACT (ACT writing optional), application essay required
- 55% graduate within 6 years; 20% enter graduate study

General. Founded in 1906. Regionally accredited. Three schools and two colleges of the University are located on New York City and Pleasantville campuses: Dyson College of Arts and Sciences, College of Health Professions, School of Education, Lubin School of Business, and Seidenberg School of Computer Science and Information Systems. The School of Law and Lubin Graduate Center are located in White Plains. **Degrees:** 1,481 bachelor's, 49 associate awarded; master's, professional, doctoral offered. **ROTC:** Army, Air Force. **Calendar:** Semester, limited summer session. **Full-time faculty:** 452 total; 85% have terminal degrees, 17% minority, 44% women. **Part-time faculty:** 827 total; 24% have terminal degrees, 15% minority, 51% women. **Class size:** 47% < 20, 50% 20-39, 2% 40-49, less than 1% 50-99, less than 1% >100. **Special facilities:** Art galleries, multimedia language laboratories, speech and hearing center, studio theater.

Freshman class profile. 11,778 applied, 9,918 admitted, 1,594 enrolled.

Mid 50% test scores			
SAT critical reading:	490-590	Rank in top tenth:	20%
SAT math:	510-600	End year in good standing:	96%
ACT composite:	23-26	Return as sophomores:	79%
GPA 3.75 or higher:	17%	Out-of-state:	38%
GPA 3.50-3.74:	21%	Live on campus:	69%
GPA 3.0-3.49:	49%	International:	4%
GPA 2.0-2.99:	13%	Fraternities:	2%
Rank in top quarter:	53%	Sororities:	2%

Basis for selection. 85 high school GPA, rank in top half of class, test scores, recommendations, personal statement important. Extracurricular activities also considered. Non-native speakers of English are required to take TOEFL. Official scores must be sent directly to the school. Notarized copies are not acceptable. Audition required for dance, dramatic arts, theater; portfolio recommended for art programs. Applicants to Lienhard School of Nursing must be certified in CPR. **Home schooled:** The transcript should be from a program and/or a detailed roster of academic course work at the secondary level. **Learning Disabled:** Diagnostic tests recommended.

High school preparation. College-preparatory program recommended. 16 units required; 20 recommended. Required and recommended units include English 4, mathematics 3-4, social studies 1-2, history 2-3, science 2 (laboratory 2), foreign language 2-3 and academic electives 2.

2011-2012 Annual costs. Tuition/fees: $35,032. Room/board: $14,230. Books/supplies: $800. Personal expenses: $1,470.

2011-2012 Financial aid. Need-based: 1,408 full-time freshmen applied for aid; 1,312 were judged to have need; 1,311 of these received aid. Average need met was 77%. Average scholarship/grant was $25,747; average loan $3,864. 76% of total undergraduate aid awarded as scholarships/grants, 24% as loans/jobs. **Non-need-based:** Awarded to 1,589 full-time undergraduates,

including 343 freshmen. Scholarships awarded for academics, alumni affiliation, athletics.

Application procedures. Admission: Closing date 2/15 (postmark date). $50 fee, may be waived for applicants with need. Admission notification on a rolling basis beginning on or about 12/15. Must reply by May 1 or within 2 week(s) if notified thereafter. **Financial aid:** Priority date 2/15; no closing date. FAFSA required. Applicants notified on a rolling basis starting 3/1; must reply by 5/1 or within 2 week(s) of notification.

Academics. Adult undergraduate degrees in liberal/general studies, business and computer science. **Special study options:** Accelerated study, combined bachelor's/graduate degree, cooperative education, cross-registration, distance learning, double major, dual enrollment of high school students, ESL, honors, independent study, internships, study abroad, teacher certification program. Evening and freshman studies programs, pre-freshman summer program, learning communities and service learning. **Credit/placement by examination:** AP, CLEP, IB, institutional tests. 30 credit hours maximum toward associate degree, 96 toward bachelor's. **Support services:** Learning center, reduced course load, remedial instruction, study skills assistance, tutoring, writing center.

Honors college/program. Honors Program requires entering freshmen have 90 or higher high school GPA, SAT verbal minimum of 550, SAT math minimum of 550 and a combined SAT score of 1200 (exclusive of Writing). Honors program students may be enrolled in any of undergraduate schools at University.

Majors. Area/ethnic studies: American, Latin American, women's. **Biology:** General, biochemistry. **Business:** General, accounting, entrepreneurial studies, finance, hotel/motel admin, human resources, international, international marketing, marketing. **Communications:** Advertising, communications/speech/rhetoric, media studies. **Computer sciences:** General, computer science, information systems, IT project management. **Conservation:** Environmental science, environmental studies. **Education:** Biology, chemistry, early childhood, earth science, elementary, English, foreign languages, history, mathematics, social studies, Spanish, special ed, speech impaired. **English:** British lit, English lit. **Foreign languages:** General, Spanish. **Health services:** Communication disorders, nursing (RN), preoccupational therapy, prephysical therapy. **History:** General. **Liberal arts:** Arts/sciences. **Math:** General. **Philosophy/religion:** General. **Physical sciences:** Chemistry. **Protective services:** Forensics, law enforcement admin. **Psychology:** General, applied, personality, psychobiology. **Social sciences:** General, economics, political science, sociology/anthropology. **Visual/performing arts:** Acting, art, art history/conservation, film/cinema/video, musical theater, studio arts, theater arts management.

Most popular majors. Business/marketing 38%, communications/journalism 10%, health sciences 11%, psychology 8%.

Computing on campus. 268 workstations in library, computer center. Dormitories linked to campus network. Commuter students can connect to campus network. Online library, helpline, wireless network available.

Student life. Freshman orientation: Mandatory, $40 fee. Preregistration for classes offered. 2 days for freshmen. Orientation held at different times during the summer. International students attend orientation for 3 days prior to the start of the fall term. 1-day program for transfer students ($25). **Policies:** No parking available on the New York City campus. All cars brought on the Pleasantville campus must be registered. Students must register their vehicles at the beginning of each academic year and will be issued a permit. Parking is in designated areas only. **Housing:** Coed dorms, apartments, wellness housing available. $500 partly refundable deposit, deadline 5/1. Apartment style housing for upperclassmen available. **Activities:** Choral groups, dance, drama, film society, international student organizations, literary magazine, Model UN, musical theater, radio station, student government, student newspaper, TV station, Collegiate Italian American Organization, Desi Heritage of Southeast Asia, International Student Club, Hillel, Pace Christian fellowship, Caribbean Students Association, African Students at Pace, Sabor Latino, Project Pericles, NATURE (environmental club).

Athletics. NCAA. **Intercollegiate:** Baseball M, basketball, cross-country, equestrian W, football (tackle) M, golf M, lacrosse M, soccer W, softball W, swimming, tennis, track and field, volleyball W. **Intramural:** Football (non-tackle), soccer, softball, volleyball. **Team name:** Setters.

Student services. Adult student services, career counseling, student employment services, health services, personal counseling, placement for graduates, veterans' counselor. **Physically disabled:** Services for visually, speech, hearing impaired.

Contact. E-mail: infoctr@pace.edu
Phone: (212) 346-1323 Toll-free number: (800) 874-7223
Fax: (212) 346-1040
Donna Grand Pre, Dean of Admissions, Pace University, 1 Pace Plaza, New York, NY 10038-1598

Pace University: Pleasantville/Briarcliff
Pleasantville, New York
www.pace.edu CB code: 2685

▶ Private 4-year university
▶ Residential campus in small town
▶ SAT or ACT (ACT writing optional), application essay required

General. Regionally accredited. Four schools and one college of the university are located on the Pleasantville campus: Dyson College of Arts and Sciences, Lienhard School of Nursing, School of Education, Lubin School of Business, and Seidenberg School of Computer Science and Information Systems. Pace School of Law and Lubin Graduate Center are located in White Plains. **ROTC:** Army. **Location:** 7 miles from White Plains, 30 miles from New York City. **Calendar:** Semester, limited summer session. **Special facilities:** Fitness center, environmental center.

Basis for selection. 85 high school GPA, rank in top half of class, test scores, recommendations, personal statement important. Extracurricular activities also considered. Non-native speakers of English are required to take TOEFL. Official scores must be sent directly to school. Notarized copies are not acceptable. Interview strongly recommended; audition required for dance, dramatic arts, theater; portfolio recommended for art programs. Applicants to Lienhard School of Nursing must be certified in CPR. **Learning Disabled:** Diagnostic tests recommended.

High school preparation. 16 units required; 20 recommended. Required and recommended units include English 4, mathematics 3-4, social studies 1-2, history 2-3, science 2 (laboratory 2), foreign language 2-3 and academic electives 2.

2011-2012 Annual costs. Tuition/fees: $35,147. Room/board: $12,110. Books/supplies: $800. Personal expenses: $1,470.

Financial aid. Non-need-based: Scholarships awarded for academics, athletics. **Additional information:** Tuition at time of first enrollment is guaranteed to matriculated undergraduate students for 5 continuous academic years.

Application procedures. Admission: Closing date 3/1 (postmark date). $45 fee, may be waived for applicants with need. Admission notification on a rolling basis beginning on or about 12/15. Must reply by May 1 or within 2 week(s) if notified thereafter. **Financial aid:** Priority date 2/15; no closing date. FAFSA required. Applicants notified on a rolling basis starting 2/28; must reply by 5/1 or within 2 week(s) of notification.

Academics. Adult undergraduate degrees in liberal/general studies, business, and computer science. **Special study options:** Accelerated study, combined bachelor's/graduate degree, cooperative education, cross-registration, distance learning, double major, dual enrollment of high school students, ESL, honors, independent study, internships, study abroad, teacher certification program. Evening and freshman studies programs, pre-freshman summer program. **Credit/placement by examination:** AP, CLEP, IB, institutional tests. 30 credit hours maximum toward associate degree, 96 toward bachelor's. **Support services:** Learning center, reduced course load, remedial instruction, study skills assistance, tutoring, writing center.

Majors. Area/ethnic studies: Women's. **Biology:** General, biochemistry. **Business:** General, accounting, business admin, e-commerce, entrepreneurial studies, finance, hotel/motel admin, human resources, international, international marketing, management science, marketing, nonprofit/public. **Communications:** Advertising, communications/speech/rhetoric, media studies. **Computer sciences:** General, computer science, data processing, information systems, systems analysis. **Conservation:** Environmental studies. **Education:** Biology, business, chemistry, computer, early childhood, elementary, English, French, history, mathematics, physics, science, social science, social studies, Spanish, speech impaired. **English:** English lit, rhetoric/composition. **Foreign languages:** General, French, Spanish. **Health services:** Clinical lab science, communication disorders, nursing (RN), physician assistant, speech pathology. **History:** General. **Human services:** Community org/advocacy. **Liberal arts:** Arts/sciences. **Math:** General. **Philosophy/religion:** Philosophy, religion. **Physical sciences:** Chemistry, geology, physics. **Protective services:** Forensics, law enforcement admin. **Psychology:** General. **Social sciences:** General, economics, political science. **Visual/performing arts:** Art, art history/conservation, dramatic.

Computing on campus. 190 workstations in library, computer center. Dormitories linked to campus network. Commuter students can connect to campus network. Online library, helpline, wireless network available.

Student life. Freshman orientation: Available, $75 fee. Preregistration for classes offered. New students may register in the summer. Orientation held in fall before classes start. **Housing:** Coed dorms, apartments, wellness housing available. $400 deposit, deadline 5/1. Townhouses available for upperclassmen. Each unit houses 8 students in 4 double rooms. **Activities:** Choral groups, dance, drama, film society, literary magazine, radio station,

student government, student newspaper, Black student union, collegiate Italian-American organization, Asian cultural society, international student organization, Jewish student association, Indo American society, Pace Christian fellowhip, Caribbean student association, NAACP.

Athletics. NCAA. **Intercollegiate:** Baseball M, basketball, cross-country, equestrian, football (tackle) M, golf, lacrosse M, soccer W, softball W, swimming, tennis, track and field, volleyball W. **Intramural:** Basketball, football (tackle) M, soccer, softball, volleyball. **Team name:** Setters.

Student services. Adult student services, career counseling, student employment services, health services, personal counseling, placement for graduates, veterans' counselor. **Physically disabled:** Services for visually, speech, hearing impaired.

Contact. E-mail: infoctr@pace.edu
Phone: (914) 773-3746 Toll-free number: (800) 874-7223
Fax: (914) 773-3851
Joanna Broda, Director of Admission, Pace University: Pleasantville/ Briarcliff, 861 Bedford Road, Pleasantville, NY 10570

Parsons The New School for Design
New York, New York
www.parsons.edu　　　　　　　　　　　**CB code: 2638**

⧫ Private 4-year visual arts college
⧫ Commuter campus in very large city
⧫ 4,254 degree-seeking undergraduates: 10% part-time, 79% women, 4% African American, 16% Asian American, 9% Hispanic American, 36% international
⧫ 582 degree-seeking graduate students
⧫ 70% of applicants admitted
⧫ SAT or ACT (ACT writing optional) required
⧫ 69% graduate within 6 years

General. Founded in 1896. Regionally accredited. Division of The New School. **Degrees:** 655 bachelor's, 447 associate awarded; master's offered. **Location:** Located in Manhattan. **Calendar:** Semester, extensive summer session. **Full-time faculty:** 152 total; 59% have terminal degrees, 14% minority, 47% women. **Part-time faculty:** 918 total; less than 1% have terminal degrees, 17% minority, 50% women. **Class size:** 91% < 20, 8% 20-39, less than 1% 50-99, less than 1% >100. **Special facilities:** Architecture studio, labs, galleries, Parsons Institute for Information Mapping, Tishman Environment and Design Center, Vera List Center for Art and Politics.

Freshman class profile. 2,590 applied, 1,825 admitted, 711 enrolled.

Mid 50% test scores			
SAT critical reading:	490-600	GPA 2.0-2.99:	20%
SAT math:	500-640	Rank in top quarter:	50%
SAT writing:	500-620	Rank in top tenth:	25%
ACT composite:	21-27	Return as sophomores:	86%
GPA 3.75 or higher:	21%	Out-of-state:	76%
GPA 3.50-3.74:	18%	Live on campus:	67%
GPA 3.0-3.49:	40%	International:	37%

Basis for selection. Portfolio and home examination most important, followed by school achievement record and test scores. Activities, leadership, motivation considered. Portfolio required, essay recommended for all; interview recommended, required for those geographically close.

2011-2012 Annual costs. Tuition/fees: $39,350. Room/board: $15,260. Books/supplies: $920. Personal expenses: $1,550.

2011-2012 Financial aid. Need-based: 377 full-time freshmen applied for aid; 333 were judged to have need; 324 of these received aid. Average need met was 52%. Average scholarship/grant was $20,040; average loan $7,220. 74% of total undergraduate aid awarded as scholarships/grants, 26% as loans/jobs. **Non-need-based:** Awarded to 284 full-time undergraduates, including 106 freshmen. Scholarships awarded for art.

Application procedures. Admission: Priority date 4/1; deadline 4/1. $50 fee, may be waived for applicants with need. Admission notification by 5/1. Admission notification on a rolling basis. Must reply by May 1 or within 2 week(s) if notified thereafter. **Financial aid:** Priority date 3/1; no closing date. FAFSA required. Applicants notified on a rolling basis starting 4/1; must reply within 4 week(s) of notification.

Academics. Special study options: Accelerated study, cross-registration, distance learning, double major, dual enrollment of high school students, ESL, exchange student, independent study, internships, liberal arts/career combination, student-designed major, study abroad. Five-year combined BA/ BFA, New York Studio Program. **Credit/placement by examination:** AP,

CLEP, IB. **Support services:** Pre-admission summer program, remedial instruction, tutoring, writing center.

Majors. Architecture: Architecture, environmental design, interior, landscape. **Business:** Fashion. **Conservation:** Environmental studies. **Visual/ performing arts:** Design, fashion design, illustration, industrial design, interior design, photography, studio arts.

Most popular majors. Visual/performing arts 97%.

Computing on campus. Dormitories wired for high-speed internet access and linked to campus network. Commuter students can connect to campus network. Online course registration, helpline, student web hosting, wireless network available.

Student life. Freshman orientation: Mandatory. Preregistration for classes offered. Orientation to school, programs, services, and New York City. **Housing:** Guaranteed on-campus for all undergraduates. Coed dorms, special housing for disabled, apartments, wellness housing available. $250 nonrefundable deposit, deadline 7/1. **Activities:** Jazz band, choral groups, dance, drama, international student organizations, literary magazine, music ensembles, opera, radio station, student government, student newspaper, symphony orchestra, Sustainable Design Review, New School Styling Club, Roots & Shoots, Radical student union, Global Health student organization, international club, PHOTOfeast, the Theatre Collective, Jewish student union, New School Remnant Christian Fellowship.

Student services. Career counseling, services for economically disadvantaged, student employment services, financial aid counseling, health services, minority student services, personal counseling, placement for graduates.

Contact. E-mail: thinkparsons@newschool.edu
Phone: (212) 229-8910 Toll-free number: (877) 528-3321
Fax: (212) 229-8975
Carolina Wheat, Director of Undergraduate Admission, Parsons The New School for Design, 72 Fifth Avenue, New York, NY 10011

Paul Smith's College
Paul Smiths, New York　　　　　　　　**CB member**
www.paulsmiths.edu　　　　　　　　　　**CB code: 2640**

⧫ Private 4-year liberal arts college
⧫ Residential campus in rural community
⧫ 1,060 degree-seeking undergraduates: 3% part-time, 34% women, 3% African American, 3% Hispanic American, 1% Native American
⧫ 75% of applicants admitted
⧫ 50% graduate within 6 years

General. Founded in 1937. Regionally accredited. **Degrees:** 127 bachelor's, 69 associate awarded. **Location:** 25 miles from Lake Placid, 143 miles from Albany. **Calendar:** Semester, limited summer session. **Full-time faculty:** 54 total. **Part-time faculty:** 21 total. **Class size:** 43% < 20, 48% 20-39, 6% 40-49, 2% 50-99, less than 1% >100. **Special facilities:** Sugar maple plantation, sawmill, on-campus restaurant, 14,200-acre forest, on-campus retail bakery, mini-palm training restaurant, woodman/lumberjack training area.

Freshman class profile. 1,152 applied, 861 admitted, 326 enrolled.

Mid 50% test scores			
SAT critical reading:	430-530	GPA 3.0-3.49:	25%
SAT math:	440-530	GPA 2.0-2.99:	52%
SAT writing:	410-500	Rank in top quarter:	18%
ACT composite:	18-23	Rank in top tenth:	5%
GPA 3.75 or higher:	5%	Return as sophomores:	62%
GPA 3.50-3.74:	11%	Out-of-state:	38%
		Live on campus:	99%

Basis for selection. Most consideration given to high school or college course work as well as SAT/ACT scores. Personal essays, letters of recommendation, relevant experience and SAT/ACT scores highly encouraged. Interview recommended. **Home schooled:** Statement describing home school structure and mission, transcript of courses and grades, interview, letter of recommendation (nonparent) required.

High school preparation. College-preparatory program recommended. 4 units required; 8 recommended. Required and recommended units include English 4, mathematics 2, science 2 (laboratory 2) and foreign language 2. High school subject requirements vary according to program.

2011-2012 Annual costs. Tuition/fees: $21,505. Program fees range from $680 to $2,190 depending on program. Room/board: $9,670. Books/supplies: $1,000. Personal expenses: $1,000.

2011-2012 Financial aid. Need-based: 309 full-time freshmen applied for aid; 286 were judged to have need; 286 of these received aid. Average

need met was 74%. Average scholarship/grant was $13,976; average loan $4,065. 58% of total undergraduate aid awarded as scholarships/grants, 42% as loans/jobs. **Non-need-based:** Awarded to 226 full-time undergraduates, including 62 freshmen. Scholarships awarded for academics. **Additional information:** Merit aid only for international students; no financial aid application required.

Application procedures. Admission: No deadline. $30 fee, may be waived for applicants with need. Admission notification on a rolling basis beginning on or about 10/1. **Financial aid:** Priority date 3/31; no closing date. FAFSA required. Applicants notified on a rolling basis starting 3/5; must reply within 4 week(s) of notification.

Academics. Special study options: Combined bachelor's/graduate degree, double major, dual enrollment of high school students, honors, independent study, internships, liberal arts/career combination, study abroad. **Credit/placement by examination:** AP, CLEP, IB, institutional tests. 15 credit hours maximum toward associate degree, 15 toward bachelor's. **Support services:** Learning center, reduced course load, remedial instruction, study skills assistance, tutoring, writing center.

Majors. Biology: General. **Business:** General, business admin, entrepreneurial studies, hospitality admin, hospitality/recreation, hotel/motel admin, resort management, restaurant/food services, tourism promotion, tourism/travel. **Conservation:** General, environmental science, fisheries, forest management, forest resources, forest sciences, forestry, management/policy, wildlife/wilderness. **Health services:** Predental, premedicine, preveterinary. **Liberal arts:** Arts/sciences. **Parks/recreation:** General, facilities management.

Most popular majors. Business/marketing 18%, natural resources/environmental science 46%, parks/recreation 11%, personal/culinary services 19%.

Computing on campus. 140 workstations in library, computer center. Dormitories wired for high-speed internet access and linked to campus network. Commuter students can connect to campus network. Online library, helpline, student web hosting, wireless network available.

Student life. Freshman orientation: Mandatory, $125 fee. Preregistration for classes offered. **Housing:** Guaranteed on-campus for all undergraduates. Coed dorms, single-sex dorms, wellness housing available. $100 nonrefundable deposit, deadline 5/1. **Activities:** Choral groups, literary magazine, radio station, student government, student newspaper, gaming and Anime, conservation club, Junior American Culinary Federation, Christian Fellowship, fiber arts, campus council.

Athletics. USCAA. **Intercollegiate:** Basketball, cross-country, rugby, skiing, soccer, volleyball W. **Intramural:** Basketball, ice hockey M, rugby, soccer, volleyball, water polo. **Team name:** Bobcats.

Student services. Adult student services, alcohol/substance abuse counseling, chaplain/spiritual director, career counseling, services for economically disadvantaged, student employment services, financial aid counseling, health services, personal counseling, placement for graduates, veterans' counselor. **Physically disabled:** Services for visually, hearing impaired.

Contact. E-mail: admissions@paulsmiths.edu
Phone: (518) 327-6227 Toll-free number: (800) 421-2605
Fax: (518) 327-6016
Eric Felver, Vice President of Enrollment Management, Paul Smith's College, PO Box 265, Routes 30 & 86, Paul Smiths, NY 12970-0265

Polytechnic Institute of New York University
Brooklyn, New York   **CB member**
www.poly.edu   **CB code: 2668**

- Private 4-year university
- Residential campus in very large city
- 1,765 degree-seeking undergraduates: 4% part-time, 21% women, 8% African American, 34% Asian American, 11% Hispanic American, 11% international
- 2,474 degree-seeking graduate students
- 68% of applicants admitted
- SAT or ACT, application essay required
- 54% graduate within 6 years

General. Founded in 1854. Regionally accredited. **Degrees:** 301 bachelor's awarded; master's, doctoral offered. **ROTC:** Army, Air Force. **Location:** 2 miles from New York City. **Calendar:** Semester, extensive summer session. **Full-time faculty:** 156 total; 88% have terminal degrees, 27% minority, 17% women. **Part-time faculty:** 213 total; 54% have terminal degrees, 18% minority, 22% women. **Class size:** 49% < 20, 40% 20-39, 4% 40-49, 6%

50-99, less than 1% >100. **Special facilities:** Library of science and technology, center for advanced technology in telecommunications, institute of imaging sciences, center for construction management technology, transportation research institute, wireless research institute, urban infrastructure institute.

Freshman class profile. 3,116 applied, 2,124 admitted, 416 enrolled.

Mid 50% test scores			
SAT critical reading:	560-660	Rank in top quarter:	88%
SAT math:	650-730	Rank in top tenth:	56%
SAT writing:	560-650	Return as sophomores:	84%
ACT composite:	26-31	Out-of-state:	27%
GPA 3.75 or higher:	29%	Live on campus:	50%
GPA 3.50-3.74:	37%	International:	10%
GPA 3.0-3.49:	25%	Fraternities:	3%
GPA 2.0-2.99:	9%	Sororities:	2%

Basis for selection. School achievement record, class rank, test scores, recommendations required. Special emphasis on mathematics and science areas. Interview recommended.

High school preparation. College-preparatory program required. Required and recommended units include English 4, mathematics 4, social studies 3, science 4, foreign language 2 and academic electives 2. Requirements include 1 chemistry, pre-calculus, calculus.

2011-2012 Annual costs. Tuition/fees: $37,882. Room/board: $10,080. Books/supplies: $1,500. Personal expenses: $1,900.

2010-2011 Financial aid. Need-based: 298 full-time freshmen applied for aid; 238 were judged to have need; 236 of these received aid. Average need met was 94%. Average scholarship/grant was $16,265; average loan $3,823. 79% of total undergraduate aid awarded as scholarships/grants, 21% as loans/jobs. **Non-need-based:** Awarded to 1,076 full-time undergraduates, including 243 freshmen. Scholarships awarded for academics.

Application procedures. Admission: Priority date 2/1; no deadline. $65 fee, may be waived for applicants with need. Admission notification on a rolling basis beginning on or about 2/1. Must reply by May 1 or within 4 week(s) if notified thereafter. **Financial aid:** Priority date 3/1; no closing date. FAFSA required. Applicants notified on a rolling basis starting 3/15; must reply within 2 week(s) of notification.

Academics. Special study options: Accelerated study, combined bachelor's/graduate degree, cooperative education, distance learning, double major, honors, internships, study abroad. Joint master's degree program in dental materials science with New York University. **Credit/placement by examination:** AP, CLEP, IB, institutional tests. 16 credit hours maximum toward bachelor's degree. Students with outstanding record or specialized competence may establish 16 credits maximum toward baccalaureate degree by passing comprehensive examinations. Each department determines courses in which examination available and examination format. **Support services:** Learning center, pre-admission summer program, remedial instruction, study skills assistance, tutoring, writing center.

Honors college/program. Students selected for Honors College must have superior high school academic records and interview with member of Honors College Faculty Governing Board.

Majors. Biology: Molecular biochemistry. **Business:** Construction management, management information systems. **Computer sciences:** Computer science, web page design. **Engineering:** Chemical, civil, computer, electrical, mechanical. **History:** Science/technology. **Liberal arts:** Arts/sciences. **Math:** Applied. **Physical sciences:** Chemistry, physics. **Social sciences:** Urban studies.

Most popular majors. Business/marketing 10%, computer/information sciences 9%, engineering/engineering technologies 71%.

Computing on campus. PC or laptop required. 104 workstations in dormitories, library, computer center, student center. Dormitories wired for high-speed internet access and linked to campus network. Commuter students can connect to campus network. Online course registration, online library, helpline, repair service, student web hosting, wireless network available.

Student life. Freshman orientation: Available. Preregistration for classes offered. **Policies:** Freshmen not permitted cars on campus. **Housing:** Guaranteed on-campus for freshmen. Coed dorms, fraternity/sorority housing, wellness housing available. $400 nonrefundable deposit. **Activities:** Film society, literary magazine, radio station, student government, student newspaper, Society of Women Engineers, Society of Black Engineers, Ambassador Society, ethnic and service organizations, Society of Hispanic Professional Engineers, Alpha Phi Omega service fraternity.

Athletics. NCAA. **Intercollegiate:** Baseball M, basketball, cross-country, judo M, soccer, softball W, tennis, track and field W, volleyball. **Intramural:** Basketball, bowling, football (non-tackle), golf, handball M, ice hockey M,

racquetball, skiing, soccer, softball W, table tennis, track and field, volleyball, weight lifting. **Team name:** Blue Jays.

Student services. Career counseling, student employment services, placement for graduates.

Contact. E-mail: uadmit@poly.edu
Phone: (718) 260-3100 Toll-free number: (800) 765-9832
Fax: (718) 260-3446
Joy Colelli, Dean of Admissions and New Students, Polytechnic Institute of New York University, 6 Metrotech Center, Brooklyn, NY 11201-2999

Pratt Institute

Brooklyn, New York
www.pratt.edu

CB member
CB code: 2669

- Private 4-year university and visual arts college
- Residential campus in very large city
- 2,996 degree-seeking undergraduates: 5% part-time, 64% women, 4% African American, 18% Asian American, 9% Hispanic American, 17% international
- 1,683 degree-seeking graduate students
- 60% of applicants admitted
- SAT or ACT with writing, application essay required
- 62% graduate within 6 years

General. Founded in 1887. Regionally accredited. Additional campus located in Manhattan with associate degree programs, bachelor's degree in construction management program, and various graduate programs. **Degrees:** 527 bachelor's, 49 associate awarded; master's offered. **Location:** 2 miles from Manhattan. **Calendar:** Semester, extensive summer session. **Full-time faculty:** 130 total; 72% have terminal degrees, 15% minority, 40% women. **Part-time faculty:** 875 total; 17% minority, 42% women. **Class size:** 74% < 20, 23% 20-39, 2% 40-49, less than 1% 50-99, less than 1% >100. **Special facilities:** Wood and metal workshops, ceramics kiln studios and casting foundry, digital arts labs, printmaking workshop, fine arts center, center for community development.

Freshman class profile. 4,247 applied, 2,541 admitted, 608 enrolled.

Mid 50% test scores			
SAT critical reading:	530-640	**GPA 3.0-3.49:**	29%
SAT math:	550-660	**GPA 2.0-2.99:**	10%
SAT writing:	540-650	**Return as sophomores:**	83%
ACT composite:	25-28	**Out-of-state:**	78%
GPA 3.75 or higher:	39%	**Live on campus:**	90%
GPA 3.50-3.74:	22%	**International:**	21%

Basis for selection. Admissions committee considers overall academic record which includes academic performance, portfolio, curriculum, test scores, recommendation, and essay. SAT Subject Test Math level 1 recommended for applicants to architecture program. Interview not required. Letter of recommendation required for all applicants. Portfolio required for architecture, art and design programs.

High school preparation. College-preparatory program recommended. 16 units recommended. Recommended units include English 4, mathematics 4, social studies 1, science 2 and academic electives 5. 4 math required for architecture and construction management applicants.

2012-2013 Annual costs. Tuition/fees: $41,092. Room/board: $10,506. Books/supplies: $3,000. Personal expenses: $1,800.

2011-2012 Financial aid. Need-based: 395 full-time freshmen applied for aid; 352 were judged to have need; 352 of these received aid. Average scholarship/grant was $9,610; average loan $3,877. 61% of total undergraduate aid awarded as scholarships/grants, 39% as loans/jobs. **Non-need-based:** Awarded to 2,109 full-time undergraduates, including 464 freshmen. Scholarships awarded for academics.

Application procedures. Admission: Closing date 1/5 (postmark date). $50 fee, may be waived for applicants with need. Admission notification by 4/1. Must reply by May 1 or within 2 week(s) if notified thereafter. **Financial aid:** Closing date 2/1. FAFSA required. Applicants notified on a rolling basis starting 3/10; must reply within 2 week(s) of notification.

Academics. Special study options: ESL, exchange student, independent study, internships, study abroad, teacher certification program. **Credit/placement by examination:** AP, CLEP, institutional tests. **Support services:** Learning center, pre-admission summer program, reduced course load, study skills assistance, tutoring, writing center.

Majors. Architecture: Architecture. **Business:** Construction management. **Communications technology:** Animation/special effects. **Computer sciences:** Computer graphics. **Education:** Art. **English:** Creative writing. **Visual/performing arts:** Art history/conservation, cinematography, design, digital arts, fashion design, industrial design, interior design, photography, studio arts.

Most popular majors. Architecture 15%, visual/performing arts 78%.

Computing on campus. 300 workstations in dormitories, library, computer center, student center. Dormitories wired for high-speed internet access and linked to campus network. Commuter students can connect to campus network. Online course registration, helpline, repair service, student web hosting, wireless network available.

Student life. Freshman orientation: Available. Preregistration for classes offered. **Housing:** Guaranteed on-campus for freshmen. Coed dorms, special housing for disabled, apartments, wellness housing available. $300 partly refundable deposit, deadline 5/1. Global learning, healthy choice and quiet floors available. **Activities:** Campus ministries, film society, international student organizations, literary magazine, music ensembles, radio station, student government, student newspaper, TV station, Christian Fellowship, Jewish student union, Muslim student association, Asian student organization, The Agenda, Korean student association, environmental resource group, Gay/Lesbian at Pratt, New York Public Interest Research Group, Pratt Projects (socially conscious project design and creation).

Athletics. NCAA. **Intercollegiate:** Basketball M, cross-country, soccer, tennis, track and field, volleyball W. **Intramural:** Badminton, basketball, football (non-tackle) M, weight lifting. **Team name:** Canonneers.

Student services. Alcohol/substance abuse counseling, chaplain/spiritual director, career counseling, student employment services, financial aid counseling, health services, minority student services, personal counseling, placement for graduates, veterans' counselor. **Physically disabled:** Services for visually, speech, hearing impaired.

Contact. E-mail: visit@pratt.edu
Phone: (718) 636-3514 Toll-free number: (800) 331-0834
Fax: (718) 636-3670
William Swan, Director of Admissions, Pratt Institute, 200 Willoughby Avenue, Brooklyn, NY 11205-3817

Rabbinical Academy Mesivta Rabbi Chaim Berlin

Brooklyn, New York

CB code: 0719

- Private 4-year rabbinical college for men affiliated with Jewish faith
- Very large city
- 122 degree-seeking undergraduates

General. Accredited by AARTS. **Degrees:** 20 bachelor's awarded; master's, doctoral offered. **Calendar:** Differs by program. **Full-time faculty:** 12 total. **Part-time faculty:** 3 total.

2011-2012 Annual costs. Tuition/fees: $10,850. Room/board: $3,000.

Application procedures. Admission: No deadline. No application fee.

Academics. Credit/placement by examination: AP, CLEP.

Majors. Theology: Talmudic.

Contact. Phone: (718) 377-0777
Eli Rabinowitz, Admissions Director, Rabbinical Academy Mesivta Rabbi Chaim Berlin, 1605 Coney Island Avenue, Brooklyn, NY 11230

Rabbinical College Beth Shraga

Monsey, New York

- Private 4-year rabbinical college for men affiliated with Jewish faith
- Commuter campus in large town
- 39 degree-seeking undergraduates

General. **Degrees:** 1 bachelor's awarded. **Calendar:** Differs by program.

2011-2012 Annual costs. Tuition/fees: $10,050. Room/board: $4,500.

Application procedures. Admission: No deadline.

Academics. Credit/placement by examination: AP, CLEP.

Majors. Theology: Talmudic.

Contact. Phone: (845) 356-1980
Schraga Schiff, Admissions Director, Rabbinical College Beth Shraga, PO Box 412, Monsey, NY 10952

Rabbinical College Bobover Yeshiva B'nei Zion
Brooklyn, New York
CB code: 7011

- Private 5-year rabbinical college for men affiliated with Jewish faith
- Very large city
- 255 degree-seeking undergraduates

General. Accredited by AARTS. **Degrees:** 56 bachelor's awarded; master's offered. **Calendar:** Differs by program.

Basis for selection. Approximately 150 folio pages of Talmud, courses on Pentateuch with commentaries, Orach Cham Codes of Jewish Law.

2011-2012 Annual costs. Tuition/fees: $8,960. Room/board: $4,500. Books/supplies: $400. Personal expenses: $500.

Application procedures. Admission: No deadline.

Academics. Credit/placement by examination: AP, CLEP.

Majors. Theology: Talmudic.

Contact. Phone: (718) 438-2018
Rabbinical College Bobover Yeshiva B'nei Zion, 1577 48th Street, Brooklyn, NY 11219

Rabbinical College Ch'san Sofer of New York
Brooklyn, New York
CB code: 0714

- Private 4-year rabbinical college for men affiliated with Jewish faith
- Very large city
- Interview required

General. Founded in 1940. Accredited by AARTS. Ordination and First Talmudic degree available. **Degrees:** 14 bachelor's awarded; master's offered. **Calendar:** Semester.

Basis for selection. Religious commitment, school achievement record, and interview most important.

2011-2012 Annual costs. Tuition/fees: $8,500. Room/board: $4,000.

Application procedures. Admission: Closing date 9/1. Admission notification on a rolling basis.

Academics. Credit/placement by examination: AP, CLEP.

Majors. Theology: Talmudic.

Student life. Policies: Religious observance required.

Contact. Phone: (718) 236-1171
Rabbinical College Ch'san Sofer of New York, 1876 50th Street, Brooklyn, NY 11204

Rabbinical College of Long Island
Long Beach, New York
CB code: 0675

- Private 4-year rabbinical and teachers college for men affiliated with Jewish faith
- Large town
- 97 degree-seeking undergraduates
- Interview required

General. Founded in 1965. Accredited by AARTS. Ordination and First Talmudic degree available. **Calendar:** Trimester. **Full-time faculty:** 4 total. **Part-time faculty:** 2 total.

Basis for selection. Religious commitment, interview, and recommendations most important.

2011-2012 Annual costs. Tuition/fees: $8,900. Room/board: $4,900.

Application procedures. Admission: No deadline. No application fee. Admission notification on a rolling basis.

Academics. Credit/placement by examination: AP, CLEP.

Majors. Theology: Talmudic.

Student life. Policies: Religious observance required.

Contact. Phone: (516) 255-4700
Rabbi Chaim Hoberman, Director of Admissions, Rabbinical College of Long Island, 205 West Beech Street, Long Beach, NY 11561

Rabbinical College of Ohr Shimon Yisroel
Brooklyn, New York

- Private 4-year rabbinical college for men
- Very large city
- 119 degree-seeking undergraduates

General. Accredited by AARTS. **Degrees:** 25 bachelor's awarded. **Calendar:** Semester.

Application procedures. Admission: No deadline.

Academics. Credit/placement by examination: AP, CLEP.

Majors. Theology: Talmudic.

Contact. Phone: (718) 855-4092
Rabbinical College of Ohr Shimon Yisroel, 215-217 Hewes Street, Brooklyn, NY 11211

Rabbinical Seminary of America
Flushing, New York
CB code: 2776

- Private 5-year rabbinical and seminary college for men affiliated with Jewish faith
- Very large city
- 263 degree-seeking undergraduates
- Interview required

General. Founded in 1933. Accredited by AARTS. Ordination available. 4-and 5-year undergraduate programs as well as graduate study. Campus in Jerusalem enrolls 50 students. **Degrees:** 25 bachelor's awarded; master's, doctoral offered. **Calendar:** Semester.

Freshman class profile.

Out-of-state: 40%   **Live on campus:** 70%

Basis for selection. Interview most important. School record and test scores considered.

High school preparation. Diploma from Hebrew high school required.

2011-2012 Annual costs. Tuition/fees: $8,000. Room/board: $6,000.

Application procedures. Admission: Closing date 7/1. Admission notification on a rolling basis. **Financial aid:** No deadline. Applicants notified on a rolling basis.

Academics. Special study options: Independent study, internships. **Credit/placement by examination:** AP, CLEP.

Majors. Theology: Talmudic.

Contact. E-mail: registrar@rabbinical.org
Phone: (718) 268-4700 Fax: (718) 268-4684
Abraham Semmel, Registrar, Rabbinical Seminary of America, 76-01 147th Street, Flushing, NY 11367

Rensselaer Polytechnic Institute
Troy, New York
www.rpi.edu

CB member
CB code: 2757

- Private 4-year university
- Residential campus in small city
- 5,240 degree-seeking undergraduates: 29% women, 2% African American, 10% Asian American, 6% Hispanic American, 5% international
- 1,551 degree-seeking graduate students
- 40% of applicants admitted
- SAT or ACT with writing, application essay required
- 82% graduate within 6 years; 18% enter graduate study

General. Founded in 1824. Regionally accredited. **Degrees:** 1,281 bachelor's awarded; master's, doctoral offered. **ROTC:** Army, Naval, Air Force. **Location:** 10 miles from Albany, 150 miles from New York City. **Calendar:** Semester, extensive summer session. **Full-time faculty:** 377 total; 98% have terminal degrees, 28% minority, 20% women. **Part-time faculty:** 105 total; 58% have terminal degrees, 10% minority, 28% women. **Special facilities:** Spectrometer; performing arts center with concert hall; computational center for nanotechnology innovations; wind tunnel; geotechnical centrifuge; clean room; electron linear accelerator; plasma dynamics lab, lighting research center; athletic village; center for terahertz research; nanoscale science and engineering center; linear accelerator lab; astronomical observatory; business incubation center; fresh water institute; social and behavioral research lab; center for game studies research; artificial intelligence and reasoning lab; human-level intelligence lab.

Freshman class profile. 14,584 applied, 5,779 admitted, 1,186 enrolled.

Mid 50% test scores			
SAT critical reading:	620-710	End year in good standing:	95%
SAT math:	670-760	Return as sophomores:	93%
SAT writing:	590-700	Out-of-state:	69%
ACT composite:	26-30	Live on campus:	100%
Rank in top quarter:	94%	International:	7%
Rank in top tenth:	65%	Fraternities:	14%
		Sororities:	10%

Basis for selection. School achievement record important, test scores and essay required, activities considered. SAT Subject Tests in a math and a science required for accelerated program applicants only, or ACT (which must include the optional writing component in lieu of SAT and SAT Subject Tests); students applying from countries (such as China) that do not offer our required standardized tests will be considered without testing on a case-by-case basis. Portfolio required for electronic arts, highly recommended for architecture.

High school preparation. College-preparatory program required. 15 units required. Required and recommended units include English 4, mathematics 4, social studies 2-3 and science 3-4. Best suited applicants will have completed 4 math through pre-calculus, 3 science, and 2 social studies and/or history.

2011-2012 Annual costs. Tuition/fees: $42,704. Freshmen required to have a laptop. Students can purchase a university-subsidized laptop costing $1,800 that is preloaded with software, or can bring one with them but it must comply with mandatory technology and software specifications. Room/board: $11,975. Books/supplies: $2,500.

2011-2012 Financial aid. **Need-based:** 957 full-time freshmen applied for aid; 820 were judged to have need; 820 of these received aid. Average need met was 88%. Average scholarship/grant was $26,269; average loan $4,975. 76% of total undergraduate aid awarded as scholarships/grants, 24% as loans/jobs. **Non-need-based:** Awarded to 2,008 full-time undergraduates, including 464 freshmen. Scholarships awarded for academics, alumni affiliation, art, athletics, leadership, minority status, music/drama, ROTC.

Application procedures. **Admission:** Closing date 1/15 (postmark date). $70 fee, may be waived for applicants with need. Admission notification by 3/12. Must reply by 5/1. **Financial aid:** Priority date 2/1; no closing date. FAFSA, CSS PROFILE required. Applicants notified by 3/12.

Academics. Extensive accelerated program offerings available in virtually all Science departments including Computer Science, Physics, Applied Physics, Biology, Biochemistry and Biophysics, Geology and Hydrology, leading to the BS-PhD. **Special study options:** Accelerated study, combined bachelor's/graduate degree, cooperative education, cross-registration, double major, dual enrollment of high school students, exchange student, honors, independent study, internships, liberal arts/career combination, student-designed major, study abroad. BS/MD with Albany Medical College; BS/JD with Columbia University and Albany Law School. **Credit/placement by examination:** AP, CLEP, IB. **Support services:** Learning center, pre-admission summer program, reduced course load, remedial instruction, study skills assistance, tutoring, writing center.

Majors. Architecture: Architecture. **Biology:** General, Biochemistry/molecular biology, bioinformatics. **Business:** Business admin. **Communications:** Communications/speech/rhetoric, digital media. **Computer sciences:** Computer science, information technology. **Conservation:** Environmental science. **Engineering:** General, aerospace, applied physics, biomedical, chemical, civil, computer, electrical, engineering science, environmental, materials, mechanical, nuclear. **Health services:** Premedicine. **Math:** General. **Philosophy/religion:** Philosophy. **Physical sciences:** Chemistry, geology, hydrology, physics. **Psychology:** General. **Social sciences:** Economics. **Visual/performing arts:** Studio arts.

Most popular majors. Business/marketing 8%, computer/information sciences 9%, engineering/engineering technologies 58%.

Computing on campus. PC or laptop required. 400 workstations in dormitories, library, computer center, student center. Dormitories wired for high-speed internet access and linked to campus network. Commuter students can connect to campus network. Online course registration, online library, helpline, repair service, student web hosting, wireless network available.

Student life. Freshman orientation: Mandatory, $175 fee. Preregistration for classes offered. Held over 2-day period in July or August. **Policies:** College housing required of all freshmen unless student lives within 50-mile radius of campus with parent(s) or legal guardian(s). **Housing:** Guaranteed on-campus for freshmen. Coed dorms, special housing for disabled, apartments, fraternity/sorority housing available. **Activities:** Bands, campus ministries, choral groups, dance, drama, film society, international student organizations, literary magazine, music ensembles, musical theater, radio station, student government, student newspaper, symphony orchestra, TV station, student-run union; more than 185 athletic, service, media, multicultural, performing arts, visual arts, religious clubs and organizations.

Athletics. NCAA. **Intercollegiate:** Baseball M, basketball, cross-country, diving, field hockey W, football (tackle) M, golf M, ice hockey, lacrosse, soccer, softball W, swimming, tennis, track and field. **Intramural:** Basketball, football (non-tackle), golf, racquetball, soccer, softball, swimming, tennis, track and field, volleyball. **Team name:** Redhawks, Engineers.

Student services. Alcohol/substance abuse counseling, chaplain/spiritual director, career counseling, services for economically disadvantaged, student employment services, financial aid counseling, health services, legal services, minority student services, personal counseling, placement for graduates, women's services. **Physically disabled:** Services for visually, speech, hearing impaired.

Contact. E-mail: admissions@rpi.edu
Phone: (518) 276-6216 Fax: (518) 276-4072
Paul Marthers, Vice President for Enrollment, Rensselaer Polytechnic Institute, 110 Eighth Street, Troy, NY 12180-3590

Roberts Wesleyan College
Rochester, New York
www.roberts.edu

CB member
CB code: 2759

- Private 4-year liberal arts college affiliated with Free Methodist Church of North America
- Residential campus in large city
- 1,357 degree-seeking undergraduates: 9% part-time, 71% women, 11% African American, 1% Asian American, 4% Hispanic American, 2% international
- 423 degree-seeking graduate students
- 51% of applicants admitted
- SAT or ACT (ACT writing recommended), application essay required
- 63% graduate within 6 years

General. Founded in 1866. Regionally accredited. **Degrees:** 394 bachelor's awarded; master's offered. **ROTC:** Army, Air Force. **Location:** 8 miles from downtown. **Calendar:** Semester, limited summer session. **Full-time faculty:** 103 total; 69% have terminal degrees, 9% minority, 50% women. **Part-time faculty:** 152 total; 16% have terminal degrees, 4% minority, 59% women. **Class size:** 67% < 20, 28% 20-39, 3% 40-49, 2% 50-99.

Freshman class profile. 1,834 applied, 940 admitted, 240 enrolled.

Mid 50% test scores			
		GPA 2.0-2.99:	17%
SAT critical reading:	470-620	Rank in top quarter:	49%
SAT math:	470-600	Rank in top tenth:	20%
SAT writing:	440-590	Return as sophomores:	73%
ACT composite:	23-29	Out-of-state:	12%
GPA 3.75 or higher:	31%	Live on campus:	64%
GPA 3.50-3.74:	18%	International:	1%
GPA 3.0-3.49:	34%		

Basis for selection. Rank in top 30% of high school class, 2.9 GPA, recommendations, test scores, and interview important. Students expected to recognize Christian perspectives and values college upholds. Audition required for music program; portfolio required for art education, studio art. **Home schooled:** Transcript of courses and grades, state high school equivalency certificate, letter of recommendation (nonparent) required. Strongly recommend applicants visit.

High school preparation. College-preparatory program recommended. 12 units required. Required and recommended units include English 4, mathematics 2-4, social studies 2-3, history 3, science 4 (laboratory 3) and foreign language 3. Biology and chemistry required of nursing applicants.

2011-2012 Annual costs. Tuition/fees: $25,683. Room/board: $9,076. Books/supplies: $1,000. Personal expenses: $1,800.

2011-2012 Financial aid. Need-based: Average need met was 79%. Average scholarship/grant was $17,657; average loan $4,206. 59% of total undergraduate aid awarded as scholarships/grants, 41% as loans/jobs. **Non-need-based:** Scholarships awarded for academics, alumni affiliation, art, athletics, music/drama, religious affiliation, ROTC. **Additional information:** Dollars for Scholars offer matching grants of up to $750.

Application procedures. Admission: Priority date 2/1; deadline 8/15 (postmark date). $35 fee, may be waived for applicants with need, free for online applicants. Admission notification on a rolling basis. Must reply by May 1 or within 2 week(s) if notified thereafter. **Financial aid:** Priority date 3/15; no closing date. FAFSA required. Applicants notified on a rolling basis starting 3/15; must reply by 5/1 or within 2 week(s) of notification.

Academics. Special study options: Accelerated study, combined bachelor's/graduate degree, cross-registration, distance learning, double major, dual enrollment of high school students, ESL, honors, independent study, internships, student-designed major, study abroad, teacher certification program, Washington semester. **Credit/placement by examination:** AP, CLEP, IB. 30 credit hours maximum toward bachelor's degree. **Support services:** Learning center, reduced course load, remedial instruction, study skills assistance, tutoring, writing center.

Majors. Biology: General, biochemistry. **Business:** Accounting, business admin, human resources, marketing. **Communications:** Communications/speech/rhetoric. **Computer sciences:** General, computer science. **Education:** Art, biology, chemistry, early childhood, early childhood special, English, history, mathematics, music, physical, physics, science, social science, social studies, Spanish, special ed. **English:** English lit. **Foreign languages:** Spanish. **Health services:** Health care admin, nursing (RN), preop/surgical nursing. **History:** General. **Human services:** Social work. **Liberal arts:** Arts/sciences, humanities. **Math:** General. **Philosophy/religion:** General. **Physical sciences:** Chemistry, physics. **Protective services:** Forensics, law enforcement admin. **Psychology:** General. **Social sciences:** General, sociology. **Theology:** Bible, preministerial. **Visual/performing arts:** Music, piano/keyboard, studio arts, voice/opera.

Most popular majors. Business/marketing 24%, education 17%, health sciences 27%.

Computing on campus. 250 workstations in library, computer center, student center. Dormitories wired for high-speed internet access and linked to campus network. Commuter students can connect to campus network. Online course registration, online library, helpline, wireless network available.

Student life. Freshman orientation: Mandatory. Preregistration for classes offered. **Policies:** Religious observance required. **Housing:** Guaranteed on-campus for freshmen. Coed dorms, single-sex dorms, special housing for disabled, apartments available. $100 fully refundable deposit, deadline 5/1. **Activities:** Bands, campus ministries, choral groups, dance, drama, international student organizations, music ensembles, Model UN, musical theater, student government, student newspaper, symphony orchestra, chapel, mission trips, At the Foot of the Cross service, Habitat for Humanity, In Jesus' Name, bible studies, SIFE (Student in Free Enterprise), Acting on AIDS, senate, And He Made Me.

Athletics. NAIA, NCCAA. **Intercollegiate:** Basketball, cross-country, golf M, lacrosse, soccer, tennis, track and field, volleyball W. **Intramural:** Basketball, cross-country, football (non-tackle), racquetball, skiing, soccer, softball, table tennis, tennis, track and field, volleyball, water polo. **Team name:** Raiders.

Student services. Adult student services, alcohol/substance abuse counseling, chaplain/spiritual director, career counseling, student employment services, financial aid counseling, health services, personal counseling, placement for graduates, veterans' counselor. **Physically disabled:** Services for visually, hearing impaired.

Contact. E-mail: admissions@roberts.edu
Phone: (585) 594-6400 Toll-free number: (800) 777-4792
Fax: (585) 594-6371
Linda Hoffman, Vice President for Admissions and Marketing, Roberts Wesleyan College, 2301 Westside Drive, Rochester, NY 14624-1997

Rochester Institute of Technology

Rochester, New York — CB member
www.rit.edu — CB code: 2760

- Private 4-year university
- Residential campus in large city
- 13,048 degree-seeking undergraduates: 6% part-time, 32% women
- 2,530 degree-seeking graduate students
- 59% of applicants admitted
- SAT or ACT (ACT writing optional), application essay required
- 64% graduate within 6 years; 14% enter graduate study

General. Founded in 1829. Regionally accredited. University comprised of 9 colleges, including National Technical Institute for the Deaf. RIT also maintains campuses in Croatia, Dubai, and Kosovo. **Degrees:** 2,546 bachelor's, 313 associate awarded; master's, doctoral offered. **ROTC:** Army, Naval, Air Force. **Location:** 5 miles from downtown, 70 miles from Buffalo. **Calendar:** Quarter, extensive summer session. **Full-time faculty:** 966 total; 68% have terminal degrees, 16% minority, 34% women. **Part-time faculty:** 509 total; 1% have terminal degrees, 8% minority, 41% women. **Class size:** 49% < 20, 43% 20-39, 3% 40-49, 3% 50-99, less than 1% >100. **Special facilities:** Laser optics laboratory, observatory, animal care facility, color and black-and-white photography darkrooms, electronic prepress and publishing equipment, ceramic kilns, glass furnaces, blacksmithing area, student-operated restaurant, computer graphics and robotic labs, microelectronic, telecommunications, and computer engineering facilities, access to Internet 2 research network.

Freshman class profile. 15,806 applied, 9,266 admitted, 2,692 enrolled.

Mid 50% test scores			
SAT critical reading:	530-650	Rank in top tenth:	37%
SAT math:	570-680	Return as sophomores:	91%
SAT writing:	520-630	Out-of-state:	48%
Rank in top quarter:	68%	Live on campus:	95%

Basis for selection. Primary emphasis on high school grades in required courses, which vary by major. SAT or ACT given considerable weight. Class rank important. Candidates allowed to apply for up to 3 majors. ACT preferred for applicants to National Technical Institute for the Deaf. Interview recommended for all; portfolio required for art, crafts, and design programs. **Home schooled:** Transcript of courses and grades required. Applicants should provide state certification of graduation if available.

High school preparation. College-preparatory program required. 16 units required; 18 recommended. Required and recommended units include English 4, mathematics 3, social studies 3, science 2-3 (laboratory 1-3), foreign language 2 and academic electives 4. Units required for social studies may be met with history courses. College of Engineering requires 4 math including precalculus.

2011-2012 Annual costs. Tuition/fees: $32,037. Room/board: $10,413. Books/supplies: $1,050. Personal expenses: $725.

Financial aid. Non-need-based: Scholarships awarded for academics, art, leadership, ROTC. **Additional information:** Most juniors and seniors participate in cooperative education program, earning an average $4,500-$6,500 per 3-month employment period through paid employment in jobs related to major.

Application procedures. Admission: Priority date 2/1; no deadline. $50 fee, may be waived for applicants with need. Admission notification on a rolling basis beginning on or about 3/1. Must reply by May 1 or within 2 week(s) if notified thereafter. Applications received after March 15 will be processed if space available. **Financial aid:** Priority date 3/1; no closing date. FAFSA required. Applicants notified on a rolling basis starting 3/15; must reply by 5/1.

Academics. Special study options: Accelerated study, combined bachelor's/graduate degree, cooperative education, cross-registration, distance learning, double major, ESL, exchange student, honors, independent study, internships, liberal arts/career combination, student-designed major, study abroad, teacher certification program, weekend college. Accelerated bachelor's/master's degree programs, England semester, Japan semester, summer program in Croatia. **Credit/placement by examination:** AP, CLEP, IB, SAT, ACT, institutional tests. 45 credit hours maximum toward associate degree. **Support services:** Learning center, pre-admission summer program, reduced course load, study skills assistance, tutoring, writing center.

Majors. Biology: General, biochemistry, bioinformatics, biomedical sciences, biotechnology. **Business:** General, accounting, accounting/business management, business admin, finance, hospitality admin, hotel/motel admin, international, management information systems, market research, marketing, resort management, restaurant/food services, special products marketing, statistics, tourism promotion, tourism/travel, travel services. **Communications:**

Advertising, communications/speech/rhetoric, digital media, journalism, photojournalism, public relations. **Communications technology:** Animation/special effects, desktop publishing, graphics, photo/film/video, printing management. **Computer sciences:** General, computer graphics, computer science, database management, information technology, LAN/WAN management, networking, security, system admin, systems analysis, web page design, webmaster. **Conservation:** Environmental science. **Engineering:** Aerospace, biomedical, chemical, computer, electrical, industrial, manufacturing, mechanical, polymer, software, systems. **Foreign languages:** American Sign Language, sign language interpretation. **Health services:** Medical illustrating, physician assistant, predental, premedicine, prepharmacy, preveterinary, sonography. **Human services:** Public policy. **Math:** Applied, computational, probability, statistics. **Philosophy/religion:** Philosophy. **Physical sciences:** Chemistry, physics, polymer chemistry. **Protective services:** Law enforcement admin. **Psychology:** General. **Social sciences:** Economics, international relations, urban studies. **Visual/performing arts:** Ceramics, cinematography, commercial photography, commercial/advertising art, crafts, design, game design, graphic design, illustration, industrial design, interior design, metal/jewelry, multimedia, painting, photography, printmaking, sculpture, studio arts. **Work/family studies:** Consumer economics, food/nutrition, human nutrition.

Most popular majors. Biology 6%, business/marketing 11%, computer/information sciences 15%, engineering/engineering technologies 26%, interdisciplinary studies 8%, visual/performing arts 16%.

Computing on campus. 2,500 workstations in dormitories, library, computer center. Dormitories wired for high-speed internet access and linked to campus network. Commuter students can connect to campus network. Online course registration, online library, helpline, repair service, student web hosting, wireless network available.

Student life. Freshman orientation: Mandatory, $165 fee. Preregistration for classes offered. Orientation in September prior to start of classes. **Policies:** Alcohol prohibited in campus residence halls. **Housing:** Guaranteed on-campus for freshmen. Coed dorms, special housing for disabled, apartments, fraternity/sorority housing, wellness housing available. $300 nonrefundable deposit, deadline 5/1. Special interest houses for students in selected majors or groups, single-sex floors within coed dorms, special honors program floor available. **Activities:** Bands, campus ministries, choral groups, dance, drama, film society, international student organizations, literary magazine, music ensembles, musical theater, radio station, student government, student newspaper, Asian Culture Society, Electronic Gaming Society, Gospel Ensemble, Society of Women Engineers, Society of Hispanic Engineers, National Society of Black Engineers, Emerging Black Artists, Feminist Action, Catholic Newman Network, Outing club.

Athletics. NCAA. **Intercollegiate:** Baseball M, basketball, cheerleading, cross-country, diving, ice hockey, lacrosse, rowing (crew), soccer, softball W, swimming, tennis, track and field, volleyball W, wrestling M. **Intramural:** Badminton, basketball, bowling, football (non-tackle) M, golf, ice hockey, racquetball, soccer, softball, table tennis, tennis, volleyball. **Team name:** Tigers.

Student services. Adult student services, alcohol/substance abuse counseling, chaplain/spiritual director, career counseling, services for economically disadvantaged, student employment services, financial aid counseling, health services, legal services, minority student services, on-campus daycare, personal counseling, placement for graduates, veterans' counselor, women's services. **Physically disabled:** Services for visually, speech, hearing impaired.

Contact. E-mail: admissions@rit.edu
Phone: (585) 475-6631 Fax: (585) 475-7424
Daniel Shelley, Assistant Vice President and Director of Undergraduate Admission, Rochester Institute of Technology, 60 Lomb Memorial Drive, Rochester, NY 14623-5604

Russell Sage College

Troy, New York
www.sage.edu/rsc

CB member
CB code: 2764

- Private 4-year health science and liberal arts college for women
- Residential campus in small city
- 763 degree-seeking undergraduates: 3% part-time, 99% women, 10% African American, 2% Asian American, 4% Hispanic American
- 69% of applicants admitted
- Application essay required
- 66% graduate within 6 years; 37% enter graduate study

General. Founded in 1916. Regionally accredited. Liberal arts and professional degree programs in business, nursing and health sciences, education, performing arts offered. RSC is a member of The Sage Colleges, including the coeducational Sage College of Albany and Sage Graduate School.

Degrees: 185 bachelor's awarded. **ROTC:** Army, Naval, Air Force. **Location:** 10 miles from Albany, 150 miles from New York City. **Calendar:** Semester, extensive summer session. **Full-time faculty:** 61 total; 88% have terminal degrees, 5% minority, 72% women. **Part-time faculty:** 54 total; 24% have terminal degrees, 6% minority, 72% women. **Class size:** 41% < 20, 56% 20-39, less than 1% 40-49, 2% 50-99. **Special facilities:** Center for women's studies, theater institute, nanotechnology business incubator.

Freshman class profile. 718 applied, 494 admitted, 153 enrolled.

Mid 50% test scores			
SAT critical reading:	420-570	GPA 2.0-2.99:	32%
SAT math:	420-560	Rank in top quarter:	47%
ACT composite:	19-25	Rank in top tenth:	23%
GPA 3.75 or higher:	23%	End year in good standing:	93%
GPA 3.50-3.74:	13%	Return as sophomores:	81%
GPA 3.0-3.49:	29%	Out-of-state:	8%
		Live on campus:	76%

Basis for selection. High school record, recommendations of school officials, intended major, school and community activities considered. SAT scores required for some joint programs that are linked with another external institution. Interview recommended. **Home schooled:** Statement describing home school structure and mission, transcript of courses and grades, interview, letter of recommendation (nonparent) required. **Learning Disabled:** Students seeking accommodations are required to present a recent evaluation of their disability conducted by a licensed professional. Upon admission, those requesting accommodations must contact the Coordinator of Disability Services in the Campus Life Office.

High school preparation. College-preparatory program required. 16 units required. Required and recommended units include English 4, mathematics 3-4, social studies 4, science 3-4 (laboratory 2-3) and foreign language 2-3. Nursing program applicants must have 6 math/science combination including chemistry. Physical and occupational therapy students must have 4 math/science.

2011-2012 Annual costs. Tuition/fees: $28,000. Room/board: $10,675. Books/supplies: $1,200. Personal expenses: $1,225.

2011-2012 Financial aid. Need-based: 152 full-time freshmen applied for aid; 141 were judged to have need; 141 of these received aid. Average scholarship/grant was $12,633; average loan $3,082. 70% of total undergraduate aid awarded as scholarships/grants, 30% as loans/jobs. **Non-need-based:** Awarded to 674 full-time undergraduates, including 110 freshmen. Scholarships awarded for academics, alumni affiliation, leadership, music/drama.

Application procedures. Admission: Priority date 3/1; no deadline. $30 fee, may be waived for applicants with need, free for online applicants. Admission notification on a rolling basis beginning on or about 12/15. Must reply by May 1 or within 2 week(s) if notified thereafter. **Financial aid:** Priority date 3/1; no closing date. FAFSA required. Applicants notified on a rolling basis starting 3/1; must reply by 5/1 or within 2 week(s) of notification.

Academics. All students complete internship, field experience, or clinical experience. All students engage in service learning through 2 required courses: Women in the World (first year) and Women Changing the World (senior year). **Special study options:** Accelerated study, combined bachelor's/graduate degree, cross-registration, distance learning, double major, honors, independent study, internships, liberal arts/career combination, student-designed major, study abroad, teacher certification program. Early College for high school juniors, combined bachelor's/master's, bachelor's/doctoral programs with Sage Graduate School, 3+3 BA/JD with Albany Law School, 3+2 BS/BSE with Rensselaer Polytechnic Institute, BA/MS Accelerated Physician Assistant Program, BA/MS Early Assurance Program and BA/MD Early Assurance Program with Albany Medical College. **Credit/placement by examination:** AP, CLEP, IB, SAT, ACT, institutional tests. 30 credit hours maximum toward bachelor's degree. **Support services:** Learning center, preadmission summer program, reduced course load, remedial instruction, study skills assistance, tutoring, writing center.

Majors. Area/ethnic studies: American. **Biology:** General, biochemistry. **Conservation:** Environmental studies. **Education:** Elementary. **English:** English lit. **History:** General. **Liberal arts:** Arts/sciences. **Math:** General. **Physical sciences:** Chemistry. **Protective services:** Forensics. **Psychology:** General. **Social sciences:** International relations, political science, sociology. **Visual/performing arts:** Dramatic.

Most popular majors. Business/marketing 6%, education 8%, health sciences 31%, interdisciplinary studies 6%, liberal arts 10%, psychology 8%, visual/performing arts 11%.

Computing on campus. 165 workstations in library, computer center, student center. Dormitories wired for high-speed internet access and linked to campus network. Commuter students can connect to campus network. Online course registration, online library, helpline, wireless network available.

Student life. Freshman orientation: Mandatory, $200 fee. Preregistration for classes offered. 1-day welcome programs offered in June. 4-day orientation

in September. **Policies:** Zero tolerance for drugs, harassment, or violence on campus. **Housing:** Guaranteed on-campus for all undergraduates. Wellness housing available. $100 partly refundable deposit, deadline 5/1. Special houses available for honor students and students interested in language/international awareness activities. Over-21 residence hall available for seniors. 19th-century brownstone residences available. **Activities:** Campus ministries, choral groups, dance, drama, literary magazine, music ensembles, musical theater, student government, student newspaper, black and Latina student alliance, gay and lesbian alliance, Christian students club, Muslim student association, Circle K, Habitat for Humanity.

Athletics. NCAA. **Intercollegiate:** Basketball W, soccer W, softball W, tennis W, volleyball. **Intramural:** Volleyball W. **Team name:** Gators.

Student services. Adult student services, alcohol/substance abuse counseling, chaplain/spiritual director, career counseling, services for economically disadvantaged, student employment services, financial aid counseling, health services, minority student services, personal counseling, placement for graduates, women's services.

Contact. E-mail: rscadm@sage.edu
Phone: (518) 244-2217 Toll-free number: (888) 837-9724
Fax: (518) 244-6880
Andrew Palumbo, Director of Undergraduate Admission, Russell Sage College, 65 1st Street, Troy, NY 12180-4115

Sage College of Albany
Albany, New York
www.sage.edu   **CB code: 2343**

▶ Private 4-year business and liberal arts college
▶ Commuter campus in small city
▶ 875 degree-seeking undergraduates: 24% part-time, 61% women, 16% African American, 2% Asian American, 9% Hispanic American
▶ 58% of applicants admitted
▶ Application essay required
▶ 37% graduate within 6 years; 24% enter graduate study

General. Founded in 1957. Regionally accredited. **Degrees:** 217 bachelor's awarded. **ROTC:** Army, Air Force. **Location:** 150 miles from New York City. **Calendar:** Semester, extensive summer session. **Full-time faculty:** 42 total; 86% have terminal degrees, 5% minority, 48% women. **Part-time faculty:** 60 total; 37% have terminal degrees, 5% minority, 50% women. **Class size:** 60% < 20, 40% 20-39. **Special facilities:** Fine arts studio, graphic design and interior design studios.

Freshman class profile. 1,083 applied, 629 admitted, 154 enrolled.

Mid 50% test scores			
SAT critical reading:	390-530	Rank in top quarter:	40%
SAT math:	410-530	Rank in top tenth:	11%
ACT composite:	17-23	End year in good standing:	93%
GPA 3.75 or higher:	8%	Return as sophomores:	68%
GPA 3.50-3.74:	15%	Out-of-state:	10%
GPA 3.0-3.49:	28%	Live on campus:	86%
GPA 2.0-2.99:	48%	International:	1%

Basis for selection. Recommendation of high school guidance counselor or teacher and academic record considered for all applicants. Applications reviewed on individual basis. SAT scores required for some joint programs that are linked with another external institution. Interview recommended for all; portfolio required for art and design programs. **Home schooled:** Statement describing home school structure and mission, transcript of courses and grades, interview, letter of recommendation (nonparent) required. Students who have written evaluations must submit SAT or ACT.

High school preparation. College-preparatory program required. 16 units required. Required and recommended units include English 4, mathematics 3-4, social studies 4, science 3-4 and foreign language 2. Students applying to Visual Art programs should have significant class experience.

2011-2012 Annual costs. Tuition/fees: $28,000. Room/board: $10,675. Books/supplies: $1,200. Personal expenses: $1,225.

2011-2012 Financial aid. Need-based: 154 full-time freshmen applied for aid; 151 were judged to have need; 151 of these received aid. Average scholarship/grant was $6,216; average loan $3,407. 76% of total undergraduate aid awarded as scholarships/grants, 24% as loans/jobs. **Non-need-based:** Awarded to 334 full-time undergraduates, including 95 freshmen. Scholarships awarded for academics, art, leadership.

Application procedures. Admission: Priority date 3/1; no deadline. $30 fee, may be waived for applicants with need, free for online applicants.

Admission notification on a rolling basis beginning on or about 11/1. Must reply by May 1 or within 2 week(s) if notified thereafter. **Financial aid:** Priority date 3/1; no closing date. FAFSA required. Applicants notified on a rolling basis starting 3/1; must reply by 5/1 or within 2 week(s) of notification.

Academics. College of Applied Studies offers specialties in art and design, business and communications, computer technologies, legal studies, creative studies. Four programs in fine arts (photography, graphic design, interior design, and fine arts) accredited by National Association of Schools of Art and Design. Flexible transfer policy; joint degrees in clinical biology and cytotechnology with Albany College of Pharmacy. Ease of transfer for community college graduates. **Special study options:** Combined bachelor's/graduate degree, cross-registration, distance learning, double major, honors, independent study, internships, liberal arts/career combination, student-designed major, study abroad. **Credit/placement by examination:** AP, CLEP, IB, institutional tests. 30 credit hours maximum toward associate degree, 30 toward bachelor's. **Support services:** Learning center, pre-admission summer program, reduced course load, remedial instruction, study skills assistance, tutoring, writing center.

Majors. Business: Accounting, business admin. **Computer sciences:** Information systems. **Education:** Physical. **Health services:** Nursing (RN). **Human services:** Public policy. **Liberal arts:** Arts/sciences, humanities. **Protective services:** Law enforcement admin. **Psychology:** General. **Social sciences:** General. **Visual/performing arts:** Graphic design, interior design, studio arts.

Most popular majors. Business/marketing 22%, computer/information sciences 6%, education 13%, health sciences 10%, liberal arts 6%, social sciences 6%, visual/performing arts 25%.

Computing on campus. 205 workstations in library, computer center. Dormitories wired for high-speed internet access and linked to campus network. Commuter students can connect to campus network. Online course registration, online library, helpline, wireless network available.

Student life. Freshman orientation: Mandatory, $200 fee. Preregistration for classes offered. New students may receive academic advising and register for classes (summer, fall, spring) beginning March 1st each year. One-day welcome programs offered in June. 4-day orientation in September. **Policies:** Zero tolerance for drugs, harassment or violence on campus. **Housing:** Guaranteed on-campus for freshmen. Coed dorms, apartments, wellness housing available. $100 partly refundable deposit, deadline 5/1. Apartment-style suites available on adjacent campus. **Activities:** Literary magazine, student government, student newspaper, SALANA (African, Latino, Asian and Native American), Sage Votes, Association of Campus Events, Sage SPECTRUMS, Campus Crusade for Christ.

Athletics. NCAA. **Intercollegiate:** Basketball, cross-country M, golf M, lacrosse W, soccer, softball W, tennis, volleyball. **Intramural:** Badminton, football (non-tackle). **Team name:** Gators.

Student services. Adult student services, alcohol/substance abuse counseling, chaplain/spiritual director, career counseling, services for economically disadvantaged, student employment services, financial aid counseling, health services, minority student services, personal counseling, placement for graduates, veterans' counselor.

Contact. E-mail: scaadm@sage.adm
Phone: (518) 292-1730 Toll-free number: (888) 837-9724
Fax: (518) 292-1912
Andrew Palumbo, Director of Undergraduate Admission, Sage College of Albany, 140 New Scotland Avenue, Albany, NY 12208

Saint Bonaventure University
St. Bonaventure, New York   **CB member**
www.sbu.edu   **CB code: 2793**

▶ Private 4-year university affiliated with Roman Catholic Church
▶ Residential campus in large town
▶ 1,894 degree-seeking undergraduates: 1% part-time, 52% women, 5% African American, 2% Asian American, 4% Hispanic American, 1% Native American, 2% international
▶ 486 degree-seeking graduate students
▶ 80% of applicants admitted
▶ SAT or ACT (ACT writing optional) required
▶ 63% graduate within 6 years; 57% enter graduate study

General. Founded in 1858. Regionally accredited. Catholic institution in Franciscan tradition. **Degrees:** 414 bachelor's awarded; master's offered. **ROTC:** Army. **Location:** 75 miles from Buffalo. **Calendar:** Semester, limited summer session. **Full-time faculty:** 154 total; 79% have terminal degrees,

8% minority, 36% women. **Part-time faculty:** 69 total; 7% have terminal degrees, 4% minority, 55% women. **Class size:** 53% < 20, 47% 20-39, less than 1% 40-49. **Special facilities:** Observatory, digital media laboratory, permanent art collection, retreat facility, rare books collection.

Freshman class profile. 2,545 applied, 2,045 admitted, 489 enrolled.

Mid 50% test scores			
SAT critical reading:	470-590	GPA 2.0-2.99:	36%
SAT math:	480-590	Rank in top quarter:	45%
SAT writing:	450-570	Rank in top tenth:	20%
ACT composite:	20-26	End year in good standing:	89%
GPA 3.75 or higher:	15%	Return as sophomores:	80%
GPA 3.50-3.74:	24%	Out-of-state:	25%
GPA 3.0-3.49:	25%	Live on campus:	99%
		International:	2%

Basis for selection. Interview, high school GPA and curriculum most important. Recommendation, class rank, test scores, extracurricular activities also considered. Applicants to dual admission premed program with George Washington University or SUNY Upstate Medical University must submit Biology SAT Subject Test score. Essay recommended for all. **Home schooled:** Statement describing home school structure and mission, transcript of courses and grades, letter of recommendation (nonparent) required. Course syllabus, book titles, and all course evaluations required to be considered for admission.

High school preparation. College-preparatory program recommended. 19 units recommended. Recommended units include English 4, mathematics 3, social studies 4, science 3 (laboratory 3) and foreign language 2. Science majors must have 4 science, 4 math. Business majors need 4 math. Recommend 3 science lab.

2011-2012 Annual costs. Tuition/fees: $27,890. Room/board: $9,840. Books/supplies: $800. Personal expenses: $650.

2010-2011 Financial aid. Need-based: 456 full-time freshmen applied for aid; 383 were judged to have need; 383 of these received aid. Average need met was 79%. Average scholarship/grant was $19,696; average loan $3,384. 65% of total undergraduate aid awarded as scholarships/grants, 35% as loans/jobs. **Non-need-based:** Awarded to 2,024 full-time undergraduates, including 523 freshmen. Scholarships awarded for academics, athletics, minority status, ROTC. **Additional information:** Families experiencing financial difficulties not adequately reflected by the FAFSA should contact the Office of Financial Assistance. Outside scholarships do not reduce other financial aid unless, when added to total aid, the new total exceeds need. If it exceeds need, then loans and work are reduced first.

Application procedures. Admission: Priority date 2/15; deadline 7/1 (postmark date). $30 fee, may be waived for applicants with need, free for online applicants. Admission notification on a rolling basis beginning on or about 10/15. Must reply by May 1 or within 1 week(s) if notified thereafter. Applications considered until housing is closed. **Financial aid:** Priority date 2/15; no closing date. FAFSA required. Applicants notified on a rolling basis starting 3/1; must reply by 5/1 or within 2 week(s) of notification.

Academics. Special study options: Combined bachelor's/graduate degree, cross-registration, distance learning, double major, dual enrollment of high school students, exchange student, honors, independent study, internships, liberal arts/career combination, student-designed major, study abroad, teacher certification program, Washington semester. **Credit/placement by examination:** AP, CLEP, IB, SAT, ACT. 30 credit hours maximum toward bachelor's degree. **Support services:** Learning center, pre-admission summer program, reduced course load, remedial instruction, study skills assistance, tutoring, writing center.

Majors. Area/ethnic studies: Women's. **Biology:** General, biochemistry, bioinformatics. **Business:** Accounting, finance, management information systems, management science. **Communications:** Journalism, media studies. **Computer sciences:** General, computer science. **Conservation:** General. **Education:** Elementary, physical, special ed. **English:** British lit, English lit. **Foreign languages:** Classics, French, Latin, Spanish. **History:** General. **Math:** General. **Parks/recreation:** Sports admin. **Philosophy/religion:** Philosophy. **Physical sciences:** Chemistry, physics. **Psychology:** General. **Social sciences:** General, political science, sociology. **Theology:** Theology. **Visual/performing arts:** General, art history/conservation, dramatic, music.

Most popular majors. Biology 8%, business/marketing 29%, communications/journalism 15%, education 13%, psychology 6%, social sciences 9%.

Computing on campus. 225 workstations in dormitories, library, computer center. Dormitories wired for high-speed internet access and linked to campus network. Online course registration, online library, helpline, student web hosting, wireless network available.

Student life. Freshman orientation: Mandatory, $415 fee. Preregistration for classes offered. 2-day session held in July. **Housing:** Guaranteed on-campus for all undergraduates. Coed dorms, apartments, wellness housing available. $200 partly refundable deposit, deadline 5/1. **Activities:** Bands,

campus ministries, choral groups, dance, drama, international student organizations, literary magazine, music ensembles, Model UN, radio station, student government, student newspaper, TV station, Students in Free Enterprise, College Republicans, College Democrats, Alpha Phi Omega, BonaResponds, Students for the Mountain, Center for Community Engagement.

Athletics. NCAA. **Intercollegiate:** Baseball M, basketball, cross-country, diving, golf M, lacrosse W, soccer, softball W, swimming, tennis. **Intramural:** Basketball, football (non-tackle), football (tackle) M, golf, racquetball, soccer, softball, table tennis, tennis, volleyball. **Team name:** Bonnies.

Student services. Alcohol/substance abuse counseling, chaplain/spiritual director, career counseling, services for economically disadvantaged, student employment services, financial aid counseling, health services, personal counseling, placement for graduates, veterans' counselor. **Physically disabled:** Services for visually, hearing impaired.

Contact. E-mail: admissions@sbu.edu
Phone: (716) 375-2400 Toll-free number: (800) 462-5050
Fax: (716) 375-4005
Monica Emery, Director of Recruitment, Saint Bonaventure University, Route 417, St. Bonaventure, NY 14778-2284

Sarah Lawrence College
Bronxville, New York
www.slc.edu

CB member
CB code: 2810

- Private 4-year liberal arts college
- Residential campus in small city
- 1,328 degree-seeking undergraduates
- Application essay required

General. Founded in 1926. Regionally accredited. **Degrees:** 341 bachelor's awarded; master's offered. **Location:** 15 miles from midtown Manhattan. **Calendar:** Semester, limited summer session. **Full-time faculty:** 102 total; 18% minority, 50% women. **Part-time faculty:** 207 total; 19% minority, 56% women. **Class size:** 93% < 20, 4% 20-39, 2% 40-49, less than 1% 50-99. **Special facilities:** Visual arts center, student-run theater, early childhood center, greenhouse.

Freshman class profile.

GPA 3.75 or higher:	39%	Rank in top quarter:	79%
GPA 3.50-3.74:	29%	Rank in top tenth:	46%
GPA 3.0-3.49:	25%	Out-of-state:	75%
GPA 2.0-2.99:	7%	Live on campus:	100%

Basis for selection. Student essays (one of which is a graded, analytical writing sample) and transcript most important. Letters of recommendation and extracurricular commitments also important. Interview considered. Students interested in visual art or music encouraged to submit slides, cassette tapes, or compositions. If on-campus interview not possible, applicant may arrange interview with an alumna/us or counselor.

High school preparation. College-preparatory program recommended. Required and recommended units include English 4, mathematics 2-4, social studies 4, history 2-4, science 2-4 and foreign language 2-4.

2011-2012 Annual costs. Tuition/fees: $45,212. Room/board: $13,958. Books/supplies: $600. Personal expenses: $800.

Financial aid. All financial aid based on need.

Application procedures. Admission: Closing date 1/1 (postmark date). $60 fee, may be waived for applicants with need. Admission notification by 4/1. Must reply by 5/1. **Financial aid:** Closing date 2/1. FAFSA, CSS PROFILE required. Applicants notified by 4/1; must reply by 5/1.

Academics. 90% of classes are seminars with 11-12 students. Individual biweekly conferences with professors and self-designed independent study available. Students design own course of study with advisor. Although there are no formal majors, students may de facto create double majors. Course work required in 3 of 4 divisions: humanities, history and the social sciences, natural sciences and mathematics, creative and performing arts. **Special study options:** Combined bachelor's/graduate degree, double major, exchange student, independent study, internships, student-designed major, study abroad, teacher certification program. Academic year in Oxford, Paris, Florence, Catania (Sicily), Havana (Cuba), theater year with British American Drama Academy in London; guest year at Reed College (OR), Eugene Lang College The New School (NY), Spelman College (GA), Pitzer College (CA), California Institute of the Arts, or Dartington College of Art at the University of Falmouth, England. **Credit/placement by examination:** AP, CLEP, IB. **Support services:** Tutoring, writing center.

Majors. Liberal arts: Arts/sciences.

Computing on campus. 110 workstations in library, computer center. Dormitories wired for high-speed internet access and linked to campus network. Commuter students can connect to campus network. Online library, helpline, student web hosting, wireless network available.

Student life. Freshman orientation: Mandatory. Preregistration for classes offered. 9-day program held just before fall semester. **Housing:** Guaranteed on-campus for all undergraduates. Coed dorms, single-sex dorms, wellness housing available. $500 nonrefundable deposit, deadline 5/1. First-year students required to live on campus unless living at home. **Activities:** Jazz band, campus ministries, choral groups, dance, drama, film society, international student organizations, literary magazine, music ensembles, Model UN, musical theater, radio station, student government, student newspaper, symphony orchestra, Amnesty International, Harambe (students of African descent), Hillel, Queer Voice Coalition, Beyond Compliance, Asian-Pacific Islander Coalition to Advance Diversity, Unidad (students of Latino descent), FLUX (Feminist Liberation Union), Transaction, Sarah Lawrence Christian Union.

Athletics. Intercollegiate: Basketball M, cross-country, equestrian, rowing (crew), soccer M, softball W, swimming W, tennis, volleyball W. **Intramural:** Basketball W. **Team name:** Gryphons.

Student services. Adult student services, alcohol/substance abuse counseling, career counseling, student employment services, financial aid counseling, health services, minority student services, personal counseling, placement for graduates, veterans' counselor. **Physically disabled:** Services for visually, speech, hearing impaired.

Contact. E-mail: slcadmit@sarahlawrence.edu
Phone: (914) 395-2510 Toll-free number: (800) 888-2858
Fax: (914) 395-2515
Amy Abrams, Dean of Admission and Financial Aid, Sarah Lawrence College, 1 Mead Way, Bronxville, NY 10708-5999

School of Visual Arts
New York, New York
www.sva.edu

CB member
CB code: 2835

- For-profit 4-year visual arts college
- Commuter campus in very large city
- 3,496 degree-seeking undergraduates: 4% part-time, 59% women, 4% African American, 13% Asian American, 11% Hispanic American, 1% Native American, 22% international
- 606 degree-seeking graduate students
- 74% of applicants admitted
- SAT or ACT (ACT writing optional), application essay required
- 70% graduate within 6 years

General. Founded in 1947. Regionally accredited. Faculty composed entirely of working professionals. **Degrees:** 661 bachelor's awarded; master's offered. **Calendar:** Semester, limited summer session. **Full-time faculty:** 149 total; 9% have terminal degrees, 6% minority, 39% women. **Part-time faculty:** 883 total; 8% have terminal degrees, 11% minority, 38% women. **Class size:** 75% < 20, 24% 20-39, less than 1% 40-49, less than 1% 50-99, less than 1% >100. **Special facilities:** Visual arts museum, Milton Glaser design study center and archives, 8 student galleries including 9,000-square-foot gallery.

Freshman class profile. 3,331 applied, 2,450 admitted, 647 enrolled.

Mid 50% test scores		GPA 3.0-3.49:	36%
SAT critical reading:	460-590	GPA 2.0-2.99:	38%
SAT math:	450-580	Return as sophomores:	79%
SAT writing:	460-580	Out-of-state:	46%
ACT composite:	19-25	Live on campus:	68%
GPA 3.75 or higher:	11%	International:	17%
GPA 3.50-3.74:	14%		

Basis for selection. Portfolio, academic record, interview important. Character and professional recommendations optional. Interview optional. Portfolio required for all programs. **Home schooled:** Statement describing home school structure and mission, transcript of courses and grades, state high school equivalency certificate, interview, letter of recommendation (non-parent) required. GED.

High school preparation. College-preparatory program recommended. Recommended units include English 4, history 4, foreign language 4 and visual/performing arts 2.

2011-2012 Annual costs. Tuition/fees: $29,550. Additional fees vary by department. Room only: $12,800. Books/supplies: $2,100. Personal expenses: $1,600.

2011-2012 Financial aid. Need-based: 465 full-time freshmen applied for aid; 405 were judged to have need; 392 of these received aid. Average need met was 44%. Average scholarship/grant was $9,647; average loan $3,509. 38% of total undergraduate aid awarded as scholarships/grants, 62% as loans/jobs. **Non-need-based:** Awarded to 653 full-time undergraduates, including 147 freshmen. Scholarships awarded for art.

Application procedures. Admission: No deadline. $50 fee, may be waived for applicants with need. Admission notification on a rolling basis beginning on or about 2/1. Admitted applicants are encouraged to reply by May 1. **Financial aid:** Priority date 2/1, closing date 3/1. FAFSA required. Applicants notified on a rolling basis starting 2/15; must reply within 4 week(s) of notification.

Academics. Curriculum designed to prepare students to graduate as working professionals in the arts. **Special study options:** ESL, exchange student, honors, independent study, internships, liberal arts/career combination, study abroad. **Credit/placement by examination:** AP, CLEP, IB. **Support services:** Learning center, pre-admission summer program, reduced course load, remedial instruction, study skills assistance, tutoring, writing center.

Honors college/program. Additional application component.

Majors. Communications technology: Animation/special effects. **Visual/performing arts:** Art history/conservation, commercial/advertising art, interior design, photography, studio arts.

Most popular majors. Communication technologies 7%, computer/information sciences 7%, visual/performing arts 81%.

Computing on campus. 728 workstations in library, computer center, student center. Dormitories wired for high-speed internet access and linked to campus network. Commuter students can connect to campus network. Online library, helpline, wireless network available.

Student life. Freshman orientation: Mandatory. Preregistration for classes offered. Comprehensive 5-day program. **Housing:** Coed dorms, single-sex dorms, wellness housing available. $800 nonrefundable deposit, deadline 5/1. **Activities:** Film society, literary magazine, radio station, student government, student newspaper, Korean Christian, animal rights, international film club, Campus Crusade for Christ, political, anime film club, fine art club, MFA Speakers, wrestling club.

Athletics. Intramural: Baseball, tennis.

Student services. Alcohol/substance abuse counseling, career counseling, student employment services, financial aid counseling, health services, personal counseling, placement for graduates, veterans' counselor, women's services. **Physically disabled:** Services for hearing impaired.

Contact. E-mail: admissions@sva.edu
Phone: (212) 592-2100 Toll-free number: (800) 436-4204
Fax: (212) 592-2116
Adam Rogers, Director of Admissions, School of Visual Arts, 209 East 23rd Street, New York, NY 10010-3994

Shor Yoshuv Rabbinical College
Lawrence, New York
www.shoryoshuv.org

CB code: 7129

- Private 4-year rabbinical college for men affiliated with Jewish faith
- Very large city
- 177 degree-seeking undergraduates

General. Accredited by AARTS. **Degrees:** 24 bachelor's awarded; master's offered. **Calendar:** Differs by program. **Full-time faculty:** 23 total.

2011-2012 Annual costs. Tuition/fees: $9,460. Room/board: $6,000.

Application procedures. Admission: Priority date 8/1; no deadline. $460 fee.

Academics. Credit/placement by examination: AP, CLEP.

Majors. Theology: Talmudic.

Contact. E-mail: info@shoryoshuv.org
Phone: (516) 239-9002
Shlomo Krasnow, Admissions Director, Shor Yoshuv Rabbinical College, One Cedar Lawn Avenue, Lawrence, NY 11559

Siena College

Loudonville, New York
www.siena.edu

CB member
CB code: 2814

- Private 4-year liberal arts college affiliated with Roman Catholic Church
- Residential campus in large town
- 3,244 degree-seeking undergraduates: 4% part-time, 52% women, 3% African American, 3% Asian American, 5% Hispanic American, 1% international
- 50 degree-seeking graduate students
- 48% of applicants admitted
- SAT or ACT with writing, application essay required
- 74% graduate within 6 years; 24% enter graduate study

General. Founded in 1937. Regionally accredited. Affiliated with the Franciscan Friars. **Degrees:** 786 bachelor's awarded; master's offered. **ROTC:** Army, Naval, Air Force. **Location:** 2 miles from Albany. **Calendar:** Semester, limited summer session. **Full-time faculty:** 218 total; 90% have terminal degrees, 10% minority, 39% women. **Part-time faculty:** 135 total; 44% have terminal degrees, 4% minority, 42% women. **Class size:** 46% < 20, 54% 20-39. **Special facilities:** Financial technology center featuring real-time capital market trading room, accounting lab, stock ticker, plasma data screens, 24 multimedia workstations.

Freshman class profile. 9,723 applied, 4,714 admitted, 782 enrolled.

Mid 50% test scores			
SAT critical reading:	510-610	GPA 2.0-2.99:	15%
SAT math:	530-630	Rank in top quarter:	66%
SAT writing:	510-610	Rank in top tenth:	23%
ACT composite:	24-29	Return as sophomores:	85%
GPA 3.75 or higher:	28%	Out-of-state:	23%
GPA 3.50-3.74:	24%	Live on campus:	93%
GPA 3.0-3.49:	33%	International:	1%

Basis for selection. School achievement record most important, priority given to students with challenging courses. Test scores, activities, recommendations also important. Interview required for Albany Medical School program finalists; recommended for all others. **Home schooled:** Transcript of courses and grades required.

High school preparation. College-preparatory program required. 13 units required; 19 recommended. Required and recommended units include English 4, mathematics 3-4, social studies 1, history 2-3, science 3-4 (laboratory 3-4) and foreign language 3.

2011-2012 Annual costs. Tuition/fees: $28,985. Room/board: $11,434. Books/supplies: $1,215. Personal expenses: $1,200.

2010-2011 Financial aid. Need-based: 703 full-time freshmen applied for aid; 580 were judged to have need; 577 of these received aid. Average need met was 72%. Average scholarship/grant was $14,720; average loan $3,455. 77% of total undergraduate aid awarded as scholarships/grants, 23% as loans/jobs. **Non-need-based:** Awarded to 2,216 full-time undergraduates, including 700 freshmen. Scholarships awarded for academics, athletics, leadership, minority status, ROTC, state residency.

Application procedures. Admission: Closing date 2/15 (postmark date). $50 fee, may be waived for applicants with need. Admission notification by 3/15. Must reply by 5/1. **Financial aid:** Priority date 2/15, closing date 5/1. FAFSA required. Applicants notified by 4/1; must reply by 5/1.

Academics. Extensive internship program in capital district with state legislature, businesses, social agencies, libraries, and museums. **Special study options:** Combined bachelor's/graduate degree, cooperative education, cross-registration, double major, ESL, honors, independent study, internships, study abroad, teacher certification program, Washington semester. Semester in Washington, Gettysburg semester. **Credit/placement by examination:** AP, CLEP, IB, institutional tests. 36 credit hours maximum toward bachelor's degree. 36 total credits permitted by proficiency examination, non-collegiate-sponsored instructional/experiential learning combined. **Support services:** Tutoring, writing center.

Majors. Area/ethnic studies: American. **Biology:** General, biochemistry. **Business:** Accounting, actuarial science, business admin, finance, marketing. **Computer sciences:** General. **Conservation:** Environmental studies. **English:** English lit. **Foreign languages:** Classics, French, Spanish. **History:** General. **Human services:** Social work. **Math:** General. **Philosophy/religion:** Philosophy, religion. **Physical sciences:** Chemistry, physics. **Psychology:** General. **Social sciences:** Economics, political science, sociology. **Visual/performing arts:** General.

Most popular majors. Biology 10%, business/marketing 44%, English 8%, psychology 11%, social sciences 11%.

Computing on campus. 456 workstations in library, computer center, student center. Dormitories wired for high-speed internet access and linked to campus network. Commuter students can connect to campus network. Online course registration, online library, helpline, wireless network available.

Student life. Freshman orientation: Mandatory, $220 fee. Preregistration for classes offered. Preregistration for classes takes place remotely during the summer. **Housing:** Guaranteed on-campus for freshmen. Coed dorms, special housing for disabled, apartments available. On-campus townhouses, quiet living area. **Activities:** Pep band, campus ministries, choral groups, dance, drama, international student organizations, literary magazine, music ensembles, Model UN, musical theater, radio station, student government, student newspaper, TV station, approximately 70 clubs and organizations.

Athletics. NCAA. **Intercollegiate:** Baseball M, basketball, cross-country, diving W, field hockey W, golf, lacrosse, soccer, softball W, swimming W, tennis, volleyball W, water polo W. **Intramural:** Basketball, football (non-tackle), golf, soccer, softball, volleyball. **Team name:** Saints.

Student services. Alcohol/substance abuse counseling, chaplain/spiritual director, career counseling, services for economically disadvantaged, student employment services, financial aid counseling, health services, minority student services, personal counseling, placement for graduates, women's services. **Physically disabled:** Services for visually, speech, hearing impaired.

Contact. E-mail: admissions@siena.edu
Phone: (518) 783-2423 Toll-free number: (888) 287-4362
Fax: (518) 783-2436
Heather Renault, Assistant Vice President for Admissions, Siena College, 515 Loudon Road, Loudonville, NY 12211-1462

Skidmore College

Saratoga Springs, New York
www.skidmore.edu

CB member
CB code: 2815

- Private 4-year liberal arts college
- Residential campus in large town
- 2,655 degree-seeking undergraduates: 1% part-time, 61% women, 3% African American, 5% Asian American, 7% Hispanic American, 4% international
- 41 degree-seeking graduate students
- 42% of applicants admitted
- SAT or ACT with writing, application essay required
- 84% graduate within 6 years; 20% enter graduate study

General. Founded in 1903. Regionally accredited. **Degrees:** 666 bachelor's awarded; master's offered. **ROTC:** Army, Air Force. **Location:** 30 miles from Albany. **Calendar:** Semester, limited summer session. **Full-time faculty:** 238 total; 88% have terminal degrees, 13% minority, 57% women. **Part-time faculty:** 101 total; 37% have terminal degrees, 11% minority, 56% women. **Class size:** 69% < 20, 30% 20-39, less than 1% 40-49, less than 1% 50-99, less than 1% >100. **Special facilities:** Fine and performing arts facilities, equestrian center, 400 acres of woodlands and trails, teaching museum.

Freshman class profile. 5,780 applied, 2,431 admitted, 663 enrolled.

Mid 50% test scores			
SAT critical reading:	570-680	Rank in top tenth:	42%
SAT math:	580-670	Return as sophomores:	95%
SAT writing:	580-680	Out-of-state:	65%
ACT composite:	26-30	Live on campus:	100%
Rank in top quarter:	75%	International:	6%

Basis for selection. Rigor of school record very important. Class rank, GPA, recommendations, and test scores also important. SAT Subject Tests recommended. 2 SAT Subject Tests recommended of all applicants. Interview recommended for all.

High school preparation. College-preparatory program required. Recommended units include English 4, mathematics 4, social studies 4, science 4 (laboratory 3) and foreign language 4.

2011-2012 Annual costs. Tuition/fees: $42,380. Room/board: $11,304. Books/supplies: $1,300. Personal expenses: $1,216.

2011-2012 Financial aid. Need-based: 351 full-time freshmen applied for aid; 273 were judged to have need; 273 of these received aid. Average need met was 100%. Average scholarship/grant was $32,249; average loan $3,612. 89% of total undergraduate aid awarded as scholarships/grants, 11% as loans/jobs. **Non-need-based:** Awarded to 135 full-time undergraduates, including 30 freshmen. Scholarships awarded for music/drama.

Application procedures. Admission: Closing date 1/15 (postmark date). $65 fee, may be waived for applicants with need. Admission notification by 4/1. Must reply by 5/1. Enrollment deposit of $500 required on or before May 1. **Financial aid:** Closing date 2/1. FAFSA, CSS PROFILE required. Applicants notified by 4/1; must reply by 5/1.

Academics. Special study options: Accelerated study, combined bachelor's/graduate degree, cross-registration, distance learning, double major, dual enrollment of high school students, exchange student, honors, independent study, internships, liberal arts/career combination, student-designed major, study abroad, teacher certification program, Washington semester. 3+2 programs in engineering with Dartmouth College and Clarkson University, 4+1 MAT with Union College, 4+1 MBA with Clarkson University and the Graduate College at Union University, Master of Science in Occupational Therapy 4+2 program and a Doctor of Physical Therapy 4+3 program with Sage College, second baccalaureate degree in Nursing from NYU in either an accelerated 15-month program or an 18-month program. **Credit/placement by examination:** AP, CLEP, IB, SAT, ACT, institutional tests. 16 credit hours maximum toward bachelor's degree. Up to 60 hours may be counted toward degree. Maximum of 12 semester hours may be granted in credit through CLEP subject examinations. **Support services:** Pre-admission summer program, reduced course load, study skills assistance, tutoring, writing center.

Majors. Area/ethnic studies: American, Asian, French. **Biology:** General, neuroscience. **Business:** General. **Computer sciences:** General. **Conservation:** Environmental science, environmental studies. **Education:** General, elementary. **English:** English lit. **Foreign languages:** Classics, French, German, Spanish. **History:** General. **Human services:** Social work. **Liberal arts:** Arts/sciences. **Math:** General. **Parks/recreation:** Exercise sciences. **Philosophy/religion:** Philosophy, religion. **Physical sciences:** Chemistry, geology, physics. **Psychology:** General. **Social sciences:** Anthropology, economics, international relations, political science, sociology. **Visual/performing arts:** Art history/conservation, dance, dramatic, music history.

Most popular majors. Business/marketing 10%, English 10%, psychology 8%, social sciences 19%, visual/performing arts 16%.

Computing on campus. 600 workstations in dormitories, library, computer center, student center. Dormitories wired for high-speed internet access and linked to campus network. Commuter students can connect to campus network. Online course registration, online library, helpline, student web hosting, wireless network available.

Student life. Freshman orientation: Mandatory. Preregistration for classes offered. Programs on and off campus. Fee for off-campus programs. **Housing:** Guaranteed on-campus for all undergraduates. Coed dorms, single-sex dorms, special housing for disabled, apartments available. $500 nonrefundable deposit, deadline 5/1. Gender neutral wing. **Activities:** Bands, campus ministries, choral groups, dance, drama, international student organizations, literary magazine, music ensembles, Model UN, musical theater, opera, radio station, student government, student newspaper, symphony orchestra, TV station, 80 clubs and organizations.

Athletics. NCAA. **Intercollegiate:** Baseball M, basketball, diving, equestrian W, field hockey W, golf M, ice hockey M, lacrosse, rowing (crew), soccer, softball W, swimming, tennis, volleyball W. **Intramural:** Basketball, football (tackle) M, racquetball, soccer, softball, tennis, volleyball, water polo. **Team name:** Thoroughbreds.

Student services. Alcohol/substance abuse counseling, chaplain/spiritual director, career counseling, services for economically disadvantaged, student employment services, financial aid counseling, health services, minority student services, on-campus daycare, personal counseling, placement for graduates, veterans' counselor. **Physically disabled:** Services for visually, speech, hearing impaired.

Contact. E-mail: admissions@skidmore.edu
Phone: (518) 580-5570 Toll-free number: (800) 867-6007
Fax: (518) 580-5584
Mary Lou Bates, Dean of Admissions and Financial Aid, Skidmore College, 815 North Broadway, Saratoga Springs, NY 12866

St. Francis College
Brooklyn Heights, New York
www.sfc.edu

CB member
CB code: 2796

- Private 4-year liberal arts college affiliated with Roman Catholic Church
- Commuter campus in very large city
- 2,648 degree-seeking undergraduates: 10% part-time, 55% women
- 47 degree-seeking graduate students
- 70% of applicants admitted
- SAT, application essay required
- 50% graduate within 6 years

General. Founded in 1884. Regionally accredited. **Degrees:** 375 bachelor's, 10 associate awarded; master's offered. **ROTC:** Army, Air Force. **Calendar:** Semester, limited summer session. **Full-time faculty:** 85 total; 89% have terminal degrees, 14% minority, 47% women. **Part-time faculty:** 196 total; 25% have terminal degrees, 26% minority, 35% women. **Class size:** 44% < 20, 53% 20-39, 3% 40-49, 1% 50-99. **Special facilities:** Television production and editing facility with 3 Ikegami cameras and 17 Mac G5 digital editing stations.

Freshman class profile. 2,201 applied, 1,551 admitted, 489 enrolled.

Mid 50% test scores			
SAT critical reading:	420-510	GPA 3.0-3.49:	21%
SAT math:	420-510	GPA 2.0-2.99:	47%
SAT writing:	410-500	Return as sophomores:	80%
GPA 3.75 or higher:	6%	Out-of-state:	2%
GPA 3.50-3.74:	8%	Live on campus:	3%

Basis for selection. Academic achievement, test scores, counselor's recommendation, school and community activities, admissions interview important. Degree-seeking students who do not meet criteria may be admitted after review and assessment of their educational background. SAT/ACT scores must be received by first day of class for fall-term admission. Interview required of academically weak applicants. **Home schooled:** Statement describing home school structure and mission, state high school equivalency certificate required.

High school preparation. 18.5 units recommended. Required and recommended units include English 4, mathematics 2, social studies 4, science 2, visual/performing arts 1, academic electives 5.5.

2011-2012 Annual costs. Tuition/fees: $18,100. Books/supplies: $1,000. Personal expenses: $4,000.

2011-2012 Financial aid. Need-based: 308 full-time freshmen applied for aid; 272 were judged to have need; 272 of these received aid. Average need met was 69%. Average scholarship/grant was $11,235; average loan $3,295. 66% of total undergraduate aid awarded as scholarships/grants, 34% as loans/jobs. **Non-need-based:** Awarded to 1,257 full-time undergraduates, including 333 freshmen. Scholarships awarded for academics, athletics.

Application procedures. Admission: No deadline. $35 fee, may be waived for applicants with need. Admission notification on a rolling basis. Must reply by May 1 or within 2 week(s) if notified thereafter. **Financial aid:** Priority date 2/15; no closing date. FAFSA required. Applicants notified on a rolling basis starting 3/15; must reply within 2 week(s) of notification.

Academics. Special study options: Accelerated study, combined bachelor's/graduate degree, cooperative education, cross-registration, double major, dual enrollment of high school students, exchange student, honors, independent study, internships, student-designed major, study abroad, teacher certification program. Accelerated biomedical science program with New York College of Podiatric Medicine, medical technology program with St. Vincent Catholic Medical Centers of New York and New York Methodist Hospital, joint affiliation program with St. Vincent Catholic Medical Centers of New York in radiologic sciences. **Credit/placement by examination:** AP, CLEP, IB, SAT, ACT, institutional tests. 32 credit hours maximum toward associate degree, 98 toward bachelor's. **Support services:** Learning center, pre-admission summer program, remedial instruction, study skills assistance, tutoring, writing center.

Majors. Biology: General, biomedical sciences. **Business:** Accounting, business admin. **Communications:** Communications/speech/rhetoric, digital media, public relations, radio/TV. **Computer sciences:** System admin. **Education:** Biology, chemistry, elementary, English, mathematics, physical, social studies, visually handicapped. **English:** English lit. **Foreign languages:** Spanish. **Health services:** Clinical lab science, medical radiologic technology/radiation therapy, nursing (RN), physician assistant. **History:** General. **Liberal arts:** Arts/sciences. **Math:** General. **Philosophy/religion:** Philosophy, religion. **Physical sciences:** Chemistry. **Protective services:** Criminal justice. **Psychology:** General. **Social sciences:** Economics, political science, sociology.

Most popular majors. Business/marketing 23%, communications/journalism 13%, education 10%, health sciences 8%, liberal arts 10%, psychology 9%, social sciences 7%.

Computing on campus. 600 workstations in library, computer center, student center. Commuter students can connect to campus network. Helpline, wireless network available.

Student life. Freshman orientation: Mandatory. Preregistration for classes offered. **Housing:** St. Francis has partnered with Educational Housing Services and offers a limited amount of student housing. **Activities:** Campus

ministries, choral groups, dance, drama, literary magazine, Model UN, student government, student newspaper, Latin American Society, Haitian Alliance, Caribbean student association, Christian club, Arab-American Society, French club, College Republicans, History and Political Science Society, Italian Historical Society.

Athletics. NCAA. **Intercollegiate:** Basketball, cross-country, diving, soccer M, swimming, tennis, track and field, volleyball W, water polo. **Intramural:** Basketball, football (tackle) M, soccer M, volleyball. **Team name:** Terriers.

Student services. Adult student services, chaplain/spiritual director, career counseling, services for economically disadvantaged, student employment services, financial aid counseling, health services, personal counseling, placement for graduates, veterans' counselor. **Physically disabled:** Services for visually, speech, hearing impaired.

Contact. E-mail: admissions@sfc.edu
Phone: (718) 489-3473 Fax: (718) 802-0453
Lisa Esposito, Associate Director, St. Francis College, 180 Remsen Street, Brooklyn Heights, NY 11201-9902

St. John Fisher College
Rochester, New York   **CB member**
www.sjfc.edu   **CB code: 2798**

- Private 4-year liberal arts college affiliated with Roman Catholic Church
- Residential campus in large town
- 2,853 degree-seeking undergraduates: 6% part-time, 58% women, 4% African American, 2% Asian American, 4% Hispanic American
- 1,097 degree-seeking graduate students
- 66% of applicants admitted
- SAT or ACT (ACT writing optional), application essay required
- 73% graduate within 6 years; 50% enter graduate study

General. Founded in 1948. Regionally accredited. **Degrees:** 726 bachelor's awarded; master's, professional, doctoral offered. **ROTC:** Army, Naval, Air Force. **Location:** 6 miles from downtown. **Calendar:** Semester, extensive summer session. **Full-time faculty:** 215 total; 88% have terminal degrees, 15% minority, 50% women. **Part-time faculty:** 199 total; 2% minority, 60% women. **Class size:** 41% < 20, 56% 20-39, 3% 40-49, less than 1% 50-99.

Freshman class profile. 3,460 applied, 2,300 admitted, 555 enrolled.

Mid 50% test scores		GPA 2.0-2.99:	13%
SAT critical reading:	480-580	Rank in top quarter:	57%
SAT math:	510-610	Rank in top tenth:	23%
SAT writing:	460-560	End year in good standing:	89%
ACT composite:	22-27	Return as sophomores:	83%
GPA 3.75 or higher:	32%	Out-of-state:	4%
GPA 3.50-3.74:	23%	Live on campus:	85%
GPA 3.0-3.49:	32%		

Basis for selection. GED not accepted. Admission based primarily on student's high school academic record, SAT or ACT scores, course curriculum, extracurricular activities, counselor and teacher recommendations, and personal statement or essay or graded paper. Interview recommended for all. **Home schooled:** Transcript of courses and grades, letter of recommendation (nonparent) required. **Learning Disabled:** Admission standards and procedures for students with disabilities are the same as for all applicants.

High school preparation. College-preparatory program required. 16 units required. Required and recommended units include English 4, mathematics 4, social studies 4, science 4 and foreign language 3.

2011-2012 Annual costs. Tuition/fees: $26,260. Room/board: $10,510. Books/supplies: $900. Personal expenses: $600.

2010-2011 Financial aid. Need-based: 609 full-time freshmen applied for aid; 539 were judged to have need; 539 of these received aid. Average need met was 83%. Average scholarship/grant was $16,354; average loan $3,875. 59% of total undergraduate aid awarded as scholarships/grants, 41% as loans/jobs. **Non-need-based:** Awarded to 1,379 full-time undergraduates, including 439 freshmen. Scholarships awarded for academics, leadership.

Application procedures. Admission: Priority date 12/1; no deadline. $30 fee, may be waived for applicants with need. Admission notification on a rolling basis beginning on or about 12/1. Must reply by May 1 or within 3 week(s) if notified thereafter. **Financial aid:** Priority date 2/15; no closing date. FAFSA required. Applicants notified on a rolling basis starting 3/21; must reply by 5/1 or within 3 week(s) of notification.

Academics. All entering first-year students participate in an integrative learning community designed to examine a topic from multiple perspectives, discover connections between different disciplines and develop close working relationships with other students. **Special study options:** Accelerated study, cross-registration, distance learning, double major, exchange student, honors, independent study, internships, liberal arts/career combination, student-designed major, study abroad, teacher certification program, Washington semester, weekend college. 3-4 optometry program with Pennsylvania College of Optometry, 3-2 pre-engineering program with affiliated engineering schools, 2-2 pre-engineering program with University of Detroit and Manhattan College, 4-2 pre-engineering program with Columbia University. **Credit/placement by examination:** AP, CLEP, IB, institutional tests. 66 credit hours maximum toward bachelor's degree. **Support services:** Reduced course load, study skills assistance, tutoring, writing center.

Majors. Area/ethnic studies: American. **Biology:** General. **Business:** Accounting, business admin, finance, human resources, marketing. **Communications:** General. **Computer sciences:** General, information technology. **Education:** General, biology, chemistry, elementary, English, French, history, mathematics, physics, secondary, social studies, Spanish, special ed. **English:** English lit. **Foreign languages:** French, Spanish. **Health services:** Nursing (RN). **History:** General. **Liberal arts:** Arts/sciences. **Math:** General, statistics. **Parks/recreation:** Sports admin. **Philosophy/religion:** Philosophy, religion. **Physical sciences:** Chemistry, physics. **Psychology:** General. **Social sciences:** Anthropology, economics, international relations, political science, sociology.

Most popular majors. Biology 7%, business/marketing 26%, communications/journalism 7%, education 16%, health sciences 17%, psychology 6%, social sciences 7%.

Computing on campus. 550 workstations in library, computer center, student center. Dormitories wired for high-speed internet access and linked to campus network. Commuter students can connect to campus network. Online course registration, online library, helpline, student web hosting, wireless network available.

Student life. Freshman orientation: Available. Preregistration for classes offered. 3-day program in late August. **Policies:** All housing is smoke-free. Freshmen not permitted cars on campus. **Housing:** Guaranteed on-campus for freshmen. Coed dorms, single-sex dorms, special housing for disabled available. $300 nonrefundable deposit, deadline 5/1. All residence halls accessible to students with disabilities. **Activities:** Campus ministries, choral groups, dance, drama, literary magazine, musical theater, student government, student newspaper, TV station, Circle K, Latino student union, black student union, Asian student union, Fisher Players, gospel choir, resident student association, commuter council, student activities board, Fisher Pride.

Athletics. NCAA. **Intercollegiate:** Baseball M, basketball, cross-country, field hockey W, football (tackle) M, golf, lacrosse, soccer, softball W, tennis, track and field, volleyball W. **Intramural:** Basketball, football (non-tackle) M, soccer, volleyball. **Team name:** Cardinals.

Student services. Adult student services, alcohol/substance abuse counseling, chaplain/spiritual director, career counseling, services for economically disadvantaged, student employment services, financial aid counseling, health services, on-campus daycare, personal counseling, placement for graduates, veterans' counselor. **Physically disabled:** Services for visually, hearing impaired.

Contact. E-mail: admissions@sjfc.edu
Phone: (585) 385-8064 Toll-free number: (800) 444-4640
Fax: (585) 385-8386
Stacy Ledermann, Director of Freshman Admissions, St. John Fisher College, 3690 East Avenue, Rochester, NY 14618-3597

St. John's University
Queens, New York   **CB member**
www.stjohns.edu   **CB code: 2799**

- Private 4-year university affiliated with Roman Catholic Church
- Commuter campus in very large city
- 11,764 degree-seeking undergraduates: 3% part-time, 53% women, 19% African American, 18% Asian American, 16% Hispanic American, 5% international
- 5,130 degree-seeking graduate students
- 49% of applicants admitted
- SAT or ACT (ACT writing optional) required
- 58% graduate within 6 years; 36% enter graduate study

General. Founded in 1870. Regionally accredited. Full degree programs offered on four campuses: Queens, Staten Island, Manhattan, and Rome, Italy;

selected degree programs offered through distance learning. Coursework, but not full degrees, are offered at Oakdale, Long Island, and at a study abroad site in Paris, France. **Degrees:** 2,173 bachelor's, 31 associate awarded; master's, professional, doctoral offered. **ROTC:** Army. **Location:** 10 miles from mid-town Manhattan. **Calendar:** Semester, extensive summer session. **Full-time faculty:** 629 total; 90% have terminal degrees, 22% minority, 43% women. **Part-time faculty:** 861 total; 25% have terminal degrees, 19% minority, 41% women. **Class size:** 37% < 20, 50% 20-39, 6% 40-49, 6% 50-99, less than 1% >100. **Special facilities:** Speech and hearing clinic, instructional media center, health education resource center, writing institute, institute of Asian studies.

Freshman class profile. 52,972 applied, 25,998 admitted, 2,763 enrolled.

Mid 50% test scores			
SAT critical reading:	480-580	GPA 2.0-2.99:	34%
SAT math:	490-610	Rank in top quarter:	30%
ACT composite:	21-27	Rank in top tenth:	11%
GPA 3.75 or higher:	18%	Return as sophomores:	79%
GPA 3.50-3.74:	13%	Out-of-state:	40%
GPA 3.0-3.49:	34%	Live on campus:	59%
		International:	4%

Basis for selection. School achievement record, standardized test scores, counselor/teacher recommendations, extracurricular activities, personal essay used. ACCUPLACER is necessary for those out of school for a number of years, or for those who have never taken an ACT or SAT. ACT or SAT Writing section required for PharmD applicants and must be received by February 1 for the fall term. Personal statement, essay recommended for all; portfolio required for creative photography, fine art, graphic design, illustration programs. Audition required for dramatic arts. Essay required for 3-year degree programs. Essay, letter of recommendation, resume of activities required for applicants to the 6-year Doctor of Pharmacy (PharmD) program. **Home schooled:** Statement describing home school structure and mission, transcript of courses and grades, state high school equivalency certificate required.

High school preparation. College-preparatory program recommended. 13 units required; 19 recommended. Required and recommended units include English 4, mathematics 2-3, history 1, science 1, foreign language 2 and academic electives 5-8.

2011-2012 Annual costs. Tuition/fees: $33,875. Tuition may vary by program and class year. A four-year fixed rate tuition plan is available for incoming freshmen. Full-time freshman or transfer students are provided with a laptop for their entire St. John's career. Room/board: $14,600. Books/supplies: $1,015. Personal expenses: $2,740.

2010-2011 Financial aid. Need-based: 2,827 full-time freshmen applied for aid; 2,666 were judged to have need; 2,666 of these received aid. Average need met was 83%. Average scholarship/grant was $13,403; average loan $3,680. 70% of total undergraduate aid awarded as scholarships/grants, 30% as loans/jobs. **Non-need-based:** Awarded to 7,813 full-time undergraduates, including 2,461 freshmen. Scholarships awarded for academics, alumni affiliation, art, athletics, leadership, music/drama, religious affiliation, ROTC.

Application procedures. Admission: Priority date 2/1; no deadline. $50 fee, may be waived for applicants with need, free for online applicants. Admission notification on a rolling basis beginning on or about 12/1. Must reply by May 1 or within 2 week(s) if notified thereafter. Application closing date for pharmacy students February 1. **Financial aid:** Priority date 2/1; no closing date. FAFSA required. Applicants notified on a rolling basis starting 3/15; must reply within 2 week(s) of notification.

Academics. Special study options: Accelerated study, combined bachelor's/graduate degree, cross-registration, distance learning, double major, dual enrollment of high school students, ESL, honors, independent study, internships, liberal arts/career combination, study abroad, teacher certification program, weekend college. Semester Study Abroad opportunities in Paris, France; Rome, Italy; Seville, Spain. Summer Study Abroad programs in Vietnam, China, Bermuda, England, Argentina, Spain, France, Italy, Russia, South Africa, Turkey, and elsewhere. Available Winter Study Abroad programs include Galapagos Islands, Brazil, India, Italy. 3-year degree programs offered at the Staten Island campus. **Credit/placement by examination:** AP, CLEP, IB, SAT, ACT, institutional tests. Students must complete at least 50 percent of major courses and at least 30 credits on campus. **Support services:** Learning center, pre-admission summer program, reduced course load, study skills assistance, tutoring, writing center.

Majors. Area/ethnic studies: Asian. **Biology:** General, toxicology. **Business:** Accounting, actuarial science, business admin, finance, hospitality admin, insurance, management information systems, marketing. **Communications:** Advertising, communications/speech/rhetoric, journalism, photojournalism. **Communications technology:** Photo/film/video. **Computer sciences:** General, security. **Conservation:** Environmental studies. **Education:** Biology, elementary, English, mathematics, physics, social studies, Spanish, special ed. **English:** English lit. **Foreign languages:** French, Italian, Spanish. **Health services:** Audiology/speech pathology, clinical lab science, health care admin, medical records technology, pathology assistant, physician assistant, radiologic technology/medical imaging. **History:** General. **Human services:** General. **Liberal arts:** Arts/sciences. **Math:** General. **Parks/recreation:** Sports admin. **Philosophy/religion:** Philosophy. **Physical sciences:** General, chemistry, physics. **Protective services:** Law enforcement admin, security management. **Psychology:** General. **Social sciences:** General, anthropology, economics, political science, sociology. **Theology:** Theology. **Visual/performing arts:** Dramatic, graphic design, illustration, photography.

Most popular majors. Biology 7%, business/marketing 27%, communications/journalism 9%, education 7%, health sciences 7%, psychology 6%, security/protective services 6%.

Computing on campus. PC or laptop required. 1,224 workstations in dormitories, library, computer center, student center. Dormitories wired for high-speed internet access and linked to campus network. Commuter students can connect to campus network. Online course registration, online library, helpline, repair service, student web hosting, wireless network available.

Student life. Freshman orientation: Mandatory, $250 fee. Preregistration for classes offered. 3-day orientation program includes trip to Manhattan. **Policies:** Freshmen not permitted cars on campus. **Housing:** Coed dorms, apartments available. $400 nonrefundable deposit, deadline 5/1. Limited off-campus apartments available. **Activities:** Bands, campus ministries, choral groups, dance, drama, film society, international student organizations, literary magazine, music ensembles, Model UN, musical theater, radio station, student government, student newspaper, TV station, over 180 organizations on all campuses.

Athletics. NCAA. **Intercollegiate:** Baseball M, basketball, cross-country W, fencing, golf, lacrosse M, soccer, softball W, tennis, track and field W, volleyball W. **Intramural:** Badminton, basketball, cheerleading, football (non-tackle), soccer, softball, table tennis, tennis, volleyball, weight lifting. **Team name:** Red Storm.

Student services. Adult student services, alcohol/substance abuse counseling, chaplain/spiritual director, career counseling, services for economically disadvantaged, student employment services, financial aid counseling, health services, minority student services, personal counseling, placement for graduates, veterans' counselor. **Physically disabled:** Services for visually, speech, hearing impaired.

Contact. E-mail: admhelp@stjohns.edu
Phone: (718) 990-2000 Toll-free number: (888) 978-5646
Fax: (718) 990-5827
Karen Vahey, Director of Admission, St. John's University, 8000 Utopia Parkway, Queens, NY 11439

St. Joseph's College, New York

Brooklyn, New York   CB member
www.sjcny.edu   CB code: 2802

- Private 4-year liberal arts and teachers college
- Commuter campus in very large city
- 1,238 degree-seeking undergraduates: 24% part-time, 72% women, 32% African American, 6% Asian American, 17% Hispanic American
- 242 degree-seeking graduate students
- 72% of applicants admitted
- SAT or ACT (ACT writing optional) required
- 62% graduate within 6 years

General. Founded in 1916. Regionally accredited. **Degrees:** 242 bachelor's awarded; master's offered. **Location:** 5 miles from midtown Manhattan. **Calendar:** Semester, limited summer session. **Full-time faculty:** 59 total; 80% have terminal degrees, 17% minority, 54% women. **Part-time faculty:** 121 total; 12% have terminal degrees, 23% minority, 52% women. **Class size:** 76% < 20, 24% 20-39, less than 1% 40-49. **Special facilities:** On-campus laboratory preschool for children 3-6 years old, model school for prospective teachers, Molloy outdoor theater.

Freshman class profile. 1,012 applied, 732 admitted, 208 enrolled.

Mid 50% test scores			
SAT critical reading:	430-540	GPA 3.50-3.74:	13%
SAT math:	440-550	GPA 3.0-3.49:	40%
SAT writing:	420-550	GPA 2.0-2.99:	31%
ACT composite:	18-24	Return as sophomores:	82%
GPA 3.75 or higher:	15%	Out-of-state:	6%
		Live on campus:	5%

Basis for selection. High school achievement record, SAT/ACT scores, class rank, activities, recommendations important. Personal statements

encouraged. Notification of admission decision within 30 days. Essay, interview recommended. **Home schooled:** Statement describing home school structure and mission, transcript of courses and grades required.

High school preparation. 18 units required. Required units include English 4, mathematics 3, social studies 4, science 2, foreign language 2 and academic electives 3. 3 units science recommended for science majors. No specific course requirements for general studies applicants.

2011-2012 Annual costs. Tuition/fees: $18,415. Books/supplies: $1,000.

2011-2012 Financial aid. Need-based: 194 full-time freshmen applied for aid; 161 were judged to have need; 161 of these received aid. Average need met was 73%. Average scholarship/grant was $12,794; average loan $3,149. 72% of total undergraduate aid awarded as scholarships/grants, 28% as loans/jobs. **Non-need-based:** Awarded to 707 full-time undergraduates, including 76 freshmen. Scholarships awarded for academics, alumni affiliation, leadership.

Application procedures. Admission: Closing date 8/15. $25 fee, may be waived for applicants with need. Admission notification on a rolling basis beginning on or about 11/1. Must reply by May 1 or within 2 week(s) if notified thereafter. **Financial aid:** Priority date 2/25; no closing date. FAFSA required. Applicants notified on a rolling basis starting 3/15; must reply by 5/1 or within 2 week(s) of notification.

Academics. Special study options: Accelerated study, combined bachelor's/graduate degree, distance learning, double major, honors, independent study, internships, study abroad, teacher certification program, weekend college. Accelerated biomedical program with New York College of Podiatric Medicine. **Credit/placement by examination:** AP, CLEP, IB, institutional tests. **Support services:** Learning center, pre-admission summer program, reduced course load, study skills assistance, tutoring, writing center.

Majors. Biology: General. **Business:** Accounting, business admin, marketing. **Computer sciences:** General, information systems. **Education:** General, biology, chemistry, elementary, English, history, mathematics, social studies, Spanish, special ed. **English:** English lit, rhetoric/composition. **Foreign languages:** General, Spanish. **Health services:** Clinical lab science, facilities admin, health care admin, staff services technology. **History:** General. **Liberal arts:** Arts/sciences. **Math:** General. **Parks/recreation:** Facilities management. **Philosophy/religion:** General. **Physical sciences:** Chemistry. **Protective services:** Law enforcement admin. **Psychology:** General. **Social sciences:** General. **Work/family studies:** Family studies.

Most popular majors. Business/marketing 19%, education 24%, English 7%, health sciences 26%.

Computing on campus. 222 workstations in library, computer center, student center. Dormitories wired for high-speed internet access. Online course registration, online library, wireless network available.

Student life. Freshman orientation: Mandatory. Preregistration for classes offered. **Housing:** Coed dorms available. **Activities:** Jazz band, campus ministries, choral groups, dance, drama, film society, international student organizations, literary magazine, music ensembles, musical theater, student government, student newspaper, symphony orchestra, Gaelic society, Hispanic awareness club, heritage gallery, Asian awareness, Japanese animation, political affairs, student ambassador club.

Athletics. NCAA, USCAA. **Intercollegiate:** Baseball M, basketball, cross-country, soccer M, softball W, swimming W, tennis, volleyball. **Intramural:** Basketball, bowling, football (non-tackle), table tennis. **Team name:** Bears.

Student services. Adult student services, chaplain/spiritual director, career counseling, student employment services, financial aid counseling, health services, personal counseling.

Contact. E-mail: asinfob@sjcny.edu
Phone: (718) 940-5800 Fax: (718) 636-8303
Theresa LaRocca-Meyer, Vice President for Enrollment Management, St. Joseph's College, New York, 245 Clinton Avenue, Brooklyn, NY 11205-3602

St. Joseph's College: Suffolk Campus
Patchogue, New York
www.sjcny.edu

CB member
CB code: 2841

- Private 4-year branch campus, liberal arts and teachers college
- Commuter campus in large town
- 3,676 degree-seeking undergraduates: 18% part-time, 71% women, 4% African American, 2% Asian American, 8% Hispanic American
- 549 degree-seeking graduate students

- 78% of applicants admitted
- SAT or ACT (ACT writing recommended) required
- 66% graduate within 6 years

General. Founded in 1916. Regionally accredited. **Degrees:** 952 bachelor's awarded; master's offered. **Location:** 55 miles from midtown Manhattan. **Calendar:** Semester, limited summer session. **Full-time faculty:** 119 total; 74% have terminal degrees, 15% minority, 60% women. **Part-time faculty:** 317 total; 13% have terminal degrees, 11% minority, 50% women. **Class size:** 63% < 20, 37% 20-39, less than 1% 40-49. **Special facilities:** The Clare Rose Playhouse.

Freshman class profile. 1,425 applied, 1,116 admitted, 448 enrolled.

Mid 50% test scores			
SAT critical reading:	480-580	GPA 3.75 or higher:	24%
SAT math:	490-600	GPA 3.50-3.74:	19%
SAT writing:	470-570	GPA 3.0-3.49:	44%
ACT composite:	20-26	GPA 2.0-2.99:	13%
		Return as sophomores:	89%

Basis for selection. Grades in high school academic classes, GPA and rank in class most important. Performance on standardized tests important. Strongly factored in are letters of recommendation, personal statement and school/community activities. TOEFL may be used in place of SAT for international students. Interview recommended. Essays required of scholarship candidates, strongly recommended for all others. **Home schooled:** Transcript of courses and grades required. SAT or ACT required. Interview strongly recommended.

High school preparation. College-preparatory program required. 19 units required. Required and recommended units include English 4, mathematics 3, social studies 4, history 4, science 3 (laboratory 3), foreign language 2, computer science 1, visual/performing arts 1 and academic electives 2. Social science unit must be American history.

2011-2012 Annual costs. Tuition/fees: $18,415. Books/supplies: $1,000.

2011-2012 Financial aid. Need-based: 437 full-time freshmen applied for aid; 314 were judged to have need; 314 of these received aid. Average need met was 76%. Average scholarship/grant was $10,287; average loan $3,149. 64% of total undergraduate aid awarded as scholarships/grants, 36% as loans/jobs. **Non-need-based:** Awarded to 2,074 full-time undergraduates, including 200 freshmen. Scholarships awarded for academics, alumni affiliation, leadership.

Application procedures. Admission: Priority date 8/15; deadline 8/15. $25 fee, may be waived for applicants with need. Application must be submitted on paper. Admission notification on a rolling basis beginning on or about 11/1. Must reply by May 1 or within 2 week(s) if notified thereafter. Notification to applicants of admission decision made ASAP or within 30 days. **Financial aid:** Priority date 2/25; no closing date. FAFSA required. Applicants notified on a rolling basis starting 3/15; must reply by 5/1 or within 2 week(s) of notification.

Academics. Special study options: Accelerated study, combined bachelor's/graduate degree, distance learning, double major, honors, independent study, internships, New York semester, study abroad, teacher certification program, weekend college. Bio-medical program with New York College of Pediatric Medicine. **Credit/placement by examination:** AP, CLEP, IB, institutional tests. **Support services:** Learning center, reduced course load, study skills assistance, tutoring, writing center.

Majors. Biology: General. **Business:** Accounting, business admin, marketing. **Computer sciences:** General, information systems. **Education:** General, biology, elementary, English, history, mathematics, social studies, Spanish, special ed. **English:** English lit, rhetoric/composition. **Foreign languages:** Spanish. **Health services:** Clinical lab science, facilities admin, health care admin, licensed practical nurse, staff services technology. **History:** General. **Liberal arts:** Arts/sciences. **Math:** General, statistics. **Parks/recreation:** Facilities management. **Philosophy/religion:** General. **Protective services:** Law enforcement admin. **Psychology:** General. **Social sciences:** General. **Work/family studies:** Family studies.

Most popular majors. Business/marketing 19%, education 42%, English 10%, psychology 6%, social sciences 6%.

Computing on campus. 257 workstations in library, computer center. Online course registration, online library, wireless network available.

Student life. Freshman orientation: Mandatory, $50 fee. Preregistration for classes offered. 1-day orientation in August just prior to start of classes. **Policies:** 2.7 average required to run for student government. **Activities:** Jazz band, campus ministries, choral groups, dance, drama, film society, literary magazine, music ensembles, musical theater, student government, student newspaper, symphony orchestra, Amnesty International, student volunteer services, Circle K, Students Taking an Active Role in Society, Spanish club, Diversity Union, Habitat for Humanity, social sciences club, Lion's Club.

Athletics. NCAA. **Intercollegiate:** Baseball M, basketball, cross-country, equestrian W, golf M, lacrosse W, soccer, softball W, swimming W, tennis, track and field, volleyball W. **Intramural:** Football (non-tackle). **Team name:** Golden Eagles.

Student services. Adult student services, alcohol/substance abuse counseling, chaplain/spiritual director, career counseling, student employment services, financial aid counseling, health services, minority student services, personal counseling, veterans' counselor. **Physically disabled:** Services for visually, hearing impaired.

Contact. E-mail: asinfob@sjcny.edu
Phone: (631) 687-4500 Fax: (631) 447-3624
Gigi Lamens, Director of Admissions and Enrollment Planning, St. Joseph's College: Suffolk Campus, 155 West Roe Boulevard, Patchogue, NY 11772-2325

St. Lawrence University
Canton, New York
www.stlawu.edu

CB member
CB code: 2805

- Private 4-year liberal arts college
- Residential campus in small town
- 2,335 degree-seeking undergraduates: 54% women, 3% African American, 1% Asian American, 4% Hispanic American, 6% international
- 73 degree-seeking graduate students
- 43% of applicants admitted
- Application essay required
- 80% graduate within 6 years; 22% enter graduate study

General. Founded in 1856. Regionally accredited. **Degrees:** 541 bachelor's awarded; master's offered. **ROTC:** Army, Air Force. **Location:** 70 miles from Ottawa, Canada. **Calendar:** Semester, limited summer session. **Full-time faculty:** 171 total; 98% have terminal degrees, 13% minority, 47% women. **Part-time faculty:** 21 total; 33% have terminal degrees, 52% women. **Class size:** 62% < 20, 36% 20-39, 1% 40-49, 1% 50-99. **Special facilities:** 1,000 contiguous acres include woods and river habitat for conducting primary research, science facility, center for arts technology, golf course, crew boathouse, Adirondack Semester yurt village.

Freshman class profile. 4,273 applied, 1,855 admitted, 647 enrolled.

Mid 50% test scores			
SAT critical reading:	570-660	Rank in top quarter:	76%
SAT math:	580-660	Rank in top tenth:	44%
SAT writing:	570-660	End year in good standing:	96%
ACT composite:	25-29	Return as sophomores:	90%
GPA 3.75 or higher:	37%	Out-of-state:	55%
GPA 3.50-3.74:	25%	Live on campus:	100%
GPA 3.0-3.49:	27%	International:	5%
GPA 2.0-2.99:	11%		

Basis for selection. Academic record most important; test scores, extracurricular activities, seriousness of purpose and intellectual promise important. Students for whom English is not the native language must provide proof of language proficiency. Accepted documentation includes official TOEFL results, SAT Critical Reading scores, and IB Higher Level English A1 or A2 exams. Interview recommended.

High school preparation. College-preparatory program required. 20 units recommended. Recommended units include English 4, mathematics 4, social studies 2, history 2, science 4 and foreign language 3.

2011-2012 Annual costs. Tuition/fees: $42,735. Room/board: $11,005. Books/supplies: $750. Personal expenses: $500.

2011-2012 Financial aid. Need-based: 493 full-time freshmen applied for aid; 409 were judged to have need; 408 of these received aid. Average need met was 91%. Average scholarship/grant was $28,044; average loan $3,356. 87% of total undergraduate aid awarded as scholarships/grants, 13% as loans/jobs. **Non-need-based:** Awarded to 651 full-time undergraduates, including 276 freshmen. Scholarships awarded for academics, alumni affiliation, athletics, leadership, minority status, ROTC, state residency.

Application procedures. Admission: Closing date 2/1 (postmark date). $60 fee, may be waived for applicants with need. Admission notification by 3/31. Must reply by May 1 or within 2 week(s) if notified thereafter. **Financial aid:** Closing date 2/1. FAFSA, CSS PROFILE required. Applicants notified by 3/31; must reply by 5/1 or within 2 week(s) of notification.

Academics. Quantitative Resource Center for math assistance. **Special study options:** Combined bachelor's/graduate degree, cross-registration, double major, exchange student, independent study, internships, New York semester, student-designed major, study abroad, teacher certification program,

Washington semester. Community-based learning; 3-2 program in engineering with Clarkson University, Columbia University, Rensselaer Polytechnic Institute, University of Rochester, University of Southern California, Washington University in St. Louis; early assurance programs in medicine with SUNY Health Science Center at Syracuse and in dentistry with SUNY at Buffalo; combined bachelor's/graduate degree program in business administration with Clarkson University, Union College and Rochester Institute of Technology; 17 study abroad programs in Europe, Kenya, Japan, Costa Rica, India, Canada, Czech Republic, Trinidad and Tobago, China, Thailand, Australia and New Zealand. **Credit/placement by examination:** AP, CLEP, IB, institutional tests. 60 credit hours maximum toward bachelor's degree. **Support services:** Pre-admission summer program, reduced course load, study skills assistance, tutoring, writing center.

Majors. Area/ethnic studies: African, Asian, Canadian. **Biology:** General, biochemistry, biophysics, conservation, neuroscience. **Communications:** Communications/speech/rhetoric. **Computer sciences:** General. **Conservation:** Environmental studies. **English:** American lit, British lit, creative writing. **Foreign languages:** French, German, Spanish. **History:** General. **Liberal arts:** Arts/sciences, humanities. **Math:** General. **Philosophy/religion:** Philosophy, religion. **Physical sciences:** Chemistry, geology, geophysics, physics. **Psychology:** General. **Social sciences:** Anthropology, econometrics, economics, political science, sociology. **Visual/performing arts:** Music, studio arts.

Most popular majors. Biology 9%, English 9%, mathematics 6%, psychology 13%, social sciences 30%, visual/performing arts 7%.

Computing on campus. 608 workstations in dormitories, library, computer center, student center. Dormitories wired for high-speed internet access and linked to campus network. Commuter students can connect to campus network. Online course registration, helpline, repair service, student web hosting, wireless network available.

Student life. Freshman orientation: Mandatory. Preregistration for classes offered. Orientation is three days preceding the start of fall classes. Programs are focused on academic introductions to the liberal arts, to the living-learning community concept, and St. Lawrence traditions. **Policies:** Residential living-learning program. First-year students live together in a residential college their first semester. Students required to live on campus all four years. **Housing:** Guaranteed on-campus for all undergraduates. Coed dorms, apartments, fraternity/sorority housing, wellness housing available. Townhouse apartments for senior leaders, some suites available. Students can petition to have quiet or single-sex halls within dormitory. **Activities:** Bands, campus ministries, choral groups, dance, drama, film society, international student organizations, literary magazine, music ensembles, radio station, student government, student newspaper, Jewish Student organization, Black student union, Muslim students organization, environmental awareness organization, Habitat for Humanity, outing club, academic honorary societies, Circle K, Amnesty International.

Athletics. NCAA. **Intercollegiate:** Baseball M, basketball, cross-country, diving, equestrian, field hockey W, football (tackle) M, golf, ice hockey, lacrosse, rowing (crew), skiing, soccer, softball W, squash, swimming, tennis, track and field, volleyball W. **Intramural:** Basketball, football (non-tackle) M, football (tackle) M, ice hockey, soccer, softball W, triathlon. **Team name:** Saints.

Student services. Alcohol/substance abuse counseling, chaplain/spiritual director, career counseling, services for economically disadvantaged, student employment services, financial aid counseling, health services, minority student services, personal counseling, placement for graduates, women's services. **Physically disabled:** Services for visually, hearing impaired.

Contact. E-mail: admissions@stlawu.edu
Phone: (315) 229-5261 Toll-free number: (800) 285-1856
Fax: (315) 229-5818
Jeffrey Rickey, Vice President and Dean of Admissions and Financial Aid, St. Lawrence University, Payson Hall, Canton, NY 13617

St. Thomas Aquinas College
Sparkill, New York
www.stac.edu

CB code: 2807

- Private 4-year liberal arts college
- Commuter campus in large town
- 1,352 degree-seeking undergraduates: 6% part-time, 56% women, 6% African American, 2% Asian American, 17% Hispanic American, 1% international
- 176 degree-seeking graduate students
- 81% of applicants admitted

- SAT or ACT (ACT writing optional) required
- 49% graduate within 6 years

General. Founded in 1952. Regionally accredited. **Degrees:** 281 bachelor's, 4 associate awarded; master's offered. **ROTC:** Air Force. **Location:** 15 miles from New York City. **Calendar:** Semester, extensive summer session. **Full-time faculty:** 64 total; 73% have terminal degrees, 9% minority, 44% women. **Part-time faculty:** 65 total; 22% have terminal degrees, 12% minority, 54% women. **Class size:** 48% < 20, 34% 20-39, 4% 40-49, 8% 50-99, 5% >100. **Special facilities:** Arts, sciences and technology center, digital imaging laboratory.

Freshman class profile. 1,669 applied, 1,350 admitted, 305 enrolled.

Mid 50% test scores			
SAT critical reading:	410-520	GPA 3.0-3.49:	27%
SAT math:	420-530	GPA 2.0-2.99:	47%
SAT writing:	420-510	Return as sophomores:	80%
ACT composite:	18-25	Out-of-state:	24%
GPA 3.75 or higher:	12%	Live on campus:	74%
GPA 3.50-3.74:	10%	International:	2%

Basis for selection. School achievement record, test scores, recommendation, and interview considered. Applicants should be in top half of class and have GPA above 3.0. Essay, interview recommended for all; portfolio recommended for art program. **Home schooled:** Statement describing home school structure and mission, transcript of courses and grades, state high school equivalency certificate, letter of recommendation (nonparent) required.

High school preparation. 20 units required. Required units include English 4, mathematics 3, social studies 4, science 3 (laboratory 2) and foreign language 3.

2011-2012 Annual costs. Tuition/fees: $23,720. Room/board: $10,650. Books/supplies: $1,000. Personal expenses: $1,500.

Financial aid. **Non-need-based:** Scholarships awarded for academics, athletics.

Application procedures. **Admission:** No deadline. $30 fee. Admission notification on a rolling basis beginning on or about 10/1. **Financial aid:** Priority date 2/15; no closing date. FAFSA required. Applicants notified on a rolling basis starting 3/1; must reply by 5/1 or within 4 week(s) of notification.

Academics. **Special study options:** Accelerated study, combined bachelor's/graduate degree, cooperative education, cross-registration, double major, dual enrollment of high school students, ESL, exchange student, honors, independent study, internships, liberal arts/career combination, study abroad, teacher certification program, Washington semester. **Credit/placement by examination:** AP, CLEP, IB, SAT, ACT, institutional tests. 15 credit hours maximum toward associate degree, 30 toward bachelor's. **Support services:** Learning center, pre-admission summer program, reduced course load, remedial instruction, study skills assistance, tutoring, writing center.

Majors. **Biology:** General. **Business:** General, accounting, business admin, finance, international marketing, marketing. **Communications:** Broadcast journalism, communications/speech/rhetoric, journalism. **Computer sciences:** General. **Education:** General, art, biology, chemistry, elementary, English, foreign languages, history, mathematics, multi-level teacher, physics, science, secondary, social studies, Spanish, special ed. **English:** English lit. **Foreign languages:** General, French, Spanish. **Health services:** Art therapy, predental, premedicine, prenursing, prepharmacy, preveterinary. **History:** General. **Liberal arts:** Arts/sciences. **Math:** General, applied. **Parks/recreation:** Facilities management. **Philosophy/religion:** Philosophy, religion. **Physical sciences:** Chemistry, physics. **Protective services:** Forensics, law enforcement admin. **Psychology:** General. **Social sciences:** General. **Visual/performing arts:** Art, commercial/advertising art, graphic design, studio arts.

Most popular majors. Business/marketing 20%, communications/journalism 8%, education 16%, legal studies 7%, parks/recreation 6%, psychology 6%, security/protective services 10%, social sciences 13%.

Computing on campus. 200 workstations in dormitories, library, computer center, student center. Dormitories wired for high-speed internet access and linked to campus network. Commuter students can connect to campus network. Online library, helpline, wireless network available.

Student life. **Freshman orientation:** Mandatory, $75 fee. Preregistration for classes offered. **Housing:** Guaranteed on-campus for freshmen. Single-sex dorms, apartments, wellness housing available. $250 nonrefundable deposit, deadline 5/1. **Activities:** Choral groups, dance, drama, literary magazine, music ensembles, musical theater, opera, radio station, student government, student newspaper, TV station, political union, business association, community service organization.

Athletics. NAIA, NCAA. **Intercollegiate:** Baseball M, basketball, cross-country, golf, lacrosse W, soccer, softball W, tennis, track and field. **Intramural:** Basketball, skiing, softball, tennis. **Team name:** Spartans.

Student services. Adult student services, alcohol/substance abuse counseling, chaplain/spiritual director, career counseling, student employment services, financial aid counseling, health services, personal counseling, placement for graduates, veterans' counselor, women's services. **Physically disabled:** Services for visually, speech, hearing impaired.

Contact. E-mail: admissions@stac.edu
Phone: (845) 398-4100 Toll-free number: (800) 999-7822
Fax: (845) 398-4114
Danielle Mac Kay, Director of Admissions, St. Thomas Aquinas College, 125 Route 340, Sparkill, NY 10976-1041

SUNY College at Brockport
Brockport, New York
www.brockport.edu

CB member
CB code: 2537

- Public 4-year liberal arts college
- Residential campus in small town
- 7,142 degree-seeking undergraduates: 10% part-time, 55% women, 8% African American, 2% Asian American, 4% Hispanic American, 1% Native American
- 1,144 degree-seeking graduate students
- 46% of applicants admitted
- SAT or ACT (ACT writing optional), application essay required
- 65% graduate within 6 years

General. Founded in 1867. Regionally accredited. **Degrees:** 1,813 bachelor's awarded; master's offered. **ROTC:** Army, Naval, Air Force. **Location:** 16 miles from Rochester. **Calendar:** Semester, limited summer session. **Full-time faculty:** 335 total; 89% have terminal degrees, 15% minority, 48% women. **Part-time faculty:** 260 total; 21% have terminal degrees, 7% minority, 51% women. **Class size:** 40% < 20, 52% 20-39, 5% 40-49, 2% 50-99, less than 1% >100. **Special facilities:** Aquaculture ponds, unidata weather information system, weather radio receiver, nuclear laboratory, high resolution germanium detector, research vessel on Lake Ontario, electron microscope, two supercomputers, Doppler radar system, hydrotherapy room, parallel supercomputer, ultramodern dance facilities including green room.

Freshman class profile. 8,575 applied, 3,956 admitted, 1,050 enrolled.

Mid 50% test scores			
SAT critical reading:	480-570	GPA 3.0-3.49:	39%
SAT math:	500-580	GPA 2.0-2.99:	13%
SAT writing:	460-550	Rank in top quarter:	43%
ACT composite:	21-25	Rank in top tenth:	12%
GPA 3.75 or higher:	26%	Return as sophomores:	84%
GPA 3.50-3.74:	22%	Out-of-state:	3%
		Live on campus:	89%

Basis for selection. High school academic record including number of academic units, GPA, class rank, test scores important. Recommendations, essay, extracurricular activities and personal circumstance(s) also considered. Recommend student take SAT or ACT for the first time in junior year of high school. Interview recommended in some cases; auditions required for dance major and dance minor. **Home schooled:** Statement describing home school structure and mission, transcript of courses and grades, state high school equivalency certificate, letter of recommendation (nonparent) required. Outline of courses completed at high school level, official test scores (SAT/ACT), personal essay, 2 letters of recommendation, letter from local superintendent indicating local graduation requirements have been fulfilled, and bibliography of books read during high school program.

High school preparation. College-preparatory program recommended. 18 units required. Required and recommended units include English 4, mathematics 3-4, social studies 4, science 3-4 (laboratory 1), foreign language 3, computer science 1, visual/performing arts 1 and academic electives 3.

2011-2012 Annual costs. Tuition/fees: $6,508; $15,558 out-of-state. Room/board: $10,320. Books/supplies: $1,200. Personal expenses: $1,532.

2010-2011 Financial aid. **Need-based:** 905 full-time freshmen applied for aid; 698 were judged to have need; 695 of these received aid. Average need met was 75%. Average scholarship/grant was $5,934; average loan $4,235. 50% of total undergraduate aid awarded as scholarships/grants, 50% as loans/jobs. **Non-need-based:** Awarded to 1,009 full-time undergraduates, including 326 freshmen. Scholarships awarded for academics, alumni affiliation, art, leadership, minority status, music/drama, ROTC.

Application procedures. **Admission:** Priority date 7/1; no deadline. $50 fee, may be waived for applicants with need. Admission notification on a

rolling basis beginning on or about 11/15. Must reply by May 1 or within 3 week(s) if notified thereafter. **Financial aid:** Priority date 2/15; no closing date. FAFSA required. Applicants notified on a rolling basis starting 3/1; must reply by 5/1 or within 4 week(s) of notification.

Academics. Time/credit-shortened B.S. degree, experiential learning, domestic and international internships through Delta College. 3-1-3 program allows 30 college credits to be earned during student's senior year of high school. **Special study options:** Accelerated study, combined bachelor's/graduate degree, cross-registration, distance learning, double major, dual enrollment of high school students, honors, independent study, internships, New York semester, semester at sea, student-designed major, study abroad, teacher certification program, Washington semester. **Credit/placement by examination:** AP, CLEP, IB, institutional tests. 90 credit hours maximum toward bachelor's degree. **Support services:** Learning center, pre-admission summer program, reduced course load, study skills assistance, tutoring, writing center.

Honors college/program. Freshman applicants should have high school average of at least a 91 and SAT of 1150 (exclusive of Writing) or ACT of 25. The average honors student has a 93 GPA and a 1220 SAT and/or 27 ACT.

Majors. **Area/ethnic studies:** African, African-American, women's. **Biology:** General, aquatic, biochemistry, biotechnology, cellular/molecular, environmental, exercise physiology. **Business:** Accounting, business admin, finance, international, international marketing. **Communications:** Broadcast journalism, communications/speech/rhetoric, journalism, media studies. **Computer sciences:** General, computer science. **Conservation:** General, environmental science, environmental studies. **Education:** General, bilingual, biology, chemistry, developmentally delayed, elementary, English, health, history, mathematics, physical, physics, science, secondary, social studies, Spanish, special ed. **English:** Creative writing, English lit. **Foreign languages:** General, French, Spanish. **Health services:** Athletic training, clinical lab technology, health care admin, nursing (RN), predental, premedicine, preveterinary. **History:** General. **Human services:** Social work. **Math:** General. **Parks/recreation:** General, facilities management, sports admin. **Philosophy/religion:** Philosophy. **Physical sciences:** Atmospheric science, chemistry, geology, hydrology, meteorology, physics, planetary. **Protective services:** Police science, security management. **Psychology:** General. **Social sciences:** Anthropology, international relations, political science, sociology. **Visual/performing arts:** General, art, dance, dramatic, studio arts.

Most popular majors. Business/marketing 18%, communications/journalism 7%, education 9%, English 7%, health sciences 14%, psychology 8%, security/protective services 7%, social sciences 6%.

Computing on campus. 1,000 workstations in dormitories, library, computer center, student center. Dormitories wired for high-speed internet access and linked to campus network. Commuter students can connect to campus network. Online course registration, online library, helpline, wireless network available.

Student life. **Freshman orientation:** Available, $145 fee. Preregistration for classes offered. 24-hour program held in late June and early July. Students are given their course schedule and take a required Computer Skills Exam. A parent/family program runs parallel to the student orientation. **Housing:** Guaranteed on-campus for freshmen. Coed dorms, special housing for disabled, apartments, wellness housing available. $100 nonrefundable deposit, deadline 5/1. Special living options available include freshman first-year experience program, transfer student program, health club, scholar floors, single-sex areas, adult, 24-hour quiet, academic excellence floors. **Activities:** Pep band, campus ministries, choral groups, dance, drama, international student organizations, literary magazine, musical theater, radio station, student government, student newspaper, symphony orchestra, TV station, Organization for Students of African Descent, Association of Latin American Students, Alpha Chi Honor Society, Caribbean club, women's center, Brockport Adult Student Organization, peer counseling, student alumni association, Native American student organization.

Athletics. NCAA. **Intercollegiate:** Baseball M, basketball, cross-country, diving, field hockey W, football (tackle) M, gymnastics W, ice hockey M, lacrosse, soccer, softball W, swimming, tennis W, track and field, volleyball W, wrestling M. **Intramural:** Badminton, basketball, bowling, football (non-tackle), racquetball, soccer, softball, table tennis, volleyball. **Team name:** Golden Eagles.

Student services. Alcohol/substance abuse counseling, chaplain/spiritual director, career counseling, services for economically disadvantaged, student employment services, financial aid counseling, health services, legal services, minority student services, on-campus daycare, personal counseling, placement for graduates, veterans' counselor, women's services. **Physically disabled:** Services for visually, speech, hearing impaired.

Contact. E-mail: admit@brockport.edu
Phone: (585) 395-2751 Fax: (585) 395-5452
Bernard Valento, Director of Undergraduate Admissions, SUNY College at Brockport, 350 New Campus Drive, Brockport, NY 14420-2915

SUNY College at Buffalo
Buffalo, New York
www.buffalostate.edu

CB member
CB code: 2533

- Public 4-year liberal arts and teachers college
- Commuter campus in large city
- 9,806 degree-seeking undergraduates: 10% part-time, 58% women, 16% African American, 2% Asian American, 7% Hispanic American, 1% Native American, 1% international
- 2,192 graduate students
- SAT or ACT (ACT writing optional), SAT Subject Tests required

General. Founded in 1867. Regionally accredited. **Degrees:** 1,841 bachelor's awarded; master's offered. **ROTC:** Army. **Location:** 450 miles from New York City, 250 miles from Cleveland. **Calendar:** Semester, limited summer session. **Full-time faculty:** 402 total; 90% have terminal degrees, 17% minority, 46% women. **Part-time faculty:** 408 total; 32% have terminal degrees, 6% minority, 55% women. **Special facilities:** Planetarium, performing arts center, center for environmental research and education, child care center, art center, Great Lakes research facility.

Freshman class profile. 1,427 enrolled.

Mid 50% test scores		Rank in top quarter:	32%
SAT critical reading:	440-530	Rank in top tenth:	8%
SAT math:	450-540	Out-of-state:	2%
SAT writing:	430-520	Live on campus:	47%
GPA 3.75 or higher:	6%	International:	1%
GPA 3.50-3.74:	12%	Fraternities:	1%
GPA 3.0-3.49:	49%	Sororities:	1%
GPA 2.0-2.99:	33%		

Basis for selection. High school GPA, class rank, test scores important. Recommendations, essay, interview, volunteer work, work experience and extracurricular activities also considered. Portfolio required for fine arts program.

High school preparation. College-preparatory program recommended. 17 units recommended. Required and recommended units include English 4, mathematics 2-3, science 2-3, foreign language 3 and academic electives 4.

2011-2012 Annual costs. Tuition/fees: $6,353; $15,403 out-of-state. Room/board: $10,240. Books/supplies: $900. Personal expenses: $1,000.

Financial aid. All financial aid based on need.

Application procedures. Admission: No deadline. $40 fee, may be waived for applicants with need. Admission notification on a rolling basis beginning on or about 12/15. Must reply by May 1 or within 4 week(s) if notified thereafter. **Financial aid:** Priority date 3/15, closing date 5/1. FAFSA required. Applicants notified on a rolling basis starting 5/1; must reply within 4 week(s) of notification.

Academics. Special study options: Cooperative education, cross-registration, distance learning, double major, dual enrollment of high school students, ESL, exchange student, honors, independent study, internships, liberal arts/career combination, New York semester, study abroad, teacher certification program, Washington semester. **Credit/placement by examination:** AP, CLEP, IB, institutional tests. 30 credit hours maximum toward bachelor's degree. **Support services:** Learning center, pre-admission summer program, reduced course load, remedial instruction, study skills assistance, tutoring.

Honors college/program. High school students must have GPA of 90 or higher (or rank within the top 10 percent of their graduating class) and SAT scores of 1100 (exclusive of Writing) or higher. Advanced Placement courses with grades of B or better, cocurricular activities, and community involvement also considered.

Majors. Architecture: Urban/community planning. **Biology:** General. **Business:** General, business admin, fashion, hospitality admin, hospitality/recreation, office management. **Communications:** Broadcast journalism, communications/speech/rhetoric, journalism, media studies. **Computer sciences:** General, information systems, programming. **Education:** General, art, biology, business, chemistry, early childhood, elementary, emotionally handicapped, English, foreign languages, French, health occupations, kindergarten/preschool, mathematics, mentally handicapped, music, physical, physically handicapped, physics, reading, sales/marketing, science, secondary, social studies, Spanish, speech impaired, technology/industrial arts, trade/industrial, voc/tech. **English:** English lit. **Foreign languages:** French, Spanish. **Health services:** Speech pathology. **History:** General. **Human services:** Social work. **Liberal arts:** Humanities. **Math:** General. **Parks/recreation:**

Health/fitness. **Philosophy/religion:** Philosophy. **Physical sciences:** Chemistry, geology, physics, planetary. **Protective services:** Criminal justice, forensics. **Psychology:** General. **Social sciences:** Anthropology, economics, geography, political science, sociology. **Visual/performing arts:** General, art history/conservation, commercial/advertising art, dramatic, fashion design, fiber arts, interior design, metal/jewelry, music, painting, photography, printmaking, sculpture, studio arts, theater arts management. **Work/family studies:** Clothing/textiles, food/nutrition.

Most popular majors. Business/marketing 14%, communications/journalism 7%, education 24%, security/protective services 7%, social sciences 8%, visual/performing arts 7%.

Computing on campus. 900 workstations in dormitories, library, computer center, student center. Dormitories wired for high-speed internet access and linked to campus network. Commuter students can connect to campus network. Online course registration, online library, helpline, repair service, wireless network available.

Student life. Freshman orientation: Mandatory, $175 fee. Preregistration for classes offered. **Housing:** Coed dorms, apartments, wellness housing available. $100 fully refundable deposit, deadline 7/1. Apartments for students with dependent children available. **Activities:** Bands, campus ministries, choral groups, dance, drama, film society, international student organizations, literary magazine, music ensembles, radio station, student government, student newspaper, TV station, Newman Club, Amnesty International, public interest groups, African American student organization, Adelante Estudiantes, Native American student organization, Muslim student organization, Caribbean student organization.

Athletics. NCAA. **Intercollegiate:** Basketball, cross-country, diving, football (tackle) M, ice hockey M, lacrosse W, soccer, softball W, swimming, tennis W, track and field, volleyball W. **Intramural:** Basketball, football (tackle) M, racquetball, soccer, softball, volleyball. **Team name:** Bengals.

Student services. Adult student services, career counseling, student employment services, health services, minority student services, on-campus daycare, personal counseling, placement for graduates, veterans' counselor. **Physically disabled:** Services for visually, speech, hearing impaired.

Contact. E-mail: admissions@buffalostate.edu
Phone: (716) 878-4017 Fax: (716) 878-6100
Carmela Thompson, Director of Admissions, SUNY College at Buffalo, 1300 Elmwood Avenue, Moot Hall, Buffalo, NY 14222-1095

SUNY College at Cortland

Cortland, New York
www.cortland.edu

CB member
CB code: 2538

- Public 4-year liberal arts and teachers college
- Residential campus in large town
- 6,344 degree-seeking undergraduates: 2% part-time, 57% women, 3% African American, 1% Asian American, 8% Hispanic American, 1% international
- 882 degree-seeking graduate students
- 41% of applicants admitted
- SAT or ACT (ACT writing recommended), application essay required
- 67% graduate within 6 years

General. Founded in 1868. Regionally accredited. **Degrees:** 1,445 bachelor's awarded; master's offered. **ROTC:** Army, Air Force. **Location:** 35 miles from Syracuse, 20 miles from Ithaca. **Calendar:** Semester, limited summer session. **Full-time faculty:** 284 total; 75% have terminal degrees, 13% minority, 53% women. **Part-time faculty:** 338 total; 17% have terminal degrees, 4% minority, 51% women. **Class size:** 36% < 20, 53% 20-39, 5% 40-49, 5% 50-99, 1% >100. **Special facilities:** Raquette Lake outdoor education complex, education center (geology field station), Hoxie Gorge Nature Preserve, science museum, ethnographic teaching museum, center for speech and hearing disorders.

Freshman class profile. 12,348 applied, 5,057 admitted, 1,205 enrolled.

Mid 50% test scores			
SAT critical reading:	490-560	GPA 2.0-2.99:	13%
SAT math:	520-600	Rank in top quarter:	45%
ACT composite:	20-24	Rank in top tenth:	10%
GPA 3.75 or higher:	25%	Return as sophomores:	85%
GPA 3.50-3.74:	22%	Out-of-state:	5%
GPA 3.0-3.49:	39%	Live on campus:	98%

Basis for selection. Primary consideration given to course selection and performance. SAT/ACT scores, class rank, extracurricular activities, personal statement/essay, recommendations also enter into decision. Additional consideration for special talents, interview, alumni relation, geographical residence, minority status, volunteer work, work experience. Audition required for musical theater program; portfolio required for art studio program.

High school preparation. College-preparatory program required. Required and recommended units include English 4, mathematics 3-4, social studies 4, science 3-4 (laboratory 3) and foreign language 3-4. 2 units in math, science, or foreign language can be compensated for by 4+ units or advanced course work in another one of the three areas.

2011-2012 Annual costs. Tuition/fees: $6,574; $15,624 out-of-state. Room/board: $11,060. Books/supplies: $1,000. Personal expenses: $1,622.

2010-2011 Financial aid. Need-based: 1,106 full-time freshmen applied for aid; 720 were judged to have need; 685 of these received aid. Average need met was 70%. Average scholarship/grant was $4,872; average loan $3,619. 46% of total undergraduate aid awarded as scholarships/grants, 54% as loans/jobs. **Non-need-based:** Awarded to 1,192 full-time undergraduates, including 392 freshmen. Scholarships awarded for academics, art, leadership, minority status, music/drama, state residency.

Application procedures. Admission: Priority date 12/1; no deadline. $50 fee, may be waived for applicants with need. Admission notification on a rolling basis beginning on or about 1/2. Must reply by May 1 or within 4 week(s) if notified thereafter. **Financial aid:** Priority date 3/1; no closing date. FAFSA required. Applicants notified on a rolling basis starting 3/15; must reply by 5/1 or within 4 week(s) of notification.

Academics. Special study options: Combined bachelor's/graduate degree, cooperative education, cross-registration, distance learning, double major, dual enrollment of high school students, exchange student, honors, independent study, internships, liberal arts/career combination, student-designed major, study abroad, teacher certification program, Washington semester. **Credit/placement by examination:** AP, CLEP, IB, institutional tests. 30 credit hours maximum toward bachelor's degree. **Support services:** Learning center, pre-admission summer program, reduced course load, study skills assistance, tutoring, writing center.

Honors college/program. Open to entering fall freshmen and rising sophomores. Applicants should have exceptional academic record based on grades, standardized tests, course selection and extracurricular activities. To complete Honors Program, students must take at least 24 credits of honors-level courses, by taking combination of specially designated honors courses, contract courses and a course in which they complete the required honors thesis. Students also may use maximum of 2 Writing Intensive (WRIT) courses beyond the all-college requirements toward completion of the honors program.

Majors. Area/ethnic studies: African-American. **Biology:** General, biomedical sciences. **Communications:** Communications/speech/rhetoric, organizational. **Education:** Biology, chemistry, elementary, English, ESL, French, health, kindergarten/preschool, mathematics, physical, physics, science, social studies, Spanish, special ed, speech impaired. **English:** English lit. **Foreign languages:** French, Spanish. **Health services:** Athletic training, audiology/speech pathology, recreational therapy. **History:** General. **Human services:** Community org/advocacy. **Math:** General. **Parks/recreation:** General, exercise sciences, facilities management, sports admin. **Philosophy/religion:** Philosophy. **Physical sciences:** Chemistry, geology, physics. **Psychology:** General. **Social sciences:** Anthropology, criminology, economics, geography, international relations, political science, sociology. **Visual/performing arts:** Art, commercial/advertising art, music, studio arts.

Most popular majors. Communications/journalism 7%, education 41%, parks/recreation 16%, social sciences 13%.

Computing on campus. 838 workstations in dormitories, library, computer center, student center. Dormitories wired for high-speed internet access and linked to campus network. Commuter students can connect to campus network. Online course registration, online library, helpline, repair service, wireless network available.

Student life. Freshman orientation: Mandatory, $140 fee. Preregistration for classes offered. 1-1/2 day program during the summer includes overnight with faculty, staff and other students. **Policies:** All students must agree to abide by Code of Student Conduct. Freshmen, sophomores, transfers required to live on campus. **Housing:** Guaranteed on-campus for freshmen. Coed dorms, special housing for disabled, apartments, cooperative housing, wellness housing available. $150 deposit, deadline 5/1. Leadership house, quiet atmosphere, transfer floor available. **Activities:** Campus ministries, choral groups, dance, drama, film society, international student organizations, literary magazine, music ensembles, Model UN, musical theater, radio station, student government, student newspaper, symphony orchestra, TV station, Agape, Hillel, Black student union, Caribbean student association, La Familia Latina, Habitat for Humanity, AIDS Prevention & Awareness, Colleges Against Cancer, Cortland Against All Rape, New York public interest research group.

Athletics. NCAA. **Intercollegiate:** Baseball M, basketball, cross-country, diving, field hockey W, football (non-tackle) M, football (tackle) M, golf W, gymnastics W, ice hockey, lacrosse, racquetball, soccer, softball W, swimming, tennis W, track and field, volleyball W, wrestling M. **Intramural:** Archery, badminton, basketball, bowling, football (non-tackle), golf, racquetball, soccer, softball, table tennis, tennis, volleyball, water polo, weight lifting. **Team name:** Red Dragons.

Student services. Adult student services, alcohol/substance abuse counseling, chaplain/spiritual director, career counseling, student employment services, financial aid counseling, health services, on-campus daycare, personal counseling, placement for graduates, veterans' counselor. **Physically disabled:** Services for visually, speech, hearing impaired.

Contact. E-mail: admissions@cortland.edu
Phone: (607) 753-4712 Fax: (607) 753-5998
Mark Yacavone, Director of Admissions, SUNY College at Cortland, PO Box 2000, Cortland, NY 13045-0900

SUNY College at Fredonia

Fredonia, New York
www.fredonia.edu

CB member
CB code: 2539

- Public 4-year liberal arts college
- Residential campus in large town
- 5,347 degree-seeking undergraduates: 2% part-time, 56% women, 3% African American, 1% Asian American, 4% Hispanic American, 1% international
- 333 degree-seeking graduate students
- 53% of applicants admitted
- SAT or ACT (ACT writing optional), application essay required
- 63% graduate within 6 years

General. Founded in 1826. Regionally accredited. **Degrees:** 1,259 bachelor's awarded; master's offered. **ROTC:** Army. **Location:** 45 miles from Buffalo, 50 miles from Erie, Pennsylvania. **Calendar:** Semester, limited summer session. **Full-time faculty:** 253 total; 90% have terminal degrees, 13% minority, 46% women. **Part-time faculty:** 229 total; 14% have terminal degrees, 6% minority, 51% women. **Class size:** 59% < 20, 32% 20-39, 3% 40-49, 4% 50-99, 2% >100. **Special facilities:** Arts center, theater, communication lab, sound recording studios, education and local history museums.

Freshman class profile. 5,918 applied, 3,163 admitted, 1,112 enrolled.

Mid 50% test scores			
SAT critical reading:	480-590	Rank in top quarter:	41%
SAT math:	490-570	Rank in top tenth:	13%
ACT composite:	21-25	End year in good standing:	86%
GPA 3.75 or higher:	12%	Return as sophomores:	83%
GPA 3.50-3.74:	24%	Out-of-state:	3%
GPA 3.0-3.49:	46%	Live on campus:	95%
GPA 2.0-2.99:	18%	Fraternities:	1%
		Sororities:	1%

Basis for selection. Academic achievement, test results, and subjects taken given priority. Counselor recommendations, resume with supporting materials important when priority credentials marginal. Audition required for acting, music, musical performance, musical theater, production design. Portfolio required for all Visual Arts and New Media programs. **Home schooled:** State high school equivalency certificate required. Letter from superintendent of school district in which the student resides, attesting to the student's completion of program of home instruction meeting requirements of Section 100.10 of the Regulations of the Commission of Education.

High school preparation. College-preparatory program recommended. 20 units required; 25 recommended. Required and recommended units include English 4, mathematics 3-4, social studies 4, science 3-4 (laboratory 3-4), foreign language 3-4 and academic electives 1.

2011-2012 Annual costs. Tuition/fees: $6,688; $15,738 out-of-state. Room/board: $10,590. Books/supplies: $1,200. Personal expenses: $700.

2010-2011 Financial aid. Need-based: 974 full-time freshmen applied for aid; 723 were judged to have need; 708 of these received aid. Average need met was 64%. Average scholarship/grant was $4,541; average loan $54,767. 89% of total undergraduate aid awarded as scholarships/grants, 11% as loans/jobs. **Non-need-based:** Awarded to 928 full-time undergraduates, including 291 freshmen. Scholarships awarded for academics, alumni affiliation, art, minority status, music/drama, state residency.

Application procedures. Admission: No deadline. $50 fee, may be waived for applicants with need. Admission notification on a rolling basis beginning on or about 12/1. Must reply by May 1 or within 4 week(s) if

notified thereafter. **Financial aid:** No deadline. FAFSA required. Applicants notified on a rolling basis starting 3/1; must reply by 5/1.

Academics. B.S. in Business Administration contains Music Business track. Liberal Arts First Year program attracts students undecided about their major (typically 20% of incoming class). B.S. and B.A. programs in Interdisciplinary Studies house programs in International Studies, Environmental Sciences, Arts Administration, American Studies (pop culture), and Women's Studies. **Special study options:** Accelerated study, combined bachelor's/graduate degree, cooperative education, cross-registration, distance learning, double major, ESL, exchange student, honors, independent study, internships, student-designed major, study abroad, teacher certification program, urban semester, Washington semester, Albany semester, over 90 exchange programs within SUNY system, 13 universities in engineering. **Credit/placement by examination:** AP, CLEP, IB. 30 credit hours maximum toward bachelor's degree. **Support services:** Learning center, study skills assistance, tutoring, writing center.

Majors. Area/ethnic studies: American. **Biology:** General, biochemistry, molecular genetics. **Business:** Accounting, business admin, finance, management information systems, management science. **Communications:** Broadcast journalism, communications/speech/rhetoric, public relations. **Communications technology:** Recording arts. **Computer sciences:** General. **Conservation:** Environmental studies. **Education:** General, biology, chemistry, early childhood, earth science, elementary, English, foreign languages, French, mathematics, music, physics, secondary, social studies, Spanish, speech impaired. **English:** English lit. **Foreign languages:** French, Spanish. **Health services:** Audiology/speech pathology, clinical lab technology, communication disorders, music therapy. **History:** General. **Human services:** Social work. **Math:** General. **Parks/recreation:** Sports admin. **Philosophy/religion:** Philosophy. **Physical sciences:** Chemistry, geology, geophysics, physics. **Protective services:** Criminal justice. **Psychology:** General. **Social sciences:** Economics, political science, sociology. **Visual/performing arts:** Art, art history/conservation, ceramics, dance, dramatic, drawing, music, music management, music performance, music theory/composition, painting, sculpture, studio arts, theater design.

Most popular majors. Business/marketing 12%, communications/journalism 6%, education 20%, interdisciplinary studies 8%, psychology 6%, visual/performing arts 10%.

Computing on campus. 500 workstations in dormitories, library, computer center. Dormitories wired for high-speed internet access and linked to campus network. Commuter students can connect to campus network. Online course registration, online library, helpline, repair service, wireless network available.

Student life. Freshman orientation: Available, $140 fee. Preregistration for classes offered. 2-day program with students and parents held late June and early July; attendance strongly recommended. Fee includes cost of program, meals, housing, entertainment, orientation materials. **Housing:** Guaranteed on-campus for all undergraduates. Coed dorms, single-sex dorms, apartments, wellness housing available. $50 fully refundable deposit, deadline 5/1. **Activities:** Bands, campus ministries, choral groups, dance, drama, film society, international student organizations, literary magazine, music ensembles, musical theater, opera, radio station, student government, student newspaper, symphony orchestra, TV station, Newman Club, Black student union, Young Republicans, service fraternities and sororities, Jewish student union, Young Democrats, Native American Student Association, Latinos Unidos, Intervarsity Christian Fellowship, Strive Ministries, Inner Room, Alpha Phi Omega.

Athletics. NCAA. **Intercollegiate:** Baseball M, basketball, cheerleading M, cross-country, diving, football (tackle), ice hockey M, lacrosse W, soccer, softball W, swimming, tennis W, track and field, volleyball W, water polo. **Intramural:** Basketball, field hockey, handball, ice hockey, lacrosse M, racquetball, soccer, softball, tennis, volleyball, water polo. **Team name:** Blue Devils.

Student services. Alcohol/substance abuse counseling, chaplain/spiritual director, career counseling, services for economically disadvantaged, student employment services, financial aid counseling, health services, legal services, minority student services, on-campus daycare, personal counseling, placement for graduates, veterans' counselor. **Physically disabled:** Services for visually, speech, hearing impaired.

Contact. E-mail: admissions.office@fredonia.edu
Phone: (716) 673-3251 Toll-free number: (800) 252-1212
Fax: (716) 673-3249
Christopher Dearth, Director of Admissions, SUNY College at Fredonia, 178 Central Avenue, Fredonia, NY 14063-1136

SUNY College at Geneseo

Geneseo, New York
www.geneseo.edu

CB member
CB code: 2540

- Public 4-year liberal arts college
- Residential campus in small town

- 5,454 degree-seeking undergraduates: 2% part-time, 57% women, 2% African American, 6% Asian American, 5% Hispanic American, 4% international
- 188 degree-seeking graduate students
- 43% of applicants admitted
- SAT or ACT (ACT writing optional), application essay required
- 81% graduate within 6 years

General. Founded in 1871. Regionally accredited. **Degrees:** 1,303 bachelor's awarded; master's offered. **ROTC:** Army, Air Force. **Location:** 30 miles from Rochester. **Calendar:** Semester, limited summer session. **Full-time faculty:** 241 total; 88% have terminal degrees, 11% minority, 41% women. **Part-time faculty:** 111 total; 26% have terminal degrees, 7% minority, 53% women. **Class size:** 26% <20, 55% 20-39, 10% 40-49, 6% 50-99, 3% >100. **Special facilities:** Nuclear accelerator, planetarium, 4 theaters, ice arena, arboretum.

Freshman class profile. 9,569 applied, 4,136 admitted, 1,010 enrolled.

Mid 50% test scores			
SAT critical reading:	590-690	GPA 2.0-2.99:	4%
SAT math:	600-690	Rank in top quarter:	85%
ACT composite:	27-30	Rank in top tenth:	47%
GPA 3.75 or higher:	47%	Return as sophomores:	91%
GPA 3.50-3.74:	32%	Out-of-state:	2%
GPA 3.0-3.49:	17%	Live on campus:	99%
		International:	6%

Basis for selection. Rigor of high school preparation, high school GPA, class rank, test scores, school and community activities, special talent, leadership, personal essay important. Special consideration given to minority applicants, children and grandchildren of alumni. Audition required for dramatic arts, music programs; portfolio required for art programs. **Home schooled:** Statement describing home school structure and mission, transcript of courses and grades, state high school equivalency certificate, letter of recommendation (nonparent) required. Letter from high school official or home school agency indicating the student is meeting production requirements.

High school preparation. College-preparatory program recommended. 20 units recommended. Recommended units include English 4, mathematics 4, social studies 4, science 4 and foreign language 4. Music, art also recommended. 4 math required for computer science and business majors.

2011-2012 Annual costs. Tuition/fees: $6,733; $15,783 out-of-state. Room/board: $10,476. Books/supplies: $950. Personal expenses: $100.

2011-2012 Financial aid. **Need-based:** 826 full-time freshmen applied for aid; 418 were judged to have need; 382 of these received aid. Average need met was 62%. Average scholarship/grant was $4,372; average loan $3,250. 49% of total undergraduate aid awarded as scholarships/grants, 51% as loans/jobs. **Non-need-based:** Awarded to 1,463 full-time undergraduates, including 77 freshmen. Scholarships awarded for academics, art, leadership, minority status, music/drama, religious affiliation, ROTC, state residency.

Application procedures. **Admission:** Closing date 1/1 (postmark date). $50 fee, may be waived for applicants with need. Admission notification on a rolling basis beginning on or about 3/1. Must reply by 5/1. **Financial aid:** Closing date 2/15. FAFSA required. Applicants notified on a rolling basis starting 3/15; must reply by 5/1.

Academics. **Special study options:** Combined bachelor's/graduate degree, cross-registration, double major, dual enrollment of high school students, ESL, honors, independent study, internships, study abroad, teacher certification program, Washington semester. Albany semester, 3-2 engineering, 3-3 engineering, 4-1 MBA, 3-4 dentistry, 3-4 optometry, 3-4 osteopathic medicine, 3-2 or 3-1 nursing, 3-3 physical therapy, pre-med and pre-law advisory program. **Credit/placement by examination:** AP, CLEP, IB, SAT, ACT, institutional tests. 30 credit hours maximum toward bachelor's degree. **Support services:** Learning center, pre-admission summer program, reduced course load, study skills assistance, tutoring, writing center.

Majors. **Area/ethnic studies:** African-American, American. **Biology:** General, biochemistry, biophysics. **Business:** General, accounting, business admin. **Communications:** Communications/speech/rhetoric. **Education:** Biology, chemistry, early childhood, elementary, English, French, mathematics, physics, science, social studies, Spanish, special ed. **English:** English lit. **Foreign languages:** Comparative lit, French, Spanish. **History:** General. **Math:** General. **Philosophy/religion:** Philosophy. **Physical sciences:** Chemistry, geochemistry, geology, geophysics, physics. **Psychology:** General. **Social sciences:** Anthropology, economics, geography, international relations, political science, sociology. **Visual/performing arts:** Art history/conservation, dramatic, music performance.

Most popular majors. Biology 11%, business/marketing 13%, education 10%, English 6%, psychology 10%, social sciences 15%.

Computing on campus. PC or laptop required. 675 workstations in dormitories, library, computer center, student center. Dormitories wired for high-speed internet access and linked to campus network. Commuter students can connect to campus network. Online course registration, helpline, student web hosting, wireless network available.

Student life. **Freshman orientation:** Available, $145 fee. Preregistration for classes offered. 5 sessions, 2 days each, during June and July. **Housing:** Guaranteed on-campus for all undergraduates. Coed dorms, special housing for disabled, wellness housing available. $150 fully refundable deposit, deadline 5/1. Special interest housing available. Some fraternities/sororities have housing independent of college. **Activities:** Bands, campus ministries, choral groups, dance, drama, international student organizations, literary magazine, music ensembles, Model UN, musical theater, radio station, student government, student newspaper, symphony orchestra, TV station, 187 organizations and clubs, interfaith center.

Athletics. NCAA. **Intercollegiate:** Basketball, cross-country, diving, equestrian W, field hockey W, ice hockey M, lacrosse, soccer, softball W, swimming, tennis W, track and field, volleyball W. **Intramural:** Badminton, basketball, football (non-tackle), racquetball, skiing, soccer, softball, squash, table tennis, tennis, volleyball, water polo M. **Team name:** Blue Knights, Lady Knights.

Student services. Alcohol/substance abuse counseling, chaplain/spiritual director, career counseling, services for economically disadvantaged, student employment services, financial aid counseling, health services, legal services, minority student services, on-campus daycare, personal counseling, placement for graduates, veterans' counselor, women's services. **Physically disabled:** Services for visually, speech, hearing impaired.

Contact. E-mail: admissions@geneseo.edu
Phone: (585) 245-5571 Toll-free number: (866) 245-5211
Fax: (585) 245-5550
Kristine Shay, Director of Admissions, SUNY College at Geneseo, 1 College Circle, Geneseo, NY 14454-1401

SUNY College at New Paltz

New Paltz, New York
www.newpaltz.edu

CB member
CB code: 2541

- Public 4-year liberal arts college
- Residential campus in large town
- 6,559 degree-seeking undergraduates: 6% part-time, 62% women, 5% African American, 4% Asian American, 12% Hispanic American, 2% international
- 1,065 degree-seeking graduate students
- 40% of applicants admitted
- SAT or ACT with writing, application essay required
- 70% graduate within 6 years

General. Founded in 1828. Regionally accredited. More than 16 percent of undergraduates participate in international education each academic year. **Degrees:** 1,596 bachelor's awarded; master's offered. **Location:** 65 miles from Albany, 96 miles from New York City. **Calendar:** Semester, extensive summer session. **Special facilities:** 3 theaters, recital hall, speech and hearing clinical center, music therapy training center, observatory, planetarium, theater collection, electronic classrooms.

Freshman class profile. 14,161 applied, 5,708 admitted, 1,162 enrolled.

Mid 50% test scores			
SAT critical reading:	520-610	GPA 2.0-2.99:	9%
SAT math:	520-610	Rank in top quarter:	76%
SAT writing:	520-610	Rank in top tenth:	26%
GPA 3.75 or higher:	9%	Return as sophomores:	88%
GPA 3.50-3.74:	34%	Out-of-state:	1%
GPA 3.0-3.49:	48%	Live on campus:	96%

Basis for selection. Secondary school curriculum and achievement, standardized test scores most important. Applicants, especially academically marginal, encouraged to send personal statements regarding academic work, recommendations from academic teachers, and any other pertinent information. One letter of recommendation required; audition required for music, music therapy, theater arts programs; portfolio required for art education, scenography, studio art, and visual arts programs. **Home schooled:** Must submit all data as required by NYS Commissioner of Education's regulations (Section 100.10).

High school preparation. College-preparatory program required. 17 units required; 21 recommended. Required and recommended units include English 4, mathematics 3-4, social studies 4, history 1, science 3-4 (laboratory 2-4) and foreign language 2-4.

2011-2012 Annual costs. Tuition/fees: $6,458; $15,508 out-of-state. Room/board: $9,950. Books/supplies: $1,300. Personal expenses: $1,100.

Financial aid. All financial aid based on need.

Application procedures. Admission: Closing date 4/1 (receipt date). $50 fee, may be waived for applicants with need. Admission notification on a rolling basis beginning on or about 1/15. Must reply by May 1 or within 2 week(s) if notified thereafter. **Financial aid:** Priority date 3/15; no closing date. FAFSA required. Applicants notified on a rolling basis starting 4/1; must reply within 6 week(s) of notification.

Academics. Special study options: Accelerated study, combined bachelor's/graduate degree, cross-registration, distance learning, double major, dual enrollment of high school students, ESL, external degree, honors, independent study, internships, New York semester, student-designed major, study abroad, teacher certification program, United Nations semester. Student exchange programs in Australia, Brazil, Cuba, Czech Republic, Denmark, Ecuador, England, France, Greece, Ireland, Italy, Japan, The Netherlands, New Zealand, Spain, Uzbekistan, U.S. Virgin Islands and Zimbabwe. **Credit/placement by examination:** AP, CLEP, IB, SAT, institutional tests. 30 credit hours maximum toward bachelor's degree. **Support services:** Learning center, reduced course load, remedial instruction, study skills assistance, tutoring, writing center.

Majors. Area/ethnic studies: African-American, Asian, Latin American, women's. **Biology:** General. **Business:** General, accounting, business admin, finance, international. **Communications:** Communications/speech/rhetoric, digital media, journalism, public relations. **Computer sciences:** General. **Education:** Art, biology, chemistry, elementary, English, French, learning disabled, mathematics, physics, science, social studies, Spanish. **Engineering:** Computer, electrical. **English:** English lit. **Foreign languages:** French, German, Spanish. **History:** General. **Liberal arts:** Arts/sciences. **Math:** General. **Philosophy/religion:** Philosophy. **Physical sciences:** Chemistry, geochemistry, geology, physics. **Psychology:** General. **Social sciences:** Anthropology, economics, geography, international relations, political science, sociology. **Visual/performing arts:** General, art, art history/conservation, ceramics, commercial/advertising art, dramatic, metal/jewelry, music, painting, photography, printmaking, sculpture, studio arts.

Most popular majors. Business/marketing 14%, communications/journalism 9%, education 22%, psychology 6%, social sciences 11%, visual/performing arts 12%.

Computing on campus. 950 workstations in dormitories, library, computer center, student center. Dormitories wired for high-speed internet access and linked to campus network. Commuter students can connect to campus network. Online course registration, online library, helpline, student web hosting, wireless network available.

Student life. Freshman orientation: Available, $215 fee. Preregistration for classes offered. 3-day academic and transition program in the summer. **Policies:** Freshmen not permitted cars on campus. **Housing:** Guaranteed on-campus for freshmen. Coed dorms, single-sex dorms, special housing for disabled available. $100 fully refundable deposit, deadline 5/1. First-year initiative, honors, art program housing. **Activities:** Bands, campus ministries, choral groups, dance, drama, international student organizations, literary magazine, music ensembles, Model UN, musical theater, radio station, student government, student newspaper, symphony orchestra, TV station, Black Student Union, Queer Action Coalition, Asian Student Association, NYPIRG, Hillel, Muslim Student Association, Latina Unidas, Students for Sustainable Agriculture, Student Alliance for Social Service, Invisible Children Club.

Athletics. NCAA. **Intercollegiate:** Baseball M, basketball, cross-country, field hockey W, lacrosse W, soccer, softball W, swimming, tennis W, volleyball. **Intramural:** Badminton, basketball, field hockey, football (non-tackle), golf, handball, racquetball, soccer, softball, tennis, volleyball. **Team name:** Hawks.

Student services. Alcohol/substance abuse counseling, chaplain/spiritual director, career counseling, services for economically disadvantaged, student employment services, financial aid counseling, health services, legal services, minority student services, on-campus daycare, personal counseling, placement for graduates, veterans' counselor, women's services. **Physically disabled:** Services for visually, speech, hearing impaired.

Contact. E-mail: admissions@newpaltz.edu
Phone: (845) 257-3200 Toll-free number: (888) 639-7589
Fax: (845) 257-3209
Kimberly Strano, Director of Freshmen Admissions, SUNY College at New Paltz, 100 Hawk Drive, New Paltz, NY 12561-2443

SUNY College at Old Westbury
Old Westbury, New York
www.oldwestbury.edu

CB member
CB code: 2866

- Public 4-year business and liberal arts college
- Commuter campus in small city
- 4,112 degree-seeking undergraduates: 14% part-time, 58% women, 31% African American, 8% Asian American, 20% Hispanic American
- 228 degree-seeking graduate students
- 45% of applicants admitted
- SAT or ACT with writing required
- 35% graduate within 6 years; 58% enter graduate study

General. Founded in 1965. Regionally accredited. Curricular focus on interdisciplinary and multicultural academic programs. **Degrees:** 745 bachelor's awarded; master's offered. **ROTC:** Army, Air Force. **Location:** 25 miles from New York City. **Calendar:** Semester, extensive summer session. **Full-time faculty:** 143 total; 82% have terminal degrees, 37% minority, 53% women. **Part-time faculty:** 165 total; 22% have terminal degrees, 22% minority, 56% women. **Class size:** 23% < 20, 74% 20-39, 3% 40-49. **Special facilities:** Language lab, performing arts theater, recital hall, science laboratories, athletic center, writing center, math labs.

Freshman class profile. 3,914 applied, 1,755 admitted, 400 enrolled.

Mid 50% test scores			
SAT critical reading:	450-530	Rank in top quarter:	45%
SAT math:	460-540	Rank in top tenth:	12%
SAT writing:	430-510	Return as sophomores:	76%
ACT composite:	19-22	Out-of-state:	1%
GPA 3.75 or higher:	3%	Live on campus:	58%
GPA 3.50-3.74:	14%	International:	1%
GPA 3.0-3.49:	42%	Fraternities:	1%
GPA 2.0-2.99:	39%	Sororities:	1%

Basis for selection. High school GPA, SAT scores, letters of recommendation, interview, personal essay important. SAT Subject Tests recommended. Essay and interview recommended for academically weak students. **Home schooled:** Statement describing home school structure and mission required. Letter from superintendent of local school district verifying home schooling equivalent to high school curriculum required.

High school preparation. College-preparatory program recommended. 18 units required; 21 recommended. Required and recommended units include English 4, mathematics 3, social studies 4, science 3 (laboratory 2-3), foreign language 2-3, computer science 1 and academic electives 2-3. Health and physical education.

2011-2012 Annual costs. Tuition/fees: $6,324; $15,374 out-of-state. Room/board: $9,700. Books/supplies: $1,000. Personal expenses: $1,210.

2010-2011 Financial aid. Need-based: 345 full-time freshmen applied for aid; 342 were judged to have need; 276 of these received aid. Average need met was 56%. Average scholarship/grant was $7,763; average loan $3,517. 57% of total undergraduate aid awarded as scholarships/grants, 43% as loans/jobs. **Non-need-based:** Awarded to 89 full-time undergraduates, including 22 freshmen. Scholarships awarded for academics, alumni affiliation, state residency.

Application procedures. Admission: Priority date 12/1; no deadline. $50 fee, may be waived for applicants with need. Admission notification on a rolling basis beginning on or about 1/7. Must reply by May 1 or within 2 week(s) if notified thereafter. **Financial aid:** Priority date 4/1; no closing date. FAFSA, institutional form required. Applicants notified on a rolling basis starting 4/15; must reply within 2 week(s) of notification.

Academics. All freshmen enroll in First-Year Experience program. **Special study options:** Combined bachelor's/graduate degree, cross-registration, distance learning, double major, ESL, exchange student, honors, independent study, internships, liberal arts/career combination, study abroad, teacher certification program, Washington semester. Minority access to research centers, Minority biomedical research. **Credit/placement by examination:** AP, CLEP, IB, SAT, institutional tests. 30 credit hours maximum toward bachelor's degree. Each department has own policy for accepting credit by examination in fulfillment of departmental requirements. 8 credits awarded for minimum of 2 years of active duty in any branch of military service. Veterans may also apply for credit based on specific formal courses of instruction given by military services. **Support services:** Learning center, pre-admission summer program, reduced course load, remedial instruction, study skills assistance, tutoring, writing center.

Honors college/program. High school GPA 90 or above, SAT scores 1100 or higher. The Honors curriculum will be comprised of 24 credits: First-year Seminar; Gen Ed Linked Course; English Composition 2; Internship

or Study Abroad or Directed Research (Independent Study) or Civic Engagement Honors Course; Major Course Requirement with Research Component and Capstone Honors Course.

Majors. Area/ethnic studies: American. **Biology:** General, biochemistry. **Business:** Accounting, business admin, finance, labor relations, marketing. **Communications:** Communications/speech/rhetoric. **Computer sciences:** General, information systems. **Education:** Bilingual, biology, chemistry, elementary, mathematics, middle, science, secondary, social studies, Spanish, special ed. **English:** English lit. **Foreign languages:** Comparative lit, Spanish. **Liberal arts:** Arts/sciences, humanities. **Math:** General. **Philosophy/religion:** Philosophy. **Physical sciences:** Chemistry. **Psychology:** General. **Social sciences:** General, criminology, sociology. **Visual/performing arts:** General.

Most popular majors. Business/marketing 29%, communications/journalism 6%, education 16%, psychology 13%, social sciences 18%.

Computing on campus. 462 workstations in library, computer center, student center. Dormitories wired for high-speed internet access. Commuter students can connect to campus network. Online course registration, online library, helpline, wireless network available.

Student life. Freshman orientation: Mandatory, $150 fee. Preregistration for classes offered. Held prior to fall term for 2 days and 1 night; 1-day parent orientation. Three 1-day sessions held prior to spring term ($50). **Housing:** Guaranteed on-campus for all undergraduates. Coed dorms, wellness housing available. $50 fully refundable deposit, deadline 5/1. Honors wing available. **Activities:** Campus ministries, choral groups, dance, drama, film society, international student organizations, radio station, student government, student newspaper, women's center, Alianza Latina, African People's Organization, Big Brother/Big Sister club, Asian club, Access for All, Council for Unity, Shekinah Chorale.

Athletics. NCAA. **Intercollegiate:** Baseball M, basketball, cross-country, golf M, soccer, softball W, swimming, volleyball W. **Intramural:** Badminton, basketball, racquetball, soccer, softball W, squash, volleyball, weight lifting. **Team name:** Panthers.

Student services. Alcohol/substance abuse counseling, chaplain/spiritual director, career counseling, services for economically disadvantaged, student employment services, financial aid counseling, health services, on-campus daycare, personal counseling, women's services. **Physically disabled:** Services for visually, hearing impaired.

Contact. E-mail: enroll@oldwestbury.edu
Phone: (516) 876-3073 Fax: (516) 876-3307
Mary Marquez Bell, Vice President of Enrollment Services, SUNY College at Old Westbury, Box 307, Old Westbury, NY 11568-0307

SUNY College at Oneonta
Oneonta, New York
www.oneonta.edu/home/default.asp

CB member
CB code: 2542

- Public 4-year liberal arts college
- Residential campus in large town
- 5,808 degree-seeking undergraduates: 2% part-time, 59% women, 3% African American, 2% Asian American, 4% Hispanic American, 2% international
- 153 degree-seeking graduate students
- 43% of applicants admitted
- SAT or ACT (ACT writing optional), application essay required
- 67% graduate within 6 years

General. Founded in 1887. Regionally accredited. **Degrees:** 1,384 bachelor's awarded; master's offered. **Location:** 75 miles from Albany, 175 miles from New York City. **Calendar:** Semester, extensive summer session. **Full-time faculty:** 253 total; 86% have terminal degrees, 19% minority, 42% women. **Part-time faculty:** 230 total; 58% women. **Class size:** 39% < 20, 46% 20-39, 11% 40-49, 4% 50-99, less than 1% >100. **Special facilities:** Digital planetarium/theater, observatory, biological field station in Cooperstown, science discovery center, music recording studio with tunable walls, computer art lab, DNA computing and genomics lab, children's center, volunteer center.

Freshman class profile. 12,338 applied, 5,359 admitted, 1,164 enrolled.

Mid 50% test scores		Return as sophomores:	84%
SAT critical reading:	500-580	Out-of-state:	1%
SAT math:	520-600	Live on campus:	98%
ACT composite:	22-25	International:	1%

Basis for selection. School achievement record, curriculum, test scores most important. Personal experiences, motivations, awards, honors and recommendations considered. Students scoring below 420 on SAT Math or 450 on SAT Verbal must take placement tests. High school writing sample can be submitted in place of essay; interview recommended. **Home schooled:** Statement describing home school structure and mission, transcript of courses and grades, state high school equivalency certificate, interview, letter of recommendation (nonparent) required.

High school preparation. College-preparatory program required. 19 units required. Required and recommended units include English 4, mathematics 4, social studies 4, science 4 and foreign language 3-4.

2011-2012 Annual costs. Tuition/fees: $6,596; $15,646 out-of-state. Room/board: $9,720. Books/supplies: $1,200. Personal expenses: $1,100.

2011-2012 Financial aid. Need-based: 1,043 full-time freshmen applied for aid; 676 were judged to have need; 645 of these received aid. Average need met was 37%. Average scholarship/grant was $5,575; average loan $1,764. 57% of total undergraduate aid awarded as scholarships/grants, 43% as loans/jobs. **Non-need-based:** Awarded to 690 full-time undergraduates, including 162 freshmen. Scholarships awarded for academics, alumni affiliation, leadership, minority status, music/drama, state residency.

Application procedures. Admission: No deadline. $50 fee, may be waived for applicants with need. Admission notification on a rolling basis. Must reply by May 1 or within 4 week(s) if notified thereafter. **Financial aid:** Priority date 3/1; no closing date. FAFSA required. Applicants notified on a rolling basis starting 3/1; must reply by 5/1 or within 4 week(s) of notification.

Academics. Special study options: Combined bachelor's/graduate degree, cross-registration, distance learning, double major, ESL, honors, independent study, internships, liberal arts/career combination, New York semester, study abroad, teacher certification program, Washington semester. 3-1 program in fashion with Fashion Institute of Technology; 3-2 program in engineering with Alfred University, Clarkson University, Georgia Institute of Technology, Polytechnic Institute of New York, Rensselaer Polytechnic Institute, SUNY at Binghamton, SUNY Buffalo, Syracuse University; 2-2 program in forestry with SUNY College of Environmental Science and Forestry; 2-2 programs in physical therapy, medical technology, respiratory care, and cytotechnology with SUNY Upstate Medical University, combined bachelor's/graduate degree programs in accounting and management with SUNY Binghamton; 4-1 MBA program with Rochester Institute of Technology; 2-3 option in physical therapy with SUNY Upstate Medical University; 3-1 option in fashion marketing and 2-2 option in fashion design with American Intercontinental University in London. **Credit/placement by examination:** AP, CLEP, IB, SAT, ACT. 36 credit hours maximum toward bachelor's degree. **Support services:** Learning center, reduced course load, remedial instruction, study skills assistance, tutoring, writing center.

Majors. Area/ethnic studies: African-American, Chicano/Hispanic-American/Latino. **Biology:** General, biochemistry. **Business:** Accounting, fashion, managerial economics. **Communications:** Communications/speech/rhetoric, media studies. **Communications technology:** Animation/special effects. **Computer sciences:** General, computer graphics, computer science. **Conservation:** Environmental science. **Education:** Biology, chemistry, early childhood, elementary, English, family/consumer sciences, foreign languages, French, history, mathematics, multi-level teacher, physics, science, social science, Spanish. **English:** English lit, rhetoric/composition. **Foreign languages:** French, Spanish. **History:** General. **Math:** General, statistics. **Philosophy/religion:** Philosophy. **Physical sciences:** Atmospheric science, chemistry, geology, hydrology, physics. **Protective services:** Criminal justice. **Psychology:** General. **Social sciences:** Anthropology, economics, geography, political science, sociology. **Visual/performing arts:** Art history/conservation, digital arts, dramatic, multimedia, music, music management, studio arts. **Work/family studies:** General, child development, clothing/textiles, family studies, food/nutrition.

Most popular majors. Business/marketing 9%, communications/journalism 10%, education 21%, family/consumer sciences 8%, psychology 8%, visual/performing arts 16%.

Computing on campus. 700 workstations in dormitories, library, computer center, student center. Dormitories wired for high-speed internet access and linked to campus network. Commuter students can connect to campus network. Online course registration, online library, helpline, student web hosting, wireless network available.

Student life. Freshman orientation: Available, $100 fee. Preregistration for classes offered. Meet adviser, select courses, register for classes. **Housing:** Guaranteed on-campus for freshmen. Coed dorms, wellness housing available. $100 fully refundable deposit, deadline 5/1. Special interest housing options and apartment-style suites available within residence halls. **Activities:** Bands, campus ministries, choral groups, dance, drama, film society, international student organizations, literary magazine, music ensembles, Model UN, musical theater, opera, radio station, student government, student newspaper,

symphony orchestra, TV station, Campus Ambassadors, Newman club, Hillel, HOLA Hispanic/Latino organization, Indian cultural club, Muslim student association, Students of Color Coalition, international students organization, Democracy Matters, Center for Social Responsibility and Community.

Athletics. NCAA. **Intercollegiate:** Baseball M, basketball, cross-country, field hockey W, lacrosse, soccer, softball W, swimming, tennis, track and field, volleyball W, wrestling M. **Intramural:** Basketball, football (non-tackle) W, soccer, softball, volleyball. **Team name:** Red Dragons.

Student services. Adult student services, alcohol/substance abuse counseling, career counseling, services for economically disadvantaged, student employment services, financial aid counseling, health services, minority student services, on-campus daycare, personal counseling, placement for graduates, veterans' counselor, women's services. **Physically disabled:** Services for visually, speech, hearing impaired.

Contact. E-mail: admissions@oneonta.edu
Phone: (607) 436-2524 Toll-free number: (800) 786-9123
Fax: (607) 436-3074
Karen Brown, Director of Admissions, SUNY College at Oneonta, Admissions Office, 116 Alumni Hall, Oneonta, NY 13820-4016

SUNY College at Oswego
Oswego, New York
www.oswego.edu

CB member
CB code: 2543

> Public 4-year university
> Residential campus in large town
> 7,342 degree-seeking undergraduates: 5% part-time, 52% women, 5% African American, 2% Asian American, 6% Hispanic American, 1% international
> 671 degree-seeking graduate students
> 48% of applicants admitted
> SAT or ACT (ACT writing optional), application essay required
> 63% graduate within 6 years; 25% enter graduate study

General. Founded in 1861. Regionally accredited. **Degrees:** 1,533 bachelor's awarded; master's offered. **ROTC:** Army, Air Force. **Location:** 35 miles from Syracuse, 65 miles from Rochester. **Calendar:** Semester, limited summer session. **Full-time faculty:** 313 total; 88% have terminal degrees, 15% minority, 44% women. **Part-time faculty:** 249 total; 23% have terminal degrees, 6% minority, 52% women. **Class size:** 55% < 20, 31% 20-39, 8% 40-49, 4% 50-99, 2% >100. **Special facilities:** Weather facsimile machine, planetarium, cross-country ski facilities, advanced technology classrooms, biological field station.

Freshman class profile. 9,743 applied, 4,707 admitted, 1,347 enrolled.

Mid 50% test scores			
SAT critical reading:	530-600	Rank in top tenth:	16%
SAT math:	530-600	End year in good standing:	92%
ACT composite:	21-25	Return as sophomores:	79%
GPA 3.75 or higher:	26%	Out-of-state:	2%
GPA 3.50-3.74:	23%	Live on campus:	95%
GPA 3.0-3.49:	40%	International:	1%
GPA 2.0-2.99:	11%	Fraternities:	6%
Rank in top quarter:	55%	Sororities:	5%

Basis for selection. High school GPA and curriculum most important, followed by test scores, supplemental portion of application and letters of recommendation. Special talents considered. Applicants recommended to send both SAT and ACT; higher score accepted. Interview recommended for all; portfolio required for graphic design and fine arts (BFA). **Home schooled:** Proof of high school graduation or GED recognized by state of residency required. **Learning Disabled:** Advised to contact Office of Learning Services and/or Disability Services with copy of IEP if applicable.

High school preparation. College-preparatory program required. 18 units required; 20 recommended. Required and recommended units include English 4, mathematics 3-4, social studies 4, science 3-4 (laboratory 2-3) and foreign language 2-4. Combined minimum of 7 units of college prep math and science recommended.

2011-2012 Annual costs. Tuition/fees: $6,510; $15,560 out-of-state. Room/board: $12,310. Books/supplies: $800. Personal expenses: $800.

2011-2012 Financial aid. **Need-based:** Average need met was 80%. Average scholarship/grant was $6,524; average loan $3,846. 43% of total undergraduate aid awarded as scholarships/grants, 57% as loans/jobs. **Non-need-based:** Scholarships awarded for academics, state residency.

Application procedures. Admission: Priority date 1/15; no deadline. $50 fee, may be waived for applicants with need. Admission notification on a rolling basis beginning on or about 1/15. Must reply by May 1 or within 4 week(s) if notified thereafter. **Financial aid:** Priority date 3/1; no closing date. FAFSA required. Applicants notified on a rolling basis starting 3/1; must reply by 5/1 or within 3 week(s) of notification.

Academics. Special study options: Accelerated study, combined bachelor's/graduate degree, cooperative education, cross-registration, distance learning, double major, dual enrollment of high school students, ESL, exchange student, external degree, honors, independent study, internships, liberal arts/career combination, study abroad, teacher certification program, Washington semester. **Credit/placement by examination:** AP, CLEP, IB, SAT. 30 credit hours maximum toward bachelor's degree. **Support services:** Learning center, pre-admission summer program, reduced course load, remedial instruction, study skills assistance, tutoring, writing center.

Honors college/program. Approximately 80 freshmen enroll annually, distinct program of general education classes held in small class settings.

Majors. Area/ethnic studies: American, women's. **Biology:** General, zoology. **Business:** Accounting, business admin, finance, human resources, management science. **Communications:** Broadcast journalism, communications/speech/rhetoric, journalism, public relations. **Computer sciences:** Computer science, information systems. **Education:** Agricultural, biology, business, chemistry, elementary, English, French, German, health occupations, history, mathematics, physics, science, secondary, social studies, Spanish, technology/industrial arts, trade/industrial, voc/tech. **Engineering:** Software. **English:** English lit. **Foreign languages:** French, German, linguistics, Spanish. **Health services:** Medical radiologic technology/radiation therapy, perfusion technology, public health ed. **History:** General. **Math:** General, applied. **Philosophy/religion:** Philosophy. **Physical sciences:** Chemistry, geochemistry, geology, meteorology, physics. **Psychology:** General. **Social sciences:** Anthropology, econometrics, economics, political science, sociology. **Visual/performing arts:** Art, commercial/advertising art, dramatic, music. **Work/family studies:** Child development.

Most popular majors. Biology 6%, business/marketing 22%, communications/journalism 11%, education 23%, psychology 8%, visual/performing arts 7%.

Computing on campus. 900 workstations in dormitories, library, computer center, student center. Dormitories wired for high-speed internet access and linked to campus network. Commuter students can connect to campus network. Online course registration, online library, helpline, student web hosting, wireless network available.

Student life. Freshman orientation: Mandatory, $180 fee. Preregistration for classes offered. 2-day program for incoming students and families. **Housing:** Guaranteed on-campus for all undergraduates. Coed dorms, wellness housing available. $100 fully refundable deposit, deadline 5/1. Pets allowed in dorm rooms. Global living and learning center, suites for upperclassmen, nontraditional student housing, first-year experience residence hall for incoming freshmen only, housing for 21 and over single suites available. **Activities:** Bands, choral groups, dance, drama, film society, international student organizations, literary magazine, music ensembles, musical theater, radio station, student government, student newspaper, symphony orchestra, TV station, Christian, Jewish, Catholic, and Baptist groups, Black student union, Latin student union, Caribbean student association, international student association, Native American Heritage Association, Students Educating Everyone About Disabilities.

Athletics. NCAA. **Intercollegiate:** Baseball M, basketball, cross-country, diving, field hockey W, golf M, ice hockey, lacrosse, soccer, softball W, swimming, tennis, track and field, volleyball W, wrestling M. **Intramural:** Badminton, basketball, football (non-tackle), golf, skiing, soccer, softball, swimming, table tennis, tennis, triathlon, volleyball, water polo. **Team name:** Lakers.

Student services. Adult student services, alcohol/substance abuse counseling, career counseling, services for economically disadvantaged, student employment services, financial aid counseling, health services, minority student services, on-campus daycare, personal counseling, placement for graduates, veterans' counselor, women's services. **Physically disabled:** Services for visually, speech, hearing impaired.

Contact. E-mail: admiss@oswego.edu
Phone: (315) 312-2250 Fax: (315) 312-3260
Joseph Grant, Vice President for Student Affairs and Enrollment, SUNY College at Oswego, 229 Sheldon Hall, Oswego, NY 13126-3599

SUNY College at Plattsburgh

Plattsburgh, New York
www.plattsburgh.edu

CB member
CB code: 2544

- Public 4-year liberal arts and teachers college
- Residential campus in large town
- 5,733 degree-seeking undergraduates: 5% part-time, 55% women, 5% African American, 2% Asian American, 4% Hispanic American, 6% international
- 499 degree-seeking graduate students
- 48% of applicants admitted
- SAT or ACT (ACT writing optional), application essay required
- 59% graduate within 6 years

General. Founded in 1889. Regionally accredited. Residential satellite campus for biotechnology and environmental science majors. **Degrees:** 1,325 bachelor's awarded; master's offered. **ROTC:** Army. **Location:** 60 miles from Montreal, Canada, 30 miles from Burlington, Vermont. **Calendar:** Semester, extensive summer session. **Full-time faculty:** 283 total; 84% have terminal degrees, 12% minority, 45% women. **Part-time faculty:** 221 total; 23% have terminal degrees, 6% minority, 59% women. **Class size:** 41% < 20, 44% 20-39, 10% 40-49, 4% 50-99, less than 1% >100. **Special facilities:** Center for art, music, and theater; access to 8,000 acre wilderness and agricultural tract; planetarium; NMR spectrophotometer; computer-operated spectrophotometer; liquid scintillation counter; auditory research labs; speech and hearing clinic; Alzheimer's disease assistance center; program for children with Asperger's; literacy lab; traumatic brain injury lab; nursing skills lab with bedside computers and a high-fidelity simulator; student laboratory restaurant.

Freshman class profile. 7,368 applied, 3,541 admitted, 961 enrolled.

Mid 50% test scores			
SAT critical reading:	480-570	Rank in top quarter:	42%
SAT math:	500-580	Rank in top tenth:	14%
ACT composite:	21-25	Return as sophomores:	81%
GPA 3.75 or higher:	6%	Out-of-state:	4%
GPA 3.50-3.74:	18%	Live on campus:	93%
GPA 3.0-3.49:	52%	International:	4%
GPA 2.0-2.99:	24%		

Basis for selection. Curriculum, high school GPA, class rank, test scores most important. Trend of grades, school and community activities, personal interview, and recommendations also considered. Educational opportunity program for academically and financially disadvantaged students. Interview recommended; portfolio required for bachelor of fine arts programs. **Home schooled:** Letter of recommendation (nonparent) required. Letter from superintendent of the school district in which the student resides attesting to the completion of program of home instruction meeting the requirements of the state of residence.

High school preparation. College-preparatory program required. 14 units required; 21 recommended. Required and recommended units include English 4, mathematics 3-4, social studies 3, history 1, science 3-4, foreign language 3 and academic electives 2.

2011-2012 Annual costs. Tuition/fees: $6,482; $15,532 out-of-state. Room/board: $9,750.

2010-2011 Financial aid. Need-based: 860 full-time freshmen applied for aid; 633 were judged to have need; 626 of these received aid. Average need met was 91%. Average scholarship/grant was $6,408; average loan $5,893. 44% of total undergraduate aid awarded as scholarships/grants, 56% as loans/jobs. **Non-need-based:** Awarded to 2,269 full-time undergraduates, including 486 freshmen. Scholarships awarded for academics, alumni affiliation, art, leadership, minority status, music/drama, ROTC, state residency.

Application procedures. Admission: Priority date 12/1; no deadline. $50 fee, may be waived for applicants with need. Admission notification on a rolling basis beginning on or about 1/15. Must reply by May 1 or within 4 week(s) if notified thereafter. **Financial aid:** Priority date 2/15; no closing date. FAFSA required. Applicants notified on a rolling basis starting 3/1; must reply by 5/1.

Academics. Credit for military experience, pass/fail option. **Special study options:** Combined bachelor's/graduate degree, cooperative education, cross-registration, distance learning, double major, dual enrollment of high school students, ESL, exchange student, honors, independent study, internships, liberal arts/career combination, student-designed major, study abroad, teacher certification program, Washington semester. Semester and academic year programs in Canada, study opportunities abroad in Australia, Canada, Chile, China, England, Italy, Mexico, Spain, and Switzerland. Students may also apply to more than 400 programs in more than 60 countries through other SUNY institutions. 3-4 BA/OD with SUNY College of Optometry, 4-1 BS/MBA with Clarkson University. **Credit/placement by examination:** AP, CLEP, IB, SAT, ACT, institutional tests. 30 credit hours maximum toward

bachelor's degree. **Support services:** Learning center, pre-admission summer program, reduced course load, remedial instruction, study skills assistance, tutoring, writing center.

Majors. Area/ethnic studies: Latin American, women's. **Biology:** General, biochemistry, cell/histology, ecology. **Business:** General, accounting, business admin, entrepreneurial studies, finance, hotel/motel admin, international, management information systems, marketing, restaurant/food services, tourism/travel. **Communications:** Journalism, media studies, organizational, radio/TV. **Computer sciences:** General. **Conservation:** General, environmental science. **Education:** Biology, chemistry, computer, early childhood, elementary, English, foreign languages, French, history, mathematics, multi-level teacher, physics, science, social science, social studies, Spanish, special ed. **English:** English lit, rhetoric/composition. **Foreign languages:** French, Spanish. **Health services:** Audiology/speech pathology, clinical lab science, cytotechnology, nursing (RN). **History:** General. **Human services:** Social work. **Liberal arts:** Arts/sciences. **Math:** General. **Parks/recreation:** General. **Philosophy/religion:** Philosophy. **Physical sciences:** Chemistry, geology, physics. **Protective services:** Criminal justice. **Psychology:** General. **Social sciences:** Anthropology, economics, geography, political science, sociology. **Visual/performing arts:** General, art, dramatic, music. **Work/family studies:** Family studies, food/nutrition.

Most popular majors. Business/marketing 27%, communications/journalism 8%, education 11%, psychology 8%, security/protective services 7%, social sciences 6%.

Computing on campus. 566 workstations in dormitories, library, computer center, student center. Dormitories wired for high-speed internet access and linked to campus network. Commuter students can connect to campus network. Online course registration, online library, helpline, repair service, student web hosting, wireless network available.

Student life. Freshman orientation: Available, $125 fee. Preregistration for classes offered. 2-night stay with meals included; simultaneous program for parents and siblings. **Housing:** Guaranteed on-campus for all undergraduates. Coed dorms, special housing for disabled, wellness housing available. $100 fully refundable deposit, deadline 5/1. Living/learning communities available. **Activities:** Bands, campus ministries, choral groups, dance, drama, film society, international student organizations, literary magazine, music ensembles, Model UN, musical theater, radio station, student government, student newspaper, TV station, Akeba, El Pueblo, environmental action committee, Hillel, Inter-Varsity Christian Fellowship, Newman association, Points of View, College Democrats, College Republicans, Feurza.

Athletics. NCAA. **Intercollegiate:** Baseball M, basketball, cross-country, ice hockey, lacrosse M, soccer, softball W, tennis W, track and field, volleyball W. **Intramural:** Basketball, field hockey, football (non-tackle) M, racquetball, soccer, softball, tennis, volleyball. **Team name:** Cardinals.

Student services. Adult student services, alcohol/substance abuse counseling, chaplain/spiritual director, career counseling, services for economically disadvantaged, student employment services, financial aid counseling, health services, legal services, minority student services, on-campus daycare, personal counseling, placement for graduates, veterans' counselor, women's services. **Physically disabled:** Services for visually, speech, hearing impaired.

Contact. E-mail: admissions@plattsburgh.edu
Phone: (518) 564-2040 Toll-free number: (888) 673-0012
Fax: (518) 564-2045
Richard Higgins, Associate Vice President for Enrollment Management, SUNY College at Plattsburgh, Kehoe Administration Building, Plattsburgh, NY 12901

SUNY College at Potsdam

Potsdam, New York
www.potsdam.edu

CB member
CB code: 2545

- Public 4-year liberal arts and teachers college
- Residential campus in large town
- 3,918 degree-seeking undergraduates: 2% part-time, 58% women, 4% African American, 1% Asian American, 6% Hispanic American, 1% Native American, 2% international
- 416 degree-seeking graduate students
- 63% of applicants admitted
- 51% graduate within 6 years; 35% enter graduate study

General. Founded in 1816. Regionally accredited. **Degrees:** 693 bachelor's awarded; master's offered. **ROTC:** Army, Air Force. **Location:** 80 miles from Montreal, Canada, 140 miles from Syracuse. **Calendar:** Semester, limited summer session. **Full-time faculty:** 258 total; 73% have terminal degrees, 10% minority, 45% women. **Part-time faculty:** 105 total; 13% have

terminal degrees, 3% minority, 62% women. **Class size:** 62% < 20, 33% 20-39, 2% 40-49, 2% 50-99, less than 1% >100. **Special facilities:** Electronic music and recording studios, performance halls, planetarium, seismographic laboratory, anthropology museum, biology museum, fine arts studios, art museum, rock climbing wall.

Freshman class profile. 5,099 applied, 3,237 admitted, 897 enrolled.

GPA 3.75 or higher:	17%	Return as sophomores:	80%
GPA 3.50-3.74:	14%	Live on campus:	94%
GPA 3.0-3.49:	35%	International:	1%
GPA 2.0-2.99:	33%	Fraternities:	2%
Rank in top quarter:	30%	Sororities:	5%
Rank in top tenth:	9%		

Basis for selection. Admissions decisions based on secondary school record and standardized test scores. Class rank, talent, ability, activities and community service also important. Most applicants will not need to submit a standardized test score for admission consideration. Essays and interviews required for some. Auditions required for music majors. Auditions encouraged for dance and theater majors. Portfolios encouraged for art majors. **Home schooled:** Need either a letter of recommendation from local school superintendent that the curriculum is equal to high school diploma, or GED.

High school preparation. College-preparatory program recommended. 14 units required; 19 recommended. Required and recommended units include English 4, mathematics 2-3, social studies 4, science 2-3 (laboratory 1), foreign language 3 and visual/performing arts 1.

2011-2012 Annual costs. Tuition/fees: $6,506; $15,556 out-of-state. Room/board: $10,270. Books/supplies: $1,200. Personal expenses: $1,100.

2011-2012 Financial aid. Need-based: 846 full-time freshmen applied for aid; 653 were judged to have need; 645 of these received aid. Average need met was 88%. Average scholarship/grant was $7,944; average loan $3,920. 55% of total undergraduate aid awarded as scholarships/grants, 45% as loans/jobs. **Non-need-based:** Awarded to 1,106 full-time undergraduates, including 304 freshmen. Scholarships awarded for academics, art, leadership, minority status, music/drama, ROTC. **Additional information:** Apply early to access limited, need-based awards.

Application procedures. Admission: No deadline. $50 fee, may be waived for applicants with need. Admission notification on a rolling basis beginning on or about 10/1. Must reply by May 1 for guaranteed enrollment. **Financial aid:** Priority date 3/1, closing date 5/1. FAFSA required. Applicants notified on a rolling basis starting 2/1; must reply by 5/1 or within 4 week(s) of notification.

Academics. Programs available that incorporate cross-registering with other local colleges. **Special study options:** Combined bachelor's/graduate degree, cross-registration, distance learning, double major, dual enrollment of high school students, exchange student, honors, independent study, internships, liberal arts/career combination, student-designed major, study abroad, teacher certification program. First-year students may enroll in interdisciplinary program to study art, literature, science, and sociology of the Adirondacks. Extension offers undergraduate and graduate courses with emphasis on teacher education. Combined degree options in engineering with Clarkson University and SUNY Binghamton; accounting, engineering or management with SUNY Institute of Technology. **Credit/placement by examination:** AP, CLEP, IB. Credit awarded for International Baccalaureate on course-by-course evaluation. **Support services:** Learning center, pre-admission summer program, reduced course load, study skills assistance, tutoring, writing center.

Majors. Area/ethnic studies: Women's. **Biology:** General, biochemistry. **Business:** Business admin, labor relations, managerial economics. **Computer sciences:** General, computer science. **Conservation:** Environmental studies. **Education:** Biology, chemistry, early childhood, earth science, elementary, English, foreign languages, French, kindergarten/preschool, mathematics, music, physical, physics, Spanish. **English:** Creative writing, English lit, rhetoric/composition. **Foreign languages:** French, Spanish. **Health services:** Public health ed. **History:** General. **Liberal arts:** Arts/sciences, humanities. **Math:** General. **Philosophy/religion:** Philosophy. **Physical sciences:** Chemistry, geology, physics. **Protective services:** Criminal justice. **Psychology:** General. **Social sciences:** Anthropology, archaeology, economics, political science, sociology. **Visual/performing arts:** General, art, art history/conservation, dramatic, music, music management, music performance, music theory/composition.

Most popular majors. Biology 6%, business/marketing 10%, computer/information sciences 6%, education 23%, English 12%, history 6%, psychology 7%, social sciences 11%, visual/performing arts 11%.

Computing on campus. 730 workstations in dormitories, library, computer center, student center. Dormitories wired for high-speed internet access and linked to campus network. Commuter students can connect to campus network. Online course registration, online library, helpline, student web hosting, wireless network available.

Student life. Freshman orientation: Available, $195 fee. Preregistration for classes offered. 2-day summer orientation, available on-campus and online. Fee for spring term orientation is $35. International freshmen fee is $145. **Policies:** Academic honor code outlines expectations for academic honesty and integrity; code of student rights, responsibilities, and conduct can be found in student handbook. **Housing:** Guaranteed on-campus for all undergraduates. Coed dorms, special housing for disabled, apartments, wellness housing available. $50 fully refundable deposit, deadline 5/1. First-year experience, quiet study, international house, transfer student housing, sustainability housing. **Activities:** Bands, campus ministries, choral groups, dance, drama, international student organizations, literary magazine, music ensembles, musical theater, opera, radio station, student government, student newspaper, symphony orchestra, inter-varsity Christian fellowship, black student alliance, Potsdam Association of Native Americans, Caribbean Latin American student society, political student association, Circle K, lesbian/gay/bisexual and transgendered association, students for peaceful alternatives, philosophy forum, pagan studies, College Republicans.

Athletics. NCAA. **Intercollegiate:** Basketball, cross-country, diving M, equestrian W, golf M, ice hockey, lacrosse, soccer, softball W, swimming, volleyball W. **Intramural:** Basketball, football (non-tackle), racquetball, soccer, softball, volleyball. **Team name:** Bears.

Student services. Adult student services, alcohol/substance abuse counseling, chaplain/spiritual director, career counseling, services for economically disadvantaged, student employment services, financial aid counseling, health services, legal services, minority student services, on-campus daycare, personal counseling, placement for graduates, veterans' counselor, women's services. **Physically disabled:** Services for visually, speech, hearing impaired.

Contact. E-mail: admissions@potsdam.edu
Phone: (315) 267-2180 Toll-free number: (877) 768-7326
Fax: (315) 267-2163
Thomas Nesbitt, Director of Admissions, SUNY College at Potsdam, 44 Pierrepont Avenue, Potsdam, NY 13676

SUNY College at Purchase
Purchase, New York
www.purchase.edu   CB code: 2878

- Public 4-year university
- Residential campus in large town
- 3,884 degree-seeking undergraduates: 6% part-time, 56% women, 6% African American, 2% Asian American, 14% Hispanic American, 2% international
- 120 degree-seeking graduate students
- 34% of applicants admitted
- SAT or ACT (ACT writing optional) required
- 57% graduate within 6 years

General. Founded in 1967. Regionally accredited. **Degrees:** 944 bachelor's awarded; master's offered. **Location:** 25 miles from New York City, 5 miles from White Plains. **Calendar:** Semester, extensive summer session. **Full-time faculty:** 166 total; 48% have terminal degrees, 15% minority, 55% women. **Part-time faculty:** 222 total; 21% have terminal degrees, 12% minority, 43% women. **Class size:** 72% < 20, 24% 20-39, 1% 40-49, 2% 50-99, less than 1% >100. **Special facilities:** Performing arts center, children's center, electron microscope, Neuberger Museum of Art.

Freshman class profile. 8,949 applied, 3,011 admitted, 797 enrolled.

Mid 50% test scores			
SAT critical reading:	500-620	GPA 2.0-2.99:	32%
SAT math:	480-580	Rank in top quarter:	36%
SAT writing:	500-600	Rank in top tenth:	11%
ACT composite:	21-26	Return as sophomores:	81%
GPA 3.75 or higher:	10%	Out-of-state:	21%
GPA 3.50-3.74:	15%	Live on campus:	90%
GPA 3.0-3.49:	43%	International:	3%

Basis for selection. For liberal arts and sciences programs, high school achievement record or test scores important. For conservatory, performing arts and visual arts applicants, audition, interview, or portfolio most important. SAT recommended. Interview and essay required for film, theater design/technology programs; audition required for acting, dance, music programs; portfolio required for visual arts program.

High school preparation. College-preparatory program recommended. 20 units recommended. Recommended units include English 4, mathematics 4, social studies 4, science 3, foreign language 3 and computer science 2.

2011-2012 Annual costs. Tuition/fees: $6,839; $15,889 out-of-state. Room/board: $11,058. Books/supplies: $1,138. Personal expenses: $1,990.

2011-2012 Financial aid. Need-based: 664 full-time freshmen applied for aid; 492 were judged to have need; 492 of these received aid. Average need met was 50%. Average scholarship/grant was $5,843; average loan $3,726. 41% of total undergraduate aid awarded as scholarships/grants, 59% as loans/jobs. **Non-need-based:** Scholarships awarded for academics, art, minority status, music/drama. **Additional information:** All applicants automatically considered for scholarship upon review of applications, essays, auditions, and/or portfolio.

Application procedures. Admission: Priority date 3/1; deadline 7/15 (postmark date). $40 fee, may be waived for applicants with need. Admission notification by 5/1. Must reply by May 1 or within 2 week(s) if notified thereafter. Application deadlines vary by program. Priority date of 1/30 for students applying to acting, design/technology, and film programs. **Financial aid:** Priority date 2/1; no closing date. FAFSA required. Applicants notified on a rolling basis starting 3/1; must reply within 2 week(s) of notification.

Academics. Special study options: Cross-registration, distance learning, double major, ESL, independent study, internships, liberal arts/career combination, student-designed major, study abroad. Conservatory master-apprentice training in dance, music, acting, film, theater design technology, visual arts. **Credit/placement by examination:** AP, CLEP, institutional tests. 30 credit hours maximum toward bachelor's degree. **Support services:** Learning center, pre-admission summer program, remedial instruction, tutoring, writing center.

Majors. Area/ethnic studies: Women's. **Biology:** General, ecology. **Communications:** Journalism, media studies. **Conservation:** Environmental science, environmental studies. **English:** American lit, British lit, creative writing. **Foreign languages:** General. **History:** General. **Liberal arts:** Arts/sciences. **Math:** General. **Philosophy/religion:** Philosophy. **Physical sciences:** Chemistry. **Psychology:** General. **Social sciences:** Anthropology, economics, political science, sociology. **Visual/performing arts:** Art history/conservation, cinematography, commercial/advertising art, dance, dramatic, drawing, graphic design, music performance, music theory/composition, painting, photography, play/screenwriting, printmaking, sculpture, studio arts management, theater design, theater history.

Most popular majors. Communications/journalism 6%, English 6%, liberal arts 22%, social sciences 11%, visual/performing arts 37%.

Computing on campus. 600 workstations in dormitories, library, computer center. Dormitories wired for high-speed internet access and linked to campus network. Commuter students can connect to campus network. Online course registration, online library, helpline, repair service, wireless network available.

Student life. Freshman orientation: Mandatory, $120 fee. Preregistration for classes offered. **Housing:** Coed dorms, special housing for disabled, apartments, wellness housing available. $100 fully refundable deposit. Freshman residence, non-traditional age hall, presidential scholars, learning community. **Activities:** Jazz band, choral groups, dance, drama, film society, international student organizations, literary magazine, music ensembles, musical theater, radio station, student government, student newspaper, TV station, philosophy club, chemistry society, literature club, dance club, ski club, Purchase Experimental Theatre, Organization of African People in America (OAPIA), Latinos Unidos, Gay/Lesbian/Bisexual and Transgendered Union.

Athletics. NCAA. **Intercollegiate:** Baseball M, basketball, cross-country, golf M, soccer, softball W, swimming W, tennis, volleyball. **Intramural:** Badminton, basketball, bowling, cross-country, fencing, golf, racquetball, skiing, soccer, softball, squash, swimming, table tennis, tennis, volleyball, water polo, weight lifting. **Team name:** Panthers.

Student services. Adult student services, alcohol/substance abuse counseling, career counseling, services for economically disadvantaged, student employment services, financial aid counseling, health services, on-campus daycare, personal counseling, placement for graduates, veterans' counselor, women's services. **Physically disabled:** Services for visually, hearing impaired.

Contact. E-mail: admissions@purchase.edu
Phone: (914) 251-6300 Fax: (914) 251-6314
Stephanie McCaine, Admissions Director, SUNY College at Purchase, 735 Anderson Hill Road, Purchase, NY 10577-1400

SUNY College of Environmental Science and Forestry

Syracuse, New York
www.esf.edu

CB member
CB code: 2530

- Public 4-year university
- Residential campus in small city

- 1,652 degree-seeking undergraduates: 1% part-time, 44% women, 2% African American, 4% Asian American, 3% Hispanic American, 2% international
- 501 degree-seeking graduate students
- 47% of applicants admitted
- SAT or ACT (ACT writing optional), application essay required
- 66% graduate within 6 years; 20% enter graduate study

General. Founded in 1911. Regionally accredited. Doctoral granting; focused on the science, engineering, design and management of the environment and natural resources. **Degrees:** 349 bachelor's, 44 associate awarded; master's, doctoral offered. **ROTC:** Army, Air Force. **Location:** 1 mile from downtown. **Calendar:** Semester, limited summer session. **Full-time faculty:** 145 total; 94% have terminal degrees, 13% minority, 29% women. **Part-time faculty:** 32 total; 38% have terminal degrees, 6% minority, 34% women. **Class size:** 68% < 20, 16% 20-39, 8% 40-49, 5% 50-99, 3% >100. **Special facilities:** Six regional campuses and field stations used for field study and research, 25,000-acre multi-campus forest system, ecological center, Roosevelt Wildlife Museum, semi-commercial paper mill.

Freshman class profile. 1,865 applied, 872 admitted, 287 enrolled.

Mid 50% test scores			
SAT critical reading:	540-640	Rank in top tenth:	37%
SAT math:	560-630	End year in good standing:	83%
ACT composite:	24-28	Return as sophomores:	82%
Rank in top quarter:	73%	Out-of-state:	25%
		Live on campus:	95%

Basis for selection. High school record most important, test scores, essay, and recommendations also important. Applicant should have strong college preparatory program with focus on mathematics and science for most programs and design background preferred for Landscape Architecture. Interview or participation in informational program recommended for all; portfolio required for some landscape architecture applicants. **Home schooled:** Statement describing home school structure and mission, transcript of courses and grades, state high school equivalency certificate required. If no superintendent's statement provided, student must have GED to enroll.

High school preparation. College-preparatory program required. 14 units required; 19 recommended. Required and recommended units include English 4, mathematics 3-4, social studies 3, history 1, science 3-4 (laboratory 3-4) and foreign language 3.

2011-2012 Annual costs. Tuition/fees: $6,241; $15,291 out-of-state. Room/board: $14,032. Books/supplies: $1,200. Personal expenses: $450.

2011-2012 Financial aid. Need-based: 260 full-time freshmen applied for aid; 201 were judged to have need; 201 of these received aid. Average need met was 91%. Average scholarship/grant was $5,000; average loan $4,750. 52% of total undergraduate aid awarded as scholarships/grants, 48% as loans/jobs. **Non-need-based:** Awarded to 550 full-time undergraduates, including 165 freshmen. Scholarships awarded for academics, alumni affiliation, leadership, minority status, ROTC, state residency.

Application procedures. Admission: Priority date 1/15; no deadline. $50 fee, may be waived for applicants with need. Application must be submitted online. Admission notification on a rolling basis beginning on or about 2/1. Must reply by May 1 or within 4 week(s) if notified thereafter. Applications submitted after the 1/15 priority date will be considered on a space-available basis. **Financial aid:** Priority date 3/1; no closing date. FAFSA required. Applicants notified on a rolling basis starting 3/15; must reply within 2 week(s) of notification.

Academics. Special study options: Combined bachelor's/graduate degree, cooperative education, cross-registration, double major, honors, independent study, internships, study abroad, teacher certification program. Associate degree programs in forest technology, land surveying technology and environmental and natural resources conservation offered through The Ranger School in Adirondack Mountains. **Credit/placement by examination:** AP, CLEP, IB, institutional tests. **Support services:** Learning center, pre-admission summer program, reduced course load, study skills assistance, tutoring, writing center.

Majors. Architecture: Landscape. **Biology:** Aquatic, biochemistry, biotechnology, conservation, environmental, wildlife. **Business:** Construction management. **Conservation:** General, environmental science, environmental studies, fisheries, forest management, forest resources, forest sciences, forestry, management/policy, wildlife/wilderness, wood science. **Education:** Biology, chemistry, science. **Engineering:** General, environmental. **General:** Animal sciences, plant protection. **Physical sciences:** Chemistry.

Most popular majors. Architecture 10%, biology 43%, engineering/engineering technologies 15%, natural resources/environmental science 31%.

Computing on campus. 250 workstations in dormitories, library, computer center, student center. Dormitories wired for high-speed internet access

and linked to campus network. Commuter students can connect to campus network. Online course registration, online library, helpline, repair service, student web hosting, wireless network available.

Student life. Freshman orientation: Mandatory, $60 fee. Preregistration for classes offered. 4-day program prior to start of fall classes. **Policies:** First-year students required to live on campus or in Syracuse University housing unless they live within commuting distance. Freshmen not permitted cars on campus. **Housing:** Guaranteed on-campus for freshmen. Coed dorms, special housing for disabled, apartments, fraternity/sorority housing, wellness housing available. $400 nonrefundable deposit, deadline 5/1. **Activities:** Bands, campus ministries, choral groups, dance, drama, film society, international student organizations, literary magazine, music ensembles, musical theater, radio station, student government, student newspaper, symphony orchestra, TV station, Undergraduate Student Association, Alpha Xi Sigma honor society, Wildlife Society, Multicultural student organization, Environmental Action Coalition, Woodsmen's Team, Creative Minds club, Green Campus Initiative, Habitat for Humanity, Alphi Chi Omega Service Fraternity.

Athletics. USCAA. **Intercollegiate:** Basketball M, cross-country, golf, soccer. **Intramural:** Basketball, football (non-tackle), racquetball, soccer, softball, tennis. **Team name:** The Mighty Oaks.

Student services. Alcohol/substance abuse counseling, chaplain/spiritual director, career counseling, services for economically disadvantaged, student employment services, financial aid counseling, health services, legal services, minority student services, on-campus daycare, personal counseling, placement for graduates, veterans' counselor, women's services. **Physically disabled:** Services for visually, speech, hearing impaired.

Contact. E-mail: esfinfo@esf.edu
Phone: (315) 470-6600 Fax: (315) 470-6933
Susan Sanford, Director of Admissions & Inter-Institutional Relations, SUNY College of Environmental Science and Forestry, 106 Bray Hall, Syracuse, NY 13210

SUNY Downstate Medical Center
Brooklyn, New York
www.downstate.edu
CB code: 2534

◗ Public two-year upper-division health science and nursing college
◗ Commuter campus in very large city
◗ Application essay, interview required

General. Founded in 1858. Regionally accredited. **Degrees:** 152 bachelor's awarded; master's, professional, doctoral offered. **Articulation:** Agreements with St. Francis College, CUNY Medgar Evers College. **Location:** 4 miles from downtown Brooklyn, 6 miles from downtown Manhattan. **Calendar:** Semester, limited summer session. **Full-time faculty:** 720 total. **Part-time faculty:** 160 total.

Student profile. 336 degree-seeking undergraduates. 100% entered as juniors. 80% transferred from two-year, 20% transferred from four-year institutions.

Out-of-state:	4%	25 or older:	72%

Basis for selection. College transcript, application essay, interview required. College of Medicine applicants apply through AMCAS: $65 application fee. Rolling admissions for College of Nursing and College of Health-Related Professions: $30 fee. Each program has different admission requirements. RN/BS program requires New York State Registered Nurse license. Prerequisite courses vary by program. Transfer accepted as juniors.

2011-2012 Annual costs. Tuition/fees: $5,820; $14,870 out-of-state. Room only: $4,750. Books/supplies: $1,484.

Application procedures. Admission: Deadline 4/1. $40 fee, may be waived for applicants with need. Application must be submitted on paper. Closing dates for applications differ, depending on program, and begin December 15. **Financial aid:** FAFSA required.

Academics. Special study options: Accelerated study, combined bachelor's/graduate degree, liberal arts/career combination. **Credit/placement by examination:** AP, CLEP.

Majors. Health services: Nursing (RN), physician assistant, sonography.

Computing on campus. Dormitories wired for high-speed internet access. Online library available.

Student life. Housing: Coed dorms available. **Activities:** Student government, student newspaper.

Athletics. Intramural: Basketball M.

Student services. Health services.

Contact. E-mail: admissions@downstate.edu
Phone: (718) 270-2446 Fax: (718) 270-7592
Shushawna DeOliveira, Director of Admissions & Enrollment, SUNY Downstate Medical Center, 450 Clarkson Avenue, Box 60, Brooklyn, NY 11203-2098

SUNY Empire State College
Saratoga Springs, New York
www.esc.edu
CB member
CB code: 2214

◗ Public 4-year liberal arts college
◗ Commuter campus in large town
◗ 10,010 degree-seeking undergraduates: 57% part-time, 61% women, 18% African American, 2% Asian American, 5% Hispanic American, 1% Native American
◗ 841 degree-seeking graduate students
◗ 80% of applicants admitted
◗ Application essay required

General. Founded in 1971. Regionally accredited. Empire State College has 34 locations in seven regions throughout New York state and abroad. Through the Center for Distance Learning (CDL), students can take a few courses or earn their entire degree online. **Degrees:** 2,502 bachelor's, 652 associate awarded; master's offered. **Calendar:** Differs by program, extensive summer session. **Full-time faculty:** 199 total; 94% have terminal degrees, 19% minority, 64% women. **Part-time faculty:** 1,119 total.

Freshman class profile. 1,562 applied, 1,252 admitted, 843 enrolled.

Basis for selection. Requirements for undergraduate admission: completed application, possession of high school diploma or equivalent, ability to pursue college-level work, payment of nonrefundable orientation fee, and completion of the college's orientation process.

2011-2012 Annual costs. Tuition/fees: $5,545; $14,595 out-of-state. Books/supplies: $1,502. Personal expenses: $1,326.

Financial aid. All financial aid based on need.

Application procedures. Admission: Priority date 6/1; no deadline. No application fee. Admission notification on a rolling basis. **Financial aid:** Priority date 4/1; no closing date. FAFSA required. Applicants notified on a rolling basis; must reply within 3 week(s) of notification.

Academics. Special study options: Accelerated study, combined bachelor's/graduate degree, cross-registration, distance learning, double major, external degree, independent study, internships, student-designed major, teacher certification program. Weekend residencies for some specialized programs. **Credit/placement by examination:** AP, CLEP, IB. 40 credit hours maximum toward associate degree, 96 toward bachelor's. **Support services:** Study skills assistance, tutoring, writing center.

Majors. Business: General, labor relations. **Education:** General. **Health services:** Nursing (RN). **History:** General. **Human services:** Community org/advocacy. **Liberal arts:** Arts/sciences. **Psychology:** General. **Social sciences:** General, economics. **Visual/performing arts:** Studio arts.

Most popular majors. Business/marketing 40%, English 7%, interdisciplinary studies 7%, physical sciences 6%, psychology 7%, public administration/social services 22%.

Computing on campus. 100 workstations in computer center. Commuter students can connect to campus network. Online course registration, online library, helpline available.

Student life. Freshman orientation: Mandatory, $50 fee. Preregistration for classes offered.

Student services. Adult student services, career counseling, student employment services, veterans' counselor. **Physically disabled:** Services for visually, speech, hearing impaired.

Contact. E-mail: admissions@esc.edu
Phone: (518) 587-2100 Toll-free number: (800) 847-3000
Fax: (518) 587-9759
Jennifer D'Agostino, Assistant Vice President for Enrollment Management, SUNY Empire State College, Two Union Avenue, Saratoga Springs, NY 12866

SUNY Farmindale State College

Farmingdale, New York

CB member

www.farmingdale.edu

CB code: 2526

- Public 4-year technical college
- Commuter campus in large town
- 6,753 degree-seeking undergraduates: 23% part-time, 41% women, 6% African American, 3% Asian American, 6% Hispanic American, 1% international
- 47% of applicants admitted
- 40% graduate within 6 years; 30% enter graduate study

General. Founded in 1912. Regionally accredited. **Degrees:** 869 bachelor's, 484 associate awarded. **Location:** 30 miles from New York City. **Calendar:** Semester, extensive summer session. **Full-time faculty:** 191 total; 62% have terminal degrees, 19% minority, 45% women. **Part-time faculty:** 378 total; 18% have terminal degrees, 14% minority, 47% women. **Class size:** 5% < 20, 72% 20-39, 20% 40-49, 3% 50-99. **Special facilities:** CAD/CAM laboratory, fleet of single-engine and multi-engine aircraft, dental and health care laboratories, bioscience labs, Cold Spring Harbor Research lab on campus, manufacturing labs with plasmajet and advanced robotic technology, solar cell and hydrogen fuel cell research.

Freshman class profile. 5,373 applied, 2,520 admitted, 1,013 enrolled.

Mid 50% test scores			
SAT critical reading:	450-530	Rank in top quarter:	37%
SAT math:	490-570	Rank in top tenth:	6%
SAT writing:	430-520	End year in good standing:	92%
GPA 3.75 or higher:	9%	Return as sophomores:	79%
GPA 3.50-3.74:	18%	Out-of-state:	1%
GPA 3.0-3.49:	59%	Live on campus:	17%
GPA 2.0-2.99:	14%	International:	1%

Basis for selection. School achievement record of primary importance. Applicants apply to and are accepted into a specific curriculum. Requirements vary according to program. SAT required for bachelor's degree students. Interview and portfolio required for advertising art and design, visual communications programs.

High school preparation. 20.5 units required. Required and recommended units include English 4, mathematics 2-4, social studies 4, science 2-4 and foreign language 2. Requirements vary by curriculum.

2011-2012 Annual costs. Tuition/fees: $6,444; $15,494 out-of-state. Room/board: $12,160.

2011-2012 Financial aid. Need-based: 738 full-time freshmen applied for aid; 522 were judged to have need; 479 of these received aid. Average need met was 64%. Average scholarship/grant was $6,018; average loan $3,530. 62% of total undergraduate aid awarded as scholarships/grants, 38% as loans/jobs. **Non-need-based:** Awarded to 1,695 full-time undergraduates, including 327 freshmen. Scholarships awarded for academics.

Application procedures. Admission: No deadline. $50 fee, may be waived for applicants with need. Admission notification on a rolling basis beginning on or about 11/1. Must reply by May 1 or within 4 week(s) if notified thereafter. Priority given to applications received by January 15 for dental hygiene program and nursing program. **Financial aid:** Priority date 4/1; no closing date. FAFSA, institutional form required. Applicants notified on a rolling basis starting 4/1.

Academics. Special study options: Distance learning, double major, honors, internships, study abroad. **Credit/placement by examination:** AP, CLEP, institutional tests. **Support services:** Learning center, remedial instruction, study skills assistance, tutoring, writing center.

Majors. Biology: General. **Business:** Business admin, operations. **Communications:** Media studies. **Computer sciences:** Programming. **English:** Technical writing. **General:** Horticulture. **Health services:** Dental hygiene, nursing (RN). **Math:** Applied. **Parks/recreation:** Sports admin. **Protective services:** Security management, security services. **Psychology:** Industrial. **Social sciences:** Applied economics.

Most popular majors. Biology 8%, business/marketing 37%, communications/journalism 9%, computer/information sciences 6%, engineering/engineering technologies 16%, interdisciplinary studies 10%.

Computing on campus. 950 workstations in dormitories, library, computer center, student center. Dormitories wired for high-speed internet access and linked to campus network. Commuter students can connect to campus network. Online course registration, online library, wireless network available.

Student life. Freshman orientation: Mandatory, $150 fee. Preregistration for classes offered. **Housing:** Coed dorms available. $175 deposit. **Activities:** Choral groups, drama, international student organizations, literary magazine, radio station, student government, student newspaper, African student association, Asian student alliance, Caribbean student organization, Christian fellowship.

Athletics. NCAA. **Intercollegiate:** Baseball M, basketball, cross-country, golf M, lacrosse, soccer, softball W, tennis M, track and field, volleyball W. **Intramural:** Basketball, golf, racquetball, soccer, softball, squash, tennis, volleyball, weight lifting. **Team name:** Rams.

Student services. Alcohol/substance abuse counseling, career counseling, services for economically disadvantaged, student employment services, financial aid counseling, health services, on-campus daycare, personal counseling, placement for graduates, veterans' counselor. **Physically disabled:** Services for visually, speech, hearing impaired.

Contact. E-mail: admissions@farmingdale.edu
Phone: (631) 420-2200 Toll-free number: (800) 432-7646
Fax: (631) 420-2633
Jim Hall, Director of Admissions, SUNY Farmindale State College, 2350 Broadhollow Road, Farmingdale, NY 11735-1021

SUNY Institute of Technology at Utica/Rome

Utica, New York

CB member

www.sunyit.edu

CB code: 0755

- Public 4-year business and engineering college
- Commuter campus in small city
- 1,731 degree-seeking undergraduates: 23% part-time, 44% women, 8% African American, 3% Asian American, 5% Hispanic American, 1% international
- 598 degree-seeking graduate students
- 38% of applicants admitted
- SAT or ACT (ACT writing optional), application essay required
- 47% graduate within 6 years

General. Founded in 1966. Regionally accredited. **Degrees:** 425 bachelor's awarded; master's offered. **ROTC:** Army. **Location:** 50 miles from Syracuse, 90 miles from Albany. **Calendar:** Semester, limited summer session. **Full-time faculty:** 77 total; 87% have terminal degrees, 30% minority, 38% women. **Part-time faculty:** 107 total; 23% have terminal degrees, 8% minority, 38% women. **Class size:** 55% < 20, 43% 20-39, 2% 40-49, less than 1% 50-99.

Freshman class profile. 1,549 applied, 583 admitted, 198 enrolled.

Mid 50% test scores			
SAT critical reading:	470-560	Rank in top quarter:	44%
SAT math:	490-590	Rank in top tenth:	13%
ACT composite:	21-25	End year in good standing:	58%
GPA 3.75 or higher:	15%	Return as sophomores:	71%
GPA 3.50-3.74:	20%	Out-of-state:	2%
GPA 3.0-3.49:	45%	Live on campus:	82%
GPA 2.0-2.99:	20%	International:	1%

Basis for selection. Students must meet minimum SAT/ACT score ranges with competitive high school averages as well as minimum high school unit requirements; letters of recommendation and an untimed essay required to determine admissibility. International students without access to SAT/ACT testing may be admitted based on alternate criteria. Interview recommended for all. **Home schooled:** Statement describing home school structure and mission, transcript of courses and grades, state high school equivalency certificate, letter of recommendation (nonparent) required. Statement from local public school superintendent that verifies home school curriculum matches NYS Regents Curriculum required.

High school preparation. College-preparatory program required. 17 units required; 25 recommended. Required and recommended units include English 4, mathematics 3-4, social studies 2, history 2, science 3-4 (laboratory 3-4), foreign language 3 and academic electives 2.

2012-2013 Annual costs. Tuition/fees (projected): $6,810; $17,920 out-of-state. Room/board: $10,985. Books/supplies: $1,200. Personal expenses: $1,500.

2010-2011 Financial aid. Need-based: 192 full-time freshmen applied for aid; 156 were judged to have need; 154 of these received aid. Average need met was 3600%. Average scholarship/grant was $3,344; average loan $1,322. 29% of total undergraduate aid awarded as scholarships/grants, 71% as loans/jobs. **Non-need-based:** Scholarships awarded for academics.

Application procedures. Admission: Priority date 2/1; deadline 8/1 (postmark date). $50 fee, may be waived for applicants with need. Admission notification on a rolling basis beginning on or about 1/15. Must reply by May 1 or within 4 week(s) if notified thereafter. **Financial aid:** Priority date 3/1; no closing date. FAFSA required. Applicants notified on a rolling basis starting 3/17; must reply within 2 week(s) of notification.

Academics. Special study options: Accelerated study, combined bachelor's/graduate degree, cooperative education, cross-registration, distance learning, double major, dual enrollment of high school students, independent study, internships, liberal arts/career combination, study abroad. Study abroad is coordinated through SUNY Study Abroad, offering 500 overseas programs in more than 51 countries. **Credit/placement by examination:** AP, CLEP, IB, SAT, ACT, institutional tests. Credit awarded for International Baccalaureate varies by academic department. **Support services:** Learning center, preadmission summer program, reduced course load, remedial instruction, study skills assistance, tutoring, writing center.

Majors. Biology: General. **Business:** General, accounting, business admin, finance. **Communications technology:** General. **Computer sciences:** General, information systems. **Engineering:** Electrical. **Health services:** Health care admin, medical records admin, nursing (RN). **Liberal arts:** Arts/sciences. **Math:** Applied. **Protective services:** Criminal justice. **Psychology:** General. **Social sciences:** Sociology.

Most popular majors. Business/marketing 23%, computer/information sciences 13%, engineering/engineering technologies 20%, health sciences 20%, psychology 10%.

Computing on campus. 241 workstations in dormitories, library, computer center, student center. Dormitories wired for high-speed internet access and linked to campus network. Commuter students can connect to campus network. Online course registration, online library, helpline, student web hosting, wireless network available.

Student life. Freshman orientation: Mandatory, $150 fee. Preregistration for classes offered. Weekend prior to start of the fall semester. Wednesday arrival through opening weekend. **Housing:** Guaranteed on-campus for freshmen. Single-sex dorms available. $150 fully refundable deposit, deadline 5/1. **Activities:** Campus ministries, drama, international student organizations, radio station, student government, student newspaper, TV station, Black, Latino, American student union, Muslim student association, international student association, Students of Christ, Xplosivo (Latin dance group).

Athletics. NCAA. Intercollegiate: Baseball M, basketball, bowling W, cricket, cross-country, lacrosse, soccer, softball W, swimming, volleyball. **Intramural:** Badminton, basketball, bowling, cricket, cross-country, golf, racquetball, soccer, softball, tennis, volleyball. **Team name:** Wildcats.

Student services. Alcohol/substance abuse counseling, chaplain/spiritual director, career counseling, student employment services, financial aid counseling, health services, personal counseling, placement for graduates, veterans' counselor, women's services. **Physically disabled:** Services for visually, speech, hearing impaired.

Contact. E-mail: admissions@sunyit.edu
Phone: (315) 792-7500 Toll-free number: (866) 278-6948
Fax: (315) 792-7837
Jennifer Phelan-Ninh, Director of Admissions, SUNY Institute of Technology at Utica/Rome, 100 Seymour Road, Utica, NY 13502

SUNY Maritime College
Throggs Neck, New York

CB member
CB code: 2536

www.sunymaritime.edu

- Public 4-year maritime college
- Residential campus in very large city
- 1,638 degree-seeking undergraduates: 4% part-time, 11% women, 4% African American, 3% Asian American, 8% Hispanic American, 4% international
- 159 degree-seeking graduate students
- 67% of applicants admitted
- SAT or ACT (ACT writing optional) required
- 51% graduate within 6 years; 7% enter graduate study

General. Founded in 1874. Regionally accredited. Graduates eligible for commission as officers in Navy, Marine Corps, Coast Guard, Air Force, and commissioned Corps of the National Oceanic and Atmospheric Administration. 3 summer semesters at sea and regiment option required for students interested in obtaining U.S. Merchant Marine Officer's License. **Degrees:** 229 bachelor's, 1 associate awarded; master's offered. **ROTC:** Army, Naval.

Location: 10 miles from New York City. **Calendar:** Semester, limited summer session. **Full-time faculty:** 94 total; 42% have terminal degrees, 10% minority, 21% women. **Part-time faculty:** 54 total; 20% have terminal degrees, 24% minority, 32% women. **Class size:** 46% < 20, 44% 20-39, 6% 40-49, 2% 50-99, less than 1% >100. **Special facilities:** 565-foot training ship, training tanker, Center for Simulated Marine Operations, bridge simulator, model basin and towing tank, CAD-CAM facilities, diesel propulsion simulators, maritime museum, sailing center including several 1-ton ocean racers.

Freshman class profile. 1,348 applied, 907 admitted, 368 enrolled.

Mid 50% test scores			
SAT critical reading:	470-560		
SAT math:	510-600		
ACT composite:	20-26		
GPA 3.75 or higher:	6%		
GPA 3.50-3.74:	12%		
GPA 3.0-3.49:	37%		
GPA 2.0-2.99:		44%	
End year in good standing:		84%	
Return as sophomores:		80%	
Out-of-state:		23%	
Live on campus:		90%	
International:		2%	

Basis for selection. Quality and strength of preparation, school achievement record, including first semester senior grades, class rank, test scores, extracurricular activities considered. Interview and essay recommended. Interviews and essays are not required but highly recommended. **Home schooled:** Statement describing home school structure and mission, transcript of courses and grades, state high school equivalency certificate, letter of recommendation (nonparent) required. Accreditation of home school.

High school preparation. College-preparatory program recommended. 18 units required. Required and recommended units include English 3-4, mathematics 3-4, social studies 3, history 3, science 3-4 (laboratory 1) and foreign language 1-3. Math requirement includes algebra, geometry, trigonometry; math beyond trigonometry recommended. Chemistry or physics required; both strongly recommended.

2011-2012 Annual costs. Tuition/fees: $6,457; $15,507 out-of-state. Students from Alabama, Connecticut, Delaware, Florida, Georgia, Louisiana, Mississippi, Maryland, New Jersey, North Carolina, Pennsylvania, Rhode Island, South Carolina, Virginia, Washington DC pay in-state rates. Room/board: $10,090. Books/supplies: $1,300. Personal expenses: $2,060.

2010-2011 Financial aid. Need-based: 202 full-time freshmen applied for aid; 195 were judged to have need; 189 of these received aid. Average need met was 49%. Average scholarship/grant was $5,838; average loan $3,660. 40% of total undergraduate aid awarded as scholarships/grants, 60% as loans/jobs. **Non-need-based:** Awarded to 108 full-time undergraduates, including 15 freshmen. Scholarships awarded for academics, leadership, ROTC, state residency. **Additional information:** All cadets who are United States citizens, physically qualified for Merchant Marine license, and not yet 25 at time of enrollment eligible to apply for Student Incentive Payment (SIP) of $3,000 per year from Maritime Administration of the Department of Transportation. Out-of-state students who elect to participate in SIP pay in-state tuition fees.

Application procedures. Admission: Priority date 3/15; no deadline. $40 fee, may be waived for applicants with need. Admission notification on a rolling basis beginning on or about 9/15. Waitlist begins March 1st. **Financial aid:** Priority date 3/15, closing date 7/15. FAFSA, institutional form required. Applicants notified on a rolling basis starting 3/15.

Academics. Cadets acquire technical, professional, and leadership experience on training cruises to foreign and domestic ports during annual summer sea terms, while preparing for U.S. Merchant Marine Officer's License. **Special study options:** Cooperative education, distance learning, double major, dual enrollment of high school students, ESL, honors, independent study, internships. United States Coast Guard-issued deck and engine license program. **Credit/placement by examination:** AP, CLEP, IB, institutional tests. 18 credit hours maximum toward associate degree, 18 toward bachelor's. **Support services:** Learning center, pre-admission summer program, reduced course load, remedial instruction, study skills assistance, tutoring, writing center.

Majors. Business: General, business admin, marketing, tourism/travel. **Engineering:** General, electrical, industrial, marine, mechanical. **Liberal arts:** Arts/sciences. **Physical sciences:** Atmospheric science.

Most popular majors. Business/marketing 52%, engineering/engineering technologies 41%.

Computing on campus. 140 workstations in dormitories, library, computer center, student center. Dormitories wired for high-speed internet access and linked to campus network. Online course registration, online library, helpline, student web hosting, wireless network available.

Student life. Freshman orientation: Mandatory, $110 fee. Preregistration for classes offered. 2-day, overnight program held in July and August, focusing on small group interaction (each session limited to 85 participants) with the goals of campus knowledge, student networking, and registration. Parents

and families can attend an informational brunch. Regimental students required to additionally attend INDOC, a two-week long training period prior to the start of classes. **Policies:** Students can choose from two lifestyle options on campus, either traditional college or Regiment of Cadets. All students governed by the College Code of Conduct and within that all Cadets are governed by the Regimental Rules and Regulations. All students have access to and can participate in student organizations, athletics, student government, and recreation facilities. **Housing:** Coed dorms, special housing for disabled available. $100 fully refundable deposit, deadline 5/1. Most undergraduates required to live in on-campus housing. **Activities:** Bands, campus ministries, choral groups, international student organizations, music ensembles, student government, Newman club, Eagle Scout Fraternity, culture club, Afro-Caribbean club, Emerald Society, Pershing Rifles, honor guard, Turkish club, Jewish club.

Athletics. NCAA. **Intercollegiate:** Baseball M, basketball, cross-country, football (tackle) M, ice hockey M, lacrosse, rifle, rowing (crew) W, sailing, soccer, softball W, swimming, volleyball W. **Intramural:** Basketball, cross-country, football (tackle) M, soccer, softball, volleyball. **Team name:** Privateers.

Student services. Alcohol/substance abuse counseling, chaplain/spiritual director, career counseling, services for economically disadvantaged, student employment services, financial aid counseling, health services, legal services, personal counseling, placement for graduates, veterans' counselor, women's services. **Physically disabled:** Services for visually, speech, hearing impaired.

Contact. E-mail: admissions@sunymaritime.edu
Phone: (718) 409-7221 Toll-free number: (800) 654-1874
Fax: (718) 409-7465
Jonathan White, Dean of Admissions, SUNY Maritime College, 6 Pennyfield Avenue, Throggs Neck, NY 10465-4198

SUNY University at Albany
Albany, New York
www.albany.edu

CB member
CB code: 2532

- Public 4-year university
- Residential campus in small city
- 12,425 degree-seeking undergraduates: 5% part-time, 48% women, 12% African American, 7% Asian American, 11% Hispanic American, 3% international
- 4,087 degree-seeking graduate students
- 51% of applicants admitted
- SAT or ACT with writing, application essay required
- 65% graduate within 6 years

General. Founded in 1844. Regionally accredited. Extensive internships in New York's Capital Region. International center for research and development in nanotechnology. **Degrees:** 3,103 bachelor's awarded; master's, doctoral offered. **ROTC:** Army, Air Force. **Location:** 4 miles from downtown. **Calendar:** Semester, extensive summer session. **Full-time faculty:** 590 total; 96% have terminal degrees, 20% minority, 38% women. **Part-time faculty:** 677 total; 12% minority, 50% women. **Class size:** 23% < 20, 44% 20-39, 12% 40-49, 8% 50-99, 12% >100. **Special facilities:** Northeast Regional Forensic Institute, atmospheric science research center and Whiteface Mountain observation facility, microbeam analysis facility, large fine arts work areas, peptide synthesis facility, recombinant DNA sequencing laboratories, nanoscale science and engineering facilities.

Freshman class profile. 21,054 applied, 10,810 admitted, 2,422 enrolled.

Mid 50% test scores			
SAT critical reading:	500-580	GPA 2.0-2.99:	19%
SAT math:	520-610	Rank in top quarter:	51%
ACT composite:	22-26	Rank in top tenth:	16%
GPA 3.75 or higher:	12%	Return as sophomores:	84%
GPA 3.50-3.74:	20%	Out-of-state:	7%
GPA 3.0-3.49:	48%	Live on campus:	95%
		International:	4%

Basis for selection. High school record, class rank, GPA, standardized test scores very important; essay, recommendations important. **Home schooled:** Statement describing home school structure and mission, state high school equivalency certificate required.

High school preparation. College-preparatory program required. 18 units required. Required and recommended units include English 4, mathematics 2-4, social studies 3, history 2, science 2-3 (laboratory 2-3), foreign language 1-3 and academic electives 4.

2011-2012 Annual costs. Tuition/fees: $7,172; $16,622 out-of-state. Room/board: $10,958. Books/supplies: $1,200. Personal expenses: $1,065.

Financial aid. **Non-need-based:** Scholarships awarded for academics, athletics, state residency.

Application procedures. **Admission:** Closing date 3/1 (receipt date). $50 fee, may be waived for applicants with need. Must reply by May 1 or within 2 week(s) if notified thereafter. Decisions sent after January 1. **Financial aid:** Priority date 3/15; no closing date. FAFSA required. Applicants notified on a rolling basis starting 3/20.

Academics. **Special study options:** Accelerated study, combined bachelor's/graduate degree, cross-registration, distance learning, double major, dual enrollment of high school students, ESL, honors, independent study, internships, liberal arts/career combination, student-designed major, study abroad, Washington semester. Accelerated 5-year bachelor's/master's in 40 fields, internships with New York State Legislature, 3+3 program with Albany Law School, biology/dental program with Boston University Goldman School of Dental Medicine, bachelor's/doctor of optometry with SUNY State College, early assurance program with Albany Medical College and SUNY Upstate Medical University. **Credit/placement by examination:** AP, CLEP, IB. 60 credit hours maximum toward bachelor's degree. **Support services:** Pre-admission summer program, remedial instruction, study skills assistance, tutoring, writing center.

Honors college/program. Applicants admitted as Presidential Scholars & Frederick Douglass Scholars invited to apply to the Honors College. Approximately 125 freshmen will be admitted each fall. An additional 25 current University at Albany students will be admitted at the end of their first year.

Majors. **Architecture:** Urban/community planning. **Area/ethnic studies:** African-American, Asian, Caribbean, Chinese, East Asian, Japanese, Latin American, women's. **Biology:** General, biochemistry, molecular. **Business:** Accounting, business admin. **Communications:** Communications/speech/rhetoric, journalism. **Computer sciences:** General, information systems. **Conservation:** Environmental science. **Engineering:** Materials. **English:** English lit, rhetoric/composition. **Foreign languages:** Linguistics, Spanish. **Health services:** Predental, premedicine, prepharmacy, preveterinary. **History:** General. **Human services:** Public policy, social work. **Math:** General, applied. **Philosophy/religion:** Philosophy, religion. **Physical sciences:** Atmospheric science, chemistry, materials science, physics. **Protective services:** Criminal justice. **Psychology:** General. **Social sciences:** Anthropology, economics, geography, political science, sociology, urban studies. **Visual/performing arts:** Art history/conservation, music, music performance, music theory/composition, studio arts.

Most popular majors. Biology 9%, business/marketing 13%, English 16%, history 6%, mathematics 6%, psychology 12%, social sciences 23%.

Computing on campus. 500 workstations in library. Dormitories wired for high-speed internet access and linked to campus network. Commuter students can connect to campus network. Online course registration, online library, helpline, student web hosting, wireless network available.

Student life. **Freshman orientation:** Mandatory, $200 fee. Preregistration for classes offered. 2 days in summer with parental participation, 2 days in fall without parental participation. **Housing:** Guaranteed on-campus for freshmen. Coed dorms, wellness housing available. $125 fully refundable deposit. Individualized services for disabled students available, including accessible housing information. **Activities:** Bands, campus ministries, choral groups, dance, drama, film society, international student organizations, literary magazine, music ensembles, Model UN, musical theater, radio station, student government, student newspaper, symphony orchestra, TV station, over 200 student groups.

Athletics. NCAA. **Intercollegiate:** Baseball M, basketball, cross-country, field hockey W, football (tackle) M, golf W, lacrosse, rugby, soccer, softball W, tennis W, track and field, volleyball W. **Intramural:** Basketball, football (non-tackle), racquetball, soccer, softball, tennis, track and field, volleyball. **Team name:** Great Danes.

Student services. Alcohol/substance abuse counseling, chaplain/spiritual director, career counseling, services for economically disadvantaged, student employment services, financial aid counseling, health services, legal services, minority student services, on-campus daycare, personal counseling, placement for graduates, women's services. **Physically disabled:** Services for visually, speech, hearing impaired.

Contact. E-mail: ugadmissions@albany.edu
Phone: (518) 442-5435 Fax: (518) 442-5383
Robert Andrea, Director of Undergraduate Admissions, SUNY University at Albany, Office of Undergraduate Admissions, University Hall, Albany, NY 12222

SUNY University at Binghamton

Binghamton, New York   CB member
www.binghamton.edu   CB code: 2535

- Public 4-year university
- Residential campus in small city
- 11,828 degree-seeking undergraduates: 3% part-time, 47% women, 5% African American, 13% Asian American, 9% Hispanic American, 10% international
- 2,763 degree-seeking graduate students
- 41% of applicants admitted
- SAT or ACT with writing, application essay required
- 78% graduate within 6 years; 39% enter graduate study

General. Founded in 1946. Regionally accredited. **Degrees:** 2,990 bachelor's awarded; master's, professional, doctoral offered. **ROTC:** Army, Air Force. **Location:** 50 miles from Ithaca, 70 miles from Syracuse, 180 miles from New York City. **Calendar:** Semester, extensive summer session. **Full-time faculty:** 580 total; 89% have terminal degrees, 25% minority, 39% women. **Part-time faculty:** 268 total; 14% minority, 47% women. **Class size:** 39% < 20, 39% 20-39, 6% 40-49, 9% 50-99, 7% >100. **Special facilities:** 190-acre nature preserve, 4-climate greenhouse, performing arts center (5 theaters), art/dance studios, sculpture foundry, research centers, electron microscopy laboratories, geographic information systems core facility, public archeology facility, integrated electronics engineering center, institute for child development, information commons, events center, kosher kitchen, Innovative Technologies Complex, NYS Center of Excellence, art museum.

Freshman class profile. 28,101 applied, 11,440 admitted, 2,516 enrolled.

Mid 50% test scores			
SAT critical reading:	600-680	GPA 2.0-2.99:	3%
SAT math:	620-710	Rank in top quarter:	87%
SAT writing:	580-670	Rank in top tenth:	57%
ACT composite:	27-31	End year in good standing:	91%
GPA 3.75 or higher:	60%	Return as sophomores:	91%
GPA 3.50-3.74:	20%	Out-of-state:	17%
GPA 3.0-3.49:	17%	Live on campus:	98%
		International:	10%

Basis for selection. Quality of courses, grades and grade trend, and test scores. Evidence of intellectual curiosity, interest in others, and nonacademic pursuits sought through application. Geographic, socioeconomic, and ethnic diversity considered. SAT or ACT scores accepted on a rolling basis for fall term admissions. Audition offered for music; portfolio review offered for art; theater, speech and debate talent also considered. **Home schooled:** State high school equivalency certificate required. Students required to obtain documentation of equivalency from local school boards.

High school preparation. College-preparatory program required. 16 units required. Required and recommended units include English 4, mathematics 3-4, social studies 2-4, history 4, science 2-4 and foreign language 3. 3 units of 1 foreign language or 2 each of 2 foreign languages required of liberal arts applicants. Academic electives units required to fulfill high school requirements.

2012-2013 Annual costs. Tuition/fees (projected): $7,216; $15,326 out-of-state. All undergraduate School of Management students required to pay $125/semester non-credit placement program fee. Room/board: $11,810. Books/supplies: $1,000. Personal expenses: $750.

2011-2012 Financial aid. Need-based: 1,994 full-time freshmen applied for aid; 1,187 were judged to have need; 1,186 of these received aid. Average need met was 72%. Average scholarship/grant was $6,995; average loan $4,191. 37% of total undergraduate aid awarded as scholarships/grants, 63% as loans/jobs. **Non-need-based:** Awarded to 1,105 full-time undergraduates, including 283 freshmen. Scholarships awarded for academics, art, athletics, leadership, minority status, music/drama, state residency. **Additional information:** Most institutional aid awarded on a first-come first-served basis while considering student's ability to pay (determined by use of the FAFSA application) and the student's academic achievement.

Application procedures. Admission: Priority date 1/15; no deadline. $50 fee, may be waived for applicants with need. Rolling notification: 2/1, 3/1, 4/1. Must reply by May 1 or within 3 week(s) if notified thereafter. **Financial aid:** Priority date 2/1; no closing date. FAFSA required. Applicants notified on a rolling basis starting 3/4; must reply within 2 week(s) of notification.

Academics. . **Special study options:** Accelerated study, combined bachelor's/graduate degree, cross-registration, distance learning, double major, dual enrollment of high school students, ESL, exchange student, honors, independent study, internships, liberal arts/career combination, student-designed major, study abroad, teacher certification program, Washington semester. Individualized majors programs; pre-health program prepares students for careers in medicine, dentistry, optometry, veterinary medicine, podiatry, nutrition, physical or occupational therapy and chiropractic; early assurance program guarantees graduate admission at partner SUNY schools: Buffalo, Upstate Medical-Syracuse and College of Optometry; 3-2 and 4-1 combined BA or BS/MA, MS, MAT, MBA, or MPA degree programs; teacher certification program is graduate only. **Credit/placement by examination:** AP, CLEP, IB, institutional tests. 32 credit hours maximum toward bachelor's degree. **Support services:** Learning center, pre-admission summer program, study skills assistance, tutoring, writing center.

Majors. Area/ethnic studies: African-American, Asian, Asian-American, East Asian, Latin American, South Asian. **Biology:** General, biochemistry, cellular/molecular. **Business:** Accounting, actuarial science, business admin, entrepreneurial studies, finance, international, logistics, management information systems, marketing. **Computer sciences:** General, computer science. **Conservation:** Environmental studies. **Engineering:** General, biomedical, computer, electrical, industrial, mechanical. **English:** Creative writing, English lit. **Foreign languages:** Arabic, classics, comparative lit, French, German, Hebrew, Italian, Latin, linguistics, Spanish. **Health services:** Nursing (RN), predental, premedicine, preoptometry, preveterinary. **History:** General. **Math:** General. **Philosophy/religion:** Judaic, philosophy. **Physical sciences:** Chemistry, geology, physics. **Psychology:** General, psychobiology. **Social sciences:** General, anthropology, applied economics, economics, geography, GIS/cartography, international relations, political science, sociology. **Visual/performing arts:** Acting, art, art history/conservation, cinematography, directing/producing, dramatic, music, music performance, theater design.

Most popular majors. Biology 8%, business/marketing 12%, engineering/engineering technologies 8%, English 9%, health sciences 7%, psychology 9%, social sciences 22%.

Computing on campus. 1,190 workstations in dormitories, library, computer center, student center. Dormitories wired for high-speed internet access and linked to campus network. Commuter students can connect to campus network. Online course registration, online library, helpline, student web hosting, wireless network available.

Student life. Freshman orientation: Available, $210 fee. Preregistration for classes offered. 2-day session held in summer for fall semester. Parents invited to participate. 2-day session held in January for students entering spring semester. **Policies:** Student code of conduct and academic honesty policy. Freshmen not permitted cars on campus. **Housing:** Guaranteed on-campus for freshmen. Coed dorms, special housing for disabled, apartments, wellness housing available. $350 nonrefundable deposit, deadline 5/1. **Activities:** Bands, campus ministries, choral groups, dance, drama, film society, international student organizations, literary magazine, music ensembles, Model UN, musical theater, opera, radio station, student government, student newspaper, symphony orchestra, TV station, College Democrats, College Republicans, College Libertarians, Hillel, gospel choir, Asian student union, Black student union, Campus Climate Challenge, Circle K, Engineers Without Borders.

Athletics. NCAA. **Intercollegiate:** Baseball M, basketball, cross-country, diving, golf M, lacrosse, soccer, softball W, swimming, tennis, track and field, volleyball W, wrestling M. **Intramural:** Basketball, bowling, football (non-tackle), racquetball, soccer, softball, tennis, volleyball. **Team name:** Bearcats.

Student services. Adult student services, alcohol/substance abuse counseling, chaplain/spiritual director, career counseling, services for economically disadvantaged, student employment services, financial aid counseling, health services, legal services, minority student services, on-campus daycare, personal counseling, placement for graduates, veterans' counselor, women's services. **Physically disabled:** Services for visually, speech, hearing impaired.

Contact. E-mail: admit@binghamton.edu
Phone: (607) 777-2171 Fax: (607) 777-4445
Sandra Starke, Vice Provost for Enrollment Management, SUNY University at Binghamton, Box 6001, Binghamton, NY 13902-6001

SUNY University at Buffalo

Buffalo, New York   CB member
www.buffalo.edu   CB code: 2925

- Public 4-year university
- Commuter campus in large city
- 18,994 degree-seeking undergraduates: 8% part-time, 46% women, 7% African American, 11% Asian American, 7% Hispanic American, 1% Native American, 16% international
- 9,075 degree-seeking graduate students
- 53% of applicants admitted

▶ SAT or ACT with writing required

▶ 69% graduate within 6 years; 40% enter graduate study

General. Founded in 1846. Regionally accredited. **Degrees:** 4,345 bachelor's awarded; master's, professional, doctoral offered. **ROTC:** Army. **Location:** 10 miles from downtown. **Calendar:** Semester, extensive summer session. **Full-time faculty:** 1,159 total; 95% have terminal degrees, 24% minority, 36% women. **Part-time faculty:** 517 total; 55% have terminal degrees, 8% minority, 49% women. **Class size:** 33% < 20, 37% 20-39, 8% 40-49, 13% 50-99, 8% >100. **Special facilities:** Center for the arts, concert hall, anthropology research museum, multidisciplinary center for earthquake engineering research, center of excellence in bioinformatics and life sciences, center for computational research, poetry and rare books collection, center for document analysis and recognition, center for engineering design and industrial innovation, pharmacy museum, virtual site museum, archaeological survey center.

Freshman class profile. 21,357 applied, 11,363 admitted, 3,255 enrolled.

Mid 50% test scores		GPA 2.0-2.99:	14%
SAT critical reading:	500-600	Rank in top quarter:	63%
SAT math:	550-650	Rank in top tenth:	26%
ACT composite:	23-28	Return as sophomores:	88%
GPA 3.75 or higher:	21%	Out-of-state:	5%
GPA 3.50-3.74:	26%	Live on campus:	74%
GPA 3.0-3.49:	38%	International:	12%

Basis for selection. Secondary school performance, strength of curriculum, standardized test scores, and, in some cases, supplemental application. SAT Subject Test considered for placement for foreign language. Architecture requires a portfolio; dance, music theater, theater & music require an audition. **Home schooled:** Transcript of courses and grades, letter of recommendation (nonparent) required. Essay describing educational program, special projects, extracurricular activities, and special accomplishments required as well as 2 letters of recommendation: 1 from parent or other person providing education, 1 from person involved with other activities. If admitted, will need to submit letter from superintendent of local school district attesting to completion of program of home instruction meeting requirements of Section 100.10 of the Regulations of the Commissioner of Education, or passing score on GED. **Learning Disabled:** No separate admissions process: eligibility for services must be established by provision of disability documentation that meets institutional standards.

High school preparation. College-preparatory program recommended. 17 units recommended. Recommended units include English 4, mathematics 3, social studies 4, science 3 and foreign language 3.

2011-2012 Annual costs. Tuition/fees: $7,482; $16,932 out-of-state. Room/board: $10,728.

2010-2011 Financial aid. Need-based: 3,131 full-time freshmen applied for aid; 2,280 were judged to have need; 2,218 of these received aid. Average need met was 65%. Average scholarship/grant was $5,767; average loan $3,543. 39% of total undergraduate aid awarded as scholarships/grants, 61% as loans/jobs. **Non-need-based:** Awarded to 2,418 full-time undergraduates, including 593 freshmen. Scholarships awarded for academics, job skills, minority status, music/drama, state residency.

Application procedures. Admission: Priority date 11/1; no deadline. $50 fee, may be waived for applicants with need. Admission notification on a rolling basis beginning on or about 2/1. Must reply by May 1 or within 2 week(s) if notified thereafter. **Financial aid:** Priority date 3/1; no closing date. FAFSA required. Applicants notified on a rolling basis starting 2/1; must reply by 5/1.

Academics. Over 300 baccalaureate, master's and doctoral degree programs. Comprehensive College of Arts and Sciences plus 11 professional schools including Law, Medicine and Dentistry. **Special study options:** Accelerated study, combined bachelor's/graduate degree, cooperative education, cross-registration, distance learning, double major, dual enrollment of high school students, ESL, exchange student, honors, independent study, internships, liberal arts/career combination, student-designed major, study abroad, teacher certification program, Washington semester. Certificate programs, combined degree programs, early assurance program with School of Medicine and Dentistry, Honors College, undergraduate academies and learning communities. **Credit/placement by examination:** AP, CLEP, IB, SAT, ACT, institutional tests. Maximum of 30 credits from International Baccalaureate. **Support services:** Learning center, pre-admission summer program, reduced course load, remedial instruction, study skills assistance, tutoring, writing center.

Honors college/program. Minimum 93 high school average, 1300 SAT combined reading and math, 29 ACT. Enroll approximately 325 freshmen a year. Program requirements include completion of colloquium and two honors seminars plus 16 credits of advanced study opportunities.

Majors. Architecture: Architecture, environmental design. **Area/ethnic studies:** African-American, American, Asian. **Biology:** General, biochemistry, bioinformatics, biomedical sciences, biophysics, biostatistics, biotechnology, ecology, exercise physiology, pharmacology/toxicology. **Business:** Accounting, business admin. **Communications:** Communications/speech/rhetoric, media studies. **Computer sciences:** Computer science, information systems. **Engineering:** General, aerospace, applied physics, biomedical, chemical, civil, computer, electrical, environmental, industrial, mechanical, structural. **English:** English lit. **Foreign languages:** Classics, French, German, Italian, linguistics, Spanish. **Health services:** Audiology/speech pathology, clinical lab science, nuclear medical technology, nursing (RN), occupational therapy. **History:** General. **Math:** General, applied. **Philosophy/religion:** Philosophy. **Physical sciences:** Chemistry, geology, physics, theoretical physics. **Psychology:** General. **Social sciences:** General, anthropology, economics, geography, political science, sociology. **Visual/performing arts:** Art, art history/conservation, dance, dramatic, film/cinema/video, music, music performance, studio arts.

Most popular majors. Biology 9%, business/marketing 22%, communications/journalism 8%, engineering/engineering technologies 11%, health sciences 6%, psychology 10%, social sciences 14%.

Computing on campus. 2,303 workstations in dormitories, library, computer center, student center. Dormitories wired for high-speed internet access and linked to campus network. Commuter students can connect to campus network. Online course registration, online library, helpline, repair service, student web hosting, wireless network available.

Student life. Freshman orientation: Available, $190 fee. Preregistration for classes offered. One-and-a-half-day program. **Policies:** University standards, administrative regulations and student conduct rules apply. **Housing:** Guaranteed on-campus for all undergraduates. Coed dorms, special housing for disabled, apartments, wellness housing available. $300 fully refundable deposit, deadline 5/1. Academic interest, honors, freshman, shared interest housing available. **Activities:** Bands, campus ministries, choral groups, dance, drama, film society, international student organizations, literary magazine, music ensembles, musical theater, radio station, student government, student newspaper, symphony orchestra, TV station, over 300 registered organizations.

Athletics. NCAA. **Intercollegiate:** Baseball M, basketball, cross-country, diving, football (tackle) M, rowing (crew) W, soccer, softball W, swimming, tennis, track and field, volleyball W, wrestling M. **Intramural:** Badminton, basketball, cross-country, football (non-tackle), racquetball, soccer, softball, tennis, volleyball. **Team name:** Bulls.

Student services. Adult student services, alcohol/substance abuse counseling, chaplain/spiritual director, career counseling, services for economically disadvantaged, student employment services, financial aid counseling, health services, legal services, minority student services, on-campus daycare, personal counseling, placement for graduates, veterans' counselor. **Physically disabled:** Services for visually, speech, hearing impaired.

Contact. E-mail: ub-admissions@buffalo.edu
Phone: (716) 645-6900 Toll-free number: (888) 822-3648
Fax: (716) 645-6411
Patricia Armstrong, Director of Admissions, SUNY University at Buffalo, 12 Capen Hall, Buffalo, NY 14260-1660

SUNY University at Stony Brook
Stony Brook, New York **CB member**
www.stonybrook.edu **CB code: 2548**

▶ Public 4-year university

▶ Residential campus in large town

▶ 15,655 degree-seeking undergraduates: 7% part-time, 47% women, 6% African American, 24% Asian American, 10% Hispanic American, 8% international

▶ 7,345 degree-seeking graduate students

▶ 38% of applicants admitted

▶ SAT or ACT with writing, application essay required

▶ 67% graduate within 6 years

General. Founded in 1957. Regionally accredited. **Degrees:** 3,643 bachelor's awarded; master's, professional, doctoral offered. **ROTC:** Army, Air Force. **Location:** 60 miles from New York City. **Calendar:** Semester, limited summer session. **Full-time faculty:** 972 total; 98% have terminal degrees, 19% minority, 34% women. **Part-time faculty:** 510 total; 79% have terminal degrees, 13% minority, 42% women. **Class size:** 33% < 20, 37% 20-39, 7% 40-49, 14% 50-99, 9% >100. **Special facilities:** Brookhaven National Laboratory, supercomputer, Van de Graaf accelerator, Centers for Molecular Medicine and Biology Learning Laboratories, Museum of Long Island Natural

Sciences, Stony Brook University Medical Center, observatory, marine station, marine and atmospheric sciences research vessel, nature preserve, center for the arts.

Freshman class profile. 27,822 applied, 10,536 admitted, 2,521 enrolled.

Mid 50% test scores			
SAT critical reading:	540-640	GPA 2.0-2.99:	3%
SAT math:	590-690	Rank in top quarter:	73%
SAT writing:	530-640	Rank in top tenth:	40%
ACT composite:	25-29	Return as sophomores:	92%
GPA 3.75 or higher:	43%	Out-of-state:	13%
GPA 3.50-3.74:	21%	Live on campus:	82%
GPA 3.0-3.49:	33%	International:	9%

Basis for selection. High school GPA, test scores and level of high school curriculum most important factors. One letter of recommendation and supplemental application, including an essay, are required. Class rank, interview, extracurricular activities, considered. Notification by 4/1. Applications accepted after priority deadline are on a space-available basis. SAT Subject Tests recommended. Audition and musicianship examination required for major in music. Two essays required for admission to Scholars for Medicine, Engineering Scholars for Medicine, and Scholar for Dental Medicine. **Home schooled:** State high school equivalency certificate required. Applicants required to take 5 Regents exams through their home district or have their home district verify that they have fulfilled high school graduation requirements. **Learning Disabled:** Applicants required to submit documentation of learning disability. Psychological and educational evaluation also required.

High school preparation. College-preparatory program required. 16 units required; 19 recommended. Required and recommended units include English 4, mathematics 3-4, social studies 4, science 3-4 and foreign language 2-3. 4 math and 4 science recommended for applicants to science, engineering, and math programs.

2011-2012 Annual costs. Tuition/fees: $6,994; $16,444 out-of-state. Room/board: $10,574. Books/supplies: $900. Personal expenses: $1,368.

Financial aid. **Non-need-based:** Scholarships awarded for academics, alumni affiliation, art, athletics, job skills, leadership, music/drama.

Application procedures. **Admission:** Closing date 2/1 (postmark date). $50 fee, may be waived for applicants with need. Admission notification on a rolling basis beginning on or about 4/1. Must reply by May 1 or within 2 week(s) if notified thereafter. **Financial aid:** Priority date 3/1; no closing date. FAFSA required. Applicants notified on a rolling basis starting 3/1; must reply by 5/1 or within 2 week(s) of notification.

Academics. **Special study options:** Combined bachelor's/graduate degree, cross-registration, distance learning, double major, dual enrollment of high school students, ESL, exchange student, honors, independent study, internships, New York semester, student-designed major, study abroad, teacher certification program, Washington semester. Sequential and combined Bachelor/Master degree programs. **Credit/placement by examination:** AP, CLEP, IB, SAT, ACT, institutional tests. 30 credit hours maximum toward bachelor's degree. **Support services:** Learning center, reduced course load, remedial instruction, tutoring, writing center.

Honors college/program. High grades in major subject areas, minimum cumulative unweighted high school average of 93, minimum combined SAT (exclusive of Writing) of 1300 or ACT score of 30, record of advanced or college-level course work, and evidence of writing ability required.

Majors. **Architecture:** Environmental design. **Area/ethnic studies:** African-American, American, Asian, Asian-American, European, women's. **Biology:** General, biochemistry, ecology, marine, pharmacology. **Business:** Business admin. **Communications:** Journalism. **Computer sciences:** Computer science, information systems. **Conservation:** Environmental studies, water/wetlands/marine. **Engineering:** General, biomedical, chemical, civil, computer, computer hardware, electrical, mechanical. **English:** English lit. **Foreign languages:** Comparative lit, French, German, Italian, linguistics, Russian, Spanish. **Health services:** Athletic training, clinical lab science, nursing (RN), respiratory therapy technology. **History:** General. **Human services:** Social work. **Liberal arts:** Humanities. **Math:** General, applied. **Philosophy/religion:** Philosophy, religion. **Physical sciences:** Astronomy, atmospheric science, chemistry, geology, physics, planetary. **Psychology:** General. **Social sciences:** Anthropology, economics, political science, sociology. **Visual/performing arts:** Art history/conservation, dramatic, film/cinema/video, music, studio arts.

Most popular majors. Biology 13%, business/marketing 9%, health sciences 17%, psychology 11%, social sciences 17%.

Computing on campus. 2,300 workstations in dormitories, library, computer center, student center. Dormitories wired for high-speed internet access and linked to campus network. Commuter students can connect to campus network. Online course registration, online library, helpline, repair service, student web hosting, wireless network available.

Student life. **Freshman orientation:** Mandatory, $180 fee. Preregistration for classes offered. 1-day session held June through August. 1-day program prior to first day of classes. **Housing:** Coed dorms, special housing for disabled, apartments, wellness housing available. $200 fully refundable deposit, deadline 5/1. Single sex floors in coed dorms available. **Activities:** Bands, choral groups, dance, drama, film society, literary magazine, music ensembles, musical theater, opera, radio station, student government, student newspaper, symphony orchestra, Jewish, Protestant, Catholic, Islamic Society, Baha'i religious organizations, Inter-Varsity Christian Fellowship, international club, Chinese association, Indian student association, Pakistan club, African students association.

Athletics. NCAA. **Intercollegiate:** Baseball M, basketball, cross-country, diving, football (tackle) M, lacrosse, soccer, softball W, swimming, tennis, track and field, volleyball W. **Intramural:** Basketball, softball. **Team name:** Seawolves.

Student services. Adult student services, alcohol/substance abuse counseling, chaplain/spiritual director, career counseling, services for economically disadvantaged, student employment services, financial aid counseling, health services, minority student services, on-campus daycare, personal counseling, placement for graduates, veterans' counselor, women's services. **Physically disabled:** Services for visually, speech, hearing impaired.

Contact. E-mail: enroll@stonybrook.edu
Phone: (631) 632-6868 Toll-free number: (800) 872-7869
Fax: (631) 632-9898
Judith Burke-Berhannan, Dean of Admissions, SUNY University at Stony Brook, 118 Administration Building, Stony Brook, NY 11794-1901

SUNY Upstate Medical University
Syracuse, New York
www.upstate.edu   **CB code: 2547**

▸ Public two-year upper-division health science and nursing college
▸ Residential campus in small city
▸ 34% of applicants admitted
▸ Application essay, interview required

General. Founded in 1834. Regionally accredited. Undergraduate level consists of upper-division programs. Affiliated with Crouse-Irving Memorial Hospital, Veteran's Administration Medical Center, Community General Hospital of Greater Syracuse, St. Joseph's Hospital Health Center, Hutchings Psychiatric Center. **Degrees:** 112 bachelor's awarded; master's, professional, doctoral offered. **Articulation:** Agreements with SUNY Alfred, SUNY Canton, SUNY Cobleskill, SUNY Cortland, SUNY Delhi, SUNY Geneseo, SUNY Morrisville, SUNY Oswego, SUNY Oneonta, Cayuga CC, Columbia-Greene CC, Finger Lakes CC, Genesee CC, Jefferson CC, Mohawk Valley CC, Monroe CC, Niagara County CC, North Country CC, Onondaga CC, Sullivan CC, Tompkins Cortland CC. **ROTC:** Army. **Location:** 250 miles from New York City, 150 miles from Buffalo. **Calendar:** Semester, limited summer session. **Full-time faculty:** 47 total; 55% have terminal degrees, 4% minority, 68% women. **Part-time faculty:** 7 total; 71% women. **Class size:** 82% < 20, 14% 20-39, 3% 40-49, less than 1% 50-99. **Special facilities:** Institutionally owned and operated 350-bed teaching hospital and Level 1 trauma center.

Student profile. 288 degree-seeking undergraduates, 1,473 degree-seeking graduate students. 478 applied as first time-transfer students, 163 admitted, 128 enrolled. 100% entered as juniors. 61% transferred from two-year, 39% transferred from four-year institutions.

Women:	70%	International:	3%
African American:	4%	Part-time:	26%
Asian American:	3%	Out-of-state:	9%
Hispanic American:	5%	25 or older:	52%

Basis for selection. College transcript, application essay, interview required. Evaluation of academic performance in courses required for admission. Personal interviews, recommendations, essay also important. Applicants must complete admissions course requirements prior to enrolling. Final decision made at discretion of admissions committee, regardless of applicant's prior academic standing. Transfer accepted as juniors.

2011-2012 Annual costs. Tuition/fees: $5,910; $15,360 out-of-state. Room only: $4,127. Books/supplies: $1,065. Personal expenses: $1,665.

Financial aid. 242 applied for aid; 242 were judged to have need; 242 of these received aid. Average need met was 100%. 40% of total undergraduate aid awarded as scholarships/grants, 60% as loans/jobs.

Application procedures. Admission: Rolling admission. $50 fee, may be waived for applicants with need. Application must be submitted online. High school seniors may apply for admission two years prior to intended date of entry. Application deadline for 3+3 and 4+3 Physical Therapy (DPT) Early Admission program February 1. Early Admission deadline for bachelor's programs March 1. Preference to New York residents. Transfer students apply in fall one year prior to intended date of entry. **Financial aid:** Applicants notified on a rolling basis starting 4/15; must reply within 2 weeks of notification. FAFSA required.

Academics. Special study options: Accelerated study, combined bachelor's/graduate degree, distance learning, independent study, internships. Distance Learning available for the Respiratory Therapy program at the SUNY Jefferson Community College campus. Accelerated 3+3 Doctor of Physical Therapy program available in conjunction with SUNY Brockport, SUNY Oneonta, SUNY Geneseo, SUNY Oswego, SUNY ESF, Syracuse University and LeMoyne College. Accelerated RN to MS nursing program. **Credit/placement by examination:** AP, CLEP, institutional tests. 60 credit hours maximum toward bachelor's degree.

Majors. Health services: Clinical lab science, nursing (RN), perfusion technology, respiratory therapy technology, sonography.

Computing on campus. 150 workstations in dormitories, library, computer center, student center. Dormitories wired for high-speed internet access and linked to campus network. Commuter students can connect to campus network. Helpline, student web hosting, wireless network available.

Student life. Policies: Students under 21 required to live on campus unless living at home. **Housing:** Coed dorms, apartments available. $150 nonrefundable deposit, deadline 7/1. **Activities:** International student organizations, student government, campus activities governing board, Chinese student association, Adopt-a-School, Christian medical fellowship, Community Outreach Preventive Education (COPE), Jewish medical association, Muslim student association.

Athletics. Intramural: Basketball, racquetball, soccer, softball, table tennis, tennis, volleyball.

Student services. Alcohol/substance abuse counseling, career counseling, financial aid counseling, health services, minority student services, on-campus daycare, personal counseling, placement for graduates, veterans' counselor.

Contact. E-mail: admiss@upstate.edu
Phone: (315) 464-4570 Fax: (315) 464-8867
Jennifer Welch, Director of Admissions, SUNY Upstate Medical University, 766 Irving Avenue, Syracuse, NY 13210

Syracuse University

Syracuse, New York	CB member
www.syr.edu	CB code: 2823

- Private 4-year university
- Residential campus in small city
- 14,220 degree-seeking undergraduates: 4% part-time, 56% women, 8% African American, 9% Asian American, 9% Hispanic American, 1% Native American, 8% international
- 5,828 degree-seeking graduate students
- 49% of applicants admitted
- SAT or ACT with writing, application essay required
- 82% graduate within 6 years; 23% enter graduate study

General. Founded in 1870. Regionally accredited. **Degrees:** 3,122 bachelor's, 7 associate awarded; master's, professional, doctoral offered. **ROTC:** Army, Air Force. **Location:** 150 miles from Albany, 250 miles from New York City. **Calendar:** Semester, extensive summer session. **Full-time faculty:** 987 total; 87% have terminal degrees, 13% minority, 36% women. **Part-time faculty:** 572 total; 7% minority, 51% women. **Class size:** 61% < 20, 26% 20-39, 4% 40-49, 6% 50-99, 3% >100. **Special facilities:** Global Collaboratory, connects students via satellite to sites all over the world; life sciences complex, media labs, digital convergence center, technology center, environmental and energy facilities, advanced flight simulator, Ballentine investment institute, darkrooms, professional equity theater, child development laboratory school, audio laboratory and archive, speech and hearing clinic.

Freshman class profile. 25,884 applied, 12,779 admitted, 3,410 enrolled.

Mid 50% test scores			
SAT critical reading:	510-620	Rank in top quarter:	73%
SAT math:	540-650	Rank in top tenth:	40%
SAT writing:	520-630	End year in good standing:	91%
ACT composite:	23-28	Return as sophomores:	92%
GPA 3.75 or higher:	43%	Out-of-state:	59%
GPA 3.50-3.74:	20%	Live on campus:	99%
GPA 3.0-3.49:	30%	International:	8%
GPA 2.0-2.99:	7%	Fraternities:	11%
		Sororities:	18%

Basis for selection. Important factors include strong performance in a rigorous college preparatory curriculum, good citizenship, personal characteristics and talents. Other factors include standardized test scores, academic recommendations and counselor evaluation. Applicants not admitted to their first-choice program may be considered for an alternate offer of admission on a space-available basis if second/third choice options are indicated on the SU Supplement to the Common Application. Priority given to those applying to first-choice programs. Portfolio required of applicants to art and architecture programs; audition required of applicants to drama and music programs. Interviews made available, but are not required. **Home schooled:** Transcript of courses and grades, interview, letter of recommendation (nonparent) required. Submit detailed course descriptions/syllabus used. Two recommendations from someone outside the home are required. For financial aid eligibility, letter from local school district must be submitted acknowledging that curriculum taught at home is substantially equivalent to that of the school district, or GED.

High school preparation. College-preparatory program required. 19 units required. Required units include English 4, mathematics 4, social studies 4, science 4 (laboratory 4) and foreign language 3.

2011-2012 Annual costs. Tuition/fees: $37,667. Room/board: $13,254. Books/supplies: $1,308. Personal expenses: $900.

2011-2012 Financial aid. Need-based: 2,545 full-time freshmen applied for aid; 1,999 were judged to have need; 1,999 of these received aid. Average need met was 96%. Average scholarship/grant was $24,030; average loan $6,600. 74% of total undergraduate aid awarded as scholarships/grants, 26% as loans/jobs. **Non-need-based:** Awarded to 2,227 full-time undergraduates, including 512 freshmen. Scholarships awarded for academics, art, athletics, music/drama, ROTC, state residency.

Application procedures. Admission: Closing date 1/1 (postmark date). $70 fee, may be waived for applicants with need. Admission notification on a rolling basis beginning on or about 3/16. Must reply by 5/1. **Financial aid:** Closing date 2/1. FAFSA, CSS PROFILE required. Applicants notified by 3/15; must reply by 5/1.

Academics. Special study options: Accelerated study, cooperative education, cross-registration, distance learning, double major, dual enrollment of high school students, ESL, honors, independent study, internships, liberal arts/career combination, New York semester, student-designed major, study abroad, teacher certification program, Washington semester. **Credit/placement by examination:** AP, CLEP, IB, institutional tests. **Support services:** Learning center, pre-admission summer program, study skills assistance, tutoring, writing center.

Majors. Architecture: Architecture. **Area/ethnic studies:** African-American, American, Latin American, Near/Middle Eastern, Russian/Slavic, women's. **Biology:** General, biochemistry, biotechnology, neuroscience. **Business:** Accounting, business admin, entrepreneurial studies, finance, logistics, marketing, real estate. **Communications:** Advertising, broadcast journalism, communications/speech/rhetoric, journalism, photojournalism, public relations, radio/TV. **Computer sciences:** General, information systems. **Education:** Art, biology, chemistry, early childhood special, elementary special ed, English, mathematics, music, physical, physics, social studies. **Engineering:** General, aerospace, biomedical, chemical, civil, computer, electrical, environmental, mechanical. **English:** English lit. **Foreign languages:** General, classics, comparative lit, French, German, Italian, linguistics, Russian, Spanish. **Health services:** Communication disorders, predental, premedicine, preveterinary. **History:** General. **Human services:** General, social work. **Liberal arts:** Arts/sciences. **Math:** General, applied. **Parks/recreation:** Exercise sciences, health/fitness, sports admin. **Philosophy/religion:** Ethics, philosophy, religion. **Physical sciences:** Chemistry, geology, physics. **Protective services:** Forensics. **Psychology:** General. **Social sciences:** Anthropology, economics, geography, international relations, political science, sociology. **Visual/performing arts:** Acting, art history/conservation, ceramics, cinematography, commercial/advertising art, design, digital arts, documentaries, dramatic, fashion design, illustration, industrial design, interior design, metal/jewelry, music, music history, music management, music performance, music theory/composition, musical theater, painting, percussion instruments, photography, piano/keyboard, printmaking, sculpture, stringed instruments, studio arts, theater design, voice/opera. **Work/family studies:** General, family studies, human nutrition, merchandising.

Most popular majors. Business/marketing 16%, communications/journalism 15%, engineering/engineering technologies 6%, social sciences 13%, visual/performing arts 11%.

Computing on campus. 3,500 workstations in dormitories, library, computer center, student center. Dormitories wired for high-speed internet access and linked to campus network. Commuter students can connect to campus network. Online course registration, online library, helpline, repair service, student web hosting, wireless network available.

Student life. Freshman orientation: Mandatory. Preregistration for classes offered. Offered two times a year, in August (4 to 5 days) and January (2 days) and provides both traditional programming (convocations, course registration and advising) as well as activities designed to build community. **Policies:** Freshmen and sophomores required to live on campus. Students must adhere to the Code of Student Conduct. Freshmen not permitted cars on campus. **Housing:** Guaranteed on-campus for freshmen. Coed dorms, special housing for disabled, apartments, fraternity/sorority housing, wellness housing available. $400 fully refundable deposit, deadline 5/1. Single-sex floors and wings, numerous learning communities and special interest housing available. **Activities:** Bands, campus ministries, choral groups, dance, drama, film society, international student organizations, literary magazine, music ensembles, musical theater, opera, radio station, student government, student newspaper, symphony orchestra, TV station, more than 300 recognized student organizations.

Athletics. NCAA. **Intercollegiate:** Basketball, cheerleading, cross-country, field hockey W, football (tackle) M, ice hockey W, lacrosse, rowing (crew), soccer, softball W, tennis W, track and field, volleyball W. **Intramural:** Basketball, football (non-tackle), racquetball, soccer, softball, tennis, volleyball. **Team name:** Orange.

Student services. Adult student services, alcohol/substance abuse counseling, chaplain/spiritual director, career counseling, services for economically disadvantaged, student employment services, financial aid counseling, health services, legal services, minority student services, on-campus daycare, personal counseling, placement for graduates, veterans' counselor, women's services. **Physically disabled:** Services for visually, speech, hearing impaired.

Contact. E-mail: orange@syr.edu
Phone: (315) 443-3611 Fax: (315) 443-4226
Office of Admissions, Syracuse University, 100 Crouse-Hinds Hall, Syracuse, NY 13244-2130

Talmudical Institute of Upstate New York
Rochester, New York
www.tiuny.org　　　　　　　　　　　　**CB code: 1426**

▶ Private 5-year rabbinical and seminary college for men affiliated with Jewish faith
▶ Residential campus in large city
▶ 22 degree-seeking undergraduates
▶ Interview required

General. Founded in 1974. Accredited by AARTS. First Talmudic degree offered. **Degrees:** 1 bachelor's awarded; doctoral offered. **Calendar:** Semester. **Full-time faculty:** 3 total. **Part-time faculty:** 3 total.

Freshman class profile.

Out-of-state:	35%	**Live on campus:**	100%

Basis for selection. Interview and school achievement record important.

2011-2012 Annual costs. Tuition/fees: $5,500. Room/board: $4,000.

Application procedures. Admission: Closing date 9/1. Admission notification on a rolling basis. **Financial aid:** No deadline. Applicants notified on a rolling basis.

Academics. Special study options: Dual enrollment of high school students. **Credit/placement by examination:** AP, CLEP.

Majors. Philosophy/religion: Judaic. **Theology:** Talmudic.

Computing on campus. 2 workstations in computer center.

Student life. Policies: Religious observance required. **Housing:** Guaranteed on-campus for all undergraduates.

Contact. Phone: (585) 473-2810 Fax: (585) 442-0417
Talmudical Institute of Upstate New York, 769 Park Avenue, Rochester, NY 14607

Talmudical Seminary Oholei Torah
Brooklyn, New York
　　　　　　　　　　　　　　　　CB code: 0712

▶ Private 4-year rabbinical and seminary college for men affiliated with Jewish faith
▶ Very large city
▶ Interview required

General. Founded in 1956. Accredited by AARTS. First Talmudic degree offered. **Degrees:** 5 bachelor's awarded. **ROTC:** Army, Naval. **Calendar:** Semester, limited summer session.

Basis for selection. Interview and institutional entrance examinations important.

2011-2012 Annual costs. Tuition/fees: $9,350. Room/board: $2,900.

Application procedures. Admission: No deadline. Admission notification on a rolling basis. **Financial aid:** No deadline. Applicants notified on a rolling basis starting 5/21.

Academics. Credit/placement by examination: AP, CLEP, institutional tests. **Support services:** Tutoring.

Majors. Theology: Talmudic.

Student life. Policies: Religious observance required. **Activities:** TV station, Lubavitcher Youth Organization.

Student services. Career counseling, personal counseling.

Contact. Phone: (718) 774-5215
Talmudical Seminary Oholei Torah, 667 Eastern Parkway, Brooklyn, NY 11213-3397

Torah Temimah Talmudical Seminary
Brooklyn, New York
　　　　　　　　　　　　　　　　CB code: 7132

▶ Private 4-year rabbinical and seminary college for men affiliated with Jewish faith
▶ Very large city
▶ 222 degree-seeking undergraduates

General. Accredited by AARTS. **Degrees:** 4 bachelor's awarded; doctoral offered. **Calendar:** Differs by program.

2011-2012 Annual costs. Tuition/fees: $9,550. Room/board: $3,000.

Application procedures. Admission: No deadline.

Academics. Credit/placement by examination: AP, CLEP.

Majors. Theology: Talmudic.

Contact. Phone: (718) 853-8500
Torah Temimah Talmudical Seminary, 555 Ocean Parkway, Brooklyn, NY 11218

Touro College
New York, New York
www.touro.edu　　　　　　　　　　　**CB code: 2902**

▶ Private 4-year liberal arts college
▶ Commuter campus in very large city
▶ 8,153 degree-seeking undergraduates

General. Founded in 1970. Regionally accredited. School of General Studies provides programs for part-time and adult students. **Degrees:** 1,445 bachelor's, 672 associate awarded; master's, professional offered. **Calendar:** Semester, limited summer session. **Full-time faculty:** 619 total; 50% women. **Part-time faculty:** 970 total; 50% women. **Class size:** 84% < 20, 15% 20-39, less than 1% 40-49, less than 1% 50-99.

Basis for selection. For College of Liberal Arts and Sciences, 3.0 high school GPA, SAT verbal and math scores of 500 preferred. Recommendations from high school teachers and counselors and motivation important. High

school experience less important for applicants to associate degree programs who take institutional admissions test. SAT or ACT recommended. SAT or ACT required for applicants to school of Health Sciences. Essay and interview recommended for College of Liberal Arts and Sciences.

High school preparation. 17 units recommended. Recommended units include English 4, mathematics 3, social studies 3, science 3 and foreign language 3. Requirements may vary by division.

2011-2012 Annual costs. Tuition/fees: $12,600. Tuition and fees vary by program. Reported costs are for the New York School of Career and Applied Studies. Room and board available only for students in the Lander College of Arts and Sciences. Room/board: $7,200. Books/supplies: $750. Personal expenses: $1,764.

Application procedures. Admission: No deadline. $50 fee, may be waived for applicants with need. Admission notification on a rolling basis. **Financial aid:** Priority date 5/15, closing date 6/1. FAFSA required. Applicants notified by 8/15.

Academics. Special study options: Accelerated study, combined bachelor's/graduate degree, distance learning, dual enrollment of high school students, ESL, honors, independent study, internships, liberal arts/career combination, student-designed major, study abroad, teacher certification program. **Credit/placement by examination:** AP, CLEP, institutional tests. **Support services:** Learning center, reduced course load, remedial instruction, tutoring.

Majors. Biology: General. **Business:** General, accounting, business admin, management information systems, managerial economics, marketing. **Communications:** Communications/speech/rhetoric. **Computer sciences:** General. **Education:** Special ed. **English:** English lit, rhetoric/composition. **Foreign languages:** General, Hebrew. **Health services:** Communication disorders, medical records technology, nursing (RN), physician assistant, predental, premedicine, prepharmacy, preveterinary. **History:** General. **Liberal arts:** Arts/sciences. **Math:** General. **Philosophy/religion:** Judaic, philosophy. **Physical sciences:** Chemistry. **Psychology:** General. **Social sciences:** General, economics, political science, sociology.

Computing on campus. 400 workstations in library, computer center.

Student life. Freshman orientation: Available. Preregistration for classes offered. **Housing:** Single-sex dorms available. $50 deposit. No board or meal plan available. Kitchen facilities in student housing. **Activities:** Literary magazine, student government, student newspaper, accounting and business society, biology club, debating society, Jewish Affairs Committee, foreign students association, Omicron Delta.

Student services. Adult student services, career counseling, student employment services, personal counseling, placement for graduates, veterans' counselor.

Contact. E-mail: lasadmit@adminm.touro.edu
Phone: (718) 252-7800 ext. 299 Fax: (718) 253-9455
Arthur Wigfall, Director of Admissions, Touro College, 1602 Avenue J, Brooklyn, NY 11230

U.T.A. Mesivta-Kiryas Jocl
Monroe, New York

♦ Private 4-year rabbinical college for men affiliated with Jewish faith
♦ Large town
♦ 1,315 degree-seeking undergraduates

General. Accredited by AARTS. **Degrees:** 225 bachelor's awarded. **Calendar:** Semester. **Full-time faculty:** 120 total.

Basis for selection. Religious commitment most important.

2011-2012 Annual costs. Tuition/fees: $7,500. Room/board: $4,000.

Application procedures. Admission: No deadline.

Academics. Credit/placement by examination: AP, CLEP.

Majors. Theology: Talmudic.

Contact. Phone: (845) 783-9901
U.T.A. Mesivta-Kiryas Jocl, 9 Nickelsburg Road, #312, Monroe, NY 10950-2169

Union College
Schenectady, New York
www.union.edu

CB member
CB code: 2920

♦ Private 4-year engineering and liberal arts college
♦ Residential campus in small city
♦ 2,174 degree-seeking undergraduates: 47% women, 5% African American, 6% Asian American, 6% Hispanic American, 5% international
♦ 43% of applicants admitted
♦ Application essay required
♦ 86% graduate within 6 years; 35% enter graduate study

General. Founded in 1795. Regionally accredited. **Degrees:** 529 bachelor's awarded. **ROTC:** Army, Naval, Air Force. **Location:** 15 miles from Albany, 175 miles from New York City. **Calendar:** Trimester, limited summer session. **Full-time faculty:** 202 total; 98% have terminal degrees, 11% minority, 39% women. **Part-time faculty:** 35 total; 37% have terminal degrees, 54% women. **Class size:** 68% < 20, 29% 20-39, 3% 40-49, less than 1% 50-99. **Special facilities:** Horticultural garden, superconducting nuclear magnetic resonance spectrometer, electron scanning microscope, tandem pelletron positive ion accelerator, X-ray diffraction equipment, remote-controlled telescope.

Freshman class profile. 5,151 applied, 2,197 admitted, 572 enrolled.

Mid 50% test scores			
SAT critical reading:	590-680	GPA 2.0-2.99:	13%
SAT math:	610-700	Rank in top quarter:	85%
SAT writing:	600-680	Rank in top tenth:	57%
ACT composite:	28-31	End year in good standing:	99%
GPA 3.75 or higher:	31%	Return as sophomores:	94%
GPA 3.50-3.74:	17%	Out-of-state:	64%
GPA 3.0-3.49:	39%	Live on campus:	100%
		International:	5%

Basis for selection. GED not accepted. Course selection and grades closely considered along with recommendations from high school and extracurricular record. Ethnic and geographic diversity sought in student body. Testing optional except for combined programs. Leadership in Medicine program applicants must submit SAT and SAT Subject Test; Law and Public Policy program applicants must submit SAT or ACT. Applicants to these programs must complete necessary tests no later than December of senior year. International students required to submit SAT or ACT, and TOEFL or IELTS if English is not their first language. Portfolio recommended for art programs. **Home schooled:** Interview required.

High school preparation. College-preparatory program required. 16 units required; 24 recommended. Required and recommended units include English 4, mathematics 3-4, social studies 1-2, history 1-2, science 2-4 (laboratory 2-4) and foreign language 2-4.

2011-2012 Annual costs. Comprehensive fee: $54,273. Rebates offered to students living off-campus and/or not using a meal plan.

2011-2012 Financial aid. Need-based: 393 full-time freshmen applied for aid; 313 were judged to have need; 311 of these received aid. Average need met was 100%. Average scholarship/grant was $30,513; average loan $3,365. 96% of total undergraduate aid awarded as scholarships/grants, 4% as loans/jobs. **Non-need-based:** Awarded to 429 full-time undergraduates, including 150 freshmen. Scholarships awarded for academics, ROTC.

Application procedures. Admission: Closing date 1/15 (postmark date). $50 fee, may be waived for applicants with need, free for online applicants. Admission notification by 4/1. Must reply by 5/1. We recommend that transfer students who have less than one year's worth of credits submit standardized test scores. **Financial aid:** Priority date 2/1; no closing date. FAFSA, CSS PROFILE required. Applicants notified by 3/25; must reply by 5/1.

Academics. Special study options: Accelerated study, combined bachelor's/graduate degree, cross-registration, double major, dual enrollment of high school students, honors, independent study, internships, liberal arts/career combination, student-designed major, study abroad, teacher certification program. **Credit/placement by examination:** AP, CLEP, IB, institutional tests. 4 credit hours maximum toward bachelor's degree. **Support services:** Study skills assistance, tutoring, writing center.

Majors. Area/ethnic studies: American, Asian, Latin American/Caribbean. **Biology:** General, biochemistry, neuroscience. **Computer sciences:** General. **Conservation:** Environmental science. **Engineering:** Biomedical, electrical, mechanical. **English:** English lit. **Foreign languages:** General, classics, French, German, Spanish. **History:** General. **Liberal arts:** Arts/sciences, humanities. **Math:** General. **Philosophy/religion:** Philosophy, religion. **Physical sciences:** Astronomy, chemistry, geology, physics. **Psychology:** General. **Social sciences:** General, anthropology, economics, political science, sociology. **Visual/performing arts:** General, studio arts.

Most popular majors. Biology 15%, engineering/engineering technologies 12%, English 7%, history 6%, liberal arts 6%, physical sciences 8%, psychology 10%, social sciences 26%.

Computing on campus. 535 workstations in dormitories, library, computer center, student center. Dormitories wired for high-speed internet access and linked to campus network. Commuter students can connect to campus network. Online course registration, online library, helpline, repair service, student web hosting, wireless network available.

Student life. Freshman orientation: Mandatory, $250 fee. Preregistration for classes offered. Begins Thursday and ends Sunday before classes begin. Orientation fee included in Admission and Security deposit. **Policies:** All students expected to live on campus during undergraduate years, provided housing is available. Freshmen not permitted cars on campus. **Housing:** Guaranteed on-campus for freshmen. Coed dorms, apartments, fraternity/sorority housing, wellness housing available. Minerva Houses. Up to 45 students live in each. All students and faculty members have house affiliations. Each house contributes intellectual, cultural, and social events to the campus. **Activities:** Bands, campus ministries, choral groups, dance, drama, film society, international student organizations, literary magazine, music ensembles, Model UN, radio station, student government, student newspaper, symphony orchestra, TV station, African and Latino Alliance of Students, Asian Student Union, Big Brothers/Big Sisters, College Republicans, Intervarsity Christian Fellowship, Jewish Student Union, Middle Eastern Civilization and Culture Association, Newman Club, UCARE-a community action club, Union College Democrats.

Athletics. NCAA. **Intercollegiate:** Baseball M, basketball, cross-country, diving, field hockey W, football (tackle) M, ice hockey, lacrosse, rowing (crew), soccer, softball W, swimming, tennis, track and field, volleyball W. **Intramural:** Basketball, football (non-tackle) M, football (tackle), lacrosse, soccer, softball, squash, tennis, volleyball. **Team name:** Dutchmen, Dutchwomen.

Student services. Alcohol/substance abuse counseling, chaplain/spiritual director, career counseling, services for economically disadvantaged, student employment services, financial aid counseling, health services, minority student services, personal counseling, placement for graduates. **Physically disabled:** Services for visually, hearing impaired.

Contact. E-mail: admissions@union.edu
Phone: (518) 388-6112 Toll-free number: (888) 843-6688
Fax: (518) 388-6986
Ann Brown, Director of Admissions, Union College, Grant Hall, 807 Union Street, Schenectady, NY 12308-3107

United States Merchant Marine Academy
Kings Point, New York
www.usmma.edu   CB code: 2923

- Public 4-year military and maritime college
- Residential campus in large town
- 1,058 degree-seeking undergraduates: 13% women
- 24 degree-seeking graduate students
- 20% of applicants admitted
- SAT or ACT (ACT writing optional), application essay required

General. Founded in 1943. Regionally accredited. Accepted applicants appointed to academy as midshipmen, USNR. **Degrees:** 207 bachelor's awarded; master's offered. **Location:** 20 miles from midtown Manhattan. **Calendar:** Trimester, limited summer session. **Full-time faculty:** 88 total. **Part-time faculty:** 1 total. **Class size:** 45% < 20, 54% 20-39, less than 1% 40-49, less than 1% 50-99. **Special facilities:** US Merchant Marine Museum, computer-aided operational research facility.

Freshman class profile. 2,076 applied, 412 admitted, 285 enrolled.

Mid 50% test scores			
SAT critical reading:	560-640	Rank in top tenth:	24%
SAT math:	600-680	Out-of-state:	89%
ACT composite:	25-29	Live on campus:	100%
Rank in top quarter:	62%	International:	1%

Basis for selection. Nomination by U.S. representatives or senators. Competitive standing determined by test scores, high school GPA, class rank, motivation, extracurricular activities, interest in academy, industry, citizenship, and recommendations from counselors, teachers, school principal. Must also meet medical requirements and pass physical fitness exercise regimen. Untimed test results not acceptable. Interview recommended. **Home schooled:** Letter of recommendation (nonparent) required. Must have completed chemistry with lab or physics with lab through state-certified instructor.

High school preparation. College-preparatory program recommended. 18 units required. Required and recommended units include English 4, mathematics 3-4, social studies 4, science 3-4 (laboratory 2-3), foreign language 2 and academic electives 8.

2011-2012 Annual costs. All midshipmen receive full tuition, room, board, and medical and dental expenses from the federal government. Total required freshmen fees ($2,905) include purchase of laptop computer, color printer, and PDA. International freshmen students pay required fees plus additional international student fee ($13,125 total). Books/supplies: $767.

2010-2011 Financial aid. Need-based: 91% of total undergraduate aid awarded as scholarships/grants, 9% as loans/jobs. **Additional information:** Students paid by steamship companies while at sea.

Application procedures. Admission: Closing date 3/1 (receipt date). No application fee. Admission notification on a rolling basis beginning on or about 11/1. Must reply by May 1 or within 2 week(s) if notified thereafter. **Financial aid:** Priority date 5/1; no closing date. FAFSA, institutional form required. Applicants notified on a rolling basis starting 1/31.

Academics. Special study options: Honors, independent study, internships, semester at sea, study abroad. Sea training on merchant vessels. **Credit/placement by examination:** AP, CLEP, institutional tests. **Support services:** Learning center, remedial instruction, study skills assistance, tutoring.

Majors. Engineering: Marine, systems.

Most popular majors. Engineering/engineering technologies 51%, trade and industry 49%.

Computing on campus. PC or laptop required. 1,200 workstations in dormitories, library. Dormitories wired for high-speed internet access and linked to campus network. Helpline, wireless network available.

Student life. Freshman orientation: Mandatory. Preregistration for classes offered. 2-week orientation starting in early July. **Policies:** All regulated within the Regiment of Midshipmen. Freshmen not permitted cars on campus. **Housing:** Guaranteed on-campus for all undergraduates. Coed dorms, wellness housing available. Students required to live on campus. **Activities:** Bands, choral groups, drama, musical theater, student government, student newspaper, Christian Fellowship Community, Newman Club.

Athletics. NCAA. **Intercollegiate:** Baseball M, basketball, cross-country, diving, football (tackle) M, golf, lacrosse M, rowing (crew), sailing, soccer M, softball W, swimming, tennis, track and field, volleyball W, wrestling M. **Intramural:** Baseball M, basketball, boxing, cross-country, football (tackle) M, racquetball, rowing (crew), soccer, softball, tennis, track and field, volleyball, water polo, weight lifting. **Team name:** Mariners.

Student services. Alcohol/substance abuse counseling, chaplain/spiritual director, career counseling, student employment services, financial aid counseling, health services, personal counseling, placement for graduates.

Contact. E-mail: admissions@usmma.edu
Phone: (516) 773-5391 Toll-free number: (866) 546-4778
Fax: (516) 773-5390
Capt. Robert Johnson, Director of Admissions, United States Merchant Marine Academy, 300 Steamboat Road, Admissions Center, Kings Point, NY 11024-1699

United States Military Academy
West Point, New York   CB member
www.westpoint.edu   CB code: 2924

- Public 4-year military college
- Residential campus in small town
- 4,624 degree-seeking undergraduates: 16% women, 7% African American, 5% Asian American, 9% Hispanic American, 1% Native American, 1% international
- 11% of applicants admitted
- SAT or ACT with writing, application essay required
- 83% graduate within 6 years; 3% enter graduate study

General. Founded in 1802. Regionally accredited. **Degrees:** 1,067 bachelor's awarded. **Location:** 50 miles from New York City. **Calendar:** Semester, limited summer session. **Full-time faculty:** 613 total; 46% have terminal degrees, 10% minority, 19% women. **Class size:** 94% < 20, 6% 20-39, less than 1% 40-49. **Special facilities:** West Point museum, American Revolutionary-era Fort Putnam, 4,500-seat Eisenhower Hall, golf course, ski slope, 500,000 square-foot Arvin Cadet Physical Development Center, Jefferson Hall Library and learning center.

Freshman class profile. 13,954 applied, 1,473 admitted, 1,231 enrolled.

Mid 50% test scores			
SAT critical reading:	560-680	Rank in top tenth:	48%
SAT math:	590-690	End year in good standing:	95%
SAT writing:	550-660	Return as sophomores:	94%
ACT composite:	25-31	Out-of-state:	93%
Rank in top quarter:	75%	Live on campus:	100%
		International:	1%

Basis for selection. All applicants must obtain a nomination from an approved source (Congress, the President, Vice President, or Department of the Army). Applicants must be at least 17 but not yet 23 years of age by July 1 of year of entry. They must also be an unmarried U.S. citizen (foreign national with approval) in good health, with no parental obligations or responsibilities, and must demonstrate leadership ability. Applicants should seek nomination and submit Service Academies Pre-candidate Questionnaire in spring of junior year. Applicants advised to seek nominations from as many sources as possible and to contact Admissions office between July 1 and January 15 of senior year. All new cadets must pass Cadet Basic Training before being admitted into West Point. Interview recommended. **Learning Disabled:** Students admitted into West Point are commissioned as officers in the U.S. Army at graduation. Therefore, students must meet certain requirements specified by public law in order to be considered for admission to West Point. Students must be in good physical and mental health and pass a Department of Defense qualifying medical examination.

High school preparation. 19 units recommended. Recommended units include English 4, mathematics 4, social studies 1, history 1, science 4 (laboratory 2), foreign language 2 and academic electives 3. English units should have strong emphasis on composition, grammar, literature and speech; math should include algebra, geometry, intermediate algebra, and trigonometry; U.S. history should include courses in geography, government and economics. Precalculus, calculus and basic computing course helpful.

2011-2012 Annual costs. Tuition covered by a full scholarship. All students are on Active Duty Status as members of the U.S. Army and receive an annual salary of approximately $10,150. Room and board, medical and dental care provided by the U.S. Army. However, a one-time deposit of $2,000 required upon admission to help pay for the initial issue of uniforms, books, supplies, equipment and fees. If needed, loans of $100 to $2,000 are available for the deposit. Graduates incur a 5-year Active Duty service obligation.

Financial aid. **Additional information:** Cadets are permitted to receive scholarships, but since there are no tuition, room or board charges, scholarships stipulated for tuition, room or board that are based only on need rather than merit cannot be accepted. Scholarships may be used for textbooks, uniforms and other expenses, or used dollar for dollar to offset initial $2,000 deposit.

Application procedures. Admission: Closing date 2/28 (receipt date). No application fee. Application must be submitted online. Admission notification on a rolling basis beginning on or about 11/15. Must reply by 5/1.

Academics. West Point's core curriculum provides a foundation in mathematics, basic sciences, engineering sciences, information technology, humanities, behavioral sciences and social sciences. This core curriculum, ranging in size from 26 to 30 courses depending on the major, represents the essential broad base of knowledge necessary for success as a commissioned officer, while also supporting each cadet's choice of academic specialization. **Special study options:** Double major, exchange student, honors, independent study, internships, study abroad. Opportunities to attend Army Schools (Airborne, Air Assault, etc.) to learn special skills and to intern with an Army organization during the summer. **Credit/placement by examination:** AP, CLEP, institutional tests. Entering freshmen may be excused from certain core courses if they have sufficient knowledge of a subject to meet the appropriate standards. Credit earned at other colleges, Advanced Placement examination scores, and tests administered at West Point are considered in the validation decision. Validation of a course allows a student to substitute an additional elective in place of the validated course. If a student shows unusual ability or has prior knowledge of a subject but cannot validate it, he or she may be enrolled in an advanced or accelerated program. **Support services:** Learning center, reduced course load, remedial instruction, study skills assistance, tutoring.

Majors. Area/ethnic studies: African, East Asian, European, Latin American, Near/Middle Eastern, regional, Russian/Slavic. **Biology:** General. **Business:** Business admin, organizational behavior. **Computer sciences:** General, information systems, information technology. **Conservation:** Environmental science, environmental studies. **Engineering:** Chemical, civil, electrical, environmental, mechanical, nuclear, operations research, systems. **Foreign languages:** Arabic, Chinese, French, German, Portuguese, Russian, Spanish. **History:** American, military. **Liberal arts:** Humanities. **Math:** General. **Parks/recreation:** Exercise sciences. **Physical sciences:** General, chemistry, physics. **Psychology:** General. **Social sciences:** Economics, geography, international relations, political science, sociology, U.S. government.

Most popular majors. Business/marketing 6%, engineering/engineering technologies 27%, foreign language 9%, social sciences 18%.

Computing on campus. PC or laptop required. 5,195 workstations in dormitories, library, computer center. Dormitories wired for high-speed internet access and linked to campus network. Commuter students can connect to campus network. Online library, helpline, repair service, wireless network available.

Student life. Freshman orientation: Mandatory. Preregistration for classes offered. Cadet basic training (CBT) is an initial, 6-week cadet program held over the summer, designed to help new cadets make a rapid transition to the military lifestyle. CBT focuses on basic soldier skills and courtesies, discipline, personal appearance, military drill and ceremonies, and physical fitness. Extensive demands are made on new cadets as a test of their emotional stability, perseverance, and abiltiy to organize and perform under stress. **Policies:** Through a formal system cadets enforce the Honor Code with power to recommend dismissal. Military dress required. All cadets participate in intercollegiate, club or intramural level sport each semester. Seniors and juniors (after spring break) permitted to maintain cars. Freshmen not permitted cars on campus. **Housing:** Guaranteed on-campus for all undergraduates. Coed dorms, wellness housing available. **Activities:** Pep band, campus ministries, choral groups, dance, drama, film society, international student organizations, literary magazine, music ensembles, Model UN, musical theater, radio station, student government, Arabic language club, Asian-Pacific club, Catholic cadet catechists, Big Brothers & Big Sisters, cadet alcohol and drug intervention council, Jewish chapel choir, cultural affairs group, domestic affairs forum, student conference on US Affairs, scoutmaster's council.

Athletics. NCAA. **Intercollegiate:** Baseball M, basketball, cheerleading, cross-country, diving, football (tackle) M, golf M, gymnastics M, ice hockey M, lacrosse M, rifle, soccer, softball W, swimming, tennis, track and field, volleyball W, wrestling M. **Intramural:** Basketball, boxing, football (tackle), rugby, soccer, squash, swimming, wrestling M. **Team name:** Black Knights.

Student services. Alcohol/substance abuse counseling, chaplain/spiritual director, career counseling, health services, legal services, personal counseling, placement for graduates, women's services.

Contact. E-mail: admissions@usma.edu
Phone: (845) 938-5760
Col. Deborah McDonald, Director of Admissions, United States Military Academy, 646 Swift Road, West Point, NY 10996-1905

United Talmudical Seminary
Brooklyn, New York

CB code: 0696

- Private 5-year rabbinical college for men affiliated with Jewish faith
- Very large city
- 1,454 degree-seeking undergraduates

General. Founded in 1949. Accredited by AARTS. First Talmudic degree and ordination available. **Degrees:** 170 bachelor's awarded; master's offered. **Calendar:** Semester. **Full-time faculty:** 41 total. **Part-time faculty:** 96 total.

Basis for selection. Institutional examination.

Application procedures. Admission: No deadline.

Academics. Credit/placement by examination: AP, CLEP.

Majors. Theology: Talmudic.

Contact. Phone: (718) 963-9260
Moses Greenfield, Director of Admissions, United Talmudical Seminary, 82 Lee Avenue, Brooklyn, NY 11211

University of Rochester
Rochester, New York
www.rochester.edu

CB member
CB code: 2928

- Private 4-year university
- Residential campus in large city
- 5,457 degree-seeking undergraduates: 2% part-time, 51% women, 4% African American, 11% Asian American, 5% Hispanic American, 11% international
- 4,186 degree-seeking graduate students
- 37% of applicants admitted
- SAT or ACT (ACT writing optional), application essay required

General. Founded in 1850. Regionally accredited. **Degrees:** 1,517 bachelor's awarded; master's, professional, doctoral offered. **ROTC:** Army, Naval,

Air Force. **Location:** 2 miles from downtown. **Calendar:** Semester, extensive summer session. **Full-time faculty:** 530 total; 89% have terminal degrees, 14% minority, 27% women. **Part-time faculty:** 291 total; 6% minority, 51% women. **Class size:** 69% < 20, 16% 20-39, 3% 40-49, 8% 50-99, 4% >100. **Special facilities:** Theater, art gallery, music library, laboratory for laser energetics, nuclear structure research laboratory, Frederick Douglass Institute for African and African-American Studies, Susan B. Anthony Institute for Gender and Women's Studies, Mees Observatory, dental center, center for visual sciences, institute for optics, interfaith chapel, VR lab, MRI scanner.

Freshman class profile. 13,678 applied, 5,001 admitted, 1,152 enrolled.

Mid 50% test scores			
SAT critical reading:	600-700	Rank in top quarter:	92%
SAT math:	650-740	Rank in top tenth:	74%
SAT writing:	610-700	Out-of-state:	58%
ACT composite:	28-32	International:	15%

Basis for selection. School achievement record, personal qualities, recommendations most important. Test scores, academic GPA, extracurricular activities important. Alumni relationship, minority status, special talents considered. An audition is required for music programs at Eastman School of Music. **Home schooled:** Statement describing home school structure and mission, transcript of courses and grades, interview, letter of recommendation (nonparent) required. Must submit comprehensive description of the program of study (including syllabi with textbooks, where applicable), complete list of all literary texts completed, method of instruction (specifically for laboratory sciences) and assessment (written essays/multiple choice examinations, homework, etc.), and a personal statement reflecting on the value of the homeschooling experience. Most students who successfully gain admission to the University of Rochester have completed four years of English, four years of mathematics, four years of history/social studies, three years of laboratory science, and three years of foreign language study.

High school preparation. College-preparatory program required. 32 units required.

2011-2012 Annual costs. Tuition/fees: $41,802. Room/board: $12,120.

2011-2012 Financial aid. Need-based: Average need met was 100%. Average scholarship/grant was $32,304; average loan $4,095. 78% of total undergraduate aid awarded as scholarships/grants, 22% as loans/jobs. **Non-need-based:** Scholarships awarded for academics, alumni affiliation, art, leadership, music/drama, ROTC. **Additional information:** Alternative loans and financing information available.

Application procedures. Admission: Priority date 12/1; deadline 1/1 (postmark date). $60 fee, may be waived for applicants with need. Admission notification by 4/1. Admission notification on a rolling basis beginning on or about 2/15. Must reply by 5/1. **Financial aid:** Closing date 2/1. FAFSA, CSS PROFILE required. Applicants notified by 4/1; must reply by 5/1.

Academics. Rochester Curriculum: imposes minimal requirements, students can take advantage of flexibility in the curriculum to complete an education that reflects their interests and passions. Senior Scholars Program: allows selected undergraduates to devote their entire final year to work on a single intellectual project--a year-long independent study. Take Five Scholars Program: provides additional semester or year, tuition-free, where students can explore offerings of another department. **Special study options:** Accelerated study, combined bachelor's/graduate degree, cooperative education, cross-registration, double major, dual enrollment of high school students, ESL, honors, independent study, internships, liberal arts/career combination, New York semester, semester at sea, student-designed major, study abroad, teacher certification program, urban semester, Washington semester. **Credit/placement by examination:** AP, CLEP, IB, institutional tests. Students who prepare a course by independent study without registering for it and who pass an examination in that course may receive degree credit for it upon petition to their Administrative Committee. A letter of support from the chair of the department, or from his or her authorized delegate, is required. **Support services:** Learning center, pre-admission summer program, reduced course load, study skills assistance, tutoring, writing center.

Majors. Area/ethnic studies: African-American, American, Russian/Slavic, women's. **Biology:** General, biochemistry, cell/histology, ecology, embryology, evolutionary, microbiology, molecular genetics, neuroscience. **Business:** Business admin, managerial economics. **Communications:** Digital media, media studies. **Computer sciences:** Computer science. **Conservation:** Environmental science, environmental studies. **Engineering:** General, biomedical, chemical, electrical, engineering science, geological, laser/optical, mechanical. **English:** Creative writing, English lit. **Foreign languages:** General, American Sign Language, classics, comparative lit, French, German, Japanese, linguistics, Russian, Spanish. **Health services:** Nursing (RN). **History:** General. **Liberal arts:** Arts/sciences. **Math:** General, applied, statistics. **Philosophy/religion:** Philosophy, religion. **Physical sciences:** Chemistry, geology, optics, physics. **Psychology:** General, experimental. **Social sciences:** Anthropology, economics, international relations, political science. **Visual/performing arts:** Art history/conservation, film/cinema/video, jazz, music, music performance, music theory/composition, studio arts.

Most popular majors. Biology 14%, engineering/engineering technologies 9%, health sciences 13%, psychology 10%, social sciences 19%, visual/performing arts 11%.

Computing on campus. 447 workstations in dormitories, library, computer center, student center. Dormitories wired for high-speed internet access. Commuter students can connect to campus network. Online course registration, online library, helpline, repair service, wireless network available.

Student life. Freshman orientation: Mandatory. Preregistration for classes offered. Held one week prior to first day of classes. **Policies:** Freshmen not permitted cars on campus. **Housing:** Guaranteed on-campus for freshmen. Coed dorms, single-sex dorms, special housing for disabled, apartments, fraternity/sorority housing, wellness housing available. Freshman housing, special-interest floors, suite-style living, single-gender floors available. **Activities:** Bands, campus ministries, choral groups, dance, drama, film society, international student organizations, literary magazine, music ensembles, Model UN, musical theater, opera, radio station, student government, student newspaper, symphony orchestra, TV station, campus activities board, Black student union, grassroots (environmental group, women's caucus, Hillel, Catholic Newman society, debate union, UR Bhangra, Charles Drew pre-health society, Colleges Against Cancer.

Athletics. NCAA. **Intercollegiate:** Baseball M, basketball, cross-country, diving, field hockey W, football (tackle) M, golf M, lacrosse W, rowing (crew), soccer, softball W, squash, swimming, tennis, track and field, volleyball W. **Intramural:** Basketball, bowling, boxing, fencing, football (tackle) M, golf M, judo, racquetball, rugby, soccer, softball, squash, table tennis, tennis, volleyball, weight lifting. **Team name:** Yellowjackets.

Student services. Adult student services, alcohol/substance abuse counseling, chaplain/spiritual director, career counseling, services for economically disadvantaged, student employment services, financial aid counseling, health services, minority student services, personal counseling, placement for graduates, veterans' counselor, women's services. **Physically disabled:** Services for visually, hearing impaired.

Contact. E-mail: admit@admissions.rochester.edu
Phone: (585) 275-3221 Toll-free number: (888) 822-2256
Fax: (585) 461-4595
Jonathan Burdick, Dean of Admissions and Financial Aid, University of Rochester, 300 Wilson Boulevard, Rochester, NY 14627-0251

Utica College
Utica, New York
www.utica.edu

CB member
CB code: 2932

- Private 4-year liberal arts college
- Residential campus in small city
- 2,624 degree-seeking undergraduates: 19% part-time, 58% women, 11% African American, 2% Asian American, 7% Hispanic American, 3% international
- 1,009 degree-seeking graduate students
- 78% of applicants admitted
- Application essay required
- 44% graduate within 6 years

General. Founded in 1946. Regionally accredited. **Degrees:** 484 bachelor's awarded; master's, professional offered. **ROTC:** Army, Air Force. **Location:** 50 miles from Syracuse. **Calendar:** Semester, limited summer session. **Full-time faculty:** 149 total; 85% have terminal degrees, 14% minority, 48% women. **Part-time faculty:** 214 total; 44% women. **Class size:** 70% < 20, 29% 20-39, less than 1% 40-49, less than 1% 50-99.

Freshman class profile. 3,605 applied, 2,823 admitted, 532 enrolled.

Mid 50% test scores			
SAT critical reading:	430-510	GPA 2.0-2.99:	31%
SAT math:	440-540	Rank in top quarter:	30%
SAT writing:	410-510	Rank in top tenth:	8%
ACT composite:	16-24	Return as sophomores:	63%
GPA 3.75 or higher:	8%	Out-of-state:	15%
GPA 3.50-3.74:	10%	Live on campus:	76%
GPA 3.0-3.49:	50%	International:	4%

Basis for selection. Academic record, high school course of study, rank in class most important. Extracurricular activities, essay, interview, recommendations also important. SAT or ACT scores required only for freshmen applying to BS Health Studies/DPT Physical Therapy, BS Health Studies/MS Occupational Therapy, Nursing, or joint health professions programs, Higher Education Opportunity Program (HEOP), or for academic merit scholarships. Interview recommended. **Home schooled:** Applicants must receive GED within first year of attendance. **Learning Disabled:** Written evaluation

required, including discrepancy analysis completed by licensed psychologist or certified learning disability specialist indicating specific learning disability or disabilities.

High school preparation. College-preparatory program recommended. 16 units required. Required units include English 4, mathematics 3, social studies 3, science 3, foreign language 2 and academic electives 1.

2011-2012 Annual costs. Tuition/fees: $30,516. Room/board: $11,650. Books/supplies: $1,180. Personal expenses: $900.

2011-2012 Financial aid. Need-based: 496 full-time freshmen applied for aid; 457 were judged to have need; 457 of these received aid. Average need met was 71%. Average scholarship/grant was $6,337; average loan $3,417. 60% of total undergraduate aid awarded as scholarships/grants, 40% as loans/jobs. **Non-need-based:** Awarded to 211 full-time undergraduates, including 80 freshmen. Scholarships awarded for academics.

Application procedures. Admission: No deadline. $40 fee, may be waived for applicants with need. Admission notification on a rolling basis beginning on or about 9/1. January 15 application deadline for all joint medical programs, BS in Health Studies/ MS in Occupational Therapy program, and BS in Health Studies/DPT in Physical Therapy program. February 15 application deadline for nursing program. **Financial aid:** Priority date 2/15; no closing date. FAFSA required. Applicants notified on a rolling basis starting 2/1; must reply by 5/1 or within 4 week(s) of notification.

Academics. Special study options: Accelerated study, combined bachelor's/graduate degree, distance learning, double major, honors, independent study, internships, study abroad, teacher certification program, United Nations semester, Washington semester. Economic Crime Investigation online program for transfer students. **Credit/placement by examination:** AP, CLEP, IB, institutional tests. 30 credit hours maximum toward bachelor's degree. **Support services:** Learning center, pre-admission summer program, reduced course load, remedial instruction, study skills assistance, tutoring, writing center.

Majors. Biology: General. **Business:** Accounting, business admin, managerial economics. **Communications:** Communications/speech/rhetoric, journalism, public relations. **Computer sciences:** General. **Education:** Early childhood, elementary, ESL, secondary, special ed. **English:** English lit. **Foreign languages:** General. **Health services:** Facilities admin, nursing (RN), recreational therapy. **History:** General. **Liberal arts:** Arts/sciences. **Math:** General. **Philosophy/religion:** Philosophy. **Physical sciences:** Chemistry, physics. **Protective services:** Criminal justice. **Psychology:** General. **Social sciences:** Economics, international relations, political science, sociology.

Most popular majors. Biology 6%, business/marketing 10%, communications/journalism 6%, education 6%, health sciences 27%, psychology 9%, security/protective services 19%.

Computing on campus. 430 workstations in library, computer center, student center. Dormitories wired for high-speed internet access and linked to campus network. Online course registration, helpline available.

Student life. Freshman orientation: Available, $50 fee. Preregistration for classes offered. Summer program for freshmen and parents held during the third week of July. **Policies:** All freshmen required to live in college residence for first 2 years, unless residing at home. **Housing:** Guaranteed on-campus for freshmen. Coed dorms, special housing for disabled, apartments, wellness housing available. $200 deposit, deadline 7/1. **Activities:** Bands, campus ministries, choral groups, dance, drama, international student organizations, literary magazine, music ensembles, musical theater, radio station, student government, student newspaper, Latin American student union, Jewish student union, College Republicans, Womyn's resource center, Asian association, gospel choir, Africa in Motion, Christian Fellowship, West Indian Connection, UC Pride.

Athletics. NCAA. **Intercollegiate:** Baseball M, basketball, cross-country, diving, field hockey W, football (tackle) M, golf M, ice hockey, lacrosse, soccer, softball W, swimming, tennis, track and field, volleyball W, water polo W. **Intramural:** Badminton, basketball, bowling, football (non-tackle), racquetball, soccer, softball, tennis, volleyball. **Team name:** Pioneers.

Student services. Adult student services, alcohol/substance abuse counseling, chaplain/spiritual director, career counseling, services for economically disadvantaged, student employment services, financial aid counseling, health services, minority student services, personal counseling, placement for graduates, veterans' counselor, women's services. **Physically disabled:** Services for visually, speech, hearing impaired.

Contact. E-mail: admiss@utica.edu
Phone: (315) 792-3006 Toll-free number: (800) 782-8884
Fax: (315) 792-3003
Patrick Quinn, Vice President for Enrollment Management, Utica College, 1600 Burrstone Road, Utica, NY 13502-4892

Vassar College
Poughkeepsie, New York
www.vassar.edu

CB member
CB code: 2956

- Private 4-year liberal arts college
- Residential campus in small city
- 2,345 degree-seeking undergraduates: 1% part-time, 56% women, 5% African American, 9% Asian American, 10% Hispanic American, 6% international
- 23% of applicants admitted
- SAT and SAT Subject Tests or ACT with writing, application essay required
- 91% graduate within 6 years; 35% enter graduate study

General. Founded in 1861. Regionally accredited. **Degrees:** 660 bachelor's awarded; master's offered. **Location:** 75 miles from New York City. **Calendar:** Semester, limited summer session. **Full-time faculty:** 280 total; 88% have terminal degrees, 25% minority, 47% women. **Part-time faculty:** 43 total; 63% have terminal degrees, 16% minority, 56% women. **Class size:** 68% < 20, 31% 20-39, 1% 40-49, less than 1% 50-99. **Special facilities:** Environmental nature center, observatory, electron microscope, nursery school, experimental theater, art center and geology museum, intercultural center and outdoor amphitheater.

Freshman class profile. 7,985 applied, 1,798 admitted, 671 enrolled.

Mid 50% test scores			
SAT critical reading:	670-740	Rank in top tenth:	74%
SAT math:	650-730	End year in good standing:	99%
SAT writing:	660-750	Return as sophomores:	98%
ACT composite:	30-33	Out-of-state:	74%
Rank in top quarter:	95%	Live on campus:	99%
		International:	7%

Basis for selection. Academic credentials most important. Personal achievements, essay, and recommendations also considered carefully. Evidence that students have elected most demanding program available crucial. Disadvantaged status considered. 2 SAT Subject Tests of student's choice required. Optional interviews available with alumni.

High school preparation. College-preparatory program recommended. 20 units recommended. Recommended units include English 4, mathematics 4, social studies 2, history 2, science 4 (laboratory 3) and foreign language 4. Advanced and accelerated courses recommended whenever possible. Minimum of 20 units recommended with additional unit in science, foreign language, and studies.

2011-2012 Annual costs. Tuition/fees: $44,705. Room/board: $10,430.

2011-2012 Financial aid. All financial aid based on need. 484 full-time freshmen applied for aid; 411 were judged to have need; 411 of these received aid. Average need met was 100%. Average scholarship/grant was $40,146; average loan $1,434. 91% of total undergraduate aid awarded as scholarships/grants, 9% as loans/jobs. **Additional information:** No loans in the initial financial aid packages for students from families with total income used in need analysis of $60,000 or less.

Application procedures. Admission: Closing date 1/1 (postmark date). $65 fee, may be waived for applicants with need. Admission notification by 4/1. Must reply by 5/1. **Financial aid:** Closing date 2/15. FAFSA, CSS PROFILE required. Applicants notified by 3/30; must reply by 5/1.

Academics. Introductory-level college course emphasizing written and oral communication required for freshmen. Majors declared through department, interdepartmental programs, multidisciplinary programs, and independent programs. Summer research with faculty. **Special study options:** Combined bachelor's/graduate degree, cooperative education, cross-registration, double major, exchange student, independent study, internships, liberal arts/career combination, semester at sea, student-designed major, study abroad, teacher certification program, urban semester, Washington semester. Independently designed junior year abroad programs; exchange programs with institutions in 12-college exchange as well as Fisk University, Hampton Institute, Howard University, Morehouse College, and Spelman College; 3-2 engineering program with Dartmouth College. **Credit/placement by examination:** AP, CLEP, IB, institutional tests. 4 credit hours maximum toward bachelor's degree. **Support services:** Learning center, reduced course load, study skills assistance, tutoring, writing center.

Majors. Area/ethnic studies: African, American, Asian, Latin American, women's. **Biology:** General, biochemistry, neuroscience. **Communications:** Media studies. **Computer sciences:** General. **Conservation:** Environmental studies. **English:** English lit. **Foreign languages:** Chinese, French, German, Italian, Japanese, Russian, Spanish. **History:** General. **Liberal arts:** Arts/sciences. **Math:** General. **Philosophy/religion:** Judaic, philosophy, religion. **Physical sciences:** Astronomy, chemistry, geology, physics. **Psychology:**

General. **Social sciences:** Anthropology, economics, geography, international relations, political science, sociology, urban studies. **Visual/performing arts:** Art, dramatic, film/cinema/video, music.

Most popular majors. Biology 9%, English 10%, foreign language 8%, psychology 8%, social sciences 25%, visual/performing arts 14%.

Computing on campus. 432 workstations in dormitories, library, computer center, student center. Dormitories wired for high-speed internet access and linked to campus network. Commuter students can connect to campus network. Online course registration, helpline, repair service, student web hosting, wireless network available.

Student life. Freshman orientation: Mandatory. Preregistration for classes offered. Held one week prior to start of classes. **Housing:** Guaranteed on-campus for all undergraduates. Coed dorms, single-sex dorms, special housing for disabled, apartments, cooperative housing, wellness housing available. $500 nonrefundable deposit, deadline 5/1. Quiet housing. **Activities:** Bands, campus ministries, choral groups, dance, drama, film society, international student organizations, literary magazine, music ensembles, Model UN, musical theater, opera, radio station, student government, student newspaper, symphony orchestra, TV station, Catholic community, Jewish union, Promoting Equality and Community Everywhere, Amnesty International, Young Socialists, Republican/Libertarian Coalition, AIDS education committee, Habitat for Humanity, Step Beyond (community service), African students union, Buddhist Sangha.

Athletics. NCAA. **Intercollegiate:** Baseball M, basketball, cross-country, diving, fencing, field hockey W, golf W, lacrosse, rowing (crew), soccer, squash, swimming, tennis, track and field, volleyball. **Intramural:** Badminton, basketball, bowling, football (non-tackle), golf, handball, soccer, softball, squash, tennis, volleyball, water polo. **Team name:** Brewers.

Student services. Alcohol/substance abuse counseling, chaplain/spiritual director, career counseling, student employment services, financial aid counseling, health services, minority student services, on-campus daycare, personal counseling, placement for graduates, veterans' counselor, women's services. **Physically disabled:** Services for visually, hearing impaired.

Contact. E-mail: admissons@vassar.edu
Phone: (845) 437-7300 Toll-free number: (800) 827-7270
Fax: (845) 437-7063
David Borus, Dean of Admission and Financial Aid, Vassar College, Box 10, 124 Raymond Avenue, Poughkeepsie, NY 12604-0077

Vaughn College of Aeronautics and Technology
Flushing, New York — **CB member**
www.vaughn.edu — **CB code: 2001**

- Private 4-year engineering college
- Commuter campus in very large city
- 1,654 degree-seeking undergraduates: 27% part-time, 13% women, 20% African American, 12% Asian American, 36% Hispanic American, 1% Native American, 3% international
- 16 degree-seeking graduate students
- 83% of applicants admitted
- SAT or ACT (ACT writing recommended), application essay, interview required
- 50% graduate within 6 years; 10% enter graduate study

General. Founded in 1932. Regionally accredited. **Degrees:** 103 bachelor's, 159 associate awarded; master's offered. **ROTC:** Army, Air Force. **Location:** 5 miles from Manhattan. **Calendar:** Semester, extensive summer session. **Full-time faculty:** 35 total; 49% have terminal degrees, 37% minority, 14% women. **Part-time faculty:** 127 total; 12% have terminal degrees, 53% minority, 16% women. **Class size:** 61% < 20, 39% 20-39. **Special facilities:** 65-foot observation tower overlooking LaGuardia Airport, two Redbird FMX full motion flight simulators, Frasca 241 flight simulator, Frasca 142 flight simulator, CRJ-200 flight simulator, mechatronic engineering laboratory, nondestructive testing laboratory, composite materials laboratory and computerized engine test-cell.

Freshman class profile. 626 applied, 521 admitted, 308 enrolled.

Mid 50% test scores			
SAT critical reading:	420-530	GPA 2.0-2.99:	45%
SAT math:	470-580	End year in good standing:	56%
GPA 3.75 or higher:	11%	Return as sophomores:	73%
GPA 3.50-3.74:	10%	Out-of-state:	12%
GPA 3.0-3.49:	30%	Live on campus:	20%
		International:	1%

Basis for selection. High school transcripts or GED scores most important followed by SAT, ACT, or TOEFL. B.S. programs require strong performance in high school math and sciences courses. Open admissions to associate degree programs. Interview required for all applicants to the Bachelor of Science program in Aircraft Operations (Flight). **Home schooled:** Statement describing home school structure and mission, transcript of courses and grades, state high school equivalency certificate required. **Learning Disabled:** IEP documentation required.

High school preparation. College-preparatory program recommended. 14 units required; 18 recommended. Required and recommended units include English 4, mathematics 3-4, social studies 1-4 and science 2-4.

2011-2012 Annual costs. Tuition/fees: $18,400. Tuition does not include the cost of individual flying lessons for the aircraft operations program. Room/board: $11,900. Books/supplies: $2,100. Personal expenses: $3,340.

2011-2012 Financial aid. Need-based: 280 full-time freshmen applied for aid; 272 were judged to have need; 264 of these received aid. Average need met was 93%. Average scholarship/grant was $1,100; average loan $1,750. 51% of total undergraduate aid awarded as scholarships/grants, 49% as loans/jobs. **Non-need-based:** Awarded to 320 full-time undergraduates, including 95 freshmen. Scholarships awarded for academics, alumni affiliation, job skills, leadership, ROTC, state residency.

Application procedures. Admission: Priority date 3/1; no deadline. $40 fee, may be waived for applicants with need. Admission notification on a rolling basis beginning on or about 2/1. **Financial aid:** Priority date 3/1; no closing date. FAFSA required. Applicants notified on a rolling basis starting 4/15; must reply within 2 week(s) of notification.

Academics. Academic programs centered around engineering, engineering technology, aviation, and management. Engineering technology programs accredited by the Accreditation Board for Engineering and Technology. Management programs accredited by the International Assembly of Collegiate Business Education. **Special study options:** Accelerated study, distance learning, double major, independent study, internships, liberal arts/career combination. **Credit/placement by examination:** AP, CLEP, IB, SAT, ACT, institutional tests. 30 credit hours maximum toward associate degree, 30 toward bachelor's. **Support services:** Learning center, pre-admission summer program, reduced course load, remedial instruction, study skills assistance, tutoring, writing center.

Majors. Business: General.

Most popular majors. Engineering/engineering technologies 28%, trade and industry 68%.

Computing on campus. 225 workstations in dormitories, library, computer center, student center. Dormitories wired for high-speed internet access and linked to campus network. Commuter students can connect to campus network. Online library, helpline, repair service, wireless network available.

Student life. Freshman orientation: Mandatory, $160 fee. Preregistration for classes offered. Two-day orientation with one-night stay in residence hall. Offered on several dates throughout the summer. **Housing:** Guaranteed on-campus for freshmen. Coed dorms available. $250 partly refundable deposit, deadline 6/15. **Activities:** Dance, drama, international student organizations, student government, Robotics Club, American Institute of Aeronautics and Astronautics, American Association of Airport Executives, inc., Institute of Electrical and Electronics Engineers, Red Tail Pilots Club, Women in Aviation-International, Circle K.

Athletics. Intercollegiate: Basketball, cross-country, soccer M, tennis W. **Intramural:** Basketball, soccer, table tennis, tennis. **Team name:** Warriors.

Student services. Alcohol/substance abuse counseling, chaplain/spiritual director, career counseling, services for economically disadvantaged, student employment services, financial aid counseling, minority student services, personal counseling, placement for graduates, veterans' counselor.

Contact. E-mail: admitme@vaughn.edu
Phone: (718) 429-6600 ext. 118 Toll-free number: (800) 866-6828
Fax: (718) 779-2231
Celso Alvarez, Director of Admissions, Vaughn College of Aeronautics and Technology, 86-01 23rd Avenue, Flushing, NY 11369

Wagner College
Staten Island, New York — **CB member**
www.wagner.edu — **CB code: 2966**

- Private 4-year liberal arts college affiliated with Lutheran Church in America
- Residential campus in very large city

- 1,840 degree-seeking undergraduates: 4% part-time, 64% women, 6% African American, 2% Asian American, 8% Hispanic American, 2% international
- 369 degree-seeking graduate students
- 69% of applicants admitted
- Application essay required
- 67% graduate within 6 years; 83% enter graduate study

General. Founded in 1883. Regionally accredited. **Degrees:** 414 bachelor's awarded; master's offered. **ROTC:** Army. **Location:** 10 miles from New York City. **Calendar:** Semester, limited summer session. **Full-time faculty:** 96 total; 90% have terminal degrees, 9% minority, 50% women. **Part-time faculty:** 165 total; 8% minority, 55% women. **Class size:** 61% < 20, 38% 20-39, 1% 40-49. **Special facilities:** Planetarium, electron microscopes.

Freshman class profile. 3,001 applied, 2,079 admitted, 470 enrolled.

Mid 50% test scores			
SAT critical reading:	530-640	GPA 2.0-2.99:	10%
SAT math:	520-640	Rank in top quarter:	71%
SAT writing:	520-630	Rank in top tenth:	14%
ACT composite:	22-28	Return as sophomores:	79%
GPA 3.75 or higher:	17%	Out-of-state:	59%
GPA 3.50-3.74:	26%	Live on campus:	80%
GPA 3.0-3.49:	47%	International:	2%

Basis for selection. School achievement, test scores, recommendations, interview, special talents, essay all considered. Interview recommended for all; audition required for music, theater programs; portfolio recommended for art programs. Interview required for Physician Assistant program. **Home schooled:** Transcript of courses and grades required.

High school preparation. College-preparatory program required. 21 units required. Required units include English 4, mathematics 3, social studies 1, history 3, science 2 (laboratory 1), foreign language 2 and academic electives 6. 4 economics, arts, computers, or other elective areas of study required.

2011-2012 Annual costs. Tuition/fees: $35,820. Room/board: $10,680. Books/supplies: $757. Personal expenses: $1,316.

2011-2012 Financial aid. Need-based: 388 full-time freshmen applied for aid; 338 were judged to have need; 338 of these received aid. Average need met was 74%. Average scholarship/grant was $15,060; average loan $2,462. 60% of total undergraduate aid awarded as scholarships/grants, 40% as loans/jobs. **Non-need-based:** Awarded to 500 full-time undergraduates, including 114 freshmen. Scholarships awarded for academics, athletics, music/drama.

Application procedures. Admission: Priority date 12/15; deadline 2/15 (postmark date). $50 fee, may be waived for applicants with need. Admission notification on a rolling basis beginning on or about 2/15. Must reply by May 1 or within 2 week(s) if notified thereafter. **Financial aid:** Priority date 2/15; no closing date. FAFSA required. Applicants notified on a rolling basis starting 3/1; must reply within 3 week(s) of notification.

Academics. Special study options: Combined bachelor's/graduate degree, double major, exchange student, honors, independent study, internships, New York semester, semester at sea, study abroad, teacher certification program, United Nations semester, Washington semester. Learning community. **Credit/placement by examination:** AP, CLEP, IB, institutional tests. 9 credit hours maximum toward bachelor's degree. Up to 9 units may be awarded for credit by exam and prior experience. Each unit is equivalent to 3.3 credit hours. **Support services:** Reduced course load, study skills assistance, tutoring, writing center.

Majors. Biology: General, bacteriology. **Business:** Accounting, business admin, finance, international, managerial economics, marketing. **Computer sciences:** Computer science. **Education:** General, early childhood, middle, secondary. **English:** English lit. **Foreign languages:** French, Spanish. **Health services:** Nursing (RN), physician assistant, predental, premedicine, preoptometry, preveterinary. **History:** General. **Human services:** Public policy. **Liberal arts:** Arts/sciences. **Math:** General. **Philosophy/religion:** Philosophy. **Physical sciences:** Chemistry, physics. **Psychology:** General. **Social sciences:** Anthropology, economics, political science, sociology. **Visual/performing arts:** Dramatic, music performance, studio arts, studio arts management, theater design.

Most popular majors. Business/marketing 23%, health sciences 18%, psychology 6%, social sciences 12%, visual/performing arts 15%.

Computing on campus. 230 workstations in dormitories, library, computer center. Dormitories wired for high-speed internet access and linked to campus network. Commuter students can connect to campus network. Online course registration, online library, helpline, wireless network available.

Student life. Freshman orientation: Mandatory. Preregistration for classes offered. Freshmen move on-campus 3 days prior to start of fall semester. Orientation involves academic advisement and registration, social activities, and trip to Manhattan. **Housing:** Guaranteed on-campus for all undergraduates. Coed dorms, fraternity/sorority housing, wellness housing available. $300 nonrefundable deposit, deadline 5/1. Separate housing for senior year students. **Activities:** Bands, campus ministries, choral groups, dance, drama, international student organizations, literary magazine, music ensembles, Model UN, musical theater, radio station, student government, student newspaper, Lutheran student club, Newman Society, Hillel, national honor societies, Amnesty International, Young Democrats, Young Republicans, Nubian Society, Muslim student association, Habitat for Humanity.

Athletics. NCAA. **Intercollegiate:** Baseball M, basketball, cross-country, football (tackle) M, golf, lacrosse, soccer W, softball W, swimming W, tennis, track and field, water polo W. **Intramural:** Basketball, bowling, cheerleading W, football (non-tackle), football (tackle) M, soccer, softball, table tennis, tennis, volleyball. **Team name:** Seahawks.

Student services. Alcohol/substance abuse counseling, chaplain/spiritual director, career counseling, student employment services, financial aid counseling, health services, personal counseling, placement for graduates, women's services. **Physically disabled:** Services for visually, hearing impaired.

Contact. E-mail: adm@wagner.edu
Phone: (718) 390-3411 Toll-free number: (800) 221-1010
Fax: (718) 390-3105
Robert Herr, Dean of Admissions, Wagner College, One Campus Road, Staten Island, NY 10301-4495

Webb Institute
Glen Cove, New York   **CB member**
www.webb-institute.edu   **CB code: 2970**

- Private 4-year engineering college
- Residential campus in large town
- 81 degree-seeking undergraduates: 16% women, 9% Asian American, 2% Hispanic American
- 37% of applicants admitted
- SAT, SAT Subject Tests, interview required
- 80% graduate within 6 years; 30% enter graduate study

General. Founded in 1889. Regionally accredited. All students participate in 2-month paid winter work program in marine industry each year. **Degrees:** 21 bachelor's awarded. **Location:** 22 miles from New York City. **Calendar:** Semester. **Full-time faculty:** 10 total; 60% have terminal degrees, 10% women. **Part-time faculty:** 2 total; 50% have terminal degrees. **Class size:** 52% < 20, 48% 20-39. **Special facilities:** Adjoining nature preserve, model testing tank.

Freshman class profile. 73 applied, 27 admitted, 22 enrolled.

Mid 50% test scores			
SAT critical reading:	630-740	GPA 3.0-3.49:	5%
SAT math:	700-770	End year in good standing:	83%
SAT writing:	620-730	Return as sophomores:	83%
GPA 3.75 or higher:	81%	Out-of-state:	68%
GPA 3.50-3.74:	14%	Live on campus:	100%

Basis for selection. GED not accepted. High school record, class rank, test scores, and interview with President of college most important. Character, motivation, and outside activities considered. **Home schooled:** Statement describing home school structure and mission, transcript of courses and grades, letter of recommendation (nonparent) required.

High school preparation. College-preparatory program recommended. 16 units required. Required units include English 4, mathematics 4, social studies 2, science 2 (laboratory 2) and academic electives 4.

2012-2013 Annual costs. All students receive 4-year, full-tuition scholarships. Room/board: $13,200. Books/supplies: $1,670. Personal expenses: $4,450.

2011-2012 Financial aid. All financial aid based on need.

Application procedures. Admission: Closing date 2/15 (postmark date). $25 fee, may be waived for applicants with need. Application must be submitted on paper. Admission notification on a rolling basis beginning on or about 3/15. Must reply by May 1 or within 2 week(s) if notified thereafter. **Financial aid:** Closing date 7/1. FAFSA required. Applicants notified by 8/1; must reply within 2 week(s) of notification.

Academics. Intensive single curriculum program demands high career motivation. **Special study options:** Double major, independent study, internships, study abroad. **Credit/placement by examination:** AP, CLEP. **Support services:** Study skills assistance.

Majors. Engineering: Marine.

Computing on campus. PC or laptop required. 25 workstations in dormitories, library, computer center, student center. Dormitories wired for high-speed internet access and linked to campus network. Commuter students can connect to campus network. Repair service, wireless network available.

Student life. Freshman orientation: Mandatory. Preregistration for classes offered. Held 1 week before classes start. **Housing:** Guaranteed on-campus for all undergraduates. Coed dorms, single-sex dorms, wellness housing available. $150 deposit. **Activities:** Choral groups, music ensembles, student government, free membership available to local YMCA, women engineers, Society of American Naval Engineers, WebbWomen, Society of Naval Architects and Marine Engineers, Marine Technology Society.

Athletics. Intercollegiate: Basketball, cross-country, sailing, soccer, tennis, track and field, volleyball. **Intramural:** Basketball, cross-country, soccer, volleyball.

Student services. Alcohol/substance abuse counseling, career counseling, student employment services, financial aid counseling, health services, personal counseling, placement for graduates.

Contact. E-mail: admissions@webb-institute.edu
Phone: (516) 671-2213 Toll-free number: (866) 708-9322
Fax: (516) 674-9838
William Murray, Director of Enrollment Management, Webb Institute, 298 Crescent Beach Road, Glen Cove, NY 11542-1398

Wells College
Aurora, New York
www.wells.edu

CB member
CB code: 2971

◗ Private 4-year liberal arts college
◗ Residential campus in rural community
◗ 493 degree-seeking undergraduates: 2% part-time, 69% women, 10% African American, 2% Asian American, 6% Hispanic American, 1% international
◗ 79% of applicants admitted
◗ SAT or ACT (ACT writing optional), application essay required
◗ 55% graduate within 6 years

General. Founded in 1868. Regionally accredited. Cross registration with Cornell University and Ithaca College allows up to four courses per year. **Degrees:** 127 bachelor's awarded. **ROTC:** Army, Air Force. **Location:** 27 miles from Ithaca, 45 miles from Syracuse. **Calendar:** Semester. **Full-time faculty:** 45 total; 93% have terminal degrees, 11% minority, 56% women. **Part-time faculty:** 29 total; 62% have terminal degrees, 10% minority, 38% women. **Class size:** 88% < 20, 11% 20-39, 1% 40-49. **Special facilities:** Book arts center, lithography presses, digital imaging laboratory, boathouse with access to Cayuga Lake, indoor tennis courts, 9-hole golf course, science facility with growth chamber, cold room, horse stables, campus in France, SHARE farm, center for study of art in Paris.

Freshman class profile. 1,610 applied, 1,264 admitted, 137 enrolled.

Mid 50% test scores			
SAT critical reading:	480-600	GPA 2.0-2.99:	31%
SAT math:	470-580	Rank in top quarter:	61%
SAT writing:	470-570	Rank in top tenth:	26%
ACT composite:	22-27	End year in good standing:	74%
GPA 3.75 or higher:	31%	Return as sophomores:	69%
GPA 3.50-3.74:	15%	Out-of-state:	31%
GPA 3.0-3.49:	23%	Live on campus:	81%

Basis for selection. Academic achievement, writing skills, school/community involvement weighed heavily in admissions process. Test scores, class rank, teacher recommendations also highly valuable. Evidence of leadership ability, intellectual curiosity, character fitness also considered. Holistic approach to each student's application for admission. Require all students to submit their standardized test scores as part of their application. Interviews are highly recommended. **Home schooled:** Statement describing home school structure and mission, transcript of courses and grades, state high school equivalency certificate required. Please contact Admissions Office for additional information.

High school preparation. College-preparatory program recommended. 17 units required; 23 recommended. Required and recommended units include

English 4, mathematics 3-4, social studies 1, history 3, science 2-3 (laboratory 2-3), foreign language 1-2 and academic electives 2-3. Students encouraged to complete 2 computer science, art, and/or music course. AP and honors courses recommended.

2011-2012 Annual costs. Tuition/fees: $32,180. Room/board: $11,000. Books/supplies: $800. Personal expenses: $800.

2011-2012 Financial aid. Need-based: 126 full-time freshmen applied for aid; 121 were judged to have need; 121 of these received aid. Average need met was 84%. Average scholarship/grant was $27,956; average loan $3,587. 81% of total undergraduate aid awarded as scholarships/grants, 19% as loans/jobs. **Non-need-based:** Awarded to 388 full-time undergraduates, including 109 freshmen. Scholarships awarded for academics, alumni affiliation, leadership.

Application procedures. Admission: Priority date 12/15; deadline 3/1 (postmark date). $40 fee, may be waived for applicants with need. Admission notification by 4/1. Must reply by 5/1. **Financial aid:** Priority date 2/15; no closing date. FAFSA required. CSS PROFILE required of early decision candidates only. Applicants notified on a rolling basis starting 3/1; must reply by 5/1.

Academics. Individualized majors offered. Experiential learning requirement fulfilled through internship and off-campus study programs, study abroad, research with professors, community service. January term. **Special study options:** Accelerated study, combined bachelor's/graduate degree, cross-registration, double major, independent study, internships, student-designed major, study abroad, teacher certification program, Washington semester. **Credit/placement by examination:** AP, CLEP, IB, SAT, ACT, institutional tests. 6 credit hours maximum toward bachelor's degree. **Support services:** Learning center, reduced course load, study skills assistance, tutoring, writing center.

Majors. Area/ethnic studies: American, women's. **Biology:** General, biochemistry, molecular. **Business:** Managerial economics. **Computer sciences:** Computer science. **Conservation:** Environmental studies. **English:** English lit. **Foreign languages:** General, Spanish. **Health services:** Predental, premedicine, preveterinary. **History:** General. **Math:** General. **Philosophy/religion:** Philosophy. **Physical sciences:** Chemistry. **Psychology:** General. **Social sciences:** Anthropology, economics, international relations, political science, sociology. **Visual/performing arts:** General, art history/conservation.

Most popular majors. Biology 10%, English 11%, history 8%, psychology 15%, public administration/social services 7%, social sciences 14%, visual/performing arts 12%.

Computing on campus. 85 workstations in dormitories, library, computer center. Dormitories wired for high-speed internet access and linked to campus network. Commuter students can connect to campus network. Online course registration, online library, repair service, wireless network available.

Student life. Freshman orientation: Mandatory. Preregistration for classes offered. 5-day program before classes begin. Incorporates traditions (bonfire, quilt making, convocation, etc.) with integrating students into a rigorous academic environment. **Policies:** Honor code governs academic and co-curricular life. Student code of conduct. **Housing:** Guaranteed on-campus for all undergraduates. Coed dorms, single-sex dorms, apartments, wellness housing available. $300 nonrefundable deposit, deadline 5/1. Social justice learning community. **Activities:** Campus ministries, choral groups, dance, drama, international student organizations, literary magazine, music ensembles, Model UN, student government, student newspaper, Amnesty International, American Red Cross club, College Democrats, College Republicans, Praising Our Work Ethnicity and Race (P.O.W.E.R.), Spanish culture club, Japanese culture club, Women in Life-Long Learning, Inclusive and Intercultural Excellence Committee, international student association, Sexuality and Gender Activists, Sex Collective, Campus Greens.

Athletics. NCAA. **Intercollegiate:** Basketball, cross-country, field hockey W, golf, lacrosse, soccer, softball W, swimming, tennis W, volleyball M. **Intramural:** Basketball, field hockey, golf, sailing, skiing, soccer, tennis, volleyball. **Team name:** The Express.

Student services. Adult student services, chaplain/spiritual director, career counseling, financial aid counseling, health services, minority student services, personal counseling, women's services.

Contact. E-mail: admissions@wells.edu
Phone: (315) 364-3264 Toll-free number: (800) 952-9355
Fax: (315) 364-3227
Susan Sloan, Director of Admissions, Wells College, 170 Main Street, Aurora, NY 13026

Yeshiva and Kolel Bais Medrash Elyon
Monsey, New York

- Private 4-year rabbinical college for men affiliated with Jewish faith
- Small city
- 24 degree-seeking undergraduates

General. Accredited by AARTS. **Degrees:** 1 bachelor's awarded; doctoral offered. **Calendar:** Semester. **Full-time faculty:** 3 total. **Part-time faculty:** 2 total.

Basis for selection. Commitment to Jewish tenet.

2011-2012 Annual costs. Tuition/fees: $7,800.

Application procedures. Admission: No deadline. No application fee. Admission notification on a rolling basis.

Academics. Credit/placement by examination: AP, CLEP.

Majors. Theology: Talmudic.

Contact. Phone: (845) 356-7064
Rabbi Israel Falk, Admissions Director, Yeshiva and Kolel Bais Medrash Elyon, 73 Main Street, Monsey, NY 10952

Yeshiva and Kollel Harbotzas Torah
Brooklyn, New York

- Private 4-year rabbinical college for men affiliated with Jewish faith
- Very large city

General. Accredited by AARTS. **Degrees:** 3 bachelor's awarded; doctoral offered. **Calendar:** Semester.

2011-2012 Annual costs. Tuition/fees: $6,200.

Application procedures. Admission: No deadline.

Academics. Credit/placement by examination: AP, CLEP.

Majors. Theology: Talmudic.

Contact. Phone: (718) 692-0208
Yeshiva and Kollel Harbotzas Torah, 1049 East 15th Street, Brooklyn, NY 11230

Yeshiva Derech Chaim
Brooklyn, New York
CB code: 0552

- Private 5-year rabbinical college for men affiliated with Jewish faith
- Very large city
- 100 degree-seeking undergraduates
- Interview required

General. Founded in 1975. Accredited by AARTS. First and advanced Talmudic degrees available. **Degrees:** 12 bachelor's awarded; doctoral offered. **Calendar:** Semester. **Full-time faculty:** 12 total. **Part-time faculty:** 7 total.

Basis for selection. Dean interviews each applicant. Recommendations very important. Applicants without high school diplomas may be admitted on basis of national AARTS exam.

2011-2012 Annual costs. Tuition/fees: $9,400. Tuition includes board expenses. Room only: $3,600. Books/supplies: $400.

Financial aid. Additional information: Financial aid interview held with each admitted student.

Application procedures. Admission: Priority date 8/20; no deadline. No application fee. Admission notification on a rolling basis. **Financial aid:** No deadline. Applicants notified on a rolling basis.

Academics. Credit/placement by examination: AP, CLEP.

Majors. Theology: Talmudic.

Student life. Policies: Religious observance required. **Activities:** Choral groups, TV station.

Contact. Phone: (718) 438-3070
Rabbi Mordechai Rennert, Admissions Director, Yeshiva Derech Chaim, 1573 39th Street, Brooklyn, NY 11218

Yeshiva D'Monsey Rabbinical College
Monsey, New York

- Private 4-year rabbinical college for men affiliated with Jewish faith
- Large town
- 37 degree-seeking undergraduates

General. Accredited by AARTS. **Degrees:** 8 bachelor's awarded; doctoral offered. **Calendar:** Semester.

Application procedures. Admission: No deadline.

Academics. Credit/placement by examination: AP, CLEP.

Majors. Theology: Talmudic.

Contact. Phone: (845) 352-5852
Yeshiva D'Monsey Rabbinical College, 2 Roman Boulevard, Monsey, NY 10952

Yeshiva Gedolah Imrei Yosef D'Spinka
Brooklyn, New York

- Private 4-year rabbinical college for men affiliated with Jewish faith
- Very large city
- 109 degree-seeking undergraduates

General. Accredited by AARTS. **Degrees:** 13 bachelor's awarded. **Calendar:** Semester. **Full-time faculty:** 9 total.

Application procedures. Admission: Priority date 8/18; deadline 9/28. No application fee.

Academics. Credit/placement by examination: AP, CLEP.

Majors. Theology: Talmudic.

Contact. Phone: (718) 851-1600
Yeshiva Gedolah Imrei Yosef D'Spinka, 1466 56th Street, Brooklyn, NY 11219

Yeshiva Gedolah Zichron Moshe
South Fallsburg, New York
CB code: 0750

- Private 4-year rabbinical college for men affiliated with Jewish faith
- Small town
- 175 degree-seeking undergraduates

General. Founded in 1969. Accredited by AARTS. First Talmudic degree and ordination available. **Degrees:** 4 bachelor's awarded; doctoral offered. **Calendar:** Semester.

Basis for selection. Institutional examination.

2011-2012 Annual costs. Tuition/fees: $10,900. Room/board: $3,200. Books/supplies: $200. Personal expenses: $3,003.

Application procedures. Admission: No deadline.

Academics. Credit/placement by examination: AP, CLEP.

Majors. Theology: Talmudic.

Contact. Phone: (845) 434-5240 Fax: (845) 434-1009
Abba Gorelick, Dean of Admissions, Yeshiva Gedolah Zichron Moshe, 84 Laurel Park Road, South Fallsburg, NY 12779

Yeshiva Karlin Stolin
Brooklyn, New York

CB code: 1582

- Private 4-year rabbinical college for men affiliated with Jewish faith
- Very large city
- 89 degree-seeking undergraduates

General. Accredited by AARTS. **Degrees:** 4 bachelor's awarded. **Calendar:** Semester.

2011-2012 Annual costs. Tuition/fees: $6,900. Room/board: $3,200.

Application procedures. Admission: No deadline.

Academics. Credit/placement by examination: AP, CLEP.

Majors. Theology: Talmudic.

Contact. Phone: (718) 232-7800
Yeshiva Karlin Stolin, 1818 54th Street, Brooklyn, NY 11204-1545

Yeshiva of Nitra
Mount Kisco, New York

CB code: 7131

- Private 4-year rabbinical college for men affiliated with Jewish faith
- Small city

General. Accredited by AARTS. **Degrees:** 14 bachelor's awarded; master's offered. **Calendar:** Differs by program.

2011-2012 Annual costs. Tuition/fees: $7,300. Room/board: $3,700.

Application procedures. Admission: No deadline.

Academics. Credit/placement by examination: AP, CLEP.

Majors. Theology: Talmudic.

Contact. Phone: (718) 387-0422
Yeshiva of Nitra, Pine Bridge Road, Mount Kisco, NY 10549

Yeshiva of the Telshe Alumni
Riverdale, New York

- Private 4-year rabbinical college for men affiliated with Jewish faith
- Very large city

General. Accredited by AARTS. **Calendar:** Semester.

2011-2012 Annual costs. Tuition/fees: $7,900. Room/board: $4,600.

Application procedures. Admission: No deadline. $50 fee.

Academics. Credit/placement by examination: AP, CLEP.

Majors. Theology: Talmudic.

Contact. Phone: (718) 601-3523
Yeshiva of the Telshe Alumni, 4904 Independence Avenue, Riverdale, NY 10471

Yeshiva Shaar Hatorah
Kew Gardens, New York

CB code: 0743

- Private 4-year rabbinical college for men affiliated with Jewish faith
- Very large city
- 90 degree-seeking undergraduates
- Interview required

General. Founded in 1976. Accredited by AARTS. Ordination and first rabbinic degree available. **Degrees:** 3 bachelor's awarded; master's offered. **Calendar:** Semester. **Full-time faculty:** 1 total. **Part-time faculty:** 1 total.

Basis for selection. Religious commitment, school achievement record, recommendations, and interview most important.

2011-2012 Annual costs. Comprehensive fee: $15,400.

Application procedures. Admission: No deadline. $100 fee.

Academics. Special study options: Double major. **Credit/placement by examination:** AP, CLEP.

Majors. Theology: Talmudic.

Student life. Policies: Religious observance required.

Contact. Phone: (718) 846-1940
Yoel Yankelewitz, Admissions Director, Yeshiva Shaar Hatorah, 117-06 84th Avenue, Kew Gardens, NY 11418

Yeshiva Shaarei Torah of Rockland
Suffern, New York

- Private 4-year rabbinical college for men affiliated with Jewish faith
- Commuter campus in large town
- 70 degree-seeking undergraduates

General. Accredited by AARTS. **Degrees:** 5 bachelor's awarded. **Calendar:** Semester. **Full-time faculty:** 7 total. **Part-time faculty:** 4 total.

2011-2012 Annual costs. Tuition/fees: $9,000. Room/board: $3,000.

Application procedures. Admission: No deadline. $250 fee.

Academics. Credit/placement by examination: AP, CLEP.

Majors. Theology: Talmudic.

Contact. Phone: (845) 352-3431
Rabbi Avraham Posner, Admissions Director, Yeshiva Shaarei Torah of Rockland, 91 West Carlton Road, Suffern, NY 10901

Yeshiva University
New York, New York
www.yu.edu

CB member
CB code: 2990

- Private 4-year university
- Residential campus in very large city
- 2,787 degree-seeking undergraduates: 3% part-time, 47% women, 1% Hispanic American, 6% international
- 3,730 degree-seeking graduate students
- 69% of applicants admitted
- SAT or ACT with writing, application essay, interview required
- 77% graduate within 6 years

General. Founded in 1886. Regionally accredited. Campus locations in Manhattan and the Bronx. **Degrees:** 672 bachelor's, 330 associate awarded; master's, professional, doctoral offered. **Calendar:** Semester, limited summer session. **Full-time faculty:** 985 total, 38% women. **Part-time faculty:** 383 total; 44% women. **Class size:** 66% < 20, 31% 20-39, 2% 40-49, less than 1% 50-99.

Freshman class profile. 1,818 applied, 1,262 admitted, 870 enrolled.

Mid 50% test scores			
SAT critical reading:	550-680	GPA 3.0-3.49:	27%
SAT math:	540-680	GPA 2.0-2.99:	15%
SAT writing:	540-670	Return as sophomores:	90%
ACT composite:	23-29	Out-of-state:	34%
GPA 3.75 or higher:	36%	Live on campus:	90%
GPA 3.50-3.74:	21%	International:	4%

Basis for selection. Equal weight given to high school GPA, test scores, ability and motivation as indicated in interview, school and community activities, recommendations of principal, guidance counselor, and/or employer. **Home schooled:** Statement describing home school structure and mission, transcript of courses and grades, state high school equivalency certificate, interview required.

High school preparation. College-preparatory program required. 16 units recommended. Recommended units include English 4, mathematics 2, social studies 2, science 2 and foreign language 2.

2011-2012 Annual costs. Tuition/fees: $35,200. Room/board: $10,650. Books/supplies: $1,166. Personal expenses: $3,101.

2010-2011 Financial aid. Need-based: 82% of total undergraduate aid awarded as scholarships/grants, 18% as loans/jobs. **Additional information:** Essays required of Distinguished Scholarship applicants.

Application procedures. Admission: Priority date 2/1; no deadline. $65 fee, may be waived for applicants with need. Admission notification on a rolling basis beginning on or about 12/15. Must reply by May 1 or within 2 week(s) if notified thereafter. **Financial aid:** Priority date 4/15, closing date 5/1. FAFSA, institutional form required. Applicants notified on a rolling basis starting 4/1.

Academics. Special study options: Combined bachelor's/graduate degree, cross-registration, double major, dual enrollment of high school students, exchange student, honors, independent study, internships, student-designed major, study abroad, teacher certification program. **Credit/placement by examination:** AP, CLEP, institutional tests. 44 credit hours maximum toward bachelor's degree. **Support services:** Reduced course load, tutoring, writing center.

Honors college/program. 1400 SAT (exclusive of Writing) or ACT equivalent, 2 nominations, interview required.

Majors. Biology: General, biochemistry, molecular. **Business:** Accounting, business admin, finance, international, management information systems, marketing. **Computer sciences:** General. **Education:** Early childhood, elementary. **Engineering:** Pre-engineering. **English:** Creative writing, English lit, general lit, rhetoric/composition, technical writing. **Foreign languages:** Hebrew. **Health services:** Audiology/speech pathology. **History:** General. **Math:** General. **Philosophy/religion:** Philosophy. **Physical sciences:** Chemistry, physics. **Psychology:** General. **Social sciences:** Economics, political science, sociology. **Visual/performing arts:** Music.

Most popular majors. Biology 15%, business/marketing 29%, English 7%, foreign language 6%, psychology 15%, social sciences 9%.

Computing on campus. 350 workstations in library, computer center, student center. Dormitories wired for high-speed internet access and linked to campus network. Online library, helpline, repair service, wireless network available.

Student life. Freshman orientation: Mandatory. Preregistration for classes offered. Held the week before classes. **Policies:** Students participate in university governance through college senates. **Housing:** Guaranteed on-campus for all undergraduates. Single-sex dorms, apartments available. $250 nonrefundable deposit, deadline 6/1. **Activities:** Jazz band, choral groups, drama, literary magazine, music ensembles, musical theater, radio station, student government, student newspaper, neighborhood social service, pre-professional, special interest, and political clubs.

Athletics. NCAA. **Intercollegiate:** Baseball M, basketball, cross-country M, fencing M, soccer M, tennis M, volleyball M, wrestling M. **Intramural:** Basketball, tennis M, volleyball W. **Team name:** Macs.

Student services. Career counseling, student employment services, health services, personal counseling, placement for graduates.

Contact. E-mail: yuadmit@yu.edu
Phone: (212) 960-5277 Fax: (212) 960-0086
Michael Kranzler, Director of Undergraduate Admissions, Yeshiva University, 500 West 185th Street, New York, NY 10033

Yeshivas Novominsk
Brooklyn, New York

♦ Private 4-year rabbinical college for men affiliated with Jewish faith
♦ Very large city
♦ 123 degree-seeking undergraduates

General. Accredited by AARTS. **Calendar:** Semester.

2011-2012 Annual costs. Tuition/fees: $9,000. Room/board: $3,500.

Application procedures. Admission: No deadline. $100 fee.

Academics. Credit/placement by examination: AP, CLEP.

Majors. Theology: Talmudic.

Contact. Phone: (718) 438-2727
Yeshivas Novominsk, 1569 47th Street, Brooklyn, NY 11219

Yeshivat Mikdash Melech
Brooklyn, New York
www.mikdashmelech.net
CB code: 1432

♦ Private 5-year rabbinical college for men affiliated with Jewish faith
♦ Residential campus in very large city
♦ 102 degree-seeking undergraduates: 6% international
♦ 18 degree-seeking graduate students
♦ Interview required

General. Accredited by AARTS. **Degrees:** 8 bachelor's awarded; master's offered. **Calendar:** Semester, extensive summer session. **Full-time faculty:** 6 total; 67% have terminal degrees. **Class size:** 100% < 20.

Freshman class profile.

End year in good standing:	100%	**Live on campus:**	80%
Out-of-state:	5%		

Basis for selection. Open admission, but selective for some programs. Recommendations, school record, test scores, and class rank considered. **Home schooled:** Statement describing home school structure and mission required.

High school preparation. Required units include English 3, mathematics 3, social studies 1, history 1, science 2 (laboratory 1), foreign language 1 and academic electives 1.

2012-2013 Annual costs. Tuition/fees (projected): $7,500. Room/board: $4,300. Personal expenses: $4,000.

2010-2011 Financial aid. Need-based: 99% of total undergraduate aid awarded as scholarships/grants, 1% as loans/jobs. **Non-need-based:** Scholarships awarded for academics, leadership, religious affiliation.

Application procedures. Admission: No deadline. $400 fee, may be waived for applicants with need. Application must be submitted on paper. Admission notification on a rolling basis. **Financial aid:** No deadline. FAFSA, institutional form required. Applicants notified on a rolling basis starting 5/1.

Academics. Special study options: Independent study, study abroad. **Credit/placement by examination:** AP, CLEP. **Support services:** Remedial instruction, tutoring.

Majors. Philosophy/religion: Judaic. **Theology:** Talmudic.

Computing on campus. Wireless network available.

Student life. Freshman orientation: Available. Preregistration for classes offered. **Policies:** Religious observance required. **Housing:** Guaranteed on-campus for freshmen. Wellness housing available.

Student services. Adult student services, chaplain/spiritual director, financial aid counseling.

Contact. E-mail: mikdashmelech@verizon.net
Phone: (718) 339-1090 Fax: (718) 998-9321
Rabbi Hillel Strouse, Admissions Director, Yeshivat Mikdash Melech, 1326 Ocean Parkway, Brooklyn, NY 11230

Yeshivath Viznitz
Monsey, New York

♦ Private 4-year rabbinical college for men
♦ Large town

General. Accredited by AARTS. **Degrees:** 45 bachelor's awarded; doctoral offered. **Calendar:** Semester.

Application procedures. Admission: No deadline.

Academics. Credit/placement by examination: AP, CLEP.

Majors. Theology: Talmudic.

Contact. Phone: (914) 356-1010
Yeshivath Viznitz, 25 Phyllis Terrace, Monsey, NY 10952

North Carolina

Apex School of Theology
Durham, North Carolina
www.apexsot.edu

- Private 4-year Bible college
- Small city
- 519 degree-seeking undergraduates
- 148 graduate students

General. Regionally accredited; also accredited by TRACS. **Degrees:** 456 bachelor's, 63 associate awarded; master's, doctoral offered. **Calendar:** Semester. **Full-time faculty:** 8 total. **Part-time faculty:** 20 total.

Basis for selection. Open admission.

2011-2012 Annual costs. Tuition/fees: $6,200. Books/supplies: $300.

Application procedures. Admission: No deadline. $25 fee.

Academics. Special study options: Distance learning, dual enrollment of high school students, independent study, internships. **Credit/placement by examination:** AP, CLEP.

Majors. Theology: Theology.

Student life. Activities: Student newspaper.

Contact. E-mail: registrar@apexsot.edu
Phone: (919) 572-1625 ext. 7025
Sandra Manning, Director of Admissions, Apex School of Theology, 2945 South Miami Boulevard, Suite 114, Durham, NC 27703

Appalachian State University
Boone, North Carolina
www.appstate.edu

CB member
CB code: 5010

- Public 4-year university
- Residential campus in large town
- 15,282 degree-seeking undergraduates: 4% part-time, 52% women, 3% African American, 1% Asian American, 3% Hispanic American, 1% international
- 1,727 degree-seeking graduate students
- 62% of applicants admitted
- SAT or ACT with writing required
- 65% graduate within 6 years

General. Founded in 1899. Regionally accredited. **Degrees:** 3,010 bachelor's awarded; master's, doctoral offered. **ROTC:** Army. **Location:** 87 miles from Winston-Salem, 100 miles from Asheville. **Calendar:** Semester, extensive summer session. **Full-time faculty:** 871 total; 99% have terminal degrees, 12% minority, 47% women. **Part-time faculty:** 309 total; 71% have terminal degrees, 5% minority, 50% women. **Class size:** 40% < 20, 46% 20-39, 6% 40-49, 7% 50-99, 1% >100. **Special facilities:** Dark sky observatory, visual arts center, year round outdoor adventure camp.

Freshman class profile. 12,959 applied, 8,006 admitted, 2,972 enrolled.

Mid 50% test scores			
SAT critical reading:	520-610	Rank in top quarter:	55%
SAT math:	530-620	Rank in top tenth:	18%
SAT writing:	500-590	End year in good standing:	88%
ACT composite:	22-26	Return as sophomores:	88%
GPA 3.75 or higher:	67%	Out-of-state:	11%
GPA 3.50-3.74:	18%	Live on campus:	99%
GPA 3.0-3.49:	14%	International:	1%
GPA 2.0-2.99:	1%	Fraternities:	4%
		Sororities:	8%

Basis for selection. GED not accepted. Satisfactory combination of grades and/or class rank and required test scores. SAT Math used for placement. Audition required for music majors; portfolio required for art majors.

High school preparation. College-preparatory program required. 13 units required. Required units include English 4, mathematics 4, social studies 1, history 1, science 3 (laboratory 1) and foreign language 2. Specific math units required.

2011-2012 Annual costs. Tuition/fees: $5,538; $17,586 out-of-state. Room/board: $6,810. Books/supplies: $700. Personal expenses: $1,500.

2010-2011 Financial aid. Need-based: 1,335 full-time freshmen applied for aid; 1,319 were judged to have need; 1,246 of these received aid. Average need met was 78%. Average scholarship/grant was $7,178; average loan $3,116. 56% of total undergraduate aid awarded as scholarships/grants, 44% as loans/jobs. **Non-need-based:** Awarded to 4,267 full-time undergraduates, including 792 freshmen. Scholarships awarded for academics, alumni affiliation, art, athletics, job skills, leadership, minority status, music/drama, religious affiliation, ROTC, state residency.

Application procedures. Admission: No deadline. $55 fee, may be waived for applicants with need. Postponement allowed on individual basis for one term during academic year. **Financial aid:** Priority date 3/1; no closing date. FAFSA required. Applicants notified on a rolling basis starting 4/1; must reply within 3 week(s) of notification.

Academics. Special study options: Distance learning, double major, dual enrollment of high school students, ESL, exchange student, honors, independent study, internships, liberal arts/career combination, student-designed major, study abroad, teacher certification program. **Credit/placement by examination:** AP, CLEP, IB, SAT, ACT, institutional tests. **Support services:** Learning center, pre-admission summer program, remedial instruction, study skills assistance, tutoring, writing center.

Honors college/program. Successful applicants will generally be in the top 5% of their high school class, with combined Math and Verbal SAT scores of at least 1250 (29 for the ACT) on average. The application process includes an essay (500 words as described on the website), two letters of recommendation, and a resume. The deadline for application for Fall 2012 is May 1, 2012. Application review will begin in January and letters of acceptance will be sent starting in February. 200 students matriculate.

Majors. Architecture: Urban/community planning. **Area/ethnic studies:** Women's. **Biology:** General, ecology. **Business:** Accounting, actuarial science, business admin, construction management, finance, hospitality admin, insurance, international, management information systems, marketing. **Communications:** Advertising, communications/speech/rhetoric, journalism, public relations, radio/TV. **Computer sciences:** Computer science. **Conservation:** Environmental science, environmental studies. **Education:** Art, biology, business, chemistry, drama/dance, elementary, English, family/consumer sciences, French, health, history, kindergarten/preschool, learning disabled, mathematics, middle, music, physical, physics, Spanish, technology/industrial arts. **English:** English lit. **Foreign languages:** French, Spanish. **Health services:** Athletic training, communication disorders, dietetics, health care admin, music therapy, nursing (RN), public health ed. **History:** General. **Human services:** Social work. **Liberal arts:** Arts/sciences. **Math:** General, statistics. **Parks/recreation:** Exercise sciences, facilities management. **Philosophy/religion:** Philosophy, religion. **Physical sciences:** Chemistry, geology, physics. **Protective services:** Criminal justice. **Psychology:** General. **Social sciences:** Anthropology, economics, geography, political science, sociology. **Visual/performing arts:** Art, commercial photography, dance, dramatic, graphic design, industrial design, interior design, music management, music performance, studio arts, studio arts management. **Work/family studies:** Child development, clothing/textiles.

Most popular majors. Business/marketing 18%, communications/journalism 9%, education 18%, psychology 7%, social sciences 8%, visual/performing arts 8%.

Computing on campus. 2,500 workstations in dormitories, library, computer center, student center. Dormitories wired for high-speed internet access and linked to campus network. Commuter students can connect to campus network. Online course registration, online library, helpline, repair service, wireless network available.

Student life. Freshman orientation: Mandatory. Preregistration for classes offered. 2-day program throughout summer and at beginning of each semester and summer school session. **Policies:** Student must be full-time and live on campus to join a fraternity or sorority. **Housing:** Guaranteed on-campus for freshmen. Coed dorms, single-sex dorms, special housing for disabled, wellness housing available. Sorority housing available. **Activities:** Bands, campus ministries, choral groups, dance, drama, film society, international student organizations, literary magazine, music ensembles, Model UN, musical theater, opera, radio station, student government, student newspaper, symphony orchestra, Campus Crusade for Christ, Habitat for Humanity, Order of the Black and Gold, ACLU, College Democrats/Republicans, Wesley Foundation, Westminster Canterbury Fellowship, Circle K.

Athletics. NCAA. **Intercollegiate:** Baseball M, basketball, cross-country, field hockey W, football (tackle) M, golf, soccer, softball W, tennis, track

and field, volleyball W, wrestling M. **Intramural:** Badminton, basketball, bowling, cross-country, football (non-tackle), golf, soccer, synchronized swimming, table tennis, triathlon, volleyball. **Team name:** Mountaineers.

Student services. Adult student services, alcohol/substance abuse counseling, chaplain/spiritual director, career counseling, student employment services, financial aid counseling, health services, minority student services, on-campus daycare, personal counseling, placement for graduates, veterans' counselor, women's services. **Physically disabled:** Services for visually, speech, hearing impaired.

Contact. E-mail: admissions@appstate.edu
Phone: (828) 262-2000 Fax: (828) 262-3296
Lloyd Scott, Director of Admissions, Appalachian State University, ASU Box 32004, Boone, NC 28608

Art Institute of Charlotte
Charlotte, North Carolina
www.artinstitutes.edu/charlotte   **CB code: 3834**

- For-profit 4-year visual arts and career college
- Commuter campus in very large city
- 1,331 degree-seeking undergraduates
- Application essay, interview required

General. Accredited by ACICS. **Degrees:** 85 bachelor's, 103 associate awarded. **Location:** 8 miles from Center City. **Calendar:** Quarter, extensive summer session. **Full-time faculty:** 42 total; 50% have terminal degrees, 29% minority, 48% women. **Part-time faculty:** 37 total; 24% have terminal degrees, 24% minority, 54% women. **Class size:** 94% < 20, 6% 20-39. **Special facilities:** Computer labs, interior design lighting laboratory, photography studio, audio/video production studios, teaching restaurant open to the public.

Basis for selection. Open admission, but selective for some programs. Interviews required. Applicant must provide a written essay, high school transcripts, and are required to take Accuplacer placement test. **Home schooled:** Statement describing home school structure and mission, transcript of courses and grades, interview required.

2012-2013 Annual costs. Tuition/fees (projected): $21,285. Fees for culinary students $300; for all other students: application fee $50, enrollment fee $100. Kit pricing varies by major. Housing security deposit: $200. Room only: $5,250. Books/supplies: $1,500. Personal expenses: $3,435.

2011-2012 Financial aid. Need-based: 208 full-time freshmen applied for aid; 208 were judged to have need; 208 of these received aid. Average need met was 58%. Average scholarship/grant was $4,221; average loan $3,500. 31% of total undergraduate aid awarded as scholarships/grants, 69% as loans/jobs.

Application procedures. Admission: No deadline. $50 fee. Admission notification on a rolling basis. **Financial aid:** No deadline. FAFSA required. Applicants notified on a rolling basis starting 7/1; must reply within 1 week(s) of notification.

Academics. Students begin studies in the majors alongside general education classes from the first quarter. **Special study options:** Distance learning, internships, study abroad. **Credit/placement by examination:** AP, CLEP. **Support services:** Learning center, remedial instruction, study skills assistance, tutoring, writing center.

Majors. Business: Apparel. **Computer sciences:** Web page design. **Visual/ performing arts:** Graphic design, interior design.

Computing on campus. 224 workstations in library, computer center, student center. Commuter students can connect to campus network. Online library, helpline, student web hosting, wireless network available.

Student life. Freshman orientation: Mandatory. Preregistration for classes offered. Orientation is held the Saturday prior to the first day of classes which is typically on Monday. **Policies:** No weapons, drugs, or alcohol permitted on campus or in on-campus housing. **Housing:** Apartments available. $200 fully refundable deposit. **Activities:** Campus ministries, choral groups, student newspaper, VerseOne.

Student services. Alcohol/substance abuse counseling, career counseling, student employment services, financial aid counseling, personal counseling, placement for graduates, veterans' counselor.

Contact. E-mail: aichadm@aii.edu
Phone: (704) 357-8020 Toll-free number: (800) 872-4417
Fax: (704) 357-1133
Michelle Idle, Senior Director of Admissions, Art Institute of Charlotte, Three LakePointe Plaza, Charlotte, NC 28217-4536

Barton College
Wilson, North Carolina   **CB member**
www.barton.edu   **CB code: 5016**

- Private 4-year liberal arts college affiliated with Christian Church (Disciples of Christ)
- Residential campus in large town
- 1,149 degree-seeking undergraduates: 22% part-time, 72% women, 27% African American, 1% Asian American, 3% Hispanic American, 2% international
- 15 degree-seeking graduate students
- 52% of applicants admitted
- SAT or ACT (ACT writing optional) required
- 47% graduate within 6 years

General. Founded in 1902. Regionally accredited. **Degrees:** 203 bachelor's awarded; master's offered. **Location:** 45 miles from Raleigh. **Calendar:** 4-1-4, limited summer session. **Full-time faculty:** 70 total; 66% have terminal degrees, 11% minority, 50% women. **Part-time faculty:** 38 total; 13% have terminal degrees, 5% minority, 63% women. **Class size:** 65% < 20, 34% 20-39, less than 1% 40-49, less than 1% 50-99. **Special facilities:** Lula E. Rackley Gallery and the Virginia Thompson Graves Gallery of the Barton Museum, greenhouse, TV and music recording studios, photo developing labs and darkroom.

Freshman class profile. 2,598 applied, 1,352 admitted, 236 enrolled.

Mid 50% test scores			
SAT critical reading:	390-540	Rank in top quarter:	31%
SAT math:	430-570	Rank in top tenth:	7%
GPA 3.75 or higher:	7%	Return as sophomores:	68%
GPA 3.50-3.74:	10%	Out-of-state:	16%
GPA 3.0-3.49:	37%	Live on campus:	87%
GPA 2.0-2.99:	46%	International:	1%

Basis for selection. High school GPA, test scores, strong academic course study important. Interview recommended for marginal students; portfolio recommended for art students. **Home schooled:** State high school equivalency certificate required.

High school preparation. 13 units required. Required and recommended units include English 4, mathematics 3, social studies 2, science 2 (laboratory 1), foreign language 2 and academic electives 1.

2011-2012 Annual costs. Tuition/fees: $22,982. Room/board: $7,632.

2011-2012 Financial aid. Non-need-based: Scholarships awarded for academics, alumni affiliation, art, athletics, leadership, minority status, music/ drama, religious affiliation, state residency.

Application procedures. Admission: No deadline. $25 fee, may be waived for applicants with need, free for online applicants. Admission notification on a rolling basis. Must reply by May 1 or within 2 week(s) if notified thereafter. **Financial aid:** Priority date 4/1; no closing date. FAFSA required. Applicants notified on a rolling basis starting 5/1; must reply within 2 week(s) of notification.

Academics. Special study options: Accelerated study, cooperative education, double major, ESL, honors, independent study, internships, liberal arts/ career combination, study abroad, teacher certification program, Washington semester, weekend college. **Credit/placement by examination:** AP, CLEP, IB, SAT, ACT, institutional tests. 30 credit hours maximum toward bachelor's degree. **Support services:** Remedial instruction, study skills assistance, tutoring, writing center.

Majors. Biology: General. **Business:** Accounting, business admin, human resources. **Communications:** Media studies. **Computer sciences:** General. **Conservation:** Environmental science. **Education:** Art, Deaf/hearing impaired, elementary, learning disabled, middle, physical, social studies. **English:** English lit. **Foreign languages:** Spanish. **Health services:** Athletic training, nursing (RN). **History:** General. **Human services:** Social work. **Liberal arts:** Arts/sciences. **Math:** General. **Parks/recreation:** Health/fitness, sports admin. **Philosophy/religion:** Religion. **Physical sciences:** Chemistry. **Protective services:** Criminal justice. **Psychology:** General. **Social sciences:** Political science. **Visual/performing arts:** Dramatic, studio arts.

Most popular majors. Business/marketing 26%, education 15%, health sciences 11%, interdisciplinary studies 6%, public administration/social services 10%.

Computing on campus. 176 workstations in dormitories, library, computer center, student center. Dormitories wired for high-speed internet access

and linked to campus network. Commuter students can connect to campus network. Online library, helpline, wireless network available.

Student life. Freshman orientation: Mandatory, $75 fee. Preregistration for classes offered. Two-day sessions held during June. **Housing:** Guaranteed on-campus for freshmen. Coed dorms, single-sex dorms, special housing for disabled, fraternity/sorority housing, wellness housing available. $150 nonrefundable deposit, deadline 5/1. Full-time freshmen and sophomores not living with parents required to live on campus. Special permission required for students under 23 to live off-campus. **Activities:** Pep band, campus ministries, choral groups, dance, drama, literary magazine, musical theater, student government, student newspaper, symphony orchestra, TV station, Disciples on Campus, Fellowship of Christian Athletes, Habitat for Humanity, Alpha Phi Omega, Campus Conservatives, College Democrats, diversity education team, political science club, Campus Crusade for Christ.

Athletics. NCAA. Intercollegiate: Baseball M, basketball, cross-country, golf M, soccer, softball W, tennis, track and field, volleyball. **Intramural:** Badminton, basketball, football (non-tackle), soccer, softball, tennis, volleyball. **Team name:** Bulldogs.

Student services. Adult student services, chaplain/spiritual director, career counseling, student employment services, financial aid counseling, health services, personal counseling, placement for graduates. **Physically disabled:** Services for visually, speech, hearing impaired.

Contact. E-mail: enroll@barton.edu
Phone: (252) 399-6317 Toll-free number: (800) 345-4973
Fax: (252) 399-6572
Amanda Metts, Director of Admissions, Barton College, Box 5000, Wilson, NC 27893-7000

Belmont Abbey College
Belmont, North Carolina   **CB member**
www.belmontabbeycollege.edu   **CB code: 5055**

▶ Private 4-year liberal arts college affiliated with Roman Catholic Church
▶ Residential campus in small town
▶ 1,693 degree-seeking undergraduates: 7% part-time, 62% women, 28% African American, 1% Asian American, 3% Hispanic American, 2% international
▶ 64% of applicants admitted
▶ 37% graduate within 6 years

General. Founded in 1876. Regionally accredited. **Degrees:** 294 bachelor's awarded. **ROTC:** Army, Naval, Air Force. **Location:** 10 miles from Charlotte. **Calendar:** Semester, limited summer session. **Full-time faculty:** 67 total; 69% have terminal degrees, 57% women. **Part-time faculty:** 72 total; 17% have terminal degrees, 57% women. **Class size:** 64% < 20, 36% 20-39, less than 1% 40-49. **Special facilities:** Monastery, basillica, adoration chapel.

Freshman class profile. 1,944 applied, 1,250 admitted, 271 enrolled.

Mid 50% test scores		Rank in top quarter:	29%
SAT critical reading:	440-550	Rank in top tenth:	10%
SAT math:	440-570	Return as sophomores:	64%
ACT composite:	19-26	Out-of-state:	43%
GPA 3.75 or higher:	12%	Live on campus:	85%
GPA 3.50-3.74:	13%	International:	4%
GPA 3.0-3.49:	22%	Fraternities:	20%
GPA 2.0-2.99:	52%	Sororities:	20%

Basis for selection. GPA, class rank, high school curriculum, and test scores most important. Personal accomplishments, extracurricular activities, and letters of recommendation strongly considered. Students with a strong academic record and high school GPA above 3.0 are not required to submit SAT/ACT scores.

High school preparation. College-preparatory program recommended. 16 units required. Required and recommended units include English 4, mathematics 3-4, social studies 1, history 1, science 2, foreign language 2-3 and academic electives 3. For science majors 4 math, 1 chemistry, 1 physics, 1 additional science recommended.

2011-2012 Annual costs. Tuition/fees: $26,182. Books included in the cost of tuition for new incoming students, including transfers. Room/board: $10,403. Books/supplies: $1,000. Personal expenses: $2,000.

2010-2011 Financial aid. Need-based: 288 full-time freshmen applied for aid; 253 were judged to have need; 253 of these received aid. Average need met was 70%. Average scholarship/grant was $15,366; average loan $3,074. 73% of total undergraduate aid awarded as scholarships/grants, 27% as loans/jobs. **Non-need-based:** Awarded to 485 full-time undergraduates,

including 148 freshmen. Scholarships awarded for academics, athletics, state residency.

Application procedures. Admission: Closing date 8/1 (postmark date). $35 fee, may be waived for applicants with need, free for online applicants. Admission notification on a rolling basis beginning on or about 9/15. Must reply by May 1 or within 3 week(s) if notified thereafter. **Financial aid:** Priority date 4/1; no closing date. FAFSA required. Applicants notified on a rolling basis starting 3/1; must reply within 2 week(s) of notification.

Academics. Special study options: Double major, dual enrollment of high school students, honors, independent study, internships, liberal arts/career combination, study abroad, teacher certification program, weekend college. **Credit/placement by examination:** AP, CLEP, IB. 30 credit hours maximum toward bachelor's degree. **Support services:** Learning center, remedial instruction, study skills assistance, tutoring, writing center.

Honors college/program. Students with the following considered for The Honors Institute: 3.70 or higher high school GPA (unweighted); 1200 SAT score (minimum verbal score of 600); Honors Institute application including an essay and personal interview. Honors Institute includes expanded 4-year core curriculum based on Great Books, $3,500 travel stipend for summer study in Europe or The Washington Experience, a week in the nation's capital, beach/mountain retreats with faculty, and extensive cultural appreciation opportunities.

Majors. Biology: General. **Business:** Accounting, business admin. **Education:** General, elementary. **English:** English lit. **Health services:** Predental, premedicine, prepharmacy, preveterinary. **History:** General. **Liberal arts:** Arts/sciences. **Math:** General. **Protective services:** Criminal justice. **Psychology:** General. **Social sciences:** Political science. **Theology:** Theology.

Most popular majors. Business/marketing 46%, education 25%, liberal arts 6%, psychology 6%.

Computing on campus. 56 workstations in library, computer center, student center. Dormitories wired for high-speed internet access and linked to campus network. Commuter students can connect to campus network. Online course registration, online library, helpline, repair service, wireless network available.

Student life. Freshman orientation: Mandatory. Preregistration for classes offered. 4 days prior to class start. **Housing:** Guaranteed on-campus for all undergraduates. Coed dorms, single-sex dorms, special housing for disabled, apartments available. $400 deposit, deadline 8/24. 24-hour quiet (honors) dorm available. **Activities:** Pep band, campus ministries, choral groups, dance, drama, international student organizations, literary magazine, musical theater, student government, student newspaper, BAC College Republicans, Belmont Abbey College Democrats, Delta Psi Theta Sorority, international club, Crusaders for Life.

Athletics. NCAA. Intercollegiate: Baseball M, basketball, cross-country, golf, lacrosse, soccer, softball W, tennis, track and field, volleyball W, wrestling M. **Intramural:** Basketball, bowling, cross-country, football (non-tackle) M, golf, softball, table tennis, volleyball. **Team name:** Crusaders.

Student services. Adult student services, alcohol/substance abuse counseling, chaplain/spiritual director, career counseling, student employment services, financial aid counseling, health services, personal counseling, placement for graduates, veterans' counselor. **Physically disabled:** Services for visually, speech, hearing impaired.

Contact. E-mail: admissions@bac.edu
Phone: (704) 461-6665 Toll-free number: (888) 222-0110
Fax: (704) 461-6220
Roger Jones, Director of Admissions, Belmont Abbey College, 100 Belmont - Mt. Holly Road, Belmont, NC 28012-2795

Bennett College for Women
Greensboro, North Carolina   **CB member**
www.bennett.edu   **CB code: 5058**

▶ Private 4-year liberal arts college for women affiliated with United Methodist Church
▶ Residential campus in large city
▶ 678 degree-seeking undergraduates: 1% part-time, 100% women, 93% African American, 3% Hispanic American
▶ 63% of applicants admitted
▶ Application essay required
▶ 39% graduate within 6 years

General. Founded in 1873. Regionally accredited. There have been recent additions to the campus that include three new buildings (The Martin Dixon

Intergenerational Center, the Global Leaning Center and the honors dorm) and a wellness complex. **Degrees:** 109 bachelor's awarded. **ROTC:** Army, Air Force. **Location:** 26 miles from Winston-Salem, 80 miles from Raleigh. **Calendar:** Semester. **Full-time faculty:** 61 total; 64% have terminal degrees, 70% minority, 77% women. **Part-time faculty:** 28 total; 29% have terminal degrees, 64% minority, 61% women. **Class size:** 72% < 20, 27% 20-39, less than 1% 40-49, less than 1% 50-99.

Freshman class profile. 1,433 applied, 900 admitted, 158 enrolled.

Mid 50% test scores		
SAT critical reading:	350-430	
SAT math:	350-420	
GPA 3.75 or higher:	5%	
GPA 3.50-3.74:	7%	
GPA 3.0-3.49:	23%	
GPA 2.0-2.99:		62%
Rank in top quarter:		12%
Rank in top tenth:		8%
Return as sophomores:		73%
Out-of-state:		65%
Live on campus:		99%

Basis for selection. Admission decisions are made by assessing school achievement record(s), test scores, recommendations and applicant's personal statement. SAT or ACT recommended. Test scores are not required of applicants, but they will be considered if they are submitted. Interview recommended for borderline students. **Home schooled:** Transcript of courses and grades, letter of recommendation (nonparent) required.

High school preparation. College-preparatory program recommended. 18 units required. Required units include English 4, mathematics 3, social studies 2, science 2, foreign language 2 and academic electives 5.

2011-2012 Annual costs. Tuition/fees: $16,794. Room/board: $7,428. Books/supplies: $1,000. Personal expenses: $2,100.

2010-2011 Financial aid. **Need-based:** 208 full-time freshmen applied for aid; 201 were judged to have need; 201 of these received aid. Average need met was 48%. Average scholarship/grant was $10,149; average loan $3,583. 50% of total undergraduate aid awarded as scholarships/grants, 50% as loans/jobs. **Non-need-based:** Awarded to 18 full-time undergraduates, including 3 freshmen. Scholarships awarded for state residency.

Application procedures. **Admission:** No deadline. $35 fee, may be waived for applicants with need. Admission notification on a rolling basis. **Financial aid:** Closing date 4/15. FAFSA, institutional form required. Applicants notified by 7/15.

Academics. Accepted students who do not meet required SAT or ACT score admitted to Academic Enrichment Program which provides tutoring, counseling and other support services. **Special study options:** Accelerated study, cooperative education, cross-registration, double major, dual enrollment of high school students, exchange student, honors, independent study, internships, liberal arts/career combination, New York semester, student-designed major, study abroad, teacher certification program, Washington semester. Dual degree programs in engineering with North Carolina Agricultural and Technical State University, Collaborative program in nursing with Howard University. **Credit/placement by examination:** AP, CLEP, IB, SAT, ACT, institutional tests. **Support services:** Learning center, pre-admission summer program, reduced course load, remedial instruction, study skills assistance, tutoring, writing center.

Majors. **Biology:** General. **Business:** Accounting, business admin. **Communications:** Journalism. **Computer sciences:** General. **Education:** Elementary, English, mathematics, mentally handicapped. **English:** English lit. **Human services:** Social work. **Math:** General. **Physical sciences:** Chemistry. **Psychology:** General. **Social sciences:** Political science. **Visual/performing arts:** General, arts management.

Most popular majors. Biology 20%, business/marketing 10%, communications/journalism 24%, education 7%, English 6%, interdisciplinary studies 7%, psychology 13%, public administration/social services 7%, visual/performing arts 7%.

Computing on campus. Dormitories wired for high-speed internet access and linked to campus network. Commuter students can connect to campus network. Online course registration, online library, helpline, wireless network available.

Student life. **Freshman orientation:** Mandatory, $125 fee. Preregistration for classes offered. **Policies:** Freshmen not permitted cars on campus. **Housing:** Guaranteed on-campus for all undergraduates. Wellness housing available. $250 nonrefundable deposit. Students with GPA of 3.0 may reside in honors residence hall. **Activities:** Campus ministries, choral groups, dance, drama, film society, international student organizations, literary magazine, music ensembles, Model UN, radio station, student government, student newspaper, TV station, Student Christian Fellowship, NAACP, social work club, Women in Communications, student teachers association, psychology club, political science club.

Athletics. USCAA. **Intercollegiate:** Basketball W. **Team name:** Belles.

Student services. Chaplain/spiritual director, career counseling, student employment services, financial aid counseling, health services, on-campus daycare, personal counseling, placement for graduates.

Contact. E-mail: admiss@bennett.edu
Phone: (336) 370-8624 Toll-free number: (800) 413-5323
Fax: (336) 517-2166
Taunya Monroe, Director of Admissions, Bennett College for Women, 900 East Washington Street, Greensboro, NC 27401-3239

Brevard College
Brevard, North Carolina
www.brevard.edu

CB member
CB code: 5067

- ◆ Private 4-year liberal arts college affiliated with United Methodist Church
- ◆ Residential campus in small town
- ◆ 625 degree-seeking undergraduates: 2% part-time, 40% women, 11% African American, 1% Native American, 5% international
- ◆ 55% of applicants admitted
- ◆ SAT or ACT (ACT writing recommended), application essay required
- ◆ 35% graduate within 6 years

General. Founded in 1853. Regionally accredited. **Degrees:** 133 bachelor's awarded. **Location:** 33 miles from Asheville. **Calendar:** Semester. **Full-time faculty:** 53 total; 77% have terminal degrees, 45% women. **Part-time faculty:** 33 total; 30% have terminal degrees, 42% women. **Class size:** 82% < 20, 18% 20-39. **Special facilities:** Climbing wall, ropes challenge course, Appalachian Center for Environmental Education, fitness appraisal lab, performing arts center, academic enrichment center.

Freshman class profile. 1,329 applied, 734 admitted, 190 enrolled.

Mid 50% test scores		
SAT critical reading:	440-520	
SAT math:	410-520	
ACT composite:	18-22	
GPA 3.75 or higher:	6%	
GPA 3.50-3.74:	9%	
GPA 3.0-3.49:	32%	
GPA 2.0-2.99:	51%	
Rank in top quarter:		20%
Rank in top tenth:		5%
End year in good standing:		74%
Return as sophomores:		65%
Out-of-state:		42%
Live on campus:		93%
International:		9%

Basis for selection. High school record, class rank, SAT/ACT scores, references, extracurricular activities, recommendations, essay, interview, talent/ability, character/personal qualities, volunteer work important. Essay, interview recommended for all students; portfolio required for art students; audition required for music students. **Home schooled:** Statement describing home school structure and mission, transcript of courses and grades required. Legal documentation from home school agency, local school district, or State Department of Education and admissions interview required. **Learning Disabled:** Evaluation by licensed professional within past 3 years.

High school preparation. College-preparatory program recommended. 22 units recommended. Recommended units include English 4, mathematics 3, social studies 4, history 1, science 3 (laboratory 1), foreign language 2 and academic electives 4. Math units should include 2 algebra and 1 geometry.

2011-2012 Annual costs. Tuition/fees: $22,700. Room/board: $7,950. Books/supplies: $1,000. Personal expenses: $1,000.

2010-2011 Financial aid. **Need-based:** 178 full-time freshmen applied for aid; 121 were judged to have need; 121 of these received aid. Average need met was 60%. Average scholarship/grant was $14,898; average loan $3,850. 71% of total undergraduate aid awarded as scholarships/grants, 29% as loans/jobs. **Non-need-based:** Awarded to 840 full-time undergraduates, including 235 freshmen. Scholarships awarded for academics, art, athletics, leadership, music/drama, religious affiliation, state residency.

Application procedures. **Admission:** No deadline. $30 fee, may be waived for applicants with need, free for online applicants. Admission notification on a rolling basis beginning on or about 7/1. **Financial aid:** Priority date 2/1; no closing date. FAFSA required. Applicants notified on a rolling basis starting 2/1; must reply by 5/1 or within 4 week(s) of notification.

Academics. **Special study options:** Double major, dual enrollment of high school students, honors, independent study, internships, student-designed major, study abroad, teacher certification program. **Credit/placement by examination:** AP, CLEP, IB, SAT, ACT, institutional tests. 92 credit hours maximum toward bachelor's degree. **Support services:** Learning center, reduced course load, remedial instruction, study skills assistance, tutoring, writing center.

Majors. **Biology:** General. **Business:** Business admin. **Conservation:** Environmental science, environmental studies. **Education:** Music. **English:**

English lit. **Health services:** Predental, premedicine, prenursing, preveterinary. **History:** General. **Liberal arts:** Arts/sciences. **Math:** General. **Parks/recreation:** Exercise sciences, facilities management. **Philosophy/religion:** Religion. **Protective services:** Law enforcement admin. **Psychology:** General. **Visual/performing arts:** Art, dramatic, music, music performance.

Most popular majors. Business/marketing 16%, interdisciplinary studies 18%, parks/recreation 23%, psychology 6%, visual/performing arts 15%.

Computing on campus. 100 workstations in dormitories, library, computer center, student center. Dormitories wired for high-speed internet access and linked to campus network. Online library, helpline, wireless network available.

Student life. Freshman orientation: Mandatory. Preregistration for classes offered. Orientations held in August prior to start of classes. **Housing:** Guaranteed on-campus for all undergraduates. Coed dorms, single-sex dorms, special housing for disabled, wellness housing available. All non-county or non-adjacent-county residents required to live on campus until age 21. **Activities:** Bands, campus ministries, choral groups, dance, drama, literary magazine, music ensembles, musical theater, opera, student government, student newspaper, Recycling Club, Fellowship of Christian Athletes, Omicron Delta Kappa, Outing Club, Environmental Educators, History Club, Young Politicians of America, Business Club, Debate Society.

Athletics. NCAA. **Intercollegiate:** Baseball M, basketball, cheerleading M, cross-country, football (tackle) M, golf, soccer, softball W, tennis, track and field, volleyball W. **Intramural:** Archery, badminton, basketball, bowling, cross-country, equestrian, football (tackle) M, golf, skiing, soccer, softball, swimming, tennis, track and field, volleyball. **Team name:** Tornados.

Student services. Alcohol/substance abuse counseling, chaplain/spiritual director, career counseling, student employment services, financial aid counseling, health services, personal counseling, placement for graduates, veterans' counselor. **Physically disabled:** Services for visually, speech, hearing impaired.

Contact. E-mail: admissions@brevard.edu
Phone: (828) 883-8292 Toll-free number: (800) 527-9090
Fax: (828) 884-3790
Mathew Cox, Vice President of Admissions, Brevard College, One Brevard College Drive, Brevard, NC 28712

Cabarrus College of Health Sciences
Concord, North Carolina
www.cabarruscollege.edu   CB code: 5136

- Private 4-year health science and nursing college
- Commuter campus in small city
- 466 degree-seeking undergraduates
- 68% of applicants admitted
- Application essay required

General. Regionally accredited. The Institution is part of a large public hospital system. Our programs specialize in healthcare careers such as nursing, medical assisting, occupational therapy assistant, medical imaging, leadership management and surgical technology. **Degrees:** 15 bachelor's, 117 associate awarded. **Location:** 25 miles from Charlotte. **Calendar:** Semester, limited summer session. **Full-time faculty:** 27 total; 11% have terminal degrees, 7% minority, 93% women. **Part-time faculty:** 9 total; 67% have terminal degrees, 44% minority. **Class size:** 59% < 20, 32% 20-39, 4% 40-49, 5% 50-99.

Freshman class profile. 53 applied, 36 admitted, 24 enrolled.

Mid 50% test scores			
SAT critical reading:	440-510	GPA 3.50-3.74:	17%
SAT math:	440-550	GPA 3.0-3.49:	33%
ACT composite:	19-20	GPA 2.0-2.99:	11%
GPA 3.75 or higher:	39%	Rank in top quarter:	40%
		Rank in top tenth:	20%

Basis for selection. School record, class rank, essay, test scores, and recommendations most important.

High school preparation. Required and recommended units include English 4, mathematics 3, science 2 (laboratory 2) and foreign language 2.

2011-2012 Annual costs. Tuition/fees: $10,740. Books/supplies: $1,300.

Application procedures. Admission: Priority date 3/1; no deadline. $50 fee, may be waived for applicants with need.

Academics. Special study options: Cross-registration, distance learning, liberal arts/career combination. **Credit/placement by examination:** AP,

CLEP, institutional tests. 15 credit hours maximum toward associate degree, 15 toward bachelor's. **Support services:** Learning center, study skills assistance.

Majors. Health services: Health care admin, health services admin, nursing (RN).

Computing on campus. 24 workstations in library, computer center, student center. Commuter students can connect to campus network. Online course registration, online library, wireless network available.

Student life. Freshman orientation: Mandatory. Preregistration for classes offered. 2-day orientation before start of first semester. **Activities:** Student government, student newspaper, Christian student union, association of nursing students, Rotaract.

Student services. Career counseling, financial aid counseling, on-campus daycare, personal counseling. **Physically disabled:** Services for hearing impaired.

Contact. E-mail: admissions@cabarruscollege.edu
Phone: (704) 403-1556 Fax: (704) 403-2077
Mark Ellison, Director of Admissions, Cabarrus College of Health Sciences, 401 Medical Park Drive, Concord, NC 28025-2405

Campbell University
Buies Creek, North Carolina   CB member
www.campbell.edu   CB code: 5100

- Private 4-year university and liberal arts college affiliated with Baptist faith
- Residential campus in rural community
- 4,539 degree-seeking undergraduates: 25% part-time, 51% women, 16% African American, 3% Hispanic American, 1% Native American, 2% international
- 1,643 degree-seeking graduate students
- 41% of applicants admitted
- SAT or ACT (ACT writing recommended) required
- 48% graduate within 6 years

General. Founded in 1887. Regionally accredited. **Degrees:** 884 bachelor's, 100 associate awarded; master's, professional offered. **ROTC:** Army. **Location:** 30 miles from Raleigh, 30 miles from Fayetteville. **Calendar:** Semester, extensive summer session. **Full-time faculty:** 215 total; 84% have terminal degrees, 37% women. **Part-time faculty:** 102 total; 42% have terminal degrees, 48% women. **Class size:** 55% < 20, 27% 20-39, 7% 40-49, 10% 50-99, less than 1% >100. **Special facilities:** Golf course, animal museum, drug information center, nature trail.

Freshman class profile. 8,835 applied, 3,582 admitted, 925 enrolled.

Mid 50% test scores			
SAT critical reading:	450-590	GPA 3.0-3.49:	24%
SAT math:	470-580	GPA 2.0-2.99:	13%
SAT writing:	430-550	Return as sophomores:	77%
ACT composite:	19-26	Out-of-state:	20%
GPA 3.75 or higher:	54%	Live on campus:	91%
GPA 3.50-3.74:	9%	International:	1%

Basis for selection. SAT, GPA, course selection, class rank, and standardized test scores considered. Students with less than the acceptable threshold may be considered for probational admission. Candidates reviewed on an individual basis. Interview recommended on a case by case basis. Essay recommended for all students; audition recommended for music programs.

High school preparation. College-preparatory program recommended. 13 units recommended. Recommended units include English 4, mathematics 3, social studies 2, science 2 (laboratory 1) and foreign language 2. One social science should be U.S. History. Math units must include algebra I and II as well as geometry.

2011-2012 Annual costs. Tuition/fees: $23,720. Room/board: $8,300. Books/supplies: $1,500.

2010-2011 Financial aid. Need-based: 773 full-time freshmen applied for aid; 690 were judged to have need; 690 of these received aid. Average need met was 80%. Average scholarship/grant was $12,922; average loan $5,149. 73% of total undergraduate aid awarded as scholarships/grants, 27% as loans/jobs. **Non-need-based:** Awarded to 3,331 full-time undergraduates, including 765 freshmen. Scholarships awarded for academics, athletics, music/drama, religious affiliation, ROTC, state residency.

Application procedures. Admission: No deadline. $35 fee, may be waived for applicants with need, free for online applicants. Admission notification on a rolling basis. **Financial aid:** Priority date 3/1; no closing date. FAFSA required. Applicants notified on a rolling basis starting 2/1; must reply within 2 week(s) of notification.

Academics. Special study options: Accelerated study, combined bachelor's/graduate degree, cooperative education, distance learning, double major, exchange student, honors, independent study, internships, liberal arts/career combination, study abroad, teacher certification program, Washington semester. **Credit/placement by examination:** AP, CLEP, IB, SAT, ACT. **Support services:** Reduced course load, remedial instruction, study skills assistance, tutoring, writing center.

Majors. Biology: General, biochemistry. **Business:** General, accounting, business admin, financial planning, international, management information systems. **Communications:** Advertising, broadcast journalism, journalism, public relations, radio/TV. **Computer sciences:** Computer graphics, computer science, information systems. **Education:** General, biology, early childhood, elementary, English, French, history, mathematics, middle, music, physical, secondary, social studies, Spanish. **English:** British lit, English lit. **Foreign languages:** French, Spanish. **Health services:** Athletic training, predental, premedicine, prepharmacy, preveterinary. **History:** General. **Human services:** General, social work. **Math:** General. **Parks/recreation:** Exercise sciences, health/fitness, sports admin. **Philosophy/religion:** Religion. **Physical sciences:** Chemistry. **Protective services:** Criminal justice. **Psychology:** General. **Social sciences:** Economics, international relations, political science. **Theology:** Religious ed, sacred music, theology. **Visual/performing arts:** Commercial/advertising art, dramatic, music, piano/keyboard, studio arts, voice/opera. **Work/family studies:** Child development, family studies.

Most popular majors. Business/marketing 25%, health sciences 10%, psychology 7%, social sciences 8%.

Computing on campus. Dormitories wired for high-speed internet access and linked to campus network. Commuter students can connect to campus network. Online course registration, online library, helpline, repair service, wireless network available.

Student life. Freshman orientation: Mandatory, $50 fee. Preregistration for classes offered. Two weekend sessions in summer available to incoming freshmen and their families for students entering in Fall. Short program before classes start for students entering in Spring. **Policies:** Religious observance required. **Housing:** Guaranteed on-campus for all undergraduates. Single-sex dorms, special housing for disabled, apartments available. $100 fully refundable deposit. **Activities:** Bands, campus ministries, choral groups, drama, international student organizations, literary magazine, music ensembles, musical theater, student government, student newspaper, symphony orchestra, Baptist Student Union, College Democrats/Republicans, Fellowship of Christian Athletes, North Carolina Student Legislators, Campus Crusade, Christians in Action, Campbell Catholic Community, Circle K.

Athletics. NCAA. **Intercollegiate:** Baseball M, basketball, cheerleading, cross-country, football (tackle) M, golf, soccer, softball W, swimming W, tennis, track and field, volleyball W, wrestling M. **Intramural:** Basketball, football (non-tackle), golf, soccer, softball, table tennis, tennis, volleyball, water polo. **Team name:** Fighting Camels.

Student services. Adult student services, alcohol/substance abuse counseling, chaplain/spiritual director, career counseling, student employment services, financial aid counseling, health services, personal counseling, placement for graduates, veterans' counselor. **Physically disabled:** Services for visually, speech, hearing impaired.

Contact. E-mail: theorangeadvantage@campbell.edu
Phone: (910) 893-1290 ext. 1290
Toll-free number: (800) 334-4111 ext. 1290 Fax: (910) 893-1288
Jason Hall, Assistant Vice President for Admissions, Campbell University, PO Box 546, Buies Creek, NC 27506

Carolina Christian College
Winston-Salem, North Carolina
www.carolina.edu

- Private 4-year Bible college affiliated with nondenominational tradition
- Commuter campus in large city
- 64 degree-seeking undergraduates: 12% part-time, 58% women
- 7 degree-seeking graduate students
- Application essay required

General. Accredited by ABHE. **Degrees:** 8 bachelor's, 4 associate awarded; master's offered. **Calendar:** Continuous, limited summer session. **Full-time

faculty: 1 total. **Part-time faculty:** 6 total; 33% have terminal degrees, 83% minority.

Freshman class profile. 15 applied, 15 admitted, 15 enrolled.

Basis for selection. Open admission. COMPASS test required.

2011-2012 Annual costs. Tuition/fees: $4,700. Books/supplies: $500.

Application procedures. Admission: No deadline. $50 fee, may be waived for applicants with need. Application must be submitted on paper. Admission notification on a rolling basis. **Financial aid:** No deadline. FAFSA required. Applicants notified on a rolling basis.

Academics. Special study options: Accelerated study, independent study. **Credit/placement by examination:** AP, CLEP. 12 credit hours maximum toward associate degree, 24 toward bachelor's. **Support services:** Remedial instruction.

Majors. Theology: Bible.

Computing on campus. 8 workstations in library. Wireless network available.

Student life. Freshman orientation: Mandatory. Preregistration for classes offered. **Activities:** Campus ministries, student government.

Contact. Phone: (336) 744-0900 Fax: (336) 744-0901
LaTanya Lucas, Academic Dean, Carolina Christian College, Box 777, Winston-Salem, NC 27102

Catawba College
Salisbury, North Carolina
www.catawba.edu

CB member
CB code: 5103

- Private 4-year liberal arts college affiliated with United Church of Christ
- Residential campus in large town
- 1,278 degree-seeking undergraduates: 5% part-time, 52% women, 21% African American, 1% Asian American, 3% Hispanic American, 1% Native American, 2% international
- 25 degree-seeking graduate students
- 42% of applicants admitted
- Application essay required
- 54% graduate within 6 years

General. Founded in 1851. Regionally accredited. **Degrees:** 282 bachelor's awarded; master's offered. **ROTC:** Army. **Location:** 30 miles from Charlotte, 50 miles from Greensboro. **Calendar:** Semester, limited summer session. **Full-time faculty:** 67 total; 88% have terminal degrees, 4% minority, 42% women. **Part-time faculty:** 39 total; 10% have terminal degrees, 13% minority, 56% women. **Class size:** 56% < 20, 43% 20-39, 1% 40-49. **Special facilities:** Comprehensive three-manual Casavant pipe-organ, observatory, 45-acre outdoor biological laboratory, nature preserve.

Freshman class profile. 2,427 applied, 1,010 admitted, 307 enrolled.

Mid 50% test scores			
SAT critical reading:	390-530	Rank in top quarter:	36%
SAT math:	410-540	Rank in top tenth:	11%
GPA 3.75 or higher:	32%	Return as sophomores:	71%
GPA 3.50-3.74:	13%	Out-of-state:	20%
GPA 3.0-3.49:	30%	Live on campus:	85%
GPA 2.0-2.99:	24%	International:	2%

Basis for selection. School achievement record, class rank, standardized test scores, school recommendations important. SAT preferred, but ACT also accepted. Interview recommended for all students; audition recommended for drama, music programs.

High school preparation. College-preparatory program required. 13 units required. Required and recommended units include English 4, mathematics 3, social studies 3, science 3 and foreign language 2. Required credits must be academic subjects at college preparatory level.

2011-2012 Annual costs. Tuition/fees: $25,160. Room/board: $8,700. Books/supplies: $1,400. Personal expenses: $1,300.

Financial aid. Non-need-based: Scholarships awarded for academics, athletics, music/drama, state residency.

Application procedures. Admission: Priority date 8/1; no deadline. $25 fee, may be waived for applicants with need, free for online applicants. Admission notification on a rolling basis beginning on or about 9/15. Must

reply by May 1 or within 2 week(s) if notified thereafter. **Financial aid:** Priority date 3/15; no closing date. FAFSA required. Applicants notified on a rolling basis starting 11/1; must reply within 2 week(s) of notification.

Academics. Special study options: Cross-registration, distance learning, double major, dual enrollment of high school students, honors, independent study, internships, student-designed major, study abroad, teacher certification program. **Credit/placement by examination:** AP, CLEP, IB, SAT, ACT. 30 credit hours maximum toward bachelor's degree. **Support services:** Study skills assistance, tutoring, writing center.

Majors. Biology: General. **Business:** Accounting, business admin, management information systems. **Communications:** Communications/speech/rhetoric. **Conservation:** Environmental science, environmental studies. **Education:** Elementary, middle, music, physical. **English:** English lit. **Foreign languages:** French, Spanish. **Health services:** Athletic training, recreational therapy. **History:** General. **Human services:** General. **Math:** General. **Parks/recreation:** General, health/fitness, sports admin. **Philosophy/religion:** Religion. **Physical sciences:** Chemistry. **Protective services:** Law enforcement admin. **Psychology:** General. **Social sciences:** Political science, sociology. **Visual/performing arts:** Dramatic, music, music performance, studio arts management.

Most popular majors. Business/marketing 32%, education 20%, parks/recreation 9%, visual/performing arts 12%.

Computing on campus. 125 workstations in dormitories, library, computer center. Dormitories wired for high-speed internet access and linked to campus network. Commuter students can connect to campus network. Online library, helpline, repair service, wireless network available.

Student life. Freshman orientation: Mandatory. Preregistration for classes offered. Held week prior to start of fall classes. **Housing:** Guaranteed on-campus for all undergraduates. Coed dorms, single-sex dorms available. $250 nonrefundable deposit. **Activities:** Bands, campus ministries, choral groups, dance, drama, literary magazine, music ensembles, musical theater, student government, student newspaper, Alpha program, Athenian society, Helen Foil Beard Society, political science association, environmental service clubs, Fellowship of Christian Athletes, multi-cultural club, Philomathean club, volunteer club.

Athletics. NCAA. **Intercollegiate:** Baseball M, basketball, cross-country, football (tackle) M, golf, lacrosse M, soccer, softball W, swimming, tennis, volleyball W. **Intramural:** Basketball, cross-country, football (tackle) M, golf, handball, racquetball, soccer, softball, table tennis, tennis, volleyball. **Team name:** Catawba Indians.

Student services. Adult student services, alcohol/substance abuse counseling, chaplain/spiritual director, career counseling, student employment services, financial aid counseling, health services, personal counseling, placement for graduates. **Physically disabled:** Services for visually, hearing impaired.

Contact. E-mail: admissions@catawba.edu
Phone: (704) 637-4402 Toll-free number: (800) 228-2922
Fax: (704) 637-4222
Lois Williams, Vice President for Enrollment Services, Catawba College, 2300 West Innes Street, Salisbury, NC 28144-2488

Chowan University
Murfreesboro, North Carolina
www.chowan.edu

CB member
CB code: 5107

- Private 4-year university and liberal arts college affiliated with Southern Baptist Convention
- Residential campus in rural community
- 1,282 degree-seeking undergraduates: 4% part-time, 51% women, 67% African American, 2% Hispanic American, 1% international
- 41 degree-seeking graduate students
- 59% of applicants admitted
- SAT or ACT (ACT writing optional) required
- 30% graduate within 6 years; 8% enter graduate study

General. Founded in 1848. Regionally accredited. **Degrees:** 123 bachelor's awarded; master's offered. **Location:** 40 miles from Hampton Roads, Virginia. **Calendar:** Semester, limited summer session. **Full-time faculty:** 59 total; 68% have terminal degrees, 12% minority, 48% women. **Part-time faculty:** 62 total; 16% have terminal degrees, 21% minority, 37% women. **Class size:** 51% < 20, 39% 20-39, 8% 40-49, 1% 50-99, less than 1% >100. **Special facilities:** Graphic Communication Center.

Freshman class profile. 4,273 applied, 2,518 admitted, 683 enrolled.

GPA 3.75 or higher:	2%	End year in good standing:	65%
GPA 3.50-3.74:	3%	Return as sophomores:	43%
GPA 3.0-3.49:	16%	Out-of-state:	53%
GPA 2.0-2.99:	62%	Live on campus:	90%
Rank in top quarter:	13%	Fraternities:	1%
Rank in top tenth:	2%	Sororities:	1%

Basis for selection. School achievement record, standardized test score (SAT or ACT score), student "fit" with the institution as determined by information from the application for admission. Interview and campus visit is recommended for all students; audition required for music majors; portfolio required for graphic design and studio art majors. **Home schooled:** State high school equivalency certificate required.

High school preparation. College-preparatory program recommended. Recommended units include English 4, mathematics 3, social studies 2, science 2 (laboratory 2) and academic electives 7.

2012-2013 Annual costs. Tuition/fees (projected): $21,020. Room/board: $7,530. Books/supplies: $1,000. Personal expenses: $1,000.

2010-2011 Financial aid. Need-based: 559 full-time freshmen applied for aid; 533 were judged to have need; 527 of these received aid. Average need met was 69%. Average scholarship/grant was $12,973; average loan $2,999. 77% of total undergraduate aid awarded as scholarships/grants, 23% as loans/jobs. **Non-need-based:** Awarded to 1,284 full-time undergraduates, including 577 freshmen. Scholarships awarded for academics, athletics, leadership, music/drama, religious affiliation, state residency.

Application procedures. Admission: No deadline. $20 fee, may be waived for applicants with need. Admission notification on a rolling basis. **Financial aid:** Priority date 3/1; no closing date. FAFSA required. Applicants notified on a rolling basis starting 3/1; must reply within 2 week(s) of notification.

Academics. Special study options: Distance learning, double major, dual enrollment of high school students, honors, independent study, internships, liberal arts/career combination, study abroad, teacher certification program. **Credit/placement by examination:** AP, CLEP, IB, SAT. 15 credit hours maximum toward associate degree, 15 toward bachelor's. **Support services:** Learning center, reduced course load, study skills assistance, tutoring, writing center.

Majors. Biology: General. **Business:** Accounting/business management, business admin, information resources management, marketing, small business admin. **Communications technology:** Graphics. **Education:** General, elementary, English, history, music, physical, secondary. **English:** English lit. **Health services:** Athletic training, predental, premedicine, prenursing, prepharmacy, preveterinary. **History:** General. **Liberal arts:** Arts/sciences. **Parks/recreation:** Exercise sciences, health/fitness, sports admin. **Philosophy/religion:** Religion. **Physical sciences:** General. **Protective services:** Law enforcement admin. **Psychology:** General. **Social sciences:** General. **Visual/performing arts:** Graphic design, music performance, studio arts.

Most popular majors. Biology 12%, business/marketing 11%, communications/journalism 12%, education 17%, history 8%, parks/recreation 7%, psychology 7%, security/protective services 10%, visual/performing arts 10%.

Computing on campus. 219 workstations in library, computer center. Dormitories wired for high-speed internet access and linked to campus network. Commuter students can connect to campus network. Online course registration, online library, helpline, repair service, wireless network available.

Student life. Freshman orientation: Mandatory. Preregistration for classes offered. **Policies:** No alcohol on campus; restricted dorm visitation; academic honor code. Religious observance required. **Housing:** Guaranteed on-campus for all undergraduates. Single-sex dorms, wellness housing available. $100 nonrefundable deposit. Apartments and suites available. **Activities:** Bands, campus ministries, choral groups, drama, international student organizations, music ensembles, student government, international students club, Instruments of Praise Gospel Choir, Student National Education Association, Fellowship of Christian Athletes and various academic area clubs.

Athletics. NCAA, NCCAA. **Intercollegiate:** Baseball M, basketball, bowling W, cheerleading, cross-country W, football (tackle) M, golf M, soccer, softball W, tennis, volleyball W. **Intramural:** Basketball, football (nontackle) M, soccer, softball, table tennis, tennis, volleyball W. **Team name:** Hawks.

Student services. Alcohol/substance abuse counseling, chaplain/spiritual director, career counseling, student employment services, financial aid counseling, health services, personal counseling, placement for graduates, veterans' counselor.

Contact. E-mail: enroll@chowan.edu
Phone: (252) 398-1236 Toll-free number: (888) 424-6926
Fax: (252) 398-1190
R. Chad Holt, Vice President for Enrollment Management, Chowan
University, One University Place, Murfreesboro, NC 27855-9901

Davidson College
Davidson, North Carolina
www.davidson.edu

CB member
CB code: 5150

- Private 4-year liberal arts college affiliated with Presbyterian Church (USA)
- Residential campus in small town
- 1,750 degree-seeking undergraduates: 49% women, 7% African American, 4% Asian American, 5% Hispanic American, 4% international
- 28% of applicants admitted
- SAT or ACT (ACT writing optional), application essay required
- 92% graduate within 6 years

General. Founded in 1837. Regionally accredited. **Degrees:** 445 bachelor's awarded. **ROTC:** Army, Air Force. **Location:** 19 miles from Charlotte. **Calendar:** Semester. **Full-time faculty:** 162 total; 96% have terminal degrees, 15% minority, 40% women. **Part-time faculty:** 5 total; 60% have terminal degrees, 20% minority, 40% women. **Class size:** 69% < 20, 30% 20-39, less than 1% 40-49. **Special facilities:** Laser facility, electron microscope, campus arboretum.

Freshman class profile. 4,309 applied, 1,208 admitted, 488 enrolled.

Mid 50% test scores			
SAT critical reading:	630-730	GPA 2.0-2.99:	1%
SAT math:	640-720	Rank in top quarter:	98%
SAT writing:	630-730	Rank in top tenth:	82%
ACT composite:	29-33	Return as sophomores:	96%
GPA 3.75 or higher:	79%	Out-of-state:	79%
GPA 3.50-3.74:	15%	Live on campus:	100%
GPA 3.0-3.49:	5%	International:	5%

Basis for selection. GED not accepted. Course selection, rigor of program, grades, recommendations, essays, test scores, class rank considered. SAT and SAT Subject Tests or ACT recommended. Campus visit strongly recommended.

High school preparation. College-preparatory program required. 16 units required. Required and recommended units include English 4, mathematics 3-4, science 2-4 and foreign language 2-4. Foreign language units should be in same language. 2 required, 4 recommended for social studies or history units.

2012-2013 Annual costs. Tuition/fees: $40,809. Room/board: $11,346. Books/supplies: $1,000. Personal expenses: $1,325.

2010-2011 Financial aid. Need-based: 284 full-time freshmen applied for aid; 226 were judged to have need; 226 of these received aid. Average need met was 100%. Average scholarship/grant was $30,083; average loan $2,420. 93% of total undergraduate aid awarded as scholarships/grants, 7% as loans/jobs. **Non-need-based:** Awarded to 473 full-time undergraduates, including 89 freshmen. Scholarships awarded for academics, art, athletics, leadership, minority status, music/drama, ROTC. **Additional information:** The college has increased the money it provides for grants in financial aid packages and eliminated mandatory loans, allowing all students, regardless of socio-economic background, to graduate debt-free.

Application procedures. Admission: Closing date 1/2 (postmark date). $50 fee, may be waived for applicants with need. Admission notification by 4/1. Must reply by 5/1. **Financial aid:** Priority date 3/15, closing date 2/15. FAFSA, CSS PROFILE required. Applicants notified by 4/7; must reply by 5/1.

Academics. 2-year interdisciplinary course in humanities available for freshmen and sophomores. Center for Special Studies supervises student-designed majors. **Special study options:** Cross-registration, double major, exchange student, honors, independent study, student-designed major, study abroad, teacher certification program, Washington semester. Visiting student program with Howard University and Morehouse College; Dean Rusk program in International Studies. **Credit/placement by examination:** AP, CLEP, IB, institutional tests. **Support services:** Tutoring, writing center.

Majors. Biology: General. **English:** English lit. **Foreign languages:** Classics, French, German, Spanish. **History:** General. **Math:** General. **Philosophy/religion:** Philosophy, religion. **Physical sciences:** Chemistry, physics. **Psychology:** General. **Social sciences:** Anthropology, economics, political science, sociology. **Visual/performing arts:** Art, dramatic, music.

Most popular majors. Biology 11%, English 11%, foreign language 9%, history 9%, psychology 11%, social sciences 28%, visual/performing arts 6%.

Computing on campus. 142 workstations in dormitories, library, computer center, student center. Dormitories wired for high-speed internet access and linked to campus network. Commuter students can connect to campus network. Online course registration, online library, helpline, repair service, wireless network available.

Student life. Freshman orientation: Mandatory, $100 fee. Preregistration for classes offered. **Housing:** Guaranteed on-campus for freshmen. Coed dorms, apartments, cooperative housing, wellness housing available. Substance-free, suite/apartment-style housing available. **Activities:** Bands, campus ministries, choral groups, dance, drama, international student organizations, literary magazine, music ensembles, musical theater, radio station, student government, student newspaper, symphony orchestra, black student coalition, Amnesty International, Young Democrats, College Republicans, Habitat for Humanity, Asia 3D, gender resource center.

Athletics. NCAA. **Intercollegiate:** Baseball M, basketball, cross-country, diving, field hockey W, football (tackle) M, golf M, lacrosse W, soccer, swimming, tennis, track and field, volleyball W, wrestling M. **Intramural:** Basketball, football (non-tackle), soccer, softball, volleyball. **Team name:** Wildcats.

Student services. Alcohol/substance abuse counseling, chaplain/spiritual director, career counseling, financial aid counseling, health services, minority student services, personal counseling, placement for graduates. **Physically disabled:** Services for visually, hearing impaired.

Contact. E-mail: admission@davidson.edu
Phone: (704) 894-2230 Toll-free number: (800) 768-0380
Fax: (704) 894-2016
Christopher Gruber, Vice President and Dean of Admission and Financial Aid, Davidson College, Box 7156, Davidson, NC 28035-7156

Duke University
Durham, North Carolina
www.duke.edu

CB member
CB code: 5156

- Private 4-year university affiliated with United Methodist Church
- Residential campus in large city
- 6,534 degree-seeking undergraduates: 50% women, 10% African American, 21% Asian American, 7% Hispanic American, 1% Native American, 8% international
- 8,575 degree-seeking graduate students
- 14% of applicants admitted
- SAT and SAT Subject Tests or ACT with writing, application essay required
- 94% graduate within 6 years

General. Founded in 1838. Regionally accredited. **Degrees:** 1,751 bachelor's awarded; master's, professional, doctoral offered. **ROTC:** Army, Naval, Air Force. **Location:** 30 miles from Raleigh, 170 miles from Richmond, Virginia. **Calendar:** Semester, extensive summer session. **Full-time faculty:** 1,173 total; 96% have terminal degrees, 20% minority, 34% women. **Class size:** 72% < 20, 20% 20-39, 3% 40-49, 4% 50-99, 2% >100. **Special facilities:** Marine laboratory, museum of art, forest, teaching and research center, herbarium, science research center, French science center, global health institute, institute for genome sciences and policy, humanities institute, institute for ethics, phytotron, institute for environmental policy solutions, social science research institute, center for black culture.

Freshman class profile. 28,145 applied, 3,938 admitted, 1,724 enrolled.

Mid 50% test scores			
SAT critical reading:	660-750	Rank in top tenth:	90%
SAT math:	690-780	Return as sophomores:	97%
SAT writing:	670-770	Out-of-state:	89%
ACT composite:	30-34	Live on campus:	100%
Rank in top quarter:	97%	International:	8%

Basis for selection. GED not accepted. Courses, school achievement record, school and community activities, essays, recommendations, test scores considered. Special consideration to alumni children and minority applicants. Applicants requesting alumni interview must submit Part I of application by 10/1 for Early Decision or by 12/1 for regular decision. Students using ACT for admission need to submit SAT Subject Tests or AP scores for foreign language and mathematics placement. Applicants to Arts and Sciences submitting SAT must submit 2 SAT Subject Tests. Applicants to School of Engineering submitting SAT must take SAT Subject Test in mathematics and 1 other subject. Interview with alumnus/a in student's home area recommended, but not required; audition recommended for drama, music majors; portfolio

recommended for art majors. **Home schooled:** Transcript of courses and grades, letter of recommendation (nonparent) required.

High school preparation. College-preparatory program required. Recommended units include English 4, mathematics 4, social studies 4, science 4 and foreign language 4. 4 math and 1 physics or chemistry required for engineering applicants, with calculus required before enrolling.

2011-2012 Annual costs. Tuition/fees: $41,938. Room/board: $11,967.

Financial aid. Non-need-based: Scholarships awarded for academics, alumni affiliation, art, athletics, leadership, minority status, religious affiliation, ROTC, state residency.

Application procedures. Admission: Closing date 1/2 (postmark date). $75 fee, may be waived for applicants with need. Admission notification by 4/2. Must reply by 5/1. **Financial aid:** Closing date 3/1. FAFSA, CSS PROFILE required. Applicants notified by 4/1; must reply by 5/1 or within 4 week(s) of notification.

Academics. International comparative studies with an emphasis in one or more areas. Special Focus Program for freshmen: engineering frontiers, evolution and humankind, forging social ideals, genome revolution, global health, memory and invention, visions of freedom. **Special study options:** Combined bachelor's/graduate degree, cross-registration, double major, exchange student, independent study, internships, New York semester, semester at sea, student-designed major, study abroad, teacher certification program, Washington semester. Art program/internship in New York City, marine biology semester in Beaufort. **Credit/placement by examination:** AP, CLEP, IB. **Support services:** Learning center, pre-admission summer program, tutoring, writing center.

Majors. Area/ethnic studies: African-American, Asian, women's. **Biology:** General, anatomy, neuroscience. **Computer sciences:** General. **Conservation:** General. **Engineering:** Biomedical, civil, electrical, mechanical. **English:** British lit, English lit. **Foreign languages:** Ancient Greek, classics, East Asian, French, German, Italian, Latin, Russian, Slavic, Spanish. **History:** General. **Human services:** Public policy. **Math:** General, statistics. **Philosophy/religion:** Philosophy, religion. **Physical sciences:** Chemistry, geology, physics. **Psychology:** General. **Social sciences:** Anthropology, economics, political science, sociology. **Visual/performing arts:** Art history/conservation, dance, design, dramatic, music.

Most popular majors. Biology 9%, engineering/engineering technologies 14%, psychology 7%, public administration/social services 9%, social sciences 21%.

Computing on campus. 450 workstations in dormitories, library, computer center, student center. Dormitories wired for high-speed internet access and linked to campus network. Commuter students can connect to campus network. Online course registration, online library, helpline, repair service, student web hosting, wireless network available.

Student life. Freshman orientation: Mandatory. Preregistration for classes offered. Held week prior to start of classes. **Housing:** Guaranteed on-campus for freshmen. Coed dorms, single-sex dorms, apartments, wellness housing available. $300 nonrefundable deposit, deadline 5/1. Special interest housing available for students in women's studies, the arts, languages, service (Alpha Phi Omega). All first-year students live together on East Campus. Most first-year residence halls have a faculty member in residence. All sophomores must live on West Campus. **Activities:** Bands, campus ministries, choral groups, dance, drama, film society, international student organizations, literary magazine, music ensembles, Model UN, musical theater, opera, radio station, student government, student newspaper, symphony orchestra, TV station, Black Student Alliance, Asian Student Association, Duke Muslim Association, Arab Student Association, Mi Gente: La Asociacion de Estudiantes Latinos, Freeman Center for Jewish Life, Volunteers for Youth, Campus Crusade for Christ, Habitat for Humanity, Blue Devils United (the Alliance of Queer Undergraduates).

Athletics. NCAA. **Intercollegiate:** Baseball M, basketball, cross-country, diving, fencing, field hockey W, football (tackle) M, golf, lacrosse, rowing (crew) W, soccer, swimming, tennis, track and field, volleyball W, wrestling M. **Intramural:** Badminton, baseball, basketball, football (tackle) M, golf, racquetball, soccer M, softball, squash, swimming, table tennis, tennis, volleyball. **Team name:** Blue Devils.

Student services. Adult student services, alcohol/substance abuse counseling, chaplain/spiritual director, career counseling, student employment services, financial aid counseling, health services, minority student services, on-campus daycare, personal counseling, placement for graduates, veterans' counselor, women's services. **Physically disabled:** Services for visually, speech, hearing impaired.

Contact. E-mail: undergrad-admissions@duke.edu
Phone: (919) 684-3214 Fax: (919) 681-8941
Christoph Guttentag, Dean of Undergraduate Admissions, Duke University, 2138 Campus Drive, Durham, NC 27708

East Carolina University
Greenville, North Carolina
www.ecu.edu

CB member
CB code: 5180

- Public 4-year university
- Residential campus in small city
- 20,738 degree-seeking undergraduates: 11% part-time, 58% women, 15% African American, 2% Asian American, 3% Hispanic American
- 5,750 degree-seeking graduate students
- 61% of applicants admitted
- SAT or ACT with writing required
- 59% graduate within 6 years

General. Founded in 1907. Regionally accredited. **Degrees:** 3,855 bachelor's awarded; master's, professional, doctoral offered. **ROTC:** Army, Air Force. **Location:** 80 miles from Raleigh. **Calendar:** Semester, extensive summer session. **Full-time faculty:** 1,198 total; 80% have terminal degrees, 11% minority, 48% women. **Part-time faculty:** 265 total; 40% have terminal degrees, 10% minority, 58% women. **Class size:** 34% < 20, 42% 20-39, 10% 40-49, 9% 50-99, 5% >100. **Special facilities:** 2 accelerators, climbing wall, ropes course, global classroom, field station.

Freshman class profile. 15,299 applied, 9,283 admitted, 3,891 enrolled.

Mid 50% test scores			
SAT critical reading:	480-560	GPA 3.0-3.49:	29%
SAT math:	500-570	GPA 2.0-2.99:	12%
SAT writing:	460-540	Rank in top quarter:	44%
ACT composite:	20-24	Rank in top tenth:	14%
GPA 3.75 or higher:	41%	Return as sophomores:	81%
GPA 3.50-3.74:	18%	Out-of-state:	14%
		Live on campus:	86%

Basis for selection. Freshman admission decisions based on a formula that weighs class rank, high school GPA (unweighted), and standardized test scores. GED accepted for non-traditional freshmen. SAT preferred, ACT also accepted. Audition, statement of purpose and letter of recommendation required for music programs. **Home schooled:** Transcript of courses and grades required.

High school preparation. College-preparatory program required. 16 units required; 18 recommended. Required and recommended units include English 4, mathematics 4, social studies 2, history 1, science 3 (laboratory 1), foreign language 2, computer science 1 and visual/performing arts 1.

2011-2012 Annual costs. Tuition/fees: $5,317; $17,896 out-of-state. All campus-based students are required to prove that they have health insurance or will be required to purchase the student health insurance plan. The "per hour" charge noted above is tuition and mandatory fees divided by 12 hours. Room/board: $8,220. Books/supplies: $1,106. Personal expenses: $3,038.

2011-2012 Financial aid. Need-based: 3,121 full-time freshmen applied for aid; 2,292 were judged to have need; 2,175 of these received aid. Average need met was 66%. Average scholarship/grant was $7,619; average loan $3,405. 41% of total undergraduate aid awarded as scholarships/grants, 59% as loans/jobs. **Non-need-based:** Awarded to 1,537 full-time undergraduates, including 267 freshmen. Scholarships awarded for academics, alumni affiliation, art, athletics, music/drama, ROTC.

Application procedures. Admission: Closing date 3/15 (postmark date). $70 fee, may be waived for applicants with need. Admission notification on a rolling basis beginning on or about 9/8. Must reply by 5/1. Out-of-state freshman enrollment limited to 18% of incoming freshman class, and processed on space-available basis. Applications received prior to December 31 receive priority. **Financial aid:** Priority date 3/1; no closing date. FAFSA required. Applicants notified on a rolling basis starting 4/1; must reply within 3 week(s) of notification.

Academics. Special study options: Accelerated study, combined bachelor's/graduate degree, cooperative education, distance learning, double major, dual enrollment of high school students, exchange student, honors, independent study, internships, student-designed major, study abroad, teacher certification program, Washington semester. **Credit/placement by examination:** AP, CLEP, IB, SAT, ACT, institutional tests. **Support services:** Learning center, reduced course load, remedial instruction, study skills assistance, tutoring, writing center.

Honors college/program. Admission is competitive and by invitation. Minimum eligibility criteria: Apply to (ECU) by December 1, minimum math/verbal combined SAT score of 1200 or minimum ACT score of 26, minimum un-weighted HS GPA of 3.5 or minimum weighted GPA of 4.0, completion of Honors College application.

Majors. Architecture: Urban/community planning. **Area/ethnic studies:** African-American, women's. **Biology:** General, biochemistry, exercise physiology. **Business:** Accounting, accounting/business management, business

admin, finance, hotel/motel admin, management information systems, marketing, office technology. **Communications:** Broadcast journalism, communications/speech/rhetoric. **Computer sciences:** Computer science, information technology. **Education:** Art, business, drama/dance, elementary, English, family/consumer sciences, French, German, health, kindergarten/preschool, learning disabled, mathematics, middle, music, physical, sales/marketing, science, social studies, Spanish, special ed. **Engineering:** General. **English:** English lit. **Foreign languages:** French, German, Spanish. **Health services:** Athletic training, audiology/speech pathology, clinical lab science, clinical nutrition, dietetics, environmental health, marriage/family therapy, medical records admin, music therapy, nursing (RN), public health ed, recreational therapy, vocational rehab counseling. **History:** General, applied. **Human services:** Social work. **Liberal arts:** Arts/sciences. **Math:** General. **Parks/recreation:** Exercise sciences, facilities management, sports admin. **Philosophy/religion:** Philosophy. **Physical sciences:** Chemistry, geology, physics. **Protective services:** Criminal justice. **Psychology:** General. **Social sciences:** Anthropology, economics, geography, political science, sociology. **Visual/performing arts:** Acting, art, art history/conservation, ceramics, cinematography, dance, directing/producing, dramatic, drawing, fiber arts, graphic design, illustration, interior design, jazz, metal/jewelry, music, music performance, music theory/composition, painting, photography, piano/keyboard, printmaking, sculpture, stringed instruments, studio arts, voice/opera. **Work/family studies:** Child development, clothing/textiles, family/community services.

Most popular majors. Biology 6%, business/marketing 19%, communications/journalism 7%, education 12%, engineering/engineering technologies 9%, health sciences 16%.

Computing on campus. 2,188 workstations in dormitories, library, computer center, student center. Dormitories wired for high-speed internet access and linked to campus network. Commuter students can connect to campus network. Online course registration, online library, helpline, repair service, student web hosting, wireless network available.

Student life. Freshman orientation: Mandatory, $100 fee. Preregistration for classes offered. 2-phase program: 1 summer session (overnight stay) and 1 session the day prior to start of classes. **Housing:** Guaranteed on-campus for freshmen. Coed dorms, single-sex dorms, special housing for disabled, fraternity/sorority housing, wellness housing available. $200 partly refundable deposit, deadline 5/1. Suite-style, summer on-campus, honors housing available. **Activities:** Bands, campus ministries, choral groups, dance, drama, film society, international student organizations, literary magazine, music ensembles, Model UN, musical theater, opera, radio station, student government, student newspaper, symphony orchestra, TV station, 280 registered organizations.

Athletics. NCAA. **Intercollegiate:** Baseball M, basketball, cheerleading, cross-country, diving, football (tackle) M, golf, soccer W, softball W, swimming, tennis, track and field, volleyball. **Intramural:** Basketball, bowling, cross-country, football (non-tackle), golf, racquetball, softball, table tennis, tennis, volleyball. **Team name:** Pirates.

Student services. Adult student services, alcohol/substance abuse counseling, chaplain/spiritual director, career counseling, student employment services, financial aid counseling, health services, minority student services, personal counseling, placement for graduates, veterans' counselor. **Physically disabled:** Services for visually, speech, hearing impaired.

Contact. E-mail: admis@ecu.edu
Phone: (252) 328-6640 Fax: (252) 328-6945
Anthony Britt, Director of Admissions, East Carolina University, Office of Undergraduate Admissions, Greenville, NC 27858-4353

Elizabeth City State University
Elizabeth City, North Carolina　　　　　**CB member**
www.ecsu.edu　　　　　　　　　　　　　**CB code: 5629**

▶ Public 4-year liberal arts college
▶ Residential campus in large town
▶ 2,836 degree-seeking undergraduates: 10% part-time, 61% women, 75% African American, 1% Hispanic American
▶ 92 degree-seeking graduate students
▶ 50% of applicants admitted
▶ SAT or ACT (ACT writing optional) required
▶ 42% graduate within 6 years

General. Founded in 1891. Regionally accredited. **Degrees:** 430 bachelor's awarded; master's offered. **ROTC:** Army. **Location:** 50 miles from Norfolk, VA. **Calendar:** Semester, extensive summer session. **Full-time faculty:** 165 total; 70% have terminal degrees, 74% minority, 62% women. **Part-time faculty:** 82 total; 26% have terminal degrees, 57% minority, 55% women. **Class size:** 50% < 20, 39% 20-39, 8% 40-49, 4% 50-99. **Special facilities:**

Recording studio, boardwalk in nature preserves/wetlands, golf driving range.

Freshman class profile. 2,894 applied, 1,458 admitted, 683 enrolled.

Mid 50% test scores		Rank in top quarter:	14%
SAT critical reading:	380-460	Rank in top tenth:	13%
SAT math:	400-470	End year in good standing:	93%
SAT writing:	370-440	Return as sophomores:	77%
ACT composite:	15-18	Out-of-state:	10%
GPA 3.75 or higher:	6%	Live on campus:	80%
GPA 3.50-3.74:	6%	Fraternities:	3%
GPA 3.0-3.49:	21%	Sororities:	6%
GPA 2.0-2.99:	66%		

Basis for selection. GPA and test scores considered. Special consideration given to residents from 21 neighboring counties. All applicants to any campus in the UNC system, except those exempted by current campus policies, must submit standardized test scores. SAT preferred, ACT accepted. **Home schooled:** Statement describing home school structure and mission, transcript of courses and grades, letter of recommendation (nonparent) required. **Learning Disabled:** Important to ascertain in advance the extent of the learning disability in order to provide the available service(s).

High school preparation. College-preparatory program recommended. 20 units required. Required units include English 4, mathematics 3, social studies 2, science 2 (laboratory 1) and foreign language 2. One additional laboratory science also required. Mathematics must include 1 algebra and 1 geometry. Social science must include 1 history.

2011-2012 Annual costs. Tuition/fees: $3,829; $13,572 out-of-state. Books are rented for $170 per semester. Room/board: $6,283. Books/supplies: $620. Personal expenses: $1,500.

Financial aid. Non-need-based: Scholarships awarded for academics, athletics, minority status, ROTC, state residency.

Application procedures. Admission: Priority date 5/1; deadline 6/30. $30 fee. Admission notification on a rolling basis. **Financial aid:** Priority date 3/15, closing date 6/1. FAFSA required. Applicants notified on a rolling basis starting 6/1; must reply by 6/30 or within 3 week(s) of notification.

Academics. Special study options: Combined bachelor's/graduate degree, cooperative education, distance learning, double major, honors, independent study, internships, liberal arts/career combination, teacher certification program, weekend college. **Credit/placement by examination:** AP, CLEP, IB, SAT. 48 credit hours maximum toward bachelor's degree. **Support services:** Learning center, pre-admission summer program, reduced course load, remedial instruction, study skills assistance, tutoring, writing center.

Majors. Biology: General. **Business:** Accounting, business admin. **Communications:** Communications/speech/rhetoric. **Computer sciences:** Computer science. **Education:** Art, biology, chemistry, elementary, English, history, kindergarten/preschool, mathematics, middle, physical, special ed. **English:** English lit. **History:** General. **Human services:** Social work. **Math:** General. **Physical sciences:** Chemistry, geology, oceanography, physics. **Protective services:** Criminal justice. **Psychology:** General. **Social sciences:** Political science, sociology. **Visual/performing arts:** Graphic design, music management, studio arts.

Most popular majors. Biology 8%, business/marketing 25%, education 24%, English 7%, psychology 6%, public administration/social services 6%, security/protective services 9%, social sciences 7%.

Computing on campus. 350 workstations in dormitories, library, computer center, student center. Dormitories wired for high-speed internet access and linked to campus network. Commuter students can connect to campus network. Online course registration, online library, helpline, repair service, wireless network available.

Student life. Freshman orientation: Mandatory, $100 fee. Preregistration for classes offered. Three sessions held during summer months covering 2 1/2 days each. **Housing:** Guaranteed on-campus for freshmen. Coed dorms, single-sex dorms, apartments, wellness housing available. $100 deposit, deadline 8/1. College-leased housing available. **Activities:** Bands, choral groups, dance, drama, literary magazine, music ensembles, radio station, student government, student newspaper, symphony orchestra, TV station, United Campus Religious Fellowship, honor and recognition societies in education, science, dramatics, journalism, student union program.

Athletics. NCAA. **Intercollegiate:** Baseball M, basketball, bowling M, cheerleading M, cross-country, football (tackle) M, golf M, softball W, tennis W, volleyball W. **Team name:** Vikings.

Student services. Alcohol/substance abuse counseling, chaplain/spiritual director, career counseling, student employment services, financial aid counseling, health services, personal counseling, placement for graduates, veterans' counselor. **Physically disabled:** Services for visually, speech, hearing impaired.

Contact. E-mail: mdwilliams2@mail.ecsu.edu
Phone: (252) 335-3305 Toll-free number: (800) 347-3278
Fax: (252) 335-3537
Monette Williams, Director of Enrollment Management and Retention,
Elizabeth City State University, 1704 Weeksville Road, Campus Box 901,
Elizabeth City, NC 27909

Elon University
Elon, North Carolina

CB member
CB code: 5183
www.elon.edu

- Private 4-year university and liberal arts college
- Residential campus in large town
- 5,225 degree-seeking undergraduates: 2% part-time, 59% women, 6% African American, 2% Asian American, 4% Hispanic American, 1% international
- 691 degree-seeking graduate students
- 58% of applicants admitted
- SAT or ACT with writing, application essay required
- 82% graduate within 6 years; 16% enter graduate study

General. Founded in 1889. Regionally accredited. **Degrees:** 1,284 bachelor's awarded; master's, professional offered. **ROTC:** Army, Air Force. **Location:** 15 miles from Greensboro. **Calendar:** 4-1-4, extensive summer session. **Full-time faculty:** 364 total; 88% have terminal degrees, 13% minority, 48% women. **Part-time faculty:** 158 total; 36% have terminal degrees, 9% minority, 42% women. **Class size:** 51% < 20, 49% 20-39, less than 1% 40-49, less than 1% 50-99. **Special facilities:** Fine arts center, science center, academic pavilions.

Freshman class profile. 9,079 applied, 5,252 admitted, 1,417 enrolled.

Mid 50% test scores			
SAT critical reading:	560-660	GPA 2.0-2.99:	6%
SAT math:	560-660	Rank in top quarter:	67%
SAT writing:	560-660	Rank in top tenth:	32%
ACT composite:	25-29	End year in good standing:	97%
GPA 3.75 or higher:	62%	Return as sophomores:	90%
GPA 3.50-3.74:	12%	Out-of-state:	80%
GPA 3.0-3.49:	20%	Live on campus:	100%
		International:	2%

Basis for selection. School achievement record most important, followed by test scores. Class rank, school and community activities, personal statement, recommendations also considered. Audition required for all performing arts programs. **Home schooled:** Statement describing home school structure and mission, transcript of courses and grades, state high school equivalency certificate, letter of recommendation (nonparent) required.

High school preparation. College-preparatory program required. 16 units required; 19 recommended. Required and recommended units include English 4, mathematics 3-4, social studies 1, history 3, science 3 (laboratory 1) and foreign language 2-3. Algebra I, II and geometry required.

2011-2012 Annual costs. Tuition/fees: $27,881. Room/board: $9,090. Books/supplies: $900. Personal expenses: $1,500.

2011-2012 Financial aid. Need-based: 864 full-time freshmen applied for aid; 548 were judged to have need; 544 of these received aid. Average need met was 69%. Average scholarship/grant was $13,829; average loan $3,896. 64% of total undergraduate aid awarded as scholarships/grants, 36% as loans/jobs. **Non-need-based:** Awarded to 2,577 full-time undergraduates, including 510 freshmen. Scholarships awarded for academics, art, athletics, leadership, music/drama, ROTC, state residency.

Application procedures. Admission: Priority date 11/1; deadline 1/10 (postmark date). $50 fee, may be waived for applicants with need. Admission notification by 3/15. Must reply by May 1 or within 2 week(s) if notified thereafter. **Financial aid:** Priority date 2/15; no closing date. FAFSA, institutional form, CSS PROFILE required. Applicants notified on a rolling basis starting 3/30.

Academics. Special study options: Accelerated study, combined bachelor's/graduate degree, cross-registration, distance learning, double major, dual enrollment of high school students, ESL, exchange student, honors, independent study, internships, liberal arts/career combination, student-designed major, study abroad, teacher certification program, Washington semester. **Credit/placement by examination:** AP, CLEP, IB, SAT, ACT, institutional tests. **Support services:** Learning center, reduced course load, remedial instruction, study skills assistance, tutoring, writing center.

Majors. Biology: General, biochemistry, biophysics. **Business:** Accounting, business admin, entrepreneurial studies, finance, international, management

information systems, marketing. **Communications:** General, broadcast journalism, journalism. **Computer sciences:** General, computer science, information systems. **Conservation:** Environmental studies. **Education:** General, curriculum, elementary, middle, secondary, special ed. **Engineering:** General, applied physics, chemical, computer, environmental. **English:** Creative writing, English lit, general lit, rhetoric/composition. **Foreign languages:** General, French, Spanish. **Health services:** Predental, premedicine, staff services technology. **History:** General. **Human services:** General. **Math:** General, applied. **Parks/recreation:** Exercise sciences, facilities management, sports admin. **Philosophy/religion:** Philosophy, religion. **Physical sciences:** Chemistry, physics. **Protective services:** Criminal justice. **Psychology:** General. **Social sciences:** Anthropology, economics, international relations, political science, sociology. **Visual/performing arts:** Art, art history/conservation, ceramics, dance, digital arts, dramatic, music, music performance, musical theater, painting, photography, theater design.

Most popular majors. Business/marketing 22%, communications/journalism 19%, education 6%, parks/recreation 6%, social sciences 14%, visual/performing arts 7%.

Computing on campus. 850 workstations in dormitories, library, computer center, student center. Dormitories wired for high-speed internet access and linked to campus network. Commuter students can connect to campus network. Online course registration, online library, helpline, repair service, student web hosting, wireless network available.

Student life. Freshman orientation: Mandatory. Preregistration for classes offered. Optional orientation during spring of high school senior year. Required orientation in August. **Policies:** Freshmen and sophomores are required to live on campus; housing is guaranteed. **Housing:** Guaranteed on-campus for freshmen. Coed dorms, single-sex dorms, apartments, fraternity/sorority housing, wellness housing available. $500 fully refundable deposit, deadline 5/1. **Activities:** Bands, campus ministries, choral groups, dance, drama, film society, international student organizations, literary magazine, music ensembles, Model UN, musical theater, radio station, student government, student newspaper, symphony orchestra, TV station, Intervarsity Christian Fellowship, Young Republicans, Black cultural society, Epsilon Sigma Alpha, liberal arts forum, Hillel, student media, Habitat for Humanity.

Athletics. NCAA. **Intercollegiate:** Baseball M, basketball, cheerleading, cross-country, football (tackle) M, golf, soccer, softball W, tennis, track and field W, volleyball W. **Intramural:** Basketball, bowling, football (non-tackle), golf, racquetball, soccer, table tennis, tennis, volleyball. **Team name:** Phoenix.

Student services. Adult student services, alcohol/substance abuse counseling, chaplain/spiritual director, career counseling, student employment services, financial aid counseling, health services, minority student services, personal counseling, placement for graduates, veterans' counselor, women's services. **Physically disabled:** Services for visually, speech, hearing impaired.

Contact. E-mail: admissions@elon.edu
Phone: (336) 278-3566 Toll-free number: (800) 334-8448
Fax: (336) 278-7699
Greg Zaiser, Dean of Admissions, Elon University, 2700 Campus Box, Elon, NC 27244-2010

Fayetteville State University
Fayetteville, North Carolina

CB member
CB code: 5212
www.uncfsu.edu

- Public 4-year university
- Commuter campus in small city
- 4,930 degree-seeking undergraduates: 21% part-time, 68% women, 70% African American, 1% Asian American, 5% Hispanic American, 2% Native American, 1% international
- 517 degree-seeking graduate students
- 64% of applicants admitted
- SAT or ACT with writing, application essay required
- 31% graduate within 6 years

General. Founded in 1867. Regionally accredited. Courses leading to bachelor's degree also available at the Fort Bragg/Pope AFB Center, Seymour Johnson AFB, and online. **Degrees:** 902 bachelor's awarded; master's, doctoral offered. **ROTC:** Army, Air Force. **Location:** 60 miles from Raleigh. **Calendar:** Semester, limited summer session. **Full-time faculty:** 282 total; 87% have terminal degrees, 65% minority, 45% women. **Part-time faculty:** 49 total; 37% have terminal degrees, 67% minority, 61% women. **Class size:** 38% < 20, 56% 20-39, 6% 40-49, less than 1% 50-99. **Special facilities:** Greenhouse, observatory, planetarium, microprobe.

Freshman class profile. 3,062 applied, 1,970 admitted, 655 enrolled.

Mid 50% test scores			
SAT critical reading:	380-460	GPA 3.0-3.49:	27%
SAT math:	400-470	GPA 2.0-2.99:	57%
SAT writing:	360-430	Rank in top quarter:	20%
ACT composite:	15-19	Rank in top tenth:	3%
GPA 3.75 or higher:	8%	Return as sophomores:	70%
GPA 3.50-3.74:	8%	Out-of-state:	8%
		Live on campus:	80%

Basis for selection. 2.3 GPA, SAT scores, completion of 19 prescribed high school units required. All applicants, except those exempted by current campus policies, must submit a standardized test score. SAT preferred, ACT also accepted.

High school preparation. 19 units required. Required and recommended units include English 4, mathematics 4, social studies 2, history 1, science 3, foreign language 2 and academic electives 6. Foreign language units can be used as academic elective units.

2011-2012 Annual costs. Tuition/fees: $4,459; $15,071 out-of-state. Car registration $60, insurance $902, room breakage deposit $125, late registration $20. Room/board: $5,500. Books/supplies: $1,000. Personal expenses: $750.

2010-2011 Financial aid. Need-based: 739 full-time freshmen applied for aid; 679 were judged to have need; 671 of these received aid. Average need met was 88%. Average scholarship/grant was $8,094; average loan $2,585. 51% of total undergraduate aid awarded as scholarships/grants, 49% as loans/jobs. **Non-need-based:** Awarded to 2,075 full-time undergraduates, including 422 freshmen. Scholarships awarded for academics, alumni affiliation, athletics, music/drama, ROTC, state residency.

Application procedures. Admission: Closing date 7/1 (postmark date). $35 fee, may be waived for applicants with need. Admission notification on a rolling basis beginning on or about 1/15. Must reply by 7/1. **Financial aid:** Priority date 3/1, closing date 3/1. FAFSA required. Applicants notified on a rolling basis starting 4/15; must reply within 2 week(s) of notification.

Academics. Special study options: Accelerated study, combined bachelor's/graduate degree, cooperative education, distance learning, double major, dual enrollment of high school students, honors, independent study, internships, study abroad, teacher certification program, weekend college. **Credit/placement by examination:** AP, CLEP, SAT, institutional tests. 30 credit hours maximum toward bachelor's degree. **Support services:** Learning center, pre-admission summer program, remedial instruction, tutoring.

Majors. Biology: General, biotechnology. **Business:** Accounting, business admin, finance, management information systems. **Communications:** Communications/speech/rhetoric. **Computer sciences:** General. **Education:** Art, biology, early childhood, elementary, English, mathematics, middle, music, physical, social science. **English:** English lit. **Foreign languages:** Spanish. **Health services:** Nursing (RN). **History:** General. **Human services:** General. **Math:** General. **Physical sciences:** Chemistry. **Protective services:** Criminal justice, fire services admin, forensics. **Psychology:** General. **Social sciences:** Geography, political science, sociology. **Visual/performing arts:** General, art, dramatic, music.

Most popular majors. Business/marketing 20%, education 11%, psychology 14%, security/protective services 14%, social sciences 15%.

Computing on campus. 600 workstations in dormitories, library, computer center, student center. Dormitories wired for high-speed internet access and linked to campus network. Commuter students can connect to campus network. Online course registration, online library, helpline, wireless network available.

Student life. Freshman orientation: Mandatory, $45 fee. Preregistration for classes offered. 3 Saturdays in July and August. **Policies:** Freshmen not permitted cars on campus. **Housing:** Coed dorms, single-sex dorms, apartments available. $125 nonrefundable deposit, deadline 7/1. **Activities:** Bands, choral groups, dance, drama, music ensembles, radio station, student government, student newspaper, symphony orchestra, TV station, Baptist student union, Federation of Young Democrats, NAACP, NCNW, Honda Campus All-Stars, art guild, Illusions modeling club.

Athletics. NCAA. **Intercollegiate:** Basketball, bowling W, cross-country, football (tackle) M, golf, softball W, tennis, track and field, volleyball W. **Intramural:** Baseball M, basketball, bowling, football (tackle) M, golf, gymnastics, swimming, tennis M, volleyball. **Team name:** Broncos.

Student services. Alcohol/substance abuse counseling, career counseling, student employment services, financial aid counseling, health services, on-campus daycare, personal counseling, placement for graduates, veterans' counselor. **Physically disabled:** Services for visually impaired.

Contact. E-mail: admissions@uncfsu.edu
Phone: (910) 672-1371 Toll-free number: (800) 222-2594
Fax: (910) 672-1414
Ulisa Bowles, Director of Admissions, Fayetteville State University, 1200 Murchison Road, Fayetteville, NC 28301-4298

Gardner-Webb University
Boiling Springs, North Carolina
www.gardner-webb.edu

CB member
CB code: 5242

- Private 4-year university and liberal arts college affiliated with Southern Baptist Convention
- Residential campus in small town
- 2,774 degree-seeking undergraduates: 16% part-time, 66% women, 20% African American, 1% Asian American, 2% Hispanic American, 1% international
- 1,931 degree-seeking graduate students
- 59% of applicants admitted
- SAT or ACT (ACT writing optional) required
- 55% graduate within 6 years

General. Founded in 1905. Regionally accredited. **Degrees:** 613 bachelor's, 47 associate awarded; master's, professional, doctoral offered. **ROTC:** Army, Air Force. **Location:** 55 miles from Charlotte, 60 miles from Greenville, SC. **Calendar:** Semester, extensive summer session. **Full-time faculty:** 154 total; 76% have terminal degrees, 7% minority, 49% women. **Part-time faculty:** 268 total. **Class size:** 71% < 20, 28% 20-39, less than 1% 50-99, less than 1% >100. **Special facilities:** Observatory, adventure and ropes course, Lake Hollifield and Carillon.

Freshman class profile. 4,544 applied, 2,696 admitted, 453 enrolled.

Mid 50% test scores			
SAT critical reading:	450-580	Rank in top quarter:	41%
SAT math:	430-550	Rank in top tenth:	19%
ACT composite:	18-24	End year in good standing:	89%
GPA 3.75 or higher:	38%	Return as sophomores:	57%
GPA 3.50-3.74:	18%	Out-of-state:	31%
GPA 3.0-3.49:	22%	Live on campus:	94%
GPA 2.0-2.99:	22%	International:	2%

Basis for selection. School achievement record most important, followed by test scores, recommendations, and school and community activities. Expected 2.5 GPA. The Accuplacer placement test is required of students whose SAT or ACT scores fall below a certain minimum. This test will be used to determine whether the student is to be placed in remedial courses or college level English and Math courses. Interview, portfolio, essay recommended for all students; audition required for music scholarships. Interview may be required for conditionally admitted students.

High school preparation. College-preparatory program recommended. Recommended units include English 4, mathematics 3, social studies 1, science 3 (laboratory 2) and foreign language 2.

2011-2012 Annual costs. Tuition/fees: $23,510. Room/board: $7,570. Books/supplies: $1,000.

2010-2011 Financial aid. Need-based: 434 full-time freshmen applied for aid; 388 were judged to have need; 388 of these received aid. Average need met was 87%. Average scholarship/grant was $10,141; average loan $3,210. 67% of total undergraduate aid awarded as scholarships/grants, 33% as loans/jobs. **Non-need-based:** Awarded to 1,323 full-time undergraduates, including 390 freshmen. Scholarships awarded for academics, athletics, leadership, music/drama, religious affiliation, ROTC, state residency.

Application procedures. Admission: No deadline. $40 fee, may be waived for applicants with need, free for online applicants. Admission notification on a rolling basis. **Financial aid:** Priority date 3/1; no closing date. FAFSA required. Applicants notified on a rolling basis starting 3/1; must reply within 2 week(s) of notification.

Academics. Special program offerings possible (including interpreters, notetakers) for students who have tested learning disabled or physically disabled. **Special study options:** Accelerated study, combined bachelor's/graduate degree, distance learning, double major, dual enrollment of high school students, ESL, honors, independent study, internships, liberal arts/career combination, study abroad, teacher certification program. Costa Rica and Quebec for language trips. **Credit/placement by examination:** AP, CLEP, IB, SAT, ACT, institutional tests. 64 credit hours maximum toward bachelor's degree. **Support services:** Learning center, pre-admission summer program, reduced course load, remedial instruction, study skills assistance, tutoring, writing center.

Honors college/program. Students participating in the Honors program have an average SAT of 1850 and an average GPA of 3.8. Students must complete 24 semester hours of course work designated as honors (six of which is comprised of an Honors Thesis during the junior and/or senior year).

Majors. Biology: General, ecology. **Business:** General, accounting, business admin, finance, international, management information systems. **Communications:** Broadcast journalism, communications/speech/rhetoric, journalism, public relations. **Computer sciences:** General, computer science. **Conservation:** Environmental science. **Education:** General, biology, chemistry, elementary, English, foreign languages, French, health, history, mathematics, middle, multi-level teacher, music, physical, science, secondary, social science, Spanish. **English:** Creative writing, English lit, technical writing, writing. **Foreign languages:** General, American Sign Language, French, sign language interpretation, Spanish. **Health services:** Athletic training, health care admin, nursing (RN), predental, premedicine, prepharmacy, prephysical therapy, preveterinary. **History:** General. **Math:** General. **Parks/recreation:** Health/fitness, sports admin. **Philosophy/religion:** Philosophy, religion. **Physical sciences:** Chemistry. **Psychology:** General. **Social sciences:** General, political science, sociology. **Theology:** Missionary, religious ed, sacred music, youth ministry. **Visual/performing arts:** Art, ceramics, dramatic, drawing, music, music management, music performance, music theory/composition, painting, photography, piano/keyboard, printmaking, sculpture, stringed instruments, studio arts, voice/opera.

Most popular majors. Business/marketing 30%, health sciences 18%, social sciences 21%.

Computing on campus. 150 workstations in library, computer center. Dormitories wired for high-speed internet access and linked to campus network. Commuter students can connect to campus network. Online library, helpline, wireless network available.

Student life. Freshman orientation: Mandatory, $100 fee. Preregistration for classes offered. One-day programs held throughout the summer months. **Policies:** Limited visitation hours: noon to midnight in dorm rooms. Lobbies open for visitation until 2:00 am., no alcohol or tobacco allowed on campus, quiet hours observed from 10 pm through 10 am. **Housing:** Guaranteed on-campus for all undergraduates. Single-sex dorms, special housing for disabled, apartments, wellness housing available. $300 nonrefundable deposit. Honors student residence hall available. **Activities:** Bands, campus ministries, choral groups, drama, international student organizations, literary magazine, music ensembles, musical theater, opera, radio station, student government, student newspaper, symphony orchestra, The Verge, Fellowship of Christian Athletes, student volunteer groups, prison ministry, student YMCA, gospel choir, Bible studies, College Republicans, College Democrats.

Athletics. NCAA. Intercollegiate: Baseball M, basketball, cheerleading, cross-country, football (tackle) M, golf, soccer, softball W, swimming, tennis, track and field, volleyball W, wrestling M. **Intramural:** Badminton, baseball, basketball, football (non-tackle), racquetball, skiing, soccer, softball, swimming, table tennis, tennis, volleyball. **Team name:** Runnin' Bulldogs.

Student services. Alcohol/substance abuse counseling, chaplain/spiritual director, career counseling, student employment services, financial aid counseling, personal counseling, placement for graduates, veterans' counselor. **Physically disabled:** Services for visually, speech, hearing impaired.

Contact. E-mail: admissions@gardner-webb.edu
Phone: (704) 406-4498 Toll-free number: (800) 253-6472
Fax: (704) 406-4488
Kristen Setzer, Associate Vice President of Undergraduate Admissions, Gardner-Webb University, PO Box 817, Boiling Springs, NC 28017

Greensboro College
Greensboro, North Carolina
www.greensboro.edu

CB member
CB code: 5260

- Private 4-year liberal arts college affiliated with United Methodist Church
- Residential campus in large city
- 1,029 degree-seeking undergraduates
- 50 graduate students
- 51% of applicants admitted
- SAT or ACT with writing, application essay required
- 40% graduate within 6 years

General. Founded in 1838. Regionally accredited. **Degrees:** 157 bachelor's awarded; master's offered. **ROTC:** Army, Air Force. **Location:** 90 miles from Charlotte, 75 miles from Raleigh. **Calendar:** Semester, limited summer session. **Full-time faculty:** 59 total; 8% minority. **Part-time faculty:** 62 total. **Class size:** 88% < 20, 12% 20-39. **Special facilities:** Historical museum, computerized music laboratories.

Freshman class profile. 1,953 applied, 995 admitted, 233 enrolled.

Mid 50% test scores			
SAT critical reading:	430-540	GPA 3.50-3.74:	13%
SAT math:	400-490	GPA 3.0-3.49:	28%
SAT writing:	390-490	GPA 2.0-2.99:	37%
ACT composite:	17-23	Return as sophomores:	64%
GPA 3.75 or higher:	22%	Out-of-state:	27%
		Live on campus:	93%

Basis for selection. High school curriculum most important, followed by grades, class rank, test scores, personal statement, school and community activities, high school caliber. Recommendations, interview considered. Interview recommended for all students. Audition required for music, theater majors; portfolio required for art majors. **Home schooled:** Interview highly recommended and SAT/ACT required. **Learning Disabled:** Students wishing to receive accommodations facilitated by the Office of Disability Services are responsible for disclosure of physical, psychological, and learning disabilities. Accommodation of learning and psychological disabilities must be accompanied by appropriate documentation that includes professional evaluation, diagnosis, and recommendations.

High school preparation. College-preparatory program recommended. Recommended units include English 4, mathematics 3, social studies 2, history 2, science 2 (laboratory 1) and foreign language 2. Remaining units must be selected from art, music, social science and physical education.

2012-2013 Annual costs. Tuition/fees: $25,600. Room/board: $9,400. Books/supplies: $1,200. Personal expenses: $900.

Financial aid. Non-need-based: Scholarships awarded for academics, alumni affiliation, art, leadership, music/drama, religious affiliation, state residency.

Application procedures. Admission: Priority date 12/15; no deadline. $35 fee, may be waived for applicants with need. Admission notification on a rolling basis. Must reply by May 1 or within 4 week(s) if notified thereafter. **Financial aid:** Priority date 4/15; no closing date. FAFSA, institutional form required. Applicants notified on a rolling basis starting 2/1; must reply within 2 week(s) of notification.

Academics. Special study options: Accelerated study, cross-registration, double major, dual enrollment of high school students, ESL, honors, independent study, internships, liberal arts/career combination, student-designed major, study abroad, teacher certification program, weekend college. Academic success program, minor in ethics across the curriculum, minor in women's and gender studies, minor in computer science. **Credit/placement by examination:** AP, CLEP, IB, institutional tests. 45 credit hours maximum toward bachelor's degree. **Support services:** Learning center, reduced course load, study skills assistance, tutoring, writing center.

Majors. Biology: General. **Business:** Accounting, managerial economics. **Education:** General, art, biology, drama/dance, early childhood, elementary, emotionally handicapped, English, history, learning disabled, mathematics, mentally handicapped, middle, multiple handicapped, music, physical, social studies, Spanish, special ed. **English:** English lit. **Foreign languages:** French, Spanish. **Health services:** Athletic training. **History:** General. **Liberal arts:** Arts/sciences. **Math:** General. **Parks/recreation:** Exercise sciences, health/fitness, sports admin. **Philosophy/religion:** Religion. **Physical sciences:** Chemistry. **Psychology:** General. **Social sciences:** Political science, sociology. **Visual/performing arts:** Dramatic, music, music performance, studio arts, theater design.

Most popular majors. Biology 7%, business/marketing 25%, education 15%, social sciences 12%, visual/performing arts 16%.

Computing on campus. 152 workstations in dormitories, library, computer center, student center. Dormitories wired for high-speed internet access and linked to campus network. Commuter students can connect to campus network. Online library, helpline, repair service, wireless network available.

Student life. Freshman orientation: Mandatory. Preregistration for classes offered. Orientations held in May, June, July and August. **Housing:** Guaranteed on-campus for all undergraduates. Coed dorms, single-sex dorms, apartments, wellness housing available. $200 partly refundable deposit. All students who have earned less than 58 credit hours required to live in college housing unless married, veterans, or residing with parents. All students encouraged to do so. **Activities:** Bands, choral groups, dance, drama, international student organizations, literary magazine, music ensembles, Model UN, musical theater, opera, student government, student newspaper, Student Christian Fellowship, United African American Society, Student National Education Association, campus activity board, Fellowship of Christian Athletes, Los Amigos.

Athletics. NCAA. Intercollegiate: Baseball M, basketball, cheerleading, cross-country, football (tackle) M, golf M, lacrosse, soccer, softball W, swimming, tennis, volleyball W. **Intramural:** Baseball M, basketball, football (non-tackle), softball W. **Team name:** The Pride.

Student services. Adult student services, alcohol/substance abuse counseling, chaplain/spiritual director, career counseling, student employment services, financial aid counseling, health services, personal counseling, placement for graduates. **Physically disabled:** Services for visually, speech, hearing impaired.

Contact. E-mail: admissions@greensboro.edu
Phone: (336) 272-7102 ext. 211 Toll-free number: (800) 346-8226
Fax: (336) 378-0154
Julie Schatz, Director of Admissions, Greensboro College, 815 West Market Street, Greensboro, NC 27401-1875

Guilford College
Greensboro, North Carolina　　　　　　　**CB member**
www.guilford.edu　　　　　　　　　　　　**CB code: 5261**

◗ Private 4-year liberal arts college affiliated with Society of Friends (Quaker)
◗ Residential campus in small city
◗ 2,581 degree-seeking undergraduates: 17% part-time, 58% women, 27% African American, 1% Asian American, 4% Hispanic American, 1% Native American, 1% international
◗ 64% of applicants admitted
◗ Application essay required
◗ 58% graduate within 6 years

General. Founded in 1837. Regionally accredited. **Degrees:** 538 bachelor's awarded. **Location:** 90 miles from Raleigh, 100 miles from Charlotte. **Calendar:** Semester, limited summer session. **Full-time faculty:** 124 total; 90% have terminal degrees, 12% minority, 47% women. **Part-time faculty:** 90 total; 50% have terminal degrees, 18% minority, 53% women. **Class size:** 49% < 20, 51% 20-39, less than 1% 40-49. **Special facilities:** Observatory, multimedia learning center for cultures and languages, telecommunications center, photography studio, outdoor sculpture studio, computer visualization laboratory.

Freshman class profile. 3,054 applied, 1,963 admitted, 382 enrolled.

Mid 50% test scores			
SAT critical reading:	470-620	GPA 3.0-3.49:	41%
SAT math:	480-590	GPA 2.0-2.99:	32%
SAT writing:	460-600	Rank in top quarter:	41%
ACT composite:	21-26	Rank in top tenth:	14%
GPA 3.75 or higher:	12%	Return as sophomores:	76%
GPA 3.50-3.74:	15%	Out-of-state:	48%
		Live on campus:	90%

Basis for selection. School achievement record and essay most important. Test scores, interview, recommendations, interests, leadership ability also important. Minimum SAT composite score of 1000 (exclusive of Writing) or ACT score of 22 recommended. Applicant may choose to submit portfolio instead of standardized test scores. Portfolio should reflect student's academic, creative, and personal interests and accomplishments. It must include, but is not limited to, 3-5 writing samples (at least one should be a graded expository written work) and, if available, a junior/senior reading list. Auditions and portfolios recommended in music, theater and art. **Home schooled:** Interview required. Provide reason for homeschooling.

High school preparation. College-preparatory program required. 18 units recommended. Recommended units include English 4, mathematics 3, social studies 3, history 3, science 3 and foreign language 2.

2011-2012 Annual costs. Tuition/fees: $30,430. Room/board: $8,270. Books/supplies: $1,250. Personal expenses: $1,220.

2011-2012 Financial aid. Need-based: 327 full-time freshmen applied for aid; 327 were judged to have need; 327 of these received aid. Average need met was 80%. Average scholarship/grant was $18,232; average loan $5,000. 67% of total undergraduate aid awarded as scholarships/grants, 33% as loans/jobs. **Non-need-based:** Awarded to 1,957 full-time undergraduates, including 276 freshmen. Scholarships awarded for academics.

Application procedures. Admission: Priority date 2/15; deadline 8/10 (postmark date). $25 fee, may be waived for applicants with need, free for online applicants. Admission notification on a rolling basis beginning on or about 10/1. Must reply by May 1 or within 4 week(s) if notified thereafter. **Financial aid:** Priority date 3/1; no closing date. FAFSA required. Applicants notified on a rolling basis starting 2/15; must reply within 2 week(s) of notification.

Academics. Faculty tutoring for skills development and student tutoring for course-specific help available. Assistance available for non-remedial writing, organizational/time-management skills, and students with learning disabilities. Remedial assistance and reader service for the blind available. **Special**

study options: Accelerated study, combined bachelor's/graduate degree, cross-registration, double major, honors, independent study, internships, student-designed major, study abroad, teacher certification program, Washington semester. 3-2 degree programs available in forestry and environmental studies with Duke University, and in physician assistant training with Bowman Gray School of Medicine at Wake Forest University. Many internships, work-study programs, accelerated degree programs in business management, computer information systems, psychology, and biology, dual majors, student-designed majors, study abroad in 9 countries, and cross-registration with members of the Greater Greensboro Consortium (8 colleges/universities). **Credit/placement by examination:** AP, CLEP, IB, SAT, ACT, institutional tests. 32 credit hours maximum toward bachelor's degree. **Support services:** Learning center, pre-admission summer program, reduced course load, remedial instruction, study skills assistance, tutoring, writing center.

Majors. Area/ethnic studies: African-American, German, women's. **Biology:** General, biomedical sciences. **Business:** Accounting, business admin. **Computer sciences:** General, information systems, information technology. **Conservation:** Environmental studies. **Education:** Elementary, physical, secondary. **English:** English lit. **Foreign languages:** French, German, Germanic, Spanish. **Health services:** Athletic training. **History:** General. **Math:** General. **Parks/recreation:** Exercise sciences, health/fitness, sports admin. **Philosophy/religion:** Philosophy, religion. **Physical sciences:** Chemistry, geology, physics. **Protective services:** Criminal justice, forensics. **Psychology:** General. **Social sciences:** Economics, international relations, political science, sociology. **Visual/performing arts:** Art, dramatic, music, theater arts management.

Most popular majors. Biology 8%, business/marketing 20%, English 6%, psychology 9%, security/protective services 9%, social sciences 10%, visual/performing arts 6%.

Computing on campus. 348 workstations in dormitories, library, computer center, student center. Dormitories wired for high-speed internet access and linked to campus network. Commuter students can connect to campus network. Online course registration, helpline, repair service, wireless network available.

Student life. Freshman orientation: Mandatory, $75 fee. Preregistration for classes offered. One-day event in Spring; parents invited. **Policies:** Consistent with its Quaker heritage, college promotes and encourages student involvement in community service projects. **Housing:** Guaranteed on-campus for freshmen. Coed dorms, single-sex dorms, apartments, cooperative housing available. $400 fully refundable deposit, deadline 5/1. Special interest housing available. **Activities:** Bands, campus ministries, choral groups, dance, drama, film society, literary magazine, music ensembles, radio station, student government, student newspaper, African American cultural society, Amnesty International, Project Community, community senate, Christian fellowship, Native American club, Hillel, Quaker Concerns, Guilford Action Network.

Athletics. NCAA. **Intercollegiate:** Baseball, basketball, cross-country, football (tackle) M, golf M, lacrosse, rugby, soccer, softball W, swimming W, tennis, volleyball W. **Intramural:** Baseball, basketball, cheerleading W, football (non-tackle), soccer, softball, table tennis, tennis, volleyball, water polo. **Team name:** Quakers.

Student services. Adult student services, alcohol/substance abuse counseling, chaplain/spiritual director, career counseling, student employment services, financial aid counseling, health services, minority student services, personal counseling, placement for graduates, veterans' counselor, women's services. **Physically disabled:** Services for visually, speech, hearing impaired.

Contact. E-mail: admission@guilford.edu
Phone: (336) 316-2100 Toll-free number: (800) 992-7759
Fax: (336) 316-2954
Randy Doss, Vice President for Enrollment Services, Guilford College, Admissions, New Garden Hall, Greensboro, NC 27410-4108

High Point University
High Point, North Carolina　　　　　　　**CB member**
www.highpoint.edu　　　　　　　　　　　**CB code: 5293**

◗ Private 4-year university and liberal arts college affiliated with United Methodist Church
◗ Residential campus in small city
◗ 3,932 degree-seeking undergraduates: 3% part-time, 60% women, 6% African American, 1% Asian American, 2% Hispanic American, 2% Native American, 1% international
◗ 239 degree-seeking graduate students
◗ 59% of applicants admitted
◗ SAT or ACT with writing, application essay required
◗ 61% graduate within 6 years; 30% enter graduate study

General. Founded in 1924. Regionally accredited. High Point University in England (at Leeds University); exchange program in Oxford Brookes University (Oxford, England); opportunities for study abroad in Canada, Ecuador, England, France, Germany, Italy, Mexico, Scotland, Spain, and Wales. **Degrees:** 659 bachelor's awarded; master's, professional offered. **ROTC:** Army, Air Force. **Location:** 15 miles from Greensboro, 15 miles from Winston Salem. **Calendar:** Semester, limited summer session. **Full-time faculty:** 209 total; 73% have terminal degrees, 12% minority, 48% women. **Part-time faculty:** 133 total; 14% have terminal degrees, 47% women. **Class size:** 57% < 20, 42% 20-39, less than 1% 40-49, less than 1% 50-99, less than 1% >100. **Special facilities:** Athletic/convocation center with arena, indoor 25 meter competition pool, racquetball courts, sports medicine center, MAC design labs, Linux labs, CAD labs, tutoring center, fine arts center, international home furnishings center, university center.

Freshman class profile. 6,866 applied, 4,030 admitted, 1,292 enrolled.

Mid 50% test scores		GPA 2.0-2.99:	32%
SAT critical reading:	490-590	Rank in top quarter:	47%
SAT math:	510-600	Rank in top tenth:	20%
SAT writing:	500-590	End year in good standing:	92%
ACT composite:	21-26	Return as sophomores:	78%
GPA 3.75 or higher:	16%	Live on campus:	99%
GPA 3.50-3.74:	16%	International:	1%
GPA 3.0-3.49:	36%		

Basis for selection. The most important factors are the academic transcript, including grades received and course selection, followed by standardized test scores (SAT or ACT). Other important factors are demonstrated leadership, extracurricular and community involvement, and special talent. Test scores are required for all applicants.

High school preparation. College-preparatory program required. 15 units required; 17 recommended. Required and recommended units include English 4, mathematics 3-4, social studies 3, science 3 (laboratory 2) and foreign language 2-3.

2011-2012 Annual costs. Comprehensive fee: $37,800. Books/supplies: $1,300. Personal expenses: $2,000.

Financial aid. Non-need-based: Scholarships awarded for academics, alumni affiliation, art, athletics, leadership, music/drama, religious affiliation, state residency.

Application procedures. Admission: Priority date 3/15; deadline 7/1 (postmark date). $50 fee, may be waived for applicants with need. Admission notification on a rolling basis beginning on or about 12/11. Must reply by 5/1. **Financial aid:** Priority date 3/1; no closing date. FAFSA required. Applicants notified on a rolling basis starting 4/1; must reply within 3 week(s) of notification.

Academics. Special study options: Accelerated study, combined bachelor's/graduate degree, cooperative education, cross-registration, double major, dual enrollment of high school students, ESL, honors, independent study, internships, liberal arts/career combination, student-designed major, study abroad, teacher certification program. Dual degree programs with Duke University (forestry and environmental science) and Wake Forest University School of Medicine (medical technology). **Credit/placement by examination:** AP, CLEP, IB, SAT, ACT, institutional tests. 32 credit hours maximum toward bachelor's degree. Credit by Examination is offered through 1) examinations written and administered by University faculty and 2) national test programs. A maximum of 32 credits may be earned by such examinations. If a student earns a significant number of credits through examination, no more than 8 of these credits will be applied to any given semester. **Support services:** Learning center, pre-admission summer program, reduced course load, study skills assistance, tutoring, writing center.

Majors. Biology: General, biochemistry. **Business:** Accounting, actuarial science, business admin, international, nonprofit/public, organizational behavior. **Communications:** General. **Computer sciences:** Computer science. **Education:** Elementary, middle, physical, secondary, special ed. **English:** English lit. **Foreign languages:** French, Spanish. **Health services:** Athletic training. **History:** General. **Math:** General. **Parks/recreation:** Exercise sciences. **Philosophy/religion:** Philosophy, religion. **Physical sciences:** Chemistry, physics. **Protective services:** Criminal justice. **Psychology:** General. **Social sciences:** Econometrics, international relations, political science, sociology. **Visual/performing arts:** Dramatic, graphic design, interior design, music, studio arts, theater design.

Most popular majors. Business/marketing 42%, communications/journalism 8%, education 7%, parks/recreation 8%, visual/performing arts 6%.

Computing on campus. 225 workstations in dormitories, library, computer center, student center. Dormitories wired for high-speed internet access and linked to campus network. Commuter students can connect to campus network. Online course registration, online library, helpline, repair service, student web hosting, wireless network available.

Student life. Freshman orientation: Mandatory. Preregistration for classes offered. 3-5 days during move-in weekend and comprised of social activities, advising sessions, residence hall meetings and an activities fair. **Policies:** Outlined fully in Student Guide to Campus Life. **Housing:** Guaranteed on-campus for freshmen. Coed dorms, single-sex dorms, special housing for disabled, apartments, fraternity/sorority housing, wellness housing available. $500 fully refundable deposit, deadline 5/1. **Activities:** Bands, campus ministries, choral groups, dance, drama, film society, international student organizations, literary magazine, music ensembles, Model UN, musical theater, opera, radio station, student government, student newspaper, symphony orchestra, TV station, College Democrats, College Republicans, debate club, Society for History and Political Awareness, BCA, Black Script, Alpha Phi Omega, Rotaract, Big Brothers Big Sisters, Habitat for Humanity.

Athletics. NCAA. **Intercollegiate:** Baseball M, basketball, cheerleading, cross-country, golf, lacrosse W, soccer, tennis, track and field, volleyball W. **Intramural:** Badminton, basketball, bowling, golf, racquetball, soccer, softball, swimming, table tennis, tennis, track and field M, volleyball, water polo. **Team name:** Panthers.

Student services. Adult student services, alcohol/substance abuse counseling, chaplain/spiritual director, career counseling, student employment services, financial aid counseling, health services, personal counseling, placement for graduates, veterans' counselor.

Contact. E-mail: admiss@highpoint.edu
Phone: (336) 841-9216 Toll-free number: (800) 345-6993
Fax: (336) 888-6382
Andy Bills, Vice President for Enrollment, High Point University, 833 Montlieu Avenue, High Point, NC 27262-3598

Johnson & Wales University: Charlotte
Charlotte, North Carolina
www.jwu.edu   CB code: 4360

- Private 4-year university
- Residential campus in very large city
- 2,537 degree-seeking undergraduates: 2% part-time, 61% women, 28% African American, 2% Asian American, 4% Hispanic American, 2% international
- 64% of applicants admitted
- 44% graduate within 6 years

General. Degrees: 344 bachelor's, 526 associate awarded. **Location:** Downtown. **Calendar:** Quarter. **Full-time faculty:** 91 total; 45% women. **Part-time faculty:** 23 total; 56% women. **Class size:** 43% < 20, 50% 20-39, 6% 40-49.

Freshman class profile. 5,177 applied, 3,338 admitted, 666 enrolled.

GPA 3.75 or higher:	14%	Return as sophomores:	73%
GPA 3.50-3.74:	11%	Out-of-state:	46%
GPA 3.0-3.49:	29%	Live on campus:	89%
GPA 2.0-2.99:	45%		

Basis for selection. Academic record, secondary school curriculum, class rank, GPA, test scores and interview important. Student motivation and interest given strong consideration. SAT or ACT required for applicants to the honors programs. **Home schooled:** Transcript of courses and grades, state high school equivalency certificate required. SAT (verbal and math) or ACT required.

High school preparation. College-preparatory program recommended. Required units include English 4, mathematics 3, social studies 2 and science 3.

2012-2013 Annual costs. Tuition/fees: $26,412. Room/board: $10,728. Books/supplies: $1,800. Personal expenses: $1,065.

Financial aid. Non-need-based: Scholarships awarded for academics, alumni affiliation, leadership, state residency.

Application procedures. Admission: No deadline. No application fee. Admission notification on a rolling basis. Must reply by May 1 or within 2 week(s) if notified thereafter. **Financial aid:** No deadline. FAFSA required. Applicants notified on a rolling basis starting 3/1.

Academics. Math center. **Special study options:** Accelerated study, cooperative education, dual enrollment of high school students, ESL, exchange student, honors, independent study, internships, study abroad. **Credit/placement by examination:** AP, CLEP, institutional tests. **Support services:** Learning center, pre-admission summer program, reduced course load, remedial instruction, study skills assistance, tutoring, writing center.

Majors. Business: Accounting, business admin, fashion, hotel/motel admin, management science, marketing, restaurant/food services. **Parks/recreation:** Facilities management, sports admin.

Most popular majors. Business/marketing 38%, family/consumer sciences 52%, parks/recreation 11%.

Computing on campus. 160 workstations in library. Dormitories wired for high-speed internet access and linked to campus network. Commuter students can connect to campus network. Online library, helpline, wireless network available.

Student life. Freshman orientation: Available. Preregistration for classes offered. **Housing:** Coed dorms, apartments available. **Activities:** Campus ministries, international student organizations, student government, student newspaper.

Athletics. Team name: Wildcats.

Student services. Career counseling, student employment services, financial aid counseling, health services, personal counseling, veterans' counselor. **Physically disabled:** Services for visually, speech, hearing impaired.

Contact. E-mail: Admissions.clt@jwu.edu
Phone: (980) 598-1100 Toll-free number: (866) 598-2427
Fax: (980) 598-1111
Joseph Campos, Director of Admissions, Johnson & Wales University: Charlotte, 801 West Trade Street, Charlotte, NC 28202

Johnson C. Smith University
Charlotte, North Carolina
www.jcsu.edu

CB member
CB code: 5333

▶ Private 4-year university and liberal arts college
▶ Residential campus in very large city
▶ 1,541 degree-seeking undergraduates: 3% part-time, 60% women, 80% African American, 2% Hispanic American, 3% international
▶ 30% of applicants admitted
▶ SAT or ACT (ACT writing optional), application essay required
▶ 37% graduate within 6 years; 23% enter graduate study

General. Founded in 1867. Regionally accredited. **Degrees:** 260 bachelor's awarded. **ROTC:** Army, Air Force. **Location:** 244 miles from Atlanta. **Calendar:** Semester, limited summer session. **Full-time faculty:** 93 total; 81% have terminal degrees, 71% minority, 58% women. **Part-time faculty:** 51 total; 20% have terminal degrees, 69% minority, 49% women. **Class size:** 57% < 20, 42% 20-39, less than 1% 40-49, less than 1% 50-99.

Freshman class profile. 5,099 applied, 1,507 admitted, 373 enrolled.

Mid 50% test scores			
SAT critical reading:	370-480	Rank in top quarter:	25%
SAT math:	380-480	Rank in top tenth:	12%
ACT composite:	17-19	End year in good standing:	88%
GPA 3.75 or higher:	9%	Return as sophomores:	74%
GPA 3.50-3.74:	9%	Out-of-state:	53%
GPA 3.0-3.49:	26%	Live on campus:	88%
GPA 2.0-2.99:	50%	International:	3%

Basis for selection. Competitive test scores and grade point averages (GPA) taken into account in admissions decisions. Two letters of recommendations, a resume or list of extra-curricular activities, personal statement required. **Home schooled:** Statement describing home school structure and mission required.

High school preparation. 16 units required. Required units include English 4, mathematics 3, social studies 2, science 2 (laboratory 1), foreign language 2 and academic electives 3.

2011-2012 Annual costs. Tuition/fees: $17,368. Room/board: $6,762. Books/supplies: $1,700. Personal expenses: $3,250.

2011-2012 Financial aid. Need-based: 336 full-time freshmen applied for aid; 328 were judged to have need; 325 of these received aid. Average need met was 51%. Average scholarship/grant was $10,367; average loan $4,095. 47% of total undergraduate aid awarded as scholarships/grants, 53% as loans/jobs. **Non-need-based:** Awarded to 164 full-time undergraduates, including 67 freshmen. Scholarships awarded for academics, athletics, ROTC, state residency.

Application procedures. Admission: Priority date 3/15; no deadline. $25 fee, may be waived for applicants with need. Admission notification on a rolling basis. **Financial aid:** Priority date 3/1; no closing date. FAFSA

---

required. Applicants notified on a rolling basis starting 3/1; must reply within 2 week(s) of notification.

Academics. Special study options: Accelerated study, cooperative education, cross-registration, double major, exchange student, honors, independent study, internships, liberal arts/career combination, student-designed major, study abroad, teacher certification program. **Credit/placement by examination:** AP, CLEP, institutional tests. **Support services:** Learning center, pre-admission summer program, reduced course load, study skills assistance, tutoring, writing center.

Majors. Biology: General. **Business:** Business admin. **Communications:** Media studies. **Computer sciences:** General, information technology. **Education:** Elementary, English, mathematics, physical, social studies. **Engineering:** Computer. **English:** English lit. **Foreign languages:** French, Spanish. **Health services:** General. **History:** General. **Human services:** Social work. **Liberal arts:** Arts/sciences. **Math:** General. **Parks/recreation:** Sports admin. **Physical sciences:** Chemistry. **Psychology:** General. **Social sciences:** Criminology, economics, political science. **Visual/performing arts:** General, music.

Most popular majors. Business/marketing 15%, communications/journalism 12%, computer/information sciences 12%, liberal arts 9%, parks/recreation 6%, public administration/social services 6%, social sciences 15%.

Computing on campus. PC or laptop required. 335 workstations in dormitories, library, computer center. Dormitories wired for high-speed internet access and linked to campus network. Commuter students can connect to campus network. Online library, helpline, repair service, wireless network available.

Student life. Freshman orientation: Available. Preregistration for classes offered. **Policies:** Freshmen not permitted cars on campus. **Housing:** Guaranteed on-campus for freshmen. Coed dorms, single-sex dorms available. $150 nonrefundable deposit, deadline 5/1. **Activities:** Bands, campus ministries, choral groups, dance, drama, international student organizations, music ensembles, student government, student newspaper, Alpha Phi Omega National Service Fraternity, Caribbean Club, Democracy Matters, Catholics on Campus Ministry, LGBTQ Alliance, NAACP, Spiritual Life Center.

Athletics. NCAA. **Intercollegiate:** Basketball, bowling W, cheerleading M, cross-country, football (tackle) M, golf M, softball W, tennis, track and field, volleyball W. **Team name:** Golden Bulls.

Student services. Adult student services, alcohol/substance abuse counseling, chaplain/spiritual director, career counseling, services for economically disadvantaged, student employment services, financial aid counseling, health services, minority student services, personal counseling, veterans' counselor. **Physically disabled:** Services for visually, speech, hearing impaired.

Contact. E-mail: admissions@jcsu.edu
Phone: (704) 378-1010 Toll-free number: (800) 782-7303
Fax: (704) 378-1242
Johnson C. Smith University, 100 Beatties Ford Road, Charlotte, NC 28216-5398

Laurel University
High Point, North Carolina
www.laureluniversity.edu

CB code: 5348

▶ Private 4-year university and Bible college affiliated with interdenominational tradition
▶ Commuter campus in small city
▶ 174 degree-seeking undergraduates: 26% part-time, 52% women
▶ 19 degree-seeking graduate students
▶ 44% of applicants admitted
▶ Application essay, interview required
▶ 31% graduate within 6 years

General. Founded in 1932. Regionally accredited; also accredited by ABHE. **Degrees:** 33 bachelor's, 1 associate awarded; master's offered. **Location:** 15 miles from Greensboro, 60 miles from Charlotte. **Calendar:** Semester, limited summer session. **Full-time faculty:** 3 total; 100% have terminal degrees. **Part-time faculty:** 27 total. **Class size:** 98% < 20, 2% 20-39.

Freshman class profile. 73 applied, 32 admitted, 13 enrolled.

Return as sophomores:	80%	Live on campus:	7%
Out-of-state:	1%		

Basis for selection. Future career in church-related vocations and motivation; religious commitment and personal statement very important. Positive

personal testimony required. Finding and following God's will foremost. **Home schooled:** Transcript of courses and grades required. Junior or higher standing, GPA 3.2 or higher, 16 or older, and recommendation from high school administrator or guidance counselor required.

High school preparation. 20 units recommended. Recommended units include English 4, mathematics 3, social studies 2, science 2 (laboratory 2).

2011-2012 Annual costs. Tuition/fees: $10,730. Room only: $2,344. Books/supplies: $1,200. Personal expenses: $2,700.

Financial aid. Additional information: Early Acceptance Scholarships, Academic Honor Scholarships, Married Student Credit and Minister/Missionary Dependent Scholarship available.

Application procedures. Admission: Closing date 8/8 (postmark date). $35 fee, may be waived for applicants with need. Admission notification on a rolling basis. **Financial aid:** Priority date 3/15; no closing date. FAFSA required. Applicants notified on a rolling basis starting 6/1; must reply within 3 week(s) of notification.

Academics. All students major in Bible; second major optional. **Special study options:** Accelerated study, cooperative education, distance learning, double major, dual enrollment of high school students, independent study, internships, student-designed major. **Credit/placement by examination:** AP, CLEP, IB, institutional tests. 15 credit hours maximum toward associate degree, 30 toward bachelor's. **Support services:** Reduced course load.

Majors. Business: Business admin. **Education:** Elementary. **Theology:** Pastoral counseling, religious ed, theology.

Most popular majors. Business/marketing 50%, philosophy/religious studies 50%.

Computing on campus. 6 workstations in library, computer center. Dormitories wired for high-speed internet access. Online library available.

Student life. Freshman orientation: Mandatory. Preregistration for classes offered. Orientation activities held 2 business days before classes begin. **Policies:** Religious observance required. **Housing:** Apartments, wellness housing available. $50 deposit, deadline 7/15. **Activities:** Campus ministries, drama, literary magazine, student government, evangelistic ministries, prison ministry, gospel music team, foreign missions involvement team.

Student services. Chaplain/spiritual director, student employment services, financial aid counseling, personal counseling, veterans' counselor.

Contact. E-mail: admissions@laureluniversity.edu
Phone: (336) 887-3000 ext. 127
Toll-free number: (855) 528-7358 ext. 127 Fax: (336) 889-2261
Jeremy Reese, Director of Enrollment Management, Laurel University, 1215 Eastchester Drive, High Point, NC 27265-3115

Lees-McRae College
Banner Elk, North Carolina
www.lmc.edu

CB member
CB code: 5364

- Private 4-year liberal arts college affiliated with Presbyterian Church (USA)
- Residential campus in rural community
- 886 degree-seeking undergraduates: 62% women, 7% African American, 1% Hispanic American, 3% international
- 87% of applicants admitted
- SAT or ACT (ACT writing optional) required

General. Founded in 1900. Regionally accredited. **Degrees:** 228 bachelor's awarded. **Location:** 17 miles from Boone, 40 miles from Johnson City, TN. **Calendar:** Semester, limited summer session. **Full-time faculty:** 46 total; 59% have terminal degrees, 56% women. **Part-time faculty:** 53 total; 17% have terminal degrees, 57% women. **Class size:** 71% < 20, 28% 20-39, less than 1% 40-49. **Special facilities:** Wireless campus, biology field station, Blue Ridge Wildlife Rehabilitation Institute.

Freshman class profile. 1,242 applied, 1,077 admitted, 199 enrolled.

Mid 50% test scores			
SAT critical reading:	410-530	GPA 2.0-2.99:	35%
SAT math:	420-520	Rank in top quarter:	28%
ACT composite:	16-22	Rank in top tenth:	6%
GPA 3.75 or higher:	20%	Return as sophomores:	67%
GPA 3.50-3.74:	11%	Out-of-state:	39%
GPA 3.0-3.49:	31%	Live on campus:	99%

Basis for selection. High school record and rank in top half of class preferred. Test scores optional. Recommendations considered. Interview recommended for all students; portfolio recommended for performing arts programs. Audition required for athletic, performing arts programs.

High school preparation. College-preparatory program recommended. 10 units required. Required and recommended units include English 4, mathematics 3, social studies 2, history 1, science 2 and foreign language 2.

2011-2012 Annual costs. Tuition/fees: $22,164. Room/board: $8,000. Books/supplies: $1,000. Personal expenses: $1,945.

2011-2012 Financial aid. Need-based: 186 full-time freshmen applied for aid; 174 were judged to have need; 174 of these received aid. Average need met was 70%. Average scholarship/grant was $9,545; average loan $3,500. 72% of total undergraduate aid awarded as scholarships/grants, 28% as loans/jobs. **Non-need-based:** Awarded to 943 full-time undergraduates, including 258 freshmen. Scholarships awarded for academics, athletics, leadership, music/drama, religious affiliation, state residency.

Application procedures. Admission: No deadline. $35 fee, may be waived for applicants with need. Admission notification on a rolling basis beginning on or about 11/1. **Financial aid:** Priority date 4/15; no closing date. FAFSA required. Applicants notified on a rolling basis starting 3/1; must reply within 2 week(s) of notification.

Academics. Special study options: Accelerated study, cross-registration, double major, dual enrollment of high school students, ESL, exchange student, honors, independent study, internships, student-designed major, study abroad, teacher certification program. 3-2 program Environmental Science/Forestry with Duke University. **Credit/placement by examination:** AP, CLEP, IB, SAT, ACT, institutional tests. 16 credit hours maximum toward bachelor's degree. **Support services:** Learning center, remedial instruction, study skills assistance, tutoring, writing center.

Majors. Biology: General. **Business:** Business admin. **Communications:** Communications/speech/rhetoric. **Computer sciences:** Computer science, information systems. **Education:** Drama/dance, elementary, physical. **English:** English lit. **Health services:** Predental, premedicine, preveterinary. **Liberal arts:** Arts/sciences. **Math:** General. **Philosophy/religion:** Religion. **Protective services:** Criminal justice. **Psychology:** General. **Social sciences** International relations, sociology. **Visual/performing arts:** General, art, dramatic, musical theater, studio arts management, theater design.

Most popular majors. Biology 7%, business/marketing 11%, education 25%, health sciences 18%, parks/recreation 9%, psychology 6%, social sciences 9%.

Computing on campus. 125 workstations in dormitories, library, computer center, student center. Dormitories wired for high-speed internet access and linked to campus network. Commuter students can connect to campus network. Online course registration, online library, helpline, wireless network available.

Student life. Freshman orientation: Mandatory. Preregistration for classes offered. 6 summer Freshmen Experience sessions (1 required) followed by August orientation. **Housing:** Guaranteed on-campus for freshmen. Coed dorms, single-sex dorms, apartments, wellness housing available. $250 fully refundable deposit, deadline 5/1. Suite style village/houses available. **Activities:** Campus ministries, dance, drama, international student organizations, musical theater, student government, Order of the Tower, student ambassadors, residence hall association, sports medicine club, Phi Beta Lambda, Circle K, campus after the class hours, EMS club.

Athletics. NCAA. **Intercollegiate:** Basketball, cheerleading, cross-country, lacrosse, soccer, softball W, tennis, track and field, volleyball. **Intramural:** Basketball, cross-country, football (non-tackle), golf, skiing, soccer, softball, table tennis, tennis, volleyball. **Team name:** Bobcats.

Student services. Alcohol/substance abuse counseling, chaplain/spiritual director, career counseling, student employment services, financial aid counseling, health services, personal counseling, veterans' counselor.

Contact. E-mail: admissions@lmc.edu
Phone: (828) 898-5241 Toll-free number: (800) 280-4562
Fax: (828) 898-8707
Steve Parrish, Associate Director of Admissions, Lees-McRae College, Box 128, Banner Elk, NC 28604

Lenoir-Rhyne University
Hickory, North Carolina
www.lr.edu

CB member
CB code: 5365

- Private 4-year university and liberal arts college affiliated with Evangelical Lutheran Church in America
- Residential campus in large town

- 1,506 degree-seeking undergraduates: 3% part-time, 61% women
- 265 degree-seeking graduate students
- 87% of applicants admitted
- SAT or ACT (ACT writing recommended) required

General. Founded in 1891. Regionally accredited. **Degrees:** 310 bachelor's awarded; master's offered. **ROTC:** Army, Air Force. **Location:** 50 miles from Charlotte. **Calendar:** Semester, limited summer session. **Full-time faculty:** 89 total; 84% have terminal degrees, 4% minority. **Part-time faculty:** 53 total; 58% have terminal degrees, 8% minority. **Class size:** 68% < 20, 30% 20-39, 1% 40-49, less than 1% 50-99. **Special facilities:** Observatory, multimedia classrooms, outdoor classroom.

Freshman class profile. 3,336 applied, 2,888 admitted, 400 enrolled.

Mid 50% test scores			
SAT critical reading:	430-540	GPA 2.0-2.99:	14%
SAT math:	460-560	Rank in top quarter:	46%
ACT composite:	18-24	Rank in top tenth:	18%
GPA 3.75 or higher:	44%	Out-of-state:	25%
GPA 3.50-3.74:	14%	Live on campus:	82%
GPA 3.0-3.49:	28%	International:	1%

Basis for selection. School achievement record and courses taken most important. Interview recommended for all students; audition required for music majors. **Home schooled:** Transcript of courses and grades required.

High school preparation. College-preparatory program recommended. 13 units required. Required units include English 4, mathematics 3, social studies 1, history 1, science 1 (laboratory 1) and foreign language 2. Chemistry required for nursing program. History refers to U.S. History; mathematics needs to include algebra I, algebra II, geometry.

2011-2012 Annual costs. Tuition/fees: $26,524. Room/board: $9,370. Books/supplies: $1,100. Personal expenses: $1,500.

2011-2012 Financial aid. Need-based: 370 full-time freshmen applied for aid; 346 were judged to have need; 346 of these received aid. Average need met was 82%. Average scholarship/grant was $22,521; average loan $3,057. 75% of total undergraduate aid awarded as scholarships/grants, 25% as loans/jobs. **Non-need-based:** Awarded to 483 full-time undergraduates, including 153 freshmen. Scholarships awarded for academics, alumni affiliation, athletics, leadership, minority status, music/drama, religious affiliation, state residency.

Application procedures. Admission: Priority date 8/1; no deadline. $35 fee, may be waived for applicants with need. Admission notification on a rolling basis beginning on or about 6/15. Must reply by May 1 or within 4 week(s) if notified thereafter. Students will not be put on the housing roster until the deposit is received. **Financial aid:** Priority date 3/15; no closing date. FAFSA required. Applicants notified on a rolling basis starting 3/1.

Academics. Special program for deaf, hearing-impaired and disabled students. **Special study options:** Accelerated study, combined bachelor's/graduate degree, cross-registration, distance learning, double major, dual enrollment of high school students, ESL, honors, independent study, internships, liberal arts/career combination, student-designed major, study abroad, teacher certification program, Washington semester. **Credit/placement by examination:** AP, CLEP, IB, SAT, ACT, institutional tests. 16 credit hours maximum toward bachelor's degree. **Support services:** Learning center, remedial instruction, study skills assistance, tutoring, writing center.

Majors. Area/ethnic studies: American. **Biology:** General. **Business:** Accounting, finance, international, management information systems, management science, marketing. **Communications:** General, broadcast journalism, communications/speech/rhetoric, digital media, journalism, media studies. **Computer sciences:** General, information systems. **Conservation:** Environmental studies, forestry. **Education:** Art, biology, chemistry, Deaf/hearing impaired, early childhood, elementary, English, ESL, history, mathematics, middle, music, physical, psychology, science, social science, social studies. **English:** English lit. **Foreign languages:** French, German, Latin, Spanish. **Health services:** Athletic training, clinical lab science, nursing (RN), pre-medicine. **History:** General. **Liberal arts:** Arts/sciences. **Math:** General. **Parks/recreation:** Sports admin. **Philosophy/religion:** Philosophy, religion. **Physical sciences:** Chemistry, physics. **Psychology:** General. **Social sciences:** Economics, international relations, political science, sociology. **Theology:** Sacred music, youth ministry. **Visual/performing arts:** Dramatic, graphic design, music, music performance, studio arts management.

Most popular majors. Business/marketing 14%, education 18%, health sciences 24%, psychology 8%.

Computing on campus. 112 workstations in library, computer center, student center. Dormitories wired for high-speed internet access and linked to campus network. Commuter students can connect to campus network. Online course registration, online library, helpline, wireless network available.

Student life. Freshman orientation: Mandatory. Preregistration for classes offered. Day-long orientation program held in June. On-campus orientation held 4 days before start of classes. **Housing:** Guaranteed on-campus for all undergraduates. Coed dorms, fraternity/sorority housing available. $200 fully refundable deposit, deadline 8/1. Men or women only floors in dorms available. **Activities:** Bands, campus ministries, choral groups, drama, literary magazine, music ensembles, Model UN, musical theater, radio station, student government, student newspaper, symphony orchestra, Black Student Alliance, Campus Crusade for Christ, Fellowship of Christian Athletes, North Carolina Student Legislature, Intervarsity Christian Fellowship, College Democrats, Lutheran Student Movement, Student Occupational Therapy Association, Gay Straight Alliance, College Republicans, College Democrats.

Athletics. NCAA. **Intercollegiate:** Baseball M, basketball, cheerleading, cross-country, football (tackle) M, golf, lacrosse, soccer, softball W, swimming, tennis, track and field, volleyball W. **Intramural:** Basketball, football (non-tackle), lacrosse, soccer, softball, volleyball. **Team name:** Bears.

Student services. Adult student services, chaplain/spiritual director, career counseling, student employment services, financial aid counseling, health services, minority student services, personal counseling, veterans' counselor. **Physically disabled:** Services for hearing impaired.

Contact. E-mail: admission@lr.edu
Phone: (828) 328-7300 Toll-free number: (800) 277-5721
Fax: (828) 328-7378
Karen Feezor, Director of Admissions, Lenoir-Rhyne University, LR Box 7227, Hickory, NC 28603

Livingstone College
Salisbury, North Carolina
www.livingstone.edu

CB member
CB code: 5367

- Private 4-year liberal arts college affiliated with African Methodist Episcopal Zion Church
- Residential campus in large town
- 1,140 degree-seeking undergraduates
- 54% of applicants admitted
- SAT or ACT (ACT writing optional) required

General. Founded in 1879. Regionally accredited. **Degrees:** 108 bachelor's awarded. **ROTC:** Army. **Location:** 44 miles from Charlotte. **Calendar:** Semester. **Full-time faculty:** 59 total. **Part-time faculty:** 22 total. **Class size:** 64% < 20, 28% 20-39, 4% 40-49, 1% 50-99, 2% >100. **Special facilities:** Center for Negro and African life, literature and international studies.

Freshman class profile. 2,714 applied, 1,466 admitted, 337 enrolled.

Mid 50% test scores			
SAT critical reading:	330-400	Rank in top quarter:	6%
SAT math:	340-420	Rank in top tenth:	4%
SAT writing:	320-390	Out-of-state:	59%
ACT composite:	13-18	Live on campus:	85%

Basis for selection. School achievement record, test scores, recommendations important. College's placement test, instead of ELPT, used for advising and placement. Audition required for music majors; interview recommended for academically weak students.

High school preparation. 10 units required. Required and recommended units include English 4, mathematics 3, social studies 2, history 1, science 2 and foreign language 2.

2011-2012 Annual costs. Tuition/fees: $15,408. Room/board: $6,342. Books/supplies: $300. Personal expenses: $3,000.

Financial aid. Non-need-based: Scholarships awarded for academics, alumni affiliation, athletics, leadership, music/drama, religious affiliation, ROTC, state residency.

Application procedures. Admission: Priority date 5/15; no deadline. $25 fee, may be waived for applicants with need. Admission notification on a rolling basis. Must reply by May 1 or within 4 week(s) if notified thereafter. **Financial aid:** Priority date 3/15, closing date 6/30. FAFSA required. Applicants notified by 5/1; must reply within 4 week(s) of notification.

Academics. Special study options: Accelerated study, cross-registration, double major, independent study, internships, teacher certification program. **Credit/placement by examination:** AP, CLEP, institutional tests. **Support services:** Learning center, reduced course load, study skills assistance, tutoring.

Majors. Biology: General. **Business:** Accounting, business admin. **Computer sciences:** General. **Education:** Elementary. **Engineering:** General.

English: English lit. **Health services:** Predental, prepharmacy. **History:** General. **Human services:** Social work. **Math:** General. **Parks/recreation:** Sports admin. **Physical sciences:** Chemistry. **Protective services:** Criminal justice. **Psychology:** General. **Social sciences:** General, political science, sociology. **Theology:** Theology. **Visual/performing arts:** Dramatic, music.

Most popular majors. Business/marketing 30%, parks/recreation 11%, psychology 21%, security/protective services 15%, social sciences 16%.

Computing on campus. 200 workstations in dormitories, library, computer center. Dormitories wired for high-speed internet access and linked to campus network.

Student life. Freshman orientation: Mandatory, $100 fee. Preregistration for classes offered. **Housing:** Single-sex dorms, special housing for disabled, apartments available. $100 deposit. **Activities:** Bands, choral groups, dance, drama, film society, music ensembles, musical theater, radio station, student government, pre-theological union, AME Zion Council.

Athletics. NCAA. **Intercollegiate:** Basketball, bowling, cross-country, football (tackle) M, softball W, tennis, track and field, volleyball W. **Intramural:** Basketball. **Team name:** Blue Bears.

Student services. Career counseling, student employment services, health services, personal counseling, placement for graduates, veterans' counselor.

Contact. E-mail: admissions@livingstone.edu
Phone: (704) 216-6001 Toll-free number: (800) 835-3435
Fax: (704) 216-6215
Nicole Daniels, Director of Enrollment Management and Admission, Livingstone College, 701 West Monroe Street, Salisbury, NC 28144-5213

Mars Hill College
Mars Hill, North Carolina
www.mhc.edu
CB member
CB code: 5395

- Private 4-year liberal arts college affiliated with Baptist faith
- Residential campus in small town
- 1,258 degree-seeking undergraduates: 7% part-time, 50% women, 17% African American, 1% Asian American, 3% Hispanic American, 2% Native American
- 14 degree-seeking graduate students
- 68% of applicants admitted
- SAT or ACT (ACT writing optional) required
- 35% graduate within 6 years; 25% enter graduate study

General. Founded in 1856. Regionally accredited. **Degrees:** 192 bachelor's awarded; master's offered. **Location:** 17 miles from Asheville. **Calendar:** Semester, extensive summer session. **Full-time faculty:** 75 total; 56% have terminal degrees, 3% minority. **Part-time faculty:** 85 total; 62% have terminal degrees, 1% minority. **Class size:** 77% < 20, 22% 20-39, less than 1% 40-49, less than 1% 50-99. **Special facilities:** Appalachian archives and artifacts museum.

Freshman class profile. 2,356 applied, 1,597 admitted, 385 enrolled.

Mid 50% test scores				
SAT critical reading:	410-520	GPA 2.0-2.99:		45%
SAT math:	420-530	Rank in top quarter:		28%
ACT composite:	17-22	Rank in top tenth:		9%
GPA 3.75 or higher:	20%	End year in good standing:		87%
GPA 3.50-3.74:	11%	Return as sophomores:		60%
GPA 3.0-3.49:	24%	Out-of-state:		32%

Basis for selection. School achievement record, test scores, school and community activities, recommendations from school officials all important. Students interested in early admission must apply as full-time students, achieve A average in courses, minimum SAT 1000 (exclusive of Writing) or ACT 22, and submit 2 recommendations from high school personnel. Audition required for music, theater programs. Essay, portfolio recommended; interview recommended for students who do not meet other admissions criteria. **Home schooled:** Transcript of courses and grades required. **Learning Disabled:** Letter of documentation required.

High school preparation. 11 units required. Required and recommended units include English 4, mathematics 3, social studies 2, history 2, science 2, foreign language 2 and computer science 1.

2011-2012 Annual costs. Tuition/fees: $23,318. Room/board: $8,082. Books/supplies: $1,300. Personal expenses: $1,100.

Financial aid. Non-need-based: Scholarships awarded for academics, athletics, state residency.

Application procedures. Admission: No deadline. $25 fee, may be waived for applicants with need. Admission notification on a rolling basis. **Financial aid:** Priority date 3/15; no closing date. FAFSA required. Applicants notified on a rolling basis; must reply within 2 week(s) of notification.

Academics. Special study options: Accelerated study, cross-registration, distance learning, double major, dual enrollment of high school students, ESL, exchange student, independent study, internships, liberal arts/career combination, student-designed major, study abroad, teacher certification program. **Credit/placement by examination:** AP, CLEP, IB, SAT, ACT, institutional tests. 32 credit hours maximum toward bachelor's degree. **Support services:** Learning center, reduced course load, remedial instruction, study skills assistance, tutoring, writing center.

Majors. Biology: General, botany, zoology. **Business:** General, accounting, business admin, finance, international. **Communications:** Communications/speech/rhetoric. **Computer sciences:** Computer science. **Education:** General, art, elementary, English, middle, music, physical, secondary. **English:** English lit. **Foreign languages:** Spanish. **Health services:** Athletic training, clinical lab assistant, physician assistant, predental, premedicine, prepharmacy, preveterinary. **History:** General. **Human services:** Social work. **Liberal arts:** Arts/sciences. **Math:** General. **Parks/recreation:** Facilities management, health/fitness. **Philosophy/religion:** Religion. **Physical sciences:** Chemistry. **Psychology:** General. **Social sciences:** International relations, political science, sociology. **Visual/performing arts:** Art, dramatic, fashion design, music, music performance.

Most popular majors. Business/marketing 26%, education 23%, psychology 8%, public administration/social services 7%, visual/performing arts 9%.

Computing on campus. 180 workstations in library, computer center, student center. Dormitories wired for high-speed internet access and linked to campus network. Commuter students can connect to campus network. Online course registration, online library, helpline, repair service, wireless network available.

Student life. Freshman orientation: Mandatory. Preregistration for classes offered. **Housing:** Guaranteed on-campus for all undergraduates. Single-sex dorms, special housing for disabled, apartments available. $250 deposit. College townhouses and apartments available to upperclassmen. **Activities:** Bands, campus ministries, choral groups, dance, drama, literary magazine, music ensembles, musical theater, student government, student newspaper, Christian Student Movement, Fellowship of Christian Athletes, Ethos, Black student association, Green Students United, Bailey Mountain Cloggers, outdoor club, Blueprint, student ambassadors.

Athletics. NCAA. **Intercollegiate:** Baseball M, basketball, cross-country, football (tackle) M, golf, lacrosse M, soccer, softball W, swimming, tennis, track and field, volleyball W. **Intramural:** Badminton, basketball, football (non-tackle), soccer, softball, tennis, volleyball, water polo M. **Team name:** Lions.

Student services. Adult student services, chaplain/spiritual director, career counseling, services for economically disadvantaged, student employment services, financial aid counseling, health services, personal counseling, veterans' counselor.

Contact. E-mail: admissions@mhc.edu
Phone: (828) 689-1201 Toll-free number: (866) 642-4968
Fax: (828) 689-1473
Craig Goforth, Dean of Admissions, Mars Hill College, Blackwell Hall, Box 370, Mars Hill, NC 28754

Meredith College
Raleigh, North Carolina
www.meredith.edu
CB member
CB code: 5410

- Private 4-year liberal arts college for women
- Residential campus in large city
- 1,665 degree-seeking undergraduates: 5% part-time, 100% women, 12% African American, 2% Asian American, 3% Hispanic American, 1% Native American, 3% international
- 239 degree-seeking graduate students
- 61% of applicants admitted
- SAT or ACT (ACT writing optional) required
- 59% graduate within 6 years

General. Founded in 1891. Regionally accredited. **Degrees:** 418 bachelor's awarded; master's offered. **ROTC:** Army, Air Force. **Location:** 250 miles from Washington, DC, 375 miles from Atlanta. **Calendar:** Semester, limited summer session. **Full-time faculty:** 121 total; 93% have terminal degrees, 10% minority, 67% women. **Part-time faculty:** 86 total; 30% have terminal

degrees, 7% minority, 76% women. **Class size:** 63% < 20, 35% 20-39, 2% 40-49. **Special facilities:** Amphitheatre, child care laboratory, experimental and clinical psychology laboratories, autism laboratory, astronomy observation deck, electron microscope suite, 15 student/faculty research laboratories, greenhouse.

Freshman class profile. 1,599 applied, 976 admitted, 398 enrolled.

Mid 50% test scores		GPA 2.0-2.99:	43%
SAT critical reading:	450-560	Rank in top quarter:	48%
SAT math:	460-560	Rank in top tenth:	20%
ACT composite:	18-24	Return as sophomores:	77%
GPA 3.75 or higher:	11%	Out-of-state:	15%
GPA 3.50-3.74:	14%	Live on campus:	93%
GPA 3.0-3.49:	32%	International:	3%

Basis for selection. GED not accepted. School record (courses taken, grades on academic subjects, and class rank), test scores, and recommendations important. Meredith seeks to enroll qualified students of varying backgrounds, interests and talents and has a need-blind admission policy. Essay and/or interview may be required of some; audition recommended for music majors; portfolio recommended for art majors. **Home schooled:** Interview, letter of recommendation (nonparent) required.

High school preparation. 16 units required. Required units include English 4, mathematics 3, science 3, foreign language 2 and academic electives 1. 3 units required in social studies or history. At least 1 elective required, preferably from core academic subjects.

2011-2012 Annual costs. Tuition/fees: $27,770. Tuition includes a new laptop computer for each full-time freshman, which will be replaced with a new laptop during her junior year. Upon graduation from Meredith, the laptop remains the property of the student. Room/board: $7,950. Books/supplies: $750. Personal expenses: $1,250.

Financial aid. **Non-need-based:** Scholarships awarded for academics, art, leadership, minority status, music/drama, religious affiliation, state residency.

Application procedures. Admission: Closing date 2/15. $40 fee, may be waived for applicants with need. Admission notification on a rolling basis beginning on or about 11/1. Must reply by 5/1. **Financial aid:** Priority date 2/15; no closing date. FAFSA required. Applicants notified on a rolling basis starting 3/15; must reply by 5/1 or within 2 week(s) of notification.

Academics. Undergraduate research program available to students in all disciplines. Post-baccalaureate dietetic internship program and post-baccalaureate certificate in paralegal studies available. **Special study options:** Accelerated study, combined bachelor's/graduate degree, cooperative education, cross-registration, double major, dual enrollment of high school students, honors, independent study, internships, liberal arts/career combination, New York semester, student-designed major, study abroad, teacher certification program, United Nations semester, Washington semester. Study Abroad includes summer programs, semester/year abroad opportunities, and individually-tailored semesters. 3-2 in engineering with NC State University. **Credit/placement by examination:** AP, CLEP, IB, institutional tests. **Support services:** Learning center, reduced course load, remedial instruction, study skills assistance, tutoring, writing center.

Majors. Biology: General, molecular. **Business:** Accounting, business admin, fashion. **Communications:** Communications/speech/rhetoric, media studies. **Computer sciences:** General, computer science. **Conservation:** Environmental science, environmental studies. **Education:** Art, drama/dance, music, physical. **English:** English lit. **Foreign languages:** Spanish. **Health services:** Dietetics. **History:** General. **Human services:** Social work. **Math:** General. **Parks/recreation:** Exercise sciences, health/fitness. **Philosophy/religion:** Religion. **Physical sciences:** Chemistry. **Psychology:** General. **Social sciences:** Economics, international relations, political science, sociology, U.S. government. **Visual/performing arts:** Dance, dramatic, fashion design, graphic design, interior design, music, music pedagogy, music performance, studio arts. **Work/family studies:** General, child development, food/nutrition.

Most popular majors. Business/marketing 18%, communications/journalism 6%, family/consumer sciences 10%, psychology 10%, social sciences 6%, visual/performing arts 15%.

Computing on campus. PC or laptop required. 145 workstations in dormitories, library, computer center, student center. Dormitories wired for high-speed internet access and linked to campus network. Commuter students can connect to campus network. Online course registration, online library, helpline, repair service, wireless network available.

Student life. Freshman orientation: Mandatory. Preregistration for classes offered. 4-day program before start of classes with extra day for athletes, international students, and students with disabilities. **Policies:** Honor Code is a longstanding tradition that requires individual integrity and community responsibility of all students. Traditional-aged freshmen and sophomores must live on campus except if married or living with parents or other relatives

by special permission. **Housing:** Guaranteed on-campus for freshmen. Apartments, wellness housing available. $100 nonrefundable deposit, deadline 5/1. Pets allowed in dorm rooms. Campus housing available for all 4 years. All on-campus housing is wellness housing. **Activities:** Concert band, choral groups, dance, drama, international student organizations, literary magazine, music ensembles, Model UN, musical theater, student government, student newspaper, symphony orchestra, association for cultural awareness, unity council, service council, Habitat for Humanity, Angels for the Environment, College Democrats, College Republicans, Christian Association, Catholic Angels.

Athletics. NCAA. **Intercollegiate:** Basketball W, cross-country W, lacrosse W, soccer W, softball W, tennis W, volleyball W. **Team name:** Avenging Angels.

Student services. Adult student services, alcohol/substance abuse counseling, chaplain/spiritual director, career counseling, student employment services, financial aid counseling, health services, minority student services, personal counseling, placement for graduates. **Physically disabled:** Services for visually, speech, hearing impaired.

Contact. E-mail: admissions@meredith.edu
Phone: (919) 760-8581 Toll-free number: (800) 637-3348
Fax: (919) 760-2348
Jen Miller-Hogg, Co-Director of Admissions, Meredith College, 3800 Hillsborough Street, Raleigh, NC 27607-5298

Methodist University
Fayetteville, North Carolina
www.methodist.edu   CB code: 5426

‣ Private 4-year liberal arts college affiliated with United Methodist Church
‣ Residential campus in small city
‣ 2,226 degree-seeking undergraduates
‣ 62% of applicants admitted
‣ SAT or ACT (ACT writing optional) required

General. Founded in 1956. Regionally accredited. **Degrees:** 297 bachelor's, 8 associate awarded; master's offered. **ROTC:** Army, Air Force. **Location:** 50 miles from Raleigh-Durham. **Calendar:** Semester, extensive summer session. **Full-time faculty:** 142 total; 69% have terminal degrees, 11% minority. **Part-time faculty:** 62 total; 24% minority. **Class size:** 74% < 20, 25% 20-39, less than 1% 40-49, less than 1% 50-99. **Special facilities:** Computer-assisted English composition laboratory, psychology computer-experimental laboratory, nature trail, professional golf and tennis management center, 18-hole golf course and driving range, environmental simulation center (virtual reality laboratory).

Freshman class profile. 3,591 applied, 2,226 admitted, 557 enrolled.

Mid 50% test scores		GPA 2.0-2.99:	35%
SAT critical reading:	430-530	Rank in top quarter:	33%
SAT math:	450-550	Rank in top tenth:	12%
SAT writing:	400-500	Out-of-state:	47%
ACT composite:	17-22	Live on campus:	91%
GPA 3.75 or higher:	22%	Fraternities:	3%
GPA 3.50-3.74:	10%	Sororities:	3%
GPA 3.0-3.49:	33%		

Basis for selection. High school record (GPA), curriculum, test scores carefully considered. All prospective student files reviewed on individual basis. Extracurricular achievements and teacher/counselor recommendations also considered. Students who transfer English 101 credits must take institutional English Placement Exam. SAT/ACT scores not required of transfer students with more than 31 semester hours of transferable credit. Essay and interview recommended for all students; audition recommended for drama and music majors; portfolio recommended for art majors. **Home schooled:** Transcript of courses and grades required.

High school preparation. College-preparatory program required. 16 units required; 20 recommended. Required and recommended units include English 4, mathematics 3-4, social studies 2, history 1-2, science 2-3 (laboratory 1-2), foreign language 2 and academic electives 4.

2011-2012 Annual costs. Tuition/fees: $25,625. Professional golf management, professional tennis management, and music students have additional fees. Room/board: $9,454. Books/supplies: $1,200. Personal expenses: $4,372.

Financial aid. Non-need-based: Scholarships awarded for academics, alumni affiliation, leadership, music/drama, religious affiliation, ROTC, state residency.

Application procedures. Admission: No deadline. $25 fee, may be waived for applicants with need, free for online applicants. Admission notification on a rolling basis beginning on or about 9/1. Must reply by May 1 or within 2 week(s) if notified thereafter. **Financial aid:** Priority date 5/1; no closing date. FAFSA required. Applicants notified on a rolling basis starting 3/1; must reply within 2 week(s) of notification.

Academics. Special study options: Accelerated study, distance learning, double major, dual enrollment of high school students, ESL, exchange student, honors, independent study, internships, liberal arts/career combination, student-designed major, study abroad, teacher certification program, Washington semester, weekend college. **Credit/placement by examination:** AP, CLEP, IB, SAT, ACT, institutional tests. 45 credit hours maximum toward associate degree, 45 toward bachelor's. **Support services:** Learning center, reduced course load, remedial instruction, study skills assistance, tutoring, writing center.

Majors. Biology: General, botany, cellular/molecular, conservation, ecology, exercise physiology, microbiology, zoology. **Business:** Accounting, business admin, finance, hospitality admin, hospitality/recreation, management information systems, marketing, resort management, tourism/travel. **Communications:** Communications/speech/rhetoric, journalism, media studies, organizational. **Computer sciences:** General, computer graphics, computer science, web page design. **Education:** General, art, biology, chemistry, elementary, English, foreign languages, mathematics, middle, music, physical, secondary, social studies, special ed. **English:** English lit, rhetoric/composition. **Foreign languages:** French, Spanish. **Health services:** Athletic training, facilities admin, health care admin, nursing (RN), physician assistant, predental, premedicine, prenursing, prepharmacy, preveterinary. **History:** General. **Human services:** Social work. **Liberal arts:** Arts/sciences. **Math:** General. **Parks/recreation:** Exercise sciences, facilities management, golf management, health/fitness, sports admin. **Philosophy/religion:** Philosophy, religion. **Physical sciences:** Chemistry, forensic chemistry. **Protective services:** Criminal justice, forensics, homeland security, law enforcement admin. **Psychology:** General. **Social sciences:** Political science, sociology. **Theology:** Religious ed. **Visual/performing arts:** General, art, ceramics, graphic design, music, music performance, painting, printmaking, sculpture, studio arts.

Most popular majors. Biology 6%, business/marketing 44%, education 7%, parks/recreation 8%, social sciences 8%.

Computing on campus. 220 workstations in library, computer center, student center. Dormitories wired for high-speed internet access and linked to campus network. Commuter students can connect to campus network. Online course registration, online library, helpline, wireless network available.

Student life. Freshman orientation: Available. Preregistration for classes offered. Typically held the weekend before classes begin in Fall. **Housing:** Guaranteed on-campus for all undergraduates. Coed dorms, single-sex dorms, apartments, wellness housing available. $100 nonrefundable deposit, deadline 5/1. Health/wellness hall, first-year experience hall available. **Activities:** Bands, campus ministries, choral groups, dance, drama, international student organizations, literary magazine, music ensembles, Model UN, musical theater, radio station, student government, student newspaper, symphony orchestra, Fellowship of Christian Athletes, Young Democrats/Republicans, African American culture society, student activities committee, commuting student organization.

Athletics. NCAA. **Intercollegiate:** Baseball M, basketball, cheerleading, cross-country, football (tackle) M, golf, lacrosse W, soccer, softball W, tennis, track and field, volleyball W. **Intramural:** Basketball, cheerleading W, football (non-tackle), golf, racquetball, soccer, softball, table tennis, tennis, volleyball. **Team name:** Monarchs.

Student services. Alcohol/substance abuse counseling, chaplain/spiritual director, career counseling, student employment services, financial aid counseling, health services, personal counseling, placement for graduates, veterans' counselor, women's services. **Physically disabled:** Services for visually impaired.

Contact. E-mail: admissions@methodist.edu
Phone: (910) 630-7027 Toll-free number: (800) 488-7110
Fax: (910) 630-7285
Jamie Legg, Dean of Admissions, Methodist University, 5400 Ramsey Street, Fayetteville, NC 28311-1498

Mid-Atlantic Christian University
Elizabeth City, North Carolina
www.macuniversity.edu   CB code: 5597

- Private 4-year university and Bible college affiliated with Church of Christ
- Residential campus in large town

- 165 degree-seeking undergraduates: 21% part-time, 44% women, 19% African American, 4% Hispanic American
- 34% of applicants admitted
- SAT or ACT (ACT writing optional), application essay required

General. Founded in 1948. Regionally accredited; also accredited by ABHE. **Degrees:** 21 bachelor's, 5 associate awarded. **ROTC:** Army. **Location:** 50 miles from Norfolk, Virginia. **Calendar:** Semester, limited summer session. **Full-time faculty:** 9 total; 67% have terminal degrees, 11% women. **Part-time faculty:** 32 total; 41% have terminal degrees, 6% minority, 28% women. **Class size:** 78% < 20, 22% 20-39.

Freshman class profile. 114 applied, 39 admitted, 27 enrolled.

Mid 50% test scores			
SAT critical reading:	400-560	GPA 2.0-2.99:	52%
SAT math:	390-530	Rank in top quarter:	17%
GPA 3.75 or higher:	9%	Rank in top tenth:	1%
GPA 3.50-3.74:	17%	Return as sophomores:	63%
GPA 3.0-3.49:	18%	Out-of-state:	56%
		Live on campus:	56%

Basis for selection. Evidence of Christian character, school achievement record, test scores, school and community activities, recommendations important. Interview recommended if questions arise from references or academic record. **Home schooled:** Transcript of courses and grades, state high school equivalency certificate required.

High school preparation. 20 units required. Required and recommended units include English 4, mathematics 3, social studies 2, history 2, science 3 (laboratory 2), foreign language 6, computer science 1 and academic electives 4.

2011-2012 Annual costs. Tuition/fees: $10,500. Room/board: $7,000. Books/supplies: $1,000. Personal expenses: $2,500.

2010-2011 Financial aid. Need-based: 23 full-time freshmen applied for aid; 19 were judged to have need; 19 of these received aid. Average need met was 41%. Average scholarship/grant was $5,876; average loan $3,391. 42% of total undergraduate aid awarded as scholarships/grants, 58% as loans/jobs. **Non-need-based:** Awarded to 12 full-time undergraduates, including 2 freshmen. Scholarships awarded for academics, alumni affiliation, leadership, music/drama, religious affiliation.

Application procedures. Admission: No deadline. $50 fee, may be waived for applicants with need. Admission notification on a rolling basis beginning on or about 9/1. Must reply by May 1 or within 2 week(s) if notified thereafter. **Financial aid:** Priority date 2/1; no closing date. FAFSA, institutional form required. Applicants notified on a rolling basis starting 5/1; must reply within 2 week(s) of notification.

Academics. Special study options: Distance learning, double major, dual enrollment of high school students, internships. Semester-long mission intern class overseas. **Credit/placement by examination:** AP, CLEP, institutional tests. 8 credit hours maximum toward associate degree, 16 toward bachelor's. **Support services:** Learning center, reduced course load, remedial instruction, study skills assistance, writing center.

Majors. Business: Organizational leadership. **Education:** Elementary. **Foreign languages:** Applied linguistics. **Psychology:** Counseling. **Theology:** Bible, missionary, pastoral counseling, preministerial, religious ed, theology, youth ministry. **Work/family studies:** Family systems.

Most popular majors. Business/marketing 15%, education 10%, psychology 10%, theological studies 62%.

Computing on campus. 24 workstations in dormitories, library, computer center. Dormitories wired for high-speed internet access and linked to campus network. Commuter students can connect to campus network.

Student life. Freshman orientation: Mandatory, $130 fee. Preregistration for classes offered. **Policies:** All students have opportunity to travel in choral group throughout country. Religious observance required. **Housing:** Guaranteed on-campus for all undergraduates. Single-sex dorms, special housing for disabled, apartments, wellness housing available. $75 nonrefundable deposit, deadline 4/1. **Activities:** Campus ministries, choral groups, drama, music ensembles, musical theater, student government.

Athletics. Intercollegiate: Basketball, volleyball W. **Intramural:** Basketball, football (non-tackle), golf, soccer, table tennis, tennis, volleyball. **Team name:** Mustangs.

Student services. Career counseling, student employment services, financial aid counseling, personal counseling, placement for graduates. **Physically disabled:** Services for hearing impaired.

Contact. E-mail: admissions@macuniversity.edu
Phone: (252) 334-2028 Toll-free number: (866) 996-MACU
Fax: (252) 334-2064
Ken Greene, VP Enrollment Services, Mid-Atlantic Christian University,
715 North Poindexter Street, Elizabeth City, NC 27909

Miller-Motte College: Wilmington
Wilmington, North Carolina
www.miller-motte.edu   CB code: 3342

▶ For-profit 4-year technical college
▶ Commuter campus in small city
▶ 953 degree-seeking undergraduates
▶ Interview required

General. Accredited by ACICS. **Degrees:** 24 bachelor's, 151 associate
awarded. **Location:** 145 miles from Raleigh. **Calendar:** Quarter, extensive
summer session. **Full-time faculty:** 13 total. **Part-time faculty:** 29 total.

Freshman class profile. 383 applied, 383 admitted, 241 enrolled.

Basis for selection. Open admission, but selective for some programs.
Minimum test score of 15 on Wonderlic test for admission, 18 for Medical
Assisting, 21 for Surgical Technology, 20 for Computer Systems Network
Administrator, 18 for Criminal Justice, 18 for Paralegal, and 18 for Dental
Assisting. **Home schooled:** Transcript of courses and grades required.

High school preparation. 17 units recommended. Recommended units
include English 4, mathematics 4, social studies 4, science 4 (laboratory 1).

2011-2012 Annual costs. Tuition/fees: $11,925. Quoted tuition and per-
credit-hour charge are for Associate programs. $300 per-credit-hour charge
for Bachelor programs. $11-$31 per-credit-hour required fees for all programs. Books/supplies: $1,800. Personal expenses: $3,350.

Financial aid. All financial aid based on need.

Application procedures. Admission: No deadline. $40 fee. Application
must be submitted on paper. Admission notification on a rolling basis. **Financial aid:** No deadline. FAFSA, institutional form required.

Academics. Special study options: Distance learning, double major,
internships. **Credit/placement by examination:** AP, CLEP, institutional
tests. 46 credit hours maximum toward associate degree. **Support services:**
Learning center, reduced course load, remedial instruction, study skills assistance, tutoring.

Majors. Business: Business admin. **Protective services:** Law enforcement admin.

Most popular majors. Business/marketing 50%, health sciences 50%.

Computing on campus. 120 workstations in library, computer center.
Commuter students can connect to campus network. Online library, repair
service, student web hosting available.

Student life. Freshman orientation: Mandatory. Preregistration for
classes offered. **Activities:** Student newspaper.

Athletics. Team name: Marlin.

Student services. Career counseling, financial aid counseling, placement
for graduates.

Contact. Phone: (910) 392-4660 Toll-free number: (800) 784-2110
Fax: (910) 799-6224
Adam Merritt, Director of Admissions, Miller-Motte College: Wilmington,
5000 Market Street, Wilmington, NC 28405

Montreat College
Montreat, North Carolina
www.montreat.edu   CB member
                                  CB code: 5423

▶ Private 4-year liberal arts college affiliated with Presbyterian Church
  Reformed and Independent
▶ Residential campus in small town
▶ 656 degree-seeking undergraduates: 2% part-time, 57% women, 21%
  African American, 2% Hispanic American, 1% Native American, 2%
  international

▶ 82 degree-seeking graduate students
▶ 51% of applicants admitted
▶ SAT or ACT (ACT writing optional), application essay required
▶ 45% graduate within 6 years

General. Founded in 1916. Regionally accredited. North Carolina's only
member institute of the Council for Christian Colleges and Universities.
Degrees: 247 bachelor's, 73 associate awarded; master's offered. **Location:**
16 miles from Asheville. **Calendar:** Semester, limited summer session. **Full-
time faculty:** 34 total; 79% have terminal degrees, 9% minority, 26% women.
Part-time faculty: 35 total; 20% have terminal degrees, 40% women. **Class
size:** 36% < 20, 63% 20-39, less than 1% 40-49. **Special facilities:** Ropes
course, climbing wall, chapel of the prodigal, Black Mountain Campus.

Freshman class profile. 553 applied, 280 admitted, 84 enrolled.

Mid 50% test scores			
SAT critical reading:	420-530	GPA 2.0-2.99:	32%
SAT math:	440-560	Rank in top quarter:	30%
ACT composite:	18-25	Rank in top tenth:	13%
GPA 3.75 or higher:	12%	Return as sophomores:	51%
GPA 3.50-3.74:	16%	Out-of-state:	61%
GPA 3.0-3.49:	40%	Live on campus:	43%
		International:	7%

Basis for selection. Decisions are criteria-based, using GPA and SAT/
ACT scores as initial qualifiers. Essay, recommendation, and extracurricular
activities also considered. Interview required for students who do not meet
standard admission requirements. **Home schooled:** Transcript of courses and
grades, letter of recommendation (nonparent) required. **Learning Disabled:**
Students with documented learning disabilities are referred to the Director
of Student Success before an admissions decision is made.

High school preparation. College-preparatory program required. 14 units
required; 16 recommended. Required and recommended units include English
4, mathematics 3-4, social studies 3, science 3 and foreign language 1-2.

2012-2013 Annual costs. Tuition/fees: $23,198. Room/board: $7,494.
Books/supplies: $1,000. Personal expenses: $1,000.

2011-2012 Financial aid. Need-based: 71% of total undergraduate aid
awarded as scholarships/grants, 29% as loans/jobs. **Non-need-based:** Scholarships awarded for academics, alumni affiliation, athletics, leadership, music/
drama, religious affiliation, state residency.

Application procedures. Admission: Priority date 5/15; deadline 8/15
(postmark date). No application fee. Admission notification on a rolling basis
beginning on or about 9/1. **Financial aid:** No deadline. FAFSA required.
Applicants notified on a rolling basis starting 3/1; must reply within 2 week(s)
of notification.

Academics. Special study options: Accelerated study, double major, dual
enrollment of high school students, internships, liberal arts/career combination, student-designed major, study abroad, teacher certification program,
Washington semester. **Credit/placement by examination:** AP, CLEP, IB,
institutional tests. 15 credit hours maximum toward associate degree, 30
toward bachelor's. **Support services:** Reduced course load, study skills assistance, tutoring, writing center.

Majors. Area/ethnic studies: American. **Biology:** General. **Business:** Business admin, international, marketing. **Communications:** Media studies.
Computer sciences: General. **Conservation:** Environmental studies. **Education:** Elementary. **English:** English lit. **History:** General. **Parks/recreation:**
General. **Philosophy/religion:** General, Christian. **Psychology:** General.
Theology: Bible, missionary, religious ed, youth ministry. **Visual/per-
forming arts:** Music management, music performance.

Most popular majors. Biology 10%, business/marketing 58%, parks/rec-
reation 6%, social sciences 6%.

Computing on campus. 60 workstations in library, computer center,
student center. Dormitories wired for high-speed internet access and linked
to campus network. Helpline, repair service, wireless network available.

Student life. Freshman orientation: Mandatory. Preregistration for
classes offered. 5 days before classes start; pre-orientation program, Wilderness Journey, available at extra cost. **Policies:** No alcohol on campus. Religious observance required. **Housing:** Guaranteed on-campus for all undergraduates. Single-sex dorms, apartments available. $100 nonrefundable
deposit, deadline 8/15. 351 spaces available for undergraduate students.
Activities: Campus ministries, choral groups, drama, literary magazine, music
ensembles, student government, student newspaper, missions club, Fellowship of Christian Athletes, Young Life.

Athletics. NAIA. **Intercollegiate:** Baseball M, basketball, cross-country,
golf, soccer, softball W, track and field, volleyball W. **Intramural:** Basketball, football (non-tackle), soccer, softball, table tennis, tennis, volleyball.
Team name: Cavaliers.

Student services. Adult student services, alcohol/substance abuse counseling, chaplain/spiritual director, career counseling, student employment services, financial aid counseling, health services, personal counseling, placement for graduates, veterans' counselor. **Physically disabled:** Services for visually, speech, hearing impaired.

Contact. E-mail: admissions@montreat.edu
Phone: (828) 669-8011 Toll-free number: (800) 622-6968
Fax: (828) 669-0120
Tony Robinson, Director of Enrollment Development & Outreach, Montreat College, 310 Gaither Circle, Montreat, NC 28757

Mount Olive College

Mount Olive, North Carolina   **CB member**
www.moc.edu   **CB code: 5435**

- Private 4-year business and liberal arts college affiliated with Free Will Baptists
- Residential campus in small town
- 3,494 degree-seeking undergraduates: 53% part-time, 69% women
- 54% of applicants admitted

General. Founded in 1951. Regionally accredited. **Degrees:** 756 bachelor's, 200 associate awarded. **ROTC:** Air Force. **Location:** 13 miles from Goldsboro. **Calendar:** Semester, extensive summer session. **Full-time faculty:** 92 total; 86% have terminal degrees, 36% women. **Part-time faculty:** 258 total; 24% have terminal degrees, 48% women. **Class size:** 81% < 20, 19% 20-39.

Freshman class profile. 1,660 applied, 897 admitted, 275 enrolled.

Mid 50% test scores			
SAT critical reading:	400-490	GPA 3.0-3.49:	25%
SAT math:	430-520	GPA 2.0-2.99:	44%
SAT writing:	400-490	Rank in top quarter:	47%
ACT composite:	17-21	Rank in top tenth:	10%
GPA 3.75 or higher:	13%	Out-of-state:	12%
GPA 3.50-3.74:	8%	Live on campus:	45%

Basis for selection. School record, test scores, class rank important. Personal recommendations considered. Interview recommended for all students; portfolio recommended for art majors. Audition required for music majors.

High school preparation. College-preparatory program recommended. 17 units required. Required units include English 4, mathematics 3, social studies 3, science 3 (laboratory 1) and academic electives 3.

2011-2012 Annual costs. Tuition/fees: $15,500. Room/board: $6,200. Books/supplies: $1,350.

2010-2011 Financial aid. Non-need-based: Scholarships awarded for academics, art, athletics, leadership, music/drama, religious affiliation.

Application procedures. Admission: Closing date 8/18. $20 fee, may be waived for applicants with need, free for online applicants. Admission notification on a rolling basis beginning on or about 1/9. Must reply by May 1 or within 2 week(s) if notified thereafter. **Financial aid:** Priority date 3/15; no closing date. FAFSA required. Applicants notified on a rolling basis starting 2/14.

Academics. Special study options: Accelerated study, cooperative education, distance learning, double major, dual enrollment of high school students, external degree, honors, independent study, internships, liberal arts/career combination, teacher certification program. Accelerated extension program at Seymour Johnson Air Force Base in Goldsboro; 55-week degree completion program in business offered in New Bern, Wilmington, and Raleigh-Research Triangle Park. **Credit/placement by examination:** AP, CLEP, SAT, ACT, institutional tests. 15 credit hours maximum toward associate degree, 30 toward bachelor's. **Support services:** Learning center, reduced course load, remedial instruction, study skills assistance, tutoring, writing center.

Majors. Biology: General. **Business:** Accounting/business management, business admin, human resources, management information systems. **Computer sciences:** Information systems. **Conservation:** Environmental science. **Education:** Early childhood, elementary, middle, music, secondary. **English:** English lit, technical writing. **General:** Business. **Health services:** Health care admin. **History:** General. **Math:** General. **Parks/recreation:** General. **Philosophy/religion:** Religion. **Physical sciences:** Chemistry. **Protective services:** Criminal justice. **Psychology:** General. **Visual/performing arts:** Art, conducting, piano/keyboard, stringed instruments, voice/opera.

Most popular majors. Business/marketing 36%, education 17%, health sciences 18%, security/protective services 12%.

Computing on campus. 50 workstations in library, computer center. Dormitories wired for high-speed internet access and linked to campus network. Commuter students can connect to campus network. Online library, repair service, wireless network available.

Student life. Freshman orientation: Available. Preregistration for classes offered. **Policies:** Religious observance required. **Housing:** Guaranteed on-campus for freshmen. Single-sex dorms, apartments available. $50 nonrefundable deposit, deadline 2/26. **Activities:** Concert band, campus ministries, choral groups, international student organizations, music ensembles, musical theater, student government, student newspaper, English society, political forum, recreation majors club, Fellowship of Christian Athletes, Phi Beta Lambda, minority students' organization, Fellowship of Christian Students, Free Spirit.

Athletics. NCAA. **Intercollegiate:** Baseball M, basketball, cross-country, golf, soccer, softball W, tennis, volleyball. **Intramural:** Badminton, baseball M, basketball, football (tackle) M, handball, racquetball, softball, table tennis, tennis, volleyball. **Team name:** Trojans.

Student services. Adult student services, career counseling, student employment services, health services, personal counseling, placement for graduates, veterans' counselor.

Contact. E-mail: admissions@moc.edu
Phone: (919) 658-2502 Toll-free number: (800) 653-0854
Fax: (919) 658-9816
Tim Woodard, Director of Admissions, Mount Olive College, 634 Henderson Street, Mount Olive, NC 28365

North Carolina Agricultural and Technical State University

Greensboro, North Carolina   **CB member**
www.ncat.edu   **CB code: 5003**

- Public 4-year university
- Residential campus in small city
- 8,921 degree-seeking undergraduates: 8% part-time, 54% women, 89% African American, 1% Asian American, 2% Hispanic American, 1% international
- 1,675 graduate students
- 66% of applicants admitted
- SAT or ACT with writing, SAT Subject Tests required
- 43% graduate within 6 years; 42% enter graduate study

General. Founded in 1891. Regionally accredited. **Degrees:** 1,306 bachelor's awarded; master's, doctoral offered. **ROTC:** Army, Air Force. **Location:** 60 miles from Raleigh, 91 miles from Charlotte. **Calendar:** Semester. **Full-time faculty:** 532 total; 77% have terminal degrees, 73% minority, 44% women. **Part-time faculty:** 142 total; 40% have terminal degrees, 68% minority, 49% women. **Class size:** 37% < 20, 45% 20-39, 10% 40-49, 8% 50-99, less than 1% >100. **Special facilities:** University galleries (including African heritage collection and African American artists' collection), planetarium, Olympic track.

Freshman class profile. 6,692 applied, 4,446 admitted, 1,875 enrolled.

Mid 50% test scores			
SAT critical reading:	400-500	GPA 3.50-3.74:	11%
SAT math:	410-500	GPA 3.0-3.49:	34%
SAT writing:	370-470	GPA 2.0-2.99:	42%
ACT composite:	17-21	Rank in top quarter:	6%
GPA 3.75 or higher:	13%	Return as sophomores:	74%
		International:	1%

Basis for selection. High school GPA, class rank, test scores, recommendations, course selection reviewed. SAT preferred, but ACT accepted. Audition recommended for music programs; portfolio recommended for art programs. **Home schooled:** State high school equivalency certificate required.

High school preparation. College-preparatory program required. 19 units required. Required units include English 4, mathematics 4, social studies 1, history 1, science 3 (laboratory 1), foreign language 2 and academic electives 4.

2011-2012 Annual costs. Tuition/fees: $4,668; $14,302 out-of-state. Room/board: $7,225. Books/supplies: $1,400. Personal expenses: $1,500.

2010-2011 Financial aid. Need-based: 2,020 full-time freshmen applied for aid; 1,831 were judged to have need; 1,814 of these received aid. Average need met was 84%. Average scholarship/grant was $6,119; average loan $3,259. 51% of total undergraduate aid awarded as scholarships/grants, 49%

as loans/jobs. **Non-need-based:** Awarded to 6,331 full-time undergraduates, including 1,799 freshmen. Scholarships awarded for academics.

Application procedures. Admission: Priority date 2/15; no deadline. $45 fee. Application must be submitted on paper. Admission notification on a rolling basis. Must reply by May 1 or within 2 week(s) if notified thereafter. Please apply for housing immediately upon being accepted for admissions. Housing is filled on a first-come, first-served basis. **Financial aid:** Priority date 3/1; no closing date. FAFSA required. Must reply within 2 week(s) of notification.

Academics. Free tutoring in math, science, business, and more. Student Athlete Academic Enhancement Program (SAAE). **Special study options:** Accelerated study, cooperative education, cross-registration, distance learning, double major, dual enrollment of high school students, honors, internships, liberal arts/career combination, study abroad, teacher certification program. **Credit/placement by examination:** AP, CLEP, IB, institutional tests. **Support services:** Learning center, reduced course load, remedial instruction, study skills assistance, tutoring, writing center.

Majors. Architecture: Landscape. **Biology:** General. **Business:** Accounting, business admin, finance, marketing, transportation. **Communications:** Media studies. **Computer sciences:** Computer science. **Education:** General, agricultural, biology, business, chemistry, driver/safety, early childhood, elementary, English, family/consumer sciences, foreign languages, French, history, kindergarten/preschool, mathematics, music, physics, science, secondary, social science, Spanish, special ed, speech, technology/industrial arts, trade/industrial. **Engineering:** General, agricultural, architectural, biomedical, chemical, civil, computer, electrical, industrial, mechanical, surveying. **English:** English lit, rhetoric/composition. **Foreign languages:** French. **General:** Animal sciences, economics, plant sciences. **Health services:** Occupational health. **History:** General. **Human services:** Social work. **Liberal arts:** Arts/sciences. **Math:** General, applied. **Parks/recreation:** Facilities management, health/fitness, sports admin. **Physical sciences:** Atmospheric science, chemistry, physics. **Protective services:** Criminal justice. **Psychology:** General. **Social sciences:** General, political science, sociology. **Visual/performing arts:** General, art, dramatic, graphic design, music. **Work/family studies:** General, child development, food/nutrition.

Most popular majors. Business/marketing 15%, communications/journalism 9%, education 6%, engineering/engineering technologies 19%, liberal arts 7%, psychology 6%.

Computing on campus. 675 workstations in library, computer center. Dormitories wired for high-speed internet access and linked to campus network. Commuter students can connect to campus network. Online course registration, online library, helpline, wireless network available.

Student life. Freshman orientation: Mandatory, $140 fee. Preregistration for classes offered. **Housing:** Guaranteed on-campus for freshmen. Coed dorms, single-sex dorms, wellness housing available. $150 deposit. Housing provided by North Carolina A&T University Foundation, Inc. **Activities:** Bands, campus ministries, choral groups, dance, drama, international student organizations, music ensembles, radio station, student government, student newspaper, symphony orchestra, TV station, National Society of Black Engineers, gospel choir, Toastmasters International, karate team, Caribbean student association, Chinese student association, environmental science club, Progressive Republicans, Students Against Driving Drunk, Young Democrats.

Athletics. NCAA. **Intercollegiate:** Baseball M, basketball, bowling W, cross-country, football (tackle) M, softball W, swimming W, tennis W, track and field, volleyball W. **Intramural:** Badminton, baseball M, basketball, bowling W, cross-country, football (tackle) M, golf, handball, racquetball, soccer, softball W, swimming, table tennis, tennis, track and field, volleyball. **Team name:** Aggies.

Student services. Adult student services, alcohol/substance abuse counseling, career counseling, student employment services, financial aid counseling, health services, minority student services, personal counseling, placement for graduates, veterans' counselor. **Physically disabled:** Services for visually, speech, hearing impaired.

Contact. E-mail: uadmit@ncat.edu
Phone: (336) 334-7946 Toll-free number: (800) 443-8964
Fax: (336) 334-7478
Keyana Scales, Director of Admissions, North Carolina Agricultural and Technical State University, Webb Hall, Greensboro, NC 27411-0002

North Carolina Central University
Durham, North Carolina   **CB member**
www.nccu.edu   **CB code: 5495**

- Public 4-year university
- Commuter campus in small city

- 5,985 degree-seeking undergraduates: 13% part-time, 67% women, 86% African American, 1% Asian American, 2% Hispanic American
- 1,816 degree-seeking graduate students
- 52% of applicants admitted
- SAT or ACT with writing required
- 38% graduate within 6 years

General. Founded in 1910. Regionally accredited. Historically, the majority of students have been African American. **Degrees:** 914 bachelor's awarded; master's, professional offered. **ROTC:** Army, Air Force. **Location:** 23 miles from Raleigh. **Calendar:** Semester, extensive summer session. **Full-time faculty:** 433 total; 74% have terminal degrees, 72% minority, 51% women. **Part-time faculty:** 175 total; 36% have terminal degrees, 68% minority, 67% women. **Class size:** 39% < 20, 52% 20-39, 6% 40-49, 3% 50-99. **Special facilities:** Collection of primary resources on black life and culture, art museum with works of Afro-American culture.

Freshman class profile. 9,240 applied, 4,782 admitted, 1,258 enrolled.

Mid 50% test scores			
SAT critical reading:	390-460	GPA 3.0-3.49:	28%
SAT math:	400-480	GPA 2.0-2.99:	53%
SAT writing:	370-450	Rank in top quarter:	20%
ACT composite:	15-19	Rank in top tenth:	6%
GPA 3.75 or higher:	10%	Return as sophomores:	68%
GPA 3.50-3.74:	9%	Out-of-state:	11%
		Live on campus:	94%

Basis for selection. Academic achievement, class rank, test scores important. SAT and SAT Subject Tests or ACT recommended. SAT preferred, ACT also accepted. Audition required for music programs. **Home schooled:** Transcript of courses and grades, state high school equivalency certificate required.

High school preparation. College-preparatory program required. 20 units required. Required units include English 4, mathematics 4, social studies 2, history 1, science 3 (laboratory 1), foreign language 2 and academic electives 3. Social studies units must include 1 U.S. history. One foreign language, and 1 math recommended during 12th grade. Students who graduate high school in and after 2006 must have one additional math course from the following: pre-calculus, AP statistics, AP calculus, IB math level II, integrated math IV, discrete math, advanced models and functions.

2011-2012 Annual costs. Tuition/fees: $4,720; $15,293 out-of-state. Room/board: $7,196. Books/supplies: $1,500. Personal expenses: $1,575.

2010-2011 Financial aid. Need-based: 1,138 full-time freshmen applied for aid; 1,061 were judged to have need; 1,059 of these received aid. Average need met was 68%. Average scholarship/grant was $7,866; average loan $3,246. 80% of total undergraduate aid awarded as scholarships/grants, 20% as loans/jobs. **Non-need-based:** Awarded to 3,930 full-time undergraduates, including 982 freshmen. Scholarships awarded for academics, alumni affiliation, art, athletics, leadership, music/drama, ROTC. **Additional information:** Departmental grants based on need plus other available criteria.

Application procedures. Admission: Priority date 8/1; no deadline. $40 fee. Admission notification on a rolling basis beginning on or about 10/15. Early admission available with permission from high school principal and academic dean. **Financial aid:** Priority date 3/1; no closing date. FAFSA required. Must reply within 2 week(s) of notification.

Academics. Special study options: Accelerated study, distance learning, double major, dual enrollment of high school students, ESL, exchange student, honors, independent study, internships, study abroad, teacher certification program, weekend college. **Credit/placement by examination:** AP, CLEP, institutional tests. 30 credit hours maximum toward bachelor's degree. **Support services:** Learning center, remedial instruction, study skills assistance, tutoring, writing center.

Majors. Biology: General. **Business:** Accounting, business admin, hospitality admin. **Communications:** Media studies. **Computer sciences:** Computer science, information systems. **Conservation:** Environmental science. **Education:** Art, biology, chemistry, drama/dance, elementary, English, family/consumer sciences, French, health, history, kindergarten/preschool, mathematics, middle, music, physical, physics, Spanish. **English:** English lit. **Foreign languages:** French, Spanish. **Health services:** Athletic training, nursing (RN), public health ed. **History:** General. **Human services:** Social work. **Math:** General. **Parks/recreation:** Facilities management, health/fitness. **Physical sciences:** Chemistry, physics. **Protective services:** Law enforcement admin. **Psychology:** General. **Social sciences:** Geography, political science, sociology. **Visual/performing arts:** Art, dramatic, jazz, music. **Work/family studies:** General.

Most popular majors. Biology 6%, business/marketing 15%, family/consumer sciences 11%, health sciences 10%, psychology 8%, security/protective services 10%, social sciences 8%.

Computing on campus. 400 workstations in dormitories, library, computer center. Dormitories wired for high-speed internet access and linked to campus network. Commuter students can connect to campus network. Online course registration, online library, helpline, repair service, wireless network available.

Student life. Freshman orientation: Mandatory, $125 fee. Preregistration for classes offered. **Housing:** Coed dorms, single-sex dorms available. $150 nonrefundable deposit, deadline 5/1. Coed honors dormitory available. **Activities:** Bands, campus ministries, choral groups, dance, drama, literary magazine, music ensembles, radio station, student government, student newspaper.

Athletics. NAIA, NCAA. **Intercollegiate:** Basketball, bowling, cheerleading W, cross-country, football (tackle) M, golf, softball W, tennis, track and field, volleyball W. **Team name:** Eagles.

Student services. Career counseling, student employment services, health services, on-campus daycare, personal counseling, placement for graduates, veterans' counselor.

Contact. E-mail: admissions@nccu.edu
Phone: (919) 560-6298 Toll-free number: (877) 667-7533
Fax: (919) 530-7625
Anthony Brooks, Director of Admissions, North Carolina Central University, PO Box 19717, Durham, NC 27707

North Carolina State University
Raleigh, North Carolina CB member
www.ncsu.edu CB code: 5496

- Public 4-year university
- Residential campus in large city
- 23,514 degree-seeking undergraduates: 7% part-time, 43% women, 8% African American, 5% Asian American, 4% Hispanic American, 1% international
- 8,550 degree-seeking graduate students
- 52% of applicants admitted
- SAT or ACT with writing required
- 73% graduate within 6 years

General. Founded in 1887. Regionally accredited. **Degrees:** 5,182 bachelor's, 127 associate awarded; master's, professional, doctoral offered. **ROTC:** Army, Naval, Air Force. **Location:** One mile from downtown. **Calendar:** Semester, extensive summer session. **Full-time faculty:** 1,733 total; 88% have terminal degrees, 17% minority, 31% women. **Part-time faculty:** 148 total; 61% have terminal degrees, 16% minority, 42% women. **Class size:** 21% < 20, 47% 20-39, 10% 40-49, 14% 50-99, 8% >100. **Special facilities:** 3 electron microscopes, phytotron, research farms, 2 campus theaters, craft center, stable isotope laboratory, teaching forest, wood products laboratory, coastal marine science laboratory, 80,000 acres of research forests and research farm lands, fiber, fabric, and garment manufacturing equipment.

Freshman class profile. 19,863 applied, 10,395 admitted, 4,564 enrolled.

Mid 50% test scores			
SAT critical reading:	530-620	Rank in top quarter:	83%
SAT math:	560-660	Rank in top tenth:	43%
SAT writing:	510-610	Return as sophomores:	91%
ACT composite:	23-28	Out-of-state:	11%
GPA 3.75 or higher:	95%	Live on campus:	76%
GPA 3.50-3.74:	3%	International:	1%
GPA 3.0-3.49:	2%	Fraternities:	8%
		Sororities:	14%

Basis for selection. GED not accepted. School academic record, standardized test scores important. Counselor evaluations, extracurricular activities also considered. Preference given to students with exceptionally strong high school record. Level and difficulty of courses considered. Weighted grades for advanced, honors, AP courses considered. All applicants to the UNC system, except those exempted by current campus policies, must submit standardized test scores. SAT preferred, ACT also accepted. Essay recommended for all students. Interview and portfolio required for College of Design applicants. Verification of golf playing ability required for Professional Golf Management Program.

High school preparation. College-preparatory program required. 16 units required; 20 recommended. Required and recommended units include English 4, mathematics 4, social studies 1, history 1, science 3-4 (laboratory 1-2), foreign language 2 and academic electives 1-4. Science units should include 1 life or biological science, 1 physical science, and 1 laboratory science. Honors, advanced, AP and IB courses given extra weight.

2011-2012 Annual costs. Tuition/fees: $7,018; $19,853 out-of-state. Room/board: $8,536. Books/supplies: $1,000. Personal expenses: $833.

2011-2012 Financial aid. Need-based: 3,566 full-time freshmen applied for aid; 2,347 were judged to have need; 2,314 of these received aid. Average need met was 88%. Average scholarship/grant was $9,218; average loan $3,007. 64% of total undergraduate aid awarded as scholarships/grants, 36% as loans/jobs. **Non-need-based:** Awarded to 2,595 full-time undergraduates, including 756 freshmen. Scholarships awarded for academics, alumni affiliation, athletics, leadership, ROTC, state residency. **Additional information:** Freshman Merit Scholarships; students submitting complete admissions application by the November 1 Early Action deadline automatically considered, additional information may be required after initial review.

Application procedures. Admission: Priority date 11/1; deadline 2/1 (postmark date). $70 fee, may be waived for applicants with need. Must reply by 5/1. Students applying under regular admission to College of Design must submit application by 12/1. Selected candidates will be invited to interview. **Financial aid:** Priority date 3/1; no closing date. FAFSA required. Applicants notified on a rolling basis starting 4/1.

Academics. Special study options: Accelerated study, combined bachelor's/graduate degree, cooperative education, cross-registration, distance learning, double major, dual enrollment of high school students, exchange student, honors, independent study, internships, liberal arts/career combination, student-designed major, study abroad, teacher certification program. 2+2 Engineering with University of North Carolina-Asheville and selected community colleges. **Credit/placement by examination:** AP, CLEP, IB, SAT, ACT, institutional tests. **Support services:** Learning center, preadmission summer program, reduced course load, remedial instruction, study skills assistance, tutoring, writing center.

Majors. Architecture: Architecture, environmental design. **Area/ethnic studies:** African-American, German, women's. **Biology:** General, biochemistry, botany, genetics, microbiology, zoology. **Business:** Accounting, business admin, managerial economics. **Communications:** Communications/speech/rhetoric. **Computer sciences:** Computer science. **Conservation:** General, environmental science, forest management, forestry, management/policy, wood science. **Education:** General, agricultural, elementary, English, French, mathematics, middle, sales/marketing, science, social studies, Spanish, technology/industrial arts. **Engineering:** General, aerospace, agricultural, biomedical, chemical, civil, computer, construction, electrical, environmental, industrial, materials, mechanical, nuclear, textile. **English:** English lit. **Foreign languages:** French, Spanish. **General:** Agribusiness operations, agronomy, animal sciences, education services, food science, horticultural science, mechanization, poultry. **History:** General. **Human services:** Social work. **Liberal arts:** Arts/sciences. **Math:** General, applied, statistics. **Parks/recreation:** Facilities management, sports admin. **Philosophy/religion:** Philosophy, religion. **Physical sciences:** Atmospheric science, chemistry, geology, oceanography, physics. **Psychology:** General. **Social sciences:** Anthropology, criminology, geography, political science, sociology. **Visual/performing arts:** Art history/conservation, design, graphic design, industrial design, studio arts management.

Most popular majors. Agriculture 6%, biology 11%, business/marketing 14%, engineering/engineering technologies 24%, social sciences 6%.

Computing on campus. 3,000 workstations in dormitories, library, computer center, student center. Dormitories wired for high-speed internet access and linked to campus network. Commuter students can connect to campus network. Online course registration, helpline, repair service, student web hosting, wireless network available.

Student life. Freshman orientation: Mandatory, $150 fee. Preregistration for classes offered. 2-day program. **Housing:** Coed dorms, single-sex dorms, special housing for disabled, apartments, fraternity/sorority housing available. Living/learning dormitories available. **Activities:** Bands, campus ministries, choral groups, dance, drama, film society, international student organizations, literary magazine, music ensembles, Model UN, musical theater, radio station, student government, student newspaper, symphony orchestra, Alpha Phi Omega, Baptist Student Union, Campus Crusade for Christ, Circle-K, international student board, Young Democrats, Young Republicans, Society of Afro-American Culture, YMCA.

Athletics. NCAA. **Intercollegiate:** Baseball M, basketball, cheerleading, cross-country, diving, football (tackle) M, golf, gymnastics W, rifle, soccer, softball W, swimming, tennis, track and field, volleyball W, wrestling M. **Intramural:** Archery, badminton, baseball M, basketball, bowling, cross-country, fencing, field hockey W, football (non-tackle), golf, gymnastics, handball, ice hockey M, lacrosse M, racquetball, rugby M, sailing, skiing, skin diving, soccer, softball, squash, swimming, table tennis, tennis, track and field, volleyball, wrestling M. **Team name:** Wolfpack.

Student services. Adult student services, alcohol/substance abuse counseling, chaplain/spiritual director, career counseling, student employment services, financial aid counseling, health services, legal services, minority student services, on-campus daycare, personal counseling, placement for graduates, veterans' counselor, women's services. **Physically disabled:** Services for visually, speech, hearing impaired.

Contact. E-mail: undergrad_admissions@ncsu.edu
Phone: (919) 515-2434 Fax: (919) 515-5039
Thomas Griffin, Director of Undergraduate Admissions, North Carolina State University, Campus Box 7103, Raleigh, NC 27695-7103

North Carolina Wesleyan College
Rocky Mount, North Carolina
www.ncwc.edu   **CB code: 5501**

‣ Private 4-year liberal arts college affiliated with United Methodist Church
‣ Residential campus in small city
‣ 1,402 degree-seeking undergraduates: 21% part-time, 62% women
‣ 54% of applicants admitted
‣ SAT or ACT (ACT writing optional) required

General. Founded in 1956. Regionally accredited. Adult students, 22 and older, can attend classes at sites in Raleigh, Goldsboro, and Rocky Mount. Free Silver Scholars program for age 60 and above. **Degrees:** 392 bachelor's awarded. **ROTC:** Army. **Location:** 57 miles from Raleigh. **Calendar:** Semester, extensive summer session. **Full-time faculty:** 46 total; 83% have terminal degrees, 6% minority. **Part-time faculty:** 144 total; 35% have terminal degrees, 15% minority. **Class size:** 82% < 20, 18% 20-39. **Special facilities:** Black Mountain archival collection, center for the performing arts.

Freshman class profile. 1,501 applied, 804 admitted, 194 enrolled.

Mid 50% test scores			
SAT math:	390-490	GPA 2.0-2.99:	56%
ACT composite:	15-22	Rank in top quarter:	12%
GPA 3.75 or higher:	13%	Rank in top tenth:	4%
GPA 3.50-3.74:	8%	Return as sophomores:	51%
GPA 3.0-3.49:	23%	Out-of-state:	37%
		International:	9%

Basis for selection. High school GPA most important, followed by SAT or ACT score, rigor of high school curriculum, and recommendations. Essay, school and community activities considered. SAT preferred. Essay, interview recommended for all students. **Home schooled:** Statement describing home school structure and mission, interview required.

High school preparation. College-preparatory program recommended. Recommended units include English 4, mathematics 3, social studies 2, science 2 (laboratory 2) and foreign language 2.

2011-2012 Annual costs. Tuition/fees: $24,890. Room/board: $8,180. Books/supplies: $1,000. Personal expenses: $1,200.

Financial aid. All financial aid based on need. **Additional information:** Scholarships based on GPA. Various scholarship and leadership awards available.

Application procedures. Admission: No deadline. $25 fee, may be waived for applicants with need. Admission notification on a rolling basis. **Financial aid:** Priority date 3/1; no closing date. FAFSA required. Applicants notified on a rolling basis starting 1/1; must reply within 2 week(s) of notification.

Academics. Special study options: Accelerated study, cooperative education, cross-registration, distance learning, double major, dual enrollment of high school students, honors, independent study, internships, liberal arts/career combination, teacher certification program, weekend college. **Credit/placement by examination:** AP, CLEP, institutional tests. **Support services:** Learning center, pre-admission summer program, reduced course load, remedial instruction, study skills assistance, tutoring, writing center.

Majors. Biology: General. **Business:** Accounting, business admin. **Computer sciences:** Information systems. **Conservation:** General. **Education:** Elementary, middle, physical. **English:** English lit. **Health services:** Premedicine. **History:** General. **Math:** General. **Philosophy/religion:** Religion. **Physical sciences:** Chemistry. **Protective services:** Criminal justice. **Psychology:** General. **Social sciences:** Political science, sociology. **Visual/performing arts:** Dramatic.

Most popular majors. Business/marketing 41%, computer/information sciences 10%, legal studies 14%, psychology 15%, social sciences 6%.

Computing on campus. 223 workstations in dormitories, library, computer center, student center. Dormitories wired for high-speed internet access and linked to campus network. Commuter students can connect to campus network. Online course registration, helpline, repair service available.

Student life. Freshman orientation: Mandatory. Preregistration for classes offered. Takes place prior to start of fall classes. **Housing:** Guaranteed on-campus for freshmen. Coed dorms, single-sex dorms, special housing for disabled, wellness housing available. $100 deposit, deadline 7/15. **Activities:**

Bands, choral groups, drama, literary magazine, music ensembles, student government, student newspaper, Black Student Association, Fellowship of Christian Athletes, College Republicans, Wesleyan Christian Fellowship.

Athletics. NCAA. **Intercollegiate:** Baseball M, basketball, cheerleading M, cross-country, football (tackle) M, golf M, lacrosse W, soccer, softball W, tennis, volleyball W. **Intramural:** Basketball, football (tackle) M, lacrosse W, soccer, softball, table tennis, tennis, volleyball. **Team name:** Bishops.

Student services. Adult student services, alcohol/substance abuse counseling, chaplain/spiritual director, career counseling, student employment services, financial aid counseling, health services, personal counseling, placement for graduates, veterans' counselor. **Physically disabled:** Services for visually, hearing impaired.

Contact. E-mail: adm@ncwc.edu
Phone: (252) 985-5200 Toll-free number: (800) 488-6292
Fax: (252) 985-5295
William Allen, Director of Admissions, North Carolina Wesleyan College, 3400 North Wesleyan Boulevard, Rocky Mount, NC 27804

Pfeiffer University
Misenheimer, North Carolina   **CB member**
www.pfeiffer.edu   **CB code: 5536**

‣ Private 4-year university and liberal arts college affiliated with United Methodist Church
‣ Residential campus in rural community
‣ 1,016 degree-seeking undergraduates: 8% part-time, 57% women, 9% African American, 1% Asian American, 3% Hispanic American, 3% international
‣ 1,002 degree-seeking graduate students
‣ 59% of applicants admitted
‣ SAT or ACT (ACT writing optional) required
‣ 45% graduate within 6 years

General. Founded in 1885. Regionally accredited. **Degrees:** 246 bachelor's awarded; master's offered. **ROTC:** Army. **Location:** 42 miles from Charlotte, 55 miles from Winston-Salem, 60 miles from Greensboro. **Calendar:** Semester, limited summer session. **Full-time faculty:** 87 total; 75% have terminal degrees, 15% minority, 46% women. **Part-time faculty:** 70 total; 13% minority, 41% women. **Class size:** 76% < 20, 23% 20-39, 1% 40-49. **Special facilities:** Center for Servant Leadership.

Freshman class profile. 1,411 applied, 836 admitted, 187 enrolled.

Mid 50% test scores			
SAT critical reading:	420-530	Rank in top quarter:	40%
SAT math:	430-540	Rank in top tenth:	11%
ACT composite:	12-23	End year in good standing:	91%
GPA 3.75 or higher:	9%	Return as sophomores:	67%
GPA 3.50-3.74:	10%	Out-of-state:	32%
GPA 3.0-3.49:	32%	Live on campus:	76%
GPA 2.0-2.99:	48%	International:	4%

Basis for selection. Academic GPA, standardized test scores required. Level of interest in attending Pfeiffer, character considered. Essay tests for both SAT and ACT are used in scholarship/merit competitions. Interview recommended for all students; audition required for music programs.

High school preparation. College-preparatory program recommended. 12 units required; 16 recommended. Required and recommended units include English 4, mathematics 3, social studies 2-4, history 2, science 2-3 (laboratory 1) and foreign language 2. Math should include algebra. 2 units of either history or social studies required.

2012-2013 Annual costs. Tuition/fees: $22,900. Room/board: $9,310. Books/supplies: $2,000. Personal expenses: $1,000.

2010-2011 Financial aid. Need-based: 58% of total undergraduate aid awarded as scholarships/grants, 42% as loans/jobs. **Non-need-based:** Scholarships awarded for academics, alumni affiliation, athletics, leadership, music/drama, religious affiliation, state residency.

Application procedures. Admission: No deadline. $35 fee, may be waived for applicants with need. Admission notification on a rolling basis beginning on or about 9/1. **Financial aid:** Priority date 5/1; no closing date. FAFSA required. Applicants notified on a rolling basis starting 3/1; must reply within 2 week(s) of notification.

Academics. Special study options: Accelerated study, combined bachelor's/graduate degree, cooperative education, distance learning, double major,

dual enrollment of high school students, honors, independent study, internships, liberal arts/career combination, study abroad, teacher certification program, Washington semester. **Credit/placement by examination:** AP, CLEP, IB, SAT, ACT, institutional tests. **Support services:** Learning center, reduced course load, remedial instruction, study skills assistance, tutoring, writing center.

Majors. Biology: General. **Business:** Accounting, business admin, international, management information systems. **Communications:** General, journalism, organizational. **Computer sciences:** General. **Conservation:** Environmental studies. **Education:** Elementary, music, physical, science, secondary, social studies, special ed. **Engineering:** General. **English:** English lit. **Health services:** Health care admin, nurse practitioner, premedicine. **History:** General. **Liberal arts:** Arts/sciences. **Math:** General. **Parks/recreation:** Exercise sciences, sports admin. **Philosophy/religion:** Religion. **Physical sciences:** Chemistry. **Protective services:** Police science. **Psychology:** General. **Social sciences:** Economics, political science. **Theology:** Religious ed, youth ministry. **Visual/performing arts:** Music, studio arts management.

Most popular majors. Biology 8%, business/marketing 28%, education 13%, health sciences 7%, security/protective services 11%.

Computing on campus. 70 workstations in library, computer center, student center. Dormitories wired for high-speed internet access and linked to campus network. Commuter students can connect to campus network. Online course registration, online library, helpline, repair service, wireless network available.

Student life. Freshman orientation: Available. Preregistration for classes offered. **Housing:** Guaranteed on-campus for all undergraduates. Coed dorms, single-sex dorms, special housing for disabled, apartments, wellness housing available. $150 partly refundable deposit. Apartment-style housing with shared kitchen and bath available for older students not married. **Activities:** Bands, campus ministries, choral groups, drama, international student organizations, literary magazine, music ensembles, musical theater, student government, student newspaper, religious organizations, political groups, service clubs, professional clubs.

Athletics. NCAA. **Intercollegiate:** Baseball M, basketball, cross-country, golf, lacrosse, soccer, softball W, swimming, tennis, volleyball. **Intramural:** Basketball, lacrosse, soccer, softball, table tennis, tennis, volleyball. **Team name:** Falcons.

Student services. Adult student services, alcohol/substance abuse counseling, chaplain/spiritual director, career counseling, student employment services, financial aid counseling, health services, personal counseling, placement for graduates, veterans' counselor. **Physically disabled:** Services for visually impaired.

Contact. E-mail: admiss@pfeiffer.edu
Phone: (704) 463-1360 ext. 2060 Toll-free number: (800) 338-2060
Fax: (704) 463-1363
Terry Parker-Jeffries, Director, Admissions, Pfeiffer University, PO Box 960, Misenheimer, NC 28109

Piedmont International University
Winston-Salem, North Carolina
www.piedmontu.edu   CB code: 5555

- Private 4-year Bible and seminary college affiliated with Baptist faith
- Small city
- 269 degree-seeking undergraduates: 27% part-time, 46% women
- 118 degree-seeking graduate students
- 50% of applicants admitted
- ACT (writing optional), application essay required

General. Founded in 1945. Regionally accredited; also accredited by TRACS. **Degrees:** 48 bachelor's, 5 associate awarded; master's, doctoral offered. **Location:** 75 miles from Charlotte, 100 miles from Raleigh. **Calendar:** Semester, limited summer session. **Full-time faculty:** 27 total. **Part-time faculty:** 19 total. **Class size:** 77% < 20, 17% 20-39, 4% 40-49, 1% 50-99. **Special facilities:** Restored 18th Century Moravian community, Old Salem.

Freshman class profile. 107 applied, 54 admitted, 43 enrolled.

Out-of-state:	44%	Live on campus:	61%

Basis for selection. Student's life objectives and previous academic record important. Interview recommended for all students; audition required for music program.

High school preparation. Recommended units include English 4, mathematics 3, social studies 3, science 3 and foreign language 2.

2012-2013 Annual costs. Tuition/fees: $12,395. Room/board: $6,410. Books/supplies: $500. Personal expenses: $2,052.

Application procedures. Admission: Priority date 7/31; no deadline. $50 fee. Admission notification on a rolling basis beginning on or about 12/1. Must reply by May 1 or within 2 week(s) if notified thereafter. **Financial aid:** No deadline. Institutional form required. Applicants notified on a rolling basis starting 3/1.

Academics. Special study options: Cooperative education, distance learning, double major, dual enrollment of high school students, independent study, internships, teacher certification program. **Credit/placement by examination:** AP, CLEP, institutional tests. **Support services:** Learning center, reduced course load, remedial instruction, study skills assistance, tutoring.

Majors. Education: Elementary, English, music, physical. **Theology:** Bible, missionary, youth ministry. **Visual/performing arts:** Music.

Most popular majors. Education 33%, philosophy/religious studies 60%.

Computing on campus. 26 workstations in library, computer center, student center. Dormitories linked to campus network. Commuter students can connect to campus network. Online course registration, online library, helpline, wireless network available.

Student life. Freshman orientation: Mandatory. Preregistration for classes offered. Held 2 days prior to registration. **Policies:** Religious observance required. **Housing:** Guaranteed on-campus for freshmen. Single-sex dorms, apartments available. **Activities:** Choral groups, drama, music ensembles, student government, student newspaper, missions fellowship, preachers' fellowship, youth leaders' fellowship, educators' fellowship, music fellowship.

Athletics. NCCAA. **Intercollegiate:** Basketball, soccer M, volleyball W. **Team name:** Conquerors.

Student services. Chaplain/spiritual director, career counseling, financial aid counseling, health services, personal counseling, placement for graduates, veterans' counselor.

Contact. E-mail: admissions@piedmontu.edu
Phone: (336) 725-8344 ext. 7924 Toll-free number: (800) 937-5097
Fax: (336) 725-5522
Angela Hoover, Director of Admissions, Piedmont International University, 420 South Boad Street, Winston-Salem, NC 27101-5133

Queens University of Charlotte
Charlotte, North Carolina   CB member
www.queens.edu   CB code: 5560

- Private 4-year university affiliated with Presbyterian Church (USA)
- Residential campus in very large city
- 1,911 degree-seeking undergraduates: 24% part-time, 76% women, 16% African American, 2% Asian American, 3% Hispanic American, 1% Native American, 8% international
- 471 degree-seeking graduate students
- 74% of applicants admitted
- SAT or ACT with writing required
- 59% graduate within 6 years

General. Founded in 1857. Regionally accredited. **Degrees:** 397 bachelor's, 88 associate awarded; master's offered. **ROTC:** Army, Air Force. **Calendar:** Semester, limited summer session. **Full-time faculty:** 123 total; 72% have terminal degrees, 6% minority, 68% women. **Part-time faculty:** 135 total; 26% have terminal degrees, 17% minority, 67% women. **Class size:** 60% < 20, 37% 20-39, 2% 40-49, 1% 50-99. **Special facilities:** Rare books museum, recital hall.

Freshman class profile. 2,199 applied, 1,618 admitted, 359 enrolled.

Mid 50% test scores		GPA 2.0-2.99:	15%
SAT critical reading:	470-580	Rank in top quarter:	39%
SAT math:	460-570	Rank in top tenth:	14%
SAT writing:	460-560	Return as sophomores:	70%
ACT composite:	20-25	Live on campus:	88%
GPA 3.75 or higher:	39%	International:	6%
GPA 3.50-3.74:	16%	Fraternities:	2%
GPA 3.0-3.49:	30%	Sororities:	12%

Basis for selection. High school courses taken, school achievement record, class rank, test scores important. Extracurricular activities, recommendations also considered. Official test scores must be received prior to admission (rolling admissions). Interview recommended for all students. Audition required for drama, music, music therapy programs; portfolio recommended

for art program. **Home schooled:** Transcript of courses and grades required. Evidence of Home School registration in the home state (copy of Home School License) required.

High school preparation. College-preparatory program required. Required units include English 4, mathematics 3, social studies 2, science 2 (laboratory 1) and foreign language 2. Chemistry recommended for nursing majors.

2011-2012 Annual costs. Tuition/fees: $25,356. Room/board: $10,188. Books/supplies: $1,200. Personal expenses: $1,500.

2011-2012 Financial aid. Need-based: 291 full-time freshmen applied for aid; 246 were judged to have need; 246 of these received aid. Average need met was 75%. Average scholarship/grant was $17,380; average loan $3,280. 59% of total undergraduate aid awarded as scholarships/grants, 41% as loans/jobs. **Non-need-based:** Awarded to 656 full-time undergraduates, including 178 freshmen. Scholarships awarded for academics, art, athletics, leadership, minority status, music/drama, religious affiliation.

Application procedures. Admission: Priority date 12/1; no deadline. $40 fee, may be waived for applicants with need. Application must be submitted online. Admission notification on a rolling basis beginning on or about 9/15. Must reply by May 1 or within 3 week(s) if notified thereafter. Admission can be deferred up to one year. **Financial aid:** Priority date 3/1; no closing date. FAFSA required. Applicants notified on a rolling basis starting 3/15; must reply by 5/1 or within 3 week(s) of notification.

Academics. 6 credit hours of internships required to enhance job placement and career opportunities. **Special study options:** Accelerated study, cross-registration, distance learning, double major, honors, independent study, internships, liberal arts/career combination, study abroad, teacher certification program, Washington semester, weekend college. John Belk International Program (3-week study tours in Europe and Asia), interdisciplinary core curriculum, professional golf management, Harvard Model UN, European internship program offered. **Credit/placement by examination:** AP, CLEP, IB, institutional tests. 43 credit hours maximum toward bachelor's degree. **Support services:** Learning center, reduced course load, study skills assistance, tutoring, writing center.

Majors. Area/ethnic studies: American, European. **Biology:** General, biochemistry, environmental. **Business:** Business admin, international, marketing. **Communications:** General, communications/speech/rhetoric, journalism, media studies, organizational, sports. **Computer sciences:** Information systems. **Conservation:** Environmental science, environmental studies. **Education:** General, elementary, English, foreign languages, secondary. **English:** British lit, creative writing, English lit. **Foreign languages:** General, French, Spanish. **Health services:** Music therapy, nursing (RN), predental, premedicine, preop/surgical nursing, prepharmacy, preveterinary. **History:** General. **Math:** General, statistics. **Parks/recreation:** Golf management. **Philosophy/religion:** Religion. **Physical sciences:** Chemistry. **Psychology:** General. **Social sciences:** Political science, sociology. **Visual/performing arts:** Dramatic, music, music performance, studio arts.

Most popular majors. Biology 6%, business/marketing 14%, communications/journalism 9%, health sciences 38%, psychology 9%.

Computing on campus. Dormitories wired for high-speed internet access and linked to campus network. Commuter students can connect to campus network. Online library, helpline, wireless network available.

Student life. Freshman orientation: Mandatory. Preregistration for classes offered. 2-day program held at beginning of academic year. Preorientation held in spring for all deposited freshmen. **Housing:** Guaranteed on-campus for freshmen. Coed dorms, special housing for disabled, apartments, wellness housing available. $300 fully refundable deposit, deadline 5/1. Apartment style residence hall available for traditional undergraduates only. All residence hall facilities are smoke-free. **Activities:** Concert band, campus ministries, choral groups, dance, drama, international student organizations, literary magazine, music ensembles, Model UN, musical theater, student government, student newspaper, Students for Black Awareness, College Republicans, College Democrats, North Carolina Student Legislature, Justinian Society.

Athletics. NCAA. **Intercollegiate:** Basketball, cheerleading, cross-country, golf, lacrosse, soccer, softball W, swimming, tennis, track and field, volleyball W. **Intramural:** Basketball, football (non-tackle) M, soccer, softball, swimming, volleyball. **Team name:** Royals.

Student services. Alcohol/substance abuse counseling, chaplain/spiritual director, career counseling, student employment services, financial aid counseling, health services, minority student services, personal counseling, placement for graduates. **Physically disabled:** Services for visually impaired.

Contact. E-mail: admissions@queens.edu
Phone: (704) 337-2212 Toll-free number: (800) 849-0202 ext. 2212
Fax: (704) 337-2403
William Lee, Director of Admissions, Queens University of Charlotte, 1900 Selwyn Ave, Charlotte, NC 28274-0001

Salem College
Winston-Salem, North Carolina   **CB member**
www.salem.edu   **CB code: 5607**

- Private 4-year liberal arts college for women affiliated with Moravian Church in America
- Residential campus in small city
- 912 degree-seeking undergraduates
- 60% of applicants admitted
- SAT or ACT (ACT writing optional), application essay required

General. Founded in 1772. Regionally accredited. Male students age 23 and over may enroll in adult program only; male students may not reside at the college. **Degrees:** 128 bachelor's awarded; master's offered. **ROTC:** Army. **Location:** 80 miles from Charlotte, 25 miles from Greensboro. **Calendar:** 4-1-4, limited summer session. **Full-time faculty:** 60 total; 83% have terminal degrees, 8% minority. **Part-time faculty:** 47 total; 38% have terminal degrees, 13% minority. **Class size:** 84% < 20, 16% 20-39. **Special facilities:** Center for women writers.

Freshman class profile. 661 applied, 397 admitted, 186 enrolled.

Mid 50% test scores			
SAT critical reading:	460-600	GPA 3.0-3.49:	24%
SAT math:	450-580	GPA 2.0-2.99:	6%
SAT writing:	450-580	Rank in top quarter:	67%
ACT composite:	19-27	Rank in top tenth:	39%
GPA 3.75 or higher:	48%	Out-of-state:	35%
GPA 3.50-3.74:	22%	Live on campus:	98%

Basis for selection. School achievement record, essay or personal statement, test scores important. Recommendations, interview, extracurricular and community activities, talent, minority status considered. Interview recommended for all students. Audition required for music program; portfolio recommended for art program.

High school preparation. College-preparatory program required. 16 units required. Required units include English 4, mathematics 3, social studies 2, science 3, foreign language 2 and academic electives 3. Math requirement includes 2 algebra and 1 geometry. On a case by case basis, a portion of this requirement may be waived for adult students.

2011-2012 Annual costs. Tuition/fees: $22,720. Traditional-age students must enroll full-time. Students registering through the Fleer Center for Adult Education pay $1,208 tuition per course. Graduate students pay $340 per credit hour. Room/board: $11,764. Books/supplies: $1,000. Personal expenses: $985.

Financial aid. Non-need-based: Scholarships awarded for academics, alumni affiliation, leadership, minority status, music/drama, state residency.

Application procedures. Admission: Priority date 3/1; no deadline. $30 fee, may be waived for applicants with need, free for online applicants. Admission notification on a rolling basis beginning on or about 10/1. Must reply by May 1 or within 2 week(s) if notified thereafter. **Financial aid:** Priority date 3/1; no closing date. FAFSA required. Applicants notified on a rolling basis starting 3/1; must reply by 5/1 or within 2 week(s) of notification.

Academics. Special study options: Accelerated study, cross-registration, double major, dual enrollment of high school students, exchange student, honors, independent study, internships, liberal arts/career combination, student-designed major, study abroad, teacher certification program, Washington semester. 3-1 clinical laboratory sciences/medical technology program with Wake Forest University's Baptist Medical Center; various study abroad options available through Brethren Colleges of America (BCA); St. Peters, Oxford; and St. Clare's, Oxford. **Credit/placement by examination:** AP, CLEP, IB, SAT, institutional tests. **Support services:** Learning center, reduced course load, study skills assistance, tutoring, writing center.

Majors. Area/ethnic studies: American. **Biology:** General. **Business:** Accounting, business admin, international, nonprofit/public. **Communications:** Communications/speech/rhetoric. **Education:** Elementary, music, secondary. **English:** Creative writing, English lit, writing. **Foreign languages:** French, Spanish. **Health services:** Clinical lab technology. **History:** General. **Math:** General. **Philosophy/religion:** Philosophy, religion. **Physical sciences:** Chemistry. **Psychology:** General. **Social sciences:** Economics, international relations, sociology. **Visual/performing arts:** Art history/conservation, interior design, music, music performance, studio arts, studio arts management.

Most popular majors. Biology 9%, business/marketing 12%, communications/journalism 9%, English 12%, foreign language 7%, psychology 9%, social sciences 18%, visual/performing arts 9%.

Computing on campus. 54 workstations in library, computer center. Dormitories wired for high-speed internet access and linked to campus network. Commuter students can connect to campus network. Online library, helpline, wireless network available.

Student life. Freshman orientation: Mandatory. Preregistration for classes offered. 3 days before fall term begins. Separate orientation program for adult students. **Housing:** Guaranteed on-campus for freshmen. Apartments, wellness housing available. $250 nonrefundable deposit, deadline 5/1. All full-time students under 23 years required to reside on-campus unless they reside with family within a 30 mile radius of the college. **Activities:** Marching band, campus ministries, choral groups, dance, drama, international student organizations, literary magazine, music ensembles, Model UN, musical theater, student government, student newspaper, College Democrats, College Republicans, Green Party, Catholic Student Association, Campus Activities Council, Intervarsity Fellowship, Habitat for Humanity.

Athletics. NCAA. **Intercollegiate:** Basketball W, cross-country W, soccer W, swimming W, tennis W, volleyball W. **Team name:** Spirits.

Student services. Adult student services, chaplain/spiritual director, career counseling, financial aid counseling, health services, personal counseling, placement for graduates, women's services.

Contact. E-mail: admissions@salem.edu
Phone: (336) 721-2621 Toll-free number: (800) 327-2536
Fax: (336) 917-5572
Katherine Watts, Dean of Admissions and Financial Aid, Salem College, 601 South Church Street, Winston-Salem, NC 27108

Shaw University
Raleigh, North Carolina
www.shawu.edu

CB member
CB code: 5612

- Private 4-year university and liberal arts college affiliated with Baptist faith
- Residential campus in large city
- 2,257 degree-seeking undergraduates: 9% part-time, 60% women, 84% African American, 2% international
- 140 degree-seeking graduate students
- 48% of applicants admitted
- SAT or ACT (ACT writing optional), application essay required

General. Founded in 1865. Regionally accredited. **Degrees:** 395 bachelor's, 9 associate awarded; master's offered. **ROTC:** Army, Air Force. **Location:** 168 miles from Charlotte. **Calendar:** Semester, limited summer session. **Full-time faculty:** 120 total; 70% have terminal degrees, 79% minority, 42% women. **Part-time faculty:** 120 total; 36% have terminal degrees, 88% minority, 42% women. **Class size:** 64% < 20, 34% 20-39, 1% 40-49, less than 1% 50-99.

Freshman class profile. 6,763 applied, 3,259 admitted, 548 enrolled.

Mid 50% test scores			
SAT critical reading:	320-390	GPA 2.0-2.99:	71%
SAT math:	320-400	Rank in top quarter:	4%
SAT writing:	310-390	Rank in top tenth:	1%
ACT composite:	13-16	Return as sophomores:	51%
GPA 3.75 or higher:	1%	Out-of-state:	35%
GPA 3.50-3.74:	1%	Live on campus:	81%
GPA 3.0-3.49:	6%	International:	1%

Basis for selection. 2.0 high school GPA desired. Interview, portfolio recommended for some. **Home schooled:** Transcript of courses and grades, state high school equivalency certificate required.

High school preparation. 18 units required. Required units include English 3, mathematics 2, social studies 2, science 2 and academic electives 9. .

2011-2012 Annual costs. Tuition/fees: $13,226. Room/board: $7,560. Books/supplies: $1,100. Personal expenses: $2,040.

Financial aid. Non-need-based: Scholarships awarded for academics, athletics, music/drama.

Application procedures. Admission: Closing date 7/30 (receipt date). $25 fee. Admission notification on a rolling basis beginning on or about 8/1. **Financial aid:** Priority date 3/1, closing date 6/30. FAFSA required. Applicants notified on a rolling basis starting 3/15.

Academics. Special study options: Accelerated study, cross-registration, distance learning, double major, dual enrollment of high school students,

---

honors, independent study, internships, liberal arts/career combination, student-designed major, study abroad, teacher certification program. **Credit/placement by examination:** AP, CLEP, institutional tests. 30 credit hours maximum toward associate degree, 60 toward bachelor's. **Support services:** Learning center, reduced course load, study skills assistance, tutoring, writing center.

Majors. Biology: General. **Business:** Business admin, international. **Communications:** Media studies. **Computer sciences:** General, computer science. **Conservation:** General. **Education:** Elementary, English, mathematics. **English:** English lit. **Health services:** Athletic training, audiology/speech pathology, recreational therapy. **Human services:** General, social work. **Liberal arts:** Arts/sciences. **Math:** General. **Parks/recreation:** General, exercise sciences. **Philosophy/religion:** Religion. **Physical sciences:** Chemistry, physics. **Protective services:** Criminal justice. **Psychology:** General. **Social sciences:** International relations, political science, sociology. **Visual/performing arts:** Dramatic, music.

Most popular majors. Business/marketing 25%, communications/journalism 6%, psychology 8%, public administration/social services 14%, security/protective services 15%, social sciences 8%.

Computing on campus. Dormitories wired for high-speed internet access and linked to campus network. Commuter students can connect to campus network. Online course registration, online library, helpline, repair service, student web hosting, wireless network available.

Student life. Freshman orientation: Available. Preregistration for classes offered. **Policies:** Religious observance required. Freshmen not permitted cars on campus. **Housing:** Single-sex dorms available. $150 nonrefundable deposit, deadline 7/1. **Activities:** Bands, campus ministries, choral groups, dance, drama, international student organizations, music ensembles, musical theater, radio station, student government, student newspaper, NAACP, business, sociology, criminal justice, accounting clubs, Christian Fellowship, northern exposure, Order of the Eastern Star.

Athletics. NCAA. **Intercollegiate:** Baseball M, basketball, bowling W, cross-country, football (tackle) M, softball W, tennis, track and field, volleyball W. **Intramural:** Basketball, tennis, volleyball. **Team name:** Bears.

Student services. Adult student services, alcohol/substance abuse counseling, chaplain/spiritual director, career counseling, student employment services, financial aid counseling, health services, personal counseling, placement for graduates, veterans' counselor. **Physically disabled:** Services for visually, speech, hearing impaired.

Contact. E-mail: admissions@shawu.edu
Phone: (919) 546-8275 Toll-free number: (800) 214-6683
Fax: (919) 546-8271
Sherlock McDougald, Director of Admissions, Shaw University, 118 East South Street, Raleigh, NC 27601

Southeastern Baptist Theological Seminary
Wake Forest, North Carolina
www.sebts.edu

CB code: 7050

- Private 4-year Bible and seminary college affiliated with Southern Baptist Convention
- Small town
- 503 degree-seeking undergraduates

General. Founded in 1950. Regionally accredited. **Degrees:** 43 bachelor's, 2 associate awarded; master's, professional, doctoral offered. **Location:** 20 miles from Raleigh, 30 miles from Durham. **Calendar:** Semester, limited summer session. **Full-time faculty:** 53 total. **Part-time faculty:** 38 total.

Freshman class profile.

Out-of-state:	40%	Live on campus:	80%

Basis for selection. Open admission, but selective for some programs. Recommendations most important.

2011-2012 Annual costs. Tuition/fees: $8,090. Non-Southern Baptist students per credit hour charge is $514. On-campus room only is $215 per month. Books/supplies: $400.

Financial aid. Additional information: Special endowment awards $300 to all freshmen.

Application procedures. Admission: No deadline. $30 fee.

Academics. Special study options: Internships. **Credit/placement by examination:** AP, CLEP. **Support services:** Remedial instruction.

Majors. Theology: Bible.

Computing on campus. 4 workstations in library.

Student life. Freshman orientation: Available, $80 fee. Preregistration for classes offered. **Activities:** Concert band, choral groups, music ensembles, student government, student newspaper.

Athletics. Intramural: Basketball, golf, racquetball, softball, tennis, volleyball.

Student services. Adult student services, career counseling, student employment services, health services, on-campus daycare, personal counseling, placement for graduates, veterans' counselor.

Contact. E-mail: admissions@sebts.edu
Phone: (919) 761-2280 Toll-free number: (800) 284-6317
Fax: (919) 556-0998
Shane Baker, Dean of Students, Southeastern Baptist Theological Seminary, PO Box 1889, Wake Forest, NC 27588

St. Andrews University
Laurinburg, North Carolina
www.sapc.edu

CB member
CB code: 5214

- Private 4-year liberal arts college affiliated with Presbyterian Church (USA)
- Residential campus in large town
- 448 degree-seeking undergraduates: 3% part-time, 52% women, 16% African American, 1% Asian American, 2% Hispanic American, 2% Native American, 5% international
- 74% of applicants admitted
- SAT or ACT (ACT writing optional) required
- 43% graduate within 6 years

General. Founded in 1958. Regionally accredited. **Degrees:** 119 bachelor's awarded. **Location:** 40 miles from Fayetteville, 20 miles from Pinehurst. **Calendar:** Semester, limited summer session. **Full-time faculty:** 28 total; 57% have terminal degrees, 43% women. **Part-time faculty:** 27 total; 52% have terminal degrees, 7% minority, 37% women. **Class size:** 77% < 20, 22% 20-39, 1% 40-49. **Special facilities:** Psychology laboratory complex, equestrian facilities, nature preserve, electronic fine arts center.

Freshman class profile. 599 applied, 442 admitted, 142 enrolled.

Mid 50% test scores			
SAT critical reading:	410-530	GPA 3.0-3.49:	30%
SAT math:	420-550	GPA 2.0-2.99:	48%
SAT writing:	410-520	Rank in top quarter:	36%
ACT composite:	16-21	Rank in top tenth:	26%
GPA 3.75 or higher:	10%	Out-of-state:	60%
GPA 3.50-3.74:	10%	Live on campus:	95%
		International:	11%

Basis for selection. High school GPA, test scores, curriculum, type of high school very important. Recommendations important. Interview required for academically weak students, recommended for all other applicants. **Home schooled:** Transcript of courses and grades, state high school equivalency certificate required. Standardized test scores and interview required.

High school preparation. College-preparatory program recommended. Required units include English 3, mathematics 3, social studies 3, science 3 and foreign language 1.

2011-2012 Annual costs. Tuition/fees: $21,614. Room/board: $8,938. Books/supplies: $1,300. Personal expenses: $2,000.

2010-2011 Financial aid. Need-based: 102 full-time freshmen applied for aid; 83 were judged to have need; 82 of these received aid. Average need met was 67%. Average scholarship/grant was $15,142; average loan $3,546. 67% of total undergraduate aid awarded as scholarships/grants, 33% as loans/jobs. **Non-need-based:** Awarded to 181 full-time undergraduates, including 45 freshmen. Scholarships awarded for academics, alumni affiliation, art, athletics, leadership, music/drama.

Application procedures. Admission: Priority date 5/1; no deadline. $30 fee, may be waived for applicants with need. Admission notification on a rolling basis beginning on or about 8/15. Housing deposit fully refundable until May 1st. **Financial aid:** Priority date 5/1; no closing date. FAFSA required. Applicants notified on a rolling basis starting 10/1; must reply within 2 week(s) of notification.

Academics. Academic programs include St. Andrew's General Education. **Special study options:** Double major, honors, independent study, internships,

---

liberal arts/career combination, study abroad, teacher certification program. Courses offered abroad during winter or summer in Britain, Greece, India, Switzerland, Venezuela, China, Hawaii, former Soviet Union; exchange programs with Stirling University, Scotland and Kansai Gaidai University, Japan; study at Brunnenburg Castle, Italy, and Beijing Normal College of Foreign Languages. **Credit/placement by examination:** AP, CLEP, IB, institutional tests. 30 credit hours maximum toward bachelor's degree. **Support services:** Reduced course load, tutoring, writing center.

Majors. Area/ethnic studies: Asian. **Biology:** General. **Business:** General, business admin, international. **Communications:** Media studies. **Education:** Elementary, physical. **English:** Creative writing, English lit. **General:** Equestrian studies. **Health services:** Premedicine, preveterinary, recreational therapy. **History:** General, applied. **Liberal arts:** Arts/sciences. **Math:** General. **Parks/recreation:** Health/fitness. **Philosophy/religion:** Philosophy, religion. **Physical sciences:** Chemistry. **Psychology:** General. **Social sciences:** Political science. **Visual/performing arts:** General, art.

Most popular majors. Biology 7%, business/marketing 23%, education 15%, interdisciplinary studies 10%, parks/recreation 9%, psychology 6%, social sciences 6%.

Computing on campus. 100 workstations in library, computer center, student center. Dormitories wired for high-speed internet access and linked to campus network. Online library, repair service available.

Student life. Freshman orientation: Mandatory, $100 fee. Preregistration for classes offered. 3 days prior to start of fall term. **Policies:** Honor code enforced. **Housing:** Guaranteed on-campus for all undergraduates. Coed dorms, single-sex dorms available. $250 deposit, deadline 8/25. **Activities:** Choral groups, literary magazine, student government, student newspaper, Christian Student Fellowship, Black student union, women's issues group, writer's forum, world culture club, Eco-Action, student activities union.

Athletics. NAIA. **Intramural:** Basketball, bowling, racquetball, soccer, softball W, table tennis, volleyball. **Team name:** Knights.

Student services. Adult student services, alcohol/substance abuse counseling, career counseling, student employment services, financial aid counseling, health services, personal counseling, placement for graduates, women's services. **Physically disabled:** Services for visually, speech, hearing impaired.

Contact. E-mail: admissions@sapc.edu
Phone: (910) 277-5555 Toll-free number: (800) 763-0198
Fax: (910) 277-5087
Kirsten Simmons, Director of Admission, St. Andrews University, 1700 Dogwood Mile, Laurinburg, NC 28352

St. Augustine's College
Raleigh, North Carolina
www.st-aug.edu

CB member
CB code: 5596

- Private 4-year liberal arts college affiliated with Episcopal Church
- Residential campus in large city
- 1,506 degree-seeking undergraduates: 3% part-time, 49% women, 97% African American, 1% Hispanic American, 2% international
- 60% of applicants admitted
- SAT or ACT (ACT writing optional) required
- 32% graduate within 6 years

General. Founded in 1867. Regionally accredited. **Degrees:** 249 bachelor's awarded. **ROTC:** Army. **Location:** One mile from downtown. **Calendar:** Semester, limited summer session. **Full-time faculty:** 82 total; 50% have terminal degrees, 78% minority, 44% women. **Part-time faculty:** 57 total. **Class size:** 68% < 20, 30% 20-39, 2% 40-49, less than 1% 50-99. **Special facilities:** Archival collection tracing history of African-Americans in North Carolina and Delany family.

Freshman class profile. 3,209 applied, 1,928 admitted, 460 enrolled.

Mid 50% test scores			
SAT critical reading:	340-450	Rank in top tenth:	15%
SAT math:	330-420	Return as sophomores:	51%
ACT composite:	15-19	Out-of-state:	49%
Rank in top quarter:	44%	Live on campus:	95%
		International:	1%

Basis for selection. High school record (GPA and rank), standardized test scores and letters of recommendation reviewed. Institutionally administered Accuplacer test is used for pre- and post-testing evaluation and placement purposes. Essay recommended. Auditions and interviews required of music majors. **Home schooled:** Transcript of courses and grades required. **Learning Disabled:** Students must self-identify. ADA Coordinator will assess level of disability and arrange for student to access the needed equipment or tutorials.

High school preparation. College-preparatory program recommended. 20 units required. Required units include English 4, mathematics 3, social studies 2, science 2 and academic electives 9. One unit of algebra required, 2 units of laboratory recommended.

2011-2012 Annual costs. Tuition/fees: $17,160. Room/board: $7,340. Books/supplies: $1,500. Personal expenses: $4,080.

2010-2011 Financial aid. Need-based: 325 full-time freshmen applied for aid; 305 were judged to have need; 305 of these received aid. Average need met was 92%. Average scholarship/grant was $1,853; average loan $1,769. 62% of total undergraduate aid awarded as scholarships/grants, 38% as loans/jobs. **Non-need-based:** Awarded to 955 full-time undergraduates, including 255 freshmen. Scholarships awarded for academics, art, athletics, leadership, minority status, music/drama, religious affiliation, ROTC, state residency.

Application procedures. Admission: No deadline. $25 fee, may be waived for applicants with need. Application must be submitted online. Admission notification on a rolling basis beginning on or about 11/1. **Financial aid:** Closing date 3/15. FAFSA, institutional form required. Applicants notified on a rolling basis starting 5/1; must reply within 2 week(s) of notification.

Academics. Required Learning Community program for all new freshmen and transfers. First-year program includes skills enhancement, college survival tips. Community service requirement part of course. **Special study options:** Accelerated study, cooperative education, cross-registration, double major, dual enrollment of high school students, honors, independent study, internships, liberal arts/career combination, semester at sea, study abroad, teacher certification program, weekend college. **Credit/placement by examination:** AP, CLEP, IB, institutional tests. 15 credit hours maximum toward bachelor's degree. **Support services:** Learning center, pre-admission summer program, reduced course load, remedial instruction, study skills assistance, tutoring, writing center.

Majors. Area/ethnic studies: African-American. **Biology:** General, biomedical sciences. **Business:** Accounting, business admin, management science, real estate. **Communications:** Communications/speech/rhetoric. **Computer sciences:** General, computer science. **Education:** Elementary. **Engineering:** General. **English:** English lit. **Health services:** Occupational health, premedicine. **History:** General. **Liberal arts:** Arts/sciences. **Math:** General. **Parks/recreation:** Health/fitness, sports admin. **Philosophy/religion:** Religion. **Physical sciences:** Chemistry. **Protective services:** Criminal justice, forensics. **Psychology:** General. **Social sciences:** Political science, sociology. **Visual/performing arts:** General, art, cinematography, music performance.

Most popular majors. Business/marketing 27%, communications/journalism 8%, parks/recreation 18%, security/protective services 6%, social sciences 8%.

Computing on campus. 250 workstations in dormitories, library, computer center, student center. Dormitories wired for high-speed internet access and linked to campus network. Commuter students can connect to campus network. Online course registration, online library, helpline, repair service, wireless network available.

Student life. Freshman orientation: Mandatory, $75 fee. Preregistration for classes offered. 2-day orientations held in June, July, and August with students and parents. **Policies:** Smoking is not allowed within the administrative buildings and dorms. There is an alcohol, drug and firearm free policy. Students may be accountable to both civil authorities and to the College for their conduct. Freshmen not permitted cars on campus. **Housing:** Guaranteed on-campus for freshmen. Coed dorms, single-sex dorms, wellness housing available. $160 nonrefundable deposit, deadline 7/15. **Activities:** Bands, campus ministries, choral groups, dance, drama, film society, international student organizations, literary magazine, music ensembles, musical theater, radio station, student government, student newspaper, symphony orchestra, TV station, Christian Fellowship Organization, Young Democrats of America, Falcons for the Cause, NAACP, Foreign Language Club, Falcon Battalion/Army ROTC, Student Service Corps, SAC Association for Black Journalists, International Student Association, Latin American Students Organization.

Athletics. NCAA. **Intercollegiate:** Baseball M, basketball, bowling W, cheerleading M, cross-country, football (tackle) M, golf M, softball W, tennis, track and field, volleyball W. **Intramural:** Basketball, football (non-tackle). **Team name:** Falcons.

Student services. Adult student services, alcohol/substance abuse counseling, chaplain/spiritual director, career counseling, services for economically disadvantaged, student employment services, financial aid counseling, health services, minority student services, personal counseling, placement for graduates, veterans' counselor. **Physically disabled:** Services for visually, hearing impaired.

Contact. E-mail: admissions@st-aug.edu
Phone: (919) 516-4012 Toll-free number: (800) 948-1126
Fax: (919) 516-5805
Jorge Sousa, Director of Admissions, St. Augustine's College, 1315 Oakwood Avenue, Raleigh, NC 27610-2298

University of North Carolina at Asheville

Asheville, North Carolina   **CB member**
www.unca.edu   **CB code: 5013**

- Public 4-year university and liberal arts college
- Residential campus in small city
- 3,334 degree-seeking undergraduates: 10% part-time, 57% women, 3% African American, 1% Asian American, 4% Hispanic American, 1% international
- 47 degree-seeking graduate students
- 68% of applicants admitted
- SAT or ACT with writing, application essay required
- 61% graduate within 6 years; 20% enter graduate study

General. Founded in 1927. Regionally accredited. **Degrees:** 685 bachelor's awarded; master's offered. **Location:** 130 miles from Charlotte, 200 miles from Atlanta. **Calendar:** Semester, limited summer session. **Full-time faculty:** 211 total; 87% have terminal degrees, 15% minority, 45% women. **Part-time faculty:** 65 total; 40% have terminal degrees, 9% minority, 49% women. **Class size:** 53% < 20, 44% 20-39, 1% 40-49, 1% 50-99, less than 1% >100. **Special facilities:** Electronic music studio, North Carolina Center for Health and Wellness, Jewish studies center, distance learning facility, National Environmental Modeling and Analysis Center (NEMAC), Pisgah Astronomical Research Institute (PARI), National Climatic Data Center, botanical gardens.

Freshman class profile. 2,947 applied, 2,018 admitted, 540 enrolled.

Mid 50% test scores			
SAT critical reading:	540-640	Rank in top quarter:	55%
SAT math:	530-620	Rank in top tenth:	20%
SAT writing:	510-630	End year in good standing:	93%
ACT composite:	24-28	Return as sophomores:	81%
GPA 3.75 or higher:	73%	Out-of-state:	14%
GPA 3.50-3.74:	16%	Live on campus:	93%
GPA 3.0-3.49:	10%	Fraternities:	2%
GPA 2.0-2.99:	1%	Sororities:	3%

Basis for selection. GED not accepted. High school curriculum, GPA, and class rank (top third), most important. Test scores important. Counselor recommendation and essay question required. Interview, extracurricular activities that support academic achievement considered. Students expected to have completed advanced coursework. Personal statements helpful. Interviews recommended. **Home schooled:** Must provide a transcript documenting all courses taken, particularly UNC system minimum admissions requirements, units of credit received. Transcript must be signed by home school administrator, and notarized. For North Carolina residents, a copy of the school's registration with the North Carolina Department of Non-Public Instruction is required. **Learning Disabled:** Untimed SAT accepted.

High school preparation. College-preparatory program required. 15 units required. Required and recommended units include English 4, mathematics 4, social studies 1, history 1, science 3 (laboratory 1), foreign language 2 and academic electives 4. Science units should include biology and physical science such as chemistry or physics. One unit US history, 1 unit other social studies required. Math must include algebra I, II and geometry and 1 math course with algebra II as pre-requisite.

2011-2012 Annual costs. Tuition/fees: $5,393; $19,025 out-of-state. Room/board: $7,302. Books/supplies: $950. Personal expenses: $2,383.

2010-2011 Financial aid. Need-based: 482 full-time freshmen applied for aid; 314 were judged to have need; 312 of these received aid. Average need met was 83%. Average scholarship/grant was $7,009; average loan $3,066. 64% of total undergraduate aid awarded as scholarships/grants, 36% as loans/jobs. **Non-need-based:** Awarded to 465 full-time undergraduates, including 81 freshmen. Scholarships awarded for academics, alumni affiliation, art, athletics, job skills, leadership, minority status, music/drama, state residency.

Application procedures. Admission: Priority date 11/15; deadline 2/15 (postmark date). $50 fee, may be waived for applicants with need. Admission notification by 3/15. Admission notification on a rolling basis. Must reply by 5/1. **Financial aid:** Priority date 3/1; no closing date. FAFSA required. Applicants notified on a rolling basis starting 3/15.

Academics. Special study options: Cross-registration, distance learning, double major, dual enrollment of high school students, exchange student, honors, independent study, internships, liberal arts/career combination, semester at sea, student-designed major, study abroad, teacher certification program. **Credit/placement by examination:** AP, CLEP, IB, institutional tests. 30 credit hours maximum toward bachelor's degree. AP and CLEP exam grades required for credit are subject to change. **Support services:** Learning center, reduced course load, study skills assistance, tutoring, writing center.

Majors. Area/ethnic studies: Women's. **Biology:** General. **Business:** Accounting, business admin, operations. **Communications:** Media studies. **Computer sciences:** Computer science, web page design. **Conservation:** Environmental studies. **Engineering:** General. **English:** English lit. **Foreign languages:** Classics, French, German, Spanish. **Health services:** Public health ed. **History:** General. **Liberal arts:** Arts/sciences. **Math:** General. **Philosophy/religion:** Philosophy, religion. **Physical sciences:** Atmospheric science, chemistry, physics. **Psychology:** General. **Social sciences:** Anthropology, economics, political science, sociology. **Visual/performing arts:** Art, dramatic, music, music technology, studio arts.

Most popular majors. Business/marketing 12%, English 7%, health sciences 6%, psychology 14%, social sciences 11%, visual/performing arts 11%.

Computing on campus. 400 workstations in dormitories, library, computer center, student center. Dormitories wired for high-speed internet access and linked to campus network. Commuter students can connect to campus network. Online course registration, online library, helpline, repair service, student web hosting, wireless network available.

Student life. Freshman orientation: Mandatory, $55 fee. Preregistration for classes offered. 2-day program for incoming freshmen held in June; 1-day program for transfer students held in June and August. Additional 3-day orientation plus 1-day transfer orientation conducted immediately prior to the start of classes. **Housing:** Guaranteed on-campus for freshmen. Coed dorms, single-sex dorms, special housing for disabled available. $150 deposit, deadline 5/1. 24-hour quiet, substance free floors available. **Activities:** Bands, campus ministries, choral groups, dance, drama, international student organizations, literary magazine, music ensembles, musical theater, radio station, student government, student newspaper, Baptist Student Union, International Student Association, InterVarsity Christian Fellowship, Black Student Association, Campus Crusade for Christ, Active Students for a Healthy Environment, University Ambassadors, Jewish Student Association, Asian Students in Asheville, Students for a Democratic Society.

Athletics. NCAA. **Intercollegiate:** Baseball M, basketball, cheerleading, cross-country, soccer, tennis, track and field, volleyball W. **Intramural:** Badminton, basketball, football (non-tackle), racquetball, soccer, tennis, volleyball, water polo. **Team name:** Bulldogs.

Student services. Adult student services, alcohol/substance abuse counseling, chaplain/spiritual director, career counseling, student employment services, financial aid counseling, health services, minority student services, personal counseling, placement for graduates, veterans' counselor, women's services. **Physically disabled:** Services for visually, hearing impaired.

Contact. E-mail: admissions@unca.edu
Phone: (828) 251-6481 Toll-free number: (800) 531-9842
Fax: (828) 251-6482
Patrice Mitchell, Dean of Admissions and Financial Aid, University of North Carolina at Asheville, CPO#1320, UNCA, Asheville, NC 28804-8502

University of North Carolina at Chapel Hill
Chapel Hill, North Carolina   **CB member**
www.unc.edu   **CB code: 5816**

- Public 4-year university
- Residential campus in large town
- 17,791 degree-seeking undergraduates: 2% part-time, 58% women, 9% African American, 7% Asian American, 9% Hispanic American, 1% Native American, 3% international
- 9,650 degree-seeking graduate students
- 33% of applicants admitted
- SAT or ACT with writing, application essay required
- 90% graduate within 6 years; 26% enter graduate study

General. Founded in 1789. Regionally accredited. **Degrees:** 4,596 bachelor's awarded; master's, professional, doctoral offered. **ROTC:** Army, Naval, Air Force. **Location:** 8 miles from Durham, 26 miles from Raleigh. **Calendar:** Semester, extensive summer session. **Full-time faculty:** 1,671 total; 90% have terminal degrees, 24% minority, 43% women. **Part-time faculty:** 139

total; 67% have terminal degrees, 9% minority, 48% women. **Class size:** 34% < 20, 44% 20-39, 9% 40-49, 7% 50-99, 7% >100. **Special facilities:** Planetarium, observatory, arboretum, botanical garden, art museum.

Freshman class profile. 22,652 applied, 7,469 admitted, 4,026 enrolled.

Mid 50% test scores		Rank in top quarter:	97%
SAT critical reading:	590-700	Rank in top tenth:	80%
SAT math:	610-700	End year in good standing:	99%
SAT writing:	590-690	Return as sophomores:	97%
ACT composite:	27-32	Out-of-state:	17%
GPA 3.75 or higher:	95%	Live on campus:	100%
GPA 3.50-3.74:	3%	International:	2%
GPA 3.0-3.49:	1%	Fraternities:	14%
GPA 2.0-2.99:	1%	Sororities:	14%

Basis for selection. GED not accepted. High school record, including course selection and performance, very important. Test scores, essays, activities, and recommendations also receive strong consideration. Separate consideration given to out-of-state children of alumni. Audition required for drama and music programs; portfolio recommended for art program. **Home schooled:** SAT Subject Tests recommended. Students should follow curriculum equivalent to that of high school students taking Advanced Placement and honors courses. **Learning Disabled:** Students may voluntarily supply documentation regarding disability and impact on educational experiences with application.

High school preparation. College-preparatory program required. 16 units required. Required units include English 4, mathematics 4, social studies 1, history 1, science 3 (laboratory 1), foreign language 2 and academic electives 1. History course must be U.S. history. Both foreign language units must be for the same language.

2011-2012 Annual costs. Tuition/fees: $7,008; $26,834 out-of-state. Room/board: $9,470.

2010-2011 Financial aid. Need-based: 2,775 full-time freshmen applied for aid; 1,649 were judged to have need; 1,649 of these received aid. Average need met was 100%. Average scholarship/grant was $12,901; average loan $3,293. 79% of total undergraduate aid awarded as scholarships/grants, 21% as loans/jobs. **Non-need-based:** Awarded to 1,454 full-time undergraduates, including 359 freshmen. Scholarships awarded for academics, alumni affiliation, art, athletics, leadership, music/drama, religious affiliation, state residency. **Additional information:** Carolina meets 100% of all need documented for both resident and non-resident undergraduates who quality for need based aid, with a favorable mix of approximately 2/3 grants and scholarships and 1/3 loans and work study. No-loan program for qualifying low-income students (whether in-state or out-of-state) where the family's adjusted gross income does not exceed 200% of the federal poverty standard, indexed by family size.

Application procedures. Admission: Closing date 1/5 (postmark date). $80 fee, may be waived for applicants with need. Notification on or around 1/31 for early notification; on or around 3/31 for regular notification. Must reply by 5/1. **Financial aid:** Priority date 3/1; no closing date. FAFSA, CSS PROFILE required. Applicants notified on a rolling basis starting 3/15; must reply by 5/1.

Academics. Entering first-year students are required to own laptop meeting university specifications, as a part of the Carolina Computing Initiative; qualified students will receive special loans or grants. **Special study options:** Combined bachelor's/graduate degree, cross-registration, distance learning, double major, dual enrollment of high school students, honors, independent study, internships, student-designed major, study abroad, teacher certification program, Washington semester. **Credit/placement by examination:** AP, CLEP, IB, SAT, ACT, institutional tests. Credit by examination is non-transferable. **Support services:** Learning center, pre-admission summer program, reduced course load, study skills assistance, tutoring, writing center.

Honors college/program. Students chosen based on academic merits, intellectual curiosity, and desire to embrace challenges and solve problems. Honors Carolina offers over 100 Honors courses each year in disciplines across the College of Arts & Sciences. Nearly all of these courses fulfill some General Education requirement. Honors Carolina students are required to complete the same General Education requirements as other students. To remain members in good standing of Honors Carolina, they must also take at least two Honors courses per academic year and maintain at least a 3.0 cumulative grade point average. In Fall 2011, 300 incoming first year students were invited to participate.

Majors. Area/ethnic studies: African-American, American, Asian, European, Latin American, women's. **Biology:** General, biostatistics, pathology. **Business:** Business admin, human resources. **Communications:** Communications/speech/rhetoric, media studies. **Computer sciences:** Computer science, information systems. **Conservation:** Environmental science, environmental studies. **Education:** Early childhood, elementary, middle. **English:** English lit. **Foreign languages:** Classics, comparative lit, German, linguistics, Romance, Slavic. **Health services:** Clinical lab science, dental hygiene,

environmental health, health care admin, medical radiologic technology/radiation therapy, nursing (RN), pharmaceutical sciences. **History:** General. **Human services:** Public policy. **Liberal arts:** Arts/sciences. **Math:** General, applied. **Parks/recreation:** Facilities management, health/fitness. **Philosophy/religion:** Philosophy, religion. **Physical sciences:** Chemistry, geology, physics. **Psychology:** General. **Social sciences:** Anthropology, archaeology, economics, geography, political science, sociology. **Visual/performing arts:** Art history/conservation, dramatic, music, music performance, studio arts. **Work/family studies:** Food/nutrition.

Most popular majors. Area/ethnic studies 7%, biology 8%, business/marketing 8%, communications/journalism 11%, health sciences 7%, psychology 8%, social sciences 17%.

Computing on campus. PC or laptop required. 800 workstations in dormitories, library, computer center, student center. Dormitories wired for high-speed internet access and linked to campus network. Commuter students can connect to campus network. Online course registration, online library, helpline, repair service, student web hosting, wireless network available.

Student life. Freshman orientation: Mandatory, $210 fee. Preregistration for classes offered. Two-day sessions held throughout June, July, and August; includes parent/family orientation. **Policies:** Policies exist regarding: illegal drugs, honor code, student organizations, non-discrimination policy, no smoking policy, student possession and consumption of alcoholic beverages in facilities, harassment, facilities use policy, student grievance policy, and FERPA. Freshmen not permitted cars on campus. **Housing:** Guaranteed on-campus for freshmen. Coed dorms, single-sex dorms, special housing for disabled, apartments, fraternity/sorority housing, wellness housing available. Special options: living-learning communities such as language houses (Spanish and Chinese), The Carolina Experience (1st year emphasis), W.E.L.L. (Women Experiencing Learning and Leadership), substance free environments, sustainability, UNITAS (exploring cultural differences), SYNC (Sophomore Year Navigating Carolina) available. **Activities:** Bands, campus ministries, choral groups, dance, drama, film society, international student organizations, literary magazine, music ensembles, Model UN, musical theater, opera, radio station, student government, student newspaper, symphony orchestra, TV station, Alpha Phi Omega co-ed service fraternity, Asian students association, Black Student Movement, Campus Crusade for Christ, College Republicans, Habitat for Humanity, Young Democrats.

Athletics. NCAA. **Intercollegiate:** Baseball M, basketball, cross-country, diving, fencing, field hockey W, football (tackle) M, golf, gymnastics W, lacrosse, rowing (crew) W, soccer, softball W, swimming, tennis, track and field, volleyball W, wrestling M. **Intramural:** Badminton, basketball, football (non-tackle), golf, racquetball, soccer, softball, swimming, table tennis, tennis, triathlon, volleyball, water polo. **Team name:** Tarheels.

Student services. Alcohol/substance abuse counseling, chaplain/spiritual director, career counseling, student employment services, financial aid counseling, health services, legal services, minority student services, personal counseling, placement for graduates, veterans' counselor, women's services. **Physically disabled:** Services for visually, speech, hearing impaired.

Contact. E-mail: unchelp@admissions.unc.edu
Phone: (919) 966-3621 Fax: (919) 962-3045
Stephen Farmer, Vice Provost for Enrollment and Undergraduate Admissions, University of North Carolina at Chapel Hill, Jackson Hall, Chapel Hill, NC 27599-2200

University of North Carolina at Charlotte
Charlotte, North Carolina CB member
www.uncc.edu CB code: 5105

- Public 4-year university
- Residential campus in very large city
- 20,179 degree-seeking undergraduates: 15% part-time, 50% women, 17% African American, 5% Asian American, 6% Hispanic American, 1% Native American, 3% international
- 3,739 degree-seeking graduate students
- 70% of applicants admitted
- SAT or ACT with writing required
- 55% graduate within 6 years

General. Founded in 1946. Regionally accredited. **Degrees:** 3,795 bachelor's awarded; master's, doctoral offered. **ROTC:** Army, Air Force. **Location:** 8 miles from downtown. **Calendar:** Semester, limited summer session. **Full-time faculty:** 1,003 total; 85% have terminal degrees, 17% minority, 43% women. **Part-time faculty:** 365 total; 30% have terminal degrees, 13% minority, 57% women. **Class size:** 26% < 20, 41% 20-39, 11% 40-49, 15% 50-99, 7% >100. **Special facilities:** Bioinformatics research center, center

for performing arts, proscenium-style theater, lab theater, 200,000-square-foot student union.

Freshman class profile. 12,306 applied, 8,570 admitted, 3,169 enrolled.

Mid 50% test scores			
SAT critical reading:	420-640	Rank in top quarter:	53%
SAT math:	450-670	Rank in top tenth:	19%
SAT writing:	410-650	End year in good standing:	80%
ACT composite:	19-29	Return as sophomores:	77%
GPA 3.75 or higher:	44%	Out-of-state:	10%
GPA 3.50-3.74:	19%	Live on campus:	75%
GPA 3.0-3.49:	29%	International:	2%
GPA 2.0-2.99:	8%	Fraternities:	15%
		Sororities:	22%

Basis for selection. Overall performance in high school academic courses and SAT scores considered. SAT preferred, but ACT also accepted. An audition is required for music, an interview required for art, architecture, and music programs. A portfolio is also required for art and architecture programs. **Learning Disabled:** Students can submit documentation of their learning disability in the admissions process if they choose to disclose.

High school preparation. College-preparatory program required. 16 units required. Required and recommended units include English 4, mathematics 4, social studies 1, history 1, science 3 (laboratory 1), foreign language 2-3, computer science 1 and academic electives 1. English should emphasize grammar, composition & literature; science should include at least 1 unit in a life or biological science and at least 1 unit in a physical science and 1 lab; foreign language units should be in same language. 2 social studies unit includes 1 U.S. history. Health education and a computer course are also recommended.

2011-2012 Annual costs. Tuition/fees: $5,440; $17,205 out-of-state. Room/board: $7,742. Books/supplies: $1,200. Personal expenses: $1,500.

2010-2011 Financial aid. Need-based: 2,333 full-time freshmen applied for aid; 1,723 were judged to have need; 1,682 of these received aid. Average need met was 73%. Average scholarship/grant was $6,802; average loan $3,116. 50% of total undergraduate aid awarded as scholarships/grants, 50% as loans/jobs. **Non-need-based:** Awarded to 1,143 full-time undergraduates, including 180 freshmen. Scholarships awarded for academics, athletics, music/drama, state residency.

Application procedures. Admission: Closing date 7/1 (postmark date). $50 fee, may be waived for applicants with need. Admission notification by 5/1. Admission notification on a rolling basis. Must reply by May 1 or within 2 week(s) if notified thereafter. **Financial aid:** Priority date 3/1; no closing date. FAFSA required. Applicants notified on a rolling basis starting 3/1; must reply within 3 week(s) of notification.

Academics. Special study options: Accelerated study, cooperative education, cross-registration, distance learning, double major, dual enrollment of high school students, ESL, honors, independent study, internships, study abroad, teacher certification program, Washington semester, weekend college. Wilderness exploration program. **Credit/placement by examination:** AP, CLEP, IB, institutional tests. 30 credit hours maximum toward bachelor's degree. **Support services:** Learning center, pre-admission summer program, reduced course load, study skills assistance, tutoring, writing center.

Honors college/program. A minimum 3.0 GPA or high school rank and SAT scores predictive of 3.0 GPA. Potential freshmen must submit a 2-3 page essay describing educational goals and objectives, as well as one letter of recommendation from a person who can address potential for success in Honors Program. A brief interview may be scheduled.

Majors. Architecture: Architecture. **Area/ethnic studies:** African-American, Latin American, women's. **Biology:** General. **Business:** Accounting, business admin, finance, international, management information systems, managerial economics, marketing, operations. **Communications:** Communications/speech/rhetoric, organizational. **Computer sciences:** Computer science. **Education:** Art, drama/dance, elementary, English, kindergarten/preschool, mathematics, middle, music, special ed. **Engineering:** Civil, computer, electrical, mechanical, systems. **English:** English lit. **Foreign languages:** French, German, Japanese, Spanish. **Health services:** Athletic training, clinical lab science, nursing (RN), public health ed, respiratory therapy technology. **History:** General. **Human services:** Social work. **Math:** General. **Parks/recreation:** Health/fitness. **Philosophy/religion:** Philosophy, religion. **Physical sciences:** Chemistry, geology, meteorology, physics. **Protective services:** Criminal justice, fire services admin. **Psychology:** General. **Social sciences:** Anthropology, economics, geography, political science, sociology. **Visual/performing arts:** Art, art history/conservation, dance, dramatic, music, music performance, studio arts. **Work/family studies:** Family studies.

Most popular majors. Business/marketing 20%, education 17%, engineering/engineering technologies 10%, health sciences 7%, social sciences 6%.

Computing on campus. 1,500 workstations in dormitories, library, computer center, student center. Dormitories wired for high-speed internet access and linked to campus network. Commuter students can connect to campus network. Online course registration, online library, helpline, repair service, student web hosting, wireless network available.

Student life. Freshman orientation: Available, $85 fee. Preregistration for classes offered. 2-day program for freshmen and parents. Parents fee $32. **Policies:** Students must follow a code of student responsibility, code of student academic integrity, and university policy statements. **Housing:** Coed dorms, single-sex dorms, special housing for disabled, apartments, fraternity/sorority housing, wellness housing available. $200 fully refundable deposit. Housing for disabled students is limited. Suite housing, honors housing, learning communities, and Greek village housing is available. **Activities:** Bands, campus ministries, choral groups, dance, drama, international student organizations, literary magazine, music ensembles, Model UN, musical theater, opera, radio station, student government, student newspaper, symphony orchestra, TV station, Campus Crusade for Christ, Hillel, College Democrats, College Republicans, Feminist union, Black student union, Latin American student organization, Muslim student association, Native American student organization, Asian student union.

Athletics. NCAA. **Intercollegiate:** Baseball M, basketball, cross-country, golf M, soccer, softball W, tennis, track and field, volleyball W. **Intramural:** Badminton, basketball, bowling, field hockey, football (non-tackle), golf, handball, lacrosse, racquetball, rugby, soccer, softball, swimming, table tennis, tennis, track and field, volleyball, water polo. **Team name:** Fortyniners.

Student services. Adult student services, alcohol/substance abuse counseling, chaplain/spiritual director, career counseling, services for economically disadvantaged, student employment services, financial aid counseling, health services, minority student services, personal counseling, placement for graduates, veterans' counselor, women's services. **Physically disabled:** Services for visually, speech, hearing impaired.

Contact. E-mail: unccadm@uncc.edu
Phone: (704) 687-2213 Fax: (704) 687-6483
Claire Kirby, Director of Admissions, University of North Carolina at Charlotte, Undergraduate Admissions- Cato Hall, Charlotte, NC 28223-0001

University of North Carolina at Greensboro
Greensboro, North Carolina — **CB member**
www.uncg.edu — **CB code: 5913**

- Public 4-year university
- Residential campus in large city
- 14,554 degree-seeking undergraduates
- SAT or ACT with writing required

General. Founded in 1891. Regionally accredited. **Degrees:** 2,762 bachelor's awarded; master's, doctoral offered. **ROTC:** Army, Air Force. **Location:** 90 miles from Raleigh. **Calendar:** Semester, extensive summer session. **Full-time faculty:** 838 total; 73% have terminal degrees, 14% minority, 50% women. **Part-time faculty:** 347 total; 39% have terminal degrees, 12% minority, 62% women. **Class size:** 41% < 20, 41% 20-39, 5% 40-49, 10% 50-99, 3% >100. **Special facilities:** Weatherspoon art museum, Silva cello music collection, Randall Jarrell collection, women's studies collection.

Freshman class profile.

GPA 3.75 or higher:	42%	Rank in top quarter:	48%
GPA 3.50-3.74:	20%	Rank in top tenth:	18%
GPA 3.0-3.49:	32%	Out-of-state:	8%
GPA 2.0-2.99:	6%	Live on campus:	81%

Basis for selection. GED not accepted. Combined test scores and high school GPA based on academic courses most important. High school recommendations and activities considered. SAT preferred, but ACT accepted. Audition required for music program.

High school preparation. College-preparatory program recommended. 15 units required. Required units include English 4, mathematics 4, social studies 2, science 3 (laboratory 1) and foreign language 2.

2011-2012 Annual costs. Tuition/fees: $5,493; $18,018 out-of-state. Room/board: $7,210. Books/supplies: $1,282. Personal expenses: $2,196.

Financial aid. Non-need-based: Scholarships awarded for academics, alumni affiliation, art, athletics, leadership, music/drama, state residency.

Application procedures. Admission: Priority date 11/1; deadline 3/1 (postmark date). $45 fee, may be waived for applicants with need. Application must be submitted on paper. Admission notification on a rolling basis beginning on or about 3/1. Must reply by May 1 or within 4 week(s) if notified thereafter. **Financial aid:** Priority date 3/1; no closing date. FAFSA required. Applicants notified on a rolling basis starting 3/15; must reply within 3 week(s) of notification.

Academics. Special study options: Accelerated study, combined bachelor's/graduate degree, cross-registration, distance learning, double major, dual enrollment of high school students, honors, independent study, internships, study abroad, teacher certification program, Washington semester. **Credit/placement by examination:** AP, CLEP, IB, institutional tests. Up to 64 semester hours of any combination of transfer, correspondence, examination or other will be accepted. SAT Subject Test scores in some subjects may qualify for credit. **Support services:** Learning center, reduced course load, remedial instruction, study skills assistance, tutoring, writing center.

Majors. Area/ethnic studies: African-American, women's. **Biology:** General, biochemistry. **Business:** Accounting, business admin, finance, hospitality admin, international, managerial economics. **Communications:** Communications/speech/rhetoric, media studies. **Computer sciences:** Computer science, networking. **Education:** Art, biology, Deaf/hearing impaired, drama/dance, early childhood, elementary, English, French, mathematics, middle, music, physical, social science, social studies, Spanish, special ed. **English:** English lit. **Foreign languages:** Classics, French, German, Spanish. **Health services:** Audiology/speech pathology, clinical lab science, nursing (RN), public health ed. **History:** General. **Human services:** Social work. **Liberal arts:** Arts/sciences. **Math:** General. **Parks/recreation:** General, exercise sciences. **Philosophy/religion:** Philosophy, religion. **Physical sciences:** Chemistry, physics. **Psychology:** General. **Social sciences:** Anthropology, economics, geography, political science, sociology. **Visual/performing arts:** Art, dance, dramatic, interior design, jazz, music, music performance, music theory/composition, studio arts. **Work/family studies:** Child development, clothing/textiles, family studies.

Most popular majors. Business/marketing 15%, education 12%, English 9%, health sciences 10%, social sciences 9%, visual/performing arts 9%.

Computing on campus. 600 workstations in dormitories, library, computer center, student center. Dormitories wired for high-speed internet access and linked to campus network. Commuter students can connect to campus network. Online course registration, online library, helpline, wireless network available.

Student life. Freshman orientation: Mandatory. Preregistration for classes offered. 2-day sessions held prior to beginning of fall and spring semesters. **Housing:** Coed dorms, single-sex dorms, special housing for disabled, apartments, fraternity/sorority housing, wellness housing available. $200 fully refundable deposit, deadline 5/1. Residential college (academic/residential program), International House available. **Activities:** Bands, campus ministries, choral groups, dance, drama, film society, international student organizations, literary magazine, music ensembles, Model UN, musical theater, opera, radio station, student government, student newspaper, symphony orchestra, neo-Black society, environmental awareness foundation, political awareness club, Habitat for Humanity, Rotaract Club, gay, lesbian and bisexual student association.

Athletics. NCAA. **Intercollegiate:** Baseball M, basketball, cross-country, golf, soccer, softball W, tennis, volleyball W. **Intramural:** Badminton, basketball, bowling, golf, racquetball, soccer, softball, swimming, table tennis, tennis, track and field, volleyball. **Team name:** Spartans.

Student services. Adult student services, chaplain/spiritual director, career counseling, student employment services, financial aid counseling, health services, minority student services, personal counseling, placement for graduates, veterans' counselor. **Physically disabled:** Services for visually, speech, hearing impaired.

Contact. E-mail: admissions@uncg.edu
Phone: (336) 334-5243 Fax: (336) 334-4180
Lise Keller, Director of Admissions, University of North Carolina at Greensboro, 1400 Spring Garden Street, Greensboro, NC 27402-6170

University of North Carolina at Pembroke
Pembroke, North Carolina — **CB member**
www.uncp.edu — **CB code: 5534**

- Public 4-year university and liberal arts college
- Commuter campus in small town
- 5,289 degree-seeking undergraduates: 18% part-time, 61% women, 32% African American, 2% Asian American, 5% Hispanic American, 15% Native American, 1% international
- 725 degree-seeking graduate students
- 70% of applicants admitted

◗ SAT or ACT with writing required
◗ 38% graduate within 6 years

General. Founded in 1887. Regionally accredited. **Degrees:** 824 bachelor's awarded; master's offered. **ROTC:** Army, Air Force. **Location:** 31 miles from Fayetteville, 100 miles from Raleigh. **Calendar:** Semester, limited summer session. **Full-time faculty:** 319 total; 74% have terminal degrees, 24% minority, 47% women. **Part-time faculty:** 67 total; 31% have terminal degrees, 22% minority, 45% women. **Class size:** 46% < 20, 47% 20-39, 5% 40-49, 2% 50-99. **Special facilities:** Native American resource center, performing arts center.

Freshman class profile. 3,316 applied, 2,316 admitted, 1,028 enrolled.

Mid 50% test scores			
SAT critical reading:	410-490	GPA 3.50-3.74:	14%
SAT math:	430-510	GPA 3.0-3.49:	33%
SAT writing:	390-470	GPA 2.0-2.99:	33%
ACT composite:	17-20	Rank in top quarter:	34%
GPA 3.75 or higher:	20%	Rank in top tenth:	11%
		Out-of-state:	5%

Basis for selection. High school record, class standing, GPA, test scores, and college preparatory courses important. Auditions and interviews may be required for acceptance to obtain entry into certain programs.

High school preparation. College-preparatory program required. 15 units required. Required units include English 4, mathematics 4, social studies 1, history 1, science 3 (laboratory 1) and foreign language 2.

2011-2012 Annual costs. Tuition/fees: $4,668; $13,875 out-of-state. Room/board: $6,830. Books/supplies: $1,200. Personal expenses: $1,211.

2011-2012 Financial aid. Need-based: 913 full-time freshmen applied for aid; 765 were judged to have need; 748 of these received aid. Average need met was 80%. Average scholarship/grant was $6,656; average loan $3,341. 52% of total undergraduate aid awarded as scholarships/grants, 48% as loans/jobs. Non-need-based: Awarded to 240 full-time undergraduates, including 95 freshmen. Scholarships awarded for academics, alumni affiliation, art, athletics, music/drama.

Application procedures. Admission: Priority date 7/15; deadline 7/31. $45 fee, may be waived for applicants with need. Admission notification on a rolling basis beginning on or about 9/15. Financial aid: Priority date 3/15; no closing date. FAFSA required. Applicants notified on a rolling basis starting 4/15; must reply within 2 week(s) of notification.

Academics. Certification on secondary teaching level in English, biology, mathematics, social studies, and science education. **Special study options:** Accelerated study, cooperative education, cross-registration, distance learning, double major, dual enrollment of high school students, ESL, exchange student, external degree, honors, independent study, internships, study abroad, teacher certification program, Washington semester. **Credit/placement by examination:** AP, CLEP, SAT, ACT, institutional tests. 30 credit hours maximum toward bachelor's degree. **Support services:** Learning center, pre-admission summer program, reduced course load, remedial instruction, tutoring, writing center.

Honors college/program. Students selected based on academic achievement, leadership, and community involvement. SAT score of 1150 and GPA above 3.5 required. Approximately 35 students are chosen yearly to participate. Academic program offers interdisciplinary educational opportunities that enhance the general curriculum as well as social and cultural opportunities.

Majors. Area/ethnic studies: American, Native American. **Biology:** General, biotechnology. **Business:** Accounting, business admin. **Communications:** Media studies. **Computer sciences:** Computer science, information technology. **Conservation:** Environmental science. **Education:** Art, elementary, English, kindergarten/preschool, mathematics, middle, music, physical, science, social studies, special ed. **English:** English lit. **Foreign languages:** Spanish. **Health services:** Athletic training, nursing (RN). **History:** General. **Human services:** Social work. **Math:** General. **Parks/recreation:** Health/fitness. **Physical sciences:** Chemistry, physics. **Protective services:** Criminal justice. **Psychology:** General. **Social sciences:** Political science, sociology. **Visual/performing arts:** Dramatic, music, music performance, studio arts.

Most popular majors. Biology 9%, business/marketing 14%, communications/journalism 6%, education 12%, health sciences 6%, parks/recreation 10%, psychology 6%, security/protective services 7%, social sciences 11%.

Computing on campus. 875 workstations in dormitories, library, computer center, student center. Dormitories wired for high-speed internet access and linked to campus network. Commuter students can connect to campus network. Online course registration, online library, helpline, wireless network available.

Student life. Freshman orientation: Mandatory, $50 fee. Preregistration for classes offered. 3-day orientation session held in Fall, Spring, Summer with campus tours, advising. **Housing:** Coed dorms, single-sex dorms, apartments available. $150 fully refundable deposit, deadline 5/1. Freshmen given preference for on-campus housing. Apartments available. **Activities:** Bands, campus ministries, choral groups, dance, drama, international student organizations, literary magazine, music ensembles, Model UN, musical theater, radio station, student government, student newspaper, TV station, Native American Organization, African American Student Organization, Baptist Student Union, Methodist Campus Ministry, Fellowship of Christian Athletes, Campus Association of Social Workers, American Medical Student Association, criminal justice club.

Athletics. NCAA. **Intercollegiate:** Baseball M, basketball, cheerleading, cross-country, football (tackle) M, golf, soccer, softball W, tennis W, track and field, volleyball W, wrestling M. **Intramural:** Basketball, football (non-tackle) M, racquetball, softball, volleyball, wrestling M. **Team name:** Braves.

Student services. Alcohol/substance abuse counseling, chaplain/spiritual director, career counseling, student employment services, financial aid counseling, health services, personal counseling, veterans' counselor. **Physically disabled:** Services for visually, hearing impaired.

Contact. E-mail: admissons@uncp.edu
Phone: (910) 521-6262 Toll-free number: (800) 949-8627
Fax: (910) 521-6497
Lela Clark, Director of Admissions, University of North Carolina at Pembroke, Box 1510, Pembroke, NC 28372

University of North Carolina at Wilmington
Wilmington, North Carolina　　　　　　　**CB member**
www.uncw.edu　　　　　　　　　　　　　**CB code: 5907**

◗ Public 4-year university
◗ Residential campus in small city
◗ 11,631 degree-seeking undergraduates: 11% part-time, 60% women, 4% African American, 2% Asian American, 5% Hispanic American, 1% Native American, 1% international
◗ 1,220 degree-seeking graduate students
◗ 53% of applicants admitted
◗ SAT or ACT with writing, application essay required
◗ 66% graduate within 6 years

General. Founded in 1947. Regionally accredited. **Degrees:** 2,639 bachelor's awarded; master's, doctoral offered. **Location:** 125 miles from Raleigh. **Calendar:** Semester, extensive summer session. **Full-time faculty:** 602 total; 86% have terminal degrees, 18% minority, 46% women. **Part-time faculty:** 362 total; 35% have terminal degrees, 28% minority, 60% women. **Class size:** 32% < 20, 55% 20-39, 6% 40-49, 6% 50-99, less than 1% >100. **Special facilities:** Undersea laboratory-Aquarius, 108-acre coastal forest research and teaching station, 10-acre wildflower preserve, oyster hatchery.

Freshman class profile. 10,339 applied, 5,471 admitted, 1,980 enrolled.

Mid 50% test scores			
SAT critical reading:	540-620	Rank in top quarter:	65%
SAT math:	550-630	Rank in top tenth:	26%
SAT writing:	520-600	End year in good standing:	96%
ACT composite:	22-27	Out-of-state:	17%
GPA 3.75 or higher:	72%	Live on campus:	91%
GPA 3.50-3.74:	15%	International:	1%
GPA 3.0-3.49:	12%	Fraternities:	11%
GPA 2.0-2.99:	1%	Sororities:	7%

Basis for selection. High school record; rank in class, if provided; standardized test scores; and rigor of courses completed in high school are very important. SAT or ACT with writing required. Auditions for Music majors required. **Home schooled:** Statement describing home school structure and mission, transcript of courses and grades, letter of recommendation (nonparent) required.

High school preparation. College-preparatory program required. Required units include English 4, mathematics 4, social studies 1, history 1, science 3 (laboratory 1) and foreign language 2. History must be US History.

2011-2012 Annual costs. Tuition/fees: $5,672; $17,492 out-of-state. Room/board: $7,900. Books/supplies: $985. Personal expenses: $1,323.

2010-2011 Financial aid. Need-based: 1,466 full-time freshmen applied for aid; 935 were judged to have need; 887 of these received aid. Average need met was 78%. Average scholarship/grant was $6,692; average loan $3,027. 56% of total undergraduate aid awarded as scholarships/grants, 44% as loans/jobs. Non-need-based: Awarded to 1,491 full-time undergraduates,

including 343 freshmen. Scholarships awarded for academics, art, athletics, leadership, minority status, music/drama, state residency.

Application procedures. Admission: Priority date 11/1; deadline 2/1 (postmark date). $60 fee, may be waived for applicants with need. Admission notification on a rolling basis beginning on or about 4/1. Must reply by May 1 or within 4 week(s) if notified thereafter. **Financial aid:** Priority date 3/1; no closing date. FAFSA required. Applicants notified on a rolling basis starting 3/15; must reply within 3 week(s) of notification.

Academics. Special study options: Accelerated study, cooperative education, cross-registration, distance learning, double major, dual enrollment of high school students, ESL, exchange student, honors, independent study, internships, study abroad, teacher certification program. 2+2 Pre-Engineering programs. **Credit/placement by examination:** AP, CLEP, IB, SAT, institutional tests. **Support services:** Learning center, reduced course load, remedial instruction, study skills assistance, tutoring, writing center.

Honors college/program. 126 students admitted. Average SAT is 1310 (exclusive of Writing) and average weighted high school GPA is 3.9.

Majors. Biology: General, marine. **Business:** Accounting, business admin, finance, management information systems, managerial economics, marketing. **Communications:** Communications/speech/rhetoric. **Computer sciences:** Computer science. **Conservation:** Environmental science, environmental studies. **Education:** Biology, chemistry, elementary, emotionally handicapped, English, French, German, history, kindergarten/preschool, learning disabled, mathematics, mentally handicapped, middle, multiple handicapped, music, physical, Spanish, special ed. **English:** Creative writing, English lit. **Foreign languages:** French, German, Spanish. **Health services:** Athletic training, nursing (RN), public health ed, recreational therapy. **History:** General. **Human services:** Social work. **Math:** General, statistics. **Parks/recreation:** Facilities management, health/fitness. **Philosophy/religion:** Philosophy, religion. **Physical sciences:** Chemistry, geology, physics. **Protective services:** Criminal justice. **Psychology:** General. **Social sciences:** Anthropology, economics, geography, political science, sociology. **Visual/performing arts:** Art history/conservation, cinematography, dramatic, music, music performance, studio arts.

Most popular majors. Biology 8%, business/marketing 22%, communications/journalism 8%, education 9%, health sciences 7%, psychology 9%, social sciences 10%.

Computing on campus. 1,675 workstations in dormitories, library, computer center, student center. Dormitories wired for high-speed internet access and linked to campus network. Commuter students can connect to campus network. Online course registration, online library, helpline, repair service, student web hosting, wireless network available.

Student life. Freshman orientation: Mandatory, $130 fee. Preregistration for classes offered. **Housing:** Coed dorms, single-sex dorms, special housing for disabled, apartments, fraternity/sorority housing, wellness housing available. $105 nonrefundable deposit, deadline 5/1. **Activities:** Bands, campus ministries, choral groups, dance, drama, film society, international student organizations, literary magazine, music ensembles, Model UN, radio station, student government, student newspaper, symphony orchestra, TV station, Upperman African-American Cultural Center, surf club, Young Life, screenwriters club, High Seas A capella, Hillel, Amnesty International, PRIDE, student veteran's organization, environmental concerns organization.

Athletics. NCAA. **Intercollegiate:** Baseball M, basketball, cheerleading, cross-country, diving, golf, soccer, softball W, swimming, tennis, track and field, volleyball W. **Intramural:** Basketball, football (non-tackle), golf, soccer, softball, tennis, volleyball. **Team name:** Seahawks.

Student services. Adult student services, alcohol/substance abuse counseling, chaplain/spiritual director, career counseling, student employment services, financial aid counseling, health services, legal services, minority student services, personal counseling, placement for graduates, veterans' counselor, women's services. **Physically disabled:** Services for visually, speech, hearing impaired.

Contact. E-mail: admissions@uncw.edu
Phone: (910) 962-3243 Toll-free number: (800) 228-5571
Fax: (910) 962-3038
Janice Rockwell, Director, University of North Carolina at Wilmington, 601 South College Road, Wilmington, NC 28403-5904

University of North Carolina School of the Arts
Winston-Salem, North Carolina   **CB member**
www.uncsa.edu   **CB code: 5512**

◗ Public 4-year visual arts and performing arts college
◗ Residential campus in small city

◗ 763 degree-seeking undergraduates: 1% part-time, 39% women, 9% African American, 1% Asian American, 7% Hispanic American, 1% international
◗ 117 degree-seeking graduate students
◗ 47% of applicants admitted
◗ SAT or ACT with writing, interview required
◗ 54% graduate within 6 years

General. Founded in 1963. Regionally accredited. State Conservatory with high school, undergraduate and graduate facilities. **Degrees:** 146 bachelor's awarded; master's offered. **Location:** 90 miles from Charlotte, 75 miles from Raleigh. **Calendar:** Semester, limited summer session. **Full-time faculty:** 140 total; 1% minority, 31% women. **Part-time faculty:** 30 total; 60% women. **Class size:** 92% < 20, 8% 20-39, less than 1% 40-49, less than 1% 50-99, less than 1% >100. **Special facilities:** Stage production shop, film village with sound and recording stages.

Freshman class profile. 624 applied, 291 admitted, 178 enrolled.

Return as sophomores:	80%	International:	2%
Live on campus:	95%		

Basis for selection. Talent, achievement, career potential most important. Admission heavily dependent on audition. SAT combined score of 800 (exclusive of Writing) or ACT composite score of 19, school record, recommendations important. Interview recommended for all students. Audition required for dance, drama, music programs; portfolio required for design, filmmaking, production programs.

High school preparation. College-preparatory program required. 20 units required. Required and recommended units include English 4, mathematics 3, social studies 2, history 1, science 3 (laboratory 1), foreign language 2 and academic electives 4.

2011-2012 Annual costs. Tuition/fees: $6,908; $19,857 out-of-state. Health Insurance $738. Room/board: $7,922. Books/supplies: $1,120. Personal expenses: $1,472.

Financial aid. Non-need-based: Scholarships awarded for academics, art, leadership, music/drama, state residency.

Application procedures. Admission: Priority date 3/1; no deadline. $60 fee, may be waived for applicants with need. Admission notification on a rolling basis beginning on or about 4/1. Must reply by May 1 or within 3 week(s) if notified thereafter. Application closing date dependent upon audition. Applications must be submitted at least 2 weeks before audition date. Dance, drama and filmmaking interviews begin in January and end in early March. Music and technical theater auditions begin in November and end in early March. Decisions generally are made by April 1, or about 2 weeks after audition if later than April 1. **Financial aid:** Priority date 3/1; no closing date. FAFSA required. Applicants notified on a rolling basis starting 4/1; must reply within 2 week(s) of notification.

Academics. Professional training supplemented by strong general studies curriculum, small classes 7:1 student-teacher ratio. **Special study options:** Independent study, internships. **Credit/placement by examination:** AP, CLEP, SAT, ACT. **Support services:** Remedial instruction, study skills assistance, tutoring, writing center.

Majors. Liberal arts: Arts/sciences. **Visual/performing arts:** Cinematography, dance, dramatic, music performance, theater design.

Computing on campus. 28 workstations in dormitories, library, student center. Dormitories wired for high-speed internet access and linked to campus network. Online course registration available.

Student life. Freshman orientation: Mandatory, $75 fee. Preregistration for classes offered. Orientation is the first three days in the academic year. All art schools have separate orientations which include academic assessment. **Housing:** Guaranteed on-campus for freshmen. Coed dorms, single-sex dorms, apartments available. $200 deposit, deadline 5/1. **Activities:** Literary magazine, student government, student newspaper, spirituality committee, ADAPT-drug prevention team, C.A.R.E.-AIDS awareness and prevention team, Awareness for Gay and Lesbian Equality, Artists for Christ, Awareness of Black Arts, Minorities on the Move.

Athletics. Team name: Fighting Pickles.

Student services. Alcohol/substance abuse counseling, career counseling, student employment services, financial aid counseling, health services, personal counseling.

Contact. E-mail: admissions@uncsa.edu
Phone: (336) 770-3291 Fax: (336) 770-3370
Sheeler Lawson, Director of Admissions, University of North Carolina School of the Arts, 1533 South Main Street, Winston-Salem, NC 27127-2188

University of Phoenix: Charlotte
Charlotte, North Carolina
www.phoenix.edu

▶ For-profit 4-year university
▶ Very large city
▶ 989 degree-seeking undergraduates

General. Regionally accredited. **Degrees:** 162 bachelor's awarded; master's offered. **Calendar:** Differs by program. **Full-time faculty:** 18 total. **Part-time faculty:** 121 total.

Basis for selection. Open admission, but selective for some programs.

2011-2012 Annual costs. Estimated costs as of August 2011: per-credit-hour charge, $380 to $450, depending upon level and course of study; electronic course materials fee, $95, if applicable. Book and material charges may vary by course and program. All fees are subject to change.

Application procedures. Admission: No deadline. No application fee. **Financial aid:** No deadline.

Academics. Credit/placement by examination: AP, CLEP.

Majors. Business: Business admin, management science, marketing. **Computer sciences:** Information technology.

Contact. Marc Booker, Director of Admission and Evaluation, University of Phoenix: Charlotte, 3800 Arco Corporate Drive, Suite 100, Charlotte, NC 28273-3409

University of Phoenix: Raleigh
Raleigh, North Carolina
www.phoenix.edu

▶ For-profit 4-year university
▶ Large city
▶ 450 degree-seeking undergraduates

General. Regionally accredited. **Degrees:** 54 bachelor's awarded; master's offered. **Calendar:** Differs by program. **Full-time faculty:** 12 total. **Part-time faculty:** 101 total.

Basis for selection. Open admission, but selective for some programs.

2011-2012 Annual costs. Estimated costs as of August 2011: per-credit-hour charge, $380 to $450, depending upon level and course of study; electronic course materials fee, $95, if applicable. Book and material charges may vary by course and program. All fees are subject to change.

Application procedures. Admission: No deadline. No application fee. **Financial aid:** No deadline.

Academics. Credit/placement by examination: AP, CLEP.

Majors. Business: Business admin, management science, marketing. **Computer sciences:** Information technology.

Contact. Marc Booker, Director of Admission and Evaluation, University of Phoenix: Raleigh, 5511 Capital Center Drive, Suite 390, Raleigh, NC 27606-3380

Wake Forest University
Winston-Salem, North Carolina
CB member
www.wfu.edu
CB code: 5885

▶ Private 4-year university
▶ Residential campus in small city
▶ 4,768 degree-seeking undergraduates: 1% part-time, 52% women, 8% African American, 5% Asian American, 5% Hispanic American, 2% international
▶ 2,542 degree-seeking graduate students
▶ 40% of applicants admitted
▶ Application essay required
▶ 88% graduate within 6 years

General. Founded in 1834. Regionally accredited. First-year students receive a notebook computer. **Degrees:** 1,019 bachelor's awarded; master's, professional, doctoral offered. **ROTC:** Army. **Location:** 4 miles from downtown. **Calendar:** Semester, limited summer session. **Full-time faculty:** 516 total; 92% have terminal degrees, 15% minority, 40% women. **Part-time faculty:** 123 total; 29% women. **Class size:** 54% < 20, 38% 20-39, 5% 40-49, 3% 50-99, less than 1% >100. **Special facilities:** Museum of anthropology, center for nanotechnology and molecular materials, Reynolda house museum of American art, Charlotte and Philip Hanes art gallery, archaeology laboratory, biomechanics laboratory, laser physics laboratory, Reynolda gardens.

Freshman class profile. 9,869 applied, 3,933 admitted, 1,240 enrolled.

Mid 50% test scores			
SAT critical reading:	610-700	Return as sophomores:	93%
SAT math:	620-700	Out-of-state:	77%
ACT composite:	28-32	Live on campus:	99%
Rank in top quarter:	96%	International:	2%
Rank in top tenth:	83%	Fraternities:	35%
		Sororities:	42%

Basis for selection. High school curriculum and classroom performance combined with the student's writing ability, extracurricular activities and evidence of character and talent are the most important criteria for admission. The admissions office strongly encourages personal interviews. Audition recommended for those competing for a Presidential Scholarship (for students with special talents in music, theater, art, dance, and debate).

High school preparation. College-preparatory program required. 16 units required; 20 recommended. Required and recommended units include English 4, mathematics 3-4, social studies 2-4, science 1-4 and foreign language 2-4.

2012-2013 Annual costs. Tuition/fees: $43,200. Room/board: $11,660. Books/supplies: $1,100. Personal expenses: $1,500.

2011-2012 Financial aid. Need-based: 535 full-time freshmen applied for aid; 473 were judged to have need; 465 of these received aid. Average need met was 100%. Average scholarship/grant was $31,492; average loan $9,276. 70% of total undergraduate aid awarded as scholarships/grants, 30% as loans/jobs. **Non-need-based:** Awarded to 2,006 full-time undergraduates, including 359 freshmen. Scholarships awarded for academics, alumni affiliation, art, athletics, leadership, music/drama, religious affiliation, ROTC, state residency. **Additional information:** First-year students with an annual family income of less than $40,000 will have their student loans capped at $4,000 per year during their college years. Other financial aid to the students will come from grant and scholarship increases and work-study opportunities.

Application procedures. Admission: Closing date 1/1. $50 fee, may be waived for applicants with need. Admission notification by 4/1. Must reply by 5/1. **Financial aid:** Priority date 2/15, closing date 3/1. FAFSA, CSS PROFILE required. Applicants notified on a rolling basis starting 4/1; must reply by 5/1 or within 4 week(s) of notification.

Academics. Language courses at all levels in Russian, Greek, Italian, Hebrew; elementary and intermediate courses in Chinese, Japanese and Arabic; elementary courses in Hindi, Portuguese. **Special study options:** Combined bachelor's/graduate degree, cross-registration, double major, dual enrollment of high school students, honors, independent study, internships, study abroad, teacher certification program, Washington semester. Semester in London, Venice, or Vienna and semester at universities in Dijon, Salamanca, Berlin, Moscow, Beijing, and Japan. **Credit/placement by examination:** AP, CLEP, IB, institutional tests. **Support services:** Learning center, reduced course load, study skills assistance, tutoring, writing center.

Majors. Biology: General, bacteriology. **Business:** General, accounting, finance, management science. **Communications:** Communications/speech/rhetoric. **Computer sciences:** Computer science. **Education:** Elementary, social studies. **English:** English lit. **Foreign languages:** Ancient Greek, Chinese, classics, French, German, Japanese, Latin, Russian, Spanish. **Health services:** Clinical lab science. **History:** General. **Math:** General. **Parks/recreation:** Exercise sciences. **Philosophy/religion:** Philosophy, religion. **Physical sciences:** Chemistry, physics. **Psychology:** General. **Social sciences:** Anthropology, econometrics, economics, political science, sociology. **Visual/performing arts:** Art history/conservation, dramatic, music history, music performance, studio arts.

Most popular majors. Biology 7%, business/marketing 21%, communications/journalism 8%, English 6%, foreign language 7%, history 6%, psychology 7%, social sciences 20%.

Computing on campus. PC or laptop required. Dormitories wired for high-speed internet access and linked to campus network. Commuter students can connect to campus network. Online course registration, online library, helpline, repair service, student web hosting, wireless network available.

Student life. Freshman orientation: Mandatory. Preregistration for classes offered. **Policies:** First- and second-year students with residential status required to live on campus. **Housing:** Guaranteed on-campus for all

undergraduates. Coed dorms, apartments, fraternity/sorority housing, wellness housing available. $500 nonrefundable deposit, deadline 5/1. **Activities:** Bands, campus ministries, choral groups, dance, drama, film society, international student organizations, literary magazine, music ensembles, Model UN, radio station, student government, student newspaper, symphony orchestra, TV station, Black Student Alliance, College Democrats, College Republicans, Alpha Phi Omega, InterVarsity Christian Fellowship, Amnesty International, Habitat for Humanity, volunteer service corps.

Athletics. NCAA. **Intercollegiate:** Baseball M, basketball, cheerleading, cross-country, field hockey W, football (tackle) M, golf, soccer, tennis, track and field, volleyball W. **Intramural:** Basketball, bowling, cross-country, diving, equestrian W, football (non-tackle), golf, racquetball, soccer, softball, table tennis, tennis, volleyball, water polo, wrestling M. **Team name:** Demon Deacons.

Student services. Alcohol/substance abuse counseling, chaplain/spiritual director, career counseling, student employment services, financial aid counseling, health services, minority student services, personal counseling, placement for graduates. **Physically disabled:** Services for visually, speech, hearing impaired.

Contact. E-mail: admissions@wfu.edu
Phone: (336) 758-5201 Fax: (336) 758-4324
Martha Allman, Director of Admissions, Wake Forest University, PO Box 7305, Winston-Salem, NC 27109-7305

Warren Wilson College
Asheville, North Carolina
www.warren-wilson.edu

CB member
CB code: 5886

- Private 4-year liberal arts college affiliated with Presbyterian Church (USA)
- Residential campus in small city
- 903 degree-seeking undergraduates
- 77 graduate students
- 93% of applicants admitted
- SAT or ACT (ACT writing optional), application essay required

General. Founded in 1894. Regionally accredited. **Degrees:** 193 bachelor's awarded; master's offered. **Location:** 10 miles from downtown. **Calendar:** Semester. **Full-time faculty:** 60 total; 95% have terminal degrees, 10% minority, 43% women. **Part-time faculty:** 20 total; 30% have terminal degrees, 10% minority. **Special facilities:** 300-acre college farm, organic garden, 600 acres of forest, hiking trails, archaeological site, adventure challenge course, GIS laboratory, visual arts center and gallery.

Freshman class profile. 986 applied, 920 admitted, 228 enrolled.

Mid 50% test scores			
		ACT composite:	22-28
SAT critical reading:	540-660	**Out-of-state:**	79%
SAT math:	490-590	**Live on campus:**	99%
SAT writing:	510-630		

Basis for selection. Admission based on both the potential and academic qualifications of the applicant. All available information is considered, including previous academic records, evidence of academic and social maturity, extracurricular activities, community service, SAT or ACT, interview, essay, references, recent grade trends and general contributions to school and community. All records of examinations taken overseas plus TOEFL required of foreign applicants. Interview, portfolio recommended. **Home schooled:** Transcript of courses and grades, interview, letter of recommendation (nonparent) required. Transcript listing course titles and content, partial portfolio of sample work completed (graded papers), document that serves as diploma, copy of state rules under which school was formed or is recognized, and an interview (phone or in person) required.

High school preparation. College-preparatory program required. Required and recommended units include English 4, mathematics 3, social studies 3, science 2 (laboratory 2) and foreign language 2. Math requirement includes algebra I, algebra II and geometry. Sciences must include 2 laboratories.

2012-2013 Annual costs. Tuition/fees: $28,300. All resident students are required to work 15 hours per week in college's work program. $3,480 earnings are credited toward tuition costs. Room/board: $8,566. Books/supplies: $920. Personal expenses: $1,747.

Financial aid. Non-need-based: Scholarships awarded for academics, art, job skills, leadership, religious affiliation, state residency.

Application procedures. Admission: Priority date 1/15; deadline 2/15 (receipt date). No application fee. Admission notification on a rolling basis

---

beginning on or about 2/1. Must reply by 5/1. **Financial aid:** Priority date 4/1; no closing date. FAFSA, institutional form required. Applicants notified on a rolling basis starting 3/1; must reply within 3 week(s) of notification.

Academics. Special study options: Cross-registration, double major, dual enrollment of high school students, ESL, exchange student, honors, independent study, internships, liberal arts/career combination, student-designed major, study abroad, Washington semester. **Credit/placement by examination:** AP, CLEP, institutional tests. **Support services:** Reduced course load, study skills assistance, tutoring, writing center.

Majors. Biology: General. **Business:** Business admin. **Conservation:** Environmental studies. **English:** English lit. **Foreign languages:** General. **Health services:** Premedicine, preveterinary. **History:** General. **Human services:** Social work. **Liberal arts:** Arts/sciences. **Math:** General. **Parks/recreation:** General. **Philosophy/religion:** Philosophy, religion. **Physical sciences:** Chemistry. **Psychology:** General. **Social sciences:** Anthropology, political science, sociology. **Visual/performing arts:** Art.

Most popular majors. Area/ethnic studies 8%, English 16%, history 6%, natural resources/environmental science 28%, psychology 6%.

Computing on campus. 91 workstations in library, computer center, student center. Dormitories wired for high-speed internet access and linked to campus network. Commuter students can connect to campus network. Online course registration, online library, helpline, wireless network available.

Student life. Freshman orientation: Mandatory, $260 fee. Preregistration for classes offered. 4-day orientation (immediately before classes begin, late August) includes academic advising, registration, full day community service, dinner/discussions with faculty and peer group. **Policies:** Triad education program requires students to work 15 hours/week at an on-campus job and do 100 hours community service by graduation, in addition to academics. **Housing:** Guaranteed on-campus for freshmen. Coed dorms, single-sex dorms, apartments, cooperative housing, wellness housing available. **Activities:** Jazz band, campus ministries, choral groups, dance, drama, international student organizations, literary magazine, music ensembles, musical theater, student government, student newspaper, Amnesty International, Emmaus, Interfaith, Jewish student group, Buddhist experience, earth first, sustainable living.

Athletics. NAIA, USCAA. **Intercollegiate:** Basketball, cross-country, soccer, swimming. **Intramural:** Basketball, soccer, table tennis, tennis, triathlon. **Team name:** Owls.

Student services. Alcohol/substance abuse counseling, chaplain/spiritual director, career counseling, student employment services, financial aid counseling, health services, minority student services, personal counseling, placement for graduates, women's services.

Contact. E-mail: admit@warren-wilson.edu
Phone: (828) 771-2073 Toll-free number: (800) 934-3536
Fax: (828) 298-1440
Richard Blomgren, Vice-President for Advancement, Admission and Marketing, Warren Wilson College, Office of Admission, Asheville, NC 28815-9000

Western Carolina University
Cullowhee, North Carolina
www.wcu.edu

CB member
CB code: 5897

- Public 4-year university
- Residential campus in small town
- 7,465 degree-seeking undergraduates: 14% part-time, 53% women, 6% African American, 1% Asian American, 3% Hispanic American, 1% Native American, 1% international
- 1,564 degree-seeking graduate students
- 39% of applicants admitted
- SAT or ACT with writing required
- 49% graduate within 6 years

General. Founded in 1889. Regionally accredited. **Degrees:** 1,654 bachelor's awarded; master's, doctoral offered. **Location:** 53 miles from Asheville, 157 miles from Atlanta, GA. **Calendar:** Semester, extensive summer session. **Full-time faculty:** 448 total; 79% have terminal degrees, 8% minority, 46% women. **Part-time faculty:** 166 total; 32% have terminal degrees, 7% minority, 50% women. **Class size:** 30% < 20, 54% 20-39, 12% 40-49, 4% 50-99, less than 1% >100. **Special facilities:** Center for applied technology, fine and performing arts center, collection of historical Native American artifacts and documents, center for the advancement of teaching, public policy institute, mountain heritage center.

Freshman class profile. 13,992 applied, 5,408 admitted, 1,520 enrolled.

Mid 50% test scores			
SAT critical reading:	460-560	GPA 3.0-3.49:	29%
SAT math:	480-570	GPA 2.0-2.99:	13%
SAT writing:	440-530	Rank in top quarter:	40%
ACT composite:	19-24	Rank in top tenth:	15%
GPA 3.75 or higher:	42%	Return as sophomores:	72%
GPA 3.50-3.74:	16%	Out-of-state:	89%
		Live on campus:	97%

Basis for selection. The most important admission factors are secondary school record, class rank, GPA, standardized test scores, talent/ability, and applicant's interest. SAT recommended. All applicants, except those exempted by current campus policies, must submit standardized test scores. SAT preferred, ACT also accepted. Essays not required but will be considered if submitted. Auditions and/or portfolios are required for some art/music/theater programs. **Home schooled:** Must submit official transcript of all work completed and meet standards equivalent to those used for applicants from approved secondary schools.

High school preparation. College-preparatory program required. 20 units required; 24 recommended. Required and recommended units include English 4, mathematics 4, social studies 2, history 1, science 3 (laboratory 3), foreign language 2 and academic electives 4-8.

2011-2012 Annual costs. Tuition/fees: $5,250; $14,847 out-of-state. Room/board: $6,650. Books/supplies: $606. Personal expenses: $1,396.

2011-2012 Financial aid. **Need-based:** 1,329 full-time freshmen applied for aid; 1,032 were judged to have need; 1,008 of these received aid. Average need met was 69%. Average scholarship/grant was $6,425; average loan $3,252. 54% of total undergraduate aid awarded as scholarships/grants, 46% as loans/jobs. **Non-need-based:** Awarded to 656 full-time undergraduates, including 162 freshmen. Scholarships awarded for academics, art, athletics, leadership, music/drama, state residency.

Application procedures. **Admission:** Priority date 2/1; deadline 3/1 (postmark date). $50 fee, may be waived for applicants with need. Admission notification on a rolling basis beginning on or about 1/15. Must reply by 5/1. Housing deposit due upon receipt of student's acceptance. **Financial aid:** Priority date 3/15; no closing date. FAFSA, institutional form required. Applicants notified on a rolling basis starting 4/1.

Academics. **Special study options:** Accelerated study, combined bachelor's/graduate degree, cooperative education, distance learning, double major, dual enrollment of high school students, exchange student, honors, independent study, internships, student-designed major, study abroad, teacher certification program. Service learning. **Credit/placement by examination:** AP, CLEP, IB, institutional tests. Student may apply to be examined in any course identified by department head as available for credit by exam. Credit by exam attempts must be completed prior to semester of graduation. Catalog does not specify maximum number of hours. **Support services:** Learning center, pre-admission summer program, reduced course load, study skills assistance, tutoring, writing center.

Honors college/program. For first-year students to be considered, must meet at least one of the following: 1875 SAT or 30 ACT, 4.0 weighted cumulative high school GPA, rank in the top 10% of class. Other requirements apply to transfer students and students currently enrolled.

Majors. **Biology:** General. **Business:** Accounting, business admin, entrepreneurial studies, finance, hospitality admin, international, management information systems, marketing. **Communications:** Communications/speech/rhetoric. **Computer sciences:** Computer science. **Conservation:** Environmental science, management/policy. **Education:** Art, elementary, English, German, kindergarten/preschool, mathematics, middle, music, physical, science, social studies, Spanish, special ed. **Engineering:** Electrical. **English:** English lit. **Foreign languages:** French, German, Spanish. **Health services:** Athletic training, clinical lab science, communication disorders, dietetics, EMT paramedic, environmental health, health care admin, medical records admin, nursing (RN), recreational therapy. **History:** General. **Human services:** General, social work. **Liberal arts:** Arts/sciences. **Math:** General. **Parks/recreation:** Facilities management, sports admin. **Philosophy/religion:** Philosophy. **Physical sciences:** Chemistry, geology. **Protective services:** Criminal justice, forensics. **Psychology:** General. **Social sciences:** General, anthropology, geography, political science, sociology. **Visual/performing arts:** Art, dramatic, interior design, music, music performance, studio arts.

Most popular majors. Business/marketing 14%, education 20%, engineering/engineering technologies 8%, health sciences 16%, security/protective services 10%.

Computing on campus. PC or laptop required. 115 workstations in library, computer center, student center. Dormitories wired for high-speed internet access and linked to campus network. Commuter students can connect to campus network. Online course registration, online library, helpline, repair service, student web hosting, wireless network available.

Student life. **Freshman orientation:** Mandatory, $115 fee. Preregistration for classes offered. 2-day orientation sessions held in June and July. Sessions for both students and parents. **Housing:** Guaranteed on-campus for freshmen. Coed dorms, single-sex dorms, special housing for disabled, apartments, fraternity/sorority housing, wellness housing available. $150 nonrefundable deposit, deadline 5/1. **Activities:** Bands, campus ministries, choral groups, dance, drama, film society, international student organizations, literary magazine, music ensembles, Model UN, musical theater, radio station, student government, student newspaper, TV station, finance club, Fellowship of Christian Athletes, Black theater ensemble, Japanese animation society, Organization of Ebony Students, College Republicans, College Democrats, La Voz Latina, Pagan Student Association.

Athletics. NCAA. **Intercollegiate:** Baseball M, basketball, cheerleading, cross-country, football (tackle) M, golf, soccer W, softball W, tennis W, track and field, volleyball W. **Intramural:** Badminton, basketball, bowling, cross-country, football (non-tackle), football (tackle), racquetball, soccer, softball, swimming, table tennis, tennis, volleyball, water polo, weight lifting, wrestling. **Team name:** Catamounts.

Student services. Alcohol/substance abuse counseling, chaplain/spiritual director, career counseling, services for economically disadvantaged, student employment services, financial aid counseling, health services, minority student services, on-campus daycare, personal counseling, placement for graduates, women's services. **Physically disabled:** Services for visually, speech, hearing impaired.

Contact. E-mail: admiss@wcu.edu
Phone: (828) 227-7317 Toll-free number: (877) 928-4968
Fax: (828) 227-7319
Philip Cauley, Director of Admissions, Western Carolina University, 102 Camp Building, Cullowhee, NC 28723

William Peace University
Raleigh, North Carolina **CB member**
www.peace.edu **CB code: 5533**

- Private 4-year liberal arts college affiliated with Presbyterian Church (USA)
- Residential campus in large city
- 652 degree-seeking undergraduates: 11% part-time, 97% women, 21% African American, 3% Asian American, 4% Hispanic American, 1% Native American
- 53% of applicants admitted
- SAT or ACT (ACT writing optional) required
- 66% graduate within 6 years

General. Founded in 1857. Regionally accredited. **Degrees:** 141 bachelor's awarded. **ROTC:** Army, Naval, Air Force. **Location:** 5 miles to downtown. **Calendar:** Semester, limited summer session. **Full-time faculty:** 27 total; 82% have terminal degrees, 56% women. **Part-time faculty:** 40 total; 30% have terminal degrees, 5% minority, 62% women. **Class size:** 76% < 20, 23% 20-39, less than 1% 40-49, less than 1% 50-99, less than 1% >100.

Freshman class profile. 1,071 applied, 568 admitted, 136 enrolled.

GPA 3.75 or higher:	23%	Rank in top tenth:	4%
GPA 3.50-3.74:	21%	End year in good standing:	83%
GPA 3.0-3.49:	25%	Return as sophomores:	60%
GPA 2.0-2.99:	30%	Out-of-state:	12%
Rank in top quarter:	23%	Live on campus:	89%

Basis for selection. A holistic approach is used to look at academic records and scores in addition to the person. Interview recommended for all students. Essay or personal statement recommended. Audition required for theater, drama, and music majors; portfolio required for art programs. Essay and interview required for honors program. **Home schooled:** Statement describing home school structure and mission required. **Learning Disabled:** Students with learning disabilities are encouraged to contact disabilities resource center regarding their needs.

High school preparation. College-preparatory program recommended. 16 units required; 17 recommended. Required and recommended units include English 4, mathematics 3-4, social studies 2, history 2, science 3 and foreign language 2.

2012-2013 Annual costs. Tuition/fees: $24,025. Room/board: $9,000. Books/supplies: $1,300. Personal expenses: $2,400.

2011-2012 Financial aid. **Need-based:** 128 full-time freshmen applied for aid; 121 were judged to have need; 121 of these received aid. Average need met was 68%. Average scholarship/grant was $19,324; average loan $3,347. 69% of total undergraduate aid awarded as scholarships/grants, 31%

as loans/jobs. **Non-need-based:** Awarded to 93 full-time undergraduates, including 18 freshmen. Scholarships awarded for academics, leadership, music/drama, state residency.

Application procedures. Admission: No deadline. $25 fee, may be waived for applicants with need. Admission notification on a rolling basis. Must reply by May 1 or within 2 week(s) if notified thereafter. Prefer early admission candidates with SAT 1100 or above, 3.5 GPA in college preparatory courses, and rank in top 25% of class. On-campus interview required. **Financial aid:** Priority date 3/15; no closing date. FAFSA required. Applicants notified on a rolling basis starting 3/1; must reply by 5/1 or within 4 week(s) of notification.

Academics. Special study options: Cooperative education, cross-registration, distance learning, double major, dual enrollment of high school students, honors, independent study, internships, liberal arts/career combination, study abroad, teacher certification program, weekend college. Adult degree evening program in Business, Liberal Studies and Psychology. **Credit/placement by examination:** AP, CLEP, IB, SAT, ACT, institutional tests. 6 credit hours maximum toward bachelor's degree. CLEP credit is granted to students who have achieved the minimum score in designated subject tests. Students may petition program coordinators for additional or alternative credit, if warranted. **Support services:** Learning center, reduced course load, remedial instruction, study skills assistance, tutoring, writing center.

Majors. Biology: General. **Business:** Business admin, human resources. **Communications:** Communications/speech/rhetoric. **Education:** Early childhood, multi-level teacher. **English:** English lit. **Foreign languages:** Spanish. **History:** General. **Liberal arts:** Arts/sciences. **Psychology:** General. **Social sciences:** Anthropology, political science. **Visual/performing arts:** Design, music performance, theater arts management. **Work/family studies:** Child development.

Most popular majors. Biology 11%, business/marketing 16%, communications/journalism 11%, English 10%, liberal arts 10%, psychology 17%, visual/performing arts 7%.

Computing on campus. 180 workstations in dormitories, library, computer center, student center. Dormitories wired for high-speed internet access and linked to campus network. Commuter students can connect to campus network. Online course registration, online library, helpline, repair service, student web hosting, wireless network available.

Student life. Freshman orientation: Mandatory. Preregistration for classes offered. 2-day program offered prior to start of classes, during the summer and a four day program at the beginning with move-in. **Policies:** Honor Code and Student Code of Conduct. **Housing:** Guaranteed on-campus for freshmen. Coed dorms, single-sex dorms, special housing for disabled available. $150 nonrefundable deposit, deadline 7/1. Freshmen required to live on campus unless living with relatives within a 30-mile radius. **Activities:** Campus ministries, choral groups, dance, drama, literary magazine, music ensembles, musical theater, opera, student government, student newspaper, Christian Association, honor societies, recreation association, Young Democrats/Republicans, Phi Theta Kappa, Green Team, Helping Hands, Home Sweet Homes, Politics Club.

Athletics. NCAA. **Intercollegiate:** Basketball W, cross-country W, soccer W, softball W, tennis W, volleyball W. **Intramural:** Tennis W. **Team name:** Peace Pacers.

Student services. Adult student services, chaplain/spiritual director, career counseling, financial aid counseling, health services, minority student services, personal counseling, placement for graduates.

Contact. E-mail: admissions@peace.edu
Phone: (919) 508-2214 Toll-free number: (800) 732-2347
Fax: (919) 508-2306
Amber Stenbeck, Vice President of Enrollment, William Peace University, 15 East Peace Street, Raleigh, NC 27604-1194

Wingate University
Wingate, North Carolina
www.wingate.edu

CB member
CB code: 5908

- Private 4-year university
- Residential campus in small town
- 1,713 degree-seeking undergraduates: 2% part-time, 54% women, 13% African American, 3% Asian American, 2% Hispanic American, 1% Native American, 4% international
- 768 degree-seeking graduate students
- 81% of applicants admitted

- SAT or ACT (ACT writing optional) required
- 37% graduate within 6 years

General. Founded in 1896. Regionally accredited. **Degrees:** 291 bachelor's awarded; master's, professional, doctoral offered. **ROTC:** Army, Air Force. **Location:** 25 miles from Charlotte. **Calendar:** Semester, limited summer session. **Full-time faculty:** 126 total; 92% have terminal degrees, 2% minority, 52% women. **Part-time faculty:** 109 total; 32% have terminal degrees, 2% minority, 44% women. **Class size:** 41% < 20, 57% 20-39, less than 1% 40-49, less than 1% 50-99. **Special facilities:** Lake, performing arts center.

Freshman class profile. 4,049 applied, 3,267 admitted, 536 enrolled.

Mid 50% test scores			
SAT critical reading:	440-540	Rank in top quarter:	58%
SAT math:	470-580	Rank in top tenth:	25%
SAT writing:	430-540	Return as sophomores:	75%
ACT composite:	19-24	Out-of-state:	18%
GPA 3.75 or higher:	55%	Live on campus:	87%
GPA 3.50-3.74:	16%	International:	3%
GPA 3.0-3.49:	23%	Fraternities:	3%
GPA 2.0-2.99:	6%	Sororities:	7%

Basis for selection. Decisions based on secondary school record (GPA, class rank) and the rigor of secondary school record. Test scores are considered. SAT/ACT not required, but strongly recommended. Interview recommended for all students; portfolio recommended for art majors; audition required for music majors.

High school preparation. College-preparatory program recommended. 13 units recommended. Recommended units include English 4, mathematics 3, social studies 2, science 2 (laboratory 1) and foreign language 2.

2011-2012 Annual costs. Tuition/fees: $22,180. Room/board: $8,770. Books/supplies: $1,100. Personal expenses: $800.

2011-2012 Financial aid. Need-based: 487 full-time freshmen applied for aid; 434 were judged to have need; 417 of these received aid. Average need met was 83%. Average scholarship/grant was $17,740; average loan $3,244. 75% of total undergraduate aid awarded as scholarships/grants, 25% as loans/jobs. **Non-need-based:** Awarded to 775 full-time undergraduates, including 460 freshmen. Scholarships awarded for academics, alumni affiliation, art, athletics, music/drama, religious affiliation, state residency. **Additional information:** Institutional aid may not be available after June 1.

Application procedures. Admission: Priority date 4/1; no deadline. $30 fee, may be waived for applicants with need. Admission notification on a rolling basis beginning on or about 9/15. Must reply by May 1 or within 4 week(s) if notified thereafter. **Financial aid:** Priority date 5/1; no closing date. FAFSA required. Applicants notified on a rolling basis starting 3/15; must reply within 2 week(s) of notification.

Academics. Attendance at cultural events required as part of Lyceum program. Travel abroad available. Internships and undergraduate research under faculty supervision available. **Special study options:** Combined bachelor's/graduate degree, cross-registration, double major, dual enrollment of high school students, honors, independent study, internships, study abroad, teacher certification program. Adult Completion Program at the Wingate University School of Graduate Programs and Adult Education in downtown Matthews, NC. The program offers undergraduate courses in the evening for working adults. **Credit/placement by examination:** AP, CLEP, IB, institutional tests. 30 credit hours maximum toward bachelor's degree. **Support services:** Learning center, reduced course load, study skills assistance, tutoring, writing center.

Majors. Biology: General, environmental. **Business:** Accounting, business admin, finance, marketing. **Communications:** Communications/speech/rhetoric, journalism, public relations. **Education:** Art, biology, elementary, English, mathematics, middle, music, physical, reading, social studies. **English:** English lit. **Health services:** Athletic training, predental, premedicine, prenursing, prepharmacy, preveterinary. **History:** General. **Liberal arts:** Arts/sciences. **Math:** General. **Parks/recreation:** Facilities management, sports admin. **Philosophy/religion:** Philosophy, religion. **Physical sciences:** Chemistry. **Psychology:** General. **Social sciences:** Sociology. **Visual/performing arts:** Art, music, music performance, studio arts.

Most popular majors. Biology 10%, business/marketing 21%, communications/journalism 8%, education 12%, liberal arts 7%, parks/recreation 10%, psychology 7%, public administration/social services 7%.

Computing on campus. 75 workstations in library, computer center, student center. Dormitories wired for high-speed internet access. Commuter students can connect to campus network. Wireless network available.

Student life. Freshman orientation: Mandatory. Preregistration for classes offered. Held over the summer and right before classes begin. **Policies:**

Honor Code. **Housing:** Guaranteed on-campus for all undergraduates. Single-sex dorms, apartments available. **Activities:** Bands, campus ministries, choral groups, drama, international student organizations, literary magazine, music ensembles, musical theater, opera, student government, student newspaper, TV station, academic honors societies, Greek life, Christian Student Union, minority student association, university and community assistance network, gospel choir, College Republicans, outdoor recreation and adventure club, running club.

Athletics. NCAA. **Intercollegiate:** Baseball M, basketball, cross-country, football (tackle) M, golf, lacrosse M, soccer, softball W, swimming, tennis, track and field, volleyball W. **Intramural:** Basketball, bowling, diving, football (tackle) M, golf, lacrosse W, racquetball, soccer, softball, swimming, table tennis, tennis, volleyball, water polo. **Team name:** Bulldogs.

Student services. Chaplain/spiritual director, career counseling, student employment services, financial aid counseling, health services, minority student services, personal counseling, placement for graduates.

Contact. E-mail: admit@wingate.edu
Phone: (704) 233-8200 Toll-free number: (800) 755-5550
Fax: (704) 233-8199
Lindsey Kreis, Director of Admissions, Wingate University, Campus Box 3059, Wingate, NC 28174-0157

Winston-Salem State University
Winston-Salem, North Carolina
www.wssu.edu

CB member
CB code: 5909

- Public 4-year university and health science college
- Commuter campus in small city
- 5,627 degree-seeking undergraduates: 11% part-time, 70% women, 78% African American, 1% Asian American, 1% Hispanic American, 2% international
- 451 degree-seeking graduate students
- 56% of applicants admitted
- 41% graduate within 6 years

General. Founded in 1892. Regionally accredited. **Degrees:** 1,262 bachelor's awarded; master's, professional offered. **ROTC:** Army. **Location:** 28 miles from Greensboro, 75 miles from Charlotte. **Calendar:** Semester, limited summer session. **Full-time faculty:** 415 total; 54% minority, 57% women. **Part-time faculty:** 119 total; 46% minority, 73% women. **Class size:** 42% < 20, 50% 20-39, 7% 40-49, less than 1% 50-99.

Freshman class profile. 3,893 applied, 2,198 admitted, 807 enrolled.

Mid 50% test scores			
SAT critical reading:	400-470	Rank in top tenth:	7%
SAT math:	420-490	Return as sophomores:	80%
SAT writing:	380-460	Out-of-state:	11%
ACT composite:	16-20	Live on campus:	94%
Rank in top quarter:	27%	International:	1%

Basis for selection. Admission consideration based on submission of completed application, SAT or ACT scores, and high school transcript. Students must meet minimum course requirements, have minimum of 2.5 cumulative weighted GPA and minimum 800 SAT (Critical Reading and Math only). Interview recommended for all students; audition required for music program.

High school preparation. College-preparatory program required. 15 units required. Required units include English 4, mathematics 4, social studies 2, history 1, science 3 and foreign language 2. Mathematics units must include or exceed algebra I, geometry and algebra II. 1 science must be Biology, 1 must be a Physical Science. One Social Studies must be US History.

2011-2012 Annual costs. Tuition/fees: $4,513; $13,626 out-of-state. Room/board: $6,976. Books/supplies: $1,500. Personal expenses: $2,100.

Financial aid. Non-need-based: Scholarships awarded for academics, athletics, ROTC, state residency.

Application procedures. Admission: Priority date 11/15; deadline 3/15. $50 fee, may be waived for applicants with need. Admission notification on a rolling basis. Must reply by May 1 or within 2 week(s) if notified thereafter. **Financial aid:** Priority date 5/1; no closing date. FAFSA required. Must reply within 2 week(s) of notification.

Academics. Special study options: Accelerated study, cross-registration, distance learning, double major, ESL, honors, independent study, internships, liberal arts/career combination, study abroad, teacher certification program, Washington semester, weekend college. **Credit/placement by examination:** AP, CLEP, IB, institutional tests. 33 credit hours maximum toward bachelor's

degree. **Support services:** Learning center, reduced course load, remedial instruction, study skills assistance, tutoring, writing center.

Majors. Area/ethnic studies: African-American. **Biology:** General, biotechnology, molecular. **Business:** Accounting, business admin, managerial economics. **Communications:** Media studies. **Computer sciences:** Computer science, information technology. **Education:** Art, early childhood, elementary, English, mathematics, middle, music, physical, social studies, Spanish, special ed. **English:** English lit. **Foreign languages:** Spanish. **Health services:** Clinical lab science, nursing (RN), recreational therapy, vocational rehab counseling. **History:** General. **Human services:** Social work. **Liberal arts:** Arts/sciences. **Math:** General. **Parks/recreation:** Exercise sciences, sports admin. **Physical sciences:** Chemistry. **Protective services:** Criminal justice. **Psychology:** General. **Social sciences:** Political science, sociology. **Visual/performing arts:** Art, music, music management.

Most popular majors. Business/marketing 8%, education 6%, health sciences 51%.

Computing on campus. PC or laptop required. 500 workstations in dormitories, library, computer center, student center. Dormitories wired for high-speed internet access and linked to campus network. Commuter students can connect to campus network. Online course registration, online library, wireless network available.

Student life. Freshman orientation: Available, $165 fee. Preregistration for classes offered. Held on a summer weekend. **Housing:** Coed dorms, single-sex dorms available. $75 nonrefundable deposit, deadline 5/14. **Activities:** Bands, choral groups, dance, drama, music ensembles, radio station, student government, student newspaper, TV station, student religious council.

Athletics. NCAA. **Intercollegiate:** Basketball, bowling W, cheerleading M, cross-country, football (tackle) M, golf M, softball W, tennis, track and field, volleyball W. **Intramural:** Basketball M. **Team name:** Rams.

Student services. Adult student services, career counseling, student employment services, financial aid counseling, health services, personal counseling, veterans' counselor. **Physically disabled:** Services for visually impaired.

Contact. E-mail: admissions@wssu.edu
Phone: (336) 750-2070 Toll-free number: (800) 257-4052
Fax: (336) 750-2079
Cheryl Pollard-Burns, Associate Director of Admissions, Winston-Salem State University, 601 Martin Luther King Jr Drive, Winston-Salem, NC 27110

North Dakota

Dickinson State University
Dickinson, North Dakota
www.dsu.nodak.edu   CB code: 6477

▶ Public 4-year university
▶ Residential campus in large town
▶ 2,346 degree-seeking undergraduates

General. Founded in 1918. Regionally accredited. **Location:** 100 miles from Bismarck, 300 miles from Billings, Montana. **Calendar:** Semester, limited summer session. **Full-time faculty:** 89 total; 53% have terminal degrees, 4% minority, 49% women. **Part-time faculty:** 154 total; 8% have terminal degrees, 1% minority, 62% women. **Class size:** 64% < 20, 29% 20-39, 4% 40-49, 3% 50-99. **Special facilities:** Nature preserve.

Freshman class profile.

Rank in top quarter:	15%	Out-of-state:	45%
Rank in top tenth:	5%		

Basis for selection. Open admission, but selective for some programs. Minimum 20 ACT composite or minimum 2.0 GPA required for nursing program. **Home schooled:** Transcript of courses and grades, letter of recommendation (nonparent) required.

High school preparation. College-preparatory program required. 13 units recommended. Recommended units include English 4, mathematics 3, social studies 3 and science 3. One algebra, 1 chemistry required for nursing program.

2011-2012 Annual costs. Tuition/fees: $5,608; $12,978 out-of-state. Tuition for South Dakota, Montana, Manitoba, Saskatchewan residents: $5516. Room/board: $4,950. Books/supplies: $1,000. Personal expenses: $1,700.

Financial aid. Non-need-based: Scholarships awarded for academics, alumni affiliation, art, athletics, job skills, leadership, minority status, music/drama, religious affiliation, state residency. **Additional information:** Scholarships available to new students, priority deadline December 1.

Application procedures. Admission: No deadline. $35 fee. Admission notification on a rolling basis. **Financial aid:** Priority date 3/15; no closing date. FAFSA required. Applicants notified on a rolling basis starting 5/15; must reply within 2 week(s) of notification.

Academics. Limited evening classes available. **Special study options:** Accelerated study, combined bachelor's/graduate degree, cooperative education, distance learning, double major, dual enrollment of high school students, ESL, honors, independent study, internships, liberal arts/career combination, student-designed major, study abroad, teacher certification program. **Credit/placement by examination:** AP, CLEP, institutional tests. 8 credit hours maximum toward associate degree, 15 toward bachelor's. **Support services:** Learning center, remedial instruction, study skills assistance, tutoring, writing center.

Honors college/program. Must have a 3.5 high school GPA and/or a 26 on ACT; submit resume, essay and two letters of recommendation; 25 freshmen admitted each fall; includes special academic track that concludes with a leadership minor.

Majors. Biology: General. **Business:** General, accounting, administrative services, business admin, finance, management information systems, office management. **Communications:** Communications/speech/rhetoric. **Computer sciences:** Computer science. **Education:** Art, biology, business, chemistry, computer, drama/dance, early childhood, elementary, English, foreign languages, health, history, mathematics, middle, music, physical, reading, science, secondary, social science, Spanish, speech. **English:** Creative writing, English lit. **Foreign languages:** Spanish. **General:** Business. **Health services:** Nursing (RN), predental, premedicine, preveterinary. **History:** General. **Liberal arts:** Arts/sciences. **Math:** General. **Parks/recreation:** Health/fitness. **Physical sciences:** Chemistry. **Psychology:** General. **Social sciences:** General, political science. **Visual/performing arts:** Art, dramatic, music, studio arts, theater design.

Most popular majors. Biology 6%, business/marketing 36%, education 16%, health sciences 7%, liberal arts 13%.

Computing on campus. 235 workstations in dormitories, library, computer center, student center. Dormitories wired for high-speed internet access and linked to campus network. Commuter students can connect to campus network. Online course registration, online library, helpline, repair service, wireless network available.

Student life. Freshman orientation: Mandatory, $35 fee. Preregistration for classes offered. **Housing:** Guaranteed on-campus for all undergraduates. Coed dorms, single-sex dorms, special housing for disabled, apartments, wellness housing available. $50 fully refundable deposit. **Activities:** Bands, choral groups, dance, drama, film society, literary magazine, music ensembles, musical theater, student government, student newspaper.

Athletics. NAIA. **Intercollegiate:** Baseball M, basketball, cross-country, football (tackle) M, golf, rodeo, softball W, track and field, volleyball W, wrestling M. **Intramural:** Basketball, football (non-tackle), soccer, softball, volleyball. **Team name:** Blue Hawks.

Student services. Adult student services, career counseling, services for economically disadvantaged, student employment services, financial aid counseling, health services, minority student services, personal counseling, placement for graduates. **Physically disabled:** Services for visually, speech, hearing impaired.

Contact. E-mail: dsu.hawks@dickinsonstate.edu
Phone: (701) 483-2175 Toll-free number: (800) 279-4295
Fax: (701) 483-2409
Norman Coley, Director of Enrollment Services, Dickinson State University, 291 Campus Drive, Dickinson, ND 58601-4896

Jamestown College
Jamestown, North Dakota
www.jc.edu   CB code: 6318

▶ Private 4-year liberal arts college affiliated with Presbyterian Church (USA)
▶ Residential campus in large town
▶ 908 degree-seeking undergraduates: 4% part-time, 53% women, 3% African American, 1% Asian American, 3% Hispanic American, 1% Native American, 7% international
▶ 6 degree-seeking graduate students
▶ 63% of applicants admitted
▶ SAT or ACT (ACT writing optional) required
▶ 45% graduate within 6 years; 13% enter graduate study

General. Founded in 1883. Regionally accredited. **Degrees:** 179 bachelor's awarded; master's offered. **Location:** 100 miles from Fargo and Bismarck. **Calendar:** Semester, limited summer session. **Full-time faculty:** 58 total; 57% have terminal degrees, 7% minority, 47% women. **Part-time faculty:** 26 total; 4% minority, 50% women. **Class size:** 54% < 20, 41% 20-39, 3% 40-49, 2% 50-99.

Freshman class profile. 797 applied, 502 admitted, 240 enrolled.

Mid 50% test scores			
SAT critical reading:	430-510	GPA 2.0-2.99:	24%
SAT math:	460-560	Rank in top quarter:	46%
ACT composite:	20-25	Rank in top tenth:	19%
GPA 3.75 or higher:	31%	Return as sophomores:	73%
GPA 3.50-3.74:	18%	Out-of-state:	46%
GPA 3.0-3.49:	26%	Live on campus:	95%
		International:	11%

Basis for selection. Applicants with minimum 2.5 high school GPA or 18 ACT or 850 SAT (exclusive of Writing) generally accepted. Applicants may be admitted on standard, conditional, or probationary basis. Audition required for music program; portfolio recommended for art program. **Home schooled:** Letter of recommendation (nonparent) required.

High school preparation. College-preparatory program recommended. Recommended units include English 4, mathematics 3, social studies 3, science 4 and foreign language 2.

2012-2013 Annual costs. Tuition/fees (projected): $17,870. Room/board: $6,030. Books/supplies: $1,000. Personal expenses: $1,300.

2011-2012 Financial aid. Need-based: Average need met was 79%. Average scholarship/grant was $11,312; average loan $3,267. 53% of total undergraduate aid awarded as scholarships/grants, 47% as loans/jobs. **Non-need-based:** Scholarships awarded for academics, alumni affiliation, art, athletics, job skills, leadership, music/drama, religious affiliation. **Additional information:** FAFSA must be received by March 15th for residents to be considered for North Dakota state grants.

Application procedures. Admission: Priority date 7/1; no deadline. $35 fee, may be waived for applicants with need, free for online applicants. Admission notification on a rolling basis. **Financial aid:** Priority date 3/15; no closing date. FAFSA required. Applicants notified on a rolling basis starting 2/1; must reply within 2 week(s) of notification.

Academics. Special study options: Combined bachelor's/graduate degree, cooperative education, double major, dual enrollment of high school students, honors, independent study, internships, liberal arts/career combination, student-designed major, study abroad, teacher certification program. **Credit/ placement by examination:** AP, CLEP, IB, SAT, ACT, institutional tests. Unlimited number of hours of credit by examination may be counted toward degree. **Support services:** Learning center, reduced course load, remedial instruction, study skills assistance, tutoring, writing center.

Majors. Biology: General, biochemistry. **Business:** Accounting, business admin, finance, financial planning, hospitality admin, international, management information systems, managerial economics, marketing, tourism/travel. **Communications:** Communications/speech/rhetoric. **Computer sciences:** Computer science, information technology. **Education:** Biology, chemistry, early childhood, elementary, English, history, mathematics, music, physical, secondary, special ed. **English:** English lit, writing. **Foreign languages:** French, German, Spanish. **Health services:** Clinical lab science, nursing (RN), radiologic technology/medical imaging. **History:** General. **Math:** General, applied. **Parks/recreation:** General, sports admin. **Philosophy/religion:** Religion. **Physical sciences:** Chemistry. **Protective services:** Criminal justice. **Psychology:** General. **Social sciences:** Political science. **Visual/performing arts:** Dramatic, music, music performance, studio arts.

Most popular majors. Biology 8%, business/marketing 18%, computer/ information sciences 7%, education 8%, health sciences 16%, history 8%, parks/recreation 7%, psychology 6%.

Computing on campus. 360 workstations in dormitories, library, computer center, student center. Dormitories wired for high-speed internet access and linked to campus network. Commuter students can connect to campus network. Online course registration, online library, helpline, repair service, student web hosting, wireless network available.

Student life. Freshman orientation: Mandatory. Preregistration for classes offered. 3 days prior to classes. **Policies:** Weekly chapel service available on campus. Non-alcoholic nightclub available. **Housing:** Guaranteed on-campus for all undergraduates. Coed dorms, special housing for disabled, apartments, wellness housing available. $100 fully refundable deposit. **Activities:** Bands, campus ministries, choral groups, dance, drama, international student organizations, music ensembles, musical theater, student government, student newspaper, TV station, honor societies, Students of Service, Fellowship of Christian Athletes, Jimmie Janes, Jimmie Ambassadors, Ignition.

Athletics. NAIA. **Intercollegiate:** Baseball M, basketball, cross-country, football (tackle) M, golf, soccer, softball W, track and field, volleyball W, wrestling. **Intramural:** Basketball, bowling, football (non-tackle), volleyball. **Team name:** Jimmies.

Student services. Alcohol/substance abuse counseling, chaplain/spiritual director, career counseling, student employment services, financial aid counseling, personal counseling, placement for graduates, veterans' counselor.

Contact. E-mail: admissions@jc.edu
Phone: (701) 252-3467 ext. 5562 Toll-free number: (800) 336-2554
Fax: (701) 253-4318
Tena Lawrence, Dean of Enrollment Management, Jamestown College, 6081 College Lane, Jamestown, ND 58405

Mayville State University
Mayville, North Dakota
www.mayvillestate.edu   CB code: 6478

- Public 4-year business and teachers college
- Residential campus in small town
- 970 degree-seeking undergraduates: 41% part-time, 56% women, 4% African American, 1% Asian American, 4% Hispanic American, 2% Native American, 4% international
- 30% graduate within 6 years; 9% enter graduate study

General. Founded in 1889. Regionally accredited. Every student issued laptop computer. All students complete an Information Technology Certificate as part of their bachelor's degree. **Degrees:** 111 bachelor's, 2 associate awarded. **ROTC:** Army, Air Force. **Location:** 60 miles from Fargo, 40 miles from Grand Forks. **Calendar:** Semester, limited summer session. **Full-time faculty:** 40 total; 40% have terminal degrees, 2% minority, 35% women. **Part-time faculty:** 36 total; 11% have terminal degrees, 6% minority, 69%

women. **Class size:** 71% < 20, 27% 20-39, 2% 40-49. **Special facilities:** Head start and child development center, undergraduate research labs.

Freshman class profile.

End year in good standing:	86%	Live on campus:	86%
Return as sophomores:	52%	International:	3%
Out-of-state:	36%		

Basis for selection. Open admission, but selective for some programs. Admission to teacher education programs based on meeting GPA criteria, completion of PPST, and specific prerequisites. ACT math scores used for placement. Interview recommended. **Home schooled:** Transcript of courses and grades required. Must provide documentation equivalent to high school diploma.

High school preparation. College-preparatory program required. 17 units required; 18 recommended. Required and recommended units include English 4, mathematics 3, social studies 3, science 3 (laboratory 2) and foreign language 2. One unit of computer studies recommended.

2011-2012 Annual costs. Tuition/fees: $6,084; $8,271 out-of-state. Room/board: $4,632. Books/supplies: $900. Personal expenses: $2,800.

2011-2012 Financial aid. Need-based: 134 full-time freshmen applied for aid; 106 were judged to have need; 106 of these received aid. Average need met was 65%. Average scholarship/grant was $4,482; average loan $3,519. 39% of total undergraduate aid awarded as scholarships/grants, 61% as loans/jobs. **Non-need-based:** Awarded to 399 full-time undergraduates, including 131 freshmen. Scholarships awarded for academics, athletics, leadership, minority status, music/drama, state residency.

Application procedures. Admission: No deadline. $35 fee. Admission notification on a rolling basis beginning on or about 1/1. **Financial aid:** Priority date 2/15; no closing date. FAFSA required. Applicants notified on a rolling basis starting 5/1; must reply within 2 week(s) of notification.

Academics. Special study options: Accelerated study, cooperative education, distance learning, double major, dual enrollment of high school students, independent study, internships, student-designed major, teacher certification program. 3-year business administration degree with cooperative education internship. **Credit/placement by examination:** AP, CLEP, IB, institutional tests. 30 credit hours maximum toward bachelor's degree. **Support services:** Learning center, pre-admission summer program, remedial instruction, study skills assistance, tutoring.

Majors. Biology: General. **Business:** Business admin. **Communications:** Communications/speech/rhetoric. **Computer sciences:** General. **Education:** Biology, chemistry, early childhood, elementary, English, geography, health, history, mathematics, physical, social science, teacher assistance. **English:** English lit. **Health services:** Clinical lab science, predental, premedicine, prenursing, prepharmacy, preveterinary. **Math:** General. **Parks/recreation:** Health/fitness, sports admin. **Physical sciences:** Chemistry. **Psychology:** General. **Social sciences:** General. **Work/family studies:** Child care management.

Most popular majors. Business/marketing 29%, education 34%, family/ consumer sciences 12%, parks/recreation 9%, psychology 6%.

Computing on campus. PC or laptop required. Dormitories wired for high-speed internet access and linked to campus network. Commuter students can connect to campus network. Online course registration, online library, helpline, repair service, wireless network available.

Student life. Freshman orientation: Mandatory, $35 fee. Preregistration for classes offered. Half-day events held in June and July. **Policies:** All freshmen and sophomore who are under 21 years of age or who have completed less than 60 credits are required to live in university owned housing facilities and are required to participate in an approved board plan. **Housing:** Guaranteed on-campus for all undergraduates. Coed dorms, single-sex dorms, apartments, wellness housing available. $50 nonrefundable deposit, deadline 8/25. **Activities:** Bands, choral groups, drama, international student organizations, music ensembles, musical theater, radio station, student government, student newspaper, Campus Crusade, student education association, residence hall association, health and physical education club, student activities council, alumni ambassadors, minority/international student association, business administration club, psychology club.

Athletics. NAIA. **Intercollegiate:** Baseball M, basketball, football (tackle) M, softball W, volleyball W. **Intramural:** Badminton, basketball, football (non-tackle), golf, ice hockey M, racquetball, soccer, softball, table tennis, tennis, track and field, volleyball, weight lifting. **Team name:** Comets.

Student services. Adult student services, career counseling, student employment services, financial aid counseling, health services, on-campus daycare, personal counseling, placement for graduates, veterans' counselor. **Physically disabled:** Services for visually, hearing impaired.

Contact. E-mail: MaSU.admissions@mayvillestate.edu
Phone: (701) 788-4842 Toll-free number: (800) 437-4104
Fax: (701) 788-4748
Misti Wuori, Director of Admissions and Extended Learning, Mayville
State University, 330 Third Street, NE, Mayville, ND 58257-1299

Medcenter One College of Nursing
Bismarck, North Dakota
www.medcenterone.com/collegeofnursing   CB code: 7051

- Private two-year upper-division nursing college
- Commuter campus in small city
- 54% of applicants admitted
- Application essay, interview required

General. Founded in 1988. Regionally accredited. Small nursing college
affiliated with Medcenter One Health Systems. **Degrees:** 43 bachelor's
awarded. **Articulation:** Agreement with Bismarck State College. **Location:**
190 miles from Fargo, 105 miles from Minot. **Calendar:** Semester, limited
summer session. **Full-time faculty:** 10 total; 10% have terminal degrees,
100% women. **Part-time faculty:** 3 total; 100% women. **Class size:** 23%
< 20, 15% 20-39, 62% 40-49.

Student profile. 92 degree-seeking undergraduates. 100 applied as first
time-transfer students, 54 admitted, 48 enrolled. 100% entered as juniors.
90% transferred from two-year, 10% transferred from four-year institutions.

Women:	86%	Part-time:	2%
African American:	4%	Out-of-state:	4%
Asian American:	2%	25 or older:	32%
Hispanic American:	1%		

Basis for selection. High school transcript, college transcript, application
essay, interview required. All students must transfer with minimum 65 credits
of general education prerequisites, including 5 prerequisite science courses.
Students not required to complete all prerequisites prior to applying but must
have a minimum of 2 required sciences completed. Credits not completed
at time of application must be completed prior to starting 300 level nursing
courses in fall semester. Overall college GPA, science GPA important. Transfer accepted as sophomores, juniors, seniors.

2011-2012 Annual costs. Tuition/fees: $10,536. Books/supplies: $1,169.
Personal expenses: $1,000.

Application procedures. Admission: Priority date 11/1. $40 fee. Appli-
cation must be submitted on paper. **Financial aid:** No deadline. Applicants
notified on a rolling basis starting 6/1; must reply within 2 weeks of notification.

Academics. Special study options: Internships. **Credit/placement by
examination:** AP, CLEP, institutional tests. 30 credit hours maximum toward
bachelor's degree.

Majors. Health services: Nursing (RN).

Computing on campus. 24 workstations in library, computer center.
Online library, wireless network available.

Student life. Activities: Student government, Student Nurse Association,
Student Organization.

Student services. Financial aid counseling, placement for graduates.

Contact. E-mail: msmith@mohs.org
Phone: (701) 323-6833 Fax: (701) 323-6289
Mary Smith, Director of Student Services, Medcenter One College of
Nursing, 512 North 7th Street, Bismarck, ND 58501-4425

Minot State University
Minot, North Dakota
www.minotstateu.edu   CB code: 6479

- Public 4-year university and liberal arts college
- Commuter campus in large town
- 3,367 degree-seeking undergraduates
- SAT or ACT (ACT writing optional) required

General. Founded in 1913. Regionally accredited. **Degrees:** 488 bachelor's,
1 associate awarded; master's offered. **Location:** 105 miles from Bismarck,
225 miles from Grand Forks. **Calendar:** Semester, limited summer session.
Full-time faculty: 167 total. **Part-time faculty:** 118 total. **Special facilities:**

Natural history museum, center for persons with disabilities, Native American
collection, observatory, rural crime and justice center, Center for Extended
Teaching and Learning.

Freshman class profile.

GPA 3.75 or higher:	23%	Rank in top quarter:	35%
GPA 3.50-3.74:	20%	Rank in top tenth:	14%
GPA 3.0-3.49:	32%	Out-of-state:	15%
GPA 2.0-2.99:	24%	Live on campus:	51%

Basis for selection. Secondary school record very important; ACT/SAT
test scores, ACT composite score must be no less than 17; those below the
recommended composite score are reviewed on an individual basis.

High school preparation. 13 units required. Required units include
English 4, mathematics 3, social studies 3, science 3 (laboratory 3). Science
should include at least 3 units of biology, chemistry, physics, or physical
science. Social science should not include consumer education, cooperative
marketing, orientation to social science, or marriage/family. Math must be
algebra I or above.

2011-2012 Annual costs. Tuition/fees: $5,763; $5,763 out-of-state.
Room/board: $4,948. Books/supplies: $1,000. Personal expenses: $3,300.

Financial aid. Non-need-based: Scholarships awarded for academics,
alumni affiliation, art, athletics, minority status, music/drama, state residency.
Additional information: Scholarship application deadline is 2/15.

Application procedures. Admission: Priority date 4/1; no deadline. $35
fee. Admission notification on a rolling basis. **Financial aid:** Priority date
3/15; no closing date. FAFSA required. Applicants notified on a rolling basis
starting 5/1; must reply within 2 week(s) of notification.

Academics. Wide variety of distance courses offered. **Special study
options:** Cooperative education, distance learning, double major, dual enrollment of high school students, ESL, external degree, honors, independent
study, internships, liberal arts/career combination, student-designed major,
study abroad, teacher certification program. **Credit/placement by examination:** AP, CLEP, SAT, ACT, institutional tests. **Support services:** Learning
center, reduced course load, remedial instruction, study skills assistance,
tutoring, writing center.

Majors. Biology: General. **Business:** Accounting, business admin, finance,
international, management information systems, marketing. **Communications:** Broadcast journalism, radio/TV. **Communications technology:** General. **Computer sciences:** General. **Education:** Art, biology, business, chemistry, Deaf/hearing impaired, elementary, English, foreign languages, French,
German, history, mathematics, mentally handicapped, music, physical, physics, science, social science, Spanish, speech impaired. **English:** English lit,
rhetoric/composition. **Foreign languages:** General, French, German, Spanish. **Health services:** Clinical lab science, communication disorders, health
care admin, medical radiologic technology/radiation therapy, nursing (RN),
substance abuse counseling. **History:** General. **Human services:** Social work.
Liberal arts: Arts/sciences. **Math:** General. **Parks/recreation:** Sports
admin. **Physical sciences:** General, chemistry, geology, physics. **Protective
services:** Criminal justice. **Psychology:** General. **Social sciences:** General,
economics, geography, sociology. **Visual/performing arts:** Art, dramatic,
music, music performance, studio arts management.

Most popular majors. Business/marketing 30%, education 22%, health
sciences 14%, security/protective services 8%.

Computing on campus. 300 workstations in dormitories, library, computer center, student center. Dormitories wired for high-speed internet access
and linked to campus network. Commuter students can connect to campus
network. Online course registration, online library, helpline, repair service,
wireless network available.

Student life. Freshman orientation: Mandatory, $35 fee. Preregistration
for classes offered. **Policies:** First-year students required to live in university
housing (exceptions exist). **Housing:** Guaranteed on-campus for freshmen.
Coed dorms, single-sex dorms, special housing for disabled, apartments,
wellness housing available. $100 deposit. **Activities:** Marching band, campus
ministries, drama, international student organizations, musical theater, radio
station, student government, student newspaper, TV station, disability awareness organization, Democratic Party, Republican Party, Intervarsity Christian
Fellowship, Native American cultural awareness club, United Campus Ministries, Catholic student association, international awareness club, Student Education of Hard of Hearing/Deaf, National Student Speech/Hearing Association.

Athletics. NAIA. **Intercollegiate:** Baseball M, basketball, cheerleading M,
cross-country, football (tackle) M, golf, soccer W, softball W, track and field,
volleyball W, wrestling M. **Intramural:** Basketball, bowling, ice hockey M,
racquetball, softball, track and field, volleyball. **Team name:** Beavers.

Student services. Adult student services, alcohol/substance abuse counseling, chaplain/spiritual director, career counseling, services for economically disadvantaged, student employment services, financial aid counseling, health services, minority student services, personal counseling, placement for graduates, veterans' counselor, women's services. **Physically disabled:** Services for visually, speech, hearing impaired.

Contact. E-mail: askmsu@minotstateu.edu
Phone: (701) 858-3350 Toll-free number: (800) 777-0750
Fax: (701) 839-6933
Kevin Harmon, Dean of Admissions, Minot State University, 500 University Avenue West, Minot, ND 58707-5002

North Dakota State University
Fargo, North Dakota   **CB member**
www.ndsu.edu   **CB code: 6474**

- Public 4-year university
- Residential campus in small city
- 11,610 degree-seeking undergraduates: 8% part-time, 43% women
- 2,157 degree-seeking graduate students
- 86% of applicants admitted
- SAT or ACT (ACT writing optional) required
- 53% graduate within 6 years

General. Founded in 1890. Regionally accredited. **Degrees:** 1,912 bachelor's awarded; master's, professional, doctoral offered. **ROTC:** Army, Air Force. **Location:** 250 miles from Minneapolis-St. Paul. **Calendar:** Semester, limited summer session. **Full-time faculty:** 670 total; 79% have terminal degrees, 18% minority, 40% women. **Part-time faculty:** 183 total; 31% have terminal degrees, 8% minority, 47% women. **Class size:** 33% < 20, 41% 20-39, 7% 40-49, 12% 50-99, 8% >100. **Special facilities:** Fine arts center, regional studies institute, biotechnology institute, engineering computer center, center for writers, wellness center, technology park, downtown campus for art and architecture, business and agribusiness, equine center.

Freshman class profile. 5,096 applied, 4,383 admitted, 2,420 enrolled.

Mid 50% test scores			
SAT critical reading:	500-630	Rank in top quarter:	43%
SAT math:	490-630	Rank in top tenth:	17%
ACT composite:	21-26	End year in good standing:	77%
GPA 3.75 or higher:	27%	Return as sophomores:	76%
GPA 3.50-3.74:	20%	Out-of-state:	63%
GPA 3.0-3.49:	32%	Live on campus:	91%
GPA 2.0-2.99:	21%	Fraternities:	5%
		Sororities:	4%

Basis for selection. All applicants must have completed college preparatory program in high school. Admission based on overall performance in high school, performance in college preparatory courses and standardized test scores. Admission to electrical engineering and mechanical engineering programs based on academic record and test scores. Scores required of all applicants unless applicant is 25 or older on the first day of class or has 24 or more transferable credits. Campus visit recommended for all students. Audition required for music programs. Secondary admission requirements for many programs. **Home schooled:** Transcript of courses and grades required. Applicants advised to work with local school district for issuance of a Certificate of Graduation.

High school preparation. College-preparatory program required. 13 units required. Required units include English 4, mathematics 3, social studies 3, science 3 (laboratory 3).

2011-2012 Annual costs. Tuition/fees: $7,175; $17,421 out-of-state. MN Reciprocity Rate $6350; WUE and MSEP rate $9203; contiguous states $9230. Room/board: $7,082. Books/supplies: $1,000. Personal expenses: $3,500.

2010-2011 Financial aid. **Need-based:** 1,869 full-time freshmen applied for aid; 1,244 were judged to have need; 1,222 of these received aid. Average need met was 63%. Average scholarship/grant was $4,655; average loan $4,533. 36% of total undergraduate aid awarded as scholarships/grants, 64% as loans/jobs. **Non-need-based:** Awarded to 2,637 full-time undergraduates, including 922 freshmen. Scholarships awarded for academics, alumni affiliation, art, athletics, leadership, minority status, music/drama, ROTC, state residency.

Application procedures. **Admission:** Closing date 8/1 (receipt date). $35 fee. Admission notification on a rolling basis. **Financial aid:** Priority date 3/15; no closing date. FAFSA required. Applicants notified on a rolling basis starting 4/20.

Academics. **Special study options:** Combined bachelor's/graduate degree, cooperative education, cross-registration, distance learning, double major, dual enrollment of high school students, ESL, honors, independent study, internships, student-designed major, study abroad, teacher certification program. Tri-college, collaborative enrollment (ND University System) Pathway program with ND partner institution with remedial coursework for students not meeting admission requirements. **Credit/placement by examination:** AP, CLEP, IB, ACT, institutional tests. **Support services:** Reduced course load, remedial instruction, study skills assistance, tutoring, writing center.

Majors. **Architecture:** Environmental design, landscape. **Area/ethnic studies:** Women's. **Biology:** General, Biochemistry/molecular biology, biotechnology, botany, microbiology, zoology. **Business:** Accounting, business admin, communications, construction management, finance, hospitality admin, management information systems, marketing. **Communications:** Digital media, health, journalism, public relations. **Computer sciences:** Computer science. **Conservation:** Management/policy. **Education:** Agricultural, biology, chemistry, elementary, English, family/consumer sciences, French, health, history, mathematics, music, physical, physics, science, social science, social studies, Spanish. **Engineering:** Agricultural, civil, computer, construction, electrical, industrial, manufacturing, mechanical. **English:** English lit. **Foreign languages:** Classics, French, Spanish. **General:** Agribusiness operations, animal sciences, communications, crop production, economics, equestrian studies, food science, horticultural science, mechanization, range science, soil science, turf management. **Health services:** Clinical lab science, dietetics, nursing (RN), premedicine, preveterinary, radiologic technology/medical imaging, respiratory therapy technology, veterinary technology/assistant. **History:** General, applied. **Math:** General, statistics. **Parks/recreation:** General, sports admin. **Philosophy/religion:** Philosophy. **Physical sciences:** Chemistry, geology, physics. **Protective services:** Criminal justice, homeland security. **Psychology:** General. **Social sciences:** General, anthropology, economics, political science, sociology. **Visual/performing arts:** Art, dramatic, interior design, music. **Work/family studies:** Clothing/textiles, family studies.

Most popular majors. Agriculture 8%, biology 7%, business/marketing 19%, engineering/engineering technologies 14%, family/consumer sciences 6%, health sciences 9%.

Computing on campus. 500 workstations in dormitories, library, computer center, student center. Dormitories wired for high-speed internet access. Online course registration, online library, helpline, repair service, student web hosting, wireless network available.

Student life. **Freshman orientation:** Available. Preregistration for classes offered. Offered in June, July or August and day before classes. **Policies:** No alcoholic beverages allowed on campus, code of student conduct. **Housing:** Guaranteed on-campus for freshmen. Coed dorms, single-sex dorms, apartments, fraternity/sorority housing, wellness housing available. $50 partly refundable deposit. Housing is handicap accessible. **Activities:** Bands, campus ministries, choral groups, dance, drama, international student organizations, music ensembles, musical theater, radio station, student government, student newspaper, TV station, Newman Center, Lutheran Student Fellowship, United Campus Ministry, College Republicans, College Democrats, Circle-K, Mortar Board, Black Student Alliance, Native American student association.

Athletics. NCAA. **Intercollegiate:** Baseball M, basketball, cross-country, football (tackle) M, golf, soccer W, softball W, track and field, volleyball W, wrestling M. **Intramural:** Basketball, football (non-tackle), softball, volleyball. **Team name:** Bison.

Student services. Adult student services, alcohol/substance abuse counseling, career counseling, services for economically disadvantaged, student employment services, financial aid counseling, health services, minority student services, on-campus daycare, personal counseling, veterans' counselor. **Physically disabled:** Services for visually, speech, hearing impaired.

Contact. E-mail: ndsu.admission@ndsu.edu
Phone: (701) 231-8643 Toll-free number: (800) 488-6378
Fax: (701) 231-8802
Jobey Lichtblau, Director of Admission, North Dakota State University, Ceres Hall 114, Fargo, ND 58108-6050

Rasmussen College: Fargo
Fargo, North Dakota
www.rasmussen.edu   **CB code: 3343**

- For-profit 4-year career college
- Commuter campus in small city
- 942 degree-seeking undergraduates

General. **Degrees:** 44 bachelor's, 88 associate awarded. **Calendar:** Quarter, extensive summer session. **Full-time faculty:** 20 total. **Part-time faculty:** 25 total.

Basis for selection. Open admission, but selective for some programs. Some programs require placement examinations.

2011-2012 Annual costs. Tuition/fees: $15,750. Full-time tuition varies according to program of study. Examples of per-credit-hour charges include Early Childhood Education ($310), Medical Lab Technician, Surgical Technician, Practical Nursing ($395), Professional Nursing, Information Systems Mgmt, Multemedia Technician ($395). Personal expenses: $2,214.

Application procedures. Admission: No deadline. $40 fee. Admission notification on a rolling basis. **Financial aid:** No deadline. FAFSA, institutional form required. Applicants notified on a rolling basis.

Academics. Special study options: Distance learning, double major, independent study, internships, liberal arts/career combination. **Credit/placement by examination:** AP, CLEP, IB, institutional tests. 45 credit hours maximum toward associate degree, 90 toward bachelor's. 50% of a student's program must be completed through coursework at Rasmussen College. **Support services:** Learning center, remedial instruction, study skills assistance, tutoring, writing center.

Majors. Business: Accounting, business admin. **Protective services:** Criminal justice.

Computing on campus. 100 workstations in library, computer center, student center. Online course registration, online library, helpline, wireless network available.

Student life. Freshman orientation: Mandatory. Preregistration for classes offered. **Activities:** Student government.

Student services. Adult student services, career counseling, services for economically disadvantaged, student employment services, financial aid counseling, placement for graduates.

Contact. E-mail: peter.limvere@rasmussen.edu
Phone: (701) 277-3889 Toll-free number: (800) 817-0009
Fax: (701) 277-5604
Susan Hammerstrom, Director of Admissions, Rasmussen College: Fargo, 4012 19th Avenue SW, Fargo, ND 58103

Trinity Bible College
Ellendale, North Dakota
www.trinitybiblecollege.edu   **CB code: 0356**

- Private 4-year Bible college affiliated with Assemblies of God
- Residential campus in rural community
- 247 degree-seeking undergraduates
- ACT (writing optional), application essay required

General. Founded in 1948. Regionally accredited; also accredited by ABHE. **Degrees:** 40 bachelor's, 5 associate awarded. **Location:** 60 miles from Jamestown, 38 miles from Aberdeen. **Calendar:** Semester, limited summer session. **Full-time faculty:** 13 total. **Part-time faculty:** 17 total. **Special facilities:** Pentecostal heritage collection of rare and out-of-print works, teacher education laboratory.

Basis for selection. Criteria include ACT scores and GPA references, school record, evidence of Christian testimony and lifestyle. Interview recommended. **Home schooled:** Statement describing home school structure and mission, transcript of courses and grades, letter of recommendation (nonparent) required. Minimum ACT scores of 14 English, 15 math required.

2011-2012 Annual costs. Tuition/fees: $13,090. Room/board: $5,150. Books/supplies: $800. Personal expenses: $1,636.

Financial aid. Non-need-based: Scholarships awarded for academics, alumni affiliation, art, leadership, music/drama, religious affiliation.

Application procedures. Admission: No deadline. $25 fee, may be waived for applicants with need. Admission notification on a rolling basis. **Financial aid:** Priority date 3/1, closing date 9/1. FAFSA required. Applicants notified on a rolling basis starting 3/1; must reply within 3 week(s) of notification.

Academics. All students major or minor in Biblical studies in conjunction with another major or minor of their choice. **Special study options:** Distance learning, double major, dual enrollment of high school students, independent study, internships, liberal arts/career combination, teacher certification program. **Credit/placement by examination:** AP, CLEP, IB, SAT, ACT, institutional tests. 30 credit hours maximum toward associate degree, 30 toward bachelor's. **Support services:** Learning center, reduced course load, remedial instruction, tutoring.

Majors. Business: General. **Education:** Elementary. **Philosophy/religion:** Religion. **Theology:** Bible, missionary, religious ed, theology. **Visual/performing arts:** Dramatic, music.

Computing on campus. 30 workstations in dormitories, library, computer center, student center. Dormitories wired for high-speed internet access and linked to campus network. Online library, helpline, wireless network available.

Student life. Freshman orientation: Mandatory. Preregistration for classes offered. **Policies:** Religious observance required. **Housing:** Single-sex dorms, wellness housing available. $150 deposit, deadline 8/31. **Activities:** Bands, campus ministries, choral groups, drama, music ensembles, radio station, student government, missions, photography, ministry clubs.

Athletics. NCCAA. **Intercollegiate:** Basketball, football (tackle) M. **Intramural:** Basketball, football (tackle) M, volleyball. **Team name:** Lions.

Student services. Chaplain/spiritual director, career counseling, student employment services, financial aid counseling, personal counseling, placement for graduates, veterans' counselor.

Contact. E-mail: admissions@trinitybiblecollege.edu
Phone: (701) 349-3621 Toll-free number: (888) 822-2329
Fax: (701) 349-5786
Jan Dressander, Director of Admissions, Trinity Bible College, 50 6th Avenue South, Ellendale, ND 58436-7150

University of Mary
Bismarck, North Dakota
www.umary.edu   **CB code: 6428**

- Private 4-year university affiliated with Roman Catholic Church
- Residential campus in small city
- 1,995 degree-seeking undergraduates: 19% part-time, 63% women, 3% African American, 1% Asian American, 2% Hispanic American, 4% Native American, 1% international
- 999 degree-seeking graduate students
- 75% of applicants admitted
- SAT or ACT (ACT writing optional) required
- 52% graduate within 6 years

General. Founded in 1959. Regionally accredited. Additional centers in Bismarck, Fargo, Grand Forks; Billings, Montana; Kansas City, Missouri; Phoenix, Arizona. **Degrees:** 514 bachelor's awarded; master's, professional offered. **Location:** 6 miles from downtown. **Calendar:** Semester, extensive summer session. **Full-time faculty:** 101 total; 54% have terminal degrees, 3% minority, 59% women. **Part-time faculty:** 160 total; 24% have terminal degrees, 6% minority, 51% women. **Class size:** 66% < 20, 28% 20-39, 3% 40-49, 3% 50-99, less than 1% >100. **Special facilities:** Climbing wall, 3 art galleries.

Freshman class profile. 1,001 applied, 753 admitted, 374 enrolled.

Mid 50% test scores		Rank in top quarter:	42%
SAT critical reading:	440-570	Rank in top tenth:	16%
SAT math:	450-580	End year in good standing:	94%
ACT composite:	20-25	Return as sophomores:	72%
GPA 3.75 or higher:	32%	Out-of-state:	37%
GPA 3.50-3.74:	18%	Live on campus:	88%
GPA 3.0-3.49:	27%	International:	1%
GPA 2.0-2.99:	22%		

Basis for selection. Automatic acceptance for applicants in top half of class with 2.5 GPA and 19 ACT. Applicants not meeting these standards may be admitted with specific conditions for enrollment. Audition required for music program; interview recommended for academically weak students. **Home schooled:** State high school equivalency certificate required.

High school preparation. College-preparatory program recommended. Recommended units include English 4, mathematics 3, social studies 4 and science 3.

2011-2012 Annual costs. Tuition/fees: $13,545. Room/board: $5,340. Books/supplies: $1,100. Personal expenses: $1,056.

2010-2011 Financial aid. Need-based: 340 full-time freshmen applied for aid; 276 were judged to have need; 264 of these received aid. Average need met was 80.43%. Average scholarship/grant was $4,355; average loan $3,444. 43% of total undergraduate aid awarded as scholarships/grants, 57% as loans/jobs. **Non-need-based:** Awarded to 1,333 full-time undergraduates, including 310 freshmen. Scholarships awarded for academics, athletics, music/drama, religious affiliation, state residency.

Application procedures. Admission: No deadline. $25 fee, may be waived for applicants with need. Admission notification on a rolling basis. Must reply by May 1 or within 4 week(s) if notified thereafter. **Financial aid:** Priority date 3/1; no closing date. FAFSA required. Applicants notified on a rolling basis starting 2/1; must reply within 2 week(s) of notification.

Academics. Special study options: Accelerated study, combined bachelor's/graduate degree, distance learning, double major, dual enrollment of high school students, honors, independent study, internships, semester at sea, student-designed major, study abroad, teacher certification program. **Credit/placement by examination:** AP, CLEP, IB, SAT, ACT. **Support services:** Learning center, reduced course load, remedial instruction, study skills assistance, tutoring, writing center.

Majors. Biology: General. **Business:** Accounting, business admin, communications, finance, information resources management, management information systems, management science, marketing. **Communications:** Media studies. **Computer sciences:** General, information systems. **Education:** Biology, business, early childhood, elementary, English, history, mathematics, mentally handicapped, music, physical, reading, social science. **Engineering:** General. **English:** English lit. **Health services:** Athletic training, clinical lab science, nursing (RN), radiologic technology/medical imaging, respiratory therapy technology, substance abuse counseling. **Human services:** Social work. **Liberal arts:** Arts/sciences. **Math:** General. **Parks/recreation:** Exercise sciences, sports admin. **Philosophy/religion:** Religion. **Protective services:** Correctional facilities, criminal justice. **Psychology:** General. **Social sciences:** General. **Theology:** Sacred music, theology. **Visual/performing arts:** Music performance.

Most popular majors. Biology 6%, business/marketing 41%, education 9%, health sciences 18%, liberal arts 6%, parks/recreation 6%.

Computing on campus. 100 workstations in dormitories, library, computer center. Dormitories wired for high-speed internet access and linked to campus network. Commuter students can connect to campus network. Online course registration, online library, helpline, student web hosting, wireless network available.

Student life. Freshman orientation: Mandatory. Preregistration for classes offered. Three-day program immediately prior to the first day of classes. **Policies:** Freshmen and sophomores have an on-campus residency requirement. **Housing:** Guaranteed on-campus for freshmen. Coed dorms, single-sex dorms, special housing for disabled, apartments, wellness housing available. $100 fully refundable deposit. **Activities:** Bands, campus ministries, choral groups, dance, drama, international student organizations, literary magazine, music ensembles, musical theater, student government, student newspaper, Circle-K, Young Democrats, College Republicans, Fellowship of Christian Athletes, Lions Club, Spanish Club, Collegians for Life, Optimist Club.

Athletics. NCAA. **Intercollegiate:** Baseball M, basketball, cross-country, football (tackle) M, golf W, soccer, softball W, tennis W, track and field, volleyball W, wrestling M. **Intramural:** Badminton, basketball, football (non-tackle), golf, racquetball, soccer, softball, swimming, table tennis, tennis, triathlon, volleyball, water polo, weight lifting. **Team name:** Marauders.

Student services. Adult student services, chaplain/spiritual director, career counseling, services for economically disadvantaged, student employment services, financial aid counseling, health services, minority student services, personal counseling, placement for graduates, veterans' counselor. **Physically disabled:** Services for visually, hearing impaired.

Contact. E-mail: marauder@umary.edu
Phone: (701) 355-8030 Toll-free number: (800) 288-6279
Fax: (701) 255-7687
Mike Heitkamp, Director of Admissions, University of Mary, 7500 University Drive, Bismarck, ND 58504-9652

University of North Dakota
Grand Forks, North Dakota
www.und.edu   CB code: 6878

- Public 4-year university
- Residential campus in small city
- 11,522 degree-seeking undergraduates: 19% part-time, 45% women, 2% African American, 1% Asian American, 2% Hispanic American, 2% Native American, 6% international
- 3,175 degree-seeking graduate students
- 71% of applicants admitted
- SAT or ACT (ACT writing optional) required
- 51% graduate within 6 years; 22% enter graduate study

General. Founded in 1883. Regionally accredited. **Degrees:** 1,689 bachelor's awarded; master's, professional, doctoral offered. **ROTC:** Army, Air Force. **Location:** 320 miles from Minneapolis-St. Paul, 150 miles from Winnipeg, Canada. **Calendar:** Semester, extensive summer session. **Full-time faculty:** 638 total; 79% have terminal degrees, 7% minority, 41% women. **Part-time faculty:** 65 total; 32% have terminal degrees, 2% minority, 60% women. **Class size:** 39% < 20, 45% 20-39, 6% 40-49, 6% 50-99, 3% >100. **Special facilities:** Native media center, American Indian center, biomedical research center, climate change and CO2 center, rural health center, children and family services training center, clinical education center, environmental training institute, ecological studies institute, hydrogen technology center, Native American aging resource center, behavioral research center, Indian law center, wellness center, unmanned serial systems center.

Freshman class profile. 4,857 applied, 3,439 admitted, 2,091 enrolled.

GPA 3.75 or higher:	28%	Return as sophomores:	77%
GPA 3.50-3.74:	18%	Out-of-state:	66%
GPA 3.0-3.49:	30%	Live on campus:	88%
GPA 2.0-2.99:	24%	International:	2%
Rank in top quarter:	42%	Fraternities:	8%
Rank in top tenth:	14%	Sororities:	11%
End year in good standing:	84%		

Basis for selection. High school record and test scores most important. **Home schooled:** Transcript of courses and grades required.

High school preparation. College-preparatory program required. 13 units required. Required and recommended units include English 4, mathematics 3, social studies 3, science 3 (laboratory 3) and foreign language 1. Math must be algebra I and above.

2011-2012 Annual costs. Tuition/fees: $7,092; $16,767 out-of-state. Tuition for South Dakota, Montana, Saskatchewan, Manitoba residents: $8,690. Room/board: $6,100. Books/supplies: $800. Personal expenses: $4,356.

2010-2011 Financial aid. Need-based: 1,538 full-time freshmen applied for aid; 1,032 were judged to have need; 1,021 of these received aid. Average need met was 54%. Average scholarship/grant was $4,309; average loan $4,572. 30% of total undergraduate aid awarded as scholarships/grants, 70% as loans/jobs. **Non-need-based:** Awarded to 2,893 full-time undergraduates, including 904 freshmen. Scholarships awarded for academics, alumni affiliation, art, athletics, job skills, leadership, music/drama, religious affiliation, ROTC.

Application procedures. Admission: No deadline. $35 fee. Admission notification on a rolling basis beginning on or about 9/1. **Financial aid:** Priority date 3/15; no closing date. FAFSA required. Applicants notified on a rolling basis starting 5/15; must reply within 4 week(s) of notification.

Academics. Special study options: Accelerated study, combined bachelor's/graduate degree, cooperative education, cross-registration, distance learning, double major, dual enrollment of high school students, ESL, exchange student, external degree, honors, independent study, internships, liberal arts/career combination, semester at sea, student-designed major, study abroad, teacher certification program, weekend college. **Credit/placement by examination:** AP, CLEP, IB, ACT, institutional tests. **Support services:** Learning center, pre-admission summer program, reduced course load, remedial instruction, study skills assistance, tutoring, writing center.

Majors. Area/ethnic studies: Chinese, Native American. **Biology:** General. **Business:** Accounting, accounting/finance, business admin, entrepreneurial studies, finance, human resources, investments/securities, managerial economics, marketing, operations. **Communications:** General. **Communications technology:** Graphics. **Computer sciences:** General, systems analysis. **Conservation:** Environmental studies. **Education:** Business, early childhood, elementary, mathematics, middle, music, physical, science, social science. **Engineering:** Chemical, civil, electrical, environmental, geological, mechanical, petroleum. **English:** English lit. **Foreign languages:** General, classics, French, German, Norwegian, Spanish. **Health services:** Athletic training, clinical lab science, clinical nutrition, communication disorders, cytotechnology, dietetics, music therapy, nursing (RN), physical therapy, rehabilitation science. **History:** General. **Human services:** General, social work. **Math:** General. **Parks/recreation:** Facilities management. **Philosophy/religion:** Philosophy, religion. **Physical sciences:** General, atmospheric science, chemistry, geology, physics. **Protective services:** Criminal justice, forensics. **Psychology:** General. **Social sciences:** General, anthropology, economics, geography, political science, sociology. **Visual/performing arts:** Art, dramatic, graphic design, music, music performance, musical theater.

Most popular majors. Business/marketing 16%, education 7%, engineering/engineering technologies 9%, health sciences 12%, trade and industry 14%.

Computing on campus. 1,500 workstations in dormitories, library, computer center, student center. Dormitories wired for high-speed internet access and linked to campus network. Commuter students can connect to campus

network. Online course registration, online library, helpline, repair service, student web hosting, wireless network available.

Student life. Freshman orientation: Available, $15 fee. Preregistration for classes offered. Held weekend before school opens in August. **Housing:** Guaranteed on-campus for freshmen. Coed dorms, single-sex dorms, special housing for disabled, apartments, fraternity/sorority housing, wellness housing available. $250 partly refundable deposit, deadline 5/1. **Activities:** Bands, campus ministries, choral groups, dance, drama, film society, international student organizations, literary magazine, music ensembles, musical theater, opera, radio station, student government, student newspaper, symphony orchestra, TV station, over 275 organizations available.

Athletics. NCAA. **Intercollegiate:** Baseball M, basketball, cross-country, diving, football (tackle) M, golf, ice hockey, soccer W, softball W, swimming, tennis W, track and field, volleyball W. **Intramural:** Badminton, basketball, golf, ice hockey, racquetball, soccer W, softball W, tennis W, volleyball W. **Team name:** Fighting Sioux.

Student services. Adult student services, alcohol/substance abuse counseling, chaplain/spiritual director, career counseling, services for economically disadvantaged, student employment services, financial aid counseling, health services, legal services, minority student services, on-campus daycare, personal counseling, placement for graduates, veterans' counselor, women's services. **Physically disabled:** Services for visually, speech, hearing impaired.

Contact. E-mail: und.enrollmentservices@email.und.edu
Phone: (701) 777-3821 Toll-free number: (800) 225-5863
Fax: (701) 777-2721
Deborah Melby, Director, University of North Dakota, Twamley Hall, Room 205, Grand Forks, ND 58202-8357

Valley City State University
Valley City, North Dakota
www.vcsu.edu   CB code: 6480

▸ Public 4-year liberal arts and teachers college
▸ Residential campus in small town
▸ 1,138 undergraduates
▸ SAT or ACT (ACT writing optional) required

General. Founded in 1889. Regionally accredited. All full-time undergraduate students are provided a laptop computer. **Degrees:** 173 bachelor's awarded; master's offered. **Location:** 60 miles from Fargo. **Calendar:** Semester, limited summer session. **Full-time faculty:** 67 total; 60% have terminal degrees, 9% minority, 49% women. **Part-time faculty:** 45 total; 27% have terminal degrees, 64% women. **Special facilities:** Planetarium, medicine wheel, undergraduate research labs.

Freshman class profile.

Mid 50% test scores		Out-of-state:	36%
SAT critical reading:	450-510	Live on campus:	95%
SAT math:	420-540	Fraternities:	3%
ACT composite:	18-22	Sororities:	3%

Basis for selection. School achievement record and test scores important. **Home schooled:** Transcript of courses and grades required.

High school preparation. College-preparatory program required. 13 units required. Required and recommended units include English 4, mathematics 3, social studies 3, science 3 (laboratory 3) and foreign language 1.

2011-2012 Annual costs. Tuition/fees: $6,197; $13,783 out-of-state. Room/board: $4,910. Books/supplies: $1,000. Personal expenses: $1,840.

Financial aid. Non-need-based: Scholarships awarded for academics, alumni affiliation, art, athletics, minority status, music/drama, state residency.

Application procedures. Admission: No deadline. $35 fee. Admission notification on a rolling basis beginning on or about 9/15. **Financial aid:** Priority date 3/15; no closing date. FAFSA required. Applicants notified on a rolling basis starting 2/1; must reply within 3 week(s) of notification.

Academics. Special study options: Combined bachelor's/graduate degree, cooperative education, distance learning, double major, dual enrollment of high school students, ESL, independent study, internships, liberal arts/career combination, student-designed major, study abroad, teacher certification program. **Credit/placement by examination:** AP, CLEP, SAT, ACT, institutional tests. **Support services:** Learning center, reduced course load, study skills assistance, tutoring, writing center.

Majors. Biology: General. **Business:** Business admin, human resources, office management. **Computer sciences:** General. **Education:** Art, biology,

business, chemistry, educational technology, elementary, English, health, history, mathematics, music, physical, science, secondary, social science, Spanish, technology/industrial arts, trade/industrial, voc/tech. **English:** English lit. **Foreign languages:** Spanish. **Health services:** Predental, premedicine, prenursing, prepharmacy, preveterinary. **History:** General. **Liberal arts:** Arts/sciences. **Math:** General. **Parks/recreation:** Health/fitness. **Physical sciences:** Chemistry. **Psychology:** General. **Social sciences:** General. **Visual/performing arts:** Art, music.

Computing on campus. 995 workstations in dormitories, library, computer center, student center. Dormitories wired for high-speed internet access and linked to campus network. Commuter students can connect to campus network. Online course registration, online library, helpline, repair service, student web hosting, wireless network available.

Student life. Freshman orientation: Available, $15 fee. Preregistration for classes offered. Half-day sessions for students with concurrent sessions for parents; held on 2 separate days in both April and June. **Policies:** Tobacco-free campus. **Housing:** Guaranteed on-campus for freshmen. Coed dorms, single-sex dorms, apartments available. $50 fully refundable deposit. Apartments for students with children. **Activities:** Bands, campus ministries, choral groups, drama, international student organizations, literary magazine, music ensembles, student government, student newspaper, inter-residence hall council, inter-fraternity/sorority council, inter-varsity Christian fellowship, Music Educators National Conference, Student National Education Association, Newman Club, Association of Information Technology Professionals, Faith Lutheran student club.

Athletics. NAIA. **Intercollegiate:** Baseball M, basketball, cross-country, football (tackle) M, golf, softball W, track and field, volleyball W. **Intramural:** Basketball, bowling, football (non-tackle), golf, ice hockey, racquetball, softball, track and field, volleyball. **Team name:** Vikings.

Student services. Career counseling, student employment services, financial aid counseling, health services, on-campus daycare, personal counseling, placement for graduates, veterans' counselor.

Contact. E-mail: enrollment.services@vcsu.edu
Phone: (701) 845-7101 Toll-free number: (800) 532-8641 ext. 7101
Fax: (701) 845-7299
Charlene Stenson, Director of Enrollment Services, Valley City State University, 101 College Street SW, Valley City, ND 58072-4098

Ohio

Allegheny Wesleyan College
Salem, Ohio
www.awc.edu **CB code: 4120**

- Private 4-year Bible college affiliated with Allegheny Wesleyan Methodist Connection
- Residential campus in small town

General. Accredited by ABHE. **Location:** 2 miles from Salem. **Calendar:** Semester.

Annual costs/financial aid. Tuition/fees (2011-2012): $5,550. Room/board: $3,300. Books/supplies: $550. Personal expenses: $800.

Contact. Phone: (330) 337-6403
Director of Admissions, 2161 Woodside Road, Salem, OH 44460-9598

Antioch University Midwest
Yellow Springs, Ohio
www.midwest.antioch.edu **CB code: 4527**

- Private 4-year university and branch campus college
- Commuter campus in small town
- 142 degree-seeking undergraduates: 54% part-time, 69% women, 18% African American, 2% Asian American, 1% Hispanic American, 4% Native American
- 403 degree-seeking graduate students
- Application essay, interview required

General. Founded in 1988. Regionally accredited. **Degrees:** 62 bachelor's awarded; master's offered. **Location:** 18 miles from Dayton. **Calendar:** Quarter, limited summer session. **Full-time faculty:** 20 total. **Part-time faculty:** 30 total. **Special facilities:** Nature reserve.

Basis for selection. Applicants must be over 21.

2011-2012 Annual costs. Tuition/fees: $16,488.

Application procedures. Admission: $45 fee, may be waived for applicants with need. Admission notification on a rolling basis. **Financial aid:** No deadline. Applicants notified on a rolling basis.

Academics. Special study options: Combined bachelor's/graduate degree, cross-registration, distance learning, double major, independent study, student-designed major, teacher certification program, weekend college. **Credit/placement by examination:** AP, CLEP. 45 credit hours maximum toward bachelor's degree. **Support services:** Reduced course load, writing center.

Majors. Business: Business admin, human resources. **Education:** General, early childhood. **Liberal arts:** Arts/sciences, humanities. **Math:** General.

Most popular majors. Business/marketing 20%, education 25%, health sciences 14%, liberal arts 15%, psychology 14%, public administration/social services 12%.

Computing on campus. PC or laptop required. 35 workstations in computer center. Commuter students can connect to campus network. Online course registration, online library, helpline, wireless network available.

Student life. Freshman orientation: Mandatory, $25 fee. Preregistration for classes offered. **Activities:** Radio station.

Student services. Adult student services, financial aid counseling.

Contact. E-mail: sas.aum@antioch.edu
Phone: (937) 769-1818 Fax: (937) 769-1804
Oscar Robinson, Director of Admissions, Antioch University Midwest, 900 Dayton Street, Yellow Springs, OH 45387

Art Academy of Cincinnati
Cincinnati, Ohio
www.artacademy.edu **CB code: 1002**

- Private 4-year visual arts college
- Commuter campus in large city

General. Founded in 1869. Regionally accredited. **Location:** One mile from downtown. **Calendar:** Semester.

Annual costs/financial aid. Tuition/fees (2011-2012): $23,530. Room: $6,000. Books/supplies: $1,500. Personal expenses: $1,200. Need-based financial aid available to full-time and part-time students.

Contact. Phone: (513) 562-8740
Vice President of Enrollment Management, 1212 Jackson Street, Cincinnati, OH 45202

Ashland University
Ashland, Ohio
www.ashland.edu **CB code: 1021**

- Private 4-year university and liberal arts college affiliated with Brethren Church
- Residential campus in large town
- 2,503 degree-seeking undergraduates: 6% part-time, 60% women, 5% African American, 2% Hispanic American, 3% international
- 2,077 degree-seeking graduate students
- 72% of applicants admitted
- SAT or ACT (ACT writing optional) required
- 60% graduate within 6 years

General. Founded in 1878. Regionally accredited. **Degrees:** 611 bachelor's, 14 associate awarded; master's, doctoral offered. **Location:** 60 miles from Cleveland, 80 miles from Columbus. **Calendar:** Semester, limited summer session. **Full-time faculty:** 276 total; 82% have terminal degrees, 8% minority, 47% women. **Part-time faculty:** 284 total; 33% have terminal degrees, 3% minority, 52% women. **Class size:** 68% < 20, 31% 20-39, less than 1% 50-99. **Special facilities:** Centers for public affairs, business and economic research, convocation, numismatic, nonviolence, educational improvement, entrepreneurial studies, institute for middle level education.

Freshman class profile. 3,463 applied, 2,502 admitted, 611 enrolled.

Mid 50% test scores			
SAT critical reading:	440-540	GPA 2.0-2.99:	24%
SAT math:	450-560	Rank in top quarter:	46%
SAT writing:	440-530	Rank in top tenth:	18%
ACT composite:	20-25	End year in good standing:	84%
GPA 3.75 or higher:	27%	Return as sophomores:	72%
GPA 3.50-3.74:	16%	Out-of-state:	10%
GPA 3.0-3.49:	32%	Live on campus:	95%
		International:	2%

Basis for selection. School achievement record most important; test scores also important. Counselor's recommendation considered. Interview recommended for all; audition recommended for music, theater programs; portfolio recommended for art. **Home schooled:** Transcript of courses and grades required.

High school preparation. College-preparatory program recommended. Required and recommended units include English 3-4, mathematics 3-4, social studies 2-3, history 1, science 3, foreign language 2 and academic electives 1.

2011-2012 Annual costs. Tuition/fees: $28,582. Room/board: $9,352. Books/supplies: $900. Personal expenses: $1,801.

2011-2012 Financial aid. Need-based: 593 full-time freshmen applied for aid; 521 were judged to have need; 521 of these received aid. Average need met was 90%. Average scholarship/grant was $19,798; average loan $3,900. 65% of total undergraduate aid awarded as scholarships/grants, 35% as loans/jobs. **Non-need-based:** Awarded to 1,849 full-time undergraduates, including 581 freshmen. Scholarships awarded for academics, alumni affiliation, art, athletics, job skills, leadership, minority status, music/drama, religious affiliation.

Application procedures. Admission: Priority date 8/15; no deadline. No application fee. Admission notification on a rolling basis beginning on or about 8/1. Must reply by May 1 or within 4 week(s) if notified thereafter. **Financial aid:** Priority date 3/15; no closing date. FAFSA required. Applicants notified on a rolling basis starting 3/1.

Academics. Seminary on quarter system. **Special study options:** Distance learning, double major, dual enrollment of high school students, ESL, honors, independent study, internships, student-designed major, study abroad, teacher certification program. Pre-MBA courses for graduated nonbusiness majors, bachelor's degree completion program for RNs, teacher licensure for those with non-teaching degrees, pre-seminary. **Credit/placement by examination:** AP, CLEP, IB, SAT, ACT, institutional tests. 32 credit hours maximum toward associate degree, 32 toward bachelor's. **Support services:** Learning center, study skills assistance, tutoring, writing center.

Majors. Biology: General, biochemistry, biotechnology, exercise physiology, toxicology. **Business:** General, accounting, actuarial science, business admin, entrepreneurial studies, fashion, finance, hospitality admin, international, logistics, management information systems, marketing. **Communications:** Digital media, organizational, persuasive communications, radio/TV, sports. **Computer sciences:** Computer science. **Conservation:** Environmental science. **Education:** Art, biology, chemistry, early childhood, early childhood special, earth science, English, family/consumer sciences, French, mathematics, middle, multiple handicapped, music, physical, science, social studies, Spanish. **English:** Creative writing, English lit. **Foreign languages:** French, Spanish. **Health services:** Athletic training, dietetics. **History:** General. **Human services:** Social work. **Math:** General. **Parks/recreation:** Sports admin. **Philosophy/religion:** Philosophy, religion. **Physical sciences:** Chemistry, geology, physics. **Protective services:** Forensics, law enforcement admin. **Psychology:** General. **Social sciences:** Economics, international relations, political science. **Visual/performing arts:** Commercial/advertising art, dramatic, graphic design, music, music theory/composition, studio arts. **Work/family studies:** Family studies.

Most popular majors. Biology 6%, business/marketing 24%, education 26%, health sciences 14%.

Computing on campus. 500 workstations in dormitories, library, computer center, student center. Dormitories wired for high-speed internet access and linked to campus network. Commuter students can connect to campus network. Online course registration, online library, helpline, repair service, wireless network available.

Student life. Freshman orientation: Available, $100 fee. Preregistration for classes offered. One-day program usually held in June and July. **Housing:** Guaranteed on-campus for all undergraduates. Coed dorms, single-sex dorms, apartments, fraternity/sorority housing, wellness housing available. $300 fully refundable deposit, deadline 8/15. Scholar hall available. Apartments available to seniors. **Activities:** Bands, campus ministries, choral groups, dance, drama, international student organizations, literary magazine, music ensembles, musical theater, radio station, student government, student newspaper, symphony orchestra, TV station, Christian Fellowship, Newman Club, Fellowship of Christian Athletes, international club, black student union, campus activities board, community care, adventure club, Republican/Democratic club.

Athletics. NCAA. **Intercollegiate:** Baseball M, basketball, cheerleading M, cross-country, diving, football (tackle) M, golf, soccer, softball W, swimming, tennis W, track and field, volleyball W, wrestling M. **Intramural:** Badminton, basketball, bowling, football (non-tackle), golf, racquetball, soccer, softball, table tennis, tennis, track and field, volleyball. **Team name:** Eagles.

Student services. Adult student services, alcohol/substance abuse counseling, chaplain/spiritual director, career counseling, student employment services, financial aid counseling, health services, minority student services, personal counseling, placement for graduates, veterans' counselor. **Physically disabled:** Services for visually, speech, hearing impaired.

Contact. E-mail: enrollme@ashland.edu
Phone: (419) 289-5052 Toll-free number: (800) 882-1548 ext. 5052
Fax: (419) 289-5999
W.C. Vance, Director of Admissions, Ashland University, 401 College Avenue, Ashland, OH 44805-9981

Baldwin-Wallace College
Berea, Ohio   **CB member**
www.bw.edu   **CB code: 1050**

- Private 4-year liberal arts college affiliated with United Methodist Church
- Residential campus in large town
- 3,411 degree-seeking undergraduates: 12% part-time, 55% women, 8% African American, 1% Asian American, 4% Hispanic American, 1% international
- 611 degree-seeking graduate students
- 63% of applicants admitted
- Application essay required
- 69% graduate within 6 years; 28% enter graduate study

General. Founded in 1845. Regionally accredited. Campus in Beachwood, offering evening and Saturday classes for bachelor's and master's degrees in business, professional development and executive education. **Degrees:** 770 bachelor's awarded; master's offered. **ROTC:** Army, Air Force. **Location:** 15 miles from Cleveland. **Calendar:** Semester, limited summer session. **Full-time faculty:** 165 total; 83% have terminal degrees, 9% minority, 45% women. **Part-time faculty:** 232 total; 15% have terminal degrees, 8% minority, 50% women. **Class size:** 57% < 20, 41% 20-39, less than 1% 40-49, less than 1% 50-99. **Special facilities:** Observatory, 2 art galleries, 2 theaters, conservatory of music, 2 dance studios, cybercafe, arboretum, Lyceum Square (historical site).

Freshman class profile. 3,748 applied, 2,372 admitted, 665 enrolled.

Mid 50% test scores			
SAT critical reading:	470-610	Rank in top quarter:	54%
SAT math:	470-610	Rank in top tenth:	22%
SAT writing:	460-590	End year in good standing:	89%
ACT composite:	20-27	Return as sophomores:	81%
GPA 3.75 or higher:	33%	Out-of-state:	19%
GPA 3.50-3.74:	18%	Live on campus:	84%
GPA 3.0-3.49:	28%	International:	1%
GPA 2.0-2.99:	21%	Fraternities:	10%
		Sororities:	18%

Basis for selection. Academic achievement (preferably 3.2 GPA) and class rank (preferably top 30%) most important. Test scores used to support data from high school record. 23 ACT, 550 SAT verbal, 550 SAT math recommended. Applicants must be graduates of accredited secondary school. Test optional for full-time, first-time freshmen. In lieu of test scores, copy of recent graded school paper required. Interview recommended for all; audition required for music, music education, music theater, and music therapy programs; portfolio recommended for art program. **Home schooled:** Statement describing home school structure and mission, transcript of courses and grades, letter of recommendation (nonparent) required. Home schooled students must provide SAT/ACT.

High school preparation. College-preparatory program required. 16 units required; 23 recommended. Required and recommended units include English 4, mathematics 3-4, social studies 2-3, history 1, science 3-4 (laboratory 2), foreign language 1-2 and academic electives 3. Some flexibility in choice of subjects permitted.

2011-2012 Annual costs. Tuition/fees: $26,396. Room/board: $7,346. Books/supplies: $1,334. Personal expenses: $3,500.

2011-2012 Financial aid. Need-based: 617 full-time freshmen applied for aid; 555 were judged to have need; 555 of these received aid. Average need met was 87%. Average scholarship/grant was $17,031; average loan $3,882. 67% of total undergraduate aid awarded as scholarships/grants, 33% as loans/jobs. **Non-need-based:** Awarded to 1,007 full-time undergraduates, including 189 freshmen. Scholarships awarded for academics, alumni affiliation, art, minority status, music/drama, religious affiliation, state residency.

Application procedures. Admission: Priority date 3/1; no deadline. $25 fee, may be waived for applicants with need, free for online applicants. Admission notification on a rolling basis beginning on or about 11/1. Must reply by May 1 or within 3 week(s) if notified thereafter. New Student Fee of $200 refundable until May 1. **Financial aid:** Priority date 5/1, closing date 9/1. FAFSA required. Applicants notified on a rolling basis starting 2/14.

Academics. Weekend classes limited to nontraditional students. **Special study options:** Accelerated study, combined bachelor's/graduate degree, cross-registration, distance learning, double major, dual enrollment of high school students, ESL, exchange student, honors, independent study, internships, liberal arts/career combination, semester at sea, student-designed major, study abroad, teacher certification program, Washington semester. 3-2 in engineering with Case Western Reserve University and Columbia University (NY); 3-2 in Social Work with Case Western Reserve University; 3/2 Accounting MBA, 3/2 Human Resources MBA and 3/2 Computer Science/Info. Systems MBA Programs. **Credit/placement by examination:** AP, CLEP, IB, SAT, ACT, institutional tests. **Support services:** Learning center, reduced course load, remedial instruction, study skills assistance, tutoring, writing center.

Majors. Biology: General, exercise physiology, neuroscience. **Business:** Accounting, business admin, finance, human resources, international, marketing, organizational leadership. **Communications:** Communications/speech/rhetoric, digital media, media studies, public relations. **Computer sciences:** Computer science, networking, systems analysis. **Conservation:** Economics. **Education:** General, early childhood, learning disabled, middle, music. **Engineering:** Pre-engineering. **English:** Creative writing, English lit. **Foreign languages:** French, German, Spanish. **Health services:** Athletic training, communication disorders, health care admin, music therapy, predental, premedicine, prepharmacy, prephysical therapy, preveterinary, public health ed. **History:** General. **Math:** General. **Parks/recreation:** Health/fitness, sports admin. **Philosophy/religion:** Philosophy, religion. **Physical sciences:** Chemistry, physics. **Protective services:** Criminal justice. **Psychology:** General. **Social sciences:** Econometrics, economics, political science, sociology.

Visual/performing arts: Art, art history/conservation, dramatic, film/cinema/video, music, music history, music performance, music theory/composition, musical theater, piano/keyboard, studio arts, voice/opera.

Most popular majors. Biology 10%, business/marketing 24%, communications/journalism 6%, education 8%, parks/recreation 6%, science technologies 7%, visual/performing arts 8%.

Computing on campus. 565 workstations in dormitories, library, computer center, student center. Dormitories wired for high-speed internet access and linked to campus network. Commuter students can connect to campus network. Online course registration, online library, helpline, repair service, student web hosting, wireless network available.

Student life. Freshman orientation: Mandatory, $100 fee. Preregistration for classes offered. Two-day program held in June, July, August. **Policies:** All full-time students required to live on campus first and second year. Residency exemptions made for commuting students living with families. **Housing:** Guaranteed on-campus for freshmen. Coed dorms, special housing for disabled, apartments, fraternity/sorority housing available. Housing for single mothers and children, student-directed learning communities, living and learning center available. **Activities:** Bands, campus ministries, choral groups, dance, drama, film society, international student organizations, literary magazine, music ensembles, Model UN, musical theater, opera, radio station, student government, student newspaper, symphony orchestra, TV station, Campus Crusade for Christ, Hillel, Newman student organization, College Democrats, College Republicans, black student alliance, Hispanic American student association, Middle Eastern student alliance, Circle K International, Habitat for Humanity.

Athletics. NCAA. **Intercollegiate:** Baseball M, basketball, cross-country, diving, football (tackle) M, golf, soccer, softball W, swimming, tennis, track and field, volleyball W, wrestling M. **Intramural:** Badminton, basketball, football (non-tackle), football (tackle) M, golf, racquetball, soccer, softball, tennis, volleyball, wrestling M. **Team name:** Yellow Jackets.

Student services. Adult student services, alcohol/substance abuse counseling, chaplain/spiritual director, career counseling, student employment services, financial aid counseling, health services, minority student services, personal counseling. **Physically disabled:** Services for visually, speech, hearing impaired.

Contact. E-mail: admission@bw.edu
Phone: (440) 826-2222 Toll-free number: (877) 292-7759
Fax: (440) 826-3830
Susan Dileno, Vice President of Enrollment Management, Baldwin-Wallace College, 275 Eastland Road, Berea, OH 44017-2088

Bluffton University
Bluffton, Ohio
www.bluffton.edu   **CB code: 1067**

▶ Private 4-year liberal arts college affiliated with Mennonite Church
▶ Residential campus in small town
▶ 961 degree-seeking undergraduates: 8% part-time, 53% women, 7% African American, 2% Hispanic American, 1% international
▶ 114 degree-seeking graduate students
▶ 64% of applicants admitted
▶ SAT or ACT (ACT writing optional) required
▶ 59% graduate within 6 years

General. Founded in 1899. Regionally accredited. Christian faith, values, and service to others in the Anabaptist, peace church tradition. **Degrees:** 213 bachelor's awarded; master's offered. **Location:** 15 miles from Lima, 65 miles from Toledo. **Calendar:** Semester, limited summer session. **Full-time faculty:** 63 total; 76% have terminal degrees, 3% minority, 36% women. **Part-time faculty:** 41 total; 7% have terminal degrees, 7% minority, 37% women. **Class size:** 62% < 20, 32% 20-39, 4% 40-49, less than 1% 50-99, less than 1% >100. **Special facilities:** Nature preserve, peace arts center.

Freshman class profile. 1,915 applied, 1,226 admitted, 250 enrolled.

Mid 50% test scores			
SAT critical reading:	440-550	GPA 2.0-2.99:	29%
SAT math:	460-550	Rank in top quarter:	42%
ACT composite:	19-24	Rank in top tenth:	16%
GPA 3.75 or higher:	24%	Return as sophomores:	64%
GPA 3.50-3.74:	15%	Out-of-state:	25%
GPA 3.0-3.49:	32%	Live on campus:	95%

Basis for selection. Class rank, school achievement record, and test scores very important. Campus visit and interview strongly recommended. Essay

required for academically weak students; audition and portfolio required for scholarships in music and art. **Home schooled:** Interview required.

High school preparation. College-preparatory program recommended. 16 units recommended. Recommended units include English 4, mathematics 3, social studies 3, science 3 and foreign language 3.

2011-2012 Annual costs. Tuition/fees: $26,154. Room/board: $8,756. Books/supplies: $1,400. Personal expenses: $1,600.

2011-2012 Financial aid. Need-based: 247 full-time freshmen applied for aid; 237 were judged to have need; 237 of these received aid. Average need met was 92%. Average scholarship/grant was $18,535; average loan $4,363. 55% of total undergraduate aid awarded as scholarships/grants, 45% as loans/jobs. **Non-need-based:** Awarded to 108 full-time undergraduates, including 36 freshmen. Scholarships awarded for academics, art, job skills, minority status, music/drama, religious affiliation, state residency.

Application procedures. Admission: Priority date 5/1; deadline 8/15 (receipt date). $20 fee, may be waived for applicants with need, free for online applicants. Admission notification on a rolling basis beginning on or about 6/1. **Financial aid:** Priority date 5/1, closing date 10/1. FAFSA required. Applicants notified on a rolling basis starting 3/1; must reply within 3 week(s) of notification.

Academics. Special study options: Accelerated study, distance learning, double major, dual enrollment of high school students, honors, independent study, internships, liberal arts/career combination, student-designed major, study abroad, teacher certification program, Washington semester. Degree-completion program for working adults 25 years and older. **Credit/placement by examination:** AP, CLEP, SAT, ACT, institutional tests. 20 credit hours maximum toward bachelor's degree. **Support services:** Learning center, reduced course load, remedial instruction, study skills assistance, tutoring, writing center.

Majors. Biology: General. **Business:** Accounting, business admin, management information systems, organizational behavior. **Communications:** Communications/speech/rhetoric. **Computer sciences:** Information technology. **Education:** General, art, biology, business, chemistry, early childhood, elementary, English, health, history, kindergarten/preschool, mathematics, mentally handicapped, middle, music, physical, physics, science, secondary, social studies, special ed. **English:** English lit. **Foreign languages:** Spanish. **Health services:** Premedicine. **History:** General. **Human services:** Social work. **Math:** General. **Parks/recreation:** Facilities management, health/fitness, sports admin. **Philosophy/religion:** Religion. **Physical sciences:** Chemistry, physics. **Protective services:** Criminal justice. **Psychology:** General. **Social sciences:** General, economics, sociology. **Theology:** Youth ministry. **Visual/performing arts:** Art, music. **Work/family studies:** Clothing/textiles, food/nutrition.

Most popular majors. Business/marketing 40%, education 17%, history 6%, parks/recreation 7%, public administration/social services 6%.

Computing on campus. 125 workstations in dormitories, library, computer center, student center. Dormitories wired for high-speed internet access and linked to campus network. Commuter students can connect to campus network. Online course registration, online library, helpline, repair service, student web hosting, wireless network available.

Student life. Freshman orientation: Mandatory. Preregistration for classes offered. Fall orientation begins Friday before classes and continues through first week of classes. Additional 1-day event held over summer; students can choose 1 of 4 dates. **Policies:** No alcoholic beverages or tobacco allowed on campus. Honor system applies to all student activities. Students should feel comfortable with emphasis on faith and values. Voluntary chapel service once each week. All traditional undergraduate students required to live on campus or commute from home. **Housing:** Guaranteed on-campus for all undergraduates. Coed dorms, single-sex dorms available. **Activities:** Bands, campus ministries, choral groups, dance, drama, film society, international student organizations, literary magazine, music ensembles, musical theater, radio station, student government, student newspaper, departmental clubs, Brothers and Sisters in Christ, peace club, Habitat for Humanity, Fellowship of Christian Athletes, African American student organization, peer awareness leaders, College Republicans, Young Democrats.

Athletics. NCAA. **Intercollegiate:** Baseball M, basketball, cheerleading M, cross-country, football (tackle) M, soccer, softball W, tennis, track and field, volleyball W. **Intramural:** Basketball, bowling, football (non-tackle), softball, volleyball. **Team name:** Beavers.

Student services. Alcohol/substance abuse counseling, chaplain/spiritual director, career counseling, student employment services, financial aid counseling, health services, minority student services, personal counseling, placement for graduates. **Physically disabled:** Services for visually, hearing impaired.

Contact. E-mail: admissions@bluffton.edu
Phone: (419) 358-3257 Toll-free number: (800) 488-3257
Fax: (419) 358-3081
Chris Jebsen, Director of Admissions, Bluffton University, 1 University
Drive, Bluffton, OH 45817-2104

Bowling Green State University
Bowling Green, Ohio
www.bgsu.edu

CB member
CB code: 1069

- Public 4-year university
- Residential campus in large town
- 14,803 degree-seeking undergraduates: 7% part-time, 55% women, 11% African American, 1% Asian American, 4% Hispanic American, 2% international
- 2,209 degree-seeking graduate students
- 76% of applicants admitted
- SAT or ACT (ACT writing optional) required
- 58% graduate within 6 years

General. Founded in 1910. Regionally accredited. **Degrees:** 2,729 bachelor's awarded; master's, doctoral offered. **ROTC:** Army, Air Force. **Location:** 23 miles from Toledo. **Calendar:** Semester, limited summer session. **Full-time faculty:** 827 total; 74% have terminal degrees, 14% minority, 47% women. **Part-time faculty:** 260 total; 6% minority, 50% women. **Class size:** 34% < 20, 53% 20-39, 5% 40-49, 5% 50-99, 3% >100. **Special facilities:** Planetarium, film theater, sound recording archives, popular culture library, marine biology laboratory, educational memorabilia center.

Freshman class profile. 16,217 applied, 12,251 admitted, 3,861 enrolled.

Mid 50% test scores			
SAT critical reading:	440-570	Rank in top quarter:	35%
SAT math:	440-560	Rank in top tenth:	13%
SAT writing:	420-540	End year in good standing:	79%
ACT composite:	19-24	Return as sophomores:	72%
GPA 3.75 or higher:	18%	Out-of-state:	15%
GPA 3.50-3.74:	13%	Live on campus:	90%
GPA 3.0-3.49:	34%	International:	1%
GPA 2.0-2.99:	35%	Fraternities:	7%
		Sororities:	6%

Basis for selection. High school coursework/curriculum, cumulative grade point average, test scores, class rank very important. Interview recommended for all; audition required for music/theater; portfolio required for art programs. Essays required for honors program. **Home schooled:** Transcript of courses and grades required. **Learning Disabled:** Prospective students encouraged to arrange an interview with Disability Services.

High school preparation. College-preparatory program recommended. Recommended units include English 4, mathematics 3, social studies 3, science 3 (laboratory 2), foreign language 2 and visual/performing arts 1.

2011-2012 Annual costs. Tuition/fees: $10,164; $17,472 out-of-state. Room/board: $7,794. Books/supplies: $1,140. Personal expenses: $2,164.

2010-2011 Financial aid. Need-based: 3,385 full-time freshmen applied for aid; 2,904 were judged to have need; 2,904 of these received aid. Average need met was 75%. Average scholarship/grant was $6,405; average loan $6,156. 44% of total undergraduate aid awarded as scholarships/grants, 56% as loans/jobs. **Non-need-based:** Awarded to 2,739 full-time undergraduates, including 980 freshmen. Scholarships awarded for academics, alumni affiliation, art, athletics, leadership, minority status, music/drama, ROTC, state residency.

Application procedures. Admission: Priority date 2/1; deadline 7/15 (postmark date). $45 fee, may be waived for applicants with need. Admission notification on a rolling basis beginning on or about 10/1. Must reply by 5/1. **Financial aid:** No deadline. FAFSA required. Applicants notified on a rolling basis starting 4/15; must reply within 3 week(s) of notification.

Academics. Evening degree programs and career counseling offered for adults in the greater community. **Special study options:** Accelerated study, combined bachelor's/graduate degree, cooperative education, cross-registration, distance learning, double major, dual enrollment of high school students, ESL, exchange student, honors, independent study, internships, liberal arts/career combination, student-designed major, study abroad, teacher certification program, Washington semester. **Credit/placement by examination:** AP, CLEP, IB, SAT, ACT, institutional tests. Students must be enrolled for at least 2 credit hours during the semester of the exam, have permission of the department and dean, the student must not have enrolled in the course previously and must present sufficient evidence of prior study or experience, and the (credit by exam) course cannot be a prerequisite for any course the student has completed. **Support services:** Learning center, pre-admission

summer program, reduced course load, remedial instruction, study skills assistance, tutoring, writing center.

Majors. Architecture: Environmental design, interior. **Area/ethnic studies:** African, African-American, American, Asian, Chicano/Hispanic-American/Latino, European, Latin American, Russian/Slavic, women's. **Biology:** General, bacteriology, biochemistry, neuroscience, parasitology. **Business:** General, accounting, actuarial science, business admin, executive assistant, fashion, finance, hospitality admin, human resources, insurance, international, labor relations, logistics, management information systems, market research, office management, operations, organizational behavior, real estate, retailing, sales/distribution, tourism promotion, tourism/travel. **Communications:** Advertising, broadcast journalism, communications/speech/rhetoric, journalism, public relations, radio/TV. **Computer sciences:** General. **Conservation:** Environmental studies, management/policy. **Education:** General, art, biology, business, chemistry, college student counseling, computer, Deaf/hearing impaired, drama/dance, educational technology, elementary, English, family/consumer sciences, foreign languages, health, history, kindergarten/preschool, learning disabled, mathematics, mentally handicapped, middle, multi-level teacher, multiple handicapped, music, physical, physics, sales/marketing, school counseling, science, social science, social studies, special ed, speech, technology/industrial arts, trade/industrial, voc/tech. **Engineering:** Operations research. **English:** Creative writing, English lit, rhetoric/composition, technical writing. **Foreign languages:** Classics, French, German, Latin, Russian, Spanish. **Health services:** Art therapy, athletic training, audiology/speech pathology, clinical lab science, communication disorders, dietetics, environmental health, health care admin, medical records admin, nursing (RN), physical therapy, predental, premedicine, vocational rehab counseling. **History:** General. **Human services:** General, social work. **Liberal arts:** Arts/sciences. **Math:** General, statistics. **Parks/recreation:** General, sports admin. **Philosophy/religion:** Philosophy. **Physical sciences:** Chemistry, geochemistry, geology, geophysics, paleontology, physics. **Protective services:** Corrections, criminal justice, fire services admin, law enforcement admin, police science. **Psychology:** General. **Social sciences:** General, economics, geography, international relations, political science, sociology. **Theology:** Sacred music. **Visual/performing arts:** Art, art history/conservation, ceramics, commercial/advertising art, crafts, design, dramatic, drawing, fashion design, fiber arts, film/cinema/video, metal/jewelry, music, music history, music performance, music theory/composition, musicology, painting, photography, piano/keyboard, printmaking, sculpture, studio arts, voice/opera. **Work/family studies:** General, aging, child development, clothing/textiles, family studies, family systems, family/community services, food/nutrition.

Most popular majors. Business/marketing 14%, education 19%, health sciences 9%, parks/recreation 6%, visual/performing arts 10%.

Computing on campus. 1,500 workstations in dormitories, library, computer center, student center. Dormitories wired for high-speed internet access and linked to campus network. Commuter students can connect to campus network. Online course registration, online library, helpline, repair service, student web hosting, wireless network available.

Student life. Freshman orientation: Available. Preregistration for classes offered. **Housing:** Guaranteed on-campus for freshmen. Coed dorms, special housing for disabled, apartments, fraternity/sorority housing, wellness housing available. $200 deposit, deadline 5/1. Honors housing, no-alcohol wings. **Activities:** Bands, campus ministries, choral groups, dance, drama, film society, international student organizations, literary magazine, music ensembles, Model UN, musical theater, opera, radio station, student government, student newspaper, symphony orchestra, TV station, Active Christians Today, African Peoples Association, Asian Communities, United Latino Student Union, world student association, women's group, College Democrats, College Republicans, Habitat for Humanity, environmental action group.

Athletics. NCAA. **Intercollegiate:** Baseball M, basketball, cross-country, football (tackle) M, golf, gymnastics W, ice hockey M, soccer, softball W, swimming W, tennis W, track and field W, volleyball W. **Intramural:** Badminton, baseball M, basketball, football (non-tackle), golf, racquetball, soccer, softball, swimming W, tennis W, track and field W, volleyball, water polo. **Team name:** Falcons.

Student services. Adult student services, alcohol/substance abuse counseling, career counseling, services for economically disadvantaged, student employment services, financial aid counseling, health services, legal services, minority student services, personal counseling, placement for graduates, veterans' counselor, women's services. **Physically disabled:** Services for visually, speech, hearing impaired.

Contact. E-mail: choosebgsu@bgsu.edu
Phone: (419) 372-BGSU Toll-free number: (866) 246-6732
Fax: (419) 372-6955
Gary Swegan, Assistant Vice President/Director of Admissions, Bowling Green State University, 110 McFall Center, Bowling Green, OH 43403-0085

Bryant & Stratton College: Eastlake
Eastlake, Ohio
www.bryantstratton.edu
CB code: 3251

- For-profit 4-year business college
- Commuter campus in small town
- 942 degree-seeking undergraduates
- Interview required

General. Degrees: 22 bachelor's, 189 associate awarded. **Location:** 15 miles from downtown Cleveland. **Calendar:** Differs by program, limited summer session. **Full-time faculty:** 23 total. **Part-time faculty:** 61 total.

Basis for selection. Open admission. Student's evaluation and diagnostic tests must show qualification for at least pre-college, preparatory math and English courses. **Learning Disabled:** Students with learning disability must provide instructional effectiveness plan from high school counselor.

2011-2012 Annual costs. Tuition/fees: $15,570. Books/supplies: $1,800. Personal expenses: $300.

Financial aid. Non-need-based: Scholarships awarded for academics.

Application procedures. Admission: Closing date 9/11 (receipt date). $35 fee. Admission notification on a rolling basis. **Financial aid:** No deadline. FAFSA required. Applicants notified on a rolling basis.

Academics. ACTIVUM learning system facilitates students in developing technical and career-based skills through field trips, portfolio presentations, computer simulations and internship opportunities. **Special study options:** Accelerated study, distance learning, double major, dual enrollment of high school students, independent study, internships. Professional skills center offers medical coding courses and computer certification. **Credit/placement by examination:** AP, CLEP, institutional tests. 12 credit hours maximum toward associate degree, 12 toward bachelor's. **Support services:** Remedial instruction, study skills assistance, tutoring.

Majors. Business: Business admin.

Computing on campus. 400 workstations in library, computer center. Commuter students can connect to campus network. Online library, helpline, repair service, wireless network available.

Student life. Freshman orientation: Mandatory. Preregistration for classes offered. Various 4-hour sessions over 1-2 days prior to start of each term. **Activities:** Student government, student newspaper, student council, Institute of Management Accountants, PC users group, campus ambassador society.

Athletics. NJCAA. **Intercollegiate:** Soccer M. **Team name:** Bobcats.

Student services. Adult student services, student employment services, financial aid counseling, placement for graduates. **Physically disabled:** Services for visually, speech, hearing impaired.

Contact. E-mail: mejohnson@bryantstratton.edu
Phone: (440) 510-1112 Fax: (440) 306-2015
Melanie Johnson, Director of Admissions, Bryant & Stratton College: Eastlake, 35350 Curtis Boulevard, Eastlake, OH 44095

Bryant & Stratton College: Parma
Parma, Ohio
www.bryantstratton.edu
CB code: 0577

- For-profit 4-year nursing and junior college
- Commuter campus in small city
- 788 degree-seeking undergraduates: 47% part-time, 83% women, 20% African American, 8% Hispanic American, 1% Native American
- Application essay, interview required
- 36% graduate within 6 years

General. Founded in 1854. Regionally accredited. On-line classes available. **Degrees:** 13 bachelor's, 187 associate awarded. **Location:** 10 miles from Cleveland. **Calendar:** Semester, extensive summer session. **Full-time faculty:** 29 total; 7% have terminal degrees, 10% minority, 41% women. **Part-time faculty:** 51 total; 4% have terminal degrees, 8% minority, 57% women. **Class size:** 78% < 20, 21% 20-39, less than 1% 40-49.

Basis for selection. Open admission, but selective for some programs. Nursing program requires either a high school transcript or a GED. Portfolio

recommended. **Home schooled:** Transcript of courses and grades required. **Learning Disabled:** IEP plan required.

2011-2012 Annual costs. Tuition/fees: $15,570. Books/supplies: $1,600. Personal expenses: $3,111.

Financial aid. All financial aid based on need.

Application procedures. Admission: No deadline. $35 fee. Application must be submitted on paper. Admission notification on a rolling basis. **Financial aid:** No deadline. FAFSA required. Applicants notified on a rolling basis starting 6/1.

Academics. Special study options: Distance learning, internships. **Credit/placement by examination:** AP, CLEP, IB, institutional tests. 30 credit hours maximum toward associate degree, 30 toward bachelor's. Students must pass Proficiency Exams with a score of 90% or higher. **Support services:** Learning center, reduced course load, study skills assistance, tutoring.

Majors. Business: Business admin. **Protective services:** Law enforcement admin.

Most popular majors. Business/marketing 50%.

Computing on campus. 107 workstations in library, computer center. Commuter students can connect to campus network. Online library, helpline, wireless network available.

Student life. Freshman orientation: Mandatory. Preregistration for classes offered. 3 hour program held week prior to start of classes.

Student services. Career counseling, student employment services, financial aid counseling, placement for graduates.

Contact. E-mail: atinman@bryantstratton.edu
Phone: (216) 265-3151 ext. 229 Fax: (216) 265-0325
Andrea Inman, Director of Admissions, Bryant & Stratton College: Parma, 12955 Snow Road, Parma, OH 44130-1013

Capital University
Columbus, Ohio
www.capital.edu
CB member
CB code: 1099

- Private 4-year university affiliated with Evangelical Lutheran Church in America
- Residential campus in very large city
- 2,582 degree-seeking undergraduates: 9% part-time, 58% women, 9% African American, 1% Asian American, 3% Hispanic American, 1% international
- 862 degree-seeking graduate students
- 76% of applicants admitted
- SAT or ACT (ACT writing optional) required
- 61% graduate within 6 years; 23% enter graduate study

General. Founded in 1830. Regionally accredited. **Degrees:** 583 bachelor's awarded; master's, professional offered. **ROTC:** Army, Air Force. **Location:** 5 miles from downtown. **Calendar:** Semester, limited summer session. **Full-time faculty:** 188 total; 76% have terminal degrees, 12% minority, 48% women. **Part-time faculty:** 241 total; 28% have terminal degrees, 9% minority, 56% women. **Class size:** 57% < 20, 39% 20-39, 2% 40-49, 1% 50-99.

Freshman class profile. 3,631 applied, 2,760 admitted, 626 enrolled.

Mid 50% test scores			
SAT critical reading:	480-610	Rank in top quarter:	53%
SAT math:	490-590	Rank in top tenth:	23%
SAT writing:	480-580	Return as sophomores:	74%
ACT composite:	21-27	Out-of-state:	11%
GPA 3.75 or higher:	32%	Live on campus:	87%
GPA 3.50-3.74:	20%	International:	1%
GPA 3.0-3.49:	29%	Fraternities:	4%
GPA 2.0-2.99:	19%	Sororities:	8%

Basis for selection. Academic achievement in college-preparatory curriculum most important. Recommendations, test scores, and extracurricular activities considered. Talent/ability considered for admission into the Conservatory of Music. Interview recommended for all; audition required for music program; portfolio recommended for art, art therapy programs. **Home schooled:** Statement describing home school structure and mission, transcript of courses and grades, letter of recommendation (nonparent) required.

High school preparation. College-preparatory program recommended. 18 units recommended. Recommended units include English 4, mathematics

3, social studies 3, science 3 (laboratory 2), foreign language 2 and visual/performing arts 1. Chemistry and algebra II for nursing applicants. One fine arts recommended.

2011-2012 Annual costs. Tuition/fees: $30,450. Room/board: $8,180. Books/supplies: $1,200. Personal expenses: $1,790.

2010-2011 Financial aid. Need-based: 671 full-time freshmen applied for aid; 625 were judged to have need; 625 of these received aid. Average need met was 95%. Average scholarship/grant was $3,451; average loan $3,447. 33% of total undergraduate aid awarded as scholarships/grants, 67% as loans/jobs. **Non-need-based:** Awarded to 2,258 full-time undergraduates, including 720 freshmen. Scholarships awarded for academics, alumni affiliation, art, leadership, minority status, music/drama, religious affiliation, state residency.

Application procedures. Admission: Priority date 12/1; deadline 5/1 (postmark date). $25 fee, may be waived for applicants with need, free for online applicants. Admission notification on a rolling basis beginning on or about 9/30. Must reply by May 1 or within 2 week(s) if notified thereafter. **Financial aid:** Priority date 3/1; no closing date. FAFSA required. Applicants notified on a rolling basis starting 3/25; must reply by 5/1.

Academics. Teacher certification for learning disabilities and reading. Paralegal certification available from law school. **Special study options:** Accelerated study, combined bachelor's/graduate degree, cooperative education, cross-registration, double major, dual enrollment of high school students, ESL, exchange student, external degree, honors, independent study, internships, liberal arts/career combination, student-designed major, study abroad, teacher certification program, Washington semester. Dual degree engineering program with Washington University, St. Louis, and Case Western Reserve; 3-2 occupational therapy program with Washington University, St. Louis. **Credit/placement by examination:** AP, CLEP, IB, SAT, ACT, institutional tests. 27 credit hours maximum toward bachelor's degree. **Support services:** Learning center, reduced course load, remedial instruction, study skills assistance, tutoring, writing center.

Majors. Biology: General, biochemistry. **Business:** Accounting, business admin, managerial economics, marketing. **Communications:** Communications/speech/rhetoric, organizational, public relations, radio/TV. **Computer sciences:** Computer science. **Conservation:** Environmental science. **Education:** Early childhood, middle, music, physical, special ed. **Engineering:** Computer. **English:** Creative writing, English lit. **Foreign languages:** French, Spanish. **Health services:** Art therapy, athletic training, nursing (RN). **History:** General. **Human services:** General, social work. **Math:** General. **Parks/recreation:** Exercise sciences, health/fitness. **Philosophy/religion:** Philosophy, religion. **Physical sciences:** Chemistry. **Psychology:** General. **Social sciences:** Criminology, economics, international relations, political science, sociology. **Visual/performing arts:** Art, dramatic, jazz, music, music management, music performance, music theory/composition, piano/keyboard, voice/opera.

Most popular majors. Business/marketing 12%, education 10%, health sciences 23%, psychology 7%, public administration/social services 8%, visual/performing arts 10%.

Computing on campus. 399 workstations in dormitories, library, computer center, student center. Dormitories wired for high-speed internet access and linked to campus network. Commuter students can connect to campus network. Online course registration, online library, helpline, wireless network available.

Student life. Freshman orientation: Mandatory. Preregistration for classes offered. One-day program in summer, 5-day program before start of classes. **Housing:** Guaranteed on-campus for freshmen. Coed dorms, special housing for disabled, apartments, fraternity/sorority housing, wellness housing available. $100 fully refundable deposit, deadline 5/1. Honors housing, self-governing areas, and group cluster housing available. **Activities:** Bands, campus ministries, choral groups, dance, drama, film society, international student organizations, literary magazine, music ensembles, musical theater, radio station, student government, student newspaper, black student union, Young Republicans, Campus Democrats, Circle K, Ebony Brotherhood Association, international student association, Capateers (volunteers), Habitat for Humanity, university programming.

Athletics. NCAA. **Intercollegiate:** Baseball M, basketball, cross-country, football (tackle) M, golf, soccer, softball W, tennis, track and field, volleyball W. **Intramural:** Basketball, bowling, football (non-tackle), softball, volleyball. **Team name:** Crusaders.

Student services. Chaplain/spiritual director, career counseling, student employment services, financial aid counseling, health services, minority student services, personal counseling, placement for graduates, veterans' counselor.

Contact. E-mail: admissions@capital.edu
Phone: (614) 236-6101 Toll-free number: (866) 544-6175
Fax: (614) 236-6926
Amanda Steiner, Director of Admission, Capital University, 1 College and Main, Columbus, OH 43209-2394

Case Western Reserve University
Cleveland, Ohio
www.case.edu

CB member
CB code: 1105

- Private 4-year university
- Residential campus in very large city
- 3,929 degree-seeking undergraduates: 1% part-time, 43% women, 4% African American, 17% Asian American, 3% Hispanic American, 7% international
- 5,380 degree-seeking graduate students
- 51% of applicants admitted
- SAT or ACT with writing, application essay required
- 78% graduate within 6 years; 41% enter graduate study

General. Founded in 1826. Regionally accredited. **Degrees:** 1,038 bachelor's awarded; master's, professional, doctoral offered. **ROTC:** Army, Air Force. **Location:** 4 miles from downtown. **Calendar:** Semester, extensive summer session. **Full-time faculty:** 758 total; 91% have terminal degrees, 18% minority, 42% women. **Part-time faculty:** 198 total; 71% have terminal degrees, 7% minority, 38% women. **Class size:** 62% < 20, 23% 20-39, 6% 40-49, 6% 50-99, 3% >100. **Special facilities:** Biology field station, observatory, interdisciplinary research centers, natural history museum, historical society, botanical garden.

Freshman class profile. 13,543 applied, 6,942 admitted, 902 enrolled.

Mid 50% test scores		Return as sophomores:	93%
SAT critical reading:	590-700	Out-of-state:	62%
SAT math:	650-740	Live on campus:	97%
SAT writing:	590-690	International:	8%
ACT composite:	28-32	Fraternities:	38%
Rank in top quarter:	92%	Sororities:	35%
Rank in top tenth:	63%		

Basis for selection. School achievement record and test scores most important. School and community activities, essays, recommendations, and interview also considered. Special consideration to applicants from culturally, educationally, or economically disadvantaged backgrounds. IELTS, AP International English test, or TOEFL required for all international students. Interview recommended for all; audition required for music, music education programs; portfolio required for art education program. **Home schooled:** Transcript of courses and grades, interview required. At least 3 SAT Subject Tests highly recommended. Students encouraged to submit at least 2 letters from outside instructors or employers.

High school preparation. College-preparatory program required. 16 units required. Required and recommended units include English 4, mathematics 3-4, social studies 3-4, science 3 (laboratory 2-3) and foreign language 2-3. 3 laboratory science recommended. 4 math, 1 chemistry and physics recommended for engineering. 3 laboratory science (1 chemistry) recommended for science, math, and premedical.

2011-2012 Annual costs. Tuition/fees: $39,120. Room/board: $11,938.

2011-2012 Financial aid. Need-based: 743 full-time freshmen applied for aid; 619 were judged to have need; 619 of these received aid. Average need met was 92%. Average scholarship/grant was $27,347; average loan $5,483. 69% of total undergraduate aid awarded as scholarships/grants, 31% as loans/jobs. **Non-need-based:** Awarded to 3,070 full-time undergraduates, including 764 freshmen. Scholarships awarded for academics, alumni affiliation, art, leadership, music/drama.

Application procedures. Admission: Closing date 1/15 (postmark date). No application fee. Application must be submitted online. Admission notification by 3/20. Must reply by 5/1. **Financial aid:** Priority date 2/15; no closing date. FAFSA, institutional form, CSS PROFILE required. Applicants notified on a rolling basis starting 3/15; must reply within 2 week(s) of notification.

Academics. Preprofessional Scholars Program gives talented undergraduates conditional acceptances to graduate schools of medicine, dentistry, law, and social work. Most programs allow students to pursue combined bachelor's/master's degrees. **Special study options:** Accelerated study, combined bachelor's/graduate degree, cooperative education, cross-registration, double major, dual enrollment of high school students, ESL, exchange student, honors, independent study, internships, liberal arts/career combination, student-designed major, study abroad, teacher certification program, Washington semester. Exchange program with Fisk University and Waseda University

(Japan), 3-2 binary program in engineering, biochemistry, and astronomy. **Credit/placement by examination:** AP, CLEP, IB, institutional tests. **Support services:** Learning center, pre-admission summer program, reduced course load, study skills assistance, tutoring, writing center.

Majors. Area/ethnic studies: American, Asian, French, German, Japanese, women's. **Biology:** General, biochemistry, computational, evolutionary. **Business:** Accounting, business admin. **Computer sciences:** General, computer science. **Conservation:** Environmental studies. **Education:** Art, music. **Engineering:** General, aerospace, applied physics, biomedical, chemical, civil, computer, electrical, materials, mechanical, polymer, systems. **English:** English lit. **Foreign languages:** Classics, comparative lit, French, German, Spanish. **Health services:** Communication disorders, dietetics, nursing (RN). **History:** General, science/technology. **Math:** General, applied, statistics. **Philosophy/religion:** Philosophy, religion. **Physical sciences:** Astronomy, chemistry, geology, materials science, physics. **Psychology:** General. **Social sciences:** Anthropology, economics, international relations, political science, sociology. **Visual/performing arts:** Art history/conservation, dramatic, music. **Work/family studies:** Human nutrition.

Most popular majors. Biology 12%, business/marketing 9%, engineering/ engineering technologies 28%, health sciences 8%, psychology 6%, social sciences 11%.

Computing on campus. 219 workstations in dormitories, library, computer center, student center. Dormitories wired for high-speed internet access and linked to campus network. Commuter students can connect to campus network. Online course registration, online library, helpline, repair service, student web hosting, wireless network available.

Student life. Freshman orientation: Mandatory, $450 fee. Preregistration for classes offered. Three-day session held in August. **Policies:** Only approved small caged, nonpoisonous animals or fish permitted in residence halls. Dogs, cats, and ferrets strictly prohibited. **Housing:** Guaranteed on-campus for freshmen. Coed dorms, apartments, fraternity/sorority housing, wellness housing available. **Activities:** Bands, campus ministries, choral groups, dance, drama, film society, international student organizations, literary magazine, music ensembles, Model UN, musical theater, radio station, student government, student newspaper, symphony orchestra, University Christian Movement, Hillel Foundation, InterVarsity Christian Fellowship, African-American society, College Democrats, College Republicans, Habitat for Humanity, International Student Fellowship, Global Medical Initiative.

Athletics. NCAA. Intercollegiate: Baseball M, basketball, cross-country, diving, football (tackle) M, soccer, softball W, swimming, tennis, track and field, volleyball W, wrestling M. **Intramural:** Badminton, basketball, bowling, cross-country, football (non-tackle), golf, handball, racquetball, soccer, softball, swimming, table tennis, tennis, track and field, volleyball, weight lifting, wrestling M. **Team name:** Spartans.

Student services. Adult student services, alcohol/substance abuse counseling, chaplain/spiritual director, career counseling, student employment services, financial aid counseling, health services, legal services, minority student services, personal counseling, placement for graduates, veterans' counselor, women's services. **Physically disabled:** Services for visually, speech, hearing impaired.

Contact. E-mail: admission@case.edu
Phone: (216) 368-4450 Fax: (216) 368-5111
Robert McCullough, Director, Case Western Reserve University, Wolstein Hall, Cleveland, OH 44106-7055

Cedarville University
Cedarville, Ohio
www.cedarville.edu
CB code: 1151

- Private 4-year university and liberal arts college affiliated with Baptist faith
- Residential campus in small town
- 3,111 degree-seeking undergraduates: 3% part-time, 54% women, 2% African American, 1% Asian American, 2% Hispanic American, 1% international
- 71 degree-seeking graduate students
- 75% of applicants admitted
- SAT or ACT (ACT writing recommended), application essay required
- 68% graduate within 6 years

General. Founded in 1887. Regionally accredited. **Degrees:** 627 bachelor's awarded; master's, professional offered. **ROTC:** Army, Air Force. **Location:** 12 miles from Springfield, 20 miles from Dayton. **Calendar:** Semester, limited summer session. **Full-time faculty:** 201 total; 77% have terminal degrees, 9% minority, 33% women. **Part-time faculty:** 97 total; 2% have terminal degrees, 3% minority, 47% women. **Class size:** 65% < 20, 27% 20-39, 3% 40-49, 4% 50-99, 2% >100.

Freshman class profile. 3,143 applied, 2,369 admitted, 851 enrolled.

Mid 50% test scores			
SAT critical reading:	540-650	GPA 2.0-2.99:	6%
SAT math:	530-640	Rank in top quarter:	65%
SAT writing:	510-640	Rank in top tenth:	33%
ACT composite:	23-28	End year in good standing:	94%
GPA 3.75 or higher:	47%	Return as sophomores:	85%
GPA 3.50-3.74:	25%	Out-of-state:	66%
GPA 3.0-3.49:	22%	Live on campus:	98%
		International:	1%

Basis for selection. Clear testimony of personal faith in Jesus Christ, evidence of consistent Christian lifestyle, above-average academic performance (academic records, class rank, test scores), personal references considered. Applications reviewed on a rolling basis. SAT and SAT Subject Tests or ACT recommended. Audition required for music majors; interview recommended for academically marginal students. Interview required for pre-pharmacy students. **Home schooled:** Statement describing home school structure and mission required. Applicants must provide an explanation of their course of study and their educator's teaching methods along with answers to the following: Who is ultimately responsible for setting up curriculum and selecting materials? What type of curriculum and materials did the student's educator(s) use? Who was responsible for providing instruction? Did the student have tutors in some areas and not in others, etc? Who recorded grades and how? What type of independent, standardized testing was used to measure the student's progress against a larger population? (Include copies of this information with the student's transcript.). **Learning Disabled:** Students encouraged to contact Coordinator of Disabilities Services.

High school preparation. College-preparatory program recommended. Recommended units include English 4, mathematics 3, social studies 3, science 3 (laboratory 3) and foreign language 3. Additional math and science recommended for nursing, science, engineering, and math applicants.

2012-2013 Annual costs. Tuition/fees (projected): $25,496. Room/board: $5,540. Books/supplies: $1,100. Personal expenses: $1,700.

2010-2011 Financial aid. Need-based: 812 full-time freshmen applied for aid; 677 were judged to have need; 675 of these received aid. Average need met was 31%. Average scholarship/grant was $4,181; average loan $4,289. 56% of total undergraduate aid awarded as scholarships/grants, 44% as loans/jobs. **Non-need-based:** Awarded to 2,204 full-time undergraduates, including 772 freshmen. Scholarships awarded for academics, alumni affiliation, athletics, leadership, minority status, music/drama, ROTC, state residency.

Application procedures. Admission: Priority date 3/1; no deadline. $30 fee, may be waived for applicants with need. Admission notification on a rolling basis beginning on or about 8/1. Must reply by May 1 or within 2 week(s) if notified thereafter. **Financial aid:** Priority date 3/1; no closing date. FAFSA required. Applicants notified on a rolling basis starting 3/1; must reply within 4 week(s) of notification.

Academics. Special study options: Accelerated study, cooperative education, distance learning, double major, dual enrollment of high school students, honors, independent study, internships, liberal arts/career combination, student-designed major, study abroad, teacher certification program, Washington semester. Academic enrichment. **Credit/placement by examination:** AP, CLEP, IB, SAT, ACT, institutional tests. 40 credit hours maximum toward bachelor's degree. **Support services:** Learning center, reduced course load, remedial instruction, study skills assistance, tutoring, writing center.

Honors college/program. 29 ACT/1290 SAT, 3.0 unweighted GPA in college-preparatory curriculum required.

Majors. Area/ethnic studies: American. **Biology:** General, cellular/molecular, environmental. **Business:** Accounting, business admin, finance, international, management information systems, marketing. **Communications:** Communications/speech/rhetoric, journalism, media studies, organizational, political, radio/TV. **Communications technology:** General. **Computer sciences:** Computer science. **Conservation:** Environmental science. **Education:** Biology, chemistry, early childhood, elementary, English, mathematics, middle, music, physical, physics, science, social studies, Spanish, special ed. **Engineering:** Computer, electrical, mechanical. **English:** English lit, technical writing. **Foreign languages:** Spanish. **Health services:** Athletic training, clinical lab science, nursing (RN), predental, premedicine, prepharmacy, preveterinary. **History:** General. **Human services:** General, social work. **Math:** General. **Parks/recreation:** Exercise sciences, health/fitness, sports admin. **Philosophy/religion:** Philosophy. **Physical sciences:** Chemistry, geology, physics. **Protective services:** Forensics, law enforcement admin. **Psychology:** General. **Social sciences:** General, political science, sociology. **Theology:** Missionary, pastoral counseling, religious ed, sacred music, theology, youth ministry. **Visual/performing arts:** Dramatic, graphic design, industrial design, music, music pedagogy, music performance, music theory/composition, studio arts.

Most popular majors. Business/marketing 13%, communications/journalism 6%, education 12%, engineering/engineering technologies 8%, health sciences 13%, theological studies 11%, visual/performing arts 6%.

Computing on campus. 3,000 workstations in dormitories, library, student center. Dormitories wired for high-speed internet access and linked to campus network. Commuter students can connect to campus network. Online course registration, online library, helpline, repair service, wireless network available.

Student life. Freshman orientation: Mandatory, $105 fee. Preregistration for classes offered. **Policies:** Alcohol, tobacco, and drugs prohibited. Religious observance required. **Housing:** Guaranteed on-campus for all undergraduates. Single-sex dorms, apartments available. $250 nonrefundable deposit, deadline 5/1. **Activities:** Bands, campus organizations, choral groups, dance, drama, international student organizations, music ensembles, musical theater, opera, radio station, student government, student newspaper, symphony orchestra, emergency medical squad, Earth stewardship organization, Fellowship for World Missions, students for social justice, Society for Technical Communicators, Society of Automotive Engineers International, College Democrats, College Republicans, student films organization, branch of National Social Work Honor Society.

Athletics. NCAA, NCCAA. **Intercollegiate:** Baseball M, basketball, cheerleading, cross-country, golf M, soccer, softball W, tennis, track and field, volleyball W. **Intramural:** Badminton, basketball, bowling, cross-country, football (tackle) M, golf, racquetball, soccer, softball, table tennis, tennis, volleyball. **Team name:** Yellow Jackets.

Student services. Chaplain/spiritual director, career counseling, student employment services, financial aid counseling, health services, personal counseling, placement for graduates, veterans' counselor. **Physically disabled:** Services for visually, speech, hearing impaired.

Contact. E-mail: admissions@cedarville.edu
Phone: (937) 766-7700 Toll-free number: (800) 233-2784
Fax: (937) 766-7575
Mark Weinstein, Director of Admissions, Cedarville University, 251 North Main Street, Cedarville, OH 45314-0601

Central State University
Wilberforce, Ohio
www.centralstate.edu

CB member
CB code: 1107

▶ Public 4-year university and liberal arts college
▶ Residential campus in rural community
▶ 2,419 degree-seeking undergraduates: 7% part-time, 51% women, 95% African American, 1% Hispanic American
▶ 45 degree-seeking graduate students
▶ 32% of applicants admitted
▶ SAT or ACT (ACT writing optional) required

General. Founded in 1887. Regionally accredited. Ohio's only public historically black university. **Degrees:** 231 bachelor's awarded; master's offered. **ROTC:** Army, Air Force. **Location:** 18 miles from Dayton. **Calendar:** Semester, limited summer session. **Full-time faculty:** 109 total; 69% have terminal degrees, 72% minority, 38% women. **Part-time faculty:** 115 total; 8% have terminal degrees, 82% minority, 50% women. **Class size:** 58% < 20, 39% 20-39, 3% 40-49, less than 1% 50-99. **Special facilities:** Afro-American museum, hydraulics laboratory, computer numerically controlled equipment for machining and robotic welding, business incubator.

Freshman class profile. 7,971 applied, 2,572 admitted, 725 enrolled.

Mid 50% test scores			
SAT critical reading:	350-420	GPA 3.0-3.49:	11%
SAT math:	340-430	GPA 2.0-2.99:	57%
ACT composite:	14-17	End year in good standing:	63%
GPA 3.75 or higher:	1%	Return as sophomores:	55%
GPA 3.50-3.74:	3%	Out-of-state:	57%
		Live on campus:	95%

Basis for selection. Out-of-state residents must have 2.5 GPA and 19 ACT or 910 SAT. Ohio residents must have 2.0 GPA and 15 ACT or 720 SAT. Interview recommended. Personal essay required for admissions appeal process. **Home schooled:** Transcript of courses and grades, state high school equivalency certificate, interview, letter of recommendation (nonparent) required. Ohio students need ONGP test results or OGT.

High school preparation. 16 units recommended. Recommended units include English 4, mathematics 3, social studies 3, science 3 and foreign language 2. 1 art recommended.

2011-2012 Annual costs. Tuition/fees: $5,672; $12,648 out-of-state. Required fees include annual health fee $500.00. Room/board: $8,484. Books/supplies: $1,200. Personal expenses: $1,500.

Financial aid. Non-need-based: Scholarships awarded for academics, alumni affiliation, art, athletics, leadership, music/drama, religious affiliation, ROTC.

Application procedures. Admission: No deadline. $20 fee, may be waived for applicants with need. Admission notification on a rolling basis. **Financial aid:** Priority date 2/15; no closing date. FAFSA, institutional form required. Applicants notified on a rolling basis starting 5/1.

Academics. Special study options: Cooperative education, cross-registration, double major, honors, independent study, internships, study abroad, teacher certification program. **Credit/placement by examination:** AP, CLEP, SAT, ACT, institutional tests. 30 credit hours maximum toward bachelor's degree. **Support services:** Learning center, pre-admission summer program, reduced course load, remedial instruction, study skills assistance, tutoring, writing center.

Majors. Biology: General. **Business:** General, accounting. **Communications:** Broadcast journalism, journalism. **Computer sciences:** Computer science. **Education:** Early childhood, middle, multi-level teacher, secondary, special ed. **Engineering:** Environmental, manufacturing, water resource. **English:** English lit. **History:** General. **Human services:** Social work. **Math:** General. **Parks/recreation:** General. **Physical sciences:** Chemistry, geology. **Protective services:** Criminal justice. **Psychology:** General. **Social sciences:** Economics, geography, political science, sociology. **Visual/performing arts:** Art, jazz, music performance.

Most popular majors. Business/marketing 25%, communications/journalism 12%, education 19%, psychology 7%, social sciences 6%.

Computing on campus. 400 workstations in library, computer center, student center. Dormitories wired for high-speed internet access and linked to campus network. Online course registration, online library, helpline, repair service, wireless network available.

Student life. Freshman orientation: Mandatory, $125 fee. Preregistration for classes offered. **Housing:** Guaranteed on-campus for freshmen. Coed dorms, single-sex dorms available. $195 fully refundable deposit, deadline 8/1. **Activities:** Bands, campus ministries, choral groups, dance, drama, music ensembles, radio station, student government, student newspaper, TV station.

Athletics. NCAA. **Intercollegiate:** Basketball, cross-country, football (tackle) M, golf W, tennis, track and field, volleyball. **Intramural:** Basketball, cross-country, football (non-tackle) M, racquetball, tennis. **Team name:** Marauders.

Student services. Alcohol/substance abuse counseling, chaplain/spiritual director, career counseling, services for economically disadvantaged, student employment services, financial aid counseling, health services, on-campus daycare, personal counseling, placement for graduates.

Contact. E-mail: admissions@centralstate.edu
Phone: (937) 376-6348 Toll-free number: (800) 388-2781
Fax: (937) 376-6648
Robin Rucker, Associate Director of Admissions, Central State University, PO Box 1004, Wilberforce, OH 45384-1004

Chamberlain College of Nursing: Columbus
Columbus, Ohio
www.chamberlain.edu

▶ For-profit 4-year nursing college
▶ Large city
▶ SAT or ACT required

General. Regionally accredited. **Degrees:** 183 bachelor's, 78 associate awarded. **Calendar:** Semester. **Full-time faculty:** 18 total. **Part-time faculty:** 68 total.

Basis for selection. Test scores, GPA, class rank very important.

2011-2012 Annual costs. Tuition/fees: $15,600. Books/supplies: $1,400. Personal expenses: $3,718.

Application procedures. Admission: No deadline. $95 fee. Admission notification on a rolling basis.

Academics. Special study options: Accelerated study, distance learning. **Credit/placement by examination:** AP, CLEP.

Majors. Health services: Nursing (RN).

Contact. Chamberlain College of Nursing: Columbus, 1350 Alum Creek Drive, Columbus, OH 43209

Chancellor University
Cleveland, Ohio
www.chancelloru.edu   **CB code: 1178**

- For-profit 4-year university
- Commuter campus in very large city

General. Founded in 1848. Regionally accredited. **Location:** Downtown. **Calendar:** Semester.

Annual costs/financial aid. Books/supplies: $1,250. Personal expenses: $2,596.

Contact. Phone: (216) 432-8992
Executive Director of Enrollment Management, 3921 Chester Avenue, Cleveland, OH 44114

Cincinnati Christian University
Cincinnati, Ohio
www.ccuniversity.edu   **CB code: 1091**

- Private 4-year university affiliated with Christian Church
- Residential campus in very large city
- 714 degree-seeking undergraduates: 14% part-time, 43% women, 12% African American, 1% Hispanic American, 1% international
- 261 degree-seeking graduate students
- 74% of applicants admitted
- SAT or ACT (ACT writing optional), application essay required
- 32% graduate within 6 years

General. Founded in 1924. Regionally accredited; also accredited by ABHE. Member of Greater Cincinnati Consortium of Colleges and Universities. **Degrees:** 142 bachelor's, 14 associate awarded; master's offered. **Location:** 10 miles from downtown. **Calendar:** Semester, limited summer session. **Full-time faculty:** 32 total; 72% have terminal degrees, 9% minority, 25% women. **Part-time faculty:** 59 total; 29% have terminal degrees, 3% minority, 29% women. **Class size:** 79% < 20, 14% 20-39, 4% 40-49, 3% 50-99.

Freshman class profile. 192 applied, 143 admitted, 121 enrolled.

Mid 50% test scores			
SAT critical reading:	450-550	GPA 2.0-2.99:	31%
SAT math:	440-530	Rank in top quarter:	28%
SAT writing:	430-530	Rank in top tenth:	9%
ACT composite:	18-24	Return as sophomores:	62%
GPA 3.75 or higher:	14%	Out-of-state:	35%
GPA 3.50-3.74:	12%	Live on campus:	79%
GPA 3.0-3.49:	37%	International:	2%

Basis for selection. High school academic record and standardized test scores important. 2.5 GPA, 17 ACT/1215 SAT required for unconditional admission. Applicants age 25 or older can substitute English proficiency test and essay for SAT/ACT requirement. Audition required for music programs.

2012-2013 Annual costs. Tuition/fees (projected): $15,266. Room/board: $6,560. Books/supplies: $900. Personal expenses: $2,348.

2010-2011 Financial aid. Need-based: 140 full-time freshmen applied for aid; 131 were judged to have need; 131 of these received aid. Average need met was 52%. Average scholarship/grant was $7,593; average loan $3,039. 43% of total undergraduate aid awarded as scholarships/grants, 57% as loans/jobs. **Non-need-based:** Awarded to 104 full-time undergraduates, including 20 freshmen. Scholarships awarded for academics, alumni affiliation, athletics, leadership, music/drama, religious affiliation.

Application procedures. Admission: Priority date 3/1; deadline 7/1 (postmark date). $40 fee, may be waived for applicants with need. Admission notification on a rolling basis. **Financial aid:** Priority date 3/1; no closing date. FAFSA required. Applicants notified on a rolling basis starting 4/1.

Academics. Special study options: Accelerated study, cooperative education, cross-registration, distance learning, double major, dual enrollment of high school students, honors, independent study, internships, teacher certification program. Adult degree completion program. **Credit/placement by examination:** AP, CLEP, IB, institutional tests. 15 credit hours maximum toward associate degree, 30 toward bachelor's. **Support services:** Learning center, reduced course load, remedial instruction, study skills assistance, tutoring, writing center.

Majors. Computer sciences: Data processing, information technology, LAN/WAN management, programming. **Education:** Early childhood, elementary, middle, secondary, special ed. **Philosophy/religion:** Christian. **Psychology:** General. **Theology:** Bible, missionary, religious ed, sacred music.

Most popular majors. Business/marketing 20%, education 7%, psychology 12%, theological studies 61%.

Computing on campus. 57 workstations in dormitories, library, computer center, student center. Dormitories wired for high-speed internet access and linked to campus network. Online library, helpline, repair service, wireless network available.

Student life. Freshman orientation: Mandatory. Preregistration for classes offered. **Policies:** Religious observance required. **Housing:** Guaranteed on-campus for all undergraduates. Single-sex dorms, apartments, wellness housing available. $35 nonrefundable deposit, deadline 7/1. **Activities:** Concert band, campus ministries, choral groups, drama, international student organizations, literary magazine, music ensembles, musical theater, student government.

Athletics. NCCAA. **Intercollegiate:** Baseball M, basketball, soccer, volleyball W. **Intramural:** Basketball, cheerleading, football (tackle) M, soccer, track and field, volleyball. **Team name:** Eagles.

Student services. Career counseling, student employment services, financial aid counseling, health services, personal counseling. **Physically disabled:** Services for hearing impaired.

Contact. E-mail: cbcadmission@ccuniversity.edu
Phone: (513) 244-8100 Toll-free number: (800) 949-4228
Fax: (513) 244-8140
Admissions Director, Cincinnati Christian University, 2700 Glenway Avenue, Cincinnati, OH 45204-3200

Cleveland Institute of Art
Cleveland, Ohio   **CB member**
www.cia.edu   **CB code: 1152**

- Private 4-year visual arts college
- Commuter campus in very large city
- 536 degree-seeking undergraduates: 1% part-time, 54% women, 10% African American, 4% Asian American, 3% Hispanic American, 2% international
- 71% of applicants admitted
- SAT or ACT (ACT writing optional), application essay required
- 59% graduate within 6 years; 4% enter graduate study

General. Founded in 1882. Regionally accredited. **Degrees:** 84 bachelor's awarded. **ROTC:** Army, Naval, Air Force. **Location:** 4 miles from downtown. **Calendar:** Semester, limited summer session. **Full-time faculty:** 51 total; 78% have terminal degrees, 10% minority, 37% women. **Part-time faculty:** 47 total; 60% have terminal degrees, 8% minority, 40% women. **Class size:** 87% < 20, 13% 20-39. **Special facilities:** Individual studio spaces, exhibition spaces, ceramics studio, wood shop, metal shop, glass shop, cInematheque, rapid 3-D prototype machines, blau kiln, lunchbox capture system.

Freshman class profile. 615 applied, 435 admitted, 127 enrolled.

Mid 50% test scores			
SAT critical reading:	460-610	Rank in top quarter:	27%
SAT math:	440-570	Rank in top tenth:	15%
ACT composite:	18-25	End year in good standing:	93%
GPA 3.75 or higher:	13%	Return as sophomores:	79%
GPA 3.50-3.74:	13%	Out-of-state:	27%
GPA 3.0-3.49:	26%	Live on campus:	70%
GPA 2.0-2.99:	44%	International:	1%

Basis for selection. Portfolio of 12 to 20 pieces, high school transcripts, statement of purpose, test scores, and 1 letter of recommendation required. Interview strongly recommended. **Home schooled:** Transcript of courses and grades, state high school equivalency certificate, letter of recommendation (nonparent) required. GED required.

High school preparation. 20 units recommended. Recommended units include English 4, mathematics 3, social studies 3, science 3 and academic electives 6. 2 years of art recommended.

2011-2012 Annual costs. Tuition/fees: $33,882. Room/board: $11,354. Books/supplies: $2,050. Personal expenses: $1,986.

2010-2011 Financial aid. Need-based: 139 full-time freshmen applied for aid; 128 were judged to have need; 128 of these received aid. Average need met was 58%. Average scholarship/grant was $18,320; average loan $4,022. 64% of total undergraduate aid awarded as scholarships/grants, 36% as loans/jobs. **Non-need-based:** Awarded to 91 full-time undergraduates, including 36 freshmen. Scholarships awarded for academics, art.

Application procedures. Admission: Priority date 7/1; no deadline. $30 fee, may be waived for applicants with need. Admission notification on a rolling basis beginning on or about 10/1. Must reply by May 1 or within 2 week(s) if notified thereafter. **Financial aid:** Priority date 3/15; no closing date. FAFSA, institutional form required. Applicants notified on a rolling basis starting 3/16.

Academics. Special study options: Cross-registration, double major, exchange student, independent study, internships, New York semester, study abroad. Study for up to 2 semesters at any Alliance of Independent Colleges of Art and Design. **Credit/placement by examination:** AP, CLEP, IB. 63 credit hours maximum toward bachelor's degree. **Support services:** Reduced course load, study skills assistance, tutoring, writing center.

Majors. Health services: Medical illustrating. **Visual/performing arts:** Ceramics, cinematography, commercial/advertising art, design, digital arts, drawing, fiber arts, film/cinema/video, game design, graphic design, illustration, industrial design, interior design, metal/jewelry, multimedia, painting, photography, printmaking, sculpture.

Computing on campus. 303 workstations in dormitories, library, computer center. Dormitories wired for high-speed internet access. Online course registration, online library, student web hosting, wireless network available.

Student life. Freshman orientation: Mandatory, $175 fee. Preregistration for classes offered. Summer overnight program for students/parents and fall orientation for students only. **Policies:** Freshmen not permitted cars on campus. **Housing:** Coed dorms, apartments, fraternity/sorority housing available. $150 nonrefundable deposit, deadline 6/1. **Activities:** Marching band, campus ministries, drama, film society, musical theater, student government, student artist association, student leadership council, student activities program board, student independent exhibition committee, gay/lesbian association, Artists for Christ, cinema club, community service club.

Athletics. Intramural: Basketball, bowling, football (non-tackle), softball, volleyball.

Student services. Alcohol/substance abuse counseling, chaplain/spiritual director, career counseling, student employment services, financial aid counseling, health services, legal services, personal counseling. **Physically disabled:** Services for visually, speech, hearing impaired.

Contact. E-mail: admissions@cia.edu
Phone: (216) 421-7418 Toll-free number: (800) 223-4700
Fax: (216) 754-3634
Joanne Landers, Director of Admissions, Cleveland Institute of Art, 11141 East Boulevard, Cleveland, OH 44106-1710

Cleveland Institute of Music
Cleveland, Ohio
www.cim.edu   **CB code: 1124**

- Private 4-year music college
- Residential campus in very large city
- 247 degree-seeking undergraduates
- SAT or ACT (ACT writing optional), application essay required

General. Founded in 1920. Regionally accredited. **Degrees:** 39 bachelor's awarded; master's, doctoral offered. **Location:** 5 miles from downtown. **Calendar:** Semester, limited summer session. **Full-time faculty:** 39 total. **Part-time faculty:** 61 total. **Special facilities:** Electronic music studios, audio recording and distance learning facilities, large CD/DVD, record, and tape library, technology learning center.

Freshman class profile.

Out-of-state:	75%	Live on campus:	100%

Basis for selection. Audition most important. High school record, test scores, and letters of recommendation also reviewed. Required institutional examinations include ear training and theory. Additional testing includes sight singing and keyboard proficiency. Audition required. **Home schooled:** Transcript of courses and grades required.

High school preparation. College-preparatory program recommended. 16 units recommended. Recommended units include English 4, mathematics 3, social studies 3, science 3 and foreign language 3.

2011-2012 Annual costs. Tuition/fees: $39,808. Room/board: $11,637. Books/supplies: $600. Personal expenses: $1,254.

Financial aid. Non-need-based: Scholarships awarded for academics, music/drama.

Application procedures. Admission: Closing date 12/1 (receipt date). $100 fee. Application must be submitted online. Admission notification by 4/1. Admission notification on a rolling basis. Must reply by 5/1. Deferred admission from fall to spring semesters is dependent upon space availability. **Financial aid:** Priority date 2/15; no closing date. FAFSA, CSS PROFILE required. Applicants notified on a rolling basis starting 4/1; must reply by 5/1 or within 2 week(s) of notification.

Academics. Special study options: Cross-registration, double major, ESL, independent study, study abroad. **Credit/placement by examination:** AP, CLEP, IB, SAT, ACT, institutional tests. **Support services:** Learning center, reduced course load, remedial instruction, study skills assistance, tutoring, writing center.

Majors. Communications technology: Recording arts. **Visual/performing arts:** Music performance, music theory/composition, voice/opera.

Computing on campus. 36 workstations in dormitories, library, computer center, student center. Dormitories wired for high-speed internet access and linked to campus network. Helpline, repair service, wireless network available.

Student life. Freshman orientation: Mandatory, $100 fee. Preregistration for classes offered. Held before the start of classes. **Policies:** Library privileges available through Case Western Reserve University. **Housing:** Coed dorms, wellness housing available. **Activities:** Jazz band, choral groups, dance, drama, music ensembles, opera, student government, student newspaper, symphony orchestra, most student organizations available through Case Western Reserve University.

Student services. Alcohol/substance abuse counseling, career counseling, student employment services, financial aid counseling, health services, personal counseling, placement for graduates, veterans' counselor.

Contact. E-mail: admission@cim.edu
Phone: (216) 795-3107
William Fay, Director of Admission, Cleveland Institute of Music, 11021 East Boulevard, Cleveland, OH 44106

Cleveland State University
Cleveland, Ohio   **CB member**
www.csuohio.edu   **CB code: 1221**

- Public 4-year university
- Commuter campus in large city
- 10,819 degree-seeking undergraduates: 24% part-time, 55% women, 22% African American, 2% Asian American, 4% Hispanic American, 3% international
- 4,883 degree-seeking graduate students
- 47% of applicants admitted
- SAT or ACT (ACT writing optional) required
- 30% graduate within 6 years

General. Founded in 1964. Regionally accredited. **Degrees:** 1,919 bachelor's awarded; master's, professional, doctoral offered. **ROTC:** Army, Air Force. **Location:** Downtown. **Calendar:** Semester, extensive summer session. **Full-time faculty:** 524 total; 92% have terminal degrees, 23% minority, 40% women. **Part-time faculty:** 508 total; 9% have terminal degrees, 15% minority, 52% women. **Class size:** 34% < 20, 46% 20-39, 11% 40-49, 8% 50-99, 1% >100. **Special facilities:** Poetry center, bioethics center, rooftop garden, Center for Healing Across Cultures, Center for Poverty Studies.

Freshman class profile. 5,113 applied, 2,389 admitted, 1,377 enrolled.

Mid 50% test scores			
SAT critical reading:	440-580	GPA 3.0-3.49:	31%
SAT math:	450-570	GPA 2.0-2.99:	40%
ACT composite:	18-24	Rank in top quarter:	35%
GPA 3.75 or higher:	16%	Rank in top tenth:	11%
GPA 3.50-3.74:	11%	Out-of-state:	7%
		Live on campus:	38%

Basis for selection. 2.3 GPA, 16 ACT/750 SAT, and successful completion of 13 core academic units required. 2.5 GPA and 20 ACT/950 SAT

required for education applicants; 2.7 GPA and 23 ACT/1070 SAT required for engineering applicants. SAT scores exclusive of Writing. Audition required for music majors.

High school preparation. College-preparatory program required. 13 units required. Required and recommended units include English 4, mathematics 3, social studies 3, science 3, foreign language 2 and visual/performing arts 1.

2011-2012 Annual costs. Tuition/fees: $9,002; $12,024 out-of-state. Room/board: $10,398. Books/supplies: $800. Personal expenses: $2,500.

2011-2012 Financial aid. Need-based: 1,188 full-time freshmen applied for aid; 1,093 were judged to have need; 1,082 of these received aid. Average need met was 35%. Average scholarship/grant was $6,512; average loan $3,662. 36% of total undergraduate aid awarded as scholarships/grants, 64% as loans/jobs. **Non-need-based:** Awarded to 605 full-time undergraduates, including 123 freshmen. Scholarships awarded for academics, alumni affiliation, art, athletics, leadership, minority status, music/drama, religious affiliation, ROTC.

Application procedures. Admission: Priority date 7/15; deadline 8/15. $30 fee, may be waived for applicants with need. Admission notification on a rolling basis beginning on or about 9/1. **Financial aid:** Priority date 2/15; no closing date. FAFSA required. Applicants notified on a rolling basis starting 3/15; must reply within 4 week(s) of notification.

Academics. Special study options: Accelerated study, combined bachelor's/graduate degree, cooperative education, cross-registration, distance learning, double major, dual enrollment of high school students, ESL, honors, independent study, internships, liberal arts/career combination, student-designed major, study abroad, teacher certification program, weekend college. **Credit/placement by examination:** AP, CLEP, IB, SAT, ACT, institutional tests. 90 credit hours maximum toward bachelor's degree. Unlimited AP exam credits accepted. **Support services:** Learning center, reduced course load, remedial instruction, study skills assistance, tutoring, writing center.

Majors. Area/ethnic studies: Women's. **Biology:** General. **Business:** Accounting, finance, international, labor relations, management information systems, managerial economics, marketing, statistics. **Communications:** Communications/speech/rhetoric, public relations. **Computer sciences:** General. **Conservation:** Environmental science, environmental studies. **Education:** General, early childhood, elementary, kindergarten/preschool, middle, physical, special ed. **Engineering:** Chemical, civil, computer, electrical, engineering science, industrial, mechanical, metallurgical. **English:** English lit. **Foreign languages:** French, Germanic, linguistics, Spanish. **Health services:** Audiology/hearing, music therapy, nursing (RN), physician assistant. **History:** General. **Human services:** Social work. **Liberal arts:** Arts/sciences. **Math:** General. **Philosophy/religion:** Philosophy, religion. **Physical sciences:** Chemistry, geology, physics. **Psychology:** General. **Social sciences:** General, anthropology, criminology, economics, international relations, political science, sociology, urban studies. **Visual/performing arts:** Art, cinematography, dramatic, music.

Most popular majors. Business/marketing 23%, communications/journalism 8%, education 7%, health sciences 12%, psychology 8%, social sciences 14%.

Computing on campus. 711 workstations in dormitories, library, computer center, student center. Dormitories wired for high-speed internet access and linked to campus network. Commuter students can connect to campus network. Online course registration, online library, helpline, repair service, wireless network available.

Student life. Freshman orientation: Available, $25 fee. Preregistration for classes offered. All-day program during summer. **Housing:** Coed dorms, special housing for disabled, apartments, fraternity/sorority housing available. $150 nonrefundable deposit, deadline 1/19. **Activities:** Bands, campus ministries, choral groups, dance, drama, film society, international student organizations, literary magazine, music ensembles, musical theater, opera, radio station, student government, student newspaper, symphony orchestra, Newman Center, Los Latinos Unidos, Hillel, University Christian Movement, Organization for Afro-American Unity, NAACP, environmental action group, College Democrats and Republicans.

Athletics. NCAA. **Intercollegiate:** Basketball, cross-country W, diving, fencing, golf, soccer, softball W, swimming, tennis, track and field W, volleyball W, wrestling M. **Intramural:** Badminton, basketball, bowling, cross-country, fencing, field hockey W, golf, handball, racquetball, rowing (crew), sailing, soccer, squash, swimming, table tennis, tennis, track and field, volleyball, water polo, wrestling M. **Team name:** Vikings.

Student services. Adult student services, alcohol/substance abuse counseling, career counseling, services for economically disadvantaged, student employment services, financial aid counseling, health services, legal services, minority student services, on-campus daycare, personal counseling, placement for graduates, veterans' counselor, women's services. **Physically disabled:** Services for visually, speech, hearing impaired.

Contact. E-mail: admissions@csuohio.edu
Phone: (216) 687-2100 Toll-free number: (800) 278-6446
Robert Spademan, Assistant Vice-President, Marketing & Admissions, Cleveland State University, 2121 Euclid Avenue, Cleveland, OH 44115-2214

College of Mount St. Joseph

Cincinnati, Ohio   **CB member**
www.msj.edu   **CB code: 1129**

▸ Private 4-year liberal arts college affiliated with Roman Catholic Church
▸ Commuter campus in very large city
▸ 1,774 degree-seeking undergraduates: 28% part-time, 64% women, 10% African American, 2% Hispanic American
▸ 408 degree-seeking graduate students
▸ 63% of applicants admitted
▸ SAT or ACT (ACT writing recommended) required
▸ 60% graduate within 6 years

General. Founded in 1920. Regionally accredited. **Degrees:** 385 bachelor's, 17 associate awarded; master's, professional offered. **ROTC:** Army, Air Force. **Location:** 7 miles from downtown. **Calendar:** Semester, extensive summer session. **Full-time faculty:** 123 total; 99% have terminal degrees, 3% minority, 58% women. **Part-time faculty:** 124 total; 70% have terminal degrees, 3% minority, 71% women. **Class size:** 58% < 20, 41% 20-39, less than 1% 40-49.

Freshman class profile. 1,621 applied, 1,021 admitted, 300 enrolled.

Mid 50% test scores			
SAT critical reading:	450-540	GPA 2.0-2.99:	26%
SAT math:	450-560	Rank in top quarter:	39%
ACT composite:	19-24	Rank in top tenth:	13%
GPA 3.75 or higher:	20%	Return as sophomores:	69%
GPA 3.50-3.74:	19%	Out-of-state:	22%
GPA 3.0-3.49:	35%	Live on campus:	56%

Basis for selection. Criteria for admission include college prep high school curriculum, strong GPA, standardized test scores, evidence of leadership and extracurricular involvement, and personal background. Essays, recommendations and interviews may be required for some students. Audition required for music programs. Portfolio recommended for art programs. **Home schooled:** Letter of recommendation (nonparent) required. Transcripts required along with any documentation from state or national home schooling accreditation agency. Description of completed courses required.

High school preparation. College-preparatory program recommended. 19 units required; 21 recommended. Required and recommended units include English 4, mathematics 3-4, social studies 3, history 3, science 3-4 (laboratory 1-2), foreign language 2 and visual/performing arts 1. May substitute 2 additional credits from other subjects in place of foreign language.

2011-2012 Annual costs. Tuition/fees: $24,400. Room/board: $7,632. Books/supplies: $800. Personal expenses: $600.

2011-2012 Financial aid. Need-based: 285 full-time freshmen applied for aid; 253 were judged to have need; 253 of these received aid. Average need met was 80%. Average scholarship/grant was $13,628; average loan $3,946. 55% of total undergraduate aid awarded as scholarships/grants, 45% as loans/jobs. **Non-need-based:** Awarded to 300 full-time undergraduates, including 78 freshmen. Scholarships awarded for academics, alumni affiliation, art, leadership, music/drama, ROTC, state residency.

Application procedures. Admission: Priority date 4/1; deadline 8/1 (postmark date). $25 fee, may be waived for applicants with need. Admission notification on a rolling basis beginning on or about 10/1. Must reply by May 1 or within 4 week(s) if notified thereafter. **Financial aid:** Priority date 3/1; no closing date. FAFSA required. Applicants notified on a rolling basis starting 1/31; must reply by 5/1 or within 4 week(s) of notification.

Academics. Special study options: Accelerated study, cooperative education, cross-registration, distance learning, double major, dual enrollment of high school students, honors, independent study, internships, liberal arts/career combination, study abroad, teacher certification program. **Credit/placement by examination:** AP, CLEP, IB, SAT, ACT, institutional tests. 32 credit hours maximum toward associate degree, 64 toward bachelor's. **Support services:** Learning center, reduced course load, remedial instruction, study skills assistance, tutoring, writing center.

Majors. Biology: General, biochemistry. **Business:** Accounting, business admin. **Communications:** Communications/speech/rhetoric. **Computer sciences:** General. **Education:** Art, early childhood, middle, special ed. **English:**

English lit. **Health services:** Athletic training, nursing (RN). **History:** General. **Human services:** Social work. **Liberal arts:** Arts/sciences. **Math:** General. **Parks/recreation:** Sports admin. **Philosophy/religion:** Religion. **Physical sciences:** Chemistry. **Psychology:** General. **Social sciences:** Criminology, sociology. **Theology:** Pastoral counseling, religious ed. **Visual/performing arts:** Art, design, graphic design, interior design, music, studio arts.

Most popular majors. Business/marketing 6%, education 8%, health sciences 29%, liberal arts 11%, parks/recreation 8%, visual/performing arts 12%.

Computing on campus. 191 workstations in library, computer center, student center. Commuter students can connect to campus network. Online course registration, online library, helpline, repair service, student web hosting, wireless network available.

Student life. Freshman orientation: Mandatory, $150 fee. Preregistration for classes offered. Two-part orientation: summer session, which includes a 2-day, 1-night stay in dorms, and welcome weekend consisting of service learning event and river cruise over the weekend before start of classes. **Policies:** Smoke-free campus. All unmarried freshmen and sophomores under age 21 who live outside 35-mile radius of college required to live on campus and participate in meal program. **Housing:** Guaranteed on-campus for freshmen. Coed dorms, special housing for disabled available. $100 fully refundable deposit, deadline 8/15. **Activities:** Bands, campus ministries, choral groups, dance, drama, international student organizations, literary magazine, music ensembles, musical theater, student government, student newspaper, Circle K International, environmental awareness club, Japanese cultural appreciation club, black student union, Alpha Phi Omega service organization, Lions for Life, Habitat for Humanity.

Athletics. NCAA. **Intercollegiate:** Baseball M, basketball, cheerleading M, cross-country, football (tackle) M, golf, lacrosse, soccer, softball W, tennis, track and field, volleyball, wrestling M. **Intramural:** Basketball, football (non-tackle), handball, racquetball, soccer, softball, tennis, volleyball. **Team name:** Lions.

Student services. Adult student services, alcohol/substance abuse counseling, chaplain/spiritual director, career counseling, services for economically disadvantaged, student employment services, financial aid counseling, health services, minority student services, on-campus daycare, personal counseling, placement for graduates, veterans' counselor, women's services. **Physically disabled:** Services for visually, speech, hearing impaired.

Contact. E-mail: admissions@mail.msj.edu
Phone: (513) 244-4531 Toll-free number: (800) 654-9314
Fax: (513) 244-4629
Peggy Minnich, Director of Admission, College of Mount St. Joseph, 5701 Delhi Road, Cincinnati, OH 45233-1670

College of Wooster
Wooster, Ohio
www.wooster.edu

CB member
CB code: 1134

- Private 4-year liberal arts college
- Residential campus in large town
- 1,990 degree-seeking undergraduates: 1% part-time, 54% women, 8% African American, 3% Asian American, 3% Hispanic American, 1% Native American, 6% international
- 61% of applicants admitted
- SAT or ACT (ACT writing recommended), application essay required
- 75% graduate within 6 years; 35% enter graduate study

General. Founded in 1866. Regionally accredited. **Degrees:** 441 bachelor's awarded. **Location:** 55 miles from Cleveland, 30 miles from Akron. **Calendar:** Semester, limited summer session. **Full-time faculty:** 141 total; 96% have terminal degrees, 14% minority, 48% women. **Part-time faculty:** 38 total; 34% have terminal degrees, 5% minority, 58% women. **Class size:** 67% < 20, 30% 20-39, 2% 40-49, less than 1% 50-99, less than 1% >100.

Freshman class profile. 4,893 applied, 2,968 admitted, 571 enrolled.

Mid 50% test scores			
SAT critical reading:	550-670	Rank in top quarter:	74%
SAT math:	550-660	Rank in top tenth:	39%
SAT writing:	550-650	End year in good standing:	95%
ACT composite:	24-30	Return as sophomores:	90%
GPA 3.75 or higher:	40%	Out-of-state:	65%
GPA 3.50-3.74:	21%	Live on campus:	100%
GPA 3.0-3.49:	28%	International:	5%
GPA 2.0-2.99:	11%	Fraternities:	12%
		Sororities:	13%

Basis for selection. Course pattern and academic performance most important. Recommendations, extracurricular activities, class rank, test scores, interview important. Auditions required for music programs. **Home schooled:** Statement describing home school structure and mission, transcript of courses and grades, interview, letter of recommendation (nonparent) required. Submit detailed course descriptions and/or syllabi for academic work completed and 2 letters of recommendation, including 1 from a person who has provided academic instruction and at least 1 from someone outside student's home.

High school preparation. College-preparatory program required. 16 units required. Required units include English 4, mathematics 3, social studies 3, science 3 (laboratory 1), foreign language 2 and academic electives 1.

2011-2012 Annual costs. Tuition/fees: $38,290. Room/board: $9,310. Books/supplies: $1,000.

2011-2012 Financial aid. Need-based: 441 full-time freshmen applied for aid; 384 were judged to have need; 384 of these received aid. Average need met was 98.5%. Average scholarship/grant was $27,331; average loan $2,992. 85% of total undergraduate aid awarded as scholarships/grants, 15% as loans/jobs. **Non-need-based:** Awarded to 874 full-time undergraduates, including 215 freshmen. Scholarships awarded for academics, minority status, music/drama, religious affiliation.

Application procedures. Admission: Closing date 2/15 (postmark date). $40 fee, may be waived for applicants with need, free for online applicants. Admission notification by 3/15. Admission notification on a rolling basis. Must reply by May 1 or within 2 week(s) if notified thereafter. **Financial aid:** Priority date 2/15; no closing date. FAFSA, institutional form required. Either CSS PROFILE or institution application from prospective students. Applicants notified on a rolling basis starting 2/15; must reply by 5/1.

Academics. Special study options: Combined bachelor's/graduate degree, double major, exchange student, independent study, internships, New York semester, student-designed major, study abroad, teacher certification program, United Nations semester, urban semester, Washington semester. **Credit/placement by examination:** AP, CLEP, IB, institutional tests. 16 credit hours maximum toward bachelor's degree. **Support services:** Learning center, study skills assistance, tutoring, writing center.

Majors. Area/ethnic studies: African, African-American, East Asian, gay/lesbian, Latin American, Near/Middle Eastern, Russian/Slavic, South Asian, Western European, women's. **Biology:** General, Biochemistry/molecular biology, neuroscience. **Business:** Managerial economics. **Communications:** Communications/speech/rhetoric. **Computer sciences:** General. **Education:** Music. **English:** English lit. **Foreign languages:** General, classics, comparative lit, French, German, Russian, Spanish. **Health services:** Audiology/speech pathology, music therapy. **History:** General. **Math:** General. **Philosophy/religion:** Philosophy, religion. **Physical sciences:** Chemical physics, chemistry, geology, physics. **Psychology:** General. **Social sciences:** Anthropology, archaeology, economics, international relations, political science, sociology, urban studies. **Visual/performing arts:** Art history/conservation, dance, dramatic, music, music history, music performance, music theory/composition, studio arts.

Most popular majors. Biology 9%, English 9%, history 9%, philosophy/religious studies 7%, physical sciences 7%, psychology 8%, social sciences 26%, visual/performing arts 6%.

Computing on campus. PC or laptop required. 75 workstations in library, student center. Dormitories wired for high-speed internet access and linked to campus network. Commuter students can connect to campus network. Online course registration, online library, helpline, student web hosting, wireless network available.

Student life. Freshman orientation: Mandatory. Preregistration for classes offered. Two-day program, held during summer prior to start of classes. **Housing:** Guaranteed on-campus for all undergraduates. Coed dorms, special housing for disabled, apartments, fraternity/sorority housing available. Service related housing, cultural living experiences housing, housing for foreign language programs. **Activities:** Bands, campus ministries, choral groups, dance, drama, film society, international student organizations, literary magazine, music ensembles, Model UN, musical theater, radio station, student government, student newspaper, symphony orchestra, variety of organizations available.

Athletics. NCAA. **Intercollegiate:** Baseball M, basketball, cross-country, diving, field hockey W, football (tackle) M, golf, lacrosse, soccer, softball W, swimming, tennis, track and field, volleyball W. **Intramural:** Badminton, basketball, bowling, football (non-tackle), golf, racquetball, soccer, softball, swimming, tennis, volleyball. **Team name:** Fighting Scots.

Student services. Alcohol/substance abuse counseling, chaplain/spiritual director, career counseling, student employment services, financial aid counseling, health services, minority student services, personal counseling, placement for graduates. **Physically disabled:** Services for visually impaired.

Contact. E-mail: admissions@wooster.edu
Phone: (330) 263-2322 Toll-free number: (800) 877-9905
Fax: (330) 263-2621
Jennifer Winge, Dean of Admissions, College of Wooster, Gault
Admissions Center, Wooster, OH 44691-2363

Columbus College of Art and Design
Columbus, Ohio
www.ccad.edu
CB code: 1085

- Private 4-year visual arts college
- Commuter campus in very large city
- 1,345 degree-seeking undergraduates: 5% part-time, 60% women, 8% African American, 4% Asian American, 4% Hispanic American, 5% international
- 20 degree-seeking graduate students
- 69% of applicants admitted
- SAT or ACT (ACT writing optional), application essay required
- 61% graduate within 6 years

General. Founded in 1879. Regionally accredited. **Degrees:** 277 bachelor's awarded. **Location:** Downtown. **Calendar:** Semester, limited summer session. **Full-time faculty:** 72 total; 61% have terminal degrees, 7% minority, 39% women. **Part-time faculty:** 133 total; 36% have terminal degrees, 8% minority, 53% women. **Class size:** 82% < 20, 17% 20-39, less than 1% 50-99. **Special facilities:** Student exhibition hall.

Freshman class profile. 627 applied, 432 admitted, 287 enrolled.

Mid 50% test scores			
SAT critical reading:	470-580	GPA 2.0-2.99:	57%
SAT math:	430-550	Rank in top quarter:	14%
SAT writing:	440-560	Rank in top tenth:	2%
ACT composite:	19-25	End year in good standing:	66%
GPA 3.75 or higher:	4%	Return as sophomores:	80%
GPA 3.50-3.74:	11%	Out-of-state:	32%
GPA 3.0-3.49:	28%	Live on campus:	79%

Basis for selection. Portfolio and 2.0 GPA important. Portfolio required; interview recommended.

High school preparation. Recommended units include English 4, mathematics 2, science 2 and foreign language 2. 4 units art recommended.

2011-2012 Annual costs. Tuition/fees: $26,112. Room/board: $7,260. Books/supplies: $4,000. Personal expenses: $200.

2010-2011 Financial aid. Need-based: 298 full-time freshmen applied for aid; 280 were judged to have need; 279 of these received aid. Average need met was 65%. Average scholarship/grant was $16,321; average loan $4,199. 64% of total undergraduate aid awarded as scholarships/grants, 36% as loans/jobs. **Non-need-based:** Awarded to 235 full-time undergraduates, including 63 freshmen. Scholarships awarded for academics, art, ROTC, state residency.

Application procedures. Admission: No deadline. $30 fee, may be waived for applicants with need. Application must be submitted online. Admission notification on a rolling basis. **Financial aid:** Closing date 3/1. FAFSA required. Applicants notified on a rolling basis starting 3/15; must reply within 2 week(s) of notification.

Academics. Special study options: Accelerated study, cooperative education, cross-registration, distance learning, double major, ESL, exchange student, honors, independent study, internships, New York semester, study abroad. **Credit/placement by examination:** AP, CLEP, IB, SAT, ACT, institutional tests. **Support services:** Learning center, reduced course load, remedial instruction, study skills assistance, tutoring, writing center.

Majors. Visual/performing arts: Commercial/advertising art, fashion design, illustration, industrial design, interior design, photography, studio arts.

Computing on campus. PC or laptop required. 485 workstations in dormitories, library, student center. Dormitories wired for high-speed internet access. Online library, helpline, wireless network available.

Student life. Freshman orientation: Mandatory. Preregistration for classes offered. Three 2-day sessions in June, 1-day session in August. **Housing:** Guaranteed on-campus for freshmen. Coed dorms, special housing for disabled, apartments, wellness housing available. $300 fully refundable deposit, deadline 5/11. **Activities:** Film society, international student organizations, student government, student newspaper, student Bible study, gay/lesbian/bisexual group, environmental awareness group, black student organization, international student organization, secular student alliance, give back, melting pot.

Student services. Adult student services, alcohol/substance abuse counseling, career counseling, student employment services, financial aid counseling, minority student services, personal counseling. **Physically disabled:** Services for visually, speech, hearing impaired.

Contact. E-mail: admissions@ccad.edu
Phone: (614) 224-9101 ext. 3261 Toll-free number: (877) 997-2223
Fax: (614) 232-8344
Thomas Green, Director of Admissions, Columbus College of Art and Design, 60 Cleveland Avenue, Columbus, OH 43215-3875

Defiance College
Defiance, Ohio
www.defiance.edu
CB code: 1162

- Private 4-year liberal arts college affiliated with United Church of Christ
- Residential campus in large town
- 998 degree-seeking undergraduates: 10% African American, 1% Asian American, 5% Hispanic American, 1% Native American, 1% international
- 84 degree-seeking graduate students
- 67% of applicants admitted
- SAT or ACT (ACT writing optional) required
- 51% graduate within 6 years

General. Founded in 1850. Regionally accredited. **Degrees:** 179 bachelor's, 6 associate awarded; master's offered. **Location:** 55 miles from Toledo; 45 miles from Fort Wayne, Indiana. **Calendar:** Semester, extensive summer session. **Full-time faculty:** 41 total; 73% have terminal degrees, 12% minority, 37% women. **Part-time faculty:** 66 total; 18% have terminal degrees, 3% minority, 48% women. **Class size:** 70% < 20, 30% 20-39, less than 1% 40-49, less than 1% 50-99. **Special facilities:** Wildlife sanctuary, greenhouse/genetics center.

Freshman class profile. 1,854 applied, 1,248 admitted, 295 enrolled.

Mid 50% test scores			
SAT critical reading:	400-520	Rank in top quarter:	25%
SAT math:	430-530	Rank in top tenth:	8%
SAT writing:	370-500	Return as sophomores:	59%
ACT composite:	18-23	Out-of-state:	39%
GPA 3.75 or higher:	12%	Live on campus:	86%
GPA 3.50-3.74:	10%	International:	1%
GPA 3.0-3.49:	31%	Fraternities:	4%
GPA 2.0-2.99:	44%	Sororities:	4%

Basis for selection. School achievement record, test scores, college preparatory curriculum important. 2.25 GPA, 18 ACT or 860 SAT (exclusive of Writing) required. **Home schooled:** Transcript of courses and grades required.

High school preparation. College-preparatory program recommended. 16 units recommended. Recommended units include English 4, mathematics 3, social studies 2, science 3, foreign language 2 and visual/performing arts 2. One unit fine arts and 1 unit of computer proficiency recommended.

2011-2012 Annual costs. Tuition/fees: $25,890. Room/board: $8,450. Books/supplies: $1,350. Personal expenses: $1,200.

Financial aid. Non-need-based: Scholarships awarded for academics, alumni affiliation, leadership, minority status, religious affiliation.

Application procedures. Admission: No deadline. $25 fee, may be waived for applicants with need, free for online applicants. Admission notification on a rolling basis beginning on or about 9/1. Must reply by May 1 or within 4 week(s) if notified thereafter. **Financial aid:** Priority date 4/1; no closing date. FAFSA required. Applicants notified on a rolling basis starting 3/1; must reply within 3 week(s) of notification.

Academics. Evening sessions available in many areas. Weekend college program for nontraditional students to pursue bachelor's or master's degree in several business majors. **Special study options:** Accelerated study, cooperative education, distance learning, double major, dual enrollment of high school students, honors, independent study, internships, liberal arts/career combination, student-designed major, study abroad, teacher certification program, weekend college. **Credit/placement by examination:** AP, CLEP, IB, institutional tests. 15 credit hours maximum toward associate degree, 30 toward bachelor's. **Support services:** Learning center, reduced course load, study skills assistance, tutoring, writing center.

Majors. Biology: General. **Business:** General, accounting, business admin, management information systems. **Communications:** Communications/speech/rhetoric, journalism, public relations. **Conservation:** General, environmental studies. **Education:** General, art, biology, business, chemistry, early childhood, elementary, English, health, history, mathematics, middle, multi-level teacher, physical, science, secondary, social science, social studies, speech. **English:** English lit, rhetoric/composition. **Health services:** Athletic training, clinical lab technology, predental, premedicine, preveterinary. **History:** General. **Human services:** Social work. **Liberal arts:** Arts/sciences. **Math:** General. **Parks/recreation:** Health/fitness, sports admin. **Philosophy/religion:** Religion. **Protective services:** Computer forensics, forensics. **Psychology:** General. **Social sciences:** General, criminology. **Theology:** Religious ed. **Visual/performing arts:** Art, commercial/advertising art, graphic design.

Most popular majors. Business/marketing 25%, education 15%, health sciences 8%, parks/recreation 9%, public administration/social services 7%, security/protective services 12%, visual/performing arts 7%.

Computing on campus. 150 workstations in dormitories, library, computer center, student center. Dormitories wired for high-speed internet access and linked to campus network. Commuter students can connect to campus network. Online library, helpline, wireless network available.

Student life. Freshman orientation: Mandatory. Preregistration for classes offered. One-day sessions held in April, May, June, July, and August. **Policies:** Students must live and take meals on campus unless they are seniors, married, veterans, or living with parents or close relatives within approved commuting distance. **Housing:** Guaranteed on-campus for all undergraduates. Coed dorms, apartments, wellness housing available. ADA-compliant rooms available. **Activities:** Bands, campus ministries, choral groups, dance, drama, literary magazine, music ensembles, musical theater, student government, student newspaper, black action student association, campus activities board, criminal justice society, Fellowship of Christian Athletes, student ecology club, Habitat for Humanity, Alpha Phi Omega Service Fraternity, social work organization.

Athletics. NCAA. Intercollegiate: Baseball M, basketball, cross-country, diving, football (tackle) M, golf, soccer, softball W, swimming, tennis, track and field, volleyball W. **Intramural:** Basketball, bowling, football (nontackle), racquetball, softball, table tennis, volleyball. **Team name:** Yellow Jackets.

Student services. Adult student services, alcohol/substance abuse counseling, chaplain/spiritual director, career counseling, student employment services, financial aid counseling, health services, minority student services, personal counseling, placement for graduates. **Physically disabled:** Services for hearing impaired.

Contact. E-mail: admissions@defiance.edu
Phone: (419) 783-2359 Toll-free number: (800) 520-4632
Fax: (419) 783-2468
Brad Harsha, Director of Admissions, Defiance College, 701 North Clinton Street, Defiance, OH 43512-1695

Denison University
Granville, Ohio
www.denison.edu

CB member
CB code: 1164

- Private 4-year liberal arts college
- Residential campus in small town
- 2,266 degree-seeking undergraduates: 57% women, 7% African American, 3% Asian American, 6% Hispanic American, 7% international
- 48% of applicants admitted
- Application essay required
- 79% graduate within 6 years

General. Founded in 1831. Regionally accredited. **Degrees:** 481 bachelor's awarded. **ROTC:** Army. **Location:** 27 miles from Columbus. **Calendar:** Semester. **Full-time faculty:** 211 total; 99% have terminal degrees, 18% minority, 46% women. **Part-time faculty:** 22 total; 41% have terminal degrees, 14% minority, 46% women. **Class size:** 68% < 20, 31% 20-39, less than 1% 50-99. **Special facilities:** Field research station in 350-acre biological reserve, high resolution spectrometer lab, nuclear magnetic resonance spectrometer, planetarium, economics computer lab, harmonic systems lab, digital media lab, fine and performing arts MIX lab (intermedia experimental lab), geographic information systems lab.

Freshman class profile. 4,772 applied, 2,304 admitted, 606 enrolled.

Mid 50% test scores			
SAT critical reading:	600-690	Rank in top quarter:	86%
SAT math:	590-670	Rank in top tenth:	55%
ACT composite:	27-30	Return as sophomores:	90%
GPA 3.75 or higher:	30%	Out-of-state:	73%
GPA 3.50-3.74:	25%	Live on campus:	100%
GPA 3.0-3.49:	36%	International:	7%
GPA 2.0-2.99:	9%	Fraternities:	23%
		Sororities:	36%

Basis for selection. Academic record, recommendations, talent and ability, character and personal qualities most important. School and community activities, essay and personal potential also important. Test scores considered. Interview recommended for all; audition required for visual and performing arts program; portfolio recommended for studio art programs.

High school preparation. College-preparatory program required. 19 units required. Required units include English 4, mathematics 4, social studies 2, history 1, science 4, foreign language 3 and academic electives 1.

2011-2012 Annual costs. Tuition/fees: $40,200. Room/board: $9,960. Books/supplies: $650. Personal expenses: $300.

2011-2012 Financial aid. Need-based: 392 full-time freshmen applied for aid; 326 were judged to have need; 326 of these received aid. Average need met was 96%. Average scholarship/grant was $29,591; average loan $3,705. 68% of total undergraduate aid awarded as scholarships/grants, 32% as loans/jobs. **Non-need-based:** Awarded to 2,023 full-time undergraduates, including 557 freshmen. Scholarships awarded for academics, alumni affiliation, art, leadership, minority status, music/drama, state residency.

Application procedures. Admission: Closing date 1/15 (postmark date). $40 fee, may be waived for applicants with need, free for online applicants. Admission notification by 4/1. Must reply by May 1 or within 2 week(s) if notified thereafter. **Financial aid:** Priority date 3/15; no closing date. FAFSA required. Applicants notified on a rolling basis starting 3/28.

Academics. Special study options: Double major, independent study, internships, New York semester, semester at sea, student-designed major, study abroad, teacher certification program, Washington semester. 3-2 Duke U. Environmental Management; 3-2 U. of Michigan Natural Resources; 3-4 Case Western Reserve Dental; 3-2 Rensselaer Poly., Washington U. (St. Louis), Case Western Reserve, Columbia U. Engineering; Washington U. (St. Louis) Occupational Therapy. **Credit/placement by examination:** AP, CLEP, IB, institutional tests. **Support services:** Learning center, reduced course load, study skills assistance, tutoring, writing center.

Majors. Area/ethnic studies: African-American, East Asian, gay/lesbian, Latin American, Western European, women's. **Biology:** General, biochemistry. **Business:** Organizational behavior. **Communications:** Communications/speech/rhetoric, digital media. **Computer sciences:** General. **Conservation:** General. **Education:** General, physical. **English:** British lit, English lit. **Foreign languages:** Classics, French, German, Spanish. **History:** General. **Math:** General. **Philosophy/religion:** Philosophy, religion. **Physical sciences:** Chemistry, geology, physics. **Psychology:** General. **Social sciences:** Anthropology, economics, political science, sociology. **Visual/performing arts:** Art history/conservation, dance, dramatic, film/cinema/video, music, studio arts.

Most popular majors. Biology 10%, communications/journalism 7%, English 9%, psychology 9%, social sciences 27%, visual/performing arts 6%.

Computing on campus. Dormitories wired for high-speed internet access and linked to campus network. Commuter students can connect to campus network. Online library, helpline, student web hosting, wireless network available.

Student life. Freshman orientation: Mandatory. Preregistration for classes offered. Mandatory no-fee August orientation program and optional but highly recommended June program costing $175. **Housing:** Guaranteed on-campus for all undergraduates. Coed dorms, single-sex dorms, apartments, cooperative housing, wellness housing available. **Activities:** Jazz band, campus ministries, choral groups, dance, drama, film society, international student organizations, literary magazine, music ensembles, musical theater, radio station, student government, student newspaper, TV station, over 130 organizations available.

Athletics. NCAA. Intercollegiate: Baseball M, basketball, cross-country, diving, field hockey W, football (tackle) M, golf M, lacrosse, soccer, softball W, swimming, tennis, track and field, volleyball W. **Intramural:** Basketball, equestrian, football (non-tackle), golf, ice hockey M, lacrosse M, racquetball, rifle, rugby, skiing, soccer, softball, squash, tennis, volleyball, water polo, wrestling M. **Team name:** Big Red.

Student services. Alcohol/substance abuse counseling, chaplain/spiritual director, career counseling, student employment services, financial aid counseling, health services, minority student services, personal counseling, placement for graduates.

Contact. E-mail: admissions@denison.edu
Phone: (740) 587-6276 Toll-free number: (800) 336-4766
Fax: (740) 587-6306
Perry Robinson, Vice President and Director of Admissions, Denison
University, 100 West College PO Box B, Granville, OH 43023

DeVry University: Columbus

Columbus, Ohio — CB member
www.devry.edu — CB code: 1605

- For-profit 4-year university
- Commuter campus in very large city
- Interview required

General. Founded in 1952. Regionally accredited. Additional locations:
Columbus North, Cincinnati, Dayton, Cleveland; Indianapolis (IN); Louisville (KY); Southfield (MI). **Degrees:** 339 bachelor's, 169 associate awarded;
master's offered. **ROTC:** Army. **Location:** 5 miles from downtown. **Calendar:** Semester, extensive summer session. **Full-time faculty:** 37 total. **Part-
time faculty:** 65 total.

Basis for selection. Applicants must have high school diploma or equivalent, demonstrate proficiency in basic college-level skills through SAT or
ACT scores or institution-administered placement examinations, and be 17
years of age. New students may enter at beginning of any semester. SAT or
ACT recommended. CPT also accepted.

High school preparation. Required units include mathematics 1. Math
unit must be algebra or higher.

2011-2012 Annual costs. Tuition/fees: $15,294. Books/supplies: $1,300.
Personal expenses: $3,574.

Financial aid. All financial aid based on need.

Application procedures. Admission: No deadline. $50 fee. Admission
notification on a rolling basis. **Financial aid:** No deadline. FAFSA required.
Applicants notified on a rolling basis.

Academics. Special study options: Accelerated study, distance learning.
Credit/placement by examination: AP, CLEP, institutional tests. **Support
services:** Learning center, tutoring.

Majors. Business: Business admin. **Computer sciences:** Networking, systems analysis.

Most popular majors. Business/marketing 49%, computer/information
sciences 35%, engineering/engineering technologies 16%.

Computing on campus. 408 workstations in library, computer center,
student center. Online course registration, online library, helpline available.

Student life. Freshman orientation: Mandatory. Preregistration for
classes offered. **Housing:** Private apartments, student-plan housing, private
rooms available. **Activities:** Student association, Tau Alpha Pi, Christian
Alliance, Asian American student association, Future Accounting Society,
Institute of Electrical and Electronics Engineers, Association of IT Professionals, minority student union.

Athletics. Intramural: Basketball, soccer, volleyball.

Student services. Career counseling, student employment services, financial aid counseling, placement for graduates, veterans' counselor. **Physically
disabled:** Services for visually, hearing impaired.

Contact. E-mail: admissions@devry.edu
Phone: (614) 253-1525 Toll-free number: (800) 426-2206
Fax: (614) 253-0843
Bill Holtry, Dean of Admissions, DeVry University: Columbus, 1350
Alum Creek Drive, Columbus, OH 43209-2705

Franciscan University of Steubenville

Steubenville, Ohio — CB member
www.franciscan.edu — CB code: 1133

- Private 4-year university affiliated with Roman Catholic Church
- Residential campus in large town
- 2,070 degree-seeking undergraduates: 4% part-time, 62% women, 1%
  Asian American, 8% Hispanic American, 1% international
- 664 degree-seeking graduate students

- 76% of applicants admitted
- SAT or ACT (ACT writing optional) required
- 70% graduate within 6 years; 22% enter graduate study

General. Founded in 1946. Regionally accredited. **Degrees:** 480 bachelor's,
44 associate awarded; master's offered. **ROTC:** Army, Air Force. **Location:**
40 miles from Pittsburgh. **Calendar:** Semester, limited summer session. **Full-
time faculty:** 115 total; 79% have terminal degrees, less than 1% minority,
26% women. **Part-time faculty:** 108 total; 23% have terminal degrees, 36%
women. **Class size:** 44% < 20, 45% 20-39, 9% 40-49, 2% 50-99, less than
1% >100. **Special facilities:** Replica of Portiuncula (St. Mary of the Angels)
Chapel as rebuilt by St. Francis of Assisi in 1207, Tomb of the Unborn Child.

Freshman class profile. 1,739 applied, 1,329 admitted, 449 enrolled.

Mid 50% test scores			
SAT critical reading:	550-650	GPA 2.0-2.99:	8%
SAT math:	510-610	Rank in top quarter:	60%
SAT writing:	520-630	Rank in top tenth:	29%
ACT composite:	23-29	Return as sophomores:	85%
GPA 3.75 or higher:	51%	Out-of-state:	78%
GPA 3.50-3.74:	18%	Live on campus:	93%
GPA 3.0-3.49:	23%	International:	1%

Basis for selection. Admission requirements include 2.4 GPA, recommendations, interview when available, 1000 SAT (exclusive of Writing) or
21 ACT. Interview recommended. **Home schooled:** Applicants should contact
Admissions Office for requirements.

High school preparation. College-preparatory program recommended.
15 units required. Required and recommended units include English 4, mathematics 3, social studies 2, history 2, science 3, foreign language 3 and
academic electives 1. 10 units in 4 of the following fields: English, foreign
language, social science, math, natural sciences. Remaining 5 units may be
in other subjects counted toward graduation. Majors in chemistry, engineering
science, or math should have 2 units algebra and 2 units geometry/trigonom-
etry.

2011-2012 Annual costs. Tuition/fees: $21,220. Room/board: $7,100.
Books/supplies: $1,200. Personal expenses: $1,200.

Financial aid. Non-need-based: Scholarships awarded for academics,
leadership, religious affiliation.

Application procedures. Admission: Priority date 1/31; no deadline.
$20 fee, may be waived for applicants with need, free for online applicants.
Admission notification on a rolling basis beginning on or about 9/1. **Financial
aid:** Priority date 4/1; no closing date. FAFSA required. Applicants notified
on a rolling basis starting 3/1; must reply within 3 week(s) of notification.

Academics. Special study options: Accelerated study, combined bachelor's/graduate degree, distance learning, double major, dual enrollment of
high school students, honors, independent study, internships, study abroad,
teacher certification program. **Credit/placement by examination:** AP,
CLEP, IB, institutional tests. 30 credit hours maximum toward associate
degree, 30 toward bachelor's. **Support services:** Learning center, reduced
course load, study skills assistance, tutoring, writing center.

Honors college/program. 1180 SAT (exclusive of Writing) or 26 ACT,
3.4 GPA, and series of essays required. 40 freshmen admitted. Academic
program consists of a great books seminar sequence.

Majors. Biology: General. **Business:** Accounting, business admin. **Communications:** Communications/speech/rhetoric. **Computer sciences:** General, computer science. **Education:** Elementary. **English:** English lit. **Foreign
languages:** Classics, French, German, Spanish. **Health services:** Nursing
(RN). **History:** General. **Human services:** Social work. **Liberal arts:**
Humanities. **Math:** General. **Philosophy/religion:** Philosophy. **Physical sciences:** Chemistry. **Psychology:** General. **Social sciences:** Anthropology, economics, political science, sociology. **Theology:** Religious ed, sacred music,
theology. **Visual/performing arts:** Dramatic.

Most popular majors. Business/marketing 11%, education 9%, English
6%, health sciences 13%, philosophy/religious studies 6%, theological studies 30%.

Computing on campus. 126 workstations in library, computer center.
Dormitories wired for high-speed internet access and linked to campus network. Commuter students can connect to campus network. Online library,
helpline available.

Student life. Freshman orientation: Available. Preregistration for classes
offered. Held the weekend before fall classes begin, from Friday morning
to Sunday afternoon. **Policies:** Freshmen not permitted cars on campus.
Housing: Guaranteed on-campus for freshmen. Single-sex dorms, apartments
available. $300 nonrefundable deposit. Household groups of 10-20 students
in residence halls may develop distinctive environment for their group within

the context of Christian and Franciscan perspective. **Activities:** Campus ministries, choral groups, drama, international student organizations, literary magazine, music ensembles, radio station, student government, student newspaper, international student organization, Human Life Concerns (pro-life), Works of Mercy Program (social justice), leadership development.

Athletics. NCAA. **Intercollegiate:** Basketball, cross-country, rugby M, soccer, softball W, tennis, track and field, volleyball W. **Intramural:** Basketball, football (non-tackle), racquetball, soccer, softball, volleyball, weight lifting. **Team name:** Barons.

Student services. Chaplain/spiritual director, career counseling, student employment services, financial aid counseling, health services, personal counseling, veterans' counselor. **Physically disabled:** Services for visually, speech, hearing impaired.

Contact. E-mail: admissions@franciscan.edu
Phone: (740) 283-6226 Toll-free number: (800) 783-6220
Fax: (740) 284-5456
Margaret Weber, Director of Admissions, Franciscan University of Steubenville, 1235 University Boulevard, Steubenville, OH 43952-1763

Franklin University
Columbus, Ohio
www.franklin.edu
CB code: 1229

▶ Private 4-year university and business college
▶ Commuter campus in very large city
▶ 6,439 degree-seeking undergraduates

General. Founded in 1902. Regionally accredited. Credit courses offered at suburban campuses and online. **Degrees:** 1,559 bachelor's, 79 associate awarded; master's offered. **ROTC:** Army. **Location:** Downtown. **Calendar:** Trimester, extensive summer session. **Full-time faculty:** 64 total. **Part-time faculty:** 702 total. **Class size:** 82% < 20, 18% 20-39. **Special facilities:** Student learning center.

Basis for selection. Open admission, but selective for some programs. Admission tests not required but considered for placement if submitted. Selective admission for international (nonresident alien) students.

High school preparation. Recommended units include mathematics 3.

2011-2012 Annual costs. Tuition/fees: $11,250. Books/supplies: $960. Personal expenses: $2,550.

Financial aid. Non-need-based: Scholarships awarded for academics, leadership, minority status.

Application procedures. Admission: No deadline. No application fee. Admission notification on a rolling basis. **Financial aid:** Priority date 6/15; no closing date. FAFSA required. Applicants notified on a rolling basis; must reply within 2 week(s) of notification.

Academics. Accelerated 6-week course offerings in addition to 12- and 15-week formats. **Special study options:** Accelerated study, combined bachelor's/graduate degree, cooperative education, cross-registration, distance learning, double major, dual enrollment of high school students, ESL, independent study, internships, study abroad, weekend college. **Credit/placement by examination:** AP, CLEP, IB, institutional tests. 32 credit hours maximum toward associate degree, 84 toward bachelor's. **Support services:** Learning center, reduced course load, remedial instruction, study skills assistance, tutoring, writing center.

Majors. Business: Accounting, business admin, finance, financial planning, human resources, management information systems, management science, marketing, nonprofit/public, operations. **Communications:** Organizational, public relations. **Computer sciences:** Computer science, information technology, web page design. **Health services:** Health care admin, medical records technology. **Psychology:** Applied. **Social sciences:** Economics. **Visual/performing arts:** Game design.

Computing on campus. 370 workstations in library, computer center, student center. Commuter students can connect to campus network. Online course registration, online library, helpline, wireless network available.

Student life. Freshman orientation: Available, $25 fee. Preregistration for classes offered. **Activities:** International student association.

Student services. Adult student services, career counseling, financial aid counseling, veterans' counselor. **Physically disabled:** Services for visually, speech, hearing impaired.

Contact. E-mail: info@franklin.edu
Phone: (614) 797-4700 Toll-free number: (877) 341-6300
Fax: (614) 224-8027
Lynne Hull, Assistant Director of New Student Enrollment, Franklin University, 201 South Grant Avenue, Columbus, OH 43215-5399

God's Bible School and College
Cincinnati, Ohio
www.gbs.edu
CB code: 1238

▶ Private 4-year Bible college affiliated with interdenominational tradition
▶ Residential campus in large city

General. Founded in 1900. Accredited by ABHE. **Location:** One mile from downtown. **Calendar:** Semester.

Annual costs/financial aid. Tuition/fees (2011-2012): $6,560. Room/board: $3,650. Books/supplies: $725. Personal expenses: $2,600. Need-based financial aid available to full-time and part-time students.

Contact. Phone: (513) 721-7944 ext. 205
Director of Admissions, 1810 Young Street, Cincinnati, OH 45202-6838

Heidelberg University
Tiffin, Ohio
www.heidelberg.edu
CB member
CB code: 1292

▶ Private 4-year liberal arts college affiliated with United Church of Christ
▶ Residential campus in large town
▶ 1,101 degree-seeking undergraduates
▶ SAT or ACT (ACT writing optional) required

General. Founded in 1850. Regionally accredited. **Degrees:** 250 bachelor's awarded; master's offered. **ROTC:** Army, Air Force. **Location:** 52 miles from Toledo, 80 miles from Cleveland. **Calendar:** Semester, limited summer session. **Full-time faculty:** 65 total; 88% have terminal degrees, 11% minority, 46% women. **Part-time faculty:** 78 total; 33% have terminal degrees, 10% minority, 45% women. **Class size:** 66% < 20, 31% 20-39, 2% 40-49, 1% 50-99. **Special facilities:** National center for water quality research, cadaver laboratory, four wooded lots for science research, archaeology laboratory, historic and military archaeology center.

Freshman class profile.

GPA 3.75 or higher:	18%	Rank in top quarter:	38%
GPA 3.50-3.74:	14%	Rank in top tenth:	12%
GPA 3.0-3.49:	33%	Out-of-state:	20%
GPA 2.0-2.99:	35%	Live on campus:	86%

Basis for selection. School achievement record most important, followed by test scores. Positive trend in grades and college prep coursework also important. Special talents, community activities, and leadership qualities considered. Audition required for music; interview recommended for academically challanged students. **Learning Disabled:** Students with learning disabilities are strongly encouraged to self-report to the Academic Success Center after acceptance to the University. Appointments to discuss possible services/accommodations are welcome.

High school preparation. College-preparatory program recommended. 21 units recommended. Recommended units include English 4, mathematics 3, social studies 3, history 2, science 3 (laboratory 1), foreign language 2 and academic electives 3.

2011-2012 Annual costs. Tuition/fees: $23,670. Room/board: $8,974. Books/supplies: $1,500. Personal expenses: $500.

Financial aid. Non-need-based: Scholarships awarded for academics, music/drama, religious affiliation, state residency.

Application procedures. Admission: Priority date 1/1; deadline 8/1. $25 fee, may be waived for applicants with need, free for online applicants. Admission notification on a rolling basis beginning on or about 10/15. Must reply by May 1 or within 2 week(s) if notified thereafter. **Financial aid:** Priority date 3/1; no closing date. FAFSA required. Applicants notified on a rolling basis starting 3/1; must reply by 5/1 or within 2 week(s) of notification.

Academics. Special study options: Accelerated study, combined bachelor's/graduate degree, cooperative education, cross-registration, double major, dual enrollment of high school students, ESL, exchange student, honors, independent study, internships, liberal arts/career combination, study abroad, teacher certification program, Washington semester. **Credit/placement by**

examination: AP, CLEP, IB, SAT, ACT, institutional tests. 30 credit hours maximum toward bachelor's degree. **Support services:** Learning center, reduced course load, study skills assistance, tutoring.

Majors. Biology: General, environmental. **Business:** Accounting, business admin, management science. **Communications:** Communications/speech/rhetoric, public relations. **Computer sciences:** General, computer science. **Conservation:** Management/policy. **Education:** Music, physical. **English:** English lit. **Foreign languages:** German, Spanish. **Health services:** Athletic training, health care admin, predental, premedicine, prenursing, preveterinary. **History:** General. **Human services:** General. **Math:** General. **Parks/recreation:** Sports admin. **Philosophy/religion:** Religion. **Physical sciences:** Chemistry, physics. **Protective services:** Law enforcement admin. **Psychology:** General. **Social sciences:** General, anthropology, economics, political science. **Visual/performing arts:** Music, music management, music performance, music theory/composition, musical theater.

Most popular majors. Business/marketing 26%, communications/journalism 7%, education 14%, parks/recreation 9%, psychology 8%, social sciences 7%.

Computing on campus. 125 workstations in dormitories, library, computer center, student center. Dormitories wired for high-speed internet access and linked to campus network. Online course registration, helpline, repair service, wireless network available.

Student life. Freshman orientation: Mandatory. Preregistration for classes offered. Five 2-day summer sessions offered. **Housing:** Guaranteed on-campus for all undergraduates. Coed dorms, single-sex dorms, special housing for disabled, apartments, cooperative housing, wellness housing available. $250 fully refundable deposit, deadline 8/1. Undergraduate specialty houses by major, interest, service groups available. **Activities:** Bands, campus ministries, choral groups, dance, drama, film society, international student organizations, literary magazine, music ensembles, Model UN, musical theater, opera, radio station, student government, student newspaper, symphony orchestra, TV station, campus fellowship, Black student union, Young Democrats, Young Republicans, world student union, Alpha Phi Omega, political science organization, Amigos de ARISE.

Athletics. NCAA. **Intercollegiate:** Baseball M, basketball, cheerleading, cross-country, football (tackle) M, golf, soccer, softball W, tennis, track and field, volleyball W, wrestling M. **Intramural:** Archery, baseball M, basketball, bowling, golf, soccer, softball, table tennis, volleyball. **Team name:** Student Princes.

Student services. Adult student services, alcohol/substance abuse counseling, chaplain/spiritual director, career counseling, student employment services, financial aid counseling, health services, minority student services, personal counseling, placement for graduates, women's services. **Physically disabled:** Services for visually, hearing impaired.

Contact. E-mail: adminfo@heidelberg.edu
Phone: (419) 448-2330 Toll-free number: (800) 434-3352
Fax: (419) 448-2334
Lindsay Sooy, Director of Admission, Heidelberg University, 310 East Market Street, Tiffin, OH 44883-2462

Herzing University: Toledo
Toledo, Ohio
www.herzing.edu

- For-profit 4-year business and technical college
- Large city
- 308 degree-seeking undergraduates

General. Regionally accredited. **Degrees:** 27 associate awarded. **Calendar:** Semester. **Full-time faculty:** 5 total. **Part-time faculty:** 25 total.

Basis for selection. Wonderlic exam required for some programs.

2011-2012 Annual costs. Tuition/fees: $10,560. Reported annual tuition is representative. Actual costs vary by program with nursing programs somewhat more expensive.

Academics. Credit/placement by examination: AP, CLEP.

Majors. Business: Accounting, business admin.

Contact. E-mail: info@tol.herzing.edu
Joe Guziolek, Director of Admissions, Herzing University: Toledo, 5212 Hill Avenue, Toledo, OH 43615

Hiram College
Hiram, Ohio
www.hiram.edu

CB member
CB code: 1297

- Private 4-year liberal arts college affiliated with Christian Church (Disciples of Christ)
- Residential campus in rural community
- 1,334 degree-seeking undergraduates
- 63% of applicants admitted
- SAT or ACT (ACT writing optional), application essay required

General. Founded in 1850. Regionally accredited. Affiliated with John Cabot University in Rome (Italy), Shoals Marine Laboratory (Appledore Island near Maine/New Hampshire coast), Institute of European Studies (Chicago). Exchange programs with Kansai University of Foreign Studies in Osaka (Japan) and Bosphorus University in Istanbul (Turkey). **Degrees:** 300 bachelor's awarded; master's offered. **Location:** 35 miles from Cleveland. **Calendar:** Semester, limited summer session. **Full-time faculty:** 80 total. **Part-time faculty:** 58 total. **Class size:** 74% < 20, 23% 20-39, 3% 40-49, less than 1% 50-99. **Special facilities:** 2 nature/science field research stations, observatory, center for literature and medicine.

Freshman class profile. 2,273 applied, 1,432 admitted, 309 enrolled.

Mid 50% test scores			
SAT critical reading:	450-660	GPA 3.0-3.49:	31%
SAT math:	450-600	GPA 2.0-2.99:	33%
SAT writing:	440-570	Rank in top quarter:	44%
ACT composite:	19-25	Rank in top tenth:	17%
GPA 3.75 or higher:	20%	Out-of-state:	17%
GPA 3.50-3.74:	16%	Live on campus:	93%

Basis for selection. School record, test scores, counselor and teacher recommendations emphasized. Extracurricular participation, alumni relationship considered. Interview required for scholarship candidates or academically marginal applicants; recommended for all others.

High school preparation. College-preparatory program recommended. 16 units required; 18 recommended. Required and recommended units include English 4, mathematics 4, social studies 1, history 1, science 3 (laboratory 1), foreign language 1-2 and academic electives 1-2. One course in fine arts recommended.

2011-2012 Annual costs. Tuition/fees: $28,950. The Hiram College Tuition Guarantee ensures that the annual cost for tuition will not increase between the first year a student is enrolled at Hiram and the student's senior year. Room/board: $9,460. Books/supplies: $700. Personal expenses: $1,404.

Financial aid. Non-need-based: Scholarships awarded for academics, alumni affiliation, music/drama, religious affiliation, state residency.

Application procedures. Admission: Priority date 2/15; no deadline. $35 fee, may be waived for applicants with need, free for online applicants. Admission notification on a rolling basis beginning on or about 10/1. Must reply by May 1 or within 2 week(s) if notified thereafter. **Financial aid:** Priority date 2/15; no closing date. FAFSA required. Applicants notified on a rolling basis starting 2/15; must reply by 5/1 or within 2 week(s) of notification.

Academics. Prelaw, premed and preveterinary programs offered. **Special study options:** Accelerated study, combined bachelor's/graduate degree, cross-registration, distance learning, double major, ESL, exchange student, independent study, internships, liberal arts/career combination, student-designed major, study abroad, teacher certification program, Washington semester, weekend college. **Credit/placement by examination:** AP, CLEP, IB, institutional tests. 60 credit hours maximum toward bachelor's degree. **Support services:** Reduced course load, study skills assistance, tutoring, writing center.

Majors. Biology: General, biochemistry, biomedical sciences. **Business:** Accounting/finance, business admin. **Communications:** Communications/speech/rhetoric. **Computer sciences:** General, computer science. **Conservation:** Environmental studies. **Education:** General, elementary. **English:** Creative writing, English lit. **Foreign languages:** Classics, French, German, Spanish. **History:** General. **Math:** General. **Philosophy/religion:** Philosophy, religion. **Physical sciences:** Chemistry, physics. **Psychology:** General. **Social sciences:** General, economics, political science, sociology. **Visual/performing arts:** Art history/conservation, dramatic, music, studio arts.

Most popular majors. Biology 14%, business/marketing 27%, communications/journalism 6%, education 7%, social sciences 17%.

Computing on campus. 100 workstations in dormitories, library, computer center, student center. Dormitories wired for high-speed internet access and linked to campus network. Commuter students can connect to campus

network. Online course registration, online library, helpline, student web hosting, wireless network available.

Student life. Freshman orientation: Mandatory, $240 fee. Preregistration for classes offered. Several orientation sessions held throughout late spring and summer. **Housing:** Guaranteed on-campus for all undergraduates. Coed dorms, single-sex dorms, special housing for disabled, wellness housing available. $200 nonrefundable deposit, deadline 5/1. Dormitories include 24-hour and 12-hour quiet floors. **Activities:** Bands, campus ministries, choral groups, dance, drama, international student organizations, literary magazine, music ensembles, Model UN, opera, radio station, student government, student newspaper, symphony orchestra, African-American Students United, environmental awareness club, Christian Fellowship, Network for Progressive Action, conservative student forum, volunteer association, international organization, Intercultural Forum, Newman Club, Islamic Society.

Athletics. NCAA. **Intercollegiate:** Baseball M, basketball, cross-country, diving, football (tackle) M, golf, soccer, softball W, swimming, tennis, track and field, volleyball W. **Intramural:** Archery, basketball, football (non-tackle), soccer, softball, tennis, volleyball, water polo. **Team name:** Terriers.

Student services. Chaplain/spiritual director, career counseling, student employment services, health services, minority student services, personal counseling, placement for graduates, veterans' counselor.

Contact. E-mail: admission@hiram.edu
Phone: (330) 569-5169 Toll-free number: (800) 362-5280
Fax: (330) 569-5944
Sherman Dean, Director of Admission, Hiram College, Teachout Price Hall, Hiram, OH 44234

John Carroll University
University Heights, Ohio
www.jcu.edu

CB member
CB code: 1342

- Private 4-year university affiliated with Roman Catholic Church
- Residential campus in large town
- 2,956 degree-seeking undergraduates: 2% part-time, 49% women, 5% African American, 2% Asian American, 4% Hispanic American
- 699 degree-seeking graduate students
- 84% of applicants admitted
- SAT or ACT (ACT writing recommended), application essay required
- 71% graduate within 6 years

General. Founded in 1886. Regionally accredited. **Degrees:** 636 bachelor's awarded; master's offered. **ROTC:** Army. **Location:** 10 miles east of Cleveland. **Calendar:** Semester, extensive summer session. **Full-time faculty:** 192 total; 97% have terminal degrees, 13% minority, 41% women. **Part-time faculty:** 161 total; 39% have terminal degrees, 8% minority, 48% women. **Class size:** 44% < 20, 56% 20-39. **Special facilities:** Science and technology center.

Freshman class profile. 3,309 applied, 2,772 admitted, 747 enrolled.

Mid 50% test scores			
SAT critical reading:	480-600	Rank in top quarter:	46%
SAT math:	490-600	Rank in top tenth:	22%
SAT writing:	490-590	Out-of-state:	36%
ACT composite:	22-27	Live on campus:	95%
GPA 3.75 or higher:	29%	Fraternities:	6%
GPA 3.50-3.74:	17%	Sororities:	15%
GPA 3.0-3.49:	33%		
GPA 2.0-2.99:	21%		

Basis for selection. High school academic record, rigor of curricula most important. Other criteria include test scores, extracurricular activities, essay. **Home schooled:** State high school equivalency certificate, interview, letter of recommendation (nonparent) required. Extra emphasis placed on standardized testing. Encourage SAT subject testing if possible.

High school preparation. College-preparatory program recommended. 16 units required; 21 recommended. Required and recommended units include English 4, mathematics 3-4, social studies 2-4, science 2-3 (laboratory 2-3), foreign language 2-3 and academic electives 3. 2-4 units among social studies, history, social science, or religion.

2011-2012 Annual costs. Tuition/fees: $31,710. Room/board: $9,150. Books/supplies: $1,200. Personal expenses: $1,000.

2010-2011 Financial aid. Need-based: 647 full-time freshmen applied for aid; 578 were judged to have need; 578 of these received aid. Average need met was 86%. Average scholarship/grant was $21,447; average loan $2,866. **Non-need-based:** Awarded to 2,730 full-time undergraduates, including 687 freshmen. Scholarships awarded for academics, alumni affiliation,

leadership, minority status, ROTC, state residency. **Additional information:** John Carroll grant combined with federal and state grant aid, and the Federal Stafford Loan program to meet the published flat, full-time tuition cost for Pell-eligible Ohio families.

Application procedures. Admission: Priority date 12/1; no deadline. No application fee. Admission notification on a rolling basis beginning on or about 12/15. Must reply by May 1 or within 4 week(s) if notified thereafter. **Financial aid:** Priority date 2/15, closing date 3/15. FAFSA required. Applicants notified on a rolling basis starting 2/1; must reply by 5/1 or within 4 week(s) of notification.

Academics. Special study options: Accelerated study, combined bachelor's/graduate degree, cooperative education, cross-registration, double major, dual enrollment of high school students, exchange student, honors, independent study, internships, liberal arts/career combination, student-designed major, study abroad, teacher certification program, Washington semester. **Credit/placement by examination:** AP, CLEP, IB, SAT, ACT, institutional tests. 30 credit hours maximum toward bachelor's degree. **Support services:** Learning center, reduced course load, study skills assistance, tutoring, writing center.

Majors. Area/ethnic studies: East Asian, women's. **Biology:** General, biochemistry. **Business:** Accounting, business admin, finance, human resources, international, logistics, managerial economics. **Communications:** Communications/speech/rhetoric. **Computer sciences:** General, computer science. **Conservation:** Environmental science, environmental studies. **Education:** Elementary, mathematics, physical. **Engineering:** Applied physics. **English:** English lit. **Foreign languages:** Ancient Greek, comparative lit, French, German, Latin, Spanish. **Health services:** Predental, premedicine, preveterinary. **History:** General. **Liberal arts:** Arts/sciences. **Math:** General. **Philosophy/religion:** Philosophy, religion. **Physical sciences:** Chemistry, physics. **Psychology:** General. **Social sciences:** Economics, political science, sociology. **Visual/performing arts:** Art history/conservation.

Most popular majors. Biology 11%, business/marketing 31%, communications/journalism 10%, education 9%, psychology 9%, social sciences 7%.

Computing on campus. 200 workstations in dormitories, library, computer center, student center. Dormitories wired for high-speed internet access and linked to campus network. Commuter students can connect to campus network. Online course registration, online library, helpline, repair service, student web hosting, wireless network available.

Student life. Freshman orientation: Mandatory, $325 fee. Preregistration for classes offered. Two-day, one overnight for parents and students. Variety of dates offered throughout June and July. **Policies:** Students must adhere to Student Code of Conduct. All incoming freshman not commuting from home required to live on campus freshman and sophomore years. **Housing:** Guaranteed on-campus for all undergraduates. Coed dorms, special housing for disabled, apartments, fraternity/sorority housing, wellness housing available. $300 fully refundable deposit, deadline 5/1. Suite-style housing available. **Activities:** Bands, campus ministries, choral groups, dance, drama, film society, international student organizations, literary magazine, music ensembles, radio station, student government, student newspaper, TV station, Christian Life Community, African American Alliance, EMS Association, Habitat for Humanity, Labre Project, Students in Free Enterprise, Public Relations Student Society of America.

Athletics. NCAA. **Intercollegiate:** Baseball M, basketball, cheerleading M, cross-country, diving, football (tackle) M, golf, soccer, softball W, swimming, tennis, track and field, volleyball W, wrestling M. **Intramural:** Basketball, football (non-tackle), golf, racquetball, soccer, softball, table tennis, tennis, volleyball, water polo. **Team name:** Blue Streaks.

Student services. Adult student services, alcohol/substance abuse counseling, chaplain/spiritual director, career counseling, student employment services, financial aid counseling, health services, minority student services, personal counseling, placement for graduates, veterans' counselor, women's services. **Physically disabled:** Services for visually, speech, hearing impaired.

Contact. E-mail: admission@jcu.edu
Phone: (216) 397-4294 Toll-free number: (888) 335-6800
Fax: (216) 397-4981
Steve Vitatoe, Executive Director of Enrollment, John Carroll University, Office of Admission, University Heights, OH 44118-4581

Kent State University
Kent, Ohio
www.kent.edu

CB member
CB code: 1367

- Public 4-year university
- Residential campus in large town

♦ 21,547 degree-seeking undergraduates: 12% part-time, 59% women, 9% African American, 1% Asian American, 3% Hispanic American, 4% international

♦ 5,240 degree-seeking graduate students

♦ 87% of applicants admitted

♦ SAT or ACT with writing required

♦ 50% graduate within 6 years

General. Founded in 1910. Regionally accredited. **Degrees:** 3,999 bachelor's awarded; master's, doctoral offered. **ROTC:** Army, Air Force. **Location:** 50 miles from Cleveland, 11 miles from Akron. **Calendar:** Semester, extensive summer session. **Full-time faculty:** 878 total; 6% minority, 50% women. **Part-time faculty:** 714 total; 4% minority, 56% women. **Class size:** 45% < 20, 40% 20-39, 5% 40-49, 6% 50-99, 4% >100. **Special facilities:** 287-acre airport, liquid crystal institute, fashion museum, planetarium, ice arena, 18-hole golf course.

Freshman class profile. 13,980 applied, 12,231 admitted, 4,351 enrolled.

Mid 50% test scores			
SAT critical reading:	440-570	Rank in top quarter:	36%
SAT math:	450-580	Rank in top tenth:	13%
SAT writing:	430-560	Return as sophomores:	75%
ACT composite:	20-25	Out-of-state:	17%
GPA 3.75 or higher:	16%	Live on campus:	82%
GPA 3.50-3.74:	15%	International:	4%
GPA 3.0-3.49:	37%	Fraternities:	10%
GPA 2.0-2.99:	32%	Sororities:	9%

Basis for selection. Academic record, course work, test scores important. Varying criteria for nursing, education, flight, fashion design and merchandising, architecture, interior design, journalism and mass communication, 6-year medical program, music, dance, and honors college applicants. Interview required for 6-year medical program, recommended for all others. Audition required for dance, music, and musical theater students.

High school preparation. College-preparatory program recommended. 16 units recommended. Recommended units include English 4, mathematics 3, social studies 3, science 3 (laboratory 2), foreign language 2 and visual/performing arts 1. One fine arts or third unit of foreign language recommended.

2011-2012 Annual costs. Tuition/fees: $9,496; $17,456 out-of-state. Room/board: $8,330. Books/supplies: $1,320. Personal expenses: $2,430.

2011-2012 Financial aid. **Need-based:** 3,759 full-time freshmen applied for aid; 3,151 were judged to have need; 3,148 of these received aid. Average need met was 52%. Average scholarship/grant was $6,086; average loan $3,254. 52% of total undergraduate aid awarded as scholarships/grants, 48% as loans/jobs. **Non-need-based:** Awarded to 4,356 full-time undergraduates, including 1,487 freshmen. Scholarships awarded for academics, alumni affiliation, art, athletics, leadership, minority status, music/drama, ROTC, state residency. **Additional information:** Participant in US Department of Education's Quality Assurance Program and Experimental Sites Program.

Application procedures. **Admission:** Priority date 5/1; no deadline. $40 fee, may be waived for applicants with need. Admission notification on a rolling basis beginning on or about 8/15. Must reply by May 1 or within 6 week(s) if notified thereafter. **Financial aid:** Priority date 3/1; no closing date. FAFSA required. Applicants notified on a rolling basis starting 3/15; must reply within 2 week(s) of notification.

Academics. **Special study options:** Accelerated study, combined bachelor's/graduate degree, cooperative education, cross-registration, distance learning, double major, dual enrollment of high school students, ESL, exchange student, external degree, honors, independent study, internships, liberal arts/career combination, New York semester, student-designed major, study abroad, teacher certification program, Washington semester, weekend college. BS/MD. **Credit/placement by examination:** AP, CLEP, IB, SAT, ACT, institutional tests. 30 credit hours maximum toward bachelor's degree. **Support services:** Learning center, pre-admission summer program, reduced course load, remedial instruction, study skills assistance, tutoring, writing center.

Honors college/program. Approximately 250 incoming freshman admitted; based on class rank within top 15%; 3.5 GPA; 26 ACT/1170 SAT (exclusive of Writing); small interactive classes (20 maximum); eight courses culminating with thesis project, portfolio, or course; two study abroad programs.

Majors. Architecture: Architecture. **Area/ethnic studies:** African-American, American, Latin American, Russian/Slavic. **Biology:** General, biotechnology, botany, zoology. **Business:** Accounting, business admin, fashion, finance, management information systems, management science, managerial economics, marketing. **Communications:** Advertising, broadcast journalism, communications/speech/rhetoric, digital media, journalism, photojournalism, public relations, radio/TV. **Computer sciences:** Systems analysis. **Conservation:** General. **Education:** General, art, business, chemistry, early childhood, health, mathematics, middle, music, physical, science, social studies, special ed, technology/industrial arts, trade/industrial. **Engineering:** General, industrial. **English:** English lit, rhetoric/composition. **Foreign languages:** French, German, Latin, Russian, sign language interpretation, Spanish. **Health services:** Athletic training, audiology/speech pathology, clinical lab science, nursing (RN), predental, premedicine, preveterinary. **History:** General. **Liberal arts:** Arts/sciences, humanities. **Math:** General, applied. **Parks/recreation:** Facilities management. **Philosophy/religion:** Philosophy. **Physical sciences:** Chemistry, geology, physics. **Protective services:** Criminal justice. **Psychology:** General. **Social sciences:** Anthropology, geography, international relations, political science, sociology. **Visual/performing arts:** Art history/conservation, commercial/advertising art, crafts, dance, dramatic, fashion design, interior design, music, painting. **Work/family studies:** Family studies, food/nutrition.

Most popular majors. Business/marketing 20%, communications/journalism 8%, education 9%, health sciences 14%, visual/performing arts 7%.

Computing on campus. 2,100 workstations in dormitories, library, computer center, student center. Dormitories wired for high-speed internet access and linked to campus network. Commuter students can connect to campus network. Online course registration, online library, helpline, repair service, student web hosting, wireless network available.

Student life. Freshman orientation: Mandatory. Preregistration for classes offered. **Housing:** Guaranteed on-campus for freshmen. Coed dorms, single-sex dorms, special housing for disabled, apartments, fraternity/sorority housing available. $200 fully refundable deposit, deadline 6/1. Single undergraduate students must live in college housing first 4 semesters with some exemptions granted. Learning communities available. **Activities:** Bands, campus ministries, choral groups, dance, drama, international student organizations, literary magazine, music ensembles, Model UN, musical theater, opera, radio station, student government, student newspaper, TV station, many additional organizations available.

Athletics. NCAA. **Intercollegiate:** Baseball M, basketball, cross-country, field hockey W, football (tackle) M, golf, gymnastics W, soccer W, softball W, track and field, volleyball W, wrestling M. **Intramural:** Badminton, basketball, bowling, football (non-tackle), golf, racquetball, soccer, softball, table tennis, tennis, water polo, wrestling M. **Team name:** Golden Flashes.

Student services. Adult student services, alcohol/substance abuse counseling, chaplain/spiritual director, career counseling, services for economically disadvantaged, student employment services, financial aid counseling, health services, legal services, minority student services, personal counseling, placement for graduates, veterans' counselor, women's services. **Physically disabled:** Services for visually, speech, hearing impaired.

Contact. E-mail: admissions@kent.edu
Phone: (330) 672-2444 Toll-free number: (800) 988-5368
Fax: (330) 672-2499
Nancy DellaVecchia, Director of Admissions, Kent State University, PO Box 5190, Kent, OH 44242-0001

Kenyon College
Gambier, Ohio   **CB member**
www.kenyon.edu   **CB code: 1370**

♦ Private 4-year liberal arts college affiliated with nondenominational tradition

♦ Residential campus in rural community

♦ 1,647 degree-seeking undergraduates: 54% women, 3% African American, 6% Asian American, 5% Hispanic American, 1% Native American, 3% international

♦ 33% of applicants admitted

♦ SAT or ACT (ACT writing optional), application essay required

♦ 87% graduate within 6 years

General. Founded in 1824. Regionally accredited. **Degrees:** 419 bachelor's awarded. **Location:** 50 miles from Columbus. **Calendar:** Semester. **Full-time faculty:** 156 total; 100% have terminal degrees, 22% minority, 42% women. **Part-time faculty:** 10 total; 90% have terminal degrees, 40% minority, 20% women. **Class size:** 64% < 20, 33% 20-39, 2% 40-49, less than 1% 50-99. **Special facilities:** Observatory, environmental center and nature preserve, science center.

Freshman class profile. 4,272 applied, 1,429 admitted, 468 enrolled.

Mid 50% test scores			
SAT critical reading:	640-740	GPA 3.0-3.49:	7%
SAT math:	610-690	Rank in top quarter:	86%
SAT writing:	640-730	Rank in top tenth:	59%
ACT composite:	28-32	Return as sophomores:	94%
GPA 3.75 or higher:	82%	Out-of-state:	85%
GPA 3.50-3.74:	11%	Live on campus:	100%
		International:	3%

Basis for selection. Secondary school record and personal character most important followed by test scores, class rank, recommendations, essay, talent, activities and interview. Alumni relationship, ethnicity, geographical residence and work experience considered. **Home schooled:** Provide complete curriculum with texts and books used.

High school preparation. College-preparatory program required. 21 units required; 24 recommended. Required and recommended units include English 4, mathematics 3-4, social studies 1, history 2-3, science 3-4 (laboratory 3), foreign language 3-4 and academic electives 3. 1 fine arts recommended.

2012-2013 Annual costs. Tuition/fees: $44,420. Room/board: $10,340. Books/supplies: $1,800.

2011-2012 Financial aid. Need-based: 230 full-time freshmen applied for aid; 165 were judged to have need; 165 of these received aid. Average need met was 98%. Average scholarship/grant was $32,973; average loan $2,604. 87% of total undergraduate aid awarded as scholarships/grants, 13% as loans/jobs. **Non-need-based:** Scholarships awarded for academics, art, minority status, music/drama. **Additional information:** Financial aid incentive guarantees a loan-free education for 25 students with the greatest need who bring the qualities of creativity, community service, and leadership.

Application procedures. Admission: Closing date 1/15 (postmark date). $50 fee, may be waived for applicants with need, free for online applicants. Admission notification by 4/1. Must reply by 5/1. **Financial aid:** Closing date 2/15. FAFSA, CSS PROFILE required. Applicants notified by 4/1; must reply by 5/1.

Academics. Special study options: Accelerated study, combined bachelor's/graduate degree, double major, exchange student, honors, independent study, liberal arts/career combination, semester at sea, student-designed major, study abroad, Washington semester. Cooperative 3-2 or 4-1 masters and teacher certification program with Bank Street College of Education; 3-2 engineering program with Case Western Reserve, Rensselaer Polytechnic Institute and Washington University; 3-2 environmental studies program with Duke University. Special off-campus study includes: Semester in Environmental Science (SES); Bard Globalization & International Affairs Program (BGIA); Historically Black Colleges & Universities; Earlham College; SEA Semester; American University (AU); The Philadelphia Center (TPC); New York Arts program (NYAP); National Theater Institute; Newberry Seminar. **Credit/placement by examination:** AP, CLEP, IB, institutional tests. 3 credit hours maximum toward bachelor's degree. Credit determined for AP, IB or School Articulation Program (SCAP) counts toward 16 units required for graduation. No diversification requirements may be satisfied with AP credit. Maximum of 3 units of advanced placement credit is accepted by Kenyon. **Support services:** Study skills assistance, tutoring, writing center.

Majors. Area/ethnic studies: American, women's. **Biology:** General, biochemistry, molecular, neuroscience. **English:** English lit. **Foreign languages:** General, ancient Greek, classics, French, German, Latin, Spanish. **History:** General. **Math:** General. **Philosophy/religion:** Philosophy, religion. **Physical sciences:** Chemistry, physics. **Psychology:** General. **Social sciences:** Anthropology, economics, international relations, political science, sociology. **Visual/performing arts:** Art history/conservation, dance, dramatic, music, studio arts.

Most popular majors. Biology 8%, English 17%, foreign language 8%, history 6%, psychology 8%, social sciences 29%, visual/performing arts 11%.

Computing on campus. 400 workstations in dormitories, library, computer center. Dormitories wired for high-speed internet access and linked to campus network. Commuter students can connect to campus network. Online library, helpline, student web hosting, wireless network available.

Student life. Freshman orientation: Mandatory. Preregistration for classes offered. Held 4 days prior to start of classes. **Housing:** Guaranteed on-campus for all undergraduates. Coed dorms, single-sex dorms, special housing for disabled, apartments, fraternity/sorority housing, wellness housing available. $350 nonrefundable deposit, deadline 5/1. Special accommodations can be made for married, international and disabled students. Fraternity and sorority housing available in room blocks only. Wellness and community service and social group halls on campus. **Activities:** Bands, campus ministries, choral groups, dance, drama, film society, international student organizations, literary magazine, music ensembles, Model UN, musical theater, opera, radio station, student government, student newspaper, symphony orchestra, Black student union, Saturday Night Fellowship, Hillel, Asian awareness

club, community service organization, allied sexual orientations, Amnesty International, political affairs clubs, Circle K.

Athletics. NCAA. **Intercollegiate:** Baseball M, basketball, cross-country, diving, field hockey W, football (tackle) M, golf M, lacrosse, soccer, softball W, swimming, tennis, track and field, volleyball W. **Intramural:** Basketball, football (non-tackle), racquetball, soccer, softball W, squash, tennis, volleyball. **Team name:** Lords/Ladies.

Student services. Alcohol/substance abuse counseling, chaplain/spiritual director, career counseling, student employment services, financial aid counseling, health services, minority student services, personal counseling, placement for graduates, women's services. **Physically disabled:** Services for visually, hearing impaired.

Contact. E-mail: admissions@kenyon.edu
Phone: (740) 427-5776 Toll-free number: (800) 848-2468
Fax: (740) 427-5770
Jennifer Delahunty, Dean of Admissions, Kenyon College, Ransom Hall-Admissions, Gambier, OH 43022-9623

Kettering College of Medical Arts
Kettering, Ohio
www.kc.edu   **CB code: 0602**

- Private 4-year health science and nursing college affiliated with Seventh-day Adventists
- Commuter campus in large city
- 839 degree-seeking undergraduates: 44% part-time, 79% women, 5% African American, 2% Asian American, 3% Hispanic American
- 77 degree-seeking graduate students
- 26% of applicants admitted
- Application essay required
- 53% graduate within 6 years

General. Founded in 1967. Regionally accredited. **Degrees:** 57 bachelor's, 168 associate awarded; master's offered. **Location:** 5 miles from Dayton. **Calendar:** Semester, limited summer session. **Full-time faculty:** 59 total; 27% have terminal degrees, 10% minority, 66% women. **Part-time faculty:** 30 total; 7% have terminal degrees, 13% minority, 80% women. **Class size:** 49% < 20, 33% 20-39, 11% 40-49, 7% 50-99.

Freshman class profile. 403 applied, 105 admitted, 85 enrolled.

Mid 50% test scores			
SAT critical reading:	550-590	GPA 2.0-2.99:	12%
SAT math:	470-560	Rank in top quarter:	60%
SAT writing:	490-600	Rank in top tenth:	19%
ACT composite:	21-25	End year in good standing:	80%
GPA 3.75 or higher:	28%	Return as sophomores:	78%
GPA 3.50-3.74:	23%	Out-of-state:	15%
GPA 3.0-3.49:	37%	Live on campus:	39%

Basis for selection. High school GPA, test scores, personal statements important. Interview required for physician assistant applicants.

High school preparation. 14 units recommended. Recommended units include English 4, mathematics 2 and science 3. Strong mathematics and science background recommended.

2011-2012 Annual costs. Tuition/fees: $11,460. $200 program fee per semester for areas of study with clinical requirements. Room only: $3,300. Books/supplies: $1,085. Personal expenses: $2,857.

Financial aid. Non-need-based: Scholarships awarded for academics.

Application procedures. Admission: No deadline. $25 fee, may be waived for applicants with need. Application must be submitted online. Admission notification on a rolling basis. **Financial aid:** Priority date 3/31; no closing date. FAFSA, institutional form required. Applicants notified on a rolling basis starting 5/15; must reply within 3 week(s) of notification.

Academics. Special study options: Distance learning, double major, dual enrollment of high school students, honors. **Credit/placement by examination:** AP, CLEP, SAT, ACT, institutional tests. **Support services:** Learning center, reduced course load, study skills assistance, tutoring, writing center.

Majors. Health services: Nursing (RN), predental, premedicine, sonography.

Computing on campus. 52 workstations in library, computer center. Dormitories wired for high-speed internet access and linked to campus network. Online library, helpline, wireless network available.

Student life. Freshman orientation: Mandatory. Preregistration for classes offered. **Policies:** Religious observance required. **Housing:** Single-sex dorms, wellness housing available. $75 nonrefundable deposit. **Activities:** Campus ministries, religious life organizations.

Athletics. Intramural: Basketball, volleyball.

Student services. Chaplain/spiritual director, career counseling, student employment services, financial aid counseling, health services, personal counseling, placement for graduates, veterans' counselor.

Contact. E-mail: studentadmissions@kc.edu
Phone: (937) 395-8628 Toll-free number: (800) 433-5262
Fax: (937) 395-8338
Becky McDonald, Director of Enrollment Services, Kettering College of Medical Arts, 3737 Southern Boulevard, Kettering, OH 45429-1299

Lake Erie College
Painesville, Ohio
www.lec.edu
CB member
CB code: 1391

- Private 4-year liberal arts college
- Residential campus in large town
- 908 degree-seeking undergraduates: 4% part-time, 48% women
- 164 degree-seeking graduate students
- 59% of applicants admitted
- SAT or ACT (ACT writing optional), application essay required
- 47% graduate within 6 years

General. Founded in 1856. Regionally accredited. **Degrees:** 170 bachelor's awarded; master's offered. **Location:** 30 miles from Cleveland. **Calendar:** Semester, limited summer session. **Full-time faculty:** 46 total; 76% have terminal degrees, 2% minority, 61% women. **Part-time faculty:** 75 total; 4% minority, 39% women. **Class size:** 68% < 20, 32% 20-39. **Special facilities:** Equestrian center.

Freshman class profile. 1,459 applied, 860 admitted, 215 enrolled.

Mid 50% test scores			
SAT critical reading:	450-560	GPA 2.0-2.99:	40%
SAT math:	450-580	Rank in top quarter:	31%
SAT writing:	420-570	Rank in top tenth:	10%
ACT composite:	19-24	End year in good standing:	76%
GPA 3.75 or higher:	15%	Return as sophomores:	62%
GPA 3.50-3.74:	15%	Out-of-state:	32%
GPA 3.0-3.49:	30%	International:	3%

Basis for selection. School achievement record, test scores, essay, reference letters and interview strongly considered. Special consideration of test scores for some applicants. Interview strongly recommended. **Home schooled:** Statement describing home school structure and mission, transcript of courses and grades, interview, letter of recommendation (nonparent) required. **Learning Disabled:** Documentation of learning disability required.

High school preparation. College-preparatory program recommended. 17 units required. Required units include English 4, mathematics 3, social studies 3, science 3 (laboratory 2) and foreign language 2.

2011-2012 Annual costs. Tuition/fees: $26,550. Equestrian fee $1,039 per course. Room/board: $8,192. Books/supplies: $1,100. Personal expenses: $2,110.

2011-2012 Financial aid. Need-based: Average need met was 70%. Average scholarship/grant was $17,116; average loan $3,104. 68% of total undergraduate aid awarded as scholarships/grants, 32% as loans/jobs. **Non-need-based:** Scholarships awarded for academics, art, leadership, music/drama, state residency. **Additional information:** Twins' scholarship, sibling discount.

Application procedures. Admission: Priority date 5/1; deadline 8/1. $30 fee, may be waived for applicants with need, free for online applicants. Admission notification on a rolling basis beginning on or about 9/1. Must reply by 8/1. **Financial aid:** No deadline. FAFSA required. Applicants notified on a rolling basis starting 2/15; must reply by 5/1 or within 4 week(s) of notification.

Academics. Special study options: Accelerated study, combined bachelor's/graduate degree, cross-registration, double major, dual enrollment of high school students, honors, independent study, internships, liberal arts/career combination, student-designed major, study abroad, teacher certification program. **Credit/placement by examination:** AP, CLEP, IB, SAT, ACT, institutional tests. 32 credit hours maximum toward bachelor's degree.

Support services: Learning center, reduced course load, study skills assistance, tutoring, writing center.

Majors. Biology: General. **Business:** Accounting, business admin, entrepreneurial studies, international, marketing, training/development. **Communications:** Communications/speech/rhetoric. **Conservation:** General, environmental studies. **Education:** General, curriculum, elementary, reading, secondary. **English:** English lit. **Foreign languages:** General, French, German, Italian, Spanish. **General:** Animal breeding, equestrian studies, equine science, farm/ranch. **History:** General. **Math:** General. **Physical sciences:** Chemistry. **Protective services:** Law enforcement admin. **Psychology:** General. **Social sciences:** General, sociology. **Visual/performing arts:** General, dance, music, studio arts, theater arts management.

Most popular majors. Agriculture 12%, business/marketing 36%, education 11%, parks/recreation 8%, psychology 6%.

Computing on campus. 75 workstations in dormitories, library, computer center, student center. Dormitories wired for high-speed internet access and linked to campus network. Online course registration, wireless network available.

Student life. Freshman orientation: Available, $200 fee. Preregistration for classes offered. One-day program during summer; extended 3-day orientation for freshman a week prior to start of classes. **Housing:** Guaranteed on-campus for freshmen. Coed dorms, single-sex dorms, apartments available. $150 fully refundable deposit, deadline 5/1. Residence halls equipped with laundry and kitchen areas available. **Activities:** Marching band, choral groups, dance, drama, music ensembles, student government, honor association, academic association, athletic association, foreign language clubs, professional organizations, equestrian clubs, student activities council.

Athletics. NCAA. Intercollegiate: Baseball M, basketball, cross-country, equestrian, football (tackle) M, golf, lacrosse, soccer, softball W, swimming, tennis, track and field, volleyball W, wrestling M. **Intramural:** Basketball, football (tackle), soccer, softball, volleyball. **Team name:** Storm.

Student services. Adult student services, career counseling, student employment services, financial aid counseling, placement for graduates, veterans' counselor. **Physically disabled:** Services for visually, hearing impaired.

Contact. E-mail: admissions@lec.edu
Phone: (440) 375-7050 Toll-free number: (800) 916-0904
Fax: (440) 375-7005
Christopher Harris, Dean of Admission and Financial Aid, Lake Erie College, 391 West Washington Street, Painesville, OH 44077-3389

Laura and Alvin Siegal College of Judaic Studies
Cleveland, Ohio
www.siegalcollege.edu
CB code: 1190

- Private 4-year liberal arts and teachers college affiliated with Jewish faith
- Commuter campus in large town

General. Founded in 1963. Regionally accredited. **Location:** 10 miles from Cleveland. **Calendar:** Semester.

Annual costs/financial aid. Tuition/fees (2011-2012): $17,160. Books/supplies: $500. Need-based financial aid available to full-time and part-time students.

Contact. Phone: (216) 464-4050
Director of Student Services, 26500 Shaker Boulevard, Cleveland, OH 44122

Lourdes University
Sylvania, Ohio
www.lourdes.edu
CB member
CB code: 1427

- Private 4-year university and liberal arts college affiliated with Roman Catholic Church
- Commuter campus in large town
- 1,995 degree-seeking undergraduates: 43% part-time, 78% women, 16% African American, 6% Hispanic American
- 311 degree-seeking graduate students
- 74% of applicants admitted
- 35% graduate within 6 years

General. Founded in 1958. Regionally accredited. **Degrees:** 287 bachelor's, 32 associate awarded; master's offered. **ROTC:** Army, Air Force. **Location:** 10 miles from Toledo. **Calendar:** Semester, limited summer session. **Full-time faculty:** 94 total; 55% have terminal degrees, 7% minority, 70% women. **Part-time faculty:** 163 total; 19% have terminal degrees, 10% minority, 68% women. **Class size:** 61% < 20, 39% 20-39. **Special facilities:** Planetarium, life lab.

Freshman class profile. 894 applied, 664 admitted, 214 enrolled.

Mid 50% test scores			
SAT critical reading:	390-500	GPA 2.0-2.99:	46%
SAT math:	310-520	Rank in top quarter:	21%
ACT composite:	17-22	Rank in top tenth:	7%
GPA 3.75 or higher:	10%	End year in good standing:	66%
GPA 3.50-3.74:	12%	Return as sophomores:	55%
GPA 3.0-3.49:	27%	Out-of-state:	12%
		Live on campus:	40%

Basis for selection. Academic GPA very important, interview considered. Conditional admission may be granted to high school graduates with no prior college experience who have below a 2.0 GPA. **Home schooled:** Transcript of courses and grades required.

High school preparation. College-preparatory program recommended. 17 units recommended. Recommended units include English 4, mathematics 3, social studies 3, science 3, foreign language 2 and visual/performing arts 1. 1 unit Physical Education/Health recommended.

2011-2012 Annual costs. Tuition/fees: $16,470. Room/board: $7,800. Books/supplies: $1,008. Personal expenses: $3,700.

2011-2012 Financial aid. Need-based: 190 full-time freshmen applied for aid; 166 were judged to have need; 166 of these received aid. Average scholarship/grant was $5,660; average loan $3,181. 39% of total undergraduate aid awarded as scholarships/grants, 61% as loans/jobs. **Non-need-based:** Awarded to 538 full-time undergraduates, including 163 freshmen. Scholarships awarded for academics, art, athletics, minority status, religious affiliation, ROTC, state residency.

Application procedures. Admission: No deadline. $25 fee, may be waived for applicants with need, free for online applicants. Admission notification on a rolling basis. **Financial aid:** Priority date 3/1; no closing date. FAFSA required. Applicants notified on a rolling basis starting 3/1; must reply within 4 week(s) of notification.

Academics. Special study options: Distance learning, double major, dual enrollment of high school students, independent study, internships, liberal arts/career combination, student-designed major, study abroad, teacher certification program. **Credit/placement by examination:** AP, CLEP, SAT, ACT, institutional tests. 15 credit hours maximum toward associate degree, 30 toward bachelor's. **Support services:** Learning center, reduced course load, remedial instruction, study skills assistance, tutoring, writing center.

Majors. Biology: General. **Business:** Accounting/finance, business admin, human resources, management science, marketing. **Conservation:** Environmental science. **Education:** Early childhood, middle, secondary. **English:** English lit. **Health services:** Health care admin, nursing (RN). **History:** General. **Human services:** Social work. **Philosophy/religion:** Religion. **Protective services:** Criminal justice. **Psychology:** General. **Social sciences:** Sociology. **Visual/performing arts:** Art, art history/conservation.

Most popular majors. Business/marketing 16%, education 9%, health sciences 40%, interdisciplinary studies 9%, public administration/social services 8%.

Computing on campus. 181 workstations in dormitories, library, computer center, student center. Dormitories wired for high-speed internet access. Commuter students can connect to campus network. Online course registration, online library, helpline, wireless network available.

Student life. Freshman orientation: Mandatory. Preregistration for classes offered. **Housing:** Guaranteed on-campus for freshmen. Coed dorms, apartments available. $100 fully refundable deposit. **Activities:** Pep band, campus ministries, choral groups, drama, literary magazine, student government, black student union, Latino student union, LINK, Arab American student association.

Athletics. NAIA. **Intercollegiate:** Baseball M, basketball, golf, softball W, volleyball W. **Intramural:** Football (non-tackle), volleyball. **Team name:** Gray Wolves.

Student services. Adult student services, alcohol/substance abuse counseling, chaplain/spiritual director, career counseling, services for economically disadvantaged, financial aid counseling, personal counseling, veterans' counselor. **Physically disabled:** Services for visually, speech, hearing impaired.

Contact. E-mail: AdmissionsLCAdmits@lourdes.edu
Phone: (419) 885-5291 ext. 3680
Toll-free number: (800) 878-3210 ext. 3680 Fax: (419) 824-3916
Amy Mergen, Dean of Enrollment, Lourdes University, 6832 Convent Boulevard, Sylvania, OH 43560-2898

Malone University
Canton, Ohio
www.malone.edu CB code: 1439

- Private 4-year university affiliated with Evangelical Friends Church-Eastern Region
- Residential campus in small city
- 1,882 degree-seeking undergraduates: 9% part-time, 57% women, 8% African American, 1% Asian American, 2% Hispanic American, 1% international
- 461 degree-seeking graduate students
- 75% of applicants admitted
- SAT or ACT (ACT writing optional) required
- 58% graduate within 6 years; 19% enter graduate study

General. Founded in 1892. Regionally accredited. Interdenominational Christian environment. **Degrees:** 468 bachelor's awarded; master's offered. **ROTC:** Army, Air Force. **Location:** 55 miles from Cleveland. **Calendar:** Semester, limited summer session. **Full-time faculty:** 107 total; 70% have terminal degrees, 6% minority, 50% women. **Part-time faculty:** 128 total; 18% have terminal degrees, 2% minority, 57% women. **Class size:** 58% < 20, 37% 20-39, 5% 40-49, 1% 50-99. **Special facilities:** Child development center.

Freshman class profile. 1,600 applied, 1,201 admitted, 362 enrolled.

Mid 50% test scores			
SAT critical reading:	450-580	Rank in top quarter:	46%
SAT math:	450-560	Rank in top tenth:	20%
ACT composite:	20-26	End year in good standing:	88%
GPA 3.75 or higher:	27%	Return as sophomores:	71%
GPA 3.50-3.74:	16%	Out-of-state:	20%
GPA 3.0-3.49:	30%	Live on campus:	90%
GPA 2.0-2.99:	25%	International:	1%

Basis for selection. Rigor of high school record, GPA, and test scores most important. Interview considered and encouraged. Audition required for entrance into music programs; portfolio required during first semester for art programs. **Home schooled:** Transcript of courses and grades required. **Learning Disabled:** Students disclosing learning disabilities must interview with Director of Student Accessibility Services.

High school preparation. College-preparatory program required. 18 units required. Required units include English 4, mathematics 3, social studies 2, history 1, science 3 (laboratory 1), foreign language 2, visual/performing arts 1 and academic electives 2.

2011-2012 Annual costs. Tuition/fees: $23,420. Room/board: $8,090. Books/supplies: $930. Personal expenses: $1,330.

2011-2012 Financial aid. Need-based: 350 full-time freshmen applied for aid; 319 were judged to have need; 319 of these received aid. Average need met was 80%. Average scholarship/grant was $18,148; average loan $4,238. 59% of total undergraduate aid awarded as scholarships/grants, 41% as loans/jobs. **Non-need-based:** Awarded to 1,438 full-time undergraduates, including 342 freshmen. Scholarships awarded for academics, alumni affiliation, athletics, leadership, music/drama, religious affiliation. **Additional information:** Prepayment discounts and employer deferred payments available for students in adult degree-completion programs. Employer deferred payment plan is available for traditional undergraduate students.

Application procedures. Admission: No deadline. $20 fee, may be waived for applicants with need, free for online applicants. Admission notification on a rolling basis beginning on or about 9/1. **Financial aid:** Priority date 3/1, closing date 7/31. FAFSA required. Applicants notified on a rolling basis starting 3/1; must reply within 2 week(s) of notification.

Academics. 50-56 hours of general education courses organized under the 3 areas of Foundations of Faith and Learning, Foundational Skills, and Engaging God's World. **Special study options:** Accelerated study, cross-registration, distance learning, double major, dual enrollment of high school students, exchange student, honors, independent study, internships, student-designed major, study abroad, teacher certification program, Washington semester, weekend college. 2 degree-completion programs for adult students in management and nursing, American Studies Program (Washington, D.C.), Australia Studies Centre (Sydney), China Studies Program (Shanghai), Latin American Studies Program (San Jose, Costa Rica), Middle East Studies

Program (Cairo, Egypt), Ugandan Studies Program, Los Angeles Film Studies Center, Contemporary Music Center (Martha's Vineyard), Washington Journalism Center, Daystar University in Kenya. **Credit/placement by examination:** AP, CLEP, SAT, ACT, institutional tests. 62 credit hours maximum toward bachelor's degree. External credit by exam limit is 20, excluding AP credit for which an additional 30 credits are available. Other credits available by in-house exams. **Support services:** Reduced course load, remedial instruction, study skills assistance, tutoring, writing center.

Majors. **Biology:** General, zoology. **Business:** Accounting, business admin, marketing, nonprofit/public, project management. **Communications:** Communications/speech/rhetoric, journalism, public relations, radio/TV. **Communications technology:** Recording arts. **Computer sciences:** Computer science. **Education:** Art, early childhood, English, health, learning disabled, middle, music, physical, science, social studies, Spanish. **English:** English lit. **Foreign languages:** Spanish. **Health services:** Clinical lab science, health care admin, nursing (RN), public health ed. **History:** General. **Human services:** Social work. **Liberal arts:** Arts/sciences. **Math:** General. **Parks/recreation:** Exercise sciences, sports admin. **Philosophy/religion:** Philosophy. **Physical sciences:** Chemistry. **Psychology:** General. **Social sciences:** Political science. **Theology:** Bible, pastoral counseling, sacred music, theology, youth ministry. **Visual/performing arts:** Dramatic, music, studio arts.

Most popular majors. Business/marketing 37%, education 13%, health sciences 19%.

Computing on campus. 232 workstations in dormitories, library, computer center. Dormitories wired for high-speed internet access and linked to campus network. Commuter students can connect to campus network. Online course registration, online library, helpline, student web hosting, wireless network available.

Student life. Freshman orientation: Mandatory. Preregistration for classes offered. Held 5 days prior to start of semester; some on-campus events, community service, relationship-building activities. **Policies:** Christian institution with conservative campus lifestyle. Full-time students required to live on campus unless 22 or older, holding senior status, married or commuting from home; exceptions considered. Religious observance required. **Housing:** Single-sex dorms, special housing for disabled, wellness housing available. $100 nonrefundable deposit, deadline 8/15. **Activities:** Bands, campus ministries, choral groups, drama, film society, international student organizations, literary magazine, music ensembles, musical theater, radio station, student government, student newspaper, TV station, Helping Hands service organization, multicultural student union, Nurses Christian Fellowship, Rotaract Club, spiritual life committee, One Voice gospel choir, Worldview Forum Council, be:Justice, Council for Exceptional Children.

Athletics. NCCAA. **Intercollegiate:** Baseball M, basketball, cheerleading, cross-country, diving, football (tackle) M, golf, soccer, softball W, swimming, tennis, track and field, volleyball W. **Intramural:** Basketball, bowling, football (non-tackle), skiing, soccer, softball, table tennis, volleyball, weight lifting. **Team name:** Pioneers.

Student services. Adult student services, chaplain/spiritual director, career counseling, student employment services, financial aid counseling, health services, minority student services, personal counseling, placement for graduates. **Physically disabled:** Services for visually, speech, hearing impaired.

Contact. E-mail: admissions@malone.edu
Phone: (330) 471-8100 ext. 8145 Toll-free number: (800) 521-1146
Fax: (330) 471-8149
David Kleffman, Director of Admissions, Malone University, 2600 Cleveland Avenue NW, Canton, OH 44709-3897

Marietta College

Marietta, Ohio   **CB member**
www.marietta.edu   **CB code: 1444**

- Private 4-year liberal arts college
- Residential campus in large town
- 1,448 degree-seeking undergraduates: 3% part-time, 46% women, 5% African American, 1% Asian American, 2% Hispanic American, 12% international
- 135 degree-seeking graduate students
- 70% of applicants admitted
- SAT or ACT (ACT writing optional) required
- 51% graduate within 6 years; 20% enter graduate study

General. Founded in 1835. Regionally accredited. **Degrees:** 325 bachelor's, 2 associate awarded; master's offered. **Location:** 120 miles from Columbus, 110 miles from Pittsburgh. **Calendar:** Semester, limited summer session.

Full-time faculty: 109 total; 89% have terminal degrees, 6% minority, 46% women. **Part-time faculty:** 38 total; 71% have terminal degrees, 5% minority, 53% women. **Class size:** 77% < 20, 23% 20-39, less than 1% 40-49. **Special facilities:** Observatory, center for leadership development, greenhouse, cadaver lab, extensive fossil collection, many historically important documents from the beginning of the old Northwest Territory, planetarium.

Freshman class profile. 4,099 applied, 2,871 admitted, 368 enrolled.

Mid 50% test scores			
SAT critical reading:	480-620	Rank in top quarter:	56%
SAT math:	500-630	Rank in top tenth:	30%
SAT writing:	470-600	End year in good standing:	90%
ACT composite:	21-27	Return as sophomores:	78%
GPA 3.75 or higher:	33%	Out-of-state:	48%
GPA 3.50-3.74:	18%	Live on campus:	95%
GPA 3.0-3.49:	29%	International:	5%
GPA 2.0-2.99:	20%	Fraternities:	6%
		Sororities:	11%

Basis for selection. High school curriculum, GPA, test scores most important. Recommendations and essay important. Interview recommended for all. Portfolio recommended for arts programs. Auditions required for some music programs. **Home schooled:** Statement describing home school structure and mission, transcript of courses and grades, interview required. Chronicle of study required.

High school preparation. College-preparatory program recommended. 16 units required. Required units include English 4, mathematics 3, social studies 2, history 2, science 3 (laboratory 2), foreign language 2 and academic electives 1.

2011-2012 Annual costs. Tuition/fees: $29,690. Room/board: $9,090. Books/supplies: $1,104. Personal expenses: $688.

2011-2012 Financial aid. Need-based: 361 full-time freshmen applied for aid; 297 were judged to have need; 297 of these received aid. Average need met was 87%. Average scholarship/grant was $15,716; average loan $3,440. 74% of total undergraduate aid awarded as scholarships/grants, 26% as loans/jobs. **Non-need-based:** Awarded to 901 full-time undergraduates, including 339 freshmen. Scholarships awarded for academics, alumni affiliation, art, leadership, minority status, music/drama, state residency. **Additional information:** Auditions/portfolios for art, creative writing, music and theater required for competitive fine art scholarships.

Application procedures. Admission: Priority date 3/1; deadline 5/1 (postmark date). $25 fee, may be waived for applicants with need, free for online applicants. Admission notification on a rolling basis beginning on or about 9/1. Must reply by May 1 or within 2 week(s) if notified thereafter. **Financial aid:** Priority date 3/1, closing date 4/15. FAFSA, institutional form required. Applicants notified on a rolling basis starting 3/15; must reply by 5/1 or within 2 week(s) of notification.

Academics. Early Alert Program whereby professors can contact the Academic Resource Center to assist those students demonstrating need for additional academic support. **Special study options:** Combined bachelor's/graduate degree, double major, dual enrollment of high school students, ESL, exchange student, honors, independent study, internships, liberal arts/career combination, student-designed major, study abroad, teacher certification program, Washington semester. Leadership program, investigative studies. **Credit/placement by examination:** AP, CLEP, IB, SAT, ACT, institutional tests. 36 credit hours maximum toward bachelor's degree. **Support services:** Learning center, reduced course load, remedial instruction, study skills assistance, tutoring, writing center.

Majors. **Area/ethnic studies:** Asian. **Biology:** General, biochemistry. **Business:** Accounting, communications, finance, human resources, international, management information systems, marketing. **Communications:** Advertising, broadcast journalism, communications/speech/rhetoric, journalism, organizational, public relations, radio/TV. **Computer sciences:** General, computer science, information systems. **Conservation:** Environmental science, environmental studies. **Education:** General, early childhood, elementary, middle, multi-level teacher, music, secondary. **Engineering:** Petroleum. **English:** English lit. **Foreign languages:** Spanish. **Health services:** Athletic training. **History:** General. **Math:** General. **Parks/recreation:** Sports admin. **Physical sciences:** Chemistry, geology, physics. **Psychology:** General. **Social sciences:** Economics, political science. **Visual/performing arts:** Commercial/advertising art, dramatic, music, studio arts.

Most popular majors. Biology 10%, business/marketing 19%, communications/journalism 10%, education 6%, engineering/engineering technologies 11%, psychology 7%, social sciences 6%.

Computing on campus. 400 workstations in library, computer center, student center. Dormitories wired for high-speed internet access and linked to campus network. Commuter students can connect to campus network. Online library, helpline, wireless network available.

Student life. Freshman orientation: Mandatory, $250 fee. Preregistration for classes offered. Four-and-one-half day program. Culminating event either white-water rafting trip or dinner theater production. **Policies:** Student code of conduct, judicial system, no alcohol policy for students under age of 21. **Housing:** Guaranteed on-campus for freshmen. Coed dorms, single-sex dorms, special housing for disabled, apartments, fraternity/sorority housing, wellness housing available. $200 fully refundable deposit, deadline 5/1. Special interest theme housing (honors, arts and humanities house) available. **Activities:** Bands, campus ministries, choral groups, dance, drama, international student organizations, literary magazine, music ensembles, Model UN, musical theater, radio station, student government, student newspaper, TV station, InterVarsity Christian Fellowship, Circle K, MC Democrats, MC Republicans, Rotoract, Feminist Rainbow Alliance, VOICE, American International Association, student global AIDS campaign.

Athletics. NCAA. **Intercollegiate:** Baseball M, basketball, cross-country, football (tackle) M, rowing (crew), soccer, softball W, tennis, track and field, volleyball W. **Intramural:** Badminton, basketball, bowling, football (nontackle), golf, handball, racquetball, soccer, softball, table tennis, tennis, volleyball. **Team name:** Pioneers.

Student services. Adult student services, alcohol/substance abuse counseling, career counseling, student employment services, financial aid counseling, health services, minority student services, personal counseling, placement for graduates. **Physically disabled:** Services for visually, speech, hearing impaired.

Contact. E-mail: admit@marietta.edu
Phone: (740) 376-4600 Toll-free number: (800) 331-7896
Fax: (740) 376-8888
Jason Turley, Director of Admission, Marietta College, 215 Fifth Street, Marietta, OH 45750-4005

Mercy College of Ohio
Toledo, Ohio
www.mercycollege.edu   CB code: 4685

- Private 4-year health science and nursing college affiliated with Roman Catholic Church
- Commuter campus in large city
- 1,206 degree-seeking undergraduates: 7% African American, 1% Asian American, 4% Hispanic American, 1% Native American
- 75% of applicants admitted

General. Degrees: 90 bachelor's, 176 associate awarded. **Calendar:** Semester, limited summer session. **Full-time faculty:** 65 total; 29% have terminal degrees, 6% minority, 86% women. **Part-time faculty:** 94 total; 6% have terminal degrees, 6% minority, 81% women. **Class size:** 62% < 20, 27% 20-39, 9% 40-49, 2% 50-99.

Freshman class profile. 87 applied, 65 admitted, 39 enrolled.

GPA 3.75 or higher:	10%	Return as sophomores:	77%
GPA 3.50-3.74:	25%	Out-of-state:	9%
GPA 3.0-3.49:	55%	Live on campus:	3%
GPA 2.0-2.99:	10%		

Basis for selection. Students reviewed by admission, progression and graduation committee. 2.3 GPA required. Admission to programs of study may have higher GPA and specific course grade requirements. ACT, SAT and/or TEAS test required for some programs of study.

High school preparation. College-preparatory program recommended. 11 units required; 15 recommended. Required and recommended units include English 3-4, mathematics 2-3, social studies 2, science 2-3 (laboratory 1), foreign language 1 and computer science 1.

2011-2012 Annual costs. Tuition/fees: $10,440. Books/supplies: $2,400. Personal expenses: $3,368.

2010-2011 Financial aid. Need-based: 45 full-time freshmen applied for aid; 38 were judged to have need; 38 of these received aid. Average need met was 35%. Average scholarship/grant was $4,585; average loan $3,155. 44% of total undergraduate aid awarded as scholarships/grants, 56% as loans/jobs. **Non-need-based:** Awarded to 92 full-time undergraduates, including 23 freshmen. Scholarships awarded for academics, alumni affiliation, leadership, religious affiliation, state residency.

Application procedures. Admission: Priority date 1/15; deadline 8/1. $25 fee, may be waived for applicants with need. Admission notification on a rolling basis. Must reply by May 1 or within 2 week(s) if notified thereafter. **Financial aid:** Priority date 3/1; no closing date. FAFSA required. Applicants notified on a rolling basis starting 3/1; must reply within 2 week(s) of notification.

Academics. Special study options: Accelerated study, combined bachelor's/graduate degree, distance learning, double major, independent study, internships. **Credit/placement by examination:** AP, CLEP, institutional tests. **Support services:** Learning center, reduced course load, remedial instruction, study skills assistance, tutoring, writing center.

Majors. Health services: Health care admin, nursing (RN).

Computing on campus. 24 workstations in library, computer center, student center. Online course registration, online library, wireless network available.

Student life. Freshman orientation: Mandatory. Preregistration for classes offered. **Housing:** Apartments available. $100 fully refundable deposit. **Activities:** Campus ministries, literary magazine, student government, student newspaper, Student Senate, Phi Theta Kappa, National Student Nurses Association, Sigma Theta Tau, College Ambassadors, American Society of Radiologic Technologists.

Student services. Adult student services, alcohol/substance abuse counseling, chaplain/spiritual director, career counseling, services for economically disadvantaged, student employment services, financial aid counseling, personal counseling. **Physically disabled:** Services for visually, speech, hearing impaired.

Contact. E-mail: admissions@mercycollege.edu
Phone: (419) 251-1313 Toll-free number: (888) 806-3729
Fax: (419) 251-1462
Shelly McCoy Grissom, Chief Admissions Officer, Mercy College of Ohio, 2221 Madison Avenue, Toledo, OH 43604

Miami University: Oxford
Oxford, Ohio   CB member
www.muohio.edu   CB code: 1463

- Public 4-year university
- Residential campus in large town
- 14,831 degree-seeking undergraduates: 2% part-time, 52% women, 5% African American, 2% Asian American, 3% Hispanic American, 5% international
- 1,831 degree-seeking graduate students
- 74% of applicants admitted
- SAT or ACT (ACT writing optional), application essay required
- 81% graduate within 6 years

General. Founded in 1809. Regionally accredited. Bachelor degree programs, associate degree programs and certificates offered at regional campuses in Hamilton and Middletown, with degrees conferred by main (Oxford) campus. **Degrees:** 4,105 bachelor's, 351 associate awarded; master's, doctoral offered. **ROTC:** Army, Naval, Air Force. **Location:** 35 miles from Cincinnati, 46 miles from Dayton. **Calendar:** Semester, extensive summer session. **Full-time faculty:** 851 total; 91% have terminal degrees, 17% minority, 43% women. **Part-time faculty:** 283 total; 31% have terminal degrees, 7% minority, 47% women. **Class size:** 30% < 20, 50% 20-39, 8% 40-49, 8% 50-99, 4% >100. **Special facilities:** Zoology museum.

Freshman class profile. 18,482 applied, 13,702 admitted, 3,581 enrolled.

Mid 50% test scores			
		GPA 2.0-2.99:	6%
SAT critical reading:	530-620	Rank in top quarter:	68%
SAT math:	560-660	Rank in top tenth:	32%
ACT composite:	24-29	Return as sophomores:	89%
GPA 3.75 or higher:	41%	Out-of-state:	35%
GPA 3.50-3.74:	22%	Live on campus:	98%
GPA 3.0-3.49:	31%	International:	4%

Basis for selection. Admission based upon academic performance, test scores, secondary school experience, community activities, and recommendations from the high school. Diversity of student body, applicant's special abilities, talents and achievements also considered. Audition required for music, theater programs; portfolio required for art, architecture programs. **Home schooled:** Submit a list of educational resources and a curriculum description in addition to transcript.

High school preparation. College-preparatory program recommended. 16 units recommended. Recommended units include English 4, mathematics 3, social studies 2, history 1, science 3, foreign language 2 and visual/performing arts 1.

2011-2012 Annual costs. Tuition/fees: $13,213; $28,385 out-of-state. Room/board: $10,640.

2010-2011 Financial aid. Need-based: 2,703 full-time freshmen applied for aid; 1,791 were judged to have need; 1,774 of these received aid. Average need met was 58%. Average scholarship/grant was $6,272; average loan $4,276. 50% of total undergraduate aid awarded as scholarships/grants, 50% as loans/jobs. **Non-need-based:** Awarded to 6,321 full-time undergraduates, including 2,417 freshmen. Scholarships awarded for academics, art, athletics, leadership, minority status, music/drama, ROTC, state residency. **Additional information:** The Miami Access Initiative guarantees eligible students with scholarships and/or grants that meet or exceed the cost of tuition and academic fees. One of the eligibility requirements includes a total family income equal to or less than $35,000.

Application procedures. Admission: Priority date 12/1; deadline 2/1 (postmark date). $50 fee, may be waived for applicants with need. Admission notification by 3/15. Must reply by 5/1. **Financial aid:** Priority date 2/15; no closing date. FAFSA required. Applicants notified on a rolling basis starting 3/20; must reply by 5/1 or within 3 week(s) of notification.

Academics. Special study options: Combined bachelor's/graduate degree, cooperative education, cross-registration, distance learning, double major, ESL, exchange student, honors, independent study, internships, liberal arts/career combination, semester at sea, student-designed major, study abroad, teacher certification program, Washington semester. Undergraduate associates, undergraduate research program, science and engineering research semester, 3-2 engineering with Case Western Reserve University and Columbia University, 3-2 forestry/environmental studies with Duke University, 3-1 and 4-1 in Clinical Laboratory Science, 3-1 Arts/Professional A.B./Professional degree. **Credit/placement by examination:** AP, CLEP, IB, institutional tests. 32 credit hours maximum toward associate degree, 32 toward bachelor's. **Support services:** Learning center, study skills assistance, tutoring, writing center.

Majors. Architecture: Architecture, interior, urban/community planning. **Area/ethnic studies:** African-American, American, East Asian, Italian, Latin American, women's. **Biology:** Biochemistry, biophysics, botany, microbiology, zoology. **Business:** Accounting, business admin, finance, management information systems, management science, managerial economics, marketing, operations. **Communications:** Digital media, journalism, media studies, public relations. **Computer sciences:** General, information technology. **Conservation:** Environmental science. **Education:** Art, biology, chemistry, early childhood, English, family/consumer sciences, foreign languages, French, German, Latin, mathematics, middle, music, physics, science, social studies, Spanish, special ed. **Engineering:** General, applied physics, biomedical, chemical, computer, electrical, manufacturing, mechanical, software. **English:** Creative writing, English lit, rhetoric/composition, technical writing. **Foreign languages:** Classics, French, German, linguistics, Spanish. **Health services:** Athletic training, audiology/speech pathology, clinical lab science, dietetics, nursing (RN). **History:** General. **Human services:** General, social work. **Liberal arts:** Arts/sciences. **Math:** General, statistics. **Parks/recreation:** Exercise sciences, health/fitness, sports admin. **Philosophy/religion:** Philosophy, religion. **Physical sciences:** Chemistry, geology, physics. **Psychology:** General. **Social sciences:** Anthropology, economics, geography, international relations, political science, sociology. **Visual/performing arts:** Art, art history/conservation, commercial/advertising art, dramatic, music, music performance. **Work/family studies:** Family studies.

Most popular majors. Biology 7%, business/marketing 24%, education 9%, psychology 6%, social sciences 10%.

Computing on campus. 1,200 workstations in dormitories, library, computer center, student center. Dormitories wired for high-speed internet access and linked to campus network. Commuter students can connect to campus network. Online course registration, online library, helpline, repair service, student web hosting, wireless network available.

Student life. Freshman orientation: Mandatory, $95 fee. Preregistration for classes offered. One-and-a-half day program held throughout June. **Policies:** Freshmen not permitted cars on campus. **Housing:** Guaranteed on-campus for freshmen. Coed dorms, single-sex dorms, special housing for disabled, apartments, cooperative housing, fraternity/sorority housing, wellness housing available. $425 nonrefundable deposit, deadline 5/1. Special arrangements include sorority suites in residence halls. **Activities:** Bands, campus ministries, choral groups, dance, drama, film society, international student organizations, literary magazine, music ensembles, Model UN, musical theater, opera, radio station, student government, student newspaper, symphony orchestra, TV station, Campus Crusade for Christ, Hillel: Association of Jewish Students, College Democrats/College Republicans, Asian-American association, Alpha Phi Omega, Black Student Action Association, international student organization, Oxfam Miami University, Green Oxford.

Athletics. NCAA. **Intercollegiate:** Baseball M, basketball, cross-country, diving, field hockey W, football (tackle) M, golf M, ice hockey M, soccer W, softball W, swimming, tennis W, track and field, volleyball W. **Intramural:** Baseball, basketball, football (non-tackle), ice hockey, racquetball, soccer, softball, tennis, volleyball. **Team name:** Red Hawks.

Student services. Alcohol/substance abuse counseling, career counseling, services for economically disadvantaged, student employment services, financial aid counseling, health services, legal services, minority student services, on-campus daycare, personal counseling, placement for graduates, veterans' counselor, women's services. **Physically disabled:** Services for visually, speech, hearing impaired.

Contact. E-mail: admission@muohio.edu
Phone: (513) 529-2531 Fax: (513) 529-1550
Ann Larson, Senior Associate Director/Director of Admission, Miami University: Oxford, 301 South Campus Avenue, Oxford, OH 45056

Mount Carmel College of Nursing

Columbus, Ohio   **CB member**
www.mccn.edu   **CB code: 1502**

- Private 4-year nursing college affiliated with Roman Catholic Church
- Very large city
- 808 degree-seeking undergraduates: 19% part-time, 89% women, 5% African American, 1% Asian American, 1% Hispanic American
- 102 degree-seeking graduate students
- 75% of applicants admitted

General. Regionally accredited. **Degrees:** 245 bachelor's awarded; master's offered. **ROTC:** Army, Air Force. **Location:** Downtown. **Calendar:** Semester, limited summer session. **Full-time faculty:** 44 total; 16% have terminal degrees, 14% minority, 93% women. **Part-time faculty:** 45 total; 11% have terminal degrees, 7% minority, 87% women. **Class size:** 26% < 20, 34% 20-39, 25% 40-49, 13% 50-99, 1% >100.

Freshman class profile. 171 applied, 129 admitted, 91 enrolled.

Mid 50% test scores			
ACT composite:	20-24	GPA 2.0-2.99:	3%
GPA 3.75 or higher:	28%	Return as sophomores:	87%
GPA 3.50-3.74:	32%	Out-of-state:	1%
GPA 3.0-3.49:	37%	Live on campus:	35%

Basis for selection. High school record and standardized test score most important. **Home schooled:** Transcript of courses and grades required.

High school preparation. College-preparatory program required. 16 units required. Required units include English 4, mathematics 3, social studies 3, science 3 (laboratory 3) and foreign language 2.

2011-2012 Annual costs. Tuition/fees: $9,390. Books/supplies: $750. Personal expenses: $1,614.

2010-2011 Financial aid. Need-based: 74 full-time freshmen applied for aid; 74 were judged to have need; 74 of these received aid. Average need met was 52%. Average scholarship/grant was $1,200; average loan $3,500. 27% of total undergraduate aid awarded as scholarships/grants, 73% as loans/jobs. **Non-need-based:** Awarded to 115 full-time undergraduates, including 65 freshmen. Scholarships awarded for academics, leadership, minority status.

Application procedures. Admission: Closing date 4/1. $30 fee. Must reply by 5/1. **Financial aid:** Priority date 3/1; no closing date. FAFSA, institutional form required. Applicants notified on a rolling basis starting 9/1; must reply within 2 week(s) of notification.

Academics. Special study options: Accelerated study, cross-registration, honors. **Credit/placement by examination:** AP, CLEP.

Majors. Health services: Nursing (RN).

Student life. Housing: Coed dorms, apartments available. $200 nonrefundable deposit. **Activities:** Campus ministries, student government.

Contact. E-mail: mccnadmissions@mchs.com
Phone: (614) 234-1085 Toll-free number: (800) 556-6942
Fax: (614) 234-2875
Kim Campbell, Director of Admissions, Mount Carmel College of Nursing, 127 South Davis Avenue, Columbus, OH 43222-1589

Mount Vernon Nazarene University

Mount Vernon, Ohio   **CB member**
www.mvnu.edu   **CB code: 1531**

- Private 4-year university affiliated with Church of the Nazarene
- Residential campus in large town

- 1,866 degree-seeking undergraduates: 9% part-time, 64% women
- 550 degree-seeking graduate students
- 72% of applicants admitted
- SAT or ACT (ACT writing optional), application essay required
- 57% graduate within 6 years; 13% enter graduate study

General. Founded in 1964. Regionally accredited. **Degrees:** 496 bachelor's, 10 associate awarded; master's offered. **Location:** 45 miles from Columbus. **Calendar:** 4-1-4, limited summer session. **Full-time faculty:** 104 total; 58% have terminal degrees, 5% minority, 40% women. **Part-time faculty:** 137 total; 23% have terminal degrees, 4% minority, 47% women. **Class size:** 75% < 20, 20% 20-39, 3% 40-49, 3% 50-99. **Special facilities:** 70-acre biological research area and nature center, weather station.

Freshman class profile. 1,034 applied, 748 admitted, 354 enrolled.

Mid 50% test scores			
SAT critical reading:	480-610	GPA 2.0-2.99:	19%
SAT math:	450-600	Rank in top quarter:	49%
ACT composite:	20-26	Rank in top tenth:	23%
GPA 3.75 or higher:	31%	End year in good standing:	84%
GPA 3.50-3.74:	18%	Return as sophomores:	71%
GPA 3.0-3.49:	31%	Out-of-state:	12%
		Live on campus:	94%

Basis for selection. High school record, ACT or SAT scores, recommendations important. Interview recommended. **Home schooled:** Transcript of courses and grades, letter of recommendation (nonparent) required. Family members cannot complete either academic or character references. Employer can complete academic reference. Students who participate in accredited program must provide transcript from accrediting agency; otherwise, must provide a list of classes completed.

High school preparation. College-preparatory program recommended. 21 units recommended. Required and recommended units include English 4, mathematics 4, social studies 3, science 3 (laboratory 3), foreign language 2-3, visual/performing arts 1 and academic electives 3. 1 health and physical education.

2011-2012 Annual costs. Tuition/fees: $23,069. Room/board: $6,430. Books/supplies: $1,300. Personal expenses: $2,080.

2011-2012 Financial aid. Need-based: 352 full-time freshmen applied for aid; 320 were judged to have need; 320 of these received aid. Average need met was 85%. Average scholarship/grant was $17,365; average loan $3,316. 63% of total undergraduate aid awarded as scholarships/grants, 37% as loans/jobs. **Non-need-based:** Awarded to 961 full-time undergraduates, including 313 freshmen. Scholarships awarded for academics, athletics, minority status, music/drama, religious affiliation, state residency.

Application procedures. Admission: Priority date 3/15; deadline 7/15 (receipt date). $25 fee, may be waived for applicants with need. Admission notification on a rolling basis beginning on or about 9/1. **Financial aid:** Priority date 3/15; no closing date. FAFSA, institutional form required. Applicants notified on a rolling basis starting 3/15; must reply within 2 week(s) of notification.

Academics. Off-campus January term offers unique educational opportunities, including urban and international studies. **Special study options:** Combined bachelor's/graduate degree, cooperative education, cross-registration, distance learning, double major, dual enrollment of high school students, honors, independent study, internships, liberal arts/career combination, study abroad, teacher certification program, Washington semester. Cooperative pre-engineering program with Olivet Nazarene University, cooperative pre-occupational therapy/physical therapy/physician's assistant programs with Chatham College, and articulation agreements with Zane State College, Central Ohio Technical College, and North Central State College. Several opportunities for students to participate in service learning or mission trips. During the academic year, students may participate in one of the following trips: Germany, Hungary, Venezuela, Costa Rica, Nicaragua, Belize, Benin, Romania, or several out-of-state USA trips. **Credit/placement by examination:** AP, CLEP, IB, SAT, ACT, institutional tests. 30 credit hours maximum toward bachelor's degree. **Support services:** Reduced course load, study skills assistance.

Majors. Biology: General. **Business:** Accounting, administrative services, business admin, finance, international, management information systems, marketing, organizational behavior. **Communications:** Communications/speech/rhetoric, journalism, public relations. **Computer sciences:** General, computer science, networking. **Education:** General, art, biology, business, chemistry, early childhood, elementary, English, family/consumer sciences, health, history, mathematics, middle, music, physical, physics, science, secondary, social studies, Spanish, special ed. **English:** English lit. **Foreign languages:** Spanish. **Health services:** Clinical lab science, nursing (RN). **History:** General. **Human services:** Social work. **Math:** General. **Parks/recreation:** Exercise sciences, health/fitness, sports admin. **Philosophy/religion:** Philosophy, religion. **Physical sciences:** General, chemistry, physics.

Protective services: Criminal justice, law enforcement admin. **Psychology:** General. **Social sciences:** Sociology. **Theology:** Bible, missionary, pastoral counseling, religious ed, sacred music, theology, youth ministry. **Visual/performing arts:** Art, dramatic, graphic design, music, music performance. **Work/family studies:** General.

Most popular majors. Business/marketing 47%, education 9%, health sciences 7%, public administration/social services 7%.

Computing on campus. 232 workstations in dormitories, library, computer center, student center. Dormitories wired for high-speed internet access and linked to campus network. Commuter students can connect to campus network. Online course registration, online library, helpline, wireless network available.

Student life. Freshman orientation: Mandatory. Preregistration for classes offered. Sessions held in June, July, and August. **Policies:** Students expected to comply with university's published lifestyle guidelines. Religious observance required. **Housing:** Guaranteed on-campus for freshmen. Single-sex dorms, special housing for disabled, apartments, wellness housing available. $150 fully refundable deposit, deadline 5/1. **Activities:** Bands, campus ministries, choral groups, drama, international student organizations, literary magazine, music ensembles, musical theater, opera, radio station, student government, student newspaper, Students in Free Enterprise, Fellowship of Christian Athletes, Young Republicans club, Young Democratic club, men's association, women's association, computing machinery association, American Sign Language club, Students with Concern, Mandate.

Athletics. NAIA, NCCAA. **Intercollegiate:** Baseball M, basketball, cross-country, golf, soccer, softball W, volleyball W. **Intramural:** Basketball, bowling, football (non-tackle), soccer, softball, volleyball. **Team name:** Cougars.

Student services. Adult student services, alcohol/substance abuse counseling, chaplain/spiritual director, career counseling, student employment services, financial aid counseling, health services, minority student services, personal counseling, placement for graduates. **Physically disabled:** Services for visually, speech, hearing impaired.

Contact. E-mail: admissions@mvnu.edu
Phone: (740) 392-6868 ext. 4510 Toll-free number: (866) 462-6868
Fax: (740) 393-0511
James Smith, Director of Admissions, Mount Vernon Nazarene University, 800 Martinsburg Road, Mount Vernon, OH 43050

Muskingum University
New Concord, Ohio
www.muskingum.edu
CB member
CB code: 1496

- Private 4-year university and liberal arts college affiliated with Presbyterian Church (USA)
- Residential campus in small town
- 1,718 degree-seeking undergraduates: 9% part-time, 53% women, 6% African American, 1% Asian American, 1% Hispanic American, 3% international
- 362 degree-seeking graduate students
- 77% of applicants admitted
- SAT or ACT (ACT writing optional) required

General. Founded in 1837. Regionally accredited. **Degrees:** 269 bachelor's awarded; master's offered. **Location:** 70 miles from Columbus, 125 miles from Pittsburgh. **Calendar:** Semester, extensive summer session. **Full-time faculty:** 101 total; 90% have terminal degrees, 13% minority, 45% women. **Part-time faculty:** 80 total; 5% have terminal degrees, 4% minority, 59% women. **Class size:** 67% < 20, 32% 20-39, 1% 40-49, less than 1% 50-99. **Special facilities:** Biology field station, conservation facility.

Freshman class profile. 2,101 applied, 1,618 admitted, 424 enrolled.

Mid 50% test scores			
SAT critical reading:	420-560	GPA 2.0-2.99:	34%
SAT math:	430-560	Rank in top quarter:	43%
SAT writing:	430-540	Rank in top tenth:	18%
ACT composite:	19-24	Out-of-state:	10%
GPA 3.75 or higher:	17%	Live on campus:	92%
GPA 3.50-3.74:	16%	International:	4%
GPA 3.0-3.49:	31%	Fraternities:	15%
		Sororities:	26%

Basis for selection. School achievement record most important. Strength of curriculum, standardized test scores, recommendations, extracurricular activities, interview considered. Special consideration to children of alumni. Essay and interview recommended for all; audition recommended for music

programs; portfolio recommended for art programs. **Home schooled:** Transcript of courses and grades, state high school equivalency certificate required. Portfolio of curriculum; statement of compliance with state truancy laws in cases where state certificate is not issued. **Learning Disabled:** PLUS Program available for students with disabilities that affect learning. Students must indicate interest in program when applying for admission, and must submit psychoeducational evaluations to complete application process. Preferred application filing date of March 1.

High school preparation. College-preparatory program required. 12 units required; 15 recommended. Required and recommended units include English 4, mathematics 2-3, social studies 2-3, science 2-3 (laboratory 2) and foreign language 2-3.

2012-2013 Annual costs. Tuition/fees (projected): $22,996. Room/board: $8,950. Books/supplies: $1,100. Personal expenses: $900.

Financial aid. Non-need-based: Scholarships awarded for academics, alumni affiliation, art, leadership, minority status, music/drama, religious affiliation, state residency. **Additional information:** Scholarship priority date February 1.

Application procedures. Admission: Closing date 8/1. No application fee. Admission notification on a rolling basis beginning on or about 10/1. Must reply by May 1 or within 2 week(s) if notified thereafter. **Financial aid:** Priority date 3/1, closing date 8/1. FAFSA required. Applicants notified on a rolling basis starting 3/1; must reply by 5/1 or within 2 week(s) of notification.

Academics. Special study options: Accelerated study, distance learning, double major, dual enrollment of high school students, ESL, exchange student, honors, independent study, internships, liberal arts/career combination, student-designed major, study abroad, teacher certification program, United Nations semester, Washington semester, weekend college. **Credit/placement by examination:** AP, CLEP, IB, SAT, ACT, institutional tests. **Support services:** Learning center, pre-admission summer program, reduced course load, study skills assistance, tutoring, writing center.

Majors. Biology: General, conservation, molecular, neuroscience. **Business:** General, accounting, international marketing, managerial economics. **Communications:** Communications/speech/rhetoric, digital media, journalism. **Computer sciences:** General, computer science, information systems. **Conservation:** Environmental science. **Education:** Early childhood, elementary, middle, secondary, special ed. **Engineering:** General, engineering science. **English:** English lit. **Foreign languages:** French, German, Spanish. **Health services:** Clinical lab technology, community health services, health care admin, nursing (RN), predental, premedicine, prepharmacy, preveterinary, speech pathology. **History:** General. **Liberal arts:** Humanities. **Math:** General. **Philosophy/religion:** Philosophy, religion. **Physical sciences:** Chemistry, geology, physics, planetary. **Protective services:** Police science. **Psychology:** General. **Social sciences:** Anthropology, economics, international relations, political science, sociology. **Theology:** Religious ed. **Visual/performing arts:** Art, dramatic, music.

Most popular majors. Biology 10%, business/marketing 23%, communications/journalism 6%, education 18%, psychology 6%, security/protective services 7%, social sciences 9%.

Computing on campus. 223 workstations in dormitories, library, computer center, student center. Dormitories wired for high-speed internet access and linked to campus network. Commuter students can connect to campus network. Online course registration, online library, helpline, repair service, student web hosting, wireless network available.

Student life. Freshman orientation: Available. Preregistration for classes offered. Six 1-day sessions held on weekdays in June. **Housing:** Guaranteed on-campus for freshmen. Coed dorms, single-sex dorms, apartments, fraternity/sorority housing, wellness housing available. $200 fully refundable deposit, deadline 5/1. **Activities:** Bands, campus ministries, choral groups, dance, drama, international student organizations, literary magazine, music ensembles, Model UN, musical theater, radio station, student government, student newspaper, symphony orchestra, TV station, Christian Fellowship, Fellowship of Christian Athletes, political awareness program, SADD, Habitat for Humanity, Young Democrats, Young Republicans, Animal Rights and Environmental Awareness.

Athletics. NCAA. **Intercollegiate:** Baseball M, basketball, cheerleading, cross-country, football (tackle) M, golf, soccer, softball W, tennis, track and field, volleyball W, wrestling M. **Intramural:** Basketball, bowling, cross-country, football (non-tackle), golf, lacrosse, racquetball, rugby, soccer, softball, table tennis M, tennis, track and field, volleyball, wrestling M. **Team name:** Muskies.

Student services. Alcohol/substance abuse counseling, chaplain/spiritual director, career counseling, student employment services, financial aid counseling, health services, minority student services, on-campus daycare, personal counseling, placement for graduates, veterans' counselor. **Physically disabled:** Services for visually, hearing impaired.

Contact. E-mail: adminfo@muskingum.edu
Phone: (740) 826-8137 Toll-free number: (800) 752-6082
Fax: (740) 826-8100
Beth DaLonzo, Senior Director of Admissions and Student Financial Services, Muskingum University, 163 Stormont Street, New Concord, OH 43762-1199

Notre Dame College
Cleveland, Ohio   **CB member**
www.notredamecollege.edu   **CB code: 1566**

- Private 4-year liberal arts college affiliated with Roman Catholic Church
- Residential campus in very large city
- 1,699 degree-seeking undergraduates: 22% part-time, 54% women, 21% African American, 1% Asian American, 2% Hispanic American, 2% international
- 285 degree-seeking graduate students
- 89% of applicants admitted
- SAT or ACT (ACT writing optional), application essay required
- 43% graduate within 6 years

General. Founded in 1922. Regionally accredited. **Degrees:** 162 bachelor's, 1 associate awarded; master's offered. **ROTC:** Army. **Location:** 10 miles from downtown Cleveland. **Calendar:** Semester, limited summer session. **Full-time faculty:** 61 total; 5% minority, 61% women. **Part-time faculty:** 242 total; 13% minority, 66% women. **Class size:** 55% < 20, 45% 20-39, less than 1% 40-49, less than 1% 50-99.

Freshman class profile. 2,322 applied, 2,064 admitted, 406 enrolled.

Mid 50% test scores			
SAT critical reading:	410-490	GPA 2.0-2.99:	46%
SAT math:	410-510	Rank in top quarter:	23%
ACT composite:	18-22	Rank in top tenth:	4%
GPA 3.75 or higher:	10%	Return as sophomores:	64%
GPA 3.50-3.74:	9%	Out-of-state:	9%
GPA 3.0-3.49:	31%	Live on campus:	84%
		International:	3%

Basis for selection. School achievement record and test scores most important. Applicants should be in top half of class and have 2.5 high school GPA for unconditional admission. Extracurricular activities also considered. Interview recommended.

High school preparation. College-preparatory program recommended. Recommended units include English 4, mathematics 3, social studies 2, history 1, science 3 (laboratory 3) and foreign language 3.

2011-2012 Annual costs. Tuition/fees: $24,652. Room/board: $8,054. Books/supplies: $2,150. Personal expenses: $910.

Financial aid. Non-need-based: Scholarships awarded for academics, state residency.

Application procedures. Admission: No deadline. No application fee. Admission notification on a rolling basis. **Financial aid:** Closing date 5/1. FAFSA required. Applicants notified on a rolling basis starting 1/1; must reply within 2 week(s) of notification.

Academics. Special study options: Cooperative education, cross-registration, distance learning, double major, dual enrollment of high school students, exchange student, honors, independent study, internships, liberal arts/career combination, student-designed major, study abroad, teacher certification program. **Credit/placement by examination:** AP, CLEP, SAT, ACT, institutional tests. **Support services:** Learning center, reduced course load, remedial instruction, study skills assistance, tutoring, writing center.

Honors college/program. Students are selected on the basis of ACT/SAT scores and high school GPA placing them in the top 5% of the entering freshman class.

Majors. Biology: General, biochemistry, environmental. **Business:** Accounting, business admin, human resources, international, management information systems, marketing. **Communications:** Communications/speech/rhetoric, digital media, public relations. **Communications technology:** Graphics. **Education:** Early childhood, elementary, secondary. **English:** English lit. **Health services:** Nursing (RN), prenursing. **History:** General. **Math:** General. **Physical sciences:** Chemistry. **Psychology:** General. **Social sciences:** Criminology, political science. **Theology:** Theology. **Visual/performing arts:** General, graphic design, studio arts.

Most popular majors. Business/marketing 36%, education 22%, health sciences 15%.

Computing on campus. 100 workstations in dormitories, library, computer center. Dormitories wired for high-speed internet access. Wireless network available.

Student life. Freshman orientation: Mandatory, $100 fee. Preregistration for classes offered. One-day program held from May through July. **Housing:** Coed dorms, single-sex dorms, wellness housing available. $200 fully refundable deposit, deadline 5/1. **Activities:** Bands, campus ministries, choral groups, drama, literary magazine, music ensembles, musical theater, student government, student newspaper, campus ministry board, Black Scholars, multicultural student advisory board, St. Julie Scholars, psychology council, science and business clubs, Achievement in Research and Scholarship.

Athletics. NCAA. **Intercollegiate:** Baseball M, basketball, cross-country, diving, football (tackle) M, golf, lacrosse W, soccer, softball W, swimming, track and field, volleyball W, water polo, wrestling M. **Intramural:** Water polo. **Team name:** Falcons.

Student services. Adult student services, alcohol/substance abuse counseling, chaplain/spiritual director, career counseling, student employment services, financial aid counseling, health services, personal counseling, placement for graduates, veterans' counselor.

Contact. E-mail: admissions@ndc.edu
Phone: (216) 373-5355 Toll-free number: (877) 632-6446 ext. 5355
Fax: (216) 381-3802
Beth Ford, Dean of Admissions, Notre Dame College, 4545 College Road, Cleveland, OH 44121-4293

Oberlin College
Oberlin, Ohio   **CB member**
www.oberlin.edu   **CB code: 1587**

- Private 4-year music and liberal arts college
- Residential campus in small town
- 2,959 degree-seeking undergraduates: 2% part-time, 55% women, 6% African American, 4% Asian American, 6% Hispanic American, 6% international
- 24 degree-seeking graduate students
- 30% of applicants admitted
- SAT or ACT with writing, application essay required
- 87% graduate within 6 years

General. Founded in 1833. Regionally accredited. **Degrees:** 700 bachelor's awarded; master's offered. **Location:** 35 miles from Cleveland. **Calendar:** 4-1-4. **Full-time faculty:** 285 total; 96% have terminal degrees, 11% minority, 39% women. **Class size:** 70% < 20, 25% 20-39, 2% 40-49, 3% 50-99, less than 1% >100. **Special facilities:** Observatory, art museum, environmental studies building, arboretum.

Freshman class profile. 7,395 applied, 2,192 admitted, 751 enrolled.

GPA 3.75 or higher:	38%	Rank in top tenth:	68%
GPA 3.50-3.74:	30%	Return as sophomores:	94%
GPA 3.0-3.49:	29%	Out-of-state:	92%
GPA 2.0-2.99:	3%	Live on campus:	100%
Rank in top quarter:	90%	International:	7%

Basis for selection. GED not accepted. For college of arts and sciences: school achievement record, test scores, school and community leadership activities, recommendations, and interview important. Special consideration to applicants from minority and first generation college families and to foreign applicants. For conservatory: audition most important factor; admission selective. SAT Subject Tests recommended. Interview required for early admission and home schooled candidates; recommended for all others. Audition required of applicants to conservatory; essay required of applicants to college of arts and sciences. **Home schooled:** Interview, letter of recommendation (nonparent) required. SAT Subject Tests, interview, and detailed portfolio also required.

High school preparation. College-preparatory program required. Required and recommended units include English 4, mathematics 3-4, social studies 3, science 3-4 and foreign language 3.

2011-2012 Annual costs. Tuition/fees: $43,210. Room/board: $11,550. Books/supplies: $830. Personal expenses: $978.

2011-2012 Financial aid. Need-based: 484 full-time freshmen applied for aid; 434 were judged to have need; 434 of these received aid. Average need met was 100%. Average scholarship/grant was $28,509; average loan $4,284. 79% of total undergraduate aid awarded as scholarships/grants, 21% as loans/jobs. **Non-need-based:** Awarded to 1,786 full-time undergraduates, including 453 freshmen. Scholarships awarded for academics, music/drama.

Application procedures. Admission: Closing date 1/15 (postmark date). $35 fee, may be waived for applicants with need. Admission notification by 4/1. Must reply by May 1 or within 2 week(s) if notified thereafter. 12/1 application closing date for Conservatory of Music; $100 application fee. 1/15 application closing date for College of Arts and Sciences; $35 application fee. **Financial aid:** Priority date 1/15, closing date 2/1. FAFSA, institutional form, CSS PROFILE required. Applicants notified by 4/1; must reply by 5/1 or within 2 week(s) of notification.

Academics. No core curriculum. Students required to take 9 credit hours in each academic division (Humanities, Social Sciences, and Math and Natural Science) and 9 hours related to cultural diversity. Students must also complete 3 Winter Term credits. **Special study options:** Combined bachelor's/graduate degree, cross-registration, double major, dual enrollment of high school students, ESL, exchange student, honors, independent study, internships, New York semester, student-designed major, study abroad, teacher certification program, urban semester, Washington semester. 5-year dual degree program with music conservatory and liberal arts college, 3-2 engineering. **Credit/placement by examination:** AP, CLEP, IB, institutional tests. 30 credit hours maximum toward bachelor's degree. **Support services:** Learning center, remedial instruction, study skills assistance, tutoring, writing center.

Majors. Area/ethnic studies: African, African-American, American, East Asian, Latin American, Russian/Slavic, women's. **Biology:** General, biochemistry, neuroscience. **Computer sciences:** General. **Conservation:** Environmental studies. **Education:** Music. **English:** Creative writing, English lit. **Foreign languages:** Ancient Greek, classics, comparative lit, French, German, Latin, Russian, Spanish. **Health services:** Predental, premedicine, preveterinary. **History:** General. **Math:** General. **Philosophy/religion:** Judaic, philosophy, religion. **Physical sciences:** Chemistry, geology, physics. **Psychology:** General. **Social sciences:** Anthropology, economics, political science, sociology. **Visual/performing arts:** Art history/conservation, conducting, dance, dramatic, film/cinema/video, jazz, music, music history, music theory/composition, piano/keyboard, stringed instruments, studio arts, voice/opera.

Most popular majors. Area/ethnic studies 8%, biology 12%, English 12%, physical sciences 6%, social sciences 11%, visual/performing arts 28%.

Computing on campus. 340 workstations in dormitories, library, computer center. Dormitories wired for high-speed internet access and linked to campus network. Commuter students can connect to campus network. Online course registration, online library, helpline, repair service, student web hosting, wireless network available.

Student life. Freshman orientation: Mandatory. Preregistration for classes offered. Held week prior to fall classes. Includes day of service. **Policies:** Students agree to follow honor code. **Housing:** Guaranteed on-campus for all undergraduates. Coed dorms, single-sex dorms, apartments, cooperative housing, wellness housing available. **Activities:** Bands, campus ministries, choral groups, dance, drama, film society, international student organizations, literary magazine, music ensembles, musical theater, opera, radio station, student government, student newspaper, symphony orchestra, religious organization, political organization, inter-cultural organization, ethnic organization, social service organization, gay/lesbian/bisexual organization.

Athletics. NCAA. **Intercollegiate:** Baseball M, basketball, cross-country, diving, field hockey W, football (tackle) M, golf M, lacrosse, soccer, softball W, swimming, tennis, track and field, volleyball W. **Intramural:** Baseball M, basketball, bowling, football (non-tackle), handball, racquetball, rugby M, skin diving, soccer, softball, squash, table tennis, tennis, track and field, volleyball, weight lifting. **Team name:** Yeomen & Yeowomen.

Student services. Alcohol/substance abuse counseling, chaplain/spiritual director, career counseling, services for economically disadvantaged, student employment services, financial aid counseling, health services, minority student services, personal counseling, placement for graduates, women's services. **Physically disabled:** Services for visually, speech, hearing impaired.

Contact. E-mail: college.admissions@oberlin.edu
Phone: (440) 775-8411 Toll-free number: (800) 622-6243
Fax: (440) 775-6905
Debra Chermonte, Dean of Admissions and Financial Aid, Oberlin College, Carnegie Building, 101 North Professor Street, Oberlin, OH 44074-1075

Ohio Christian University
Circleville, Ohio
www.ohiochristian.edu   **CB code: 1088**

- Private 4-year university and Bible college affiliated with Churches of Christ in Christian Union
- Residential campus in large town

▶ 2,127 degree-seeking undergraduates: 24% part-time, 58% women
▶ 38 degree-seeking graduate students
▶ 63% of applicants admitted
▶ SAT or ACT (ACT writing optional), application essay required

General. Founded in 1948. Candidate for regional accreditation; also accredited by ABHE. **Degrees:** 147 bachelor's, 77 associate awarded; master's offered. **Location:** 25 miles from Columbus. **Calendar:** Semester, limited summer session. **Full-time faculty:** 102 total. **Part-time faculty:** 202 total. **Class size:** 75% < 20, 15% 20-39, 5% 40-49, 5% 50-99.

Freshman class profile. 1,311 applied, 828 admitted, 355 enrolled.

Mid 50% test scores			
		SAT writing:	410-530
SAT critical reading:	420-570	**ACT composite:**	17-23
SAT math:	390-610	**Out-of-state:**	10%

Basis for selection. Positive Christian testimony, potential for Christian service, sound academic performance, and personal character references important. Students without SAT or ACT may be admitted conditionally but must meet test requirement at earliest opportunity. Interview recommended for all; audition required for music majors. **Home schooled:** Transcript of courses and grades, letter of recommendation (nonparent) required.

High school preparation. 15 units recommended. Recommended units include English 4, mathematics 3, social studies 3, science 3 and foreign language 2.

2012-2013 Annual costs. Tuition/fees: $17,750. Room/board: $6,886. Books/supplies: $1,000. Personal expenses: $6,400.

2010-2011 Financial aid. Need-based: 52% of total undergraduate aid awarded as scholarships/grants, 48% as loans/jobs. **Non-need-based:** Scholarships awarded for academics, alumni affiliation, religious affiliation, state residency. **Additional information:** Religious affiliation tuition discount.

Application procedures. Admission: No deadline. $25 fee, may be waived for applicants with need. Admission notification on a rolling basis. Must reply by May 1 or within 2 week(s) if notified thereafter. **Financial aid:** Priority date 5/7; no closing date. FAFSA, institutional form required. Applicants notified on a rolling basis starting 5/1; must reply within 2 week(s) of notification.

Academics. Every student required to complete minimum of 30 hours in Bible and theology courses. **Special study options:** Accelerated study, combined bachelor's/graduate degree, distance learning, double major, dual enrollment of high school students, honors, independent study, internships, liberal arts/career combination, student-designed major, study abroad, teacher certification program, weekend college. **Credit/placement by examination:** AP, CLEP, SAT, ACT, institutional tests. **Support services:** Reduced course load, remedial instruction, study skills assistance, tutoring, writing center.

Majors. Business: General, business admin. **Education:** Early childhood, elementary, music, secondary. **Philosophy/religion:** Religion. **Psychology:** General. **Theology:** Missionary, pastoral counseling, religious ed, sacred music, theology, youth ministry.

Most popular majors. Business/marketing 28%, education 7%, interdisciplinary studies 6%, psychology 30%, theological studies 19%.

Computing on campus. 75 workstations in dormitories, library, computer center. Dormitories wired for high-speed internet access and linked to campus network. Commuter students can connect to campus network. Online library, helpline, repair service, wireless network available.

Student life. Freshman orientation: Mandatory. Preregistration for classes offered. Held 2-days prior to start of classes. **Policies:** Curfew of 11:30 pm (Monday-Thursday), 1:00 am (Friday), 12:00 am (Saturday-Sunday); dress code. Religious observance required. **Housing:** Guaranteed on-campus for freshmen. Single-sex dorms available. $50 deposit, deadline 8/1. **Activities:** Concert band, campus ministries, choral groups, student government, ministerial association, prison ministries, S.H.I.N.E., world gospel mission student involvement, summer camp ministries, drama team.

Athletics. NCCAA. **Intercollegiate:** Baseball, basketball, cross-country, soccer, softball W, volleyball W. **Intramural:** Basketball, table tennis. **Team name:** Trailblazers.

Student services. Adult student services, chaplain/spiritual director, career counseling, student employment services, financial aid counseling, health services, minority student services, veterans' counselor. **Physically disabled:** Services for visually impaired.

Contact. E-mail: enroll@ohiochristian.edu
Phone: (740) 477-7701 Toll-free number: (877) 762-8669
Fax: (740) 420-5921
Mike Egenreider, Director of Admissions, Ohio Christian University, 1476 Lancaster Pike, Circleville, OH 43113

Ohio Dominican University
Columbus, Ohio   **CB member**
www.ohiodominican.edu   **CB code: 1131**

▶ Private 4-year university and liberal arts college affiliated with Roman Catholic Church
▶ Commuter campus in very large city
▶ 1,680 degree-seeking undergraduates: 9% part-time, 59% women, 28% African American, 1% Asian American, 2% Hispanic American, 1% international
▶ 620 degree-seeking graduate students
▶ 61% of applicants admitted
▶ SAT or ACT (ACT writing optional), application essay required
▶ 48% graduate within 6 years

General. Founded in 1911. Regionally accredited. **Degrees:** 365 bachelor's, 51 associate awarded; master's offered. **ROTC:** Army. **Location:** 4 miles from downtown. **Calendar:** Semester, limited summer session. **Full-time faculty:** 71 total; 90% have terminal degrees, 7% minority, 48% women. **Part-time faculty:** 94 total; 26% have terminal degrees, 7% minority, 37% women. **Class size:** 48% < 20, 52% 20-39.

Freshman class profile. 1,821 applied, 1,110 admitted, 312 enrolled.

Mid 50% test scores			
		GPA 2.0-2.99:	36%
SAT critical reading:	430-560	**Rank in top quarter:**	31%
SAT math:	450-520	**Rank in top tenth:**	14%
ACT composite:	19-24	**Return as sophomores:**	57%
GPA 3.75 or higher:	14%	**Out-of-state:**	8%
GPA 3.50-3.74:	13%	**Live on campus:**	75%
GPA 3.0-3.49:	36%		

Basis for selection. High school GPA, curriculum most important, followed by class rank, test scores, interview, recommendations, and activities. Interview required for in-state applicants; recommended for out-of-state. **Home schooled:** Transcript of courses and grades, state high school equivalency certificate required.

High school preparation. College-preparatory program recommended. 16 units recommended. Recommended units include English 4, mathematics 4, social studies 3, science 3 and foreign language 3.

2011-2012 Annual costs. Tuition/fees: $26,760. Room/board: $8,738. Books/supplies: $1,100. Personal expenses: $1,470.

Financial aid. Non-need-based: Scholarships awarded for academics, athletics, state residency.

Application procedures. Admission: Priority date 4/1; no deadline. $25 fee, may be waived for applicants with need, free for online applicants. Admission notification on a rolling basis beginning on or about 9/1. **Financial aid:** Priority date 4/1; no closing date. FAFSA required. Applicants notified on a rolling basis starting 3/1; must reply within 2 week(s) of notification.

Academics. Special study options: Cross-registration, distance learning, double major, dual enrollment of high school students, honors, independent study, internships, study abroad, teacher certification program, Washington semester. **Credit/placement by examination:** AP, CLEP, IB, ACT, institutional tests. No limit on credit hours by examination, but residency requirement must be met. **Support services:** Learning center, pre-admission summer program, reduced course load, remedial instruction, study skills assistance, tutoring, writing center.

Majors. Biology: General. **Business:** Accounting, business admin, communications, finance, international. **Communications:** Communications/speech/rhetoric, public relations. **Computer sciences:** Information systems. **Conservation:** Environmental studies. **Education:** Art, biology, chemistry, elementary, English, mathematics, middle, multiple handicapped, physics, science, secondary, social studies, special ed. **English:** English lit. **History:** General. **Human services:** Social work. **Liberal arts:** Arts/sciences. **Math:** General. **Parks/recreation:** Sports admin. **Philosophy/religion:** Philosophy. **Physical sciences:** Chemistry. **Protective services:** Criminal justice. **Psychology:** General. **Social sciences:** Economics, political science, sociology. **Theology:** Theology. **Visual/performing arts:** Art, graphic design.

Most popular majors. Business/marketing 53%, education 16%, social sciences 7%.

Computing on campus. 380 workstations in dormitories, library, computer center, student center. Dormitories wired for high-speed internet access and linked to campus network. Commuter students can connect to campus network. Online course registration, online library, helpline, student web hosting available.

Student life. Freshman orientation: Mandatory, $175 fee. Preregistration for classes offered. Held 2 days in August. **Housing:** Coed dorms available. $150 partly refundable deposit, deadline 8/15. **Activities:** Bands, campus ministries, choral groups, drama, literary magazine, music ensembles, Model UN, radio station, student government, student newspaper, black student union, resident student association, commuter student association, social work club, psychology club, association of commuter students, association of resident students, Amigos Latinos, College Republicans and Conservatives, Young Democrats and Progressive club.

Athletics. NCAA. **Intercollegiate:** Baseball M, basketball, cross-country, football (tackle) M, golf, soccer, softball W, tennis, track and field, volleyball W. **Intramural:** Basketball, table tennis, volleyball. **Team name:** Panthers.

Student services. Adult student services, chaplain/spiritual director, career counseling, student employment services, financial aid counseling, health services, minority student services, personal counseling, placement for graduates, veterans' counselor.

Contact. E-mail: admissions@ohiodominican.edu
Phone: (614) 251-4500 Toll-free number: (800) 955-6446
Fax: (614) 251-4772
Nicole Evans, Director of Admissions, Ohio Dominican University, 1216 Sunbury Road, Columbus, OH 43219

Ohio Mid-Western College
Cincinnati, Ohio
www.omw.edu

- Private 4-year liberal arts college affiliated with Baptist faith
- Very large city
- 56 degree-seeking undergraduates

General. Regionally accredited; also accredited by TRACS. **Degrees:** 10 bachelor's awarded. **Location:** 16 miles from Cincinnati. **Calendar:** Quarter, limited summer session. **Full-time faculty:** 6 total. **Part-time faculty:** 15 total.

Basis for selection. Open admission.

High school preparation. Recommended units include English 4, mathematics 3, science 3 (laboratory 1).

2011-2012 Annual costs. Tuition/fees: $11,655.

Application procedures. Admission: No deadline. $35 fee. Admission notification on a rolling basis. **Financial aid:** Closing date 10/1.

Academics. Credit/placement by examination: AP, CLEP.

Majors. Business: Business admin. **Education:** General, elementary. **Theology:** Religious ed.

Computing on campus. Dormitories wired for high-speed internet access. Wireless network available.

Student life. Freshman orientation: Mandatory. Preregistration for classes offered. **Housing:** Single-sex dorms, apartments, wellness housing available. **Activities:** Campus ministries, student government.

Athletics. USCAA. **Intercollegiate:** Basketball, football (tackle) M, soccer, wrestling M. **Team name:** Rams.

Contact. E-mail: rams@omw.edu
Phone: (513) 772-9888 Fax: (513) 771-0702
Heather Fischer, Dean of Student Affairs, Ohio Mid-Western College, 19 Triangle Park Drive, Cincinnati, OH 45246

Ohio Northern University
Ada, Ohio
www.onu.edu

CB member
CB code: 1591

- Private 4-year university affiliated with United Methodist Church
- Residential campus in small town
- 2,262 degree-seeking undergraduates

- 82% of applicants admitted
- SAT or ACT (ACT writing optional) required

General. Founded in 1871. Regionally accredited. **Degrees:** 479 bachelor's awarded; master's, professional offered. **ROTC:** Army, Air Force. **Location:** 15 miles from Lima, 80 miles from Columbus. **Calendar:** Quarter, limited summer session. **Full-time faculty:** 225 total. **Part-time faculty:** 83 total. **Class size:** 57% < 20, 40% 20-39, 2% 40-49, less than 1% 50-99, less than 1% >100. **Special facilities:** Nature center, drug information center (College of Pharmacy), pharmacy museum.

Freshman class profile. 3,136 applied, 2,572 admitted, 694 enrolled.

Mid 50% test scores			
SAT critical reading:	520-620	GPA 2.0-2.99:	9%
SAT math:	550-660	Rank in top quarter:	74%
SAT writing:	510-620	Rank in top tenth:	50%
ACT composite:	24-29	Out-of-state:	20%
GPA 3.75 or higher:	58%	Live on campus:	96%
GPA 3.50-3.74:	14%	Fraternities:	19%
GPA 3.0-3.49:	19%	Sororities:	19%

Basis for selection. 20 ACT preferred; secondary school record very important. Colleges of Pharmacy and Engineering have higher test score credentials for consideration. GPA, class rank, test scores, college prep curriculum, extracurricular activities considered. Essay required for all freshmen. Interview recommended for all. Audition required for music, music education, musical theatre, and performance. Portfolio required for advertising design, art education, graphic design and studio arts. Interview required for international theatre production. **Home schooled:** Statement describing home school structure and mission required.

High school preparation. College-preparatory program required. 16 units required; 24 recommended. Required and recommended units include English 4, mathematics 2-4, social studies 2-3, history 2, science 2-3 (laboratory 2), foreign language 2, computer science 1, visual/performing arts 1 and academic electives 4. 4 units math and science required for engineering and pharmacy applicants.

2011-2012 Annual costs. Tuition/fees: $34,380. Room/board: $9,844. Books/supplies: $1,800. Personal expenses: $1,229.

Financial aid. Non-need-based: Scholarships awarded for academics, alumni affiliation, art, leadership, minority status, music/drama, ROTC, state residency.

Application procedures. Admission: Priority date 12/1; deadline 8/1 (postmark date). $30 fee, may be waived for applicants with need, free for online applicants. Admission notification on a rolling basis. Priority date for scholarship eligibility December 1. Pharmacy deadline is November 1 of senior year. **Financial aid:** Closing date 4/15. FAFSA, institutional form required. Applicants notified on a rolling basis starting 2/15; must reply within 2 week(s) of notification.

Academics. Pharmacy students admitted directly to 6-year PharmD. program. **Special study options:** Combined bachelor's/graduate degree, cooperative education, distance learning, double major, dual enrollment of high school students, ESL, exchange student, honors, independent study, internships, liberal arts/career combination, study abroad, teacher certification program, Washington semester. **Credit/placement by examination:** AP, CLEP, IB, SAT, ACT, institutional tests. 30 credit hours maximum toward bachelor's degree. **Support services:** Pre-admission summer program, reduced course load, remedial instruction, study skills assistance, tutoring, writing center.

Majors. Biology: General, biochemistry, exercise physiology, molecular. **Business:** Accounting, business admin, construction management, finance, international, management science, marketing. **Communications:** Communications/speech/rhetoric, journalism, organizational, persuasive communications, radio/TV. **Computer sciences:** Computer science. **Conservation:** Environmental studies. **Education:** General, early childhood, English, health, middle, music, physical, social studies, technology/industrial arts. **Engineering:** General, civil, computer, electrical, mechanical. **English:** British lit, creative writing, English lit, technical writing. **Foreign languages:** French, German, Germanic, Spanish. **Health services:** Athletic training, clinical lab science, nursing (RN), pharmaceutical marketing/management, predental, premedicine, preveterinary. **History:** General. **Liberal arts:** Arts/sciences. **Math:** General, statistics. **Parks/recreation:** Exercise sciences, health/fitness, sports admin. **Philosophy/religion:** Philosophy, religion. **Physical sciences:** Chemistry, physics. **Protective services:** Criminal justice, forensics, law enforcement admin. **Psychology:** General. **Social sciences:** Political science, sociology. **Theology:** Youth ministry. **Visual/performing arts:** General, art, commercial/advertising art, dramatic, music, music management, music performance, music theory/composition, studio arts.

Most popular majors. Biology 6%, business/marketing 16%, education 8%, engineering/engineering technologies 22%, health sciences 8%, parks/recreation 6%.

Computing on campus. 550 workstations in dormitories, library, computer center, student center. Dormitories wired for high-speed internet access and linked to campus network. Commuter students can connect to campus network. Online course registration, online library, helpline, repair service, wireless network available.

Student life. Freshman orientation: Mandatory. Preregistration for classes offered. Three 1-day sessions held in June and July on Fridays. **Policies:** All students must reside on campus until senior status reached. No smoking in residence halls. **Housing:** Guaranteed on-campus for freshmen. Coed dorms, single-sex dorms, special housing for disabled, apartments, cooperative housing, fraternity/sorority housing, wellness housing available. $200 fully refundable deposit, deadline 5/1. Honors residence halls available. **Activities:** Bands, campus ministries, choral groups, dance, drama, international student organizations, literary magazine, music ensembles, Model UN, musical theater, opera, radio station, student government, student newspaper, symphony orchestra, TV station, Christian legal society, Fellowship of Christian Athletes, University Religious Association Council, Black student union, Amnesty International, College Republicans, Black law student association, Habitat for Humanity, world student organization.

Athletics. NCAA. **Intercollegiate:** Baseball M, basketball, cross-country, diving, football (tackle) M, golf, soccer, softball W, swimming, tennis, track and field, volleyball W, wrestling M. **Intramural:** Badminton, basketball, bowling, football (non-tackle) M, racquetball, soccer, softball, swimming, table tennis M, tennis, track and field, volleyball, wrestling M. **Team name:** Polar Bears.

Student services. Alcohol/substance abuse counseling, chaplain/spiritual director, career counseling, student employment services, financial aid counseling, health services, legal services, minority student services, on-campus daycare, personal counseling, placement for graduates. **Physically disabled:** Services for visually, speech, hearing impaired.

Contact. E-mail: admissions-ug@onu.edu
Phone: (419) 772-2260 Toll-free number: (888) 408-4668
Fax: (419) 772-2821
Deborah Miller, Director of Admissions, Ohio Northern University, 525 South Main Street, Ada, OH 45810

Ohio State University: Columbus Campus

Columbus, Ohio	CB member
www.osu.edu	CB code: 1592

- Public 4-year university
- Residential campus in very large city
- 41,709 degree-seeking undergraduates: 6% part-time, 47% women, 6% African American, 5% Asian American, 3% Hispanic American, 6% international
- 13,961 degree-seeking graduate students
- 63% of applicants admitted
- SAT or ACT with writing, application essay required
- 80% graduate within 6 years

General. Founded in 1870. Regionally accredited. Additional campuses in Wooster, Marion, Lima, Newark, Mansfield. **Degrees:** 10,667 bachelor's, 465 associate awarded; master's, professional, doctoral offered. **ROTC:** Army, Naval, Air Force. **Location:** 2 miles from downtown. **Calendar:** Quarter, extensive summer session. **Full-time faculty:** 3,400 total; 99% have terminal degrees, 22% minority, 34% women. **Part-time faculty:** 1,363 total; 14% minority, 53% women. **Class size:** 31% < 20, 39% 20-39, 10% 40-49, 13% 50-99, 8% >100. **Special facilities:** Radio telescope, dance notation bureau, extension center for educational research, biological science laboratory on Lake Erie, campus airport, environmental studies center, research vessel on Lake Erie, nuclear research reactor, supercomputer facility, arts center, cultural center, public service and public policy institute, polar research center, health policy studies center, mapping center, materials research center.

Freshman class profile. 26,100 applied, 16,546 admitted, 7,089 enrolled.

Mid 50% test scores			
SAT critical reading:	540-660	Rank in top tenth:	55%
SAT math:	600-700	End year in good standing:	95%
SAT writing:	550-650	Return as sophomores:	93%
ACT composite:	26-30	Out-of-state:	18%
Rank in top quarter:	89%	Live on campus:	92%
		International:	6%

Basis for selection. Secondary school record, class rank, test scores most important. Audition required for dance, music programs; portfolio required for art programs. **Home schooled:** May be required to provide GED.

High school preparation. College-preparatory program recommended. 19 units required; 22 recommended. Required and recommended units include

English 4, mathematics 3-4, social studies 2-3, science 3 (laboratory 3), foreign language 2-3, visual/performing arts 1 and academic electives 1.

2011-2012 Annual costs. Tuition/fees: $9,735; $24,630 out-of-state. Room/board: $9,180. Books/supplies: $1,602. Personal expenses: $4,554.

2011-2012 Financial aid. Need-based: 5,780 full-time freshmen applied for aid; 4,093 were judged to have need; 4,039 of these received aid. Average need met was 59%. Average scholarship/grant was $8,776; average loan $3,687. 44% of total undergraduate aid awarded as scholarships/grants, 56% as loans/jobs. **Non-need-based:** Awarded to 7,645 full-time undergraduates, including 1,962 freshmen. Scholarships awarded for academics, alumni affiliation, art, athletics, job skills, leadership, minority status, music/drama, ROTC, state residency.

Application procedures. Admission: Closing date 2/1 (postmark date). $60 fee, may be waived for applicants with need. Admission notification on a rolling basis beginning on or about 11/15. Must reply by May 1 or within 3 week(s) if notified thereafter. **Financial aid:** Priority date 2/15; no closing date. FAFSA required. Must reply by 5/1 or within 4 week(s) of notification.

Academics. Special study options: Accelerated study, combined bachelor's/graduate degree, cooperative education, cross-registration, distance learning, double major, dual enrollment of high school students, ESL, exchange student, honors, independent study, internships, liberal arts/career combination, semester at sea, student-designed major, study abroad, teacher certification program, Washington semester. **Credit/placement by examination:** AP, CLEP, IB, SAT, ACT, institutional tests. 45 credit hours maximum toward bachelor's degree. **Support services:** Learning center, pre-admission summer program, reduced course load, remedial instruction, study skills assistance, tutoring, writing center.

Majors. Architecture: Architecture, environmental design, interior, landscape. **Area/ethnic studies:** African, African-American, East Asian, Latin American, Near/Middle Eastern, Russian/Eastern European/Eurasian, Russian/Slavic, Western European, women's. **Biology:** General, biochemistry, biomedical sciences, botany, ecology, entomology, genetics, microbiology, molecular genetics, plant pathology, zoology. **Business:** General, accounting, actuarial science, business admin, fashion, finance, hospitality admin, hospitality/recreation, hotel/motel admin, human resources, insurance, international, logistics, management information systems, managerial economics, marketing, operations, real estate, transportation. **Communications:** Communications/speech/rhetoric, journalism, public relations. **Computer sciences:** General, computer science, information systems. **Conservation:** General, environmental studies, fisheries, forestry, management/policy, wildlife/wilderness. **Education:** General, agricultural, art, family/consumer sciences, music, physical, special ed, technology/industrial arts, trade/industrial, voc/tech. **Engineering:** Aerospace, agricultural, applied physics, biomedical, ceramic, chemical, civil, computer, electrical, industrial, materials, mechanical, metallurgical, systems. **English:** English lit, writing. **Foreign languages:** Arabic, Chinese, classics, comparative lit, French, German, Hebrew, Italian, Japanese, Korean, Latin, linguistics, modern Greek, Portuguese, Russian, Spanish. **General:** Agronomy, animal sciences, business, communications, economics, food processing, food science, landscaping, ornamental horticulture, plant protection, plant sciences, products processing, turf management. **Health services:** Athletic training, audiology/hearing, audiology/speech pathology, clinical lab science, dental hygiene, dietetics, medical radiologic technology/radiation therapy, medical records admin, nursing (RN), perfusion technology, pharmaceutical sciences, respiratory therapy technology. **History:** General. **Human services:** Social work. **Liberal arts:** Arts/sciences. **Math:** General. **Parks/recreation:** Exercise sciences, facilities management, health/fitness, sports admin. **Philosophy/religion:** Islamic, Judaic, philosophy, religion. **Physical sciences:** Astronomy, chemistry, geology, geophysics, materials science, optics, physics. **Psychology:** General. **Social sciences:** General, anthropology, criminology, economics, geography, international relations, political science, sociology, urban studies. **Visual/performing arts:** Art, art history/conservation, ceramics, dance, design, dramatic, drawing, film/cinema/video, industrial design, interior design, jazz, music, music history, music performance, music theory/composition, painting, photography, piano/keyboard, printmaking, sculpture, studio arts, voice/opera. **Work/family studies:** General, clothing/textiles, family resources, family studies, family/community services, food/nutrition, human nutrition.

Most popular majors. Biology 6%, business/marketing 16%, engineering/engineering technologies 10%, family/consumer sciences 7%, health sciences 8%, psychology 7%, social sciences 12%.

Computing on campus. 800 workstations in dormitories, library, computer center, student center. Dormitories wired for high-speed internet access and linked to campus network. Commuter students can connect to campus network. Online course registration, online library, helpline, wireless network available.

Student life. Freshman orientation: Mandatory, $50 fee. Preregistration for classes offered. Two-day programs held June-August. **Policies:** Student organizations need to have 5 student members, faculty or staff advisor, constitution, and purpose statement to register. Freshmen not permitted cars

on campus. **Housing:** Guaranteed on-campus for freshmen. Coed dorms, single-sex dorms, special housing for disabled, apartments, cooperative housing, fraternity/sorority housing, wellness housing available. $200 partly refundable deposit. **Activities:** Bands, choral groups, dance, drama, film society, international student organizations, literary magazine, music ensembles, musical theater, opera, radio station, student government, student newspaper, symphony orchestra, TV station, over 1,000 organizations.

Athletics. NCAA. **Intercollegiate:** Baseball M, basketball, cheerleading M, cross-country, diving, fencing, field hockey W, football (tackle) M, golf, gymnastics, ice hockey, lacrosse, rifle, rowing (crew) W, soccer, softball W, swimming, synchronized swimming W, tennis, track and field, volleyball, wrestling M. **Intramural:** Badminton, baseball, basketball, cricket, football (non-tackle), golf, ice hockey, racquetball, soccer, softball, table tennis, tennis, volleyball, water polo, weight lifting, wrestling. **Team name:** Buckeyes.

Student services. Adult student services, alcohol/substance abuse counseling, career counseling, services for economically disadvantaged, student employment services, financial aid counseling, health services, legal services, minority student services, on-campus daycare, personal counseling, veterans' counselor, women's services. **Physically disabled:** Services for visually, speech, hearing impaired.

Contact. E-mail: askabuckeye@osu.edu
Phone: (614) 292-3980 Fax: (614) 292-4818
Mabel Freeman, Assistant Vice President for Undergraduate Admissions and First Year Experience, Ohio State University: Columbus Campus, 110 Enarson Hall, Columbus, OH 43210

Ohio State University: Lima Campus
Lima, Ohio
www.lima.ohio-state.edu   **CB code: 1541**

▶ Public 4-year university and branch campus college
▶ Commuter campus in large town
▶ 1,193 degree-seeking undergraduates: 12% part-time, 52% women, 4% African American, 1% Asian American, 3% Hispanic American
▶ 66 degree-seeking graduate students
▶ Application essay required
▶ 45% graduate within 6 years

General. Founded in 1960. Regionally accredited. Branch campus of Ohio State University; all degrees awarded through main campus. **Degrees:** 100 bachelor's, 45 associate awarded; master's offered. **ROTC:** Army, Naval, Air Force. **Location:** 78 miles from Toledo. **Calendar:** Quarter, limited summer session. **Full-time faculty:** 39 total; 97% have terminal degrees, 18% minority, 41% women. **Part-time faculty:** 48 total; 10% minority, 48% women. **Class size:** 48% < 20, 42% 20-39, 3% 40-49, 7% 50-99, less than 1% >100. **Special facilities:** Greenhouse, nature trails, dinosaur museum.

Freshman class profile.

Mid 50% test scores			
SAT critical reading:	420-540	**ACT composite:**	19-24
SAT math:	460-610	**Rank in top quarter:**	24%
SAT writing:	420-530	**Rank in top tenth:**	6%
		Return as sophomores:	60%

Basis for selection. Open admission, but selective for out-of-state students. Out-of-state students evaluated on basis of GPA, class rank, principal/counselor recommendation. **Home schooled:** May be required to provide GED.

High school preparation. College-preparatory program recommended.

2011-2012 Annual costs. Tuition/fees: $6,327; $21,222 out-of-state. Books/supplies: $1,602. Personal expenses: $4,140.

2011-2012 Financial aid. Need-based: 432 full-time freshmen applied for aid; 363 were judged to have need; 361 of these received aid. Average need met was 49%. Average scholarship/grant was $3,701; average loan $3,671. 33% of total undergraduate aid awarded as scholarships/grants, 67% as loans/jobs. **Non-need-based:** Awarded to 94 full-time undergraduates, including 60 freshmen. Scholarships awarded for academics, alumni affiliation, art, athletics, job skills, leadership, minority status, music/drama, ROTC, state residency.

Application procedures. Admission: Closing date 7/1 (postmark date). $60 fee, may be waived for applicants with need. Admission notification on a rolling basis beginning on or about 11/15. Must reply by May 1 or within 3 week(s) if notified thereafter. **Financial aid:** Priority date 2/15; no closing date. FAFSA required. Applicants notified on a rolling basis starting 4/5; must reply by 5/1 or within 4 week(s) of notification.

Academics. Students often leave campus after 1-3 years and complete bachelor's degree on Columbus campus. **Special study options:** Accelerated study, cooperative education, cross-registration, distance learning, double major, dual enrollment of high school students, ESL, exchange student, honors, independent study, internships, liberal arts/career combination, student-designed major, study abroad, teacher certification program, weekend college. **Credit/placement by examination:** AP, CLEP, IB, institutional tests. 45 credit hours maximum toward bachelor's degree. **Support services:** Learning center, remedial instruction, tutoring, writing center.

Majors. Biology: General. **Business:** General, financial planning, hospitality admin. **Education:** General, elementary. **English:** English lit. **History:** General. **Math:** General. **Psychology:** General. **Visual/performing arts:** Dramatic. **Work/family studies:** Family resources.

Computing on campus. 150 workstations in library, computer center. Commuter students can connect to campus network. Online course registration, online library, helpline, wireless network available.

Student life. Freshman orientation: Mandatory. Preregistration for classes offered. Orientation services available throughout year, days and evenings. **Housing:** Coed dorms, apartments available. **Activities:** Pep band, campus ministries, choral groups, literary magazine, music ensembles, musical theater, student government, Campus Crusade for Christ, College Republicans, Students for Obama, Newman Catholic Association, Stars and Stripes Vet club, outreach and engagment, human service club, multi-cultural club, French and Japanese club, global club.

Athletics. Intramural: Basketball, football (non-tackle), soccer, volleyball. **Team name:** Barons.

Student services. Adult student services, chaplain/spiritual director, career counseling, student employment services, financial aid counseling, on-campus daycare, personal counseling, placement for graduates. **Physically disabled:** Services for visually, speech, hearing impaired.

Contact. E-mail: admissions@lima.ohio-state.edu
Phone: (419) 995-8396 Fax: (419) 995-8483
Beth Keehn, Director of Admissions, Ohio State University: Lima Campus, 4240 Campus Drive, Lima, OH 45804-3596

Ohio State University: Mansfield Campus
Mansfield, Ohio
www.mansfield.ohio-state.edu   **CB code: 0744**

▶ Public 4-year university and branch campus college
▶ Commuter campus in large town
▶ 1,252 degree-seeking undergraduates: 14% part-time, 54% women, 7% African American, 1% Asian American, 2% Hispanic American
▶ 78 degree-seeking graduate students
▶ Application essay required
▶ 39% graduate within 6 years

General. Founded in 1958. Regionally accredited. Branch campus of Ohio State University; all degrees awarded through main campus. **ROTC:** Army, Naval, Air Force. **Location:** 67 miles from Columbus. **Calendar:** Quarter, limited summer session. **Full-time faculty:** 41 total; 98% have terminal degrees, 10% minority, 44% women. **Part-time faculty:** 54 total; 11% minority, 63% women. **Class size:** 47% < 20, 43% 20-39, 6% 40-49, 4% 50-99. **Special facilities:** Archives and reading room, educational enrichment laboratory, language laboratory, elementary education suite.

Freshman class profile. 1,500 applied, 1,484 admitted, 502 enrolled.

Mid 50% test scores			
SAT critical reading:	460-570	**Rank in top quarter:**	31%
SAT math:	450-570	**Rank in top tenth:**	11%
SAT writing:	430-550	**End year in good standing:**	78%
ACT composite:	20-25	**Return as sophomores:**	71%
		Live on campus:	35%

Basis for selection. Open admission, but selective for out-of-state students. Out-of-state applicants evaluated on basis of GPA, class rank, principal/counselor recommendations and SAT/ACT. **Home schooled:** May be required to provide GED.

High school preparation. College-preparatory program recommended.

2011-2012 Annual costs. Tuition/fees: $6,327; $21,222 out-of-state. Room/board: $5,205. Books/supplies: $1,602. Personal expenses: $4,554.

2011-2012 Financial aid. Need-based: Average need met was 48%. Average scholarship/grant was $4,638; average loan $3,698. 35% of total undergraduate aid awarded as scholarships/grants, 65% as loans/jobs. **Non-need-based:** Scholarships awarded for academics, alumni affiliation, art, athletics,

job skills, leadership, minority status, music/drama, ROTC, state residency.

Application procedures. Admission: Closing date 7/1 (postmark date). $60 fee, may be waived for applicants with need. Admission notification on a rolling basis beginning on or about 11/15. Must reply by May 1 or within 3 week(s) if notified thereafter. **Financial aid:** Priority date 2/15; no closing date. FAFSA required. Applicants notified on a rolling basis starting 4/5; must reply within 4 week(s) of notification.

Academics. Students often leave campus after 1-3 years and complete bachelor's degree on Columbus campus. **Special study options:** Accelerated study, cooperative education, cross-registration, distance learning, double major, dual enrollment of high school students, ESL, exchange student, honors, independent study, internships, liberal arts/career combination, student-designed major, study abroad, teacher certification program. **Credit/ placement by examination:** AP, CLEP, institutional tests. 45 credit hours maximum toward bachelor's degree. **Support services:** Learning center, remedial instruction, tutoring, writing center.

Majors. Business: Business admin. **Education:** Elementary. **English:** English lit. **History:** General. **Psychology:** General.

Computing on campus. 260 workstations in library, computer center, student center. Commuter students can connect to campus network. Online course registration, online library, helpline, wireless network available.

Student life. Freshman orientation: Mandatory. Preregistration for classes offered. **Housing:** Special housing for disabled, apartments, wellness housing available. $200 partly refundable deposit. **Activities:** Campus ministries, choral groups, drama, film society, international student organizations, music ensembles, musical theater, student government, multicultural student association, campus activities board, Campus Crusade for Christ, College Republicans, Habitat for Humanity, Theta Alpha Phi, Catholic young adults, paralegal association, OutLoud, history club.

Athletics. Intramural: Basketball, equestrian W, football (non-tackle), softball, table tennis, tennis, volleyball. **Team name:** Mavericks.

Student services. Adult student services, career counseling, student employment services, financial aid counseling, minority student services, personal counseling, placement for graduates. **Physically disabled:** Services for visually, speech, hearing impaired.

Contact. E-mail: admissions@mansfield.ohio-state.edu
Phone: (419) 755-4226 Fax: (419) 755-4241
Ken Sigler, Director of Admissions & Financial Aid, Ohio State University: Mansfield Campus, 1680 University Drive, Mansfield, OH 44906

Ohio State University: Marion Campus
Marion, Ohio
www.osumarion.osu.edu   **CB code: 0752**

- Public 4-year university and branch campus college
- Commuter campus in large town
- 1,397 degree-seeking undergraduates: 21% part-time, 53% women, 10% African American, 4% Asian American, 2% Hispanic American
- 80 degree-seeking graduate students
- Application essay required
- 37% graduate within 6 years

General. Founded in 1958. Regionally accredited. Branch campus of Ohio State University; all degrees awarded through main campus. **Degrees:** 91 bachelor's, 167 associate awarded; master's offered. **ROTC:** Army, Naval, Air Force. **Location:** 44 miles from Columbus. **Calendar:** Quarter, limited summer session. **Full-time faculty:** 36 total; 100% have terminal degrees, 11% minority, 36% women. **Part-time faculty:** 65 total; 8% minority, 55% women. **Class size:** 46% < 20, 48% 20-39, 6% 40-49, less than 1% 50-99.

Freshman class profile. 964 applied, 944 admitted, 473 enrolled.

Mid 50% test scores			
SAT critical reading:	470-560	Rank in top quarter:	36%
SAT math:	490-590	Rank in top tenth:	10%
SAT writing:	430-550	End year in good standing:	78%
ACT composite:	20-25	Return as sophomores:	67%

Basis for selection. Open admission, but selective for out-of-state students. Out-of-state students evaluated on basis of GPA, class rank, principal/ counselor recommendation. **Home schooled:** May be required to provide GED.

High school preparation. College-preparatory program recommended. 19 units required; 22 recommended. Required and recommended units include

English 4, mathematics 3-4, social studies 2-3, science 3 (laboratory 3), foreign language 2-3, visual/performing arts 1 and academic electives 1.

2011-2012 Annual costs. Tuition/fees: $6,327; $21,222 out-of-state. Books/supplies: $1,602. Personal expenses: $4,140.

2011-2012 Financial aid. Need-based: 346 full-time freshmen applied for aid; 289 were judged to have need; 288 of these received aid. Average need met was 52%. Average scholarship/grant was $4,532; average loan $3,664. 37% of total undergraduate aid awarded as scholarships/grants, 63% as loans/jobs. **Non-need-based:** Awarded to 84 full-time undergraduates, including 43 freshmen. Scholarships awarded for academics, alumni affiliation, art, athletics, job skills, leadership, minority status, music/drama, ROTC, state residency.

Application procedures. Admission: Closing date 7/1 (postmark date). $60 fee, may be waived for applicants with need. Admission notification on a rolling basis beginning on or about 11/15. Must reply by May 1 or within 3 week(s) if notified thereafter. **Financial aid:** Priority date 2/15; no closing date. FAFSA required. Must reply by 5/1 or within 4 week(s) of notification.

Academics. Students often leave campus after 1-3 years and complete bachelor's degree on Columbus campus. **Special study options:** Accelerated study, cooperative education, cross-registration, distance learning, double major, dual enrollment of high school students, ESL, exchange student, honors, independent study, internships, liberal arts/career combination, student-designed major, study abroad, teacher certification program, weekend college. **Credit/placement by examination:** AP, CLEP, institutional tests. 45 credit hours maximum toward bachelor's degree. **Support services:** Learning center, reduced course load, remedial instruction, tutoring, writing center.

Majors. Business: Business admin. **Education:** Elementary. **English:** English lit. **History:** General. **Psychology:** General.

Computing on campus. 163 workstations in library, computer center. Commuter students can connect to campus network. Online course registration, online library, helpline, wireless network available.

Student life. Freshman orientation: Mandatory. Preregistration for classes offered. **Activities:** Marching band, choral groups, literary magazine, student government, Buckeye Ambassador, Christian and Pagan religious organizations, Democratic/Republican political organizations, education society, honors organizations, language organizations, theater and improv troupe, diversity student organization.

Athletics. USCAA. **Intercollegiate:** Basketball M, golf M, volleyball W. **Team name:** Scarlet Wave.

Student services. Career counseling, student employment services, financial aid counseling, legal services, on-campus daycare, personal counseling, placement for graduates. **Physically disabled:** Services for visually, speech, hearing impaired.

Contact. E-mail: moreau.1@osu.edu
Phone: (740) 389-6786 ext. 6242 Fax: (740) 386-2439
Matt Moreau, Coordinator of Admissions, Ohio State University: Marion Campus, 1465 Mount Vernon Avenue, Marion, OH 43302

Ohio State University: Newark Campus
Newark, Ohio
www.newark.osu.edu   **CB code: 0824**

- Public 4-year university and branch campus college
- Commuter campus in large town
- 2,503 degree-seeking undergraduates: 12% part-time, 52% women, 14% African American, 3% Asian American, 2% Hispanic American
- 109 degree-seeking graduate students
- Application essay required
- 38% graduate within 6 years

General. Founded in 1957. Regionally accredited. Branch campus of Ohio State University; all degrees awarded through main campus. **Degrees:** 130 bachelor's, 180 associate awarded; master's offered. **ROTC:** Army, Naval, Air Force. **Location:** 40 miles from Columbus. **Calendar:** Quarter, limited summer session. **Full-time faculty:** 53 total; 98% have terminal degrees, 17% minority, 38% women. **Part-time faculty:** 87 total; 6% minority, 53% women. **Class size:** 34% < 20, 52% 20-39, 8% 40-49, 6% 50-99. **Special facilities:** Math laboratory, writing laboratory.

Freshman class profile.

Mid 50% test scores		Rank in top quarter:	21%
SAT critical reading:	450-540	Rank in top tenth:	4%
SAT math:	460-570	End year in good standing:	66%
SAT writing:	430-530	Return as sophomores:	63%
ACT composite:	19-24	Live on campus:	13%

Basis for selection. Open admission, but selective for out-of-state students. Out of state applicants evaluated on basis of GPA, class rank, principal/counselor recommendations. **Home schooled:** May be required to provide GED.

High school preparation. College-preparatory program recommended. 19 units required. Required units include English 4, mathematics 3, social studies 2, science 3 (laboratory 3), foreign language 2, visual/performing arts 1 and academic electives 1.

2011-2012 Annual costs. Tuition/fees: $6,327; $21,222 out-of-state. Room only: $7,185. Books/supplies: $1,602. Personal expenses: $4,554.

2011-2012 Financial aid. Need-based: 1,054 full-time freshmen applied for aid; 867 were judged to have need; 841 of these received aid. Average need met was 46%. Average scholarship/grant was $4,627; average loan $3,751. 35% of total undergraduate aid awarded as scholarships/grants, 65% as loans/jobs. **Non-need-based:** Awarded to 30 full-time undergraduates, including 13 freshmen. Scholarships awarded for academics, alumni affiliation, art, athletics, job skills, leadership, minority status, music/drama, ROTC, state residency.

Application procedures. Admission: Closing date 7/1 (postmark date). $60 fee, may be waived for applicants with need. Admission notification on a rolling basis beginning on or about 11/15. Must reply by May 1 or within 3 week(s) if notified thereafter. **Financial aid:** Priority date 2/15; no closing date. FAFSA required. Must reply by 5/1 or within 4 week(s) of notification.

Academics. Students often leave campus after 1-3 years and complete bachelor's degree on Columbus campus. **Special study options:** Accelerated study, cooperative education, cross-registration, distance learning, double major, dual enrollment of high school students, ESL, exchange student, honors, independent study, internships, liberal arts/career combination, student-designed major, study abroad, teacher certification program, weekend college. **Credit/placement by examination:** AP, CLEP, institutional tests. 45 credit hours maximum toward bachelor's degree. **Support services:** Learning center, remedial instruction, tutoring, writing center.

Majors. Business: Business admin. **Education:** General, multicultural. **English:** English lit. **History:** General. **Psychology:** General.

Computing on campus. 1,100 workstations in library, computer center. Dormitories wired for high-speed internet access and linked to campus network. Commuter students can connect to campus network. Online course registration, online library, helpline, wireless network available.

Student life. Freshman orientation: Mandatory. Preregistration for classes offered. **Housing:** Apartments, wellness housing available. **Activities:** Choral groups, drama, literary magazine, music ensembles, student government, campus ministry, support groups, minority organization, international multicultural association, ski club, gay/straight alliance, academic and honors organizations.

Athletics. Team name: Titans.

Student services. Career counseling, student employment services, financial aid counseling, minority student services, on-campus daycare, personal counseling, placement for graduates. **Physically disabled:** Services for visually, speech, hearing impaired.

Contact. E-mail: barclay.3@osu.edu
Phone: (740) 366-9333 Fax: (740) 364-9645
Ann Donahue, Coordinator of Admissions, Ohio State University: Newark Campus, 1179 University Drive, Newark, OH 43055

Ohio University
Athens, Ohio   CB member
www.ohio.edu   CB code: 1593

- Public 4-year university
- Residential campus in large town
- 21,784 degree-seeking undergraduates: 21% part-time, 58% women, 5% African American, 1% Asian American, 2% Hispanic American, 4% international
- 4,555 degree-seeking graduate students

- 86% of applicants admitted
- SAT or ACT (ACT writing recommended) required
- 65% graduate within 6 years; 28% enter graduate study

General. Founded in 1804. Regionally accredited. **Degrees:** 4,630 bachelor's, 688 associate awarded; master's, professional, doctoral offered. **ROTC:** Army, Air Force. **Location:** 75 miles from Columbus. **Calendar:** Quarter, extensive summer session. **Full-time faculty:** 898 total; 85% have terminal degrees, 15% minority, 38% women. **Part-time faculty:** 283 total; 58% have terminal degrees, 5% minority, 47% women. **Class size:** 40% < 20, 39% 20-39, 7% 40-49, 9% 50-99, 5% >100. **Special facilities:** University airport, academic and research center, nuclear accelerator, biotechnology research center, greenhouse, ridges land lab, innovation center, museum of American art, cartography and meteorology centers, contemporary history institute.

Freshman class profile. 13,251 applied, 11,415 admitted, 3,886 enrolled.

Mid 50% test scores		Rank in top quarter:	39%
SAT critical reading:	480-600	Rank in top tenth:	15%
SAT math:	480-590	End year in good standing:	92%
SAT writing:	470-570	Return as sophomores:	80%
ACT composite:	21-26	Out-of-state:	11%
GPA 3.75 or higher:	18%	Live on campus:	95%
GPA 3.50-3.74:	18%	International:	2%
GPA 3.0-3.49:	42%	Fraternities:	13%
GPA 2.0-2.99:	22%	Sororities:	8%

Basis for selection. High school record as represented by rank in class, GPA, and curriculum completed most important. Secondary criteria test scores and recommendation. Rank in top third of class preferred. Audition required for dance and music programs. Interview required for Honors Tutorial College. Interview and portfolio review required for Visual Communications. **Home schooled:** Statement describing home school structure and mission, transcript of courses and grades, interview required. Copy of academic assessment report, curriculum outline, and documentation from school district.

High school preparation. College-preparatory program recommended. 16 units required. Required units include English 4, mathematics 3, social studies 3, science 3, foreign language 2 and visual/performing arts 1.

2011-2012 Annual costs. Tuition/fees: $9,936; $18,900 out-of-state. Room/board: $9,753. Books/supplies: $885. Personal expenses: $1,032.

2011-2012 Financial aid. Need-based: 3,256 full-time freshmen applied for aid; 2,402 were judged to have need; 2,402 of these received aid. Average scholarship/grant was $5,192; average loan $3,370. 37% of total undergraduate aid awarded as scholarships/grants, 63% as loans/jobs. **Non-need-based:** Scholarships awarded for academics, art, athletics, minority status, music/drama, religious affiliation, ROTC.

Application procedures. Admission: Closing date 2/1 (receipt date). $45 fee, may be waived for applicants with need. Admission notification on a rolling basis beginning on or about 9/15. Must reply by 5/1. **Financial aid:** Priority date 3/15, closing date 4/1. FAFSA required. Applicants notified on a rolling basis starting 4/1; must reply within 3 week(s) of notification.

Academics. Extensive learning community opportunities. **Special study options:** Accelerated study, combined bachelor's/graduate degree, cooperative education, cross-registration, distance learning, double major, dual enrollment of high school students, ESL, external degree, honors, independent study, internships, liberal arts/career combination, student-designed major, study abroad, teacher certification program. **Credit/placement by examination:** AP, CLEP, IB, ACT, institutional tests. Sophomore standing available by earning 45 quarter hours of credit based on AP scores. **Support services:** Learning center, pre-admission summer program, remedial instruction, study skills assistance, tutoring, writing center.

Honors college/program. Honors Tutorial College application deadline December 15, interview required.

Majors. Area/ethnic studies: African, African-American, Asian, European, Latin American, women's. **Biology:** General, botany, cellular/molecular, microbiology, neuroscience, wildlife, zoology. **Business:** Accounting, actuarial science, business admin, finance, human resources, international, management information systems, managerial economics, marketing. **Communications:** Broadcast journalism, communications/speech/rhetoric, digital media, health, journalism, organizational, photojournalism, radio/TV. **Computer sciences:** General, computer science, information technology, networking. **Education:** Art, early childhood, family/consumer sciences, French, German, physical, secondary, Spanish, special ed. **Engineering:** Chemical, civil, electrical, industrial, mechanical. **English:** Creative writing, English lit, rhetoric/composition. **Foreign languages:** Classics, French, German, linguistics, Russian, Spanish. **Health services:** Athletic training, audiology/speech pathology, community health services, dietetics, environmental health, health care admin, nursing (RN), occupational health. **History:** General. **Human services:** Social work. **Math:** General, applied. **Parks/recreation:** General,

exercise sciences, health/fitness. **Philosophy/religion:** Philosophy, religion. **Physical sciences:** Astrophysics, atmospheric science, chemistry, geology, physics. **Psychology:** General. **Social sciences:** Anthropology, criminology, economics, geography, international relations, political science, sociology, urban studies. **Visual/performing arts:** Acting, art, art history/conservation, ceramics, cinematography, dance, dramatic, graphic design, music history, music performance, music theory/composition, painting, photography, piano/keyboard, play/screenwriting, printmaking, sculpture, studio arts, voice/opera. **Work/family studies:** Child development, clothing/textiles, family resources, family studies, food/nutrition, housing, institutional food production.

Most popular majors. Business/marketing 13%, communications/journalism 16%, education 9%, health sciences 17%, social sciences 7%.

Computing on campus. 1,000 workstations in library, computer center, student center. Dormitories wired for high-speed internet access and linked to campus network. Commuter students can connect to campus network. Online course registration, online library, helpline, repair service, student web hosting, wireless network available.

Student life. Freshman orientation: Mandatory, $140 fee. Preregistration for classes offered. One-and-a-half day program in late July and early August. **Policies:** Student organizations required to register annually. Freshmen not permitted cars on campus. **Housing:** Guaranteed on-campus for freshmen. Coed dorms, single-sex dorms, special housing for disabled, apartments, wellness housing available. $200 nonrefundable deposit, deadline 5/1. Intensive-study residence halls available. **Activities:** Bands, campus ministries, choral groups, dance, drama, film society, international student organizations, literary magazine, music ensembles, opera, radio station, student government, student newspaper, symphony orchestra, TV station, over 300 organizations available.

Athletics. NCAA. Intercollegiate: Baseball M, basketball, cheerleading, cross-country, diving W, field hockey W, football (tackle) M, golf, soccer W, softball W, swimming W, track and field W, volleyball W, wrestling M. **Intramural:** Badminton, basketball, football (non-tackle), golf, racquetball, soccer, softball, tennis, volleyball. **Team name:** Bobcats.

Student services. Adult student services, alcohol/substance abuse counseling, career counseling, services for economically disadvantaged, student employment services, financial aid counseling, health services, legal services, minority student services, personal counseling, placement for graduates, veterans' counselor, women's services. **Physically disabled:** Services for visually, speech, hearing impaired.

Contact. E-mail: admissions@ohio.edu
Phone: (740) 593-4100 Fax: (740) 593-0560
Candace Boeninger, Director, Undergraduate Admissions, Ohio University, 120 Chubb Hall, Athens, OH 45701-2979

Ohio University: Chillicothe Campus
Chillicothe, Ohio
www.chillicothe.ohiou.edu   CB code: 0775

- Public 4-year branch campus college
- Commuter campus in large town
- 2,350 degree-seeking undergraduates

General. Founded in 1946. Regionally accredited. **Degrees:** 201 associate awarded; master's offered. **Location:** 45 miles from Columbus. **Calendar:** Quarter, limited summer session. **Full-time faculty:** 46 total. **Part-time faculty:** 100 total.

Basis for selection. Open admission, but selective for some programs. Business, communications, education, and engineering colleges require high school GPA and ACT/SAT test scores. **Home schooled:** State high school equivalency certificate required. Passing scores on Ohio graduation test or GED required.

High school preparation. Recommended units include English 4, mathematics 3, social studies 3, science 3 and foreign language 2. College-preparatory program strongly recommended including 1 visual or performing art.

2011-2012 Annual costs. Tuition/fees: $4,713; $9,036 out-of-state. Books/supplies: $848.

Application procedures. Admission: No deadline. $20 fee, may be waived for applicants with need. Admission notification on a rolling basis. **Financial aid:** No deadline. FAFSA required. Applicants notified on a rolling basis.

Academics. Bachelor's programs in management, elementary education, criminal justice, nursing, technical and applied studies and self-designed

major. Degree granted by Ohio University main campus. **Special study options:** Distance learning, double major, dual enrollment of high school students, external degree, independent study, internships, student-designed major, study abroad, teacher certification program. **Credit/placement by examination:** AP, CLEP, institutional tests. **Support services:** Learning center, pre-admission summer program, remedial instruction, study skills assistance, tutoring, writing center.

Majors. Business: Business admin. **Communications:** Organizational. **Education:** Early childhood, middle. **Health services:** Nursing (RN). **Protective services:** Criminal justice. **Psychology:** General.

Computing on campus. 275 workstations in library, computer center, student center. Commuter students can connect to campus network. Online course registration, online library, helpline, student web hosting, wireless network available.

Student life. Freshman orientation: Available. Preregistration for classes offered. One-day session conducted prior to fall, winter and spring quarters. **Activities:** Drama, student government, student newspaper, National Communication Association, Ross County Association of Future Teachers, anime club, nursing student club, student programming club, human services association, law enforcement association, psychology club.

Athletics. Team name: Hilltoppers.

Student services. Adult student services, career counseling, services for economically disadvantaged, student employment services, financial aid counseling, personal counseling. **Physically disabled:** Services for visually, hearing impaired.

Contact. E-mail: lowej@ohio.edu
Phone: (740) 774-7240 Toll-free number: (877) 462-6824 ext. 240
Fax: (740) 774-7295
Jaime Lowe, Coordinator of Enrollment Services, Ohio University: Chillicothe Campus, 101 University Drive, Chillicothe, OH 45601

Ohio University: Eastern Campus
St. Clairsville, Ohio
www.eastern.ohiou.edu   CB code: 0828

- Public 4-year branch campus college
- Commuter campus in small town
- 1,017 degree-seeking undergraduates

General. Founded in 1957. Regionally accredited. **Degrees:** 77 bachelor's, 14 associate awarded; master's offered. **Location:** 7 miles from downtown; 14 miles from Wheeling, West Virginia. **Calendar:** Quarter, limited summer session. **Full-time faculty:** 20 total. **Part-time faculty:** 40 total. **Special facilities:** Primeval oak forest laboratory, Great Western School (Little Red Schoolhouse).

Basis for selection. Open admission, but selective for some programs. Special requirements for education, business, communication programs. SAT/ACT scores required for admission to education program.

High school preparation. Recommended units include English 4, mathematics 4, social studies 3, science 3 and foreign language 2.

2011-2012 Annual costs. Tuition/fees: $4,527; $5,847 out-of-state.

Financial aid. Non-need-based: Scholarships awarded for academics, alumni affiliation, minority status.

Application procedures. Admission: No deadline. $20 fee, may be waived for applicants with need. Admission notification on a rolling basis. **Financial aid:** Priority date 3/15; no closing date. FAFSA required.

Academics. Several degree programs offered through cross-registration with main campus. **Special study options:** Accelerated study, cooperative education, cross-registration, distance learning, double major, dual enrollment of high school students, external degree, independent study, internships, student-designed major, teacher certification program. **Credit/placement by examination:** AP, CLEP, institutional tests. **Support services:** Learning center, reduced course load, remedial instruction, study skills assistance, tutoring, writing center.

Majors. Education: Elementary. **Liberal arts:** Arts/sciences.

Computing on campus. 11 workstations in library, computer center. Online course registration available.

Student life. Freshman orientation: Available. Preregistration for classes offered. **Activities:** Drama.

Athletics. Intercollegiate: Basketball, golf M, volleyball W. **Intramural:** Basketball. **Team name:** Panthers.

Student services. Adult student services, career counseling, on-campus daycare, personal counseling.

Contact. E-mail: admissions@ohio.edu
Phone: (740) 695-1720 Fax: (740) 695-7077
Kevin Chenoweth, Student Services Manager, Ohio University: Eastern Campus, 45425 National Road West, St. Clairsville, OH 43950-9724

Ohio University: Lancaster Campus
Lancaster, Ohio
www.lancaster.ohiou.edu   CB code: 0826

- Public 4-year branch campus college
- Large town
- 2,514 undergraduates

General. Founded in 1968. Regionally accredited. Some bachelor's and master's degrees available, awarded through Athens campus. **Degrees:** 90 associate awarded; master's offered. **ROTC:** Army, Naval, Air Force. **Location:** 30 miles from Columbus. **Calendar:** Quarter, extensive summer session. **Full-time faculty:** 31 total. **Part-time faculty:** 112 total.

Basis for selection. Open admission, but selective for some programs. Special requirements for business, education, engineering and communication programs. ACT or SAT scores used in admission decisions to colleges of education, engineering. International students must take English fluency test through Ohio Program of Intensive English.

2011-2012 Annual costs. Tuition/fees: $4,713; $9,036 out-of-state. Books/supplies: $500.

Financial aid. Additional information: Scholarship application deadline April 1.

Application procedures. Admission: No deadline. $20 fee, may be waived for applicants with need. Admission notification on a rolling basis. **Financial aid:** Priority date 2/15; no closing date. FAFSA required. Applicants notified on a rolling basis; must reply within 2 week(s) of notification.

Academics. Special study options: Combined bachelor's/graduate degree, cross-registration, double major, independent study, internships, student-designed major. **Credit/placement by examination:** AP, CLEP, institutional tests. **Support services:** Learning center, remedial instruction, tutoring.

Computing on campus. 98 workstations in library, computer center, student center. Online course registration, online library, helpline, student web hosting available.

Student life. Freshman orientation: Available. Preregistration for classes offered. **Activities:** Choral groups, drama, student government, outdoor club, Young Democrats, Young Republicans, Christian Fellowship, adult support group.

Athletics. Intercollegiate: Baseball M, basketball, golf, softball W, tennis. **Intramural:** Skiing, table tennis, volleyball. **Team name:** Cougars.

Student services. Career counseling, student employment services, financial aid counseling, on-campus daycare, placement for graduates, veterans' counselor. **Physically disabled:** Services for visually, speech, hearing impaired.

Contact. E-mail: admissions@ohio.edu
Phone: (740) 654-6711 ext. 215 Toll-free number: (888) 446-4468
Fax: (740) 687-9497
Pat Fox, Enrollment Manager, Ohio University: Lancaster Campus, 1570 Granville Pike, Lancaster, OH 43130

Ohio University: Southern Campus at Ironton
Ironton, Ohio
www.southern.ohiou.edu   CB code: 1912

- Public 4-year branch campus college
- Commuter campus in large town
- 2,199 undergraduates

General. Founded in 1956. Regionally accredited. Student body reflects both traditional (65%) and non-traditional (45%) students who commute to classes from 3-state area (OH, KY, WV). **Degrees:** 161 associate awarded;

master's offered. **Location:** 20 miles from Huntington, West Virginia. **Calendar:** Quarter. **Full-time faculty:** 28 total. **Part-time faculty:** 105 total. **Special facilities:** Microwave link with main campus and other regional campuses, Ohio horse park, nature center, Proctorville center.

Basis for selection. Open admission. **Home schooled:** Transcript of courses and grades, state high school equivalency certificate required. Written verification from appropriate school district excusing attendance, personal statement discussing academic preparation for college, ACT, SAT required.

High school preparation. College-preparatory program recommended.

2011-2012 Annual costs. Tuition/fees: $4,527; $5,847 out-of-state. Books/supplies: $873. Personal expenses: $1,257.

Financial aid. Non-need-based: Scholarships awarded for academics, state residency.

Application procedures. Admission: No deadline. $20 fee, may be waived for applicants with need. Admission notification on a rolling basis. **Financial aid:** Priority date 3/15; no closing date. FAFSA required. Applicants notified on a rolling basis starting 4/1.

Academics. Special study options: Distance learning, double major, dual enrollment of high school students, teacher certification program. **Credit/placement by examination:** AP, CLEP, institutional tests. **Support services:** Learning center, remedial instruction, study skills assistance, tutoring, writing center.

Majors. Business: Business admin. **Communications:** Communications/speech/rhetoric, health, organizational, political. **Health services:** Nursing (RN). **History:** General. **Protective services:** Criminal justice. **Psychology:** General.

Computing on campus. Online course registration, online library, helpline, wireless network available.

Student life. Freshman orientation: Mandatory. Preregistration for classes offered. Summer and online orientations available. **Activities:** Concert band, international student organizations, literary magazine, music ensembles, radio station, student government, TV station, Phi Alpha Xi service honor society, Los Amigos Internacionales club, diversity student council, student nurses association, psychology club, art club.

Athletics. Intercollegiate: Equestrian.

Student services. Adult student services, career counseling, financial aid counseling, personal counseling, veterans' counselor. **Physically disabled:** Services for visually, speech, hearing impaired.

Contact. E-mail: askousc@ohiou.edu
Phone: (740) 533-4600 Toll-free number: (800) 626-0513
Fax: (740) 533-4632
Robert Pleasant, Director of Enrollment and Student Services, Ohio University: Southern Campus at Ironton, 1804 Liberty Avenue, Ironton, OH 45638

Ohio University: Zanesville Campus
Zanesville, Ohio
www.zanesville.ohiou.edu   CB code: 0846

- Public 4-year branch campus college
- Commuter campus in large town
- 1,982 degree-seeking undergraduates: 47% part-time, 70% women, 4% African American, 1% Hispanic American, 1% international

General. Founded in 1946. Regionally accredited. **Degrees:** 120 bachelor's, 135 associate awarded. **Location:** 55 miles from Columbus. **Calendar:** Quarter, limited summer session. **Full-time faculty:** 35 total. **Part-time faculty:** 75 total.

Freshman class profile. 556 applied, 496 admitted, 282 enrolled.

Basis for selection. Open admission, but selective for some programs. Nursing admissions based on National League for Nursing test scores, high school GPA, and class rank. Admission to Colleges of Business, Engineering, and Communication based on high school rank and ACT scores. Essay, audition, and portfolio recommended for all; interview recommended for nursing program. **Home schooled:** Transcript of courses and grades required.

High school preparation. College-preparatory program recommended. Recommended units include English 4, mathematics 3, social studies 3, science 3, foreign language 2 and visual/performing arts 1. One year of visual or performing arts recommended.

2011-2012 Annual costs. Tuition/fees: $4,728; $9,198 out-of-state. Books/supplies: $1,200. Personal expenses: $879.

Application procedures. Admission: No deadline. $20 fee, may be waived for applicants with need. Admission notification on a rolling basis. **Financial aid:** Priority date 3/15; no closing date. FAFSA required. Applicants notified on a rolling basis starting 4/15; must reply within 2 week(s) of notification.

Academics. Special study options: Cross-registration, double major, dual enrollment of high school students, independent study, internships, student-designed major, study abroad, teacher certification program. **Credit/placement by examination:** AP, CLEP, institutional tests. **Support services:** Learning center, reduced course load, remedial instruction, tutoring.

Majors. Communications: Health, organizational. **Education:** Early childhood, middle. **Health services:** Health services admin. **History:** General. **Human services:** Social work. **Protective services:** Police science.

Computing on campus. 50 workstations in library, computer center. Commuter students can connect to campus network. Online course registration, online library, wireless network available.

Student life. Freshman orientation: Mandatory. Preregistration for classes offered. **Activities:** Literary magazine, radio station, student government, cultural events committee, student nursing association.

Athletics. Intercollegiate: Baseball M, basketball, golf, tennis, volleyball W. **Intramural:** Badminton, basketball, bowling, golf, skiing, table tennis, tennis, volleyball. **Team name:** Tracers.

Student services. Chaplain/spiritual director, career counseling, student employment services, personal counseling, placement for graduates, veterans' counselor.

Contact. E-mail: ouzservices@ohio.edu
Phone: (740) 588-1439 Fax: (740) 588-1444
Jason Howard, Associate Director of Student Services, Ohio University: Zanesville Campus, 1425 Newark Road, Zanesville, OH 43701

Ohio Wesleyan University
Delaware, Ohio
www.owu.edu

CB member
CB code: 1594

- Private 4-year liberal arts college affiliated with United Methodist Church
- Residential campus in large town
- 1,819 degree-seeking undergraduates: 56% women, 4% African American, 2% Asian American, 2% Hispanic American, 8% international
- 70% of applicants admitted
- SAT or ACT (ACT writing optional), application essay required
- 61% graduate within 6 years

General. Founded in 1842. Regionally accredited. **Degrees:** 375 bachelor's awarded. **ROTC:** Army, Air Force. **Location:** 25 miles from Columbus. **Calendar:** Semester, limited summer session. **Full-time faculty:** 139 total; 98% have terminal degrees, 6% minority, 40% women. **Part-time faculty:** 81 total; 5% minority, 48% women. **Class size:** 70% < 20, 28% 20-39, 1% 40-49, less than 1% 50-99. **Special facilities:** 2 observatories, US Department of Agriculture laboratories, 2 nature field study preserves, science center, art museum.

Freshman class profile. 4,226 applied, 2,950 admitted, 483 enrolled.

Mid 50% test scores			
SAT critical reading:	520-650	GPA 2.0-2.99:	19%
SAT math:	510-650	Rank in top quarter:	61%
ACT composite:	22-29	Rank in top tenth:	29%
GPA 3.75 or higher:	29%	Return as sophomores:	82%
GPA 3.50-3.74:	21%	Out-of-state:	48%
GPA 3.0-3.49:	30%	Live on campus:	97%
		International:	7%

Basis for selection. High school record (level of challenge and success) most important, followed by class rank, recommendations, test scores, essay, extracurricular activities, general aptitude, character, volunteerism, alumni affiliation. Special consideration given to music, fine art and theater talent. Interview recommended for all. Audition required for music programs. Portfolio recommended for art programs. Essay required of all applicants. **Home schooled:** Statement describing home school structure and mission, state high school equivalency certificate, letter of recommendation (nonparent) required.

High school preparation. College-preparatory program required. 15 units required. Required and recommended units include English 4, mathematics 3-4, social studies 3-4, science 3-4 and foreign language 2-3.

2011-2012 Annual costs. Tuition/fees: $37,820. Room/board: $10,404. Books/supplies: $1,000.

Financial aid. Non-need-based: Scholarships awarded for academics, alumni affiliation, art, minority status, music/drama, religious affiliation, state residency.

Application procedures. Admission: Priority date 3/1; deadline 5/1 (postmark date). $35 fee, may be waived for applicants with need, free for online applicants. Admission notification on a rolling basis beginning on or about 3/1. Must reply by May 1 or within 2 week(s) if notified thereafter. **Financial aid:** Priority date 3/1, closing date 5/1. FAFSA, institutional form required. Applicants notified on a rolling basis starting 2/15; must reply by 5/1 or within 2 week(s) of notification.

Academics. Quantitative Skills Center provides individualized and alternative modes of instruction and tutoring to students who need assistance with math skills in any area of study. **Special study options:** Double major, dual enrollment of high school students, exchange student, honors, independent study, internships, New York semester, student-designed major, study abroad, teacher certification program, United Nations semester, urban semester, Washington semester. 3-2 engineering programs with Washington University (MO), Case Western Reserve University, California Institute of Technology (CA), Rensselaer Polytechnic Institute (NY), Alfred College of Ceramics (NY), and Polytechnic Institute of New York. **Credit/placement by examination:** AP, CLEP, IB, SAT, ACT, institutional tests. International Baccalaureate credit given for specific performance levels on higher exams. Students may receive exemption from certain requirements for test scores on SAT, SAT Subject Tests or ACT. **Support services:** Learning center, reduced course load, study skills assistance, tutoring, writing center.

Majors. Area/ethnic studies: African-American, East Asian, women's. **Biology:** General, bacteriology, biochemistry, botany, genetics, microbiology, neuroscience, zoology. **Business:** Accounting, international, managerial economics. **Communications:** Broadcast journalism, journalism. **Computer sciences:** General, computer science. **Conservation:** Environmental studies. **Education:** General, art, biology, chemistry, drama/dance, early childhood, elementary, foreign languages, French, German, health, kindergarten/preschool, Latin, mathematics, middle, multi-level teacher, music, physical, physics, science, secondary, social science, social studies, Spanish. **English:** American lit, British lit, creative writing, English lit, writing. **Foreign languages:** Biblical, classics, comparative lit, French, German, Latin, Spanish. **Health services:** Predental, premedicine, preveterinary. **History:** General. **Liberal arts:** Arts/sciences. **Math:** General, statistics. **Philosophy/religion:** Philosophy, religion. **Physical sciences:** Astronomy, chemistry, geology, physics. **Psychology:** General. **Social sciences:** Anthropology, economics, geography, international relations, political science, sociology, U.S. government, urban studies. **Theology:** Preministerial. **Visual/performing arts:** Art history/conservation, dance, dramatic, music, music performance, studio arts.

Most popular majors. Biology 11%, business/marketing 11%, foreign language 8%, psychology 8%, social sciences 17%, visual/performing arts 10%.

Computing on campus. 300 workstations in dormitories, library, computer center, student center. Dormitories wired for high-speed internet access and linked to campus network. Commuter students can connect to campus network. Online library, helpline, repair service, student web hosting, wireless network available.

Student life. Freshman orientation: Mandatory. Preregistration for classes offered. Two-day session held in June and during the week before classes begin in August. **Housing:** Guaranteed on-campus for all undergraduates. Coed dorms, single-sex dorms, apartments, fraternity/sorority housing, wellness housing available. $400 nonrefundable deposit, deadline 5/1. Pets allowed in dorm rooms. Small living units for groups of 10-15 students. **Activities:** Bands, campus ministries, choral groups, dance, drama, international student organizations, literary magazine, music ensembles, Model UN, musical theater, opera, radio station, student government, student newspaper, symphony orchestra, B'nai B'rith Hillel Chapter, Christian Fellowship, Young Democrats, College Republicans, student union on black awareness, Sisters United, Tauheed, gay/lesbian/bisexual/transgender center, women's resource center, Habitat for Humanity.

Athletics. NCAA. Intercollegiate: Baseball M, basketball, cross-country, diving, field hockey W, football (tackle) M, golf M, lacrosse, soccer, softball W, swimming, tennis, track and field, volleyball W. **Intramural:** Badminton, basketball, equestrian, football (non-tackle) M, golf, handball, lacrosse, racquetball, soccer, softball, squash, swimming, tennis, track and field, volleyball, water polo. **Team name:** Battling Bishops.

Student services. Alcohol/substance abuse counseling, chaplain/spiritual director, career counseling, student employment services, financial aid counseling, health services, minority student services, on-campus daycare, personal counseling.

Contact. E-mail: owuadmit@owu.edu
Phone: (740) 368-3020 Toll-free number: (800) 922-8953
Fax: (740) 368-3314
Carol DelPropost, Assistant Vice President of Admission and Financial Aid, Ohio Wesleyan University, 75 South Sandusky Street, Delaware, OH 43015-2398

Otterbein University
Westerville, Ohio — CB member
www.otterbein.edu — CB code: 1597

- Private 4-year university and liberal arts college affiliated with United Methodist Church
- Residential campus in large town
- 2,484 degree-seeking undergraduates: 9% part-time, 63% women
- 422 graduate students
- 82% of applicants admitted
- SAT or ACT (ACT writing optional), application essay required
- 62% graduate within 6 years; 18% enter graduate study

General. Founded in 1847. Regionally accredited. **Degrees:** 617 bachelor's awarded; master's, professional offered. **ROTC:** Army, Air Force. **Location:** 12 miles from Columbus. **Calendar:** 4-1-4, limited summer session. **Full-time faculty:** 174 total; 54% women. **Part-time faculty:** 163 total; 48% women. **Class size:** 78% < 20, 18% 20-39, 2% 40-49, 2% 50-99, less than 1% >100. **Special facilities:** Horse stables and riding facility, 3 performance stages, 3 art galleries.

Freshman class profile. 3,381 applied, 2,774 admitted, 653 enrolled.

Mid 50% test scores			
SAT critical reading:	480-600	GPA 3.0-3.49:	28%
SAT math:	490-600	GPA 2.0-2.99:	21%
SAT writing:	460-590	Rank in top quarter:	55%
ACT composite:	21-26	Rank in top tenth:	26%
GPA 3.75 or higher:	30%	Return as sophomores:	75%
GPA 3.50-3.74:	21%	Live on campus:	80%

Basis for selection. School achievement record most important; test scores also important. Recommendations, essay, interview, and extracurricular activities considered. Visit recommended for all; audition required for music and theater programs; portfolio recommended for visual art program. Essays required for scholarships. **Home schooled:** Statement describing home school structure and mission, transcript of courses and grades required. Submit written documentation of successful completion of college preparatory high school equivalency. Transcripts from cooperating school district preferred. **Learning Disabled:** Students with diagnosed learning disabilities recommended to send documentation with admission application.

High school preparation. College-preparatory program recommended. Recommended units include English 4, mathematics 3, social studies 3, science 3 and foreign language 2. One unit in fine arts recommended.

2011-2012 Annual costs. Tuition/fees: $29,550. Room/board: $8,252. Books/supplies: $1,174. Personal expenses: $1,514.

Financial aid. Non-need-based: Scholarships awarded for academics, alumni affiliation, art, leadership, minority status, music/drama, state residency.

Application procedures. Admission: Priority date 2/1; no deadline. No application fee. Admission notification on a rolling basis beginning on or about 10/1. Must reply by May 1 or within 4 week(s) if notified thereafter. Students applying between May 1 and June 1 accepted on space-available basis. **Financial aid:** Priority date 4/1; no closing date. FAFSA required. Applicants notified on a rolling basis starting 2/15.

Academics. Special study options: Combined bachelor's/graduate degree, cross-registration, double major, dual enrollment of high school students, ESL, exchange student, honors, independent study, internships, liberal arts/career combination, student-designed major, study abroad, teacher certification program, Washington semester. BA/BS in engineering with Washington University (MO) or Case Western Reserve University. **Credit/placement by examination:** AP, CLEP, IB, SAT, ACT, institutional tests. 60 credit hours maximum toward bachelor's degree. **Support services:** Learning center, reduced course load, remedial instruction, study skills assistance, tutoring, writing center.

Honors college/program. Presidential Scholars or must be in top 10% of high school class and have 25 ACT.

Majors. Biology: General, biochemistry, molecular. **Business:** General, accounting, actuarial science, business admin, finance, managerial economics. **Communications:** Broadcast journalism, communications/speech/rhetoric, journalism, organizational, public relations. **Computer sciences:** Computer science. **Conservation:** General, environmental studies, management/policy. **Education:** General, art, biology, chemistry, early childhood, elementary, English, foreign languages, French, health, history, mathematics, middle, multi-level teacher, music, physical, physics, science, secondary, social studies, Spanish, special ed. **English:** Creative writing, English lit, writing. **Foreign languages:** French, Spanish. **General:** Equestrian studies. **Health services:** Athletic training, nursing (RN), predental, premedicine, prepharmacy, preveterinary. **History:** General. **Math:** General. **Parks/recreation:** Health/fitness, sports admin. **Philosophy/religion:** Philosophy, religion. **Physical sciences:** Chemistry, physics. **Psychology:** General. **Social sciences:** Economics, international relations, political science, sociology. **Visual/performing arts:** General, acting, art, dramatic, music, music history, music performance, music theory/composition, theater design.

Most popular majors. Business/marketing 14%, communications/journalism 12%, education 11%, health sciences 13%, psychology 6%, social sciences 7%, visual/performing arts 15%.

Computing on campus. 124 workstations in dormitories, library, computer center. Dormitories wired for high-speed internet access and linked to campus network. Commuter students can connect to campus network. Online course registration, helpline, wireless network available.

Student life. Freshman orientation: Mandatory, $150 fee. Preregistration for classes offered. One-day orientation held in July or August. **Housing:** Guaranteed on-campus for freshmen. Coed dorms, single-sex dorms, apartments, fraternity/sorority housing available. **Activities:** Bands, campus ministries, choral groups, dance, drama, international student organizations, literary magazine, music ensembles, musical theater, opera, radio station, student government, student newspaper, symphony orchestra, TV station, Fellowship of Christian Athletes, Christian support group, Afro-American student union, Asian American student union, international students association, religious life council.

Athletics. NCAA. **Intercollegiate:** Baseball M, basketball, cross-country, equestrian, football (tackle) M, golf, lacrosse, soccer, softball W, tennis, track and field, volleyball W. **Intramural:** Basketball, bowling, football (non-tackle) M, handball, racquetball, soccer, softball, volleyball. **Team name:** Cardinals.

Student services. Adult student services, alcohol/substance abuse counseling, chaplain/spiritual director, career counseling, student employment services, financial aid counseling, health services, minority student services, personal counseling, veterans' counselor.

Contact. E-mail: uotterb@otterbein.edu
Phone: (614) 823-1500 Toll-free number: (800) 488-8144
Fax: (614) 823-1200
Ben Shoemaker, Director of Admission, Otterbein University, One Otterbein College, Westerville, OH 43081

Pontifical College Josephinum
Columbus, Ohio
www.pcj.edu — CB code: 1348

- Private 4-year liberal arts and seminary college for men affiliated with Roman Catholic Church
- Residential campus in very large city
- 85 degree-seeking undergraduates
- 68 degree-seeking graduate students
- 96% of applicants admitted
- SAT or ACT (ACT writing optional), application essay, interview required
- 50% graduate within 6 years; 95% enter graduate study

General. Founded in 1892. Regionally accredited; also accredited by ATS. **Degrees:** 29 bachelor's awarded; master's offered. **Location:** 11 miles from downtown. **Calendar:** Semester. **Full-time faculty:** 17 total; 65% have terminal degrees, 35% women. **Part-time faculty:** 3 total; 67% have terminal degrees, 100% women. **Class size:** 80% < 20, 19% 20-39, 2% 50-99.

Freshman class profile. 25 applied, 24 admitted, 24 enrolled.

Mid 50% test scores			
SAT critical reading:	560-730	End year in good standing:	95%
SAT math:	470-680	Return as sophomores:	92%
SAT writing:	500-650	Out-of-state:	64%
ACT composite:	20-27	Live on campus:	100%

Basis for selection. School achievement record, recommendations from pastor and director of vocations required. **Home schooled:** Transcript of courses and grades required.

High school preparation. College-preparatory program recommended. 10 units required; 18 recommended. Required and recommended units include English 4, mathematics 2-4, social studies 2-4, science 1-4 and foreign language 1-2.

2011-2012 Annual costs. Tuition/fees: $18,999. Room/board: $8,390. Books/supplies: $1,000.

2010-2011 Financial aid. All financial aid based on need. 12 full-time freshmen applied for aid; 12 were judged to have need; 8 of these received aid. Average need met was 62%. Average scholarship/grant was $4,200; average loan $1,990. 59% of total undergraduate aid awarded as scholarships/grants, 41% as loans/jobs.

Application procedures. **Admission:** Priority date 8/1; no deadline. $25 fee, may be waived for applicants with need. Application must be submitted on paper. Admission notification on a rolling basis beginning on or about 5/1. **Financial aid:** Priority date 9/2; no closing date. FAFSA, institutional form required. Applicants notified on a rolling basis starting 8/15; must reply within 2 week(s) of notification.

Academics. Students participate in supervised field experience and clinical pastoral education. **Special study options:** Double major, ESL, honors, independent study. **Credit/placement by examination:** AP, CLEP, IB, institutional tests. 30 credit hours maximum toward bachelor's degree. **Support services:** Learning center, reduced course load, remedial instruction, tutoring, writing center.

Majors. **Area/ethnic studies:** Chicano/Hispanic-American/Latino, Latin American. **English:** English lit. **History:** General. **Liberal arts:** Humanities. **Philosophy/religion:** Philosophy, religion.

Most popular majors. Philosophy/religious studies 83%.

Computing on campus. 16 workstations in library, computer center. Dormitories wired for high-speed internet access and linked to campus network. Commuter students can connect to campus network. Online course registration, online library, helpline, wireless network available.

Student life. Freshman orientation: Mandatory. Preregistration for classes offered. **Policies:** Daily chapel, morning and evening prayer. Religious observance required. **Activities:** Choral groups, music ensembles, student government.

Athletics. Intramural: Basketball M, soccer M, softball M.

Student services. Chaplain/spiritual director, career counseling, financial aid counseling, health services, personal counseling.

Contact. E-mail: acrawford@pcj.edu
Phone: (614) 985-2241 Toll-free number: (888) 252-5812
Fax: (614) 885-2307
V. Rev. James Wehner, Director of Admissions, Pontifical College Josephinum, 7625 North High Street, Columbus, OH 43235-1499

Rabbinical College of Telshe
Wickliffe, Ohio

CB code: 1660

- Private 4-year rabbinical and teachers college for men affiliated with Jewish faith
- Small city

General. Founded in 1941. Accredited by AARTS. **Degrees:** 3 bachelor's awarded; master's offered. **Calendar:** Semester. **Full-time faculty:** 10 total. **Part-time faculty:** 15 total.

Basis for selection. GED not accepted. Personal interview and religious commitment most important. **Home schooled:** Interview required.

2011-2012 Annual costs. Books/supplies: $300.

Application procedures. Admission: Closing date 8/15. $100 fee.

Academics. Credit/placement by examination: AP, CLEP.

Majors. Theology: Talmudic.

Student life. Freshman orientation: Mandatory. Preregistration for classes offered.

Contact. Phone: (440) 943-5300 ext. 17 Fax: (440) 943-5303
Rabbi Abraham Matitia, Registrar, Rabbinical College of Telshe, 28400 Euclid Avenue, Wickliffe, OH 44092-2584

Shawnee State University
Portsmouth, Ohio
www.shawnee.edu

CB member
CB code: 1790

- Public 4-year university
- Commuter campus in large town
- 4,436 degree-seeking undergraduates: 14% part-time, 57% women, 5% African American, 1% Hispanic American, 1% Native American, 1% international
- 93 degree-seeking graduate students

General. Founded in 1986. Regionally accredited. **Degrees:** 361 bachelor's, 200 associate awarded; master's offered. **Location:** 90 miles from Columbus, 90 miles from Cincinnati. **Calendar:** Semester, extensive summer session. **Full-time faculty:** 145 total; 57% have terminal degrees, 8% minority, 46% women. **Part-time faculty:** 171 total; 2% minority, 46% women. **Class size:** 43% < 20, 48% 20-39, 5% 40-49, 3% 50-99, less than 1% >100. **Special facilities:** Planetarium, motion capture studio.

Freshman class profile. 4,451 applied, 3,766 admitted, 1,187 enrolled.

Mid 50% test scores		End year in good standing:	56%
SAT critical reading:	390-540	Return as sophomores:	52%
SAT math:	410-560	Out-of-state:	10%
ACT composite:	17-23	Live on campus:	40%
Rank in top quarter:	30%	Fraternities:	1%
Rank in top tenth:	10%	Sororities:	1%

Basis for selection. Open admission, but selective for some programs. ACT required, interview recommended for admission to allied health programs. SAT/ACT may be used in lieu of university-developed placement test. **Home schooled:** State high school equivalency certificate required. GED required.

High school preparation. College-preparatory program recommended. 16 units recommended. Recommended units include English 4, mathematics 3, social studies 3, science 3 and foreign language 2. Algebra, biology, chemistry required for allied health programs.

2011-2012 Annual costs. Tuition/fees: $6,762; $11,568 out-of-state. Room/board: $8,698. Books/supplies: $1,440. Personal expenses: $2,350.

Financial aid. Non-need-based: Scholarships awarded for academics. **Additional information:** ACT recommended for scholarship applicants.

Application procedures. Admission: No deadline. No application fee. Admission notification on a rolling basis. Applicants to allied health programs advised to apply by February 1. **Financial aid:** Priority date 6/15; no closing date. FAFSA, institutional form required. Applicants notified on a rolling basis starting 5/1; must reply within 4 week(s) of notification.

Academics. Special study options: Accelerated study, combined bachelor's/graduate degree, distance learning, double major, dual enrollment of high school students, ESL, honors, independent study, internships, student-designed major, study abroad, teacher certification program. **Credit/placement by examination:** AP, CLEP, institutional tests. SAT/ACT may be used in lieu of university-developed placement test. **Support services:** Learning center, reduced course load, remedial instruction, study skills assistance, tutoring, writing center.

Majors. Biology: General. **Business:** Business admin. **Education:** General, art, early childhood, elementary special ed, mathematics, multi-level teacher, science, social science, special ed. **English:** English lit. **Health services:** Athletic training, nursing (RN). **History:** General. **Math:** General. **Parks/recreation:** Health/fitness, sports admin. **Physical sciences:** Chemistry, geology. **Psychology:** General. **Social sciences:** General, international relations, sociology. **Visual/performing arts:** Game design, studio arts.

Most popular majors. Biology 9%, business/marketing 17%, education 12%, engineering/engineering technologies 7%, health sciences 7%, parks/recreation 6%, psychology 7%, social sciences 13%, visual/performing arts 7%.

Computing on campus. 620 workstations in library, computer center, student center. Dormitories wired for high-speed internet access. Online course registration, online library, helpline, wireless network available.

Student life. Freshman orientation: Mandatory. Preregistration for classes offered. One-day programs held throughout the summer. **Housing:** Coed dorms available. $150 partly refundable deposit. **Activities:** Campus

ministries, choral groups, drama, international student organizations, literary magazine, music ensembles, musical theater, student government, student newspaper, health executives and administrators learning society, student programming board, Habitat for Humanity.

Athletics. NAIA. **Intercollegiate:** Baseball M, basketball, cross-country, golf M, soccer, softball W, tennis W, volleyball W. **Intramural:** Basketball, bowling, golf, racquetball, softball M, swimming, table tennis, tennis, volleyball. **Team name:** Bears.

Student services. Alcohol/substance abuse counseling, career counseling, services for economically disadvantaged, student employment services, financial aid counseling, health services, on-campus daycare, personal counseling, placement for graduates, veterans' counselor. **Physically disabled:** Services for visually, speech, hearing impaired.

Contact. E-mail: to_ssu@shawnee.edu
Phone: (740) 351-4778 Toll-free number: (800) 959-2778
Fax: (740) 351-3111
Bob Trusz, Director of Admissions, Shawnee State University, 940 Second Street, Portsmouth, OH 45662

Tiffin University
Tiffin, Ohio
www.tiffin.edu

CB member
CB code: 1817

▶ Private 4-year university and liberal arts college
▶ Residential campus in large town
▶ 5,361 degree-seeking undergraduates: 54% part-time, 63% women, 32% African American, 1% Asian American, 4% Hispanic American, 1% Native American, 1% international
▶ 1,144 degree-seeking graduate students
▶ 51% of applicants admitted
▶ 47% graduate within 6 years

General. Founded in 1888. Regionally accredited. Off-campus courses offered in Cleveland, Lorain, Columbus, Elyria, Toledo, Fremont, and Cincinnati. **Degrees:** 339 bachelor's, 19 associate awarded; master's offered. **ROTC:** Army, Air Force. **Location:** 50 miles from Toledo, 90 miles from Columbus. **Calendar:** Semester, limited summer session. **Full-time faculty:** 77 total; 60% have terminal degrees, 12% minority, 44% women. **Part-time faculty:** 369 total; 22% have terminal degrees, 8% minority, 50% women. **Class size:** 51% < 20, 46% 20-39, 3% 40-49. **Special facilities:** Nature preserve.

Freshman class profile. 7,082 applied, 3,615 admitted, 1,682 enrolled.

Mid 50% test scores			
SAT critical reading:	420-510	Rank in top quarter:	23%
SAT math:	420-540	Rank in top tenth:	8%
ACT composite:	18-23	Return as sophomores:	69%
GPA 3.75 or higher:	7%	Out-of-state:	66%
GPA 3.50-3.74:	11%	Live on campus:	26%
GPA 3.0-3.49:	35%	Fraternities:	1%
GPA 2.0-2.99:	46%	Sororities:	1%

Basis for selection. Test scores, GPA very important. Students with below 2.0 GPA may be admitted conditionally into Learning Assistance Program. SAT or ACT recommended. Interview required for academically weak applicants.

High school preparation. College-preparatory program recommended. Recommended units include English 4, mathematics 3, social studies 3, science 3 and foreign language 2.

2012-2013 Annual costs. Tuition/fees (projected): $19,890. Room/board: $9,202. Books/supplies: $1,500. Personal expenses: $2,700.

2011-2012 Financial aid. Need-based: 709 full-time freshmen applied for aid; 680 were judged to have need; 679 of these received aid. Average need met was 58%. Average scholarship/grant was $9,844; average loan $4,089. 51% of total undergraduate aid awarded as scholarships/grants, 49% as loans/jobs. **Non-need-based:** Awarded to 181 full-time undergraduates, including 47 freshmen. Scholarships awarded for academics, alumni affiliation, athletics, leadership, music/drama, state residency.

Application procedures. Admission: No deadline. $20 fee, may be waived for applicants with need, free for online applicants. Admission notification on a rolling basis beginning on or about 9/15. **Financial aid:** No deadline. FAFSA required. Applicants notified on a rolling basis starting 1/15; must reply within 2 week(s) of notification.

Academics. Special study options: Accelerated study, cross-registration, distance learning, double major, dual enrollment of high school students,

ESL, exchange student, external degree, honors, independent study, internships, study abroad, teacher certification program, Washington semester. **Credit/placement by examination:** AP, CLEP, IB, SAT, ACT, institutional tests. 15 credit hours maximum toward associate degree, 30 toward bachelor's. **Support services:** Learning center, pre-admission summer program, reduced course load, remedial instruction, study skills assistance, tutoring, writing center.

Majors. Business: Accounting, business admin, e-commerce, finance, hospitality admin, human resources, international, logistics, marketing, nonprofit/public, operations, organizational behavior. **Communications:** Communications/speech/rhetoric, digital media, journalism, media studies, public relations. **Computer sciences:** General, information systems, information technology. **Education:** General, English, history, science. **English:** English lit. **General:** Equine science. **Health services:** Health care admin, health services admin, long term care admin, substance abuse counseling. **History:** General. **Liberal arts:** Arts/sciences. **Parks/recreation:** Sports admin. **Protective services:** Computer forensics, corrections, counterterrorism, forensics, homeland security, law enforcement admin, special ops. **Psychology:** General, experimental, forensic, industrial. **Social sciences:** Criminology, international relations. **Visual/performing arts:** Art, music, music management, studio arts management.

Most popular majors. Business/marketing 51%, psychology 8%, security/protective services 32%.

Computing on campus. 300 workstations in dormitories, library, computer center, student center. Dormitories wired for high-speed internet access and linked to campus network. Commuter students can connect to campus network. Online course registration, online library, helpline, repair service, wireless network available.

Student life. Freshman orientation: Available. Preregistration for classes offered. Three-part program; first part occurs on a Saturday in April or May, or on a Friday in June; second part is a weekend in late July; third part occurs during first weekend of classes. **Policies:** Lower-division residential students required to be on meal plan. All undergraduates complete 26 hours of co-curricular credit. **Housing:** Guaranteed on-campus for freshmen. Coed dorms, single-sex dorms, special housing for disabled, apartments, fraternity/sorority housing available. $49 partly refundable deposit, deadline 4/9. Theme housing, performing arts, leadership society, junior/senior house units. **Activities:** Bands, campus ministries, choral groups, dance, drama, international student organizations, literary magazine, music ensembles, musical theater, student government, student newspaper, symphony orchestra, Black United Students, World Student Organization, Greek Council, H2O, Delta Sigma Kappa, gospel choir, Circle K, residence life council, Student African-American Brotherhood, Student African-American Sisterhood for Excellence.

Athletics. NCAA. **Intercollegiate:** Baseball M, basketball, cross-country, equestrian, football (tackle) M, golf, lacrosse W, soccer, softball W, tennis, track and field, volleyball W, wrestling M. **Intramural:** Basketball, cross-country. **Team name:** Dragons.

Student services. Adult student services, career counseling, student employment services, financial aid counseling, health services, minority student services, personal counseling, placement for graduates, veterans' counselor, women's services.

Contact. E-mail: admissions@tiffin.edu
Phone: (419) 447-6443 ext. 3423
Toll-free number: (800) 968-6446 ext. 3423 Fax: (419) 443-5006
Ronald Schumacher, Vice President for Enrollment Management, Tiffin University, 155 Miami Street, Tiffin, OH 44883

Tri-State Bible College
South Point, Ohio
www.tsbc.edu

▶ Private 4-year Bible college
▶ Commuter campus in rural community
▶ 60 degree-seeking undergraduates

General. Accredited by ABHE. **Degrees:** 5 bachelor's awarded. **Location:** 150 miles from Cincinnati, 150 miles from Columbus, 50 miles from Charleston, WV. **Calendar:** Semester, limited summer session. **Full-time faculty:** 6 total. **Part-time faculty:** 14 total.

Basis for selection. Open admission. **Home schooled:** State high school equivalency certificate required.

High school preparation. College-preparatory program recommended.

2011-2012 Annual costs. Tuition/fees: $9,500. Books/supplies: $530. Personal expenses: $2,016.

Application procedures. Admission: Closing date 9/15 (postmark date). $25 fee.

Academics. Credit/placement by examination: AP, CLEP.

Student life. Activities: Student newspaper.

Contact. E-mail: cmark@zoominternet.net
Phone: (740) 377-2520 Fax: (740) 377-0001
Ken Law, Director of Admission, Tri-State Bible College, 506 Margaret Street, South Point, OH 45680-0445

Union Institute & University
Cincinnati, Ohio   **CB member**
www.myunion.edu

- Private 4-year university
- Commuter campus in very large city
- 1,101 degree-seeking undergraduates: 37% part-time, 53% women, 28% African American, 1% Asian American, 14% Hispanic American, 1% Native American
- 488 degree-seeking graduate students
- Application essay required

General. Founded in 1964. Regionally accredited. Academic centers in Montpelier and Brattleboro, Vermont; North Miami Beach, Florida; Los Angeles and Sacramento, California. **Degrees:** 525 bachelor's awarded; master's, doctoral offered. **Location:** 2 miles from downtown. **Calendar:** Continuous, extensive summer session. **Full-time faculty:** 31 total; 90% have terminal degrees, 19% minority, 52% women. **Part-time faculty:** 320 total; 51% have terminal degrees, 22% minority, 51% women.

Freshman class profile.

Return as sophomores:	71%	Out-of-state:	2%

Basis for selection. Maturity and evidence of ability to engage in self-directed learning is important. Programs designed for adult learners; majority are over age 25.

2011-2012 Annual costs. Tuition/fees: $14,310. Books/supplies: $1,000.

Financial aid. Non-need-based: Scholarships awarded for academics, state residency.

Application procedures. Admission: No deadline. No application fee. Admission notification on a rolling basis. **Financial aid:** No deadline. FAFSA required. Must reply within 4 week(s) of notification.

Academics. Many courses available through online learning. Serves adult learners, and offers both standardized curricula (B.S.) and individualized learning (B.A.) programs. **Special study options:** Accelerated study, distance learning, double major, independent study, internships, teacher certification program, weekend college. **Credit/placement by examination:** AP, CLEP, IB. 30 credit hours maximum toward bachelor's degree. **Support services:** Reduced course load, tutoring, writing center.

Majors. Business: Business admin. **Education:** General, elementary, ESL, mathematics, multi-level teacher, reading, secondary, social studies, special ed. **Health services:** Maternal/child health. **Human services:** General, social work. **Liberal arts:** Arts/sciences. **Protective services:** Disaster management, law enforcement admin. **Work/family studies:** Child development.

Most popular majors. Business/marketing 8%, family/consumer sciences 11%, liberal arts 13%, security/protective services 49%.

Computing on campus. 74 workstations in computer center. Commuter students can connect to campus network. Online course registration, online library, helpline, wireless network available.

Student life. Freshman orientation: Available. Preregistration for classes offered. **Housing:** Short term on-campus housing provided for B.A. program in Montpelier, Vermont for students participating in brief residencies.

Student services. Adult student services, career counseling, financial aid counseling, veterans' counselor. **Physically disabled:** Services for visually, speech, hearing impaired.

Contact. E-mail: admissions@myunion.edu
Phone: (800) 486-3116 Toll-free number: (800) 486-3116
Fax: (802) 828-8565
Jon Mays, Vice President, Enrollment Management, Union Institute & University, 440 East McMillan Street, Cincinnati, OH 45206

University of Akron
Akron, Ohio   **CB member**
www.uakron.edu   **CB code: 1829**

- Public 4-year university
- Commuter campus in small city
- 21,445 degree-seeking undergraduates: 19% part-time, 48% women, 17% African American, 2% Asian American, 2% Hispanic American, 1% international
- 4,343 degree-seeking graduate students
- 74% of applicants admitted
- SAT or ACT (ACT writing recommended) required
- 35% graduate within 6 years

General. Founded in 1870. Regionally accredited. **Degrees:** 2,815 bachelor's, 495 associate awarded; master's, professional, doctoral offered. **ROTC:** Army, Air Force. **Location:** 40 miles from Cleveland. **Calendar:** Semester, limited summer session. **Full-time faculty:** 776 total; 82% have terminal degrees, 16% minority, 42% women. **Part-time faculty:** 955 total; 29% have terminal degrees, 9% minority, 53% women. **Class size:** 39% < 20, 49% 20-39, 5% 40-49, 5% 50-99, 2% >100. **Special facilities:** Polymer training center, bath nature preserve field station, gas turbine testing facility, training center for fire and hazardous materials.

Freshman class profile. 14,413 applied, 10,673 admitted, 4,464 enrolled.

Mid 50% test scores			
SAT critical reading:	440-570	GPA 2.0-2.99:	38%
SAT math:	430-590	Rank in top quarter:	30%
ACT composite:	18-24	Rank in top tenth:	12%
GPA 3.75 or higher:	16%	Return as sophomores:	73%
GPA 3.50-3.74:	11%	Out-of-state:	5%
GPA 3.0-3.49:	24%	Live on campus:	48%
		International:	1%

Basis for selection. School record, class rank, GPA, and test scores most important. Open access to Summit College Student Success Program and Wayne College. Essay, interview required for honors program; audition required for dance, music programs. **Home schooled:** Students required to obtain letter of exemption from school district.

High school preparation. College-preparatory program recommended. 15 units recommended. Recommended units include English 4, mathematics 3, social studies 3, science 3 and foreign language 2.

2011-2012 Annual costs. Tuition/fees: $9,545; $17,468 out-of-state. Room/board: $9,586. Books/supplies: $900. Personal expenses: $1,520.

2010-2011 Financial aid. Need-based: 4,090 full-time freshmen applied for aid; 3,627 were judged to have need; 3,627 of these received aid. Average need met was 64%. Average scholarship/grant was $5,300; average loan $3,274. 47% of total undergraduate aid awarded as scholarships/grants, 53% as loans/jobs. **Non-need-based:** Scholarships awarded for academics, art, athletics, leadership, music/drama, ROTC, state residency.

Application procedures. Admission: Closing date 7/15 (receipt date). $40 fee, may be waived for applicants with need. Admission notification on a rolling basis beginning on or about 9/15. **Financial aid:** Priority date 2/1; no closing date. FAFSA, institutional form required. Applicants notified on a rolling basis starting 4/1; must reply within 2 week(s) of notification.

Academics. Special study options: Accelerated study, combined bachelor's/graduate degree, cooperative education, distance learning, double major, ESL, external degree, honors, independent study, internships, student-designed major, study abroad, teacher certification program, weekend college. Undergraduates may take graduate level classes. Co-op programs in arts, business, computer science, engineering, family & consumer sciences, humanities, natural science, technologies. Dual enrollment offered for select graduate level programs. **Credit/placement by examination:** AP, CLEP, IB, SAT, ACT, institutional tests. 38 credit hours maximum toward associate degree, 38 toward bachelor's. **Support services:** Learning center, reduced course load, remedial instruction, study skills assistance, tutoring, writing center.

Honors college/program. Must have 2 out of 3 of following criteria: 3.5 GPA; high school class rank in highest 10%; 27 ACT or 1200 SAT (exclusive of Writing). Some students with other unique qualifications may be admitted.

Majors. Architecture: Urban/community planning. **Biology:** General, animal physiology, biochemistry, botany, ecology, microbiology, zoology. **Business:** Accounting, business admin, e-commerce, financial planning, hotel/motel admin, human resources, international, management information systems, marketing, operations, sales/distribution. **Communications:** Broadcast journalism, media studies, organizational, public relations, radio/TV. **Computer sciences:** Computer science, networking. **Education:** Art, drama/

dance, early childhood, early childhood special, English, family/consumer sciences, French, mathematics, middle, music, physical, science, social studies, Spanish, special ed, voc/tech. **Engineering:** General, biomedical, chemical, civil, computer, electrical, mechanical, polymer. **English:** English lit. **Foreign languages:** Classics, French, Spanish. **Health services:** Athletic training, audiology/speech pathology, communication disorders, dietetics, licensed practical nurse, nursing (RN), recreational therapy, respiratory therapy technology. **History:** General. **Human services:** Social work. **Liberal arts:** Arts/sciences, humanities. **Math:** General, applied, statistics. **Parks/recreation:** Exercise sciences, sports admin. **Philosophy/religion:** Philosophy. **Physical sciences:** Chemistry, geology, geophysics, physics, polymer chemistry. **Protective services:** Criminal justice, fire safety technology. **Psychology:** General. **Social sciences:** General, anthropology, criminology, economics, geography, GIS/cartography, international relations, sociology, U.S. government. **Visual/performing arts:** Art history/conservation, ceramics, dance, dramatic, graphic design, jazz, metal/jewelry, music, music history, music performance, music theory/composition, photography, piano/keyboard, printmaking, sculpture, stringed instruments, studio arts, voice/opera. **Work/family studies:** Child development, clothing/textiles, family systems, housing.

Most popular majors. Business/marketing 18%, communications/journalism 11%, education 10%, engineering/engineering technologies 12%, health sciences 15%.

Computing on campus. 3,100 workstations in dormitories, library, student center. Dormitories wired for high-speed internet access and linked to campus network. Commuter students can connect to campus network. Online course registration, online library, helpline, repair service, student web hosting, wireless network available.

Student life. Freshman orientation: Mandatory, $50 fee. Preregistration for classes offered. One-day program. **Policies:** All student organizations make own criteria for members, but some criteria stipulated through university, such as 2.0 GPA requirement and good standing within university. **Housing:** Coed dorms, single-sex dorms, special housing for disabled, fraternity/sorority housing available. $150 nonrefundable deposit, deadline 5/15. Honors student dormitory. **Activities:** Bands, campus ministries, choral groups, dance, drama, international student organizations, music ensembles, musical theater, radio station, student government, student newspaper, symphony orchestra, TV station, Chinese students and scholars association, Indian students association, Muslim students association, black united students, H.O.L.A., Hillel, College Republicans, College Democrats, Campus Focus, gospel choir.

Athletics. NCAA. **Intercollegiate:** Baseball M, basketball, cheerleading, cross-country, diving W, football (tackle) M, golf M, rifle, soccer, softball W, swimming W, tennis W, track and field, volleyball W. **Intramural:** Badminton, basketball, bowling, cross-country, golf, racquetball, skiing, soccer, softball, swimming, table tennis, track and field, volleyball W, wrestling M. **Team name:** Zips.

Student services. Adult student services, alcohol/substance abuse counseling, career counseling, student employment services, financial aid counseling, health services, minority student services, on-campus daycare, personal counseling, placement for graduates, veterans' counselor, women's services. **Physically disabled:** Services for visually, speech, hearing impaired.

Contact. E-mail: admissions@uakron.edu
Phone: (330) 972-7100 Toll-free number: (800) 655-4884
Fax: (330) 972-7022
Diane Raybuck, Director of Admissions, University of Akron, Simmons Hall, Akron, OH 44325-2001

University of Cincinnati

Cincinnati, Ohio　　　　　　　　**CB member**
www.uc.edu　　　　　　　　**CB code: 1833**

♦ Public 4-year university
♦ Commuter campus in large city
♦ 22,543 degree-seeking undergraduates: 14% part-time, 51% women, 8% African American, 3% Asian American, 2% Hispanic American, 3% international
♦ 9,778 degree-seeking graduate students
♦ 65% of applicants admitted
♦ SAT or ACT with writing, application essay required
♦ 59% graduate within 6 years

General. Founded in 1819. Regionally accredited. **Degrees:** 4,277 bachelor's, 114 associate awarded; master's, professional, doctoral offered. **ROTC:** Army, Air Force. **Location:** 2 miles from downtown. **Calendar:** Quarter, extensive summer session. **Full-time faculty:** 1,160 total; 80% have terminal degrees, 17% minority, 42% women. **Part-time faculty:** 41 total; 15% have terminal degrees, 10% minority, 61% women. **Class size:** 41% < 20, 42% 20-39, 7% 40-49, 7% 50-99, 3% >100.

Freshman class profile. 17,020 applied, 11,020 admitted, 4,268 enrolled.

Mid 50% test scores			
SAT critical reading:	500-620	GPA 3.0-3.49:	37%
SAT math:	520-640	GPA 2.0-2.99:	15%
SAT writing:	480-590	Rank in top quarter:	50%
ACT composite:	22-27	Rank in top tenth:	22%
GPA 3.75 or higher:	27%	Out-of-state:	12%
GPA 3.50-3.74:	21%	Live on campus:	76%
		International:	3%

Basis for selection. Secondary school record, test scores most important. Interview required for music programs; audition required for dance, music programs. **Home schooled:** Transcript of courses and grades required. Release for home schooling from local Board of Education required.

High school preparation. College-preparatory program recommended. 16 units required. Required and recommended units include English 4, mathematics 3-4, social studies 2, science 2, foreign language 2 and academic electives 2. Specific requirements may vary for each college.

2011-2012 Annual costs. Tuition/fees: $10,419; $24,942 out-of-state. Room/board: $9,780. Books/supplies: $1,275. Personal expenses: $5,090.

2011-2012 Financial aid. Need-based: 3,571 full-time freshmen applied for aid; 2,804 were judged to have need; 2,752 of these received aid. Average need met was 68%. Average scholarship/grant was $5,801; average loan $3,792. 42% of total undergraduate aid awarded as scholarships/grants, 58% as loans/jobs. **Non-need-based:** Awarded to 6,988 full-time undergraduates, including 1,966 freshmen. Scholarships awarded for academics, alumni affiliation, art, athletics, leadership, minority status, music/drama, ROTC, state residency.

Application procedures. Admission: Priority date 12/1; deadline 2/1 (postmark date). $50 fee, may be waived for applicants with need. Admission notification on a rolling basis beginning on or about 10/1. **Financial aid:** No deadline. FAFSA required. Applicants notified on a rolling basis starting 4/4; must reply within 2 week(s) of notification.

Academics. Some engineering programs require students to acquire personal computers. **Special study options:** Accelerated study, combined bachelor's/graduate degree, cooperative education, distance learning, double major, ESL, honors, independent study, internships, liberal arts/career combination, study abroad, teacher certification program, Washington semester, weekend college. Learning at Large (students earn college credit without attending regularly scheduled classes). **Credit/placement by examination:** AP, CLEP, institutional tests. **Support services:** Pre-admission summer program, remedial instruction, study skills assistance, tutoring, writing center.

Majors. Architecture: Architecture, urban/community planning. **Area/ethnic studies:** African-American, Asian, French, German, Latin American, Spanish/Iberian. **Biology:** General, neuroscience. **Business:** Accounting, business admin, finance, management information systems, management science, operations, real estate. **Communications:** Communications/speech/rhetoric, radio/TV. **Computer sciences:** General. **Education:** Art, early childhood, elementary, health, music, secondary. **Engineering:** General, aerospace, chemical, civil, computer, electrical, engineering mechanics, mechanical, metallurgical, nuclear. **English:** British lit, English lit. **Foreign languages:** Classics, comparative lit, French, German, Latin, linguistics, Spanish. **Health services:** Audiology/speech pathology, clinical lab science, health care admin, nuclear medical technology, nursing (RN), predental, premedicine, prepharmacy, preveterinary. **History:** General. **Human services:** Social work. **Liberal arts:** Arts/sciences. **Math:** General. **Philosophy/religion:** Judaic, philosophy. **Physical sciences:** Chemistry, geology, physics. **Protective services:** Criminal justice. **Psychology:** General. **Social sciences:** Anthropology, economics, geography, international relations, political science, sociology, urban studies. **Visual/performing arts:** Art history/conservation, commercial/advertising art, conducting, dance, dramatic, fashion design, industrial design, interior design, jazz, music, music history, music performance, music theory/composition, piano/keyboard, studio arts, theater design, voice/opera. **Work/family studies:** Food/nutrition.

Most popular majors. Business/marketing 16%, communications/journalism 7%, education 8%, engineering/engineering technologies 11%, health sciences 17%, visual/performing arts 9%.

Computing on campus. 560 workstations in library, computer center. Dormitories wired for high-speed internet access and linked to campus network. Commuter students can connect to campus network. Online course registration, helpline, repair service, student web hosting, wireless network available.

Student life. Freshman orientation: Available. Preregistration for classes offered. **Housing:** Guaranteed on-campus for freshmen. Coed dorms, single-sex dorms, apartments, fraternity/sorority housing available. **Activities:**

Bands, choral groups, dance, drama, film society, music ensembles, musical theater, opera, radio station, student government, student newspaper, symphony orchestra, women's initiative network, College Democrats, College Republicans.

Athletics. NCAA. **Intercollegiate:** Baseball M, basketball, cross-country, diving, football (tackle) M, golf, lacrosse W, soccer, swimming, tennis W, track and field, volleyball W. **Intramural:** Basketball, football (non-tackle), racquetball, soccer, softball, volleyball. **Team name:** Bearcats.

Student services. Adult student services, alcohol/substance abuse counseling, career counseling, services for economically disadvantaged, student employment services, financial aid counseling, health services, minority student services, personal counseling, placement for graduates, women's services. **Physically disabled:** Services for visually, speech, hearing impaired.

Contact. E-mail: admissions@uc.edu
Phone: (513) 556-1100 Toll-free number: (800) 827-8728
Fax: (513) 556-1105
Thomas Canepa, Associate Vice President, Admissions, University of Cincinnati, PO Box 210091, Cincinnati, OH 45221-0091

University of Dayton

Dayton, Ohio
www.udayton.edu
CB member
CB code: 1834

- Private 4-year university affiliated with Roman Catholic Church
- Residential campus in small city
- 7,597 degree-seeking undergraduates: 4% part-time, 49% women, 4% African American, 1% Asian American, 3% Hispanic American, 3% international
- 2,684 degree-seeking graduate students
- 76% of applicants admitted
- SAT or ACT (ACT writing optional), application essay required
- 74% graduate within 6 years

General. Founded in 1850. Regionally accredited. **Degrees:** 1,820 bachelor's awarded; master's, professional, doctoral offered. **ROTC:** Army, Air Force. **Location:** 2 miles from downtown, 50 miles from Cincinnati. **Calendar:** Semester, extensive summer session. **Full-time faculty:** 503 total; 90% have terminal degrees, 16% minority, 36% women. **Part-time faculty:** 438 total; 7% minority, 44% women. **Class size:** 38% < 20, 52% 20-39, 6% 40-49, 2% 50-99, 1% >100. **Special facilities:** Research institute, portfolio management center, learning-teaching center, information sciences center, student-operated stores and coffee shops, RISE Symposium.

Freshman class profile. 12,041 applied, 9,106 admitted, 1,970 enrolled.

Mid 50% test scores			
SAT critical reading:	510-610	GPA 2.0-2.99:	11%
SAT math:	520-640	Rank in top quarter:	56%
SAT writing:	510-610	Rank in top tenth:	26%
ACT composite:	24-29	End year in good standing:	92%
GPA 3.75 or higher:	36%	Return as sophomores:	86%
GPA 3.50-3.74:	20%	Out-of-state:	45%
GPA 3.0-3.49:	32%	Live on campus:	96%
		International:	2%

Basis for selection. Selection of courses in preparation for college, grade record and pattern in high school, class rank, SAT or ACT, character, and record of leadership and service. Will review PAA if presented. Interview recommended for all; audition required for all music programs. **Home schooled:** Transcript of courses and grades required. Description of courses taken required, including bibliography of texts used for instruction. Examples of projects, homework or writing samples helpful. **Learning Disabled:** Prefer applicant provide documentation explaining disability for assessment.

High school preparation. College-preparatory program required. 16 units recommended. Recommended units include English 4, mathematics 4, social studies 4, history 4, science 4 (laboratory 1), foreign language 2, computer science 4 and visual/performing arts 4. 2 units of foreign language required for admission to the College of Arts and Sciences.

2011-2012 Annual costs. Tuition/fees: $31,640. Room/board: $9,950. Books/supplies: $2,500. Personal expenses: $1,000.

2011-2012 Financial aid. **Need-based:** 1,590 full-time freshmen applied for aid; 1,160 were judged to have need; 1,160 of these received aid. Average need met was 79%. Average scholarship/grant was $16,754; average loan $2,709. 61% of total undergraduate aid awarded as scholarships/grants, 39% as loans/jobs. **Non-need-based:** Awarded to 3,655 full-time undergraduates, including 1,009 freshmen. Scholarships awarded for academics, alumni affiliation, art, athletics, job skills, leadership, minority status, music/drama, religious affiliation, ROTC, state residency.

Application procedures. **Admission:** Priority date 12/15; deadline 3/1 (postmark date). $50 fee, may be waived for applicants with need. Application must be submitted online. Admission notification on a rolling basis beginning on or about 2/1. Must reply by May 1 or within 2 week(s) if notified thereafter. **Financial aid:** Priority date 3/1; no closing date. FAFSA required. Applicants notified on a rolling basis starting 3/15; must reply by 5/1 or within 3 week(s) of notification.

Academics. **Special study options:** Accelerated study, combined bachelor's/graduate degree, cooperative education, cross-registration, distance learning, double major, dual enrollment of high school students, ESL, exchange student, honors, independent study, internships, liberal arts/career combination, semester at sea, study abroad, teacher certification program, Washington semester. Domestic exchange program with other Marianist institutions; student-designed major in general studies only. **Credit/placement by examination:** AP, CLEP, IB, SAT, ACT, institutional tests. 24 credit hours maximum toward bachelor's degree. **Support services:** Learning center, pre-admission summer program, reduced course load, remedial instruction, study skills assistance, tutoring, writing center.

Majors. **Area/ethnic studies:** American. **Biology:** General, biochemistry, environmental. **Business:** General, accounting, business admin, entrepreneurial studies, finance, international, management information systems, managerial economics, marketing, operations. **Communications:** Communications/speech/rhetoric, digital media, journalism, media studies, public relations. **Computer sciences:** General, computer science. **Conservation:** Environmental science. **Education:** Art, early childhood, foreign languages, French, German, middle, multi-level teacher, music, physical, secondary, Spanish, special ed. **Engineering:** Chemical, civil, computer, electrical, mechanical. **English:** English lit. **Foreign languages:** French, German, Spanish. **Health services:** Dietetics, music therapy, predental, premedicine. **History:** General. **Math:** General. **Parks/recreation:** Exercise sciences, facilities management, sports admin. **Philosophy/religion:** Philosophy, religion. **Physical sciences:** General, chemistry, geology, physics. **Protective services:** Criminal justice. **Psychology:** General. **Social sciences:** Econometrics, economics, political science, sociology. **Visual/performing arts:** Art history/conservation, design, dramatic, music, music performance, music theory/composition, photography, studio arts. **Work/family studies:** Food/nutrition.

Most popular majors. Business/marketing 28%, communications/journalism 7%, education 9%, engineering/engineering technologies 17%.

Computing on campus. PC or laptop required. Dormitories wired for high-speed internet access and linked to campus network. Commuter students can connect to campus network. Online course registration, online library, helpline, repair service, student web hosting, wireless network available.

Student life. **Freshman orientation:** Mandatory, $160 fee. Preregistration for classes offered. Held 2-3 days preceding the first day of classes. Virtual orientation also available online. **Policies:** Freshmen not permitted cars on campus. **Housing:** Guaranteed on-campus for freshmen. Coed dorms, single-sex dorms, special housing for disabled, apartments, fraternity/sorority housing, wellness housing available. $400 nonrefundable deposit, deadline 5/1. University-owned houses available. **Activities:** Bands, campus ministries, choral groups, dance, drama, international student organizations, literary magazine, music ensembles, Model UN, musical theater, opera, radio station, student government, student newspaper, symphony orchestra, TV station, Catholic Life, Campus Crusade for Christ, College Democrats, College Republicans, diversity discussion group, Indian student association, NAACP, Irish club, Italian club.

Athletics. NCAA. **Intercollegiate:** Baseball M, basketball, cheerleading, cross-country, football (tackle) M, golf, rowing (crew) W, soccer, softball W, tennis, track and field W, volleyball W. **Intramural:** Badminton, basketball, bowling, football (non-tackle), golf, racquetball, soccer, softball, tennis, volleyball, water polo, wrestling. **Team name:** Flyers.

Student services. Adult student services, alcohol/substance abuse counseling, chaplain/spiritual director, career counseling, services for economically disadvantaged, student employment services, financial aid counseling, health services, minority student services, on-campus daycare, personal counseling, placement for graduates, veterans' counselor, women's services. **Physically disabled:** Services for visually, speech, hearing impaired.

Contact. E-mail: admission@udayton.edu
Phone: (937) 229-4411 Toll-free number: (800) 837-7433
Fax: (937) 229-4729
Kathy McEuen Harmon, Dean of Admission and Financial Aid, University of Dayton, 300 College Park, Dayton, OH 45469-1300

University of Findlay

Findlay, Ohio
www.findlay.edu
CB code: 1223

- Private 4-year university and health science college affiliated with Church of God
- Residential campus in small city

- 2,760 degree-seeking undergraduates: 8% part-time, 65% women, 3% African American, 1% Asian American, 2% Hispanic American, 6% international
- 782 degree-seeking graduate students
- 69% of applicants admitted
- SAT or ACT (ACT writing optional) required
- 55% graduate within 6 years

General. Founded in 1882. Regionally accredited. **Degrees:** 495 bachelor's, 41 associate awarded; master's, professional offered. **ROTC:** Army, Air Force. **Location:** 45 miles from Toledo, 90 miles from Columbus. **Calendar:** Semester, limited summer session. **Full-time faculty:** 203 total; 61% have terminal degrees, 10% minority, 48% women. **Part-time faculty:** 85 total; 8% minority, 45% women. **Class size:** 58% < 20, 35% 20-39, 3% 40-49, 3% 50-99. **Special facilities:** Two equestrian farms, animal science facility, cadaver lab, environmental resource training center, planetarium, habitat studies center, museum.

Freshman class profile. 2,570 applied, 1,769 admitted, 606 enrolled.

Mid 50% test scores			
SAT critical reading:	460-570	Rank in top quarter:	56%
SAT math:	480-590	Rank in top tenth:	30%
SAT writing:	480-580	End year in good standing:	87%
ACT composite:	20-26	Return as sophomores:	78%
GPA 3.75 or higher:	34%	Out-of-state:	22%
GPA 3.50-3.74:	18%	Live on campus:	92%
GPA 3.0-3.49:	30%	Fraternities:	2%
GPA 2.0-2.99:	18%	Sororities:	2%

Basis for selection. School achievement record, curriculum, class rank, and recommendations. Interview required for special admission programs. **Home schooled:** Statement describing home school structure and mission, state high school equivalency certificate, letter of recommendation (nonparent) required. Greater weight placed on standardized entrance exam scores for admission, evaluation of GED if taken. **Learning Disabled:** Strongly encourage interview or campus visit.

High school preparation. College-preparatory program recommended. 16 units recommended. Recommended units include English 4, mathematics 3, social studies 3, history 1, science 4, foreign language 3 and academic electives 1. One fine arts unit recommended. Additional 1 math and 1 science for preveterinary and environmental programs.

2011-2012 Annual costs. Tuition/fees: $28,104. Room/board: $9,074. Books/supplies: $1,100.

2011-2012 Financial aid. Need-based: 558 full-time freshmen applied for aid; 489 were judged to have need; 489 of these received aid. Average need met was 67%. Average scholarship/grant was $1,906; average loan $2,963. 66% of total undergraduate aid awarded as scholarships/grants, 34% as loans/jobs. **Non-need-based:** Awarded to 2,561 full-time undergraduates, including 591 freshmen. Scholarships awarded for academics, alumni affiliation, athletics, music/drama, state residency.

Application procedures. Admission: Closing date 8/1 (receipt date). No application fee. Admission notification on a rolling basis beginning on or about 9/1. Must reply by May 1 or within 4 week(s) if notified thereafter. Part-time applicants may be admitted year round to any of the six different program start dates. **Financial aid:** Priority date 8/1, closing date 9/1. FAFSA required. Applicants notified on a rolling basis starting 3/1; must reply within 2 week(s) of notification.

Academics. Special study options: Accelerated study, combined bachelor's/graduate degree, cooperative education, distance learning, double major, dual enrollment of high school students, ESL, external degree, honors, independent study, internships, liberal arts/career combination, semester at sea, student-designed major, study abroad, teacher certification program, Washington semester, weekend college. BS in nursing with Mount Carmel College of Nursing and Lourdes College. **Credit/placement by examination:** AP, CLEP, ACT, institutional tests. 15 credit hours maximum toward associate degree, 30 toward bachelor's. **Support services:** Learning center, reduced course load, remedial instruction, study skills assistance, tutoring, writing center.

Majors. Biology: General. **Business:** General, accounting, business admin, entrepreneurial studies, finance, hospitality admin, hospitality/recreation, human resources, international, marketing. **Communications:** Communications/speech/rhetoric, journalism, public relations. **Computer sciences:** General, computer science, systems analysis. **Education:** General, art, bilingual, biology, curriculum, developmentally delayed, drama/dance, driver/safety, early childhood, early childhood special, emotionally handicapped, English, ESL, evaluation, foreign languages, foundations, geography, health, history, kindergarten/preschool, learning disabled, mathematics, mentally handicapped, middle, multi-level teacher, multicultural, multiple handicapped,

physical, psychology, reading, science, secondary, social science, social studies, Spanish, special ed, speech, testing/assessment. **English:** Creative writing, English lit. **Foreign languages:** Japanese, Spanish. **General:** Animal sciences, equestrian studies, farm/ranch. **Health services:** Athletic training, environmental health, health care admin, nuclear medical technology, occupational health, prenursing, preveterinary. **History:** General. **Human services:** Social work. **Math:** General. **Parks/recreation:** Exercise sciences, health/fitness, sports admin. **Philosophy/religion:** Philosophy, religion. **Protective services:** Law enforcement admin. **Psychology:** General. **Social sciences:** General, economics, political science, sociology. **Theology:** Theology. **Visual/performing arts:** Art, commercial/advertising art, dramatic, theater design.

Most popular majors. Agriculture 13%, business/marketing 20%, education 12%, health sciences 25%.

Computing on campus. 400 workstations in dormitories, library, computer center, student center. Dormitories wired for high-speed internet access and linked to campus network. Commuter students can connect to campus network. Online course registration, online library, helpline, repair service, student web hosting, wireless network available.

Student life. Freshman orientation: Mandatory, $100 fee. Preregistration for classes offered. One-day registrations for students and orientation for parents during summer. 2-day orientation for students 2 days before classes begin. **Policies:** All freshmen, sophomores, and juniors under the age of 22 required to live on-campus. **Housing:** Guaranteed on-campus for freshmen. Coed dorms, single-sex dorms, special housing for disabled, apartments, fraternity/sorority housing, wellness housing available. $150 nonrefundable deposit, deadline 7/1. Honors house and special interest houses. **Activities:** Bands, campus ministries, choral groups, dance, drama, international student organizations, literary magazine, music ensembles, musical theater, opera, radio station, student government, student newspaper, symphony orchestra, TV station, Circle-K, black student union, wilderness club, Campus Compact, College Democrats, College Republicans, Fellowship of Christian Athletes, Habitat for Humanity, international club.

Athletics. NCAA. **Intercollegiate:** Baseball M, basketball, cheerleading, cross-country, diving, equestrian, football (tackle) M, golf, soccer, softball W, swimming, tennis, track and field, volleyball W, wrestling M. **Intramural:** Basketball, bowling, cricket, football (non-tackle), golf, skiing, soccer, softball, table tennis, tennis, volleyball, water polo. **Team name:** Oilers.

Student services. Adult student services, alcohol/substance abuse counseling, chaplain/spiritual director, career counseling, services for economically disadvantaged, student employment services, financial aid counseling, health services, minority student services, personal counseling, placement for graduates, veterans' counselor, women's services. **Physically disabled:** Services for visually, speech, hearing impaired.

Contact. E-mail: admissions@findlay.edu
Phone: (419) 434-4540 Toll-free number: (800) 548-0932
Fax: (419) 434-4898
Donna Gruber, Director of Undergraduate Admissions, University of Findlay, 1000 North Main Street, Findlay, OH 45840-3653

University of Mount Union

Alliance, Ohio
www.mountunion.edu

CB member
CB code: 1492

- Private 4-year university affiliated with United Methodist Church
- Residential campus in large town
- 2,122 degree-seeking undergraduates: 48% women, 6% African American, 1% Asian American, 1% Hispanic American, 3% international
- 57 degree-seeking graduate students
- 73% of applicants admitted
- SAT or ACT (ACT writing optional), application essay required
- 65% graduate within 6 years; 30% enter graduate study

General. Founded in 1846. Regionally accredited. **Degrees:** 448 bachelor's awarded; master's offered. **ROTC:** Army, Air Force. **Location:** 55 miles from Cleveland, 75 miles from Pittsburgh. **Calendar:** Semester, limited summer session. **Full-time faculty:** 129 total; 85% have terminal degrees, 13% minority, 40% women. **Part-time faculty:** 111 total; 9% minority, 49% women. **Class size:** 55% < 20, 43% 20-39, less than 1% 40-49, 1% 50-99. **Special facilities:** 2 astronomical observatories, 141-acre nature center for ecological studies, bird observatory, scanning electron microscope facility.

Freshman class profile. 2,579 applied, 1,880 admitted, 618 enrolled.

Mid 50% test scores		Rank in top tenth:	12%
SAT critical reading:	450-540	End year in good standing:	95%
SAT math:	460-570	Return as sophomores:	72%
ACT composite:	20-25	Out-of-state:	15%
GPA 3.75 or higher:	16%	Live on campus:	92%
GPA 3.50-3.74:	15%	International:	2%
GPA 3.0-3.49:	33%	Fraternities:	4%
GPA 2.0-2.99:	36%	Sororities:	6%
Rank in top quarter:	32%		

Basis for selection. Class rank, rigor of secondary school record, standardized test scores, academic GPA very important. Rolling deadline for SAT/ACT scores. Interview recommended for all. Audition recommended for communications, music, and theater programs. Portfolio recommended for art and communications programs. **Home schooled:** Statement describing home school structure and mission required.

High school preparation. 18 units recommended. Recommended units include English 4, mathematics 3, social studies 3, science 3 (laboratory 2), foreign language 2 and academic electives 1.

2011-2012 Annual costs. Tuition/fees: $25,700. Room/board: $8,150. Books/supplies: $1,100. Personal expenses: $800.

2010-2011 Financial aid. Need-based: 591 full-time freshmen applied for aid; 552 were judged to have need; 552 of these received aid. Average need met was 71%. Average scholarship/grant was $14,412; average loan $4,297. 64% of total undergraduate aid awarded as scholarships/grants, 36% as loans/jobs. **Non-need-based:** Awarded to 442 full-time undergraduates, including 119 freshmen. Scholarships awarded for academics, alumni affiliation, art, job skills, leadership, minority status, music/drama, religious affiliation, ROTC, state residency.

Application procedures. Admission: Priority date 3/1; no deadline. No application fee. Admission notification on a rolling basis beginning on or about 10/1. Admission determined by space availability after May 1. **Financial aid:** No deadline. FAFSA required. Applicants notified on a rolling basis starting 3/15; must reply within 4 week(s) of notification.

Academics. All freshmen must take Liberal Studies Experience course. **Special study options:** Accelerated study, combined bachelor's/graduate degree, cooperative education, double major, ESL, honors, independent study, internships, student-designed major, study abroad, teacher certification program. **Credit/placement by examination:** AP, CLEP, IB, institutional tests. 15 credit hours maximum toward bachelor's degree. **Support services:** Learning center, reduced course load, study skills assistance, tutoring, writing center.

Majors. Area/ethnic studies: American, Asian. **Biology:** General, biochemistry, neuroscience. **Business:** Accounting, business admin, international. **Communications:** Communications/speech/rhetoric, digital media, media studies. **Computer sciences:** Programming, web page design. **Conservation:** Environmental science. **Education:** Early childhood, health, middle, music, physical, special ed. **Engineering:** Civil, mechanical. **English:** Creative writing, English lit. **Foreign languages:** French, German, Japanese, Spanish. **Health services:** Athletic training, clinical lab science. **History:** General. **Math:** General, financial. **Parks/recreation:** Exercise sciences, sports admin. **Philosophy/religion:** Philosophy, religion. **Physical sciences:** Chemistry, geology, physics. **Protective services:** Criminalistics. **Psychology:** General. **Social sciences:** Criminology, economics, international relations, political science, sociology. **Visual/performing arts:** Dramatic, music, music performance, studio arts.

Most popular majors. Biology 9%, business/marketing 24%, education 15%, foreign language 7%, parks/recreation 12%.

Computing on campus. 220 workstations in dormitories, library, computer center, student center. Dormitories wired for high-speed internet access and linked to campus network. Commuter students can connect to campus network. Online course registration, online library, helpline, repair service, student web hosting, wireless network available.

Student life. Freshman orientation: Available. Preregistration for classes offered. Two-day summer orientation includes program for parents. Fall orientation held week before registration for students only. **Housing:** Guaranteed on-campus for all undergraduates. Coed dorms, single-sex dorms, special housing for disabled, apartments, fraternity/sorority housing, wellness housing available. **Activities:** Bands, campus ministries, choral groups, dance, drama, literary magazine, music ensembles, Model UN, musical theater, radio station, student government, student newspaper, academic clubs, academic honoraries, religious clubs, service organizations, Alpha Phi Omega, black student union, international students association, women students association, religious life council, student activities council.

Athletics. NCAA. **Intercollegiate:** Baseball M, basketball, cheerleading, cross-country, diving, football (tackle) M, golf, lacrosse, soccer, softball W, swimming, tennis, track and field, volleyball W, wrestling M. **Intramural:** Badminton, basketball, bowling, diving, football (non-tackle), golf, gymnastics, lacrosse, racquetball, soccer, softball, swimming, tennis, volleyball, water polo, weight lifting. **Team name:** Purple Raiders.

Student services. Adult student services, alcohol/substance abuse counseling, chaplain/spiritual director, career counseling, student employment services, financial aid counseling, health services, minority student services, personal counseling, placement for graduates, women's services. **Physically disabled:** Services for visually impaired.

Contact. E-mail: admission@mountunion.edu
Phone: (330) 823-2590 Toll-free number: (800) 334-6682
Fax: (330) 823-5097
Grace Chalker, Director of Admissions, University of Mount Union, 1972 Clark Avenue, Alliance, OH 44601-3993

University of Phoenix: Cincinnati
West Chester, Ohio
www.phoenix.edu

▸ For-profit 4-year university
▸ Large city
▸ 164 degree-seeking undergraduates

General. Regionally accredited. **Degrees:** 25 bachelor's awarded; master's offered. **Calendar:** Differs by program. **Full-time faculty:** 10 total. **Part-time faculty:** 87 total.

Basis for selection. Open admission, but selective for some programs.

2011-2012 Annual costs. Estimated costs as of August 2011: per-credit-hour charge, $380 to $480, depending upon level and course of study; electronic course materials fee, $95, if applicable. Book and material charges may vary by course and program. All fees are subject to change.

Application procedures. Admission: No deadline. No application fee.

Academics. Credit/placement by examination: AP, CLEP.

Majors. Business: Accounting, business admin, marketing.

Contact. Toll-free number: (866) 766-0766
Marc Booker, Director of Admission and Evaluation, University of Phoenix: Cincinnati, 9050 Centre Point, Ste 250, West Chester, OH 4874

University of Phoenix: Cleveland
Independence, Ohio
www.phoenix.edu

▸ For-profit 4-year university
▸ Large city
▸ 513 degree-seeking undergraduates

General. Regionally accredited. **Degrees:** 82 bachelor's awarded; master's offered. **Calendar:** Differs by program. **Full-time faculty:** 14 total. **Part-time faculty:** 137 total.

Basis for selection. Open admission.

2011-2012 Annual costs. Estimated costs as of August 2011: per-credit-hour charge, $465 to $480, depending upon level and course of study; electronic course materials fee, $95, if applicable. Book and material charges may vary by course and program. All fees are subject to change.

Application procedures. Admission: No deadline. No application fee. **Financial aid:** No deadline.

Academics. Credit/placement by examination: AP, CLEP.

Majors. Business: Business admin. **Computer sciences:** Information technology.

Contact. Marc Booker, Director of Admission and Evaluation, University of Phoenix: Cleveland, 5005 Rockside Road, Suite 130, Independence, OH 44131-6808

University of Phoenix: Columbus Ohio
Columbus, Ohio
www.phoenix.edu

- For-profit 4-year university
- Very large city
- 189 degree-seeking undergraduates

General. Regionally accredited. **Degrees:** 28 bachelor's awarded; master's offered. **Calendar:** Differs by program. **Full-time faculty:** 7 total. **Part-time faculty:** 72 total.

Basis for selection. Open admission, but selective for some programs.

2011-2012 Annual costs. Estimated costs as of August 2011: per-credit-hour charge, $465 to $480, depending upon level and course of study; electronic course materials fee, $95, if applicable. Book and material charges may vary by course and program. All fees are subject to change.

Application procedures. Admission: No deadline. No application fee. **Financial aid:** No deadline.

Academics. Credit/placement by examination: AP, CLEP.

Majors. Business: Accounting, business admin, finance, retail management. **Health services:** Health services admin.

Contact. Marc Booker, Director of Admission and Evaluation, University of Phoenix: Columbus Ohio, 8415 Pulsar Place, Columbus, OH 43240-4032

University of Rio Grande
Rio Grande, Ohio
www.rio.edu   CB code: 1663

- Private 4-year community and liberal arts college
- Commuter campus in rural community
- 1,482 degree-seeking undergraduates: 18% part-time, 61% women
- 88 degree-seeking graduate students
- 61% graduate within 6 years

General. Founded in 1876. Regionally accredited. Institution is both public and private. First 2 years are state subsidized, second 2 years are private, with higher tuition. Affiliated with Rio Grande Community College. **Degrees:** 184 bachelor's, 207 associate awarded; master's offered. **Location:** 12 miles from Gallipolis. **Calendar:** Semester, limited summer session. **Full-time faculty:** 89 total; 52% have terminal degrees, 7% minority, 46% women. **Part-time faculty:** 91 total; 4% have terminal degrees, 3% minority, 57% women. **Class size:** 68% < 20, 29% 20-39, 2% 40-49, 1% 50-99. **Special facilities:** Early childhood care center.

Freshman class profile. 2,078 applied, 1,620 admitted, 558 enrolled.

GPA 3.75 or higher:	9%	End year in good standing:	69%
GPA 3.50-3.74:	11%	Return as sophomores:	54%
GPA 3.0-3.49:	28%	Out-of-state:	8%
GPA 2.0-2.99:	45%	Live on campus:	27%
Rank in top quarter:	27%	International:	1%
Rank in top tenth:	8%		

Basis for selection. Open admission, but selective for some programs. ACT required for nursing, medical laboratory technician, radiologic technology, diagnostic medical sonography, respiratory therapy, and education programs. Deferred admission for students demonstrating need for remedial work. Acceptance to Education department occurs at end of sophomore year. **Learning Disabled:** Students with any kind of special needs asked to meet with Director of Accessibility to determine education plan and for academic advising purposes.

High school preparation. College-preparatory program recommended. 21 units recommended. Recommended units include English 4, mathematics 3, social studies 3, history 2, science 3 (laboratory 2), foreign language 2 and academic electives 9. Chemistry, algebra, biology required for nursing applicants.

2011-2012 Annual costs. Tuition/fees: $19,520. Tuition reported is for private university sector of institution. Public community college in-state in-district tuition: $3,090 ($103 per credit hour); in-state out-of-district, $3,690 ($123 per credit hour). All public community college undergraduates pay $750 in required fees. Out-of-state community college students charged private tuition rate. Room/board: $8,220. Books/supplies: $1,000. Personal expenses: $1,571.

2010-2011 Financial aid. Need-based: 317 full-time freshmen applied for aid; 317 were judged to have need; 302 of these received aid. Average need met was 78%. Average scholarship/grant was $5,522. 26% of total undergraduate aid awarded as scholarships/grants, 74% as loans/jobs. **Non-need-based:** Awarded to 760 full-time undergraduates, including 162 freshmen. Scholarships awarded for academics, alumni affiliation, athletics, leadership, music/drama, state residency.

Application procedures. Admission: No deadline. $25 fee, may be waived for applicants with need, free for online applicants. Admission notification on a rolling basis. **Financial aid:** Priority date 3/15; no closing date. FAFSA, institutional form required. Applicants notified on a rolling basis starting 1/15; must reply within 3 week(s) of notification.

Academics. Special study options: Accelerated study, combined bachelor's/graduate degree, cooperative education, distance learning, double major, dual enrollment of high school students, ESL, honors, independent study, internships, liberal arts/career combination, student-designed major, study abroad, teacher certification program. **Credit/placement by examination:** AP, CLEP, institutional tests. **Support services:** Learning center, pre-admission summer program, reduced course load, remedial instruction, tutoring, writing center.

Majors. Area/ethnic studies: American. **Biology:** General. **Business:** Accounting, business admin, marketing, office technology, retailing. **Communications:** Communications/speech/rhetoric, journalism, media studies, public relations. **Computer sciences:** General, applications programming, computer science. **Conservation:** General, environmental studies, wildlife/wilderness. **Education:** General, art, biology, business, chemistry, early childhood, elementary, English, health, history, mathematics, middle, multi-level teacher, music, physical, physics, reading, science, secondary, social science, special ed, speech. **English:** English lit. **Foreign languages:** Spanish. **Health services:** Facilities admin, health care admin, nursing (RN), prenursing, sonography. **History:** General. **Human services:** General, social work. **Liberal arts:** Humanities. **Math:** General. **Parks/recreation:** Sports admin. **Physical sciences:** Chemistry. **Psychology:** General. **Social sciences:** General, archaeology, economics. **Visual/performing arts:** General, graphic design, multimedia, music, music management.

Most popular majors. Area/ethnic studies 6%, business/marketing 13%, education 22%, health sciences 9%, natural resources/environmental science 6%, parks/recreation 8%, public administration/social services 7%.

Computing on campus. 300 workstations in library, computer center, student center. Dormitories wired for high-speed internet access and linked to campus network. Online course registration, online library, repair service, student web hosting, wireless network available.

Student life. Freshman orientation: Available, $50 fee. Preregistration for classes offered. One-day program held in April, May, June, July, and August. **Policies:** Smoke free dorms and buildings. **Housing:** Guaranteed on-campus for all undergraduates. Coed dorms, single-sex dorms, wellness housing available. $200 fully refundable deposit, deadline 7/15. **Activities:** Bands, campus ministries, choral groups, dance, drama, literary magazine, music ensembles, musical theater, radio station, student government, student newspaper, symphony orchestra, TV station, international student organization, Valley Artist Services, Handicapped Coalition, Young Republicans, Rio Christian Fellowship, Student Ambassadors, Students in Free Enterprise.

Athletics. NAIA. **Intercollegiate:** Baseball M, basketball, cheerleading, cross-country, soccer, softball W, track and field, volleyball W. **Intramural:** Archery, badminton, basketball, equestrian, handball, racquetball, softball, swimming, tennis, water polo, wrestling M. **Team name:** Redstorm.

Student services. Career counseling, student employment services, financial aid counseling, health services, on-campus daycare, personal counseling, placement for graduates, veterans' counselor. **Physically disabled:** Services for visually, speech, hearing impaired.

Contact. E-mail: admissions@rio.edu
Phone: (740) 245-7208 Toll-free number: (800) 282-7201
Fax: (740) 245-7260
Thomas Mansperger, Admissions Director, University of Rio Grande, 218 North College Avenue, Rio Grande, OH 45674

University of Toledo
Toledo, Ohio   CB member
www.utoledo.edu   CB code: 1845

- Public 4-year university
- Commuter campus in large city

- 17,365 degree-seeking undergraduates: 17% part-time, 49% women, 17% African American, 2% Asian American, 4% Hispanic American, 4% international
- 4,582 degree-seeking graduate students
- 46% graduate within 6 years

General. Founded in 1872. Regionally accredited. **Degrees:** 2,684 bachelor's, 155 associate awarded; master's, professional, doctoral offered. **ROTC:** Army, Air Force. **Location:** 6 miles from downtown. **Calendar:** Semester, extensive summer session. **Special facilities:** 2 observatories, ion accelerator, arboretum, planetarium, linear laser and nuclear physics laboratory, Lake Erie research center.

Freshman class profile. 11,633 applied, 11,131 admitted, 3,837 enrolled.

Mid 50% test scores		GPA 2.0-2.99:	32%
ACT composite:	18-25	Return as sophomores:	65%
GPA 3.75 or higher:	19%	Out-of-state:	11%
GPA 3.50-3.74:	13%	Live on campus:	59%
GPA 3.0-3.49:	28%	International:	2%

Basis for selection. Open admission, but selective for some programs and for out-of-state students. Out-of-state students need 2.0 GPA and 21 ACT or 980 SAT. Applicants to BS program in engineering need 3.0 GPA and 22 ACT or 1020 SAT. For admission to premedicine, predentistry, or preveterinary programs, 3.0 GPA and 25 ACT or 1130 SAT required. Applicants to computer science-engineering program need 3.0 GPA and 25 ACT or 1130 SAT, engineering technology 2.0 GPA and 21 ACT or 980 SAT, business college 2.25 GPA and 25 ACT or 1130 SAT. All SAT scores exclusive of Writing. Audition required for music program. **Home schooled:** Official recognized transcript required. **Learning Disabled:** Registering with the Office of Accessibility recommended.

High school preparation. College-preparatory program required.

2011-2012 Annual costs. Tuition/fees: $8,926; $18,046 out-of-state. Room/board: $9,776. Books/supplies: $750. Personal expenses: $2,204.

Financial aid. Non-need-based: Scholarships awarded for academics, alumni affiliation, art, athletics, leadership, minority status, music/drama, ROTC. **Additional information:** March priority date for federal aid. Students encouraged to apply as early as December for priority consideration for institutional aid.

Application procedures. Admission: No deadline. $40 fee, may be waived for applicants with need. Admission notification on a rolling basis beginning on or about 10/1. Freshman applicants desiring on-campus housing encouraged to apply early. **Financial aid:** Priority date 3/1; no closing date. FAFSA required. Applicants notified on a rolling basis starting 3/1.

Academics. Special study options: Accelerated study, combined bachelor's/graduate degree, cooperative education, cross-registration, distance learning, double major, dual enrollment of high school students, ESL, exchange student, external degree, honors, independent study, internships, liberal arts/career combination, student-designed major, study abroad, teacher certification program, weekend college. **Credit/placement by examination:** AP, CLEP, institutional tests. 30 credit hours maximum toward associate degree, 30 toward bachelor's. **Support services:** Learning center, pre-admission summer program, reduced course load, remedial instruction, study skills assistance, tutoring, writing center.

Majors. Area/ethnic studies: African-American, American, Asian, European, Latin American, Near/Middle Eastern, women's. **Biology:** General. **Business:** General, accounting, business admin, entrepreneurial studies, finance, human resources, international, logistics, management information systems, management science, market research, marketing, operations, organizational behavior. **Communications:** Communications/speech/rhetoric, media studies. **Computer sciences:** Information systems, information technology. **Conservation:** Environmental studies. **Education:** General, art, business, English, French, German, health, kindergarten/preschool, mathematics, music, physical, science, secondary, social studies, Spanish, speech impaired, trade/industrial. **Engineering:** General, biomedical, chemical, civil, computer, electrical, industrial, mechanical. **English:** English lit. **Foreign languages:** French, German, linguistics, Spanish. **Health services:** Facilities admin, medical records admin, nursing (RN), pharmaceutical sciences, predental, premedicine, preveterinary, public health ed, recreational therapy, respiratory therapy technology. **History:** General. **Human services:** Social work. **Liberal arts:** Arts/sciences, humanities. **Math:** General. **Parks/recreation:** General, exercise sciences, health/fitness. **Philosophy/religion:** Philosophy, religion. **Physical sciences:** Astronomy, chemistry, geology, physics. **Protective services:** Criminal justice. **Psychology:** General. **Social sciences:** Anthropology, economics, geography, international relations, political science, sociology, urban studies. **Visual/performing arts:** Art, art history/conservation, dramatic, film/cinema/video, music, studio arts.

Most popular majors. Business/marketing 21%, education 9%, engineering/engineering technologies 14%, health sciences 15%, interdisciplinary studies 7%.

Computing on campus. 5,000 workstations in dormitories, library, computer center, student center. Dormitories linked to campus network. Commuter students can connect to campus network. Online course registration, online library, helpline, repair service, wireless network available.

Student life. Freshman orientation: Mandatory, $60 fee. Preregistration for classes offered. **Housing:** Coed dorms, special housing for disabled, fraternity/sorority housing available. $200 partly refundable deposit, deadline 4/1. **Activities:** Bands, campus ministries, choral groups, dance, drama, international student organizations, literary magazine, music ensembles, musical theater, radio station, student government, student newspaper, TV station, black student union, Campus Crusade for Christ, Hillel, Latino student union, University YMCA, gay and lesbian student union, international student association, Habitat for Humanity, Toledo Campus Ministry Fellowship.

Athletics. NCAA. **Intercollegiate:** Baseball M, basketball, cross-country, diving W, football (tackle) M, golf, soccer W, softball W, swimming W, tennis, track and field W, volleyball W. **Intramural:** Badminton, basketball, bowling, cheerleading W, diving W, fencing, football (tackle), golf, lacrosse, racquetball, soccer, softball, swimming W, table tennis, tennis, track and field W, volleyball, weight lifting. **Team name:** Rockets.

Student services. Adult student services, alcohol/substance abuse counseling, chaplain/spiritual director, career counseling, services for economically disadvantaged, student employment services, financial aid counseling, health services, legal services, minority student services, on-campus daycare, personal counseling, placement for graduates, veterans' counselor, women's services. **Physically disabled:** Services for visually, speech, hearing impaired.

Contact. E-mail: enroll@utoledo.edu
Phone: (419) 530-8700 Toll-free number: (800) 586-5336
Fax: (419) 530-4504
Cathi Kwapich, Director of Admission, University of Toledo, 2801 West Bancroft Street, Toledo, OH 43606-3398

Urbana University
Urbana, Ohio
www.urbana.edu   **CB code: 1847**

- Private 4-year liberal arts college
- Commuter campus in large town

General. Founded in 1850. Regionally accredited. **Location:** 42 miles from Columbus, 49 miles from Dayton. **Calendar:** Semester.

Annual costs/financial aid. Tuition/fees (2011-2012): $21,725. Room/board: $8,120. Books/supplies: $650. Personal expenses: $666. Need-based financial aid available to full-time and part-time students.

Contact. Phone: (937) 484-1356
Director of Admissions, 579 College Way, Urbana, OH 43078

Ursuline College
Pepper Pike, Ohio   **CB member**
www.ursuline.edu   **CB code: 1848**

- Private 4-year liberal arts college for women affiliated with Roman Catholic Church
- Commuter campus in small town
- 938 degree-seeking undergraduates: 38% part-time, 91% women, 28% African American, 1% Asian American, 2% Hispanic American, 1% international
- 531 degree-seeking graduate students
- 57% of applicants admitted
- SAT or ACT (ACT writing optional) required
- 54% graduate within 6 years

General. Founded in 1871. Regionally accredited. Primarily women's college, but some men admitted. **Degrees:** 254 bachelor's awarded; master's, professional offered. **ROTC:** Army. **Location:** 10 miles from Cleveland. **Calendar:** Semester, limited summer session. **Full-time faculty:** 69 total; 62% have terminal degrees, 9% minority, 83% women. **Part-time faculty:** 146 total; 23% have terminal degrees, 10% minority, 81% women. **Class size:** 86% < 20, 14% 20-39.

Freshman class profile. 457 applied, 260 admitted, 78 enrolled.

Mid 50% test scores			
SAT critical reading:	400-540	GPA 2.0-2.99:	31%
SAT math:	390-540	Rank in top quarter:	46%
SAT writing:	390-550	Rank in top tenth:	21%
ACT composite:	19-24	End year in good standing:	86%
GPA 3.75 or higher:	16%	Return as sophomores:	72%
GPA 3.50-3.74:	22%	Out-of-state:	10%
GPA 3.0-3.49:	31%	Live on campus:	79%
		International:	1%

Basis for selection. Secondary school record and standardized test scores are very important. Interview recommended for all. **Home schooled:** Transcript of courses and grades, state high school equivalency certificate required. Official transcript from accrediting agency needed.

High school preparation. College-preparatory program recommended. 18 units recommended. Recommended units include English 4, mathematics 3, social studies 3, science 3 (laboratory 2), foreign language 2 and visual/performing arts 1. One physical education unit recommended. Nursing students should have chemistry.

2011-2012 Annual costs. Tuition/fees: $24,910. Room/board: $8,288. Books/supplies: $1,150. Personal expenses: $800.

2010-2011 Financial aid. Need-based: 79 full-time freshmen applied for aid; 77 were judged to have need; 77 of these received aid. Average need met was 83%. Average scholarship/grant was $17,890; average loan $3,749. 46% of total undergraduate aid awarded as scholarships/grants, 54% as loans/jobs. **Non-need-based:** Awarded to 92 full-time undergraduates, including 21 freshmen. Scholarships awarded for academics, art, athletics, leadership, religious affiliation, ROTC.

Application procedures. Admission: Closing date 2/14 (postmark date). $25 fee, may be waived for applicants with need, free for online applicants. Applicants notified within 3 weeks of application. Must reply by May 1 or within 4 week(s) if notified thereafter. **Financial aid:** Priority date 3/15; no closing date. FAFSA required. Applicants notified on a rolling basis starting 3/1; must reply within 2 week(s) of notification.

Academics. Special study options: Accelerated study, combined bachelor's/graduate degree, cross-registration, double major, independent study, internships, New York semester, teacher certification program. Optional junior year program in fashion merchandising or design at Fashion Institute of Technology in New York City for enrichment electives only. **Credit/placement by examination:** AP, CLEP, SAT, ACT, institutional tests. 43 credit hours maximum toward bachelor's degree. **Support services:** Learning center, reduced course load, remedial instruction, study skills assistance, tutoring, writing center.

Majors. Biology: General, biotechnology. **Business:** Accounting, business admin, fashion, human resources, management information systems, marketing. **Communications:** Public relations. **Education:** Art, early childhood, English, mathematics, middle, science, social studies, special ed. **English:** English lit. **Health services:** Facilities admin, health care admin, nursing (RN), prenursing, preop/surgical nursing. **History:** General. **Human services:** Social work. **Liberal arts:** Humanities. **Math:** General. **Philosophy/religion:** Christian, philosophy. **Psychology:** General. **Social sciences:** Sociology. **Visual/performing arts:** Art history/conservation, fashion design, graphic design, interior design, studio arts.

Most popular majors. Business/marketing 20%, health sciences 53%, legal studies 9%, psychology 7%, visual/performing arts 6%.

Computing on campus. 72 workstations in dormitories, library, computer center, student center. Dormitories wired for high-speed internet access and linked to campus network. Online library, wireless network available.

Student life. Freshman orientation: Available. Preregistration for classes offered. Three-day program offered prior to start of fall semester. **Housing:** Coed dorms available. $100 fully refundable deposit. **Activities:** Campus ministries, drama, literary magazine, student government, student nurses, education association, campus service and spiritual life committees, ethnic groups, public relations society, peer mentors.

Athletics. Intercollegiate: Basketball W, bowling W, cross-country W, golf W, soccer W, softball W, swimming W, tennis W, track and field W, volleyball W. **Team name:** Arrows.

Student services. Adult student services, chaplain/spiritual director, career counseling, student employment services, financial aid counseling, minority student services, personal counseling. **Physically disabled:** Services for visually, speech, hearing impaired.

Contact. E-mail: admission@ursuline.edu
Phone: (440) 449-4203 Toll-free number: (888) 877-8546
Fax: (440) 684-6138
Matthew McCaffrey, Director of Admissions, Ursuline College, 2550 Lander Road, Pepper Pike, OH 44124-4398

Walsh University
North Canton, Ohio
www.walsh.edu

CB member
CB code: 1926

- Private 4-year university and liberal arts college affiliated with Roman Catholic Church
- Residential campus in small city
- 2,308 degree-seeking undergraduates: 17% part-time, 63% women
- 501 degree-seeking graduate students
- 77% of applicants admitted
- SAT or ACT (ACT writing optional) required
- 56% graduate within 6 years; 23% enter graduate study

General. Founded in 1958. Regionally accredited. Campus in Rome, Italy; program in Kisubi, Uganda. **Degrees:** 456 bachelor's, 1 associate awarded; master's, professional offered. **Location:** 20 miles from Akron, 55 miles from Cleveland. **Calendar:** Semester, limited summer session. **Full-time faculty:** 114 total; 75% have terminal degrees, 9% minority, 53% women. **Part-time faculty:** 200 total; 14% have terminal degrees, 3% minority, 47% women. **Class size:** 66% < 20, 34% 20-39, less than 1% 40-49, less than 1% 50-99. **Special facilities:** Bioinformatics laboratory, prayer garden, environmental education center.

Freshman class profile. 1,650 applied, 1,269 admitted, 512 enrolled.

Mid 50% test scores			
SAT critical reading:	450-550	Rank in top quarter:	42%
SAT math:	480-580	Rank in top tenth:	14%
ACT composite:	20-24	End year in good standing:	92%
GPA 3.75 or higher:	23%	Return as sophomores:	75%
GPA 3.50-3.74:	20%	Out-of-state:	4%
GPA 3.0-3.49:	34%	Live on campus:	78%
GPA 2.0-2.99:	23%	International:	1%

Basis for selection. Secondary school record and standardized test scores very important; class rank, recommendations, essay, and character important. Essay, interview recommended for all. **Home schooled:** Transcript of courses and grades required.

High school preparation. College-preparatory program recommended. 16 units recommended. Recommended units include English 4, mathematics 3, social studies 3, science 3, foreign language 2 and academic electives 1. Algebra, biology, and chemistry required for nursing applicants.

2011-2012 Annual costs. Tuition/fees: $23,550. Room/board: $8,640. Books/supplies: $1,062. Personal expenses: $1,212.

2011-2012 Financial aid. Need-based: 497 full-time freshmen applied for aid; 456 were judged to have need; 456 of these received aid. Average need met was 67%. Average scholarship/grant was $5,847; average loan $4,282. 60% of total undergraduate aid awarded as scholarships/grants, 40% as loans/jobs. **Non-need-based:** Awarded to 1,947 full-time undergraduates, including 515 freshmen. Scholarships awarded for academics, alumni affiliation, athletics, music/drama, religious affiliation, state residency.

Application procedures. Admission: Closing date 8/15 (postmark date). $25 fee, may be waived for applicants with need. Admission notification on a rolling basis beginning on or about 10/1. **Financial aid:** Priority date 5/1; no closing date. FAFSA required. Applicants notified on a rolling basis starting 2/15.

Academics. Accelerated degree completion program for adults with evening and weekend classes. **Special study options:** Accelerated study, combined bachelor's/graduate degree, distance learning, double major, dual enrollment of high school students, ESL, exchange student, external degree, honors, independent study, internships, liberal arts/career combination, study abroad, teacher certification program, Washington semester. CCSA Consortium for Study Abroad, Rome Experience, Uganda experience. **Credit/placement by examination:** AP, CLEP, SAT, ACT, institutional tests. 45 credit hours maximum toward bachelor's degree. Credit and placement are based on each division's evaluation of test information. **Support services:** Learning center, remedial instruction, study skills assistance, tutoring, writing center.

Honors college/program. Admissions based on 3.75 GPA, 27 ACT or 1200 SAT (exclusive of Writing), graduation in top 10% of class. Writing sample and interview required. 35 freshmen admitted each fall.

Majors. Biology: General. **Business:** General, accounting, business admin, communications, international, management information systems, marketing. **Communications:** Communications/speech/rhetoric. **Computer sciences:** Computer science. **Education:** Early childhood, elementary, emotionally handicapped, English, mathematics, mentally handicapped, middle, multiple handicapped, physical, reading, science, secondary, social science, social studies. **English:** English lit. **Foreign languages:** French, Spanish. **Health**

services: Nursing (RN), predental, premedicine, preveterinary. **History:** General. **Math:** General. **Parks/recreation:** Health/fitness. **Philosophy/religion:** Philosophy. **Physical sciences:** Chemistry. **Psychology:** General. **Social sciences:** Political science, sociology. **Theology:** Theology.

Most popular majors. Biology 9%, business/marketing 33%, education 15%, health sciences 21%, psychology 9%.

Computing on campus. 371 workstations in dormitories, library, student center. Dormitories wired for high-speed internet access and linked to campus network. Commuter students can connect to campus network. Online course registration, online library, helpline, repair service, wireless network available.

Student life. Freshman orientation: Mandatory, $200 fee. Preregistration for classes offered. Held on 5 separate weekends during the summer before classes begin in August. **Policies:** All full-time undergraduate students 23 and younger must live on campus (some exceptions permitted). **Housing:** Guaranteed on-campus for all undergraduates. Coed dorms, single-sex dorms, special housing for disabled, apartments, wellness housing available. $200 nonrefundable deposit, deadline 8/15. **Activities:** Bands, campus ministries, choral groups, dance, drama, international student organizations, literary magazine, music ensembles, radio station, student government, student newspaper, Circle-K, black student union, Habitat for Humanity, College Democrats, College Republicans, international club, Students for Life, justice and peace club.

Athletics. NCAA. **Intercollegiate:** Baseball M, basketball, cheerleading, cross-country, football (tackle) M, golf, soccer, softball W, tennis, track and field, volleyball W. **Intramural:** Basketball, bowling, football (non-tackle), golf, soccer, table tennis, tennis, volleyball. **Team name:** Cavaliers.

Student services. Adult student services, alcohol/substance abuse counseling, chaplain/spiritual director, career counseling, student employment services, financial aid counseling, health services, minority student services, personal counseling, placement for graduates, veterans' counselor. **Physically disabled:** Services for visually, speech, hearing impaired.

Contact. E-mail: admissions@walsh.edu
Phone: (330) 490-7172 Toll-free number: (800) 362-9846
Fax: (330) 490-7165
Brett Freshour, Vice President for Enrollment Management, Walsh University, 2020 East Maple Street, North Canton, OH 44720-3396

Wilberforce University
Wilberforce, Ohio CB member
www.wilberforce.edu CB code: 1906

- Private 4-year liberal arts college affiliated with African Methodist Episcopal Church
- Residential campus in rural community
- 599 degree-seeking undergraduates

General. Founded in 1856. Regionally accredited. Cooperative education program required of all students. **Degrees:** 102 bachelor's awarded; master's offered. **ROTC:** Army, Air Force. **Location:** 18 miles from Dayton. **Calendar:** Semester, extensive summer session. **Full-time faculty:** 38 total. **Part-time faculty:** 34 total. **Special facilities:** African Methodist Episcopal Church archives.

Freshman class profile.

Out-of-state:	67%	**Live on campus:**	94%

Basis for selection. Class rank (top two-thirds), high school GPA, test scores most important. SAT or ACT recommended. Essay, interview recommended.

High school preparation. College-preparatory program recommended. 15 units required. Required and recommended units include English 4, mathematics 2-3, social studies 2, science 2-3 and foreign language 2.

2011-2012 Annual costs. Tuition/fees: $12,470. Room/board: $5,700. Books/supplies: $1,000. Personal expenses: $1,500.

Application procedures. Admission: Priority date 1/1; deadline 5/1. $25 fee, may be waived for applicants with need. Admission notification on a rolling basis. **Financial aid:** Priority date 3/15, closing date 6/30. FAFSA, institutional form required. Applicants notified on a rolling basis starting 3/15; must reply within 2 week(s) of notification.

Academics. Special study options: Cooperative education, cross-registration, honors, internships, study abroad. **Credit/placement by examination:** AP, CLEP, institutional tests. 30 credit hours maximum toward bachelor's degree. **Support services:** Remedial instruction, tutoring.

Majors. Biology: General. **Business:** Accounting, business admin, finance, managerial economics. **Communications:** Journalism. **Computer sciences:** General, information systems. **Engineering:** Chemical, civil, electrical, mechanical. **English:** English lit. **Foreign languages:** Comparative lit. **Health services:** Health care admin. **Liberal arts:** Arts/sciences. **Math:** General. **Physical sciences:** Chemistry. **Psychology:** General. **Social sciences:** Economics, political science, sociology. **Visual/performing arts:** Music, studio arts.

Computing on campus. 49 workstations in library, computer center.

Student life. Housing: Guaranteed on-campus for freshmen. Single-sex dorms, apartments available. **Activities:** Choral groups, dance, drama, music ensembles, radio station, student government, student newspaper, Inter-Faith Fellowship, Interdenominational Ministerial Alliance, Alpha-Omega.

Athletics. NAIA. **Intercollegiate:** Basketball, cross-country, golf, track and field. **Intramural:** Baseball M, basketball, softball, table tennis, tennis, volleyball.

Student services. Career counseling, student employment services, health services, personal counseling, placement for graduates, veterans' counselor.

Contact. E-mail: admissions@wilberforce.edu
Phone: (937) 708-5721 Toll-free number: (800) 367-8568
Fax: (937) 376-4751
Juan Alexander, Admissions Director, Wilberforce University, 1055 North Bickett Road, Wilberforce, OH 45384-1001

Wilmington College
Wilmington, Ohio CB member
www.wilmington.edu CB code: 1909

- Private 4-year liberal arts college affiliated with Society of Friends (Quaker)
- Residential campus in large town
- 1,274 degree-seeking undergraduates: 16% part-time, 56% women, 11% African American, 1% Hispanic American, 1% Native American, 1% international
- 26 degree-seeking graduate students
- 90% of applicants admitted
- SAT or ACT (ACT writing optional) required
- 52% graduate within 6 years

General. Founded in 1870. Regionally accredited. Affiliated with Wilmington Yearly Meeting of the Religious Society of Friends. Branch campuses in Cincinnati and other locations. BA in business offered at Cincinnati branch and Wilmington evening program. **Degrees:** 316 bachelor's awarded; master's offered. **Location:** 50 miles from Cincinnati, 60 miles from Columbus. **Calendar:** Semester, limited summer session. **Full-time faculty:** 66 total. **Part-time faculty:** 53 total. **Class size:** 71% < 20, 28% 20-39, less than 1% 40-49, less than 1% 50-99. **Special facilities:** Greenhouse, herbarium, observatory, electron microscope, live animal area, sports medicine center, Peace Resource Center containing Hiroshima/Nagasaki Memorial collection.

Freshman class profile. 1,614 applied, 1,453 admitted, 291 enrolled.

Mid 50% test scores			
SAT critical reading:	440-560	GPA 2.0-2.99:	33%
SAT math:	420-550	Rank in top quarter:	36%
ACT composite:	18-23	Rank in top tenth:	11%
GPA 3.75 or higher:	20%	Return as sophomores:	67%
GPA 3.50-3.74:	16%	Out-of-state:	9%
GPA 3.0-3.49:	31%	Live on campus:	80%
		International:	1%

Basis for selection. Previous academic record, test scores, counselor recommendation, and interview important. Essay, interview recommended for all.

High school preparation. College-preparatory program recommended. 16 units required. Required and recommended units include English 4, mathematics 2, social studies 2, science 2 (laboratory 2), foreign language 2 and academic electives 4. 6 art units recommended.

2011-2012 Annual costs. Tuition/fees: $26,840. Room/board: $8,870. Books/supplies: $500. Personal expenses: $450.

Financial aid. Non-need-based: Scholarships awarded for academics, alumni affiliation, religious affiliation, state residency.

Application procedures. Admission: Closing date 8/1. No application fee. Admission notification on a rolling basis beginning on or about 11/1. Online application does not require application fee. **Financial aid:** Priority date 3/31, closing date 6/1. FAFSA required. Applicants notified on a rolling basis starting 3/1; must reply by 5/1 or within 2 week(s) of notification.

Academics. Special study options: Cross-registration, double major, dual enrollment of high school students, honors, independent study, internships, liberal arts/career combination, student-designed major, study abroad, teacher certification program, Washington semester, weekend college. **Credit/placement by examination:** AP, CLEP, IB, SAT, ACT, institutional tests. 30 credit hours maximum toward bachelor's degree. **Support services:** Learning center, reduced course load, remedial instruction, study skills assistance, tutoring, writing center.

Majors. Biology: General, bacteriology, biochemistry, environmental. **Business:** Accounting, business admin, management science, marketing, sales/distribution. **Communications:** Communications/speech/rhetoric, journalism, media studies, public relations. **Computer sciences:** General, computer science. **Education:** General, agricultural, biology, chemistry, early childhood, elementary, English, health, history, mathematics, middle, multi-level teacher, physical, science, secondary, social science, social studies. **English:** English lit. **Foreign languages:** Spanish. **General:** Agribusiness operations, agronomy, animal sciences, business, equine science, farm/ranch, production. **History:** General. **Human services:** Social work. **Liberal arts:** Arts/sciences. **Math:** General. **Parks/recreation:** Sports admin. **Physical sciences:** Astronomy, chemistry, geology, planetary. **Protective services:** Criminal justice. **Psychology:** General. **Social sciences:** General, economics, political science, sociology. **Visual/performing arts:** Art, commercial/advertising art, dramatic, music.

Most popular majors. Agriculture 9%, business/marketing 30%, education 18%, parks/recreation 6%, psychology 6%.

Computing on campus. 156 workstations in library, computer center. Dormitories wired for high-speed internet access and linked to campus network. Commuter students can connect to campus network. Online course registration, helpline, student web hosting available.

Student life. Freshman orientation: Mandatory. Preregistration for classes offered. Held 3 days prior to start of fall semester. **Housing:** Guaranteed on-campus for all undergraduates. Coed dorms, single-sex dorms, apartments, fraternity/sorority housing available. $100 nonrefundable deposit, deadline 8/1. Living/learning units available. **Activities:** Pep band, campus ministries, choral groups, drama, music ensembles, musical theater, student government, student newspaper, social service, international club, education club, agriculture club, Christian Students, Young Friends (Quaker-Christian group), sports medicine association.

Athletics. NCAA. **Intercollegiate:** Baseball M, basketball, cheerleading, cross-country, football (tackle), golf, soccer, softball W, swimming, tennis, track and field, volleyball W, wrestling M. **Intramural:** Basketball, football (non-tackle), racquetball, soccer, softball, squash, table tennis, tennis, volleyball, weight lifting. **Team name:** Quakers.

Student services. Adult student services, alcohol/substance abuse counseling, chaplain/spiritual director, career counseling, student employment services, financial aid counseling, health services, minority student services, personal counseling, placement for graduates, veterans' counselor.

Contact. E-mail: admissions@wilmington.edu
Phone: (800) 341-9318 ext. 260 Fax: (937) 382-7077
Tina Garland, Director of Admission, Wilmington College, Box 1325 Pyle Center, Wilmington, OH 45177

Wittenberg University
Springfield, Ohio
www.wittenberg.edu

CB member
CB code: 1922

- Private 4-year liberal arts college affiliated with Evangelical Lutheran Church in America
- Residential campus in small city
- 1,735 degree-seeking undergraduates: 1% part-time, 56% women
- 6 degree-seeking graduate students
- 85% of applicants admitted
- Application essay required
- 71% graduate within 6 years

General. Founded in 1845. Regionally accredited. **Degrees:** 386 bachelor's awarded; master's offered. **ROTC:** Army, Air Force. **Location:** 25 miles from Dayton, 45 miles from Columbus. **Calendar:** Semester, limited summer session. **Full-time faculty:** 142 total; 94% have terminal degrees, 9% minority, 40% women. **Part-time faculty:** 58 total; 38% have terminal degrees, 10% minority, 52% women. **Class size:** 69% < 20, 31% 20-39, less than 1% 50-99, less than 1% >100. **Special facilities:** Observatory, East Asian art collection, Martin Luther library collection, humanities and technology center.

Freshman class profile. 4,412 applied, 3,735 admitted, 535 enrolled.

Mid 50% test scores			
SAT critical reading:	510-630	Rank in top quarter:	54%
SAT math:	510-630	Rank in top tenth:	27%
ACT composite:	22-30	End year in good standing:	99%
GPA 3.75 or higher:	37%	Return as sophomores:	79%
GPA 3.50-3.74:	16%	Out-of-state:	34%
GPA 3.0-3.49:	31%	Live on campus:	95%
GPA 2.0-2.99:	16%	International:	2%

Basis for selection. In order of importance: school achievement record, courses taken, school attended, trend in work, test scores, counselor recommendation, extracurricular activities, and interview. Special consideration for children of alumni, minorities, Lutherans, residents of Clark County, and international students. Math and foreign language placement tests required. Interview recommended for all; portfolio required for art program; audition recommended for dance, music, theater programs. **Home schooled:** On-campus interview.

High school preparation. College-preparatory program recommended. 16 units required; 21 recommended. Required and recommended units include English 4, mathematics 3-4, history 2-3, science 3-5 (laboratory 2) and foreign language 2-3.

2011-2012 Annual costs. Tuition/fees: $36,434. Room/board: $9,294.

2010-2011 Financial aid. All financial aid based on need. 455 full-time freshmen applied for aid; 407 were judged to have need; 407 of these received aid. Average need met was 88%. Average scholarship/grant was $24,818; average loan $3,825. 68% of total undergraduate aid awarded as scholarships/grants, 32% as loans/jobs. **Additional information:** Auditions required from applicants for music, theater, and dance scholarships. Portfolio required of applicants for art scholarships.

Application procedures. Admission: Priority date 3/15; no deadline. $40 fee, may be waived for applicants with need. Admission notification on a rolling basis. Must reply by May 1 or within 2 week(s) if notified thereafter. **Financial aid:** Priority date 3/1; no closing date. FAFSA required. Applicants notified on a rolling basis starting 3/1; must reply by 5/1 or within 2 week(s) of notification.

Academics. Special study options: Combined bachelor's/graduate degree, cross-registration, double major, dual enrollment of high school students, honors, independent study, internships, liberal arts/career combination, student-designed major, study abroad, teacher certification program, urban semester, Washington semester. Semester programs with Duke University (marine biology), School of Visual Arts in New York, Camarillo Hospital in California, National Institutes of Health in Washington, D.C., Washington University (MO) (occupational therapy), Johns Hopkins Nursing Program; 3-2 engineering with Washington University (MO), Case Western Reserve University. **Credit/placement by examination:** AP, CLEP, IB, institutional tests. **Support services:** Learning center, pre-admission summer program, reduced course load, study skills assistance, tutoring, writing center.

Majors. Area/ethnic studies: American, East Asian, European, Russian/Slavic. **Biology:** General, biochemistry, molecular. **Business:** General. **Communications:** Communications/speech/rhetoric. **Computer sciences:** Computer science. **Conservation:** Environmental studies. **Education:** General, early childhood, middle. **English:** English lit. **Foreign languages:** French, German, Spanish. **History:** General. **Liberal arts:** Arts/sciences. **Math:** General. **Philosophy/religion:** Philosophy, religion. **Physical sciences:** General, chemistry, geology, physics. **Psychology:** General. **Social sciences:** General, economics, geography, international relations, political science, sociology. **Visual/performing arts:** General, art, music.

Most popular majors. Biology 14%, business/marketing 14%, communications/journalism 6%, education 8%, English 8%, psychology 8%, social sciences 13%.

Computing on campus. 900 workstations in dormitories, library, computer center, student center. Dormitories wired for high-speed internet access and linked to campus network. Commuter students can connect to campus network. Online course registration, online library, helpline, student web hosting, wireless network available.

Student life. Freshman orientation: Mandatory. Preregistration for classes offered. Pre-orientation days offered 3 times during the summer. Full orientation held 3 days before the beginning of fall classes. **Housing:** Guaranteed on-campus for all undergraduates. Coed dorms, single-sex dorms, apartments, fraternity/sorority housing, wellness housing available. $400

deposit, deadline 7/1. Pets allowed in dorm rooms. Substance-free residence hall, honors residence hall, special theme halls available. **Activities:** Bands, campus ministries, choral groups, dance, drama, international student organizations, literary magazine, music ensembles, Model UN, musical theater, opera, radio station, student government, student newspaper, symphony orchestra, Newman club, Concerned Black Students, community volunteer service, Weaver Chapel Association, Project Woman, East Asian studies club, Hillel, Amnesty International, Habitat for Humanity.

Athletics. NCAA. **Intercollegiate:** Baseball M, basketball, cheerleading, cross-country, diving, field hockey W, football (tackle) M, golf, lacrosse, soccer, softball W, swimming, tennis, track and field, volleyball W. **Intramural:** Badminton, basketball, bowling, cricket M, diving, fencing, football (non-tackle), golf, gymnastics, handball M, ice hockey M, judo, racquetball, rugby, sailing, skiing, skin diving, soccer, softball, squash, swimming, table tennis, tennis, track and field, volleyball, water polo M, weight lifting. **Team name:** Tigers.

Student services. Adult student services, alcohol/substance abuse counseling, chaplain/spiritual director, career counseling, student employment services, financial aid counseling, health services, minority student services, personal counseling, placement for graduates, veterans' counselor, women's services.

Contact. E-mail: admission@wittenberg.edu
Phone: (937) 327-6314 Toll-free number: (877) 206-0332 ext. 6314
Fax: (937) 327-6379
Karen Hunt, Director of Admission, Wittenberg University, Ward Street and North Wittenberg, Springfield, OH 45501-0720

Wright State University

Dayton, Ohio
www.wright.edu

CB member
CB code: 1179

- Public 4-year university
- Commuter campus in small city
- 13,883 degree-seeking undergraduates: 14% part-time, 54% women, 15% African American, 2% Asian American, 3% Hispanic American, 2% international
- 3,591 degree-seeking graduate students
- 75% of applicants admitted
- SAT or ACT (ACT writing optional) required
- 40% graduate within 6 years

General. Founded in 1964. Regionally accredited. **Degrees:** 2,292 bachelor's, 67 associate awarded; master's, professional, doctoral offered. **ROTC:** Army, Air Force. **Location:** 10 miles from downtown. **Calendar:** Quarter, extensive summer session. **Full-time faculty:** 654 total; 14% minority, 46% women. **Part-time faculty:** 4 total; 50% women. **Class size:** 34% < 20, 44% 20-39, 9% 40-49, 11% 50-99, 2% >100. **Special facilities:** Biological preserve, disabled-accessible, garden of the senses.

Freshman class profile. 8,333 applied, 6,273 admitted, 2,713 enrolled.

Mid 50% test scores			
SAT critical reading:	440-570	Rank in top quarter:	33%
SAT math:	430-570	Rank in top tenth:	14%
SAT writing:	410-550	End year in good standing:	72%
ACT composite:	18-24	Return as sophomores:	62%
GPA 3.75 or higher:	14%	Out-of-state:	3%
GPA 3.50-3.74:	11%	Live on campus:	54%
GPA 3.0-3.49:	27%	International:	2%
GPA 2.0-2.99:	43%	Fraternities:	1%
		Sororities:	3%

Basis for selection. Liberal admission policy. College-preparatory curriculum. 2.0 GPA required. Test scores important for selected programs. Audition required for acting, dance, directing/stage management, music programs; portfolio required for art, art education programs. **Learning Disabled:** Students encouraged to contact Office of Disability Services to fill out application to qualify for support services.

High school preparation. College-preparatory program required. 16 units required. Required units include English 4, mathematics 3, social studies 3, science 3 (laboratory 3), foreign language 2 and visual/performing arts 1. Math requirement includes 2 algebra. Art, music or theater recommended. Students not meeting course recommendations must make up deficiency prior to admission to program.

2011-2012 Annual costs. Tuition/fees: $8,070; $15,633 out-of-state. Room/board: $8,387.

2011-2012 Financial aid. **Need-based:** 2,354 full-time freshmen applied for aid; 2,024 were judged to have need; 2,010 of these received aid. Average

need met was 53%. Average scholarship/grant was $5,729; average loan $3,610. 33% of total undergraduate aid awarded as scholarships/grants, 67% as loans/jobs. **Non-need-based:** Awarded to 1,234 full-time undergraduates, including 361 freshmen. Scholarships awarded for academics, alumni affiliation, art, athletics, leadership, minority status, music/drama, ROTC.

Application procedures. **Admission:** No deadline. $30 fee. Admission notification on a rolling basis beginning on or about 10/1. Application by January recommended for students desiring on-campus housing. **Financial aid:** Priority date 2/15; no closing date. FAFSA required. Applicants notified on a rolling basis starting 3/15.

Academics. **Special study options:** Cooperative education, cross-registration, distance learning, double major, dual enrollment of high school students, ESL, honors, independent study, internships, semester at sea, student-designed major, study abroad, teacher certification program, weekend college. **Credit/placement by examination:** AP, CLEP, institutional tests. **Support services:** Learning center, pre-admission summer program, reduced course load, remedial instruction, study skills assistance, tutoring, writing center.

Majors. **Area/ethnic studies:** African-American, women's. **Biology:** General, bacteriology. **Business:** Accounting, business admin, finance, human resources, international, logistics, management information systems, managerial economics, marketing. **Communications:** Communications/speech/rhetoric, media studies, public relations. **Computer sciences:** General. **Education:** Business, early childhood, middle, music, physical, sales/marketing, science, voc/tech. **Engineering:** Applied physics, biomedical, computer, electrical, engineering science, materials, mechanical. **English:** English lit. **Foreign languages:** General, classics, French, German, Latin, modern Greek, sign language interpretation, Spanish. **Health services:** Clinical lab science, environmental health, nursing (RN), prenursing, public health nursing, vocational rehab counseling. **History:** General. **Human services:** Social work. **Liberal arts:** Arts/sciences. **Math:** General, statistics. **Parks/recreation:** Health/fitness. **Philosophy/religion:** Philosophy, religion. **Physical sciences:** Chemistry, geology, physics. **Psychology:** General. **Social sciences:** Anthropology, criminology, economics, geography, international relations, political science, sociology, urban studies. **Visual/performing arts:** Acting, art, art history/conservation, dance, dramatic, film/cinema/video, music, music history, music performance, theater design.

Most popular majors. Business/marketing 32%, education 7%, engineering/engineering technologies 6%, health sciences 13%, psychology 8%, social sciences 8%.

Computing on campus. 1,700 workstations in dormitories, library, computer center, student center. Dormitories wired for high-speed internet access and linked to campus network. Commuter students can connect to campus network. Online course registration, online library, helpline, repair service, student web hosting, wireless network available.

Student life. **Freshman orientation:** Available, $75 fee. Preregistration for classes offered. **Housing:** Coed dorms, special housing for disabled, apartments, wellness housing available. $150 fully refundable deposit. Honors dorm, institutional apartments. **Activities:** Bands, campus ministries, choral groups, dance, drama, international student organizations, literary magazine, music ensembles, Model UN, musical theater, opera, radio station, student government, student newspaper, symphony orchestra, TV station, black student union, Baptist student union, student association for escorts, College Students for Special Wish, Fellowship of Christian Students, Circle-K, Campus Crusade for Christ, Ohio College Democrats, Jewish student union.

Athletics. NCAA. **Intercollegiate:** Baseball M, basketball, cheerleading, cross-country, diving, golf M, soccer, softball W, swimming, tennis, track and field W, volleyball W. **Intramural:** Archery, baseball M, basketball, cricket M, cross-country, football (tackle), golf, handball, lacrosse M, soccer, softball, squash, tennis, volleyball W. **Team name:** Raiders.

Student services. Adult student services, chaplain/spiritual director, career counseling, student employment services, financial aid counseling, health services, legal services, minority student services, on-campus daycare, personal counseling, placement for graduates, veterans' counselor, women's services. **Physically disabled:** Services for visually, speech, hearing impaired.

Contact. E-mail: admissions@wright.edu
Phone: (937) 775-5700 Toll-free number: (800) 247-1770
Fax: (937) 775-5795
Cathy Davis, Assistant Vice President for Undergraduate Admissions, Wright State University, 3640 Colonel Glenn Highway, Dayton, OH 45435

Xavier University
Cincinnati, Ohio
www.xavier.edu

CB member
CB code: 1965

- Private 4-year university affiliated with Roman Catholic Church
- Residential campus in large city
- 4,355 degree-seeking undergraduates: 8% part-time, 53% women, 10% African American, 2% Asian American, 4% Hispanic American, 1% international
- 2,219 degree-seeking graduate students
- 70% of applicants admitted
- SAT or ACT (ACT writing optional), application essay required
- 79% graduate within 6 years; 57% enter graduate study

General. Founded in 1831. Regionally accredited. **Degrees:** 945 bachelor's, 17 associate awarded; master's, professional offered. **ROTC:** Army, Air Force. **Location:** 5 miles from downtown. **Calendar:** Semester, limited summer session. **Full-time faculty:** 352 total; 75% have terminal degrees, 14% minority, 50% women. **Part-time faculty:** 338 total; 9% minority, 56% women. **Class size:** 42% < 20, 55% 20-39, 2% 40-49, 1% 50-99, less than 1% >100. **Special facilities:** Observatory.

Freshman class profile. 9,783 applied, 6,865 admitted, 1,123 enrolled.

Mid 50% test scores			
SAT critical reading:	480-600	Rank in top quarter:	54%
SAT math:	500-610	Rank in top tenth:	22%
ACT composite:	22-27	End year in good standing:	91%
GPA 3.75 or higher:	34%	Return as sophomores:	84%
GPA 3.50-3.74:	20%	Out-of-state:	48%
GPA 3.0-3.49:	32%	Live on campus:	87%
GPA 2.0-2.99:	14%	International:	1%

Basis for selection. Rigor of curriculum, class rank, grades, ACT/SAT, counselor recommendations, essay, and activities important. Campus visit recommended for all students.

High school preparation. College-preparatory program recommended. 21 units recommended. Recommended units include English 4, mathematics 3, social studies 3, science 3, foreign language 2 and academic electives 5. 1 health/physical education recommended.

2011-2012 Annual costs. Tuition/fees: $31,160. Room/board: $10,130. Books/supplies: $1,000. Personal expenses: $1,000.

2011-2012 Financial aid. Need-based: 940 full-time freshmen applied for aid; 742 were judged to have need; 741 of these received aid. Average need met was 74%. Average scholarship/grant was $15,327; average loan $4,121. 65% of total undergraduate aid awarded as scholarships/grants, 35% as loans/jobs. **Non-need-based:** Awarded to 1,736 full-time undergraduates, including 501 freshmen. Scholarships awarded for academics, alumni affiliation, art, athletics, leadership, music/drama, religious affiliation.

Application procedures. Admission: Closing date 2/1. $35 fee, may be waived for applicants with need, free for online applicants. Admission notification on a rolling basis beginning on or about 10/15. Must reply by 5/1. **Financial aid:** Priority date 2/15; no closing date. FAFSA required. Applicants notified on a rolling basis starting 2/15; must reply by 5/1.

Academics. Strong emphasis on ethics and values in core curriculum. **Special study options:** Combined bachelor's/graduate degree, cooperative education, cross-registration, double major, dual enrollment of high school students, ESL, honors, independent study, internships, semester at sea, study abroad, teacher certification program, urban semester, Washington semester, weekend college. Cooperative science-engineering program (physics and chemistry) with University of Cincinnati, forestry program and environmental management programs with Duke University, Service Learning Semester. **Credit/placement by examination:** AP, CLEP, IB, institutional tests. 30 credit hours maximum toward associate degree, 60 toward bachelor's. **Support services:** Learning center, pre-admission summer program, reduced course load, remedial instruction, study skills assistance, tutoring, writing center.

Majors. Biology: General. **Business:** General, accounting, actuarial science, business admin, entrepreneurial studies, finance, human resources, international, management information systems, managerial economics, marketing. **Communications:** Advertising, organizational, public relations, radio/TV. **Computer sciences:** Computer science. **Conservation:** Environmental science, management/policy. **Education:** Biology, chemistry, early childhood, elementary, middle, Montessori teacher, music, physics, science, special ed. **Engineering:** Applied physics, chemical. **English:** English lit. **Foreign languages:** Classics, French, German, Spanish. **Health services:** Athletic training, clinical lab science, nursing (RN). **History:** General. **Human services:** Social work. **Liberal arts:** Arts/sciences. **Math:** General. **Parks/recreation:**

Sports admin. **Philosophy/religion:** Philosophy, religion. **Physical sciences:** Chemistry, physics. **Protective services:** Criminal justice. **Psychology:** General. **Social sciences:** Economics, international relations, political science, sociology. **Visual/performing arts:** Art, music, studio arts.

Most popular majors. Business/marketing 29%, health sciences 7%, liberal arts 16%, social sciences 8%.

Computing on campus. 334 workstations in dormitories, library, computer center, student center. Dormitories wired for high-speed internet access and linked to campus network. Commuter students can connect to campus network. Online course registration, online library, helpline, repair service, student web hosting, wireless network available.

Student life. Freshman orientation: Mandatory, $190 fee. Preregistration for classes offered. Held the weekend before the start of classes. **Policies:** Student handbook, responsible computer use, university alcohol policy, harassment code accountability procedures. **Housing:** Guaranteed on-campus for freshmen. Coed dorms, special housing for disabled, apartments available. $200 fully refundable deposit, deadline 5/1. **Activities:** Bands, campus ministries, choral groups, dance, drama, film society, international student organizations, literary magazine, music ensembles, musical theater, opera, student government, student newspaper, symphony orchestra, TV station, Life after Sunday, Xavier Interfaith, South Asian society, St. Vincent de Paul society, Natural Ties, black student association, College Republicans, College Democrats, Voices of Solidarity, Latino student organization.

Athletics. NCAA. **Intercollegiate:** Baseball M, basketball, cheerleading, cross-country, golf, soccer, swimming, tennis, track and field, volleyball W. **Intramural:** Basketball, bowling, football (non-tackle), racquetball, soccer, softball, tennis, volleyball. **Team name:** Musketeers.

Student services. Adult student services, alcohol/substance abuse counseling, chaplain/spiritual director, career counseling, services for economically disadvantaged, student employment services, financial aid counseling, health services, minority student services, personal counseling, placement for graduates, veterans' counselor, women's services. **Physically disabled:** Services for visually, speech, hearing impaired.

Contact. E-mail: xuadmit@xavier.edu
Phone: (513) 745-3301 Toll-free number: (877) 982-3648
Fax: (513) 745-4319
Aaron Meis, Dean of Admissions, Xavier University, 3800 Victory Parkway, Cincinnati, OH 45207-5311

Youngstown State University
Youngstown, Ohio
www.ysu.edu

CB member
CB code: 1975

- Public 4-year university
- Commuter campus in small city
- 13,032 degree-seeking undergraduates: 21% part-time, 52% women, 17% African American, 1% Asian American, 3% Hispanic American, 1% international
- 1,083 degree-seeking graduate students
- 35% graduate within 6 years

General. Founded in 1908. Regionally accredited. **Degrees:** 1,468 bachelor's, 201 associate awarded; master's, professional, doctoral offered. **ROTC:** Army, Air Force. **Location:** 65 miles from Cleveland, 60 miles from Pittsburgh. **Calendar:** Semester, limited summer session. **Full-time faculty:** 441 total; 85% have terminal degrees, 17% minority, 41% women. **Part-time faculty:** 625 total; 7% minority, 53% women. **Class size:** 35% < 20, 50% 20-39, 8% 40-49, 6% 50-99, 2% >100. **Special facilities:** Planetarium, historic preservation center.

Freshman class profile. 5,274 applied, 4,530 admitted, 2,571 enrolled.

Mid 50% test scores			
		GPA 2.0-2.99:	44%
SAT critical reading:	400-540	Rank in top quarter:	25%
SAT math:	410-550	Rank in top tenth:	10%
SAT writing:	380-520	Return as sophomores:	65%
ACT composite:	17-24	Out-of-state:	11%
GPA 3.75 or higher:	11%	Live on campus:	18%
GPA 3.50-3.74:	10%	Fraternities:	2%
GPA 3.0-3.49:	25%	Sororities:	3%

Basis for selection. Open admission, but selective for some programs and for out-of-state students. Out-of-state applicants must be in top two-thirds of class, or have 17 ACT or 820 SAT exclusive of Writing. Open admission policy for Ohio residents and Mercer and Lawrence County, Pennsylvania residents. Special requirements for nursing, engineering and some other programs. Interview required for BS/MD program; audition required

for music, BFA theater programs. **Home schooled:** Transcript of courses and grades required. ACT/SAT required unless out of high school 2 or more years. Official transcript showing documentation of coursework completed for grades 9-12 and indicating date of completion of studies or graduation must be sent to Admissions. Any relevant supporting documents required by applicant's home state verifying home school curriculum required. Curriculum outline, detailing course content, textbooks used, any other relevant information regarding coursework must be submitted. Copy of the Superintendent's Exemption Notice showing the student is excused to receive home schooling also required.

High school preparation. College-preparatory program recommended.

2011-2012 Annual costs. Tuition/fees: $7,451; $13,408 out-of-state. Room/board: $7,900. Books/supplies: $1,237. Personal expenses: $1,776.

2010-2011 Financial aid. Need-based: 2,456 full-time freshmen applied for aid; 2,178 were judged to have need; 2,172 of these received aid. Average need met was 31%. Average scholarship/grant was $5,517; average loan $3,248. 54% of total undergraduate aid awarded as scholarships/grants, 46% as loans/jobs. **Non-need-based:** Awarded to 3,148 full-time undergraduates, including 813 freshmen. Scholarships awarded for academics, alumni affiliation, athletics, ROTC, state residency.

Application procedures. Admission: Priority date 2/15; deadline 8/1 (postmark date). $30 fee, may be waived for applicants with need. Admission notification on a rolling basis. Students who apply by February 15 eligible for early registration and orientation. **Financial aid:** Priority date 2/15; no closing date. FAFSA, institutional form required. Applicants notified on a rolling basis starting 5/30; must reply within 2 week(s) of notification.

Academics. Special study options: Accelerated study, combined bachelor's/graduate degree, cooperative education, cross-registration, distance learning, double major, dual enrollment of high school students, ESL, exchange student, honors, independent study, internships, semester at sea, student-designed major, study abroad, teacher certification program, urban semester, Washington semester. Off-campus study with Lorain County Community College. **Credit/placement by examination:** AP, CLEP, IB, institutional tests. In select CLEP and AP tests, higher grade may make student eligible for more credits. **Support services:** Learning center, pre-admission summer program, reduced course load, remedial instruction, study skills assistance, tutoring, writing center.

Majors. Area/ethnic studies: African-American, American. **Biology:** General. **Business:** General, accounting, apparel, banking/financial services, business admin, fashion, finance, financial planning, hospitality admin, hospitality/recreation, human resources, management information systems, managerial economics, marketing, merchandising, operations, public finance, retailing, sales/distribution, selling, tourism promotion, tourism/travel. **Communications:** Advertising, communications/speech/rhetoric, journalism, public relations, radio/TV. **Computer sciences:** General, computer science, information systems, information technology, programming. **Conservation:** Environmental science. **Education:** General, art, autistic, biology, business, chemistry, computer, early childhood, elementary, emotionally handicapped, English, family/consumer sciences, foreign languages, French, health, history, kindergarten/preschool, learning disabled, mathematics, mentally handicapped, middle, multi-level teacher, multiple handicapped, music, physical, physics, science, secondary, social science, social studies, Spanish, special ed, speech. **Engineering:** General, chemical, civil, computer, electrical, industrial, mechanical. **English:** English lit, rhetoric/composition, technical writing. **Foreign languages:** General, French, Italian, Spanish. **Health services:** Athletic training, clinical lab science, community health, community health services, dental hygiene, dietetics, facilities admin, nursing (RN), predental, premedicine, prepharmacy, preveterinary, public health ed, respiratory therapy technology. **History:** General. **Human services:** General, social work. **Liberal arts:** Arts/sciences. **Math:** General. **Parks/recreation:** Exercise sciences, health/fitness, sports admin. **Philosophy/religion:** Philosophy, religion. **Physical sciences:** General, astronomy, chemistry, geology, physics, planetary. **Protective services:** Corrections, criminal justice, forensics, law enforcement admin, security services. **Psychology:** General. **Social sciences:** General, anthropology, econometrics, economics, geography, international economics, political science, sociology. **Visual/performing arts:** General, acting, art, art history/conservation, commercial/advertising art, dance, dramatic, jazz, music, music history, music performance, music theory/composition, painting, photography, piano/keyboard, printmaking, stringed instruments, studio arts, theater design, voice/opera. **Work/family studies:** General, clothing/textiles, family/community services, food/nutrition.

Most popular majors. Business/marketing 17%, education 14%, engineering/engineering technologies 9%, health sciences 10%, liberal arts 7%, security/protective services 6%.

Computing on campus. 170 workstations in dormitories, library, student center. Dormitories wired for high-speed internet access and linked to campus network. Commuter students can connect to campus network. Online course registration, online library, helpline, repair service, student web hosting, wireless network available.

Student life. Freshman orientation: Available, $75 fee. Preregistration for classes offered. Held in March, June, July, and August. **Policies:** All activities and events governed by student code of conduct and all organization members must be currently registered students. **Housing:** Guaranteed on-campus for all undergraduates. Coed dorms, single-sex dorms, apartments, fraternity/sorority housing, wellness housing available. $200 deposit. University scholars program honors facility available. **Activities:** Bands, campus ministries, choral groups, dance, drama, international student organizations, literary magazine, music ensembles, Model UN, musical theater, opera, radio station, student government, student newspaper, symphony orchestra, College Republicans, College Democrats, black student union, Latino organization, student athlete advisory council, Interfraternity Council, Golden Key, Omicron Delta Kappa, gospel choir, Panhellenic Council.

Athletics. NCAA. **Intercollegiate:** Baseball M, basketball, cross-country, football (tackle) M, golf, soccer W, softball W, swimming W, tennis, track and field, volleyball W. **Intramural:** Badminton, basketball, football (non-tackle), handball, racquetball, soccer, softball, swimming, table tennis, volleyball. **Team name:** Penguins.

Student services. Adult student services, alcohol/substance abuse counseling, chaplain/spiritual director, career counseling, student employment services, financial aid counseling, health services, minority student services, on-campus daycare, personal counseling, placement for graduates, veterans' counselor, women's services. **Physically disabled:** Services for visually, speech, hearing impaired.

Contact. E-mail: enroll@ysu.edu
Phone: (330) 941-2000 Toll-free number: (877) 468-6978
Fax: (330) 941-3674
Sue Davis, Director of Undergraduate Admissions, Youngstown State University, One University Plaza, Youngstown, OH 44555-0001

Oklahoma

Bacone College
Muskogee, Oklahoma
www.bacone.edu
CB code: 6030

▶ Private 4-year liberal arts college affiliated with American Baptist Churches in the USA
▶ Residential campus in large town
▶ 1,140 degree-seeking undergraduates
▶ SAT or ACT required

General. Founded in 1880. Regionally accredited. American Indian heritage and commitment to serving Native Americans. Guided by Christian principles. **Degrees:** 76 bachelor's, 64 associate awarded. **Location:** 50 miles from Tulsa. **Calendar:** Semester, limited summer session. **Full-time faculty:** 23 total. **Part-time faculty:** 58 total. **Class size:** 70% < 20, 25% 20-39, 5% 40-49. **Special facilities:** Native American museum and collection.

Freshman class profile.

GPA 3.75 or higher:	6%	Rank in top quarter:	17%
GPA 3.50-3.74:	10%	Rank in top tenth:	5%
GPA 3.0-3.49:	26%	Out-of-state:	39%
GPA 2.0-2.99:	56%	Live on campus:	78%

Basis for selection. Student must meet two of the following: 2.0 GPA, top 50% of graduating class and/or 18 ACT. Additional standards for admission to nursing and radiography programs applied after student has been admitted. ACT used for counseling. Interview recommended for nursing, radiologic technology programs. **Home schooled:** Official transcript from accredited homeschool organization or GED required.

High school preparation. College-preparatory program recommended. Recommended units include English 4, mathematics 3, history 2, science 2 (laboratory 2).

2011-2012 Annual costs. Tuition/fees: $12,900. Room/board: $8,550. Books/supplies: $1,400. Personal expenses: $500.

Financial aid. All financial aid based on need.

Application procedures. Admission: No deadline. $25 fee, may be waived for applicants with need, free for online applicants. Admission notification on a rolling basis. **Financial aid:** Priority date 3/31; no closing date. FAFSA required. Applicants notified on a rolling basis starting 4/1; must reply within 2 week(s) of notification.

Academics. Special study options: Accelerated study, cross-registration, double major, dual enrollment of high school students, independent study, internships, liberal arts/career combination, student-designed major, teacher certification program. **Credit/placement by examination:** AP, CLEP, SAT, ACT, institutional tests. 15 credit hours maximum toward associate degree. **Support services:** Learning center, pre-admission summer program, remedial instruction, study skills assistance, tutoring.

Majors. Area/ethnic studies: Native American. **Business:** Business admin. **Education:** Early childhood, elementary, health, physical. **Health services:** Medical radiologic technology/radiation therapy, nursing (RN). **Parks/recreation:** Exercise sciences, facilities management, sports admin. **Protective services:** Criminal justice.

Most popular majors. Business/marketing 12%, education 61%, parks/recreation 13%, social sciences 11%.

Computing on campus. 84 workstations in library, computer center. Dormitories wired for high-speed internet access and linked to campus network. Commuter students can connect to campus network. Online library, wireless network available.

Student life. Freshman orientation: Mandatory, $100 fee. Preregistration for classes offered. **Policies:** No alcohol or tobacco products allowed on campus. **Housing:** Single-sex dorms available. $100 deposit. **Activities:** Campus ministries, choral groups, dance, drama, student government, student newspaper, Native American learning work community, Native American students of promise, journalism club, praise team club, praise band, American Indian stickball club, criminal justice studies club, Native American student association, black student association, American Indian dance and song.

Athletics. NAIA. **Intercollegiate:** Baseball M, basketball, cheerleading, cross-country, football (tackle) M, golf, rodeo, soccer, softball W, tennis, track and field, volleyball W, wrestling M. **Intramural:** Basketball, football (tackle) M, soccer, softball, table tennis. **Team name:** Warriors.

Student services. Chaplain/spiritual director, career counseling, student employment services, financial aid counseling, health services, personal counseling, placement for graduates. **Physically disabled:** Services for visually, speech, hearing impaired.

Contact. E-mail: admissionsoffice@bacone.edu
Phone: (918) 683-4581 ext. 7342
Toll-free number: (888) 682-5514 ext. 7342 Fax: (918) 781-7416
Mike Jackson, Director of Admissions, Bacone College, 2299 Old Bacone Road, Muskogee, OK 74403

Cameron University
Lawton, Oklahoma
www.cameron.edu
CB member
CB code: 6080

▶ Public 4-year university
▶ Commuter campus in small city
▶ 5,599 degree-seeking undergraduates: 30% part-time, 61% women, 17% African American, 2% Asian American, 6% Hispanic American, 7% Native American, 5% international
▶ 497 degree-seeking graduate students
▶ 99% of applicants admitted
▶ SAT or ACT (ACT writing optional) required

General. Founded in 1909. Regionally accredited. **Degrees:** 539 bachelor's, 184 associate awarded; master's offered. **ROTC:** Army. **Location:** 90 miles from Oklahoma City. **Calendar:** Semester, limited summer session. **Full-time faculty:** 173 total; 72% have terminal degrees, 17% minority, 41% women. **Part-time faculty:** 153 total; 16% have terminal degrees, 14% minority, 50% women. **Class size:** 36% < 20, 54% 20-39, 7% 40-49, 2% 50-99, less than 1% >100.

Freshman class profile. 1,490 applied, 1,479 admitted, 1,100 enrolled.

Mid 50% test scores		**End year in good standing:**	55%
ACT composite:	16-22	**Return as sophomores:**	52%
GPA 3.75 or higher:	13%	**Out-of-state:**	6%
GPA 3.50-3.74:	15%	**Live on campus:**	20%
GPA 3.0-3.49:	30%	**International:**	3%
GPA 2.0-2.99:	38%	**Fraternities:**	3%
Rank in top quarter:	15%	**Sororities:**	2%
Rank in top tenth:	4%		

Basis for selection. All applicants must be graduates of accredited high school or possess GED (student's high school class must have graduated). Associate of science and baccalaureate degree requirements: 20 ACT/890 SAT OR rank in top 50% of high school class with 2.7 GPA.

High school preparation. College-preparatory program recommended. 15 units required; 17 recommended. Required and recommended units include English 4, mathematics 3, history 3, science 3 (laboratory 3), foreign language 1, computer science 1 and academic electives 2.

2011-2012 Annual costs. Tuition/fees: $4,590; $11,198 out-of-state. Room/board: $3,754. Books/supplies: $810. Personal expenses: $300.

2010-2011 Financial aid. Need-based: 819 full-time freshmen applied for aid; 653 were judged to have need; 584 of these received aid. Average need met was 61%. Average scholarship/grant was $5,607; average loan $3,029. 70% of total undergraduate aid awarded as scholarships/grants, 30% as loans/jobs. **Non-need-based:** Awarded to 867 full-time undergraduates, including 255 freshmen. Scholarships awarded for academics, alumni affiliation, art, athletics, leadership, music/drama, ROTC.

Application procedures. Admission: No deadline. $15 fee, may be waived for applicants with need. Admission notification on a rolling basis. **Financial aid:** Priority date 4/1; no closing date. FAFSA required. Applicants notified on a rolling basis starting 4/1; must reply by 8/7 or within 2 week(s) of notification.

Academics. Special study options: Accelerated study, distance learning, double major, dual enrollment of high school students, honors, independent study, internships, liberal arts/career combination, student-designed major, study abroad, teacher certification program. **Credit/placement by examination:** AP, CLEP, IB, institutional tests. **Support services:** Learning center, pre-admission summer program, remedial instruction, study skills assistance, tutoring, writing center.

Majors. Biology: General. **Business:** Accounting, business admin. **Communications:** Communications/speech/rhetoric. **Computer sciences:** General, computer science, information technology. **Education:** General, chemistry, early childhood, educational technology, elementary, English, foreign languages, mathematics, music, physical, science, social studies. **English:** English lit. **Foreign languages:** General. **Health services:** Clinical lab science. **History:** General. **Math:** General. **Parks/recreation:** Health/fitness. **Physical sciences:** Chemistry, physics. **Psychology:** General. **Social sciences:** Political science, sociology. **Visual/performing arts:** Art, music.

Most popular majors. Business/marketing 17%, communications/journalism 6%, computer/information sciences 6%, education 19%, liberal arts 10%.

Computing on campus. 277 workstations in dormitories, library, computer center. Dormitories wired for high-speed internet access and linked to campus network. Commuter students can connect to campus network. Online library, helpline, student web hosting, wireless network available.

Student life. Freshman orientation: Mandatory. Preregistration for classes offered. Two-part orientation requirement for students with less than 15 hours of credit. First part held throughout the summer and before classes start in the fall; second part held the weekend before classes start. **Policies:** Student code of conduct; no alcohol on campus. **Housing:** Single-sex dorms, special housing for disabled, apartments available. $200 partly refundable deposit. Quiet areas available. **Activities:** Bands, campus ministries, choral groups, dance, drama, film society, international student organizations, literary magazine, music ensembles, musical theater, opera, student government, student newspaper, symphony orchestra, TV station, programming activities council, biology club, Alpha Phi, Sigma Tau Gamma, health professions student society, Fellowship of Christian Athletes, Students of the Caribbean Alliance, Nigerian student association.

Athletics. NCAA. **Intercollegiate:** Baseball M, basketball, cross-country M, golf, softball W, tennis, volleyball W. **Intramural:** Archery, badminton, basketball, bowling, football (non-tackle), golf, racquetball, soccer, swimming, table tennis, tennis, volleyball. **Team name:** Aggies.

Student services. Adult student services, alcohol/substance abuse counseling, career counseling, services for economically disadvantaged, student employment services, financial aid counseling, health services, personal counseling, veterans' counselor. **Physically disabled:** Services for visually, speech, hearing impaired.

Contact. E-mail: admissions@cameron.edu
Phone: (580) 581-2289 Toll-free number: (888) 454-7600
Fax: (580) 581-5416
Zoe DuRant, Director of Admissions, Cameron University, 2800 West Gore Boulevard, Lawton, OK 73505-6377

East Central University
Ada, Oklahoma
www.ecok.edu   **CB code: 6186**

▶ Public 4-year university
▶ Residential campus in large town
▶ 3,879 degree-seeking undergraduates: 19% part-time, 58% women, 4% African American, 4% Hispanic American, 18% Native American, 5% international
▶ 949 degree-seeking graduate students
▶ 92% of applicants admitted
▶ SAT or ACT (ACT writing optional) required

General. Founded in 1909. Regionally accredited. **Degrees:** 679 bachelor's awarded; master's offered. **Location:** 86 miles from Oklahoma City. **Calendar:** Semester, extensive summer session. **Full-time faculty:** 170 total; 63% have terminal degrees, 14% minority, 44% women. **Part-time faculty:** 100 total; 13% have terminal degrees, 18% minority, 68% women. **Class size:** 38% < 20, 51% 20-39, 9% 40-49, 3% 50-99. **Special facilities:** Outdoor sculpture garden, 2 theatres, TV studio, photography studio.

Freshman class profile. 946 applied, 869 admitted, 622 enrolled.

Mid 50% test scores		GPA 2.0-2.99:	21%
SAT critical reading:	380-480	Rank in top quarter:	45%
SAT math:	480-620	Rank in top tenth:	22%
ACT composite:	18-23	Return as sophomores:	65%
GPA 3.75 or higher:	26%	Out-of-state:	8%
GPA 3.50-3.74:	20%	Live on campus:	60%
GPA 3.0-3.49:	32%	International:	5%

Basis for selection. Rank in top 50% of graduating class, 20 ACT or SAT equivalent, 2.7 GPA and required course work important.

High school preparation. 15 units required. Required units include English 4, mathematics 3, social studies 2, history 1, science 3 (laboratory 1) and academic electives 2. Additional courses from English, math, science, history, social sciences, foreign language, or computer science.

2011-2012 Annual costs. Tuition/fees: $4,653; $11,285 out-of-state. Room/board: $4,574. Books/supplies: $1,200. Personal expenses: $1,880.

Financial aid. Non-need-based: Scholarships awarded for academics, athletics.

Application procedures. Admission: No deadline. $20 fee. Admission notification on a rolling basis. **Financial aid:** Closing date 3/1. FAFSA required. Applicants notified on a rolling basis starting 4/15; must reply within 2 week(s) of notification.

Academics. Special study options: Distance learning, double major, dual enrollment of high school students, exchange student, honors, independent study, internships, study abroad, teacher certification program. **Credit/placement by examination:** AP, CLEP, ACT, institutional tests. 94 credit hours maximum toward bachelor's degree. Students do not receive CLEP or AP credit until 12 hours completed in residence with 2.0 GPA. **Support services:** Learning center, pre-admission summer program, reduced course load, remedial instruction, study skills assistance, tutoring, writing center.

Majors. Area/ethnic studies: Native American. **Biology:** General. **Business:** General, accounting, business admin, finance, human resources. **Communications:** Communications/speech/rhetoric, journalism, media studies. **Computer sciences:** General. **Education:** Art, biology, chemistry, drama/dance, early childhood, elementary, English, family/consumer sciences, history, mathematics, music, physical, physics, science, social studies, special ed, speech. **English:** English lit, rhetoric/composition. **Health services:** Athletic training, clinical lab science, environmental health, nursing (RN), vocational rehab counseling. **History:** General. **Human services:** Social work. **Math:** General, applied. **Parks/recreation:** General, exercise sciences. **Physical sciences:** Chemistry, physics. **Protective services:** Police science. **Psychology:** General. **Social sciences:** GIS/cartography, political science, sociology. **Theology:** Sacred music. **Visual/performing arts:** Art, dramatic, graphic design, music, piano/keyboard, voice/opera. **Work/family studies:** General, child care service, clothing/textiles.

Most popular majors. Biology 7%, business/marketing 13%, education 11%, health sciences 13%, parks/recreation 6%, public administration/social services 14%.

Computing on campus. 677 workstations in library, computer center. Online library, helpline, repair service, wireless network available.

Student life. Freshman orientation: Mandatory. Preregistration for classes offered. **Housing:** Coed dorms, single-sex dorms, special housing for disabled, apartments, fraternity/sorority housing available. $40 nonrefundable deposit. **Activities:** Bands, choral groups, dance, drama, film society, literary magazine, music ensembles, musical theater, student government, student newspaper, association of black students, Native American student association, Baptist student union, united campus ministry, students with disabilities, Church of Christ Bible Chair, Life House, Sigma Society, Panhellenic, silent friends club.

Athletics. NCAA. **Intercollegiate:** Baseball M, basketball, cross-country, football (tackle) M, golf, soccer W, softball W, tennis, volleyball W. **Intramural:** Basketball, soccer, softball, volleyball. **Team name:** Tigers.

Student services. Adult student services, career counseling, student employment services, financial aid counseling, health services, minority student services, on-campus daycare, personal counseling, placement for graduates, veterans' counselor. **Physically disabled:** Services for visually, speech, hearing impaired.

Contact. E-mail: parmstro@ecok.edu
Phone: (580) 332-8000 Fax: (580) 559-5432
Pamla Armstrong, Registrar and Director of Admissions, East Central University, PMBJ8, 1100 East 14th Street, Ada, OK 74820

Family of Faith College
Shawnee, Oklahoma
www.familyoffaithcollege.edu

▶ Private 4-year Bible college
▶ Residential campus in rural community
▶ 18 degree-seeking undergraduates
▶ Application essay required

General. Regionally accredited; also accredited by ABHE. **Degrees:** 5 bachelor's awarded. **Location:** 6 miles from Shawnee, 30 miles from Oklahoma

City. **Calendar:** Semester, limited summer session. **Full-time faculty:** 3 total. **Part-time faculty:** 3 total.

Basis for selection. SAT/ACT not required for certificate programs. Academic and personal references required. SAT or ACT recommended. **Home schooled:** Transcript of courses and grades, state high school equivalency certificate, letter of recommendation (nonparent) required.

2011-2012 Annual costs. Tuition/fees: $5,410. Room only: $1,600.

Application procedures. Admission: Closing date 4/1 (receipt date). $25 fee.

Academics. Credit/placement by examination: AP, CLEP.

Majors. Education: Multi-level teacher. **Theology:** Bible, theology.

Student life. Freshman orientation: Mandatory. Preregistration for classes offered. **Policies:** Religious observance required. **Housing:** Single-sex dorms available. $50 fully refundable deposit. **Activities:** Campus ministries, choral groups, student government.

Athletics. Intramural: Volleyball.

Student services. Adult student services, alcohol/substance abuse counseling, chaplain/spiritual director, financial aid counseling, personal counseling.

Contact. E-mail: info@familyoffaithcollege.edu
Phone: (405) 273-5331 Fax: (405) 273-8535
Rhonda Gaines, Vice President of Student Affairs, Family of Faith College, PO Box 1805, Shawnee, OK 74802-1805

Hillsdale Free Will Baptist College
Moore, Oklahoma
www.hc.edu   CB code: 0927

- Private 4-year liberal arts college
- Residential campus in small city
- 202 degree-seeking undergraduates
- SAT or ACT (ACT writing recommended) required

General. Regionally accredited; also accredited by TRACS. **Degrees:** 26 bachelor's, 24 associate awarded; master's offered. **Location:** 2 miles from Oklahoma City, 2 miles from Norman. **Calendar:** Semester, limited summer session. **Full-time faculty:** 14 total. **Part-time faculty:** 35 total.

Basis for selection. Academic GPA and test scores most important.

2011-2012 Annual costs. Tuition/fees: $10,410. Room/board: $5,750.

Application procedures. Admission: No deadline. $50 fee. **Financial aid:** No deadline.

Academics. Special study options: Distance learning, double major, independent study. **Credit/placement by examination:** AP, CLEP, ACT. **Support services:** Remedial instruction, tutoring.

Majors. Biology: Exercise physiology. **Business:** General. **Education:** Multi-level teacher. **Psychology:** General. **Theology:** Bible, missionary, theology. **Visual/performing arts:** Music.

Student life. Freshman orientation: Mandatory, $100 fee. Preregistration for classes offered. **Housing:** Single-sex dorms, apartments available. **Activities:** Campus ministries, drama, music ensembles, student government.

Athletics. NCCAA. **Intercollegiate:** Baseball M, basketball, cross-country M, soccer M, softball W. **Team name:** Saints.

Contact. E-mail: recruitment@hc.edu
Phone: (415) 912-9011
Lyndsey Braisher, Admissions Counselor, Hillsdale Free Will Baptist College, PO Box 7208, Moore, OK 73153

ITT Technical Institute: Tulsa
Tulsa, Oklahoma
www.itt-tech.edu

- For-profit 4-year business and technical college
- Large city

- 602 undergraduates
- Interview required

General. Accredited by ACICS. **Degrees:** 21 bachelor's, 127 associate awarded. **Calendar:** Quarter. **Full-time faculty:** 10 total. **Part-time faculty:** 74 total.

Basis for selection. Satisfactory scores from on-site tests in English and math required.

2011-2012 Annual costs. Estimated costs as of June 2011: per-credit-hour charge, $493, depending upon level and course of study; academic fee, $200. Certain programs of study require purchase of tools, which could cost an additional $100 to $655. All costs are subject to change.

Application procedures. Admission: No deadline. No application fee. Admission notification on a rolling basis.

Academics. Credit/placement by examination: AP, CLEP.

Majors. Business: Business admin, construction management. **Computer sciences:** Programming, security. **Protective services:** Law enforcement admin.

Contact. ITT Technical Institute: Tulsa, 8421 East 61st Street, Suite U, Tulsa, OK 74133

Langston University
Langston, Oklahoma   CB member
www.lunet.edu   CB code: 6361

- Public 4-year university and liberal arts college
- Residential campus in rural community
- 2,237 degree-seeking undergraduates: 13% part-time, 57% women, 89% African American, 1% Asian American, 1% Hispanic American, 1% Native American, 3% international
- 355 degree-seeking graduate students
- 63% of applicants admitted
- SAT or ACT (ACT writing optional), application essay required

General. Founded in 1897. Regionally accredited. Branch campuses in Oklahoma City, Tulsa. **Degrees:** 290 bachelor's, 17 associate awarded; master's, doctoral offered. **ROTC:** Army, Air Force. **Location:** 40 miles from Oklahoma City, 90 miles from Tulsa. **Calendar:** Semester, limited summer session. **Full-time faculty:** 140 total; 66% minority, 48% women. **Part-time faculty:** 65 total; 48% minority, 58% women. **Class size:** 62% < 20, 31% 20-39, 3% 40-49, 3% 50-99. **Special facilities:** International dairy goat research facility.

Freshman class profile. 3,113 applied, 1,966 admitted, 493 enrolled.

GPA 3.75 or higher:	1%	Rank in top quarter:	31%
GPA 3.50-3.74:	2%	Rank in top tenth:	12%
GPA 3.0-3.49:	14%	Out-of-state:	62%
GPA 2.0-2.99:	64%	International:	1%

Basis for selection. 2.7 GPA, 20 ACT or SAT equivalent required. March 1 priority date for SAT or ACT scores. Audition recommended for music program.

High school preparation. Required units include English 4, mathematics 3, history 3, (laboratory 3) and academic electives 2. Remaining units must be additional work in these areas or in computer science, speech, economics, geography, government, psychology, or sociology. Required units must begin with algebra I. Required social sciences units must include 1 US history.

2011-2012 Annual costs. Tuition/fees: $4,112; $10,265 out-of-state. Apartment-style housing, includes 4 private bedrooms with shared living room and kitchen. Room/board: $7,880. Books/supplies: $800. Personal expenses: $2,037.

2011-2012 Financial aid. All financial aid based on need. 39% of total undergraduate aid awarded as scholarships/grants, 61% as loans/jobs.

Application procedures. Admission: Priority date 6/15; deadline 8/17. $25 fee. Admission notification on a rolling basis beginning on or about 8/11. **Financial aid:** Priority date 3/1, closing date 5/1. FAFSA required. Applicants notified on a rolling basis starting 7/15; must reply within 2 week(s) of notification.

Academics. Special study options: Accelerated study, distance learning, double major, dual enrollment of high school students, ESL, exchange student, honors, independent study, internships, liberal arts/career combination, study

abroad, weekend college. **Credit/placement by examination:** AP, CLEP, SAT, ACT, institutional tests. 16 credit hours maximum toward associate degree, 30 toward bachelor's. **Support services:** Learning center, reduced course load, remedial instruction, tutoring, writing center.

Majors. Biology: General, zoology. **Business:** Accounting, administrative services, business admin, human resources. **Communications:** Broadcast journalism, communications/speech/rhetoric, journalism. **Communications technology:** General. **Computer sciences:** General. **Education:** General, business, elementary, family/consumer sciences, mathematics, music, physical, secondary, social studies, special ed, technology/industrial arts. **English:** English lit. **General:** Animal sciences, business, economics, farm/ranch. **Health services:** Health care admin, preveterinary. **History:** General. **Math:** General. **Physical sciences:** Chemistry. **Protective services:** Corrections, police science. **Psychology:** General. **Social sciences:** General, economics, geography, sociology, urban studies. **Visual/performing arts:** Art, music, music performance. **Work/family studies:** General, clothing/textiles, family studies, food/nutrition.

Most popular majors. Business/marketing 19%, education 8%, health sciences 24%, liberal arts 6%, psychology 11%, security/protective services 8%.

Computing on campus. 300 workstations in library, computer center. Dormitories wired for high-speed internet access and linked to campus network. Commuter students can connect to campus network. Online library, helpline, repair service, wireless network available.

Student life. Freshman orientation: Mandatory. Preregistration for classes offered. Begins 7 days prior to fall enrollment; includes social, cultural, and institutional activities along with registration and enrollment processes. **Policies:** All freshman and sophomore students required to live on campus. Students must have 2.0 GPA to join student organizations. Students must have 2.5 GPA to be in student government, campus royalty, or fraternities and sororities. **Housing:** Guaranteed on-campus for all undergraduates. Single-sex dorms, special housing for disabled, apartments available. $200 fully refundable deposit. **Activities:** Bands, campus ministries, choral groups, dance, drama, film society, international student organizations, literary magazine, music ensembles, Model UN, musical theater, opera, radio station, student government, student newspaper, symphony orchestra, TV station, Pan Hellenic fraternities and sororities, NAACP, NCNW.

Athletics. NAIA. **Intercollegiate:** Basketball, cheerleading, cross-country, football (tackle) M, softball W, track and field, volleyball W. **Intramural:** Basketball, football (non-tackle), track and field, volleyball. **Team name:** Lions.

Student services. Alcohol/substance abuse counseling, chaplain/spiritual director, career counseling, services for economically disadvantaged, student employment services, financial aid counseling, health services, on-campus daycare, personal counseling, placement for graduates, veterans' counselor. **Physically disabled:** Services for visually, speech, hearing impaired.

Contact. E-mail: gtrobertson@lunet.edu
Phone: (405) 466-3428 Fax: (405) 466-3391
Josita Baker, Director of Enrollment Management, Langston University, Box 728, Langston, OK 73050

Mid-America Christian University
Oklahoma City, Oklahoma
www.macu.edu   **CB code: 0918**

- Private 4-year university and liberal arts college affiliated with Church of God
- Residential campus in very large city
- 335 degree-seeking undergraduates: 14% African American, 10% Hispanic American, 6% Native American, 1% international

General. Founded in 1953. Regionally accredited. Free YMCA membership for all students. **Degrees:** 183 bachelor's, 2 associate awarded; master's offered. **Location:** 10 miles from downtown. **Calendar:** Semester, limited summer session. **Full-time faculty:** 22 total; 4% minority, 59% women. **Part-time faculty:** 20 total; 5% minority, 40% women. **Class size:** 67% < 20, 26% 20-39, 2% 40-49, 4% 50-99. **Special facilities:** On-campus nature reserve.

Freshman class profile.

Out-of-state:	39%	Live on campus:	48%

Basis for selection. Open admission. Two references required. Interview, audition recommended. **Home schooled:** Transcript of courses and grades, letter of recommendation (nonparent) required. Applicants without GED must have 15 ACT English and 14 ACT math.

2011-2012 Annual costs. Tuition/fees: $14,730. Laptop purchase required. Room/board: $5,985. Books/supplies: $1,200. Personal expenses: $2,200.

Financial aid. Non-need-based: Scholarships awarded for academics, athletics, leadership, minority status, music/drama, religious affiliation.

Application procedures. Admission: Priority date 8/15; no deadline. $25 fee, may be waived for applicants with need, free for online applicants. Admission notification on a rolling basis beginning on or about 2/1. Students may provisionally enroll without graduation posted in senior year. **Financial aid:** Priority date 5/1; no closing date. FAFSA required. Applicants notified on a rolling basis starting 5/1.

Academics. Special study options: Combined bachelor's/graduate degree, double major, dual enrollment of high school students, external degree, independent study, internships, liberal arts/career combination, teacher certification program, weekend college. **Credit/placement by examination:** AP, CLEP, SAT, ACT, institutional tests. **Support services:** Remedial instruction, tutoring, writing center.

Majors. Business: Business admin, marketing. **Communications:** Persuasive communications. **Education:** Elementary, English, mathematics, music, secondary, social science, social studies. **English:** English lit. **Math:** General. **Philosophy/religion:** Religion. **Physical sciences:** Physics. **Psychology:** General. **Social sciences:** General. **Theology:** Bible, pastoral counseling, sacred music, theology. **Visual/performing arts:** Music performance.

Computing on campus. 40 workstations in library, computer center, student center. Dormitories wired for high-speed internet access and linked to campus network. Online library, wireless network available.

Student life. Freshman orientation: Mandatory. Preregistration for classes offered. Held several consecutive days prior to start of classes. **Policies:** No smoking or drinking allowed on campus. Students under 22 must live on-campus unless they are married or live with parent/guardian within 40 mile radius. Students who are 22 and older must have lived on campus for at least 6 semesters, maintain 2.5 GPA, and have clean discipline history with Student Life. Maximum age for living on campus is 26. Religious observance required. **Housing:** Guaranteed on-campus for freshmen. Single-sex dorms, wellness housing available. $50 nonrefundable deposit. **Activities:** Concert band, campus ministries, choral groups, drama, music ensembles, musical theater, student government, missions club, Student Ministerial Fellowship, Ministry Refresher Institute.

Athletics. NAIA, NCCAA. **Intercollegiate:** Baseball M, basketball, cheerleading, golf M, soccer, softball W, volleyball W. **Intramural:** Basketball, bowling, softball W, table tennis, volleyball. **Team name:** Evangels.

Student services. Chaplain/spiritual director, career counseling, student employment services, financial aid counseling, health services, personal counseling, placement for graduates, veterans' counselor. **Physically disabled:** Services for speech impaired.

Contact. E-mail: info@macu.edu
Toll-free number: (888) 436-3035 Fax: (405) 692-3165
Dustin Rowton, Director of Admissions, Mid-America Christian University, 3500 SW 119th Street, Oklahoma City, OK 73170

Northeastern State University
Tahlequah, Oklahoma
www.nsuok.edu   **CB code: 6485**

- Public 4-year university
- Commuter campus in large town
- 8,106 degree-seeking undergraduates: 27% part-time, 61% women, 6% African American, 2% Asian American, 2% Hispanic American, 29% Native American, 2% international
- 1,245 degree-seeking graduate students
- ACT (writing optional) required

General. Founded in 1851. Regionally accredited. **Degrees:** 1,434 bachelor's awarded; master's, professional offered. **ROTC:** Army. **Location:** 60 miles from Tulsa, 30 miles from Muskogee. **Calendar:** Semester, extensive summer session. **Full-time faculty:** 287 total; 74% have terminal degrees, 19% minority, 47% women. **Part-time faculty:** 226 total; 27% have terminal degrees, 21% minority, 52% women. **Class size:** 53% < 20, 39% 20-39, 4% 40-49, 4% 50-99. **Special facilities:** Literacy study center, tribal studies center, Oklahoma Institute for Learning Styles.

Freshman class profile.

Mid 50% test scores			
ACT composite:	18-23	End year in good standing:	54%
GPA 3.75 or higher:	21%	Return as sophomores:	65%
GPA 3.50-3.74:	14%	Out-of-state:	6%
GPA 3.0-3.49:	35%	Live on campus:	61%
GPA 2.0-2.99:	28%	International:	1%
Rank in top quarter:	46%	Fraternities:	4%
Rank in top tenth:	19%	Sororities:	12%

Basis for selection. Admissions based on secondary school record, class rank, and standardized test scores. Audition required, interview recommended for music program. Interview recommended for drama program; portfolio recommended for graphic art program. Interview required for alternative admission. **Home schooled:** Transcript of courses and grades required.

High school preparation. College-preparatory program required. 15 units required. Required and recommended units include English 4, mathematics 3, social studies 2, history 1, science 2 (laboratory 2) and foreign language 2. 3 from English, lab science, math, history, social studies, computer science, or foreign language.

2011-2012 Annual costs. Tuition/fees: $4,627; $11,152 out-of-state. Room/board: $5,370. Books/supplies: $1,200. Personal expenses: $1,120.

2010-2011 Financial aid. Need-based: 1,103 full-time freshmen applied for aid; 469 were judged to have need; 464 of these received aid. Average need met was 80%. Average scholarship/grant was $5,051; average loan $2,212. 54% of total undergraduate aid awarded as scholarships/grants, 46% as loans/jobs. **Non-need-based:** Awarded to 3,978 full-time undergraduates, including 638 freshmen. Scholarships awarded for academics, alumni affiliation, art, athletics, leadership, minority status, music/drama, religious affiliation, ROTC, state residency. **Additional information:** Participates in off-campus job location and development program to assist students with off-campus employers to earn money for college expenses.

Application procedures. Admission: Priority date 8/1; no deadline. $25 fee, may be waived for applicants with need. Admission notification on a rolling basis. **Financial aid:** Priority date 3/1; no closing date. FAFSA required. Applicants notified on a rolling basis starting 4/1.

Academics. NSU College of Optometry on campus. **Special study options:** Combined bachelor's/graduate degree, distance learning, double major, dual enrollment of high school students, honors, independent study, internships, student-designed major, teacher certification program, weekend college. **Credit/placement by examination:** AP, CLEP, IB, ACT, institutional tests. 30 credit hours maximum toward bachelor's degree. **Support services:** Learning center, pre-admission summer program, reduced course load, remedial instruction, study skills assistance, tutoring, writing center.

Majors. Area/ethnic studies: Native American. **Biology:** General, cell/histology, wildlife. **Business:** Accounting, business admin, entrepreneurial studies, finance, human resources, international, logistics, management information systems, marketing, operations, organizational leadership, tourism/travel. **Communications:** Advertising, communications/speech/rhetoric, journalism, public relations. **Computer sciences:** Computer science. **Conservation:** Environmental science. **Education:** Art, biology, chemistry, early childhood, elementary, English, learning disabled, mathematics, music, Native American, physical, physics, science, social studies, Spanish. **English:** English lit. **Foreign languages:** Spanish. **Health services:** Audiology/speech pathology, clinical lab science, facilities admin, nursing (RN). **History:** General. **Human services:** Social work. **Math:** General. **Parks/recreation:** Exercise sciences. **Physical sciences:** Chemistry. **Protective services:** Homeland security, law enforcement admin. **Psychology:** General, developmental. **Social sciences:** Geography, political science, sociology. **Visual/performing arts:** Art, commercial/advertising art, design, dramatic, jazz, music, photography, studio arts. **Work/family studies:** General, food/nutrition.

Most popular majors. Business/marketing 18%, education 27%, health sciences 7%, psychology 9%, security/protective services 7%.

Computing on campus. 1,160 workstations in dormitories, library, computer center, student center. Dormitories wired for high-speed internet access and linked to campus network. Commuter students can connect to campus network. Online library, helpline, student web hosting, wireless network available.

Student life. Freshman orientation: Mandatory. Preregistration for classes offered. **Housing:** Guaranteed on-campus for freshmen. Coed dorms, single-sex dorms, special housing for disabled, apartments, fraternity/sorority housing available. $75 nonrefundable deposit. Living learning communities available. **Activities:** Bands, campus ministries, choral groups, dance, drama, international student organizations, literary magazine, music ensembles, Model UN, musical theater, student government, student newspaper, symphony orchestra, TV station, Native American student association, American Indian science and engineering society, Association of Black Collegians, government and international studies society, Campus Christian Fellowship,

Baptist campus ministries, Chi Alpha campus ministries, Habitat for Humanity, Sigma Theta Epsilon, RiverHawks for Christ.

Athletics. NCAA. **Intercollegiate:** Baseball M, basketball, football (tackle) M, golf, soccer, softball W, tennis W. **Intramural:** Basketball, football (non-tackle), golf, racquetball, soccer, softball, tennis, volleyball. **Team name:** RiverHawks.

Student services. Adult student services, alcohol/substance abuse counseling, career counseling, services for economically disadvantaged, student employment services, financial aid counseling, health services, personal counseling, placement for graduates, veterans' counselor. **Physically disabled:** Services for visually, speech, hearing impaired.

Contact. E-mail: nsuinfo@nsuok.edu
Phone: (918) 444-2200 Toll-free number: (800) 722-9614
Fax: (918) 458-2342
Dawn Cain, Director of Admissions, Northeastern State University, 600 North Grand Avenue, Tahlequah, OK 74464-2399

Northwestern Oklahoma State University
Alva, Oklahoma
www.nwosu.edu   **CB code: 6493**

- Public 4-year university and teachers college
- Commuter campus in rural community
- 2,005 degree-seeking undergraduates: 23% part-time, 55% women, 5% African American, 6% Hispanic American, 6% Native American, 2% international
- 144 degree-seeking graduate students
- 100% of applicants admitted
- SAT or ACT (ACT writing optional) required

General. Founded in 1897. Regionally accredited. **Degrees:** 320 bachelor's awarded; master's offered. **Location:** 160 miles from Oklahoma City, 70 miles from Enid. **Calendar:** Semester, limited summer session. **Full-time faculty:** 91 total; 50% have terminal degrees, 7% minority, 53% women. **Part-time faculty:** 82 total; 8% have terminal degrees, 8% minority, 60% women. **Special facilities:** Agriculture farm, natural history museum.

Freshman class profile. 882 applied, 882 admitted, 423 enrolled.

Mid 50% test scores			
ACT composite:	17-23	Rank in top quarter:	35%
GPA 3.75 or higher:	23%	Rank in top tenth:	12%
GPA 3.50-3.74:	15%	Out-of-state:	22%
GPA 3.0-3.49:	36%	Live on campus:	81%
GPA 2.0-2.99:	25%	International:	4%

Basis for selection. Applicants with 2.7 GPA and in top 50% of class or with 19 ACT admitted unconditionally. Others admitted provisionally. Audition recommended for music program. **Home schooled:** Transcript of courses and grades required.

High school preparation. 15 units required. Required and recommended units include English 4, mathematics 3, history 3, science 3 (laboratory 3), foreign language 2 and academic electives 3. 1 unit required from either government, economics, geography or non-Western culture.

2011-2012 Annual costs. Tuition/fees: $4,591; $10,141 out-of-state. Room/board: $3,820. Books/supplies: $1,200. Personal expenses: $2,000.

Financial aid. Non-need-based: Scholarships awarded for academics, alumni affiliation, art, athletics, leadership, music/drama.

Application procedures. Admission: No deadline. $15 fee. Admission notification on a rolling basis. **Financial aid:** No deadline. FAFSA required. Applicants notified on a rolling basis starting 5/1.

Academics. Special study options: Distance learning, double major, dual enrollment of high school students, honors, independent study, internships, study abroad, teacher certification program. 2-2 programs in many professional fields. **Credit/placement by examination:** AP, CLEP, SAT, ACT, institutional tests. **Support services:** Learning center, reduced course load, remedial instruction, tutoring, writing center.

Majors. Biology: General. **Business:** Accounting, business admin, e-commerce. **Communications:** Media studies. **Computer sciences:** General. **Education:** General, agricultural, business, early childhood, elementary, English, health, learning disabled, mathematics, mentally handicapped, middle, music, physical, science, secondary, social science, Spanish, special ed, technology/industrial arts. **English:** English lit. **General:** Agribusiness

operations. **Health services:** Nursing (RN). **History:** General. **Human services:** Social work. **Math:** General. **Parks/recreation:** Health/fitness. **Physical sciences:** Chemistry. **Protective services:** Police science. **Psychology:** General. **Social sciences:** General, political science, sociology. **Visual/performing arts:** Dramatic, music.

Most popular majors. Agriculture 8%, business/marketing 20%, education 19%, health sciences 6%, parks/recreation 6%, psychology 12%.

Computing on campus. 218 workstations in library, computer center, student center. Commuter students can connect to campus network. Online library, helpline, wireless network available.

Student life. Freshman orientation: Mandatory. Preregistration for classes offered. **Housing:** Single-sex dorms, special housing for disabled available. $75 fully refundable deposit. **Activities:** Bands, campus ministries, choral groups, drama, international student organizations, music ensembles, radio station, student government, student newspaper, TV station, Conserving Our Ranger Environment, Spanish club, social sciences organization, Baptist student union, Wesley House, art society, Oklahoma Broadcast Education Association, Aggie club.

Athletics. NAIA. **Intercollegiate:** Baseball M, basketball, cross-country, football (tackle) M, golf, rodeo, soccer W, softball W. **Intramural:** Basketball, bowling, football (non-tackle), racquetball, softball, volleyball. **Team name:** Rangers.

Student services. Adult student services, career counseling, student employment services, financial aid counseling, health services, personal counseling, placement for graduates, veterans' counselor, women's services. **Physically disabled:** Services for visually, speech, hearing impaired.

Contact. E-mail: recruit@nwosu.edu
Phone: (580) 327-8546 Fax: (580) 327-8413
Matt Adair, Director of Recruitment, Northwestern Oklahoma State University, 709 Oklahoma Boulevard, Alva, OK 73717-2799

Oklahoma Baptist University
Shawnee, Oklahoma
www.okbu.edu

CB code: 6541

♦ Private 4-year university and liberal arts college affiliated with Southern Baptist Convention
♦ Residential campus in large town
♦ 1,594 degree-seeking undergraduates: 2% part-time, 61% women, 5% African American, 1% Asian American, 4% Hispanic American, 8% Native American, 3% international
♦ 69 degree-seeking graduate students
♦ 66% of applicants admitted
♦ SAT or ACT (ACT writing optional) required
♦ 51% graduate within 6 years

General. Founded in 1910. Regionally accredited. Each summer approximately 250 students, faculty and staff serve in projects around the world. About 300 students participate in local service projects during the year. **Degrees:** 304 bachelor's, 4 associate awarded; master's offered. **ROTC:** Air Force. **Location:** 35 miles from Oklahoma City, 90 miles from Tulsa. **Calendar:** Semester, limited summer session. **Full-time faculty:** 105 total. **Part-time faculty:** 55 total. **Class size:** 72% < 20, 22% 20-39, 3% 40-49, 3% 50-99. **Special facilities:** Planetarium (operated by students), greenhouse, music technology laboratory, biblical research library.

Freshman class profile. 4,790 applied, 3,158 admitted, 476 enrolled.

Mid 50% test scores			
SAT critical reading:	480-590	GPA 2.0-2.99:	7%
SAT math:	490-600	Rank in top quarter:	62%
ACT composite:	21-27	Rank in top tenth:	33%
GPA 3.75 or higher:	53%	Return as sophomores:	76%
GPA 3.50-3.74:	17%	Out-of-state:	36%
GPA 3.0-3.49:	23%	Live on campus:	93%
		International:	3%

Basis for selection. 20 ACT or 950 SAT (exclusive of Writing), 3.0 GPA or class rank in top half required. Interview recommended for borderline applicants; audition recommended for drama, music programs; portfolio recommended for art program.

High school preparation. 17 units recommended. Recommended units include English 4, mathematics 3, social studies 2, history 1, science 3 (laboratory 2), foreign language 2 and academic electives 2. Math recommendation includes 2 algebra and 1 plane geometry.

2012-2013 Annual costs. Tuition/fees: $20,796. Room/board: $6,200. Books/supplies: $1,200. Personal expenses: $1,894.

2010-2011 Financial aid. Need-based: 350 full-time freshmen applied for aid; 306 were judged to have need; 306 of these received aid. Average need met was 81%. Average scholarship/grant was $6,746; average loan $3,928. 64% of total undergraduate aid awarded as scholarships/grants, 36% as loans/jobs. **Non-need-based:** Awarded to 1,447 full-time undergraduates, including 222 freshmen. Scholarships awarded for academics, alumni affiliation, art, athletics, job skills, leadership, minority status, music/drama, religious affiliation, ROTC, state residency.

Application procedures. Admission: Priority date 4/1; deadline 8/1 (postmark date). No application fee. Admission notification on a rolling basis beginning on or about 6/1. **Financial aid:** Priority date 3/1; no closing date. FAFSA required. Applicants notified on a rolling basis starting 2/1.

Academics. Opportunities for January-term travel to Europe, Russia, South America; also opportunity to teach English in China and Hungary. **Special study options:** Accelerated study, combined bachelor's/graduate degree, cooperative education, double major, ESL, exchange student, honors, independent study, internships, liberal arts/career combination, student-designed major, study abroad, teacher certification program. Exchange program with Seinan Gakuin University, Japan, and Hong Kong Baptist College; opportunities for January-term travel to Europe, Russia, South America. **Credit/placement by examination:** AP, CLEP, IB, SAT, ACT, institutional tests. 32 credit hours maximum toward bachelor's degree. Essay required for English, government, history exams; oral exam required for French, German and Spanish; lab exam required for information systems. **Support services:** Learning center, reduced course load, remedial instruction, study skills assistance, tutoring, writing center.

Majors. Biology: General, biochemistry. **Business:** General, accounting, business admin, finance, international, international finance, management information systems, management science, marketing. **Communications:** Broadcast journalism, communications/speech/rhetoric, journalism, public relations. **Computer sciences:** General, applications programming, computer science, information systems, systems analysis. **Education:** Art, biology, chemistry, early childhood, elementary, English, foreign languages, French, German, health, history, learning disabled, mathematics, mentally handicapped, music, physical, physics, science, secondary, social science, social studies, Spanish, special ed, speech. **English:** English lit, rhetoric/composition. **Foreign languages:** General, French, German, Spanish. **Health services:** Athletic training, nursing (RN). **History:** General. **Human services:** Social work. **Liberal arts:** Arts/sciences. **Math:** General. **Parks/recreation:** Exercise sciences, facilities management, health/fitness, sports admin. **Philosophy/religion:** Philosophy, religion. **Physical sciences:** Chemistry, physics. **Psychology:** General. **Social sciences:** General, anthropology, political science, sociology. **Theology:** Bible, missionary, religious ed, sacred music, theology. **Visual/performing arts:** Art, dramatic, music, music performance, music theory/composition, piano/keyboard, studio arts, voice/opera.

Most popular majors. Business/marketing 9%, education 16%, health sciences 19%, social sciences 7%, theological studies 6%, visual/performing arts 10%.

Computing on campus. 200 workstations in dormitories, library, computer center, student center. Dormitories wired for high-speed internet access and linked to campus network. Commuter students can connect to campus network. Online course registration, online library, helpline, wireless network available.

Student life. Freshman orientation: Mandatory. Preregistration for classes offered. Held during the 3 days immediately prior to start of fall semester. **Policies:** Campus is alcohol/drug/smoke free. **Housing:** Guaranteed on-campus for all undergraduates. Single-sex dorms, apartments, wellness housing available. $125 partly refundable deposit, deadline 8/1. **Activities:** Bands, choral groups, drama, literary magazine, music ensembles, musical theater, opera, student government, student newspaper, symphony orchestra, TV station, Campus Crusade, FCA, Baptist Collegiate Ministries, Collegiate Republicans, Young Democrats, black student fellowship, international student union, Native American heritage association, residence hall association.

Athletics. NAIA. **Intercollegiate:** Baseball M, basketball, cross-country, diving, golf, soccer, softball W, swimming, tennis, track and field. **Intramural:** Badminton, basketball, bowling, racquetball, soccer, softball, swimming, table tennis, tennis, volleyball. **Team name:** Bison.

Student services. Chaplain/spiritual director, career counseling, student employment services, financial aid counseling, health services, personal counseling, placement for graduates, veterans' counselor. **Physically disabled:** Services for visually, hearing impaired.

Contact. E-mail: admissions@mail.okbu.edu
Phone: (405) 878-2033 Toll-free number: (800) 654-3285
Fax: (405) 878-2068
Bruce Perkins, Dean of Enrollment Management, Oklahoma Baptist University, 500 West University, Shawnee, OK 74804

Oklahoma Christian University
Oklahoma City, Oklahoma
www.oc.edu — CB code: 6086

- Private 4-year liberal arts college affiliated with Church of Christ
- Residential campus in very large city
- 1,854 degree-seeking undergraduates: 4% part-time, 49% women, 5% African American, 2% Asian American, 4% Hispanic American, 4% Native American, 9% international
- 340 degree-seeking graduate students
- 55% of applicants admitted
- SAT or ACT (ACT writing optional) required
- 48% graduate within 6 years

General. Founded in 1950. Regionally accredited. Every student receives MacBook and choice of iPhone, iPod touch or iPad upon enrollment. **Degrees:** 351 bachelor's awarded; master's offered. **ROTC:** Army, Air Force. **Calendar:** Semester, extensive summer session. **Full-time faculty:** 112 total; 69% have terminal degrees, 30% women. **Part-time faculty:** 95 total; 67% have terminal degrees, 33% women. **Class size:** 63% < 20, 29% 20-39, 2% 40-49, 5% 50-99, less than 1% >100.

Freshman class profile. 1,786 applied, 991 admitted, 463 enrolled.

Mid 50% test scores			
SAT critical reading:	450-620	GPA 2.0-2.99:	18%
SAT math:	470-610	Rank in top quarter:	50%
SAT writing:	470-580	Rank in top tenth:	27%
ACT composite:	20-27	End year in good standing:	77%
GPA 3.75 or higher:	36%	Return as sophomores:	77%
GPA 3.50-3.74:	15%	Live on campus:	90%
GPA 3.0-3.49:	30%	International:	5%

Basis for selection. Students evaluated on both merit and character. Interview/campus visit strongly recommended.

High school preparation. College-preparatory program recommended. 15 units recommended. Required and recommended units include English 4, mathematics 4, social studies 3, science 4 (laboratory 2) and foreign language 2.

2011-2012 Annual costs. Tuition/fees: $18,456. Additional $900 annually for 8 GB IPod Touch and MacBook configured with Mac OS X and Windows 7, MS Office. Room/board: $6,825. Books/supplies: $1,000. Personal expenses: $1,700.

2010-2011 Financial aid. **Need-based:** 438 full-time freshmen applied for aid; 358 were judged to have need; 358 of these received aid. Average need met was 71%. Average scholarship/grant was $2,446; average loan $2,296. 48% of total undergraduate aid awarded as scholarships/grants, 52% as loans/jobs. **Non-need-based:** Awarded to 1,501 full-time undergraduates, including 427 freshmen. Scholarships awarded for academics, art, athletics, music/drama, religious affiliation, ROTC.

Application procedures. **Admission:** Priority date 5/1; no deadline. $25 fee, may be waived for applicants with need. Admission notification on a rolling basis beginning on or about 9/1. Must reply by May 1 or within 2 week(s) if notified thereafter. **Financial aid:** Priority date 3/15, closing date 8/31. FAFSA required. Applicants notified on a rolling basis starting 1/15; must reply within 4 week(s) of notification.

Academics. **Special study options:** Accelerated study, combined bachelor's/graduate degree, cross-registration, distance learning, double major, dual enrollment of high school students, ESL, honors, independent study, internships, liberal arts/career combination, study abroad, teacher certification program. **Credit/placement by examination:** AP, CLEP, IB, SAT, ACT, institutional tests. 60 credit hours maximum toward bachelor's degree. **Support services:** Learning center, reduced course load, remedial instruction, study skills assistance, tutoring, writing center.

Majors. **Architecture:** Interior. **Biology:** General, biochemistry. **Business:** General, accounting, business admin, finance, international, management science, market research, marketing, merchandising. **Communications:** Advertising, broadcast journalism, communications/speech/rhetoric, journalism, media studies, public relations. **Communications technology:** Animation/special effects. **Computer sciences:** General, computer science, information systems, programming. **Education:** Art, early childhood, elementary, English, ESL, mathematics, middle, music, physical, science, secondary, social studies, speech. **Engineering:** Computer, electrical, mechanical. **English:** Creative writing, English lit, writing. **Foreign languages:** Spanish. **Health services:** Clinical lab science, nursing (RN), predental, premedicine, prenursing, prepharmacy, preveterinary. **History:** General. **Liberal arts:** Arts/sciences. **Math:** General. **Parks/recreation:** Health/fitness. **Philosophy/religion:** Christian, religion. **Physical sciences:** Chemistry, physics. **Psychology:** General. **Social sciences:** Political science. **Theology:** Bible, missionary, religious ed, theology, youth ministry. **Visual/performing arts:** Art, commercial/advertising art, design, dramatic, game design, graphic design, interior design, music, music performance, piano/keyboard, studio arts, voice/opera. **Work/family studies:** Family studies.

Most popular majors. Business/marketing 17%, communications/journalism 7%, education 12%, engineering/engineering technologies 10%, health sciences 6%, interdisciplinary studies 9%.

Computing on campus. PC or laptop required. 1,850 workstations in dormitories, library, computer center, student center. Dormitories wired for high-speed internet access and linked to campus network. Commuter students can connect to campus network. Online course registration, online library, helpline, repair service, student web hosting, wireless network available.

Student life. **Freshman orientation:** Mandatory, $200 fee. Preregistration for classes offered. Two-part program includes 1-day summer event and week-long event the week before school starts. **Policies:** Single students must live on campus or with parents. Special arrangements considered. Religious observance required. **Housing:** Guaranteed on-campus for all undergraduates. Single-sex dorms, special housing for disabled, apartments, wellness housing available. $100 partly refundable deposit, deadline 5/1. **Activities:** Bands, campus ministries, choral groups, drama, international student organizations, literary magazine, music ensembles, musical theater, opera, radio station, student government, student newspaper, symphony orchestra, TV station.

Athletics. NAIA. **Intercollegiate:** Baseball M, basketball, cheerleading W, cross-country, golf M, soccer, softball W, tennis, track and field. **Intramural:** Basketball, bowling, cross-country, football (non-tackle), golf M, soccer, softball, swimming, table tennis, tennis, track and field, volleyball. **Team name:** Eagles.

Student services. Alcohol/substance abuse counseling, chaplain/spiritual director, career counseling, student employment services, financial aid counseling, health services, minority student services, personal counseling, placement for graduates, veterans' counselor, women's services. **Physically disabled:** Services for visually, speech, hearing impaired.

Contact. E-mail: info@oc.edu
Phone: (405) 425-5050 Toll-free number: (800) 877-5050
Fax: (405) 425-5069
Darci Thompson, Director of Admissions, Oklahoma Christian University, Box 11000, Oklahoma City, OK 73136-1100

Oklahoma City University
Oklahoma City, Oklahoma
www.okcu.edu — CB member — CB code: 6543

- Private 4-year university and liberal arts college affiliated with United Methodist Church
- Residential campus in very large city
- 2,227 degree-seeking undergraduates: 16% part-time, 63% women, 7% African American, 2% Asian American, 6% Hispanic American, 3% Native American, 16% international
- 1,319 degree-seeking graduate students
- 74% of applicants admitted
- SAT or ACT (ACT writing optional), application essay required
- 60% graduate within 6 years

General. Founded in 1904. Regionally accredited. **Degrees:** 593 bachelor's awarded; master's, professional, doctoral offered. **ROTC:** Army, Air Force. **Location:** 180 miles from Dallas, 350 miles from Kansas City. **Calendar:** Semester, limited summer session. **Full-time faculty:** 215 total; 77% have terminal degrees, 11% minority, 49% women. **Part-time faculty:** 127 total; 61% have terminal degrees, 8% minority, 48% women. **Class size:** 69% < 20, 30% 20-39, less than 1% 40-49, less than 1% 50-99. **Special facilities:** Art center, entrepreneurship center, urban wilderness laboratory.

Freshman class profile. 1,329 applied, 977 admitted, 332 enrolled.

Mid 50% test scores			
SAT critical reading:	510-610	Rank in top tenth:	31%
SAT math:	520-620	End year in good standing:	79%
ACT composite:	23-28	Return as sophomores:	79%
GPA 3.75 or higher:	37%	Out-of-state:	50%
GPA 3.50-3.74:	24%	Live on campus:	89%
GPA 3.0-3.49:	31%	International:	4%
GPA 2.0-2.99:	8%	Fraternities:	29%
Rank in top quarter:	59%	Sororities:	22%

Basis for selection. School achievement record, which includes class rank, and test scores most important. Counselor recommendations, essays, and activities also considered. Interview recommended for all; audition required for dance, music programs; portfolio required for art, graphic design programs. **Home schooled:** Must demonstrate that individual is graduating no earlier than their class in the public school system.

High school preparation. College-preparatory program recommended. 15 units required. Required units include English 4, mathematics 3, social studies 3, science 3 (laboratory 1) and foreign language 2. Math requirement includes 2 algebra and 1 geometry, trigonometry, math analysis, or calculus. Social studies requirement includes 1 world history, 1 state history or civics, and 1 U.S. history.

2011-2012 Annual costs. Tuition/fees: $28,190. Room/board: $7,880. Books/supplies: $1,500. Personal expenses: $1,000.

Financial aid. Non-need-based: Scholarships awarded for academics, alumni affiliation, art, athletics, leadership, music/drama, religious affiliation, ROTC, state residency. **Additional information:** Four year, fixed rate tuition plan available to any undergraduate student who elects to enroll in the plan prior to start of fall term. To be eligible, student must matriculate in or before Fall semester. Fixed rate applies to block of 12-16 hours for fall/spring and summer semesters. The required fees charged each semester not fixed and subject to increases.

Application procedures. Admission: Priority date 11/15; deadline 3/1 (postmark date). $50 fee, may be waived for applicants with need. Admission notification on a rolling basis beginning on or about 10/15. Must reply by May 1 or within 2 week(s) if notified thereafter. **Financial aid:** Priority date 3/1, closing date 6/30. FAFSA, institutional form required. Applicants notified on a rolling basis starting 2/20; must reply within 2 week(s) of notification.

Academics. Special study options: Accelerated study, combined bachelor's/graduate degree, cooperative education, distance learning, double major, dual enrollment of high school students, ESL, exchange student, external degree, honors, independent study, internships, liberal arts/career combination, New York semester, student-designed major, study abroad, teacher certification program, Washington semester. **Credit/placement by examination:** AP, CLEP, IB, SAT, ACT, institutional tests. 30 credit hours maximum toward bachelor's degree. **Support services:** Learning center, pre-admission summer program, reduced course load, study skills assistance, tutoring, writing center.

Majors. Area/ethnic studies: American. **Biology:** General, biochemistry, biomedical sciences, cell/histology. **Business:** General, accounting, business admin, finance, international, management information systems, management science, managerial economics, marketing. **Communications:** Advertising, broadcast journalism, journalism, media studies, public relations, radio/TV. **Computer sciences:** General, computer science. **Conservation:** Environmental science. **Education:** General, art, business, early childhood, elementary, English, foreign languages, French, German, health, history, mathematics, Montessori teacher, music, physical, science, secondary, social studies, Spanish, speech. **English:** English lit, rhetoric/composition. **Foreign languages:** French, German, Spanish. **Health services:** Athletic training, nursing (RN), predental, premedicine, prepharmacy, preveterinary. **History:** General. **Human services:** Social work. **Liberal arts:** Arts/sciences, humanities. **Math:** General. **Parks/recreation:** Exercise sciences, health/fitness. **Philosophy/religion:** Philosophy, religion. **Physical sciences:** Chemistry, physics. **Protective services:** Corrections, law enforcement admin, police science. **Psychology:** General. **Social sciences:** Economics, political science, sociology. **Theology:** Bible, religious ed, sacred music, youth ministry. **Visual/performing arts:** General, acting, art, art history/conservation, cinematography, dance, dramatic, film/cinema/video, graphic design, music, music management, music performance, music theory/composition, photography, piano/keyboard, stringed instruments, studio arts, studio arts management, theater arts management, theater design, voice/opera.

Most popular majors. Health sciences 21%, liberal arts 28%, social sciences 6%, visual/performing arts 22%.

Computing on campus. 378 workstations in dormitories, library, computer center, student center. Dormitories wired for high-speed internet access and linked to campus network. Commuter students can connect to campus network. Online course registration, online library, helpline, repair service, student web hosting, wireless network available.

Student life. Freshman orientation: Mandatory, $50 fee. Preregistration for classes offered. **Housing:** Guaranteed on-campus for all undergraduates. Coed dorms, single-sex dorms, apartments, fraternity/sorority housing, wellness housing available. $100 deposit. Learning communities available. **Activities:** Bands, campus ministries, choral groups, dance, drama, international student organizations, literary magazine, music ensembles, musical theater, opera, student government, student newspaper, symphony orchestra, TV station, Kappa Phi, Sigma Theta Epsilon, association for people of color, United

Methodist student fellowship, students of arts management, Alpha Phi sorority, Gamma Phi Beta sorority, Lambda Chi Alpha fraternity, Kappa Sigma fraternity.

Athletics. NAIA. **Intercollegiate:** Baseball M, basketball, cheerleading, cross-country, golf, soccer, softball W, volleyball W, wrestling. **Intramural:** Basketball, fencing, football (non-tackle) M, golf, softball, table tennis, volleyball. **Team name:** Stars.

Student services. Adult student services, chaplain/spiritual director, career counseling, services for economically disadvantaged, student employment services, financial aid counseling, health services, minority student services, personal counseling, placement for graduates, veterans' counselor. **Physically disabled:** Services for visually, hearing impaired.

Contact. E-mail: uadmissions@okcu.edu
Phone: (405) 208-5050 Toll-free number: (800) 633-7242
Fax: (405) 208-5916
Michelle Cook, Director of Admission, Oklahoma City University, 2501 North Blackwelder Avenue, Oklahoma City, OK 73106-1493

Oklahoma Panhandle State University
Goodwell, Oklahoma
www.opsu.edu   CB code: 6571

◗ Public 4-year university and liberal arts college
◗ Residential campus in rural community
◗ 1,376 degree-seeking undergraduates: 13% part-time, 47% women, 11% African American, 1% Asian American, 15% Hispanic American, 4% Native American, 2% international
◗ 89% of applicants admitted
◗ 39% graduate within 6 years

General. Founded in 1909. Regionally accredited. **Degrees:** 205 bachelor's, 62 associate awarded. **Location:** 110 miles from Amarillo, Texas, 10 miles from Guymon. **Calendar:** Semester, limited summer session. **Full-time faculty:** 70 total. **Part-time faculty:** 35 total. **Class size:** 72% < 20, 23% 20-39, 2% 40-49, 3% 50-99, less than 1% >100. **Special facilities:** Agronomy experiment station, historical museum, livestock facilities, farming area, rodeo arena, meat lab.

Freshman class profile. 785 applied, 699 admitted, 434 enrolled.

Mid 50% test scores			
SAT critical reading:	340-450	GPA 3.0-3.49:	33%
SAT math:	370-500	GPA 2.0-2.99:	37%
ACT composite:	16-19	Out-of-state:	54%
GPA 3.75 or higher:	18%	Live on campus:	90%
GPA 3.50-3.74:	9%	International:	2%

Basis for selection. Secondary school record, test scores and class rank most important. SAT or ACT recommended. Incoming students without ACT, or with score of 19 or below, must take ACCUPLACER test. **Home schooled:** Transcript of courses and grades required.

High school preparation. 15 units required. Required units include English 4, mathematics 3, social studies 2, history 1, science 2 (laboratory 2) and academic electives 3.

2011-2012 Annual costs. Tuition/fees: $6,189; $11,748 out-of-state. Room/board: $3,734. Books/supplies: $240.

Financial aid. All financial aid based on need.

Application procedures. Admission: No deadline. No application fee. Admission notification on a rolling basis. **Financial aid:** Priority date 3/15; no closing date. FAFSA, institutional form required.

Academics. Special study options: Cooperative education, distance learning, double major, ESL, independent study, internships, teacher certification program. **Credit/placement by examination:** AP, CLEP, SAT, ACT, institutional tests. 34 credit hours maximum toward associate degree, 60 toward bachelor's. **Support services:** Learning center, reduced course load, remedial instruction, study skills assistance, tutoring, writing center.

Majors. Biology: General. **Business:** Accounting, business admin. **Computer sciences:** General. **Education:** Agricultural, business, elementary. **English:** English lit. **General:** Agribusiness operations, agronomy, animal sciences, equine science. **Health services:** Nursing (RN). **History:** General. **Liberal arts:** Arts/sciences. **Math:** General. **Parks/recreation:** Health/fitness. **Physical sciences:** Chemistry. **Psychology:** General. **Social sciences:** General. **Visual/performing arts:** Art, music.

Most popular majors. Agriculture 20%, biology 12%, business/marketing 17%, health sciences 12%, parks/recreation 6%, psychology 9%, visual/performing arts 6%.

Computing on campus. 150 workstations in dormitories, library, computer center, student center. Dormitories wired for high-speed internet access. Online library, wireless network available.

Student life. Freshman orientation: Mandatory. Preregistration for classes offered. **Housing:** Guaranteed on-campus for freshmen. Single-sex dorms, apartments available. **Activities:** Bands, choral groups, drama, music ensembles, musical theater, radio station, student government, student newspaper, Wesley Foundation, Baptist student union, Church of Christ student center, Circle-K, Newman club, Methodist student center.

Athletics. NCAA. **Intercollegiate:** Baseball M, basketball, cheerleading, cross-country, football (tackle) M, golf, softball W, volleyball W. **Intramural:** Basketball, football (non-tackle), golf, soccer, softball, table tennis, volleyball. **Team name:** Aggies.

Student services. Adult student services, alcohol/substance abuse counseling, career counseling, student employment services, financial aid counseling, health services, minority student services, personal counseling, placement for graduates. **Physically disabled:** Services for visually, speech, hearing impaired.

Contact. E-mail: dshort@opsu.edu
Phone: (580) 349-1312 Toll-free number: (800) 664-6778
Fax: (580) 349-1371
Bobby Jenkins, Registrar and Director of Admissions, Oklahoma Panhandle State University, OPSU Admissions, Goodwell, OK 73939-0430

Oklahoma State University
Stillwater, Oklahoma
www.okstate.edu

CB member
CB code: 6546

- Public 4-year university
- Residential campus in large town
- 18,762 degree-seeking undergraduates: 13% part-time, 49% women, 5% African American, 1% Asian American, 4% Hispanic American, 7% Native American, 2% international
- 4,943 degree-seeking graduate students
- 82% of applicants admitted
- SAT or ACT (ACT writing optional) required
- 62% graduate within 6 years

General. Founded in 1890. Regionally accredited. Campuses in Oklahoma City, Okmulgee, Tulsa and Center for Health Sciences (includes College of Osteopathic Medicine) at Tulsa. Stillwater campus includes the Center for Veterinary Health Sciences. **Degrees:** 3,649 bachelor's awarded; master's, professional, doctoral offered. **ROTC:** Army, Air Force. **Location:** 65 miles from Tulsa, 65 miles from Oklahoma City. **Calendar:** Semester, extensive summer session. **Full-time faculty:** 986 total; 87% have terminal degrees, 11% minority, 33% women. **Part-time faculty:** 314 total; 22% have terminal degrees, 10% minority, 52% women. **Class size:** 39% < 20, 39% 20-39, 10% 40-49, 8% 50-99, 4% >100. **Special facilities:** Laser research center with 8 laboratories and 30 laser systems, biotechnology and genetic engineering research center, telecommunication center.

Freshman class profile. 9,914 applied, 8,099 admitted, 3,896 enrolled.

Mid 50% test scores		Rank in top quarter:	54%
SAT critical reading:	490-600	Rank in top tenth:	26%
SAT math:	510-620	Return as sophomores:	80%
ACT composite:	22-27	Out-of-state:	34%
GPA 3.75 or higher:	33%	Live on campus:	94%
GPA 3.50-3.74:	22%	International:	1%
GPA 3.0-3.49:	33%	Fraternities:	22%
GPA 2.0-2.99:	12%	Sororities:	34%

Basis for selection. Applicants must have 3.0 GPA and rank in top 33% of class, or 24 ACT/1090 SAT (exclusive of Writing), or 3.0 GPA in 15 required curricular units and 21 ACT/980 SAT(exclusive of Writing), or 3.0 GPA in 15 required curricular units, or 22 ACT/1020 SAT and answer 7 undergraduate application questions. Early application encouraged. Test scores must be received no later than Friday before classes begin for fall-term admission. Interview recommended for academically borderline students.

High school preparation. College-preparatory program required. 15 units required; 18 recommended. Required and recommended units include English 4, mathematics 3, social studies 2, history 1, science 2 (laboratory 2), foreign language 2, computer science 1 and academic electives 3.

2011-2012 Annual costs. Tuition/fees: $7,418; $18,765 out-of-state. Room/board: $6,527. Books/supplies: $1,040. Personal expenses: $2,610.

2011-2012 Financial aid. Need-based: Average need met was 82%. Average scholarship/grant was $7,258; average loan $3,197. 52% of total undergraduate aid awarded as scholarships/grants, 48% as loans/jobs. **Non-need-based:** Scholarships awarded for academics, alumni affiliation, art, athletics, leadership, minority status, music/drama, ROTC, state residency. **Additional information:** Students benefiting from the state funded Oklahoma's Promise program do not have to pay out of pocket for tuition, mandatory fees, or books.

Application procedures. Admission: No deadline. $40 fee, may be waived for applicants with need. Admission notification on a rolling basis. Deferred admission allowed based on military deployments. **Financial aid:** Priority date 2/1; no closing date. FAFSA required. Applicants notified on a rolling basis starting 4/1; must reply within 2 week(s) of notification.

Academics. Special study options: Accelerated study, combined bachelor's/graduate degree, cross-registration, distance learning, double major, dual enrollment of high school students, ESL, exchange student, honors, independent study, internships, semester at sea, student-designed major, study abroad, teacher certification program, Washington semester. **Credit/placement by examination:** AP, CLEP, IB, SAT, ACT. Maximum number of credit hours towards degree is subject to university "residence credit" policy. **Support services:** Learning center, pre-admission summer program, reduced course load, remedial instruction, study skills assistance, tutoring, writing center.

Honors college/program. 27 ACT/1220 SAT (exclusive of Writing) and 3.75 GPA required.

Majors. Architecture: Architecture, landscape. **Area/ethnic studies:** American. **Biology:** General, biochemistry, botany, ecology, entomology, microbiology, physiology, zoology. **Business:** Accounting, business admin, entrepreneurial studies, finance, hospitality admin, international, management information systems, managerial economics, marketing. **Communications:** Journalism, sports. **Computer sciences:** General. **Conservation:** Environmental science, forestry. **Education:** General, agricultural, elementary, music, physical, secondary, voc/tech. **Engineering:** Aerospace, agricultural, architectural, chemical, civil, computer, electrical, industrial, mechanical. **English:** English lit. **Foreign languages:** French, German, Russian, Spanish. **General:** Animal sciences, business, communications, economics, food science, horticultural science, landscaping, soil science. **Health services:** Athletic training, public health ed, speech pathology. **History:** General. **Liberal arts:** Arts/sciences. **Math:** General, statistics. **Parks/recreation:** General. **Philosophy/religion:** Philosophy. **Physical sciences:** Chemistry, geology, physics. **Protective services:** Fire safety technology. **Psychology:** General. **Social sciences:** Economics, geography, political science, sociology. **Visual/performing arts:** Art, dramatic, music. **Work/family studies:** Family studies, food/nutrition, housing.

Most popular majors. Agriculture 8%, business/marketing 30%, education 7%, engineering/engineering technologies 11%, family/consumer sciences 8%.

Computing on campus. Dormitories wired for high-speed internet access and linked to campus network. Commuter students can connect to campus network. Online course registration, online library, helpline, repair service, wireless network available.

Student life. Freshman orientation: Mandatory. Preregistration for classes offered. One-day programs in June. Additional program held week before classes begin each fall semester for a fee. **Housing:** Guaranteed on-campus for freshmen. Coed dorms, single-sex dorms, special housing for disabled, apartments, fraternity/sorority housing, wellness housing available. $150 fully refundable deposit. **Activities:** Bands, campus ministries, choral groups, dance, drama, international student organizations, literary magazine, music ensembles, musical theater, opera, radio station, student government, student newspaper, symphony orchestra, TV station, Campus Crusade for Christ, Flying Aggies, rodeo club, Young Democrats, Young Republicans, fire protection society, Alpha Pi Omega, National Organization for Women, African American student association, Hispanic student association.

Athletics. NCAA. **Intercollegiate:** Baseball M, basketball, cross-country, equestrian W, football (tackle) M, golf, soccer W, softball W, tennis, track and field, wrestling M. **Intramural:** Archery, badminton, basketball, bowling, cross-country, football (tackle), golf, racquetball, soccer, softball, squash, swimming, table tennis, tennis, track and field, volleyball, water polo, weight lifting, wrestling M. **Team name:** Cowboys, Cowgirls.

Student services. Adult student services, alcohol/substance abuse counseling, career counseling, student employment services, financial aid counseling, health services, legal services, minority student services, personal counseling, placement for graduates, veterans' counselor, women's services. **Physically disabled:** Services for visually, speech, hearing impaired.

Contact. E-mail: admissions@okstate.edu
Phone: (405) 744-5358 Toll-free number: (800) 233-5019 ext. 1
Fax: (405) 744-7092
Christine Crenshaw, Director of Undergraduate Admissions, Oklahoma
State University, 219 Student Union, Stillwater, OK 74078

Oklahoma Wesleyan University
Bartlesville, Oklahoma
www.okwu.edu
CB code: 6135

- Private 4-year university and liberal arts college affiliated with Wesleyan Church
- Residential campus in large town
- 1,048 degree-seeking undergraduates: 43% part-time, 60% women
- 98 degree-seeking graduate students
- 66% of applicants admitted
- SAT or ACT (ACT writing optional) required

General. Founded in 1909. Regionally accredited. **Degrees:** 310 bachelor's, 35 associate awarded; master's offered. **Location:** 40 miles from Tulsa. **Calendar:** Continuous, limited summer session. **Full-time faculty:** 30 total; 57% have terminal degrees, 33% women. **Part-time faculty:** 39 total; 56% women. **Class size:** 89% < 20, 9% 20-39, 1% 40-49. **Special facilities:** Historic La Quinta mansion, fine arts center, hiking and biking trail.

Freshman class profile. 1,880 applied, 1,240 admitted, 133 enrolled.

GPA 3.75 or higher:	23%	Rank in top tenth:	13%
GPA 3.50-3.74:	16%	Return as sophomores:	66%
GPA 3.0-3.49:	31%	Out-of-state:	48%
GPA 2.0-2.99:	28%	Live on campus:	77%
Rank in top quarter:	33%		

Basis for selection. In addition to required high school study, students must fulfill 2 of the following: rank in top half of class, 2.0 GPA, 18 ACT. **Home schooled:** Statement describing home school structure and mission, transcript of courses and grades required.

High school preparation. 15 units required. Required units include English 4, mathematics 2, social studies 2, science 1 (laboratory 1).

2012-2013 Annual costs. Tuition/fees: $21,140. Room/board: $7,240. Books/supplies: $900. Personal expenses: $1,690.

2011-2012 Financial aid. **Need-based:** Average need met was 14%. Average scholarship/grant was $9,135; average loan $3,311. 46% of total undergraduate aid awarded as scholarships/grants, 54% as loans/jobs. **Non-need-based:** Scholarships awarded for academics, alumni affiliation, athletics, leadership, music/drama, religious affiliation, state residency.

Application procedures. **Admission:** No deadline. $25 fee, may be waived for applicants with need, free for online applicants. Admission notification on a rolling basis. Students must be accepted prior to beginning of classes. **Financial aid:** Priority date 4/1; no closing date. FAFSA, institutional form required. Applicants notified on a rolling basis starting 4/1; must reply by 5/1 or within 2 week(s) of notification.

Academics. **Special study options:** Distance learning, double major, dual enrollment of high school students, independent study, internships, student-designed major, study abroad, teacher certification program, Washington semester. **Credit/placement by examination:** AP, CLEP, SAT, ACT, institutional tests. 30 credit hours maximum toward associate degree, 36 toward bachelor's. **Support services:** Learning center, reduced course load, remedial instruction, study skills assistance, tutoring, writing center.

Majors. **Biology:** General. **Business:** General, business admin. **Communications:** Communications/speech/rhetoric. **Computer sciences:** General, computer science. **Education:** Business, elementary, English, mathematics, music, physical, science, social studies. **English:** English lit. **History:** General. **Math:** General. **Parks/recreation:** Exercise sciences. **Philosophy/religion:** Christian. **Physical sciences:** Chemistry. **Psychology:** General. **Social sciences:** General, political science. **Theology:** Bible, missionary, sacred music, theology.

Computing on campus. 40 workstations in library, computer center, student center. Dormitories wired for high-speed internet access and linked to campus network. Commuter students can connect to campus network. Online course registration, online library, helpline, repair service, wireless network available.

Student life. **Freshman orientation:** Mandatory, $100 fee. Preregistration for classes offered. **Policies:** Religious observance required. **Housing:** Guaranteed on-campus for all undergraduates. Single-sex dorms, apartments available. $250 partly refundable deposit. **Activities:** Bands, campus ministries,

choral groups, music ensembles, student government, student newspaper, campus missionary fellowship, theology fellowship, Fellowship of Christian Athletes, Operation Saturation, Sudan fellowship, College Republicans.

Athletics. NAIA, NCCAA. **Intercollegiate:** Baseball M, basketball, cheerleading M, cross-country, golf M, soccer, softball W, tennis, track and field, volleyball W. **Intramural:** Basketball, football (non-tackle), racquetball, softball W, table tennis, volleyball. **Team name:** Eagles.

Student services. Adult student services, chaplain/spiritual director, career counseling, student employment services, financial aid counseling, health services, placement for graduates, veterans' counselor.

Contact. E-mail: admissions@okwu.edu
Phone: (918) 335-6219 Toll-free number: (800) 468-6292
Fax: (918) 335-6229
John Means, Vice President of Enrollment Services, Oklahoma Wesleyan University, 2201 Silver Lake Road, Bartlesville, OK 74006

Oral Roberts University
Tulsa, Oklahoma
www.oru.edu
CB member
CB code: 6552

- Private 4-year university and liberal arts college affiliated with nondenominational tradition
- Residential campus in large city
- 2,676 degree-seeking undergraduates: 12% part-time, 59% women, 15% African American, 6% Hispanic American, 2% Native American, 5% international
- 583 degree-seeking graduate students
- 59% of applicants admitted
- SAT or ACT (ACT writing optional), application essay required

General. Founded in 1965. Regionally accredited. Integrated math and science academy sponsored by Oklahoma State Regents for Higher Education. **Degrees:** 424 bachelor's awarded; master's, professional, doctoral offered. **ROTC:** Air Force. **Location:** 7 miles from downtown. **Calendar:** Semester, limited summer session. **Full-time faculty:** 172 total; 62% have terminal degrees, 12% minority, 36% women. **Part-time faculty:** 91 total; 19% have terminal degrees, 15% minority, 58% women. **Special facilities:** Prayer tower, mineralogical museum.

Freshman class profile. 1,163 applied, 690 admitted, 405 enrolled.

GPA 3.75 or higher:	31%	Rank in top tenth:	23%
GPA 3.50-3.74:	16%	Out-of-state:	63%
GPA 3.0-3.49:	29%	Live on campus:	75%
GPA 2.0-2.99:	24%	International:	2%
Rank in top quarter:	45%		

Basis for selection. Academic record, test scores, personal essay, minister's recommendation, other recommendations, extracurricular activities considered. Students must provide immunization records. Interview recommended for all; audition required for music program; portfolio recommended for art program. **Home schooled:** Under special circumstances, applicants may be required to submit additional curricular information and/or proof of high school equivalency.

High school preparation. College-preparatory program recommended. 16 units recommended. Recommended units include English 4, mathematics 2, social studies 2, science 1 (laboratory 1), foreign language 2 and academic electives 4. Students matriculating in bachelor of science program may substitute additional math units for foreign language.

2011-2012 Annual costs. Tuition/fees: $20,746. Room/board: $8,594. Books/supplies: $1,500. Personal expenses: $1,500.

Financial aid. **Non-need-based:** Scholarships awarded for academics, alumni affiliation, art, athletics, leadership, music/drama.

Application procedures. **Admission:** Priority date 11/15; no deadline. $35 fee, may be waived for applicants with need. Admission notification on a rolling basis. **Financial aid:** Priority date 3/15; no closing date. FAFSA required. Applicants notified on a rolling basis starting 3/15; must reply by 7/15.

Academics. **Special study options:** Accelerated study, combined bachelor's/graduate degree, distance learning, double major, dual enrollment of high school students, ESL, external degree, honors, independent study, internships, liberal arts/career combination, student-designed major, study abroad, teacher

certification program, Washington semester, weekend college. **Credit/placement by examination:** AP, CLEP, institutional tests. 30 credit hours maximum toward associate degree, 30 toward bachelor's. **Support services:** Learning center, reduced course load, remedial instruction, study skills assistance, tutoring.

Majors. Biology: General, biochemistry. **Business:** Accounting, business admin, finance, international, international marketing, management information systems, management science, marketing, organizational behavior, organizational leadership. **Communications:** Communications/speech/rhetoric. **Computer sciences:** General, computer science. **Education:** Art, business, early childhood, elementary, English, foreign languages, health, mathematics, music, physical, science, social studies, Spanish, special ed. **Engineering:** General, applied physics, biomedical, computer, electrical, environmental, mechanical. **English:** English lit, writing. **Foreign languages:** French, Spanish. **Health services:** Clinical lab science, nursing (RN). **History:** General. **Human services:** Social work. **Liberal arts:** Arts/sciences. **Math:** General. **Parks/recreation:** Exercise sciences, facilities management, health/fitness. **Physical sciences:** Chemistry, physics. **Psychology:** General. **Social sciences:** International relations, political science. **Theology:** Bible, missionary, pastoral counseling, preministerial, religious ed, sacred music, theology. **Visual/performing arts:** Acting, art, commercial/advertising art, dance, design, dramatic, graphic design, music, music performance, music theory/composition, piano/keyboard, studio arts, theater design, voice/opera.

Most popular majors. Business/marketing 22%, communications/journalism 9%, psychology 8%, theological studies 16%, visual/performing arts 7%.

Computing on campus. 382 workstations in library, computer center. Dormitories linked to campus network. Commuter students can connect to campus network. Online course registration, online library, wireless network available.

Student life. Freshman orientation: Mandatory. Preregistration for classes offered. **Policies:** Single undergraduate students under 25 years of age must live in university housing or with parents. Religious observance required. **Housing:** Guaranteed on-campus for all undergraduates. Single-sex dorms available. $125 nonrefundable deposit, deadline 8/8. **Activities:** Bands, campus ministries, choral groups, dance, drama, international student organizations, music ensembles, Model UN, musical theater, radio station, student government, student newspaper, TV station, Community Outreach, missions club, Young Republicans, Young Democrats, student activist society, Students in Free Enterprise, Oklahoma Intercollegiate Legislature.

Athletics. NCAA. **Intercollegiate:** Baseball M, basketball, cross-country, golf, soccer, tennis, track and field, volleyball W. **Intramural:** Badminton, basketball, bowling, cross-country, football (non-tackle), golf, racquetball, softball, swimming, table tennis, tennis, volleyball, wrestling M. **Team name:** Golden Eagles.

Student services. Chaplain/spiritual director, career counseling, student employment services, financial aid counseling, health services, personal counseling, placement for graduates, veterans' counselor. **Physically disabled:** Services for visually, speech, hearing impaired.

Contact. E-mail: admissions@oru.edu
Phone: (918) 496-6518 Toll-free number: (800) 678-8876
Fax: (918) 495-6222
Chris Belcher, Director of Admissions, Oral Roberts University, 7777 South Lewis Avenue, Tulsa, OK 74171

Rogers State University
Claremore, Oklahoma
www.rsu.edu   **CB code: 6545**

▸ Public 4-year university
▸ Commuter campus in large town
▸ 4,587 degree-seeking undergraduates: 38% part-time, 63% women, 3% African American, 1% Asian American, 4% Hispanic American, 13% Native American, 1% international
▸ 54% of applicants admitted

General. Founded in 1909. Regionally accredited. **Degrees:** 269 bachelor's, 276 associate awarded. **Location:** 25 miles from Tulsa. **Calendar:** Semester, limited summer session. **Full-time faculty:** 105 total; 65% have terminal degrees, 15% minority, 44% women. **Part-time faculty:** 163 total; 18% have terminal degrees, 15% minority, 68% women. **Class size:** 43% < 20, 53% 20-39, 3% 40-49, less than 1% 50-99. **Special facilities:** Conservation education reserve, Oklahoma military academy museum, innovation center.

Freshman class profile. 1,925 applied, 1,043 admitted, 888 enrolled.

Mid 50% test scores			
ACT composite:	18-23	Rank in top tenth:	13%
GPA 3.75 or higher:	16%	End year in good standing:	74%
GPA 3.50-3.74:	14%	Return as sophomores:	55%
GPA 3.0-3.49:	32%	Out-of-state:	4%
GPA 2.0-2.99:	34%	Live on campus:	28%
Rank in top quarter:	19%	Sororities:	3%

Basis for selection. Bachelor degree programs require 20 ACT and no curricular deficiencies. Open admission for associate degree programs only. ACT recommended. Essay required for returning suspension students only.

High school preparation. College-preparatory program recommended. 15 units required; 19 recommended. Required and recommended units include English 4, mathematics 3-4, history 3, science 3 (laboratory 3), foreign language 2, computer science 1, visual/performing arts 2 and academic electives 2. Math should include algebra I and II; 1 computer science also recommended; history should include 1 unit of U.S. history and 1 of citizenship (government, geography, etc.).

2011-2012 Annual costs. Tuition/fees: $4,927; $10,972 out-of-state. Apartment-style housing. All residents required to purchase $200 per semester declining balance meal plan. Room only: $4,855. Books/supplies: $2,130. Personal expenses: $1,848.

2011-2012 Financial aid. Need-based: 645 full-time freshmen applied for aid; 531 were judged to have need; 519 of these received aid. Average need met was 46%. Average scholarship/grant was $5,924; average loan $3,432. 52% of total undergraduate aid awarded as scholarships/grants, 48% as loans/jobs. **Non-need-based:** Awarded to 551 full-time undergraduates, including 178 freshmen. Scholarships awarded for academics, art, athletics, leadership, music/drama, state residency.

Application procedures. Admission: No deadline. No application fee. Admission notification on a rolling basis beginning on or about 2/1. Housing deposit refundable through July 1. **Financial aid:** Priority date 6/1; no closing date. FAFSA, institutional form required. Applicants notified on a rolling basis starting 4/1; must reply within 1 week(s) of notification.

Academics. Special study options: Distance learning, honors, independent study, internships, study abroad, Washington semester. **Credit/placement by examination:** AP, CLEP, IB, SAT, ACT, institutional tests. 30 credit hours maximum toward associate degree, 45 toward bachelor's. **Support services:** Learning center, reduced course load, remedial instruction, study skills assistance, tutoring, writing center.

Majors. Biology: General. **Business:** Business admin, nonprofit/public. **Communications:** Communications/speech/rhetoric. **Computer sciences:** Computer graphics. **Health services:** Nursing (RN). **History:** Military. **Human services:** General. **Liberal arts:** Arts/sciences. **Parks/recreation:** Sports admin. **Protective services:** Law enforcement admin. **Psychology:** Community. **Social sciences:** General. **Visual/performing arts:** General.

Most popular majors. Biology 15%, business/marketing 29%, engineering/engineering technologies 7%, interdisciplinary studies 6%, liberal arts 6%, security/protective services 6%, social sciences 10%.

Computing on campus. 254 workstations in dormitories, library, student center. Dormitories wired for high-speed internet access and linked to campus network. Online library, helpline, wireless network available.

Student life. Freshman orientation: Available. Preregistration for classes offered. **Housing:** Special housing for disabled, apartments, wellness housing available. $200 fully refundable deposit. **Activities:** Bands, campus ministries, choral groups, drama, international student organizations, literary magazine, radio station, student government, student newspaper, TV station, Native American student association, Baptist collegiate ministry, student art association, student nursing association, Campus Crusade for Christ, College Republicans.

Athletics. NAIA. **Intercollegiate:** Baseball M, basketball, cheerleading, cross-country, golf, soccer, softball W. **Intramural:** Football (non-tackle), volleyball. **Team name:** Hillcats.

Student services. Adult student services, alcohol/substance abuse counseling, career counseling, services for economically disadvantaged, financial aid counseling, health services, on-campus daycare, personal counseling, veterans' counselor. **Physically disabled:** Services for visually, speech, hearing impaired.

Contact. E-mail: admissions@rsu.edu
Phone: (918) 343-7546 Toll-free number: (800) 256-7511
Fax: (918) 343-7595
Julie Rampey, Director of Admissions, Rogers State University, 1701 West Will Rogers Boulevard, Claremore, OK 74017

Southeastern Oklahoma State University
Durant, Oklahoma
www.se.edu   CB code: 6657

▶ Public 4-year liberal arts and teachers college
▶ Commuter campus in large town
▶ 3,690 degree-seeking undergraduates: 22% part-time, 56% women, 6% African American, 1% Asian American, 3% Hispanic American, 30% Native American, 3% international
▶ 335 degree-seeking graduate students
▶ 78% of applicants admitted
▶ SAT or ACT (ACT writing optional) required

General. Founded in 1909. Regionally accredited. Degree programs offered through satellite campus at Idabel and Higher Education Centers at Ardmore, McAlester, Tinker Air Force Base, Oklahoma City Community College, and Grayson County College. **Degrees:** 625 bachelor's awarded; master's offered. **Location:** 90 miles from Dallas. **Calendar:** Semester, extensive summer session. **Full-time faculty:** 142 total; 78% have terminal degrees, 13% minority, 42% women. **Part-time faculty:** 120 total; 22% have terminal degrees, 21% minority, 58% women. **Class size:** 49% < 20, 41% 20-39, 7% 40-49, 3% 50-99, less than 1% >100. **Special facilities:** Herbarium, equestrian facilities.

Freshman class profile. 1,143 applied, 886 admitted, 635 enrolled.

Mid 50% test scores			
ACT composite:	18-22	Rank in top quarter:	40%
GPA 3.75 or higher:	20%	Rank in top tenth:	15%
GPA 3.50-3.74:	16%	Return as sophomores:	54%
GPA 3.0-3.49:	36%	Out-of-state:	27%
GPA 2.0-2.99:	26%	Live on campus:	53%
		International:	2%

Basis for selection. High school transcript and test scores important. Must have 2.7 GPA and rank in top half of class, 20 ACT or 940 SAT (exclusive of Writing), score in top half of applicants on ACT scores, or attain 2.7 GPA in 15 core units. Audition required for drama, music programs. Interview required for alternative admissions. **Home schooled:** 20 ACT required.

High school preparation. College-preparatory program recommended. 15 units required. Required and recommended units include English 4, mathematics 3, history 3, science 3 (laboratory 3), foreign language 1, computer science 1 and academic electives 2.

2011-2012 Annual costs. Tuition/fees: $4,904; $12,117 out-of-state. Room/board: $5,160. Books/supplies: $800. Personal expenses: $1,447.

2010-2011 Financial aid. Need-based: 564 full-time freshmen applied for aid; 488 were judged to have need; 482 of these received aid. Average need met was 27%. Average scholarship/grant was $1,422; average loan $1,295. 62% of total undergraduate aid awarded as scholarships/grants, 38% as loans/jobs. **Non-need-based:** Awarded to 873 full-time undergraduates, including 249 freshmen. Scholarships awarded for academics, alumni affiliation, art, athletics, leadership, minority status, music/drama, state residency.

Application procedures. Admission: No deadline. $20 fee. Admission notification on a rolling basis. Open admission for adults over 21. **Financial aid:** Priority date 3/1; no closing date. FAFSA, institutional form required. Applicants notified on a rolling basis starting 4/1.

Academics. Programs in aviation, ecology, energy, health-related sciences, and criminology. **Special study options:** Combined bachelor's/graduate degree, distance learning, double major, honors, independent study, internships, teacher certification program. **Credit/placement by examination:** AP, CLEP, IB, SAT, ACT, institutional tests. 60 credit hours maximum toward bachelor's degree. **Support services:** Learning center, pre-admission summer program, reduced course load, remedial instruction, study skills assistance, tutoring, writing center.

Majors. Biology: General, biotechnology. **Business:** Accounting, business admin, finance, management science, marketing, organizational leadership. **Communications:** Communications/speech/rhetoric. **Computer sciences:** General, information systems. **Conservation:** General. **Education:** Art, elementary, English, mathematics, music, physical, science, social studies, Spanish, special ed. **Engineering:** Aerospace. **English:** English lit. **Foreign languages:** Spanish. **History:** General. **Math:** General. **Parks/recreation:** General. **Physical sciences:** Chemistry. **Protective services:** Criminal justice. **Psychology:** General. **Social sciences:** Political science, sociology. **Visual/performing arts:** Art, dramatic, graphic design, music, music performance.

Most popular majors. Business/marketing 10%, communications/journalism 7%, education 22%, engineering/engineering technologies 12%, liberal arts 9%, parks/recreation 6%, psychology 8%.

Computing on campus. 2,138 workstations in dormitories, library, computer center, student center. Dormitories wired for high-speed internet access and linked to campus network. Commuter students can connect to campus network. Online course registration, online library, helpline, student web hosting, wireless network available.

Student life. Freshman orientation: Available, $20 fee. Preregistration for classes offered. **Policies:** No alcohol at university events on/off campus. **Housing:** Coed dorms, single-sex dorms, special housing for disabled available. $100 nonrefundable deposit. **Activities:** Bands, campus ministries, choral groups, dance, drama, international student organizations, literary magazine, music ensembles, musical theater, opera, radio station, student government, student newspaper, Black American society, Wesley Center, student Bible center, Chi Alpha, Young Democrats, College Republicans, Muslim student association.

Athletics. NCAA. **Intercollegiate:** Baseball M, basketball, cross-country W, football (tackle) M, golf M, rodeo, softball W, tennis, volleyball W. **Intramural:** Basketball, football (non-tackle), football (tackle) M, soccer, softball, volleyball. **Team name:** Savage Storm.

Student services. Adult student services, alcohol/substance abuse counseling, chaplain/spiritual director, career counseling, student employment services, financial aid counseling, health services, minority student services, personal counseling, placement for graduates, veterans' counselor. **Physically disabled:** Services for visually, speech, hearing impaired.

Contact. E-mail: admissions@se.edu
Phone: (580) 745-2060 Toll-free number: (800) 435-1327
Fax: (580) 745-7502
Kristie Luke, Associate Dean of Admissions and Records/Registrar, Southeastern Oklahoma State University, 1405 North Fourth Avenue, PMB 4225, Durant, OK 74701-0607

Southern Nazarene University
Bethany, Oklahoma   CB member
www.snu.edu   CB code: 6036

▶ Private 4-year university and liberal arts college affiliated with Church of the Nazarene
▶ Residential campus in large town
▶ 1,468 degree-seeking undergraduates: 4% part-time, 52% women
▶ 527 graduate students
▶ SAT or ACT required

General. Founded in 1899. Regionally accredited. **Degrees:** 537 bachelor's, 1 associate awarded; master's offered. **ROTC:** Army, Air Force. **Location:** 10 miles from Oklahoma City. **Calendar:** Semester, limited summer session. **Full-time faculty:** 85 total. **Part-time faculty:** 60 total. **Special facilities:** Human cadaver laboratory, physics laser laboratory, laboratory school for children.

Freshman class profile.

GPA 3.75 or higher:	32%	Rank in top quarter:	45%
GPA 3.50-3.74:	16%	Rank in top tenth:	22%
GPA 3.0-3.49:	27%	Live on campus:	85%
GPA 2.0-2.99:	24%		

Basis for selection. 2.0 GPA and 19 ACT or SAT equivalent required for unconditional admissions. Students who do not meet requirements may be granted provisional acceptance by committee review. Higher TOEFL score requirement of 79 (internet-based test) for pre-med and nursing programs. Interview recommended for all; audition recommended for music program. **Home schooled:** Transcript of courses and grades required.

High school preparation. 13 units recommended. Recommended units include English 4, mathematics 3, social studies 2, science 2 and foreign language 2. One computer course recommended.

2011-2012 Annual costs. Tuition/fees: $19,794. Room/board: $7,900. Books/supplies: $600. Personal expenses: $1,200.

Financial aid. Non-need-based: Scholarships awarded for academics, athletics, ROTC, state residency.

Application procedures. Admission: Priority date 5/1; deadline 8/1. $35 fee, may be waived for applicants with need. Admission notification on a rolling basis. **Financial aid:** Priority date 3/1; no closing date. FAFSA, institutional form required. Applicants notified on a rolling basis starting 5/1; must reply within 2 week(s) of notification.

Academics. Special study options: Combined bachelor's/graduate degree, distance learning, double major, dual enrollment of high school students,

external degree, honors, independent study, internships, liberal arts/career combination, student-designed major, study abroad, teacher certification program, urban semester, Washington semester. **Credit/placement by examination:** AP, CLEP, IB, institutional tests. 30 credit hours maximum toward bachelor's degree. **Support services:** Remedial instruction, study skills assistance, tutoring, writing center.

Majors. Area/ethnic studies: American. **Biology:** General, biochemistry. **Business:** General, accounting, business admin, finance, marketing. **Communications:** Communications/speech/rhetoric, journalism. **Communications technology:** General. **Computer sciences:** General, networking. **Conservation:** General. **Education:** General, early childhood, elementary, English, history, mathematics, music, physical, reading, science, secondary, Spanish, speech. **English:** English lit, rhetoric/composition. **Foreign languages:** Spanish. **Health services:** Athletic training, clinical lab technology. **History:** General. **Liberal arts:** Arts/sciences. **Math:** General. **Parks/recreation:** Exercise sciences. **Philosophy/religion:** Philosophy, religion. **Physical sciences:** Chemistry, physics. **Protective services:** Criminal justice. **Psychology:** General. **Social sciences:** General, political science, sociology. **Theology:** Missionary, religious ed, sacred music, theology. **Visual/performing arts:** General, graphic design, music.

Most popular majors. Business/marketing 54%, computer/information sciences 6%, education 6%, family/consumer sciences 9%, health sciences 7%.

Computing on campus. 120 workstations in library, computer center. Dormitories wired for high-speed internet access and linked to campus network. Helpline, repair service, wireless network available.

Student life. Freshman orientation: Mandatory. Preregistration for classes offered. **Policies:** Single students under 23 required to live on campus or with relatives. Religious observance required. **Housing:** Guaranteed on-campus for freshmen. Single-sex dorms, apartments available. $50 deposit, deadline 8/1. **Activities:** Bands, choral groups, drama, film society, music ensembles, student government, student newspaper, symphony orchestra, TV station, Gospel team, Mission Crusaders, Circle-K, Spanish club, Mortar Board.

Athletics. NAIA. **Intercollegiate:** Baseball M, basketball, cheerleading, cross-country, equestrian, football (tackle) M, golf, soccer, softball W, tennis, track and field, volleyball W. **Intramural:** Basketball, football (non-tackle), football (tackle) M, softball, tennis, track and field, volleyball. **Team name:** Crimson Storm.

Student services. Alcohol/substance abuse counseling, chaplain/spiritual director, career counseling, services for economically disadvantaged, student employment services, financial aid counseling, health services, personal counseling, placement for graduates. **Physically disabled:** Services for visually, speech, hearing impaired.

Contact. E-mail: lcantwell@snu.edu
Phone: (405) 491-6324 Toll-free number: (800) 648-9899
Fax: (405) 491-6320
Linda Cantwell, Director of Admissions, Southern Nazarene University, 6729 NW 39th Expressway, Bethany, OK 73008

Southwestern Christian University
Bethany, Oklahoma
www.swcu.edu   **CB code: 1433**

- Private 4-year liberal arts college affiliated with Pentecostal Holiness Church
- Residential campus in large town
- 635 degree-seeking undergraduates
- 83% of applicants admitted
- SAT or ACT with writing, application essay, interview required

General. Founded in 1946. Regionally accredited. Adult degree-completion program offered. Lockstep program allows for degree completion in 18 months or less. **Degrees:** 60 bachelor's, 7 associate awarded; master's offered. **ROTC:** Army. **Location:** 10 miles from Oklahoma City. **Calendar:** Semester, limited summer session. **Full-time faculty:** 16 total. **Part-time faculty:** 42 total.

Freshman class profile. 300 applied, 250 admitted, 243 enrolled.

Mid 50% test scores			
SAT critical reading:	410-510	GPA 3.0-3.49:	32%
SAT math:	430-530	GPA 2.0-2.99:	36%
ACT composite:	17-23	Rank in top quarter:	27%
GPA 3.75 or higher:	5%	Rank in top tenth:	8%
GPA 3.50-3.74:	25%	Out-of-state:	4%
		Live on campus:	48%

Basis for selection. 2.5 GPA or 19 ACT required. Additional materials and interview may be requested.

High school preparation. Required units include English 4, mathematics 2, social studies 2, history 2, science 2 (laboratory 2).

2011-2012 Annual costs. Tuition/fees: $12,350. Room/board: $5,100. Books/supplies: $750. Personal expenses: $1,100.

Financial aid. Non-need-based: Scholarships awarded for academics, alumni affiliation, leadership, music/drama, religious affiliation.

Application procedures. Admission: No deadline. No application fee. Application must be submitted on paper. Admission notification on a rolling basis. **Financial aid:** Priority date 8/1; no closing date. FAFSA required. Applicants notified on a rolling basis starting 5/1; must reply within 2 week(s) of notification.

Academics. Applied Biblical Leadership Education (ABLE), an adult studies completion program. **Special study options:** Accelerated study, cross-registration, double major, dual enrollment of high school students, honors, independent study, internships, liberal arts/career combination. **Credit/placement by examination:** AP, CLEP, institutional tests. 30 credit hours maximum toward bachelor's degree. **Support services:** Learning center, reduced course load, remedial instruction, tutoring.

Majors. Business: Business admin. **Philosophy/religion:** Religion. **Theology:** Bible, missionary, pastoral counseling, religious ed, sacred music, theology, youth ministry. **Visual/performing arts:** Music performance.

Computing on campus. 9 workstations in library. Dormitories wired for high-speed internet access and linked to campus network. Online library, wireless network available.

Student life. Freshman orientation: Mandatory. Preregistration for classes offered. Held the week prior to classes; includes academic, financial aid and spiritual life orientation. **Policies:** Extracurricular Christian programs and activities emphasized. Mandatory dress code. Students sign lifestyle covenant agreeing to certain behaviors. Religious observance required. **Housing:** Single-sex dorms available. $100 nonrefundable deposit, deadline 8/15. **Activities:** Campus ministries, choral groups, drama, music ensembles, musical theater, student government, student newspaper, Southwestern Ministerial Association, missionary society, Christian education association.

Athletics. NCCAA. **Intercollegiate:** Basketball M, cross-country, golf M, soccer M, softball, volleyball W. **Intramural:** Baseball M, basketball, cheerleading, football (non-tackle) M, softball, table tennis, volleyball. **Team name:** Eagles.

Student services. Adult student services, chaplain/spiritual director, career counseling, student employment services, financial aid counseling, personal counseling, veterans' counselor.

Contact. E-mail: admissions@swcu.edu
Phone: (405) 789-7661 ext. 3442 Toll-free number: (888) 418-9272
Fax: (405) 495-0078
Chad Pugh, Recruitment/Admissions, Southwestern Christian University, Box 340, Bethany, OK 73008

Southwestern Oklahoma State University
Weatherford, Oklahoma   **CB member**
www.swosu.edu   **CB code: 6673**

- Public 4-year university
- Residential campus in large town
- 4,374 degree-seeking undergraduates: 15% part-time, 58% women, 6% African American, 2% Asian American, 6% Hispanic American, 6% Native American, 2% international
- 823 degree-seeking graduate students
- 92% of applicants admitted
- SAT or ACT (ACT writing optional) required

General. Founded in 1901. Regionally accredited. Campus at Sayre offers lower division and remedial courses, as well as associate degrees. **Degrees:** 563 bachelor's, 98 associate awarded; master's, professional offered. **Location:** 75 miles from Oklahoma City. **Calendar:** Semester, extensive summer session. **Full-time faculty:** 215 total; 62% have terminal degrees, 13% minority, 47% women. **Part-time faculty:** 19 total. **Class size:** 44% < 20, 40% 20-39, 11% 40-49, 5% 50-99.

Freshman class profile. 1,717 applied, 1,585 admitted, 986 enrolled.

Mid 50% test scores		Rank in top quarter:	44%
ACT composite:	18-24	Rank in top tenth:	20%
GPA 3.75 or higher:	30%	Return as sophomores:	57%
GPA 3.50-3.74:	16%	Out-of-state:	10%
GPA 3.0-3.49:	30%	Live on campus:	56%
GPA 2.0-2.99:	22%		

Basis for selection. Bachelor degree programs require 19 ACT and no curricular deficiencies. Open admission for associate degree programs. Last date to submit test scores is first day of classes. Essay required for returning suspension students only.

High school preparation. College-preparatory program required. 15 units required; 17 recommended. Required and recommended units include English 4, mathematics 3, social studies 1, history 2, science 2 (laboratory 2), computer science 1 and academic electives 2-4. Social studies unit must be citizenship. Academic electives should be in fine arts. 3 units computer science or foreign language required.

2011-2012 Annual costs. Tuition/fees: $4,590; $10,650 out-of-state. Room/board: $4,600. Books/supplies: $1,230. Personal expenses: $996.

2011-2012 Financial aid. Need-based: 765 full-time freshmen applied for aid; 627 were judged to have need; 616 of these received aid. Average need met was 92%. Average scholarship/grant was $1,456; average loan $1,416. 45% of total undergraduate aid awarded as scholarships/grants, 55% as loans/jobs. **Non-need-based:** Awarded to 2,839 full-time undergraduates, including 601 freshmen. Scholarships awarded for academics, alumni affiliation, art, athletics, leadership, music/drama, state residency.

Application procedures. Admission: No deadline. $15 fee. Admission notification on a rolling basis. **Financial aid:** Closing date 3/1. FAFSA, institutional form required. Applicants notified by 3/15.

Academics. Special study options: Accelerated study, combined bachelor's/graduate degree, distance learning, double major, independent study, internships, student-designed major, study abroad, teacher certification program. **Credit/placement by examination:** AP, CLEP, IB, ACT, institutional tests. 62 credit hours maximum toward bachelor's degree. **Support services:** Pre-admission summer program, reduced course load, remedial instruction, study skills assistance, tutoring, writing center.

Majors. Biology: General, biophysics. **Business:** General, accounting, business admin, human resources, management information systems. **Communications:** Communications/speech/rhetoric. **Computer sciences:** General, computer science, information systems. **Education:** Art, early childhood, elementary, English, health, history, learning disabled, mathematics, mentally handicapped, music, physical, science, social science, special ed, technology/industrial arts. **Engineering:** General, applied physics. **English:** English lit. **Health services:** Athletic training, clinical lab technology, health care admin, medical records admin, music therapy, nursing (RN). **History:** General. **Human services:** Social work. **Math:** General. **Parks/recreation:** General, facilities management. **Physical sciences:** Chemistry, physics. **Protective services:** Criminal justice. **Psychology:** General. **Social sciences:** Political science, sociology. **Theology:** Sacred music. **Visual/performing arts:** Commercial/advertising art, music, music management, music performance, music theory/composition, piano/keyboard, voice/opera.

Most popular majors. Business/marketing 17%, education 14%, health sciences 24%, parks/recreation 9%.

Computing on campus. 200 workstations in library, computer center. Dormitories wired for high-speed internet access. Commuter students can connect to campus network. Online library, wireless network available.

Student life. Freshman orientation: Mandatory, $60 fee. Preregistration for classes offered. **Housing:** Guaranteed on-campus for all undergraduates. Single-sex dorms, apartments available. $100 fully refundable deposit, deadline 8/1. **Activities:** Bands, campus ministries, choral groups, drama, international student organizations, literary magazine, music ensembles, Model UN, musical theater, opera, student government, student newspaper, symphony orchestra, 7 religious organizations, 4 political organizations, and approximately 75 social and professional clubs.

Athletics. NCAA. **Intercollegiate:** Baseball M, basketball, cheerleading, cross-country W, football (tackle) M, golf, rodeo, soccer, softball W. **Intramural:** Basketball, bowling, football (non-tackle), golf, racquetball, soccer, softball, swimming, tennis, volleyball. **Team name:** Bulldogs.

Student services. Adult student services, alcohol/substance abuse counseling, career counseling, student employment services, financial aid counseling, health services, personal counseling, placement for graduates, veterans' counselor. **Physically disabled:** Services for visually, hearing impaired.

Contact. E-mail: admissions@swosu.edu
Phone: (580) 774-3009 Fax: (580) 774-3795
Todd Boyd, Director of Admissions, Southwestern Oklahoma State University, 100 Campus Drive, Weatherford, OK 73096

Spartan College of Aeronautics and Technology
Tulsa, Oklahoma
www.spartan.edu   CB code: 0336

- For-profit 4-year technical college
- Commuter campus in large city
- 957 degree-seeking undergraduates
- 87 graduate students
- 90% of applicants admitted
- Interview required

General. Founded in 1928. Accredited by ACCSC. Multi-campus institution with technical campuses at Tulsa International Airport and R.L Jones Airport in South Tulsa. **Degrees:** 23 bachelor's, 169 associate awarded. **Location:** 100 miles from Oklahoma City. **Calendar:** Continuous, extensive summer session. **Full-time faculty:** 65 total; 2% have terminal degrees, 14% women. **Part-time faculty:** 34 total; 3% have terminal degrees, 12% women. **Class size:** 60% < 20, 40% 20-39.

Freshman class profile. 1,315 applied, 1,186 admitted, 462 enrolled.

Out-of-state:	83%	Live on campus:	25%

Basis for selection. Applicants must demonstrate proficiency in college-level skills by submission of examination scores deemed appropriate for the chosen program of study. Students wishing to attend flight training must obtain FAA Class II flight certificate and pass TSA screening. SAT or ACT recommended. **Home schooled:** Statement describing home school structure and mission, transcript of courses and grades, state high school equivalency certificate, interview required. Any student graduating from a non-accredited high school must submit ACT/SAT.

2011-2012 Annual costs. Tuition/fees: $15,000. Room only: $3,510. Books/supplies: $2,000.

Application procedures. Admission: No deadline. $100 fee. Admission notification on a rolling basis. **Financial aid:** No deadline. FAFSA, institutional form required. Applicants notified on a rolling basis starting 2/1; must reply within 2 week(s) of notification.

Academics. Special study options: Distance learning, independent study. **Credit/placement by examination:** AP, CLEP, institutional tests. No more than half of credits required for degree may be earned through examination. **Support services:** Remedial instruction, tutoring.

Computing on campus. 100 workstations in library, student center. Dormitories wired for high-speed internet access. Online library, wireless network available.

Student life. Freshman orientation: Mandatory. Preregistration for classes offered. Usually held on Friday immediately preceding start of classes. **Policies:** All students subject to random drug testing. **Housing:** Apartments, wellness housing available. **Activities:** Student government.

Student services. Career counseling, student employment services, financial aid counseling, personal counseling, placement for graduates, veterans' counselor.

Contact. E-mail: spartan@mail.spartan.edu
Phone: (918) 836-6886 ext. 242
Toll-free number: (800) 331-1204 ext. 242 Fax: (918) 831-8609
Damon Bowling, Vice President, Marketing, Spartan College of Aeronautics and Technology, 8820 East Pine Street, Tulsa, OK 74158-2833

St. Gregory's University
Shawnee, Oklahoma
www.stgregorys.edu   CB code: 6621

- Private 4-year university and liberal arts college affiliated with Roman Catholic Church
- Residential campus in large town
- 688 degree-seeking undergraduates
- SAT or ACT (ACT writing optional), application essay required

General. Founded in 1875. Regionally accredited. Roman Catholic and Benedictine tradition. **Degrees:** 79 bachelor's, 38 associate awarded; master's offered. **ROTC:** Air Force. **Location:** 30 miles from Oklahoma City. **Calendar:** Semester, limited summer session. **Full-time faculty:** 28 total. **Part-time faculty:** 144 total. **Class size:** 93% < 20, 7% 20-39. **Special facilities:** Benedictine abbey, art museum.

Basis for selection. Core classes, GPA most important; test scores, class rank important. Interview required for students admitted on probation; audition required for dance, drama, and choral scholarships; portfolio required for art scholarships. **Home schooled:** Interview required. **Learning Disabled:** Students with need beyond ADA standards may apply to Partners in Learning Program. Additional fee of approximately $7,000 required if admitted.

High school preparation. 17 units recommended. Recommended units include English 4, mathematics 3, social studies 2, history 2, science 2 (laboratory 2) and foreign language 2.

2011-2012 Annual costs. Tuition/fees: $19,305. Room/board: $6,880. Books/supplies: $900. Personal expenses: $1,914.

Financial aid. **Non-need-based:** Scholarships awarded for academics, alumni affiliation, art, athletics, job skills, leadership, music/drama, religious affiliation.

Application procedures. **Admission:** Priority date 8/1; no deadline. $25 fee, may be waived for applicants with need. Admission notification on a rolling basis. **Financial aid:** Priority date 4/1; no closing date. FAFSA, institutional form required. Applicants notified on a rolling basis starting 2/15; must reply within 3 week(s) of notification.

Academics. Discussion-based seminars on Western and Catholic intellectual traditions required of all freshmen and sophomore students. Special accelerated programs for non-traditional students in Shawnee, Oklahoma City, and Tulsa. **Special study options:** Accelerated study, cooperative education, double major, ESL, honors, independent study, internships, student-designed major, study abroad, teacher certification program. **Credit/placement by examination:** AP, CLEP, IB, SAT, ACT. 12 credit hours maximum toward associate degree, 30 toward bachelor's. Course proficiency exams available in areas where no CLEP exams offered. **Support services:** Remedial instruction, study skills assistance, tutoring.

Majors. **Biology:** General, biomedical sciences. **Business:** Business admin. **Communications:** Communications/speech/rhetoric. **Conservation:** General. **Education:** General, elementary, secondary. **English:** English lit. **History:** General. **Liberal arts:** Arts/sciences, humanities. **Math:** General. **Parks/recreation:** Exercise sciences. **Protective services:** Criminal justice. **Psychology:** General. **Social sciences:** General, political science, sociology. **Theology:** Theology. **Visual/performing arts:** General, art, dance.

Most popular majors. Biology 8%, business/marketing 59%, family/consumer sciences 13%, social sciences 8%.

Computing on campus. 60 workstations in dormitories, library, computer center, student center. Dormitories wired for high-speed internet access and linked to campus network. Commuter students can connect to campus network. Online library, helpline, repair service, student web hosting, wireless network available.

Student life. Freshman orientation: Mandatory. Preregistration for classes offered. Three-day program held prior to start of fall term, plus evenings in first week of fall semester. **Policies:** Smoke-free; alcohol/drug-free; on-campus residency required under age 22. **Housing:** Guaranteed on-campus for freshmen. Single-sex dorms, wellness housing available. $100 fully refundable deposit. **Activities:** Jazz band, campus ministries, choral groups, dance, drama, international student organizations, student government, Knights of Columbus, Fellowship of Christian Athletes, history club, student alumni council, Students in Free Enterprise, Hispanic awareness student association, human rights action committee, pro-life team.

Athletics. NAIA. **Intercollegiate:** Baseball M, basketball, soccer, softball W, volleyball W. **Intramural:** Basketball, football (non-tackle), football (tackle) M, racquetball, soccer, softball, table tennis, tennis, volleyball. **Team name:** Cavaliers.

Student services. Adult student services, alcohol/substance abuse counseling, chaplain/spiritual director, career counseling, services for economically disadvantaged, student employment services, financial aid counseling, minority student services, personal counseling, placement for graduates, veterans' counselor.

Contact. E-mail: admissions@stgregorys.edu
Phone: (405) 878-5444 Toll-free number: (888) 784-7347
Fax: (405) 878-5198
William Kuehl, Director of Admissions, St. Gregory's University, 1900 West MacArthur Drive, Shawnee, OK 74804

University of Central Oklahoma
Edmond, Oklahoma — CB member
www.uco.edu — CB code: 6091

- Public 4-year university
- Commuter campus in small city
- 15,158 degree-seeking undergraduates: 27% part-time, 57% women, 10% African American, 3% Asian American, 6% Hispanic American, 4% Native American, 6% international
- 1,782 degree-seeking graduate students
- 80% of applicants admitted
- SAT or ACT (ACT writing optional) required

General. Founded in 1890. Regionally accredited. **Degrees:** 2,305 bachelor's, 58 associate awarded; master's offered. **ROTC:** Army. **Location:** 12 miles from Oklahoma City. **Calendar:** Semester, extensive summer session. **Full-time faculty:** 449 total; 77% have terminal degrees, 13% minority, 46% women. **Part-time faculty:** 486 total; 18% have terminal degrees, 11% minority, 52% women. **Class size:** 31% < 20, 55% 20-39, 11% 40-49, 3% 50-99, less than 1% >100. **Special facilities:** Jazz lab.

Freshman class profile. 4,742 applied, 3,792 admitted, 2,195 enrolled.

GPA 3.75 or higher:	20%	Out-of-state:	4%
GPA 3.50-3.74:	17%	Live on campus:	43%
GPA 3.0-3.49:	36%	International:	6%
GPA 2.0-2.99:	26%	Fraternities:	9%
Rank in top quarter:	34%	Sororities:	10%
Rank in top tenth:	13%		

Basis for selection. 2.7 GPA and rank in top 50% of class, or 2.7 GPA in 15 unit high school core, or 20 ACT required.

High school preparation. College-preparatory program recommended. 15 units required; 18 recommended. Required and recommended units include English 4, mathematics 3-4, social studies 1, history 3, science 3 (laboratory 3), foreign language 2 and computer science 1. 2 additional units of math, science, English, history or 2 units computer science and/or foreign language required.

2011-2012 Annual costs. Tuition/fees: $4,718; $11,905 out-of-state. Room/board: $6,475. Books/supplies: $1,200. Personal expenses: $2,000.

Financial aid. **Non-need-based:** Scholarships awarded for academics, alumni affiliation, art, athletics, leadership, minority status, music/drama, ROTC, state residency.

Application procedures. **Admission:** No deadline. $25 fee. Admission notification on a rolling basis beginning on or about 4/1. **Financial aid:** Priority date 5/31; no closing date. FAFSA, institutional form required. Applicants notified on a rolling basis starting 5/1; must reply by 6/30 or within 4 week(s) of notification.

Academics. **Special study options:** Accelerated study, distance learning, double major, dual enrollment of high school students, ESL, honors, independent study, internships, teacher certification program, weekend college. **Credit/placement by examination:** AP, CLEP, ACT, institutional tests. 94 credit hours maximum toward bachelor's degree. **Support services:** Learning center, reduced course load, remedial instruction, tutoring, writing center.

Majors. **Biology:** General. **Business:** Accounting, actuarial science, apparel, business admin, finance, human resources, insurance, management information systems, managerial economics, marketing, nonprofit/public, operations. **Communications:** Advertising, broadcast journalism, communications/speech/rhetoric, journalism, photojournalism, public relations. **Computer sciences:** General, information technology. **Education:** General, art, biology, business, chemistry, curriculum, drama/dance, early childhood, educational technology, elementary, ESL, family/consumer sciences, French, German, health occupations, history, mathematics, music, physical, physics, reading, science, social studies, Spanish, special ed, technology/industrial arts. **Engineering:** Applied physics, biomedical. **English:** English lit, writing. **Foreign languages:** French, German, Spanish. **Health services:** Audiology/speech pathology, clinical lab science, nursing (RN), public health ed, speech pathology. **History:** General. **Liberal arts:** Arts/sciences. **Math:** General, applied, statistics. **Parks/recreation:** General, exercise sciences. **Philosophy/religion:** Philosophy. **Physical sciences:** Chemistry, physics. **Protective services:** Corrections, criminal justice, forensics, juvenile corrections, police science. **Psychology:** General. **Social sciences:** Applied economics, economics, geography, political science, sociology, urban studies. **Visual/performing arts:** Art, art history/conservation, dance, dramatic, graphic design, interior design, music, music performance, piano/keyboard, stringed instruments, voice/opera. **Work/family studies:** General, aging, child development, family systems, food/nutrition.

Most popular majors. Business/marketing 26%, communications/journalism 6%, education 16%, health sciences 6%, liberal arts 12%.

Computing on campus. 450 workstations in dormitories, library, computer center, student center. Dormitories wired for high-speed internet access. Commuter students can connect to campus network. Helpline, wireless network available.

Student life. Freshman orientation: Mandatory, $35 fee. Preregistration for classes offered. Three-day orientation held the week before classes start in August. **Housing:** Coed dorms, single-sex dorms, apartments, fraternity/sorority housing, wellness housing available. $150 fully refundable deposit. **Activities:** Bands, choral groups, dance, drama, international student organizations, music ensembles, musical theater, radio station, student government, student newspaper, symphony orchestra, TV station, Baptist student union, Fellowship of Christian Athletes, Young Democrats, Collegiate Republicans, black student association, Malaysian student association, association of women students, Webmasters.

Athletics. NCAA. **Intercollegiate:** Baseball M, basketball, cross-country, football (tackle) M, golf, ice hockey M, soccer W, softball W, tennis, track and field, volleyball W, wrestling M. **Intramural:** Badminton, baseball M, basketball, bowling, football (non-tackle), golf, handball, soccer, softball, swimming, table tennis, tennis, track and field, volleyball, wrestling M. **Team name:** Bronchos.

Student services. Career counseling, student employment services, health services, personal counseling, placement for graduates, veterans' counselor. **Physically disabled:** Services for visually, speech, hearing impaired.

Contact. E-mail: 4ucoinfo@uco.edu
Phone: (405) 974-2338 Fax: (405) 341-4964
Linda Lofton, Director, Admissions & Records, University of Central Oklahoma, 100 North University Drive, Edmond, OK 73034-0151

University of Oklahoma
Norman, Oklahoma
www.ou.edu

CB member
CB code: 6879

- Public 4-year university
- Residential campus in small city
- 21,041 degree-seeking undergraduates: 12% part-time, 52% women, 5% African American, 5% Asian American, 6% Hispanic American, 5% Native American, 3% international
- 9,330 graduate students
- 82% of applicants admitted
- SAT or ACT (ACT writing optional) required
- 68% graduate within 6 years

General. Founded in 1890. Regionally accredited. Faculty-in-residence program has faculty live in student dorms and mix with students. **Degrees:** 4,648 bachelor's awarded; master's, professional, doctoral offered. **ROTC:** Army, Naval, Air Force. **Location:** 20 miles from Oklahoma City, 200 miles from Dallas. **Calendar:** Semester, extensive summer session. **Full-time faculty:** 1,487 total; 84% have terminal degrees, 19% minority, 41% women. **Part-time faculty:** 331 total; 56% have terminal degrees, 12% minority, 43% women. **Class size:** 40% < 20, 41% 20-39, 7% 40-49, 8% 50-99, 4% >100. **Special facilities:** Art museum, natural history museum, national weather center, national severe storms laboratory, biological station, history of science collection, western history collection, Oklahoma geological survey.

Freshman class profile. 11,456 applied, 9,377 admitted, 4,053 enrolled.

Mid 50% test scores			
SAT critical reading:	510-650	Rank in top quarter:	70%
SAT math:	540-660	Rank in top tenth:	36%
ACT composite:	23-29	Return as sophomores:	85%
GPA 3.75 or higher:	43%	Out-of-state:	38%
GPA 3.50-3.74:	27%	Live on campus:	82%
GPA 3.0-3.49:	27%	International:	3%
GPA 2.0-2.99:	3%	Fraternities:	16%
		Sororities:	21%

Basis for selection. Standardized test scores, class rank, and secondary school records very important. Prescribed set of requirements that guarantee admission vary for state residents/nonresidents. Applicants who do not meet requirements for guaranteed admission, but do meet certain performance minimums, will be placed on wait list and admitted on space-available basis, with preference given to most academically qualified. SAT/ACT not required for first-time freshman who are active duty military. Audition required for dance, drama and music programs. **Home schooled:** Transcript of courses and grades required. **Learning Disabled:** Students must self-identify after admission and provide documentation to receive special services.

High school preparation. College-preparatory program required. 15 units required. Required and recommended units include English 4, mathematics 3-4, social studies 2, history 1, science 3 (laboratory 3), foreign language 2, computer science 1 and academic electives 2. Must have 1 U.S. history and 2 additional units from history, economics, geography, government, or non-western culture.

2011-2012 Annual costs. Tuition/fees: $8,325; $19,278 out-of-state. Room/board: $8,060. Books/supplies: $1,043. Personal expenses: $2,785.

2010-2011 Financial aid. Need-based: 2,658 full-time freshmen applied for aid; 1,855 were judged to have need; 1,802 of these received aid. Average need met was 82%. Average scholarship/grant was $6,378; average loan $3,315. 40% of total undergraduate aid awarded as scholarships/grants, 60% as loans/jobs. **Non-need-based:** Awarded to 5,623 full-time undergraduates, including 1,512 freshmen. Scholarships awarded for academics, alumni affiliation, art, athletics, leadership, music/drama, religious affiliation, ROTC.

Application procedures. Admission: Closing date 4/1 (receipt date). $40 fee, may be waived for applicants with need. Admission notification on a rolling basis. Admitted applicants should reply as soon as possible. Applicants encouraged to apply at end junior year or by scholarship deadline of February 1. **Financial aid:** Priority date 3/1; no closing date. FAFSA required. Applicants notified on a rolling basis starting 3/15; must reply within 6 week(s) of notification.

Academics. College of Liberal Studies, through distance learning, provides non-traditional students with interdisciplinary liberal arts programs. **Special study options:** Accelerated study, combined bachelor's/graduate degree, cooperative education, distance learning, double major, dual enrollment of high school students, ESL, external degree, honors, independent study, internships, liberal arts/career combination, semester at sea, student-designed major, study abroad, teacher certification program, Washington semester, weekend college. **Credit/placement by examination:** AP, CLEP, IB, SAT, ACT, institutional tests. Credit for prior work/life experience awarded according to recommendations of American Council on Education. Applicability of credits toward a degree vary depending on the college. Credit by examination may be counted toward bachelor's degree, but total number of hours that may be applied vary depending on college. **Support services:** Learning center, pre-admission summer program, remedial instruction, study skills assistance, tutoring, writing center.

Honors college/program. 30 ACT/1330 SAT, rank in top 10% of high school class, or 3.75 GPA required; approximately 500 freshmen admitted each year.

Majors. Architecture: Architecture, environmental design. **Area/ethnic studies:** African-American, Native American, women's. **Biology:** Biochemistry, botany, microbiology, zoology. **Business:** Accounting, business admin, construction management, finance, management information systems, managerial economics, marketing, organizational behavior. **Communications:** Advertising, broadcast journalism, communications/speech/rhetoric, journalism. **Computer sciences:** Computer science, information systems. **Conservation:** Environmental science, environmental studies. **Education:** Early childhood, elementary, English, foreign languages, mathematics, music, science, social studies, special ed. **Engineering:** General, aerospace, applied physics, architectural, chemical, civil, computer, electrical, environmental, geological, industrial, mechanical, petroleum. **English:** English lit. **Foreign languages:** Arabic, Chinese, classics, French, Germanic, Italian, linguistics, Russian, Spanish. **Health services:** Clinical lab science, communication disorders, dental hygiene, medical radiologic technology/radiation therapy, nuclear medical technology, nursing (RN), pharmaceutical sciences, sonography. **History:** General, science/technology. **Human services:** General, social work. **Liberal arts:** Arts/sciences, humanities. **Math:** General. **Parks/recreation:** Exercise sciences. **Philosophy/religion:** Judaic, philosophy, religion. **Physical sciences:** Astronomy, astrophysics, chemistry, geology, geophysics, meteorology, physics. **Protective services:** Law enforcement admin. **Psychology:** General. **Social sciences:** Anthropology, economics, geography, GIS/cartography, political science, sociology. **Visual/performing arts:** Art history/conservation, dance, dramatic, film/cinema/video, interior design, music, music pedagogy, musical theater, studio arts.

Most popular majors. Business/marketing 16%, communications/journalism 8%, engineering/engineering technologies 7%, health sciences 16%, interdisciplinary studies 11%, social sciences 6%.

Computing on campus. 4,500 workstations in dormitories, library, computer center, student center. Dormitories wired for high-speed internet access and linked to campus network. Commuter students can connect to campus network. Online course registration, online library, helpline, repair service, student web hosting, wireless network available.

Student life. Freshman orientation: Available, $60 fee. Preregistration for classes offered. **Housing:** Guaranteed on-campus for freshmen. Coed dorms, single-sex dorms, special housing for disabled, apartments, fraternity/sorority housing available. $190 fully refundable deposit. Honors, cultural,

scholastic, National Merit housing available. **Activities:** Bands, campus ministries, choral groups, dance, drama, film society, international student organizations, literary magazine, music ensembles, Model UN, musical theater, opera, radio station, student government, student newspaper, symphony orchestra, TV station, American Indian student association, black student association, Hispanic American student association, Asian American student association, College Republicans, Young Democrats, Hillel Jewish student organization, Chi Alpha campus ministries, Muslim student association, Alpha Phi Omega.

Athletics. NCAA. **Intercollegiate:** Baseball M, basketball, cheerleading, cross-country, football (tackle) M, golf, gymnastics, rowing (crew) W, soccer W, softball W, tennis, track and field, volleyball W, wrestling M. **Intramural:** Badminton, basketball, cross-country, football (non-tackle), golf, racquetball, soccer, softball, swimming, table tennis, tennis, volleyball, water polo. **Team name:** Sooners.

Student services. Adult student services, alcohol/substance abuse counseling, career counseling, services for economically disadvantaged, student employment services, financial aid counseling, health services, legal services, minority student services, on-campus daycare, personal counseling, placement for graduates, veterans' counselor, women's services. **Physically disabled:** Services for visually, speech, hearing impaired.

Contact. E-mail: admrec@ou.edu
Phone: (405) 325-2252 Toll-free number: (800) 234-6868
Fax: (405) 325-7124
Mark McMasters, Director of Admissions, University of Oklahoma, 1000 Asp Avenue, Room 127, Norman, OK 73019-4076

University of Phoenix: Oklahoma City
Oklahoma City, Oklahoma
www.phoenix.edu

- For-profit 4-year university
- Very large city
- 649 degree-seeking undergraduates

General. Regionally accredited. **Degrees:** 135 bachelor's awarded; master's offered. **Calendar:** Differs by program. **Full-time faculty:** 17 total. **Part-time faculty:** 151 total.

Basis for selection. Open admission, but selective for some programs.

2011-2012 Annual costs. Estimated costs as of August 2011: per-credit-hour charge, $380 to $415, depending upon level and course of study; electronic course materials fee, $95, if applicable. Book and material charges may vary by course and program. All fees are subject to change.

Application procedures. Admission: No deadline. No application fee. **Financial aid:** No deadline.

Academics. Credit/placement by examination: AP, CLEP.

Majors. Business: Accounting, business admin, e-commerce, human resources, marketing. **Computer sciences:** General. **Health services:** Facilities admin, health care admin. **Protective services:** Law enforcement admin. **Psychology:** General.

Contact. Marc Booker, Director of Admission and Evaluation, University of Phoenix: Oklahoma City, 6501 North Broadway, Suite 100, Oklahoma City, OK 73116-8244

University of Phoenix: Tulsa
Tulsa, Oklahoma
www.phoenix.edu

- For-profit 4-year university
- Large city
- 627 degree-seeking undergraduates

General. Regionally accredited. **Degrees:** 114 bachelor's awarded; master's offered. **Calendar:** Differs by program. **Full-time faculty:** 19 total. **Part-time faculty:** 155 total.

Basis for selection. Open admission, but selective for some programs.

2011-2012 Annual costs. Estimated costs as of August 2011: per-credit-hour charge, $380 to $415, depending upon level and course of study; electronic course materials fee, $95, if applicable. Book and material charges may vary by course and program. All fees are subject to change.

Application procedures. Admission: No deadline. No application fee. **Financial aid:** No deadline.

Academics. Credit/placement by examination: AP, CLEP.

Majors. Business: Accounting, business admin, marketing. **Computer sciences:** General. **Health services:** Facilities admin, health care admin, long term care admin, medical records technology, nursing (RN). **Protective services:** Law enforcement admin, security management.

Contact. Marc Booker, Director of Admission and Evaluation, University of Phoenix: Tulsa, 14002 East 21st Street, Suite 1000, Tulsa, OK 74134-1412

University of Science and Arts of Oklahoma
Chickasha, Oklahoma
www.usao.edu   CB code: 6544

- Public 4-year university and liberal arts college
- Residential campus in large town
- 999 degree-seeking undergraduates: 10% part-time, 62% women, 5% African American, 1% Asian American, 5% Hispanic American, 13% Native American, 5% international
- 27% of applicants admitted
- SAT or ACT (ACT writing optional) required
- 38% graduate within 6 years; 20% enter graduate study

General. Founded in 1908. Regionally accredited. Offers trimester system classes, allowing for graduation in 3 years. **Degrees:** 212 bachelor's awarded. **Location:** 45 miles from Oklahoma City. **Calendar:** Trimester, extensive summer session. **Full-time faculty:** 54 total; 85% have terminal degrees, 11% minority, 50% women. **Part-time faculty:** 33 total; 15% have terminal degrees, 6% minority, 52% women. **Class size:** 64% < 20, 29% 20-39, 2% 40-49, 4% 50-99, less than 1% >100. **Special facilities:** Speech and hearing clinic, herbarium, child development center, school for the deaf.

Freshman class profile. 866 applied, 236 admitted, 211 enrolled.

Mid 50% test scores		End year in good standing:	80%
ACT composite:	20-26	Return as sophomores:	63%
GPA 3.75 or higher:	30%	Out-of-state:	4%
GPA 3.50-3.74:	19%	Live on campus:	74%
GPA 3.0-3.49:	29%	International:	6%
GPA 2.0-2.99:	21%	Fraternities:	1%
Rank in top quarter:	49%	Sororities:	1%
Rank in top tenth:	23%		

Basis for selection. One of the following required: 24 ACT/1090 SAT, 3.0 GPA and ranking in top 25% of high school graduating class, or 3.0 GPA in the 15-unit high school core curriculum and 22 ACT/1020 SAT. All SAT scores exclusive of Writing. **Home schooled:** Transcript of courses and grades required.

High school preparation. College-preparatory program required. 15 units required; 20 recommended. Required and recommended units include English 4, mathematics 3-4, social studies 2, history 1, science 3 (laboratory 3), foreign language 2, computer science 1, visual/performing arts 2 and academic electives 2. 2 units of fine arts, drama and/or speech recommended.

2011-2012 Annual costs. Tuition/fees: $5,065; $12,025 out-of-state. Room/board: $5,140. Books/supplies: $1,200. Personal expenses: $1,520.

2011-2012 Financial aid. Need-based: 174 full-time freshmen applied for aid; 141 were judged to have need; 138 of these received aid. Average need met was 68%. Average scholarship/grant was $7,425; average loan $2,835. 60% of total undergraduate aid awarded as scholarships/grants, 40% as loans/jobs. **Non-need-based:** Awarded to 222 full-time undergraduates, including 45 freshmen. Scholarships awarded for academics, art, athletics, leadership, music/drama, state residency.

Application procedures. Admission: Closing date 9/2 (postmark date). $25 fee, may be waived for applicants with need, free for online applicants. Admission notification on a rolling basis beginning on or about 1/2. **Financial aid:** Priority date 3/15; no closing date. FAFSA, institutional form required. Applicants notified on a rolling basis starting 3/15.

Academics. Special study options: Accelerated study, double major, dual enrollment of high school students, independent study, internships, student-designed major, study abroad, teacher certification program. **Credit/placement by examination:** AP, CLEP, SAT, ACT, institutional tests. 62 credit hours maximum toward bachelor's degree. **Support services:** Learning center, pre-admission summer program, reduced course load, remedial instruction, study skills assistance, tutoring, writing center.

Majors. Area/ethnic studies: Native American. **Biology:** General. **Business:** Business admin. **Communications:** Communications/speech/rhetoric. **Computer sciences:** Computer science. **Education:** Deaf/hearing impaired, early childhood, elementary. **English:** English lit. **Health services:** Speech pathology. **History:** General. **Math:** General. **Parks/recreation:** Health/fitness. **Physical sciences:** Chemistry, physics. **Psychology:** General. **Social sciences:** Economics, political science, sociology. **Visual/performing arts:** Art, dramatic, music, studio arts.

Most popular majors. Business/marketing 21%, education 12%, history 6%, parks/recreation 6%, psychology 11%, social sciences 7%, visual/performing arts 13%.

Computing on campus. 175 workstations in library, computer center, student center. Dormitories wired for high-speed internet access and linked to campus network. Online library, helpline, repair service, student web hosting, wireless network available.

Student life. Freshman orientation: Mandatory. Preregistration for classes offered. Held the week prior to start of fall trimester. **Housing:** Guaranteed on-campus for freshmen. Coed dorms, special housing for disabled, apartments available. $200 nonrefundable deposit, deadline 5/1. **Activities:** Bands, campus ministries, choral groups, dance, drama, international student organizations, literary magazine, music ensembles, musical theater, student government, student newspaper, TV station, Ameslan culture club, Chi Alpha Christian Fellowship, College Democrats, College Republicans, African American student association, international student association, intertribal heritage club, student ambassadors, students with children club, feminist collective.

Athletics. NAIA. **Intercollegiate:** Baseball M, basketball, cheerleading, soccer, softball W. **Intramural:** Basketball, golf, softball M, volleyball. **Team name:** Drovers.

Student services. Alcohol/substance abuse counseling, career counseling, services for economically disadvantaged, student employment services, financial aid counseling, health services, minority student services, personal counseling, placement for graduates, veterans' counselor. **Physically disabled:** Services for visually, hearing impaired.

Contact. E-mail: usao-admissions@usao.edu
Phone: (405) 574-1357 Toll-free number: (800) 933-8726
Fax: (405) 574-1220
Kellee Johnson, Director of Admissions, University of Science and Arts of Oklahoma, 1727 West Alabama, Chickasha, OK 73018-5322

University of Tulsa
Tulsa, Oklahoma CB member
www.utulsa.edu CB code: 6883

- Private 4-year university affiliated with Presbyterian Church (USA)
- Residential campus in large city
- 2,948 degree-seeking undergraduates: 3% part-time, 45% women, 6% African American, 3% Asian American, 4% Hispanic American, 4% Native American, 18% international
- 1,076 degree-seeking graduate students
- 41% of applicants admitted
- SAT or ACT (ACT writing optional) required
- 68% graduate within 6 years; 33% enter graduate study

General. Founded in 1894. Regionally accredited. **Degrees:** 637 bachelor's awarded; master's, professional, doctoral offered. **ROTC:** Air Force. **Location:** 100 miles from Oklahoma City. **Calendar:** Semester, limited summer session. **Full-time faculty:** 315 total; 96% have terminal degrees, 16% minority, 33% women. **Part-time faculty:** 97 total; 96% have terminal degrees, 11% minority, 43% women. **Class size:** 61% <20, 31% 20-39, 5% 40-49, 2% 50-99, less than 1% >100. **Special facilities:** Biotechnology institute, communicative disorders center, communication lab, tall grass prairie preserve, art museum.

Freshman class profile. 6,257 applied, 2,564 admitted, 617 enrolled.

Mid 50% test scores			
SAT critical reading:	550-690	Rank in top tenth:	74%
SAT math:	570-690	End year in good standing:	92%
ACT composite:	24-31	Return as sophomores:	86%
GPA 3.75 or higher:	58%	Out-of-state:	48%
GPA 3.50-3.74:	15%	Live on campus:	85%
GPA 3.0-3.49:	20%	International:	18%
GPA 2.0-2.99:	7%	Fraternities:	21%
Rank in top quarter:	86%	Sororities:	23%

Basis for selection. Primary requirements are school achievement records and test scores. High school guidance counselor recommendation required. Extracurricular activities, community involvement, and talents considered. Essays and interviews recommended for all; audition required for music, theater programs; portfolio required for art program. **Home schooled:** Statement describing home school structure and mission, transcript of courses and grades, letter of recommendation (nonparent) required.

High school preparation. College-preparatory program recommended. 16 units recommended. Recommended units include English 4, mathematics 3, social studies 1, history 2, science 3 (laboratory 2), foreign language 2 and computer science 1. 4 math and 4 physical science recommended for engineering and natural science students.

2011-2012 Annual costs. Tuition/fees: $31,126. First-time students pay a one time student services fee of $425, which includes orientation fee, graduation fee, all course drop/add fees, and unlimited transcript request fees. Room/board: $9,464. Books/supplies: $1,200. Personal expenses: $3,016.

2010-2011 Financial aid. Need-based: 621 full-time freshmen applied for aid; 350 were judged to have need; 350 of these received aid. Average need met was 85%. Average scholarship/grant was $7,398; average loan $4,225. 40% of total undergraduate aid awarded as scholarships/grants, 60% as loans/jobs. **Non-need-based:** Awarded to 2,668 full-time undergraduates, including 654 freshmen. Scholarships awarded for academics, alumni affiliation, athletics, leadership, minority status, music/drama, religious affiliation, ROTC.

Application procedures. Admission: Priority date 2/1; no deadline. $35 fee, may be waived for applicants with need. Admission notification on a rolling basis beginning on or about 10/1. Must reply by May 1 or within 2 week(s) if notified thereafter. **Financial aid:** Priority date 3/1; no closing date. FAFSA required. Applicants notified on a rolling basis starting 3/1; must reply by 5/1 or within 2 week(s) of notification.

Academics. Special study options: Accelerated study, combined bachelor's/graduate degree, double major, ESL, honors, independent study, internships, liberal arts/career combination, student-designed major, study abroad, teacher certification program, Washington semester. **Credit/placement by examination:** AP, CLEP, IB, SAT, ACT, institutional tests. 36 credit hours maximum toward bachelor's degree. **Support services:** Learning center, reduced course load, study skills assistance, tutoring, writing center.

Majors. Area/ethnic studies: Russian/Slavic. **Biology:** General, biochemistry. **Business:** Accounting, business admin, finance, international, management information systems, marketing, organizational behavior. **Communications:** Communications/speech/rhetoric. **Computer sciences:** General, computer science, information technology. **Conservation:** Environmental studies. **Education:** Chemistry, Deaf/hearing impaired, early childhood, elementary, mathematics, music. **Engineering:** Applied physics, chemical, electrical, mechanical, petroleum. **English:** English lit. **Foreign languages:** French, German, Spanish. **Health services:** Athletic training, audiology/speech pathology, communication disorders, nursing (RN). **History:** General. **Liberal arts:** Arts/sciences. **Math:** General, applied. **Parks/recreation:** Exercise sciences. **Philosophy/religion:** Philosophy, religion. **Physical sciences:** Chemistry, geology, geophysics, physics. **Psychology:** General. **Social sciences:** Anthropology, economics, political science, sociology. **Visual/performing arts:** Art, art history/conservation, dramatic, film/cinema/video, music, music performance, music theory/composition, piano/keyboard, studio arts management, voice/opera.

Most popular majors. Business/marketing 20%, engineering/engineering technologies 26%, health sciences 6%, social sciences 8%, visual/performing arts 8%.

Computing on campus. 900 workstations in dormitories, library, computer center, student center. Dormitories wired for high-speed internet access and linked to campus network. Commuter students can connect to campus network. Online course registration, online library, helpline, student web hosting, wireless network available.

Student life. Freshman orientation: Available. Preregistration for classes offered. Held the week prior to fall term. **Housing:** Guaranteed on-campus for freshmen. Coed dorms, single-sex dorms, special housing for disabled, apartments, fraternity/sorority housing, wellness housing available. $250 partly refundable deposit, deadline 3/1. Honors and language houses available. **Activities:** Bands, campus ministries, choral groups, dance, drama, international student organizations, literary magazine, music ensembles, Model UN, musical theater, opera, radio station, student government, student newspaper, symphony orchestra, TV station, Baptist student union, Fellowship of Christian Athletes, Jewish student association, Young Democrats, women's law caucus, Hispanic student association, College Republicans, International Fellowship House, Association of Black Collegians, volunteer income tax assistance project.

Athletics. NCAA. **Intercollegiate:** Basketball, cheerleading, cross-country, football (tackle) M, golf, rowing (crew) W, soccer, softball W, tennis, track

and field, volleyball W. **Intramural:** Badminton, basketball, bowling, cross-country, diving, football (non-tackle), golf, racquetball, soccer, softball, squash, swimming, table tennis, tennis, track and field, volleyball, water polo, wrestling M. **Team name:** Golden Hurricane.

Student services. Adult student services, alcohol/substance abuse counseling, chaplain/spiritual director, career counseling, student employment services, financial aid counseling, health services, legal services, minority student services, on-campus daycare, personal counseling, placement for graduates, veterans' counselor, women's services. **Physically disabled:** Services for visually, speech, hearing impaired.

Contact. E-mail: admission@utulsa.edu
Phone: (918) 631-2307 Toll-free number: (800) 331-3050
Fax: (918) 631-5003
Earl Johnson, Associate Vice President of Enrollment and Student Services, University of Tulsa, 800 South Tucker Drive, Tulsa, OK 74104-3189

Oregon

Art Institute of Portland

Portland, Oregon
www.aipd.artinstitutes.edu

CB member
CB code: 4231

▶ For-profit 4-year visual arts and liberal arts college
▶ Commuter campus in large city

General. Founded in 1963. Regionally accredited. **Calendar:** Quarter.

Annual costs/financial aid. Tuition/fees (2011-2012): $21,695. Room: $9,564. Books/supplies: $2,208. Personal expenses: $4,020. Need-based financial aid available to full-time and part-time students.

Contact. Phone: (503) 228-6528
Director of Admissions, 1122 Northwest Davis Street, Portland, OR 97209-2911

Concordia University

Portland, Oregon
www.cu-portland.edu

CB code: 4079

▶ Private 4-year liberal arts and teachers college affiliated with Lutheran Church - Missouri Synod
▶ Commuter campus in very large city
▶ 1,257 degree-seeking undergraduates
▶ SAT or ACT (ACT writing optional) required

General. Founded in 1905. Regionally accredited. **Degrees:** 268 bachelor's awarded; master's offered. **ROTC:** Air Force. **Location:** 5 miles from downtown. **Calendar:** Semester, limited summer session. **Full-time faculty:** 57 total. **Part-time faculty:** 158 total. **Class size:** 68% < 20, 30% 20-39, 1% 40-49, less than 1% 50-99. **Special facilities:** Environmental research center, children's literature center, Shakespeare authorship research center.

Freshman class profile.

GPA 3.75 or higher:	28%	Rank in top quarter:	48%
GPA 3.50-3.74:	19%	Rank in top tenth:	20%
GPA 3.0-3.49:	34%	Out-of-state:	54%
GPA 2.0-2.99:	19%	Live on campus:	78%

Basis for selection. 2.5 GPA, 480 SAT verbal, or 18 ACT required. **Home schooled:** Statement describing home school structure and mission, state high school equivalency certificate, letter of recommendation (nonparent) required. Interview may be required.

High school preparation. College-preparatory program recommended. 19 units recommended. Recommended units include English 4, mathematics 3, social studies 3, science 3, foreign language 2 and academic electives 3. One computer/keyboarding recommended.

2011-2012 Annual costs. Tuition/fees: $25,650. Room/board: $7,450. Books/supplies: $900. Personal expenses: $1,600.

Financial aid. Non-need-based: Scholarships awarded for academics, athletics, leadership, music/drama, religious affiliation.

Application procedures. Admission: Priority date 3/1; deadline 7/1 (postmark date). $20 fee, may be waived for applicants with need, free for online applicants. Admission notification on a rolling basis beginning on or about 1/1. Must reply by May 1 or within 2 week(s) if notified thereafter. Official high school transcripts, 2 letters of recommendation required. **Financial aid:** No deadline. FAFSA required. Applicants notified on a rolling basis.

Academics. Special study options: Accelerated study, cross-registration, distance learning, double major, dual enrollment of high school students, ESL, exchange student, honors, independent study, internships, liberal arts/career combination, semester at sea, student-designed major, study abroad, teacher certification program, weekend college. **Credit/placement by examination:** AP, CLEP, institutional tests. **Support services:** Learning center, remedial instruction, tutoring, writing center.

Majors. Biology: General. **Business:** General, business admin, international. **Education:** General, biology, business, chemistry, early childhood, elementary, English, health, history, mathematics, middle, multi-level teacher, physical, science, secondary, social studies. **English:** English lit. **Health services:** Athletic training, health care admin, nursing (RN), premedicine. **History:** General. **Human services:** Social work. **Parks/recreation:** Health/fitness, sports admin. **Philosophy/religion:** Religion. **Physical sciences:** Chemistry. **Psychology:** General. **Social sciences:** General. **Theology:** Religious ed, theology. **Visual/performing arts:** Music.

Most popular majors. Biology 8%, business/marketing 28%, education 20%, health sciences 17%, psychology 6%, public administration/social services 7%, theological studies 8%.

Computing on campus. PC or laptop required. 100 workstations in dormitories, library, computer center, student center. Dormitories wired for high-speed internet access and linked to campus network. Commuter students can connect to campus network. Online course registration, online library, helpline, repair service, wireless network available.

Student life. Freshman orientation: Mandatory. Preregistration for classes offered. Usually held the day before classes begin. **Policies:** Optional attendance for chapel services. Lutheran format, mixture of traditional and contemporary services offered. **Housing:** Guaranteed on-campus for freshmen. Coed dorms, single-sex dorms, special housing for disabled, apartments, wellness housing available. $50 nonrefundable deposit, deadline 5/1. Homestay option for international students. **Activities:** Campus ministries, choral groups, drama, international student organizations, literary magazine, music ensembles, student government, student newspaper, Christian Life Ministries, Teacher Corps, Hawaii club, Invisible Children, missions club, multi-cultural club, ONE Voice, peace club, Stop Human Trafficking, world club.

Athletics. NAIA. **Intercollegiate:** Baseball M, basketball, cross-country, golf, soccer, softball W, track and field, volleyball W. **Intramural:** Basketball, bowling, football (non-tackle), soccer, softball, table tennis, tennis, volleyball. **Team name:** Cavaliers.

Student services. Adult student services, alcohol/substance abuse counseling, chaplain/spiritual director, career counseling, financial aid counseling, health services, personal counseling, placement for graduates, veterans' counselor.

Contact. E-mail: admission@cu-portland.edu
Phone: (503) 280-8501 Toll-free number: (800) 321-9371
Fax: (503) 280-8531
Bobi Swan, Dean of Admission, Concordia University, 2811 Northeast Holman Street, Portland, OR 97211-6099

Corban University

Salem, Oregon
www.corban.edu

CB code: 4956

▶ Private 4-year liberal arts college affiliated with Baptist faith
▶ Residential campus in small city
▶ 983 degree-seeking undergraduates: 9% part-time, 63% women
▶ 225 degree-seeking graduate students
▶ 43% of applicants admitted
▶ SAT or ACT (ACT writing recommended), application essay required
▶ 50% graduate within 6 years

General. Founded in 1935. Regionally accredited. **Degrees:** 293 bachelor's, 2 associate awarded; master's offered. **ROTC:** Army, Air Force. **Location:** 45 miles from Portland. **Calendar:** Semester, limited summer session. **Full-time faculty:** 48 total; 54% have terminal degrees, 2% minority, 25% women. **Part-time faculty:** 69 total; 16% have terminal degrees, 36% women. **Class size:** 49% < 20, 38% 20-39, 9% 40-49, 4% 50-99. **Special facilities:** Archaeological museum.

Freshman class profile. 2,551 applied, 1,104 admitted, 275 enrolled.

Mid 50% test scores			
SAT critical reading:	490-610	GPA 2.0-2.99:	11%
SAT math:	460-580	Rank in top quarter:	60%
SAT writing:	470-580	Rank in top tenth:	33%
ACT composite:	20-26	Return as sophomores:	77%
GPA 3.75 or higher:	43%	Out-of-state:	53%
GPA 3.50-3.74:	20%	Live on campus:	91%
GPA 3.0-3.49:	26%	International:	5%

Basis for selection. Commitment to Christianity, GPA, test scores, recommendations, essays, school and community activities considered. Audition

required for music program. **Home schooled:** Transcript of courses and grades, state high school equivalency certificate required.

High school preparation. College-preparatory program recommended. 14 units recommended. Recommended units include English 4, mathematics 3, social studies 3, science 2 and foreign language 2.

2011-2012 Annual costs. Tuition/fees: $25,405. Room/board: $7,980. Books/supplies: $900. Personal expenses: $1,602.

2011-2012 Financial aid. Need-based: Average need met was 62%. Average scholarship/grant was $16,671; average loan $3,428. 68% of total undergraduate aid awarded as scholarships/grants, 32% as loans/jobs. **Non-need-based:** Scholarships awarded for academics, alumni affiliation, athletics, leadership, music/drama, ROTC.

Application procedures. Admission: Priority date 3/1; deadline 8/1 (receipt date). $35 fee, may be waived for applicants with need. Admission notification on a rolling basis beginning on or about 12/1. **Financial aid:** Priority date 2/15; no closing date. FAFSA required. Applicants notified on a rolling basis starting 3/1.

Academics. Special study options: Accelerated study, combined bachelor's/graduate degree, cross-registration, distance learning, double major, dual enrollment of high school students, honors, independent study, internships, liberal arts/career combination, study abroad, teacher certification program, Washington semester, weekend college. **Credit/placement by examination:** AP, CLEP, IB, institutional tests. 20 credit hours maximum toward associate degree, 32 toward bachelor's. **Support services:** Learning center, reduced course load, tutoring, writing center.

Majors. Business: General, accounting, accounting/business management, accounting/finance, business admin, communications, finance, information resources management, management information systems. **Communications:** Communications/speech/rhetoric, journalism. **Education:** General, biology, business, elementary, English, history, mathematics, middle, multilevel teacher, music, physical, science, secondary, social science, social studies. **English:** English lit. **Health services:** Predental, premedicine, prenursing, prepharmacy, preveterinary. **History:** General. **Human services:** Community org/advocacy. **Liberal arts:** Arts/sciences, humanities. **Math:** General. **Parks/recreation:** Health/fitness, sports admin. **Philosophy/religion:** Religion. **Protective services:** Criminal justice. **Psychology:** General. **Social sciences:** General. **Theology:** Bible, missionary, pastoral counseling, preministerial, religious ed, sacred music, theology, youth ministry. **Visual/performing arts:** Music, music performance, piano/keyboard, voice/opera.

Most popular majors. Business/marketing 27%, education 10%, English 6%, psychology 30%, social sciences 6%, theological studies 9%.

Computing on campus. 34 workstations in dormitories, library, computer center, student center. Dormitories wired for high-speed internet access and linked to campus network. Commuter students can connect to campus network. Online library, helpline, repair service, wireless network available.

Student life. Freshman orientation: Mandatory. Preregistration for classes offered. **Policies:** Religious observance required. **Housing:** Guaranteed on-campus for freshmen. Single-sex dorms, apartments available. $100 nonrefundable deposit, deadline 8/1. **Activities:** Bands, campus ministries, choral groups, drama, music ensembles, radio station, student government, student newspaper, symphony orchestra, Christian fellowships.

Athletics. NAIA, NCCAA. **Intercollegiate:** Baseball M, basketball, cross-country, golf, soccer, softball W, volleyball W. **Intramural:** Basketball, football (non-tackle), soccer, softball, volleyball, weight lifting. **Team name:** Warriors.

Student services. Adult student services, chaplain/spiritual director, career counseling, student employment services, financial aid counseling, health services, personal counseling, placement for graduates. **Physically disabled:** Services for visually, hearing impaired.

Contact. E-mail: admissions@corban.edu
Phone: (503) 375-7005 Toll-free number: (800) 845-3005
Fax: (503) 585-4316
Marty Ziesemer, Director of Admissions, Corban University, 5000 Deer Park Drive SE, Salem, OR 97317-9392

Eastern Oregon University
La Grande, Oregon   **CB member**
www.eou.edu   **CB code: 4300**

- Public 4-year university and liberal arts college
- Residential campus in large town

- 3,546 degree-seeking undergraduates: 33% part-time, 61% women, 2% African American, 2% Asian American, 5% Hispanic American, 2% Native American, 1% international
- 310 degree-seeking graduate students
- 65% of applicants admitted
- SAT or ACT (ACT writing optional) required
- 32% graduate within 6 years

General. Founded in 1929. Regionally accredited. **Degrees:** 540 bachelor's, 6 associate awarded; master's offered. **ROTC:** Army. **Location:** 260 miles from Portland; 180 miles from Boise, Idaho. **Calendar:** Quarter, limited summer session. **Full-time faculty:** 117 total; 80% have terminal degrees, 6% minority, 39% women. **Part-time faculty:** 11 total; 64% have terminal degrees, 18% minority, 91% women. **Class size:** 66% < 20, 28% 20-39, 3% 40-49, 3% 50-99, less than 1% >100. **Special facilities:** Wildlife habitat laboratory, agriculture experiment station.

Freshman class profile. 1,296 applied, 843 admitted, 385 enrolled.

Mid 50% test scores			
SAT critical reading:	420-550	GPA 2.0-2.99:	25%
SAT math:	410-550	Rank in top quarter:	40%
SAT writing:	400-520	Rank in top tenth:	15%
ACT composite:	19-24	Return as sophomores:	72%
GPA 3.75 or higher:	16%	Out-of-state:	35%
GPA 3.50-3.74:	21%	Live on campus:	63%
GPA 3.0-3.49:	36%	International:	2%

Basis for selection. Secondary school record most important; 3.0 GPA in 14 subject areas required. Students not meeting requirements must submit portfolio including essay and 2 letters of recommendation. Limited number of students not meeting requirements may be admitted. **Home schooled:** State high school equivalency certificate, letter of recommendation (nonparent) required. Applicants must present certificate of completion and portfolio including essay, letters of recommendation, standardized test scores.

High school preparation. College-preparatory program required. Required and recommended units include English 4, mathematics 3, social studies 3, science 2 (laboratory 1) and foreign language 2.

2011-2012 Annual costs. Tuition/fees: $7,046; $7,046 out-of-state. Room/board: $7,185. Books/supplies: $1,350. Personal expenses: $1,500.

2011-2012 Financial aid. Need-based: 319 full-time freshmen applied for aid; 250 were judged to have need; 247 of these received aid. Average need met was 49%. Average scholarship/grant was $5,368; average loan $2,900. 49% of total undergraduate aid awarded as scholarships/grants, 51% as loans/jobs. **Non-need-based:** Awarded to 697 full-time undergraduates, including 173 freshmen. Scholarships awarded for academics, art, leadership, minority status, music/drama, state residency.

Application procedures. Admission: Priority date 12/1; deadline 8/15 (postmark date). No application fee. Admission notification on a rolling basis beginning on or about 10/1. **Financial aid:** Priority date 3/1; no closing date. FAFSA required. Applicants notified on a rolling basis starting 4/1; must reply within 4 week(s) of notification.

Academics. Regional advisers for distance education students. **Special study options:** Combined bachelor's/graduate degree, cooperative education, cross-registration, distance learning, double major, dual enrollment of high school students, exchange student, external degree, honors, independent study, internships, liberal arts/career combination, semester at sea, student-designed major, study abroad, teacher certification program, weekend college. **Credit/placement by examination:** AP, CLEP, IB, institutional tests. 45 credit hours maximum toward bachelor's degree. **Support services:** Learning center, study skills assistance, tutoring, writing center.

Majors. Biology: General, biomedical sciences. **Business:** General, business admin. **Communications:** Media studies. **Computer sciences:** General. **Education:** Health. **English:** English lit. **History:** General. **Liberal arts:** Arts/sciences. **Math:** General. **Parks/recreation:** Health/fitness. **Physical sciences:** Chemistry. **Protective services:** Fire services admin. **Psychology:** General. **Visual/performing arts:** Art, dramatic, music.

Most popular majors. Business/marketing 33%, education 14%, liberal arts 20%.

Computing on campus. 150 workstations in dormitories, library, computer center, student center. Dormitories wired for high-speed internet access and linked to campus network. Commuter students can connect to campus network. Online course registration, online library, helpline, repair service, wireless network available.

Student life. Freshman orientation: Available. Preregistration for classes offered. **Housing:** Guaranteed on-campus for freshmen. Coed dorms, apartments available. **Activities:** Bands, choral groups, dance, drama, international

student organizations, literary magazine, music ensembles, musical theater, radio station, student government, student newspaper, symphony orchestra, international relations club, outdoor club, biology club, Fellowship of Christian Athletes, Latter-day Saints student association.

Athletics. NAIA. **Intercollegiate:** Basketball, cheerleading, cross-country, football (tackle) M, rodeo, soccer W, softball W, track and field, volleyball W. **Intramural:** Badminton, basketball, football (non-tackle), racquetball, softball, swimming, tennis, volleyball. **Team name:** Mountaineers.

Student services. Alcohol/substance abuse counseling, career counseling, student employment services, financial aid counseling, health services, minority student services, personal counseling, placement for graduates, veterans' counselor, women's services. **Physically disabled:** Services for visually, hearing impaired.

Contact. E-mail: admissions@eou.edu
Phone: (541) 962-3393 Toll-free number: (800) 452-8639
Fax: (541) 962-3418
Arlyn Love, Director of Admissions, Eastern Oregon University, One University Boulevard, La Grande, OR 97850

George Fox University
Newberg, Oregon
www.georgefox.edu
CB member
CB code: 4325

- Private 4-year university and seminary college affiliated with Society of Friends (Quaker)
- Residential campus in large town
- 2,155 degree-seeking undergraduates: 12% part-time, 59% women, 2% African American, 4% Asian American, 7% Hispanic American, 1% Native American, 6% international
- 1,218 degree-seeking graduate students
- 80% of applicants admitted
- SAT or ACT (ACT writing optional), application essay required
- 62% graduate within 6 years; 21% enter graduate study

General. Founded in 1891. Regionally accredited. Volunteer service encouraged through all-campus Serve Day and serve trips during school breaks. **Degrees:** 520 bachelor's awarded; master's, professional offered. **ROTC:** Air Force. **Location:** 23 miles from Portland. **Calendar:** Semester, limited summer session. **Full-time faculty:** 175 total; 76% have terminal degrees, 9% minority, 40% women. **Part-time faculty:** 213 total; 28% have terminal degrees, 4% minority, 50% women. **Class size:** 57% < 20, 36% 20-39, 5% 40-49, 2% 50-99, less than 1% >100. **Special facilities:** Electron microscope, art galleries, Hess Creek Canyon.

Freshman class profile. 2,547 applied, 2,028 admitted, 460 enrolled.

Mid 50% test scores			
SAT critical reading:	490-630	Rank in top quarter:	73%
SAT math:	490-610	Rank in top tenth:	36%
SAT writing:	480-610	End year in good standing:	89%
ACT composite:	21-27	Return as sophomores:	80%
GPA 3.75 or higher:	47%	Out-of-state:	42%
GPA 3.50-3.74:	23%	Live on campus:	93%
GPA 3.0-3.49:	21%	International:	3%
GPA 2.0-2.99:	8%		

Basis for selection. Decision based on grade transcript; test scores; recommendations from teacher and counselor; church, school, and community activities. Interview recommended for all; audition recommended for drama, music programs. **Home schooled:** Transcript of courses and grades, letter of recommendation (nonparent) required.

High school preparation. College-preparatory program recommended. 16 units recommended. Recommended units include English 4, mathematics 2, social studies 3, history 2, science 2 (laboratory 2) and foreign language 2. 1 unit health and physical education recommended.

2011-2012 Annual costs. Tuition/fees: $29,380. Room/board: $9,050.

2011-2012 Financial aid. Need-based: 394 full-time freshmen applied for aid; 352 were judged to have need; 352 of these received aid. Average need met was 89%. Average scholarship/grant was $11,355; average loan $3,099. 68% of total undergraduate aid awarded as scholarships/grants, 32% as loans/jobs. **Non-need-based:** Awarded to 1,257 full-time undergraduates, including 329 freshmen. Scholarships awarded for academics, alumni affiliation, art, job skills, leadership, minority status, music/drama, religious affiliation. **Additional information:** Audition required for music and drama scholarships.

Application procedures. Admission: Priority date 2/1; no deadline. $40 fee, may be waived for applicants with need. Admission notification on a

rolling basis beginning on or about 10/1. Must reply by May 1 or within 2 week(s) if notified thereafter. **Financial aid:** Priority date 2/1; no closing date. FAFSA required. Applicants notified on a rolling basis starting 3/1; must reply within 6 week(s) of notification.

Academics. Special study options: Accelerated study, cross-registration, distance learning, double major, dual enrollment of high school students, ESL, exchange student, honors, independent study, internships, New York semester, student-designed major, study abroad, teacher certification program, Washington semester. **Credit/placement by examination:** AP, CLEP, IB, SAT, ACT, institutional tests. 32 credit hours maximum toward bachelor's degree. **Support services:** Learning center, reduced course load, remedial instruction, study skills assistance, tutoring, writing center.

Majors. Biology: General. **Business:** Accounting/business management, business admin, entrepreneurial studies, finance, international, management information systems, marketing. **Communications:** Communications/speech/rhetoric, journalism, organizational. **Computer sciences:** General, information systems. **Education:** Elementary, music. **Engineering:** General, civil, computer, electrical, mechanical. **English:** English lit. **Foreign languages:** Spanish. **Health services:** Athletic training, nursing (RN). **History:** General. **Human services:** Social work. **Math:** General. **Parks/recreation:** Health/fitness. **Philosophy/religion:** Philosophy. **Physical sciences:** Chemistry. **Psychology:** General. **Social sciences:** Economics, political science, sociology. **Theology:** Bible. **Visual/performing arts:** Art, cinematography, dramatic, music. **Work/family studies:** General.

Most popular majors. Business/marketing 29%, education 6%, health sciences 7%, interdisciplinary studies 12%, visual/performing arts 8%.

Computing on campus. 130 workstations in dormitories, library, computer center, student center. Dormitories wired for high-speed internet access and linked to campus network. Commuter students can connect to campus network. Online course registration, online library, helpline, repair service, wireless network available.

Student life. Freshman orientation: Mandatory. Preregistration for classes offered. One-day programs available during summer. New students attend three-day program at start of semester. **Policies:** Three-year residency requirement for undergraduates. Required spiritual formation program and chapel program. Religious observance required. **Housing:** Single-sex dorms, special housing for disabled, apartments, wellness housing available. Pets allowed in dorm rooms. Houses. **Activities:** Bands, campus ministries, choral groups, drama, international student organizations, literary magazine, music ensembles, musical theater, radio station, student government, student newspaper, symphony orchestra, Christian services committee, associated student community, multicultural club, Student Nurses Association, Young Life, leadership development program, Little Bruin, urban services, College Republicans, College Democrats.

Athletics. NCAA. **Intercollegiate:** Baseball M, basketball, cross-country, football (tackle) M, golf, lacrosse W, soccer, softball W, tennis, track and field, volleyball W. **Intramural:** Badminton, basketball, football (non-tackle), golf, racquetball, skiing, soccer, table tennis, tennis, volleyball. **Team name:** Bruins.

Student services. Adult student services, alcohol/substance abuse counseling, chaplain/spiritual director, career counseling, student employment services, financial aid counseling, health services, minority student services, personal counseling, veterans' counselor. **Physically disabled:** Services for visually, speech, hearing impaired.

Contact. E-mail: admissions@georgefox.edu
Phone: (503) 554-2240 Toll-free number: (800) 765-4369 ext. 2240
Fax: (503) 554-3110
Ryan Dougherty, Director of Undergraduate Admissions, George Fox University, 414 North Meridian Street #6089, Newberg, OR 97132-2697

Gutenberg College
Eugene, Oregon
www.gutenberg.edu
CB code: 2605

- Private 4-year liberal arts college
- Small city
- 29 degree-seeking undergraduates
- SAT, application essay required

General. Candidate for regional accreditation; also accredited by TRACS. "Great Books" education from a biblical worldview. **Degrees:** 8 bachelor's awarded. **Calendar:** Quarter. **Full-time faculty:** 8 total. **Part-time faculty:** 2 total.

Basis for selection. Admissions decision based on application, essays, 2 references (academic and character), SAT, transcripts, and course of study. 2 written essays required.

2011-2012 Annual costs. Tuition/fees: $11,853. Estimated annual cost of on-campus room and meal program is $5,000. Books/supplies: $650. Personal expenses: $500.

Application procedures. Admission: Closing date 3/1. $40 fee. Late applications after 3/1 may be considered; application fee is $60 for late applicants. **Financial aid:** Closing date 6/1. CSS PROFILE required.

Academics. Credit/placement by examination: AP, CLEP.

Majors. Liberal arts: Arts/sciences.

Student life. Freshman orientation: Mandatory. Preregistration for classes offered. **Housing:** Single-sex dorms available.

Contact. E-mail: admissions@gutenberg.edu
Phone: (541) 683-5141
Tim McIntosh, Director of Admissions, Gutenberg College, 1883 University Street, Eugene, OR 97403

ITT Technical Institute: Portland
Portland, Oregon
www.itt-tech.edu   **CB code: 0947**

- For-profit 4-year technical college
- Commuter campus in large city
- 953 undergraduates
- Interview required

General. Founded in 1979. Accredited by ACICS. **Degrees:** 46 bachelor's, 197 associate awarded. **Location:** 10 miles from downtown. **Calendar:** Quarter, extensive summer session. **Full-time faculty:** 15 total. **Part-time faculty:** 55 total.

Basis for selection. Satisfactory scores from on-site tests in English and math required.

2011-2012 Annual costs. Estimated costs as of June 2011: per-credit-hour charge, $493, depending upon level and course of study; academic fee, $200. Certain programs of study require purchase of tools, which could cost an additional $100 to $500. All costs are subject to change.

Application procedures. Admission: No deadline. No application fee. Admission notification on a rolling basis. **Financial aid:** No deadline. FAFSA, institutional form required. Applicants notified on a rolling basis.

Academics. Credit/placement by examination: AP, CLEP. **Support services:** Learning center, tutoring.

Majors. Business: Business admin, construction management. **Communications technology:** Animation/special effects. **Computer sciences:** Security, system admin. **Protective services:** Law enforcement admin.

Computing on campus. Online library available.

Student life. Freshman orientation: Available. Preregistration for classes offered.

Student services. Career counseling, student employment services, placement for graduates.

Contact. Phone: (503) 255-6500 Toll-free number: (800) 234-5488
Fax: (503) 255-6500
Cliff Custer, Director of Recruitment, ITT Technical Institute: Portland, 9500 NE Cascades Parkway, Portland, OR 97220

Lewis & Clark College
Portland, Oregon   **CB member**
www.lclark.edu   **CB code: 4384**

- Private 4-year liberal arts college
- Residential campus in very large city
- 2,030 degree-seeking undergraduates: 1% part-time, 59% women, 2% African American, 4% Asian American, 7% Hispanic American, 1% Native American, 5% international
- 1,572 degree-seeking graduate students

- 66% of applicants admitted
- Application essay required
- 75% graduate within 6 years

General. Founded in 1867. Regionally accredited. **Degrees:** 429 bachelor's awarded; master's, professional, doctoral offered. **Calendar:** Semester, limited summer session. **Full-time faculty:** 232 total; 97% have terminal degrees, 11% minority, 47% women. **Part-time faculty:** 128 total; 57% have terminal degrees, 10% minority, 58% women. **Class size:** 61% < 20, 37% 20-39, less than 1% 40-49, 1% 50-99. **Special facilities:** DIC and fluorescence microscopes, time-lapse deconvolution microscope, high-resolution oxygen analyzer, carbon dioxide gas exchange analyzer, end-point and real-time PCR equipment, multi-capacity lyophilizer, gel electrophoresis and imaging facilities, solar telescope with spectrograph, imaging laboratory with high resolution optical microscope, research astronomical observatory, holographic laboratory, electro-acoustic music studio, 85-rank Casavant organ, multi-media foreign language lab, human-computer interaction laboratory, climate-controlled greenhouse, GIS lab running ArcGIS for environmental research.

Freshman class profile. 5,901 applied, 3,922 admitted, 607 enrolled.

Mid 50% test scores			
SAT critical reading:	610-710	GPA 2.0-2.99:	2%
SAT math:	580-680	Rank in top quarter:	77%
SAT writing:	610-710	Rank in top tenth:	41%
ACT composite:	27-31	Return as sophomores:	88%
GPA 3.75 or higher:	55%	Out-of-state:	84%
GPA 3.50-3.74:	22%	Live on campus:	97%
GPA 3.0-3.49:	21%	International:	4%

Basis for selection. School curriculum and achievement most important. Standardized tests, recommendations, extracurricular involvement, essay, and interview also considered. Students may apply using Portfolio Path, where test scores are optional. In addition to the Common Application and Supplement, Portfolio Path applicants submit 3 academic teacher recommendations and academic portfolio. Applicants may choose whether to submit standardized test scores. All other admission requirements remain the same. Interviews optional. Audition recommended for music scholarships. **Home schooled:** School's Portfolio Path for admissions recommended. GED required, interview recommended.

High school preparation. College-preparatory program recommended. Recommended units include English 4, mathematics 4, social studies 4, science 3 (laboratory 2) and foreign language 3. One unit fine arts recommended.

2011-2012 Annual costs. Tuition/fees: $38,500. Room/board: $10,014. Books/supplies: $1,050. Personal expenses: $990.

2010-2011 Financial aid. Non-need-based: Scholarships awarded for academics.

Application procedures. Admission: Closing date 2/1 (postmark date). $50 fee, may be waived for applicants with need, free for online applicants. Admission notification by 4/1. Must reply by 5/1. **Financial aid:** Priority date 2/15; no closing date. FAFSA, CSS PROFILE required. Applicants notified on a rolling basis starting 3/1.

Academics. Special study options: Accelerated study, combined bachelor's/graduate degree, cross-registration, double major, dual enrollment of high school students, ESL, honors, independent study, internships, New York semester, student-designed major, study abroad, Washington semester. 3-2 engineering program with Columbia University, University of Southern California, Oregon Graduate Institute of Science and Engineering at OHSU, Washington University (St. Louis). **Credit/placement by examination:** AP, CLEP, IB, institutional tests. Up to 24 semester hours awarded for International Baccalaureate full diploma with score of 36 (16 hours for diploma with 32-35). Scores of 5 on higher level AP exams get 4 credits. **Support services:** Learning center, reduced course load, study skills assistance, tutoring, writing center.

Majors. Area/ethnic studies: East Asian. **Biology:** General, biochemistry. **Communications:** Communications/speech/rhetoric. **Computer sciences:** Computer science. **Conservation:** Environmental studies. **English:** English lit. **Foreign languages:** General, French, German, Spanish. **History:** General. **Liberal arts:** Arts/sciences. **Math:** General. **Philosophy/religion:** Philosophy, religion. **Physical sciences:** Chemistry, physics. **Psychology:** General. **Social sciences:** Anthropology, economics, international relations, political science, sociology. **Visual/performing arts:** Art, dramatic, music, music performance, studio arts.

Most popular majors. Biology 7%, communications/journalism 18%, English 6%, foreign language 7%, psychology 11%, social sciences 21%, visual/performing arts 8%.

Computing on campus. 158 workstations in library, computer center, student center. Dormitories wired for high-speed internet access and linked to campus network. Commuter students can connect to campus network. Online course registration, online library, helpline, repair service, student web hosting, wireless network available.

Student life. Freshman orientation: Mandatory. Preregistration for classes offered. Held 4 days preceding class in late August. **Policies:** Students required to live on-campus for 2 years. **Housing:** Guaranteed on-campus for freshmen. Coed dorms, single-sex dorms available. Apartment-style residence halls available for upperclassmen. **Activities:** Bands, campus ministries, choral groups, dance, drama, international student organizations, literary magazine, music ensembles, Model UN, musical theater, radio station, student government, student newspaper, symphony orchestra, TV station, Jewish student union, InterVarsity Christian Fellowship, Fellowship of Christian Athletes, Hawaii club, Amnesty International, black student union, Circle K, forensics, Gringos y Latinos.

Athletics. NCAA. **Intercollegiate:** Baseball M, basketball, cross-country, football (tackle) M, golf, rowing (crew), soccer W, softball W, swimming, tennis, track and field, volleyball W. **Intramural:** Badminton, basketball, cross-country, softball, swimming, table tennis, tennis, volleyball, water polo. **Team name:** Pioneers, Pios.

Student services. Adult student services, alcohol/substance abuse counseling, chaplain/spiritual director, career counseling, services for economically disadvantaged, student employment services, financial aid counseling, health services, legal services, minority student services, personal counseling, placement for graduates, veterans' counselor, women's services. **Physically disabled:** Services for visually, speech, hearing impaired.

Contact. E-mail: admissions@lclark.edu
Phone: (503) 768-7040 Toll-free number: (800) 444-4111
Fax: (503) 768-7055
Lisa Meyer, Dean of Admissions and Financial Aid, Lewis & Clark College, 0615 SW Palatine Hill Road, Portland, OR 97219-7899

Linfield College
McMinnville, Oregon
www.linfield.edu

CB member
CB code: 4387

- Private 4-year liberal arts college affiliated with American Baptist Churches in the USA
- Residential campus in large town
- 1,658 degree-seeking undergraduates: 1% part-time, 61% women, 2% African American, 7% Asian American, 7% Hispanic American, 1% Native American, 4% international
- 76% of applicants admitted
- SAT or ACT (ACT writing optional), application essay required
- 72% graduate within 6 years; 20% enter graduate study

General. Founded in 1849. Regionally accredited. Students interested in nursing or health sciences major may begin studies on the McMinnville Campus and then transfer to the Portland Campus to complete their degrees. Part-time students who wish to complete bachelor's degree online are served through Division of Continuing Education. **Degrees:** 323 bachelor's awarded. **ROTC:** Air Force. **Location:** 38 miles from Portland. **Calendar:** 4-1-4, limited summer session. **Full-time faculty:** 115 total; 94% have terminal degrees, 9% minority, 45% women. **Part-time faculty:** 79 total; 32% have terminal degrees, 6% minority, 47% women. **Class size:** 67% < 20, 29% 20-39, 2% 40-49, less than 1% 50-99, less than 1% >100. **Special facilities:** Cadaver lab, anthropology museum, music technology lab, interactive writing laboratory, speaking center.

Freshman class profile. 2,376 applied, 1,811 admitted, 459 enrolled.

Mid 50% test scores		Rank in top quarter:	65%
SAT critical reading:	490-610	Rank in top tenth:	31%
SAT math:	510-610	End year in good standing:	95%
SAT writing:	480-590	Return as sophomores:	84%
ACT composite:	22-28	Out-of-state:	46%
GPA 3.75 or higher:	35%	Live on campus:	99%
GPA 3.50-3.74:	33%	International:	3%
GPA 3.0-3.49:	28%	Fraternities:	10%
GPA 2.0-2.99:	4%	Sororities:	25%

Basis for selection. High school academic performance, writing sample, recommendations from teachers and counselors, and pre-college test results important. Non-academic community and school activities considered. Interview recommended. **Home schooled:** Transcript of courses and grades required. Home school supplement to the Common Application required.

High school preparation. College-preparatory program recommended. 17 units recommended. Recommended units include English 4, mathematics 4, social studies 3, science 3 and foreign language 2.

2011-2012 Annual costs. Tuition/fees: $32,416. Room/board: $9,090. Books/supplies: $750. Personal expenses: $1,100.

2011-2012 Financial aid. Need-based: 405 full-time freshmen applied for aid; 347 were judged to have need; 347 of these received aid. Average need met was 81%. Average scholarship/grant was $10,974; average loan $3,693. 71% of total undergraduate aid awarded as scholarships/grants, 29% as loans/jobs. **Non-need-based:** Awarded to 412 full-time undergraduates, including 246 freshmen. Scholarships awarded for academics, minority status, music/drama.

Application procedures. Admission: Priority date 2/15; no deadline. No application fee. Must reply by May 1 or within 2 week(s) if notified thereafter. **Financial aid:** Priority date 2/1; no closing date. FAFSA required.

Academics. Special study options: Cross-registration, distance learning, double major, ESL, external degree, independent study, internships, liberal arts/career combination, semester at sea, student-designed major, study abroad, teacher certification program, Washington semester. Semester abroad programs at Linfield centers in Australia, Austria, China (Beijing and Hong Kong), Costa Rica, Ecuador, England, France, Ireland, Japan, Korea, Mexico, New Zealand, Norway, and Senegal; shorter term study abroad opportunities through one-month January term. **Credit/placement by examination:** AP, CLEP, IB, institutional tests. 30 credit hours maximum toward bachelor's degree. **Support services:** Learning center, reduced course load, study skills assistance, tutoring, writing center.

Majors. Area/ethnic studies: German. **Biology:** General. **Business:** General, accounting, finance, international. **Communications:** Communications/speech/rhetoric, media studies. **Computer sciences:** Computer science. **Conservation:** Environmental studies. **Education:** Elementary, music. **Engineering:** Applied physics. **English:** Creative writing, English lit. **Foreign languages:** French, German, Japanese, Spanish. **Health services:** Athletic training, nursing (RN). **History:** General. **Math:** General. **Parks/recreation:** Exercise sciences, health/fitness. **Philosophy/religion:** Philosophy, religion. **Physical sciences:** General, chemistry, physics. **Psychology:** General. **Social sciences:** Anthropology, economics, political science, sociology. **Visual/performing arts:** Art, design, dramatic, music, music performance, music theory/composition, studio arts.

Most popular majors. Business/marketing 26%, communications/journalism 7%, education 7%, parks/recreation 10%, social sciences 10%, visual/performing arts 6%.

Computing on campus. 250 workstations in dormitories, library, computer center, student center. Dormitories wired for high-speed internet access and linked to campus network. Commuter students can connect to campus network. Online course registration, online library, helpline, repair service, student web hosting, wireless network available.

Student life. Freshman orientation: Mandatory. Preregistration for classes offered. Four-day program held at beginning of fall semester; includes advising, peer mentoring. **Policies:** All students required to live on-campus unless they are of senior standing, married, or living with parents locally. **Housing:** Guaranteed on-campus for all undergraduates. Coed dorms, single-sex dorms, special housing for disabled, apartments, fraternity/sorority housing, wellness housing available. **Activities:** Bands, campus ministries, choral groups, dance, drama, international student organizations, literary magazine, music ensembles, musical theater, opera, radio station, student government, student newspaper, symphony orchestra, multicultural student club, Greenfield, Hawaiian club, Fellowship of Christian Athletes, progressive student union, Circle-K, Habitat for Humanity, gay straight alliance, Republican club.

Athletics. NCAA. **Intercollegiate:** Baseball M, basketball, cross-country, football (tackle) M, golf, lacrosse W, soccer, softball, swimming, tennis, track and field, volleyball W. **Intramural:** Basketball, bowling, soccer, softball, volleyball. **Team name:** Wildcats.

Student services. Adult student services, alcohol/substance abuse counseling, chaplain/spiritual director, career counseling, student employment services, financial aid counseling, health services, minority student services, personal counseling, placement for graduates, veterans' counselor, women's services. **Physically disabled:** Services for visually, speech, hearing impaired.

Contact. E-mail: admission@linfield.edu
Phone: (503) 883-2213 Toll-free number: (800) 640-2287
Fax: (503) 883-2472
Lisa Knodle-Bragiel, Director of Admission, Linfield College, 900 Southeast Baker Street, McMinnville, OR 97128-3725

Marylhurst University
Marylhurst, Oregon
www.marylhurst.edu   CB code: 0440

- Private 4-year university and liberal arts college affiliated with Roman Catholic Church
- Commuter campus in large town
- 839 degree-seeking undergraduates: 73% part-time, 71% women
- 883 degree-seeking graduate students
- 70% of applicants admitted
- Application essay, interview required

General. Founded in 1893. Regionally accredited. **Degrees:** 206 bachelor's awarded; master's, professional offered. **Location:** 10 miles from Portland. **Calendar:** Quarter, extensive summer session. **Full-time faculty:** 57 total; 54% have terminal degrees, 9% minority, 49% women. **Part-time faculty:** 203 total; 29% have terminal degrees, 9% minority, 51% women. **Class size:** 96% < 20, 4% 20-39.

Freshman class profile. 33 applied, 23 admitted, 15 enrolled.

Basis for selection. Bachelor's programs with special requirements include all music degree programs and accelerated online degree programs.

2011-2012 Annual costs. Tuition/fees: $18,405. Books/supplies: $2,250. Personal expenses: $1,860.

2011-2012 Financial aid. Non-need-based: Scholarships awarded for academics.

Application procedures. Admission: No deadline. $40 fee, may be waived for applicants with need. Admission notification on a rolling basis. **Financial aid:** Priority date 3/1; no closing date. FAFSA, institutional form required. Applicants notified on a rolling basis starting 5/1.

Academics. Special study options: Accelerated study, cooperative education, cross-registration, distance learning, double major, dual enrollment of high school students, ESL, independent study, internships, liberal arts/career combination, student-designed major, teacher certification program, weekend college. **Credit/placement by examination:** AP, CLEP, IB, institutional tests. 45 credit hours maximum toward bachelor's degree. **Support services:** Learning center, reduced course load, study skills assistance, tutoring, writing center.

Majors. Business: General, business admin, communications, real estate. **Communications:** Communications/speech/rhetoric. **Conservation:** Environmental studies. **Liberal arts:** Arts/sciences. **Philosophy/religion:** Religion. **Psychology:** General. **Social sciences:** General. **Visual/performing arts:** Art, interior design, music, studio arts.

Most popular majors. Business/marketing 39%, communications/journalism 10%, English 8%, interdisciplinary studies 13%, liberal arts 6%, visual/performing arts 11%.

Computing on campus. 41 workstations in library. Commuter students can connect to campus network. Online course registration, helpline, wireless network available.

Student life. Activities: Jazz band, campus ministries, choral groups, literary magazine, music ensembles, student newspaper, symphony orchestra.

Student services. Adult student services, career counseling, financial aid counseling, personal counseling, veterans' counselor. **Physically disabled:** Services for visually, hearing impaired.

Contact. E-mail: admissions@marylhurst.edu
Phone: (503) 699-6268 Toll-free number: (800) 634-9982 ext. 6268
Fax: (503) 699-6320
Chris Sweet, Director of Admissions, Marylhurst University, PO Box 261, Marylhurst, OR 97036-0261

Mount Angel Seminary
St. Benedict, Oregon
www.mountangelabbey.org   CB code: 4491

- Private 4-year seminary college for men affiliated with Roman Catholic Church
- Residential campus in small town
- 103 degree-seeking undergraduates: 3% African American, 10% Asian American, 38% Hispanic American
- 128 degree-seeking graduate students
- 85% of applicants admitted

General. Founded in 1887. Regionally accredited; also accredited by ATS. All undergraduates candidates for Roman Catholic priesthood. **Degrees:** 15 bachelor's awarded; master's offered. **Location:** 40 miles from Portland. **Calendar:** Semester. **Full-time faculty:** 34 total; 29% have terminal degrees, 6% minority, 29% women. **Part-time faculty:** 11 total; 46% have terminal degrees, 36% women.

Freshman class profile. 20 applied, 17 admitted, 17 enrolled.

Out-of-state: 55%   **Live on campus:**   100%

Basis for selection. Primarily recommendations from sponsoring dioceses or clergymen, personal interview important. Test scores considered. SAT or ACT recommended. Interview recommended. **Home schooled:** State high school equivalency certificate required.

2012-2013 Annual costs. Tuition/fees (projected): $14,562. Formation fee of $3,365. Room/board: $10,148. Books/supplies: $900. Personal expenses: $1,000.

Application procedures. Admission: Closing date 7/1 (postmark date). $29 fee, may be waived for applicants with need. Admission notification on a rolling basis beginning on or about 7/31. **Financial aid:** Priority date 4/30, closing date 6/30. FAFSA, institutional form required. Applicants notified on a rolling basis; must reply within 2 week(s) of notification.

Academics. Special study options: Cross-registration, double major, ESL. Inter-divisional program, 3-week full-time pursuit of single approved course of study. **Credit/placement by examination:** AP, CLEP, institutional tests. **Support services:** Study skills assistance, tutoring, writing center.

Majors. Liberal arts: Arts/sciences. **Philosophy/religion:** Philosophy. **Theology:** Theology.

Computing on campus. 10 workstations in dormitories, library, computer center. Dormitories wired for high-speed internet access and linked to campus network. Online library, helpline, wireless network available.

Student life. Freshman orientation: Mandatory. Preregistration for classes offered. One-week program held the week before classes begin. **Policies:** All full-time students working toward priesthood required to live on campus. Religious observance required. **Housing:** Guaranteed on-campus for all undergraduates. **Activities:** Student government.

Athletics. Intramural: Basketball M, racquetball M, soccer M, swimming M, volleyball M.

Student services. Chaplain/spiritual director, financial aid counseling, health services, personal counseling.

Contact. Phone: (503) 845-3951 Fax: (503) 845-3128
Rev. Ralph Recker, Admissions Director, Mount Angel Seminary, One Abbey Drive, St. Benedict, OR 97373

Multnomah University
Portland, Oregon
www.multnomah.edu   CB code: 4496

- Private 4-year Bible and seminary college affiliated with interdenominational tradition
- Residential campus in very large city
- 583 degree-seeking undergraduates: 16% part-time, 42% women, 3% African American, 2% Asian American, 5% Hispanic American, 1% Native American, 1% international
- 356 degree-seeking graduate students
- 73% of applicants admitted
- SAT or ACT (ACT writing optional), application essay required
- 39% graduate within 6 years

General. Founded in 1936. Regionally accredited; also accredited by ABHE. Emphasis on preparation for Christian ministries. **Degrees:** 124 bachelor's awarded; master's offered. **Location:** 5 miles from downtown. **Calendar:** Semester, limited summer session. **Full-time faculty:** 33 total; 76% have terminal degrees, 24% women. **Part-time faculty:** 57 total; 39% have terminal degrees, 32% women. **Class size:** 73% < 20, 21% 20-39, 5% 40-49, less than 1% 50-99, less than 1% >100.

Freshman class profile. 135 applied, 99 admitted, 65 enrolled.

Mid 50% test scores				
SAT critical reading:	470-630	GPA 3.0-3.49:		32%
SAT math:	460-560	GPA 2.0-2.99:		23%
SAT writing:	460-590	Rank in top quarter:		48%
ACT composite:	17-25	Rank in top tenth:		7%
GPA 3.75 or higher:	29%	Return as sophomores:		62%
GPA 3.50-3.74:	15%	Out-of-state:		72%
		Live on campus:		67%

Basis for selection. School achievement record, test scores, recommendations most important. **Home schooled:** If official transcript cannot be supplied, parental statement verifying student has met high school graduation requirements for home schoolers for their home state or GED test scores required.

High school preparation. College-preparatory program recommended. Recommended units include English 4, mathematics 2, social studies 3, history 2, science 3 (laboratory 1) and foreign language 2.

2011-2012 Annual costs. Tuition/fees: $20,240. Room/board: $6,800. Books/supplies: $1,000. Personal expenses: $3,200.

2010-2011 Financial aid. **Need-based:** 65 full-time freshmen applied for aid; 58 were judged to have need; 58 of these received aid. Average need met was 48%. Average scholarship/grant was $6,661; average loan $3,123. 42% of total undergraduate aid awarded as scholarships/grants, 58% as loans/jobs. **Non-need-based:** Awarded to 29 full-time undergraduates, including 11 freshmen. Scholarships awarded for academics, leadership, music/drama, religious affiliation.

Application procedures. Admission: Priority date 3/1; deadline 7/15 (postmark date). $40 fee. Admission notification on a rolling basis. Must reply by 8/15. **Financial aid:** Priority date 4/1, closing date 8/1. FAFSA required. Applicants notified on a rolling basis starting 3/15; must reply within 2 week(s) of notification.

Academics. **Special study options:** Cooperative education, distance learning, double major, internships, liberal arts/career combination, teacher certification program. **Credit/placement by examination:** AP, CLEP, IB, institutional tests. 20 credit hours maximum toward bachelor's degree. **Support services:** Reduced course load, study skills assistance, tutoring, writing center.

Majors. **Communications:** Communications/speech/rhetoric, journalism. **Education:** Elementary. **Foreign languages:** Ancient Greek, Hebrew. **History:** General. **Psychology:** General. **Theology:** Bible, missionary, pastoral counseling, religious ed, sacred music, theology, youth ministry.

Computing on campus. 42 workstations in dormitories, library, computer center, student center. Dormitories wired for high-speed internet access and linked to campus network. Commuter students can connect to campus network. Online course registration, online library, helpline, wireless network available.

Student life. **Freshman orientation:** Mandatory. Preregistration for classes offered. Held 3 days before start of classes. **Policies:** No alcohol, smoking, gambling. Religious observance required. **Housing:** Guaranteed on-campus for freshmen. Single-sex dorms, special housing for disabled, apartments available. $100 fully refundable deposit, deadline 7/15. Houses for students with spouses or dependents. **Activities:** Campus ministries, choral groups, music ensembles, student government, student newspaper.

Athletics. NCCAA. **Intercollegiate:** Basketball M, volleyball W. **Intramural:** Basketball, soccer, volleyball. **Team name:** Lions.

Student services. Chaplain/spiritual director, career counseling, student employment services, financial aid counseling, health services, personal counseling, placement for graduates.

Contact. E-mail: admiss@multnomah.edu
Phone: (503) 255-0332 ext. 485 Toll-free number: (800) 275-4672
Fax: (503) 254-1268
John Mayner, Director of Admissions, Multnomah University, 8435 Northeast Glisan Street, Portland, OR 97220-5898

New Hope Christian College
Eugene, Oregon
www.newhope.edu   CB code: 4274

▪ Private 4-year Bible college affiliated with nondenominational tradition
▪ Residential campus in small city
▪ 143 degree-seeking undergraduates: 6% part-time, 39% women, 3% African American, 1% Asian American, 3% Hispanic American, 1% international

---

▪ 47% of applicants admitted
▪ Application essay required

General. Founded in 1925. Regionally accredited; also accredited by ABHE. **Degrees:** 18 bachelor's awarded. **Location:** 100 miles from Portland. **Calendar:** Semester, limited summer session. **Full-time faculty:** 9 total; 44% have terminal degrees, 33% minority, 33% women. **Part-time faculty:** 16 total; 19% have terminal degrees, 12% minority, 38% women. **Class size:** 76% < 20, 18% 20-39, 4% 40-49, 2% 50-99. **Special facilities:** Pentecostal historical archives.

Freshman class profile. 118 applied, 55 admitted, 43 enrolled.

GPA 3.75 or higher:	10%	Rank in top quarter:	25%
GPA 3.50-3.74:	20%	Rank in top tenth:	5%
GPA 3.0-3.49:	45%	Out-of-state:	40%
GPA 2.0-2.99:	25%		

Basis for selection. School achievement and activities, test scores, recommendations, personal essay most important. Religious affiliation or commitment important factor. **Home schooled:** CAT test, SAT Subject Test, or ITBS recommended.

2011-2012 Annual costs. Tuition/fees: $13,190. Room/board: $6,260. Books/supplies: $900. Personal expenses: $2,052.

2010-2011 Financial aid. **Need-based:** 30 full-time freshmen applied for aid; 30 were judged to have need; 30 of these received aid. Average need met was 50%. Average scholarship/grant was $6,500; average loan $3,500. 42% of total undergraduate aid awarded as scholarships/grants, 58% as loans/jobs. **Non-need-based:** Awarded to 68 full-time undergraduates, including 29 freshmen. Scholarships awarded for academics, art, athletics, job skills, leadership, music/drama, religious affiliation, state residency. **Additional information:** Some early acceptance awards possible for those admitted by May 15. Distance awards to those coming from over 1,000 miles away. Some awards for husbands and wives enrolled at same time.

Application procedures. Admission: Priority date 1/1; deadline 8/1 (receipt date). $35 fee. Admission notification on a rolling basis beginning on or about 10/1. **Financial aid:** Priority date 4/1, closing date 8/1. FAFSA, institutional form required. Applicants notified on a rolling basis starting 2/1; must reply within 4 week(s) of notification.

Academics. Transfer-track programs available in elementary education: first 2 years at college, final 2-3 years at other institutions. **Special study options:** Accelerated study, distance learning, double major, dual enrollment of high school students, independent study, internships. **Credit/placement by examination:** AP, CLEP, institutional tests. **Support services:** Reduced course load, remedial instruction, study skills assistance, tutoring.

Majors. **Philosophy/religion:** Christian, religion. **Theology:** Bible, missionary, pastoral counseling, religious ed, sacred music, theology, youth ministry.

Computing on campus. 18 workstations in dormitories, library, computer center, student center. Dormitories wired for high-speed internet access. Repair service available.

Student life. **Freshman orientation:** Mandatory. Preregistration for classes offered. Week-long program ends with camping retreat to mountains with fellow students and faculty. **Policies:** Students required to sign Code of Conduct agreement. Student ministry/community service required. Religious observance required. **Housing:** Guaranteed on-campus for freshmen. Single-sex dorms, apartments available. $150 fully refundable deposit, deadline 8/1. **Activities:** Campus ministries, choral groups, dance, drama, music ensembles, musical theater, student government, student newspaper.

Athletics. **Intramural:** Basketball, soccer, volleyball. **Team name:** Deacons.

Student services. Chaplain/spiritual director, student employment services, financial aid counseling, personal counseling, placement for graduates, veterans' counselor.

Contact. E-mail: admissions@newhope.edu
Phone: (541) 485-1780 Toll-free number: (800) 322-2638
Fax: (541) 343-5801
Sarah Huntoon, Director of Admissions/Registrar, New Hope Christian College, 2155 Bailey Hill Road, Eugene, OR 97405

Northwest Christian University
Eugene, Oregon
www.nwcu.edu   CB code: 4543

▶ Private 4-year university affiliated with Christian Church (Disciples of Christ)
▶ Commuter campus in small city
▶ 471 degree-seeking undergraduates: 20% part-time, 62% women
▶ 129 degree-seeking graduate students
▶ 66% of applicants admitted
▶ SAT or ACT (ACT writing recommended), application essay required

General. Founded in 1895. Regionally accredited. **Degrees:** 135 bachelor's, 6 associate awarded; master's offered. **Location:** 110 miles from Portland. **Calendar:** Semester, limited summer session. **Full-time faculty:** 22 total; 68% have terminal degrees, 4% minority, 36% women. **Part-time faculty:** 54 total; 26% have terminal degrees, 2% minority, 59% women. **Class size:** 76% < 20, 24% 20-39.

Freshman class profile. 256 applied, 168 admitted, 58 enrolled.

GPA 3.75 or higher:	41%	Rank in top quarter:	45%
GPA 3.50-3.74:	3%	Rank in top tenth:	21%
GPA 3.0-3.49:	37%	Out-of-state:	31%
GPA 2.0-2.99:	19%	Live on campus:	75%

Basis for selection. Overall grade performance; adherence to College Preparation Standards; content and difficulty of courses taken; standardized test scores; quality of involvement in applicant's church, community, and school activities important. Additional information may be requested, including updated transcripts, additional essays, and interview. Interview recommended, personal statement required.

High school preparation. College-preparatory program recommended. 14 units recommended. Recommended units include English 4, mathematics 3, social studies 3, science 2 (laboratory 1) and foreign language 2.

2011-2012 Annual costs. Tuition/fees: $23,600. Room/board: $7,400. Books/supplies: $900. Personal expenses: $2,340.

2011-2012 Financial aid. **Need-based:** 66% of total undergraduate aid awarded as scholarships/grants, 34% as loans/jobs. **Non-need-based:** Scholarships awarded for academics, athletics, leadership, music/drama, religious affiliation.

Application procedures. **Admission:** Priority date 7/1; no deadline. No application fee. Admission notification on a rolling basis beginning on or about 9/15. **Financial aid:** Priority date 3/1; no closing date. FAFSA required. Applicants notified on a rolling basis starting 3/1; must reply within 2 week(s) of notification.

Academics. **Special study options:** Accelerated study, distance learning, double major, ESL, exchange student, internships, study abroad, teacher certification program. **Credit/placement by examination:** AP, CLEP, IB, SAT, ACT. No limit on credit by examination. **Support services:** Reduced course load, remedial instruction, study skills assistance, tutoring, writing center.

Majors. **Biology:** Exercise physiology. **Business:** Accounting, business admin. **Communications:** Communications/speech/rhetoric. **Education:** Multi-level teacher. **English:** English lit. **Health services:** Health services admin. **History:** General. **Math:** General. **Psychology:** General. **Theology:** Bible, missionary, pastoral counseling, sacred music, theology, youth ministry. **Visual/performing arts:** Music management.

Most popular majors. Business/marketing 34%, education 7%, interdisciplinary studies 12%, psychology 25%, theological studies 7%.

Computing on campus. 55 workstations in dormitories, library, computer center. Dormitories wired for high-speed internet access and linked to campus network. Commuter students can connect to campus network. Online library, helpline, wireless network available.

Student life. Freshman orientation: Mandatory. Preregistration for classes offered. 4 day program; includes excursion trip. **Policies:** Attendance at chapel required. Religious observance required. **Housing:** Guaranteed on-campus for freshmen. Coed dorms, apartments available. $100 fully refundable deposit, deadline 5/1. Pets allowed in dorm rooms. **Activities:** Pep band, campus ministries, choral groups, dance, drama, literary magazine, music ensembles, student government, student newspaper, Parable, Circle K, Believers Building Bonds through Boardgames, community life groups.

Athletics. NAIA. **Intercollegiate:** Basketball, cross-country, golf, soccer, softball W, track and field, volleyball W. **Intramural:** Badminton, basketball, football (non-tackle) M, handball, skiing, volleyball. **Team name:** Beacons.

Student services. Adult student services, alcohol/substance abuse counseling, chaplain/spiritual director, career counseling, student employment services, financial aid counseling, personal counseling, placement for graduates, veterans' counselor. **Physically disabled:** Services for hearing impaired.

Contact. E-mail: admissions@nwcu.edu
Phone: (541) 684-7201 Toll-free number: (877) 463-6622
Fax: (541) 684-7317
Kacie Gerdrum, Associate Director of Undergraduate Admissions, Northwest Christian University, 828 East 11th Avenue, Eugene, OR 97401-3745

Oregon College of Art & Craft
Portland, Oregon
www.ocac.edu   CB code: 4236

▶ Private 4-year visual arts college
▶ Commuter campus in very large city
▶ 151 degree-seeking undergraduates: 26% part-time, 73% women, 2% Asian American, 5% Hispanic American, 3% Native American
▶ 92% of applicants admitted
▶ Application essay required
▶ 59% graduate within 6 years; 9% enter graduate study

General. Candidate for regional accreditation. **Degrees:** 26 bachelor's awarded. **Calendar:** Semester. **Full-time faculty:** 10 total; 90% have terminal degrees, 10% minority, 50% women. **Part-time faculty:** 20 total; 80% have terminal degrees, 5% minority, 70% women. **Class size:** 95% < 20, 5% 20-39. **Special facilities:** Galleries and gift shop.

Freshman class profile. 60 applied, 55 admitted, 26 enrolled.

GPA 3.75 or higher:	23%	End year in good standing:	85%
GPA 3.50-3.74:	20%	Return as sophomores:	65%
GPA 3.0-3.49:	31%	Out-of-state:	70%
GPA 2.0-2.99:	24%	Live on campus:	23%

Basis for selection. Talent and ability, GPA, essay, and test scores are all considered. SAT or ACT recommended. Portfolio required. **Home schooled:** Statement describing home school structure and mission required.

High school preparation. Recommended units include English 4, mathematics 3, social studies 1, history 3, science 3, foreign language 2 and visual/performing arts 4.

2011-2012 Annual costs. Tuition/fees: $24,271. Required fees vary by area of concentration. Books/supplies: $1,000.

2011-2012 Financial aid. **Need-based:** 18 full-time freshmen applied for aid; 17 were judged to have need; 17 of these received aid. Average need met was 20%. Average scholarship/grant was $3,496; average loan $3,107. 48% of total undergraduate aid awarded as scholarships/grants, 52% as loans/jobs. **Non-need-based:** Awarded to 92 full-time undergraduates, including 19 freshmen. Scholarships awarded for academics, art.

Application procedures. **Admission:** No deadline. $35 fee, may be waived for applicants with need. Admission notification on a rolling basis beginning on or about 1/1. Must reply by May 1 or within 4 week(s) if notified thereafter. **Financial aid:** Priority date 3/1; no closing date. FAFSA required. Applicants notified on a rolling basis starting 3/1.

Academics. **Special study options:** Cross-registration, exchange student, independent study, internships, study abroad. **Credit/placement by examination:** AP, CLEP, IB, institutional tests. **Support services:** Study skills assistance, tutoring.

Majors. **Visual/performing arts:** Ceramics, drawing, fiber arts, metal/jewelry, painting, photography.

Computing on campus. 15 workstations in dormitories, library, computer center. Dormitories wired for high-speed internet access. Helpline, wireless network available.

Student life. Freshman orientation: Mandatory. Preregistration for classes offered. Two-day orientation includes field trip to Portland Art Museum. Guided kayaking trip also offered. **Housing:** Cooperative housing available. $150 nonrefundable deposit, deadline 5/1. Small number of on-campus housing units available for first-time freshman. **Activities:** Student government, student newspaper.

Student services. Career counseling, financial aid counseling, personal counseling.

Contact. E-mail: admissions@ocac.edu
Phone: (971) 255-4192 Toll-free number: (800) 390-0632
Fax: (503) 297-9651
Anne Boerner, Chief Enrollment Officer and Director of Admissions,
Oregon College of Art & Craft, 8245 SW Barnes Road, Portland, OR
97225-6349

Oregon Health & Science University
Portland, Oregon
www.ohsu.edu

CB member
CB code: 4900

- Public 3-year university and health science college
- Commuter campus in very large city
- 780 degree-seeking undergraduates

General. Founded in 1887. Regionally accredited. **Degrees:** 317 bachelor's
awarded; master's, professional, doctoral offered. **Calendar:** Quarter, limited
summer session. **Full-time faculty:** 2,215 total. **Part-time faculty:** 515 total.

Basis for selection. Admission requirements vary by program.

2011-2012 Annual costs. Tuition/fees: $19,444; $31,144 out-of-state.
Tuition shown is for undergraduate nursing program; costs for other programs
vary. Books/supplies: $1,368.

Financial aid. Non-need-based: Scholarships awarded for academics,
minority status, state residency.

Application procedures. Admission: Closing date 1/15 (postmark date).
$120 fee, may be waived for applicants with need. Application must be
submitted online. Admission notification on a rolling basis. Must reply by
5/1. **Financial aid:** Closing date 3/1.

Academics. Special study options: Accelerated study, combined bachelor's/graduate degree, distance learning. **Credit/placement by examination:**
AP, CLEP. **Support services:** Pre-admission summer program, study skills
assistance, tutoring.

Majors. Health services: Clinical lab science, EMT paramedic, medical
radiologic technology/radiation therapy, nursing (RN).

Computing on campus. 60 workstations in library, computer center,
student center. Commuter students can connect to campus network. Online
library, helpline, wireless network available.

Student life. Freshman orientation: Mandatory. Preregistration for
classes offered. Orientation varies by program. **Activities:** Student government, student newspaper.

Athletics. Intramural: Basketball, soccer, swimming, table tennis, tennis, volleyball.

Student services. Career counseling, financial aid counseling, health services, personal counseling.

Contact. E-mail: proginfo@ohsu.edu
Phone: (503) 494-7800 Toll-free number: (800) 775-5460
Fax: (503) 494-4629
Jennifer Anderson, Director of Admissions, Oregon Health & Science
University, 3181 SW Sam Jackson Park Road, Portland, OR 97239-3098

Oregon Institute of Technology
Klamath Falls, Oregon
www.oit.edu

CB member
CB code: 4587

- Public 4-year career college
- Commuter campus in small city
- 3,135 degree-seeking undergraduates: 31% part-time, 46% women, 1%
  African American, 4% Asian American, 6% Hispanic American, 1%
  Native American, 2% international
- 30 degree-seeking graduate students
- 93% of applicants admitted
- SAT or ACT with writing required
- 45% graduate within 6 years

General. Founded in 1947. Regionally accredited. Upper-division courses
offered in electronics engineering technology, manufacturing engineering
technology. Software engineering technology offered at OIT Portland West
in Beaverton area. **Degrees:** 531 bachelor's, 50 associate awarded; master's

offered. **ROTC:** Army. **Location:** 280 miles from Portland; 270 miles from
Reno, Nevada. **Calendar:** Quarter, limited summer session. **Full-time faculty:** 134 total; 8% minority, 40% women. **Part-time faculty:** 113 total; 8%
minority, 34% women. **Class size:** 53% < 20, 40% 20-39, 3% 40-49, 4%
50-99. **Special facilities:** Center for research on geothermal energy, renewable
energy center, center for health professions.

Freshman class profile. 713 applied, 664 admitted, 299 enrolled.

Mid 50% test scores			
SAT critical reading:	430-560	GPA 2.0-2.99:	13%
SAT math:	450-580	Rank in top quarter:	51%
SAT writing:	420-530	Rank in top tenth:	23%
ACT composite:	19-26	Return as sophomores:	73%
GPA 3.75 or higher:	28%	Out-of-state:	9%
GPA 3.50-3.74:	20%	Live on campus:	57%
GPA 3.0-3.49:	39%	International:	1%

Basis for selection. Secondary school record and standardized test scores
very important. Class rank, recommendations, essay, interview, character/
personal qualities and work experience all considered. Applicants from nonstandard or unaccredited high schools must take 3 SAT Subject Tests: 1
English, 1 math, 1 other of student's choice. **Learning Disabled:** Tech
opportunities available.

High school preparation. 14 units required. Required units include
English 4, mathematics 3, social studies 3, science 2 (laboratory 1) and
foreign language 2.

2011-2012 Annual costs. Tuition/fees: $7,889; $22,212 out-of-state.
Room/board: $8,145. Books/supplies: $1,000. Personal expenses: $2,438.

2010-2011 Financial aid. Need-based: 288 full-time freshmen applied
for aid; 228 were judged to have need; 226 of these received aid. Average
need met was 19%. Average scholarship/grant was $5,341; average loan
$3,347. 36% of total undergraduate aid awarded as scholarships/grants, 64%
as loans/jobs. **Non-need-based:** Awarded to 126 full-time undergraduates,
including 30 freshmen. Scholarships awarded for academics, athletics, leadership, minority status.

Application procedures. Admission: Priority date 2/1; deadline 10/1.
$50 fee. Admission notification on a rolling basis beginning on or about
10/15. Must reply by May 1 or within 4 week(s) if notified thereafter.
Application deadline for dual enrollment is 3 weeks before term starts. **Financial aid:** Priority date 2/1; no closing date. FAFSA required. Applicants
notified on a rolling basis starting 4/1; must reply within 3 week(s) of notification.

Academics. Special study options: Combined bachelor's/graduate degree,
cooperative education, cross-registration, distance learning, double major,
dual enrollment of high school students, external degree, internships, liberal
arts/career combination, study abroad. **Credit/placement by examination:**
AP, CLEP, SAT, ACT, institutional tests. No more than 25% of credits
submitted for graduation may be credit by examination. **Support services:**
Learning center, reduced course load, remedial instruction, study skills assistance, tutoring.

Majors. Biology: General. **Business:** Accounting, management information
systems, marketing, operations, small business admin. **Communications:**
Communications/speech/rhetoric. **Computer sciences:** Information technology. **Conservation:** Environmental science. **Engineering:** Civil, electrical,
mechanical. **Health services:** Clinical lab science, dental hygiene, health
care admin, medical records admin, nuclear medical technology, radiologic
technology/medical imaging, respiratory therapy technology, sonography.
Math: Applied. **Psychology:** General.

Most popular majors. Business/marketing 17%, engineering/engineering
technologies 33%, health sciences 31%, psychology 11%.

Computing on campus. 656 workstations in dormitories, library, computer center. Dormitories wired for high-speed internet access. Commuter
students can connect to campus network. Online course registration, online
library, helpline, repair service, student web hosting, wireless network available.

Student life. Freshman orientation: Mandatory. Preregistration for
classes offered. **Housing:** Coed dorms available. $150 partly refundable
deposit, deadline 5/1. **Activities:** Pep band, choral groups, radio station,
student government, student newspaper, symphony orchestra, TV station,
Newman club, Latter-day Saints, Christian Fellowship, Native American
club, international student club, Circle K, Latin American club, residence
hall association, Phi Delta Theta, College Republicans.

Athletics. NAIA. **Intercollegiate:** Baseball M, basketball, cross-country,
soccer W, softball W, track and field, volleyball W. **Intramural:** Basketball,
cheerleading, cross-country, football (tackle) M, lacrosse M, soccer, softball,
track and field, volleyball. **Team name:** Owls.

Student services. Adult student services, alcohol/substance abuse counseling, career counseling, student employment services, financial aid counseling, health services, personal counseling, placement for graduates, veterans' counselor. **Physically disabled:** Services for visually, hearing impaired.

Contact. E-mail: oit@oit.edu
Phone: (541) 885-1150 Toll-free number: (800) 422-2017
Fax: (541) 885-1115
Ginny Gardiner, Director of Admissions, Oregon Institute of Technology, 3201 Campus Drive, Klamath Falls, OR 97601

Oregon State University
Corvallis, Oregon
CB member
www.oregonstate.edu
CB code: 4586

- Public 4-year university
- Residential campus in small city
- 19,501 degree-seeking undergraduates
- 81% of applicants admitted
- SAT or ACT with writing, application essay required

General. Founded in 1868. Regionally accredited. **Degrees:** 3,484 bachelor's awarded; master's, professional, doctoral offered. **ROTC:** Army, Naval, Air Force. **Location:** 80 miles from Portland, 45 miles from Eugene. **Calendar:** Quarter, extensive summer session. **Full-time faculty:** 893 total. **Part-time faculty:** 657 total. **Class size:** 36% < 20, 37% 20-39, 6% 40-49, 13% 50-99, 7% >100. **Special facilities:** Arboretum, 13,429-acre forest, radiation center (with TRIGA Mark II Nuclear Reactor), wave research facility, marine science center museum and aquarium.

Freshman class profile. 11,428 applied, 9,257 admitted, 3,703 enrolled.

Mid 50% test scores			
SAT critical reading:	470-600	GPA 2.0-2.99:	8%
SAT math:	490-620	Rank in top quarter:	51%
ACT composite:	21-26	Rank in top tenth:	19%
GPA 3.75 or higher:	30%	Out-of-state:	22%
GPA 3.50-3.74:	23%	Live on campus:	79%
GPA 3.0-3.49:	39%	Fraternities:	16%
		Sororities:	11%

Basis for selection. Secondary school record, GPA, essay most important. Students not meeting admission requirements may petition for exception. Students who do not meet subject requirements, who graduated from nonstandard or unaccredited high schools, or who graduated prior to 1987 must submit SAT Subject Test scores in addition to SAT or ACT. Applicants with GED not required to submit test scores. **Home schooled:** Must submit SAT Subject Tests or GED.

High school preparation. College-preparatory program required. 14 units required. Required and recommended units include English 4, mathematics 3, social studies 3, science 2 (laboratory 1-2) and foreign language 2.

2011-2012 Annual costs. Tuition/fees: $7,600; $21,316 out-of-state. Room/board: $10,464.

Financial aid. **Non-need-based:** Scholarships awarded for academics, athletics, job skills, leadership, minority status, ROTC, state residency.

Application procedures. **Admission:** Priority date 2/1; deadline 8/27. $50 fee. Admission notification on a rolling basis beginning on or about 10/1. Must reply by May 1 or within 3 week(s) if notified thereafter. **Financial aid:** Priority date 2/1, closing date 5/1. FAFSA required. Applicants notified on a rolling basis starting 4/1; must reply within 4 week(s) of notification.

Academics. **Special study options:** Accelerated study, cooperative education, cross-registration, distance learning, double major, dual enrollment of high school students, ESL, exchange student, external degree, honors, independent study, internships, liberal arts/career combination, student-designed major, study abroad, teacher certification program. **Credit/placement by examination:** AP, CLEP, IB, institutional tests. **Support services:** Learning center, remedial instruction, study skills assistance, tutoring.

Majors. **Area/ethnic studies:** General, American. **Biology:** General, bacteriology, biochemistry, biophysics, biotechnology, botany, entomology, zoology. **Business:** Business admin. **Computer sciences:** General. **Conservation:** General, environmental science, fisheries, forest management, forest resources, management/policy, wildlife/wilderness. **Education:** Technology/industrial arts. **Engineering:** Applied physics, biomedical, chemical, civil, computer, construction, electrical, environmental, forest, industrial, manufacturing, mechanical, mining, nuclear. **English:** English lit, rhetoric/composition. **Foreign languages:** French, German, Spanish. **General:** Agronomy, animal sciences, business, economics, food science, horticultural science, plant sciences, range science. **Health services:** Clinical lab technology, environmental health, health care admin, physics/radiologic health, public health

ed. **History:** General. **Liberal arts:** Arts/sciences. **Math:** General. **Parks/recreation:** General, health/fitness. **Philosophy/religion:** Philosophy. **Physical sciences:** Chemistry, geology, physics. **Psychology:** General. **Social sciences:** Anthropology, economics, geography, political science, sociology. **Visual/performing arts:** General, art, fashion design, interior design, music. **Work/family studies:** Clothing/textiles, family studies, food/nutrition, housing, merchandising.

Most popular majors. Biology 7%, business/marketing 11%, education 6%, engineering/engineering technologies 19%, family/consumer sciences 8%, interdisciplinary studies 8%, natural resources/environmental science 7%, parks/recreation 6%.

Computing on campus. 1,660 workstations in dormitories, library, computer center. Dormitories wired for high-speed internet access and linked to campus network. Commuter students can connect to campus network. Online course registration, helpline, repair service, student web hosting, wireless network available.

Student life. **Freshman orientation:** Available, $400 fee. Preregistration for classes offered. **Housing:** Coed dorms, special housing for disabled, apartments, cooperative housing, fraternity/sorority housing available. $45 nonrefundable deposit. **Activities:** Bands, campus ministries, choral groups, dance, drama, film society, international student organizations, literary magazine, music ensembles, Model UN, musical theater, opera, radio station, student government, student newspaper, symphony orchestra, TV station, 253 student organizations, 47 student honor and recognition societies.

Athletics. NCAA. **Intercollegiate:** Baseball M, basketball, cheerleading, cross-country W, football (tackle) M, golf, gymnastics W, rowing (crew), soccer, softball W, swimming W, track and field M, volleyball W, wrestling M. **Intramural:** Badminton, basketball, bowling, cross-country, football (tackle) M, golf, racquetball, soccer, softball, swimming, tennis, track and field, volleyball, water polo, wrestling M. **Team name:** Beavers.

Student services. Adult student services, career counseling, student employment services, financial aid counseling, health services, legal services, minority student services, on-campus daycare, personal counseling, placement for graduates, veterans' counselor, women's services. **Physically disabled:** Services for visually, speech, hearing impaired.

Contact. E-mail: osuadmit@orst.edu
Phone: (541) 737-4411 Toll-free number: (800) 291-4192
Fax: (541) 737-2482
Noah Buckley, Director of Admissions, Oregon State University, 104 Kerr Administration Building, Corvallis, OR 97331-2130

Pacific Northwest College of Art
Portland, Oregon
www.pnca.edu
CB code: 4504

- Private 4-year visual arts college
- Commuter campus in large city
- 521 degree-seeking undergraduates: 8% part-time, 65% women, 2% African American, 3% Asian American, 4% Hispanic American, 2% Native American, 1% international
- 75 degree-seeking graduate students
- 52% of applicants admitted
- Application essay required
- 42% graduate within 6 years

General. Founded in 1909. Regionally accredited. **Degrees:** 90 bachelor's awarded; master's offered. **Calendar:** Semester, limited summer session. **Full-time faculty:** 28 total; 82% have terminal degrees, 18% minority, 43% women. **Part-time faculty:** 75 total; 56% have terminal degrees, 4% minority, 51% women. **Class size:** 95% < 20, 5% 20-39. **Special facilities:** Contemporary craft museum, student art galleries, printmaking center, individual studio spaces for seniors.

Freshman class profile. 392 applied, 205 admitted, 76 enrolled.

GPA 3.75 or higher:	15%	Return as sophomores:	56%
GPA 3.50-3.74:	15%	Out-of-state:	52%
GPA 3.0-3.49:	24%	Live on campus:	58%
GPA 2.0-2.99:	38%		

Basis for selection. Portfolio, essays important. 2.0 GPA recommended for academic courses. Greater emphasis on portfolio. Interview recommended. **Home schooled:** Statement describing home school structure and mission, transcript of courses and grades, state high school equivalency certificate, letter of recommendation (nonparent) required. SAT/ACT exam recommended.

High school preparation. College-preparatory program recommended. Recommended units include English 4, mathematics 3, social studies 3 and science 3. Visual arts classes recommended.

2011-2012 Annual costs. Tuition/fees: $29,532. Off-campus housing available, approximately one mile from campus. Annual cost is $4,374 for shared bedroom. Books/supplies: $1,000. Personal expenses: $615.

Financial aid. Non-need-based: Scholarships awarded for academics, art.

Application procedures. Admission: Priority date 3/1; no deadline. No application fee. Admission notification on a rolling basis. Must reply by May 1 or within 4 week(s) if notified thereafter. **Financial aid:** Priority date 3/1; no closing date. FAFSA required. Applicants notified on a rolling basis starting 4/1; must reply by 5/1 or within 4 week(s) of notification.

Academics. Thesis required during fourth year. **Special study options:** Cooperative education, cross-registration, dual enrollment of high school students, exchange student, independent study, internships, New York semester, student-designed major, study abroad. 5-year BA/BFA program with Reed College. **Credit/placement by examination:** AP, CLEP. **Support services:** Study skills assistance, tutoring, writing center.

Majors. Visual/performing arts: Digital arts, graphic design, illustration, multimedia, painting, photography, printmaking, sculpture, studio arts.

Computing on campus. 130 workstations in library, computer center, student center. Commuter students can connect to campus network. Online course registration, online library, helpline, wireless network available.

Student life. Freshman orientation: Available. Preregistration for classes offered. 3 day program held prior to start of semester. **Housing:** Coed dorms available. $450 partly refundable deposit, deadline 6/15. Pets allowed in dorm rooms. Student housing available through partnership with College Housing Northwest. **Activities:** Film society, radio station, student government.

Student services. Career counseling, financial aid counseling, personal counseling.

Contact. E-mail: admissions@pnca.edu
Phone: (503) 821-8972 Fax: (503) 821-8978
Kavin Buck, Vice President of Enrollment, Pacific Northwest College of Art, 1241 NW Johnson Street, Portland, OR 97209

Pacific University
Forest Grove, Oregon
www.pacificu.edu   CB code: 4601

- Private 4-year university affiliated with United Church of Christ
- Residential campus in large town
- 1,555 degree-seeking undergraduates: 2% part-time, 58% women, 2% African American, 14% Asian American, 8% Hispanic American, 1% Native American, 2% international
- 1,641 degree-seeking graduate students
- 75% of applicants admitted
- SAT or ACT (ACT writing optional), application essay required
- 61% graduate within 6 years

General. Founded in 1849. Regionally accredited. Branch campuses in Hillsboro, Portland, and Eugene for selected professional programs. **Degrees:** 373 bachelor's awarded; master's, professional offered. **ROTC:** Army, Air Force. **Location:** 25 miles from Portland. **Calendar:** Semester, limited summer session. **Full-time faculty:** 215 total; 83% have terminal degrees, 15% minority, 51% women. **Part-time faculty:** 170 total; 14% have terminal degrees, 14% minority, 55% women. **Class size:** 60% < 20, 34% 20-39, 3% 40-49, 3% 50-99, less than 1% >100. **Special facilities:** Permaculture project, wildlife refuge, performing arts center, arboretum, center for Internet studies, English language institute, humanitarian center, institute for ethics and social policy, center for gender equity.

Freshman class profile. 2,487 applied, 1,868 admitted, 374 enrolled.

Mid 50% test scores			
SAT critical reading:	490-600	Rank in top quarter:	66%
SAT math:	510-610	Rank in top tenth:	34%
ACT composite:	21-26	Return as sophomores:	75%
GPA 3.75 or higher:	43%	Out-of-state:	59%
GPA 3.50-3.74:	23%	Live on campus:	96%
GPA 3.0-3.49:	26%	International:	1%
GPA 2.0-2.99:	8%	Fraternities:	5%
		Sororities:	6%

Basis for selection. Strength of high school program, GPA, test scores, course selection, interview most important. 1000 SAT (exclusive of Writing) plus 3.0 GPA recommended. Recommendation, essay, extracurricular activities, leadership involvement also important. Audition required for music program; portfolio recommended for art program. **Home schooled:** Statement describing home school structure and mission, transcript of courses and grades, state high school equivalency certificate, interview, letter of recommendation (nonparent) required.

High school preparation. College-preparatory program recommended. 21 units recommended. Recommended units include English 4, mathematics 3, social studies 3, history 1, science 3 (laboratory 1), foreign language 2 and academic electives 4.

2011-2012 Annual costs. Tuition/fees: $33,612. Room/board: $9,208. Books/supplies: $1,000. Personal expenses: $900.

Financial aid. Non-need-based: Scholarships awarded for academics, alumni affiliation, art, music/drama.

Application procedures. Admission: Priority date 2/15; deadline 8/15. $40 fee, may be waived for applicants with need. Admission notification on a rolling basis beginning on or about 11/1. Must reply by May 1 or within 2 week(s) if notified thereafter. **Financial aid:** Priority date 3/1; no closing date. FAFSA required. Applicants notified on a rolling basis starting 3/1.

Academics. Special study options: Combined bachelor's/graduate degree, cross-registration, double major, ESL, independent study, internships, liberal arts/career combination, study abroad, teacher certification program, Washington semester. 3-2 engineering programs with Oregon Graduate Institute and Washington University, 3-2 applied physics program, 4-1 computer science, 4-1 environmental science programs with Oregon Graduate Institute, exchange programs with University of Vienna, Beijing Normal University, University of Edinburgh, other institutions in Europe and Asia; cooperative arrangement with Northwest Film Center. **Credit/placement by examination:** AP, CLEP, IB, SAT, ACT, institutional tests. **Support services:** Learning center, reduced course load, tutoring, writing center.

Majors. Area/ethnic studies: American, Asian, Latin American, Western European, women's. **Biology:** General, biochemistry, bioinformatics. **Business:** Business admin. **Communications:** Communications/speech/rhetoric, journalism. **Computer sciences:** General. **Conservation:** Environmental science, environmental studies. **Education:** General. **English:** Creative writing, English lit. **Foreign languages:** General, Chinese, French, German, Japanese, Spanish. **History:** General. **Human services:** Social work. **Liberal arts:** Arts/sciences. **Math:** General. **Parks/recreation:** Exercise sciences. **Philosophy/religion:** Philosophy. **Physical sciences:** Chemistry, physics. **Psychology:** General. **Social sciences:** Economics, international relations, political science, sociology. **Visual/performing arts:** General, art, dramatic, multimedia, music, music performance.

Most popular majors. Biology 11%, business/marketing 10%, communications/journalism 6%, education 7%, health sciences 14%, parks/recreation 12%, social sciences 11%, visual/performing arts 6%.

Computing on campus. 200 workstations in dormitories, library, computer center, student center. Dormitories wired for high-speed internet access and linked to campus network. Commuter students can connect to campus network. Online library, helpline, repair service, student web hosting, wireless network available.

Student life. Freshman orientation: Mandatory. Preregistration for classes offered. **Policies:** Unmarried freshmen and sophomores under age 21 must live on campus unless living near campus with family. **Housing:** Guaranteed on-campus for freshmen. Coed dorms, special housing for disabled, apartments available. $100 fully refundable deposit, deadline 5/1. 1 wing designated for females. **Activities:** Bands, campus ministries, choral groups, dance, drama, film society, international student organizations, literary magazine, music ensembles, musical theater, radio station, student government, student newspaper, symphony orchestra, Hawaii club, Christian Fellowship, politics and law forum, Circle K, humanitarian center, gay and lesbian support group, ethnic diversity appreciation club, United Church of Christ student organization.

Athletics. NCAA. **Intercollegiate:** Baseball M, basketball, cheerleading, cross-country, golf, lacrosse W, soccer, softball W, swimming, tennis, track and field, volleyball W, wrestling. **Intramural:** Basketball, football (tackle), golf, handball, racquetball, soccer, softball, tennis, volleyball. **Team name:** Boxers.

Student services. Alcohol/substance abuse counseling, career counseling, student employment services, financial aid counseling, health services, minority student services, personal counseling, placement for graduates, veterans' counselor.

Contact. E-mail: admissions@pacificu.edu
Phone: (503) 352-2218 Toll-free number: (800) 677-6712
Fax: (503) 352-2975
Karen Dunston, Executive Director of Undergraduate Admission, Pacific
University, 2043 College Way, Forest Grove, OR 97116-1797

Portland State University
Portland, Oregon
www.pdx.edu

CB member
CB code: 4610

- Public 4-year university
- Commuter campus in very large city
- 20,119 degree-seeking undergraduates: 30% part-time, 53% women, 3% African American, 8% Asian American, 8% Hispanic American, 2% Native American, 4% international
- 5,804 graduate students
- 70% of applicants admitted
- 35% graduate within 6 years

General. Founded in 1946. Regionally accredited. Courses offered at off-campus locations. **Degrees:** 4,358 bachelor's awarded; master's, doctoral offered. **ROTC:** Army, Air Force. **Location:** Downtown. **Calendar:** Quarter, extensive summer session. **Full-time faculty:** 885 total; 76% have terminal degrees, 16% minority, 46% women. **Part-time faculty:** 696 total; 16% have terminal degrees, 11% minority, 54% women. **Class size:** 38% < 20, 39% 20-39, 10% 40-49, 11% 50-99, 3% >100. **Special facilities:** Native American center.

Freshman class profile. 4,954 applied, 3,471 admitted, 1,354 enrolled.

Mid 50% test scores			
SAT critical reading:	450-580	GPA 3.0-3.49:	47%
SAT math:	460-580	GPA 2.0-2.99:	14%
SAT writing:	430-560	End year in good standing:	72%
ACT composite:	18-25	Return as sophomores:	73%
GPA 3.75 or higher:	18%	Out-of-state:	24%
GPA 3.50-3.74:	21%	International:	6%

Basis for selection. 3.0 GPA required. If GPA requirement is not met, specific combination of test scores and GPA may qualify under special action by admissions committee. Test scores considered for students who do not meet GPA requirement. Interview recommended for those who do not meet regular admission requirement. **Home schooled:** State high school equivalency certificate required.

High school preparation. 14 units required. Required and recommended units include English 4, mathematics 3, social studies 2, history 1, science 2 (laboratory 1) and foreign language 2. One unit laboratory science recommended.

2011-2012 Annual costs. Tuition/fees: $7,764; $22,983 out-of-state. Room/board: $9,459. Books/supplies: $1,854. Personal expenses: $1,932.

Financial aid. **Non-need-based:** Scholarships awarded for academics, art, athletics, music/drama, state residency.

Application procedures. **Admission:** Priority date 6/1; no deadline. $50 fee. Admission notification on a rolling basis. **Financial aid:** Priority date 2/28; no closing date. FAFSA required. Applicants notified on a rolling basis; must reply within 4 week(s) of notification.

Academics. Community based service and research projects offered in Portland area. All students required to complete 45 credit hour multidisciplinary core curriculum, including community service learning experience. Teaching certification only offered at graduate level. **Special study options:** Accelerated study, combined bachelor's/graduate degree, cooperative education, distance learning, double major, ESL, exchange student, honors, independent study, internships, liberal arts/career combination, study abroad, teacher certification program, Washington semester. **Credit/placement by examination:** AP, CLEP, institutional tests. 45 credit hours maximum toward bachelor's degree. **Support services:** Pre-admission summer program, reduced course load, tutoring, writing center.

Honors college/program. 1200 SAT (exclusive of Writing) and 3.5 GPA required. Limited to 200 participants.

Majors. **Architecture:** Architecture, urban/community planning. **Area/ethnic studies:** African, East Asian, European, Latin American, Near/Middle Eastern, Russian/Eastern European/Eurasian, women's. **Biology:** General, biochemistry. **Business:** General, accounting, business admin, finance, human resources, logistics, management information systems, marketing. **Computer sciences:** Computer science. **Conservation:** General. **Education:** Health. **Engineering:** Civil, computer, electrical, mechanical. **English:** English lit,

rhetoric/composition. **Foreign languages:** Chinese, French, German, Japanese, linguistics, Russian, Spanish. **Health services:** Audiology/hearing, public health ed. **History:** General. **Human services:** Social work. **Liberal arts:** Arts/sciences. **Math:** General. **Philosophy/religion:** Philosophy. **Physical sciences:** Chemistry, geology, physics. **Protective services:** Criminal justice, law enforcement admin. **Psychology:** General. **Social sciences:** General, anthropology, economics, geography, international relations, political science, sociology, urban studies. **Visual/performing arts:** Art, art history/conservation, commercial/advertising art, design, dramatic, drawing, music, music performance, painting, printmaking, sculpture, studio arts. **Work/family studies:** Family studies.

Most popular majors. Business/marketing 17%, health sciences 6%, liberal arts 9%, psychology 7%, social sciences 17%, visual/performing arts 6%.

Computing on campus. 925 workstations in dormitories, library, computer center, student center. Dormitories wired for high-speed internet access and linked to campus network. Commuter students can connect to campus network. Online course registration, online library, helpline, repair service, student web hosting, wireless network available.

Student life. **Freshman orientation:** Mandatory. Preregistration for classes offered. **Policies:** Meal service available on campus. **Housing:** Coed dorms, special housing for disabled, apartments, fraternity/sorority housing available. $150 nonrefundable deposit. Pets allowed in dorm rooms. **Activities:** Bands, campus ministries, choral groups, dance, drama, film society, international student organizations, literary magazine, music ensembles, musical theater, opera, radio station, student government, student newspaper, symphony orchestra, student public interest research group, black cultural affairs board, United Indian Students in Higher Education, women's union, outdoor program, disabled student union, Hispanic student union.

Athletics. NCAA. **Intercollegiate:** Baseball M, basketball, cross-country, football (tackle) M, golf W, soccer W, softball W, tennis, track and field, volleyball W. **Intramural:** Archery, basketball, football (tackle) M, golf, racquetball, soccer W, softball, volleyball. **Team name:** Vikings.

Student services. Adult student services, alcohol/substance abuse counseling, chaplain/spiritual director, career counseling, student employment services, financial aid counseling, health services, legal services, minority student services, on-campus daycare, personal counseling, placement for graduates, veterans' counselor, women's services. **Physically disabled:** Services for visually, speech, hearing impaired.

Contact. E-mail: admissions@pdx.edu
Phone: (503) 725-3511 Toll-free number: (800) 547-8887 ext. 3511
Fax: (503) 725-5525
Agnes Hoffman, Vice Provost for Enrollment Management, Portland State University, PO Box 751-ADM, Portland, OR 97207-0751

Reed College
Portland, Oregon
www.reed.edu

CB member
CB code: 4654

- Private 4-year liberal arts college
- Residential campus in very large city
- 1,426 degree-seeking undergraduates: 54% women, 2% African American, 6% Asian American, 8% Hispanic American, 6% international
- 17 degree-seeking graduate students
- 40% of applicants admitted
- SAT or ACT (ACT writing optional), application essay required
- 79% graduate within 6 years

General. Founded in 1909. Regionally accredited. **Degrees:** 328 bachelor's awarded; master's offered. **Location:** 5 miles from downtown. **Calendar:** Semester. **Full-time faculty:** 140 total. **Part-time faculty:** 13 total. **Class size:** 76% < 20, 19% 20-39, 1% 40-49, 2% 50-99, 2% >100. **Special facilities:** Nuclear research reactor, wildlife refuge, fish ladder.

Freshman class profile. 3,059 applied, 1,219 admitted, 374 enrolled.

Mid 50% test scores			
SAT critical reading:	670-750	GPA 2.0-2.99:	1%
SAT math:	630-720	Rank in top quarter:	90%
SAT writing:	650-740	Rank in top tenth:	65%
ACT composite:	29-33	Return as sophomores:	92%
GPA 3.75 or higher:	69%	Out-of-state:	91%
GPA 3.50-3.74:	19%	Live on campus:	99%
GPA 3.0-3.49:	11%	International:	6%

Basis for selection. Academic achievement, essay, recommendations, test scores most important. Qualities of character, such as motivation, intellectual curiosity, individual responsibility, social consciousness are important. SAT

Subject Tests recommended. Interview recommended. **Home schooled:** Transcript of courses and grades, letter of recommendation (nonparent) required. High school diploma waived in some cases. Must be above age of compulsory education in home state, submit writing sample, essay.

High school preparation. College-preparatory program recommended. Recommended units include English 4, mathematics 3, social studies 1, history 3, science 3 and foreign language 3.

2011-2012 Annual costs. Tuition/fees: $42,800. Room/board: $11,050. Books/supplies: $950. Personal expenses: $900.

2011-2012 Financial aid. All financial aid based on need. 226 full-time freshmen applied for aid; 178 were judged to have need; 178 of these received aid. Average need met was 100%. Average scholarship/grant was $36,321; average loan $2,890. 87% of total undergraduate aid awarded as scholarships/grants, 13% as loans/jobs. **Additional information:** College meets demonstrated need of continuing students who have attended Reed minimum of 2 semesters, who file financial aid applications on time, and who maintain satisfactory academic progress. Institutional aid consideration is for total of 8 semesters.

Application procedures. Admission: Closing date 1/15 (postmark date). $50 fee, may be waived for applicants with need. Admission notification by 4/1. Must reply by May 1 or within 2 week(s) if notified thereafter. **Financial aid:** Closing date 2/1. FAFSA, CSS PROFILE required. Applicants notified by 4/1; must reply by 5/1 or within 2 week(s) of notification.

Academics. All students take a 1-year course in the humanities. After declaring their major, students must pass a junior qualifying examination prior to senior year. Seniors engage in a 1-year research project in their major field writing a senior thesis and orally defending it before a committee of faculty members. **Special study options:** Combined bachelor's/graduate degree, cross-registration, double major, dual enrollment of high school students, exchange student, independent study, internships, liberal arts/career combination, study abroad. Computer science program with University of Washington; engineering arrangement with California Institute of Technology, Columbia University School of Engineering and Applied Sciences, Rensselaer Polytechnic Institute; forestry-environmental sciences degree arrangement with Nicholas School of the Environment of Duke University; joint 5-year art program with Pacific Northwest College of Art. **Credit/placement by examination:** AP, CLEP, IB, institutional tests. 30 credit hours maximum toward bachelor's degree. **Support services:** Learning center, study skills assistance, tutoring, writing center.

Majors. Area/ethnic studies: American. **Biology:** General, biochemistry, molecular. **Conservation:** Environmental studies. **English:** Creative writing, English lit. **Foreign languages:** Chinese, classics, comparative lit, French, German, linguistics, Russian, Spanish. **History:** General. **Math:** General. **Philosophy/religion:** Philosophy, religion. **Physical sciences:** Chemistry, physics. **Psychology:** General. **Social sciences:** Anthropology, economics, international relations, political science, sociology. **Visual/performing arts:** Art, dramatic, music.

Most popular majors. Biology 10%, English 9%, foreign language 15%, history 8%, philosophy/religious studies 8%, physical sciences 7%, psychology 10%, social sciences 20%.

Computing on campus. 434 workstations in dormitories, library, computer center, student center. Dormitories wired for high-speed internet access and linked to campus network. Commuter students can connect to campus network. Online course registration, online library, helpline, repair service, student web hosting, wireless network available.

Student life. Freshman orientation: Mandatory. Preregistration for classes offered. Held 5 days before start of classes. **Policies:** Honor code in effect. First-year students required to live on campus. **Housing:** Guaranteed on-campus for freshmen. Coed dorms, special housing for disabled, apartments, cooperative housing, wellness housing available. $100 partly refundable deposit, deadline 6/15. Chinese, French, German, Russian, and Spanish language houses available for upper division students. **Activities:** Campus ministries, choral groups, dance, drama, film society, international student organizations, literary magazine, music ensembles, Model UN, radio station, student government, student newspaper, symphony orchestra, Christian Fellowship, Jewish student union, women's center, environmental coalition, politically active student groups, volunteer tutoring, language and outing clubs, poetry forum.

Athletics. Intramural: Archery, badminton, basketball M, equestrian, fencing, golf, judo, rowing (crew), rugby, sailing, skiing, soccer, softball, squash, swimming, tennis, volleyball. **Team name:** Griffins.

Student services. Adult student services, alcohol/substance abuse counseling, career counseling, student employment services, financial aid counseling, health services, minority student services, personal counseling, placement for graduates. **Physically disabled:** Services for visually, speech, hearing impaired.

Contact. E-mail: admission@reed.edu
Phone: (503) 777-7511 Toll-free number: (800) 547-4750
Fax: (503) 777-7553
Keith Todd, Dean of Admission, Reed College, 3203 SE Woodstock Boulevard, Portland, OR 97202-8199

Southern Oregon University
Ashland, Oregon   CB member
www.sou.edu   CB code: 4702

- Public 4-year university and liberal arts college
- Residential campus in large town
- 4,802 degree-seeking undergraduates: 20% part-time, 56% women, 2% African American, 2% Asian American, 8% Hispanic American, 2% Native American, 2% international
- 477 degree-seeking graduate students
- 94% of applicants admitted
- SAT or ACT (ACT writing recommended), application essay required

General. Founded in 1926. Regionally accredited. Designated by National Aeronautics and Space Administration to cooperate in NASA-directed joint space research by undergraduates. **Degrees:** 736 bachelor's awarded; master's offered. **ROTC:** Army. **Location:** 180 miles from Eugene, 285 miles from Portland. **Calendar:** Quarter, extensive summer session. **Full-time faculty:** 203 total; 82% have terminal degrees, 13% minority, 41% women. **Part-time faculty:** 143 total; 5% minority, 48% women. **Class size:** 46% < 20, 46% 20-39, 4% 40-49, 3% 50-99, less than 1% >100. **Special facilities:** Herbarium, U.S. Fish and Wildlife forensics laboratory, public radio network studios, preschool and kindergarten, community television studio, center for visual arts, biotechnology center, institute for environmental economic and civic studies.

Freshman class profile. 1,447 applied, 1,356 admitted, 697 enrolled.

Mid 50% test scores			
SAT critical reading:	450-590	GPA 3.0-3.49:	39%
SAT math:	440-560	GPA 2.0-2.99:	32%
SAT writing:	420-550	Return as sophomores:	69%
ACT composite:	19-25	Out-of-state:	37%
GPA 3.75 or higher:	15%	Live on campus:	79%
GPA 3.50-3.74:	14%	International:	2%

Basis for selection. Admission based on 2.75 GPA from regionally accredited high school, 21 ACT, 1010 SAT (exclusive of Writing), and 14 required high school academic units. Requests for special admission for undergraduates reviewed individually. **Home schooled:** 1010 combined scores on SAT Critical Reading and Math, 470 on SAT Writing, and 2 SAT Subject Tests (Math Level I or Math Level II and one other subject area of student's choice) required.

High school preparation. College-preparatory program required. 15 units required. Required units include English 4, mathematics 3, social studies 3, science 2 (laboratory 1) and foreign language 2.

2011-2012 Annual costs. Tuition/fees: $7,215; $20,490 out-of-state. Room/board: $9,918. Books/supplies: $1,155. Personal expenses: $2,475.

Financial aid. Non-need-based: Scholarships awarded for academics, alumni affiliation, art, athletics, leadership, minority status, music/drama, religious affiliation, state residency.

Application procedures. Admission: Priority date 2/15; no deadline. $50 fee, may be waived for applicants with need. Admission notification on a rolling basis beginning on or about 9/15. **Financial aid:** No deadline. FAFSA required. Applicants notified on a rolling basis starting 3/1; must reply within 2 week(s) of notification.

Academics. Special study options: Accelerated study, combined bachelor's/graduate degree, cross-registration, distance learning, double major, dual enrollment of high school students, ESL, exchange student, honors, independent study, internships, student-designed major, study abroad, teacher certification program. **Credit/placement by examination:** AP, CLEP, IB, institutional tests. 24 credit hours maximum toward bachelor's degree. **Support services:** Learning center, reduced course load, remedial instruction, study skills assistance, tutoring, writing center.

Majors. Biology: General. **Business:** General, accounting, business admin, hospitality admin, marketing. **Communications:** Communications/speech/rhetoric, journalism, public relations. **Computer science:** General, computer science, programming, security. **Conservation:** Environmental studies. **Education:** General. **English:** English lit, rhetoric/composition. **Foreign languages:** General, Spanish. **Health services:** Athletic training, nursing (RN), predental, premedicine, preop/surgical nursing, prepharmacy, preveterinary.

History: General. **Math:** General. **Parks/recreation:** Health/fitness, sports admin. **Physical sciences:** Chemistry, geology, physics. **Protective services:** Criminal justice, law enforcement admin, police science. **Psychology:** General. **Social sciences:** General, anthropology, criminology, economics, geography, political science, sociology. **Visual/performing arts:** Art, dramatic, music, music management.

Most popular majors. Business/marketing 18%, communications/journalism 7%, education 9%, psychology 9%, security/protective services 10%, social sciences 8%, visual/performing arts 12%.

Computing on campus. 750 workstations in dormitories, library, computer center, student center. Dormitories wired for high-speed internet access and linked to campus network. Commuter students can connect to campus network. Online course registration, online library, helpline, student web hosting, wireless network available.

Student life. Freshman orientation: Mandatory. Preregistration for classes offered. Early registration in July; orientation few days before start of classes. **Housing:** Guaranteed on-campus for freshmen. Coed dorms, special housing for disabled, apartments, wellness housing available. $50 deposit. Special quiet, nonsmoking, older student or freshmen residence halls available. **Activities:** Bands, campus ministries, choral groups, dance, drama, film society, international student organizations, literary magazine, music ensembles, musical theater, opera, radio station, student government, student newspaper, symphony orchestra, TV station, 100 clubs available.

Athletics. NAIA. **Intercollegiate:** Basketball, cross-country, football (tackle) M, soccer W, softball W, tennis W, track and field, volleyball W, wrestling M. **Intramural:** Badminton, baseball M, basketball, bowling, golf, racquetball, rugby, sailing, skiing, soccer, softball, swimming, table tennis, tennis, track and field, volleyball, water polo. **Team name:** Raiders.

Student services. Adult student services, alcohol/substance abuse counseling, career counseling, services for economically disadvantaged, student employment services, financial aid counseling, health services, legal services, minority student services, on-campus daycare, personal counseling, placement for graduates, veterans' counselor, women's services. **Physically disabled:** Services for visually, speech, hearing impaired.

Contact. E-mail: admissions@sou.edu
Phone: (541) 552-6411 Toll-free number: (800) 482-7672 ext. 6411
Fax: (541) 552-8403
Mark Bottorff, Director of Admissions, Southern Oregon University, 1250 Siskiyou Boulevard, Ashland, OR 97520-5032

University of Oregon
Eugene, Oregon
www.uoregon.edu

CB member
CB code: 4846

- Public 4-year university
- Residential campus in small city
- 20,248 degree-seeking undergraduates: 8% part-time, 52% women, 2% African American, 5% Asian American, 6% Hispanic American, 1% Native American, 8% international
- 3,478 degree-seeking graduate students
- 73% of applicants admitted
- SAT or ACT with writing, application essay required
- 67% graduate within 6 years; 28% enter graduate study

General. Founded in 1876. Regionally accredited. **Degrees:** 4,202 bachelor's awarded; master's, professional, doctoral offered. **ROTC:** Army, Air Force. **Location:** 110 miles from Portland. **Calendar:** Quarter, extensive summer session. **Full-time faculty:** 1,002 total; 91% have terminal degrees, 16% minority, 44% women. **Part-time faculty:** 443 total; 78% have terminal degrees, 14% minority, 50% women. **Class size:** 37% < 20, 41% 20-39, 5% 40-49, 10% 50-99, 7% >100. **Special facilities:** Art museum, natural and cultural history museum, sports marketing center, entrepreneurship center, Many Nations Longhouse, green chemistry laboratory, instrumentation center, computer music center, mountain observatory, marine biology institute.

Freshman class profile. 23,012 applied, 16,790 admitted, 4,167 enrolled.

Mid 50% test scores			
SAT critical reading:	490-610	Rank in top tenth:	28%
SAT math:	500-610	End year in good standing:	88%
GPA 3.75 or higher:	31%	Return as sophomores:	86%
GPA 3.50-3.74:	28%	Out-of-state:	45%
GPA 3.0-3.49:	38%	Live on campus:	80%
GPA 2.0-2.99:	3%	International:	6%
Rank in top quarter:	63%	Fraternities:	15%
		Sororities:	18%

Basis for selection. Standard admissions based on 3.0 GPA, graduation from accredited high school, C- or higher in 15 college preparatory courses, submission of SAT or ACT scores, and application essay. Applications will be evaluated based on strength of academic course work, grades earned, grade trend, class rank, standardized test scores, senior course load, academic motivation as demonstrated in application essay, extracurricular activities ability to enhance the diversity of the university, academic potential, and special talents. Low test scores will not keep students from being admitted, however, test submission is required. Applicants to architecture or interior architecture must submit SAT Reasoning Test or ACT scores regardless of class level. Audition required for music programs. Portfolio required for arts, architecture, and interior architecture programs. **Home schooled:** Must submit SAT with a minimum score of 1540 for critical reading, mathematics and writing scores combined or submit the ACT with optional writing component with a minimum score of 22. SAT Subject Tests in Math I or II, and a second test of student's choice in a subject other than math required. Must earn a minimum score of 470 on each of the two tests, with a total score of at least 940. Must demonstrate proficiency in second language; standardized test strongly recommended to meet second language proficiency requirements. **Learning Disabled:** If student does not meet admission requirements and has self-identified a documented disability, a secondary review will take place by disability review committee.

High school preparation. College-preparatory program required. 15 units required; 16 recommended. Required and recommended units include English 4, mathematics 3, social studies 3, science 3 (laboratory 1) and foreign language 2.

2011-2012 Annual costs. Tuition/fees: $8,789; $27,653 out-of-state. Room/board: $9,801. Books/supplies: $1,050. Personal expenses: $2,412.

2011-2012 Financial aid. Need-based: 2,899 full-time freshmen applied for aid; 2,005 were judged to have need; 1,822 of these received aid. Average need met was 44%. Average scholarship/grant was $6,044; average loan $4,065. 44% of total undergraduate aid awarded as scholarships/grants, 56% as loans/jobs. **Non-need-based:** Awarded to 4,104 full-time undergraduates, including 1,301 freshmen. Scholarships awarded for academics, athletics, leadership, minority status, music/drama, ROTC, state residency.

Application procedures. Admission: Priority date 11/1; deadline 1/15 (postmark date). $50 fee. Admission notification on a rolling basis beginning on or about 9/15. Must reply by May 1 or within 4 week(s) if notified thereafter. Additional academic deadlines: Architecture, 1/15 (priority deadline, 12/1); Interior Architecture, 1/15; Digital Arts, 2/1; Landscape Architecture, 1/15; Art, 2/1; Product Design, 1/15; School of Music and Dance, 1/15; Clark Honors College, 11/1 early notification, 1/15 standard notification. **Financial aid:** Priority date 3/1; no closing date. FAFSA required. Applicants notified on a rolling basis starting 4/15; must reply within 4 week(s) of notification.

Academics. Special study options: Cross-registration, distance learning, double major, ESL, exchange student, honors, independent study, internships, liberal arts/career combination, semester at sea, student-designed major, study abroad, teacher certification program. Dual enrollment program with Lane Community College and Southwestern Oregon Community College. Professional distinctions program (certificate program) in which students gain direct professional preparation through internships, special courses, professional mentor, and development of electronic resume and portfolio. **Credit/placement by examination:** AP, CLEP, IB, SAT, ACT, institutional tests. For some courses, departments have authorized the use of subject examinations prepared by the College Level Examination Program (CLEP). Once a student is admitted, successfully completed CLEP subject exams are accepted as transfer credit. **Support services:** Learning center, remedial instruction, study skills assistance, tutoring.

Honors college/program. Admissions based on short self-introduction, admission essay, 2 teacher evaluations, description of accomplishments, SAT or ACT, GPA, depth and breadth of high school curriculum, and ways in which applicant will add to diversity of honors community. Around 200 freshmen admitted each year.

Majors. Architecture: Architecture, interior, landscape. **Area/ethnic studies:** General, Asian, Latin American, Russian/Slavic, women's. **Biology:** General, biochemistry, marine, physiology. **Business:** General, accounting. **Communications:** Advertising, journalism, media studies, public relations. **Computer sciences:** General. **Conservation:** Environmental science, environmental studies. **Education:** General, music. **English:** English lit. **Foreign languages:** Chinese, classics, comparative lit, French, German, Italian, Japanese, linguistics, Romance, Spanish. **Health services:** Communication disorders. **History:** General. **Human services:** General. **Liberal arts:** Humanities. **Math:** General. **Philosophy/religion:** Judaic, philosophy, religion. **Physical sciences:** Chemistry, geology, physics. **Psychology:** General. **Social sciences:** General, anthropology, economics, geography, political science, sociology. **Visual/performing arts:** Art, art history/conservation, ceramics, cinematography, dance, digital arts, dramatic, fiber arts, jazz, metal/jewelry, music, music performance, music theory/composition, painting, photography, printmaking, sculpture, studio arts.

Most popular majors. Biology 6%, business/marketing 13%, communications/journalism 8%, foreign language 7%, psychology 7%, social sciences 22%, visual/performing arts 7%.

Computing on campus. 1,237 workstations in dormitories, library, computer center, student center. Dormitories wired for high-speed internet access and linked to campus network. Commuter students can connect to campus network. Online course registration, online library, helpline, repair service, student web hosting, wireless network available.

Student life. Freshman orientation: Mandatory. Preregistration for classes offered. Two-day session held during summer for students and family members. **Housing:** Coed dorms, apartments, cooperative housing, fraternity/sorority housing, wellness housing available. $250 partly refundable deposit. Residence halls have separate men's and women's floors, family housing available. **Activities:** Bands, campus ministries, choral groups, dance, drama, film society, international student organizations, literary magazine, music ensembles, musical theater, opera, radio station, student government, student newspaper, symphony orchestra, Jewish student union, Muslim student association, College Democrats, College Republicans, black student union, Asian/Pacific American student union, non-traditional student union, Coalition Against Environmental Racism, service based fraternities and sororities.

Athletics. NCAA. **Intercollegiate:** Baseball M, basketball, cross-country, football (tackle) M, golf, lacrosse W, soccer W, softball W, tennis, track and field, volleyball W. **Intramural:** Badminton, basketball, cross-country, football (non-tackle), golf, racquetball, soccer, softball, swimming, tennis, track and field, volleyball. **Team name:** Ducks.

Student services. Adult student services, alcohol/substance abuse counseling, career counseling, services for economically disadvantaged, student employment services, financial aid counseling, health services, legal services, minority student services, on-campus daycare, personal counseling, veterans' counselor, women's services. **Physically disabled:** Services for visually, speech, hearing impaired.

Contact. E-mail: uoadmit@uoregon.edu
Phone: (541) 346-3201 Toll-free number: (800) 232-3825
Fax: (541) 346-5815
Brian Henley, Director of Admissions, University of Oregon, 1217 University of Oregon, Eugene, OR 97403-1217

University of Phoenix: Oregon
Tigard, Oregon
www.phoenix.edu   **CB code: 7856**

- For-profit 4-year university
- Commuter campus in very large city
- 1,020 degree-seeking undergraduates

General. Regionally accredited. **Degrees:** 213 bachelor's awarded; master's offered. **Calendar:** Differs by program. **Full-time faculty:** 21 total. **Part-time faculty:** 215 total.

Basis for selection. Open admission.

2011-2012 Annual costs. Estimated costs as of August 2011: per-credit-hour charge, $420 to $450, depending upon level and course of study; electronic course materials fee, $95, if applicable. Book and material charges may vary by course and program. All fees are subject to change.

Application procedures. Admission: No deadline. No application fee. **Financial aid:** No deadline.

Academics. Credit/placement by examination: AP, CLEP.

Majors. Business: Accounting, business admin, credit management, human resources, marketing, operations. **Computer sciences:** General, programming. **Health services:** Facilities admin. **Human services:** General. **Protective services:** Law enforcement admin. **Psychology:** General.

Contact. Marc Booker, Director of Admission and Evaluation, University of Phoenix: Oregon, 13221 Southwest 68th Parkway, Suite 500, Tigard, OR 97223-8328

University of Portland
Portland, Oregon   **CB member**
www.up.edu   **CB code: 4847**

- Private 4-year university affiliated with Roman Catholic Church
- Residential campus in large city

- 3,332 degree-seeking undergraduates: 1% part-time, 60% women, 1% African American, 9% Asian American, 8% Hispanic American, 2% international
- 555 degree-seeking graduate students
- 64% of applicants admitted
- SAT or ACT (ACT writing optional), application essay required
- 76% graduate within 6 years; 18% enter graduate study

General. Founded in 1901. Regionally accredited. **Degrees:** 759 bachelor's awarded; master's, professional offered. **ROTC:** Army, Air Force. **Calendar:** Semester, limited summer session. **Full-time faculty:** 205 total; 92% have terminal degrees, 3% minority, 43% women. **Part-time faculty:** 132 total; 4% have terminal degrees, 7% minority, 48% women. **Class size:** 34% < 20, 58% 20-39, 5% 40-49, 3% 50-99.

Freshman class profile. 8,307 applied, 5,300 admitted, 836 enrolled.

Mid 50% test scores			
SAT critical reading:	550-670	Rank in top quarter:	78%
SAT math:	560-650	Rank in top tenth:	46%
GPA 3.75 or higher:	51%	End year in good standing:	98%
GPA 3.50-3.74:	26%	Return as sophomores:	91%
GPA 3.0-3.49:	21%	Out-of-state:	68%
GPA 2.0-2.99:	2%	Live on campus:	96%
		International:	2%

Basis for selection. School achievement record, test scores, counselor recommendation, essay important. **Home schooled:** Transcript of courses and grades required. Interview strongly encouraged.

High school preparation. College-preparatory program recommended. Required and recommended units include English 3-4, mathematics 2-3, social studies 2, history 2, science 2 and academic electives 7. Engineering, math, and some science majors require additional math and science courses.

2011-2012 Annual costs. Tuition/fees: $33,780. Room/board: $9,965. Books/supplies: $1,000. Personal expenses: $800.

2011-2012 Financial aid. Need-based: 724 full-time freshmen applied for aid; 563 were judged to have need; 561 of these received aid. Average need met was 74%. Average scholarship/grant was $21,481; average loan $3,526. 72% of total undergraduate aid awarded as scholarships/grants, 28% as loans/jobs. **Non-need-based:** Awarded to 2,796 full-time undergraduates, including 784 freshmen. Scholarships awarded for academics, athletics, music/drama, religious affiliation, ROTC.

Application procedures. Admission: Closing date 1/15 (postmark date). $50 fee, may be waived for applicants with need. Admission notification on a rolling basis beginning on or about 9/1. Must reply by May 1 or within 2 week(s) if notified thereafter. **Financial aid:** Priority date 3/1; no closing date. FAFSA required. Applicants notified on a rolling basis starting 2/28; must reply within 3 week(s) of notification.

Academics. Special study options: Cross-registration, double major, honors, independent study, internships, liberal arts/career combination, study abroad, teacher certification program, Washington semester. **Credit/placement by examination:** AP, CLEP, IB, institutional tests. 45 credit hours maximum toward bachelor's degree. **Support services:** Learning center, study skills assistance, tutoring, writing center.

Majors. Biology: General. **Business:** Accounting, business admin, finance, international, marketing. **Communications:** Media studies, organizational. **Computer sciences:** Computer science. **Conservation:** Environmental science, environmental studies. **Education:** Elementary, music, secondary. **Engineering:** Civil, computer, electrical, environmental, mechanical. **English:** English lit. **Foreign languages:** French, German, Spanish. **Health services:** Nursing (RN). **History:** General. **Human services:** Social work. **Math:** General. **Philosophy/religion:** Philosophy. **Physical sciences:** Chemistry, physics. **Psychology:** General. **Social sciences:** Political science, sociology. **Theology:** Theology. **Visual/performing arts:** Dramatic, music, theater arts management.

Most popular majors. Biology 8%, business/marketing 16%, engineering/engineering technologies 11%, foreign language 7%, health sciences 26%.

Computing on campus. 400 workstations in dormitories, library, computer center, student center. Dormitories wired for high-speed internet access and linked to campus network. Commuter students can connect to campus network. Online course registration, online library, helpline, student web hosting, wireless network available.

Student life. Freshman orientation: Available. Preregistration for classes offered. Held 3 days before classes begin. **Policies:** Freshmen not permitted cars on campus. **Housing:** Guaranteed on-campus for freshmen. Coed dorms, single-sex dorms available. $100 nonrefundable deposit, deadline 5/1. **Activities:** Bands, campus ministries, choral groups, dance, drama, film society, international student organizations, literary magazine, music ensembles,

musical theater, radio station, student government, student newspaper, symphony orchestra, volunteer services, black student union, international club, Hawaiian club, Engineers Without Borders, feminist discussion group, Bible study group, Movimiento Estudiantil de Chicanos de Astlan, ecology club, student-led unity garden.

Athletics. NCAA. **Intercollegiate:** Baseball M, basketball, cross-country, rowing (crew), soccer, tennis, track and field, volleyball W. **Intramural:** Basketball, bowling, football (non-tackle), skiing, soccer, softball, swimming, table tennis, tennis, volleyball, weight lifting. **Team name:** Pilots.

Student services. Adult student services, alcohol/substance abuse counseling, chaplain/spiritual director, career counseling, student employment services, financial aid counseling, health services, personal counseling, placement for graduates, veterans' counselor. **Physically disabled:** Services for visually, speech, hearing impaired.

Contact. E-mail: admissions@up.edu
Phone: (503) 943-7147 Toll-free number: (888) 627-5601
Fax: (503) 943-7315
Jason McDonald, Dean of Admissions, University of Portland, 5000 North Willamette Boulevard, Portland, OR 97203-5798

Warner Pacific College
Portland, Oregon
www.warnerpacific.edu   CB code: 4595

- Private 4-year liberal arts college affiliated with Church of God
- Residential campus in very large city
- 1,551 degree-seeking undergraduates
- 61% of applicants admitted
- SAT or ACT (ACT writing recommended), application essay required

General. Founded in 1937. Regionally accredited. **Degrees:** 298 bachelor's, 59 associate awarded; master's offered. **ROTC:** Army, Naval, Air Force. **Location:** 44 miles from Salem; 10 miles from Vancouver, Washington. **Calendar:** Semester, limited summer session. **Full-time faculty:** 29 total. **Part-time faculty:** 110 total. **Class size:** 80% < 20, 19% 20-39, 1% 40-49. **Special facilities:** Field station for wildlife observation and study.

Freshman class profile. 1,090 applied, 665 admitted, 100 enrolled.

Mid 50% test scores			
SAT critical reading:	430-550	GPA 3.50-3.74:	17%
SAT math:	450-540	GPA 3.0-3.49:	34%
SAT writing:	420-520	GPA 2.0-2.99:	34%
ACT composite:	16-22	Out-of-state:	38%
GPA 3.75 or higher:	15%	Live on campus:	69%

Basis for selection. High school GPA important; test scores, essay, and signed lifestyle agreement required. **Home schooled:** Statement describing home school structure and mission, transcript of courses and grades, state high school equivalency certificate, interview, letter of recommendation (non-parent) required. **Learning Disabled:** Students are extended extra services to assist them to be successful.

High school preparation. 11 units recommended. Recommended units include English 4, mathematics 2, social studies 3 and science 2.

2011-2012 Annual costs. Tuition/fees: $18,290. Room/board: $7,320. Books/supplies: $1,100. Personal expenses: $1,634.

Financial aid. **Non-need-based:** Scholarships awarded for academics, alumni affiliation, athletics, leadership, minority status, music/drama, religious affiliation.

Application procedures. **Admission:** No deadline. $50 fee, may be waived for applicants with need. Admission notification on a rolling basis. **Financial aid:** Priority date 3/1, closing date 8/1. FAFSA required. Applicants notified on a rolling basis starting 3/1; must reply within 2 week(s) of notification.

Academics. **Special study options:** Accelerated study, cooperative education, cross-registration, double major, independent study, internships, liberal arts/career combination, student-designed major, study abroad, teacher certification program, Washington semester. 2-2 nursing program with Walla Walla School of Nursing. **Credit/placement by examination:** AP, CLEP, institutional tests. 30 credit hours maximum toward associate degree, 30 toward bachelor's. No more than 45 total alternative credits (maximum 30 of any one type). **Support services:** Learning center, reduced course load, remedial instruction, study skills assistance, tutoring.

Majors. **Area/ethnic studies:** American. **Biology:** General. **Business:** Business admin, international. **Communications:** Communications/speech/rhetoric. **Education:** Elementary, music, physical, secondary. **English:** English lit. **History:** General. **Human services:** Social work. **Liberal arts:** Arts/sciences. **Parks/recreation:** Exercise sciences, health/fitness, sports admin. **Philosophy/religion:** Religion. **Physical sciences:** General. **Psychology:** General, developmental. **Social sciences:** General, urban studies. **Theology:** Preministerial. **Visual/performing arts:** Music. **Work/family studies:** Family studies.

Most popular majors. Business/marketing 30%, education 15%, family/consumer sciences 39%.

Computing on campus. 30 workstations in dormitories, library, computer center. Dormitories wired for high-speed internet access and linked to campus network. Online library, helpline, wireless network available.

Student life. **Freshman orientation:** Available. Preregistration for classes offered. **Policies:** Religious observance required. **Housing:** Guaranteed on-campus for freshmen. Single-sex dorms, special housing for disabled, apartments available. $100 deposit. **Activities:** Bands, campus ministries, choral groups, drama, literary magazine, music ensembles, student government.

Athletics. NAIA, NCCAA. **Intercollegiate:** Basketball, cross-country, golf, soccer, track and field, volleyball W. **Intramural:** Badminton, basketball, football (non-tackle), volleyball. **Team name:** Knights.

Student services. Adult student services, chaplain/spiritual director, career counseling, student employment services, financial aid counseling, health services, minority student services, personal counseling, placement for graduates.

Contact. E-mail: admissions@warnerpacific.edu
Phone: (503) 517-1020 Toll-free number: (800) 804-1510
Fax: (503) 517-1352
Shannon Mackey, Executive Director of Enrollment Management, Warner Pacific College, 2219 SE 68th Avenue, Portland, OR 97215-4026

Western Oregon University
Monmouth, Oregon   CB member
www.wou.edu   CB code: 4585

- Public 4-year liberal arts and teachers college
- Residential campus in small town
- 5,370 degree-seeking undergraduates: 13% part-time, 59% women, 3% African American, 2% Asian American, 11% Hispanic American, 2% Native American, 5% international
- 678 degree-seeking graduate students
- 88% of applicants admitted
- SAT or ACT with writing required
- 38% graduate within 6 years

General. Founded in 1856. Regionally accredited. **Degrees:** 843 bachelor's awarded; master's offered. **ROTC:** Army, Naval, Air Force. **Location:** 15 miles from Salem, 60 miles from Portland. **Calendar:** Quarter, limited summer session. **Full-time faculty:** 203 total; 84% have terminal degrees, 13% minority, 46% women. **Part-time faculty:** 241 total; 4% have terminal degrees, 11% minority, 53% women. **Class size:** 49% < 20, 41% 20-39, 6% 40-49, 3% 50-99, less than 1% >100. **Special facilities:** Arctic museum, teaching research institute, early childhood and training development center.

Freshman class profile. 2,693 applied, 2,362 admitted, 1,011 enrolled.

Mid 50% test scores			
SAT critical reading:	410-490	GPA 3.0-3.49:	37%
SAT math:	420-530	GPA 2.0-2.99:	34%
SAT writing:	400-500	Rank in top quarter:	27%
ACT composite:	16-21	Rank in top tenth:	9%
GPA 3.75 or higher:	13%	Return as sophomores:	68%
GPA 3.50-3.74:	16%	Out-of-state:	12%
		Live on campus:	100%

Basis for selection. 2.75 GPA required. 1000 SAT (exclusive of Writing) strongly recommended, but only used in admissions decision if applicant does not meet GPA or college preparation requirements. If applicant does not meet academic requirements, other evidence of potential in the form of interviews, portfolios, auditions, and essays considered. **Home schooled:** 1000 SAT (exclusive of Writing) or 21 ACT or 1410 SAT Subject Tests combined score in 3 subjects required; must take 1 SAT Reasoning Test, 1 SAT Subject Test in math, and second exam in foreign language.

High school preparation. College-preparatory program required. 14 units required. Required and recommended units include English 4, mathematics 3, social studies 2, history 1, science 2 (laboratory 1) and foreign language 2.

2011-2012 Annual costs. Tuition/fees: $8,076; $19,986 out-of-state. Resident tuition reflects WOU "Promise 2010," a four-year tuition commitment for resident undergraduate students. Nonresident rate shown is for non-Promise students. Room/board: $8,620. Books/supplies: $1,125. Personal expenses: $2,475.

2011-2012 Financial aid. **Need-based:** Average need met was 61%. Average scholarship/grant was $7,263; average loan $3,310. 40% of total undergraduate aid awarded as scholarships/grants, 60% as loans/jobs. **Non-need-based:** Scholarships awarded for academics, alumni affiliation, art, athletics, leadership, music/drama.

Application procedures. **Admission:** No deadline. $50 fee. Admission notification on a rolling basis. **Financial aid:** Priority date 2/1; no closing date. FAFSA required. Applicants notified on a rolling basis starting 2/28; must reply within 3 week(s) of notification.

Academics. **Special study options:** Combined bachelor's/graduate degree, distance learning, double major, dual enrollment of high school students, ESL, exchange student, honors, independent study, internships, student-designed major, study abroad, teacher certification program. Pre-professional studies, interdisciplinary studies, non-degree licensure programs, service learning and career development. **Credit/placement by examination:** AP, CLEP, IB, SAT, ACT, institutional tests. 48 credit hours maximum toward bachelor's degree. **Support services:** Learning center, remedial instruction, study skills assistance, tutoring, writing center.

Majors. **Area/ethnic studies:** Deaf. **Biology:** General. **Business:** General. **Communications:** Communications/speech/rhetoric. **Computer sciences:** General. **Education:** General, biology, chemistry, educational technology, elementary, health, middle, multi-level teacher, physical, reading, science, secondary, social studies, Spanish. **English:** English lit, rhetoric/composition. **Foreign languages:** Sign language interpretation, Spanish. **Health services:** Nursing (RN). **History:** General. **Human services:** General. **Liberal arts:** Arts/sciences, humanities. **Math:** General. **Philosophy/religion:** Philosophy. **Physical sciences:** Chemistry, geology, planetary. **Protective services:** Corrections, fire services admin, law enforcement admin. **Psychology:** General, geropsychology. **Social sciences:** General, anthropology, economics, geography, international relations, political science, sociology. **Visual/performing arts:** General, art, dance, dramatic, music, studio arts, theater arts management.

Most popular majors. Business/marketing 15%, education 11%, interdisciplinary studies 10%, parks/recreation 6%, psychology 10%, social sciences 8%.

Computing on campus. 411 workstations in dormitories, library, computer center, student center. Dormitories wired for high-speed internet access and linked to campus network. Commuter students can connect to campus network. Online course registration, online library, helpline, repair service, wireless network available.

Student life. **Freshman orientation:** Available. Preregistration for classes offered. Held last weekend in June and 2nd and 3rd weekends in July on Friday and/or Saturday. **Policies:** No alcohol permitted in residence halls. **Housing:** Guaranteed on-campus for freshmen. Coed dorms, special housing for disabled, apartments, wellness housing available. Family housing, housing by learning communities, community living options available. **Activities:** Bands, campus ministries, choral groups, dance, drama, international student organizations, literary magazine, music ensembles, Model UN, musical theater, radio station, student government, student newspaper, symphony orchestra, TV station, Baptist student union, Big Brother/Big Sister, multicultural student union, Campus Crusade for Christ, Circle K, environmental action committee.

Athletics. NCAA. **Intercollegiate:** Baseball M, basketball, cheerleading, cross-country, football (tackle) M, soccer W, softball W, track and field, volleyball W. **Intramural:** Basketball, bowling, cross-country, football (non-tackle), football (tackle) M, golf, racquetball, rifle, skiing, soccer, softball, swimming, table tennis, tennis, track and field, triathlon, volleyball, water polo, weight lifting, wrestling. **Team name:** Wolves.

Student services. Adult student services, alcohol/substance abuse counseling, chaplain/spiritual director, career counseling, services for economically disadvantaged, student employment services, financial aid counseling, health services, minority student services, on-campus daycare, personal counseling, placement for graduates, veterans' counselor, women's services. **Physically disabled:** Services for visually, speech, hearing impaired.

Contact. E-mail: wolfgram@wou.edu
Phone: (503) 838-8211 Toll-free number: (877) 877-1593
Fax: (503) 838-8067
Rob Findtner, Director of Admissions, Western Oregon University, 345 North Monmouth Avenue, Monmouth, OR 97361

Willamette University

Salem, Oregon
www.willamette.edu

CB member
CB code: 4954

- Private 4-year university and liberal arts college affiliated with United Methodist Church
- Residential campus in small city
- 1,967 degree-seeking undergraduates: 1% part-time, 56% women, 2% African American, 6% Asian American, 6% Hispanic American, 1% Native American, 1% international
- 824 degree-seeking graduate students
- 57% of applicants admitted
- SAT or ACT with writing, application essay required
- 77% graduate within 6 years; 27% enter graduate study

General. Founded in 1842. Regionally accredited. Sister school to Tokyo International University of America. **Degrees:** 404 bachelor's awarded; master's, professional offered. **ROTC:** Army, Air Force. **Location:** 45 miles from Portland. **Calendar:** Semester. **Full-time faculty:** 246 total; 94% have terminal degrees, 13% minority, 47% women. **Part-time faculty:** 91 total; 85% have terminal degrees, 8% minority, 48% women. **Class size:** 67% < 20, 32% 20-39, less than 1% 40-49. **Special facilities:** Art museum, American headquarters for International Debate Education Association, papers and memorabilia of Senator Mark O. Hatfield, botanical gardens, Japanese gardens, rose gardens, rural retreat center, wildlife refuge field station, digital art and music studios, 2 electron microscopes (scanning and transmission), 500 MHz Nuclear Magnetic Resonance spectrometer, 305 acre Zena research forest.

Freshman class profile. 8,175 applied, 4,685 admitted, 617 enrolled.

Mid 50% test scores			
SAT critical reading:	560-670	GPA 2.0-2.99:	6%
SAT math:	540-650	Rank in top quarter:	74%
SAT writing:	540-650	Rank in top tenth:	41%
ACT composite:	26-30	End year in good standing:	92%
GPA 3.75 or higher:	35%	Return as sophomores:	88%
GPA 3.50-3.74:	23%	Out-of-state:	73%
GPA 3.0-3.49:	36%	Live on campus:	97%

Basis for selection. School record most important, followed by test scores, essay, recommendations, school and community activities, and interview. Audition recommended for music, theater programs; portfolio recommended for art program. **Home schooled:** Recommend submission of accredited transcript from governing agency, if available.

High school preparation. College-preparatory program recommended. 20 units recommended. Recommended units include English 4, mathematics 4, social studies 1, history 2, science 3 (laboratory 3), foreign language 4 and academic electives 2.

2011-2012 Annual costs. Tuition/fees: $39,012. Room/board: $9,350. Books/supplies: $900.

2011-2012 Financial aid. **Need-based:** 615 full-time freshmen applied for aid; 404 were judged to have need; 404 of these received aid. Average need met was 87%. Average scholarship/grant was $24,876; average loan $3,684. 76% of total undergraduate aid awarded as scholarships/grants, 24% as loans/jobs. **Non-need-based:** Awarded to 894 full-time undergraduates, including 357 freshmen. Scholarships awarded for academics, alumni affiliation, leadership, minority status, music/drama, religious affiliation.

Application procedures. **Admission:** Priority date 2/1; no deadline. $50 fee, may be waived for applicants with need, free for online applicants. Admission notification on a rolling basis beginning on or about 10/1. Must reply by May 1 or within 2 week(s) if notified thereafter. **Financial aid:** Priority date 2/1; no closing date. FAFSA required. CSS PROFILE recommended of early action applicants. Applicants notified on a rolling basis starting 4/1; must reply by 5/1 or within 2 week(s) of notification.

Academics. **Special study options:** Accelerated study, combined bachelor's/graduate degree, cross-registration, double major, dual enrollment of high school students, exchange student, independent study, internships, student-designed major, study abroad, teacher certification program, urban semester, Washington semester. Interdisciplinary freshman study program, undergraduate research grants, field studies program in ecology in Hawaii, Ecuador, American Southwest, Oregon; 3-2 program, master's degree in management; 3-2 program, bachelor's degree in computer science with Oregon Graduate Institute, University of Oregon; 3-2 program, master's degree in forestry with Duke University. **Credit/placement by examination:** AP, CLEP, IB, institutional tests. 32 credit hours maximum toward bachelor's degree. **Support services:** Reduced course load, study skills assistance, tutoring, writing center.

Majors. Area/ethnic studies: American, Asian, Japanese, Latin American, women's. **Biology:** General. **Computer sciences:** General. **Conservation:** Environmental science. **Education:** Music. **English:** English lit, rhetoric/composition. **Foreign languages:** Classics, comparative lit, French, German, Spanish. **History:** General. **Liberal arts:** Humanities. **Math:** General. **Parks/recreation:** Exercise sciences. **Philosophy/religion:** Philosophy, religion. **Physical sciences:** Chemistry, physics. **Psychology:** General. **Social sciences:** Anthropology, economics, political science, sociology. **Visual/performing arts:** Art history/conservation, dramatic, film/cinema/video, music performance, music theory/composition, piano/keyboard, stringed instruments, studio arts, voice/opera.

Most popular majors. English 8%, foreign language 10%, history 6%, psychology 6%, social sciences 28%, visual/performing arts 7%.

Computing on campus. 400 workstations in dormitories, library, computer center, student center. Dormitories wired for high-speed internet access and linked to campus network. Commuter students can connect to campus network. Online course registration, online library, helpline, repair service, student web hosting, wireless network available.

Student life. Freshman orientation: Mandatory. Preregistration for classes offered. 5 day program held prior to start of semester. **Housing:** Guaranteed on-campus for freshmen. Coed dorms, apartments, fraternity/sorority housing, wellness housing available. $400 nonrefundable deposit, deadline 5/1. Environmental, intensive study residences available. **Activities:** Bands, campus ministries, choral groups, dance, drama, film society, international student organizations, literary magazine, music ensembles, Model UN, musical theater, opera, student government, student newspaper, symphony orchestra, more than 100 student organizations available.

Athletics. NCAA. **Intercollegiate:** Baseball M, basketball, cross-country, football (tackle) M, golf, rowing (crew) W, soccer, softball W, swimming, tennis, track and field, volleyball W. **Intramural:** Badminton, basketball, football (non-tackle), golf, racquetball, soccer, softball, table tennis, tennis, volleyball, weight lifting. **Team name:** Bearcats.

Student services. Alcohol/substance abuse counseling, chaplain/spiritual director, career counseling, student employment services, financial aid counseling, health services, minority student services, personal counseling, veterans' counselor, women's services. **Physically disabled:** Services for visually, speech, hearing impaired.

Contact. E-mail: libarts@willamette.edu
Phone: (503) 370-6303 Toll-free number: (877) 542-2787
Fax: (503) 375-5363
Madeleine Rhyneer, Vice President for Admissions and Financial Aid, Willamette University, 900 State Street, Salem, OR 97301-3922

Pennsylvania

Albright College
Reading, Pennsylvania
www.albright.edu

CB member
CB code: 2004

- Private 4-year liberal arts college affiliated with United Methodist Church
- Residential campus in small city
- 2,304 degree-seeking undergraduates: 57% women, 13% African American, 2% Asian American, 8% Hispanic American, 1% Native American, 3% international
- 23 degree-seeking graduate students
- 43% of applicants admitted
- Application essay required
- 61% graduate within 6 years

General. Founded in 1856. Regionally accredited. **Degrees:** 499 bachelor's awarded; master's offered. **ROTC:** Army. **Location:** 50 miles from Philadelphia. **Calendar:** 4-1-4, limited summer session. **Full-time faculty:** 114 total; 83% have terminal degrees, 13% minority, 47% women. **Part-time faculty:** 52 total; 25% have terminal degrees, 2% minority, 60% women. **Class size:** 60% < 20, 38% 20-39, 2% 40-49, less than 1% 50-99. **Special facilities:** Satellite dish for foreign language program, transmission and scanning electron microscopes, Holocaust resource center, center for local government, center for cultural ecology, center for Latin American studies.

Freshman class profile. 7,060 applied, 3,011 admitted, 517 enrolled.

Mid 50% test scores			
SAT critical reading:	480-570	GPA 2.0-2.99:	37%
SAT math:	480-580	Rank in top quarter:	40%
ACT composite:	21-25	Rank in top tenth:	17%
GPA 3.75 or higher:	16%	Return as sophomores:	74%
GPA 3.50-3.74:	18%	Out-of-state:	38%
GPA 3.0-3.49:	29%	Live on campus:	89%
		International:	3%

Basis for selection. High school performance (with emphasis on difficulty of curriculum pursued), personal statement, and recommendations most important. Community service, extracurricular activity and test scores considered. Interview recommended.

High school preparation. College-preparatory program required. 16 units required; 20 recommended. Required and recommended units include English 4, mathematics 2-3, social studies 2, history 1-2, science 3-4 (laboratory 1-2), foreign language 2-3 and computer science 2. Bachelor of science applicants should have 1 additional unit in science and 1 in math. 2 units of laboratory science recommended.

2011-2012 Annual costs. Tuition/fees: $33,990. Room/board: $9,200. Books/supplies: $1,000. Personal expenses: $1,100.

Financial aid. Non-need-based: Scholarships awarded for academics, alumni affiliation, art, leadership, minority status, music/drama, religious affiliation.

Application procedures. Admission: Priority date 3/1; no deadline. $25 fee, may be waived for applicants with need. Admission notification on a rolling basis beginning on or about 10/1. Must reply by May 1 or within 2 week(s) if notified thereafter. **Financial aid:** Priority date 3/1; no closing date. FAFSA required. Applicants notified on a rolling basis starting 2/15; must reply by 5/1 or within 2 week(s) of notification.

Academics. Flexible curriculum combines liberal arts education with hands-on experiences. Institution emphasizes faculty-student collaboration and has an active undergraduate research program, which also funds summer projects with faculty. **Special study options:** Accelerated study, combined bachelor's/graduate degree, cross-registration, double major, dual enrollment of high school students, ESL, exchange student, honors, independent study, internships, liberal arts/career combination, semester at sea, student-designed major, study abroad, teacher certification program, urban semester, Washington semester. **Credit/placement by examination:** AP, CLEP, IB, institutional tests. 28 credit hours maximum toward bachelor's degree. **Support services:** Learning center, pre-admission summer program, reduced course load, study skills assistance, tutoring, writing center.

Majors. Area/ethnic studies: American, Latin American, women's. **Biology:** General, biochemistry. **Business:** Accounting, business admin, finance, international, marketing. **Communications:** Communications/speech/rhetoric. **Computer sciences:** General, information systems. **Conservation:** General, environmental science, environmental studies. **Education:** Art, early childhood, elementary, secondary, special ed. **English:** English lit. **Foreign languages:** French, Spanish. **Health services:** Predental, premedicine, preveterinary. **History:** General. **Math:** General. **Philosophy/religion:** Philosophy, religion. **Physical sciences:** Chemistry, optics, physics. **Psychology:** General. **Social sciences:** Anthropology, criminology, economics, political science, sociology. **Visual/performing arts:** Dramatic, fashion design, music, studio arts. **Work/family studies:** Clothing/textiles.

Most popular majors. Business/marketing 27%, psychology 14%, social sciences 17%, visual/performing arts 10%.

Computing on campus. 270 workstations in dormitories, library, computer center, student center. Dormitories wired for high-speed internet access and linked to campus network. Online course registration, online library, helpline, wireless network available.

Student life. Freshman orientation: Mandatory. Preregistration for classes offered. Held 4 days prior to start of fall classes. **Policies:** Freshmen not permitted cars on campus. **Housing:** Guaranteed on-campus for all undergraduates. Coed dorms, apartments, wellness housing available. $100 nonrefundable deposit, deadline 6/1. Honors housing, break housing suite, all freshmen housing, all-female floors, all-male floors, single rooms, single-sex suites/apartments/wings. **Activities:** Bands, campus ministries, choral groups, dance, drama, international student organizations, literary magazine, music ensembles, Model UN, musical theater, radio station, student government, student newspaper, TV station, Newman, Hillel, Christian Fellowship, African American society, Asian American society, environmental action group, American Association of University Women, human services organization.

Athletics. NCAA. **Intercollegiate:** Baseball M, basketball, cheerleading, cross-country, field hockey W, football (tackle) M, golf, lacrosse, soccer, softball W, swimming, tennis, track and field, volleyball W. **Intramural:** Basketball, bowling, football (non-tackle), soccer, softball, triathlon, volleyball. **Team name:** Lions.

Student services. Adult student services, chaplain/spiritual director, career counseling, student employment services, financial aid counseling, health services, minority student services, personal counseling, women's services. **Physically disabled:** Services for visually, hearing impaired.

Contact. E-mail: admission@albright.edu
Phone: (610) 921-7700 Toll-free number: (800) 252-1856
Fax: (610) 921-7729
Gregory Eichhorn, Vice-President for Enrollment Management and Dean of Admissions, Albright College, 13th and Bern Streets, Reading, PA 19612-5234

Allegheny College
Meadville, Pennsylvania
www.allegheny.edu

CB member
CB code: 2006

- Private 4-year liberal arts college affiliated with United Methodist Church
- Residential campus in large town
- 2,094 degree-seeking undergraduates: 53% women, 5% African American, 3% Asian American, 5% Hispanic American, 1% international
- 58% of applicants admitted
- SAT or ACT (ACT writing recommended), application essay required
- 80% graduate within 6 years; 34% enter graduate study

General. Founded in 1815. Regionally accredited. **Degrees:** 509 bachelor's awarded. **Location:** 90 miles from Pittsburgh and Cleveland. **Calendar:** Semester, limited summer session. **Full-time faculty:** 164 total; 95% have terminal degrees, 15% minority, 42% women. **Part-time faculty:** 32 total; 19% have terminal degrees, 6% minority, 50% women. **Class size:** 63% < 20, 35% 20-39, 1% 40-49, less than 1% 50-99. **Special facilities:** Planetarium, observatory, Geographic Information Systems learning lab, solid-volume glass sculpture grouping, environmental research reserve, 80-acre protected forest, seismographic network station, art studios, art galleries, dance studio and performance area, Center for Political Participation, Center for Economic and Environmental Development, environmental roof garden, Center for Experiential Learning, theater and communication arts center, Learning Commons, language learning center.

Freshman class profile. 4,770 applied, 2,747 admitted, 559 enrolled.

Mid 50% test scores			
SAT critical reading:	530-660	Rank in top quarter:	73%
SAT math:	540-640	Rank in top tenth:	43%
SAT writing:	520-640	End year in good standing:	98%
ACT composite:	23-29	Return as sophomores:	87%
GPA 3.75 or higher:	50%	Out-of-state:	41%
GPA 3.50-3.74:	23%	Live on campus:	99%
GPA 3.0-3.49:	19%	International:	1%
GPA 2.0-2.99:	8%	Fraternities:	19%
		Sororities:	24%

Basis for selection. Rigor of high school program most important, followed by high school achievement. Test scores important. Essay, minority status, alumni ties, geography considered. One recommendation from guidance counselor and one from teacher required. Interview recommended. **Home schooled:** Campus visit and individual interview with admissions counselor to discuss portfolios recommended. Recommendation from a non-family member, description of the level of instruction. **Learning Disabled:** Recommended interview with Director of Student Support Services.

High school preparation. College-preparatory program required. 16 units required. Required units include English 4, mathematics 3, social studies 3, science 3, foreign language 2 and academic electives 1.

2012-2013 Annual costs. Tuition/fees: $37,610. Room/board: $9,540. Books/supplies: $1,000. Personal expenses: $1,000.

2011-2012 Financial aid. Need-based: 500 full-time freshmen applied for aid; 430 were judged to have need; 430 of these received aid. Average need met was 91%. Average scholarship/grant was $25,411; average loan $4,479. 79% of total undergraduate aid awarded as scholarships/grants, 21% as loans/jobs. **Non-need-based:** Awarded to 783 full-time undergraduates, including 191 freshmen. Scholarships awarded for academics, leadership, minority status, state residency.

Application procedures. Admission: Closing date 2/15 (postmark date). $35 fee, may be waived for applicants with need, free for online applicants. Admission notification by 4/1. Must reply by 5/1. **Financial aid:** Priority date 2/15; no closing date. FAFSA required. Applicants notified on a rolling basis starting 3/1; must reply by 5/1 or within 4 week(s) of notification.

Academics. Special study options: Combined bachelor's/graduate degree, double major, dual enrollment of high school students, ESL, exchange student, independent study, internships, student-designed major, study abroad, Washington semester. Graduate school partnerships, marine biology study program, combined degree programs (3-2, 3-4), Experiential Learning Term (summer study program), double minor, pre-professional programs, domestic off-campus semester away study programs, accelerated master's and doctorate programs, New York Arts Program, Oak Ridge Science Semester, The Philadelphia Center, Newberry Seminar Research in the Humanities, Ecosystems Center, MA. **Credit/placement by examination:** AP, CLEP, IB, institutional tests. 20 credit hours maximum toward bachelor's degree. Up to 32 prematriculation credits, includes credit by examination, may be earned for college-level courses offered at high schools by accredited colleges or universities. **Support services:** Learning center, reduced course load, study skills assistance, tutoring, writing center.

Majors. Area/ethnic studies: Women's. **Biology:** General, biochemistry, neuroscience. **Business:** Managerial economics. **Communications:** Communications/speech/rhetoric, journalism, media studies. **Computer sciences:** Computer science. **Conservation:** Environmental science, environmental studies. **Education:** General. **Engineering:** Software. **English:** Creative writing, English lit. **Foreign languages:** French, German, Spanish. **Health services:** Predental, premedicine, prenursing, prepharmacy, preveterinary. **History:** General. **Math:** General. **Philosophy/religion:** Philosophy, religion. **Physical sciences:** Chemistry, geology, physics. **Psychology:** General. **Social sciences:** Applied economics, economics, international relations, political science. **Visual/performing arts:** Art, art history/conservation, dramatic, music, music performance, studio arts.

Most popular majors. Biology 22%, communications/journalism 6%, English 8%, natural resources/environmental science 9%, psychology 13%, social sciences 18%.

Computing on campus. 205 workstations in library, computer center, student center. Dormitories wired for high-speed internet access and linked to campus network. Commuter students can connect to campus network. Online course registration, online library, helpline, repair service, student web hosting, wireless network available.

Student life. Freshman orientation: Mandatory. Preregistration for classes offered. 4-day session held 4 days directly before fall classes begin. **Policies:** Honor code. **Housing:** Guaranteed on-campus for all undergraduates. Coed dorms, single-sex dorms, special housing for disabled, apartments, fraternity/sorority housing, wellness housing available. Environmentally-sensitive townhouses, LEED certified, low fume material; quiet study floors, civic engagement hall, living/learning residential communities. **Activities:**

Bands, campus ministries, choral groups, dance, drama, international student organizations, literary magazine, music ensembles, Model UN, musical theater, radio station, student government, student newspaper, symphony orchestra, TV station, Association for Asian and Asian-American awareness, Advancement of Black Culture, Union Latina, Habitat for Humanity, Newman Association, Hillel, Christian Outreach, Alpha Phi Omega, Americorps Bonner Leaders, College Democrats, College Republicans.

Athletics. NCAA. **Intercollegiate:** Baseball M, basketball, cross-country, diving, football (tackle) M, golf, lacrosse W, soccer, softball W, swimming, tennis, track and field, volleyball W. **Intramural:** Basketball, soccer, volleyball. **Team name:** Gators.

Student services. Adult student services, chaplain/spiritual director, career counseling, student employment services, financial aid counseling, health services, minority student services, personal counseling, placement for graduates. **Physically disabled:** Services for visually, hearing impaired.

Contact. E-mail: admissions@allegheny.edu
Phone: (814) 332-4351 Toll-free number: (800) 521-5293
Fax: (814) 337-0431
Sheryle Proper, Dean of Enrollment and Financial Aid, Allegheny College, Box 5, 520 North Main Street, Meadville, PA 16335

Alvernia University
Reading, Pennsylvania
www.alvernia.edu

CB member
CB code: 2431

◆ Private 4-year university and liberal arts college affiliated with Roman Catholic Church
◆ Residential campus in small city
◆ 2,135 degree-seeking undergraduates: 21% part-time, 68% women, 10% African American, 1% Asian American, 7% Hispanic American
◆ 570 degree-seeking graduate students
◆ 75% of applicants admitted
◆ SAT or ACT (ACT writing optional), application essay required
◆ 53% graduate within 6 years

General. Founded in 1958. Regionally accredited. Affiliated with Bernardine Sisters, Third Order of St. Francis. **Degrees:** 398 bachelor's, 5 associate awarded; master's, doctoral offered. **ROTC:** Army. **Location:** 60 miles from Philadelphia. **Calendar:** Semester, limited summer session. **Full-time faculty:** 98 total; 64% have terminal degrees, 6% minority, 56% women. **Part-time faculty:** 226 total; 22% have terminal degrees, 10% minority, 47% women. **Class size:** 62% < 20, 38% 20-39, less than 1% 50-99.

Freshman class profile. 1,814 applied, 1,364 admitted, 376 enrolled.

Mid 50% test scores			
		GPA 3.0-3.49:	33%
SAT critical reading:	440-530	GPA 2.0-2.99:	32%
SAT math:	440-550	Rank in top quarter:	28%
SAT writing:	420-520	Rank in top tenth:	7%
ACT composite:	18-23	Return as sophomores:	72%
GPA 3.75 or higher:	18%	Out-of-state:	27%
GPA 3.50-3.74:	17%	Live on campus:	79%

Basis for selection. Important factors include academic performance, standardized test scores, class rank, extracurricular activities, and community involvement. Interview recommended for all. Interview required of nursing, occupational therapy and physical therapist assistant applicants. Recommendation letters required of nursing applicants.

High school preparation. College-preparatory program recommended. 16 units recommended. Recommended units include English 4, mathematics 4, social studies 3, science 2, foreign language 2 and computer science 1.

2012-2013 Annual costs. Tuition/fees: $27,950. Room/board: $10,010. Books/supplies: $1,500.

2011-2012 Financial aid. Need-based: 375 full-time freshmen applied for aid; 336 were judged to have need; 336 of these received aid. Average need met was 63%. Average scholarship/grant was $13,865; average loan $3,340. 56% of total undergraduate aid awarded as scholarships/grants, 44% as loans/jobs. **Non-need-based:** Awarded to 245 full-time undergraduates, including 68 freshmen. Scholarships awarded for academics, ROTC.

Application procedures. Admission: No deadline. $25 fee, may be waived for applicants with need. Admission notification on a rolling basis beginning on or about 10/1. Must reply by May 1 or within 2 week(s) if notified thereafter. **Financial aid:** Priority date 5/1; no closing date. FAFSA required. Applicants notified on a rolling basis starting 2/20; must reply within 2 week(s) of notification.

Academics. **Special study options:** Accelerated study, combined bachelor's/graduate degree, cross-registration, distance learning, double major, dual enrollment of high school students, ESL, honors, independent study, internships, student-designed major, study abroad, teacher certification program, Washington semester. **Credit/placement by examination:** AP, CLEP, IB, institutional tests. 30 credit hours maximum toward associate degree, 30 toward bachelor's. Total of 30 credits allowed for all experiential credit, CLEP, life experience, challenge exam. **Support services:** Learning center, pre-admission summer program, reduced course load, remedial instruction, study skills assistance, tutoring, writing center.

Majors. **Biology:** General, biochemistry. **Business:** General, accounting, human resources, marketing. **Communications:** Communications/speech/rhetoric. **Computer sciences:** General. **Education:** General, biology, chemistry, computer, early childhood, elementary, English, mathematics, science, social studies, special ed. **English:** English lit. **Health services:** Athletic training, nursing (RN), substance abuse counseling. **History:** General. **Human services:** Social work. **Liberal arts:** Arts/sciences. **Math:** General. **Parks/recreation:** Sports admin. **Philosophy/religion:** Religion. **Physical sciences:** Chemistry. **Protective services:** Forensics, law enforcement admin. **Psychology:** General. **Social sciences:** General, political science. **Theology:** Theology. **Visual/performing arts:** Dramatic.

Most popular majors. Business/marketing 18%, education 11%, health sciences 34%, security/protective services 14%.

Computing on campus. 460 workstations in dormitories, library, computer center, student center. Dormitories wired for high-speed internet access and linked to campus network. Commuter students can connect to campus network. Online course registration, online library, helpline, wireless network available.

Student life. **Freshman orientation:** Mandatory. Preregistration for classes offered. Held weekend before classes start. **Housing:** Guaranteed on-campus for freshmen. Coed dorms, special housing for disabled, apartments available. $250 nonrefundable deposit, deadline 6/1. Single-sex townhouses available. Single-sex floors in dorms. **Activities:** Concert band, campus ministries, choral groups, dance, drama, literary magazine, music ensembles, student government, student newspaper.

Athletics. NCAA. **Intercollegiate:** Baseball M, basketball, cross-country, field hockey W, golf M, ice hockey M, lacrosse, soccer, softball W, tennis, track and field, volleyball W. **Intramural:** Basketball, cheerleading W, football (non-tackle), soccer. **Team name:** Crusaders.

Student services. Adult student services, chaplain/spiritual director, career counseling, services for economically disadvantaged, student employment services, financial aid counseling, health services, minority student services, personal counseling, placement for graduates, veterans' counselor. **Physically disabled:** Services for visually impaired.

Contact. E-mail: admissions@alvernia.edu
Phone: (610) 796-8269 Toll-free number: (888) 258-3764
Fax: (610) 796-2873
Stacey Perry, Dean of Admissions and Student Financial Planning, Alvernia University, 400 St. Bernardine Street, Reading, PA 19607-1799

Arcadia University
Glenside, Pennsylvania
www.arcadia.edu

CB member
CB code: 2039

- Private 4-year university affiliated with Presbyterian Church (USA)
- Residential campus in large town
- 2,151 degree-seeking undergraduates: 7% part-time, 71% women, 7% African American, 4% Asian American, 5% Hispanic American, 1% international
- 1,561 degree-seeking graduate students
- 54% of applicants admitted
- SAT or ACT with writing, application essay required
- 61% graduate within 6 years

General. Founded in 1853. Regionally accredited. **Degrees:** 406 bachelor's awarded; master's, professional, doctoral offered. **ROTC:** Army. **Location:** 10 miles from Philadelphia. **Calendar:** Semester, limited summer session. **Full-time faculty:** 161 total. **Part-time faculty:** 318 total. **Class size:** 76% < 20, 19% 20-39, 2% 40-49, 2% 50-99. **Special facilities:** Observatory housing 14-inch Schmidt-Cassegrain telescope with extensive astrophotography capabilities, Grey Towers Castle (national historic landmark) used as residence hall.

Freshman class profile. 7,673 applied, 4,108 admitted, 511 enrolled.

Mid 50% test scores			
SAT critical reading:	510-600	GPA 2.0-2.99:	9%
SAT math:	510-600	Rank in top quarter:	57%
SAT writing:	500-600	Rank in top tenth:	26%
ACT composite:	22-27	Return as sophomores:	78%
GPA 3.75 or higher:	38%	Out-of-state:	43%
GPA 3.50-3.74:	27%	Live on campus:	75%
GPA 3.0-3.49:	26%	International:	1%

Basis for selection. Emphasis placed on academic records, including type of program followed, courses taken, grades earned, class rank. Standardized test scores, counselor/teacher recommendations, participation in school and community activities important. Character references also considered. Supplementary materials demonstrating student's talents and potential recommended. Portfolio review required for fine arts department. Auditions required for BFA in acting. **Home schooled:** Statement describing home school structure and mission, letter of recommendation (nonparent) required. Portfolio representing academic record/work and level of achievement for grades 9-12 required.

High school preparation. College-preparatory program required. 19 units recommended. Recommended units include English 4, mathematics 3, social studies 2, history 2, science 3 (laboratory 3) and foreign language 2. Additional units in foreign language, math, and/or laboratory science recommended. Math includes algebra II and geometry.

2011-2012 Annual costs. Tuition/fees: $34,150. Room/board: $11,640. Books/supplies: $1,400. Personal expenses: $850.

2011-2012 Financial aid. **Need-based:** 497 full-time freshmen applied for aid; 481 were judged to have need; 435 of these received aid. Average need met was 72%. Average scholarship/grant was $21,925; average loan $3,336. 68% of total undergraduate aid awarded as scholarships/grants, 32% as loans/jobs. **Non-need-based:** Scholarships awarded for academics, alumni affiliation, art, leadership, music/drama. **Additional information:** Automatic $1,000 renewable FAFSA Early Filer Grant for new incoming full-time undergraduates who file FAFSA by March 1, listing Arcadia as a recipient school on the form, and have a completed admissions application on file by March 1.

Application procedures. **Admission:** Priority date 1/15; deadline 3/1. $30 fee, may be waived for applicants with need, free for online applicants. Admission notification on a rolling basis beginning on or about 9/1. Must reply by May 1 or within 2 week(s) if notified thereafter. **Financial aid:** Priority date 3/1; no closing date. FAFSA, institutional form required. Applicants notified on a rolling basis starting 2/1; must reply by 5/1.

Academics. **Special study options:** Accelerated study, combined bachelor's/graduate degree, cooperative education, cross-registration, distance learning, double major, dual enrollment of high school students, exchange student, honors, independent study, internships, liberal arts/career combination, student-designed major, study abroad, teacher certification program, Washington semester. Combined programs leading to graduate degrees in physical therapy, physician assistant studies (option to combine with public health), forensic science, international peace and conflict resolution. Combined with other universities for degrees in engineering, nursing, optometry. **Credit/placement by examination:** AP, CLEP, IB, institutional tests. 64 credit hours maximum toward bachelor's degree. **Support services:** Learning center, pre-admission summer program, reduced course load, remedial instruction, study skills assistance, tutoring, writing center.

Majors. **Area/ethnic studies:** Italian, Spanish/Iberian. **Biology:** General. **Business:** General, accounting, business admin, finance, human resources, international, management information systems, management science, marketing. **Communications:** Communications/speech/rhetoric, media studies, radio/TV. **Computer sciences:** General, computer science, programming. **Conservation:** Environmental studies. **Education:** General, art, biology, chemistry, early childhood, elementary, English, mathematics, multi-level teacher, science, secondary, social science, social studies, special ed. **Engineering:** General. **English:** Creative writing, English lit. **Foreign languages:** French, Spanish. **Health services:** Art therapy, facilities admin, health care admin, health services admin, medical illustrating. **History:** General. **Liberal arts:** Arts/sciences. **Math:** General. **Philosophy/religion:** Philosophy. **Physical sciences:** Chemistry, physics. **Psychology:** General. **Social sciences:** Criminology, international relations, political science, sociology. **Visual/performing arts:** General, acting, art, art history/conservation, ceramics, commercial/advertising art, dramatic, graphic design, illustration, interior design, metal/jewelry, painting, photography, printmaking, studio arts, theater history.

Most popular majors. Biology 11%, business/marketing 13%, education 7%, history 6%, interdisciplinary studies 10%, psychology 11%, social sciences 9%, visual/performing arts 14%.

Computing on campus. 200 workstations in library, computer center. Dormitories wired for high-speed internet access and linked to campus network. Commuter students can connect to campus network. Online course registration, helpline, repair service, wireless network available.

Student life. Freshman orientation: Mandatory. Preregistration for classes offered. **Housing:** Guaranteed on-campus for all undergraduates. Coed dorms, single-sex dorms, special housing for disabled, apartments, wellness housing available. $400 nonrefundable deposit, deadline 5/1. Living and learning community available. **Activities:** Choral groups, dance, drama, literary magazine, music ensembles, musical theater, radio station, student government, student newspaper, TV station, approximately 45 clubs and organizations.

Athletics. NCAA. **Intercollegiate:** Baseball M, basketball, equestrian, field hockey W, golf, lacrosse W, soccer, softball W, swimming, tennis, volleyball W. **Intramural:** Basketball, field hockey W, football (non-tackle), skiing, soccer, softball, swimming M, tennis, volleyball, weight lifting. **Team name:** Scarlet Knights.

Student services. Adult student services, alcohol/substance abuse counseling, career counseling, services for economically disadvantaged, student employment services, financial aid counseling, health services, minority student services, personal counseling, placement for graduates. **Physically disabled:** Services for visually, speech, hearing impaired.

Contact. E-mail: admiss@arcadia.edu
Phone: (215) 572-2910 Toll-free number: (877) 272-2342
Fax: (215) 881-8767
Mark Laprezioza, Associate Vice President of Enrollment Management, Arcadia University, 450 South Easton Road, Glenside, PA 19038-3295

Art Institute of Philadelphia
Philadelphia, Pennsylvania
www.artinstitutes.edu/Philadelphia   CB code: 2033

▶ For-profit 4-year visual arts college
▶ Commuter campus in very large city
▶ 3,242 degree-seeking undergraduates
▶ Application essay, interview required

General. Founded in 1966. Accredited by ACICS. **Degrees:** 477 bachelor's, 172 associate awarded. **Calendar:** Quarter, extensive summer session. **Full-time faculty:** 95 total. **Part-time faculty:** 110 total. **Special facilities:** Recording studio utilizing Pro-tools software, digital photography laboratory, nonlinear digital editing suites, and full-service chef instructor/student-run restaurant.

Basis for selection. High school transcript most important. Essay and interview required. Portfolio recommended. **Home schooled:** Transcript of courses and grades, state high school equivalency certificate required.

High school preparation. Background or strong interest in chosen major preferred.

2011-2012 Annual costs. Books/supplies: $1,200.

Financial aid. Additional information: Institute-sponsored scholarships available. May 1st application deadline for Pennsylvania State Grant.

Application procedures. Admission: No deadline. $50 fee. Admission notification on a rolling basis. **Financial aid:** No deadline. FAFSA, institutional form required. Applicants notified on a rolling basis starting 3/1; must reply within 2 week(s) of notification.

Academics. Academic program designed to simulate working environment, focusing course work on job-related skills. **Special study options:** Independent study, internships. **Credit/placement by examination:** AP, CLEP, IB, SAT, ACT, institutional tests. **Support services:** Learning center, reduced course load, remedial instruction, study skills assistance, tutoring.

Majors. Communications technology: Animation/special effects. **Computer sciences:** Web page design. **Visual/performing arts:** Cinematography, commercial/advertising art, design, fashion design, industrial design, interior design, photography.

Computing on campus. 507 workstations in dormitories, library, computer center. Dormitories wired for high-speed internet access. Online library, student web hosting available.

Student life. Freshman orientation: Mandatory. Preregistration for classes offered. **Housing:** Guaranteed on-campus for all undergraduates. Coed dorms, apartments available. **Activities:** Student government.

Student services. Career counseling, student employment services, financial aid counseling, personal counseling, placement for graduates.

Contact. E-mail: aiphadm@aii.edu
Phone: (215) 567-7080 Toll-free number: (800) 275-2474
Fax: (215) 405-6399
Steven Cohen, Director of Admissions, Art Institute of Philadelphia, 1622 Chestnut Street, Philadelphia, PA 19103-5198

Art Institute of Pittsburgh
Pittsburgh, Pennsylvania
www.artinstitutes.edu/pittsburgh   CB code: 2029

▶ For-profit 4-year culinary school and visual arts college
▶ Commuter campus in large city
▶ 2,194 degree-seeking undergraduates
▶ Application essay, interview required

General. Founded in 1921. Regionally accredited. **Degrees:** 422 bachelor's, 93 associate awarded. **Calendar:** Differs by program, extensive summer session. **Full-time faculty:** 292 total. **Part-time faculty:** 1,095 total. **Special facilities:** Photography laboratory, art gallery, traveling exhibits, 24-track recording studio.

Freshman class profile.

Out-of-state:	50%	**Live on campus:**	50%

Basis for selection. High school transcript most important. Limited portfolio required for some programs. **Home schooled:** Statement describing home school structure and mission, transcript of courses and grades, state high school equivalency certificate, letter of recommendation (nonparent) required.

High school preparation. Prefer students with demonstrated interest in chosen major.

2011-2012 Annual costs. Tuition/fees: $22,015. Culinary lab fee for food courses, $250; $100 lab fee per online course. Room only: $7,092. Books/supplies: $1,445.

Application procedures. Admission: No deadline. $50 fee. Admission notification on a rolling basis. **Financial aid:** No deadline. FAFSA, institutional form required. Applicants notified on a rolling basis starting 4/15.

Academics. Special study options: Distance learning, internships, study abroad. **Credit/placement by examination:** AP, CLEP, institutional tests. **Support services:** Learning center, remedial instruction, tutoring, writing center.

Majors. Business: Fashion. **Communications technology:** Animation/special effects. **Computer sciences:** Web page design. **Visual/performing arts:** Cinematography, commercial/advertising art, design, industrial design, interior design, photography.

Computing on campus. 447 workstations in dormitories, library, computer center. Dormitories wired for high-speed internet access and linked to campus network. Commuter students can connect to campus network. Online course registration, online library, helpline, student web hosting, wireless network available.

Student life. Freshman orientation: Mandatory. Preregistration for classes offered. One-day program held before start of classes. **Housing:** Coed dorms, apartments, wellness housing available. $100 deposit. **Activities:** Drama, film society, international student organizations, student government, student newspaper, community relations activities, student success task force, student council.

Student services. Alcohol/substance abuse counseling, career counseling, student employment services, financial aid counseling, personal counseling, placement for graduates, veterans' counselor. **Physically disabled:** Services for visually, speech, hearing impaired.

Contact. E-mail: aipadm@aii.edu
Phone: (412) 263-6600 Toll-free number: (800) 275-2470
Fax: (412) 263-6667
Lee Colker, Director of Admissions, Art Institute of Pittsburgh, 420 Boulevard of the Allies, Pittsburgh, PA 15219-1328

Baptist Bible College of Pennsylvania
Clarks Summit, Pennsylvania
www.bbc.edu CB code: 2036

- Private 4-year Bible and teachers college affiliated with Baptist faith
- Residential campus in small city
- 722 degree-seeking undergraduates: 21% part-time, 50% women
- 279 degree-seeking graduate students
- 81% of applicants admitted
- SAT or ACT (ACT writing optional), application essay required
- 36% graduate within 6 years; 6% enter graduate study

General. Founded in 1932. Regionally accredited; also accredited by ABHE. Part of each student's curriculum includes ministry/service experiences in churches or social agencies. **Degrees:** 116 bachelor's, 20 associate awarded; master's, professional, doctoral offered. **ROTC:** Army. **Location:** 7 miles from Scranton, 20 miles from Wilkes-Barre. **Calendar:** Semester, limited summer session. **Full-time faculty:** 41 total; 68% have terminal degrees, 24% women. **Part-time faculty:** 36 total; 42% have terminal degrees, 28% women. **Class size:** 70% < 20, 20% 20-39, 4% 40-49, 6% 50-99, 1% >100.

Freshman class profile. 834 applied, 676 admitted, 151 enrolled.

Mid 50% test scores			
SAT critical reading:	460-580	GPA 3.50-3.74:	24%
SAT math:	430-580	GPA 3.0-3.49:	25%
SAT writing:	450-580	GPA 2.0-2.99:	22%
ACT composite:	20-25	Return as sophomores:	47%
GPA 3.75 or higher:	24%	Out-of-state:	68%
		Live on campus:	64%

Basis for selection. Academic record, test scores, references/recommendations most important. Audition required, interview recommended for all; portfolio required for music programs. **Home schooled:** Transcript of courses and grades required.

2011-2012 Annual costs. Tuition/fees: $18,240. Room/board: $6,650. Books/supplies: $600. Personal expenses: $2,630.

2010-2011 Financial aid. Need-based: 137 full-time freshmen applied for aid; 134 were judged to have need; 134 of these received aid. Average scholarship/grant was $11,449. 75% of total undergraduate aid awarded as scholarships/grants, 25% as loans/jobs. **Non-need-based:** Awarded to 115 full-time undergraduates, including 30 freshmen. Scholarships awarded for academics, leadership, music/drama, religious affiliation.

Application procedures. Admission: Priority date 5/1; deadline 8/15 (postmark date). $30 fee. Admission notification on a rolling basis. Must reply by May 1 or within 4 week(s) if notified thereafter. **Financial aid:** Closing date 5/1. FAFSA, institutional form required. Applicants notified on a rolling basis starting 4/1.

Academics. Special study options: Combined bachelor's/graduate degree, distance learning, double major, dual enrollment of high school students, independent study, internships, study abroad, teacher certification program. **Credit/placement by examination:** AP, CLEP, IB, SAT, ACT, institutional tests. **Support services:** Reduced course load, remedial instruction, study skills assistance, tutoring, writing center.

Majors. Business: Administrative services. **Communications:** Communications/speech/rhetoric. **Education:** Early childhood, elementary, health, mathematics, multi-level teacher, music, physical, science, secondary, social studies. **Liberal arts:** Arts/sciences. **Parks/recreation:** Health/fitness. **Philosophy/religion:** General. **Psychology:** Counseling. **Theology:** Missionary, preministerial, sacred music, youth ministry. **Visual/performing arts:** Music.

Most popular majors. Education 27%, liberal arts 21%, psychology 12%, theological studies 33%.

Computing on campus. 30 workstations in library, computer center. Dormitories wired for high-speed internet access and linked to campus network. Online course registration, online library, helpline, wireless network available.

Student life. Freshman orientation: Mandatory. Preregistration for classes offered. Parent and student orientation weekend includes sessions on academics, student life, finances, and interaction with faculty. **Policies:** Students must abide by standard given in the student handbook. Religious observance required. **Housing:** Guaranteed on-campus for all undergraduates. Single-sex dorms, special housing for disabled, wellness housing available. $250 deposit, deadline 5/1. **Activities:** Choral groups, drama, music ensembles, student government, student newspaper, several religious and service groups.

Athletics. NCAA, NCCAA. **Intercollegiate:** Baseball M, basketball, cheerleading M, cross-country, golf M, soccer, softball W, tennis W, track and field, volleyball. **Intramural:** Basketball, soccer, softball M, volleyball. **Team name:** Defenders.

Student services. Adult student services, alcohol/substance abuse counseling, chaplain/spiritual director, career counseling, student employment services, financial aid counseling, health services, personal counseling, placement for graduates, women's services.

Contact. E-mail: admissions@bbc.edu
Phone: (570) 586-2400 ext. 9271 Toll-free number: (800) 451-7664
Fax: (570) 585-9299
Ken Shepard, Vice President for Enrollment and Marketing Services, Baptist Bible College of Pennsylvania, 538 Venard Road, Clarks Summit, PA 18411-1297

Bloomsburg University of Pennsylvania
Bloomsburg, Pennsylvania CB member
www.bloomu.edu CB code: 2646

- Public 4-year university and liberal arts college
- Residential campus in large town
- 9,065 degree-seeking undergraduates: 5% part-time, 57% women, 7% African American, 1% Asian American, 4% Hispanic American, 1% international
- 848 degree-seeking graduate students
- 63% of applicants admitted
- SAT or ACT (ACT writing optional) required
- 61% graduate within 6 years; 25% enter graduate study

General. Founded in 1839. Regionally accredited. **Degrees:** 1,670 bachelor's awarded; master's, professional offered. **ROTC:** Army, Air Force. **Location:** 40 miles from Wilkes-Barre, 80 miles from Harrisburg. **Calendar:** Semester, extensive summer session. **Full-time faculty:** 397 total; 83% have terminal degrees, 11% minority, 42% women. **Part-time faculty:** 93 total; 10% have terminal degrees, 2% minority, 66% women. **Class size:** 16% < 20, 69% 20-39, 7% 40-49, 4% 50-99, 4% >100.

Freshman class profile. 11,423 applied, 7,188 admitted, 1,981 enrolled.

Mid 50% test scores			
SAT critical reading:	450-540	GPA 2.0-2.99:	25%
SAT math:	460-560	Rank in top quarter:	30%
SAT writing:	440-530	Rank in top tenth:	8%
ACT composite:	19-24	Return as sophomores:	80%
GPA 3.75 or higher:	18%	Out-of-state:	13%
GPA 3.50-3.74:	21%	Live on campus:	90%
GPA 3.0-3.49:	35%	International:	1%

Basis for selection. High school work, achievement, SAT or ACT test scores, personal characteristics and enrollment capacity considered. To be considered for nursing, application must be complete by November 15 of your senior year. **Home schooled:** Statement describing home school structure and mission, transcript of courses and grades, state high school equivalency certificate required.

High school preparation. College-preparatory program recommended. 16 units required; 21 recommended. Required and recommended units include English 4, mathematics 3-4, social studies 2, history 2, science 3-4, foreign language 2, computer science 1 and academic electives 2.

2011-2012 Annual costs. Tuition/fees: $8,082; $17,442 out-of-state. Room/board: $7,216. Books/supplies: $1,200. Personal expenses: $3,000.

Financial aid. Non-need-based: Scholarships awarded for academics, art, athletics, job skills, leadership, minority status, music/drama, ROTC, state residency.

Application procedures. Admission: Priority date 12/1; no deadline. $35 fee, may be waived for applicants with need. Admission notification on a rolling basis beginning on or about 9/18. Must reply by May 1 or within 2 week(s) if notified thereafter. **Financial aid:** Priority date 3/15; no closing date. FAFSA required. Applicants notified on a rolling basis starting 4/1.

Academics. Special study options: Combined bachelor's/graduate degree, cooperative education, cross-registration, distance learning, double major, dual enrollment of high school students, ESL, exchange student, honors, independent study, internships, liberal arts/career combination, study abroad, teacher certification program. B.S. Computer Forensics 2+2+2. Program to program articulation agreements in Early Childhood Education with Luzerne County Community College, Lehigh Carbon Community College, Northampton Area Community College, and Harrisburg Area Community College.

Credit/placement by examination: AP, CLEP, SAT, institutional tests. 64 credit hours maximum toward bachelor's degree. **Support services:** Learning center, pre-admission summer program, reduced course load, remedial instruction, study skills assistance, tutoring, writing center.

Majors. Biology: General. **Business:** General, accounting, business admin. **Communications:** Communications/speech/rhetoric, media studies. **Computer sciences:** General, computer science. **Education:** Early childhood, middle, special ed. **Engineering:** Electrical. **English:** English lit. **Foreign languages:** General, sign language interpretation. **Health services:** Audiology/speech pathology, clinical lab science, medical radiologic technology/radiation therapy, nursing (RN), physics/radiologic health. **History:** General. **Human services:** Social work. **Math:** General. **Philosophy/religion:** Philosophy. **Physical sciences:** Chemistry, geology, physics. **Protective services:** Criminal justice. **Psychology:** General. **Social sciences:** Anthropology, economics, geography, political science, sociology. **Visual/performing arts:** Art history/conservation, dramatic, music, studio arts.

Most popular majors. Business/marketing 22%, education 15%, English 7%, health sciences 14%, social sciences 9%.

Computing on campus. 1,557 workstations in dormitories, library, computer center, student center. Dormitories wired for high-speed internet access and linked to campus network. Commuter students can connect to campus network. Online course registration, online library, helpline, wireless network available.

Student life. Freshman orientation: Mandatory, $95 fee. Preregistration for classes offered. Preview day program in June and a 3-day program prior to start of classes. **Housing:** Guaranteed on-campus for freshmen. Coed dorms, apartments, cooperative housing, wellness housing available. $100 partly refundable deposit, deadline 5/1. Eleven living and learning communities available: Business, Civic Engagement, Education, Fine Arts and Humanities, Frederick Douglass, Helping Professions, Honors, International Studies, Presidential Leadership, Science & Health Sciences, and Social Justice & Sustainability. **Activities:** Bands, campus ministries, choral groups, dance, drama, international student organizations, literary magazine, music ensembles, Model UN, radio station, student government, student newspaper, symphony orchestra, TV station, Bloomsburg Christian Fellowship, Hillel, University Democrats, College Republicans, Black Cultural Society, Student Organization of Latinos, Habitat for Humanity.

Athletics. NCAA. **Intercollegiate:** Baseball M, basketball, cross-country, field hockey W, football (tackle) M, lacrosse W, soccer, softball W, swimming, tennis, track and field, wrestling M. **Intramural:** Basketball, field hockey W, football (non-tackle) M, racquetball, soccer, softball, tennis, volleyball, wrestling M. **Team name:** Huskies.

Student services. Adult student services, alcohol/substance abuse counseling, chaplain/spiritual director, career counseling, services for economically disadvantaged, student employment services, financial aid counseling, health services, legal services, minority student services, on-campus daycare, personal counseling, placement for graduates, veterans' counselor, women's services. **Physically disabled:** Services for visually, speech, hearing impaired.

Contact. E-mail: buadmiss@bloomu.edu
Phone: (570) 389-4316 Fax: (570) 389-4741
Christopher Keller, Director of Admissions, Bloomsburg University of Pennsylvania, 104 Student Service Center, Bloomsburg, PA 17815

Bryn Athyn College of the New Church
Bryn Athyn, Pennsylvania
www.brynathyn.edu
CB member
CB code: 2002

- Private 4-year liberal arts college affiliated with General Church of the New Jerusalem (Swedenborgian)
- Residential campus in small town
- 233 degree-seeking undergraduates: 3% part-time, 59% women, 12% African American, 1% Asian American, 3% Hispanic American, 13% international
- 12 degree-seeking graduate students
- 44% of applicants admitted
- SAT or ACT with writing, application essay required

General. Founded in 1876. Regionally accredited. **Degrees:** 30 bachelor's, 18 associate awarded; master's offered. **ROTC:** Army, Air Force. **Location:** 15 miles from Philadelphia. **Calendar:** Trimester, limited summer session. **Full-time faculty:** 26 total; 69% have terminal degrees, 4% minority, 46% women. **Part-time faculty:** 18 total; 11% have terminal degrees, 61% women. **Class size:** 85% < 20, 15% 20-39. **Special facilities:** Performing arts center, local and church archives, ecological restoration trust, cathedral, ice rink and pavillion, social center, Cairnwood Estate, outdoor sanctuary, Glencairn Museum.

Freshman class profile. 833 applied, 370 admitted, 82 enrolled.

Mid 50% test scores			
SAT critical reading:	480-600	GPA 3.0-3.49:	36%
SAT math:	460-580	GPA 2.0-2.99:	30%
SAT writing:	470-580	Return as sophomores:	71%
ACT composite:	21-27	Out-of-state:	41%
GPA 3.75 or higher:	18%	Live on campus:	78%
GPA 3.50-3.74:	16%	International:	8%

Basis for selection. Applicants expected to have interest in the New Church. School achievement record important; test scores considered. TOEFL required of non-native English speakers. SAT may be required of some Canadian applicants. Interview recommended; may be required. **Home schooled:** SAT Subject Tests in literature and math recommended.

High school preparation. 15 units recommended. Recommended units include English 4, mathematics 4, social studies 2, history 2, science 2 (laboratory 2), foreign language 2, computer science 2, visual/performing arts 2 and academic electives 2.

2012-2013 Annual costs. Tuition/fees: $16,878. Room/board: $9,771. Books/supplies: $750. Personal expenses: $1,000.

2010-2011 Financial aid. Need-based: 62 full-time freshmen applied for aid; 59 were judged to have need; 59 of these received aid. Average need met was 100%. Average scholarship/grant was $13,154; average loan $2,604. 78% of total undergraduate aid awarded as scholarships/grants, 22% as loans/jobs. **Non-need-based:** Awarded to 96 full-time undergraduates, including 41 freshmen. Scholarships awarded for academics, religious affiliation.

Application procedures. Admission: Priority date 2/1; deadline 7/1 (receipt date). No application fee. Admission notification on a rolling basis beginning on or about 2/1. Must reply by 8/1. **Financial aid:** Priority date 2/15, closing date 6/1. FAFSA required. Applicants notified on a rolling basis starting 3/1; must reply within 3 week(s) of notification.

Academics. Academic Career Excellence: peer tutoring and supported self-study, math center and research center. **Special study options:** Accelerated study, cooperative education, cross-registration, distance learning, ESL, independent study, internships, student-designed major, study abroad, teacher certification program. Students can combine multiple curricular areas to design an educational program tailored to meet their particular interests, abilities, and needs. **Credit/placement by examination:** AP, CLEP, IB, institutional tests. **Support services:** Remedial instruction, study skills assistance, tutoring, writing center.

Majors. Biology: General. **Business:** General. **Computer sciences:** General. **Education:** General, English. **English:** English lit. **History:** General. **Math:** General. **Philosophy/religion:** Religion. **Theology:** Theology.

Most popular majors. Biology 10%, education 10%, English 10%, history 27%, interdisciplinary studies 30%, philosophy/religious studies 13%.

Computing on campus. PC or laptop required. 24 workstations in dormitories, library, computer center, student center. Dormitories wired for high-speed internet access and linked to campus network. Commuter students can connect to campus network. Online library, helpline, repair service, wireless network available.

Student life. Freshman orientation: Mandatory. Preregistration for classes offered. **Policies:** No alcohol on campus, restricted dorm visiting, required chapel attendance. Religious observance required. **Housing:** Guaranteed on-campus for all undergraduates. Single-sex dorms available. $100 nonfundable deposit, deadline 7/15. Satellite housing available. All housing on-campus is alcohol and smoke free. **Activities:** Choral groups, dance, drama, international student organizations, musical theater, student government, student newspaper, CARE.

Athletics. Intercollegiate: Ice hockey M, lacrosse M, soccer M, tennis, volleyball W. **Team name:** Lions.

Student services. Chaplain/spiritual director, career counseling, student employment services, financial aid counseling, health services, personal counseling.

Contact. E-mail: admissions@brynathyn.edu
Phone: (267) 502-2511 Fax: (267) 502-2593
Allen Linnell, Director of Admissions, Bryn Athyn College of the New Church, PO Box 462, Bryn Athyn, PA 19009-0462

Bryn Mawr College
Bryn Mawr, Pennsylvania
www.brynmawr.edu

CB member
CB code: 2049

- Private 4-year liberal arts college for women
- Residential campus in very large city
- 1,302 degree-seeking undergraduates: 1% part-time, 100% women, 4% African American, 13% Asian American, 9% Hispanic American, 16% international
- 457 degree-seeking graduate students
- 46% of applicants admitted
- SAT and SAT Subject Tests or ACT (ACT writing optional), application essay required
- 87% graduate within 6 years; 26% enter graduate study

General. Founded in 1885. Regionally accredited. Academic exchange with Haverford College, Swarthmore College, and University of Pennsylvania. Extracurricular and social coordination with Haverford College. **Degrees:** 322 bachelor's awarded; master's, doctoral offered. **ROTC:** Air Force. **Location:** 11 miles from Philadelphia. **Calendar:** Semester, limited summer session. **Full-time faculty:** 157 total; 98% have terminal degrees, 16% minority, 54% women. **Part-time faculty:** 53 total; 68% have terminal degrees, 8% minority, 66% women. **Class size:** 74% < 20, 19% 20-39, 4% 40-49, 3% 50-99. **Special facilities:** Collections of minerals, archaeological and anthropological artifacts.

Freshman class profile. 2,335 applied, 1,080 admitted, 361 enrolled.

Mid 50% test scores			
SAT critical reading:	600-710	Rank in top tenth:	60%
SAT math:	600-720	Return as sophomores:	90%
SAT writing:	630-710	Out-of-state:	84%
ACT composite:	26-31	Live on campus:	100%
Rank in top quarter:	89%	International:	21%

Basis for selection. School achievement record, recommendations, essay most important. Test scores, school and community activities, extracurricular achievements important. For those submitting SAT, 2 SAT Subject Tests required. Interview recommended. **Home schooled:** Statement describing home school structure and mission, transcript of courses and grades, state high school equivalency certificate, interview, letter of recommendation (non-parent) required. Interview required, but may be completed with admissions officer or alumna.

High school preparation. 16 units recommended. Recommended units include English 4, mathematics 3, social studies 2, history 2, science 2 (laboratory 1) and foreign language 3.

2011-2012 Annual costs. Tuition/fees: $40,824. Room/board: $12,890. Books/supplies: $1,000. Personal expenses: $1,000.

2011-2012 Financial aid. All financial aid based on need. 234 full-time freshmen applied for aid; 199 were judged to have need; 199 of these received aid. Average need met was 100%. Average scholarship/grant was $30,642; average loan $4,556. 86% of total undergraduate aid awarded as scholarships/grants, 14% as loans/jobs.

Application procedures. Admission: Closing date 1/15 (postmark date). $50 fee, may be waived for applicants with need, free for online applicants. Admission notification by 4/1. Must reply by 5/1. **Financial aid:** Priority date 2/5, closing date 3/1. FAFSA, CSS PROFILE required. Applicants notified by 3/23; must reply by 5/1.

Academics. Most examinations self-scheduled. **Special study options:** Accelerated study, combined bachelor's/graduate degree, cross-registration, double major, dual enrollment of high school students, exchange student, independent study, internships, liberal arts/career combination, student-designed major, study abroad, teacher certification program. 3-2 Program in City and Regional Planning with the University of Pennsylvania. A.B./B.S. 3-2 engineering programs with University of Pennsylvania. **Credit/placement by examination:** AP, CLEP, IB, institutional tests. 32 credit hours maximum toward bachelor's degree. **Support services:** Pre-admission summer program, reduced course load, study skills assistance, tutoring, writing center.

Majors. Architecture: Urban/community planning. **Area/ethnic studies:** East Asian. **Biology:** General. **Computer sciences:** Computer science. **English:** English lit. **Foreign languages:** Ancient Greek, classics, comparative lit, French, German, Italian, Latin, Russian, Spanish. **History:** General. **Math:** General. **Philosophy/religion:** Philosophy, religion. **Physical sciences:** Astronomy, chemistry, geology, physics. **Psychology:** General. **Social sciences:** Anthropology, archaeology, economics, political science, sociology, urban studies. **Visual/performing arts:** Art history/conservation, music, studio arts.

Most popular majors. Biology 8%, English 10%, foreign language 9%, history 6%, mathematics 7%, physical sciences 7%, psychology 8%, social sciences 33%.

Computing on campus. 200 workstations in dormitories, library, computer center, student center. Dormitories linked to campus network. Commuter students can connect to campus network. Online course registration, online library, helpline, repair service, student web hosting, wireless network available.

Student life. Freshman orientation: Mandatory. Preregistration for classes offered. Week-long program; students divided into groups of 10-20 students based on residence hall assignments. **Policies:** Self-governing student body, academic and social honor code, Customs and Traditions programs. **Housing:** Guaranteed on-campus for all undergraduates. Coed dorms, apartments, cooperative housing, wellness housing available. $200 fully refundable deposit, deadline 6/1. Students may live at Haverford. Foreign language houses available (Chinese, French, German, Hebrew, Italian, Russian, Spanish). Special housing available for non-traditional-aged students. **Activities:** Jazz band, campus ministries, choral groups, dance, drama, film society, international student organizations, literary magazine, music ensembles, Model UN, musical theater, radio station, student government, student newspaper, Mujeres, Rainbow Alliance, investment group, Jewish student union.

Athletics. NCAA. **Intercollegiate:** Badminton W, basketball W, cross-country W, field hockey W, lacrosse W, rowing (crew) W, soccer W, swimming W, tennis W, track and field W, volleyball W. **Intramural:** Tennis W, volleyball W. **Team name:** Owls.

Student services. Adult student services, alcohol/substance abuse counseling, chaplain/spiritual director, career counseling, services for economically disadvantaged, student employment services, financial aid counseling, health services, minority student services, personal counseling, placement for graduates, women's services. **Physically disabled:** Services for visually, speech, hearing impaired.

Contact. E-mail: admissions@brynmawr.edu
Phone: (610) 526-5152 Toll-free number: (800) 262-1885
Fax: (610) 526-7471
Laurie Koehler, Dean of Admissions, Bryn Mawr College, 101 North Merion Avenue, Bryn Mawr, PA 19010-2899

Bucknell University
Lewisburg, Pennsylvania
www.bucknell.edu

CB member
CB code: 2050

- Private 4-year university
- Residential campus in small town
- 3,535 degree-seeking undergraduates: 52% women, 3% African American, 3% Asian American, 4% Hispanic American, 5% international
- 53 degree-seeking graduate students
- 28% of applicants admitted
- SAT or ACT with writing, application essay required
- 91% graduate within 6 years; 27% enter graduate study

General. Founded in 1846. Regionally accredited. **Degrees:** 839 bachelor's awarded; master's offered. **ROTC:** Army. **Location:** 75 miles from Harrisburg, 195 miles from Philadelphia. **Calendar:** Semester, limited summer session. **Full-time faculty:** 358 total; 97% have terminal degrees, 14% minority, 41% women. **Part-time faculty:** 21 total; 48% have terminal degrees, 5% minority, 57% women. **Class size:** 57% < 20, 40% 20-39, 1% 40-49, 2% 50-99, less than 1% >100. **Special facilities:** Observatory, 63-acre nature preserve, center for performing arts, poetry center, greenhouse, outdoor naturalistic primate facility, engineering structural test lab, gas chromatograph/mass spectrometer, nuclear magnetic resonance spectrometer, herbarium, 18-hole golf course, small business development center, environmental center, center for public policy, high ropes course.

Freshman class profile. 7,940 applied, 2,188 admitted, 916 enrolled.

Mid 50% test scores			
SAT critical reading:	590-680	GPA 2.0-2.99:	7%
SAT math:	630-720	Rank in top quarter:	91%
SAT writing:	600-700	Rank in top tenth:	60%
ACT composite:	27-31	End year in good standing:	97%
GPA 3.75 or higher:	28%	Return as sophomores:	94%
GPA 3.50-3.74:	24%	Out-of-state:	76%
GPA 3.0-3.49:	41%	Live on campus:	100%
		International:	5%

Basis for selection. Emphasis on school achievement. Test scores, recommendations, special talents and abilities, evidence of volunteer work, personal qualities important. If English is not student's first language and student submits SAT scores with Critical Reading score below 550, TOEFL required.

Audition required for music program; portfolio recommended for art program. **Home schooled:** Statement describing home school structure and mission required. SAT, graded English paper, writing sample (not from English class), program description or certification from home schooler's accrediting agency or school district, name/address/phone number of home school supervisor required. Important: personal qualities, extracurriculars, and evidence of volunteer work.

High school preparation. College-preparatory program required. 16 units required; 20 recommended. Required and recommended units include English 4, mathematics 3-4, social studies 2, history 2, science 2-3, foreign language 2-4 and academic electives 1.

2011-2012 Annual costs. Tuition/fees: $43,866. Room/board: $10,374. Books/supplies: $900. Personal expenses: $2,000.

2011-2012 Financial aid. Need-based: 527 full-time freshmen applied for aid; 422 were judged to have need; 422 of these received aid. Average need met was 95%. Average scholarship/grant was $24,500; average loan $4,200. 79% of total undergraduate aid awarded as scholarships/grants, 21% as loans/jobs. **Non-need-based:** Awarded to 422 full-time undergraduates, including 111 freshmen. Scholarships awarded for academics, art, athletics, leadership, music/drama, ROTC.

Application procedures. Admission: Closing date 1/15 (postmark date). $60 fee, may be waived for applicants with need. Admission notification by 4/1. Must reply by 5/1. **Financial aid:** Closing date 1/15. FAFSA, CSS PROFILE required. Applicants notified by 4/1; must reply by 5/1.

Academics. Special study options: Combined bachelor's/graduate degree, double major, dual enrollment of high school students, honors, independent study, internships, liberal arts/career combination, semester at sea, student-designed major, study abroad, teacher certification program, Washington semester. Pass/Fail option. **Credit/placement by examination:** AP, CLEP, IB, institutional tests. No policy limit on number of credits; only a few courses offer this option. **Support services:** Learning center, study skills assistance, tutoring, writing center.

Majors. Area/ethnic studies: East Asian, Italian, Latin American, women's. **Biology:** General, animal behavior, biochemistry, cellular/molecular, neuroscience. **Business:** Accounting/finance, business admin, international, marketing. **Computer sciences:** General. **Conservation:** Environmental studies. **Education:** General, early childhood, elementary, music, secondary. **Engineering:** Biomedical, chemical, civil, computer, electrical, mechanical. **English:** Creative writing, English lit. **Foreign languages:** Classics, French, German, Russian, Spanish. **History:** General. **Liberal arts:** Humanities. **Math:** General. **Philosophy/religion:** Philosophy, religion. **Physical sciences:** Chemistry, geology, physics. **Psychology:** General. **Social sciences:** Anthropology, econometrics, economics, geography, international relations, political science, sociology. **Visual/performing arts:** General, art history/conservation, dramatic, music, music history, music performance, music theory/composition, studio arts.

Most popular majors. Biology 8%, business/marketing 12%, engineering/engineering technologies 14%, English 6%, foreign language 6%, psychology 6%, social sciences 26%.

Computing on campus. 970 workstations in dormitories, library, computer center, student center. Dormitories wired for high-speed internet access and linked to campus network. Commuter students can connect to campus network. Online course registration, online library, helpline, repair service, wireless network available.

Student life. Freshman orientation: Mandatory, $100 fee. Preregistration for classes offered. Held 5 days prior to start of classes. **Policies:** All first-year students must sign statement of student responsibility. Freshmen not permitted cars on campus. **Housing:** Guaranteed on-campus for all undergraduates. Coed dorms, single-sex dorms, special housing for disabled, apartments, cooperative housing, fraternity/sorority housing, wellness housing available. Seven residential colleges with themes: arts, humanities, global, environment, social justice, technology and society; language and culture. Quiet floors available. **Activities:** Bands, campus ministries, choral groups, dance, drama, film society, international student organizations, literary magazine, music ensembles, Model UN, musical theater, opera, radio station, student government, student newspaper, symphony orchestra, Hillel, Chinese culture association, Japan society, Muslim student association, OHLAS, College Democrats, College Republicans, Habitat for Humanity, Bucknell Brigade, Rooke Chapel Congregation.

Athletics. NCAA. **Intercollegiate:** Baseball M, basketball, cross-country, diving, field hockey W, football (tackle) M, golf, lacrosse, rowing (crew) W, soccer, softball W, swimming, tennis, track and field, volleyball W, water polo, wrestling M. **Intramural:** Badminton, basketball, bowling, cross-country, football (non-tackle), golf, racquetball, soccer, softball, squash, table tennis, tennis, volleyball, weight lifting M. **Team name:** Bison.

Student services. Alcohol/substance abuse counseling, chaplain/spiritual director, career counseling, financial aid counseling, health services, minority student services, personal counseling, placement for graduates, women's services. **Physically disabled:** Services for visually, hearing impaired.

Contact. E-mail: admissions@bucknell.edu
Phone: (570) 577-1101 Fax: (570) 577-3538
Robert Springall, Dean of Admissions, Bucknell University, Office of Admissions, Bucknell University, Lewisburg, PA 17837-9988

Cabrini College
Radnor, Pennsylvania
www.cabrini.edu

CB member
CB code: 2071

- Private 4-year liberal arts college affiliated with Roman Catholic Church
- Residential campus in large town
- 1,341 degree-seeking undergraduates: 6% part-time, 64% women, 9% African American, 1% Asian American, 6% Hispanic American
- 1,662 degree-seeking graduate students
- 72% of applicants admitted
- SAT or ACT (ACT writing optional) required
- 56% graduate within 6 years; 16% enter graduate study

General. Founded in 1957. Regionally accredited. College sponsored by Missionary Sisters of the Sacred Heart of Jesus (international religious order serving six continents). **Degrees:** 327 bachelor's awarded; master's offered. **ROTC:** Army, Air Force. **Location:** 18 miles from Philadelphia, 5 miles from King of Prussia. **Calendar:** Semester, limited summer session. **Full-time faculty:** 71 total; 86% have terminal degrees, 8% minority, 63% women. **Part-time faculty:** 231 total; 23% have terminal degrees, 11% minority, 56% women. **Class size:** 72% < 20, 27% 20-39, less than 1% 40-49. **Special facilities:** College-operated preschool (off-campus), human performance lab, video studio, graphic design lab.

Freshman class profile. 2,397 applied, 1,720 admitted, 346 enrolled.

Mid 50% test scores			
SAT critical reading:	410-510	GPA 2.0-2.99:	43%
SAT math:	400-510	Rank in top quarter:	20%
SAT writing:	400-510	Rank in top tenth:	8%
GPA 3.75 or higher:	14%	End year in good standing:	83%
GPA 3.50-3.74:	12%	Return as sophomores:	73%
GPA 3.0-3.49:	30%	Out-of-state:	43%
		Live on campus:	90%

Basis for selection. School achievement record, test scores, academic potential, and personal qualities most important. Special consideration for children of alumni and students with special backgrounds, skills or abilities. Community action required. Non-English-speaking international students may take TOEFL instead of SAT/ACT. Interview recommended for all. **Home schooled:** Transcript of courses and grades, state high school equivalency certificate required. Provide as much external testing data as possible. Standardized test scores given more weight for homeschooled students.

High school preparation. College-preparatory program required. 18 units required; 21 recommended. Required and recommended units include English 4, mathematics 3-4, social studies 3, science 3, foreign language 2 and academic electives 2. Two arts and humanities also recommended. Additional math and science units recommended for science students.

2011-2012 Annual costs. Tuition/fees: $33,176. Room/board: $11,742.

Financial aid. Non-need-based: Scholarships awarded for academics.

Application procedures. Admission: Priority date 5/1; no deadline. $35 fee, may be waived for applicants with need. Admission notification on a rolling basis. **Financial aid:** Closing date 4/1. FAFSA required. Applicants notified on a rolling basis starting 2/15.

Academics. Education fieldwork opportunities provided to education majors from sophomore to senior years. Students participate in community service. Internship or co-op programs offered in all majors. **Special study options:** Combined bachelor's/graduate degree, cooperative education, cross-registration, double major, honors, independent study, internships, liberal arts/career combination, student-designed major, study abroad, teacher certification program, Washington semester. Exchange programs with Eastern University, Rosemont College, Valley Forge Military College; cross-registration with Southeastern Pennsylvania Consortium for Higher Education (8-member consortium of private colleges/universities). **Credit/placement by examination:** AP, CLEP, IB, SAT, institutional tests. 30 credit hours maximum toward bachelor's degree. DANTES. **Support services:** Learning center, reduced course load, remedial instruction, study skills assistance, tutoring, writing center.

Majors. Area/ethnic studies: American. **Biology:** General. **Business:** Accounting, business admin, finance, human resources, marketing. **Communications:** Communications/speech/rhetoric. **Computer sciences:** Information technology. **Education:** General, elementary, kindergarten/preschool, special ed. **English:** English lit. **Foreign languages:** French, Spanish. **History:** General. **Human services:** Social work. **Liberal arts:** Arts/sciences. **Math:** General. **Parks/recreation:** Exercise sciences. **Philosophy/religion:** Philosophy, religion. **Physical sciences:** Chemistry. **Psychology:** General. **Social sciences:** Criminology, political science, sociology. **Visual/performing arts:** Graphic design.

Most popular majors. Biology 6%, business/marketing 23%, communications/journalism 10%, education 16%, psychology 10%, social sciences 7%.

Computing on campus. 469 workstations in dormitories, library, computer center. Dormitories wired for high-speed internet access and linked to campus network. Commuter students can connect to campus network. Online course registration, online library, helpline, student web hosting, wireless network available.

Student life. Freshman orientation: Mandatory, $220 fee. Preregistration for classes offered. 3-day program prior to beginning of fall semester. **Housing:** Coed dorms, single-sex dorms, special housing for disabled, apartments available. $150 fully refundable deposit, deadline 5/1. Special interest housing options designated for intensified study, honors, Hispanic culture and community service. **Activities:** Campus ministries, choral groups, dance, drama, film society, international student organizations, literary magazine, musical theater, radio station, student government, student newspaper, TV station, black student union, Habitat for Humanity, Cavaliers for Life, La Raza, campus ministry activities council, search club, CRS ambassadors, sanctuary.

Athletics. NCAA. **Intercollegiate:** Basketball, cross-country, field hockey W, golf M, lacrosse, soccer, softball W, swimming, tennis, volleyball W. **Intramural:** Basketball, cricket, football (non-tackle), soccer, squash, volleyball. **Team name:** Cavaliers.

Student services. Adult student services, alcohol/substance abuse counseling, chaplain/spiritual director, career counseling, student employment services, financial aid counseling, health services, minority student services, personal counseling, placement for graduates. **Physically disabled:** Services for visually, hearing impaired.

Contact. E-mail: admit@cabrini.edu
Phone: (610) 902-8552 Toll-free number: (800) 848-1003
Fax: (610) 902-8508
Eugene Soltys, Director of Admissions, Cabrini College, 610 King of Prussia Road, Radnor, PA 19087-3698

California University of Pennsylvania

California, Pennsylvania — CB member
www.calu.edu — CB code: 2647

- Public 4-year university
- Commuter campus in small town
- 7,341 degree-seeking undergraduates: 11% part-time, 52% women, 7% African American, 2% Hispanic American, 1% international
- 1,878 degree-seeking graduate students
- 59% of applicants admitted
- SAT required
- 54% graduate within 6 years

General. Founded in 1852. Regionally accredited. Green-oriented; utilizes geothermal technologies to reduce energy consumption. **Degrees:** 1,348 bachelor's, 44 associate awarded; master's offered. **ROTC:** Army. **Location:** 38 miles from Pittsburgh. **Calendar:** Semester, limited summer session. **Full-time faculty:** 246 total; 82% have terminal degrees, 13% minority, 48% women. **Part-time faculty:** 167 total; 7% minority, 47% women. **Class size:** 14% < 20, 47% 20-39, 17% 40-49, 20% 50-99, 1% >100. **Special facilities:** International corporate art collection, 98-acre farm with recreational facilities.

Freshman class profile. 4,400 applied, 2,602 admitted, 1,346 enrolled.

Mid 50% test scores			
SAT critical reading:	440-530	Rank in top tenth:	6%
SAT math:	450-530	Return as sophomores:	73%
GPA 3.75 or higher:	12%	Out-of-state:	9%
GPA 3.50-3.74:	15%	Live on campus:	76%
GPA 3.0-3.49:	32%	International:	1%
GPA 2.0-2.99:	40%	Fraternities:	6%
Rank in top quarter:	25%	Sororities:	6%

Basis for selection. School achievement record, test scores, activities, recommendations, interview considered. Essay recommended. **Home schooled:** Transcript of courses and grades required.

High school preparation. College-preparatory program recommended. 19 units required; 21 recommended. Required and recommended units include English 4, mathematics 3, social studies 2, history 2, science 1 (laboratory 1), foreign language 2 and academic electives 6.

2011-2012 Annual costs. Tuition/fees: $8,912; $12,656 out-of-state. Room/board: $9,934. Books/supplies: $1,000. Personal expenses: $2,076.

2011-2012 Financial aid. Need-based: 988 full-time freshmen applied for aid; 834 were judged to have need; 834 of these received aid. Average need met was 85%. Average scholarship/grant was $8,707; average loan $7,069. 47% of total undergraduate aid awarded as scholarships/grants, 53% as loans/jobs. **Non-need-based:** Awarded to 1,008 full-time undergraduates, including 319 freshmen. Scholarships awarded for academics, athletics, leadership, minority status, music/drama, state residency.

Application procedures. Admission: Priority date 5/1; no deadline. $25 fee, may be waived for applicants with need. Admission notification on a rolling basis. **Financial aid:** Priority date 5/1; no closing date. FAFSA required. Applicants notified on a rolling basis starting 4/1; must reply within 2 week(s) of notification.

Academics. Special study options: Accelerated study, combined bachelor's/graduate degree, cooperative education, cross-registration, distance learning, double major, dual enrollment of high school students, ESL, exchange student, external degree, honors, independent study, internships, liberal arts/career combination, student-designed major, study abroad, teacher certification program, urban semester, Washington semester, weekend college. **Credit/placement by examination:** AP, CLEP, IB, SAT, institutional tests. **Support services:** Learning center, pre-admission summer program, reduced course load, remedial instruction, study skills assistance, tutoring, writing center.

Honors college/program. Minimum 1100 SAT (exclusive of Writing), 3.0 GPA, letter of recommendation required. Admitted students work with adviser and dean to design course of study.

Majors. Biology: General. **Business:** Accounting, business admin. **Communications:** Communications/speech/rhetoric. **Computer sciences:** General. **Conservation:** Environmental science. **Education:** General, elementary, kindergarten/preschool, special ed. **English:** English lit. **Foreign languages:** General, French, German, Russian, Spanish. **Health services:** Athletic training, clinical lab technology, communication disorders, nursing (RN). **History:** General. **Human services:** Social work. **Liberal arts:** Arts/sciences. **Math:** General. **Parks/recreation:** Facilities management, sports admin. **Philosophy/religion:** Philosophy. **Physical sciences:** General, chemistry, geology, physics. **Protective services:** Criminal justice. **Psychology:** General. **Social sciences:** General, geography, political science. **Visual/performing arts:** Art, commercial/advertising art, dramatic, graphic design.

Most popular majors. Business/marketing 15%, education 11%, health sciences 10%, liberal arts 6%, parks/recreation 11%, security/protective services 8%.

Computing on campus. 1,220 workstations in dormitories, library, computer center, student center. Dormitories wired for high-speed internet access and linked to campus network. Commuter students can connect to campus network. Online course registration, online library, helpline available.

Student life. Freshman orientation: Mandatory. Preregistration for classes offered. One-day session held in July or August. **Policies:** Freshman students under 21 and not commuting from parental home required to live in dormitory. **Housing:** Coed dorms, single-sex dorms, special housing for disabled, apartments, cooperative housing, fraternity/sorority housing, wellness housing available. $235 deposit. **Activities:** Bands, campus ministries, choral groups, dance, drama, international student organizations, literary magazine, music ensembles, musical theater, opera, radio station, student government, student newspaper, symphony orchestra, TV station.

Athletics. NCAA. **Intercollegiate:** Baseball M, basketball, cheerleading, cross-country, football (tackle) M, golf, rugby, soccer, softball, swimming W, tennis W, track and field, volleyball. **Intramural:** Archery, badminton, baseball M, basketball, bowling, cheerleading, cross-country, fencing, football (non-tackle), football (tackle), golf, gymnastics, handball, ice hockey, judo, lacrosse, racquetball, rugby, skiing, skin diving M, soccer, softball W, swimming W, table tennis, tennis W, track and field, triathlon, volleyball, weight lifting, wrestling M. **Team name:** Vulcans.

Student services. Adult student services, alcohol/substance abuse counseling, chaplain/spiritual director, career counseling, services for economically disadvantaged, student employment services, financial aid counseling, health services, legal services, minority student services, personal counseling,

placement for graduates, veterans' counselor, women's services. **Physically disabled:** Services for visually, speech, hearing impaired.

Contact. E-mail: inquiry@calu.edu
Phone: (724) 938-4404 Toll-free number: (888) 412-0479
Fax: (724) 938-4564
William Edmonds, Dean of Admissions, California University of Pennsylvania, 250 University Avenue, California, PA 15419-1394

Carlow University
Pittsburgh, Pennsylvania
www.carlow.edu

CB member
CB code: 2421

- Private 4-year university and liberal arts college affiliated with Roman Catholic Church
- Residential campus in large city
- 1,441 degree-seeking undergraduates: 23% part-time, 93% women, 17% African American, 1% Asian American, 1% Hispanic American
- 895 degree-seeking graduate students
- 65% of applicants admitted
- SAT or ACT (ACT writing optional) required
- 51% graduate within 6 years; 23% enter graduate study

General. Founded in 1929. Regionally accredited. Founded by the Sisters of Mercy in 1929 and member of the Conference for Mercy Higher Education. **Degrees:** 291 bachelor's awarded; master's, professional offered. **ROTC:** Army, Naval, Air Force. **Location:** 3 miles from downtown. **Calendar:** Semester, limited summer session. **Full-time faculty:** 92 total; 67% have terminal degrees, 9% minority, 78% women. **Part-time faculty:** 188 total; 25% have terminal degrees, 4% minority, 76% women. **Class size:** 79% < 20, 20% 20-39, less than 1% 50-99. **Special facilities:** Early Learning Center, Campus School (preK-12), science and technology research labs, cadaver lab, communications lab, math lab, greenhouse, herbarium, biochamber, tissue culture lab, children's science lab, International Poetry Forum archives, Women of Spirit Institute.

Freshman class profile. 1,072 applied, 696 admitted, 224 enrolled.

Mid 50% test scores			
SAT critical reading:	430-530	GPA 2.0-2.99:	26%
SAT math:	420-510	Rank in top quarter:	38%
SAT writing:	430-520	Rank in top tenth:	12%
ACT composite:	18-23	End year in good standing:	82%
GPA 3.75 or higher:	21%	Return as sophomores:	74%
GPA 3.50-3.74:	17%	Out-of-state:	7%
GPA 3.0-3.49:	36%	Live on campus:	71%

Basis for selection. Secondary school GPA, rank, record, and course work most important. SAT or ACT also considered. 2.5 GPA and class ranking in upper two-fifths of graduating class strengthen the application. International students must take TOEFL and ACT or SAT exams. Essay, interview recommended for all and in some cases required. Portfolio recommended for all art programs. **Home schooled:** Transcript of courses and grades required. Personal interview and portfolio from most recent year highly recommended.

High school preparation. College-preparatory program recommended. 18 units required. Required and recommended units include English 4, mathematics 3-4, social studies 2, history 2, science 3-4 (laboratory 2) and academic electives 4. Applicants to professional nursing programs must have 4 units English, 3 units social sciences, 2 units math (1 must be algebra), and 2 units laboratory science, including chemistry.

2012-2013 Annual costs. Tuition/fees: $24,438. Undergraduate adult students pay $585 per-credit-hour. Room/board: $9,630. Books/supplies: $1,020. Personal expenses: $1,300.

Application procedures. Admission: No deadline. $20 fee, may be waived for applicants with need, free for online applicants. Admission notification on a rolling basis. Must reply by May 1 or within 4 week(s) if notified thereafter. **Financial aid:** Priority date 4/1; no closing date. FAFSA required. Applicants notified on a rolling basis starting 2/15; must reply within 4 week(s) of notification.

Academics. Special study options: Accelerated study, combined bachelor's/graduate degree, cross-registration, distance learning, double major, dual enrollment of high school students, honors, independent study, internships, liberal arts/career combination, semester at sea, study abroad, teacher certification program, weekend college. 3+2 programs: biology/environmental engineering, chemistry/chemical engineering, math/engineering with Carnegie Mellon University, Biology/environmental science and management, 3+3 JD Law Program with Duquesne University, First Year Seminar for freshmen. **Credit/placement by examination:** AP, CLEP, IB, institutional tests. 30

credit hours maximum toward bachelor's degree. **Support services:** Learning center, reduced course load, remedial instruction, study skills assistance, tutoring, writing center.

Majors. Biology: General. **Business:** Accounting, auditing, business admin. **Communications:** Media studies. **Education:** Art, early childhood, middle, special ed. **English:** Creative writing, English lit, technical writing. **Health services:** Art therapy, health care admin, nursing (RN). **History:** General. **Human services:** Social work. **Liberal arts:** Arts/sciences. **Math:** General. **Philosophy/religion:** Philosophy. **Physical sciences:** Chemistry. **Psychology:** General. **Social sciences:** Political science, sociology. **Theology:** Theology. **Visual/performing arts:** Studio arts.

Most popular majors. Biology 6%, business/marketing 12%, education 24%, health sciences 26%, psychology 9%.

Computing on campus. 212 workstations in library, computer center, student center. Dormitories wired for high-speed internet access and linked to campus network. Commuter students can connect to campus network. Online course registration, online library, helpline, wireless network available.

Student life. Freshman orientation: Mandatory. Preregistration for classes offered. Held for several days prior to Fall semester, includes seminars, team-building activities, social events. **Housing:** Single-sex dorms available. $100 fully refundable deposit, deadline 5/1. **Activities:** Pep band, campus ministries, choral groups, dance, drama, international student organizations, literary magazine, music ensembles, musical theater, student government, student newspaper, Community Outreach, Alpha Phi Omega, Commuter Student Organization, Social Work Association, Black Student Union, FEMME, LGBT and Allies, Chi Eta Phi, Women in Communications.

Athletics. NAIA, USCAA. **Intercollegiate:** Basketball W, soccer W, softball W, tennis W, volleyball W. **Team name:** Celtics.

Student services. Adult student services, alcohol/substance abuse counseling, chaplain/spiritual director, career counseling, student employment services, financial aid counseling, health services, minority student services, on-campus daycare, personal counseling, placement for graduates, women's services. **Physically disabled:** Services for visually, speech, hearing impaired.

Contact. E-mail: admissions@carlow.edu
Phone: (412) 578-6059 Toll-free number: (800) 333-2275
Fax: (412) 578-6321
Susan Winstel, Director of Admissions, Carlow University, 3333 Fifth Avenue, Pittsburgh, PA 15213-3165

Carnegie Mellon University
Pittsburgh, Pennsylvania
www.cmu.edu

CB member
CB code: 2074

- Private 4-year university
- Residential campus in large city
- 6,178 degree-seeking undergraduates: 2% part-time, 42% women, 5% African American, 22% Asian American, 3% Hispanic American, 17% international
- 5,777 degree-seeking graduate students
- 30% of applicants admitted
- SAT or ACT with writing, SAT Subject Tests, application essay required
- 87% graduate within 6 years

General. Founded in 1900. Regionally accredited. **Degrees:** 1,415 bachelor's awarded; master's, doctoral offered. **ROTC:** Army, Naval, Air Force. **Location:** 5 miles from downtown. **Calendar:** Semester, limited summer session. **Class size:** 67% < 20, 18% 20-39, 4% 40-49, 8% 50-99, 4% >100. **Special facilities:** Botanical institute, rare books collection, recording studios, design studios, photo shoot studio, music halls.

Freshman class profile. 16,527 applied, 5,030 admitted, 1,436 enrolled.

Mid 50% test scores			
SAT critical reading:	630-730	GPA 2.0-2.99:	2%
SAT math:	680-780	Rank in top quarter:	92%
SAT writing:	640-740	Rank in top tenth:	75%
ACT composite:	29-34	Return as sophomores:	95%
GPA 3.75 or higher:	52%	Out-of-state:	84%
GPA 3.50-3.74:	28%	Live on campus:	99%
GPA 3.0-3.49:	18%	International:	9%

Basis for selection. Academic and artistic potential, standardized tests, activities, jobs, interests, and other personalized information important. Applicants to art, architecture, design, drama, and music programs should submit Common Application and Carnegie Mellon Supplement by regular decision fine arts deadline of December 1. SAT subject tests are not required for

drama, design, art, or music applicants. All other students/applicants must take appropriate tests, preferably by December, but no later than January. All other applicants must take appropriate tests, preferably by December, but no later than January. College of Fine Arts deadline for application December 1. CMU uses AP, SAT/ACT, SAT/ACT subject tests and institutional exams for placement. Interview recommended for all; audition required for drama, music programs; portfolio required for art, design programs. **Home schooled:** Transcript of courses and grades, letter of recommendation (nonparent) required. Submit syllabus/course descriptions of work done; transcript of grades/evaluations; recommendation from counselor, representative of state board of education, homeschool association, or other person of authority.

High school preparation. College-preparatory program required. Required and recommended units include English 4, mathematics 4, science 3 (laboratory 3), foreign language 2 and academic electives 3-4. Requirements vary by program.

2011-2012 Annual costs. Tuition/fees: $43,812. Room/board: $11,110. Books/supplies: $1,000. Personal expenses: $1,400.

2011-2012 Financial aid. Need-based: 1,108 full-time freshmen applied for aid; 840 were judged to have need; 828 of these received aid. Average need met was 83%. Average scholarship/grant was $25,810; average loan $4,617. 74% of total undergraduate aid awarded as scholarships/grants, 26% as loans/jobs. **Non-need-based:** Awarded to 1,557 full-time undergraduates, including 424 freshmen. Scholarships awarded for academics, art, leadership, minority status, music/drama, state residency. **Additional information:** Early need analysis offered; merit awards available. Students notified within week to 10 days of receipt of financial aid application.

Application procedures. Admission: Closing date 1/1 (postmark date). $70 fee, may be waived for applicants with need. Admission notification by 4/15. Admission notification on a rolling basis. Must reply by 5/1. Application closing date December 1 for College of Fine Arts. **Financial aid:** Priority date 2/15, closing date 5/1. FAFSA, institutional form, CSS PROFILE required. Applicants notified by 3/15.

Academics. Special study options: Combined bachelor's/graduate degree, cooperative education, cross-registration, distance learning, double major, dual enrollment of high school students, exchange student, independent study, internships, liberal arts/career combination, student-designed major, study abroad, teacher certification program, Washington semester. **Credit/placement by examination:** AP, CLEP, IB, SAT, institutional tests. **Support services:** Learning center, pre-admission summer program, study skills assistance, tutoring, writing center.

Majors. Architecture: Architecture, history/criticism, technology. **Area/ethnic studies:** European, Russian/Slavic. **Biology:** General, biometrics, biophysics. **Business:** Business admin, managerial economics. **Computer sciences:** Computer science, information systems, information technology. **Conservation:** Management/policy. **Education:** Multicultural. **Engineering:** General, biomedical, chemical, civil, computer, electrical, materials, mechanical, operations research. **English:** Creative writing, English lit, technical writing. **Foreign languages:** General, Chinese, French, German, Japanese, linguistics, Russian, Spanish. **History:** General. **Human services:** Public policy. **Liberal arts:** Arts/sciences. **Math:** General, applied, computational, financial, probability, statistics. **Philosophy/religion:** Ethics, logic, philosophy, professional ethics. **Physical sciences:** Astrophysics, chemical physics, chemistry, physics, theoretical physics. **Psychology:** General. **Social sciences:** General, anthropology, econometrics, economics, international relations. **Visual/performing arts:** Art, design, dramatic, industrial design, jazz, music performance, music theory/composition, piano/keyboard, stringed instruments, voice/opera.

Most popular majors. Business/marketing 10%, computer/information sciences 12%, engineering/engineering technologies 23%, interdisciplinary studies 9%, physical sciences 8%, visual/performing arts 11%.

Computing on campus. 384 workstations in dormitories, library, computer center, student center. Dormitories wired for high-speed internet access and linked to campus network. Commuter students can connect to campus network. Online course registration, online library, helpline, repair service, student web hosting, wireless network available.

Student life. Freshman orientation: Mandatory, $198 fee. Preregistration for classes offered. Week-long program held one week before start of classes. **Policies:** Freshmen required to live on campus. **Housing:** Guaranteed on-campus for freshmen. Coed dorms, single-sex dorms, special housing for disabled, apartments, fraternity/sorority housing, wellness housing available. $800 nonrefundable deposit, deadline 5/1. Special interest group housing available. **Activities:** Bands, campus ministries, choral groups, dance, drama, film society, international student organizations, literary magazine, music ensembles, Model UN, musical theater, radio station, student government, student newspaper, symphony orchestra, TV station, Alpha Phi Omega, Hillel, minority women's club, service clubs, National Society of Black Engineers, Society of Women Engineers, Phi Beta Kappa.

Athletics. NCAA. **Intercollegiate:** Basketball, cheerleading, cross-country, diving, football (tackle) M, golf M, soccer, swimming, tennis, track and field, volleyball W. **Intramural:** Badminton, basketball, bowling, cross-country, fencing, football (non-tackle), golf, racquetball, soccer, softball, squash, swimming, table tennis, tennis, track and field, volleyball, water polo. **Team name:** Tartans.

Student services. Alcohol/substance abuse counseling, chaplain/spiritual director, career counseling, student employment services, financial aid counseling, health services, minority student services, on-campus daycare, personal counseling, placement for graduates, women's services. **Physically disabled:** Services for visually, speech, hearing impaired.

Contact. E-mail: undergraduate-admissions@andrew.cmu.edu
Phone: (412) 268-2082 Fax: (412) 268-7838
Michael Steidel, Director of Admissions, Carnegie Mellon University, 5000 Forbes Avenue, Pittsburgh, PA 15213-3890

Cedar Crest College
Allentown, Pennsylvania   CB member
www.cedarcrest.edu   CB code: 2079

- Private 4-year liberal arts college for women
- Residential campus in small city
- 1,370 degree-seeking undergraduates: 47% part-time, 96% women, 9% African American, 3% Asian American, 10% Hispanic American, 1% international
- 206 degree-seeking graduate students
- 62% of applicants admitted
- SAT or ACT (ACT writing optional), application essay required
- 50% graduate within 6 years

General. Founded in 1867. Regionally accredited. Men admitted to evening and weekend classes and daytime programs in nursing and nuclear medicine. **Degrees:** 363 bachelor's awarded; master's offered. **ROTC:** Army. **Location:** 55 miles from Philadelphia, 100 miles from New York City. **Calendar:** Semester, extensive summer session. **Full-time faculty:** 83 total; 76% have terminal degrees, 5% minority, 66% women. **Part-time faculty:** 88 total; 19% have terminal degrees, 7% minority, 73% women. **Class size:** 76% < 20, 20% 20-39, 2% 40-49, 2% 50-99. **Special facilities:** Wildlife sanctuary, outdoor Greek theater, arboretum, sculpture garden, aquatic center, college-operated museums, media convergence lab.

Freshman class profile. 924 applied, 576 admitted, 117 enrolled.

Mid 50% test scores			
SAT critical reading:	460-560	GPA 2.0-2.99:	39%
SAT math:	440-540	Rank in top quarter:	39%
SAT writing:	430-540	Rank in top tenth:	10%
ACT composite:	20-23	End year in good standing:	89%
GPA 3.75 or higher:	7%	Return as sophomores:	76%
GPA 3.50-3.74:	12%	Out-of-state:	17%
GPA 3.0-3.49:	42%	Live on campus:	67%
		International:	1%

Basis for selection. Secondary school curriculum and grades most important. Test scores important. Special talents, potential for academic and personal growth considered. Interview and essay recommended for all. **Home schooled:** Transcript of courses and grades, letter of recommendation (nonparent) required.

High school preparation. College-preparatory program required. 20 units required. Required units include English 4, mathematics 3, social studies 3, history 3, science 2 (laboratory 2), foreign language 2 and academic electives 3. Special natural science requirements for nuclear medicine and nursing.

2011-2012 Annual costs. Tuition/fees: $30,110. Room/board: $9,804. Books/supplies: $1,000. Personal expenses: $850.

2011-2012 Financial aid. Need-based: 111 full-time freshmen applied for aid; 111 were judged to have need; 111 of these received aid. Average need met was 75%. Average scholarship/grant was $21,856; average loan $3,410. 70% of total undergraduate aid awarded as scholarships/grants, 30% as loans/jobs. **Non-need-based:** Scholarships awarded for academics, alumni affiliation, art, leadership, music/drama.

Application procedures. Admission: Priority date 2/15; no deadline. $35 fee, may be waived for applicants with need, free for online applicants. Admission notification on a rolling basis beginning on or about 9/15. Must reply by May 1 or within 2 week(s) if notified thereafter. **Financial aid:** Priority date 5/1; no closing date. FAFSA required. Applicants notified on a rolling basis starting 1/1; must reply within 2 week(s) of notification.

Academics. Special study options: Combined bachelor's/graduate degree, cross-registration, distance learning, double major, honors, independent study, internships, liberal arts/career combination, student-designed major, study abroad, teacher certification program, Washington semester. **Credit/placement by examination:** AP, CLEP, IB, SAT, ACT. 18 credit hours maximum toward bachelor's degree. **Support services:** Learning center, pre-admission summer program, remedial instruction, study skills assistance, tutoring, writing center.

Majors. Biology: General, biochemistry, environmental, genetics, neuroscience. **Business:** Accounting, business admin, marketing. **Communications:** Communications/speech/rhetoric. **Computer sciences:** General. **Education:** Elementary, secondary. **English:** English lit. **Foreign languages:** Spanish. **Health services:** Nuclear medical technology, nursing (RN). **History:** General. **Human services:** Social work. **Math:** General. **Physical sciences:** Chemistry. **Psychology:** General. **Social sciences:** Criminology, political science. **Visual/performing arts:** General, art, dance, dramatic, music, studio arts. **Work/family studies:** Food/nutrition.

Most popular majors. Biology 8%, business/marketing 10%, education 9%, health sciences 31%, psychology 16%, public administration/social services 6%, visual/performing arts 6%.

Computing on campus. 287 workstations in dormitories, library, computer center, student center. Dormitories wired for high-speed internet access and linked to campus network. Online course registration, online library, helpline, repair service, wireless network available.

Student life. Freshman orientation: Mandatory. Preregistration for classes offered. 5-day academic and social program in August mandatory. 2-day academic testing and advising program in June mandatory. **Policies:** Drinking under age 21 prohibited; honor philosophy exists. **Housing:** Guaranteed on-campus for all undergraduates. $100 nonrefundable deposit, deadline 7/1. **Activities:** Campus ministries, choral groups, dance, drama, international student organizations, literary magazine, music ensembles, musical theater, radio station, student government, student newspaper, Amnesty International, Black Student Union, Best Buddies, Cedar Crest Christian Fellowship, Hillel Society, Muslim student association, Sisters Inc, Global Eyes, Take Back the Night.

Athletics. NCAA. **Intercollegiate:** Basketball W, cross-country W, field hockey W, lacrosse W, soccer W, softball W, tennis W, volleyball W. **Intramural:** Badminton W, basketball W, football (non-tackle) W, soccer W, softball W, triathlon W. **Team name:** Falcons.

Student services. Adult student services, alcohol/substance abuse counseling, chaplain/spiritual director, career counseling, services for economically disadvantaged, student employment services, financial aid counseling, health services, minority student services, personal counseling, placement for graduates, women's services. **Physically disabled:** Services for visually, hearing impaired.

Contact. E-mail: admissions@cedarcrest.edu
Phone: (610) 740-3780 Toll-free number: (800) 360-1222
Fax: (610) 606-4647
Mariea Noblitt, Vice President for Enrollment Management, Cedar Crest College, 100 College Drive, Allentown, PA 18104-6196

Central Pennsylvania College
Summerdale, Pennsylvania
www.centralpenn.edu   **CB code: 1061**

▸ For-profit 4-year technical and career college
▸ Commuter campus in rural community
▸ 1,471 degree-seeking undergraduates: 50% part-time, 65% women, 20% African American, 1% Asian American, 4% Hispanic American
▸ 43% of applicants admitted
▸ Application essay, interview required
▸ 60% graduate within 6 years

General. Founded in 1881. Regionally accredited. **Degrees:** 214 bachelor's, 82 associate awarded. **Location:** 5 miles from Harrisburg. **Calendar:** Trimester, extensive summer session. **Full-time faculty:** 24 total. **Part-time faculty:** 88 total. **Special facilities:** Student-staffed restaurant, mock courtroom, multimedia lab, child-care facility, advanced technology education center, conference facility, crime lab.

Freshman class profile. 2,987 applied, 1,298 admitted, 210 enrolled.

Return as sophomores:	68%	Live on campus:	64%
Out-of-state:	20%		

Basis for selection. High school achievement record very important for admission to physical therapist assistant program. Minimum GPA of 2.5 (3.0

---

preferred) and two references required for entrance into the physical therapy assistant program. **Home schooled:** Provide transcript of courses completed with grades and include parent/teacher/academy signatures. **Learning Disabled:** Students meet with academic dean to discuss provisions needed for individual learning experience.

2011-2012 Annual costs. Tuition/fees: $18,550. Room/board: $6,570. Books/supplies: $1,500. Personal expenses: $1,000.

Financial aid. Non-need-based: Scholarships awarded for academics, alumni affiliation, job skills, leadership, minority status, state residency.

Application procedures. Admission: Priority date 5/1; no deadline. No application fee. Admission notification on a rolling basis. **Financial aid:** Priority date 3/15; no closing date. FAFSA, institutional form required. Applicants notified on a rolling basis starting 2/1; must reply within 2 week(s) of notification.

Academics. Special study options: Distance learning, double major, dual enrollment of high school students, honors, independent study, internships, study abroad. **Credit/placement by examination:** AP, CLEP, IB, institutional tests. 15 credit hours maximum toward associate degree, 15 toward bachelor's. **Support services:** Learning center, reduced course load, remedial instruction, study skills assistance, tutoring, writing center.

Majors. Business: Accounting, business admin. **Communications:** Communications/speech/rhetoric. **Computer sciences:** Computer science. **Protective services:** Criminal justice, homeland security.

Most popular majors. Business/marketing 73%, computer/information sciences 21%, security/protective services 27%.

Computing on campus. 150 workstations in library, computer center. Dormitories wired for high-speed internet access and linked to campus network. Commuter students can connect to campus network. Online course registration, online library, helpline, wireless network available.

Student life. Freshman orientation: Mandatory. Preregistration for classes offered. **Policies:** Dress code, mandatory attendance, ethics policies, no alcohol or drugs. **Housing:** Guaranteed on-campus for freshmen. Apartments, wellness housing available. $250 deposit. All resident housing is either single-gender townhouses or apartments. **Activities:** Choral groups, literary magazine, student government, student newspaper, Gamma Beta Phi, Delta Epsilon Chi, technology club, Club MED, Toastmasters, Young Republicans.

Athletics. USCAA. **Intercollegiate:** Basketball, bowling, golf. **Intramural:** Basketball, football (non-tackle), softball, tennis, volleyball. **Team name:** Silver Knights.

Student services. Adult student services, alcohol/substance abuse counseling, chaplain/spiritual director, career counseling, student employment services, financial aid counseling, on-campus daycare, personal counseling, placement for graduates, veterans' counselor.

Contact. E-mail: admissions@centralpenn.edu
Phone: (717) 728-2201 Toll-free number: (800) 759-2727
Fax: (717) 732-5254
Stacy Scott, Director of Admissions, Central Pennsylvania College, College Hill and Valley Roads, Summerdale, PA 17093-0309

Chatham University
Pittsburgh, Pennsylvania   **CB member**
www.chatham.edu   **CB code: 2081**

▸ Private 4-year university and liberal arts college for women
▸ Residential campus in large city
▸ 723 degree-seeking undergraduates: 14% part-time, 98% women, 13% African American, 2% Asian American, 3% Hispanic American, 8% international
▸ 1,317 degree-seeking graduate students
▸ 62% of applicants admitted
▸ Application essay required
▸ 60% graduate within 6 years

General. Founded in 1869. Regionally accredited. **Degrees:** 199 bachelor's awarded; master's, professional offered. **ROTC:** Army, Naval, Air Force. **Location:** 5 miles from downtown. **Calendar:** 4-1-4, limited summer session. **Full-time faculty:** 100 total; 90% have terminal degrees, 62% women. **Part-time faculty:** 193 total. **Class size:** 82% < 20, 17% 20-39, less than 1% 50-99. **Special facilities:** Broadcast studio, science complex and greenhouse, proscenium theater, arboretum.

Freshman class profile. 693 applied, 429 admitted, 130 enrolled.

Mid 50% test scores			
SAT critical reading:	480-600	GPA 2.0-2.99:	16%
SAT math:	460-560	Rank in top quarter:	48%
SAT writing:	460-580	Rank in top tenth:	26%
ACT composite:	19-27	Return as sophomores:	70%
GPA 3.75 or higher:	31%	Out-of-state:	18%
GPA 3.50-3.74:	24%	Live on campus:	74%
GPA 3.0-3.49:	29%	International:	8%

Basis for selection. School achievement record, essays, and test scores most important, though test scores are not required. Students who do not submit SAT/ACT scores required to submit a graded writing sample and resume/list of activities. Portfolios may also be submitted. Activities, talents, volunteer work, paid work, alumnae relationship, class rank, recommendations considered. TOEFL or IELTS required for international students. Campus visit or interviews recommended for all.

High school preparation. College-preparatory program recommended. 11 units required; 15 recommended. Required and recommended units include English 4, mathematics 2-3, science 2-3 and foreign language 2. Require 3 units of social science.

2012-2013 Annual costs. Tuition/fees: $31,532. Required fees ($1,150) cover technology fee, which includes cost of a MacBook Pro (required for all first-time first-year students) and the campus fee. Room/board: $9,692. Books/supplies: $860. Personal expenses: $2,862.

Financial aid. Non-need-based: Scholarships awarded for academics, alumni affiliation, leadership, minority status.

Application procedures. Admission: Priority date 3/15; deadline 8/1. $35 fee, may be waived for applicants with need, free for online applicants. Admission notification on a rolling basis beginning on or about 10/15. Must reply by May 1 or within 2 week(s) if notified thereafter. **Financial aid:** Priority date 5/1; no closing date. FAFSA required. Applicants notified on a rolling basis starting 2/15; must reply by 5/1 or within 2 week(s) of notification.

Academics. All students eligible through PACE Center to receive free tutoring in every course offered. Specialized courses offered for students having academic difficulties, as well as career preparation courses to help students choose a career path. **Special study options:** Accelerated study, combined bachelor's/graduate degree, cooperative education, cross-registration, distance learning, double major, dual enrollment of high school students, ESL, exchange student, honors, independent study, internships, liberal arts/career combination, semester at sea, student-designed major, study abroad, teacher certification program, Washington semester. Five-year bachelor's/master's programs on campus and with other institutions. **Credit/placement by examination:** AP, CLEP, IB. 12 credit hours maximum toward bachelor's degree. **Support services:** Learning center, reduced course load, remedial instruction, study skills assistance, tutoring, writing center.

Majors. Architecture: Interior. **Area/ethnic studies:** Women's. **Biology:** General, biochemistry. **Business:** Accounting, business admin, international, managerial economics, marketing. **Communications:** Broadcast journalism, communications/speech/rhetoric, journalism, public relations. **Conservation:** Environmental science, environmental studies. **Education:** Early childhood, elementary. **Engineering:** General. **English:** Creative writing, English lit. **Foreign languages:** French, Spanish. **Health services:** Nursing (RN). **History:** General. **Human services:** Public policy, social work. **Liberal arts:** Arts/sciences. **Math:** General. **Parks/recreation:** Exercise sciences. **Physical sciences:** Chemistry, physics. **Protective services:** Forensics. **Psychology:** General. **Social sciences:** Economics, international relations, political science. **Visual/performing arts:** Art history/conservation, music, photography, studio arts, studio arts management.

Most popular majors. Biology 9%, business/marketing 8%, English 8%, health sciences 13%, physical sciences 8%, psychology 13%, social sciences 6%, visual/performing arts 11%.

Computing on campus. PC or laptop required. 300 workstations in dormitories, library, computer center. Dormitories wired for high-speed internet access and linked to campus network. Commuter students can connect to campus network. Online course registration, online library, helpline, repair service, student web hosting, wireless network available.

Student life. Freshman orientation: Mandatory. Preregistration for classes offered. Held immediately before classes begin in late August. Mini-orientations held during late spring and summer when students can register for courses. **Policies:** Honor code. **Housing:** Guaranteed on-campus for all undergraduates. Apartments, wellness housing available. $150 nonrefundable deposit, deadline 5/1. Intercultural residence hall, community service floor and environmental floor within larger residence hall available. **Activities:** Choral groups, dance, drama, international student organizations, literary magazine, music ensembles, musical theater, student government, student newspaper, Black student union, Christian Fellowship, Jewish organization, Feminist collective, Gateway student association, Green Horizons, Mortar Board, Students Against Sexual Oppression.

Athletics. NCAA. **Intercollegiate:** Basketball W, cross-country W, ice hockey W, soccer W, softball W, swimming W, tennis W, volleyball W, water polo W. **Team name:** Cougars.

Student services. Adult student services, chaplain/spiritual director, career counseling, services for economically disadvantaged, student employment services, financial aid counseling, health services, personal counseling, placement for graduates, women's services. **Physically disabled:** Services for visually, speech, hearing impaired.

Contact. E-mail: admissions@chatham.edu
Phone: (412) 365-1825 Toll-free number: (800) 837-1290
Fax: (412) 365-1609
Marylyn Scott, Director of Undergraduate Admissions, Chatham University, Woodland Road, Pittsburgh, PA 15232

Chestnut Hill College
Philadelphia, Pennsylvania
www.chc.edu

CB member
CB code: 2082

- Private 4-year liberal arts college affiliated with Roman Catholic Church
- Residential campus in very large city
- 1,535 degree-seeking undergraduates: 18% part-time, 72% women, 32% African American, 3% Asian American, 6% Hispanic American, 3% international
- 759 degree-seeking graduate students
- 64% of applicants admitted
- SAT or ACT (ACT writing optional) required
- 44% graduate within 6 years

General. Founded in 1924. Regionally accredited. Extended campus at adjacent Sugar Loaf Hill. **Degrees:** 276 bachelor's, 1 associate awarded; master's, professional offered. **Location:** 17 miles from Center City. **Calendar:** Semester, limited summer session. **Full-time faculty:** 86 total; 84% have terminal degrees, 6% minority, 72% women. **Part-time faculty:** 268 total; 28% have terminal degrees, 10% minority, 52% women. **Class size:** 82% < 20, 18% 20-39. **Special facilities:** Observatory, planetarium, Irish literature collection, multimedia center, smart classrooms.

Freshman class profile. 2,294 applied, 1,467 admitted, 238 enrolled.

Mid 50% test scores			
SAT critical reading:	430-530	GPA 2.0-2.99:	30%
SAT math:	430-520	Rank in top quarter:	29%
SAT writing:	430-530	Rank in top tenth:	6%
ACT composite:	18-22	End year in good standing:	83%
GPA 3.75 or higher:	14%	Return as sophomores:	75%
GPA 3.50-3.74:	22%	Out-of-state:	48%
GPA 3.0-3.49:	34%	Live on campus:	82%

Basis for selection. Secondary school record, essay very important. Standardized test scores, recommendations, character, interview, extracurricular activities important. Alumni connection, talent, volunteer activity, work experience considered. Open admissions to accelerated program in the School of Continuing and Professional Studies. Students are placed in writing, math, and language courses on basis of placement tests administered by the college. **Home schooled:** Must subscribe to a homeschool agency.

High school preparation. College-preparatory program recommended. 16 units recommended. Recommended units include English 4, mathematics 3, social studies 4, science 3 and foreign language 2.

2011-2012 Annual costs. Tuition/fees: $29,200. Room/board: $9,340. Books/supplies: $1,000. Personal expenses: $1,400.

2011-2012 Financial aid. Need-based: 235 full-time freshmen applied for aid; 228 were judged to have need; 227 of these received aid. Average need met was 72%. Average scholarship/grant was $19,524; average loan $4,130. 61% of total undergraduate aid awarded as scholarships/grants, 39% as loans/jobs. **Non-need-based:** Awarded to 153 full-time undergraduates, including 45 freshmen. Scholarships awarded for academics, athletics.

Application procedures. Admission: Priority date 5/1; no deadline. $35 fee, may be waived for applicants with need. Admission notification on a rolling basis beginning on or about 10/1. Housing deposit refunded if requested in writing prior to May 1. **Financial aid:** Priority date 4/1; no closing date. FAFSA required. Applicants notified on a rolling basis starting 2/15.

Academics. Montessori certification available. Secondary education certification available in major field of study. Interdisciplinary bachelor's degree in international business, language, and culture. **Special study options:** Combined bachelor's/graduate degree, cross-registration, distance learning, double major, dual enrollment of high school students, ESL, exchange student, honors, independent study, internships, student-designed major, study abroad, teacher certification program. 2-2 double bachelor's program in biology or chemistry and medical technology with Thomas Jefferson University School of Allied Health Sciences, 3-2 BA/MS psychology, 3-2 BS/MS applied technology, 5-year BS/MEd elementary education with emphasis in special education, dual degree bachelor's in biology or chemistry, master's in physician assistant at Arcadia University, dual degree bachelor's in biology or chemistry, Doctor of Podiatric Medicine at Temple University. **Credit/placement by examination:** AP, CLEP, IB, SAT, ACT, institutional tests. 15 credit hours maximum toward bachelor's degree. **Support services:** Learning center, reduced course load, remedial instruction, study skills assistance, tutoring, writing center.

Majors. Biology: General, biochemistry, molecular. **Business:** Accounting/business management, business admin, communications, human resources, international, marketing. **Communications:** Media studies. **Computer sciences:** General. **Conservation:** Environmental science. **Education:** Early childhood, elementary, music. **English:** English lit. **Foreign languages:** French, Spanish. **Health services:** Health care admin. **History:** General. **Liberal arts:** Arts/sciences. **Math:** General. **Physical sciences:** Chemistry, forensic chemistry. **Protective services:** Forensics, law enforcement admin. **Psychology:** General. **Social sciences:** Political science, sociology. **Visual/performing arts:** Music. **Work/family studies:** Child care management.

Most popular majors. Business/marketing 18%, education 13%, psychology 9%, public administration/social services 21%, security/protective services 10%.

Computing on campus. 53 workstations in library, computer center. Dormitories wired for high-speed internet access and linked to campus network. Commuter students can connect to campus network. Online course registration, helpline, wireless network available.

Student life. Freshman orientation: Available. Preregistration for classes offered. Held 2 or 3 times during the summer. Additional program held the few days before classes begin. **Policies:** Freshmen not permitted cars on campus. **Housing:** Coed dorms, apartments available. $500 nonrefundable deposit, deadline 5/1. **Activities:** Bands, campus ministries, choral groups, dance, drama, international student organizations, literary magazine, music ensembles, musical theater, radio station, student government, student newspaper, TV station, African-American awareness society, Caribbean Culture Club, ecology club, gay/straight alliance, hospitality club, Hispanics in Action, Mosaic of Cultures club, Students for Peace and Justice, College Democrats, College Republicans.

Athletics. NCAA. **Intercollegiate:** Baseball M, basketball, cross-country, golf M, lacrosse, soccer, softball W, tennis, volleyball W. **Team name:** Griffins.

Student services. Adult student services, alcohol/substance abuse counseling, chaplain/spiritual director, career counseling, financial aid counseling, health services, personal counseling, veterans' counselor. **Physically disabled:** Services for visually impaired.

Contact. E-mail: chcapply@chc.edu
Phone: (215) 248-7001 Toll-free number: (800) 248-0052
Fax: (215) 248-7082
Lori Boccuzzi, Director of Admissions, School of Undergraduate Studies, Chestnut Hill College, 9601 Germantown Avenue, Philadelphia, PA 19118-2693

Cheyney University of Pennsylvania
Cheyney, Pennsylvania   **CB member**
www.cheyney.edu   **CB code: 2648**

▶ Public 4-year university
▶ Residential campus in small town
▶ 1,114 degree-seeking undergraduates: 4% part-time, 52% women
▶ 61 degree-seeking graduate students
▶ 81% of applicants admitted
▶ SAT or ACT, application essay required

General. Founded in 1837. Regionally accredited. Courses offered at Philadelphia Urban Center. **Degrees:** 136 bachelor's awarded; master's offered. **ROTC:** Army. **Location:** 25 miles from Philadelphia. **Calendar:** Semester, limited summer session. **Full-time faculty:** 79 total. **Part-time faculty:** 26 total. **Special facilities:** Planetarium, weather station, theater arts center.

Freshman class profile. 1,736 applied, 1,403 admitted, 220 enrolled.

Mid 50% test scores		Out-of-state:	33%
SAT critical reading:	350-420	Live on campus:	89%
SAT math:	340-420		

Basis for selection. Test scores, class rank, GPA, counselor recommendation, extracurricular activities important. 830 SAT (exclusive of Writing) or 17 ACT required. SAT Subject Tests recommended. Interview recommended.

High school preparation. College-preparatory program recommended. 13 units required. Required units include English 4, mathematics 3, history 2, science 2 and foreign language 2.

2011-2012 Annual costs. Tuition/fees: $8,404; $17,764 out-of-state. Tuition for residents of MD, NY, NJ and DE is $12,480. Room/board: $8,588. Books/supplies: $1,300.

Financial aid. Non-need-based: Scholarships awarded for academics, athletics.

Application procedures. Admission: Closing date 3/31. $20 fee, may be waived for applicants with need. Admission notification on a rolling basis. Must reply by 3/31. **Financial aid:** Priority date 3/15; no closing date. FAFSA required. Applicants notified on a rolling basis starting 4/1; must reply within 2 week(s) of notification.

Academics. Health and physical education courses required of most students. **Special study options:** Cooperative education, cross-registration, distance learning, double major, honors, independent study, internships, study abroad, teacher certification program. **Credit/placement by examination:** AP, CLEP, institutional tests. 23 credit hours maximum toward bachelor's degree. **Support services:** Learning center, pre-admission summer program, reduced course load, remedial instruction, tutoring.

Majors. Biology: General. **Business:** Business admin, hospitality admin. **Communications:** Communications/speech/rhetoric. **Computer sciences:** General. **Education:** Early childhood, elementary, special ed. **English:** English lit. **Foreign languages:** French, Spanish. **Health services:** Clinical lab science. **Math:** General. **Parks/recreation:** Facilities management. **Physical sciences:** Chemistry. **Psychology:** General. **Social sciences:** General, economics, political science, sociology. **Visual/performing arts:** Art, dramatic, music. **Work/family studies:** Clothing/textiles.

Most popular majors. Biology 10%, business/marketing 22%, education 7%, psychology 16%, social sciences 22%.

Computing on campus. 296 workstations in dormitories, library, computer center, student center. Dormitories wired for high-speed internet access and linked to campus network. Online course registration, helpline, repair service available.

Student life. Freshman orientation: Mandatory. Preregistration for classes offered. **Policies:** Ecumenical services held on campus. **Housing:** Guaranteed on-campus for freshmen. Coed dorms, single-sex dorms available. $100 fully refundable deposit, deadline 5/11. Honors dorm available. **Activities:** Bands, choral groups, drama, film society, music ensembles, radio station, student government, student newspaper, TV station, Shades of Unity, Toastmasters, business club, education club, NAACP, Latino Students in Action, LaOriginale, Commuter Students Association.

Athletics. NCAA. **Intercollegiate:** Basketball, bowling W, cross-country, football (tackle) M, tennis W, track and field, volleyball W. **Intramural:** Basketball, football (tackle) M. **Team name:** Wolves.

Student services. Adult student services, career counseling, student employment services, health services, personal counseling, placement for graduates, veterans' counselor.

Contact. E-mail: admissions@cheyney.edu
Phone: (610) 399-2275 Toll-free number: (800) 243-9639 ext. 2275
Fax: (610) 399-2099
Angela Brown, Assistant Director of Admissions, Cheyney University of Pennsylvania, 1837 University Circle, Cheyney, PA 19319-0019

Clarion University of Pennsylvania
Clarion, Pennsylvania
www.clarion.edu   **CB code: 2649**

▶ Public 4-year business and teachers college
▶ Residential campus in small town
▶ 5,716 degree-seeking undergraduates: 12% part-time, 62% women, 7% African American, 1% Asian American, 1% Hispanic American, 1% international

- 1,083 degree-seeking graduate students
- 71% of applicants admitted
- SAT or ACT (ACT writing optional) required
- 54% graduate within 6 years

General. Founded in 1867. Regionally accredited. **Degrees:** 983 bachelor's, 146 associate awarded; master's offered. **ROTC:** Army. **Location:** 80 miles from Pittsburgh, 90 miles from Erie. **Calendar:** Semester, limited summer session. **Full-time faculty:** 247 total; 2% have terminal degrees, 10% minority, 49% women. **Part-time faculty:** 96 total; 5% minority, 60% women. **Class size:** 24% < 20, 53% 20-39, 12% 40-49, 9% 50-99, 2% >100. **Special facilities:** Planetarium.

Freshman class profile. 3,795 applied, 2,700 admitted, 1,239 enrolled.

Mid 50% test scores			
		GPA 3.0-3.49:	32%
SAT critical reading:	410-510	GPA 2.0-2.99:	33%
SAT math:	470-520	Rank in top quarter:	25%
SAT writing:	400-500	Rank in top tenth:	8%
ACT composite:	17-22	Return as sophomores:	70%
GPA 3.75 or higher:	16%	Out-of-state:	5%
GPA 3.50-3.74:	16%	Live on campus:	80%

Basis for selection. School achievement record, class rank, GPA, test scores considered. Audition required of music program applicants; Nursing students must complete NLN entrance exam. **Home schooled:** Transcript of courses and grades required.

High school preparation. College-preparatory program required. 13 units required; 20 recommended. Required and recommended units include English 4, mathematics 3-4, social studies 3-4, history 1, science 3-4 (laboratory 1) and foreign language 2.

2011-2012 Annual costs. Tuition/fees: $8,828; $15,068 out-of-state. Tuition for incoming out-of-state residents with SAT of 1000 or higher and at least a 3.0 GPA or the top 30% of their graduating class is $9,360. Room/board: $6,932. Books/supplies: $1,000. Personal expenses: $3,000.

2010-2011 Financial aid. **Need-based:** 1,231 full-time freshmen applied for aid; 1,065 were judged to have need; 1,036 of these received aid. Average need met was 57%. Average scholarship/grant was $6,008; average loan $3,227. 56% of total undergraduate aid awarded as scholarships/grants, 44% as loans/jobs. **Non-need-based:** Awarded to 1,318 full-time undergraduates, including 396 freshmen. Scholarships awarded for academics, alumni affiliation, art, athletics, job skills, leadership, minority status, music/drama, state residency.

Application procedures. Admission: No deadline. $30 fee, may be waived for applicants with need. Admission notification on a rolling basis beginning on or about 9/1. **Financial aid:** Priority date 5/1; no closing date. FAFSA required. Applicants notified on a rolling basis starting 3/15; must reply within 4 week(s) of notification.

Academics. Special study options: Accelerated study, combined bachelor's/graduate degree, cooperative education, distance learning, double major, dual enrollment of high school students, ESL, honors, independent study, internships, liberal arts/career combination, study abroad, teacher certification program. Co-op program in engineering with two participating schools; co-op in speech pathology and audiology with Gallaudet University. Joint and collaborative programs in MSLS/JD, pharmacy, osteopathic medicine, nanotechnology, master of nursing, language, radiologic science, respiratory care and industrial technology. **Credit/placement by examination:** AP, CLEP, IB, SAT, ACT, institutional tests. 38 credit hours maximum toward bachelor's degree. **Support services:** Learning center, pre-admission summer program, remedial instruction, study skills assistance, tutoring, writing center.

Majors. Biology: General, ecology, environmental, molecular. **Business:** Business admin, finance, international, labor relations, managerial economics, marketing, real estate. **Communications:** Journalism, media studies. **Computer sciences:** General, information systems. **Conservation:** Environmental science. **Education:** Early childhood, elementary, special ed. **English:** English lit. **Foreign languages:** French, Spanish. **Health services:** Clinical lab technology, medical radiologic technology/radiation therapy, nursing (RN), rehabilitation science, speech pathology. **History:** General. **Liberal arts:** Arts/sciences, library science. **Math:** General. **Philosophy/religion:** Philosophy. **Physical sciences:** Chemistry, geology, physics. **Psychology:** General, social. **Social sciences:** Anthropology, economics, political science, sociology. **Visual/performing arts:** Art, dramatic, music.

Most popular majors. Business/marketing 17%, communications/journalism 7%, education 14%, health sciences 14%, liberal arts 11%, social sciences 6%.

Computing on campus. 1,143 workstations in dormitories, library, computer center, student center. Dormitories wired for high-speed internet access and linked to campus network. Commuter students can connect to campus network. Online course registration, online library, helpline, student web hosting, wireless network available.

Student life. Freshman orientation: Mandatory, $150 fee. Preregistration for classes offered. One-day session held in January, spring and summer. **Policies:** Students who live on campus have first option of returning to their same housing following year. **Housing:** Guaranteed on-campus for freshmen. Coed dorms, single-sex dorms, special housing for disabled, apartments, fraternity/sorority housing, wellness housing available. $125 nonrefundable deposit. Pets allowed in dorm rooms. **Activities:** Bands, campus ministries, choral groups, dance, drama, international student organizations, literary magazine, music ensembles, musical theater, radio station, student government, student newspaper, symphony orchestra, TV station, Koinonia Christian Fellowship, African American Caucus, Newman Association, Hip Hop Dance Team, NAACP, Young Democrats, Eagle Ambassadors, People Reaching Out and Understanding Disabilities, Students Together Against Rape, University Activities Board.

Athletics. NCAA. **Intercollegiate:** Baseball M, basketball, cross-country, diving, football (tackle) M, golf M, soccer W, softball W, swimming, tennis W, track and field W, volleyball W, wrestling M. **Intramural:** Badminton, basketball, bowling, football (non-tackle), golf, racquetball, soccer, softball, swimming, table tennis, tennis, track and field, volleyball, water polo, wrestling. **Team name:** Golden Eagles.

Student services. Adult student services, alcohol/substance abuse counseling, chaplain/spiritual director, career counseling, services for economically disadvantaged, student employment services, financial aid counseling, health services, minority student services, personal counseling, placement for graduates, veterans' counselor, women's services. **Physically disabled:** Services for visually, speech, hearing impaired.

Contact. E-mail: admissions@clarion.edu
Phone: (814) 393-2306 Toll-free number: (800) 672-7171
Fax: (814) 393-2030
William Bailey, Dean of Enrollment Management, Clarion University of Pennsylvania, 840 Wood Street, Clarion, PA 16214

Curtis Institute of Music
Philadelphia, Pennsylvania
www.curtis.edu   CB code: 2100

- Private 4-year music college
- Residential campus in very large city
- 123 degree-seeking undergraduates: 48% women, 2% African American, 15% Asian American, 2% Hispanic American, 43% international
- 42 degree-seeking graduate students
- 5% of applicants admitted
- SAT, application essay required
- 83% graduate within 6 years

General. Founded in 1924. Regionally accredited. **Degrees:** 25 bachelor's awarded; master's offered. **Calendar:** Semester. **Full-time faculty:** 2 total; 50% have terminal degrees, 50% women. **Part-time faculty:** 96 total; 8% have terminal degrees, 17% minority, 33% women. **Special facilities:** More than 82,000 titles in audiovisual materials, sheet music, and books.

Freshman class profile. 279 applied, 14 admitted, 8 enrolled.

End year in good standing:	96%	Out-of-state:	100%
Return as sophomores:	91%	Live on campus:	88%

Basis for selection. Admission based on audition. Test scores considered for applicants to bachelor's degree program. **Home schooled:** Transcript of courses and grades, state high school equivalency certificate required.

High school preparation. Major emphasis on applied music activities.

2012-2013 Annual costs. All students receive a full-tuition scholarship. Bachelor of Music students pay $2,300 in required fees. Students who do not have comprehensive health insurance are required to purchase insurance through Curtis; the approximate cost is $2,500 for 12 months of coverage. Room/board: $13,505. Books/supplies: $1,575. Personal expenses: $2,810.

2011-2012 Financial aid. All financial aid based on need. 4 full-time freshmen applied for aid; 2 were judged to have need; 2 of these received aid. Average need met was 92%. Average scholarship/grant was $11,723; average loan $2,514. 67% of total undergraduate aid awarded as scholarships/grants, 33% as loans/jobs. **Additional information:** All admitted students receive a full tuition scholarship. The estimated value of this scholarship is $33,500.

Application procedures. Admission: Closing date 12/13 (postmark date). $150 fee, may be waived for applicants with need. Admission notification by 4/1. Must reply by 5/1. **Financial aid:** Closing date 3/1. FAFSA, institutional form required. Applicants notified on a rolling basis starting 4/1; must reply by 5/1 or within 2 week(s) of notification.

Academics. Special study options: Double major, ESL, independent study. **Credit/placement by examination:** AP, CLEP, SAT, institutional tests. **Support services:** Remedial instruction, study skills assistance, tutoring.

Majors. Visual/performing arts: Music performance, music theory/composition.

Computing on campus. 16 workstations in library, computer center, student center. Dormitories linked to campus network. Commuter students can connect to campus network. Online library, repair service, wireless network available.

Student life. Freshman orientation: Mandatory. Preregistration for classes offered. Orientation for international students usually begins 3 to 4 days prior to the general orientation program. The general orientation for all students (including international students) begins 1 week before classes begin. A program for parents is offered on the opening day. **Policies:** Students should refer to our web site for specific information on housing requirements for new students. Freshmen not permitted cars on campus. **Housing:** Guaranteed on-campus for freshmen. Coed dorms, apartments available. We now house approximately 80 students in Lenfest Hall. All suites are single-gender, but the floors are coed. Most are single rooms, but there are a number of doubles. **Activities:** Music ensembles, opera, student government, symphony orchestra.

Student services. Alcohol/substance abuse counseling, career counseling, financial aid counseling, health services, personal counseling, veterans' counselor, women's services.

Contact. E-mail: admissions@curtis.edu
Phone: (215) 717-3117 Fax: (215) 893-9065
Christopher Hodges, Admissions Officer, Curtis Institute of Music, 1726 Locust Street, Philadelphia, PA 19103-6187

Delaware Valley College
Doylestown, Pennsylvania
www.delval.edu

CB member
CB code: 2510

- Private 4-year agricultural and liberal arts college
- Residential campus in large town
- 1,913 degree-seeking undergraduates: 11% part-time, 60% women
- 257 degree-seeking graduate students
- 74% of applicants admitted
- SAT or ACT (ACT writing optional), application essay required
- 55% graduate within 6 years

General. Founded in 1896. Regionally accredited. **Degrees:** 386 bachelor's, 2 associate awarded; master's offered. **Location:** 20 miles from Philadelphia, 70 miles from New York City. **Calendar:** Semester, extensive summer session. **Full-time faculty:** 83 total; 59% have terminal degrees, 8% minority, 40% women. **Part-time faculty:** 122 total; 5% minority, 40% women. **Class size:** 52% < 20, 36% 20-39, 8% 40-49, 4% 50-99. **Special facilities:** Equine facility with indoor and outdoor arenas, animal farms, dairy, farm market, arboretum greenhouses, tissue culture laboratories.

Freshman class profile. 1,652 applied, 1,215 admitted, 424 enrolled.

Mid 50% test scores			
SAT critical reading:	450-560	GPA 2.0-2.99:	9%
SAT math:	460-560	Rank in top quarter:	42%
SAT writing:	430-540	Rank in top tenth:	15%
ACT composite:	20-27	Return as sophomores:	75%
GPA 3.75 or higher:	43%	Out-of-state:	43%
GPA 3.50-3.74:	18%	Live on campus:	88%
GPA 3.0-3.49:	30%	Fraternities:	4%
		Sororities:	5%

Basis for selection. Academic achievement, class rank, test scores, letters of recommendation from math or science teacher and guidance counselor, grades in math and science considered. Interview, essay recommended. A score of 500 on the SAT Critical Reading section or a score of 21 on the ACT English and Reading sections may substitute for the TOEFL or IELTS. **Home schooled:** State high school equivalency certificate required.

High school preparation. College-preparatory program required. 15 units required. Required units include English 3, mathematics 2, social studies 2, science 2 (laboratory 1) and academic electives 6. Business administration

computer information systems management, criminal justice, or English majors and students applying for the equine science program need only one unit of science: biology, chemistry or physics.

2011-2012 Annual costs. Tuition/fees: $30,796. Room/board: $10,742. Books/supplies: $1,000. Personal expenses: $900.

Financial aid. Non-need-based: Scholarships awarded for academics, alumni affiliation, music/drama, state residency.

Application procedures. Admission: Closing date 5/1. $50 fee, may be waived for applicants with need, free for online applicants. Admission notification on a rolling basis beginning on or about 10/31. Must reply by May 1 or within 4 week(s) if notified thereafter. **Financial aid:** Priority date 4/15; no closing date. FAFSA required. Applicants notified on a rolling basis starting 2/15; must reply by 5/1 or within 2 week(s) of notification.

Academics. Students complete 500-hour employment program related to major. **Special study options:** Accelerated study, combined bachelor's/graduate degree, distance learning, double major, dual enrollment of high school students, honors, independent study, internships, student-designed major, study abroad, teacher certification program, weekend college. **Credit/placement by examination:** AP, CLEP, institutional tests. Credit for 5 courses may be granted through examination. **Support services:** Learning center, pre-admission summer program, reduced course load, remedial instruction, study skills assistance, tutoring, writing center.

Majors. Biology: General, zoology. **Business:** Accounting, business admin, management information systems, marketing. **Computer sciences:** General. **Conservation:** Wildlife/wilderness. **Education:** Secondary. **English:** English lit. **General:** Agribusiness operations, agronomy, animal sciences, crop production, dairy, food science, horticultural science, ornamental horticulture, turf management. **Math:** General. **Physical sciences:** Chemistry. **Protective services:** Law enforcement admin. **Psychology:** Counseling.

Most popular majors. Agriculture 47%, biology 14%, business/marketing 18%, natural resources/environmental science 7%.

Computing on campus. 150 workstations in dormitories, library, computer center, student center. Dormitories wired for high-speed internet access and linked to campus network. Online library, helpline, repair service, wireless network available.

Student life. Freshman orientation: Mandatory. Preregistration for classes offered. **Housing:** Guaranteed on-campus for freshmen. Coed dorms, single-sex dorms available. $200 fully refundable deposit, deadline 5/1. **Activities:** Concert band, choral groups, drama, literary magazine, music ensembles, radio station, student government, student newspaper, Intervarsity Christian Fellowship, Hillel, Students for Diversity, Lions Club, Alpha Phi Omega, Habitat for Humanity, Project EARTH, Students in Free Enterprise, Animal Lifeline, Positive Awareness of Wildlife and Zoos.

Athletics. NCAA. **Intercollegiate:** Baseball M, basketball, cheerleading M, cross-country, equestrian, field hockey W, football (tackle) M, golf M, soccer, softball W, track and field, volleyball W, wrestling M. **Intramural:** Basketball, equestrian, football (tackle) M, softball, volleyball. **Team name:** Aggies.

Student services. Adult student services, career counseling, student employment services, health services, personal counseling, placement for graduates. **Physically disabled:** Services for visually, speech, hearing impaired.

Contact. E-mail: AdmitMe@delval.edu
Phone: (215) 489-2211 Toll-free number: (800) 233-5825
Fax: (215) 230-2968
Norm Jones, Vice President, Enrollment and Athletics, Delaware Valley College, 700 East Butler Avenue, Doylestown, PA 18901-2697

DeSales University
Center Valley, Pennsylvania
www.desales.edu

CB member
CB code: 2021

- Private 4-year university affiliated with Roman Catholic Church
- Residential campus in small town
- 2,375 degree-seeking undergraduates: 25% part-time, 59% women, 3% African American, 2% Asian American, 6% Hispanic American, 1% Native American
- 795 degree-seeking graduate students
- 73% of applicants admitted
- SAT or ACT required
- 65% graduate within 6 years

General. Founded in 1964. Regionally accredited. **Degrees:** 496 bachelor's awarded; master's, doctoral offered. **ROTC:** Army. **Location:** 7 miles from Allentown and Bethlehem; 50 miles from Philadelphia. **Calendar:** Semester, limited summer session. **Full-time faculty:** 103 total; 6% minority, 48% women. **Part-time faculty:** 179 total. **Class size:** 89% < 20, 11% 20-39.

Freshman class profile. 2,207 applied, 1,603 admitted, 446 enrolled.

Mid 50% test scores			
SAT critical reading:	480-590	GPA 2.0-2.99:	31%
SAT math:	480-600	Rank in top quarter:	45%
ACT composite:	20-26	Rank in top tenth:	33%
GPA 3.75 or higher:	16%	Return as sophomores:	81%
GPA 3.50-3.74:	19%	Out-of-state:	36%
GPA 3.0-3.49:	33%	Live on campus:	82%

Basis for selection. High school achievement most important. Test scores and recommendations also considered. Essay, interview recommended for all; audition required for dance, theater programs. Interview required for physician assistant program.

High school preparation. College-preparatory program required. 16 units required; 18 recommended. Required and recommended units include English 4, mathematics 3-4, social studies 3-4, science 2 (laboratory 2) and foreign language 2. Biology, chemistry, 3 math recommended for biology major. 3 math, including 2 algebra, recommended for business major. Chemistry, physics, 3 math recommended for chemistry major. Biology, chemistry, physics, 2 math recommended for nursing major. 2 biology, chemistry, or physics, and 3 math recommended for pre-med major. 4 math recommended for math major.

2011-2012 Annual costs. Tuition/fees: $29,000. Room/board: $10,520. Books/supplies: $1,526. Personal expenses: $4,216.

2011-2012 Financial aid. **Need-based:** 415 full-time freshmen applied for aid; 374 were judged to have need; 374 of these received aid. Average need met was 72%. Average scholarship/grant was $17,703; average loan $3,358. 61% of total undergraduate aid awarded as scholarships/grants, 39% as loans/jobs. **Non-need-based:** Awarded to 1,258 full-time undergraduates, including 397 freshmen. Scholarships awarded for academics, alumni affiliation, art, leadership, music/drama, religious affiliation, ROTC.

Application procedures. **Admission:** Priority date 3/1; deadline 8/1. $30 fee, may be waived for applicants with need. Admission notification on a rolling basis. Must reply by May 1 or within 2 week(s) if notified thereafter. **Financial aid:** Priority date 2/1, closing date 5/1. FAFSA required. Applicants notified on a rolling basis starting 2/15; must reply by 5/1 or within 2 week(s) of notification.

Academics. **Special study options:** Accelerated study, combined bachelor's/graduate degree, cross-registration, distance learning, double major, dual enrollment of high school students, ESL, external degree, honors, independent study, internships, liberal arts/career combination, semester at sea, study abroad, teacher certification program, weekend college. BS in medical studies, MS in physician assistant studies; 5 year BS/MBA in accounting, 5 year BA/MACJ in criminal justice, cross-registration at consortium schools: Cedar Crest, Moravian, Muhlenberg, Lafayette, Lehigh. **Credit/placement by examination:** AP, CLEP, institutional tests. 24 credit hours maximum toward bachelor's degree. For AP credit for Physics B must complete lab component. Must submit research paper for CLEP English Composition with Essay to obtain 6 credits. **Support services:** Learning center, pre-admission summer program, reduced course load, study skills assistance, tutoring.

Majors. **Biology:** General, biochemistry, molecular. **Business:** General, accounting, business admin, e-commerce, finance, human resources, international, management information systems, marketing, personal/financial services. **Communications:** General. **Computer sciences:** General, information technology. **Education:** Early childhood, elementary. **English:** English lit. **Foreign languages:** Spanish. **Health services:** Clinical lab science, nursing (RN), pharmaceutical marketing/management. **History:** General. **Liberal arts:** Arts/sciences. **Math:** General. **Parks/recreation:** Exercise sciences, sports admin. **Philosophy/religion:** Philosophy. **Physical sciences:** Chemistry. **Protective services:** Criminal justice. **Psychology:** General. **Social sciences:** Political science. **Theology:** Theology. **Visual/performing arts:** Dance, dramatic, film/cinema/video.

Most popular majors. Business/marketing 25%, health sciences 21%, visual/performing arts 12%.

Computing on campus. 200 workstations in library, computer center, student center. Dormitories wired for high-speed internet access and linked to campus network. Commuter students can connect to campus network. Online course registration, online library, helpline, student web hosting, wireless network available.

Student life. **Freshman orientation:** Mandatory, $200 fee. Preregistration for classes offered. One-day academic orientation in May or June; 3-day social and academic orientation in August. **Policies:** Students under 21 cannot possess or be in presence of alcohol. Access to dorm rooms of opposite sex restricted during certain hours (overnight), social gathering policy. **Housing:** Guaranteed on-campus for all undergraduates. Single-sex dorms, special housing for disabled, wellness housing available. Town houses for upperclassmen, and graduate student housing available. **Activities:** Bands, campus ministries, choral groups, dance, drama, film society, international student organizations, literary magazine, music ensembles, Model UN, musical theater, radio station, student government, student newspaper, TV station, prolife club, Habitat For Humanity, Best Buddies, Esto Vir, Lion's club, natural science club, Rotoract, St. Thomas More Society, American marketing association, criminal justice association.

Athletics. NCAA. **Intercollegiate:** Baseball M, basketball, cross-country, field hockey W, golf M, lacrosse M, soccer, softball W, track and field, volleyball W. **Intramural:** Basketball, football (non-tackle), soccer, softball, volleyball. **Team name:** Bulldogs.

Student services. Adult student services, alcohol/substance abuse counseling, chaplain/spiritual director, career counseling, services for economically disadvantaged, student employment services, financial aid counseling, health services, minority student services, personal counseling, veterans' counselor. **Physically disabled:** Services for visually, speech, hearing impaired.

Contact. E-mail: admiss@desales.edu
Phone: (610) 282-4443 Toll-free number: (877) 433-7253
Fax: (610) 282-0131
Derrick Wetzell, Director of Admissions, DeSales University, 2755 Station Avenue, Center Valley, PA 18034-9568

DeVry University: Fort Washington
Fort Washington, Pennsylvania
www.devry.edu   **CB code: 3866**

- For-profit 4-year university
- Commuter campus in large town
- 837 degree-seeking undergraduates
- Interview required

General. Additional locations: Philadelphia, King of Prussia, Pittsburgh. **Degrees:** 117 bachelor's, 40 associate awarded; master's offered. **Location:** 35 miles from Philadelphia. **Calendar:** Semester, extensive summer session. **Full-time faculty:** 20 total. **Part-time faculty:** 104 total.

Basis for selection. Applicants must have high school diploma or equivalent, or a degree from accredited postsecondary institution, demonstrate proficiency in basic college-level skills through SAT or ACT scores or institution-administered placement exams, and be at least 17 years of age on the first day of classes. New students may enter at beginning of any semester. CPT also accepted.

High school preparation. College-preparatory program recommended. Math unit must be algebra or higher.

2011-2012 Annual costs. Tuition/fees: $15,294. Books/supplies: $1,310. Personal expenses: $3,270.

Financial aid. All financial aid based on need.

Application procedures. **Admission:** No deadline. $50 fee. Admission notification on a rolling basis. **Financial aid:** No deadline. FAFSA required. Applicants notified on a rolling basis.

Academics. **Special study options:** Accelerated study, distance learning. **Credit/placement by examination:** AP, CLEP. **Support services:** Learning center, remedial instruction, tutoring.

Majors. **Business:** Business admin. **Computer sciences:** Networking, systems analysis. **Engineering:** Software.

Most popular majors. Business/marketing 63%, computer/information sciences 28%, engineering/engineering technologies 10%.

Computing on campus. 407 workstations in library, computer center. Online course registration, online library, helpline available.

Student life. **Freshman orientation:** Mandatory. Preregistration for classes offered. **Activities:** Campus Crusade for Christ, electronic gamers club, creative arts club.

Athletics. **Intramural:** Volleyball.

Student services. Career counseling, student employment services, financial aid counseling, placement for graduates, veterans' counselor. **Physically disabled:** Services for visually, hearing impaired.

Contact. E-mail: admissions@phi.devry.edu
Phone: (215) 591-5701 Toll-free number: (866) 303-3879
Fax: (215) 591-5745
Steve Cohen, Director of Admission, DeVry University: Fort Washington, 1140 Virginia Drive, Fort Washington, PA 19034-3204

Dickinson College

Carlisle, Pennsylvania
www.dickinson.edu

CB member
CB code: 2186

- Private 4-year liberal arts college
- Residential campus in large town
- 2,358 degree-seeking undergraduates: 1% part-time, 56% women, 4% African American, 3% Asian American, 6% Hispanic American, 7% international
- 42% of applicants admitted
- Application essay required
- 84% graduate within 6 years; 29% enter graduate study

General. Founded in 1783. Regionally accredited. **Degrees:** 575 bachelor's awarded. **ROTC:** Army. **Location:** 100 miles from Philadelphia, 90 miles from Washington, DC. **Calendar:** Semester, limited summer session. **Full-time faculty:** 209 total; 95% have terminal degrees, 10% minority, 46% women. **Part-time faculty:** 43 total; 51% have terminal degrees, 7% minority, 42% women. **Class size:** 74% < 20, 25% 20-39, 2% 40-49. **Special facilities:** Arts center, planetarium and multiple telescope observatory, intercontinental satellite communications for study-abroad programs, study of contemporary issues center.

Freshman class profile. 6,063 applied, 2,543 admitted, 652 enrolled.

Mid 50% test scores			
SAT critical reading:	600-690	Rank in top tenth:	52%
SAT math:	590-680	End year in good standing:	99%
SAT writing:	600-690	Return as sophomores:	90%
ACT composite:	27-30	Out-of-state:	78%
Rank in top quarter:	82%	Live on campus:	100%
		International:	6%

Basis for selection. Academic potential as shown by school achievement record most important. Extracurricular activities very important. Counselor recommendation required. Motivation, personal character considered. Special consideration given to applicants of color. Preference given to academically qualified children of alumni if they satisfy above criteria. Standardized tests optional. SAT or ACT recommended. Submission of standardized tests scores is optional. Interview recommended.

High school preparation. College-preparatory program recommended. 16 units required. Required and recommended units include English 4, mathematics 3, social studies 2, science 3 (laboratory 2), foreign language 2-3 and academic electives 2.

2012-2013 Annual costs. Tuition/fees: $44,576. Room/board: $11,178. Books/supplies: $1,000. Personal expenses: $1,200.

2011-2012 Financial aid. Need-based: 433 full-time freshmen applied for aid; 355 were judged to have need; 350 of these received aid. Average need met was 97%. Average scholarship/grant was $28,764; average loan $4,928. 81% of total undergraduate aid awarded as scholarships/grants, 19% as loans/jobs. **Non-need-based:** Awarded to 343 full-time undergraduates, including 116 freshmen. Scholarships awarded for academics, leadership, ROTC.

Application procedures. Admission: Closing date 2/1 (postmark date). $65 fee, may be waived for applicants with need. Admission notification by 3/20. Must reply by May 1 or within 2 week(s) if notified thereafter. **Financial aid:** Priority date 11/15, closing date 2/1. FAFSA, CSS PROFILE required. Applicants notified by 3/20; must reply by 5/1 or within 2 week(s) of notification.

Academics. Certificates offered in ballet, health studies, and security studies. Prebusiness, prelaw and premedical preparation available in conjunction with majors listed. **Special study options:** Accelerated study, combined bachelor's/graduate degree, cross-registration, double major, ESL, exchange student, independent study, internships, liberal arts/career combination, student-designed major, study abroad, teacher certification program, Washington semester. 3-2 engineering programs with University of Pennsylvania, Case Western Reserve University, Rensselaer Polytechnic Institute; 3-3 law degree with Dickinson School of Law of Penn State University. **Credit/**

placement by examination: AP, CLEP, IB, institutional tests. **Support services:** Tutoring, writing center.

Majors. Area/ethnic studies: African, American, East Asian, Italian, Latin American, Near/Middle Eastern, women's. **Biology:** General, biochemistry, neuroscience. **Business:** International. **Computer sciences:** General. **Conservation:** Environmental science, environmental studies. **English:** English lit. **Foreign languages:** Classics, French, German, Italian, Russian, Spanish. **History:** General. **Human services:** Public policy. **Math:** General. **Philosophy/religion:** Judaic, philosophy, religion. **Physical sciences:** Chemistry, geology, physics. **Psychology:** General. **Social sciences:** Anthropology, archaeology, economics, international relations, political science, sociology. **Visual/performing arts:** Dance, dramatic, music, studio arts.

Most popular majors. Area/ethnic studies 11%, biology 9%, business/marketing 12%, foreign language 8%, psychology 6%, social sciences 25%.

Computing on campus. 1,041 workstations in dormitories, library, computer center, student center. Dormitories wired for high-speed internet access and linked to campus network. Commuter students can connect to campus network. Online course registration, online library, helpline, repair service, wireless network available.

Student life. Freshman orientation: Mandatory. Preregistration for classes offered. **Policies:** Freshmen not permitted cars on campus. **Housing:** Guaranteed on-campus for all undergraduates. Coed dorms, special housing for disabled, apartments, fraternity/sorority housing available. **Activities:** Bands, choral groups, dance, drama, film society, international student organizations, literary magazine, music ensembles, Model UN, musical theater, radio station, student government, student newspaper, symphony orchestra, public affairs, social service, religious, multicultural, College Democrats, Young Republicans, debate club, foreign language.

Athletics. NCAA. **Intercollegiate:** Baseball M, basketball, cross-country, field hockey W, football (tackle) M, golf, lacrosse, soccer, softball W, swimming, tennis, track and field, volleyball W. **Intramural:** Badminton, basketball, field hockey W, football (non-tackle) M, racquetball, soccer, softball M, tennis, volleyball. **Team name:** Red Devils.

Student services. Adult student services, alcohol/substance abuse counseling, career counseling, student employment services, financial aid counseling, health services, minority student services, on-campus daycare, personal counseling, placement for graduates. **Physically disabled:** Services for visually, speech, hearing impaired.

Contact. E-mail: admit@dickinson.edu
Phone: (717) 245-1231 Toll-free number: (800) 644-1773
Fax: (717) 245-1442
Stephanie Balmer, VP for Enrollment, Marketing and Communications and Dean of Admissions, Dickinson College, PO Box 1773, Carlisle, PA 17013-2896

Drexel University

Philadelphia, Pennsylvania
www.drexel.edu

CB member
CB code: 2194

- Private 5-year university
- Residential campus in very large city
- 14,727 degree-seeking undergraduates: 16% part-time, 46% women, 8% African American, 12% Asian American, 6% Hispanic American, 1% Native American, 9% international
- 9,734 degree-seeking graduate students
- 58% of applicants admitted
- SAT or ACT (ACT writing optional) required

General. Founded in 1891. Regionally accredited. Most undergraduate programs require up to 18 months work experience within 5-year program of study. **Degrees:** 2,666 bachelor's, 27 associate awarded; master's, professional, doctoral offered. **ROTC:** Army, Naval, Air Force. **Calendar:** Quarter, extensive summer session. **Full-time faculty:** 1,011 total; 83% have terminal degrees, 15% minority, 44% women. **Part-time faculty:** 625 total; 13% minority, 45% women. **Class size:** 60% < 20, 32% 20-39, 3% 40-49, 3% 50-99, 2% >100. **Special facilities:** Art collection, observatory.

Freshman class profile. 48,450 applied, 27,861 admitted, 3,141 enrolled.

Mid 50% test scores			
SAT critical reading:	530-630	GPA 2.0-2.99:	16%
SAT math:	570-680	Rank in top quarter:	69%
SAT writing:	520-630	Rank in top tenth:	37%
ACT composite:	24-29	Return as sophomores:	85%
GPA 3.75 or higher:	29%	Out-of-state:	54%
GPA 3.50-3.74:	25%	Live on campus:	89%
GPA 3.0-3.49:	30%	International:	12%

Basis for selection. Academic average, counselor's recommendation and test scores most important, followed by class rank, school, community and church activities. Employment also considered. Essay required for most majors for media arts and design programs. Portfolio required for graphic design, music industry, photography and fashion design. Audition required for dance.

High school preparation. College-preparatory program recommended. Required and recommended units include mathematics 3, science 1 (laboratory 1) and foreign language 1. Engineering applicants required to have 4 units math (including algebra I and II, geometry, trigonometry, and pre-calculus) and 2 units lab science (including chemistry and physics). Science applicants required to have 4 units math (including algebra I and II, geometry, and trigonometry) and 2 units lab science (including biology, chemistry, or physics). Most other applicants must have algebra I and II and geometry as required math units and one lab science.

2012-2013 Annual costs. Tuition/fees (projected): $36,100. Room/board: $14,175. Books/supplies: $2,000. Personal expenses: $3,000.

Financial aid. Non-need-based: Scholarships awarded for academics, alumni affiliation, art, athletics, leadership, music/drama, ROTC.

Application procedures. Admission: Closing date 3/1 (postmark date). $75 fee, may be waived for applicants with need, free for online applicants. Admission notification on a rolling basis. Must reply by May 1 or within 2 week(s) if notified thereafter. **Financial aid:** Closing date 3/1. FAFSA, CSS PROFILE required. Applicants notified on a rolling basis starting 3/15.

Academics. Special study options: Accelerated study, combined bachelor's/graduate degree, cooperative education, distance learning, double major, dual enrollment of high school students, ESL, honors, independent study, internships, semester at sea, study abroad, teacher certification program, weekend college. 3-3 programs in engineering with Lincoln University and Indiana University of Pennsylvania. **Credit/placement by examination:** AP, CLEP, IB, institutional tests. 30 credit hours maximum toward bachelor's degree. **Support services:** Learning center, pre-admission summer program, reduced course load, remedial instruction, study skills assistance, tutoring, writing center.

Majors. Architecture: Architecture. **Biology:** General. **Business:** General, hotel/motel admin, managerial economics. **Computer sciences:** Computer science, information systems, security, web page design. **Conservation:** Environmental science, environmental studies. **Education:** Elementary. **Engineering:** Architectural, biomedical, chemical, civil, computer, construction, electrical, environmental, industrial, materials, mechanical, software. **English:** English lit, technical writing. **Health services:** Clinical lab assistant, health care admin, nursing (RN), physician assistant, substance abuse counseling. **History:** General. **Liberal arts:** Humanities. **Math:** General. **Parks/recreation:** Sports admin. **Physical sciences:** General, chemistry, physics. **Protective services:** Law enforcement admin. **Psychology:** General. **Social sciences:** Anthropology, economics, international relations, political science, sociology. **Visual/performing arts:** Cinematography, dance, design, fashion design, graphic design, interior design, music, photography, play/screenwriting, theater arts management.

Most popular majors. Business/marketing 22%, computer/information sciences 7%, engineering/engineering technologies 19%, health sciences 19%, visual/performing arts 11%.

Computing on campus. PC or laptop required. 610 workstations in dormitories, library, computer center, student center. Dormitories wired for high-speed internet access and linked to campus network. Commuter students can connect to campus network. Online course registration, online library, helpline, repair service, student web hosting, wireless network available.

Student life. Freshman orientation: Available. Preregistration for classes offered. 2-day overnight sessions held in July; 3-day program prior to start of classes. **Housing:** Guaranteed on-campus for freshmen. Coed dorms, special housing for disabled, apartments, fraternity/sorority housing available. $200 nonrefundable deposit, deadline 6/15. Freshmen required to live on campus unless living with parents. **Activities:** Bands, campus ministries, choral groups, dance, drama, film society, literary magazine, music ensembles, musical theater, radio station, student government, student newspaper, TV station, Newman Center, Hillel, Alpha Phi Omega, NAACP, Eye Openers, Disciples in Deed, Drexel Christian Fellowship, Jewish Heritage Program.

Athletics. NCAA. **Intercollegiate:** Basketball, cheerleading, diving, field hockey W, golf M, lacrosse, rowing (crew), soccer, softball W, swimming, tennis, wrestling M. **Intramural:** Badminton, basketball, football (non-tackle), soccer, softball, squash, table tennis, tennis, volleyball. **Team name:** Dragons.

Student services. Adult student services, career counseling, student employment services, financial aid counseling, health services, minority student services, personal counseling, placement for graduates. **Physically disabled:** Services for visually, speech, hearing impaired.

Contact. E-mail: enroll@drexel.edu
Phone: (215) 895-2400 Toll-free number: (800) 237-3935
Fax: (215) 895-5939
Joan McDonald, Senior Vice President of Enrollment Management, Drexel University, 3141 Chestnut Street, Philadelphia, PA 19104-2876

Duquesne University
Pittsburgh, Pennsylvania

CB member

www.duq.edu

CB code: 2196

- Private 4-year university affiliated with Roman Catholic Church
- Residential campus in large city
- 5,639 degree-seeking undergraduates: 3% part-time, 57% women, 5% African American, 2% Asian American, 3% Hispanic American, 3% international
- 4,256 graduate students
- 70% of applicants admitted
- SAT or ACT with writing, application essay required
- 75% graduate within 6 years; 33% enter graduate study

General. Founded in 1878. Regionally accredited. **Degrees:** 1,285 bachelor's awarded; master's, professional, doctoral offered. **ROTC:** Army, Naval, Air Force. **Calendar:** Semester, extensive summer session. **Full-time faculty:** 480 total; 91% have terminal degrees, 7% minority, 44% women. **Part-time faculty:** 512 total; 8% minority, 49% women. **Class size:** 50% < 20, 40% 20-39, 5% 40-49, 3% 50-99, 3% >100. **Special facilities:** Recording complex, recital hall, music technology center, music control lab, phenomenology center, health sciences cadaver lab, nurse managed wellness center, business school investment center, center for nursing research, confocal microscopes, mass spectrometry facilities, 400- and 500- MHZ NMR spectrometers, single crystal and powder x-ray diffraction spectrometers, academic research center for pharmacy care, pharmacy wellness and disease management program, patient simulation lab, digital media center, center for health care diversity, center for performance/innovation, biomechanics lab, exercise physiology lab, scanning/transmission electron microscopes.

Freshman class profile. 6,528 applied, 4,578 admitted, 1,343 enrolled.

Mid 50% test scores			
SAT critical reading:	520-600	Rank in top quarter:	60%
SAT math:	520-610	Rank in top tenth:	29%
SAT writing:	510-600	End year in good standing:	95%
ACT composite:	23-27	Return as sophomores:	87%
GPA 3.75 or higher:	45%	Out-of-state:	26%
GPA 3.50-3.74:	20%	Live on campus:	92%
GPA 3.0-3.49:	28%	International:	2%
GPA 2.0-2.99:	7%	Fraternities:	19%
		Sororities:	12%

Basis for selection. School achievement record, standardized test scores, recommendations, and essay. Decisions based on overall GPA, standardized test scores, curriculum, volunteer activities, and leadership roles. Interview recommended for all, audition required for music program, 40 hours shadowing for physical therapy. **Home schooled:** Transcript of courses and grades required. **Learning Disabled:** Documentation of learning disabilities may be required.

High school preparation. College-preparatory program required. 16 units recommended. Recommended units include English 4, mathematics 2, social studies 2, science 2, foreign language 2 and academic electives 4.

2011-2012 Annual costs. Tuition/fees: $28,671. Room/board: $9,806. Books/supplies: $1,000. Personal expenses: $750.

2010-2011 Financial aid. Need-based: 1,266 full-time freshmen applied for aid; 1,052 were judged to have need; 1,052 of these received aid. Average need met was 89%. Average scholarship/grant was $15,213; average loan $3,778. 51% of total undergraduate aid awarded as scholarships/grants, 49% as loans/jobs. **Non-need-based:** Awarded to 5,172 full-time undergraduates, including 1,451 freshmen. Scholarships awarded for academics, alumni affiliation, athletics, music/drama, ROTC.

Application procedures. Admission: Priority date 11/1; deadline 7/1 (receipt date). $50 fee, may be waived for applicants with need. Admission notification on a rolling basis beginning on or about 10/1. Must reply by May 1 or within 2 week(s) if notified thereafter. **Financial aid:** Closing date 5/1. FAFSA, institutional form required. Applicants notified on a rolling basis starting 3/1; must reply by 5/1 or within 3 week(s) of notification.

Academics. Special study options: Accelerated study, combined bachelor's/graduate degree, cross-registration, distance learning, double major, dual enrollment of high school students, ESL, exchange student, external degree, honors, independent study, internships, liberal arts/career combination, semester at sea, student-designed major, study abroad, teacher certification

program, Washington semester, weekend college. **Credit/placement by examination:** AP, CLEP, IB, institutional tests. 60 credit hours maximum toward bachelor's degree. **Support services:** Learning center, pre-admission summer program, reduced course load, remedial instruction, study skills assistance, tutoring, writing center.

Honors college/program. Admissions are based on a constellation of factors; Generally the top 5 - 7 % of applicants invited. Students not receiving an invitation letter from University Honors College after general application, may apply via our website.

Majors. Biology: General, biochemistry. **Business:** Accounting, communications, entrepreneurial studies, finance, international, logistics, management information systems, management science, managerial economics, marketing. **Communications:** Communications/speech/rhetoric, journalism, public relations. **Computer sciences:** Computer science, web page design. **Conservation:** Environmental science. **Education:** General, early childhood, English, Latin, mathematics, middle, music, secondary, social studies, Spanish. **English:** English lit, rhetoric/composition. **Foreign languages:** General, ancient Greek, classics, Latin, Spanish. **Health services:** Athletic training, music therapy, nursing (RN). **History:** General. **Liberal arts:** Arts/sciences. **Math:** General. **Philosophy/religion:** Philosophy. **Physical sciences:** Chemistry, physics. **Psychology:** General. **Social sciences:** Economics, international relations, political science, sociology. **Theology:** Theology. **Visual/performing arts:** Art history/conservation, dramatic, music performance.

Most popular majors. Biology 6%, business/marketing 26%, communications/journalism 8%, education 9%, health sciences 20%, social sciences 6%.

Computing on campus. 1,000 workstations in dormitories, library, computer center, student center. Dormitories wired for high-speed internet access and linked to campus network. Commuter students can connect to campus network. Online course registration, online library, helpline, repair service, student web hosting, wireless network available.

Student life. Freshman orientation: Mandatory, $156 fee. Preregistration for classes offered. 5 day program in August; includes volunteer opportunities. **Policies:** All recognized student organizations must have faculty or staff adviser, have purpose consistent with University mission, and abide by Code of Rights, Responsibilities and Conduct. **Housing:** Guaranteed on-campus for freshmen. Coed dorms, special housing for disabled, apartments, fraternity/sorority housing, wellness housing available. $500 nonrefundable deposit, deadline 5/1. Club wings, fraternity and sorority wings, and international wings available. **Activities:** Bands, campus ministries, choral groups, dance, drama, film society, international student organizations, literary magazine, music ensembles, Model UN, musical theater, opera, radio station, student government, student newspaper, symphony orchestra, TV station, Black Student Union, Duquesne University Volunteers, Latin American Student Association, Evergreen, Indian Student Association, St. Vincent de Paul Society, College Republicans, Asian Student Association, Young Democrats, Knights of Columbus.

Athletics. NCAA. **Intercollegiate:** Basketball, cross-country, football (tackle) M, lacrosse W, rowing (crew) W, soccer, swimming W, tennis, track and field, volleyball W. **Intramural:** Basketball, football (non-tackle), racquetball, soccer, volleyball. **Team name:** Dukes.

Student services. Adult student services, alcohol/substance abuse counseling, chaplain/spiritual director, career counseling, services for economically disadvantaged, student employment services, financial aid counseling, health services, minority student services, on-campus daycare, personal counseling, placement for graduates, veterans' counselor, women's services. **Physically disabled:** Services for visually, speech, hearing impaired.

Contact. E-mail: admissions@duq.edu
Phone: (412) 396-6222 Toll-free number: (800) 456-0590
Fax: (412) 396-6223
Debra Zugates, Director, Admissions, Duquesne University, 600 Forbes Avenue, Administration Building, Pittsburgh, PA 15282-0201

East Stroudsburg University of Pennsylvania

East Stroudsburg, Pennsylvania	CB member
www4.esu.edu	CB code: 2650

- Public 4-year university
- Residential campus in large town
- 6,610 degree-seeking undergraduates: 8% part-time, 55% women, 7% African American, 2% Asian American, 4% Hispanic American, 1% international
- 592 degree-seeking graduate students
- 81% of applicants admitted

- SAT or ACT with writing required
- 59% graduate within 6 years

General. Founded in 1893. Regionally accredited. Marine science consortium provides students within marine science and similar disciplines access to a marine station for field trips, summer courses, and research. The consortium field stations at Wallops Island, VA is near Chincoteague and Assateague Islands, well known for their abundant wildlife. **Degrees:** 1,134 bachelor's awarded; master's offered. **ROTC:** Army, Air Force. **Location:** 40 miles from Allentown and Scranton. **Calendar:** Semester, extensive summer session. **Full-time faculty:** 262 total; 86% have terminal degrees, 16% minority, 47% women. **Part-time faculty:** 57 total; 16% have terminal degrees, 5% minority, 65% women. **Class size:** 15% < 20, 52% 20-39, 19% 40-49, 10% 50-99, 3% >100. **Special facilities:** 30-acre ecological studies area, business accelerator program, college-operated planetarium.

Freshman class profile. 6,520 applied, 5,256 admitted, 1,412 enrolled.

Mid 50% test scores		
SAT critical reading:	440-520	
SAT math:	450-540	
SAT writing:	430-520	
GPA 3.75 or higher:	1%	
GPA 3.50-3.74:	11%	
GPA 3.0-3.49:	49%	

GPA 2.0-2.99:	26%
Rank in top quarter:	24%
Rank in top tenth:	8%
Return as sophomores:	78%
Out-of-state:	30%
Live on campus:	79%

Basis for selection. Academic achievement primary factor in selection process. Whole-person assessment also used, taking into account school and community activities, achievements and aspirations.

High school preparation. College-preparatory program recommended. 16 units recommended. Recommended units include English 4, mathematics 4, social studies 3, science 3 (laboratory 2) and foreign language 2.

2011-2012 Annual costs. Tuition/fees: $8,350; $17,710 out-of-state. Tuition for incoming out-of-state residents who are high achieving science and technology majors (biology, chemistry, computer science, mathematics, and physics) is $9,360. Room/board: $6,858. Books/supplies: $1,200. Personal expenses: $2,369.

2010-2011 Financial aid. Need-based: 974 full-time freshmen applied for aid; 742 were judged to have need; 742 of these received aid. Average need met was 76%. Average scholarship/grant was $4,705; average loan $3,250. 44% of total undergraduate aid awarded as scholarships/grants, 56% as loans/jobs. **Non-need-based:** Awarded to 1,238 full-time undergraduates, including 275 freshmen. Scholarships awarded for academics, alumni affiliation, art, athletics, leadership, minority status, music/drama, religious affiliation, state residency.

Application procedures. Admission: Closing date 4/1 (postmark date). $45 fee, may be waived for applicants with need. Admission notification on a rolling basis beginning on or about 12/1. Must reply by May 1 or within 3 week(s) if notified thereafter. **Financial aid:** Closing date 3/1. FAFSA required. Applicants notified by 4/1; must reply by 5/1.

Academics. Special study options: Accelerated study, combined bachelor's/graduate degree, cross-registration, distance learning, double major, dual enrollment of high school students, exchange student, honors, independent study, internships, student-designed major, study abroad, teacher certification program. **Credit/placement by examination:** AP, CLEP, SAT, ACT, institutional tests. 24 credit hours maximum toward bachelor's degree. **Support services:** Learning center, pre-admission summer program, reduced course load, remedial instruction, study skills assistance, tutoring, writing center.

Majors. Biology: General, biochemistry, biotechnology, ecology, marine. **Business:** Business admin, hospitality admin. **Communications:** Communications/speech/rhetoric. **Communications technology:** General. **Computer sciences:** General, security. **Education:** Early childhood, elementary, health, physical, special ed. **English:** English lit. **Foreign languages:** French, Spanish. **Health services:** Athletic training, audiology/speech pathology, clinical lab science, health services admin, nursing (RN). **History:** General. **Liberal arts:** Arts/sciences, humanities. **Math:** General. **Parks/recreation:** Exercise sciences, facilities management. **Philosophy/religion:** Philosophy. **Physical sciences:** General, chemistry, geology, physics. **Psychology:** General. **Social sciences:** General, economics, geography, political science, sociology. **Visual/performing arts:** General, dramatic, graphic design.

Most popular majors. Biology 7%, business/marketing 13%, education 28%, health sciences 13%, parks/recreation 9%, psychology 6%, social sciences 9%.

Computing on campus. 397 workstations in dormitories, library, computer center, student center. Dormitories linked to campus network. Online course registration, helpline, wireless network available.

Student life. Freshman orientation: Available, $65 fee. Preregistration for classes offered. 2-day event during summer with joint and separate sessions

for parents. **Housing:** Guaranteed on-campus for freshmen. Coed dorms available. $150 nonrefundable deposit, deadline 6/1. **Activities:** Bands, choral groups, dance, drama, international student organizations, literary magazine, music ensembles, radio station, student government, student newspaper, symphony orchestra, Latin American Students Association, Campus Democrats, Young Republicans, African American Student Alliance, Fellowship of Christian Athletes, Newman Club, Women for Awareness.

Athletics. NCAA. **Intercollegiate:** Baseball M, basketball, cross-country, field hockey W, football (tackle) M, golf W, lacrosse W, soccer, softball W, swimming W, tennis W, track and field, volleyball W, wrestling M. **Intramural:** Badminton, basketball, football (non-tackle), racquetball, soccer, softball, tennis, water polo. **Team name:** Warriors.

Student services. Adult student services, chaplain/spiritual director, career counseling, student employment services, financial aid counseling, health services, minority student services, on-campus daycare, personal counseling, placement for graduates, veterans' counselor, women's services. **Physically disabled:** Services for visually, speech, hearing impaired.

Contact. E-mail: undergrads@esu.edu
Phone: (570) 422-3542 Toll-free number: (877) 230-5547
Fax: (570) 422-3933
Jeff Jones, Director of Admissions, East Stroudsburg University of Pennsylvania, 200 Prospect Street, East Stroudsburg, PA 18301-2999

Eastern University
St. Davids, Pennsylvania
www.eastern.edu   **CB code: 2220**

- Private 4-year university affiliated with American Baptist Churches in the USA
- Residential campus in small town
- 2,733 degree-seeking undergraduates: 19% part-time, 71% women
- 1,441 degree-seeking graduate students
- 70% of applicants admitted
- SAT or ACT (ACT writing recommended), application essay required
- 67% graduate within 6 years; 19% enter graduate study

General. Founded in 1952. Regionally accredited. **Degrees:** 546 bachelor's, 101 associate awarded; master's, doctoral offered. **ROTC:** Army, Air Force. **Location:** 10 miles from Philadelphia. **Calendar:** Semester, limited summer session. **Full-time faculty:** 146 total. **Part-time faculty:** 392 total. **Class size:** 70% < 20, 29% 20-39, less than 1% 40-49, less than 1% 50-99, less than 1% >100. **Special facilities:** Planetarium, observatory.

Freshman class profile. 1,506 applied, 1,050 admitted, 399 enrolled.

GPA 3.75 or higher:	28%	Rank in top tenth:	16%
GPA 3.50-3.74:	15%	Return as sophomores:	80%
GPA 3.0-3.49:	38%	Out-of-state:	52%
GPA 2.0-2.99:	18%	Live on campus:	91%
Rank in top quarter:	44%		

Basis for selection. SAT, GPA, and class rank most important. Interest in school mission, slope of grades, attendance, interviews also evaluated. Interview recommended.

High school preparation. Recommended units include English 4, mathematics 3, science 3 and foreign language 2.

2011-2012 Annual costs. Tuition/fees: $25,850. $50 required fee is for a lifetime transcript fee. Room/board: $9,330. Books/supplies: $1,200. Personal expenses: $1,700.

Application procedures. Admission: No deadline. $25 fee, may be waived for applicants with need. Admission notification on a rolling basis. **Financial aid:** No deadline. FAFSA, institutional form required. Applicants notified on a rolling basis starting 4/1.

Academics. Special study options: Cross-registration, double major, ESL, exchange student, honors, independent study, internships, liberal arts/career combination, student-designed major, study abroad, teacher certification program, Washington semester. **Credit/placement by examination:** AP, CLEP, IB, SAT, ACT. 30 credit hours maximum toward associate degree, 60 toward bachelor's. **Support services:** Pre-admission summer program, remedial instruction, study skills assistance, tutoring, writing center.

Honors college/program. Students must be in top 9% of class and have 1300 SAT (exclusive of Writing) or 30 ACT, or have extraordinary leadership abilities with significant academic achievements.

Majors. Biology: General, biochemistry, environmental. **Business:** Accounting/finance, business admin, entrepreneurial studies, international, organizational leadership. **Communications:** Communications/speech/rhetoric. **Education:** Early childhood, elementary, middle, secondary. **Foreign languages:** Spanish. **Health services:** Athletic training, nursing (RN), nursing practice. **History:** General. **Human services:** Social work. **Math:** General. **Parks/recreation:** Exercise sciences. **Philosophy/religion:** Philosophy. **Physical sciences:** Chemistry. **Psychology:** General. **Social sciences:** Political science, sociology. **Theology:** Bible, missionary, theology, youth ministry. **Visual/performing arts:** Dance, music.

Most popular majors. Business/marketing 28%, education 20%, health sciences 11%, theological studies 10%.

Computing on campus. 131 workstations in dormitories, library, computer center, student center. Dormitories wired for high-speed internet access and linked to campus network. Commuter students can connect to campus network. Repair service, wireless network available.

Student life. Freshman orientation: Mandatory. Preregistration for classes offered. Held 3 days before fall semester. **Policies:** Smoke-free campus. Freshmen not permitted cars on campus. **Housing:** Coed dorms, apartments, wellness housing available. $150 nonrefundable deposit, deadline 8/1. Students required to live on campus unless they receive permission from Dean of Students Office. **Activities:** Bands, choral groups, dance, drama, literary magazine, music ensembles, musical theater, student government, student newspaper, Black student league, Penn State Education Association, yacht club, gospel outreach, Fellowship of Christian Athletes, Habitat for Humanity, Evangelicals for Social Action, students organized against racism, prison ministry, Latinos Unidos.

Athletics. NCAA. **Intercollegiate:** Baseball M, basketball, cross-country, field hockey W, golf, lacrosse, soccer, softball W, tennis, volleyball W. **Intramural:** Basketball, soccer, volleyball. **Team name:** Eagles.

Student services. Adult student services, alcohol/substance abuse counseling, chaplain/spiritual director, career counseling, financial aid counseling, health services, legal services, minority student services, personal counseling, veterans' counselor, women's services. **Physically disabled:** Services for visually, speech, hearing impaired.

Contact. E-mail: ugadm@eastern.edu
Phone: (610) 341-5967 Toll-free number: (800) 452-0996
Fax: (610) 341-1723
Michael Dziedziak, Director of Admissions, Eastern University, 1300 Eagle Road, St. Davids, PA 19087-3696

Edinboro University of Pennsylvania
Edinboro, Pennsylvania   **CB member**
www.edinboro.edu   **CB code: 2651**

- Public 4-year university
- Commuter campus in small town
- 6,553 degree-seeking undergraduates: 8% part-time, 58% women, 7% African American, 1% Asian American, 2% Hispanic American, 1% international
- 1,441 degree-seeking graduate students
- 75% of applicants admitted
- 54% graduate within 6 years

General. Founded in 1857. Regionally accredited. **Degrees:** 985 bachelor's, 65 associate awarded; master's offered. **ROTC:** Army. **Location:** 18 miles from Erie. **Calendar:** Semester, extensive summer session. **Full-time faculty:** 323 total; 5% minority, 48% women. **Part-time faculty:** 71 total; 61% women. **Class size:** 27% < 20, 52% 20-39, 9% 40-49, 12% 50-99, 1% >100. **Special facilities:** Observatory, planetarium, natural wildlife museum, robotics laboratory, center for performing arts, speech and hearing clinic.

Freshman class profile. 4,852 applied, 3,660 admitted, 1,512 enrolled.

Mid 50% test scores			
SAT critical reading:	420-520	GPA 2.0-2.99:	32%
SAT math:	420-520	Rank in top quarter:	14%
ACT composite:	17-22	Rank in top tenth:	4%
GPA 3.75 or higher:	19%	Return as sophomores:	74%
GPA 3.50-3.74:	17%	Out-of-state:	17%
GPA 3.0-3.49:	30%	Live on campus:	79%
		International:	1%

Basis for selection. High school curriculum, test scores, GPA, and class rank most important. Recommendations and activities record also reviewed. Interview and essay recommended; audition required for music program.

Home schooled: Transcript of courses and grades, interview, letter of recommendation (nonparent) required. Students out of high school less than two years also need test scores.

High school preparation. College-preparatory program recommended. 15 units recommended. Recommended units include English 4, mathematics 3, social studies 4, science 3, foreign language 2 and computer science 1.

2011-2012 Annual costs. Tuition/fees: $8,359; $11,479 out-of-state. Room/board: $7,514. Books/supplies: $1,000. Personal expenses: $1,300.

2010-2011 Financial aid. Need-based: 1,401 full-time freshmen applied for aid; 1,218 were judged to have need; 1,185 of these received aid. Average need met was 61%. Average scholarship/grant was $2,569; average loan $3,579. 58% of total undergraduate aid awarded as scholarships/grants, 42% as loans/jobs. **Non-need-based:** Awarded to 4,603 full-time undergraduates, including 1,208 freshmen. Scholarships awarded for academics, alumni affiliation, art, athletics, job skills, leadership, minority status, music/drama, religious affiliation, ROTC, state residency.

Application procedures. Admission: No deadline. $30 fee, may be waived for applicants with need. Admission notification on a rolling basis beginning on or about 9/15. Must reply by May 1 or within 4 week(s) if notified thereafter. **Financial aid:** Priority date 3/15, closing date 5/1. FAFSA required. Applicants notified on a rolling basis starting 3/22; must reply within 2 week(s) of notification.

Academics. 60 credits of general education electives required for bachelor's degree. Associate degree counseling, peer tutoring, peer mentors, academic advising center, and trial admissions program offered. **Special study options:** Combined bachelor's/graduate degree, cooperative education, cross-registration, distance learning, double major, dual enrollment of high school students, honors, independent study, internships, liberal arts/career combination, student-designed major, study abroad, teacher certification program. Extensive programs and services for physically and learning disabled students available. Credit courses, continuing education, workshops, and seminars offered at Porreco Extension Center in Erie and Buba Center in Meadville. **Credit/placement by examination:** AP, CLEP, SAT, ACT, institutional tests. 30 credit hours maximum toward associate degree, 30 toward bachelor's. **Support services:** Learning center, pre-admission summer program, reduced course load, remedial instruction, study skills assistance, tutoring, writing center.

Majors. Area/ethnic studies: Latin American, women's. **Biology:** General. **Business:** Business admin. **Communications:** Broadcast journalism, communications/speech/rhetoric, journalism, media studies. **Computer sciences:** General. **Conservation:** Environmental science. **Education:** Elementary, special ed. **English:** English lit. **Foreign languages:** German, Spanish. **Health services:** Clinical lab assistant, clinical lab technology, communication disorders, nursing (RN), prepharmacy. **History:** General. **Human services:** Social work. **Liberal arts:** Arts/sciences, humanities. **Math:** General. **Philosophy/religion:** Philosophy. **Physical sciences:** Chemistry, geology, physics, planetary. **Protective services:** Criminal justice. **Psychology:** General. **Social sciences:** General, anthropology, economics, geography, political science, sociology. **Visual/performing arts:** Art, art history/conservation, dramatic, music, studio arts.

Most popular majors. Business/marketing 9%, communications/journalism 8%, education 10%, health sciences 10%, liberal arts 6%, parks/recreation 6%, psychology 7%, security/protective services 7%, social sciences 7%, visual/performing arts 14%.

Computing on campus. 1,055 workstations in dormitories, library, computer center, student center. Dormitories wired for high-speed internet access and linked to campus network. Commuter students can connect to campus network. Online course registration, online library, helpline, repair service, student web hosting, wireless network available.

Student life. Freshman orientation: Mandatory. Preregistration for classes offered. Summer and spring programs. **Policies:** Zero tolerance policy for alcohol and drugs on campus. **Housing:** Guaranteed on-campus for freshmen. Coed dorms, special housing for disabled available. $75 fully refundable deposit, deadline 5/1. Living-learning and suite style housing available. **Activities:** Bands, campus ministries, choral groups, dance, drama, film society, international student organizations, literary magazine, music ensembles, opera, radio station, student government, student newspaper, TV station.

Athletics. NCAA. **Intercollegiate:** Basketball, cross-country, football (tackle) M, lacrosse W, soccer W, softball W, swimming, tennis, track and field, volleyball W, wrestling M. **Intramural:** Basketball, football (non-tackle), racquetball, soccer, softball, volleyball, wrestling M. **Team name:** The Fighting Scots.

Student services. Adult student services, alcohol/substance abuse counseling, chaplain/spiritual director, career counseling, student employment services, financial aid counseling, health services, minority student services,

personal counseling, placement for graduates, veterans' counselor. **Physically disabled:** Services for visually, speech, hearing impaired.

Contact. E-mail: eup_admissions@edinboro.edu
Phone: (814) 732-2761 Toll-free number: (888) 846-2676
Fax: (814) 732-2420
Craig Grooms, Director of Undergraduate Admissions, Edinboro University of Pennsylvania, 200 East Normal Street, Edinboro, PA 16444

Elizabethtown College
Elizabethtown, Pennsylvania
www.etown.edu
CB member
CB code: 2225

- Private 4-year liberal arts college affiliated with Church of the Brethren
- Residential campus in large town
- 2,290 degree-seeking undergraduates: 19% part-time, 64% women, 4% African American, 2% Asian American, 3% Hispanic American, 2% international
- 28 degree-seeking graduate students
- 66% of applicants admitted
- SAT or ACT (ACT writing optional), application essay required
- 78% graduate within 6 years

General. Founded in 1899. Regionally accredited. **Degrees:** 503 bachelor's, 32 associate awarded; master's, doctoral offered. **Location:** 20 miles from Harrisburg, 90 miles from Philadelphia. **Calendar:** Semester, limited summer session. **Full-time faculty:** 130 total; 90% have terminal degrees, 8% minority, 42% women. **Part-time faculty:** 120 total; 14% have terminal degrees, less than 1% minority, 48% women. **Class size:** 72% < 20, 25% 20-39, 2% 40-49, less than 1% 50-99. **Special facilities:** Anabaptist and Pietist groups center, global citizenship center, Brethren Colleges Abroad headquarters, Center for Community and Civic Engagement.

Freshman class profile. 3,665 applied, 2,411 admitted, 523 enrolled.

Mid 50% test scores			
SAT critical reading:	490-610	**Rank in top tenth:**	38%
SAT math:	510-620	**Return as sophomores:**	84%
ACT composite:	21-27	**Out-of-state:**	32%
Rank in top quarter:	66%	**Live on campus:**	95%
		International:	3%

Basis for selection. School achievement record most important. College preparatory program strongly recommended. Co-curricular activities also considered, particularly service-oriented activities. Applicants should be in top quarter of class. Students may waive SAT/ACT score from admissions and merit-based scholarship decisions if they are ranked in top 10% of class or have 3.5 GPA if school does not rank. Interview required for occupational therapy and honors program. For international business applicants, essay must demonstrate interest in that subject area. Audition required for music, music education, music therapy programs; portfolio required for art program. **Home schooled:** Letter of recommendation (nonparent) required.

High school preparation. 15 units required; 20 recommended. Required and recommended units include English 4, mathematics 3-4, social studies 2, history 2, science 2-4 (laboratory 2-3), foreign language 2 and academic electives 2.

2012-2013 Annual costs. Tuition/fees: $36,550. Room/board: $9,050. Books/supplies: $1,000. Personal expenses: $800.

2011-2012 Financial aid. Need-based: 456 full-time freshmen applied for aid; 406 were judged to have need; 406 of these received aid. Average need met was 83%. Average scholarship/grant was $20,706; average loan $3,425. 73% of total undergraduate aid awarded as scholarships/grants, 27% as loans/jobs. **Non-need-based:** Awarded to 578 full-time undergraduates, including 194 freshmen. Scholarships awarded for academics, art, music/drama, religious affiliation.

Application procedures. Admission: Priority date 3/1; no deadline. $30 fee, may be waived for applicants with need, free for online applicants. Admission notification on a rolling basis beginning on or about 11/1. December 15 closing date for occupational therapy program. March 1 closing date for international business. January 15 closing date for honors program. **Financial aid:** Priority date 3/15; no closing date. FAFSA, institutional form required. Applicants notified on a rolling basis starting 3/1; must reply by 5/1 or within 2 week(s) of notification.

Academics. Special study options: Combined bachelor's/graduate degree, distance learning, double major, dual enrollment of high school students, ESL, exchange student, external degree, honors, independent study, internships, study abroad, teacher certification program, Washington semester. 3-3 program in physical therapy (DPT) with Thomas Jefferson University: 3-2 in engineering with Penn State; 3-2 with Duke University in forestry and

environmental management; 3-3 in physical therapy with Widener University and University of Maryland, Baltimore; 3+4 in dentistry with Temple University; agreements for MBA programs at Lehigh University, Rutgers University, Loyola College (MD), Penn State University, Harrisburg. **Credit/placement by examination:** AP, CLEP, IB, SAT, ACT, institutional tests. Credit by examination unlimited provided student is able to fulfill residency requirement. Credit for International Baccalaureate awarded only for subject exams and only for earned scores from 4-7. **Support services:** Learning center, pre-admission summer program, reduced course load, study skills assistance, tutoring, writing center.

Majors. Biology: General, biochemistry, biotechnology, environmental. **Business:** Accounting, business admin, international, management information systems, managerial economics, marketing. **Computer sciences:** General, information systems. **Conservation:** Forest management. **Education:** Early childhood, middle, science. **Engineering:** General, computer, industrial. **English:** English lit, technical writing. **Foreign languages:** French, German, Japanese, Spanish. **Health services:** Music therapy. **History:** General. **Human services:** General, social work. **Math:** General. **Philosophy/religion:** Philosophy, religion. **Physical sciences:** Chemistry, physics. **Protective services:** Criminal justice. **Psychology:** General. **Social sciences:** General, criminology, economics, political science. **Visual/performing arts:** Art history/conservation, dramatic, music, studio arts.

Most popular majors. Biology 6%, business/marketing 30%, communications/journalism 8%, education 8%, English 6%, psychology 6%, social sciences 9%.

Computing on campus. 200 workstations in dormitories, library, computer center, student center. Dormitories wired for high-speed internet access and linked to campus network. Commuter students can connect to campus network. Online course registration, online library, helpline, student web hosting, wireless network available.

Student life. Freshman orientation: Mandatory. Preregistration for classes offered. One-day summer program in June and multi-day program at beginning of fall semester. **Policies:** All residence halls are smoke-free. **Housing:** Guaranteed on-campus for all undergraduates. Coed dorms, single-sex dorms, special housing for disabled, apartments, wellness housing available. $200 nonrefundable deposit, deadline 5/1. Special housing available for students involved in service learning and community service, and FY Honors Learning Community. **Activities:** Bands, campus ministries, choral groups, dance, drama, international student organizations, literary magazine, music ensembles, musical theater, radio station, student government, student newspaper, symphony orchestra, TV station, Newman club, Intervarsity Christian Fellowship, Hillel, Circle-K, Habitat for Humanity, Amnesty International, College Democrats, Republican club.

Athletics. NCAA. Intercollegiate: Baseball M, basketball, cross-country, field hockey W, golf M, lacrosse, soccer, softball W, swimming, tennis, track and field, volleyball W, wrestling M. **Intramural:** Badminton, basketball, racquetball, soccer, softball, tennis, volleyball, water polo. **Team name:** Blue Jays.

Student services. Adult student services, alcohol/substance abuse counseling, chaplain/spiritual director, career counseling, student employment services, financial aid counseling, health services, minority student services, personal counseling, placement for graduates, veterans' counselor, women's services. **Physically disabled:** Services for visually, hearing impaired.

Contact. E-mail: admissions@etown.edu
Phone: (717) 361-1400 Fax: (717) 361-1365
Debra Murray, Director of Admissions, Elizabethtown College, One Alpha Drive, Elizabethtown, PA 17022-2298

Franklin & Marshall College

Lancaster, Pennsylvania
www.fandm.edu

CB member
CB code: 2261

- Private 4-year liberal arts college
- Residential campus in small city
- 2,324 degree-seeking undergraduates: 52% women, 3% African American, 3% Asian American, 6% Hispanic American, 9% international
- 38% of applicants admitted
- Application essay required
- 85% graduate within 6 years; 25% enter graduate study

General. Founded in 1787. Regionally accredited. **Degrees:** 541 bachelor's awarded. **Location:** 60 miles from Philadelphia, 120 miles from Washington, DC. **Calendar:** Semester, limited summer session. **Full-time faculty:** 213 total; 95% have terminal degrees, 11% minority, 43% women. **Part-time faculty:** 55 total; 66% have terminal degrees, 9% minority, 60% women. **Class size:** 51% < 20, 48% 20-39, less than 1% 40-49, less than 1% 50-99.

Special facilities: Observatory, science library, retail sales complex, bronze casting foundry, field house, planetarium, museum of art, concert hall, performing arts center, Writers House.

Freshman class profile. 5,105 applied, 1,965 admitted, 597 enrolled.

Mid 50% test scores			
SAT critical reading:	610-680	GPA 2.0-2.99:	7%
SAT math:	630-710	Rank in top quarter:	87%
ACT composite:	28-31	Rank in top tenth:	59%
GPA 3.75 or higher:	28%	Return as sophomores:	93%
GPA 3.50-3.74:	34%	Out-of-state:	72%
GPA 3.0-3.49:	31%	Live on campus:	100%
		International:	12%

Basis for selection. School achievement record, test scores or graded writing samples, extracurricular activities, recommendations, essay considered. Submission of standardized test scores optional for all students. If student choose to omit scores, two recent graded writing samples must be submitted instead. Interview required for early decision applicants, strongly recommended for others. Auditions and portfolios recommended for all students who wish to demonstrate particular talent. **Home schooled:** Transcript of courses and grades required. Students should present a transcript from either a parent or outside evaluating agency. If a parent serves as the primary source of evaluation, he or she may submit the School Report and Counselor Recommendation. The Office of Admission recommends that home schooled students also submit a reading list and have an on-campus interview. It is strongly recommended that home schooled students submit standardized test scores for best admission consideration.

High school preparation. College-preparatory program required. Required and recommended units include English 4, mathematics 3-4, social studies 1-3, history 2-3, science 2-3 (laboratory 2-3), foreign language 2-4 and visual/performing arts 1.

2011-2012 Annual costs. Tuition/fees: $42,610. Room/board: $11,500. Books/supplies: $1,200. Personal expenses: $1,270.

2011-2012 Financial aid. Need-based: 376 full-time freshmen applied for aid; 296 were judged to have need; 296 of these received aid. Average need met was 100%. Average scholarship/grant was $35,712; average loan $3,272. 82% of total undergraduate aid awarded as scholarships/grants, 18% as loans/jobs. **Non-need-based:** Scholarships awarded for leadership, minority status, music/drama.

Application procedures. Admission: Closing date 2/1 (postmark date). $60 fee, may be waived for applicants with need. Admission notification by 4/1. Must reply by May 1 or within 2 week(s) if notified thereafter. **Financial aid:** Closing date 2/15. FAFSA, CSS PROFILE required. Applicants notified by 4/1; must reply by 5/1.

Academics. Special study options: Accelerated study, combined bachelor's/graduate degree, cross-registration, double major, dual enrollment of high school students, exchange student, honors, independent study, internships, liberal arts/career combination, New York semester, student-designed major, study abroad, teacher certification program, Washington semester. 3-2 programs in forestry, engineering, environmental studies; Columbia University's New York/Paris program. **Credit/placement by examination:** AP, CLEP, IB, institutional tests. 64 credit hours maximum toward bachelor's degree. **Support services:** Pre-admission summer program, reduced course load, tutoring, writing center.

Majors. Area/ethnic studies: African, African-American, American. **Biology:** General, animal behavior, biochemistry, neuroscience. **Business:** Business admin. **Conservation:** Environmental science, environmental studies. **English:** Creative writing, English lit. **Foreign languages:** Ancient Greek, classics, French, German, Latin, Spanish. **History:** General. **Math:** General. **Philosophy/religion:** Philosophy, religion. **Physical sciences:** Astronomy, astrophysics, chemistry, geology, physics. **Psychology:** General. **Social sciences:** Anthropology, economics, political science, sociology. **Visual/performing arts:** Art history/conservation, dance, dramatic, music, studio arts.

Most popular majors. Biology 10%, business/marketing 12%, foreign language 6%, interdisciplinary studies 7%, physical sciences 6%, psychology 7%, social sciences 29%.

Computing on campus. 125 workstations in library, computer center. Dormitories wired for high-speed internet access and linked to campus network. Commuter students can connect to campus network. Online course registration, online library, helpline, student web hosting, wireless network available.

Student life. Freshman orientation: Mandatory, $200 fee. Preregistration for classes offered. 5 days prior to start of classes. **Policies:** All students required to live in college-approved housing. Freshmen not permitted cars on campus. **Housing:** Guaranteed on-campus for freshmen. Coed dorms, special housing for disabled, apartments, fraternity/sorority housing, wellness housing available. French house, arts house, international house, community outreach house, sustainability house, and men's and women's floors available.

Activities: Bands, campus ministries, choral groups, dance, drama, international student organizations, literary magazine, music ensembles, musical theater, opera, radio station, student government, student newspaper, symphony orchestra, TV station, East Asian society, Catholic Campus Community, Hillel, Christian Fellowship, Habitat for Humanity, Voices for Women, Coalition for Choice, Environmental Action Alliance, Black student union, Mi Gente Latina.

Athletics. NCAA. **Intercollegiate:** Baseball M, basketball, cross-country, field hockey W, football (tackle) M, golf, lacrosse, rowing (crew), soccer, softball W, squash, swimming, tennis, track and field, volleyball W, wrestling M. **Intramural:** Basketball, football (non-tackle), soccer, softball. **Team name:** Diplomats.

Student services. Alcohol/substance abuse counseling, chaplain/spiritual director, career counseling, student employment services, financial aid counseling, health services, minority student services, on-campus daycare, personal counseling, placement for graduates, women's services. **Physically disabled:** Services for visually, hearing impaired.

Contact. E-mail: admission@fandm.edu
Phone: (717) 291-3953 Toll-free number: (877) 678-9111
Fax: (717) 291-4389
Daniel Lugo, Vice President and Dean of Admission and Financial Aid, Franklin & Marshall College, PO Box 3003, Lancaster, PA 17604-3003

Gannon University
Erie, Pennsylvania
www.gannon.edu

CB member
CB code: 2270

- Private 4-year university affiliated with Roman Catholic Church
- Residential campus in small city
- 2,652 degree-seeking undergraduates: 4% part-time, 59% women, 7% African American, 1% Asian American, 2% Hispanic American, 4% international
- 1,142 degree-seeking graduate students
- 85% of applicants admitted
- SAT or ACT (ACT writing optional) required
- 69% graduate within 6 years; 43% enter graduate study

General. Founded in 1925. Regionally accredited. **Degrees:** 484 bachelor's, 28 associate awarded; master's, professional, doctoral offered. **ROTC:** Army. **Location:** 120 miles from Pittsburgh, 90 miles from Cleveland. **Calendar:** Semester, extensive summer session. **Full-time faculty:** 197 total; 74% have terminal degrees, 10% minority, 46% women. **Part-time faculty:** 159 total; 12% have terminal degrees, 3% minority, 52% women. **Class size:** 55% < 20, 44% 20-39, less than 1% 40-49, less than 1% 50-99. **Special facilities:** Environmental studies center, computer integrated enterprise manufacturing center, floating laboratory providing hands-on environmental study on Lake Erie, patient simulation center for health sciences.

Freshman class profile. 3,633 applied, 3,095 admitted, 684 enrolled.

Mid 50% test scores			
SAT critical reading:	450-570	**GPA 2.0-2.99:**	17%
SAT math:	460-580	**Rank in top quarter:**	52%
ACT composite:	20-25	**Rank in top tenth:**	22%
GPA 3.75 or higher:	39%	**Return as sophomores:**	79%
GPA 3.50-3.74:	20%	**Out-of-state:**	27%
GPA 3.0-3.49:	24%	**Live on campus:**	75%
		International:	4%

Basis for selection. High school record important, including course selection, GPA, class rank, standardized test scores, recommendations, personal statement. Admission requirements vary by program. Limited number of students who do not meet all admissions requirements may be accepted into General Studies program. **Home schooled:** State high school equivalency certificate required. **Learning Disabled:** Applicants screened through director or must be interviewed.

High school preparation. College-preparatory program required. 16 units required; 25 recommended. Required and recommended units include English 4, mathematics 2-4, social studies 2, history 1, science 2-4 (laboratory 2-3), foreign language 2, computer science 1, visual/performing arts 1 and academic electives 3.

2011-2012 Annual costs. Tuition/fees: $25,522. Room/board: $10,230.

2011-2012 Financial aid. Need-based: 624 full-time freshmen applied for aid; 571 were judged to have need; 571 of these received aid. Average need met was 75%. Average scholarship/grant was $18,021; average loan $3,378. 66% of total undergraduate aid awarded as scholarships/grants, 34% as loans/jobs. **Non-need-based:** Awarded to 719 full-time undergraduates, including 138 freshmen. Scholarships awarded for academics, athletics, leadership, music/drama, religious affiliation, ROTC.

Application procedures. Admission: Priority date 1/15; no deadline. $25 fee, may be waived for applicants with need. Admission notification on a rolling basis beginning on or about 9/15. Early application especially recommended for health science programs since space is limited. Charleston, Duquesne, LECOM and LECOM Pharmacy Programs all have application deadlines of 1/15. **Financial aid:** Priority date 3/15; no closing date. FAFSA required. Applicants notified on a rolling basis starting 11/1.

Academics. Preferred admission to doctorate physical therapy program granted to students with bachelor's degree from Gannon in physical therapy. Occupational therapy and physician assistant programs are 5-year master's degree programs. **Special study options:** Accelerated study, combined bachelor's/graduate degree, cooperative education, distance learning, double major, dual enrollment of high school students, ESL, honors, independent study, internships, liberal arts/career combination, semester at sea, study abroad, teacher certification program, Washington semester, weekend college. **Credit/placement by examination:** AP, CLEP, IB. **Support services:** Learning center, reduced course load, remedial instruction, study skills assistance, tutoring, writing center.

Honors college/program. The Honors Program requires a minimum 1150 SAT score (exclusive of Writing), 3.5 GPA, rank in top tenth of high school class, extracurricular activities, community service. Recommendation, interview and essay required. Approximately 50 freshmen admitted per year.

Majors. Biology: General, bioinformatics. **Business:** Accounting, business admin, entrepreneurial studies, finance, insurance, international, management information systems, marketing. **Communications:** Advertising, journalism. **Communications technology:** Radio/TV. **Computer sciences:** General, programming. **Conservation:** Environmental science. **Education:** Early childhood, elementary, foreign languages, secondary, social studies. **Engineering:** Chemical, electrical, environmental, mechanical. **English:** English lit. **Foreign languages:** General. **Health services:** Clinical lab science, nursing (RN), premedicine, respiratory therapy technology. **History:** General. **Human services:** Social work. **Liberal arts:** Arts/sciences. **Math:** General. **Parks/recreation:** Exercise sciences, sports admin. **Philosophy/religion:** Philosophy. **Physical sciences:** Chemistry. **Protective services:** Criminal justice. **Psychology:** General. **Social sciences:** Political science. **Theology:** Theology. **Visual/performing arts:** General, dramatic.

Most popular majors. Biology 7%, business/marketing 11%, education 6%, health sciences 27%, parks/recreation 11%.

Computing on campus. 386 workstations in dormitories, library, computer center, student center. Dormitories wired for high-speed internet access and linked to campus network. Commuter students can connect to campus network. Online library, helpline, wireless network available.

Student life. Freshman orientation: Mandatory, $65 fee. Preregistration for classes offered. 4 sessions during summer; open to parents and students. One fall session held prior to first day of classes. Fee includes overnight accomodations; students who commute to campus during orientation charged $40. **Housing:** Guaranteed on-campus for freshmen. Coed dorms, special housing for disabled, apartments available. $100 fully refundable deposit, deadline 5/1. **Activities:** Bands, campus ministries, choral groups, dance, drama, international student organizations, literary magazine, music ensembles, Model UN, musical theater, radio station, student government, student newspaper, Social Concerns, Multi-Cultures United, Campus Conservatives, GU Habitat for Humanity campus chapter, GU Students for Life, KnightLife, Ichthi, Adelphai, The Zone.

Athletics. NCAA. **Intercollegiate:** Baseball M, basketball, cross-country, diving, football (tackle) M, golf, lacrosse W, soccer, softball W, swimming, volleyball W, water polo, wrestling M. **Intramural:** Basketball, football (non-tackle), handball, racquetball, soccer, volleyball, wrestling M. **Team name:** Golden Knights.

Student services. Adult student services, alcohol/substance abuse counseling, chaplain/spiritual director, career counseling, services for economically disadvantaged, student employment services, financial aid counseling, health services, minority student services, personal counseling, placement for graduates, veterans' counselor. **Physically disabled:** Services for speech, hearing impaired.

Contact. E-mail: admissions@gannon.edu
Phone: (814) 871-7240 Toll-free number: (800) 426-6668
Fax: (814) 871-5803
Terrance Kizina, Director of Admissions, Gannon University, 109 University Square, Erie, PA 16541-0001

Geneva College
Beaver Falls, Pennsylvania
www.geneva.edu

CB member
CB code: 2273

- Private 4-year liberal arts college affiliated with Reformed Presbyterian Church of North America
- Residential campus in large town
- 1,353 degree-seeking undergraduates: 1% part-time, 49% women
- 263 graduate students
- 79% of applicants admitted
- SAT or ACT (ACT writing optional), application essay required
- 61% graduate within 6 years

General. Founded in 1848. Regionally accredited. **Degrees:** 306 bachelor's, 2 associate awarded; master's offered. **ROTC:** Army. **Location:** 35 miles from Pittsburgh. **Calendar:** Semester, limited summer session. **Full-time faculty:** 86 total; 74% have terminal degrees, 7% minority, 35% women. **Part-time faculty:** 92 total. **Class size:** 64% < 20, 31% 20-39, 2% 40-49, 1% 50-99, 2% >100. **Special facilities:** Collection of artifacts and records of Pittsburgh steel industry, technology development center, high adventure ropes course.

Freshman class profile. 1,373 applied, 1,084 admitted, 313 enrolled.

Mid 50% test scores			
SAT critical reading:	480-600	Rank in top quarter:	51%
SAT math:	480-590	Rank in top tenth:	20%
SAT writing:	460-580	Return as sophomores:	75%
ACT composite:	21-27	Out-of-state:	31%
GPA 3.75 or higher:	40%	Live on campus:	87%
GPA 3.50-3.74:	19%	International:	2%
GPA 3.0-3.49:	32%		
GPA 2.0-2.99:	9%		

Basis for selection. Academic performance and test scores most important. Recommendations and extracurricular activities considered. Placement tests in English and math required if the student does not perform well enough on the relevant SAT or ACT examinations. For students with high SAT or ACT scores, placement tests used to determine if students should be placed in more advanced courses. Interview recommended for all; audition required for music program. **Home schooled:** Transcript of courses and grades required. Help in preparing homeschooler's transcript available if necessary.

High school preparation. College-preparatory program required. 16 units required. Required units include English 4, mathematics 2, social studies 3, science 1, foreign language 2 and academic electives 4. Engineering students should have 1 unit of chemistry and physics, 4 units of college-preparatory mathematics including trigonometry or precalculus.

2011-2012 Annual costs. Tuition/fees: $23,330. Room/board: $8,560. Books/supplies: $900. Personal expenses: $1,150.

2010-2011 Financial aid. **Need-based:** 394 full-time freshmen applied for aid; 363 were judged to have need; 362 of these received aid. Average need met was 77%. Average scholarship/grant was $14,587; average loan $3,502. 68% of total undergraduate aid awarded as scholarships/grants, 32% as loans/jobs. **Non-need-based:** Awarded to 329 full-time undergraduates, including 76 freshmen. Scholarships awarded for academics, alumni affiliation, music/drama, religious affiliation.

Application procedures. **Admission:** No deadline. $40 fee, may be waived for applicants with need, free for online applicants. Admission notification on a rolling basis beginning on or about 9/1. Must reply by May 1 or within 3 week(s) if notified thereafter. **Financial aid:** Priority date 3/15; no closing date. FAFSA required. Applicants notified on a rolling basis starting 3/1; must reply by 5/1 or within 4 week(s) of notification.

Academics. **Special study options:** Accelerated study, cooperative education, cross-registration, double major, dual enrollment of high school students, honors, independent study, internships, liberal arts/career combination, student-designed major, study abroad, teacher certification program, Washington semester. **Credit/placement by examination:** AP, CLEP, IB, SAT, ACT, institutional tests. 30 credit hours maximum toward bachelor's degree. **Support services:** Reduced course load, remedial instruction, study skills assistance, tutoring, writing center.

Majors. **Biology:** General, biochemistry. **Business:** Accounting, business admin. **Communications:** Communications/speech/rhetoric. **Computer sciences:** General. **Conservation:** Environmental science. **Education:** General, elementary, mathematics, middle, music, special ed. **Engineering:** General, chemical. **English:** English lit, writing. **Foreign languages:** Biblical. **Health services:** Speech pathology. **History:** General. **Math:** Applied. **Parks/recreation:** Sports admin. **Philosophy/religion:** Philosophy. **Physical sciences:** Chemistry, physics. **Psychology:** General. **Social sciences:** Political science,

sociology. **Theology:** Bible, youth ministry. **Visual/performing arts:** Music, music management, music performance.

Most popular majors. Business/marketing 22%, education 9%, engineering/engineering technologies 10%, psychology 6%, public administration/social services 6%, theological studies 11%.

Computing on campus. 150 workstations in dormitories, library, computer center, student center. Dormitories wired for high-speed internet access and linked to campus network. Commuter students can connect to campus network. Online course registration, online library, helpline, repair service, wireless network available.

Student life. **Freshman orientation:** Mandatory. Preregistration for classes offered. Held 5 days prior to start of classes. **Policies:** Smoking, drinking, social or ballroom dancing not permitted on campus. Students must live on campus unless married, commuting, or over age 24. Religious observance required. **Housing:** Guaranteed on-campus for all undergraduates. Single-sex dorms, apartments, wellness housing available. $150 fully refundable deposit. **Activities:** Bands, campus ministries, choral groups, drama, international student organizations, literary magazine, music ensembles, radio station, student government, student newspaper, Acting on Aids, American Society of Civil Engineering, American Society of Mechanical Engineers, Black student organization, Business and Professional Women, Creation Stewardship Club, International Justice Mission, Young Republicans, Young Democrats.

Athletics. NCAA, NCCAA. **Intercollegiate:** Baseball M, basketball, cross-country, football (tackle) M, soccer, softball W, tennis W, track and field, volleyball W. **Intramural:** Basketball, football (non-tackle), racquetball, soccer, softball, volleyball. **Team name:** Golden Tornadoes.

Student services. Alcohol/substance abuse counseling, chaplain/spiritual director, career counseling, student employment services, financial aid counseling, health services, minority student services, personal counseling, placement for graduates. **Physically disabled:** Services for visually, hearing impaired.

Contact. E-mail: admissions@geneva.edu
Phone: (724) 847-6500 Toll-free number: (800) 847-8255
Fax: (724) 847-6776
Dave Layton, Dean of Undergraduate Enrollment, Geneva College, 3200 College Avenue, Beaver Falls, PA 15010

Gettysburg College
Gettysburg, Pennsylvania
www.gettysburg.edu

CB member
CB code: 2275

- Private 4-year liberal arts college affiliated with Evangelical Lutheran Church in America
- Residential campus in large town
- 2,500 degree-seeking undergraduates: 51% women
- 40% of applicants admitted
- SAT or ACT (ACT writing optional), application essay required
- 85% graduate within 6 years

General. Founded in 1832. Regionally accredited. **Degrees:** 609 bachelor's awarded. **ROTC:** Army. **Location:** 36 miles from Harrisburg, 80 miles from Washington, DC. **Calendar:** Semester. **Full-time faculty:** 215 total; 93% have terminal degrees, 14% minority, 42% women. **Part-time faculty:** 77 total; 44% have terminal degrees, 6% minority, 40% women. **Class size:** 69% < 20, 29% 20-39, 2% 40-49, less than 1% 50-99. **Special facilities:** Sunderman Conservatory of Music, intercultural resource center, women's resource center, child study center, public service center, optics and plasma physics laboratories, infrared and NMR spectrometers, proton accelerator, science center, indoor and outdoor climbing walls, observatory, planetarium.

Freshman class profile. 5,662 applied, 2,257 admitted, 732 enrolled.

Mid 50% test scores			
		Rank in top tenth:	71%
SAT critical reading:	610-690	Out-of-state:	74%
SAT math:	610-690	Live on campus:	100%
Rank in top quarter:	89%		

Basis for selection. Academic record, recommendations, activities are most important. Audition required for the Sunderman Conservatory of Music; portfolio recommended for art program. Interview strongly recommended. **Home schooled:** Statement describing home school structure and mission, transcript of courses and grades, interview, letter of recommendation (nonparent) required.

High school preparation. College-preparatory program required. Required and recommended units include English 4, mathematics 3-4, history

3-4, science 3-4 (laboratory 3-4) and foreign language 3-4. History requirement can be fulfilled with social studies units, depending on available high school courses.

2011-2012 Annual costs. Tuition/fees: $42,610. Room/board: $10,180. Books/supplies: $500.

2011-2012 Financial aid. Need-based: 508 full-time freshmen applied for aid; 421 were judged to have need; 409 of these received aid. Average need met was 100%. Average scholarship/grant was $28,891; average loan $4,279. 86% of total undergraduate aid awarded as scholarships/grants, 14% as loans/jobs. **Non-need-based:** Scholarships awarded for academics, music/drama, religious affiliation.

Application procedures. Admission: Closing date 2/1 (postmark date). $55 fee, may be waived for applicants with need. Admission notification by 4/1. Must reply by May 1 or within 2 week(s) if notified thereafter. **Financial aid:** Closing date 2/15. FAFSA, CSS PROFILE required. Applicants notified by 3/26; must reply by 5/1.

Academics. Special study options: Combined bachelor's/graduate degree, double major, independent study, internships, semester at sea, student-designed major, study abroad, teacher certification program, United Nations semester, Washington semester. 3-2 programs in engineering with Columbia University, Rensselaer Polytechnic Institute, and Washington University in St. Louis; 3-2 program in nursing with Johns Hopkins University; pre-law and health professions advising available. **Credit/placement by examination:** AP, CLEP, IB, SAT, institutional tests. **Support services:** Study skills assistance, tutoring, writing center.

Majors. Area/ethnic studies: African-American, American, Asian, Asian-American, East Asian, Japanese, Latin American, women's. **Biology:** General, biochemistry, conservation, molecular, neuroscience. **Business:** Business admin, finance, international, management science, marketing, nonprofit/public. **Communications:** Communications/speech/rhetoric, journalism. **Computer sciences:** General, computer science. **Conservation:** General, environmental science, environmental studies, forestry, management/policy, water/wetlands/marine. **Education:** Music. **English:** American lit, British lit, creative writing, English lit. **Foreign languages:** Chinese, classics, comparative lit, French, German, Italian, Japanese, Latin, Spanish. **Health services:** Nursing (RN), predental, premedicine, prepharmacy, preveterinary. **History:** General, American, Asian, European. **Liberal arts:** Arts/sciences. **Math:** General. **Parks/recreation:** Exercise sciences, health/fitness, sports admin. **Philosophy/religion:** Philosophy, religion. **Physical sciences:** Astronomy, chemistry, physics. **Psychology:** General. **Social sciences:** Anthropology, economics, international relations, political science, sociology, U.S. government. **Theology:** Preministerial. **Visual/performing arts:** General, art, art history/conservation, dramatic, film/cinema/video, music, music performance, music theory/composition, piano/keyboard, studio arts, theater arts management, voice/opera.

Most popular majors. Biology 13%, business/marketing 11%, English 9%, history 7%, interdisciplinary studies 6%, psychology 7%, social sciences 20%.

Computing on campus. 620 workstations in library, computer center, student center. Dormitories wired for high-speed internet access and linked to campus network. Commuter students can connect to campus network. Online course registration, online library, helpline, repair service, student web hosting, wireless network available.

Student life. Freshman orientation: Mandatory. Preregistration for classes offered. Held 5 days prior to the start of fall semester. **Housing:** Guaranteed on-campus for all undergraduates. Coed dorms, single-sex dorms, apartments, fraternity/sorority housing, wellness housing available. $500 nonrefundable deposit, deadline 5/1. **Activities:** Bands, choral groups, dance, drama, film society, international student organizations, literary magazine, music ensembles, musical theater, opera, radio station, student government, student newspaper, symphony orchestra, TV station, over 120 clubs available.

Athletics. NCAA. **Intercollegiate:** Baseball M, basketball, cheerleading, cross-country, field hockey W, football (tackle) M, golf, lacrosse, soccer, softball W, swimming, tennis, track and field, volleyball W, wrestling M. **Intramural:** Basketball, field hockey, football (non-tackle), lacrosse W, soccer, softball, tennis, volleyball, water polo. **Team name:** Bullets.

Student services. Chaplain/spiritual director, career counseling, student employment services, financial aid counseling, health services, minority student services, personal counseling, placement for graduates, women's services.

Contact. E-mail: admiss@gettysburg.edu
Phone: (717) 337-6100 Toll-free number: (800) 431-0803
Fax: (717) 337-6145
Gail Sweezey, Director of Admissions, Gettysburg College, 300 North Washington Street, Gettysburg, PA 17325-1400

Gratz College
Melrose Park, Pennsylvania
www.gratz.edu   CB code: 2280

▸ Private 4-year liberal arts college affiliated with Jewish faith
▸ Commuter campus in very large city
▸ 19 degree-seeking undergraduates
▸ Application essay required

General. Founded in 1895. Regionally accredited. **Degrees:** 4 bachelor's awarded; master's, professional offered. **Location:** 6 miles from Philadelphia. **Calendar:** Semester, limited summer session. **Full-time faculty:** 7 total. **Special facilities:** Jewish music library and rare book collection, oral history Holocaust archives.

Basis for selection. Application, personal statement, transcripts, and two recommendations are used in evaluating applicants. Interview recommended. **Learning Disabled:** Students seeking accommodations should submit written documentation to the Office of Disability Services.

2011-2012 Annual costs. Tuition/fees: $16,050. Books/supplies: $1,000. Personal expenses: $3,000.

Application procedures. Admission: No deadline. $50 fee, may be waived for applicants with need. Admission notification on a rolling basis. **Financial aid:** Priority date 6/1; no closing date. FAFSA, institutional form required. Applicants notified on a rolling basis starting 11/1.

Academics. Special study options: Cross-registration, distance learning, double major, independent study, internships, study abroad, teacher certification program. **Credit/placement by examination:** AP, CLEP, institutional tests. **Support services:** Reduced course load.

Majors. Philosophy/religion: Judaic, religion.

Computing on campus. 4 workstations in library, student center. Commuter students can connect to campus network. Wireless network available.

Student life. Freshman orientation: Available. Preregistration for classes offered. **Activities:** Student government.

Student services. Adult student services, career counseling, financial aid counseling, personal counseling, placement for graduates.

Contact. E-mail: admissions@gratz.edu
Phone: (215) 635-7300 ext. 140
Toll-free number: (800) 475-4635 ext. 140 Fax: (215) 635-7399
Joanna Bratton, Director of Admissions, Gratz College, 7605 Old York Road, Melrose Park, PA 19027

Grove City College
Grove City, Pennsylvania   **CB member**
www.gcc.edu   **CB code: 2277**

▸ Private 4-year liberal arts college affiliated with Presbyterian Church (USA)
▸ Residential campus in small town
▸ 2,452 degree-seeking undergraduates: 1% part-time, 50% women, 1% African American, 2% Asian American, 2% Hispanic American, 1% international
▸ 76% of applicants admitted
▸ SAT or ACT (ACT writing optional), application essay, interview required
▸ 82% graduate within 6 years; 24% enter graduate study

General. Founded in 1876. Regionally accredited. We do not accept federal monies (Pell Grant, Stafford Loan, Parent Plus Loan, GI Bill, or any other government scholarship or loan program). **Degrees:** 562 bachelor's awarded. **Location:** 60 miles from Pittsburgh. **Calendar:** Semester, extensive summer session. **Full-time faculty:** 129 total; 95% have terminal degrees, 3% minority, 27% women. **Part-time faculty:** 88 total; 22% have terminal degrees, 1% minority, 43% women. **Class size:** 46% < 20, 41% 20-39, 7% 40-49, 4% 50-99, 2% >100. **Special facilities:** Observatory.

Freshman class profile. 1,592 applied, 1,205 admitted, 619 enrolled.

Mid 50% test scores			
SAT critical reading:	560-690	Rank in top quarter:	79%
SAT math:	560-680	Rank in top tenth:	48%
ACT composite:	25-30	End year in good standing:	89%
GPA 3.75 or higher:	52%	Return as sophomores:	88%
GPA 3.50-3.74:	30%	Out-of-state:	52%
GPA 3.0-3.49:	16%	Live on campus:	96%
GPA 2.0-2.99:	2%	International:	1%

Basis for selection. Highly selective admissions process considers the following: High school GPA, rigor of curriculum, class rank, test scores, recommendations, interview, essay, character, and extracurricular activities very important. Audition required for music program. **Home schooled:** Transcript of courses and grades, interview, letter of recommendation (nonparent) required. Outside activities important.

High school preparation. College-preparatory program recommended. 17 units recommended. Recommended units include English 4, mathematics 3, social studies 2, history 2, science 3 (laboratory 2) and foreign language 3. Engineering, science, and math applicants must have 4 math and 4 science.

2011-2012 Annual costs. Tuition/fees: $13,598. Room/board: $7,410. Books/supplies: $1,000. Personal expenses: $350.

2010-2011 Financial aid. Need-based: 399 full-time freshmen applied for aid; 309 were judged to have need; 309 of these received aid. Average need met was 53%. Average scholarship/grant was $6,489. 60% of total undergraduate aid awarded as scholarships/grants, 40% as loans/jobs. **Non-need-based:** Awarded to 290 full-time undergraduates, including 44 freshmen. Scholarships awarded for academics, leadership. **Additional information:** Institutional aid applications required for institutional scholarships, loans, and student employment.

Application procedures. Admission: Closing date 2/1 (postmark date). $50 fee, may be waived for applicants with need. Decision letters mailed 3/15. Must reply by 5/1. **Financial aid:** Closing date 4/15. Institutional form required. Applicants notified on a rolling basis starting 3/15; must reply by 5/1.

Academics. All students required to complete general education core that includes 3-year humanities sequence, with emphasis in religion, philosophy, history, philosophy of science, science/faith/technology, literature, art, and music, as well as courses in social sciences, quantitative/logical reasoning, natural sciences (with labs), physical education, and a foreign language. **Special study options:** Accelerated study, double major, independent study, internships, study abroad, teacher certification program, Washington semester. **Credit/placement by examination:** AP, CLEP, IB. **Support services:** Reduced course load, study skills assistance, tutoring, writing center.

Majors. Biology: General, biochemistry, exercise physiology, molecular. **Business:** Accounting, business admin, communications, entrepreneurial studies, finance, international, managerial economics, marketing. **Communications:** Communications/speech/rhetoric. **Computer sciences:** General, applications programming, systems analysis. **Education:** Biology, chemistry, early childhood, elementary, English, French, history, mathematics, music, physics, science, secondary, social studies, Spanish, special ed. **Engineering:** Electrical, mechanical. **English:** English lit. **Foreign languages:** French, Spanish. **Health services:** Predental, premedicine, prenursing, prepharmacy, prephysical therapy, preveterinary. **History:** General. **Math:** General. **Philosophy/religion:** Philosophy, religion. **Physical sciences:** Chemistry, physics. **Psychology:** General. **Social sciences:** Economics, political science, sociology. **Visual/performing arts:** Music, music management, music performance.

Most popular majors. Biology 11%, business/marketing 21%, communications/journalism 7%, education 7%, engineering/engineering technologies 9%, English 6%, foreign language 6%, social sciences 9%.

Computing on campus. PC or laptop required. 50 workstations in library, computer center. Dormitories wired for high-speed internet access and linked to campus network. Commuter students can connect to campus network. Online course registration, online library, helpline, repair service, student web hosting, wireless network available.

Student life. Freshman orientation: Available, $25 fee. Preregistration for classes offered. One-day programs in June and a 3-1/2-day program in August prior to the beginning of the fall semester. **Policies:** Alcohol not permitted on campus. Chapel program consists of lectures, vespers, and seminars. Students must attend 16 chapels per semester out of 50 opportunities. Religious observance required. Freshmen not permitted cars on campus. **Housing:** Guaranteed on-campus for all undergraduates. Single-sex dorms, apartments, wellness housing available. **Activities:** Bands, campus ministries, choral groups, dance, drama, international student organizations, literary magazine, music ensembles, musical theater, opera, radio station, student government, student newspaper, symphony orchestra, TV station, Fellowship of Christian Athletes, Salt Company, Warriors for Christ, Young Life, Newman club, College Republicans, College Democrats, outing club, orientation board, Life Advocates.

Athletics. NCAA. **Intercollegiate:** Baseball M, basketball, cheerleading M, cross-country, diving, football (tackle) M, golf, soccer, softball W, swimming, tennis, track and field, volleyball W, water polo W. **Intramural:** Badminton, basketball, bowling, football (non-tackle), football (tackle), golf M, handball M, racquetball, soccer W, softball, swimming W, tennis, volleyball. **Team name:** Wolverines.

Student services. Alcohol/substance abuse counseling, chaplain/spiritual director, career counseling, student employment services, financial aid counseling, health services, minority student services, personal counseling, placement for graduates.

Contact. E-mail: admissions@gcc.edu
Phone: (724) 458-2100 Fax: (724) 458-3395
Jeffrey Mincey, Director of Admissions, Grove City College, 100 Campus Drive, Grove City, PA 16127-2104

Gwynedd-Mercy College
Gwynedd Valley, Pennsylvania
www.gmc.edu

CB member
CB code: 2278

▸ Private 4-year nursing and liberal arts college affiliated with Roman Catholic Church
▸ Residential campus in large town
▸ 2,300 degree-seeking undergraduates: 8% part-time, 76% women, 27% African American, 3% Asian American, 3% Hispanic American
▸ 349 degree-seeking graduate students
▸ 87% of applicants admitted
▸ SAT or ACT (ACT writing optional) required
▸ 52% graduate within 6 years

General. Founded in 1948. Regionally accredited. Affiliated with the Religious Sisters of Mercy. 8-week evening sessions running 12 months for business and accounting majors. Accelerated degree program begins every 6 weeks. **Degrees:** 425 bachelor's, 199 associate awarded; master's offered. **Location:** 20 miles from Philadelphia. **Calendar:** Semester, limited summer session. **Full-time faculty:** 80 total; 50% have terminal degrees, 69% women. **Part-time faculty:** 192 total; 20% have terminal degrees, 6% minority, 66% women. **Class size:** 67% < 20, 29% 20-39, 2% 40-49, 2% 50-99, less than 1% >100. **Special facilities:** Lincoln-era collection, nursery laboratory school for early childhood education.

Freshman class profile. 1,187 applied, 1,035 admitted, 297 enrolled.

Mid 50% test scores			
		GPA 2.0-2.99:	26%
SAT critical reading:	420-530	Rank in top quarter:	21%
SAT math:	410-520	Rank in top tenth:	4%
GPA 3.75 or higher:	16%	Return as sophomores:	81%
GPA 3.50-3.74:	15%	Out-of-state:	17%
GPA 3.0-3.49:	42%	Live on campus:	73%

Basis for selection. School achievement record most important, followed by test scores and recommendations. Extracurricular activities considered. Nursing program very competitive.

High school preparation. College-preparatory program recommended. 16 units required. Required units include English 4, mathematics 3, history 1, science 3 and academic electives 3. Chemistry required for applicants to nursing, cardiovascular, biology, medical technology programs. Biology required for cardiovascular, health information technology programs. Physics required for radiation therapy, medical technology, biology programs. Chemistry or physics required for respiratory therapy.

2011-2012 Annual costs. Tuition/fees: $27,870. Room/board: $10,025. Books/supplies: $1,000. Personal expenses: $600.

2010-2011 Financial aid. Need-based: 289 full-time freshmen applied for aid; 252 were judged to have need; 252 of these received aid. Average need met was 69%. Average scholarship/grant was $15,456; average loan $3,383. 63% of total undergraduate aid awarded as scholarships/grants, 37% as loans/jobs. **Non-need-based:** Awarded to 327 full-time undergraduates, including 61 freshmen. Scholarships awarded for academics, alumni affiliation, leadership, minority status.

Application procedures. Admission: Closing date 8/20 (receipt date). $25 fee, may be waived for applicants with need, free for online applicants. Admission notification on a rolling basis beginning on or about 9/15. Must reply by May 1 or within 3 week(s) if notified thereafter. Nursing program usually filled by May 1. **Financial aid:** Priority date 3/15, closing date 5/1.

FAFSA, institutional form required. Applicants notified on a rolling basis starting 2/15; must reply by 5/1 or within 2 week(s) of notification.

Academics. Special study options: Accelerated study, cross-registration, double major, ESL, honors, independent study, internships, liberal arts/career combination, study abroad, teacher certification program, weekend college. **Credit/placement by examination:** AP, CLEP, institutional tests. Credit by examination cannot be applied to open electives. **Support services:** Learning center, reduced course load, remedial instruction, study skills assistance, tutoring, writing center.

Majors. Biology: General. **Business:** Accounting, business admin. **Computer sciences:** General. **Education:** Biology, business, elementary, mathematics, special ed. **English:** English lit. **Health services:** Cardiovascular technology, clinical lab science, medical radiologic technology/radiation therapy, medical records admin, nursing (RN), premedicine, preveterinary, respiratory therapy technology. **History:** General. **Math:** General. **Protective services:** Law enforcement admin. **Psychology:** General. **Social sciences:** Sociology. **Work/family studies:** Aging.

Most popular majors. Business/marketing 41%, education 14%, health sciences 31%.

Computing on campus. 217 workstations in library, computer center, student center. Dormitories wired for high-speed internet access and linked to campus network. Commuter students can connect to campus network. Online course registration, online library, helpline, wireless network available.

Student life. Freshman orientation: Available. Preregistration for classes offered. Multiple full-day sessions offered during the summer. **Housing:** Coed dorms available. $250 deposit, deadline 5/1. **Activities:** Campus ministries, choral groups, literary magazine, student government, student newspaper, Kappa Delta Pi, business society, honor societies, Mercy Corps, resident council, student nurses' association, education club, peer counseling, psychology/sociology club, biology student association.

Athletics. NCAA. **Intercollegiate:** Baseball M, basketball, cross-country, field hockey W, golf M, lacrosse W, soccer, softball W, tennis, track and field, volleyball W. **Intramural:** Volleyball. **Team name:** Griffins.

Student services. Adult student services, chaplain/spiritual director, career counseling, student employment services, financial aid counseling, health services, minority student services, on-campus daycare, personal counseling, placement for graduates.

Contact. E-mail: admissions@gmc.edu
Phone: (215) 646-7300 ext. 530 Toll-free number: (800) 342-5462
Fax: (215) 641-5556
Michele Diehl, Director of Undergraduate Admissions, Gwynedd-Mercy College, 1325 Sumneytown Pike, Gwynedd Valley, PA 19437-0901

Harrisburg University of Science and Technology
Harrisburg, Pennsylvania
www.HarrisburgU.edu   **CB code: 4511**

- Private 4-year university
- Commuter campus in small city
- 220 degree-seeking undergraduates: 8% part-time, 46% women, 25% African American, 7% Asian American, 10% Hispanic American
- 77 degree-seeking graduate students
- 48% of applicants admitted

General. Regionally accredited. **Degrees:** 20 bachelor's awarded; master's offered. **Location:** Located in Central Pennsylvania. **Calendar:** Trimester, limited summer session. **Full-time faculty:** 10 total; 90% have terminal degrees, 40% minority, 50% women. **Part-time faculty:** 25 total; 20% have terminal degrees, 28% women. **Class size:** 95% < 20, 5% 20-39.

Freshman class profile. 1,472 applied, 708 admitted, 93 enrolled.

Mid 50% test scores			
SAT critical reading:	420-520	End year in good standing:	67%
SAT math:	420-550	Return as sophomores:	60%
SAT writing:	400-500	Out-of-state:	10%
ACT composite:	19-22	Live on campus:	59%

Basis for selection. Admissions based on high school record. SAT or ACT recommended. Interview and essay or personal statement strongly recommended. **Home schooled:** Statement describing home school structure and mission, transcript of courses and grades, letter of recommendation (nonparent) required.

2011-2012 Annual costs. Tuition/fees: $22,500. Room only: $5,775. Books/supplies: $1,500.

2010-2011 Financial aid. Need-based: 38% of total undergraduate aid awarded as scholarships/grants, 62% as loans/jobs. **Non-need-based:** Scholarships awarded for academics, leadership, state residency.

Application procedures. Admission: No deadline. No application fee. Admission notification on a rolling basis. **Financial aid:** No deadline. FAFSA required. Applicants notified on a rolling basis; must reply within 2 week(s) of notification.

Academics. Special study options: Double major, dual enrollment of high school students, internships, student-designed major. **Credit/placement by examination:** AP, CLEP, IB, institutional tests. 18 credit hours maximum toward bachelor's degree. **Support services:** Reduced course load, remedial instruction, study skills assistance, tutoring.

Majors. Biology: Biotechnology. **Business:** E-commerce. **Computer sciences:** General, information technology. **Conservation:** Environmental science. **Physical sciences:** General, chemistry. **Social sciences:** Geography.

Most popular majors. Computer/information sciences 37%, physical sciences 48%, science technologies 15%.

Computing on campus. PC or laptop required. 12 workstations in computer center. Commuter students can connect to campus network. Online library, repair service, wireless network available.

Student life. Freshman orientation: Mandatory. Preregistration for classes offered. **Housing:** Guaranteed on-campus for freshmen. Coed dorms available. **Activities:** Student government, student newspaper.

Student services. Financial aid counseling.

Contact. E-mail: admissions@HarrisburgU.edu
Phone: (717) 901-5101 Fax: (717) 901-3101
Timothy Dawson, Director of Admissions and Enrollment Systems, Harrisburg University of Science and Technology, 326 Market Street, Harrisburg, PA 17101-2208

Haverford College
Haverford, Pennsylvania
www.haverford.edu   **CB member**
                                   CB code: 2289

- Private 4-year liberal arts college
- Residential campus in large town
- 1,198 degree-seeking undergraduates: 54% women
- 25% of applicants admitted
- SAT and SAT Subject Tests or ACT with writing, application essay required
- 93% graduate within 6 years; 18% enter graduate study

General. Founded in 1833. Regionally accredited. Founded by the Society of Friends (Quakers), but now independent. **Degrees:** 299 bachelor's awarded. **Location:** 10 miles from Philadelphia. **Calendar:** Semester. **Full-time faculty:** 117 total; 97% have terminal degrees, 24% minority, 44% women. **Part-time faculty:** 21 total; 67% have terminal degrees, 19% minority, 67% women. **Class size:** 74% < 20, 24% 20-39, 2% 40-49, less than 1% 50-99. **Special facilities:** Observatory, arboretum, fine arts foundry.

Freshman class profile. 3,470 applied, 870 admitted, 335 enrolled.

Mid 50% test scores			
SAT critical reading:	650-750	Rank in top tenth:	94%
SAT math:	650-750	Return as sophomores:	96%
SAT writing:	660-760	Out-of-state:	86%
ACT composite:	30-33	Live on campus:	100%
Rank in top quarter:	99%	International:	6%

Basis for selection. School record, test scores, extracurricular achievements, and recommendations important. College seeks diversity of social, economic, and geographic backgrounds. Some preference given to children of alumni. First-year applicants must take SAT or ACT plus 2 SAT Subject Tests before deadline for decision plan chosen. Interview required of applicants living within 150 miles of college, recommended for others. **Home schooled:** Statement describing home school structure and mission, transcript of courses and grades, interview, letter of recommendation (nonparent) required.

High school preparation. College-preparatory program recommended. No specific high school curriculum required, but recommend 4 years of

English; at least 3 years of mathematics, the sciences, history; 2 years of social studies; 1 or 2 foreign languages and coursework in art and music.

2011-2012 Annual costs. Tuition/fees: $42,208. In addition to the $378 required fee, First-year students pay a $200 orientation fee. Room/board: $12,842. Books/supplies: $1,194. Personal expenses: $1,468.

2011-2012 Financial aid. All financial aid based on need. 191 full-time freshmen applied for aid; 153 were judged to have need; 153 of these received aid. Average need met was 100%. Average scholarship/grant was $37,737; average loan $946. 96% of total undergraduate aid awarded as scholarships/grants, 4% as loans/jobs.

Application procedures. Admission: Closing date 1/15. $60 fee, may be waived for applicants with need. Admission notification by 4/15. Must reply by May 1 or within 2 week(s) if notified thereafter. **Financial aid:** Closing date 2/1. FAFSA, CSS PROFILE required. Applicants notified by 4/1; must reply by 5/1.

Academics. Academic Flexibility Program allows for advanced independent work and interdepartmental majors. Ample opportunity for student-faculty research. Senior seminars, comprehensive examination and/or senior thesis required for completion of all major programs. **Special study options:** Combined bachelor's/graduate degree, cross-registration, double major, exchange student, independent study, internships, liberal arts/career combination, student-designed major, study abroad, teacher certification program. Exchange programs with Spelman College (GA), Claremont McKenna College and Pitzer College (CA), Fisk University (TN); cross-registration with Bryn Mawr College, Swarthmore College, noncredit internships also available; 3-2 engineering program with California Institute of Technology. **Credit/placement by examination:** AP, CLEP, IB. **Support services:** Learning center, study skills assistance, tutoring, writing center.

Majors. Architecture: Urban/community planning. **Area/ethnic studies:** East Asian. **Biology:** General. **Computer sciences:** General. **English:** English lit. **Foreign languages:** Ancient Greek, classics, comparative lit, French, German, Italian, Latin, Russian, Spanish. **History:** General. **Liberal arts:** Arts/sciences. **Math:** General. **Philosophy/religion:** Philosophy, religion. **Physical sciences:** Astronomy, chemistry, geology, physics. **Psychology:** General. **Social sciences:** Anthropology, archaeology, economics, political science, sociology, urban studies. **Visual/performing arts:** Art history/conservation, music, studio arts.

Most popular majors. Biology 11%, English 12%, foreign language 7%, history 7%, philosophy/religious studies 7%, physical sciences 10%, psychology 9%, social sciences 24%.

Computing on campus. 300 workstations in dormitories, library, computer center, student center. Dormitories wired for high-speed internet access and linked to campus network. Commuter students can connect to campus network. Online course registration, online library, helpline, student web hosting, wireless network available.

Student life. Freshman orientation: Mandatory, $200 fee. Preregistration for classes offered. Directly precedes the start of the fall semester. **Policies:** Student conduct regulated by academic and social honor code, which allows for unsupervised examinations. Students serve on campus governance and policy-making committees. Freshmen not permitted cars on campus. **Housing:** Guaranteed on-campus for all undergraduates. Coed dorms, single-sex dorms, apartments, wellness housing available. Students may live at Bryn Mawr College through dormitory exchange program. Students at both colleges may eat meals on either campus. **Activities:** Campus ministries, choral groups, dance, drama, international student organizations, literary magazine, music ensembles, musical theater, radio station, student government, student newspaper, Quaker activities committee, Hillel, Christian Fellowship, environmental action committee, black students league, Puerto Rican students association, Asian students association, Bisexual/Gay/Lesbian alliance, Eighth Dimension Volunteer Service Program.

Athletics. NCAA. **Intercollegiate:** Baseball M, basketball, cricket, cross-country, fencing, field hockey W, lacrosse, soccer, softball W, squash, tennis, track and field, volleyball W. **Intramural:** Basketball, soccer, tennis.

Student services. Alcohol/substance abuse counseling, career counseling, student employment services, financial aid counseling, health services, minority student services, personal counseling, placement for graduates, women's services. **Physically disabled:** Services for visually, speech, hearing impaired.

Contact. E-mail: admission@haverford.edu
Phone: (610) 896-1350 Fax: (610) 896-1338
Jess Lord, Dean of Admissions and Financial Aid, Haverford College, 370 Lancaster Avenue, Haverford, PA 19041-1392

Holy Family University
Philadelphia, Pennsylvania
www.holyfamily.edu

CB member
CB code: 2297

- Private 4-year university affiliated with Roman Catholic Church
- Commuter campus in very large city
- 2,031 degree-seeking undergraduates: 21% part-time, 73% women, 7% African American, 4% Asian American, 7% Hispanic American, 1% international
- 1,031 degree-seeking graduate students
- 71% of applicants admitted
- SAT or ACT (ACT writing optional) required
- 61% graduate within 6 years

General. Founded in 1954. Regionally accredited. Additional instructional sites in Newtown, Bensalem and Quakertown. **Degrees:** 432 bachelor's, 18 associate awarded; master's, doctoral offered. **Location:** 12 miles from downtown. **Calendar:** Semester, extensive summer session. **Full-time faculty:** 94 total; 76% have terminal degrees, 13% minority, 66% women. **Part-time faculty:** 276 total; 26% have terminal degrees, 6% minority, 50% women. **Class size:** 73% < 20, 27% 20-39. **Special facilities:** Early childhood center with nursery school and kindergarten.

Freshman class profile. 1,270 applied, 896 admitted, 289 enrolled.

Mid 50% test scores			
SAT critical reading:	430-510	GPA 2.0-2.99:	46%
SAT math:	420-500	Rank in top quarter:	32%
SAT writing:	420-500	Rank in top tenth:	10%
GPA 3.75 or higher:	11%	Return as sophomores:	79%
GPA 3.50-3.74:	9%	Out-of-state:	21%
GPA 3.0-3.49:	31%	Live on campus:	26%

Basis for selection. High school record most important, followed by recommendations, interview and test scores. Motivation, schoolwork and community activities considered. Essay, interview recommended. **Home schooled:** State-issued equivalency diploma required. **Learning Disabled:** Students must meet with Counseling Center to be evaluated. Results and formal report shared with Admission department and acceptance decision is made. Results discussed with student.

High school preparation. College-preparatory program required. 16 units required. Required units include English 4, mathematics 3, history 2, science 2, foreign language 2 and academic electives 3. All students must have algebra I, algebra II, and geometry. Math majors need trigonometry. Nursing requires biology, chemistry, and science electives. Science requires biology, chemistry, and trigonometry.

2011-2012 Annual costs. Tuition/fees: $24,640. Room/board: $11,750. Books/supplies: $1,030.

2011-2012 Financial aid. Non-need-based: Scholarships awarded for academics, alumni affiliation, athletics.

Application procedures. Admission: No deadline. $25 fee, may be waived for applicants with need. Admission notification on a rolling basis beginning on or about 9/15. Must reply by May 1 or within 2 week(s) if notified thereafter. **Financial aid:** Priority date 3/1; no closing date. FAFSA, institutional form required. Applicants notified on a rolling basis starting 3/15; must reply within 2 week(s) of notification.

Academics. Special study options: Accelerated study, cooperative education, cross-registration, distance learning, double major, honors, independent study, internships, liberal arts/career combination, teacher certification program, weekend college. **Credit/placement by examination:** AP, CLEP, SAT, institutional tests. 30 credit hours maximum toward bachelor's degree. **Support services:** Learning center, pre-admission summer program, reduced course load, remedial instruction, study skills assistance, tutoring, writing center.

Majors. Biology: General, biochemistry. **Business:** Accounting, accounting/finance, business admin, finance, human resources, international, management information systems. **Communications:** Media studies. **Education:** Art, biology, chemistry, early childhood, elementary, English, French, history, mathematics, social science, social studies, Spanish, special ed. **English:** English lit. **Foreign languages:** French, Spanish. **Health services:** Clinical lab science, nursing (RN), radiologic technology/medical imaging. **History:** General. **Human services:** Social work. **Liberal arts:** Humanities. **Math:** General. **Parks/recreation:** Sports admin. **Philosophy/religion:** Religion. **Physical sciences:** Chemistry. **Protective services:** Criminal justice, fire services admin. **Psychology:** General, industrial. **Social sciences:** Economics, sociology. **Visual/performing arts:** Studio arts.

Most popular majors. Business/marketing 23%, education 20%, health sciences 28%, psychology 8%, security/protective services 6%.

Computing on campus. 475 workstations in dormitories, library, computer center. Dormitories wired for high-speed internet access and linked to campus network. Commuter students can connect to campus network. Online course registration, online library, helpline, repair service, wireless network available.

Student life. Freshman orientation: Mandatory. Preregistration for classes offered. **Policies:** Mature and intelligent student conduct expected in accordance with college's interests, standards, and ideals. **Housing:** Guaranteed on-campus for freshmen. Coed dorms, special housing for disabled, apartments, wellness housing available. $300 fully refundable deposit, deadline 3/15. On-campus housing available for some athletes. **Activities:** Campus ministries, choral groups, drama, literary magazine, musical theater, radio station, student government, student newspaper, TV station, community health and welfare organizations, social and departmental clubs, honor societies, ministry team, Habitat for Humanity.

Athletics. NCAA. **Intercollegiate:** Basketball, cross-country, golf M, lacrosse W, soccer, softball W, tennis W, track and field, volleyball W. **Intramural:** Basketball, bowling, cheerleading W, football (non-tackle), racquetball, table tennis, volleyball. **Team name:** Tigers.

Student services. Adult student services, alcohol/substance abuse counseling, chaplain/spiritual director, career counseling, student employment services, financial aid counseling, health services, minority student services, personal counseling, placement for graduates. **Physically disabled:** Services for visually, speech, hearing impaired.

Contact. E-mail: admissions@holyfamily.edu
Phone: (215) 637-3050 Fax: (215) 281-1022
Lauren Campbell, Director of Admissions, Holy Family University, 9801 Frankford Avenue, Philadelphia, PA 19114-2009

Immaculata University
Immaculata, Pennsylvania — **CB member**
www.immaculata.edu — **CB code: 2320**

- Private 4-year university and liberal arts college affiliated with Roman Catholic Church
- Residential campus in large town
- 2,904 degree-seeking undergraduates: 58% part-time, 78% women, 17% African American, 3% Asian American, 3% Hispanic American, 1% international
- 1,095 degree-seeking graduate students
- 80% of applicants admitted
- SAT or ACT (ACT writing recommended) required
- 47% graduate within 6 years

General. Founded in 1920. Regionally accredited. **Degrees:** 650 bachelor's, 9 associate awarded; master's, doctoral offered. **ROTC:** Army. **Location:** 20 miles from Philadelphia. **Calendar:** Semester, limited summer session. **Full-time faculty:** 113 total; 79% have terminal degrees, 6% minority, 77% women. **Part-time faculty:** 295 total; 20% have terminal degrees, 4% minority, 60% women. **Class size:** 84% < 20, 15% 20-39, less than 1% 40-49, less than 1% 50-99.

Freshman class profile. 1,426 applied, 1,140 admitted, 242 enrolled.

Mid 50% test scores			
SAT critical reading:	420-520	GPA 3.50-3.74:	18%
SAT math:	420-520	GPA 3.0-3.49:	28%
SAT writing:	430-530	GPA 2.0-2.99:	38%
ACT composite:	17-23	Return as sophomores:	83%
GPA 3.75 or higher:	15%	Out-of-state:	32%
		Live on campus:	80%

Basis for selection. Class rank, academic program, test scores, counselor recommendation important. Minimum 2.3 GPA preferred. Interviews, essay recommended. Audition required for music program. **Home schooled:** Transcript of courses and grades required. **Learning Disabled:** Proof of psychological or educational testing date must be supplied.

High school preparation. College-preparatory program required. 16 units required. Required units include English 4, mathematics 2, social studies 2, science 2 (laboratory 1) and foreign language 2. 4 electives required; music required for music majors.

2011-2012 Annual costs. Tuition/fees: $28,850. Immaculata University has a fixed rate tuition plan. Students will pay the same rate for all four years of undergraduate study. Room/board: $11,460. Books/supplies: $1,695. Personal expenses: $2,880.

Financial aid. Non-need-based: Scholarships awarded for academics, alumni affiliation, art, job skills, leadership, minority status, music/drama, religious affiliation, state residency.

Application procedures. Admission: No deadline. $35 fee, may be waived for applicants with need, free for online applicants. Admission notification on a rolling basis beginning on or about 9/15. Must reply by May 1 or within 2 week(s) if notified thereafter. **Financial aid:** Priority date 2/15, closing date 4/15. FAFSA required. Applicants notified on a rolling basis starting 2/1; must reply within 2 week(s) of notification.

Academics. Special study options: Accelerated study, combined bachelor's/graduate degree, cross-registration, distance learning, double major, dual enrollment of high school students, honors, independent study, internships, liberal arts/career combination, semester at sea, study abroad, teacher certification program, Washington semester. **Credit/placement by examination:** AP, CLEP, IB, SAT, ACT, institutional tests. 30 credit hours maximum toward associate degree, 63 toward bachelor's. **Support services:** Learning center, reduced course load, remedial instruction, study skills assistance, tutoring, writing center.

Majors. Biology: General. **Business:** Accounting, business admin, fashion, finance, human resources, marketing. **Communications:** Communications/speech/rhetoric. **Computer sciences:** Information systems. **Conservation:** Environmental studies. **Education:** Business, elementary, family/consumer sciences, mathematics, music. **English:** English lit. **Foreign languages:** French, German, Spanish. **Health services:** Dietetics, health care admin, music therapy, nursing (RN), premedicine. **History:** General. **Human services:** Public policy. **Liberal arts:** Arts/sciences. **Math:** General. **Parks/recreation:** Exercise sciences. **Physical sciences:** Chemistry. **Protective services:** Criminal justice. **Psychology:** General. **Social sciences:** Economics, international relations, political science, sociology. **Theology:** Theology. **Visual/performing arts:** Music, music performance.

Most popular majors. Business/marketing 28%, health sciences 44%, psychology 6%.

Computing on campus. 326 workstations in dormitories, library, computer center, student center. Dormitories wired for high-speed internet access and linked to campus network. Commuter students can connect to campus network. Online course registration, online library, helpline, wireless network available.

Student life. Freshman orientation: Mandatory. Preregistration for classes offered. 2-day session held in summer. **Housing:** Coed dorms, single-sex dorms, special housing for disabled, apartments available. $250 partly refundable deposit, deadline 5/1. **Activities:** Bands, campus ministries, choral groups, dance, drama, international student organizations, literary magazine, music ensembles, musical theater, student government, student newspaper, symphony orchestra, African American cultural society, American Music Therapy Association, Modern Foreign Language Association.

Athletics. NCAA. **Intercollegiate:** Basketball, cross-country W, field hockey W, golf, lacrosse, soccer, softball W, tennis, track and field M, volleyball W. **Intramural:** Basketball, cross-country W, field hockey W, lacrosse W, soccer W, softball W, swimming W, tennis W, volleyball W. **Team name:** Mighty Macs.

Student services. Adult student services, alcohol/substance abuse counseling, chaplain/spiritual director, career counseling, student employment services, financial aid counseling, health services, minority student services, personal counseling, placement for graduates. **Physically disabled:** Services for visually, hearing impaired.

Contact. E-mail: admiss@immaculata.edu
Phone: (610) 647-4400 ext. 3060 Toll-free number: (877) 428-6329
Fax: (610) 640-0836
Rebecca Bowlby, Director of Admission, Immaculata University, 1145 King Road, Immaculata, PA 19345

Indiana University of Pennsylvania
Indiana, Pennsylvania — **CB member**
www.iup.edu — **CB code: 2652**

- Public 4-year university
- Residential campus in large town
- 12,660 degree-seeking undergraduates: 5% part-time, 57% women, 10% African American, 1% Asian American, 3% Hispanic American, 2% international
- 2,113 degree-seeking graduate students
- 58% of applicants admitted

- SAT or ACT (ACT writing optional) required
- 54% graduate within 6 years

General. Founded in 1875. Regionally accredited. Branch campuses located in Punxsutawney and Armstrong County. **Degrees:** 2,156 bachelor's, 16 associate awarded; master's, doctoral offered. **ROTC:** Army. **Location:** 50 miles from Pittsburgh. **Calendar:** Semester, extensive summer session. **Full-time faculty:** 623 total; 14% minority, 47% women. **Part-time faculty:** 78 total; 5% minority, 58% women. **Class size:** 30% < 20, 46% 20-39, 9% 40-49, 12% 50-99, 2% >100. **Special facilities:** Museums, ski slopes, nature preserve, lodge, and sailing base.

Freshman class profile. 12,735 applied, 7,428 admitted, 2,928 enrolled.

Mid 50% test scores			
SAT critical reading:	450-540	Rank in top tenth:	2%
SAT math:	450-540	Return as sophomores:	77%
SAT writing:	430-520	Out-of-state:	9%
Rank in top quarter:	12%	Live on campus:	85%
		International:	1%

Basis for selection. School achievement record, recommendations and extracurricular activities considered, test scores, and high school rank important. Audition required for music program; portfolio required for art program. **Home schooled:** Transcript of courses and grades required.

High school preparation. College-preparatory program recommended. Recommended units include English 4, mathematics 3, social studies 2, history 2, science 3 (laboratory 2) and foreign language 2. Additional .5 unit computer science recommended.

2011-2012 Annual costs. Tuition/fees: $8,361; $17,721 out-of-state. Additional fees of $1,132 for out-of-state students. Tuition is $9,360 for students in any of these categories: OH, VA, WV, IN and MI residents; branch campus students from any state; out-of-state students with high school GPA of at least 3.0; any transfer student with GPA of at least 3.0. Room/board: $9,782. Books/supplies: $1,100. Personal expenses: $3,358.

2010-2011 Financial aid. **Need-based:** 2,742 full-time freshmen applied for aid; 2,202 were judged to have need; 2,162 of these received aid. Average need met was 63%. Average scholarship/grant was $6,067; average loan $3,668. 47% of total undergraduate aid awarded as scholarships/grants, 53% as loans/jobs. **Non-need-based:** Awarded to 2,248 full-time undergraduates, including 787 freshmen. Scholarships awarded for academics, alumni affiliation, art, athletics, job skills, leadership, music/drama, ROTC, state residency.

Application procedures. Admission: Priority date 12/31; no deadline. $45 fee, may be waived for applicants with need. Admission notification on a rolling basis beginning on or about 9/1. Must reply by May 1 or within 2 week(s) if notified thereafter. **Financial aid:** Priority date 4/25; no closing date. FAFSA required. Applicants notified on a rolling basis starting 3/15.

Academics. Special study options: Accelerated study, combined bachelor's/graduate degree, cooperative education, cross-registration, distance learning, double major, dual enrollment of high school students, ESL, exchange student, external degree, honors, independent study, internships, liberal arts/career combination, student-designed major, study abroad, teacher certification program, urban semester, Washington semester, weekend college. **Credit/placement by examination:** AP, CLEP, IB, institutional tests. Unlimited number of hours of credit by examination may be counted toward degree. **Support services:** Learning center, pre-admission summer program, remedial instruction, study skills assistance, tutoring, writing center.

Honors college/program. Average SAT of 1300 and are in top 10% of high school class.

Majors. Architecture: Urban/community planning. **Area/ethnic studies:** Asian. **Biology:** General, biochemistry. **Business:** General, accounting, business admin, fashion, finance, hospitality admin, human resources, international, management information systems, marketing, office management. **Communications:** Communications/speech/rhetoric, journalism. **Computer sciences:** General. **Education:** Deaf/hearing impaired, early childhood, early childhood special, elementary, middle, special ed, trade/industrial. **Engineering:** Applied physics. **English:** English lit. **Foreign languages:** Spanish. **Health services:** Athletic training, clinical lab science, environmental health, nuclear medical technology, nursing (RN), respiratory therapy technology. **History:** General. **Math:** General, applied. **Parks/recreation:** Health/fitness. **Philosophy/religion:** Philosophy, religion. **Physical sciences:** Chemistry, geology, physics. **Psychology:** General. **Social sciences:** Anthropology, criminology, economics, geography, international relations, political science, sociology. **Visual/performing arts:** General, art, dramatic, interior design, multimedia, music, music performance, studio arts. **Work/family studies:** General, family studies, food/nutrition.

Most popular majors. Business/marketing 25%, communications/journalism 6%, education 6%, family/consumer sciences 6%, health sciences 8%, parks/recreation 6%, social sciences 18%, visual/performing arts 7%.

Computing on campus. 2,263 workstations in dormitories, library, computer center. Dormitories wired for high-speed internet access and linked to campus network. Commuter students can connect to campus network. Online course registration, helpline, repair service, student web hosting, wireless network available.

Student life. Freshman orientation: Mandatory, $140 fee. Preregistration for classes offered. **Housing:** Guaranteed on-campus for freshmen. Coed dorms, special housing for disabled, apartments, wellness housing available. $80 nonrefundable deposit, deadline 5/15. Honors college dormitory, substance-free housing, academic specialty floors available. **Activities:** Bands, campus ministries, choral groups, dance, drama, international student organizations, literary magazine, music ensembles, musical theater, radio station, student government, student newspaper, symphony orchestra, TV station, Alpha Phi Omega National Service Fraternity (coeducational), Gamma Sigma Sigma Service Sorority, African American Cultural Center, Campus Crusade for Christ, Coalition for Christian Outreach, Newman Center, Panhellenic Association, NAACP.

Athletics. NCAA. **Intercollegiate:** Baseball M, basketball, cross-country, field hockey W, football (tackle) M, golf M, lacrosse W, soccer W, softball W, swimming, tennis W, track and field, volleyball W. **Intramural:** Basketball, bowling, football (non-tackle), golf, racquetball, soccer, softball, tennis, track and field, volleyball. **Team name:** Crimson Hawks.

Student services. Adult student services, alcohol/substance abuse counseling, chaplain/spiritual director, career counseling, services for economically disadvantaged, student employment services, financial aid counseling, health services, legal services, minority student services, on-campus daycare, personal counseling, placement for graduates, veterans' counselor, women's services. **Physically disabled:** Services for visually, speech, hearing impaired.

Contact. E-mail: admissions_inquiry@iup.edu
Phone: (724) 357-2230 Toll-free number: (800) 442-6830
Fax: (724) 357-6281
Rhonda Luckey, Vice President for Student Affairs, Indiana University of Pennsylvania, 117 John Sutton Hall, 1011 South Drive, Indiana, PA 15705-1088

Juniata College
Huntingdon, Pennsylvania
www.juniata.edu

CB member
CB code: 2341

- Private 4-year liberal arts college
- Residential campus in small town
- 1,469 degree-seeking undergraduates: 56% women, 3% African American, 2% Asian American, 3% Hispanic American, 5% international
- 71% of applicants admitted
- Application essay required
- 76% graduate within 6 years

General. Founded in 1876. Regionally accredited. **Degrees:** 326 bachelor's awarded. **Location:** 30 miles from Altoona and State College. **Calendar:** Semester, limited summer session. **Full-time faculty:** 104 total; 90% have terminal degrees, 7% minority, 38% women. **Part-time faculty:** 43 total; 14% minority, 56% women. **Class size:** 68% < 20, 27% 20-39, 3% 40-49, 2% 50-99, less than 1% >100. **Special facilities:** Nature preserve, environmental studies field station, observatory, early childhood education center.

Freshman class profile. 2,144 applied, 1,528 admitted, 363 enrolled.

Mid 50% test scores			
SAT critical reading:	540-640	Rank in top quarter:	77%
SAT math:	540-640	Rank in top tenth:	40%
GPA 3.75 or higher:	65%	Return as sophomores:	85%
GPA 3.50-3.74:	16%	Out-of-state:	33%
GPA 3.0-3.49:	17%	Live on campus:	99%
GPA 2.0-2.99:	2%	International:	7%

Basis for selection. School achievement record most important. Standardized test scores, school and community activities, recommendations and essay also important. SAT or ACT recommended. Students may submit SAT or ACT scores either directly from the testing agency or from the guidance counselor. If a student chooses not to submit standardized test scores, then must submit two graded papers. Interview recommended. **Home schooled:** Interview required.

High school preparation. College-preparatory program required. 16 units required; 18 recommended. Required and recommended units include English 4, mathematics 3-4, social studies 1, history 3, science 3-4 (laboratory 2) and foreign language 2.

2012-2013 Annual costs. Tuition/fees: $35,780. Room/board: $9,800. Books/supplies: $600. Personal expenses: $1,000.

2011-2012 Financial aid. **Need-based:** 302 full-time freshmen applied for aid; 260 were judged to have need; 260 of these received aid. Average need met was 86%. Average scholarship/grant was $22,736; average loan $4,043. 76% of total undergraduate aid awarded as scholarships/grants, 24% as loans/jobs. **Non-need-based:** Awarded to 550 full-time undergraduates, including 151 freshmen. Scholarships awarded for academics, alumni affiliation, art, minority status, music/drama.

Application procedures. **Admission:** Priority date 11/15; deadline 3/15 (postmark date). $35 fee, may be waived for applicants with need, free for online applicants. Admission notification on a rolling basis beginning on or about 9/15. Must reply by May 1 or within 2 week(s) if notified thereafter. **Financial aid:** Closing date 3/1. FAFSA required. Applicants notified on a rolling basis starting 3/1; must reply by 5/1.

Academics. **Special study options:** Combined bachelor's/graduate degree, double major, dual enrollment of high school students, ESL, exchange student, honors, independent study, internships, student-designed major, study abroad, teacher certification program, urban semester, Washington semester. Marine biology with Oregon Marine Program; 3-3 law with Duquesne University; 3-2 engineering with Columbia University, Pennsylvania State University, Clarkson University, Washington University; 3-4 dentistry with Temple University; 3-4 medicine with Tulane University School of Medicine, Lake Erie College of Osteopathic Medicine, Temple University School of Medicine; 3-4 optometry with Pennsylvania College of Optometry; 3-4 podiatry with Temple University School of Podiatric Medicine and Ohio College of Podiatric Medicine; nursing with Johns Hopkins University, Case Western Reserve University; biotechnology, cytotechnology with Jefferson School of Health Professions; physical therapy with Widener University, Drexel University, Jefferson School of Health Professions; medical technology with Jefferson College of Health Professions, Altoona Regional Health Systems; chiropractic medicine with New York Chiropractic College; pharmacy with Lake Erie College of Osteopathic Medicine School of Pharmacy at Erie Campus, and Lake Erie College of Osteopathic Medicine School of Pharmacy at Bradenton Campus; Physician Assistant with Saint Francis University. **Credit/placement by examination:** AP, CLEP, IB, institutional tests. Unlimited number of hours of credit by examination may be counted toward degree. **Support services:** Reduced course load, study skills assistance, tutoring, writing center.

Majors. **Biology:** General, biochemistry, botany, cell/histology, ecology, marine, microbiology, molecular, zoology. **Business:** General, accounting, business admin, entrepreneurial studies, finance, human resources, information resources management, international, marketing. **Communications:** Communications/speech/rhetoric, digital media, health. **Computer sciences:** General, information technology. **Conservation:** Economics, environmental science, environmental studies, wildlife/wilderness. **Education:** General, biology, chemistry, early childhood, early childhood special, elementary, English, French, German, mathematics, multi-level teacher, physics, science, secondary, social studies, Spanish. **Engineering:** General, applied physics. **English:** English lit, technical writing. **Foreign languages:** General, French, German, Russian, Spanish. **Health services:** Predental, premedicine, prenursing, prepharmacy, preveterinary. **History:** General. **Human services:** General, social work. **Liberal arts:** Arts/sciences, humanities. **Math:** General. **Philosophy/religion:** Philosophy, religion. **Physical sciences:** General, chemistry, geology, physics. **Psychology:** General. **Social sciences:** General, anthropology, criminology, economics, international relations, political science, sociology. **Visual/performing arts:** Art, art history/conservation, directing/producing, dramatic, studio arts.

Most popular majors. Biology 15%, business/marketing 21%, communications/journalism 6%, education 7%, interdisciplinary studies 6%, natural resources/environmental science 6%, psychology 8%, social sciences 7%.

Computing on campus. PC or laptop required. 340 workstations in library, computer center, student center. Dormitories wired for high-speed internet access and linked to campus network. Commuter students can connect to campus network. Online course registration, online library, helpline, repair service, wireless network available.

Student life. **Freshman orientation:** Available. Preregistration for classes offered. 2 days in summer, parallel programs for new students and their parents. **Housing:** Guaranteed on-campus for all undergraduates. Coed dorms, single-sex dorms, apartments, wellness housing available. $400 nonrefundable deposit, deadline 5/1. Special interest housing available. **Activities:** Bands, campus ministries, choral groups, dance, drama, international student organizations, music ensembles, Model UN, musical theater, radio station, student government, student newspaper, symphony orchestra, TV station, Christian Ministry Board, Catholic Council, Hillel, Muslim student association, United Spiritual Council, Brethren Student Fellowship, Habitat for Humanity, Colleges Against Cancer, African American Student Alliance.

Athletics. NCAA. **Intercollegiate:** Baseball M, basketball, cross-country, field hockey W, football (tackle) M, soccer, softball W, swimming W, tennis, track and field, volleyball. **Intramural:** Basketball, soccer, volleyball. **Team name:** Eagles.

Student services. Adult student services, alcohol/substance abuse counseling, chaplain/spiritual director, career counseling, student employment services, financial aid counseling, health services, minority student services, personal counseling, placement for graduates. **Physically disabled:** Services for visually, hearing impaired.

Contact. E-mail: admissions@juniata.edu
Phone: (814) 641-3420 Toll-free number: (877) 586-4282
Fax: (814) 641-3100
Michelle Bartol, Dean of Enrollment, Juniata College, 1700 Moore Street, Huntingdon, PA 16652-2196

Keystone College

La Plume, Pennsylvania — **CB member**
www.keystone.edu — **CB code: 2351**

- Private 4-year liberal arts college
- Residential campus in rural community
- 1,688 degree-seeking undergraduates: 18% part-time, 61% women, 5% African American, 1% Asian American, 3% Hispanic American
- 26 graduate students
- 93% of applicants admitted
- SAT or ACT (ACT writing optional), application essay required
- 43% graduate within 6 years

General. Founded in 1868. Regionally accredited. Students may enroll in up to 12 credits as nonmatriculating prior to making formal application to college. Trimester system for Adult Weekender Program. **Degrees:** 251 bachelor's, 68 associate awarded. **ROTC:** Army, Air Force. **Location:** Northeastern region of Pennsylvania; 15 miles from the city of Scranton. **Calendar:** Semester, limited summer session. **Full-time faculty:** 67 total; 49% have terminal degrees, 3% minority, 60% women. **Part-time faculty:** 193 total; 11% have terminal degrees, 2% minority, 56% women. **Class size:** 80% < 20, 19% 20-39, less than 1% 40-49. **Special facilities:** Observatory, children's center, Microsoft-certified systems engineer training site, Linder art gallery, Willary Water Resource center, U.S. Mid-Atlantic Urban Forestry Center, restaurant (operated by culinary students), delayed harvest trout stream, Countryside Conservancy, PRAXIS testing location, Nightshade Press, nature trails, maple sugar shack.

Freshman class profile. 1,144 applied, 1,062 admitted, 351 enrolled.

Mid 50% test scores			
SAT critical reading:	400-490	Rank in top tenth:	3%
SAT math:	390-490	Return as sophomores:	71%
SAT writing:	380-470	Out-of-state:	23%
ACT composite:	15-20	Live on campus:	66%
Rank in top quarter:	13%	International:	1%

Basis for selection. School achievement record, extracurricular activities, test scores, recommendations, class rank, preparation in proposed major area of study considered. Portfolio and interview required for all art and art education applications. Admissions interview required for some on a case-by-case basis. **Home schooled:** Interview required. Portfolio of high school level work and homeschool supplement to the Common Application's secondary school report required. **Learning Disabled:** Current psychological report and Individualized Educational Program or 504 plan should be submitted at time of application. On-campus interview generally required to ensure that the college provides a level of support needed for the student to be academically successful.

High school preparation. College-preparatory program recommended. 17 units required; 22 recommended. Required and recommended units include English 4, mathematics 3-4, social studies 2, history 1, science 2-3 (laboratory 1), foreign language 2, computer science 1, visual/performing arts 1 and academic electives 4. Foreign language recommended for art, communications, and liberal arts curricula. 4 math and 3 science (including 2 lab) recommended for allied health, environmental sciences, biology, pre-medical tracks, and forensic biology.

2012-2013 Annual costs. Tuition/fees (projected): $20,675. Room/board: $9,500. Books/supplies: $1,900. Personal expenses: $2,000.

2010-2011 Financial aid. **Need-based:** Average need met was 79%. Average scholarship/grant was $3,317; average loan $3,379. 65% of total undergraduate aid awarded as scholarships/grants, 35% as loans/jobs. **Non-need-based:** Scholarships awarded for academics, alumni affiliation, art, ROTC.

Application procedures. **Admission:** Priority date 5/1; deadline 7/15 (receipt date). $30 fee, may be waived for applicants with need. Admission notification on a rolling basis beginning on or about 10/1. Must reply by May 1 or within 3 week(s) if notified thereafter. **Financial aid:** Closing date

5/1. FAFSA required. Applicants notified on a rolling basis starting 2/2; must reply within 2 week(s) of notification.

Academics. Students in good academic and financial standing who have not received at least 1 job offer or acceptance into a transfer or graduate program within 6 months after graduating and fulfilling requirements of Career Development Center will be provided with additional courses and career counseling at no extra charge. **Special study options:** Combined bachelor's/graduate degree, cooperative education, cross-registration, distance learning, double major, dual enrollment of high school students, honors, independent study, internships, semester at sea, study abroad, teacher certification program, weekend college. 2+2, 2+3, 3+3, 4+3 programs with various 4-year institutions and graduate programs for students studying allied health, health sciences, and environmental sciences. **Credit/placement by examination:** AP, CLEP, IB, SAT, ACT, institutional tests. 12 credit hours maximum toward associate degree, 18 toward bachelor's. Maximum of 32 credits for associate degree-seekers and 64 credits for bachelor's degree-seekers awarded for prior work and/or life experience. **Support services:** Learning center, reduced course load, remedial instruction, study skills assistance, tutoring, writing center.

Majors. Biology: General, environmental, wildlife. **Business:** Accounting, business admin, organizational behavior. **Communications:** General. **Computer sciences:** Information technology. **Conservation:** Management/policy. **Education:** General, art, early childhood, mathematics, middle, social studies, special ed. **Health services:** Predental, premedicine, prepharmacy, prephysical therapy, preveterinary. **Liberal arts:** Humanities. **Parks/recreation:** Facilities management, sports admin. **Protective services:** Criminalistics, forensics, law enforcement admin. **Psychology:** General. **Social sciences:** General. **Visual/performing arts:** Studio arts. **Work/family studies:** General.

Most popular majors. Business/marketing 19%, communications/journalism 7%, computer/information sciences 6%, education 13%, interdisciplinary studies 13%, parks/recreation 7%, public administration/social services 8%, security/protective services 20%, social sciences 7%, visual/performing arts 8%.

Computing on campus. 120 workstations in dormitories, library, computer center, student center. Dormitories wired for high-speed internet access and linked to campus network. Commuter students can connect to campus network. Online course registration, online library, helpline, repair service, wireless network available.

Student life. Freshman orientation: Mandatory, $150 fee. Preregistration for classes offered. One-day program during summer for scheduling classes. 2-day overnight adventure program, at off-campus venues, prior to start of classes. **Policies:** Alcohol and drug-free campus. **Housing:** Guaranteed on-campus for freshmen. Coed dorms, single-sex dorms, special housing for disabled, apartments available. $200 nonrefundable deposit, deadline 5/1. **Activities:** Campus ministries, choral groups, drama, international student organizations, literary magazine, musical theater, radio station, student government, student newspaper, multicultural affairs student association, Opposing Prejudice Ending Negativity, Keystone service club, Key Choices, Winner's Circle.

Athletics. NCAA. **Intercollegiate:** Baseball M, basketball, cross-country, field hockey W, golf M, soccer, softball W, tennis, track and field, volleyball W. **Intramural:** Basketball, football (non-tackle), soccer, volleyball. **Team name:** Giants.

Student services. Adult student services, alcohol/substance abuse counseling, chaplain/spiritual director, career counseling, services for economically disadvantaged, student employment services, financial aid counseling, health services, minority student services, on-campus daycare, personal counseling, placement for graduates, veterans' counselor, women's services.

Contact. E-mail: admissions@keystone.edu
Phone: (570) 945-8111 Toll-free number: (800) 824-2764 ext. 1
Fax: (570) 945-7916
Kathryn Reilly, Director of Admissions, Keystone College, One College Green, La Plume, PA 18440-1099

King's College
Wilkes-Barre, Pennsylvania
www.kings.edu

CB member
CB code: 2353

- Private 4-year business and liberal arts college affiliated with Roman Catholic Church
- Residential campus in small city
- 2,090 degree-seeking undergraduates: 4% part-time, 49% women, 3% African American, 2% Asian American, 5% Hispanic American
- 285 degree-seeking graduate students

- 72% of applicants admitted
- 63% graduate within 6 years; 26% enter graduate study

General. Founded in 1946. Regionally accredited. **Degrees:** 500 bachelor's, 1 associate awarded; master's offered. **ROTC:** Army, Air Force. **Location:** 110 miles from Philadelphia, 140 miles from New York City. **Calendar:** Semester, extensive summer session. **Full-time faculty:** 132 total; 78% have terminal degrees, 4% minority, 43% women. **Part-time faculty:** 103 total; 27% have terminal degrees, 54% women. **Class size:** 57% < 20, 42% 20-39, 1% 40-49. **Special facilities:** Rooftop greenhouse, molecular biology laboratory.

Freshman class profile. 2,561 applied, 1,850 admitted, 551 enrolled.

Mid 50% test scores			
SAT critical reading:	460-570	GPA 2.0-2.99:	26%
SAT math:	460-570	Rank in top quarter:	38%
SAT writing:	450-560	Rank in top tenth:	12%
GPA 3.75 or higher:	28%	Return as sophomores:	79%
GPA 3.50-3.74:	13%	Out-of-state:	35%
GPA 3.0-3.49:	33%	Live on campus:	70%

Basis for selection. Class rank and academic GPA very important. Standardized test scores important. SAT or ACT recommended. Students may choose a standardized test option/essay choice in which an official graded writing sample from either junior or senior year is submitted and notarized by the high school guidance office. Students choosing this option are required to notify the Office of Admission on the application. A student's decision is non-reversible and must be made prior to application review. Interview recommended. **Home schooled:** Transcript of courses and grades, state high school equivalency certificate required. **Learning Disabled:** Must submit supplemental application with appropriate documentation, contact Director of Academic Skills Center.

High school preparation. College-preparatory program required. 16 units required; 24 recommended. Required and recommended units include English 4, mathematics 3-4, social studies 3, history 1, science 3-4 (laboratory 2), foreign language 2-4 and computer science 2.

2011-2012 Annual costs. Tuition/fees: $27,680. Room/board: $10,470. Books/supplies: $1,250. Personal expenses: $1,300.

2011-2012 Financial aid. Need-based: 526 full-time freshmen applied for aid; 469 were judged to have need; 469 of these received aid. Average need met was 76%. Average scholarship/grant was $17,808; average loan $3,758. 70% of total undergraduate aid awarded as scholarships/grants, 30% as loans/jobs. **Non-need-based:** Awarded to 521 full-time undergraduates, including 149 freshmen. Scholarships awarded for academics, leadership, ROTC. **Additional information:** Any minority student with financial need may receive some aid in the form of a diversity scholarship.

Application procedures. Admission: No deadline. $30 fee, may be waived for applicants with need, free for online applicants. Admission notification on a rolling basis beginning on or about 10/1. Must reply by May 1 or within 2 week(s) if notified thereafter. **Financial aid:** Priority date 2/15; no closing date. FAFSA, institutional form required. Applicants notified on a rolling basis starting 3/1; must reply within 2 week(s) of notification.

Academics. Special study options: Accelerated study, cross-registration, distance learning, double major, dual enrollment of high school students, ESL, honors, independent study, internships, student-designed major, study abroad, teacher certification program, Washington semester, weekend college. Pre-professional programs in dentistry, medicine, pharmacy, veterinary science. **Credit/placement by examination:** AP, CLEP, IB, SAT, ACT, institutional tests. 15 credit hours maximum toward associate degree, 30 toward bachelor's. **Support services:** Learning center, pre-admission summer program, reduced course load, study skills assistance, tutoring, writing center.

Majors. Biology: General, neuroscience. **Business:** Accounting, business admin, finance, human resources, international, marketing. **Communications:** Media studies. **Computer sciences:** General, computer science. **Conservation:** Environmental science, environmental studies. **Education:** Early childhood, elementary, special ed. **English:** English lit. **Foreign languages:** French, Spanish. **Health services:** Athletic training, clinical lab science. **History:** General. **Math:** General. **Philosophy/religion:** Philosophy. **Physical sciences:** Chemistry. **Protective services:** Criminal justice. **Psychology:** General. **Social sciences:** Economics, political science, sociology. **Theology:** Theology. **Visual/performing arts:** Dramatic.

Most popular majors. Biology 7%, business/marketing 33%, education 12%, health sciences 9%, security/protective services 11%.

Computing on campus. 470 workstations in dormitories, library, computer center, student center. Dormitories wired for high-speed internet access and linked to campus network. Commuter students can connect to campus network. Online course registration, helpline, repair service, student web hosting, wireless network available.

Student life. Freshman orientation: Mandatory, $165 fee. Preregistration for classes offered. Held the 4 days prior to start of fall classes. **Housing:** Guaranteed on-campus for all undergraduates. Coed dorms, single-sex dorms, apartments available. $200 nonrefundable deposit. **Activities:** Campus ministries, choral groups, dance, drama, literary magazine, music ensembles, radio station, student government, student newspaper, association of campus events, organizations of various majors, Campion Society, Blood Council, Circle K, politics society, environmental awareness and outdoors club, residence hall council, service fraternity and sorority.

Athletics. NCAA. **Intercollegiate:** Baseball M, basketball, cheerleading, cross-country, field hockey W, football (tackle) M, golf M, lacrosse, soccer, softball W, swimming, tennis, volleyball W, wrestling M. **Intramural:** Basketball, football (non-tackle) M, soccer. **Team name:** Monarchs.

Student services. Adult student services, chaplain/spiritual director, career counseling, student employment services, financial aid counseling, health services, on-campus daycare, personal counseling, placement for graduates.

Contact. E-mail: admissions@kings.edu
Phone: (570) 208-5858 Toll-free number: (888) 546-4772
Fax: (570) 208-5971
James Anderson, Director of Admissions, King's College, 133 North River Street, Wilkes-Barre, PA 18711

Kutztown University of Pennsylvania
Kutztown, Pennsylvania
www.kutztown.edu

CB member
CB code: 2653

- Public 4-year university
- Residential campus in small town
- 9,147 degree-seeking undergraduates: 6% part-time, 57% women, 7% African American, 1% Asian American, 6% Hispanic American, 1% international
- 730 degree-seeking graduate students
- 67% of applicants admitted
- SAT or ACT (ACT writing optional) required
- 54% graduate within 6 years; 21% enter graduate study

General. Founded in 1866. Regionally accredited. **Degrees:** 1,831 bachelor's awarded; master's offered. **ROTC:** Army. **Location:** 20 miles from Allentown and Reading. **Calendar:** Semester, extensive summer session. **Full-time faculty:** 429 total; 82% have terminal degrees, 15% minority, 46% women. **Part-time faculty:** 32 total; 19% have terminal degrees, 6% minority, 47% women. **Class size:** 27% < 20, 60% 20-39, 4% 40-49, 5% 50-99, 4% >100. **Special facilities:** Observatory, Pennsylvania German heritage cultural center, planetarium.

Freshman class profile. 10,087 applied, 6,760 admitted, 2,037 enrolled.

Mid 50% test scores			
SAT critical reading:	430-530	Rank in top quarter:	24%
SAT math:	430-530	Rank in top tenth:	6%
SAT writing:	420-520	End year in good standing:	84%
ACT composite:	17-21	Return as sophomores:	77%
GPA 3.75 or higher:	9%	Out-of-state:	13%
GPA 3.50-3.74:	13%	Live on campus:	91%
GPA 3.0-3.49:	33%	Fraternities:	8%
GPA 2.0-2.99:	45%	Sororities:	6%

Basis for selection. School records and academic aptitude tests most important. Recommendations, essays, extracurricular activities considered. SAT Subject Tests (biology and chemistry) required for medical technology program. Audition required for music program; portfolio and/or art test required for art education, communication design, crafts, and fine arts programs. **Home schooled:** Applicants must submit supporting data from Pennsylvania Home Schooling Association.

High school preparation. College-preparatory program recommended. 18 units recommended. Recommended units include English 4, mathematics 4, social studies 4, science 4 and foreign language 2. Course recommendations vary for specific programs.

2011-2012 Annual costs. Tuition/fees: $8,359; $17,719 out-of-state. Room/board: $8,536. Books/supplies: $1,100. Personal expenses: $2,600.

2010-2011 Financial aid. Need-based: 1,877 full-time freshmen applied for aid; 1,430 were judged to have need; 1,376 of these received aid. Average need met was 50%. Average scholarship/grant was $6,066; average loan $3,234. 34% of total undergraduate aid awarded as scholarships/grants, 66% as loans/jobs. **Non-need-based:** Awarded to 816 full-time undergraduates, including 120 freshmen. Scholarships awarded for academics, art, athletics, leadership, minority status, music/drama.

Application procedures. Admission: Priority date 12/1; no deadline. $35 fee, may be waived for applicants with need. Admission notification on a rolling basis beginning on or about 10/1. Must reply by May 1 or by date stated on notification letter. **Financial aid:** Priority date 3/1; no closing date. FAFSA required. Applicants notified on a rolling basis starting 3/30; must reply by 5/1 or within 4 week(s) of notification.

Academics. Special study options: Combined bachelor's/graduate degree, cross-registration, distance learning, double major, dual enrollment of high school students, honors, independent study, internships, liberal arts/career combination, student-designed major, study abroad, teacher certification program. **Credit/placement by examination:** AP, CLEP, IB, SAT, ACT, institutional tests. **Support services:** Learning center, pre-admission summer program, remedial instruction, study skills assistance, tutoring, writing center.

Majors. Area/ethnic studies: German. **Biology:** General, biochemistry. **Business:** Accounting, business admin, finance, human resources, international, marketing. **Communications:** Digital media. **Computer sciences:** Information technology. **Conservation:** Environmental science. **Education:** Early childhood, elementary, kindergarten/preschool, middle, special ed, speech impaired, visually handicapped. **English:** English lit, rhetoric/composition, technical writing. **Foreign languages:** French, German, Spanish. **Health services:** Clinical lab science, nursing (RN). **History:** General. **Human services:** General, social work. **Liberal arts:** Library science. **Math:** General. **Parks/recreation:** General. **Philosophy/religion:** Philosophy. **Physical sciences:** Chemistry, geology, oceanography, physics. **Protective services:** Criminal justice. **Psychology:** General. **Social sciences:** General, anthropology, geography, political science, sociology. **Visual/performing arts:** Art, commercial/advertising art, crafts, dramatic, music, studio arts.

Most popular majors. Business/marketing 18%, education 16%, English 8%, psychology 9%, social sciences 7%, visual/performing arts 11%.

Computing on campus. 800 workstations in dormitories, library, computer center, student center. Dormitories wired for high-speed internet access and linked to campus network. Commuter students can connect to campus network. Online course registration, online library, helpline, student web hosting, wireless network available.

Student life. Freshman orientation: Mandatory, $115 fee. Preregistration for classes offered. 2-day, one overnight session in June, plus 1-day informational program preceding fall semester. **Policies:** No alcohol or drugs. **Housing:** Guaranteed on-campus for freshmen. Coed dorms, single-sex dorms, apartments, cooperative housing available. $50 nonrefundable deposit, deadline 5/1. **Activities:** Bands, campus ministries, choral groups, dance, drama, film society, international student organizations, literary magazine, music ensembles, Model UN, musical theater, radio station, student government, student newspaper, symphony orchestra, TV station, Student Alliance for Learning, Success and Achievement, black student union, Minority Achievement Coalition, Brothers and Sisters Seeking Excellence, Feminist Majority Leadership Alliance, Circle K, volunteer center, social work club.

Athletics. NCAA. **Intercollegiate:** Baseball M, basketball, bowling W, cheerleading M, cross-country, field hockey W, football (tackle) M, golf W, lacrosse W, soccer W, softball W, swimming W, tennis, track and field, volleyball W, wrestling M. **Intramural:** Basketball, football (non-tackle), racquetball, soccer, softball, table tennis, tennis, volleyball. **Team name:** Golden Bears.

Student services. Adult student services, alcohol/substance abuse counseling, career counseling, services for economically disadvantaged, student employment services, financial aid counseling, health services, minority student services, on-campus daycare, personal counseling, veterans' counselor, women's services. **Physically disabled:** Services for visually, speech, hearing impaired.

Contact. E-mail: admission@kutztown.edu
Phone: (610) 683-4060 Toll-free number: (877) 628-1915
Fax: (610) 683-1375
Valerie Reidout, Director of Admissions, Kutztown University of Pennsylvania, Admissions Office, Kutztown, PA 19530-0730

La Roche College
Pittsburgh, Pennsylvania
www.laroche.edu

CB member
CB code: 2379

- Private 4-year liberal arts college affiliated with Roman Catholic Church
- Commuter campus in large city

♦ 1,291 degree-seeking undergraduates: 15% part-time, 58% women, 8% African American, 1% Asian American, 1% Hispanic American, 10% international
♦ 107 degree-seeking graduate students
♦ 51% of applicants admitted
♦ SAT or ACT (ACT writing optional) required
♦ 52% graduate within 6 years

General. Founded in 1963. Regionally accredited. Founded and sponsored by Sisters of Divine Providence. **Degrees:** 242 bachelor's, 15 associate awarded; master's offered. **ROTC:** Army, Air Force. **Calendar:** Semester, limited summer session. **Full-time faculty:** 62 total; 77% have terminal degrees, 8% minority, 58% women. **Part-time faculty:** 116 total; 9% have terminal degrees, less than 1% minority, 48% women. **Class size:** 66% < 20, 33% 20-39, less than 1% 40-49.

Freshman class profile. 1,845 applied, 948 admitted, 262 enrolled.

Mid 50% test scores				
SAT critical reading:	420-520	GPA 2.0-2.99:		38%
SAT math:	410-510	Rank in top quarter:		18%
SAT writing:	410-500	Rank in top tenth:		6%
ACT composite:	17-21	End year in good standing:		83%
GPA 3.75 or higher:	11%	Return as sophomores:		74%
GPA 3.50-3.74:	15%	Out-of-state:		13%
GPA 3.0-3.49:	35%	Live on campus:		79%
		International:		11%

Basis for selection. Depth and rigor of curriculum considered. Standardized test scores considered in relation to other factors. Recommendation from guidance counselor important. Extracurricular involvement considered. Essay, interview recommended.

High school preparation. College-preparatory program recommended. 16 units required; 18 recommended. Required and recommended units include English 4, mathematics 3, social studies 3, history 3, science 3 (laboratory 2) and foreign language 2.

2011-2012 Annual costs. Tuition/fees: $23,160. Room/board: $9,182. Books/supplies: $1,200. Personal expenses: $1,512.

2011-2012 Financial aid. **Need-based:** 226 full-time freshmen applied for aid; 210 were judged to have need; 210 of these received aid. Average need met was 96%. Average scholarship/grant was $3,768; average loan $3,433. 54% of total undergraduate aid awarded as scholarships/grants, 46% as loans/jobs. **Non-need-based:** Awarded to 863 full-time undergraduates, including 213 freshmen. Scholarships awarded for academics.

Application procedures. **Admission:** No deadline. $50 fee, may be waived for applicants with need. Admission notification on a rolling basis beginning on or about 10/1. **Financial aid:** Priority date 2/15, closing date 5/1. FAFSA required. Applicants notified on a rolling basis starting 3/1; must reply within 2 week(s) of notification.

Academics. **Special study options:** Accelerated study, combined bachelor's/graduate degree, cross-registration, distance learning, double major, ESL, honors, independent study, internships, student-designed major, study abroad, teacher certification program. **Credit/placement by examination:** AP, CLEP, IB, institutional tests. 60 credit hours maximum toward bachelor's degree. **Support services:** Learning center, pre-admission summer program, reduced course load, remedial instruction, study skills assistance, tutoring, writing center.

Majors. **Architecture:** Interior. **Biology:** General. **Business:** Accounting, finance, international, management science, marketing, real estate. **Communications:** Media studies. **Computer sciences:** General, computer science, information technology. **Education:** Elementary, English. **English:** English lit, writing. **Foreign languages:** Spanish. **Health services:** Medical radiologic technology/radiation therapy, nursing (RN). **History:** General. **Liberal arts:** Arts/sciences. **Math:** General. **Philosophy/religion:** Religion. **Physical sciences:** Chemistry. **Protective services:** Criminal justice. **Psychology:** General. **Social sciences:** International relations, national security policy, political science, sociology. **Visual/performing arts:** Dance, design. **Work/family studies:** Family/community services.

Most popular majors. Business/marketing 30%, education 10%, health sciences 15%, psychology 8%, visual/performing arts 11%.

Computing on campus. 200 workstations in library, computer center. Dormitories wired for high-speed internet access and linked to campus network. Commuter students can connect to campus network. Online course registration, online library, helpline, wireless network available.

Student life. Freshman orientation: Mandatory. Preregistration for classes offered. **Housing:** Coed dorms available. $100 nonrefundable deposit, deadline 5/1. **Activities:** Campus ministries, choral groups, dance, drama, international student organizations, literary magazine, radio station, student government, student newspaper, professional organizations, environment club, black student coalition, African Student Forum, Rotaract club, community service.

Athletics. NCAA. **Intercollegiate:** Baseball M, basketball, cross-country, golf M, lacrosse M, soccer, softball W, tennis W, volleyball W. **Intramural:** Basketball, racquetball, soccer, softball, table tennis, tennis, volleyball. **Team name:** Redhawks.

Student services. Adult student services, alcohol/substance abuse counseling, chaplain/spiritual director, career counseling, services for economically disadvantaged, student employment services, financial aid counseling, health services, minority student services, personal counseling, placement for graduates, veterans' counselor. **Physically disabled:** Services for visually impaired.

Contact. E-mail: admissions@laroche.edu
Phone: (412) 536-1271 Toll-free number: (800) 838-4572
Fax: (412) 536-1048
Director of Admissions, La Roche College, 9000 Babcock Boulevard, Pittsburgh, PA 15237

La Salle University
Philadelphia, Pennsylvania
www.lasalle.edu

CB member
CB code: 2363

♦ Private 4-year university and liberal arts college affiliated with Roman Catholic Church
♦ Residential campus in very large city
♦ 4,328 degree-seeking undergraduates: 19% part-time, 63% women, 19% African American, 5% Asian American, 12% Hispanic American, 1% Native American, 1% international
♦ 2,101 degree-seeking graduate students
♦ 73% of applicants admitted
♦ SAT or ACT (ACT writing optional), application essay required
♦ 67% graduate within 6 years

General. Founded in 1863. Regionally accredited. **Degrees:** 849 bachelor's, 45 associate awarded; master's, doctoral offered. **ROTC:** Army, Air Force. **Location:** 6 miles from Center City Philadelphia. **Calendar:** Semester, extensive summer session. **Full-time faculty:** 234 total; 77% have terminal degrees, 8% minority, 52% women. **Part-time faculty:** 207 total; 8% minority, 45% women. **Class size:** 41% < 20, 55% 20-39, 2% 40-49, 1% 50-99. **Special facilities:** Art museum, campus includes the restored home and gardens of 18th-century American portrait painter Charles Wilson Peale.

Freshman class profile. 5,838 applied, 4,279 admitted, 957 enrolled.

Mid 50% test scores			
SAT critical reading:	440-540	Rank in top quarter:	39%
SAT math:	440-550	Rank in top tenth:	16%
ACT composite:	19-25	Return as sophomores:	81%
GPA 3.75 or higher:	25%	Out-of-state:	42%
GPA 3.50-3.74:	17%	Live on campus:	80%
GPA 3.0-3.49:	30%	International:	2%
GPA 2.0-2.99:	28%	Fraternities:	7%
		Sororities:	18%

Basis for selection. Criteria include college preparatory high school curriculum, SAT and/or ACT score, involvement in extracurricular high school athletics/clubs/activities. Other factors include evidence of commitment and maturity. Interview recommended. **Home schooled:** Statement describing home school structure and mission required.

High school preparation. College-preparatory program required. 16 units required. Required units include English 4, mathematics 3, history 1, science 1 (laboratory 1), foreign language 2 and academic electives 5.

2011-2012 Annual costs. Tuition/fees: $35,240. Room/board: $11,680. Books/supplies: $500. Personal expenses: $1,119.

2010-2011 Financial aid. **Need-based:** 908 full-time freshmen applied for aid; 761 were judged to have need; 761 of these received aid. Average need met was 74%. Average scholarship/grant was $20,694; average loan $3,624. 69% of total undergraduate aid awarded as scholarships/grants, 31% as loans/jobs. **Non-need-based:** Awarded to 973 full-time undergraduates, including 297 freshmen. Scholarships awarded for academics, athletics, ROTC.

Application procedures. **Admission:** No deadline. $35 fee, may be waived for applicants with need, free for online applicants. Admission notification on a rolling basis beginning on or about 12/15. Must reply by May 1 or within 2 week(s) if notified thereafter. **Financial aid:** Priority date 2/15;

no closing date. FAFSA required. Applicants notified on a rolling basis starting 3/15; must reply by 5/1 or within 2 week(s) of notification.

Academics. **Special study options:** Accelerated study, combined bachelor's/graduate degree, cooperative education, double major, dual enrollment of high school students, ESL, honors, independent study, internships, study abroad, teacher certification program. 2+3 Program with Thomas Jefferson University in Medical Technology and Occupational Therapy. **Credit/placement by examination:** AP, CLEP, SAT, ACT, institutional tests. 70 credit hours maximum toward bachelor's degree. **Support services:** Learning center, pre-admission summer program, reduced course load, remedial instruction, study skills assistance, tutoring, writing center.

Majors. **Area/ethnic studies:** Regional, Russian/Eastern European/Eurasian, Russian/Slavic. **Biology:** General, biochemistry. **Business:** General, accounting, banking/financial services, business admin, communications, finance, human resources, insurance, international, international marketing, labor relations, management science, managerial economics, market research, marketing, nonprofit/public, operations, organizational behavior, statistics. **Communications:** Broadcast journalism, communications/speech/rhetoric, digital media, journalism, media studies, public relations, radio/TV. **Communications technology:** Desktop publishing, radio/TV. **Computer sciences:** General, applications programming, computer graphics, computer science, database management, information systems, information technology, programming, web page design. **Conservation:** General, environmental science. **Education:** General, bilingual, biology, chemistry, developmentally delayed, early childhood, early childhood special, elementary, emotionally handicapped, English, foreign languages, French, German, history, mathematics, mentally handicapped, middle, multi-level teacher, physically handicapped, science, secondary, social science, social studies, Spanish, special ed. **English:** American lit, British lit, English lit, rhetoric/composition, technical writing, writing. **Foreign languages:** General, Biblical, classics, comparative lit, French, German, Italian, Latin, Spanish. **Health services:** Audiology/ hearing, audiology/speech pathology, nursing (RN), predental, premedicine, preveterinary, speech pathology. **History:** General, American. **Human services:** General, social work. **Liberal arts:** Arts/sciences. **Math:** General, applied, statistics. **Philosophy/religion:** Philosophy, religion. **Physical sciences:** Chemistry, geology, planetary. **Protective services:** Criminal justice. **Psychology:** General. **Social sciences:** General, criminology, economics, international economics, international relations, political science, sociology, U.S. government. **Theology:** Religious ed. **Visual/performing arts:** Art history/conservation, cinematography, film/cinema/video, music, music history, studio arts.

Most popular majors. Business/marketing 19%, communications/journalism 10%, health sciences 33%, psychology 8%, social sciences 7%.

Computing on campus. 344 workstations in library, computer center, student center. Dormitories wired for high-speed internet access and linked to campus network. Commuter students can connect to campus network. Online course registration, online library, helpline, repair service, student web hosting, wireless network available.

Student life. **Freshman orientation:** Mandatory, $100 fee. Preregistration for classes offered. **Policies:** Nonalcoholic nightclub and eatery available 7 days a week. **Housing:** Guaranteed on-campus for all undergraduates. Coed dorms, special housing for disabled, apartments, wellness housing available. $200 nonrefundable deposit, deadline 5/1. Campus owned and operated townhouses available. **Activities:** Jazz band, campus ministries, choral groups, dance, drama, film society, international student organizations, literary magazine, musical theater, radio station, student government, student newspaper, TV station, black student union, Hillel, women's center, social work association, veterans club, Young Socialist Alliance, student council for exceptional children, urban center.

Athletics. NCAA. **Intercollegiate:** Baseball M, basketball, cheerleading, cross-country, diving, field hockey W, golf, lacrosse W, rowing (crew), soccer, softball W, swimming, tennis, track and field, volleyball W. **Intramural:** Basketball, football (non-tackle), football (tackle), rugby M, softball, volleyball. **Team name:** Explorers.

Student services. Adult student services, alcohol/substance abuse counseling, chaplain/spiritual director, career counseling, services for economically disadvantaged, student employment services, health services, minority student services, on-campus daycare, personal counseling, placement for graduates, veterans' counselor.

Contact. E-mail: admiss@lasalle.edu
Phone: (215) 951-1500 Toll-free number: (800) 328-1910
Fax: (215) 951-1656
James Plunkett, Executive Director of Admission, La Salle University, 1900 West Olney Avenue, Philadelphia, PA 19141-1199

Lafayette College
Easton, Pennsylvania
www.lafayette.edu

CB member
CB code: 2361

▶ Private 4-year engineering and liberal arts college
▶ Residential campus in large town
▶ 2,443 degree-seeking undergraduates: 1% part-time, 47% women, 5% African American, 4% Asian American, 5% Hispanic American, 6% international
▶ 40% of applicants admitted
▶ SAT or ACT with writing, application essay required
▶ 88% graduate within 6 years

General. Founded in 1826. Regionally accredited. **Degrees:** 551 bachelor's awarded. **ROTC:** Army. **Location:** 80 miles from New York City, 60 miles from Philadelphia. **Calendar:** Semester, limited summer session. **Full-time faculty:** 214 total; 98% have terminal degrees, 12% minority, 33% women. **Part-time faculty:** 47 total; 53% have terminal degrees, 8% minority, 40% women. **Class size:** 57% < 20, 38% 20-39, 4% 40-49, 1% 50-99. **Special facilities:** Advanced computer-aided design laboratory, satellite downlink capability.

Freshman class profile. 5,716 applied, 2,304 admitted, 638 enrolled.

Mid 50% test scores			
SAT critical reading:	590-680	GPA 2.0-2.99:	10%
SAT math:	620-700	Rank in top quarter:	89%
SAT writing:	580-680	Rank in top tenth:	65%
ACT composite:	26-31	End year in good standing:	95%
GPA 3.75 or higher:	27%	Return as sophomores:	95%
GPA 3.50-3.74:	24%	Out-of-state:	79%
GPA 3.0-3.49:	39%	Live on campus:	100%
		International:	6%

Basis for selection. Academic performance, class rank, quality of courses taken, personal qualities, extracurricular record, recommendations, and standardized test results important. Special consideration to applicants who will contribute diversity to student body. SAT Subject Tests recommended. SAT Subject Tests, if submitted, may be considered for placement in math and foreign languages. Interview highly recommended for all; portfolio recommended for art program.

High school preparation. College-preparatory program recommended. 18 units recommended. Recommended units include English 4, mathematics 3, science 2 (laboratory 2), foreign language 2 and academic electives 5. 4 math, chemistry, physics required of bachelor of science degree candidates.

2011-2012 Annual costs. Tuition/fees: $41,358. Room/board: $12,362. Books/supplies: $1,000. Personal expenses: $900.

2011-2012 Financial aid. **Need-based:** 429 full-time freshmen applied for aid; 298 were judged to have need; 298 of these received aid. Average need met was 99%. Average scholarship/grant was $32,539; average loan $3,619. 85% of total undergraduate aid awarded as scholarships/grants, 15% as loans/jobs. **Non-need-based:** Awarded to 478 full-time undergraduates, including 139 freshmen. Scholarships awarded for academics, athletics, leadership, ROTC. **Additional information:** Parent loans, up to $7,500 annually, available with college absorbing interest while student is enrolled. Family has 8 years after graduation to repay. Not limited to those demonstrating need.

Application procedures. **Admission:** Closing date 1/15 (postmark date). $65 fee, may be waived for applicants with need. Admission notification by 3/25. Must reply by May 1 or within 2 week(s) if notified thereafter. **Financial aid:** Priority date 1/15, closing date 3/1. FAFSA, CSS PROFILE required. Applicants notified by 4/1; must reply by 5/1.

Academics. Examples of students' self-designed interdisciplinary majors include Management Science, Studies in Human Rights, Asian Studies, Computational Biology, and Community Development among many others. Interdisciplinary minors also offered. **Special study options:** Cross-registration, double major, dual enrollment of high school students, exchange student, honors, independent study, internships, New York semester, semester at sea, student-designed major, study abroad, urban semester, Washington semester. Interim-session courses abroad and on campus. **Credit/placement by examination:** AP, CLEP, IB, institutional tests. **Support services:** Reduced course load, study skills assistance, tutoring, writing center.

Majors. **Area/ethnic studies:** African, American, Asian, Russian/Slavic. **Biology:** General, biochemistry, neuroscience. **Computer sciences:** General. **Engineering:** General, chemical, civil, electrical, mechanical. **English:** English lit. **Foreign languages:** French, German, Spanish. **History:** General. **Human services:** Public policy. **Math:** General. **Philosophy/religion:** Philosophy, religion. **Physical sciences:** Chemistry, geology, physics. **Psychology:** General. **Social sciences:** Anthropology, econometrics, economics, international economics, international relations, political science, sociology.

Visual/performing arts: Art, music, music history, studio arts, theater arts management.

Most popular majors. Biology 10%, engineering/engineering technologies 19%, English 8%, psychology 8%, social sciences 33%.

Computing on campus. 600 workstations in library, computer center, student center. Dormitories wired for high-speed internet access and linked to campus network. Commuter students can connect to campus network. Online course registration, online library, helpline, repair service, student web hosting, wireless network available.

Student life. Freshman orientation: Mandatory. Preregistration for classes offered. 4-day program before fall classes begin. **Policies:** Freshmen not permitted cars on campus. **Housing:** Guaranteed on-campus for all undergraduates. Coed dorms, single-sex dorms, special housing for disabled, apartments, fraternity/sorority housing, wellness housing available. Scholars houses, Hillel House, arts houses. **Activities:** Bands, campus ministries, choral groups, dance, drama, film society, international student organizations, literary magazine, music ensembles, Model UN, musical theater, radio station, student government, student newspaper, symphony orchestra, Hillel Society, Muslim student association, Newman Association, Association of Black Collegians, Association for Lafayette Feminists, Lafayette Environmental Awareness and Protection, College Democrats, College Republicans, Students for Social Justice.

Athletics. NCAA. **Intercollegiate:** Baseball M, basketball, cheerleading, cross-country, diving, fencing, field hockey W, football (tackle) M, golf, lacrosse, soccer, softball W, swimming, tennis, track and field, volleyball W. **Intramural:** Badminton, basketball, bowling, football (non-tackle), golf, racquetball, soccer, softball, squash, table tennis, tennis, volleyball, water polo. **Team name:** Leopards.

Student services. Adult student services, alcohol/substance abuse counseling, chaplain/spiritual director, career counseling, services for economically disadvantaged, student employment services, financial aid counseling, health services, minority student services, personal counseling, placement for graduates, women's services. **Physically disabled:** Services for visually impaired.

Contact. E-mail: admissions@lafayette.edu
Phone: (610) 330-5100 Fax: (610) 330-5355
Matt Hyde, Director of Admissions, Lafayette College, 118 Markle Hall, Easton, PA 18042

Lancaster Bible College
Lancaster, Pennsylvania
www.lbc.edu   CB code: 2388

- Private 4-year Bible college affiliated with nondenominational tradition
- Residential campus in small city
- 918 degree-seeking undergraduates
- 169 graduate students
- SAT or ACT (ACT writing recommended), application essay required

General. Founded in 1933. Regionally accredited; also accredited by ABHE. **Degrees:** 148 bachelor's, 14 associate awarded; master's, doctoral offered. **Location:** 64 miles from Philadelphia. **Calendar:** Semester, limited summer session. **Full-time faculty:** 29 total; 62% have terminal degrees, 10% minority, 31% women. **Part-time faculty:** 55 total; 49% have terminal degrees, 34% women. **Class size:** 65% < 20, 29% 20-39, 5% 40-49, less than 1% 50-99.

Freshman class profile.

Out-of-state:	17%	Live on campus:	78%

Basis for selection. Application must include personal spiritual testimony, academic transcripts, SAT or ACT scores, and 3 references. Interview recommended for all; audition required for music program. **Home schooled:** Yearly evaluations should be included with application.

2011-2012 Annual costs. Tuition/fees: $17,160. Students required to purchase Logos Bible Software: Scholars Library $325 (minimum requirement); Scholar's Silver Library $510 (recommended); Scholar's Gold Library $700. Room/board: $7,470. Books/supplies: $1,000. Personal expenses: $1,500.

2010-2011 Financial aid. Non-need-based: Scholarships awarded for academics, alumni affiliation, leadership, music/drama.

Application procedures. Admission: Priority date 8/1; no deadline. $25 fee, may be waived for applicants with need. Admission notification on a rolling basis. **Financial aid:** Priority date 5/1; no closing date. FAFSA

---

required. Applicants notified on a rolling basis starting 3/1; must reply within 3 week(s) of notification.

Academics. Special study options: Accelerated study, distance learning, double major, independent study, internships, study abroad, teacher certification program. **Credit/placement by examination:** AP, CLEP, SAT, ACT, institutional tests. 15 credit hours maximum toward associate degree, 30 toward bachelor's. **Support services:** Learning center, reduced course load, remedial instruction, study skills assistance, tutoring, writing center.

Majors. Education: Elementary, physical. **Theology:** Bible.

Most popular majors. Education 8%, theological studies 92%.

Computing on campus. 35 workstations in dormitories, library, computer center, student center. Dormitories wired for high-speed internet access and linked to campus network. Commuter students can connect to campus network. Online course registration, online library, helpline, repair service, wireless network available.

Student life. Freshman orientation: Mandatory, $125 fee. Preregistration for classes offered. 2 days prior to start of classes. **Policies:** Religious observance required. **Housing:** Guaranteed on-campus for freshmen. Single-sex dorms available. **Activities:** Bands, choral groups, drama, international student organizations, music ensembles, musical theater, student government, student newspaper, Christian Counseling Fellowship, married couples fellowship, Helpers in Service teams, student missionary fellowship, resident affairs council, commuter affairs council.

Athletics. NCAA, NCCAA. **Intercollegiate:** Baseball M, basketball, cheerleading, cross-country, lacrosse W, soccer, tennis, volleyball. **Intramural:** Basketball, football (non-tackle) M, soccer, softball, table tennis, tennis, volleyball. **Team name:** Chargers.

Student services. Chaplain/spiritual director, career counseling, student employment services, financial aid counseling, health services, personal counseling, placement for graduates.

Contact. E-mail: admissions@lbc.edu
Phone: (717) 560-8271 Toll-free number: (800) 544-7335
Fax: (717) 560-8213
Scott Boyer, Director, Admissions, Lancaster Bible College, 901 Eden Road, Lancaster, PA 17601-5036

Lebanon Valley College
Annville, Pennsylvania   CB member
www.lvc.edu   CB code: 2364

- Private 4-year liberal arts college affiliated with United Methodist Church
- Residential campus in small town
- 1,697 degree-seeking undergraduates: 5% part-time, 56% women, 2% African American, 1% Asian American, 4% Hispanic American
- 272 degree-seeking graduate students
- 67% of applicants admitted
- 73% graduate within 6 years; 30% enter graduate study

General. Founded in 1866. Regionally accredited. **Degrees:** 425 bachelor's, 2 associate awarded; master's, professional offered. **ROTC:** Army. **Location:** 7 miles from Hershey, 25 miles from Harrisburg. **Calendar:** Semester, limited summer session. **Full-time faculty:** 102 total; 87% have terminal degrees, 7% minority, 41% women. **Part-time faculty:** 125 total; 27% have terminal degrees, 4% minority, 40% women. **Class size:** 55% < 20, 42% 20-39, 2% 40-49, 1% 50-99. **Special facilities:** Electronic pianos, sound recording studio, transmission electron microscope, scanning electron microscope, Fourier transform infrared spectrometer, atomic absorption spectrometer, nuclear magnetic resonance spectrometer, molecular modeling lab, physical therapy wellness pool, Steinway grand piano, new piano lab with Mac computers.

Freshman class profile. 3,534 applied, 2,385 admitted, 468 enrolled.

Mid 50% test scores		Rank in top tenth:	35%
SAT critical reading:	480-590	End year in good standing:	92%
SAT math:	500-610	Return as sophomores:	86%
SAT writing:	470-580	Out-of-state:	22%
ACT composite:	20-25	Live on campus:	90%
Rank in top quarter:	71%		

Basis for selection. Record of high school achievement in challenging college prep courses is most important. Recommendations, test scores (optional), school and community activities evaluated. Submission of standardized test scores is optional for all applicants. Essay and interview recommended for all; audition required for music program.

High school preparation. College-preparatory program required. 16 units required. Required and recommended units include English 4, mathematics 3, social studies 3, history 2, science 3 (laboratory 2) and foreign language 2-3.

2011-2012 Annual costs. Tuition/fees: $33,200. Room/board: $8,800. Books/supplies: $1,100. Personal expenses: $1,300.

2011-2012 Financial aid. Need-based: 450 full-time freshmen applied for aid; 408 were judged to have need; 407 of these received aid. Average need met was 75%. Average scholarship/grant was $20,787; average loan $3,802. 78% of total undergraduate aid awarded as scholarships/grants, 22% as loans/jobs. **Non-need-based:** Awarded to 341 full-time undergraduates, including 85 freshmen. Scholarships awarded for academics, alumni affiliation, music/drama, ROTC. **Additional information:** Students and families impacted by the struggling economy are encouraged to contact the Financial Aid Office.

Application procedures. Admission: No deadline. $30 fee, may be waived for applicants with need. Admission notification on a rolling basis beginning on or about 10/15. Must reply by May 1 or within 2 week(s) if notified thereafter. **Financial aid:** Priority date 3/1; no closing date. FAFSA, institutional form required. Applicants notified on a rolling basis starting 3/1; must reply by 5/1 or within 2 week(s) of notification.

Academics. Special study options: Combined bachelor's/graduate degree, double major, dual enrollment of high school students, independent study, internships, liberal arts/career combination, student-designed major, study abroad, teacher certification program, urban semester, Washington semester. **Credit/placement by examination:** AP, CLEP, IB, institutional tests. 15 credit hours maximum toward associate degree, 30 toward bachelor's. **Support services:** Reduced course load, study skills assistance, tutoring, writing center.

Majors. Biology: General, Biochemistry/molecular biology. **Business:** Accounting, actuarial science, business admin. **Communications:** Digital media. **Communications technology:** Recording arts. **Computer sciences:** Computer science. **Education:** Early childhood, music, special ed. **English:** English lit. **Foreign languages:** French, German, Spanish. **Health services:** Clinical lab science, health care admin. **History:** General. **Math:** General. **Philosophy/religion:** Philosophy, religion. **Physical sciences:** Chemistry, physics. **Psychology:** General, psychobiology. **Social sciences:** Criminology, economics, political science, sociology. **Visual/performing arts:** Art, music management, music performance.

Most popular majors. Biology 6%, business/marketing 18%, education 19%, health sciences 8%, psychology 7%, social sciences 6%, visual/performing arts 10%.

Computing on campus. 189 workstations in library, computer center, student center. Dormitories wired for high-speed internet access and linked to campus network. Commuter students can connect to campus network. Online course registration, online library, helpline, student web hosting, wireless network available.

Student life. Freshman orientation: Mandatory. Preregistration for classes offered. 2 programs in May and July; 3-day program in August. **Policies:** Four Loko is a prohibited beverage; four-year residency requirement. **Housing:** Guaranteed on-campus for all undergraduates. Coed dorms, single-sex dorms, special housing for disabled, apartments available. Suite style and small houses available. **Activities:** Bands, campus ministries, choral groups, drama, literary magazine, music ensembles, musical theater, radio station, student government, student newspaper, symphony orchestra, College Conservatives, College Democrats, Best Buddies, Student Action for Earth, The F Word, Down to Earth, A.S.I.A., Habitat for Humanity, College Against Cancer, Community Dutchmen.

Athletics. NCAA. **Intercollegiate:** Baseball M, basketball, cross-country, field hockey W, football (tackle) M, golf M, lacrosse, soccer, softball W, swimming, tennis, track and field, volleyball W. **Intramural:** Basketball, football (non-tackle), racquetball, softball, table tennis, volleyball. **Team name:** Flying Dutchmen.

Student services. Alcohol/substance abuse counseling, chaplain/spiritual director, career counseling, student employment services, financial aid counseling, health services, minority student services, personal counseling, placement for graduates. **Physically disabled:** Services for visually, speech impaired.

Contact. E-mail: admission@lvc.edu
Phone: (717) 867-6181 Toll-free number: (866) 582-4236
Fax: (717) 867-6026
William Brown, Vice President of Enrollment, Lebanon Valley College, 101 North College Avenue, Annville, PA 17003-1400

Lehigh University
Bethlehem, Pennsylvania   **CB member**
www.lehigh.edu   **CB code: 2365**

▸ Private 4-year university
▸ Residential campus in small city
▸ 4,851 degree-seeking undergraduates: 1% part-time, 43% women, 4% African American, 6% Asian American, 8% Hispanic American, 5% international
▸ 2,039 degree-seeking graduate students
▸ 33% of applicants admitted
▸ SAT or ACT with writing, application essay required
▸ 87% graduate within 6 years; 27% enter graduate study

General. Founded in 1865. Regionally accredited. **Degrees:** 1,113 bachelor's awarded; master's, doctoral offered. **ROTC:** Army. **Location:** 50 miles from Philadelphia, 75 miles from New York City. **Calendar:** Semester, limited summer session. **Full-time faculty:** 482 total; 96% have terminal degrees, 18% minority, 29% women. **Part-time faculty:** 199 total; 10% minority, 47% women. **Class size:** 48% < 20, 38% 20-39, 5% 40-49, 6% 50-99, 4% >100. **Special facilities:** Two aberration-corrected electron microscopes, financial service laboratory, broadband seismic station, multidirectional experimental laboratory, electron optical labs, particle accelerator, rock climbing wall, golf driving range, STEPS green building.

Freshman class profile. 11,578 applied, 3,864 admitted, 1,207 enrolled.

Mid 50% test scores			
SAT critical reading:	580-680	Rank in top tenth:	96%
SAT math:	640-720	Return as sophomores:	95%
ACT composite:	28-31	Out-of-state:	74%
Rank in top quarter:	99%	Live on campus:	99%
		International:	5%

Basis for selection. Recommendations and school record very important. All submitted material considered. Applicants whose native language is not English must take the TOEFL. Minimum target score of 570 on the paper-pencil test, or 90 on the Internet-based TOEFL is recommended for admission. IELTS results accepted in place of TOEFL with a recommended minimum score of 7.0. Students scoring 570 or higher on the Critical Reading section of the SAT not required to submit TOEFL/IELTS scores, but it is highly recommended. Campus visit recommended.

High school preparation. 16 units required. Required units include English 4, mathematics 3, social studies 2, science 2 (laboratory 2), foreign language 2 and academic electives 3. Chemistry required, physics recommended for engineering and science candidates. Waivers in math granted by some departments to well-qualified candidates.

2011-2012 Annual costs. Tuition/fees: $40,960. Room/board: $10,840. Books/supplies: $1,000. Personal expenses: $1,220.

2011-2012 Financial aid. Need-based: 828 full-time freshmen applied for aid; 568 were judged to have need; 568 of these received aid. Average need met was 96%. Average scholarship/grant was $30,309; average loan $3,420. 83% of total undergraduate aid awarded as scholarships/grants, 17% as loans/jobs. **Non-need-based:** Awarded to 542 full-time undergraduates, including 113 freshmen. Scholarships awarded for academics, art, athletics, leadership, music/drama, ROTC. **Additional information:** Loans eliminated in financial aid packages for students eligible for financial aid and whose calculated total family income is less than $50,000. Loans limited to $3,000 in financial aid packages for students eligible for financial aid and who have a calculated total family income between $50,000 and $75,000.

Application procedures. Admission: Closing date 1/1 (postmark date). $70 fee, may be waived for applicants with need. Admission notification by 4/1. Must reply by 5/1. **Financial aid:** Closing date 2/15. FAFSA, CSS PROFILE required. Applicants notified by 3/30; must reply by 5/1 or within 3 week(s) of notification.

Academics. Special study options: Accelerated study, combined bachelor's/graduate degree, cooperative education, cross-registration, distance learning, double major, ESL, exchange student, external degree, honors, independent study, internships, liberal arts/career combination, study abroad, Washington semester. **Credit/placement by examination:** AP, CLEP. **Support services:** Learning center, study skills assistance, tutoring, writing center.

Majors. Architecture: Architecture, history/criticism. **Area/ethnic studies:** African, American, Asian, women's. **Biology:** General, biochemistry, molecular, neuroscience. **Business:** Accounting, finance, logistics, management information systems, management science, managerial economics, marketing. **Communications:** Journalism, technical/scientific. **Computer sciences:** Computer science, information systems. **Conservation:** Environmental studies. **Engineering:** Applied physics, biomedical, chemical, civil, computer,

electrical, engineering mechanics, environmental, industrial, materials, mechanical. **English:** English lit. **Foreign languages:** Chinese, classics, French, German, Spanish. **History:** General. **Math:** General, statistics. **Philosophy/religion:** Philosophy, religion. **Physical sciences:** Astronomy, astrophysics, chemistry, physics. **Psychology:** General. **Social sciences:** Anthropology, international relations, political science, sociology. **Visual/performing arts:** Art, art history/conservation, design, dramatic, music, music history.

Most popular majors. Biology 6%, business/marketing 31%, engineering/engineering technologies 27%, social sciences 9%.

Computing on campus. 638 workstations in dormitories, library, computer center, student center. Dormitories wired for high-speed internet access and linked to campus network. Commuter students can connect to campus network. Online course registration, online library, helpline, repair service, student web hosting, wireless network available.

Student life. Freshman orientation: Mandatory, $270 fee. Preregistration for classes offered. 4-day program held prior to first day of classes. **Policies:** Freshmen not permitted cars on campus. **Housing:** Guaranteed on-campus for freshmen. Coed dorms, special housing for disabled, apartments, fraternity/sorority housing, wellness housing available. $500 nonrefundable deposit, deadline 5/1. **Activities:** Bands, campus ministries, choral groups, dance, drama, film society, international student organizations, literary magazine, music ensembles, Model UN, musical theater, radio station, student government, student newspaper, symphony orchestra, Global Union, Asian cultural society, Fellowship of Christian Athletes, Omicron Delta Kappa, Chinese culture club, Black student union, Muslim students association, Alpha Phi Omega Service Fraternity, Best Buddies.

Athletics. NCAA. **Intercollegiate:** Baseball M, basketball, cross-country, diving, field hockey W, football (tackle) M, golf, lacrosse, rowing (crew) W, soccer, softball W, swimming, tennis, track and field, volleyball W, wrestling M. **Intramural:** Basketball, cross-country, football (non-tackle), soccer, softball, volleyball. **Team name:** Mountain Hawks.

Student services. Alcohol/substance abuse counseling, chaplain/spiritual director, career counseling, student employment services, financial aid counseling, health services, minority student services, on-campus daycare, personal counseling, placement for graduates, women's services. **Physically disabled:** Services for visually, speech, hearing impaired.

Contact. E-mail: admissions@lehigh.edu
Phone: (610) 758-3100 Fax: (610) 758-4361
Bruce Bunnick, Director of Admissions, Lehigh University, 27 Memorial Drive West, Bethlehem, PA 18015-3094

Lincoln University
Lincoln University, Pennsylvania   **CB member**
www.lincoln.edu   **CB code: 2367**

- Public 4-year university and liberal arts college
- Residential campus in small town

General. Founded in 1854. Regionally accredited. **Location:** 45 miles from Philadelphia. **Calendar:** Semester.

Annual costs/financial aid. Tuition/fees (2011-2012): $9,600; $14,566 out-of-state. Out-of-state students pay additional $666 in fees, which are included in out-of-state tuition figure. Room/board: $8,404. Books/supplies: $1,475. Personal expenses: $1,280. Need-based financial aid available to full-time and part-time students.

Contact. Phone: (484) 365-7206
Director of Admissions, 1570 Baltimore Pike, Lincoln University, PA 19352-0999

Lock Haven University of Pennsylvania
Lock Haven, Pennsylvania   **CB member**
www.lhup.edu   **CB code: 2654**

- Public 4-year university and liberal arts college
- Residential campus in small town
- 4,917 degree-seeking undergraduates: 6% part-time, 57% women, 6% African American, 1% Asian American, 2% Hispanic American, 1% international
- 318 degree-seeking graduate students
- 61% of applicants admitted

- SAT or ACT (ACT writing optional) required
- 46% graduate within 6 years

General. Founded in 1870. Regionally accredited. Branch campus in Clearfield. **Degrees:** 781 bachelor's, 92 associate awarded; master's offered. **ROTC:** Army. **Location:** 26 miles from Williamsport, 35 miles from State College. **Calendar:** Semester, limited summer session. **Full-time faculty:** 231 total; 77% have terminal degrees, 13% minority, 47% women. **Part-time faculty:** 19 total; 21% minority, 79% women. **Class size:** 26% < 20, 52% 20-39, 12% 40-49, 8% 50-99, 2% >100. **Special facilities:** Rural retreat conference center, cadaver dissection laboratory, electron microscope, primate laboratory.

Freshman class profile. 5,072 applied, 3,118 admitted, 1,261 enrolled.

Mid 50% test scores			
SAT critical reading:	420-510	GPA 2.0-2.99:	24%
SAT math:	430-530	Rank in top quarter:	28%
ACT composite:	17-23	Rank in top tenth:	8%
GPA 3.75 or higher:	15%	End year in good standing:	60%
GPA 3.50-3.74:	26%	Return as sophomores:	69%
GPA 3.0-3.49:	35%	Out-of-state:	7%
		Live on campus:	86%

Basis for selection. Course selection, grades received, and test scores most important. Preferred test score report date February 1. Interview required for nursing program; audition required for music programs. **Home schooled:** Provide as much documentation as possible.

High school preparation. College-preparatory program required. 16 units required; 21 recommended. Required and recommended units include English 4, mathematics 3-4, social studies 2, history 2, science 3-4 (laboratory 2-3) and foreign language 2. 4 units math required for math, computer science, biology, physics, and chemistry majors. 1 unit each biology, chemistry, physics required for health science majors. 1 unit each biology, anatomy and physiology, chemistry recommended for health and physical education majors.

2011-2012 Annual costs. Tuition/fees: $8,239; $15,599 out-of-state. All freshman students are required to have a laptop computer for use in the classroom. Computers can be purchased through the university; cost of computer is not included in mandatory fees. The university has a small number of laptops available to students who cannot afford to make such a purchase. Room/board: $7,056. Books/supplies: $1,260. Personal expenses: $2,045.

Financial aid. Non-need-based: Scholarships awarded for academics, art, athletics, leadership, minority status, music/drama, ROTC, state residency.

Application procedures. Admission: Priority date 3/1; no deadline. $25 fee, may be waived for applicants with need. Admission notification on a rolling basis beginning on or about 10/1. Must reply by May 1 or within 2 week(s) if notified thereafter. **Financial aid:** Closing date 3/15. FAFSA required. Applicants notified on a rolling basis starting 4/1; must reply within 2 week(s) of notification.

Academics. Special study options: Combined bachelor's/graduate degree, cross-registration, distance learning, double major, dual enrollment of high school students, honors, independent study, internships, student-designed major, study abroad, teacher certification program. Exchange program with institutions in Taiwan, Russia, Australia, France, England, Poland, Germany, Scotland, Costa Rica, China, Japan, Croatia, Italy, Kenya, Mexico. 2-2 program in music education with Clarion University of Pennsylvania and Millersville University of Pennsylvania. **Credit/placement by examination:** AP, CLEP, IB, SAT, institutional tests. 30 credit hours maximum toward bachelor's degree. **Support services:** Learning center, pre-admission summer program, reduced course load, remedial instruction, study skills assistance, tutoring, writing center.

Majors. Biology: General. **Business:** Accounting, business admin. **Communications:** Media studies. **Computer sciences:** General. **Education:** Early childhood special, kindergarten/preschool, middle, secondary. **English:** English lit. **Foreign languages:** French, German, Spanish. **History:** General. **Human services:** Social work. **Liberal arts:** Arts/sciences. **Math:** General. **Parks/recreation:** Facilities management, sports admin. **Philosophy/religion:** Philosophy. **Physical sciences:** Chemistry, geology, physics. **Protective services:** Law enforcement admin. **Psychology:** General. **Social sciences:** General, international relations, political science, sociology. **Visual/performing arts:** Art, dramatic, music, studio arts.

Most popular majors. Business/marketing 12%, education 12%, health sciences 12%, parks/recreation 22%, security/protective services 11%, social sciences 7%.

Computing on campus. PC or laptop required. 290 workstations in dormitories, library, computer center, student center. Dormitories wired for high-speed internet access and linked to campus network. Commuter students can connect to campus network. Online course registration, online library, helpline, repair service, student web hosting, wireless network available.

Student life. Freshman orientation: Available, $75 fee. Preregistration for classes offered. Overnight new student and parent programs, run concurrently, held during June. **Housing:** Guaranteed on-campus for freshmen. Coed dorms, apartments available. $200 nonrefundable deposit, deadline 5/1. **Activities:** Bands, campus ministries, choral groups, dance, drama, international student organizations, literary magazine, music ensembles, musical theater, radio station, student government, student newspaper, symphony orchestra, TV station, Newman Club, Black Cultural Society, Campus Crusade, Commonwealth Association of Students, Fellowship of Christian Athletes, social service society, Full Gospel Fellowship, New Life Student Fellowship.

Athletics. NCAA. **Intercollegiate:** Baseball M, basketball, boxing, cheerleading, cross-country, field hockey W, football (tackle) M, lacrosse W, soccer, softball W, swimming W, track and field, volleyball W, wrestling M. **Intramural:** Badminton, basketball, cross-country, field hockey W, golf, racquetball, skiing, soccer, softball, tennis, volleyball, water polo, wrestling M. **Team name:** Bald Eagles, Lady Eagles.

Student services. Adult student services, alcohol/substance abuse counseling, chaplain/spiritual director, career counseling, student employment services, financial aid counseling, health services, minority student services, personal counseling, placement for graduates, veterans' counselor, women's services. **Physically disabled:** Services for visually, speech impaired.

Contact. E-mail: admissions@lhup.edu
Phone: (570) 484-2027 Fax: (570) 484-2201
Robin Rockey, Director of Admissions, Lock Haven University of Pennsylvania, LHU Office of Admissions, Lock Haven, PA 17745

Lycoming College

Williamsport, Pennsylvania
www.lycoming.edu

CB member
CB code: 2372

- Private 4-year liberal arts college affiliated with United Methodist Church
- Residential campus in small city
- 1,346 degree-seeking undergraduates: 56% women, 5% African American, 1% Asian American, 3% Hispanic American, 2% international
- 70% of applicants admitted
- Application essay required
- 70% graduate within 6 years; 20% enter graduate study

General. Founded in 1812. Regionally accredited. **Degrees:** 278 bachelor's awarded. **ROTC:** Army. **Location:** 90 miles from Harrisburg, 170 miles from Philadelphia. **Calendar:** Semester, limited summer session. **Full-time faculty:** 82 total; 94% have terminal degrees, 5% minority, 39% women. **Part-time faculty:** 37 total; 14% have terminal degrees, 3% minority, 43% women. **Class size:** 65% < 20, 33% 20-39, 1% 40-49, less than 1% >100. **Special facilities:** Planetarium, clean water institute, graphics computer lab, polling institute.

Freshman class profile. 1,868 applied, 1,299 admitted, 417 enrolled.

Mid 50% test scores			
SAT critical reading:	470-590	Rank in top quarter:	47%
SAT math:	480-580	Rank in top tenth:	17%
SAT writing:	450-570	End year in good standing:	88%
ACT composite:	20-26	Return as sophomores:	86%
GPA 3.75 or higher:	32%	Out-of-state:	33%
GPA 3.50-3.74:	24%	Live on campus:	92%
GPA 3.0-3.49:	30%	International:	2%
GPA 2.0-2.99:	14%		

Basis for selection. Academic achievement as reflected in school record, class rank, and test scores most important. Curriculum, counselor and teacher recommendations also considered. SAT or ACT recommended. Interview recommended for all; portfolio recommended for art program and creative writing program; audition recommended for music and theater programs.

High school preparation. College-preparatory program required. 17 units required; 21 recommended. Required and recommended units include English 4, mathematics 3-4, social studies 3-4, science 3, foreign language 2-3 and academic electives 2-3.

2011-2012 Annual costs. Tuition/fees: $31,818. Room/board: $8,970. Books/supplies: $1,000. Personal expenses: $1,200.

2011-2012 Financial aid. Need-based: 390 full-time freshmen applied for aid; 351 were judged to have need; 351 of these received aid. Average need met was 83%. Average scholarship/grant was $22,058; average loan $3,913. 77% of total undergraduate aid awarded as scholarships/grants, 23% as loans/jobs. **Non-need-based:** Awarded to 284 full-time undergraduates, including 109 freshmen. Scholarships awarded for academics, art, minority status, music/drama, ROTC.

Application procedures. Admission: Priority date 12/1; deadline 3/1 (receipt date). $35 fee, may be waived for applicants with need, free for online applicants. Admission notification on a rolling basis beginning on or about 12/15. Must reply by May 1 or within 4 week(s) if notified thereafter. **Financial aid:** Priority date 5/1; no closing date. FAFSA, institutional form required. Applicants notified on a rolling basis starting 3/1; must reply by 5/1.

Academics. Teacher certification offered on elementary and secondary levels; special education certification as part of bachelor of arts program. **Special study options:** Accelerated study, combined bachelor's/graduate degree, cross-registration, double major, dual enrollment of high school students, honors, independent study, internships, student-designed major, study abroad, teacher certification program, United Nations semester, urban semester, Washington semester. **Credit/placement by examination:** AP, CLEP, IB, institutional tests. 64 credit hours maximum toward bachelor's degree. **Support services:** Learning center, study skills assistance, tutoring, writing center.

Majors. Area/ethnic studies: American. **Biology:** General, anatomy, ecology, molecular. **Business:** Accounting, actuarial science, business admin, communications, finance, international finance, managerial economics, marketing. **Communications:** Communications/speech/rhetoric, digital media. **English:** Creative writing, English lit. **Foreign languages:** French, German, Spanish. **History:** General, American, European. **Math:** General. **Philosophy/religion:** Philosophy, religion. **Physical sciences:** Astronomy, chemistry, physics. **Protective services:** Criminal justice. **Psychology:** General. **Social sciences:** Anthropology, archaeology, criminology, econometrics, economics, political science, sociology, U.S. government. **Visual/performing arts:** General, acting, art, art history/conservation, commercial/advertising art, directing/producing, dramatic, music, painting, photography, printmaking, sculpture, studio arts.

Most popular majors. Biology 10%, business/marketing 22%, history 9%, interdisciplinary studies 6%, psychology 16%, social sciences 15%, visual/performing arts 8%.

Computing on campus. 165 workstations in library, computer center, student center. Dormitories wired for high-speed internet access and linked to campus network. Commuter students can connect to campus network. Online course registration, online library, helpline, repair service, student web hosting, wireless network available.

Student life. Freshman orientation: Mandatory, $200 fee. Preregistration for classes offered. 2-day, one-night event for students and parents. Choose one of 3 dates. **Policies:** Students must live in college-owned residence halls or apartments. **Housing:** Guaranteed on-campus for all undergraduates. Coed dorms, single-sex dorms, special housing for disabled, apartments, fraternity/sorority housing, wellness housing available. $100 nonrefundable deposit, deadline 5/1. Study-intensive housing, Creative Arts Society housing available. **Activities:** Bands, campus ministries, choral groups, dance, drama, film society, international student organizations, literary magazine, music ensembles, musical theater, radio station, student government, student newspaper, TV station, Circle K, Habitat for Humanity, College Democrats, College Republicans, environmental awareness foundation, Black Student Union, Big Brothers/Big Sisters, Colleges Against Cancer, Religious Experiences at Lycoming.

Athletics. NCAA. **Intercollegiate:** Basketball, cross-country, football (tackle) M, golf, lacrosse, soccer, softball W, swimming, tennis, volleyball W, wrestling M. **Intramural:** Basketball, football (non-tackle), soccer, softball, table tennis, volleyball. **Team name:** Warriors.

Student services. Alcohol/substance abuse counseling, chaplain/spiritual director, career counseling, student employment services, financial aid counseling, health services, personal counseling, placement for graduates, women's services. **Physically disabled:** Services for visually, hearing impaired.

Contact. E-mail: admissions@lycoming.edu
Phone: (570) 321-4026 Toll-free number: (800) 345-3920 ext. 4026
Fax: (570) 321-4317
James Spencer, Vice President for Admissions and Financial Aid, Lycoming College, 700 College Place, Williamsport, PA 17701

Mansfield University of Pennsylvania

Mansfield, Pennsylvania
www.mansfield.edu

CB code: 2655

- Public 4-year university
- Residential campus in small town
- 2,819 degree-seeking undergraduates: 6% part-time, 59% women, 8% African American, 1% Asian American, 2% Hispanic American, 1% Native American, 1% international
- 373 degree-seeking graduate students

- 77% of applicants admitted
- SAT or ACT (ACT writing optional) required
- 54% graduate within 6 years

General. Founded in 1857. Regionally accredited. **Degrees:** 557 bachelor's, 23 associate awarded; master's offered. **ROTC:** Army. **Location:** 50 miles from Williamsport, 30 miles from Corning, New York. **Calendar:** Semester, limited summer session. **Full-time faculty:** 132 total; 62% have terminal degrees, 15% minority. **Part-time faculty:** 46 total; 44% have terminal degrees, 6% minority. **Class size:** 29% < 20, 50% 20-39, 12% 40-49, 9% 50-99, less than 1% >100. **Special facilities:** Planetarium, solar collector, science museum, animal collection, fisheries research boat, leadership institute.

Freshman class profile. 2,338 applied, 1,798 admitted, 624 enrolled.

Mid 50% test scores			
SAT critical reading:	420-530	Rank in top quarter:	31%
SAT math:	410-530	Rank in top tenth:	9%
SAT writing:	390-500	End year in good standing:	72%
GPA 3.75 or higher:	30%	Out-of-state:	16%
GPA 3.50-3.74:	16%	Live on campus:	83%
GPA 3.0-3.49:	25%	Fraternities:	7%
GPA 2.0-2.99:	27%	Sororities:	10%

Basis for selection. Class rank, high school curriculum, test scores important; counselor's recommendation, extracurricular activities considered. Special consideration given to applicants eligible for Equal Education Opportunity Program. Entry competitive in X-ray technology, respiratory therapy, fisheries, music, art programs, premed, nursing, biology, chemistry. Essay recommended for all; interview required for radiology program; audition required for music program; portfolio required for art program. **Home schooled:** Statement describing home school structure and mission, transcript of courses and grades required.

High school preparation. College-preparatory program recommended. 21 units required; 25 recommended. Required and recommended units include English 4, mathematics 3-4, history 4, science 2-3 (laboratory 2-3), foreign language 2-4 and academic electives 6.

2011-2012 Annual costs. Tuition/fees: $8,654; $18,014 out-of-state. Reduced out-of-state tuition for NY and NJ residents: $10,296 for the academic year; $429 per-credit hour for part-time students. Room/board: $8,078. Books/supplies: $1,200. Personal expenses: $2,000.

Financial aid. **Non-need-based:** Scholarships awarded for academics, art, athletics, leadership, music/drama, state residency.

Application procedures. **Admission:** No deadline. $25 fee, may be waived for applicants with need. Admission notification on a rolling basis beginning on or about 7/1. Must reply by May 1 or within 2 week(s) if notified thereafter. Applicants to competitive programs should apply by January 15. **Financial aid:** Priority date 3/15; no closing date. FAFSA, institutional form required. Applicants notified on a rolling basis starting 3/15; must reply within 2 week(s) of notification.

Academics. **Special study options:** Cross-registration, distance learning, double major, dual enrollment of high school students, ESL, exchange student, honors, independent study, internships, liberal arts/career combination, student-designed major, study abroad, teacher certification program, Washington semester. Online programs. **Credit/placement by examination:** AP, CLEP, IB, SAT, ACT, institutional tests. **Support services:** Learning center, pre-admission summer program, reduced course load, remedial instruction, study skills assistance, tutoring, writing center.

Majors. **Architecture:** Urban/community planning. **Biology:** General, biochemistry, cell/histology, marine, molecular. **Business:** Accounting, actuarial science, business admin, human resources, international, marketing, tourism promotion, tourism/travel. **Communications:** Broadcast journalism, communications/speech/rhetoric, journalism, public relations. **Computer sciences:** General, computer science, information systems. **Conservation:** General, environmental studies, fisheries. **Education:** Art, biology, chemistry, early childhood, elementary, English, foreign languages, French, German, history, mathematics, middle, multi-level teacher, music, physics, secondary, social studies, Spanish, special ed. **English:** English lit, rhetoric/composition. **Foreign languages:** French, German, Spanish. **Health services:** Clinical lab science, clinical lab technology, music therapy, predental, premedicine, preop/surgical nursing, prepharmacy, preveterinary. **History:** General. **Human services:** Social work. **Liberal arts:** Arts/sciences. **Math:** General. **Philosophy/religion:** Philosophy. **Physical sciences:** Chemistry, geology, physics. **Protective services:** Law enforcement admin. **Psychology:** General. **Social sciences:** General, anthropology, economics, geography, political science, sociology. **Visual/performing arts:** Art, art history/conservation, dramatic, graphic design, music, music management, music performance, piano/keyboard, studio arts, voice/opera.

Most popular majors. Business/marketing 11%, communications/journalism 8%, education 11%, English 8%, health sciences 8%, psychology 11%, security/protective services 12%, social sciences 6%, visual/performing arts 13%.

Computing on campus. 840 workstations in dormitories, library, computer center, student center. Dormitories wired for high-speed internet access and linked to campus network. Commuter students can connect to campus network. Online course registration, online library, helpline, wireless network available.

Student life. **Freshman orientation:** Mandatory, $65 fee. Preregistration for classes offered. 2-day program for students and parents. **Housing:** Guaranteed on-campus for all undergraduates. Coed dorms, fraternity/sorority housing available. $200 partly refundable deposit. **Activities:** Bands, campus ministries, choral groups, dance, drama, international student organizations, literary magazine, music ensembles, Model UN, musical theater, radio station, student government, student newspaper, symphony orchestra, TV station, Black Awareness Association, Inter-Varsity Christian Fellowship, Commonwealth Association of Students.

Athletics. NCAA. **Intercollegiate:** Baseball M, basketball, cross-country, diving W, field hockey W, soccer W, softball W, swimming W, track and field. **Intramural:** Basketball, football (non-tackle) M, soccer, softball, tennis, volleyball, water polo. **Team name:** Mounties.

Student services. Adult student services, alcohol/substance abuse counseling, chaplain/spiritual director, career counseling, services for economically disadvantaged, student employment services, financial aid counseling, health services, minority student services, on-campus daycare, personal counseling, placement for graduates, veterans' counselor, women's services. **Physically disabled:** Services for visually, speech, hearing impaired.

Contact. E-mail: admissions@mansfield.edu
Phone: (570) 662-4243 Toll-free number: (800) 577-6826
Fax: (570) 662-4121
Brian Barden, Executive Director of Enrollment Services, Mansfield University of Pennsylvania, South Hall, Mansfield, PA 16933

Marywood University
Scranton, Pennsylvania
www.marywood.edu

CB member
CB code: 2407

- Private 4-year university affiliated with Roman Catholic Church
- Residential campus in small city
- 2,190 degree-seeking undergraduates: 4% part-time, 70% women, 1% African American, 2% Asian American, 4% Hispanic American
- 1,050 degree-seeking graduate students
- 70% of applicants admitted
- SAT or ACT (ACT writing optional) required
- 63% graduate within 6 years

General. Founded in 1915. Regionally accredited. Marywood University has four colleges and one school: Insalaco College of Creative and Performing Arts, Reap College of Education and Human Development, College of Health and Human Services, College of Liberal Arts and Sciences, and the School of Architecture. **Degrees:** 478 bachelor's awarded; master's, professional, doctoral offered. **ROTC:** Army, Air Force. **Location:** 110 miles from Philadelphia, 120 miles from New York City. **Calendar:** Semester, extensive summer session. **Full-time faculty:** 153 total; 94% have terminal degrees, 52% women. **Part-time faculty:** 229 total; 4% minority. **Class size:** 55% < 20, 43% 20-39, 1% 40-49, less than 1% 50-99. **Special facilities:** Academic excellence center, human physiology lab, human development (counseling, psychology) labs, biotechnology lab, communication sciences and disorders clinic, nutrition and dietetics lab, computer labs, television editing suites, studio art center, visual arts center (including graphic design and interior architecture computer labs, Maslow Collection of Contemporary Art and Maslow Study Gallery), performance theater, black box theater, NCAA regulation pool and aquatics center, hydro-therapy room, arboretum.

Freshman class profile. 2,203 applied, 1,543 admitted, 466 enrolled.

Mid 50% test scores			
SAT critical reading:	470-560	GPA 3.0-3.49:	32%
SAT math:	480-570	GPA 2.0-2.99:	32%
SAT writing:	460-560	Rank in top quarter:	54%
ACT composite:	20-26	Rank in top tenth:	20%
GPA 3.75 or higher:	16%	Return as sophomores:	84%
GPA 3.50-3.74:	20%	Out-of-state:	37%
		Live on campus:	73%

Basis for selection. Class rank, high school achievement weighed alongside SAT/ACT scores. Course selection, achievement outside classroom, involvement in activities in and out of school, and letters of recommendations

also considered. TOEFL used for admission of non-native English speakers. Essay and interviews recommended for all. Audition for music program; portfolio for art program required after acceptance. **Learning Disabled:** Students may request accommodation by submitting documentation to admissions office or coordinator of services for students with disabilities.

High school preparation. College-preparatory program recommended. 16 units required. Required units include English 4, mathematics 2, social studies 3, science 1 (laboratory 1) and academic electives 6. Biological science must be laboratory science.

2011-2012 Annual costs. Tuition/fees: $28,175. Room/board: $12,520. Books/supplies: $1,200. Personal expenses: $500.

2011-2012 Financial aid. **Need-based:** 69% of total undergraduate aid awarded as scholarships/grants, 31% as loans/jobs. **Non-need-based:** Scholarships awarded for academics, art, leadership, music/drama, ROTC.

Application procedures. **Admission:** No deadline. $35 fee, may be waived for applicants with need, free for online applicants. Admission notification on a rolling basis beginning on or about 10/1. Must reply by May 1 or within 3 week(s) if notified thereafter. No refunds of housing deposit after May 1; for returning students deposit is not refundable. Students applying for early admission must submit letter from their high school principal recommending them for early admission. **Financial aid:** Closing date 2/15. FAFSA, institutional form required. Applicants notified on a rolling basis starting 2/15; must reply by 5/1 or within 3 week(s) of notification.

Academics. Healthy Family Center provides opportunities for study and research in nutrition, dietetics, and athletic performance; Robert J. Mellow Center for Athletics and Wellness provides full support for athletic training program. **Special study options:** Combined bachelor's/graduate degree, cross-registration, double major, dual enrollment of high school students, ESL, honors, independent study, internships, semester at sea, student-designed major, study abroad, teacher certification program. Students may study in any accredited school in any country that is approved by Marywood, or Marywood also has faculty-led, short-term study abroad programs. **Credit/placement by examination:** AP, CLEP, IB. 30 credit hours maximum toward associate degree, 66 toward bachelor's. **Support services:** Learning center, reduced course load, study skills assistance, tutoring, writing center.

Majors. **Architecture:** Architecture, environmental design. **Biology:** General, biotechnology. **Business:** Accounting, business admin, financial planning, hospitality admin, international, marketing. **Communications:** Broadcast journalism, digital media. **Conservation:** Environmental science. **Education:** Art, biology, elementary, English, family/consumer sciences, French, mathematics, music, science, social science, Spanish, special ed. **English:** English lit. **Foreign languages:** French, Spanish. **Health services:** Art therapy, athletic training, audiology/speech pathology, clinical lab science, dietetics, health care admin, music therapy. **History:** General. **Human services:** Social work. **Math:** General. **Parks/recreation:** Health/fitness. **Philosophy/religion:** Philosophy, religion. **Protective services:** Criminal justice. **Psychology:** General. **Social sciences:** General. **Visual/performing arts:** Ceramics, dramatic, graphic design, illustration, interior design, music performance, musical theater, painting, photography, sculpture.

Most popular majors. Business/marketing 12%, education 15%, health sciences 24%, psychology 6%, visual/performing arts 15%.

Computing on campus. 460 workstations in dormitories, library, computer center, student center. Dormitories wired for high-speed internet access and linked to campus network. Commuter students can connect to campus network. Online course registration, online library, helpline, repair service, student web hosting, wireless network available.

Student life. **Freshman orientation:** Available, $225 fee. Preregistration for classes offered. 3-day program held in July, for student and family. Additional 3-day program prior to start of classes. **Policies:** First- and second-year students under 21 not living at home with families in area required to live on campus. **Housing:** Guaranteed on-campus for freshmen. Coed dorms, single-sex dorms, special housing for disabled, apartments, wellness housing available. $300 fully refundable deposit. Volunteer services residential community. **Activities:** Bands, campus ministries, choral groups, dance, drama, international student organizations, literary magazine, music ensembles, musical theater, radio station, student government, student newspaper, TV station, environmental club, volunteers in action, peer educators, education club, criminal justice club, social work club, students to uphold life, Irish dancers club, diversity united, politically active students united.

Athletics. NCAA. **Intercollegiate:** Baseball M, basketball, cross-country, diving, field hockey W, golf M, lacrosse, soccer, softball W, swimming, tennis, volleyball W. **Intramural:** Badminton, basketball, football (non-tackle), racquetball, soccer, softball, table tennis, tennis, volleyball, water polo. **Team name:** Pacers.

Student services. Adult student services, alcohol/substance abuse counseling, chaplain/spiritual director, career counseling, services for economically disadvantaged, student employment services, financial aid counseling, health services, minority student services, on-campus daycare, personal counseling, placement for graduates, women's services. **Physically disabled:** Services for visually, speech, hearing impaired.

Contact. E-mail: yourfuture@marywood.edu
Phone: (570) 348-6234 Toll-free number: (866) 279-9663
Fax: (570) 961-4763
Christian DiGregorio, Director of University Admissions, Marywood University, 2300 Adams Avenue, Scranton, PA 18509-1598

Mercyhurst University

Erie, Pennsylvania   **CB member**
www.mercyhurst.edu   **CB code: 2410**

- Private 4-year liberal arts college affiliated with Roman Catholic Church
- Residential campus in small city
- 3,872 degree-seeking undergraduates: 13% part-time, 59% women, 7% African American, 1% Asian American, 2% Hispanic American, 5% international
- 345 degree-seeking graduate students
- 76% of applicants admitted
- SAT or ACT (ACT writing recommended), application essay required
- 67% graduate within 6 years; 31% enter graduate study

General. Founded in 1926. Regionally accredited. **Degrees:** 575 bachelor's, 268 associate awarded; master's offered. **ROTC:** Army. **Location:** 100 miles from Pittsburgh; 90 miles from Buffalo, NY. **Calendar:** Trimester, limited summer session. **Full-time faculty:** 192 total; 53% have terminal degrees, 5% minority, 48% women. **Part-time faculty:** 119 total; 13% have terminal degrees, 6% minority. **Class size:** 60% < 20, 39% 20-39, less than 1% 40-49. **Special facilities:** Observatory, archaeological materials preservation laboratory, principal center for forensic geoarchelogical studies for various federal agencies managing Archaeological Resources Protection Act cases.

Freshman class profile. 2,965 applied, 2,260 admitted, 671 enrolled.

Mid 50% test scores			
SAT critical reading:	470-580	GPA 2.0-2.99:	23%
SAT math:	480-580	Rank in top quarter:	41%
SAT writing:	460-570	Rank in top tenth:	17%
ACT composite:	21-26	End year in good standing:	89%
GPA 3.75 or higher:	23%	Return as sophomores:	81%
GPA 3.50-3.74:	22%	Out-of-state:	53%
GPA 3.0-3.49:	32%	Live on campus:	93%
		International:	8%

Basis for selection. Admissions based on secondary school record. Class rank, standardized test scores, talent, ability, character, and personal qualities also important. Audition required for dance and music programs; portfolio required for art program. **Home schooled:** SAT/ACT and transcript preferred.

High school preparation. College-preparatory program recommended. 16 units required. Required and recommended units include English 4, mathematics 2-3, social studies 5, science 2-3 (laboratory 1-2) and foreign language 2-3.

2011-2012 Annual costs. Tuition/fees: $27,657. Room/board: $9,738. Books/supplies: $1,000. Personal expenses: $600.

2011-2012 Financial aid. **Need-based:** 67% of total undergraduate aid awarded as scholarships/grants, 33% as loans/jobs. **Non-need-based:** Scholarships awarded for academics, alumni affiliation, art, athletics, leadership, minority status, music/drama, religious affiliation, ROTC.

Application procedures. **Admission:** Priority date 3/15; no deadline. $30 fee, may be waived for applicants with need, free for online applicants. Admission notification on a rolling basis beginning on or about 11/15. Must reply by May 1 or within 2 week(s) if notified thereafter. **Financial aid:** Priority date 3/1; no closing date. FAFSA required. Applicants notified on a rolling basis starting 2/15; must reply by 5/1 or within 2 week(s) of notification.

Academics. Education department offers graduate student-taught special education programs for learning disabled students. Asperger Initiative program offered. **Special study options:** Combined bachelor's/graduate degree, cooperative education, cross-registration, distance learning, double major, honors, independent study, internships, liberal arts/career combination, New York semester, semester at sea, student-designed major, study abroad, teacher certification program, Washington semester. **Credit/placement by examination:** AP, CLEP, IB, SAT, ACT, institutional tests. 30 credit hours maximum toward bachelor's degree. **Support services:** Learning center, pre-admission

summer program, reduced course load, remedial instruction, study skills assistance, tutoring, writing center.

Majors. Area/ethnic studies: Russian/Slavic. **Biology:** General, biochemistry. **Business:** Accounting, business admin, fashion, finance, hospitality admin, human resources, international, managerial economics, market research, marketing. **Communications:** Communications/speech/rhetoric. **Computer sciences:** General. **Education:** Art, biology, business, chemistry, early childhood, elementary, English, foreign languages, mathematics, music, science, secondary, social science, special ed. **English:** English lit. **Foreign languages:** General. **Health services:** Art therapy, medical records technology, nursing (RN). **History:** General. **Human services:** Health policy, social work. **Liberal arts:** Arts/sciences. **Math:** General. **Philosophy/religion:** Philosophy, religion. **Physical sciences:** Chemistry, geology. **Protective services:** Criminal justice, forensics. **Psychology:** General. **Social sciences:** Anthropology, political science, sociology. **Theology:** Religious ed. **Visual/performing arts:** Dance, graphic design, interior design, music, music performance, studio arts.

Most popular majors. Biology 6%, business/marketing 28%, education 9%, health sciences 6%, interdisciplinary studies 13%, security/protective services 8%, visual/performing arts 8%.

Computing on campus. 375 workstations in dormitories, library, computer center, student center. Dormitories wired for high-speed internet access and linked to campus network. Commuter students can connect to campus network. Online course registration, online library, helpline, repair service, student web hosting, wireless network available.

Student life. Freshman orientation: Mandatory, $150 fee. Preregistration for classes offered. 3 days prior to start of classes. **Policies:** Freshmen not permitted cars on campus. **Housing:** Guaranteed on-campus for all undergraduates. Coed dorms, single-sex dorms, apartments, wellness housing available. $350 fully refundable deposit, deadline 8/1. **Activities:** Bands, campus ministries, chaplain groups, dance, drama, international student organizations, literary magazine, music ensembles, musical theater, opera, radio station, student government, student newspaper, symphony orchestra, Association of Black Collegians, Habitat for Humanity, Amnesty International, ambassadors club.

Athletics. NCAA. **Intercollegiate:** Baseball M, basketball, cheerleading, cross-country, field hockey W, football (tackle) M, golf, ice hockey, lacrosse, rowing (crew), soccer, softball W, tennis, volleyball W, water polo, wrestling M. **Intramural:** Basketball, bowling, football (non-tackle) M, ice hockey, skiing, soccer, softball. **Team name:** Lakers.

Student services. Adult student services, alcohol/substance abuse counseling, chaplain/spiritual director, career counseling, services for economically disadvantaged, student employment services, financial aid counseling, health services, personal counseling, placement for graduates, veterans' counselor. **Physically disabled:** Services for hearing impaired.

Contact. E-mail: admissions@mercyhurst.edu
Phone: (814) 824-2202 Toll-free number: (800) 825-1926
Fax: (814) 824-2071
Christopher Coons, Director of Undergraduate Admissions, Mercyhurst University, 501 East 38th Street, Erie, PA 16546-0001

Messiah College
Grantham, Pennsylvania   CB member
www.messiah.edu   CB code: 2411

▸ Private 4-year liberal arts college affiliated with interdenominational tradition

▸ Residential campus in small town

▸ 2,751 degree-seeking undergraduates: 1% part-time, 61% women, 2% African American, 1% Asian American, 2% Hispanic American, 2% international

▸ 167 degree-seeking graduate students

▸ 64% of applicants admitted

▸ Application essay required

▸ 74% graduate within 6 years; 20% enter graduate study

General. Founded in 1909. Regionally accredited. Students able to take coursework at Temple University. **Degrees:** 608 bachelor's awarded; master's offered. **Location:** 10 miles from Harrisburg, 20 miles from Gettysburg. **Calendar:** Semester, limited summer session. **Full-time faculty:** 177 total; 81% have terminal degrees, 6% minority, 43% women. **Part-time faculty:** 111 total; 25% have terminal degrees, 4% minority, 56% women. **Class size:** 44% < 20, 50% 20-39, 3% 40-49, 2% 50-99, 1% >100. **Special facilities:** Historical library and archives, natural history museum, service and learning center, community-supported agriculture, solar panel array and pavilion.

Freshman class profile. 3,154 applied, 2,032 admitted, 694 enrolled.

Mid 50% test scores			
SAT critical reading:	520-630	GPA 2.0-2.99:	5%
SAT math:	520-640	Rank in top quarter:	68%
SAT writing:	500-620	Rank in top tenth:	39%
ACT composite:	22-29	End year in good standing:	94%
GPA 3.75 or higher:	58%	Return as sophomores:	83%
GPA 3.50-3.74:	19%	Out-of-state:	43%
GPA 3.0-3.49:	18%	Live on campus:	97%
		International:	1%

Basis for selection. Admitted students normally in top third of class and have B average or better. Statement of Christian commitment required. SAT or ACT recommended. Tests required of standard choice applicants. Students in the top 20% of high school class may apply without test scores, but must submit graded writing sample and have on-campus interview. Interview required for students who apply by the "Write Choice" application method, strongly recommended for all others. **Home schooled:** Comprehensive transcript of senior year academic program as well as courses and course evaluations of 9th through 11th grades required. Include independent evaluation by qualified educator if available. **Learning Disabled:** Autobiographical statement required. Psychoeducational report (done within last 4 years) and interview required only after admissions decision. High school IEP recommended.

High school preparation. College-preparatory program required. 16 units required; 20 recommended. Required and recommended units include English 4, mathematics 2-3, social studies 2, history 2, science 2-3 (laboratory 2-3), foreign language 2 and academic electives 4.

2012-2013 Annual costs. Tuition/fees: $29,460. Room/board: $8,760. Books/supplies: $1,220. Personal expenses: $1,380.

2011-2012 Financial aid. Need-based: 627 full-time freshmen applied for aid; 532 were judged to have need; 532 of these received aid. Average need met was 74%. Average scholarship/grant was $15,663; average loan $3,566. 66% of total undergraduate aid awarded as scholarships/grants, 34% as loans/jobs. **Non-need-based:** Awarded to 923 full-time undergraduates, including 226 freshmen. Scholarships awarded for academics, art, leadership, music/drama, religious affiliation.

Application procedures. Admission: Priority date 5/1; no deadline. $30 fee, may be waived for applicants with need. Admission notification on a rolling basis beginning on or about 7/1. Must reply by May 1 or within 4 week(s) if notified thereafter. **Financial aid:** Priority date 4/1; no closing date. FAFSA required. Applicants notified on a rolling basis starting 3/15; must reply by 5/1 or within 4 week(s) of notification.

Academics. Supplemental instructional support available. **Special study options:** Accelerated study, combined bachelor's/graduate degree, double major, dual enrollment of high school students, ESL, exchange student, honors, independent study, internships, student-designed major, study abroad, teacher certification program, urban semester, Washington semester. Pass/Fail option. **Credit/placement by examination:** AP, CLEP, IB, institutional tests. 32 credit hours maximum toward bachelor's degree. **Support services:** Learning center, pre-admission summer program, reduced course load, remedial instruction, study skills assistance, tutoring, writing center.

Majors. Biology: General, biochemistry, molecular. **Business:** Accounting, business admin, entrepreneurial studies, human resources, international, managerial economics, marketing, restaurant/food services. **Communications:** Communications/speech/rhetoric, journalism, radio/TV. **Computer sciences:** Computer science, information systems. **Conservation:** Environmental science, environmental studies. **Education:** Art, biology, chemistry, early childhood, elementary, English, family/consumer sciences, French, German, mathematics, music, physical, physics, social studies, Spanish. **Engineering:** General. **English:** English lit. **Foreign languages:** French, German, Spanish. **Health services:** Athletic training, clinical nutrition, nursing (RN). **History:** General. **Human services:** Social work. **Liberal arts:** General. **Parks/recreation:** General, exercise sciences, sports admin. **Philosophy/religion:** Philosophy. **Physical sciences:** Chemistry, physics. **Protective services:** Criminal justice. **Psychology:** General. **Social sciences:** Economics, political science, sociology. **Theology:** Bible, religious ed. **Visual/performing arts:** Art history/conservation, dramatic, music, music performance, studio arts, studio arts management. **Work/family studies:** Child care management, family/community services.

Most popular majors. Biology 6%, business/marketing 13%, education 19%, health sciences 11%, psychology 7%.

Computing on campus. 571 workstations in dormitories, library, computer center, student center. Dormitories wired for high-speed internet access and linked to campus network. Commuter students can connect to campus network. Online course registration, online library, helpline, student web hosting, wireless network available.

Student life. Freshman orientation: Mandatory. Preregistration for classes offered. 4-day orientation for students and parents during fall welcome

weekend; includes placement exams and service day. **Policies:** Students generally required to live on campus unless married or living with relatives. Religious observance required. **Housing:** Guaranteed on-campus for all undergraduates. Coed dorms, single-sex dorms, special housing for disabled, apartments, wellness housing available. $200 partly refundable deposit, deadline 5/1. **Activities:** Bands, campus ministries, choral groups, dance, drama, film society, international student organizations, literary magazine, music ensembles, musical theater, radio station, student government, student newspaper, symphony orchestra, outreach teams, World Christian Fellowship, Nurses Christian Fellowship, Newman Club, Powerhouse band, Acclamation dance, Alliance of Confessing Theologies.

Athletics. NCAA. **Intercollegiate:** Baseball M, basketball, cross-country, field hockey W, golf M, lacrosse, soccer, softball W, swimming, tennis, track and field, volleyball W, wrestling M. **Intramural:** Basketball, football (non-tackle), racquetball, soccer, softball, volleyball. **Team name:** Falcons.

Student services. Chaplain/spiritual director, career counseling, student employment services, financial aid counseling, health services, minority student services, on-campus daycare, personal counseling, placement for graduates. **Physically disabled:** Services for visually, speech, hearing impaired.

Contact. E-mail: admiss@messiah.edu
Phone: (717) 691-6000 Toll-free number: (800) 233-4220
Fax: (717) 691-2307
John Chopka, Vice President of Enrollment Management, Messiah College, PO Box 3005, Grantham, PA 17027-0800

Millersville University of Pennsylvania
Millersville, Pennsylvania   **CB member**
www.millersville.edu   **CB code: 2656**

▶ Public 4-year university and liberal arts college
▶ Residential campus in small town
▶ 7,536 degree-seeking undergraduates: 10% part-time, 56% women, 8% African American, 2% Asian American, 6% Hispanic American
▶ 731 degree-seeking graduate students
▶ 58% of applicants admitted
▶ SAT or ACT (ACT writing recommended) required
▶ 65% graduate within 6 years

General. Founded in 1855. Regionally accredited. **Degrees:** 1,536 bachelor's, 4 associate awarded; master's offered. **ROTC:** Army. **Location:** 5 miles from Lancaster, 35 miles from Harrisburg. **Calendar:** 4-1-4, limited summer session. **Full-time faculty:** 299 total; 97% have terminal degrees, 15% minority, 48% women. **Part-time faculty:** 132 total; 32% have terminal degrees, 4% minority, 52% women. **Class size:** 15% < 20, 64% 20-39, 11% 40-49, 8% 50-99, 3% >100. **Special facilities:** Teleconferencing center, weather station, foreign language lab, art galleries.

Freshman class profile. 6,974 applied, 4,023 admitted, 1,304 enrolled.

Mid 50% test scores		Rank in top quarter:	42%
SAT critical reading:	470-570	Rank in top tenth:	15%
SAT math:	480-580	Return as sophomores:	81%
SAT writing:	450-560	Out-of-state:	6%
ACT composite:	19-24	Live on campus:	85%

Basis for selection. High school record most important, followed by class rank, test scores, and recommendations. Special consideration to students with special talents. All students required to take Basic Skills Test for placement purposes. All incoming students must take at least one math course; math placement test required. Some students may also be required to take a chemistry and/or a foreign language placement test. Educationally and economically disadvantaged students may be admitted to Aim for Success enrichment program if they demonstrate potential for college success. Submit all SAT/ACT scores. Highest combination of scores from multiple sittings for the SAT and highest composite ACT used. Applicants without SAT scores may enroll as non-degree students and be admitted to degree-seeking status after completing 12 credits with 2.0 GPA. The University uses a rolling date by which SAT or ACT scores must be received for fall-term admission. Interview required for applicants to disadvantaged program; recommended for all others. Audition required for music applicants; portfolio required for art applicants. RN required for nursing program. Letters of reference and personal statement are recommended.

High school preparation. College-preparatory program required. 15 units required; 21 recommended. Required and recommended units include English 4, mathematics 3, social studies 3, history 2, science 3 (laboratory 2), foreign language 2 and academic electives 4.

2011-2012 Annual costs. Tuition/fees: $8,361; $17,721 out-of-state. Room/board: $8,732. Books/supplies: $1,000. Personal expenses: $1,888.

2010-2011 Financial aid. **Need-based:** 1,193 full-time freshmen applied for aid; 854 were judged to have need; 828 of these received aid. Average need met was 71%. Average scholarship/grant was $5,765; average loan $3,200. 48% of total undergraduate aid awarded as scholarships/grants, 52% as loans/jobs. **Non-need-based:** Awarded to 701 full-time undergraduates, including 186 freshmen. Scholarships awarded for academics, athletics, minority status.

Application procedures. **Admission:** Priority date 1/1; no deadline. $50 fee, may be waived for applicants with need. Admission notification on a rolling basis beginning on or about 9/15. Extensions of reply date for accepted applicants granted upon request until May 1. **Financial aid:** Closing date 3/15. FAFSA required. Applicants notified on a rolling basis starting 3/19; must reply within 2 week(s) of notification.

Academics. **Special study options:** Accelerated study, combined bachelor's/graduate degree, cooperative education, cross-registration, distance learning, double major, dual enrollment of high school students, honors, independent study, internships, study abroad, teacher certification program. Off-campus study, learning disabilities services, adult and continuing education (ACE) program. **Credit/placement by examination:** AP, CLEP, IB, institutional tests. No limit to the hours of credit examination that may be counted toward an associate or bachelor's degree. Students may challenge most courses in which they have not received a grade, and which have not been waived because of demonstrated competency or advanced placement. Because of content and structure, some courses may not be challenged by examination. **Support services:** Learning center, reduced course load, remedial instruction, study skills assistance, tutoring, writing center.

Majors. **Biology:** General. **Business:** Business admin. **Communications:** Communications/speech/rhetoric. **Computer sciences:** General. **Education:** Elementary, secondary, special ed. **English:** English lit. **Foreign languages:** French, German, Spanish. **Health services:** Nursing (RN). **History:** General. **Human services:** Social work. **Math:** General. **Philosophy/religion:** Philosophy. **Physical sciences:** Atmospheric science, chemistry, geology, oceanography, physics. **Psychology:** General. **Social sciences:** Anthropology, economics, geography, international relations, political science, sociology. **Visual/performing arts:** Art, music.

Most popular majors. Biology 6%, business/marketing 12%, communications/journalism 7%, education 16%, engineering/engineering technologies 8%, psychology 7%, social sciences 12%, visual/performing arts 6%.

Computing on campus. 430 workstations in dormitories, library, computer center, student center. Dormitories wired for high-speed internet access and linked to campus network. Commuter students can connect to campus network. Online course registration, online library, helpline, repair service, wireless network available.

Student life. **Freshman orientation:** Mandatory, $290 fee. Preregistration for classes offered. All incoming new students with less than 30 credits required to attend 6-day program in August. Parents invited to attend a separate orientation session. **Policies:** All residence hall students required to purchase a meal plan. 24 hour visitation, must adhere to housing guidelines. Freshmen not permitted cars on campus. **Housing:** Guaranteed on-campus for freshmen. Coed dorms, apartments, wellness housing available. $125 nonrefundable deposit, deadline 5/1. Academic interest housing. University-affiliated apartments and dormitory for single students adjacent to campus. **Activities:** Bands, campus ministries, choral groups, dance, drama, international student organizations, literary magazine, music ensembles, musical theater, radio station, student government, student newspaper, symphony orchestra, TV station, Black student union, commuting student association, Circle-K, College Republicans, Marauder Graphics, Asian and Friends Affiliation, College Democrats, NAACP, Society on Latino Affairs.

Athletics. NCAA. **Intercollegiate:** Baseball M, basketball, cheerleading M, cross-country, field hockey W, football (tackle) M, golf M, lacrosse W, soccer, softball W, swimming W, tennis, track and field, volleyball W, wrestling M. **Intramural:** Badminton, basketball, golf, racquetball, soccer, softball, tennis, volleyball, water polo. **Team name:** Marauders.

Student services. Adult student services, alcohol/substance abuse counseling, chaplain/spiritual director, career counseling, services for economically disadvantaged, student employment services, financial aid counseling, health services, minority student services, personal counseling, placement for graduates, veterans' counselor, women's services. **Physically disabled:** Services for visually, speech, hearing impaired.

Contact. E-mail: admissions@millersville.edu
Phone: (717) 872-3371 Toll-free number: (800) 682-3648
Fax: (717) 871-2147
Jose Aviles, Associate Provost for Enrollment Management, Millersville University of Pennsylvania, PO Box 1002, Millersville, PA 17551-0302

Misericordia University
Dallas, Pennsylvania
www.misericordia.edu

CB member
CB code: 2087

- Private 4-year health science and liberal arts college affiliated with Roman Catholic Church
- Residential campus in large town
- 2,335 degree-seeking undergraduates: 28% part-time, 71% women, 1% African American, 1% Asian American, 2% Hispanic American
- 444 degree-seeking graduate students
- 57% of applicants admitted
- SAT or ACT (ACT writing optional) required
- 67% graduate within 6 years; 18% enter graduate study

General. Founded in 1924. Regionally accredited. Guaranteed Placement Program (within six months of graduation); Women with Children program for single women. **Degrees:** 537 bachelor's awarded; master's, professional offered. **ROTC:** Army, Air Force. **Location:** 9 miles from Wilkes-Barre, 20 miles from Scranton. **Calendar:** Semester, limited summer session. **Full-time faculty:** 109 total; 81% have terminal degrees, 7% minority, 54% women. **Part-time faculty:** 207 total; 13% have terminal degrees, 3% minority, 53% women. **Class size:** 54% < 20, 44% 20-39, 1% 40-49.

Freshman class profile. 2,013 applied, 1,153 admitted, 368 enrolled.

Mid 50% test scores			
SAT critical reading:	480-570	Rank in top quarter:	60%
SAT math:	500-590	Rank in top tenth:	25%
ACT composite:	22-25	End year in good standing:	94%
GPA 3.75 or higher:	18%	Return as sophomores:	86%
GPA 3.50-3.74:	27%	Out-of-state:	29%
GPA 3.0-3.49:	37%	Live on campus:	82%
GPA 2.0-2.99:	18%		

Basis for selection. In order of importance: high school achievement, test scores, character, recommendations from school teachers or counselors. Test scores weighed more heavily for health science programs. Essay required for occupational therapy and speech language pathology applicants. **Home schooled:** Transcript of courses and grades required. If applicant not affiliated with specific organization, college will accept transcript from home schooling parent that shows course work completed and grades achieved. GED not required. **Learning Disabled:** Essay, 3 letters of recommendation, documentation of disability, test results (i.e., WAIS) required. SAT/ACT not required.

High school preparation. College-preparatory program recommended. 16 units required. Required units include English 4, mathematics 4, social studies 4 and science 4. 2 units science and algebra required for allied health applicants. Strong math background required for computer science, physical therapy, chemistry and biology applicants.

2011-2012 Annual costs. Tuition/fees: $25,990. Room/board: $10,760. Books/supplies: $1,000. Personal expenses: $500.

2011-2012 Financial aid. Need-based: 355 full-time freshmen applied for aid; 310 were judged to have need; 310 of these received aid. Average need met was 80%. Average scholarship/grant was $13,669; average loan $7,005. 59% of total undergraduate aid awarded as scholarships/grants, 41% as loans/jobs. **Non-need-based:** Awarded to 375 full-time undergraduates, including 103 freshmen. Scholarships awarded for academics, alumni affiliation, leadership, minority status, state residency.

Application procedures. Admission: No deadline. $25 fee, may be waived for applicants with need. Admission notification on a rolling basis beginning on or about 9/1. Must reply by May 1 or within 4 week(s) if notified thereafter. **Financial aid:** Priority date 3/1, closing date 5/1. FAFSA, institutional form required. Applicants notified on a rolling basis starting 3/15.

Academics. Special study options: Accelerated study, combined bachelor's/graduate degree, cross-registration, distance learning, double major, dual enrollment of high school students, honors, independent study, internships, student-designed major, study abroad, teacher certification program, weekend college. **Credit/placement by examination:** AP, CLEP, IB, SAT, ACT, institutional tests. 40 credit hours maximum toward bachelor's degree. **Support services:** Learning center, pre-admission summer program, study skills assistance, tutoring, writing center.

Majors. Biology: General, biochemistry. **Business:** Accounting, business admin, marketing. **Communications:** General. **Computer sciences:** General, information technology. **Education:** Biology, chemistry, early childhood, elementary, English, mathematics, middle, social studies, special ed. **English:** English lit. **Health services:** Clinical lab science, health care admin, medical radiologic technology/radiation therapy, nursing (RN), nursing practice, sonography. **History:** General. **Human services:** Social work. **Liberal arts:** Arts/sciences. **Math:** General. **Parks/recreation:** Sports admin. **Philosophy/religion:** Philosophy. **Physical sciences:** Chemistry. **Psychology:** General. **Social sciences:** General, U.S. government.

Most popular majors. Business/marketing 16%, education 9%, health sciences 41%, liberal arts 8%.

Computing on campus. 100 workstations in dormitories, library, computer center, student center. Dormitories wired for high-speed internet access and linked to campus network. Commuter students can connect to campus network. Online course registration, online library, helpline, repair service, wireless network available.

Student life. Freshman orientation: Mandatory, $200 fee. Preregistration for classes offered. One-day testing for math and English placement. **Policies:** Freshmen not permitted cars on campus. **Housing:** Coed dorms available. $100 nonrefundable deposit, deadline 5/1. Leadership house, 2 apartment buildings for women with children located adjacent to campus. **Activities:** Jazz band, campus ministries, choral groups, dance, drama, literary magazine, music ensembles, radio station, student government, student newspaper, TV station, student nurses association, Council for Exceptional Children, Circle-K, Peer Associates, Diversity Institute.

Athletics. NCAA. **Intercollegiate:** Baseball M, basketball, cross-country, field hockey W, golf, lacrosse, soccer, softball W, swimming, tennis, track and field, volleyball W. **Intramural:** Basketball, cross-country, football (non-tackle), racquetball, soccer, softball, tennis, volleyball. **Team name:** Cougars.

Student services. Adult student services, alcohol/substance abuse counseling, chaplain/spiritual director, career counseling, services for economically disadvantaged, student employment services, financial aid counseling, health services, minority student services, personal counseling, placement for graduates, women's services. **Physically disabled:** Services for visually, speech, hearing impaired.

Contact. E-mail: admiss@misericordia.edu
Phone: (570) 674-6264 Toll-free number: (866) 262-6363
Fax: (570) 675-2441
Glenn Bozinski, Director of Admissions, Misericordia University, 301 Lake Street, Dallas, PA 18612-1098

Moore College of Art and Design
Philadelphia, Pennsylvania
www.moore.edu

CB code: 2417

- Private 4-year visual arts college for women
- Commuter campus in very large city
- 468 degree-seeking undergraduates: 6% part-time, 100% women, 15% African American, 4% Asian American, 4% Hispanic American, 1% Native American, 3% international
- 58 degree-seeking graduate students
- 67% of applicants admitted
- Interview required
- 57% graduate within 6 years

General. Founded in 1848. Regionally accredited. Moore is the first and only women's visual arts college in the nation. The College thrives on the premise of empowering women to achieve financial independence by providing quality, career-focused education. The graduate programs at Moore prepare men and women with the skills, knowledge and resources to become professional artists, designers and educators. **Degrees:** 129 bachelor's awarded; master's offered. **Location:** 90 miles from New York City. **Calendar:** Semester, limited summer session. **Full-time faculty:** 24 total; 50% have terminal degrees, 8% minority, 62% women. **Part-time faculty:** 112 total; 40% have terminal degrees, 15% minority, 55% women. **Class size:** 86% < 20, 14% 20-39. **Special facilities:** Professional and student galleries.

Freshman class profile. 493 applied, 329 admitted, 99 enrolled.

Mid 50% test scores			
SAT critical reading:	440-580	GPA 3.0-3.49:	31%
SAT math:	420-530	GPA 2.0-2.99:	33%
ACT composite:	16-26	Return as sophomores:	84%
GPA 3.75 or higher:	16%	Out-of-state:	44%
GPA 3.50-3.74:	19%	International:	4%

Basis for selection. High school record, interview, portfolio, and test scores important. 850 SAT (exclusive of Writing) or 18 ACT and 2.5 GPA required. First-time degree seeking students must complete writing placement essay. Transfer students may participate in the Directed Self-Placement program for English courses. Portfolio required; essay recommended for all. **Home schooled:** State high school equivalency certificate required. **Learning Disabled:** Students who request accommodations must provide qualifying documentation on professional letterhead and contain dates of assessment,

signatures, titles, and license/certification numbers of diagnosing professionals. Documentation should be no more than 3 years old.

High school preparation. College-preparatory program recommended. 14 units recommended. Recommended units include English 4, mathematics 2, social studies 4, science 2, foreign language 2 and visual/performing arts 3. Portfolio review required.

2011-2012 Annual costs. Tuition/fees: $31,626. Room/board: $11,823. Books/supplies: $2,060. Personal expenses: $2,000.

2010-2011 Financial aid. Non-need-based: Scholarships awarded for academics, art, leadership.

Application procedures. Admission: $40 fee, may be waived for applicants with need. Admission notification on a rolling basis beginning on or about 11/15. Must reply by May 1 or within 3 week(s) if notified thereafter. **Financial aid:** Priority date 3/1, closing date 5/1. FAFSA required. Applicants notified on a rolling basis starting 2/15; must reply within 2 week(s) of notification.

Academics. Writing Center available. Students who need support services on the weekends and in the evenings can get assistance via email. **Special study options:** Double major, exchange student, independent study, internships, study abroad, teacher certification program. **Credit/placement by examination:** AP, CLEP, IB, institutional tests. 6 credit hours maximum toward bachelor's degree. **Support services:** Pre-admission summer program, reduced course load, study skills assistance, tutoring, writing center.

Majors. Education: Art. **Visual/performing arts:** Art history/conservation, fashion design, graphic design, illustration, interior design, photography, studio arts.

Most popular majors. Education 6%, visual/performing arts 94%.

Computing on campus. PC or laptop required. 125 workstations in dormitories, library, computer center. Dormitories wired for high-speed internet access. Commuter students can connect to campus network. Online course registration, wireless network available.

Student life. Freshman orientation: Mandatory, $55 fee. Preregistration for classes offered. Held 4 days prior to beginning of semester. **Housing:** Guaranteed on-campus for freshmen. $200 partly refundable deposit, deadline 7/15. **Activities:** Drama, student government, student-run gallery, Student Orientation staff, Emerging Leaders in the Arts, student judiciary committee, residence life staff, Moore Magazine, Business Scholars in the Arts.

Student services. Adult student services, career counseling, financial aid counseling, health services, personal counseling.

Contact. E-mail: admiss@moore.edu
Phone: (215) 965-4014 Toll-free number: (800) 523-2025
Fax: (215) 568-3547
Heeseung Lee, Director of Admissions, Moore College of Art and Design, The Parkway at 20th Street, Philadelphia, PA 19103-1179

Moravian College
Bethlehem, Pennsylvania   **CB member**
www.moravian.edu   **CB code: 2418**

◗ Private 4-year liberal arts college affiliated with Moravian Church in America
◗ Residential campus in small city
◗ 1,551 degree-seeking undergraduates: 3% part-time, 59% women, 4% African American, 2% Asian American, 9% Hispanic American
◗ 150 degree-seeking graduate students
◗ 80% of applicants admitted
◗ Application essay required
◗ 76% graduate within 6 years; 21% enter graduate study

General. Founded in 1742. Regionally accredited. Member of Lehigh Valley Association of Independent Colleges Consortium. Sixth oldest college in country. **Degrees:** 396 bachelor's awarded; master's, professional offered. **ROTC:** Army. **Location:** 60 miles from Philadelphia, 90 miles from New York City. **Calendar:** Semester, extensive summer session. **Full-time faculty:** 113 total; 88% have terminal degrees, 7% minority, 57% women. **Part-time faculty:** 79 total; 35% have terminal degrees, 4% minority, 56% women. **Class size:** 64% < 20, 35% 20-39, 1% 40-49.

Freshman class profile. 1,940 applied, 1,546 admitted, 375 enrolled.

Mid 50% test scores		
SAT critical reading:	470-580	
SAT math:	480-590	
SAT writing:	470-580	
Rank in top quarter:	49%	
Rank in top tenth:	19%	

End year in good standing:	95%
Return as sophomores:	78%
Out-of-state:	44%
Live on campus:	87%
International:	1%

Basis for selection. High school record and standardized test scores important. Academic credentials, character, extracurricular involvement, volunteer work and potential for contribution considered. SAT and SAT Subject Tests or ACT recommended. Interviews strongly recommended; audition required for music applicants; portfolio required for art applicants. **Home schooled:** Letter of recommendation (nonparent) required. Interview strongly encouraged in order to share educational background in detail.

High school preparation. College-preparatory program required. 16 units required; 18 recommended. Required and recommended units include English 4, mathematics 3-4, social studies 4, science 3 (laboratory 2) and foreign language 2-3. 4 math units recommended for business, science, or math students.

2011-2012 Annual costs. Tuition/fees: $33,446. Room/board: $9,623. Books/supplies: $1,000. Personal expenses: $1,406.

2011-2012 Financial aid. Need-based: 349 full-time freshmen applied for aid; 316 were judged to have need; 316 of these received aid. Average need met was 77%. Average scholarship/grant was $20,468; average loan $3,950. 67% of total undergraduate aid awarded as scholarships/grants, 33% as loans/jobs. **Non-need-based:** Awarded to 279 full-time undergraduates, including 75 freshmen. Scholarships awarded for academics, alumni affiliation, leadership, minority status, music/drama, religious affiliation, ROTC.

Application procedures. Admission: Closing date 3/1 (postmark date). $40 fee, may be waived for applicants with need, free for online applicants. Admission notification by 3/15. Must reply by 5/1. **Financial aid:** Priority date 2/14, closing date 3/15. FAFSA, institutional form required. Applicants notified on a rolling basis starting 4/1; must reply by 5/1 or within 2 week(s) of notification.

Academics. Learning Center offers partial but responsive program for learning disabled students. **Special study options:** Combined bachelor's/graduate degree, cooperative education, cross-registration, double major, honors, independent study, internships, student-designed major, study abroad, teacher certification program, Washington semester. Allied health program with Thomas Jefferson University, forestry program cooperative with Duke University, engineering programs cooperative with Lehigh University and Washington University (MO), dental program cooperative with Temple University. **Credit/placement by examination:** AP, CLEP, IB, SAT, ACT, institutional tests. Some courses not included in credit-by-examination option. **Support services:** Learning center, study skills assistance, tutoring, writing center.

Majors. Area/ethnic studies: German. **Biology:** General, biochemistry, neuroscience. **Business:** Accounting, business admin, international. **Computer sciences:** Computer science. **Conservation:** Environmental science, environmental studies. **Education:** Music, science, social science. **English:** Creative writing, English lit. **Foreign languages:** Classics, French, German, Spanish. **Health services:** Clinical lab science, nursing (RN). **History:** General. **Math:** General. **Philosophy/religion:** Philosophy, religion. **Physical sciences:** Chemistry, geology, physics. **Protective services:** Criminal justice. **Psychology:** General. **Social sciences:** Economics, political science, sociology. **Theology:** Sacred music. **Visual/performing arts:** Art, art history/conservation, dramatic, graphic design, music, music performance, music theory/composition, studio arts.

Most popular majors. Biology 8%, business/marketing 20%, English 7%, health sciences 13%, history 6%, psychology 9%, social sciences 12%, visual/performing arts 9%.

Computing on campus. 263 workstations in library, computer center. Dormitories wired for high-speed internet access and linked to campus network. Commuter students can connect to campus network. Online library, helpline, repair service, student web hosting, wireless network available.

Student life. Freshman orientation: Mandatory, $100 fee. Preregistration for classes offered. 3-day program held immediately prior to fall semester. **Policies:** Freshmen not permitted cars on campus. **Housing:** Guaranteed on-campus for all undergraduates. Coed dorms, single-sex dorms, special housing for disabled, apartments, fraternity/sorority housing available. $400 nonrefundable deposit, deadline 5/1. Townhouses and suites available. **Activities:** Bands, campus ministries, choral groups, dance, drama, international student organizations, literary magazine, music ensembles, Model UN, opera, radio station, student government, student newspaper, symphony orchestra, Hillel Society, Newman Association, Moravian College Christian Fellowship, Catacombs, Campus Community Connection (C3), The Forum, multicultural club, The Learning Connection, Gamma Sigma Sigma.

Athletics. NCAA. **Intercollegiate:** Baseball M, basketball, cross-country, field hockey W, football (tackle) M, golf M, soccer, softball W, tennis, track and field, volleyball W. **Intramural:** Basketball, football (non-tackle), soccer, softball, table tennis, tennis, volleyball. **Team name:** Greyhounds.

Student services. Adult student services, alcohol/substance abuse counseling, chaplain/spiritual director, career counseling, student employment services, financial aid counseling, health services, minority student services, personal counseling, placement for graduates. **Physically disabled:** Services for visually, speech, hearing impaired.

Contact. E-mail: admissions@moravian.edu
Phone: (610) 861-1320 Toll-free number: (800) 441-3191
Fax: (610) 625-7930
Erika Mondok, Director of Enrollment, Moravian College, 1200 Main Street, Bethlehem, PA 18018

Mount Aloysius College
Cresson, Pennsylvania
www.mtaloy.edu

CB member
CB code: 2420

- Private 4-year liberal arts college affiliated with Roman Catholic Church
- Residential campus in small town
- 1,493 degree-seeking undergraduates: 18% part-time, 71% women, 2% African American, 1% Hispanic American
- 53 degree-seeking graduate students
- 76% of applicants admitted
- SAT or ACT (ACT writing optional), application essay required
- 36% graduate within 6 years

General. Founded in 1939. Regionally accredited. **Degrees:** 174 bachelor's, 174 associate awarded; master's offered. **Location:** 12 miles from Altoona, 90 miles from Pittsburgh. **Calendar:** Semester, limited summer session. **Full-time faculty:** 66 total; 47% have terminal degrees, 3% minority, 67% women. **Part-time faculty:** 114 total; 8% have terminal degrees, less than 1% minority, 54% women. **Class size:** 62% < 20, 38% 20-39. **Special facilities:** Health and science center with mock operating room, telehealth/telenursing, ecumenical library.

Freshman class profile. 1,323 applied, 1,004 admitted, 373 enrolled.

Mid 50% test scores			
SAT critical reading:	410-500	GPA 3.50-3.74:	21%
SAT math:	410-500	GPA 3.0-3.49:	40%
SAT writing:	400-490	GPA 2.0-2.99:	27%
ACT composite:	17-21	Return as sophomores:	62%
GPA 3.75 or higher:	11%	Out-of-state:	5%
		Live on campus:	50%

Basis for selection. School record, test scores, activities, talent, and character most important. Application priority date for health and nursing applicants for the fall semester is June 1st. Nursing entrance test not required for students with SAT of 900 (exclusive of Writing) or higher. Placement test waived if student scores 500 or higher in either section. Interview required for students with lower SAT scores and GPA. Interviews and essays required for physical therapist assistant majors. **Learning Disabled:** Admission interview required.

High school preparation. College-preparatory program recommended. 16 units required. Required and recommended units include English 4, mathematics 3, social studies 3, history 3, science 3, foreign language 2 and academic electives 3. Algebra and 2 lab sciences required for nursing. Algebra, chemistry required for physical therapist assistant, radiography and medical imaging applicants. Biology required for occupational therapy assistant applicants.

2011-2012 Annual costs. Tuition/fees: $18,750. Room/board: $8,120. Books/supplies: $2,500. Personal expenses: $3,000.

2011-2012 Financial aid. Need-based: 362 full-time freshmen applied for aid; 315 were judged to have need; 315 of these received aid. Average need met was 30%. Average scholarship/grant was $6,000; average loan $3,700. 54% of total undergraduate aid awarded as scholarships/grants, 46% as loans/jobs. **Non-need-based:** Awarded to 112 full-time undergraduates, including 94 freshmen. Scholarships awarded for academics, art, leadership, music/drama, religious affiliation, state residency.

Application procedures. Admission: No deadline. $30 fee, may be waived for applicants with need. Admission notification on a rolling basis beginning on or about 8/1. Must reply by May 1 or within 4 week(s) if notified thereafter. **Financial aid:** Priority date 4/1; no closing date. FAFSA required. Applicants notified on a rolling basis starting 3/15; must reply within 2 week(s) of notification.

Academics. Special study options: Accelerated study, combined bachelor's/graduate degree, distance learning, double major, dual enrollment of high school students, honors, independent study, internships, student-designed major, study abroad, teacher certification program. **Credit/placement by examination:** AP, CLEP, SAT, institutional tests. 15 credit hours maximum toward associate degree, 30 toward bachelor's. **Support services:** Learning center, pre-admission summer program, reduced course load, remedial instruction, study skills assistance, tutoring, writing center.

Majors. Business: Accounting, accounting/business management, business admin. **Computer sciences:** General, information technology. **Education:** Early childhood, elementary. **English:** English lit. **Foreign languages:** Sign language interpretation. **Health services:** Nursing (RN), physician assistant, radiologic technology/medical imaging. **History:** General. **Liberal arts:** Arts/sciences, humanities. **Protective services:** Criminal justice. **Psychology:** General. **Social sciences:** General, criminology, political science.

Most popular majors. Business/marketing 19%, education 6%, health sciences 40%, liberal arts 14%, security/protective services 6%.

Computing on campus. 175 workstations in dormitories, library, computer center, student center. Dormitories linked to campus network. Helpline, repair service available.

Student life. Freshman orientation: Mandatory. Preregistration for classes offered. **Housing:** Guaranteed on-campus for all undergraduates. Coed dorms available. $125 nonrefundable deposit. **Activities:** Campus ministries, choral groups, dance, drama, student government, student newspaper, nursing, occupational therapy assistant, business, Phi Theta Kappa, student programming council.

Athletics. NCAA. **Intercollegiate:** Baseball M, basketball, cross-country, golf, soccer, softball W, volleyball W. **Intramural:** Baseball M, basketball, football (tackle), golf, skiing, soccer, softball W, table tennis, tennis, volleyball. **Team name:** Mounties.

Student services. Alcohol/substance abuse counseling, chaplain/spiritual director, career counseling, student employment services, financial aid counseling, health services, on-campus daycare, personal counseling, placement for graduates, veterans' counselor. **Physically disabled:** Services for hearing impaired.

Contact. E-mail: admissions@mtaloy.edu
Phone: (814) 886-6383 Toll-free number: (888) 823-2220
Fax: (814) 886-6441
Frank Crouse, Vice President for Enrollment Management/Dean of Admissions, Mount Aloysius College, 7373 Admiral Peary Highway, Cresson, PA 16630

Muhlenberg College
Allentown, Pennsylvania
www.muhlenberg.edu

CB member
CB code: 2424

- Private 4-year liberal arts college affiliated with Evangelical Lutheran Church in America
- Residential campus in small city
- 2,384 degree-seeking undergraduates: 4% part-time, 58% women, 3% African American, 3% Asian American, 4% Hispanic American
- 43% of applicants admitted
- Application essay required
- 86% graduate within 6 years; 30% enter graduate study

General. Founded in 1848. Regionally accredited. **Degrees:** 573 bachelor's, 1 associate awarded. **ROTC:** Army. **Location:** 55 miles from Philadelphia, 90 miles from New York City. **Calendar:** Semester, limited summer session. **Full-time faculty:** 172 total; 89% have terminal degrees, 5% minority, 50% women. **Part-time faculty:** 103 total; 23% have terminal degrees, 10% minority, 48% women. **Class size:** 62% < 20, 35% 20-39, 1% 40-49, less than 1% 50-99, less than 1% >100. **Special facilities:** 3-theater complex, electronic music studio, natural history museum, 38-acre environmental field station, greenhouse, two electron microscopes, isolation laboratories, DNA sequencer, 20-foot boat for marine studies, 60-acre arboretum.

Freshman class profile. 4,876 applied, 2,109 admitted, 584 enrolled.

Mid 50% test scores			
SAT critical reading:	560-670	GPA 2.0-2.99:	20%
SAT math:	560-670	Rank in top quarter:	78%
SAT writing:	560-670	Rank in top tenth:	51%
ACT composite:	25-31	End year in good standing:	97%
GPA 3.75 or higher:	13%	Return as sophomores:	90%
GPA 3.50-3.74:	27%	Out-of-state:	78%
GPA 3.0-3.49:	40%	Live on campus:	99%

Basis for selection. High school courses, grades, class rank, test scores, personal qualities, essay, recommendations, special talents and activities important. Interview strongly recommended. Test scores optional for admission. SAT or ACT required for merit scholarships, honors programs, and cooperative programs (i.e. 4-4 medical program, 3-4 dental program, etc.). Audition recommended for dance, drama, music programs; portfolio recommended for art program. **Home schooled:** Statement describing home school structure and mission, transcript of courses and grades, state high school equivalency certificate, letter of recommendation (nonparent) required. Interview strongly recommended.

High school preparation. College-preparatory program required. 16 units required; 20 recommended. Required and recommended units include English 4, mathematics 3-4, social studies 2, history 2, science 2-3 (laboratory 2-3), foreign language 2-4 and academic electives 1-3. Advanced placement and accelerated courses encouraged.

2011-2012 Annual costs. Tuition/fees: $39,915. Room/board: $9,040.

2011-2012 Financial aid. Need-based: 413 full-time freshmen applied for aid; 293 were judged to have need; 287 of these received aid. Average need met was 94%. Average scholarship/grant was $23,395; average loan $4,111. 80% of total undergraduate aid awarded as scholarships/grants, 20% as loans/jobs. **Non-need-based:** Awarded to 925 full-time undergraduates, including 275 freshmen. Scholarships awarded for academics, art, leadership, music/drama, ROTC.

Application procedures. Admission: Closing date 2/15 (postmark date). $50 fee, may be waived for applicants with need. Admission notification by 3/15. Must reply by 5/1. **Financial aid:** Closing date 2/15. FAFSA, institutional form, CSS PROFILE required. Applicants notified by 3/20; must reply by 5/1.

Academics. Special study options: Accelerated study, combined bachelor's/graduate degree, cross-registration, double major, exchange student, honors, independent study, internships, student-designed major, study abroad, teacher certification program, Washington semester. Study abroad with Lehigh Valley Association of Independent Colleges; over 60 agreements with foreign universities for study abroad; 3-2 or 4-2 combined Degree Program in Engineering with Columbia University or Washington University. MC/Penn Dental Program-University of Pennsylvania. Combined program with Drexel University College of Medicine. 7-year Optometry Program-State University of New York 3-2 or 4-2. Combined Degree Program in Environmental Science or Forestry. **Credit/placement by examination:** AP, CLEP, IB, SAT, ACT, institutional tests. 68 credit hours maximum toward bachelor's degree. 68 credit hours equivalent to 17 course units. **Support services:** Learning center, reduced course load, study skills assistance, tutoring, writing center.

Majors. Area/ethnic studies: American, German, Russian/Slavic. **Biology:** General, biochemistry, neuroscience. **Business:** Accounting, business admin, finance, human resources, management information systems. **Communications:** Communications/speech/rhetoric. **Computer sciences:** General. **Conservation:** Environmental science. **English:** English lit. **Foreign languages:** General, French, German, Spanish. **History:** General. **Math:** General. **Philosophy/religion:** Philosophy, religion. **Physical sciences:** General, chemistry, physics. **Psychology:** General. **Social sciences:** Anthropology, economics, international relations, political science, sociology. **Visual/performing arts:** Art, dance, dramatic, film/cinema/video, music.

Most popular majors. Biology 8%, business/marketing 25%, communications/journalism 9%, psychology 11%, social sciences 11%, visual/performing arts 14%.

Computing on campus. 490 workstations in dormitories, library, computer center, student center. Dormitories wired for high-speed internet access and linked to campus network. Commuter students can connect to campus network. Online course registration, helpline, repair service, wireless network available.

Student life. Freshman orientation: Mandatory, $120 fee. Preregistration for classes offered. 3-day program prior to start of classes in August. **Policies:** Students share responsibility for maintaining high standards and must pledge to abide by Academic Behavior Code. Freshmen not permitted cars on campus. **Housing:** Guaranteed on-campus for all undergraduates. Coed dorms, single-sex dorms, special housing for disabled, apartments, fraternity/sorority housing, wellness housing available. $400 partly refundable deposit, deadline 5/1. College-owned houses in neighborhood surrounding campus. **Activities:** Bands, campus ministries, choral groups, dance, drama, film society, international student organizations, literary magazine, music ensembles, musical theater, radio station, student government, student newspaper, symphony orchestra, TV station, over 100 clubs and organizations.

Athletics. NCAA. **Intercollegiate:** Baseball M, basketball, cheerleading, cross-country, field hockey W, football (tackle) M, golf, lacrosse, soccer, softball W, tennis, track and field, volleyball W, wrestling M. **Intramural:** Basketball, cross-country, football (non-tackle) M, racquetball, soccer, softball, swimming, tennis, volleyball. **Team name:** Mules.

Student services. Adult student services, alcohol/substance abuse counseling, chaplain/spiritual director, career counseling, student employment services, financial aid counseling, health services, minority student services, personal counseling, placement for graduates, women's services. **Physically disabled:** Services for visually, speech, hearing impaired.

Contact. E-mail: admissions@muhlenberg.edu
Phone: (484) 664-3200 Fax: (484) 664-3234
Christopher Hooker-Haring, Dean of Admission and Financial Aid, Muhlenberg College, 2400 Chew Street, Allentown, PA 18104

Neumann University
Aston, Pennsylvania
www.neumann.edu

CB member
CB code: 2628

- Private 4-year university affiliated with Roman Catholic Church
- Residential campus in large town
- 2,531 degree-seeking undergraduates: 17% African American, 1% Asian American, 3% Hispanic American, 1% international
- 399 degree-seeking graduate students
- 90% of applicants admitted
- SAT or ACT (ACT writing optional) required
- 55% graduate within 6 years; 19% enter graduate study

General. Founded in 1965. Regionally accredited. Franciscan studies institute. **Degrees:** 444 bachelor's, 13 associate awarded; master's, professional, doctoral offered. **ROTC:** Army. **Location:** 19 miles from Philadelphia. **Calendar:** Semester, limited summer session. **Full-time faculty:** 97 total. **Part-time faculty:** 224 total. **Class size:** 49% < 20, 49% 20-39, less than 1% 40-49, 1% 50-99, less than 1% >100. **Special facilities:** Betty Neumann archives.

Freshman class profile. 2,660 applied, 2,401 admitted, 575 enrolled.

Mid 50% test scores			
SAT critical reading:	400-490	GPA 2.0-2.99:	53%
SAT math:	400-490	End year in good standing:	85%
GPA 3.75 or higher:	1%	Return as sophomores:	73%
GPA 3.50-3.74:	14%	Out-of-state:	8%
GPA 3.0-3.49:	32%	Live on campus:	28%

Basis for selection. Acceptance depends on major applied for, SAT scores and high school GPA. Interview recommended. **Home schooled:** State high school equivalency certificate required.

High school preparation. College-preparatory program recommended. 16 units required; 17 recommended. Required and recommended units include English 4, mathematics 2, social studies 2, science 2-3, foreign language 2 and academic electives 4.

2011-2012 Annual costs. Tuition/fees: $23,350. Room/board: $10,644. Books/supplies: $1,500. Personal expenses: $2,000.

Financial aid. All financial aid based on need.

Application procedures. Admission: No deadline. $40 fee, may be waived for applicants with need, free for online applicants. Admission notification on a rolling basis beginning on or about 9/15. Must reply by May 1 or within 2 week(s) if notified thereafter. **Financial aid:** No deadline. FAFSA required. Applicants notified on a rolling basis; must reply within 2 week(s) of notification.

Academics. Special study options: Accelerated study, combined bachelor's/graduate degree, cooperative education, distance learning, double major, exchange student, honors, independent study, internships, liberal arts/career combination, study abroad, teacher certification program, weekend college. **Credit/placement by examination:** AP, CLEP, SAT, ACT, institutional tests. 15 credit hours maximum toward associate degree, 30 toward bachelor's. **Support services:** Learning center, pre-admission summer program, reduced course load, remedial instruction, study skills assistance, tutoring, writing center.

Majors. Biology: General. **Business:** Accounting, business admin, human resources, international, marketing, organizational behavior. **Communications:** General. **Computer sciences:** General. **Conservation:** Environmental studies. **Education:** Early childhood, elementary. **English:** English lit. **Liberal arts:** Arts/sciences. **Parks/recreation:** Sports admin. **Protective services:** Criminal justice. **Psychology:** General. **Social sciences:** Political science. **Visual/performing arts:** Dramatic.

Most popular majors. Business/marketing 15%, education 12%, health sciences 15%, liberal arts 18%, parks/recreation 7%, psychology 9%, security/protective services 7%.

Computing on campus. 400 workstations in dormitories, library, computer center. Dormitories wired for high-speed internet access and linked to campus network. Commuter students can connect to campus network. Online library, helpline, wireless network available.

Student life. Freshman orientation: Mandatory. Preregistration for classes offered. Held the last weekend before classes begin. **Policies:** Alcohol-free campus. **Housing:** Guaranteed on-campus for all undergraduates. Coed dorms, special housing for disabled, apartments available. $200 nonrefundable deposit, deadline 8/1. **Activities:** Bands, campus ministries, choral groups, dance, drama, literary magazine, music ensembles, musical theater, radio station, student government, student newspaper, symphony orchestra, TV station, Black student union, environmental club, bio/sci club, business association, professional education society, student nurses association, psychology club.

Athletics. NCAA. **Intercollegiate:** Baseball M, basketball, cross-country, field hockey W, golf M, ice hockey, lacrosse, soccer, softball W, tennis, track and field, volleyball W. **Intramural:** Basketball, lacrosse M, soccer, softball W, table tennis, tennis, volleyball. **Team name:** Knights.

Student services. Adult student services, alcohol/substance abuse counseling, chaplain/spiritual director, career counseling, services for economically disadvantaged, student employment services, financial aid counseling, health services, on-campus daycare, personal counseling, placement for graduates.

Contact. E-mail: neumann@neumann.edu
Phone: (610) 558-5616 Toll-free number: (800) 963-8626
Fax: (610) 558-5652
Dennis Murphy, Vice President for Enrollment Management, Neumann University, Office of Admissions, Aston, PA 19014-1298

Peirce College
Philadelphia, Pennsylvania
www.peirce.edu

CB member
CB code: 2674

- Private 4-year business and technical college
- Commuter campus in very large city
- 2,267 degree-seeking undergraduates: 68% part-time, 72% women, 65% African American, 1% Asian American, 6% Hispanic American
- 78% graduate within 6 years; 17% enter graduate study

General. Founded in 1865. Regionally accredited. **Degrees:** 275 bachelor's, 157 associate awarded. **Calendar:** Semester, limited summer session. **Full-time faculty:** 36 total; 58% have terminal degrees, 36% minority, 58% women. **Part-time faculty:** 122 total; 22% have terminal degrees, 27% minority, 46% women. **Class size:** 77% < 20, 23% 20-39.

Freshman class profile.

End year in good standing:	46%	Out-of-state:	8%

Basis for selection. Open admission, but selective for some programs. Official high school transcript or copy of GED scores, cumulative GPA of 2.0 or higher, and minimum of 30 transferable credits required for Business Administration with a concentration in Professional Studies for Bachelor of Science degree program. Nonmatriculated students may take up to 15 credits while waiting for official transcripts and other documents to be evaluated.

2011-2012 Annual costs. Tuition/fees: $15,900.

2010-2011 Financial aid. Need-based: 16 full-time freshmen applied for aid; 16 were judged to have need; 16 of these received aid. Average need met was 33%. Average scholarship/grant was $7,127; average loan $3,716. 29% of total undergraduate aid awarded as scholarships/grants, 71% as loans/jobs. **Non-need-based:** Scholarships awarded for academics, alumni affiliation, leadership. **Additional information:** Tuition discounts available for US students serving in US military and in protect-and-serve fields.

Application procedures. Admission: No deadline. $50 fee, may be waived for applicants with need. Admission notification on a rolling basis. **Financial aid:** Priority date 5/1; no closing date. FAFSA required. Applicants notified on a rolling basis starting 5/1.

Academics. Through the Walker Center for Academic Excellence, students are able to participate in workshops on campus or online. In addition, students can participate in tutoring services on campus, via telephone or online through Smarthinking. **Special study options:** Accelerated study, cooperative education, distance learning, internships. **Credit/placement by examination:** AP,

CLEP, institutional tests. 30 credit hours maximum toward associate degree, 90 toward bachelor's. **Support services:** Learning center, study skills assistance, tutoring.

Majors. Business: Accounting, business admin, human resources. **Computer sciences:** Information technology. **Health services:** Health care admin, medical records admin.

Most popular majors. Business/marketing 58%, computer/information sciences 18%, legal studies 24%.

Computing on campus. PC or laptop required. 44 workstations in library, student center. Commuter students can connect to campus network. Online course registration, online library, helpline, repair service, wireless network available.

Student life. Freshman orientation: Mandatory, $565 fee. Preregistration for classes offered. 3-credit orientation course for students with less than 15 college credits; the cost is the same as a regular college course. **Activities:** Chi Alpha Epsilon Honor Society, Delta Mu Delta Honor Society, Lambda Epsilon Chi Honor Society, paralegal student association, information technology student association, health program student association, Students for Free Enterprise and student leadership program.

Student services. Adult student services, career counseling, services for economically disadvantaged, student employment services, financial aid counseling, health services. **Physically disabled:** Services for visually, hearing impaired.

Contact. E-mail: info@peirce.edu
Phone: (215) 670-9214 Toll-free number: (888) 467-3472 ext. 9214
Fax: (215) 670-9366
Nadine Maher, Dean of Enrollment Management, Peirce College, 1420 Pine Street, Philadelphia, PA 19102-4699

Penn State Abington
Abington, Pennsylvania
www.abington.psu.edu

CB code: 2660

- Public 4-year branch campus college
- Commuter campus in small city
- 3,033 degree-seeking undergraduates: 12% part-time, 47% women, 15% African American, 15% Asian American, 8% Hispanic American, 2% international
- 78% of applicants admitted
- SAT or ACT with writing required
- 44% graduate within 6 years

General. Founded in 1950. Regionally accredited. Certain bachelor degree programs must be completed at another Penn State campus. **Degrees:** 384 bachelor's, 38 associate awarded. **ROTC:** Army, Air Force. **Location:** 15 miles from Philadelphia. **Calendar:** Semester, limited summer session. **Full-time faculty:** 109 total; 66% have terminal degrees, 12% minority, 48% women. **Part-time faculty:** 121 total; 26% have terminal degrees, 12% minority, 48% women. **Class size:** 34% < 20, 55% 20-39, 5% 40-49, 4% 50-99, 1% >100.

Freshman class profile. 3,363 applied, 2,629 admitted, 811 enrolled.

Mid 50% test scores			
SAT critical reading:	410-520	GPA 2.0-2.99:	43%
SAT math:	420-550	Rank in top quarter:	28%
SAT writing:	400-510	Rank in top tenth:	10%
GPA 3.75 or higher:	8%	Return as sophomores:	74%
GPA 3.50-3.74:	11%	Out-of-state:	9%
GPA 3.0-3.49:	37%	International:	3%

Basis for selection. Admission decisions based upon high school GPA, standardized test scores, class rank, personal statements, activities. Essay considered if submitted; portfolios required for select majors. **Home schooled:** Provide complete documentation showing courses studied and all evaluations presented from home school evaluator or supervisor assigned to student in cooperation with local school district or evaluator approved through program.

High school preparation. College-preparatory program recommended. Required units include English 4, mathematics 3, social studies 3, science 3 and foreign language 2.

2011-2012 Annual costs. Tuition/fees: $13,102; $19,542 out-of-state. Books/supplies: $1,536. Personal expenses: $1,854.

2010-2011 Financial aid. Need-based: 734 full-time freshmen applied for aid; 606 were judged to have need; 593 of these received aid. Average need met was 62%. Average scholarship/grant was $7,256; average loan $3,358. 48% of total undergraduate aid awarded as scholarships/grants, 52% as loans/jobs. **Non-need-based:** Awarded to 554 full-time undergraduates, including 312 freshmen. Scholarships awarded for academics, alumni affiliation, ROTC.

Application procedures. Admission: Priority date 11/30; no deadline. $50 fee, may be waived for applicants with need. Admission notification on a rolling basis beginning on or about 11/1. All freshmen applications processed at University Park Campus. **Financial aid:** Priority date 2/15; no closing date. FAFSA required. Applicants notified on a rolling basis.

Academics. Special study options: Accelerated study, combined bachelor's/graduate degree, cooperative education, distance learning, double major, dual enrollment of high school students, ESL, exchange student, external degree, honors, independent study, internships, liberal arts/career combination, student-designed major, study abroad, teacher certification program, weekend college. **Credit/placement by examination:** AP, CLEP, IB, SAT. 60 credit hours maximum toward bachelor's degree. **Support services:** Learning center, pre-admission summer program, remedial instruction, study skills assistance, tutoring, writing center.

Majors. Area/ethnic studies: African-American, American, Asian, Latin American, women's. **Biology:** General, bacteriology, biochemistry, toxicology. **Business:** General, accounting, actuarial science, communications, finance, labor relations, management information systems, marketing, organizational behavior. **Communications:** Advertising, communications/speech/rhetoric, journalism. **Computer sciences:** General, information systems. **Conservation:** General, environmental studies, forest sciences, forest technology. **Education:** Adult ed admin, agricultural, art, elementary, foreign languages, secondary, special ed. **Engineering:** Aerospace, agricultural, architectural, biomedical, chemical, civil, computer, electrical, engineering science, environmental, industrial, mechanical, mining, nuclear, petroleum. **English:** English lit. **Foreign languages:** Chinese, classics, comparative lit, French, German, Italian, Japanese, Russian, Spanish. **General:** Agribusiness operations, animal sciences, food science, horticultural science, landscaping, mechanization, plant protection, turf management. **Health services:** Athletic training, communication disorders, health care admin, nursing (RN), premedicine, preveterinary. **History:** General. **Liberal arts:** Arts/sciences. **Math:** General, statistics. **Parks/recreation:** Exercise sciences, facilities management. **Philosophy/religion:** Judaic, philosophy, religion. **Physical sciences:** Astronomy, atmospheric science, chemistry, geology, materials science, physics. **Protective services:** Criminal justice, forensics, law enforcement admin. **Psychology:** General, social. **Social sciences:** Anthropology, archaeology, economics, geography, international relations, political science, sociology. **Visual/performing arts:** General, acting, art, art history/conservation, film/cinema/video, graphic design, music, theater design. **Work/family studies:** Family studies, human nutrition.

Most popular majors. Business/marketing 37%, English 7%, psychology 23%, security/protective services 12%.

Computing on campus. 150 workstations in library, computer center. Commuter students can connect to campus network. Online course registration, online library, helpline, repair service, student web hosting, wireless network available.

Student life. Freshman orientation: Mandatory, $30 fee. Preregistration for classes offered. 3-part process before classes start: one-day orientation, advising appointment, and new student day. **Policies:** Acts of intolerance and high-risk drinking discouraged at all locations. All facilities designated smoke-free. Students expected to abide by The Penn State Principles. **Activities:** Campus ministries, choral groups, dance, drama, film society, literary magazine, student government, student newspaper, Christian Fellowship, Asian club, Black student union, Hillel, lesbian and gay alliance, Latino student association, Italian American organization, Muslim student association, Praise and Worship gospel association.

Athletics. USCAA. **Intercollegiate:** Baseball M, basketball, golf, lacrosse, soccer, softball, tennis, volleyball W. **Intramural:** Basketball, cross-country, football (non-tackle) M, handball, soccer, softball, tennis, volleyball. **Team name:** Nittany Lions.

Student services. Adult student services, alcohol/substance abuse counseling, career counseling, services for economically disadvantaged, student employment services, financial aid counseling, health services, minority student services, personal counseling, placement for graduates, veterans' counselor. **Physically disabled:** Services for visually, speech, hearing impaired.

Contact. E-mail: abingtonadmissions@psu.edu
Phone: (215) 881-7600 Fax: (215) 881-7655
Anne Rohrbach, Executive Director for Undergraduate Admissions, Penn State Abington, 106 Sutherland, Abingdon, PA 19001-3990

Penn State Altoona
Altoona, Pennsylvania
www.aa.psu.edu **CB code: 2660**

- Public 4-year branch campus college
- Residential campus in small city
- 4,016 degree-seeking undergraduates: 4% part-time, 47% women, 7% African American, 2% Asian American, 4% Hispanic American, 1% international
- 84% of applicants admitted
- SAT or ACT with writing required
- 65% graduate within 6 years

General. Founded in 1929. Regionally accredited. Certain bachelor degree programs must be completed at another Penn State campus. **Degrees:** 329 bachelor's, 89 associate awarded. **ROTC:** Army, Air Force. **Location:** 2 miles from downtown. **Calendar:** Semester, limited summer session. **Full-time faculty:** 173 total; 72% have terminal degrees, 9% minority, 44% women. **Part-time faculty:** 126 total; 22% have terminal degrees, 3% minority, 47% women. **Class size:** 40% < 20, 46% 20-39, 5% 40-49, 9% 50-99, less than 1% >100. **Special facilities:** MAC lab, CAD lab, robotics lab, manufacturing lab, automation lab, environmental studies lab, comprehensive art studio space.

Freshman class profile. 6,083 applied, 5,138 admitted, 1,585 enrolled.

Mid 50% test scores			
SAT critical reading:	440-540	GPA 2.0-2.99:	46%
SAT math:	460-560	Rank in top quarter:	27%
SAT writing:	440-530	Rank in top tenth:	6%
GPA 3.75 or higher:	4%	Return as sophomores:	86%
GPA 3.50-3.74:	9%	Out-of-state:	24%
GPA 3.0-3.49:	41%	International:	1%

Basis for selection. Admission decisions based upon high school GPA, test scores, class rank, personal statements, and activities. Essay considered if submitted; portfolios required for select majors. **Home schooled:** Provide complete documentation showing courses studied and all evaluations presented from home school evaluator or supervisor assigned to student in cooperation with local school district or evaluator approved through program.

High school preparation. College-preparatory program recommended. Required units include English 4, mathematics 3, social studies 3, science 3 and foreign language 2.

2011-2012 Annual costs. Tuition/fees: $13,636; $20,408 out-of-state. Room/board: $9,420. Books/supplies: $1,536. Personal expenses: $3,222.

2010-2011 Financial aid. Need-based: 1,222 full-time freshmen applied for aid; 999 were judged to have need; 957 of these received aid. Average need met was 60%. Average scholarship/grant was $5,979; average loan $3,360. 38% of total undergraduate aid awarded as scholarships/grants, 62% as loans/jobs. **Non-need-based:** Awarded to 955 full-time undergraduates, including 360 freshmen. Scholarships awarded for academics, alumni affiliation, ROTC.

Application procedures. Admission: Priority date 11/30; no deadline. $50 fee, may be waived for applicants with need. Admission notification on a rolling basis beginning on or about 11/1. All freshmen applications processed at University Park Campus. **Financial aid:** Priority date 2/15; no closing date. FAFSA required. Applicants notified on a rolling basis.

Academics. Special study options: Accelerated study, cooperative education, cross-registration, distance learning, double major, dual enrollment of high school students, ESL, exchange student, honors, independent study, internships, liberal arts/career combination, student-designed major, study abroad, teacher certification program, weekend college. **Credit/placement by examination:** AP, CLEP, IB, SAT. 60 credit hours maximum toward bachelor's degree. **Support services:** Learning center, remedial instruction, study skills assistance, tutoring, writing center.

Majors. Area/ethnic studies: African-American, Asian, Latin American, women's. **Biology:** General, bacteriology, biochemistry, toxicology. **Business:** General, accounting, actuarial science, finance, labor relations, management information systems, marketing, organizational behavior. **Communications:** Advertising, communications/speech/rhetoric, journalism. **Computer sciences:** General, information systems, security. **Conservation:** General, environmental studies, forest sciences, forest technology. **Education:** Adult ed admin, agricultural, art, elementary, foreign languages, secondary, special ed. **Engineering:** Aerospace, agricultural, architectural, biomedical, chemical, civil, computer, electrical, engineering science, environmental, industrial, mechanical, mining, nuclear, petroleum. **English:** English lit. **Foreign languages:** Chinese, classics, comparative lit, French, German, Italian, Japanese, Russian, Spanish. **General:** Agribusiness operations, animal sciences, food

science, horticultural science, landscaping, mechanization, plant protection, turf management. **Health services:** Athletic training, communication disorders, health care admin, nursing (RN), premedicine, preveterinary. **History:** General. **Liberal arts:** Arts/sciences. **Math:** General, statistics. **Parks/recreation:** Exercise sciences, facilities management. **Philosophy/religion:** Judaic, philosophy, religion. **Physical sciences:** Astronomy, atmospheric science, chemistry, geology, materials science, physics. **Protective services:** Criminal justice, forensics, law enforcement admin. **Psychology:** General. **Social sciences:** Anthropology, archaeology, economics, geography, international relations, political science, sociology. **Visual/performing arts:** General, acting, art, art history/conservation, film/cinema/video, graphic design, music, theater design. **Work/family studies:** Family studies, human nutrition.

Most popular majors. Business/marketing 18%, communications/journalism 8%, education 8%, engineering/engineering technologies 9%, family/consumer sciences 8%, health sciences 9%, psychology 6%, security/protective services 13%.

Computing on campus. 450 workstations in dormitories, library, computer center. Dormitories wired for high-speed internet access and linked to campus network. Commuter students can connect to campus network. Online course registration, online library, helpline, student web hosting, wireless network available.

Student life. Freshman orientation: Mandatory. Preregistration for classes offered. Begins Saturday prior to start of classes and runs 2 weeks. **Policies:** Acts of intolerance and high-risk drinking discouraged at all locations. All facilities designated as smoke-free. **Housing:** Coed dorms, special housing for disabled, wellness housing available. $100 partly refundable deposit, deadline 5/1. Suites, special interest housing available. **Activities:** Bands, campus ministries, choral groups, dance, drama, film society, international student organizations, literary magazine, music ensembles, student government, student newspaper, Black student union, Circle K, Latin American student association, Catholic campus community, Students About Living Truth, Jewish student association, Asian student association, German club, Eco-Action, Being United for Social Transformation.

Athletics. NCAA. Intercollegiate: Baseball M, basketball, cross-country, diving, golf, soccer, softball W, swimming, tennis, volleyball W. **Intramural:** Badminton, basketball, football (non-tackle), football (tackle), racquetball, soccer, softball, table tennis, track and field, triathlon, volleyball, weight lifting. **Team name:** Nittany Lions.

Student services. Adult student services, alcohol/substance abuse counseling, chaplain/spiritual director, career counseling, services for economically disadvantaged, student employment services, financial aid counseling, health services, minority student services, personal counseling, placement for graduates, veterans' counselor, women's services. **Physically disabled:** Services for visually, speech, hearing impaired.

Contact. E-mail: aaadmit@psu.edu
Phone: (814) 949-5466 Toll-free number: (800) 848-9843
Fax: (814) 949-5564
Anne Rohrbach, Executive Director of Undergraduate Admissions, Penn State Altoona, E108 Smith Building, Altoona, PA 16801-3760

Penn State Beaver
Monaca, Pennsylvania
www.br.psu.edu   **CB code: 2660**

♦ Public 4-year branch campus college
♦ Residential campus in small town
♦ 724 degree-seeking undergraduates: 5% part-time, 45% women, 11% African American, 2% Asian American, 4% Hispanic American, 1% international
♦ 86% of applicants admitted
♦ SAT or ACT with writing required
♦ 47% graduate within 6 years

General. Founded in 1964. Regionally accredited. Certain bachelor degree programs must be completed at another Penn State campus. **Degrees:** 66 bachelor's, 5 associate awarded; master's offered. **Location:** 30 miles from Pittsburgh. **Calendar:** Semester, limited summer session. **Full-time faculty:** 34 total; 65% have terminal degrees, 21% minority, 53% women. **Part-time faculty:** 27 total; 22% have terminal degrees, 48% women. **Class size:** 50% < 20, 44% 20-39, 4% 40-49, 2% 50-99.

Freshman class profile. 737 applied, 637 admitted, 251 enrolled.

Mid 50% test scores		
SAT critical reading:	420-520	
SAT math:	410-550	
SAT writing:	400-520	
GPA 3.75 or higher:	5%	
GPA 3.50-3.74:	6%	
GPA 3.0-3.49:	32%	

GPA 2.0-2.99:	57%
Rank in top quarter:	27%
Rank in top tenth:	7%
Return as sophomores:	71%
Out-of-state:	13%
International:	2%

Basis for selection. Admission decisions based upon high school GPA as well as other factors, including standardized verbal and math test scores, class rank, personal statements, activities lists. Essay considered if submitted; portfolios required for select majors. **Home schooled:** Helpful if applicants provide complete documentation showing courses studied and all evaluations from home school evaluator or supervisor assigned to student in cooperation with local school district or evaluator approved through program.

High school preparation. College-preparatory program recommended. Required units include English 4, mathematics 3, social studies 3, science 3 and foreign language 2.

2011-2012 Annual costs. Tuition/fees: $13,102; $19,542 out-of-state. Room/board: $9,420. Books/supplies: $1,536. Personal expenses: $3,222.

2010-2011 Financial aid. Need-based: 249 full-time freshmen applied for aid; 216 were judged to have need; 215 of these received aid. Average need met was 66%. Average scholarship/grant was $6,582; average loan $3,258. 47% of total undergraduate aid awarded as scholarships/grants, 53% as loans/jobs. **Non-need-based:** Awarded to 224 full-time undergraduates, including 117 freshmen. Scholarships awarded for academics, alumni affiliation, ROTC.

Application procedures. Admission: Priority date 11/30; no deadline. $50 fee, may be waived for applicants with need. Admission notification on a rolling basis beginning on or about 11/1. All freshmen applications processed at University Park Campus. **Financial aid:** Priority date 2/15; no closing date. FAFSA required. Applicants notified on a rolling basis.

Academics. Special study options: Cross-registration, distance learning, double major, dual enrollment of high school students, ESL, honors, independent study, internships, semester at sea, study abroad. **Credit/placement by examination:** AP, CLEP, IB, SAT. 60 credit hours maximum toward bachelor's degree. **Support services:** Learning center, pre-admission summer program, reduced course load, remedial instruction, study skills assistance, tutoring, writing center.

Majors. Area/ethnic studies: African-American, Asian, Latin American, women's. **Biology:** General, bacteriology, biochemistry, toxicology. **Business:** Accounting, actuarial science, business admin, finance, labor relations, management information systems, marketing, organizational behavior. **Communications:** Advertising, communications/speech/rhetoric, journalism. **Computer sciences:** General, information systems. **Conservation:** General, environmental studies, forest sciences, forest technology. **Education:** Adult ed admin, agricultural, art, elementary, foreign languages, secondary, special ed. **Engineering:** Aerospace, agricultural, architectural, biomedical, chemical, civil, computer, electrical, engineering science, environmental, industrial, mechanical, mining, nuclear, petroleum. **English:** English lit. **Foreign languages:** Chinese, classics, comparative lit, French, German, Italian, Japanese, Russian, Spanish. **General:** Agribusiness operations, animal sciences, food science, horticultural science, landscaping, mechanization, plant protection, turf management. **Health services:** Athletic training, communication disorders, health care admin, nursing (RN), premedicine, preveterinary. **History:** General. **Liberal arts:** Arts/sciences. **Math:** General, statistics. **Parks/recreation:** Exercise sciences, facilities management. **Philosophy/religion:** Judaic, philosophy, religion. **Physical sciences:** Astronomy, atmospheric science, chemistry, geology, materials science, physics. **Protective services:** Criminal justice, forensics, law enforcement admin. **Psychology:** General. **Social sciences:** Anthropology, archaeology, economics, geography, international relations, political science, sociology. **Visual/performing arts:** General, acting, art, art history/conservation, film/cinema/video, graphic design, music, theater design. **Work/family studies:** Family studies, human nutrition.

Most popular majors. Business/marketing 55%, communications/journalism 20%, psychology 26%.

Computing on campus. 127 workstations in library, computer center, student center. Dormitories wired for high-speed internet access and linked to campus network. Commuter students can connect to campus network. Online course registration, online library, helpline, repair service, student web hosting, wireless network available.

Student life. Freshman orientation: Mandatory, $30 fee. Preregistration for classes offered. One-day orientation session just before classes begin. **Policies:** Acts of intolerance and high-risk drinking discouraged at all locations. All facilities designated as smoke-free. **Housing:** Coed dorms, special housing for disabled available. $100 partly refundable deposit, deadline 5/1. Townhouses available. **Activities:** Campus ministries, choral groups, drama,

literary magazine, radio station, student government, student newspaper, Common Ground Christian club, Big Brothers/Big Sisters.

Athletics. USCAA. **Intercollegiate:** Baseball M, basketball, soccer M, softball W, volleyball W. **Intramural:** Basketball, bowling, football (non-tackle), table tennis, volleyball. **Team name:** Nittany Lions.

Student services. Adult student services, alcohol/substance abuse counseling, chaplain/spiritual director, career counseling, services for economically disadvantaged, student employment services, financial aid counseling, health services, personal counseling, placement for graduates, veterans' counselor. **Physically disabled:** Services for visually, speech, hearing impaired.

Contact. E-mail: br-admissions@psu.edu
Phone: (724) 773-3800 Toll-free number: (877) 564-6778
Fax: (724) 773-3658
Anne Rohrbach, Executive Director for Undergraduate Admissions, Penn State Beaver, 100 University Drive, Monaca, PA 15061-2799

Penn State Berks
Reading, Pennsylvania
www.bk.psu.edu   CB code: 2660

- Public 4-year branch campus college
- Residential campus in small city
- 2,666 degree-seeking undergraduates: 7% part-time, 44% women, 8% African American, 4% Asian American, 8% Hispanic American, 1% international
- 82% of applicants admitted
- SAT or ACT with writing required
- 55% graduate within 6 years

General. Founded in 1924. Regionally accredited. Certain bachelor degree programs must be completed at another Penn State campus. **Degrees:** 224 bachelor's, 56 associate awarded. **ROTC:** Army. **Location:** 5 miles from downtown. **Calendar:** Semester, limited summer session. **Full-time faculty:** 118 total; 65% have terminal degrees, 12% minority, 51% women. **Part-time faculty:** 99 total; 11% have terminal degrees, 4% minority, 52% women. **Class size:** 39% < 20, 44% 20-39, 8% 40-49, 10% 50-99.

Freshman class profile. 2,788 applied, 2,280 admitted, 855 enrolled.

Mid 50% test scores			
SAT critical reading:	430-530	Rank in top quarter:	25%
SAT math:	440-560	Rank in top tenth:	5%
SAT writing:	420-520	Return as sophomores:	79%
GPA 3.75 or higher:	4%	Out-of-state:	12%
GPA 3.50-3.74:	7%	International:	2%
GPA 3.0-3.49:	37%		
GPA 2.0-2.99:	50%		

Basis for selection. Admission decisions based upon high school GPA, test scores, class rank, personal statements, and activities. Essay considered if submitted; portfolios required for select majors. **Home schooled:** Complete documentation showing courses studied and all evaluations presented from home school evaluator or supervisor assigned to student in cooperation with local school district or evaluator approved through program required.

High school preparation. College-preparatory program recommended. Required units include English 4, mathematics 3, social studies 3, science 3 and foreign language 2.

2011-2012 Annual costs. Tuition/fees: $13,636; $20,408 out-of-state. Room/board: $10,250. Books/supplies: $1,536. Personal expenses: $3,222.

2010-2011 Financial aid. Need-based: 769 full-time freshmen applied for aid; 609 were judged to have need; 587 of these received aid. Average need met was 56%. Average scholarship/grant was $6,131; average loan $3,353. 39% of total undergraduate aid awarded as scholarships/grants, 61% as loans/jobs. **Non-need-based:** Awarded to 395 full-time undergraduates, including 171 freshmen. Scholarships awarded for academics, alumni affiliation, ROTC.

Application procedures. Admission: Priority date 11/30; no deadline. $50 fee, may be waived for applicants with need. Admission notification on a rolling basis beginning on or about 11/1. All freshmen applications processed at University Park Campus. **Financial aid:** Priority date 2/15; no closing date. FAFSA required. Applicants notified on a rolling basis.

Academics. Special study options: Accelerated study, cooperative education, cross-registration, distance learning, dual enrollment of high school students, ESL, honors, independent study, internships, study abroad, teacher certification program. **Credit/placement by examination:** AP, CLEP, IB, SAT. 60 credit hours maximum toward bachelor's degree. **Support services:**

Learning center, pre-admission summer program, remedial instruction, study skills assistance, tutoring, writing center.

Majors. Area/ethnic studies: African-American, American, Asian, Latin American, women's. **Biology:** General, bacteriology, biochemistry, toxicology. **Business:** General, accounting, actuarial science, finance, human resources, labor relations, management information systems, marketing, organizational behavior. **Communications:** Advertising, communications/speech/rhetoric, journalism. **Computer sciences:** General, information systems, security. **Conservation:** General, environmental studies, forest sciences, forest technology. **Education:** Adult ed admin, agricultural, art, elementary, foreign languages, secondary, special ed. **Engineering:** Aerospace, agricultural, architectural, biomedical, chemical, civil, computer, electrical, engineering science, environmental, industrial, mechanical, mining, nuclear, petroleum. **English:** English lit, technical writing. **Foreign languages:** General, Chinese, classics, comparative lit, French, German, Italian, Japanese, Russian, Spanish. **General:** Agribusiness operations, animal sciences, food science, horticultural science, landscaping, mechanization, plant protection, turf management. **Health services:** Athletic training, communication disorders, health care admin, nursing (RN), premedicine, preveterinary. **History:** General. **Liberal arts:** Arts/sciences. **Math:** General, statistics. **Parks/recreation:** Exercise sciences, facilities management. **Philosophy/religion:** Judaic, philosophy, religion. **Physical sciences:** Astronomy, atmospheric science, chemistry, geology, materials science, physics. **Protective services:** Forensics, law enforcement admin. **Psychology:** General. **Social sciences:** Anthropology, archaeology, economics, geography, international relations, political science, sociology. **Visual/performing arts:** General, acting, art, art history/conservation, film/cinema/video, graphic design, music, theater design. **Work/family studies:** Family studies, human nutrition.

Most popular majors. Biology 6%, business/marketing 26%, communications/journalism 9%, education 16%, engineering/engineering technologies 9%, interdisciplinary studies 6%, parks/recreation 13%, psychology 6%.

Computing on campus. 311 workstations in dormitories, library, computer center, student center. Dormitories wired for high-speed internet access and linked to campus network. Commuter students can connect to campus network. Online course registration, online library, helpline, repair service, student web hosting, wireless network available.

Student life. Freshman orientation: Mandatory. Preregistration for classes offered. Week prior to the start of classes. **Policies:** All facilities smoke-free. **Housing:** Coed dorms, special housing for disabled available. $100 partly refundable deposit, deadline 5/1. Honor students, suites, special interest houses available. **Activities:** Choral groups, dance, drama, film society, literary magazine, radio station, student government, student newspaper, Christian fellowship, Dimensions-the Ethnic Society, multicultural dance group, Substance Free, Rainbow Alliance, political science club, Spiritual Praise Choir, yoga and meditation society.

Athletics. NCAA. **Intercollegiate:** Baseball M, basketball, cross-country, golf M, soccer, softball W, tennis, volleyball W. **Intramural:** Badminton, basketball, football (non-tackle), golf, table tennis, volleyball. **Team name:** NIttany Lions.

Student services. Adult student services, alcohol/substance abuse counseling, career counseling, services for economically disadvantaged, student employment services, financial aid counseling, health services, minority student services, personal counseling, placement for graduates, veterans' counselor. **Physically disabled:** Services for visually, speech, hearing impaired.

Contact. E-mail: admissionsbk@psu.edu
Phone: (610) 396-6060 Fax: (610) 396-6077
Anne Rohrbach, Executive Director for Undergraduate Admissions, Penn State Berks, Tulpehocken Road, Reading, PA 19610-6009

Penn State Brandywine
Media, Pennsylvania
www.brandywine.psu.edu   CB code: 2660

- Public 4-year branch campus college
- Commuter campus in small town
- 1,438 degree-seeking undergraduates: 11% part-time, 43% women, 11% African American, 8% Asian American, 4% Hispanic American, 1% international
- 83% of applicants admitted
- SAT or ACT with writing required
- 37% graduate within 6 years

General. Founded in 1966. Regionally accredited. Certain bachelor degree programs must be completed at another Penn State campus. **Degrees:** 174 bachelor's, 1 associate awarded. **ROTC:** Army, Air Force. **Location:** 20

miles from Philadelphia. **Calendar:** Semester, limited summer session. **Full-time faculty:** 56 total; 70% have terminal degrees, 11% minority, 57% women. **Part-time faculty:** 72 total; 26% have terminal degrees, 8% minority, 58% women. **Class size:** 42% < 20, 52% 20-39, 4% 40-49, 2% 50-99, less than 1% >100.

Freshman class profile. 1,260 applied, 1,050 admitted, 402 enrolled.

Mid 50% test scores		GPA 3.0-3.49:	24%
SAT critical reading:	420-530	GPA 2.0-2.99:	60%
SAT math:	440-550	Rank in top quarter:	19%
SAT writing:	410-510	Rank in top tenth:	3%
GPA 3.75 or higher:	6%	Return as sophomores:	72%
GPA 3.50-3.74:	8%	Out-of-state:	7%

Basis for selection. Admission decisions based on high school GPA, as well as other factors, which may include standardized verbal and math test scores, class rank, personal statements, and list of activities. Essay considered if submitted; portfolios required for select majors. **Home schooled:** Applicants should provide complete documentation showing courses studied and all evaluations presented from evaluator or supervisor assigned to student in cooperation with local school district or evaluator approved through program.

High school preparation. College-preparatory program recommended. Required units include English 4, mathematics 3, social studies 3, science 3 and foreign language 2.

2011-2012 Annual costs. Tuition/fees: $13,102; $19,542 out-of-state. Books/supplies: $1,536. Personal expenses: $1,854.

2010-2011 Financial aid. Need-based: 335 full-time freshmen applied for aid; 247 were judged to have need; 241 of these received aid. Average need met was 61%. Average scholarship/grant was $6,407; average loan $3,170. 45% of total undergraduate aid awarded as scholarships/grants, 55% as loans/jobs. **Non-need-based:** Awarded to 359 full-time undergraduates, including 160 freshmen. Scholarships awarded for academics, alumni affiliation, ROTC.

Application procedures. Admission: Priority date 11/30; no deadline. $50 fee, may be waived for applicants with need. Admission notification on a rolling basis beginning on or about 11/1. All freshmen applications processed at University Park Campus. **Financial aid:** Priority date 2/15; no closing date. FAFSA required. Applicants notified on a rolling basis.

Academics. Special study options: Combined bachelor's/graduate degree, distance learning, double major, dual enrollment of high school students, ESL, honors, independent study, internships, study abroad, teacher certification program. **Credit/placement by examination:** AP, CLEP, IB, SAT. 60 credit hours maximum toward bachelor's degree. **Support services:** Learning center, pre-admission summer program, reduced course load, remedial instruction, study skills assistance, tutoring, writing center.

Majors. Area/ethnic studies: African-American, American, Asian, Latin American, women's. **Biology:** General, bacteriology, biochemistry, toxicology. **Business:** Accounting, actuarial science, business admin, finance, labor relations, management information systems, marketing, organizational behavior. **Communications:** Advertising, communications/speech/rhetoric, journalism. **Computer sciences:** General, information systems. **Conservation:** General, environmental studies, forest sciences, forest technology. **Education:** Adult ed admin; agricultural, art, elementary, foreign languages, secondary, special ed. **Engineering:** Aerospace, agricultural, architectural, biomedical, chemical, civil, computer, electrical, engineering science, environmental, industrial, mechanical, mining, nuclear, petroleum. **English:** English lit. **Foreign languages:** Chinese, classics, comparative lit, French, German, Italian, Japanese, Russian, Spanish. **General:** Agribusiness operations, animal sciences, food science, horticultural science, landscaping, mechanization, plant protection, turf management. **Health services:** Athletic training, communication disorders, health care admin, nursing (RN), premedicine, preveterinary. **History:** General. **Liberal arts:** Arts/sciences. **Math:** General, statistics. **Parks/recreation:** Exercise sciences, facilities management. **Philosophy/religion:** Judaic, philosophy, religion. **Physical sciences:** Astronomy, atmospheric science, chemistry, geology, materials science, physics. **Protective services:** Forensics, law enforcement admin. **Psychology:** General. **Social sciences:** Anthropology, archaeology, economics, geography, international relations, political science, sociology. **Visual/performing arts:** General, acting, art, art history/conservation, film/cinema/video, graphic design, music, theater design. **Work/family studies:** Family studies, human nutrition.

Most popular majors. Area/ethnic studies 11%, business/marketing 30%, communications/journalism 25%, family/consumer sciences 26%.

Computing on campus. 142 workstations in library, computer center, student center. Commuter students can connect to campus network. Online course registration, online library, helpline, repair service, student web hosting, wireless network available.

Student life. Freshman orientation: Available. Preregistration for classes offered. Held in summer, prior to fall semester. **Policies:** Acts of intolerance

and high-risk drinking discouraged at all locations. All facilities designated smoke-free. **Activities:** Choral groups, dance, film society, literary magazine, student government, student newspaper, Black Student League, Nittany Christian Fellowship, Gay-Straight Alliance, gospel ensemble, Jewish Student League.

Athletics. USCAA. **Intercollegiate:** Baseball M, basketball, soccer, tennis, volleyball W. **Intramural:** Basketball, soccer. **Team name:** Nittany Lions.

Student services. Adult student services, alcohol/substance abuse counseling, career counseling, services for economically disadvantaged, student employment services, financial aid counseling, health services, minority student services, personal counseling, placement for graduates, veterans' counselor, women's services. **Physically disabled:** Services for visually, speech, hearing impaired.

Contact. E-mail: bwadmissions@psu.edu
Phone: (610) 892-1200 Fax: (610) 892-1320
Anne Rohrbach, Executive Director for Undergraduate Admissions, Penn State Brandywine, 25 Yearsley Mill Road, Media, PA 19063-5596

Penn State DuBois
DuBois, Pennsylvania
www.ds.psu.edu   **CB code: 2660**

- Public 4-year branch campus college
- Commuter campus in small town
- 641 degree-seeking undergraduates: 13% part-time, 49% women, 2% African American, 1% Asian American, 2% Hispanic American
- 88% of applicants admitted
- SAT or ACT with writing required
- 60% graduate within 6 years

General. Founded in 1935. Regionally accredited. Certain bachelor degree programs must be completed at another Penn State campus. We also offer additional certificates in the following areas: family literacy, wellness leadership, addiction studies, health policy and administration, project management communication, communication and leadership, digital arts, and writing instruction specialist. **Degrees:** 50 bachelor's, 132 associate awarded; master's offered. **Location:** 120 miles from Pittsburgh. **Calendar:** Semester, limited summer session. **Full-time faculty:** 46 total; 65% have terminal degrees, 15% minority, 52% women. **Part-time faculty:** 30 total; 17% have terminal degrees, 43% women. **Class size:** 63% < 20, 33% 20-39, 2% 40-49, 2% 50-99, less than 1% >100.

Freshman class profile. 433 applied, 379 admitted, 165 enrolled.

Mid 50% test scores		GPA 3.0-3.49:	36%
SAT critical reading:	410-510	GPA 2.0-2.99:	54%
SAT math:	420-540	Rank in top quarter:	19%
SAT writing:	390-480	Rank in top tenth:	3%
GPA 3.75 or higher:	2%	Return as sophomores:	74%
GPA 3.50-3.74:	5%	Out-of-state:	4%

Basis for selection. Admission decisions based upon high school GPA, as well as other factors, which may include standardized verbal and math test scores, class rank, personal statements, and list of activities. Essay considered if submitted; portfolios required for select majors. **Home schooled:** Applicants should provide complete documentation showing the courses studied and all evaluations presented from evaluator or supervisor assigned to student in cooperation with local school district or evaluator who is approved through the program.

High school preparation. College-preparatory program recommended. Required units include English 4, mathematics 3, social studies 3, science 3 and foreign language 2.

2011-2012 Annual costs. Tuition/fees: $12,994; $19,434 out-of-state. Books/supplies: $1,536. Personal expenses: $1,854.

2010-2011 Financial aid. Need-based: 194 full-time freshmen applied for aid; 177 were judged to have need; 175 of these received aid. Average need met was 62%. Average scholarship/grant was $6,275; average loan $3,235. 51% of total undergraduate aid awarded as scholarships/grants, 49% as loans/jobs. **Non-need-based:** Awarded to 224 full-time undergraduates, including 79 freshmen. Scholarships awarded for academics, alumni affiliation, ROTC.

Application procedures. Admission: Priority date 11/30; no deadline. $50 fee, may be waived for applicants with need. Admission notification on a rolling basis beginning on or about 11/1. All freshmen applications processed at University Park Campus. **Financial aid:** Priority date 2/15; no closing date. FAFSA required. Applicants notified on a rolling basis.

Academics. **Special study options:** Accelerated study, cross-registration, distance learning, double major, dual enrollment of high school students, honors, independent study, internships, student-designed major, study abroad. **Credit/placement by examination:** AP, CLEP, IB, SAT. 60 credit hours maximum toward bachelor's degree. **Support services:** Learning center, reduced course load, remedial instruction, study skills assistance, tutoring, writing center.

Majors. **Area/ethnic studies:** African-American, Asian, Latin American, women's. **Biology:** General, bacteriology, biochemistry, toxicology. **Business:** Accounting, actuarial science, business admin, finance, labor relations, management information systems, marketing, organizational behavior. **Communications:** Advertising, communications/speech/rhetoric, journalism. **Computer sciences:** General, information systems. **Conservation:** General, environmental studies, forest sciences, forest technology. **Education:** Adult ed admin, agricultural, art, elementary, foreign languages, secondary, special ed. **Engineering:** General, aerospace, agricultural, architectural, biomedical, chemical, civil, computer, electrical, engineering science, environmental, industrial, mechanical, mining, nuclear, petroleum. **English:** English lit. **Foreign languages:** Chinese, classics, comparative lit, French, German, Italian, Japanese, Russian, Spanish. **General:** Agribusiness operations, animal sciences, food science, horticultural science, landscaping, mechanization, plant protection, turf management. **Health services:** Athletic training, communication disorders, health care admin, nursing (RN), premedicine, preveterinary. **History:** General. **Liberal arts:** Arts/sciences. **Math:** General, statistics. **Parks/recreation:** Exercise sciences, facilities management. **Philosophy/religion:** Judaic, philosophy, religion. **Physical sciences:** Astronomy, atmospheric science, chemistry, geology, materials science, physics. **Protective services:** Forensics, law enforcement admin. **Psychology:** General. **Social sciences:** Anthropology, archaeology, economics, geography, international relations, political science, sociology. **Visual/performing arts:** General, acting, art, art history/conservation, film/cinema/video, graphic design, music, theater design. **Work/family studies:** Family studies, human nutrition.

Most popular majors. Business/marketing 38%, family/consumer sciences 40%, liberal arts 22%.

Computing on campus. 212 workstations in computer center, student center. Commuter students can connect to campus network. Online course registration, online library, helpline, repair service, student web hosting available.

Student life. **Freshman orientation:** Available. Preregistration for classes offered. Both fall and spring orientations available. **Policies:** Acts of intolerance and high risk drinking discouraged at all locations. All facilities designated smoke free. Students expected to abide by The Penn State Principles. **Housing:** Independently owned housing nearby. **Activities:** Choral groups, drama, film society, literary magazine, student government, student newspaper, diversity club, women's liaison committee, veterans club, adult learner student organization, environmental conservation and outing club, Campus Crusade for Christ, world cultures club.

Athletics. USCAA. **Intercollegiate:** Basketball M, cross-country, volleyball W. **Intramural:** Basketball, table tennis, volleyball. **Team name:** Nittany Lions.

Student services. Adult student services, alcohol/substance abuse counseling, career counseling, services for economically disadvantaged, student employment services, financial aid counseling, health services, personal counseling, placement for graduates, veterans' counselor, women's services. **Physically disabled:** Services for visually, speech, hearing impaired.

Contact. E-mail: duboisinfo@psu.edu
Phone: (814) 375-4720 Toll-free number: (800) 346-7627
Fax: (814) 375-4784
Anne Rohrbach, Executive Director for Undergraduate Admissions, Penn State DuBois, Enrollment Services House, DuBois, PA 15801-3199

Penn State Erie, The Behrend College
Erie, Pennsylvania
www.erie.psu.edu   CB code: 2660

- Public 4-year branch campus college
- Residential campus in small city
- 3,940 degree-seeking undergraduates: 5% part-time, 36% women, 3% African American, 2% Asian American, 3% Hispanic American, 2% international
- 91 degree-seeking graduate students
- 83% of applicants admitted
- SAT or ACT with writing required
- 66% graduate within 6 years

General. Founded in 1926. Regionally accredited. **Degrees:** 754 bachelor's, 63 associate awarded; master's offered. **ROTC:** Army. **Calendar:** Semester, limited summer session. **Full-time faculty:** 232 total; 63% have terminal degrees, 10% minority, 36% women. **Part-time faculty:** 70 total; 13% have terminal degrees, 6% minority, 41% women. **Class size:** 33% < 20, 43% 20-39, 19% 40-49, 4% 50-99, 1% >100. **Special facilities:** Observatory, natural area for science field trips and experimentation, hiking trails, cross-country skiing.

Freshman class profile. 3,367 applied, 2,778 admitted, 1,082 enrolled.

Mid 50% test scores			
SAT critical reading:	460-560	GPA 2.0-2.99:	31%
SAT math:	490-610	Rank in top quarter:	43%
SAT writing:	440-550	Rank in top tenth:	15%
GPA 3.75 or higher:	9%	Return as sophomores:	82%
GPA 3.50-3.74:	17%	Out-of-state:	13%
GPA 3.0-3.49:	43%	International:	3%

Basis for selection. Admission decisions based on high school GPA, standardized test scores, class rank, personal statements, and activities. Essay considered if submitted; portfolios required for select majors. **Home schooled:** Complete documentation helpful, showing courses studied and all evaluations presented from home school evaluator, supervisor assigned to student in cooperation with local school district, or evaluator approved through program.

High school preparation. College-preparatory program recommended. Required units include English 4, mathematics 3, social studies 3, science 3 and foreign language 2.

2011-2012 Annual costs. Tuition/fees: $13,636; $20,408 out-of-state. Room/board: $9,420. Books/supplies: $1,536. Personal expenses: $3,222.

2010-2011 Financial aid. **Need-based:** 891 full-time freshmen applied for aid; 755 were judged to have need; 737 of these received aid. Average need met was 60%. Average scholarship/grant was $6,208; average loan $3,384. 38% of total undergraduate aid awarded as scholarships/grants, 62% as loans/jobs. **Non-need-based:** Awarded to 879 full-time undergraduates, including 241 freshmen. Scholarships awarded for academics, alumni affiliation, ROTC.

Application procedures. **Admission:** Priority date 11/30; no deadline. $50 fee, may be waived for applicants with need. Admission notification on a rolling basis beginning on or about 11/1. All freshmen applications processed at University Park Campus. **Financial aid:** Priority date 2/15; no closing date. FAFSA required. Applicants notified on a rolling basis.

Academics. **Special study options:** Accelerated study, combined bachelor's/graduate degree, cooperative education, distance learning, double major, dual enrollment of high school students, honors, independent study, internships, liberal arts/career combination, semester at sea, study abroad, teacher certification program. **Credit/placement by examination:** AP, CLEP, IB, SAT, institutional tests. 60 credit hours maximum toward bachelor's degree. **Support services:** Learning center, pre-admission summer program, remedial instruction, study skills assistance, tutoring, writing center.

Majors. **Area/ethnic studies:** African-American, Asian, Latin American, women's. **Biology:** General, bacteriology, biochemistry, toxicology. **Business:** Accounting, actuarial science, business admin, finance, international, labor relations, management information systems, managerial economics, marketing, organizational behavior. **Communications:** Advertising, communications/speech/rhetoric, journalism. **Computer sciences:** General, computer science, information systems. **Conservation:** General, environmental studies, forest sciences, forest technology. **Education:** Adult ed admin, agricultural, art, elementary, foreign languages, secondary, special ed. **Engineering:** Aerospace, agricultural, architectural, biomedical, chemical, civil, computer, electrical, engineering science, environmental, industrial, mechanical, mining, nuclear, petroleum, polymer, software. **English:** Creative writing, English lit. **Foreign languages:** Chinese, classics, comparative lit, French, German, Italian, Japanese, Russian, Spanish. **General:** Agribusiness operations, animal sciences, food science, horticultural science, landscaping, mechanization, plant protection, turf management. **Health services:** Athletic training, communication disorders, health care admin, nursing (RN), premedicine, preveterinary. **History:** General. **Liberal arts:** Arts/sciences. **Math:** General, statistics. **Parks/recreation:** Exercise sciences, facilities management. **Philosophy/religion:** Judaic, philosophy, religion. **Physical sciences:** General, astronomy, atmospheric science, chemistry, geology, materials science, physics. **Protective services:** Forensics, law enforcement admin. **Psychology:** General. **Social sciences:** Anthropology, archaeology, economics, geography, international relations, political science, sociology. **Visual/performing arts:** General, acting, art, art history/conservation, film/cinema/video, graphic design, music, theater design. **Work/family studies:** Family studies, human nutrition.

Most popular majors. Biology 7%, business/marketing 37%, engineering/engineering technologies 25%, psychology 7%.

Computing on campus. 778 workstations in dormitories, library, computer center, student center. Dormitories wired for high-speed internet access and linked to campus network. Commuter students can connect to campus network. Online course registration, online library, helpline, repair service, student web hosting, wireless network available.

Student life. Freshman orientation: Mandatory. Preregistration for classes offered. Held during the 3 days before start of classes. **Policies:** Acts of intolerance and high-risk drinking discouraged at all locations. All facilities designated as smoke-free. **Housing:** Coed dorms, single-sex dorms, special housing for disabled, apartments available. $100 partly refundable deposit, deadline 5/1. Suites, special interest housing available. **Activities:** Bands, campus ministries, choral groups, dance, drama, film society, international student organizations, literary magazine, music ensembles, radio station, student government, student newspaper, Asian student organization, Association of Black Collegians, National Society of Black Engineers, human relations programming council, multicultural council, Irish American society, Women Today, College Republicans, InterVarsity Christian fellowship, gospel choir.

Athletics. NCAA. **Intercollegiate:** Baseball M, basketball, cross-country, golf, soccer, softball W, swimming, tennis, track and field, volleyball, water polo. **Intramural:** Badminton, basketball, bowling, football (non-tackle), golf, soccer, softball, swimming, table tennis, track and field, triathlon, volleyball. **Team name:** Behrend Lions.

Student services. Adult student services, alcohol/substance abuse counseling, chaplain/spiritual director, career counseling, services for economically disadvantaged, student employment services, financial aid counseling, health services, minority student services, on-campus daycare, personal counseling, placement for graduates, veterans' counselor, women's services. **Physically disabled:** Services for visually, speech, hearing impaired.

Contact. E-mail: behrend.admissions@psu.edu
Phone: (814) 898-6100 Toll-free number: (866) 374-3378
Fax: (814) 898-6044
Anne Rohrbach, Executive Director for Undergraduate Admissions, Penn State Erie, The Behrend College, 4701 College Drive, Erie, PA 16563-0105

Penn State Fayette, The Eberly Campus
Uniontown, Pennsylvania
www.fe.psu.edu   CB code: 2660

▸ Public 4-year branch campus college
▸ Commuter campus in large town
▸ 889 degree-seeking undergraduates: 16% part-time, 58% women, 5% African American, 1% Asian American, 1% Hispanic American, 1% international
▸ 90% of applicants admitted
▸ SAT or ACT with writing required
▸ 42% graduate within 6 years

General. Founded in 1934. Regionally accredited. Certain bachelor degree programs must be completed at another Penn State campus. **Degrees:** 85 bachelor's, 107 associate awarded. **ROTC:** Army. **Location:** 40 miles from Pittsburgh. **Calendar:** Semester, limited summer session. **Full-time faculty:** 55 total; 47% have terminal degrees, 6% minority, 42% women. **Part-time faculty:** 35 total; 26% have terminal degrees, 3% minority, 46% women. **Class size:** 54% < 20, 44% 20-39, 2% 40-49, less than 1% 50-99.

Freshman class profile. 555 applied, 497 admitted, 232 enrolled.

Mid 50% test scores			
SAT critical reading:	390-500	GPA 2.0-2.99:	46%
SAT math:	400-530	Rank in top quarter:	30%
SAT writing:	380-490	Rank in top tenth:	11%
GPA 3.75 or higher:	5%	Return as sophomores:	74%
GPA 3.50-3.74:	12%	Out-of-state:	7%
GPA 3.0-3.49:	36%	International:	1%

Basis for selection. Admission decisions based on high school GPA, as well as other factors, which may include standardized verbal and math test scores, class rank, personal statements, and activities lists. Essay considered if submitted; portfolios required for select majors. **Home schooled:** Complete documentation helpful, showing courses studied and all evaluations presented from home school evaluator, supervisor assigned to student in cooperation with local school district, or evaluator approved through program. **Learning Disabled:** Contact or visit the Office for Disability Services in junior or senior year of high school.

High school preparation. College-preparatory program recommended. Required units include English 4, mathematics 3, social studies 3, science 3 and foreign language 2.

2011-2012 Annual costs. Tuition/fees: $13,040; $19,480 out-of-state. Books/supplies: $1,536. Personal expenses: $1,854.

2010-2011 Financial aid. Need-based: 229 full-time freshmen applied for aid; 200 were judged to have need; 199 of these received aid. Average need met was 65%. Average scholarship/grant was $6,453; average loan $3,413. 45% of total undergraduate aid awarded as scholarships/grants, 55% as loans/jobs. **Non-need-based:** Awarded to 222 full-time undergraduates, including 84 freshmen. Scholarships awarded for academics, alumni affiliation, ROTC.

Application procedures. Admission: Priority date 11/30; no deadline. $50 fee, may be waived for applicants with need. Admission notification on a rolling basis beginning on or about 11/1. All freshmen applications processed at University Park Campus. **Financial aid:** Priority date 2/15; no closing date. FAFSA required. Applicants notified on a rolling basis.

Academics. Special study options: Accelerated study, cross-registration, distance learning, double major, dual enrollment of high school students, honors, independent study, internships, student-designed major, study abroad, weekend college. **Credit/placement by examination:** AP, CLEP, IB, SAT. 60 credit hours maximum toward bachelor's degree. **Support services:** Learning center, remedial instruction, study skills assistance, tutoring, writing center.

Majors. Area/ethnic studies: African-American, Asian, Latin American, women's. **Biology:** General, bacteriology, biochemistry, toxicology. **Business:** Accounting, actuarial science, business admin, finance, labor relations, management information systems, marketing, organizational behavior. **Communications:** Advertising, communications/speech/rhetoric, journalism. **Computer sciences:** General, information systems. **Conservation:** General, environmental studies, forest sciences, forest technology. **Education:** Adult ed admin, agricultural, art, elementary, foreign languages, secondary, special ed. **Engineering:** Aerospace, agricultural, architectural, biomedical, chemical, civil, computer, electrical, engineering science, environmental, industrial, mechanical, mining, nuclear, petroleum. **English:** English lit. **Foreign languages:** Chinese, classics, comparative lit, French, German, Italian, Japanese, Russian, Spanish. **General:** Agribusiness operations, animal sciences, food science, horticultural science, landscaping, mechanization, plant protection, turf management. **Health services:** Athletic training, communication disorders, health care admin, nursing (RN), premedicine, preveterinary. **History:** General. **Liberal arts:** Arts/sciences. **Math:** General, statistics. **Parks/recreation:** Exercise sciences, facilities management. **Philosophy/religion:** Judaic, philosophy, religion. **Physical sciences:** Astronomy, atmospheric science, chemistry, geology, materials science, physics. **Protective services:** Criminal justice, forensics, law enforcement admin. **Psychology:** General. **Social sciences:** Anthropology, archaeology, economics, geography, international relations, political science, sociology. **Visual/performing arts:** General, acting, art, art history/conservation, film/cinema/video, graphic design, music, theater design. **Work/family studies:** Family studies, human nutrition.

Most popular majors. Business/marketing 19%, family/consumer sciences 12%, health sciences 39%, security/protective services 11%.

Computing on campus. 196 workstations in library, computer center, student center. Commuter students can connect to campus network. Online course registration, online library, helpline, repair service, student web hosting available.

Student life. Freshman orientation: Available. Preregistration for classes offered. **Policies:** Acts of intolerance and high-risk drinking discouraged at all locations. All facilities designated smoke-free. **Housing:** Privately owned, off-campus housing available. **Activities:** Choral groups, drama, literary magazine, musical theater, student government, student newspaper, adult student organization, humanities society, Christian club, minority students association, Women in Science Engineering and Technology, Students Against Destructive Decisions.

Athletics. USCAA. **Intercollegiate:** Baseball M, basketball, golf M, softball W, volleyball W. **Intramural:** Basketball, football (non-tackle), racquetball, softball, tennis. **Team name:** Nittany Lions.

Student services. Adult student services, alcohol/substance abuse counseling, career counseling, services for economically disadvantaged, student employment services, financial aid counseling, health services, on-campus daycare, personal counseling, placement for graduates, veterans' counselor. **Physically disabled:** Services for visually, speech, hearing impaired.

Contact. E-mail: feadm@psu.edu
Phone: (724) 430-4130 Toll-free number: (877) 568-4130
Fax: (724) 430-4175
Anne Rohrbach, Executive Director for Undergraduate Admissions, Penn State Fayette, The Eberly Campus, PO Box 519, Route 119 North, Uniontown, PA 15401-0519

Penn State Greater Allegheny
McKeesport, Pennsylvania
www.ga.psu.edu

▶ Public 4-year branch campus college

▶ Residential campus in large town

▶ 647 degree-seeking undergraduates: 7% part-time, 47% women, 29% African American, 2% Asian American, 3% Hispanic American, 3% international

▶ 81% of applicants admitted

▶ SAT or ACT with writing required

▶ 47% graduate within 6 years

General. Founded in 1947. Regionally accredited. Certain bachelor degree programs must be completed at another Penn State campus. **Degrees:** 49 bachelor's, 3 associate awarded; master's offered. **Location:** 15 miles from Pittsburgh. **Calendar:** Semester, limited summer session. **Full-time faculty:** 36 total; 75% have terminal degrees, 22% minority, 50% women. **Part-time faculty:** 33 total; 15% have terminal degrees, 9% minority, 46% women. **Class size:** 58% < 20, 39% 20-39, 3% 40-49. **Special facilities:** Computer-based lab science equipment, special computer labs for systems integration and networking.

Freshman class profile. 719 applied, 583 admitted, 234 enrolled.

Mid 50% test scores			
SAT critical reading:	380-500	GPA 2.0-2.99:	60%
SAT math:	380-530	Rank in top quarter:	30%
SAT writing:	370-490	Rank in top tenth:	8%
GPA 3.75 or higher:	2%	Return as sophomores:	70%
GPA 3.50-3.74:	7%	Out-of-state:	14%
GPA 3.0-3.49:	28%	International:	3%

Basis for selection. Admission decisions based upon high school GPA, as well as other factors, which may include standardized verbal and math test scores, class rank, personal statements, and list of activities. Essay considered if submitted; portfolios required for select majors. **Home schooled:** Complete documentation showing the courses studied and all evaluations presented from evaluator or supervisor assigned to student in cooperation with local school district or evaluator who is approved through the program.

High school preparation. College-preparatory program recommended. Required units include English 4, mathematics 3, social studies 3, science 3 and foreign language 2.

2011-2012 Annual costs. Tuition/fees: $13,102; $19,542 out-of-state. Room/board: $9,420. Books/supplies: $1,536. Personal expenses: $3,222.

2010-2011 Financial aid. Need-based: 260 full-time freshmen applied for aid; 240 were judged to have need; 240 of these received aid. Average need met was 70%. Average scholarship/grant was $8,066; average loan $3,277. 53% of total undergraduate aid awarded as scholarships/grants, 47% as loans/jobs. **Non-need-based:** Awarded to 262 full-time undergraduates, including 155 freshmen. Scholarships awarded for academics, alumni affiliation, ROTC.

Application procedures. Admission: Priority date 11/30; no deadline. $50 fee, may be waived for applicants with need. Admission notification on a rolling basis beginning on or about 11/1. **Financial aid:** Priority date 2/15; no closing date. FAFSA required. Applicants notified on a rolling basis.

Academics. Special study options: Cross-registration, distance learning, double major, dual enrollment of high school students, ESL, honors, independent study, internships, liberal arts/career combination, student-designed major, study abroad. **Credit/placement by examination:** AP, CLEP, IB, SAT. 60 credit hours maximum toward bachelor's degree. **Support services:** Learning center, pre-admission summer program, reduced course load, remedial instruction, study skills assistance, tutoring, writing center.

Majors. Area/ethnic studies: African-American, Asian, Latin American, women's. **Biology:** General, bacteriology, biochemistry, toxicology. **Business:** Accounting, actuarial science, business admin, finance, labor relations, management information systems, marketing, organizational behavior. **Communications:** Advertising, communications/speech/rhetoric, journalism. **Computer sciences:** General, information systems. **Conservation:** General, environmental studies, forest sciences, forest technology. **Education:** Adult ed admin, adult/continuing, agricultural, art, elementary, foreign languages, secondary, special ed. **Engineering:** Aerospace, agricultural, architectural, biomedical, chemical, civil, computer, electrical, engineering science, environmental, industrial, mechanical, mining, nuclear, petroleum. **English:** English lit. **Foreign languages:** Chinese, classics, comparative lit, French, German, Italian, Japanese, Russian, Spanish. **General:** Agribusiness operations, animal sciences, food science, horticultural science, landscaping, mechanization, plant protection, turf management. **Health services:** Athletic training, communication disorders, health care admin, nursing (RN), premedicine,

preveterinary. **History:** General. **Liberal arts:** Arts/sciences. **Math:** General, statistics. **Parks/recreation:** Exercise sciences, facilities management. **Philosophy/religion:** Judaic, philosophy, religion. **Physical sciences:** Astronomy, atmospheric science, chemistry, geology, materials science, physics. **Protective services:** Forensics, law enforcement admin. **Psychology:** General. **Social sciences:** Anthropology, archaeology, economics, geography, international relations, political science, sociology. **Visual/performing arts:** General, acting, art, art history/conservation, film/cinema/video, graphic design, music, theater design. **Work/family studies:** Family studies, human nutrition.

Most popular majors. Business/marketing 39%, communications/journalism 16%, liberal arts 6%, psychology 37%.

Computing on campus. 203 workstations in dormitories, library, computer center, student center. Dormitories wired for high-speed internet access and linked to campus network. Commuter students can connect to campus network. Online course registration, online library, helpline, student web hosting, wireless network available.

Student life. Freshman orientation: Mandatory. Preregistration for classes offered. Orientation held prior to start of semester. **Policies:** Acts of intolerance and high-risk drinking discouraged at all locations. All facilities designated as smoke-free. Students expected to abide by The Penn State Principles. **Housing:** Coed dorms, special housing for disabled, wellness housing available. $100 partly refundable deposit, deadline 5/1. **Activities:** Campus ministries, choral groups, dance, drama, literary magazine, music ensembles, radio station, student government, student newspaper, TV station, Black student union, Christian fellowship, gospel choir, Spanish club, multicultural organization.

Athletics. USCAA. **Intercollegiate:** Baseball M, basketball, golf, soccer M, softball W, volleyball W. **Intramural:** Basketball, football (non-tackle), soccer, softball, volleyball.

Student services. Adult student services, alcohol/substance abuse counseling, chaplain/spiritual director, career counseling, services for economically disadvantaged, student employment services, financial aid counseling, health services, minority student services, personal counseling, placement for graduates, veterans' counselor, women's services. **Physically disabled:** Services for visually, speech, hearing impaired.

Contact. E-mail: psuga@psu.edu
Phone: (412) 675-9010 Toll-free number: (800) 248-5466
Fax: (412) 675-9046
Anne Rohrbach, Executive Director for Undergraduate Admissions, Penn State Greater Allegheny, 101 Frable Building, McKeesport, PA 15132-7698

Penn State Harrisburg
Middletown, Pennsylvania
www.hbg.psu.edu   CB code: 2660

▶ Public 4-year branch campus college

▶ Residential campus in small town

▶ 3,008 degree-seeking undergraduates: 13% part-time, 44% women, 10% African American, 7% Asian American, 6% Hispanic American, 3% international

▶ 1,024 degree-seeking graduate students

▶ 79% of applicants admitted

▶ SAT or ACT with writing required

▶ 63% graduate within 6 years

General. Founded in 1966. Regionally accredited. Certain bachelor degree programs must be completed at another Penn State campus. **Degrees:** 546 bachelor's, 7 associate awarded; master's, doctoral offered. **ROTC:** Army. **Location:** 8 miles from Harrisburg. **Calendar:** Semester, limited summer session. **Full-time faculty:** 206 total; 86% have terminal degrees, 19% minority, 39% women. **Part-time faculty:** 115 total; 25% have terminal degrees, 5% minority, 45% women. **Class size:** 45% < 20, 50% 20-39, 3% 40-49, 2% 50-99. **Special facilities:** Black cultural arts center, humanities gallery, American studies archives.

Freshman class profile. 2,482 applied, 1,964 admitted, 543 enrolled.

Mid 50% test scores			
SAT critical reading:	440-560	GPA 2.0-2.99:	38%
SAT math:	470-590	Rank in top quarter:	37%
SAT writing:	430-540	Rank in top tenth:	9%
GPA 3.75 or higher:	5%	Return as sophomores:	44%
GPA 3.50-3.74:	8%	Out-of-state:	27%
GPA 3.0-3.49:	49%	International:	6%

Basis for selection. Admissions based on secondary school record and standardized test scores.

High school preparation. College-preparatory program recommended. Required units include English 4, mathematics 3, social studies 3, science 3 and foreign language 2.

2011-2012 Annual costs. Tuition/fees: $13,628; $20,400 out-of-state. Room/board: $10,690. Books/supplies: $1,536. Personal expenses: $3,222.

2010-2011 Financial aid. Need-based: 429 full-time freshmen applied for aid; 348 were judged to have need; 337 of these received aid. Average need met was 59%. Average scholarship/grant was $6,495; average loan $3,423. 39% of total undergraduate aid awarded as scholarships/grants, 61% as loans/jobs. **Non-need-based:** Awarded to 490 full-time undergraduates, including 127 freshmen. Scholarships awarded for academics, alumni affiliation, ROTC.

Application procedures. Admission: Priority date 11/30; no deadline. $50 fee, may be waived for applicants with need. Admission notification on a rolling basis beginning on or about 11/1. All freshmen applications processed at University Park Campus. **Financial aid:** Priority date 2/15; no closing date. FAFSA required. Applicants notified on a rolling basis.

Academics. Special study options: Cooperative education, cross-registration, distance learning, double major, dual enrollment of high school students, honors, independent study, internships, student-designed major, study abroad, teacher certification program. **Credit/placement by examination:** AP, CLEP, IB, SAT. 60 credit hours maximum toward bachelor's degree. **Support services:** Learning center, study skills assistance, tutoring, writing center.

Majors. Area/ethnic studies: American. **Business:** Business admin, finance, international, management information systems, marketing, organizational behavior. **Communications:** Communications/speech/rhetoric. **Computer sciences:** General, information systems. **Education:** Elementary, social studies. **Engineering:** Civil, electrical, environmental, mechanical, structural. **English:** English lit. **Health services:** Nursing (RN). **Human services:** Public policy. **Liberal arts:** Arts/sciences, humanities. **Math:** Applied. **Protective services:** Criminal justice. **Psychology:** General. **Social sciences:** Sociology. **Work/family studies:** Family studies.

Most popular majors. Business/marketing 34%, communications/journalism 7%, engineering/engineering technologies 23%, psychology 8%.

Computing on campus. 520 workstations in library, computer center. Dormitories wired for high-speed internet access and linked to campus network. Commuter students can connect to campus network. Online course registration, online library, helpline, repair service, student web hosting, wireless network available.

Student life. Freshman orientation: Available. Preregistration for classes offered. Held 2 days prior to the start of classes. **Policies:** Acts of intolerance and high-risk drinking discouraged at all locations. All facilities designated smoke-free. **Housing:** Special housing for disabled, apartments available. $100 partly refundable deposit, deadline 5/1. Special interest housing available. **Activities:** Choral groups, dance, drama, literary magazine, music ensembles, radio station, student government, student newspaper, black student union, Christian Fellowship, resident community council.

Athletics. NCAA. **Intercollegiate:** Baseball M, basketball, cross-country, golf, soccer, softball W, tennis, volleyball W. **Intramural:** Badminton, basketball, racquetball, tennis. **Team name:** Nittany Lions.

Student services. Adult student services, alcohol/substance abuse counseling, career counseling, services for economically disadvantaged, student employment services, financial aid counseling, health services, minority student services, on-campus daycare, personal counseling, placement for graduates, veterans' counselor, women's services. **Physically disabled:** Services for visually, speech, hearing impaired.

Contact. E-mail: hbgadmit@psu.edu
Phone: (717) 948-6250 Toll-free number: (800) 222-2056
Fax: (717) 948-6325
Anne Rohrbach, Executive Director for Undergraduate Admissions, Penn State Harrisburg, Swatara Building, Middletown, PA 17057-4898

Penn State Hazleton
Hazleton, Pennsylvania
www.hn.psu.edu   **CB code: 2660**

- Public 4-year branch campus college
- Residential campus in large town

1064

- 1,133 degree-seeking undergraduates: 4% part-time, 46% women, 13% African American, 4% Asian American, 15% Hispanic American, 1% international
- 87% of applicants admitted
- SAT or ACT (ACT writing optional) required
- 52% graduate within 6 years

General. Founded in 1934. Regionally accredited. Certain bachelor degree programs must be completed at another Penn State campus. **Degrees:** 38 bachelor's, 48 associate awarded. **ROTC:** Army, Air Force. **Location:** 4 miles from Hazleton. **Calendar:** Semester, limited summer session. **Full-time faculty:** 55 total; 60% have terminal degrees, 7% minority, 44% women. **Part-time faculty:** 28 total; 25% have terminal degrees, 7% minority, 54% women. **Class size:** 39% < 20, 51% 20-39, 4% 40-49, 5% 50-99. **Special facilities:** Weather station.

Freshman class profile. 1,268 applied, 1,100 admitted, 458 enrolled.

Mid 50% test scores		GPA 2.0-2.99:	56%
SAT critical reading:	410-510	Rank in top quarter:	30%
SAT math:	420-530	Rank in top tenth:	7%
SAT writing:	390-500	Return as sophomores:	76%
GPA 3.75 or higher:	2%	Out-of-state:	33%
GPA 3.50-3.74:	6%	International:	1%
GPA 3.0-3.49:	31%		

Basis for selection. Admission decisions based on high school GPA, as well as other factors, which may include standardized verbal and math test scores, class rank, personal statements, and activities lists. Essay considered if submitted; portfolios required for select majors. **Home schooled:** Complete documentation helpful, showing courses studied and all evaluations presented from home school evaluator, supervisor assigned to student in cooperation with local school district, or evaluator approved through program.

High school preparation. College-preparatory program recommended. Required units include English 4, mathematics 3, social studies 3, science 3 and foreign language 2.

2011-2012 Annual costs. Tuition/fees: $13,102; $19,542 out-of-state. Room/board: $9,420. Books/supplies: $1,536. Personal expenses: $3,222.

2010-2011 Financial aid. Need-based: 503 full-time freshmen applied for aid; 431 were judged to have need; 417 of these received aid. Average need met was 61%. Average scholarship/grant was $6,777; average loan $3,329. 45% of total undergraduate aid awarded as scholarships/grants, 55% as loans/jobs. **Non-need-based:** Awarded to 397 full-time undergraduates, including 189 freshmen. Scholarships awarded for academics, alumni affiliation, ROTC.

Application procedures. Admission: Priority date 11/30; no deadline. $50 fee, may be waived for applicants with need. Admission notification on a rolling basis beginning on or about 11/1. All freshmen applications processed at University Park Campus. **Financial aid:** Priority date 2/15; no closing date. FAFSA required. Applicants notified on a rolling basis.

Academics. Special study options: Accelerated study, cross-registration, distance learning, double major, dual enrollment of high school students, ESL, honors, independent study, internships, student-designed major, study abroad. **Credit/placement by examination:** AP, CLEP, IB, SAT. 60 credit hours maximum toward bachelor's degree. **Support services:** Learning center, remedial instruction, study skills assistance, tutoring, writing center.

Honors college/program. 300 admitted university-wide each year.

Majors. Area/ethnic studies: African-American, Asian, Latin American, women's. **Biology:** General, bacteriology, biochemistry, toxicology. **Business:** Accounting, actuarial science, business admin, finance, labor relations, management information systems, marketing, organizational behavior. **Communications:** Advertising, communications/speech/rhetoric, journalism. **Computer sciences:** General, information systems. **Conservation:** General, environmental studies, forest sciences, forest technology. **Education:** Adult ed admin, agricultural, art, elementary, foreign languages, secondary, special ed. **Engineering:** General, aerospace, agricultural, architectural, biomedical, chemical, civil, computer, electrical, engineering science, environmental, industrial, mechanical, mining, nuclear, petroleum. **English:** English lit. **Foreign languages:** Chinese, classics, comparative lit, French, German, Italian, Japanese, Russian, Spanish. **General:** Agribusiness operations, animal sciences, food science, horticultural science, landscaping, mechanization, plant protection, turf management. **Health services:** Athletic training, communication disorders, health care admin, nursing (RN), premedicine, preveterinary. **History:** General. **Liberal arts:** Arts/sciences. **Math:** General, statistics. **Parks/recreation:** Exercise sciences, facilities management. **Philosophy/religion:** Judaic, philosophy, religion. **Physical sciences:** Astronomy, atmospheric science, chemistry, geology, materials science, physics. **Protective services:** Forensics, law enforcement admin. **Psychology:** General. **Social sciences:** Anthropology, archaeology, economics, geography, international

relations, political science, sociology. **Visual/performing arts:** General, acting, art, art history/conservation, film/cinema/video, graphic design, music, theater design. **Work/family studies:** Family studies, human nutrition.

Most popular majors. Business/marketing 61%, liberal arts 26%, psychology 11%.

Computing on campus. 166 workstations in library, student center. Dormitories wired for high-speed internet access and linked to campus network. Commuter students can connect to campus network. Online course registration, online library, helpline, repair service, student web hosting, wireless network available.

Student life. Freshman orientation: Available. Preregistration for classes offered. Testing and academic advising in June; formal orientation in August and September. **Policies:** Acts of intolerance and high-risk drinking discouraged at all locations. All facilities designated as smoke-free. Students expected to abide by The Penn State Principles. **Housing:** Coed dorms available. $100 partly refundable deposit, deadline 5/1. Townhouses, suites available. **Activities:** Choral groups, dance, drama, literary magazine, radio station, student government, student newspaper, multicultural club, Circle K, Allies, Fellowship of Christian Athletes, Helping Hands.

Athletics. USCAA. **Intercollegiate:** Baseball M, basketball, cheerleading, golf, soccer M, softball W, tennis, volleyball W. **Intramural:** Rifle, softball, table tennis, tennis, volleyball. **Team name:** Nittany Lions.

Student services. Adult student services, alcohol/substance abuse counseling, chaplain/spiritual director, career counseling, services for economically disadvantaged, student employment services, financial aid counseling, health services, legal services, minority student services, personal counseling, placement for graduates, veterans' counselor, women's services. **Physically disabled:** Services for visually, speech, hearing impaired.

Contact. E-mail: admissions-hn@psu.edu
Phone: (570) 450-3142 Toll-free number: (800) 279-8495
Fax: (570) 450-3182
Anne Rohrbach, Executive Director for Undergraduate Admissions, Penn State Hazleton, 110 Administration Building, University Park, PA 18202-1291

Penn State Lehigh Valley
Center Valley, Pennsylvania
www.lv.psu.edu   **CB code: 2660**

- Public 4-year branch campus college
- Commuter campus in rural community
- 785 degree-seeking undergraduates: 11% part-time, 44% women, 4% African American, 9% Asian American, 14% Hispanic American, 1% international
- 87% of applicants admitted
- SAT or ACT with writing required
- 47% graduate within 6 years

General. Regionally accredited. Certain bachelor degree programs must be completed at another Penn State campus. **Degrees:** 63 bachelor's, 6 associate awarded. **ROTC:** Army. **Location:** 15 miles from Allentown, 30 miles from Easton. **Calendar:** Semester, limited summer session. **Full-time faculty:** 33 total; 76% have terminal degrees, 12% minority, 54% women. **Part-time faculty:** 56 total; 21% have terminal degrees, 5% minority, 50% women. **Class size:** 60% < 20, 35% 20-39, 4% 40-49, less than 1% 50-99.

Freshman class profile. 951 applied, 831 admitted, 260 enrolled.

Mid 50% test scores			
SAT critical reading:	420-540	Rank in top quarter:	29%
SAT math:	440-560	Rank in top tenth:	5%
SAT writing:	410-520	Return as sophomores:	76%
GPA 3.75 or higher:	4%	Out-of-state:	6%
GPA 3.50-3.74:	9%	International:	1%
GPA 3.0-3.49:	27%		
GPA 2.0-2.99:	57%		

Basis for selection. Admission decisions based on high school GPA, standardized test scores, class rank, personal statements, and activities. Essay considered if submitted; portfolios required for select majors. **Home schooled:** Applicants should provide complete documentation showing courses studied and all evaluations presented from evaluator or supervisor assigned to student in cooperation with local school district or evaluator approved through program.

High school preparation. College-preparatory program recommended. Required units include English 4, mathematics 3, social studies 3, science 3 and foreign language 2.

2011-2012 Annual costs. Tuition/fees: $13,094; $19,534 out-of-state. Books/supplies: $1,536. Personal expenses: $1,854.

2010-2011 Financial aid. Need-based: 239 full-time freshmen applied for aid; 181 were judged to have need; 174 of these received aid. Average need met was 62%. Average scholarship/grant was $6,923; average loan $3,331. 46% of total undergraduate aid awarded as scholarships/grants, 54% as loans/jobs. **Non-need-based:** Awarded to 137 full-time undergraduates, including 68 freshmen. Scholarships awarded for academics, alumni affiliation, ROTC.

Application procedures. Admission: Priority date 11/30; no deadline. $50 fee, may be waived for applicants with need. Admission notification on a rolling basis beginning on or about 11/1. All freshmen applications processed at University Park Campus. **Financial aid:** Priority date 2/15; no closing date. FAFSA required. Applicants notified on a rolling basis.

Academics. Special study options: Accelerated study, cooperative education, cross-registration, distance learning, dual enrollment of high school students, honors, independent study, internships, liberal arts/career combination, study abroad, teacher certification program. **Credit/placement by examination:** AP, CLEP, IB, SAT. 60 credit hours maximum toward bachelor's degree. **Support services:** Learning center, reduced course load, study skills assistance, tutoring, writing center.

Majors. Area/ethnic studies: African-American, Asian, Latin American, women's. **Biology:** General, bacteriology, biochemistry, toxicology. **Business:** General, accounting, actuarial science, business admin, finance, labor relations, management information systems, marketing, organizational behavior. **Communications:** Advertising, communications/speech/rhetoric, journalism. **Computer sciences:** General, information systems. **Conservation:** General, environmental studies, forest sciences, forest technology. **Education:** Adult ed admin, agricultural, art, elementary, foreign languages, secondary, special ed. **Engineering:** Aerospace, agricultural, architectural, biomedical, chemical, civil, computer, electrical, engineering science, environmental, industrial, mechanical, mining, nuclear, petroleum. **English:** English lit, technical writing. **Foreign languages:** General, Chinese, classics, comparative lit, French, German, Italian, Japanese, Russian, Spanish. **General:** Agribusiness operations, animal sciences, food science, horticultural science, landscaping, mechanization, plant protection, turf management. **Health services:** Athletic training, communication disorders, health care admin, nursing (RN), premedicine, preveterinary. **History:** General. **Liberal arts:** Arts/sciences. **Math:** General, statistics. **Parks/recreation:** Exercise sciences, facilities management. **Philosophy/religion:** Judaic, philosophy, religion. **Physical sciences:** Astronomy, atmospheric science, chemistry, geology, materials science, physics. **Protective services:** Forensics, law enforcement admin. **Psychology:** General. **Social sciences:** Anthropology, archaeology, economics, geography, international relations, political science, sociology. **Visual/performing arts:** General, acting, art, art history/conservation, film/cinema/video, graphic design, music, theater design. **Work/family studies:** Family studies, human nutrition.

Most popular majors. Business/marketing 46%, education 29%, psychology 21%.

Computing on campus. 155 workstations in dormitories, library, computer center, student center. Commuter students can connect to campus network. Online course registration, online library, helpline, repair service, student web hosting, wireless network available.

Student life. Freshman orientation: Mandatory. Preregistration for classes offered. One-day program held prior to start of classes. **Policies:** Acts of intolerance and high-risk drinking discouraged at all locations. All facilities designated as smoke-free. Students expected to abide by The Penn State Principles. **Activities:** Dance, drama, literary magazine, student government, student newspaper, Asian club, Christian Fellowship, Habitat for Humanity.

Athletics. USCAA. **Intercollegiate:** Golf, tennis. **Intramural:** Basketball, football (non-tackle), soccer. **Team name:** Nittany Lions.

Student services. Adult student services, alcohol/substance abuse counseling, career counseling, services for economically disadvantaged, student employment services, financial aid counseling, health services, minority student services, personal counseling, placement for graduates, veterans' counselor. **Physically disabled:** Services for visually, speech, hearing impaired.

Contact. E-mail: admissions-lv@psu.edu
Phone: (610) 285-5000 Fax: (610) 285-5220
Anne Rohrbach, Executive Director for Undergraduate Admissions, Penn State Lehigh Valley, 2809 Saucon Valley Road, Center Vally, PA 18034-8447

Penn State Mont Alto
Mont Alto, Pennsylvania
www.ma.psu.edu   CB code: 2660

- Public 4-year branch campus college
- Residential campus in rural community
- 1,130 degree-seeking undergraduates: 17% part-time, 59% women, 12% African American, 2% Asian American, 5% Hispanic American
- 85% of applicants admitted
- SAT or ACT with writing required
- 52% graduate within 6 years

General. Founded in 1929. Regionally accredited. Certain bachelor degree programs must be completed at another Penn State campus. **Degrees:** 28 bachelor's, 116 associate awarded. **ROTC:** Army. **Location:** 12 miles from Chambersburg. **Calendar:** Semester, limited summer session. **Full-time faculty:** 56 total; 46% have terminal degrees, 7% minority, 54% women. **Part-time faculty:** 58 total; 19% have terminal degrees, 5% minority, 66% women. **Class size:** 54% < 20, 41% 20-39, 4% 40-49, 2% 50-99.

Freshman class profile. 947 applied, 803 admitted, 394 enrolled.

Mid 50% test scores			
SAT critical reading:	410-520	GPA 3.0-3.49:	35%
		GPA 2.0-2.99:	49%
SAT math:	410-530	Rank in top quarter:	32%
SAT writing:	400-500	Rank in top tenth:	9%
GPA 3.75 or higher:	4%	Return as sophomores:	76%
GPA 3.50-3.74:	9%	Out-of-state:	26%

Basis for selection. Admission decisions based upon high school GPA, as well as other factors, which may include standardized verbal and math test scores, class rank, personal statements, and list of activities. Essay considered if submitted; portfolios required for select majors. **Home schooled:** Applicants should provide complete documentation showing courses studied and all evaluations presented from evaluator or supervisor assigned to student in cooperation with local school district or evaluator who is approved through the program.

High school preparation. College-preparatory program recommended. Required units include English 4, mathematics 3, social studies 3, science 3 and foreign language 2.

2011-2012 Annual costs. Tuition/fees: $13,102; $19,542 out-of-state. Room/board: $9,420. Books/supplies: $1,536. Personal expenses: $3,222.

2010-2011 Financial aid. **Need-based:** 372 full-time freshmen applied for aid; 318 were judged to have need; 317 of these received aid. Average need met was 66%. Average scholarship/grant was $6,828; average loan $3,390. 44% of total undergraduate aid awarded as scholarships/grants, 56% as loans/jobs. **Non-need-based:** Awarded to 317 full-time undergraduates, including 168 freshmen. Scholarships awarded for academics, alumni affiliation, ROTC.

Application procedures. **Admission:** Priority date 11/30; no deadline. $50 fee, may be waived for applicants with need. Admission notification on a rolling basis beginning on or about 11/1. All freshmen applications processed at University Park Campus. **Financial aid:** Priority date 2/15; no closing date. FAFSA required. Applicants notified on a rolling basis starting 3/1.

Academics. **Special study options:** Accelerated study, cross-registration, distance learning, double major, dual enrollment of high school students, honors, independent study, internships, liberal arts/career combination, student-designed major, study abroad, weekend college. **Credit/placement by examination:** AP, CLEP, IB, SAT. 60 credit hours maximum toward bachelor's degree. **Support services:** Learning center, pre-admission summer program, remedial instruction, study skills assistance, tutoring, writing center.

Majors. **Area/ethnic studies:** African-American, Asian, Latin American, women's. **Biology:** General, bacteriology, biochemistry, toxicology. **Business:** Accounting, actuarial science, business admin, finance, labor relations, management information systems, marketing, organizational behavior. **Communications:** Advertising, communications/speech/rhetoric, journalism. **Computer sciences:** General, information systems. **Conservation:** General, environmental studies, forest sciences, forest technology. **Education:** Adult ed admin, agricultural, art, elementary, foreign languages, secondary, special ed. **Engineering:** Aerospace, agricultural, architectural, biomedical, chemical, civil, computer, electrical, engineering science, environmental, industrial, mechanical, mining, nuclear, petroleum. **English:** English lit. **Foreign languages:** Chinese, classics, comparative lit, French, German, Italian, Japanese, Russian, Spanish. **General:** Agribusiness operations, animal sciences, food science, horticultural science, landscaping, mechanization, plant protection, turf management. **Health services:** Athletic training, communication disorders, health care admin, nursing (RN), premedicine, preveterinary. **History:** General. **Liberal arts:** Arts/sciences. **Math:** General, statistics. **Parks/recreation:** Exercise sciences, facilities management. **Philosophy/religion:** Judaic,

philosophy, religion. **Physical sciences:** Astronomy, atmospheric science, chemistry, geology, materials science, physics. **Protective services:** Forensics, law enforcement admin. **Psychology:** General. **Social sciences:** Anthropology, archaeology, economics, geography, international relations, political science, sociology. **Visual/performing arts:** General, acting, art, art history/conservation, film/cinema/video, graphic design, music, theater design. **Work/family studies:** Family studies, human nutrition.

Most popular majors. Business/marketing 21%, English 21%, family/consumer sciences 36%, health sciences 14%, liberal arts 7%.

Computing on campus. 164 workstations in computer center, student center. Dormitories wired for high-speed internet access and linked to campus network. Commuter students can connect to campus network. Online course registration, online library, helpline, repair service, student web hosting, wireless network available.

Student life. **Freshman orientation:** Available. Preregistration for classes offered. **Policies:** Acts of intolerance and high-risk drinking discouraged at all locations. All facilities designated as smoke-free. **Housing:** Coed dorms, special housing for disabled available. $100 partly refundable deposit, deadline 5/1. Suites, special interest housing, townhouses available. **Activities:** Jazz band, choral groups, dance, drama, student government, student newspaper, Christian fellowship, language club, multicultural club, volunteer club, Black student union, Asian student association.

Athletics. USCAA. **Intercollegiate:** Basketball, cheerleading, cross-country, golf, soccer, softball W, tennis, volleyball W. **Intramural:** Badminton, basketball, racquetball, soccer, softball, volleyball. **Team name:** Nittany Lions.

Student services. Adult student services, alcohol/substance abuse counseling, chaplain/spiritual director, career counseling, services for economically disadvantaged, student employment services, financial aid counseling, health services, minority student services, placement for graduates, veterans' counselor, women's services. **Physically disabled:** Services for visually, speech, hearing impaired.

Contact. E-mail: psuma@psu.edu
Phone: (717) 749-6130 Toll-free number: (800) 392-6173
Fax: (717) 749-6132
Anne Rohrbach, Executive Director for Undergraduate Admissions, Penn State Mont Alto, 1 Campus Drive, Mont Alto, PA 17237-9703

Penn State New Kensington
New Kensington, Pennsylvania
www.nk.psu.edu   CB code: 2660

- Public 4-year branch campus college
- Commuter campus in large town
- 694 degree-seeking undergraduates: 18% part-time, 39% women, 5% African American, 1% Asian American, 2% Hispanic American
- 1 graduate students
- 80% of applicants admitted
- SAT or ACT with writing required
- 40% graduate within 6 years

General. Founded in 1958. Regionally accredited. Certain bachelor degree programs must be completed at another Penn State campus. **Degrees:** 62 bachelor's, 33 associate awarded; master's offered. **ROTC:** Air Force. **Location:** 22 miles from Pittsburgh. **Calendar:** Semester, limited summer session. **Full-time faculty:** 37 total; 62% have terminal degrees, 16% minority, 40% women. **Part-time faculty:** 42 total; 29% have terminal degrees, 14% minority, 31% women. **Class size:** 66% < 20, 30% 20-39, 2% 40-49, 1% 50-99.

Freshman class profile. 528 applied, 422 admitted, 195 enrolled.

Mid 50% test scores			
SAT critical reading:	400-510	GPA 3.0-3.49:	30%
		GPA 2.0-2.99:	53%
SAT math:	430-540	Rank in top quarter:	34%
SAT writing:	390-490	Rank in top tenth:	16%
GPA 3.75 or higher:	8%	Return as sophomores:	74%
GPA 3.50-3.74:	8%	Out-of-state:	6%

Basis for selection. Admission decisions based upon high school GPA, as well as other factors, which may include standardized verbal and math test scores, class rank, personal statements, and list of activities. Essay considered if submitted; portfolios required for select majors. **Home schooled:** Applicants should provide complete documentation showing the courses studied and all evaluations presented from evaluator or supervisor assigned to student in cooperation with local school district or evaluator who is approved through the program.

High school preparation. College-preparatory program recommended. Required units include English 4, mathematics 3, social studies 3, science 3 and foreign language 2.

2011-2012 Annual costs. Tuition/fees: $13,102; $19,542 out-of-state. Books/supplies: $1,536. Personal expenses: $1,854.

2010-2011 Financial aid. Need-based: 201 full-time freshmen applied for aid; 171 were judged to have need; 167 of these received aid. Average need met was 65%. Average scholarship/grant was $6,389; average loan $3,254. 43% of total undergraduate aid awarded as scholarships/grants, 57% as loans/jobs. **Non-need-based:** Awarded to 157 full-time undergraduates, including 81 freshmen. Scholarships awarded for academics, alumni affiliation, ROTC.

Application procedures. Admission: Priority date 11/30; no deadline. $50 fee, may be waived for applicants with need. Admission notification on a rolling basis beginning on or about 11/1. All freshmen applications processed at University Park Campus. **Financial aid:** Priority date 2/15; no closing date. FAFSA required. Applicants notified on a rolling basis.

Academics. Special study options: Cross-registration, distance learning, double major, dual enrollment of high school students, external degree, honors, independent study, internships, study abroad. **Credit/placement by examination:** AP, CLEP, IB, SAT. 60 credit hours maximum toward bachelor's degree. **Support services:** Learning center, pre-admission summer program, remedial instruction, study skills assistance, tutoring, writing center.

Majors. Area/ethnic studies: African-American, Asian, Latin American, women's. **Biology:** General, bacteriology, biochemistry, toxicology. **Business:** Accounting, actuarial science, business admin, finance, labor relations, management information systems, marketing, organizational behavior. **Communications:** Advertising, communications/speech/rhetoric, journalism. **Computer sciences:** General, information systems. **Conservation:** General, environmental studies, forest sciences, forest technology. **Education:** Adult ed admin, agricultural, art, elementary, foreign languages, secondary, special ed. **Engineering:** Aerospace, agricultural, architectural, biomedical, chemical, civil, computer, electrical, engineering science, environmental, industrial, mechanical, mining, nuclear, petroleum. **English:** English lit. **Foreign languages:** Chinese, classics, comparative lit, French, German, Italian, Japanese, Russian, Spanish. **General:** Agribusiness operations, animal sciences, food science, horticultural science, landscaping, mechanization, plant protection, turf management. **Health services:** Athletic training, communication disorders, health care admin, medical radiologic technology/radiation therapy, nursing (RN), premedicine, preveterinary. **History:** General. **Liberal arts:** Arts/sciences. **Math:** General, statistics. **Parks/recreation:** Exercise sciences, facilities management. **Philosophy/religion:** Judaic, philosophy, religion. **Physical sciences:** Astronomy, atmospheric science, chemistry, geology, materials science, physics. **Protective services:** Criminal justice, forensics, law enforcement admin. **Psychology:** General. **Social sciences:** Anthropology, archaeology, economics, geography, international relations, political science, sociology. **Visual/performing arts:** General, acting, art, art history/conservation, film/cinema/video, graphic design, music, theater design. **Work/family studies:** Family studies, human nutrition.

Most popular majors. Business/marketing 34%, communications/journalism 14%, engineering/engineering technologies 14%, health sciences 16%, psychology 21%.

Computing on campus. 265 workstations in computer center. Commuter students can connect to campus network. Online course registration, online library, helpline, repair service, student web hosting, wireless network available.

Student life. Freshman orientation: Mandatory, $25 fee. Preregistration for classes offered. 2-day program held prior to beginning of classes. **Policies:** Acts of intolerance and high-risk drinking discouraged at all locations. All facilities designated as smoke-free. Students expected to abide by The Penn State Principles. **Housing:** Privately owned apartment complex adjacent to campus and multiple single apartments within 30 minutes available. **Activities:** Jazz band, dance, drama, literary magazine, musical theater, student government, student newspaper, multicultural club, Society of Women Engineers, Spanish culture club.

Athletics. USCAA. **Intercollegiate:** Basketball, cheerleading, golf, volleyball W. **Intramural:** Basketball, football (non-tackle), racquetball, soccer, softball, table tennis, volleyball. **Team name:** Nittany Lions.

Student services. Adult student services, alcohol/substance abuse counseling, chaplain/spiritual director, career counseling, services for economically disadvantaged, student employment services, financial aid counseling, health services, minority student services, placement for graduates, veterans' counselor, women's services. **Physically disabled:** Services for visually, speech, hearing impaired.

Contact. E-mail: nkadmissions@psu.edu
Phone: (724) 334-5466 Toll-free number: (888) 968-7297
Fax: (724) 334-6111
Anne Rohrbach, Executive Director for Undergraduate Admissions, Penn State New Kensington, 3550 Seventh Street Road, Route 780, New Kensington, PA 15068-1765

Penn State Schuylkill
Schuylkill Haven, Pennsylvania
www.sl.psu.edu   **CB code: 2660**

▶ Public 4-year branch campus college
▶ Residential campus in small town
▶ 956 degree-seeking undergraduates: 14% part-time, 54% women, 30% African American, 2% Asian American, 7% Hispanic American, 1% international
▶ 79% of applicants admitted
▶ SAT or ACT with writing required
▶ 47% graduate within 6 years

General. Founded in 1934. Regionally accredited. Certain bachelor degree programs must be completed at another Penn State campus. **Degrees:** 45 bachelor's, 28 associate awarded. **Location:** 4 miles from Pottsville. **Calendar:** Semester, limited summer session. **Full-time faculty:** 45 total; 76% have terminal degrees, 2% minority, 42% women. **Part-time faculty:** 29 total; 10% have terminal degrees, 45% women. **Class size:** 48% < 20, 46% 20-39, 5% 40-49, less than 1% 50-99, less than 1% >100.

Freshman class profile. 834 applied, 663 admitted, 332 enrolled.

Mid 50% test scores			
SAT critical reading:	380-500	GPA 2.0-2.99:	71%
SAT math:	370-490	Rank in top quarter:	18%
SAT writing:	370-470	Rank in top tenth:	4%
GPA 3.75 or higher:	1%	Return as sophomores:	71%
GPA 3.50-3.74:	3%	Out-of-state:	29%
GPA 3.0-3.49:	19%	International:	1%

Basis for selection. Admission decisions based upon high school GPA, standardized test scores, class rank, personal statements, and activities. Essay considered if submitted; portfolios required for select majors. **Home schooled:** Complete documentation showing courses studied and all evaluations presented from evaluator or supervisor assigned to student in cooperation with local school district or evaluator approved through program.

High school preparation. College-preparatory program recommended. Required units include English 4, mathematics 3, social studies 3, science 3 and foreign language 2.

2011-2012 Annual costs. Tuition/fees: $12,994; $19,434 out-of-state. Books/supplies: $1,536. Personal expenses: $1,854.

2010-2011 Financial aid. Need-based: 360 full-time freshmen applied for aid; 338 were judged to have need; 337 of these received aid. Average need met was 60%. Average scholarship/grant was $6,825; average loan $3,370. 49% of total undergraduate aid awarded as scholarships/grants, 51% as loans/jobs. **Non-need-based:** Awarded to 274 full-time undergraduates, including 164 freshmen. Scholarships awarded for academics, alumni affiliation, ROTC.

Application procedures. Admission: Priority date 11/30; no deadline. $50 fee, may be waived for applicants with need. Admission notification on a rolling basis beginning on or about 11/1. All freshmen applications processed at University Park Campus. **Financial aid:** Priority date 2/15; no closing date. FAFSA required. Applicants notified on a rolling basis.

Academics. Special study options: Distance learning, double major, dual enrollment of high school students, ESL, honors, independent study, internships, student-designed major, study abroad. **Credit/placement by examination:** AP, CLEP, IB, SAT. 60 credit hours maximum toward bachelor's degree. **Support services:** Learning center, remedial instruction, study skills assistance, tutoring, writing center.

Majors. Area/ethnic studies: African-American, Asian, Latin American, women's. **Biology:** General, bacteriology, biochemistry, toxicology. **Business:** Accounting, actuarial science, business admin, finance, labor relations, management information systems, marketing, organizational behavior. **Communications:** Advertising, communications/speech/rhetoric, journalism. **Computer sciences:** General, information systems. **Conservation:** General, environmental studies, forest sciences, forest technology. **Education:** Adult ed admin, agricultural, art, elementary, foreign languages, secondary, special ed. **Engineering:** Aerospace, agricultural, architectural, biomedical, chemical, civil, computer, electrical, engineering science, environmental, industrial,

mechanical, mining, nuclear, petroleum. **English:** English lit. **Foreign languages:** Chinese, classics, comparative lit, French, German, Italian, Japanese, Russian, Spanish. **General:** Agribusiness operations, animal sciences, food science, horticultural science, landscaping, mechanization, plant protection, turf management. **Health services:** Athletic training, clinical lab technology, communication disorders, health care admin, nursing (RN), premedicine, preveterinary. **History:** General. **Liberal arts:** Arts/sciences, humanities. **Math:** General, statistics. **Parks/recreation:** Exercise sciences, facilities management. **Philosophy/religion:** Judaic, philosophy, religion. **Physical sciences:** Astronomy, atmospheric science, chemistry, geology, materials science, physics. **Protective services:** Criminal justice, forensics, law enforcement admin. **Psychology:** General. **Social sciences:** Anthropology, archaeology, economics, geography, international relations, political science, sociology. **Visual/performing arts:** General, acting, art, art history/conservation, film/cinema/video, graphic design, music, theater design. **Work/family studies:** Family studies, human nutrition.

Most popular majors. Business/marketing 20%, health sciences 7%, psychology 38%, security/protective services 33%.

Computing on campus. 165 workstations in computer center, student center. Dormitories wired for high-speed internet access and linked to campus network. Commuter students can connect to campus network. Online course registration, online library, helpline, repair service, student web hosting, wireless network available.

Student life. Freshman orientation: Available. Preregistration for classes offered. 3-day program held prior to start of classes. **Policies:** Acts of intolerance and high-risk drinking discouraged at all locations. All facilities designated as smoke-free. Students expected to abide by The Penn State Principles. **Housing:** Special housing for disabled, apartments available. $100 partly refundable deposit, deadline 5/1. **Activities:** Campus ministries, choral groups, dance, drama, international student organizations, musical theater, student government, student newspaper, Campus Crusade for Christ, criminal justice club, religious and philosophical forum, united minority leaders, Keystone honor society.

Athletics. USCAA. **Intercollegiate:** Basketball, cross-country, golf M, soccer M, softball W, volleyball W. **Intramural:** Basketball, football (non-tackle) M, soccer, softball, table tennis, volleyball. **Team name:** Nittany Lions.

Student services. Adult student services, career counseling, services for economically disadvantaged, student employment services, financial aid counseling, health services, minority student services, personal counseling, placement for graduates, veterans' counselor. **Physically disabled:** Services for visually, speech, hearing impaired.

Contact. E-mail: sl-admissions@psu.edu
Phone: (570) 385-6252 Fax: (570) 385-6272
Anne Rohrbach, Executive Director for Undergraduate Admissions, Penn State Schuylkill, 200 University Drive, Schuylkill Haven, PA 17972-2208

Penn State Shenango
Sharon, Pennsylvania
www.shenango.psu.edu   CB code: 2660

- Public 4-year branch campus college
- Commuter campus in large town
- 542 degree-seeking undergraduates: 32% part-time, 64% women, 7% African American, 2% Hispanic American
- 74% of applicants admitted
- SAT or ACT with writing required
- 43% graduate within 6 years

General. Founded in 1965. Regionally accredited. Certain bachelor degree programs must be completed at another Penn State campus. **Degrees:** 64 bachelor's, 53 associate awarded. **Location:** 17 miles from Youngstown, Ohio. **Calendar:** Semester, limited summer session. **Full-time faculty:** 28 total; 68% have terminal degrees, 11% minority, 61% women. **Part-time faculty:** 40 total; 20% have terminal degrees, 40% women. **Class size:** 64% < 20, 28% 20-39, 5% 40-49, 3% 50-99. **Special facilities:** Scanning electron microscope.

Freshman class profile. 254 applied, 189 admitted, 101 enrolled.

Mid 50% test scores			
SAT critical reading:	380-480	GPA 3.0-3.49:	28%
SAT math:	380-510	GPA 2.0-2.99:	58%
SAT writing:	340-450	Rank in top quarter:	24%
GPA 3.75 or higher:	3%	Rank in top tenth:	6%
GPA 3.50-3.74:	10%	Return as sophomores:	63%
		Out-of-state:	14%

Basis for selection. Admission decisions based upon GPA, as well as other factors which may include standardized verbal and math test scores, class rank, personal statements, and activities lists. Essay considered if submitted; portfolios required for select majors. **Home schooled:** Complete documentation showing courses studied and all evaluations presented from home school evaluator or supervisor assigned to the student in cooperation with the local school district or evaluator who is approved through the program.

High school preparation. College-preparatory program recommended. Required units include English 4, mathematics 3, social studies 3, science 3 and foreign language 2.

2011-2012 Annual costs. Tuition/fees: $12,994; $19,434 out-of-state. Books/supplies: $1,536. Personal expenses: $1,854.

2010-2011 Financial aid. Need-based: 99 full-time freshmen applied for aid; 94 were judged to have need; 93 of these received aid. Average need met was 63%. Average scholarship/grant was $6,176; average loan $3,238. 47% of total undergraduate aid awarded as scholarships/grants, 53% as loans/jobs. **Non-need-based:** Awarded to 180 full-time undergraduates, including 57 freshmen. Scholarships awarded for academics, alumni affiliation, ROTC.

Application procedures. Admission: Priority date 11/30; no deadline. $50 fee, may be waived for applicants with need. Admission notification on a rolling basis beginning on or about 11/1. All freshmen applications processed at University Park Campus. **Financial aid:** Priority date 2/15; no closing date. FAFSA required. Applicants notified on a rolling basis.

Academics. Special study options: Accelerated study, cross-registration, distance learning, double major, dual enrollment of high school students, honors, independent study, internships, student-designed major, study abroad. **Credit/placement by examination:** AP, CLEP, IB, SAT. 60 credit hours maximum toward bachelor's degree. **Support services:** Learning center, remedial instruction, study skills assistance, tutoring, writing center.

Majors. Area/ethnic studies: African-American, Asian, Latin American, women's. **Biology:** General, bacteriology, biochemistry, toxicology. **Business:** Accounting, actuarial science, business admin, finance, labor relations, management information systems, marketing, organizational behavior. **Communications:** Advertising, communications/speech/rhetoric, journalism. **Computer sciences:** General, information systems. **Conservation:** General, environmental studies, forest sciences, forest technology. **Education:** Adult ed admin, agricultural, art, elementary, foreign languages, secondary, special ed. **Engineering:** Aerospace, agricultural, architectural, biomedical, chemical, civil, computer, electrical, engineering science, environmental, industrial, mechanical, mining, nuclear, petroleum. **English:** English lit. **Foreign languages:** Chinese, classics, comparative lit, French, German, Italian, Japanese, Russian, Spanish. **General:** Agribusiness operations, animal sciences, food science, horticultural science, landscaping, mechanization, plant protection, turf management. **Health services:** Athletic training, communication disorders, health care admin, nursing (RN), premedicine, preveterinary. **History:** General. **Liberal arts:** Arts/sciences. **Math:** General, statistics. **Parks/recreation:** Exercise sciences, facilities management. **Philosophy/religion:** Judaic, philosophy, religion. **Physical sciences:** Astronomy, atmospheric science, chemistry, geology, materials science, physics. **Protective services:** Criminal justice, forensics, law enforcement admin. **Psychology:** General. **Social sciences:** Anthropology, archaeology, economics, geography, international relations, political science, sociology. **Visual/performing arts:** General, acting, art, art history/conservation, film/cinema/video, graphic design, music, theater design. **Work/family studies:** Family studies, human nutrition.

Most popular majors. Business/marketing 30%, family/consumer sciences 50%, health sciences 17%.

Computing on campus. 132 workstations in library, computer center, student center. Commuter students can connect to campus network. Online course registration, online library, helpline, repair service, student web hosting, wireless network available.

Student life. Freshman orientation: Mandatory. Preregistration for classes offered. One-day program held prior to start of semester. **Policies:** Acts of intolerance and high-risk drinking discouraged at all locations. All facilities designated as smoke-free. Students expected to abide by The Penn State Principles. **Activities:** Choral groups, drama, literary magazine, student government, environmental club, students for cultural diversity, Women in Transition, Word of God Bible study club, Adults Seeking Knowledge.

Athletics. USCAA. **Intramural:** Basketball, golf, softball, volleyball. **Team name:** Nittany Lions.

Student services. Adult student services, alcohol/substance abuse counseling, career counseling, student employment services, financial aid counseling, health services, minority student services, placement for graduates, veterans' counselor, women's services. **Physically disabled:** Services for visually, speech, hearing impaired.

Contact. E-mail: psushenango@psu.edu
Phone: (724) 983-2800 Fax: (724) 983-2820
Anne Rohrbach, Executive Director for Undergraduate Admissions, Penn State Shenango, 147 Shenango Avenue, Room 206, Sharon, PA 16146-1597

Penn State University Park
University Park, Pennsylvania **CB member**
www.psu.edu **CB code: 2660**

- Public 4-year university
- Residential campus in large town
- 38,229 degree-seeking undergraduates: 2% part-time, 46% women, 4% African American, 5% Asian American, 5% Hispanic American, 7% international
- 6,507 degree-seeking graduate students
- 54% of applicants admitted
- SAT or ACT with writing required
- 87% graduate within 6 years; 20% enter graduate study

General. Founded in 1855. Regionally accredited. **Degrees:** 11,438 bachelor's, 147 associate awarded; master's, professional, doctoral offered. **ROTC:** Army, Naval, Air Force. **Location:** 90 miles from Harrisburg. **Calendar:** Semester, extensive summer session. **Full-time faculty:** 2,481 total; 79% have terminal degrees, 16% minority, 38% women. **Part-time faculty:** 399 total; 33% have terminal degrees, 6% minority, 47% women. **Class size:** 30% < 20, 41% 20-39, 10% 40-49, 10% 50-99, 8% >100. **Special facilities:** Art museum, earth and mineral science museum and art gallery, anthropology museum, entomological museum, sports museum, land-grant frescoes, agricultural museum, Pennsylvania space grant consortium, botanic gardens and arboretum.

Freshman class profile. 44,502 applied, 23,855 admitted, 7,366 enrolled.

Mid 50% test scores			
SAT critical reading:	530-630	Rank in top quarter:	87%
SAT math:	560-670	Rank in top tenth:	45%
SAT writing:	540-640	Return as sophomores:	92%
GPA 3.75 or higher:	28%	Out-of-state:	40%
GPA 3.50-3.74:	29%	International:	9%
GPA 3.0-3.49:	38%		
GPA 2.0-2.99:	5%		

Basis for selection. Admission decisions based upon high school GPA, standardized test scores, class rank, personal statements, and activities. Essay considered if submitted; portfolios required for select majors. **Home schooled:** Complete documentation showing courses studied and all evaluations presented from evaluator or supervisor assigned to student in cooperation with local school district or evaluator approved through program.

High school preparation. College-preparatory program recommended. Required units include English 4, mathematics 3, social studies 3, science 3 and foreign language 2. 3 units required in arts and humanities. Additional requirements for some programs.

2011-2012 Annual costs. Tuition/fees: $15,984; $28,066 out-of-state. Room/board: $9,420. Books/supplies: $1,536. Personal expenses: $3,222.

2010-2011 Financial aid. Need-based: 5,300 full-time freshmen applied for aid; 3,721 were judged to have need; 3,486 of these received aid. Average need met was 60%. Average scholarship/grant was $6,592; average loan $3,381. 36% of total undergraduate aid awarded as scholarships/grants, 64% as loans/jobs. **Non-need-based:** Awarded to 9,741 full-time undergraduates, including 2,137 freshmen. Scholarships awarded for academics, alumni affiliation, athletics, ROTC.

Application procedures. Admission: Priority date 11/30; no deadline. $50 fee, may be waived for applicants with need. Admission notification on a rolling basis beginning on or about 11/1. **Financial aid:** Priority date 2/15; no closing date. FAFSA required. Applicants notified on a rolling basis.

Academics. Special study options: Accelerated study, combined bachelor's/graduate degree, cooperative education, cross-registration, distance learning, double major, dual enrollment of high school students, ESL, exchange student, external degree, honors, independent study, internships, liberal arts/career combination, semester at sea, student-designed major, study abroad, teacher certification program, Washington semester, weekend college. **Credit/placement by examination:** AP, CLEP, IB, SAT, institutional tests. 60 credit hours maximum toward bachelor's degree. **Support services:** Learning center, pre-admission summer program, study skills assistance, tutoring, writing center.

Honors college/program. Candidates will be assessed based on the academic and extracurricular documents submitted with the application, as well as responses to essay questions and letters of recommendation.

Majors. Architecture: Architecture, landscape. **Area/ethnic studies:** African-American, Asian, Latin American, women's. **Biology:** General, bacteriology, biochemistry, toxicology. **Business:** General, accounting, actuarial science, finance, labor relations, management information systems, marketing, organizational behavior. **Communications:** Advertising, communications/speech/rhetoric, journalism. **Computer sciences:** General, information systems. **Conservation:** General, environmental studies, forest sciences, forest technology. **Education:** Adult ed admin, agricultural, art, elementary, foreign languages, music, secondary, special ed. **Engineering:** Aerospace, agricultural, architectural, biomedical, chemical, civil, computer, electrical, engineering science, environmental, industrial, mechanical, mining, nuclear, petroleum. **English:** English lit. **Foreign languages:** Chinese, classics, comparative lit, French, German, Italian, Japanese, Russian, Spanish. **General:** Agribusiness operations, animal sciences, food science, horticultural science, landscaping, mechanization, plant protection, turf management. **Health services:** Athletic training, communication disorders, health care admin, nursing (RN), premedicine, preveterinary. **History:** General. **Liberal arts:** Arts/sciences. **Math:** General, statistics. **Parks/recreation:** Exercise sciences, facilities management. **Philosophy/religion:** Judaic, philosophy, religion. **Physical sciences:** Astronomy, atmospheric science, chemistry, geology, materials science, physics. **Protective services:** Criminal justice, forensics, law enforcement admin. **Psychology:** General. **Social sciences:** Anthropology, archaeology, economics, geography, international relations, political science, sociology. **Visual/performing arts:** General, acting, art, art history/conservation, film/cinema/video, graphic design, music, music performance, theater design. **Work/family studies:** Family studies, human nutrition.

Most popular majors. Business/marketing 16%, communications/journalism 9%, computer/information sciences 7%, engineering/engineering technologies 12%, health sciences 6%, social sciences 7%.

Computing on campus. 6,150 workstations in dormitories, library, computer center, student center. Dormitories wired for high-speed internet access and linked to campus network. Commuter students can connect to campus network. Online course registration, online library, helpline, repair service, student web hosting, wireless network available.

Student life. Freshman orientation: Mandatory. Preregistration for classes offered. Held the 2 days prior to start of classes. **Policies:** Acts of intolerance and high-risk drinking discouraged at all locations. All facilites designated as smoke-free. Freshmen not permitted cars on campus. **Housing:** Coed dorms, single-sex dorms, special housing for disabled, apartments, fraternity/sorority housing available. $100 partly refundable deposit, deadline 5/1. Suites, special interest housing available. **Activities:** Bands, campus ministries, choral groups, dance, drama, film society, international student organizations, literary magazine, music ensembles, Model UN, musical theater, opera, radio station, student government, student newspaper, symphony orchestra, TV station, Adult learners, eco-action, Habitat for Humanity, minorities in agriculture and natural resources, National Society of Black Engineers, College Democrats, College Libertarians, Black Caucus, Alliance Christian Fellowship, Commission for Women.

Athletics. NCAA. **Intercollegiate:** Baseball M, basketball, cheerleading, cross-country, diving, fencing, field hockey W, football (tackle) M, golf, gymnastics, lacrosse, soccer, softball W, swimming, tennis, track and field, volleyball, wrestling M. **Intramural:** Badminton, basketball, bowling, cross-country, diving, football (non-tackle), football (tackle), golf, gymnastics, racquetball, soccer, softball, squash, swimming, tennis, track and field, volleyball, wrestling. **Team name:** Nittany Lions.

Student services. Adult student services, alcohol/substance abuse counseling, chaplain/spiritual director, career counseling, services for economically disadvantaged, student employment services, financial aid counseling, health services, legal services, minority student services, on-campus daycare, personal counseling, placement for graduates, veterans' counselor, women's services. **Physically disabled:** Services for visually, speech, hearing impaired.

Contact. E-mail: admissions@psu.edu
Phone: (814) 865-5471 Fax: (814) 863-7590
Anne Rohrbach, Executive Director for Undergraduate Admissions, Penn State University Park, 201 Shields Building, University Park, PA 16804-3000

Penn State Wilkes-Barre
Lehman, Pennsylvania
www.wb.psu.edu **CB code: 2660**

- Public 4-year branch campus college
- Commuter campus in small city

- 601 degree-seeking undergraduates: 7% part-time, 34% women, 5% African American, 2% Asian American, 3% Hispanic American
- 88% of applicants admitted
- SAT or ACT with writing required
- 47% graduate within 6 years

General. Founded in 1916. Regionally accredited. Certain bachelor degree programs must be completed at another Penn State campus. **Degrees:** 46 bachelor's, 16 associate awarded. **ROTC:** Army, Air Force. **Location:** 10 miles from Wilkes-Barre. **Calendar:** Semester, limited summer session. **Full-time faculty:** 34 total; 71% have terminal degrees, 18% minority, 24% women. **Part-time faculty:** 23 total; 17% have terminal degrees, 61% women. **Class size:** 55% < 20, 42% 20-39, 2% 40-49, 2% 50-99.

Freshman class profile. 549 applied, 482 admitted, 191 enrolled.

Mid 50% test scores		GPA 3.0-3.49:	38%
SAT critical reading:	430-540	GPA 2.0-2.99:	44%
SAT math:	450-560	Rank in top quarter:	32%
SAT writing:	410-530	Rank in top tenth:	10%
GPA 3.75 or higher:	5%	Return as sophomores:	73%
GPA 3.50-3.74:	11%	Out-of-state:	7%

Basis for selection. Admission decisions based upon high school GPA, standardized test scores, class rank, personal statements, and activities. Essay considered if submitted; portfolios required for select majors. **Home schooled:** Complete documentation showing courses studied and all evaluations presented from evaluator or supervisor assigned to student in cooperation with local school district or evaluator approved through program. **Learning Disabled:** Contact or visit the Office for Disability Services in junior or senior year in high school.

High school preparation. College-preparatory program recommended. Required units include English 4, mathematics 3, social studies 3, science 3 and foreign language 2.

2011-2012 Annual costs. Tuition/fees: $12,994; $19,434 out-of-state. Books/supplies: $1,536. Personal expenses: $1,854.

2010-2011 Financial aid. Need-based: 189 full-time freshmen applied for aid; 150 were judged to have need; 147 of these received aid. Average need met was 65%. Average scholarship/grant was $6,202; average loan $3,296. 47% of total undergraduate aid awarded as scholarships/grants, 53% as loans/jobs. **Non-need-based:** Awarded to 193 full-time undergraduates, including 75 freshmen. Scholarships awarded for academics, alumni affiliation, ROTC.

Application procedures. Admission: Priority date 11/30; no deadline. $50 fee, may be waived for applicants with need. Admission notification on a rolling basis beginning on or about 11/1. All freshmen applications processed at University Park Campus. **Financial aid:** Priority date 2/15; no closing date. FAFSA required. Applicants notified on a rolling basis.

Academics. Special study options: Accelerated study, cross-registration, distance learning, double major, dual enrollment of high school students, honors, independent study, internships, student-designed major, study abroad. **Credit/placement by examination:** AP, CLEP, IB, SAT. 60 credit hours maximum toward bachelor's degree. **Support services:** Learning center, study skills assistance, tutoring, writing center.

Majors. Area/ethnic studies: African-American, Asian, Latin American, women's. **Biology:** General, bacteriology, biochemistry, toxicology. **Business:** Accounting, actuarial science, business admin, finance, labor relations, management information systems, marketing, organizational behavior. **Communications:** Advertising, communications/speech/rhetoric, journalism. **Computer sciences:** General, information systems. **Conservation:** General, environmental studies, forest sciences, forest technology. **Education:** Adult ed admin, agricultural, art, elementary, foreign languages, secondary, special ed. **Engineering:** Aerospace, agricultural, architectural, biomedical, chemical, civil, computer, electrical, engineering science, environmental, industrial, mechanical, mining, nuclear, petroleum, surveying. **English:** English lit. **Foreign languages:** Chinese, classics, comparative lit, French, German, Italian, Japanese, Russian, Spanish. **General:** Agribusiness operations, animal sciences, food science, horticultural science, landscaping, mechanization, plant protection, turf management. **Health services:** Athletic training, communication disorders, health care admin, nursing (RN), premedicine, preveterinary. **History:** General. **Liberal arts:** Arts/sciences. **Math:** General, statistics. **Parks/recreation:** Exercise sciences, facilities management. **Philosophy/religion:** Judaic, philosophy, religion. **Physical sciences:** Astronomy, atmospheric science, chemistry, geology, materials science, physics. **Protective services:** Criminal justice, forensics, law enforcement admin. **Psychology:** General. **Social sciences:** Anthropology, archaeology, economics, geography, international relations, political science, sociology. **Visual/performing arts:** General, acting, art, art history/conservation, film/cinema/video, graphic design, music, theater design. **Work/family studies:** Family studies, human nutrition.

Most popular majors. Business/marketing 41%, English 17%, security/protective services 35%.

Computing on campus. 196 workstations in library, computer center, student center. Commuter students can connect to campus network. Online course registration, online library, helpline, repair service, student web hosting, wireless network available.

Student life. Freshman orientation: Mandatory. Preregistration for classes offered. One-day session held prior to start of classes. **Policies:** Acts of intolerance and high-risk drinking discouraged at all locations. All facilities designated smoke-free. Students expected to abide by The Penn State Principles. **Activities:** Dance, radio station, student government, student newspaper, students for justice club.

Athletics. USCAA. **Intercollegiate:** Baseball M, basketball M, cross-country, golf, soccer, volleyball W. **Intramural:** Basketball, football (tackle), racquetball, softball, volleyball. **Team name:** Nittany Lions.

Student services. Adult student services, alcohol/substance abuse counseling, chaplain/spiritual director, career counseling, services for economically disadvantaged, student employment services, financial aid counseling, health services, minority student services, personal counseling, placement for graduates. **Physically disabled:** Services for visually, hearing impaired.

Contact. E-mail: wbadmissions@psu.edu
Phone: (570) 675-9238 Toll-free number: (800) 966-6613
Fax: (570) 675-9113
Anne Rohrbach, Executive Director for Undergraduate Admissions, Penn State Wilkes-Barre, Hayfield House 101, Lehman, PA 18627-0217

Penn State Worthington Scranton
Dunmore, Pennsylvania
www.sn.psu.edu   CB code: 2660

- Public 4-year branch campus college
- Commuter campus in large town
- 1,166 degree-seeking undergraduates: 17% part-time, 52% women, 1% African American, 4% Asian American, 4% Hispanic American
- 82% of applicants admitted
- SAT or ACT with writing required
- 46% graduate within 6 years

General. Founded in 1923. Regionally accredited. Certain bachelor degree programs must be completed at another Penn State campus. **Degrees:** 106 bachelor's, 73 associate awarded. **ROTC:** Army, Air Force. **Location:** 1 mile from Scranton. **Calendar:** Semester, limited summer session. **Full-time faculty:** 52 total; 64% have terminal degrees, 10% minority, 52% women. **Part-time faculty:** 48 total; 15% have terminal degrees, 58% women. **Class size:** 42% < 20, 50% 20-39, 6% 40-49, 2% 50-99.

Freshman class profile. 799 applied, 653 admitted, 318 enrolled.

Mid 50% test scores		GPA 3.0-3.49:	31%
SAT critical reading:	400-530	GPA 2.0-2.99:	62%
SAT math:	420-530	Rank in top quarter:	19%
SAT writing:	400-500	Rank in top tenth:	4%
GPA 3.75 or higher:	1%	Return as sophomores:	71%
GPA 3.50-3.74:	4%	Out-of-state:	3%

Basis for selection. Admission decisions based upon high school GPA, as well as other factors, which may include standardized verbal and math test scores, class rank, personal statements, and list of activities. Essay considered if submitted; portfolios required for select majors. **Home schooled:** Provide complete documentation showing courses studied and all evaluations presented from evaluator or supervisor assigned to student in cooperation with local school district or evaluator who is approved through the program.

High school preparation. College-preparatory program recommended. Required units include English 4, mathematics 3, social studies 3, science 3 and foreign language 2.

2011-2012 Annual costs. Tuition/fees: $12,966; $19,406 out-of-state. Books/supplies: $1,536. Personal expenses: $1,854.

2010-2011 Financial aid. Need-based: 339 full-time freshmen applied for aid; 298 were judged to have need; 295 of these received aid. Average need met was 62%. Average scholarship/grant was $6,066; average loan $3,302. 42% of total undergraduate aid awarded as scholarships/grants, 58% as loans/jobs. **Non-need-based:** Awarded to 199 full-time undergraduates, including 82 freshmen. Scholarships awarded for academics, alumni affiliation, ROTC.

Application procedures. Admission: Priority date 11/30; no deadline. $50 fee, may be waived for applicants with need. Admission notification on a rolling basis beginning on or about 11/1. All freshmen applications processed at University Park Campus. **Financial aid:** Priority date 2/15; no closing date. FAFSA required. Applicants notified on a rolling basis.

Academics. Special study options: Accelerated study, cooperative education, cross-registration, distance learning, double major, dual enrollment of high school students, honors, independent study, internships, study abroad. **Credit/placement by examination:** AP, CLEP, IB, SAT. 60 credit hours maximum toward bachelor's degree. **Support services:** Learning center, remedial instruction, study skills assistance, tutoring, writing center.

Majors. Area/ethnic studies: African-American, American, Asian, Latin American, women's. **Biology:** General, bacteriology, biochemistry, toxicology. **Business:** Accounting, actuarial science, business admin, finance, labor relations, management information systems, marketing, organizational behavior. **Communications:** Advertising, communications/speech/rhetoric, journalism. **Computer sciences:** General, information systems. **Conservation:** General, environmental studies, forest sciences, forest technology. **Education:** Adult ed admin, agricultural, art, elementary, foreign languages, secondary, special ed. **Engineering:** Aerospace, agricultural, architectural, biomedical, chemical, civil, computer, electrical, engineering science, environmental, industrial, mechanical, mining, nuclear, petroleum. **English:** English lit. **Foreign languages:** Chinese, classics, comparative lit, French, German, Italian, Japanese, Russian, Spanish. **General:** Agribusiness operations, animal sciences, food science, horticultural science, landscaping, mechanization, plant protection, turf management. **Health services:** Athletic training, communication disorders, health care admin, nursing (RN), premedicine, preveterinary. **History:** General. **Liberal arts:** Arts/sciences. **Math:** General, statistics. **Parks/recreation:** Exercise sciences, facilities management. **Philosophy/religion:** Judaic, philosophy, religion. **Physical sciences:** Astronomy, atmospheric science, chemistry, geology, materials science, physics. **Protective services:** Forensics, law enforcement admin. **Psychology:** General. **Social sciences:** Anthropology, archaeology, economics, geography, international relations, political science, sociology. **Visual/performing arts:** General, acting, art, art history/conservation, film/cinema/video, graphic design, music, theater design. **Work/family studies:** Family studies, human nutrition.

Most popular majors. Area/ethnic studies 7%, business/marketing 54%, family/consumer sciences 17%, health sciences 14%, liberal arts 8%.

Computing on campus. 180 workstations in library, computer center, student center. Commuter students can connect to campus network. Online course registration, online library, helpline, repair service, student web hosting, wireless network available.

Student life. Freshman orientation: Available. Preregistration for classes offered. **Policies:** Acts of intolerance and high-risk drinking discouraged at all locations. All facilities designated as smoke-free. Students expected to abide by The Penn State Principles. **Activities:** Jazz band, choral groups, drama, literary magazine, music ensembles, student government, student newspaper, community human service organization, Faith and Values, German club, lighthouse club, multicultural club, veterans club, public affairs club.

Athletics. USCAA. **Intercollegiate:** Baseball M, basketball, cross-country, soccer M, softball W. **Intramural:** Basketball, soccer, softball, volleyball, weight lifting. **Team name:** Nittany Lions.

Student services. Adult student services, alcohol/substance abuse counseling, career counseling, services for economically disadvantaged, student employment services, financial aid counseling, health services, personal counseling, placement for graduates, veterans' counselor, women's services. **Physically disabled:** Services for visually, speech, hearing impaired.

Contact. E-mail: wsadmissions@psu.edu
Phone: (570) 963-2500 Fax: (570) 963-2524
Anne Rohrbach, Executive Director for Undergraduate Admissions, Penn State Worthington Scranton, 120 Ridge View Drive, Dunmore, PA 18512-1602

Penn State York
York, Pennsylvania
www.yk.psu.edu   CB code: 2660

- Public 4-year branch campus college
- Commuter campus in large town
- 1,063 degree-seeking undergraduates: 22% part-time, 43% women, 8% African American, 5% Asian American, 6% Hispanic American, 4% international
- 20 degree-seeking graduate students
- 79% of applicants admitted

- SAT or ACT with writing required
- 45% graduate within 6 years

General. Founded in 1926. Regionally accredited. Certain bachelor degree programs must be completed at another Penn State campus. **Degrees:** 98 bachelor's, 44 associate awarded; master's offered. **Calendar:** Semester, extensive summer session. **Full-time faculty:** 56 total; 62% have terminal degrees, 14% minority, 43% women. **Part-time faculty:** 54 total; 26% have terminal degrees, 4% minority, 46% women. **Class size:** 53% < 20, 43% 20-39, 3% 40-49, 1% 50-99.

Freshman class profile. 1,200 applied, 947 admitted, 282 enrolled.

Mid 50% test scores			
SAT critical reading:	430-540	GPA 2.0-2.99:	56%
SAT math:	430-570	Rank in top quarter:	25%
SAT writing:	410-520	Rank in top tenth:	7%
GPA 3.75 or higher:	4%	Return as sophomores:	77%
GPA 3.50-3.74:	7%	Out-of-state:	18%
GPA 3.0-3.49:	31%	International:	4%

Basis for selection. Admission decisions based upon high school GPA and other factors, which may include standardized verbal and math test scores, class rank, personal statements, activities lists. Essay considered if submitted; portfolios required for select majors. **Home schooled:** Complete documentation showing courses studied and all evaluations from home school evaluator or supervisor assigned to student in cooperation with local school district or evaluator approved through program.

High school preparation. College-preparatory program recommended. Required units include English 4, mathematics 3, social studies 3, science 3 and foreign language 2.

2011-2012 Annual costs. Tuition/fees: $12,966; $19,406 out-of-state. Books/supplies: $1,536. Personal expenses: $1,854.

2010-2011 Financial aid. Need-based: 282 full-time freshmen applied for aid; 222 were judged to have need; 218 of these received aid. Average need met was 60%. Average scholarship/grant was $5,822; average loan $3,196. 43% of total undergraduate aid awarded as scholarships/grants, 57% as loans/jobs. **Non-need-based:** Awarded to 252 full-time undergraduates, including 115 freshmen. Scholarships awarded for academics, alumni affiliation, ROTC.

Application procedures. Admission: Priority date 11/30; no deadline. $50 fee, may be waived for applicants with need. Admission notification on a rolling basis beginning on or about 11/1. All freshmen applications processed at University Park Campus. **Financial aid:** Priority date 2/15; no closing date. FAFSA required. Applicants notified on a rolling basis.

Academics. Special study options: Accelerated study, cross-registration, distance learning, double major, dual enrollment of high school students, ESL, honors, independent study, internships, student-designed major, study abroad. **Credit/placement by examination:** AP, CLEP, IB, SAT. 60 credit hours maximum toward bachelor's degree. **Support services:** Learning center, pre-admission summer program, reduced course load, remedial instruction, study skills assistance, tutoring, writing center.

Majors. Area/ethnic studies: African-American, Asian, Latin American, women's. **Biology:** General, bacteriology, biochemistry, toxicology. **Business:** Accounting, actuarial science, business admin, finance, labor relations, management information systems, marketing, organizational behavior. **Communications:** Advertising, communications/speech/rhetoric, journalism. **Computer sciences:** General, information systems. **Conservation:** General, environmental studies, forest sciences, forest technology. **Education:** Adult ed admin, agricultural, art, elementary, foreign languages, secondary, special ed. **Engineering:** Aerospace, agricultural, architectural, biomedical, chemical, civil, computer, electrical, engineering science, environmental, industrial, mechanical, mining, nuclear, petroleum. **English:** English lit. **Foreign languages:** Chinese, classics, comparative lit, French, German, Italian, Japanese, Russian, Spanish. **General:** Agribusiness operations, animal sciences, food science, horticultural science, landscaping, mechanization, plant protection, turf management. **Health services:** Athletic training, communication disorders, health care admin, nursing (RN), premedicine, preveterinary. **History:** General. **Liberal arts:** Arts/sciences. **Math:** General, statistics. **Parks/recreation:** Exercise sciences, facilities management. **Philosophy/religion:** Judaic, philosophy, religion. **Physical sciences:** Astronomy, atmospheric science, chemistry, geology, materials science, physics. **Protective services:** Forensics, law enforcement admin. **Psychology:** General. **Social sciences:** Anthropology, archaeology, economics, geography, international relations, political science, sociology. **Visual/performing arts:** General, acting, art, art history/conservation, film/cinema/video, graphic design, music, theater design. **Work/family studies:** Family studies, human nutrition.

Most popular majors. Business/marketing 33%, communications/journalism 11%, engineering/engineering technologies 16%, English 6%, family/consumer sciences 26%.

Computing on campus. 169 workstations in computer center. Commuter students can connect to campus network. Online course registration, online library, helpline, repair service, student web hosting, wireless network available.

Student life. Freshman orientation: Mandatory. Preregistration for classes offered. Full-day event in August. **Policies:** Acts of intolerance and high-risk drinking discouraged at all locations. All facilities designated as smoke-free. Students expected to abide by The Penn State Principles. **Housing:** Room, apartment, house rentals in the local community available. **Activities:** Dance, drama, literary magazine, student government, student newspaper, Black student union, Christian fellowship, Hispanic students association, Rainbow Alliance, veterans club, Asian culture club, foreign policy club, debate club.

Athletics. Intercollegiate: Baseball M, basketball, soccer, tennis, volleyball. **Intramural:** Badminton, basketball, football (non-tackle) M, handball, soccer, softball, table tennis, tennis, volleyball. **Team name:** Nittany Lions.

Student services. Adult student services, alcohol/substance abuse counseling, chaplain/spiritual director, career counseling, services for economically disadvantaged, student employment services, financial aid counseling, health services, minority student services, personal counseling, placement for graduates, veterans' counselor, women's services. **Physically disabled:** Services for visually, speech, hearing impaired.

Contact. E-mail: ykadmissions@psu.edu
Phone: (717) 771-4040 Toll-free number: (800) 778-6227
Fax: (717) 771-4005
Anne Rohrbach, Executive Director for Undergraduate Admissions, Penn State York, 1031 Edgecomb Avenue, York, PA 17403-3398

Pennsylvania Academy of the Fine Arts
Philadelphia, Pennsylvania
www.pafa.edu   CB code: 3038

- Private 4-year visual arts college
- Commuter campus in very large city
- 247 degree-seeking undergraduates: 6% part-time, 58% women
- 106 degree-seeking graduate students
- 92% of applicants admitted
- Application essay required

General. Candidate for regional accreditation. PAFA is both a school of fine art and an museum of American art. **Degrees:** 51 bachelor's awarded; master's offered. **Calendar:** Semester, limited summer session. **Full-time faculty:** 21 total; 52% have terminal degrees, 29% women. **Part-time faculty:** 52 total; 46% have terminal degrees, 4% minority, 38% women.

Freshman class profile. 90 applied, 83 admitted, 21 enrolled.

Basis for selection. Admission to all program based on committee review of all credentials: application, personal statement, recommendations, transcripts, and artistic portfolio. If considered for admission, applicants are also considered for merit-based scholarships on a competitive basis. Interviews not required but are encouraged. Portfolios are required. **Home schooled:** Transcript of courses and grades, state high school equivalency certificate, letter of recommendation (nonparent) required.

2011-2012 Annual costs. Tuition/fees: $27,270. Books/supplies: $1,365. Personal expenses: $1,205.

2010-2011 Financial aid. Need-based: 43% of total undergraduate aid awarded as scholarships/grants, 57% as loans/jobs. **Non-need-based:** Scholarships awarded for academics, art.

Application procedures. Admission: Priority date 3/1; no deadline. $50 fee, may be waived for applicants with need. Admission notification on a rolling basis. **Financial aid:** Priority date 3/1; no closing date. FAFSA required. Applicants notified on a rolling basis; must reply by 5/1 or within 14 week(s) of notification.

Academics. Special study options: Dual enrollment of high school students, independent study, internships. In addition to its own BFA, the Pennsylvania Academy of the Fine Arts has a Coordinated BFA with the University of Pennsylvania which dates from 1929. **Credit/placement by examination:** AP, CLEP, IB, institutional tests. **Support services:** Pre-admission summer program, study skills assistance, tutoring, writing center.

Majors. Visual/performing arts: Drawing, painting, printmaking, sculpture.

Computing on campus. 20 workstations in computer center. Online library, wireless network available.

Student life. Freshman orientation: Mandatory. Preregistration for classes offered. **Housing:** $200 nonrefundable deposit. Agreement with International House-Philadelphia to house certain percentage of first-year students. **Activities:** Film society, student government.

Student services. Career counseling, financial aid counseling, personal counseling.

Contact. E-mail: admissions@pafa.edu
Phone: (215) 972-7625 Fax: (215) 972-0839
David Sigman, Director of Admissions, Pennsylvania Academy of the Fine Arts, 128 North Broad Street, Philadelphia, PA 19102

Pennsylvania College of Art and Design
Lancaster, Pennsylvania
www.pcad.edu   CB code: 2681

- Private 4-year visual arts college
- Commuter campus in small city
- 259 degree-seeking undergraduates: 6% part-time, 66% women, 3% African American, 2% Asian American, 5% Hispanic American
- 38% of applicants admitted
- Application essay, interview required
- 38% graduate within 6 years

General. Regionally accredited. **Degrees:** 50 bachelor's awarded. **Location:** 75 miles from Philadelphia, 75 miles from Baltimore. **Calendar:** Semester, limited summer session. **Full-time faculty:** 15 total; 7% have terminal degrees, 33% women. **Part-time faculty:** 38 total; 3% minority, 29% women. **Class size:** 84% < 20, 16% 20-39. **Special facilities:** Visual arts gallery.

Freshman class profile. 357 applied, 134 admitted, 65 enrolled.

GPA 3.75 or higher:	9%	End year in good standing:	76%
GPA 3.50-3.74:	6%	Return as sophomores:	66%
GPA 3.0-3.49:	30%	Out-of-state:	23%
GPA 2.0-2.99:	53%		

Basis for selection. Portfolio review, interview, personal statement, and high school transcripts required. Students with GPA below 2.5 required to submit two letters of recommendation. Portfolio required. **Home schooled:** Transcript of courses and grades, state high school equivalency certificate, interview required.

High school preparation. College-preparatory program required.

2011-2012 Annual costs. Tuition/fees: $18,980.

2010-2011 Financial aid. Need-based: 54 full-time freshmen applied for aid; 47 were judged to have need; 47 of these received aid. 99% of total undergraduate aid awarded as scholarships/grants, 1% as loans/jobs.

Application procedures. Admission: No deadline. $40 fee, may be waived for applicants with need. Admission notification on a rolling basis. Must reply by May 1 or within 2 week(s) if notified thereafter. **Financial aid:** No deadline. FAFSA required. Applicants notified on a rolling basis starting 4/15.

Academics. Special study options: Dual enrollment of high school students, internships. **Credit/placement by examination:** AP, CLEP, institutional tests.

Majors. Visual/performing arts: Digital arts, graphic design, illustration, photography, studio arts.

Computing on campus. Online library, wireless network available.

Student life. Freshman orientation: Mandatory. Preregistration for classes offered. **Housing:** Housing referral service available. **Activities:** Student government.

Student services. Career counseling, student employment services, financial aid counseling.

Contact. E-mail: admissions@pcad.edu
Phone: (717) 396-7833 Toll-free number: (800) 689-0379
Fax: (717) 396-1339
Natalie Lascek-Speakman, Director of Admission Marketing and Recruitment, Pennsylvania College of Art and Design, PO Box 59, Lancaster, PA 17608-0059

Pennsylvania College of Technology
Williamsport, Pennsylvania   **CB member**
www.pct.edu   **CB code: 2989**

- Public 4-year technical college
- Commuter campus in small city
- 5,850 degree-seeking undergraduates: 16% part-time, 36% women, 4% African American, 1% Asian American, 2% Hispanic American
- 53% graduate within 6 years; 40% enter graduate study

General. Founded in 1965. Regionally accredited. **Degrees:** 581 bachelor's, 991 associate awarded. **ROTC:** Army. **Location:** 85 miles from Harrisburg, 70 miles from Wilkes-Barre. **Calendar:** Semester, limited summer session. **Full-time faculty:** 298 total; 6% minority, 30% women. **Part-time faculty:** 182 total; 2% minority, 61% women. **Class size:** 62% < 20, 38% 20-39. **Special facilities:** Automotive technology center, aviation center, plastics manufacturing center, community arts center, earth science center.

Freshman class profile. 3,384 applied, 3,112 admitted, 1,279 enrolled.

Basis for selection. Open admission, but selective for some programs. Competitive admissions to health science programs, using GPA, SAT scores, high school rank, selected course grades, completed developmental course work. Some programs have more specific requirements. SAT recommended for all bachelor's programs, dental hygiene, radiography, occupational therapy assistant, nursing applicants; college placement exams required for all applicants. **Home schooled:** Transcript of courses and grades, state high school equivalency certificate required. Must provide proof of graduation from an organization governed by the State Board of Education, such as Pennsylvania Home Schoolers Accreditation Agency. Otherwise must present GED.

2011-2012 Annual costs. Tuition/fees: $13,590; $17,010 out-of-state. Room/board: $9,766. Books/supplies: $1,200. Personal expenses: $2,795.

Financial aid. Non-need-based: Scholarships awarded for academics, alumni affiliation.

Application procedures. Admission: Closing date 7/1 (postmark date). $50 fee, may be waived for applicants with need. Admission notification on a rolling basis. **Financial aid:** Priority date 4/1; no closing date. FAFSA, institutional form required. Applicants notified on a rolling basis starting 6/1; must reply by 7/1 or within 4 week(s) of notification.

Academics. Special study options: Accelerated study, cooperative education, cross-registration, distance learning, dual enrollment of high school students, exchange student, independent study, internships, student-designed major, study abroad, weekend college. **Credit/placement by examination:** AP, CLEP, institutional tests. 30 credit hours maximum toward associate degree, 30 toward bachelor's. **Support services:** Learning center, preadmission summer program, reduced course load, remedial instruction, study skills assistance, tutoring.

Majors. Architecture: Building sciences. **Business:** Accounting, business admin. **Computer sciences:** Networking, programming, security, web page design. **Health services:** Adult health nursing, cardiovascular technology, dental hygiene, EMT paramedic, medical records admin, physician assistant. **Visual/performing arts:** Commercial/advertising art, industrial design.

Most popular majors. Business/marketing 17%, computer/information sciences 10%, engineering/engineering technologies 28%, health sciences 19%, trade and industry 15%.

Computing on campus. 1,794 workstations in dormitories, library, computer center, student center. Dormitories wired for high-speed internet access and linked to campus network. Commuter students can connect to campus network. Online course registration, online library, helpline, repair service, student web hosting, wireless network available.

Student life. Freshman orientation: Available. Preregistration for classes offered. 2-day sessions offered throughout the summer and between fall and spring semesters for new students planning to begin in the spring. **Policies:** No alcohol or illegal drugs on campus. Smoke-free buildings and housing environments. **Housing:** Coed dorms, wellness housing available. $300 partly refundable deposit. Academic theme housing offers a living-learning atmosphere. **Activities:** Campus ministries, dance, international student organizations, radio station, student government, Alpha Omega Fellowship, Campus Crusade for Christ, Campus Ministry International, Earth Smart, Human Services Club, Multicultural Society, Skills USA, Student Government Association, Students Making a Contribution, United Campus Ministries, US Green Building Council Students of Penn College.

Athletics. USCAA. **Intercollegiate:** Archery, baseball M, basketball, bowling, cross-country, golf, soccer, softball W, tennis, volleyball, wrestling M. **Intramural:** Archery, badminton, basketball, bowling, football (non-tackle), golf, soccer, softball, table tennis, tennis, volleyball, weight lifting. **Team name:** Wildcats.

Student services. Adult student services, alcohol/substance abuse counseling, career counseling, student employment services, financial aid counseling, health services, on-campus daycare, personal counseling, placement for graduates. **Physically disabled:** Services for visually, speech, hearing impaired.

Contact. E-mail: admissions@pct.edu
Phone: (570) 327-4761 Toll-free number: (800) 367-9222
Fax: (570) 321-5551
Dennis Correll, Associate Dean for Admissions and Financial Aid, Pennsylvania College of Technology, One College Avenue, Williamsport, PA 17701-5799

Philadelphia Biblical University
Langhorne, Pennsylvania
www.pbu.edu   **CB code: 2661**

- Private 4-year university and Bible college affiliated with Protestant Evangelical tradition
- Residential campus in small town
- 937 degree-seeking undergraduates: 7% part-time, 53% women, 14% African American, 4% Asian American, 5% Hispanic American, 1% Native American, 2% international
- 246 degree-seeking graduate students
- 74% of applicants admitted
- SAT or ACT (ACT writing optional), application essay, interview required
- 63% graduate within 6 years; 30% enter graduate study

General. Founded in 1913. Regionally accredited; also accredited by ABHE. **Degrees:** 294 bachelor's awarded; master's offered. **ROTC:** Air Force. **Location:** 17 miles from Philadelphia; 5 miles from Trenton, New Jersey. **Calendar:** Semester, limited summer session. **Full-time faculty:** 50 total; 70% have terminal degrees, 18% minority, 30% women. **Part-time faculty:** 78 total; 19% have terminal degrees, 10% minority, 37% women. **Class size:** 70% < 20, 27% 20-39, 2% 40-49, 1% 50-99, less than 1% >100.

Freshman class profile. 482 applied, 358 admitted, 148 enrolled.

Mid 50% test scores			
SAT critical reading:	470-590	GPA 2.0-2.99:	22%
SAT math:	450-580	Rank in top quarter:	39%
ACT composite:	17-24	Rank in top tenth:	18%
GPA 3.75 or higher:	30%	End year in good standing:	99%
GPA 3.50-3.74:	16%	Return as sophomores:	78%
GPA 3.0-3.49:	29%	Out-of-state:	52%
		Live on campus:	80%

Basis for selection. High school GPA, pastor's references, writing sample, SAT or ACT scores required for some. Some applicants not meeting academic admissions requirements may be admitted and placed in a remedial program. Audition required for music program. **Home schooled:** Letter of recommendation (nonparent) required.

High school preparation. College-preparatory program recommended. 15 units recommended. Recommended units include English 4, mathematics 1, social studies 3, science 2 and foreign language 2.

2012-2013 Annual costs. Tuition/fees: $21,705. Room/board: $8,525. Books/supplies: $1,200. Personal expenses: $1,700.

2011-2012 Financial aid. Need-based: 140 full-time freshmen applied for aid; 129 were judged to have need; 129 of these received aid. Average need met was 75%. Average scholarship/grant was $15,594; average loan $3,644. 58% of total undergraduate aid awarded as scholarships/grants, 42% as loans/jobs. **Non-need-based:** Awarded to 161 full-time undergraduates, including 21 freshmen. Scholarships awarded for academics, leadership, music/drama.

Application procedures. Admission: No deadline. $25 fee, may be waived for applicants with need. Admission notification on a rolling basis beginning on or about 7/1. Housing deposit refundable in full if requested before May 1. **Financial aid:** Priority date 3/1; no closing date. FAFSA required. Applicants notified on a rolling basis starting 2/15; must reply within 2 week(s) of notification.

Academics. Students may participate in semester studies in Israel or in the 'Best Semester' program. **Special study options:** Accelerated study, combined bachelor's/graduate degree, double major, honors, internships, study abroad, teacher certification program. **Credit/placement by examination:** AP,

CLEP, IB, SAT, ACT, institutional tests. 12 credit hours maximum toward bachelor's degree. **Support services:** Learning center, reduced course load, remedial instruction, study skills assistance, tutoring, writing center.

Majors. Business: Business admin. **Education:** Early childhood, elementary, English, mathematics, music, physical, social studies. **Human services:** Social work. **Parks/recreation:** Health/fitness. **Theology:** Bible, missionary, pastoral counseling, religious ed, sacred music, theology. **Visual/performing arts:** Music, music performance, music theory/composition.

Most popular majors. Business/marketing 9%, education 13%, philosophy/religious studies 69%, public administration/social services 7%.

Computing on campus. 79 workstations in dormitories, library, student center. Dormitories wired for high-speed internet access and linked to campus network. Commuter students can connect to campus network. Online course registration, online library, helpline, wireless network available.

Student life. Freshman orientation: Mandatory. Preregistration for classes offered. **Policies:** Religious observance required. **Housing:** Guaranteed on-campus for freshmen. Single-sex dorms, special housing for disabled, apartments available. $250 deposit. **Activities:** Concert band, campus ministries, choral groups, drama, international student organizations, music ensembles, musical theater, opera, student government, student newspaper, symphony orchestra, student missionary fellowship, commuter council, resident council, student theological society, cultural awareness association, student business club, social committee.

Athletics. NCAA, NCCAA. **Intercollegiate:** Baseball M, basketball, cross-country, golf M, soccer, softball W, tennis W, volleyball. **Intramural:** Basketball, football (non-tackle), soccer, tennis, volleyball. **Team name:** Eagles.

Student services. Alcohol/substance abuse counseling, chaplain/spiritual director, career counseling, student employment services, financial aid counseling, health services, personal counseling, placement for graduates. **Physically disabled:** Services for visually, hearing impaired.

Contact. E-mail: admissions@pbu.edu
Phone: (215) 702-4235 Toll-free number: (800) 366-0049
Fax: (215) 702-4248
Eric Rivera, Assistant Director of Admissions, Philadelphia Biblical University, 200 Manor Avenue, Langhorne, PA 19047-2990

Philadelphia University
Philadelphia, Pennsylvania
www.philau.edu

CB member
CB code: 2666

- Private 4-year university
- Residential campus in very large city
- 2,943 degree-seeking undergraduates: 6% part-time, 65% women, 11% African American, 4% Asian American, 6% Hispanic American, 2% international
- 618 degree-seeking graduate students
- 71% of applicants admitted
- SAT or ACT (ACT writing optional) required
- 58% graduate within 6 years

General. Founded in 1884. Regionally accredited. **Degrees:** 634 bachelor's, 2 associate awarded; master's, doctoral offered. **Location:** 6 miles from Center City. **Calendar:** Semester, extensive summer session. **Full-time faculty:** 115 total; 73% have terminal degrees, 15% minority, 40% women. **Part-time faculty:** 384 total; 11% minority, 45% women. **Class size:** 66% < 20, 33% 20-39, less than 1% 40-49, less than 1% 50-99. **Special facilities:** Center for sustainability, energy efficiency and design, laboratory for engineered human protection, Institute for Textile and Apparel Product Safety, Engineering and Design Institute (a partnership with Ben Franklin Technology Partners), computer-aided design laboratories in architecture, graphic design and fashion design, CAD facilities, university design center, rapid prototyping.

Freshman class profile. 4,136 applied, 2,929 admitted, 1,298 enrolled.

Mid 50% test scores			
SAT critical reading:	480-580	Rank in top quarter:	27%
SAT math:	500-600	Rank in top tenth:	18%
SAT writing:	470-570	Return as sophomores:	71%
ACT composite:	22-26	Out-of-state:	58%
GPA 3.75 or higher:	35%	Live on campus:	92%
GPA 3.50-3.74:	18%	International:	3%
GPA 3.0-3.49:	29%	Fraternities:	1%
GPA 2.0-2.99:	18%	Sororities:	1%

Basis for selection. Academic record, GPA, and test scores most important. Extracurricular activities, counselor's recommendation and interview considered. Interview, essay recommended.

High school preparation. College-preparatory program recommended. 15 units required; 19 recommended. Required and recommended units include English 4, mathematics 3-4, social studies 2-3, history 1-2, science 3-4 (laboratory 2), foreign language 2 and academic electives 2.

2011-2012 Annual costs. Tuition/fees: $30,446. Room/board: $9,834. Books/supplies: $1,600. Personal expenses: $1,789.

2011-2012 Financial aid. Need-based: 581 full-time freshmen applied for aid; 531 were judged to have need; 531 of these received aid. Average need met was 81%. Average scholarship/grant was $24,479; average loan $4,021. 62% of total undergraduate aid awarded as scholarships/grants, 38% as loans/jobs. **Non-need-based:** Awarded to 703 full-time undergraduates, including 163 freshmen. Scholarships awarded for academics, athletics.

Application procedures. Admission: No deadline. $40 fee, may be waived for applicants with need. Admission notification on a rolling basis. Must reply by May 1 or within 1 week(s) if notified thereafter. Housing deposit not refundable after May 1st. **Financial aid:** Closing date 4/15. FAFSA required. Applicants notified on a rolling basis starting 2/10; must reply by 5/1.

Academics. Special study options: Accelerated study, combined bachelor's/graduate degree, distance learning, double major, honors, independent study, internships, liberal arts/career combination, semester at sea, study abroad. **Credit/placement by examination:** AP, CLEP, SAT, ACT, institutional tests. 60 credit hours maximum toward bachelor's degree. **Support services:** Learning center, reduced course load, remedial instruction, study skills assistance, tutoring, writing center.

Majors. Architecture: Architecture, interior, landscape. **Biology:** General, biochemistry, environmental. **Business:** Accounting, apparel, business admin, fashion, finance, international, management information systems, marketing. **Communications:** Digital media. **Communications technology:** Animation/special effects, graphics. **Conservation:** Environmental studies. **Engineering:** General, architectural, industrial, mechanical, textile. **Health services:** Health care admin, premedicine. **Physical sciences:** Chemistry. **Psychology:** General. **Visual/performing arts:** Fashion design, fiber arts, graphic design, industrial design, interior design. **Work/family studies:** Apparel marketing, clothing/textiles, textile science.

Most popular majors. Architecture 20%, business/marketing 33%, health sciences 11%, visual/performing arts 22%.

Computing on campus. PC or laptop required. 600 workstations in library, computer center, student center. Dormitories wired for high-speed internet access and linked to campus network. Commuter students can connect to campus network. Online course registration, online library, helpline, student web hosting, wireless network available.

Student life. Freshman orientation: Mandatory, $100 fee. Preregistration for classes offered. 3-day residential program in summer. **Housing:** Guaranteed on-campus for freshmen. Coed dorms, single-sex dorms, special housing for disabled, apartments available. $250 fully refundable deposit. Townhouses available. **Activities:** Campus ministries, choral groups, dance, drama, international student organizations, student government, student newspaper, professional (major-related) organizations, Black awareness society, Hillel, Christian fellowship, community service corps, Minaret, Gemini Theatre, Phila Capella, Gay Lesbian Bisexual Allies Coalition.

Athletics. NCAA. **Intercollegiate:** Baseball M, basketball, cross-country, golf M, lacrosse W, rowing (crew), soccer, softball W, tennis, track and field M, volleyball W. **Intramural:** Basketball, cross-country, football (tackle) M, skiing, soccer, softball, swimming, tennis, volleyball W. **Team name:** Rams.

Student services. Adult student services, alcohol/substance abuse counseling, career counseling, student employment services, financial aid counseling, health services, personal counseling, placement for graduates. **Physically disabled:** Services for visually, hearing impaired.

Contact. E-mail: admissions@philau.edu
Phone: (215) 951-2800 Toll-free number: (800) 951-7287
Fax: (215) 951-2907
Greg Potts, Director of Admissions, Philadelphia University, School House Lane and Henry Avenue, Philadelphia, PA 19144-5497

Point Park University
Pittsburgh, Pennsylvania
www.pointpark.edu

CB member
CB code: 2676

- Private 4-year university
- Commuter campus in large city

- 3,316 degree-seeking undergraduates: 20% part-time, 58% women, 18% African American, 1% Asian American, 3% Hispanic American, 1% international
- 532 degree-seeking graduate students
- 75% of applicants admitted
- SAT or ACT (ACT writing optional), application essay, interview required
- 50% graduate within 6 years

General. Founded in 1960. Regionally accredited. **Degrees:** 676 bachelor's, 6 associate awarded; master's offered. **ROTC:** Army, Air Force. **Location:** Downtown. **Calendar:** Semester, extensive summer session. **Full-time faculty:** 129 total; 71% have terminal degrees, 15% minority, 62% women. **Part-time faculty:** 304 total. **Class size:** 74% < 20, 25% 20-39, less than 1% 40-49, less than 1% 50-99. **Special facilities:** Pittsburgh Playhouse, 3-theater performing arts center.

Freshman class profile. 3,357 applied, 2,503 admitted, 491 enrolled.

Mid 50% test scores		**GPA 2.0-2.99:**	31%
SAT critical reading:	470-570	**Rank in top quarter:**	31%
SAT math:	440-540	**Rank in top tenth:**	9%
SAT writing:	450-560	**Return as sophomores:**	75%
ACT composite:	20-25	**Out-of-state:**	35%
GPA 3.75 or higher:	14%	**Live on campus:**	82%
GPA 3.50-3.74:	14%	**International:**	3%
GPA 3.0-3.49:	41%		

Basis for selection. High school record, class rank, test scores most important. Recommendations, extracurricular activities, talent, character also important. Test scores must be received by the first day of class. Audition required for some majors, portfolio recommended for multimedia, technical theater, stage management programs.

High school preparation. Recommended units include English 4, mathematics 4, social studies 3, history 3, science 4, foreign language 2 and visual/performing arts 2.

2011-2012 Annual costs. Tuition/fees: $23,720. Students in the Conservatory of Performing Arts (COPA) pay full-time tuition of $28,900 per year and $815 per-credit hour. Mandatory fees, room and board are the same as listed above for non-COPA students. Room/board: $9,720. Books/supplies: $1,000. Personal expenses: $1,100.

2011-2012 Financial aid. Need-based: Average need met was 67%. Average scholarship/grant was $15,279; average loan $4,614. 57% of total undergraduate aid awarded as scholarships/grants, 43% as loans/jobs. **Non-need-based:** Scholarships awarded for academics, athletics, music/drama.

Application procedures. Admission: No deadline. $40 fee, may be waived for applicants with need, free for online applicants. Admission notification on a rolling basis beginning on or about 10/1. Must reply by May 1 or within 2 week(s) if notified thereafter. **Financial aid:** Priority date 3/15; no closing date. FAFSA required. Applicants notified on a rolling basis starting 2/15; must reply by 8/30 or within 2 week(s) of notification.

Academics. Special study options: Accelerated study, cooperative education, cross-registration, distance learning, double major, dual enrollment of high school students, ESL, exchange student, honors, independent study, internships, liberal arts/career combination, student-designed major, study abroad, teacher certification program, weekend college. Numerous off-campus programs for college credits. Several accelerated programs available. Offers professionally oriented programs in arts, business, communications, and technology. **Credit/placement by examination:** AP, CLEP, IB. 30 credit hours maximum toward associate degree, 60 toward bachelor's. **Support services:** Learning center, pre-admission summer program, reduced course load, remedial instruction, study skills assistance, tutoring.

Majors. Biology: General, biotechnology. **Business:** Accounting, business admin, human resources. **Communications:** Advertising, broadcast journalism, digital media, journalism, media studies, photojournalism. **Computer sciences:** Information technology. **Conservation:** Environmental science. **Education:** Biology, drama/dance, early childhood, elementary, English, mathematics. **English:** English lit. **History:** General. **Human services:** General. **Liberal arts:** Arts/sciences. **Protective services:** Criminal justice, law enforcement admin. **Psychology:** General. **Social sciences:** General, economics, international relations, political science. **Visual/performing arts:** Cinematography, dance, dramatic, photography, play/screenwriting.

Most popular majors. Business/marketing 23%, communications/journalism 16%, education 7%, security/protective services 13%, visual/performing arts 26%.

Computing on campus. 371 workstations in dormitories, library, computer center, student center. Dormitories wired for high-speed internet access and linked to campus network. Commuter students can connect to campus network. Online course registration, online library, helpline, repair service, student web hosting, wireless network available.

Student life. Freshman orientation: Mandatory. Preregistration for classes offered. Held in summer months, includes placement testing if needed for major. **Policies:** Policies regarding student conduct, plagiarism and resident life. **Housing:** Guaranteed on-campus for all undergraduates. Coed dorms, special housing for disabled, apartments available. $400 fully refundable deposit. Living & learning communities; suite style housing. **Activities:** Campus ministries, dance, drama, film society, international student organizations, literary magazine, musical theater, radio station, student government, student newspaper, TV station, Black student union, Amnesty International.

Athletics. NAIA. **Intercollegiate:** Baseball M, basketball, cross-country, golf, soccer, softball W, volleyball W. **Intramural:** Basketball M, tennis, volleyball, weight lifting M. **Team name:** Pioneers.

Student services. Adult student services, alcohol/substance abuse counseling, career counseling, student employment services, financial aid counseling, health services, on-campus daycare, personal counseling, placement for graduates, veterans' counselor. **Physically disabled:** Services for visually, speech, hearing impaired.

Contact. E-mail: enroll@pointpark.edu
Phone: (412) 392-3430 Toll-free number: (800) 321-0129
Fax: (412) 392-3902
Joell Minford, Director of Admissions, Point Park University, 201 Wood Street, Pittsburgh, PA 15222-1984

Restaurant School at Walnut Hill College

Philadelphia, Pennsylvania
www.walnuthillcollege.edu **CB code: 4883**

- For-profit 4-year culinary school and business college
- Commuter campus in very large city
- 515 degree-seeking undergraduates: 15% African American, 2% Asian American, 5% Hispanic American
- Application essay, interview required

General. Accredited by ACCSC. Emphasis on fine dining and upscale hotels. **Degrees:** 42 bachelor's, 82 associate awarded. **Calendar:** Quarter. **Full-time faculty:** 21 total. **Part-time faculty:** 3 total. **Special facilities:** Students interact with numerous food and beverage outlets open to public. 4 uniquely themed restaurants and pastry shop/cafe.

Freshman class profile.

Out-of-state:	51%	**Live on campus:**	30%

Basis for selection. All students must interview with admissions representative, submit two letters of reference, 250-word essay, SAT/ACT scores and/or take a basic skills evaluation. Students who score below 900 combined on SAT/ACT Math and Critical Reading, or who did not take either test, must take in-house assessment test. Decisions are based on all information received, however the interview is the most heavily weighted. SAT or ACT recommended. **Home schooled:** Interview required.

Financial aid. Non-need-based: Scholarships awarded for leadership.

Application procedures. Admission: No deadline. $50 fee. Admission notification on a rolling basis. **Financial aid:** No deadline. FAFSA, institutional form required.

Academics. Special study options: Independent study, internships. **Credit/placement by examination:** AP, CLEP. **Support services:** Study skills assistance, tutoring.

Majors. Business: Hotel/motel admin, restaurant/food services.

Most popular majors. Business/marketing 15%, personal/culinary services 75%.

Computing on campus. 48 workstations in library, computer center. Dormitories wired for high-speed internet access and linked to campus network. Online library, wireless network available.

Student life. Freshman orientation: Mandatory. Preregistration for classes offered. 3-day orientation held week prior to start of classes. **Housing:** Guaranteed on-campus for all undergraduates. Coed dorms available. $850 fully refundable deposit. **Activities:** Literary magazine, music ensembles, student newspaper.

Student services. Career counseling, student employment services, financial aid counseling.

Contact. E-mail: info@walnuthillcollege.edu
Phone: (215) 222-4200 ext. 3011
Toll-free number: (877) 925-6884 ext. 3011 Fax: (215) 222-2811
Toni Morelli, Director of Admissions, Restaurant School at Walnut Hill
College, 4207 Walnut Street, Philadelphia, PA 19104

Robert Morris University
Moon Township, Pennsylvania
CB member
www.rmu.edu
CB code: 2769

- Private 4-year university
- Commuter campus in large town
- 3,882 degree-seeking undergraduates: 11% part-time, 45% women, 8% African American, 1% Asian American, 2% Hispanic American, 3% international
- 1,043 degree-seeking graduate students
- 79% of applicants admitted
- SAT or ACT (ACT writing optional) required
- 59% graduate within 6 years

General. Founded in 1921. Regionally accredited. **Degrees:** 779 bachelor's awarded; master's, professional offered. **ROTC:** Army, Air Force. **Location:** 17 miles from Pittsburgh. **Calendar:** Semester, limited summer session. **Full-time faculty:** 194 total; 87% have terminal degrees, 9% minority, 42% women. **Part-time faculty:** 215 total; 33% have terminal degrees, 7% minority, 50% women. **Class size:** 48% < 20, 42% 20-39, 6% 40-49, 4% 50-99.

Freshman class profile. 5,354 applied, 4,233 admitted, 787 enrolled.

Mid 50% test scores			
SAT critical reading:	450-550	Rank in top quarter:	37%
SAT math:	460-570	Rank in top tenth:	14%
SAT writing:	430-540	Return as sophomores:	81%
ACT composite:	20-24	Out-of-state:	19%
GPA 3.75 or higher:	25%	Live on campus:	82%
GPA 3.50-3.74:	19%	International:	4%
GPA 3.0-3.49:	32%	Fraternities:	3%
GPA 2.0-2.99:	24%	Sororities:	9%

Basis for selection. Academic potential, high school GPA, class rank, test scores, and evidence of motivation important. Interview required of restricted-status applicants, recommended for all others.

High school preparation. College-preparatory program required. 16 units required; 19 recommended. Required and recommended units include English 4, mathematics 3-4, social studies 4, science 2, foreign language 2 and academic electives 3.

2011-2012 Annual costs. Tuition/fees: $23,038. Room/board: $11,030. Books/supplies: $1,200. Personal expenses: $1,500.

2011-2012 Financial aid. Need-based: 716 full-time freshmen applied for aid; 654 were judged to have need; 654 of these received aid. Average need met was 73%. Average scholarship/grant was $14,511; average loan $4,059. 53% of total undergraduate aid awarded as scholarships/grants, 47% as loans/jobs. **Non-need-based:** Awarded to 826 full-time undergraduates, including 191 freshmen. Scholarships awarded for academics, athletics, ROTC.

Application procedures. Admission: Priority date 4/1; no deadline. $30 fee, may be waived for applicants with need, free for online applicants. Admission notification on a rolling basis beginning on or about 9/1. Must reply by May 1 or within 2 week(s) if notified thereafter. **Financial aid:** No deadline. FAFSA required. Applicants notified on a rolling basis starting 3/1.

Academics. Special study options: Combined bachelor's/graduate degree, cooperative education, cross-registration, distance learning, double major, honors, independent study, internships, study abroad, teacher certification program, weekend college. **Credit/placement by examination:** AP, CLEP, SAT, ACT, institutional tests. 30 credit hours maximum toward bachelor's degree. **Support services:** Pre-admission summer program, reduced course load, remedial instruction, study skills assistance, tutoring.

Majors. Biology: General. **Business:** Accounting, actuarial science, business admin, finance, hospitality admin, management information systems, marketing, organizational behavior. **Communications:** Communications/speech/rhetoric. **Computer sciences:** Information systems. **Conservation:** Environmental science. **Education:** Business, elementary. **Engineering:** Manufacturing, software. **English:** English lit. **Health services:** Health services admin, medical radiologic technology/radiation therapy, nursing (RN). **Math:** Applied. **Parks/recreation:** Sports admin. **Psychology:** General. **Social sciences:** General, economics. **Visual/performing arts:** Design.

Most popular majors. Business/marketing 53%, communications/journalism 7%, health sciences 9%.

Computing on campus. 300 workstations in dormitories, library, computer center, student center. Dormitories wired for high-speed internet access and linked to campus network. Commuter students can connect to campus network. Online course registration, online library, helpline, wireless network available.

Student life. Freshman orientation: Mandatory, $100 fee. Preregistration for classes offered. 3-day program. **Housing:** Coed dorms, single-sex dorms, special housing for disabled, apartments, wellness housing available. $100 fully refundable deposit, deadline 5/1. **Activities:** Bands, campus ministries, choral groups, drama, international student organizations, literary magazine, music ensembles, musical theater, radio station, student government, student newspaper, TV station, minority student organizations, campus activities board, inter-residence hall council, inter-fraternity council/Panhellenic council, honor societies, major-related organizations, campus Republicans and Democrats, community service and volunteer organizations.

Athletics. NCAA. **Intercollegiate:** Basketball, field hockey W, football (tackle) M, golf, ice hockey, lacrosse, rowing (crew) W, soccer, softball W, tennis, track and field, volleyball W. **Intramural:** Basketball, football (non-tackle) M, softball, volleyball W. **Team name:** Colonials.

Student services. Adult student services, alcohol/substance abuse counseling, chaplain/spiritual director, career counseling, services for economically disadvantaged, student employment services, financial aid counseling, health services, minority student services, personal counseling, placement for graduates, veterans' counselor, women's services. **Physically disabled:** Services for visually, speech, hearing impaired.

Contact. E-mail: admissionsoffice@rmu.edu
Phone: (412) 397-5200 Toll-free number: (800) 762-0097
Fax: (412) 397-2425
Kellie Laurenzi, Dean of Admissions, Robert Morris University, 6001
University Boulevard, Moon Township, PA 15108-1189

Rosemont College
Rosemont, Pennsylvania
CB member
www.rosemont.edu
CB code: 2763

- Private 4-year liberal arts college affiliated with Roman Catholic Church
- Residential campus in small town
- 519 degree-seeking undergraduates: 17% part-time, 69% women, 40% African American, 4% Asian American, 6% Hispanic American, 2% international
- 364 degree-seeking graduate students
- 54% of applicants admitted
- SAT or ACT required
- 58% graduate within 6 years; 35% enter graduate study

General. Founded in 1921. Regionally accredited. **Degrees:** 85 bachelor's awarded; master's offered. **ROTC:** Army, Air Force. **Location:** 11 miles from Philadelphia. **Calendar:** Semester, limited summer session. **Full-time faculty:** 28 total; 75% have terminal degrees, 11% minority, 64% women. **Part-time faculty:** 120 total; 75% have terminal degrees, 17% minority, 61% women. **Class size:** 81% < 20, 19% 20-39. **Special facilities:** Our administration building "Rathalla" has recently been historically certified.

Freshman class profile. 1,032 applied, 553 admitted, 107 enrolled.

Mid 50% test scores			
SAT critical reading:	430-550	GPA 3.0-3.49:	39%
SAT math:	420-540	GPA 2.0-2.99:	28%
SAT writing:	430-520	End year in good standing:	97%
ACT composite:	18-22	Return as sophomores:	67%
GPA 3.75 or higher:	19%	Out-of-state:	30%
GPA 3.50-3.74:	14%	Live on campus:	90%
		International:	1%

Basis for selection. School achievement record and curriculum, recommendations, test scores, extracurricular activities strongly considered. Interview recommended. **Home schooled:** Statement describing home school structure and mission, transcript of courses and grades, letter of recommendation (nonparent) required.

High school preparation. College-preparatory program recommended. 18 units required. Required units include English 4, mathematics 2, social studies 2, history 2, science 2 (laboratory 2), foreign language 2 and academic electives 2.

2011-2012 Annual costs. Tuition/fees: $29,050. Room/board: $11,440. Books/supplies: $1,500. Personal expenses: $1,000.

2011-2012 Financial aid. Need-based: Average need met was 81%. Average scholarship/grant was $23,703; average loan $3,253. 71% of total undergraduate aid awarded as scholarships/grants, 29% as loans/jobs. **Non-need-based:** Scholarships awarded for academics, alumni affiliation, art, religious affiliation.

Application procedures. Admission: No deadline. $35 fee, may be waived for applicants with need, free for online applicants. Admission notification on a rolling basis. Must reply by May 1 or within 2 week(s) if notified thereafter. $350 deposit required if student plans to live on campus. $200 deposit if student plans to commute to campus. **Financial aid:** Priority date 2/15; no closing date. FAFSA required. Applicants notified on a rolling basis starting 3/1; must reply within 4 week(s) of notification.

Academics. Special study options: Accelerated study, combined bachelor's/graduate degree, cross-registration, distance learning, double major, ESL, exchange student, honors, independent study, internships, liberal arts/career combination, student-designed major, study abroad, teacher certification program, Washington semester. **Credit/placement by examination:** AP, CLEP, IB, SAT, ACT, institutional tests. 30 credit hours maximum toward bachelor's degree. Students may be exempted if they demonstrate mastery of subject as determined by particular department. **Support services:** Learning center, pre-admission summer program, reduced course load, remedial instruction, study skills assistance, tutoring, writing center.

Majors. Area/ethnic studies: Women's. **Biology:** General, biochemistry. **Business:** General, accounting, business admin, communications, hospitality admin, human resources, management science, managerial economics, marketing, organizational behavior. **Communications:** Communications/speech/rhetoric. **Conservation:** Environmental science. **Education:** Elementary, secondary. **English:** English lit. **Foreign languages:** General, French, German, Italian, Spanish. **History:** General. **Liberal arts:** Arts/sciences, humanities. **Math:** General. **Philosophy/religion:** Philosophy, religion. **Physical sciences:** Chemistry. **Protective services:** Criminal justice. **Psychology:** General. **Social sciences:** General, economics, political science, sociology. **Visual/performing arts:** Art history/conservation, studio arts.

Most popular majors. Biology 9%, business/marketing 38%, communications/journalism 12%, English 7%, psychology 11%, security/protective services 12%, social sciences 7%.

Computing on campus. 100 workstations in dormitories, library, computer center, student center. Dormitories wired for high-speed internet access and linked to campus network. Commuter students can connect to campus network. Online course registration, online library, helpline, student web hosting, wireless network available.

Student life. Freshman orientation: Mandatory, $280 fee. Preregistration for classes offered. Orientation approximately 3 days; includes academics component. **Housing:** Guaranteed on-campus for all undergraduates. Single-sex dorms, wellness housing available. Honors housing. **Activities:** Bands, campus ministries, choral groups, dance, drama, international student organizations, literary magazine, music ensembles, Model UN, musical theater, opera, radio station, student government, student newspaper, premed club, politics club, Rosemont Alcohol and Drug Awareness Resource, multicultural society, Best Buddies, Triad, art society.

Athletics. NCAA. **Intercollegiate:** Basketball, golf M, lacrosse, soccer, tennis, volleyball W. **Team name:** The Ravens.

Student services. Adult student services, alcohol/substance abuse counseling, chaplain/spiritual director, career counseling, student employment services, financial aid counseling, health services, legal services, minority student services, on-campus daycare, personal counseling, placement for graduates, veterans' counselor, women's services. **Physically disabled:** Services for visually, speech, hearing impaired.

Contact. E-mail: admissions@rosemont.edu
Phone: (610) 526-2966 Toll-free number: (800) 331-0708
Fax: (610) 520-4399
Kevin McIntyre, Vice President for Enrollment Management, Rosemont College, 1400 Montgomery Avenue, Rosemont, PA 19010-1699

Saint Joseph's University
Philadelphia, Pennsylvania
www.sju.edu

CB member
CB code: 2801

- Private 4-year university affiliated with Roman Catholic Church
- Residential campus in very large city
- 5,324 degree-seeking undergraduates: 14% part-time, 53% women, 7% African American, 2% Asian American, 4% Hispanic American, 1% international
- 3,205 degree-seeking graduate students

- 78% of applicants admitted
- SAT or ACT (ACT writing optional), application essay required
- 76% graduate within 6 years; 23% enter graduate study

General. Founded in 1851. Regionally accredited. **Degrees:** 1,044 bachelor's, 6 associate awarded; master's, doctoral offered. **ROTC:** Army, Naval, Air Force. **Location:** 8 miles from downtown. **Calendar:** Semester, extensive summer session. **Full-time faculty:** 299 total; 90% have terminal degrees, 14% minority, 42% women. **Part-time faculty:** 475 total; 10% minority, 45% women. **Class size:** 37% < 20, 56% 20-39, 6% 40-49, less than 1% 50-99.

Freshman class profile. 7,401 applied, 5,752 admitted, 1,133 enrolled.

Mid 50% test scores		
SAT critical reading:	510-600	
SAT math:	520-610	
SAT writing:	520-610	
ACT composite:	22-26	
GPA 3.75 or higher:	33%	
GPA 3.50-3.74:	20%	
GPA 3.0-3.49:	29%	

GPA 2.0-2.99:	18%
Rank in top quarter:	53%
Rank in top tenth:	22%
Return as sophomores:	89%
Out-of-state:	60%
Live on campus:	97%
International:	1%

Basis for selection. Careful consideration given to applicant's academic GPA and rigor of high school record. Important factors include application essay, counselor or teacher recommendations, character and personal qualities.

High school preparation. College-preparatory program recommended. 12 units required. Required units include English 4, mathematics 3, history 1, science 2 (laboratory 1) and foreign language 2.

2011-2012 Annual costs. Tuition/fees: $36,640. Traditional undergraduate day students taking additional credits over 5 courses pay an additional per-credit-hour fee of $1,156. Part-time, adult undergraduate evening division per-credit-hour fee is $480 (non-traditional, adult continuing education). Business and Psychology majors are required have a laptop but are not required to purchase from the University. Room/board: $12,206.

Financial aid. Non-need-based: Scholarships awarded for academics, alumni affiliation, art, athletics, minority status, music/drama, ROTC.

Application procedures. Admission: Closing date 2/1 (postmark date). $60 fee, may be waived for applicants with need. Admission notification by 3/15. Must reply by May 1 or within 2 week(s) if notified thereafter. **Financial aid:** Priority date 2/15; no closing date. FAFSA required. Applicants notified on a rolling basis starting 3/31; must reply by 5/1.

Academics. Special study options: Accelerated study, combined bachelor's/graduate degree, cooperative education, distance learning, double major, dual enrollment of high school students, ESL, exchange student, honors, independent study, internships, student-designed major, study abroad, teacher certification program, Washington semester, weekend college, Jesuit student exchange. **Credit/placement by examination:** AP, CLEP, IB, institutional tests. **Support services:** Learning center, pre-admission summer program, reduced course load, study skills assistance, tutoring, writing center.

Majors. Area/ethnic studies: Asian, European, French. **Biology:** General, biochemistry. **Business:** Accounting, actuarial science, business admin, finance, financial planning, human resources, insurance, international, knowledge management, management information systems, marketing, organizational behavior, purchasing, small business admin, special products marketing. **Communications:** General, communications/speech/rhetoric. **Computer sciences:** General, information systems. **Conservation:** Environmental studies. **Education:** Art, biology, chemistry, elementary, English, ESL, foreign languages, French, history, Latin, mathematics, physics, science, secondary, Spanish. **English:** English lit. **Foreign languages:** French, German, Italian, Latin, Spanish. **Health services:** Facilities admin. **History:** General. **Human services:** General. **Liberal arts:** Arts/sciences. **Math:** General. **Philosophy/religion:** Philosophy, religion. **Physical sciences:** Chemistry, physics. **Psychology:** General, industrial. **Social sciences:** Criminology, economics, international relations, political science, sociology. **Visual/performing arts:** General, music.

Most popular majors. Business/marketing 46%, education 7%, social sciences 12%.

Computing on campus. 725 workstations in dormitories, library, computer center, student center. Dormitories wired for high-speed internet access and linked to campus network. Commuter students can connect to campus network. Online course registration, online library, helpline, repair service, student web hosting, wireless network available.

Student life. Freshman orientation: Available, $225 fee. Preregistration for classes offered. **Policies:** Freshmen not permitted cars on campus. **Housing:** Guaranteed on-campus for freshmen. Coed dorms, single-sex dorms,

special housing for disabled, apartments, cooperative housing, wellness housing available. $500 nonrefundable deposit, deadline 5/1. **Activities:** Bands, campus ministries, choral groups, dance, drama, film society, international student organizations, literary magazine, music ensembles, musical theater, radio station, student government, student newspaper, Black student union, Caribbean students association, Hand-in-Hand, College Democrats, College Republicans, Habitat for Humanity, Students for Life, community service weekly programs.

Athletics. NCAA. **Intercollegiate:** Baseball M, basketball, cross-country, field hockey W, golf M, lacrosse, rowing (crew), soccer, softball W, tennis, track and field. **Intramural:** Basketball, football (non-tackle), racquetball, soccer, softball, tennis, volleyball. **Team name:** Hawks.

Student services. Adult student services, alcohol/substance abuse counseling, chaplain/spiritual director, career counseling, services for economically disadvantaged, student employment services, financial aid counseling, health services, minority student services, personal counseling, women's services. **Physically disabled:** Services for visually, speech, hearing impaired.

Contact. E-mail: admit@sju.edu
Phone: (610) 660-1300 Toll-free number: (888) 232-4295
Fax: (610) 660-1314
Maureen Mathis, Executive Director of Undergraduate Admissions, Saint Joseph's University, 5600 City Avenue, Philadelphia, PA 19131

Seton Hill University
Greensburg, Pennsylvania
www.setonhill.edu

CB member
CB code: 2812

- Private 4-year university and liberal arts college affiliated with Roman Catholic Church
- Residential campus in large town
- 1,610 degree-seeking undergraduates: 9% part-time, 64% women
- 437 degree-seeking graduate students
- 44% of applicants admitted
- Application essay required
- 44% graduate within 6 years; 30% enter graduate study

General. Founded in 1918. Regionally accredited. **Degrees:** 301 bachelor's awarded; master's offered. **ROTC:** Army. **Location:** 35 miles from Pittsburgh. **Calendar:** Semester, limited summer session. **Full-time faculty:** 95 total; 84% have terminal degrees, 5% minority, 54% women. **Part-time faculty:** 97 total; 32% have terminal degrees, 2% minority, 61% women. **Class size:** 56% < 20, 41% 20-39, 3% 40-49. **Special facilities:** Performing arts center, child development center, kindergarten, women in business center, Catholic Holocaust education center.

Freshman class profile. 2,975 applied, 1,322 admitted, 356 enrolled.

Mid 50% test scores			
SAT critical reading:	450-560	Rank in top quarter:	47%
SAT math:	450-570	Rank in top tenth:	19%
SAT writing:	440-550	End year in good standing:	94%
ACT composite:	19-26	Return as sophomores:	75%
GPA 3.75 or higher:	34%	Out-of-state:	26%
GPA 3.50-3.74:	18%	Live on campus:	86%
GPA 3.0-3.49:	29%		
GPA 2.0-2.99:	19%		

Basis for selection. School achievement record most important, followed by test scores and recommendations. Applicants from minorities or low-income families encouraged, accepted on basis of motivation and potential. SAT or ACT recommended. Students who have not taken SAT or ACT may submit 2 graded writing samples for consideration. Interview recommended for all; audition required for music, theater programs; portfolio required for art program. Additional application required for physician assistant and BS/DO and BS/DPharm programs. **Home schooled:** Must provide SAT/ACT scores and official transcript issued by a school district or agency approving the curriculum, or GED.

High school preparation. College-preparatory program recommended. 15 units required. Required and recommended units include English 4, mathematics 2, social studies 2, science 1 (laboratory 1), foreign language 2 and academic electives 4. 4 math units recommended for science majors.

2011-2012 Annual costs. Tuition/fees: $28,354. Required fees vary from $700 to $1,100 according to what technology plan student chooses and by number of credits if part-time. Various options available for room and board. Room/board: $9,126. Books/supplies: $1,000. Personal expenses: $2,500.

2011-2012 Financial aid. Need-based: 339 full-time freshmen applied for aid; 316 were judged to have need; 314 of these received aid. Average need met was 77%. Average scholarship/grant was $19,713; average loan

$5,093. 69% of total undergraduate aid awarded as scholarships/grants, 31% as loans/jobs. **Non-need-based:** Scholarships awarded for academics, alumni affiliation, art, athletics, job skills, music/drama, religious affiliation.

Application procedures. Admission: Priority date 5/1; deadline 8/15 (postmark date). $35 fee, may be waived for applicants with need, free for online applicants. Admission notification on a rolling basis beginning on or about 9/1. **Financial aid:** Priority date 5/1; no closing date. FAFSA, institutional form required. Applicants notified on a rolling basis starting 11/20.

Academics. Special study options: Accelerated study, combined bachelor's/graduate degree, cross-registration, distance learning, double major, dual enrollment of high school students, ESL, honors, independent study, internships, liberal arts/career combination, New York semester, semester at sea, student-designed major, study abroad, teacher certification program, United Nations semester, Washington semester, weekend college. **Credit/placement by examination:** AP, CLEP, IB, SAT, ACT. 30 credit hours maximum toward bachelor's degree. **Support services:** Learning center, pre-admission summer program, reduced course load, remedial instruction, study skills assistance, tutoring, writing center.

Majors. Biology: General, biochemistry. **Business:** Accounting, actuarial science, business admin, entrepreneurial studies, hospitality admin, human resources, international, management information systems, marketing, sales/distribution. **Communications:** Communications/speech/rhetoric, journalism. **Computer sciences:** Computer science. **Education:** Art, biology, chemistry, English, family/consumer sciences, foreign languages, mathematics, music, Spanish. **Engineering:** General. **English:** Creative writing, English lit. **Foreign languages:** Spanish. **Health services:** Art therapy, clinical lab science, dietetics, music therapy, physician assistant. **History:** General. **Human services:** Social work. **Math:** General. **Parks/recreation:** Sports admin. **Philosophy/religion:** Religion. **Physical sciences:** Chemistry. **Protective services:** Criminal justice, forensics. **Psychology:** General. **Social sciences:** Economics, international relations, political science, sociology. **Theology:** Sacred music. **Visual/performing arts:** Acting, art history/conservation, ceramics, commercial/advertising art, dramatic, drawing, metal/jewelry, music, music performance, painting, printmaking, sculpture, studio arts, studio arts management, theater arts management, theater design. **Work/family studies:** General, child care management, child development.

Most popular majors. Business/marketing 24%, health sciences 7%, history 6%, psychology 8%, public administration/social services 8%, security/protective services 7%, visual/performing arts 10%.

Computing on campus. PC or laptop required. 153 workstations in dormitories, library, computer center, student center. Dormitories wired for high-speed internet access and linked to campus network. Online course registration, helpline, repair service, student web hosting, wireless network available.

Student life. Freshman orientation: Mandatory, $25 fee. Preregistration for classes offered. One-day, on-campus family orientation in summer. 4-day orientation during weekend and weekdays prior to start of classes. **Policies:** Residence hall students involved in setting community standards. **Housing:** Guaranteed on-campus for all undergraduates. Coed dorms, single-sex dorms available. $250 deposit, deadline 7/1. Housing for honors students. **Activities:** Bands, campus ministries, choral groups, dance, drama, international student organizations, literary magazine, music ensembles, musical theater, student government, student newspaper, symphony orchestra, social work club, liturgical groups, Respect Life, Operation Christmas Basket, Association of Black Collegians, National Coalition Building Institute, Helping Hands, Habitat for Humanity.

Athletics. NCAA. **Intercollegiate:** Baseball M, basketball, cross-country, equestrian W, field hockey W, football (tackle) M, golf W, lacrosse, soccer, softball W, tennis W, track and field, volleyball W, wrestling M. **Intramural:** Basketball W, equestrian W, soccer W, softball W, volleyball W. **Team name:** Griffins.

Student services. Adult student services, alcohol/substance abuse counseling, chaplain/spiritual director, career counseling, services for economically disadvantaged, student employment services, financial aid counseling, health services, minority student services, on-campus daycare, personal counseling, placement for graduates, veterans' counselor. **Physically disabled:** Services for visually, speech, hearing impaired.

Contact. E-mail: admit@setonhill.edu
Phone: (724) 838-4255 Toll-free number: (800) 826-6234
Fax: (724) 830-1294
Ashley Josay, Assistant Director of Admissions, Seton Hill University, 1 Seton Hill Drive, Greensburg, PA 15601

Shippensburg University of Pennsylvania
Shippensburg, Pennsylvania
www.ship.edu

CB member
CB code: 2657

- Public 4-year university
- Residential campus in small town
- 7,066 degree-seeking undergraduates: 4% part-time, 52% women, 6% African American, 1% Asian American, 3% Hispanic American
- 917 degree-seeking graduate students
- 80% of applicants admitted
- SAT or ACT (ACT writing optional) required
- 60% graduate within 6 years

General. Founded in 1871. Regionally accredited. **Degrees:** 1,297 bachelor's awarded; master's offered. **ROTC:** Army. **Location:** 40 miles from Harrisburg. **Calendar:** Semester, extensive summer session. **Full-time faculty:** 323 total; 91% have terminal degrees, 15% minority, 43% women. **Part-time faculty:** 96 total; 32% have terminal degrees, 3% minority, 50% women. **Class size:** 23% < 20, 55% 20-39, 14% 40-49, 8% 50-99. **Special facilities:** On-campus elementary school for student teachers, planetarium, vertebrate museum, greenhouse, herbarium, electron microscope, NMR spectrometer, fashion archives, interfaith spiritual center, women's center, performing arts center.

Freshman class profile. 6,883 applied, 5,504 admitted, 1,752 enrolled.

Mid 50% test scores			
SAT critical reading:	440-530	GPA 2.0-2.99:	37%
SAT math:	440-540	Rank in top quarter:	21%
SAT writing:	420-510	Rank in top tenth:	7%
ACT composite:	17-22	End year in good standing:	72%
GPA 3.75 or higher:	14%	Return as sophomores:	70%
GPA 3.50-3.74:	13%	Out-of-state:	7%
GPA 3.0-3.49:	35%	Live on campus:	87%

Basis for selection. Secondary school record and test scores important. Summer Bridge Program provides access and academic support to students who do not meet regular admission criteria but have demonstrated potential, desire, and motivation to succeed in college. Interviews advisable in some situations. **Home schooled:** Transcript of courses and grades, state high school equivalency certificate required. Those working with accredited agency must submit copy of both annual evaluation and homeschool diploma. All others encouraged to schedule interview and present portfolio, and must provide GED results. Grade transcripts required (if available). **Learning Disabled:** Students must register with Office of Disability Services and provide documentation from qualified professional and must be less than 3 years old. Reasonable accommodations provided.

High school preparation. College-preparatory program required. 16 units recommended. Recommended units include English 4, mathematics 3, social studies 3, science 3 (laboratory 3) and foreign language 3.

2011-2012 Annual costs. Tuition/fees: $8,856; $18,216 out-of-state. Tuition for transfer students from five neighboring MD community colleges with dual admission agreements is $9,360. Tuition for all MD residents not covered by the aforementioned differential for transfer students is $14,040. Room/board: $7,620. Books/supplies: $1,200. Personal expenses: $1,914.

2011-2012 Financial aid. **Need-based:** Average need met was 55%. Average scholarship/grant was $5,996; average loan $3,196. 38% of total undergraduate aid awarded as scholarships/grants, 62% as loans/jobs. **Non-need-based:** Scholarships awarded for academics, athletics.

Application procedures. **Admission:** No deadline. $30 fee, may be waived for applicants with need. Admission notification on a rolling basis. Must reply by April 1 or request a May 1 extension in writing. **Financial aid:** Priority date 3/15; no closing date. FAFSA required. Applicants notified on a rolling basis; must reply within 2 week(s) of notification.

Academics. Web-based online courses and programs also available. **Special study options:** Accelerated study, combined bachelor's/graduate degree, cooperative education, distance learning, double major, dual admission of high school students, honors, independent study, internships, semester at sea, study abroad, teacher certification program, Washington semester. Raider Plan. **Credit/placement by examination:** AP, CLEP, IB, SAT, ACT, institutional tests. 30 credit hours maximum toward bachelor's degree. **Support services:** Learning center, pre-admission summer program, reduced course load, remedial instruction, study skills assistance, tutoring, writing center.

Majors. Biology: General. **Business:** Accounting, business admin, finance, logistics, management science, marketing. **Communications:** Journalism. **Computer sciences:** General, systems analysis. **Conservation:** Environmental studies. **Education:** Early childhood, middle. **Engineering:** Software.

English: English lit, rhetoric/composition. **Foreign languages:** French, Spanish. **Health services:** Health care admin. **History:** General. **Human services:** General, social work. **Math:** General. **Parks/recreation:** Exercise sciences. **Physical sciences:** Chemistry, geology, physics. **Protective services:** Criminal justice. **Psychology:** General. **Social sciences:** Economics, geography, political science, sociology. **Visual/performing arts:** Art.

Most popular majors. Business/marketing 24%, communications/journalism 6%, education 14%, psychology 9%, security/protective services 6%, social sciences 6%.

Computing on campus. 800 workstations in library, computer center, student center. Dormitories wired for high-speed internet access and linked to campus network. Commuter students can connect to campus network. Online course registration, online library, helpline, repair service, student web hosting, wireless network available.

Student life. **Freshman orientation:** Mandatory, $150 fee. Preregistration for classes offered. Orientation held in summer and prior to fall and spring semesters. **Policies:** University student code of conduct in effect. **Housing:** Guaranteed on-campus for freshmen. Coed dorms, apartments, wellness housing available. $100 partly refundable deposit, deadline 4/1. **Activities:** Bands, campus ministries, choral groups, dance, drama, international student organizations, literary magazine, music ensembles, musical theater, radio station, student government, student newspaper, symphony orchestra, TV station, African American Organization, Fellowship of Christian Athletes, Christian Fellowship, College Republicans, nontraditional student organization, Latino student organization, Asian-American association, College Democrats, Bridge for Kids, multi-ethnic student association.

Athletics. NCAA. **Intercollegiate:** Baseball M, basketball, cross-country, field hockey W, football (tackle) M, lacrosse W, soccer, softball W, swimming, tennis W, track and field, volleyball W, wrestling M. **Intramural:** Basketball, soccer, softball, volleyball. **Team name:** Raiders.

Student services. Adult student services, chaplain/spiritual director, career counseling, student employment services, financial aid counseling, health services, minority student services, on-campus daycare, personal counseling, placement for graduates, veterans' counselor, women's services. **Physically disabled:** Services for visually, hearing impaired.

Contact. E-mail: admiss@ship.edu
Phone: (717) 477-1231 Toll-free number: (800) 822-8028
Fax: (717) 477-4016
Thomas Speakman, Dean of Enrollment Services, Shippensburg University of Pennsylvania, 1871 Old Main Drive, Shippensburg, PA 17257-2299

Slippery Rock University of Pennsylvania
Slippery Rock, Pennsylvania
www.sru.edu

CB member
CB code: 2658

- Public 4-year university
- Residential campus in small town
- 7,881 degree-seeking undergraduates: 5% part-time, 57% women, 5% African American, 1% Asian American, 2% Hispanic American, 1% international
- 663 degree-seeking graduate students
- 61% of applicants admitted
- SAT or ACT (ACT writing optional) required
- 59% graduate within 6 years; 23% enter graduate study

General. Founded in 1889. Regionally accredited. **Degrees:** 1,548 bachelor's awarded; master's, professional offered. **ROTC:** Army. **Location:** 50 miles from Pittsburgh. **Calendar:** Semester, extensive summer session. **Full-time faculty:** 350 total; 89% have terminal degrees, 17% minority, 48% women. **Part-time faculty:** 49 total; 35% have terminal degrees, 18% minority, 57% women. **Class size:** 17% < 20, 58% 20-39, 16% 40-49, 7% 50-99, 3% >100. **Special facilities:** Environmental education centers, crime scene investigation house, planetarium.

Freshman class profile. 6,418 applied, 3,943 admitted, 1,536 enrolled.

Mid 50% test scores			
SAT critical reading:	450-540	Rank in top quarter:	41%
SAT math:	450-540	Rank in top tenth:	14%
SAT writing:	430-530	End year in good standing:	86%
ACT composite:	18-23	Return as sophomores:	81%
GPA 3.75 or higher:	23%	Out-of-state:	13%
GPA 3.50-3.74:	21%	Live on campus:	95%
GPA 3.0-3.49:	39%	Fraternities:	10%
GPA 2.0-2.99:	17%	Sororities:	7%

Basis for selection. Recommended minimum 2.5 GPA, or 76 percent or higher average. Minimum score of 900 SAT (exclusive of Writing) or 20 ACT recommended. Audition required for music and dance majors. **Home schooled:** Documentation of homeschool diploma or certification information regarding how homeschool material was covered.

High school preparation. College-preparatory program recommended. 16 units recommended. Recommended units include English 4, mathematics 3, social studies 3, history 3, science 3 (laboratory 1) and foreign language 2.

2011-2012 Annual costs. Tuition/fees: $8,506; $11,626 out-of-state. Tuition for out-of-state students with at least 3.0 GPA is $9,360; all out-of-state undergraduates pay an additional $178 in required fees. Room/board: $9,150. Books/supplies: $1,425. Personal expenses: $952.

2011-2012 Financial aid. **Need-based:** 1,444 full-time freshmen applied for aid; 1,137 were judged to have need; 1,132 of these received aid. Average need met was 59%. Average scholarship/grant was $5,644; average loan $3,398. 48% of total undergraduate aid awarded as scholarships/grants, 52% as loans/jobs. **Non-need-based:** Awarded to 1,755 full-time undergraduates, including 571 freshmen. Scholarships awarded for academics, alumni affiliation, art, athletics, job skills, leadership, minority status, music/drama, ROTC, state residency. **Additional information:** May 1 closing date for Pennsylvania state grants.

Application procedures. **Admission:** No deadline. $30 fee, may be waived for applicants with need. Admission notification on a rolling basis beginning on or about 6/15. Must reply by May 1 or within 2 week(s) if notified thereafter. **Financial aid:** Priority date 5/1; no closing date. FAFSA required. Applicants notified on a rolling basis starting 3/15.

Academics. Exploratory Program for undecided majors, First Year Student Seminar, Living-Learning Environments in the Residence Halls, Learning Communities based on academic majors. **Special study options:** Combined bachelor's/graduate degree, distance learning, double major, dual enrollment of high school students, exchange student, honors, independent study, internships, liberal arts/career combination, student-designed major, study abroad, teacher certification program. **Credit/placement by examination:** AP, CLEP, IB, SAT, ACT, institutional tests. 45 credit hours maximum toward bachelor's degree. **Support services:** Learning center, pre-admission summer program, reduced course load, remedial instruction, study skills assistance, tutoring, writing center.

Majors. **Biology:** General, biochemistry, biomedical sciences. **Business:** Accounting, actuarial science, business admin, finance, management science, marketing. **Communications:** Communications/speech/rhetoric, digital media, journalism, public relations. **Computer sciences:** Computer science, information systems, information technology. **Education:** Elementary, secondary, special ed. **English:** Creative writing, English lit, technical writing. **Foreign languages:** French, Spanish. **Health services:** Athletic training, cytotechnology, health services admin, music therapy, nursing (RN), recreational therapy. **History:** General. **Human services:** Social work. **Math:** General, statistics. **Parks/recreation:** Exercise sciences, facilities management, health/fitness, sports admin. **Philosophy/religion:** Philosophy. **Physical sciences:** Chemistry, forensic chemistry, geology, physics. **Psychology:** General. **Social sciences:** Criminology, economics, geography, political science. **Visual/performing arts:** Acting, art, dance, music, music performance, play/screenwriting, studio arts, theater arts management, theater design.

Most popular majors. Business/marketing 13%, education 16%, engineering/engineering technologies 6%, health sciences 13%, parks/recreation 11%, social sciences 7%.

Computing on campus. 1,323 workstations in dormitories, library, computer center, student center. Dormitories wired for high-speed internet access and linked to campus network. Commuter students can connect to campus network. Online course registration, online library, helpline, repair service, wireless network available.

Student life. **Freshman orientation:** Mandatory, $90 fee. Preregistration for classes offered. Several sessions held during summer months. **Housing:** Guaranteed on-campus for freshmen. Coed dorms, special housing for disabled, apartments available. $175 partly refundable deposit. Living-learning communities available. **Activities:** Bands, campus ministries, choral groups, dance, drama, film society, international student organizations, literary magazine, music ensembles, Model UN, musical theater, radio station, student government, student newspaper, symphony orchestra, TV station, Campus Crusade for Christ, Black Action Society, Latino Student Organization, Council for Exceptional Children, American Sign Language Club, Adapted Physical Activity Council, RockOUT, Rock Catholic, Student Union for Multicultural Affairs, Fellowship of Christian Athletes.

Athletics. NCAA. **Intercollegiate:** Baseball M, basketball, cross-country, field hockey W, football (tackle) M, lacrosse W, soccer, softball W, tennis W, track and field, volleyball W. **Intramural:** Badminton, basketball, bowling, football (non-tackle), racquetball, soccer, softball, table tennis, tennis, volleyball, water polo. **Team name:** The Rock.

Student services. Adult student services, alcohol/substance abuse counseling, chaplain/spiritual director, career counseling, services for economically disadvantaged, student employment services, financial aid counseling, health services, legal services, minority student services, on-campus daycare, personal counseling, placement for graduates, veterans' counselor, women's services. **Physically disabled:** Services for visually, speech, hearing impaired.

Contact. E-mail: asktherock@sru.edu
Phone: (724) 738-2015 Toll-free number: (800) 929-4778
Fax: (724) 738-2913
Mimi Campbell, Associate Director of Admissions, Slippery Rock University of Pennsylvania, 1 Morrow Way, Slippery Rock, PA 16057-1383

St. Charles Borromeo Seminary - Overbrook
Wynnewood, Pennsylvania
www.scs.edu CB code: 2794

- Private 4-year seminary college for men affiliated with Roman Catholic Church
- Residential campus in large town
- 54 degree-seeking undergraduates: 2% Asian American, 7% Hispanic American
- 101 degree-seeking graduate students
- 100% of applicants admitted
- Application essay, interview required
- 50% graduate within 6 years

General. Founded in 1832. Regionally accredited; also accredited by ATS. College and theology divisions enroll full-time seminary students. Religious studies division enrolls part-time undergraduate and graduate students who wish to pursue theological studies. Part-time programs open to men and women. **Degrees:** 14 bachelor's awarded; master's offered. **Location:** 4 miles from central Philadelphia. **Calendar:** Semester, limited summer session. **Full-time faculty:** 17 total; 82% have terminal degrees, 24% women. **Part-time faculty:** 14 total; 43% have terminal degrees, 36% women. **Class size:** 94% < 20, 6% 20-39. **Special facilities:** Rare book collection.

Freshman class profile. 9 applied, 9 admitted, 9 enrolled.

Mid 50% test scores			
SAT critical reading:	590-750	Rank in top tenth:	50%
SAT math:	550-690	End year in good standing:	100%
SAT writing:	590-630	Return as sophomores:	76%
Rank in top quarter:	67%	Out-of-state:	33%
		Live on campus:	100%

Basis for selection. Sponsorship by diocese or religious community required for admission to college and theology divisions. SAT or ACT recommended. **Home schooled:** Transcript of courses and grades, letter of recommendation (nonparent) required.

High school preparation. College-preparatory program recommended. 20 units recommended. Recommended units include English 4, mathematics 3, social studies 3, science 3 and foreign language 3. 3 to 4 units of religious education recommended. GED accepted on individual basis.

2012-2013 Annual costs. Tuition/fees (projected): $18,775. Room/board: $11,820. Books/supplies: $1,200. Personal expenses: $3,000.

2011-2012 Financial aid. **Need-based:** 6 full-time freshmen applied for aid; 4 were judged to have need; 4 of these received aid. Average need met was 80%. Average scholarship/grant was $5,000; average loan $3,000. 88% of total undergraduate aid awarded as scholarships/grants, 12% as loans/jobs. **Non-need-based:** Awarded to 33 full-time undergraduates, including 4 freshmen. Scholarships awarded for religious affiliation.

Application procedures. **Admission:** Priority date 3/1; deadline 7/15. No application fee. Application must be submitted on paper. Admission notification on a rolling basis beginning on or about 4/1. Level of admission dependent on academic background in philosophy, theology, and classical languages. **Financial aid:** Closing date 4/15. FAFSA, institutional form required. Applicants notified on a rolling basis starting 6/1; must reply by 6/1 or within 4 week(s) of notification.

Academics. Strong emphasis on philosophy, theology, classical languages, and liberal arts. **Special study options:** Accelerated study, ESL, independent study. **Credit/placement by examination:** AP, CLEP, institutional tests. 12 credit hours maximum toward bachelor's degree. **Support services:** Reduced course load, study skills assistance, tutoring.

Majors. **Philosophy/religion:** Philosophy.

Computing on campus. 60 workstations in library, computer center. Online library available.

Student life. Freshman orientation: Mandatory. Preregistration for classes offered. **Policies:** Religious observance required. **Housing:** Guaranteed on-campus for all undergraduates. Wellness housing available. **Activities:** Choral groups, music ensembles, student government, student newspaper, Seminarians for Life.

Athletics. Intramural: Basketball M, football (non-tackle) M, soccer M, volleyball M.

Student services. Chaplain/spiritual director, financial aid counseling, health services, personal counseling.

Contact. E-mail: jbongard@scs.edu
Phone: (610) 785-6271 Fax: (610) 617-9267
Rev. Joseph Bongard, Vice Rector, St. Charles Borromeo Seminary - Overbrook, 100 East Wynnewood Road, Wynnewood, PA 19096

St. Francis University

Loretto, Pennsylvania **CB member**
www.francis.edu **CB code: 2797**

- Private 4-year university and liberal arts college affiliated with Roman Catholic Church
- Residential campus in rural community
- 1,719 degree-seeking undergraduates: 6% part-time, 60% women, 6% African American, 1% Asian American, 2% Hispanic American, 4% international
- 630 degree-seeking graduate students
- 95% of applicants admitted
- SAT or ACT (ACT writing recommended), application essay required
- 66% graduate within 6 years; 39% enter graduate study

General. Founded in 1847. Regionally accredited. Saint Francis University welcomes students of all faiths; has extensive faith based opportunities for both Catholic and non-Catholic students. The Franciscan mission is deeply woven throughout the academic programs and campus offerings. **Degrees:** 358 bachelor's, 2 associate awarded; master's, professional offered. **ROTC:** Army. **Location:** 90 miles from Pittsburgh, 20 miles from Altoona. **Calendar:** Semester, limited summer session. **Full-time faculty:** 114 total; 66% have terminal degrees, 4% minority, 55% women. **Part-time faculty:** 78 total; 4% minority, 46% women. **Class size:** 48% < 20, 47% 20-39, 2% 40-49, 3% 50-99. **Special facilities:** Rural health and wellness Institute, small business development center, global competitiveness center, Southern Alleghenies art museum, center for remote and medically underserved areas, nature trail, field station, university owned study abroad campus in France.

Freshman class profile. 1,358 applied, 1,293 admitted, 430 enrolled.

Mid 50% test scores		Rank in top quarter:	53%
SAT critical reading:	450-550	Rank in top tenth:	21%
SAT math:	460-570	End year in good standing:	89%
SAT writing:	440-550	Return as sophomores:	84%
ACT composite:	19-24	Out-of-state:	24%
GPA 3.75 or higher:	36%	Live on campus:	89%
GPA 3.50-3.74:	18%	International:	5%
GPA 3.0-3.49:	30%	Fraternities:	13%
GPA 2.0-2.99:	16%	Sororities:	19%

Basis for selection. High school record most important, followed by test scores, counselor's recommendations, major area of interest, activities, honors. Relationship to alumni also considered. Campus visit highly recommended. Admission to professional track programs places more weight on test scores. SAT Subject Tests recommended. Essay must be a minimum of 250 words; essay topics may be found on the application for admission. Physician assistant and physical therapy students must complete essay directed towards their chosen discipline. Interviews recommended. **Learning Disabled:** Send official documentation to the Office of Disability Services.

High school preparation. College-preparatory program recommended. 16 units required. Required and recommended units include English 4, mathematics 2-4, social studies 2, history 1, science 1-4, foreign language 2, computer science 1, visual/performing arts 1 and academic electives 7. One natural science for nonscience majors, 2 for science majors also required. One science unit must include laboratory. Remaining units in academic electives. 4 math and 2 science required for physician assistant and occupational therapy. 4 math and 4 science required for physical therapy.

2011-2012 Annual costs. Tuition/fees: $27,808. Required fees cover purchase of mandatory laptop computer for full-time junior students and incoming full-time freshmen. Room/board: $9,520. Books/supplies: $1,650. Personal expenses: $2,500.

2010-2011 Financial aid. Need-based: 402 full-time freshmen applied for aid; 357 were judged to have need; 357 of these received aid. Average need met was 86%. Average scholarship/grant was $5,619; average loan $3,533. 58% of total undergraduate aid awarded as scholarships/grants, 42% as loans/jobs. **Non-need-based:** Awarded to 1,886 full-time undergraduates, including 474 freshmen. Scholarships awarded for academics, alumni affiliation, athletics, music/drama, religious affiliation.

Application procedures. Admission: Priority date 3/1; deadline 7/30 (postmark date). $30 fee, may be waived for applicants with need. Admission notification on a rolling basis beginning on or about 9/1. Must reply by May 1 or within 2 week(s) if notified thereafter. Physician assistant students must submit a refundable tuition deposit by March 1. Application closing date for physical therapy, occupational therapy, and physician assistant programs January 15. Notification by February 1. **Financial aid:** Priority date 5/1; no closing date. FAFSA required. Applicants notified on a rolling basis starting 3/1.

Academics. Special study options: Combined bachelor's/graduate degree, cooperative education, distance learning, double major, honors, independent study, internships, liberal arts/career combination, semester at sea, student-designed major, study abroad, teacher certification program, Washington semester. **Credit/placement by examination:** AP, CLEP, IB, SAT, ACT, institutional tests. 15 credit hours maximum toward associate degree, 30 toward bachelor's. **Support services:** Learning center, pre-admission summer program, reduced course load, remedial instruction, study skills assistance, tutoring, writing center.

Honors college/program. 3.25 GPA, 1150 SAT (580 Critical Reading, exclusive of Writing), position in top 20% of high school class required. Approximately 40 applicants admitted.

Majors. Area/ethnic studies: American, French. **Biology:** General, marine. **Business:** Accounting, business admin, finance, management information systems, marketing. **Communications:** Communications/speech/rhetoric, public relations. **Computer sciences:** General, computer science, information systems, programming. **Conservation:** Environmental science, environmental studies, forest management, forestry. **Education:** General, biology, chemistry, elementary, English, foreign languages, French, history, mathematics, multi-level teacher, psychology, secondary, social science, social studies, Spanish, speech. **Engineering:** General, environmental. **English:** English lit. **Foreign languages:** General, French, Spanish. **Health services:** Clinical lab technology, nursing (RN), physician assistant, public health nursing. **History:** General. **Human services:** General, social work. **Math:** General. **Philosophy/religion:** Philosophy, religion. **Physical sciences:** Chemistry. **Psychology:** General. **Social sciences:** Economics, political science, sociology.

Most popular majors. Biology 8%, business/marketing 29%, education 7%, health sciences 28%.

Computing on campus. PC or laptop required. 40 workstations in dormitories, library, computer center, student center. Dormitories wired for high-speed internet access and linked to campus network. Commuter students can connect to campus network. Online library, helpline, repair service, wireless network available.

Student life. Freshman orientation: Mandatory. Preregistration for classes offered. Held at various times during spring and summer. **Policies:** All students required to live in campus-owned housing to receive institutional financial aid unless commuting from home (within 30 mile radius). **Housing:** Guaranteed on-campus for all undergraduates. Coed dorms, single-sex dorms, special housing for disabled, apartments, fraternity/sorority housing, wellness housing available. $100 partly refundable deposit, deadline 5/1. **Activities:** Bands, campus ministries, choral groups, drama, music ensembles, musical theater, radio station, student government, student newspaper, TV station, Secular Franciscan Order, student activities organization, multicultural awareness club, Historians' Round Table, Habitat for Humanity, Peace and Justice Center, current affairs club, prelaw club.

Athletics. NCAA. **Intercollegiate:** Basketball, bowling W, cross-country, field hockey W, football (tackle) M, golf, lacrosse W, soccer, softball W, swimming W, tennis, track and field, volleyball. **Intramural:** Basketball, cross-country, football (non-tackle), ice hockey, skiing, soccer, softball, swimming, table tennis, tennis, track and field, volleyball. **Team name:** Red Flash.

Student services. Adult student services, alcohol/substance abuse counseling, chaplain/spiritual director, career counseling, student employment services, financial aid counseling, health services, minority student services, personal counseling, placement for graduates, veterans' counselor.

Contact. E-mail: admissions@francis.edu
Phone: (814) 472-3100 Toll-free number: (800) 342-5732
Fax: (814) 472-3335
Erin McCloskey, Vice President for Enrollment Management, St. Francis University, Box 600, Loretto, PA 15940

St. Vincent College

Latrobe, Pennsylvania	CB member
www.stvincent.edu	CB code: 2808

- Private 4-year liberal arts college affiliated with Roman Catholic Church
- Residential campus in large town
- 1,619 degree-seeking undergraduates: 1% part-time, 45% women, 6% African American, 1% Asian American, 3% Hispanic American, 1% international
- 215 degree-seeking graduate students
- 67% of applicants admitted
- SAT or ACT (ACT writing optional), application essay required
- 72% graduate within 6 years

General. Founded in 1846. Regionally accredited. Affiliated with Order of Saint Benedict. **Degrees:** 375 bachelor's awarded; master's offered. **ROTC:** Army, Air Force. **Location:** 35 miles from Pittsburgh. **Calendar:** Semester, extensive summer session. **Full-time faculty:** 101 total; 89% have terminal degrees, 31% women. **Part-time faculty:** 94 total; 32% have terminal degrees, 42% women. **Class size:** 50% < 20, 50% 20-39. **Special facilities:** Planetarium, observatory, radio telescope, wetlands program, rare book collection, spectrophotometer, spectrometer, physiograph workstations, nature reserve, digital imaging lab, Fred Rogers archives.

Freshman class profile. 1,863 applied, 1,249 admitted, 411 enrolled.

Mid 50% test scores			
SAT critical reading:	470-580	GPA 2.0-2.99:	14%
SAT math:	500-590	Rank in top quarter:	55%
SAT writing:	450-570	Rank in top tenth:	26%
GPA 3.75 or higher:	38%	Return as sophomores:	84%
GPA 3.50-3.74:	23%	Out-of-state:	18%
GPA 3.0-3.49:	25%	Live on campus:	88%
		International:	1%

Basis for selection. High school curriculum and grades most important; class rank, test scores, and essay important. Recommendations from school counselor considered. Interview recommended for all; audition required for music programs; portfolio required for art programs. **Learning Disabled:** All prior test results related to learning disability should be submitted.

High school preparation. College-preparatory program recommended. 16 units required; 20 recommended. Required and recommended units include English 4, mathematics 3, social studies 3, science 1-3 (laboratory 1), foreign language 2 and academic electives 5. One plane geometry, 1 intermediate algebra, .5 trigonometry, and 1 physics required for 3-2 engineering program applicants.

2011-2012 Annual costs. Tuition/fees: $28,370. Room/board: $9,248. Books/supplies: $1,200. Personal expenses: $1,600.

Financial aid. Non-need-based: Scholarships awarded for academics, alumni affiliation, leadership, minority status, religious affiliation.

Application procedures. Admission: Priority date 2/1; deadline 4/1 (postmark date). $25 fee, may be waived for applicants with need, free for online applicants. Admission notification on a rolling basis beginning on or about 10/1. Must reply by May 1 or within 3 week(s) if notified thereafter. **Financial aid:** Priority date 3/1, closing date 5/1. FAFSA required. Applicants notified on a rolling basis starting 3/1; must reply within 2 week(s) of notification.

Academics. College attempts to place career orientation in context of broader human and religious values with emphasis on liberal arts core curriculum. **Special study options:** Accelerated study, combined bachelor's/graduate degree, cooperative education, cross-registration, double major, dual enrollment of high school students, ESL, external degree, honors, independent study, internships, study abroad, teacher certification program. 3-2 engineering BA/BS program with University of Pittsburgh, Catholic University of America, Pennsylvania State; 4-1 BS/MBA, 3-3 BA/JD, 3-2 occupational therapy, physical therapy, and physician's assistant, 2-4 pharmacy programs with Duquesne University; 3-4 podiatry with Ohio College of Pediatric Medicine and Pennsylvania College of Pediatric Medicine. **Credit/placement by examination:** AP, CLEP, IB, institutional tests. 62 credit hours maximum toward bachelor's degree. **Support services:** Learning center, pre-admission summer program, remedial instruction, study skills assistance, tutoring, writing center.

Majors. Biology: General, biochemistry, bioinformatics. **Business:** Accounting, business admin, finance, international, marketing. **Communications:** Communications/speech/rhetoric. **Computer sciences:** General. **Conservation:** Environmental science, management/policy. **Education:** Art, business, elementary, physics, psychology. **Engineering:** General. **English:** English lit. **Foreign languages:** French, Spanish. **Health services:** Predental, premedicine, prepharmacy, preveterinary. **History:** General. **Human services:** Public policy. **Liberal arts:** Arts/sciences. **Math:** General. **Philosophy/religion:** Philosophy. **Physical sciences:** Chemistry, physics. **Psychology:** General, educational. **Social sciences:** Anthropology, economics, political science, sociology. **Theology:** Religious ed, theology. **Visual/performing arts:** Art history/conservation, dramatic, graphic design, music, music performance, studio arts, studio arts management.

Most popular majors. Biology 12%, business/marketing 27%, communications/journalism 6%, education 8%, history 7%, mathematics 8%, psychology 9%, social sciences 10%.

Computing on campus. 286 workstations in dormitories, library, computer center, student center. Dormitories wired for high-speed internet access and linked to campus network. Online course registration, helpline, repair service, wireless network available.

Student life. Freshman orientation: Mandatory, $125 fee. Preregistration for classes offered. 4-weeks of activities are planned to acclimate students to college on academic and social levels. Upperclassmen volunteer to serve as mentors to first-year students through the program. **Housing:** Guaranteed on-campus for freshmen. Coed dorms, apartments available. $200 nonrefundable deposit, deadline 5/1. **Activities:** Bands, campus ministries, choral groups, dance, drama, international student organizations, literary magazine, music ensembles, musical theater, radio station, student government, student newspaper, TV station, Respect for Life club, Democrats club, College Republicans, Students for Social Justice, pre-law society, Student Council for Exceptional Children, Italian club, Habitat for Humanity.

Athletics. NCAA. **Intercollegiate:** Baseball M, basketball, cross-country, field hockey W, football (tackle) M, golf, lacrosse, soccer, softball W, swimming, tennis, track and field M, volleyball W. **Intramural:** Basketball, football (non-tackle), soccer, softball, table tennis, volleyball. **Team name:** Bearcats.

Student services. Adult student services, alcohol/substance abuse counseling, chaplain/spiritual director, career counseling, student employment services, financial aid counseling, health services, minority student services, personal counseling, placement for graduates. **Physically disabled:** Services for visually, speech, hearing impaired.

Contact. E-mail: admission@stvincent.edu
Phone: (724) 805-2500 Toll-free number: (800) 782-5549
Fax: (724) 532-5069
David Collins, Assistant Vice President of Admission and Financial Aid, St. Vincent College, 300 Fraser Purchase Road, Latrobe, PA 15650-2690

Susquehanna University

Selinsgrove, Pennsylvania	CB member
www.susqu.edu	CB code: 2820

- Private 4-year university and liberal arts college affiliated with Evangelical Lutheran Church in America
- Residential campus in small town
- 2,190 degree-seeking undergraduates: 1% part-time, 54% women, 3% African American, 1% Asian American, 4% Hispanic American, 1% international
- 73% of applicants admitted
- Application essay required
- 77% graduate within 6 years; 22% enter graduate study

General. Founded in 1858. Regionally accredited. **Degrees:** 484 bachelor's awarded. **ROTC:** Army. **Location:** 50 miles from Harrisburg. **Calendar:** Semester, limited summer session. **Full-time faculty:** 142 total; 92% have terminal degrees, 21% minority, 47% women. **Part-time faculty:** 110 total; 28% have terminal degrees, 4% minority, 48% women. **Class size:** 53% < 20, 46% 20-39, less than 1% 40-49. **Special facilities:** Ecology field station, film library, music library, rare book room, 24-hour study center, arboretum, observatory, 450-seat teaching theater, child development center, satellite dishes, distribution system for foreign language broadcasts, video conferencing facility, high technology center for business and communications.

Freshman class profile. 3,610 applied, 2,644 admitted, 599 enrolled.

Mid 50% test scores			
SAT critical reading:	510-610	GPA 2.0-2.99:	29%
SAT math:	510-610	Rank in top quarter:	52%
SAT writing:	490-600	Rank in top tenth:	25%
ACT composite:	23-28	End year in good standing:	92%
GPA 3.75 or higher:	28%	Return as sophomores:	84%
GPA 3.50-3.74:	12%	Out-of-state:	51%
GPA 3.0-3.49:	31%	Live on campus:	97%
		International:	1%

Basis for selection. School record and class rank most important, test scores secondary. Application essay, interview, teacher and counselor evaluations, activities, and interest in the university considered. Students have option of submitting 2 graded writing samples in place of SAT or ACT scores. Interview highly recommended for all. Audition required for music majors. Portfolio required for writing and graphic design majors. **Home schooled:** Student should have detailed description of course work taken.

High school preparation. College-preparatory program required. 18 units required; 25 recommended. Required and recommended units include English 4, mathematics 3-4, social studies 2-4, history 2, science 2-3 (laboratory 2-3), foreign language 2-4 and academic electives 2-3.

2011-2012 Annual costs. Tuition/fees: $35,860. Room/board: $9,600. Books/supplies: $850. Personal expenses: $750.

2011-2012 Financial aid. Need-based: 520 full-time freshmen applied for aid; 452 were judged to have need; 452 of these received aid. Average need met was 83%. Average scholarship/grant was $22,631; average loan $3,464. 75% of total undergraduate aid awarded as scholarships/grants, 25% as loans/jobs. **Non-need-based:** Awarded to 754 full-time undergraduates, including 179 freshmen. Scholarships awarded for academics, alumni affiliation, leadership, minority status, music/drama, ROTC. **Additional information:** Graduated pay scale for federal work-study program.

Application procedures. Admission: Closing date 3/1 (postmark date). $35 fee, may be waived for applicants with need, free for online applicants. Admission notification on a rolling basis beginning on or about 12/15. Must reply by 5/1. **Financial aid:** Priority date 3/1, closing date 5/1. FAFSA, CSS PROFILE required. Applicants notified on a rolling basis starting 3/15.

Academics. Special study options: Accelerated study, combined bachelor's/graduate degree, cross-registration, distance learning, double major, dual enrollment of high school students, exchange student, honors, independent study, internships, semester at sea, student-designed major, study abroad, teacher certification program, United Nations semester, urban semester, Washington semester. **Credit/placement by examination:** AP, CLEP, IB, SAT, ACT, institutional tests. 65 credit hours maximum toward bachelor's degree. **Support services:** Reduced course load, study skills assistance, tutoring, writing center.

Majors. Biology: General, biochemistry, ecology. **Business:** Accounting, business admin. **Communications:** Communications/speech/rhetoric. **Computer sciences:** Computer science, information systems. **Conservation:** Environmental science. **Education:** Early childhood, elementary, music. **English:** Creative writing, English lit. **Foreign languages:** French, German, Italian, Spanish. **History:** General. **Liberal arts:** Arts/sciences. **Math:** General. **Philosophy/religion:** Philosophy, religion. **Physical sciences:** Chemistry, physics. **Psychology:** General. **Social sciences:** Economics, political science, sociology. **Visual/performing arts:** Art, art history/conservation, dramatic, graphic design, music, music performance.

Most popular majors. Biology 6%, business/marketing 24%, communications/journalism 14%, English 9%, history 6%, psychology 6%, social sciences 10%, visual/performing arts 7%.

Computing on campus. 489 workstations in dormitories, library, student center. Dormitories wired for high-speed internet access and linked to campus network. Commuter students can connect to campus network. Online course registration, online library, helpline, repair service, student web hosting, wireless network available.

Student life. Freshman orientation: Mandatory. Preregistration for classes offered. 4-day program; includes community service projects. **Housing:** Guaranteed on-campus for all undergraduates. Coed dorms, special housing for disabled, apartments, fraternity/sorority housing available. $400 nonrefundable deposit, deadline 5/1. Volunteer services living groups, scholars' house, townhouses available. **Activities:** Bands, campus ministries, choral groups, dance, drama, film society, international student organizations, literary magazine, music ensembles, Model UN, musical theater, opera, radio station, student government, student newspaper, symphony orchestra, TV station, Habitat for Humanity, Big Brothers/Big Sisters, Lutheran Student Movement, College Democrats, College Republicans, Asian Cultural Association, Gender and Sexuality Alliance, Hispanic Organization for Latino Awareness, Student Awareness of the Value of the Environment.

Athletics. NCAA. **Intercollegiate:** Baseball M, basketball, cheerleading, cross-country, field hockey W, football (tackle) M, golf, lacrosse, soccer, softball W, swimming, tennis, track and field, volleyball W. **Intramural:** Basketball, football (non-tackle), racquetball, soccer, softball, volleyball. **Team name:** Crusaders.

Student services. Adult student services, alcohol/substance abuse counseling, chaplain/spiritual director, career counseling, student employment services, financial aid counseling, health services, minority student services, on-campus daycare, personal counseling, placement for graduates, veterans' counselor, women's services. **Physically disabled:** Services for visually, speech, hearing impaired.

Contact. E-mail: suadmiss@susqu.edu
Phone: (570) 372-4260 Toll-free number: (800) 326-9672
Fax: (570) 372-2722
Chris Markle, Director of Admissions, Susquehanna University, 514 University Avenue, Selinsgrove, PA 17870-1164

Swarthmore College
Swarthmore, Pennsylvania
www.swarthmore.edu

CB member
CB code: 2821

- Private 4-year liberal arts college
- Residential campus in small town
- 1,536 degree-seeking undergraduates: 51% women, 7% African American, 14% Asian American, 13% Hispanic American, 8% international
- 15% of applicants admitted
- SAT and SAT Subject Tests or ACT with writing, application essay required
- 95% graduate within 6 years; 27% enter graduate study

General. Founded in 1864. Regionally accredited. Swarthmore is a nonsectarian institution, though the community continues to value the principles of the College's Quaker founders. The Lang Center for Civic and Social Responsibility supports service, community based learning, social action, and social justice projects. **Degrees:** 372 bachelor's awarded. **ROTC:** Army, Naval, Air Force. **Location:** 11 miles from Philadelphia. **Calendar:** Semester. **Full-time faculty:** 169 total; 100% have terminal degrees, 17% minority, 43% women. **Part-time faculty:** 39 total; 56% have terminal degrees, 20% minority, 49% women. **Class size:** 74% < 20, 22% 20-39, 2% 40-49, 2% 50-99, less than 1% >100. **Special facilities:** Campus is a 425-acre arboretum, about half of which is undeveloped mature forest used for recreation and research; art galleries, dance studios, cinema, and theater, distinctive library facilities include the Friends Historical Library and Peace Collection, indoor tennis courts, science center is LEED. certified; includes an observatory, robotics, and solar energy labs.

Freshman class profile. 6,547 applied, 987 admitted, 386 enrolled.

Mid 50% test scores			
SAT critical reading:	680-770	Rank in top tenth:	84%
SAT math:	670-760	End year in good standing:	97%
SAT writing:	680-770	Out-of-state:	87%
ACT composite:	30-34	Live on campus:	100%
Rank in top quarter:	98%	International:	9%

Basis for selection. Applications for admission are reviewed holistically. The admissions committee considers high school transcript, essays, standardized test scores, recommendations, and any supplemental materials submitted. Each application is read within the context of the student's life experiences and considers what they have accomplished with the opportunities available to them. Applicants required to submit scores for one of three testing scenarios: SAT and any two SAT subject tests; ACT with writing; or SAT and ACT (with or without Writing). Prospective engineers, regardless of whether they opt for the SAT or ACT, encouraged to take the Math Level 2 SAT Subject Test. TOEFL or IELTS strongly recommended for non-U.S. citizens whose first language is not English. Personal interview is highly recommended for all first-year applicants. Both on and off-campus interviews are available to prospective students. Students may submit supplemental materials for review by the creative writing, dance, music, theater, and/or visual arts faculty. **Home schooled:** Application may need to be adapted to specific experiences of homeschooler. Include transcripts from any formal classes; examples of research projects, papers, etc. and personal interview recommended. **Learning Disabled:** Proper documentation required.

High school preparation. Recommended units include English 4, mathematics 3, social studies 3, history 3, science 3 and foreign language 3. Four years of English and at least three years each of mathematics, the sciences, history and social studies, study of one or two foreign languages, coursework in art and music recommended.

2011-2012 Annual costs. Tuition/fees: $41,150. Room/board: $12,100. Books/supplies: $1,150. Personal expenses: $1,120.

2011-2012 Financial aid. Need-based: 276 full-time freshmen applied for aid; 221 were judged to have need; 221 of these received aid. Average need met was 100%. Average scholarship/grant was $37,379. 96% of total undergraduate aid awarded as scholarships/grants, 4% as loans/jobs. **Non-need-based:** Scholarships awarded for academics, job skills. **Additional information:** Need-blind admissions policy for U.S. citizens and permanent residents, wherein admission and financial aid decisions are made independently. Financial aid is also available for some international students. All Swarthmore aid awards are loan-free and are packaged to meet the full demonstrated need for admitted students.

Application procedures. Admission: Closing date 1/1 (postmark date). $60 fee, may be waived for applicants with need. Admission notification by 4/1. Must reply by 5/1. **Financial aid:** Closing date 2/15. FAFSA, institutional form, CSS PROFILE required. Applicants notified by 4/1; must reply by 5/1.

Academics. Special study options: Accelerated study, cross-registration, double major, exchange student, honors, independent study, internships, student-designed major, study abroad, teacher certification program. Honors Program features small groups of students working closely with faculty and peers; an emphasis on independent learning; and a final examination by outside scholars. Cross-registration is available at Bryn Mawr and Haverford colleges, and the University of Pennsylvania. Cooperative exchange programs are available with Rice and Tufts universities and Harvey Mudd, Pomona, Mills, and Middlebury colleges. Study abroad is encouraged and is available to students of all academic majors. **Credit/placement by examination:** AP, CLEP, IB, institutional tests. **Support services:** Reduced course load, study skills assistance, tutoring, writing center.

Majors. Area/ethnic studies: African-American, Asian, Latin American, Near/Middle Eastern, women's. **Biology:** General, biochemistry. **Computer sciences:** General. **Education:** General. **Engineering:** General. **English:** English lit. **Foreign languages:** Ancient Greek, Chinese, classics, comparative lit, French, German, Japanese, Latin, linguistics, Russian, Spanish. **History:** General. **Math:** General. **Philosophy/religion:** Islamic, philosophy, religion. **Physical sciences:** Astronomy, astrophysics, chemical physics, chemistry, physics. **Psychology:** General. **Social sciences:** Economics, political science, sociology/anthropology. **Visual/performing arts:** Art history/conservation, dance, dramatic, music, studio arts.

Most popular majors. Biology 12%, English 7%, foreign language 8%, philosophy/religious studies 6%, physical sciences 6%, psychology 7%, social sciences 29%, visual/performing arts 6%.

Computing on campus. 332 workstations in dormitories, library, computer center, student center. Dormitories wired for high-speed internet access and linked to campus network. Commuter students can connect to campus network. Online course registration, online library, helpline, repair service, student web hosting, wireless network available.

Student life. Freshman orientation: Mandatory. Preregistration for classes offered. 4-day orientation program is held in August; optional pre-orientation programs are available. **Policies:** New students are required to live on campus. **Housing:** Guaranteed on-campus for all undergraduates. Coed dorms, single-sex dorms available. Gender-neutral housing (students of any gender may share rooms and/or bathrooms), special housing for disabled students available on individual basis. **Activities:** Jazz band, campus ministries, choral groups, dance, drama, film society, international student organizations, literary magazine, music ensembles, radio station, student government, student newspaper, symphony orchestra, more than 100 clubs and organizations.

Athletics. NCAA. **Intercollegiate:** Badminton W, baseball M, basketball, cross-country, field hockey W, golf M, lacrosse, soccer, softball W, swimming, tennis, track and field, volleyball W. **Intramural:** Basketball, football (non-tackle), soccer, softball, table tennis, tennis, volleyball. **Team name:** Garnet.

Student services. Alcohol/substance abuse counseling, chaplain/spiritual director, career counseling, services for economically disadvantaged, student employment services, financial aid counseling, health services, minority student services, personal counseling, placement for graduates, women's services. **Physically disabled:** Services for visually, speech, hearing impaired.

Contact. E-mail: admissions@swarthmore.edu
Phone: (610) 328-8300 Toll-free number: (800) 667-3110
Fax: (610) 328-8580
James Bock, Dean of Admissions and Financial Aid, Swarthmore College, 500 College Avenue, Swarthmore, PA 19081

Talmudical Yeshiva of Philadelphia
Philadelphia, Pennsylvania

CB code: 1037

- Private 4-year rabbinical college for men affiliated with Jewish faith
- Residential campus in very large city
- 118 degree-seeking undergraduates: 3% international
- 74% of applicants admitted
- Interview required

General. Founded in 1953. Accredited by AARTS. First Talmudic degree and ordination available. **Degrees:** 20 bachelor's awarded. **Calendar:** Trimester, extensive summer session. **Full-time faculty:** 5 total. **Part-time faculty:** 1 total.

Freshman class profile. 53 applied, 39 admitted, 38 enrolled.

End year in good standing:	86%	Out-of-state:	92%
Return as sophomores:	82%	Live on campus:	100%

Basis for selection. Institutional examinations required.

High school preparation. 20 units required. Required and recommended units include English 4, social studies 3, science 3 and foreign language 2.

2011-2012 Annual costs. Tuition/fees: $8,100. Room/board: $6,800. Books/supplies: $900.

2010-2011 Financial aid. All financial aid based on need. 97% of total undergraduate aid awarded as scholarships/grants, 3% as loans/jobs.

Application procedures. Admission: Priority date 1/15; no deadline. No application fee. Admission notification on a rolling basis beginning on or about 7/15. **Financial aid:** Priority date 8/1, closing date 5/1. FAFSA, institutional form required. Applicants notified on a rolling basis starting 3/15; must reply within 2 week(s) of notification.

Academics. Credit/placement by examination: AP, CLEP, IB, institutional tests. **Support services:** Tutoring.

Majors. Theology: Talmudic.

Student life. Policies: Religious observance required. Freshmen not permitted cars on campus. **Housing:** Guaranteed on-campus for all undergraduates.

Student services. Career counseling, health services, personal counseling, placement for graduates.

Contact. Phone: (215) 477-1000 Fax: (215) 477-5065
Rabbi Sholom Kamenetsky, Admissions Director, Talmudical Yeshiva of Philadelphia, 6063 Drexel Road, Philadelphia, PA 19131

Temple University
Philadelphia, Pennsylvania
www.temple.edu

CB member
CB code: 2906

- Public 4-year university
- Commuter campus in very large city
- 27,171 degree-seeking undergraduates: 10% part-time, 52% women, 14% African American, 10% Asian American, 4% Hispanic American, 2% international
- 8,204 degree-seeking graduate students
- 63% of applicants admitted
- SAT or ACT with writing, application essay required
- 67% graduate within 6 years; 24% enter graduate study

General. Founded in 1884. Regionally accredited. Campuses in Ambler, Fort Washington, downtown Philadelphia, Harrisburg, Rome, Japan and other international locations. **Degrees:** 5,665 bachelor's, 3 associate awarded; master's, professional, doctoral offered. **ROTC:** Army, Naval, Air Force. **Location:** 2 miles from downtown. **Calendar:** Semester, extensive summer session. **Full-time faculty:** 1,451 total; 85% have terminal degrees, 18% minority, 40% women. **Part-time faculty:** 1,443 total; 16% minority, 43% women. **Class size:** 37% < 20, 51% 20-39, 7% 40-49, 3% 50-99, 2% >100. **Special facilities:** Arboretum, Charles L. Blockson Afro-American Collection, observatory, planetarium, technology center, Temple Gallery at Tyler School of Art.

Freshman class profile. 18,977 applied, 11,926 admitted, 4,276 enrolled.

Mid 50% test scores				
SAT critical reading:	500-600	GPA 2.0-2.99:	12%
SAT math:	510-610	Rank in top quarter:	53%
SAT writing:	500-600	Rank in top tenth:	18%
ACT composite:	21-26	Return as sophomores:	87%
GPA 3.75 or higher:	20%	Out-of-state:	22%
GPA 3.50-3.74:	25%	Live on campus:	75%
GPA 3.0-3.49:	43%	International:	2%

Basis for selection. Admissions process holistic; every aspect of student's academic history considered. Audition required for dance, music programs; portfolio required for art. **Home schooled:** Statement describing home school structure and mission, transcript of courses and grades, letter of recommendation (nonparent) required.

High school preparation. College-preparatory program required. 16 units required; 22 recommended. Required and recommended units include English 4, mathematics 3-4, social studies 2, history 1-2, science 2-3 (laboratory 1-2), foreign language 2 and academic electives 1-3.

2011-2012 Annual costs. Tuition/fees: $13,596; $23,422 out-of-state. Room/board: $9,886. Books/supplies: $1,000. Personal expenses: $4,480.

2011-2012 Financial aid. **Need-based:** 4,056 full-time freshmen applied for aid; 3,051 were judged to have need; 2,991 of these received aid. Average need met was 84%. Average scholarship/grant was $5,146; average loan $3,040. 56% of total undergraduate aid awarded as scholarships/grants, 44% as loans/jobs. **Non-need-based:** Awarded to 9,524 full-time undergraduates, including 2,304 freshmen. Scholarships awarded for academics, art, athletics, music/drama, ROTC.

Application procedures. **Admission:** Closing date 3/1 (postmark date). $50 fee, may be waived for applicants with need. Admission notification on a rolling basis beginning on or about 10/15. Must reply by May 1 or within 2 week(s) if notified thereafter. **Financial aid:** Closing date 3/1. FAFSA required. Applicants notified on a rolling basis starting 2/15; must reply by 5/1 or within 3 week(s) of notification.

Academics. **Special study options:** Accelerated study, combined bachelor's/graduate degree, cooperative education, cross-registration, distance learning, double major, dual enrollment of high school students, ESL, exchange student, external degree, honors, independent study, internships, liberal arts/career combination, study abroad, teacher certification program. Programs in Japan, Italy, Costa Rica, France, Germany, Ghana, India, Spain, Turkey, United Kingdom and Brazil. **Credit/placement by examination:** AP, CLEP, IB, institutional tests. **Support services:** Learning center, pre-admission summer program, reduced course load, remedial instruction, study skills assistance, tutoring, writing center.

Majors. **Architecture:** Architecture, landscape, urban/community planning. **Area/ethnic studies:** African-American, American, Asian, Latin American, women's. **Biology:** General, biochemistry, biophysics, neuroscience. **Business:** Accounting, actuarial science, business admin, entrepreneurial studies, finance, hospitality admin, insurance, international, labor relations, management information systems, marketing, real estate. **Communications:** Advertising, broadcast journalism, journalism, organizational, public relations, radio/TV. **Computer sciences:** General, information technology. **Conservation:** Environmental science, environmental studies. **Education:** Art, business, elementary, English, foreign languages, mathematics, music, science, social studies, trade/industrial. **Engineering:** Biomedical, civil, computer, electrical, mechanical. **English:** English lit, rhetoric/composition. **Foreign languages:** Classics, French, German, Hebrew, Italian, linguistics, Russian, Spanish. **General:** Horticultural science. **Health services:** Athletic training, audiology/speech pathology, medical records admin, music therapy, nursing (RN), public health ed, recreational therapy. **History:** General. **Human services:** Social work. **Math:** General. **Parks/recreation:** Exercise sciences, facilities management. **Philosophy/religion:** Judaic, philosophy, religion. **Physical sciences:** Chemistry, geology, physics. **Protective services:** Criminal justice. **Psychology:** General. **Social sciences:** Anthropology, economics, international relations, political science, sociology, urban studies. **Visual/performing arts:** Acting, art, art history/conservation, ceramics, dance, directing/producing, dramatic, fiber arts, film/cinema/video, graphic design, jazz, metal/jewelry, music, music history, music pedagogy, music performance, music theory/composition, painting, photography, printmaking, sculpture, voice/opera.

Most popular majors. Business/marketing 23%, communications/journalism 10%, education 8%, health sciences 6%, parks/recreation 6%, social sciences 6%, visual/performing arts 10%.

Computing on campus. 3,670 workstations in dormitories, library, computer center, student center. Dormitories wired for high-speed internet access and linked to campus network. Commuter students can connect to campus network. Online library, helpline, student web hosting, wireless network available.

Student life. **Freshman orientation:** Mandatory. Preregistration for classes offered. Includes some placement testing. **Housing:** Guaranteed on-campus for freshmen. Coed dorms, special housing for disabled, apartments, wellness housing available. $250 fully refundable deposit, deadline 5/1. Living/learning centers available. **Activities:** Bands, campus ministries, choral groups, dance, drama, film society, international student organizations, literary magazine, music ensembles, Model UN, musical theater, opera, radio station, student government, student newspaper, symphony orchestra, TV station, National Society for Leadership and Success, Asian student association, Asociacion de Estudiantes Latinos, Greek American student association, organization of African students, Progressive NAACP, American Society of Mechanical Engineers, Cherry Crusade, Habitat for Humanity, Student Peace Alliance.

Athletics. NCAA. **Intercollegiate:** Baseball M, basketball, cheerleading, cross-country, fencing W, field hockey W, football (tackle) M, golf M, gymnastics, lacrosse W, rowing (crew), soccer, softball W, tennis, track and field, volleyball W. **Intramural:** Basketball, football (non-tackle), racquetball, soccer, softball, volleyball. **Team name:** Owls.

Student services. Adult student services, alcohol/substance abuse counseling, career counseling, services for economically disadvantaged, student employment services, financial aid counseling, health services, legal services, personal counseling, placement for graduates, veterans' counselor. **Physically disabled:** Services for visually, speech, hearing impaired.

Contact. E-mail: tuadm@temple.edu
Phone: (215) 204-7200 Toll-free number: (888) 340-2222
Fax: (215) 204-5694
Karin Mormando, Director, Undergraduate Admissions, Temple University, 103 Conwell Hall, Philadelphia, PA 19122-6096

Thiel College

Greenville, Pennsylvania   **CB member**
www.thiel.edu   **CB code: 2910**

- Private 4-year liberal arts college affiliated with Evangelical Lutheran Church in America
- Residential campus in small town
- 1,056 degree-seeking undergraduates: 1% part-time, 47% women, 9% African American, 2% Hispanic American, 1% Native American, 3% international
- 64% of applicants admitted
- SAT or ACT (ACT writing optional), application essay required
- 39% graduate within 6 years

General. Founded in 1866. Regionally accredited. **Degrees:** 173 bachelor's, 1 associate awarded. **Location:** 75 miles from Pittsburgh, 75 miles from Cleveland. **Calendar:** Semester, limited summer session. **Full-time faculty:** 78 total; 60% have terminal degrees, 6% minority, 30% women. **Part-time faculty:** 55 total; 14% have terminal degrees, 71% women. **Class size:** 68% < 20, 31% 20-39, less than 1% 40-49, less than 1% 50-99. **Special facilities:** Wildlife sanctuary, black box theater.

Freshman class profile. 2,596 applied, 1,654 admitted, 375 enrolled.

Mid 50% test scores				
SAT critical reading:	430-520	Rank in top quarter:	28%
SAT math:	420-520	Rank in top tenth:	9%
ACT composite:	18-23	Return as sophomores:	59%
GPA 3.75 or higher:	13%	Out-of-state:	42%
GPA 3.50-3.74:	13%	Live on campus:	95%
GPA 3.0-3.49:	29%	Fraternities:	20%
GPA 2.0-2.99:	43%	Sororities:	31%

Basis for selection. High school GPA, standardized test scores, class rank, curriculum, and recommendation important. SAT or ACT scores received for fall admission on rolling basis. **Home schooled:** Transcript of courses and grades, letter of recommendation (nonparent) required. Proof of graduation required. **Learning Disabled:** Students with disabilities must submit evidence of disability to Office of Special Needs.

High school preparation. College-preparatory program recommended. 16 units recommended. Recommended units include English 4, mathematics 2, social studies 3, science 2 (laboratory 2), foreign language 2 and academic electives 1. Engineering, math, and science majors should complete 3 years of college preparatory math and science.

2011-2012 Annual costs. Tuition/fees: $25,156. Required fees include a $900 technology fee; a part of this fee is for the laptop computer entering freshmen are required to purchase. Entering freshmen also pay an additional fee for FYE activities. Room/board: $9,652. Books/supplies: $1,000. Personal expenses: $1,300.

2010-2011 Financial aid. Need-based: 348 full-time freshmen applied for aid; 330 were judged to have need; 330 of these received aid. Average need met was 67%. Average scholarship/grant was $15,033; average loan $3,961. 66% of total undergraduate aid awarded as scholarships/grants, 34% as loans/jobs. **Non-need-based:** Awarded to 164 full-time undergraduates, including 51 freshmen. Scholarships awarded for academics, alumni affiliation, leadership, music/drama, religious affiliation.

Application procedures. Admission: Priority date 4/1; no deadline. $35 fee, may be waived for applicants with need, free for online applicants. Admission notification on a rolling basis beginning on or about 8/1. Must reply by May 1 or within 2 week(s) if notified thereafter. **Financial aid:** Priority date 3/15; no closing date. FAFSA required. Applicants notified on a rolling basis starting 2/15; must reply within 2 week(s) of notification.

Academics. Academic counseling, career/major exploration. **Special study options:** Combined bachelor's/graduate degree, cooperative education, distance learning, double major, dual enrollment of high school students, ESL, honors, independent study, internships, liberal arts/career combination, semester at sea, student-designed major, study abroad, teacher certification program, United Nations semester, Washington semester. 3-2 engineering with Case Western Reserve University and University of Pittsburgh, cooperative program with the Art Institute of Pittsburgh, exchange with Duke University in forestry, cooperative program with Pittsburgh Institute of Mortuary Science. Affiliation program with Lake Erie College of Osteopathic Medicine. **Credit/placement by examination:** AP, CLEP, IB, SAT, ACT, institutional tests. 30 credit hours maximum toward bachelor's degree. **Support services:** Learning center, reduced course load, remedial instruction, study skills assistance, tutoring, writing center.

Majors. Biology: General, neuroscience. **Business:** Accounting, actuarial science, business admin, communications, e-commerce, international, management information systems. **Communications:** Communications/speech/rhetoric. **Communications technology:** Radio/TV. **Computer sciences:** General, information systems. **Conservation:** General, environmental studies. **Education:** Biology, chemistry, elementary, English, history, mathematics, physics, science, social studies. **English:** English lit, writing. **Health services:** Audiology/speech pathology, clinical lab technology, cytotechnology. **History:** General. **Math:** General. **Philosophy/religion:** Philosophy, religion. **Physical sciences:** Chemistry, physics. **Protective services:** Criminal justice. **Psychology:** General. **Social sciences:** Political science, sociology. **Theology:** Religious ed. **Visual/performing arts:** Art, commercial/advertising art.

Most popular majors. Biology 8%, business/marketing 38%, psychology 12%, security/protective services 6%, social sciences 6%.

Computing on campus. PC or laptop required. 130 workstations in library, computer center, student center. Dormitories wired for high-speed internet access and linked to campus network. Commuter students can connect to campus network. Online course registration, online library, helpline, repair service, student web hosting, wireless network available.

Student life. Freshman orientation: Mandatory, $300 fee. Preregistration for classes offered. Weekend before classes start. **Housing:** Guaranteed on-campus for all undergraduates. Coed dorms, apartments, fraternity/sorority housing available. $100 fully refundable deposit, deadline 7/1. **Activities:** Bands, campus ministries, choral groups, dance, drama, international student organizations, literary magazine, music ensembles, musical theater, radio station, student government, student newspaper, symphony orchestra, TV station, organization of black collegiates, Lutheran student movement, Circle K, commuter student organization, Rainbow Alliance, Safe Zone Program, English club.

Athletics. NCAA. **Intercollegiate:** Baseball M, basketball, cheerleading, cross-country, football (tackle) M, golf, lacrosse, soccer, softball W, tennis, track and field, volleyball, wrestling M. **Intramural:** Basketball, football (non-tackle), softball, table tennis, volleyball. **Team name:** Tomcats.

Student services. Alcohol/substance abuse counseling, chaplain/spiritual director, career counseling, financial aid counseling, health services, minority student services, personal counseling, placement for graduates. **Physically disabled:** Services for visually, speech, hearing impaired.

Contact. E-mail: admissions@thiel.edu
Phone: (724) 589-2345 Toll-free number: (800) 248-4435
Fax: (724) 589-2013
Amy Becher, Dean of Enrollment, Thiel College, 75 College Avenue, Greenville, PA 16125-2181

Thomas Jefferson University: College of Health Professions
Philadelphia, Pennsylvania
www.jefferson.edu
CB code: 2903

▶ Private two-year upper-division health science and nursing college
▶ Residential campus in very large city

General. Founded in 1824. Regionally accredited. **Calendar:** Semester.

Annual costs/financial aid. Tuition/fees (2011-2012): $27,707. Quoted annual tuition is for the occupational therapy undergraduate program. Annual costs for other programs vary by program. Books/supplies: $1,495. Personal expenses: $1,125. Need-based financial aid available for full-time students.

Contact. Phone: (215) 503-8890
Assistant Dean for Admission, 130 South Ninth Street, Edison Building, Suite 100, Philadelphia, PA 19107

University of Pennsylvania
Philadelphia, Pennsylvania
www.upenn.edu
CB member
CB code: 2926

▶ Private 4-year university
▶ Residential campus in very large city
▶ 9,779 degree-seeking undergraduates: 3% part-time, 51% women, 7% African American, 19% Asian American, 8% Hispanic American, 11% international
▶ 10,140 degree-seeking graduate students
▶ 12% of applicants admitted
▶ SAT and SAT Subject Tests or ACT with writing, application essay required
▶ 96% graduate within 6 years; 21% enter graduate study

General. Founded in 1740. Regionally accredited. **Degrees:** 2,891 bachelor's, 2 associate awarded; master's, professional, doctoral offered. **ROTC:** Army, Naval, Air Force. **Location:** 1 mile from downtown. **Calendar:** Semester, extensive summer session. **Full-time faculty:** 1,397 total; 100% have terminal degrees, 18% minority, 36% women. **Part-time faculty:** 799 total; 100% have terminal degrees, 11% minority, 42% women. **Class size:** 71% < 20, 17% 20-39, 3% 40-49, 7% 50-99, 2% >100. **Special facilities:** Archaeology and anthropology museum, institute of contemporary art, arboretum, theater, astronomical observatory, large animal research center, equine sports medicine and imaging center, women's center, undergraduate research center, wind tunnel, cyclotron facility, dairy.

Freshman class profile. 31,663 applied, 3,935 admitted, 2,467 enrolled.

Mid 50% test scores			
SAT critical reading:	660-750	Rank in top tenth:	96%
SAT math:	690-780	End year in good standing:	99%
SAT writing:	670-770	Return as sophomores:	97%
ACT composite:	30-34	Out-of-state:	81%
GPA 3.75 or higher:	88%	Live on campus:	100%
GPA 3.50-3.74:	7%	International:	12%
GPA 3.0-3.49:	5%	Fraternities:	30%
Rank in top quarter:	99%	Sororities:	27%

Basis for selection. Transcript indicating rigor of course work and achievement/evaluation most important criteria. Co-curricular involvements and testing strongly considered, as are counselor and faculty recommendations. Personal commentary (essays) and interview considered as well. Penn is interested in a diverse geographic, economic, racial, and ethnic student body. Penn requests students submit their entire ACT and/or SAT test score history. Portfolio strongly suggested for those applying to Architecture, Digital Media Design, Music, or Fine Arts majors. **Home schooled:** Statement describing home school structure and mission, transcript of courses and grades, letter of recommendation (nonparent) required. Commentary from primary instructor most important, and at least 1 other academic reference highly recommended. SAT subject tests in major academic areas highly recommended.

High school preparation. College-preparatory program recommended. 20 units recommended. Recommended units include English 4, mathematics 4, social studies 2, history 3, science 3 (laboratory 3) and foreign language 4.

2011-2012 Annual costs. Tuition/fees: $42,098. Room/board: $11,878. Books/supplies: $1,160. Personal expenses: $2,224.

2010-2011 Financial aid. All financial aid based on need. 1,590 full-time freshmen applied for aid; 1,126 were judged to have need; 1,126 of these received aid. Average need met was 100%. Average scholarship/grant was $36,522; average loan $201. 90% of total undergraduate aid awarded as scholarships/grants, 10% as loans/jobs. **Additional information:** All loans have been eliminated from need-based aid packages.

Application procedures. Admission: Closing date 1/1 (postmark date). $75 fee, may be waived for applicants with need. Admission notification by 4/1. Must reply by 5/1. **Financial aid:** Priority date 2/15; no closing date. FAFSA, institutional form, CSS PROFILE required. Applicants notified by 4/1; must reply by 5/1.

Academics. **Special study options:** Accelerated study, combined bachelor's/graduate degree, cross-registration, distance learning, double major, dual enrollment of high school students, ESL, exchange student, honors, independent study, internships, liberal arts/career combination, student-designed major, study abroad, teacher certification program, Washington semester. **Credit/placement by examination:** AP, CLEP, IB, institutional tests. **Support services:** Learning center, pre-admission summer program, remedial instruction, study skills assistance, tutoring, writing center.

Majors. **Architecture:** Architecture, environmental design. **Area/ethnic studies:** African, African-American, American, East Asian, South Asian, women's. **Biology:** General, biochemistry, bioinformatics, biomedical sciences, biophysics, neuroscience. **Business:** Accounting, actuarial science, business admin, e-commerce, finance, human resources, insurance, international, management information systems, marketing, operations, real estate, sales/distribution, transportation. **Communications:** Communications/speech/rhetoric. **Computer sciences:** General, computer graphics, networking. **Conservation:** Environmental studies. **Education:** General, elementary. **Engineering:** Biomedical, chemical, computer, electrical, environmental, materials, mechanical, systems. **English:** English lit. **Foreign languages:** Classics, comparative lit, East Asian, French, German, Italian, linguistics, Russian, Semitic, Spanish. **Health services:** Community health services, health care admin, nursing (RN). **History:** General, science/technology. **Human services:** Public policy. **Liberal arts:** Arts/sciences, humanities. **Math:** General, statistics. **Philosophy/religion:** Judaic, logic, philosophy, religion. **Physical sciences:** Chemistry, geology, materials science, physics. **Psychology:** General. **Social sciences:** General, anthropology, economics, international relations, political science, sociology, urban studies. **Visual/performing arts:** General, art history/conservation, dramatic, film/cinema/video, music, studio arts.

Most popular majors. Biology 9%, business/marketing 23%, engineering/engineering technologies 9%, health sciences 9%, social sciences 17%.

Computing on campus. Dormitories wired for high-speed internet access and linked to campus network. Commuter students can connect to campus network. Online course registration, online library, helpline, repair service, student web hosting, wireless network available.

Student life. **Freshman orientation:** Mandatory, $205 fee. Preregistration for classes offered. **Housing:** Guaranteed on-campus for freshmen. Coed dorms, special housing for disabled, apartments, fraternity/sorority housing, wellness housing available. $200 nonrefundable deposit, deadline 5/1. Private off-campus housing available. **Activities:** Bands, campus ministries, choral groups, dance, drama, film society, international student organizations, literary magazine, music ensembles, Model UN, musical theater, opera, radio station, student government, student newspaper, symphony orchestra, TV station, various religious, political, ethnic, social service, performing arts, cultural, and organizations.

Athletics. NCAA. **Intercollegiate:** Baseball M, basketball, cross-country, diving, fencing, field hockey W, football (tackle) M, golf, gymnastics W, lacrosse, rowing (crew), soccer, softball W, squash, swimming, tennis, track and field, volleyball W, wrestling M. **Intramural:** Basketball, football (non-tackle), soccer, tennis, volleyball. **Team name:** Quakers.

Student services. Adult student services, alcohol/substance abuse counseling, chaplain/spiritual director, career counseling, services for economically disadvantaged, student employment services, financial aid counseling, health services, legal services, minority student services, on-campus daycare, personal counseling, placement for graduates, veterans' counselor, women's services. **Physically disabled:** Services for visually, speech, hearing impaired.

Contact. E-mail: info@admissions.upenn.edu
Phone: (215) 898-7507 Fax: (215) 898-9670
Eric Furda, Dean of Admissions, University of Pennsylvania, 1 College Hall, Philadelphia, PA 19104-6376

University of Phoenix: Harrisburg
Harrisburg, Pennsylvania
www.phoenix.edu

- For-profit 4-year university
- Commuter campus in large town
- 113 degree-seeking undergraduates

General. Regionally accredited. **Degrees:** 3 bachelor's awarded; master's offered. **Calendar:** Differs by program. **Full-time faculty:** 5 total. **Part-time faculty:** 27 total.

Basis for selection. Open admission.

2011-2012 Annual costs. Estimated costs as of August 2011: per-credit-hour charge, $380 to $520, depending upon level and course of study; electronic course materials fee, $95, if applicable. Book and material charges may vary by course and program. All fees are subject to change.

Application procedures. **Admission:** No deadline. No application fee. **Financial aid:** No deadline.

Academics. **Credit/placement by examination:** AP, CLEP.

Majors. **Business:** Accounting, business admin, human resources, marketing. **Health services:** Facilities admin, health care admin. **Protective services:** Law enforcement admin.

Most popular majors. Business/marketing 67%, security/protective services 33%.

Contact. Toll-free number: (866) 766-0766
Marc Booker, Director of Admission and Evaluation, University of Phoenix: Harrisburg, 4050 Crums Mill Road, Harrisburg, PA 17112-2894

University of Phoenix: Philadelphia
Wayne, Pennsylvania
www.phoenix.edu

- For-profit 4-year university
- Commuter campus in very large city
- 780 degree-seeking undergraduates

General. Regionally accredited. **Degrees:** 164 bachelor's awarded; master's offered. **Calendar:** Differs by program. **Full-time faculty:** 12 total. **Part-time faculty:** 91 total.

Basis for selection. Open admission.

2011-2012 Annual costs. Estimated costs as of August 2011: per-credit-hour charge, $380 to $520, depending upon level and course of study; electronic course materials fee, $95, if applicable. Book and material charges may vary by course and program. All fees are subject to change.

Application procedures. **Admission:** No deadline. No application fee. **Financial aid:** No deadline.

Academics. **Credit/placement by examination:** AP, CLEP.

Majors. **Business:** Business admin, credit management, marketing. **Computer sciences:** General, information technology, networking, programming, security, systems analysis, web page design, webmaster. **Engineering:** Software. **Health services:** Facilities admin. **Protective services:** Law enforcement admin.

Most popular majors. Business/marketing 75%, computer/information sciences 9%, security/protective services 14%.

Contact. Toll-free number: (866) 766-0766
Marc Booker, Director of Admission and Evaluation, University of Phoenix: Philadelphia, 1170 Devon Park Drive, Wayne, PA 19087-2121

University of Phoenix: Pittsburgh
Pittsburgh, Pennsylvania
www.phoenix.edu

- For-profit 4-year university
- Commuter campus in large city
- 131 degree-seeking undergraduates

General. Regionally accredited. **Degrees:** 12 bachelor's awarded; master's offered. **Calendar:** Differs by program. **Full-time faculty:** 2 total. **Part-time faculty:** 45 total.

Basis for selection. Open admission.

2011-2012 Annual costs. Estimated costs as of August 2011: per-credit-hour charge, $380 to $520, depending upon level and course of study; electronic course materials fee, $95, if applicable. Book and material charges may vary by course and program. All fees are subject to change.

Application procedures. **Admission:** No deadline. No application fee. **Financial aid:** No deadline.

Academics. **Credit/placement by examination:** AP, CLEP.

Majors. Business: Accounting, business admin, credit management, human resources, marketing. **Computer sciences:** General, networking, programming, security, systems analysis, web page design, webmaster. **Health services:** Facilities admin, health care admin. **Protective services:** Law enforcement admin.

Most popular majors. Business/marketing 67%, computer/information sciences 17%, security/protective services 14%.

Contact. Toll-free number: (866) 766-0766
Marc Booker, Director of Admission and Evaluation, University of Phoenix: Pittsburgh, Penn Center West, Building 6, Suite 100, Pittsburgh, PA 15276-0119

University of Pittsburgh
Pittsburgh, Pennsylvania
www.pitt.edu
CB member
CB code: 2927

- Public 4-year university
- Residential campus in large city
- 18,092 degree-seeking undergraduates: 5% part-time, 50% women, 7% African American, 6% Asian American, 2% Hispanic American, 3% international
- 10,100 degree-seeking graduate students
- 58% of applicants admitted
- SAT or ACT with writing required
- 79% graduate within 6 years; 36% enter graduate study

General. Founded in 1787. Regionally accredited. Regional campuses in Johnstown, Bradford, Titusville, and Greensburg. **Degrees:** 4,212 bachelor's awarded; master's, professional, doctoral offered. **ROTC:** Army, Naval, Air Force. **Location:** 3 miles from downtown. **Calendar:** Semester, extensive summer session. **Full-time faculty:** 1,670 total; 93% have terminal degrees, 16% minority, 41% women. **Part-time faculty:** 645 total; 9% minority, 50% women. **Class size:** 40% < 20, 33% 20-39, 7% 40-49, 13% 50-99, 7% >100. **Special facilities:** Observatory, nationality rooms, performance hall, ecology laboratory.

Freshman class profile. 23,409 applied, 13,544 admitted, 3,768 enrolled.

Mid 50% test scores			
SAT critical reading:	570-690	Rank in top quarter:	86%
SAT math:	600-690	Rank in top tenth:	54%
SAT writing:	560-660	Return as sophomores:	90%
ACT composite:	25-30	Out-of-state:	32%
GPA 3.75 or higher:	71%	Live on campus:	97%
GPA 3.50-3.74:	15%	International:	3%
GPA 3.0-3.49:	12%	Fraternities:	12%
GPA 2.0-2.99:	2%	Sororities:	10%

Basis for selection. GED not accepted. High school record, class rank, test scores, and activities considered. College of General Studies applicants must apply directly to that college, not through Admissions and Financial Aid. Students admitted as freshmen into the Dietrich School of Arts and Sciences, Swanson School of Engineering, School of Nursing, and College of Business Administration. Students may be conditionally accepted into the School of Pharmacy, PharmD program with the provision that they successfully complete 4 terms (2 years) of preprofessional study in School of Arts and Sciences. Interview and essay recommended for all; audition required for music program; portfolio recommended for studio art program; essay required for pharmacy applicants. **Home schooled:** Statement describing home school structure and mission, transcript of courses and grades required.

High school preparation. College-preparatory program required. 17 units required; 23 recommended. Required and recommended units include English 4, mathematics 3-4, social studies 2-3, science 3-4 (laboratory 3-4), foreign language 2-3 and academic electives 3-5.

2011-2012 Annual costs. Tuition/fees: $16,132; $25,540 out-of-state. Room/board: $9,430.

2010-2011 Financial aid. Need-based: 3,067 full-time freshmen applied for aid; 2,162 were judged to have need; 2,074 of these received aid. Average need met was 59%. Average scholarship/grant was $8,274; average loan $4,160. 39% of total undergraduate aid awarded as scholarships/grants, 61% as loans/jobs. **Non-need-based:** Awarded to 977 full-time undergraduates, including 389 freshmen. Scholarships awarded for academics, athletics.

Application procedures. Admission: No deadline. $45 fee, may be waived for applicants with need. Admission notification on a rolling basis beginning on or about 10/1. Must reply by May 1 or within 3 week(s) if notified thereafter. **Financial aid:** Priority date 3/1; no closing date. FAFSA required. Applicants notified on a rolling basis starting 3/15.

Academics. Accelerated high school program enables students to take courses in School of Arts and Sciences while in high school. **Special study options:** Accelerated study, combined bachelor's/graduate degree, cooperative education, cross-registration, distance learning, double major, dual enrollment of high school students, ESL, exchange student, external degree, honors, independent study, internships, liberal arts/career combination, student-designed major, study abroad, teacher certification program. Freshman seminars, early admission to some graduate programs for exceptional students. **Credit/placement by examination:** AP, CLEP, IB, SAT, ACT, institutional tests. 60 credit hours maximum toward bachelor's degree. Dietrich School of Arts and Sciences does not accept CLEP. **Support services:** Learning center, pre-admission summer program, reduced course load, remedial instruction, study skills assistance, tutoring, writing center.

Honors college/program. In order to enroll in honors courses a 1400 combined SAT Math and Critical Reading scores required.

Majors. Area/ethnic studies: African-American. **Biology:** General, bioinformatics, ecology/evolutionary, microbiology, molecular, neuroscience. **Business:** Accounting, business admin, finance, international, marketing. **Communications:** Media studies. **Computer sciences:** Computer science, information systems. **Education:** Physical. **Engineering:** Applied physics, biomedical, chemical, civil, computer, electrical, industrial, materials, mechanical. **English:** British lit, creative writing, rhetoric/composition. **Foreign languages:** Chinese, classics, French, German, Italian, Japanese, linguistics, Polish, Russian, Slavic, Spanish. **Health services:** Audiology/speech pathology, dental hygiene, dietetics, health services admin, medical records admin, nursing (RN), occupational therapy, orthotics/prosthetics, rehabilitation science. **History:** General, science/technology. **Human services:** General, social work. **Liberal arts:** Arts/sciences, humanities. **Math:** General, applied, statistics. **Philosophy/religion:** Philosophy, religion. **Physical sciences:** General, chemistry, geology, physics. **Protective services:** Corrections. **Psychology:** General, educational. **Social sciences:** General, anthropology, economics, political science, sociology, urban studies. **Visual/performing arts:** Art history/conservation, dramatic, film/cinema/video, music, studio arts.

Most popular majors. Biology 7%, business/marketing 15%, engineering/engineering technologies 9%, English 10%, health sciences 11%, psychology 8%, social sciences 14%.

Computing on campus. 2,000 workstations in library, computer center, student center. Dormitories wired for high-speed internet access and linked to campus network. Commuter students can connect to campus network. Online course registration, online library, helpline, repair service, student web hosting, wireless network available.

Student life. Freshman orientation: Available. Preregistration for classes offered. Held during first week of classes; open to parents and family. **Policies:** Students must abide by the Student Code of Conduct rules provided by the school. **Housing:** Guaranteed on-campus for freshmen. Coed dorms, single-sex dorms, special housing for disabled, apartments, fraternity/sorority housing, wellness housing available. $325 fully refundable deposit. Rooms can be adapted to meet disabled students' particular needs. **Activities:** Bands, campus ministries, choral groups, dance, drama, film society, international student organizations, literary magazine, music ensembles, Model UN, musical theater, radio station, student government, student newspaper, TV station, approximately 460 student organizations.

Athletics. NCAA. **Intercollegiate:** Baseball M, basketball, cross-country, diving, football (tackle) M, gymnastics W, soccer, softball W, swimming, tennis W, track and field, volleyball W, wrestling M. **Intramural:** Badminton, basketball, football (tackle) M, handball, racquetball, soccer, squash, volleyball. **Team name:** Panthers.

Student services. Adult student services, alcohol/substance abuse counseling, chaplain/spiritual director, career counseling, services for economically disadvantaged, student employment services, financial aid counseling, health services, minority student services, personal counseling, placement for graduates, veterans' counselor. **Physically disabled:** Services for visually, speech, hearing impaired.

Contact. E-mail: oafa@pitt.edu
Phone: (412) 624-7488 Fax: (412) 648-8815
Betsy Porter, Director, Office of Admissions and Financial Aid, University of Pittsburgh, 4227 Fifth Avenue, 1st Floor, Alumni Hall, Pittsburgh, PA 15260

University of Pittsburgh at Bradford
Bradford, Pennsylvania
www.upb.pitt.edu
CB member
CB code: 2935

- Public 4-year university
- Residential campus in large town

- 1,557 degree-seeking undergraduates: 8% part-time, 55% women, 8% African American, 3% Asian American, 2% Hispanic American, 2% international
- 69% of applicants admitted
- SAT or ACT (ACT writing optional) required
- 40% graduate within 6 years; 20% enter graduate study

General. Founded in 1963. Regionally accredited. Campus located in the Allegheny National Forest. **Degrees:** 280 bachelor's, 46 associate awarded. **ROTC:** Army. **Location:** 160 miles from Pittsburgh, 79 miles from Buffalo, New York. **Calendar:** Semester, extensive summer session. **Full-time faculty:** 74 total; 68% have terminal degrees, 14% minority, 36% women. **Part-time faculty:** 83 total; 14% have terminal degrees, 2% minority, 55% women. **Class size:** 54% < 20, 39% 20-39, 5% 40-49, 2% 50-99.

Freshman class profile. 961 applied, 660 admitted, 369 enrolled.

Mid 50% test scores			
SAT critical reading:	420-540	Rank in top quarter:	27%
SAT math:	430-540	Rank in top tenth:	2%
SAT writing:	410-510	End year in good standing:	81%
ACT composite:	19-23	Return as sophomores:	72%
GPA 3.75 or higher:	19%	Out-of-state:	18%
GPA 3.50-3.74:	16%	Live on campus:	84%
GPA 3.0-3.49:	35%	International:	3%

GPA 2.0-2.99: 30%

Basis for selection. School achievement record, test scores, interview most important. Essay and recommendations considered. **Home schooled:** Required: Complete listing of courses taken/completed/in progress, syllabus for each course, textbook used, 1 recommendation from educator, 1 outside recommendation, personal essay, personal interview, state requirement satisfaction.

High school preparation. College-preparatory program recommended. 15 units required. Required and recommended units include English 4, mathematics 2-2.5, history 1, science 1-2 (laboratory 1-2), foreign language 2 and academic electives 5. Engineering and math students must have trigonometry and physics with a lab. Nursing majors must have 3 social science and 1 each of chemistry and biology with labs in both.

2011-2012 Annual costs. Tuition/fees: $12,496; $22,688 out-of-state. Room/board: $7,804. Books/supplies: $1,110. Personal expenses: $1,660.

2010-2011 Financial aid. Need-based: 343 full-time freshmen applied for aid; 343 were judged to have need; 343 of these received aid. Average need met was 82%. Average scholarship/grant was $8,141; average loan $3,468. 44% of total undergraduate aid awarded as scholarships/grants, 56% as loans/jobs. **Non-need-based:** Awarded to 505 full-time undergraduates, including 245 freshmen. Scholarships awarded for academics, alumni affiliation, ROTC, state residency.

Application procedures. Admission: Priority date 5/1; no deadline. $45 fee, may be waived for applicants with need. Admission notification on a rolling basis beginning on or about 11/2. Must reply by May 1 or within 2 week(s) if notified thereafter. **Financial aid:** Priority date 3/1; no closing date. FAFSA required. Applicants notified on a rolling basis starting 4/1; must reply within 2 week(s) of notification.

Academics. Student services include: on-going individual academic, personal and career counseling; strategies for maintaining and improving GPA; assistance with study skills and life management issues; cultural enrichment activities; computer learning lab services; graduate school assistance. **Special study options:** Combined bachelor's/graduate degree, cross-registration, distance learning, double major, dual enrollment of high school students, external degree, honors, independent study, internships, semester at sea, study abroad, teacher certification program. 3-4 pre-optometry program with Pennsylvania College of Optometry, 1-4 pharmacy program with Oakland campus, 3+4 program with LECOM in Osteopathic Medicine. **Credit/placement by examination:** AP, CLEP, IB, SAT, ACT, institutional tests. 30 credit hours maximum toward associate degree, 90 toward bachelor's. **Support services:** Learning center, reduced course load, remedial instruction, study skills assistance, tutoring, writing center.

Majors. Biology: General. **Business:** General, accounting, business admin, entrepreneurial studies, hospitality admin. **Communications:** Public relations, radio/TV. **Computer sciences:** Applications programming, computer science. **Conservation:** Environmental studies. **Education:** General, elementary, physical, secondary, social science. **Engineering:** General, chemical, civil, electrical, engineering science, industrial, mechanical. **English:** Creative writing, English lit, rhetoric/composition. **Health services:** Athletic training, nursing (RN), radiologic technology/medical imaging. **Liberal arts:** Humanities. **Math:** Applied. **Parks/recreation:** General, sports admin. **Physical sciences:** General, chemistry. **Protective services:** Corrections, law enforcement admin. **Psychology:** General. **Social sciences:** General, demography, economics, political science, sociology. **Visual/performing arts:** General.

Most popular majors. Business/marketing 23%, education 12%, health sciences 13%, security/protective services 9%, social sciences 11%.

Computing on campus. 120 workstations in library, computer center, student center. Dormitories wired for high-speed internet access and linked to campus network. Commuter students can connect to campus network. Online course registration, online library, helpline, repair service, student web hosting, wireless network available.

Student life. Freshman orientation: Mandatory, $90 fee. Preregistration for classes offered. 2-day program for students and parents in July; additional 3-day program immediately prior to start of classes. **Housing:** Guaranteed on-campus for freshmen. Coed dorms, special housing for disabled, apartments available. $125 nonrefundable deposit, deadline 5/1. Townhouse/apartment style housing available. **Activities:** Campus ministries, choral groups, dance, drama, literary magazine, music ensembles, radio station, student government, student newspaper, Black Action Committee, Christ in Action, Collegiate Liberals of America, Conservative Union, Habitat for Humanity, Ideology Expression Club.

Athletics. NCAA. **Intercollegiate:** Baseball M, basketball, cross-country, golf M, soccer, softball W, swimming, tennis, volleyball W. **Intramural:** Basketball, football (non-tackle), golf, ice hockey, soccer, softball, swimming, table tennis, volleyball, water polo. **Team name:** Panthers.

Student services. Adult student services, alcohol/substance abuse counseling, chaplain/spiritual director, career counseling, student employment services, financial aid counseling, health services, personal counseling, placement for graduates, veterans' counselor. **Physically disabled:** Services for visually, speech, hearing impaired.

Contact. E-mail: admissions@upb.pitt.edu
Phone: (814) 362-7555 Toll-free number: (800) 872-1787
Fax: (814) 362-5150
Alexander Nazemetz, Director of Admissions, University of Pittsburgh at Bradford, 300 Campus Drive, Bradford, PA 16701

University of Pittsburgh at Greensburg
Greensburg, Pennsylvania
www.greensburg.pitt.edu
CB code: 2936

- Public 4-year branch campus and liberal arts college
- Commuter campus in large town
- 1,852 degree-seeking undergraduates: 9% part-time, 49% women, 5% African American, 2% Asian American, 3% Hispanic American, 1% international
- 86% of applicants admitted
- SAT or ACT with writing required
- 58% graduate within 6 years

General. Founded in 1963. Regionally accredited. **Degrees:** 259 bachelor's awarded. **ROTC:** Army, Air Force. **Location:** 35 miles from Pittsburgh. **Calendar:** Semester, limited summer session. **Full-time faculty:** 74 total. **Part-time faculty:** 60 total. **Class size:** 23% < 20, 50% 20-39, 18% 40-49, 3% 50-99, 6% >100.

Freshman class profile. 1,468 applied, 1,256 admitted, 454 enrolled.

Mid 50% test scores			
SAT critical reading:	460-550	Rank in top quarter:	38%
SAT math:	470-570	Rank in top tenth:	10%
SAT writing:	450-540	Return as sophomores:	78%
ACT composite:	19-23	Out-of-state:	4%
GPA 3.75 or higher:	25%	Live on campus:	66%
GPA 3.50-3.74:	24%	International:	4%
GPA 3.0-3.49:	39%		

GPA 2.0-2.99: 12%

Basis for selection. High school curriculum and grades most important, followed by class rank and SAT/ACT scores. Interviews, essays and letters of recommendation all optional. **Home schooled:** Transcript of courses and grades required.

High school preparation. College-preparatory program required. 15 units required; 20 recommended. Required and recommended units include English 4, mathematics 2-4, social studies 2, history 2, science 1-2 (laboratory 1), foreign language 4, computer science 1 and academic electives 1-3.

2011-2012 Annual costs. Tuition/fees: $12,626; $22,818 out-of-state. Room/board: $8,410. Books/supplies: $1,098. Personal expenses: $1,642.

2010-2011 Financial aid. Need-based: 384 full-time freshmen applied for aid; 327 were judged to have need; 322 of these received aid. Average need met was 62%. Average scholarship/grant was $6,629; average loan

$3,448. 40% of total undergraduate aid awarded as scholarships/grants, 60% as loans/jobs. **Non-need-based:** Awarded to 558 full-time undergraduates, including 196 freshmen. Scholarships awarded for academics, leadership, minority status.

Application procedures. Admission: No deadline. $45 fee, may be waived for applicants with need. Admission notification on a rolling basis beginning on or about 9/15. Must reply by May 1 or within 3 week(s) if notified thereafter. **Financial aid:** Priority date 2/15; no closing date. FAFSA required. Applicants notified on a rolling basis starting 3/15; must reply within 3 week(s) of notification.

Academics. Special study options: Combined bachelor's/graduate degree, cross-registration, double major, dual enrollment of high school students, exchange student, independent study, internships, liberal arts/career combination, student-designed major, study abroad. **Credit/placement by examination:** AP, CLEP, SAT, ACT, institutional tests. 30 credit hours maximum toward bachelor's degree. **Support services:** Learning center, reduced course load, remedial instruction, study skills assistance, tutoring, writing center.

Majors. Area/ethnic studies: American. **Biology:** General. **Business:** Accounting, business admin, management information systems. **Communications:** Communications/speech/rhetoric, journalism, public relations. **Computer sciences:** Information systems. **Education:** Biology, chemistry, early childhood, elementary, English, history, mathematics, multi-level teacher, science, secondary, social science, social studies. **English:** English lit, writing. **Foreign languages:** Spanish. **Health services:** Predental, premedicine, prepharmacy, preveterinary. **History:** General. **Liberal arts:** Arts/sciences. **Math:** Applied. **Physical sciences:** Chemistry. **Protective services:** Law enforcement admin. **Psychology:** General. **Social sciences:** General, anthropology, criminology, political science. **Visual/performing arts:** General.

Most popular majors. Biology 12%, business/marketing 24%, English 12%, psychology 27%, security/protective services 6%.

Computing on campus. 400 workstations in dormitories, library, computer center. Dormitories wired for high-speed internet access and linked to campus network. Commuter students can connect to campus network. Online course registration, online library, helpline, repair service, student web hosting, wireless network available.

Student life. Freshman orientation: Mandatory, $55 fee. Preregistration for classes offered. **Housing:** Coed dorms available. $150 fully refundable deposit, deadline 5/1. **Activities:** Campus ministries, choral groups, dance, drama, international student organizations, literary magazine, musical theater, radio station, student government, student newspaper, student activities board, honor societies, academic societies, Alpha Phi Omega, Circle K, Amnesty International, Christian fellowship club, College Republicans, College Democrats.

Athletics. NCAA. **Intercollegiate:** Baseball M, basketball, bowling W, cross-country, golf, soccer, softball W, tennis, volleyball W. **Intramural:** Baseball M, basketball, golf, racquetball, skiing, soccer, softball, table tennis, tennis, volleyball. **Team name:** Bobcats.

Student services. Adult student services, alcohol/substance abuse counseling, career counseling, student employment services, financial aid counseling, health services, personal counseling, placement for graduates, veterans' counselor. **Physically disabled:** Services for visually, hearing impaired.

Contact. E-mail: upgadmit@pitt.edu
Phone: (724) 836-9880 Fax: (724) 836-7471
Heather Kabala, Director of Admissions, University of Pittsburgh at Greensburg, 150 Finoli Drive, Greensburg, PA 15601

University of Pittsburgh at Johnstown
Johnstown, Pennsylvania   **CB member**
www.upj.pitt.edu   **CB code: 2934**

▶ Public 4-year engineering and liberal arts college
▶ Residential campus in small city
▶ 2,956 degree-seeking undergraduates: 4% part-time, 46% women, 3% African American, 1% Asian American, 2% Hispanic American, 1% international
▶ 88% of applicants admitted
▶ SAT or ACT (ACT writing recommended) required
▶ 60% graduate within 6 years

General. Founded in 1927. Regionally accredited. **Degrees:** 489 bachelor's, 27 associate awarded. **Location:** 70 miles from Pittsburgh. **Calendar:** Semester, limited summer session. **Class size:** 30% < 20, 58% 20-39, 9% 40-49, 3% 50-99, less than 1% >100. **Special facilities:** 40-acre nature preserve maintained by biology department, performing arts center.

Freshman class profile. 1,613 applied, 1,418 admitted, 745 enrolled.

Mid 50% test scores			
SAT critical reading:	450-540	GPA 2.0-2.99:	23%
SAT math:	460-560	Rank in top quarter:	34%
SAT writing:	430-530	Rank in top tenth:	11%
ACT composite:	20-24	Return as sophomores:	74%
GPA 3.75 or higher:	30%	Out-of-state:	3%
GPA 3.50-3.74:	16%	Live on campus:	77%
GPA 3.0-3.49:	31%	International:	3%

Basis for selection. College preparatory curriculum, high school achievement, test scores, and class rank very important. Recommendations and essay considered. Interview recommended.

High school preparation. College-preparatory program recommended. 15 units required. Required units include English 4, mathematics 2, social studies 4, science 2 (laboratory 1) and foreign language 2. One each of trigonometry, physics, and chemistry required for engineering technology program.

2011-2012 Annual costs. Tuition/fees: $12,528; $22,720 out-of-state. Room/board: $8,054.

2010-2011 Financial aid. Need-based: 690 full-time freshmen applied for aid; 589 were judged to have need; 583 of these received aid. Average need met was 56%. Average scholarship/grant was $6,523; average loan $3,790. 45% of total undergraduate aid awarded as scholarships/grants, 55% as loans/jobs. **Non-need-based:** Awarded to 826 full-time undergraduates, including 251 freshmen. Scholarships awarded for academics, athletics, leadership, minority status, state residency.

Application procedures. Admission: No deadline. $45 fee, may be waived for applicants with need. Admission notification on a rolling basis beginning on or about 8/15. Must reply by May 1 or within 2 week(s) if notified thereafter. **Financial aid:** Priority date 4/1; no closing date. FAFSA required. Applicants notified on a rolling basis starting 4/1; must reply within 2 week(s) of notification.

Academics. Special study options: Accelerated study, combined bachelor's/graduate degree, cooperative education, cross-registration, double major, dual enrollment of high school students, independent study, internships, liberal arts/career combination, student-designed major, study abroad, teacher certification program. **Credit/placement by examination:** AP, CLEP, IB, SAT, ACT, institutional tests. 90 credit hours maximum toward bachelor's degree. **Support services:** Learning center, reduced course load, study skills assistance, tutoring, writing center.

Majors. Area/ethnic studies: American. **Biology:** General. **Business:** General, accounting, finance, managerial economics, marketing. **Communications:** Communications/speech/rhetoric, journalism. **Computer sciences:** General. **Conservation:** Environmental studies. **Education:** Biology, chemistry, elementary, English, mathematics, science, secondary, social science, social studies. **English:** American lit, British lit, creative writing. **Health services:** Nursing (RN), predental, premedicine, preveterinary. **History:** General. **Liberal arts:** Arts/sciences. **Math:** General. **Physical sciences:** Chemistry, geology. **Psychology:** General. **Social sciences:** General, economics, geography, political science, sociology. **Visual/performing arts:** Dramatic.

Most popular majors. Biology 8%, business/marketing 25%, communications/journalism 9%, education 16%, engineering/engineering technologies 14%, social sciences 7%.

Computing on campus. 150 workstations in library, computer center. Dormitories wired for high-speed internet access and linked to campus network. Commuter students can connect to campus network. Online course registration, online library, helpline, student web hosting, wireless network available.

Student life. Freshman orientation: Mandatory, $55 fee. Preregistration for classes offered. One-day program. **Policies:** To be eligible to hold office within group or organization, student must be full-time and have minimum 2.0 GPA. **Housing:** Guaranteed on-campus for all undergraduates. Coed dorms, special housing for disabled, apartments, fraternity/sorority housing available. $150 fully refundable deposit. Townhouses, lodges, and single-sex residences available. **Activities:** Concert band, campus ministries, choral groups, dance, drama, literary magazine, music ensembles, Model UN, musical theater, radio station, student government, student newspaper, TV station, Newman Association, Black Action Society, Student Outreach Through Service, Time Out Christian Fellowship, Student Council on World Affairs, political science club, Habitat for Humanity.

Athletics. NCAA. **Intercollegiate:** Baseball M, basketball, cross-country W, golf, soccer, track and field W, volleyball W, wrestling M. **Intramural:** Basketball, football (non-tackle), softball, volleyball. **Team name:** Mountain Cats.

Student services. Adult student services, alcohol/substance abuse counseling, chaplain/spiritual director, career counseling, student employment services, financial aid counseling, health services, personal counseling, placement for graduates, veterans' counselor. **Physically disabled:** Services for visually, speech, hearing impaired.

Contact. E-mail: upjadmit@pitt.edu
Phone: (814) 269-7050 Toll-free number: (800) 765-4875
Fax: (814) 269-7044
Bernard Sarneso, Director of Admissions, University of Pittsburgh at Johnstown, 450 Schoolhouse Road, 157 Blackington Hall, Johnstown, PA 15904-1200

University of Scranton
Scranton, Pennsylvania
www.scranton.edu

CB member
CB code: 2929

- Private 4-year university and liberal arts college affiliated with Roman Catholic Church
- Residential campus in small city
- 3,967 degree-seeking undergraduates: 3% part-time, 55% women, 2% African American, 2% Asian American, 7% Hispanic American
- 1,952 degree-seeking graduate students
- 72% of applicants admitted
- SAT or ACT (ACT writing optional), application essay required
- 77% graduate within 6 years; 37% enter graduate study

General. Founded in 1888. Regionally accredited. **Degrees:** 969 bachelor's, 2 associate awarded; master's, professional offered. **ROTC:** Army, Air Force. **Location:** 125 miles from Philadelphia, 125 miles from New York City. **Calendar:** Semester, limited summer session. **Full-time faculty:** 278 total; 78% have terminal degrees, 10% minority, 41% women. **Part-time faculty:** 216 total; 12% have terminal degrees, 3% minority, 56% women. **Class size:** 50% < 20, 48% 20-39, 2% 40-49, less than 1% 50-99. **Special facilities:** New science center with vivarium and rooftop greehouse and observation deck, cyber cafe, conference and retreat center at Chapman Lake, performing arts center with seating for 700.

Freshman class profile. 9,047 applied, 6,531 admitted, 1,054 enrolled.

Mid 50% test scores			
SAT critical reading:	510-600	**GPA 2.0-2.99:**	21%
SAT math:	520-610	**Rank in top quarter:**	59%
ACT composite:	22-26	**Rank in top tenth:**	26%
GPA 3.75 or higher:	19%	**Return as sophomores:**	88%
GPA 3.50-3.74:	20%	**Out-of-state:**	64%
GPA 3.0-3.49:	40%	**Live on campus:**	88%

Basis for selection. Program taken, GPA, SAT scores, class rank most important. Essay, extracurricular/leadership activities, recommendations important. **Home schooled:** State high school equivalency certificate required.

High school preparation. College-preparatory program recommended. 16 units required. Required and recommended units include English 4, mathematics 3-4, history 2-3, science 1-2, foreign language 2 and academic electives 4. Science and business students should have 4 math; science students should have 4 science.

2011-2012 Annual costs. Tuition/fees: $36,042. Room/board: $12,432.

2010-2011 Financial aid. Need-based: 823 full-time freshmen applied for aid; 685 were judged to have need; 679 of these received aid. Average need met was 67%. Average scholarship/grant was $19,740; average loan $6,664. 68% of total undergraduate aid awarded as scholarships/grants, 32% as loans/jobs. **Non-need-based:** Awarded to 817 full-time undergraduates, including 218 freshmen. Scholarships awarded for academics, ROTC.

Application procedures. Admission: Closing date 3/1 (postmark date). No application fee. Application must be submitted online. Admission notification on a rolling basis beginning on or about 12/15. Must reply by May 1 or within 2 week(s) if notified thereafter. **Financial aid:** Priority date 2/15; no closing date. FAFSA required. Applicants notified on a rolling basis starting 3/15; must reply by 5/1 or within 2 week(s) of notification.

Academics. Special study options: Accelerated study, combined bachelor's/graduate degree, cross-registration, distance learning, double major, dual enrollment of high school students, ESL, exchange student, honors, independent study, internships, semester at sea, student-designed major, study abroad, teacher certification program, United Nations semester, Washington semester. Baccalaureate/master's degree programs available. **Credit/placement by examination:** AP, CLEP, IB, institutional tests. 30 credit hours maximum

toward bachelor's degree. **Support services:** Learning center, remedial instruction, study skills assistance, tutoring, writing center.

Majors. Area/ethnic studies: Chicano/Hispanic-American/Latino, French, German, Italian, women's. **Biology:** General, biochemistry, biophysics, molecular, molecular pharmacology, neuroscience. **Business:** Accounting, business admin, e-commerce, finance, human resources, international, marketing, operations. **Communications:** Communications/speech/rhetoric, digital media. **Computer sciences:** Computer science, information systems. **Conservation:** Environmental science. **Education:** Early childhood, elementary, middle, secondary. **Engineering:** Computer, electrical, pre-engineering. **English:** English lit. **Foreign languages:** Ancient Greek, classics, French, German, Latin, Spanish. **Health services:** Clinical lab science, health care admin, nursing (RN), public health ed. **History:** General. **Liberal arts:** Arts/sciences. **Math:** General. **Parks/recreation:** Exercise sciences. **Philosophy/religion:** Philosophy, religion. **Physical sciences:** Chemistry, physics. **Protective services:** Criminal justice, forensics. **Psychology:** General. **Social sciences:** Economics, international relations, political science, sociology. **Visual/performing arts:** Dramatic.

Most popular majors. Biology 12%, business/marketing 22%, communications/journalism 7%, education 9%, health sciences 12%, parks/recreation 7%, psychology 6%.

Computing on campus. PC or laptop required. 935 workstations in dormitories, library, computer center, student center. Dormitories wired for high-speed internet access and linked to campus network. Commuter students can connect to campus network. Online course registration, online library, helpline, repair service, student web hosting, wireless network available.

Student life. Freshman orientation: Mandatory, $275 fee. Preregistration for classes offered. Overnight program for students and parents, held between end of June and mid-July. **Policies:** Freshmen not permitted cars on campus. **Housing:** Guaranteed on-campus for all undergraduates. Coed dorms, single-sex dorms, special housing for disabled, apartments, wellness housing available. $150 nonrefundable deposit, deadline 5/1. **Activities:** Bands, campus ministries, choral groups, dance, drama, international student organizations, literary magazine, music ensembles, musical theater, radio station, student government, student newspaper, symphony orchestra, TV station, College Democrats, College Republicans, Colleges Against Cancer, Habitat for Humanity,environmental awareness Club, Spirit of Scranton, Students for Life, United Colors, University of Scranton Political Society.

Athletics. NCAA. **Intercollegiate:** Baseball M, basketball, cross-country, field hockey W, golf M, lacrosse, soccer, softball W, swimming, tennis, volleyball W, wrestling M. **Intramural:** Badminton, basketball, football (non-tackle), racquetball, skiing, soccer, softball, table tennis, tennis, volleyball. **Team name:** Royals.

Student services. Adult student services, alcohol/substance abuse counseling, chaplain/spiritual director, career counseling, student employment services, health services, personal counseling, placement for graduates, veterans' counselor. **Physically disabled:** Services for visually, hearing impaired.

Contact. E-mail: admissions@scranton.edu
Phone: (570) 941-7540 Toll-free number: (888) 727-2686
Fax: (570) 941-5928
Joseph Roback, Assistant Vice President for Admissions and Enrollment, University of Scranton, 800 Linden Street, Scranton, PA 18510-4699

University of the Arts
Philadelphia, Pennsylvania
www.uarts.edu

CB member
CB code: 2664

- Private 4-year visual arts and performing arts college
- Residential campus in very large city
- 1,971 degree-seeking undergraduates: 2% part-time, 56% women, 12% African American, 3% Asian American, 7% Hispanic American, 1% Native American, 6% international
- 244 degree-seeking graduate students
- 46% of applicants admitted
- Application essay required
- 66% graduate within 6 years

General. Founded in 1870. Regionally accredited. **Degrees:** 466 bachelor's awarded; master's offered. **Calendar:** Semester, limited summer session. **Full-time faculty:** 126 total. **Part-time faculty:** 367 total. **Class size:** 81% < 20, 19% 20-39, less than 1% 50-99, less than 1% >100. **Special facilities:** 12 individual gallery spaces, including student-run art gallery, 7 performance venues including a black box theater and a 1874-seat theater, specialized music library, extensive Visual Resource Collection and digital electronic resources, multimedia laboratories, Oxberry animation stand, MIDI and

recording studios, analog and digital electronic music studios, music calligraphy laboratory, center for publication arts, industrial design computer-aided product design center.

Freshman class profile. 2,399 applied, 1,095 admitted, 432 enrolled.

Mid 50% test scores			
SAT critical reading:	440-580	GPA 3.0-3.49:	30%
SAT math:	430-550	GPA 2.0-2.99:	53%
SAT writing:	450-570	Return as sophomores:	79%
GPA 3.75 or higher:	6%	Out-of-state:	69%
GPA 3.50-3.74:	7%	Live on campus:	85%
		International:	6%

Basis for selection. Academic records, art work portfolio, audition very important. SAT or ACT scores considered; no minimum score required. Statement of purpose and letters of recommendation also important; a minimum GPA of 2.0 or better is recommended. Class placement in English composition through SAT/ACT scores. August 15 score deadline for placement, counseling and/or credit. For international students: English proficiency demonstrated by TOEFL (80 ibt), IELTS (6.0), PTE (54), or UArts ESL Institute Completion. Interview recommended for all; audition or portfolio required for performing arts programs; portfolio required for design, visual arts, film programs; essay required for all programs. **Home schooled:** Statement describing home school structure and mission, transcript of courses and grades, state high school equivalency certificate, letter of recommendation (nonparent) required. Interview not required but recommended; GED accepted in lieu of state high school equivalency certificate.

High school preparation. College-preparatory program recommended. Required and recommended units include English 4, mathematics 3, social studies 2, history 2, science 2 and foreign language 2. Coursework in art, dance, music, creative writing, or theater as appropriate for specific programs recommended.

2011-2012 Annual costs. Tuition/fees: $33,500. Room/board: $12,300. Books/supplies: $2,100. Personal expenses: $1,665.

Financial aid. Non-need-based: Scholarships awarded for academics, art, music/drama.

Application procedures. Admission: Priority date 3/15; no deadline. $60 fee, may be waived for applicants with need. Admission notification on a rolling basis beginning on or about 11/1. Must reply by May 1 or within 3 week(s) if notified thereafter. **Financial aid:** Priority date 3/1; no closing date. FAFSA required. Applicants notified on a rolling basis starting 3/15; must reply within 2 week(s) of notification.

Academics. Special study options: Accelerated study, cross-registration, double major, dual enrollment of high school students, ESL, exchange student, independent study, internships, liberal arts/career combination, study abroad, teacher certification program. **Credit/placement by examination:** AP, CLEP, IB, SAT, ACT, institutional tests. Credit by examination counted toward bachelor's degree varies by program. **Support services:** Learning center, pre-admission summer program, reduced course load, remedial instruction, study skills assistance, tutoring, writing center.

Majors. Communications: Digital media. **Communications technology:** Animation/special effects. **Education:** Drama/dance. **Visual/performing arts:** Acting, cinematography, crafts, dance, directing/producing, graphic design, illustration, industrial design, multimedia, music performance, music theory/composition, musical theater, painting, photography, play/screenwriting, printmaking, sculpture, studio arts, theater design.

Most popular majors. Visual/performing arts 95%.

Computing on campus. PC or laptop required. 400 workstations in library, computer center, student center. Dormitories wired for high-speed internet access and linked to campus network. Commuter students can connect to campus network. Online course registration, online library, helpline, wireless network available.

Student life. Freshman orientation: Available. Preregistration for classes offered. Offers practical skills for being a successful college student-artist. Experience first-hand Philadelphia sights and sounds and get to know fellow classmates and faculty. **Policies:** Campus code of conduct. **Housing:** Coed dorms, apartments, wellness housing available. $200 nonrefundable deposit, deadline 5/1. All housing in apartment-style units. **Activities:** Jazz band, choral groups, dance, drama, film society, international student organizations, literary magazine, music ensembles, musical theater, radio station, student government, Student Council, GLBTS Student Union, African Diaspora Collective, African American Student Union, Friends not Food, Global Exchange, JewArts, Ladies of Service, Latino Student Union, UArts Christian Fellowship.

Student services. Adult student services, alcohol/substance abuse counseling, career counseling, services for economically disadvantaged, student employment services, financial aid counseling, health services, personal counseling, placement for graduates, veterans' counselor. **Physically disabled:** Services for visually, speech, hearing impaired.

Contact. E-mail: admissions@uarts.edu
Phone: (215) 717-6030 Toll-free number: (800) 616-2787
Fax: (215) 717-6045
Susan Gandy, Dean of Admissions, University of the Arts, 320 South Broad Street, Philadelphia, PA 19102

University of the Sciences in Philadelphia
Philadelphia, Pennsylvania — CB member
www.usp.edu — CB code: 2663

- Private 4-year health science and pharmacy college
- Residential campus in very large city
- 2,478 degree-seeking undergraduates: 1% part-time, 61% women, 5% African American, 38% Asian American, 2% Hispanic American, 2% international
- 296 degree-seeking graduate students
- 63% of applicants admitted
- SAT or ACT with writing required
- 65% graduate within 6 years

General. Founded in 1821. Regionally accredited. **Degrees:** 241 bachelor's awarded; master's, professional, doctoral offered. **ROTC:** Army, Air Force. **Calendar:** Semester, limited summer session. **Full-time faculty:** 170 total; 81% have terminal degrees, 16% minority, 47% women. **Part-time faculty:** 158 total; 18% minority, 58% women. **Class size:** 40% < 20, 43% 20-39, 5% 40-49, 5% 50-99, 7% >100. **Special facilities:** History of pharmacy museum, advanced pharmacy studies lab, research labs, science and technology center, wet labs.

Freshman class profile. 3,723 applied, 2,358 admitted, 483 enrolled.

Mid 50% test scores			
SAT critical reading:	510-600	GPA 2.0-2.99:	9%
SAT math:	550-650	Rank in top quarter:	77%
SAT writing:	510-610	Rank in top tenth:	39%
ACT composite:	23-27	End year in good standing:	86%
GPA 3.75 or higher:	43%	Return as sophomores:	83%
GPA 3.50-3.74:	19%	Out-of-state:	52%
GPA 3.0-3.49:	29%	Live on campus:	86%
		International:	1%

Basis for selection. High school curriculum, GPA, class rank if provided by high school, and SAT or ACT test scores most important criteria. ACT recommended. Essay and/or letters of recommendation not required, but reviewed if provided. **Home schooled:** Transcript of courses and grades, state high school equivalency certificate required.

High school preparation. College-preparatory program required. 16 units required. Required and recommended units include English 4, mathematics 3-4, social studies 1, history 1, science 3 (laboratory 2-3) and academic electives 4.

2011-2012 Annual costs. Tuition/fees: $32,148. Room/board: $12,564. Books/supplies: $1,050. Personal expenses: $2,660.

Financial aid. Non-need-based: Scholarships awarded for academics, athletics.

Application procedures. Admission: No deadline. $45 fee, may be waived for applicants with need, free for online applicants. Admission notification on a rolling basis beginning on or about 10/1. Must reply by May 1 or within 3 week(s) if notified thereafter. **Financial aid:** Closing date 3/15. FAFSA required. Applicants notified on a rolling basis starting 1/15; must reply by 5/1 or within 2 week(s) of notification.

Academics. Direct-entry admission for freshman pharmacy, DPT and MPT physical therapy program, occupational therapy and physician assistant programs. Students not required to reapply to professional phase of their majors. **Special study options:** Combined bachelor's/graduate degree, cross-registration, double major, honors, independent study, internships, study abroad. **Credit/placement by examination:** AP, CLEP, IB, institutional tests. **Support services:** Learning center, pre-admission summer program, reduced course load, remedial instruction, study skills assistance, tutoring, writing center.

Majors. Biology: General, biochemistry, bioinformatics, microbiology, pharmacology/toxicology. **Business:** Marketing. **Computer sciences:** Computer science. **Conservation:** Environmental science. **Health services:** Clinical lab science, physician assistant. **Parks/recreation:** Exercise sciences,

sports admin. **Physical sciences:** Chemistry, physics. **Psychology:** General, medical.

Most popular majors. Biology 14%, health sciences 77%.

Computing on campus. 190 workstations in dormitories, library, computer center, student center. Dormitories wired for high-speed internet access and linked to campus network. Commuter students can connect to campus network. Online course registration, online library, helpline, repair service, wireless network available.

Student life. Freshman orientation: Mandatory. Preregistration for classes offered. Programs for parents and students; placement testing. **Policies:** Campus alcohol free. Freshmen not permitted cars on campus. **Housing:** Guaranteed on-campus for freshmen. Coed dorms, apartments, fraternity/sorority housing, wellness housing available. $200 nonrefundable deposit. Honor halls. **Activities:** Concert band, choral groups, dance, drama, literary magazine, musical theater, student government, student newspaper, professional organizations, Greek letter organizations, religious groups, honor societies, student community involvement program, ethnic/diversity groups, student chapters of scientific organizations, student publications.

Athletics. NAIA, NCAA. **Intercollegiate:** Baseball M, basketball, cross-country, golf, rifle, softball W, tennis, volleyball W. **Intramural:** Archery, badminton, basketball, bowling, rifle, table tennis, volleyball. **Team name:** Devils.

Student services. Adult student services, alcohol/substance abuse counseling, career counseling, student employment services, financial aid counseling, health services, personal counseling, placement for graduates, veterans' counselor. **Physically disabled:** Services for visually, speech, hearing impaired.

Contact. E-mail: admit@usciences.edu
Phone: (215) 596-8810 Toll-free number: (888) 996-8747
Fax: (215) 596-8821
Dianna Collins, Executive Director of Admission and Enrollment Services, University of the Sciences in Philadelphia, 600 South 43rd Street, Philadelphia, PA 19104-4495

Ursinus College
Collegeville, Pennsylvania
www.ursinus.edu
CB member
CB code: 2931

- Private 4-year liberal arts college
- Residential campus in small town
- 1,741 degree-seeking undergraduates: 53% women, 6% African American, 4% Asian American, 4% Hispanic American, 1% international
- 70% of applicants admitted
- Application essay required
- 80% graduate within 6 years

General. Founded in 1869. Regionally accredited. All freshmen receive laptop computers (updated at beginning of junior year). **Degrees:** 387 bachelor's awarded. **Location:** 28 miles from Philadelphia. **Calendar:** Semester. **Full-time faculty:** 125 total; 90% have terminal degrees, 14% minority, 48% women. **Part-time faculty:** 69 total; 41% have terminal degrees, 13% minority, 58% women. **Class size:** 79% < 20, 20% 20-39, less than 1% 50-99. **Special facilities:** Performing arts center, art museum, observatory, outdoor sculpture collection, public walking trails.

Freshman class profile. 3,851 applied, 2,703 admitted, 428 enrolled.

Mid 50% test scores		Rank in top quarter:	70%
SAT critical reading:	550-650	Rank in top tenth:	33%
SAT math:	560-670	Return as sophomores:	89%
SAT writing:	540-640	Out-of-state:	50%
ACT composite:	25-30	Live on campus:	99%
GPA 3.75 or higher:	40%	International:	1%
GPA 3.50-3.74:	25%	Fraternities:	20%
GPA 3.0-3.49:	27%	Sororities:	30%
GPA 2.0-2.99:	8%		

Basis for selection. Academic achievement, including course rigor and results are most important. Motivation and leadership are considered. Test scores are optional. SAT/ACT optional for students ranking in top 10% of class, or with minimum 3.5 GPA from non-ranking school. Interview recommended.

High school preparation. College-preparatory program required. 16 units required; 21 recommended. Required and recommended units include English 4, mathematics 3-4, social studies 2, history 1-2, science 3-4 (laboratory 1-2), foreign language 2-4 and academic electives 1.

2011-2012 Annual costs. Tuition/fees: $41,650. Required $170 laptop insurance fee. Room/board: $10,300. Books/supplies: $1,000. Personal expenses: $1,500.

Financial aid. Non-need-based: Scholarships awarded for academics, alumni affiliation, art, leadership, music/drama.

Application procedures. Admission: Closing date 2/15 (receipt date). $50 fee, may be waived for applicants with need, free for online applicants. Admission notification by 4/1. Must reply by May 1 or within 2 week(s) if notified thereafter. Rolling notification for Early Action within 7 weeks of receipt of application. **Financial aid:** Priority date 2/15, closing date 5/1. FAFSA, institutional form, CSS PROFILE required. Applicants notified by 4/1; must reply by 5/1 or within 2 week(s) of notification.

Academics. Summer undergraduate research fellowships available. Independent Learning Experience required of all. Study abroad encouraged. All first-year students complete overview of human thought, creativity, culture, history in a 2-semester seminar called the Common Intellectual Experience (CIE). **Special study options:** Combined bachelor's/graduate degree, double major, dual enrollment of high school students, ESL, exchange student, independent study, internships, semester at sea, student-designed major, study abroad, teacher certification program, United Nations semester, Washington semester. Howard University semester. **Credit/placement by examination:** AP, CLEP, IB, institutional tests. **Support services:** Pre-admission summer program, reduced course load, tutoring, writing center.

Majors. Area/ethnic studies: American, East Asian. **Biology:** General, neuroscience. **Communications:** Communications/speech/rhetoric. **Computer sciences:** Computer science. **Conservation:** Environmental studies. **English:** English lit. **Foreign languages:** Classics, French, German, Spanish. **History:** General. **Math:** General. **Parks/recreation:** Health/fitness. **Philosophy/religion:** Philosophy. **Physical sciences:** Chemistry, physics. **Psychology:** General. **Social sciences:** Anthropology, economics, international relations, political science, sociology. **Visual/performing arts:** Art, art history/conservation, dance, dramatic.

Most popular majors. Biology 19%, English 8%, parks/recreation 8%, psychology 11%, social sciences 25%.

Computing on campus. 1,655 workstations in dormitories, library, computer center, student center. Dormitories wired for high-speed internet access and linked to campus network. Commuter students can connect to campus network. Online course registration, online library, helpline, repair service, student web hosting, wireless network available.

Student life. Freshman orientation: Mandatory. Preregistration for classes offered. 2-day session in June and 4-day session in August before start of classes. **Housing:** Guaranteed on-campus for all undergraduates. Coed dorms, single-sex dorms, special housing for disabled, wellness housing available. $500 nonrefundable deposit, deadline 5/1. Multicultural, community service, art, physical science, literature houses and quiet halls, other special interest housing available. **Activities:** Bands, campus ministries, choral groups, dance, drama, film society, literary magazine, music ensembles, Model UN, musical theater, radio station, student government, student newspaper, TV station, Relay for Life, Association of Latinos Motivated to Achieve, Best Buddies, College Democrats, College Republicans, Hillel, Inter-Faith Outreach, Buddhist meditation group.

Athletics. NCAA. **Intercollegiate:** Baseball M, basketball, cross-country, field hockey W, football (tackle) M, golf, gymnastics W, lacrosse, soccer, softball W, swimming, tennis, track and field, volleyball W, wrestling M. **Intramural:** Basketball, football (non-tackle) M, soccer, softball, squash, swimming, tennis, volleyball. **Team name:** Bears.

Student services. Adult student services, alcohol/substance abuse counseling, chaplain/spiritual director, career counseling, student employment services, financial aid counseling, health services, minority student services, personal counseling, placement for graduates. **Physically disabled:** Services for visually, speech, hearing impaired.

Contact. E-mail: admissions@ursinus.edu
Phone: (610) 409-3200 Fax: (610) 409-3662
Richard Floyd, Director of Admission, Ursinus College, PO Box 1000, Collegeville, PA 19426-1000

Valley Forge Christian College
Phoenixville, Pennsylvania
www.vfcc.edu
CB code: 2579

- Private 4-year liberal arts college affiliated with Assemblies of God
- Residential campus in large town
- 886 degree-seeking undergraduates: 10% part-time, 52% women, 13% African American, 2% Asian American, 10% Hispanic American

- 26 degree-seeking graduate students
- 77% of applicants admitted
- SAT or ACT with writing, application essay required
- 44% graduate within 6 years

General. Founded in 1938. Regionally accredited. **Degrees:** 144 bachelor's, 8 associate awarded; master's offered. **Location:** 25 miles from Philadelphia. **Calendar:** Semester, extensive summer session. **Full-time faculty:** 33 total; 42% have terminal degrees, 9% minority, 36% women. **Part-time faculty:** 45 total; 16% have terminal degrees, 11% minority, 36% women. **Class size:** 70% < 20, 23% 20-39, 2% 40-49, 4% 50-99.

Freshman class profile. 356 applied, 274 admitted, 156 enrolled.

Mid 50% test scores			
SAT critical reading:	420-550	GPA 3.0-3.49:	26%
SAT math:	400-530	GPA 2.0-2.99:	32%
SAT writing:	400-520	End year in good standing:	79%
ACT composite:	17-24	Return as sophomores:	63%
GPA 3.75 or higher:	17%	Out-of-state:	49%
GPA 3.50-3.74:	17%	Live on campus:	96%

Basis for selection. School achievement record, pastor recommendation, written essay, test scores important. Bible test required for all; music, computer, English, and math tests required for some. **Home schooled:** Statement describing home school structure and mission, transcript of courses and grades required. Student must sign and date a VFCC home schooled self-certification form. **Learning Disabled:** Academic recommendation from counselor IEP or other.

High school preparation. College-preparatory program recommended. 16 units recommended. Recommended units include English 4, mathematics 2, social studies 4, science 4 and foreign language 2.

2011-2012 Annual costs. Tuition/fees: $17,302. Cost of mandatory laptop is included in the required fees. Room/board: $7,236. Books/supplies: $818. Personal expenses: $1,816.

2011-2012 Financial aid. **Need-based:** Average need met was 52%. Average scholarship/grant was $8,470; average loan $3,350. 49% of total undergraduate aid awarded as scholarships/grants, 51% as loans/jobs. **Non-need-based:** Scholarships awarded for academics, leadership, music/drama, religious affiliation, state residency.

Application procedures. Admission: Priority date 5/1; deadline 8/1 (receipt date). $25 fee, may be waived for applicants with need, free for online applicants. Admission notification by 8/15. Admission notification on a rolling basis. **Financial aid:** Priority date 5/1; no closing date. FAFSA required. Applicants notified on a rolling basis starting 3/15; must reply within 3 week(s) of notification.

Academics. Special study options: Accelerated study, distance learning, double major, dual enrollment of high school students, ESL, honors, independent study, internships, liberal arts/career combination, study abroad, teacher certification program. **Credit/placement by examination:** AP, CLEP, IB, SAT, ACT, institutional tests. 15 credit hours maximum toward associate degree, 30 toward bachelor's. **Support services:** Learning center, reduced course load, remedial instruction, study skills assistance, tutoring, writing center.

Majors. Business: Business admin. **Communications:** Digital media. **Education:** Early childhood, elementary, music. **Foreign languages:** Translation. **Human services:** Social work. **Theology:** Bible, missionary, pastoral counseling, religious ed, sacred music, theology. **Visual/performing arts:** Music performance.

Most popular majors. Business/marketing 10%, education 20%, psychology 16%, theological studies 42%.

Computing on campus. PC or laptop required. 86 workstations in library, computer center. Dormitories wired for high-speed internet access and linked to campus network. Commuter students can connect to campus network. Online course registration, online library, helpline, repair service, student web hosting, wireless network available.

Student life. Freshman orientation: Mandatory, $75 fee. Preregistration for classes offered. 3-day program held weekend prior to beginning of classes. **Policies:** Religious observance required. **Housing:** Guaranteed on-campus for all undergraduates. Single-sex dorms, apartments available. $100 nonrefundable deposit. **Activities:** Bands, campus ministries, choral groups, dance, drama, music ensembles, student government, student newspaper.

Athletics. NCCAA. **Intercollegiate:** Baseball M, basketball, cross-country, golf M, soccer, volleyball W. **Intramural:** Basketball, bowling, football (non-tackle), soccer, softball. **Team name:** Patriots.

Student services. Chaplain/spiritual director, career counseling, student employment services, financial aid counseling, health services, personal counseling, placement for graduates.

Contact. E-mail: admission@vfcc.edu
Phone: (610) 935-0450 Toll-free number: (800) 432-8322
Fax: (610) 917-2069
Rev. William Chenco, Director of Admissions, Valley Forge Christian College, 1401 Charlestown Road, Phoenixville, PA 19460

Villanova University
Villanova, Pennsylvania
www.villanova.edu

CB member
CB code: 2959

- Private 4-year university affiliated with Roman Catholic Church
- Residential campus in large town
- 6,898 degree-seeking undergraduates: 4% part-time, 51% women, 5% African American, 6% Asian American, 7% Hispanic American, 3% international
- 3,440 degree-seeking graduate students
- 44% of applicants admitted
- SAT or ACT with writing, application essay required
- 91% graduate within 6 years; 23% enter graduate study

General. Founded in 1842. Regionally accredited. **Degrees:** 1,865 bachelor's, 1 associate awarded; master's, professional, doctoral offered. **ROTC:** Army, Naval, Air Force. **Location:** 12 miles from Philadelphia. **Calendar:** Semester, extensive summer session. **Full-time faculty:** 590 total; 88% have terminal degrees, 15% minority, 38% women. **Part-time faculty:** 361 total; 36% have terminal degrees, 8% minority, 44% women. **Class size:** 42% < 20, 53% 20-39, 1% 40-49, 3% 50-99, less than 1% >100. **Special facilities:** Astronomy and astrophysics observatories, electron microscope, structural engineering teaching and research laboratory, nursing simulation labs.

Freshman class profile. 15,394 applied, 6,768 admitted, 1,644 enrolled.

Mid 50% test scores			
SAT critical reading:	590-680	Rank in top quarter:	89%
SAT math:	620-710	Rank in top tenth:	64%
ACT composite:	28-31	End year in good standing:	97%
GPA 3.75 or higher:	66%	Return as sophomores:	94%
GPA 3.50-3.74:	20%	Out-of-state:	82%
GPA 3.0-3.49:	12%	Live on campus:	98%
GPA 2.0-2.99:	2%	International:	3%

Basis for selection. High school record, class rank, standardized test scores, counselor recommendation, essay, extracurricular activities considered. Interview required for finalists of health affiliation programs and Presidential Scholarship consideration. **Home schooled:** Objective third-party evaluation (state high school association, for example), including syllabi, required.

High school preparation. College-preparatory program required. 22 units required; 25 recommended. Required and recommended units include English 4, mathematics 4, science 4 (laboratory 2-3), foreign language 2-4 and academic electives 2. 4 social studies and/or history required. Total units required varies by academic college. 3 laboratory science recommended.

2011-2012 Annual costs. Tuition/fees: $41,260. Full-time tuition includes laptop for all students. Room/board: $10,940. Books/supplies: $950. Personal expenses: $900.

2011-2012 Financial aid. Need-based: 1,153 full-time freshmen applied for aid; 846 were judged to have need; 829 of these received aid. Average need met was 82%. Average scholarship/grant was $26,383; average loan $3,198. 67% of total undergraduate aid awarded as scholarships/grants, 33% as loans/jobs. **Non-need-based:** Awarded to 1,540 full-time undergraduates, including 428 freshmen. Scholarships awarded for academics, alumni affiliation, athletics, leadership, minority status, religious affiliation, ROTC.

Application procedures. Admission: Closing date 1/7 (receipt date). $80 fee, may be waived for applicants with need. Application must be submitted online. Admission notification by 4/1. Must reply by 5/1. November 1 priority application date for scholarship consideration. **Financial aid:** Closing date 2/7. FAFSA, CSS PROFILE required. Applicants notified by 4/1; must reply by 5/1 or within 2 week(s) of notification.

Academics. Special study options: Accelerated study, combined bachelor's/graduate degree, cooperative education, cross-registration, distance learning, double major, dual enrollment of high school students, ESL, exchange student, honors, independent study, internships, liberal arts/career

combination, study abroad, teacher certification program, Washington semester. Cooperative certification programs in elementary education with Rosemont College. **Credit/placement by examination:** AP, CLEP, IB, institutional tests. 30 credit hours maximum toward bachelor's degree. Deans make decisions regarding prior work and life experiences on individual basis. **Support services:** Reduced course load, study skills assistance, tutoring, writing center.

Majors. Area/ethnic studies: Latin American, women's. **Biology:** General, biochemistry. **Business:** Accounting, business admin, finance, international, management information systems, managerial economics, marketing, real estate. **Communications:** Media studies. **Computer sciences:** Computer science. **Conservation:** Environmental science, environmental studies. **Education:** General, secondary. **Engineering:** Chemical, civil, computer, electrical, mechanical. **English:** English lit. **Foreign languages:** Classics, French, German, Italian, Spanish. **Health services:** Nursing (RN), predental, premedicine. **History:** General. **Liberal arts:** Arts/sciences, humanities. **Math:** General. **Philosophy/religion:** Islamic, philosophy, religion. **Physical sciences:** General, astronomy, astrophysics, chemistry, physics. **Protective services:** Law enforcement admin. **Psychology:** General. **Social sciences:** Economics, geography, political science, sociology. **Visual/performing arts:** Art history/conservation.

Most popular majors. Business/marketing 31%, communications/journalism 8%, engineering/engineering technologies 12%, health sciences 12%, social sciences 10%.

Computing on campus. PC or laptop required. 1,200 workstations in dormitories, library, computer center, student center. Dormitories wired for high-speed internet access and linked to campus network. Commuter students can connect to campus network. Online course registration, online library, helpline, repair service, student web hosting, wireless network available.

Student life. Freshman orientation: Mandatory, $125 fee. Preregistration for classes offered. 4-day on-campus program prior to start of fall term. **Housing:** Guaranteed on-campus for freshmen. Coed dorms, single-sex dorms, special housing for disabled, apartments, wellness housing available. $700 nonrefundable deposit, deadline 5/1. On-campus housing available for transfer students on space-available basis; themed learning communities. **Activities:** Bands, campus ministries, choral groups, dance, drama, film society, international student organizations, literary magazine, music ensembles, Model UN, musical theater, radio station, student government, student newspaper, symphony orchestra, TV station, Special Olympics, Amnesty International, Villanovans for Life, Black Cultural Society, Big Brother/Sister, Committee for the Homeless, Project Sunshine, Habitat for Humanity, Blue Key Society.

Athletics. NCAA. **Intercollegiate:** Baseball M, basketball, bowling W, cheerleading, cross-country, diving, field hockey W, football (tackle) M, golf M, lacrosse, rowing (crew) W, soccer, softball W, swimming, tennis, track and field, volleyball W, water polo W. **Intramural:** Basketball, cross-country, field hockey W, football (non-tackle), skiing, soccer, softball, tennis, volleyball. **Team name:** Wildcats.

Student services. Adult student services, alcohol/substance abuse counseling, chaplain/spiritual director, career counseling, services for economically disadvantaged, student employment services, financial aid counseling, health services, minority student services, personal counseling, placement for graduates. **Physically disabled:** Services for visually, hearing impaired.

Contact. E-mail: gotovu@villanova.edu
Phone: (610) 519-4000 Fax: (610) 519-6450
Michael Gaynor, Director of University Admission, Villanova University, Autsin Hall, 800 Lancaster Avenue, Villanova, PA 19085-1672

Washington & Jefferson College
Washington, Pennsylvania
www.washjeff.edu

CB member
CB code: 2967

- Private 4-year liberal arts college
- Residential campus in large town
- 1,418 degree-seeking undergraduates: 1% part-time, 50% women, 3% African American, 2% Asian American, 2% Hispanic American, 1% Native American
- 43% of applicants admitted
- Application essay required
- 74% graduate within 6 years; 39% enter graduate study

General. Founded in 1781. Regionally accredited. **Degrees:** 343 bachelor's awarded. **ROTC:** Army, Air Force. **Location:** 27 miles from Pittsburgh. **Calendar:** 4-1-4, limited summer session. **Full-time faculty:** 113 total; 93% have terminal degrees, 13% minority, 42% women. **Part-time faculty:** 47 total; 30% have terminal degrees, 17% minority, 32% women. **Class size:** 70% < 20, 29% 20-39, less than 1% 40-49. **Special facilities:** Microplate

reader, cell culture labs, isolator lab, X-ray diffraction unit, neuropsychology lab, atomic absorption unit, nuclear magnetic resonance lab, refrigerated centrifuge, global learning unit, language lab, spectrometers, laser scanning confocal microscope facility, Abernathy field station, atomic force microscope, fine arts center.

Freshman class profile. 6,643 applied, 2,855 admitted, 387 enrolled.

Mid 50% test scores			
SAT critical reading:	510-610	Rank in top quarter:	65%
SAT math:	530-620	Rank in top tenth:	34%
ACT composite:	23-28	End year in good standing:	95%
GPA 3.75 or higher:	22%	Return as sophomores:	88%
GPA 3.50-3.74:	23%	Out-of-state:	31%
GPA 3.0-3.49:	34%	Live on campus:	94%
GPA 2.0-2.99:	21%	International:	1%

Basis for selection. Entire high school record including difficulty of schedule, GPA, class rank, extracurricular activities, essay, letters of recommendation important. Interviews required of some students. **Home schooled:** Letter of recommendation (nonparent) required.

High school preparation. College-preparatory program required. 15 units required. Required and recommended units include English 3-4, mathematics 3-4, science 1-2 (laboratory 1-2), foreign language 2-3 and academic electives 6. Six or more academic elective courses from English, math, foreign language, history, and social or natural history required.

2011-2012 Annual costs. Tuition/fees: $36,420. Room/board: $9,756. Books/supplies: $800. Personal expenses: $700.

2011-2012 Financial aid. Need-based: 355 full-time freshmen applied for aid; 316 were judged to have need; 316 of these received aid. Average need met was 78%. Average scholarship/grant was $11,407; average loan $34,332. 71% of total undergraduate aid awarded as scholarships/grants, 29% as loans/jobs. **Non-need-based:** Awarded to 1,222 full-time undergraduates, including 364 freshmen. Scholarships awarded for academics, alumni affiliation, leadership.

Application procedures. Admission: Priority date 1/15; deadline 3/1 (postmark date). $25 fee, may be waived for applicants with need, free for online applicants. Admission notification on a rolling basis beginning on or about 10/1. Must reply by 5/1. **Financial aid:** Priority date 2/15; no closing date. FAFSA required. Applicants notified on a rolling basis starting 3/1; must reply by 5/1.

Academics. Magellan Project supports students who want to do independent research and study either domestically or abroad during the summer. **Special study options:** Accelerated study, combined bachelor's/graduate degree, double major, dual enrollment of high school students, honors, independent study, internships, liberal arts/career combination, student-designed major, study abroad, teacher certification program, Washington semester. **Credit/placement by examination:** AP, CLEP, IB, SAT, ACT, institutional tests. 64 credit hours maximum toward bachelor's degree. **Support services:** Learning center, reduced course load, study skills assistance, tutoring.

Majors. Biology: General, biochemistry, biophysics, cellular/anatomical. **Business:** General, accounting, international. **Communications:** Communications/speech/rhetoric. **Computer sciences:** Information technology. **Conservation:** Environmental studies. **Education:** General, art. **English:** English lit. **Foreign languages:** French, German, Spanish. **History:** General. **Math:** General. **Philosophy/religion:** Philosophy. **Physical sciences:** Chemistry, physics. **Psychology:** General. **Social sciences:** Economics, political science, sociology. **Visual/performing arts:** Art, music, theater history.

Most popular majors. Biology 10%, business/marketing 24%, English 8%, foreign language 8%, psychology 13%, social sciences 12%.

Computing on campus. 450 workstations in library, computer center, student center. Dormitories wired for high-speed internet access and linked to campus network. Commuter students can connect to campus network. Online course registration, online library, helpline, repair service, student web hosting, wireless network available.

Student life. Freshman orientation: Mandatory. Preregistration for classes offered. Planned summer events and 3-day series of sessions/activities held at beginning of fall semester. **Policies:** All students required to live in campus housing unless granted written approval or living with parents 15 miles or less from the college. Students not permitted to smoke in rooms, hallways, or lounges. **Housing:** Guaranteed on-campus for all undergraduates. Coed dorms, single-sex dorms, special housing for disabled, apartments, fraternity/sorority housing, wellness housing available. Pets allowed in dorm rooms. On-campus suites available. **Activities:** Bands, campus ministries, choral groups, dance, drama, film society, international student organizations, literary magazine, music ensembles, Model UN, musical theater, radio station, student government, student newspaper, Newman club, Hillel Society, Young Republicans, College Democrats, Black student union, Alpha Phi Omega, Get

Involved in Volunteer Experiences, Asian culture association, Gay Straight Alliance, Indian student association.

Athletics. NCAA. **Intercollegiate:** Baseball M, basketball, cross-country, diving, field hockey W, football (tackle) M, golf, lacrosse, soccer, softball W, swimming, tennis, track and field, volleyball W, water polo, wrestling M. **Intramural:** Basketball, bowling, football (non-tackle), racquetball, soccer, softball, squash, table tennis, tennis, volleyball. **Team name:** Presidents.

Student services. Adult student services, alcohol/substance abuse counseling, chaplain/spiritual director, career counseling, student employment services, financial aid counseling, health services, minority student services, personal counseling, placement for graduates, women's services.

Contact. E-mail: admission@washjeff.edu
Phone: (724) 223-6025 Toll-free number: (888) 926-3529
Fax: (724) 223-6534
Alton Newell, Vice President for Enrollment, Washington & Jefferson College, 60 South Lincoln Street, Washington, PA 15301

Waynesburg University
Waynesburg, Pennsylvania — CB member
www.waynesburg.edu — CB code: 2969

- Private 4-year liberal arts college affiliated with Presbyterian Church (USA)
- Residential campus in small town
- 1,600 degree-seeking undergraduates: 5% part-time, 60% women, 4% African American, 1% Asian American, 2% Hispanic American
- 719 degree-seeking graduate students
- 75% of applicants admitted
- SAT or ACT with writing required
- 58% graduate within 6 years

General. Founded in 1849. Regionally accredited. Member of the Council for Christian Colleges and Universities. **Degrees:** 385 bachelor's awarded; master's, professional offered. **ROTC:** Army. **Location:** 50 miles from Pittsburgh. **Calendar:** Semester, limited summer session. **Full-time faculty:** 78 total; 65% have terminal degrees, 9% minority, 47% women. **Part-time faculty:** 181 total; 16% have terminal degrees, 62% women. **Class size:** 72% < 20, 25% 20-39, 2% 40-49, less than 1% 50-99. **Special facilities:** Geological museum, historical museum, constitutional studies and moral leadership center, research and economic development center, service leadership center.

Freshman class profile. 2,066 applied, 1,541 admitted, 397 enrolled.

Mid 50% test scores			
SAT critical reading:	450-550	Rank in top quarter:	44%
SAT math:	460-560	Rank in top tenth:	19%
ACT composite:	20-24	Return as sophomores:	78%
GPA 3.75 or higher:	33%	Out-of-state:	28%
GPA 3.50-3.74:	19%	Live on campus:	88%
GPA 3.0-3.49:	40%		
GPA 2.0-2.99:	8%		

Basis for selection. High school classes taken, grades, test scores, activities, community activities, interview, and recommendations considered. Essay, interview recommended. **Home schooled:** Statement describing home school structure and mission, transcript of courses and grades, state high school equivalency certificate required. College should be apprised if applicant enrolled in program approved by state's department of education.

High school preparation. College-preparatory program required. 16 units required. Required and recommended units include English 4, mathematics 3, social studies 2, science 2-3, foreign language 2 and academic electives 5.

2011-2012 Annual costs. Tuition/fees: $19,090. Room/board: $7,930. Books/supplies: $1,300. Personal expenses: $180.

2011-2012 Financial aid. **Need-based:** Average need met was 77%. Average scholarship/grant was $12,001; average loan $3,070. 65% of total undergraduate aid awarded as scholarships/grants, 35% as loans/jobs. **Non-need-based:** Scholarships awarded for academics, alumni affiliation, job skills, leadership, religious affiliation, state residency.

Application procedures. **Admission:** No deadline. $20 fee, may be waived for applicants with need. Admission notification on a rolling basis. Rolling date as specified in deposit letter. **Financial aid:** Priority date 3/15; no closing date. FAFSA required. Applicants notified on a rolling basis starting 2/15; must reply within 2 week(s) of notification.

Academics. **Special study options:** Accelerated study, combined bachelor's/graduate degree, distance learning, double major, dual enrollment of high school students, ESL, honors, independent study, internships, liberal arts/career combination, student-designed major, study abroad, teacher certification program, Washington semester. 3-2 program in engineering with Penn State University in State College, PA and Washington University in St. Louis; 3-1 program in marine biology with Florida Institute of Technology and University of North Carolina, Wilmington; 3-3 law program with Duquesne University. **Credit/placement by examination:** AP, CLEP, SAT, ACT, institutional tests. 15 credit hours maximum toward bachelor's degree. **Support services:** Learning center, reduced course load, study skills assistance, tutoring, writing center.

Majors. **Biology:** General, environmental, marine. **Business:** General, accounting, business admin, finance, international, international marketing. **Communications:** Advertising, broadcast journalism, communications/speech/rhetoric, digital media, journalism, public relations. **Computer sciences:** General, computer science, information technology, networking. **Education:** Art, biology, chemistry, elementary, English, history, mathematics, science, secondary, social studies, special ed. **English:** British lit, creative writing, English lit. **Health services:** Athletic training, nursing (RN), predental, premedicine, preveterinary. **History:** General. **Math:** General. **Parks/recreation:** Exercise sciences, sports admin. **Philosophy/religion:** Religion. **Physical sciences:** Chemistry. **Protective services:** Forensics, law enforcement admin. **Psychology:** General. **Social sciences:** General, political science, sociology. **Theology:** Theology. **Visual/performing arts:** Art, studio arts management. **Work/family studies:** Family studies.

Most popular majors. Biology 7%, business/marketing 17%, communications/journalism 8%, education 7%, health sciences 33%, security/protective services 10%.

Computing on campus. 160 workstations in dormitories, library, computer center, student center. Dormitories wired for high-speed internet access and linked to campus network. Commuter students can connect to campus network. Online course registration, online library, helpline, wireless network available.

Student life. **Freshman orientation:** Mandatory. Preregistration for classes offered. One-day summer program for parents and students; 2-day program prior to start of classes. **Policies:** No alcohol or drugs permitted on campus. **Housing:** Guaranteed on-campus for all undergraduates. Single-sex dorms available. $150 partly refundable deposit. **Activities:** Bands, campus ministries, choral groups, dance, drama, literary magazine, music ensembles, musical theater, radio station, student government, student newspaper, TV station, Fellowship of Christian Athletes, Newman Club, Black student union, Waynesburg Christian Fellowship, Bonner Scholars, Alpha Phi Omega, Habitat for Humanity, leadership program.

Athletics. NCAA. **Intercollegiate:** Baseball M, basketball, cross-country, football (tackle) M, golf, lacrosse W, soccer, softball W, tennis, track and field, volleyball W, wrestling M. **Intramural:** Basketball, bowling, football (non-tackle), racquetball, softball, table tennis, volleyball W. **Team name:** Yellow Jackets.

Student services. Adult student services, chaplain/spiritual director, career counseling, student employment services, financial aid counseling, health services, minority student services, personal counseling, placement for graduates.

Contact. E-mail: admissions@waynesburg.edu
Phone: (724) 852-3248 Toll-free number: (800) 225-7393
Fax: (724) 627-8124
Sarah Zwinger, Director of Admissions, Waynesburg University, 51 West College Street, Waynesburg, PA 15370-1222

West Chester University of Pennsylvania
West Chester, Pennsylvania — CB member
www.wcupa.edu — CB code: 2659

- Public 4-year university
- Commuter campus in large town
- 12,521 degree-seeking undergraduates: 7% part-time, 59% women, 10% African American, 2% Asian American, 4% Hispanic American, 1% Native American
- 1,746 degree-seeking graduate students
- 47% of applicants admitted
- SAT or ACT with writing, application essay required
- 68% graduate within 6 years

General. Founded in 1871. Regionally accredited. **Degrees:** 2,556 bachelor's awarded; master's offered. **ROTC:** Army, Air Force. **Location:** 25 miles from Philadelphia. **Calendar:** Semester, extensive summer session. **Special facilities:** Planetarium, herbarium, speech and hearing clinic, autism clinic,

center for government and community affairs, 151-acre natural area for environmental studies, mineral museum, music library, fully-equipped food preparation laboratory for nutrition and dietetics program, nursing skills laboratory, athletic training rooms, HEAT (Heat Illness Evaluation Avoidance and Treatment) Institute, dance studio, poetry center.

Freshman class profile. 15,080 applied, 7,013 admitted, 2,292 enrolled.

Mid 50% test scores		Rank in top quarter:	43%
SAT critical reading:	490-580	Rank in top tenth:	12%
SAT math:	500-580	Return as sophomores:	86%
SAT writing:	480-570	Out-of-state:	16%
GPA 3.75 or higher:	32%	Live on campus:	92%
GPA 3.50-3.74:	20%	Fraternities:	10%
GPA 3.0-3.49:	35%	Sororities:	15%
GPA 2.0-2.99:	12%		

Basis for selection. College preparatory curriculum in high school, standardized test scores, and personal statement are required and evaluated. Specific course prerequisites depend on major selection. Committee review for special admissions programs and additional documentation is required of candidates for the summer academic development program. SAT or ACT scores are required for all first-time, first-year, degree-seeking applicants unless they have been out of high school for 5 years or more. Interview required for athletic training, premedical, pharmaceutical product development and respiratory care programs. Audition required for music applicants. **Home schooled:** Students must have work certified by PA Homeschoolers' Association or their high school. **Learning Disabled:** By law, we cannot ask about any disabilities on the admissions application so they are not considered in decision making.

High school preparation. College-preparatory program required. 16 units required; 21 recommended. Required and recommended units include English 4, mathematics 3-4, social studies 2, history 2, science 3 (laboratory 2), foreign language 2, computer science 1, visual/performing arts 1 and academic electives 2.

2011-2012 Annual costs. Tuition/fees: $8,274; $17,634 out-of-state. Room/board: $7,784. Books/supplies: $1,464. Personal expenses: $2,208.

Financial aid. **Non-need-based:** Scholarships awarded for academics, art, athletics, leadership, music/drama.

Application procedures. **Admission:** Priority date 2/1; no deadline. $45 fee, may be waived for applicants with need. Admission notification on a rolling basis beginning on or about 10/1. Must reply by May 1 or within 4 week(s) if notified thereafter. **Financial aid:** Priority date 3/1; no closing date. FAFSA required. Must reply within 4 week(s) of notification.

Academics. **Special study options:** Accelerated study, cross-registration, distance learning, double major, dual enrollment of high school students, exchange student, honors, independent study, internships, liberal arts/career combination, student-designed major, study abroad, teacher certification program, Washington semester. **Credit/placement by examination:** AP, CLEP, SAT, institutional tests. 32 credit hours maximum toward bachelor's degree. **Support services:** Learning center, pre-admission summer program, reduced course load, remedial instruction, study skills assistance, tutoring, writing center.

Honors college/program. The Honors College has three distinct academic programs. The Honors Program for incoming first-year students with a maximum of 40 seats offered each fall; the Honors Seminar Certification Program geared toward transfer students and WCU students with a minimum of 30 earned credits; and the Undergraduate Certificate Program in Leadership and Civic Engagement (UCP-LCE) which challenges students from multiple disciplines to develop their academic gifts for leadership and apply them within the larger community.

Majors. **Area/ethnic studies:** American, women's. **Biology:** General, biochemistry. **Business:** General, accounting, business admin, finance, managerial economics, sales/distribution. **Computer sciences:** General. **Education:** Early childhood, elementary, middle, special ed. **English:** English lit. **Foreign languages:** French, German, Latin, Russian, Spanish. **Health services:** Athletic training, audiology/speech pathology, dietetics, health care admin, premedicine. **History:** General. **Human services:** Social work. **Liberal arts:** Arts/sciences. **Math:** General. **Parks/recreation:** Health/fitness. **Philosophy/religion:** Philosophy. **Physical sciences:** Analytical chemistry, chemistry, geology, physics. **Protective services:** Criminal justice. **Psychology:** General. **Social sciences:** Anthropology, geography, political science, sociology. **Visual/performing arts:** Art, dance, dramatic, music, music performance, studio arts.

Most popular majors. Business/marketing 13%, education 19%, English 9%, health sciences 14%, liberal arts 7%, psychology 6%.

Computing on campus. 1,800 workstations in dormitories, library, computer center, student center. Dormitories wired for high-speed internet access and linked to campus network. Commuter students can connect to campus

network. Online course registration, online library, helpline, repair service, wireless network available.

Student life. **Freshman orientation:** Mandatory, $155 fee. Preregistration for classes offered. One-day program in late June/early July followed by 3-day program prior to start of classes in August. **Policies:** Code of conduct applicable on and off campus. Freshmen not permitted cars on campus. **Housing:** Coed dorms, special housing for disabled, apartments, wellness housing available. $200 nonrefundable deposit, deadline 5/1. **Activities:** Bands, campus ministries, choral groups, dance, drama, international student organizations, literary magazine, music ensembles, Model UN, musical theater, opera, radio station, student government, student newspaper, symphony orchestra, TV station, Crusade for Christ, Hillel Jewish Student Union, College Democrats, College Republicans, Black student union, Latino American student organization, Best Buddies, Travelling Across Generations.

Athletics. NCAA. **Intercollegiate:** Baseball M, basketball, cheerleading M, cross-country, diving, field hockey W, football (tackle) M, golf, gymnastics W, lacrosse W, rugby W, soccer, softball W, swimming, tennis, track and field, volleyball W. **Intramural:** Basketball, field hockey, football (non-tackle), soccer, softball, tennis, volleyball. **Team name:** Golden Rams.

Student services. Adult student services, alcohol/substance abuse counseling, chaplain/spiritual director, career counseling, services for economically disadvantaged, student employment services, financial aid counseling, health services, legal services, minority student services, on-campus daycare, personal counseling, placement for graduates, veterans' counselor, women's services. **Physically disabled:** Services for visually, speech, hearing impaired.

Contact. E-mail: ugadmiss@wcupa.edu
Phone: (610) 436-3411 Toll-free number: (877) 315-2165
Fax: (610) 436-2907
Marsha Haug, Director of Admissions, West Chester University of Pennsylvania, Emil H. Messikomer Hall, West Chester, PA 19383

Westminster College
New Wilmington, Pennsylvania CB member
www.westminster.edu CB code: 2975

- Private 4-year liberal arts college affiliated with Presbyterian Church (USA)
- Residential campus in small town
- 2,376 degree-seeking undergraduates: 5% part-time, 55% women
- 798 degree-seeking graduate students
- 68% of applicants admitted
- SAT or ACT (ACT writing recommended), application essay required
- 66% graduate within 6 years

General. Founded in 1852. Regionally accredited. General studies curriculum with a freshman common experience. Semester at Oxford. **Degrees:** 461 bachelor's awarded; master's offered. **ROTC:** Army, Naval, Air Force. **Location:** 60 miles from Pittsburgh. **Calendar:** Semester, limited summer session. **Full-time faculty:** 147 total; 94% have terminal degrees, 6% minority, 48% women. **Part-time faculty:** 249 total; 20% have terminal degrees, 3% minority, 57% women. **Class size:** 58% < 20, 41% 20-39, 1% 40-49. **Special facilities:** Observatory, environmental outdoor laboratory, planetarium, electron microscopes, radar defractor.

Freshman class profile. 3,414 applied, 2,321 admitted, 513 enrolled.

Mid 50% test scores		GPA 2.0-2.99:	14%
SAT critical reading:	490-620	Rank in top quarter:	56%
SAT math:	500-620	Rank in top tenth:	23%
ACT composite:	22-27	Return as sophomores:	80%
GPA 3.75 or higher:	36%	Out-of-state:	53%
GPA 3.50-3.74:	25%	Live on campus:	71%
GPA 3.0-3.49:	25%	International:	5%

Basis for selection. Class rank most important. Test scores also important. Interview recommended for all; audition recommended for music; portfolio recommended for art.

High school preparation. College-preparatory program required. 16 units required. Required units include English 4, mathematics 3, social studies 2, history 1, science 2 (laboratory 2), foreign language 2 and academic electives 3.

2011-2012 Annual costs. Tuition/fees: $30,310. Room/board: $9,200. Books/supplies: $1,000. Personal expenses: $2,304.

2011-2012 Financial aid. **Need-based:** 426 full-time freshmen applied for aid; 341 were judged to have need; 341 of these received aid. Average need met was 84%. Average scholarship/grant was $17,628; average loan

$3,716. 61% of total undergraduate aid awarded as scholarships/grants, 39% as loans/jobs. **Non-need-based:** Awarded to 882 full-time undergraduates, including 178 freshmen. Scholarships awarded for academics, alumni affiliation, art, athletics, minority status, music/drama, ROTC.

Application procedures. Admission: Priority date 3/1; deadline 8/27. $50 fee, may be waived for applicants with need, free for online applicants. Admission notification on a rolling basis beginning on or about 9/1. Must reply by May 1 or within 3 week(s) if notified thereafter. **Financial aid:** Priority date 4/15; no closing date. FAFSA required. Applicants notified on a rolling basis starting 3/1; must reply by 5/1 or within 3 week(s) of notification.

Academics. Special study options: Accelerated study, cooperative education, distance learning, double major, dual enrollment of high school students, ESL, honors, independent study, internships, liberal arts/career combination, semester at sea, student-designed major, study abroad, teacher certification program, Washington semester, weekend college. 3-2 engineering programs with Case Western Reserve University (OH), Penn State, Washington University (MO), 3-2 law program with Duquesne University. **Credit/placement by examination:** AP, CLEP, SAT, ACT, institutional tests. **Support services:** Learning center, reduced course load, tutoring.

Majors. Biology: General, biochemistry, biophysics, ecology, molecular. **Business:** Accounting, business admin, finance, international, international finance, management science, managerial economics, organizational behavior. **Communications:** Broadcast journalism, public relations. **Computer sciences:** General, computer science, programming. **Education:** General, elementary, English, foreign languages, middle, multi-level teacher, secondary, social studies. **Engineering:** General. **English:** American lit, British lit, creative writing, English lit. **Foreign languages:** General, classics, French, German, Latin, Spanish. **Health services:** Predental, premedicine, prepharmacy, preveterinary. **History:** General. **Human services:** Social work. **Math:** General. **Philosophy/religion:** Philosophy, religion. **Physical sciences:** Chemistry, physics. **Protective services:** Criminal justice. **Psychology:** General. **Social sciences:** Economics, international relations, political science, sociology. **Theology:** Religious ed. **Visual/performing arts:** Art, dramatic, music, music performance, music theory/composition, piano/keyboard, studio arts, voice/opera.

Most popular majors. Biology 6%, business/marketing 26%, English 7%, health sciences 19%, psychology 7%, social sciences 9%.

Computing on campus. 160 workstations in library, computer center. Dormitories linked to campus network. Commuter students can connect to campus network. Helpline available.

Student life. Freshman orientation: Mandatory, $105 fee. Preregistration for classes offered. 4-day general social and academic orientation. **Housing:** Guaranteed on-campus for freshmen. Coed dorms, single-sex dorms, special housing for disabled, apartments, cooperative housing available. $200 nonrefundable deposit, deadline 6/1. **Activities:** Jazz band, campus ministries, choral groups, dance, drama, film society, international student organizations, literary magazine, music ensembles, musical theater, student government, student newspaper, symphony orchestra, Fellowship of Christian Athletes, mock convention, service organizations, social awareness and action groups, Students in Action Who Value the Environment, Habitat for Humanity, Alpha Phi Omega.

Athletics. NCAA. **Intercollegiate:** Baseball M, basketball, cross-country, football (tackle) M, golf, soccer, softball W, swimming, tennis, track and field, volleyball W. **Intramural:** Archery, badminton, basketball, equestrian, racquetball, rugby M, softball, track and field W, volleyball. **Team name:** Titans.

Student services. Adult student services, career counseling, student employment services, health services, personal counseling, placement for graduates.

Contact. E-mail: admis@westminster.edu
Phone: (724) 946-7100 Toll-free number: (800) 942-8033
Fax: (724) 946-7171
Bradley Tokar, Dean of Admissions, Westminster College, Admissions, Westminster College, New Wilmington, PA 16172-0001

Widener University
Chester, Pennsylvania
www.widener.edu

CB member
CB code: 2642

- Private 4-year university
- Residential campus in large town
- 3,253 degree-seeking undergraduates: 17% part-time, 56% women, 16% African American, 3% Asian American, 4% Hispanic American, 2% international

- 2,979 degree-seeking graduate students
- 66% of applicants admitted
- SAT or ACT (ACT writing optional) required
- 54% graduate within 6 years

General. Founded in 1821. Regionally accredited. **Degrees:** 623 bachelor's, 24 associate awarded; master's, professional, doctoral offered. **ROTC:** Army, Naval, Air Force. **Location:** 10 miles from Philadelphia. **Calendar:** Semester, limited summer session. **Full-time faculty:** 326 total; 90% have terminal degrees, 14% minority, 51% women. **Part-time faculty:** 355 total; 41% have terminal degrees, 12% minority, 48% women. **Class size:** 60% < 20, 38% 20-39, less than 1% 40-49, less than 1% 50-99, less than 1% >100. **Special facilities:** Astronomical observatory, rock climbing wall, restaurant lab, executive seminar facility, child development center, recording studio, education lab, commercial graphics lab, physical therapy lab.

Freshman class profile. 5,336 applied, 3,538 admitted, 762 enrolled.

Mid 50% test scores			
SAT critical reading:	440-520	Rank in top quarter:	37%
SAT math:	450-550	Rank in top tenth:	12%
GPA 3.75 or higher:	26%	Return as sophomores:	72%
GPA 3.50-3.74:	20%	Out-of-state:	45%
GPA 3.0-3.49:	33%	Live on campus:	84%
GPA 2.0-2.99:	21%	Fraternities:	9%
		Sororities:	8%

Basis for selection. Strength of curriculum, GPA, standardized test scores, class rank most important; recommendations, strength of character important. Interview recommended. **Home schooled:** Transcript of courses and grades required. Curriculum validation and interview with director of admissions required.

High school preparation. College-preparatory program required. 18 units required; 23 recommended. Required and recommended units include English 4, mathematics 3-4, social studies 3-4, science 3-4 (laboratory 2), foreign language 2 and academic electives 3.

2011-2012 Annual costs. Tuition/fees: $34,762. Room/board: $11,896. Books/supplies: $1,200. Personal expenses: $1,170.

2011-2012 Financial aid. Need-based: 729 full-time freshmen applied for aid; 687 were judged to have need; 684 of these received aid. Average need met was 77%. Average scholarship/grant was $10,100; average loan $4,093. 63% of total undergraduate aid awarded as scholarships/grants, 37% as loans/jobs. **Non-need-based:** Awarded to 2,180 full-time undergraduates, including 671 freshmen. Scholarships awarded for academics, leadership, music/drama, ROTC.

Application procedures. Admission: Priority date 2/15; no deadline. $35 fee, may be waived for applicants with need, free for online applicants. Admission notification on a rolling basis beginning on or about 10/1. Must reply by May 1 or within 2 week(s) if notified thereafter. **Financial aid:** Priority date 2/15; no closing date. FAFSA required. Applicants notified on a rolling basis starting 3/15; must reply within 4 week(s) of notification.

Academics. Special study options: Accelerated study, combined bachelor's/graduate degree, cooperative education, distance learning, double major, ESL, honors, independent study, internships, liberal arts/career combination, student-designed major, study abroad, teacher certification program, weekend college. **Credit/placement by examination:** AP, CLEP, IB, institutional tests. Students can earn up to 2 years of credit in some fields via CLEP, challenge exams, and Advanced Placement exams. **Support services:** Learning center, pre-admission summer program, reduced course load, remedial instruction, study skills assistance, tutoring, writing center.

Majors. Area/ethnic studies: Women's. **Biology:** General, biochemistry. **Business:** Accounting, business admin, finance, financial planning, hospitality admin, human resources, international, management information systems, managerial economics, operations. **Communications:** Communications/speech/rhetoric. **Computer sciences:** General, computer science, information systems. **Conservation:** Environmental science. **Education:** Early childhood, elementary, science, special ed. **Engineering:** General, biomedical, chemical, civil, electrical, mechanical. **English:** Creative writing, English lit. **Foreign languages:** General, French, Spanish. **Health services:** Facilities admin, nursing (RN), predental, premedicine, prenursing, preveterinary. **History:** General. **Human services:** Social work. **Liberal arts:** Arts/sciences, humanities. **Math:** General. **Physical sciences:** Chemistry, physics. **Protective services:** Law enforcement admin. **Psychology:** General. **Social sciences:** Anthropology, economics, international relations, political science, sociology. **Visual/performing arts:** Studio arts.

Most popular majors. Business/marketing 28%, engineering/engineering technologies 12%, health sciences 22%, psychology 8%.

Computing on campus. 710 workstations in library, student center. Dormitories wired for high-speed internet access and linked to campus network.

Commuter students can connect to campus network. Online course registration, online library, helpline, repair service, student web hosting, wireless network available.

Student life. Freshman orientation: Mandatory. Preregistration for classes offered. **Housing:** Guaranteed on-campus for freshmen. Coed dorms, single-sex dorms, apartments, cooperative housing, fraternity/sorority housing, wellness housing available. $100 nonrefundable deposit, deadline 5/1. **Activities:** Bands, campus ministries, choral groups, dance, drama, film society, international student organizations, literary magazine, music ensembles, radio station, student government, student newspaper, TV station, Hillel, black student union, political affairs club, Young Republicans, Young Democrats, environmental society, Widener Big Friends, Crusade for Christ, Alpha Phi Omega, Asian student association, presidential service corps.

Athletics. NCAA. **Intercollegiate:** Baseball M, basketball, cheerleading M, cross-country, field hockey W, football (tackle) M, golf M, lacrosse, soccer, softball W, swimming, track and field, volleyball W. **Intramural:** Basketball, football (non-tackle), skiing, soccer, softball, volleyball. **Team name:** Pride.

Student services. Adult student services, alcohol/substance abuse counseling, chaplain/spiritual director, career counseling, services for economically disadvantaged, student employment services, financial aid counseling, health services, minority student services, on-campus daycare, personal counseling, placement for graduates, veterans' counselor, women's services. **Physically disabled:** Services for visually, speech, hearing impaired.

Contact. E-mail: admissions.office@widener.edu
Phone: (610) 499-4126 Toll-free number: (888) 943-3637
Fax: (610) 499-4676
Edwin Wright, Director of Admissions, Widener University, One University Place, Chester, PA 19013

Wilkes University
Wilkes-Barre, Pennsylvania
www.wilkes.edu
CB member
CB code: 2977

- Private 4-year university
- Residential campus in small city
- 2,171 degree-seeking undergraduates: 7% part-time, 49% women, 3% African American, 2% Asian American, 3% Hispanic American, 3% international
- 2,952 degree-seeking graduate students
- 76% of applicants admitted
- SAT or ACT required
- 58% graduate within 6 years

General. Founded in 1933. Regionally accredited. **Degrees:** 462 bachelor's awarded; master's, professional, doctoral offered. **ROTC:** Army, Air Force. **Location:** 100 miles from Philadelphia, 140 miles from New York City. **Calendar:** Semester, extensive summer session. **Full-time faculty:** 157 total; 89% have terminal degrees, 8% minority, 46% women. **Part-time faculty:** 259 total; 3% minority, 46% women. **Class size:** 52% < 20, 40% 20-39, 3% 40-49, 5% 50-99, less than 1% >100. **Special facilities:** Performing arts center, field station, telecommunications center, indoor recreation and athletic center.

Freshman class profile. 2,811 applied, 2,146 admitted, 545 enrolled.

Mid 50% test scores		Rank in top tenth:	27%
SAT critical reading:	470-560	Return as sophomores:	82%
SAT math:	470-590	Out-of-state:	19%
SAT writing:	460-560	Live on campus:	74%
Rank in top quarter:	55%	International:	1%

Basis for selection. 920 SAT (exclusive of Writing) and/or rank in top 50% of high school class required for unconditional admission. Conditional admission may be offered to some applicants who do not meet these standards; must attend summer program prior to first semester. Interview recommended for all; audition required for theater arts programs.

High school preparation. Recommended units include English 4, mathematics 3, social studies 3, science 2 (laboratory 2) and computer science 1.

2011-2012 Annual costs. Tuition/fees: $28,210. Room/board: $11,698. Books/supplies: $1,500. Personal expenses: $1,500.

2011-2012 Financial aid. Need-based: 517 full-time freshmen applied for aid; 480 were judged to have need; 480 of these received aid. Average need met was 75%. Average scholarship/grant was $18,344; average loan $3,450. 63% of total undergraduate aid awarded as scholarships/grants, 37% as loans/jobs. **Non-need-based:** Awarded to 1,545 full-time undergraduates,

including 454 freshmen. Scholarships awarded for academics, leadership, minority status, music/drama.

Application procedures. Admission: No deadline. $40 fee, may be waived for applicants with need. Admission notification on a rolling basis. Must reply by May 1 or within 2 week(s) if notified thereafter. **Financial aid:** Priority date 3/1; no closing date. FAFSA required. Applicants notified on a rolling basis starting 3/1.

Academics. Special study options: Combined bachelor's/graduate degree, cooperative education, cross-registration, distance learning, double major, dual enrollment of high school students, ESL, external degree, honors, independent study, internships, student-designed major, study abroad, teacher certification program, weekend college. **Credit/placement by examination:** AP, CLEP, institutional tests. Credit by examination may be given to within 30 credits of graduation. **Support services:** Learning center, pre-admission summer program, reduced course load, remedial instruction, study skills assistance, tutoring, writing center.

Majors. Biology: General, biochemistry. **Business:** Accounting, business admin, entrepreneurial studies. **Communications:** Communications/speech/rhetoric, digital media. **Computer sciences:** General, information systems. **Education:** Elementary, special ed. **Engineering:** Electrical, environmental, mechanical. **English:** English lit. **Foreign languages:** Spanish. **Health services:** Clinical lab science, nursing (RN). **History:** General. **Liberal arts:** Arts/sciences. **Math:** General. **Philosophy/religion:** Philosophy. **Physical sciences:** Chemistry, geology. **Protective services:** Criminal justice. **Psychology:** General. **Social sciences:** International relations, political science, sociology. **Visual/performing arts:** Dramatic.

Most popular majors. Business/marketing 19%, communications/journalism 8%, education 7%, engineering/engineering technologies 11%, health sciences 11%, liberal arts 14%, psychology 7%.

Computing on campus. 709 workstations in library, computer center, student center. Dormitories wired for high-speed internet access and linked to campus network. Commuter students can connect to campus network. Online course registration, online library, helpline, wireless network available.

Student life. Freshman orientation: Mandatory, $135 fee. Preregistration for classes offered. **Housing:** Guaranteed on-campus for all undergraduates. Coed dorms, single-sex dorms, apartments available. $100 nonrefundable deposit. **Activities:** Bands, campus ministries, choral groups, dance, drama, international student organizations, literary magazine, music ensembles, musical theater, radio station, student government, student newspaper, TV station.

Athletics. NCAA. **Intercollegiate:** Baseball M, basketball, cross-country, field hockey W, football (tackle) M, golf M, lacrosse W, soccer, softball W, tennis, volleyball W, wrestling M. **Intramural:** Basketball M, bowling, football (tackle) M, ice hockey M, racquetball, rowing (crew), rugby M, skiing, softball, table tennis, volleyball. **Team name:** Colonels.

Student services. Adult student services, career counseling, student employment services, financial aid counseling, health services, personal counseling, placement for graduates, veterans' counselor. **Physically disabled:** Services for visually, hearing impaired.

Contact. E-mail: admissions@wilkes.edu
Phone: (570) 408-4400 Toll-free number: (800) 945-5378
Fax: (570) 408-4904
Melanie Mickelson, Vice President of Enrollment Services, Wilkes University, 84 West South Street, Wilkes-Barre, PA 18766

Wilson College
Chambersburg, Pennsylvania
www.wilson.edu
CB member
CB code: 2979

- Private 4-year liberal arts college for women affiliated with Presbyterian Church (USA)
- Residential campus in large town
- 322 degree-seeking undergraduates: 100% women
- 48 graduate students
- 56% of applicants admitted
- Application essay required

General. Founded in 1869. Regionally accredited. Undergraduate residential program for single mothers and their children; childcare provided when mother is in classes. **Degrees:** 87 bachelor's, 5 associate awarded; master's offered. **ROTC:** Army. **Location:** 90 miles from Washington, DC; 145 miles from Philadelphia. **Calendar:** Semester, limited summer session. **Full-time faculty:** 45 total; 82% have terminal degrees, 7% minority, 56% women. **Part-time faculty:** 40 total; 18% have terminal degrees, 5% minority, 70%

women. **Class size:** 82% < 20, 18% 20-39, less than 1% 40-49. **Special facilities:** Equestrian center with two indoor and one outdoor arenas, barns for horse boarding, equestrian cross country course, center for sustainable living, classics gallery, veterinary medical technology facilities, college archives.

Freshman class profile. 407 applied, 226 admitted, 70 enrolled.

GPA 3.75 or higher:	30%	Rank in top quarter:	52%
GPA 3.50-3.74:	14%	Rank in top tenth:	21%
GPA 3.0-3.49:	41%	Out-of-state:	31%
GPA 2.0-2.99:	15%	Live on campus:	76%

Basis for selection. Admissions based on record of college preparatory classes, recommendation from 11th or 12th grade teacher of a college preparatory subject; graded English paper as a writing sample, and rank in class are all considered in admissions decisions. SAT/ACT optional for students with 3.0 GPA in specified college prep curriculum from a regionally accredited secondary school. **Home schooled:** Transcript of courses and grades, state high school equivalency certificate, letter of recommendation (nonparent) required. If the state of residence and/or the home school program does not issue a diploma, the student must pursue a GED.

High school preparation. College-preparatory program required. 15 units required. Required units include English 4, mathematics 3, social studies 4, science 2 (laboratory 2) and foreign language 2.

2011-2012 Annual costs. Tuition/fees: $29,340. Room/board: $9,710. Books/supplies: $1,200. Personal expenses: $800.

2011-2012 Financial aid. Need-based: Average need met was 76%. Average scholarship/grant was $21,075; average loan $3,912. 70% of total undergraduate aid awarded as scholarships/grants, 30% as loans/jobs. **Non-need-based:** Scholarships awarded for academics, alumni affiliation, religious affiliation, state residency.

Application procedures. Admission: Priority date 4/30; deadline 7/31. No application fee. Admission notification on a rolling basis beginning on or about 9/15. Must reply by May 1 or within 3 week(s) if notified thereafter. **Financial aid:** Priority date 4/30; no closing date. FAFSA, institutional form required. Applicants notified on a rolling basis starting 2/15.

Academics. Special study options: Cross-registration, distance learning, double major, dual enrollment of high school students, ESL, exchange student, honors, independent study, internships, liberal arts/career combination, student-designed major, study abroad, teacher certification program, Washington semester. **Credit/placement by examination:** AP, CLEP, IB, SAT, ACT, institutional tests. 4 credit hours maximum toward associate degree, 4 toward bachelor's. **Support services:** Learning center, reduced course load, remedial instruction, study skills assistance, tutoring, writing center.

Majors. Biology: General. **Business:** Accounting, business admin, management information systems. **Communications:** Media studies. **Conservation:** Environmental science, environmental studies. **Education:** Elementary. **English:** English lit. **Foreign languages:** French, Spanish. **General:** Equestrian studies. **Health services:** Veterinary technology/assistant. **History:** General. **Math:** General. **Parks/recreation:** Exercise sciences, sports admin. **Philosophy/religion:** Philosophy, religion. **Physical sciences:** Chemistry. **Psychology:** General, psychobiology. **Social sciences:** General, economics, international relations, sociology. **Visual/performing arts:** Art.

Most popular majors. Agriculture 6%, business/marketing 6%, education 11%, English 6%, health sciences 31%, philosophy/religious studies 10%, social sciences 10%.

Computing on campus. 105 workstations in dormitories, library, computer center, student center. Dormitories wired for high-speed internet access and linked to campus network. Commuter students can connect to campus network. Online course registration, online library, helpline, repair service, wireless network available.

Student life. Freshman orientation: Mandatory, $265 fee. Preregistration for classes offered. Week-long program held in August prior to arrival of upperclass students. Two days of orientation program are held off-campus. **Policies:** Honor principle, shared governance observed. **Housing:** Guaranteed on-campus for all undergraduates. Wellness housing available. $400 nonrefundable deposit, deadline 5/1. Pets allowed in dorm rooms. Single rooms available to all students on a space-available basis. Housing for single mothers with children available. Adult female students have on-campus residency options. **Activities:** Campus ministries, choral groups, dance, drama, international student organizations, literary magazine, student government, student newspaper, religious activities committee, language clubs, interfaith support group, Black student union, Curran Scholars, Alternative Spring Break, Agape Christian Fellowship, Habitat for Humanity, Muhibbah International Club, Political Science Association.

Athletics. NCAA. **Intercollegiate:** Basketball W, field hockey W, gymnastics W, lacrosse W, soccer W, softball W. **Team name:** Phoenix.

Student services. Adult student services, alcohol/substance abuse counseling, chaplain/spiritual director, career counseling, student employment services, financial aid counseling, health services, on-campus daycare, personal counseling, placement for graduates, women's services.

Contact. E-mail: admissions@wilson.edu
Phone: (717) 262-2002 Toll-free number: (800) 421-8402
Fax: (717) 262-2546
Mary Ann Naso, Vice President for Enrollment, Wilson College, 1015 Philadelphia Avenue, Chambersburg, PA 17201-1285

Yeshivath Beth Moshe
Scranton, Pennsylvania

CB code: 1657

- Private 4-year rabbinical college for men affiliated with Jewish faith
- Small city

General. Founded in 1965. Accredited by AARTS. First and second Talmudic degrees offered. Ordination available. **Degrees:** 1 bachelor's awarded; master's offered. **Calendar:** Differs by program. **Full-time faculty:** 6 total.

Basis for selection. Open admission.

2011-2012 Annual costs. Tuition/fees: $8,300.

Application procedures. Admission: No deadline. No application fee. Admission notification on a rolling basis. **Financial aid:** No deadline. Applicants notified on a rolling basis.

Academics. Credit/placement by examination: AP, CLEP.

Majors. Theology: Talmudic.

Student life. Activities: Choral groups, TV station.

Contact. Phone: (717) 346-1747 Fax: (717) 346-2251
Rabbi Chaim Bressler, Admissions Director, Yeshivath Beth Moshe, 930 Hickory Street, Scranton, PA 18505

York College of Pennsylvania
York, Pennsylvania
www.ycp.edu

CB member
CB code: 2991

- Private 4-year liberal arts college
- Residential campus in small city
- 5,168 degree-seeking undergraduates: 9% part-time, 56% women, 4% African American, 1% Asian American, 4% Hispanic American
- 240 degree-seeking graduate students
- 73% of applicants admitted
- SAT or ACT (ACT writing optional) required
- 60% graduate within 6 years

General. Founded in 1787. Regionally accredited. **Degrees:** 934 bachelor's, 26 associate awarded; master's, professional offered. **ROTC:** Army. **Location:** 46 miles from Baltimore, 95 miles from Philadelphia. **Calendar:** Semester, limited summer session. **Full-time faculty:** 181 total; 79% have terminal degrees, 42% women. **Part-time faculty:** 376 total; 56% women. **Class size:** 42% < 20, 55% 20-39, 3% 40-49, less than 1% 50-99. **Special facilities:** Engineering innovation center, telecommunications center, rare books collection, oral history room, video production studios, nursing education center.

Freshman class profile. 10,888 applied, 7,911 admitted, 1,176 enrolled.

Mid 50% test scores			
SAT critical reading:	480-570	GPA 3.0-3.49:	32%
SAT math:	500-590	GPA 2.0-2.99:	20%
SAT writing:	470-560	Rank in top quarter:	37%
ACT composite:	20-25	Rank in top tenth:	11%
GPA 3.75 or higher:	29%	Return as sophomores:	78%
GPA 3.50-3.74:	19%	Out-of-state:	55%
		Live on campus:	67%

Basis for selection. High school record, standardized test results, personal qualities most important. Interviews, essays recommended for academically borderline students; audition required for music programs; portfolio recommended for art programs. **Home schooled:** Statement describing home school structure and mission, transcript of courses and grades, state high school equivalency certificate, letter of recommendation (nonparent) required. Diploma required from home school association or local school district; portfolio evaluation conducted by certified teacher; syllabus for each course.

High school preparation. College-preparatory program recommended. 15 units required. Required and recommended units include English 4, mathematics 3-4, social studies 3, science 3 and foreign language 2. One biology, 2 chemistry, and 2 algebra required of nursing applicants.

2011-2012 Annual costs. Tuition/fees: $15,880. Room/board: $8,920. Books/supplies: $1,200. Personal expenses: $1,000.

2011-2012 Financial aid. Need-based: 1,103 full-time freshmen applied for aid; 850 were judged to have need; 847 of these received aid. Average need met was 66%. Average scholarship/grant was $5,216; average loan $5,243. 60% of total undergraduate aid awarded as scholarships/grants, 40% as loans/jobs. **Non-need-based:** Awarded to 2,587 full-time undergraduates, including 1,161 freshmen. Scholarships awarded for academics, alumni affiliation, minority status, music/drama.

Application procedures. Admission: No deadline. $30 fee, may be waived for applicants with need, free for online applicants. Admission notification on a rolling basis beginning on or about 10/1. **Financial aid:** No deadline. FAFSA required. Applicants notified on a rolling basis starting 3/1; must reply within 4 week(s) of notification.

Academics. Special study options: Combined bachelor's/graduate degree, cooperative education, double major, dual enrollment of high school students, independent study, internships, liberal arts/career combination, student-designed major, study abroad, teacher certification program. **Credit/placement by examination:** AP, CLEP, IB, SAT, ACT, institutional tests. 30 credit hours maximum toward associate degree, 60 toward bachelor's. **Support services:** Learning center, reduced course load, remedial instruction, study skills assistance, tutoring, writing center.

Majors. Biology: General. **Business:** Accounting, business admin, entrepreneurial studies, finance, logistics, management information systems, marketing. **Communications:** Communications/speech/rhetoric, media studies, public relations. **Communications technology:** Recording arts. **Computer sciences:** Computer science. **Education:** Biology, early childhood, early childhood special, English, mathematics, music, science, social studies, Spanish. **Engineering:** Computer, electrical, mechanical. **English:** English lit, technical writing. **Foreign languages:** Spanish. **Health services:** Clinical lab science, licensed practical nurse, nuclear medical technology, nursing (RN), radiologic technology/medical imaging, respiratory therapy technology. **History:** General. **Math:** General. **Parks/recreation:** General, sports admin. **Philosophy/religion:** Philosophy. **Physical sciences:** Chemistry. **Protective services:** Forensics, law enforcement admin. **Psychology:** General. **Social sciences:** Economics, international relations, political science, sociology. **Visual/performing arts:** Commercial/advertising art, dramatic, music, studio arts.

Most popular majors. Business/marketing 20%, communications/journalism 7%, education 13%, health sciences 14%, parks/recreation 7%, security/protective services 9%.

Computing on campus. 893 workstations in library, computer center. Dormitories wired for high-speed internet access and linked to campus network. Commuter students can connect to campus network. Online course registration, online library, helpline, wireless network available.

Student life. Freshman orientation: Mandatory. Preregistration for classes offered. 4-day program prior to fall semester. **Housing:** Guaranteed on-campus for freshmen. Coed dorms, special housing for disabled, apartments, fraternity/sorority housing, wellness housing available. $200 fully refundable deposit. **Activities:** Bands, campus ministries, choral groups, dance, drama, international student organizations, literary magazine, music ensembles, Model UN, musical theater, radio station, student government, student newspaper, symphony orchestra, TV station, over 80 student organizations.

Athletics. NCAA. **Intercollegiate:** Baseball M, basketball, cheerleading, cross-country, field hockey W, golf M, lacrosse, soccer, softball W, swimming, tennis, track and field, volleyball W, wrestling M. **Intramural:** Badminton, basketball, football (non-tackle), racquetball, soccer, softball, table tennis, tennis, volleyball. **Team name:** Spartans.

Student services. Adult student services, alcohol/substance abuse counseling, chaplain/spiritual director, career counseling, services for economically disadvantaged, student employment services, financial aid counseling, health services, minority student services, personal counseling, placement for graduates, veterans' counselor. **Physically disabled:** Services for visually, hearing impaired.

Contact. E-mail: admissions@ycp.edu
Phone: (717) 849-1600 Toll-free number: (800) 455-8018
Fax: (717) 849-1607
Nancy Spataro, Director of Admissions, York College of Pennsylvania, 441 Country Club Road, York, PA 17403-3651

Puerto Rico

American University of Puerto Rico
Bayamon, Puerto Rico CB member
www.aupr.edu CB code: 0961

▶ Private 4-year university and business college
▶ Commuter campus in large city
▶ 2,260 degree-seeking undergraduates

General. Founded in 1963. Regionally accredited. Branch campus at Manati. **Degrees:** 214 bachelor's, 45 associate awarded; master's offered. **ROTC:** Army. **Location:** 12 miles from San Juan. **Calendar:** Semester, limited summer session. **Full-time faculty:** 53 total. **Part-time faculty:** 120 total. **Special facilities:** Fully computerized classrooms.

Basis for selection. SAT required for English-speaking applicants and NCAA student athletes. Interview recommended. **Home schooled:** Transcript of courses and grades, state high school equivalency certificate required.

High school preparation. 18 units recommended. Recommended units include English 3, mathematics 2, social studies 2, history 1, science 2, foreign language 3 and academic electives 5.

2011-2012 Annual costs. Books/supplies: $900.

Financial aid. All financial aid based on need.

Application procedures. Admission: No deadline. $25 fee, may be waived for applicants with need. Admission notification on a rolling basis. **Financial aid:** Priority date 4/30, closing date 5/31. FAFSA, institutional form required. Applicants notified by 6/1; must reply within 2 week(s) of notification.

Academics. Special study options: Honors, independent study, internships, liberal arts/career combination. **Credit/placement by examination:** AP, CLEP, institutional tests. **Support services:** Learning center, reduced course load, tutoring.

Majors. Business: General, accounting, administrative services, business admin, office technology, office/clerical, purchasing. **Communications:** Communications/speech/rhetoric. **Communications technology:** General. **Computer sciences:** Programming. **Education:** General, elementary, ESL, mathematics, physical, secondary, Spanish, special ed. **Protective services:** Criminal justice.

Most popular majors. Security/protective services 30%.

Computing on campus. 75 workstations in computer center.

Student life. Freshman orientation: Mandatory. Preregistration for classes offered. **Activities:** Student government.

Athletics. NCAA. **Intercollegiate:** Basketball, cross-country, swimming, tennis, track and field, volleyball. **Intramural:** Basketball, cross-country, softball M, table tennis, track and field, volleyball. **Team name:** Pirates.

Student services. Career counseling, student employment services, health services, personal counseling, veterans' counselor. **Physically disabled:** Services for speech impaired.

Contact. E-mail: oficinaadmisiones@aupr.edu
Phone: (787) 620-2040 ext. 2020 Fax: (787) 785-7377
Keren Llanos, Director of Admissions, American University of Puerto Rico, PO Box 2037, Bayamon, PR 00960-2037

Atlantic College
Guaynabo, Puerto Rico
www.atlanticcollege.edu CB code: 7137

▶ Private 4-year liberal arts college
▶ Commuter campus in small city
▶ 1,251 degree-seeking undergraduates

General. Founded in 1983. Accredited by ACICS. **Degrees:** 128 bachelor's, 18 associate awarded; master's offered. **Location:** 20 miles from San Juan. **Calendar:** Quarter, extensive summer session. **Full-time faculty:** 23 total. **Part-time faculty:** 32 total. **Special facilities:** Motion caption laboratories, audio laboratories (for study of digital graphic design, computerized animation technology).

Basis for selection. Open admission.

High school preparation. 16 units recommended. Recommended units include English 3, mathematics 2, social studies 1, history 2, science 2, foreign language 3 and academic electives 3.

2011-2012 Annual costs. Books/supplies: $800.

Financial aid. All financial aid based on need.

Application procedures. Admission: No deadline. $30 fee. Admission notification on a rolling basis. **Financial aid:** Closing date 6/30. FAFSA, institutional form required. Applicants notified on a rolling basis starting 4/1; must reply within 2 week(s) of notification.

Academics. Special study options: Combined bachelor's/graduate degree, honors, internships, liberal arts/career combination, student-designed major. **Credit/placement by examination:** AP, CLEP. **Support services:** Learning center, pre-admission summer program, remedial instruction, tutoring.

Majors. Business: Accounting, administrative services, business admin. **Computer sciences:** Security. **Education:** Early childhood special. **Visual/performing arts:** Commercial/advertising art, game design.

Most popular majors. Business/marketing 6%, computer/information sciences 12%, visual/performing arts 74%.

Computing on campus. 16 workstations in library, computer center. Online library, repair service, wireless network available.

Student life. Freshman orientation: Available. Preregistration for classes offered. **Activities:** Dance, drama, student government, student newspaper.

Athletics. Intercollegiate: Basketball. **Intramural:** Basketball, volleyball.

Student services. Alcohol/substance abuse counseling, career counseling, financial aid counseling, health services, personal counseling, placement for graduates. **Physically disabled:** Services for hearing impaired.

Contact. E-mail: admisiones@atlanticcollege.edu
Phone: (787) 720-1022 ext. 1027 Fax: (787) 720-1092
Zaida Perez, Admissions Officer, Atlantic College, PO Box 3918, Guaynabo, PR 00970

Bayamon Central University
Bayamon, Puerto Rico CB member
www.ucb.edu.pr CB code: 0840

▶ Private 4-year university affiliated with Roman Catholic Church
▶ Commuter campus in large city
▶ 938 degree-seeking undergraduates: 9% part-time, 67% women
▶ 264 degree-seeking graduate students
▶ 47% of applicants admitted

General. Founded in 1970. Regionally accredited. Member of consortium of U.S. and South American universities. Virtually all students come from Spanish-speaking backgrounds. **Degrees:** 345 bachelor's, 15 associate awarded; master's offered. **ROTC:** Army, Air Force. **Location:** 9 miles from San Juan. **Calendar:** Semester, limited summer session. **Full-time faculty:** 39 total. **Part-time faculty:** 114 total. **Special facilities:** Library of Dominican Order.

Freshman class profile. 1,578 applied, 747 admitted, 710 enrolled.

Basis for selection. School achievement record and test scores most important. Minimum 2.0 high school GPA. Fluency in Spanish, basic knowledge of English necessary. Conditional admission to those identified as having underdeveloped academic potential. SAT or ACT recommended. SAT or ACT accepted from English-speaking students. Score report must be received by 4/15. Essay recommended for all; interview recommended for academically weak. **Home schooled:** Transcript of courses and grades required. **Learning Disabled:** Details of protocol for students with physical or learning disabilities available at the Admission Office and the Counseling and Orientation Office.

High school preparation. Required units include English 3, mathematics 3, social studies 3 and science 1. 3 units of Spanish required.

2012-2013 Annual costs. Tuition/fees (projected): $8,200. Books/supplies: $1,504. Personal expenses: $3,816.

2010-2011 Financial aid. All financial aid based on need.

Application procedures. Admission: Priority date 12/6; deadline 5/6 (postmark date). $25 fee, may be waived for applicants with need. Application must be submitted on paper. Admission notification on a rolling basis beginning on or about 3/4. **Financial aid:** Priority date 5/31, closing date 7/2. FAFSA, institutional form required. Applicants notified on a rolling basis starting 5/31; must reply within 6 week(s) of notification.

Academics. All classroom instruction conducted in Spanish. Core curriculum includes courses in Spanish. Course in methodology of learning must be satisfactorily completed. **Special study options:** Double major, independent study, teacher certification program. **Credit/placement by examination:** AP, CLEP. **Support services:** Learning center, reduced course load, remedial instruction, tutoring.

Majors. Biology: General. **Business:** General, accounting, administrative services, business admin, finance, human resources, management information systems, management science, marketing. **Communications:** Journalism. **Conservation:** General. **Education:** Early childhood, educational technology, elementary, English, mathematics, physical, science, secondary, Spanish, special ed. **English:** English lit. **Foreign languages:** Spanish. **Health services:** Occupational health. **Human services:** General, social work. **Philosophy/religion:** Philosophy, religion. **Physical sciences:** Chemistry. **Psychology:** General.

Most popular majors. Business/marketing 26%, education 23%, health sciences 17%, psychology 8%, public administration/social services 14%.

Computing on campus. 200 workstations in library, computer center, student center. Online library available.

Student life. Freshman orientation: Mandatory. Preregistration for classes offered. **Activities:** Drama, student government, student newspaper.

Athletics. Intercollegiate: Basketball, cross-country, swimming, table tennis, track and field, volleyball. **Intramural:** Basketball, track and field, volleyball. **Team name:** Halcones.

Student services. Alcohol/substance abuse counseling, chaplain/spiritual director, career counseling, student employment services, financial aid counseling, health services, on-campus daycare, personal counseling, placement for graduates. **Physically disabled:** Services for visually, speech, hearing impaired.

Contact. E-mail: chernandez@ucb.edu.pr
Phone: (787) 786-3030 ext. 2100 Fax: (787) 740-2200
Cristina Hernandez, Director of Admissions, Bayamon Central University, PO Box 1725, Bayamon, PR 00960-1725

Caribbean University
Bayamon, Puerto Rico
www.caribbean.edu

CB member
CB code: 0779

- Private 4-year university
- Commuter campus in large city
- 4,745 degree-seeking undergraduates: 25% part-time, 59% women
- 1,098 degree-seeking graduate students

General. Founded in 1969. Regionally accredited. Extension centers in Carolina, Vega Baja, and Ponce. **Degrees:** 322 bachelor's, 104 associate awarded; master's offered. **ROTC:** Army, Naval, Air Force. **Location:** 12 miles from San Juan. **Calendar:** Continuous, extensive summer session. **Full-time faculty:** 77 total; 23% have terminal degrees, 100% minority, 46% women. **Part-time faculty:** 347 total; 19% have terminal degrees, 100% minority, 53% women. **Special facilities:** College-operated museum program at Bayamon campus.

Freshman class profile.

Return as sophomores:	72%	Out-of-state:	5%

Basis for selection. Open admission, but selective for some programs. School achievement record, test scores important, and interview considered. SAT required of English-speaking applicants. PAA score reports by August 15. Interview recommended for academically weak. **Home schooled:** State high school equivalency certificate required.

High school preparation. College-preparatory program recommended.

2011-2012 Annual costs. Books/supplies: $1,053. Personal expenses: $2,500.

Financial aid. All financial aid based on need.

Application procedures. Admission: No deadline. $25 fee, may be waived for applicants with need. Admission notification on a rolling basis beginning on or about 3/1. **Financial aid:** Priority date 5/30; no closing date. FAFSA required. Applicants notified on a rolling basis starting 7/30; must reply within 2 week(s) of notification.

Academics. Special study options: Distance learning, honors, liberal arts/career combination, teacher certification program, weekend college. **Credit/placement by examination:** AP, CLEP, institutional tests. **Support services:** Learning center, remedial instruction, tutoring.

Majors. Biology: General. **Business:** Accounting, administrative services, business admin. **Computer sciences:** General. **Education:** Business, elementary, English, mathematics, science, secondary, special ed. **Engineering:** Civil, petroleum. **Foreign languages:** Spanish. **Health services:** Nursing (RN), premedicine, speech pathology. **Human services:** Social work. **Parks/recreation:** General. **Social sciences:** General, criminology.

Most popular majors. Business/marketing 16%, education 15%, engineering/engineering technologies 16%, health sciences 29%, public administration/social services 14%.

Computing on campus. 100 workstations in library, computer center, student center. Online course registration, online library, student web hosting, wireless network available.

Student life. Freshman orientation: Mandatory. Preregistration for classes offered. **Activities:** Choral groups, drama, music ensembles, student government, student newspaper.

Athletics. Intercollegiate: Cheerleading. **Intramural:** Basketball, cross-country, football (tackle), gymnastics, judo, table tennis, tennis, track and field, volleyball. **Team name:** Gryphons.

Student services. Alcohol/substance abuse counseling, career counseling, services for economically disadvantaged, student employment services, financial aid counseling, health services, personal counseling, placement for graduates, veterans' counselor. **Physically disabled:** Services for visually, speech, hearing impaired.

Contact. E-mail: jtorres@caribbean.edu
Phone: (787) 780-0070 ext. 1111 Toll-free number: (888) 780-0070
Fax: (787) 785-0101
Jannette Torres, Admissions Director, Caribbean University, PO Box 493, Bayamon, PR 00960-0493

Carlos Albizu University: San Juan
San Juan, Puerto Rico
www.albizu.edu

CB code: 2104

- Private two-year upper-division university
- Large town
- Test scores, application essay, interview required

General. Regionally accredited. **Degrees:** 52 bachelor's awarded; master's, professional, doctoral offered. **Calendar:** Semester, limited summer session. **Full-time faculty:** 22 total. **Part-time faculty:** 4 total.

Student profile. 150 degree-seeking undergraduates.

Basis for selection. College transcript, application essay, interview, standardized test scores required. Transfer accepted as sophomores.

2011-2012 Annual costs. Books/supplies: $2,606. Personal expenses: $3,681.

Application procedures. Admission: $75 fee. Application must be submitted on paper.

Academics. Special study options: Combined bachelor's/graduate degree, distance learning. **Credit/placement by examination:** AP, CLEP.

Majors. Education: Speech impaired.

Computing on campus. 30 workstations in computer center.

Contact. Phone: (787) 725-6500 ext. 21 Fax: (787) 721-7187
Carlos Rodriguez-Irizarry, Director of Admissions, Carlos Albizu
University: San Juan, 151 Tanca Street, San Juan, PR 00902-3711

Columbia Centro Universitario: Caguas
Caguas, Puerto Rico
www.columbiaco.edu   CB code: 2315

- For-profit 4-year business and technical college
- Commuter campus in small city
- 1,329 degree-seeking undergraduates: 49% part-time, 74% women
- 100 degree-seeking graduate students
- Interview required

General. Founded in 1966. Regionally accredited. **Degrees:** 136 bachelor's,
232 associate awarded; master's offered. **Location:** 18 miles from San Juan.
Calendar: Continuous, extensive summer session. **Full-time faculty:** 17
total; 18% have terminal degrees, 65% women. **Part-time faculty:** 87 total;
15% have terminal degrees, 61% women. **Class size:** 57% < 20, 43% 20-39.

Basis for selection. Open admission, but selective for some programs.
For nursing program, applicants must have 1.90 GPA. Otherwise, applicants
will be admitted under the conditional enrollment option. Parent signature
and vaccination certificate required for students under age 21. Portfolio
required for adult education students. **Home schooled:** Transcript of courses
and grades, state high school equivalency certificate required.

High school preparation. 15 units required. Required units include
English 3, mathematics 2, social studies 2, history 2, science 3 and academic
electives 3.

2011-2012 Annual costs. Books/supplies: $862. Personal expenses:
$1,500.

2010-2011 Financial aid. All financial aid based on need. 231 full-time
freshmen applied for aid; 208 were judged to have need; 208 of these received
aid. 99% of total undergraduate aid awarded as scholarships/grants, 1% as
loans/jobs.

Application procedures. Admission: No deadline. $50 fee. Application
must be submitted on paper. Admission notification on a rolling basis. **Financial aid:** FAFSA, institutional form required.

Academics. Credit/placement by examination: AP, CLEP. **Support services:** Tutoring.

Majors. Business: Business admin. **Health services:** Nursing (RN).

Most popular majors. Business/marketing 26%, health sciences 74%.

Computing on campus. 27 workstations in library, computer center.

Student life. Freshman orientation: Mandatory. Preregistration for
classes offered.

Student services. Career counseling, student employment services, financial aid counseling, personal counseling, placement for graduates, veterans' counselor.

Contact. E-mail: info@columbiaco.edu
Phone: (787) 743-4041 ext. 240
Toll-free number: (800) 981-4877 ext. 240 Fax: (787) 744-7031
Xiomara Sánchez, Admissions Coordinator, Columbia Centro
Universitario: Caguas, PO Box 8517, Caguas, PR 00726-8517

Conservatory of Music of Puerto Rico
San Juan, Puerto Rico
www.cmpr.edu   CB code: 1115

- Public 4-year music college
- Commuter campus in large city
- 420 degree-seeking undergraduates: 29% part-time, 30% women, 91%
  Hispanic American, 8% international
- 42 degree-seeking graduate students
- 55% of applicants admitted
- Interview required
- 76% graduate within 6 years; 17% enter graduate study

General. Founded in 1959. Regionally accredited. **Degrees:** 35 bachelor's
awarded; master's offered. **Calendar:** Semester, limited summer session.
Full-time faculty: 50 total; 12% have terminal degrees, 94% minority, 24%
women. **Part-time faculty:** 41 total; 17% have terminal degrees, 95% minority, 27% women. **Class size:** 90% < 20, 7% 20-39, less than 1% 40-49, 2%
50-99. **Special facilities:** Library with more than 26,000 musical scores,
technology lab (computers applied to music), piano lab, theater.

Freshman class profile. 152 applied, 83 admitted, 77 enrolled.

GPA 3.75 or higher:	30%	End year in good standing:	88%
GPA 3.50-3.74:	30%	Return as sophomores:	70%
GPA 3.0-3.49:	23%	Out-of-state:	1%
GPA 2.0-2.99:	17%		

Basis for selection. Musical ability very important. School achievement
record, test scores important. Recommendations considered. Must take
entrance examination in both theory and instrument. SAT accepted from US
mainland applicants. Audition required for music performance. Essays and
interview also required for music education. **Home schooled:** State high
school equivalency certificate required.

High school preparation. College-preparatory program recommended.
Required and recommended units include English 3, mathematics 3, history
3, science 3, foreign language 3 and academic electives 3.

2012-2013 Annual costs. Tuition/fees (projected): $2,770. Books/sup-
plies: $1,800. Personal expenses: $1,250.

Financial aid. All financial aid based on need.

Application procedures. Admission: Closing date 12/19 (receipt date).
$75 fee. Application must be submitted on paper. Admission notification by
4/30. **Financial aid:** Priority date 12/15; no closing date. FAFSA required.
Applicants notified on a rolling basis starting 4/30.

Academics. Special study options: Cross-registration, dual enrollment of
high school students, liberal arts/career combination, teacher certification
program. **Credit/placement by examination:** AP, CLEP, IB, institutional
tests. 12 credit hours maximum toward bachelor's degree. **Support services:**
Learning center, pre-admission summer program, reduced course load, remedial instruction, tutoring.

Majors. Education: Music. **Visual/performing arts:** Jazz, music performance, piano/keyboard, stringed instruments, voice/opera.

Most popular majors. Education 18%, visual/performing arts 82%.

Computing on campus. 17 workstations in library, computer center.
Online library, wireless network available.

Student life. Freshman orientation: Mandatory. Preregistration for
classes offered. **Activities:** Bands, choral groups, music ensembles, opera,
student government, symphony orchestra.

Student services. Career counseling, student employment services, financial aid counseling, personal counseling, placement for graduates.

Contact. E-mail: admisiones@cmpr.edu
Phone: (787) 751-0160 ext. 275 Fax: (787) 764-3581
Ilsamar Hernandez, Director of Admissions, Conservatory of Music of
Puerto Rico, 951 Ave. Ponce de Leon, San Juan, PR 00907-3373

Electronic Data Processing College of Puerto Rico
Hato Rey, Puerto Rico
www.edpcollege.edu   CB code: 2243

- For-profit 4-year business and technical college
- Commuter campus in very large city

General. Founded in 1968. Candidate for regional accreditation. **Calendar:** Semester.

Annual costs/financial aid. Books/supplies: $465. Personal expenses:
$1,455.

Contact. Phone: (787) 765-3560
Admissions Director, PO Box 1923, Hato Rey, PR 00919-2303

Electronic Data Processing College: San Sebastian
San Sebastian, Puerto Rico
www.edpcollege.edu   CB code: 3219

- For-profit 4-year business and health science college
- Commuter campus in small city
- 650 full-time, degree-seeking undergraduates
- 100% of applicants admitted
- Application essay, interview required

General. **Degrees:** 6 bachelor's, 7 associate awarded. **Location:** 28 miles from Mayaguez. **Calendar:** Semester, extensive summer session. **Full-time faculty:** 19 total; 100% minority, 68% women. **Part-time faculty:** 70 total; 9% have terminal degrees, 100% minority, 71% women. **Class size:** 78% < 20, 22% 20-39.

Freshman class profile. 239 applied, 239 admitted, 178 enrolled.

Basis for selection. 2.5 GPA required for Health Academic Area Programs. Interview required for Physical Therapy Technology. Candidates for admission must take either College Entrance Examination Board tests or placement test offered by institution. **Home schooled:** State high school equivalency certificate required. Seal of the Secondary School which validates diploma required. **Learning Disabled:** Interview with student doctor, vocational rehabilitation program, or other government agencies required.

High school preparation. 18 units required. Required units include English 3, mathematics 3, history 3, science 3, foreign language 3 and academic electives 3.

2010-2011 Financial aid. All financial aid based on need. 306 full-time freshmen applied for aid; 305 were judged to have need; 305 of these received aid. Average need met was 42%. Average scholarship/grant was $2,689; average loan $1,754.

Application procedures. **Admission:** No deadline. $15 fee. Application must be submitted on paper. Admission notification on a rolling basis. **Financial aid:** Closing date 6/30.

Academics. **Special study options:** Cooperative education, internships. **Credit/placement by examination:** AP, CLEP, institutional tests. **Support services:** Learning center, reduced course load, remedial instruction, tutoring.

Computing on campus. 103 workstations in library, computer center.

Student life. **Freshman orientation:** Mandatory. Preregistration for classes offered.

Athletics. **Intercollegiate:** Softball M, volleyball. **Team name:** Zoros.

Student services. Alcohol/substance abuse counseling, career counseling, services for economically disadvantaged, student employment services, financial aid counseling, personal counseling, placement for graduates.

Contact. E-mail: zolavarria@edpcollege.edu
Phone: (787) 896-2252 ext. 300 Fax: (787) 896-0066
Zenaida Olavarria, Admissions Officer, Electronic Data Processing College: San Sebastian, PO Box 1674, San Sebastian, PR 00685

Escuela de Artes Plasticas de Puerto Rico
San Juan, Puerto Rico
www.eap.edu   CB code: 7036

- Public 4-year visual arts college
- Commuter campus in large city
- 527 degree-seeking undergraduates: 39% part-time, 59% women, 100% Hispanic American
- 72% of applicants admitted
- Application essay, interview required
- 54% graduate within 6 years; 15% enter graduate study

General. Founded in 1965. Regionally accredited. Institution participates in Year Round Pell and the program is accelerated. 1.5 academic years may be completed in each calendar year (3 terms of 15 weeks each); academic year defined as any two terms. **Degrees:** 51 bachelor's awarded. **Location:** 12 miles from Carolina and Bayamón. **Calendar:** Semester. **Full-time faculty:** 16 total; 69% have terminal degrees, 44% women. **Part-time faculty:** 44 total; 54% have terminal degrees, 66% women. **Class size:** 82% < 20, 15% 20-39, 3% 40-49. **Special facilities:** Art gallery and student design center.

Freshman class profile. 119 applied, 86 admitted, 77 enrolled.

GPA 3.75 or higher:	10%	End year in good standing:	67%
GPA 3.50-3.74:	5%	Return as sophomores:	79%
GPA 3.0-3.49:	49%	International:	1%
GPA 2.0-2.99:	36%		

Basis for selection. Applicants must satisfy two pre-admission evaluation requirements regarding artistic skills through a portfolio or seminar and academic achievements. First evaluation consists of a committee interview and the review of portfolio or seminar outcomes. Second evaluation consists of high school GPA of at least 2.0 and standardized test scores. Candidates that satisfy both evaluation requirements must complete the security seminar. SAT recommended for U.S. mainland applicants. **Home schooled:** An attorney must certify that the student is home schooled.

High school preparation. College-preparatory program required.

2012-2013 Annual costs. Tuition/fees (projected): $3,921; $6,621 out-of-state. Books/supplies: $3,000. Personal expenses: $1,000.

2010-2011 Financial aid. All financial aid based on need. 99% of total undergraduate aid awarded as scholarships/grants, 1% as loans/jobs.

Application procedures. **Admission:** Closing date 7/2 (receipt date). $25 fee. Application must be submitted on paper. Admission notification on a rolling basis beginning on or about 1/10. **Financial aid:** Priority date 4/25, closing date 5/18. FAFSA required. Applicants notified by 7/11.

Academics. **Special study options:** Accelerated study, independent study, internships, liberal arts/career combination, teacher certification program. **Credit/placement by examination:** AP, CLEP. **Support services:** Learning center, reduced course load, study skills assistance.

Majors. **Education:** Art. **Visual/performing arts:** General, design, fashion design, industrial design, painting, printmaking, sculpture.

Most popular majors. Education 22%, visual/performing arts 78%.

Computing on campus. 110 workstations in library, computer center. Wireless network available.

Student life. **Freshman orientation:** Mandatory. Preregistration for classes offered. Orientation consists of 1-day seminar; offered 3 times during academic year. **Policies:** Policies in effect regarding drugs and alcohol, academic progress, sexual harassment; security workshops; handicap policies. **Activities:** Literary magazine, music ensembles, student government, student newspaper.

Student services. Adult student services, alcohol/substance abuse counseling, career counseling, student employment services, financial aid counseling, personal counseling, placement for graduates. **Physically disabled:** Services for visually, speech, hearing impaired.

Contact. E-mail: nmelendez@eap.edu
Phone: (787) 725-8120 ext. 333 Fax: (787) 721-3798
Nitza Meléndez, Officer of Admissions, Escuela de Artes Plasticas de Puerto Rico, PO Box 9021112, San Juan, PR 00902-1112

Inter American University of Puerto Rico: Aguadilla Campus
Aguadilla, Puerto Rico
www.aguadilla.inter.edu   CB code: 2042

- Private 4-year university and liberal arts college
- Commuter campus in small city
- 4,675 degree-seeking undergraduates: 13% part-time, 54% women, 99% Hispanic American
- 251 degree-seeking graduate students
- 55% of applicants admitted

General. Founded in 1957. Regionally accredited. Adult higher education and continuing education programs. **Degrees:** 315 bachelor's, 79 associate awarded; master's offered. **ROTC:** Army, Air Force. **Location:** 10 miles from Aguadilla City, 17 miles from Mayaguez. **Calendar:** Semester, extensive summer session. **Full-time faculty:** 79 total; 100% have terminal degrees, 60% women. **Part-time faculty:** 163 total; 100% have terminal degrees, 45% women. **Class size:** 56% < 20, 35% 20-39, 9% 40-49. **Special facilities:** Manuel Mendez Bellester literary collection.

Freshman class profile. 1,926 applied, 1,067 admitted, 1,041 enrolled.

GPA 3.75 or higher:	12%	GPA 2.0-2.99:	48%
GPA 3.50-3.74:	11%	End year in good standing:	84%
GPA 3.0-3.49:	21%	Return as sophomores:	70%

Basis for selection. Regular program requires 2.0 GPA from accredited secondary school and 800 SAT (exclusive of Writing) or PAA. SAT accepted for English-speaking applicants. School achievement record, test scores very important. Pilot Program requires 1.75 GPA from accredited secondary school and College Board examination.

High school preparation. 18 units required. Required units include English 3, mathematics 2, history 2, science 2, foreign language 3 and academic electives 6.

2011-2012 Annual costs. Tuition/fees: $5,582. Books/supplies: $900.

Financial aid. Non-need-based: Scholarships awarded for academics.

Application procedures. Admission: Priority date 5/1; deadline 5/15 (receipt date). No application fee. Admission notification on a rolling basis. **Financial aid:** Closing date 4/30. FAFSA required. Applicants notified by 6/15; must reply by 8/8.

Academics. Special study options: Accelerated study, cross-registration, distance learning, honors, independent study, internships, study abroad, teacher certification program, weekend college. **Credit/placement by examination:** AP, CLEP. **Support services:** Learning center, remedial instruction, study skills assistance, tutoring.

Majors. Biology: General, biotechnology, microbiology. **Business:** Accounting, entrepreneurial studies, hotel/motel admin, human resources, management information systems, marketing, office management. **Computer sciences:** Computer science, networking. **Education:** Biology, early childhood special, elementary, ESL, kindergarten/preschool, physical, Spanish. **Health services:** Nursing (RN), radiologic technology/medical imaging. **Human services:** Social work. **Protective services:** Criminal justice, forensics. **Psychology:** General.

Most popular majors. Biology 6%, business/marketing 23%, computer/information sciences 9%, education 21%, health sciences 11%, public administration/social services 13%, security/protective services 16%.

Computing on campus. 700 workstations in library, computer center. Commuter students can connect to campus network. Online course registration, online library, wireless network available.

Student life. Freshman orientation: Mandatory. Preregistration for classes offered. One-day program in August. **Activities:** Choral groups, dance, drama, student government, student newspaper, Juventud Universitaria Catolica, Asociacion Evangelica Universitaria, Future Teachers Association, Criminal Justice Association, Secretarial Sciences Association, Psychosocial Human Services Association, Hotel Management Association, Marketing Association, Honors Society.

Athletics. Intercollegiate: Baseball M, basketball, cheerleading, cross-country, judo, soccer M, softball, table tennis, tennis, track and field, volleyball, weight lifting. **Intramural:** Basketball, cheerleading, cross-country, soccer, softball, table tennis, tennis, track and field, volleyball, weight lifting. **Team name:** Tigers.

Student services. Adult student services, chaplain/spiritual director, career counseling, student employment services, financial aid counseling, health services, personal counseling, placement for graduates, veterans' counselor.

Contact. Phone: (787) 891-0925 ext. 2101 Fax: (787) 882-3020 Doris Perez, Director of Admissions, Inter American University of Puerto Rico: Aguadilla Campus, Box 20000, Aguadilla, PR 00605

Inter American University of Puerto Rico: Arecibo Campus
Arecibo, Puerto Rico
www.arecibo.inter.edu   **CB code: 1411**

- Private 4-year liberal arts college
- Commuter campus in small city
- 5,066 degree-seeking undergraduates
- 52% of applicants admitted

General. Founded in 1957. Regionally accredited. **Degrees:** 355 bachelor's, 87 associate awarded; master's offered. **ROTC:** Army. **Location:** 45 miles from San Juan. **Calendar:** Semester, limited summer session. **Full-time faculty:** 95 total. **Part-time faculty:** 213 total.

Freshman class profile. 2,912 applied, 1,524 admitted, 1,501 enrolled.

Basis for selection. 2.0 GPA required. Test scores important; minimum admission index of 800 required. Special admissions policies apply to adults 21 years or older. SAT required of English-speaking applicants. Score reports by August 3. Interview recommended for academically weak.

High school preparation. 15 units required. Required units include English 3, mathematics 3, social studies 3, science 3 and foreign language 3.

2011-2012 Annual costs. Tuition/fees: $5,620. Books/supplies: $890. Personal expenses: $880.

Financial aid. Non-need-based: Scholarships awarded for academics, athletics.

Application procedures. Admission: Priority date 5/1; no deadline. No application fee. Admission notification on a rolling basis. **Financial aid:** Closing date 5/15. FAFSA, institutional form required. Applicants notified on a rolling basis.

Academics. Special study options: Cooperative education, distance learning, honors, independent study, internships, study abroad, teacher certification program. **Credit/placement by examination:** AP, CLEP, institutional tests. 15 credit hours maximum toward associate degree, 15 toward bachelor's. **Support services:** Pre-admission summer program, remedial instruction, study skills assistance, tutoring.

Majors. Biology: General, bacteriology. **Business:** Accounting, administrative services, business admin, management science. **Computer sciences:** General, computer science. **Education:** Biology, chemistry, early childhood, elementary, secondary, Spanish, special ed. **Health services:** Nursing (RN). **Human services:** Social work. **Physical sciences:** Chemistry. **Protective services:** Criminal justice.

Computing on campus. 350 workstations in library, computer center. Commuter students can connect to campus network. Helpline, wireless network available.

Student life. Freshman orientation: Mandatory. Preregistration for classes offered. **Activities:** Drama, student government, Baptist Unity, Young Catholics Association, Criminal Justice Association, Haziel Evangelical Association, Future Social Workers Association, Bahai Association, Student Counseling Association, Society for Human Resources.

Athletics. Intercollegiate: Basketball, soccer, softball, table tennis, tennis, track and field, volleyball. **Intramural:** Basketball, cheerleading, soccer, softball, table tennis, tennis, track and field, volleyball. **Team name:** Tigers.

Student services. Adult student services, alcohol/substance abuse counseling, chaplain/spiritual director, career counseling, student employment services, health services, personal counseling, veterans' counselor. **Physically disabled:** Services for visually, hearing impaired.

Contact. E-mail: pmontalvo@arecibo.inter.edu
Phone: (787) 878-5195 Fax: (787) 880-1624
Provi Montalvo, Director of Admissions, Inter American University of Puerto Rico: Arecibo Campus, PO Box 4050, Arecibo, PR 00614-4050

Inter American University of Puerto Rico: Barranquitas Campus
Barranquitas, Puerto Rico
www.br.inter.edu   **CB code: 2067**

- Private 4-year university and branch campus college
- Commuter campus in large town
- 2,316 undergraduates

General. Founded in 1957. Regionally accredited. **Degrees:** 202 bachelor's, 87 associate awarded; master's offered. **Location:** 35 miles from San Juan. **Calendar:** Semester, extensive summer session. **Full-time faculty:** 42 total. **Part-time faculty:** 134 total. **Special facilities:** Nature preserve, 35 e-classrooms.

Basis for selection. 2.0 GPA and minimum PAA or SAT score required. Interview, portfolio, essay recommended. **Home schooled:** Transcript of courses and grades, state high school equivalency certificate required.

High school preparation. 15 units required. Required units include English 3, mathematics 2, social studies 2 and science 3. 3 units of Spanish

required for Puerto Rican high school graduates, 2 units liberal arts recommended.

2011-2012 Annual costs. Tuition/fees: $5,582. Books/supplies: $900. Personal expenses: $2,731.

Financial aid. All financial aid based on need.

Application procedures. Admission: No deadline. No application fee. Admission notification on a rolling basis. **Financial aid:** Closing date 4/30. FAFSA required. Applicants notified on a rolling basis; must reply within 2 week(s) of notification.

Academics. Special study options: Accelerated study, combined bachelor's/graduate degree, cross-registration, distance learning, ESL, honors, independent study, internships, liberal arts/career combination, teacher certification program, Washington semester, weekend college. **Credit/placement by examination:** AP, CLEP. **Support services:** Learning center, pre-admission summer program, remedial instruction, study skills assistance, tutoring.

Majors. Biology: General, biotechnology. **Business:** General, accounting, administrative services, business admin. **Computer sciences:** General, computer science, information systems. **Education:** General, biology, early childhood, elementary, English, mathematics, secondary, social studies, Spanish, visually handicapped. **Engineering:** General. **Health services:** Audiology/speech pathology, nursing (RN), radiologic technology/medical imaging. **Protective services:** Law enforcement admin.

Most popular majors. Business/marketing 16%, education 56%, health sciences 8%, social sciences 11%.

Computing on campus. 43 workstations in library, computer center, student center. Commuter students can connect to campus network. Online course registration, online library, helpline, wireless network available.

Student life. Freshman orientation: Mandatory. Preregistration for classes offered. **Activities:** Concert band, dance, drama, literary magazine, musical theater, student government, student newspaper.

Athletics. NAIA. **Intercollegiate:** Baseball M, basketball M, cross-country, softball, tennis, volleyball. **Team name:** Tigers.

Student services. Adult student services, career counseling, personal counseling, veterans' counselor. **Physically disabled:** Services for visually, speech, hearing impaired.

Contact. E-mail: mdiaz@br.inter.edu
Phone: (787) 857-3600 ext. 2011 Fax: (787) 857-2125
Maribel Pena, Director of Admissions, Inter American University of Puerto Rico: Barranquitas Campus, PO Box 517, Barranquitas, PR 00794

Inter American University of Puerto Rico: Bayamon Campus
Bayamon, Puerto Rico
www.bayamon.inter.edu
CB code: 2043

- Private 4-year university and engineering college
- Commuter campus in small city
- 5,081 degree-seeking undergraduates: 14% part-time, 44% women, 99% Hispanic American
- 121 degree-seeking graduate students
- 36% of applicants admitted

General. Founded in 1912. Regionally accredited. **Degrees:** 413 bachelor's, 54 associate awarded; master's offered. **ROTC:** Army, Naval, Air Force. **Location:** 15 miles from San Juan. **Calendar:** Semester, limited summer session. **Full-time faculty:** 103 total; 39% have terminal degrees, 45% women. **Part-time faculty:** 205 total; 17% have terminal degrees, 49% women. **Class size:** 37% < 20, 55% 20-39, 7% 40-49, 1% 50-99. **Special facilities:** Wetland used as a natural laboratory, mata de platano field station.

Freshman class profile. 3,397 applied, 1,222 admitted, 1,217 enrolled.

GPA 3.75 or higher:	14%	GPA 2.0-2.99:	43%
GPA 3.50-3.74:	13%	End year in good standing:	83%
GPA 3.0-3.49:	27%	Return as sophomores:	73%

Basis for selection. High school GPA and test scores most important. 2.0 GPA, 800 admission index (based on college formula) required. Achievement tests required for placement in math, English, and Spanish. Interview recommended.

High school preparation. Required units include English 3, mathematics 3, social studies 1, history 2, science 3 and foreign language 3.

2011-2012 Annual costs. Tuition/fees: $5,620. Books/supplies: $993.

2010-2011 Financial aid. All financial aid based on need. 1,278 full-time freshmen applied for aid; 1,259 were judged to have need; 718 of these received aid. Average need met was 2%. Average scholarship/grant was $225; average loan $157. 19% of total undergraduate aid awarded as scholarships/grants, 81% as loans/jobs.

Application procedures. Admission: Closing date 5/1 (receipt date). No application fee. Admission notification on a rolling basis. Must reply by 8/1. **Financial aid:** Priority date 6/30; no closing date. FAFSA required. Applicants notified on a rolling basis starting 5/10.

Academics. Special study options: Accelerated study, cooperative education, distance learning, honors, independent study, internships, study abroad. **Credit/placement by examination:** AP, CLEP. 225 credit hours maximum toward associate degree, 225 toward bachelor's. **Support services:** Learning center, pre-admission summer program, study skills assistance, tutoring.

Majors. Biology: General, biotechnology. **Business:** Accounting, auditing, business admin, entrepreneurial studies, finance, human resources, logistics, management information systems, managerial economics, marketing, office management. **Communications:** Digital media. **Communications technology:** General. **Computer sciences:** Computer science. **Conservation:** Environmental science. **Engineering:** Computer, electrical, industrial, mechanical. **General:** Food processing. **Health services:** Licensed practical nurse, nursing (RN). **Human services:** General. **Math:** General. **Parks/recreation:** Sports admin. **Philosophy/religion:** Religion. **Physical sciences:** Chemistry. **Protective services:** Correctional facilities, criminal justice, forensics. **Psychology:** General.

Most popular majors. Biology 6%, business/marketing 38%, communications/journalism 7%, computer/information sciences 11%, engineering/engineering technologies 14%, health sciences 11%, trade and industry 7%.

Computing on campus. 610 workstations in library, computer center. Dormitories wired for high-speed internet access. Commuter students can connect to campus network. Online course registration, online library, repair service, wireless network available.

Student life. Freshman orientation: Mandatory. Preregistration for classes offered. **Housing:** Coed dorms, wellness housing available. **Activities:** Concert band, choral groups, drama, student council, business administration students association, Catholic students association, Christian University Brotherhood Association, Society of Joined Students for Science, photography club, ANCLA group, senior class association, engineering students association.

Athletics. Intercollegiate: Baseball M, basketball, cross-country, soccer M, softball, swimming, table tennis, tennis, track and field, volleyball, wrestling M. **Intramural:** Basketball, cross-country, softball, swimming, table tennis, tennis, track and field, volleyball, wrestling M. **Team name:** Tigers.

Student services. Adult student services, alcohol/substance abuse counseling, chaplain/spiritual director, career counseling, student employment services, financial aid counseling, health services, on-campus daycare, personal counseling, placement for graduates, veterans' counselor. **Physically disabled:** Services for visually, speech, hearing impaired.

Contact. E-mail: calicea@bayamon.inter.edu
Phone: (787) 279-1912 ext. 2017 Fax: (787) 279-2205
Carlos Alicea, Director of Students Services, Inter American University of Puerto Rico: Bayamon Campus, 500 Dr. John Will Harris Road, Bayamon, PR 00957

Inter American University of Puerto Rico: Fajardo Campus
Fajardo, Puerto Rico
www.fajardo.inter.edu
CB code: 2065

- Private 4-year university and branch campus college
- Commuter campus in large town
- 2,163 degree-seeking undergraduates: 100% Hispanic American
- 29 degree-seeking graduate students
- 50% of applicants admitted

General. Regionally accredited. **Degrees:** 195 bachelor's, 22 associate awarded; master's offered. **ROTC:** Air Force. **Location:** 34 miles from San Juan. **Calendar:** Semester, limited summer session. **Full-time faculty:** 40

total; 30% have terminal degrees, 60% women. **Part-time faculty:** 74 total; 51% women. **Class size:** 58% < 20, 32% 20-39, 10% 40-49.

Freshman class profile. 909 applied, 453 admitted, 453 enrolled.

GPA 3.75 or higher:	21%	GPA 2.0-2.99:	47%
GPA 3.50-3.74:	27%		

Basis for selection. High school students must have 2.0 GPA and average of 400 on first three parts of PAA. Special admissions policies apply to adults age 21 or older. PAA test required for Spanish-speaking applicants; SAT or ACT required for English-speaking applicants. **Home schooled:** Statement describing home school structure and mission required.

High school preparation. 15 units required. Required units include English 3, mathematics 2, social studies 2 and science 3. 3 units Spanish required for Puerto Rican students.

2011-2012 Annual costs. Tuition/fees: $5,620. Books/supplies: $985.

Application procedures. Admission: Closing date 5/15. No application fee. Admission notification on a rolling basis. **Financial aid:** Closing date 4/30. FAFSA, institutional form required. Applicants notified on a rolling basis.

Academics. Special study options: Cross-registration, distance learning, double major, dual enrollment of high school students, ESL, honors, independent study, internships, teacher certification program, Washington semester. Adult education program. **Credit/placement by examination:** AP, CLEP, institutional tests. 15 credit hours maximum toward bachelor's degree. Maximum 24 credit hours counted for adult education students. **Support services:** Tutoring.

Majors. Business: General, accounting, administrative services, business admin. **Education:** General, biology, early childhood, elementary, ESL, secondary, social studies, Spanish. **Protective services:** Criminal justice.

Computing on campus. 188 workstations in library, computer center. Commuter students can connect to campus network. Online course registration, online library, wireless network available.

Student life. Freshman orientation: Mandatory. Preregistration for classes offered. **Activities:** Dance, drama, student government, future teacher club, muiltilingual club, Christian students club, future social work club, criminal justice club, computer science club, speech and language therapy club, marketing club, accounting club, psychology club.

Athletics. Intramural: Baseball M, basketball, boxing M, cheerleading W, judo M, softball, table tennis, tennis, track and field, volleyball. **Team name:** Tigers.

Student services. Adult student services, chaplain/spiritual director, career counseling, student employment services, financial aid counseling, health services, personal counseling, placement for graduates, veterans' counselor.

Contact. E-mail: ada.caraballo@fajardo.inter.edu
Phone: (787) 860-3100 Fax: (787) 860-3470
Ada Caraballo, Admissions Director, Inter American University of Puerto Rico: Fajardo Campus, Call Box 70003, Fajardo, PR 00738-7003

Inter American University of Puerto Rico: Guayama Campus
Guayama, Puerto Rico
www.guayama.inter.edu   CB code: 2077

- Private 4-year university
- Commuter campus in large town
- 2,334 degree-seeking undergraduates: 16% part-time, 66% women, 99% Hispanic American
- 87 degree-seeking graduate students
- 71% of applicants admitted
- Interview required

General. Founded in 1957. Regionally accredited. **Degrees:** 202 bachelor's, 75 associate awarded; master's offered. **ROTC:** Army. **Location:** 18 miles from Ponce. **Calendar:** Semester, limited summer session. **Full-time faculty:** 42 total; 29% have terminal degrees, 52% women. **Part-time faculty:** 158 total; 14% have terminal degrees, 60% women. **Class size:** 49% < 20, 42% 20-39, 8% 40-49, less than 1% 50-99.

Freshman class profile. 290 applied, 207 admitted, 200 enrolled.

GPA 3.75 or higher:	5%	GPA 2.0-2.99:	55%
GPA 3.50-3.74:	10%	End year in good standing:	83%
GPA 3.0-3.49:	19%	Return as sophomores:	70%

Basis for selection. High school graduates must have 2.0 GPA and 800 admission index.

2011-2012 Annual costs. Tuition/fees: $5,582. Books/supplies: $905. Personal expenses: $3,928.

2011-2012 Financial aid. All financial aid based on need. Average need met was 1%. Average scholarship/grant was $30; average loan $178. 9% of total undergraduate aid awarded as scholarships/grants, 91% as loans/jobs.

Application procedures. Admission: Priority date 5/15; no deadline. No application fee. Admission notification on a rolling basis beginning on or about 4/1. **Financial aid:** Closing date 4/29. FAFSA, institutional form required. Applicants notified by 6/15; must reply by 7/30.

Academics. Special study options: Accelerated study, distance learning, dual enrollment of high school students, exchange student, external degree, honors, internships, study abroad, teacher certification program, weekend college. **Credit/placement by examination:** AP, CLEP. **Support services:** Learning center, remedial instruction, tutoring.

Majors. Biology: General, biotechnology. **Business:** Accounting, business admin, human resources, office management. **Education:** Early childhood special, elementary, ESL, kindergarten/preschool, physical. **Health services:** Nursing (RN), respiratory therapy technology. **Protective services:** Law enforcement admin.

Most popular majors. Biology 8%, business/marketing 36%, computer/information sciences 6%, education 18%, health sciences 8%, security/protective services 7%.

Computing on campus. 232 workstations in library, computer center, student center. Online course registration, online library, wireless network available.

Student life. Freshman orientation: Mandatory. Preregistration for classes offered. **Activities:** Choral groups, dance, student government, CONFRA religious organization.

Athletics. Intercollegiate: Baseball M, basketball, cross-country, soccer M, swimming M. **Intramural:** Baseball M, basketball, cross-country M, softball, swimming M, table tennis W, tennis W, track and field. **Team name:** Tigers.

Student services. Adult student services, chaplain/spiritual director, career counseling, student employment services, health services, personal counseling, placement for graduates, veterans' counselor. **Physically disabled:** Services for visually impaired.

Contact. E-mail: lferrer@inter.edu
Phone: (787) 864-7059 Fax: (787) 864-8232
Laura Ferrer-Sanchez, Director of Admissions, Inter American University of Puerto Rico: Guayama Campus, PO Box 10004, Guayama, PR 00785

Inter American University of Puerto Rico: Metropolitan Campus
San Juan, Puerto Rico   CB member
www.metro.inter.edu   CB code: 0873

- Private 4-year branch campus college
- Commuter campus in large city
- 7,451 degree-seeking undergraduates: 22% part-time, 55% women, 96% Hispanic American
- 2,854 degree-seeking graduate students
- 25% of applicants admitted

General. Founded in 1962. Regionally accredited. **Degrees:** 790 bachelor's, 126 associate awarded; master's, doctoral offered. **ROTC:** Army, Air Force. **Location:** 9 miles from San Juan. **Calendar:** Trimester, limited summer session. **Full-time faculty:** 215 total; 56% have terminal degrees, 54% women. **Part-time faculty:** 357 total; 33% have terminal degrees, 52% women. **Class size:** 44% < 20, 47% 20-39, 7% 40-49, 3% 50-99.

Freshman class profile. 3,847 applied, 976 admitted, 898 enrolled.

GPA 3.75 or higher:	11%	GPA 2.0-2.99:	41%
GPA 3.50-3.74:	15%	End year in good standing:	95%
GPA 3.0-3.49:	33%	Return as sophomores:	73%

Basis for selection. School grade average and test scores important. 2.0 GPA plus score average of 400 in SAT. Special admissions policies apply to adults 21 years of age or older. SAT required of English-speaking applicants. **Home schooled:** Statement describing home school structure and mission, state high school equivalency certificate required. In addition to a sworn statement declaring that studies were completed by homeschooling, such students must submit satisfactory College Board test scores (English, Spanish, mathematics).

High school preparation. Required units include English 3, mathematics 3 and science 3.

2011-2012 Annual costs. Tuition/fees: $5,620.

2010-2011 Financial aid. **Need-based:** 1,149 full-time freshmen applied for aid; 1,120 were judged to have need; 971 of these received aid. Average need met was 3%. Average scholarship/grant was $319; average loan $438. 26% of total undergraduate aid awarded as scholarships/grants, 74% as loans/jobs. **Non-need-based:** Awarded to 46 full-time undergraduates, including 10 freshmen.

Application procedures. Admission: Closing date 5/15 (receipt date). No application fee. Admission notification on a rolling basis. Must reply by 8/15. **Financial aid:** Closing date 4/30. FAFSA required. Applicants notified on a rolling basis.

Academics. Adult education programs available. **Special study options:** Accelerated study, distance learning, ESL, honors, independent study, internships. **Credit/placement by examination:** AP, CLEP. 12 credit hours maximum toward associate degree, 12 toward bachelor's. Departmental convalidation test. **Support services:** Learning center, pre-admission summer program, remedial instruction, study skills assistance, tutoring, writing center.

Majors. Biology: General, biomedical sciences. **Business:** Accounting, administrative services, business admin, entrepreneurial studies, finance, human resources, management information systems, managerial economics, marketing, office management, office/clerical. **Computer sciences:** General. **Education:** Bilingual, chemistry, elementary, ESL, health, history, mathematics, physical, science, Spanish, special ed. **Foreign languages:** Spanish. **Health services:** Clinical lab science, nursing (RN). **Human services:** Social work. **Math:** General. **Physical sciences:** Chemistry. **Protective services:** Correctional facilities, criminal justice. **Psychology:** General. **Social sciences:** General, anthropology, political science, sociology. **Theology:** Religious ed. **Visual/performing arts:** Music performance.

Most popular majors. Biology 6%, business/marketing 27%, education 13%, health sciences 12%, psychology 12%, public administration/social services 6%, security/protective services 14%.

Computing on campus. 679 workstations in library, computer center. Commuter students can connect to campus network. Online course registration, online library, helpline, wireless network available.

Student life. Freshman orientation: Mandatory. Preregistration for classes offered. Held 2 weeks before regular classes begin. **Activities:** Jazz band, choral groups, drama, international student organizations, music ensembles, student government, student newspaper, intercultural student association, Club ROTARACT, Alpha Phi Omega, criminal justice club, biological science club, premedical studies student association, psychology student association, chemistry student association, professional counseling student association, Finance for a Better Future.

Athletics. Intercollegiate: Baseball M, basketball, judo M, softball, swimming, tennis, track and field, volleyball. **Intramural:** Basketball, softball, table tennis, tennis, volleyball. **Team name:** Tigres.

Student services. Adult student services, alcohol/substance abuse counseling, chaplain/spiritual director, career counseling, student employment services, financial aid counseling, health services, on-campus daycare, personal counseling, placement for graduates, veterans' counselor. **Physically disabled:** Services for visually, speech, hearing impaired.

Contact. E-mail: jolivieri@metro.inter.edu
Phone: (787) 250-1912 ext. 2188 Fax: (787) 250-1025
Janies Olivieri, Admissions Officer, Inter American University of Puerto Rico: Metropolitan Campus, Box 191293, San Juan, PR 00919-1293

Inter American University of Puerto Rico: Ponce Campus
Mercedita, Puerto Rico
www.ponce.inter.edu   CB code: 3531

▶ Private 4-year university
▶ Large town

▶ 5,966 degree-seeking undergraduates: 16% part-time, 60% women, 98% Hispanic American
▶ 317 degree-seeking graduate students
▶ 38% of applicants admitted

General. Regionally accredited. **Degrees:** 565 bachelor's, 132 associate awarded; master's offered. **ROTC:** Naval. **Calendar:** Semester. **Full-time faculty:** 99 total; 35% have terminal degrees, 52% women. **Part-time faculty:** 248 total; 12% have terminal degrees, 62% women. **Class size:** 30% < 20, 55% 20-39, 14% 40-49, less than 1% 50-99.

Freshman class profile. 2,903 applied, 1,101 admitted, 1,070 enrolled.

GPA 3.75 or higher:	7%	GPA 2.0-2.99:	50%
GPA 3.50-3.74:	13%	End year in good standing:	83%
GPA 3.0-3.49:	26%	Return as sophomores:	73%

Basis for selection. 2.0 GPA and average of 400 on first three parts of PAA. Interview required for AVANCE program.

High school preparation. 18 units required. Required units include English 3, mathematics 3, social studies 1, history 3, science 3 (laboratory 1), foreign language 3 and academic electives 1.

2011-2012 Annual costs. Tuition/fees: $5,620. Books/supplies: $905. Personal expenses: $3,928.

2010-2011 Financial aid. All financial aid based on need. 1,387 full-time freshmen applied for aid; 1,380 were judged to have need; 1,164 of these received aid. Average need met was 3%. Average scholarship/grant was $271; average loan $451. 78% of total undergraduate aid awarded as scholarships/grants, 22% as loans/jobs.

Application procedures. Admission: Closing date 5/15 (receipt date). No application fee. Admission notification on a rolling basis. **Financial aid:** No deadline. FAFSA required.

Academics. Special study options: Cooperative education, distance learning, honors, independent study, internships, study abroad, teacher certification program. Adult programs (AVANCE), development programs, PREAD program. **Credit/placement by examination:** AP, CLEP. **Support services:** Learning center, study skills assistance, tutoring.

Majors. Biology: General, biomedical sciences, biotechnology, microbiology. **Business:** Accounting, administrative services, business admin, finance, hotel/motel admin, human resources, international, management information systems, management science, marketing, office technology, operations, training/development. **Communications:** Journalism, public relations. **Computer sciences:** Computer science, information systems. **Conservation:** General. **Education:** Biology, early childhood, elementary, ESL, secondary, special ed. **Health services:** Nursing (RN). **Protective services:** Forensics, law enforcement admin. **Psychology:** General.

Most popular majors. Biology 8%, business/marketing 33%, education 17%, health sciences 22%, security/protective services 17%.

Computing on campus. PC or laptop required. 983 workstations in library, computer center, student center. Commuter students can connect to campus network. Online course registration, online library, helpline available.

Student life. Freshman orientation: Available. Preregistration for classes offered. Includes workshops, seminars, and social activities. **Activities:** Concert band, choral groups, dance, student government, student newspaper.

Athletics. Intercollegiate: Baseball M, basketball, cross-country M, judo, softball, table tennis M, track and field, weight lifting, wrestling. **Intramural:** Baseball M, basketball, cross-country M, softball, table tennis M, track and field, weight lifting, wrestling. **Team name:** Tigers.

Student services. Adult student services, alcohol/substance abuse counseling, chaplain/spiritual director, career counseling, student employment services, financial aid counseling, health services, on-campus daycare, personal counseling, placement for graduates, women's services. **Physically disabled:** Services for visually, speech, hearing impaired.

Contact. E-mail: fldiaz@poce.inter.edu
Phone: (787) 841-0110 Fax: (787) 841-0103
Franco Diaz Vega, Director of Admissions, Inter American University of Puerto Rico: Ponce Campus, 104 Turpo Industrial Park Road #1, Mercedita, PR 00715-1602

Inter American University of Puerto Rico: San German Campus
San German, Puerto Rico
www.sg.inter.edu　　　　　　　　　　**CB code: 0946**

- Private 4-year university
- Commuter campus in large town
- 4,722 degree-seeking undergraduates: 10% part-time, 53% women, 100% Hispanic American
- 800 degree-seeking graduate students
- 70% of applicants admitted
- 35% graduate within 6 years; 9% enter graduate study

General. Founded in 1912. Regionally accredited. San German Inter American School (pre-school to grade 12). **Degrees:** 475 bachelor's, 51 associate awarded; master's, doctoral offered. **ROTC:** Army, Air Force. **Location:** 14 miles from Mayaguez, 104 miles from San Juan. **Calendar:** Semester, extensive summer session. **Full-time faculty:** 122 total; 51% have terminal degrees, 100% minority, 58% women. **Part-time faculty:** 204 total; 23% have terminal degrees, 100% minority, 57% women. **Class size:** 54% < 20, 44% 20-39, 1% 40-49, 1% 50-99. **Special facilities:** Nature preserve, museums.

Freshman class profile. 1,584 applied, 1,107 admitted, 1,070 enrolled.

GPA 3.75 or higher:	12%	GPA 2.0-2.99:	40%
GPA 3.50-3.74:	14%	End year in good standing:	88%
GPA 3.0-3.49:	27%	Return as sophomores:	75%

Basis for selection. High school GPA and test scores important. SAT or ACT recommended. SAT required of English-speaking applicants. Essay, interview recommended for all; audition recommended for music; portfolio recommended for art programs. **Home schooled:** Statement describing home school structure and mission, transcript of courses and grades, state high school equivalency certificate required.

High school preparation. 11 units required; 18 recommended. Required and recommended units include English 3, mathematics 2-3, social studies 2-3, history 2-3, science 2-3, foreign language 3 and academic electives 3. 3 units of Spanish required of Spanish-speaking students.

2011-2012 Annual costs. Tuition/fees: $5,620. Room/board: $2,500. Books/supplies: $894. Personal expenses: $880.

2010-2011 Financial aid. Need-based: 1,036 full-time freshmen applied for aid; 1,011 were judged to have need; 785 of these received aid. Average need met was 3%. Average scholarship/grant was $312; average loan $189. 78% of total undergraduate aid awarded as scholarships/grants, 22% as loans/jobs. **Non-need-based:** Awarded to 102 full-time undergraduates, including 37 freshmen. Scholarships awarded for academics, athletics.

Application procedures. Admission: Closing date 5/15 (receipt date). No application fee. Admission notification on a rolling basis beginning on or about 2/15. **Financial aid:** Closing date 5/14. FAFSA, institutional form required. Applicants notified on a rolling basis; must reply by 8/1.

Academics. Bilingual program enables students to learn English or Spanish while taking courses in their native language. **Special study options:** Accelerated study, cooperative education, cross-registration, distance learning, double major, dual enrollment of high school students, ESL, honors, independent study, internships, liberal arts/career combination, study abroad, teacher certification program, weekend college. Weekend college in some graduate programs. **Credit/placement by examination:** AP, CLEP, institutional tests. 12 credit hours maximum toward associate degree, 18 toward bachelor's. **Support services:** Learning center, reduced course load, remedial instruction, tutoring.

Majors. Biology: General, microbiology. **Business:** Accounting, business admin, entrepreneurial studies, finance, human resources, management information systems, marketing, office management. **Computer sciences:** Computer science. **Conservation:** Environmental science. **Education:** General, art, biology, chemistry, early childhood, elementary, English, ESL, health, history, kindergarten/preschool, mathematics, music, physical, science, secondary, social studies, Spanish, special ed, voc/tech. **English:** English lit. **Health services:** Clinical lab science, licensed practical nurse, nursing (RN), radiologic technology/medical imaging. **Math:** General. **Parks/recreation:** Health/fitness. **Physical sciences:** Chemistry. **Psychology:** General. **Social sciences:** Political science, sociology. **Visual/performing arts:** General, ceramics, drawing, music performance, painting, photography, sculpture.

Most popular majors. Biology 19%, business/marketing 21%, education 23%, health sciences 9%, psychology 10%, visual/performing arts 6%.

Computing on campus. 1,250 workstations in dormitories, library, computer center, student center. Dormitories wired for high-speed internet access and linked to campus network. Commuter students can connect to campus network. Online course registration, online library, wireless network available.

Student life. Freshman orientation: Mandatory. Preregistration for classes offered. General orientation program offered in spring, summer, and fall. **Housing:** Single-sex dorms, apartments, wellness housing available. $25 fully refundable deposit, deadline 6/30. **Activities:** Bands, choral groups, dance, drama, international student organizations, music ensembles, student government, student newspaper, Catholic students organization, asociacion ciencias politicas, Yashab y Taller Blessed.

Athletics. Intercollegiate: Baseball M, basketball, cross-country, soccer M, softball, swimming, table tennis, tennis, track and field, volleyball, weight lifting. **Intramural:** Basketball, cross-country, softball, table tennis, tennis, track and field, volleyball. **Team name:** Tigers.

Student services. Adult student services, alcohol/substance abuse counseling, chaplain/spiritual director, career counseling, student employment services, financial aid counseling, health services, on-campus daycare, personal counseling, placement for graduates, veterans' counselor.

Contact. E-mail: milcama@sg.inter.edu
Phone: (787) 892-3090 Fax: (787) 892-6350
Mildred Camacho, Director of Admissions, Inter American University of Puerto Rico: San German Campus, Box 5100, San German, PR 00683-9801

National University College: Arecibo
Arecibo, Puerto Rico
www.nuc.edu　　　　　　　　　　**CB code: 3222**

- For-profit 3-year career college
- Commuter campus in small city
- 1,681 degree-seeking undergraduates: 31% part-time, 63% women, 100% Hispanic American
- 97% of applicants admitted
- Interview required

General. Regionally accredited; also accredited by ACICS. Additional campuses in Bayamon, Arecibo, Rio Grande, Ponce; learning center in Caguas. **Degrees:** 100 bachelor's, 256 associate awarded. **Calendar:** Trimester. **Full-time faculty:** 30 total; 70% women. **Part-time faculty:** 48 total; 67% women. **Class size:** 58% < 20, 39% 20-39, 3% 40-49.

Freshman class profile. 715 applied, 693 admitted, 637 enrolled.

GPA 3.0-3.49:	10%	End year in good standing:	95%
GPA 2.0-2.99:	80%	Return as sophomores:	57%

Basis for selection. Admissions based on high school record and institutional admissions or SAT test. College Entrance Examination Board test, institutional tests, or SAT required.

High school preparation. 18 units required. Required units include English 3, mathematics 3, history 3, science 3, foreign language 3 and academic electives 3.

2011-2012 Annual costs. Books/supplies: $908. Personal expenses: $2,050.

2011-2012 Financial aid. Need-based: 232 full-time freshmen applied for aid; 232 were judged to have need; 232 of these received aid. Average scholarship/grant was $3,255; average loan $3,437. 84% of total undergraduate aid awarded as scholarships/grants, 16% as loans/jobs.

Application procedures. Admission: Priority date 8/12; deadline 3/12. $25 fee. Application must be submitted on paper. Admission notification on a rolling basis. **Financial aid:** Priority date 12/31, closing date 4/30. FAFSA required. Applicants notified on a rolling basis starting 5/2; must reply by 5/15 or within 2 week(s) of notification.

Academics. Special study options: Independent study, internships. **Credit/placement by examination:** AP, CLEP, SAT, institutional tests. 50 credit hours maximum toward associate degree, 50 toward bachelor's. **Support services:** Tutoring.

Majors. BACHELOR'S. Business: Accounting/business management, banking/financial services, executive assistant. **Computer sciences:** Networking. **Education:** Early childhood, health. **Health services:** Nursing (RN). **Protective services:** Law enforcement admin. **ASSOCIATE. Business:** Accounting/business management, entrepreneurial studies, office technology, tourism/travel. **Computer sciences:** Networking. **Health services:**

Dental assistant, medical secretary, nursing (RN), pharmacy assistant. **Protective services:** Law enforcement admin.

Most popular majors. Business/marketing 15%, communications/journalism 7%, health sciences 44%, liberal arts 12%, personal/culinary services 22%.

Computing on campus. 175 workstations in library, computer center, student center. Online library, student web hosting, wireless network available.

Student life. Freshman orientation: Mandatory. Preregistration for classes offered. **Activities:** Student newspaper, CONFRA.

Athletics. Intramural: Basketball M.

Student services. Alcohol/substance abuse counseling, career counseling, financial aid counseling, personal counseling, placement for graduates.

Contact. E-mail: mepagan@nuc.edu
Phone: (787) 879-5044 ext. 5203 Toll-free number: (800) 780-5134
Fax: (787) 879-5047
Mercedes Pagán, Admissions Director, National University College: Arecibo, PO Box 4035, MSC 452, Arecibo, PR 00614

National University College: Bayamon
Bayamon, Puerto Rico   **CB member**
www.nuc.edu   **CB code: 7135**

▶ For-profit 3-year career college
▶ Commuter campus in large town
▶ 2,846 degree-seeking undergraduates: 35% part-time, 71% women, 100% African American
▶ 16 degree-seeking graduate students
▶ 86% of applicants admitted

General. Regionally accredited; also accredited by ACICS. Additional campuses in Arecibo, Rio Grande, Ponce; learning center in Caguas. **Degrees:** 153 bachelor's, 341 associate awarded; master's offered. **Location:** 25 miles from San Juan. **Calendar:** Trimester. **Full-time faculty:** 62 total; 68% women. **Part-time faculty:** 94 total; 63% women. **Class size:** 53% < 20, 47% 20-39, less than 1% 40-49.

Freshman class profile. 1,833 applied, 1,574 admitted, 1,333 enrolled.

End year in good standing: 97%   **Return as sophomores:** 53%

Basis for selection. High school transcript, College Entrance Examination Board test or institutional test required for admissions.

High school preparation. 18 units required. Required units include English 3, mathematics 3, history 3, science 3, foreign language 3 and academic electives 3.

2011-2012 Annual costs. Books/supplies: $908. Personal expenses: $2,050.

2011-2012 Financial aid. All financial aid based on need. 331 full-time freshmen applied for aid; 331 were judged to have need; 331 of these received aid. Average scholarship/grant was $5,244; average loan $3,058.

Application procedures. Admission: $25 fee. Application must be submitted on paper. Admission notification by 8/9. Admission notification on a rolling basis. **Financial aid:** Priority date 12/31, closing date 4/30. FAFSA required. Applicants notified on a rolling basis starting 5/2; must reply by 5/15 or within 2 week(s) of notification.

Academics. Special study options: Distance learning, independent study, internships. **Credit/placement by examination:** AP, CLEP, institutional tests. 50 credit hours maximum toward associate degree, 50 toward bachelor's. **Support services:** Tutoring.

Majors. BACHELOR'S. Business: Accounting/business management, banking/financial services, executive assistant. **Computer sciences:** Networking. **Education:** Early childhood, health. **Health services:** Nursing (RN). **Protective services:** Law enforcement admin. **ASSOCIATE. Business:** Accounting/business management, entrepreneurial studies, information resources management, office technology, tourism/travel. **Computer sciences:** Networking. **Health services:** Dental assistant, medical secretary, nursing (RN), pharmacy assistant. **Protective services:** Law enforcement admin.

Most popular majors. Computer/information sciences 9%, education 9%, health sciences 36%.

Computing on campus. 200 workstations in library, computer center, student center. Online library, student web hosting, wireless network available.

Student life. Freshman orientation: Available. Preregistration for classes offered. **Housing:** Wellness housing available. **Activities:** Student newspaper.

Athletics. Intercollegiate: Basketball, softball, table tennis, track and field, volleyball. **Intramural:** Basketball, softball, table tennis, track and field, volleyball.

Student services. Alcohol/substance abuse counseling, career counseling, student employment services, financial aid counseling, personal counseling, placement for graduates.

Contact. E-mail: srubio@nuc.edu
Phone: (787) 780-5134 ext. 4000 Toll-free number: (800) 780-5134
Fax: (787) 779-4909
Suzette Rubio, Admissions and Marketing Director, National University College: Bayamon, PO Box 2036, Bayamon, PR 00960

National University College: Ponce
Coto Laurel, Puerto Rico
www.nuc.edu

▶ For-profit 3-year career college
▶ Commuter campus in large city
▶ 803 degree-seeking undergraduates: 32% part-time, 76% women

General. Regionally accredited; also accredited by ACICS. Additional campuses in Bayamon, Arecibo, Rio Grande, Ponce; learning center in Caguas. **Degrees:** 86 bachelor's, 83 associate awarded. **Calendar:** Trimester. **Full-time faculty:** 13 total; 77% women. **Part-time faculty:** 47 total; 70% women. **Class size:** 70% < 20, 30% 20-39.

Freshman class profile.

End year in good standing: 98%   **Return as sophomores:** 77%

Basis for selection. School record, GPA, and test scores important.

High school preparation. 18 units required. Required units include English 3, mathematics 3, science 3, foreign language 3, computer science 3 and academic electives 3.

2011-2012 Annual costs. Books/supplies: $908. Personal expenses: $2,050.

2011-2012 Financial aid. All financial aid based on need. 101 full-time freshmen applied for aid; 101 were judged to have need; 101 of these received aid. Average scholarship/grant was $5,716; average loan $3,648. 73% of total undergraduate aid awarded as scholarships/grants, 27% as loans/jobs.

Application procedures. Admission: Closing date 9/30. $25 fee. Application must be submitted on paper. **Financial aid:** Closing date 4/30.

Academics. Special study options: Distance learning, independent study, internships. **Credit/placement by examination:** AP, CLEP. 50 credit hours maximum toward associate degree, 50 toward bachelor's. **Support services:** Tutoring.

Majors. BACHELOR'S. Business: Accounting/business management, executive assistant. **Health services:** Nursing (RN). **ASSOCIATE. Business:** Accounting/business management. **Health services:** Medical secretary, nursing (RN), pharmacy assistant.

Computing on campus. 45 workstations in library, computer center. Online library, student web hosting, wireless network available.

Student life. Freshman orientation: Mandatory. Preregistration for classes offered. Four-hour session held before semester begins. **Activities:** Student newspaper.

Student services. Alcohol/substance abuse counseling, career counseling, financial aid counseling, personal counseling, placement for graduates.

Contact. E-mail: mbermudez@nuc.edu
Phone: (787) 840-4474 ext. 7001 Fax: (787) 841-1360
Mayra Bermudez Sanchez, Director of Admissions, National University College: Ponce, PO Box 801243, Coto Laurel, PR 00780-1243

National University College: Rio Grande
Rio Grande, Puerto Rico
www.nuc.edu

- For-profit 3-year career college
- Commuter campus in small town
- 1,474 degree-seeking undergraduates: 34% part-time, 70% women
- 94% of applicants admitted
- Interview required

General. Regionally accredited; also accredited by ACICS. Additional campuses in Bayamon, Arecibo, Ponce; learning center in Caguas. **Degrees:** 86 bachelor's, 122 associate awarded. **Calendar:** Trimester. **Full-time faculty:** 22 total; 68% women. **Part-time faculty:** 64 total; 72% women. **Class size:** 68% < 20, 32% 20-39, less than 1% 40-49.

Freshman class profile. 1,049 applied, 987 admitted, 781 enrolled.

End year in good standing: 96%   **Return as sophomores:**   51%

Basis for selection. College Entrance Examination Board test or institutional tests required for admissions.

High school preparation. 18 units required. Required units include English 3, mathematics 3, history 3, science 3, foreign language 3 and academic electives 3.

2011-2012 Annual costs. Books/supplies: $908. Personal expenses: $2,050.

2010-2011 Financial aid. All financial aid based on need. 94 full-time freshmen applied for aid; 94 were judged to have need; 94 of these received aid. Average scholarship/grant was $5,576; average loan $3,060. 86% of total undergraduate aid awarded as scholarships/grants, 14% as loans/jobs.

Application procedures. Admission: Priority date 8/15; deadline 3/21. $25 fee. Application must be submitted on paper. Admission notification by 8/9. Admission notification on a rolling basis. **Financial aid:** Priority date 12/31, closing date 4/30. FAFSA required. Must reply by 5/15 or within 2 week(s) of notification.

Academics. Special study options: Independent study, internships, weekend college. **Credit/placement by examination:** AP, CLEP, institutional tests. 50 credit hours maximum toward associate degree, 50 toward bachelor's. **Support services:** Tutoring.

Majors. BACHELOR'S. Business: Accounting/business management, executive assistant. **Computer sciences:** Networking. **Education:** Early childhood. **Health services:** Nursing (RN). **Protective services:** Law enforcement admin. **ASSOCIATE. Business:** Accounting/business management, entrepreneurial studies, office technology, tourism/travel. **Computer sciences:** Networking. **Health services:** Dental assistant, medical secretary, nursing (RN), pharmacy assistant. **Protective services:** Law enforcement admin.

Most popular majors. Business/marketing 9%, computer/information sciences 6%, education 12%, health sciences 66%, legal studies 7%.

Computing on campus. 129 workstations in library, computer center, student center. Online library, student web hosting, wireless network available.

Student life. Freshman orientation: Mandatory. Preregistration for classes offered. Three-hour sessions available. **Housing:** Wellness housing available. **Activities:** Dance, student newspaper, AMISADAI-Asociacion Cristiana de Estudiantes de National University College.

Athletics. Intramural: Basketball, cross-country, softball, table tennis, volleyball.

Student services. Alcohol/substance abuse counseling, career counseling, financial aid counseling, personal counseling, placement for graduates, women's services.

Contact. E-mail: rnavarro@nuc.edu
Phone: (800) 981-0812 Fax: (787) 888-8280
Suzette Rubio, Admissions Director, National University College: Rio Grande, PO Box 3064, Rio Grande, PR 00745

Pontifical Catholic University of Puerto Rico
Ponce, Puerto Rico   CB member
www.pucpr.edu   CB code: 0910

- Private 4-year university affiliated with Roman Catholic Church
- Commuter campus in small city
- 6,235 degree-seeking undergraduates: 7% part-time, 59% women, 99% Hispanic American, 1% international
- 2,435 degree-seeking graduate students
- 73% of applicants admitted
- SAT or ACT (ACT writing optional) required

General. Founded in 1948. Regionally accredited. Branch campuses in Arecibo and Mayaguez. **Degrees:** 647 bachelor's, 29 associate awarded; master's, professional, doctoral offered. **ROTC:** Army, Air Force. **Location:** 60 miles from San Juan. **Calendar:** Semester, limited summer session. **Full-time faculty:** 214 total; 41% have terminal degrees, 100% minority, 55% women. **Part-time faculty:** 236 total; 26% have terminal degrees, 100% minority, 44% women. **Class size:** 46% < 20, 43% 20-39, 9% 40-49, 1% 50-99.

Freshman class profile. 2,752 applied, 2,012 admitted, 1,416 enrolled.

GPA 3.75 or higher:	24%	Return as sophomores:	84%
GPA 3.50-3.74:	14%	Live on campus:	4%
GPA 3.0-3.49:	28%	Fraternities:	1%
GPA 2.0-2.99:	32%	Sororities:	1%

Basis for selection. School achievement record, test scores important. Admission index will be determined by GPA, math and verbal scores on aptitude test. SAT required of English-speaking applicants. Interview required for special program; essay or personal statement for some programs. **Home schooled:** Transcript of courses and grades, state high school equivalency certificate required. Home-schooled legal certification required.

High school preparation. College-preparatory program required. 15 units required. Required units include English 4, mathematics 3, history 2, science 2 and foreign language 4.

2011-2012 Annual costs. Tuition/fees: $5,618. Room only: $1,326. Books/supplies: $1,535. Personal expenses: $2,049.

Financial aid. Non-need-based: Scholarships awarded for academics, athletics.

Application procedures. Admission: Priority date 3/15; deadline 7/15 (receipt date). $15 fee, may be waived for applicants with need. Admission notification on a rolling basis beginning on or about 2/15. **Financial aid:** Closing date 5/15. FAFSA, institutional form required. Applicants notified by 6/15; must reply within 4 week(s) of notification.

Academics. Special study options: Accelerated study, combined bachelor's/graduate degree, double major, dual enrollment of high school students, ESL, exchange student, honors, independent study, internships, liberal arts/career combination, study abroad, teacher certification program. **Credit/placement by examination:** AP, CLEP, institutional tests. 30 credit hours maximum toward bachelor's degree. **Support services:** Learning center, preadmission summer program, reduced course load, remedial instruction, tutoring.

Majors. Architecture: Architecture. **Area/ethnic studies:** Chicano/Hispanic-American/Latino. **Biology:** General. **Business:** General, accounting, administrative services, business admin, communications, entrepreneurial studies, finance, human resources, international, management information systems, managerial economics, marketing, tourism/travel, transportation. **Communications:** Communications/speech/rhetoric. **Conservation:** General, environmental studies. **Education:** Art, biology, business, chemistry, early childhood, elementary, English, ESL, family/consumer sciences, history, mathematics, music, physical, science, secondary, social studies, Spanish, special ed. **English:** English lit. **Foreign languages:** Spanish. **Health services:** Cardiovascular technology, clinical lab science, nursing (RN), premedicine. **History:** General. **Human services:** General, social work. **Liberal arts:** Arts/sciences. **Math:** General. **Philosophy/religion:** Philosophy. **Physical sciences:** Chemistry, physics. **Psychology:** General. **Social sciences:** Criminology, political science, sociology. **Visual/performing arts:** Music, studio arts. **Work/family studies:** General.

Most popular majors. Business/marketing 17%, education 18%, health sciences 22%, liberal arts 7%, psychology 6%, public administration/social services 9%, social sciences 6%.

Computing on campus. 470 workstations in library, computer center, student center. Commuter students can connect to campus network. Online course registration, online library, wireless network available.

Student life. Freshman orientation: Mandatory. Preregistration for classes offered. **Housing:** Single-sex dorms available. $25 nonrefundable deposit. **Activities:** Choral groups, dance, drama, musical theater, radio station, student government, student newspaper, TV station, Pi Gamma Mu, Phi Alpha Theta, Beta Beta Beta, Alpha Beta Chi, Phi Delta Kappa, honor society for business students, Pioneer Students in Christ and Mary, Miles Jesu, Knights of Columbus, Phi Sigma Kappa.

Athletics. Intercollegiate: Basketball, cross-country, diving, judo, soccer, softball M, swimming, table tennis, tennis, track and field, volleyball, water polo M, wrestling M. **Intramural:** Archery, basketball, cross-country, diving, softball, swimming, table tennis, tennis, track and field, volleyball, wrestling M. **Team name:** Pioneers.

Student services. Chaplain/spiritual director, career counseling, student employment services, health services, on-campus daycare, personal counseling, placement for graduates, veterans' counselor.

Contact. E-mail: admisiones@pucpr.edu
Phone: (787) 841-2000 ext. 1000 Fax: (787) 651-2044
Ana Bonilla, Director of Admissions, Pontifical Catholic University of Puerto Rico, 2250 Las Americas Avenue, Suite 284, Ponce, PR 00717-9777

Theological University of the Caribbean
Saint Just, Puerto Rico
www.cbp.edu

- Private 4-year Bible and seminary college
- Small city

General. Accredited by ABHE. **Calendar:** Semester.

Contact. Phone: (787) 761-0808
Registrar, PO Box 901, Saint Just, PR 00978-0901

Turabo University
Gurabo, Puerto Rico
www.suagm.edu/ut   **CB code: 0780**

- Private 4-year university
- Commuter campus in small city
- 13,817 degree-seeking undergraduates: 23% part-time, 59% women, 100% Hispanic American
- 2,788 degree-seeking graduate students
- 46% of applicants admitted

General. Founded in 1972. Regionally accredited. 5 off-campus sites. **Degrees:** 1,264 bachelor's, 106 associate awarded; master's, professional, doctoral offered. **ROTC:** Army. **Location:** 17 miles from San Juan. **Calendar:** Semester, limited summer session. **Full-time faculty:** 194 total; 55% have terminal degrees, 48% women. **Part-time faculty:** 1,131 total; 20% have terminal degrees, 54% women. **Class size:** 50% < 20, 47% 20-39, 3% 40-49.

Freshman class profile. 9,581 applied, 4,406 admitted, 2,985 enrolled.

GPA 3.75 or higher:	10%	GPA 2.0-2.99:	47%
GPA 3.50-3.74:	11%	Return as sophomores:	74%
GPA 3.0-3.49:	26%		

Basis for selection. SAT required for admission to honors and science programs. Minimum 2.0 GPA required for program in business administration; for biology, 2.5; health, 2.5; education, 2.5; engineering, 2.5.

High school preparation. 15 units required. Required units include English 3, mathematics 3, social studies 2, science 2 and foreign language 3.

2011-2012 Annual costs. Tuition/fees: $5,064. Books/supplies: $1,600. Personal expenses: $3,481.

2010-2011 Financial aid. All financial aid based on need.

Application procedures. Admission: No deadline. $15 fee, may be waived for applicants with need. Admission notification on a rolling basis beginning on or about 3/1. **Financial aid:** Priority date 5/30; no closing date. FAFSA required. Applicants notified by 8/30.

Academics. Special study options: Accelerated study, distance learning, honors, independent study, internships, liberal arts/career combination, weekend college. **Credit/placement by examination:** AP, CLEP, institutional

tests. **Support services:** Remedial instruction, study skills assistance, tutoring.

Majors. Biology: General. **Business:** Accounting, business admin, management information systems, marketing, office management. **Communications:** Communications/speech/rhetoric. **Education:** Biology, chemistry, early childhood, elementary, English, history, mathematics, physical, science, social science, Spanish, special ed, trade/industrial. **Engineering:** Computer, electrical, mechanical. **Foreign languages:** Sign language interpretation. **Health services:** Dietetics, nursing (RN), speech pathology. **Human services:** General, social work. **Liberal arts:** Humanities. **Physical sciences:** Chemistry. **Psychology:** General, counseling. **Social sciences:** General, criminology, sociology. **Visual/performing arts:** Graphic design, industrial design, interior design.

Most popular majors. Business/marketing 40%, education 20%, health sciences 8%, social sciences 13%.

Computing on campus. Commuter students can connect to campus network. Online library, helpline available.

Student life. Freshman orientation: Available. Preregistration for classes offered. **Activities:** Choral groups, dance, drama, music ensembles, radio station, student government, student newspaper, TV station.

Athletics. NAIA. **Intercollegiate:** Baseball M, basketball, cross-country, judo, soccer M, softball, swimming, tennis, track and field, volleyball, weight lifting. **Intramural:** Basketball, softball, table tennis, tennis W, volleyball, weight lifting. **Team name:** Taínos.

Student services. Adult student services, alcohol/substance abuse counseling, career counseling, services for economically disadvantaged, student employment services, financial aid counseling, health services, personal counseling, placement for graduates, veterans' counselor. **Physically disabled:** Services for visually, speech, hearing impaired.

Contact. E-mail: admisiones_ut@suagm.edu
Phone: (787) 746-3009 Toll-free number: (800) 747-8362
Fax: (787) 743-7940
Virginia Gonzalez, Associate Director of Admissions and Financial Aid, Turabo University, PO Box 3030, Gurabo, PR 00778

Universidad Adventista de las Antillas
Mayaguez, Puerto Rico   **CB member**
www.uaa.edu   **CB code: 1020**

- Private 4-year university and liberal arts college affiliated with Seventh-day Adventists
- Commuter campus in small city
- 1,124 degree-seeking undergraduates
- 50 graduate students

General. Founded in 1957. Regionally accredited. **Degrees:** 111 bachelor's, 13 associate awarded; master's offered. **Location:** 100 miles from San Juan. **Calendar:** Semester, limited summer session. **Full-time faculty:** 42 total; 26% have terminal degrees, 45% women. **Part-time faculty:** 51 total; 31% have terminal degrees, 31% women.

Basis for selection. Open admission, but selective for some programs. SAT or ACT recommended for English-speaking applicants. Interview required for admission to nursing and theology programs. **Home schooled:** Transcript of courses and grades, interview, letter of recommendation (nonparent) required. Unless homeschool program is accredited, applicant must take GED. If necessary, especially in the case of nonresident students, state high school equivalency certificate will be requested.

High school preparation. 18 units recommended. Recommended units include English 3, mathematics 3, social studies 3, science 3 and academic electives 3. 3 Spanish units recommended.

2011-2012 Annual costs. Books/supplies: $1,000. Personal expenses: $550.

Application procedures. Admission: No deadline. $20 fee, may be waived for applicants with need. Admission notification on a rolling basis. **Financial aid:** No deadline. FAFSA, institutional form required. Applicants notified on a rolling basis starting 8/15; must reply within 3 week(s) of notification.

Academics. Federal programs known as TRIO SSS Regular and TRIO ESL, which provide assistance to students who are weak in Spanish, English, or mathematics. **Special study options:** Combined bachelor's/graduate degree, cooperative education, double major, ESL, internships, liberal arts/

career combination, teacher certification program. **Credit/placement by examination:** AP, CLEP, institutional tests. 12 credit hours maximum toward associate degree, 12 toward bachelor's. **Support services:** Learning center, reduced course load, remedial instruction, study skills assistance, tutoring.

Majors. Biology: General. **Business:** General, administrative services. **Computer sciences:** General, computer science, information systems. **Education:** Elementary, music, secondary. **Foreign languages:** Spanish. **Health services:** Respiratory therapy technology. **History:** General. **Physical sciences:** Chemistry. **Psychology:** General. **Theology:** Theology. **Visual/performing arts:** Music.

Most popular majors. Business/marketing 7%, education 6%, health sciences 21%, theological studies 6%.

Computing on campus. 62 workstations in dormitories, library, computer center. Commuter students can connect to campus network. Online course registration, online library, repair service available.

Student life. Freshman orientation: Mandatory. Preregistration for classes offered. 2-day program at beginning of each semester. Counselors available to help students with enrollment. **Policies:** Religious environment designed for Seventh-day Adventist students. Religious observance required. **Housing:** Guaranteed on-campus for freshmen. Single-sex dorms, apartments available. **Activities:** Concert band, choral groups, drama, international student organizations, music ensembles, student government, student newspaper, L.I.F.E., S.C.O.R., international club, ministerial club, office administration club.

Athletics. Intramural: Basketball, bowling, gymnastics, soccer, softball M, swimming, table tennis, tennis, track and field, volleyball. **Team name:** Eagles Gym Team.

Student services. Alcohol/substance abuse counseling, chaplain/spiritual director, career counseling, services for economically disadvantaged, student employment services, financial aid counseling, health services, personal counseling, veterans' counselor.

Contact. E-mail: admissions@uaa.edu
Phone: (787) 834-9595 ext. 2208 Fax: (787) 834-9597
Yolanda Ferrer, Director of Admissions, Universidad Adventista de las Antillas, PO Box 118, Mayaguez, PR 00681-0118

Universidad Central del Caribe
Bayamon, Puerto Rico
www.uccaribe.edu/   CB code: 1549

- Private 4-year university
- Small city
- 138 full-time, degree-seeking undergraduates

General. Regionally accredited. Many student interest groups focus on community service. **Degrees:** 17 bachelor's, 37 associate awarded; master's, professional, doctoral offered. **Calendar:** Continuous. **Full-time faculty:** 19 total. **Part-time faculty:** 1 total.

Basis for selection. GPA, school records, and recommendations most important.

2011-2012 Annual costs. Books/supplies: $600.

Application procedures. Admission: Closing date 4/1. $25 fee. No application fee.

Academics. Credit/placement by examination: AP, CLEP.

Majors. Health services: Radiologic technology/medical imaging.

Contact. E-mail: icordero@uccaribe.edu
Phone: (787) 740-1611 Fax: (787) 269-7550
Omar Perez, Dean for Student Affairs, Universidad Central del Caribe, Decanato de Admisiones y Asuntos Estudiantiles, Bayamon, PR 00960-6032

Universidad del Este
Carolina, Puerto Rico   CB member
www.suagm.edu/une   CB code: 0883

- Private 4-year university and liberal arts college
- Commuter campus in small city

- 12,666 degree-seeking undergraduates: 27% part-time, 63% women, 100% Hispanic American
- 1,109 degree-seeking graduate students

General. Founded in 1949. Regionally accredited. Accelerated undergraduate programs for adult students with work experience. **Degrees:** 924 bachelor's, 213 associate awarded; master's offered. **ROTC:** Army. **Location:** 5 miles from San Juan. **Calendar:** Semester, limited summer session. **Full-time faculty:** 106 total; 38% have terminal degrees, 100% minority, 59% women. **Part-time faculty:** 1,007 total; 12% have terminal degrees, 100% minority, 60% women. **Class size:** 49% < 20, 47% 20-39, 4% 40-49.

Freshman class profile. 8,743 applied, 3,852 admitted, 2,676 enrolled.

GPA 3.75 or higher:	7%	GPA 2.0-2.99:	52%
GPA 3.50-3.74:	9%	Return as sophomores:	74%
GPA 3.0-3.49:	23%		

Basis for selection. Open admission, but selective for some programs. Special requirements for health, hospitality, and science programs; interview recommended. SAT required for English-speaking freshman applicants. **Home schooled:** Statement describing home school structure and mission, letter of recommendation (nonparent) required.

2011-2012 Annual costs. Tuition/fees: $5,064. Books/supplies: $1,600.

2010-2011 Financial aid. All financial aid based on need. 92% of total undergraduate aid awarded as scholarships/grants, 8% as loans/jobs.

Application procedures. Admission: No deadline. $15 fee, may be waived for applicants with need. Admission notification on a rolling basis. **Financial aid:** Priority date 5/30; no closing date. FAFSA, institutional form required. Applicants notified by 7/30.

Academics. Special study options: Accelerated study, cross-registration, distance learning, double major, honors, independent study, internships, liberal arts/career combination, teacher certification program, weekend college. Accelerated program for working adults only. **Credit/placement by examination:** AP, CLEP. **Support services:** Learning center, reduced course load, remedial instruction, study skills assistance, tutoring.

Majors. Biology: General, biotechnology, microbiology. **Business:** Accounting, administrative services, business admin, event planning, hotel/motel admin, insurance, management information systems, marketing. **Communications:** Digital media. **Education:** Biology, early childhood, ESL, health, kindergarten/preschool, physical, science, special ed. **Health services:** Health care admin, medical radiologic technology/radiation therapy, nursing (RN), sonography. **Human services:** Social work. **Protective services:** Criminal justice. **Psychology:** General. **Work/family studies:** Facilities/event planning.

Most popular majors. Business/marketing 42%, education 8%, health sciences 10%, psychology 6%, public administration/social services 14%, security/protective services 15%.

Computing on campus. Commuter students can connect to campus network. Online library, helpline, wireless network available.

Student life. Freshman orientation: Available. Preregistration for classes offered. **Activities:** Choral groups, dance, drama, international student organizations, student government, student newspaper, Phi Theta Kappa, Future Secretaries of America, nursing club.

Athletics. Intercollegiate: Baseball M, basketball, cheerleading, cross-country, softball W, track and field, volleyball, weight lifting M. **Intramural:** Basketball, volleyball. **Team name:** Pitirre.

Student services. Adult student services, alcohol/substance abuse counseling, career counseling, services for economically disadvantaged, student employment services, financial aid counseling, health services, personal counseling, placement for graduates, veterans' counselor. **Physically disabled:** Services for visually, speech, hearing impaired.

Contact. E-mail: admisiones_une@suagm.edu
Phone: (787) 257-8080 Toll-free number: (800) 981-6570
Fax: (787) 257-8601 ext. 3307
Magda Ostolaza, Associate Vice Chancellor of Marketing and Recruitment, Universidad del Este, PO Box 2010, Carolina, PR 00984-2010

Universidad Metropolitana
Rio Piedras, Puerto Rico   CB member
www.suagm.edu/umet   CB code: 1519

- Private 4-year university and liberal arts college
- Commuter campus in large city

▶ 11,278 degree-seeking undergraduates: 100% Hispanic American

▶ 2,170 graduate students

▶ 44% of applicants admitted

General. Founded in 1985. Regionally accredited. **Degrees:** 1,118 bachelor's, 108 associate awarded; master's, professional, doctoral offered. **ROTC:** Army, Naval, Air Force. **Location:** 3 miles from San Juan. **Calendar:** Semester, limited summer session. **Full-time faculty:** 106 total; 40% have terminal degrees, 100% minority, 64% women. **Part-time faculty:** 882 total; 18% have terminal degrees, 57% women. **Class size:** 53% < 20, 43% 20-39, 3% 40-49, less than 1% 50-99, less than 1% >100.

Freshman class profile. 10,346 applied, 4,578 admitted, 2,591 enrolled.

GPA 3.75 or higher:	9%	GPA 2.0-2.99:	49%
GPA 3.50-3.74:	10%	Return as sophomores:	76%
GPA 3.0-3.49:	22%		

Basis for selection. School achievement record and test scores considered. SAT required of English-speaking applicants. Interview required for academically weak. **Home schooled:** State high school equivalency certificate required.

2011-2012 Annual costs. Tuition/fees: $5,064. Books/supplies: $1,600.

Financial aid. All financial aid based on need.

Application procedures. Admission: Closing date 8/15 (receipt date). $15 fee, may be waived for applicants with need. Admission notification on a rolling basis. **Financial aid:** Priority date 5/30; no closing date. FAFSA required. Applicants notified by 7/30.

Academics. Special study options: Accelerated study, combined bachelor's/graduate degree, distance learning, honors, independent study, internships, liberal arts/career combination, teacher certification program, Washington semester, weekend college. Off-campus full-degree sites. **Credit/placement by examination:** AP, CLEP. **Support services:** Learning center, preadmission summer program, remedial instruction, tutoring.

Majors. Biology: General, molecular. **Business:** Accounting, banking/financial services, business admin, management information systems, managerial economics, marketing, office management, sales/distribution. **Communications:** General, digital media, media studies, public relations. **Computer sciences:** Computer science. **Conservation:** Enforcement, environmental science. **Education:** Early childhood, elementary, elementary special ed, kindergarten/preschool, multi-level teacher, physical, secondary, special ed. **Health services:** Cardiovascular technology, environmental health, nursing (RN), respiratory therapy technology, speech pathology. **Human services:** Social work. **Math:** Applied. **Physical sciences:** General, chemistry. **Protective services:** Criminal justice. **Psychology:** General.

Most popular majors. Business/marketing 41%, education 20%, health sciences 14%, public administration/social services 9%, security/protective services 11%.

Computing on campus. Commuter students can connect to campus network. Online library, helpline, repair service, wireless network available.

Student life. Freshman orientation: Mandatory. Preregistration for classes offered. Held 4 weeks before the beginning of the academic year. **Activities:** Choral groups, dance, drama, radio station, student government, student newspaper, TV station, business students association, social work students association, communication students association.

Athletics. Intercollegiate: Baseball M, basketball, cheerleading, cross-country, judo, soccer, softball W, table tennis, tennis, track and field, volleyball, weight lifting. **Intramural:** Basketball, cross-country, table tennis, volleyball. **Team name:** Cocodrilo.

Student services. Adult student services, alcohol/substance abuse counseling, career counseling, services for economically disadvantaged, student employment services, financial aid counseling, health services, on-campus daycare, personal counseling, placement for graduates, veterans' counselor, women's services. **Physically disabled:** Services for visually, hearing impaired.

Contact. E-mail: admisiones-umet@suagm.edu
Phone: (787) 766-1717 ext. 6657 Toll-free number: (787) 747-8362
Fax: (787) 751-0992
Yadira Rivera Lugo, Director of Admission, Universidad Metropolitana, Apartado 21150, San Juan, PR 00928

Universidad Pentecostal Mizpa
San Juan, Puerto Rico
www.colmizpa.edu

▶ Private 4-year university and Bible college affiliated with Pentecostal Holiness Church

▶ Commuter campus in very large city

▶ 339 degree-seeking undergraduates: 65% part-time, 40% women, 100% Hispanic American

▶ 97% of applicants admitted

▶ Interview required

General. Accredited by ABHE. **Degrees:** 8 bachelor's, 19 associate awarded; master's offered. **Calendar:** Continuous, limited summer session. **Full-time faculty:** 5 total; 20% women. **Part-time faculty:** 26 total; 19% have terminal degrees, 50% women. **Class size:** 89% < 20, 11% 20-39.

Freshman class profile. 116 applied, 112 admitted, 109 enrolled.

Basis for selection. Religious affiliation very important; rigor of secondary school record considered. **Home schooled:** State high school equivalency certificate, interview, letter of recommendation (nonparent) required. **Learning Disabled:** Certified information concerning disability must be provided by student.

2012-2013 Annual costs. Tuition/fees (projected): $3,400. Room only: $1,280. Books/supplies: $500. Personal expenses: $3,440.

2011-2012 Financial aid. All financial aid based on need. 9 full-time freshmen applied for aid; 9 were judged to have need; 9 of these received aid. 95% of total undergraduate aid awarded as scholarships/grants, 5% as loans/jobs.

Application procedures. Admission: No deadline. $45 fee ($45 out-of-state). Application must be submitted on paper. **Financial aid:** No deadline. FAFSA required.

Academics. Special study options: External degree, weekend college. **Credit/placement by examination:** AP, CLEP, institutional tests. **Support services:** Learning center, writing center.

Majors. Theology: Bible, pastoral counseling, religious ed.

Computing on campus. Dormitories linked to campus network. Online library, wireless network available.

Student life. Freshman orientation: Mandatory. Preregistration for classes offered. **Policies:** Religious observance required. **Housing:** Single-sex dorms, wellness housing available. $150 fully refundable deposit. **Activities:** Campus ministries, radio station, student government, student newspaper, TV station.

Athletics. Intramural: Basketball M, softball, table tennis.

Student services. Adult student services, chaplain/spiritual director, career counseling, services for economically disadvantaged, student employment services, financial aid counseling, personal counseling.

Contact. E-mail: decanatoestudiante@colmizpa.edu
Phone: (787) 720-4476 Fax: (787) 720-2012
Jorge Burgos, Admissions Director and Dean of Students, Universidad Pentecostal Mizpa, PO Box 20966, San Juan, PR 00928-0966

Universidad Politecnica de Puerto Rico
Hato Rey, Puerto Rico   CB member
www.pupr.edu   CB code: 0614

▶ Private 5-year university and engineering college

▶ Commuter campus in large city

▶ 3,800 degree-seeking undergraduates: 53% part-time, 23% women

▶ 729 degree-seeking graduate students

▶ 95% of applicants admitted

General. Founded in 1966. Regionally accredited. **Degrees:** 510 bachelor's awarded; master's offered. **ROTC:** Army, Air Force. **Location:** 3 miles from San Juan. **Calendar:** Trimester, extensive summer session. **Full-time faculty:** 161 total; 30% have terminal degrees, 6% minority, 35% women. **Part-time faculty:** 104 total; 24% have terminal degrees, 25% women. **Class size:** 21% < 20, 78% 20-39, less than 1% 40-49, less than 1% 50-99.

Freshman class profile. 737 applied, 697 admitted, 505 enrolled.

GPA 3.75 or higher:	17%	GPA 2.0-2.99:	35%
GPA 3.50-3.74:	16%	Return as sophomores:	72%
GPA 3.0-3.49:	31%		

Basis for selection. Flexible admissions policy that provides an opportunity to high school graduates or individuals who have passed a state high school equivalency examination to enroll in university credit courses and programs. SAT in English or Spanish required. **Home schooled:** Transcript of courses and grades, state high school equivalency certificate, letter of recommendation (nonparent) required. College Board scores required.

High school preparation. College-preparatory program required. 15 units required. Required units include English 3, mathematics 3, social studies 3, science 3, foreign language 3 and academic electives 3.

2011-2012 Annual costs. Academic year consists of three consecutive terms (from August to July). Undergraduate per-credit-hour charge (tuition only), $185; required fees per term, $225. Books/supplies: $2,312. Personal expenses: $5,696.

Financial aid. **Non-need-based:** Scholarships awarded for academics, music/drama.

Application procedures. **Admission:** No deadline. $30 fee. Application must be submitted on paper. Admission notification on a rolling basis. **Financial aid:** Priority date 5/15, closing date 6/30. FAFSA required. Applicants notified by 7/15.

Academics. **Special study options:** Cooperative education, distance learning, exchange student, honors, internships. PEES (Programa Especial de Escuela Superior). **Credit/placement by examination:** AP, CLEP, institutional tests. **Support services:** Learning center, pre-admission summer program, remedial instruction, tutoring.

Majors. **Architecture:** Architecture. **Business:** General, business admin. **Computer sciences:** Computer science. **Engineering:** Chemical, civil, computer, electrical, industrial, mechanical.

Most popular majors. Architecture 10%, business/marketing 10%, engineering/engineering technologies 75%.

Computing on campus. 550 workstations in library, computer center. Online course registration, online library, helpline, wireless network available.

Student life. **Freshman orientation:** Available. Preregistration for classes offered. Week-long orientation offered each trimester. **Activities:** Choral groups, international student organizations, student government, University Bible Association, drugs and alcohol committee, student association.

Athletics. **Intercollegiate:** Basketball, bowling, cross-country, judo, soccer M, table tennis, tennis, track and field, volleyball, wrestling M. **Intramural:** Basketball, bowling, cross-country W, judo, table tennis, tennis, track and field, volleyball. **Team name:** Beavers.

Student services. Alcohol/substance abuse counseling, career counseling, student employment services, financial aid counseling, health services, personal counseling, placement for graduates, veterans' counselor. **Physically disabled:** Services for hearing impaired.

Contact. E-mail: admissions@pupr.edu
Phone: (787) 622-8000 ext. 310 Fax: (787) 764-8712
Teresa Cardona, Director of Admissions, Universidad Politecnica de Puerto Rico, PO Box 192017, San Juan, PR 00919-2017

University College of San Juan
San Juan, Puerto Rico   **CB member**
www.cunisanjuan.edu   **CB code: 0391**

▸ Public 4-year university and community college
▸ Commuter campus in large city
▸ 1,608 degree-seeking undergraduates: 16% part-time, 54% women, 100% Hispanic American

General. Founded in 1972. Regionally accredited. **Degrees:** 90 bachelor's, 178 associate awarded. **Calendar:** Semester, limited summer session. **Full-time faculty:** 31 total; 16% have terminal degrees, 100% minority, 68% women. **Part-time faculty:** 86 total; 100% minority. **Special facilities:** Language laboratory, learning resource center, amphitheater.

Basis for selection. Combined College Board PAA test scores of 2000 and 2.0 GPA required for regular students. Special consideration and priority to applicants from low-income families. SAT/ACT accepted from US applicants. Interview required for nursing program.

High school preparation. College-preparatory program required. 16 units required. Required units include English 3, mathematics 2, social studies 2, history 2, science 1 and academic electives 2. 3 Spanish courses required.

2011-2012 Annual costs. Tuition/fees: $3,150; $3,150 out-of-state. Books/supplies: $1,200. Personal expenses: $920.

2010-2011 Financial aid. All financial aid based on need. 98% of total undergraduate aid awarded as scholarships/grants, 2% as loans/jobs.

Application procedures. **Admission:** Closing date 5/1. $15 fee. Application must be submitted on paper. Admission notification by 6/1. Admission after July 31 on space-available basis. **Financial aid:** Closing date 9/30. FAFSA, institutional form required. Applicants notified by 10/30.

Academics. **Special study options:** Cooperative education, double major, exchange student, honors, independent study, study abroad, weekend college. **Credit/placement by examination:** AP, CLEP. 9 credit hours maximum toward associate degree, 4 toward bachelor's. **Support services:** Reduced course load, remedial instruction, tutoring.

Majors. **Business:** Accounting. **Computer sciences:** General. **Health services:** Nursing (RN). **Protective services:** Police science.

Most popular majors. Business/marketing 11%, computer/information sciences 6%, health sciences 45%, security/protective services 29%.

Computing on campus. 281 workstations in library, computer center. Commuter students can connect to campus network. Online library, wireless network available.

Student life. **Freshman orientation:** Mandatory. Preregistration for classes offered. One-day program in summer that offers opportunity to meet faculty and staff. **Activities:** Choral groups, dance, drama, student government.

Athletics. **Intercollegiate:** Basketball M, cross-country, softball, table tennis, tennis, track and field, volleyball, weight lifting. **Intramural:** Basketball, bowling, cross-country, handball, racquetball, softball M, table tennis, tennis, track and field, volleyball. **Team name:** Falcons.

Student services. Career counseling, services for economically disadvantaged, student employment services, financial aid counseling, health services, minority student services, personal counseling, placement for graduates, veterans' counselor. **Physically disabled:** Services for visually, speech, hearing impaired.

Contact. E-mail: admisiones@cts.sanjuancapital.com
Phone: (787) 250-7375 Fax: (787) 274-1388
Victor Rivera, Enrollment Management Director, University College of San Juan, 180 Jose R. Oliver Avenue, San Juan, PR 00918

University of Phoenix: Puerto Rico
Guaynabo, Puerto Rico
www.phoenix.edu

▸ For-profit 4-year university
▸ Small city
▸ 897 degree-seeking undergraduates

General. Regionally accredited. **Degrees:** 181 bachelor's awarded; master's offered. **Calendar:** Differs by program. **Full-time faculty:** 26 total. **Part-time faculty:** 282 total.

Basis for selection. Open admission, but selective for some programs.

2011-2012 Annual costs. Estimated costs as of August 2011: per-credit-hour charge, $245, depending upon level and course of study; electronic course materials fee, $95, if applicable. Book and material charges may vary by course and program. All fees are subject to change.

Application procedures. **Admission:** No deadline. No application fee. **Financial aid:** No deadline.

Academics. **Credit/placement by examination:** AP, CLEP.

Majors. **Business:** Business admin, marketing. **Protective services:** Law enforcement admin.

Contact. Marc Booker, Director of Admission and Evaluation, University of Phoenix: Puerto Rico, B7 Calle Tabonuco, Guaynabo, PR 00968-3003

University of Puerto Rico: Aguadilla
Aguadilla, Puerto Rico
www.uprag.edu   CB code: 0983

- Public 4-year liberal arts and technical college
- Commuter campus in small city
- 2,754 degree-seeking undergraduates: 6% part-time, 60% women, 96% Hispanic American
- 54% of applicants admitted
- 33% graduate within 6 years

General. Founded in 1972. Regionally accredited. **Degrees:** 273 bachelor's, 11 associate awarded. **ROTC:** Army. **Location:** 81 miles from San Juan. **Calendar:** Semester, limited summer session. **Full-time faculty:** 115 total; 25% have terminal degrees, 99% minority, 56% women. **Part-time faculty:** 37 total; 19% have terminal degrees, 100% minority, 46% women. **Class size:** 18% < 20, 82% 20-39.

Freshman class profile. 1,400 applied, 762 admitted, 684 enrolled.

Mid 50% test scores		End year in good standing:	81%
SAT critical reading:	450-560	Return as sophomores:	77%
SAT math:	470-520		

Basis for selection. Admissions based on secondary school record and standardized test scores. Talent and ability considered. SAT and SAT Subject Tests in Spanish and math level I required of English-speaking applicants. **Home schooled:** Copy of curriculum required.

High school preparation. Recommended units include English 3, mathematics 2 and social studies 2. 3 Spanish recommended.

2011-2012 Annual costs. Tuition/fees: $2,534. Nonresidents who are U.S. citizens will be charged amount that will be equal to the rate for nonresidents at a state university in their home state. In second year of residency in Puerto Rico, such students will be charged in-state rate. Books/supplies: $1,825. Personal expenses: $1,200.

Financial aid. All financial aid based on need.

Application procedures. **Admission:** Priority date 11/17; deadline 1/30 (receipt date). $20 fee, may be waived for applicants with need. Application must be submitted on paper. Admission notification by 4/2. Admission notification on a rolling basis. Must reply by 4/30. **Financial aid:** Closing date 5/6. FAFSA, institutional form required. Applicants notified on a rolling basis starting 4/1; must reply within 1 week(s) of notification.

Academics. **Special study options:** Combined bachelor's/graduate degree, honors, liberal arts/career combination, teacher certification program. **Credit/placement by examination:** AP, CLEP, institutional tests. **Support services:** Learning center, remedial instruction, tutoring.

Majors. **Biology:** General. **Business:** General, accounting, executive assistant, finance, hotel/motel admin, human resources, management information systems, marketing. **Communications technology:** Radio/TV. **Education:** Elementary, English.

Most popular majors. Biology 24%, business/marketing 43%, education 26%, engineering/engineering technologies 7%.

Computing on campus. 547 workstations in library, computer center, student center. Online library, student web hosting, wireless network available.

Student life. **Freshman orientation:** Available. Preregistration for classes offered. **Housing:** Family community housing and private guest house available. **Activities:** Concert band, choral groups, drama, student government, Organizacion Juventud en Cristo, Estudiantes Orientadores, Teatro Experimental 80, Bio-Study, Kayukembo Association, Companeros Alertas Ante Un Mundo Buscando Alternativas, alcohol and drug prevention organization, Centro de Reciclaje y Orientación Ambiental.

Athletics. **Intercollegiate:** Baseball M, basketball, cross-country, softball W, table tennis, tennis, track and field, volleyball, weight lifting. **Intramural:** Baseball M, basketball, cross-country, softball W, table tennis, tennis, track and field, volleyball, weight lifting. **Team name:** Tiburones.

Student services. Alcohol/substance abuse counseling, career counseling, student employment services, financial aid counseling, health services, personal counseling, placement for graduates. **Physically disabled:** Services for visually impaired.

Contact. E-mail: meserrano@uprag.edu
Phone: (787) 890-2681 ext. 280
Melba Serrano, Admissions Officer, University of Puerto Rico: Aguadilla, Box 6150, Aguadilla, PR 00604-6150

University of Puerto Rico: Arecibo
Arecibo, Puerto Rico
www.upra.edu   CB code: 0911

- Public 4-year university
- Commuter campus in small city
- 3,488 degree-seeking undergraduates: 5% part-time, 63% women
- 84% of applicants admitted

General. Founded in 1967. Regionally accredited. **Degrees:** 462 bachelor's awarded. **ROTC:** Army. **Location:** 48 miles from San Juan. **Calendar:** Semester, limited summer session. **Full-time faculty:** 202 total; 35% have terminal degrees, 53% women. **Part-time faculty:** 60 total; 10% have terminal degrees, 75% women. **Class size:** 25% < 20, 75% 20-39.

Freshman class profile. 947 applied, 795 admitted, 672 enrolled.

Basis for selection. Admissions considered according to admission index (defined and published for each academic program) based equally on high school GPA and SAT scores. Applicants must take Academic Aptitude Test and Achievement Test offered by the College Entrance Examination Board (CEEB). Interviews sometimes required. **Home schooled:** State high school equivalency certificate required.

2011-2012 Annual costs. Tuition/fees: $2,534. Nonresidents who are U.S. citizens will be charged amount that will be equal to the rate for nonresidents at a state university in their home state. In second year of residency in Puerto Rico, such students will be charged in-state rate. Books/supplies: $1,825. Personal expenses: $1,000.

Financial aid. All financial aid based on need.

Application procedures. **Admission:** Closing date 1/31. $20 fee. Admission notification by 4/15. **Financial aid:** Closing date 4/27. FAFSA, institutional form required.

Academics. **Special study options:** ESL, exchange student, honors, internships, liberal arts/career combination, study abroad, Washington semester. Evening college, continuing education program, and professional improvement program. **Credit/placement by examination:** AP, CLEP, IB. **Support services:** Learning center, pre-admission summer program, remedial instruction, study skills assistance, tutoring, writing center.

Majors. **Biology:** Bacteriology. **Business:** Accounting, administrative services, business admin, finance, marketing. **Communications:** Radio/TV. **Communications technology:** Radio/TV. **Computer sciences:** Computer science. **Education:** Elementary, physical. **Health services:** Nursing (RN). **Psychology:** Industrial.

Most popular majors. Business/marketing 27%, communications/journalism 15%, education 7%, health sciences 23%, psychology 20%.

Computing on campus. 269 workstations in library, computer center. Commuter students can connect to campus network. Online library, student web hosting, wireless network available.

Student life. **Freshman orientation:** Mandatory. Preregistration for classes offered. Four-day program held (mornings) in summer. **Activities:** Concert band, choral groups, dance, drama, film society, music ensembles, student government, student newspaper, Cheerleaders UPRA, Rhythm Busters, Federacion de Estudiantes de Iberoamericana, Asociación de Estudiantes Coro de Concierto, Asociación Nacional de Estudiantes de Educación, writers club, Capítulo de Estudiantes de Microbiología, Asociación Intercesores Cristiana, ACTRE.

Athletics. **Intercollegiate:** Baseball M, basketball, cross-country, judo, softball W, track and field, volleyball, weight lifting, wrestling M. **Intramural:** Basketball, softball W, volleyball. **Team name:** Los Lobos (Wolves).

Student services. Alcohol/substance abuse counseling, career counseling, services for economically disadvantaged, student employment services, financial aid counseling, health services, personal counseling, placement for graduates, women's services. **Physically disabled:** Services for visually, hearing impaired.

Contact. E-mail: mmendez@upra.edu
Phone: (787) 815-0000 ext. 4110 Fax: (787) 817-3461
Magaly Mendez, Admissions Officer, University of Puerto Rico: Arecibo,
PO Box 4010, Arecibo, PR 00614-4010

University of Puerto Rico: Bayamon University College
Bayamon, Puerto Rico
www.uprb.edu   CB code: 0852

▶ Public 4-year university and technical college
▶ Commuter campus in small city
▶ 4,948 degree-seeking undergraduates: 13% part-time, 52% women, 100% Hispanic American
▶ 30% of applicants admitted
▶ 35% graduate within 6 years

General. Founded in 1971. Regionally accredited. **Degrees:** 435 bachelor's, 44 associate awarded. **ROTC:** Army. **Location:** 9 miles from San Juan. **Calendar:** Semester, limited summer session. **Full-time faculty:** 166 total; 40% have terminal degrees, 100% minority, 51% women. **Part-time faculty:** 80 total; 22% have terminal degrees, 100% minority, 61% women. **Special facilities:** Multimedia laboratory.

Freshman class profile. 4,400 applied, 1,305 admitted, 1,145 enrolled.

End year in good standing:	71%	Out-of-state:	1%
Return as sophomores:	88%		

Basis for selection. High school GPA and test scores most important. Higher scores required of applicants to bachelor's programs. Special consideration given to applicants with special talents or handicaps. SAT and 2 SAT Subject Tests (Spanish, mathematics) accepted for English-speaking applicants from U.S. mainland. PAA required of Spanish-speaking applicants.

High school preparation. 12 units required. Required and recommended units include English 2, mathematics 2, social studies 1-2 and science 1. 3 units Spanish also required.

2011-2012 Annual costs. Tuition/fees: $2,534. Nonresidents who are U.S. citizens will be charged amount that will be equal to the rate for nonresidents at a state university in their home state. In second year of residency in Puerto Rico, such students will be charged in-state rate. Books/supplies: $1,825. Personal expenses: $1,200.

Financial aid. All financial aid based on need.

Application procedures. Admission: Priority date 12/10; deadline 1/31 (receipt date). $15 fee. Application must be submitted on paper. Admission notification on a rolling basis beginning on or about 4/25. Must reply by 5/30. **Financial aid:** Closing date 6/15. Institutional form required. Applicants notified by 7/12; must reply within 4 week(s) of notification.

Academics. Special study options: Cooperative education, cross-registration, double major, ESL, exchange student, honors, internships. **Credit/placement by examination:** AP, CLEP. **Support services:** Pre-admission summer program, reduced course load, study skills assistance, tutoring.

Majors. Biology: General. **Business:** Accounting, business admin, executive assistant, finance, logistics, marketing. **Computer sciences:** General. **Education:** Multi-level teacher, physically handicapped.

Most popular majors. Biology 12%, business/marketing 49%, education 31%.

Computing on campus. 370 workstations in computer center. Commuter students can connect to campus network. Wireless network available.

Student life. Freshman orientation: Available. Preregistration for classes offered. **Activities:** Bands, choral groups, drama, student government, student newspaper, Confraternidad de Cristianos Unidos, Asociacion Juventud Catolica, Society for Human Resource Management, Asociacion de Estudiantes Orientadores, American Marketing Association, Asociacion de Estudiantes de Computadoras, Asociacion de Gerencia de Materiales.

Athletics. NCAA. **Intercollegiate:** Baseball M, basketball, cheerleading, cross-country, swimming, table tennis, tennis, track and field, volleyball, weight lifting, wrestling M. **Intramural:** Table tennis, tennis, volleyball. **Team name:** Vaqueros.

Student services. Adult student services, career counseling, student employment services, health services, personal counseling, placement for graduates.

Contact. E-mail: cmontes@uprb.edu
Phone: (787) 993-8952 Fax: (787) 993-8929
Carmen Montes, Director of Admissions, University of Puerto Rico: Bayamon University College, 174 Street #170 Minillas Industrial Park, Bayamon, PR 00959-1919

University of Puerto Rico: Carolina Regional College
Carolina, Puerto Rico
www.uprc.edu   CB code: 3891

▶ Public 4-year university
▶ Commuter campus in small city
▶ 3,444 degree-seeking undergraduates: 19% part-time, 62% women, 88% Hispanic American
▶ 93% of applicants admitted
▶ 41% graduate within 6 years

General. Founded in 1974. Regionally accredited. **Degrees:** 490 bachelor's, 126 associate awarded. **Location:** 10 miles from San Juan. **Calendar:** Quarter, limited summer session. **Full-time faculty:** 20 total; 10% have terminal degrees, 50% women. **Part-time faculty:** 83 total; 14% have terminal degrees, 51% women.

Freshman class profile. 1,024 applied, 948 admitted, 736 enrolled.

Mid 50% test scores		GPA 3.50-3.74:	2%
SAT critical reading:	470-570	GPA 3.0-3.49:	19%
SAT math:	460-610	GPA 2.0-2.99:	75%
GPA 3.75 or higher:	4%	End year in good standing:	84%

Basis for selection. High school GPA and test scores important. SAT and SAT Subject Tests in Spanish, Math Level 1 required of English-speaking applicants. Interview recommended for those with exceptional ability; portfolio recommended for art. **Home schooled:** Transcript of courses and grades, state high school equivalency certificate required. SAT or CEEB required.

High school preparation. 15 units required; 17 recommended. Required and recommended units include English 3, mathematics 3, social studies 3, history 2, science 2, foreign language 3 and academic electives 1.

2011-2012 Annual costs. Tuition/fees: $3,401. Nonresidents who are U.S. citizens will be charged amount that will be equal to the rate for nonresidents at a state university in their home state. In second year of residency in Puerto Rico, such students will be charged in-state rate. Books/supplies: $2,735. Personal expenses: $1,200.

Financial aid. All financial aid based on need.

Application procedures. Admission: Closing date 1/31 (postmark date). $20 fee ($20 out-of-state). Must reply by 6/12. **Financial aid:** Closing date 5/15. FAFSA, institutional form required. Applicants notified by 6/30; Applicants notified on a rolling basis starting 6/10.

Academics. Special study options: Double major, exchange student, honors, independent study, internships, liberal arts/career combination, study abroad. **Credit/placement by examination:** AP, CLEP, SAT. 12 credit hours maximum toward associate degree, 12 toward bachelor's. **Support services:** Learning center, pre-admission summer program, remedial instruction, study skills assistance, tutoring, writing center.

Majors. Business: Administrative services, business admin, finance, hotel/motel admin, tourism promotion. **Communications:** Advertising. **Communications technology:** Graphic/printing. **Protective services:** Forensics, law enforcement admin.

Most popular majors. Business/marketing 48%, communications/journalism 12%, communication technologies 12%, security/protective services 25%.

Computing on campus. 163 workstations in library, computer center. Online course registration, online library, wireless network available.

Student life. Freshman orientation: Mandatory. Preregistration for classes offered. **Activities:** Concert band, choral groups, dance, drama, international student organizations, student government, consejo de estudiantes, cruz roja capitulo PR-UPRCA, asociacion estudiantil de coro, capitulo estudiantil ambiente marino, asociacion estudiantil de banda, juventud universitaria progresista, circulo teatral universitario, estudiantes de sistemas de oficina,

universitarios cristianos en accion, ASL (American sign language) jaguares.

Athletics. Intercollegiate: Baseball M, basketball, cheerleading, cross-country, soccer M, softball W, tennis, track and field, volleyball, weight lifting. **Intramural:** Basketball M. **Team name:** Jaguar.

Student services. Alcohol/substance abuse counseling, career counseling, services for economically disadvantaged, student employment services, financial aid counseling, health services, on-campus daycare, personal counseling, veterans' counselor. **Physically disabled:** Services for visually impaired.

Contact. Phone: (787) 757-1485 Fax: (787) 750-7940
Celia Méndez, Director of Admissions, University of Puerto Rico: Carolina Regional College, PO Box 4800, Carolina, PR 00984-4800

University of Puerto Rico: Cayey University College

Cayey, Puerto Rico
www.cayey.upr.edu   **CB code: 0981**

▶ Public 4-year university and liberal arts college
▶ Commuter campus in large town
▶ 3,528 degree-seeking undergraduates: 7% part-time, 69% women, 100% Hispanic American
▶ 86% of applicants admitted
▶ 43% graduate within 6 years

General. Founded in 1967. Regionally accredited. Located on former military base. **Degrees:** 434 bachelor's awarded. **ROTC:** Army. **Location:** 30 miles from San Juan. **Calendar:** Semester, limited summer session. **Full-time faculty:** 101 total; 38% have terminal degrees, 100% minority, 48% women. **Part-time faculty:** 16 total; 44% have terminal degrees, 100% minority, 50% women. **Class size:** 31% < 20, 68% 20-39, less than 1% 40-49. **Special facilities:** Pio Lopez museum, Las Sombras eco-park, ecological learning center, interdisciplinary research center, womens violence prevention center.

Freshman class profile. 954 applied, 818 admitted, 752 enrolled.

Mid 50% test scores			
SAT critical reading:	510-570	GPA 3.0-3.49:	21%
SAT math:	500-570	GPA 2.0-2.99:	3%
GPA 3.75 or higher:	50%	End year in good standing:	93%
GPA 3.50-3.74:	24%	Return as sophomores:	85%

Basis for selection. School achievement record, College Board's verbal and mathematics test scores most important. SAT required for English-speaking applicants. Students from Puerto Rico must submit their CEEB test scores for math and verbal aptitude. SAT critical reading will be used to evaluate verbal aptitude. Audition, portfolio required for admission of candidates based on special talents such as sports; interview recommended for music, theater programs. **Home schooled:** Transcript of courses and grades, state high school equivalency certificate required.

High school preparation. College-preparatory program required. 18 units required. Required units include English 3, mathematics 3, social studies 3, history 3, science 2 and academic electives 3. 3 units of Spanish required.

2011-2012 Annual costs. Tuition/fees: $2,534. Nonresidents who are U.S. citizens will be charged amount that will be equal to the rate for nonresidents at a state university in their home state. In second year of residency in Puerto Rico, such students will be charged in-state rate. Books/supplies: $2,735. Personal expenses: $1,200.

2011-2012 Financial aid. All financial aid based on need.

Application procedures. Admission: Closing date 1/31 (postmark date). $20 fee. Admission notification by 4/4. Must reply by 5/4. **Financial aid:** Closing date 6/30. FAFSA required. Applicants notified by 7/30.

Academics. Special study options: Accelerated study, combined bachelor's/graduate degree, double major, ESL, exchange student, honors, liberal arts/career combination, study abroad, teacher certification program. **Credit/placement by examination:** AP, CLEP, institutional tests. 72 credit hours maximum toward associate degree, 135 toward bachelor's. **Support services:** Learning center, pre-admission summer program, remedial instruction, tutoring, writing center.

Majors. Biology: General. **Business:** General, accounting, administrative services, business admin, office/clerical. **Education:** English, history, mathematics, physical, science, social science, social studies, Spanish, special ed. **English:** English lit. **Foreign languages:** Spanish. **History:** General. **Liberal arts:** Humanities. **Math:** General. **Physical sciences:** Chemistry. **Psychology:** General. **Social sciences:** General, economics, sociology.

Most popular majors. Biology 12%, business/marketing 25%, education 23%, interdisciplinary studies 12%, psychology 14%.

Computing on campus. 1,100 workstations in library, computer center. Online course registration, wireless network available.

Student life. Freshman orientation: Mandatory. Preregistration for classes offered. **Housing:** Housing available for some athletes and exchange students. **Activities:** Bands, choral groups, dance, drama, literary magazine, radio station, student government, student newspaper, Asociación de Estudiantes del Programa de Estudios de Honor, Asociación de Estudiantes de Psicología, Psy-Chi, Círculo de Historia, English Club, Círculo de Química, American Medical Student Association, GAIA, Círculo de Matemática, Asociación de Estudiantes de Contabilidad, Club de Leones UPR de Cayey.

Athletics. Intercollegiate: Baseball M, basketball, cross-country, soccer, softball W, swimming M, table tennis, tennis, volleyball, weight lifting, wrestling. **Intramural:** Baseball M, basketball, cross-country, soccer, softball W, swimming M, table tennis, tennis, volleyball, weight lifting, wrestling. **Team name:** Toritos.

Student services. Alcohol/substance abuse counseling, career counseling, services for economically disadvantaged, student employment services, financial aid counseling, health services, on-campus daycare, personal counseling, placement for graduates, veterans' counselor, women's services. **Physically disabled:** Services for visually impaired.

Contact. E-mail: admisiones@cayey.upr.edu
Phone: (787) 738-2161 ext. 2233 Fax: (787) 738-5633
Jesus Martinez, Director of Admissions, University of Puerto Rico: Cayey University College, Oficina de Admisiones UPR- Cayey, Cayey, PR 00737-2230

University of Puerto Rico: Humacao

Humacao, Puerto Rico   **CB member**
www.uprh.edu   **CB code: 0874**

▶ Public 4-year university and liberal arts college
▶ Commuter campus in small city
▶ 3,669 degree-seeking undergraduates: 6% part-time, 66% women, 88% Hispanic American
▶ 40% of applicants admitted
▶ 39% graduate within 6 years

General. Founded in 1962. Regionally accredited. **Degrees:** 490 bachelor's, 110 associate awarded. **Location:** 30 miles from San Juan. **Calendar:** Semester, limited summer session. **Full-time faculty:** 219 total; 54% have terminal degrees, 68% minority, 53% women. **Part-time faculty:** 38 total; 24% have terminal degrees, 45% minority, 47% women. **Special facilities:** Observatory, census data center, communication competencies center, Casa Roig Museum.

Freshman class profile. 1,913 applied, 766 admitted, 656 enrolled.

Mid 50% test scores			
SAT critical reading:	500-600	GPA 3.50-3.74:	26%
SAT math:	490-610	GPA 3.0-3.49:	20%
GPA 3.75 or higher:	52%	GPA 2.0-2.99:	2%
		Out-of-state:	1%

Basis for selection. High school achievement record, test scores important. Non-native speakers of Spanish required to prove fluency through institutional examinations, interviews. SAT scores accepted from U.S. mainland students. Spanish version of Puerto Rico CEEB of the College Board: aptitude test (verbal and mathematics) and achievement test battery (Spanish, English and mathematics). In lieu of the above, applicants may take SAT and SAT Subject Tests (Spanish Composition and Spanish Reading). SAT Subject Test (Spanish and Mathematics level) required for English speaking applicant. **Home schooled:** Sworn statement indicating that student received formal education at home. **Learning Disabled:** Director of Disabled Students Services Office (SERPI) evaluates learning disabled students to determine if they qualify for special admission.

High school preparation. 18 units recommended. Recommended units include English 3, mathematics 3, social studies 1, history 2, science 3, foreign language 3 and academic electives 3. Foreign language must be Spanish.

2011-2012 Annual costs. Tuition/fees: $2,534. Nonresidents who are U.S. citizens will be charged amount that will be equal to the rate for nonresidents at a state university in their home state. In second year of residency in Puerto Rico, such students will be charged in-state rate. Books/supplies: $1,825. Personal expenses: $1,200.

2010-2011 Financial aid. Need-based: 91% of total undergraduate aid awarded as scholarships/grants, 9% as loans/jobs. **Non-need-based:** Scholarships awarded for academics, athletics, music/drama.

Application procedures. Admission: Priority date 12/15; deadline 1/31 (receipt date). $20 fee. Admission notification by 4/15. Admission notification on a rolling basis. Must reply by 5/1. **Financial aid:** Priority date 3/1, closing date 6/30. FAFSA required. Applicants notified on a rolling basis starting 4/30; must reply by 7/31.

Academics. Course work conducted in Spanish. **Special study options:** Exchange student, honors, internships, teacher certification program. **Credit/ placement by examination:** AP, CLEP. **Support services:** Learning center, remedial instruction, study skills assistance, tutoring, writing center.

Majors. Biology: General, marine, microbiology. **Business:** Accounting, administrative services, business admin, human resources, international. **Conservation:** Wildlife/wilderness. **Education:** Elementary, ESL. **Health services:** Nursing (RN). **Human services:** Social work. **Math:** Computational. **Physical sciences:** Chemistry, physics. **Social sciences:** General.

Most popular majors. Biology 13%, business/marketing 46%, education 12%, health sciences 10%, public administration/social services 10%.

Computing on campus. 1,000 workstations in library, computer center. Online course registration, online library available.

Student life. Freshman orientation: Available. Preregistration for classes offered. One-day program that describes student services and undergraduate curriculum. **Activities:** Marching band, choral groups, dance, student government, various religious and social service organizations available.

Athletics. Intercollegiate: Baseball M, basketball, cheerleading, cross-country, judo, softball W, swimming, table tennis, tennis, track and field, volleyball, weight lifting, wrestling. **Intramural:** Basketball, softball W, volleyball. **Team name:** Buhos.

Student services. Alcohol/substance abuse counseling, career counseling, student employment services, financial aid counseling, health services, personal counseling, women's services. **Physically disabled:** Services for visually, speech, hearing impaired.

Contact. E-mail: elizabeth.gerena@upr.edu
Phone: (787) 850-9301 Fax: (787) 850-9428
Elizabeth Gerena, Director of Admissions, University of Puerto Rico: Humacao, Call Box 860, Humacao, PR 00792

University of Puerto Rico: Mayaguez

Mayaguez, Puerto Rico	**CB member**
www.uprm.edu	**CB code: 0912**

- Public 5-year university and engineering college
- Commuter campus in small city
- 11,319 degree-seeking undergraduates: 5% part-time, 48% women, 100% Hispanic American
- 939 degree-seeking graduate students
- 66% of applicants admitted
- 42% graduate within 6 years

General. Founded in 1911. Regionally accredited. Most courses conducted in Spanish. Students must have working knowledge of Spanish and English. **Degrees:** 1,431 bachelor's awarded; master's, doctoral offered. **ROTC:** Army, Air Force. **Location:** 100 miles from San Juan. **Calendar:** Semester, limited summer session. **Full-time faculty:** 668 total; 75% have terminal degrees, 87% minority, 37% women. **Part-time faculty:** 7 total; 14% have terminal degrees, 100% minority, 57% women. **Class size:** 36% < 20, 57% 20-39, 2% 40-49, 5% 50-99, less than 1% >100. **Special facilities:** Planetarium, botanical garden, agricultural extension service, agricultural experimental station, natural history collection, resource center for science and engineering.

Freshman class profile. 2,880 applied, 1,891 admitted, 1,774 enrolled.

Mid 50% test scores			
SAT critical reading:	540-650	GPA 3.0-3.49:	19%
SAT math:	560-690	GPA 2.0-2.99:	5%
GPA 3.75 or higher:	55%	Return as sophomores:	86%
GPA 3.50-3.74:	21%	Out-of-state:	1%

Basis for selection. Applicants must have high school diploma or its equivalent from educational institution duly accredited by Department of Education of Puerto Rico. Prospective applicants must take University Evaluation and Admissions Tests (PEAU in Spanish) administered by the College Board. First-year applicants only considered for admission in August of first

semester. Applications should be submitted before November 30 of year prior to admission. SAT and SAT Subject Tests required for English-speaking applicants. Students from Puerto Rico required to submit scores from College Board Entrance Examination aptitude tests. **Home schooled:** Must supply notarized document (sworn statement) that functions as certification of student educated in home.

High school preparation. 18 units recommended. Recommended units include English 3, mathematics 2, social studies 2, history 2, science 2, foreign language 3 and academic electives 4.

2011-2012 Annual costs. Tuition/fees: $2,534. Nonresidents who are U.S. citizens will be charged amount that will be equal to the rate for nonresidents at a state university in their home state. In second year of residency in Puerto Rico, such students will be charged in-state rate. Books/ supplies: $1,825. Personal expenses: $1,200.

2010-2011 Financial aid. All financial aid based on need. Average need met was 71%. Average scholarship/grant was $11,350; average loan $3,500. 83% of total undergraduate aid awarded as scholarships/grants, 17% as loans/jobs.

Application procedures. Admission: Closing date 12/15 (postmark date). $20 fee. Admission notification on a rolling basis beginning on or about 4/1. Must reply by 4/15. **Financial aid:** Priority date 1/30, closing date 6/30. FAFSA, institutional form required. Applicants notified on a rolling basis starting 5/30.

Academics. Online support available. Spanish language skills (reading, writing) required to read most online course materials. **Special study options:** Cooperative education, distance learning, double major, ESL, exchange student, honors, internships, study abroad, teacher certification program. **Credit/ placement by examination:** AP, CLEP, institutional tests. 22 credit hours maximum toward bachelor's degree. **Support services:** Reduced course load, remedial instruction, tutoring, writing center.

Majors. Biology: General, biotechnology, marine, microbiology. **Business:** Accounting, administrative services, business admin, finance, human resources, marketing, office management, organizational behavior, sales/distribution. **Computer sciences:** General, computer science, systems analysis. **Education:** Agricultural, mathematics, physical. **Engineering:** General, chemical, civil, computer, electrical, industrial, mechanical. **English:** English lit. **Foreign languages:** Comparative lit, French, Spanish. **General:** Agribusiness operations, agronomy, animal sciences, business, economics, education services, horticultural science, plant protection, soil science. **Health services:** Athletic training, nursing (RN), premedicine. **History:** General. **Math:** General. **Parks/recreation:** Facilities management, health/fitness. **Philosophy/ religion:** Philosophy. **Physical sciences:** General, chemistry, geology, physics. **Psychology:** General. **Social sciences:** General, economics, political science, sociology. **Visual/performing arts:** Art history/conservation, studio arts.

Most popular majors. Biology 19%, business/marketing 12%, engineering/engineering technologies 37%.

Computing on campus. 1,000 workstations in library, computer center, student center. Commuter students can connect to campus network. Online library, wireless network available.

Student life. Freshman orientation: Mandatory. Preregistration for classes offered. Four-day session held during week preceding start of Fall classes. **Housing:** Housing available near campus. **Activities:** Bands, choral groups, dance, drama, literary magazine, radio station, student government, student newspaper, Asociación de Colegiales Evangelicos, Federación Adventista de Universitarios, Grupo de Apostolado Católico, Hermandad Colegial de Avivamiento, Jóvenes Cristianos del Parque, Asociación de Colombianos del RUM, Asociación de Estudiantes Dominicanos del RUM, Juventud Popular Universitaria, Universitarios Estadístas en Acción.

Athletics. NCAA. **Intercollegiate:** Baseball M, basketball, cross-country, gymnastics, soccer M, softball W, swimming, table tennis, tennis, track and field, volleyball, water polo M, wrestling M. **Intramural:** Archery, baseball M, basketball, cross-country, racquetball, soccer M, softball, swimming, table tennis, tennis, volleyball, water polo M, wrestling M. **Team name:** Tarzanes "Bulldogs".

Student services. Alcohol/substance abuse counseling, career counseling, student employment services, health services, personal counseling, placement for graduates, veterans' counselor, women's services. **Physically disabled:** Services for visually, speech, hearing impaired.

Contact. E-mail: admisiones@upr.edu
Phone: (787) 265-3811 Fax: (787) 834-5265
Norma Torres, Director of Admissions, University of Puerto Rico: Mayaguez, Admissions Office, Mayaguez, PR 00681-9000

University of Puerto Rico: Medical Sciences
San Juan, Puerto Rico
www.rcm.upr.edu
CB code: 0631

- Public 4-year university
- Commuter campus in large city
- 522 degree-seeking undergraduates: 8% part-time, 80% women, 100% Hispanic American
- 1,779 degree-seeking graduate students

General. Founded in 1950. Regionally accredited. First-time freshmen not admitted. **Degrees:** 144 bachelor's, 44 associate awarded; master's, professional, doctoral offered. **Calendar:** Continuous, limited summer session. **Full-time faculty:** 667 total. **Part-time faculty:** 187 total. **Class size:** 70% < 20, 28% 20-39, 1% 40-49, 1% 50-99.

Basis for selection. Candidates are admitted on a competitive basis. Applicants must present evidence of successful completion of all admission requirements for the program in which they are interested. In most programs, an admissions committee will also consider nonacademic factors as additional criteria in screening applicants.

2011-2012 Annual costs. Tuition/fees: $2,534. Nonresidents who are U.S. citizens will be charged amount that will be equal to the rate for nonresidents at a state university in their home state. In second year of residency in Puerto Rico, such students will be charged in-state rate. Books/supplies: $1,825. Personal expenses: $800.

Financial aid. All financial aid based on need.

Application procedures. Admission: Closing date 2/15 (receipt date). $20 fee. Application must be submitted online. **Financial aid:** Priority date 4/30, closing date 6/15. FAFSA, institutional form required. Applicants notified on a rolling basis starting 8/1; must reply within 2 week(s) of notification.

Academics. Special study options: Combined bachelor's/graduate degree, exchange student, honors, internships. **Credit/placement by examination:** AP, CLEP. **Support services:** Tutoring.

Majors. Health services: Clinical lab science, clinical lab technology, nuclear medical technology, nursing (RN), public health ed, veterinary technology/assistant.

Computing on campus. 216 workstations in library, computer center. Commuter students can connect to campus network. Helpline, repair service available.

Student life. Activities: Choral groups, dance, drama, student government.

Athletics. Intramural: Basketball M, soccer M, softball M, volleyball.

Student services. Career counseling, student employment services, financial aid counseling, health services, legal services, personal counseling, women's services. **Physically disabled:** Services for visually impaired.

Contact. E-mail: margarita.rivera4@upr.edu
Phone: (787) 758-2525 ext. 5211 Fax: (787) 282-7117
Margarita Rivera, Director, Central Office of Admissions, University of Puerto Rico: Medical Sciences, PO Box 365067, San Juan, PR 00936-5067

University of Puerto Rico: Ponce
Ponce, Puerto Rico
www.uprp.edu
CB code: 0836

- Public 4-year university and branch campus college
- Commuter campus in small city
- 2,909 degree-seeking undergraduates: 5% part-time, 59% women, 100% Hispanic American
- 78% of applicants admitted
- 45% graduate within 6 years

General. Founded in 1970. Regionally accredited. **Degrees:** 316 bachelor's, 116 associate awarded. **ROTC:** Army. **Location:** 68 miles from San Juan, 46 miles from Mayaguez. **Calendar:** Semester, limited summer session. **Full-time faculty:** 114 total; 36% have terminal degrees, 100% minority, 59% women. **Part-time faculty:** 35 total; 29% have terminal degrees, 100% minority, 51% women. **Class size:** 29% < 20, 71% 20-39.

Freshman class profile. 1,042 applied, 812 admitted, 615 enrolled.

Mid 50% test scores		
SAT critical reading:	470-600	
SAT math:	480-600	

End year in good standing:	72%
Return as sophomores:	77%

Basis for selection. Admission based on general application index (GAI), combination of high school GPA and College Board test scores (50% each). Programs have their own GAI requirements. Interview required for academically weak and special ability. **Home schooled:** State high school equivalency certificate required.

High school preparation. 18 units required. Required units include English 3, mathematics 3, social studies 3, science 3 and academic electives 2. 3 units Spanish, 1 unit fine arts.

2011-2012 Annual costs. Tuition/fees: $2,534. Nonresidents who are U.S. citizens will be charged amount that will be equal to the rate for nonresidents at a state university in their home state. In second year of residency in Puerto Rico, such students will be charged in-state rate. Books/supplies: $1,825. Personal expenses: $800.

2010-2011 Financial aid. All financial aid based on need. 88% of total undergraduate aid awarded as scholarships/grants, 12% as loans/jobs.

Application procedures. Admission: Closing date 11/30. $20 fee. Admission notification on a rolling basis beginning on or about 4/15. Must reply by May 1 or within 3 week(s) if notified thereafter. **Financial aid:** Closing date 5/30. FAFSA, institutional form required.

Academics. Special study options: Dual enrollment of high school students, honors, internships. **Credit/placement by examination:** AP, CLEP. **Support services:** Remedial instruction, tutoring.

Majors. Biology: General. **Business:** Accounting, administrative services, business admin, finance, marketing. **Computer sciences:** General. **Education:** Elementary. **Health services:** Athletic training. **Math:** General. **Protective services:** Forensics. **Psychology:** General.

Most popular majors. Biology 15%, business/marketing 38%, education 12%, health sciences 8%, psychology 23%.

Computing on campus. 344 workstations in library, computer center, student center. Wireless network available.

Student life. Freshman orientation: Mandatory. Preregistration for classes offered. **Activities:** Bands, choral groups, dance, drama, student government, Christian youth organizations.

Athletics. Intercollegiate: Basketball, cross-country, softball, table tennis, tennis, track and field, volleyball. **Intramural:** Basketball, cross-country, gymnastics, softball, table tennis, tennis, track and field, volleyball.

Student services. Career counseling, student employment services, health services, on-campus daycare, personal counseling, placement for graduates, veterans' counselor. **Physically disabled:** Services for visually impaired.

Contact. E-mail: avelazquez@uprp.edu
Phone: (787) 844-8181 ext. 2531 Fax: (787) 840-8108
Acmin Rivera, Director of Admissions, University of Puerto Rico: Ponce, Box 7186, Ponce, PR 00732

University of Puerto Rico: Rio Piedras
San Juan, Puerto Rico
CB member
www.uprrp.edu
CB code: 0979

- Public 4-year university
- Commuter campus in very large city
- 12,058 degree-seeking undergraduates: 9% part-time, 64% women, 51% Hispanic American
- 3,068 degree-seeking graduate students
- 24% of applicants admitted
- 53% graduate within 6 years

General. Founded in 1903. Regionally accredited. Most courses conducted in Spanish. Students must have working knowledge of Spanish and English. **Degrees:** 1,847 bachelor's awarded; master's, professional, doctoral offered. **ROTC:** Army, Air Force. **Calendar:** Semester, limited summer session. **Full-time faculty:** 852 total; 84% have terminal degrees, 47% women. **Part-time faculty:** 264 total; 18% have terminal degrees, 44% women. **Class size:** 44% < 20, 53% 20-39, 1% 40-49, 2% 50-99, less than 1% >100. **Special facilities:** Theater, warm-blooded animal house, herbarium, biology museum,

high-technology microscopy facility, nanotechnology lasers, virtual astronomy lab; museum of history, anthropology and art.

Freshman class profile. 7,749 applied, 1,889 admitted, 1,708 enrolled.

Mid 50% test scores		GPA 3.0-3.49:	25%
SAT critical reading:	560-660	GPA 2.0-2.99:	7%
SAT math:	550-680	Return as sophomores:	86%
GPA 3.75 or higher:	44%	Live on campus:	10%
GPA 3.50-3.74:	24%		

Basis for selection. Admissions based on secondary school record and standardized test scores. Talent and ability considered. Verbal and math Academic Aptitude Test offered by the College Entrance Examination Board required. Environmental Design requires separate application form and school test; Fine Arts requires departmental test. **Home schooled:** Transcript of courses and grades required. Notarized homeschooling certificate required.

High school preparation. Required and recommended units include English 3, mathematics 2, social studies 1, history 1, science 2 and academic electives 6. 3 units Spanish required.

2011-2012 Annual costs. Tuition/fees: $2,534. Nonresidents who are U.S. citizens will be charged amount that will be equal to the rate for nonresidents at a state university in their home state. In second year of residency in Puerto Rico, such students will be charged in-state rate. Room/board: $8,280. Books/supplies: $1,825. Personal expenses: $1,200.

Financial aid. All financial aid based on need. **Additional information:** Tuition waived for honor students, athletes, members of chorus, and others with special talents.

Application procedures. Admission: Closing date 12/15 (postmark date). $20 fee. Admission notification by 4/15. Admission notification on a rolling basis. Must reply by 3/1. **Financial aid:** Closing date 4/1. FAFSA required.

Academics. Special study options: Combined bachelor's/graduate degree, cooperative education, double major, exchange student, external degree, honors, internships, liberal arts/career combination, semester at sea, student-designed major, study abroad, teacher certification program, Washington semester. **Credit/placement by examination:** AP, CLEP, institutional tests. 30 credit hours maximum toward bachelor's degree. **Support services:** Remedial instruction, study skills assistance, tutoring, writing center.

Majors. Architecture: Environmental design. **Biology:** General. **Business:** General, accounting, administrative services, finance, human resources, labor relations, management information systems, managerial economics, marketing, operations, statistics. **Communications:** Digital media, journalism, media studies, public relations. **Computer sciences:** Computer science. **Conservation:** Environmental science. **Education:** Elementary, family/consumer sciences, secondary. **English:** English lit. **Foreign languages:** General, comparative lit, French, Spanish. **History:** American, European. **Human services:** Social work. **Liberal arts:** Arts/sciences. **Math:** General. **Philosophy/religion:** Philosophy. **Physical sciences:** Chemistry, physics. **Psychology:** General. **Social sciences:** General, anthropology, economics, geography, political science, sociology. **Visual/performing arts:** General, art, art history/conservation, dramatic, drawing, multimedia, music, painting, photography, sculpture, studio arts. **Work/family studies:** General, food/nutrition.

Most popular majors. Business/marketing 20%, communications/journalism 6%, education 19%, interdisciplinary studies 11%, psychology 7%, social sciences 11%.

Computing on campus. 154 workstations in dormitories, library, computer center, student center. Dormitories wired for high-speed internet access and linked to campus network. Commuter students can connect to campus network. Online library, wireless network available.

Student life. Freshman orientation: Available. Preregistration for classes offered. Session held for 1 day in summer. **Policies:** Students represented in university administration. **Housing:** Coed dorms, wellness housing available. $35 fully refundable deposit, deadline 5/31. **Activities:** Jazz band, choral groups, dance, drama, literary magazine, musical theater, opera, radio station, student government, student newspaper, Club Avanza, Confraternidad Universitaria de Avivamiento, Jovenes Cristianos Universitarios, Juventud Universitaria Popular, Club de la Cruz Roja Americana del Recinto de Rio Piedras.

Athletics. NAIA, NCAA. **Intercollegiate:** Basketball W, cross-country, soccer M, swimming, tennis, track and field, volleyball. **Intramural:** Basketball, cross-country, gymnastics, soccer M, softball, swimming, table tennis, tennis, track and field, volleyball, water polo, wrestling M. **Team name:** Gallitos/Jerezanas.

Student services. Adult student services, alcohol/substance abuse counseling, career counseling, student employment services, health services, on-campus daycare, personal counseling, placement for graduates, veterans'

counselor. **Physically disabled:** Services for visually, speech, hearing impaired.

Contact. E-mail: admisiones@uprrp.edu
Phone: (787) 764-0000 ext. 85700 Fax: (787) 764-3680
Cruz Valentin, Director of Admissions, University of Puerto Rico: Rio Piedras, Box 21907, San Juan, PR 00931-1907

University of Puerto Rico: Utuado
Utuado, Puerto Rico
www.uprutuado.edu/UPRU/
CB member
CB code: 3893

- Public 4-year agricultural college
- Commuter campus in large town
- 1,207 degree-seeking undergraduates: 2% part-time, 54% women
- 52% of applicants admitted
- Interview required
- 39% graduate within 6 years

General. Founded in 1979. Regionally accredited. **Degrees:** 68 bachelor's, 111 associate awarded. **ROTC:** Army. **Location:** 20 miles from Arecibo. **Calendar:** Semester, limited summer session. **Full-time faculty:** 64 total; 53% have terminal degrees, 100% minority, 41% women. **Part-time faculty:** 21 total; 19% have terminal degrees, 100% minority, 48% women. **Special facilities:** 118-acre farm.

Freshman class profile. 1,226 applied, 638 admitted, 446 enrolled.

Mid 50% test scores		SAT math:	390-490
SAT critical reading:	370-490	Return as sophomores:	61%

Basis for selection. GED not accepted. High school GPA, test scores important. SAT required of English-speaking students.

High school preparation. College-preparatory program required. Required units include English 3, mathematics 2, history 3, science 2 and foreign language 3. 3 fine arts required.

2011-2012 Annual costs. Tuition/fees: $2,534. Nonresidents who are U.S. citizens will be charged amount that will be equal to the rate for nonresidents at a state university in their home state. In second year of residency in Puerto Rico, such students will be charged in-state rate. Books/supplies: $1,825. Personal expenses: $1,200.

2010-2011 Financial aid. All financial aid based on need.

Application procedures. Admission: Priority date 11/15; no deadline. $20 fee, may be waived for applicants with need. Must reply by May 1 or within 2 week(s) if notified thereafter. **Financial aid:** Priority date 5/31; no closing date. FAFSA required. Applicants notified on a rolling basis starting 9/30; must reply within 4 week(s) of notification.

Academics. Special study options: Cooperative education, honors, internships, teacher certification program. **Credit/placement by examination:** AP, CLEP. **Support services:** Learning center, reduced course load, remedial instruction, tutoring.

Majors. Business: Accounting, executive assistant. **Education:** Elementary.

Most popular majors. Business/marketing 65%, education 35%.

Computing on campus. 90 workstations in library. Online library, wireless network available.

Student life. Freshman orientation: Mandatory. Preregistration for classes offered. **Housing:** Wellness housing available. Private housing near college available. **Activities:** Choral groups, student government.

Athletics. Intercollegiate: Baseball M, basketball M, cross-country M, soccer M, softball M, track and field, volleyball, weight lifting. **Intramural:** Baseball M, basketball M, cross-country M, soccer M, softball M, track and field, volleyball, weight lifting. **Team name:** Guaraguao.

Student services. Alcohol/substance abuse counseling, career counseling, financial aid counseling, health services, personal counseling, placement for graduates, veterans' counselor.

Contact. Phone: (787) 894-2316 Fax: (787) 894-2891
Erika Medina, Admissions Officer, University of Puerto Rico: Utuado, PO Box 2500, Utuado, PR 00641

University of the Sacred Heart
San Juan, Puerto Rico

CB member
CB code: 0913

www.sagrado.edu

- Private 4-year university and liberal arts college affiliated with Roman Catholic Church
- Commuter campus in large city
- 5,428 degree-seeking undergraduates: 13% part-time, 61% women, 100% Hispanic American
- 964 degree-seeking graduate students
- 37% of applicants admitted
- 40% graduate within 6 years

General. Founded in 1935. Regionally accredited. **Degrees:** 603 bachelor's, 125 associate awarded; master's offered. **Calendar:** Semester, extensive summer session. **Full-time faculty:** 126 total; 66% women. **Part-time faculty:** 296 total; 49% women. **Special facilities:** Jardin Escultorico, Museo de la Radio, Pabellon de las Artes, Patio de las Artes, Galeria Jose (Pepin) Mendez y Teatro Emilio S. Belaval.

Freshman class profile. 4,932 applied, 1,834 admitted, 1,116 enrolled.

GPA 3.75 or higher:	15%	**GPA 2.0-2.99:**	36%
GPA 3.50-3.74:	14%	**Return as sophomores:**	72%
GPA 3.0-3.49:	35%		

Basis for selection. High school GPA and highest score CEEB important. SAT scores accepted in place of CEEB. Interview required for nursing program.

High school preparation. 15 units required. Required and recommended units include English 3, mathematics 3, social studies 2, science 3, foreign language 3 and academic electives 3.

2011-2012 Annual costs. Tuition/fees: $6,250. Room only: $2,700. Books/supplies: $1,978. Personal expenses: $4,595.

Financial aid. **Non-need-based:** Scholarships awarded for academics, athletics.

Application procedures. **Admission:** Priority date 12/15; deadline 6/30. $15 fee, may be waived for applicants with need. Admission notification on a rolling basis. **Financial aid:** Priority date 4/30, closing date 5/30. FAFSA, institutional form required. Applicants notified on a rolling basis starting 6/15; must reply by 8/30.

Academics. **Special study options:** Combined bachelor's/graduate degree, cooperative education, cross-registration, double major, dual enrollment of high school students, exchange student, external degree, honors, independent study, internships, liberal arts/career combination, semester at sea, teacher certification program. International programs with universities in Mexico and Spain. **Credit/placement by examination:** AP, CLEP, institutional tests. **Support services:** Pre-admission summer program, reduced course load, remedial instruction, tutoring.

Majors. **Biology:** General. **Business:** Accounting, business admin, tourism promotion. **Communications:** Advertising, communications/speech/rhetoric, journalism. **Computer sciences:** Computer science, information systems. **Education:** General, bilingual, elementary, secondary. **Health services:** Nursing (RN). **Human services:** Social work. **Math:** General. **Parks/recreation:** Health/fitness. **Physical sciences:** Chemistry. **Psychology:** General. **Social sciences:** General. **Visual/performing arts:** General, dramatic, photography.

Most popular majors. Business/marketing 16%, communications/journalism 44%, health sciences 15%.

Computing on campus. 500 workstations in dormitories, library, computer center, student center. Commuter students can connect to campus network. Repair service available.

Student life. **Freshman orientation:** Available. Preregistration for classes offered. **Housing:** Single-sex dorms available. $150 deposit, deadline 6/15. **Activities:** Choral groups, drama, film society, literary magazine, radio station, student government, student newspaper, TV station, pastoral services organization, health and allied sciences organization, student council, senior class organization, judo club, soccer club, nursing club, Christian club, microbioloby club, psychology club, chemistry club, justice system, telecommunication club.

Athletics. **Intercollegiate:** Basketball M, cross-country, swimming, tennis, track and field, volleyball, wrestling M. **Intramural:** Basketball M, swimming, volleyball. **Team name:** Dolphins.

Student services. Alcohol/substance abuse counseling, career counseling, student employment services, financial aid counseling, health services, personal counseling, placement for graduates, veterans' counselor. **Physically disabled:** Services for visually, hearing impaired.

Contact. E-mail: admision@sagrado.edu
Phone: (787) 728-1515 ext. 3236 Fax: (787) 728-2066
Lilia Planell, Institutional Statistician, University of the Sacred Heart, Universidad del Sagrado Corazon Oficina de Nuevo Ingreso, San Juan, PR 00914-0383

Rhode Island

Brown University

Providence, Rhode Island
www.brown.edu

CB member
CB code: 3094

- Private 4-year university and liberal arts college
- Residential campus in small city
- 6,118 degree-seeking undergraduates: 51% women, 6% African American, 14% Asian American, 10% Hispanic American, 11% international
- 2,336 degree-seeking graduate students
- 9% of applicants admitted
- SAT and SAT Subject Tests or ACT with writing, application essay required

General. Founded in 1764. Regionally accredited. **Degrees:** 1,554 bachelor's awarded; master's, professional, doctoral offered. **ROTC:** Army. **Location:** 45 miles from Boston. **Calendar:** Semester, limited summer session. **Full-time faculty:** 792 total; 94% have terminal degrees, 17% minority, 36% women. **Part-time faculty:** 184 total; 65% have terminal degrees, 10% minority, 40% women. **Class size:** 70% < 20, 17% 20-39, 3% 40-49, 6% 50-99, 4% >100. **Special facilities:** Museum of anthropology, observatory, center for the performing arts, center for information technology, institute for education, institute for international studies, center for the humanities.

Freshman class profile. 30,944 applied, 2,757 admitted, 1,507 enrolled.

Rank in top quarter:	99%	Out-of-state:	86%
Rank in top tenth:	93%	Live on campus:	100%
Return as sophomores:	98%	International:	11%

Basis for selection. Strength of academic course load and student's achievement in courses most important. Extracurricular activities, recommendations, personal essay important; test scores strongly considered. Students submitting SAT should submit scores of any 2 SAT Subject Tests. Portfolio recommended for art, music programs. Alumni interviews available, but not required, for all applicants. **Home schooled:** Statement describing home school structure and mission required. **Learning Disabled:** Special accommodations for standardized tests accepted.

High school preparation. 19 units recommended. Recommended units include English 4, mathematics 4, history 2, science 4 (laboratory 3), foreign language 4 and academic electives 1. At least 1 art unit (music or art) recommended. Familiarity with computers recommended. Physics, chemistry, and advanced mathematics recommended for prospective science or engineering majors.

2011-2012 Annual costs. Tuition/fees: $42,230. Room/board: $10,906. Books/supplies: $2,902. Personal expenses: $1,636.

2010-2011 Financial aid. All financial aid based on need. 812 full-time freshmen applied for aid; 736 were judged to have need; 736 of these received aid. Average need met was 100%. Average scholarship/grant was $34,611; average loan $4,876. 88% of total undergraduate aid awarded as scholarships/grants, 12% as loans/jobs. **Additional information:** Financial aid initiatives: 1) Undergraduate financial aid applicants with total parent incomes less than $100,000 do not have a loan component in their awards. Students with family earnings above $100,000 have moderate loans ($3,000, $4,000, or $5,000) depending on family total income level; 2) Families with total parent earnings less than $60,000 and assets less than $100,000 are not required to make a contribution toward the cost of education; 3) Families with total parent earnings less than $60,000 and assets greater than $100,000 have a significantly reduced contribution (from assets only); 4) Students are able to use outside scholarships to eliminate all of the self-help components in their awards including the summer savings expectation. These University initiatives are determined based on a family's calculated total income.

Application procedures. Admission: Closing date 1/1 (postmark date). $75 fee, may be waived for applicants with need. Admission notification by 4/1. Must reply by 5/1. **Financial aid:** Closing date 2/1. FAFSA, CSS PROFILE required. Applicants notified by 4/1; must reply by 5/1.

Academics. Students must complete course requirements in major(s) of choice, but are free to choose courses without a core curriculum prior to designating a major. **Special study options:** Combined bachelor's/graduate degree, cross-registration, double major, exchange student, honors, independent study, internships, student-designed major, study abroad, teacher certification program. 8-year medical program, 5-year dual degree program with Rhode Island School of Design, cross-registration with Rhode Island School of Design, early childhood certification (in teaching) program via Wheaton College courses. **Credit/placement by examination:** AP, CLEP, institutional tests. **Support services:** Reduced course load, study skills assistance, tutoring, writing center.

Majors. Architecture: History/criticism. **Area/ethnic studies:** African, African-American, American, Asian, Chicano/Hispanic-American/Latino, East Asian, European, French, German, Italian, Latin American, Near/Middle Eastern, Slavic, South Asian, women's. **Biology:** General, aquatic, biochemistry, biophysics, cell/histology, molecular, neuroscience. **Computer sciences:** Computer science. **Conservation:** Environmental science, environmental studies. **Education:** General. **Engineering:** Applied physics, biomedical, chemical, civil, computer, electrical, materials, mechanical. **English:** American lit, British lit, English lit. **Foreign languages:** Ancient Greek, classics, comparative lit, French, German, Italian, Latin, linguistics, Portuguese, Slavic, Spanish. **Health services:** Community health services. **History:** General. **Human services:** Public policy. **Math:** General, applied, statistics. **Philosophy/religion:** Judaic, philosophy, religion. **Physical sciences:** Chemical physics, chemistry, geochemistry, geology, geophysics, physics. **Psychology:** General. **Social sciences:** Anthropology, archaeology, economics, international economic development, international relations, political science, sociology, urban studies. **Visual/performing arts:** General, art history/conservation, dramatic, music, musicology, studio arts.

Most popular majors. Biology 10%, English 6%, foreign language 6%, social sciences 23%, visual/performing arts 7%.

Computing on campus. 500 workstations in dormitories, library, computer center, student center. Dormitories wired for high-speed internet access and linked to campus network. Commuter students can connect to campus network. Online course registration, online library, helpline, repair service, wireless network available.

Student life. Freshman orientation: Mandatory. Preregistration for classes offered. 5-day program, beginning Wednesday prior to Labor Day. **Policies:** Students must live in on-campus housing for first 3 years; those entering 7th semester may request off-campus residence. Freshmen not permitted cars on campus. **Housing:** Guaranteed on-campus for all undergraduates. Coed dorms, special housing for disabled, apartments, cooperative housing, fraternity/sorority housing, wellness housing available. Language houses, social dormitories, cultural houses, special program housing (international students, technology students, environmental studies) available. **Activities:** Bands, campus ministries, choral groups, dance, drama, film society, international student organizations, literary magazine, music ensembles, Model UN, musical theater, opera, radio station, student government, student newspaper, symphony orchestra, TV station, African American students association, ACLU, Amnesty International, Asian American students association, Big Brothers, community outreach, Catholic pastoral council, Latino American students association, Canadian club.

Athletics. NCAA. **Intercollegiate:** Baseball M, basketball, cross-country, diving, equestrian W, fencing, field hockey W, football (tackle) M, golf, gymnastics W, ice hockey, lacrosse, rowing (crew), skiing W, soccer, softball W, squash, swimming, tennis, track and field, volleyball W, water polo, wrestling M. **Intramural:** Badminton, basketball, fencing, field hockey W, ice hockey, lacrosse, racquetball, soccer, softball, squash, swimming, tennis, volleyball, water polo. **Team name:** Bears.

Student services. Adult student services, alcohol/substance abuse counseling, chaplain/spiritual director, career counseling, student employment services, financial aid counseling, health services, minority student services, personal counseling, placement for graduates, women's services. **Physically disabled:** Services for visually, speech, hearing impaired.

Contact. E-mail: admission_undergraduate@brown.edu
Phone: (401) 863-2378 Fax: (401) 863-9300
James Miller, Dean of Admission, Brown University, 45 Prospect Street, Providence, RI 02912

Bryant University

Smithfield, Rhode Island
www.bryant.edu

CB member
CB code: 3095

- Private 4-year business and liberal arts college
- Residential campus in large town
- 3,312 degree-seeking undergraduates: 3% part-time, 41% women, 4% African American, 3% Asian American, 5% Hispanic American, 6% international
- 258 degree-seeking graduate students

▶ 77% of applicants admitted

▶ Application essay required

▶ 77% graduate within 6 years; 24% enter graduate study

General. Founded in 1863. Regionally accredited. Academic programs integrate business and liberal arts to develop the skills essential to every profession. **Degrees:** 853 bachelor's awarded; master's offered. **ROTC:** Army. **Location:** 12 miles from Providence, 40 miles from Boston. **Calendar:** Semester, extensive summer session. **Full-time faculty:** 166 total; 83% have terminal degrees, 18% minority, 38% women. **Part-time faculty:** 140 total; 16% have terminal degrees, 10% minority, 51% women. **Class size:** 23% < 20, 76% 20-39, less than 1% 40-49. **Special facilities:** Financial markets center connected to worldwide financial markets, communications complex & center with TV studio, control room and editing suite.

Freshman class profile. 5,177 applied, 3,971 admitted, 814 enrolled.

Mid 50% test scores		GPA 2.0-2.99:	25%
SAT critical reading:	500-590	Rank in top quarter:	52%
SAT math:	540-630	Rank in top tenth:	20%
SAT writing:	500-590	End year in good standing:	94%
ACT composite:	22-26	Return as sophomores:	86%
GPA 3.75 or higher:	18%	Out-of-state:	89%
GPA 3.50-3.74:	16%	Live on campus:	95%
GPA 3.0-3.49:	40%	International:	8%

Basis for selection. Secondary school curriculum, GPA, guidance counselor's recommendation, personal essay very important. Standardized test optional policy. **Home schooled:** Must complete a state-accredited program. Course descriptions and progress reports required as part of application process. **Learning Disabled:** Foreign language requirement may be waived.

High school preparation. College-preparatory program required. 16 units required; 18 recommended. Required and recommended units include English 4, mathematics 4, history 2-3, science 2-3 (laboratory 2) and foreign language 2. Mathematics must include a year beyond algebra II, with a preference for pre-calculus or calculus in senior year. History includes social sciences.

2012-2013 Annual costs. Tuition/fees: $35,940. Room/board: $13,240. Books/supplies: $1,300. Personal expenses: $1,000.

Financial aid. Non-need-based: Scholarships awarded for academics, athletics, minority status, ROTC.

Application procedures. Admission: Closing date 2/1 (postmark date). $50 fee, may be waived for applicants with need. Admission notification by 3/23. Must reply by 5/1. **Financial aid:** Closing date 2/15. FAFSA required. Applicants notified by 3/24; must reply by 5/1.

Academics. Students in College of Business earn a liberal arts minor that complements their business studies; students in College of Arts and Sciences earn a business administration minor that enhances the value of their liberal arts education. All students required to complete a minor. New students complete a one-credit Foundations for Learning course to ease the transition to higher learning. International Business majors share residence and must complete 12 credit hours of study abroad. **Special study options:** Double major, ESL, honors, independent study, internships, study abroad, Washington semester. Service learning. **Credit/placement by examination:** AP, CLEP, IB, institutional tests. 30 credit hours maximum toward bachelor's degree. **Support services:** Learning center, study skills assistance, tutoring, writing center.

Majors. Biology: General. **Business:** Accounting, actuarial science, business admin, entrepreneurial studies, finance, financial planning, human resources, international, marketing. **Communications:** Communications/speech/rhetoric. **Computer sciences:** General, information technology. **Conservation:** Environmental science. **English:** English lit. **Foreign languages:** Chinese, Spanish. **History:** General. **Human services:** Community org/advocacy. **Math:** Applied, statistics. **Psychology:** General. **Social sciences:** Applied economics, economics, political science, sociology.

Most popular majors. Business/marketing 77%, communications/journalism 6%.

Computing on campus. PC or laptop required. 478 workstations in library, computer center. Dormitories wired for high-speed internet access and linked to campus network. Commuter students can connect to campus network. Online course registration, online library, helpline, repair service, student web hosting, wireless network available.

Student life. Freshman orientation: Available, $75 fee. Preregistration for classes offered. Two-day program in late June during which students and parents/guardians are housed in campus residence halls overnight. Students also register for elective courses. **Policies:** All residence halls are smoke free. Students ages 21 and over may possess alcohol for their personal consumption in the privacy of their room. Quiet study hour policy in effect throughout the academic year. **Housing:** Guaranteed on-campus for freshmen.

Coed dorms, single-sex dorms, special housing for disabled, apartments available. Honors, international business communities. **Activities:** Bands, campus ministries, choral groups, dance, drama, international student organizations, literary magazine, music ensembles, musical theater, radio station, student government, student newspaper, TV station, Bryant Christian Fellowship, Hillel, Fellowship of the Unashamed, multicultural student union, international student organization, Alliance for Women's Awareness, Amnesty International, Bryant Helps, Bryant Democrats, Bryant Republicans.

Athletics. NCAA. **Intercollegiate:** Baseball M, basketball, cross-country, diving W, field hockey W, football (tackle) M, golf M, lacrosse, soccer, softball W, swimming, tennis, track and field, volleyball W. **Intramural:** Basketball, football (non-tackle), soccer, softball, table tennis, tennis, volleyball. **Team name:** Bulldogs.

Student services. Adult student services, alcohol/substance abuse counseling, chaplain/spiritual director, career counseling, services for economically disadvantaged, student employment services, financial aid counseling, health services, minority student services, personal counseling, placement for graduates, veterans' counselor, women's services. **Physically disabled:** Services for visually, hearing impaired.

Contact. E-mail: admission@bryant.edu
Phone: (401) 232-6100 Toll-free number: (800) 622-7001
Fax: (401) 232-6741
Michelle Beauregard, Director of Admission, Bryant University, 1150 Douglas Pike, Smithfield, RI 02917-1291

Johnson & Wales University: Providence

Providence, Rhode Island **CB member**
www.jwu.edu **CB code: 3465**

▶ Private 4-year university

▶ Residential campus in small city

▶ 9,756 degree-seeking undergraduates: 7% part-time, 56% women, 8% African American, 2% Asian American, 8% Hispanic American, 10% international

▶ 266 degree-seeking graduate students

▶ 76% of applicants admitted

▶ 51% graduate within 6 years

General. Founded in 1914. Regionally accredited. **Degrees:** 1,583 bachelor's, 1,070 associate awarded; master's, doctoral offered. **ROTC:** Army. **Location:** 200 miles from New York City, 50 miles from Boston. **Calendar:** Quarter, limited summer session. **Full-time faculty:** 308 total; 42% women. **Part-time faculty:** 194 total; 48% women. **Class size:** 47% < 20, 40% 20-39, 13% 40-49, less than 1% 50-99. **Special facilities:** 3 university-operated hotels and restaurants, banquet facilities, information kiosk, culinary museum, equine center.

Freshman class profile. 11,830 applied, 9,049 admitted, 2,392 enrolled.

GPA 3.75 or higher:	14%	Return as sophomores:	74%
GPA 3.50-3.74:	11%	Out-of-state:	89%
GPA 3.0-3.49:	33%	Live on campus:	84%
GPA 2.0-2.99:	42%	International:	5%

Basis for selection. Academic record, secondary school curriculum, GPA, class rank, test scores important; student motivation and interest given strong consideration. SAT or ACT required for admission to honors program. Interview and letter of recommendation generally required of students in bottom quarter of class; essay and interview recommended for others. **Home schooled:** Transcript of courses and grades, state high school equivalency certificate required. SAT (exclusive of Writing) or ACT required.

High school preparation. College-preparatory program recommended. Required units include English 4, mathematics 3, social studies 2 and science 3.

2011-2012 Annual costs. Tuition/fees: $25,107. Room/board: $9,603. Books/supplies: $1,800. Personal expenses: $1,065.

Financial aid. Non-need-based: Scholarships awarded for academics, alumni affiliation, leadership, state residency.

Application procedures. Admission: No deadline. No application fee. Admission notification on a rolling basis. Must reply by May 1 or within 2 week(s) if notified thereafter. **Financial aid:** No deadline. FAFSA required. Applicants notified on a rolling basis starting 3/1; must reply within 2 week(s) of notification.

Academics. Special study options: Accelerated study, cooperative education, dual enrollment of high school students, ESL, exchange student, honors,

independent study, internships, study abroad. Externships, practicums (hands-on learning). **Credit/placement by examination:** AP, CLEP, institutional tests. **Support services:** Learning center, pre-admission summer program, reduced course load, remedial instruction, study skills assistance, tutoring, writing center.

Majors. Business: Accounting, business admin, entrepreneurial studies, fashion, finance, hospitality admin, hotel/motel admin, international, investments/securities, marketing, public finance, tourism promotion, tourism/travel. **Communications:** Advertising. **Computer sciences:** Information systems, systems analysis, web page design, webmaster. **Engineering:** Computer, electrical, systems. **General:** Equestrian studies, equine science, farm/ranch. **Parks/recreation:** Facilities management, sports admin. **Protective services:** Law enforcement admin, security management. **Psychology:** Counseling.

Most popular majors. Business/marketing 43%, family/consumer sciences 13%, parks/recreation 12%, personal/culinary services 16%.

Computing on campus. 400 workstations in library, computer center. Dormitories wired for high-speed internet access and linked to campus network. Commuter students can connect to campus network. Online library, helpline, wireless network available.

Student life. Freshman orientation: Mandatory, $276 fee. Preregistration for classes offered. **Housing:** Guaranteed on-campus for freshmen. Coed dorms, special housing for disabled, apartments, wellness housing available. $300 deposit. **Activities:** Campus ministries, dance, international student organizations, student government, student newspaper, Hillel, Christian student union, ACLU, T.R.U.E. (Together Realizing Unity Can Exist), College Republicans.

Athletics. NCAA. **Intercollegiate:** Baseball M, basketball, cross-country, equestrian, golf M, ice hockey M, sailing, soccer, softball W, tennis, volleyball, wrestling M. **Intramural:** Basketball, soccer, softball, tennis. **Team name:** Wildcats.

Student services. Career counseling, student employment services, financial aid counseling, health services, personal counseling, placement for graduates, veterans' counselor, women's services. **Physically disabled:** Services for visually, speech, hearing impaired.

Contact. E-mail: pvd@admissions.jwu.edu
Phone: (401) 598-2310 Toll-free number: (800) 342-5598
Fax: (401) 598-2948
Amy Podbelski, Director of Undergraduate Admissions, Johnson & Wales University: Providence, 8 Abbott Park Place, Providence, RI 02903-3703

New England Institute of Technology
Warwick, Rhode Island
www.neit.edu   CB code: 0339

- Private 4-year technical college
- Commuter campus in small city
- 2,894 degree-seeking undergraduates: 13% part-time, 24% women
- 39 degree-seeking graduate students
- Interview required

General. Founded in 1940. Regionally accredited. **Degrees:** 276 bachelor's, 1,009 associate awarded; master's offered. **Location:** 10 miles from Providence, 50 miles from Boston. **Calendar:** Quarter, extensive summer session. **Full-time faculty:** 118 total; 8% have terminal degrees. **Part-time faculty:** 180 total; 6% have terminal degrees.

Basis for selection. Open admission. Basic skills testing, Ronald P. Carver reading test used for placement. Portfolio recommended for drafting program.

2011-2012 Annual costs. Tuition/fees: $19,640. Books/supplies: $1,464. Personal expenses: $2,250.

Financial aid. Non-need-based: Scholarships awarded for academics. **Additional information:** Tuition at time of first enrollment guaranteed all students for 2 years.

Application procedures. Admission: No deadline. $25 fee. Admission notification on a rolling basis. Must reply by May 1 or within 4 week(s) if notified thereafter. **Financial aid:** No deadline. FAFSA, institutional form required. Applicants notified on a rolling basis.

Academics. Special study options: Accelerated study, cooperative education, distance learning, double major, internships, student-designed major. **Credit/placement by examination:** AP, CLEP, institutional tests. 51 credit hours maximum toward associate degree. **Support services:** Learning center,

pre-admission summer program, reduced course load, remedial instruction, study skills assistance, tutoring, writing center.

Majors. Business: General. **Communications technology:** Recording arts. **Computer sciences:** General, computer science, information technology, programming, systems analysis. **Engineering:** Architectural, manufacturing, mechanical. **Protective services:** Law enforcement admin. **Visual/performing arts:** Interior design.

Computing on campus. 850 workstations in library, computer center. Online course registration, online library, helpline, student web hosting, wireless network available.

Student life. Freshman orientation: Mandatory. Preregistration for classes offered. **Activities:** Radio station, student newspaper.

Student services. Career counseling, student employment services, financial aid counseling, personal counseling, placement for graduates, veterans' counselor.

Contact. E-mail: neit@neit.edu
Phone: (401) 467-7744 Toll-free number: (800) 736-7744 ext. 3357
Fax: (401) 886-0868
Mark Blondin, Director of Admissions, New England Institute of Technology, 2500 Post Road, Warwick, RI 02886-2286

Providence College
Providence, Rhode Island   CB member
www.providence.edu   CB code: 3693

- Private 4-year liberal arts college affiliated with Roman Catholic Church
- Residential campus in small city
- 3,840 degree-seeking undergraduates: 58% women, 4% African American, 1% Asian American, 4% Hispanic American, 2% international
- 452 degree-seeking graduate students
- 61% of applicants admitted
- Application essay required
- 85% graduate within 6 years

General. Founded in 1917. Regionally accredited. Has community-oriented evening school for part-time students, in addition to traditional undergraduate college. **Degrees:** 917 bachelor's, 2 associate awarded; master's, doctoral offered. **ROTC:** Army. **Location:** 50 miles from Boston, 180 miles from New York City. **Calendar:** Semester, limited summer session. **Full-time faculty:** 299 total; 94% have terminal degrees, 10% minority, 38% women. **Part-time faculty:** 102 total; 37% have terminal degrees, 5% minority, 50% women. **Class size:** 48% < 20, 47% 20-39, 1% 40-49, 3% 50-99.

Freshman class profile. 9,873 applied, 5,979 admitted, 982 enrolled.

Mid 50% test scores			
SAT critical reading:	520-620	GPA 2.0-2.99:	15%
SAT math:	530-640	Rank in top quarter:	71%
SAT writing:	540-640	Rank in top tenth:	40%
ACT composite:	23-27	Return as sophomores:	90%
GPA 3.75 or higher:	21%	Out-of-state:	89%
GPA 3.50-3.74:	19%	Live on campus:	98%
GPA 3.0-3.49:	45%	International:	2%

Basis for selection. GED not accepted. Emphasis placed on scholastic ability, motivation, character, and seriousness of purpose. Recommendations and essay considered. Strength of curriculum and grades are the most important factors. Standardized tests scores are optional. Prospective students who choose not to submit standardized test scores will receive full consideration, without penalty, for admission. Audition recommended for music programs; portfolio recommended for art programs. **Home schooled:** Statement describing home school structure and mission, transcript of courses and grades, state high school equivalency certificate, letter of recommendation (nonparent) required. If not associated with a particular program or institution, the applicant is encouraged to submit a descriptive resume that outlines the student's high school work, level of challenge, and depth and breadth of curriculum, including reading lists and a graded writing sample. **Learning Disabled:** Students must provide documentation of disability. Accommodations are then made as deemed appropriate.

High school preparation. College-preparatory program required. Required and recommended units include English 4, mathematics 4, social studies 2, history 2, science 3-4 (laboratory 2) and foreign language 3.

2012-2013 Annual costs. Tuition/fees (projected): $40,975. Room/board: $12,140. Books/supplies: $900. Personal expenses: $1,500.

2011-2012 Financial aid. Need-based: 760 full-time freshmen applied for aid; 597 were judged to have need; 597 of these received aid. Average need met was 86%. Average scholarship/grant was $21,557; average loan $4,776. 77% of total undergraduate aid awarded as scholarships/grants, 23% as loans/jobs. **Non-need-based:** Awarded to 714 full-time undergraduates, including 224 freshmen. Scholarships awarded for academics, athletics, leadership, music/drama, ROTC.

Application procedures. Admission: Closing date 1/15 (postmark date). $55 fee, may be waived for applicants with need. Admission notification by 4/1. Must reply by 5/1. **Financial aid:** Closing date 2/1. FAFSA, CSS PROFILE required. Applicants notified by 4/1.

Academics. Special study options: Combined bachelor's/graduate degree, distance learning, double major, dual enrollment of high school students, honors, independent study, internships, liberal arts/career combination, semester at sea, student-designed major, study abroad, teacher certification program, Washington semester. **Credit/placement by examination:** AP, CLEP, IB, SAT, ACT, institutional tests. International Baccalaureate credit restricted to 5-7 higher level exams. **Support services:** Learning center, reduced course load, study skills assistance, tutoring, writing center.

Majors. Area/ethnic studies: American, women's. **Biology:** General, biochemistry. **Business:** Accounting, business admin, finance, labor relations, marketing, organizational behavior. **Computer sciences:** Computer science. **Education:** Mathematics, music, secondary, special ed. **Engineering:** Applied physics, systems. **English:** English lit. **Foreign languages:** French, Italian, Spanish. **Health services:** Health care admin. **History:** General. **Human services:** Community org/advocacy, social work. **Liberal arts:** Arts/sciences, humanities. **Math:** General. **Philosophy/religion:** Philosophy. **Physical sciences:** Chemistry. **Psychology:** General. **Social sciences:** General, economics, political science, sociology. **Theology:** Theology. **Visual/performing arts:** General, art history/conservation, ceramics, digital arts, drawing, music, painting, photography, sculpture, studio arts.

Most popular majors. Biology 8%, business/marketing 30%, education 8%, English 7%, health sciences 6%, psychology 6%, social sciences 14%.

Computing on campus. 338 workstations in library, computer center, student center. Dormitories wired for high-speed internet access and linked to campus network. Commuter students can connect to campus network. Online course registration, online library, helpline, repair service, student web hosting, wireless network available.

Student life. Freshman orientation: Mandatory. Preregistration for classes offered. Six-day program held the week before classes begin. **Policies:** Freshmen not permitted cars on campus. **Housing:** Guaranteed on-campus for freshmen. Coed dorms, single-sex dorms, special housing for disabled, apartments available. $200 nonrefundable deposit, deadline 5/1. **Activities:** Bands, campus ministries, choral groups, dance, drama, international student organizations, literary magazine, music ensembles, musical theater, radio station, student government, student newspaper, TV station, Afro-American society, Amnesty International, Big Brothers and Sisters, Pastoral Service Organization, PC Pals, Best Buddies, College Democrats, College Republicans.

Athletics. NCAA. **Intercollegiate:** Basketball, cross-country, diving, field hockey W, ice hockey, lacrosse M, soccer, softball W, swimming, tennis W, track and field, volleyball W. **Intramural:** Basketball, field hockey, football (non-tackle), ice hockey, lacrosse, racquetball, soccer, softball, tennis, volleyball. **Team name:** Friars.

Student services. Adult student services, alcohol/substance abuse counseling, chaplain/spiritual director, career counseling, services for economically disadvantaged, student employment services, financial aid counseling, health services, minority student services, personal counseling, placement for graduates. **Physically disabled:** Services for visually, hearing impaired.

Contact. E-mail: pcadmiss@providence.edu
Phone: (401) 865-2535 Toll-free number: (800) 721-6444
Fax: (401) 865-2826
Raul Fonts, Dean of Admissions, Providence College, Harkins Hall 103, One Cunningham Square, Providence, RI 02918-0001

Rhode Island College
Providence, Rhode Island

www.ric.edu

CB member
CB code: 3724

- Public 4-year liberal arts college
- Commuter campus in small city
- 7,488 degree-seeking undergraduates: 24% part-time, 65% women, 7% African American, 2% Asian American, 9% Hispanic American
- 750 degree-seeking graduate students

- 73% of applicants admitted
- SAT or ACT with writing, application essay required
- 44% graduate within 6 years; 15% enter graduate study

General. Founded in 1854. Regionally accredited. **Degrees:** 1,212 bachelor's awarded; master's, doctoral offered. **ROTC:** Army. **Location:** 4 miles from downtown Providence. **Calendar:** Semester, extensive summer session. **Full-time faculty:** 327 total; 90% have terminal degrees, 12% minority, 57% women. **Part-time faculty:** 427 total; 58% women. **Class size:** 45% < 20, 54% 20-39, less than 1% 40-49, less than 1% 50-99, less than 1% >100. **Special facilities:** Center for the performing arts, art gallery.

Freshman class profile. 3,349 applied, 2,445 admitted, 974 enrolled.

Mid 50% test scores			
SAT critical reading:	420-520	Rank in top quarter:	35%
SAT math:	410-520	Rank in top tenth:	11%
SAT writing:	420-520	Return as sophomores:	76%
ACT composite:	17-21	Out-of-state:	20%
		Live on campus:	45%

Basis for selection. High school academic record, GPA and class rank most important, followed by test scores, essay, and references. TOEFL required for all applicants who have been in the country for less than 5 years and are not native speakers of English. SAT scores required of non-native speakers of English who have been in the United States for more than 5 years. Interview available but not required. Audition required for music; portfolio required for bachelor of fine arts. **Home schooled:** Transcript of courses and grades, state high school equivalency certificate, interview required. Must submit GED scores unless their home school curriculum is provided by an accredited agency.

High school preparation. College-preparatory program required. 18 units required. Required units include English 4, mathematics 3, social studies 2, science 2 (laboratory 2), foreign language 2 and academic electives 5. Biology and either chemistry or physics are recommended lab sciences; 2 years of same foreign language required. Algebra I, II and geometry required. All units must be college-preparatory level.

2011-2012 Annual costs. Tuition/fees: $7,268; $17,554 out-of-state. Connecticut and Massachusetts students whose permanent address is within a 50-mile radius of RIC pay the in-state tuition rate plus 50%. Room/board: $9,256. Books/supplies: $1,000. Personal expenses: $1,000.

2011-2012 Financial aid. Need-based: 872 full-time freshmen applied for aid; 673 were judged to have need; 657 of these received aid. Average need met was 75%. Average scholarship/grant was $6,988; average loan $3,405. 42% of total undergraduate aid awarded as scholarships/grants, 58% as loans/jobs. **Non-need-based:** Awarded to 174 full-time undergraduates, including 65 freshmen. Scholarships awarded for academics, alumni affiliation, art, music/drama.

Application procedures. Admission: Closing date 3/15 (postmark date). $50 fee, may be waived for applicants with need. Admission notification on a rolling basis beginning on or about 12/15. Must reply by May 1 or within 2 week(s) if notified thereafter. **Financial aid:** Priority date 3/1; no closing date. FAFSA, institutional form required. Applicants notified on a rolling basis starting 3/15; must reply within 3 week(s) of notification.

Academics. Special study options: Combined bachelor's/graduate degree, double major, dual enrollment of high school students, exchange student, honors, independent study, internships, student-designed major, study abroad, teacher certification program. **Credit/placement by examination:** AP, CLEP, SAT, ACT, institutional tests. **Support services:** Learning center, pre-admission summer program, reduced course load, remedial instruction, study skills assistance, tutoring, writing center.

Majors. Area/ethnic studies: African-American, French, Latin American, women's. **Biology:** General. **Business:** General, accounting, business admin, finance, management information systems, managerial economics, marketing. **Communications:** Communications/speech/rhetoric. **Computer sciences:** General. **Education:** Art, biology, chemistry, early childhood, elementary, English, foreign languages, French, geography, health, history, mathematics, multi-level teacher, music, physical, physics, science, secondary, social science, social studies, Spanish, special ed, technology/industrial arts, voc/tech. **English:** Creative writing, English lit. **Foreign languages:** French, Portuguese, Spanish. **Health services:** Clinical lab science, health care admin, medical radiologic technology/radiation therapy, nursing (RN), predental, premedicine, preveterinary, substance abuse counseling. **History:** General. **Human services:** General, social work. **Liberal arts:** Arts/sciences. **Math:** General. **Philosophy/religion:** Philosophy. **Physical sciences:** Chemistry, physics. **Protective services:** Criminal justice. **Psychology:** General. **Social sciences:** General, anthropology, economics, geography, political science, sociology. **Visual/performing arts:** Art history/conservation, dance, dramatic, film/cinema/video, music, music performance, studio arts.

Most popular majors. Business/marketing 17%, communications/journalism 7%, education 21%, health sciences 11%, psychology 12%, visual/performing arts 8%.

Computing on campus. 220 workstations in library, computer center, student center. Dormitories wired for high-speed internet access and linked to campus network. Commuter students can connect to campus network. Online course registration, online library, helpline, repair service, student web hosting, wireless network available.

Student life. Freshman orientation: Mandatory, $150 fee. Preregistration for classes offered. Two-day programs offered in June and/or July. **Housing:** Coed dorms, single-sex dorms, special housing for disabled available. $220 partly refundable deposit, deadline 5/15. **Activities:** Bands, campus ministries, choral groups, dance, drama, film society, international student organizations, literary magazine, music ensembles, musical theater, radio station, student government, student newspaper, symphony orchestra, TV station, Advocacy and Beyond, Asian student association, Feminists United, HOPE (Helping Others Promote Equality), intra-varsity student fellowship, Iota Phi Theta, Inc., Harambee, LIFE (Live, Inspire, Fight, Educate), Latin American student organization, Women of Color.

Athletics. NCAA. **Intercollegiate:** Baseball M, basketball, cross-country, golf, gymnastics W, lacrosse W, soccer, softball W, swimming W, tennis, track and field, volleyball W, wrestling M. **Intramural:** Badminton, basketball, football (non-tackle) M, golf, gymnastics W, sailing, skin diving, soccer, softball, swimming, tennis, volleyball, water polo. **Team name:** Anchormen, Anchorwomen.

Student services. Adult student services, alcohol/substance abuse counseling, chaplain/spiritual director, career counseling, student employment services, financial aid counseling, health services, minority student services, on-campus daycare, personal counseling, placement for graduates, veterans' counselor, women's services. **Physically disabled:** Services for visually, speech, hearing impaired.

Contact. E-mail: admissions@ric.edu
Phone: (401) 456-8234 Toll-free number: (800) 669-5760
Fax: (401) 456-8817
Lucille Saunders, Director of Admissions, Rhode Island College, 600 Mount Pleasant Avenue, Providence, RI 02908

Rhode Island School of Design
Providence, Rhode Island   **CB member**
www.risd.edu   **CB code: 3726**

- Private 4-year visual arts college
- Residential campus in small city
- 1,972 degree-seeking undergraduates: 68% women
- 424 degree-seeking graduate students
- 34% of applicants admitted
- SAT or ACT with writing, application essay required
- 87% graduate within 6 years

General. Founded in 1877. Regionally accredited. **Degrees:** 515 bachelor's awarded; master's offered. **Location:** 52 miles from Boston, 180 miles from New York City. **Calendar:** 4-1-4, limited summer session. **Full-time faculty:** 148 total; 70% have terminal degrees, 13% minority, 42% women. **Part-time faculty:** 394 total; 68% have terminal degrees, 16% minority, 46% women. **Class size:** 73% < 20, 26% 20-39, less than 1% 40-49, less than 1% 50-99. **Special facilities:** Fine art and design museum, extensive photograph and clipping collections, slide collection, recreational farm on Narragansett Bay, nature laboratory.

Freshman class profile. 2,666 applied, 899 admitted, 453 enrolled.

Mid 50% test scores			
		ACT composite:	24-30
SAT critical reading:	560-680	**Return as sophomores:**	95%
SAT math:	590-660	**Out-of-state:**	96%
SAT writing:	580-640	**Live on campus:**	99%

Basis for selection. Academic history, visual portfolio, and 2 required drawings most important. Portfolio required for all applicants. **Home schooled:** Proof of high school equivalency/GED required.

High school preparation. College-preparatory program recommended. Architecture, interior architecture, landscape architecture, and industrial design applicants must have 2 algebra, .5 trigonometry, 1 science.

2011-2012 Annual costs. Tuition/fees: $39,777. Room/board: $11,652. Books/supplies: $2,600. Personal expenses: $2,415.

2011-2012 Financial aid. Need-based: Average need met was 50%. Average scholarship/grant was $20,333; average loan $3,366. 50% of total undergraduate aid awarded as scholarships/grants, 50% as loans/jobs.

Application procedures. Admission: Closing date 2/1 (receipt date). $60 fee, may be waived for applicants with need. Admission notification by 3/15. Must reply by 5/1. **Financial aid:** Closing date 2/15. FAFSA, CSS PROFILE required. Applicants notified by 3/31; must reply by 5/1.

Academics. Special study options: Cross-registration, double major, exchange student, independent study, internships, study abroad, teacher certification program. **Credit/placement by examination:** AP, CLEP, IB. **Support services:** Remedial instruction, tutoring, writing center.

Majors. Architecture: Architecture, interior, landscape. **Visual/performing arts:** Ceramics, fiber arts, graphic design, illustration, industrial design, metal/jewelry, painting, photography, printmaking, sculpture. **Work/family studies:** Clothing/textiles.

Most popular majors. Architecture 18%, visual/performing arts 73%.

Computing on campus. 425 workstations in dormitories, library, computer center, student center. Dormitories wired for high-speed internet access and linked to campus network. Commuter students can connect to campus network. Online course registration, helpline, repair service, student web hosting, wireless network available.

Student life. Freshman orientation: Mandatory. Preregistration for classes offered. **Policies:** Freshmen not permitted cars on campus. **Housing:** Guaranteed on-campus for freshmen. Coed dorms, apartments, wellness housing available. $175 nonrefundable deposit, deadline 5/1. **Activities:** Dance, drama, film society, international student organizations, literary magazine, student government, student newspaper.

Athletics. Intramural: Basketball, football (non-tackle), ice hockey.

Student services. Alcohol/substance abuse counseling, chaplain/spiritual director, career counseling, financial aid counseling, health services, legal services, minority student services, personal counseling, placement for graduates. **Physically disabled:** Services for hearing impaired.

Contact. E-mail: admissions@risd.edu
Phone: (401) 454-6300 Toll-free number: (800) 364-7473
Fax: (401) 454-6309
Edward Newhall, Director of Admissions, Rhode Island School of Design, 2 College Street, Providence, RI 02903-2784

Roger Williams University
Bristol, Rhode Island   **CB member**
www.rwu.edu   **CB code: 3729**

- Private 4-year university and liberal arts college
- Residential campus in large town
- 3,785 degree-seeking undergraduates: 1% part-time, 50% women, 1% African American, 1% Asian American, 3% Hispanic American, 5% international
- 375 degree-seeking graduate students
- 77% of applicants admitted
- SAT or ACT (ACT writing recommended), application essay required
- 62% graduate within 6 years

General. Founded in 1956. Regionally accredited. Certificate and associate programs offered only in School of Continuing Studies in Providence and Bristol. **Degrees:** 904 bachelor's, 2 associate awarded; master's, professional offered. **ROTC:** Army. **Location:** 18 miles from Providence, 10 miles from Newport. **Calendar:** Semester, limited summer session. **Full-time faculty:** 205 total; 12% minority, 42% women. **Part-time faculty:** 343 total; 5% minority, 42% women. **Special facilities:** Marine and natural sciences building with marine biology wetlab.

Freshman class profile. 9,202 applied, 7,081 admitted, 1,174 enrolled.

Mid 50% test scores			
		GPA 2.0-2.99:	29%
SAT critical reading:	490-580	**Rank in top quarter:**	38%
SAT math:	510-600	**Rank in top tenth:**	14%
SAT writing:	490-580	**Return as sophomores:**	80%
ACT composite:	22-26	**Out-of-state:**	91%
GPA 3.75 or higher:	14%	**Live on campus:**	96%
GPA 3.50-3.74:	14%	**International:**	4%
GPA 3.0-3.49:	43%		

Basis for selection. Admissions based on high school performance and SAT or ACT scores. Audition required for dance; portfolio required for

art, architecture programs. **Home schooled:** State high school equivalency certificate required. Students must submit portfolio of their work.

High school preparation. College-preparatory program required. 22 units required; 26 recommended. Required and recommended units include English 4, mathematics 3-4, social studies 2-3, history 2-3, science 2-4 (laboratory 2), foreign language 2 and academic electives 2-3. Specific subject requirements vary with intended major.

2011-2012 Annual costs. Tuition/fees: $30,908. Tuition differential for architecture program. Room/board: $13,220. Books/supplies: $900. Personal expenses: $794.

Financial aid. Non-need-based: Scholarships awarded for academics, ROTC.

Application procedures. Admission: Closing date 2/1. $50 fee. Application must be submitted online. Admission notification on a rolling basis beginning on or about 3/15. Must reply by 5/1. **Financial aid:** Priority date 1/1, closing date 2/1. FAFSA, CSS PROFILE required. Applicants notified on a rolling basis starting 3/20; must reply by 5/1.

Academics. All students graduate with two areas of specialization: one in their major and a second in a liberal arts discipline; most students may complete two majors. **Special study options:** Combined bachelor's/graduate degree, cooperative education, distance learning, double major, dual enrollment of high school students, ESL, exchange student, external degree, honors, independent study, internships, liberal arts/career combination, semester at sea, student-designed major, study abroad, teacher certification program, Washington semester, weekend college. **Credit/placement by examination:** AP, CLEP, IB, SAT, institutional tests. 15 credit hours maximum toward associate degree, 30 toward bachelor's. Students can test out of no more than 25% of the credits required for a degree. **Support services:** Learning center, reduced course load, study skills assistance, tutoring, writing center.

Honors college/program. Applicants must have 1250 SAT (exclusive of Writing) and 3.3 GPA; 1300 SAT required for architecture and marine biology. Application deadline, February 1st.

Majors. Architecture: Architecture, history/criticism. **Area/ethnic studies:** American. **Biology:** General, marine. **Business:** Accounting, business admin, finance, international, management information systems, marketing, operations. **Communications:** Journalism, media studies. **Communications technology:** Graphics. **Computer sciences:** General, computer science. **Conservation:** General, environmental science. **Education:** General, elementary, secondary. **Engineering:** General. **English:** British lit, creative writing. **Foreign languages:** General. **History:** General. **Human services:** General. **Math:** General. **Philosophy/religion:** Philosophy. **Physical sciences:** Chemistry. **Protective services:** Law enforcement admin. **Psychology:** General. **Social sciences:** Anthropology, economics, political science, sociology. **Visual/performing arts:** Art, art history/conservation, dance, dramatic, graphic design, studio arts.

Most popular majors. Business/marketing 20%, communications/journalism 7%, engineering/engineering technologies 9%, psychology 6%, security/protective services 13%.

Computing on campus. 540 workstations in dormitories, library, computer center. Dormitories wired for high-speed internet access and linked to campus network. Commuter students can connect to campus network. Online course registration, online library, helpline, repair service, wireless network available.

Student life. Freshman orientation: Mandatory. Preregistration for classes offered. 2-day program with overnight stay on campus during summer; separate orientations for transfer and international students. **Housing:** Guaranteed on-campus for freshmen. Coed dorms, special housing for disabled, apartments, wellness housing available. $350 fully refundable deposit, deadline 5/1. Special interest academic and honors housing available. **Activities:** Choral groups, dance, drama, film society, international student organizations, literary magazine, Model UN, musical theater, radio station, student government, student newspaper, Hillel, Inter-Varsity Christian Fellowship, multicultural student union, College Democrats, College Republicans, environmental and animal rights club, Model UN, Best Buddies of Rhode Island, Habitat for Humanity, student volunteer association.

Athletics. NCAA. **Intercollegiate:** Baseball M, basketball, cross-country, diving, equestrian, lacrosse, sailing, soccer, softball W, swimming, tennis, volleyball W, wrestling M. **Intramural:** Basketball, field hockey, football (non-tackle), golf, racquetball, skiing, soccer, softball, squash, tennis, volleyball, water polo. **Team name:** Hawks.

Student services. Chaplain/spiritual director, career counseling, student employment services, financial aid counseling, health services, minority student services, personal counseling, women's services. **Physically disabled:** Services for visually, hearing impaired.

Contact. E-mail: admit@rwu.edu
Phone: (401) 254-3500 Toll-free number: (800) 458-7144 ext. 3500
Fax: (401) 254-3557
Wesley Roy, Dean of Admissions, Roger Williams University, 1 Old Ferry Road, Bristol, RI 02809-2921

Salve Regina University
Newport, Rhode Island
www.salve.edu

CB member
CB code: 3759

- Private 4-year university and liberal arts college affiliated with Roman Catholic Church
- Residential campus in large town
- 2,015 degree-seeking undergraduates: 4% part-time, 69% women, 2% African American, 1% Asian American, 5% Hispanic American, 1% international
- 465 degree-seeking graduate students
- 70% of applicants admitted
- Application essay required
- 73% graduate within 6 years; 23% enter graduate study

General. Founded in 1934. Regionally accredited. Affiliated with Religious Sisters of Mercy. **Degrees:** 420 bachelor's awarded; master's, doctoral offered. **ROTC:** Army. **Location:** 30 miles from Providence. **Calendar:** Semester, limited summer session. **Full-time faculty:** 116 total; 67% have terminal degrees, 6% minority, 55% women. **Part-time faculty:** 150 total; 21% have terminal degrees, 2% minority, 54% women. **Class size:** 50% < 20, 50% 20-39, less than 1% 40-49. **Special facilities:** International relations and public policy center.

Freshman class profile. 4,686 applied, 3,258 admitted, 547 enrolled.

Mid 50% test scores			
SAT critical reading:	510-590	GPA 2.0-2.99:	33%
SAT math:	520-600	Rank in top quarter:	46%
SAT writing:	500-590	Rank in top tenth:	15%
ACT composite:	22-27	End year in good standing:	98%
GPA 3.75 or higher:	10%	Return as sophomores:	79%
GPA 3.50-3.74:	14%	Out-of-state:	88%
GPA 3.0-3.49:	43%	Live on campus:	99%
		International:	1%

Basis for selection. High school achievement most important, followed by rank in top half of high school class, test scores for nursing and teacher education programs (test scores for others are optional), recommendations, essay, activities, interview. Special consideration given to applicants from minority and low-income families. SAT or TOEFL required for international applicants. SAT or ACT is required for applicants to 4-year nursing and teacher education programs and for homeschooled applicants. Audition and portfolio considered. **Home schooled:** Statement describing home school structure and mission, transcript of courses and grades, letter of recommendation (nonparent) required. Require two recommendations, one of which must be academic. Course syllabus required for each course; results of SAT or ACT examinations; portfolio of academic accomplishments including a reading list, course descriptions and list of extra-curricular/community involvement.

High school preparation. College-preparatory program required. 16 units required. Required units include English 4, mathematics 3, social studies 1, science 2 (laboratory 2), foreign language 2 and academic electives 4. Additional course work may be required of students who have not completed recommended units. Social studies includes history.

2011-2012 Annual costs. Tuition/fees: $32,800. Room/board: $11,600. Books/supplies: $900. Personal expenses: $1,000.

2011-2012 Financial aid. Need-based: 493 full-time freshmen applied for aid; 414 were judged to have need; 412 of these received aid. Average need met was 71%. Average scholarship/grant was $19,034; average loan $3,408. 69% of total undergraduate aid awarded as scholarships/grants, 31% as loans/jobs. **Non-need-based:** Awarded to 379 full-time undergraduates, including 175 freshmen. Scholarships awarded for academics, alumni affiliation, ROTC.

Application procedures. Admission: Priority date 2/1; no deadline. $50 fee, may be waived for applicants with need. Application must be submitted online. Must reply by May 1 or within 2 week(s) if notified thereafter. **Financial aid:** Priority date 3/1; no closing date. FAFSA, CSS PROFILE required. Applicants notified by 12/25; must reply by 5/1 or within 2 week(s) of notification.

Academics. Credit may be awarded for learning associated with life experience. **Special study options:** Accelerated study, combined bachelor's/graduate degree, distance learning, double major, dual enrollment of high school

students, ESL, honors, independent study, internships, liberal arts/career combination, study abroad, teacher certification program, Washington semester. **Credit/placement by examination:** AP, CLEP, IB, institutional tests. **Support services:** Learning center, reduced course load, study skills assistance, tutoring, writing center.

Majors. Area/ethnic studies: American. **Biology:** General. **Business:** Accounting, business admin, finance, information resources management, management science, marketing. **Education:** Early childhood, elementary, secondary, special ed. **English:** English lit. **Foreign languages:** French, Spanish. **Health services:** Clinical lab science, nursing (RN). **History:** General. **Human services:** Social work. **Liberal arts:** Arts/sciences. **Math:** General. **Philosophy/religion:** Philosophy, religion. **Physical sciences:** Chemistry. **Protective services:** Law enforcement admin. **Psychology:** General. **Social sciences:** Economics, international economics, political science, sociology. **Visual/performing arts:** Art history/conservation, ceramics, dramatic, graphic design, music, painting, photography, studio arts.

Most popular majors. Business/marketing 23%, education 18%, health sciences 10%, psychology 9%, security/protective services 8%.

Computing on campus. PC or laptop required. 300 workstations in library, computer center, student center. Dormitories wired for high-speed internet access and linked to campus network. Commuter students can connect to campus network. Online course registration, online library, helpline, repair service, student web hosting, wireless network available.

Student life. Freshman orientation: Mandatory, $300 fee. Preregistration for classes offered. 2-day sessions during June and July for full-time freshmen; separate sessions for international and transfer students. **Policies:** Freshmen not permitted cars on campus. **Housing:** Guaranteed on-campus for freshmen. Coed dorms, single-sex dorms, special housing for disabled, apartments, wellness housing available. $500 nonrefundable deposit, deadline 5/1. Off-campus housing available to upperclassmen. **Activities:** Bands, campus ministries, choral groups, dance, drama, film society, international student organizations, literary magazine, music ensembles, Model UN, radio station, student government, student newspaper, Artist's Guild, Circle K, environmental club, Student Outdoor Adventures, Volunteers Interested in Researching and Guiding, Women's Issues Now, Stagefright Theater Company, College Democrats, College Republicans.

Athletics. NCAA. **Intercollegiate:** Baseball M, basketball, cross-country, field hockey W, football (tackle) M, ice hockey, lacrosse, soccer, softball W, tennis, track and field W, volleyball W. **Intramural:** Basketball, field hockey W, football (non-tackle) W, football (tackle) M, racquetball, soccer, softball, tennis, track and field W, volleyball, weight lifting. **Team name:** Seahawks.

Student services. Adult student services, alcohol/substance abuse counseling, chaplain/spiritual director, career counseling, financial aid counseling, health services, minority student services, personal counseling, veterans' counselor. **Physically disabled:** Services for visually, hearing impaired.

Contact. E-mail: sruadmis@salve.edu
Phone: (401) 341-2908 Toll-free number: (888) 467-2583
Fax: (401) 848-2823
Colleen Emerson, Dean of Undergraduate Admissions, Salve Regina University, 100 Ochre Point Avenue, Newport, RI 02840-4192

University of Rhode Island
Kingston, Rhode Island **CB member**
www.uri.edu **CB code: 3919**

- Public 4-year university
- Residential campus in small town
- 12,943 degree-seeking undergraduates: 10% part-time, 55% women, 5% African American, 3% Asian American, 7% Hispanic American
- 2,730 degree-seeking graduate students
- 76% of applicants admitted
- SAT or ACT (ACT writing recommended), application essay required
- 63% graduate within 6 years

General. Founded in 1892. Regionally accredited. College of Continuing Education in Providence offers credit-bearing courses for degree and non-degree students. **Degrees:** 2,670 bachelor's awarded; master's, professional, doctoral offered. **ROTC:** Army. **Location:** 30 miles from Providence. **Calendar:** Semester, extensive summer session. **Full-time faculty:** 684 total; 86% have terminal degrees, 18% minority, 42% women. **Part-time faculty:** 522 total; 56% women. **Class size:** 33% < 20, 52% 20-39, 6% 40-49, 5% 50-99, 4% >100. **Special facilities:** Inner space center, center for robotics research, animal science farm, planetarium, marine sciences campus, American historic textiles museum, aquaculture center, fisheries and marine technology laboratory, biotechnology center, human performance laboratory.

Freshman class profile. 20,012 applied, 15,211 admitted, 3,215 enrolled.

Mid 50% test scores			
SAT critical reading:	490-590	GPA 2.0-2.99:	27%
SAT math:	500-610	Rank in top quarter:	49%
SAT writing:	490-590	Rank in top tenth:	18%
ACT composite:	21-26	Return as sophomores:	82%
GPA 3.75 or higher:	17%	Out-of-state:	54%
GPA 3.50-3.74:	17%	Live on campus:	90%
GPA 3.0-3.49:	39%	Fraternities:	9%
		Sororities:	14%

Basis for selection. School record primary, test scores secondary; extracurricular activities considered. Economically and socially disadvantaged students from Rhode Island admitted through special program for talent development.

High school preparation. College-preparatory program required. 18 units required. Required units include English 4, mathematics 3, social studies 2, science 2 (laboratory 1), foreign language 2 and academic electives 5.

2011-2012 Annual costs. Tuition/fees: $11,366; $27,454 out-of-state. Room/board: $10,796. Books/supplies: $1,200. Personal expenses: $1,440.

2011-2012 Financial aid. Need-based: 2,434 full-time freshmen applied for aid; 2,013 were judged to have need; 1,828 of these received aid. Average need met was 63%. Average scholarship/grant was $9,566; average loan $5,080. 56% of total undergraduate aid awarded as scholarships/grants, 44% as loans/jobs. **Non-need-based:** Awarded to 1,100 full-time undergraduates, including 395 freshmen. Scholarships awarded for academics, alumni affiliation, art, athletics, music/drama, ROTC.

Application procedures. Admission: Closing date 2/1 (postmark date). $65 fee, may be waived for applicants with need. Admission notification by 3/31. Admission notification on a rolling basis beginning on or about 2/3. Must reply by 5/1. **Financial aid:** Priority date 3/1; no closing date. FAFSA required. Applicants notified on a rolling basis starting 3/31; must reply by 5/1.

Academics. Special study options: Combined bachelor's/graduate degree, cross-registration, distance learning, double major, dual enrollment of high school students, exchange student, honors, independent study, internships, liberal arts/career combination, semester at sea, study abroad, teacher certification program, weekend college. **Credit/placement by examination:** AP, CLEP, IB, SAT, ACT, institutional tests. 45 credit hours maximum toward bachelor's degree. **Support services:** Pre-admission summer program, reduced course load, remedial instruction, study skills assistance, tutoring, writing center.

Honors college/program. Open to all continuing students with a cumulative grade point average of 3.20 or higher. Transfer students with GPA of 3.20 from their previous institution and incoming freshmen who graduated in the top 10% of their high school class are also eligible to enroll in honors courses.

Majors. Architecture: Landscape. **Area/ethnic studies:** African-American, Latin American, women's. **Biology:** General, marine, microbiology, zoology. **Business:** General, accounting, apparel, business admin, finance, international, marketing. **Communications:** Communications/speech/rhetoric, journalism, public relations. **Computer sciences:** General. **Conservation:** Environmental studies, fisheries, management/policy, water/wetlands/marine, wildlife/wilderness. **Education:** Elementary, music, physical, secondary. **Engineering:** Biomedical, chemical, civil, computer, electrical, industrial, mechanical, ocean. **English:** English lit. **Foreign languages:** Classics, comparative lit, French, German, Italian, Spanish. **General:** Animal sciences. **Health services:** Clinical lab science, communication disorders, dietetics, health care admin, nursing (RN). **History:** General. **Human services:** Public policy. **Math:** General. **Parks/recreation:** Exercise sciences. **Philosophy/religion:** Philosophy. **Physical sciences:** Chemistry, forensic chemistry, geology, oceanography, physics. **Psychology:** General. **Social sciences:** Anthropology, applied economics, econometrics, economics, political science, sociology. **Visual/performing arts:** Art history/conservation, cinematography, dramatic, music, music performance, music theory/composition, studio arts. **Work/family studies:** Clothing/textiles, family studies, food/nutrition.

Most popular majors. Biology 6%, business/marketing 15%, communications/journalism 10%, education 8%, engineering/engineering technologies 9%, health sciences 11%, psychology 6%, social sciences 8%.

Computing on campus. Dormitories wired for high-speed internet access and linked to campus network. Commuter students can connect to campus network. Online course registration, online library, helpline, repair service, wireless network available.

Student life. Freshman orientation: Mandatory, $175 fee. Preregistration for classes offered. 2-day programs throughout June. Family members encouraged to attend. **Housing:** Guaranteed on-campus for freshmen. Coed dorms, special housing for disabled, apartments, fraternity/sorority housing, wellness housing available. $200 partly refundable deposit, deadline 5/1. Learning

communities for undecided majors, honor program, health sciences, engineering, environment majors, and nursing. **Activities:** Bands, campus ministries, choral groups, dance, drama, film society, international student organizations, literary magazine, music ensembles, musical theater, radio station, student government, student newspaper, TV station, Hillel, Newman Club, College Democrats, College Republicans, Uhuru Sasa, NAACP, Latin American student association, Habitat for Humanity, Asian student association, club sports council.

Athletics. NCAA. **Intercollegiate:** Baseball M, basketball, cheerleading, cross-country, diving W, football (tackle) M, golf M, rowing (crew) W, soccer, softball W, swimming W, tennis W, track and field, volleyball W. **Intramural:** Football (non-tackle) M, soccer, volleyball M. **Team name:** Rams.

Student services. Adult student services, alcohol/substance abuse counseling, chaplain/spiritual director, career counseling, services for economically disadvantaged, student employment services, financial aid counseling, health services, legal services, minority student services, personal counseling, placement for graduates, veterans' counselor, women's services. **Physically disabled:** Services for visually, speech, hearing impaired.

Contact. E-mail: admission@uri.edu
Phone: (401) 874-7000 Fax: (401) 874-5523
Cynthia Bonn, Dean of Admission, University of Rhode Island, Newman Hall, Kingston, RI 02881-1322

South Carolina

Allen University
Columbia, South Carolina
www.allenuniversity.edu

CB code: 5006

▸ Private 4-year university and liberal arts college affiliated with African Methodist Episcopal Church
▸ Residential campus in large city
▸ 644 degree-seeking undergraduates: 1% part-time, 59% women, 99% African American
▸ 60% of applicants admitted

General. Founded in 1870. Regionally accredited. **Degrees:** 80 bachelor's awarded. **ROTC:** Army, Naval. **Location:** 112 miles from Charleston, 72 miles from Charlotte, NC. **Calendar:** Semester, limited summer session. **Full-time faculty:** 43 total; 46% have terminal degrees, 84% minority, 54% women. **Part-time faculty:** 19 total; 5% have terminal degrees, 79% women.

Freshman class profile. 1,391 applied, 841 admitted, 180 enrolled.

GPA 3.75 or higher:	3%	GPA 3.0-3.49:	19%
GPA 3.50-3.74:	6%	GPA 2.0-2.99:	69%

Basis for selection. Applicants reviewed by admission committee. Decision provided to applicant in writing. SAT or ACT recommended. Interview, campus visit recommended. **Home schooled:** Statement describing home school structure and mission, transcript of courses and grades, state high school equivalency certificate, interview, letter of recommendation (nonparent) required.

High school preparation. College-preparatory program recommended. Recommended units include English 4, mathematics 4, social studies 3, history 3, science 3, foreign language 1 and computer science 1.

2012-2013 Annual costs. Tuition/fees (projected): $12,340. Room/board: $5,560. Books/supplies: $1,000. Personal expenses: $800.

Financial aid. **Non-need-based:** Scholarships awarded for academics, athletics, music/drama, ROTC.

Application procedures. **Admission:** Priority date 6/30; deadline 7/31 (receipt date). No application fee. Admission notification on a rolling basis. Must reply by May 1 or within 2 week(s) if notified thereafter. **Financial aid:** Priority date 4/15, closing date 7/20. FAFSA required. Applicants notified on a rolling basis starting 4/1; must reply within 2 week(s) of notification.

Academics. **Special study options:** Combined bachelor's/graduate degree, cooperative education, honors, independent study, internships, teacher certification program, weekend college. Nontraditional program for returning students. **Credit/placement by examination:** AP, CLEP, SAT, ACT, institutional tests. 3 credit hours maximum toward bachelor's degree. **Support services:** Learning center, pre-admission summer program, reduced course load, study skills assistance, tutoring, writing center.

Majors. **Biology:** General. **Business:** Business admin. **English:** English lit. **Math:** General. **Philosophy/religion:** Religion. **Physical sciences:** Chemistry. **Social sciences:** General.

Most popular majors. Biology 11%, business/marketing 43%, English 9%, mathematics 6%, social sciences 24%, theological studies 9%.

Computing on campus. Dormitories wired for high-speed internet access and linked to campus network. Commuter students can connect to campus network. Online course registration, online library, helpline, wireless network available.

Student life. **Freshman orientation:** Mandatory. Preregistration for classes offered. Week-long session. Students complete financial aid forms, receive dorm assignments, and complete the registration process. **Housing:** Guaranteed on-campus for freshmen. Single-sex dorms, apartments available. $250 nonrefundable deposit, deadline 7/31. **Activities:** Bands, campus ministries, choral groups, dance, international student organizations, music ensembles, student government, social science club, NAACP, BASIC, global ministries, chic republic, Voices of Praise, National Black MBA Association, Spirit Club, ICONIC Arts, Men Armed with Knowledge.

Athletics. NAIA. **Intercollegiate:** Basketball, cross-country. **Team name:** Yellow Jackets.

Student services. Adult student services, chaplain/spiritual director, career counseling, student employment services, financial aid counseling, health services, personal counseling, placement for graduates, veterans' counselor.

Contact. Phone: (803) 376-5735 Toll-free number: (877) 625-5368 Fax: (803) 376-5731
Director of Admissions, Allen University, 1530 Harden Street, Columbia, SC 29204

Anderson University
Anderson, South Carolina
www.andersonuniversity.edu

CB member
CB code: 5008

▸ Private 4-year university affiliated with Southern Baptist Convention
▸ Residential campus in large town
▸ 2,479 degree-seeking undergraduates: 20% part-time, 66% women
▸ 230 degree-seeking graduate students
▸ 75% of applicants admitted
▸ SAT or ACT (ACT writing optional) required
▸ 47% graduate within 6 years

General. Founded in 1911. Regionally accredited. **Degrees:** 323 bachelor's awarded; master's offered. **ROTC:** Army, Air Force. **Location:** 32 miles from Greenville, 100 miles from Atlanta. **Calendar:** Semester, limited summer session. **Full-time faculty:** 87 total; 71% have terminal degrees, 8% minority, 46% women. **Part-time faculty:** 155 total; 24% have terminal degrees, 7% minority, 54% women. **Class size:** 50% < 20, 43% 20-39, 6% 40-49, less than 1% 50-99, less than 1% >100. **Special facilities:** Audio recording studio.

Freshman class profile. 2,118 applied, 1,586 admitted, 603 enrolled.

Mid 50% test scores			
SAT critical reading:	470-590	GPA 3.0-3.49:	37%
SAT math:	470-580	GPA 2.0-2.99:	10%
SAT writing:	460-570	Rank in top quarter:	52%
ACT composite:	20-25	Rank in top tenth:	29%
GPA 3.75 or higher:	29%	Return as sophomores:	72%
GPA 3.50-3.74:	24%	Out-of-state:	6%
		Live on campus:	91%

Basis for selection. High school achievement record, test scores important; recommendations considered. Minimum high school GPA of 2.5 and SAT (exclusive of Writing) combined score of 1000 preferred. Each applicant considered individually. Applicants not meeting these guidelines may be admitted into developmental studies program. Recommendations, further grades or interview may be required for academically weak applicants. Interview recommended for some; audition required for art, music, theater programs. **Learning Disabled:** Applicants with diagnosed learning disabilities must meet regular requirements and supply summary of recent (within 1 year of enrollment) diagnostic testing.

High school preparation. College-preparatory program recommended. 20 units required. Required and recommended units include English 4, mathematics 3-4, social studies 2, history 2, science 3-4 (laboratory 2), foreign language 2 and academic electives 4.

2011-2012 Annual costs. Tuition/fees: $20,910. Room/board: $7,725. Books/supplies: $1,500. Personal expenses: $1,600.

2011-2012 Financial aid. **Need-based:** 499 full-time freshmen applied for aid; 436 were judged to have need; 436 of these received aid. Average need met was 9%. Average scholarship/grant was $16,793; average loan $3,881. 67% of total undergraduate aid awarded as scholarships/grants, 33% as loans/jobs. **Non-need-based:** Awarded to 715 full-time undergraduates, including 226 freshmen. Scholarships awarded for academics, alumni affiliation, art, athletics, leadership, minority status, music/drama, religious affiliation, state residency.

Application procedures. **Admission:** No deadline. $25 fee, may be waived for applicants with need. Admission notification on a rolling basis beginning on or about 9/1. **Financial aid:** Priority date 3/1, closing date 6/30. FAFSA required. Applicants notified on a rolling basis starting 3/15; must reply within 2 week(s) of notification.

Academics. **Special study options:** Accelerated study, cooperative education, distance learning, double major, dual enrollment of high school students, ESL, honors, independent study, internships, liberal arts/career combination, study abroad, teacher certification program, Washington semester. **Credit/ placement by examination:** AP, CLEP, IB, institutional tests. 24 credit

hours maximum toward bachelor's degree. **Support services:** Learning center, reduced course load, remedial instruction, study skills assistance, tutoring, writing center.

Majors. Biology: General. **Business:** General, business admin, finance, human resources, marketing, organizational behavior, retailing. **Communications:** Communications/speech/rhetoric. **Education:** Art, early childhood, elementary, English, history, mathematics, music, physical, special ed. **English:** English lit. **Foreign languages:** Spanish. **History:** General. **Liberal arts:** Arts/sciences. **Math:** General. **Parks/recreation:** Exercise sciences. **Philosophy/religion:** Christian. **Protective services:** Law enforcement admin. **Psychology:** General. **Theology:** Bible. **Visual/performing arts:** Art, dramatic, interior design, music, music performance, musical theater.

Most popular majors. Business/marketing 32%, education 28%, parks/recreation 7%, psychology 6%, visual/performing arts 11%.

Computing on campus. 130 workstations in library, computer center. Dormitories wired for high-speed internet access and linked to campus network. Commuter students can connect to campus network. Online course registration, online library, helpline, wireless network available.

Student life. Freshman orientation: Mandatory. Preregistration for classes offered. 2 orientation sessions held during summer. **Housing:** Guaranteed on-campus for freshmen. Single-sex dorms, apartments, wellness housing available. $250 fully refundable deposit, deadline 5/1. **Activities:** Bands, campus ministries, choral groups, dance, drama, literary magazine, music ensembles, musical theater, student government, student newspaper, symphony orchestra, Gamma Beta Phi, campus activities board, Fellowship of Christian Athletes, Minorities for Change, student alumni council, Reformed University Fellowship, Young Life.

Athletics. NCAA. **Intercollegiate:** Baseball M, basketball, cheerleading M, cross-country, golf, soccer, softball W, tennis, track and field, volleyball W, wrestling M. **Intramural:** Basketball, football (non-tackle), racquetball, softball, table tennis, tennis, volleyball, weight lifting M. **Team name:** Trojans.

Student services. Adult student services, chaplain/spiritual director, career counseling, student employment services, financial aid counseling, health services, on-campus daycare, personal counseling, placement for graduates. **Physically disabled:** Services for visually impaired.

Contact. E-mail: admissions@andersonuniversity.edu
Phone: (864) 231-2030 Toll-free number: (800) 542-3594
Fax: (864) 231-2033
Pam Bryant, Director of Admissions, Anderson University, 316 Boulevard, Anderson, SC 29621-4002

Benedict College
Columbia, South Carolina   **CB member**
www.benedict.edu   **CB code: 5056**

- Private 4-year liberal arts college affiliated with American Baptist Churches in the USA
- Residential campus in very large city
- 3,224 degree-seeking undergraduates
- SAT or ACT required

General. Founded in 1870. Regionally accredited. Benedict College is a historically black institution. **Degrees:** 339 bachelor's awarded. **ROTC:** Army, Air Force. **Location:** 110 miles from Greenville, 120 miles from Charleston. **Calendar:** Semester, limited summer session. **Full-time faculty:** 145 total. **Part-time faculty:** 39 total. **Class size:** 46% < 20, 33% 20-39, 13% 40-49, 8% 50-99.

Freshman class profile.

GPA 3.75 or higher:	4%	Rank in top quarter:	15%
GPA 3.50-3.74:	6%	Rank in top tenth:	5%
GPA 3.0-3.49:	19%	Out-of-state:	50%
GPA 2.0-2.99:	51%	Live on campus:	93%

Basis for selection. High school GPA and test scores important.

High school preparation. College-preparatory program recommended. 20 units recommended. Recommended units include English 4, mathematics 3, social studies 3 and science 2.

2011-2012 Annual costs. Tuition/fees: $17,190. Room/board: $7,906. Books/supplies: $1,000. Personal expenses: $1,400.

Application procedures. Admission: No deadline. $25 fee. Admission notification on a rolling basis. **Financial aid:** Priority date 4/15; no closing

---

date. FAFSA required. Applicants notified on a rolling basis starting 4/15.

Academics. Special study options: Accelerated study, double major, dual enrollment of high school students, external degree, honors, internships, teacher certification program, weekend college. **Credit/placement by examination:** AP, CLEP, institutional tests. 24 credit hours maximum toward bachelor's degree. **Support services:** Learning center, pre-admission summer program, reduced course load, remedial instruction, study skills assistance, tutoring, writing center.

Majors. Biology: General. **Business:** Accounting, business admin. **Computer sciences:** General, computer science. **Conservation:** Environmental science. **Education:** Early childhood, elementary. **English:** English lit. **History:** General. **Human services:** Social work. **Math:** General. **Parks/recreation:** Health/fitness. **Physical sciences:** Chemistry, physics. **Social sciences:** Economics, political science. **Visual/performing arts:** Art, multimedia. **Work/family studies:** Family studies.

Most popular majors. Biology 10%, business/marketing 20%, communications/journalism 7%, family/consumer sciences 9%, health sciences 9%, liberal arts 6%, psychology 6%, public administration/social services 6%, security/protective services 10%.

Computing on campus. 385 workstations in dormitories, library, computer center, student center. Dormitories wired for high-speed internet access and linked to campus network. Commuter students can connect to campus network. Online library, helpline, repair service, wireless network available.

Student life. Freshman orientation: Mandatory. Preregistration for classes offered. **Housing:** Guaranteed on-campus for freshmen. Single-sex dorms available. **Activities:** Bands, choral groups, dance, drama, music ensembles, radio station, student government, student newspaper, Gordon-Jenkins Theological Association.

Athletics. NAIA. **Intercollegiate:** Baseball M, basketball, cross-country, football (tackle) M, golf, soccer M, softball, tennis, track and field, volleyball W, wrestling M. **Intramural:** Baseball M, basketball, softball W, volleyball W. **Team name:** Tigers.

Student services. Adult student services, chaplain/spiritual director, career counseling, student employment services, financial aid counseling, health services, minority student services, on-campus daycare, personal counseling, placement for graduates, veterans' counselor.

Contact. E-mail: admissions@benedict.edu
Phone: (803) 705-4491 Toll-free number: (800) 868-6598
Fax: (803) 253-5167
Phyllis Thompson, Director of Admissions, Benedict College, 1600 Harden Street, Columbia, SC 29204

Bob Jones University
Greenville, South Carolina
www.bju.edu   **CB code: 5065**

- Private 4-year Bible and liberal arts college affiliated with nondenominational tradition
- Residential campus in small city
- 3,023 degree-seeking undergraduates: 2% part-time, 57% women, 1% African American, 3% Asian American, 4% Hispanic American, 5% international
- 464 degree-seeking graduate students
- 83% of applicants admitted
- Application essay required
- 62% graduate within 6 years

General. Regionally accredited; also accredited by TRACS. **Degrees:** 751 bachelor's, 59 associate awarded; master's, doctoral offered. **Location:** 100 miles from Charlotte, NC, 128 miles from Atlanta, GA. **Calendar:** Semester, limited summer session. **Full-time faculty:** 229 total; 39% have terminal degrees, 3% minority, 40% women. **Part-time faculty:** 62 total; 34% have terminal degrees, 3% minority, 81% women.

Freshman class profile. 1,182 applied, 978 admitted, 702 enrolled.

GPA 3.75 or higher:	10%	End year in good standing:	93%
GPA 3.50-3.74:	23%	Return as sophomores:	75%
GPA 3.0-3.49:	37%	Out-of-state:	75%
GPA 2.0-2.99:	26%	Live on campus:	85%
Rank in top quarter:	17%	International:	5%

Basis for selection. Prospective applicants whose admissions fall outside of the requirements will go to the Admissions Committee for a decision. Some graduate programs require interviews, auditions, and/or portfolios.

Home schooled: Achievement test scores. **Learning Disabled:** Students with documented learning disabilities are afforded help through the Learning Resource Center and the Academic Success Center.

High school preparation. College-preparatory program recommended. 16 units required. Required and recommended units include English 3, mathematics 2, social studies 2, science 1, foreign language 2 and academic electives 6.

2012-2013 Annual costs. Tuition/fees (projected): $12,730. Room/board: $5,100. Books/supplies: $1,336. Personal expenses: $3,996.

2010-2011 Financial aid. Need-based: 70% of total undergraduate aid awarded as scholarships/grants, 30% as loans/jobs. **Non-need-based:** Scholarships awarded for state residency.

Application procedures. Admission: Closing date 8/1 (receipt date). No application fee. Admission notification on a rolling basis. **Financial aid:** Priority date 3/1; no closing date. FAFSA required. Applicants notified on a rolling basis.

Academics. Special study options: Accelerated study, distance learning, ESL, independent study, internships, teacher certification program. **Credit/placement by examination:** AP, CLEP, ACT, institutional tests. **Support services:** Learning center, pre-admission summer program, reduced course load, remedial instruction, study skills assistance, tutoring, writing center.

Majors. Biology: General, molecular biochemistry. **Business:** Accounting, actuarial science, business admin, human resources, international, office management, office/clerical, restaurant/food services. **Communications:** General. **Computer sciences:** Computer science, information technology. **Education:** Biology, early childhood, elementary, English, mathematics, middle, music, science, social studies, special ed. **Engineering:** General. **English:** Creative writing, English lit, rhetoric/composition. **Foreign languages:** Spanish. **Health services:** Communication disorders, nursing (RN), premedicine. **History:** General. **Liberal arts:** Humanities. **Math:** General. **Parks/recreation:** Health/fitness. **Physical sciences:** Chemistry, physics. **Protective services:** Criminal justice. **Psychology:** Counseling. **Social sciences:** International relations, political science. **Theology:** Bible, missionary, religious ed, sacred music. **Visual/performing arts:** Art, cinematography, dramatic, fashion design, graphic design, music pedagogy, music performance, piano/keyboard, voice/opera. **Work/family studies:** General, food/nutrition.

Most popular majors. Business/marketing 19%, education 13%, health sciences 10%, theological studies 13%, visual/performing arts 10%.

Computing on campus. 420 workstations in dormitories, library, computer center. Dormitories linked to campus network. Commuter students can connect to campus network. Online course registration, online library, helpline, repair service, wireless network available.

Student life. Freshman orientation: Available. Preregistration for classes offered. Held in June. **Policies:** Religious observance required. **Housing:** Single-sex dorms, special housing for disabled, apartments available. **Activities:** Concert band, campus ministries, choral groups, drama, music ensembles, opera, radio station, student government, student newspaper, symphony orchestra, TV station.

Student services. Chaplain/spiritual director, career counseling, student employment services, financial aid counseling, health services, on-campus daycare, personal counseling, placement for graduates, veterans' counselor. **Physically disabled:** Services for visually, speech, hearing impaired.

Contact. E-mail: admission@bju.edu
Phone: (800) 252-6363 Toll-free number: (800) 252-6363
Fax: (800) 232-9258
Gary Deedrick, Director of Admission, Bob Jones University, 1700 Wade Hampton Boulevard, Greenville, SC 29614

Charleston Southern University
Charleston, South Carolina
www.csuniv.edu   **CB code: 5079**

- Private 4-year university and liberal arts college affiliated with Southern Baptist Convention
- Commuter campus in large city
- 2,895 degree-seeking undergraduates
- 65% of applicants admitted
- SAT or ACT with writing required

General. Founded in 1964. Regionally accredited. **Degrees:** 469 bachelor's awarded; master's offered. **ROTC:** Army, Air Force. **Location:** 15 miles from downtown. **Calendar:** 4-1-4, limited summer session. **Full-time faculty:** 138

total. **Part-time faculty:** 118 total. **Special facilities:** Earthquake research center.

Freshman class profile. 3,513 applied, 2,283 admitted, 708 enrolled.

Mid 50% test scores		ACT composite:	19-24
SAT critical reading:	440-550	Out-of-state:	23%
SAT math:	440-550	Live on campus:	73%

Basis for selection. School achievement record, academic coursework, test scores, GPA most important. Interview and recommendations considered. Students may be required to take institutional math test for acceptance and/or placement. Essay, interview recommended for all; audition recommended for music programs. **Learning Disabled:** Special needs allowances require documentation and interview with Director of Special Needs.

High school preparation. College-preparatory program recommended. 23 units required. Required and recommended units include English 4, mathematics 3-4, social studies 2, history 2, science 3 (laboratory 2) and foreign language 2.

2011-2012 Annual costs. Tuition/fees: $20,600. Room/board: $8,000. Books/supplies: $1,200.

Financial aid. Non-need-based: Scholarships awarded for academics, athletics, religious affiliation, ROTC.

Application procedures. Admission: No deadline. $40 fee, may be waived for applicants with need. Admission notification on a rolling basis beginning on or about 9/1. **Financial aid:** Priority date 4/15; no closing date. FAFSA required. Applicants notified on a rolling basis starting 3/1; must reply within 2 week(s) of notification.

Academics. Special study options: Accelerated study, combined bachelor's/graduate degree, cooperative education, cross-registration, distance learning, double major, dual enrollment of high school students, honors, internships, study abroad, teacher certification program. **Credit/placement by examination:** AP, CLEP, IB, SAT, ACT, institutional tests. 30 credit hours maximum toward bachelor's degree. **Support services:** Learning center, remedial instruction, study skills assistance, tutoring, writing center.

Majors. Biology: General, biochemistry. **Business:** Accounting, business admin, finance, management information systems, marketing. **Computer sciences:** General, computer science. **Education:** Early childhood, elementary, English, mathematics, multi-level teacher, music, physical, science, social studies, Spanish. **English:** English lit. **Foreign languages:** Spanish. **Health services:** Athletic training, music therapy, nursing (RN). **History:** General, American, European. **Liberal arts:** Humanities. **Math:** General, applied. **Parks/recreation:** Health/fitness. **Philosophy/religion:** Religion. **Physical sciences:** Chemistry. **Protective services:** Criminal justice. **Psychology:** General. **Social sciences:** General, economics, political science, sociology. **Theology:** Sacred music, youth ministry. **Visual/performing arts:** Graphic design, music, music performance, voice/opera.

Most popular majors. Biology 8%, business/marketing 30%, education 9%, health sciences 10%, psychology 7%, security/protective services 9%, social sciences 9%.

Computing on campus. 150 workstations in dormitories, library, computer center, student center. Dormitories wired for high-speed internet access. Commuter students can connect to campus network. Online library, helpline, student web hosting, wireless network available.

Student life. Freshman orientation: Available. Preregistration for classes offered. **Policies:** Religious observance required. **Housing:** Guaranteed on-campus for freshmen. Single-sex dorms available. $200 fully refundable deposit, deadline 8/15. **Activities:** Bands, choral groups, dance, drama, international student organizations, literary magazine, music ensembles, musical theater, student government, student newspaper, College Republicans, Young Democrats, Afro-American society, Baptist Student Union, Fellowship of Christian Athletes, Campus Crusade, future teachers society.

Athletics. NCAA. **Intercollegiate:** Baseball M, basketball, cross-country, football (tackle) M, golf, soccer, softball W, tennis, track and field, volleyball W. **Intramural:** Basketball, soccer, softball, volleyball. **Team name:** Buccaneer.

Student services. Adult student services, chaplain/spiritual director, career counseling, student employment services, financial aid counseling, health services, personal counseling, placement for graduates, veterans' counselor. **Physically disabled:** Services for visually, speech, hearing impaired.

Contact. E-mail: enroll@csuniv.edu
Phone: (843) 863-7050 Toll-free number: (800) 947-7474
Fax: (843) 863-7070
Jim Rhoton, Director of Admissions, Charleston Southern University, 9200 University Boulevard, Charleston, SC 29423-8087

The Citadel
Charleston, South Carolina
www.citadel.edu

CB member
CB code: 5108

▶ Public 4-year military college
▶ Residential campus in large city
▶ 2,401 degree-seeking undergraduates: 4% part-time, 7% women
▶ 776 degree-seeking graduate students
▶ 77% of applicants admitted
▶ SAT or ACT with writing required
▶ 72% graduate within 6 years; 15% enter graduate study

General. Founded in 1842. Regionally accredited. **Degrees:** 491 bachelor's awarded; master's offered. **ROTC:** Army, Naval, Air Force. **Location:** 110 miles from Columbia; 120 miles from Savannah, Georgia. **Calendar:** Semester, extensive summer session. **Full-time faculty:** 178 total; 94% have terminal degrees, 16% minority, 33% women. **Part-time faculty:** 86 total; 57% have terminal degrees, 20% minority, 34% women. **Class size:** 42% < 20, 50% 20-39, 4% 40-49, 4% 50-99. **Special facilities:** Archives, museum, beach house, boating center.

Freshman class profile. 2,523 applied, 1,940 admitted, 631 enrolled.

Mid 50% test scores			
SAT critical reading:	480-580	GPA 2.0-2.99:	19%
SAT math:	500-590	Rank in top quarter:	37%
ACT composite:	21-25	Rank in top tenth:	14%
GPA 3.75 or higher:	30%	Return as sophomores:	82%
GPA 3.50-3.74:	16%	Out-of-state:	54%
GPA 3.0-3.49:	35%	Live on campus:	100%
		International:	1%

Basis for selection. Admissions based on class rank, test scores, GPA, alumni recommendations, extracurricular activities. Interview recommended.

High school preparation. College-preparatory program required. 19 units required. Required units include English 4, mathematics 4, social studies 2, history 1, science 3 (laboratory 3), foreign language 2, computer science 1, visual/performing arts 1 and academic electives 1. 1 physical education or ROTC, 1 fine arts required. 1 of the Social Studies units must be US History.

2011-2012 Annual costs. Tuition/fees: $10,216; $27,033 out-of-state. Freshmen also pay $6440 deposit and upperclassmen pay $2374 deposit for uniforms, laundry, dry cleaning charges, infirmary fees, books, and supplies. Room/board: $7,228. Books/supplies: $6,440.

2011-2012 Financial aid. Need-based: 527 full-time freshmen applied for aid; 415 were judged to have need; 393 of these received aid. Average need met was 51%. Average scholarship/grant was $12,309; average loan $3,425. 56% of total undergraduate aid awarded as scholarships/grants, 44% as loans/jobs. **Non-need-based:** Awarded to 937 full-time undergraduates, including 214 freshmen. Scholarships awarded for academics, athletics, leadership, minority status, music/drama, ROTC, state residency.

Application procedures. Admission: No deadline. $40 fee. Admission notification on a rolling basis beginning on or about 7/15. **Financial aid:** Priority date 2/28; no closing date. FAFSA, institutional form required. Applicants notified on a rolling basis starting 4/1; must reply by 4/1 or within 2 week(s) of notification.

Academics. 4 years of ROTC required. **Special study options:** Cooperative education, distance learning, double major, ESL, honors, independent study, internships, study abroad, teacher certification program. **Credit/placement by examination:** AP, CLEP, SAT, institutional tests. **Support services:** Learning center, pre-admission summer program, study skills assistance, tutoring, writing center.

Majors. Biology: General. **Business:** Business admin. **Computer sciences:** General. **Education:** Physical, secondary. **Engineering:** Civil, electrical. **English:** English lit. **Foreign languages:** General. **History:** General. **Math:** General. **Physical sciences:** Chemistry, physics. **Protective services:** Law enforcement admin. **Psychology:** General. **Social sciences:** Political science.

Most popular majors. Business/marketing 30%, education 7%, engineering/engineering technologies 16%, history 6%, security/protective services 14%, social sciences 13%.

Computing on campus. 350 workstations in dormitories, library, computer center. Dormitories wired for high-speed internet access and linked to campus network. Commuter students can connect to campus network. Online course registration, online library, helpline, repair service, wireless network available.

Student life. Freshman orientation: Mandatory. Preregistration for classes offered. **Policies:** Freshmen not permitted cars on campus. **Housing:** Guaranteed on-campus for all undergraduates. Coed dorms available. $300 partly refundable deposit. **Activities:** Bands, campus ministries, choral groups, international student organizations, literary magazine, student government, student newspaper, African American Society, American Society of Civil Engineers, Association for Computing Machinery, Alpha Phi Sigma, Summerall Guards, African Methodist Episcopal, Baptist Student Union, Campus Crusade for Christ, Knights of Columbus, Army Aviator Association of America, WISE (Women in Science & Engineering).

Athletics. NCAA. Intercollegiate: Baseball M, basketball M, cross-country, football (tackle) M, golf W, rifle, soccer W, tennis M, track and field, volleyball W, wrestling M. **Intramural:** Badminton, basketball, diving, football (non-tackle), golf, handball, racquetball, soccer, softball, swimming, table tennis, tennis, track and field, triathlon, volleyball, weight lifting, wrestling. **Team name:** Bulldogs.

Student services. Alcohol/substance abuse counseling, chaplain/spiritual director, career counseling, student employment services, financial aid counseling, health services, minority student services, personal counseling, placement for graduates, veterans' counselor.

Contact. E-mail: admissions@citadel.edu
Phone: (843) 953-5230 Toll-free number: (800) 868-1842
Fax: (843) 953-7036
Lt. Col. John Powell, Director of Admissions, The Citadel, 171 Moultrie Street, Charleston, SC 29409

Claflin University
Orangeburg, South Carolina
www.claflin.edu

CB member
CB code: 5109

▶ Private 4-year liberal arts college affiliated with United Methodist Church
▶ Residential campus in large town
▶ 1,821 degree-seeking undergraduates: 1% part-time, 65% women, 93% African American, 1% Hispanic American, 1% Native American, 2% international
▶ 66 degree-seeking graduate students
▶ 39% of applicants admitted
▶ SAT or ACT (ACT writing optional), application essay required
▶ 40% graduate within 6 years

General. Founded in 1869. Regionally accredited. **Degrees:** 319 bachelor's awarded; master's offered. **ROTC:** Army, Air Force. **Location:** 37 miles from Columbia. **Calendar:** Semester, limited summer session. **Full-time faculty:** 117 total; 78% have terminal degrees, 72% minority, 41% women. **Part-time faculty:** 41 total; 32% have terminal degrees, 73% minority, 49% women. **Class size:** 55% < 20, 42% 20-39, 3% 40-49, less than 1% 50-99. **Special facilities:** Leadership development center, South Carolina Center for Biotechnology, Arthur Rose museum, molecular science research center, chapel.

Freshman class profile. 4,037 applied, 1,578 admitted, 408 enrolled.

Mid 50% test scores			
SAT critical reading:	380-490	Rank in top quarter:	55%
SAT math:	380-490	Rank in top tenth:	13%
ACT composite:	15-20	End year in good standing:	85%
GPA 3.75 or higher:	11%	Return as sophomores:	77%
GPA 3.50-3.74:	17%	Out-of-state:	22%
GPA 3.0-3.49:	31%	Live on campus:	93%
GPA 2.0-2.99:	40%	International:	2%

Basis for selection. Secondary school record, class rank, GPA, recommendations, test scores most important. Audition required; essay, interview, portfolio recommended for certain majors.

High school preparation. 24 units required. Required units include English 4, mathematics 3, social studies 1, history 1, science 3, foreign language 1, computer science 1 and academic electives 7. 1 physical education or Junior ROTC, .5 US government, .5 economics.

2011-2012 Annual costs. Tuition/fees: $13,680. Room/board: $7,520. Books/supplies: $1,500. Personal expenses: $3,825.

2011-2012 Financial aid. Need-based: Average scholarship/grant was $2,444; average loan $3,118. 60% of total undergraduate aid awarded as scholarships/grants, 40% as loans/jobs.

Application procedures. Admission: Priority date 1/15; deadline 8/1. $25 fee, may be waived for applicants with need. Admission notification on a rolling basis beginning on or about 10/1. **Financial aid:** Priority date 4/15; no closing date. FAFSA, institutional form required. Applicants notified on a rolling basis starting 5/15; must reply within 2 week(s) of notification.

Academics. Special study options: Accelerated study, cooperative education, cross-registration, double major, dual enrollment of high school students, exchange student, honors, independent study, internships, liberal arts/career combination, study abroad, teacher certification program, weekend college. **Credit/placement by examination:** AP, CLEP, SAT, ACT. 18 credit hours maximum toward bachelor's degree. **Support services:** Learning center, pre-admission summer program, reduced course load, remedial instruction, tutoring, writing center.

Honors college/program. Based on achievement, leadership, SAT score (1100) or ACT (24) and GPA 3.3., 65 to 75 admitted.

Majors. Area/ethnic studies: African-American, American. **Biology:** General, biochemistry, bioinformatics, biotechnology. **Business:** Business admin, management information systems, marketing, organizational behavior. **Communications:** Media studies. **Computer sciences:** Computer science. **Conservation:** Environmental science. **Education:** Art, early childhood, elementary, English, mathematics, middle, music. **Engineering:** Software. **English:** English lit. **History:** General. **Math:** General. **Parks/recreation:** Health/fitness, sports admin. **Philosophy/religion:** Philosophy, religion. **Physical sciences:** Chemistry. **Protective services:** Law enforcement admin. **Social sciences:** Political science, sociology. **Visual/performing arts:** Art, music, studio arts.

Most popular majors. Biology 11%, business/marketing 29%, communications/journalism 6%, security/protective services 20%, social sciences 14%.

Computing on campus. 540 workstations in dormitories, library, computer center, student center. Dormitories wired for high-speed internet access and linked to campus network. Commuter students can connect to campus network. Online course registration, online library, helpline, repair service, wireless network available.

Student life. Freshman orientation: Mandatory, $55 fee. Preregistration for classes offered. Early registration sessions held during summer; one-week orientation held during early fall; semester-long orientation seminars held during first academic year. **Policies:** Freshmen not permitted cars on campus. **Housing:** Guaranteed on-campus for freshmen. Single-sex dorms available. $55 nonrefundable deposit, deadline 7/1. **Activities:** Bands, choral groups, dance, drama, film society, international student organizations, literary magazine, music ensembles, radio station, student government, student newspaper, TV station, Alpha Kappa Mu, literature, art and film society, Phi Beta Lambda Business Fraternity, Students in Free Enterprise, NAACP, Claflin University Women's Group, Sigma Tau Delta English Honor Society.

Athletics. NCAA. **Intercollegiate:** Baseball M, basketball, cross-country, softball W, track and field, volleyball W. **Intramural:** Basketball, softball W, volleyball W. **Team name:** Panthers.

Student services. Adult student services, chaplain/spiritual director, career counseling, student employment services, financial aid counseling, health services, minority student services, personal counseling, placement for graduates, veterans' counselor.

Contact. E-mail: admissions@claflin.edu
Phone: (803) 535-5382 Toll-free number: (800) 922-1276
Fax: (803) 535-5385
Michael Zeigler, Director of Admissions, Claflin University, 400 Magnolia Street, Orangeburg, SC 29115

Clemson University
Clemson, South Carolina   **CB member**
www.clemson.edu   **CB code: 5111**

▸ Public 4-year university and engineering college
▸ Residential campus in large town
▸ 15,697 degree-seeking undergraduates
▸ 63% of applicants admitted
▸ SAT or ACT with writing required

General. Founded in 1889. Regionally accredited. **Degrees:** 3,443 bachelor's awarded; master's, doctoral offered. **ROTC:** Army, Air Force. **Location:** 17 miles from Anderson. **Calendar:** Semester, extensive summer session. **Full-time faculty:** 1,013 total; 88% have terminal degrees, 15% minority, 34% women. **Part-time faculty:** 109 total; 65% have terminal degrees, 10% minority, 38% women. **Class size:** 52% < 20, 27% 20-39, 7% 40-49, 10% 50-99, 4% >100. **Special facilities:** Planetarium, agricultural and forestry experimental facilities, geology museum, state botanical gardens, center for sustainable living, John C. Calhoun historical site and home, performing arts center.

Freshman class profile. 17,072 applied, 10,803 admitted, 2,933 enrolled.

Mid 50% test scores			
SAT critical reading:	550-650	GPA 2.0-2.99:	1%
SAT math:	590-680	Rank in top quarter:	80%
ACT composite:	25-30	Rank in top tenth:	48%
GPA 3.75 or higher:	80%	Out-of-state:	35%
GPA 3.50-3.74:	9%	Live on campus:	98%
GPA 3.0-3.49:	10%	Fraternities:	14%
		Sororities:	27%

Basis for selection. Admission competitive and based largely on high school curriculum, performance in that curriculum, peer comparison, SAT or ACT scores, and choice of major. Campus visit recommended for all. Interview, portfolio recommended for art applicants. Audition required for performing arts program applicants. **Home schooled:** Statement describing home school structure and mission, transcript of courses and grades required. Include copies of all secondary school transcripts and course descriptions of any courses different from those traditionally offered in public school settings.

High school preparation. College-preparatory program required. 19 units required. Required and recommended units include English 4, mathematics 3-4, social studies 3-4, history 1-2, science 3 (laboratory 3-4), foreign language 3-4 and academic electives 2. Also require physical education or ROTC. 3 foreign language units must be in same language.

2011-2012 Annual costs. Tuition/fees: $12,304; $28,462 out-of-state. Laptop computer required of all entering new students. This cost has been estimated at $1,600. Room/board: $7,570. Books/supplies: $900. Personal expenses: $1,920.

2011-2012 Financial aid. Need-based: 45% of total undergraduate aid awarded as scholarships/grants, 55% as loans/jobs. **Non-need-based:** Scholarships awarded for academics, art, athletics, leadership, minority status, music/drama, ROTC, state residency.

Application procedures. Admission: Priority date 12/1; deadline 5/1 (receipt date). $60 fee, may be waived for applicants with need. Application must be submitted online. Admission notification on a rolling basis beginning on or about 2/15. Must reply by 5/1. Scholarship candidates notified on rolling basis, beginning on or about October 1 for fall admission. Preferred application date of December 1. Those who apply by that date, and whose application file is complete, will receive an admission decision on or about the week of February 15 for fall admission. **Financial aid:** Priority date 4/1; no closing date. FAFSA required. Applicants notified on a rolling basis starting 4/1; must reply within 3 week(s) of notification.

Academics. Special study options: Combined bachelor's/graduate degree, cooperative education, distance learning, double major, dual enrollment of high school students, ESL, exchange student, external degree, honors, independent study, internships, study abroad, teacher certification program, Washington semester. Cooperative language center. **Credit/placement by examination:** AP, CLEP, IB, institutional tests. Challenge examinations offered by each academic department. **Support services:** Learning center, pre-admission summer program, study skills assistance, tutoring, writing center.

Honors college/program. Less than 10 percent of freshman class invited to enroll. Minimum peer comparison must show student in top 3 percent of graduating secondary school class.

Majors. Architecture: Architecture, landscape. **Biology:** General, biochemistry, biomedical sciences, botany, entomology, genetics, microbiology, plant pathology, zoology. **Business:** General, accounting, construction management, finance, marketing, operations. **Computer sciences:** General, information systems. **Conservation:** General, forest management, forest sciences. **Education:** Agricultural, early childhood, elementary, mathematics, middle, science, secondary, special ed, technology/industrial arts. **Engineering:** Agricultural, biomedical, ceramic, chemical, civil, computer, electrical, industrial, mechanical. **English:** English lit, rhetoric/composition. **Foreign languages:** General, Spanish. **General:** Agronomy, animal sciences, aquaculture, business, economics, food science, horticultural science, horticulture, plant sciences. **Health services:** Clinical lab science, nursing (RN), predental, premedicine, prepharmacy, preveterinary. **History:** General. **Math:** General. **Parks/recreation:** Facilities management. **Philosophy/religion:** Philosophy. **Physical sciences:** Chemistry, geology, physics. **Psychology:** General. **Social sciences:** Economics, political science, sociology. **Visual/performing arts:** Art.

Most popular majors. Business/marketing 16%, engineering/engineering technologies 10%, health sciences 6%, physical sciences 30%, social sciences 6%.

Computing on campus. PC or laptop required. 875 workstations in library, computer center. Dormitories wired for high-speed internet access and linked to campus network. Commuter students can connect to campus network. Online course registration, online library, helpline, repair service, student web hosting, wireless network available.

Student life. Freshman orientation: Mandatory, $55 fee. Preregistration for classes offered. One and 1/2-day sessions held 8 times during June and July. Students must complete online mathematics placement exam prior to participating in orientation. **Policies:** All students required to submit proof of legal presence in the United States. **Housing:** Guaranteed on-campus for all undergraduates. Coed dorms, single-sex dorms, special housing for disabled, apartments, fraternity/sorority housing, wellness housing available. $100 nonrefundable deposit. Housing guaranteed so long as continuing in on-campus housing. **Activities:** Bands, choral groups, dance, drama, international student organizations, literary magazine, music ensembles, musical theater, radio station, student government, student newspaper, symphony orchestra, TV station, religious organizations, Young Democrats, Young Republicans, minority awareness organizations, Blue Key, Alpha Phi Omega, Mortarboard, Hillel, Fellowship of Christian Athletes.

Athletics. NCAA. **Intercollegiate:** Baseball M, basketball, cross-country, diving, football (tackle) M, golf M, rowing (crew) W, soccer, swimming, tennis, track and field, volleyball W. **Intramural:** Basketball, diving, fencing, field hockey W, football (non-tackle), golf, racquetball, soccer, softball, table tennis, tennis, track and field, volleyball. **Team name:** Tigers.

Student services. Alcohol/substance abuse counseling, chaplain/spiritual director, career counseling, student employment services, financial aid counseling, health services, minority student services, personal counseling, placement for graduates, veterans' counselor. **Physically disabled:** Services for visually, speech, hearing impaired.

Contact. E-mail: cuadmissions@clemson.edu
Phone: (864) 656-2287 Fax: (864) 656-2464
Robert Barkley, Director of Admissions, Clemson University, 105 Sikes Hall, Clemson, SC 29634-5124

Coastal Carolina University
Conway, South Carolina
www.coastal.edu

CB member
CB code: 5837

- Public 4-year university
- Commuter campus in large town
- 8,297 degree-seeking undergraduates: 6% part-time, 53% women, 20% African American, 1% Asian American, 3% Hispanic American, 1% international
- 383 degree-seeking graduate students
- 75% of applicants admitted
- SAT or ACT (ACT writing optional) required
- 46% graduate within 6 years

General. Founded in 1954. Regionally accredited. Barrier-reef island used for marine science field studies and research. **Degrees:** 1,379 bachelor's awarded; master's offered. **ROTC:** Army. **Location:** 9 miles from Myrtle Beach. **Calendar:** Semester, extensive summer session. **Full-time faculty:** 351 total; 79% have terminal degrees, 12% minority, 42% women. **Part-time faculty:** 268 total; 25% have terminal degrees, 8% minority, 57% women. **Class size:** 36% < 20, 49% 20-39, 11% 40-49, 3% 50-99, less than 1% >100.

Freshman class profile. 10,502 applied, 7,836 admitted, 2,137 enrolled.

Mid 50% test scores			
SAT critical reading:	450-540	Rank in top tenth:	9%
SAT math:	460-560	End year in good standing:	71%
ACT composite:	18-22	Return as sophomores:	63%
GPA 3.75 or higher:	25%	Out-of-state:	54%
GPA 3.50-3.74:	15%	Live on campus:	87%
GPA 3.0-3.49:	32%	International:	1%
GPA 2.0-2.99:	28%	Fraternities:	8%
Rank in top quarter:	32%	Sororities:	16%

Basis for selection. Secondary school record and test scores most important; class rank important. Applicants whose native language is not English must take TOEFL. Tests are not required for applicants 22 years or older. Interview recommended for all. **Home schooled:** Transcript of courses and grades required. Copy of declaration of intent to home school as filed with local board of education. **Learning Disabled:** To become eligible for support services, students with disabilities must provide documentation of disability to Service for Students with Disabilities Office.

High school preparation. College-preparatory program required. 19 units required. Required and recommended units include English 4, mathematics 4, social studies 2, history 1, science 3 (laboratory 3), foreign language 2, computer science 1, visual/performing arts 1 and academic electives 1. 1 unit of physical education or ROTC.

2011-2012 Annual costs. Tuition/fees: $9,760; $21,560 out-of-state. Room/board: $7,700.

2010-2011 Financial aid. Need-based: 1,811 full-time freshmen applied for aid; 1,467 were judged to have need; 1,453 of these received aid. Average need met was 51%. Average scholarship/grant was $5,319; average loan $8,117. 46% of total undergraduate aid awarded as scholarships/grants, 54% as loans/jobs. **Non-need-based:** Awarded to 3,013 full-time undergraduates, including 1,084 freshmen. Scholarships awarded for academics, art, athletics, leadership, music/drama, ROTC, state residency.

Application procedures. Admission: Priority date 12/1; deadline 8/1 (receipt date). $45 fee, may be waived for applicants with need. Admission notification on a rolling basis beginning on or about 9/1. Must reply by May 1 or within 2 week(s) if notified thereafter. **Financial aid:** Priority date 3/1; no closing date. FAFSA required. Applicants notified on a rolling basis starting 3/1; must reply by 5/15.

Academics. Professional golf management specialization in any program in the Wall College of Business, accredited by PGA. International tourism management specialization in resort tourism management program. CPA/CMA option in accounting. **Special study options:** Accelerated study, combined bachelor's/graduate degree, cooperative education, distance learning, double major, dual enrollment of high school students, honors, independent study, internships, liberal arts/career combination, student-designed major, study abroad, teacher certification program. 3-2 engineering program with Clemson University. **Credit/placement by examination:** AP, CLEP, IB, SAT, ACT, institutional tests. Credit by examination must be obtained prior to reaching senior classification (90 credit hours). Will not be awarded for courses previously audited, or courses that have been previously failed. Cannot be used to raise a grade previously earned in a college course. **Support services:** Learning center, reduced course load, tutoring, writing center.

Majors. Biology: General, biochemistry, marine. **Business:** Accounting, business admin, finance, managerial economics, marketing, resort management. **Communications:** Communications/speech/rhetoric. **Computer sciences:** General, information systems. **Education:** Early childhood, elementary, middle, physical, special ed. **English:** English lit. **Foreign languages:** Spanish. **Health services:** Health care admin, nursing (RN), public health ed. **History:** General. **Liberal arts:** Arts/sciences. **Math:** Applied. **Parks/recreation:** Exercise sciences, sports admin. **Philosophy/religion:** Philosophy. **Physical sciences:** Chemistry, physics. **Psychology:** General. **Social sciences:** Economics, political science, sociology. **Visual/performing arts:** Dramatic, graphic design, music, musical theater, studio arts.

Most popular majors. Biology 11%, business/marketing 29%, communications/journalism 7%, education 10%, parks/recreation 7%, psychology 6%, social sciences 6%.

Computing on campus. 700 workstations in dormitories, library, computer center, student center. Dormitories wired for high-speed internet access and linked to campus network. Commuter students can connect to campus network. Online course registration, online library, helpline, student web hosting, wireless network available.

Student life. Freshman orientation: Mandatory, $140 fee. Preregistration for classes offered. 2-day programs. **Housing:** Coed dorms, special housing for disabled, apartments available. $150 partly refundable deposit, deadline 5/1. **Activities:** Bands, campus ministries, choral groups, dance, drama, international student organizations, literary magazine, music ensembles, musical theater, radio station, student government, student newspaper, African American Association, Students Taking Active Responsibility, Refuge, Baptist collegiate ministry, Campus Democrats, College Republicans.

Athletics. NCAA. **Intercollegiate:** Baseball M, basketball, cheerleading, cross-country, football (tackle) M, golf, soccer, softball W, tennis, track and field, volleyball W. **Intramural:** Badminton, basketball, football (non-tackle), golf, soccer, softball, table tennis, tennis, volleyball, water polo. **Team name:** Chanticleers.

Student services. Adult student services, alcohol/substance abuse counseling, career counseling, student employment services, financial aid counseling, health services, minority student services, personal counseling, placement for graduates, veterans' counselor, women's services. **Physically disabled:** Services for visually, speech, hearing impaired.

Contact. E-mail: admissions@coastal.edu
Phone: (843) 349-2170 Toll-free number: (800) 277-7000
Fax: (843) 349-2127
Judy Vogt, Vice President for Enrollment Services, Coastal Carolina University, PO Box 261954, Conway, SC 29528-6054

Coker College
Hartsville, South Carolina
www.coker.edu

CB member
CB code: 5112

▸ Private 4-year liberal arts college
▸ Residential campus in large town
▸ 1,090 degree-seeking undergraduates: 12% part-time, 69% women, 40% African American, 2% Hispanic American, 1% Native American, 2% international
▸ 48% of applicants admitted
▸ SAT or ACT (ACT writing optional) required

General. Founded in 1908. Regionally accredited. **Degrees:** 247 bachelor's awarded. **Location:** 70 miles from Columbia, 80 miles from Charlotte, NC. **Calendar:** Semester, limited summer session. **Full-time faculty:** 63 total; 92% have terminal degrees, 51% women. **Part-time faculty:** 52 total; 14% have terminal degrees, 48% women. **Class size:** 75% < 20, 25% 20-39. **Special facilities:** Botanical gardens, boathouse, clubhouse, 9-hole disc golf course.

Freshman class profile. 1,278 applied, 616 admitted, 338 enrolled.

Mid 50% test scores			
SAT critical reading:	440-550	GPA 3.0-3.49:	25%
SAT math:	450-550	GPA 2.0-2.99:	20%
ACT composite:	18-24	Rank in top quarter:	38%
GPA 3.75 or higher:	38%	Rank in top tenth:	15%
GPA 3.50-3.74:	14%	Return as sophomores:	90%
		Out-of-state:	21%

Basis for selection. Each applicant evaluated based on the rigor of school record, academic GPA and/or standardized test scores. Involvement in extracurricular activities, letters of recommendation, talents and qualities are also important and are taken into consideration before an official decision is made.

High school preparation. College-preparatory program required. 15 units required. Required units include English 4, mathematics 3, social studies 3, science 3 (laboratory 1) and foreign language 2.

2011-2012 Annual costs. Tuition/fees: $22,800. Room/board: $6,950. Books/supplies: $1,200. Personal expenses: $1,091.

2011-2012 Financial aid. **Need-based:** 197 full-time freshmen applied for aid; 184 were judged to have need; 184 of these received aid. Average need met was 46%. Average scholarship/grant was $3,379; average loan $1,828. 61% of total undergraduate aid awarded as scholarships/grants, 39% as loans/jobs. **Non-need-based:** Awarded to 689 full-time undergraduates, including 206 freshmen. Scholarships awarded for academics, alumni affiliation, art, athletics, job skills, leadership, minority status, music/drama, religious affiliation, ROTC, state residency. **Additional information:** Endowed scholarship program for qualified applicants. June 1 deadline for filing South Carolina Tuition Grant forms.

Application procedures. **Admission:** Priority date 5/1; deadline 8/1. $25 fee, may be waived for applicants with need. Admission notification on a rolling basis beginning on or about 9/1. Must reply by May 1 or within 8 week(s) if notified thereafter. Juniors allowed to apply and make admissions decision during summer prior to senior year. **Financial aid:** Priority date 4/1, closing date 6/1. FAFSA required. Applicants notified on a rolling basis starting 3/1; must reply by 5/1 or within 3 week(s) of notification.

Academics. **Special study options:** Distance learning, double major, dual enrollment of high school students, honors, independent study, internships, student-designed major, study abroad, teacher certification program. 2-2 programs with two-year colleges, 3-1 program with regional medical facility. **Credit/placement by examination:** AP, CLEP, IB, SAT, ACT, institutional tests. Unlimited hours of credit by examination may be counted toward degree. **Support services:** Remedial instruction, study skills assistance, tutoring, writing center.

Majors. **Biology:** General. **Business:** General. **Communications:** Communications/speech/rhetoric. **Computer sciences:** Computer science. **Education:** General, art, biology, chemistry, early childhood, elementary, English, history, mathematics, music, physical. **English:** English lit, technical writing. **Foreign languages:** Spanish. **Health services:** Clinical lab science. **History:** General. **Human services:** Social work. **Math:** General. **Parks/recreation:** Exercise sciences, health/fitness, sports admin. **Physical sciences:** Chemistry. **Psychology:** General, counseling. **Social sciences:** Criminology, political science, sociology. **Visual/performing arts:** Acting, dance, dramatic, graphic design, music, photography, piano/keyboard, studio arts, theater design, voice/opera.

Most popular majors. Business/marketing 22%, education 14%, psychology 12%, public administration/social services 8%, social sciences 20%, visual/performing arts 6%.

Computing on campus. 116 workstations in dormitories, library, computer center. Dormitories wired for high-speed internet access and linked to campus network. Online course registration, online library, helpline, wireless network available.

Student life. **Freshman orientation:** Mandatory. Preregistration for classes offered. **Housing:** Guaranteed on-campus for freshmen. Coed dorms, special housing for disabled available. $150 partly refundable deposit, deadline 5/1. Honors housing, loft apartments. **Activities:** Campus ministries, choral groups, dance, drama, international student organizations, literary magazine, musical theater, student government, Fellowship of Christian Athletes, Pan African Sisterhood Association, Psi Chi.

Athletics. NCAA. **Intercollegiate:** Baseball M, basketball, cheerleading, cross-country, golf, lacrosse M, soccer, softball W, tennis, volleyball W. **Intramural:** Basketball, cross-country, football (non-tackle), soccer, softball, tennis, volleyball. **Team name:** Cobras.

Student services. Adult student services, career counseling, student employment services, financial aid counseling, health services, personal counseling.

Contact. E-mail: admissions@coker.edu
Phone: (843) 383-8050 Toll-free number: (800) 950-1908
Fax: (843) 383-8056
Adam Connolly, Director of Admissions, Coker College, 300 East College Avenue, Hartsville, SC 29550

College of Charleston
Charleston, South Carolina
www.cofc.edu

CB member
CB code: 5113

▸ Public 4-year liberal arts college
▸ Residential campus in large city
▸ 10,132 degree-seeking undergraduates: 5% part-time, 62% women, 6% African American, 1% Asian American, 3% Hispanic American, 1% international
▸ 585 degree-seeking graduate students
▸ 74% of applicants admitted
▸ SAT or ACT (ACT writing optional), application essay required
▸ 63% graduate within 6 years

General. Founded in 1770. Regionally accredited. **Degrees:** 2,213 bachelor's awarded; master's offered. **ROTC:** Air Force. **Calendar:** Semester, limited summer session. **Full-time faculty:** 542 total; 89% have terminal degrees, 12% minority, 42% women. **Part-time faculty:** 395 total; 33% have terminal degrees, 8% minority, 56% women. **Class size:** 32% < 20, 54% 20-39, 8% 40-49, 5% 50-99, less than 1% >100. **Special facilities:** Communications museum, early childhood development center, observatory, marine science laboratory, sculpture studio, sailing center, African-American history and culture research center, bilingual legal interpreting center, media and technology studio, center for entrepreneurship, real estate center, natural history museum.

Freshman class profile. 11,086 applied, 8,149 admitted, 2,334 enrolled.

Mid 50% test scores			
SAT critical reading:	560-650	Rank in top quarter:	63%
SAT math:	550-640	Rank in top tenth:	28%
ACT composite:	23-27	Return as sophomores:	83%
GPA 3.75 or higher:	53%	Out-of-state:	46%
GPA 3.50-3.74:	20%	Live on campus:	93%
GPA 3.0-3.49:	24%	Fraternities:	17%
GPA 2.0-2.99:	3%	Sororities:	24%

Basis for selection. School grades, class rank, curriculum most important, then test scores. Recommendations and activities are considered. Essay required and personal statement is optional. Writing portion of ACT required only if student does not also submit SAT (with mandatory Writing component). Interviews are not required. Campus visits and personal meetings with College of Charleston personnel are encouraged. **Home schooled:** Transcript of courses and grades required. Students should indicate which school district syllabus was followed during home schooling. **Learning Disabled:** Explanation of curriculum modifications are recommended. Documentation is not required in the admissions process, but must be submitted to utilize disability services if enrolled.

High school preparation. College-preparatory program required. 21 units required. Required and recommended units include English 4, mathematics 4, social studies 2, history 1-2, science 3 (laboratory 3), foreign language 3, computer science 1 and academic electives 3. Mathematics requirement includes 2 algebra. Social science recommendation .5 economics and .5 government. 2 units of same foreign language, 1 additional unit of advanced

mathematics, computer science, world history, world geography, or Western civilization required. 1 unit of five arts.

2011-2012 Annual costs. Tuition/fees: $9,616; $24,330 out-of-state. Room/board: $10,179. Books/supplies: $1,224. Personal expenses: $1,715.

2010-2011 Financial aid. Need-based: 1,392 full-time freshmen applied for aid; 987 were judged to have need; 940 of these received aid. Average need met was 56%. Average scholarship/grant was $2,942; average loan $2,887. 51% of total undergraduate aid awarded as scholarships/grants, 49% as loans/jobs. **Non-need-based:** Awarded to 3,685 full-time undergraduates, including 1,156 freshmen. Scholarships awarded for academics, alumni affiliation, art, athletics, music/drama.

Application procedures. Admission: Priority date 2/1; deadline 4/1 (receipt date). $50 fee, may be waived for applicants with need. Admission notification by 4/1. Admission notification on a rolling basis beginning on or about 12/15. Must reply by 5/1. March 1 application date recommended for residence hall students. **Financial aid:** Priority date 3/15; no closing date. FAFSA required. Applicants notified on a rolling basis starting 4/10; must reply within 8 week(s) of notification.

Academics. Special study options: Accelerated study, combined bachelor's/graduate degree, cooperative education, cross-registration, distance learning, double major, dual enrollment of high school students, ESL, exchange student, honors, independent study, internships, liberal arts/career combination, semester at sea, study abroad, teacher certification program. Internships and courses in conjunction with Spoleto US (international arts festival); 3-2 engineering program with Case Western Reserve University, Clemson University, University of South Carolina; marine engineering option with University of Michigan. **Credit/placement by examination:** AP, CLEP, IB, SAT, institutional tests. 30 credit hours maximum toward bachelor's degree. **Support services:** Learning center, pre-admission summer program, reduced course load, study skills assistance, tutoring, writing center.

Honors college/program. Students admitted to honors program are typically in top 10 percent of class, have taken numerous honors and/or AP courses, active in eHonors extracurricular activities. No minimum SAT or ACT score required but average is 1340 on the SAT Math and Reading and 30 on ACT composite. Approximately 200 entering freshmen enroll each year. Students encouraged to apply to both the College of Charleston and the Honors College (separate applications) before November 1.

Majors. Area/ethnic studies: Latin American/Caribbean, women's. **Biology:** General, marine. **Business:** Accounting, business admin, hospitality admin, international. **Communications:** Communications/speech/rhetoric. **Computer sciences:** General, information systems. **Education:** Early childhood, elementary, middle, physical, secondary, special ed. **English:** English lit. **Foreign languages:** Classics, French, German, Spanish. **Health services:** Athletic training. **History:** General. **Math:** General. **Philosophy/religion:** Judaic, philosophy, religion. **Physical sciences:** Astronomy, astrophysics, chemistry, geology, physics. **Psychology:** General. **Social sciences:** Anthropology, economics, political science, sociology, urban studies. **Visual/performing arts:** Art history/conservation, dramatic, music, studio arts, studio arts management.

Most popular majors. Biology 9%, business/marketing 23%, communications/journalism 10%, education 10%, psychology 8%, social sciences 11%, visual/performing arts 8%.

Computing on campus. 2,500 workstations in dormitories, library, computer center, student center. Dormitories wired for high-speed internet access and linked to campus network. Commuter students can connect to campus network. Online course registration, helpline, wireless network available.

Student life. Freshman orientation: Mandatory. Preregistration for classes offered. **Policies:** Honor system, student code of conduct, alcohol and drug policies, students' rights and responsibilities, and other policies and guidelines such as class attendance policies set by individual instructors. Freshmen not permitted cars on campus. **Housing:** Coed dorms, single-sex dorms, apartments, fraternity/sorority housing available. $200 nonrefundable deposit, deadline 5/1. Restored old Charleston houses used as residence halls, some with kitchen facilities in suite. **Activities:** Bands, campus ministries, choral groups, dance, drama, international student organizations, literary magazine, music ensembles, musical theater, radio station, student government, student newspaper, symphony orchestra, 175 organizations available.

Athletics. NCAA. **Intercollegiate:** Baseball M, basketball, cross-country, diving, equestrian W, golf, sailing, soccer, softball W, swimming, tennis, track and field W, volleyball W. **Intramural:** Badminton, basketball, football (non-tackle), racquetball, soccer, softball, table tennis, tennis, volleyball, weight lifting. **Team name:** Cougars.

Student services. Adult student services, alcohol/substance abuse counseling, chaplain/spiritual director, career counseling, student employment services, financial aid counseling, health services, legal services, minority student services, on-campus daycare, personal counseling, placement for graduates, veterans' counselor. **Physically disabled:** Services for visually, speech, hearing impaired.

Contact. E-mail: admissions@cofc.edu
Phone: (843) 953-5670 Fax: (843) 953-6322
Suzette Stille, Director of Admission, College of Charleston, Office of Admissions and Adult Student Services, Charleston, SC 29424-0001

Columbia College
Columbia, South Carolina   CB member
www.columbiasc.edu   CB code: 5117

- Private 4-year liberal arts college for women affiliated with United Methodist Church
- Residential campus in large city
- 1,109 degree-seeking undergraduates: 21% part-time, 98% women
- 122 degree-seeking graduate students
- 69% of applicants admitted
- SAT or ACT with writing required
- 47% graduate within 6 years

General. Founded in 1854. Regionally accredited. **Degrees:** 210 bachelor's awarded; master's offered. **ROTC:** Army. **Location:** 70 miles from Charlotte, North Carolina. **Calendar:** Semester, limited summer session. **Full-time faculty:** 71 total; 80% have terminal degrees, 14% minority, 66% women. **Part-time faculty:** 65 total; 31% have terminal degrees, 15% minority, 55% women. **Class size:** 67% < 20, 33% 20-39. **Special facilities:** Leadership center for women.

Freshman class profile. 893 applied, 617 admitted, 193 enrolled.

Mid 50% test scores		
SAT critical reading:	450-570	
SAT math:	450-550	
SAT writing:	430-530	
ACT composite:	19-24	
GPA 3.75 or higher:	48%	
GPA 3.50-3.74:	15%	
GPA 3.0-3.49:	23%	

GPA 2.0-2.99:	14%
Rank in top quarter:	53%
Rank in top tenth:	20%
End year in good standing:	87%
Return as sophomores:	69%
Out-of-state:	16%
Live on campus:	87%

Basis for selection. School record, test scores, recommendations most important. Audition recommended for dance, music programs; portfolio recommended for art programs; essay, interview recommended for borderline applicants.

High school preparation. 16 units recommended. Recommended units include English 4, mathematics 3, social studies 2, history 1, science 2 (laboratory 2), foreign language 2 and academic electives 2. 2.5 units in music, dance, art also recommended.

2011-2012 Annual costs. Tuition/fees: $25,050. Room/board: $6,638. Books/supplies: $800. Personal expenses: $2,750.

2010-2011 Financial aid. Need-based: 200 full-time freshmen applied for aid; 187 were judged to have need; 187 of these received aid. Average need met was 77%. Average scholarship/grant was $19,517; average loan $3,252. 65% of total undergraduate aid awarded as scholarships/grants, 35% as loans/jobs. **Non-need-based:** Scholarships awarded for academics, alumni affiliation, art, athletics, leadership, music/drama.

Application procedures. Admission: No deadline. $25 fee, may be waived for applicants with need, free for online applicants. Admission notification on a rolling basis beginning on or about 10/1. Must reply by May 1 or within 4 week(s) if notified thereafter. **Financial aid:** Priority date 4/1; no closing date. FAFSA required. Applicants notified on a rolling basis starting 3/15; must reply within 2 week(s) of notification.

Academics. Special study options: Double major, dual enrollment of high school students, exchange student, honors, independent study, internships, student-designed major, study abroad, teacher certification program, Washington semester. **Credit/placement by examination:** AP, CLEP, IB, SAT, ACT, institutional tests. **Support services:** Learning center, reduced course load, remedial instruction, study skills assistance, tutoring, writing center.

Majors. Biology: General, biochemistry. **Business:** Accounting, business admin. **Communications:** Communications/speech/rhetoric, journalism. **Computer sciences:** General. **Education:** Drama/dance, early childhood, elementary, middle, music, special ed. **English:** English lit. **Foreign languages:** French, Spanish. **Health services:** Speech pathology. **History:** General. **Human services:** Social work. **Liberal arts:** Arts/sciences. **Math:** General. **Philosophy/religion:** Religion. **Physical sciences:** Chemistry. **Psychology:** General. **Social sciences:** Political science. **Theology:** Religious

ed. **Visual/performing arts:** Art, dance, music, music performance, piano/keyboard, studio arts, voice/opera. **Work/family studies:** Family studies.

Most popular majors. Business/marketing 12%, communications/journalism 6%, education 20%, family/consumer sciences 7%, psychology 12%, public administration/social services 9%, visual/performing arts 9%.

Computing on campus. 165 workstations in dormitories, library, computer center, student center. Dormitories wired for high-speed internet access and linked to campus network. Online course registration, online library, helpline, repair service, wireless network available.

Student life. Freshman orientation: Available, $150 fee. Preregistration for classes offered. One-day program in June. 4-day program in August where students participate in community service project. **Policies:** All students required to live on campus during first 2 years unless living with parent or guardian. All residence halls nonsmoking. Chapel requirements in place for first-year, sophomore, and junior students. Religious observance required. **Housing:** Guaranteed on-campus for freshmen. Wellness housing available. $100 deposit, deadline 5/1. **Activities:** Concert band, choral groups, dance, drama, international student organizations, literary magazine, music ensembles, musical theater, student government, student newspaper, Young Republicans, Young Democrats, CC Serves, Sister to Sista, African-American student association, NAACP.

Athletics. NAIA. **Intercollegiate:** Basketball W, soccer W, softball W, tennis W, volleyball W. **Team name:** Koalas.

Student services. Adult student services, chaplain/spiritual director, career counseling, student employment services, financial aid counseling, health services, personal counseling, placement for graduates, veterans' counselor.

Contact. E-mail: admissions@columbiasc.edu
Phone: (803) 786-3871 Toll-free number: (800) 277-1301
Fax: (803) 786-3674
Ron White, Vice President of Enrollment Management, Columbia College, 1301 Columbia College Drive, Columbia, SC 29203

Columbia International University
Columbia, South Carolina
www.ciu.edu   **CB code: 5116**

- Private 4-year university and Bible college affiliated with multidenominational/evangelical churches
- Residential campus in small city
- 542 degree-seeking undergraduates: 4% part-time, 51% women, 8% African American, 2% Asian American, 3% Hispanic American, 4% international
- 385 degree-seeking graduate students
- 67% of applicants admitted
- SAT or ACT (ACT writing optional), application essay required
- 57% graduate within 6 years

General. Founded in 1923. Regionally accredited; also accredited by ABHE, ATS. **Degrees:** 102 bachelor's, 17 associate awarded; master's, doctoral offered. **Location:** 75 miles from Charlotte, NC, 225 miles from Atlanta. **Calendar:** Semester, limited summer session. **Full-time faculty:** 37 total. **Part-time faculty:** 36 total. **Class size:** 60% < 20, 29% 20-39, 4% 40-49, 2% 50-99, 5% >100. **Special facilities:** Prayer towers.

Freshman class profile. 246 applied, 166 admitted, 83 enrolled.

Mid 50% test scores			
SAT critical reading:	530-630	**GPA 2.0-2.99:**	8%
SAT math:	490-580	**Rank in top quarter:**	47%
SAT writing:	490-600	**Rank in top tenth:**	27%
ACT composite:	20-26	**Return as sophomores:**	81%
GPA 3.75 or higher:	58%	**Out-of-state:**	35%
GPA 3.50-3.74:	19%	**Live on campus:**	95%
GPA 3.0-3.49:	15%	**International:**	7%

Basis for selection. School achievement, recommendations, test scores, essay, school and community activities, religious commitment important. Audition required for church music program. **Home schooled:** Transcripts should include GPA.

High school preparation. Recommended units include English 4, mathematics 2, social studies 2, science 1 and foreign language 2. Thorough background in English grammar and composition required.

2011-2012 Annual costs. Tuition/fees: $18,040. Room/board: $6,670. Books/supplies: $600. Personal expenses: $2,000.

2010-2011 Financial aid. Need-based: 103 full-time freshmen applied for aid; 94 were judged to have need; 92 of these received aid. Average need met was 86%. Average scholarship/grant was $9,510; average loan $3,359. 74% of total undergraduate aid awarded as scholarships/grants, 26% as loans/jobs. **Non-need-based:** Awarded to 368 full-time undergraduates, including 75 freshmen. Scholarships awarded for academics, alumni affiliation, athletics, leadership, religious affiliation, state residency. **Additional information:** Spouse scholarship program; special short quarter scholarships for missionaries on furlough.

Application procedures. Admission: Priority date 5/1; deadline 8/1 (postmark date). $45 fee, may be waived for applicants with need. Admission notification on a rolling basis. **Financial aid:** Priority date 2/28, closing date 6/30. FAFSA, institutional form required. Applicants notified on a rolling basis starting 3/1; must reply by 6/1.

Academics. Special study options: Combined bachelor's/graduate degree, cross-registration, distance learning, double major, independent study, internships, liberal arts/career combination, study abroad, teacher certification program. **Credit/placement by examination:** AP, CLEP, IB. 15 credit hours maximum toward associate degree, 30 toward bachelor's. **Support services:** Learning center, reduced course load, remedial instruction, study skills assistance, tutoring.

Majors. Area/ethnic studies: Near/Middle Eastern. **Business:** Nonprofit/public. **Communications:** Communications/speech/rhetoric. **Education:** Multi-level teacher. **English:** English lit. **Foreign languages:** Biblical. **Liberal arts:** Humanities. **Psychology:** General. **Theology:** Bible, pastoral counseling, religious ed, sacred music, youth ministry.

Most popular majors. Interdisciplinary studies 7%, liberal arts 12%, psychology 8%, theological studies 64%.

Computing on campus. 46 workstations in library, computer center. Dormitories wired for high-speed internet access and linked to campus network. Online course registration, online library, helpline, repair service available.

Student life. Freshman orientation: Mandatory, $40 fee. Preregistration for classes offered. 3 sessions held prior to start of fall semester; 1 session held 3 days prior to start of spring semester. **Policies:** Standards of Christian living are outlined in the Biblical Standards Handbook. Religious observance required. **Housing:** Guaranteed on-campus for all undergraduates. Single-sex dorms available. $100 partly refundable deposit. Mobile home park available for married students. **Activities:** Concert band, choral groups, drama, music ensembles, radio station, student government, student newspaper, symphony orchestra, student missions committee, African-American Fellowship, student senate, student union, grad life council.

Athletics. Intramural: Basketball, football (non-tackle), soccer M, softball, table tennis, volleyball. **Team name:** Rams.

Student services. Chaplain/spiritual director, career counseling, student employment services, financial aid counseling, health services, personal counseling, placement for graduates, veterans' counselor. **Physically disabled:** Services for visually, hearing impaired.

Contact. E-mail: yesciu@ciu.edu
Phone: (803) 754-4100 ext. 5024 Toll-free number: (800) 777-2227
Fax: (803) 786-4209
Sandra Rhyne, Director of Admissions, Columbia International University, PO Box 3122, Columbia, SC 29203-3122

Converse College
Spartanburg, South Carolina   **CB member**
www.converse.edu   **CB code: 5121**

- Private 4-year liberal arts and performing arts college for women
- Residential campus in small city
- 694 degree-seeking undergraduates: 10% part-time, 100% women
- 597 graduate students
- 53% of applicants admitted
- SAT or ACT (ACT writing optional), application essay required
- 57% graduate within 6 years

General. Founded in 1889. Regionally accredited. Men admitted to graduate programs. **Degrees:** 176 bachelor's awarded; master's offered. **ROTC:** Army. **Location:** 70 miles from Charlotte, NC. **Calendar:** 4-1-4, limited summer session. **Full-time faculty:** 78 total; 96% have terminal degrees, 6% minority, 58% women. **Part-time faculty:** 7 total; 43% have terminal degrees, 57% women. **Class size:** 84% < 20, 16% 20-39. **Special facilities:** State of the art science educational facility, music library, music and performing arts auditorium.

Freshman class profile. 1,125 applied, 600 admitted, 194 enrolled.

Mid 50% test scores		Rank in top quarter:	57%
ACT composite:	19-28	Rank in top tenth:	22%
GPA 3.75 or higher:	22%	End year in good standing:	95%
GPA 3.50-3.74:	28%	Return as sophomores:	62%
GPA 3.0-3.49:	38%	Out-of-state:	26%
GPA 2.0-2.99:	12%	Live on campus:	90%

Basis for selection. School record, class rank, test scores, extracurricular activities, school recommendation considered. Interview recommended for all; audition required for music programs. **Home schooled:** Statement describing home school structure and mission, interview, letter of recommendation (nonparent) required.

High school preparation. College-preparatory program required. 16 units recommended. Recommended units include English 4, mathematics 3, social studies 2, history 2, science 3 (laboratory 1), foreign language 2 and academic electives 8.

2011-2012 Annual costs. Tuition/fees: $27,320. Room/board: $8,834. Books/supplies: $1,000. Personal expenses: $1,500.

2011-2012 Financial aid. Need-based: 187 full-time freshmen applied for aid; 172 were judged to have need; 172 of these received aid. Average need met was 81%. Average scholarship/grant was $21,612; average loan $3,877. 72% of total undergraduate aid awarded as scholarships/grants, 28% as loans/jobs. **Non-need-based:** Awarded to 204 full-time undergraduates, including 75 freshmen. Scholarships awarded for academics, art, athletics, music/drama, ROTC, state residency.

Application procedures. Admission: Priority date 3/1; no deadline. No application fee. Admission notification on a rolling basis. Must reply by May 1 or within 2 week(s) if notified thereafter. **Financial aid:** Priority date 3/15; no closing date. FAFSA required. Applicants notified on a rolling basis starting 3/1; must reply by 5/1 or within 2 week(s) of notification.

Academics. Special study options: Combined bachelor's/graduate degree, cross-registration, double major, ESL, honors, independent study, internships, liberal arts/career combination, student-designed major, study abroad, teacher certification program. Women's leadership program. **Credit/placement by examination:** AP, CLEP, IB, SAT, ACT, institutional tests. 30 credit hours maximum toward bachelor's degree. **Support services:** Learning center, remedial instruction, study skills assistance, tutoring, writing center.

Majors. Biology: General, biochemistry. **Business:** Accounting, finance, international, managerial economics, marketing, training/development. **Education:** General, Deaf/hearing impaired, early childhood, elementary, special ed. **English:** Creative writing, English lit. **Foreign languages:** General, Spanish. **Health services:** Art therapy, music therapy. **History:** General. **Math:** General. **Philosophy/religion:** Philosophy, religion. **Physical sciences:** Chemistry. **Psychology:** General. **Social sciences:** Economics, political science. **Visual/performing arts:** Art, art history/conservation, dramatic, interior design, music, music history, music pedagogy, music performance, music theory/composition, piano/keyboard, stringed instruments, studio arts, theater arts management, voice/opera.

Most popular majors. Education 22%, English 9%, foreign language 6%, health sciences 6%, psychology 13%, visual/performing arts 22%.

Computing on campus. 75 workstations in dormitories, library, computer center, student center. Dormitories wired for high-speed internet access and linked to campus network. Commuter students can connect to campus network. Online library, helpline, repair service, wireless network available.

Student life. Freshman orientation: Mandatory. Preregistration for classes offered. 3-day program immediately prior to classes beginning. Optional summer orientation. **Policies:** Strong honor tradition based on mutual trust and responsibility. **Housing:** Guaranteed on-campus for all undergraduates. Apartments, wellness housing available. $300 partly refundable deposit, deadline 8/1. **Activities:** Concert band, campus ministries, choral groups, dance, drama, international student organizations, literary magazine, music ensembles, Model UN, musical theater, opera, student government, student newspaper, symphony orchestra, Student Christian Association, student activities committee, Young Republicans, community service organizations, honor organizations, student volunteer services.

Athletics. NCAA. **Intercollegiate:** Basketball W, cross-country W, equestrian W, golf W, lacrosse W, soccer W, swimming W, tennis W, volleyball W. **Intramural:** Archery W, basketball W, football (non-tackle) W, soccer W, softball W, synchronized swimming W, volleyball W. **Team name:** Valkyries.

Student services. Adult student services, alcohol/substance abuse counseling, chaplain/spiritual director, career counseling, student employment services, financial aid counseling, health services, personal counseling, placement for graduates, women's services. **Physically disabled:** Services for hearing impaired.

Contact. E-mail: admissions@converse.edu
Phone: (864) 596-9040 Toll-free number: (800) 766-1125
Fax: (864) 596-9225
April Lewis, Director of Admissions, Converse College, 580 East Main Street, Spartanburg, SC 29302-0006

Erskine College
Due West, South Carolina   **CB member**
www.erskine.edu   **CB code: 5188**

- Private 4-year liberal arts and seminary college affiliated with Associate Reformed Presbyterian Church
- Residential campus in rural community
- 600 degree-seeking undergraduates
- 67% of applicants admitted
- SAT or ACT (ACT writing optional), application essay required

General. Founded in 1839. Regionally accredited. Affiliated with Erskine Theological Seminary. **Degrees:** 118 bachelor's awarded; master's, doctoral offered. **Location:** 18 miles from Anderson, 45 miles from Greenville. **Calendar:** 4-1-4, limited summer session. **Full-time faculty:** 58 total. **Part-time faculty:** 22 total. **Class size:** 72% < 20, 28% 20-39. **Special facilities:** Arts center.

Freshman class profile. 636 applied, 426 admitted, 166 enrolled.

Mid 50% test scores		Rank in top quarter:	65%
SAT critical reading:	440-580	Rank in top tenth:	39%
SAT math:	460-580	Out-of-state:	24%
ACT composite:	18-25	Live on campus:	96%

Basis for selection. High school transcript, testings and personal qualities considered in admissions decisions. Rigor of coursework most important. Grades, class rank, test scores, extracurricular activities, essay very important. Interview required for academically weak; audition required for music. **Home schooled:** Transcript of courses and grades, letter of recommendation (nonparent) required. High school diploma, GED, or college preparatory diploma certification required. Portfolio showing courses studied, textbooks used, course outline and extracurricular activities may be requested in some instances.

High school preparation. College-preparatory program required. 14 units required. Required units include English 4, mathematics 2, science 2 (laboratory 2). 2 social sciences and at least 4 other units earned from these subject areas: history, science, Latin, modern foreign languages, advanced math and English.

2011-2012 Annual costs. Tuition/fees: $28,160. Room/board: $9,200. Books/supplies: $2,000. Personal expenses: $1,250.

Financial aid. Non-need-based: Scholarships awarded for academics, alumni affiliation, athletics, leadership, minority status, music/drama, religious affiliation, state residency. **Additional information:** Filing deadline 5/1 for institutional form, 6/30 for state form.

Application procedures. Admission: No deadline. $25 fee, may be waived for applicants with need, free for online applicants. Admission notification on a rolling basis beginning on or about 11/15. **Financial aid:** Priority date 4/1; no closing date. FAFSA, institutional form required. Applicants notified on a rolling basis starting 12/15; must reply within 2 week(s) of notification.

Academics. Special study options: Double major, independent study, internships, study abroad, teacher certification program. **Credit/placement by examination:** AP, CLEP, IB, institutional tests. 18 credit hours maximum toward bachelor's degree. **Support services:** Pre-admission summer program, study skills assistance, tutoring, writing center.

Majors. Area/ethnic studies: American. **Biology:** General. **Business:** Business admin. **Education:** Early childhood, elementary, physical, secondary, social studies, special ed. **English:** English lit. **Foreign languages:** French, Spanish. **Health services:** Athletic training, clinical lab technology. **History:** General. **Math:** General. **Parks/recreation:** Sports admin. **Philosophy/religion:** Philosophy, religion. **Physical sciences:** Chemistry, physics. **Psychology:** General. **Social sciences:** Political science. **Theology:** Religious ed. **Visual/performing arts:** Art, music.

Most popular majors. Biology 21%, business/marketing 20%, education 13%, history 6%, parks/recreation 6%, psychology 8%.

Computing on campus. Dormitories wired for high-speed internet access and linked to campus network. Commuter students can connect to campus network. Helpline, repair service, student web hosting, wireless network available.

Student life. Freshman orientation: Mandatory. Preregistration for classes offered. Held in August prior to first day of classes. **Policies:** Religious observance required. **Housing:** Guaranteed on-campus for all undergraduates. Single-sex dorms, wellness housing available. $300 deposit. **Activities:** Bands, campus ministries, choral groups, dance, drama, literary magazine, music ensembles, musical theater, radio station, student government, student newspaper, national honor societies for academics, drama, and leadership, association of minority students, denominational organizations, judicial council, Fellowship of Christian Athletes, Habitat for Humanity, council for exceptional children.

Athletics. NCAA. **Intercollegiate:** Baseball M, basketball, cross-country, golf, lacrosse W, soccer, softball W, tennis, volleyball W. **Intramural:** Basketball, football (non-tackle) W, football (tackle) M, racquetball, soccer, softball, tennis. **Team name:** Flying Fleet.

Student services. Alcohol/substance abuse counseling, chaplain/spiritual director, career counseling, financial aid counseling, health services, personal counseling, placement for graduates.

Contact. E-mail: admissions@erskine.edu
Phone: (864) 379-8838 Toll-free number: (800) 241-8721
Fax: (864) 379-2167
Cory Young, Director of Admissions, Erskine College, PO Box 176, Due West, SC 29639-0176

Francis Marion University
Florence, South Carolina   **CB member**
www.fmarion.edu   **CB code: 5442**

- Public 4-year university and liberal arts college
- Commuter campus in small city
- 3,466 degree-seeking undergraduates: 4% part-time, 66% women, 48% African American, 1% Asian American, 1% Hispanic American, 1% Native American, 1% international
- 194 degree-seeking graduate students
- 59% of applicants admitted
- SAT or ACT (ACT writing recommended) required
- 41% graduate within 6 years

General. Founded in 1970. Regionally accredited. **Degrees:** 553 bachelor's awarded; master's offered. **ROTC:** Army. **Location:** 7 miles from downtown, 80 miles from Columbia. **Calendar:** Semester, limited summer session. **Full-time faculty:** 196 total; 81% have terminal degrees, 10% minority, 46% women. **Part-time faculty:** 91 total; 24% have terminal degrees, 8% minority, 62% women. **Class size:** 43% < 20, 49% 20-39, 2% 40-49, 6% 50-99, less than 1% >100. **Special facilities:** Planetarium, observatory, arboretum, hewn timber cabins.

Freshman class profile. 3,843 applied, 2,255 admitted, 743 enrolled.

Mid 50% test scores			
SAT critical reading:	410-530	Rank in top quarter:	42%
SAT math:	430-530	Rank in top tenth:	13%
SAT writing:	390-500	End year in good standing:	69%
ACT composite:	17-22	Return as sophomores:	67%
GPA 3.75 or higher:	33%	Out-of-state:	4%
GPA 3.50-3.74:	15%	Live on campus:	86%
GPA 3.0-3.49:	36%	International:	1%
GPA 2.0-2.99:	16%	Fraternities:	3%
		Sororities:	5%

Basis for selection. Combination of standardized test scores and high school GPA important. Borderline cases may be admitted provisionally. Proficiency in math and English required. **Learning Disabled:** Accommodations provided with documentation.

High school preparation. College-preparatory program required. 19 units required. Required units include English 4, mathematics 4, social studies 3, history 1, science 3 (laboratory 3), foreign language 2, visual/performing arts 1 and academic electives 1. Social studies should include 1 history (U.S.), 1 unit of either PE or ROTC, 2 units of same foreign language required, 1 unit of Fine Arts.

2011-2012 Annual costs. Tuition/fees: $8,802; $17,269 out-of-state. Room/board: $6,620. Books/supplies: $1,900. Personal expenses: $4,100.

2011-2012 Financial aid. Need-based: 699 full-time freshmen applied for aid; 656 were judged to have need; 656 of these received aid. Average scholarship/grant was $4,834; average loan $3,364. 43% of total undergraduate aid awarded as scholarships/grants, 57% as loans/jobs. **Non-need-based:** Awarded to 1,297 full-time undergraduates, including 571 freshmen. Scholarships awarded for academics, music/drama.

Application procedures. Admission: No deadline. $31 fee, may be waived for applicants with need. Application must be submitted on paper. Admission notification on a rolling basis beginning on or about 9/1. April 1 reply date for dormitory students. **Financial aid:** Priority date 3/1; no closing date. FAFSA required. Applicants notified on a rolling basis starting 4/15.

Academics. Special study options: Double major, dual enrollment of high school students, honors, independent study, internships, study abroad, teacher certification program, Washington semester. **Credit/placement by examination:** AP, CLEP, institutional tests. **Support services:** Reduced course load, tutoring, writing center.

Majors. Biology: General. **Business:** Accounting, business admin, finance, management information systems, managerial economics, marketing. **Communications:** Media studies. **Computer sciences:** General. **Education:** Art, early childhood, elementary, English, history, mathematics, secondary, social studies. **English:** English lit. **Foreign languages:** French, German, Spanish. **Health services:** Nursing (RN). **History:** General. **Liberal arts:** Arts/sciences. **Math:** General. **Physical sciences:** Chemistry, physics. **Psychology:** General. **Social sciences:** Economics, international relations, political science, sociology. **Visual/performing arts:** Art, dramatic, music.

Most popular majors. Biology 14%, business/marketing 24%, education 8%, health sciences 14%, psychology 10%, social sciences 11%.

Computing on campus. 624 workstations in dormitories, library, computer center, student center. Dormitories wired for high-speed internet access. Online course registration, online library, wireless network available.

Student life. Freshman orientation: Mandatory, $46 fee. Preregistration for classes offered. Held in summer for fall term. Session in January for spring. **Housing:** Single-sex dorms, special housing for disabled, apartments, wellness housing available. $250 deposit. **Activities:** Jazz band, campus ministries, choral groups, dance, drama, international student organizations, literary magazine, music ensembles, Model UN, student government, student newspaper, TV station, College Democrats, College Republicans, NAACP, psychology club, education club, First Fellowship, Baptist campus ministries, Young, Gifted, and Blessed Chorus.

Athletics. NCAA. **Intercollegiate:** Baseball M, basketball, cross-country, golf M, soccer, softball W, tennis, track and field, volleyball W. **Intramural:** Basketball, bowling, football (non-tackle), golf, racquetball, soccer, softball, table tennis, tennis, track and field, volleyball. **Team name:** Patriots.

Student services. Adult student services, chaplain/spiritual director, career counseling, student employment services, health services, minority student services, personal counseling, placement for graduates, veterans' counselor. **Physically disabled:** Services for visually, speech, hearing impaired.

Contact. E-mail: admission@fmarion.edu
Phone: (843) 661-1231 Toll-free number: (800) 368-7551
Fax: (843) 661-4635
Perry Wilson, Director of Admissions, Francis Marion University, PO Box 100547, Florence, SC 29502-0547

Furman University
Greenville, South Carolina   **CB member**
www.furman.edu   **CB code: 5222**

- Private 4-year liberal arts college
- Residential campus in small city
- 2,799 degree-seeking undergraduates: 4% part-time, 57% women, 5% African American, 2% Asian American, 3% Hispanic American, 2% international
- 144 degree-seeking graduate students
- 83% of applicants admitted
- Application essay required
- 87% graduate within 6 years; 41% enter graduate study

General. Founded in 1826. Regionally accredited. Abundant internship and collaborative research opportunities. **Degrees:** 628 bachelor's awarded; master's offered. **ROTC:** Army. **Location:** 100 miles from Charlotte, North Carolina, 140 miles from Atlanta. **Calendar:** Semester, extensive summer session. **Full-time faculty:** 238 total; 95% have terminal degrees, 11% minority, 31% women. **Part-time faculty:** 31 total; 52% have terminal degrees, 10% minority, 61% women. **Class size:** 62% < 20, 38% 20-39, less than 1% 50-99. **Special facilities:** Observatory, center for engaged learning, center for international education, center for collaborative learning and communication, center for sustainability.

Freshman class profile. 4,888 applied, 4,058 admitted, 785 enrolled.

Mid 50% test scores			
SAT critical reading:	560-670	Rank in top quarter:	77%
SAT math:	570-670	Rank in top tenth:	46%
SAT writing:	560-670	Return as sophomores:	89%
ACT composite:	25-30	Out-of-state:	72%
GPA 3.75 or higher:	40%	Live on campus:	98%
GPA 3.50-3.74:	21%	International:	3%
GPA 3.0-3.49:	25%	Fraternities:	36%
GPA 2.0-2.99:	13%	Sororities:	49%

Basis for selection. High school record including courses taken and grades most important, then SAT or ACT scores. Special talents such as fine arts, athletic ability, writing ability considered. Special consideration given to children of alumni and minorities. SAT or ACT recommended. Audition required for music scholarship applicants; portfolio required for art scholarship applicants. **Home schooled:** SAT Subject Tests including math, subject of student's choice recommended. Interview strongly recommended.

High school preparation. College-preparatory program recommended. 14 units required; 18 recommended. Required and recommended units include English 4, mathematics 3-4, science 2-3 (laboratory 2) and foreign language 3-4.

2011-2012 Annual costs. Tuition/fees: $39,560. Room/board: $10,192. Books/supplies: $1,110. Personal expenses: $1,000.

2011-2012 Financial aid. **Need-based:** 503 full-time freshmen applied for aid; 363 were judged to have need; 361 of these received aid. Average need met was 74%. Average scholarship/grant was $22,769; average loan $2,944. 87% of total undergraduate aid awarded as scholarships/grants, 13% as loans/jobs. **Non-need-based:** Awarded to 2,319 full-time undergraduates, including 693 freshmen. Scholarships awarded for academics, alumni affiliation, art, athletics, leadership, music/drama, religious affiliation, ROTC, state residency. **Additional information:** 5-point comprehensive education financing plan includes financial aid packaging, money management counseling, debt management counseling, outside scholarship coordination, summer job-match program.

Application procedures. **Admission:** Closing date 1/15 (postmark date). $50 fee, may be waived for applicants with need, free for online applicants. Admission notification by 4/2. Must reply by May 1 or within 2 week(s) if notified thereafter. **Financial aid:** Closing date 1/15. FAFSA, institutional form, CSS PROFILE required. Applicants notified by 4/2; must reply by 5/1.

Academics. Strong emphasis on research, internships and other opportunities for engaged, hands-on learning. **Special study options:** Combined bachelor's/graduate degree, double major, independent study, internships, student-designed major, study abroad, teacher certification program, United Nations semester, Washington semester. Undergraduate research program, 3-2 engineering with Auburn University, Clemson University, Georgia Institute of Technology, North Carolina State, Washington University in St. Louis, 3-2 forestry program with Duke University, 3-1 dentistry and medicine programs with any accredited medical or dental school, 3-2 nursing, pharmacy, physical therapy, and physician assistant programs with any accredited medical school. **Credit/placement by examination:** AP, CLEP, IB, institutional tests. **Support services:** Learning center, reduced course load, study skills assistance, tutoring, writing center.

Majors. **Area/ethnic studies:** Asian. **Biology:** General, neuroscience. **Business:** Accounting, business admin, management information systems. **Communications:** Communications/speech/rhetoric. **Computer sciences:** Computer science. **Education:** General, music. **English:** English lit. **Foreign languages:** Ancient Greek, French, German, Latin, Spanish. **Health services:** General, predental, premedicine, prenursing, prepharmacy, preveterinary. **History:** General. **Math:** General. **Philosophy/religion:** Philosophy, religion. **Physical sciences:** Chemistry, geology, physics. **Psychology:** General. **Social sciences:** Economics, political science, sociology, urban studies. **Theology:** Sacred music. **Visual/performing arts:** Art, dramatic, music, music history, music performance, music theory/composition.

Most popular majors. Biology 7%, business/marketing 12%, communications/journalism 6%, health sciences 7%, history 6%, physical sciences 6%, social sciences 20%, visual/performing arts 9%.

Computing on campus. 450 workstations in library, computer center, student center. Dormitories wired for high-speed internet access and linked to campus network. Commuter students can connect to campus network. Online course registration, online library, helpline, student web hosting, wireless network available.

Student life. **Freshman orientation:** Mandatory. Preregistration for classes offered. Early orientation session during the summer (charge of $150) and free session at beginning of Fall semester. **Housing:** Guaranteed on-campus for freshmen. Coed dorms, single-sex dorms, apartments, wellness housing available. $500 nonrefundable deposit, deadline 5/1. Lakeside cottages and environmentally equipped eco-cottage also available. **Activities:**

Bands, campus ministries, choral groups, dance, drama, film society, international student organizations, literary magazine, music ensembles, Model UN, musical theater, opera, radio station, student government, student newspaper, symphony orchestra, TV station, Collegiate Educational Service Corps, Young Democrats, College Republicans, Student League for Black Culture, Fellowship of Christian Athletes, Council for Exceptional Children, Habitat for Humanity, arts students league.

Athletics. NCAA. **Intercollegiate:** Baseball M, basketball, cheerleading, cross-country, football (tackle) M, golf, soccer, softball W, tennis, track and field, volleyball W. **Intramural:** Basketball, bowling, cross-country, football (non-tackle), golf, handball, racquetball, rowing (crew), soccer, softball, swimming, tennis, track and field, volleyball. **Team name:** Paladins.

Student services. Adult student services, alcohol/substance abuse counseling, chaplain/spiritual director, career counseling, student employment services, financial aid counseling, health services, minority student services, personal counseling, placement for graduates, veterans' counselor, women's services. **Physically disabled:** Services for visually, hearing impaired.

Contact. E-mail: admissions@furman.edu
Phone: (864) 294-2034 Fax: (864) 294-2018
Brad Pochard, Director of Admissions, Furman University, 3300 Poinsett Highway, Greenville, SC 29613

ITT Technical Institute: Greenville
Greenville, South Carolina
www.itt-tech.edu   **CB code: 2708**

- For-profit 4-year technical college
- Commuter campus in large city
- 690 undergraduates
- Interview required

General. Accredited by ACICS. **Degrees:** 42 bachelor's, 168 associate awarded. **Calendar:** Quarter, extensive summer session. **Full-time faculty:** 9 total. **Part-time faculty:** 30 total.

Basis for selection. Satisfactory scores from on-site tests in English and mathematics required.

2011-2012 Annual costs. Estimated costs as of June 2011: per-credit-hour charge, $493, depending upon level and course of study; academic fee, $200. Certain programs of study require purchase of tools, which could cost an additional $100 to $500. All costs are subject to change.

Application procedures. **Admission:** No deadline. No application fee. Admission notification on a rolling basis. **Financial aid:** No deadline. FAFSA, institutional form required. Applicants notified on a rolling basis.

Academics. **Credit/placement by examination:** AP, CLEP. **Support services:** Learning center, tutoring.

Majors. **Communications technology:** Animation/special effects. **Computer sciences:** Security. **Protective services:** Law enforcement admin.

Computing on campus. Online library available.

Student life. **Freshman orientation:** Available. Preregistration for classes offered.

Student services. Career counseling, student employment services, placement for graduates.

Contact. Phone: (864) 288-0777 Toll-free number: (800) 932-4488
Fax: (864) 297-0930
Joseph Fisher, Director of Recruitment, ITT Technical Institute: Greenville, 6 Independence Pointe, Greenville, SC 29615

Lander University
Greenwood, South Carolina   **CB member**
www.lander.edu   **CB code: 5363**

- Public 4-year liberal arts and teachers college
- Residential campus in large town
- 3,000 degree-seeking undergraduates
- 46% of applicants admitted
- SAT or ACT (ACT writing optional), interview required

General. Founded in 1872. Regionally accredited. **Degrees:** 430 bachelor's awarded; master's offered. **ROTC:** Army. **Location:** 55 miles from Greenville, 75 miles from Columbia. **Calendar:** Semester, limited summer session. **Full-time faculty:** 132 total. **Part-time faculty:** 108 total. **Class size:** 44% < 20, 45% 20-39, 5% 40-49, 6% 50-99.

Freshman class profile. 2,903 applied, 1,335 admitted, 681 enrolled.

Mid 50% test scores			
SAT critical reading:	410-520	GPA 3.50-3.74:	17%
SAT math:	430-540	GPA 3.0-3.49:	27%
SAT writing:	400-500	GPA 2.0-2.99:	13%
ACT composite:	18-22	Out-of-state:	4%
GPA 3.75 or higher:	43%	Live on campus:	80%

Basis for selection. Test scores, class rank, curriculum, high school GPA important. Out-of-state students must rank in top half of high school class. Selectivity of students may be based on transcripts and GED score. Audition required for music programs; interview recommended for art, music programs; portfolio recommended for art programs.

High school preparation. 20 units recommended. Recommended units include English 4, mathematics 3, social studies 2, history 1, science 3 (laboratory 3), foreign language 2 and academic electives 4. One unit physical education or ROTC also recommended.

2011-2012 Annual costs. Tuition/fees: $9,504; $17,976 out-of-state. Room/board: $7,456. Books/supplies: $1,200. Personal expenses: $1,600.

Financial aid. **Non-need-based:** Scholarships awarded for academics, art, athletics, leadership, music/drama.

Application procedures. **Admission:** No deadline. $35 fee, may be waived for applicants with need. Admission notification on a rolling basis. **Financial aid:** Priority date 4/15; no closing date. FAFSA required. Applicants notified on a rolling basis starting 4/15; must reply within 4 week(s) of notification.

Academics. **Special study options:** Combined bachelor's/graduate degree, cooperative education, distance learning, double major, dual enrollment of high school students, honors, independent study, internships, liberal arts/career combination, student-designed major, study abroad, teacher certification program. Dual degree in engineering with Clemson University, nursing (RN to BSN completion) offered online, MBA and M.Ed. in counseling/school administration from Clemson University offered on campus. **Credit/placement by examination:** AP, CLEP, IB, institutional tests. 30 credit hours maximum toward bachelor's degree. **Support services:** Learning center, pre-admission summer program, reduced course load, remedial instruction, study skills assistance, tutoring, writing center.

Majors. **Biology:** General. **Business:** Business admin. **Computer sciences:** General. **Conservation:** Environmental science. **Education:** Early childhood, elementary, Montessori teacher, physical, secondary, special ed. **English:** English lit. **Foreign languages:** Spanish. **Health services:** Athletic training, nursing (RN). **History:** General. **Liberal arts:** Arts/sciences, humanities. **Math:** General. **Parks/recreation:** Exercise sciences. **Physical sciences:** Chemistry. **Protective services:** Law enforcement admin. **Psychology:** General. **Social sciences:** Political science, sociology. **Visual/performing arts:** Art, music.

Most popular majors. Business/marketing 19%, education 15%, health sciences 10%, parks/recreation 6%, psychology 7%, social sciences 14%.

Computing on campus. PC or laptop required. 233 workstations in library, computer center. Dormitories linked to campus network. Commuter students can connect to campus network. Online course registration, online library, helpline, repair service, wireless network available.

Student life. **Freshman orientation:** Mandatory. Preregistration for classes offered. **Housing:** Coed dorms, single-sex dorms available. $175 partly refundable deposit, deadline 4/15. **Activities:** Bands, choral groups, dance, drama, literary magazine, music ensembles, student government, student newspaper, Baptist Student Union, Bible study, Young Democrats, College Republicans, Minorities on the Move, Blue Key and Alpha Kappa Gamma (honor societies).

Athletics. NCAA. **Intercollegiate:** Baseball M, basketball, golf M, soccer, softball W, tennis, volleyball W. **Intramural:** Basketball, football (non-tackle), golf, soccer, softball, volleyball. **Team name:** Bearcats.

Student services. Adult student services, alcohol/substance abuse counseling, career counseling, student employment services, financial aid counseling, health services, minority student services, personal counseling, placement for graduates, veterans' counselor. **Physically disabled:** Services for visually, speech, hearing impaired.

Contact. E-mail: admissions@lander.edu
Phone: (864) 388-8307 Fax: (864) 388-8125
Jennifer Mathis, Director of Admissions, Lander University, Stanley Avenue, Greenwood, SC 29649-2099

Limestone College
Gaffney, South Carolina
www.limestone.edu   CB code: 5366

- Private 4-year liberal arts college
- Residential campus in large town
- 857 degree-seeking undergraduates: 2% part-time, 41% women, 22% African American, 1% Asian American, 4% Hispanic American, 7% international
- 53% of applicants admitted
- SAT or ACT (ACT writing optional) required
- 40% graduate within 6 years

General. Founded in 1845. Regionally accredited. Evening classes available at 8 SC sites through Limestone's Extended Campus-Classroom Program; online classes available through Extended Campus-Internet Program. **Degrees:** 117 bachelor's, 4 associate awarded. **ROTC:** Army. **Location:** 25 miles from Spartanburg, 49 miles from Charlotte, NC. **Calendar:** Semester, extensive summer session. **Full-time faculty:** 65 total; 83% have terminal degrees, 3% minority. **Part-time faculty:** 16 total; 6% have terminal degrees, 6% minority, 56% women. **Class size:** 72% < 20, 28% 20-39, less than 1% 40-49. **Special facilities:** Computer graphics art lab, Winnie Davis Museum of Southern History.

Freshman class profile. 1,363 applied, 725 admitted, 224 enrolled.

Mid 50% test scores			
SAT critical reading:	440-520	Rank in top quarter:	18%
SAT math:	480-560	Rank in top tenth:	5%
ACT composite:	19-23	End year in good standing:	82%
GPA 3.75 or higher:	12%	Return as sophomores:	59%
GPA 3.50-3.74:	10%	Out-of-state:	45%
GPA 3.0-3.49:	27%	Live on campus:	84%
GPA 2.0-2.99:	48%	International:	6%

Basis for selection. SAT combined score of 910 (exclusive of Writing) or ACT score of 19 (exclusive of Writing) and GPA of 2.0. Admissions committee must approve all applicants who do not meet these standards. SAT requirement waived for freshmen age 21 or older or in military service. The SAT or ACT requirement is waived for students admitted into the PALS Program (Program for Alternative Learning Styles). Interview required for lower-ranking applicants, recommended for all others. Audition required of first-time, first-year freshmen for music, music education, and theater programs; portfolio required for studio art programs; essay required for Honors Program. **Learning Disabled:** Documentation required to be eligible for admission to Program for Alternative Learning Styles (PALS).

High school preparation. 12 units required. Required units include English 4, mathematics 3, social studies 3, science 2 (laboratory 2).

2011-2012 Annual costs. Tuition/fees: $20,000. Room/board: $7,500. Books/supplies: $2,304. Personal expenses: $1,640.

2011-2012 Financial aid. **Need-based:** Average need met was 59%. Average scholarship/grant was $12,716; average loan $3,431. 61% of total undergraduate aid awarded as scholarships/grants, 39% as loans/jobs. **Non-need-based:** Scholarships awarded for academics, art, athletics, job skills, leadership, music/drama, religious affiliation, ROTC, state residency.

Application procedures. **Admission:** Priority date 8/1; deadline 8/26 (receipt date). $25 fee, may be waived for applicants with need, free for online applicants. Admission notification on a rolling basis beginning on or about 6/1. **Financial aid:** Priority date 2/1; no closing date. FAFSA required. Applicants notified on a rolling basis starting 1/15; must reply within 3 week(s) of notification.

Academics. **Special study options:** Accelerated study, distance learning, double major, honors, independent study, internships, liberal arts/career combination, student-designed major, teacher certification program. **Credit/placement by examination:** AP, CLEP, institutional tests. 15 credit hours maximum toward associate degree, 30 toward bachelor's. **Support services:** Learning center, reduced course load, remedial instruction, study skills assistance, tutoring, writing center.

Majors. **Biology:** General. **Business:** General, accounting, e-commerce, finance, human resources, managerial economics, marketing, training/development. **Computer sciences:** Information technology, programming, security, webmaster. **Education:** Early childhood, elementary, English, mathematics, music, physical. **English:** English lit, writing. **Health services:** Athletic training, health care admin, predental, premedicine, prenursing,

prepharmacy, preveterinary. **History:** General. **Human services:** Social work. **Liberal arts:** Arts/sciences. **Math:** General. **Parks/recreation:** Sports admin. **Physical sciences:** Chemistry. **Protective services:** Law enforcement admin. **Psychology:** General. **Visual/performing arts:** Dramatic, graphic design, jazz, music, music performance, musical theater, studio arts.

Most popular majors. Business/marketing 21%, education 26%, liberal arts 9%, parks/recreation 14%.

Computing on campus. 141 workstations in library, computer center. Dormitories wired for high-speed internet access and linked to campus network. Commuter students can connect to campus network. Online library, helpline, repair service, wireless network available.

Student life. Freshman orientation: Mandatory. Preregistration for classes offered. 5 days prior to start of semester. **Policies:** Alcohol-free campus. Students must live on campus unless age 21, or have attained 90 credit hours, or live with immediate family within 50 miles of campus. **Housing:** Guaranteed on-campus for freshmen. Single-sex dorms, wellness housing available. $50 fully refundable deposit. **Activities:** Bands, campus ministries, choral groups, drama, international student organizations, literary magazine, music ensembles, musical theater, student government, Fellowship of Christian Athletes, Student Alumni Leadership Council, Student Organization of Social Workers, Students in Free Enterprise, Christian Education and Leadership Program, Joyful Saints Gospel Choir, criminal justice student organization, psychology club, student government association.

Athletics. NCAA. **Intercollegiate:** Baseball M, basketball, cross-country, field hockey W, golf, lacrosse, soccer, softball W, swimming, tennis, track and field, volleyball, wrestling M. **Intramural:** Basketball, racquetball, table tennis. **Team name:** Saints.

Student services. Adult student services, alcohol/substance abuse counseling, chaplain/spiritual director, career counseling, student employment services, financial aid counseling, health services, personal counseling, placement for graduates, veterans' counselor.

Contact. E-mail: cphenicie@limestone.edu
Phone: (864) 488-4554 Toll-free number: (800) 795-7151 ext. 4554
Fax: (864) 487-8706
Chris Phenicie, Vice President for Enrollment Services, Limestone College, 1115 College Drive, Gaffney, SC 29340-3799

Medical University of South Carolina
Charleston, South Carolina
www.musc.edu   **CB code: 5407**

▶ Public two-year upper-division university
▶ Commuter campus in small city

General. Founded in 1824. Regionally accredited. Upper division/graduate academic health center consisting of six colleges: dental medicine, graduate studies, health professions, medicine, nursing, and pharmacy. College offers only two undergraduate degrees. **Degrees:** 189 bachelor's awarded; master's, professional, doctoral offered. **Location:** 350 miles from Atlanta. **Calendar:** Semester, limited summer session. **Full-time faculty:** 128 total; 89% have terminal degrees, 8% minority, 61% women. **Part-time faculty:** 99 total; 65% have terminal degrees, 7% minority, 52% women. **Class size:** 47% < 20, 53% 50-99. **Special facilities:** Historical medical library, dental museum, pharmacy museum.

Student profile. 198 degree-seeking undergraduates, 2,465 degree-seeking graduate students. 100% entered as juniors.

Women:	79%	Native American:	1%
African American:	11%	Part-time:	2%
Asian American:	3%	Out-of-state:	12%
Hispanic American:	6%	25 or older:	56%

2011-2012 Annual costs. Tuition and fees for BS in nursing for in-state $14,994 out-of-state $23,824; BS in cardiovascular perfusion, in-state $14,500, out-of-state $21,610. Books/supplies: $3,840.

Financial aid. Need-based: 162 applied for aid; 158 were judged to have need; 157 of these received aid. Average need met was 38%. 25% of total undergraduate aid awarded as scholarships/grants, 75% as loans/jobs. **Non-need-based:** Awarded to 36 undergraduates. Scholarships awarded for academics, alumni affiliation, minority status, state residency.

Application procedures. Admission: $95 fee. Application must be submitted online. All admission policies and dates vary by academic program and college. **Financial aid:** FAFSA, institutional form required.

Academics. Special study options: Cross-registration, distance learning. **Credit/placement by examination:** AP, CLEP. Credit by exam policies vary by program.

Majors. Health services: Cardiovascular technology, nursing (RN).

Computing on campus. PC or laptop required. 300 workstations in library, student center. Commuter students can connect to campus network. Online library, helpline, student web hosting, wireless network available.

Student life. Activities: Campus ministries, choral groups, international student organizations, literary magazine, music ensembles, student government, Christian Medical Society, campus crusade, student union, community help initiative, South Carolina health initiative, minority student union, Student National Medical Association.

Athletics. Intramural: Basketball, football (non-tackle), softball, volleyball.

Student services. Alcohol/substance abuse counseling, chaplain/spiritual director, services for economically disadvantaged, financial aid counseling, health services, legal services, minority student services, personal counseling, veterans' counselor.

Contact. E-mail: oesadmis@musc.edu
Phone: (843) 792-3281 Fax: (843) 792-6615
Lyla Hudson, Director of Admissions, Medical University of South Carolina, 41 Bee Street, Charleston, SC 29425-2030

Morris College
Sumter, South Carolina   **CB member**
www.morris.edu   **CB code: 5418**

▶ Private 4-year liberal arts college affiliated with Baptist faith
▶ Residential campus in large town
▶ 978 degree-seeking undergraduates: 2% part-time, 57% women, 99% African American
▶ 88% of applicants admitted

General. Founded in 1908. Regionally accredited. **Degrees:** 130 bachelor's awarded. **ROTC:** Army. **Location:** 45 miles from Columbia, 110 miles from Charlotte, NC. **Calendar:** Semester, limited summer session. **Full-time faculty:** 51 total; 69% have terminal degrees, 59% minority, 45% women. **Part-time faculty:** 17 total; 24% have terminal degrees, 82% minority, 41% women. **Class size:** 55% < 20, 40% 20-39, 5% 40-49, less than 1% 50-99. **Special facilities:** Radio station/training lab, electronic learning lab, television production studio, forensics labs.

Freshman class profile. 2,177 applied, 1,919 admitted, 284 enrolled.

GPA 3.75 or higher:	1%	End year in good standing:	60%
GPA 3.50-3.74:	3%	Return as sophomores:	43%
GPA 3.0-3.49:	13%	Out-of-state:	17%
GPA 2.0-2.99:	67%	Live on campus:	91%
Rank in top quarter:	5%		

Basis for selection. High school record most important. Students with less than 2.0 high school GPA may be admitted on probation but limited to 13-credit-hour load during each of first 2 semesters and required to participate in tutorial and study sessions. SAT or ACT scores must be submitted for all degree-seeking students, except foreign students. Scores used for informational/advisement purposes only. Interview recommended, required for some students.

High school preparation. 24 units required. Required and recommended units include English 4, mathematics 4, social studies 1, history 1, science 3, foreign language 1-2, computer science 1 and academic electives 7. .5 Government, .5 Economics, 1 Physical Education or ROTC.

2011-2012 Annual costs. Tuition/fees: $10,530. Room/board: $4,696. Books/supplies: $2,100. Personal expenses: $250.

2011-2012 Financial aid. All financial aid based on need. Average need met was 49%. Average scholarship/grant was $2,138; average loan $3,195. 51% of total undergraduate aid awarded as scholarships/grants, 49% as loans/jobs.

Application procedures. Admission: Priority date 7/1; no deadline. $20 fee, may be waived for applicants with need. Admission notification on a rolling basis beginning on or about 11/1. **Financial aid:** Priority date 3/30; no closing date. FAFSA, institutional form required. Applicants notified by 6/1; Applicants notified on a rolling basis starting 6/1; must reply within 2 week(s) of notification.

Academics. Special study options: Accelerated study, cooperative education, double major, honors, internships, liberal arts/career combination, study abroad, teacher certification program. Adult Degree Program in Organizational Management offered through evening courses; students must be at least 25 years old and have earned 60 credit hours. **Credit/placement by examination:** AP, CLEP. 30 credit hours maximum toward bachelor's degree. **Support services:** Learning center, reduced course load, remedial instruction, study skills assistance, tutoring, writing center.

Majors. Biology: General. **Business:** Business admin, operations. **Communications:** Media studies. **Education:** Biology, early childhood, elementary, English, mathematics, social studies. **English:** English lit. **Health services:** Community health services. **History:** General. **Liberal arts:** Arts/sciences. **Math:** General. **Parks/recreation:** Facilities management. **Protective services:** Law enforcement admin. **Social sciences:** Political science, sociology. **Theology:** Religious ed, theology.

Most popular majors. Biology 14%, business/marketing 25%, health sciences 12%, security/protective services 12%, social sciences 13%.

Computing on campus. 252 workstations in dormitories, library, computer center. Dormitories wired for high-speed internet access and linked to campus network. Commuter students can connect to campus network. Online course registration, online library, wireless network available.

Student life. Freshman orientation: Mandatory. Preregistration for classes offered. Held during first week of fall and spring semesters, as needed during summer terms. **Policies:** Promotes drug-free, alcohol-free campus. Cigarette smoking prohibited in all buildings. **Housing:** Single-sex dorms available. $100 fully refundable deposit, deadline 8/1. **Activities:** Pep band, campus ministries, choral groups, dance, drama, radio station, student government, student newspaper, Baptist Student Union, NAACP, Alpha Phi Omega, Durham Ministerial Union, National Association of Blacks in Criminal Justice.

Athletics. NAIA. **Intercollegiate:** Baseball M, basketball, cheerleading, cross-country, golf M, softball W, tennis, track and field, volleyball W. **Intramural:** Basketball, football (non-tackle), table tennis. **Team name:** Hornets.

Student services. Adult student services, alcohol/substance abuse counseling, chaplain/spiritual director, career counseling, services for economically disadvantaged, student employment services, financial aid counseling, health services, personal counseling, placement for graduates, veterans' counselor. **Physically disabled:** Services for visually, hearing impaired.

Contact. E-mail: dcalhoun@morris.edu
Phone: (803) 934-3225 Toll-free number: (866) 853-1345
Fax: (803) 773-8241
Deborah Calhoun, Director of Admission and Records, Morris College, 100 West College Street, Sumter, SC 29150-3599

Newberry College
Newberry, South Carolina
www.newberry.edu

CB member
CB code: 5493

- Private 4-year liberal arts college affiliated with Evangelical Lutheran Church in America
- Residential campus in large town
- 1,103 degree-seeking undergraduates: 3% part-time, 45% women, 24% African American, 1% Asian American, 4% Hispanic American, 3% international
- 61% of applicants admitted
- 35% graduate within 6 years; 15% enter graduate study

General. Founded in 1856. Regionally accredited. **Degrees:** 191 bachelor's awarded. **ROTC:** Army. **Location:** 40 miles from Columbia. **Calendar:** Semester, limited summer session. **Full-time faculty:** 63 total; 57% have terminal degrees, 10% minority, 51% women. **Part-time faculty:** 36 total; 8% have terminal degrees, 8% minority, 53% women. **Class size:** 58% < 20, 40% 20-39, 2% 40-49.

Freshman class profile. 1,400 applied, 852 admitted, 282 enrolled.

Mid 50% test scores			
SAT critical reading:	430-520	Rank in top quarter:	32%
SAT math:	440-530	Rank in top tenth:	11%
SAT writing:	420-520	End year in good standing:	89%
ACT composite:	17-24	Return as sophomores:	64%
GPA 3.75 or higher:	34%	Out-of-state:	12%
GPA 3.50-3.74:	13%	Live on campus:	90%
GPA 3.0-3.49:	31%	International:	3%
GPA 2.0-2.99:	22%	Fraternities:	11%
		Sororities:	4%

Basis for selection. High school record and test scores important; recommendations and interview considered. SAT or ACT recommended. Interview recommended for all; audition required for drama, music programs; portfolio required for art. **Home schooled:** Statement describing home school structure and mission, transcript of courses and grades, state high school equivalency certificate, interview, letter of recommendation (nonparent) required. Submit transcripts from HS or home school association. If unavailable, submit major essays and course descriptions. References necessary from primary instructor and another source.

High school preparation. College-preparatory program recommended. 14 units required. Required and recommended units include English 4, mathematics 3, social studies 2, history 1, science 2 (laboratory 2) and foreign language 2.

2011-2012 Annual costs. Tuition/fees: $22,925. Room/board: $8,550. Books/supplies: $1,600.

2010-2011 Financial aid. Need-based: 234 full-time freshmen applied for aid; 217 were judged to have need; 217 of these received aid. Average need met was 71%. Average scholarship/grant was $18,842; average loan $3,886. 74% of total undergraduate aid awarded as scholarships/grants, 26% as loans/jobs. **Non-need-based:** Awarded to 373 full-time undergraduates, including 92 freshmen. Scholarships awarded for academics, alumni affiliation, athletics, leadership, music/drama, religious affiliation, ROTC, state residency.

Application procedures. Admission: No deadline. $30 fee. Admission notification on a rolling basis. **Financial aid:** Priority date 3/15; no closing date. FAFSA, institutional form required. Applicants notified on a rolling basis starting 3/1; must reply by 5/1 or within 2 week(s) of notification.

Academics. Special study options: Accelerated study, double major, dual enrollment of high school students, honors, independent study, internships, liberal arts/career combination, student-designed major, study abroad, teacher certification program, Washington semester. Medical Technology Dual Degree Program with Palmetto Baptist Medical Center. Forest and Environmental Management Dual Degree Program with Duke University. **Credit/placement by examination:** AP, CLEP, IB, SAT, ACT, institutional tests. 30 credit hours maximum toward bachelor's degree. Sophomore standing available by earning 24 credit hours based on AP exam scores. **Support services:** Learning center, reduced course load, remedial instruction, tutoring, writing center.

Majors. Biology: General. **Business:** Business admin. **Communications:** Communications/speech/rhetoric. **Education:** Early childhood, elementary, middle, music, physical. **Foreign languages:** Spanish. **Health services:** Nursing education. **History:** General. **Math:** General. **Parks/recreation:** General, sports admin. **Philosophy/religion:** Philosophy, religion. **Physical sciences:** Chemistry. **Psychology:** General. **Social sciences:** Political science, sociology. **Theology:** Sacred music. **Visual/performing arts:** Art, dramatic, music, music performance, music theory/composition.

Most popular majors. Biology 8%, business/marketing 24%, communications/journalism 7%, education 15%, health sciences 8%, parks/recreation 15%.

Computing on campus. PC or laptop required. 12 workstations in library. Dormitories wired for high-speed internet access and linked to campus network. Commuter students can connect to campus network. Online course registration, online library, helpline, student web hosting, wireless network available.

Student life. Freshman orientation: Mandatory, $125 fee. Preregistration for classes offered. 2-day event. Students stay overnight on campus. **Policies:** Residence halls are non-smoking. **Housing:** Guaranteed on-campus for freshmen. Coed dorms, single-sex dorms, fraternity/sorority housing available. $175 partly refundable deposit, deadline 5/1. **Activities:** Bands, campus ministries, choral groups, dance, drama, international student organizations, literary magazine, music ensembles, musical theater, radio station, student government, student newspaper, TV station, Lutheran Student Movement, Baptist campus ministries, Young Republicans, Fellowship of Christian Athletes, ECHO, multicultural student association, African American Student Association, Christians Living Among You.

Athletics. NCAA. **Intercollegiate:** Baseball M, basketball, cheerleading, cross-country, football (tackle) M, golf, lacrosse W, soccer, softball W, tennis, volleyball W, wrestling M. **Intramural:** Basketball, football (non-tackle). **Team name:** Wolves.

Student services. Alcohol/substance abuse counseling, chaplain/spiritual director, career counseling, student employment services, financial aid counseling, health services, personal counseling, placement for graduates.

Contact. E-mail: admissionsandfinancialaid@newberry.edu
Phone: (803) 321-5127 Toll-free number: (800) 845-4955 ext. 5127
Fax: (803) 321-5138
Sheila Wendeln, Director of Admissions, Newberry College, 2100 College Street, Newberry, SC 29108

North Greenville University
Tigerville, South Carolina

www.ngu.edu   CB code: 5498

- Private 4-year liberal arts college affiliated with Southern Baptist Convention
- Residential campus in rural community
- 1,998 degree-seeking undergraduates: 3% part-time, 50% women, 8% African American, 1% Hispanic American, 1% international
- 233 graduate students
- 58% of applicants admitted
- SAT or ACT (ACT writing optional) required
- 41% graduate within 6 years; 10% enter graduate study

General. Founded in 1891. Regionally accredited. Off-site recreation and learning center for Outdoor Leadership major. **Degrees:** 395 bachelor's awarded; master's offered. **ROTC:** Army. **Location:** 18 miles from Greenville, 54 miles from Asheville, NC. **Calendar:** Semester, limited summer session. **Full-time faculty:** 125 total; 70% have terminal degrees, 6% minority, 38% women. **Part-time faculty:** 65 total; 14% have terminal degrees, 3% minority, 49% women. **Class size:** 69% < 20, 31% 20-39, less than 1% 50-99. **Special facilities:** Bible museum.

Freshman class profile. 1,592 applied, 923 admitted, 540 enrolled.

Mid 50% test scores			
SAT critical reading:	440-670	GPA 3.0-3.49:	40%
SAT math:	450-650	GPA 2.0-2.99:	4%
SAT writing:	460-640	Rank in top quarter:	46%
ACT composite:	21-31	Rank in top tenth:	23%
GPA 3.75 or higher:	27%	Return as sophomores:	73%
GPA 3.50-3.74:	29%	Out-of-state:	14%
		Live on campus:	89%

Basis for selection. High school record, standardized test scores, class rank most important. Require 2 of the following: SAT 820 (exclusive of Writing); ACT 16; GPA 2.0; class rank top 60 percent. Computerized Placement Test required for those with SAT verbal and math scores below 500. Portfolio recommended for all; audition required for music, theater programs; essay required for English-deficient; interview recommended for music, theater programs. **Learning Disabled:** Meet with Director of Disability Services.

High school preparation. 12 units required; 18 recommended. Required and recommended units include English 4, mathematics 2-3, social studies 1, history 1-2, science 2-3 (laboratory 1), foreign language 2, computer science 1, visual/performing arts 1 and academic electives 2.

2011-2012 Annual costs. Tuition/fees: $13,396. Room/board: $7,850. Books/supplies: $1,680. Personal expenses: $3,415.

Financial aid. **Non-need-based:** Scholarships awarded for academics, athletics, leadership, music/drama, religious affiliation, state residency.

Application procedures. Admission: Priority date 6/1; deadline 8/26. $25 fee, may be waived for applicants with need. Admission notification on a rolling basis. **Financial aid:** Priority date 6/1, closing date 6/30. FAFSA required. Applicants notified on a rolling basis starting 8/1; must reply within 2 week(s) of notification.

Academics. **Special study options:** Cross-registration, double major, dual enrollment of high school students, ESL, honors, independent study, internships, student-designed major, study abroad, teacher certification program. **Credit/placement by examination:** AP, CLEP, IB, SAT, ACT, institutional tests. 16 credit hours maximum toward associate degree, 30 toward bachelor's. CLEP and other exam credits cannot exceed 25 percent of hours needed for degree. **Support services:** Learning center, reduced course load, remedial instruction, study skills assistance, tutoring, writing center.

Majors. Biology: General. **Business:** General, accounting, business admin, international, marketing. **Communications:** Broadcast journalism, journalism, media studies, radio/TV. **Education:** Early childhood, elementary, music. **English:** English lit. **Foreign languages:** Spanish. **Health services:** Predental, premedicine, prepharmacy. **History:** General. **Liberal arts:** Arts/sciences. **Math:** General. **Parks/recreation:** General, sports admin. **Psychology:** General. **Theology:** Bible, missionary, sacred music, youth ministry. **Visual/performing arts:** Dramatic, music, music performance, piano/keyboard, studio arts, voice/opera.

Most popular majors. Business/marketing 19%, communications/journalism 8%, education 16%, liberal arts 12%, parks/recreation 10%, psychology 6%, theological studies 13%.

Computing on campus. 75 workstations in library, computer center, student center. Dormitories wired for high-speed internet access and linked to campus network. Commuter students can connect to campus network. Online library, helpline, wireless network available.

Student life. Freshman orientation: Mandatory. Preregistration for classes offered. Held in August, the 5 days prior to the start of the fall semester. **Policies:** NGU is a drug, alcohol, smoke free campus. Religious observance required. **Housing:** Guaranteed on-campus for all undergraduates. Single-sex dorms, special housing for disabled, apartments, wellness housing available. $100 deposit, deadline 8/26. **Activities:** Bands, campus ministries, choral groups, drama, literary magazine, music ensembles, musical theater, radio station, student government, student newspaper, symphony orchestra, Baptist student union, athletic ministries, Etude music society, Fellowship of Christians in Service, Joyful sound, business club, Teacher Education Association, Phi Beta Lambda, Dramatis Personae Society.

Athletics. NCAA, NCCAA. **Intercollegiate:** Baseball M, basketball, cheerleading, cross-country, football (tackle) M, golf, soccer, softball W, tennis, track and field, volleyball W. **Intramural:** Basketball, football (non-tackle) M, softball, table tennis, tennis, volleyball. **Team name:** Crusaders.

Student services. Chaplain/spiritual director, career counseling, student employment services, financial aid counseling, health services, on-campus daycare, personal counseling, placement for graduates. **Physically disabled:** Services for visually impaired.

Contact. E-mail: admissions@ngu.edu
Phone: (864) 977-7001 Toll-free number: (800) 468-6642
Fax: (864) 977-7177
Keli Sewell, Vice President for Admissions and Financial Aid, North Greenville University, PO Box 1892, Tigerville, SC 29688-1892

Presbyterian College
Clinton, South Carolina

www.presby.edu	CB member
	CB code: 5540

- Private 4-year pharmacy and liberal arts college affiliated with Presbyterian Church (USA)
- Residential campus in small town
- 1,153 degree-seeking undergraduates: 1% part-time, 53% women, 10% African American, 1% Asian American, 2% Hispanic American, 1% Native American, 1% international
- 157 degree-seeking graduate students
- 67% of applicants admitted
- SAT or ACT (ACT writing optional), application essay required
- 68% graduate within 6 years; 30% enter graduate study

General. Founded in 1880. Regionally accredited. **Degrees:** 266 bachelor's awarded; professional offered. **ROTC:** Army. **Location:** 40 miles from Greenville, 35 miles from Spartanburg. **Calendar:** Semester, limited summer session. **Full-time faculty:** 99 total; 97% have terminal degrees, 9% minority, 37% women. **Part-time faculty:** 37 total; 35% have terminal degrees, 3% minority, 54% women. **Class size:** 62% < 20, 37% 20-39, less than 1% 40-49, less than 1% 50-99. **Special facilities:** Scanning electron and transmission microscopes, ecological research center, Confucius Institute.

Freshman class profile. 1,484 applied, 1,000 admitted, 359 enrolled.

Mid 50% test scores			
SAT critical reading:	500-600	Rank in top quarter:	67%
SAT math:	510-620	Rank in top tenth:	34%
ACT composite:	21-27	Return as sophomores:	76%
GPA 3.75 or higher:	35%	Out-of-state:	32%
GPA 3.50-3.74:	20%	Live on campus:	99%
GPA 3.0-3.49:	30%	International:	1%
GPA 2.0-2.99:	15%	Fraternities:	35%
		Sororities:	38%

Basis for selection. Rigor of high school curriculum most important, followed by test scores, high school GPA, and high school recommendation. Extracurricular involvement and interview considered in some cases. Interview recommended. **Home schooled:** State high school equivalency certificate required.

High school preparation. College-preparatory program recommended. 18 units required. Required and recommended units include English 4, mathematics 4, social studies 2, history 2, science 2-4 (laboratory 2), foreign language 2 and academic electives 2. 2 or more units of laboratory science recommended for science majors.

2011-2012 Annual costs. Tuition/fees: $31,280. Room/board: $8,670. Books/supplies: $1,200. Personal expenses: $2,502.

2011-2012 Financial aid. **Need-based:** 346 full-time freshmen applied for aid; 302 were judged to have need; 302 of these received aid. Average

need met was 92%. Average scholarship/grant was $28,158; average loan $2,968. 87% of total undergraduate aid awarded as scholarships/grants, 13% as loans/jobs. **Non-need-based:** Awarded to 660 full-time undergraduates, including 194 freshmen. Scholarships awarded for academics, alumni affiliation, art, athletics, job skills, leadership, minority status, music/drama, religious affiliation, ROTC, state residency.

Application procedures. Admission: Priority date 2/1; deadline 6/30 (postmark date). $40 fee, may be waived for applicants with need. Admission notification by 3/15. Must reply by 5/1. **Financial aid:** Priority date 3/15, closing date 6/30. FAFSA required. Applicants notified by 3/1; must reply by 5/1.

Academics. Special study options: Combined bachelor's/graduate degree, double major, dual enrollment of high school students, exchange student, honors, independent study, internships, semester at sea, study abroad, teacher certification program, Washington semester. 3-2 environmental science program, 3-2 engineering program, religious educational program, dual degrees offered with Auburn University (AL), Clemson University, Vanderbilt University (TN), University of South Carolina. **Credit/placement by examination:** AP, CLEP, IB, SAT, ACT, institutional tests. 40 credit hours maximum toward bachelor's degree. **Support services:** Pre-admission summer program, study skills assistance, tutoring, writing center.

Majors. Biology: General. **Business:** Business admin. **Education:** Early childhood, elementary, middle, music. **English:** English lit. **Foreign languages:** General, French, German, Spanish. **History:** General. **Math:** General. **Philosophy/religion:** Philosophy, religion. **Physical sciences:** Chemistry, physics. **Psychology:** General. **Social sciences:** Political science, sociology. **Visual/performing arts:** Art, dramatic, music.

Most popular majors. Biology 12%, business/marketing 25%, education 6%, English 8%, history 16%, psychology 6%, social sciences 12%.

Computing on campus. 100 workstations in dormitories, library, computer center, student center. Dormitories wired for high-speed internet access and linked to campus network. Commuter students can connect to campus network. Online course registration, online library, helpline, student web hosting, wireless network available.

Student life. Freshman orientation: Mandatory, $100 fee. Preregistration for classes offered. Orientation includes registration, placement testing, and organization fair. **Policies:** Honor code governs conduct inside and outside classroom, on and off campus. Cultural Enrichment Program requires students to attend 40 on-campus cultural events as part of graduation requirement. **Housing:** Guaranteed on-campus for all undergraduates. Coed dorms, single-sex dorms, apartments, fraternity/sorority housing, wellness housing available. $400 nonrefundable deposit, deadline 5/1. All full-time students, except those commuting daily from family's residence, required to live on campus. Sorority housing not available. **Activities:** Bands, campus ministries, choral groups, dance, drama, international student organizations, literary magazine, music ensembles, musical theater, opera, radio station, student government, student newspaper, symphony orchestra, Volunteer organizations, multicultural student union, Young Democrats and Republicans, interdenominational organizations, Habitat for Humanity, Amnesty International, Fellowship of Christian Athletes.

Athletics. NCAA. Intercollegiate: Baseball M, basketball, cheerleading, cross-country, football (tackle) M, golf, lacrosse W, soccer, softball W, tennis, volleyball W. **Intramural:** Basketball, football (non-tackle), golf, soccer, softball, tennis, volleyball. **Team name:** Blue Hose.

Student services. Chaplain/spiritual director, career counseling, student employment services, financial aid counseling, health services, minority student services, personal counseling, placement for graduates.

Contact. E-mail: admissions@presby.edu
Phone: (864) 833-8230 Toll-free number: (800) 960-7583
Fax: (864) 833-8195
Brian Fortman, Dean of Admissions, Presbyterian College, 503 South Broad Street, Clinton, SC 29325-2865

South Carolina State University
Orangeburg, South Carolina   CB member
www.scsu.edu   CB code: 5618

- Public 4-year university
- Residential campus in large town
- 3,708 degree-seeking undergraduates: 6% part-time, 54% women
- 571 degree-seeking graduate students
- 96% of applicants admitted
- SAT or ACT (ACT writing optional) required
- 40% graduate within 6 years; 35% enter graduate study

General. Founded in 1896. Regionally accredited. **Degrees:** 546 bachelor's awarded; master's, doctoral offered. **ROTC:** Army, Air Force. **Location:** 41 miles from Columbia, 79 miles from Charleston. **Calendar:** Semester, limited summer session. **Full-time faculty:** 217 total. **Part-time faculty:** 67 total. **Special facilities:** Planetarium, laboratory school, child development learning center.

Freshman class profile. 3,267 applied, 3,130 admitted, 826 enrolled.

Mid 50% test scores			
SAT critical reading:	380-460	GPA 2.0-2.99:	49%
SAT math:	380-460	Rank in top quarter:	17%
ACT composite:	15-19	Rank in top tenth:	9%
GPA 3.75 or higher:	9%	End year in good standing:	80%
GPA 3.50-3.74:	12%	Return as sophomores:	67%
GPA 3.0-3.49:	25%	Out-of-state:	30%
		Live on campus:	90%

Basis for selection. Admission decisions based primarily on high school record, class rank, and standardized test scores. Audition required for music education program; portfolio required for art education program. **Learning Disabled:** Student must submit documentation, which is sent to Student Health Services Center--Disabled Student Support Services.

High school preparation. College-preparatory program recommended. 20 units required. Required units include English 4, mathematics 3, social studies 3, science 3 (laboratory 3), foreign language 2 and academic electives 4. 1 physical education or ROTC required.

2011-2012 Annual costs. Tuition/fees: $9,258; $18,170 out-of-state. Room/board: $9,286. Books/supplies: $1,200. Personal expenses: $3,150.

2010-2011 Financial aid. Need-based: 60% of total undergraduate aid awarded as scholarships/grants, 40% as loans/jobs. **Non-need-based:** Scholarships awarded for academics, athletics, ROTC.

Application procedures. Admission: Closing date 7/31 (postmark date). $25 fee, may be waived for applicants with need. Admission notification on a rolling basis. **Financial aid:** Closing date 5/1. FAFSA required. Applicants notified on a rolling basis starting 3/15; must reply by 7/1 or within 2 week(s) of notification.

Academics. Special study options: Cooperative education, cross-registration, distance learning, double major, dual enrollment of high school students, exchange student, honors, independent study, internships, liberal arts/career combination, student-designed major, study abroad, teacher certification program, Washington semester. **Credit/placement by examination:** AP, CLEP, institutional tests. 30 credit hours maximum toward bachelor's degree. **Support services:** Learning center, pre-admission summer program, study skills assistance, tutoring, writing center.

Majors. Biology: General. **Business:** Accounting, business admin, managerial economics, marketing. **Communications:** Media studies. **Computer sciences:** General. **Education:** Art, business, early childhood, elementary, family/consumer sciences, middle, music, physical, special ed, technology/industrial arts. **Engineering:** Nuclear. **English:** English lit. **Foreign languages:** General. **General:** Agribusiness operations. **Health services:** Audiology/speech pathology, nursing (RN). **History:** General. **Human services:** Social work. **Math:** General. **Parks/recreation:** Health/fitness. **Physical sciences:** Chemistry, physics. **Protective services:** Law enforcement admin. **Psychology:** General. **Social sciences:** General, political science, sociology. **Visual/performing arts:** Dramatic, music management, music performance, studio arts. **Work/family studies:** General, food/nutrition.

Most popular majors. Biology 9%, business/marketing 18%, education 11%, engineering/engineering technologies 7%, family/consumer sciences 10%, health sciences 8%, psychology 6%, security/protective services 6%.

Computing on campus. 300 workstations in dormitories, library, computer center, student center. Dormitories wired for high-speed internet access and linked to campus network. Commuter students can connect to campus network. Online course registration, online library, helpline, repair service, wireless network available.

Student life. Freshman orientation: Available, $100 fee. Preregistration for classes offered. **Housing:** Guaranteed on-campus for freshmen. Single-sex dorms, apartments available. $35 deposit. **Activities:** Bands, choral groups, dance, drama, international student organizations, music ensembles, radio station, student government, student newspaper.

Athletics. NCAA. Intercollegiate: Basketball, cheerleading, cross-country, football (tackle) M, golf W, soccer W, softball W, tennis, track and field, volleyball W. **Intramural:** Basketball, bowling, softball. **Team name:** Bulldogs.

Student services. Adult student services, alcohol/substance abuse counseling, chaplain/spiritual director, career counseling, services for economically disadvantaged, student employment services, financial aid counseling, health services, minority student services, personal counseling, placement

for graduates, veterans' counselor. **Physically disabled:** Services for visually, speech, hearing impaired.

Contact. E-mail: admissions@scsu.edu
Phone: (803) 536-7185 Toll-free number: (800) 260-5956
Fax: (803) 536-8990
Antonio Boyle, Assistant Vice President of Enrollment Management and Director of Admissions, South Carolina State University, 300 College Street NE, Orangeburg, SC 29117

South University: Columbia
Columbia, South Carolina
www.southuniversity.edu   **CB code: 5097**

- For-profit 4-year university
- Commuter campus in small city
- 1,089 degree-seeking undergraduates

General. Founded in 1935. Regionally accredited. **Degrees:** 119 bachelor's, 31 associate awarded; master's, professional offered. **Location:** 5 miles from downtown. **Calendar:** Quarter, extensive summer session. **Full-time faculty:** 31 total. **Part-time faculty:** 70 total.

Freshman class profile. 26 enrolled.

Basis for selection. SAT or ACT may be submitted in place of required institutional tests for placement. **Home schooled:** Students must provide evidence that home schooling was conducted in accordance with state laws. A certificate of attendance or completion is not sufficient.

2011-2012 Annual costs. Tuition/fees: $16,035. Tuition and fees are representative of most campus degree programs.

Financial aid. All financial aid based on need.

Application procedures. Admission: No deadline. $50 fee. Admission notification on a rolling basis. **Financial aid:** No deadline. FAFSA required. Applicants notified on a rolling basis starting 5/30.

Academics. Special study options: Distance learning, internships, weekend college. **Credit/placement by examination:** AP, CLEP, institutional tests. **Support services:** Remedial instruction, study skills assistance, tutoring, writing center.

Majors. Business: Business admin. **Computer sciences:** Information technology. **Health services:** Health care admin, nursing (RN). **Protective services:** Police science. **Psychology:** General. **Visual/performing arts:** Graphic design.

Most popular majors. Business/marketing 29%, computer/information sciences 9%, health sciences 33%, legal studies 25%, security/protective services 13%.

Computing on campus. Commuter students can connect to campus network. Online library, helpline, wireless network available.

Student life. Freshman orientation: Mandatory. Preregistration for classes offered.

Student services. Adult student services, career counseling, student employment services, financial aid counseling, personal counseling, placement for graduates, veterans' counselor. **Physically disabled:** Services for visually, speech, hearing impaired.

Contact. Phone: (803) 799-9082 Toll-free number: (866) 629-3031
Fax: (803) 799-9038
Trisha Wade, Director of Admissions, South University: Columbia, 9 Science Court, Columbia, SC 29203

Southern Wesleyan University
Central, South Carolina
www.swu.edu   **CB code: 5896**

- Private 4-year university and liberal arts college affiliated with Wesleyan Church
- Residential campus in small town

General. Founded in 1906. Regionally accredited. **Location:** 20 miles from Greenville, SC; 100 miles from Atlanta, GA. **Calendar:** Semester.

Annual costs/financial aid. Tuition/fees (2011-2012): $20,550. Undergraduate tuition for adult evening program is $340 per credit hour. Graduate tuition ranges from $440 - $475 per credit hour. Room/board: $8,410. Books/supplies: $1,020. Personal expenses: $1,050. Need-based financial aid available for full-time students.

Contact. Phone: (864) 644-5550
Director of Admissions, PO Box 1020, Central, SC 29630-1020

University of Phoenix: Columbia
Columbia, South Carolina
www.phoenix.edu

- For-profit 4-year university
- Small city
- 914 degree-seeking undergraduates

General. Regionally accredited. **Degrees:** 66 bachelor's awarded; master's offered. **Calendar:** Differs by program. **Full-time faculty:** 17 total. **Part-time faculty:** 103 total.

Basis for selection. Open admission.

2011-2012 Annual costs. Estimated costs as of August 2011: per-credit-hour charge, $380 to $415; depending upon level and course of study; electronic course materials fee, $95, if applicable. Book and material charges may vary by course and program. All fees are subject to change.

Application procedures. Admission: No deadline. No application fee. **Financial aid:** No deadline.

Academics. Credit/placement by examination: AP, CLEP.

Majors. Business: Accounting, business admin. **Computer sciences:** General, web page design. **Health services:** Health care admin.

Contact. Marc Booker, Director of Admission and Evaluation, University of Phoenix: Columbia, 1001 Pinnacle Point Drive, Suite 200, Columbia, SC 29223-5727

University of South Carolina: Aiken
Aiken, South Carolina   **CB member**
www.usca.edu   **CB code: 5840**

- Public 4-year university and liberal arts college
- Residential campus in large town
- 2,955 degree-seeking undergraduates: 16% part-time, 65% women, 29% African American, 1% Asian American, 3% Hispanic American, 1% international
- 55 degree-seeking graduate students
- 36% of applicants admitted
- SAT or ACT (ACT writing recommended) required
- 42% graduate within 6 years

General. Founded in 1961. Regionally accredited. **Degrees:** 498 bachelor's awarded; master's offered. **Location:** 55 miles from Columbia; 15 miles from Augusta, Georgia. **Calendar:** Semester, limited summer session. **Full-time faculty:** 145 total; 74% have terminal degrees, 9% minority, 47% women. **Part-time faculty:** 103 total; 19% have terminal degrees, 9% minority, 58% women. **Class size:** 41% < 20, 54% 20-39, 3% 40-49, 2% 50-99. **Special facilities:** Fine arts center, science center, natatorium, planetarium, convocation center.

Freshman class profile. 2,747 applied, 1,000 admitted, 606 enrolled.

Mid 50% test scores			
SAT critical reading:	430-530	Rank in top quarter:	43%
SAT math:	440-550	Rank in top tenth:	17%
SAT writing:	410-530	End year in good standing:	67%
ACT composite:	18-23	Return as sophomores:	70%
GPA 3.75 or higher:	37%	Out-of-state:	12%
GPA 3.50-3.74:	17%	Live on campus:	58%
GPA 3.0-3.49:	31%	International:	1%
GPA 2.0-2.99:	15%	Fraternities:	6%
		Sororities:	6%

Basis for selection. Test scores, high school core GPA important. Admission based on course selection, standardized test scores and a predicted college GPA. Audition, essay, interview, portfolio recommended.

High school preparation. 21 units required. Required and recommended units include English 4, mathematics 4, social studies 2, history 1, science 3 (laboratory 3), foreign language 2, computer science 1, visual/performing arts 1 and academic electives 4. Physical education or ROTC of 1 unit; elective college preparatory credits must come from 3 different fields.

2011-2012 Annual costs. Tuition/fees: $8,750; $17,238 out-of-state. Room/board: $6,630. Books/supplies: $1,080. Personal expenses: $1,711.

2010-2011 Financial aid. **Need-based:** 576 full-time freshmen applied for aid; 423 were judged to have need; 423 of these received aid. Average need met was 83%. Average scholarship/grant was $8,881; average loan $2,334. 48% of total undergraduate aid awarded as scholarships/grants, 52% as loans/jobs. **Non-need-based:** Awarded to 736 full-time undergraduates, including 193 freshmen. Scholarships awarded for academics, alumni affiliation, art, athletics, leadership, minority status, music/drama, state residency. **Additional information:** Students must be enrolled at least half time and be able to present documentation which verifies eligibility to work in the U.S.

Application procedures. **Admission:** Priority date 7/1; deadline 8/1 (postmark date). $45 fee, may be waived for applicants with need. Admission notification on a rolling basis beginning on or about 9/1. Must reply by May 1 or within 3 week(s) if notified thereafter. **Financial aid:** Priority date 3/15; no closing date. FAFSA required. Applicants notified on a rolling basis starting 4/20; must reply within 2 week(s) of notification.

Academics. **Special study options:** Cooperative education, distance learning, double major, dual enrollment of high school students, ESL, honors, independent study, internships, student-designed major, study abroad, teacher certification program. **Credit/placement by examination:** AP, CLEP, IB, institutional tests. 30 credit hours maximum toward bachelor's degree. **Support services:** Learning center, study skills assistance, tutoring, writing center.

Majors. **Biology:** General. **Business:** Business admin. **Communications:** Communications/speech/rhetoric. **Education:** Early childhood, elementary, middle, music, secondary, special ed. **English:** English lit. **Health services:** Nursing (RN). **History:** General. **Liberal arts:** Arts/sciences. **Math:** Applied. **Parks/recreation:** Exercise sciences. **Physical sciences:** Chemistry. **Psychology:** General. **Social sciences:** Political science, sociology. **Visual/performing arts:** Studio arts.

Most popular majors. Business/marketing 25%, communications/journalism 6%, education 14%, health sciences 12%, parks/recreation 9%, social sciences 9%.

Computing on campus. 550 workstations in dormitories, library, computer center, student center. Dormitories wired for high-speed internet access and linked to campus network. Commuter students can connect to campus network. Online course registration, online library, helpline, wireless network available.

Student life. **Freshman orientation:** Mandatory, $75 fee. Preregistration for classes offered. Held in June, July, and August. June and July orientations offer registration. **Housing:** Coed dorms, special housing for disabled, apartments, wellness housing available. $125 partly refundable deposit. **Activities:** Bands, campus ministries, choral groups, dance, drama, international student organizations, literary magazine, music ensembles, musical theater, student government, student newspaper, Campus Crusade for Christ, honor societies, Pacer Union Board, African American Students' Alliance, College Republicans, Circle K, Fellowship of Christian Athletes.

Athletics. NCAA. **Intercollegiate:** Baseball M, basketball, cross-country W, golf M, soccer, softball W, tennis, volleyball W. **Intramural:** Basketball, football (non-tackle), soccer, volleyball. **Team name:** Pacers.

Student services. Adult student services, alcohol/substance abuse counseling, career counseling, student employment services, financial aid counseling, health services, minority student services, on-campus daycare, personal counseling, placement for graduates, veterans' counselor. **Physically disabled:** Services for visually, speech, hearing impaired.

Contact. E-mail: admit@usca.edu
Phone: (803) 641-3366 Toll-free number: (888) 969-8722
Fax: (803) 641-3727
Andrew Hendrix, Director of Admissions, University of South Carolina: Aiken, 471 University Parkway, Aiken, SC 29801-6399

University of South Carolina: Beaufort
Bluffton, South Carolina **CB member**
www.uscb.edu **CB code: 5845**

▶ Public 4-year university and liberal arts college
▶ Commuter campus in large town

▶ 1,773 degree-seeking undergraduates: 20% part-time, 63% women
▶ 75% of applicants admitted
▶ SAT or ACT (ACT writing optional) required

General. Founded in 1959. Regionally accredited. Two locations: Gateway to Hilton Head and historic Beaufort. **Degrees:** 216 bachelor's, 3 associate awarded. **Location:** 72 miles from Charleston, 42 miles from Savannah, GA. **Calendar:** Semester, limited summer session. **Full-time faculty:** 59 total; 76% have terminal degrees, 15% minority, 48% women. **Part-time faculty:** 82 total. **Class size:** 54% < 20, 41% 20-39, 2% 40-49, 2% 50-99. **Special facilities:** Performing arts center.

Freshman class profile. 1,434 applied, 1,070 admitted, 432 enrolled.

Return as sophomores:	54%	**Live on campus:**	40%
Out-of-state:	20%		

Basis for selection. Test scores, rigor of secondary school record important; academic GPA considered.

High school preparation. College-preparatory program required. 19 units required. Required units include English 4, mathematics 4, social studies 2, history 1, science 3 (laboratory 3), foreign language 2, visual/performing arts 1 and academic electives 2. Electives must be from 2 areas. Computer science course recommended. 1 PE or ROTC required.

2011-2012 Annual costs. Tuition/fees: $8,108; $17,220 out-of-state. Room/board: $6,850. Books/supplies: $975. Personal expenses: $1,512.

Financial aid. **Non-need-based:** Scholarships awarded for academics, art, athletics, leadership, religious affiliation, state residency.

Application procedures. **Admission:** No deadline. $40 fee, may be waived for applicants with need. Admission notification on a rolling basis beginning on or about 2/1. **Financial aid:** Priority date 4/15; no closing date. FAFSA required. Applicants notified on a rolling basis starting 5/31; must reply within 2 week(s) of notification.

Academics. **Special study options:** Cooperative education, distance learning, dual enrollment of high school students, independent study, internships, student-designed major, study abroad, teacher certification program, weekend college. **Credit/placement by examination:** AP, CLEP, institutional tests. 15 credit hours maximum toward associate degree, 30 toward bachelor's. **Support services:** Learning center, reduced course load, study skills assistance, tutoring, writing center.

Majors. **Biology:** General. **Business:** Business admin, hospitality admin. **Education:** Early childhood. **English:** English lit. **Foreign languages:** Spanish. **Health services:** Nursing (RN). **History:** General. **Liberal arts:** Arts/sciences. **Math:** Computational. **Psychology:** General. **Social sciences:** General, sociology. **Visual/performing arts:** Studio arts.

Most popular majors. Biology 8%, business/marketing 37%, education 10%, health sciences 15%, psychology 10%, social sciences 10%.

Computing on campus. 114 workstations in library, computer center. Dormitories wired for high-speed internet access. Online course registration, online library, helpline, wireless network available.

Student life. **Freshman orientation:** Mandatory. Preregistration for classes offered. **Housing:** Special housing for disabled, apartments, wellness housing available. **Activities:** Choral groups, drama, literary magazine, musical theater, student government, student newspaper, African American student association, Christian student fellowship, business club, veterans association, education club, Gamma Beta Phi honor society, psychology/sociology/anthropology club.

Athletics. NAIA. **Intercollegiate:** Baseball M, cross-country, golf, soccer W, softball W, track and field. **Intramural:** Football (non-tackle), soccer. **Team name:** Sand Sharks.

Student services. Alcohol/substance abuse counseling, career counseling, student employment services, financial aid counseling, personal counseling, veterans' counselor.

Contact. E-mail: admissions@uscb.edu
Phone: (843) 208-8000 Toll-free number: (877) 885-5271
Fax: (843) 208-8290
Joffery Blair, Director of Admissions, University of South Carolina: Beaufort, One University Boulevard, Bluffton, SC 29909

University of South Carolina: Columbia

Columbia, South Carolina | **CB member**
www.sc.edu | **CB code: 5818**

- Public 4-year university
- Residential campus in small city
- 22,222 degree-seeking undergraduates: 7% part-time, 54% women, 11% African American, 3% Asian American, 4% Hispanic American, 1% international
- 7,884 degree-seeking graduate students
- 63% of applicants admitted
- SAT or ACT with writing required
- 70% graduate within 6 years

General. Founded in 1801. Regionally accredited. **Degrees:** 4,462 bachelor's, 6 associate awarded; master's, professional, doctoral offered. **ROTC:** Army, Naval, Air Force. **Location:** 70 miles from Charlotte, North Carolina. **Calendar:** Semester, extensive summer session. **Full-time faculty:** 1,232 total; 84% have terminal degrees, 13% minority, 40% women. **Part-time faculty:** 560 total; 40% have terminal degrees, 12% minority, 53% women. **Class size:** 36% < 20, 46% 20-39, 8% 40-49, 7% 50-99, 3% >100. **Special facilities:** Observatory, arboretum, green dorm with learning center focusing on sustainability.

Freshman class profile. 21,311 applied, 13,451 admitted, 4,636 enrolled.

Mid 50% test scores			
SAT critical reading:	540-640	**Rank in top tenth:**	28%
SAT math:	560-650	**End year in good standing:**	92%
ACT composite:	24-29	**Return as sophomores:**	87%
GPA 3.75 or higher:	64%	**Out-of-state:**	43%
GPA 3.50-3.74:	16%	**Live on campus:**	94%
GPA 3.0-3.49:	17%	**International:**	1%
GPA 2.0-2.99:	3%	**Fraternities:**	23%
Rank in top quarter:	62%	**Sororities:**	34%

Basis for selection. Admission based on high school curriculum, grades in required high school courses, SAT and ACT scores. **Learning Disabled:** Diagnostic tests required for learning disabled students.

High school preparation. College-preparatory program required. 18 units required. Required units include English 4, mathematics 4, social studies 2, history 1, science 3 (laboratory 3), foreign language 2, visual/performing arts 1 and academic electives 1. 1 unit physical education or ROTC is required.

2011-2012 Annual costs. Tuition/fees: $10,168; $26,352 out-of-state. Health professions (pharmacy, health, nursing), law and medical professions have higher undergraduate and graduate fees. Room/board: $8,026. Books/supplies: $950. Personal expenses: $2,420.

2011-2012 Financial aid. **Need-based:** 3,401 full-time freshmen applied for aid; 2,177 were judged to have need; 2,177 of these received aid. Average need met was 76%. Average scholarship/grant was $5,408; average loan $2,302. 58% of total undergraduate aid awarded as scholarships/grants, 42% as loans/jobs. **Non-need-based:** Scholarships awarded for academics, alumni affiliation, art, athletics, job skills, leadership, minority status, music/drama, religious affiliation, ROTC, state residency.

Application procedures. **Admission:** Closing date 12/1 (postmark date). $50 fee, may be waived for applicants with need. Admission notification by 3/15. Admission notification on a rolling basis. Must reply by 5/1. **Financial aid:** Priority date 4/1; no closing date. FAFSA required. Applicants notified on a rolling basis starting 4/1.

Academics. One-month May term focusing on specialized topics. **Special study options:** Accelerated study, combined bachelor's/graduate degree, cooperative education, cross-registration, distance learning, double major, dual enrollment of high school students, ESL, exchange student, external degree, honors, independent study, internships, study abroad, teacher certification program, weekend college. Alternative spring break, Dobson volunteer service program, international program for students. **Credit/placement by examination:** AP, CLEP, IB, institutional tests. Maximum number of semester hours of credit by examination allowed varies according to degree and program of study. **Support services:** Learning center, reduced course load, study skills assistance, tutoring, writing center.

Honors college/program. To be competitive for admission, students must have minimum 1300 SAT score (exclusive of Writing) and minimum high school GPA of 3.5. 600 admitted to yield freshman class of 275. Two recommendations must be submitted with application. Academic program consists of 115-125 honors classes per semester across most disciplines and levels.

Majors. **Area/ethnic studies:** African-American, European, Latin American, women's. **Biology:** General, marine. **Business:** Accounting, business admin, finance, hospitality admin, insurance, management science, managerial economics, marketing, nonprofit/public, office management, real estate, retailing, tourism/travel. **Communications:** Advertising, broadcast journalism, journalism, media studies, public relations. **Computer sciences:** General, information systems. **Conservation:** Environmental science. **Education:** Art, early childhood, elementary, physical. **Engineering:** Biomedical, chemical, civil, computer, electrical, engineering science, mechanical. **English:** English lit. **Foreign languages:** Classics, comparative lit, French, German, Italian, Russian, Spanish. **Health services:** Cardiovascular technology, nursing (RN). **History:** General. **Human services:** Social work. **Liberal arts:** Arts/sciences. **Math:** General, statistics. **Parks/recreation:** Exercise sciences, sports admin. **Philosophy/religion:** Philosophy, religion. **Physical sciences:** Chemistry, geology, geophysics, physics. **Protective services:** Law enforcement admin. **Psychology:** Experimental. **Social sciences:** Anthropology, economics, geography, international relations, political science, sociology. **Visual/performing arts:** Art history/conservation, dance, dramatic, film/cinema/video, music, studio arts.

Most popular majors. Biology 10%, business/marketing 27%, communications/journalism 8%, education 6%, engineering/engineering technologies 6%, health sciences 6%, psychology 6%, social sciences 9%.

Computing on campus. 2,800 workstations in dormitories, library, computer center, student center. Dormitories wired for high-speed internet access and linked to campus network. Commuter students can connect to campus network. Online course registration, online library, helpline, wireless network available.

Student life. **Freshman orientation:** Available, $70 fee. Preregistration for classes offered. Parents may also attend to view campus for $40 fee. **Housing:** Guaranteed on-campus for freshmen. Coed dorms, single-sex dorms, special housing for disabled, apartments, fraternity/sorority housing, wellness housing available. $150 partly refundable deposit, deadline 6/1. Honors housing (undergraduate), residential college, communities for Pre-Medical, Pre-Law, French, Spanish, Journalism, Engineering, Athletic, Music, Global, and Environmentally Friendly. **Activities:** Bands, campus ministries, choral groups, dance, drama, international student organizations, literary magazine, music ensembles, musical theater, opera, radio station, student government, student newspaper, symphony orchestra, TV station, College Democrats, College Republicans, Campus Crusade for Christ, Baptist Collegiate Ministry, Dance Marathon, Association of African American Students, Habitat for Humanity, Alpha Lambda Delta.

Athletics. NCAA. **Intercollegiate:** Baseball M, basketball, cross-country W, diving, equestrian W, football (tackle) M, golf, soccer, softball W, swimming, tennis, track and field, volleyball W. **Intramural:** Basketball, bowling, football (non-tackle), golf, racquetball, soccer, softball, swimming, table tennis, tennis, volleyball, weight lifting. **Team name:** Fighting Gamecocks.

Student services. Adult student services, alcohol/substance abuse counseling, chaplain/spiritual director, career counseling, services for economically disadvantaged, student employment services, financial aid counseling, health services, minority student services, on-campus daycare, personal counseling, placement for graduates, veterans' counselor, women's services. **Physically disabled:** Services for visually, speech, hearing impaired.

Contact. E-mail: admissions-ugrad@sc.edu
Phone: (803) 777-7700 Toll-free number: (800) 868-5872
Fax: (803) 777-0101
Mary Wagner, Senior Associate Director of Undergraduate Admissions, University of South Carolina: Columbia, Office of Undergraduate Admissions, Columbia, SC 29208

University of South Carolina: Upstate

Spartanburg, South Carolina
www.uscupstate.edu | **CB code: 5850**

- Public 4-year university
- Commuter campus in small city
- 5,149 degree-seeking undergraduates: 14% part-time, 64% women, 27% African American, 2% Asian American, 4% Hispanic American, 1% international
- 10 degree-seeking graduate students
- 59% of applicants admitted
- SAT or ACT (ACT writing optional) required
- 39% graduate within 6 years

General. Founded in 1967. Regionally accredited. **Degrees:** 1,078 bachelor's awarded; master's offered. **ROTC:** Army. **Location:** 30 miles from Greenville, 70 miles from Charlotte, North Carolina. **Calendar:** Semester,

extensive summer session. **Full-time faculty:** 206 total; 80% have terminal degrees, 12% minority, 55% women. **Part-time faculty:** 200 total; 50% have terminal degrees, 12% minority, 50% women. **Class size:** 53% < 20, 44% 20-39, 3% 40-49, less than 1% 50-99. **Special facilities:** Film theater, recital hall, center for international studies and language services, audiovisual production center, digital lab, centers for interdisciplinary studies, watershed ecology center.

Freshman class profile. 3,096 applied, 1,816 admitted, 797 enrolled.

Mid 50% test scores			
SAT critical reading:	430-520	Rank in top quarter:	41%
SAT math:	450-530	Rank in top tenth:	12%
SAT writing:	420-510	Return as sophomores:	67%
ACT composite:	18-22	Out-of-state:	7%
GPA 3.75 or higher:	42%	Live on campus:	71%
GPA 3.50-3.74:	18%	International:	1%
GPA 3.0-3.49:	27%	Fraternities:	1%
GPA 2.0-2.99:	13%	Sororities:	1%

Basis for selection. Cumulative average of C or better in preparatory courses and minimum 850 SAT (exclusive of Writing), or 18 ACT required. Higher grades may offset lower SAT/ACT scores, and higher SAT/ACT scores may offset lower grades. All applicants who are 21 years of age or younger, with the exception of transfer applicants who have completed at least 30 semester hours of college credit, must submit results of the SAT or the ACT. Applicants who are 22 years of age or older are not required to submit SAT/ACT scores. Interviews recommended.

High school preparation. College-preparatory program required. 20 units required; 22 recommended. Required and recommended units include English 4, mathematics 3-4, social studies 2, history 1, science 3 (laboratory 3), foreign language 2-3 and academic electives 4. Students who graduated from high school between 1988-2000 must meet above requirements. However, these students need 2 rather than 3 laboratory sciences and 1 rather than 4 electives.

2011-2012 Annual costs. Tuition/fees: $9,686; $19,112 out-of-state. Room/board: $7,072. Books/supplies: $1,300. Personal expenses: $2,509.

2010-2011 Financial aid. Need-based: 753 full-time freshmen applied for aid; 634 were judged to have need; 630 of these received aid. Average need met was 69%. Average scholarship/grant was $5,496; average loan $3,104. 50% of total undergraduate aid awarded as scholarships/grants, 50% as loans/jobs. **Non-need-based:** Awarded to 1,690 full-time undergraduates, including 685 freshmen. Scholarships awarded for academics, athletics, minority status, ROTC, state residency. **Additional information:** Out-of-state students who are recipients of financial aid may qualify for out-of-state fee waiver. Educational benefits available to veterans and children of deceased/disabled veterans.

Application procedures. Admission: Priority date 8/15; no deadline. $40 fee, may be waived for applicants with need. Admission notification on a rolling basis beginning on or about 9/15. **Financial aid:** Priority date 3/1, closing date 7/15. FAFSA, institutional form required. Applicants notified on a rolling basis starting 5/1; must reply within 2 week(s) of notification.

Academics. Special study options: Accelerated study, cooperative education, cross-registration, distance learning, double major, ESL, exchange student, honors, independent study, internships, liberal arts/career combination, student-designed major, study abroad, teacher certification program, Washington semester. **Credit/placement by examination:** AP, CLEP, IB, institutional tests. 30 credit hours maximum toward bachelor's degree. Credit also awarded for: American College Testing Program, Defense Activity for Non-traditional Education Support, Institution Credit by Examination, Military Service School Credit, Credit for Non-collegiate Programs, and Correspondence Course Credits. **Support services:** Learning center, reduced course load, remedial instruction, study skills assistance, tutoring, writing center.

Majors. Biology: General. **Business:** Business admin, nonprofit/public. **Communications:** Communications/speech/rhetoric. **Computer sciences:** General, information systems, information technology. **Education:** Early childhood, elementary, physical, secondary, special ed. **English:** English lit. **Foreign languages:** Spanish. **Health services:** Nursing (RN). **History:** General. **Liberal arts:** Arts/sciences. **Math:** General, applied. **Physical sciences:** Chemistry. **Protective services:** Criminal justice. **Psychology:** General. **Social sciences:** Political science, sociology. **Visual/performing arts:** Commercial/advertising art, design, graphic design, music performance.

Most popular majors. Business/marketing 16%, education 20%, health sciences 26%, liberal arts 8%, psychology 6%.

Computing on campus. 725 workstations in dormitories, library, computer center, student center. Dormitories wired for high-speed internet access and linked to campus network. Commuter students can connect to campus network. Online course registration, online library, helpline, repair service, student web hosting, wireless network available.

Student life. Freshman orientation: Available. Preregistration for classes offered. **Housing:** Coed dorms, apartments, wellness housing available. $135 fully refundable deposit, deadline 6/1. **Activities:** Jazz band, campus ministries, choral groups, dance, drama, international student organizations, literary magazine, music ensembles, student government, student newspaper, African-American Association, Baptist student union, Campus Crusade for Christ, College Republicans, Young Democrats, student education association, campus activity board, Association for the Education of Young Children, environmental club.

Athletics. NCAA. **Intercollegiate:** Baseball M, basketball, cheerleading, cross-country, golf, soccer, softball W, tennis, track and field, volleyball W. **Intramural:** Badminton, basketball, bowling, football (non-tackle), racquetball, soccer, softball, table tennis, tennis, track and field, volleyball. **Team name:** Spartans.

Student services. Adult student services, alcohol/substance abuse counseling, chaplain/spiritual director, career counseling, services for economically disadvantaged, student employment services, financial aid counseling, health services, minority student services, on-campus daycare, personal counseling, placement for graduates, veterans' counselor, women's services. **Physically disabled:** Services for visually, speech, hearing impaired.

Contact. E-mail: dstewart@uscupstate.edu
Phone: (864) 503-5246 Toll-free number: (800) 277-8727
Fax: (864) 503-5727
Donette Stewart, Assistant Vice Chancellor for Enrollment Services, University of South Carolina: Upstate, 800 University Way, Spartanburg, SC 29303

Voorhees College
Denmark, South Carolina
www.voorhees.edu

CB member
CB code: 5863

- Private 4-year liberal arts college affiliated with Episcopal Church
- Residential campus in small town
- 740 degree-seeking undergraduates
- 51% of applicants admitted

General. Founded in 1897. Regionally accredited. **Degrees:** 108 bachelor's awarded. **ROTC:** Army. **Location:** 50 miles from Columbia and Augusta, Georgia. **Calendar:** Semester, limited summer session. **Full-time faculty:** 41 total. **Part-time faculty:** 20 total.

Freshman class profile. 4,349 applied, 2,218 admitted, 133 enrolled.

Rank in top quarter:	10%	Out-of-state:	10%
Rank in top tenth:	2%	Live on campus:	95%

Basis for selection. Secondary school record, GPA (2.0 or above), recommendations, and standardized test scores considered in admissions decisions.

High school preparation. 20 units recommended. Recommended units include English 4, mathematics 3, social studies 2, science 2, foreign language 2 and academic electives 7.

2011-2012 Annual costs. Tuition/fees: $10,780. Room/board: $7,346. Books/supplies: $600. Personal expenses: $1,365.

Application procedures. Admission: Priority date 4/15; no deadline. $25 fee, may be waived for applicants with need. Admission notification on a rolling basis beginning on or about 1/15. **Financial aid:** Priority date 4/15; no closing date. FAFSA, institutional form required. Applicants notified on a rolling basis starting 3/1; must reply within 2 week(s) of notification.

Academics. Special study options: Accelerated study, combined bachelor's/graduate degree, cooperative education, honors, independent study, internships, liberal arts/career combination, study abroad, weekend college. **Credit/placement by examination:** AP, CLEP, IB, institutional tests. 15 credit hours maximum toward bachelor's degree. **Support services:** Learning center, reduced course load, remedial instruction, study skills assistance, tutoring.

Majors. Biology: General. **Business:** General, accounting, accounting/finance, business admin, management information systems, organizational behavior. **Communications:** Broadcast journalism, media studies. **Computer sciences:** General, computer science. **English:** English lit. **Health services:** Predental, premedicine, prenursing. **Math:** General. **Parks/recreation:** Health/fitness. **Social sciences:** Sociology.

Computing on campus. 175 workstations in dormitories, library, computer center. Dormitories wired for high-speed internet access and linked to campus network. Commuter students can connect to campus network. Online library, helpline, wireless network available.

Student life. Freshman orientation: Mandatory. Preregistration for classes offered. One day orientation offered in June and July. One week orientation offered in August. **Housing:** Guaranteed on-campus for all undergraduates. Single-sex dorms available. $75 nonrefundable deposit, deadline 7/31. Accommodations for single mothers. **Activities:** Pep band, choral groups, dance, drama, radio station, student government, student newspaper.

Athletics. NAIA. **Intercollegiate:** Baseball M, basketball, cheerleading, cross-country, softball W, track and field, volleyball W. **Intramural:** Baseball M, basketball, softball W. **Team name:** Tigers.

Student services. Adult student services, chaplain/spiritual director, career counseling, student employment services, financial aid counseling, health services, personal counseling, placement for graduates, veterans' counselor.

Contact. E-mail: spellman@voorhees.edu
Phone: (803) 780-1031 Toll-free number: (800) 446-6250
Fax: (803) 780-1444
Benjamin Watson, Director of Admissions, Voorhees College, 213 Wiggins Road, Denmark, SC 29042

W.L. Bonner Bible College
Columbia, South Carolina
www.wlbonnercollege.org

▶ Private 4-year Bible college
▶ Small city

General. Accredited by ABHE. **Calendar:** Semester.

Contact. Phone: (803) 754-3950
Assistant Registrar, 4430 Argent Court, Columbia, SC 29203

Winthrop University
Rock Hill, South Carolina   CB member
www.winthrop.edu   CB code: 5910

▶ Public 4-year university
▶ Residential campus in small city
▶ 4,593 degree-seeking undergraduates: 8% part-time, 67% women, 28% African American, 1% Asian American, 2% Hispanic American, 3% international
▶ 932 degree-seeking graduate students
▶ 68% of applicants admitted
▶ SAT or ACT (ACT writing optional) required
▶ 60% graduate within 6 years

General. Founded in 1886. Regionally accredited. **Degrees:** 917 bachelor's awarded; master's offered. **ROTC:** Army. **Location:** 20 miles from Charlotte, NC. **Calendar:** Semester, extensive summer session. **Full-time faculty:** 286 total; 86% have terminal degrees, 13% minority, 52% women. **Part-time faculty:** 221 total; 18% have terminal degrees, 10% minority, 63% women. **Class size:** 43% < 20, 48% 20-39, 6% 40-49, 2% 50-99. **Special facilities:** Nursery laboratory, music conservatory, capital markets training and trading center.

Freshman class profile. 4,115 applied, 2,815 admitted, 983 enrolled.

Mid 50% test scores			
SAT critical reading:	470-580	**Rank in top quarter:**	47%
SAT math:	480-570	**Rank in top tenth:**	22%
ACT composite:	20-25	**End year in good standing:**	83%
GPA 3.75 or higher:	54%	**Return as sophomores:**	72%
GPA 3.50-3.74:	19%	**Out-of-state:**	9%
GPA 3.0-3.49:	24%	**Live on campus:**	88%
GPA 2.0-2.99:	3%	**International:**	2%

Basis for selection. School achievement record, test scores, counselor recommendations important, school and community activities considered. Essay, interview recommended for all; audition recommended for dance, music, theater programs.

High school preparation. College-preparatory program recommended. 19 units required. Required units include English 4, mathematics 4, social studies 2, history 1, science 3 (laboratory 3), foreign language 2, visual/performing arts 1 and academic electives 1. 1 PE or ROTC required.

2011-2012 Annual costs. Tuition/fees: $12,706; $23,846 out-of-state. Room/board: $7,004.

2010-2011 Financial aid. Need-based: 872 full-time freshmen applied for aid; 714 were judged to have need; 711 of these received aid. Average need met was 70%. Average scholarship/grant was $9,350; average loan $3,258. 49% of total undergraduate aid awarded as scholarships/grants, 51% as loans/jobs. **Non-need-based:** Awarded to 805 full-time undergraduates, including 218 freshmen. Scholarships awarded for academics, art, athletics, leadership, music/drama. **Additional information:** Academic scholarships from $1,500 to full tuition and board awarded to approximately one-third of entering freshman class each year.

Application procedures. Admission: Closing date 5/1. $40 fee, may be waived for applicants with need. Application must be submitted on paper. Admission notification on a rolling basis beginning on or about 10/21. Must reply by May 1 or within 3 week(s) if notified thereafter. 8 monthly notification dates for fall between October and May on the 21st of the month. **Financial aid:** Priority date 3/15; no closing date. FAFSA required. Applicants notified on a rolling basis starting 3/15; must reply within 2 week(s) of notification.

Academics. World Languages and Cultures Learning Center is available to students and instructors for teaching, learning, and practicing foreign languages. **Special study options:** Cooperative education, cross-registration, distance learning, double major, dual enrollment of high school students, ESL, exchange student, honors, independent study, internships, liberal arts/career combination, study abroad, teacher certification program, United Nations semester. **Credit/placement by examination:** AP, CLEP, IB, SAT, ACT, institutional tests. 30 credit hours maximum toward bachelor's degree. **Support services:** Learning center, pre-admission summer program, study skills assistance, tutoring, writing center.

Majors. Biology: General. **Business:** Business admin, e-commerce. **Communications:** Journalism, media studies, public relations. **Computer sciences:** General. **Conservation:** Environmental science, environmental studies. **Education:** Early childhood, elementary, family/consumer sciences, middle, music, physical, special ed. **English:** English lit, technical writing. **Foreign languages:** General. **Health services:** Athletic training, clinical lab science, communication disorders. **History:** General. **Human services:** Social work. **Math:** General. **Parks/recreation:** Exercise sciences, sports admin. **Philosophy/religion:** Philosophy, religion. **Physical sciences:** Chemistry. **Psychology:** General. **Social sciences:** Economics, political science, sociology. **Visual/performing arts:** Art, art history/conservation, dance, dramatic, interior design, music, studio arts. **Work/family studies:** Human nutrition.

Most popular majors. Business/marketing 25%, communications/journalism 6%, education 16%, psychology 7%, social sciences 7%, visual/performing arts 12%.

Computing on campus. 620 workstations in dormitories, library, computer center, student center. Dormitories wired for high-speed internet access and linked to campus network. Commuter students can connect to campus network. Online course registration, online library, helpline, student web hosting, wireless network available.

Student life. Freshman orientation: Mandatory. Preregistration for classes offered. 2 day residential experience held June 20-21, 23-24, 27-28, 30 and July 1, and Aug 17-18. **Policies:** First and second year students are required to live on campus unless living with parents within 50 miles. **Housing:** Guaranteed on-campus for freshmen. Coed dorms, single-sex dorms, apartments, fraternity/sorority housing available. **Activities:** Bands, campus ministries, choral groups, dance, drama, international student organizations, literary magazine, music ensembles, Model UN, musical theater, opera, radio station, student government, student newspaper, 115 clubs and organizations.

Athletics. NCAA. **Intercollegiate:** Baseball M, basketball, cross-country, golf, soccer, softball W, tennis, track and field, volleyball W. **Intramural:** Badminton, basketball, cross-country, equestrian, football (non-tackle), football (tackle) M, golf, racquetball, soccer, softball, swimming, table tennis, tennis, track and field, volleyball. **Team name:** Eagles.

Student services. Adult student services, alcohol/substance abuse counseling, career counseling, student employment services, financial aid counseling, health services, minority student services, personal counseling, placement for graduates, veterans' counselor. **Physically disabled:** Services for visually, hearing impaired.

Contact. E-mail: admissions@winthrop.edu
Phone: (803) 323-2191 Toll-free number: (800) 946-8476
Fax: (803) 323-2137
Debi Barber, Director of Admissions, Winthrop University, 701 Oakland Avenue, Rock Hill, SC 29733

Wofford College
Spartanburg, South Carolina

www.wofford.edu

CB member

CB code: 5912

- Private 4-year liberal arts college affiliated with United Methodist Church
- Residential campus in small city
- 1,515 degree-seeking undergraduates: 1% part-time, 49% women, 8% African American, 2% Asian American, 2% Hispanic American, 1% international
- 65% of applicants admitted
- SAT or ACT with writing, application essay required
- 79% graduate within 6 years; 46% enter graduate study

General. Founded in 1854. Regionally accredited. **Degrees:** 365 bachelor's awarded. **ROTC:** Army. **Location:** 70 miles from Charlotte, NC, 180 miles from Atlanta. **Calendar:** 4-1-4, limited summer session. **Full-time faculty:** 126 total; 92% have terminal degrees, 10% minority, 40% women. **Part-time faculty:** 29 total; 55% have terminal degrees, 7% minority, 52% women. **Class size:** 56% < 20, 44% 20-39, less than 1% 40-49, less than 1% 50-99. **Special facilities:** Arboretum, environmental studies center, South Carolina Methodist archives, Center for Professional Excellence, Center for Global and Community Engagement.

Freshman class profile. 2,871 applied, 1,861 admitted, 446 enrolled.

Mid 50% test scores		End year in good standing:	92%
SAT critical reading:	570-680	Return as sophomores:	88%
SAT math:	580-690	Out-of-state:	44%
SAT writing:	570-670	Live on campus:	95%
ACT composite:	23-28	International:	3%
Rank in top quarter:	85%	Fraternities:	38%
Rank in top tenth:	56%	Sororities:	60%

Basis for selection. High school record, including AP courses, most important. Test scores important. School recommendation, leadership, extra-curricular activities considered. Interview recommended. **Learning Disabled:** Prospective students with learning disabilities consult with the Dean of Health Services.

High school preparation. College-preparatory program recommended. 20 units recommended. Recommended units include English 4, mathematics 4, social studies 3, history 1, science 3 (laboratory 3), foreign language 3, computer science 1, visual/performing arts 1 and academic electives 1.

2011-2012 Annual costs. Tuition/fees: $34,270. Room/board: $9,375. Books/supplies: $1,200. Personal expenses: $1,260.

2011-2012 Financial aid. Need-based: 357 full-time freshmen applied for aid; 285 were judged to have need; 285 of these received aid. Average need met was 82%. Average scholarship/grant was $27,140; average loan $3,313. 86% of total undergraduate aid awarded as scholarships/grants, 14% as loans/jobs. **Non-need-based:** Awarded to 825 full-time undergraduates, including 236 freshmen. Scholarships awarded for academics, athletics, leadership, music/drama, religious affiliation, ROTC, state residency.

Application procedures. Admission: Closing date 2/1 (postmark date). $35 fee, may be waived for applicants with need. Admission notification by 3/15. Must reply by 5/1. **Financial aid:** Priority date 3/15; no closing date. FAFSA required. Applicants notified on a rolling basis starting 4/1; must reply by 5/1.

Academics. January Interim program devoted to internships, foreign travel, independent study, and other nontraditional academic pursuits. **Special study options:** Accelerated study, combined bachelor's/graduate degree, cross-registration, double major, dual enrollment of high school students, independent study, internships, student-designed major, study abroad, teacher certification program, Washington semester. Opportunities for studies abroad, service learning, and environmental studies. **Credit/placement by examination:** AP, CLEP, IB. 30 credit hours maximum toward bachelor's degree. **Support services:** Tutoring, writing center.

Majors. Biology: General. **Business:** Accounting, finance, managerial economics. **Computer sciences:** General, computer science. **Conservation:** Environmental studies. **English:** English lit. **Foreign languages:** Chinese, French, German, Spanish. **History:** General. **Liberal arts:** Arts/sciences. **Math:** General. **Philosophy/religion:** Philosophy, religion. **Physical sciences:** Chemistry, physics. **Psychology:** General. **Social sciences:** Economics, sociology, U.S. government. **Visual/performing arts:** Art history/conservation, theater design.

Most popular majors. Biology 17%, business/marketing 20%, English 8%, foreign language 15%, history 6%, physical sciences 6%, social sciences 12%.

Computing on campus. 156 workstations in library, computer center, student center. Dormitories wired for high-speed internet access and linked to campus network. Commuter students can connect to campus network. Online course registration, online library, helpline, student web hosting, wireless network available.

Student life. Freshman orientation: Mandatory. Preregistration for classes offered. Weekend in summer before the start of classes. **Policies:** Honor code and honor council. Students not living with immediate family member must secure permission to live off-campus. **Housing:** Guaranteed on-campus for all undergraduates. Coed dorms, apartments, wellness housing available. $300 nonrefundable deposit, deadline 5/1. **Activities:** Bands, campus ministries, choral groups, dance, drama, international student organizations, literary magazine, music ensembles, student government, student newspaper, Fellowship of Christian Athletes, Baptist Collegiate Ministry, Association of Multicultural Students, student volunteer services, Wesley Fellowship, Catholic Newman Club, College Republicans, College Democrats, Lion's Club, Rotaract Club.

Athletics. NCAA. **Intercollegiate:** Baseball M, basketball, cross-country, football (tackle) M, golf, rifle, soccer, tennis, track and field, volleyball W. **Intramural:** Basketball, football (non-tackle), racquetball, soccer, softball, tennis, volleyball. **Team name:** Terriers.

Student services. Alcohol/substance abuse counseling, chaplain/spiritual director, career counseling, student employment services, financial aid counseling, health services, minority student services, personal counseling, placement for graduates. **Physically disabled:** Services for visually, speech, hearing impaired.

Contact. E-mail: admission@wofford.edu
Phone: (864) 597-4130 Fax: (864) 597-4147
S. Wells Shepard, Director of Admission, Wofford College, 429 North Church Street, Spartanburg, SC 29303-3663

South Dakota

Support services: Reduced course load, study skills assistance, tutoring, writing center.

Majors. Biology: General, biochemistry. **Business:** General, accounting, business admin, communications. **Communications:** Communications/speech/rhetoric, journalism. **Computer sciences:** Computer science. **Education:** Art, biology, Deaf/hearing impaired, elementary, emotionally handicapped, English, French, German, history, learning disabled, mathematics, mentally handicapped, multicultural, music, physical, physically handicapped, physics, psychology, secondary, social studies, Spanish, special ed, speech, speech impaired. **Engineering:** Applied physics. **English:** English lit. **Foreign languages:** General, American Sign Language, French, German, sign language interpretation, Spanish. **Health services:** Athletic training, clinical lab science, clinical lab technology, communication disorders, nursing (RN), predental, premedicine, prepharmacy, prephysical therapy, preveterinary. **History:** General. **Math:** General. **Parks/recreation:** Exercise sciences, health/fitness, sports admin. **Philosophy/religion:** Philosophy, religion. **Physical sciences:** Chemistry, physics. **Psychology:** General. **Social sciences:** Anthropology, economics, political science, sociology. **Theology:** Sacred music. **Visual/performing arts:** Art, dramatic, music.

Most popular majors. Biology 9%, business/marketing 15%, education 19%, foreign language 7%, health sciences 15%, parks/recreation 6%.

Computing on campus. 255 workstations in dormitories, library, computer center, student center. Dormitories wired for high-speed internet access and linked to campus network. Commuter students can connect to campus network. Online library, helpline, repair service, wireless network available.

Student life. Freshman orientation: Mandatory. Preregistration for classes offered. Held 3 days before start of fall semester. **Housing:** Guaranteed on-campus for freshmen. Coed dorms, special housing for disabled, apartments available. $100 fully refundable deposit, deadline 9/1. Housing is available for students with children. **Activities:** Bands, campus ministries, choral groups, dance, drama, film society, international student organizations, literary magazine, music ensembles, musical theater, opera, student government, student newspaper, symphony orchestra, Lutheran-ELCA congregation, Fellowship of Christian Athletes, Circle K, Augie Democrats, College Republicans, Augie Green, Catholics in Action, Young Life, Colleges Against Cancer.

Athletics. NCAA. **Intercollegiate:** Baseball M, basketball, cheerleading M, cross-country, football (tackle) M, golf, soccer W, softball W, tennis, track and field, volleyball W, wrestling M. **Intramural:** Basketball, football (non-tackle), golf, racquetball, softball, triathlon, volleyball. **Team name:** Vikings.

Student services. Adult student services, alcohol/substance abuse counseling, chaplain/spiritual director, career counseling, student employment services, financial aid counseling, health services, minority student services, on-campus daycare, personal counseling, placement for graduates. **Physically disabled:** Services for visually, hearing impaired.

Contact. E-mail: admission@augie.edu
Phone: (605) 274-5516 Toll-free number: (800) 727-2844
Fax: (605) 274-5518
Adam Heinitz, Director of Admission, Augustana College, 2001 South Summit Avenue, Sioux Falls, SD 57197-9990

Augustana College
Sioux Falls, South Dakota
www.augie.edu
CB member
CB code: 6015

- Private 4-year liberal arts college affiliated with Evangelical Lutheran Church in America
- Residential campus in small city
- 1,751 degree-seeking undergraduates: 3% part-time, 62% women, 1% African American, 1% Asian American, 1% Hispanic American, 4% international
- 31 degree-seeking graduate students
- 80% of applicants admitted
- SAT or ACT (ACT writing optional), application essay required
- 65% graduate within 6 years; 27% enter graduate study

General. Founded in 1860. Regionally accredited. **Degrees:** 333 bachelor's awarded; master's offered. **ROTC:** Army, Air Force. **Location:** 160 miles from Omaha, NE; 230 miles from Minneapolis-St. Paul. **Calendar:** 4-1-4, limited summer session. **Full-time faculty:** 126 total; 79% have terminal degrees, 4% minority, 44% women. **Part-time faculty:** 80 total; 19% have terminal degrees, 2% minority, 68% women. **Class size:** 51% < 20, 45% 20-39, 3% 40-49, 2% 50-99. **Special facilities:** Western studies museum and archives, archeology lab, prairie garden, ASL laboratory, art gallery, model classroom.

Freshman class profile. 1,261 applied, 1,005 admitted, 432 enrolled.

Mid 50% test scores			
ACT composite:	23-28	Rank in top quarter:	65%
GPA 3.75 or higher:	52%	Rank in top tenth:	31%
GPA 3.50-3.74:	21%	Return as sophomores:	83%
GPA 3.0-3.49:	18%	Out-of-state:	58%
GPA 2.0-2.99:	9%	Live on campus:	97%
		International:	4%

Basis for selection. 20 ACT (or equivalent SAT), 2.7 GPA, rank in top half of class, high school transcript, recommendation, and writing sample required. Interview recommended for all.

High school preparation. College-preparatory program recommended. 19 units recommended. Recommended units include English 4, mathematics 3, social studies 3, history 2, science 3, foreign language 2, computer science 1 and visual/performing arts 1.

2011-2012 Annual costs. Tuition/fees: $26,590. Room/board: $6,400. Books/supplies: $1,000. Personal expenses: $800.

2011-2012 Financial aid. Need-based: 429 full-time freshmen applied for aid; 308 were judged to have need; 308 of these received aid. Average need met was 93%. Average scholarship/grant was $19,723; average loan $4,375. 69% of total undergraduate aid awarded as scholarships/grants, 31% as loans/jobs. **Non-need-based:** Awarded to 1,880 full-time undergraduates, including 473 freshmen. Scholarships awarded for academics, alumni affiliation, art, athletics, leadership, minority status, music/drama, religious affiliation, ROTC, state residency.

Application procedures. Admission: Priority date 1/15; no deadline. No application fee. Admission notification on a rolling basis beginning on or about 10/1. Must reply by May 1 or within 3 week(s) if notified thereafter. **Financial aid:** Priority date 3/1; no closing date. FAFSA required. Applicants notified on a rolling basis starting 4/1; must reply within 3 week(s) of notification.

Academics. Special study options: Cooperative education, cross-registration, distance learning, double major, dual enrollment of high school students, exchange student, external degree, honors, independent study, internships, liberal arts/career combination, student-designed major, study abroad, teacher certification program, urban semester, Washington semester. Metro-Urban Studies through HECUA. January Abroad program through UMAIE. Washington, DC.Semesters. Study Australia through EAN. Dual Degree Program in Engineering. Service-Learning Spring Breaks trips; Faculty-led Spring Breaks Abroad; Honors Courses in Western Civilization, Chemistry, and Religion. Civitas honors program for students with 27 ACT and 3.5 GPA. **Credit/placement by examination:** AP, CLEP, IB, SAT, ACT, institutional tests. 32 credit hours maximum toward bachelor's degree.

Black Hills State University
Spearfish, South Dakota
www.bhsu.edu
CB code: 6042

- Public 4-year liberal arts and teachers college
- Commuter campus in large town
- 3,308 degree-seeking undergraduates: 22% part-time, 62% women
- 193 degree-seeking graduate students
- 94% of applicants admitted
- SAT or ACT (ACT writing optional) required

General. Founded in 1883. Regionally accredited. Evening degree program available at Ellsworth Air Force Base campus in Rapid City. **Degrees:** 483 bachelor's, 28 associate awarded; master's offered. **ROTC:** Army. **Location:** 45 miles from Rapid City. **Calendar:** Semester, extensive summer session. **Full-time faculty:** 136 total. **Part-time faculty:** 73 total. **Class size:** 39% < 20, 50% 20-39, 5% 40-49, 4% 50-99, less than 1% >100.

Freshman class profile. 1,476 applied, 1,390 admitted, 620 enrolled.

Mid 50% test scores			
ACT composite:	19-23	GPA 2.0-2.99:	33%
GPA 3.75 or higher:	16%	Rank in top quarter:	28%
GPA 3.50-3.74:	13%	Rank in top tenth:	10%
GPA 3.0-3.49:	34%	Return as sophomores:	61%
		Out-of-state:	78%

Basis for selection. For bachelor's programs, requirements include 18 ACT or class rank in top 60% (in-state applicants), top half (out-of-state applicants) or 2.6 GPA in required courses. Portfolio recommended.

High school preparation. College-preparatory program recommended. 14 units required. Required units include English 4, mathematics 3, social studies 3, science 3 (laboratory 3) and visual/performing arts 1.

2011-2012 Annual costs. Tuition/fees: $6,960; $8,675 out-of-state. Reciprocity agreements reduce tuition for some out-of-state students. Room/board: $5,825. Books/supplies: $1,000. Personal expenses: $1,500.

Financial aid. All financial aid based on need.

Application procedures. Admission: Closing date 7/15. $20 fee. Admission notification on a rolling basis. **Financial aid:** Closing date 2/15. FAFSA required. Applicants notified on a rolling basis starting 5/15; must reply within 3 week(s) of notification.

Academics. Special study options: Distance learning, double major, dual enrollment of high school students, ESL, honors, independent study, internships, liberal arts/career combination, study abroad, teacher certification program. **Credit/placement by examination:** AP, CLEP, SAT, ACT, institutional tests. 32 credit hours maximum toward bachelor's degree. **Support services:** Learning center, remedial instruction, study skills assistance, tutoring, writing center.

Majors. Area/ethnic studies: Native American. **Biology:** General. **Business:** Accounting, business admin, entrepreneurial studies, human resources, marketing, office management, tourism/travel. **Communications:** Media studies. **Education:** Art, biology, business, chemistry, elementary, English, foreign languages, history, kindergarten/preschool, mathematics, middle, music, physical, science, social science, special ed, speech, technology/industrial arts. **English:** English lit, rhetoric/composition. **Foreign languages:** Spanish. **Health services:** Facilities admin. **History:** General. **Human services:** Community org/advocacy. **Math:** General. **Parks/recreation:** General, exercise sciences, sports admin. **Physical sciences:** General, chemistry. **Psychology:** General. **Social sciences:** General, political science, sociology. **Visual/performing arts:** Art, commercial/advertising art, music.

Most popular majors. Biology 6%, business/marketing 20%, communications/journalism 7%, education 17%, English 6%, psychology 7%, public administration/social services 6%, social sciences 10%, visual/performing arts 6%.

Computing on campus. 500 workstations in dormitories, library, student center. Dormitories wired for high-speed internet access and linked to campus network. Commuter students can connect to campus network. Online course registration, online library, helpline, wireless network available.

Student life. Freshman orientation: Available. Preregistration for classes offered. **Housing:** Guaranteed on-campus for freshmen. Coed dorms, single-sex dorms, apartments available. $100 deposit. Married student housing. **Activities:** Concert band, campus ministries, choral groups, drama, international student organizations, literary magazine, music ensembles, musical theater, opera, radio station, student government, student newspaper, TV station, Native American special services, Inter-Greek council, United Ministry, Veterans club, Young Democrats, Young Republicans.

Athletics. NAIA. **Intercollegiate:** Basketball, cross-country, football (tackle) M, golf W, softball W, track and field, volleyball W. **Intramural:** Archery, badminton, basketball, bowling, golf, skiing, soccer, softball, swimming, table tennis, tennis, volleyball. **Team name:** Yellow Jackets.

Student services. Chaplain/spiritual director, career counseling, student employment services, financial aid counseling, health services, on-campus daycare, personal counseling, placement for graduates, veterans' counselor. **Physically disabled:** Services for visually, speech, hearing impaired.

Contact. E-mail: admissions@bhsu.edu
Phone: (605) 642-6343 Toll-free number: (800) 255-2478
Fax: (605) 642-6022
Beth Oaks, Director of Admissions, Black Hills State University, 1200 University Street Box 9502, Spearfish, SD 57799-9502

Dakota State University
Madison, South Dakota
www.dsu.edu CB code: 6247

- Public 4-year university
- Residential campus in small town
- 1,691 degree-seeking undergraduates: 28% part-time, 45% women, 2% African American, 1% Asian American, 2% Hispanic American, 1% Native American, 2% international

- 207 degree-seeking graduate students
- 92% of applicants admitted
- SAT or ACT (ACT writing optional) required
- 44% graduate within 6 years

General. Founded in 1881. Regionally accredited. **Degrees:** 238 bachelor's, 42 associate awarded; master's, doctoral offered. **ROTC:** Air Force. **Location:** 45 miles from Sioux Falls. **Calendar:** Semester, limited summer session. **Full-time faculty:** 95 total; 70% have terminal degrees, 10% minority, 37% women. **Part-time faculty:** 34 total; 29% have terminal degrees, 44% women. **Class size:** 50% < 20, 47% 20-39, less than 1% 40-49, 2% 50-99.

Freshman class profile. 711 applied, 651 admitted, 319 enrolled.

Mid 50% test scores			
SAT critical reading:	440-530	Rank in top quarter:	22%
SAT math:	410-540	Rank in top tenth:	7%
ACT composite:	18-25	End year in good standing:	82%
GPA 3.75 or higher:	13%	Return as sophomores:	67%
GPA 3.50-3.74:	15%	Out-of-state:	30%
GPA 3.0-3.49:	31%	Live on campus:	86%
GPA 2.0-2.99:	38%	International:	1%

Basis for selection. Top 60% of class, 18 ACT, or 2.6 GPA required. Under-qualified applicants considered for probational acceptance. **Home schooled:** State high school equivalency certificate or ACT minimum scores required.

High school preparation. College-preparatory program recommended. Recommended units include English 4, mathematics 3, social studies 3, science 3 (laboratory 3). 1 fine arts, .5 computer studies.

2011-2012 Annual costs. Tuition/fees: $7,621; $9,336 out-of-state. All degree-seeking undergraduates participate in the Wireless Mobile Computing Initiative and provided with a TabletPC. Students are assessed a fee each semester for these services. Room/board: $5,088. Books/supplies: $1,000. Personal expenses: $2,500.

2010-2011 Financial aid. Need-based: 287 full-time freshmen applied for aid; 221 were judged to have need; 219 of these received aid. Average need met was 80%. Average scholarship/grant was $4,264; average loan $3,094. 35% of total undergraduate aid awarded as scholarships/grants, 65% as loans/jobs. **Non-need-based:** Awarded to 577 full-time undergraduates, including 226 freshmen. Scholarships awarded for academics, alumni affiliation, art, athletics, leadership, minority status, music/drama, state residency. **Additional information:** Application deadline for grants and scholarships 3/1. No deadline for loan and job applications.

Application procedures. Admission: No deadline. $20 fee. Admission notification on a rolling basis. **Financial aid:** Priority date 3/1; no closing date. FAFSA required. Applicants notified on a rolling basis starting 4/1; must reply within 2 week(s) of notification.

Academics. Special study options: Cooperative education, cross-registration, distance learning, double major, dual enrollment of high school students, ESL, honors, independent study, internships, teacher certification program. **Credit/placement by examination:** AP, CLEP, IB, SAT, ACT, institutional tests. 16 credit hours maximum toward associate degree, 32 toward bachelor's. **Support services:** Learning center, reduced course load, remedial instruction, study skills assistance, tutoring, writing center.

Majors. Business: Accounting, business admin, finance, marketing. **Computer sciences:** General, computer graphics, information systems, LAN/WAN management, security. **Education:** Biology, business, computer, elementary, English, mathematics, physical. **English:** Technical writing. **Health services:** Medical records admin, respiratory therapy technology. **Liberal arts:** Arts/sciences. **Math:** Mathematics/statistics. **Parks/recreation:** Exercise sciences. **Physical sciences:** General. **Visual/performing arts:** Game design.

Most popular majors. Business/marketing 27%, computer/information sciences 32%, education 25%.

Computing on campus. PC or laptop required. Dormitories wired for high-speed internet access and linked to campus network. Commuter students can connect to campus network. Online course registration, online library, helpline, repair service, student web hosting, wireless network available.

Student life. Freshman orientation: Mandatory. Preregistration for classes offered. **Policies:** Alcohol/drugs/smoking prohibited. 2-year live-in and meal plan requirement, residence halls in 24/7 lockdown for student safety. **Housing:** Guaranteed on-campus for freshmen. Coed dorms, single-sex dorms, apartments, wellness housing available. $50 fully refundable deposit. **Activities:** Pep band, campus ministries, choral groups, dance, drama,

international student organizations, literary magazine, Model UN, radio station, student government, student newspaper, InterVarsity Christian Fellowship, Campus Crusade for Christ, Newman club, diverse student union, Colleges Against Cancer.

Athletics. NAIA. **Intercollegiate:** Baseball M, basketball, cheerleading, cross-country, football (tackle) M, softball W, track and field, volleyball W. **Intramural:** Basketball, football (non-tackle), softball, table tennis, tennis, volleyball. **Team name:** Trojans.

Student services. Adult student services, alcohol/substance abuse counseling, chaplain/spiritual director, career counseling, student employment services, financial aid counseling, health services, minority student services, personal counseling, placement for graduates, veterans' counselor. **Physically disabled:** Services for visually, speech, hearing impaired.

Contact. E-mail: yourfuture@dsu.edu
Phone: (605) 256-5139 Toll-free number: (888) 378-9988
Fax: (605) 256-5020
Amy Crissinger, Director of Admission, Dakota State University, 820 North Washington Avenue, Madison, SD 57042

Dakota Wesleyan University
Mitchell, South Dakota
www.dwu.edu   CB code: 6155

- Private 4-year university and liberal arts college affiliated with United Methodist Church
- Residential campus in large town
- 679 degree-seeking undergraduates: 6% part-time, 55% women, 4% African American, 1% Asian American, 3% Hispanic American, 1% Native American, 1% international
- 62 degree-seeking graduate students
- 76% of applicants admitted
- SAT or ACT (ACT writing optional) required
- 45% graduate within 6 years

General. Founded in 1885. Regionally accredited. **Degrees:** 136 bachelor's, 66 associate awarded; master's offered. **ROTC:** Army. **Location:** 70 miles from Sioux Falls. **Calendar:** Semester, limited summer session. **Full-time faculty:** 51 total; 2% minority, 57% women. **Part-time faculty:** 26 total; 62% women. **Class size:** 61% < 20, 36% 20-39, 2% 40-49, 2% 50-99. **Special facilities:** Observatory.

Freshman class profile. 526 applied, 400 admitted, 169 enrolled.

Mid 50% test scores		GPA 2.0-2.99:	35%
SAT critical reading:	340-540	Rank in top quarter:	26%
SAT math:	370-620	Rank in top tenth:	9%
SAT writing:	290-540	End year in good standing:	91%
ACT composite:	17-25	Return as sophomores:	66%
GPA 3.75 or higher:	15%	Out-of-state:	31%
GPA 3.50-3.74:	14%	Live on campus:	80%
GPA 3.0-3.49:	34%	International:	2%

Basis for selection. High school record, test scores, school activities considered. Recommendations and personal interview used for marginal students. **Home schooled:** Transcript of courses and grades required. Meeting with admissions counselor and placement testing required when appropriate. **Learning Disabled:** For special assistance, documentation of student's learning disability required.

High school preparation. College-preparatory program recommended. Recommended units include English 4, mathematics 4, social studies 4, history 3, science 3 (laboratory 1) and foreign language 2.

2011-2012 Annual costs. Tuition/fees: $20,810. Room/board: $6,700. Books/supplies: $1,000. Personal expenses: $1,350.

2011-2012 Financial aid. Need-based: 148 full-time freshmen applied for aid; 134 were judged to have need; 134 of these received aid. Average need met was 67%. Average scholarship/grant was $10,383; average loan $3,300. 58% of total undergraduate aid awarded as scholarships/grants, 42% as loans/jobs. **Non-need-based:** Awarded to 186 full-time undergraduates, including 67 freshmen. Scholarships awarded for academics, alumni affiliation, art, athletics, leadership, minority status, music/drama, religious affiliation.

Application procedures. Admission: Closing date 8/25 (receipt date). $25 fee, may be waived for applicants with need. Admission notification on a rolling basis. **Financial aid:** Priority date 4/1; no closing date. FAFSA required. Applicants notified on a rolling basis starting 3/1; must reply within 2 week(s) of notification.

Academics. Special study options: Cross-registration, distance learning, double major, dual enrollment of high school students, exchange student, honors, independent study, internships, student-designed major, study abroad, teacher certification program. **Credit/placement by examination:** AP, CLEP, IB, SAT, ACT, institutional tests. 12 credit hours maximum toward associate degree, 18 toward bachelor's. **Support services:** Learning center, pre-admission summer program, reduced course load, remedial instruction, study skills assistance, tutoring, writing center.

Majors. Biology: General, biochemistry. **Business:** General, accounting. **Communications:** Communications/speech/rhetoric, journalism. **Computer sciences:** Web page design. **Conservation:** Wildlife/wilderness. **Education:** General, biology, elementary, English, history, mathematics, music, physical, special ed. **English:** Creative writing, English lit. **Health services:** Athletic training, nursing (RN). **History:** General. **Liberal arts:** Arts/sciences. **Math:** General. **Parks/recreation:** Sports admin. **Philosophy/religion:** Religion. **Protective services:** Criminal justice. **Psychology:** General. **Visual/performing arts:** Art, dramatic, music.

Most popular majors. Biology 10%, business/marketing 20%, education 13%, health sciences 10%, parks/recreation 10%.

Computing on campus. 85 workstations in dormitories, library, computer center, student center. Dormitories wired for high-speed internet access and linked to campus network. Commuter students can connect to campus network. Online course registration, online library, helpline, repair service, student web hosting, wireless network available.

Student life. Freshman orientation: Mandatory. Preregistration for classes offered. 2-day program held the weekend before classes begin. **Housing:** Guaranteed on-campus for freshmen. Coed dorms, single-sex dorms, apartments, wellness housing available. $50 fully refundable deposit. Honor housing available for upperclassmen; ADA rooms and apartments available. **Activities:** Concert band, campus ministries, choral groups, drama, literary magazine, music ensembles, student government, student newspaper, variety of organizations available.

Athletics. NAIA. **Intercollegiate:** Baseball M, basketball, cheerleading, cross-country, football (tackle) M, golf, soccer, softball W, track and field, volleyball W, wrestling M. **Intramural:** Basketball, softball, volleyball, weight lifting. **Team name:** Tigers.

Student services. Adult student services, alcohol/substance abuse counseling, chaplain/spiritual director, career counseling, services for economically disadvantaged, student employment services, financial aid counseling, health services, minority student services, on-campus daycare, personal counseling, placement for graduates. **Physically disabled:** Services for visually, hearing impaired.

Contact. E-mail: admissions@dwu.edu
Phone: (605) 995-2650 Toll-free number: (800) 333-8506
Fax: (605) 995-2699
Melissa Herr-Valburg, Director of Admissions, Dakota Wesleyan University, 1200 West University Avenue, Mitchell, SD 57301-4398

Mount Marty College
Yankton, South Dakota
www.mtmc.edu   CB code: 6416

- Private 4-year nursing and liberal arts college affiliated with Roman Catholic Church
- Residential campus in large town
- 784 degree-seeking undergraduates: 24% part-time, 61% women, 2% African American, 1% Asian American, 6% Hispanic American, 4% Native American
- 129 degree-seeking graduate students
- 69% of applicants admitted
- SAT or ACT (ACT writing optional) required
- 54% graduate within 6 years; 10% enter graduate study

General. Founded in 1936. Regionally accredited. **Degrees:** 168 bachelor's, 41 associate awarded; master's offered. **ROTC:** Army. **Location:** 75 miles from Sioux Falls; 60 miles from Sioux City, Iowa. **Calendar:** Semester, limited summer session. **Full-time faculty:** 44 total; 68% have terminal degrees, 7% minority, 46% women. **Part-time faculty:** 15 total; 20% have terminal degrees, 73% women. **Class size:** 80% < 20, 19% 20-39, less than 1% 40-49, less than 1% 50-99, less than 1% >100.

Freshman class profile. 475 applied, 330 admitted, 150 enrolled.

Mid 50% test scores		Rank in top quarter:	28%
ACT composite:	19-25	Rank in top tenth:	6%
GPA 3.75 or higher:	23%	End year in good standing:	76%
GPA 3.50-3.74:	15%	Return as sophomores:	66%
GPA 3.0-3.49:	37%	Out-of-state:	36%
GPA 2.0-2.99:	23%	Live on campus:	94%

Basis for selection. Academic record, test scores, GPA very important. 2.0 GPA and 18 ACT required for consideration. Interview recommended for all; audition required for scholarship recipients, music and theater programs. **Learning Disabled:** Students requesting disability services must submit letter and documentation to support diagnosed disability.

2011-2012 Annual costs. Tuition/fees: $20,656. Room/board: $5,918.

2011-2012 Financial aid. Need-based: 114 full-time freshmen applied for aid; 102 were judged to have need; 102 of these received aid. Average need met was 100%. Average scholarship/grant was $5,991; average loan $5,531. 62% of total undergraduate aid awarded as scholarships/grants, 38% as loans/jobs. **Non-need-based:** Awarded to 48 full-time undergraduates, including 12 freshmen. Scholarships awarded for academics, athletics, leadership, music/drama, religious affiliation. **Additional information:** Prestige scholarships application deadline 2/1.

Application procedures. Admission: Closing date 8/30 (receipt date). $35 fee, may be waived for applicants with need. Admission notification on a rolling basis. **Financial aid:** Priority date 3/1; no closing date. FAFSA, institutional form required. Applicants notified on a rolling basis starting 3/15; must reply within 2 week(s) of notification.

Academics. Special study options: Accelerated study, double major, dual enrollment of high school students, honors, independent study, internships, liberal arts/career combination, student-designed major, teacher certification program. **Credit/placement by examination:** AP, CLEP, IB, SAT, ACT, institutional tests. 88 credit hours maximum toward associate degree, 24 toward bachelor's. **Support services:** Learning center, reduced course load, remedial instruction, study skills assistance, tutoring, writing center.

Majors. Biology: General. **Business:** Accounting, business admin. **Communications:** Digital media. **Computer sciences:** Computer science, information technology, programming. **Education:** Biology, chemistry, elementary, English, health, history, mathematics, middle, music, physical, science, secondary, social science, special ed. **English:** English lit. **Health services:** Clinical lab science, medical radiologic technology/radiation therapy, nursing (RN). **History:** General. **Liberal arts:** Arts/sciences. **Math:** General. **Parks/recreation:** Facilities management. **Philosophy/religion:** Religion. **Physical sciences:** Chemistry. **Protective services:** Criminal justice, forensics. **Psychology:** General. **Social sciences:** General. **Visual/performing arts:** Dramatic, music.

Most popular majors. Business/marketing 20%, education 13%, health sciences 20%, security/protective services 6%.

Computing on campus. PC or laptop required. 53 workstations in dormitories, library, computer center, student center. Dormitories wired for high-speed internet access and linked to campus network. Commuter students can connect to campus network. Online library, helpline, repair service, wireless network available.

Student life. Freshman orientation: Mandatory. Preregistration for classes offered. Three-day intensive orientation prior to beginning of fall semester. **Policies:** Alcohol, tobacco and drug-free campus. Unmarried undergraduates under 21 required to live in college housing unless living with family. **Housing:** Guaranteed on-campus for freshmen. Single-sex dorms, special housing for disabled, wellness housing available. $50 partly refundable deposit. **Activities:** Bands, campus ministries, choral groups, drama, literary magazine, music ensembles, musical theater, student government, student newspaper, Habitat for Humanity, education club, nursing club, English club, STEP club, Raising Adam.

Athletics. NAIA. **Intercollegiate:** Baseball M, basketball, cross-country, golf, soccer, softball W, track and field, volleyball W. **Intramural:** Basketball. **Team name:** Lancers.

Student services. Adult student services, alcohol/substance abuse counseling, chaplain/spiritual director, career counseling, student employment services, financial aid counseling, health services, on-campus daycare, personal counseling, placement for graduates, veterans' counselor.

Contact. E-mail: mmcadmit@mtmc.edu
Phone: (800) 658-4552 Toll-free number: (800) 658-4552
Fax: (605) 668-1607
Paula Tacke, Vice President for Marketing and Admissions, Mount Marty College, 1105 West Eighth Street, Yankton, SD 57078

National American University: Rapid City
Rapid City, South Dakota
www.national.edu   **CB code: 6464**

- For-profit 4-year business and technical college
- Residential campus in small city

General. Founded in 1941. Regionally accredited. **Location:** 400 miles from Denver. **Calendar:** Quarter.

Annual costs/financial aid. Books/supplies: $1,200. Need-based financial aid available to full-time and part-time students.

Contact. Phone: (605) 394-4800
Director of Enrollment Management, 321 Kansas City Street, Rapid City, SD 57701

Northern State University
Aberdeen, South Dakota
www.northern.edu   **CB code: 6487**

- Public 4-year university and liberal arts college
- Residential campus in large town
- 1,806 degree-seeking undergraduates: 19% part-time, 56% women, 2% African American, 3% Hispanic American, 3% Native American, 2% international
- 149 degree-seeking graduate students
- 92% of applicants admitted
- SAT or ACT (ACT writing optional) required
- 46% graduate within 6 years

General. Founded in 1901. Regionally accredited. Technology proficiency certification available for all degree programs. Emphasis on distance delivery technology in all degree programs, especially in teacher preparation. **Degrees:** 252 bachelor's, 16 associate awarded; master's offered. **Location:** 285 miles from Minneapolis-St. Paul. **Calendar:** Semester, limited summer session. **Full-time faculty:** 90 total; 79% have terminal degrees, 12% minority, 37% women. **Class size:** 47% < 20, 44% 20-39, 4% 40-49, 3% 50-99, 1% >100. **Special facilities:** E-learning center, center of excellence for international business.

Freshman class profile. 1,134 applied, 1,043 admitted, 402 enrolled.

Mid 50% test scores		Rank in top tenth:	10%
SAT critical reading:	440-550	Out-of-state:	28%
SAT math:	460-510	Live on campus:	81%
ACT composite:	19-24	International:	1%
Rank in top quarter:	25%		

Basis for selection. Applicants to 4-year programs should have 2.6 GPA or 18 ACT or rank in top 60% of class. C average required in core courses. Applicants not meeting requirements may apply. Applicants lacking required high school units admitted provisionally. Equivalent work must be completed within 2 years. Interview recommended for borderline applicants; portfolio recommended for art program.

High school preparation. College-preparatory program recommended. 13 units required. Required units include English 4, mathematics 3, social studies 3, science 3 (laboratory 3). Mathematics units must be algebra or above; .5 fine arts required.

2011-2012 Annual costs. Tuition/fees: $6,951; $8,666 out-of-state. Reciprocity agreements reduce tuition for some out-of-state students. Room/board: $6,060. Books/supplies: $1,200. Personal expenses: $3,500.

Financial aid. Non-need-based: Scholarships awarded for academics, art, athletics, leadership, minority status, music/drama.

Application procedures. Admission: No deadline. $20 fee. Admission notification on a rolling basis. **Financial aid:** Priority date 3/1; no closing date. FAFSA required. Applicants notified on a rolling basis starting 4/15; must reply within 2 week(s) of notification.

Academics. Special study options: Accelerated study, cooperative education, cross-registration, distance learning, double major, dual enrollment of high school students, ESL, exchange student, honors, independent study, internships, liberal arts/career combination, student-designed major, study abroad, teacher certification program. International Business; E-Learning Certification. **Credit/placement by examination:** AP, CLEP, IB, SAT, ACT, institutional tests. 32 credit hours maximum toward bachelor's degree. **Support services:** Learning center, pre-admission summer program, reduced

course load, remedial instruction, study skills assistance, tutoring, writing center.

Majors. Biology: General, ecology. **Business:** General, accounting, banking/financial services, business admin, finance, international, management information systems, marketing, office/clerical. **Communications:** Communications/speech/rhetoric. **Computer sciences:** General. **Education:** General, art, business, early childhood, elementary, English, foreign languages, history, mathematics, multi-level teacher, music, physical, science, social science, special ed, speech. **English:** English lit, rhetoric/composition. **Foreign languages:** French, German, Spanish. **Health services:** Clinical lab science. **History:** General. **Human services:** Community org/advocacy, social work. **Math:** General. **Parks/recreation:** Health/fitness, sports admin. **Physical sciences:** Chemistry. **Psychology:** General. **Social sciences:** Criminology, economics, political science, sociology. **Visual/performing arts:** Art, music, musical theater.

Most popular majors. Business/marketing 34%, education 20%, parks/recreation 8%, social sciences 14%.

Computing on campus. 135 workstations in dormitories, library, computer center, student center. Dormitories wired for high-speed internet access and linked to campus network. Commuter students can connect to campus network. Online course registration, online library, helpline, repair service, student web hosting, wireless network available.

Student life. Freshman orientation: Mandatory. Preregistration for classes offered. **Housing:** Coed dorms, special housing for disabled, apartments available. $50 deposit. **Activities:** Bands, campus ministries, choral groups, dance, drama, international student organizations, literary magazine, music ensembles, musical theater, student government, student newspaper, symphony orchestra, TV station, over 100 student organizations.

Athletics. NCAA. **Intercollegiate:** Baseball M, basketball, cheerleading M, cross-country, football (tackle) M, golf, soccer W, softball W, swimming W, tennis W, track and field, volleyball W, wrestling M. **Intramural:** Basketball, football (non-tackle), softball, volleyball. **Team name:** Wolves.

Student services. Adult student services, alcohol/substance abuse counseling, chaplain/spiritual director, career counseling, services for economically disadvantaged, student employment services, financial aid counseling, health services, legal services, minority student services, on-campus daycare, personal counseling, placement for graduates, veterans' counselor, women's services. **Physically disabled:** Services for visually, speech, hearing impaired.

Contact. E-mail: admission2@northern.edu
Phone: (605) 626-2544 Toll-free number: (800) 678-5330
Fax: (605) 626-2587
Allan Vogel, Director of Admissions, Northern State University, 1200 South Jay Street, Aberdeen, SD 57401-7198

Oglala Lakota College
Kyle, South Dakota
www.olc.edu **CB code: 1430**

▶ Public 4-year liberal arts and teachers college
▶ Commuter campus in small town

General. Founded in 1971. Regionally accredited. **Location:** 90 miles from Rapid City. **Calendar:** Semester.

Annual costs/financial aid. Tuition/fees (2011-2012): $2,900. Tuition not determined by student residency. Above rates for Native Americans. Non-Native American students pay tuition rate of $2,940 and $98 per credit hour. Books/supplies: $1,200. Personal expenses: $450.

Contact. Phone: (605) 455-6000
Registrar, Box 490, Kyle, SD 57752-0490

Presentation College
Aberdeen, South Dakota
www.presentation.edu **CB code: 6582**

▶ Private 4-year business and health science college affiliated with Roman Catholic Church
▶ Commuter campus in large town

General. Founded in 1951. Regionally accredited. **Location:** 200 miles from Sioux Falls, 280 miles from Minneapolis-St. Paul. **Calendar:** Semester.

Annual costs/financial aid. Tuition/fees (2011-2012): $15,260. Room/board: $6,100. Books/supplies: $1,300. Personal expenses: $620. Need-based financial aid available to full-time and part-time students.

Contact. Phone: (605) 229-8492
Vice President for Enrollment and Student Retention Services, 1500 North Main Street, Aberdeen, SD 57401

Sinte Gleska University
Mission, South Dakota
www.sintegleska.edu **CB code: 7328**

▶ Public 4-year university and liberal arts college
▶ Commuter campus in rural community

General. Founded in 1970. Regionally accredited. **Location:** 90 miles from Pierre, 240 miles from Sioux Falls. **Calendar:** Semester.

Annual costs/financial aid. Tuition/fees (2011-2012): $3,590; $3,590 out-of-state. Books/supplies: $500. Personal expenses: $500. Need-based financial aid available to full-time and part-time students.

Contact. Phone: (605) 747-2263
Registrar, Box 105, Mission, SD 57555

South Dakota School of Mines and Technology
Rapid City, South Dakota
www.sdsmt.edu **CB code: 6652**

▶ Public 4-year university
▶ Commuter campus in small city
▶ 1,797 degree-seeking undergraduates: 10% part-time, 21% women, 1% African American, 1% Asian American, 2% Hispanic American, 2% Native American, 3% international
▶ 294 degree-seeking graduate students
▶ 88% of applicants admitted
▶ SAT or ACT (ACT writing optional) required
▶ 46% graduate within 6 years; 27% enter graduate study

General. Founded in 1885. Regionally accredited. **Degrees:** 235 bachelor's, 8 associate awarded; master's, doctoral offered. **ROTC:** Army. **Location:** 222 miles from Cheyenne, Wyoming. **Calendar:** Semester, limited summer session. **Full-time faculty:** 130 total; 92% have terminal degrees, 14% minority, 18% women. **Part-time faculty:** 23 total; 22% have terminal degrees, 4% minority, 52% women. **Class size:** 35% < 20, 53% 20-39, 4% 40-49, 7% 50-99, 1% >100. **Special facilities:** Geology/paleontology museum, engineering/mining experiment station, atmospheric science institute, CAMP-center for advanced manufacturing and production, advanced materials processing and joining lab, analytical characterization and testing laboratory, additive manufacturing laboratory, center for accelerated applications at the nanoscale, center for bioenergy, paleontology building.

Freshman class profile. 1,030 applied, 905 admitted, 419 enrolled.

Mid 50% test scores			
SAT critical reading:	520-670	GPA 2.0-2.99:	15%
SAT math:	540-660	Rank in top quarter:	54%
SAT writing:	500-640	Rank in top tenth:	20%
ACT composite:	24-29	End year in good standing:	74%
GPA 3.75 or higher:	38%	Return as sophomores:	78%
GPA 3.50-3.74:	22%	Out-of-state:	49%
GPA 3.0-3.49:	25%	Live on campus:	84%
		International:	1%

Basis for selection. Test scores, GPA or class rank very important. ACT and/or COMPASS used for placement. **Home schooled:** 225 GED with 40 on each test (paper based); or 2250 GED with 410 on each test (computer based); or submit ACT/SAT and be reviewed by admissions review committee.

High school preparation. College-preparatory program recommended. 18.5 units required. Required units include English 4, mathematics 4, social studies 3, science 4 (laboratory 3), foreign language 2, computer science .5 and visual/performing arts 1. 1 unit of fine arts is art, theatre or music appreciation, analysis, or performance.

2011-2012 Annual costs. Tuition/fees: $7,897; $9,612 out-of-state. Reciprocity agreements reduce tuition for some out-of-state students. Room/board: $5,695.

2010-2011 Financial aid. Need-based: 409 full-time freshmen applied for aid; 271 were judged to have need; 271 of these received aid. Average need met was 84%. Average scholarship/grant was $3,706; average loan $3,420. 36% of total undergraduate aid awarded as scholarships/grants, 64% as loans/jobs. **Non-need-based:** Awarded to 691 full-time undergraduates, including 263 freshmen. Scholarships awarded for academics, athletics, leadership, ROTC. **Additional information:** Closing date for scholarship applications 2/1.

Application procedures. Admission: No deadline. $20 fee. Admission notification on a rolling basis beginning on or about 11/1. High school students may be enrolled fulltime but as special (non-degree seeking) students prior to high school graduation. **Financial aid:** No deadline. FAFSA required. Applicants notified on a rolling basis starting 4/15; must reply within 3 week(s) of notification.

Academics. Undergraduate teams compete in solar vehicle, ChemE Car, unmanned aero vehicle, SAE aero design, ASCE concrete canoe and bridge, SAE Formula SAE, SAE Mini Baja, ASME human-powered vehicle, SAE clean snowmobile challenge and SAMPE Composites national competitions. Site of 2 Research Experience for undergraduates programs funded by National Science Foundation. **Special study options:** Cooperative education, cross-registration, distance learning, dual enrollment of high school students, ESL, independent study, internships, study abroad. **Credit/placement by examination:** AP, CLEP, IB, SAT, ACT, institutional tests. Credits obtained through validation other than nationally recognized exams are limited to 32 credit hours for bachelor's degrees and 16 credit hours for associate degrees. No limit to credits earned through nationally recognized exams such as CLEP, AP, or DANTES. **Support services:** Learning center, reduced course load, remedial instruction, study skills assistance, tutoring.

Majors. Computer sciences: Computer science. **Engineering:** Chemical, civil, computer, electrical, environmental, geological, industrial, mechanical, metallurgical, mining. **Math:** General. **Physical sciences:** Atmospheric science, chemistry, geology, physics.

Most popular majors. Engineering/engineering technologies 75%, interdisciplinary studies 7%, physical sciences 10%.

Computing on campus. PC or laptop required. 210 workstations in dormitories, library, computer center, student center. Dormitories wired for high-speed internet access and linked to campus network. Commuter students can connect to campus network. Online course registration, online library, helpline, repair service, student web hosting, wireless network available.

Student life. Freshman orientation: Available. Preregistration for classes offered. Held in April and May. Adventure weekends for various groups in summer. **Policies:** Dorm residents required to purchase meal plan each semester. **Housing:** Guaranteed on-campus for freshmen. Coed dorms, special housing for disabled, apartments, fraternity/sorority housing, wellness housing available. $100 fully refundable deposit, deadline 8/15. **Activities:** Bands, campus ministries, choral groups, dance, drama, international student organizations, music ensembles, radio station, student government, student newspaper, Circle K, College Republicans, College Democrats, American Indian Science & Engineering Society, Habitat for Humanity, Muslim student association, Intervarsity Christian Fellowship.

Athletics. NCAA. **Intercollegiate:** Basketball, cross-country, football (tackle) M, golf, track and field, volleyball W. **Intramural:** Basketball, golf, racquetball, skiing, softball, swimming, track and field, volleyball. **Team name:** Hardrockers.

Student services. Adult student services, alcohol/substance abuse counseling, chaplain/spiritual director, career counseling, student employment services, financial aid counseling, health services, minority student services, on-campus daycare, personal counseling, placement for graduates, veterans' counselor, women's services. **Physically disabled:** Services for visually, speech, hearing impaired.

Contact. E-mail: admissions@sdsmt.edu
Phone: (605) 394-2414 Toll-free number: (877) 877-6044
Fax: (605) 394-1979
Molly Frankl, Director of Admissions, South Dakota School of Mines and Technology, 501 East St. Joseph Street, Rapid City, SD 57701

South Dakota State University
Brookings, South Dakota
www.sdstate.edu   **CB code: 6653**

- Public 4-year university
- Commuter campus in large town
- 10,060 degree-seeking undergraduates: 14% part-time, 51% women
- 1,732 graduate students

- 92% of applicants admitted
- SAT or ACT (ACT writing optional) required
- 54% graduate within 6 years

General. Founded in 1881. Regionally accredited. **Degrees:** 1,717 bachelor's, 29 associate awarded; master's, professional, doctoral offered. **ROTC:** Army, Air Force. **Location:** 50 miles from Sioux Falls. **Calendar:** Semester, limited summer session. **Full-time faculty:** 467 total; 71% have terminal degrees, 14% minority, 46% women. **Part-time faculty:** 225 total; 15% have terminal degrees, 3% minority, 72% women. **Class size:** 30% < 20, 49% 20-39, 8% 40-49, 10% 50-99, 3% >100. **Special facilities:** Water resources research center, agricultural experiment station, cooperative extension service, Northern Great Plains biostress center, agricultural heritage museum, animal disease research and diagnostic laboratory, entrepreneur institute, GIS center of excellence, innovation research park, performing arts center.

Freshman class profile. 4,673 applied, 4,313 admitted, 2,241 enrolled.

Mid 50% test scores		Rank in top quarter:	24%
ACT composite:	19-25	Rank in top tenth:	15%
GPA 3.75 or higher:	27%	Return as sophomores:	73%
GPA 3.50-3.74:	18%	Out-of-state:	40%
GPA 3.0-3.49:	31%	Live on campus:	97%
GPA 2.0-2.99:	23%		

Basis for selection. School achievement record and test scores most important. **Home schooled:** Transcript of courses and grades required. Must take ACT and receive scores of 18 composition, 18 English, 20 math, 17 social studies/reasoning, and 17 science reasoning.

High school preparation. College-preparatory program required. 14 units required. Required and recommended units include English 4, mathematics 3, social studies 3, science 3 (laboratory 3), computer science 1 and visual/performing arts 1. 1 fine arts required of in-state applicants. Will accept noncredit fine arts activities in out-of-state schools that do not require it.

2011-2012 Annual costs. Tuition/fees: $7,209; $8,924 out-of-state. Reduced out-of-state tuition for Minnesota students. Room/board: $5,992. Books/supplies: $1,100. Personal expenses: $2,116.

2011-2012 Financial aid. Need-based: 1,749 full-time freshmen applied for aid; 1,494 were judged to have need; 1,494 of these received aid. Average need met was 93%. Average scholarship/grant was $4,830; average loan $4,810. 34% of total undergraduate aid awarded as scholarships/grants, 66% as loans/jobs. **Non-need-based:** Awarded to 7,287 full-time undergraduates, including 1,665 freshmen. Scholarships awarded for academics, art, athletics, job skills, leadership, minority status, music/drama, ROTC, state residency.

Application procedures. Admission: No deadline. $20 fee. Admission notification on a rolling basis. **Financial aid:** Priority date 3/10; no closing date. FAFSA required. Applicants notified on a rolling basis starting 3/30; must reply within 3 week(s) of notification.

Academics. Evening, weekend and other condensed degree-awarding classes available at Sioux Falls Center for Public Higher Education. **Special study options:** Accelerated study, combined bachelor's/graduate degree, cooperative education, cross-registration, distance learning, double major, dual enrollment of high school students, exchange student, honors, independent study, internships, study abroad, teacher certification program. **Credit/placement by examination:** AP, CLEP, IB, SAT, ACT, institutional tests. 16 credit hours maximum toward associate degree, 32 toward bachelor's. **Support services:** Reduced course load, remedial instruction, study skills assistance, tutoring, writing center.

Majors. Architecture: Architecture. **Biology:** General, biochemistry, biotechnology, microbiology. **Business:** Entrepreneurial studies, hotel/motel admin. **Communications:** Advertising, communications/speech/rhetoric, journalism. **Computer sciences:** General. **Conservation:** Environmental studies, management/policy, wildlife/wilderness. **Education:** Agricultural, early childhood, music, secondary, voc/tech. **Engineering:** Agricultural, applied physics, civil, electrical, mechanical, software. **English:** English lit, rhetoric/composition. **Foreign languages:** French, German, Spanish. **General:** Agribusiness operations, agronomy, animal sciences, communications, dairy, economics, horticulture, landscaping, mechanization, range science. **Health services:** Athletic training, clinical lab science, nursing (RN), pharmaceutical sciences. **History:** General. **Liberal arts:** Arts/sciences. **Math:** General. **Parks/recreation:** Facilities management, health/fitness. **Physical sciences:** Chemistry, physics. **Psychology:** General. **Social sciences:** Economics, geography, political science, sociology. **Visual/performing arts:** General, dramatic, graphic design, interior design, music, music management. **Work/family studies:** Apparel marketing, consumer economics, family resources, family studies, food/nutrition.

Most popular majors. Agriculture 13%, biology 6%, engineering/engineering technologies 11%, family/consumer sciences 7%, health sciences 22%, social sciences 10%.

Computing on campus. 437 workstations in dormitories, library, student center. Dormitories wired for high-speed internet access and linked to campus network. Commuter students can connect to campus network. Online course registration, online library, helpline, repair service, wireless network available.

Student life. Freshman orientation: Mandatory. Preregistration for classes offered. Two-day programs in June, one-day programs later in the summer. **Policies:** Students out of high school for less than 2 years required to live in campus housing unless living with family. **Housing:** Guaranteed on-campus for freshmen. Coed dorms, special housing for disabled, apartments, fraternity/sorority housing, wellness housing available. $75 fully refundable deposit. Limited single rooms with optional meal plan available for upperclassmen. **Activities:** Bands, choral groups, dance, drama, international student organizations, literary magazine, music ensembles, Model UN, musical theater, radio station, student government, student newspaper, symphony orchestra, University Program Council, Golden Key International Honor Society, Campus Crusade for Christ, Fellowship of Christian Athletes, Native American club, Circle K International, Black Student Alliance, geography club.

Athletics. NCAA. **Intercollegiate:** Baseball M, basketball, cross-country, equestrian W, football (tackle) M, golf, soccer W, softball W, swimming, tennis, track and field, volleyball W, wrestling M. **Intramural:** Badminton, basketball, football (non-tackle), golf, racquetball, soccer W, softball, swimming, table tennis, track and field, volleyball, wrestling M. **Team name:** Jackrabbits.

Student services. Adult student services, alcohol/substance abuse counseling, career counseling, student employment services, financial aid counseling, health services, legal services, minority student services, personal counseling, placement for graduates, veterans' counselor. **Physically disabled:** Services for visually, speech, hearing impaired.

Contact. E-mail: sdsu.admissions@sdstate.edu
Phone: (605) 688-4121 Toll-free number: (800) 952-3541
Fax: (605) 688-6891
Tracy Welsh, Director of Admissions and High School Relations, South Dakota State University, Box 2201 SAD 200, Brookings, SD 57007-0649

University of Sioux Falls
Sioux Falls, South Dakota
www.usiouxfalls.edu
CB code: 6651

- Private 4-year university and liberal arts college affiliated with American Baptist Churches in the USA
- Residential campus in small city
- 1,108 degree-seeking undergraduates: 14% part-time, 55% women
- 323 degree-seeking graduate students
- 88% of applicants admitted
- SAT or ACT (ACT writing optional) required
- 59% graduate within 6 years

General. Founded in 1883. Regionally accredited. **Degrees:** 285 bachelor's, 7 associate awarded; master's offered. **ROTC:** Air Force. **Location:** 180 miles from Omaha, NE. **Calendar:** 4-1-4, limited summer session. **Full-time faculty:** 63 total; 70% have terminal degrees, 2% minority, 48% women. **Part-time faculty:** 121 total; 2% minority, 64% women. **Class size:** 60% < 20, 38% 20-39, 1% 40-49, less than 1% 50-99. **Special facilities:** Rotating sculpture collection.

Freshman class profile. 624 applied, 547 admitted, 184 enrolled.

Mid 50% test scores		Return as sophomores:	74%
SAT critical reading:	390-480	Out-of-state:	35%
SAT math:	430-470	Live on campus:	95%
ACT composite:	16-26		

Basis for selection. ACT or SAT, GPA, and class rank important. Audition required for music, theater programs; portfolio recommended for art program. **Home schooled:** Statement describing home school structure and mission, transcript of courses and grades required.

High school preparation. College-preparatory program recommended. Recommended units include English 4, mathematics 3, social studies 2, science 3 (laboratory 3) and foreign language 2.

2012-2013 Annual costs. Tuition/fees: $23,740. Room/board: $6,790. Books/supplies: $900. Personal expenses: $2,440.

2010-2011 Financial aid. Need-based: Average scholarship/grant was $11,700; average loan $5,900. 32% of total undergraduate aid awarded as scholarships/grants, 68% as loans/jobs. **Non-need-based:** Scholarships

---

awarded for academics, art, athletics, music/drama. **Additional information:** USF participates in all federal and military educational programs. Priority filing date for FAFSA, March 1st.

Application procedures. Admission: No deadline. No application fee. Admission notification on a rolling basis. **Financial aid:** Priority date 3/1; no closing date. FAFSA required. Applicants notified on a rolling basis starting 3/1; must reply within 2 week(s) of notification.

Academics. Degree completion program offered for adults 25 and older with 64 hours previous college education. **Special study options:** Accelerated study, cross-registration, distance learning, double major, dual enrollment of high school students, honors, independent study, internships, liberal arts/career combination, student-designed major, study abroad, teacher certification program, Washington semester. **Credit/placement by examination:** AP, CLEP, IB, SAT, ACT. 16 credit hours maximum toward bachelor's degree. **Support services:** Learning center, reduced course load, study skills assistance, tutoring, writing center.

Majors. Biology: General. **Business:** Accounting, business admin, hospitality admin, organizational behavior. **Communications:** Journalism. **Computer sciences:** General, computer science. **Education:** Art, elementary, English, health, multi-level teacher, music. **English:** English lit, rhetoric/composition. **Foreign languages:** Spanish. **Health services:** Nursing (RN). **History:** General. **Human services:** Social work. **Liberal arts:** Arts/sciences. **Math:** General, applied. **Parks/recreation:** Exercise sciences. **Philosophy/religion:** Religion. **Physical sciences:** Chemistry. **Protective services:** Criminal justice, police science. **Psychology:** General. **Social sciences:** General, political science, sociology. **Theology:** Theology. **Visual/performing arts:** Art, dramatic, music.

Most popular majors. Business/marketing 35%, education 12%, health sciences 6%, parks/recreation 7%, psychology 9%, security/protective services 7%.

Computing on campus. 175 workstations in dormitories, library, computer center, student center. Dormitories wired for high-speed internet access and linked to campus network. Commuter students can connect to campus network. Online course registration, online library, helpline, repair service, student web hosting, wireless network available.

Student life. Freshman orientation: Available. Preregistration for classes offered. Held 2 days immediately preceding fall semester. **Policies:** No alcohol at university-sponsored events. Freshmen and sophomores required to live in college housing unless over 20 years of age or given permission by director of residence life. **Housing:** Guaranteed on-campus for all undergraduates. Coed dorms, single-sex dorms, apartments available. $50 deposit. **Activities:** Bands, campus ministries, choral groups, dance, drama, film society, international student organizations, music ensembles, Model UN, musical theater, opera, radio station, student government, student newspaper, symphony orchestra, TV station, nontraditional student association, student volunteer groups, religious organizations, Fellowship of Christian Athletes, Campus Crusade For Christ, Young Life.

Athletics. NCAA. **Intercollegiate:** Baseball M, basketball, cross-country, football (tackle) M, golf, soccer, softball W, tennis W, track and field, volleyball W. **Intramural:** Basketball, golf, ice hockey, soccer, softball, table tennis, tennis, volleyball. **Team name:** Cougars.

Student services. Adult student services, alcohol/substance abuse counseling, chaplain/spiritual director, career counseling, student employment services, financial aid counseling, health services, personal counseling, placement for graduates, veterans' counselor, women's services. **Physically disabled:** Services for visually, speech, hearing impaired.

Contact. E-mail: admissions@usiouxfalls.edu
Phone: (605) 331-6600 Toll-free number: (800) 888-1047
Fax: (605) 331-6615
Aimee Vander Feen, Director of Admissions, University of Sioux Falls, 1101 West 22nd Street, Sioux Falls, SD 57105-1699

University of South Dakota
Vermillion, South Dakota
CB member
www.usd.edu
CB code: 6881

- Public 4-year university
- Residential campus in large town
- 6,220 degree-seeking undergraduates: 28% part-time, 62% women, 2% African American, 1% Asian American, 3% Hispanic American, 2% Native American, 1% international
- 2,215 degree-seeking graduate students
- 89% of applicants admitted

▶ SAT or ACT (ACT writing optional), interview required
▶ 49% graduate within 6 years; 50% enter graduate study

General. Founded in 1862. Regionally accredited. **Degrees:** 1,031 bachelor's, 313 associate awarded; master's, professional, doctoral offered. **ROTC:** Army. **Location:** 55 miles from Sioux Falls; 35 miles from Sioux City, Iowa. **Calendar:** Semester, extensive summer session. **Full-time faculty:** 367 total; 81% have terminal degrees, 15% minority, 50% women. **Part-time faculty:** 167 total; 10% have terminal degrees, 6% minority, 64% women. **Class size:** 53% < 20, 37% 20-39, 4% 40-49, 4% 50-99, 2% >100. **Special facilities:** Center for instructional design and delivery, center for disabilities, governmental research bureau, state data center, federal technical procurement center, geological survey, archaeology lab, speech and hearing center, disaster mental health institute, wellness center.

Freshman class profile. 3,287 applied, 2,923 admitted, 1,252 enrolled.

Mid 50% test scores			
SAT critical reading:	460-550	Rank in top tenth:	13%
SAT math:	460-580	End year in good standing:	86%
ACT composite:	20-26	Return as sophomores:	76%
GPA 3.75 or higher:	26%	Out-of-state:	36%
GPA 3.50-3.74:	18%	Live on campus:	84%
GPA 3.0-3.49:	31%	International:	1%
GPA 2.0-2.99:	23%	Fraternities:	26%
Rank in top quarter:	37%	Sororities:	13%

Basis for selection. Admission in good standing granted with 2.0 GPA in required courses or 2.6 overall, rank in top 60% of class, or 20 ACT. Interview recommended for dental hygiene, nursing, physician assistant programs; audition recommended for music, theater programs; portfolio recommended for art program. **Home schooled:** State high school equivalency certificate required.

High school preparation. College-preparatory program recommended. 14 units required; 18 recommended. Required and recommended units include English 4, mathematics 3-4, social studies 3, science 3-4 (laboratory 3) and foreign language 2. 1 fine arts required.

2011-2012 Annual costs. Tuition/fees: $7,209; $8,924 out-of-state. Reciprocity agreement in place for Minnesota residents. Reduced tuition for Iowa residents. Room/board: $6,543. Books/supplies: $1,200. Personal expenses: $2,511.

2010-2011 Financial aid. Need-based: 926 full-time freshmen applied for aid; 681 were judged to have need; 604 of these received aid. Average need met was 77%. Average scholarship/grant was $4,975; average loan $3,562. 39% of total undergraduate aid awarded as scholarships/grants, 61% as loans/jobs. **Non-need-based:** Awarded to 2,891 full-time undergraduates, including 801 freshmen. Scholarships awarded for academics, art, athletics, leadership, minority status, music/drama, ROTC.

Application procedures. Admission: No deadline. $20 fee. Admission notification on a rolling basis beginning on or about 9/20. 2/15 closing date for dental hygiene and nursing programs. **Financial aid:** Priority date 3/15; no closing date. FAFSA required. Applicants notified on a rolling basis starting 5/5.

Academics. Special study options: Accelerated study, combined bachelor's/graduate degree, cross-registration, distance learning, double major, dual enrollment of high school students, ESL, exchange student, external degree, honors, independent study, internships, liberal arts/career combination, student-designed major, study abroad, teacher certification program. **Credit/placement by examination:** AP, CLEP, institutional tests. 15 credit hours maximum toward associate degree, 30 toward bachelor's. **Support services:** Learning center, pre-admission summer program, reduced course load, remedial instruction, study skills assistance, tutoring.

Honors college/program. Honors program open to students in all majors who displayed potential for honors work in high school through good grades, college preparatory curriculum, high ACT scores, and participation in school and community activities.

Majors. Area/ethnic studies: Native American. **Biology:** General. **Business:** Accounting, business admin, finance, managerial economics. **Communications:** Communications/speech/rhetoric, journalism, media studies. **Computer sciences:** General. **Education:** Biology, chemistry, drama/dance, early childhood, elementary, English, foreign languages, French, German, history, kindergarten/preschool, mathematics, music, physical, physics, science, social science, Spanish, special ed, speech. **English:** English lit, rhetoric/composition. **Foreign languages:** French, German, Spanish. **Health services:** Communication disorders, dental hygiene, health services admin, substance abuse counseling. **History:** General. **Human services:** Social work. **Liberal arts:** Arts/sciences. **Math:** General. **Parks/recreation:** General. **Philosophy/religion:** Philosophy. **Physical sciences:** Chemistry, geology, physics. **Protective services:** Criminal justice. **Psychology:** General. **Social sciences:** Anthropology, economics, political science, sociology. **Visual/performing**

arts: Art, dramatic, music, music performance, studio arts, studio arts management.

Most popular majors. Biology 6%, business/marketing 18%, education 11%, health sciences 12%, psychology 12%, security/protective services 6.68%, social sciences 7%.

Computing on campus. 995 workstations in dormitories, library, student center. Dormitories wired for high-speed internet access and linked to campus network. Commuter students can connect to campus network. Online course registration, online library, helpline, repair service, student web hosting, wireless network available.

Student life. Freshman orientation: Mandatory. Preregistration for classes offered. **Policies:** Students required to live in residence halls for first 2 years unless living in fraternity/sorority housing or commuting from home. **Housing:** Guaranteed on-campus for freshmen. Coed dorms, special housing for disabled, apartments, fraternity/sorority housing, wellness housing available. $100 partly refundable deposit, deadline 9/1. Apartments available for students with dependent children. **Activities:** Bands, choral groups, dance, drama, international student organizations, literary magazine, music ensembles, musical theater, opera, radio station, student government, student newspaper, symphony orchestra, TV station, Young Democrats, College Republicans, Campus Crusade for Christ, Chinese student association, gay/lesbian/bisexual alliance, Habitat for Humanity, nontraditional student association, political science league.

Athletics. NCAA. **Intercollegiate:** Basketball, cross-country, diving, football (tackle) M, golf, soccer W, softball W, swimming, tennis W, track and field. **Intramural:** Badminton, basketball, bowling, cross-country, football (non-tackle), golf, racquetball, soccer, softball, swimming, table tennis, tennis, track and field, volleyball. **Team name:** Coyotes.

Student services. Adult student services, alcohol/substance abuse counseling, chaplain/spiritual director, career counseling, services for economically disadvantaged, student employment services, financial aid counseling, health services, legal services, minority student services, on-campus daycare, personal counseling, placement for graduates, veterans' counselor. **Physically disabled:** Services for visually, speech, hearing impaired.

Contact. E-mail: admission@usd.edu
Phone: (605) 677-5434 Toll-free number: (877) 269-6837
Fax: (605) 677-6753
Scott Pohlson, Dean of Enrollment, University of South Dakota, 414 East Clark Street, Vermillion, SD 57069-2390

Tennessee

American Baptist College
Nashville, Tennessee
www.abcnash.edu   CB code: 2401

- Private 4-year Bible college affiliated with Baptist faith
- Commuter campus in large city

General. Founded in 1924. Accredited by ABHE. **Location:** 200 miles from Memphis. **Calendar:** Semester.

Annual costs/financial aid. Tuition/fees (2011-2012): $10,464. Room: $2,000. Books/supplies: $900. Need-based financial aid available for full-time students.

Contact. Phone: (615) 256-1463
Director of Enrollment Management, 1800 Baptist World Center Drive, Nashville, TN 37207

Aquinas College
Nashville, Tennessee   **CB member**
www.aquinascollege.edu   CB code: 7318

- Private 4-year nursing and liberal arts college affiliated with Roman Catholic Church
- Commuter campus in very large city
- 632 degree-seeking undergraduates
- SAT or ACT (ACT writing optional), application essay required

General. Founded in 1961. Regionally accredited. **Degrees:** 101 bachelor's, 134 associate awarded. **Location:** 1 mile from downtown, 195 miles from Knoxville. **Calendar:** Semester, limited summer session. **Full-time faculty:** 36 total; 33% have terminal degrees, 72% women. **Part-time faculty:** 58 total; 29% have terminal degrees, 55% women.

Basis for selection. School achievement record, test scores important. **Home schooled:** Transcript of courses and grades required. Must provide copy of transcript from accredited home school agency along with official ACT Report.

High school preparation. 20 units recommended. Recommended units include English 4, mathematics 3, social studies 3, science 3, foreign language 2 and academic electives 5.

2011-2012 Annual costs. Tuition/fees: $19,050. Books/supplies: $1,000. Personal expenses: $1,500.

Financial aid. Non-need-based: Scholarships awarded for academics, alumni affiliation, leadership, religious affiliation.

Application procedures. Admission: Priority date 2/15; no deadline. $25 fee, may be waived for applicants with need. Admission notification on a rolling basis. **Financial aid:** Priority date 2/15; no closing date. FAFSA required. Applicants notified on a rolling basis starting 2/15; must reply within 2 week(s) of notification.

Academics. WriteReason Program to ensure that students communicate ideas in writing that are clear, accurate, and effective. **Special study options:** Accelerated study, double major, dual enrollment of high school students, independent study, liberal arts/career combination, teacher certification program. **Credit/placement by examination:** AP, CLEP, SAT, ACT, institutional tests. 30 credit hours maximum toward associate degree, 60 toward bachelor's. **Support services:** Learning center, reduced course load, remedial instruction, study skills assistance, tutoring, writing center.

Majors. Business: Business admin, management information systems. **Education:** Elementary. **English:** English lit. **Health services:** Nursing (RN). **History:** General. **Liberal arts:** Arts/sciences. **Theology:** Theology.

Computing on campus. 55 workstations in library, computer center, student center. Online library, helpline, wireless network available.

Student life. Freshman orientation: Mandatory. Preregistration for classes offered. **Policies:** Drug-free/alcohol-free campus. **Activities:** Campus ministries, student government, Phi Beta Lambda, Delta Epsilon Sigma, Association of Student Nurses, Association for Supervision and Curriculum Development student chapter, Student Activities Board, Tennessee Intercollegiate State Legislature, Frassati Society, Sigma Beta Delta.

Athletics. Intramural: Tennis, volleyball. **Team name:** Cavaliers.

Student services. Alcohol/substance abuse counseling, chaplain/spiritual director, career counseling, student employment services, financial aid counseling, personal counseling.

Contact. E-mail: admissions@aquinascollege.edu
Phone: (615) 297-7545 ext. 460 Toll-free number: (800) 649-9956
Fax: (615) 279-3893
Connie Hansom, Director of Admissions, Aquinas College, 4210 Harding Road, Nashville, TN 37205-2086

Argosy University: Nashville
Nashville, Tennessee
www.argosy.edu/nashville   CB code: 5685

- For-profit 4-year university
- Very large city
- 151 degree-seeking undergraduates

General. Regionally accredited. **Degrees:** 11 bachelor's awarded; master's, professional, doctoral offered. **Calendar:** Differs by program. **Full-time faculty:** 3 total. **Part-time faculty:** 63 total.

Basis for selection. Open admission.

2011-2012 Annual costs. Tuition/fees: $17,962.

Application procedures. Admission: Closing date 9/14. $50 fee. **Financial aid:** No deadline.

Academics. Credit/placement by examination: AP, CLEP.

Majors. Business: Business admin. **Liberal arts:** Arts/sciences. **Protective services:** Police science. **Psychology:** General.

Contact. Phone: (615) 525-2800
Erica Bligen, Senior Director of Admissions, Argosy University: Nashville, 100 Centerview Drive, Suite 225, Nashville, TN 37214

Austin Peay State University
Clarksville, Tennessee   **CB member**
www.apsu.edu   CB code: 1028

- Public 4-year university and liberal arts college
- Commuter campus in small city
- 9,832 degree-seeking undergraduates: 27% part-time, 60% women, 19% African American, 2% Asian American, 6% Hispanic American, 1% Native American
- 841 degree-seeking graduate students
- 88% of applicants admitted
- SAT or ACT (ACT writing optional) required
- 35% graduate within 6 years

General. Founded in 1927. Regionally accredited. **Degrees:** 1,253 bachelor's, 226 associate awarded; master's offered. **ROTC:** Army, Air Force. **Location:** 45 miles from Nashville. **Calendar:** Semester, limited summer session. **Full-time faculty:** 347 total; 12% minority, 46% women. **Part-time faculty:** 279 total; 10% minority, 62% women. **Class size:** 47% < 20, 42% 20-39, 5% 40-49, 5% 50-99, less than 1% >100. **Special facilities:** Zoological museum.

Freshman class profile. 3,290 applied, 2,897 admitted, 1,551 enrolled.

Mid 50% test scores			
SAT critical reading:	420-560	Rank in top quarter:	38%
SAT math:	440-560	Rank in top tenth:	14%
ACT composite:	19-23	Return as sophomores:	69%
GPA 3.75 or higher:	16%	Out-of-state:	8%
GPA 3.50-3.74:	14%	Live on campus:	46%
GPA 3.0-3.49:	37%	Fraternities:	10%
GPA 2.0-2.99:	31%	Sororities:	11%

Basis for selection. Rigor of secondary school record, GPA, and test scores very important. ACT/SAT not required of active duty military. **Home schooled:** Transcript of courses and grades required.

High school preparation. College-preparatory program required. 14 units required. Required units include English 4, mathematics 3, social studies 1, history 1, science 2 (laboratory 1), foreign language 2 and visual/performing arts 1. Mathematics units should be algebra I and II, 1 geometry or advanced mathematics. Social science units should be 1 social studies, 1 US history. Foreign language units must be in 1 language.

2011-2012 Annual costs. Tuition/fees: $6,690; $20,928 out-of-state. Room/board: $6,984. Books/supplies: $1,550. Personal expenses: $2,100.

2011-2012 Financial aid. Need-based: Average scholarship/grant was $6,407; average loan $2,995. 58% of total undergraduate aid awarded as scholarships/grants, 42% as loans/jobs. **Non-need-based:** Scholarships awarded for academics, art, athletics, leadership, music/drama, ROTC, state residency.

Application procedures. Admission: Closing date 7/25. $15 fee. Admission notification on a rolling basis. **Financial aid:** Priority date 4/1; no closing date. FAFSA required. Applicants notified on a rolling basis starting 5/1.

Academics. Special study options: Accelerated study, cooperative education, distance learning, double major, dual enrollment of high school students, ESL, honors, independent study, internships, study abroad, teacher certification program. Service Members Opportunity College (associate and bachelor's degrees). **Credit/placement by examination:** AP, CLEP, SAT, ACT, institutional tests. 32 credit hours maximum toward associate degree, 64 toward bachelor's. **Support services:** Learning center, remedial instruction, study skills assistance, tutoring, writing center.

Honors college/program. Rank in top 10% of class, 26 ACT, and commendable high school record required.

Majors. Biology: General. **Business:** General, nonprofit/public. **Communications:** Media studies. **Computer sciences:** General. **Education:** Health, special ed. **English:** English lit. **Foreign languages:** General, Spanish. **Health services:** Clinical lab science, medical radiologic technology/radiation therapy, nursing (RN). **History:** General. **Human services:** Social work. **Liberal arts/sciences:** Arts/sciences. **Math:** General. **Parks/recreation:** Health/fitness. **Philosophy/religion:** Philosophy. **Physical sciences:** Chemistry, geology, physics. **Protective services:** Law enforcement admin. **Psychology:** General. **Social sciences:** Political science, sociology. **Visual/performing arts:** Art, music.

Most popular majors. Business/marketing 19%, communications/journalism 6%, health sciences 11%, liberal arts 6%, psychology 6%.

Computing on campus. 825 workstations in dormitories, library, computer center, student center. Dormitories wired for high-speed internet access and linked to campus network. Commuter students can connect to campus network. Online course registration, online library, helpline, wireless network available.

Student life. Freshman orientation: Mandatory, $75 fee. Preregistration for classes offered. **Policies:** Alcohol not permitted on campus. **Housing:** Coed dorms, single-sex dorms, special housing for disabled, apartments, fraternity/sorority housing available. $200 fully refundable deposit. **Activities:** Bands, campus ministries, choral groups, dance, drama, film society, international student organizations, literary magazine, music ensembles, musical theater, opera, radio station, student government, student newspaper, symphony orchestra, TV station, Wesley Foundation, Room In the Inn, student art league, Baptist Collegiate Ministry, Church of Christ Student Center, Hispanic Cultural Center, African American Cultural Center.

Athletics. NCAA. **Intercollegiate:** Baseball M, basketball, cross-country, football (tackle) M, golf, rifle W, soccer W, softball W, tennis, track and field W, volleyball W. **Intramural:** Basketball, football (non-tackle), racquetball, soccer, table tennis, volleyball. **Team name:** Governors.

Student services. Adult student services, alcohol/substance abuse counseling, career counseling, student employment services, financial aid counseling, health services, on-campus daycare, personal counseling, veterans' counselor. **Physically disabled:** Services for visually, speech, hearing impaired.

Contact. E-mail: admissions@apsu.edu
Phone: (931) 221-7661 Toll-free number: (800) 844-2778
Fax: (931) 221-6168
Amy Deaton, Director of Admissions, Austin Peay State University, PO Box 4548, Clarksville, TN 37044-4548

Baptist College of Health Sciences
Memphis, Tennessee
www.bchs.edu
CB code: 6548

▶ Private 4-year health science and nursing college affiliated with Baptist faith
▶ Commuter campus in very large city

General. Regionally accredited. **Calendar:** Trimester.

Annual costs/financial aid. Tuition/fees (2011-2012): $10,660. Room: $1,800. Books/supplies: $1,200.

Contact. Phone: (901) 575-2247
Manager of Admissions, 1003 Monroe Avenue, Memphis, TN 38104

Belmont University
Nashville, Tennessee
www.belmont.edu
CB code: 1058

▶ Private 4-year university affiliated with interdenominational tradition
▶ Residential campus in very large city
▶ 4,931 degree-seeking undergraduates: 7% part-time, 58% women, 4% African American, 2% Asian American, 3% Hispanic American, 1% international
▶ 1,385 degree-seeking graduate students
▶ 82% of applicants admitted
▶ SAT or ACT (ACT writing optional) required
▶ 65% graduate within 6 years; 22% enter graduate study

General. Founded in 1951. Regionally accredited. **Degrees:** 993 bachelor's awarded; master's, doctoral offered. **ROTC:** Army, Naval, Air Force. **Location:** 2 miles from downtown. **Calendar:** Semester, limited summer session. **Full-time faculty:** 316 total; 78% have terminal degrees, 7% minority, 52% women. **Part-time faculty:** 341 total; 24% have terminal degrees, 8% minority, 53% women. **Class size:** 44% < 20, 56% 20-39, less than 1% 40-49. **Special facilities:** 22-track recording studio, Studio B on Music Row, 140-year-old antebellum mansion.

Freshman class profile. 3,878 applied, 3,161 admitted, 1,163 enrolled.

Mid 50% test scores			
SAT critical reading:	530-640	Rank in top tenth:	33%
SAT math:	530-630	End year in good standing:	92%
ACT composite:	24-29	Return as sophomores:	80%
GPA 3.75 or higher:	33%	Out-of-state:	71%
GPA 3.50-3.74:	23%	Live on campus:	93%
GPA 3.0-3.49:	32%	International:	1%
GPA 2.0-2.99:	12%	Fraternities:	3%
Rank in top quarter:	62%	Sororities:	5%

Basis for selection. Admissions based on test scores, course selection, GPA, class rank, recommendations, leadership activity. Interview required for music business; audition required for music programs.

High school preparation. College-preparatory program required. 18 units required. Required and recommended units include English 4, mathematics 3-4, social studies 3, science 3-4, foreign language 2 and academic electives 3.

2011-2012 Annual costs. Tuition/fees: $24,960. Room/board: $9,390. Books/supplies: $1,400. Personal expenses: $2,550.

2010-2011 Financial aid. Need-based: 976 full-time freshmen applied for aid; 610 were judged to have need; 587 of these received aid. Average need met was 82%. Average scholarship/grant was $7,133; average loan $3,362. 46% of total undergraduate aid awarded as scholarships/grants, 54% as loans/jobs. **Non-need-based:** Awarded to 1,992 full-time undergraduates, including 570 freshmen. Scholarships awarded for academics, art, athletics, leadership, music/drama, religious affiliation, state residency.

Application procedures. Admission: Priority date 12/1; deadline 8/1. $50 fee. Admission notification on a rolling basis beginning on or about 9/1. Must reply by May 1 or within 2 week(s) if notified thereafter. **Financial aid:** Priority date 3/1; no closing date. FAFSA required. Applicants notified on a rolling basis starting 3/15; must reply by 5/1 or within 2 week(s) of notification.

Academics. Special study options: Accelerated study, combined bachelor's/graduate degree, cooperative education, cross-registration, distance learning, double major, dual enrollment of high school students, ESL, honors,

independent study, internships, liberal arts/career combination, student-designed major, study abroad, teacher certification program, Washington semester. **Credit/placement by examination:** AP, CLEP, IB, SAT, ACT, institutional tests. 24 credit hours maximum toward bachelor's degree. **Support services:** Learning center, pre-admission summer program, reduced course load, tutoring, writing center.

Majors. Biology: General, environmental, molecular, molecular biochemistry. **Business:** General, accounting, entrepreneurial studies, finance, hospitality admin, management information systems, management science, managerial economics, marketing. **Communications:** Broadcast journalism, communications/speech/rhetoric, journalism, media studies, public relations. **Computer sciences:** Computer science, information systems. **Education:** General, art, biology, chemistry, early childhood, elementary, English, French, health, health occupations, history, mathematics, middle, music, physical, physics, science, secondary, social science, social studies, Spanish. **English:** English lit, rhetoric/composition. **Foreign languages:** French, German, Spanish. **Health services:** Nursing (RN). **History:** General. **Human services:** Social work. **Liberal arts:** Arts/sciences. **Math:** General. **Parks/recreation:** Exercise sciences, health/fitness. **Philosophy/religion:** Philosophy, religion. **Physical sciences:** Chemistry, physics. **Psychology:** General. **Social sciences:** Economics, political science, sociology. **Theology:** Sacred music. **Visual/performing arts:** Art, commercial/advertising art, dramatic, music, music management, music pedagogy, music performance, music theory/composition, piano/keyboard, voice/opera. **Work/family studies:** Child care management.

Most popular majors. Business/marketing 16%, health sciences 13%, visual/performing arts 11%.

Computing on campus. 500 workstations in dormitories, library, computer center, student center. Dormitories wired for high-speed internet access and linked to campus network. Commuter students can connect to campus network. Online course registration, online library, helpline, wireless network available.

Student life. Freshman orientation: Mandatory, $60 fee. Preregistration for classes offered. 2-day program in summer or 4-day program in fall before classes start. **Housing:** Guaranteed on-campus for freshmen. Single-sex dorms, apartments, wellness housing available. $100 nonrefundable deposit, deadline 5/1. **Activities:** Bands, campus ministries, choral groups, dance, drama, international student organizations, literary magazine, music ensembles, musical theater, opera, radio station, student government, student newspaper, symphony orchestra, TV station, Baptist student union, Christian music society, Campus Crusade for Christ, Fellowship of Christian Athletes, Black Student Alliance.

Athletics. NCAA. **Intercollegiate:** Baseball M, basketball, cross-country, golf, soccer, softball W, tennis, track and field, volleyball W. **Intramural:** Basketball, bowling, golf M, racquetball, softball, table tennis, tennis, volleyball. **Team name:** Bruins.

Student services. Adult student services, alcohol/substance abuse counseling, chaplain/spiritual director, career counseling, student employment services, financial aid counseling, health services, minority student services, personal counseling, placement for graduates, veterans' counselor.

Contact. E-mail: buadmission@belmont.edu
Phone: (615) 460-6785 Fax: (615) 460-5434
David Mee, Dean of Enrollment Services, Belmont University, 1900 Belmont Boulevard, Nashville, TN 37212-3757

Bethel University
McKenzie, Tennessee
www.bethelu.edu   CB code: 1063

- Private 4-year university and liberal arts college affiliated with Cumberland Presbyterian Church
- Residential campus in small town
- 3,877 degree-seeking undergraduates
- SAT or ACT (ACT writing optional) required

General. Founded in 1842. Regionally accredited. Students provided with laptop computer upon full-time registration. **Degrees:** 433 bachelor's awarded; master's offered. **Location:** 115 miles from Nashville, 120 miles from Memphis. **Calendar:** Continuous, limited summer session. **Full-time faculty:** 97 total; 46% have terminal degrees, 7% minority, 44% women. **Part-time faculty:** 194 total. **Class size:** 72% < 20, 28% 20-39, less than 1% 40-49, less than 1% 50-99. **Special facilities:** Autism resource center.

Freshman class profile.

Mid 50% test scores		ACT composite:	16-22
SAT critical reading:	400-510	Out-of-state:	7%
SAT math:	430-530	Live on campus:	32%
SAT writing:	600-690		

Basis for selection. GPA and academic units considered. Counselor recommendation and interview considered for academically marginal applicants. **Home schooled:** 19 ACT and passing score on GED required.

High school preparation. College-preparatory program recommended. Required units include English 4, mathematics 2, social studies 2 and science 2.

2011-2012 Annual costs. Tuition/fees: $13,552. Room/board: $7,782. Books/supplies: $1,000. Personal expenses: $1,750.

Financial aid. Non-need-based: Scholarships awarded for academics, athletics, music/drama, religious affiliation, state residency.

Application procedures. Admission: Priority date 2/3; no deadline. $30 fee. Admission notification on a rolling basis. **Financial aid:** Priority date 3/3, closing date 6/30. FAFSA, institutional form required. Applicants notified on a rolling basis starting 3/1.

Academics. Special study options: Accelerated study, combined bachelor's/graduate degree, double major, honors, independent study, internships, student-designed major, study abroad, teacher certification program, weekend college. **Credit/placement by examination:** AP, CLEP, SAT, ACT, institutional tests. 30 credit hours maximum toward bachelor's degree. Accepts CLEP, DANTES, institutional exams for credit. **Support services:** Remedial instruction, study skills assistance, tutoring.

Majors. Biology: General. **Business:** Accounting/business management, business admin, management information systems. **Education:** Elementary, music, physical, special ed. **English:** English lit. **Health services:** Nursing (RN), premedicine, prepharmacy. **History:** General. **Math:** General. **Philosophy/religion:** Christian. **Physical sciences:** Chemistry. **Psychology:** General. **Social sciences:** Sociology. **Visual/performing arts:** Dramatic, music, music management.

Most popular majors. Business/marketing 80%, education 6%.

Computing on campus. PC or laptop required. 650 workstations in dormitories, library. Dormitories wired for high-speed internet access and linked to campus network. Commuter students can connect to campus network. Online library, helpline, repair service, wireless network available.

Student life. Freshman orientation: Mandatory. Preregistration for classes offered. One-day Saturday program held June-August. Week-long sessions held the week prior to start of classes. **Housing:** Guaranteed on-campus for freshmen. Coed dorms, single-sex dorms, apartments available. $175 nonrefundable deposit, deadline 8/18. **Activities:** Bands, choral groups, drama, music ensembles, musical theater, student government, Fellowship of Christian Athletes, honor societies, American Chemical Society, student education association, art club, Students in Free Enterprise, Arete, Campus Crusade for Christ, Relay for Life.

Athletics. NAIA. **Intercollegiate:** Baseball M, basketball, bowling, cheerleading, cross-country, football (tackle) M, golf, rifle, soccer, softball W, tennis, track and field, volleyball W. **Intramural:** Basketball, football (non-tackle), football (tackle) M, golf, soccer, softball, swimming, table tennis, volleyball W. **Team name:** Wildcats.

Student services. Adult student services, alcohol/substance abuse counseling, chaplain/spiritual director, career counseling, student employment services, financial aid counseling, personal counseling, veterans' counselor.

Contact. E-mail: admissions@bethelu.edu
Phone: (731) 352-4030 Fax: (731) 352-4069
Tina Hodges, Enrollment Director of Admissions and Financial Aid, Bethel University, 325 Cherry Avenue, McKenzie, TN 38201

Bryan College
Dayton, Tennessee
www.bryan.edu   CB code: 1908

- Private 4-year liberal arts college affiliated with interdenominational tradition
- Residential campus in small town
- 1,120 degree-seeking undergraduates: 6% part-time, 53% women, 5% African American, 2% Hispanic American, 2% international
- 121 degree-seeking graduate students
- 56% of applicants admitted
- SAT or ACT (ACT writing recommended), application essay required
- 56% graduate within 6 years

General. Founded in 1930. Regionally accredited. All courses taught from Christian perspective. All faculty sign statement of faith annually. **Degrees:**

353 bachelor's awarded; master's offered. **Location:** 40 miles from Chattanooga. **Calendar:** Semester, limited summer session. **Full-time faculty:** 42 total; 71% have terminal degrees, 24% women. **Part-time faculty:** 19 total; 21% have terminal degrees, 47% women. **Class size:** 62% < 20, 32% 20-39, 2% 40-49, 3% 50-99, less than 1% >100. **Special facilities:** Natural history museum.

Freshman class profile. 866 applied, 483 admitted, 233 enrolled.

Mid 50% test scores			
SAT critical reading:	500-670	GPA 2.0-2.99:	10%
SAT math:	470-600	Rank in top quarter:	48%
SAT writing:	460-640	Rank in top tenth:	20%
ACT composite:	20-26	Return as sophomores:	71%
GPA 3.75 or higher:	43%	Out-of-state:	63%
GPA 3.50-3.74:	21%	Live on campus:	88%
GPA 3.0-3.49:	26%	International:	2%

Basis for selection. High school record, Christian character supported by references, and SAT or ACT scores important. 23 ACT/SAT equivalent or Pre-Professional Skills Test required of all teacher education applicants. Interview required for marginal applicants. **Home schooled:** Detailed high school transcript of courses and grades required.

High school preparation. 18 units required. Required units include English 4, mathematics 3, social studies 3, science 3 and foreign language 2.

2011-2012 Annual costs. Tuition/fees: $19,550. Room/board: $5,720. Books/supplies: $1,400. Personal expenses: $1,500.

Financial aid. Non-need-based: Scholarships awarded for academics, alumni affiliation, art, athletics, job skills, leadership, music/drama.

Application procedures. Admission: Priority date 5/1; no deadline. $35 fee, may be waived for applicants with need. Admission notification on a rolling basis. **Financial aid:** Priority date 2/15; no closing date. FAFSA required. Applicants notified on a rolling basis starting 1/1; must reply within 2 week(s) of notification.

Academics. Special study options: Combined bachelor's/graduate degree, distance learning, double major, dual enrollment of high school students, honors, independent study, internships, study abroad, teacher certification program, Washington semester. Adult degree completion program. **Credit/placement by examination:** AP, CLEP, IB, SAT, ACT, institutional tests. 30 credit hours maximum toward associate degree, 31 toward bachelor's. **Support services:** Reduced course load, remedial instruction, study skills assistance, tutoring, writing center.

Majors. Biology: General. **Business:** Business admin. **Communications:** Communications/speech/rhetoric. **Computer sciences:** Computer science. **Education:** General. **English:** English lit. **Foreign languages:** Spanish. **History:** General. **Liberal arts:** Arts/sciences. **Math:** General. **Parks/recreation:** Exercise sciences. **Philosophy/religion:** Christian. **Psychology:** General. **Social sciences:** Political science. **Theology:** Bible, religious ed. **Visual/performing arts:** Dramatic, music.

Most popular majors. Business/marketing 58%, communications/journalism 8%, education 7%.

Computing on campus. 100 workstations in dormitories, library, computer center, student center. Dormitories wired for high-speed internet access and linked to campus network. Commuter students can connect to campus network. Online library, helpline, student web hosting, wireless network available.

Student life. Freshman orientation: Mandatory. Preregistration for classes offered. **Policies:** No alcohol, tobacco, drugs. Curfew and dress code enforced. Religious observance required. **Housing:** Guaranteed on-campus for all undergraduates. Single-sex dorms, apartments available. $100 fully refundable deposit, deadline 8/10. **Activities:** Campus ministries, choral groups, drama, music ensembles, student government, student newspaper, Christian service organizations, community tutoring program, Students for Life, Fellowship of Christian Athletes.

Athletics. NAIA, NCCAA. **Intercollegiate:** Baseball M, basketball, cheerleading M, cross-country, golf, soccer, softball W, track and field, volleyball W. **Intramural:** Basketball, football (non-tackle) M, soccer, table tennis, tennis, volleyball. **Team name:** Lions.

Student services. Adult student services, chaplain/spiritual director, career counseling, student employment services, financial aid counseling, health services, personal counseling, placement for graduates.

Contact. E-mail: admissions@bryan.edu
Phone: (423) 775-7204 Toll-free number: (800) 277-9522
Fax: (423) 775-7199
Aaron Porter, Director of Admissions, Bryan College, PO Box 7000, Dayton, TN 37321-7000

Carson-Newman College
Jefferson City, Tennessee
www.cn.edu   CB code: 1102

- Private 4-year liberal arts college affiliated with Southern Baptist Convention
- Residential campus in small town
- 1,658 degree-seeking undergraduates: 4% part-time, 54% women, 9% African American, 2% Hispanic American, 2% international
- 284 degree-seeking graduate students
- 67% of applicants admitted
- SAT or ACT required
- 45% graduate within 6 years

General. Founded in 1851. Regionally accredited. **Degrees:** 351 bachelor's awarded; master's offered. **ROTC:** Army, Air Force. **Location:** 30 miles from Knoxville. **Calendar:** Semester, extensive summer session. **Full-time faculty:** 123 total; 73% have terminal degrees. **Part-time faculty:** 81 total. **Class size:** 63% < 20, 34% 20-39, 2% 40-49. **Special facilities:** Appalachia museum.

Freshman class profile. 3,542 applied, 2,382 admitted, 446 enrolled.

Mid 50% test scores			
ACT composite:	20-25	Rank in top tenth:	27%
GPA 3.75 or higher:	36%	End year in good standing:	88%
GPA 3.50-3.74:	16%	Return as sophomores:	64%
GPA 3.0-3.49:	27%	Out-of-state:	32%
GPA 2.0-2.99:	21%	Live on campus:	90%
Rank in top quarter:	47%	International:	1%

Basis for selection. 2.5 GPA, 19 ACT or 920 SAT (exclusive of Writing), school and community activities, and recommendations important. Rank in top half of class considered. Essay required for marginal students; audition required for music; portfolio required for art; interview recommended for academically weak.

High school preparation. 20 units required. Required and recommended units include English 4, mathematics 2-3, social studies 3, history 2, science 2 (laboratory 1) and foreign language 2.

2011-2012 Annual costs. Tuition/fees: $21,774. Room/board: $6,247. Books/supplies: $1,088. Personal expenses: $1,921.

Financial aid. Non-need-based: Scholarships awarded for academics, art, athletics, leadership, minority status, music/drama, religious affiliation, ROTC.

Application procedures. Admission: Priority date 12/31; deadline 8/1. $25 fee, may be waived for applicants with need. Admission notification on a rolling basis. Must reply by May 1 or within 4 week(s) if notified thereafter. **Financial aid:** Priority date 4/1; no closing date. FAFSA, institutional form required. Applicants notified on a rolling basis starting 2/1; must reply within 2 week(s) of notification.

Academics. 3-year pre-engineering programs available. **Special study options:** Accelerated study, double major, dual enrollment of high school students, ESL, exchange student, honors, independent study, internships, liberal arts/career combination, student-designed major, study abroad, teacher certification program, Washington semester, weekend college. **Credit/placement by examination:** AP, CLEP, institutional tests. 32 credit hours maximum toward associate degree, 32 toward bachelor's. **Support services:** Learning center, pre-admission summer program, reduced course load, remedial instruction, tutoring.

Majors. Biology: General. **Business:** General, accounting, business admin, managerial economics, small business admin. **Communications:** Communications/speech/rhetoric, journalism. **Computer sciences:** General. **Education:** Early childhood, elementary, family/consumer sciences, middle, music, physical, secondary, special ed. **Engineering:** Applied physics. **English:** English lit, rhetoric/composition. **Foreign languages:** French, Spanish. **Health services:** Athletic training, health care admin, nursing (RN), predental, premedicine, prepharmacy. **History:** General. **Liberal arts:** Arts/sciences. **Math:** General. **Parks/recreation:** General, exercise sciences, health/fitness. **Philosophy/religion:** Philosophy, religion. **Physical sciences:** Chemistry, physics. **Psychology:** General. **Social sciences:** Economics, political science, sociology. **Theology:** Sacred music, theology. **Visual/performing arts:** General, art, interior design, music, music performance, music theory/composition, painting, photography. **Work/family studies:** Clothing/textiles, family/community services, food/nutrition.

Most popular majors. Business/marketing 13%, education 24%, health sciences 19%, psychology 6%.

Computing on campus. 100 workstations in dormitories, library, computer center. Dormitories wired for high-speed internet access and linked to campus network. Commuter students can connect to campus network. Helpline, repair service available.

Student life. Freshman orientation: Available. Preregistration for classes offered. **Policies:** Religious observance required. **Housing:** Guaranteed on-campus for freshmen. Single-sex dorms, apartments available. $50 deposit, deadline 8/1. Honors house available. **Activities:** Bands, choral groups, dance, drama, film society, literary magazine, music ensembles, musical theater, radio station, student government, student newspaper, TV station, Baptist student union, Fellowship of Christian Athletes, honor societies, Appalachian Outreach, Bonners Scholars community service.

Athletics. NCAA. **Intercollegiate:** Baseball M, basketball, cross-country, football (tackle) M, golf M, soccer, softball W, tennis, track and field, volleyball W. **Intramural:** Badminton, basketball, bowling, golf, racquetball, soccer, softball, swimming, table tennis, tennis, volleyball. **Team name:** Eagles.

Student services. Adult student services, career counseling, health services, personal counseling, placement for graduates, veterans' counselor. **Physically disabled:** Services for visually, hearing impaired.

Contact. E-mail: mredding@cn.edu
Phone: (865) 471-3223 Fax: (865) 471-3502
Melanie Redding, Director of Admissions, Carson-Newman College, 1646 Russell Avenue, Jefferson City, TN 37760

Christian Brothers University

Memphis, Tennessee   **CB member**
www.cbu.edu   **CB code: 1121**

- Private 4-year university affiliated with Roman Catholic Church
- Commuter campus in very large city
- 1,327 degree-seeking undergraduates: 10% part-time, 55% women, 35% African American, 5% Asian American, 5% Hispanic American, 3% international
- 346 degree-seeking graduate students
- 46% of applicants admitted
- SAT or ACT (ACT writing optional), application essay required
- 57% graduate within 6 years

General. Founded in 1871. Regionally accredited. **Degrees:** 243 bachelor's awarded; master's offered. **ROTC:** Army, Naval, Air Force. **Location:** 200 miles from Nashville; 150 miles from Little Rock, AR. **Calendar:** Semester, limited summer session. **Full-time faculty:** 106 total; 87% have terminal degrees, 14% minority, 33% women. **Part-time faculty:** 78 total; 64% have terminal degrees, 13% minority, 63% women. **Class size:** 65% < 20, 35% 20-39. **Special facilities:** Center for life sciences.

Freshman class profile. 2,130 applied, 989 admitted, 307 enrolled.

Mid 50% test scores			
ACT composite:	21-26	Rank in top tenth:	29%
GPA 3.75 or higher:	42%	Return as sophomores:	78%
GPA 3.50-3.74:	17%	Out-of-state:	23%
GPA 3.0-3.49:	30%	Live on campus:	61%
GPA 2.0-2.99:	10%	International:	5%
Rank in top quarter:	60%	Fraternities:	25%
		Sororities:	19%

Basis for selection. Graduation from approved secondary school or GED equivalent, 2.0 GPA, rank in upper 2/3 of graduating class, and satisfactory test scores required. Audition required for some programs; interview recommended for all.

High school preparation. Recommended units include English 4, mathematics 4 and science 4. College-preparatory program required of engineering applicants.

2011-2012 Annual costs. Tuition/fees: $26,110. Room/board: $6,390.

2011-2012 Financial aid. Non-need-based: Scholarships awarded for academics, alumni affiliation, athletics, music/drama, state residency. **Additional information:** ROTC scholarships available to qualified applicants.

Application procedures. Admission: Priority date 12/1; no deadline. $25 fee, may be waived for applicants with need. Admission notification on a rolling basis beginning on or about 12/1. Must reply by May 1 or within 3 week(s) if notified thereafter. **Financial aid:** Priority date 2/15; no closing date. FAFSA required. Applicants notified on a rolling basis starting 3/1; must reply within 2 week(s) of notification.

Academics. Special study options: Accelerated study, cross-registration, distance learning, double major, dual enrollment of high school students, honors, independent study, internships, liberal arts/career combination, study abroad, teacher certification program. **Credit/placement by examination:** AP, CLEP, IB, SAT, ACT, institutional tests. 30 credit hours maximum toward bachelor's degree. **Support services:** Pre-admission summer program, reduced course load, tutoring, writing center.

Majors. Biology: General, biochemistry, biomedical sciences. **Business:** General, accounting, business admin. **Computer sciences:** Computer science. **Education:** Biology, chemistry, early childhood, elementary, English, history, mathematics, physics, secondary, special ed. **Engineering:** Applied physics, chemical, civil, computer, electrical, mechanical. **English:** English lit. **Health services:** Nursing practice. **History:** General. **Liberal arts:** Arts/sciences. **Math:** General. **Philosophy/religion:** Philosophy, religion. **Physical sciences:** General, chemistry, physics. **Psychology:** General, applied. **Visual/performing arts:** Studio arts.

Most popular majors. Biology 7%, business/marketing 41%, engineering/engineering technologies 15%, English 8%, physical sciences 6%, psychology 15%.

Computing on campus. 310 workstations in dormitories, library, computer center, student center. Dormitories wired for high-speed internet access and linked to campus network. Commuter students can connect to campus network. Online course registration, online library, helpline, wireless network available.

Student life. Freshman orientation: Mandatory. Preregistration for classes offered. Held Friday-Monday before classes begin. **Housing:** Guaranteed on-campus for freshmen. Coed dorms, single-sex dorms, apartments available. $300 nonrefundable deposit, deadline 5/1. Juniors and seniors may live in on-campus apartments. Freshmen and sophomores whose permanent address is beyond a 30 mile radius required to live on-campus. **Activities:** Campus ministries, choral groups, drama, literary magazine, musical theater, student government, black student association, The Chosen Generation, intercultural club, Lasallian Volunteers, student peace association, Up 'Til Dawn.

Athletics. NCAA. **Intercollegiate:** Baseball M, basketball, cross-country, golf, soccer, softball W, tennis, volleyball W. **Intramural:** Basketball, bowling, football (non-tackle), soccer, softball, swimming, tennis, volleyball. **Team name:** Buccaneers.

Student services. Adult student services, alcohol/substance abuse counseling, chaplain/spiritual director, career counseling, student employment services, financial aid counseling, health services, minority student services, personal counseling, placement for graduates, veterans' counselor.

Contact. E-mail: admissions@cbu.edu
Phone: (901) 321-3205 Toll-free number: (800) 288-7576
Fax: (901) 321-3202
Anne Kenworthy, Dean of Admissions, Christian Brothers University, 650 East Parkway South, Memphis, TN 38104-5519

Cumberland University

Lebanon, Tennessee
www.cumberland.edu   **CB code: 1146**

- Private 4-year university and liberal arts college
- Commuter campus in large town
- 1,185 degree-seeking undergraduates: 8% part-time, 58% women, 11% African American, 1% Asian American, 2% Hispanic American, 1% Native American, 4% international
- 244 degree-seeking graduate students
- 49% of applicants admitted
- SAT or ACT (ACT writing optional), application essay required
- 34% graduate within 6 years

General. Founded in 1842. Regionally accredited. **Degrees:** 199 bachelor's, 1 associate awarded; master's offered. **ROTC:** Army. **Location:** 30 miles from Nashville. **Calendar:** Semester, limited summer session. **Full-time faculty:** 50 total; 58% have terminal degrees, 8% minority, 50% women. **Part-time faculty:** 99 total; 24% have terminal degrees, 11% minority, 63% women. **Class size:** 63% < 20, 29% 20-39, 4% 40-49, 4% 50-99.

Freshman class profile. 695 applied, 338 admitted, 191 enrolled.

Mid 50% test scores			
SAT critical reading:	430-560	Rank in top quarter:	43%
SAT math:	450-570	Rank in top tenth:	20%
SAT writing:	370-510	End year in good standing:	90%
ACT composite:	20-24	Return as sophomores:	70%
GPA 3.75 or higher:	28%	Out-of-state:	12%
GPA 3.50-3.74:	20%	Live on campus:	60%
GPA 3.0-3.49:	33%	International:	4%
GPA 2.0-2.99:	19%	Fraternities:	19%
		Sororities:	12%

Basis for selection. High school academic record and standardized test scores most important. Audition, portfolio required for some programs; interview recommended for academically weak. **Home schooled:** Transcript of courses and grades required.

High school preparation. College-preparatory program recommended. 16 units required; 19 recommended. Required and recommended units include English 4, mathematics 3-4, social studies 2, history 2, science 3 (laboratory 1-2) and foreign language 2.

2011-2012 Annual costs. Tuition/fees: $19,200. Room/board: $6,600. Books/supplies: $1,400. Personal expenses: $2,200.

Financial aid. Non-need-based: Scholarships awarded for academics, art, athletics, music/drama.

Application procedures. Admission: Priority date 2/15; no deadline. $25 fee, may be waived for applicants with need. Admission notification on a rolling basis beginning on or about 3/1. **Financial aid:** Priority date 2/1; no closing date. FAFSA, institutional form required. Applicants notified on a rolling basis starting 5/1; must reply within 2 week(s) of notification.

Academics. Selection of major or minor not required. **Special study options:** Accelerated study, combined bachelor's/graduate degree, cooperative education, distance learning, double major, dual enrollment of high school students, independent study, internships, liberal arts/career combination, teacher certification program. **Credit/placement by examination:** AP, CLEP, ACT, institutional tests. 30 credit hours maximum toward bachelor's degree. **Support services:** Learning center, pre-admission summer program, reduced course load, remedial instruction, study skills assistance, tutoring, writing center.

Majors. Area/ethnic studies: American. **Biology:** General. **Business:** General, accounting, management science. **Education:** General, biology, early childhood, elementary, English, history, mathematics, middle, multi-level teacher, music, physical, secondary, social science, special ed. **English:** English lit. **Health services:** Nursing (RN), predental, premedicine, prepharmacy, preveterinary. **History:** General. **Human services:** General. **Liberal arts:** Arts/sciences. **Math:** General. **Parks/recreation:** Health/fitness, sports admin. **Protective services:** Criminal justice. **Psychology:** General. **Social sciences:** General, political science, sociology. **Visual/performing arts:** Music, studio arts.

Most popular majors. Business/marketing 16%, education 12%, health sciences 46%, security/protective services 6%.

Computing on campus. 90 workstations in library, computer center. Dormitories linked to campus network. Commuter students can connect to campus network. Online library, helpline, repair service, wireless network available.

Student life. Freshman orientation: Mandatory, $100 fee. Preregistration for classes offered. 1-1/2 day session held in August. **Housing:** Single-sex dorms, apartments, wellness housing available. $200 fully refundable deposit, deadline 8/1. **Activities:** Bands, campus ministries, choral groups, dance, drama, music ensembles, musical theater, radio station, student government, student newspaper, Fellowship of Christian Athletes, African American student association, Campus Crusade for Christ, Champions for Christ.

Athletics. NAIA. **Intercollegiate:** Baseball M, basketball, bowling, cheerleading, cross-country, football (tackle) M, golf, soccer, softball W, tennis, volleyball W, wrestling M. **Intramural:** Basketball, football (non-tackle) M, softball, table tennis, volleyball. **Team name:** Bulldogs.

Student services. Adult student services, chaplain/spiritual director, career counseling, student employment services, financial aid counseling, health services, personal counseling, placement for graduates. **Physically disabled:** Services for visually impaired.

Contact. E-mail: admissions@cumberland.edu
Phone: (615) 444-2562 Toll-free number: (800) 467-0562
Fax: (615) 444-2569
Beatrice LaChance, Director of Enrollment Services, Cumberland University, One Cumberland Square, Lebanon, TN 37087

East Tennessee State University

Johnson City, Tennessee
www.etsu.edu

CB member
CB code: 1198

▶ Public 4-year university
▶ Commuter campus in small city
▶ 12,138 degree-seeking undergraduates: 13% part-time, 56% women, 6% African American, 1% Asian American, 2% Hispanic American, 1% international

▶ 2,587 degree-seeking graduate students
▶ 85% of applicants admitted
▶ SAT or ACT (ACT writing optional) required
▶ 44% graduate within 6 years

General. Founded in 1911. Regionally accredited. Additional campus in Kingsport. **Degrees:** 2,028 bachelor's awarded; master's, professional, doctoral offered. **ROTC:** Army. **Location:** 90 miles from Knoxville; 60 miles from Asheville, NC. **Calendar:** Semester, extensive summer session. **Full-time faculty:** 514 total. **Part-time faculty:** 296 total. **Class size:** 38% < 20, 49% 20-39, 5% 40-49, 5% 50-99, 3% >100. **Special facilities:** Appalachian archives, planetarium, observatory, arboretum.

Freshman class profile. 5,269 applied, 4,482 admitted, 2,140 enrolled.

Mid 50% test scores			
SAT critical reading:	430-550	Rank in top quarter:	43%
SAT math:	430-540	Rank in top tenth:	17%
ACT composite:	19-24	Return as sophomores:	70%
GPA 3.75 or higher:	23%	Out-of-state:	12%
GPA 3.50-3.74:	18%	Live on campus:	55%
GPA 3.0-3.49:	31%	International:	1%
GPA 2.0-2.99:	27%	Fraternities:	5%
		Sororities:	5%

Basis for selection. 2.3 GPA or 19 ACT/SAT equivelent required. COMPASS may be required if ACT/SAT scores do not meet minimums. Interview recommended for dental hygiene, health-related professions, nursing, physical therapy programs; audition required for music; portfolio recommended for art. **Home schooled:** Transcript of courses and grades required.

High school preparation. College-preparatory program required. 14 units required; 16 recommended. Required and recommended units include English 4, mathematics 3-4, social studies 1, history 1, science 2-3 (laboratory 1), foreign language 2 and visual/performing arts 1.

2011-2012 Annual costs. Tuition/fees: $6,529; $20,767 out-of-state. Room/board: $6,100. Books/supplies: $1,090. Personal expenses: $4,146.

Financial aid. Non-need-based: Scholarships awarded for academics, alumni affiliation, art, athletics, leadership, minority status, music/drama, religious affiliation, ROTC, state residency. **Additional information:** Housing costs payable by installment.

Application procedures. Admission: Priority date 7/1; no deadline. $25 fee, may be waived for applicants with need. Admission notification on a rolling basis beginning on or about 9/1. **Financial aid:** Priority date 4/15; no closing date. FAFSA required. Applicants notified on a rolling basis starting 4/15; must reply within 3 week(s) of notification.

Academics. Special study options: Combined bachelor's/graduate degree, cooperative education, distance learning, double major, dual enrollment of high school students, ESL, exchange student, external degree, honors, independent study, internships, student-designed major, study abroad, teacher certification program. **Credit/placement by examination:** AP, CLEP, IB, SAT, ACT, institutional tests. **Support services:** Learning center, reduced course load, study skills assistance, tutoring, writing center.

Honors college/program. 29 ACT/comparable SAT and 3.5 GPA required; 20 new freshmen selected each year for specifically designed courses.

Majors. Biology: General. **Business:** Accounting, business admin, finance, managerial economics, marketing. **Communications:** Media studies. **Communications technology:** Animation/special effects. **Computer sciences:** General. **Education:** Special ed. **English:** English lit, rhetoric/composition. **Foreign languages:** General. **Health services:** Dental hygiene, environmental health, nursing (RN). **History:** General. **Human services:** Social work. **Liberal arts:** Arts/sciences. **Math:** General. **Parks/recreation:** Health/fitness, sports admin. **Philosophy/religion:** Philosophy. **Physical sciences:** Chemistry, physics. **Protective services:** Law enforcement admin. **Psychology:** General. **Social sciences:** Economics, geography, political science, sociology. **Visual/performing arts:** Art, music. **Work/family studies:** General, child development, family studies.

Most popular majors. Business/marketing 15%, education 6%, health sciences 20%, liberal arts 8%.

Computing on campus. 1,400 workstations in dormitories, library, computer center, student center. Dormitories wired for high-speed internet access and linked to campus network. Commuter students can connect to campus network. Online course registration, online library, helpline, repair service, student web hosting, wireless network available.

Student life. Freshman orientation: Mandatory. Preregistration for classes offered. Five sessions during summer, each for 1-2 days. **Housing:** Coed dorms, single-sex dorms, special housing for disabled, apartments, fraternity/sorority housing, wellness housing available. $100 fully refundable

deposit. **Activities:** Bands, campus ministries, choral groups, drama, international student organizations, literary magazine, music ensembles, radio station, student government, student newspaper, TV station, Baptist student union, Campus Crusade, Catholic center, Christian student fellowship, Fellowship of Christian Athletes, Real Life Fellowship, Wesley Foundation, Black Affairs Association.

Athletics. NCAA. **Intercollegiate:** Baseball M, basketball, cross-country, golf, soccer, softball W, tennis, track and field, volleyball W. **Intramural:** Basketball, cross-country, football (non-tackle), golf, handball, racquetball, softball, tennis, volleyball W, weight lifting M. **Team name:** Buccaneers.

Student services. Adult student services, alcohol/substance abuse counseling, chaplain/spiritual director, career counseling, services for economically disadvantaged, student employment services, financial aid counseling, health services, legal services, minority student services, on-campus daycare, personal counseling, placement for graduates, veterans' counselor, women's services. **Physically disabled:** Services for visually, speech, hearing impaired.

Contact. E-mail: go2etsu@etsu.edu
Phone: (423) 439-4213 Toll-free number: (800) 462-3878
Fax: (423) 439-4630
Michael Pitts, Director of Admissions, East Tennessee State University, ETSU Box 70731, Johnson City, TN 37614

Fisk University
Nashville, Tennessee
www.fisk.edu

CB member
CB code: 1224

- Private 4-year liberal arts college affiliated with United Church of Christ
- Residential campus in very large city
- 480 degree-seeking undergraduates: 6% part-time, 64% women, 78% African American, 8% international
- 53 degree-seeking graduate students
- 100% of applicants admitted
- SAT or ACT (ACT writing optional), interview required
- 40% graduate within 6 years

General. Founded in 1866. Regionally accredited. **Degrees:** 99 bachelor's awarded; master's offered. **ROTC:** Army, Naval. **Location:** 216 miles from Memphis, 225 miles from Atlanta. **Calendar:** Semester, limited summer session. **Full-time faculty:** 49 total; 84% have terminal degrees, 69% minority, 49% women. **Part-time faculty:** 26 total; 54% have terminal degrees, 81% minority, 46% women. **Class size:** 84% < 20, 16% 20-39, less than 1% 40-49.

Freshman class profile. 1,864 applied, 1,864 admitted, 125 enrolled.

Mid 50% test scores			
SAT critical reading:	410-560	GPA 2.0-2.99:	48%
SAT math:	420-540	Rank in top quarter:	27%
SAT writing:	420-560	Rank in top tenth:	13%
ACT composite:	18-24	End year in good standing:	78%
GPA 3.75 or higher:	8%	Return as sophomores:	75%
GPA 3.50-3.74:	12%	Out-of-state:	64%
GPA 3.0-3.49:	27%	Live on campus:	91%
		International:	6%

Basis for selection. School achievement record, class rank, test scores, recommendations, activities important. Essay recommended for all; audition recommended for music. Interview required for scholarship nominees and must take place prior to 2/15.

High school preparation. College-preparatory program recommended. 20 units recommended. Recommended units include English 4, mathematics 3, social studies 3, history 1, science 3, foreign language 1 and academic electives 6. 1 Algebra I, 1 Geometry, and 1 Algebra II recommended.

2012-2013 Annual costs. Tuition/fees (projected): $20,391. Room/board: $9,546. Books/supplies: $2,000. Personal expenses: $2,000.

2010-2011 Financial aid. All financial aid based on need. 161 full-time freshmen applied for aid; 153 were judged to have need; 153 of these received aid. Average need met was 87%. Average scholarship/grant was $12,661; average loan $3,202. 60% of total undergraduate aid awarded as scholarships/grants, 40% as loans/jobs.

Application procedures. **Admission:** Priority date 3/1; no deadline. $50 fee, may be waived for applicants with need. Application must be submitted on paper. Admission notification on a rolling basis. **Financial aid:** Priority date 3/1, closing date 7/1. FAFSA required. Applicants notified on a rolling basis starting 4/1; must reply within 2 week(s) of notification.

Academics. **Special study options:** Combined bachelor's/graduate degree, cooperative education, cross-registration, double major, dual enrollment of high school students, exchange student, honors, independent study, internships, liberal arts/career combination, student-designed major, study abroad, teacher certification program. 2-2 program with Rush-Presbyterian-St. Luke's Medical Center in nursing, dual degree in science and engineering, dual degree in engineering and natural sciences in 5 years, 3-3 program with Howard University for Doctor of Pharmacy, 5-year MBA program with Vanderbilt University, 7-year MD, PhD, DDS programs with Meharry Medical College. **Credit/placement by examination:** AP, CLEP, IB, SAT, ACT, institutional tests. 30 credit hours maximum toward bachelor's degree. **Support services:** Learning center, pre-admission summer program, tutoring, writing center.

Majors. **Biology:** General. **Business:** Business admin. **Computer sciences:** Computer science. **Education:** Music, special ed. **English:** English lit. **Foreign languages:** Spanish. **Health services:** Nursing (RN). **History:** General. **Math:** General. **Physical sciences:** Chemistry, physics. **Psychology:** General. **Social sciences:** Political science, sociology. **Visual/performing arts:** Art, music, music performance.

Most popular majors. Biology 17%, business/marketing 21%, English 8%, physical sciences 9%, psychology 17%, social sciences 13%, visual/performing arts 6%.

Computing on campus. 100 workstations in dormitories, library, computer center. Dormitories wired for high-speed internet access and linked to campus network. Online course registration, helpline, student web hosting, wireless network available.

Student life. **Freshman orientation:** Mandatory, $350 fee. Preregistration for classes offered. 3-5 day orientation held 1 week before classes. **Policies:** All students required to live on-campus, with few exceptions. Freshmen have 12 am curfew. **Housing:** Guaranteed on-campus for all undergraduates. Single-sex dorms, special housing for disabled available. $100 nonrefundable deposit, deadline 7/15. **Activities:** Jazz band, campus ministries, choral groups, dance, drama, literary magazine, music ensembles, radio station, student government, student newspaper, TV station, Baptist student union, Muslim student association, Nation of Islam, Carribean student union, African student association, race relations students organization.

Athletics. NAIA. **Intercollegiate:** Basketball, cross-country, softball W, tennis, track and field, volleyball W. **Intramural:** Basketball, football (non-tackle), soccer M, tennis, volleyball W, weight lifting M. **Team name:** Bulldogs.

Student services. Career counseling, student employment services, financial aid counseling, health services, personal counseling, placement for graduates.

Contact. E-mail: admit@fisk.edu
Phone: (615) 329-8665 Toll-free number: (888) 702-0022
Fax: (615) 329-8774
Anthony Jones, Director of Recruitment and Admission, Fisk University, 1000 Seventeenth Avenue North, Nashville, TN 37208-3051

Free Will Baptist Bible College
Nashville, Tennessee
www.fwbbc.edu

CB code: 1232

- Private 4-year Bible and teachers college affiliated with Free Will Baptists
- Residential campus in very large city
- 249 degree-seeking undergraduates: 19% part-time, 50% women, 9% African American, 2% Hispanic American, 1% international
- Application essay required
- 49% graduate within 6 years

General. Founded in 1942. Regionally accredited; also accredited by ABHE. **Degrees:** 22 bachelor's, 7 associate awarded. **ROTC:** Army, Air Force. **Location:** 3 miles from downtown. **Calendar:** Semester, limited summer session. **Full-time faculty:** 21 total; 33% have terminal degrees, 24% women. **Part-time faculty:** 34 total; 35% have terminal degrees, 6% minority, 35% women. **Class size:** 92% < 20, 7% 20-39, 1% 40-49.

Freshman class profile.

Mid 50% test scores			
ACT composite:	16-27	GPA 2.0-2.99:	34%
GPA 3.75 or higher:	34%	Return as sophomores:	59%
GPA 3.50-3.74:	11%	Out-of-state:	54%
GPA 3.0-3.49:	19%	Live on campus:	84%

Basis for selection. Open admission. Applicants without high school diploma or GED must pass GED prior to receiving degree.

High school preparation. 22 units recommended. Recommended units include English 4, mathematics 4, social studies 3, history 2, science 4, foreign language 3 and academic electives 2.

2011-2012 Annual costs. Tuition/fees: $14,306. Room/board: $6,042. Books/supplies: $800. Personal expenses: $820.

2010-2011 Financial aid. Need-based: 44 full-time freshmen applied for aid; 43 were judged to have need; 43 of these received aid. Average scholarship/grant was $2,411; average loan $4,973. **Non-need-based:** Awarded to 108 full-time undergraduates, including 36 freshmen. Scholarships awarded for academics, alumni affiliation, art, music/drama.

Application procedures. Admission: Priority date 4/15; no deadline. $35 fee, may be waived for applicants with need. Admission notification on a rolling basis. **Financial aid:** Priority date 4/15; no closing date. FAFSA, institutional form required. Applicants notified on a rolling basis starting 7/1; must reply within 2 week(s) of notification.

Academics. Special study options: Distance learning, double major, dual enrollment of high school students, independent study, internships, teacher certification program. **Credit/placement by examination:** AP, CLEP, IB, institutional tests. 16 credit hours maximum toward bachelor's degree. **Support services:** Reduced course load, remedial instruction, tutoring.

Majors. Business: Business admin. **Education:** Early childhood, elementary, music, physical, secondary. **English:** English lit. **History:** General. **Parks/recreation:** Exercise sciences. **Psychology:** General. **Theology:** Bible, missionary, religious ed, theology. **Visual/performing arts:** Music.

Most popular majors. Business/marketing 15%, education 24%, psychology 15%, theological studies 37%.

Computing on campus. 34 workstations in library, computer center, student center. Commuter students can connect to campus network. Online library, repair service, wireless network available.

Student life. Freshman orientation: Mandatory. Preregistration for classes offered. **Policies:** Religious observance required. **Housing:** Single-sex dorms, apartments available. $100 fully refundable deposit, deadline 8/1. Single students required to live on campus unless living with parents or close relatives. **Activities:** Campus ministries, choral groups, drama, music ensembles, musical theater, student government, ministerial and missionary organizations, Christian service assignments, organization for business students, literary societies.

Athletics. NCCAA. **Intercollegiate:** Baseball M, basketball, cross-country, golf, volleyball W. **Intramural:** Basketball, table tennis, tennis, volleyball. **Team name:** Flames.

Student services. Career counseling, student employment services, financial aid counseling, personal counseling, placement for graduates, veterans' counselor.

Contact. E-mail: recruit@fwbbc.edu
Phone: (615) 844-5000 Toll-free number: (800) 763-9222
Fax: (615) 269-6028
Rusty Campbell, Director of Enrollment Services, Free Will Baptist Bible College, 3606 West End Avenue, Nashville, TN 37205-2403

Freed-Hardeman University
Henderson, Tennessee
www.fhu.edu

CB member
CB code: 1230

- Private 4-year university and liberal arts college affiliated with Church of Christ
- Residential campus in small town
- 1,439 degree-seeking undergraduates: 3% part-time, 56% women, 6% African American, 1% Hispanic American
- 482 graduate students
- 99% of applicants admitted
- SAT or ACT (ACT writing recommended) required
- 58% graduate within 6 years

General. Founded in 1869. Regionally accredited. Campus in Verviers, Belgium. **Degrees:** 261 bachelor's awarded; master's offered. **Location:** 15 miles from Jackson, 85 miles from Memphis. **Calendar:** Semester, limited summer session. **Full-time faculty:** 96 total. **Part-time faculty:** 50 total. **Class size:** 52% < 20, 41% 20-39, 6% 40-49, 1% 50-99.

Freshman class profile. 1,082 applied, 1,073 admitted, 387 enrolled.

Mid 50% test scores		
SAT critical reading:	480-620	
SAT math:	490-600	
ACT composite:	19-26	
GPA 3.75 or higher:	39%	
GPA 3.50-3.74:	20%	
GPA 3.0-3.49:	27%	
GPA 2.0-2.99:	14%
Rank in top quarter:	58%
Rank in top tenth:	28%
Return as sophomores:	71%
Out-of-state:	50%
Live on campus:	90%

Basis for selection. Admissions based on school achievement record, test scores, references. Applicants without minimum test score or GPA may be admitted with restrictions after further evaluation.

High school preparation. 20 units recommended. Recommended units include English 4, mathematics 2, social studies 2, science 2 and academic electives 10. Additional science and math courses recommended.

2011-2012 Annual costs. Tuition/fees: $16,958. Room/board: $7,296. Books/supplies: $1,300. Personal expenses: $2,080.

Financial aid. Non-need-based: Scholarships awarded for academics, art, athletics, leadership, minority status, music/drama.

Application procedures. Admission: No deadline. No application fee. Admission notification on a rolling basis. **Financial aid:** Priority date 2/1; no closing date. FAFSA required. Applicants notified on a rolling basis starting 3/10; must reply within 4 week(s) of notification.

Academics. Students enrolled for 12 or more undergraduate hours must register for Bible class. **Special study options:** Accelerated study, combined bachelor's/graduate degree, cooperative education, cross-registration, distance learning, double major, dual enrollment of high school students, honors, independent study, internships, liberal arts/career combination, student-designed major, study abroad, teacher certification program. 3-2 engineering co-op. **Credit/placement by examination:** AP, CLEP, IB, SAT, ACT, institutional tests. 33 credit hours maximum toward bachelor's degree. **Support services:** Learning center, reduced course load, remedial instruction, study skills assistance, tutoring.

Honors college/program. Approximately 5% of freshmen class admitted to honors course work as result of competitive application process.

Majors. Biology: General, biochemistry. **Business:** Accounting, business admin, finance, human resources, management information systems, marketing. **Communications:** Communications/speech/rhetoric, journalism, media studies, public relations. **Computer sciences:** General. **Education:** Art, biology, curriculum, early childhood, elementary, English, history, mathematics, middle, multi-level teacher, music, physical, science, secondary, special ed. **English:** English lit. **Health services:** Health care admin. **History:** General. **Human services:** Social work. **Liberal arts:** Arts/sciences. **Math:** General. **Parks/recreation:** Exercise sciences. **Philosophy/religion:** Philosophy. **Physical sciences:** General, chemistry. **Protective services:** Criminal justice. **Psychology:** General. **Social sciences:** General. **Theology:** Bible, missionary, theology. **Visual/performing arts:** Acting, art, design, interior design, music, theater design. **Work/family studies:** Family studies.

Most popular majors. Biology 10%, business/marketing 11%, education 17%, family/consumer sciences 6%, health sciences 7%, interdisciplinary studies 11%, theological studies 8%, visual/performing arts 7%.

Computing on campus. 238 workstations in dormitories, library, computer center, student center. Dormitories wired for high-speed internet access and linked to campus network. Commuter students can connect to campus network. Online course registration, online library, helpline, repair service, wireless network available.

Student life. Freshman orientation: Mandatory. Preregistration for classes offered. Held the 4 days prior to start of classes in August. **Policies:** Daily chapel is mandatory. Nightly curfew enforced. Religious observance required. **Housing:** Guaranteed on-campus for freshmen. Single-sex dorms, apartments, wellness housing available. $100 nonrefundable deposit, deadline 4/1. Housing deposit refundable up to 30 days prior to term. Some student-teacher housing available for education majors. **Activities:** Bands, choral groups, drama, music ensembles, musical theater, radio station, student government, student newspaper, TV station, evangelism forum, preachers club, student-alumni association, university student ambassadors, university program council, youth workers club, Impact Team, Young Republicans, Young Democrats.

Athletics. NAIA. **Intercollegiate:** Baseball M, basketball, cheerleading W, cross-country, soccer, softball W, volleyball W. **Intramural:** Badminton, basketball, football (non-tackle), racquetball, soccer, softball, table tennis, tennis, volleyball. **Team name:** Lions.

Student services. Alcohol/substance abuse counseling, chaplain/spiritual director, career counseling, student employment services, financial aid counseling, health services, on-campus daycare, personal counseling, placement

for graduates, veterans' counselor. **Physically disabled:** Services for visually, hearing impaired.

Contact. E-mail: admissions@fhu.edu
Phone: (731) 989-6651 Toll-free number: (800) 348-3480
Fax: (731) 989-6047
Joseph Askew, Director of Admissions, Freed-Hardeman University, 158 East Main Street, Henderson, TN 38340

International Academy of Design and Technology: Nashville
Nashville, Tennessee
www.iadtnashville.com

- For-profit 4-year branch campus and visual arts college
- Commuter campus in very large city
- 435 degree-seeking undergraduates

General. Accredited by ACICS. **Degrees:** 28 bachelor's, 129 associate awarded. **Calendar:** Quarter, extensive summer session. **Full-time faculty:** 10 total. **Part-time faculty:** 42 total.

Basis for selection. Open admission.

2011-2012 Annual costs. Tuition/fees: $12,975. Books/supplies: $1,800.

Application procedures. Admission: No deadline. $50 fee. **Financial aid:** No deadline.

Academics. Credit/placement by examination: AP, CLEP.

Majors. Business: Fashion. **Visual/performing arts:** Fashion design, graphic design, interior design.

Computing on campus. Online library available.

Student life. Freshman orientation: Available. Preregistration for classes offered.

Student services. Student employment services, financial aid counseling, placement for graduates.

Contact. E-mail: admissions@iadtnashville.com
Phone: (866) 302-4238
Sonya Flanagan-Ensign, Director of Admissions, International Academy of Design and Technology: Nashville, 1 Bridgestone Park, Nashville, TN 37214

ITT Technical Institute: Knoxville
Knoxville, Tennessee
www.itt-tech.edu   CB code: 7139

- For-profit 4-year technical college
- Commuter campus in small city
- 943 undergraduates
- Interview required

General. Accredited by ACICS. **Degrees:** 75 bachelor's, 224 associate awarded. **Calendar:** Quarter, extensive summer session. **Full-time faculty:** 12 total. **Part-time faculty:** 63 total.

Basis for selection. Satisfactory scores from on-site test in English and mathematics required.

2011-2012 Annual costs. Estimated costs as of July 2011: per-credit-hour charge, $493, depending upon level and course of study; academic fee, $200. Certain programs of study require purchase of tools, which could cost an additional $100 to $500. All costs are subject to change.

Application procedures. Admission: No deadline. No application fee. Admission notification on a rolling basis. **Financial aid:** No deadline. FAFSA, institutional form required. Applicants notified on a rolling basis.

Academics. Credit/placement by examination: AP, CLEP. **Support services:** Learning center, tutoring.

Majors. Business: Business admin, construction management, e-commerce. **Communications technology:** Animation/special effects. **Computer sciences:** Networking, security. **Protective services:** Criminal justice.

Computing on campus. Online library available.

Student life. Freshman orientation: Available. Preregistration for classes offered.

Student services. Career counseling, student employment services, placement for graduates.

Contact. Phone: (865) 671-2800 Toll-free number: (800) 671-2801
Fax: (865) 671-2811
Holly Winters, Director of Recruitment, ITT Technical Institute: Knoxville, 10208 Technology Drive, Knoxville, TN 37932

ITT Technical Institute: Memphis
Cordova, Tennessee
www.itt-tech.edu   CB code: 2731

- For-profit 4-year technical college
- Commuter campus in very large city
- 912 undergraduates
- Interview required

General. Accredited by ACICS. **Degrees:** 80 bachelor's, 173 associate awarded. **Calendar:** Quarter, extensive summer session. **Full-time faculty:** 12 total. **Part-time faculty:** 107 total.

Basis for selection. Satisfactory scores from on-site tests in English and mathematics required.

2011-2012 Annual costs. Estimated costs as of June 2011: per-credit-hour charge, $493, depending upon level and course of study; academic fee, $200. Certain programs of study require purchase of tools, which could cost an additional $100 to $500. All costs are subject to change.

Application procedures. Admission: No application fee. Admission notification on a rolling basis. **Financial aid:** No deadline. FAFSA, institutional form required. Applicants notified on a rolling basis.

Academics. Credit/placement by examination: AP, CLEP. **Support services:** Learning center, tutoring.

Majors. Business: Accounting technology, accounting/business management, business admin, construction management, e-commerce. **Computer sciences:** Security. **Protective services:** Law enforcement admin. **Visual/performing arts:** Game design.

Computing on campus. Online library available.

Student life. Freshman orientation: Available. Preregistration for classes offered.

Student services. Career counseling, student employment services, placement for graduates.

Contact. Phone: (901) 762-0556 Toll-free number: (866) 444-5141
Fax: (901) 762-0566
James Mills, Director of Recruitment, ITT Technical Institute: Memphis, 7260 Goodlett Farms Parkway, Cordova, TN 38016

ITT Technical Institute: Nashville
Nashville, Tennessee
www.itt-tech.edu   CB code: 7025

- For-profit 4-year technical college
- Commuter campus in very large city
- 1,010 undergraduates
- Interview required

General. Accredited by ACICS. **Degrees:** 93 bachelor's, 212 associate awarded. **Calendar:** Quarter, extensive summer session. **Full-time faculty:** 10 total. **Part-time faculty:** 75 total.

Basis for selection. Satisfactory scores from on-site English and mathematics tests required.

2011-2012 Annual costs. Estimated costs as of June 2011: per-credit-hour charge, $493, depending upon level and course of study; academic fee, $200. Certain programs of study require purchase of tools, which could cost an additional $100 to $500. All costs are subject to change.

Application procedures. **Admission:** No deadline. No application fee. Admission notification on a rolling basis. **Financial aid:** No deadline. FAFSA, institutional form required. Applicants notified on a rolling basis.

Academics. **Credit/placement by examination:** AP, CLEP. **Support services:** Learning center, tutoring.

Majors. **Business:** Accounting/business management, business admin, construction management, e-commerce. **Communications technology:** Animation/special effects. **Computer sciences:** Networking, security, system admin. **Protective services:** Criminal justice.

Computing on campus. Online library available.

Student life. **Freshman orientation:** Available. Preregistration for classes offered.

Student services. Career counseling, student employment services, placement for graduates.

Contact. Phone: (615) 889-8700 Toll-free number: (800) 331-8386 Fax: (615) 872-7209
James Royster, Director of Recruitment, ITT Technical Institute: Nashville, 2845 Elm Hill Pike, Nashville, TN 37214

Johnson University
Knoxville, Tennessee
www.jbc.edu   CB code: 1345

- Private 4-year Bible college affiliated with Christian Church
- Residential campus in large city
- 725 degree-seeking undergraduates
- SAT or ACT (ACT writing recommended), application essay required

General. Founded in 1893. Regionally accredited; also accredited by ABHE. **Degrees:** 135 bachelor's, 15 associate awarded; master's offered. **Location:** 7 miles from Knoxville. **Calendar:** Semester, limited summer session. **Full-time faculty:** 35 total. **Part-time faculty:** 38 total. **Class size:** 61% < 20, 20% 20-39, 9% 40-49, 8% 50-99, 2% >100.

Freshman class profile.

Mid 50% test scores			
SAT critical reading:	480-590	GPA 3.50-3.74:	13%
SAT math:	460-610	GPA 3.0-3.49:	32%
ACT composite:	20-26	GPA 2.0-2.99:	13%
GPA 3.75 or higher:	42%	Out-of-state:	72%
		Live on campus:	93%

Basis for selection. High school transcript and 3 references, 1 from minister required. Essay, combination of high school percentile rank and ACT determines initial admission criteria. 19 ACT and 1350 SAT required for teacher education. Interview recommended.

High school preparation. 16 units required. Required units include academic electives 4. 12 of the 16 units must be content courses such as English, history, mathematics, foreign language, and science.

2011-2012 Annual costs. Tuition/fees: $9,630. Room/board: $5,550. Books/supplies: $900. Personal expenses: $2,060.

Financial aid. **Non-need-based:** Scholarships awarded for academics, leadership, minority status, music/drama, religious affiliation, state residency.

Application procedures. **Admission:** Closing date 6/1 (receipt date). $35 fee. Admission notification on a rolling basis. **Financial aid:** Closing date 3/1. FAFSA, institutional form required. Applicants notified on a rolling basis starting 4/30; must reply within 2 week(s) of notification.

Academics. Majors in Bible with double major in music, teacher education, counseling, preaching, or youth ministry/preaching offered. **Special study options:** Accelerated study, combined bachelor's/graduate degree, cooperative education, distance learning, double major, ESL, honors, independent study, internships, teacher certification program. **Credit/placement by examination:** AP, CLEP, SAT, ACT, institutional tests. 32 credit hours maximum toward bachelor's degree. **Support services:** Learning center, remedial instruction, study skills assistance, tutoring.

Majors. **Business:** Nonprofit/public. **Education:** Elementary. **Psychology:** Counseling. **Theology:** Bible, sacred music.

Most popular majors. Education 29%, philosophy/religious studies 71%.

Computing on campus. 50 workstations in library, computer center. Dormitories linked to campus network. Commuter students can connect to campus network. Helpline, student web hosting, wireless network available.

Student life. **Freshman orientation:** Mandatory. Preregistration for classes offered. Held the weekend preceeding first semester. **Policies:** Religious observance required. **Housing:** Guaranteed on-campus for freshmen. Single-sex dorms, apartments, wellness housing available. $100 fully refundable deposit, deadline 8/1. Mobile homes, duplex houses, available for family housing. **Activities:** Jazz band, campus ministries, choral groups, drama, literary magazine, music ensembles, musical theater, radio station, student government.

Athletics. NCCAA. **Intercollegiate:** Baseball M, basketball, soccer, volleyball W. **Intramural:** Basketball, softball, tennis, volleyball.

Student services. Alcohol/substance abuse counseling, chaplain/spiritual director, career counseling, student employment services, financial aid counseling, health services, on-campus daycare, personal counseling, placement for graduates. **Physically disabled:** Services for visually impaired.

Contact. E-mail: twingfield@jbc.edu
Phone: (865) 251-2233 Toll-free number: (800) 827-2122
Fax: (865) 251-2336
Tim Wingfield, Director of Admissions, Johnson University, 7900 Johnson Drive, Knoxville, TN 37998-0001

King College
Bristol, Tennessee   CB member
www.king.edu   CB code: 1371

- Private 4-year nursing and liberal arts college affiliated with Presbyterian Church (USA)
- Residential campus in large town
- 1,802 degree-seeking undergraduates
- 325 graduate students
- 66% of applicants admitted
- SAT or ACT (ACT writing optional), application essay required
- 42% graduate within 6 years

General. Founded in 1867. Regionally accredited. Christian values emphasized. **Degrees:** 466 bachelor's awarded; master's offered. **ROTC:** Army. **Location:** 110 miles from Knoxville; 95 miles from Asheville, NC. **Calendar:** Semester, extensive summer session. **Full-time faculty:** 86 total; 71% have terminal degrees, 7% minority, 57% women. **Part-time faculty:** 96 total; 41% have terminal degrees, 57% women. **Class size:** 62% < 20, 34% 20-39, 3% 40-49, less than 1% 50-99. **Special facilities:** Observatory, nuclear physics laboratory.

Freshman class profile. 901 applied, 599 admitted, 174 enrolled.

Mid 50% test scores			
		GPA 2.0-2.99:	17%
SAT critical reading:	450-540	Rank in top quarter:	40%
SAT math:	430-530	Rank in top tenth:	15%
SAT writing:	400-520	Return as sophomores:	67%
ACT composite:	20-26	Out-of-state:	50%
GPA 3.75 or higher:	25%	Live on campus:	55%
GPA 3.50-3.74:	23%	International:	6%
GPA 3.0-3.49:	35%		

Basis for selection. Qualified applicants have 2.4 GPA and 19 ACT/890 SAT (exclusive of Writing). Others may be conditionally accepted. SAT Writing used for financial aid eligibility purposes only. Interview recommended.

High school preparation. College-preparatory program recommended. 16 units required; 22 recommended. Required and recommended units include English 4, mathematics 2-4, social studies 1-2, history 1-2, science 1-4 (laboratory 1-4), foreign language 2 and academic electives 4. 2 algebra (I and II); one unit of geometry; 1 natural science required.

2011-2012 Annual costs. Tuition/fees: $24,052. Tuition and fees include laptop computer. Room/board: $8,180. Books/supplies: $1,200.

2011-2012 Financial aid. **Need-based:** Average need met was 78%. Average scholarship/grant was $19,321; average loan $3,398. 57% of total undergraduate aid awarded as scholarships/grants, 43% as loans/jobs. **Non-need-based:** Scholarships awarded for academics, art, athletics, job skills, music/drama, state residency.

Application procedures. **Admission:** No deadline. $20 fee, may be waived for applicants with need, free for online applicants. Admission notification on a rolling basis beginning on or about 9/1. **Financial aid:** Priority date 3/1; no closing date. FAFSA required. Applicants notified on a rolling basis starting 3/1; must reply within 2 week(s) of notification.

Academics. Special study options: Accelerated study, combined bachelor's/graduate degree, cross-registration, double major, dual enrollment of high school students, exchange student, honors, independent study, internships, student-designed major, study abroad, teacher certification program. **Credit/placement by examination:** AP, CLEP, SAT, ACT. 30 credit hours maximum toward bachelor's degree. **Support services:** Learning center, reduced course load, remedial instruction, study skills assistance, tutoring, writing center.

Honors college/program. Specific score on entrance exam required.

Majors. Area/ethnic studies: American. **Biology:** General, biochemistry, biophysics, neuroscience. **Business:** Accounting, business admin, management information systems. **Communications:** Digital media. **Computer sciences:** Information technology. **Education:** Music, physical. **English:** English lit. **Foreign languages:** General, French, Spanish. **Health services:** Athletic training, clinical lab science, nursing (RN). **History:** General. **Math:** General. **Parks/recreation:** Health/fitness. **Philosophy/religion:** Religion. **Physical sciences:** Chemistry, physics. **Psychology:** General. **Social sciences:** Economics, political science. **Theology:** Bible, youth ministry. **Visual/performing arts:** General, photography.

Most popular majors. Business/marketing 30%, health sciences 40%.

Computing on campus. PC or laptop required. 88 workstations in library, computer center, student center. Dormitories wired for high-speed internet access and linked to campus network. Commuter students can connect to campus network. Online library, helpline, repair service, wireless network available.

Student life. Freshman orientation: Available. Preregistration for classes offered. **Policies:** Traditional undergraduates participate in Chapel and Convocation series as part of service requirements necessary to fulfill degree requirements. Religious observance required. **Housing:** Guaranteed on-campus for all undergraduates. Single-sex dorms available. $250 fully refundable deposit. **Activities:** Bands, campus ministries, choral groups, dance, drama, international student organizations, music ensembles, musical theater, student government, student newspaper, Fellowship of Christian Athletes, Young Life Leadership, student life and activities committee, Students in Free Enterprise, College Republicans, World Christian Fellowship, literary society.

Athletics. NCAA. **Intercollegiate:** Baseball M, basketball, cheerleading, cross-country, golf, soccer, softball W, swimming, tennis, track and field, volleyball W, wrestling. **Intramural:** Badminton, basketball, cross-country, football (non-tackle), golf, soccer, softball W, table tennis, track and field, volleyball. **Team name:** Tornado.

Student services. Adult student services, chaplain/spiritual director, career counseling, student employment services, financial aid counseling, health services, personal counseling, placement for graduates.

Contact. E-mail: admissions@king.edu
Phone: (423) 652-4861 Toll-free number: (800) 362-0014
Fax: (423) 652-4727
Micah Crews, Enrollment Management, King College, 1350 King College Road, Bristol, TN 37620-2699

Lane College
Jackson, Tennessee
www.lanecollege.edu
CB code: 1395

◆ Private 4-year liberal arts college affiliated with Christian Methodist Episcopal Church
◆ Residential campus in small city
◆ 2,002 degree-seeking undergraduates: 1% part-time, 52% women
◆ 33% of applicants admitted
◆ SAT or ACT (ACT writing optional) required
◆ 33% graduate within 6 years; 36% enter graduate study

General. Founded in 1882. Regionally accredited. **Degrees:** 307 bachelor's awarded. **Location:** 80 miles from Memphis, 126 miles from Nashville. **Calendar:** Semester, limited summer session. **Full-time faculty:** 95 total. **Part-time faculty:** 1 total. **Class size:** 35% < 20, 63% 20-39, 1% 40-49, less than 1% 50-99.

Freshman class profile. 6,350 applied, 2,125 admitted, 601 enrolled.

Mid 50% test scores			
ACT composite:	16-19	Rank in top quarter:	8%
GPA 3.75 or higher:	1%	Rank in top tenth:	5%
GPA 3.50-3.74:	2%	End year in good standing:	90%
GPA 3.0-3.49:	10%	Return as sophomores:	58%
GPA 2.0-2.99:	66%	Out-of-state:	44%
		Live on campus:	97%

Basis for selection. School achievement record and recommendations most important.

High school preparation. College-preparatory program recommended. 16 units recommended. Recommended units include English 4, mathematics 2, social studies 2, science 2 and foreign language 2.

2011-2012 Annual costs. Tuition/fees: $8,220. Room/board: $5,800. Books/supplies: $1,100. Personal expenses: $650.

2010-2011 Financial aid. Need-based: 589 full-time freshmen applied for aid; 582 were judged to have need; 576 of these received aid. Average need met was 62%. Average scholarship/grant was $1,570. 52% of total undergraduate aid awarded as scholarships/grants, 48% as loans/jobs. **Non-need-based:** Awarded to 60 full-time undergraduates, including 37 freshmen. Scholarships awarded for academics, athletics, religious affiliation.

Application procedures. Admission: Priority date 7/1; deadline 8/1 (postmark date). No application fee. Admission notification on a rolling basis beginning on or about 2/1. Must reply by May 1 or within 2 week(s) if notified thereafter. **Financial aid:** Priority date 3/1; no closing date. FAFSA required. Applicants notified on a rolling basis starting 3/31; must reply within 2 week(s) of notification.

Academics. Special study options: Accelerated study, independent study, internships, study abroad, teacher certification program. **Credit/placement by examination:** AP, CLEP. **Support services:** Study skills assistance, tutoring, writing center.

Majors. Biology: General. **Business:** Business admin. **Communications:** Communications/speech/rhetoric. **Computer sciences:** General. **Education:** Physical. **English:** English lit. **Foreign languages:** French. **History:** General. **Math:** General. **Philosophy/religion:** Religion. **Physical sciences:** Chemistry, physics. **Protective services:** Criminal justice. **Social sciences:** Sociology. **Visual/performing arts:** Music.

Most popular majors. Biology 14%, business/marketing 18%, communications/journalism 7%, education 9%, interdisciplinary studies 9%, security/protective services 18%, social sciences 17%.

Computing on campus. 470 workstations in library, computer center. Dormitories wired for high-speed internet access and linked to campus network. Online library, helpline, wireless network available.

Student life. Freshman orientation: Mandatory. Preregistration for classes offered. **Policies:** Religious observance required. **Housing:** Single-sex dorms available. $50 nonrefundable deposit. **Activities:** Bands, campus ministries, choral groups, dance, drama, music ensembles, student government, student newspaper, student ministerial alliance, student Christian association, pre-alumni council.

Athletics. NCAA. **Intercollegiate:** Baseball M, basketball, cheerleading M, cross-country, football (tackle) M, softball W, tennis, track and field, volleyball W. **Intramural:** Badminton, basketball, softball, swimming, table tennis, volleyball. **Team name:** Dragons.

Student services. Alcohol/substance abuse counseling, chaplain/spiritual director, career counseling, services for economically disadvantaged, student employment services, financial aid counseling, health services, personal counseling, placement for graduates, veterans' counselor.

Contact. E-mail: ebrown@lanecollege.edu
Phone: (731) 426-7533 Toll-free number: (800) 960-7533
Fax: (731) 426-7559
Evelyn Brown, Director of Admissions, Lane College, 545 Lane Avenue, Jackson, TN 38301-4598

Lee University
Cleveland, Tennessee
www.leeuniversity.edu
CB code: 1401

◆ Private 4-year university and liberal arts college affiliated with Church of God
◆ Residential campus in large town
◆ 3,723 degree-seeking undergraduates: 5% part-time, 58% women, 5% African American, 1% Asian American, 4% Hispanic American, 5% international
◆ 322 degree-seeking graduate students
◆ 61% of applicants admitted
◆ SAT or ACT (ACT writing optional) required
◆ 49% graduate within 6 years

General. Founded in 1918. Regionally accredited. **Degrees:** 658 bachelor's awarded; master's offered. **Location:** 20 miles from Chattanooga, 75 miles from Knoxville. **Calendar:** Semester, extensive summer session. **Full-time faculty:** 158 total; 73% have terminal degrees, 15% minority, 31% women. **Part-time faculty:** 222 total; 25% have terminal degrees, 6% minority, 40% women. **Class size:** 48% < 20, 39% 20-39, 6% 40-49, 6% 50-99, 1% >100.

Freshman class profile. 1,777 applied, 1,088 admitted, 875 enrolled.

Mid 50% test scores			
SAT critical reading:	470-610	Rank in top quarter:	51%
SAT math:	460-610	Rank in top tenth:	22%
ACT composite:	21-27	End year in good standing:	72%
GPA 3.75 or higher:	41%	Return as sophomores:	72%
GPA 3.50-3.74:	16%	Out-of-state:	54%
GPA 3.0-3.49:	25%	Live on campus:	93%
GPA 2.0-2.99:	17%	International:	4%

Basis for selection. School achievement record and test scores considered. Audition required for music program. **Home schooled:** Must have high school transcript with date of graduation and 17 ACT or 860 SAT (exclusive of Writing).

High school preparation. 13 units required; 14 recommended. Required and recommended units include English 4, mathematics 3, social studies 2, history 1, science 2, foreign language 1 and computer science 1.

2011-2012 Annual costs. Tuition/fees: $12,680. Room/board: $6,010.

2011-2012 Financial aid. Need-based: 774 full-time freshmen applied for aid; 632 were judged to have need; 628 of these received aid. Average need met was 67%. Average scholarship/grant was $9,806; average loan $3,494. 58% of total undergraduate aid awarded as scholarships/grants, 42% as loans/jobs. **Non-need-based:** Awarded to 948 full-time undergraduates, including 332 freshmen. Scholarships awarded for academics, alumni affiliation, athletics, leadership, minority status, music/drama, religious affiliation, state residency.

Application procedures. Admission: Closing date 9/1 (receipt date). $25 fee. Admission notification on a rolling basis beginning on or about 9/1. **Financial aid:** Priority date 3/15; no closing date. FAFSA required. Applicants notified on a rolling basis starting 2/1; must reply within 3 week(s) of notification.

Academics. Special study options: Distance learning, double major, dual enrollment of high school students, ESL, exchange student, external degree, honors, independent study, internships, liberal arts/career combination, study abroad, teacher certification program, Washington semester. **Credit/placement by examination:** AP, CLEP, IB, SAT, ACT, institutional tests. 32 credit hours maximum toward bachelor's degree. **Support services:** Learning center, pre-admission summer program, reduced course load, remedial instruction, tutoring, writing center.

Majors. Biology: General, biochemistry. **Business:** Accounting, business admin. **Communications:** Advertising, communications/speech/rhetoric, digital media, journalism, public relations. **Computer sciences:** General. **Education:** General, biology, business, chemistry, early childhood, English, French, health, history, mathematics, middle, music, physical, psychology, Spanish, special ed. **English:** English lit. **Foreign languages:** French, Spanish. **Health services:** Athletic training. **History:** General. **Liberal arts:** Humanities. **Math:** General. **Parks/recreation:** Health/fitness. **Physical sciences:** Chemistry. **Psychology:** General. **Social sciences:** Anthropology, political science, sociology. **Theology:** Bible, missionary, pastoral counseling, preministerial, religious ed, sacred music, theology, youth ministry. **Visual/performing arts:** Dramatic, music, music performance, studio arts.

Most popular majors. Business/marketing 15%, communications/journalism 12%, education 18%, psychology 10%, theological studies 16%.

Computing on campus. 410 workstations in dormitories, library, computer center, student center. Dormitories wired for high-speed internet access and linked to campus network. Online library, helpline, wireless network available.

Student life. Freshman orientation: Mandatory. Preregistration for classes offered. Held weekend before classes begin. **Policies:** Religious observance required. **Housing:** Guaranteed on-campus for freshmen. Single-sex dorms, apartments, wellness housing available. $200 fully refundable deposit, deadline 9/1. University leases apartments and houses for students. **Activities:** Bands, campus ministries, choral groups, drama, international student organizations, literary magazine, music ensembles, Model UN, musical theater, opera, student government, student newspaper, symphony orchestra, Greek councils, student leadership council, Collegiate Sertoma, married students fellowship, Pioneers for Christ, Fellowship of Christian Athletes, Missions Alive, deaf ministry association.

Athletics. NAIA, NCCAA. **Intercollegiate:** Baseball M, basketball, cross-country, golf M, soccer, softball W, tennis, volleyball W. **Intramural:** Basketball, bowling, football (non-tackle) M, racquetball, soccer, softball, table tennis, tennis, volleyball. **Team name:** Flames.

Student services. Alcohol/substance abuse counseling, chaplain/spiritual director, career counseling, student employment services, financial aid counseling, health services, personal counseling, placement for graduates, veterans' counselor.

Contact. E-mail: admissions@leeuniversity.edu
Phone: (423) 614-8500 Toll-free number: (800) 533-9930
Fax: (423) 614-8533
Phil Cook, Vice President for Enrollment, Lee University, 1120 North Ocoee Street, Cleveland, TN 37320-3450

LeMoyne-Owen College
Memphis, Tennessee
www.loc.edu

CB member
CB code: 1403

- Private 4-year liberal arts college affiliated with United Church of Christ
- Commuter campus in very large city
- 1,091 degree-seeking undergraduates: 10% part-time, 67% women, 99% African American, 1% international
- 23% of applicants admitted
- SAT or ACT (ACT writing recommended) required

General. Founded in 1862. Regionally accredited. **Degrees:** 65 bachelor's awarded. **ROTC:** Army, Air Force. **Calendar:** Semester, extensive summer session. **Full-time faculty:** 53 total; 58% have terminal degrees, 85% minority, 47% women. **Part-time faculty:** 64 total; 17% have terminal degrees, 89% minority, 45% women. **Class size:** 82% < 20, 18% 20-39, less than 1% 40-49.

Freshman class profile. 1,242 applied, 290 admitted, 183 enrolled.

Out-of-state:	5%	International:	1%
Live on campus:	20%		

Basis for selection. High school transcript, test scores, letter of recommendation, and interview important. Special consideration given to children of alumni. Essay, interview recommended.

High school preparation. 15 units required. Required units include English 4, mathematics 3, history 2, science 3, foreign language 2 and academic electives 1.

2012-2013 Annual costs. Tuition/fees (projected): $10,318. Room/board: $4,852. Books/supplies: $1,600. Personal expenses: $1,800.

Financial aid. Non-need-based: Scholarships awarded for academics, athletics, music/drama.

Application procedures. Admission: Closing date 4/15. $25 fee. Admission notification on a rolling basis. Must reply by May 1 or within 2 week(s) if notified thereafter. **Financial aid:** Priority date 4/15; no closing date. FAFSA required. Applicants notified on a rolling basis starting 4/1.

Academics. Special study options: Accelerated study, cooperative education, cross-registration, double major, dual enrollment of high school students, honors, independent study, internships, liberal arts/career combination, student-designed major, study abroad, teacher certification program, weekend college. **Credit/placement by examination:** AP, CLEP, IB, ACT, institutional tests. 24 credit hours maximum toward bachelor's degree. **Support services:** Learning center, pre-admission summer program, reduced course load, remedial instruction, tutoring.

Majors. Biology: General. **Business:** Business admin. **Computer sciences:** Computer science, information technology. **Education:** Early childhood, mathematics, science, social studies, special ed. **English:** English lit. **History:** General. **Human services:** Social work. **Liberal arts:** Humanities. **Math:** General. **Physical sciences:** Chemistry. **Protective services:** Police science. **Social sciences:** General, political science, sociology. **Visual/performing arts:** Art, music.

Most popular majors. Business/marketing 50%, education 19%, social sciences 9%.

Computing on campus. 223 workstations in dormitories, library, computer center. Dormitories wired for high-speed internet access and linked to campus network. Commuter students can connect to campus network. Online library, helpline, repair service, wireless network available.

Student life. Freshman orientation: Mandatory. Preregistration for classes offered. **Housing:** Single-sex dorms, wellness housing available. $100 deposit. **Activities:** Jazz band, campus ministries, choral groups, dance, drama, international student organizations, music ensembles, student government, student newspaper, NAACP, social work club, Students for Free Enterprise, pre-alumni council, National Student Business Organization.

Athletics. NCAA. **Intercollegiate:** Baseball M, basketball, cross-country, golf, soccer, softball W, tennis, volleyball W. **Intramural:** Basketball. **Team name:** Magicians.

Student services. Adult student services, alcohol/substance abuse counseling, chaplain/spiritual director, career counseling, student employment services, financial aid counseling, health services, personal counseling, placement for graduates, veterans' counselor.

Contact. E-mail: admission@loc.edu
Phone: (901) 435-1500 Fax: (901) 435-1524
Samuel King, Director of Admissions/Recruitment, LeMoyne-Owen College, 807 Walker Avenue, Memphis, TN 38126

Lincoln Memorial University
Harrogate, Tennessee
www.lmunet.edu

CB member
CB code: 1408

- Private 4-year university and liberal arts college
- Commuter campus in small town
- 1,754 degree-seeking undergraduates: 17% part-time, 72% women, 4% African American, 1% Hispanic American, 3% international
- 2,566 degree-seeking graduate students
- 65% of applicants admitted
- SAT or ACT (ACT writing optional) required
- 36% graduate within 6 years

General. Founded in 1897. Regionally accredited. **Degrees:** 202 bachelor's, 148 associate awarded; master's, professional, doctoral offered. **ROTC:** Army. **Location:** 50 miles from Knoxville. **Calendar:** Semester, limited summer session. **Full-time faculty:** 191 total; 65% have terminal degrees, 5% minority, 50% women. **Part-time faculty:** 84 total; 21% have terminal degrees, 4% minority, 57% women. **Class size:** 66% < 20, 31% 20-39, 2% 40-49, less than 1% 50-99. **Special facilities:** Abraham Lincoln library and museum, mountain research center, driving range.

Freshman class profile. 1,593 applied, 1,035 admitted, 318 enrolled.

Mid 50% test scores			
SAT critical reading:	450-560	GPA 3.0-3.49:	35%
SAT math:	470-550	GPA 2.0-2.99:	15%
ACT composite:	20-25	Return as sophomores:	71%
GPA 3.75 or higher:	27%	Out-of-state:	25%
GPA 3.50-3.74:	23%	Live on campus:	70%
		International:	1%

Basis for selection. Academic record, ACT or SAT very important.

High school preparation. College-preparatory program recommended. Required and recommended units include English 4, mathematics 3-4, social studies 1-2, history 1, science 2, foreign language 2 and visual/performing arts 1.

2011-2012 Annual costs. Tuition/fees: $17,720. Room/board: $6,220. Books/supplies: $1,250.

2011-2012 Financial aid. Need-based: 312 full-time freshmen applied for aid; 288 were judged to have need; 288 of these received aid. Average need met was 87%. Average scholarship/grant was $4,200; average loan $2,000. 71% of total undergraduate aid awarded as scholarships/grants, 29% as loans/jobs. **Non-need-based:** Awarded to 151 full-time undergraduates, including 58 freshmen. Scholarships awarded for academics, alumni affiliation, athletics, music/drama, ROTC.

Application procedures. Admission: Priority date 6/1; no deadline. $25 fee, may be waived for applicants with need, free for online applicants. Admission notification on a rolling basis beginning on or about 9/1. **Financial aid:** Priority date 2/15; no closing date. FAFSA required. Applicants notified on a rolling basis starting 3/15; must reply within 3 week(s) of notification.

Academics. Special study options: Distance learning, double major, dual enrollment of high school students, ESL, independent study, internships, teacher certification program. **Credit/placement by examination:** AP, CLEP, IB, SAT, ACT, institutional tests. 16 credit hours maximum toward associate degree, 32 toward bachelor's. **Support services:** Learning center, reduced course load, remedial instruction, study skills assistance, tutoring, writing center.

Majors. Area/ethnic studies: American. **Biology:** General. **Business:** General, accounting, business admin, management science, managerial economics, office/clerical. **Communications:** Communications/speech/rhetoric. **Computer sciences:** General. **Conservation:** Environmental science, wildlife/wilderness. **Education:** General, art, biology, business, chemistry, early childhood, elementary, English, health, history, mathematics, middle, physical, science, secondary, social science, social studies. **English:** English lit. **Health services:** Athletic training, clinical lab science, clinical lab technology, nursing (RN), predental, premedicine, prepharmacy, preveterinary, veterinary technology/assistant. **History:** General. **Human services:** Social work. **Liberal arts:** Humanities. **Math:** General. **Parks/recreation:** Health/fitness. **Philosophy/religion:** General. **Physical sciences:** Chemistry. **Psychology:** General. **Social sciences:** General. **Visual/performing arts:** General, art.

Most popular majors. Security/protective services 9%.

Computing on campus. Dormitories wired for high-speed internet access and linked to campus network. Commuter students can connect to campus network. Online library, helpline, wireless network available.

Student life. Freshman orientation: Mandatory. Preregistration for classes offered. **Housing:** Guaranteed on-campus for all undergraduates. Coed dorms, single-sex dorms, special housing for disabled, apartments available. $200 fully refundable deposit. Housing deposit refundable in full until 7/1. **Activities:** Pep band, campus ministries, choral groups, dance, drama, international student organizations, literary magazine, music ensembles, radio station, student government, TV station, Baptist collegiate ministries, Students in Free Enterprise, international student union, All Beliefs in Action.

Athletics. NCAA. **Intercollegiate:** Baseball M, basketball, cheerleading, cross-country, golf, soccer, softball W, tennis, volleyball W. **Intramural:** Basketball, football (non-tackle), soccer, softball, swimming, table tennis, tennis, volleyball. **Team name:** Railsplitters.

Student services. Alcohol/substance abuse counseling, chaplain/spiritual director, career counseling, student employment services, financial aid counseling, health services, personal counseling, placement for graduates. **Physically disabled:** Services for visually, hearing impaired.

Contact. E-mail: admissions@lmunet.edu
Phone: (423) 869-3611 ext. 6280
Toll-free number: (800) 325-0900 ext. 6280 Fax: (423) 869-6444
Sherry McCreary, Dean of Admissions, Lincoln Memorial University, 6965 Cumberland Gap Parkway, Harrogate, TN 37752-1901

Lipscomb University
Nashville, Tennessee
www.lipscomb.edu

CB code: 1161

- Private 4-year university and liberal arts college affiliated with Church of Christ
- Residential campus in very large city
- 2,675 degree-seeking undergraduates: 8% part-time, 58% women, 9% African American, 3% Asian American, 4% Hispanic American, 2% international
- 1,335 degree-seeking graduate students
- 51% of applicants admitted
- SAT or ACT (ACT writing recommended), interview required
- 63% graduate within 6 years

General. Founded in 1891. Regionally accredited. **Degrees:** 461 bachelor's awarded; master's, professional offered. **ROTC:** Army, Air Force. **Location:** 4 miles from downtown. **Calendar:** Semester, extensive summer session. **Full-time faculty:** 169 total; 85% have terminal degrees, 5% minority, 36% women. **Part-time faculty:** 244 total; 42% have terminal degrees, 8% minority, 54% women. **Class size:** 57% < 20, 32% 20-39, 4% 40-49, 6% 50-99, less than 1% >100.

Freshman class profile. 3,430 applied, 1,758 admitted, 629 enrolled.

Mid 50% test scores			
SAT critical reading:	480-600	GPA 2.0-2.99:	16%
SAT math:	490-610	Rank in top quarter:	52%
ACT composite:	22-28	Rank in top tenth:	27%
GPA 3.75 or higher:	40%	Return as sophomores:	71%
GPA 3.50-3.74:	18%	Out-of-state:	35%
GPA 3.0-3.49:	26%	Live on campus:	82%
		International:	1%

Basis for selection. School achievement record, test scores, educational and personal references required. Strong moral character desired. Audition required for music; portfolio required for art; interview recommended for art, honors, music programs.

High school preparation. College-preparatory program recommended. 14 units required. Required units include English 4, mathematics 2, social studies 2, science 2, foreign language 2 and academic electives 2. Math units preferably algebra I, II. Foreign language units in the same language. 2 academic electives should be selected from natural sciences, mathematics, foreign languages, or social sciences.

2012-2013 Annual costs. Tuition/fees (projected): $24,654. Room/board: $9,224. Books/supplies: $1,500. Personal expenses: $1,250.

2011-2012 Financial aid. Need-based: 622 full-time freshmen applied for aid; 475 were judged to have need; 475 of these received aid. Average need met was 60%. Average scholarship/grant was $4,533; average loan $3,999. 63% of total undergraduate aid awarded as scholarships/grants, 37% as loans/jobs. **Non-need-based:** Awarded to 1,982 full-time undergraduates, including 627 freshmen. Scholarships awarded for academics, art, athletics, leadership, minority status, music/drama, religious affiliation, state residency.

Application procedures. Admission: Priority date 10/31; no deadline. $50 fee, may be waived for applicants with need. Admission notification on a rolling basis beginning on or about 8/15. **Financial aid:** Priority date 1/31; no closing date. FAFSA required. Applicants notified on a rolling basis starting 1/31.

Academics. Special study options: Combined bachelor's/graduate degree, cross-registration, distance learning, double major, dual enrollment of high school students, honors, independent study, internships, study abroad, teacher certification program, weekend college. **Credit/placement by examination:** AP, CLEP, IB, SAT, ACT, institutional tests. 30 credit hours maximum toward bachelor's degree. **Support services:** Learning center, pre-admission summer program, reduced course load, remedial instruction, study skills assistance, tutoring, writing center.

Majors. Area/ethnic studies: American. **Biology:** General, biochemistry. **Business:** Accounting, business admin, fashion, human resources, international, management information systems, managerial economics, marketing. **Communications:** Journalism, media studies, organizational, public relations. **Computer sciences:** Computer science, information technology. **Conservation:** Environmental science. **Education:** Art, biology, chemistry, drama/dance, elementary, English, ESL, French, German, history, mathematics, music, physical, physics, Spanish. **Engineering:** Computer, engineering mechanics, engineering science, mechanical. **English:** English lit, rhetoric/composition. **Foreign languages:** French, German, Spanish. **Health services:** Athletic training, dietetics, nursing (RN), predental, premedicine, prenursing, prepharmacy, preveterinary. **History:** General. **Human services:** General, social work. **Math:** General. **Parks/recreation:** Exercise sciences. **Philosophy/religion:** Philosophy. **Physical sciences:** Chemistry, physics. **Psychology:** General. **Social sciences:** Political science, urban studies. **Theology:** Bible, missionary, youth ministry. **Visual/performing arts:** Commercial/advertising art, dramatic, music performance, music theory/composition, piano/keyboard, studio arts, voice/opera. **Work/family studies:** General, clothing/textiles, family systems, institutional food production.

Most popular majors. Biology 10%, business/marketing 24%, education 12%, health sciences 10%, psychology 6%.

Computing on campus. 203 workstations in dormitories, library, computer center, student center. Dormitories wired for high-speed internet access and linked to campus network. Commuter students can connect to campus network. Online course registration, helpline, repair service, wireless network available.

Student life. Freshman orientation: Mandatory, $110 fee. Preregistration for classes offered. **Policies:** Daily chapel service and Bible studies required. Out-of-town undergraduates required to live on campus, except for seniors, students over age of 21, married students. Religious observance required. **Housing:** Single-sex dorms, apartments available. $125 fully refundable deposit. **Activities:** Bands, campus ministries, choral groups, drama, international student organizations, literary magazine, music ensembles, musical theater, radio station, student government, student newspaper, TV station, College Republicans, Young Democrats, honorary societies, multicultural association, Circle K, Fellowship of Christian Athletes, Youth Encouragement Services, men and women's service clubs, homeless ministry, DAC (ministry to the hearing impaired).

Athletics. NCAA. **Intercollegiate:** Baseball M, basketball, cross-country, golf, soccer, softball W, tennis, track and field, volleyball W. **Intramural:** Badminton, basketball, football (non-tackle), racquetball, soccer, softball, tennis, volleyball. **Team name:** Bisons.

Student services. Adult student services, chaplain/spiritual director, career counseling, student employment services, financial aid counseling, health services, minority student services, personal counseling, placement for graduates. **Physically disabled:** Services for visually, speech, hearing impaired.

Contact. E-mail: admissions@lipscomb.edu
Phone: (615) 966-1776 Toll-free number: (877) 582-4766
Fax: (615) 966-1804
Ricky Holaway, Director of Admissions, Lipscomb University, One University Park Drive, Nashville, TN 37204-3951

Martin Methodist College
Pulaski, Tennessee
www.martinmethodist.edu   CB code: 1449

- Private 4-year liberal arts college affiliated with United Methodist Church
- Residential campus in small town
- 893 degree-seeking undergraduates: 7% part-time, 62% women, 11% African American, 1% Hispanic American, 7% international
- 54% graduate within 6 years

General. Founded in 1870. Regionally accredited. **Degrees:** 146 bachelor's, 12 associate awarded. **Location:** 70 miles from Nashville; 40 miles from Huntsville, AL. **Calendar:** Semester, limited summer session. **Full-time faculty:** 46 total; 50% have terminal degrees. **Part-time faculty:** 40 total; 20% have terminal degrees. **Class size:** 78% < 20, 21% 20-39, less than 1% 40-49.

Freshman class profile.

GPA 3.75 or higher:	15%	Out-of-state:	13%
GPA 3.50-3.74:	19%	Live on campus:	46%
GPA 3.0-3.49:	34%	International:	6%
GPA 2.0-2.99:	28%		

Basis for selection. High school record, interview, test scores important. Applicants must meet 2 of the following or apply for special circumstances admission status: 2.0 GPA, 18 ACT, or rank in upper 50% of class. Students conditionally admitted will be offered full enrollment after completion of a semester with 2.0 GPA. ACT recommended. Audition recommended for music; portfolio recommended for art.

High school preparation. 13 units required. Required and recommended units include English 4, mathematics 2-3, social studies 2, history 1, science 2 (laboratory 2), foreign language 2, computer science 1 and academic electives 4.

2011-2012 Annual costs. Tuition/fees: $20,582. Room/board: $7,000. Books/supplies: $750. Personal expenses: $1,200.

Financial aid. Non-need-based: Scholarships awarded for academics, art, athletics, leadership, music/drama, religious affiliation, state residency.

Application procedures. Admission: Priority date 5/1; deadline 8/1 (postmark date). $30 fee. Admission notification on a rolling basis. **Financial aid:** No deadline. FAFSA, institutional form required. Applicants notified on a rolling basis starting 3/1; must reply within 2 week(s) of notification.

Academics. Special study options: Dual enrollment of high school students, ESL, honors, independent study, study abroad. **Credit/placement by examination:** AP, CLEP. 30 credit hours maximum toward associate degree. **Support services:** Learning center, pre-admission summer program, reduced course load, remedial instruction, study skills assistance, tutoring, writing center.

Majors. Biology: General. **Business:** General, accounting, business admin. **Education:** Biology, business, elementary, English, history, middle, physical, secondary. **English:** English lit. **Health services:** Nursing (RN). **History:** General. **Parks/recreation:** Health/fitness, sports admin. **Philosophy/religion:** Religion. **Protective services:** Law enforcement admin. **Psychology:** General. **Theology:** Preministerial, religious ed, sacred music.

Most popular majors. Biology 10%, business/marketing 15%, education 13%, liberal arts 13%, social sciences 22%.

Computing on campus. 150 workstations in library, computer center. Dormitories wired for high-speed internet access and linked to campus network. Commuter students can connect to campus network. Online course registration, online library, helpline, wireless network available.

Student life. Freshman orientation: Mandatory. Preregistration for classes offered. Held 3 days prior to other students' arrival. **Housing:** Guaranteed on-campus for all undergraduates. Single-sex dorms, apartments available. $125 fully refundable deposit, deadline 6/1. **Activities:** Campus ministries, choral groups, drama, international student organizations, music ensembles, student government, student newspaper, student Christian association, black student union, Fellowship of Christian Athletes.

Athletics. NAIA, NJCAA. **Intercollegiate:** Baseball M, basketball, bowling, cheerleading M, golf, soccer, softball W, tennis, volleyball W. **Intramural:** Basketball, football (non-tackle), racquetball, softball, swimming, table tennis, volleyball. **Team name:** RedHawks.

Student services. Adult student services, chaplain/spiritual director, career counseling, student employment services, financial aid counseling, personal counseling, placement for graduates, veterans' counselor.

Contact. E-mail: lsmith2@martinmethodist.edu
Phone: (931) 363-9868 Toll-free number: (800) 467-1273
Fax: (931) 363-9803
Lisa Smith, Director of Admissions, Martin Methodist College, 433 West Madison, Pulaski, TN 38478-2799

Maryville College
Maryville, Tennessee
www.maryvillecollege.edu

CB member
CB code: 1454

- Private 4-year liberal arts college affiliated with Presbyterian Church (USA)
- Residential campus in small city
- 1,078 degree-seeking undergraduates: 4% part-time, 54% women
- 66% of applicants admitted
- SAT or ACT (ACT writing optional) required
- 53% graduate within 6 years; 43% enter graduate study

General. Founded in 1819. Regionally accredited. **Degrees:** 200 bachelor's awarded. **Location:** 15 miles from Knoxville. **Calendar:** 4-1-4, limited summer session. **Full-time faculty:** 72 total; 89% have terminal degrees, 4% minority, 51% women. **Part-time faculty:** 35 total; 54% have terminal degrees, 9% minority, 57% women. **Class size:** 62% < 20, 37% 20-39, less than 1% 40-49. **Special facilities:** Science center, civic arts center, college woods with ropes courses, equestrian center.

Freshman class profile. 1,998 applied, 1,325 admitted, 293 enrolled.

Mid 50% test scores			
SAT critical reading:	470-600	GPA 2.0-2.99:	12%
SAT math:	480-600	Rank in top quarter:	68%
ACT composite:	22-37	Rank in top tenth:	42%
GPA 3.75 or higher:	36%	Return as sophomores:	71%
GPA 3.50-3.74:	21%	Out-of-state:	20%
GPA 3.0-3.49:	31%	Live on campus:	85%

Basis for selection. Admissions based on academic criteria, extracurricular involvement, and personal achievement. Successful students typically follow strong college preparatory curriculums and rank in top 25% of class. Writing samples encouraged. Essay, interview recommended for all; audition required for music; portfolio recommended for art. **Home schooled:** Pursue rigorous curriculum that includes strong emphasis on writing and reasoning. **Learning Disabled:** Students must meet the same admission criteria as other students. Accommodated test scores accepted.

High school preparation. College-preparatory program required. 16 units required; 25 recommended. Required and recommended units include English 4, mathematics 3-4, social studies 2-4, history 1-2, science 2-4 (laboratory 1-2), foreign language 2-4, computer science 1 and academic electives 1.

2011-2012 Annual costs. Tuition/fees: $29,924. Room/board: $9,234. Books/supplies: $1,060. Personal expenses: $1,260.

2011-2012 Financial aid. **Need-based:** 293 full-time freshmen applied for aid; 252 were judged to have need; 252 of these received aid. Average need met was 88%. Average scholarship/grant was $26,473; average loan $3,782. 77% of total undergraduate aid awarded as scholarships/grants, 23% as loans/jobs. **Non-need-based:** Awarded to 1,005 full-time undergraduates, including 293 freshmen. Scholarships awarded for academics, art, leadership, minority status, music/drama, religious affiliation, state residency.

Application procedures. **Admission:** Priority date 3/1; no deadline. No application fee. Admission notification on a rolling basis beginning on or about 11/1. Must reply by May 1 or within 4 week(s) if notified thereafter. **Financial aid:** Priority date 2/15; no closing date. FAFSA required. Applicants notified on a rolling basis starting 3/15; must reply within 4 week(s) of notification.

Academics. All students complete 6 credit-hour research project and comprehensive examination in their major area of study. **Special study options:** Accelerated study, combined bachelor's/graduate degree, double major, dual enrollment of high school students, ESL, honors, independent study, internships, liberal arts/career combination, student-designed major, study abroad, teacher certification program, Washington semester. Undergraduate research.

Credit/placement by examination: AP, CLEP, IB, SAT, ACT, institutional tests. 32 credit hours maximum toward bachelor's degree. Students may petition individual departments for credit by examination. **Support services:** Learning center, reduced course load, remedial instruction, study skills assistance, tutoring, writing center.

Majors. Biology: General, biochemistry. **Business:** Business admin, international. **Computer sciences:** General. **Conservation:** Environmental studies. **Education:** General, biology, chemistry, drama/dance, English, ESL, health, history, mathematics, music, physical, social science, social studies, Spanish. **Engineering:** General. **English:** English lit, technical writing. **Foreign languages:** American Sign Language, sign language interpretation, Spanish. **Health services:** Nursing (RN), predental, premedicine, prenursing, prepharmacy, preveterinary. **History:** General. **Math:** General. **Parks/recreation:** General, health/fitness. **Philosophy/religion:** Philosophy, religion. **Physical sciences:** Chemical physics, chemistry. **Psychology:** General, developmental. **Social sciences:** Economics, international relations, political science, sociology. **Visual/performing arts:** Art, art history/conservation, dramatic, music, music performance, music theory/composition, studio arts.

Most popular majors. Biology 9%, business/marketing 19%, education 10%, English 7%, history 7%, psychology 12%, social sciences 14%, visual/performing arts 6%.

Computing on campus. 265 workstations in library, computer center, student center. Dormitories wired for high-speed internet access and linked to campus network. Commuter students can connect to campus network. Online course registration, online library, helpline, repair service, wireless network available.

Student life. Freshman orientation: Mandatory, $25 fee. Preregistration for classes offered. Held several days before registration; includes Mountain Challenge component. Optional 3-day wilderness experience. **Policies:** Alcohol policy prohibits consumption in company of people under legal drinking age. **Housing:** Guaranteed on-campus for all undergraduates. Coed dorms, single-sex dorms, special housing for disabled, apartments, wellness housing available. $50 fully refundable deposit, deadline 5/1. Housing deposit refundable before 5/1. **Activities:** Bands, campus ministries, choral groups, dance, drama, film society, international student organizations, literary magazine, music ensembles, Model UN, student government, student newspaper, symphony orchestra, Habitat for Humanity, Literary Corps, Fellowship of Christian Athletes, wellness council, student programming board, black student association.

Athletics. NCAA. **Intercollegiate:** Baseball M, basketball, cheerleading, cross-country, equestrian, football (tackle) M, golf M, soccer, softball W, tennis, volleyball W. **Intramural:** Archery, badminton, baseball M, basketball, bowling, football (non-tackle), golf, racquetball, rugby, skiing, soccer, softball, swimming, table tennis, tennis, track and field, volleyball, water polo. **Team name:** Scots.

Student services. Adult student services, alcohol/substance abuse counseling, chaplain/spiritual director, career counseling, student employment services, financial aid counseling, health services, minority student services, personal counseling, placement for graduates. **Physically disabled:** Services for visually, speech, hearing impaired.

Contact. E-mail: admissions@maryvillecollege.edu
Phone: (865) 981-8092 Toll-free number: (800) 597-2687
Fax: (865) 981-8005
Dolph Henry, Vice President for Enrollment Management, Maryville College, 502 East Lamar Alexander Parkway, Maryville, TN 37804-5907

Memphis College of Art
Memphis, Tennessee
www.mca.edu

CB code: 1511

- Private 4-year visual arts college
- Residential campus in very large city
- 376 degree-seeking undergraduates: 9% part-time, 65% women, 18% African American, 2% Asian American, 6% Hispanic American, 2% international
- 47 degree-seeking graduate students
- 45% of applicants admitted
- SAT or ACT (ACT writing optional) required
- 32% graduate within 6 years; 10% enter graduate study

General. Founded in 1936. Regionally accredited. Students have access to Memphis Brooks Museum of Art and Overton Park Zoo. Consortium with four other local colleges/universities. Mobility consortium with 30+ art colleges across the US and Canada. **Degrees:** 61 bachelor's awarded; master's offered. **Location:** 500 miles from New Orleans, 700 miles from Dallas.

Calendar: Semester, limited summer session. **Full-time faculty:** 26 total; 81% have terminal degrees, 19% minority, 58% women. **Part-time faculty:** 35 total; 37% have terminal degrees, 11% minority, 31% women. **Class size:** 76% < 20, 24% 20-39.

Freshman class profile. 544 applied, 247 admitted, 94 enrolled.

Mid 50% test scores		GPA 2.0-2.99:	37%
ACT composite:	19-24	Return as sophomores:	76%
GPA 3.75 or higher:	21%	Out-of-state:	53%
GPA 3.50-3.74:	10%	Live on campus:	67%
GPA 3.0-3.49:	30%		

Basis for selection. Art portfolio, high school transcript, test scores required; letter of recommendation from art teacher and essay considered, but not required. Portfolio required; essay, interview recommended for all. **Home schooled:** State high school equivalency certificate required.

High school preparation. College-preparatory program recommended. Recommended units include visual/performing arts 1. Portfolio should include 10 to 20 pieces of work, originals or slides, with focus on direct observational drawing.

2012-2013 Annual costs. Tuition/fees (projected): $26,250. Room/board: $8,500. Books/supplies: $1,650. Personal expenses: $1,500.

2010-2011 Financial aid. Need-based: 73 full-time freshmen applied for aid; 68 were judged to have need; 68 of these received aid. Average need met was 70%. Average scholarship/grant was $14,885; average loan $3,321. 68% of total undergraduate aid awarded as scholarships/grants, 32% as loans/jobs. **Non-need-based:** Awarded to 95 full-time undergraduates, including 22 freshmen. Scholarships awarded for academics, art. **Additional information:** Students considered for institutional resources through admissions application process.

Application procedures. Admission: Priority date 3/31; no deadline. $25 fee, may be waived for applicants with need. Admission notification on a rolling basis beginning on or about 11/15. Must reply by May 1 or within 3 week(s) if notified thereafter. **Financial aid:** Priority date 2/15; no closing date. FAFSA required. Applicants notified on a rolling basis starting 3/15; must reply within 3 week(s) of notification.

Academics. Special study options: Combined bachelor's/graduate degree, cross-registration, double major, exchange student, independent study, internships, New York semester, study abroad, teacher certification program. New York Studio Exchange Program. Mobility semester exchange at 30+ independent art colleges across the country (AICAD consortium). **Credit/placement by examination:** AP, CLEP, SAT, ACT, institutional tests. 15 credit hours maximum toward bachelor's degree. **Support services:** Reduced course load, remedial instruction, study skills assistance, tutoring, writing center.

Majors. Computer sciences: Computer graphics. **Visual/performing arts:** Art, commercial/advertising art, design, digital arts, drawing, graphic design, illustration, metal/jewelry, multimedia, painting, photography, printmaking, sculpture, studio arts.

Computing on campus. 200 workstations in dormitories, library, computer center. Dormitories wired for high-speed internet access. Wireless network available.

Student life. Freshman orientation: Mandatory. Preregistration for classes offered. Four-day session includes parents. **Policies:** Considerable assistance available in matching roommates and helping students find affordable housing within walking distance. **Housing:** Coed dorms, apartments, wellness housing available. $300 partly refundable deposit. **Activities:** International student organizations, student government, student newspaper, photography club, student alliance, multicultural student association, gay-straight alliance, Give-Back community service club.

Student services. Adult student services, career counseling, student employment services, financial aid counseling, personal counseling, placement for graduates, veterans' counselor.

Contact. E-mail: info@mca.edu
Phone: (901) 272-5151 Toll-free number: (800) 727-1088
Fax: (901) 272-5158
Annette Moore, Dean of Admissions, Memphis College of Art, 1930 Poplar Avenue, Memphis, TN 38104-2764

Middle Tennessee State University
Murfreesboro, Tennessee
www.mtsu.edu

CB member
CB code: 1466

- Public 4-year university
- Commuter campus in small city

- 23,173 degree-seeking undergraduates: 16% part-time, 53% women, 18% African American, 3% Asian American, 3% Hispanic American
- 3,027 degree-seeking graduate students
- 70% of applicants admitted
- SAT or ACT (ACT writing optional) required

General. Founded in 1911. Regionally accredited. **Degrees:** 3,868 bachelor's awarded; master's, doctoral offered. **ROTC:** Army, Air Force. **Location:** 32 miles from Nashville. **Calendar:** Semester, extensive summer session. **Full-time faculty:** 938 total; 16% minority, 46% women. **Part-time faculty:** 408 total; 13% minority, 55% women. **Class size:** 34% < 20, 55% 20-39, 4% 40-49, 6% 50-99, 1% >100. **Special facilities:** 3 recording studios, observatory, flight simulators, weather center, electronic music laboratory, digital audio edit laboratory, satellite mapping equipment, seismograph, 3 television studios, electronic newsroom, Centers for Historic Preservation and Popular Music.

Freshman class profile. 10,814 applied, 7,600 admitted, 3,439 enrolled.

Mid 50% test scores		Rank in top tenth:	15%
SAT critical reading:	470-590	Out-of-state:	5%
SAT math:	450-580	Live on campus:	44%
ACT composite:	20-24	Fraternities:	5%
Rank in top quarter:	42%	Sororities:	7%

Basis for selection. 3.0 GPA or 22 ACT or combination of 19 ACT and 2.7 GPA required. Personal statement required of students who do not meet standard requirements.

High school preparation. 14 units required. Required units include English 4, mathematics 3, social studies 1, history 1, science 2 (laboratory 1), foreign language 2 and visual/performing arts 1. Foreign language units must be in single language. Mathematics units must include algebra I and II, geometry or other advanced mathematics. 1 US history, 1 global studies also required.

2011-2012 Annual costs. Tuition/fees: $7,018; $21,406 out-of-state. Room/board: $7,442. Books/supplies: $1,325. Personal expenses: $3,533.

2010-2011 Financial aid. Need-based: Average need met was 74%. Average scholarship/grant was $6,691; average loan $2,966. 59% of total undergraduate aid awarded as scholarships/grants, 41% as loans/jobs. **Non-need-based:** Scholarships awarded for academics, alumni affiliation, art, athletics, leadership, music/drama, ROTC, state residency. **Additional information:** Deadline for scholarships 2/15.

Application procedures. Admission: No deadline. $25 fee. Admission notification on a rolling basis. **Financial aid:** Priority date 12/1; no closing date. FAFSA required. Applicants notified on a rolling basis starting 4/1; must reply within 2 week(s) of notification.

Academics. Special study options: Cooperative education, distance learning, double major, dual enrollment of high school students, honors, independent study, internships, study abroad, teacher certification program. Academic basic skills. **Credit/placement by examination:** AP, CLEP, IB, SAT, ACT, institutional tests. 66 credit hours maximum toward bachelor's degree. Up to 66 semester hours from correspondence study, credit-by-examination, credit for service-related experience, and flight training may be counted toward degree. **Support services:** Learning center, pre-admission summer program, reduced course load, remedial instruction, study skills assistance, tutoring, writing center.

Honors college/program. 26 ACT/1170 SAT and 3.0 GPA or 22 ACT/950 SAT and 3.5 GPA required. SAT scores exclusive of Writing.

Majors. Biology: General. **Business:** Accounting, business admin, finance, management information systems, managerial economics, marketing, office management, purchasing, sales/distribution. **Communications:** Media studies. **Computer sciences:** General, computer science. **Education:** Art, business, early childhood, health, kindergarten/preschool, sales/marketing, special ed, technology/industrial arts. **English:** English lit. **Foreign languages:** General. **General:** Agribusiness operations, animal sciences, plant sciences, soil science. **Health services:** Athletic training, nursing (RN). **History:** General. **Human services:** Social work. **Liberal arts:** Arts/sciences. **Math:** General. **Parks/recreation:** Facilities management, health/fitness. **Philosophy/religion:** Philosophy. **Physical sciences:** Chemistry, geology, physics. **Protective services:** Law enforcement admin. **Psychology:** General. **Social sciences:** Anthropology, economics, international relations, political science, sociology. **Visual/performing arts:** Art, art history/conservation, dramatic, interior design, music, music management. **Work/family studies:** Clothing/textiles, family resources, food/nutrition.

Most popular majors. Business/marketing 18%, communications/journalism 6%, interdisciplinary studies 9%, liberal arts 9%, visual/performing arts 11%.

Computing on campus. 2,300 workstations in dormitories, library, computer center, student center. Dormitories wired for high-speed internet access and linked to campus network. Commuter students can connect to campus network. Online course registration, online library, helpline, wireless network available.

Student life. Freshman orientation: Mandatory, $45 fee. Preregistration for classes offered. Offered from mid-June to mid-July. **Policies:** Parents notified when student under age of 21 found responsible for use and/or possession of drugs or alcohol. **Housing:** Coed dorms, single-sex dorms, special housing for disabled, apartments, cooperative housing, fraternity/sorority housing available. $200 partly refundable deposit. **Activities:** Bands, campus ministries, choral groups, dance, drama, film society, international student organizations, literary magazine, music ensembles, Model UN, musical theater, radio station, student government, student newspaper, TV station, Golden Key National Honor Society, African American student association, Fellowship of Christian Athletes, Collegiate Women International, Citizens for Action, Baptist student union, aerospace maintenance club, agricultural council, Student Tennessee Education Association.

Athletics. NCAA. **Intercollegiate:** Baseball M, basketball, cross-country, football (tackle) M, golf, soccer W, softball W, tennis, track and field, volleyball W. **Intramural:** Basketball M, boxing M, equestrian, football (tackle) M, racquetball, rugby M, soccer, softball, swimming, tennis, volleyball. **Team name:** Blue Raiders.

Student services. Adult student services, chaplain/spiritual director, career counseling, student employment services, financial aid counseling, health services, minority student services, on-campus daycare, personal counseling, placement for graduates, veterans' counselor, women's services. **Physically disabled:** Services for visually, speech, hearing impaired.

Contact. E-mail: admissions@mtsu.edu
Phone: (615) 898-2111 Fax: (615) 898-5478
Lynn Palmer, Director of Admissions, Middle Tennessee State University, 1301 East Main Street, Murfreesboro, TN 37132

Milligan College
Milligan College, Tennessee
www.milligan.edu   CB code: 1469

- Private 4-year liberal arts college affiliated with Christian Church
- Residential campus in small city
- 939 degree-seeking undergraduates: 4% part-time, 60% women, 6% African American, 1% Asian American, 4% Hispanic American, 3% international
- 224 degree-seeking graduate students
- 70% of applicants admitted
- SAT or ACT (ACT writing optional), application essay required
- 65% graduate within 6 years; 21% enter graduate study

General. Founded in 1866. Regionally accredited. Weekly chapels, convocation programs, vespers. **Degrees:** 197 bachelor's awarded; master's offered. **ROTC:** Army. **Location:** 3 miles from Johnson City. **Calendar:** Semester, limited summer session. **Full-time faculty:** 67 total; 79% have terminal degrees, 3% minority, 49% women. **Part-time faculty:** 65 total; 29% have terminal degrees, 2% minority, 54% women. **Class size:** 72% < 20, 25% 20-39, 1% 40-49, 1% 50-99, less than 1% >100.

Freshman class profile. 603 applied, 424 admitted, 204 enrolled.

Mid 50% test scores		GPA 2.0-2.99:	7%
SAT critical reading:	490-600	Rank in top quarter:	65%
SAT math:	490-610	Rank in top tenth:	37%
SAT writing:	480-560	Return as sophomores:	80%
ACT composite:	21-27	Out-of-state:	43%
GPA 3.75 or higher:	50%	Live on campus:	89%
GPA 3.50-3.74:	20%	International:	1%
GPA 3.0-3.49:	23%		

Basis for selection. Academic work, test scores, and references from minister/church leader and high school principal/counselor required. Audition required for music; interview recommended in some instances.

High school preparation. College-preparatory program recommended. 17 units recommended. Recommended units include English 4, mathematics 3, social studies 2, history 3, science 3 and foreign language 2.

2011-2012 Annual costs. Tuition/fees: $25,260. Room/board: $5,650. Books/supplies: $900. Personal expenses: $1,236.

2011-2012 Financial aid. Need-based: Average need met was 83%. Average scholarship/grant was $18,406; average loan $2,954. 70% of total undergraduate aid awarded as scholarships/grants, 30% as loans/jobs. **Non-need-based:** Scholarships awarded for academics, athletics, leadership, minority status, music/drama.

Application procedures. Admission: Priority date 4/1; deadline 8/1 (postmark date). $30 fee, may be waived for applicants with need. Admission notification on a rolling basis beginning on or about 10/1. Must reply by May 1 or within 2 week(s) if notified thereafter. **Financial aid:** Priority date 3/1; no closing date. FAFSA required. Applicants notified on a rolling basis starting 3/15; must reply within 2 week(s) of notification.

Academics. Special study options: Combined bachelor's/graduate degree, cross-registration, distance learning, double major, dual enrollment of high school students, independent study, internships, study abroad, teacher certification program, Washington semester. American Studies Program in Washington, DC; Australia Studies Center; China Studies Program; Contemporary Music Center in Martha's Vineyard; Latin American Studies Program in Costa Rica; Los Angeles Film Studies Center; Middle East Studies Program in Egypt; Russian Studies Program; Scholars' Semester in Oxford; Uganda Studies Program; Summer Institute of Journalism in Washington, DC; Oxford Summer Programme. **Credit/placement by examination:** AP, CLEP, IB, SAT, ACT, institutional tests. 32 credit hours maximum toward bachelor's degree. Students may not receive credit by examination upon achieving a total of 64 credit hours. **Support services:** Reduced course load, remedial instruction, study skills assistance, tutoring, writing center.

Majors. Biology: General. **Business:** Accounting, business admin. **Communications:** Communications/speech/rhetoric. **Computer sciences:** General. **Education:** General, early childhood, music. **English:** English lit. **Health services:** Nursing (RN). **History:** General. **Liberal arts:** Humanities. **Math:** General. **Parks/recreation:** Health/fitness. **Physical sciences:** Chemistry. **Psychology:** General. **Social sciences:** Sociology. **Theology:** Bible. **Visual/performing arts:** General, music.

Most popular majors. Business/marketing 21%, communications/journalism 7%, education 14%, health sciences 15%, parks/recreation 7%, psychology 10%.

Computing on campus. 102 workstations in library, computer center. Dormitories wired for high-speed internet access and linked to campus network. Commuter students can connect to campus network. Online library, helpline, repair service, student web hosting, wireless network available.

Student life. Freshman orientation: Available, $10 fee. Preregistration for classes offered. Weekend sessions available in April or June. Abbreviated version offered weekend prior to first day of fall classes. **Policies:** Smoking and alcoholic beverages not permitted on-campus. Students must live in college housing unless married or living with members of immediate family. Religious observance required. **Housing:** Guaranteed on-campus for all undergraduates. Single-sex dorms, apartments, wellness housing available. $200 nonrefundable deposit, deadline 8/15. Housing deposit refundable until 5/1. **Activities:** Bands, choral groups, drama, literary magazine, music ensembles, musical theater, radio station, student government, student newspaper, symphony orchestra, Fellowship of Christian Athletes, missions club, service seekers, College Republicans, Habitat for Humanity, political awareness group, Roteract.

Athletics. NAIA. **Intercollegiate:** Baseball M, basketball, cross-country, golf M, soccer, softball W, swimming, tennis, track and field, volleyball W. **Intramural:** Basketball, football (non-tackle), softball, table tennis, tennis, volleyball. **Team name:** Buffaloes.

Student services. Adult student services, chaplain/spiritual director, career counseling, student employment services, financial aid counseling, health services, minority student services, personal counseling, placement for graduates.

Contact. E-mail: admissions@milligan.edu
Phone: (423) 461-8730 Toll-free number: (800) 262-8337
Fax: (423) 461-8982
Tracy Brinn, Director of Enrollment Management, Milligan College, Box 210, Milligan College, TN 37682

O'More College of Design
Franklin, Tennessee
www.omorecollege.edu   CB code: 1545

- Private 4-year visual arts college
- Commuter campus in large town

► 191 degree-seeking undergraduates: 14% part-time, 87% women, 4% African American, 1% Asian American, 3% Hispanic American, 1% Native American, 2% international

► 49% of applicants admitted

► SAT or ACT (ACT writing optional), application essay required

General. Founded in 1970. Accredited by ACCSC. **Degrees:** 43 bachelor's awarded. **Location:** 15 miles from Nashville. **Calendar:** Semester, limited summer session. **Full-time faculty:** 15 total; 7% have terminal degrees, 13% minority, 60% women. **Part-time faculty:** 28 total; 4% have terminal degrees, 4% minority, 54% women. **Class size:** 99% < 20, less than 1% 20-39. **Special facilities:** Sensory garden.

Freshman class profile. 61 applied, 30 admitted, 21 enrolled.

GPA 3.75 or higher:	48%	GPA 2.0-2.99:	19%
GPA 3.50-3.74:	10%	Out-of-state:	8%
GPA 3.0-3.49:	23%		

Basis for selection. High school record most important. Test scores, grades given equal weight.

High school preparation. 18 units recommended. Recommended units include English 4, mathematics 3, social studies 1, history 2, science 3, foreign language 2 and academic electives 3. Art, mechanical drawing, and design courses are recommended.

2012-2013 Annual costs. Tuition/fees (projected): $23,952. Books/supplies: $550.

Financial aid. All financial aid based on need.

Application procedures. Admission: Closing date 8/2 (postmark date). $50 fee, may be waived for applicants with need. Admission notification on a rolling basis. **Financial aid:** Priority date 4/1; no closing date. FAFSA required. Applicants notified on a rolling basis starting 8/1.

Academics. Special study options: Double major, dual enrollment of high school students, independent study, internships, liberal arts/career combination, study abroad. Annual study-abroad program in Ireland and annual international trip. **Credit/placement by examination:** AP, CLEP, IB, institutional tests. 9 credit hours maximum toward bachelor's degree.

Majors. Visual/performing arts: Commercial/advertising art, design, fashion design, interior design.

Computing on campus. PC or laptop required. 30 workstations in library, computer center, student center. Student web hosting, wireless network available.

Student life. Freshman orientation: Available. Preregistration for classes offered. **Activities:** Film society, student government, student newspaper, American Society of Interior Designers, fashion merchandisers association, American Institute of Graphic Arts, International Interior Design Association.

Student services. Career counseling, student employment services, financial aid counseling.

Contact. E-mail: admissions@omorecollege.edu
Phone: (615) 794-4254 ext. 229
Toll-free number: (888) 662-1970 ext. 229 Fax: (615) 790-1662
Amy Shelton, Registrar, O'More College of Design, 423 South Margin Street, Franklin, TN 37064-0908

Rhodes College

Memphis, Tennessee
www.rhodes.edu

CB member
CB code: 1730

► Private 4-year liberal arts college affiliated with Presbyterian Church (USA)

► Residential campus in very large city

► 1,801 degree-seeking undergraduates: 60% women, 7% African American, 5% Asian American, 3% Hispanic American, 1% Native American, 3% international

► 10 degree-seeking graduate students

► 50% of applicants admitted

► SAT or ACT (ACT writing optional), application essay required

► 76% graduate within 6 years

General. Founded in 1848. Regionally accredited. **Degrees:** 359 bachelor's awarded; master's offered. **ROTC:** Army, Air Force. **Location:** 4 miles from

downtown. **Calendar:** Semester. **Full-time faculty:** 171 total; 96% have terminal degrees, 12% minority, 46% women. **Part-time faculty:** 34 total; 38% have terminal degrees, 18% minority, 44% women. **Class size:** 69% < 20, 29% 20-39, 1% 40-49, 1% 50-99. **Special facilities:** Arboretum, scanning electron microscope, rooftop observatory, cell culture facility, nuclear magnetic resonance instrument.

Freshman class profile. 5,211 applied, 2,617 admitted, 561 enrolled.

Mid 50% test scores			
SAT critical reading:	590-690	Rank in top quarter:	83%
SAT math:	590-680	Rank in top tenth:	51%
ACT composite:	26-31	Return as sophomores:	90%
GPA 3.75 or higher:	62%	Out-of-state:	73%
GPA 3.50-3.74:	16%	Live on campus:	97%
GPA 3.0-3.49:	18%	International:	2%
GPA 2.0-2.99:	4%	Fraternities:	30%
		Sororities:	60%

Basis for selection. Academic record, standardized test scores, class rank, recommendations, essay, school and community activities important. Applications sought from international students, minorities, and children of alumni. Interview recommended. **Home schooled:** 2 SAT Subject Tests other than math or literature required.

High school preparation. College-preparatory program required. 16 units required. Required units include English 4, mathematics 3, social studies 2, science 2 (laboratory 2), foreign language 2 and academic electives 3.

2011-2012 Annual costs. Tuition/fees: $36,464. Room/board: $8,976. Books/supplies: $1,071. Personal expenses: $1,415.

2011-2012 Financial aid. Need-based: 460 full-time freshmen applied for aid; 319 were judged to have need; 319 of these received aid. Average need met was 94%. Average scholarship/grant was $23,014; average loan $3,758. 83% of total undergraduate aid awarded as scholarships/grants, 17% as loans/jobs. **Non-need-based:** Awarded to 1,019 full-time undergraduates, including 329 freshmen. Scholarships awarded for academics, art, minority status, music/drama, religious affiliation. **Additional information:** Auditions required for theater and music achievement awards and art achievement awards. Interviews recommended for merit scholarships. Notification of admissions decision for Bellingrath Scholarship applicants by 3/15; must reply by 5/1.

Application procedures. Admission: Priority date 1/15; no deadline. $45 fee, may be waived for applicants with need, free for online applicants. **Financial aid:** Closing date 3/1. FAFSA, CSS PROFILE required. Must reply by 5/1.

Academics. Expense-paid summer internships in businesses abroad. Model United Nations program, opportunities for participation in computer-simulated international negotiating, mock trial program. **Special study options:** Combined bachelor's/graduate degree, cooperative education, cross-registration, double major, dual enrollment of high school students, exchange student, honors, independent study, internships, liberal arts/career combination, student-designed major, study abroad, Washington semester. **Credit/placement by examination:** AP, CLEP, IB, institutional tests. 28 credit hours maximum toward bachelor's degree. **Support services:** Tutoring, writing center.

Majors. Area/ethnic studies: African-American, Latin American, Russian/Slavic. **Biology:** General, Biochemistry/molecular biology, neuroscience. **Business:** Business admin, international. **Computer sciences:** Computer science. **English:** English lit. **Foreign languages:** Classics, French, German, Spanish. **History:** General. **Math:** General. **Philosophy/religion:** Philosophy, religion. **Physical sciences:** Chemistry, physics. **Psychology:** General. **Social sciences:** Anthropology, economics, international economics, international relations, political science, urban studies. **Visual/performing arts:** Art, dramatic, music.

Most popular majors. Biology 15%, business/marketing 11%, English 11%, history 6%, philosophy/religious studies 6%, physical sciences 7%, psychology 9%, social sciences 24%, visual/performing arts 7%.

Computing on campus. 220 workstations in library, computer center, student center. Dormitories wired for high-speed internet access and linked to campus network. Commuter students can connect to campus network. Online course registration, online library, helpline, repair service, wireless network available.

Student life. Freshman orientation: Mandatory, $110 fee. Preregistration for classes offered. Two-day summer program. **Policies:** Student-run honor system central to campus life. **Housing:** Guaranteed on-campus for freshmen. Coed dorms, single-sex dorms, apartments, wellness housing available. Special interest townhouses. **Activities:** Bands, campus ministries, choral groups, dance, drama, film society, international student organizations, literary magazine, music ensembles, Model UN, musical theater, radio station, student

government, student newspaper, symphony orchestra, TV station, black student association, social service club, Inter-Varsity Christian Fellowship, international house, Habitat for Humanity, interfaith circle, diversity group, College Democrats, College Republicans.

Athletics. NCAA. **Intercollegiate:** Baseball M, basketball, cross-country, field hockey W, football (tackle) M, golf, lacrosse M, soccer, softball W, swimming, tennis, track and field, volleyball W. **Intramural:** Basketball, football (non-tackle), football (tackle), racquetball, soccer, squash M, table tennis, tennis, volleyball. **Team name:** Lynx.

Student services. Alcohol/substance abuse counseling, chaplain/spiritual director, career counseling, student employment services, financial aid counseling, health services, minority student services, personal counseling, placement for graduates, women's services. **Physically disabled:** Services for visually, speech, hearing impaired.

Contact. E-mail: adminfo@rhodes.edu
Phone: (901) 843-3700 Toll-free number: (800) 844-5969
Fax: (901) 843-3631
David Wottle, Dean of Admissions and Financial Aid, Rhodes College, 2000 North Parkway, Memphis, TN 38112

South College
Knoxville, Tennessee
www.southcollegetn.edu   CB code: 0711

- For-profit 4-year liberal arts college
- Commuter campus in small city
- 1,018 degree-seeking undergraduates
- Interview required

General. Founded in 1882. Regionally accredited. **Degrees:** 88 bachelor's, 14 associate awarded; master's offered. **Location:** Downtown. **Calendar:** Quarter, extensive summer session. **Full-time faculty:** 110 total. **Part-time faculty:** 70 total.

Basis for selection. CPTS, SAT or ACT required. SAT or ACT recommended. **Home schooled:** Must provide minimum required ACT/SAT score or proof of passing GED.

2011-2012 Annual costs. Tuition/fees: $17,700. Reported annual costs are for programs in physical therapy assistance, radiography, health science. Costs of other programs vary by program. Books/supplies: $1,500. Personal expenses: $1,350.

Financial aid. All financial aid based on need.

Application procedures. Admission: No deadline. $50 fee. Admission notification on a rolling basis. **Financial aid:** No deadline. FAFSA, institutional form required. Applicants notified on a rolling basis.

Academics. Special study options: Accelerated study, double major, dual enrollment of high school students, internships, teacher certification program. **Credit/placement by examination:** AP, CLEP, institutional tests. **Support services:** Learning center, reduced course load, study skills assistance, tutoring, writing center.

Majors. Business: Business admin.

Computing on campus. 85 workstations in library, computer center. Online library, wireless network available.

Student life. Freshman orientation: Mandatory. Preregistration for classes offered. **Activities:** Literary magazine, student government, student newspaper, Collegiate Secretaries International, paralegal association, student affairs advisory council, business club, students of medical assisting, movie club, community service club.

Student services. Career counseling, student employment services, financial aid counseling, personal counseling, placement for graduates, veterans' counselor.

Contact. E-mail: admissions@southcollegetn.edu
Phone: (865) 251-1800 Fax: (865) 470-8737
Carrie Major, Admissions Director, South College, 3904 Lonas Drive, Knoxville, TN 37909

Southern Adventist University
Collegedale, Tennessee
www.southern.edu   CB code: 1727

- Private 4-year university and liberal arts college affiliated with Seventh-day Adventists
- Residential campus in small town
- 2,742 degree-seeking undergraduates
- SAT or ACT (ACT writing optional) required

General. Founded in 1892. Regionally accredited. **Degrees:** 373 bachelor's, 145 associate awarded; master's offered. **Location:** 18 miles from Chattanooga. **Calendar:** Semester, limited summer session. **Full-time faculty:** 161 total; 58% have terminal degrees, 11% minority, 44% women. **Part-time faculty:** 75 total; 64% have terminal degrees, 15% minority, 49% women. **Special facilities:** Civil War collection, Lincoln collection, Anton Memorial Organ.

Freshman class profile.

Out-of-state:	77%	Live on campus:	89%

Basis for selection. School achievement record and test scores important. SAT/ACT Writing component used in committee appeal. Interview recommended for all; audition required for music and gymnastics programs. **Home schooled:** Transcript of courses and grades required. Home school organization must be academically accredited or student must take GED. Portfolio required and must include copy of original research paper and written statement reflecting on value student received from home school experience.

High school preparation. College-preparatory program recommended. 18 units required; 24 recommended. Required and recommended units include English 3-4, mathematics 2-3, social studies 1, history 1-2, science 2-3, foreign language 2, computer science 1 and academic electives 9. One unit chemistry (2.0 GPA or better) required for nursing majors. 2 units foreign language required for BA program applicants. Computer competency strongly recommended.

2011-2012 Annual costs. Tuition/fees: $18,324. Room/board: $5,786. Books/supplies: $1,200. Personal expenses: $2,000.

Financial aid. Non-need-based: Scholarships awarded for academics, alumni affiliation, art, athletics, leadership, music/drama.

Application procedures. Admission: No deadline. $25 fee, may be waived for applicants with need. Admission notification on a rolling basis. **Financial aid:** Priority date 3/1; no closing date. FAFSA required. Applicants notified on a rolling basis starting 2/15; must reply within 2 week(s) of notification.

Academics. Special study options: Combined bachelor's/graduate degree, distance learning, double major, dual enrollment of high school students, ESL, honors, independent study, internships, study abroad, teacher certification program. **Credit/placement by examination:** AP, CLEP, SAT, ACT, institutional tests. 12 credit hours maximum toward associate degree, 12 toward bachelor's. **Support services:** Learning center, reduced course load, remedial instruction, study skills assistance, tutoring, writing center.

Majors. Biology: General, biochemistry, biophysics. **Business:** Accounting, business admin, finance, human resources, international, management information systems, management science, marketing, nonprofit/public. **Communications:** Advertising, broadcast journalism, intercultural, journalism, media studies, public relations. **Communications technology:** General. **Computer sciences:** Computer science, programming. **Education:** Art, biology, chemistry, elementary, English, French, history, mathematics, music, physical, physics, Spanish. **English:** English lit. **Foreign languages:** General, French, Spanish. **Health services:** Art therapy, clinical lab science, health care admin, nursing (RN). **History:** General, European. **Human services:** Social work. **Math:** General. **Parks/recreation:** Exercise sciences, sports admin. **Philosophy/religion:** Religion. **Physical sciences:** Chemistry, physics. **Psychology:** General, clinical, industrial, psychobiology. **Social sciences:** Archaeology. **Theology:** Missionary, pastoral counseling, religious ed, theology. **Visual/performing arts:** Art, cinematography, commercial/advertising art, graphic design, music, music performance, music theory/composition, photography. **Work/family studies:** Family systems.

Most popular majors. Business/marketing 16%, communications/journalism 7%, education 9%, health sciences 16%, theological studies 8%, visual/performing arts 7%.

Computing on campus. 200 workstations in dormitories, library, computer center. Dormitories wired for high-speed internet access and linked to campus network. Commuter students can connect to campus network. Online course registration, online library, helpline, repair service, student web hosting, wireless network available.

Student life. Freshman orientation: Mandatory. Preregistration for classes offered. Held prior to registration. Includes exams and instruction in course planning. **Policies:** Alcohol- and drug-free campus. Religious observance required. **Housing:** Guaranteed on-campus for all undergraduates. Single-sex dorms, apartments available. $250 fully refundable deposit, deadline 6/1. **Activities:** Bands, campus ministries, choral groups, drama, film society, music ensembles, radio station, student government, student newspaper, symphony orchestra, TV station, African club, Black Christian Union, Partners at Wellness, Association of South East Asian Nation Students.

Athletics. Intramural: Badminton, basketball, racquetball, soccer, softball, table tennis, tennis, volleyball.

Student services. Chaplain/spiritual director, career counseling, student employment services, financial aid counseling, health services, personal counseling, placement for graduates, veterans' counselor.

Contact. E-mail: admissions@southern.edu
Phone: (423) 236-2835 Toll-free number: (800) 768-8437
Fax: (423) 236-1835
Marc Grundy, Director of Admissions, Southern Adventist University, PO Box 370, Collegedale, TN 37315-0370

Tennessee State University

Nashville, Tennessee
www.tnstate.edu

CB member
CB code: 1803

- Public 4-year university
- Residential campus in very large city
- 6,938 degree-seeking undergraduates: 21% part-time, 62% women
- 1,871 degree-seeking graduate students
- 57% of applicants admitted
- SAT or ACT with writing required
- 40% graduate within 6 years

General. Founded in 1912. Regionally accredited. **Degrees:** 972 bachelor's, 115 associate awarded; master's, doctoral offered. **ROTC:** Air Force. **Location:** 115 miles from Chattanooga, 195 miles from Memphis. **Calendar:** Semester, limited summer session. **Full-time faculty:** 412 total; 84% have terminal degrees, 64% minority, 43% women. **Part-time faculty:** 167 total; 40% have terminal degrees, 48% minority, 56% women. **Class size:** 45% < 20, 49% 20-39, 4% 40-49, 3% 50-99, less than 1% >100. **Special facilities:** Observatory, research and demonstration farm, geospatial information systems labratory.

Freshman class profile. 5,986 applied, 3,426 admitted, 1,152 enrolled.

Mid 50% test scores			
SAT critical reading:	400-500	GPA 3.0-3.49:	26%
SAT math:	380-480	GPA 2.0-2.99:	63%
ACT composite:	15-20	Return as sophomores:	85%
GPA 3.75 or higher:	3%	Out-of-state:	28%
GPA 3.50-3.74:	7%	Live on campus:	80%

Basis for selection. School achievement record, test scores important. Interview required for health sciences, nursing, physical therapy programs. **Home schooled:** State high school equivalency certificate required.

High school preparation. 14 units required. Required units include English 4, mathematics 3, social studies 2, science 2 (laboratory 1) and foreign language 2. One unit visual and/or performing arts recommended.

2011-2012 Annual costs. Tuition/fees: $6,346; $19,498 out-of-state. Room/board: $5,910. Books/supplies: $1,250. Personal expenses: $1,500.

Financial aid. Non-need-based: Scholarships awarded for academics.

Application procedures. Admission: Closing date 8/1. $25 fee. Application must be submitted on paper. Admission notification on a rolling basis. **Financial aid:** Priority date 4/1; no closing date. FAFSA required. Applicants notified on a rolling basis starting 4/15; must reply within 3 week(s) of notification.

Academics. Special study options: Combined bachelor's/graduate degree, cooperative education, cross-registration, distance learning, double major, ESL, exchange student, honors, independent study, internships, liberal arts/career combination, study abroad, teacher certification program. **Credit/placement by examination:** AP, CLEP, SAT, ACT, institutional tests. 33 credit hours maximum toward bachelor's degree. **Support services:** Learning center, remedial instruction, study skills assistance, tutoring, writing center.

Majors. Architecture: Architecture. **Biology:** General, biochemistry. **Business:** Accounting, administrative services, business admin, managerial economics. **Communications:** Communications/speech/rhetoric, journalism.

Computer sciences: Computer science. **Education:** General, early childhood, physical, secondary, special ed. **Engineering:** General, architectural, civil, electrical. **English:** English lit. **Foreign languages:** French, Spanish. **General:** Animal sciences. **Health services:** Audiology/speech pathology, dental hygiene, health care admin, medical records admin. **History:** General. **Human services:** Social work. **Liberal arts:** Arts/sciences. **Math:** General. **Physical sciences:** Chemistry, physics. **Protective services:** Criminal justice. **Psychology:** General. **Social sciences:** General, political science, sociology, urban studies. **Visual/performing arts:** Art history/conservation, dramatic, music. **Work/family studies:** General, clothing/textiles, family studies, food/nutrition.

Most popular majors. Business/marketing 17%, health sciences 15%, liberal arts 20%, psychology 6%, visual/performing arts 7%.

Computing on campus. 450 workstations in dormitories, library, computer center, student center. Dormitories wired for high-speed internet access and linked to campus network. Commuter students can connect to campus network. Online course registration, online library, helpline, repair service, student web hosting, wireless network available.

Student life. Freshman orientation: Mandatory. Preregistration for classes offered. **Housing:** Coed dorms, single-sex dorms, apartments available. $100 fully refundable deposit, deadline 4/1. **Activities:** Bands, choral groups, dance, drama, film society, international student organizations, music ensembles, musical theater, radio station, student government, student newspaper, TV station, religious organizations, honor organization, literary organization.

Athletics. NCAA. Intercollegiate: Baseball M, basketball, cheerleading, cross-country, football (tackle) M, golf, softball W, tennis, track and field, volleyball W. **Intramural:** Basketball, bowling, football (non-tackle) M, racquetball, tennis, track and field, volleyball. **Team name:** Tigers.

Student services. Career counseling, student employment services, financial aid counseling, health services, minority student services, on-campus daycare, personal counseling, placement for graduates, veterans' counselor, women's services. **Physically disabled:** Services for visually, speech, hearing impaired.

Contact. Phone: (615) 963-5101 Fax: (615) 963-5108
Michael Freeman, Vice President of Student Affairs, Tennessee State University, 3500 John A. Merritt Boulevard, Nashville, TN 37209-1561

Tennessee Technological University

Cookeville, Tennessee
www.tntech.edu

CB member
CB code: 1804

- Public 4-year university
- Residential campus in large town
- 9,479 degree-seeking undergraduates: 7% part-time, 46% women, 4% African American, 1% Asian American, 2% Hispanic American, 3% international
- 1,483 degree-seeking graduate students
- 97% of applicants admitted
- SAT or ACT (ACT writing recommended) required
- 50% graduate within 6 years

General. Founded in 1915. Regionally accredited. **Degrees:** 1,626 bachelor's awarded; master's offered. **ROTC:** Army, Air Force. **Location:** 80 miles from Nashville, 100 miles from Knoxville. **Calendar:** Semester, extensive summer session. **Full-time faculty:** 389 total; 75% have terminal degrees, 13% minority, 40% women. **Part-time faculty:** 251 total; 25% have terminal degrees, 4% minority, 64% women. **Class size:** 34% < 20, 46% 20-39, 8% 40-49, 7% 50-99, 4% >100. **Special facilities:** Center for crafts, cooperative fishery research unit, agricultural pavilion, center for energy systems research, center for manufacturing research, center for the management, utilization and protection of water resources, childcare resource center, STEM center.

Freshman class profile. 4,447 applied, 4,318 admitted, 1,968 enrolled.

Mid 50% test scores			
SAT critical reading:	480-620	Rank in top quarter:	53%
SAT math:	500-650	Rank in top tenth:	25%
ACT composite:	20-26	Return as sophomores:	73%
GPA 3.75 or higher:	29%	Out-of-state:	2%
GPA 3.50-3.74:	20%	Live on campus:	66%
GPA 3.0-3.49:	31%	International:	4%
GPA 2.0-2.99:	20%	Fraternities:	12%
		Sororities:	17%

Basis for selection. High school classes, GPA and test scores very important. Additional requirements for engineering, computer science, nursing and

pre-professional majors. Interview recommended for all; audition recommended for music; portfolio recommended for arts, crafts. **Home schooled:** 2.5 GPA and 19 ACT or GED required.

High school preparation. 14 units required. Required units include English 4, mathematics 3, social studies 1, history 1, science 2 (laboratory 1) and foreign language 2. Math units must include algebra I and II and geometry or advanced math course. Science units must be biology, chemistry, or physics with laboratories (can include physical sciences). Foreign language units must be in single language. 1 U.S. history, 1 unit visual and/or performing arts also required. Social studies must be either world, ancient, modern, or European history, or world geography.

2011-2012 Annual costs. Tuition/fees: $6,698; $21,008 out-of-state. Room/board: $7,484. Books/supplies: $780. Personal expenses: $840.

Financial aid. Non-need-based: Scholarships awarded for academics, alumni affiliation, art, athletics, leadership, minority status, music/drama, ROTC, state residency. **Additional information:** Tuition and/or fee waivers available for children of Tennessee public school teachers.

Application procedures. Admission: Priority date 5/1; deadline 8/1 (postmark date). $25 fee. Admission notification on a rolling basis. **Financial aid:** Priority date 3/15; no closing date. FAFSA required. Applicants notified on a rolling basis starting 3/15; must reply within 2 week(s) of notification.

Academics. Special study options: Accelerated study, cooperative education, distance learning, double major, dual enrollment of high school students, ESL, honors, independent study, internships, liberal arts/career combination, study abroad, teacher certification program. **Credit/placement by examination:** AP, CLEP, IB, institutional tests. 33 credit hours maximum toward bachelor's degree. **Support services:** Learning center, pre-admission summer program, reduced course load, remedial instruction, study skills assistance, tutoring, writing center.

Majors. Biology: General, biochemistry. **Business:** General, accounting, finance, labor relations, management science, managerial economics, operations. **Communications:** Communications/speech/rhetoric, journalism. **Communications technology:** General. **Computer sciences:** General, computer science, web page design. **Conservation:** General, fisheries, wildlife/wilderness. **Education:** General, agricultural, early childhood, English, health, music, physical, secondary, special ed. **Engineering:** Chemical, civil, computer, electrical, mechanical. **English:** English lit, technical writing. **Foreign languages:** French, German, Spanish. **General:** Agribusiness operations, agronomy, animal sciences, horticultural science, horticulture, landscaping, nursery operations, soil science. **Health services:** Nursing (RN), predental, premedicine, prepharmacy, preveterinary. **History:** General. **Math:** General. **Parks/recreation:** Health/fitness. **Physical sciences:** Chemistry, geology, physics. **Psychology:** General. **Social sciences:** Economics, political science, sociology. **Visual/performing arts:** Ceramics, drawing, fiber arts, music performance, painting, sculpture, studio arts. **Work/family studies:** General, clothing/textiles, family/community services, food/nutrition, housing.

Most popular majors. Business/marketing 16%, engineering/engineering technologies 15%, interdisciplinary studies 18%, liberal arts 6%.

Computing on campus. 600 workstations in dormitories, library, computer center. Dormitories wired for high-speed internet access and linked to campus network. Commuter students can connect to campus network. Online course registration, online library, helpline, wireless network available.

Student life. Freshman orientation: Mandatory, $45 fee. Preregistration for classes offered. **Housing:** Guaranteed on-campus for freshmen. Coed dorms, single-sex dorms, special housing for disabled, apartments, fraternity/sorority housing available. $50 deposit. Learning Villages. **Activities:** Bands, campus ministries, choral groups, dance, drama, international student organizations, literary magazine, music ensembles, musical theater, opera, radio station, student government, student newspaper, symphony orchestra, TV station, over 200 organizations.

Athletics. NCAA. **Intercollegiate:** Baseball M, basketball, cheerleading, cross-country, football (tackle) M, golf, soccer W, softball W, tennis M, track and field W, volleyball W. **Intramural:** Basketball, bowling, golf M, handball, racquetball, rugby M, soccer, softball, tennis, volleyball, wrestling M. **Team name:** Golden Eagles.

Student services. Alcohol/substance abuse counseling, career counseling, student employment services, financial aid counseling, health services, minority student services, on-campus daycare, personal counseling, placement for graduates, veterans' counselor, women's services. **Physically disabled:** Services for visually, speech, hearing impaired.

Contact. E-mail: admissions@tntech.edu
Phone: (931) 372-3888 Toll-free number: (800) 255-8881
Fax: (931) 372-6250
Vanessa Palmer, Admissions, Tennessee Technological University, Office of Admissions, Cookeville, TN 38505-0001

Tennessee Temple University
Chattanooga, Tennessee
www.tntemple.edu   **CB code: 1818**

▸ Private 4-year university and seminary college affiliated with Baptist faith
▸ Residential campus in small city

General. Founded in 1946. **Location:** 120 miles from Atlanta. **Calendar:** Semester.

Annual costs/financial aid. Tuition/fees (2011-2012): $11,290. Room/board: $6,030. Books/supplies: $700. Personal expenses: $850. Need-based financial aid available to full-time and part-time students.

Contact. Phone: (423) 493-4371
Director of Enrollment Services, 1815 Union Avenue, Chattanooga, TN 37404

Tennessee Wesleyan College
Athens, Tennessee
www.twcnet.edu   **CB code: 1805**

▸ Private 4-year liberal arts and teachers college affiliated with United Methodist Church
▸ Commuter campus in large town
▸ 1,068 degree-seeking undergraduates: 8% part-time, 65% women, 5% African American, 1% Asian American, 1% Hispanic American, 2% international
▸ 82% of applicants admitted
▸ SAT or ACT (ACT writing optional) required
▸ 44% graduate within 6 years

General. Founded in 1857. Regionally accredited. Baccalaureate programs in nursing and evening business school through Knoxville campus. **Degrees:** 235 bachelor's awarded. **ROTC:** Army, Naval, Air Force. **Location:** 50 miles from Chattanooga and Knoxville. **Calendar:** Semester, extensive summer session. **Full-time faculty:** 53 total; 70% have terminal degrees, 4% minority, 47% women. **Part-time faculty:** 48 total; 27% have terminal degrees, 54% women. **Class size:** 58% < 20, 36% 20-39, 3% 40-49, 3% 50-99.

Freshman class profile. 653 applied, 538 admitted, 208 enrolled.

Mid 50% test scores				
SAT critical reading:	400-490	Rank in top quarter:	44%
SAT math:	380-490	Rank in top tenth:	25%
ACT composite:	19-24	Return as sophomores:	66%
GPA 3.75 or higher:	26%	Out-of-state:	20%
GPA 3.50-3.74:	16%	Live on campus:	59%
GPA 3.0-3.49:	31%	International:	1%
GPA 2.0-2.99:	27%	Fraternities:	2%
		Sororities:	10%

Basis for selection. Test scores, school records, recommendations and GPA very important. ACT/SAT not required if student has GED. Essay recommended for all; interview recommended for academically weak; audition required for music and theater.

High school preparation. College-preparatory program recommended. 10 units recommended. Recommended units include English 4, mathematics 2, social studies 1, history 1 and science 2.

2011-2012 Annual costs. Tuition/fees: $19,700. Room/board: $6,480. Books/supplies: $1,200. Personal expenses: $1,000.

2010-2011 Financial aid. Need-based: 224 full-time freshmen applied for aid; 209 were judged to have need; 208 of these received aid. Average need met was 65%. Average scholarship/grant was $14,604; average loan $2,831. 69% of total undergraduate aid awarded as scholarships/grants, 31% as loans/jobs. **Non-need-based:** Awarded to 279 full-time undergraduates, including 65 freshmen. Scholarships awarded for academics, alumni affiliation, athletics, minority status, music/drama, religious affiliation.

Application procedures. Admission: Closing date 8/15 (receipt date). $25 fee, may be waived for applicants with need. Admission notification on a rolling basis beginning on or about 9/1. **Financial aid:** Priority date 2/15; no closing date. FAFSA, institutional form required. Applicants notified on a rolling basis starting 2/15; must reply within 2 week(s) of notification.

Academics. Study abroad opportunities available for students wishing to extend their learning globally. **Special study options:** Accelerated study, double major, dual enrollment of high school students, exchange student,

honors, independent study, internships, student-designed major, study abroad, teacher certification program. Member of the Private College Consortium for International Studies (semester in London program). **Credit/placement by examination:** AP, CLEP, IB, SAT, ACT, institutional tests. 12 credit hours maximum toward bachelor's degree. **Support services:** Learning center, reduced course load, remedial instruction, study skills assistance, tutoring, writing center.

Majors. Area/ethnic studies: American. **Biology:** General. **Business:** Accounting, business admin, finance, human resources, marketing. **Computer sciences:** General. **Conservation:** Environmental studies. **Education:** Early childhood, elementary, multi-level teacher, secondary, special ed. **English:** English lit. **Health services:** Nursing (RN), predental, premedicine, prenursing, prepharmacy, prephysical therapy, preveterinary. **History:** General. **Math:** General. **Parks/recreation:** Health/fitness, sports admin. **Philosophy/religion:** Christian. **Physical sciences:** Chemistry. **Protective services:** Criminal justice. **Psychology:** General. **Social sciences:** Sociology. **Theology:** Preministerial. **Visual/performing arts:** Music.

Most popular majors. Business/marketing 25%, education 13%, health sciences 24%, interdisciplinary studies 8%, parks/recreation 10%.

Computing on campus. 133 workstations in dormitories, library, computer center, student center. Dormitories wired for high-speed internet access and linked to campus network. Online library, wireless network available.

Student life. Freshman orientation: Mandatory. Preregistration for classes offered. Held in August. **Policies:** All students required to live on-campus unless residing with relative within commuting distance, married, or have children. Visitation hours in dorms by opposite sex restricted. No alcohol allowed on campus. Religious observance required. **Housing:** Guaranteed on-campus for freshmen. Single-sex dorms, apartments, wellness housing available. **Activities:** Bands, campus ministries, choral groups, drama, literary magazine, music ensembles, student government, student newspaper, Circle K, Hackberry and Oak Society, National Student Nurses Association, student activities board, Education Angels, Fellowship of Christian Athletes, Wesleyan Christian Fellowship, College Democrats.

Athletics. NAIA. **Intercollegiate:** Baseball M, basketball, cross-country, golf, soccer, softball W, tennis, volleyball W. **Team name:** Bulldogs.

Student services. Adult student services, alcohol/substance abuse counseling, chaplain/spiritual director, career counseling, student employment services, financial aid counseling, personal counseling, placement for graduates, veterans' counselor. **Physically disabled:** Services for visually, hearing impaired.

Contact. E-mail: admissions@twcnet.edu
Phone: (423) 745-7504 Toll-free number: (800) 742-5892
Fax: (423) 745-9335
Kara Fox, Director of Enrollment Services, Tennessee Wesleyan College, 204 East College Street, Athens, TN 37371-0040

Trevecca Nazarene University
Nashville, Tennessee
www.trevecca.edu   CB code: 1809

- Private 4-year university and liberal arts college affiliated with Church of the Nazarene
- Residential campus in very large city
- 1,379 degree-seeking undergraduates: 14% part-time, 56% women, 8% African American, 1% Asian American, 3% Hispanic American, 1% Native American, 1% international
- 1,034 degree-seeking graduate students
- 77% of applicants admitted
- SAT or ACT (ACT writing optional) required
- 54% graduate within 6 years

General. Founded in 1901. Regionally accredited. **Degrees:** 375 bachelor's, 3 associate awarded; master's, doctoral offered. **ROTC:** Army. **Location:** 200 miles from Memphis, 175 miles from Knoxville. **Calendar:** Semester, limited summer session. **Full-time faculty:** 85 total; 86% have terminal degrees, 5% minority, 29% women. **Part-time faculty:** 145 total; 44% have terminal degrees, 4% minority, 46% women. **Class size:** 70% < 20, 26% 20-39, 2% 40-49, 2% 50-99.

Freshman class profile. 1,105 applied, 848 admitted, 269 enrolled.

Mid 50% test scores				
SAT critical reading:	450-620	GPA 2.0-2.99:		30%
SAT math:	460-600	Rank in top quarter:		52%
ACT composite:	19-26	Rank in top tenth:		20%
GPA 3.75 or higher:	29%	Return as sophomores:		69%
GPA 3.50-3.74:	19%	Out-of-state:		39%
GPA 3.0-3.49:	22%	Live on campus:		83%
		International:		3%

Basis for selection. 18 ACT/860 SAT (exclusive of Writing) or 2.5 GPA required. **Home schooled:** Transcript with all subjects and grades should be provided by correspondence-school based organization or by the parent depending on method of homeschooling. **Learning Disabled:** Students should contact Disability Services for information concerning documentation of disability and services available.

High school preparation. College-preparatory program recommended. 15 units recommended. Recommended units include English 4, mathematics 2, social studies 1, history 1, science 1, foreign language 2 and academic electives 4.

2011-2012 Annual costs. Tuition/fees: $20,590. Room/board: $7,488. Books/supplies: $1,100. Personal expenses: $405.

2010-2011 Financial aid. Need-based: 53% of total undergraduate aid awarded as scholarships/grants, 47% as loans/jobs. **Non-need-based:** Scholarships awarded for academics, alumni affiliation, athletics, leadership, minority status, music/drama, religious affiliation.

Application procedures. Admission: Priority date 4/1; deadline 8/1. $25 fee, may be waived for applicants with need, free for online applicants. Admission notification on a rolling basis. Must reply by May 1 or within 2 week(s) if notified thereafter. Enrollment deposit of $200 due by 5/1; refundable only if notification received by 5/1. **Financial aid:** Priority date 3/1, closing date 8/1. FAFSA required. Applicants notified on a rolling basis starting 3/1.

Academics. Special study options: Combined bachelor's/graduate degree, distance learning, double major, internships, study abroad, teacher certification program. 4 adult degree completion programs offer class schedules at night/online (varies by program). **Credit/placement by examination:** AP, CLEP, IB, SAT, ACT. 22 credit hours maximum toward associate degree, 45 toward bachelor's. Credit awarded after one semester and tuition paid. **Support services:** Learning center, remedial instruction, study skills assistance, tutoring.

Majors. Biology: General. **Business:** Accounting, business admin, e-commerce, marketing, nonprofit/public. **Communications:** Communications/speech/rhetoric, digital media, journalism, media studies, organizational. **Communications technology:** Radio/TV. **Computer sciences:** Information technology, web page design, webmaster. **Education:** Biology, business, chemistry, drama/dance, early childhood, elementary, English, history, mathematics, music, physical, physics, secondary, special ed, speech. **Engineering:** Applied physics. **English:** English lit. **Health services:** General, clinical lab science, medical records admin, nursing (RN). **History:** General. **Human services:** Public policy, social work. **Math:** General, applied, biological, financial. **Parks/recreation:** Physical fitness technician, sports admin, sports studies. **Physical sciences:** Chemistry, physics. **Protective services:** Law enforcement admin. **Psychology:** General. **Social sciences:** Sociology. **Theology:** Lay ministry, missionary, sacred music, youth ministry. **Visual/performing arts:** Dramatic, music management, music performance. **Work/family studies:** Food/nutrition.

Most popular majors. Business/marketing 44%, education 10%, visual/performing arts 7%.

Computing on campus. 200 workstations in dormitories, library, computer center, student center. Dormitories linked to campus network. Commuter students can connect to campus network. Online course registration, online library, helpline, wireless network available.

Student life. Freshman orientation: Mandatory. Preregistration for classes offered. **Policies:** Religious observance required. **Housing:** Single-sex dorms, apartments available. **Activities:** Bands, campus ministries, choral groups, drama, international student organizations, literary magazine, music ensembles, musical theater, student government, student newspaper, symphony orchestra, TV station, mission club, ministerial association, Phi Beta Lambda.

Athletics. NAIA. **Intercollegiate:** Baseball M, basketball, cross-country, golf, soccer, softball W, volleyball W. **Intramural:** Badminton, basketball, football (tackle) M, golf, racquetball, softball, table tennis, track and field, volleyball. **Team name:** Trojans.

Student services. Chaplain/spiritual director, career counseling, student employment services, financial aid counseling, health services, personal counseling, placement for graduates.

Contact. E-mail: admissions_und@trevecca.edu
Phone: (615) 248-1320 Toll-free number: (888) 210-4868
Fax: (615) 248-7406
Holly Whitby, Director of Admissions, Trevecca Nazarene University, 333 Murfreesboro Road, Nashville, TN 37210

Tusculum College
Greeneville, Tennessee
www.tusculum.edu
CB member
CB code: 1812

- Private 4-year liberal arts college affiliated with Presbyterian Church (USA)
- Residential campus in large town
- 1,914 degree-seeking undergraduates: 4% part-time, 58% women, 13% African American, 1% Asian American, 2% Hispanic American, 2% international
- 214 degree-seeking graduate students
- 69% of applicants admitted
- SAT or ACT (ACT writing optional), application essay required
- 38% graduate within 6 years; 12% enter graduate study

General. Founded in 1794. Regionally accredited. Strong civic arts focus and service-learning curriculum. **Degrees:** 418 bachelor's awarded; master's offered. **Location:** 70 miles from Knoxville, 30 miles from Johnson City. **Calendar:** Semester, limited summer session. **Full-time faculty:** 77 total. **Part-time faculty:** 130 total. **Class size:** 65% < 20, 35% 20-39.

Freshman class profile. 3,081 applied, 2,137 admitted, 282 enrolled.

Mid 50% test scores			
SAT critical reading:	420-520	Return as sophomores:	59%
SAT math:	430-570	Out-of-state:	33%
ACT composite:	19-24	Live on campus:	71%
		International:	4%

Basis for selection. Admissions based on secondary school record and standardized test scores. Essay also important. Math and English placement tests may be required based on ACT or SAT scores. Interview recommended. **Home schooled:** Statement describing home school structure and mission, interview required. Syllabi for all courses taken and list of textbooks required.

High school preparation. 12 units required. Required units include English 4, mathematics 3, social studies 3, science 2 (laboratory 1).

2011-2012 Annual costs. Tuition/fees: $20,910. Room/board: $8,000. Books/supplies: $1,200. Personal expenses: $1,400.

Financial aid. Non-need-based: Scholarships awarded for academics, athletics, leadership, religious affiliation, state residency.

Application procedures. Admission: No deadline. No application fee. Admission notification on a rolling basis. **Financial aid:** Closing date 2/15. FAFSA required. Applicants notified on a rolling basis starting 3/1; must reply within 3 week(s) of notification.

Academics. Semesters comprised of 4 blocks, each 3 1/2 weeks long. Students take one course per block. Intensive 16-month professional studies program designed for non-traditional students also offered. **Special study options:** Accelerated study, combined bachelor's/graduate degree, double major, honors, independent study, internships, student-designed major, study abroad, teacher certification program. **Credit/placement by examination:** AP, CLEP, SAT, ACT, institutional tests. 30 credit hours maximum toward bachelor's degree. **Support services:** Learning center, pre-admission summer program, study skills assistance, tutoring, writing center.

Majors. Biology: General. **Business:** Accounting, business admin, entrepreneurial studies. **Communications:** Journalism. **Conservation:** General, environmental studies. **Education:** Art, biology, business, early childhood, elementary, English, health, history, mathematics, middle, physical, psychology, secondary, special ed. **English:** English lit. **Health services:** Athletic training, clinical lab science, premedicine, prepharmacy. **History:** General. **Math:** General. **Parks/recreation:** Health/fitness, sports admin. **Psychology:** General. **Social sciences:** Political science. **Visual/performing arts:** General.

Computing on campus. 160 workstations in library, computer center, student center. Dormitories wired for high-speed internet access and linked to campus network. Commuter students can connect to campus network. Online library, helpline, repair service available.

Student life. Freshman orientation: Mandatory. Preregistration for classes offered. **Housing:** Guaranteed on-campus for freshmen. Single-sex dorms, apartments available. $200 nonrefundable deposit, deadline 6/1. Pets allowed in dorm rooms. **Activities:** Bands, campus ministries, choral groups,

drama, literary magazine, radio station, student government, student newspaper, TV station, Bonwandi, campus activities board, Fellowship of Christian Athletes.

Athletics. NCAA. **Intercollegiate:** Baseball M, basketball, cheerleading M, cross-country, football (tackle) M, golf, soccer, softball W, tennis, volleyball W. **Intramural:** Basketball, football (tackle), soccer, softball, table tennis, tennis, volleyball. **Team name:** Pioneers.

Student services. Adult student services, alcohol/substance abuse counseling, chaplain/spiritual director, career counseling, financial aid counseling, health services, personal counseling, placement for graduates, veterans' counselor.

Contact. E-mail: mripley@tusculum.edu
Phone: (423) 636-7300 Toll-free number: (800) 729-0256
Fax: (423) 798-1622
Melissa Ripley, Director of Admissions, Tusculum College, 60 Shiloh Road, Greeneville, TN 37743

Union University
Jackson, Tennessee
www.uu.edu
CB code: 1826

- Private 4-year university and liberal arts college affiliated with Southern Baptist Convention
- Residential campus in small city
- 2,481 degree-seeking undergraduates: 12% part-time, 60% women, 12% African American, 1% Asian American, 2% Hispanic American, 1% international
- 927 degree-seeking graduate students
- 77% of applicants admitted
- SAT or ACT (ACT writing optional) required
- 61% graduate within 6 years

General. Founded in 1823. Regionally accredited. **Degrees:** 644 bachelor's, 4 associate awarded; master's, professional, doctoral offered. **ROTC:** Army. **Location:** 80 miles from Memphis, 120 miles from Nashville. **Calendar:** Semester, extensive summer session. **Full-time faculty:** 238 total; 78% have terminal degrees, 8% minority, 48% women. **Part-time faculty:** 4 total; 25% have terminal degrees, 50% women. **Class size:** 69% < 20, 27% 20-39, 3% 40-49, 1% 50-99. **Special facilities:** Aquatic center, creative communications center.

Freshman class profile. 1,923 applied, 1,472 admitted, 487 enrolled.

Mid 50% test scores			
SAT critical reading:	530-670	Rank in top quarter:	63%
SAT math:	510-650	Rank in top tenth:	37%
ACT composite:	23-30	Return as sophomores:	94%
GPA 3.75 or higher:	53%	Out-of-state:	36%
GPA 3.50-3.74:	17%	Live on campus:	83%
GPA 3.0-3.49:	22%	Fraternities:	29%
GPA 2.0-2.99:	8%	Sororities:	20%

Basis for selection. School achievement, recommendations, special talents, test scores important. 22 ACT or 1030 SAT (exclusive of Writing), top 50% of high school class, and 2.5 GPA required. Interview recommended for all; audition required for music; portfolio recommended for art, communications. Essay required for academic and leadership scholarships. **Home schooled:** If class rank is unavailable, students may be admitted without conditions provided they meet minimum ACT/SAT scores and GPA requirements.

High school preparation. College-preparatory program required. 15 units required; 22 recommended. Required and recommended units include English 4, mathematics 3-4, social studies 2, history 1-2, science 3-4 (laboratory 2), foreign language 1-2, computer science 1, visual/performing arts 1 and academic electives 1-4.

2011-2012 Annual costs. Tuition/fees: $24,030. Room/board: $8,090. Books/supplies: $1,200. Personal expenses: $3,700.

2011-2012 Financial aid. Need-based: Average need met was 71%. Average scholarship/grant was $6,207; average loan $3,406. 62% of total undergraduate aid awarded as scholarships/grants, 38% as loans/jobs. **Non-need-based:** Scholarships awarded for academics, alumni affiliation, art, athletics, job skills, leadership, minority status, music/drama, religious affiliation, state residency.

Application procedures. Admission: Priority date 12/1; deadline 8/1 (postmark date). $35 fee, may be waived for applicants with need. Admission notification on a rolling basis beginning on or about 10/1. Must reply by

May 1 or within 2 week(s) if notified thereafter. **Financial aid:** Priority date 2/1; no closing date. FAFSA, institutional form required. Applicants notified on a rolling basis starting 3/1; must reply by 5/1 or within 2 week(s) of notification.

Academics. Special study options: Accelerated study, combined bachelor's/graduate degree, cooperative education, cross-registration, distance learning, double major, dual enrollment of high school students, ESL, exchange student, honors, independent study, internships, study abroad, teacher certification program, Washington semester. **Credit/placement by examination:** AP, CLEP, IB, SAT, ACT, institutional tests. 32 credit hours maximum toward bachelor's degree. **Support services:** Learning center, preadmission summer program, reduced course load, remedial instruction, study skills assistance, tutoring, writing center.

Majors. Biology: General, cellular/molecular, conservation, zoology. **Business:** Accounting, business admin, international, managerial economics, marketing. **Communications:** Advertising, broadcast journalism, communications/speech/rhetoric, digital media, journalism, public relations. **Computer sciences:** Computer science, web page design. **Education:** General, art, biology, business, chemistry, early childhood special, elementary, English, ESL, foreign languages, French, history, kindergarten/preschool, mathematics, middle, music, physical, science, secondary, Spanish, special ed. **Engineering:** Applied physics, electrical, mechanical. **English:** English lit, rhetoric/composition. **Foreign languages:** French, Spanish. **Health services:** Athletic training, clinical lab science, nursing (RN). **History:** General. **Human services:** Social work. **Math:** General. **Parks/recreation:** Exercise sciences, sports admin. **Philosophy/religion:** Christian, ethics, philosophy, religion. **Physical sciences:** General, chemical physics, chemistry, physics. **Psychology:** General. **Social sciences:** Economics, political science, sociology. **Theology:** Sacred music, theology, youth ministry. **Visual/performing arts:** Dramatic, music, music performance, music theory/composition, studio arts. **Work/family studies:** Family systems.

Most popular majors. Business/marketing 7%, communications/journalism 6%, education 13%, health sciences 21%, interdisciplinary studies 18%.

Computing on campus. 300 workstations in dormitories, library, computer center, student center. Dormitories wired for high-speed internet access and linked to campus network. Commuter students can connect to campus network. Online course registration, online library, helpline, repair service, wireless network available.

Student life. Freshman orientation: Available, $70 fee. Preregistration for classes offered. Held 4 days before classes begin. **Policies:** Full-time resident students required to attend 14 chapel services per semester. Smoke and alcohol-free campus. Religious observance required. **Housing:** Guaranteed on-campus for all undergraduates. Single-sex dorms, special housing for disabled, apartments available. $100 nonrefundable deposit, deadline 5/1. **Activities:** Bands, campus ministries, choral groups, drama, film society, international student organizations, literary magazine, music ensembles, student government, student newspaper, Fellowship of Christian Athletes, ministerial association, student activity council, Mu Kappa, honors student association, Tennessee Intercollegiate State Legislature, LIFE Groups, Klemata.

Athletics. NAIA, NCAA. **Intercollegiate:** Baseball M, basketball, cheerleading M, cross-country, golf, soccer, softball W, volleyball W. **Intramural:** Basketball, cheerleading W, cross-country, football (non-tackle), golf, racquetball, softball, swimming, table tennis, tennis, volleyball, weight lifting. **Team name:** Bulldogs.

Student services. Adult student services, alcohol/substance abuse counseling, chaplain/spiritual director, career counseling, student employment services, financial aid counseling, health services, personal counseling, placement for graduates, veterans' counselor. **Physically disabled:** Services for visually, speech, hearing impaired.

Contact. E-mail: info@uu.edu
Phone: (731) 661-5000 Toll-free number: (800) 338-6466
Fax: (731) 661-5017
Rich Grimm, Vice President for Enrollment Services, Union University, 1050 Union University Drive, Jackson, TN 38305-3697

University of Memphis
Memphis, Tennessee
www.memphis.edu

CB code: 1459

- Public 4-year university
- Commuter campus in very large city
- 17,283 degree-seeking undergraduates: 24% part-time, 62% women, 42% African American, 2% Asian American, 3% Hispanic American, 1% international
- 4,265 degree-seeking graduate students

- 66% of applicants admitted
- SAT or ACT (ACT writing optional) required
- 39% graduate within 6 years

General. Founded in 1912. Regionally accredited. **Degrees:** 2,680 bachelor's awarded; master's, professional, doctoral offered. **ROTC:** Army, Naval, Air Force. **Location:** 10 miles from downtown. **Calendar:** Semester, extensive summer session. **Full-time faculty:** 846 total; 79% have terminal degrees, 24% minority, 42% women. **Part-time faculty:** 651 total; 34% have terminal degrees, 22% minority, 57% women. **Class size:** 36% < 20, 47% 20-39, 6% 40-49, 8% 50-99, 2% >100. **Special facilities:** Institute of Egyptian art and archaeology, speech and hearing center, earthquake research and information center, technology institute, Chucalissa Indian village and museum, Confucius institute.

Freshman class profile. 6,710 applied, 4,452 admitted, 2,577 enrolled.

Mid 50% test scores			
ACT composite:	19-25	Rank in top quarter:	44%
GPA 3.75 or higher:	23%	Rank in top tenth:	17%
GPA 3.50-3.74:	15%	Return as sophomores:	78%
GPA 3.0-3.49:	33%	Out-of-state:	9%
GPA 2.0-2.99:	29%	Live on campus:	56%
		International:	1%

Basis for selection. GPA and test scores important. Admissions Index calculated by multiplying GPA by 30 and adding ACT score. Admissions competitive based on calculated index, and includes evaluation of high school curriculum. Interview required for university college; audition required for music; portfolio required for fine arts. **Home schooled:** Transcript of courses and grades required. Applicants must comply with state law by submitting proof of registration with local education agency.

High school preparation. College-preparatory program required. Required and recommended units include English 4, mathematics 3-4, social studies 2, history 1, science 2 (laboratory 1), foreign language 2 and visual/performing arts 1.

2011-2012 Annual costs. Tuition/fees: $7,696; $23,146 out-of-state. Room/board: $6,240. Books/supplies: $1,100. Personal expenses: $2,393.

Financial aid. Non-need-based: Scholarships awarded for academics, alumni affiliation, art, athletics, leadership, minority status, music/drama, ROTC, state residency.

Application procedures. Admission: Closing date 7/1 (postmark date). $25 fee. Admission notification on a rolling basis. Must meet registration deadline. **Financial aid:** Priority date 3/1, closing date 8/1. FAFSA required. Applicants notified on a rolling basis starting 4/1; must reply within 2 week(s) of notification.

Academics. University enables students to create non-traditional degrees. **Special study options:** Accelerated study, cooperative education, cross-registration, distance learning, double major, dual enrollment of high school students, ESL, exchange student, external degree, honors, independent study, internships, liberal arts/career combination, student-designed major, study abroad, teacher certification program. **Credit/placement by examination:** AP, CLEP, IB, SAT, ACT, institutional tests. Number of credits awarded decided by individual departments. **Support services:** Learning center, preadmission summer program, reduced course load, remedial instruction, study skills assistance, tutoring, writing center.

Honors college/program. 27 ACT or 1200 SAT (exclusive of Writing), 3.5 GPA required.

Majors. Architecture: Environmental design. **Area/ethnic studies:** African-American. **Biology:** General. **Business:** Accounting, business admin, finance, hotel/motel admin, international, logistics, management information systems, managerial economics, marketing, selling. **Communications:** Journalism, media studies. **Computer sciences:** Computer science. **Education:** Multi-level teacher, physical, special ed. **Engineering:** Biomedical, civil, computer, electrical, mechanical. **English:** English lit. **Foreign languages:** General. **History:** General. **Human services:** Social work. **Liberal arts:** Arts/sciences. **Math:** General. **Parks/recreation:** Exercise sciences, sports admin. **Philosophy/religion:** Philosophy. **Physical sciences:** Chemistry, geology, physics. **Protective services:** Law enforcement admin. **Psychology:** General. **Social sciences:** Anthropology, economics, geography, international relations, political science, sociology. **Visual/performing arts:** Art, art history/conservation, dramatic, interior design, music.

Most popular majors. Business/marketing 21%, communications/journalism 6%, education 10%, health sciences 6%, interdisciplinary studies 10%, liberal arts 6%, psychology 6%, social sciences 6%.

Computing on campus. 1,255 workstations in dormitories, library, computer center, student center. Dormitories wired for high-speed internet access and linked to campus network. Commuter students can connect to campus

network. Online course registration, online library, helpline, repair service, wireless network available.

Student life. Freshman orientation: Mandatory. Preregistration for classes offered. One- or 2-day sessions, evening program for adult students. Fees vary by program. **Housing:** Coed dorms, single-sex dorms, special housing for disabled, apartments, fraternity/sorority housing available. **Activities:** Bands, campus ministries, choral groups, dance, drama, international student organizations, literary magazine, music ensembles, musical theater, opera, radio station, student government, student newspaper, symphony orchestra.

Athletics. NCAA. **Intercollegiate:** Baseball M, basketball, cross-country, football (tackle) M, golf, rifle, soccer, softball W, tennis, track and field, volleyball W. **Intramural:** Basketball, bowling, football (non-tackle), golf, racquetball, soccer, softball, table tennis, tennis, track and field, volleyball, water polo. **Team name:** Tigers.

Student services. Adult student services, alcohol/substance abuse counseling, career counseling, student employment services, financial aid counseling, health services, legal services, minority student services, on-campus daycare, personal counseling, placement for graduates, veterans' counselor, women's services. **Physically disabled:** Services for visually, speech, hearing impaired.

Contact. E-mail: recruitment@memphis.edu
Phone: (901) 678-2111 Toll-free number: (800) 669-2678
Fax: (901) 678-3053
Gloria Moore, Associate Director of Admissions, University of Memphis, 101 Wilder Tower, Memphis, TN 38152

University of Phoenix: Chattanooga
Chattanooga, Tennessee
www.phoenix.edu

- For-profit 4-year university
- Small city
- 536 degree-seeking undergraduates

General. Regionally accredited. **Degrees:** 16 bachelor's awarded; master's offered. **Calendar:** Differs by program. **Full-time faculty:** 8 total. **Part-time faculty:** 86 total.

Basis for selection. Open admission, but selective for some programs.

2011-2012 Annual costs. Estimated costs as of August 2011: per-credit-hour charge, $420 to $450, depending upon level and course of study; electronic course materials fee, $95, if applicable. Book and material charges may vary by course and program. All fees are subject to change.

Application procedures. Admission: No deadline. No application fee. **Financial aid:** No deadline.

Academics. Credit/placement by examination: AP, CLEP.

Majors. Business: Business admin. **Computer sciences:** Information technology.

Contact. Marc Booker, Director of Admission and Evaluation, University of Phoenix: Chattanooga, 1208 Pointe Centre Drive, Chattanooga, TN 37421-3983

University of Phoenix: Knoxville
Knoxville, Tennessee
www.phoenix.edu

- For-profit 4-year branch campus college
- Small city
- 57 degree-seeking undergraduates

General. Regionally accredited. **Calendar:** Differs by program. **Part-time faculty:** 3 total.

Basis for selection. Open admission.

Academics. Credit/placement by examination: AP, CLEP.

Majors. Business: Business admin.

Contact. University of Phoenix: Knoxville, 10133 Sherrill Boulevard, Knoxville, TN 37932

University of Phoenix: Memphis
Cordova, Tennessee
www.phoenix.edu

- For-profit 4-year university
- Large city
- 1,264 degree-seeking undergraduates

General. Regionally accredited. **Degrees:** 94 bachelor's awarded; master's offered. **Calendar:** Differs by program. **Full-time faculty:** 22 total. **Part-time faculty:** 121 total.

Basis for selection. Open admission, but selective for some programs.

2011-2012 Annual costs. Estimated costs as of August 2011: per-credit-hour charge, $405 to $450, depending upon level and course of study; electronic course materials fee, $95, if applicable. Book and material charges may vary by course and program. All fees are subject to change.

Application procedures. Admission: No deadline. No application fee. **Financial aid:** No deadline.

Academics. Credit/placement by examination: AP, CLEP.

Majors. Business: Business admin. **Computer sciences:** Information technology.

Contact. Toll-free number: (877) 766-0766
Marc Booker, Director of Admission and Evaluation, University of Phoenix: Memphis, 65 Germantown Court, Suite 100, Cordova, TN 38018-7290

University of Phoenix: Nashville
Nashville, Tennessee
www.phoenix.edu

- For-profit 4-year university
- Large city
- 1,723 degree-seeking undergraduates

General. Regionally accredited. **Degrees:** 118 bachelor's awarded; master's offered. **Calendar:** Differs by program. **Full-time faculty:** 20 total. **Part-time faculty:** 186 total.

Basis for selection. Open admission, but selective for some programs. Selective admission to allied health programs.

2011-2012 Annual costs. Estimated costs as of August 2011: per-credit-hour charge, $405 to $450, depending upon level and course of study; electronic course materials fee, $95, if applicable. Book and material charges may vary by course and program. All fees are subject to change.

Application procedures. Admission: No deadline. No application fee. **Financial aid:** No deadline.

Academics. Credit/placement by examination: AP, CLEP.

Majors. Business: Accounting technology, business admin, marketing. **Computer sciences:** General, web page design. **Health services:** Facilities admin, nursing (RN). **Protective services:** Law enforcement admin.

Contact. Marc Booker, Director of Admission and Evaluation, University of Phoenix: Nashville, 616 Marriott Drive, Suite 150, Nashville, TN 37214-5048

University of Tennessee Health Science Center
Memphis, Tennessee
www.uthsc.edu   **CB code: 1850**

- Public two-year upper-division university and health science college
- Residential campus in very large city
- 56% of applicants admitted
- Application essay, interview required

General. Founded in 1911. Regionally accredited. **Degrees:** 48 bachelor's awarded; master's, professional, doctoral offered. **Location:** 220 miles from Nashville; 299 miles from St. Louis, MO. **Calendar:** Semester, limited summer session. **Full-time faculty:** 1,063 total; 21% minority, 34% women.

Part-time faculty: 441 total; 13% minority, 42% women. **Special facilities:** Computer laboratories, specialize laboratories, simulated patients.

Student profile. 88 degree-seeking undergraduates, 2,727 graduate students. 102 applied as first time-transfer students, 57 admitted, 49 enrolled. 58% entered as juniors, 42% entered as seniors.

Women:	92%	Part-time:	55%
African American:	18%	Out-of-state:	19%
Asian American:	2%	25 or older:	44%
Hispanic American:	2%		

Basis for selection. High school transcript, college transcript, application essay, interview required. Students must have 2 years of college. Admissions based on GPA, test scores, consistency in achievement, course load and content, recommendations, extracurricular performance, motivation and goals, preprofessional evaluation, and interview (if required by program). GPA requirements and application closing dates vary by program. Transfer accepted as juniors.

2011-2012 Annual costs. Tuition/fees: $7,791; $24,291 out-of-state. Above costs are for bachelor's program in Medical Technology. Other programs vary by cost. Books/supplies: $1,182.

Financial aid. Non-need-based: Scholarships awarded for academics, leadership, minority status, state residency. **Additional information:** Scholarships available to defray out-of-state portion of fees charged to out-of-state minority students.

Application procedures. Admission: Deadline 6/15. $75 fee. Application must be submitted online. Must reply by 6/30. Application deadlines vary by program. **Financial aid:** No deadline. Applicants notified on a rolling basis starting 5/1; must reply within 2 weeks of notification. FAFSA required.

Academics. Special study options: Accelerated study, combined bachelor's/graduate degree, distance learning, dual enrollment of high school students, independent study, internships. **Credit/placement by examination:** AP, CLEP.

Majors. Health services: Clinical lab science, dental hygiene, medical records admin.

Computing on campus. 147 workstations in library, computer center, student center. Online library, helpline, repair service, student web hosting, wireless network available.

Student life. Activities: Campus ministries, international student organizations, student government, Baptist student union, United Methodist fellowship, Catholic student association, black student association.

Athletics. Intramural: Basketball, racquetball, softball, tennis, volleyball, water polo.

Student services. Alcohol/substance abuse counseling, career counseling, services for economically disadvantaged, student employment services, financial aid counseling, health services, personal counseling, placement for graduates, veterans' counselor. **Physically disabled:** Services for visually impaired.

Contact. E-mail: rpatte10@uthsc.edu
Phone: (901) 448-5560 Fax: (901) 448-7772
Ron Patterson, Director, University of Tennessee Health Science Center, 910 Madison Avenue, Memphis, TN 38163

University of Tennessee: Chattanooga
Chattanooga, Tennessee
www.utc.edu   CB code: 1831

- Public 4-year university
- Commuter campus in large city
- 9,778 degree-seeking undergraduates: 12% part-time, 55% women, 12% African American, 2% Asian American, 3% Hispanic American, 1% international
- 1,451 degree-seeking graduate students
- 74% of applicants admitted
- SAT or ACT (ACT writing optional) required
- 39% graduate within 6 years

General. Founded in 1886. Regionally accredited. **Degrees:** 1,320 bachelor's awarded; master's, professional, doctoral offered. **ROTC:** Army. **Location:** 130 miles from Nashville, 118 miles from Atlanta. **Calendar:** Semester, extensive summer session. **Full-time faculty:** 431 total; 69% have terminal degrees, 15% minority, 47% women. **Part-time faculty:** 299 total; 17% have terminal degrees, 52% women. **Class size:** 32% < 20, 50% 20-39, 9% 40-49, 7% 50-99, 2% >100. **Special facilities:** Art galleries, theater, observatory, arboretum, riverwalk.

Freshman class profile. 6,703 applied, 4,938 admitted, 2,186 enrolled.

Mid 50% test scores		**GPA 3.0-3.49:**	36%
SAT critical reading:	470-600	**GPA 2.0-2.99:**	21%
SAT math:	470-580	**Return as sophomores:**	69%
ACT composite:	21-25	**Out-of-state:**	4%
GPA 3.75 or higher:	24%	**Live on campus:**	76%
GPA 3.50-3.74:	19%		

Basis for selection. High school curriculum and GPA very important. 2.75 GPA with 17 ACT (830 SAT) or 2.0 GPA with 21 ACT (990 SAT) required. SAT scores exclusive of Writing. Special talents, recommendations, essay or personal statement considered. Essay recommended. **Home schooled:** Transcript of courses and grades required. 2.75 GPA and 21 ACT/980 SAT (exclusive of Writing) required. **Learning Disabled:** Student may register for services with Office for Students with Disabilities after admission.

High school preparation. College-preparatory program recommended. 14 units required. Required units include English 4, mathematics 3, social studies 1, history 1, science 2 (laboratory 2), foreign language 2 and visual/performing arts 1. Math units must include algebra I and II, and geometry. Foreign language units must be in same language. History unit should be US history. Social studies unit should be world history, European history or world geography.

2011-2012 Annual costs. Tuition/fees: $6,618; $20,252 out-of-state. Room/board: $8,250. Books/supplies: $1,400. Personal expenses: $1,480.

2011-2012 Financial aid. Non-need-based: Scholarships awarded for academics, alumni affiliation, art, athletics, leadership, music/drama, religious affiliation, ROTC, state residency.

Application procedures. Admission: Closing date 8/1. $30 fee, may be waived for applicants with need. Admission notification on a rolling basis. May defer admission for one semester. **Financial aid:** Priority date 7/1; no closing date. FAFSA required. Applicants notified on a rolling basis starting 3/15.

Academics. Special study options: Cooperative education, cross-registration, distance learning, double major, dual enrollment of high school students, ESL, honors, independent study, internships, study abroad, teacher certification program. Washington Center Internship, Southeastern Command and Leadership Academy (SECLA), Senator Tommy Burks Victim Assistance Academy,. **Credit/placement by examination:** AP, CLEP, SAT, ACT, institutional tests. 24 credit hours maximum toward bachelor's degree. May only be used for elective credit hours. **Support services:** Learning center, pre-admission summer program, reduced course load, remedial instruction, study skills assistance, tutoring, writing center.

Honors college/program. Based on application, teacher evaluations, essay, official high school transcript, and ACT or SAT; about 45 applicants admitted each year.

Majors. Biology: General. **Business:** Business admin. **Communications:** Communications/speech/rhetoric. **Computer sciences:** Computer science. **Conservation:** Environmental science. **Education:** Art, early childhood, English, foreign languages, mathematics, middle, music, science, social studies, special ed. **Engineering:** General, electrical, mechanical. **English:** English lit. **Foreign languages:** General. **Health services:** Nursing (RN). **History:** General. **Human services:** Community org/advocacy, social work. **Liberal arts:** Humanities. **Math:** General, applied. **Parks/recreation:** Exercise sciences. **Physical sciences:** Chemistry, geology, physics. **Protective services:** Law enforcement admin. **Psychology:** General. **Social sciences:** Economics, political science, sociology. **Visual/performing arts:** Art, dramatic, interior design, music. **Work/family studies:** General.

Most popular majors. Business/marketing 22%, education 12%, engineering/engineering technologies 6%, parks/recreation 6%, psychology 8%, social sciences 6%.

Computing on campus. 965 workstations in library, computer center, student center. Dormitories wired for high-speed internet access and linked to campus network. Commuter students can connect to campus network. Online course registration, online library, helpline, repair service, wireless network available.

Student life. Freshman orientation: Mandatory, $65 fee. Preregistration for classes offered. Two-day sessions held in summer. **Housing:** Guaranteed on-campus for freshmen. Coed dorms, apartments, fraternity/sorority housing available. $75 partly refundable deposit, deadline 8/1. **Activities:** Bands, campus ministries, choral groups, dance, drama, film society, international student organizations, literary magazine, music ensembles, Model UN, radio station, student government, student newspaper, symphony orchestra, TV station, Bahai club, Baptist collegiate ministry, Campus Crusade for Christ,

Fellowship of Christian Athletes, Omega Phi Alpha, Sigma Alpha Iota, Habitat for Humanity, College Democrats, College Republicans, National Society of Black Engineers.

Athletics. NCAA. **Intercollegiate:** Basketball, cross-country, football (tackle) M, golf, soccer W, softball W, tennis, track and field, volleyball W, wrestling M. **Intramural:** Badminton, basketball, cross-country, football (non-tackle), racquetball, soccer, softball W, swimming, table tennis, tennis, volleyball, wrestling M. **Team name:** Mocs.

Student services. Adult student services, alcohol/substance abuse counseling, chaplain/spiritual director, career counseling, student employment services, financial aid counseling, health services, minority student services, on-campus daycare, personal counseling, placement for graduates, veterans' counselor, women's services. **Physically disabled:** Services for visually, speech, hearing impaired.

Contact. E-mail: yancy-freeman@utc.edu
Phone: (423) 425-4662 Toll-free number: (800) 882-6627
Fax: (423) 425-4157
Yancy Freeman, Director of Student Recruitment and Admissions, University of Tennessee: Chattanooga, 615 McCallie Avenue, Chattanooga, TN 37403

University of Tennessee: Knoxville

Knoxville, Tennessee   **CB member**
www.utk.edu   **CB code: 1843**

- Public 4-year university
- Residential campus in large city
- 20,962 degree-seeking undergraduates: 5% part-time, 49% women, 8% African American, 3% Asian American, 3% Hispanic American, 1% Native American, 1% international
- 8,731 degree-seeking graduate students
- 70% of applicants admitted
- SAT or ACT (ACT writing optional) required
- 63% graduate within 6 years

General. Founded in 1794. Regionally accredited. **Degrees:** 4,569 bachelor's awarded; master's, professional, doctoral offered. **ROTC:** Army, Air Force. **Location:** 224 miles from Atlanta, 178 miles from Nashville. **Calendar:** Semester, extensive summer session. **Full-time faculty:** 1,641 total; 14% minority, 41% women. **Part-time faculty:** 278 total; 9% minority, 46% women. **Special facilities:** 2 theaters, science/engineering research facility, International House, olympic track, baseball stadium.

Freshman class profile. 13,768 applied, 9,594 admitted, 4,188 enrolled.

Mid 50% test scores			
SAT critical reading:	520-640	GPA 2.0-2.99:	4%
SAT math:	530-640	Return as sophomores:	85%
ACT composite:	24-29	Live on campus:	90%
GPA 3.75 or higher:	64%	International:	2%
GPA 3.50-3.74:	15%	Fraternities:	27%
GPA 3.0-3.49:	17%	Sororities:	17%

Basis for selection. Admission based on holistic review of grades in core academic subjects, SAT/ACT, extracurricular school and community activities, awards, personal statement, and optional letters of recommendation that address applicant's potential for success in college. Essay not required but preferred; portfolio required for architecture and interior design; audition required for music; essay required for nursing.

High school preparation. College-preparatory program required. 17 units required. Required units include English 4, mathematics 4, social studies 2, history 1, science 3 (laboratory 3), foreign language 2 and visual/performing arts 1. Mathematics units must include algebra I & II, geometry, and 1 unit of higher math (e.g., statistics, trigonometry, precalculus, calculus). Science units must include biology, chemistry or physics, and 1 additional lab science unit. Social science units must include at least 1 unit US history, 1 world history, European history, or world geography, and 1 additional unit.

2011-2012 Annual costs. Tuition/fees: $8,396; $25,238 out-of-state. Out-of-state students pay additional required fees of $300. Room/board: $8,480. Books/supplies: $1,448. Personal expenses: $3,593.

2011-2012 Financial aid. All financial aid based on need. 3,942 full-time freshmen applied for aid; 2,496 were judged to have need; 2,494 of these received aid. Average need met was 76%. Average scholarship/grant was $3,175; average loan $3,701. 65% of total undergraduate aid awarded as scholarships/grants, 35% as loans/jobs. **Additional information:** Application priority date for scholarships 2/1.

Application procedures. **Admission:** Priority date 11/1; deadline 12/1 (postmark date). $30 fee, may be waived for applicants with need. Admission notification on a rolling basis. Must reply by May 1 or within 2 week(s) if notified thereafter. **Financial aid:** Priority date 2/15; no closing date. FAFSA required. Applicants notified on a rolling basis starting 3/15; must reply within 3 week(s) of notification.

Academics. **Special study options:** Accelerated study, combined bachelor's/graduate degree, cooperative education, distance learning, double major, dual enrollment of high school students, ESL, exchange student, external degree, honors, independent study, internships, liberal arts/career combination, student-designed major, study abroad, teacher certification program. **Credit/placement by examination:** AP, CLEP, IB, SAT, ACT, institutional tests. **Support services:** Study skills assistance, tutoring.

Majors. **Architecture:** Architecture. **Area/ethnic studies:** Women's. **Biology:** General. **Business:** Accounting, business admin, finance, hotel/motel admin, human resources, logistics, managerial economics, marketing, statistics. **Communications:** Advertising, communications/speech/rhetoric, journalism, public relations. **Computer sciences:** Computer science. **Conservation:** Economics, forestry, wildlife/wilderness. **Education:** Special ed. **Engineering:** Aerospace, agricultural, chemical, civil, computer, electrical, engineering science, industrial, materials, mechanical, nuclear. **English:** English lit. **Foreign languages:** Classics, French, German, Italian, Russian, Spanish. **General:** Animal sciences, business, education services, food science, plant sciences, soil chem/physics. **Health services:** Clinical lab science, dental hygiene, medical records admin, nursing (RN). **History:** General. **Human services:** General, social work. **Math:** General, statistics. **Parks/recreation:** Exercise sciences, sports admin. **Philosophy/religion:** Philosophy, religion. **Physical sciences:** Chemistry, geology, physics. **Psychology:** General. **Social sciences:** Anthropology, economics, geography, political science, sociology. **Visual/performing arts:** Art history/conservation, commercial/advertising art, dramatic, interior design, music, studio arts. **Work/family studies:** Consumer economics, family studies, food/nutrition.

Most popular majors. Business/marketing 20%, communications/journalism 10%, engineering/engineering technologies 8%, psychology 10%, social sciences 9%.

Computing on campus. 1,000 workstations in dormitories, library, student center. Dormitories wired for high-speed internet access and linked to campus network. Commuter students can connect to campus network. Online course registration, online library, helpline, repair service, student web hosting, wireless network available.

Student life. **Freshman orientation:** Mandatory, $99 fee. Preregistration for classes offered. Two-day session; parents may attend for $35 per parent and does not include housing. **Policies:** Freshmen must live on-campus unless residing with parent or legal guardian. **Housing:** Guaranteed on-campus for freshmen. Coed dorms, single-sex dorms, special housing for disabled, apartments, fraternity/sorority housing available. $100 nonrefundable deposit, deadline 5/1. Transfer student floors available. **Activities:** Bands, campus ministries, choral groups, drama, film society, international student organizations, literary magazine, music ensembles, Model UN, musical theater, opera, radio station, student government, student newspaper, symphony orchestra, TV station.

Athletics. NCAA. **Intercollegiate:** Baseball M, basketball, cross-country, diving, football (tackle) M, golf, rowing (crew) W, soccer W, softball W, swimming, tennis, track and field, volleyball W. **Intramural:** Badminton, basketball, bowling, field hockey, football (non-tackle), golf, racquetball, soccer, softball, table tennis, tennis, volleyball, water polo, weight lifting. **Team name:** Volunteers.

Student services. Alcohol/substance abuse counseling, career counseling, student employment services, financial aid counseling, health services, minority student services, personal counseling, placement for graduates, veterans' counselor, women's services. **Physically disabled:** Services for visually, speech, hearing impaired.

Contact. E-mail: admissions@utk.edu
Phone: (865) 974-2184
Vern Granger, Director of Admissions, University of Tennessee: Knoxville, 320 Student Services Building, Circle Park, Knoxville, TN 37996-0230

University of Tennessee: Martin

Martin, Tennessee
www.utm.edu   **CB code: 1844**

- Public 4-year university
- Residential campus in small town

- 6,825 degree-seeking undergraduates: 10% part-time, 58% women, 17% African American, 1% Asian American, 2% Hispanic American, 2% international
- 363 degree-seeking graduate students
- 73% of applicants admitted
- SAT or ACT (ACT writing optional) required
- 48% graduate within 6 years

General. Founded in 1927. Regionally accredited. Coordinates online education for UT system. **Degrees:** 1,038 bachelor's awarded; master's offered. **ROTC:** Army. **Location:** 125 miles from Memphis, 150 miles from Nashville. **Calendar:** Semester, extensive summer session. **Full-time faculty:** 282 total; 73% have terminal degrees, 7% minority, 44% women. **Part-time faculty:** 280 total; 16% have terminal degrees, 7% minority, 53% women. **Class size:** 51% <20, 38% 20-39, 6% 40-49, 6% 50-99, less than 1% >100. **Special facilities:** Teacher resource center, 680-acre agriculture, natural resources teaching, demonstration complex, teaching/research facility resort, international education center.

Freshman class profile. 3,512 applied, 2,579 admitted, 1,304 enrolled.

Mid 50% test scores		Rank in top tenth:	20%
ACT composite:	20-24	Return as sophomores:	73%
GPA 3.75 or higher:	26%	Out-of-state:	4%
GPA 3.50-3.74:	19%	Live on campus:	67%
GPA 3.0-3.49:	39%	International:	3%
GPA 2.0-2.99:	16%	Fraternities:	27%
Rank in top quarter:	49%	Sororities:	27%

Basis for selection. 2.85 GPA with 18 ACT or 2.5 GPA with 21 ACT required. Students not meeting regular admission requirements may be considered for conditional admission. Auditions required in fine and performing arts. **Home schooled:** 21 ACT and 2.85 GPA required.

High school preparation. College-preparatory program required. 15 units required. Required units include English 4, mathematics 3, history 1, science 2 (laboratory 1), foreign language 2 and visual/performing arts 1.

2011-2012 Annual costs. Tuition/fees: $6,718; $19,128 out-of-state. Room/board: $5,424. Books/supplies: $1,500. Personal expenses: $2,368.

2011-2012 Financial aid. All financial aid based on need. 1,243 full-time freshmen applied for aid; 985 were judged to have need; 983 of these received aid. Average need met was 80%. Average scholarship/grant was $6,270; average loan $3,156. 55% of total undergraduate aid awarded as scholarships/grants, 45% as loans/jobs.

Application procedures. Admission: Priority date 2/1; deadline 8/1. $30 fee. Admission notification on a rolling basis beginning on or about 9/1. **Financial aid:** Priority date 2/15; no closing date. FAFSA required. Applicants notified on a rolling basis starting 4/1; must reply within 2 week(s) of notification.

Academics. Special study options: Accelerated study, cooperative education, cross-registration, distance learning, double major, dual enrollment of high school students, ESL, exchange student, honors, independent study, internships, student-designed major, study abroad, teacher certification program. 3-1 pharmacy program, 3-1 veterinary medicine program, 3-1 dentistry program, 3-1 medicine program, 3-1 optometry program, 3-1 podiatry program, 3-1 chiropractory program. **Credit/placement by examination:** AP, CLEP, SAT, ACT, institutional tests. 30 credit hours maximum toward bachelor's degree. **Support services:** Remedial instruction, study skills assistance, tutoring, writing center.

Majors. Biology: General. **Business:** Accounting, business admin, finance, management information systems, managerial economics, marketing. **Communications:** Communications/speech/rhetoric. **Computer sciences:** Computer science. **Conservation:** Management/policy. **Education:** Secondary, special ed. **Engineering:** General. **English:** English lit. **Foreign languages:** French, Spanish. **Health services:** Nursing (RN). **History:** General. **Human services:** Social work. **Math:** General. **Parks/recreation:** Health/fitness. **Philosophy/religion:** Philosophy. **Physical sciences:** Chemistry, geology. **Protective services:** Law enforcement admin. **Psychology:** General. **Social sciences:** International relations, political science, sociology. **Visual/performing arts:** General, music. **Work/family studies:** General.

Most popular majors. Agriculture 7%, business/marketing 16%, education 14%, interdisciplinary studies 13%, parks/recreation 8%.

Computing on campus. 313 workstations in dormitories, library, student center. Dormitories wired for high-speed internet access and linked to campus network. Commuter students can connect to campus network. Online course registration, online library, helpline, repair service, student web hosting, wireless network available.

Student life. Freshman orientation: Available, $165 fee. Preregistration for classes offered. 4-day program held in August. **Policies:** Freshmen must live on-campus. **Housing:** Guaranteed on-campus for freshmen. Coed dorms, single-sex dorms, special housing for disabled, apartments, fraternity/sorority housing available. $100 fully refundable deposit, deadline 8/1. **Activities:** Bands, campus ministries, choral groups, dance, drama, international student organizations, literary magazine, music ensembles, opera, radio station, student government, student newspaper, TV station, Chi Alpha Christian Fellowship, Interfaith student center, Rotaract, Free Thinkers club, Fellowship of Christian Athletes, College Democrats, College Republicans, Reformed University Fellowship, Japanese animation research society.

Athletics. NCAA. **Intercollegiate:** Baseball M, basketball, cheerleading M, cross-country, equestrian W, football (tackle) M, golf M, rifle, rodeo, soccer W, softball W, tennis W, volleyball W. **Intramural:** Basketball, football (non-tackle), golf, racquetball, soccer, softball, tennis, volleyball, water polo. **Team name:** Skyhawks.

Student services. Adult student services, alcohol/substance abuse counseling, chaplain/spiritual director, career counseling, services for economically disadvantaged, student employment services, financial aid counseling, health services, minority student services, on-campus daycare, personal counseling, placement for graduates, veterans' counselor, women's services. **Physically disabled:** Services for visually, speech, hearing impaired.

Contact. E-mail: admitme@utm.edu
Phone: (731) 881-7020 Toll-free number: (800) 829-8861
Fax: (731) 881-7029
Judy Rayburn, Director of Admissions, University of Tennessee: Martin, 200 Hall Moody Administration Building, Martin, TN 38238

University of the South
Sewanee, Tennessee
www.sewanee.edu

CB member
CB code: 1842

- Private 4-year university affiliated with Episcopal Church
- Residential campus in rural community
- 1,454 degree-seeking undergraduates: 51% women, 4% African American, 2% Asian American, 4% Hispanic American, 2% international
- 76 degree-seeking graduate students
- 61% of applicants admitted
- Application essay required
- 42% graduate within 6 years; 27% enter graduate study

General. Founded in 1857. Regionally accredited; also accredited by ATS. **Degrees:** 335 bachelor's awarded; master's, professional offered. **Location:** 45 miles from Chattanooga; 57 miles from Huntsville, AL. **Calendar:** Semester, limited summer session. **Full-time faculty:** 137 total; 97% have terminal degrees, 14% minority, 39% women. **Part-time faculty:** 35 total; 69% have terminal degrees, 6% minority, 37% women. **Class size:** 69% < 20, 30% 20-39, less than 1% 40-49, less than 1% 50-99. **Special facilities:** Landscape analysis lab, observatory, materials analysis laboratory with electron microscopy, hiking and horseback riding trails, climbing.

Freshman class profile. 2,920 applied, 1,793 admitted, 433 enrolled.

Mid 50% test scores		GPA 2.0-2.99:	10%
SAT critical reading:	580-680	Rank in top quarter:	77%
SAT math:	560-650	Rank in top tenth:	44%
SAT writing:	560-670	Return as sophomores:	90%
ACT composite:	26-30	Out-of-state:	71%
GPA 3.75 or higher:	42%	Live on campus:	100%
GPA 3.50-3.74:	18%	International:	2%
GPA 3.0-3.49:	30%		

Basis for selection. GED not accepted. School achievement record, recommendations, extracurricular activities, test scores, and essay important. Children of alumni and minority applicants given special consideration. SAT/ACT or evaluative interview and graded academic paper required. Interview recommended.

High school preparation. College-preparatory program required. 13 units required; 20 recommended. Required and recommended units include English 4, mathematics 3-4, social studies 1-2, history 1-2, science 2-4 (laboratory 2-3) and foreign language 2-4.

2012-2013 Annual costs. Tuition/fees (projected): $34,714. Room/board: $9,916. Books/supplies: $800. Personal expenses: $900.

2011-2012 Financial aid. Need-based: 160 full-time freshmen applied for aid; 110 were judged to have need; 110 of these received aid. Average need met was 96%. Average scholarship/grant was $24,356; average loan $6,979. 80% of total undergraduate aid awarded as scholarships/grants, 20%

as loans/jobs. **Non-need-based:** Awarded to 177 full-time undergraduates, including 91 freshmen. Scholarships awarded for academics, minority status, religious affiliation.

Application procedures. Admission: Closing date 2/1 (postmark date). $45 fee, may be waived for applicants with need, free for online applicants. Admission notification by 3/17. Must reply by 5/1. **Financial aid:** Priority date 3/1; no closing date. FAFSA, institutional form required. Must reply within 4 week(s) of notification.

Academics. Special study options: Double major, independent study, internships, student-designed major, study abroad, Washington semester. **Credit/placement by examination:** AP, CLEP, IB, SAT, ACT, institutional tests. 60 credit hours maximum toward bachelor's degree. **Support services:** Tutoring.

Majors. Area/ethnic studies: American, Asian, French, German, Russian/Slavic. **Biology:** General, biochemistry. **Computer sciences:** General, computer science. **Conservation:** Environmental studies, forestry, management/policy. **English:** English lit. **Foreign languages:** Ancient Greek, comparative lit, French, German, Latin, modern Greek, Russian, Spanish. **History:** General. **Math:** General. **Philosophy/religion:** Philosophy, religion. **Physical sciences:** Chemistry, geology, physics. **Psychology:** General. **Social sciences:** Anthropology, economics, political science. **Visual/performing arts:** General, art history/conservation, music, studio arts.

Most popular majors. Biology 7%, English 14%, foreign language 8%, interdisciplinary studies 10%, psychology 11%, social sciences 17%, visual/performing arts 11%.

Computing on campus. 200 workstations in dormitories, library, computer center. Dormitories wired for high-speed internet access and linked to campus network. Commuter students can connect to campus network. Online course registration, online library, helpline, repair service, student web hosting, wireless network available.

Student life. Freshman orientation: Available. Preregistration for classes offered. Held several days before start of classes. **Policies:** Student-administered honor code strictly observed. **Housing:** Guaranteed on-campus for freshmen. Coed dorms, single-sex dorms, special housing for disabled, apartments, cooperative housing, fraternity/sorority housing, wellness housing available. $300 nonrefundable deposit, deadline 5/1. **Activities:** Bands, campus ministries, choral groups, dance, drama, film society, international student organizations, literary magazine, music ensembles, Model UN, musical theater, radio station, student government, student newspaper, symphony orchestra, tutoring center for disadvantaged youth, religious organizations, Big Brother-Big Sister program.

Athletics. NCAA. **Intercollegiate:** Baseball M, basketball, cheerleading, cross-country, diving, equestrian, field hockey W, football (tackle) M, golf, lacrosse, soccer, softball W, swimming, tennis, track and field, volleyball. **Intramural:** Badminton, basketball, football (non-tackle), racquetball, soccer, softball, squash, swimming, track and field M, volleyball. **Team name:** Tigers.

Student services. Chaplain/spiritual director, career counseling, student employment services, health services, minority student services, on-campus daycare, personal counseling, placement for graduates, women's services. **Physically disabled:** Services for visually, hearing impaired.

Contact. E-mail: admiss@sewanee.edu
Phone: (931) 598-1238 Toll-free number: (800) 522-2234
Fax: (931) 598-3248
Lee Ann Afton, Dean of Admission, University of the South, Office of Admission, Sewanee, TN 37383-1000

Vanderbilt University
Nashville, Tennessee
www.vanderbilt.edu

CB member
CB code: 1871

- Private 4-year university
- Residential campus in very large city
- 6,754 degree-seeking undergraduates: 50% women, 8% African American, 7% Asian American, 8% Hispanic American, 5% international
- 5,909 degree-seeking graduate students
- 16% of applicants admitted
- SAT or ACT (ACT writing optional), application essay required
- 92% graduate within 6 years; 47% enter graduate study

General. Founded in 1873. Regionally accredited. **Degrees:** 1,735 bachelor's awarded; master's, professional, doctoral offered. **ROTC:** Army, Naval, Air Force. **Location:** 240 miles from Atlanta, 300 miles from St. Louis. **Calendar:** Semester, limited summer session. **Full-time faculty:** 901 total;

97% have terminal degrees, 16% minority, 35% women. **Part-time faculty:** 207 total. **Class size:** 62% < 20, 27% 20-39, 3% 40-49, 6% 50-99, 2% >100. **Special facilities:** Observatory, electron microscopes, television news archive, national arboretum, video productions, black cultural center, women's center, cinema and art museum.

Freshman class profile. 24,837 applied, 4,078 admitted, 1,601 enrolled.

Mid 50% test scores			
SAT critical reading:	680-770	GPA 2.0-2.99:	2%
SAT math:	700-780	Rank in top quarter:	97%
SAT writing:	670-760	Rank in top tenth:	89%
ACT composite:	31-34	Return as sophomores:	96%
GPA 3.75 or higher:	57%	Out-of-state:	89%
GPA 3.50-3.74:	22%	Live on campus:	100%
GPA 3.0-3.49:	19%	International:	6%

Basis for selection. Academic achievement, recommendation, essay, test scores, activities important. Audition required for music program. **Home schooled:** Statement describing home school structure and mission required.

High school preparation. College-preparatory program required. 18 units required; 21 recommended. Required and recommended units include English 4, mathematics 3-4, social studies 2-3, history 1, science 3-4 (laboratory 2-3), foreign language 2 and academic electives 3. Additional unit in math and 2 in science recommended for engineering applicants. Music applicants do not require 2 units of science. Engineering program recommends 2 years of language. Education & Human Development program does not require language.

2011-2012 Annual costs. Tuition/fees: $41,996. Room/board: $13,560.

2011-2012 Financial aid. Need-based: 973 full-time freshmen applied for aid; 812 were judged to have need; 809 of these received aid. Average need met was 100%. Average scholarship/grant was $38,347; average loan $3,056. 96% of total undergraduate aid awarded as scholarships/grants, 4% as loans/jobs. **Non-need-based:** Awarded to 2,362 full-time undergraduates, including 685 freshmen. Scholarships awarded for academics, athletics, leadership, music/drama, ROTC, state residency. **Additional information:** Financial aid packages awarded to incoming and returning undergraduate students are loan-free.

Application procedures. Admission: Closing date 1/3 (postmark date). $50 fee, may be waived for applicants with need. Admission notification by 4/1. Must reply by 5/1. **Financial aid:** Priority date 2/5; no closing date. FAFSA, CSS PROFILE required.

Academics. Special study options: Accelerated study, combined bachelor's/graduate degree, double major, dual enrollment of high school students, ESL, honors, independent study, internships, liberal arts/career combination, student-designed major, study abroad, teacher certification program, Washington semester. **Credit/placement by examination:** AP, CLEP, IB, institutional tests. 30 credit hours maximum toward bachelor's degree. **Support services:** Learning center, study skills assistance, tutoring, writing center.

Majors. Area/ethnic studies: African-American, American, Asian, East Asian, European, Latin American, Western European, women's. **Biology:** General, ecology/evolutionary, molecular, neuroscience. **Communications:** Communications/speech/rhetoric. **Computer sciences:** Computer science. **Education:** General, early childhood, elementary, foreign languages, music, secondary, special ed. **Engineering:** Biomedical, chemical, civil, computer, electrical, engineering science, mechanical. **English:** English lit. **Foreign languages:** Classics, French, German, Romance, Russian, Spanish. **History:** General. **Human services:** Public policy. **Math:** General. **Philosophy/religion:** Judaic, philosophy, religion. **Physical sciences:** Chemistry, geology, physics. **Psychology:** General, developmental. **Social sciences:** General, anthropology, economics, political science, sociology. **Visual/performing arts:** Art history/conservation, brass instruments, dramatic, film/cinema/video, music theory/composition, percussion instruments, piano/keyboard, stringed instruments, studio arts, voice/opera, woodwind instruments. **Work/family studies:** Child development.

Most popular majors. Biology 6%, engineering/engineering technologies 17%, interdisciplinary studies 8%, psychology 6%, social sciences 28%.

Computing on campus. 400 workstations in library, computer center, student center. Dormitories wired for high-speed internet access and linked to campus network. Commuter students can connect to campus network. Online course registration, online library, helpline, repair service, student web hosting, wireless network available.

Student life. Freshman orientation: Mandatory, $664 fee. Preregistration for classes offered. **Policies:** Freshmen not permitted cars on campus. **Housing:** Guaranteed on-campus for freshmen. Coed dorms, single-sex dorms, special housing for disabled, apartments, fraternity/sorority housing available. **Activities:** Bands, campus ministries, choral groups, dance, drama, film society, international student organizations, literary magazine, music ensembles, Model UN, musical theater, opera, radio station, student government,

student newspaper, symphony orchestra, TV station, over 300 clubs and organizations.

Athletics. NCAA. **Intercollegiate:** Baseball M, basketball, bowling W, cheerleading, cross-country, football (tackle) M, golf, lacrosse W, soccer W, swimming W, tennis, track and field W. **Intramural:** Badminton, basketball, bowling, football (non-tackle), golf, racquetball, soccer, softball, squash, swimming, table tennis, tennis, track and field, volleyball, water polo, wrestling. **Team name:** Commodores.

Student services. Alcohol/substance abuse counseling, chaplain/spiritual director, career counseling, student employment services, financial aid counseling, health services, minority student services, on-campus daycare, personal counseling, placement for graduates, women's services. **Physically disabled:** Services for visually, speech, hearing impaired.

Contact. E-mail: admissions@vanderbilt.edu
Phone: (615) 322-2561 Toll-free number: (800) 288-0432
Fax: (615) 343-7765
John Gaines, Director, Admissions, Vanderbilt University, 2305 West End Avenue, Nashville, TN 37203-1727

Victory University
Memphis, Tennessee
www.victory.edu   CB code: 1782

- Private 4-year liberal arts college affiliated with nondenominational tradition
- Commuter campus in very large city

General. Founded in 1941. Regionally accredited. **Location:** 7 miles from downtown. **Calendar:** Semester.

Annual costs/financial aid. Tuition/fees (2011-2012): $10,620. Books/supplies: $1,608. Personal expenses: $6,651. Need-based financial aid available to full-time and part-time students.

Contact. Phone: (901) 320-9777
Director of Admissions and International Admissions, 255 North Highland Street, Memphis, TN 38111-1375

Visible Music College
Memphis, Tennessee
www.visible.edu   CB code: 5450

- Private 3-year Bible and performing arts college affiliated with Christian Church
- Very large city
- 130 degree-seeking undergraduates
- SAT or ACT (ACT writing optional), application essay, interview required

General. Candidate for regional accreditation; also accredited by TRACS. Provides practical ministry training and discipleship in addition to modern music education. **Degrees:** 20 bachelor's awarded. **Calendar:** Semester, limited summer session. **Full-time faculty:** 15 total. **Part-time faculty:** 6 total.

Basis for selection. Personal relationship with Jesus Christ required, having had a salvation experience. 18 ACT or 750 SAT (exclusive of Writing) or 1500 SAT (including Writing) required. Audition required for Modern Music Ministry program.

2011-2012 Annual costs. Tuition/fees: $20,000. Room only: $3,400. Books/supplies: $800.

Application procedures. Admission: Closing date 6/30. $40 fee, may be waived for applicants with need. Admission notification on a rolling basis.

Academics. Credit/placement by examination: AP, CLEP.

Majors. Communications: Digital media. **Theology:** Theology. **Visual/performing arts:** Music management, music performance.

Contact. E-mail: seeyourself@visible.edu
Phone: (901) 377-2992 Toll-free number: (877) 558-4742
Fax: (901) 377-0544
Heather Isaac, Admissions Coordinator, Visible Music College, 1015 South Cooper Street, Memphis, TN 38104

Watkins College of Art, Design & Film
Nashville, Tennessee
www.watkins.edu   CB code: 4927

- Private 4-year visual arts college
- Commuter campus in very large city
- 378 degree-seeking undergraduates: 31% part-time, 52% women
- 85% of applicants admitted
- SAT or ACT (ACT writing optional), application essay required

General. Regionally accredited. **Degrees:** 55 bachelor's awarded. **Calendar:** Semester, limited summer session. **Full-time faculty:** 20 total; 60% have terminal degrees, 50% women. **Part-time faculty:** 37 total; 51% have terminal degrees, 49% women. **Class size:** 88% < 20, 11% 20-39, less than 1% 40-49, less than 1% 50-99.

Freshman class profile. 126 applied, 107 admitted, 76 enrolled.

Mid 50% test scores			
ACT composite:	19-25	GPA 3.50-3.74:	16%
		GPA 3.0-3.49:	33%
GPA 3.75 or higher:	14%	GPA 2.0-2.99:	35%

Basis for selection. Admissions based on artistic exercises and academic essays, test scores, prior academic record and letter of recommendation. Additional artistic portfolio in addition to required artistic exercises highly recommended. **Home schooled:** Transcript of courses and grades, state high school equivalency certificate, letter of recommendation (nonparent) required. **Learning Disabled:** Doctor's report required.

High school preparation. Recommended units include English 4, mathematics 2, social studies 2, history 2, science 1, computer science 2 and visual/performing arts 4.

2011-2012 Annual costs. Tuition/fees: $20,460. Room only: $6,200. Books/supplies: $1,500. Personal expenses: $2,500.

Financial aid. Non-need-based: Scholarships awarded for academics, art, minority status.

Application procedures. Admission: Priority date 5/1; deadline 7/15 (postmark date). $50 fee, may be waived for applicants with need. Admission notification on a rolling basis. Must reply by 7/31. **Financial aid:** Priority date 4/1, closing date 8/1. FAFSA, institutional form required. Applicants notified on a rolling basis starting 5/1; must reply within 2 week(s) of notification.

Academics. Special study options: Cooperative education, cross-registration, dual enrollment of high school students, internships, study abroad. Cooperative agreement with all AICAD colleges; cooperative agreement with Belmont University. **Credit/placement by examination:** AP, CLEP, IB, institutional tests. **Support services:** Pre-admission summer program, study skills assistance, tutoring, writing center.

Majors. Visual/performing arts: Art, film/cinema/video, graphic design, interior design, photography, studio arts.

Computing on campus. 200 workstations in library, computer center, student center. Dormitories wired for high-speed internet access and linked to campus network. Commuter students can connect to campus network. Helpline, wireless network available.

Student life. Freshman orientation: Mandatory. Preregistration for classes offered. Two-day program held one week prior to beginning of classes. **Housing:** Guaranteed on-campus for freshmen. Coed dorms available. $300 partly refundable deposit, deadline 7/15. **Activities:** Film society, student government.

Student services. Alcohol/substance abuse counseling, career counseling, services for economically disadvantaged, financial aid counseling, personal counseling. **Physically disabled:** Services for visually, speech, hearing impaired.

Contact. E-mail: admissions@watkins.edu
Phone: (615) 383-4848 ext. 7418 Toll-free number: (866) 887-6395
Fax: (615) 383-4849
Linda Schwab, Director of Admissions, Watkins College of Art, Design & Film, 2298 Rosa L. Parks Boulevard, Nashville, TN 37228

Williamson Christian College
Franklin, Tennessee
www.williamsoncc.edu

▶ Private 4-year liberal arts college affiliated with interdenominational tradition

▶ Commuter campus in small city

▶ 118 degree-seeking undergraduates: 4% African American, 41% Asian American, 3% Hispanic American

General. Accredited by ABHE. Accelerated degree completion programs available for working adults. **Degrees:** 10 bachelor's awarded. **Location:** 15 miles from downtown. **Calendar:** Semester, limited summer session. **Full-time faculty:** 5 total; 100% have terminal degrees, 40% women. **Part-time faculty:** 20 total. **Class size:** 100% < 20.

Freshman class profile.

GPA 3.50-3.74:	33%	GPA 2.0-2.99:	33%
GPA 3.0-3.49:	34%		

Basis for selection. Open admission, but selective for some programs.

2011-2012 Annual costs. Tuition/fees: $9,830. Books/supplies: $1,000. Personal expenses: $3,843.

Application procedures. Admission: No deadline. $25 fee. Application must be submitted on paper. Admission notification on a rolling basis. **Financial aid:** No deadline. FAFSA required. Applicants notified on a rolling basis starting 7/1; must reply within 2 week(s) of notification.

Academics. Special study options: Accelerated study, distance learning, liberal arts/career combination, weekend college. **Credit/placement by examination:** AP, CLEP. 15 credit hours maximum toward associate degree, 32 toward bachelor's. **Support services:** Study skills assistance, tutoring.

Majors. Business: Nonprofit/public. **Philosophy/religion:** Religion.

Most popular majors. Business/marketing 50%, philosophy/religious studies 50%.

Computing on campus. 1 workstations in computer center. Wireless network available.

Student life. Freshman orientation: Mandatory. Preregistration for classes offered. **Activities:** Student government, student newspaper.

Student services. Adult student services, chaplain/spiritual director, financial aid counseling, personal counseling.

Contact. E-mail: info@williamsoncc.edu
Phone: (615) 771-7821 Fax: (615) 771-7810
Williamson Christian College, 200 Seaboard Lane, Franklin, TN 37067

Texas

Abilene Christian University

Abilene, Texas   **CB member**
www.acu.edu   **CB code: 6001**

▶ Private 4-year university affiliated with Church of Christ
▶ Residential campus in small city
▶ 3,730 degree-seeking undergraduates: 5% part-time, 55% women
▶ 763 degree-seeking graduate students
▶ 64% of applicants admitted
▶ SAT or ACT (ACT writing recommended), application essay required
▶ 59% graduate within 6 years; 27% enter graduate study

General. Founded in 1906. Regionally accredited. **Degrees:** 685 bachelor's, 2 associate awarded; master's, doctoral offered. **Location:** 150 miles from Dallas, Fort Worth. **Calendar:** Semester, limited summer session. **Full-time faculty:** 246 total; 83% have terminal degrees, 9% minority, 32% women. **Part-time faculty:** 108 total; 29% have terminal degrees, 7% minority, 46% women. **Class size:** 49% < 20, 39% 20-39, 5% 40-49, 5% 50-99, 1% >100. **Special facilities:** Converged media newsroom, center for restoration studies, voice institute, demonstration farm and ranch, observatory, AT&T learning studio, learning commons.

Freshman class profile. 3,470 applied, 2,234 admitted, 864 enrolled.

Mid 50% test scores			
SAT critical reading:	490-620	Rank in top quarter:	55%
SAT math:	510-610	Rank in top tenth:	25%
ACT composite:	22-28	End year in good standing:	85%
GPA 3.75 or higher:	37%	Return as sophomores:	75%
GPA 3.50-3.74:	29%	Out-of-state:	15%
GPA 3.0-3.49:	24%	Live on campus:	97%
GPA 2.0-2.99:	9%	International:	3%

Basis for selection. High school records (including courses taken, grade trends and rank in class), score on SAT or ACT, essay responses, extracurricular activities and honors. Admission or denial of admission not based on any single factor. On lieu of writing own essay, you may submit your own ACT or SAT writing score. Audition required for music and theater programs. **Home schooled:** Transcript of courses and grades required.

High school preparation. College-preparatory program required. 12 units recommended. Recommended units include English 4, mathematics 3, science 3 (laboratory 2) and foreign language 2.

2012-2013 Annual costs. Tuition/fees (projected): $26,770. Books/supplies: $1,250. Personal expenses: $1,914.

2010-2011 Financial aid. Need-based: 837 full-time freshmen applied for aid; 680 were judged to have need; 680 of these received aid. Average need met was 68%. Average scholarship/grant was $11,946; average loan $3,426. 74% of total undergraduate aid awarded as scholarships/grants, 26% as loans/jobs. **Non-need-based:** Awarded to 2,720 full-time undergraduates, including 812 freshmen. Scholarships awarded for academics, art, athletics, leadership, minority status, music/drama, religious affiliation, state residency. **Additional information:** Early estimate service available.

Application procedures. Admission: Closing date 2/15 (postmark date). $50 fee, may be waived for applicants with need. Admission notification on a rolling basis beginning on or about 2/15. Admitted students planning to enroll should confirm the offer by submitting a $250 enrollment deposit (non-refundable after May 1), along with letter of intent to the Admissions Office. Enrollment deposit is a pre-payment toward total bill. **Financial aid:** Priority date 3/1; no closing date. FAFSA, institutional form required. Applicants notified on a rolling basis starting 4/1.

Academics. Special study options: Combined bachelor's/graduate degree, cross-registration, distance learning, double major, dual enrollment of high school students, ESL, honors, independent study, internships, student-designed major, study abroad, teacher certification program. **Credit/placement by examination:** AP, CLEP, IB, SAT, ACT, institutional tests. 15 credit hours maximum toward associate degree, 30 toward bachelor's. **Support services:** Pre-admission summer program, reduced course load, remedial instruction, study skills assistance, tutoring, writing center.

Honors college/program. Must have high school GPA of 3.75 or rank in top 10 percent of high school class; SAT of 1210 (exclusive of Writing) or ACT of 27; submit satisfactory resume (achievements, awards, offices, etc.) and honors college application essay. 150 freshmen admitted. Students take 18 hours of Honors courses in their first 2 years, all general education requirements; 8 projects of which at least 2 must be 1-hour colloquia and one must be a major project in the student's major.

Majors. Biology: General, biochemistry. **Business:** Accounting, business admin, finance, information resources management, marketing. **Communications:** Communications/speech/rhetoric, digital media, journalism. **Computer sciences:** Computer science, information technology. **Conservation:** Environmental science. **Education:** Art, biology, elementary, English, history, mathematics, middle, music, physical, science, secondary, social studies, Spanish, special ed. **Engineering:** Engineering science. **English:** English lit. **Foreign languages:** Spanish. **General:** Agribusiness operations, animal sciences. **Health services:** Clinical lab science, dietetics, nursing (RN), ophthalmic lab technology, predental, premedicine, prepharmacy, preveterinary, speech pathology. **History:** General. **Human services:** Social work. **Math:** General. **Parks/recreation:** Health/fitness, sports admin. **Physical sciences:** Chemistry, physics. **Protective services:** Law enforcement admin. **Psychology:** General. **Social sciences:** Political science, sociology. **Theology:** Bible, missionary, youth ministry. **Visual/performing arts:** Dramatic, graphic design, interior design, music, piano/keyboard, studio arts, voice/opera. **Work/family studies:** Family studies.

Most popular majors. Biology 6%, business/marketing 22%, communications/journalism 8%, education 6%, health sciences 8%, interdisciplinary studies 8%, visual/performing arts 6%.

Computing on campus. 530 workstations in dormitories, library, computer center, student center. Dormitories wired for high-speed internet access and linked to campus network. Commuter students can connect to campus network. Online course registration, online library, helpline, student web hosting, wireless network available.

Student life. Freshman orientation: Mandatory, $115 fee. Preregistration for classes offered. Held twice each summer, late June and August. Overnight, two-day event open to parents. **Policies:** Religious observance required. **Housing:** Guaranteed on-campus for freshmen. Single-sex dorms, special housing for disabled, apartments available. **Activities:** Bands, campus ministries, choral groups, drama, international student organizations, literary magazine, music ensembles, Model UN, musical theater, opera, radio station, student government, student newspaper, symphony orchestra, TV station, student association, Seekers of the Word, campus activities team, Hispanos Unidos, College Democrats, African Missions Fellowship, Essence of Ebony, mission student committee, College Republicans.

Athletics. NCAA. **Intercollegiate:** Baseball M, basketball, cross-country, football (tackle) M, golf M, soccer W, softball W, tennis, track and field, volleyball W. **Intramural:** Basketball, bowling, football (non-tackle), golf, racquetball, soccer, softball, tennis, volleyball, water polo. **Team name:** Wildcats.

Student services. Adult student services, alcohol/substance abuse counseling, chaplain/spiritual director, career counseling, student employment services, financial aid counseling, health services, minority student services, personal counseling, placement for graduates, veterans' counselor. **Physically disabled:** Services for visually, speech, hearing impaired.

Contact. E-mail: info@admissions.acu.edu
Phone: (325) 674-2650 Toll-free number: (800) 460-6228
Fax: (325) 674-2130
Mark Lavender, Director of Admissions, Abilene Christian University, ACU Box 29000, Abilene, TX 79699

Amberton University

Garland, Texas
www.amberton.edu   **CB code: 6140**

▶ Private 4-year university affiliated with nondenominational tradition
▶ Commuter campus in small city
▶ 313 degree-seeking undergraduates: 43% part-time, 64% women
▶ 1,139 degree-seeking graduate students

General. Founded in 1971. Regionally accredited. Upper level and graduate institution designed for adult students. Must have previous college and be over 21 years old to attend. **Degrees:** 125 bachelor's awarded; master's offered. **Location:** 12 miles from downtown Dallas. **Calendar:** Four 10-week sessions. Extensive summer session. **Full-time faculty:** 15 total; 93% have terminal degrees. **Part-time faculty:** 60 total; 92% have terminal degrees.

Basis for selection. All students required to have previously completed college work. No first-time freshmen. Must be at least 21 years of age.

2011-2012 Annual costs. Tuition/fees: $7,050. Books/supplies: $500.

Application procedures. Admission: No deadline. No application fee. Application must be submitted on paper. Admission notification on a rolling basis. **Financial aid:** No deadline.

Academics. Special study options: Distance learning, independent study, weekend college. **Credit/placement by examination:** AP, CLEP. 30 credit hours maximum toward bachelor's degree.

Majors. Business: General, accounting, business admin. **Liberal arts:** Arts/sciences.

Most popular majors. Business/marketing 90%, liberal arts 10%.

Computing on campus. 25 workstations in library, computer center. Online library available.

Student services. Adult student services, career counseling, personal counseling, placement for graduates, veterans' counselor.

Contact. E-mail: advisor@amberton.edu
Phone: (972) 279-6511 ext. 180 Fax: (972) 279-9773
Don Hebbard, Academic Dean, Amberton University, 1700 Eastgate Drive, Garland, TX 75041-5595

Angelo State University

San Angelo, Texas
www.angelo.edu

CB member
CB code: 6644

- Public 4-year university
- Residential campus in small city
- 6,105 degree-seeking undergraduates: 15% part-time, 55% women, 7% African American, 1% Asian American, 27% Hispanic American, 1% Native American, 1% international
- 797 degree-seeking graduate students
- 93% of applicants admitted
- SAT or ACT (ACT writing optional) required
- 31% graduate within 6 years

General. Founded in 1928. Regionally accredited. More than 50 percent of ASU's undergraduates are first-generation college students with more than 26 percent Hispanic enrollment. ASU is a Hispanic-serving institution. **Degrees:** 809 bachelor's, 168 associate awarded; master's, professional offered. **ROTC:** Air Force. **Location:** 200 miles from Austin, 210 miles from San Antonio, 220 miles from Fort Worth, 250 miles from Dallas. **Calendar:** Semester, extensive summer session. **Full-time faculty:** 272 total; 76% have terminal degrees, 18% minority, 43% women. **Part-time faculty:** 76 total; 30% have terminal degrees, 5% minority, 55% women. **Class size:** 25% <20, 55% 20-39, 7% 40-49, 11% 50-99, less than 1% >100. **Special facilities:** Agricultural research center, food safety and product development lab, 6,000-acre farm/ranch, natural history collections, global immersion center/planetarium, West Texas Collection regional historical archive.

Freshman class profile. 4,527 applied, 4,202 admitted, 1,455 enrolled.

Mid 50% test scores			
SAT critical reading:	420-530	Out-of-state:	1%
SAT math:	440-550	Live on campus:	65%
ACT composite:	18-23	International:	1%
Rank in top quarter:	40%	Fraternities:	5%
Rank in top tenth:	14%	Sororities:	4%

Basis for selection. Should rank in the top half of high school class, have minimum 16 ACT or 760 SAT (exclusive of Writing). If ranked in third quartile, must have 23 ACT or 1030 SAT. If ranked in fourth quartile, must have 30 ACT or 1270 SAT. **Home schooled:** Transcript of courses and grades required. ASU recommends that students should have completed the equivalent of a high school curriculum.

High school preparation. College-preparatory program recommended. 26 units recommended. Recommended units include English 4, mathematics 4, social studies 3.5, science 4, foreign language 2, visual/performing arts 1, academic electives 5.5. Economics 0.5, speech 0.5, physical education 1; or be on track to complete the recommended units or an advanced curriculum.

2011-2012 Annual costs. Tuition/fees: $7,349; $16,739 out-of-state. Room/board: $7,964. Books/supplies: $1,150. Personal expenses: $2,025.

2010-2011 Financial aid. Need-based: 1,216 full-time freshmen applied for aid; 986 were judged to have need; 984 of these received aid. Average need met was 54%. Average scholarship/grant was $2,819; average loan $2,700. 59% of total undergraduate aid awarded as scholarships/grants, 41% as loans/jobs. **Non-need-based:** Awarded to 2,311 full-time undergraduates, including 819 freshmen. Scholarships awarded for academics, art, athletics, leadership, music/drama, ROTC, state residency. **Additional information:** ASU's Blue and Gold Guarantee provides full tuition and mandatory fees for freshmen coming from Texas families with a combined adjusted gross income of $40,000 or less. Carr Academic Scholarship program offers $1,000 to $3,000 to entering freshmen who meet qualifications.

Application procedures. Admission: Closing date 8/23 (receipt date). $35 fee, may be waived for applicants with need. Admission notification on a rolling basis beginning on or about 9/1. **Financial aid:** Priority date 4/1; no closing date. FAFSA required. Applicants notified on a rolling basis starting 4/1; must reply within 4 week(s) of notification.

Academics. Special study options: Combined bachelor's/graduate degree, distance learning, double major, dual enrollment of high school students, ESL, honors, independent study, internships, study abroad, teacher certification program. 4+1 programs in various fields with Texas Tech University allowing recipients of ASU bachelor's degree to earn a master's degree in related field in one year at TTU. 3-2 engineering-physics and 3-2 agriculture-education programs with Texas A&M and University of Texas El Paso. **Credit/placement by examination:** AP, CLEP, SAT, ACT. Unlimited credits by examination provided student meets hours required in residence. **Support services:** Learning center, reduced course load, remedial instruction, study skills assistance, tutoring, writing center.

Honors college/program. Students must have 3.25 GPA in coursework done at ASU. If enrolling from high school, must be in the top 10% of graduating class and have 27 ACT or 1200 (exclusive of Writing) SAT. Some classes are strictly honors only, but normal classes can be given honors credit by contract: student meets with professor before semester and discusses additional work necessary to qualify for honors credit.

Majors. Biology: General, biochemistry, ecology, evolutionary. **Business:** Accounting, business admin, finance, international, management information systems, marketing, real estate. **Communications:** Communications/speech/rhetoric, journalism. **Computer sciences:** General. **Conservation:** Management/policy. **Engineering:** Applied physics. **English:** English lit. **Foreign languages:** French, German, Spanish. **General:** Animal husbandry, animal sciences. **Health services:** Athletic training, clinical lab science, nursing (RN). **History:** General. **Math:** General. **Parks/recreation:** Health/fitness. **Physical sciences:** Chemistry, physics. **Protective services:** Criminal justice. **Psychology:** General. **Social sciences:** Political science, sociology. **Visual/performing arts:** Art, dramatic, music, studio arts. **Work/family studies:** Child development.

Most popular majors. Business/marketing 20%, communications/journalism 8%, health sciences 7%, interdisciplinary studies 14%, parks/recreation 10%, psychology 9%.

Computing on campus. 700 workstations in dormitories, library, computer center, student center. Dormitories wired for high-speed internet access and linked to campus network. Commuter students can connect to campus network. Online course registration, online library, helpline, student web hosting, wireless network available.

Student life. Freshman orientation: Available, $25 fee. Preregistration for classes offered. Sessions offered several times during the summer. **Policies:** Single undergraduates with 12-60 semester credit hours of college-level work who do not live with parents are required to reside in University-owned housing. **Housing:** Coed dorms, special housing for disabled, apartments available. $200 nonrefundable deposit, deadline 7/15. **Activities:** Bands, campus ministries, choral groups, dance, drama, international student organizations, literary magazine, music ensembles, musical theater, radio station, student government, student newspaper, TV station, Association of Mexican-American Students, Baptist student union, Black Organization Striving for Success, Block and Bridle, College Republicans, Newman Center, Nontraditional Student Organization, residence hall association, Young Democrats.

Athletics. NCAA. **Intercollegiate:** Baseball M, basketball, cross-country, football (tackle) M, golf W, soccer W, softball W, track and field, volleyball W. **Intramural:** Badminton, basketball, football (non-tackle), golf, racquetball, soccer, softball, table tennis, tennis, volleyball. **Team name:** Rams and Rambelles.

Student services. Adult student services, alcohol/substance abuse counseling, chaplain/spiritual director, career counseling, services for economically disadvantaged, student employment services, financial aid counseling, health services, minority student services, personal counseling, placement for graduates, veterans' counselor. **Physically disabled:** Services for visually, hearing impaired.

Contact. E-mail: admissions@angelo.edu
Phone: (325) 942-2041 Toll-free number: (800) 946-8627
Fax: (325) 942-2078
Michael Loehring, Director of Admissions, Angelo State University, ASU
Station #11014, San Angelo, TX 76909-1014

Argosy University: Dallas
Farmers Branch, Texas
www.argosy.edu/dallas

▶ For-profit 4-year university
▶ Very large city
▶ 182 degree-seeking undergraduates

General. Regionally accredited. **Degrees:** 10 bachelor's awarded; master's, professional, doctoral offered. **Calendar:** Differs by program. **Full-time faculty:** 13 total. **Part-time faculty:** 53 total.

Basis for selection. Open admission.

2011-2012 Annual costs. Tuition/fees: $17,962.

Application procedures. **Admission:** Closing date 9/13. $50 fee. **Financial aid:** No deadline.

Academics. Credit/placement by examination: AP, CLEP.

Majors. **Business:** Business admin. **Liberal arts:** Arts/sciences. **Protective services:** Law enforcement admin. **Psychology:** General.

Contact. E-mail: audadmis@argosy.edu
Phone: (214) 459-2237
Casey McMullen, Senior Director of Admissions, Argosy University: Dallas, 5001 Lyndon B. Johnson Freeway, Heritage Square, Farmers Branch, TX 75244

Arlington Baptist College
Arlington, Texas
www.arlingtonbaptistcollege.edu CB code: 6039

▶ Private 4-year Bible and teachers college affiliated with Baptist faith
▶ Commuter campus in very large city
▶ 220 degree-seeking undergraduates: 10% part-time, 45% women, 18% African American, 8% Hispanic American, 2% Native American, 1% international
▶ 21 degree-seeking graduate students
▶ Application essay required
▶ 41% graduate within 6 years; 20% enter graduate study

General. Founded in 1939. Accredited by ABHE. **Degrees:** 27 bachelor's awarded; master's offered. **Location:** 10 miles from Fort Worth, 25 miles from Dallas. **Calendar:** Semester, limited summer session. **Full-time faculty:** 12 total; 17% have terminal degrees, 25% women. **Part-time faculty:** 5 total; 20% minority, 20% women. **Class size:** 76% < 20, 19% 20-39, 3% 40-49, 1% 50-99.

Freshman class profile. 86 applied, 86 admitted, 54 enrolled.

GPA 3.75 or higher:	9%	Rank in top tenth:	4%
GPA 3.50-3.74:	11%	End year in good standing:	60%
GPA 3.0-3.49:	28%	Return as sophomores:	51%
GPA 2.0-2.99:	41%	Out-of-state:	13%
Rank in top quarter:	21%	Live on campus:	74%

Basis for selection. Open admission. Interview recommended for all; audition required for music. **Home schooled:** Transcript of courses and grades, interview required. Advised to obtain GED.

High school preparation. 16 units recommended. Recommended units include English 3, mathematics 2, social studies 3, history 3 and science 1.

2012-2013 Annual costs. Tuition/fees (projected): $7,840. Room/board: $4,800. Books/supplies: $800. Personal expenses: $720.

2011-2012 Financial aid. All financial aid based on need. 52 full-time freshmen applied for aid; 52 were judged to have need; 52 of these received aid. Average need met was 100%. Average scholarship/grant was $8,275. 39% of total undergraduate aid awarded as scholarships/grants, 61% as loans/jobs.

Application procedures. **Admission:** Priority date 8/1; no deadline. $15 fee, may be waived for applicants with need. Admission notification on a rolling basis. **Financial aid:** Closing date 8/15. FAFSA required. Applicants notified on a rolling basis starting 12/1; must reply by 8/15.

Academics. **Special study options:** Distance learning, double major, dual enrollment of high school students, external degree, teacher certification program. **Credit/placement by examination:** AP, CLEP, institutional tests. 30 credit hours maximum toward bachelor's degree. **Support services:** Reduced course load, remedial instruction, tutoring.

Majors. **Education:** General, elementary, English, kindergarten/preschool, middle, multi-level teacher, music, science, secondary, social studies. **Philosophy/religion:** Religion. **Psychology:** Counseling. **Theology:** Bible, missionary, pastoral counseling, religious ed, sacred music, youth ministry. **Visual/performing arts:** Music.

Most popular majors. Education 26%, theological studies 50%.

Computing on campus. 25 workstations in library, computer center. Online course registration, wireless network available.

Student life. **Freshman orientation:** Mandatory. Preregistration for classes offered. Orientation includes placement testing. **Policies:** Religious observance required. **Housing:** Guaranteed on-campus for freshmen. Single-sex dorms, wellness housing available. $25 nonrefundable deposit. **Activities:** Campus ministries, choral groups, music ensembles, student government, ministry teams.

Athletics. NCCAA. **Intercollegiate:** Baseball M, basketball, cross-country, volleyball W. **Team name:** Patriots.

Student services. Chaplain/spiritual director, career counseling, student employment services, financial aid counseling, personal counseling, placement for graduates, veterans' counselor.

Contact. E-mail: jtaylor@arlingtonbaptistcollege.edu
Phone: (817) 461-8741 ext. 105 Fax: (817) 274-1138
Janie Taylor, Registrar, Arlington Baptist College, 3001 West Division Street, Arlington, TX 76012

Art Institute of Dallas
Dallas, Texas
www.aid.edu CB code: 2680

▶ For-profit 4-year visual arts college
▶ Very large city
▶ 1,900 degree-seeking undergraduates

General. Regionally accredited. **Degrees:** 193 bachelor's, 131 associate awarded. **Calendar:** Quarter. **Full-time faculty:** 65 total. **Part-time faculty:** 70 total.

Basis for selection. Open admission, but selective for some programs. Some animation, art and design associate degree programs may require portfolio evaluation.

2011-2012 Annual costs. Bachelor's programs from $100,932-$104,016. Associate programs from $54,190-$58,696. Personal expenses: $2,880.

Application procedures. **Admission:** No deadline. $50 fee. Admission notification on a rolling basis. **Financial aid:** No deadline. FAFSA required. Applicants notified on a rolling basis.

Academics. Credit/placement by examination: AP, CLEP.

Majors. **Visual/performing arts:** Studio arts.

Student life. **Freshman orientation:** Available. Preregistration for classes offered.

Contact. E-mail: cwilliams@aii.edu
Phone: (214) 692-8080 Toll-free number: (800) 275-4243
Dawn Polk-Bridges, Director of Admissions, Art Institute of Dallas, Two North Park, 8080 Park Lane, Dallas, TX 75231

Art Institute of Houston
Houston, Texas
www.artinstitutes.edu/houston
CB code: 8271

- For-profit 4-year culinary school and visual arts college
- Very large city
- 2,677 degree-seeking undergraduates: 32% part-time, 54% women, 16% African American, 3% Asian American, 24% Hispanic American, 2% international

General. Regionally accredited. **Degrees:** 229 bachelor's, 179 associate awarded. **Calendar:** Quarter. **Full-time faculty:** 61 total. **Part-time faculty:** 41 total. **Special facilities:** Photography studio, video lab, 5 multi-purpose culinary lab kitchens.

Basis for selection. Proof of graduation from accredited high school, a Graduate Equivalency Diploma (GED), or foreign equivalent required for admissions. Applicants to Media Arts & Animation program must submit portfolio for approval by faculty committee. SAT or ACT recommended. Observes TASP guidelines. ASSET or COMPASS testing may be required. Remediation may be required if test scores fall below required ranges; some remediation available on campus.

2011-2012 Annual costs. Tuition/fees: $21,960.

Application procedures. Admission: No deadline. $50 fee. Admission notification on a rolling basis. **Financial aid:** Priority date 3/1; no closing date. FAFSA, institutional form required.

Academics. Special study options: Distance learning, honors, internships, study abroad. **Credit/placement by examination:** AP, CLEP, SAT, ACT, institutional tests. **Support services:** Learning center, remedial instruction, tutoring, writing center.

Majors. Visual/performing arts: Graphic design, interior design.

Student life. Activities: International student organizations.

Contact. E-mail: aihadm@aii.edu
Phone: (713) 623-2040 Toll-free number: (800) 275-4244
Fax: (713) 966-2797
Jane Chastant, Senior Director of Admissions, Art Institute of Houston, 1900 Yorktown, Houston, TX 77056-4115

Austin College
Sherman, Texas
www.austincollege.edu
CB member
CB code: 6016

- Private 4-year liberal arts and teachers college affiliated with Presbyterian Church (USA)
- Residential campus in small city
- 1,320 degree-seeking undergraduates: 53% women
- 25 degree-seeking graduate students
- 52% of applicants admitted
- SAT or ACT with writing, application essay required
- 75% graduate within 6 years

General. Founded in 1849. Regionally accredited. **Degrees:** 274 bachelor's awarded; master's offered. **Location:** 60 miles from Dallas. **Calendar:** 4-1-4, limited summer session. **Full-time faculty:** 92 total; 95% have terminal degrees, 33% women. **Part-time faculty:** 52 total; 33% have terminal degrees, 42% women. **Class size:** 71% < 20, 27% 20-39, 2% 40-49, less than 1% 50-99. **Special facilities:** Environmental research areas totaling 174 acres, lake recreation area, tissue culture facility for study of cellular molecular interactions of eukaryotic cells, high performance numeric and graphics computing facility for advanced scientific computing and 3-D graphics.

Freshman class profile. 3,309 applied, 1,737 admitted, 359 enrolled.

Mid 50% test scores			
SAT critical reading:	580-680	Return as sophomores:	84%
SAT math:	570-680	Out-of-state:	11%
SAT writing:	560-650	Live on campus:	97%
ACT composite:	24-29	Fraternities:	15%
		Sororities:	14%

Basis for selection. Academic transcript record, test scores, recommendations, extracurricular involvement, essay important. Interview considered. Interview recommended for all; audition recommended for music, theater (required for scholarship consideration); portfolio recommended for art (required for scholarship consideration). **Home schooled:** Transcript of courses and grades required.

High school preparation. College-preparatory program recommended. Required and recommended units include English 4, mathematics 3-4, social studies 2-3, science 3-4 (laboratory 2-3), foreign language 2-3, visual/performing arts 1-2 and academic electives 1.

2011-2012 Annual costs. Tuition/fees: $31,270. Room/board: $10,078. Books/supplies: $1,200. Personal expenses: $800.

2011-2012 Financial aid. Need-based: 354 full-time freshmen applied for aid; 261 were judged to have need; 261 of these received aid. Average need met was 100%. Average scholarship/grant was $22,865; average loan $3,980. 71% of total undergraduate aid awarded as scholarships/grants, 29% as loans/jobs. **Non-need-based:** Awarded to 536 full-time undergraduates, including 121 freshmen. Scholarships awarded for academics, alumni affiliation, art, leadership, music/drama, religious affiliation, state residency.

Application procedures. Admission: Priority date 1/15; deadline 5/1 (postmark date). No application fee. Admission notification on a rolling basis beginning on or about 12/15. Must reply by 5/1. **Financial aid:** Priority date 4/1; no closing date. FAFSA required. Applicants notified on a rolling basis starting 3/1; must reply by 5/1.

Academics. Special study options: Double major, exchange student, honors, independent study, internships, liberal arts/career combination, student-designed major, study abroad, teacher certification program, Washington semester. 3-2 dual degree engineering program with University of Texas Dallas, Washington University in St. Louis, Columbia University, Texas A&M University. **Credit/placement by examination:** AP, CLEP, IB, institutional tests. **Support services:** Learning center, study skills assistance, tutoring.

Majors. Area/ethnic studies: American, Latin American. **Biology:** General, biochemistry. **Business:** General. **Communications:** Communications/speech/rhetoric. **Computer sciences:** Computer science. **Conservation:** Environmental studies. **English:** English lit. **Foreign languages:** Classics, French, German, Latin, Spanish. **History:** General. **Math:** General. **Philosophy/religion:** Philosophy, religion. **Physical sciences:** Chemistry, physics. **Psychology:** General. **Social sciences:** Economics, international economics, international relations, political science, sociology. **Visual/performing arts:** Art, music.

Computing on campus. 160 workstations in dormitories, library, computer center, student center. Dormitories wired for high-speed internet access and linked to campus network. Commuter students can connect to campus network. Online library, helpline, student web hosting, wireless network available.

Student life. Freshman orientation: Mandatory. Preregistration for classes offered. Held the weekend prior to the first day of classes. **Housing:** Guaranteed on-campus for freshmen. Coed dorms, single-sex dorms, apartments available. Language emphasis residence, suite-style housing for upper-level students with private bedroom, common area, kitchenette. **Activities:** Bands, campus ministries, choral groups, dance, drama, international student organizations, literary magazine, music ensembles, Model UN, musical theater, student government, student newspaper, symphony orchestra, Alpha Phi Omega, Intervarsity Christian Fellowship, Black Expressions, Young Democrats, Service Station, Los Amigos, Habitat for Humanity, Activators, Amnesty International.

Athletics. NCAA. **Intercollegiate:** Baseball M, basketball, football (tackle) M, soccer, softball W, swimming, tennis, volleyball W. **Intramural:** Basketball, football (non-tackle), soccer, softball, volleyball. **Team name:** Roos.

Student services. Chaplain/spiritual director, career counseling, financial aid counseling, health services, personal counseling.

Contact. E-mail: admission@austincollege.edu
Phone: (903) 813-3000 Toll-free number: (800) 526-4276
Fax: (903) 813-3198
Nan Davis, Vice President for Institutional Enrollment, Austin College, 900 North Grand Avenue, Suite 6N, Sherman, TX 75090-4400

Austin Graduate School of Theology
Austin, Texas
www.austingrad.edu
CB code: 4969

- Private two-year upper-division Bible and seminary college affiliated with Church of Christ
- Commuter campus in very large city
- Application essay required

General. Founded in 1917. Regionally accredited. Highly diverse ethnic and socioeconomic student body grounded in Christian faith traditions. **Degrees:** 6 bachelor's awarded; master's offered. **Location:** 80 miles from San Antonio,

150 miles from Houston. **Calendar:** Semester, limited summer session. **Full-time faculty:** 4 total; 100% have terminal degrees. **Part-time faculty:** 7 total; 57% have terminal degrees, 14% minority. **Class size:** 90% < 20, 10% 20-39.

Student profile. 31 degree-seeking undergraduates, 28 degree-seeking graduate students.

Women:	32%	**Part-time:**	84%

Basis for selection. Open admission. College transcript, application essay required. Transcript, GPA, recommendations required. High school transcript, test scores required for applicants with fewer than 35 hours. Transfer accepted as sophomores, juniors, seniors.

2011-2012 Annual costs. Tuition/fees: $9,375. Books/supplies: $600. Personal expenses: $1,980.

Financial aid. Non-need-based: Scholarships awarded for academics, leadership. **Additional information:** Generous scholarships for students taking at least 12 hours. Federal work study program available. Institutional work study program (need-based) available.

Application procedures. Admission: Priority date 6/1. No application fee. Application must be submitted on paper. **Financial aid:** No deadline. FAFSA, institutional form required.

Academics. Special study options: Dual enrollment of high school students, liberal arts/career combination. Liberal arts/career combination program in religion; combined bachelor's/graduate program in ministry. **Credit/placement by examination:** AP, CLEP. 18 credit hours maximum toward bachelor's degree.

Majors. Theology: Bible, theology.

Computing on campus. 4 workstations in library, computer center, student center. Online library, wireless network available.

Student life. Policies: Religious observance required. **Activities:** Student government.

Student services. Financial aid counseling, personal counseling.

Contact. E-mail: admissions@austingrad.edu
Phone: (512) 476-2772 ext. 103 Toll-free number: (866) 287-4723
Fax: (512) 476-3919
Celeste Scarborough, Registrar, Austin Graduate School of Theology, 7640 Guadalupe Street, Austin, TX 78752-1333

Baptist Missionary Association Theological Seminary
Jacksonville, Texas
www.bmats.edu
CB code: 7042

- Private 4-year Bible and seminary college affiliated with Baptist faith
- Commuter campus in large town
- 54 degree-seeking undergraduates

General. Founded in 1955. Regionally accredited. **Degrees:** 14 bachelor's, 1 associate awarded; master's offered. **Location:** 120 miles from Dallas. **Calendar:** Semester, limited summer session. **Full-time faculty:** 5 total. **Part-time faculty:** 6 total.

Basis for selection. Open admission, but selective for some programs. Essay or personal statement very important. Religious commitment, interview, recommendations, school and community activities important.

2011-2012 Annual costs. Tuition/fees: $3,800. Room/board: $2,400.

Application procedures. Admission: Closing date 7/1. $35 fee.

Academics. Special study options: Internships. **Credit/placement by examination:** AP, CLEP.

Majors. Philosophy/religion: Religion. **Theology:** Theology.

Computing on campus. 2 workstations in library.

Student life. Activities: Student government.

Student services. Career counseling, personal counseling.

Contact. E-mail: bmatsem@bmats.edu
Phone: (903) 586-2501 Fax: (903) 586-0378
Philip Attebery, Dean/Registrar, Baptist Missionary Association Theological Seminary, 1530 East Pine Street, Jacksonville, TX 75766

Baptist University of the Americas
San Antonio, Texas
www.bua.edu

- Private 4-year university and Bible college affiliated with Baptist faith
- Commuter campus in very large city
- 211 degree-seeking undergraduates

General. Accredited by ABHE. Baptist University of the Americas trains cross-culturally students in Biblical/Theological Studies and Ministry Studies, at a higher education academic level, from a Hispanic context. **Degrees:** 45 bachelor's, 14 associate awarded. **Calendar:** Semester, limited summer session. **Full-time faculty:** 9 total. **Part-time faculty:** 22 total.

Basis for selection. Open admission. Observes THEA requirements.

2011-2012 Annual costs. Tuition/fees: $6,000. Room/board: $2,880. Books/supplies: $500. Personal expenses: $1,925.

Application procedures. Admission: No deadline. $25 fee. **Financial aid:** No deadline.

Academics. Special study options: ESL, independent study. **Credit/placement by examination:** AP, CLEP. **Support services:** Learning center, remedial instruction, study skills assistance, tutoring, writing center.

Majors. Business: Business admin. **Foreign languages:** Spanish. **Theology:** Bible, theology.

Computing on campus. Dormitories wired for high-speed internet access and linked to campus network. Online library, repair service available.

Student life. Freshman orientation: Available, $25 fee. Preregistration for classes offered. **Housing:** $200 deposit. **Activities:** Campus ministries, drama, international student organizations.

Contact. E-mail: mary.ranjel@bua.edu
Phone: (210) 924-4338
Mary Ranjel, Director of Admissions, Baptist University of the Americas, 8019 South Pan Am Expressway, San Antonio, TX 78224

Baylor University
Waco, Texas
www.baylor.edu
CB member
CB code: 6032

- Private 4-year university affiliated with Baptist faith
- Residential campus in small city
- 12,518 degree-seeking undergraduates: 2% part-time, 58% women, 8% African American, 6% Asian American, 13% Hispanic American, 2% international
- 2,446 degree-seeking graduate students
- 40% of applicants admitted
- SAT or ACT with writing, application essay required
- 72% graduate within 6 years

General. Founded in 1845. Regionally accredited. **Degrees:** 2,605 bachelor's awarded; master's, professional, doctoral offered. **ROTC:** Army, Air Force. **Location:** 100 miles from Dallas-Fort Worth, 100 miles from Austin. **Calendar:** Semester, extensive summer session. **Full-time faculty:** 886 total; 82% have terminal degrees, 13% minority, 38% women. **Part-time faculty:** 325 total; 10% minority, 50% women. **Class size:** 47% < 20, 37% 20-39, 8% 40-49, 6% 50-99, 3% >100. **Special facilities:** Museum of natural science, Texas collection library, Armstrong Browning library.

Freshman class profile. 38,960 applied, 15,451 admitted, 3,033 enrolled.

Mid 50% test scores			
SAT critical reading:	560-660	Rank in top tenth:	39%
SAT math:	570-680	End year in good standing:	90%
SAT writing:	530-640	Return as sophomores:	85%
ACT composite:	24-29	Out-of-state:	25%
Rank in top quarter:	74%	Live on campus:	98%
		International:	2%

Basis for selection. Competitive high school performance and competitive scores on ACT or SAT most important; above-average achievement

and potential expected. Audition required for music and theater programs; interview recommended for marginal achievers; portfolio recommended for art. **Home schooled:** Transcript of courses and grades required. If applicant graduated from home school not officially recognized by state in which school is located, applicant must be 17 years old before first day of class unless GED certificate submitted prior to registration.

High school preparation. College-preparatory program required. Required units include English 4, mathematics 4, social studies 2, history 1, science 4 (laboratory 2) and foreign language 2.

2012-2013 Annual costs. Tuition/fees: $33,716. Various options available for room and board. Room/board: $11,072. Books/supplies: $1,364. Personal expenses: $3,328.

2011-2012 Financial aid. **Need-based:** 2,370 full-time freshmen applied for aid; 1,859 were judged to have need; 1,850 of these received aid. Average need met was 68%. Average scholarship/grant was $17,793; average loan $3,132. 64% of total undergraduate aid awarded as scholarships/grants, 36% as loans/jobs. **Non-need-based:** Awarded to 10,537 full-time undergraduates, including 2,925 freshmen. Scholarships awarded for academics, alumni affiliation, art, athletics, job skills, leadership, music/drama, religious affiliation, ROTC.

Application procedures. **Admission:** Priority date 11/1; no deadline. $50 fee, may be waived for applicants with need. Application must be submitted online. Must reply by May 1 or within 2 week(s) if notified thereafter. Notification of admission decision by 1/15 for 11/1 applications and by 3/15 for 2/1 applications; after 3/15 on space available basis. $300 enrollment deposit required by May 1. **Financial aid:** Priority date 3/1; no closing date. FAFSA required. Applicants notified on a rolling basis starting 3/1; must reply by 5/1 or within 2 week(s) of notification.

Academics. Online support (website advising resources and tutoring) available. **Special study options:** Accelerated study, combined bachelor's/graduate degree, double major, honors, internships, student-designed major, study abroad, teacher certification program. Architecture program with Washington University, forestry with Duke University. **Credit/placement by examination:** AP, CLEP, IB, institutional tests. 60 credit hours maximum toward bachelor's degree. **Support services:** Learning center, pre-admission summer program, reduced course load, remedial instruction, study skills assistance, tutoring, writing center.

Honors college/program. Baylor Interdisciplinary Core: all regularly admitted students may apply, phone interview may be required; Honors Program: average SAT score for the previous class was 1375 (exclusive of Writing) and over 30 ACT Composite; University Scholars: no minimum SAT, current scores average above 1400 (exclusive of Writing); Great Texts: no specific requirements, students who declare a major in Great Texts are considered Honors College participants.

Majors. **Architecture:** Architecture. **Area/ethnic studies:** American, Asian, Latin American, Slavic. **Biology:** General, biochemistry, bioinformatics, exercise physiology, neuroscience. **Business:** General, accounting, business admin, entrepreneurial studies, fashion, finance, financial planning, human resources, insurance, international, logistics, management information systems, managerial economics, marketing, real estate, sales/distribution. **Communications:** Communications/speech/rhetoric, digital media, journalism. **Computer sciences:** Computer science, information technology. **Conservation:** Environmental science, environmental studies, forestry. **Education:** Elementary, English, health occupations, mathematics, music, physical, science, social studies, special ed. **Engineering:** General, electrical, mechanical. **English:** English lit, technical writing. **Foreign languages:** Ancient Greek, Biblical, classics, French, German, Latin, linguistics, Russian, Spanish. **Health services:** Athletic training, clinical lab science, communication disorders, environmental health, nursing (RN), predental, premedicine, prenursing, preoptometry. **History:** General. **Human services:** General, social work. **Liberal arts:** Humanities. **Math:** General, applied, statistics. **Parks/recreation:** Health/fitness. **Philosophy/religion:** Philosophy, religion. **Physical sciences:** Astronomy, astrophysics, chemistry, geology, geophysics, physics. **Psychology:** General. **Social sciences:** Anthropology, geography, international relations, political science, sociology. **Theology:** Sacred music. **Visual/performing arts:** Acting, art history/conservation, dramatic, fashion design, interior design, music, music history, music pedagogy, music performance, music theory/composition, studio arts, theater design. **Work/family studies:** General, family studies, human nutrition.

Most popular majors. Biology 11%, business/marketing 23%, communications/journalism 9%, health sciences 12%, social sciences 7%.

Computing on campus. 1,676 workstations in dormitories, library, computer center, student center. Dormitories wired for high-speed internet access and linked to campus network. Commuter students can connect to campus network. Online course registration, online library, helpline, repair service, student web hosting, wireless network available.

Student life. **Freshman orientation:** Mandatory. Preregistration for classes offered. 10 2-day sessions primarily in June. **Policies:** All students required to participate in chapel-forum for 2 semesters. **Housing:** Guaranteed on-campus for freshmen. Single-sex dorms, special housing for disabled, apartments, wellness housing available. Living-learning centers. **Activities:** Bands, campus ministries, choral groups, dance, drama, film society, international student organizations, literary magazine, music ensembles, Model UN, musical theater, opera, radio station, student government, student newspaper, symphony orchestra, TV station, Campus Crusade for Christ, College Republicans, Young Democrats, association of black students, Hispanic student association, Asian student association, Habitat for Humanity, Alpha Phi Omega, Baylor Chamber of Commerce.

Athletics. NCAA. **Intercollegiate:** Baseball M, basketball, cheerleading M, cross-country, equestrian W, football (tackle) M, golf, soccer W, softball W, tennis, track and field, volleyball W. **Intramural:** Basketball, bowling, cross-country, equestrian, football (non-tackle), golf, lacrosse, racquetball, soccer, softball, swimming, table tennis, tennis, track and field, volleyball, weight lifting. **Team name:** Bears.

Student services. Chaplain/spiritual director, career counseling, student employment services, financial aid counseling, health services, legal services, personal counseling, placement for graduates. **Physically disabled:** Services for visually, speech, hearing impaired.

Contact. E-mail: admissions@baylor.edu
Phone: (254) 710-3435 Toll-free number: (800) 229-5678
Fax: (254) 710-3436
Jennifer Carron, Assistant Vice President of Admissions Services, Baylor University, One Bear Place #97056, Waco, TX 76798-7056

College of Biblical Studies-Houston
Houston, Texas
www.cbshouston.edu   **CB code: 3946**

- Private 4-year Bible college
- Commuter campus in very large city
- 390 degree-seeking undergraduates

General. Accredited by ABHE. Multi-denominational and multi-ethnic Christian Bible college. **Degrees:** 69 bachelor's, 24 associate awarded. **Calendar:** Trimester, limited summer session. **Full-time faculty:** 10 total. **Part-time faculty:** 43 total.

Basis for selection. Open admission, but selective for some programs. ASSET testing may be required for associate or baccalaureate level programs. **Home schooled:** State high school equivalency certificate required.

2011-2012 Annual costs. Tuition/fees: $7,470. Books/supplies: $900. Personal expenses: $2,766.

Application procedures. **Admission:** No deadline. $40 fee. Admission notification on a rolling basis. **Financial aid:** No deadline.

Academics. **Special study options:** Accelerated study, dual enrollment of high school students, ESL, independent study. Associate degree in biblical studies taught in Spanish. **Credit/placement by examination:** AP, CLEP, institutional tests. **Support services:** Remedial instruction, tutoring.

Majors. **Theology:** Bible, preministerial.

Computing on campus. 14 workstations in library, computer center. Commuter students can connect to campus network. Online library, wireless network available.

Student life. **Freshman orientation:** Mandatory. Preregistration for classes offered. **Policies:** Students are expected to be Christians. Religious observance required. **Activities:** Campus ministries, student government.

Student services. Adult student services, career counseling, financial aid counseling. **Physically disabled:** Services for visually impaired.

Contact. E-mail: cbs@cbshouston.edu
Phone: (713) 785-5995 Fax: (713) 785-5998
Justin Racca, Director of Admission, College of Biblical Studies-Houston, 7000 Regency Square Boulevard, #110, Houston, TX 77036-3211

College of Saint Thomas More
Fort Worth, Texas
www.cstm.edu   **CB code: 0169**

- Private 4-year liberal arts college affiliated with Roman Catholic Church
- Residential campus in very large city

- 8 degree-seeking undergraduates
- Application essay, interview required

General. Regionally accredited. Most classes consist of close reading of the Great Books curriculum with emphasis on reading primary sources. **Degrees:** 2 bachelor's awarded. **ROTC:** Army, Air Force. **Location:** 5 miles from downtown. **Calendar:** Semester, limited summer session. **Full-time faculty:** 3 total. **Part-time faculty:** 5 total. **Class size:** 100% < 20.

Basis for selection. Secondary school record, essays, interview, test scores important; 2 letters of recommendation required. SAT recommended. **Home schooled:** Transcript of courses and grades, interview, letter of recommendation (nonparent) required.

2011-2012 Annual costs. Tuition/fees: $12,800. Each unit of on-campus housing equipped with a kitchen. Six meals a week provided by the school and is included in fees. Room only: $4,892. Books/supplies: $500. Personal expenses: $1,000.

Financial aid. **Non-need-based:** Scholarships awarded for academics.

Application procedures. **Admission:** No deadline. $35 fee. Application must be submitted on paper. Admission notification on a rolling basis. **Financial aid:** No deadline. FAFSA required. Applicants notified on a rolling basis starting 1/1.

Academics. Three inter-term courses that are part of the curriculum are presented in Rome, Greece, and Oxford, England. Rome is offered freshmen year, Greece and Oxford after sophomore, junior, or senior year. **Special study options:** Dual enrollment of high school students, study abroad. **Credit/placement by examination:** AP, CLEP. **Support services:** Remedial instruction, study skills assistance, tutoring, writing center.

Majors. **Liberal arts:** Arts/sciences.

Computing on campus. 10 workstations in library, student center. Dormitories wired for high-speed internet access and linked to campus network. Online library, wireless network available.

Student life. **Freshman orientation:** Mandatory. Preregistration for classes offered. **Housing:** Guaranteed on-campus for freshmen. Apartments available. $200 fully refundable deposit. **Activities:** Student government, Chapel of Christ the Teacher, Adoration, Culture Society.

Student services. Alcohol/substance abuse counseling, chaplain/spiritual director, career counseling, financial aid counseling, personal counseling.

Contact. E-mail: tcooper@cstm.edu
Phone: (817) 923-8459 Toll-free number: (800) 583-6489
Fax: (817) 924-3206
Peter Capani, Director of Admissions, College of Saint Thomas More, 3020 Lubbock Avenue, Fort Worth, TX 76109

Concordia University Texas
Austin, Texas
www.concordia.edu
CB code: 6127

- Private 4-year university and liberal arts college affiliated with Lutheran Church - Missouri Synod
- Commuter campus in very large city
- 1,466 degree-seeking undergraduates: 20% part-time, 64% women, 13% African American, 3% Asian American, 20% Hispanic American, 1% Native American
- 1,135 degree-seeking graduate students
- 92% of applicants admitted
- SAT or ACT (ACT writing optional) required
- 35% graduate within 6 years

General. Founded in 1926. Regionally accredited. **Degrees:** 186 bachelor's, 12 associate awarded; master's offered. **ROTC:** Army, Air Force. **Calendar:** Semester, extensive summer session. **Full-time faculty:** 67 total; 79% have terminal degrees, 6% minority, 40% women. **Part-time faculty:** 203 total; 59% have terminal degrees, 14% minority, 46% women. **Class size:** 75% < 20, 25% 20-39, less than 1% 40-49.

Freshman class profile. 813 applied, 752 admitted, 260 enrolled.

Mid 50% test scores			
SAT critical reading:	430-560	GPA 2.0-2.99:	20%
SAT math:	460-560	Rank in top quarter:	45%
GPA 3.75 or higher:	30%	Rank in top tenth:	14%
GPA 3.50-3.74:	16%	Return as sophomores:	54%
GPA 3.0-3.49:	34%	Out-of-state:	7%
		Live on campus:	90%

Basis for selection. School achievement record, test scores, and 2.5 GPA important. Interview recommended for academically weak.

2011-2012 Annual costs. Tuition/fees: $23,020. Room/board: $8,460.

2010-2011 Financial aid. **Need-based:** 205 full-time freshmen applied for aid; 170 were judged to have need; 170 of these received aid. Average need met was 71%. Average scholarship/grant was $13,323; average loan $3,570. 69% of total undergraduate aid awarded as scholarships/grants, 31% as loans/jobs. **Non-need-based:** Awarded to 252 full-time undergraduates, including 61 freshmen. Scholarships awarded for academics, music/drama, religious affiliation.

Application procedures. **Admission:** Closing date 8/1. $25 fee, may be waived for applicants with need. Admission notification on a rolling basis beginning on or about 8/15. Must reply by 8/1. Reply by August 15 if dormitory applicant. **Financial aid:** No deadline. FAFSA required. Applicants notified on a rolling basis starting 3/1; must reply within 2 week(s) of notification.

Academics. **Special study options:** Accelerated study, cross-registration, distance learning, double major, dual enrollment of high school students, independent study, internships, liberal arts/career combination, student-designed major, study abroad, teacher certification program. **Credit/placement by examination:** AP, CLEP, IB, SAT, ACT, institutional tests. 15 credit hours maximum toward associate degree, 30 toward bachelor's. **Support services:** Learning center, reduced course load, remedial instruction, study skills assistance, tutoring, writing center.

Majors. **Biology:** General. **Business:** General, business admin, training/development. **Communications:** Communications/speech/rhetoric. **Computer sciences:** Computer science. **Conservation:** Environmental studies. **Education:** Elementary, secondary. **English:** English lit. **Health services:** Health care admin. **History:** General. **Liberal arts:** Arts/sciences. **Math:** General. **Parks/recreation:** Exercise sciences. **Protective services:** Law enforcement admin. **Social sciences:** General. **Theology:** Religious ed, sacred music. **Visual/performing arts:** Conducting, piano/keyboard.

Most popular majors. Business/marketing 49%, education 9%, social sciences 8%, theological studies 6%.

Computing on campus. 45 workstations in library, computer center, student center. Dormitories wired for high-speed internet access and linked to campus network. Commuter students can connect to campus network. Online library, helpline, wireless network available.

Student life. **Freshman orientation:** Mandatory. Preregistration for classes offered. **Housing:** Guaranteed on-campus for freshmen. Coed dorms, special housing for disabled available. $275 deposit, deadline 5/1. **Activities:** Bands, campus ministries, choral groups, drama, literary magazine, music ensembles, musical theater, opera, radio station, student government, student newspaper, Sisters in Christ, Lutheran Student Fellowship, Lutheran Women's Missionary League, Pro Life, College Republicans, Pre-Sem Club (pre-seminary students), Fellowship of Christian Athletes, students active for the environment, writer's guild.

Athletics. NCAA. **Intercollegiate:** Baseball M, basketball, cross-country, golf, soccer, softball W, tennis W, volleyball W. **Intramural:** Badminton, basketball, bowling, handball, racquetball, softball, table tennis, tennis, volleyball. **Team name:** Tornados.

Student services. Adult student services, alcohol/substance abuse counseling, chaplain/spiritual director, career counseling, student employment services, financial aid counseling, personal counseling, placement for graduates, veterans' counselor. **Physically disabled:** Services for visually, speech, hearing impaired.

Contact. E-mail: admissions@concordia.edu
Phone: (512) 313-4600 Toll-free number: (800) 865-4282
Fax: (512) 313-4269
Kristin Coulter, Director of Admissions, Concordia University Texas, 11400 Concordia University Drive, Austin, TX 78726

Criswell College
Dallas, Texas
www.criswell.edu
CB code: 0794

- Private 4-year Bible and seminary college affiliated with Southern Baptist Convention
- Commuter campus in very large city
- 213 degree-seeking undergraduates
- SAT or ACT (ACT writing optional), application essay required

General. Founded in 1970. Regionally accredited. **Degrees:** 35 bachelor's awarded; master's offered. **Calendar:** Semester, limited summer session. **Full-time faculty:** 18 total. **Part-time faculty:** 13 total.

Basis for selection. Test scores, official transcripts, church endorsement and 2 letters of recommendation required. School achievement, essay, religious affiliation very important. Interview recommended.

High school preparation. Recommended units include English 4, mathematics 2, social studies 2, science 3 and foreign language 2.

2011-2012 Annual costs. Tuition/fees: $6,934. Books/supplies: $600.

Application procedures. Admission: Priority date 5/1; no deadline. $35 fee, may be waived for applicants with need. Admission notification on a rolling basis. Must reply by May 1 or within 2 week(s) if notified thereafter. **Financial aid:** Closing date 7/15. FAFSA, institutional form required. Applicants notified on a rolling basis.

Academics. Special study options: Double major, dual enrollment of high school students, independent study, internships. **Credit/placement by examination:** AP, CLEP. **Support services:** Reduced course load, study skills assistance, tutoring.

Majors. Philosophy/religion: Philosophy, religion. **Theology:** Bible, missionary, pastoral counseling, theology.

Computing on campus. 25 workstations in computer center. Online course registration available.

Student life. Policies: Religious observance required. **Activities:** Student government, student newspaper, missionary fellowship, international fellowship, student council.

Athletics. Intramural: Basketball, soccer, softball, table tennis, volleyball.

Student services. Career counseling, student employment services, personal counseling, veterans' counselor.

Contact. E-mail: tccsa@criswell.edu
Phone: (214) 818-1305 Toll-free number: (800) 899-0012
Fax: (214) 818-1310
Joe Thomas, Director of Admissions, Criswell College, 4010 Gaston Avenue, Dallas, TX 75246-1537

Dallas Baptist University
Dallas, Texas
www.dbu.edu
CB member
CB code: 6159

▸ Private 4-year university affiliated with Baptist faith
▸ Commuter campus in very large city
▸ 3,405 degree-seeking undergraduates: 32% part-time, 58% women, 17% African American, 2% Asian American, 10% Hispanic American, 1% Native American, 7% international
▸ 2,060 degree-seeking graduate students
▸ 44% of applicants admitted
▸ SAT or ACT with writing, application essay required
▸ 47% graduate within 6 years

General. Founded in 1898. Regionally accredited. **Degrees:** 793 bachelor's awarded; master's, doctoral offered. **ROTC:** Army, Air Force. **Location:** 13 miles from downtown, 29 miles from Fort Worth. **Calendar:** 4-1-4, extensive summer session. **Full-time faculty:** 126 total; 75% have terminal degrees, 14% minority, 41% women. **Part-time faculty:** 410 total; 33% have terminal degrees, 7% minority, 45% women. **Class size:** 67% <20, 28% 20-39, 2% 40-49, 2% 50-99, less than 1% >100. **Special facilities:** Corrie ten Boom collection.

Freshman class profile. 2,126 applied, 930 admitted, 444 enrolled.

Mid 50% test scores		Rank in top quarter:	58%
SAT critical reading:	470-660	Rank in top tenth:	28%
SAT math:	480-650	Return as sophomores:	73%
ACT composite:	20-28	Out-of-state:	9%
GPA 3.75 or higher:	34%	Live on campus:	96%
GPA 3.50-3.74:	23%	Fraternities:	15%
GPA 3.0-3.49:	33%	Sororities:	32%
GPA 2.0-2.99:	10%		

Basis for selection. All factors considered for admission, including test scores, class rank, essay and GPA. Interview recommended.

High school preparation. College-preparatory program recommended. 16 units recommended. Recommended units include English 4, mathematics 3, social studies 3, history 2, science 2 and foreign language 2.

2011-2012 Annual costs. Tuition/fees: $19,900. Room/board: $6,120. Books/supplies: $2,130. Personal expenses: $1,836.

2011-2012 Financial aid. Need-based: 406 full-time freshmen applied for aid; 299 were judged to have need; 297 of these received aid. Average need met was 74%. Average scholarship/grant was $3,491; average loan $3,197. 50% of total undergraduate aid awarded as scholarships/grants, 50% as loans/jobs. **Non-need-based:** Awarded to 1,821 full-time undergraduates, including 416 freshmen. Scholarships awarded for academics, athletics, job skills, leadership, music/drama, religious affiliation.

Application procedures. Admission: Priority date 1/15; no deadline. $25 fee. Admission notification on a rolling basis. **Financial aid:** Priority date 3/6, closing date 5/1. FAFSA, institutional form required. Applicants notified on a rolling basis starting 2/1.

Academics. Special study options: Accelerated study, combined bachelor's/graduate degree, distance learning, double major, dual enrollment of high school students, ESL, honors, independent study, internships, study abroad, teacher certification program, Washington semester, weekend college. **Credit/placement by examination:** AP, CLEP, IB, SAT, ACT, institutional tests. Credit by examination not counted toward residency hours. Credits recorded on permanent record after student has completed minimum of 12 hours in residence. **Support services:** Learning center, pre-admission summer program, remedial instruction, study skills assistance, tutoring, writing center.

Majors. Biology: General, cellular/anatomical. **Business:** Accounting, business admin, finance, hospitality admin, management information systems, marketing. **Communications:** Communications/speech/rhetoric. **Computer sciences:** General, computer science. **Conservation:** Environmental science. **Education:** General, early childhood, elementary, history, music, physical, reading, science, secondary. **English:** English lit. **Health services:** Health care admin. **History:** General. **Liberal arts:** Arts/sciences. **Math:** General. **Parks/recreation:** Health/fitness. **Philosophy/religion:** Philosophy. **Protective services:** Criminal justice. **Psychology:** General. **Social sciences:** Political science, sociology. **Theology:** Bible, pastoral counseling, religious ed, sacred music. **Visual/performing arts:** Art, music, music management, music performance, music theory/composition, piano/keyboard, voice/opera.

Computing on campus. 207 workstations in dormitories, library, computer center, student center. Dormitories wired for high-speed internet access and linked to campus network. Commuter students can connect to campus network. Online library, helpline, wireless network available.

Student life. Freshman orientation: Available. Preregistration for classes offered. **Policies:** Religious observance required. **Housing:** Single-sex dorms, special housing for disabled, apartments, wellness housing available. $100 fully refundable deposit. **Activities:** Campus ministries, choral groups, dance, drama, international student organizations, music ensembles, musical theater, opera, student government, College Republicans, Spanish-speaking students association, Chinese student association, Ministerial Alliance, Japanese student association, Korean student association.

Athletics. NCAA, NCCAA. **Intercollegiate:** Baseball M, cross-country, golf, soccer, tennis, track and field, volleyball W. **Intramural:** Badminton, basketball, football (non-tackle), golf M, softball, table tennis, tennis, volleyball. **Team name:** Patriots.

Student services. Adult student services, alcohol/substance abuse counseling, chaplain/spiritual director, career counseling, student employment services, financial aid counseling, health services, personal counseling, placement for graduates, veterans' counselor. **Physically disabled:** Services for visually, speech, hearing impaired.

Contact. E-mail: admiss@dbu.edu
Phone: (214) 333-5360 Toll-free number: (800) 460-1328
Fax: (214) 333-5447
Bobby Soto, Director of Undergraduate Admissions, Dallas Baptist University, 3000 Mountain Creek Parkway, Dallas, TX 75211-9299

Dallas Christian College
Dallas, Texas
www.dallas.edu
CB code: 0792

▸ Private 4-year Bible college affiliated with nondenominational tradition
▸ Commuter campus in very large city
▸ 325 degree-seeking undergraduates
▸ 64% of applicants admitted
▸ SAT or ACT (ACT writing recommended), application essay required

General. Founded in 1950. Accredited by ABHE. Special program for adult, nontraditional students. **Degrees:** 54 bachelor's, 1 associate awarded. **Location:** 10 miles from downtown. **Calendar:** 4-1-4, limited summer session. **Full-time faculty:** 8 total. **Part-time faculty:** 45 total.

Freshman class profile. 107 applied, 68 admitted, 48 enrolled.

Mid 50% test scores			
SAT critical reading:	410-550	GPA 3.50-3.74:	14%
SAT math:	400-540	GPA 3.0-3.49:	34%
SAT writing:	360-520	GPA 2.0-2.99:	40%
ACT composite:	21-24	Rank in top quarter:	22%
GPA 3.75 or higher:	6%	Rank in top tenth:	6%

Basis for selection. School record and recommendations, followed by test scores. Class rank also important. Interview recommended. **Home schooled:** Letter of recommendation (nonparent) required.

High school preparation. College-preparatory program recommended. Recommended units include English 4, mathematics 3, social studies 3, history 3, science 2 and foreign language 2.

2011-2012 Annual costs. Tuition/fees: $12,270. Room/board: $6,700. Books/supplies: $600.

Financial aid. **Non-need-based:** Scholarships awarded for leadership, music/drama.

Application procedures. **Admission:** Priority date 7/1; deadline 7/15 (postmark date). $25 fee. Admission notification on a rolling basis. Must reply by 8/15. **Financial aid:** No deadline. FAFSA, institutional form required. Applicants notified on a rolling basis; must reply within 2 week(s) of notification.

Academics. **Special study options:** Distance learning, double major, dual enrollment of high school students, independent study, internships, liberal arts/career combination, teacher certification program. Evening degree-seeking program for adults. **Credit/placement by examination:** AP, CLEP, IB, SAT, ACT, institutional tests. 15 credit hours maximum toward associate degree, 30 toward bachelor's. **Support services:** Reduced course load, remedial instruction, study skills assistance, tutoring.

Majors. **Business:** Business admin. **Education:** General, early childhood, elementary, English, history, multi-level teacher, music, secondary. **Liberal arts:** Arts/sciences. **Psychology:** General. **Theology:** Bible, religious ed, sacred music, theology.

Most popular majors. Business/marketing 23%, education 8%, theological studies 66%.

Computing on campus. 16 workstations in library, student center. Dormitories wired for high-speed internet access. Commuter students can connect to campus network. Online library, helpline, wireless network available.

Student life. **Freshman orientation:** Mandatory, $75 fee. Preregistration for classes offered. Held 3 days prior to semester start. **Policies:** All resident students and those taking 6 hours or more required to attend campus chapel services 2 times a week. **Housing:** Guaranteed on-campus for all undergraduates. Single-sex dorms, wellness housing available. $150 deposit, deadline 8/10. **Activities:** Pep band, campus ministries, choral groups, drama, music ensembles, student government, student newspaper.

Athletics. NCCAA. **Intercollegiate:** Baseball M, basketball, soccer, volleyball W. **Intramural:** Football (non-tackle), soccer, table tennis, volleyball. **Team name:** Crusaders.

Student services. Adult student services, chaplain/spiritual director, student employment services, financial aid counseling, personal counseling, placement for graduates.

Contact. E-mail: dcc@dallas.edu
Phone: (972) 241-3371 ext. 161 Toll-free number: (800) 688-1029
Fax: (972) 241-8021
Matthew Meeks, Director of Admissions, Dallas Christian College, 2700 Christian Parkway, Dallas, TX 75234-7299

DeVry University: Houston
Houston, Texas
www.devry.edu   **CB code: 4132**

- For-profit 4-year university
- Commuter campus in very large city
- 1,462 degree-seeking undergraduates

General. Additional locations: Houston Galleria, Austin, San Antonio. **Degrees:** 217 bachelor's, 41 associate awarded; master's offered. **Calendar:** Semester. **Full-time faculty:** 26 total. **Part-time faculty:** 158 total.

Basis for selection. Interview, high school GPA, and test scores most important.

High school preparation. College-preparatory program recommended.

2011-2012 Annual costs. Tuition/fees: $15,294. Books/supplies: $1,310. Personal expenses: $3,574.

Application procedures. **Admission:** No deadline. $50 fee. Admission notification on a rolling basis. **Financial aid:** No deadline. Applicants notified on a rolling basis.

Academics. **Special study options:** Accelerated study, distance learning. **Credit/placement by examination:** AP, CLEP.

Majors. **Business:** Business admin. **Computer sciences:** Networking, systems analysis.

Most popular majors. Business/marketing 81%, computer/information sciences 14%.

Student life. **Housing:** Off-campus housing available.

Contact. Phone: (713) 973-3000 Toll-free number: (866) 338-7941
Fax: (713) 896-7650
DeVry University: Houston, 11125 Equity Drive, Houston, TX 77041-8217

DeVry University: Irving
Dallas, Texas
www.devry.edu   **CB code: 6180**

- For-profit 4-year university
- Commuter campus in small city
- 1,369 degree-seeking undergraduates
- Interview required

General. Founded in 1969. Regionally accredited. Additional locations: Fort Worth, Richardson; Oklahoma City (OK). **Degrees:** 202 bachelor's, 65 associate awarded; master's offered. **Location:** 12 miles from Dallas. **Calendar:** Semester, extensive summer session. **Full-time faculty:** 41 total. **Part-time faculty:** 57 total.

Basis for selection. Applicants must have a high school diploma or equivalent or a degree from an accredited postsecondary institution, demonstrating proficiency in basic college-level skills through SAT or ACT scores or institution-administered placement examinations, and be at least 17 years of age on the first day of classes. New students may enter at beginning of any semester.

High school preparation. College-preparatory program recommended.

2011-2012 Annual costs. Tuition/fees: $15,294. Books/supplies: $1,310. Personal expenses: $3,574.

Financial aid. All financial aid based on need.

Application procedures. **Admission:** No deadline. $50 fee. Admission notification on a rolling basis. **Financial aid:** No deadline. Applicants notified on a rolling basis.

Academics. **Special study options:** Accelerated study, distance learning. **Credit/placement by examination:** AP, CLEP, institutional tests. No more than 35% of credit toward graduation requirement accepted. **Support services:** Learning center, remedial instruction, tutoring.

Majors. **Business:** Business admin. **Computer sciences:** Networking, systems analysis. **Engineering:** Software.

Most popular majors. Business/marketing 58%, computer/information sciences 23%, engineering/engineering technologies 20%.

Computing on campus. 450 workstations in library, computer center. Online course registration, online library, helpline available.

Student life. **Freshman orientation:** Mandatory. Preregistration for classes offered. **Housing:** Off-campus housing available. **Activities:** Association of Information Technology Professionals, campus Bible study, Christian Students Fellowship, Habitat for Humanity, Institute of Electrical and Electronics Engineers, Institute of Management Accountants, minority student

union, National Society of Black Engineers, Society of Women Engineers, Telecommunications Management and Associations, Society of Hispanic Professional Engineers, gamers club.

Athletics. Intramural: Basketball, football (tackle) M, volleyball.

Student services. Career counseling, student employment services, financial aid counseling, placement for graduates, veterans' counselor. **Physically disabled:** Services for visually, hearing impaired.

Contact. Phone: (972) 929-5777 Toll-free number: (800) 633-3879 Fax: (972) 929-2860
Chad Williams, Director of Admissions, DeVry University: Irving, 4800 Regent Boulevard, Dallas, TX 75063-2439

East Texas Baptist University
Marshall, Texas
www.etbu.edu   CB code: 6187

- Private 4-year university and liberal arts college affiliated with Baptist faith
- Residential campus in large town
- 1,121 degree-seeking undergraduates: 4% part-time, 52% women, 19% African American, 1% Asian American, 9% Hispanic American, 1% Native American, 2% international
- 26 degree-seeking graduate students
- 57% of applicants admitted
- SAT or ACT (ACT writing optional) required
- 43% graduate within 6 years

General. Founded in 1912. Regionally accredited. Marshall is in the center of a recreational and tourist region, and is near the Caddo Lake international wetlands. **Degrees:** 206 bachelor's awarded; master's offered. **Location:** 20 miles from Longview, 35 miles from Shreveport, Louisiana. **Calendar:** Semester, extensive summer session. **Full-time faculty:** 66 total; 88% have terminal degrees, 6% minority, 39% women. **Part-time faculty:** 38 total; 13% have terminal degrees, 5% minority, 55% women. **Class size:** 51% < 20, 43% 20-39, 5% 40-49, less than 1% 50-99.

Freshman class profile. 1,146 applied, 656 admitted, 330 enrolled.

Mid 50% test scores			
SAT critical reading:	400-510	Rank in top tenth:	16%
SAT math:	440-530	End year in good standing:	85%
ACT composite:	18-22	Return as sophomores:	59%
GPA 3.75 or higher:	18%	Out-of-state:	4%
GPA 3.50-3.74:	23%	Live on campus:	98%
GPA 3.0-3.49:	41%	International:	2%
GPA 2.0-2.99:	18%	Fraternities:	5%
Rank in top quarter:	42%	Sororities:	4%

Basis for selection. Admission granted to students scoring 18 or above on the ACT (excluding Writing) or a minimum combined 860 on the SAT in Critical Reading, Math. Admission may also be granted to those ranked in the upper 40% of their class from an accredited high school. Evidence of good character considered. Interview recommended for academically deficient; audition recommended for music program. **Learning Disabled:** Student should provide documentation of learning disability to the Student Advising and Career Development Office, which verifies documentation and assists in acquiring reasonable accommodations.

2012-2013 Annual costs. Tuition/fees: $21,530. Room/board: $6,145. Books/supplies: $920. Personal expenses: $1,477.

2010-2011 Financial aid. Need-based: 272 full-time freshmen applied for aid; 251 were judged to have need; 251 of these received aid. Average need met was 44%. Average scholarship/grant was $7,602; average loan $3,002. 57% of total undergraduate aid awarded as scholarships/grants, 43% as loans/jobs. **Non-need-based:** Awarded to 991 full-time undergraduates, including 275 freshmen. Scholarships awarded for academics, alumni affiliation, leadership, music/drama, religious affiliation.

Application procedures. Admission: Closing date 8/16. $25 fee, may be waived for applicants with need. Admission notification on a rolling basis beginning on or about 9/1. **Financial aid:** Priority date 6/1; no closing date. FAFSA, institutional form required. Applicants notified on a rolling basis starting 1/1.

Academics. Special study options: Accelerated study, cross-registration, distance learning, double major, dual enrollment of high school students, exchange student, honors, independent study, internships, student-designed major, study abroad, teacher certification program, Washington semester. **Credit/placement by examination:** AP, CLEP, IB, SAT, ACT, institutional

---

tests. ACT is used for mathematics placement. Departmental examinations administered on request upon approval of department chair. **Support services:** Reduced course load, study skills assistance, tutoring, writing center.

Majors. Biology: General. **Business:** General. **Communications:** Media studies. **Education:** General, biology, chemistry, drama/dance, elementary, English, history, mathematics, music, physical, social studies, Spanish, speech. **English:** English lit, rhetoric/composition. **Foreign languages:** Spanish. **Health services:** Athletic training, nursing (RN). **History:** General. **Math:** General. **Parks/recreation:** Health/fitness. **Philosophy/religion:** Religion. **Physical sciences:** Chemistry. **Protective services:** Law enforcement admin. **Psychology:** General, developmental. **Social sciences:** Political science, sociology. **Theology:** Bible, missionary, pastoral counseling, sacred music, youth ministry. **Visual/performing arts:** Dramatic, music, piano/keyboard, voice/opera.

Most popular majors. Business/marketing 11%, education 23%, health sciences 7%, interdisciplinary studies 20%, psychology 11%.

Computing on campus. 200 workstations in dormitories, library, computer center. Dormitories wired for high-speed internet access and linked to campus network. Commuter students can connect to campus network. Online course registration, online library, helpline, repair service, wireless network available.

Student life. Freshman orientation: Available. Preregistration for classes offered. Four days of activities, lectures, seminar sessions, community service activities. Held the week before classes begin in the fall term. **Policies:** Required chapel attendance, graded curfew, weekly clean room check. Religious observance required. **Housing:** Guaranteed on-campus for all undergraduates. Single-sex dorms, apartments, wellness housing available. **Activities:** Bands, campus ministries, choral groups, drama, international student organizations, literary magazine, music ensembles, Model UN, musical theater, radio station, student government, student newspaper, symphony orchestra, Fellowship of Christian Athletes, Political Awareness Society, Delta Pi Theta, Pi Sigma, Sigma Sigma Epsilon, Delta Chi Rho.

Athletics. NCAA. **Intercollegiate:** Baseball M, basketball, cross-country, football (tackle) M, soccer, softball W, tennis, volleyball W. **Intramural:** Basketball, football (non-tackle), racquetball, soccer, softball, volleyball. **Team name:** Tigers.

Student services. Adult student services, chaplain/spiritual director, career counseling, student employment services, financial aid counseling, personal counseling, placement for graduates, veterans' counselor.

Contact. E-mail: admissions@etbu.edu
Phone: (903) 923-2000 Toll-free number: (800) 804-3828
Fax: (903) 923-2001
Jason Soles, Director of Admissions, East Texas Baptist University, One Tiger Drive, Marshall, TX 75670-1498

Hardin-Simmons University
Abilene, Texas   CB member
www.hsutx.edu   CB code: 6268

- Private 4-year university affiliated with Baptist faith
- Residential campus in small city
- 1,891 degree-seeking undergraduates: 14% part-time, 54% women, 6% African American, 2% Asian American, 13% Hispanic American, 1% Native American, 1% international
- 448 degree-seeking graduate students
- 56% of applicants admitted
- SAT or ACT with writing required
- 47% graduate within 6 years

General. Founded in 1891. Regionally accredited. Part of 3-member consortium (with Abilene Christian University and McMurry University) comprising Abilene Intercollegiate School of Nursing. **Degrees:** 367 bachelor's awarded; master's, professional, doctoral offered. **Location:** 150 miles from Fort Worth. **Calendar:** Semester, extensive summer session. **Full-time faculty:** 138 total; 90% have terminal degrees, 4% minority, 33% women. **Part-time faculty:** 64 total; 33% have terminal degrees, 5% minority, 42% women. **Class size:** 68% < 20, 30% 20-39, 2% 40-49, less than 1% 50-99. **Special facilities:** Rare and fine book room, observatory.

Freshman class profile. 1,776 applied, 997 admitted, 397 enrolled.

Mid 50% test scores			
SAT critical reading:	450-570	GPA 2.0-2.99:	11%
SAT math:	480-580	Rank in top quarter:	46%
SAT writing:	440-550	Rank in top tenth:	21%
ACT composite:	20-26	Return as sophomores:	65%
GPA 3.75 or higher:	45%	Out-of-state:	4%
GPA 3.50-3.74:	18%	Live on campus:	89%
GPA 3.0-3.49:	25%	International:	1%

Basis for selection. Applicants admitted on basis of acceptable combination of test scores and prior academic record. Special cases considered individually. Non-native speakers of English require score of 550 on TOEFL, unless transferring 24 or more credits. Audition required for music program; interview recommended for special cases. Written essay, interview, and separate application required for honors program. **Home schooled:** GED scores required only if applicant plans to apply for federal need-based financial aid. **Learning Disabled:** No special admission requirements for students with disabilities; accepted students apply to Office for Students with Disabilities.

High school preparation. College-preparatory program recommended. 16 units required. Required units include English 3, mathematics 2, social studies 2, science 2 and academic electives 7. Math must include algebra I and above.

2011-2012 Annual costs. Tuition/fees: $22,460. Room/board: $6,804. Books/supplies: $800. Personal expenses: $1,476.

2011-2012 Financial aid. Need-based: 390 full-time freshmen applied for aid; 314 were judged to have need; 314 of these received aid. Average need met was 70%. Average scholarship/grant was $6,387; average loan $3,016. 40% of total undergraduate aid awarded as scholarships/grants, 60% as loans/jobs. **Non-need-based:** Awarded to 1,462 full-time undergraduates, including 359 freshmen. Scholarships awarded for academics, alumni affiliation, art, music/drama, religious affiliation.

Application procedures. Admission: No deadline. $50 fee, may be waived for applicants with need. Admission notification on a rolling basis beginning on or about 9/1. **Financial aid:** Priority date 3/1; no closing date. FAFSA required. Applicants notified on a rolling basis starting 2/1; must reply within 2 week(s) of notification.

Academics. Special study options: Accelerated study, cross-registration, distance learning, double major, dual enrollment of high school students, honors, independent study, internships, New York semester, study abroad, teacher certification program, United Nations semester, Washington semester. **Credit/placement by examination:** AP, CLEP, SAT, ACT, institutional tests. 32 credit hours maximum toward bachelor's degree. Maximum 14 hours in any one discipline. **Support services:** Pre-admission summer program, reduced course load, remedial instruction, study skills assistance, tutoring, writing center.

Majors. Biology: General, Biochemistry/molecular biology. **Business:** Accounting, business admin, finance, management information systems, management science, marketing. **Communications:** Broadcast journalism, communications/speech/rhetoric, media studies, public relations, radio/TV. **Computer sciences:** Programming. **Conservation:** Environmental science. **Education:** Art, business, computer, drama/dance, early childhood, English, history, mathematics, music, physical, reading, science, social studies, Spanish, speech. **English:** English lit, rhetoric/composition. **Foreign languages:** Spanish. **General:** Agronomy, animal sciences, business. **Health services:** Athletic training, audiology/speech pathology, nursing (RN), predental, premedicine. **History:** General. **Human services:** Social work. **Math:** General. **Parks/recreation:** Exercise sciences, health/fitness. **Philosophy/religion:** Philosophy. **Physical sciences:** Chemistry, geology, physics. **Protective services:** Criminal justice. **Psychology:** General. **Social sciences:** Economics, political science, sociology. **Theology:** Bible, missionary, preministerial, sacred music, theology, youth ministry. **Visual/performing arts:** Dramatic, graphic design, music, music history, music management, music performance, music theory/composition, piano/keyboard, stringed instruments, studio arts, voice/opera.

Most popular majors. Biology 10%, business/marketing 15%, education 14%, health sciences 9%, parks/recreation 9%, psychology 7%, visual/performing arts 7%.

Computing on campus. 225 workstations in dormitories, library, computer center, student center. Dormitories wired for high-speed internet access and linked to campus network. Online library, helpline, wireless network available.

Student life. Freshman orientation: Available, $10 fee. Preregistration for classes offered. Held Tuesday through Sunday the week before classes begin. **Policies:** Single, undergraduate students under 21 who have not completed 60 credit hours and are not living at home required to live in residence halls. All housing is alcohol, drug and smoke-free. Religious observance required. **Housing:** Guaranteed on-campus for freshmen. Single-sex dorms, special housing for disabled, apartments available. $100 fully refundable deposit. Single, duplex housing available with priority given to families. **Activities:** Bands, campus ministries, choral groups, drama, international student organizations, literary magazine, music ensembles, Model UN, musical theater, opera, student government, student newspaper, symphony orchestra, Sigma Alpha, Student 2 Student, Tri Phi, Alphi Phi Omega, Baptist Student Ministries, Theta Alpha Zeta, Zeta Chi, Epsilon Pi Alpha, Phi Mu Alpha.

Athletics. NCAA. **Intercollegiate:** Baseball M, basketball, cheerleading, cross-country, football (tackle) M, golf, soccer, softball W, tennis, track and field, volleyball W. **Intramural:** Badminton, basketball, bowling, football (non-tackle), football (tackle), golf, handball, racquetball, soccer, softball, tennis, volleyball. **Team name:** Cowboys/Cowgirls.

Student services. Chaplain/spiritual director, career counseling, student employment services, financial aid counseling, health services, personal counseling, placement for graduates, veterans' counselor. **Physically disabled:** Services for visually, speech, hearing impaired.

Contact. E-mail: enroll@hsutx.edu
Phone: (325) 670-1206 Toll-free number: (877) 464-7889
Fax: (325) 671-2115
Vicki House, Director of Admissions and Recruiting, Hardin-Simmons University, PO Box 16050, Abilene, TX 79698-0001

Houston Baptist University
Houston, Texas
www.hbu.edu

CB member
CB code: 6282

- Private 4-year university and liberal arts college affiliated with Baptist faith
- Commuter campus in very large city
- 2,072 degree-seeking undergraduates: 9% part-time, 66% women, 18% African American, 13% Asian American, 27% Hispanic American, 4% international
- 308 degree-seeking graduate students
- 38% of applicants admitted
- SAT or ACT (ACT writing recommended), application essay required
- 45% graduate within 6 years

General. Founded in 1960. Regionally accredited. Christian liberal arts university. **Degrees:** 329 bachelor's, 51 associate awarded; master's offered. **ROTC:** Army, Naval, Air Force. **Location:** 10 miles from downtown Houston. **Calendar:** Semester, extensive summer session. **Full-time faculty:** 110 total; 84% have terminal degrees, 19% minority, 46% women. **Part-time faculty:** 101 total; 45% have terminal degrees, 16% minority, 61% women. **Class size:** 61% < 20, 36% 20-39, less than 1% 40-49, 2% 50-99. **Special facilities:** Cultural arts center, American architecture and decorative arts museum, Bible in America museum, Southern history museum.

Freshman class profile. 9,868 applied, 3,795 admitted, 500 enrolled.

Mid 50% test scores			
SAT critical reading:	480-590	Return as sophomores:	67%
SAT math:	500-610	Out-of-state:	4%
SAT writing:	470-580	Live on campus:	50%
ACT composite:	22-27	International:	2%
Rank in top quarter:	64%	Fraternities:	8%
Rank in top tenth:	30%	Sororities:	9%

Basis for selection. School achievement record, test scores, recommendations, class rank, special talents, and skills most important. Audition required for music majors; portfolio required for art majors; interview recommended for academically weak students.

High school preparation. College-preparatory program recommended. 14 units required; 24 recommended. Required and recommended units include English 4, mathematics 3, social studies 4, history 2, science 3, foreign language 2, computer science 1, visual/performing arts 1, academic electives 3.5. 2 physical education/health, 0.5 speech.

2012-2013 Annual costs. Tuition/fees (projected): $26,795. Room/board: $6,290. Books/supplies: $1,350. Personal expenses: $1,900.

Financial aid. Non-need-based: Scholarships awarded for academics, alumni affiliation, art, athletics, music/drama, religious affiliation, ROTC.

Application procedures. Admission: No deadline. No application fee. Admission notification on a rolling basis. **Financial aid:** Priority date 3/1, closing date 4/15. FAFSA required. Applicants notified on a rolling basis starting 3/10.

Academics. Special study options: Accelerated study, combined bachelor's/graduate degree, double major, honors, internships, study abroad, teacher certification program. **Credit/placement by examination:** AP, CLEP, IB, SAT, ACT, institutional tests. CLEP credit limited to students with 63 or fewer credit hours. **Support services:** Reduced course load, remedial instruction, tutoring, writing center.

Honors college/program. Admission to the Honors College is a competitive process by application only. Students should have at least a 1250 SAT

or 27 ACT, 3.2 GPA, two letters of recommendation (one academic, one character), leadership experience and service to the church and community. Following a review of your application by the dean and the Honors College Advisory Committee, finalists will be invited for a personal interview as part of the Honors College selection process.

Majors. Biology: General, molecular. **Business:** General, accounting, business admin, entrepreneurial studies, finance, information resources management, management information systems, managerial economics, marketing. **Communications:** Communications/speech/rhetoric, media studies. **Education:** Art, early childhood, English, mathematics, middle, music, physical, science, secondary, social studies. **English:** Creative writing, English lit. **Foreign languages:** Biblical, French, Spanish. **Health services:** Nursing (RN). **History:** General. **Human services:** Public policy. **Math:** General. **Parks/recreation:** Exercise sciences, health/fitness. **Philosophy/religion:** Christian, philosophy. **Physical sciences:** Chemistry, physics. **Psychology:** General. **Social sciences:** Economics, political science, sociology. **Theology:** Pastoral counseling, sacred music. **Visual/performing arts:** Music, music performance, music theory/composition, studio arts. **Work/family studies:** Child development.

Most popular majors. Biology 13%, business/marketing 22%, education 12%, health sciences 8%, psychology 11%, social sciences 6%.

Computing on campus. 95 workstations in dormitories, library, computer center. Dormitories wired for high-speed internet access and linked to campus network. Commuter students can connect to campus network. Online course registration, online library, helpline, repair service, wireless network available.

Student life. Freshman orientation: Available. Preregistration for classes offered. 2-day overnight summer orientation and registration. 2-1/2 day camp held off campus prior to start of classes. **Policies:** Spiritual Life Program graduation requirement for all undergraduate students. **Housing:** Guaranteed on-campus for freshmen. Coed dorms, single-sex dorms, special housing for disabled, apartments available. $200 partly refundable deposit. **Activities:** Bands, campus ministries, choral groups, dance, drama, international student organizations, music ensembles, opera, student government, student newspaper, Christian Life on Campus, Psi Chi, Nursing Association, Black Student Fellowship, Toastmasters, Digital Eon, Vietnamese student association, Indian student association, Sisters for the Lord, Brothers Under Christ.

Athletics. NCAA. **Intercollegiate:** Baseball M, basketball, cheerleading, cross-country, golf, soccer, softball W, track and field, volleyball W. **Intramural:** Badminton, basketball, bowling, football (non-tackle), softball, table tennis, volleyball. **Team name:** Huskies.

Student services. Adult student services, alcohol/substance abuse counseling, chaplain/spiritual director, career counseling, student employment services, financial aid counseling, health services, placement for graduates, women's services. **Physically disabled:** Services for visually, speech, hearing impaired.

Contact. E-mail: admissions@hbu.edu
Phone: (281) 649-3211 Toll-free number: (800) 969-3210
Fax: (281) 649-3701
Ed Borges, Director of Admissions, Houston Baptist University, 7502 Fondren Road, Houston, TX 77074-3298

Howard Payne University
Brownwood, Texas
www.hputx.edu   CB code: 6278

- Private 4-year university and teachers college affiliated with Baptist faith
- Residential campus in large town
- 1,053 degree-seeking undergraduates: 8% part-time, 49% women, 7% African American, 17% Hispanic American, 1% Native American
- 18 degree-seeking graduate students
- 69% of applicants admitted
- SAT or ACT (ACT writing optional) required
- 45% graduate within 6 years

General. Founded in 1889. Regionally accredited. **Degrees:** 210 bachelor's, 3 associate awarded; master's offered. **Location:** 150 miles from Dallas, 77 miles from Abilene. **Calendar:** Semester, limited summer session. **Full-time faculty:** 85 total; 61% have terminal degrees, 4% minority, 38% women. **Part-time faculty:** 43 total; 16% have terminal degrees, 7% minority, 35% women. **Class size:** 69% < 20, 27% 20-39, 2% 40-49, less than 1% 50-99. **Special facilities:** General Douglas MacArthur Academy of Freedom, Faith and Life Leadership Center, art center, Center for Social Justice.

Freshman class profile. 971 applied, 674 admitted, 279 enrolled.

Mid 50% test scores			
SAT critical reading:	430-540	Rank in top quarter:	40%
SAT math:	450-570	Rank in top tenth:	14%
ACT composite:	18-24	End year in good standing:	76%
GPA 3.75 or higher:	22%	Return as sophomores:	57%
GPA 3.50-3.74:	23%	Out-of-state:	2%
GPA 3.0-3.49:	27%	Live on campus:	82%
GPA 2.0-2.99:	28%	Fraternities:	19%
		Sororities:	29%

Basis for selection. Average GPA of 3.0 on 4.0 scale, ACT composite score of 19, or SAT score of 910 (exclusive of Writing). ACT/SAT scores used to exempt students from placement tests in English, math, or reading. Interview may be required by admissions committee for select applicants. Audition required for music program. **Home schooled:** Transcript of courses and grades required. **Learning Disabled:** If a student meets requirements for admission, accommodations may be initiated by Student Success Services.

High school preparation. College-preparatory program recommended. 16 units required. Required and recommended units include English 4, mathematics 3, social studies 2, history 2, science 3 and foreign language 2.

2012-2013 Annual costs. Tuition/fees (projected): $22,560. Room/board: $6,382. Books/supplies: $1,000. Personal expenses: $1,500.

Financial aid. Non-need-based: Scholarships awarded for academics, alumni affiliation, art, athletics, leadership, music/drama, religious affiliation, state residency.

Application procedures. Admission: Priority date 3/15; no deadline. No application fee. Admission notification on a rolling basis. Must reply by May 1 or within 2 week(s) if notified thereafter. **Financial aid:** Priority date 3/15; no closing date. FAFSA, institutional form required. Applicants notified on a rolling basis starting 2/15; must reply within 2 week(s) of notification.

Academics. Special study options: Accelerated study, cooperative education, distance learning, double major, dual enrollment of high school students, honors, independent study, internships, liberal arts/career combination, study abroad, teacher certification program. Extension classes in El Paso. **Credit/placement by examination:** AP, CLEP, IB, SAT, ACT, institutional tests. 15 credit hours maximum toward associate degree, 30 toward bachelor's. **Support services:** Reduced course load, remedial instruction, study skills assistance, tutoring, writing center.

Honors college/program. Academy of Freedom, minimum 24 composite ACT, 1100 SAT combined Math and Critical Reading, priority application deadline 2/1, 25 students maximum at freshman level.

Majors. Biology: General. **Business:** General, accounting, business admin, finance, management information systems, marketing. **Communications:** Communications/speech/rhetoric, digital media, media studies, organizational, persuasive communications, radio/TV. **Computer sciences:** General, computer science. **Education:** Art, biology, business, computer, drama/dance, elementary, English, ESL, history, mathematics, middle, music, physical, secondary, social studies, Spanish, speech. **English:** English lit. **Foreign languages:** Ancient Greek, Biblical, Spanish. **Health services:** Athletic training, health care admin. **History:** General, American, European. **Human services:** Public policy, social work. **Liberal arts:** Arts/sciences, humanities. **Math:** General. **Parks/recreation:** Health/fitness, sports admin. **Philosophy/religion:** Christian, philosophy. **Physical sciences:** Chemistry. **Protective services:** Criminal justice. **Psychology:** General. **Social sciences:** General, anthropology, criminology, international relations, political science, sociology. **Theology:** Bible, missionary, religious ed, sacred music, theology, youth ministry. **Visual/performing arts:** Art, dramatic, music performance, piano/keyboard, studio arts, voice/opera. **Work/family studies:** Family studies.

Most popular majors. Business/marketing 13%, communications/journalism 6%, education 14%, parks/recreation 7%, psychology 6%, social sciences 7%, theological studies 13%, visual/performing arts 6%.

Computing on campus. 260 workstations in dormitories, library, computer center, student center. Dormitories wired for high-speed internet access and linked to campus network. Commuter students can connect to campus network. Online library, helpline, repair service, wireless network available.

Student life. Freshman orientation: Mandatory. Preregistration for classes offered. Held for 4-5 days before fall semester classes begin. A mini orientation (3-4 hours) is offered in January for students who begin at that time of year. **Policies:** Chapel is an important part of student life at HPU and is a required element for graduation. Four (4) semesters of Chapel credits are required to graduate. A team of University administrators, under the auspices of the Office of Student Life, direct Chapel. The mission of Chapel is to promote a vibrant relationship with Jesus Christ in a praise and worship format. Occasionally, a Student Assembly will be held for the purpose of promoting cultural awareness, academic life, student activities, and world events in a student-friendly setting that integrates faith and life. Religious

observance required. **Housing:** Guaranteed on-campus for freshmen. Single-sex dorms, apartments available. $100 nonrefundable deposit, deadline 6/1. **Activities:** Bands, campus ministries, choral groups, drama, music ensembles, Model UN, musical theater, opera, student government, student newspaper, symphony orchestra, student foundation, ministerial alliance, Fellowship of Christian Athletes, Students in Free Enterprise, social work club, Gamma Beta Phi, Baptist Student Ministry.

Athletics. NCAA. **Intercollegiate:** Baseball M, basketball, cheerleading, cross-country, football (tackle) M, soccer, softball W, tennis, volleyball W. **Intramural:** Basketball, football (non-tackle), softball, table tennis, tennis, volleyball. **Team name:** Yellow Jackets.

Student services. Adult student services, chaplain/spiritual director, career counseling, student employment services, financial aid counseling, health services, personal counseling, placement for graduates.

Contact. E-mail: enroll@hputx.edu
Phone: (325) 649-8020 Toll-free number: (800) 880-4478
Fax: (325) 649-8901
Kevin Kirk, Assistant Vice President for Enrollment Management,
Howard Payne University, 1000 Fisk Street, Brownwood, TX 76801-2794

Huston-Tillotson University

Austin, Texas	**CB member**
www.htu.edu	**CB code: 6280**

- Private 4-year business and liberal arts college affiliated with United Methodist Church and United Church of Christ
- Residential campus in very large city
- 889 degree-seeking undergraduates: 14% part-time, 50% women, 69% African American, 19% Hispanic American, 4% international
- 15 graduate students
- 90% of applicants admitted
- SAT or ACT (ACT writing optional) required

General. Founded in 1876. Regionally accredited. **Degrees:** 120 bachelor's awarded. **ROTC:** Army. **Location:** 80 miles from San Antonio. **Calendar:** Semester, extensive summer session. **Full-time faculty:** 49 total; 69% have terminal degrees, 51% minority, 51% women. **Part-time faculty:** 33 total; 12% have terminal degrees, 39% minority, 48% women. **Class size:** 55% < 20, 45% 20-39, less than 1% 40-49.

Freshman class profile. 739 applied, 665 admitted, 190 enrolled.

GPA 3.75 or higher:	6%	**Rank in top tenth:**	6%
GPA 3.50-3.74:	5%	**Return as sophomores:**	51%
GPA 3.0-3.49:	33%	**Out-of-state:**	1%
GPA 2.0-2.99:	53%	**International:**	4%
Rank in top quarter:	24%		

Basis for selection. School achievement record important. Test scores and interview considered.

High school preparation. College-preparatory program recommended. 22 units required. Required and recommended units include English 4, mathematics 3, social studies 3, science 2, foreign language 2 and computer science 1. Health, physical education recommended.

2011-2012 Annual costs. Tuition/fees: $12,430. Room/board: $6,946. Books/supplies: $1,040. Personal expenses: $2,782.

2010-2011 Financial aid. **Need-based:** 211 full-time freshmen applied for aid; 207 were judged to have need; 188 of these received aid. Average need met was 98%. Average scholarship/grant was $2,228; average loan $3,732. 61% of total undergraduate aid awarded as scholarships/grants, 39% as loans/jobs. **Non-need-based:** Awarded to 363 full-time undergraduates, including 99 freshmen. Scholarships awarded for academics, alumni affiliation, art, athletics, job skills, leadership, minority status, music/drama, religious affiliation, state residency.

Application procedures. **Admission:** Priority date 3/15; deadline 7/1 (postmark date). $25 fee, may be waived for applicants with need. Admission notification on a rolling basis beginning on or about 1/1. Must reply by May 1 or within 1 week(s) if notified thereafter. **Financial aid:** Priority date 3/15; no closing date. FAFSA required. Applicants notified on a rolling basis starting 3/1.

Academics. **Special study options:** Cooperative education, cross-registration, distance learning, double major, dual enrollment of high school students, external degree, honors, independent study, internships, liberal arts/career combination, study abroad, teacher certification program. 3-2 engineering program with Prairie View A&M University. **Credit/placement by**

examination: AP, CLEP, SAT, ACT, institutional tests. 15 credit hours maximum toward bachelor's degree. **Support services:** Learning center, pre-admission summer program, remedial instruction, tutoring, writing center.

Majors. **Biology:** General. **Business:** Accounting, business admin, international, marketing. **Computer sciences:** General, computer science. **Education:** General, physical. **English:** Writing. **History:** General. **Liberal arts:** Arts/sciences. **Math:** General. **Physical sciences:** Chemistry. **Protective services:** Criminal justice. **Psychology:** General. **Social sciences:** General, political science, sociology. **Visual/performing arts:** Music.

Most popular majors. Business/marketing 26%, English 8%, interdisciplinary studies 14%, parks/recreation 18%, psychology 6%, security/protective services 12%.

Computing on campus. 400 workstations in dormitories, library, computer center, student center. Dormitories wired for high-speed internet access and linked to campus network. Commuter students can connect to campus network. Online library, helpline, wireless network available.

Student life. **Freshman orientation:** Mandatory. Preregistration for classes offered. **Housing:** Guaranteed on-campus for all undergraduates. Single-sex dorms, wellness housing available. **Activities:** Jazz band, campus ministries, choral groups, dance, drama, film society, international student organizations, literary magazine, music ensembles, Model UN, student government, NAACP student chapter, Toastmasters.

Athletics. NAIA. **Intercollegiate:** Baseball M, basketball, soccer, track and field, volleyball W. **Intramural:** Basketball, cheerleading W, soccer, softball, table tennis, volleyball. **Team name:** Rams.

Student services. Adult student services, career counseling, student employment services, financial aid counseling, health services, personal counseling, placement for graduates, veterans' counselor. **Physically disabled:** Services for visually, hearing impaired.

Contact. E-mail: admission@htu.edu
Phone: (512) 505-3028 Toll-free number: (877) 505-3028
Fax: (512) 505-3192
Shakitha Stinson, Director of Admission, Huston-Tillotson University, 900 Chicon Street, Austin, TX 78702-2795

Jarvis Christian College

Hawkins, Texas	
www.jarvis.edu	**CB code: 6319**

- Private 4-year liberal arts and teachers college affiliated with Christian Church (Disciples of Christ)
- Residential campus in rural community
- 574 degree-seeking undergraduates: 8% part-time, 50% women, 94% African American, 4% Hispanic American

General. Founded in 1912. Regionally accredited. **Degrees:** 67 bachelor's awarded. **Location:** 100 miles from Dallas; 100 miles from Shreveport, Louisiana. **Calendar:** Semester, limited summer session. **Full-time faculty:** 23 total; 52% have terminal degrees, 44% women. **Part-time faculty:** 33 total; 27% have terminal degrees, 39% women. **Class size:** 65% < 20, 28% 20-39, 5% 40-49, 1% 50-99, less than 1% >100. **Special facilities:** Observatory, Natatorium, archives of black Christian church (Disciples of Christ).

Freshman class profile.

GPA 3.75 or higher:	2%	**Rank in top quarter:**	6%
GPA 3.50-3.74:	1%	**Return as sophomores:**	42%
GPA 3.0-3.49:	10%	**Out-of-state:**	11%
GPA 2.0-2.99:	69%	**Live on campus:**	98%

Basis for selection. Open admission. **Home schooled:** State high school equivalency certificate required.

High school preparation. 16 units recommended. Recommended units include English 3, mathematics 2, social studies 3, science 1 and academic electives 7.

2011-2012 Annual costs. Tuition/fees: $13,374. Room/board: $9,346. Books/supplies: $1,300. Personal expenses: $1,800.

2010-2011 Financial aid. All financial aid based on need. 125 full-time freshmen applied for aid; 125 were judged to have need; 125 of these received aid. Average need met was 5%. Average scholarship/grant was $7,324; average loan $3,425. 45% of total undergraduate aid awarded as scholarships/grants, 55% as loans/jobs. **Additional information:** High school transcript required for scholarship consideration.

Application procedures. Admission: No deadline. $50 fee. Admission notification on a rolling basis beginning on or about 4/1. **Financial aid:** Priority date 6/30, closing date 1/3. FAFSA required. Applicants notified on a rolling basis starting 5/1; must reply by 5/30 or within 2 week(s) of notification.

Academics. Special study options: Accelerated study, combined bachelor's/graduate degree, cooperative education, cross-registration, distance learning, double major, dual enrollment of high school students, ESL, honors, internships, liberal arts/career combination, student-designed major, teacher certification program, Washington semester. **Credit/placement by examination:** AP, CLEP, IB, institutional tests. 18 credit hours maximum toward bachelor's degree. **Support services:** Learning center, reduced course load, remedial instruction, study skills assistance, tutoring, writing center.

Majors. Biology: General. **Business:** Business admin. **Communications:** Journalism. **Education:** General, biology, business, early childhood, elementary, English, history, mathematics, middle, physical, reading, secondary, special ed. **English:** English lit. **Health services:** Premedicine. **History:** General. **Math:** General. **Philosophy/religion:** Religion. **Physical sciences:** Chemistry. **Protective services:** Criminal justice. **Social sciences:** Sociology. **Visual/performing arts:** Music.

Most popular majors. Business/marketing 24%, education 6%, interdisciplinary studies 27%, security/protective services 9%, social sciences 25%.

Computing on campus. 359 workstations in dormitories, library, computer center. Dormitories wired for high-speed internet access and linked to campus network. Commuter students can connect to campus network. Online library, helpline, repair service, wireless network available.

Student life. Freshman orientation: Mandatory. Preregistration for classes offered. **Policies:** Religious services available, regardless of denomination. Religious observance required. **Housing:** Guaranteed on-campus for all undergraduates. Coed dorms, single-sex dorms, special housing for disabled, apartments, wellness housing available. $200 nonrefundable deposit, deadline 8/1. Single parents housing available on limited basis. **Activities:** Bands, choral groups, music ensembles, student government, student ministers' association, United Campus Christian Fellowship, pre-law club, National Society of Black Accountants, Student National Educational Association, Students in Free Enterprise, Phi Beta Lambda English Club, college church.

Athletics. NAIA. **Intercollegiate:** Baseball M, basketball, cheerleading, cross-country, volleyball W. **Intramural:** Baseball M, basketball, football (non-tackle), football (tackle) M, golf, soccer, softball, swimming, table tennis, tennis, volleyball, weight lifting, wrestling M. **Team name:** Bulldogs.

Student services. Alcohol/substance abuse counseling, chaplain/spiritual director, career counseling, services for economically disadvantaged, student employment services, financial aid counseling, health services, personal counseling, placement for graduates, veterans' counselor. **Physically disabled:** Services for visually, speech, hearing impaired.

Contact. E-mail: Robert.Harper@jarvis.edu
Phone: (903) 769-5731 Fax: (903) 769-1282
Robert Harper, Director of Enrollment Management, Jarvis Christian College, PO Box 1470, Hawkins, TX 75765-1470

Lamar University
Beaumont, Texas
www.lamar.edu

CB member
CB code: 6360

▶ Public 4-year university
▶ Commuter campus in small city
▶ 9,214 degree-seeking undergraduates: 25% part-time, 59% women, 33% African American, 3% Asian American, 8% Hispanic American, 1% Native American, 1% international
▶ 3,586 degree-seeking graduate students
▶ 67% of applicants admitted
▶ SAT or ACT required
▶ 30% graduate within 6 years

General. Founded in 1923. Regionally accredited. **Degrees:** 1,341 bachelor's, 36 associate awarded; master's, professional, doctoral offered. **Location:** 75 miles from Houston. **Calendar:** Semester, limited summer session. **Full-time faculty:** 414 total; 22% minority, 46% women. **Part-time faculty:** 178 total; 18% minority, 50% women. **Class size:** 32% < 20, 48% 20-39, 12% 40-49, 7% 50-99, 1% >100. **Special facilities:** Hazardous waste research center, city museum.

Freshman class profile. 4,331 applied, 2,894 admitted, 1,564 enrolled.

Mid 50% test scores			
SAT critical reading:	430-530	End year in good standing:	88%
SAT math:	410-530	Return as sophomores:	65%
SAT writing:	410-520	Out-of-state:	2%
ACT composite:	17-23	Live on campus:	47%
Rank in top quarter:	33%	International:	1%
Rank in top tenth:	13%	Fraternities:	5%
		Sororities:	4%

Basis for selection. Admission decision based on high school class rank, SAT scores, and completion of 14 high school units of college preparatory courses. SAT Subject Tests recommended for students with strong academic background. Interview required for early entry and of students accepted with GED tests. **Home schooled:** Transcript of courses and grades required. Must submit SAT and meet state TASP testing requirements.

High school preparation. 15 units required. Required and recommended units include English 4, mathematics 3, social studies 3, science 2, foreign language 2 and academic electives 3.

2011-2012 Annual costs. Tuition/fees: $7,630; $17,020 out-of-state. Room/board: $7,682. Books/supplies: $1,468. Personal expenses: $2,164.

Financial aid. All financial aid based on need.

Application procedures. Admission: Closing date 8/1. $25 fee. Admission notification on a rolling basis. **Financial aid:** Priority date 4/1; no closing date. FAFSA, institutional form required. Applicants notified on a rolling basis starting 4/1; must reply within 2 week(s) of notification.

Academics. Special study options: Accelerated study, cooperative education, distance learning, double major, dual enrollment of high school students, ESL, honors, independent study, internships, study abroad, teacher certification program. **Credit/placement by examination:** AP, CLEP, institutional tests. 15 credit hours maximum toward associate degree, 30 toward bachelor's. **Support services:** Learning center, pre-admission summer program, reduced course load, remedial instruction, study skills assistance, tutoring, writing center.

Majors. Architecture: Interior. **Biology:** General, marine. **Business:** General, accounting, business admin, finance, human resources, management information systems, managerial economics, marketing, office management, sales/distribution. **Communications:** Advertising, communications/speech/rhetoric. **Computer sciences:** General. **Conservation:** General, environmental studies. **Education:** Art, Deaf/hearing impaired, early childhood, elementary, family/consumer sciences, health, mathematics, music, physical, school counseling, science, secondary, social studies, special ed. **Engineering:** General, chemical, civil, electrical, environmental, industrial, mechanical. **English:** English lit, rhetoric/composition. **Foreign languages:** French, Spanish. **Health services:** Audiology/speech pathology, clinical lab science, nursing (RN). **History:** General. **Human services:** Social work. **Liberal arts:** Arts/sciences. **Math:** General, applied. **Parks/recreation:** Health/fitness. **Physical sciences:** Chemistry, geology, physics, planetary. **Protective services:** Criminal justice. **Psychology:** General. **Social sciences:** Economics, political science, sociology. **Visual/performing arts:** Art, commercial/advertising art, dance, dramatic, music, voice/opera. **Work/family studies:** General, clothing/textiles, family/community services, food/nutrition.

Most popular majors. Business/marketing 18%, engineering/engineering technologies 9%, health sciences 12%, interdisciplinary studies 15%, liberal arts 9%.

Computing on campus. 644 workstations in dormitories, library, computer center, student center. Dormitories wired for high-speed internet access and linked to campus network. Commuter students can connect to campus network. Online course registration, online library, helpline, repair service, student web hosting, wireless network available.

Student life. Freshman orientation: Available, $10 fee. Preregistration for classes offered. One-day program available June-August. **Housing:** Guaranteed on-campus for freshmen. Coed dorms, single-sex dorms, special housing for disabled, wellness housing available. $150 deposit, deadline 8/1. **Activities:** Bands, choral groups, dance, drama, film society, literary magazine, music ensembles, musical theater, opera, radio station, student government, student newspaper, symphony orchestra, TV station, Catholic student union, Church of Latter-day Saints, Episcopal center, Church of Christ student center, Wesley Foundation, Vietnamese student organization.

Athletics. NCAA. **Intercollegiate:** Baseball M, basketball, cross-country, football (tackle) M, golf, soccer W, tennis, track and field, volleyball W. **Intramural:** Badminton, basketball, cross-country, racquetball, soccer, softball, swimming, table tennis, tennis, track and field, volleyball, weight lifting. **Team name:** Cardinals.

Student services. Adult student services, career counseling, student employment services, health services, on-campus daycare, personal counseling, placement for graduates, veterans' counselor. **Physically disabled:** Services for visually, speech, hearing impaired.

Contact. E-mail: admissions@hal.lamar.edu
Phone: (409) 880-8888 Fax: (409) 880-8463
James Rush, Director of Academic Services, Lamar University, Box 10009, Beaumont, TX 77705

LeTourneau University
Longview, Texas
www.letu.edu

CB code: 6365

- Private 4-year university affiliated with nondenominational tradition
- Residential campus in small city
- 2,540 degree-seeking undergraduates: 48% part-time, 52% women, 18% African American, 1% Asian American, 9% Hispanic American, 1% Native American, 2% international
- 359 degree-seeking graduate students
- SAT or ACT (ACT writing optional), application essay required
- 49% graduate within 6 years

General. Founded in 1946. Regionally accredited. Centers in Tyler, Dallas, Houston, Austin, and Bedford. **Degrees:** 687 bachelor's, 21 associate awarded; master's offered. **Location:** 120 miles from Dallas, 60 miles from Shreveport, Louisiana. **Calendar:** Semester, limited summer session. **Full-time faculty:** 70 total; 67% have terminal degrees, 10% minority, 17% women. **Part-time faculty:** 184 total; 45% have terminal degrees, 13% minority, 42% women. **Class size:** 69% < 20, 29% 20-39, 1% 40-49, less than 1% 50-99. **Special facilities:** Microprocessor and robotics laboratory, CAD laboratory, scanning electronic microscope, dynamic simulation laboratory, fleet of nine airplanes, biomedical engineering laboratory with motion analysis system.

Freshman class profile. 307 enrolled.

Mid 50% test scores			
SAT critical reading:	520-650	GPA 2.0-2.99:	9%
SAT math:	540-670	Rank in top quarter:	68%
SAT writing:	480-610	Rank in top tenth:	44%
ACT composite:	22-29	Return as sophomores:	74%
GPA 3.75 or higher:	42%	Out-of-state:	37%
GPA 3.50-3.74:	28%	Live on campus:	93%
GPA 3.0-3.49:	21%	International:	2%

Basis for selection. Applicants should rank in top half of high school graduating class, have minimum ACT of 20 or minimum SAT of 950 (exclusive of Writing), and GPA of 2.5. Interview recommended. **Home schooled:** Require SAT or ACT, transcript; recommend GED and detailed summary of curriculum used.

High school preparation. College-preparatory program recommended. 16 units required. Required and recommended units include English 4, mathematics 3, social studies 2, history 1, science 3 (laboratory 3), foreign language 1 and academic electives 2. 4 math (including trigonometry) recommended for engineering applicants.

2012-2013 Annual costs. Tuition/fees: $24,540. Room/board: $8,940. Books/supplies: $1,470. Personal expenses: $1,190.

2011-2012 Financial aid. Need-based: 261 full-time freshmen applied for aid; 219 were judged to have need; 218 of these received aid. Average need met was 73%. Average scholarship/grant was $15,666; average loan $2,780. 46% of total undergraduate aid awarded as scholarships/grants, 54% as loans/jobs. **Non-need-based:** Awarded to 297 full-time undergraduates, including 83 freshmen. Scholarships awarded for academics, alumni affiliation, leadership, minority status, religious affiliation, state residency.

Application procedures. Admission: Priority date 3/1; no deadline. $35 fee, may be waived for applicants with need. Admission notification on a rolling basis beginning on or about 9/15. **Financial aid:** Priority date 2/1; no closing date. FAFSA required. Applicants notified on a rolling basis starting 3/1; must reply within 2 week(s) of notification.

Academics. Peer advisers, student resource center, CARE committee, freshman year experience course available. **Special study options:** Accelerated study, cooperative education, distance learning, double major, dual enrollment of high school students, ESL, honors, independent study, internships, study abroad, teacher certification program, weekend college. **Credit/placement by examination:** AP, CLEP, IB, SAT, ACT, institutional tests. Credit must be established by end of student's first year at school. **Support services:** Reduced course load, remedial instruction, study skills assistance, tutoring.

Majors. Biology: General. **Business:** General, accounting, business admin, finance, human resources, international, management information systems, marketing, operations. **Computer sciences:** General, computer science, information systems. **Education:** Business, computer, elementary, English, history, mathematics, middle, multi-level teacher, physical, science, secondary, social studies. **Engineering:** General, biomedical, computer, electrical, mechanical. **English:** English lit. **Health services:** Predental, premedicine, prepharmacy, preveterinary. **History:** General. **Math:** General. **Parks/recreation:** Exercise sciences, sports admin. **Physical sciences:** Chemistry, physical chemistry. **Psychology:** General. **Social sciences:** Political science. **Theology:** Bible.

Most popular majors. Business/marketing 42%, education 23%, engineering/engineering technologies 15%, psychology 6%.

Computing on campus. 200 workstations in library, computer center. Dormitories wired for high-speed internet access and linked to campus network. Commuter students can connect to campus network. Online course registration, online library, helpline, wireless network available.

Student life. Freshman orientation: Mandatory, $80 fee. Preregistration for classes offered. 3-day event for students and parents held before classes start. **Policies:** Religious observance required. **Housing:** Guaranteed on-campus for all undergraduates. Single-sex dorms, special housing for disabled, apartments available. $100 deposit. Residential societies available. **Activities:** Bands, campus ministries, choral groups, drama, international student organizations, literary magazine, music ensembles, musical theater, student government, student newspaper, Fellowship of Christian Athletes, Student Foundation, Habitat for Humanity, summer missions, married student fellowship, student ministries, 2 CARE Council.

Athletics. NCAA, NCCAA. **Intercollegiate:** Baseball M, basketball, golf, soccer, softball W, tennis, volleyball W. **Intramural:** Badminton, basketball, cross-country, football (non-tackle), golf, racquetball, soccer, softball, swimming, table tennis, tennis, volleyball. **Team name:** YellowJackets.

Student services. Chaplain/spiritual director, career counseling, student employment services, financial aid counseling, health services, personal counseling, placement for graduates, veterans' counselor. **Physically disabled:** Services for visually, speech, hearing impaired.

Contact. E-mail: admissions@letu.edu
Phone: (903) 233-4300 Toll-free number: (800) 759-8811
Fax: (903) 233-4301
James Townsend, Director of Admissions, LeTourneau University, PO Box 7001, Longview, TX 75607-7001

Lubbock Christian University
Lubbock, Texas
www.lcu.edu

CB code: 6378

- Private 4-year university and liberal arts college affiliated with Church of Christ
- Commuter campus in small city
- 1,596 degree-seeking undergraduates: 15% part-time, 59% women, 6% African American, 1% Asian American, 18% Hispanic American, 1% Native American, 2% international
- 442 degree-seeking graduate students
- 61% of applicants admitted
- SAT or ACT (ACT writing recommended), application essay, interview required
- 48% graduate within 6 years; 32% enter graduate study

General. Founded in 1957. Regionally accredited. **Degrees:** 394 bachelor's awarded; master's offered. **ROTC:** Army, Air Force. **Location:** 300 miles from Dallas; 325 miles from Albuquerque, New Mexico. **Calendar:** Semester, limited summer session. **Full-time faculty:** 89 total; 75% have terminal degrees, 3% minority, 42% women. **Part-time faculty:** 90 total; 32% have terminal degrees, 6% minority, 48% women. **Class size:** 58% < 20, 35% 20-39, 3% 40-49, 3% 50-99. **Special facilities:** Welcome center; recreational center, golf course.

Freshman class profile. 1,485 applied, 909 admitted, 322 enrolled.

Mid 50% test scores			
SAT critical reading:	420-540	Rank in top quarter:	40%
SAT math:	440-560	Rank in top tenth:	17%
SAT writing:	410-530	End year in good standing:	85%
ACT composite:	19-24	Return as sophomores:	61%
GPA 3.75 or higher:	25%	Out-of-state:	12%
GPA 3.50-3.74:	28%	Live on campus:	80%
GPA 3.0-3.49:	32%	International:	2%
GPA 2.0-2.99:	14%	Fraternities:	36%
		Sororities:	34%

Basis for selection. ACT or SAT required and minimum scores are established; evidence of secondary completion required. For applicants applying after June 1 that have ACT of 15-17 or SAT (Critical Reading and Math) of 710-850, written appeal and essay required for consideration. For applicants applying after June 1 that have ACT of 15-17 or SAT (Critical Reading and Math) of 710-850, written appeal and essay required for consideration. **Home schooled:** Transcript of courses and grades required.

High school preparation. College-preparatory program recommended. 21 units recommended. Recommended units include English 4, mathematics 3, social studies 1, history 2, science 3 (laboratory 2), foreign language 2, computer science 1, visual/performing arts 1 and academic electives 2.

2011-2012 Annual costs. Tuition/fees: $16,870. Room/board: $5,200. Books/supplies: $1,150. Personal expenses: $2,184.

2010-2011 Financial aid. Need-based: 259 full-time freshmen applied for aid; 224 were judged to have need; 224 of these received aid. Average need met was 69%. Average scholarship/grant was $9,069; average loan $3,685. 44% of total undergraduate aid awarded as scholarships/grants, 56% as loans/jobs. **Non-need-based:** Awarded to 343 full-time undergraduates, including 85 freshmen. Scholarships awarded for academics, athletics, job skills, leadership, music/drama.

Application procedures. Admission: Closing date 6/1 (receipt date). $25 fee, may be waived for applicants with need. Admission notification on a rolling basis. $200 non-refundable tuition advance due by 6/1 or, if accepted after 6/1, within two weeks of acceptance, to register for classes. **Financial aid:** Priority date 6/1; no closing date. FAFSA, institutional form required. Applicants notified on a rolling basis starting 3/1.

Academics. Special study options: Distance learning, double major, ESL, honors, internships, liberal arts/career combination, student-designed major, study abroad, teacher certification program, weekend college. **Credit/placement by examination:** AP, CLEP, IB, SAT, ACT, institutional tests. 45 credit hours maximum toward bachelor's degree. **Support services:** Learning center, pre-admission summer program, reduced course load, remedial instruction, study skills assistance, tutoring, writing center.

Honors college/program. Minimum of 27 composite on ACT or 1210 on SAT (Critical Reading, Math); 36 honors students admitted in Fall 2010; honors designation can be obtained with any degree by completing 15 hours of honors-specific coursework.

Majors. Biology: General. **Business:** Accounting, business admin, finance, financial planning, management information systems, marketing, organizational leadership. **Communications:** Digital media, organizational. **Computer sciences:** General, information technology. **Conservation:** General. **Education:** Agricultural, art, biology, business, chemistry, computer, early childhood, elementary, English, history, mathematics, middle, music, physical, science, secondary, social studies, Spanish, special ed, speech. **Engineering:** General. **English:** English lit, technical writing. **General:** Animal sciences. **Health services:** Athletic training, music therapy, nursing (RN), predental, premedicine, prepharmacy, preveterinary. **Human services:** Social work. **Liberal arts:** Arts/sciences, humanities. **Math:** General. **Parks/recreation:** Exercise sciences, health/fitness, outdoor education, sports admin, sports studies. **Physical sciences:** Chemistry. **Protective services:** Law enforcement admin. **Psychology:** General. **Social sciences:** Economics. **Theology:** Bible, missionary, theology, youth ministry. **Visual/performing arts:** Art, design, directing/producing, music, music management, music pedagogy. **Work/family studies:** Family systems.

Most popular majors. Business/marketing 25%, education 18%, health sciences 16%, parks/recreation 7%.

Computing on campus. 235 workstations in dormitories, library, computer center, student center. Dormitories wired for high-speed internet access and linked to campus network. Commuter students can connect to campus network. Online course registration, online library, helpline, repair service, wireless network available.

Student life. Freshman orientation: Mandatory, $110 fee. Preregistration for classes offered. Week-long orientation held the week before fall semester begins. **Policies:** Chapel attendance required for full-time in-residence students age 24 or under. Religious observance required. **Housing:** Guaranteed on-campus for freshmen. Single-sex dorms, special housing for disabled, apartments, wellness housing available. **Activities:** Bands, campus ministries, choral groups, drama, international student organizations, music ensembles, musical theater, student government, student newspaper, Best Friends, Missions Club, Fellowship of Christian Athletes, Students in Free Enterprise, Social Work Outreach Association, social clubs, Organization of Latin American Students.

Athletics. NAIA. **Intercollegiate:** Baseball M, basketball, cheerleading, cross-country, golf, soccer, softball W, track and field, volleyball W. **Intramural:** Badminton, basketball, bowling, football (non-tackle), soccer, softball, table tennis, tennis, volleyball. **Team name:** Chaparrals.

Student services. Adult student services, alcohol/substance abuse counseling, chaplain/spiritual director, career counseling, services for economically disadvantaged, student employment services, financial aid counseling, health services, personal counseling, placement for graduates, veterans' counselor. **Physically disabled:** Services for visually, speech, hearing impaired.

Contact. E-mail: admissions@lcu.edu
Phone: (806) 720-7151 Toll-free number: (800) 933-7601 ext. 7151
Fax: (806) 720-7162
Charlie Webb, Director of Admissions, Lubbock Christian University, 5601 19th Street, Lubbock, TX 79407-2099

McMurry University
Abilene, Texas
www.mcm.edu   CB code: 6402

- Private 4-year university and liberal arts college affiliated with United Methodist Church
- Residential campus in small city
- 1,336 degree-seeking undergraduates: 11% part-time, 50% women, 17% African American, 1% Asian American, 20% Hispanic American, 1% Native American
- 61% of applicants admitted
- SAT or ACT (ACT writing recommended) required
- 36% graduate within 6 years; 36% enter graduate study

General. Founded in 1923. Regionally accredited. Three-week May term available; additional off-campus extension at Dyess Air Force Base; part of 3-member consortium providing collegiate nursing education in Texas. **Degrees:** 232 bachelor's awarded. **Location:** 155 miles from Fort Worth, 220 miles from Austin. **Calendar:** Semester, extensive summer session. **Full-time faculty:** 79 total; 73% have terminal degrees, 40% women. **Part-time faculty:** 40 total; 28% have terminal degrees, 52% women. **Class size:** 62% < 20, 34% 20-39, 2% 40-49, 1% 50-99. **Special facilities:** Buffalo Gap historical village.

Freshman class profile. 1,266 applied, 769 admitted, 330 enrolled.

Mid 50% test scores			
SAT critical reading:	400-510	Rank in top quarter:	36%
SAT math:	430-540	Rank in top tenth:	12%
ACT composite:	17-23	End year in good standing:	79%
GPA 3.75 or higher:	30%	Return as sophomores:	61%
GPA 3.50-3.74:	13%	Out-of-state:	6%
GPA 3.0-3.49:	26%	Live on campus:	86%
GPA 2.0-2.99:	31%	International:	1%

Basis for selection. Evaluated based on overall academic preparation including high school rank and GPA, ACT or SAT scores, and leadership and extracurricular activities. Interview recommended for all; audition required for music and theater; portfolio required for art; interview required for admission to Honors Program. **Learning Disabled:** Appropriate documentation required for students seeking special accommodations.

High school preparation. College-preparatory program recommended. 18 units required. Required units include English 4, mathematics 4, social studies 4, science 4 and foreign language 2.

2011-2012 Annual costs. Tuition/fees: $21,870. Students pay a block tuition rate for 12-18 hours per semester. Block tuition helps students take more hours at no additional cost. The cost of a tablet PC is included in tuition cost. The cost covers a tablet PC and school-related software. Room/board: $7,225. Books/supplies: $1,200. Personal expenses: $1,911.

2011-2012 Financial aid. Need-based: 319 full-time freshmen applied for aid; 288 were judged to have need; 288 of these received aid. Average need met was 84%. Average scholarship/grant was $11,504; average loan $3,522. 68% of total undergraduate aid awarded as scholarships/grants, 32% as loans/jobs. **Non-need-based:** Awarded to 774 full-time undergraduates, including 243 freshmen. Scholarships awarded for academics, art, music/drama, religious affiliation.

Application procedures. Admission: Priority date 3/15; deadline 8/15 (receipt date). $25 fee, may be waived for applicants with need. Admission notification on a rolling basis beginning on or about 9/1. Must reply by May 1 or within 2 week(s) if notified thereafter. **Financial aid:** Priority date 3/15; no closing date. FAFSA required. Applicants notified on a rolling basis starting 2/1; must reply within 3 week(s) of notification.

Academics. Students receive credit for both nontraditional and traditional courses on and off campus during 3-week May term. Opportunities for bachelor's degree after early admission to dental, medical, or veterinary

school. **Special study options:** Accelerated study, combined bachelor's/graduate degree, cross-registration, double major, dual enrollment of high school students, honors, independent study, internships, liberal arts/career combination, student-designed major, teacher certification program. **Credit/placement by examination:** AP, CLEP, IB, SAT, ACT, institutional tests. 45 credit hours maximum toward bachelor's degree. With departmental approval, examinations may be given for credit in areas not covered by AP or CLEP. **Support services:** Learning center, reduced course load, remedial instruction, study skills assistance, tutoring, writing center.

Majors. Biology: General, biochemistry, biomedical sciences. **Business:** General, accounting, business admin, finance, management information systems, marketing. **Computer sciences:** General, information technology. **Education:** Art, biology, chemistry, computer, early childhood, elementary, English, history, mathematics, middle, physical, secondary, Spanish. **English:** Creative writing, English lit. **Foreign languages:** Spanish. **Health services:** Athletic training, nursing (RN), prenursing. **History:** General, applied. **Math:** General. **Parks/recreation:** Exercise sciences. **Philosophy/religion:** Christian. **Physical sciences:** Chemistry, physics. **Psychology:** General. **Social sciences:** Political science, sociology. **Visual/performing arts:** Conducting, dramatic, music, studio arts.

Most popular majors. Biology 7%, business/marketing 19%, education 23%, psychology 7%, social sciences 7%, visual/performing arts 8%.

Computing on campus. PC or laptop required. 130 workstations in library, computer center, student center. Dormitories wired for high-speed internet access and linked to campus network. Commuter students can connect to campus network. Online library, helpline, student web hosting, wireless network available.

Student life. Freshman orientation: Available, $175 fee. Preregistration for classes offered. Summer weekend orientation plus 4-day orientation before first week of classes. **Housing:** Guaranteed on-campus for all undergraduates. Coed dorms, single-sex dorms, special housing for disabled, apartments, wellness housing available. $150 nonrefundable deposit, deadline 5/1. **Activities:** Bands, campus ministries, choral groups, drama, international student organizations, literary magazine, music ensembles, Model UN, musical theater, student government, student newspaper, Alpha Phi Omega, Fellowship of Christian Athletes, Religious Life, Servant Leadership, Kappa Delta Sigma, student ambassador board, Zeta Phi Beta, campus activities board.

Athletics. NCAA. **Intercollegiate:** Baseball M, basketball, cheerleading, cross-country, diving, football (tackle) M, golf, soccer, swimming, tennis, track and field, volleyball W. **Intramural:** Basketball, football (non-tackle), golf, racquetball, soccer, softball, tennis, volleyball. **Team name:** War Hawks.

Student services. Alcohol/substance abuse counseling, chaplain/spiritual director, career counseling, student employment services, financial aid counseling, health services, personal counseling, placement for graduates, veterans' counselor.

Contact. E-mail: admissions@mcm.edu
Phone: (325) 793-4700 Toll-free number: (800) 460-2392
Fax: (325) 793-4701
Kim Poligala, Admission Director, McMurry University, South 14th and Sayles Boulevard, Abilene, TX 79697-0001

Midwestern State University
Wichita Falls, Texas   **CB member**
www.mwsu.edu   **CB code: 6408**

▶ Public 4-year university and liberal arts college

▶ Commuter campus in small city

▶ 5,443 degree-seeking undergraduates: 26% part-time, 58% women, 12% African American, 3% Asian American, 12% Hispanic American, 1% Native American, 8% international

▶ 672 degree-seeking graduate students

▶ 52% of applicants admitted

▶ SAT or ACT (ACT writing optional) required

General. Founded in 1922. Regionally accredited. **Degrees:** 994 bachelor's, 48 associate awarded; master's offered. **ROTC:** Air Force. **Location:** 130 miles from Dallas-Fort Worth. **Calendar:** Semester, extensive summer session. **Full-time faculty:** 225 total; 78% have terminal degrees, 12% minority, 48% women. **Part-time faculty:** 112 total; 22% have terminal degrees, 12% minority, 54% women. **Class size:** 33% < 20, 48% 20-39, 7% 40-49, 11% 50-99, less than 1% >100. **Special facilities:** Kurzweil reading machine for the blind, greenhouse, 2 biologic study properties, North Texas Regional simulation center, Wichita Falls Museum of Art.

Freshman class profile. 2,751 applied, 1,436 admitted, 646 enrolled.

Mid 50% test scores		Rank in top quarter:	44%
SAT critical reading:	450-560	Rank in top tenth:	14%
SAT math:	480-580	Return as sophomores:	68%
SAT writing:	430-530	Out-of-state:	5%
ACT composite:	20-24	Live on campus:	61%
GPA 3.75 or higher:	30%	International:	3%
GPA 3.50-3.74:	25%	Fraternities:	5%
GPA 3.0-3.49:	27%	Sororities:	12%
GPA 2.0-2.99:	17%		

Basis for selection. For unconditional admission, students must graduate from accredited high school, meet requirements, submit official transcripts and ACT/SAT scores. Entrance exams determined by class rank. Texas public universities require THEA test score on file prior to enrollment unless student exempt. Audition required for applied music program. **Home schooled:** Home-schooled applicants go through individual review.

High school preparation. College-preparatory program recommended. 26 units required. Required units include English 4, mathematics 4, social studies 4, science 4, foreign language 2, visual/performing arts 1, academic electives 5.5. .5 Speech, 1 P.E.

2011-2012 Annual costs. Tuition/fees: $6,910; $7,810 out-of-state. Room/board: $5,800.

2011-2012 Financial aid. Need-based: 515 full-time freshmen applied for aid; 386 were judged to have need; 378 of these received aid. Average need met was 72%. Average scholarship/grant was $6,937; average loan $4,952. 42% of total undergraduate aid awarded as scholarships/grants, 58% as loans/jobs. **Non-need-based:** Awarded to 758 full-time undergraduates, including 130 freshmen. Scholarships awarded for academics, alumni affiliation, art, athletics, leadership, music/drama. **Additional information:** Employees offered tuition reimbursement provided they meet stated criteria. Dependents and children of faculty and staff may receive scholarship to defer local tuition and fees.

Application procedures. Admission: Priority date 3/1; deadline 8/7 (receipt date). $25 fee, may be waived for applicants with need. Admission notification on a rolling basis beginning on or about 9/1. **Financial aid:** Priority date 3/1; no closing date. FAFSA, institutional form required. Applicants notified on a rolling basis starting 4/15; must reply within 4 week(s) of notification.

Academics. Special study options: Combined bachelor's/graduate degree, distance learning, double major, dual enrollment of high school students, ESL, honors, independent study, internships, liberal arts/career combination, study abroad, teacher certification program. **Credit/placement by examination:** AP, CLEP, IB, SAT, ACT, institutional tests. 26 credit hours maximum toward associate degree, 60 toward bachelor's. **Support services:** Learning center, reduced course load, remedial instruction, study skills assistance, tutoring, writing center.

Majors. Biology: General, exercise physiology. **Business:** General, accounting, business admin, finance, management information systems, managerial economics, marketing. **Communications:** Media studies. **Computer sciences:** General. **Conservation:** Environmental science. **Education:** Bilingual, early childhood, English, mathematics, science, social studies. **Engineering:** General, mechanical. **English:** English lit. **Foreign languages:** Spanish. **Health services:** Athletic training, clinical lab science, dental hygiene, nursing (RN), predental, premedicine, prepharmacy, preveterinary, radiologic technology/medical imaging, respiratory therapy technology. **History:** General. **Human services:** Social work. **Liberal arts:** Humanities. **Math:** General. **Parks/recreation:** General, exercise sciences. **Physical sciences:** Chemistry, geology. **Protective services:** Criminal justice. **Psychology:** General. **Social sciences:** Political science, sociology. **Visual/performing arts:** Art, dramatic, music, studio arts.

Most popular majors. Business/marketing 23%, health sciences 28%, interdisciplinary studies 16%.

Computing on campus. 429 workstations in dormitories, library, computer center, student center. Dormitories wired for high-speed internet access and linked to campus network. Commuter students can connect to campus network. Online course registration, online library, wireless network available.

Student life. Freshman orientation: Mandatory. Preregistration for classes offered. Parents, family welcome. **Housing:** Guaranteed on-campus for freshmen. Coed dorms, single-sex dorms, special housing for disabled, apartments, wellness housing available. $100 fully refundable deposit. Cooperative housing units for honors students and biology students. **Activities:** Bands, campus ministries, choral groups, dance, drama, film society, international student organizations, literary magazine, music ensembles, student government, student newspaper, TV station, Methodist student foundation,

Baptist student center, Student Ambassadors, black student union, organization of Hispanic students, University Democrats, College Republicans, Amnesty International.

Athletics. NCAA. **Intercollegiate:** Basketball, cross-country W, football (tackle) M, golf, soccer, softball W, tennis, volleyball W. **Intramural:** Archery, badminton, basketball, bowling, football (non-tackle), golf, soccer, softball, table tennis, tennis, volleyball. **Team name:** Mustangs.

Student services. Alcohol/substance abuse counseling, career counseling, student employment services, financial aid counseling, health services, personal counseling, placement for graduates, veterans' counselor. **Physically disabled:** Services for visually, speech, hearing impaired.

Contact. E-mail: admissions@mwsu.edu
Phone: (940) 397-4334 Toll-free number: (800) 842-1922
Fax: (940) 397-4672
Barbara Merkle, Director of Admissions, Midwestern State University, 3410 Taft Boulevard, Wichita Falls, TX 76308-2099

National American University: Austin
Austin, Texas
www.national.edu

- For-profit 4-year university
- Very large city

General. Regionally accredited. **Calendar:** Quarter.

Contact. Phone: (512) 651-4700
Director of Admissions, 13801 Burnet Road, Suite 300, Austin, TX 78727

Northwood University: Texas
Cedar Hill, Texas
www.northwood.edu   **CB code: 6499**

- Private 4-year university and business college
- Residential campus in large town
- 406 degree-seeking undergraduates
- 45% of applicants admitted
- SAT or ACT (ACT writing optional), application essay required

General. Founded in 1966. Regionally accredited. Specialty university offering only business degrees in professional management; 3 residential campuses in Michigan, Florida, and Texas; program centers in 8 states. **Degrees:** 94 bachelor's awarded; master's offered. **Location:** 18 miles from Dallas, 28 miles from Fort Worth. **Calendar:** Semester, limited summer session. **Full-time faculty:** 16 total. **Part-time faculty:** 15 total. **Class size:** 57% < 20, 41% 20-39, 2% 40-49, less than 1% 50-99.

Freshman class profile. 509 applied, 227 admitted, 82 enrolled.

Mid 50% test scores			
SAT critical reading:	390-490	GPA 3.0-3.49:	58%
SAT math:	430-520	GPA 2.0-2.99:	15%
SAT writing:	360-470	Rank in top quarter:	34%
ACT composite:	16-20	Rank in top tenth:	8%
GPA 3.75 or higher:	7%	Out-of-state:	2%
GPA 3.50-3.74:	20%	Live on campus:	52%

Basis for selection. Minimum GPA of 2.0 and strong interest in business or related field. Test scores considered. Students with lower GPA possibly admitted on probation. Interview recommended. **Home schooled:** Transcript of courses and grades, state high school equivalency certificate required.

High school preparation. College-preparatory program recommended. 17 units recommended. Recommended units include English 4, mathematics 3, social studies 3, science 3 (laboratory 2), foreign language 1 and computer science 1.

2011-2012 Annual costs. Tuition/fees: $20,140. Room/board: $8,437. Books/supplies: $182.

Financial aid. Non-need-based: Scholarships awarded for academics, athletics, leadership, minority status, state residency.

Application procedures. Admission: No deadline. $25 fee, may be waived for applicants with need, free for online applicants. Admission notification on a rolling basis beginning on or about 10/1. **Financial aid:** No deadline. FAFSA required. Applicants notified on a rolling basis starting 3/1.

Academics. Special study options: Accelerated study, distance learning, double major, dual enrollment of high school students, external degree, honors, independent study, internships, student-designed major, study abroad, weekend college. **Credit/placement by examination:** AP, CLEP, IB, SAT, ACT, institutional tests. 12 credit hours maximum toward bachelor's degree. **Support services:** Learning center, reduced course load, remedial instruction, study skills assistance, tutoring, writing center.

Majors. Business: Accounting, business admin, marketing. **Computer sciences:** General. **Parks/recreation:** Sports admin. **Protective services:** Fire services admin.

Computing on campus. 50 workstations in library, computer center. Dormitories wired for high-speed internet access and linked to campus network. Commuter students can connect to campus network. Online course registration, online library, helpline, student web hosting, wireless network available.

Student life. Freshman orientation: Mandatory, $125 fee. Preregistration for classes offered. Multiple sessions throughout the summer. **Housing:** Guaranteed on-campus for freshmen. Single-sex dorms, apartments, wellness housing available. $100 nonrefundable deposit, deadline 8/1. **Activities:** Choral groups, dance, drama, literary magazine, student government, student newspaper, Christian Fellowship.

Athletics. NAIA. **Intercollegiate:** Baseball M, cross-country, golf, soccer, softball W, track and field. **Intramural:** Basketball, volleyball. **Team name:** Knights.

Student services. Adult student services, career counseling, student employment services, financial aid counseling, health services, personal counseling, placement for graduates.

Contact. E-mail: txadmit@northwood.edu
Phone: (972) 293-5400 Toll-free number: (800) 927-9663
Fax: (972) 291-3824
Terry Silva, Director of Admissions, Northwood University: Texas, 1114 West FM 1382, Cedar Hill, TX 75104

Our Lady of the Lake University of San Antonio
San Antonio, Texas   **CB member**
www.ollusa.edu   **CB code: 6550**

- Private 4-year university affiliated with Roman Catholic Church
- Commuter campus in very large city
- 1,455 degree-seeking undergraduates: 19% part-time, 73% women, 8% African American, 1% Asian American, 64% Hispanic American, 1% Native American, 1% international
- 1,103 degree-seeking graduate students
- 55% of applicants admitted
- SAT or ACT (ACT writing optional) required
- 33% graduate within 6 years

General. Founded in 1895. Regionally accredited. **Degrees:** 304 bachelor's awarded; master's, professional, doctoral offered. **ROTC:** Army, Air Force. **Location:** 4 miles from downtown, 80 miles from Austin. **Calendar:** Semester, limited summer session. **Full-time faculty:** 114 total; 40% minority, 60% women. **Part-time faculty:** 152 total; 43% minority, 50% women. **Class size:** 68% < 20, 32% 20-39. **Special facilities:** International center, international folk culture center, speech and hearing clinic, community counseling center, elementary school, child development center, center for social work research, center for women in church and society.

Freshman class profile. 1,883 applied, 1,042 admitted, 244 enrolled.

Mid 50% test scores			
SAT critical reading:	420-520	GPA 2.0-2.99:	13%
SAT math:	400-500	Rank in top quarter:	54%
ACT composite:	16-21	Rank in top tenth:	27%
GPA 3.75 or higher:	22%	Return as sophomores:	59%
GPA 3.50-3.74:	32%	Out-of-state:	1%
GPA 3.0-3.49:	32%	Live on campus:	58%

Basis for selection. High school academic record and test scores important. **Home schooled:** Transcript of courses and grades required.

High school preparation. College-preparatory program recommended. 14 units required. Required units include English 4, mathematics 3, social studies 3 and science 2. 2 additional credits in English, math, social sciences, or nature sciences.

2011-2012 Annual costs. Tuition/fees: $22,784. Room/board: $7,326. Books/supplies: $1,200. Personal expenses: $3,300.

Financial aid. Non-need-based: Scholarships awarded for academics, alumni affiliation, art, athletics, leadership, music/drama.

Application procedures. Admission: No deadline. $25 fee, may be waived for applicants with need. Admission notification on a rolling basis. **Financial aid:** No deadline. FAFSA, institutional form required. Applicants notified on a rolling basis starting 3/1; must reply within 2 week(s) of notification.

Academics. Special study options: Accelerated study, combined bachelor's/graduate degree, cooperative education, cross-registration, distance learning, double major, dual enrollment of high school students, exchange student, honors, independent study, internships, study abroad, teacher certification program, weekend college. **Credit/placement by examination:** AP, CLEP, IB, SAT, ACT, institutional tests. No limit to number of credit hours that may be awarded through CLEP or that may be counted towards bachelor's degree. **Support services:** Learning center, pre-admission summer program, reduced course load, remedial instruction, study skills assistance, tutoring.

Majors. Area/ethnic studies: Chicano/Hispanic-American/Latino. **Biology:** General. **Business:** Accounting, business admin, finance, human resources, international, marketing, organizational leadership. **Communications:** Broadcast journalism, communications/speech/rhetoric, journalism, public relations. **Computer sciences:** General. **Education:** General, kindergarten/preschool, special ed, speech impaired. **English:** English lit. **Foreign languages:** Spanish. **Health services:** Speech pathology. **History:** General. **Human services:** Social work. **Liberal arts:** Arts/sciences. **Math:** General. **Parks/recreation:** Exercise science. **Philosophy/religion:** Philosophy, religion. **Physical sciences:** Chemistry. **Protective services:** Criminal justice. **Psychology:** General. **Social sciences:** General, political science, sociology. **Visual/performing arts:** Art, dramatic, music. **Work/family studies:** Business.

Most popular majors. Business/marketing 23%, education 7%, family/consumer sciences 7%, health sciences 6%, liberal arts 6%, psychology 12%.

Computing on campus. 208 workstations in dormitories, library, computer center, student center. Dormitories wired for high-speed internet access and linked to campus network. Commuter students can connect to campus network. Online course registration, online library, helpline, repair service, wireless network available.

Student life. Freshman orientation: Mandatory, $50 fee. Preregistration for classes offered. Overnight program, 4 times during spring and summer, Includes assessment testing. Parent participation encouraged. **Housing:** Guaranteed on-campus for freshmen. Coed dorms, single-sex dorms available. $100 deposit. **Activities:** Bands, campus ministries, choral groups, dance, drama, film society, international student organizations, literary magazine, music ensembles, musical theater, student government, student newspaper, symphony orchestra, TV station, religious organizations, black and Hispanic clubs, service clubs.

Athletics. NAIA. **Intercollegiate:** Basketball, cross-country, golf M, soccer, softball W, tennis, volleyball W. **Intramural:** Basketball, football (non-tackle), golf, racquetball, soccer W, softball, swimming, tennis, volleyball. **Team name:** Saints.

Student services. Adult student services, alcohol/substance abuse counseling, chaplain/spiritual director, career counseling, student employment services, financial aid counseling, health services, personal counseling, placement for graduates, veterans' counselor, women's services. **Physically disabled:** Services for visually, speech, hearing impaired.

Contact. E-mail: webmaster@lake.ollusa.edu
Phone: (210) 431-3961 Toll-free number: (800) 436-6558
Fax: (210) 431-4036
Michael Acosta, Vice President, Enrollment Management, Our Lady of the Lake University of San Antonio, 411 Southwest 24th Street, San Antonio, TX 78207-4689

Paul Quinn College
Dallas, Texas
www.pqc.edu

CB member
CB code: 6577

- Private 4-year liberal arts college affiliated with African Methodist Episcopal Church
- Residential campus in very large city
- 202 undergraduates
- SAT or ACT with writing required

General. Founded in 1872. Regionally accredited. Historically Black institution. **Degrees:** 26 bachelor's awarded. **Location:** 12 miles from Dallas.

Calendar: Semester, limited summer session. **Full-time faculty:** 10 total. **Part-time faculty:** 20 total.

Freshman class profile.

Out-of-state:	10%	**Live on campus:**	80%

Basis for selection. 2.0 GPA and test scores most important.

High school preparation. Required and recommended units include English 4, mathematics 3, social studies 2, science 3 and foreign language 2.

2011-2012 Annual costs. Books/supplies: $1,000. Personal expenses: $350.

Financial aid. All financial aid based on need.

Application procedures. Admission: Priority date 7/1; deadline 8/1. $25 fee, may be waived for applicants with need. Admission notification on a rolling basis. **Financial aid:** Priority date 7/1; no closing date. FAFSA, institutional form required. Applicants notified on a rolling basis starting 7/15; must reply within 2 week(s) of notification.

Academics. Special study options: Combined bachelor's/graduate degree, cooperative education, distance learning, honors, internships, liberal arts/career combination, teacher certification program. Program with Texas State Technical Institute leading to bachelor of applied science in 24 fields. **Credit/placement by examination:** AP, CLEP. 12 credit hours maximum toward bachelor's degree. **Support services:** Reduced course load, remedial instruction, study skills assistance, tutoring.

Majors. Biology: General. **Business:** Accounting, business admin. **Communications:** General. **Computer sciences:** General. **Education:** Elementary, secondary. **Philosophy/religion:** Religion. **Protective services:** Criminal justice. **Social sciences:** Sociology.

Computing on campus. 30 workstations in computer center.

Student life. Freshman orientation: Mandatory. Preregistration for classes offered. **Policies:** Religious observance required. **Housing:** Guaranteed on-campus for all undergraduates. Single-sex dorms available. $75 deposit. **Activities:** Jazz band, choral groups, drama, student government, student newspaper, student ministerial council, Christian student organization.

Athletics. NAIA. **Intercollegiate:** Baseball M, basketball, cross-country, football (tackle) M, softball W, track and field, volleyball. **Intramural:** Basketball, softball, table tennis, volleyball. **Team name:** Tigers.

Student services. Career counseling, student employment services, health services, on-campus daycare, personal counseling, placement for graduates, veterans' counselor.

Contact. E-mail: admissions@pqc.edu
Phone: (214) 302-3575 Toll-free number: (800) 237-2648
Fax: (214) 302-3613
Nena Taylor, Director of Admissions, Paul Quinn College, 3837 Simpson Stuart Road, Dallas, TX 75241

Prairie View A&M University
Prairie View, Texas
www.pvamu.edu

CB member
CB code: 6580

- Public 4-year university
- Commuter campus in small town
- 6,813 degree-seeking undergraduates: 7% part-time, 60% women, 86% African American, 2% Asian American, 5% Hispanic American, 1% international
- 1,571 degree-seeking graduate students
- 40% of applicants admitted
- SAT or ACT (ACT writing optional) required
- 31% graduate within 6 years

General. Founded in 1876. Regionally accredited. Historically Black college. **Degrees:** 900 bachelor's awarded; master's, doctoral offered. **ROTC:** Army, Naval. **Location:** 47 miles from Houston. **Calendar:** Semester, extensive summer session. **Full-time faculty:** 394 total; 67% have terminal degrees, 80% minority, 39% women. **Part-time faculty:** 107 total; 43% have terminal degrees, 78% minority, 49% women. **Class size:** 22% < 20, 58% 20-39, 9% 40-49, 11% 50-99, less than 1% >100. **Special facilities:** Nuclear magnetic resonance spectrometric differentiator, scanning calorimeter, high pressure liquid chromatograph, solid state engineering laboratory, computer-aided design and drafting laboratory, center for learning and teaching effectiveness,

international dairy goat research center, cooperative agricultural research center, solar observatory.

Freshman class profile. 9,258 applied, 3,716 admitted, 1,703 enrolled.

Mid 50% test scores			
SAT critical reading:	370-450	GPA 3.50-3.74:	7%
SAT math:	390-480	GPA 3.0-3.49:	33%
SAT writing:	360-450	GPA 2.0-2.99:	57%
ACT composite:	15-20	Rank in top quarter:	10%
GPA 3.75 or higher:	3%	Rank in top tenth:	1%
		Return as sophomores:	64%

Basis for selection. Score on institution's entrance examination, personal qualities, high school GPA important. Students may be admitted conditionally if grades or test scores are below minimum requirement. **Home schooled:** Transcript of courses and grades, state high school equivalency certificate required.

High school preparation. 24 units required; 26 recommended. Required and recommended units include English 4, mathematics 3-4, history 4, science 3-4, foreign language 1-2, computer science 1, visual/performing arts 1, academic electives 2.5. 1 Economics, 2 Physical Education, 1 Health, 1 Speech.

2011-2012 Annual costs. Tuition/fees: $7,401; $16,702 out-of-state. Room/board: $7,321. Books/supplies: $1,000. Personal expenses: $1,000.

2011-2012 Financial aid. Need-based: Average need met was 1%. Average scholarship/grant was $4,120; average loan $3,875. 56% of total undergraduate aid awarded as scholarships/grants, 44% as loans/jobs. **Non-need-based:** Scholarships awarded for academics, athletics, ROTC.

Application procedures. Admission: Priority date 6/1; deadline 6/1 (receipt date). $25 fee, may be waived for applicants with need. Application must be submitted online. Admission notification by 8/15. Admission notification on a rolling basis. **Financial aid:** Closing date 3/15. FAFSA required. Applicants notified by 6/1; must reply by 8/1.

Academics. Special study options: Accelerated study, combined bachelor's/graduate degree, cooperative education, cross-registration, distance learning, double major, exchange student, honors, independent study, internships, study abroad, teacher certification program. **Credit/placement by examination:** AP, CLEP, SAT, ACT, institutional tests. 30 credit hours maximum toward bachelor's degree. **Support services:** Learning center, pre-admission summer program, reduced course load, remedial instruction, tutoring.

Majors. Architecture: Architecture. **Biology:** General. **Business:** Accounting, business admin, finance, management information systems. **Communications:** Communications/speech/rhetoric. **Computer sciences:** General. **Engineering:** Chemical, civil, computer, electrical, mechanical. **English:** English lit. **Foreign languages:** Spanish. **Health services:** Clinical lab science, nursing (RN). **History:** General. **Human services:** Social work. **Math:** General. **Parks/recreation:** Health/fitness. **Physical sciences:** Chemistry, physics. **Protective services:** Criminal justice. **Psychology:** General. **Social sciences:** Political science, sociology. **Visual/performing arts:** Dramatic, music, music performance. **Work/family studies:** Food/nutrition.

Most popular majors. Business/marketing 14%, engineering/engineering technologies 14%, health sciences 20%, interdisciplinary studies 6%, psychology 6%.

Computing on campus. 500 workstations in dormitories, library, computer center, student center. Dormitories wired for high-speed internet access and linked to campus network. Commuter students can connect to campus network. Online library, helpline, wireless network available.

Student life. Freshman orientation: Mandatory, $60 fee. Preregistration for classes offered. 1 day for Phase 1; 3 days for Phase 2. **Housing:** Guaranteed on-campus for freshmen. Single-sex dorms, special housing for disabled, apartments available. $150 fully refundable deposit, deadline 7/1. **Activities:** Bands, campus ministries, choral groups, dance, drama, international student organizations, music ensembles, radio station, student government, student newspaper, symphony orchestra, College Republicans, Spanish-speaking students association, Baptist student ministry, Chinese student association, ministerial alliance, Japanese student association, Korean student association.

Athletics. NAIA, NCAA. **Intercollegiate:** Baseball M, basketball, bowling W, cross-country, football (tackle) M, golf, soccer W, softball W, tennis, track and field, volleyball W. **Intramural:** Basketball, bowling W, football (tackle) M, golf, soccer W, softball, tennis, track and field, volleyball W. **Team name:** Panthers.

Student services. Adult student services, alcohol/substance abuse counseling, chaplain/spiritual director, career counseling, student employment services, financial aid counseling, health services, personal counseling, placement for graduates, veterans' counselor. **Physically disabled:** Services for hearing impaired.

Contact. E-mail: admissions@pvamu.edu
Phone: (936) 261-1000 Toll-free number: (877) 782-6830
Fax: (936) 261-1079
Mary Gooch, Director of Undergraduate Admissions, Prairie View A&M University, PO Box 519, MS 1009, Prairie View, TX 77446-0519

Rice University
Houston, Texas
www.rice.edu

CB member
CB code: 6609

▶ Private 4-year university
▶ Residential campus in very large city
▶ 3,708 degree-seeking undergraduates
▶ 19% of applicants admitted
▶ SAT and SAT Subject Tests or ACT with writing, application essay required

General. Founded in 1891. Regionally accredited. **Degrees:** 802 bachelor's awarded; master's, doctoral offered. **ROTC:** Army, Naval, Air Force. **Location:** 3 miles from downtown Houston. **Calendar:** Semester, limited summer session. **Full-time faculty:** 615 total. **Part-time faculty:** 122 total. **Special facilities:** Wetland center for biochemical research, arboretum, nanotechnology lab, center for study of languages and culture, civil engineering lab, concert hall with grand organ, institute for public policy, observatory, digital media center, Oshman engineering design kitchen.

Freshman class profile. 13,816 applied, 2,600 admitted, 1,000 enrolled.

Mid 50% test scores			
SAT critical reading:	650-750	Rank in top quarter:	96%
SAT math:	680-780	Rank in top tenth:	89%
SAT writing:	650-760	Out-of-state:	49%
ACT composite:	30-34	Live on campus:	98%

Basis for selection. High school course selection and performance, test scores, teacher and counselor recommendations, extracurricular activity, and application answers/essay most important. If student submits SAT Reasoning, two SAT Subject Tests are also required (recommend subject tests be in subjects related to student's area of interest). If student submits ACT with Writing, then no SAT Subject Tests are required. Audition required for music; portfolio required for architecture. Interview recommended for all freshman applicants. **Home schooled:** Statement describing home school structure and mission, letter of recommendation (nonparent) required.

High school preparation. College-preparatory program required. 16 units required; 20 recommended. Required and recommended units include English 4, mathematics 3-4, social studies 2-4, science 2-4 (laboratory 2-4), foreign language 2-4 and academic electives 3. Trigonometry (pre-calculus), physics, and chemistry required of engineering and natural science majors, although 2nd year of chemistry or biology may replace physics requirement.

2011-2012 Annual costs. Tuition/fees: $35,551. Room/board: $12,270. Books/supplies: $800. Personal expenses: $1,550.

2011-2012 Financial aid. Need-based: Average need met was 100%. Average scholarship/grant was $31,153; average loan $1,420. 92% of total undergraduate aid awarded as scholarships/grants, 8% as loans/jobs. **Non-need-based:** Scholarships awarded for academics, art, athletics, leadership, minority status, music/drama, ROTC, state residency.

Application procedures. Admission: Closing date 1/1 (postmark date). $70 fee, may be waived for applicants with need. Admission notification by 4/1. Must reply by 5/1. **Financial aid:** Priority date 3/1; no closing date. FAFSA, CSS PROFILE required. Applicants notified by 4/1; must reply by 5/1.

Academics. Special study options: Combined bachelor's/graduate degree, cross-registration, double major, dual enrollment of high school students, ESL, exchange student, independent study, internships, liberal arts/career combination, student-designed major, study abroad, teacher certification program. 8-year guaranteed medical school program with Baylor College of Medicine for 14 entering freshmen. **Credit/placement by examination:** AP, CLEP, IB, institutional tests. **Support services:** Study skills assistance, tutoring, writing center.

Majors. Architecture: Architecture. **Area/ethnic studies:** Asian, Chicano/Hispanic-American/Latino, German, Latin American, Slavic, women's. **Biology:** General, biochemistry, ecology, evolutionary. **Business:** Business admin. **Computer sciences:** Computer science. **Engineering:** Biomedical, chemical, civil, computer, electrical, environmental, materials, mechanical. **English:** English lit. **Foreign languages:** Ancient Greek, classics, French, German, Latin, linguistics, Slavic, Spanish. **History:** General. **Human services:** Public policy. **Math:** General, applied, statistics. **Parks/recreation:** Exercise sciences, sports admin. **Philosophy/religion:** Philosophy, religion.

Physical sciences: Astronomy, astrophysics, chemical physics, chemistry, geology, geophysics, physical chemistry, physics. **Psychology:** General. **Social sciences:** General, anthropology, economics, political science, sociology. **Visual/performing arts:** General, art, art history/conservation, music, music history, music performance, music theory/composition, studio arts.

Most popular majors. Biology 10%, engineering/engineering technologies 18%, parks/recreation 7%, social sciences 19%, visual/performing arts 6%.

Computing on campus. 543 workstations in dormitories, library, computer center, student center. Dormitories wired for high-speed internet access and linked to campus network. Commuter students can connect to campus network. Online course registration, online library, helpline, student web hosting, wireless network available.

Student life. Freshman orientation: Mandatory, $505 fee. Preregistration for classes offered. Held the week before start of classes. **Policies:** Academic honor code. All undergraduates are granted membership in one of 11 residential college communities and maintain that affiliation for their entire college career. Each college is self governing and designed to facilitate student and faculty networking, leadership development, pre-major advising, and social interaction. **Housing:** Guaranteed on-campus for freshmen. Coed dorms, special housing for disabled available. $100 nonrefundable deposit, deadline 5/1. **Activities:** Bands, campus ministries, choral groups, dance, drama, film society, international student organizations, literary magazine, music ensembles, Model UN, musical theater, opera, radio station, student government, student newspaper, symphony orchestra, TV station, Hispanic student association, Hillel, Black student association, Young Democrats, Young Republicans, Chinese student association, Baptist student union, Catholic student center, student volunteer program.

Athletics. NCAA. **Intercollegiate:** Baseball M, basketball, cheerleading, cross-country, football (non-tackle) W, football (tackle) M, golf M, soccer W, swimming W, tennis, track and field, volleyball W. **Intramural:** Badminton, basketball, racquetball, soccer, softball, swimming, table tennis, tennis, track and field, volleyball. **Team name:** Owls.

Student services. Alcohol/substance abuse counseling, chaplain/spiritual director, career counseling, student employment services, financial aid counseling, health services, minority student services, personal counseling, placement for graduates, women's services. **Physically disabled:** Services for visually, speech, hearing impaired.

Contact. E-mail: admission@rice.edu
Phone: (713) 348-7423 Toll-free number: (800) 527-6957
Fax: (713) 348-5952
Dan Warner, Director of Admission, Rice University, 6100 Main Street, Houston, TX 77251-1892

Sam Houston State University
Huntsville, Texas   **CB member**
www.shsu.edu   **CB code: 6643**

- Public 4-year university
- Residential campus in large town
- 14,992 degree-seeking undergraduates: 17% part-time, 57% women, 17% African American, 1% Asian American, 16% Hispanic American, 2% Native American, 1% international
- 2,463 degree-seeking graduate students
- 77% of applicants admitted
- SAT or ACT (ACT writing optional) required
- 47% graduate within 6 years

General. Founded in 1879. Regionally accredited. **Degrees:** 3,129 bachelor's awarded; master's, doctoral offered. **ROTC:** Army. **Location:** 69 miles from Houston, 170 miles from Dallas. **Calendar:** Semester, extensive summer session. **Full-time faculty:** 614 total; 78% have terminal degrees, 17% minority, 44% women. **Part-time faculty:** 181 total; 24% have terminal degrees, 14% minority, 58% women. **Class size:** 34% < 20, 46% 20-39, 8% 40-49, 10% 50-99, 2% >100. **Special facilities:** Sam Houston Memorial Museum, Huntsville State Park, planetarium and observatory, Texas Prison Museum.

Freshman class profile. 7,070 applied, 5,473 admitted, 2,069 enrolled.

Mid 50% test scores		Rank in top tenth:	15%
SAT critical reading:	440-540	Return as sophomores:	72%
SAT math:	460-560	Out-of-state:	1%
ACT composite:	19-23	Live on campus:	82%
Rank in top quarter:	45%	International:	1%

Basis for selection. Test scores, school achievement records very important. Students graduating in top quarter of accredited high school exempt from test requirements.

High school preparation. College-preparatory program recommended. 22 units required; 26 recommended. Required and recommended units include English 4, mathematics 3-4, social studies 4, history 3.5, science 2-4 (laboratory 1), foreign language 2, computer science 1, visual/performing arts 1, academic electives 3.5.

2011-2012 Annual costs. Tuition/fees: $7,328; $16,718 out-of-state. Room/board: $7,644. Books/supplies: $1,096. Personal expenses: $1,844.

Financial aid. Non-need-based: Scholarships awarded for academics, alumni affiliation, art, athletics, job skills, leadership, music/drama, religious affiliation, ROTC, state residency.

Application procedures. Admission: Priority date 6/15; deadline 8/1 (postmark date). $45 fee, may be waived for applicants with need. Admission notification on a rolling basis beginning on or about 9/1. **Financial aid:** Priority date 4/1; no closing date. FAFSA, institutional form required. Applicants notified on a rolling basis starting 3/1; must reply within 4 week(s) of notification.

Academics. Special study options: Combined bachelor's/graduate degree, distance learning, double major, dual enrollment of high school students, ESL, honors, independent study, internships, study abroad, teacher certification program. **Credit/placement by examination:** AP, CLEP, IB, SAT, ACT, institutional tests. 30 credit hours maximum toward bachelor's degree. **Support services:** Learning center, pre-admission summer program, reduced course load, remedial instruction, study skills assistance, tutoring, writing center.

Majors. Architecture: Interior. **Biology:** General. **Business:** General, accounting, banking/financial services, business admin, fashion, finance, human resources, international, managerial economics, marketing, operations. **Communications:** Advertising, journalism, media studies, public relations, radio/TV. **Communications technology:** Animation/special effects. **Computer sciences:** General. **Conservation:** Environmental science. **English:** English lit, rhetoric/composition. **Foreign languages:** French, Spanish. **General:** Agribusiness operations, animal sciences, horticultural science, mechanization. **Health services:** Music therapy. **History:** General. **Math:** General. **Parks/recreation:** Health/fitness. **Philosophy/religion:** Philosophy. **Physical sciences:** Chemistry, geology, physics. **Protective services:** Corrections, criminal justice. **Psychology:** General. **Social sciences:** Geography, political science, sociology. **Visual/performing arts:** Art, commercial/advertising art, dance, dramatic, music, music performance, photography, studio arts. **Work/family studies:** General, food/nutrition, institutional food production.

Most popular majors. Business/marketing 25%, communications/journalism 6%, interdisciplinary studies 13%, psychology 6%, security/protective services 17%.

Computing on campus. 552 workstations in library, computer center, student center. Dormitories wired for high-speed internet access and linked to campus network. Commuter students can connect to campus network. Online course registration, online library, helpline, repair service, student web hosting, wireless network available.

Student life. Freshman orientation: Available, $125 fee. Preregistration for classes offered. Overnight program throughout summer and before classes commence. Parent participation. **Housing:** Guaranteed on-campus for freshmen. Coed dorms, single-sex dorms, apartments, fraternity/sorority housing available. $200 deposit. **Activities:** Bands, campus ministries, choral groups, dance, drama, international student organizations, music ensembles, musical theater, radio station, student government, student newspaper, symphony orchestra, TV station, Democratic and Republican student associations, Baptist student ministry, Church of Christ student center, Lutheran student center, Hillel, Muslim students association, student Pagan association, ROTARACT, Habitat for Humanity, Wesley Foundation.

Athletics. NCAA. **Intercollegiate:** Baseball M, basketball, cross-country, equestrian, football (tackle) M, golf, rifle, rodeo, soccer, softball W, tennis, track and field, volleyball W. **Intramural:** Baseball M, basketball, bowling, diving, football (tackle) M, golf, gymnastics W, handball, lacrosse M, racquetball, rugby M, soccer, softball W, swimming, tennis, volleyball, water polo. **Team name:** Bearkats.

Student services. Alcohol/substance abuse counseling, career counseling, student employment services, financial aid counseling, health services, legal services, minority student services, on-campus daycare, personal counseling, placement for graduates, veterans' counselor. **Physically disabled:** Services for visually impaired.

Contact. E-mail: admissions@shsu.edu
Phone: (936) 294-1828 Toll-free number: (800) 232-7528
Fax: (936) 294-3758
Trevor Thorn, Director of Admissions, Sam Houston State University, Box 2418, Huntsville, TX 77341-2418

Schreiner University

Kerrville, Texas

www.schreiner.edu

CB member

CB code: 6647

⬧ Private 4-year liberal arts college affiliated with Presbyterian Church (USA)
⬧ Residential campus in large town
⬧ 1,016 degree-seeking undergraduates: 3% part-time, 59% women, 4% African American, 1% Asian American, 26% Hispanic American
⬧ 46 degree-seeking graduate students
⬧ 61% of applicants admitted
⬧ SAT or ACT with writing required
⬧ 39% graduate within 6 years

General. Founded in 1923. Regionally accredited. **Degrees:** 170 bachelor's, 1 associate awarded; master's offered. **Location:** 60 miles from San Antonio, 80 miles from Austin. **Calendar:** Semester. **Full-time faculty:** 54 total; 68% have terminal degrees, 7% minority, 43% women. **Part-time faculty:** 63 total; 36% have terminal degrees, 5% minority, 56% women. **Class size:** 56% <20, 43% 20-39, less than 1% 40-49. **Special facilities:** Hill Country Museum.

Freshman class profile. 1,109 applied, 677 admitted, 276 enrolled.

Mid 50% test scores			
SAT critical reading:	440-560	GPA 3.0-3.49:	34%
SAT math:	460-570	GPA 2.0-2.99:	2%
SAT writing:	440-540	Rank in top quarter:	43%
ACT composite:	19-24	Rank in top tenth:	13%
GPA 3.75 or higher:	13%	Return as sophomores:	64%
GPA 3.50-3.74:	51%	Out-of-state:	1%
		Live on campus:	86%

Basis for selection. High school courses taken, grades, class rank, extracurricular activities, test scores, recommendations, interviews considered. Interview recommended for all; essay required for applicants not meeting certain admissions standards; portfolio recommended for fine arts.

High school preparation. College-preparatory program recommended. 24 units recommended. Recommended units include English 4, mathematics 3, social studies 2, history 2, science 3 (laboratory 2), foreign language 2, computer science 1, visual/performing arts 1, academic electives 3.5.

2011-2012 Annual costs. Tuition/fees: $20,354. Room/board: $9,675. Books/supplies: $1,200. Personal expenses: $1,000.

2010-2011 Financial aid. Need-based: 242 full-time freshmen applied for aid; 207 were judged to have need; 207 of these received aid. Average need met was 72%. Average scholarship/grant was $13,255; average loan $2,963. 66% of total undergraduate aid awarded as scholarships/grants, 34% as loans/jobs. **Non-need-based:** Awarded to 167 full-time undergraduates, including 55 freshmen. Scholarships awarded for academics, art, job skills, leadership, music/drama, religious affiliation.

Application procedures. Admission: Priority date 5/1; deadline 8/1. $25 fee, may be waived for applicants with need. Admission notification on a rolling basis. **Financial aid:** Priority date 5/1; no closing date. FAFSA required. Applicants notified on a rolling basis starting 2/15; must reply within 2 week(s) of notification.

Academics. Special study options: Accelerated study, double major, dual enrollment of high school students, honors, independent study, internships, liberal arts/career combination, student-designed major, study abroad, teacher certification program. **Credit/placement by examination:** AP, CLEP, IB, SAT, ACT, institutional tests. **Support services:** Learning center, reduced course load, remedial instruction, study skills assistance, tutoring, writing center.

Majors. Biology: General, biochemistry. **Business:** General, accounting, business admin, finance, international, management information systems, marketing. **Communications:** Communications/speech/rhetoric. **Education:** General, biology, early childhood, elementary, English, history, mathematics, middle, music, physical, secondary. **Engineering:** General. **English:** English lit. **Health services:** Nursing (RN). **History:** General. **Liberal arts:** Arts/sciences, humanities. **Math:** General. **Parks/recreation:** Exercise sciences, sports admin. **Philosophy/religion:** Religion. **Physical sciences:** Chemistry. **Psychology:** General. **Social sciences:** Political science. **Visual/performing arts:** Commercial/advertising art, dramatic, graphic design, music.

Most popular majors. Biology 13%, business/marketing 15%, communications/journalism 6%, education 11%, parks/recreation 8%, psychology 13%, visual/performing arts 11%.

Computing on campus. 103 workstations in library, computer center, student center. Dormitories wired for high-speed internet access and linked to campus network. Commuter students can connect to campus network. Online library, helpline, repair service, student web hosting, wireless network available.

Student life. Freshman orientation: Mandatory. Preregistration for classes offered. Overnight program prior to start of classes. **Housing:** Guaranteed on-campus for all undergraduates. Coed dorms, special housing for disabled, apartments available. $100 nonrefundable deposit, deadline 5/1. **Activities:** Pep band, campus ministries, choral groups, dance, drama, literary magazine, music ensembles, musical theater, student government, student newspaper, symphony orchestra, community outreach program, pre-law society, Celtic Cross, Episcopal-Lutheran association, Fellowship of Christian Athletes, Young Catholic Adults, Young Republicans, Green society, Hispanic culture club, Asian culture club, Schreiner Democrats, Shades United.

Athletics. NCAA. **Intercollegiate:** Baseball M, basketball, cheerleading M, golf, soccer, softball W, tennis, volleyball W. **Intramural:** Basketball, football (non-tackle), football (tackle), golf, racquetball, soccer, swimming, table tennis, tennis, volleyball. **Team name:** Mountaineers.

Student services. Adult student services, chaplain/spiritual director, career counseling, student employment services, financial aid counseling, health services, personal counseling, placement for graduates. **Physically disabled:** Services for visually, speech, hearing impaired.

Contact. E-mail: admissions@schreiner.edu
Phone: (830) 792-7217 Toll-free number: (800) 343-4919
Fax: (830) 792-7226
Dean of Admissions & Financial Aid, Schreiner University, 2100 Memorial Boulevard, Kerrville, TX 78028-5697

Southern Methodist University

Dallas, Texas

www.smu.edu

CB member

CB code: 6660

⬧ Private 4-year university affiliated with United Methodist Church
⬧ Residential campus in large town
⬧ 6,150 degree-seeking undergraduates: 3% part-time, 52% women, 6% African American, 6% Asian American, 11% Hispanic American, 7% international
⬧ 4,528 degree-seeking graduate students
⬧ 55% of applicants admitted
⬧ SAT or ACT (ACT writing optional), application essay required
⬧ 75% graduate within 6 years

General. Founded in 1911. Regionally accredited. Courses also offered at SMU-in-Plano and SMU-in-Taos in New Mexico. **Degrees:** 1,625 bachelor's awarded; master's, professional, doctoral offered. **ROTC:** Army, Air Force. **Location:** 5 miles from downtown. **Calendar:** Semester, limited summer session. **Full-time faculty:** 705 total; 83% have terminal degrees, 18% minority, 38% women. **Part-time faculty:** 401 total; 47% have terminal degrees, 7% minority, 39% women. **Class size:** 59% <20, 26% 20-39, 8% 40-49, 7% 50-99, less than 1% >100. **Special facilities:** Film/video archives, New Mexico archeological dig of 13th century Indian pueblo, institute for the study of Earth and man, seismological observatory, electron microscopy laboratory, paleontology museum, business information center.

Freshman class profile. 10,338 applied, 5,641 admitted, 1,382 enrolled.

Mid 50% test scores			
SAT critical reading:	580-680	GPA 2.0-2.99:	7%
SAT math:	600-690	Rank in top quarter:	78%
SAT writing:	570-670	Rank in top tenth:	49%
ACT composite:	26-31	Return as sophomores:	89%
GPA 3.75 or higher:	49%	Out-of-state:	57%
GPA 3.50-3.74:	22%	Live on campus:	97%
GPA 3.0-3.49:	22%	International:	5%

Basis for selection. GED not accepted. Students evaluated comprehensively. High school curriculum, GPA, test scores, school/community activities, recommendations, and essay important. Special talents considered. Interview recommended for all; audition required for performing arts; portfolio recommended for studio art. **Home schooled:** SAT Subject Tests required.

High school preparation. College-preparatory program recommended. 15 units required; 20 recommended. Required and recommended units include English 4, mathematics 3-4, social studies 1-2, history 2-3, science 3-4 (laboratory 2-3) and foreign language 2-3.

2012-2013 Annual costs. Tuition/fees (projected): $41,750. Room/board: $13,539. Books/supplies: $800. Personal expenses: $1,600.

2011-2012 Financial aid. Need-based: 782 full-time freshmen applied for aid; 603 were judged to have need; 596 of these received aid. Average need met was 85%. Average scholarship/grant was $18,779; average loan $2,828. 77% of total undergraduate aid awarded as scholarships/grants, 23% as loans/jobs. **Non-need-based:** Awarded to 3,699 full-time undergraduates, including 971 freshmen. Scholarships awarded for academics, art, athletics, leadership, music/drama, religious affiliation, ROTC, state residency.

Application procedures. Admission: Priority date 1/15; deadline 3/15 (postmark date). $60 fee, may be waived for applicants with need. Admission notification on a rolling basis beginning on or about 12/31. Must reply by May 1 or within 2 week(s) if notified thereafter. **Financial aid:** Priority date 2/15; no closing date. FAFSA, CSS PROFILE required. Applicants notified on a rolling basis starting 3/15.

Academics. Special study options: Accelerated study, combined bachelor's/graduate degree, cooperative education, distance learning, double major, ESL, exchange student, honors, independent study, internships, student-designed major, study abroad, teacher certification program, Washington semester. **Credit/placement by examination:** AP, CLEP, IB, SAT, ACT, institutional tests. No limit on number of AP credits that may be counted toward bachelor's degree. Maximum of 8 hours of International Baccalaureate credits may be counted toward bachelor's degree. **Support services:** Learning center, pre-admission summer program, remedial instruction, study skills assistance, tutoring, writing center.

Majors. Area/ethnic studies: African-American, Chicano/Hispanic-American/Latino, Italian, Latin American. **Biology:** General, biochemistry. **Business:** General, accounting, business admin, finance, financial planning, insurance, marketing, real estate. **Communications:** Advertising, journalism, public relations. **Computer sciences:** Computer science. **Conservation:** Environmental studies. **Education:** Music. **Engineering:** Civil, computer, electrical, environmental, mechanical, operations research. **English:** Creative writing, English lit. **Foreign languages:** French, German, Italian, Spanish. **History:** General. **Human services:** Public policy. **Math:** General, statistics. **Philosophy/religion:** Philosophy, religion. **Physical sciences:** Chemistry, geology, geophysics, physics. **Psychology:** General. **Social sciences:** Anthropology, econometrics, economics, political science, sociology. **Visual/performing arts:** Art history/conservation, dance, dramatic, film/cinema/video, music, music performance, music theory/composition, piano/keyboard, studio arts, voice/opera.

Most popular majors. Business/marketing 24%, communications/journalism 11%, engineering/engineering technologies 7%, psychology 6%, social sciences 17%, visual/performing arts 8%.

Computing on campus. 758 workstations in dormitories, library, computer center, student center. Dormitories wired for high-speed internet access and linked to campus network. Commuter students can connect to campus network. Online course registration, online library, helpline, repair service, student web hosting, wireless network available.

Student life. Freshman orientation: Mandatory. Preregistration for classes offered. **Housing:** Guaranteed on-campus for freshmen. Coed dorms, apartments, cooperative housing, fraternity/sorority housing available. $100 nonrefundable deposit, deadline 5/1. **Activities:** Bands, campus ministries, choral groups, dance, drama, film society, international student organizations, literary magazine, music ensembles, Model UN, musical theater, opera, radio station, student government, student newspaper, symphony orchestra, TV station, over 180 student organizations available.

Athletics. NCAA. **Intercollegiate:** Basketball, cross-country W, diving, equestrian W, football (tackle) M, golf, rowing (crew) W, soccer, swimming, tennis, track and field W, volleyball W. **Intramural:** Basketball, bowling, golf, racquetball, soccer, softball, swimming, table tennis, tennis, volleyball. **Team name:** Mustangs.

Student services. Adult student services, alcohol/substance abuse counseling, chaplain/spiritual director, career counseling, student employment services, financial aid counseling, health services, minority student services, on-campus daycare, personal counseling, placement for graduates, veterans' counselor, women's services. **Physically disabled:** Services for visually, speech, hearing impaired.

Contact. E-mail: ugadmission@smu.edu
Phone: (214) 768-2058 Toll-free number: (800) 323-0672
Fax: (214) 768-0103
Wes Waggoner, Executive Director of Enrollment Services, Southern Methodist University, PO Box 750181, Dallas, TX 75275-0181

Southwestern Adventist University
Keene, Texas
www.swau.edu   **CB code: 6671**

- Private 4-year university and liberal arts college affiliated with Seventh-day Adventists
- Residential campus in small town

- 710 degree-seeking undergraduates: 9% part-time, 58% women
- 26 degree-seeking graduate students
- 37% of applicants admitted
- SAT or ACT (ACT writing optional) required
- 36% graduate within 6 years; 36% enter graduate study

General. Founded in 1893. Regionally accredited. **Degrees:** 141 bachelor's, 1 associate awarded; master's offered. **Location:** 55 miles from Dallas, 25 miles from Fort Worth. **Calendar:** Semester, limited summer session. **Full-time faculty:** 53 total; 60% have terminal degrees, 23% minority, 34% women. **Part-time faculty:** 20 total; 20% have terminal degrees, 20% minority, 60% women. **Class size:** 81% < 20, 15% 20-39, 4% 40-49, less than 1% 50-99. **Special facilities:** Observatory, museum of student life, paleontology museum.

Freshman class profile. 575 applied, 215 admitted, 127 enrolled.

Mid 50% test scores			
SAT critical reading:	440-520	GPA 2.0-2.99:	33%
SAT math:	430-520	End year in good standing:	75%
ACT composite:	17-24	Return as sophomores:	58%
GPA 3.75 or higher:	17%	Out-of-state:	34%
GPA 3.50-3.74:	15%	Live on campus:	35%
GPA 3.0-3.49:	32%	International:	13%

Basis for selection. Secondary school record, test scores important. Additional requirements for nursing and education programs. **Home schooled:** A state high school equivalency certificate is accepted instead of a high school diploma or GED. **Learning Disabled:** Prospective students must submit a letter with documentation of their learning disability.

High school preparation. College-preparatory program recommended. Recommended units include English 4, mathematics 2, social studies 2.5, science 2 and foreign language 2.

2011-2012 Annual costs. Tuition/fees: $17,080. Room/board: $7,010. Books/supplies: $1,142. Personal expenses: $1,332.

Financial aid. Non-need-based: Scholarships awarded for academics, leadership, music/drama.

Application procedures. Admission: Closing date 8/31. No application fee. Admission notification on a rolling basis. **Financial aid:** Priority date 3/15; no closing date. FAFSA, institutional form required. Applicants notified on a rolling basis starting 4/15.

Academics. Special study options: Accelerated study, cross-registration, distance learning, double major, ESL, external degree, honors, independent study, internships, liberal arts/career combination, student-designed major, study abroad, teacher certification program. **Credit/placement by examination:** AP, CLEP, IB, SAT, ACT, institutional tests. **Support services:** Reduced course load, remedial instruction, tutoring, writing center.

Majors. Biology: General, biostatistics. **Business:** Accounting, business admin, communications, finance, international, management information systems, management science. **Communications:** Broadcast journalism, communications/speech/rhetoric, journalism. **Computer sciences:** General, computer science, information systems. **Education:** Elementary, physical. **English:** English lit. **Health services:** Clinical lab technology, nursing (RN). **History:** General. **Math:** General, applied. **Parks/recreation:** Health/fitness. **Philosophy/religion:** Religion. **Physical sciences:** Chemistry, theoretical physics. **Psychology:** General. **Social sciences:** General, international relations. **Theology:** Theology. **Visual/performing arts:** Music.

Most popular majors. Business/marketing 22%, education 19%, health sciences 27%, liberal arts 10%, psychology 8%.

Computing on campus. 150 workstations in library, computer center. Dormitories wired for high-speed internet access and linked to campus network. Commuter students can connect to campus network. Helpline, repair service, student web hosting, wireless network available.

Student life. Freshman orientation: Mandatory, $125 fee. Preregistration for classes offered. Held the week prior to fall registration starting Wednesday evening through Monday noon. **Housing:** Guaranteed on-campus for all undergraduates. Single-sex dorms, apartments available. $100 fully refundable deposit, deadline 8/31. **Activities:** Concert band, campus ministries, choral groups, drama, international student organizations, music ensembles, musical theater, radio station, student government, student newspaper, symphony orchestra, TV station.

Athletics. Intramural: Badminton, basketball, football (non-tackle), gymnastics, racquetball, soccer, table tennis, tennis W, volleyball. **Team name:** Knights.

Student services. Adult student services, alcohol/substance abuse counseling, chaplain/spiritual director, career counseling, student employment

services, financial aid counseling, health services, personal counseling, placement for graduates, veterans' counselor.

Contact. E-mail: admissions@swau.edu
Phone: (817) 202-6252 Toll-free number: (800) 433-2240
Fax: (817) 556-4744
Robert Gardner, Associate Academic Vice President, Southwestern Adventist University, Box 567, Keene, TX 76059

Southwestern Assemblies of God University
Waxahachie, Texas
www.sagu.edu   CB code: 6669

- Private 4-year university and Bible college affiliated with Assemblies of God
- Residential campus in large town
- 1,691 degree-seeking undergraduates
- 32% of applicants admitted
- SAT or ACT (ACT writing optional), application essay required

General. Founded in 1927. Regionally accredited. **Degrees:** 304 bachelor's, 114 associate awarded; master's offered. **ROTC:** Army. **Location:** 20 miles from Dallas. **Calendar:** Semester, limited summer session. **Full-time faculty:** 66 total. **Part-time faculty:** 51 total.

Freshman class profile. 1,321 applied, 423 admitted, 300 enrolled.

Out-of-state:	45%	Live on campus:	80%

Basis for selection. Minister's reference and 1 personal reference required. Interview recommended. **Learning Disabled:** Enrollment with the Achievement Center indicated.

2011-2012 Annual costs. Tuition/fees: $15,730. Room/board: $5,590. Books/supplies: $612. Personal expenses: $1,479.

Application procedures. Admission: Priority date 7/1; no deadline. $35 fee. Admission notification on a rolling basis beginning on or about 3/1. **Financial aid:** Priority date 3/1; no closing date. FAFSA required. Applicants notified on a rolling basis starting 6/1; must reply within 2 week(s) of notification.

Academics. Special study options: Distance learning, double major, dual enrollment of high school students, external degree, independent study, internships, teacher certification program. **Credit/placement by examination:** AP, CLEP, institutional tests. 15 credit hours maximum toward associate degree, 30 toward bachelor's. **Support services:** Learning center, reduced course load, remedial instruction, tutoring.

Majors. Business: General, accounting, business admin, marketing. **Education:** Early childhood, elementary, English, music, reading, secondary, social studies. **English:** English lit. **Health services:** Clinical pastoral counseling. **History:** General. **Philosophy/religion:** Christian. **Theology:** Bible, missionary, pastoral counseling, religious ed, sacred music, youth ministry. **Visual/performing arts:** Music performance, piano/keyboard, voice/opera.

Computing on campus. 45 workstations in dormitories, library, computer center. Dormitories wired for high-speed internet access and linked to campus network. Online library, repair service, wireless network available.

Student life. Freshman orientation: Mandatory. Preregistration for classes offered. **Policies:** Dress code observed. Religious observance required. **Housing:** Guaranteed on-campus for freshmen. Coed dorms, single-sex dorms, apartments available. Unmarried students 23 and under required to live in college housing unless alternative arrangements agreed to upon enrollment. **Activities:** Bands, campus ministries, choral groups, drama, music ensembles, musical theater, student government, student newspaper, prayer groups, ministry labs.

Athletics. NAIA, NCCAA. **Intercollegiate:** Baseball M, basketball, cheerleading, football (tackle) M, soccer M, volleyball W. **Intramural:** Basketball, football (non-tackle) W, racquetball, softball, table tennis, volleyball. **Team name:** Lions.

Student services. Adult student services, chaplain/spiritual director, career counseling, student employment services, financial aid counseling, health services, personal counseling, placement for graduates, veterans' counselor.

Contact. E-mail: admissions@sagu.edu
Phone: (972) 937-7248 Toll-free number: (888) 937-7248
Fax: (972) 923-0006
Bryan Brooks, Director of Admissions, Southwestern Assemblies of God University, 1200 Sycamore Street, Waxahachie, TX 75165

Southwestern Baptist Theological Seminary
Fort Worth, Texas
www.swbts.edu   CB code: 4546

- Private 4-year Bible and seminary college
- Very large city
- 266 full-time, degree-seeking undergraduates

General. Regionally accredited. **Degrees:** 26 bachelor's awarded; master's, professional, doctoral offered. **Calendar:** Semester. **Full-time faculty:** 117 total.

Basis for selection. Commitment to Christian ministry important.

2011-2012 Annual costs. Tuition/fees: $6,928.

Application procedures. Admission: No deadline. $35 fee. **Financial aid:** No deadline.

Academics. Credit/placement by examination: AP, CLEP.

Majors. Liberal arts: Humanities. **Theology:** Sacred music.

Contact. E-mail: admissions@swbts.edu
Phone: (800) 792-8701
Kyle Walker, Director of Admissions, Southwestern Baptist Theological Seminary, PO Box 22000, Fort Worth, TX 76122

Southwestern Christian College
Terrell, Texas
www.swcc.edu   CB code: 6705

- Private 4-year Bible and liberal arts college affiliated with Church of Christ
- Residential campus in large town
- 250 degree-seeking undergraduates
- Application essay required

General. Founded in 1949. Regionally accredited. **Degrees:** 5 bachelor's, 26 associate awarded. **Location:** 30 miles from Dallas. **Calendar:** Semester. **Full-time faculty:** 10 total. **Part-time faculty:** 8 total.

Freshman class profile.

Out-of-state:	85%	Live on campus:	94%

Basis for selection. Open admission. Interview recommended. **Home schooled:** Transcript of courses and grades required.

2011-2012 Annual costs. Tuition/fees: $6,910. Room/board: $4,688. Books/supplies: $900. Personal expenses: $400.

Financial aid. Non-need-based: Scholarships awarded for academics, athletics, music/drama.

Application procedures. Admission: Closing date 7/31. $20 fee, may be waived for applicants with need. Admission notification on a rolling basis. **Financial aid:** Closing date 6/1. FAFSA required. Applicants notified on a rolling basis starting 7/15; must reply within 2 week(s) of notification.

Academics. Special study options: Independent study, internships. **Credit/placement by examination:** AP, CLEP, institutional tests. 8 credit hours maximum toward associate degree, 12 toward bachelor's. **Support services:** Learning center, reduced course load, remedial instruction.

Majors. Theology: Bible.

Student life. Freshman orientation: Mandatory, $10 fee. Preregistration for classes offered. **Policies:** High moral standards required. Profanity, vulgarity, gambling, drinking alcoholic beverages, attending dances or places of questionable amusement are against college's ideals and rules. **Housing:** Guaranteed on-campus for all undergraduates. Single-sex dorms available. **Activities:** Jazz band, choral groups, drama, music ensembles, student government, student newspaper.

Athletics. NJCAA. **Intercollegiate:** Basketball, track and field. **Team name:** Rams.

Student services. Career counseling, personal counseling.

Contact. E-mail: professorprice@swcc.edu
Phone: (972) 524-3341 Toll-free number: (972) 524-3341 ext. 161
Fax: (972) 563-7133
Walter Price, Director of Admissions and Retention, Southwestern
Christian College, Box 10, Terrell, TX 75160

Southwestern University
Georgetown, Texas — CB member
www.southwestern.edu — CB code: 6674

- Private 4-year liberal arts college affiliated with United Methodist Church
- Residential campus in large town
- 1,341 degree-seeking undergraduates: 1% part-time, 60% women
- 65% of applicants admitted
- SAT or ACT with writing, application essay required

General. Founded in 1840. Regionally accredited. **Degrees:** 308 bachelor's
awarded. **Location:** 28 miles from Austin. **Calendar:** Semester, limited
summer session. **Full-time faculty:** 122 total; 98% have terminal degrees,
15% minority, 52% women. **Part-time faculty:** 42 total; 62% have terminal
degrees, 14% minority, 50% women. **Class size:** 76% < 20, 24% 20-39, less
than 1% 40-49.

Freshman class profile. 2,613 applied, 1,694 admitted, 344 enrolled.

Rank in top quarter:	79%	Out-of-state:	12%
Rank in top tenth:	48%	Live on campus:	100%

Basis for selection. School record, class rank, recommendations, test
scores, essay most important. Audition required for music, theater programs;
portfolio required for art program.

High school preparation. College-preparatory program required. 17 units
required; 20 recommended. Required and recommended units include English
4, mathematics 4, social studies 2-3, history 1-2, science 3-4 (laboratory 2-
3), foreign language 2-3 and academic electives 1.

2011-2012 Annual costs. Tuition/fees: $33,440. Room/board: $9,680.
Books/supplies: $1,000. Personal expenses: $900.

2011-2012 Financial aid. Need-based: 71% of total undergraduate aid
awarded as scholarships/grants, 29% as loans/jobs. **Non-need-based:** Scholarships awarded for academics, art, minority status, music/drama, religious
affiliation.

Application procedures. Admission: Closing date 2/1 (postmark date).
$40 fee, may be waived for applicants with need. Admission notification by
4/1. Must reply by 5/1. Applicants accepted after 2/15 if space allows.
Financial aid: Priority date 3/1; no closing date. FAFSA required. Applicants
notified on a rolling basis starting 3/1; must reply by 5/1 or within 2 week(s)
of notification.

Academics. Students must demonstrate computer skills and grasp of major
through capstone project, course, or examination prior to graduation. **Special
study options:** Combined bachelor's/graduate degree, double major, honors,
independent study, internships, liberal arts/career combination, New York
semester, student-designed major, study abroad, teacher certification program,
Washington semester. **Credit/placement by examination:** AP, CLEP, IB,
institutional tests. **Support services:** Reduced course load, study skills assistance, tutoring, writing center.

Majors. Area/ethnic studies: American, Latin American, women's. **Biol-
ogy:** General, animal behavior, biochemistry. **Business:** General, accounting.
Communications: Communications/speech/rhetoric, media studies. **Computer sciences:** General. **Conservation:** Environmental studies. **Education:**
General, elementary, music, physical, science, social studies. **English:**
English lit. **Foreign languages:** Chinese, classics, French, German, Latin,
Spanish. **Health services:** Athletic training. **History:** General. **Math:** General. **Philosophy/religion:** Philosophy, religion. **Physical sciences:** General,
chemistry, physics. **Psychology:** General. **Social sciences:** Anthropology,
economics, international relations, political science, sociology. **Visual/per-
forming arts:** Art, art history/conservation, dramatic, music, music history,
music performance, music theory/composition, musicology, studio arts management.

Most popular majors. Biology 7%, business/marketing 11%, communica-
tions/journalism 10%, education 8%, English 6%, history 7%, physical sciences 6%, psychology 7%, social sciences 17%, visual/performing arts 10%.

Computing on campus. 410 workstations in dormitories, library, computer center, student center. Dormitories wired for high-speed internet access
and linked to campus network. Online course registration, online library,
helpline, repair service, student web hosting, wireless network available.

Student life. Freshman orientation: Mandatory. Preregistration for
classes offered. **Housing:** Guaranteed on-campus for freshmen. Coed dorms,
single-sex dorms, special housing for disabled, apartments, fraternity/sorority
housing available. $250 nonrefundable deposit, deadline 5/1. **Activities:**
Bands, choral groups, dance, drama, film society, literary magazine, music
ensembles, musical theater, radio station, student government, student newspaper, Alpha Phi Omega, Ebony, Mexican American student association,
political science society, international club, Equal Voice For Women's Perspective.

Athletics. NCAA. **Intercollegiate:** Baseball M, basketball, cross-country,
diving, golf, lacrosse M, soccer, softball W, swimming, tennis, track and
field, volleyball W. **Team name:** Bucs/Pirates.

Student services. Alcohol/substance abuse counseling, chaplain/spiritual
director, career counseling, student employment services, financial aid counseling, health services, minority student services, personal counseling, placement for graduates. **Physically disabled:** Services for hearing impaired.

Contact. E-mail: admission@southwestern.edu
Phone: (512) 863-1200 Toll-free number: (800) 252-3166
Fax: (512) 863-9601
Dave Voskuil, Vice President Enrollment Services, Southwestern
University, 1001 East University Avenue, Georgetown, TX 78626

St. Edward's University
Austin, Texas — CB member
www.stedwards.edu — CB code: 6619

- Private 4-year university and liberal arts college affiliated with Roman
  Catholic Church
- Residential campus in very large city
- 4,392 degree-seeking undergraduates: 19% part-time, 61% women, 4%
  African American, 2% Asian American, 33% Hispanic American, 1%
  Native American, 5% international
- 892 degree-seeking graduate students
- 64% of applicants admitted
- SAT or ACT with writing, application essay required
- 68% graduate within 6 years

General. Founded in 1885. Regionally accredited. **Degrees:** 959 bachelor's
awarded; master's offered. **ROTC:** Army, Air Force. **Location:** 80 miles
from San Antonio, 180 miles from Dallas. **Calendar:** Semester, limited
summer session. **Full-time faculty:** 204 total; 90% have terminal degrees,
14% minority, 45% women. **Part-time faculty:** 315 total; 46% have terminal
degrees, 16% minority, 52% women. **Class size:** 52% < 20, 48% 20-39, less
than 1% 40-49, less than 1% 50-99. **Special facilities:** Fine arts facility with
photography laboratory, theater, chapel, natural sciences center, interdisciplinary research laboratory at Wild Basin Wilderness Preserve, portal campus
in Angers, France at Universite Catholique de l'Ouest.

Freshman class profile. 3,886 applied, 2,475 admitted, 781 enrolled.

Mid 50% test scores			
SAT critical reading:	510-620	Rank in top tenth:	23%
SAT math:	510-610	End year in good standing:	91%
SAT writing:	490-600	Return as sophomores:	81%
ACT composite:	23-27	Out-of-state:	13%
Rank in top quarter:	59%	Live on campus:	88%
		International:	5%

Basis for selection. Holistic review process, with grades and curriculum,
class rank and test scores (both preferably in top 50th percentile) most
important components. Extracurricular activities, leadership and service,
application essay, letters of recommendation reviewed as complement to
student's academic record. Interviews recommended. **Home schooled:**
Assessment done on individual basis. **Learning Disabled:** Students are welcome to submit learning disability documentation with admission application.

High school preparation. College-preparatory program recommended.
14 units required; 20 recommended. Required and recommended units include
English 4, mathematics 3-4, social studies 1, history 2-3, science 2-3 (laboratory 2-3), foreign language 2-3, computer science 1 and academic electives 1.

2012-2013 Annual costs. Tuition/fees (projected): $31,110. Room/board:
$10,044. Books/supplies: $1,100. Personal expenses: $1,846.

2011-2012 Financial aid. Need-based: 653 full-time freshmen applied
for aid; 531 were judged to have need; 531 of these received aid. Average
need met was 71%. Average scholarship/grant was $15,825; average loan
$3,476. 74% of total undergraduate aid awarded as scholarships/grants, 26%
as loans/jobs. **Non-need-based:** Awarded to 1,866 full-time undergraduates,
including 457 freshmen. Scholarships awarded for academics, art, athletics,
leadership, music/drama, religious affiliation, state residency.

Application procedures. **Admission:** Priority date 2/1; deadline 5/1 (postmark date). $45 fee, may be waived for applicants with need. Admission notification on a rolling basis beginning on or about 11/1. Must reply by May 1 or within 2 week(s) if notified thereafter. For merit scholarship consideration, students must apply by the February 1 priority deadline. **Financial aid:** Priority date 3/1, closing date 5/1. FAFSA required. Applicants notified on a rolling basis starting 1/15; must reply by 5/1 or within 2 week(s) of notification.

Academics. Writing center, tutoring services available evenings and weekends. **Special study options:** Double major, honors, internships, New York semester, study abroad, teacher certification program, Washington semester. **Credit/placement by examination:** AP, CLEP, IB, SAT, ACT, institutional tests. **Support services:** Learning center, pre-admission summer program, reduced course load, remedial instruction, study skills assistance, tutoring, writing center.

Majors. **Area/ethnic studies:** Latin American. **Biology:** General, biochemistry, bioinformatics. **Business:** Accounting, accounting technology, business admin, entrepreneurial studies, finance, international, marketing. **Communications:** Digital media, media studies. **Computer sciences:** General, computer science. **Conservation:** Environmental studies. **Education:** Art, biology, chemistry, drama/dance, history, mathematics, multi-level teacher, physical, social studies, Spanish. **English:** English lit, writing. **Foreign languages:** French, Spanish. **Health services:** Clinical lab science. **History:** General. **Human services:** Social work. **Liberal arts:** Arts/sciences. **Math:** General. **Parks/recreation:** Exercise sciences. **Philosophy/religion:** Philosophy. **Physical sciences:** Chemistry, environmental chemistry, forensic chemistry. **Protective services:** Criminal justice, forensics. **Psychology:** General. **Social sciences:** Criminology, economics, political science, sociology. **Theology:** Theology. **Visual/performing arts:** Art, arts management, dramatic, game design, graphic design, photography.

Most popular majors. Business/marketing 29%, communications/journalism 14%, psychology 9%, social sciences 8%, visual/performing arts 8%.

Computing on campus. 790 workstations in dormitories, library, computer center, student center. Dormitories wired for high-speed internet access and linked to campus network. Commuter students can connect to campus network. Online course registration, online library, helpline, repair service, student web hosting, wireless network available.

Student life. **Freshman orientation:** Mandatory, $200 fee. Preregistration for classes offered. 2-day sessions held 6 times during summer. **Housing:** Guaranteed on-campus for freshmen. Coed dorms, single-sex dorms, special housing for disabled, apartments available. $150 nonrefundable deposit, deadline 5/1. Community-style living in casitas/casas, 6 living-learning communities available: Global Understanding, Social Justice, Honors (by invitation), Business, Natural Sciences, French Language. (A Faith and Service LLC is available for upperclassmen.). **Activities:** Jazz band, campus ministries, choral groups, dance, drama, film society, literary magazine, music ensembles, musical theater, student government, student newspaper, TV station, Approximately 115 student organizations on campus in many categories including academic/professional, political/social issues, cultural, service, religious/spiritual, programming, and social.

Athletics. NCAA. **Intercollegiate:** Baseball M, basketball, golf, soccer, softball W, tennis, volleyball W. **Intramural:** Basketball, football (non-tackle), racquetball, soccer, tennis, volleyball. **Team name:** Hilltoppers.

Student services. Adult student services, alcohol/substance abuse counseling, chaplain/spiritual director, career counseling, services for economically disadvantaged, student employment services, financial aid counseling, health services, minority student services, personal counseling, placement for graduates, veterans' counselor. **Physically disabled:** Services for visually, speech, hearing impaired.

Contact. E-mail: seu.admit@stedwards.edu
Phone: (512) 448-8500 Toll-free number: (800) 555-0164
Fax: (512) 464-8877
Tracy Manier, Associate VP and Dean of Undergraduate Admission, St. Edward's University, 3001 South Congress Avenue, Austin, TX 78704-6489

St. Mary's University
San Antonio, Texas
www.stmarytx.edu

CB member
CB code: 6637

- Private 4-year university and liberal arts college affiliated with Roman Catholic Church
- Residential campus in very large city

- 2,501 degree-seeking undergraduates: 7% part-time, 58% women, 4% African American, 2% Asian American, 71% Hispanic American, 5% international
- 1,680 degree-seeking graduate students
- 61% of applicants admitted
- SAT or ACT (ACT writing recommended) required
- 60% graduate within 6 years

General. Founded in 1852. Regionally accredited. **Degrees:** 452 bachelor's awarded; master's, professional, doctoral offered. **ROTC:** Army, Air Force. **Location:** 5 miles from downtown. **Calendar:** Semester, limited summer session. **Full-time faculty:** 198 total; 94% have terminal degrees, 21% minority, 35% women. **Part-time faculty:** 169 total; 46% have terminal degrees, 34% minority, 40% women. **Class size:** 50% < 20, 49% 20-39, less than 1% 40-49, less than 1% 50-99.

Freshman class profile. 4,372 applied, 2,672 admitted, 641 enrolled.

Mid 50% test scores			
SAT critical reading:	450-550	GPA 2.0-2.99:	15%
SAT math:	480-570	Rank in top quarter:	63%
SAT writing:	450-540	Rank in top tenth:	28%
ACT composite:	20-24	End year in good standing:	80%
GPA 3.75 or higher:	20%	Return as sophomores:	75%
GPA 3.50-3.74:	27%	Out-of-state:	7%
GPA 3.0-3.49:	37%	Live on campus:	84%
		International:	4%

Basis for selection. Balanced consideration given to all aspects of high school performance, including selection of college-preparatory courses, GPA and grade pattern throughout high school, class rank, standardized test scores, and record of service and leadership.

High school preparation. College-preparatory program recommended. 16 units required; 19 recommended. Required and recommended units include English 4, mathematics 3-4, social studies 3-4, science 3-4, foreign language 2-3 and academic electives 1. Applicants to science and engineering program should complete 4 units of math and 3 units of lab science.

2012-2013 Annual costs. Tuition/fees (projected): $24,226. Room/board: $8,428. Books/supplies: $1,300. Personal expenses: $1,900.

Financial aid. **Non-need-based:** Scholarships awarded for academics, alumni affiliation, athletics, leadership, minority status, music/drama, ROTC, state residency.

Application procedures. **Admission:** Priority date 1/15; no deadline. $30 fee, may be waived for applicants with need, free for online applicants. Admission notification on a rolling basis beginning on or about 10/20. Must reply by May 1 or within 2 week(s) if notified thereafter. **Financial aid:** Priority date 3/31; no closing date. FAFSA required. Applicants notified on a rolling basis starting 3/1; must reply by 5/1 or within 2 week(s) of notification.

Academics. Writing across the curriculum program requires students in all undergraduate programs to take writing-intensive courses. **Special study options:** Combined bachelor's/graduate degree, cross-registration, distance learning, double major, dual enrollment of high school students, ESL, exchange student, honors, independent study, internships, liberal arts/career combination, study abroad, teacher certification program, Washington semester. **Credit/placement by examination:** AP, CLEP, SAT, ACT, institutional tests. 30 credit hours maximum toward bachelor's degree. **Support services:** Learning center, pre-admission summer program, reduced course load, remedial instruction, study skills assistance, tutoring, writing center.

Majors. **Biology:** General, biochemistry, biophysics. **Business:** General, accounting, business admin, entrepreneurial studies, finance, human resources, international, management information systems, marketing. **Communications:** Communications/speech/rhetoric. **Computer sciences:** General, computer science, information technology. **Education:** General. **Engineering:** Computer, electrical, engineering science, industrial, software. **English:** English lit, rhetoric/composition. **Foreign languages:** French, Spanish. **History:** General. **Liberal arts:** Arts/sciences. **Math:** General. **Parks/recreation:** Exercise sciences. **Philosophy/religion:** Philosophy. **Physical sciences:** Chemistry, forensic chemistry, geology, physics. **Protective services:** Criminal justice, forensics. **Psychology:** General. **Social sciences:** General, criminology, economics, international relations, political science, sociology. **Theology:** Theology. **Visual/performing arts:** Music.

Most popular majors. Biology 13%, business/marketing 29%, engineering/engineering technologies 6%, English 6%, psychology 6%, social sciences 15%.

Computing on campus. PC or laptop required. 100 workstations in dormitories, library, computer center, student center. Dormitories wired for high-speed internet access and linked to campus network. Commuter students can connect to campus network. Online course registration, online library, helpline, repair service, wireless network available.

Student life. **Freshman orientation:** Mandatory, $130 fee. Preregistration for classes offered. 2-day program offered twice in June and once in August. Parallel program for parents. June program offers campus accommodations for students and parents. Transfer student orientation is a 1-day program, held once in May and once in August. **Housing:** Guaranteed on-campus for freshmen. Coed dorms available. $100 nonrefundable deposit, deadline 5/1. Nontraditional residence halls available for students 21 years old or above. **Activities:** Bands, campus ministries, choral groups, dance, drama, international student organizations, literary magazine, music ensembles, musical theater, student government, student newspaper, Circle K, Amnesty International, black student union, College Democrats, Habitat for Humanity, League of United Latin American Citizens, Youth for a United World, Environmental Conservation Organization, Mexican student association, Alpha Phi Omega.

Athletics. NCAA. **Intercollegiate:** Baseball M, basketball, cheerleading, cross-country W, golf, soccer, softball W, tennis, volleyball W. **Intramural:** Basketball, football (tackle), racquetball, soccer, softball, table tennis, tennis, volleyball. **Team name:** Rattlers.

Student services. Adult student services, alcohol/substance abuse counseling, chaplain/spiritual director, career counseling, student employment services, financial aid counseling, health services, personal counseling, placement for graduates, veterans' counselor. **Physically disabled:** Services for visually, speech, hearing impaired.

Contact. E-mail: uadm@stmarytx.edu
Phone: (210) 436-3126 Toll-free number: (800) 367-7868
Fax: (210) 431-6742
Nelson Delgado, Director of Admission, St. Mary's University, One Camino Santa Maria, San Antonio, TX 78228-8503

Stephen F. Austin State University
Nacogdoches, Texas
www.sfasu.edu

CB member
CB code: 6682

▸ Public 4-year university
▸ Residential campus in large town
▸ 11,368 degree-seeking undergraduates: 16% part-time, 63% women, 25% African American, 1% Asian American, 11% Hispanic American, 1% Native American, 1% international
▸ 1,535 degree-seeking graduate students
▸ 63% of applicants admitted
▸ SAT or ACT with writing required
▸ 43% graduate within 6 years

General. Founded in 1923. Regionally accredited. **Degrees:** 1,945 bachelor's awarded; master's, doctoral offered. **ROTC:** Army. **Location:** 140 miles from Houston, 70 miles from Longview. **Calendar:** Semester, extensive summer session. **Full-time faculty:** 459 total; 71% have terminal degrees, 8% minority, 48% women. **Part-time faculty:** 215 total; 46% have terminal degrees, 8% minority, 60% women. **Class size:** 23% < 20, 55% 20-39, 9% 40-49, 10% 50-99, 2% >100. **Special facilities:** Computerized observatory; experimental forest; arboretum; beef, poultry and swine research facilities; equine, goat and sheep centers; soil, plant and water analysis labs; biotechnology/environmental science research center; Stone Fort museum; agricultural pond; forest resources institute; geographic information systems lab; regional geospatial service center; early childhood research center.

Freshman class profile. 10,975 applied, 6,883 admitted, 2,538 enrolled.

Mid 50% test scores			
SAT critical reading:	420-530	Rank in top tenth:	12%
SAT math:	440-540	Return as sophomores:	65%
SAT writing:	410-510	Out-of-state:	1%
ACT composite:	18-23	Live on campus:	91%
Rank in top quarter:	40%	Fraternities:	21%
		Sororities:	14%

Basis for selection. Applicants must complete prescribed high school preparation and submit official transcript and SAT or ACT scores. No minimum score required for those ranking in top quartile; those in second quartile must have composite score of 850 SAT, 18 ACT; third quartile 1050 SAT, 23 ACT; fourth quartile 1250 SAT, 28 ACT (All SAT scores exclusive of Writing). Applicants not meeting rank-in-class and test requirements reviewed on individual basis. SAT or ACT scores must be received by last day of registration for fall term admission. **Home schooled:** Applicants individually assessed based on probability of success.

High school preparation. College-preparatory program required. Required units include English 4, mathematics 4, social studies 3, science 4, foreign language 2, visual/performing arts 1, academic electives 5.5. 1 physical education, .5 government, .5 economics, and .5 speech units required.

2011-2012 Annual costs. Tuition/fees: $7,344; $16,734 out-of-state. Room/board: $8,186. Books/supplies: $1,107. Personal expenses: $1,729.

2010-2011 Financial aid. **Need-based:** 1,817 full-time freshmen applied for aid; 1,504 were judged to have need; 1,483 of these received aid. Average need met was 49%. Average scholarship/grant was $7,468; average loan $2,978. 53% of total undergraduate aid awarded as scholarships/grants, 47% as loans/jobs. **Non-need-based:** Awarded to 3,058 full-time undergraduates, including 893 freshmen. Scholarships awarded for academics, alumni affiliation, athletics, leadership, music/drama, state residency. **Additional information:** Tuition guarantee program covers the remaining balance of any tuition and mandatory fees not covered by other gift aid, for 15 hours per regular semester for up to 4 years.

Application procedures. **Admission:** No deadline. $35 fee, may be waived for applicants with need. Admission notification on a rolling basis beginning on or about 9/1. **Financial aid:** Priority date 4/1; no closing date. FAFSA required. Applicants notified on a rolling basis starting 4/1.

Academics. **Special study options:** Accelerated study, combined bachelor's/graduate degree, distance learning, double major, dual enrollment of high school students, honors, independent study, internships, liberal arts/career combination, student-designed major, study abroad, teacher certification program. **Credit/placement by examination:** AP, CLEP, IB, SAT, ACT, institutional tests. 32 credit hours maximum toward bachelor's degree. **Support services:** Learning center, pre-admission summer program, reduced course load, remedial instruction, study skills assistance, tutoring, writing center.

Majors. **Architecture:** Interior. **Biology:** General, biochemistry. **Business:** General, accounting, business admin, fashion, finance, hospitality admin, international, managerial economics, marketing, special products marketing. **Communications:** Journalism, radio/TV. **Computer sciences:** General, information technology. **Conservation:** Environmental science, forest management, forestry, wildlife/wilderness. **English:** Creative writing, English lit, rhetoric/composition. **Foreign languages:** French, Hispanic and Latin American, Spanish. **General:** Agribusiness operations, animal sciences, horticultural science, mechanization, poultry, production. **Health services:** Audiology/hearing, communication disorders, nursing (RN), rehabilitation science. **History:** General. **Human services:** General, social work. **Liberal arts:** Arts/sciences. **Math:** General. **Parks/recreation:** Exercise sciences, facilities management. **Philosophy/religion:** Philosophy. **Physical sciences:** Chemistry, geology, physics. **Protective services:** Corrections, police science. **Psychology:** General. **Social sciences:** Economics, geography, GIS/cartography, political science, sociology. **Visual/performing arts:** Art, art history/conservation, dance, dramatic, music. **Work/family studies:** General, family studies, food/nutrition.

Most popular majors. Business/marketing 21%, health sciences 11%, interdisciplinary studies 17%, parks/recreation 7%, visual/performing arts 7%.

Computing on campus. 1,000 workstations in dormitories, library, computer center, student center. Dormitories wired for high-speed internet access and linked to campus network. Commuter students can connect to campus network. Online course registration, online library, helpline, repair service, student web hosting, wireless network available.

Student life. **Freshman orientation:** Available, $140 fee. Preregistration for classes offered. Five 2-day sessions held each summer for students and parents. **Housing:** Guaranteed on-campus for freshmen. Coed dorms, single-sex dorms, special housing for disabled, apartments, fraternity/sorority housing, wellness housing available. $100 fully refundable deposit, deadline 4/9. Students must live in college housing until 60 semester hours completed. Off-campus housing permitted if student is 21 or older, married, commutes from permanent address of parent or relative, or enrolls for 8 hours or less. **Activities:** Bands, campus ministries, choral groups, dance, drama, film society, international student organizations, literary magazine, music ensembles, musical theater, opera, radio station, student government, student newspaper, symphony orchestra, TV station, African American student association, Canterbury Episcopal student association, Campus Crusade for Christ, Jewish student fellowship, Habitat for Humanity, SFA Democrats, Young Republicans, social services.

Athletics. NCAA. **Intercollegiate:** Baseball M, basketball, bowling W, cross-country, football (tackle) M, golf, soccer W, softball W, tennis W, track and field, volleyball W. **Intramural:** Badminton, baseball M, basketball, cross-country, football (non-tackle), lacrosse M, racquetball, rodeo, rugby, soccer M, softball, table tennis, tennis, volleyball, water polo, wrestling M. **Team name:** Lumberjacks/Ladyjacks.

Student services. Adult student services, alcohol/substance abuse counseling, career counseling, student employment services, financial aid counseling, health services, legal services, minority student services, on-campus daycare, personal counseling, placement for graduates, veterans' counselor. **Physically disabled:** Services for visually, speech, hearing impaired.

Contact. E-mail: admissions@sfasu.edu
Phone: (936) 468-2504 Fax: (936) 468-3849
Monique Cossich, Executive Director of Enrollment Management, Stephen F. Austin State University, Box 13051, SFA Station, Nacogdoches, TX 75962-3051

Sul Ross State University
Alpine, Texas   **CB member**
www.sulross.edu   **CB code: 6685**

- Public 4-year university
- Residential campus in small town
- 1,217 full-time, degree-seeking undergraduates
- SAT or ACT (ACT writing optional) required

General. Founded in 1917. Regionally accredited. Off-campus upper-level and graduate programs also available at Rio Grande College in Del Rio, Eagle Pass, and Uvalde. **Degrees:** 398 bachelor's, 6 associate awarded; master's offered. **Location:** 140 miles from Odessa, 220 miles from El Paso. **Calendar:** Semester, limited summer session. **Full-time faculty:** 127 total; 23% minority, 65% women. **Part-time faculty:** 47 total; 21% minority, 55% women. **Class size:** 64% < 20, 31% 20-39, 4% 40-49, less than 1% 50-99. **Special facilities:** Center for Big Bend studies, materials characterization laboratory.

Freshman class profile.

GPA 3.75 or higher:	7%	Rank in top quarter:	17%
GPA 3.50-3.74:	20%	Rank in top tenth:	6%
GPA 3.0-3.49:	42%	Out-of-state:	3%
GPA 2.0-2.99:	24%	Live on campus:	81%

Basis for selection. Students must meet one of following criteria: ACT score of 20, SAT score of 800 (exclusive of Writing), or rank in top half of graduating class. Probational admission for all other applicants.

High school preparation. College-preparatory program recommended. 15 units required; 31 recommended. Required and recommended units include English 4, mathematics 3-4, history 1-2, science 2-4 (laboratory 2), foreign language 3, computer science 1 and visual/performing arts 1. 1 U.S. government, 1 world history/geography, 1 economics, 1.5 physical education, 0.5 health education required; 1 health education, 4 technical area recommended.

2011-2012 Annual costs. Tuition/fees: $5,760; $15,150 out-of-state. Room/board: $6,810. Books/supplies: $1,200. Personal expenses: $3,100.

Application procedures. Admission: No deadline. $25 fee. Admission notification on a rolling basis. **Financial aid:** Priority date 3/1, closing date 4/1. FAFSA, institutional form required. Applicants notified on a rolling basis starting 5/1; must reply within 2 week(s) of notification.

Academics. Special study options: Cross-registration, distance learning, double major, dual enrollment of high school students, honors, independent study, internships, liberal arts/career combination, teacher certification program. **Credit/placement by examination:** AP, CLEP, institutional tests. 30 credit hours maximum toward bachelor's degree. **Support services:** Learning center, pre-admission summer program, reduced course load, remedial instruction, study skills assistance, tutoring, writing center.

Majors. Biology: General. **Business:** General, accounting, administrative services, business admin, finance, marketing, office management. **Communications:** Communications/speech/rhetoric. **Computer sciences:** General. **Conservation:** General, management/policy, wildlife/wilderness. **Education:** Elementary. **English:** English lit, rhetoric/composition. **Foreign languages:** Spanish. **General:** Agribusiness operations, animal health, animal sciences, equestrian studies, food science, range science. **History:** General. **Math:** General. **Parks/recreation:** Health/fitness. **Physical sciences:** Chemistry, geology. **Protective services:** Criminal justice. **Psychology:** General. **Social sciences:** General, political science. **Visual/performing arts:** Art, dramatic, music.

Most popular majors. Agriculture 6%, biology 6%, business/marketing 11%, English 7%, interdisciplinary studies 22%, liberal arts 8%, psychology 8%, security/protective services 9%.

Computing on campus. 200 workstations in library, computer center. Dormitories wired for high-speed internet access and linked to campus network. Commuter students can connect to campus network. Online library, helpline, repair service, wireless network available.

Student life. Freshman orientation: Available, $100 fee. Preregistration for classes offered. **Housing:** Guaranteed on-campus for freshmen. Coed dorms, apartments, wellness housing available. First-year experience. **Activities:** Bands, campus ministries, choral groups, dance, drama, music ensembles, musical theater, radio station, student government, student newspaper, Wesley Foundation, Newman Club, Baptist Student Union, Fellowship of Christian Athletes, Spanish club, rodeo club, black student association, international student association, nontraditional student association.

Athletics. NCAA. **Intercollegiate:** Baseball M, basketball, cross-country, football (tackle) M, softball W, tennis, track and field, volleyball W. **Intramural:** Basketball, football (non-tackle), racquetball, soccer, softball, tennis, volleyball, water polo, weight lifting. **Team name:** Lobos.

Student services. Alcohol/substance abuse counseling, chaplain/spiritual director, career counseling, student employment services, financial aid counseling, health services, on-campus daycare, personal counseling, placement for graduates, veterans' counselor. **Physically disabled:** Services for visually, hearing impaired.

Contact. E-mail: admissions@sulross.edu
Phone: (432) 837-8050 Toll-free number: (888) 722-7778
Fax: (432) 837-8186
Gregory Schwab, Associate VP for Enrollment Management, Sul Ross State University, PO Box C-2, Alpine, TX 79832

Tarleton State University
Stephenville, Texas   **CB member**
www.tarleton.edu   **CB code: 6817**

- Public 4-year university
- Residential campus in large town
- 8,470 degree-seeking undergraduates: 22% part-time, 59% women, 6% African American, 1% Asian American, 12% Hispanic American, 1% Native American
- 1,408 degree-seeking graduate students
- 86% of applicants admitted
- SAT or ACT (ACT writing recommended) required
- 40% graduate within 6 years

General. Founded in 1899. Regionally accredited. Courses available at several off-campus locations within 150-mile radius. **Degrees:** 1,525 bachelor's, 27 associate awarded; master's, doctoral offered. **ROTC:** Army. **Location:** 65 miles from Fort Worth. **Calendar:** Semester, extensive summer session. **Full-time faculty:** 282 total; less than 1% have terminal degrees, 11% minority, 48% women. **Part-time faculty:** 253 total; less than 1% have terminal degrees, 8% minority, 54% women. **Class size:** 49% < 20, 41% 20-39, 5% 40-49, 4% 50-99, less than 1% >100. **Special facilities:** University farm and equine center, planetarium.

Freshman class profile. 3,917 applied, 3,354 admitted, 1,577 enrolled.

Rank in top quarter:	24%	Live on campus:	75%
Rank in top tenth:	9%	Fraternities:	8%
Return as sophomores:	66%	Sororities:	7%
Out-of-state:	1%		

Basis for selection. Unconditional admission requires 950 combined SAT (exclusive of Writing) or 20 ACT. Rank in top quarter of class ensures unconditional admission if student has taken 4 years English and 3 years math. **Home schooled:** Must provide proof of curriculum completed from an agency or teacher. **Learning Disabled:** Contact Director of Disability Services for appropriate accommodation.

High school preparation. College-preparatory program recommended. 19 units required. Required and recommended units include English 4, mathematics 3, social studies 2, history 1, science 2-3 (laboratory 2), foreign language 2 and computer science 2-4.

2011-2012 Annual costs. Tuition/fees: $6,359; $15,749 out-of-state. Room/board: $7,474. Books/supplies: $1,174.

2010-2011 Financial aid. Need-based: 59% of total undergraduate aid awarded as scholarships/grants, 41% as loans/jobs. **Non-need-based:** Scholarships awarded for academics, alumni affiliation, art, athletics, leadership, music/drama, ROTC. **Additional information:** Tuition guarantee program covers tuition and fees for qualified freshman.

Application procedures. Admission: Priority date 3/1; no deadline. $30 fee. Admission notification on a rolling basis beginning on or about 9/1. **Financial aid:** Priority date 4/1; no closing date. FAFSA required. Applicants notified on a rolling basis starting 2/1.

Academics. Special study options: Accelerated study, distance learning, double major, dual enrollment of high school students, honors, internships,

study abroad, teacher certification program. Specialized bachelor of applied arts and science degree for students with practical work experience in field of study; cooperative doctoral program in educational administration offered in partnership with Texas A&M University-Commerce; 2-2 engineering with Texas A&M University and University of Texas Arlington. **Credit/placement by examination:** AP, CLEP, SAT, ACT, institutional tests. Students can earn the majority of credits toward their degree by examination. **Support services:** Learning center, pre-admission summer program, reduced course load, remedial instruction, study skills assistance, tutoring, writing center.

Majors. Biology: General, zoology. **Business:** General, accounting, business admin, finance, human resources, management information systems, marketing, office management. **Communications:** Communications/speech/rhetoric. **Computer sciences:** General. **Conservation:** Wildlife/wilderness. **Education:** Computer, science. **Engineering:** Applied physics, environmental. **English:** English lit. **Foreign languages:** Spanish. **General:** Agribusiness operations, agronomy, animal husbandry, animal sciences, business, economics, livestock, mechanization, ornamental horticulture, supplies. **Health services:** Clinical lab science, nursing (RN). **History:** General. **Human services:** Social work. **Liberal arts:** Arts/sciences. **Math:** General. **Parks/recreation:** Health/fitness. **Physical sciences:** Chemistry, geology, hydrology, physics. **Protective services:** Criminal justice. **Psychology:** General. **Social sciences:** Economics, political science, sociology. **Visual/performing arts:** Dramatic, music, music performance, studio arts. **Work/family studies:** General.

Most popular majors. Agriculture 13%, business/marketing 18%, interdisciplinary studies 17%, parks/recreation 11%, psychology 6%.

Computing on campus. 1,200 workstations in dormitories, library, computer center, student center. Dormitories wired for high-speed internet access and linked to campus network. Commuter students can connect to campus network. Online course registration, online library, helpline, repair service, student web hosting, wireless network available.

Student life. Freshman orientation: Mandatory, $100 fee. Preregistration for classes offered. Held multiple times during the summer. **Housing:** Guaranteed on-campus for freshmen. Coed dorms, single-sex dorms, apartments, wellness housing available. $100 nonrefundable deposit. **Activities:** Bands, campus ministries, choral groups, dance, drama, international student organizations, literary magazine, music ensembles, musical theater, radio station, student government, student newspaper, symphony orchestra, Los Tejanos, Chinese student association, progressive united Black student organization, student social work association, Alpha Phi Omega, Circle K, Fellowship of Christian Athletes, Fellowship of Christian Cowboys, College Republicans, Young Democrats.

Athletics. NCAA. **Intercollegiate:** Baseball M, basketball, cheerleading, cross-country, football (tackle) M, golf W, rodeo, softball W, tennis W, track and field, volleyball W. **Intramural:** Archery, basketball, football (nontackle) M, football (tackle), golf, racquetball, rodeo, soccer, softball, table tennis, tennis, volleyball. **Team name:** Texans.

Student services. Adult student services, alcohol/substance abuse counseling, chaplain/spiritual director, career counseling, student employment services, financial aid counseling, health services, legal services, minority student services, on-campus daycare, personal counseling, placement for graduates, veterans' counselor. **Physically disabled:** Services for visually, speech, hearing impaired.

Contact. E-mail: uadm@tarleton.edu
Phone: (254) 968-9125 Toll-free number: (800) 687-8236
Fax: (254) 968-9951
Cindy Hess, Director of Admissions, Tarleton State University, Box T-0030, Stephenville, TX 76402

Texas A&M International University
Laredo, Texas
www.tamiu.edu

CB member
CB code: 0359

- Public 4-year university
- Commuter campus in small city
- 6,068 degree-seeking undergraduates: 37% part-time, 59% women, 1% African American, 1% Asian American, 94% Hispanic American, 2% international
- 805 degree-seeking graduate students
- 50% of applicants admitted
- SAT or ACT (ACT writing recommended) required
- 42% graduate within 6 years; 14% enter graduate study

General. Founded in 1969. Regionally accredited. **Degrees:** 777 bachelor's awarded; master's, doctoral offered. **ROTC:** Army. **Location:** 150 miles from San Antonio and Corpus Christi. **Calendar:** Semester, extensive summer

session. **Full-time faculty:** 218 total; 66% have terminal degrees, 41% minority, 45% women. **Part-time faculty:** 89 total; 15% have terminal degrees, 74% minority, 47% women. **Class size:** 33% < 20, 45% 20-39, 8% 40-49, 12% 50-99, 3% >100. **Special facilities:** Planetarium.

Freshman class profile. 4,389 applied, 2,184 admitted, 984 enrolled.

Mid 50% test scores			
SAT critical reading:	390-480	GPA 2.0-2.99:	2%
SAT math:	430-510	Rank in top quarter:	53%
SAT writing:	390-480	Rank in top tenth:	23%
ACT composite:	16-20	End year in good standing:	91%
GPA 3.75 or higher:	39%	Return as sophomores:	69%
GPA 3.50-3.74:	40%	Out-of-state:	1%
GPA 3.0-3.49:	17%	International:	2%

Basis for selection. Students in top 40% of graduating class admitted with no minimum ACT or SAT score. Students in bottom 60% need minimum score of 900 on SAT (exclusive of Writing) or 19 on ACT.

High school preparation. Required and recommended units include English 4, mathematics 3, social studies 3, history 3, science 2, foreign language 2 and academic electives 2. 1 computer technology, 1 fine arts required; three years of foreign language recommended.

2011-2012 Annual costs. Tuition/fees: $6,558; $15,858 out-of-state. Room/board: $6,918.

Financial aid. Non-need-based: Scholarships awarded for academics.

Application procedures. Admission: Closing date 7/1 (postmark date). No application fee. Admission notification on a rolling basis beginning on or about 11/1. **Financial aid:** Priority date 3/15; no closing date. FAFSA, institutional form required. Applicants notified on a rolling basis starting 4/15; must reply within 2 week(s) of notification.

Academics. Special study options: Cooperative education, cross-registration, distance learning, double major, dual enrollment of high school students, ESL, honors, independent study, internships, liberal arts/career combination, study abroad, teacher certification program. **Credit/placement by examination:** AP, CLEP, IB, SAT, ACT, institutional tests. 33 credit hours maximum toward bachelor's degree. **Support services:** Learning center, pre-admission summer program, reduced course load, remedial instruction, study skills assistance, tutoring, writing center.

Majors. Biology: General. **Business:** Accounting, business admin, finance, management information systems, managerial economics, marketing. **Communications:** Communications/speech/rhetoric. **Conservation:** General. **Education:** Bilingual, biology, early childhood, elementary, English, history, mathematics, reading, social studies, Spanish, special ed. **English:** English lit. **Foreign languages:** Spanish. **Health services:** Nursing (RN), preop/surgical nursing. **History:** General. **Math:** General. **Parks/recreation:** Health/fitness. **Physical sciences:** Chemistry. **Protective services:** Criminal justice. **Psychology:** General. **Social sciences:** General, political science, sociology, urban studies.

Most popular majors. Business/marketing 22%, health sciences 12%, interdisciplinary studies 23%, psychology 8%, security/protective services 8%.

Computing on campus. 200 workstations in dormitories, library, computer center. Dormitories wired for high-speed internet access and linked to campus network. Commuter students can connect to campus network. Wireless network available.

Student life. Freshman orientation: Mandatory, $75 fee. Preregistration for classes offered. 4 overnight sessions held June-August and 1 one-day session in August for late registrants. **Housing:** Apartments available. On-campus housing, not owned by college (private contractor) available. **Activities:** Bands, campus ministries, choral groups, dance, drama, international student organizations, literary magazine, music ensembles, student government, student newspaper, student ambassadors, Association of International Students, Tau Sigma Chi (criminal justice), High Twisters, Ballet Folklorico, student system group, student finance society, student government association.

Athletics. NCAA. **Intercollegiate:** Baseball M, basketball, cross-country, golf, soccer, softball W, volleyball W. **Intramural:** Baseball, basketball, soccer, table tennis, volleyball, weight lifting. **Team name:** Dust Devils.

Student services. Career counseling, services for economically disadvantaged, student employment services, financial aid counseling, health services, personal counseling, placement for graduates, veterans' counselor. **Physically disabled:** Services for visually, speech, hearing impaired.

Contact. E-mail: enroll@tamiu.edu
Phone: (956) 326-2200 Fax: (956) 326-2199
Rosa Dickinson, Director of Admissions, Texas A&M International
University, 5201 University Boulevard, Laredo, TX 78041-1900

Texas A&M University
College Station, Texas
CB member
www.tamu.edu
CB code: 6003

- Public 4-year university
- Residential campus in small city
- 39,751 degree-seeking undergraduates: 8% part-time, 48% women, 3% African American, 5% Asian American, 17% Hispanic American, 1% international
- 9,830 degree-seeking graduate students
- 64% of applicants admitted
- SAT or ACT with writing, application essay required
- 80% graduate within 6 years

General. Founded in 1876. Regionally accredited. **Degrees:** 8,747 bachelor's awarded; master's, professional, doctoral offered. **ROTC:** Army, Naval, Air Force. **Location:** 90 miles from Houston, 100 miles from Austin. **Calendar:** Semester, extensive summer session. **Full-time faculty:** 2,097 total; 92% have terminal degrees, 24% minority, 31% women. **Part-time faculty:** 404 total; 79% have terminal degrees, 18% minority, 29% women. **Class size:** 19% <20, 49% 20-39, 7% 40-49, 14% 50-99, 10% >100. **Special facilities:** Reactor, cyclotron, observatory, agriculture research property, 18-hole golf course, supercomputer center, oceanographic research vessel, Italian study center, George H. W. Bush Presidential Library and Museum.

Freshman class profile. 25,949 applied, 16,489 admitted, 8,254 enrolled.

Mid 50% test scores			
SAT critical reading:	530-650	Rank in top tenth:	55%
SAT math:	570-670	Return as sophomores:	92%
SAT writing:	510-620	Out-of-state:	4%
ACT composite:	23-30	Live on campus:	65%
Rank in top quarter:	90%	International:	1%

Basis for selection. Automatic admission to applicants in top 10% of Texas high school class (with completed application), as specified by state law. Strong senior year course schedule recommended. Test scores required of all applicants but not used for admission of applicants from top 10% of any Texas high school class. **Learning Disabled:** Must provide documentation from qualified professional licensed or certified to diagnose disability.

High school preparation. College-preparatory program required. 18 units required; 19 recommended. Required and recommended units include English 4, mathematics 3.5, social studies 2, history 1, science 3 (laboratory 2), foreign language 2 and computer science 1.

2011-2012 Annual costs. Tuition/fees: $8,419; $23,809 out-of-state. Room/board: $8,200. Books/supplies: $1,340. Personal expenses: $2,262.

2010-2011 Financial aid. **Need-based:** 5,531 full-time freshmen applied for aid; 3,472 were judged to have need; 3,423 of these received aid. Average need met was 78%. Average scholarship/grant was $11,310; average loan $5,200. 66% of total undergraduate aid awarded as scholarships/grants, 34% as loans/jobs. **Non-need-based:** Awarded to 2,789 full-time undergraduates, including 1,226 freshmen. Scholarships awarded for academics, alumni affiliation, art, athletics, job skills, leadership, music/drama, religious affiliation, ROTC, state residency. **Additional information:** Short-term loans available. Out-of-state students awarded academic scholarships of $1,000 or more are eligible for waiver of out-of-state tuition. Texas residents: Regents scholarship provides an additional $5,000 annually for 4 years for first-generation students incomes with >$40,000.

Application procedures. **Admission:** Priority date 12/1; deadline 1/15 (receipt date). $60 fee, may be waived for applicants with need. Admission notification on a rolling basis beginning on or about 4/1. Must reply by 5/1. Housing deposit due at time of application. **Financial aid:** Priority date 3/1; no closing date. FAFSA required. Applicants notified on a rolling basis starting 3/15.

Academics. Core curriculum requirements in foreign language and computer science may be satisfied by selected high school courses. **Special study options:** Accelerated study, combined bachelor's/graduate degree, cooperative education, distance learning, double major, dual enrollment of high school students, ESL, exchange student, honors, independent study, internships, liberal arts/career combination, study abroad, teacher certification program. Exchange programs in architecture with Instituto Tecnológico y de Estudios Superiores de Monterrey, King's College London (England), University of Lancaster (England), Denmark's international study program, Ruhr University Bochum (Germany), University of Lausanne (Switzerland). **Credit/placement by examination:** AP, CLEP, IB, institutional tests. **Support services:** Learning center, pre-admission summer program, remedial instruction, tutoring, writing center.

Majors. **Architecture:** Architecture, environmental design, landscape. **Area/ethnic studies:** American. **Biology:** General, biochemistry, biomedical sciences, botany, cellular/molecular, entomology, environmental, microbiology, molecular genetics, zoology. **Business:** Accounting, finance, management science, marketing, sales/distribution, tourism promotion, tourism/travel. **Communications:** Digital media, journalism. **Computer sciences:** Computer science. **Conservation:** General, environmental science, environmental studies, forest management, forestry, management/policy, urban forestry, wildlife/wilderness. **Engineering:** Aerospace, agricultural, biomedical, chemical, civil, computer, electrical, geological, industrial, mechanical, nuclear, ocean, petroleum. **English:** English lit, rhetoric/composition. **Foreign languages:** Classics, French, German, Russian, Spanish. **General:** Agribusiness operations, agronomy, animal husbandry, animal sciences, aquaculture, business, communications, dairy, economics, farm/ranch, food science, horticultural science, horticulture, ornamental horticulture, plant protection, plant sciences, poultry, production, range science, soil science, supplies, turf management. **Health services:** Community health services, preveterinary. **History:** General. **Human services:** Community org/advocacy. **Math:** General, applied. **Parks/recreation:** General, facilities management, health/fitness. **Philosophy/religion:** Philosophy. **Physical sciences:** Atmospheric science, chemistry, geology, geophysics, physics. **Protective services:** Forensics. **Psychology:** General. **Social sciences:** Anthropology, economics, geography, GIS/cartography, political science, sociology. **Visual/performing arts:** Dramatic, music. **Work/family studies:** Food/nutrition.

Most popular majors. Agriculture 10%, biology 8%, business/marketing 18%, engineering/engineering technologies 17%, interdisciplinary studies 9%, social sciences 7%.

Computing on campus. 1,979 workstations in dormitories, library, computer center, student center. Dormitories wired for high-speed internet access and linked to campus network. Commuter students can connect to campus network. Online course registration, online library, helpline, repair service, student web hosting, wireless network available.

Student life. **Freshman orientation:** Mandatory, $35 fee. Preregistration for classes offered. Numerous 2-1/2 day programs offered throughout the summer. **Housing:** Coed dorms, single-sex dorms, special housing for disabled, apartments, cooperative housing, fraternity/sorority housing, wellness housing available. $300 fully refundable deposit. Campus housing guaranteed to members of Corps of Cadets and recipients of major 4-year endowed academic scholarships. Freshman honors dorm available. **Activities:** Bands, campus ministries, choral groups, dance, drama, film society, international student organizations, literary magazine, music ensembles, musical theater, radio station, student government, student newspaper, symphony orchestra, TV station, Black awareness committee, committee for the awareness of Mexican American culture, student Y association, student conference on national affairs, social service organizations, College Republicans, Aggie Democrats, political forum, Aggies for Christ, Corps of Cadets.

Athletics. NCAA. **Intercollegiate:** Archery W, baseball M, basketball, cross-country, diving, equestrian W, football (tackle) M, golf, soccer W, softball W, swimming, tennis, track and field, volleyball W. **Intramural:** Archery, badminton, basketball, bowling, diving, golf, lacrosse, racquetball, rodeo, soccer, softball, squash, swimming, table tennis, track and field, volleyball. **Team name:** Aggies.

Student services. Alcohol/substance abuse counseling, career counseling, student employment services, financial aid counseling, health services, legal services, minority student services, on-campus daycare, personal counseling, placement for graduates, veterans' counselor, women's services. **Physically disabled:** Services for visually, speech, hearing impaired.

Contact. E-mail: admissions@tamu.edu
Phone: (979) 845-1060 Fax: (979) 458-1808
Lynn Barnes, Director of Recruitment, Texas A&M University, PO Box 30014, College Station, TX 77842-3014

Texas A&M University-Baylor College of Dentistry
Dallas, Texas
www.bcd.tamhsc.edu
CB code: 6059

- Public two-year upper-division health science college
- Commuter campus in very large city
- 23% of applicants admitted
- Application essay, interview required

General. Founded in 1905. Regionally accredited. **Degrees:** 28 bachelor's awarded; master's, professional, doctoral offered. **Articulation:** Agreement with Collin County Community College District. **Calendar:** Semester. **Full-time faculty:** 116 total; 97% have terminal degrees, 28% minority, 40% women. **Part-time faculty:** 128 total; 92% have terminal degrees, 23% minority, 30% women.

Student profile. 54 degree-seeking undergraduates, 519 degree-seeking graduate students. 146 applied as first time-transfer students, 33 admitted, 27 enrolled. 60% transferred from two-year, 40% transferred from four-year institutions.

Women:	98%	Hispanic American:	13%
African American:	6%	Out-of-state:	4%
Asian American:	13%	25 or older:	25%

Basis for selection. High school transcript, college transcript, application essay, interview required. School achievement most important. Essay, interview, and recommendations highly considered. Transfer accepted as juniors.

2012-2013 Annual costs. Tuition/fees (projected): $6,450; $17,450 out-of-state. Personal expenses: $2,850.

Financial aid. Need-based: 54 applied for aid; 52 were judged to have need; 52 of these received aid. Average need met was 44%. 27% of total undergraduate aid awarded as scholarships/grants, 73% as loans/jobs. **Non-need-based:** Scholarships awarded for academics.

Application procedures. Admission: Priority date 12/31. $35 fee. **Financial aid:** FAFSA, institutional form required.

Academics. Participation in research activities under faculty sponsorship and annual research fellowships awarded by college offered. **Special study options:** Combined bachelor's/graduate degree, internships. **Credit/placement by examination:** AP, CLEP.

Majors. Health services: Dental hygiene.

Computing on campus. 25 workstations in library, computer center. Commuter students can connect to campus network. Online library, helpline, wireless network available.

Student life. Housing: Baylor Medical Center nursing dormitory housing available. **Activities:** Student government.

Student services. Student employment services, financial aid counseling, health services, personal counseling.

Contact. Phone: (214) 828-8230 Fax: (214) 828-8346
Barbara Miller, Director, Texas A&M University-Baylor College of Dentistry, PO Box 660677, Dallas, TX 75266-0677

Texas A&M University-Commerce
Commerce, Texas
www.tamu-commerce.edu

CB member
CB code: 6188

- Public 4-year university
- Commuter campus in small town
- 6,618 degree-seeking undergraduates
- 4,125 graduate students
- 44% of applicants admitted
- SAT or ACT with writing required

General. Founded in 1889. Regionally accredited. **Degrees:** 1,286 bachelor's awarded; master's, doctoral offered. **Location:** 60 miles from Dallas. **Calendar:** Semester, extensive summer session. **Full-time faculty:** 287 total. **Part-time faculty:** 195 total. **Class size:** 53% < 20, 33% 20-39, 6% 40-49, 7% 50-99, less than 1% >100. **Special facilities:** Instructional university farm, planetarium.

Freshman class profile. 4,712 applied, 2,073 admitted, 809 enrolled.

Mid 50% test scores		GPA 3.0-3.49:	34%
SAT critical reading:	420-530	GPA 2.0-2.99:	34%
SAT math:	440-540	Rank in top quarter:	39%
ACT composite:	18-24	Rank in top tenth:	17%
GPA 3.75 or higher:	16%	Out-of-state:	2%
GPA 3.50-3.74:	14%		

Basis for selection. ACT or SAT scores most important, followed by high school grades and class rank. Students admitted with 20 ACT or 920 SAT (exclusive of Writing). TASP scores may exempt student from SAT or ACT tests. If student is TASP remedial, must take TASP within first semester of enrolling. Portfolio required for advertising art program; audition

recommended for music program. **Home schooled:** Must earn GED and be at least 18 years of age.

High school preparation. 12 units required. Required and recommended units include English 4, mathematics 3, science 2 and foreign language 2. 2.5 hours history/social studies required.

2011-2012 Annual costs. Tuition/fees: $6,283; $15,673 out-of-state. Room/board: $6,750. Books/supplies: $1,400. Personal expenses: $1,830.

Financial aid. Non-need-based: Scholarships awarded for academics, art, athletics, leadership, music/drama. **Additional information:** Work-study also available for full-time students.

Application procedures. Admission: Priority date 8/1; no deadline. No application fee. Admission notification on a rolling basis. High school seniors may enroll part-time before graduation with consent of high school principal if they meet requirements. **Financial aid:** Priority date 4/1, closing date 6/30. FAFSA required. Applicants notified on a rolling basis starting 4/1; must reply within 2 week(s) of notification.

Academics. Special study options: Combined bachelor's/graduate degree, cooperative education, distance learning, double major, dual enrollment of high school students, external degree, honors, independent study, internships, liberal arts/career combination, study abroad, teacher certification program, weekend college. **Credit/placement by examination:** AP, CLEP, IB, SAT, ACT, institutional tests. 6 credit hours maximum toward bachelor's degree. **Support services:** Learning center, pre-admission summer program, remedial instruction, study skills assistance, tutoring, writing center.

Majors. Biology: General, cell/histology. **Business:** General, accounting, business admin, human resources, management information systems, managerial economics, marketing, office management, office/clerical, operations, public finance. **Communications:** Advertising, broadcast journalism, communications/speech/rhetoric, digital media, journalism, public relations. **Communications technology:** Graphic/printing. **Computer sciences:** General, computer science, information systems. **Conservation:** General, environmental studies, wildlife/wilderness. **Education:** Bilingual, biology, chemistry, driver/safety, early childhood, elementary, middle, multi-level teacher, physical, special ed. **Engineering:** Operations research. **English:** American lit, British lit, English lit, rhetoric/composition, writing. **Foreign languages:** German, Spanish. **General:** Animal sciences, communications, economics, food science, plant sciences, soil science. **Health services:** Athletic training, health care admin, medical records admin, predental, premedicine, prepharmacy, preveterinary. **History:** General. **Human services:** Social work. **Liberal arts:** Arts/sciences, library science. **Math:** General. **Parks/recreation:** Health/fitness. **Physical sciences:** Chemistry, geology, organic chemistry, physics, planetary. **Protective services:** Criminal justice, law enforcement admin. **Psychology:** General. **Social sciences:** General, anthropology, criminology, economics, geography, political science, sociology. **Theology:** Preministerial. **Visual/performing arts:** General, art, ceramics, commercial photography, commercial/advertising art, design, dramatic, industrial design, metal/jewelry, music, music history, music pedagogy, music performance, music theory/composition, musicology, painting, photography, piano/keyboard, printmaking, sculpture, studio arts management, voice/opera.

Most popular majors. Business/marketing 8%, education 25%, interdisciplinary studies 33%.

Computing on campus. 1,500 workstations in dormitories, library, computer center, student center. Dormitories wired for high-speed internet access and linked to campus network. Commuter students can connect to campus network. Online course registration, online library, helpline, repair service, wireless network available.

Student life. Freshman orientation: Mandatory, $100 fee. Preregistration for classes offered. Held throughout summer; includes advising, assessment testing, and parental involvement. **Housing:** Coed dorms, single-sex dorms, special housing for disabled, apartments, fraternity/sorority housing, wellness housing available. $100 deposit, deadline 7/1. Shared freshman experience housing available. **Activities:** Bands, choral groups, dance, drama, film society, literary magazine, music ensembles, musical theater, opera, radio station, student government, student newspaper, symphony orchestra, TV station, Baptist student union, Church of Christ Bible chair, Newman Club, university Christian center, Young Democrats, association cultural de Hispanos-Americanos, Chinese student association, Muslim society, NAACP, Thai students association, Alpha Phi Omega.

Athletics. NCAA. **Intercollegiate:** Basketball, cross-country, football (tackle) M, golf, soccer W, track and field, volleyball W. **Intramural:** Archery, badminton, baseball M, basketball, bowling, cross-country, golf, racquetball, softball, swimming, table tennis, tennis, track and field, volleyball. **Team name:** Lions.

Student services. Alcohol/substance abuse counseling, chaplain/spiritual director, career counseling, student employment services, financial aid counseling, health services, legal services, on-campus daycare, personal counseling, placement for graduates, veterans' counselor. **Physically disabled:** Services for visually, speech, hearing impaired.

Contact. E-mail: hope_youngl@tamu-commerce.edu
Phone: (903) 886-5102 Toll-free number: (888) 886-2682
Fax: (903) 468-6080
Jody Todhunter, Director of Undergraduate Admissions, Texas A&M University-Commerce, Box 3011, Commerce, TX 75429-3011

Texas A&M University-Corpus Christi
Corpus Christi, Texas — **CB member**
www.tamucc.edu — **CB code: 0366**

▸ Public 4-year university
▸ Commuter campus in large city
▸ 8,254 degree-seeking undergraduates: 21% part-time, 60% women, 5% African American, 5% Asian American, 43% Hispanic American, 1% Native American, 4% international
▸ 1,799 degree-seeking graduate students
▸ 85% of applicants admitted
▸ SAT or ACT (ACT writing optional) required
▸ 36% graduate within 6 years

General. Founded in 1947. Regionally accredited. **Degrees:** 1,308 bachelor's awarded; master's, doctoral offered. **ROTC:** Army. **Location:** 150 miles from San Antonio, 200 miles from Houston. **Calendar:** Semester, extensive summer session. **Full-time faculty:** 317 total; 78% have terminal degrees, 19% minority, 45% women. **Part-time faculty:** 230 total; 78% have terminal degrees, 24% minority, 62% women. **Class size:** 22% < 20, 54% 20-39, 6% 40-49, 11% 50-99, 5% >100. **Special facilities:** National spill control school, institute for surveying and science, center for coastal studies, center for environmental studies and services, early childhood development center, South Texas Institute for the Arts.

Freshman class profile. 5,732 applied, 4,879 admitted, 1,422 enrolled.

Mid 50% test scores			
SAT critical reading:	420-520	Rank in top quarter:	39%
SAT math:	440-540	Rank in top tenth:	13%
SAT writing:	410-510	Return as sophomores:	60%
ACT composite:	17-23	Out-of-state:	2%
GPA 3.75 or higher:	13%	Live on campus:	15%
GPA 3.50-3.74:	19%	International:	3%
GPA 3.0-3.49:	42%	Fraternities:	5%
GPA 2.0-2.99:	25%	Sororities:	5%

Basis for selection. High school GPA, class rank, and course work most important. Test scores, school and community leadership activities, special talents also considered. Minimum 900 SAT (exclusive of Writing), required. Applicants not meeting minimum requirements may apply to admission committee for special consideration. Local placement exams in reading, writing and math required of all first-time freshmen.

High school preparation. 15 units required. Required units include English 4, mathematics 3, social studies 3, science 3 and foreign language 2.

2011-2012 Annual costs. Tuition/fees: $6,718; $16,133 out-of-state. Room/board: $9,500. Books/supplies: $966. Personal expenses: $1,436.

Financial aid. **Non-need-based:** Scholarships awarded for academics, art, athletics, leadership, music/drama, ROTC.

Application procedures. **Admission:** Closing date 7/1 (receipt date). $25 fee. Admission notification on a rolling basis. **Financial aid:** Priority date 3/31; no closing date. FAFSA required. Applicants notified on a rolling basis starting 4/1; must reply within 2 week(s) of notification.

Academics. **Special study options:** Combined bachelor's/graduate degree, cooperative education, distance learning, double major, dual enrollment of high school students, ESL, honors, independent study, internships, study abroad, teacher certification program. **Credit/placement by examination:** AP, CLEP, IB, SAT, ACT, institutional tests. DANTES, ACT, PEP accepted. **Support services:** Learning center, remedial instruction, study skills assistance, tutoring, writing center.

Majors. **Biology:** General, biomedical sciences. **Business:** General, accounting, business admin, finance, management information systems, managerial economics, marketing. **Communications:** Communications/speech/rhetoric. **Computer sciences:** General. **Conservation:** General. **Engineering:** Mechanical. **English:** English lit. **Foreign languages:** Spanish. **Health services:** Athletic training, clinical lab science, clinical nurse specialist, nurse practitioner, nursing (RN). **History:** General. **Math:** General. **Parks/recreation:** Health/fitness. **Physical sciences:** Chemistry, geology. **Protective services:** Criminal justice. **Psychology:** General. **Social sciences:** Economics, political science, sociology. **Visual/performing arts:** General, music, studio arts.

Most popular majors. Biology 10%, business/marketing 18%, communications/journalism 6%, health sciences 13%, interdisciplinary studies 16%, psychology 6%.

Computing on campus. 500 workstations in library, computer center. Dormitories wired for high-speed internet access and linked to campus network. Online course registration, online library, helpline, repair service, student web hosting, wireless network available.

Student life. **Freshman orientation:** Available. Preregistration for classes offered. Program held various times in summer before fall entry. **Policies:** No alcohol on campus except by adult students in their own apartments. **Housing:** Guaranteed on-campus for freshmen. Coed dorms, apartments available. $20 nonrefundable deposit. **Activities:** Bands, campus ministries, choral groups, dance, drama, international student organizations, music ensembles, student government, student newspaper, Baptist student union, Newman Club, Friends Meeting, LDS students association, Amigos, computer science club, African-American cultural society.

Athletics. NCAA. **Intercollegiate:** Baseball, basketball, cross-country, golf W, softball W, tennis, track and field, volleyball W. **Intramural:** Badminton, baseball M, basketball, cross-country, golf, racquetball, soccer, softball, swimming, table tennis, tennis, track and field, volleyball. **Team name:** Islanders.

Student services. Alcohol/substance abuse counseling, chaplain/spiritual director, career counseling, student employment services, financial aid counseling, health services, personal counseling, placement for graduates, veterans' counselor. **Physically disabled:** Services for visually, speech, hearing impaired.

Contact. E-mail: admiss@tamucc.edu
Phone: (361) 825-2624 Toll-free number: (800) 482-6822
Fax: (361) 825-5887
Christopher Fleming, Director of Admissions, Texas A&M University-Corpus Christi, 6300 Ocean Drive, Unit 5774, Corpus Christi, TX 78412-5774

Texas A&M University-Galveston
Galveston, Texas — **CB member**
www.tamug.edu — **CB code: 6835**

▸ Public 4-year university and branch campus college
▸ Residential campus in small city
▸ 1,948 degree-seeking undergraduates: 7% part-time, 38% women, 3% African American, 2% Asian American, 15% Hispanic American, 1% Native American, 1% international
▸ 83 degree-seeking graduate students
▸ 69% of applicants admitted
▸ SAT or ACT with writing, application essay required
▸ 30% graduate within 6 years

General. Founded in 1962. Regionally accredited. Institution houses Texas Maritime Academy, 1 of 5 seacoast maritime academies in the U.S. preparing graduates for licensing as officers in the Merchant Marine. **Degrees:** 250 bachelor's awarded; master's, doctoral offered. **ROTC:** Naval. **Location:** 50 miles from Houston. **Calendar:** Semester, limited summer session. **Full-time faculty:** 98 total. **Part-time faculty:** 57 total. **Class size:** 67% < 20, 23% 20-39, 4% 40-49, 4% 50-99, 2% >100. **Special facilities:** Fleet of research and training boats, 300-acre wetlands on west Galveston Bay, wetlands research center, ship bridge simulator.

Freshman class profile. 1,716 applied, 1,187 admitted, 592 enrolled.

Mid 50% test scores			
SAT critical reading:	480-580	Rank in top tenth:	11%
SAT math:	510-600	End year in good standing:	50%
ACT composite:	21-25	Return as sophomores:	47%
Rank in top quarter:	40%	Out-of-state:	14%
		Live on campus:	75%

Basis for selection. School achievement record and test scores most important. Adverse circumstances, leadership, exceptional talents, course selections, and references reviewed on individual basis. **Home schooled:** Transcript of courses and grades, letter of recommendation (nonparent) required.

High school preparation. College-preparatory program recommended. 13 units required; 19 recommended. Required and recommended units include English 4, mathematics 3-4, social studies 3, science 3-4 (laboratory 2) and foreign language 3. 1 unit computer literacy required. Science courses must be selected from biology, chemistry or physics.

2011-2012 Annual costs. Tuition/fees: $7,226; $16,616 out-of-state. Room/board: $7,126. Books/supplies: $1,340. Personal expenses: $262.

Financial aid. Non-need-based: Scholarships awarded for academics, state residency.

Application procedures. Admission: Closing date 8/1 (postmark date). $45 fee, may be waived for applicants with need. Admission notification on a rolling basis. **Financial aid:** Priority date 4/1; no closing date. FAFSA required. Applicants notified on a rolling basis starting 3/15; must reply within 3 week(s) of notification.

Academics. All academic programs are ocean-related. USCG ship officer's license may be earned through license option program. **Special study options:** Accelerated study, combined bachelor's/graduate degree, cooperative education, double major, dual enrollment of high school students, independent study, internships, liberal arts/career combination, semester at sea, study abroad, teacher certification program. Merchant marine licensing program available with marine biology, marine science, marine transportation, and marine engineering technology degrees. **Credit/placement by examination:** AP, CLEP, IB, institutional tests. **Support services:** Learning center, pre-admission summer program, remedial instruction, study skills assistance, tutoring.

Majors. Biology: General, aquatic, biomedical sciences, botany, marine, zoology. **Business:** Business admin, international, international finance, tourism/travel, transportation. **Conservation:** General, fisheries. **Education:** Biology, science. **Engineering:** Marine, ocean, systems. **General:** Aquaculture. **Liberal arts:** Arts/sciences. **Parks/recreation:** General. **Physical sciences:** General, geology, hydrology, oceanography.

Most popular majors. Biology 31%, business/marketing 21%, engineering/engineering technologies 13%, interdisciplinary studies 7%, natural resources/environmental science 11%, trade and industry 12%.

Computing on campus. 130 workstations in dormitories, library, computer center. Dormitories wired for high-speed internet access and linked to campus network. Commuter students can connect to campus network. Online library, helpline, repair service, wireless network available.

Student life. Freshman orientation: Mandatory, $75 fee. Preregistration for classes offered. 4 days in June and August. **Housing:** Coed dorms, single-sex dorms, special housing for disabled, apartments, wellness housing available. $250 fully refundable deposit. **Activities:** Choral groups, dance, drama, literary magazine, student government, student newspaper, Circle K, Campus Crusade for Christ, emergency care team, outdoor and environmental conservation, Catholic student association, SEED (Students Encouraging Ethnic Diversity), Wesley Foundation.

Athletics. Intercollegiate: Rowing (crew), sailing. **Intramural:** Basketball, football (non-tackle), racquetball, soccer, softball, tennis, volleyball, water polo. **Team name:** Aggies.

Student services. Alcohol/substance abuse counseling, chaplain/spiritual director, career counseling, student employment services, financial aid counseling, health services, minority student services, personal counseling, placement for graduates, veterans' counselor. **Physically disabled:** Services for hearing impaired.

Contact. E-mail: seaaggie@tamug.edu
Phone: (409) 740-4414 Toll-free number: (877) 322-4443
Fax: (409) 740-4731
Cheryl Moon, Executive Director of Enrollment Services, Texas A&M University-Galveston, PO Box 1675, Galveston, TX 77553-1675

Texas A&M University-Kingsville
Kingsville, Texas   **CB member**
www.tamuk.edu   **CB code: 6822**

- Public 4-year university
- Commuter campus in large town
- 5,551 degree-seeking undergraduates: 18% part-time, 49% women, 6% African American, 69% Hispanic American, 1% international
- 1,135 degree-seeking graduate students
- 37% graduate within 6 years

General. Founded in 1925. Regionally accredited. **Degrees:** 831 bachelor's awarded; master's, doctoral offered. **ROTC:** Army. **Location:** 40 miles from Corpus Christi, 250 miles from Houston. **Calendar:** Semester, extensive summer session. **Full-time faculty:** 304 total; 22% minority, 34% women. **Part-time faculty:** 84 total; 39% minority, 56% women. **Class size:** 31% < 20, 59% 20-39, 5% 40-49, 5% 50-99, less than 1% >100. **Special facilities:** Equine facilities, observatory, college-operated farms, research center for citrus, museum, venomous toxin research, greenhouses, extensive engineering facilities.

Freshman class profile.

Mid 50% test scores			
SAT critical reading:	410-520	Rank in top quarter:	25%
SAT math:	410-520	Rank in top tenth:	15%
SAT writing:	360-460	End year in good standing:	46%
ACT composite:	15-20	Return as sophomores:	56%
GPA 3.75 or higher:	15%	Out-of-state:	1%
GPA 3.50-3.74:	20%	Live on campus:	60%
GPA 3.0-3.49:	40%	Fraternities:	2%
GPA 2.0-2.99:	25%	Sororities:	2%

Basis for selection. Audition required, portfolio recommended for music program.

High school preparation. College-preparatory program recommended. 24 units recommended. Recommended units include English 4, mathematics 3, social studies 4, history 3, science 3, foreign language 3 and academic electives 3. One fine arts, 1 computer recommended.

2011-2012 Annual costs. Tuition/fees: $6,640; $16,030 out-of-state. Room/board: $6,138. Books/supplies: $614. Personal expenses: $2,108.

Financial aid. Non-need-based: Scholarships awarded for academics, alumni affiliation, art, athletics, job skills, leadership, music/drama, ROTC, state residency.

Application procedures. Admission: No deadline. $15 fee, may be waived for applicants with need. Admission notification on a rolling basis. **Financial aid:** Priority date 3/31; no closing date. FAFSA required. Applicants notified on a rolling basis starting 5/1.

Academics. Special study options: Combined bachelor's/graduate degree, cooperative education, distance learning, double major, dual enrollment of high school students, ESL, honors, internships, study abroad, teacher certification program. **Credit/placement by examination:** AP, CLEP, institutional tests. **Support services:** Remedial instruction, study skills assistance, tutoring.

Majors. Architecture: Interior. **Biology:** General. **Business:** General, accounting, finance, international, management information systems, management science, managerial economics. **Communications:** Communications/speech/rhetoric. **Conservation:** Wildlife/wilderness. **Education:** General, agricultural, art, bilingual, elementary, family/consumer sciences, health, music, physical, secondary. **Engineering:** Chemical, civil, computer, electrical, mechanical, petroleum. **English:** English lit. **Foreign languages:** Spanish. **General:** Agribusiness operations, animal sciences, business, food science, plant sciences, range science. **Health services:** Speech pathology. **History:** General. **Math:** General. **Physical sciences:** Chemistry, geology, physics. **Psychology:** General. **Social sciences:** Political science, sociology. **Visual/performing arts:** Dramatic, interior design, music, studio arts. **Work/family studies:** General, clothing/textiles, family studies, food/nutrition.

Most popular majors. Business/marketing 17%, engineering/engineering technologies 13%, interdisciplinary studies 27%, parks/recreation 6%, social sciences 7%.

Computing on campus. Dormitories linked to campus network. Commuter students can connect to campus network. Online course registration, online library, helpline, repair service, wireless network available.

Student life. Freshman orientation: Mandatory. Preregistration for classes offered. **Housing:** Guaranteed on-campus for freshmen. Coed dorms, single-sex dorms, apartments available. $150 partly refundable deposit. **Activities:** Bands, campus ministries, choral groups, dance, drama, international student organizations, music ensembles, musical theater, radio station, student government, student newspaper, TV station, Baptist student association, Catholic student organization, Chi Alpha Christian Fellowship, Fellowship of Christian Athletes, Society of Hispanic Professional Engineers, Pre-law society, The Net Fellowship, Pre-Pharmacy association, Sigma Alpha Iota Music Sorority, Indian student association.

Athletics. NCAA. **Intercollegiate:** Baseball M, basketball, cross-country, football (tackle) M, softball W, tennis, track and field, volleyball W. **Intramural:** Archery, bowling, equestrian, golf, racquetball, softball, volleyball. **Team name:** Javelinas.

Student services. Adult student services, alcohol/substance abuse counseling, career counseling, student employment services, financial aid counseling, health services, minority student services, on-campus daycare, personal counseling, placement for graduates, veterans' counselor, women's services. **Physically disabled:** Services for visually, speech, hearing impaired.

Contact. E-mail: admissions@tamuk.edu
Phone: (361) 593-2315 Toll-free number: (800) 687-6000
Fax: (361) 593-2195
Jennifer Minke, Associate Director of Admissions, Texas A&M
University-Kingsville, MSC 105, Kingsville, TX 78363-8201

Texas A&M University-Texarkana
Texarkana, Texas
www.tamut.edu **CB code: 6206**

▶ Public two-year upper-division university
▶ Commuter campus in small city
▶ Test scores required

General. Founded in 1971. Regionally accredited. **Degrees:** 330 bachelor's
awarded; master's offered. **Articulation:** Agreements with Texarkana College, Northeast Texas Community College, Panola College, Paris Junior
College, Cossatot College, Rich Mountain College, University of Arkansas
Community College at Hope. **Location:** 180 miles from Dallas, 145 miles
from Little Rock, Arkansas. **Calendar:** Semester, limited summer session.
Full-time faculty: 62 total. **Part-time faculty:** 54 total.

Student profile. 1,413 degree-seeking undergraduates, 473 graduate students.

Out-of-state:	25%	25 or older:	60%

Basis for selection. Open admission. College transcript, standardized test
scores required. Minimum 2.0 GPA; must satisfy Texas Success Initiative.
Transfer accepted as sophomores, juniors, seniors.

2011-2012 Annual costs. Tuition/fees: $5,167; $14,647 out-of-state.
Room/board: $7,002. Books/supplies: $1,160.

Financial aid. Non-need-based: Scholarships awarded for academics,
leadership, state residency.

Application procedures. Admission: Rolling admission. No application
fee. **Financial aid:** Applicants notified on a rolling basis; must reply within
10 weeks of notification. Transfer students must have completed minimum
of 54 semester hours of transferable college credit to apply for financial aid
and notified applicants must reply within 45 days from date of award letter.
Exceptions made on individual basis. April 1 financial aid deadline for scholarships.

Academics. Student academic support offices open until 7pm on Tuesdays.
Special study options: Combined bachelor's/graduate degree, cross-
registration, distance learning, dual enrollment of high school students, honors, independent study, internships, liberal arts/career combination, student-
designed major, teacher certification program. **Credit/placement by examination:** AP, CLEP, IB, institutional tests. 30 credit hours maximum toward
bachelor's degree. BAAS degree limits credit by exam to 18 semester
credit hours.

Majors. Biology: General. **Business:** General, accounting, business admin,
finance, human resources, international, management information systems,
marketing. **Communications:** Media studies. **Computer sciences:** General.
Engineering: Electrical. **English:** English lit. **Health services:** Nursing (RN).
History: General. **Math:** General. **Protective services:** Criminal justice.
Psychology: General. **Social sciences:** Political science.

Most popular majors. Business/marketing 19%, interdisciplinary studies
42%, liberal arts 10%, psychology 7%.

Computing on campus. 119 workstations in library, computer center.
Commuter students can connect to campus network. Online library, helpline,
wireless network available.

Student life. Activities: Dance, drama, student government, student newspaper, multicultural association.

Athletics. Team name: Eagles.

Student services. Career counseling, student employment services, financial aid counseling, personal counseling, placement for graduates, veterans'
counselor. **Physically disabled:** Services for visually, hearing impaired.

Contact. E-mail: admissions@tamut.edu
Phone: (903) 223-3069 Fax: (903) 223-3140
Jennifer Willis, Director of Admissions, Texas A&M University-
Texarkana, 7101 University Avenue, Texarkana, TX 75505-5518

Texas Christian University
Fort Worth, Texas
www.tcu.edu **CB member**
 CB code: 6820

▶ Private 4-year university affiliated with Christian Church (Disciples
of Christ)
▶ Residential campus in very large city
▶ 8,171 degree-seeking undergraduates: 4% part-time, 59% women, 5%
African American, 3% Asian American, 10% Hispanic American, 1%
Native American, 5% international
▶ 1,274 degree-seeking graduate students
▶ 38% of applicants admitted
▶ SAT or ACT (ACT writing optional), application essay required
▶ 74% graduate within 6 years; 29% enter graduate study

General. Founded in 1873. Regionally accredited. **Degrees:** 1,705 bachelor's awarded; master's, professional, doctoral offered. **ROTC:** Army, Air
Force. **Location:** 3 miles from downtown Fort Worth, 35 miles from Dallas.
Calendar: Semester, limited summer session. **Full-time faculty:** 544 total;
84% have terminal degrees, 12% minority, 43% women. **Part-time faculty:**
301 total; 31% have terminal degrees, 9% minority, 56% women. **Class size:**
42% < 20, 42% 20-39, 9% 40-49, 5% 50-99, 2% >100. **Special facilities:**
Geological center for remote sensing, nuclear magnetic resonance facility,
observatory, film library, performance complex, behavioral research institute,
meteorite collection, two lab schools, speech and hearing clinic, transmission
electron microscope, Beowulf computing cluster, optical spectroscopy and
microscopy laboratory.

Freshman class profile. 19,168 applied, 7,217 admitted, 1,871 enrolled.

Mid 50% test scores		End year in good standing:	89%
SAT critical reading:	520-630	Return as sophomores:	87%
SAT math:	540-650	Out-of-state:	45%
SAT writing:	540-640	Live on campus:	97%
ACT composite:	24-29	International:	4%
Rank in top quarter:	73%	Fraternities:	49%
Rank in top tenth:	38%	Sororities:	61%

Basis for selection. GED not accepted. Academic credentials most important; talents, leadership potential, and applicant's determination to make difference considered. Audition, portfolio required for fine arts students; interview
recommended for all. **Home schooled:** Interview with admissions officer
recommended, additional weight may be placed on SAT/ACT scores in
admissions process.

High school preparation. College-preparatory program required. 17 units
required; 20 recommended. Required and recommended units include English
4, mathematics 3-4, social studies 3-4, science 3-4, foreign language 2-4 and
academic electives 2.

2011-2012 Annual costs. Tuition/fees: $32,490. Room/board: $10,410.

2010-2011 Financial aid. Need-based: 1,028 full-time freshmen applied
for aid; 713 were judged to have need; 710 of these received aid. Average
need met was 68%. Average scholarship/grant was $17,342; average loan
$3,201. 63% of total undergraduate aid awarded as scholarships/grants, 37%
as loans/jobs. **Non-need-based:** Awarded to 4,085 full-time undergraduates,
including 948 freshmen. Scholarships awarded for academics, alumni affiliation, art, minority status, music/drama, religious affiliation, ROTC, state residency.

Application procedures. Admission: Closing date 2/15 (postmark date).
$40 fee, may be waived for applicants with need. Admission notification by
4/1. Admission notification on a rolling basis. Must reply by May 1 or within
2 week(s) if notified thereafter. **Financial aid:** Closing date 5/1. FAFSA
required. Applicants notified on a rolling basis starting 3/15.

Academics. Variety of academic support services available. Academic
Success workshops offered each semester. Topics include time management,
note taking, preparing for exams. Individual departments may offer group
tutoring for students enrolled in specific courses. Student Support Services
offers individual assistance to students who qualify under specific federal
guidelines. **Special study options:** Accelerated study, combined bachelor's/
graduate degree, cross-registration, distance learning, double major, dual
enrollment of high school students, ESL, honors, independent study, internships, liberal arts/career combination, New York semester, semester at sea,
study abroad, teacher certification program, Washington semester. Two comprehensive leadership programs offered. Leadership center, information and
resources related to leadership development and training. **Credit/placement
by examination:** AP, CLEP, IB, SAT, ACT, institutional tests. **Support
services:** Study skills assistance, writing center.

Honors college/program. Admission to the Honors College by invitation
only. The selection committee uses the general TCU admission application;

therefore, students do not need to submit a separate Honors College application. When evaluating students' applications, the selection committee takes into consideration various quantitative and qualitative factors, such as strength of the high school curriculum, rank in class, high school grade point average, SAT and/or ACT scores, and involvement in community service, extracurricular activities, and leadership.

Majors. **Biology:** General, biochemistry, neuroscience. **Business:** Accounting, actuarial science, business admin, e-commerce, entrepreneurial studies, fashion, finance, international, international finance, international marketing, management science, marketing. **Communications:** Broadcast journalism, communications/speech/rhetoric, journalism, radio/TV. **Computer sciences:** General, information technology. **Conservation:** Environmental science. **Education:** Art, business, computer, Deaf/hearing impaired, drama/dance, early childhood, early childhood special, elementary, English, foreign languages, French, history, mathematics, middle, multi-level teacher, music, physical, reading, science, secondary, social science, social studies, Spanish, special ed. **Engineering:** General. **English:** English lit. **Foreign languages:** French, German, Spanish. **General:** Farm/ranch. **Health services:** Athletic training, dietetics, movement therapy, nursing (RN), premedicine, speech pathology. **History:** General. **Human services:** Social work. **Liberal arts:** Arts/sciences. **Math:** General. **Parks/recreation:** Health/fitness. **Philosophy/religion:** Philosophy, religion. **Physical sciences:** Astronomy, chemistry, geology, physics. **Protective services:** Criminal justice. **Psychology:** General. **Social sciences:** Anthropology, economics, geography, international economics, international relations, political science, sociology. **Theology:** Sacred music. **Visual/performing arts:** Acting, art history/conservation, ballet, ceramics, dramatic, film/cinema/video, graphic design, interior design, music, music pedagogy, music performance, music theory/composition, musical theater, painting, photography, piano/keyboard, printmaking, sculpture, stringed instruments, studio arts, theater design, voice/opera.

Most popular majors. Business/marketing 23%, communications/journalism 18%, education 6%, health sciences 13%, social sciences 8%, visual/performing arts 6%.

Computing on campus. 1,400 workstations in dormitories, library, computer center, student center. Dormitories wired for high-speed internet access and linked to campus network. Commuter students can connect to campus network. Online course registration, online library, helpline, repair service, wireless network available.

Student life. Freshman orientation: Mandatory. Preregistration for classes offered. 10 sessions in June and August, parents encouraged to attend. **Housing:** Guaranteed on-campus for freshmen. Coed dorms, single-sex dorms, apartments, fraternity/sorority housing available. $400 partly refundable deposit, deadline 5/1. Designated rooms available for ADA needs. **Activities:** Bands, campus ministries, choral groups, dance, drama, international student organizations, literary magazine, music ensembles, Model UN, musical theater, opera, radio station, student government, student newspaper, TV station, over 200 social, religious, service, academic, and pre-professional organizations.

Athletics. NCAA. **Intercollegiate:** Baseball M, basketball, cross-country, diving, equestrian W, football (tackle) M, golf, rifle W, soccer W, swimming, tennis, track and field, volleyball W. **Intramural:** Badminton, basketball, bowling, football (non-tackle), golf, racquetball, soccer, table tennis, tennis, volleyball. **Team name:** Horned Frogs.

Student services. Adult student services, alcohol/substance abuse counseling, chaplain/spiritual director, career counseling, services for economically disadvantaged, student employment services, financial aid counseling, health services, minority student services, personal counseling, placement for graduates, veterans' counselor, women's services. **Physically disabled:** Services for visually, speech, hearing impaired.

Contact. E-mail: frogmail@tcu.edu
Phone: (817) 257-7490 Toll-free number: (800) 828-3764
Fax: (817) 257-7268
Raymond Brown, Dean of Admissions, Texas Christian University, TCU Box 297013, Fort Worth, TX 76129

Texas College
Tyler, Texas
www.texascollege.edu   CB code: 6821

- Private 4-year liberal arts college affiliated with Christian Methodist Episcopal Church
- Residential campus in small city
- 860 degree-seeking undergraduates: 3% part-time, 41% women, 87% African American, 9% Hispanic American

General. Founded in 1894. Regionally accredited. Charter member college of the United Negro College Fund. **Degrees:** 91 bachelor's, 9 associate awarded. **Location:** 90 miles from Dallas, 100 miles from Shreveport, Louisiana. **Calendar:** Semester, limited summer session. **Full-time faculty:** 34 total; 35% have terminal degrees, 76% minority, 41% women. **Part-time faculty:** 17 total; 24% have terminal degrees, 76% minority, 47% women. **Class size:** 60% < 20, 17% 20-39, 6% 40-49, 15% 50-99, 1% >100.

Freshman class profile. 218 enrolled.

GPA 3.75 or higher:	5%	GPA 2.0-2.99:	53%
GPA 3.50-3.74:	12%	International:	1%
GPA 3.0-3.49:	23%		

Basis for selection. Open admission. SAT/ACT recommended for scholarships and placement. **Home schooled:** Must submit notarized copy of home school transcript showing date of graduation and course requirements that meet state graduation requirements as approved by the Texas Board of Education. **Learning Disabled:** Students requiring special assistance should provide documentation of disability to the Records/Registrar's Office and the need for assistance to the Office of Academic Affairs.

High school preparation. 16 units required. Required units include English 4, mathematics 2, social studies 2, science 2 and academic electives 6.

2012-2013 Annual costs. Tuition/fees (projected): $9,682. Room/board: $7,000. Books/supplies: $2,300. Personal expenses: $1,500.

Financial aid. Non-need-based: Scholarships awarded for academics, athletics, leadership, music/drama.

Application procedures. Admission: No deadline. $20 fee, may be waived for applicants with need. Admission notification on a rolling basis. **Financial aid:** Priority date 6/1; no closing date. FAFSA, institutional form required. Applicants notified on a rolling basis starting 4/15.

Academics. Special study options: Accelerated study, distance learning, double major, dual enrollment of high school students, independent study, internships, teacher certification program. **Credit/placement by examination:** AP, CLEP, institutional tests. 32 credit hours maximum toward bachelor's degree. **Support services:** Learning center, reduced course load, remedial instruction, study skills assistance, tutoring.

Majors. Biology: General. **Business:** Business admin. **Computer sciences:** General. **Education:** Art, biology, elementary, history, mathematics, middle, music, physical. **English:** English lit. **History:** General. **Human services:** Social work. **Liberal arts:** Arts/sciences. **Math:** General. **Parks/recreation:** Health/fitness. **Philosophy/religion:** Religion. **Protective services:** Law enforcement admin. **Social sciences:** Political science, sociology. **Visual/performing arts:** Music, studio arts.

Most popular majors. Biology 6%, business/marketing 51%, education 8%, legal studies 6%, public administration/social services 11%, social sciences 7%, visual/performing arts 7%.

Computing on campus. 200 workstations in dormitories, library, computer center. Dormitories wired for high-speed internet access and linked to campus network. Commuter students can connect to campus network. Online library, helpline, repair service, student web hosting, wireless network available.

Student life. Freshman orientation: Mandatory. Preregistration for classes offered. Held 2-3 days prior to first day of classes each semester. **Policies:** Students required to attend chapel weekly. Religious observance required. **Housing:** Guaranteed on-campus for freshmen. Single-sex dorms, wellness housing available. $150 nonrefundable deposit. **Activities:** Bands, choral groups, dance, music ensembles, student government, Young Adults for Christ, Fellowship of Christian Athletes, pre-alumni council, Omega Psi Phi, Delta Sigma Theta, Alpha Kappa Alpha.

Athletics. NAIA. **Intercollegiate:** Baseball M, basketball, cheerleading, football (tackle) M, soccer, softball W, track and field, volleyball W. **Intramural:** Basketball, football (non-tackle), soccer, softball W, volleyball W. **Team name:** Steers.

Student services. Adult student services, alcohol/substance abuse counseling, chaplain/spiritual director, career counseling, student employment services, financial aid counseling, health services, personal counseling.

Contact. E-mail: jroberts@texascollege.edu
Phone: (903) 593-8311 ext. 2297 Toll-free number: (800) 306-6299
Fax: (903) 363-1854
John Roberts, Vice President for Admissions/ Recruitment, Texas College, 2404 North Grand Avenue, Tyler, TX 75712-4500

Texas Lutheran University

Seguin, Texas
www.tlu.edu
CB member
CB code: 6823

- Private 4-year university and liberal arts college affiliated with Evangelical Lutheran Church in America
- Residential campus in large town
- 1,353 degree-seeking undergraduates: 3% part-time, 50% women, 10% African American, 1% Asian American, 27% Hispanic American, 1% Native American, 1% international
- 65% of applicants admitted
- SAT or ACT (ACT writing optional), application essay required
- 49% graduate within 6 years

General. Founded in 1891. Regionally accredited. **Degrees:** 258 bachelor's awarded. **ROTC:** Army, Air Force. **Location:** 30 miles from San Antonio, 55 miles from Austin. **Calendar:** Semester, limited summer session. **Full-time faculty:** 68 total; 81% have terminal degrees, 10% minority, 41% women. **Part-time faculty:** 73 total; 30% have terminal degrees, 14% minority, 55% women. **Class size:** 53% < 20, 46% 20-39, less than 1% 40-49. **Special facilities:** Biology field station, Mexican-American study center, life enrichment center, geological museum, center for servant leadership.

Freshman class profile. 1,552 applied, 1,007 admitted, 398 enrolled.

Mid 50% test scores			
SAT critical reading:	440-550	Rank in top quarter:	58%
SAT math:	470-580	Rank in top tenth:	21%
ACT composite:	19-24	End year in good standing:	77%
GPA 3.75 or higher:	42%	Return as sophomores:	75%
GPA 3.50-3.74:	19%	Out-of-state:	3%
GPA 3.0-3.49:	28%	Live on campus:	87%
GPA 2.0-2.99:	11%		

Basis for selection. Quality of academic curriculum pursued and class rank most important. Academic record and test scores also important. Interview recommended. **Home schooled:** Transcript of courses and grades, letter of recommendation (nonparent) required. Greater emphasis placed on SAT or ACT scores.

High school preparation. College-preparatory program recommended. 17 units required; 23 recommended. Required and recommended units include English 4, mathematics 3-4, social studies 3-4, history 2, science 3-4 (laboratory 2), foreign language 2-3, computer science 1 and academic electives 1.

2011-2012 Annual costs. Tuition/fees: $23,930. Room/board: $7,410. Books/supplies: $950. Personal expenses: $1,100.

2011-2012 Financial aid. Need-based: 381 full-time freshmen applied for aid; 343 were judged to have need; 343 of these received aid. Average need met was 82%. Average scholarship/grant was $17,085; average loan $3,656. 64% of total undergraduate aid awarded as scholarships/grants, 36% as loans/jobs. **Non-need-based:** Awarded to 341 full-time undergraduates, including 100 freshmen. Scholarships awarded for academics, alumni affiliation, leadership, music/drama, religious affiliation.

Application procedures. Admission: Priority date 5/1; deadline 8/1 (postmark date). $40 fee, may be waived for applicants with need. Admission notification on a rolling basis beginning on or about 10/1. **Financial aid:** Priority date 3/1; no closing date. FAFSA required. Applicants notified on a rolling basis starting 3/1; must reply within 6 week(s) of notification.

Academics. Special study options: Combined bachelor's/graduate degree, double major, dual enrollment of high school students, exchange student, honors, independent study, internships, liberal arts/career combination, study abroad, teacher certification program, Washington semester. International studies curriculum, dual BS program in applied science and engineering in conjunction with Texas state institutions. **Credit/placement by examination:** AP, CLEP, IB, institutional tests. 30 credit hours maximum toward bachelor's degree. **Support services:** Study skills assistance, tutoring, writing center.

Majors. Biology: General, molecular. **Business:** General, accounting, business admin. **Communications:** Communications/speech/rhetoric. **Computer sciences:** General, computer science, information systems. **Education:** Elementary, English, history, mathematics, middle, multi-level teacher, music, physical, reading, social studies. **English:** English lit. **Foreign languages:** Spanish. **Health services:** Athletic training. **History:** General, applied. **Math:** General. **Parks/recreation:** Exercise sciences, health/fitness, sports admin. **Philosophy/religion:** Philosophy. **Physical sciences:** Chemistry, physics. **Psychology:** General. **Social sciences:** Economics, political science, sociology. **Theology:** Preministerial, youth ministry. **Visual/performing arts:** General, art, dramatic, music, music history, music performance.

Most popular majors. Biology 11%, business/marketing 25%, education 12%, parks/recreation 13%, psychology 7%, social sciences 6%.

Computing on campus. 237 workstations in dormitories, library, computer center, student center. Dormitories wired for high-speed internet access and linked to campus network. Commuter students can connect to campus network. Online course registration, online library, helpline, wireless network available.

Student life. Freshman orientation: Mandatory. Preregistration for classes offered. Held 2 days prior to start of fall semester. **Housing:** Guaranteed on-campus for freshmen. Coed dorms, single-sex dorms, apartments available. $200 fully refundable deposit, deadline 8/1. **Activities:** Bands, campus ministries, choral groups, dance, drama, international student organizations, literary magazine, music ensembles, musical theater, student government, student newspaper, symphony orchestra, black student union, Mexican American student association, Young Democrats, College Republicans, Fellowship of Christian Athletes, Students Make a Difference, Lutheran student movement, Canterbury, Catholic student organization.

Athletics. NCAA. **Intercollegiate:** Baseball M, basketball, cross-country W, football (tackle) M, golf, soccer, softball W, tennis, track and field W, volleyball W. **Intramural:** Basketball, bowling, football (non-tackle), handball, racquetball, softball, swimming, tennis, volleyball. **Team name:** Bulldogs.

Student services. Alcohol/substance abuse counseling, chaplain/spiritual director, career counseling, student employment services, financial aid counseling, health services, personal counseling, placement for graduates, veterans' counselor.

Contact. E-mail: admissions@tlu.edu
Phone: (830) 372-8050 Toll-free number: (800) 771-8521
Fax: (830) 372-8096
Mandy Owen, Director of Admissions, Texas Lutheran University, 1000 West Court Street, Seguin, TX 78155-5999

Texas Southern University

Houston, Texas
www.tsu.edu
CB member
CB code: 6824

- Public 4-year university
- Commuter campus in very large city
- 6,881 degree-seeking undergraduates: 19% part-time, 57% women, 87% African American, 2% Asian American, 5% Hispanic American, 4% international
- 2,849 degree-seeking graduate students
- 26% of applicants admitted

General. Founded in 1947. Regionally accredited. Texas Southern University is one of the nation's largest Historically Black Colleges and Universities. **Degrees:** 750 bachelor's awarded; master's, professional, doctoral offered. **ROTC:** Army. **Location:** 2 miles from downtown. **Calendar:** Semester, extensive summer session. **Full-time faculty:** 335 total; 87% minority, 47% women. **Part-time faculty:** 218 total; 92% minority, 50% women. **Class size:** 35% < 20, 41% 20-39, 11% 40-49, 12% 50-99, 1% >100. **Special facilities:** University museum.

Freshman class profile. 8,670 applied, 2,269 admitted, 1,184 enrolled.

Mid 50% test scores			
SAT critical reading:	370-450	Rank in top quarter:	15%
SAT math:	380-470	Rank in top tenth:	3%
SAT writing:	360-440	End year in good standing:	55%
ACT composite:	15-19	Return as sophomores:	61%
GPA 3.75 or higher:	5%	Out-of-state:	20%
GPA 3.50-3.74:	8%	Live on campus:	59%
GPA 3.0-3.49:	28%	International:	2%
GPA 2.0-2.99:	58%	Fraternities:	3%
		Sororities:	1%

Basis for selection. Special requirements for pharmacy, law, accounting, marketing, and computer science programs. For selective programs high school achievement, interview, essay important; test scores, individual abilities, high school activities considered.

High school preparation. College-preparatory program recommended. Recommended units include English 4, mathematics 3, social studies 4, science 2, foreign language 2 and academic electives 6.

2011-2012 Annual costs. Tuition/fees: $7,462; $16,762 out-of-state. Books/supplies: $1,400. Personal expenses: $2,293.

Financial aid. All financial aid based on need.

Application procedures. Admission: Priority date 7/31; deadline 8/15 (postmark date). $42 fee, may be waived for applicants with need. Admission

notification on a rolling basis. Must reply by 7/31. **Financial aid:** Priority date 5/15; no closing date. FAFSA required. Applicants notified on a rolling basis starting 6/1.

Academics. Special study options: Cooperative education, distance learning, double major, ESL, honors, independent study, internships, study abroad, teacher certification program, weekend college. **Credit/placement by examination:** AP, CLEP, SAT, ACT, institutional tests. **Support services:** Learning center, pre-admission summer program, remedial instruction, study skills assistance, tutoring.

Majors. Biology: General. **Business:** Accounting, banking/financial services, business admin, management information systems, marketing, operations. **Communications:** Communications/speech/rhetoric, journalism, radio/TV. **Communications technology:** Recording arts. **Computer sciences:** General. **Conservation:** Environmental studies. **English:** English lit, rhetoric/composition. **Foreign languages:** French, Spanish. **Health services:** Clinical lab science, dietetics, environmental health, health care admin, medical records admin, prepharmacy, respiratory therapy technology. **History:** General. **Human services:** General, social work. **Math:** General. **Parks/recreation:** Exercise sciences, health/fitness, sports admin. **Physical sciences:** Chemistry, physics. **Protective services:** Law enforcement admin. **Psychology:** General. **Social sciences:** Economics, political science, sociology. **Visual/performing arts:** General, dramatic, music, studio arts. **Work/family studies:** General, child development, food/nutrition.

Most popular majors. Biology 9%, business/marketing 19%, communications/journalism 7%, health sciences 16%, liberal arts 6%, security/protective services 6%.

Computing on campus. 500 workstations in library, computer center, student center. Dormitories wired for high-speed internet access and linked to campus network. Online course registration, online library, helpline, wireless network available.

Student life. Freshman orientation: Mandatory. Preregistration for classes offered. Two-day orientation held every semester during registration week. Includes participation in seminars, advising, placement test. **Housing:** Guaranteed on-campus for freshmen. Single-sex dorms, apartments available. $350 partly refundable deposit, deadline 6/1. **Activities:** Bands, choral groups, drama, film society, music ensembles, musical theater, opera, radio station, student government, student newspaper, symphony orchestra, TV station, Alpha Phi Omega, Gamma Phi Delta Christian Fraternity, Tigers for Christ, Alpha Eta Rho international aviation fraternity, sociology club, political science club, student psychological club, NAACP, association of black journalists, bilingual education association, environmental health club.

Athletics. NCAA. **Intercollegiate:** Baseball M, basketball, bowling W, cross-country, football (tackle) M, golf, soccer W, softball W, tennis, track and field, volleyball W. **Intramural:** Basketball, bowling W, cheerleading, softball W, tennis, track and field, volleyball W. **Team name:** Tigers.

Student services. Alcohol/substance abuse counseling, chaplain/spiritual director, career counseling, student employment services, financial aid counseling, health services, on-campus daycare, personal counseling, placement for graduates, veterans' counselor. **Physically disabled:** Services for speech impaired.

Contact. E-mail: admissions@tsu.edu
Phone: (713) 313-7849 Toll-free number: (866) 878-4968
Fax: (713) 313-7851
Brian Armstrong, Executive Director of Enrollment Management, Texas Southern University, 3100 Cleburne Street, Houston, TX 77004

Texas State University: San Marcos
San Marcos, Texas
www.txstate.edu

CB member
CB code: 6667

- Public 4-year university
- Commuter campus in large town
- 28,967 degree-seeking undergraduates: 18% part-time, 55% women, 7% African American, 2% Asian American, 27% Hispanic American, 1% international
- 4,311 degree-seeking graduate students
- 77% of applicants admitted
- SAT or ACT with writing, application essay required
- 56% graduate within 6 years; 24% enter graduate study

General. Founded in 1899. Regionally accredited. **Degrees:** 5,362 bachelor's awarded; master's, professional, doctoral offered. **ROTC:** Army, Air Force. **Location:** 30 miles from Austin, 49 miles from San Antonio. **Calendar:** Semester, extensive summer session. **Full-time faculty:** 1,119 total;

75% have terminal degrees, 22% minority, 46% women. **Part-time faculty:** 469 total; 40% have terminal degrees, 17% minority, 55% women. **Class size:** 19% < 20, 54% 20-39, 9% 40-49, 12% 50-99, 7% >100. **Special facilities:** Southwestern writers collection (original manuscripts), observatory, archaeological forensic lab, clean room for microchip production, sound recording studio, ranch.

Freshman class profile. 14,878 applied, 11,530 admitted, 4,347 enrolled.

Mid 50% test scores			
SAT critical reading:	470-570	Rank in top tenth:	12%
SAT math:	480-580	Return as sophomores:	79%
SAT writing:	450-540	Out-of-state:	1%
ACT composite:	21-25	Live on campus:	88%
Rank in top quarter:	48%	International:	1%

Basis for selection. Applicants who rank in top 10% of high school class have no minimum test score requirements. Otherwise score requirements are as follows: rank in next 15%, 920 SAT or 20 ACT; rank in second quarter, 1010 SAT, 22 ACT; rank in third quarter, 1180 SAT, 26 ACT; rank in bottom quarter, 1270 SAT, 29 ACT. (SAT scores exclusive of Writing). SAT Subject Tests required for placement in certain higher level courses, but not used in the admissions decision. Audition required for music program. **Home schooled:** Transcript of courses and grades required. Minimum 26 ACT or 1180 SAT (exclusive of Writing) and admissions essay.

High school preparation. College-preparatory program required. 24 units required; 26 recommended. Required and recommended units include English 4, mathematics 3-4, social studies 3.5, science 3-4 (laboratory 2-3), foreign language 2-3, computer science 1, visual/performing arts 1, academic electives 3.5. 1.5 physical education, 0.5 economics, 0.5 speech required, 0.5 health education required.

2011-2012 Annual costs. Tuition/fees: $8,232; $17,622 out-of-state. Room/board: $6,912. Books/supplies: $1,050. Personal expenses: $2,670.

2011-2012 Financial aid. Need-based: 3,820 full-time freshmen applied for aid; 2,703 were judged to have need; 2,575 of these received aid. Average scholarship/grant was $8,599; average loan $2,504. 52% of total undergraduate aid awarded as scholarships/grants, 48% as loans/jobs. **Non-need-based:** Awarded to 2,061 full-time undergraduates, including 742 freshmen. Scholarships awarded for academics, art, athletics, leadership, music/drama, ROTC, state residency. **Additional information:** To be eligible for the Bobcat Promise program you must be an entering first-time freshmen (transfer students are not eligible), be a Texas resident, have a family adjusted gross income of $25,000 or less, be enrolled full-time and complete at least 30 credit hours during each academic year (fall and spring semester), and submit a completed FAFSA no later than April 1.

Application procedures. Admission: Closing date 5/1 (receipt date). $60 fee, may be waived for applicants with need. Admission notification on a rolling basis beginning on or about 9/1. Application deadlines for McCoy College of Business and the Department of Communication Design are March 15th for fall and October 15th for spring admissions. **Financial aid:** Priority date 4/1; no closing date. FAFSA required. Applicants notified on a rolling basis starting 5/1; must reply within 3 week(s) of notification.

Academics. Special study options: Accelerated study, combined bachelor's/graduate degree, distance learning, double major, dual enrollment of high school students, ESL, exchange student, honors, independent study, internships, study abroad, teacher certification program, Washington semester, weekend college. **Credit/placement by examination:** AP, CLEP, IB, institutional tests. Credit hours earned by exam do not count as credit earned in residence, and 25% of course work must be completed in residency. **Support services:** Learning center, reduced course load, remedial instruction, study skills assistance, tutoring, writing center.

Majors. Architecture: Urban/community planning. **Area/ethnic studies:** American, Asian, European, Near/Middle Eastern. **Biology:** General, animal physiology, aquatic, biochemistry, botany, microbiology, wildlife, zoology. **Business:** Accounting, business admin, fashion, finance, management information systems, managerial economics, marketing. **Communications:** Advertising, journalism, media studies, public relations, radio/TV. **Communications technology:** Desktop publishing, recording arts. **Computer sciences:** General. **Conservation:** Environmental science, water/wetlands/marine. **Engineering:** Electrical, industrial, manufacturing. **English:** English lit, rhetoric/composition. **Foreign languages:** French, German, Spanish. **General:** Agribusiness operations, animal sciences. **Health services:** Athletic training, clinical lab science, communication disorders, health care admin, medical radiologic technology/radiation therapy, medical records admin, nursing (RN), public health ed, respiratory therapy technology. **History:** General. **Human services:** General, social work. **Math:** General, applied. **Parks/recreation:** Exercise sciences, facilities management, health/fitness, sports admin. **Philosophy/religion:** Philosophy. **Physical sciences:** Chemistry, physics. **Protective services:** Corrections, criminal justice, police science. **Psychology:** General. **Social sciences:** Anthropology, economics, geography, GIS/cartography, international relations, political science, sociology. **Visual/performing arts:** Art, dance, design, dramatic, graphic design, interior

design, jazz, music, music performance, musical theater, photography, studio arts. **Work/family studies:** General, family studies, food/nutrition.

Most popular majors. Business/marketing 20%, communications/journalism 7%, English 6%, interdisciplinary studies 11%, parks/recreation 7%, psychology 6%, social sciences 8%, visual/performing arts 8%.

Computing on campus. 1,843 workstations in dormitories, library, computer center, student center. Dormitories wired for high-speed internet access and linked to campus network. Commuter students can connect to campus network. Online course registration, helpline, repair service, student web hosting, wireless network available.

Student life. Freshman orientation: Mandatory, $60 fee. Preregistration for classes offered. 2-day program combined with welcome week prior to start of semester. **Policies:** All unmarried students under 21 with fewer than 56 credit hours must live in university housing. **Housing:** Guaranteed on-campus for freshmen. Coed dorms, single-sex dorms, apartments, fraternity/sorority housing available. $300 partly refundable deposit. **Activities:** Bands, campus ministries, choral groups, dance, drama, film society, international student organizations, literary magazine, music ensembles, Model UN, musical theater, opera, radio station, student government, student newspaper, symphony orchestra, nearly 300 social, service, religious, political, and professional organizations.

Athletics. NCAA. **Intercollegiate:** Baseball M, basketball, cheerleading, cross-country, football (tackle) M, golf, soccer W, softball W, tennis W, track and field, volleyball W. **Intramural:** Basketball, bowling, football (non-tackle), golf, racquetball, soccer, softball, tennis, volleyball. **Team name:** Bobcats.

Student services. Adult student services, alcohol/substance abuse counseling, chaplain/spiritual director, career counseling, student employment services, financial aid counseling, health services, legal services, minority student services, personal counseling, placement for graduates, veterans' counselor. **Physically disabled:** Services for visually, speech, hearing impaired.

Contact. E-mail: admissions@txstate.edu
Phone: (512) 245-2364 Fax: (512) 245-8044
Stephanie Anderson, Assistant VP for Enrollment Management, Texas State University: San Marcos, 429 North Guadalupe Street, San Marcos, TX 78666-5709

Texas Tech University
Lubbock, Texas
www.ttu.edu

CB member
CB code: 6827

- Public 4-year university
- Commuter campus in small city
- 26,004 degree-seeking undergraduates: 10% part-time, 45% women, 5% African American, 3% Asian American, 18% Hispanic American, 1% Native American, 3% international
- 5,767 degree-seeking graduate students
- 66% of applicants admitted
- SAT or ACT (ACT writing optional) required
- 61% graduate within 6 years

General. Founded in 1923. Regionally accredited. **Degrees:** 4,749 bachelor's awarded; master's, professional, doctoral offered. **ROTC:** Army, Air Force. **Location:** 348 miles from Dallas, 321 miles from Albuquerque, New Mexico. **Calendar:** Semester, extensive summer session. **Full-time faculty:** 1,153 total; 90% have terminal degrees, 26% minority, 35% women. **Part-time faculty:** 195 total; 50% have terminal degrees, 17% minority, 63% women. **Class size:** 24% < 20, 39% 20-39, 12% 40-49, 15% 50-99, 10% >100. **Special facilities:** Museum, national ranching heritage center, special collections library, archaeological dig/state park, international cultural center, international textile research center, science research laboratory, arid and semi-arid land studies center, seismological observatory, child development research center, institutes for environmental and human health, Vietnam center, planetarium, wind energy program.

Freshman class profile. 17,569 applied, 11,645 admitted, 4,464 enrolled.

Mid 50% test scores			
SAT critical reading:	490-590	Rank in top quarter:	56%
SAT math:	520-610	Rank in top tenth:	21%
SAT writing:	470-570	Return as sophomores:	82%
ACT composite:	22-27	Out-of-state:	6%
		International:	2%

Basis for selection. Class rank and test scores considered first, and students meeting the following score requirements (exclusive of Writing) eligible for unconditional admission: class rank in top 10%, no minimum test scores;

rank in next 15%, with 1140 SAT or 25 ACT; rank in second quarter, with 1230 SAT or 28 ACT; rank in third quarter, with 1270 SAT or 29 ACT. (SAT scores exclusive of Writing.) Applicants who do not meet assured admission criteria will have records reviewed in holistic manner. Auditions and portfolios required for admission to some programs.

High school preparation. College-preparatory program required. 26 units recommended. Recommended units include English 4, mathematics 4, science 4, foreign language 2, visual/performing arts 1 and academic electives 6. .5 economics, 1 physical education, 3.5 social studies and history.

2011-2012 Annual costs. Tuition/fees: $8,765; $18,155 out-of-state. Room/board: $8,095. Books/supplies: $1,200. Personal expenses: $1,890.

Financial aid. Non-need-based: Scholarships awarded for academics, art, athletics, job skills, leadership, music/drama, ROTC.

Application procedures. Admission: Priority date 3/1; deadline 8/1 (receipt date). $60 fee, may be waived for applicants with need. Admission notification on a rolling basis beginning on or about 10/1. **Financial aid:** Priority date 4/15; no closing date. FAFSA required. Applicants notified on a rolling basis; must reply within 2 week(s) of notification.

Academics. Special study options: Accelerated study, combined bachelor's/graduate degree, cooperative education, distance learning, double major, dual enrollment of high school students, ESL, external degree, honors, independent study, internships, semester at sea, student-designed major, study abroad, teacher certification program. **Credit/placement by examination:** AP, CLEP, IB, SAT, ACT, institutional tests. **Support services:** Learning center, pre-admission summer program, remedial instruction, study skills assistance, tutoring, writing center.

Honors college/program. Requires separate application, minimum 1200 SAT (exclusive of Writing) or 26 ACT, or top 10% class rank, essays, 2 teacher recommendations. Fall 2011, 351 freshmen admitted. Total enrollment 1022. Average SAT score: 1303. Two tracks offered: nondegree program working with all colleges and majors to provide honors academic, co-curricular and social program; and interdisciplinary degree program for bachelor of arts degree in natural history and humanities or Honors Arts and Letters.

Majors. Architecture: Architecture, interior, landscape. **Area/ethnic studies:** Latin American, Russian/Slavic. **Biology:** General, biochemistry, cellular/molecular, microbiology, zoology. **Business:** General, accounting, business admin, fashion, finance, hotel/motel admin, international, marketing. **Communications:** Advertising, journalism, public relations, radio/TV. **Computer sciences:** General, information systems. **Conservation:** General, enforcement, wildlife/wilderness. **Engineering:** Chemical, civil, computer, construction, electrical, environmental, industrial, mechanical, petroleum. **English:** English lit, rhetoric/composition, technical writing. **Foreign languages:** Classics, French, German, Spanish. **General:** Agronomy, animal sciences, business, communications, economics, food science, horticulture, range science. **Health services:** General, dietetics. **History:** General. **Human services:** Social work. **Liberal arts:** Arts/sciences. **Math:** General. **Parks/recreation:** Exercise sciences. **Philosophy/religion:** Philosophy. **Physical sciences:** Chemistry, geology, physics. **Psychology:** General. **Social sciences:** Anthropology, economics, geography, international economics, political science, sociology. **Visual/performing arts:** Art, dance, dramatic, fashion design, music. **Work/family studies:** General, child development, family resources, family studies, family/community services, food/nutrition.

Most popular majors. Business/marketing 23%, communications/journalism 6%, engineering/engineering technologies 11%, family/consumer sciences 8%, social sciences 6%.

Computing on campus. 3,000 workstations in dormitories, library, computer center, student center. Dormitories wired for high-speed internet access and linked to campus network. Commuter students can connect to campus network. Online course registration, online library, helpline, repair service, student web hosting, wireless network available.

Student life. Freshman orientation: Mandatory, $150 fee. Preregistration for classes offered. Three-day sessions held in January, May, June, July. One-day sessions held only for transfer students only in May and July. **Policies:** Freshmen required to live on campus. **Housing:** Guaranteed on-campus for freshmen. Coed dorms, single-sex dorms, special housing for disabled, apartments, wellness housing available. $50 nonrefundable deposit, deadline 4/1. Honors, intensive study, substance-free, freshman interest groups, learning communities. **Activities:** Bands, campus ministries, choral groups, dance, drama, film society, international student organizations, literary magazine, music ensembles, musical theater, opera, student government, student newspaper, symphony orchestra, Catholic students association, Hispanic law student association, Alpha Phi Omega, women's service organization, Tech Student Democrats, Campus Crusade for Christ, Chi Alpha Christian Fellowship, African student organization, Tech College Republicans, Vietnamese student organization.

Athletics. NCAA. **Intercollegiate:** Baseball M, basketball, cross-country, football (tackle) M, golf, soccer W, softball W, tennis, track and field, volleyball. **Intramural:** Badminton, baseball, basketball, bowling, football (non-tackle), golf, racquetball, soccer, softball, swimming, table tennis, tennis, triathlon, volleyball, weight lifting M. **Team name:** Red Raiders/ Lady Raiders.

Student services. Alcohol/substance abuse counseling, career counseling, student employment services, financial aid counseling, health services, legal services, personal counseling, placement for graduates, veterans' counselor. **Physically disabled:** Services for visually, speech, hearing impaired.

Contact. E-mail: admissions@ttu.edu
Phone: (806) 742-1480 Fax: (806) 742-0062
Ethan Logan, Managing Director of Undergraduate Recruitment and Admissions, Texas Tech University, Box 45005, Lubbock, TX 79409-5005

Texas Tech University Health Sciences Center
Lubbock, Texas
www.ttuhsc.edu   CB code: 3423

- Public two-year upper-division university
- Commuter campus in small city
- Application essay required

General. Founded in 1969. Regionally accredited. **Degrees:** 684 bachelor's awarded; master's, professional, doctoral offered. **Calendar:** Semester, limited summer session. **Full-time faculty:** 866 total; 17% minority, 44% women. **Part-time faculty:** 77 total; 18% minority, 35% women. **Class size:** 58% < 20, 30% 20-39, 4% 40-49, 6% 50-99, 2% >100.

Student profile. 1,154 degree-seeking undergraduates, 2,940 degree-seeking graduate students.

Women:	81%	Out-of-state:	5%
Part-time:	9%	25 or older:	53%

Basis for selection. College transcript, application essay required. Transfer accepted as juniors.

2011-2012 Annual costs. Tuition/fees: $7,223; $16,613 out-of-state. Reported costs are for Allied Health Sciences and School of Nursing. Books/supplies: $1,119. Personal expenses: $3,651.

Financial aid. Non-need-based: Scholarships awarded for academics.

Application procedures. Admission: $40 fee. **Financial aid:** No deadline. Applicants notified on a rolling basis.

Academics. Special study options: Combined bachelor's/graduate degree, distance learning. **Credit/placement by examination:** AP, CLEP.

Majors. Health services: Clinical lab science, communication disorders, health care admin, nursing (RN).

Computing on campus. PC or laptop required. 160 workstations in library. Commuter students can connect to campus network. Online library, wireless network available.

Student services. Physically disabled: Services for visually, speech, hearing impaired.

Contact. Phone: (806) 743-2300
Texas Tech University Health Sciences Center, 3601 Fourth Street, Lubbock, TX 79430

Texas Wesleyan University
Fort Worth, Texas
www.txwes.edu   CB code: 6828

- Private 4-year university affiliated with United Methodist Church
- Commuter campus in large city
- 1,478 degree-seeking undergraduates: 19% part-time, 63% women
- 1,423 degree-seeking graduate students
- 52% of applicants admitted
- SAT or ACT (ACT writing optional) required
- 33% graduate within 6 years

General. Founded in 1890. Regionally accredited. **Degrees:** 352 bachelor's awarded; master's, professional, doctoral offered. **ROTC:** Army, Air Force. **Location:** 2 miles from downtown. **Calendar:** Semester, limited summer session. **Full-time faculty:** 168 total; 90% have terminal degrees, 11% minority, 51% women. **Part-time faculty:** 111 total; 10% minority, 50% women. **Class size:** 73% < 20, 27% 20-39, less than 1% 40-49.

Freshman class profile. 912 applied, 477 admitted, 168 enrolled.

Mid 50% test scores		GPA 2.0-2.99:	27%
SAT critical reading:	440-530	Rank in top quarter:	40%
SAT math:	460-560	Rank in top tenth:	15%
SAT writing:	420-510	End year in good standing:	81%
ACT composite:	19-23	Return as sophomores:	59%
GPA 3.75 or higher:	27%	Out-of-state:	5%
GPA 3.50-3.74:	15%	Live on campus:	46%
GPA 3.0-3.49:	30%	International:	3%

Basis for selection. Regular freshmen admission requires minimum 2.5 high school GPA, 19 ACT or 920 SAT combined score (exclusive of Writing), top 50% ranking in senior class. **Home schooled:** Transcript of courses and grades required.

High school preparation. College-preparatory program recommended. 24 units recommended. Recommended units include English 4, mathematics 4, social studies 3, science 3, foreign language 2 and academic electives 8.

2011-2012 Annual costs. Tuition/fees: $19,760. Room/board: $7,180. Books/supplies: $1,052. Personal expenses: $2,088.

2010-2011 Financial aid. All financial aid based on need. 178 full-time freshmen applied for aid; 165 were judged to have need; 165 of these received aid. Average need met was 62%. Average scholarship/grant was $12,998; average loan $2,900. 51% of total undergraduate aid awarded as scholarships/grants, 49% as loans/jobs.

Application procedures. Admission: No deadline. No application fee. Admission notification on a rolling basis. **Financial aid:** No deadline. FAFSA required. Applicants notified on a rolling basis starting 3/1.

Academics. Special study options: Accelerated study, combined bachelor's/graduate degree, distance learning, double major, dual enrollment of high school students, ESL, exchange student, honors, independent study, internships, liberal arts/career combination, study abroad, teacher certification program, weekend college. **Credit/placement by examination:** AP, CLEP, SAT, ACT, institutional tests. 30 credit hours maximum toward bachelor's degree. **Support services:** Learning center, pre-admission summer program, reduced course load, remedial instruction, study skills assistance, tutoring, writing center.

Majors. **Biology:** General, biochemistry. **Business:** Accounting, business admin, finance, international, management information systems, management science, managerial economics, marketing, office technology. **Communications:** Communications/speech/rhetoric, journalism, public relations, radio/TV. **Computer sciences:** General, computer science, information systems. **Education:** General, bilingual, biology, business, elementary, English, history, mathematics, music, physical, reading, science, social studies, Spanish. **English:** Creative writing, English lit, rhetoric/composition. **Foreign languages:** Spanish. **Health services:** Athletic training, predental. **History:** General. **Liberal arts:** Arts/sciences, humanities. **Math:** General. **Parks/recreation:** Exercise sciences, sports admin. **Philosophy/religion:** Christian, religion. **Physical sciences:** Chemistry. **Protective services:** Criminal justice. **Psychology:** General, industrial. **Social sciences:** General, international relations, political science. **Visual/performing arts:** Art, music, theater arts management.

Most popular majors. Business/marketing 19%, education 15%, interdisciplinary studies 14%, parks/recreation 6%, psychology 13%, social sciences 9%.

Computing on campus. 418 workstations in library, computer center. Dormitories wired for high-speed internet access and linked to campus network. Commuter students can connect to campus network. Online library, helpline, repair service, wireless network available.

Student life. Freshman orientation: Mandatory. Preregistration for classes offered. **Policies:** Resident chaplain on staff. **Housing:** Coed dorms, single-sex dorms, apartments, fraternity/sorority housing, wellness housing available. $200 partly refundable deposit. **Activities:** Concert band, campus ministries, choral groups, dance, drama, international student organizations, literary magazine, music ensembles, musical theater, opera, student government, student newspaper, Methodist and Baptist student unions, Student Foundation, Alpha Phi Omega, Fellowship of Christian Athletes.

Athletics. NAIA. **Intercollegiate:** Baseball M, basketball, cross-country, golf M, soccer, softball W, table tennis M, track and field, volleyball W. **Intramural:** Badminton, basketball, bowling, diving, golf M, soccer, softball, swimming, table tennis, tennis W, volleyball. **Team name:** Rams.

Student services. Adult student services, alcohol/substance abuse counseling, chaplain/spiritual director, career counseling, student employment services, financial aid counseling, health services, personal counseling, placement for graduates, veterans' counselor.

Contact. E-mail: admissions@txwes.edu
Phone: (817) 531-4422 Toll-free number: (800) 580-8980
Fax: (817) 531-7515
Holly Kiser, Director of Freshman Admissions, Texas Wesleyan University, 1201 Wesleyan Street, Fort Worth, TX 76105-1536

Texas Woman's University
Denton, Texas
www.twu.edu

CB member
CB code: 6826

- Public 4-year university
- Residential campus in small city
- 8,781 degree-seeking undergraduates: 29% part-time, 91% women, 21% African American, 8% Asian American, 22% Hispanic American, 1% Native American, 1% international
- 5,463 degree-seeking graduate students
- 88% of applicants admitted
- 42% graduate within 6 years

General. Founded in 1901. Regionally accredited. **Degrees:** 1,795 bachelor's awarded; master's, professional, doctoral offered. **ROTC:** Army, Air Force. **Location:** 35 miles from Dallas and Fort Worth. **Calendar:** Semester, extensive summer session. **Full-time faculty:** 365 total; 18% minority, 76% women. **Part-time faculty:** 26 total; 15% minority, 81% women. **Class size:** 17% < 20, 52% 20-39, 13% 40-49, 13% 50-99, 5% >100. **Special facilities:** Art collection, Little Chapel-in-the-Woods, Texas Women's Hall of Fame, Texas First Ladies historic costume collection, woman's collection, Women Airforce Service Pilots memorabilia, botanical gardens, Gertrude Gibson Guest House, collection of children's book art, cookbook collection.

Freshman class profile. 3,364 applied, 2,972 admitted, 1,044 enrolled.

Mid 50% test scores			
SAT critical reading:	350-500	Rank in top quarter:	42%
SAT math:	370-510	Rank in top tenth:	14%
ACT composite:	17-20	Return as sophomores:	64%
GPA 3.75 or higher:	14%	Out-of-state:	2%
GPA 3.50-3.74:	16%	Live on campus:	80%
GPA 3.0-3.49:	43%	Sororities:	3%
GPA 2.0-2.99:	27%		

Basis for selection. School achievement record and test scores most important: Texas Academic Skills Program, 1000 SAT score (exclusive of Writing) or ACT of 21. Interview and audition required for drama and music programs; interview required and portfolio recommended for art program. **Home schooled:** Transcript of courses and grades required. Must submit official transcript showing completion of secondary school education and date of completion; SAT or ACT test score results. Applications missing these items will be reviewed by an admission officer and applicants given the opportunity to provide additional information to support their request for individual consideration.

High school preparation. College-preparatory program recommended. 22 units required. Required units include English 4, mathematics 3, social studies 2, science 2 and academic electives 11.

2011-2012 Annual costs. Tuition/fees: $6,587; $15,977 out-of-state. Room/board: $6,550. Books/supplies: $1,020. Personal expenses: $1,964.

Application procedures. Admission: Priority date 2/1; deadline 7/15 (receipt date). $50 fee, may be waived for applicants with need. Admission notification on a rolling basis beginning on or about 3/1. **Financial aid:** Priority date 4/1; no closing date. FAFSA required. Must reply within 3 week(s) of notification.

Academics. Special study options: Accelerated study, combined bachelor's/graduate degree, cooperative education, cross-registration, distance learning, double major, dual enrollment of high school students, external degree, honors, independent study, internships, liberal arts/career combination, study abroad, teacher certification program, weekend college. **Credit/placement by examination:** AP, CLEP, SAT, ACT, institutional tests. 30 credit hours maximum toward bachelor's degree. **Support services:** Learning center, pre-admission summer program, reduced course load, remedial instruction, study skills assistance, tutoring, writing center.

Majors. Biology: General, biochemistry, zoology. **Business:** Accounting, administrative services, business admin, fashion, finance, marketing. **Computer sciences:** General. **English:** English lit. **Health services:** Clinical lab science, dental hygiene, dietetics, music therapy, nursing (RN). **History:**

General. **Human services:** Social work. **Math:** General. **Parks/recreation:** Health/fitness. **Physical sciences:** Chemistry. **Protective services:** Criminal justice. **Psychology:** General. **Social sciences:** Political science, sociology. **Visual/performing arts:** Art, dance, dramatic, fashion design, music. **Work/family studies:** General, child development, family studies, food/nutrition.

Most popular majors. Business/marketing 7%, health sciences 32%, interdisciplinary studies 13%, liberal arts 15%.

Computing on campus. 1,000 workstations in dormitories, library, computer center, student center. Dormitories linked to campus network. Commuter students can connect to campus network. Online course registration, helpline available.

Student life. Freshman orientation: Mandatory, $25 fee. Preregistration for classes offered. Two-day event. **Housing:** Guaranteed on-campus for all undergraduates. Coed dorms, single-sex dorms, special housing for disabled, apartments, cooperative housing, fraternity/sorority housing available. $125 partly refundable deposit, deadline 7/15. Family housing, honors students housing, NET housing (neighbors educated together). **Activities:** Jazz band, campus ministries, choral groups, dance, drama, international student organizations, music ensembles, musical theater, opera, student government, student newspaper, Alpha Theta Omega, LULAC, multicultural African organization, NAACP, Alpha Kappa Alpha Sorority, Delta Sigma Theta Sorority, Zeta Phi Beta Sorority, Golden Key international honor society.

Athletics. NCAA. **Intercollegiate:** Basketball W, gymnastics W, soccer W, softball W, volleyball W. **Intramural:** Basketball, football (non-tackle), golf, racquetball, soccer, softball, swimming, table tennis M, tennis, volleyball, weight lifting. **Team name:** Pioneers.

Student services. Adult student services, alcohol/substance abuse counseling, career counseling, student employment services, financial aid counseling, health services, minority student services, personal counseling, placement for graduates, veterans' counselor, women's services. **Physically disabled:** Services for visually, speech, hearing impaired.

Contact. E-mail: admissions@twu.edu
Phone: (940) 898-3188 Toll-free number: (866) 809-6130
Fax: (940) 898-3081
Erma Nieto-Brecht, Director of Admissions, Texas Woman's University, Box 425589, Denton, TX 76204-5589

Trinity University
San Antonio, Texas
www.trinity.edu

CB member
CB code: 6831

- Private 4-year liberal arts college affiliated with Presbyterian Church (USA)
- Residential campus in very large city
- 2,404 degree-seeking undergraduates: 1% part-time, 54% women, 3% African American, 7% Asian American, 13% Hispanic American, 7% international
- 204 degree-seeking graduate students
- 61% of applicants admitted
- SAT or ACT (ACT writing optional), application essay required
- 80% graduate within 6 years

General. Founded in 1869. Regionally accredited. **Degrees:** 553 bachelor's awarded; master's offered. **ROTC:** Air Force. **Location:** 3 miles from downtown. **Calendar:** Semester, limited summer session. **Full-time faculty:** 255 total; 97% have terminal degrees, 17% minority, 39% women. **Part-time faculty:** 70 total; 26% have terminal degrees, 19% minority, 34% women. **Class size:** 62% < 20, 35% 20-39, 1% 40-49, 2% 50-99, less than 1% >100.

Freshman class profile. 4,507 applied, 2,755 admitted, 636 enrolled.

Mid 50% test scores			
SAT critical reading:	570-680	Rank in top quarter:	79%
SAT math:	590-680	Rank in top tenth:	50%
SAT writing:	570-670	End year in good standing:	87%
ACT composite:	26-31	Return as sophomores:	89%
GPA 3.75 or higher:	33%	Out-of-state:	32%
GPA 3.50-3.74:	25%	Live on campus:	100%
GPA 3.0-3.49:	34%	International:	6%
GPA 2.0-2.99:	8%		

Basis for selection. GPA, high school rank, test scores, essay, interview, recommendations, extracurricular involvement, and achievement important. **Home schooled:** At least 3 SAT Subject Tests recommended, including natural science and foreign language.

High school preparation. 15 units required; 19 recommended. Required and recommended units include English 4, mathematics 3, social studies 3,

science 3 (laboratory 2-3), foreign language 2-3 and academic electives 3.

2011-2012 Annual costs. Tuition/fees: $31,356. Room/board: $10,966. Books/supplies: $1,000. Personal expenses: $1,100.

2011-2012 Financial aid. Need-based: 448 full-time freshmen applied for aid; 333 were judged to have need; 332 of these received aid. Average need met was 90%. Average scholarship/grant was $22,584; average loan $5,514. 77% of total undergraduate aid awarded as scholarships/grants, 23% as loans/jobs. **Non-need-based:** Awarded to 1,105 full-time undergraduates, including 266 freshmen. Scholarships awarded for academics, leadership, music/drama.

Application procedures. Admission: Closing date 2/1 (postmark date). $50 fee, may be waived for applicants with need, free for online applicants. Admission notification by 4/1. Must reply by 5/1. **Financial aid:** Priority date 2/15, closing date 4/1. FAFSA required. Applicants notified by 4/1; must reply by 5/1 or within 3 week(s) of notification.

Academics. Special study options: Accelerated study, combined bachelor's/graduate degree, double major, honors, independent study, internships, liberal arts/career combination, New York semester, semester at sea, student-designed major, study abroad, teacher certification program, United Nations semester, urban semester, Washington semester. **Credit/placement by examination:** AP, CLEP, IB, institutional tests. 36 credit hours maximum toward bachelor's degree. **Support services:** Writing center.

Majors. Area/ethnic studies: Asian, European, Latin American. **Biology:** General, biochemistry. **Business:** Accounting, business admin, finance, international, management science, marketing. **Communications:** Communications/speech/rhetoric. **Computer sciences:** General. **Education:** Elementary. **Engineering:** Engineering science. **English:** English lit, rhetoric/composition. **Foreign languages:** Chinese, classics, French, German, Russian, Spanish. **History:** General. **Math:** General. **Philosophy/religion:** Philosophy, religion. **Physical sciences:** Chemistry, geology, physics. **Psychology:** General. **Social sciences:** Anthropology, economics, political science, sociology, urban studies. **Visual/performing arts:** Art, art history/conservation, dramatic, music, music performance, music theory/composition, theater design, voice/opera.

Most popular majors. Biology 6%, business/marketing 26%, communications/journalism 6%, English 7%, foreign language 10%, social sciences 15%, visual/performing arts 6%.

Computing on campus. 400 workstations in library, computer center, student center. Dormitories wired for high-speed internet access and linked to campus network. Commuter students can connect to campus network. Online course registration, online library, helpline, student web hosting, wireless network available.

Student life. Freshman orientation: Available. Preregistration for classes offered. **Housing:** Guaranteed on-campus for freshmen. Coed dorms, wellness housing available. $500 nonrefundable deposit, deadline 5/1. **Activities:** Bands, campus ministries, choral groups, dance, drama, film society, literary magazine, music ensembles, Model UN, musical theater, opera, radio station, student government, student newspaper, symphony orchestra, TV station, Phi Beta Kappa, academic honor societies, activities council, Young Democrats, Young Republicans, association of student representatives, Alpha Phi Omega, religious organizations, minority student organizations, Trinity Multicultural Network.

Athletics. NCAA. **Intercollegiate:** Baseball M, basketball, cross-country, diving, football (tackle) M, golf, soccer, softball W, swimming, tennis, track and field, volleyball W. **Intramural:** Basketball, cross-country, football (non-tackle), racquetball, soccer, softball, swimming, table tennis, tennis, volleyball, wrestling. **Team name:** Tigers.

Student services. Chaplain/spiritual director, career counseling, student employment services, financial aid counseling, health services, personal counseling, placement for graduates, veterans' counselor. **Physically disabled:** Services for visually, hearing impaired.

Contact. E-mail: admissions@trinity.edu
Phone: (210) 999-7207 Toll-free number: (800) 874-6489
Fax: (210) 999-8164
Christopher Ellertson, Dean of Admissions and Financial Aid, Trinity University, One Trinity Place, San Antonio, TX 78212-7200

University of Dallas
Irving, Texas
www.udallas.edu

CB member
CB code: 6868

- Private 4-year university and liberal arts college affiliated with Roman Catholic Church
- Residential campus in small city

- 1,356 degree-seeking undergraduates: 2% part-time, 51% women, 1% African American, 4% Asian American, 16% Hispanic American, 3% international
- 1,369 degree-seeking graduate students
- 88% of applicants admitted
- SAT or ACT with writing, application essay required
- 73% graduate within 6 years

General. Founded in 1956. Regionally accredited. Campus in Marino, Italy. **Degrees:** 271 bachelor's awarded; master's, doctoral offered. **ROTC:** Army, Air Force. **Location:** 5 miles from Dallas. **Calendar:** Semester, limited summer session. **Full-time faculty:** 127 total; 85% have terminal degrees, 11% minority, 33% women. **Part-time faculty:** 108 total; 11% minority, 34% women. **Class size:** 57% < 20, 39% 20-39, 2% 40-49, 2% 50-99, less than 1% >100.

Freshman class profile. 1,082 applied, 947 admitted, 371 enrolled.

Mid 50% test scores			
SAT critical reading:	550-700	GPA 2.0-2.99:	4%
SAT math:	530-640	Rank in top quarter:	66%
SAT writing:	550-690	Rank in top tenth:	43%
ACT composite:	24-30	Return as sophomores:	80%
GPA 3.75 or higher:	53%	Out-of-state:	55%
GPA 3.50-3.74:	19%	Live on campus:	91%
GPA 3.0-3.49:	20%	International:	2%

Basis for selection. Sufficient academic preparation and ability required along with evidence of good character. Critical writing and composition skills important. Interview recommended for academically marginal; audition recommended for theater program; portfolio recommended for art program. **Home schooled:** Transcript of courses and grades required. Transcript must be from a recognized, accredited consortium or association; or a comprehensive syllabi (including list of books used, laboratory work done, and narrative description or experiential learning) is required. Homeschool supplement and self-certification forms also required.

High school preparation. College-preparatory program recommended. Required and recommended units include English 4, mathematics 3-4, social studies 3-4, history 3-4, science 3 (laboratory 3), foreign language 2-3, visual/performing arts 2 and academic electives 4.

2012-2013 Annual costs. Tuition/fees (projected): $31,070. Room/board: $9,890. Books/supplies: $1,200. Personal expenses: $1,600.

2010-2011 Financial aid. Need-based: 309 full-time freshmen applied for aid; 267 were judged to have need; 267 of these received aid. Average need met was 78%. Average scholarship/grant was $19,933; average loan $4,147. 83% of total undergraduate aid awarded as scholarships/grants, 17% as loans/jobs. **Non-need-based:** Awarded to 449 full-time undergraduates, including 115 freshmen. Scholarships awarded for academics, alumni affiliation, art, leadership, minority status, music/drama, religious affiliation, ROTC, state residency.

Application procedures. Admission: Priority date 12/1; deadline 3/1 (postmark date). $40 fee, may be waived for applicants with need. Admission notification on a rolling basis beginning on or about 4/1. Must reply by May 1 or within 4 week(s) if notified thereafter. Two early action deadlines: November 1 and December 1. Notification is 3-4 weeks later. **Financial aid:** Priority date 1/15, closing date 3/1. FAFSA required. Applicants notified on a rolling basis starting 3/1; must reply by 5/1 or within 2 week(s) of notification.

Academics. Special study options: Combined bachelor's/graduate degree, double major, dual enrollment of high school students, independent study, internships, liberal arts/career combination, student-designed major, study abroad, teacher certification program. Intensive honors chemistry summer program for entering freshmen. **Credit/placement by examination:** AP, CLEP, IB, institutional tests. 32 credit hours maximum toward bachelor's degree. **Support services:** Pre-admission summer program, reduced course load, tutoring, writing center.

Majors. Biology: General, biochemistry. **Business:** Business admin. **Education:** General, elementary. **English:** English lit. **Foreign languages:** Classics, French, German, Spanish. **History:** General. **Math:** General. **Philosophy/religion:** Philosophy. **Physical sciences:** Chemistry, physics. **Psychology:** General. **Social sciences:** Economics, political science. **Theology:** Preministerial, theology. **Visual/performing arts:** Art history/conservation, ceramics, dramatic, painting, printmaking, sculpture.

Most popular majors. Biology 10%, business/marketing 12%, English 14%, foreign language 8%, history 10%, psychology 10%, social sciences 13%, theological studies 7%, visual/performing arts 6%.

Computing on campus. 125 workstations in library, computer center, student center. Dormitories wired for high-speed internet access and linked

to campus network. Commuter students can connect to campus network. Online library, helpline, wireless network available.

Student life. Freshman orientation: Mandatory. Preregistration for classes offered. One-day program prior to fall semester. **Housing:** Guaranteed on-campus for freshmen. Single-sex dorms, apartments available. $150 nonrefundable deposit, deadline 6/1. **Activities:** Campus ministries, choral groups, dance, drama, film society, international student organizations, literary magazine, music ensembles, musical theater, student government, student newspaper, Best Buddies, Society of St. Vincent de Paul, Alpha Phi Omega, Crusaders for Life, Asian student organization, Latin American student association, SPUD.

Athletics. NCAA. **Intercollegiate:** Baseball M, basketball, cross-country, golf M, lacrosse, soccer, softball W, track and field, volleyball W. **Intramural:** Basketball M, football (non-tackle), soccer, softball, volleyball. **Team name:** Crusaders.

Student services. Chaplain/spiritual director, career counseling, student employment services, financial aid counseling, health services, personal counseling, placement for graduates. **Physically disabled:** Services for visually impaired.

Contact. E-mail: ugadmis@udallas.edu
Phone: (972) 721-5266 Toll-free number: (800) 628-6999
Fax: (972) 721-5017
John Plotts, Associate Provost and VP of Enrollment Management, University of Dallas, 1845 East Northgate Drive, Irving, TX 75062-4736

University of Houston
Houston, Texas
www.uh.edu

CB member
CB code: 6870

- Public 4-year university
- Commuter campus in very large city
- 30,452 degree-seeking undergraduates: 25% part-time, 50% women, 13% African American, 21% Asian American, 27% Hispanic American, 4% international
- 8,056 degree-seeking graduate students
- 64% of applicants admitted
- SAT or ACT (ACT writing optional) required
- 46% graduate within 6 years

General. Founded in 1927. Regionally accredited. **Degrees:** 5,092 bachelor's awarded; master's, professional, doctoral offered. **ROTC:** Army, Naval, Air Force. **Location:** 3 miles from downtown. **Calendar:** Semester, extensive summer session. **Full-time faculty:** 1,320 total; 86% have terminal degrees, 25% minority, 37% women. **Part-time faculty:** 493 total; 49% have terminal degrees, 19% minority, 37% women. **Class size:** 29% < 20, 40% 20-39, 10% 40-49, 12% 50-99, 10% >100. **Special facilities:** Theater complex, observatory, opera house, university center, campus recreation and wellness center, Blaffer art museum.

Freshman class profile. 14,725 applied, 9,359 admitted, 3,719 enrolled.

Mid 50% test scores		End year in good standing:	84%
SAT critical reading:	480-590	Return as sophomores:	81%
SAT math:	520-630	Out-of-state:	3%
ACT composite:	21-26	Live on campus:	43%
Rank in top quarter:	63%	International:	3%
Rank in top tenth:	31%		

Basis for selection. Those ranked in top 10% of high school class are automatically accepted provided they apply by April 1. Before December 1, applicants in top 15% are admitted, applicants in the top 15%-25% with minimum combined score of 1000 SAT (exclusive of Writing) or 21 ACT composite are admitted, and applicants in the top 26%-50% with minimum combined score of 1100 SAT (exclusive of Writing) or 24 ACT composite are admitted. Students submitting after December 1 or applicants attending a school that doesn't rank are considered for admission under the school's individual/holistic review process, which examines rigor of high school curriculum, first-generation college attendance, socioeconomic background, special talents, abilities or awards, family responsibilities, leadership, public service and extracurricular activities. Audition and application required for music, theater, and dance programs; essay recommended for honors college and individual review. Portfolio suggested for architecture program. **Home schooled:** Transcript of courses and grades, state high school equivalency certificate required. Must submit minimum SAT score of 1180 (exclusive of Writing) or a 26 composite score on the ACT and transcript (can be created by parent). In order to qualify for financial aid, must pass GED exam. **Learning Disabled:** Intake appointment with counselor scheduled upon receipt of required documentation of limitations due to disability.

High school preparation. College-preparatory program recommended. Required and recommended units include English 4, mathematics 4, social studies 4, science 4 (laboratory 2), foreign language 2, computer science 1 and visual/performing arts 1.

2011-2012 Annual costs. Tuition/fees: $9,211; $18,601 out-of-state. Room/board: $8,318. Books/supplies: $1,200. Personal expenses: $2,624.

2011-2012 Financial aid. Need-based: 2,856 full-time freshmen applied for aid; 2,411 were judged to have need; 2,341 of these received aid. Average need met was 77%. Average scholarship/grant was $8,803; average loan $5,455. 43% of total undergraduate aid awarded as scholarships/grants, 57% as loans/jobs. **Non-need-based:** Awarded to 688 full-time undergraduates, including 289 freshmen. Scholarships awarded for academics, alumni affiliation, art, athletics, job skills, leadership, music/drama, ROTC, state residency. **Additional information:** The Cougar Promise guarantees free tuition and mandatory fees to new in-state freshmen with family incomes at or below $45,000. Qualifying students will have tuition and fees guaranteed for up to four years as long as students continue to meet eligibility criteria and maintain at least a 2.5 GPA. Covers tuition and fees during the fall and spring semesters only. Eligibility is determined when a student fills out the FAFSA. Those who miss the March 31st deadline will be awarded based on the availability of funds.

Application procedures. Admission: Priority date 12/1; deadline 4/1 (receipt date). $50 fee ($50 out-of-state), may be waived for applicants with need. Admission notification by 4/15. Admission notification on a rolling basis beginning on or about 9/15. Must reply by 6/1. **Financial aid:** Priority date 4/1; no closing date. FAFSA required. Applicants notified on a rolling basis starting 5/1.

Academics. Special study options: Accelerated study, combined bachelor's/graduate degree, cooperative education, cross-registration, distance learning, double major, dual enrollment of high school students, ESL, exchange student, honors, independent study, internships, study abroad, teacher certification program, Washington semester, weekend college. Academic enrichment programs, certification programs and affiliated studies. **Credit/placement by examination:** AP, CLEP, IB, institutional tests. **Support services:** Learning center, reduced course load, remedial instruction, study skills assistance, tutoring, writing center.

Honors college/program. All students encouraged to apply. High school and/or academic record, extracurricular activities, test scores, and essay of each applicant considered. No specific requirements for admission, however the average honors student is in top 10 percent of high school class with SAT score of 1270 (exclusive of Writing).

Majors. Architecture: Architecture, environmental design, interior. **Biology:** General, biochemistry, biotechnology. **Business:** Accounting, business admin, communications, entrepreneurial studies, finance, hotel/motel admin, management information systems, marketing, operations, organizational leadership, sales/distribution, training/development. **Communications:** Advertising, communications/speech/rhetoric, health, journalism, media studies, public relations, radio/TV. **Computer sciences:** General, computer graphics, information systems, systems analysis. **Conservation:** Environmental science. **Engineering:** Biomedical, chemical, civil, computer, electrical, industrial, mechanical, petroleum. **English:** Creative writing, English lit. **Foreign languages:** American Sign Language, Chinese, French, Italian, linguistics, Spanish. **Health services:** General, communication disorders, pharmaceutical sciences. **History:** General. **Liberal arts:** Arts/sciences. **Math:** General, biological. **Parks/recreation:** Exercise sciences, sports admin. **Philosophy/religion:** Philosophy. **Physical sciences:** Chemistry, geology, geophysics, physics. **Psychology:** General. **Social sciences:** Anthropology, economics, political science, sociology. **Visual/performing arts:** Art, art history/conservation, dance, dramatic, graphic design, industrial design, music, music performance, painting, photography, sculpture. **Work/family studies:** Business, family studies, human nutrition.

Most popular majors. Biology 7%, business/marketing 29%, communications/journalism 7%, engineering/engineering technologies 8%, psychology 8%, social sciences 8%.

Computing on campus. 1,110 workstations in dormitories, library, student center. Dormitories wired for high-speed internet access and linked to campus network. Commuter students can connect to campus network. Online course registration, online library, helpline, repair service, student web hosting, wireless network available.

Student life. Freshman orientation: Mandatory, $120 fee. Preregistration for classes offered. Two-day conferences include advising, placement testing, textbook orders. Held late spring through summer. **Housing:** Coed dorms, special housing for disabled, apartments, fraternity/sorority housing available. $300 partly refundable deposit. **Activities:** Bands, campus ministries, choral groups, dance, drama, film society, international student organizations, literary magazine, music ensembles, musical theater, opera, radio station, student government, student newspaper, symphony orchestra, TV station, African

Student Organization, Council of Ethnic Organizations, Indian Student Association, Bhakti Yoga Society, Asian Campus Fellowship, Catholic Student Organization, Student Government Association, Skeptics Society, National Society of Collegiate Scholars, Phi Alpha Theta-Zeta Kappa, Hispanic Business Student Association, Gamma Iota Sigma.

Athletics. NCAA. **Intercollegiate:** Baseball M, basketball, cross-country, diving W, football (tackle) M, golf M, soccer W, softball W, swimming W, tennis W, track and field, volleyball W. **Intramural:** Badminton, basketball, bowling, cross-country, football (non-tackle), golf, racquetball, soccer, softball, swimming, table tennis, tennis, track and field, volleyball. **Team name:** Cougars.

Student services. Adult student services, alcohol/substance abuse counseling, chaplain/spiritual director, career counseling, student employment services, financial aid counseling, health services, on-campus daycare, personal counseling, placement for graduates, veterans' counselor, women's services. **Physically disabled:** Services for visually, speech, hearing impaired.

Contact. E-mail: admissions@uh.edu
Phone: (713) 743-1010 Fax: (713) 743-7542
Djuana Young, Executive Director of Admissions, University of Houston, Welcome Center, Houston, TX 77204-2023

University of Houston-Clear Lake
Houston, Texas
www.uhcl.edu

CB member
CB code: 6916

- Public two-year upper-division university
- Commuter campus in very large city
- 73% of applicants admitted

General. Founded in 1971. Regionally accredited. Upper level university for undergraduates. Located 3 miles from NASA. **Degrees:** 1,183 bachelor's awarded; master's, professional offered. **Articulation:** Agreements with all community colleges in Houston metropolitan area, Houston CC, Lone Star CC, San Jacinto College, Galveston College, Alvin CC, Lee College, College of the Mainland, Wharton County Junior College. **Location:** 21 miles from Houston. **Calendar:** Semester, limited summer session. **Full-time faculty:** 242 total; 81% have terminal degrees, 24% minority, 45% women. **Part-time faculty:** 216 total; 37% have terminal degrees, 23% minority, 63% women.

Student profile. 4,568 degree-seeking undergraduates, 3,368 degree-seeking graduate students. 2,034 applied as first time-transfer students, 1,485 admitted, 1,132 enrolled. 82% entered as juniors, 18% entered as seniors.

Women:	68%	International:	1%
African American:	9%	Part-time:	53%
Asian American:	6%	25 or older:	57%
Hispanic American:	30%		

Basis for selection. College transcript required. Successful completion of college algebra or higher math. 54 hours with C or better. Must meet Texas Success Initiative. Must be in good standing. Must turn in all transcripts if degree seeking. Must have completed English composition 1 and 2 with C- or better. Transfer accepted as juniors, seniors.

2011-2012 Annual costs. Tuition/fees: $6,508; $17,346 out-of-state. Books/supplies: $1,050. Personal expenses: $3,736.

Financial aid. Non-need-based: Scholarships awarded for academics, leadership, state residency.

Application procedures. Admission: Deadline 8/1. $35 fee. **Financial aid:** Priority date 3/31, no deadline. Applicants notified on a rolling basis starting 5/15; must reply within 4 weeks of notification. FAFSA required.

Academics. Special study options: Combined bachelor's/graduate degree, cooperative education, distance learning, double major, dual enrollment of high school students, ESL, independent study, internships, student-designed major, study abroad, teacher certification program, weekend college. **Credit/placement by examination:** AP, CLEP. 18 credit hours maximum toward bachelor's degree. No more than 3 hours in history and government may be earned through CLEP.

Majors. Area/ethnic studies: Women's. **Biology:** General. **Business:** General, accounting, business admin, finance, management information systems, marketing. **Communications:** General. **Computer sciences:** General, computer science. **Conservation:** Environmental science. **Engineering:** Computer. **English:** English lit. **Health services:** Health care admin. **History:** General. **Human services:** General, social work. **Liberal arts:** Humanities. **Math:** General. **Parks/recreation:** Exercise sciences. **Physical sciences:** General, chemistry, physics. **Psychology:** General. **Social sciences:** Anthropology, criminology, geography, political science, sociology. **Visual/performing arts:** Studio arts.

Most popular majors. Business/marketing 27%, interdisciplinary studies 23%, psychology 8%.

Computing on campus. 799 workstations in library, computer center, student center. Commuter students can connect to campus network. Online library, helpline, wireless network available.

Student life. Housing: Limited apartments on campus. **Activities:** Film society, international student organizations, literary magazine, student government, student newspaper, black student association, Chinese student association, Latino and Hispanic Heritage student association, Indian student association, Muslim student association, Baptist Student Ministry, Soka Peace Group, Student Veterans of America.

Student services. Alcohol/substance abuse counseling, career counseling, student employment services, financial aid counseling, health services, minority student services, personal counseling, placement for graduates, veterans' counselor, women's services. **Physically disabled:** Services for visually, speech, hearing impaired.

Contact. E-mail: admissions@uhcl.edu
Phone: (281) 283-2500 Fax: (281) 283-2522
Rauchelle Jones, Executive Director of Admissions, University of Houston-Clear Lake, 2700 Bay Area Boulevard, Houston, TX 77058-1098

University of Houston-Downtown
Houston, Texas
www.uhd.edu

CB member
CB code: 6922

- Public 4-year university
- Commuter campus in very large city
- 12,670 degree-seeking undergraduates: 51% part-time, 61% women, 28% African American, 9% Asian American, 37% Hispanic American, 5% international
- 161 degree-seeking graduate students

General. Founded in 1974. Regionally accredited. UHD operates a campus at Lone Star College University Center. Classes are also offered at these Lone Star College (LSC) sites: LSC-Kingwood, LSC-CyFair, and LSC-Atascocita Center. UHD offers 12 undergraduate degrees for online completion and an online MS-Criminal Justice. The MBA is a hybrid program (online and face to face) developed for working professionals. **Degrees:** 2,517 bachelor's awarded; master's offered. **ROTC:** Army, Air Force. **Location:** Downtown. **Calendar:** Semester, extensive summer session. **Full-time faculty:** 327 total; 85% have terminal degrees, 33% minority, 48% women. **Part-time faculty:** 315 total; 35% have terminal degrees, 44% minority, 48% women. **Class size:** 27% < 20, 58% 20-39, 11% 40-49, 4% 50-99.

Freshman class profile. 2,883 applied, 2,794 admitted, 1,138 enrolled.

Mid 50% test scores		Rank in top quarter:	27%
SAT critical reading:	360-470	Rank in top tenth:	9%
SAT math:	400-490	Return as sophomores:	60%
ACT composite:	14-19	Out-of-state:	1%
GPA 3.75 or higher:	18%	International:	7%
GPA 3.50-3.74:	8%	Fraternities:	1%
GPA 3.0-3.49:	26%	Sororities:	1%
GPA 2.0-2.99:	44%		

Basis for selection. Open admission. **Home schooled:** Transcript of courses and grades required.

High school preparation. College-preparatory program recommended. 28.5 units recommended. Recommended units include English 4, mathematics 3, social studies 1.5, history 2, science 3, foreign language 3, computer science 1, visual/performing arts 1 and academic electives 1. 9 units recommended in economics, health education, physical education, speech and additional components.

2011-2012 Annual costs. Tuition/fees: $5,716; $15,106 out-of-state. Tuition rates for College of Business courses that could count toward a Bachelor of Business Administration degree are an additional $2 per credit hour ($157 per hour for resident and $470 per hour for nonresident students). Books/supplies: $1,100. Personal expenses: $3,800.

2010-2011 Financial aid. Need-based: 688 full-time freshmen applied for aid; 640 were judged to have need; 626 of these received aid. Average need met was 54%. Average scholarship/grant was $8,627; average loan $2,847. 50% of total undergraduate aid awarded as scholarships/grants, 50% as loans/jobs. **Non-need-based:** Awarded to 210 full-time undergraduates, including 157 freshmen. Scholarships awarded for academics, leadership.

Application procedures. Admission: Closing date 6/1 (postmark date). $35 fee, may be waived for applicants with need. Application must be

submitted online. Notified within 3-5 business days after all items received. **Financial aid:** Priority date 4/1; no closing date. FAFSA required. Applicants notified on a rolling basis starting 4/15; must reply within 4 week(s) of notification.

Academics. Special study options: Distance learning, double major, dual enrollment of high school students, ESL, honors, independent study, internships, study abroad, teacher certification program, weekend college. **Credit/ placement by examination:** AP, CLEP, IB, institutional tests. 24 credit hours maximum toward bachelor's degree. **Support services:** Learning center, reduced course load, remedial instruction, study skills assistance, tutoring, writing center.

Majors. Biology: General, biotechnology. **Business:** General, accounting, business admin, finance, insurance, international, management information systems, marketing, purchasing. **Communications:** General. **Computer sciences:** General. **English:** English lit, technical writing. **Foreign languages:** Spanish. **History:** General. **Human services:** Social work. **Liberal arts:** Arts/sciences, humanities. **Math:** General, applied. **Philosophy/religion:** Philosophy. **Physical sciences:** Chemistry. **Protective services:** Criminal justice. **Psychology:** General. **Social sciences:** General, political science, sociology. **Visual/performing arts:** General.

Most popular majors. Business/marketing 40%, interdisciplinary studies 12%, liberal arts 15%, psychology 7%, security/protective services 8%.

Computing on campus. 1,971 workstations in library, computer center, student center. Commuter students can connect to campus network. Online course registration, online library, helpline, student web hosting, wireless network available.

Student life. Freshman orientation: Mandatory, $80 fee. Preregistration for classes offered. For students starting in summer and fall semester, 2-day program for students and parents with testing and enrollment support offered, held May to July. For students starting in the spring, 1-day program for students and parents with testing support offered, held November to January. **Policies:** Students must have at least a 2.5 GPA to be an officer in student organizations and at least 2.0 GPA to be a member. **Activities:** Jazz band, campus ministries, drama, international student organizations, literary magazine, Model UN, student government, student newspaper, Black Student Alliance, Indian and Pakistan Student Association, La Tertulia Hispanic Club, Lebanese American Association, International Student Organization, Bilingual Education Student Organization, Revolution, Chariot.

Athletics. Intramural: Badminton, basketball, bowling, soccer, tennis, volleyball. **Team name:** Gators.

Student services. Alcohol/substance abuse counseling, career counseling, student employment services, financial aid counseling, health services, legal services, personal counseling, placement for graduates, veterans' counselor. **Physically disabled:** Services for visually, hearing impaired.

Contact. E-mail: uhdadmit@uhd.edu
Phone: (713) 221-8522 Fax: (713) 221-8157
Jose Cantu, Director of Admissions and Recruitment, University of Houston-Downtown, One Main Street, Suite 350-S, Houston, TX 77002

University of Houston-Victoria
Victoria, Texas
www.uhv.edu   **CB code: 6917**

▶ Public 4-year university
▶ Commuter campus in small city
▶ 2,548 degree-seeking undergraduates
▶ 40% of applicants admitted

General. Founded in 1973. Regionally accredited. **Degrees:** 578 bachelor's awarded; master's offered. **ROTC:** Air Force. **Location:** 100 miles from Houston and San Antonio. **Calendar:** Semester, limited summer session. **Full-time faculty:** 125 total. **Part-time faculty:** 83 total. **Class size:** 37% < 20, 40% 20-39, 15% 40-49, 8% 50-99.

Freshman class profile. 1,960 applied, 787 admitted, 156 enrolled.

Mid 50% test scores			
SAT critical reading:	400-490	SAT math:	420-510
		ACT composite:	18-21

Basis for selection. Admissions based on college transcript and TASP score. SAT or ACT recommended.

2011-2012 Annual costs. Tuition/fees: $5,828; $15,218 out-of-state. Books/supplies: $1,100. Personal expenses: $2,028.

Financial aid. Non-need-based: Scholarships awarded for academics, athletics, leadership, state residency. **Additional information:** Short-term loans available at registration.

Application procedures. Admission: Closing date 8/25. No application fee. Application must be submitted online. Admission notification on a rolling basis. **Financial aid:** Closing date 4/15. FAFSA required. Applicants notified on a rolling basis; must reply within 3 week(s) of notification.

Academics. Online course support. **Special study options:** Accelerated study, distance learning, double major, honors, independent study, internships, study abroad, teacher certification program. **Credit/placement by examination:** AP, CLEP.

Majors. Biology: General. **Business:** General, accounting, business admin, marketing. **Communications:** Communications/speech/rhetoric. **Computer sciences:** General, information systems. **Education:** General. **English:** English lit, rhetoric/composition. **Health services:** Nursing (RN). **History:** General. **Math:** General. **Protective services:** Law enforcement admin. **Psychology:** General.

Most popular majors. Biology 7%, business/marketing 16%, education 27%, health sciences 13%, interdisciplinary studies 12%, psychology 8%.

Computing on campus. 250 workstations in library, computer center, student center. Commuter students can connect to campus network. Online course registration, online library, helpline, repair service, wireless network available.

Student life. Housing: Coed dorms available. **Activities:** International student organizations, student government.

Athletics. NAIA. **Intercollegiate:** Baseball M, softball W. **Team name:** Jaguar.

Student services. Career counseling, student employment services, financial aid counseling, placement for graduates, veterans' counselor. **Physically disabled:** Services for visually, hearing impaired.

Contact. E-mail: admission@uhv.edu
Phone: (361) 570-4359 Toll-free number: (877) 970-4848 ext. 110
Fax: (361) 580-5500
Denee Thomas, Admission Officer, University of Houston-Victoria, 3007 North Ben Wilson, Victoria, TX 77901-4450

University of Mary Hardin-Baylor
Belton, Texas   **CB member**
www.umhb.edu   **CB code: 6396**

▶ Private 4-year university affiliated with Baptist faith
▶ Residential campus in large town
▶ 2,750 degree-seeking undergraduates: 7% part-time, 63% women, 14% African American, 2% Asian American, 14% Hispanic American, 1% Native American, 1% international
▶ 353 degree-seeking graduate students
▶ 42% of applicants admitted
▶ SAT or ACT with writing required
▶ 46% graduate within 6 years

General. Founded in 1845. Regionally accredited. **Degrees:** 494 bachelor's awarded; master's, doctoral offered. **ROTC:** Army, Air Force. **Location:** 60 miles from Austin. **Calendar:** Semester, limited summer session. **Full-time faculty:** 141 total; 70% have terminal degrees, 11% minority, 57% women. **Part-time faculty:** 120 total; 30% have terminal degrees, 7% minority, 60% women. **Class size:** 57% < 20, 35% 20-39, 5% 40-49, 3% 50-99, less than 1% >100.

Freshman class profile. 9,246 applied, 3,881 admitted, 630 enrolled.

Mid 50% test scores			
		ACT composite:	20-26
SAT critical reading:	450-570	Return as sophomores:	64%
SAT math:	470-580	Out-of-state:	2%
SAT writing:	430-550	Live on campus:	92%

Basis for selection. School achievement record and test scores important. Must either rank in top 10% of graduating class; rank in the top half of class and score 950 SAT or 20 ACT; or rank in lower half of class and score 990 SAT or 21 ACT (all SAT scores exclusive of Writing). Academically deficient students may be accepted on individual basis by approval of admissions committee. Interview recommended for academically marginal; audition recommended for music. **Home schooled:** Transcript of courses and grades required. Admission based on ACT or SAT test scores.

High school preparation. College-preparatory program recommended. 24 units required. Required units include English 4, mathematics 3, social studies 3.5, science 3 and foreign language 2.

2011-2012 Annual costs. Tuition/fees: $23,050. Room/board: $6,221. Books/supplies: $1,200. Personal expenses: $1,282.

2011-2012 Financial aid. Need-based: 523 full-time freshmen applied for aid; 465 were judged to have need; 464 of these received aid. Average need met was 62%. Average scholarship/grant was $10,884; average loan $3,353. 58% of total undergraduate aid awarded as scholarships/grants, 42% as loans/jobs. **Non-need-based:** Awarded to 419 full-time undergraduates, including 130 freshmen. Scholarships awarded for academics, art, leadership, music/drama, religious affiliation, ROTC.

Application procedures. Admission: No deadline. $35 fee, may be waived for applicants with need. Admission notification on a rolling basis. Must reply by May 1 or within 2 week(s) if notified thereafter. **Financial aid:** Priority date 3/1; no closing date. FAFSA required. Applicants notified on a rolling basis starting 2/1; must reply within 2 week(s) of notification.

Academics. Special study options: Accelerated study, combined bachelor's/graduate degree, double major, dual enrollment of high school students, ESL, honors, independent study, internships, student-designed major, study abroad, teacher certification program. Servicemember Opportunity Colleges (SOC) programs, military degree completion programs, tuition exchange program with other participating universities. **Credit/placement by examination:** AP, CLEP, IB, institutional tests. 31 credit hours maximum toward bachelor's degree. No more than one-fourth of total credit hours required for degree may be earned through credit by examination. **Support services:** Learning center, reduced course load, remedial instruction, study skills assistance, tutoring.

Majors. Biology: Biomedical sciences. **Business:** General, accounting, business admin, finance, management information systems, marketing. **Communications:** Communications/speech/rhetoric. **Computer sciences:** General, computer graphics, computer science, information systems. **Education:** Elementary, English, mathematics, music, physical, science, social studies, special ed, speech. **Engineering:** Pre-engineering. **English:** English lit. **Foreign languages:** Spanish. **Health services:** Athletic training, clinical lab science, nursing (RN). **History:** General. **Human services:** Social work. **Math:** General. **Parks/recreation:** General, sports admin. **Philosophy/religion:** Christian, religion. **Physical sciences:** Chemistry. **Protective services:** Law enforcement admin. **Psychology:** General. **Social sciences:** Political science, sociology. **Theology:** Bible, pastoral counseling, sacred music, theology. **Visual/performing arts:** Dramatic, music performance, music theory/composition, studio arts.

Most popular majors. Business/marketing 13%, education 18%, health sciences 18%, liberal arts 7%, psychology 8%.

Computing on campus. 275 workstations in dormitories, library, computer center, student center. Dormitories wired for high-speed internet access and linked to campus network. Online course registration, online library, helpline, wireless network available.

Student life. Freshman orientation: Available, $30 fee. Preregistration for classes offered. One-day orientation in summer for students and parents. Full-week orientation for students only before start of classes. **Policies:** Religious observance required. **Housing:** Guaranteed on-campus for freshmen. Single-sex dorms, special housing for disabled, apartments, wellness housing available. $300 partly refundable deposit. **Activities:** Bands, campus ministries, choral groups, drama, international student organizations, literary magazine, music ensembles, musical theater, opera, student government, student newspaper, symphony orchestra, Catholic student organization, College Democrats, College Republicans, Crusaders for Christ, Fellowship of Christian Athletes, Focus (community-wide worship), Habitat for Humanity.

Athletics. NCAA. **Intercollegiate:** Baseball M, basketball, football (tackle) M, golf, soccer, softball W, tennis, volleyball W. **Intramural:** Basketball, football (non-tackle), golf, soccer, softball, table tennis, volleyball, weight lifting. **Team name:** Crusaders.

Student services. Alcohol/substance abuse counseling, chaplain/spiritual director, career counseling, student employment services, financial aid counseling, health services, personal counseling, placement for graduates, veterans' counselor. **Physically disabled:** Services for visually, speech, hearing impaired.

Contact. E-mail: admissions@umhb.edu
Phone: (254) 295-4520 Toll-free number: (800) 727-8642 ext. 4520
Fax: (254) 295-5049
Brent Burks, Director of Admissions and Recruiting, University of Mary Hardin-Baylor, 900 College Street, Belton, TX 76513

University of North Texas

Denton, Texas   **CB member**
www.unt.edu   **CB code: 6481**

- Public 4-year university
- Residential campus in small city
- 28,325 degree-seeking undergraduates: 21% part-time, 52% women, 13% African American, 6% Asian American, 17% Hispanic American, 1% Native American, 3% international
- 1,777 degree-seeking graduate students
- 56% of applicants admitted
- SAT or ACT (ACT writing recommended) required
- 49% graduate within 6 years

General. Founded in 1890. Regionally accredited. **Degrees:** 6,575 bachelor's awarded; master's, professional, doctoral offered. **ROTC:** Army, Air Force. **Location:** 35 miles from Dallas and Fort Worth. **Calendar:** Semester, extensive summer session. **Full-time faculty:** 1,047 total; 79% have terminal degrees, 26% minority, 42% women. **Part-time faculty:** 596 total; 4% have terminal degrees, 16% minority, 60% women. **Class size:** 31% < 20, 41% 20-39, 9% 40-49, 10% 50-99, 9% >100. **Special facilities:** Laser, observatory, accelerators, environmental science facility, planetarium.

Freshman class profile. 14,563 applied, 8,113 admitted, 4,075 enrolled.

Mid 50% test scores			
SAT critical reading:	480-600	Return as sophomores:	80%
SAT math:	490-610	Out-of-state:	3%
SAT writing:	460-580	Live on campus:	83%
ACT composite:	20-26	International:	1%
Rank in top quarter:	51%	Fraternities:	7%
Rank in top tenth:	18%	Sororities:	6%

Basis for selection. It is recommended that students apply well in advance of stated application deadlines. School achievement record most important. Test score minimums vary with class rank: top 10% no minimum. High school students may be admitted on an individual basis after completion of the junior year of high school. Must rank in the top quarter of their class, have strong B average, 3 units of English and 2 units each of solid mathematics, social sciences and natural sciences, minimum SAT score of 1180 (exclusive of Writing) or ACT composite of 26, letters from high school counselor or principal recommending early admission, letter from parents or guardians stating approval, and interview with Office of Admissions. Audition required for music program. **Home schooled:** Statement describing home school structure and mission, transcript of courses and grades required. An interview, essay and letters of recommendation may be required after a review of the application.

High school preparation. College-preparatory program recommended. 22 units required. Required units include English 4, mathematics 3, social studies 2, history 2, science 3, foreign language 2 and academic electives 3. 0.5 health, 1.5 physical education, 0.5-1 computer sciences, 1 fine arts recommended.

2011-2012 Annual costs. Tuition/fees: $8,349; $17,739 out-of-state. Room/board: $6,892.

2011-2012 Financial aid. Need-based: 3,219 full-time freshmen applied for aid; 2,439 were judged to have need; 2,402 of these received aid. Average need met was 76%. Average scholarship/grant was $8,181; average loan $3,381. 45% of total undergraduate aid awarded as scholarships/grants, 55% as loans/jobs. **Non-need-based:** Awarded to 5,954 full-time undergraduates, including 1,693 freshmen.

Application procedures. Admission: Priority date 3/1; deadline 8/1 (postmark date). $60 fee, may be waived for applicants with need. Application must be submitted online. Admission notification on a rolling basis beginning on or about 10/15. **Financial aid:** Priority date 3/31; no closing date. FAFSA required. Applicants notified on a rolling basis starting 4/1.

Academics. Special study options: Accelerated study, combined bachelor's/graduate degree, cooperative education, cross-registration, distance learning, double major, dual enrollment of high school students, ESL, honors, independent study, internships, student-designed major, study abroad, teacher certification program, weekend college. **Credit/placement by examination:** AP, CLEP, IB, institutional tests. 90 credit hours maximum toward bachelor's degree. **Support services:** Learning center, pre-admission summer program, remedial instruction, study skills assistance, tutoring, writing center.

Honors college/program. 1200 or above on the SAT or 27 on ACT. GPA, class rank, advanced courses important.

Majors. **Architecture:** Interior. **Biology:** General, biochemistry. **Business:** General, accounting, banking/financial services, e-commerce, fashion, financial planning, hospitality admin, insurance, logistics, management information systems, managerial economics, marketing, operations, organizational behavior, real estate, sales/distribution, special products marketing. **Communications:** Broadcast journalism, journalism, radio/TV. **Computer sciences:** General, information systems. **Engineering:** Computer, electrical, mechanical. **English:** English lit, rhetoric/composition. **Foreign languages:** French, German, Spanish. **Health services:** Audiology/speech pathology, clinical lab science, cytotechnology, vocational rehab counseling. **History:** General. **Human services:** General, social work. **Math:** General. **Parks/recreation:** Facilities management, health/fitness. **Philosophy/religion:** Philosophy. **Physical sciences:** Chemistry, materials science, physics. **Protective services:** Criminal justice. **Psychology:** General. **Social sciences:** General, anthropology, economics, geography, political science, sociology. **Visual/performing arts:** Art, art history/conservation, commercial/advertising art, dance, dramatic, fashion design, jazz, music, music history, music performance, music theory/composition, studio arts. **Work/family studies:** Family studies.

Most popular majors. Business/marketing 21%, interdisciplinary studies 17%, social sciences 11%, visual/performing arts 9%.

Computing on campus. 735 workstations in dormitories, library, computer center, student center. Dormitories wired for high-speed internet access and linked to campus network. Commuter students can connect to campus network. Online course registration, online library, helpline, student web hosting, wireless network available.

Student life. **Freshman orientation:** Mandatory, $144 fee. Preregistration for classes offered. Nine sessions during June and July; includes overnight stay in one of the resident halls. **Housing:** Guaranteed on-campus for freshmen. Coed dorms, single-sex dorms, special housing for disabled, apartments, fraternity/sorority housing, wellness housing available. $400 fully refundable deposit. **Activities:** Bands, campus ministries, choral groups, dance, drama, film society, international student organizations, literary magazine, music ensembles, Model UN, musical theater, opera, radio station, student government, student newspaper, symphony orchestra, TV station, honorary societies; religious, ethnic, and social service organizations.

Athletics. NCAA. **Intercollegiate:** Basketball, cross-country, diving W, football (tackle) M, golf, soccer W, softball, swimming W, tennis W, track and field, volleyball W. **Intramural:** Basketball, bowling, football (non-tackle), golf, racquetball, soccer, softball, table tennis, tennis, volleyball. **Team name:** Mean Green.

Student services. Adult student services, alcohol/substance abuse counseling, career counseling, student employment services, financial aid counseling, health services, legal services, minority student services, personal counseling, placement for graduates, veterans' counselor, women's services. **Physically disabled:** Services for visually, speech, hearing impaired.

Contact. E-mail: undergrad@unt.edu
Phone: (940) 565-2681 Toll-free number: (800) 868-8211
Fax: (940) 565-2408
Rebecca Lothringer, Director of Admissions, University of North Texas, 1401 West Prairie, Suite 309, Denton, TX 76203-5017

University of Phoenix: Austin
Austin, Texas
www.phoenix.edu

- For-profit 4-year university
- Commuter campus in very large city
- 624 degree-seeking undergraduates

General. Regionally accredited. **Degrees:** 44 bachelor's awarded; master's offered. **Calendar:** Differs by program. **Full-time faculty:** 12 total. **Part-time faculty:** 71 total.

Basis for selection. Open admission.

2011-2012 Annual costs. Estimated costs as of August 2011: per-credit-hour charge, $435 to $480, depending upon level and course of study; electronic course materials fee, $95, if applicable. Book and material charges may vary by course and program. All fees are subject to change.

Application procedures. **Admission:** No deadline. No application fee. **Financial aid:** No deadline.

Academics. **Credit/placement by examination:** AP, CLEP.

Majors. **Business:** Accounting, business admin, credit management, e-commerce, entrepreneurial studies, management science, marketing, operations. **Computer sciences:** Programming. **Health services:** Health care admin, long term care admin, medical records technology. **Human services:** General. **Protective services:** Disaster management, law enforcement admin. **Psychology:** General.

Most popular majors. Business/marketing 50%, interdisciplinary studies 49%.

Contact. Toll-free number: (866) 766-0766
Marc Booker, Director of Admission and Evaluation, University of Phoenix: Austin, 10801-2 North MoPac, Suite 300, Austin, TX 78759-5459

University of Phoenix: Dallas Fort Worth
Dallas, Texas
www.phoenix.edu

- For-profit 4-year university
- Commuter campus in very large city
- 1,190 degree-seeking undergraduates

General. Regionally accredited. **Degrees:** 208 bachelor's awarded; master's offered. **Calendar:** Differs by program. **Full-time faculty:** 15 total. **Part-time faculty:** 153 total.

Basis for selection. Open admission.

2011-2012 Annual costs. Estimated costs as of August 2011: per-credit-hour charge, $435 to $480, depending upon level and course of study; electronic course materials fee, $95, if applicable. Book and material charges may vary by course and program. All fees are subject to change.

Application procedures. **Admission:** No deadline. No application fee. **Financial aid:** No deadline.

Academics. **Credit/placement by examination:** AP, CLEP.

Majors. **Business:** Accounting, business admin, credit management, e-commerce, entrepreneurial studies, marketing, operations. **Communications:** Media studies. **Computer sciences:** General. **Health services:** Long term care admin, medical records technology. **Human services:** General. **Protective services:** Disaster management, law enforcement admin.

Contact. Toll-free number: (866) 766-0766
Marc Booker, Director of Admission and Evaluation, University of Phoenix: Dallas Fort Worth, 12400 Coit Road, Suite 200, Dallas, TX 75251-2004

University of Phoenix: Houston Westside
Houston, Texas
www.phoenix.edu

- For-profit 4-year university
- Commuter campus in very large city
- 2,366 degree-seeking undergraduates

General. Regionally accredited. **Degrees:** 448 bachelor's awarded; master's offered. **Calendar:** Differs by program. **Full-time faculty:** 20 total. **Part-time faculty:** 347 total.

Basis for selection. Open admission.

2011-2012 Annual costs. Estimated costs as of August 2011: per-credit-hour charge, $435 to $480, depending upon level and course of study; electronic course materials fee, $95, if applicable. Book and material charges may vary by course and program. All fees are subject to change.

Application procedures. **Admission:** No deadline. No application fee. **Financial aid:** No deadline.

Academics. **Credit/placement by examination:** AP, CLEP.

Majors. **Business:** Accounting, business admin, credit management, e-commerce, entrepreneurial studies, human resources, marketing, operations. **Computer sciences:** General, informatics, programming. **Education:** Health. **Health services:** Facilities admin, long term care admin, medical records technology. **Human services:** General. **Protective services:** Disaster management, law enforcement admin, security management. **Psychology:** General. **Work/family studies:** Aging.

Contact. Toll-free number: (866) 766-0766
Marc Booker, Director of Admission and Evaluation, University of
Phoenix: Houston Westside, 11451 Katy Freeway, Houston, TX
77079-2004

University of Phoenix: San Antonio
San Antonio, Texas
www.phoenix.edu

- For-profit 4-year university
- Commuter campus in very large city
- 1,015 degree-seeking undergraduates

General. Regionally accredited. **Degrees:** 135 bachelor's awarded; master's offered. **Calendar:** Differs by program. **Full-time faculty:** 11 total. **Part-time faculty:** 149 total.

Basis for selection. Open admission.

2011-2012 Annual costs. Estimated costs as of August 2011: per-credit-hour charge, $435 to $480, depending upon level and course of study; electronic course materials fee, $95, if applicable. Book and material charges may vary by course and program. All fees are subject to change.

Application procedures. Admission: No deadline. No application fee. **Financial aid:** No deadline.

Academics. Credit/placement by examination: AP, CLEP.

Majors. Business: Accounting, business admin, marketing. **Education:** Special ed. **Health services:** Health care admin, long term care admin, medical records admin. **Human services:** General. **Protective services:** Disaster management, law enforcement admin. **Psychology:** General.

Most popular majors. Business/marketing 98%.

Contact. Toll-free number: (866) 766-0766
Marc Booker, Director of Admission and Evaluation, University of
Phoenix: San Antonio, 8200 IH010 West, Suite 910, San Antonio, TX
78230-3876

University of St. Thomas
Houston, Texas   **CB member**
www.stthom.edu   **CB code: 6880**

- Private 4-year university and liberal arts college affiliated with Roman Catholic Church
- Commuter campus in very large city
- 1,532 degree-seeking undergraduates: 22% part-time, 61% women, 5% African American, 11% Asian American, 38% Hispanic American, 7% international
- 2,056 degree-seeking graduate students
- 78% of applicants admitted
- SAT or ACT with writing required
- 44% graduate within 6 years

General. Founded in 1947. Regionally accredited. **Degrees:** 299 bachelor's awarded; master's, doctoral offered. **ROTC:** Army, Air Force. **Location:** 3 miles from downtown. **Calendar:** Semester, limited summer session. **Full-time faculty:** 150 total; 92% have terminal degrees, 19% minority, 38% women. **Part-time faculty:** 183 total; 55% have terminal degrees, 20% minority, 49% women. **Class size:** 67% < 20, 33% 20-39, less than 1% 40-49. **Special facilities:** Meditation garden.

Freshman class profile. 820 applied, 643 admitted, 238 enrolled.

Mid 50% test scores			
SAT critical reading:	510-610	**Rank in top quarter:**	61%
SAT math:	510-610	**Rank in top tenth:**	33%
SAT writing:	500-610	**End year in good standing:**	87%
ACT composite:	24-29	**Return as sophomores:**	82%
GPA 3.75 or higher:	41%	**Out-of-state:**	5%
GPA 3.50-3.74:	21%	**Live on campus:**	44%
GPA 3.0-3.49:	26%	**International:**	11%
GPA 2.0-2.99:	12%		

Basis for selection. School achievement record, test scores, graded essay most important. Cumulative high school GPA of 2.8 required, as well as minimum 1070 SAT (exclusive of Writing) or 23 ACT. High school class rank in upper 50%, if ranking available. International Baccalaureate exam

also used for placement. Essay or personal statement may be required of some applicants. Audition required for applied music, drama, voice programs; portfolio required for art program.

High school preparation. College-preparatory program recommended. 18 units required. Required units include English 4, mathematics 3, social studies 2, history 1, science 3 (laboratory 2) and foreign language 2. Three units of electives in college preparatory classes.

2011-2012 Annual costs. Tuition/fees: $25,300. Room/board: $7,900. Books/supplies: $1,042. Personal expenses: $1,968.

2011-2012 Financial aid. Need-based: 179 full-time freshmen applied for aid; 149 were judged to have need; 148 of these received aid. Average need met was 74%. Average scholarship/grant was $14,772; average loan $3,441. 67% of total undergraduate aid awarded as scholarships/grants, 33% as loans/jobs. **Non-need-based:** Awarded to 420 full-time undergraduates, including 108 freshmen. Scholarships awarded for academics, athletics, music/drama, religious affiliation, ROTC.

Application procedures. Admission: Closing date 5/1. $25 fee, may be waived for applicants with need. Admission notification on a rolling basis beginning on or about 11/15. Must reply by May 1 or within 2 week(s) if notified thereafter. **Financial aid:** Priority date 4/15; no closing date. FAFSA required. Applicants notified on a rolling basis starting 2/15; must reply within 2 week(s) of notification.

Academics. Special study options: Accelerated study, combined bachelor's/graduate degree, distance learning, double major, dual enrollment of high school students, honors, independent study, internships, liberal arts/career combination, student-designed major, study abroad, teacher certification program, weekend college. **Credit/placement by examination:** AP, CLEP, IB, SAT, ACT, institutional tests. 30 credit hours maximum toward bachelor's degree. Validation of credit by examination contingent upon completion of at least 24 semester hours in residence at institution. **Support services:** Learning center, reduced course load, remedial instruction, study skills assistance, tutoring, writing center.

Majors. Biology: General, biochemistry, bioinformatics. **Business:** Accounting, business admin, finance, marketing. **Communications:** Communications/speech/rhetoric. **Conservation:** Environmental science, environmental studies. **Education:** General, elementary, music, secondary. **English:** English lit. **Foreign languages:** French, Spanish. **History:** General. **Liberal arts:** Arts/sciences. **Math:** General. **Philosophy/religion:** Philosophy. **Physical sciences:** Chemistry. **Psychology:** General. **Social sciences:** International economic development, international relations, political science. **Theology:** Pastoral counseling, theology. **Visual/performing arts:** Dramatic, music, studio arts.

Most popular majors. Biology 7%, business/marketing 23%, communications/journalism 10%, education 7%, liberal arts 12%, psychology 9%, social sciences 13%.

Computing on campus. 316 workstations in dormitories, library, computer center. Dormitories wired for high-speed internet access. Online course registration, online library, helpline, wireless network available.

Student life. Freshman orientation: Available. Preregistration for classes offered. Held in August and January. **Policies:** Annual Risk Management Training reviews school's policies on alcohol, travel, speakers, and other student life issues. **Housing:** Coed dorms, apartments available. $300 fully refundable deposit. Pets allowed in dorm rooms. **Activities:** Jazz band, campus ministries, choral groups, dance, drama, international student organizations, literary magazine, music ensembles, Model UN, musical theater, student government, student newspaper, Al-Nadi cultural society, black student union, Vietnamese student association, bilingual education organization, Celts for Life, Pi Sigma Alpha, ECOS, French club, Irish club, Chi Rho.

Athletics. NAIA. **Intercollegiate:** Basketball, golf, soccer M, volleyball W. **Intramural:** Basketball, bowling, football (non-tackle), racquetball, table tennis, tennis, volleyball. **Team name:** Celts.

Student services. Adult student services, chaplain/spiritual director, career counseling, student employment services, financial aid counseling, health services, personal counseling, placement for graduates, veterans' counselor. **Physically disabled:** Services for visually, speech, hearing impaired.

Contact. E-mail: admissions@stthom.edu
Phone: (713) 525-3500 Toll-free number: (800) 856-8565
Fax: (713) 525-3558
Arthur Ortiz, Director of Freshmen Admissions, University of St. Thomas, 3800 Montrose Boulevard, Houston, TX 77006-4626

University of Texas at Arlington
Arlington, Texas
www.uta.edu

CB member
CB code: 6013

- Public 4-year university
- Commuter campus in large city
- 25,092 degree-seeking undergraduates: 37% part-time, 56% women, 15% African American, 11% Asian American, 22% Hispanic American, 4% international
- 7,737 degree-seeking graduate students
- 69% of applicants admitted
- SAT or ACT with writing required
- 42% graduate within 6 years

General. Founded in 1895. Regionally accredited. **Degrees:** 4,994 bachelor's awarded; master's, professional, doctoral offered. **ROTC:** Army, Air Force. **Location:** 15 miles from Dallas and Fort Worth. **Calendar:** 4-1-4-1 January and May terms. Extensive summer session. **Full-time faculty:** 899 total; 27% minority, 41% women. **Part-time faculty:** 417 total; 18% minority, 54% women. **Class size:** 23% < 20, 39% 20-39, 9% 40-49, 20% 50-99, 9% >100. **Special facilities:** Engineering-Science Research Building, large-scale civil engineering labs, nanoelectronics center, manufacturing automation and robotic systems facility, transonic wind tunnel, Texas microfactory, Texas Manufacturing Assistance Center, College of Nursing Smart Hospital, planetarium, Texana and Mexican war history library, kinesiology labs, studio art center with student-run gallery, workforce development center, amphibian and reptile diversity research center, urban design center partnership with the City of Arlington, service learning center, Arlington technology incubator, Optical Medical Imaging Center, Center for Renewable Energy Science and Technology, Genomics Translational Research Laboratory.

Freshman class profile. 9,559 applied, 6,593 admitted, 2,625 enrolled.

Mid 50% test scores			
SAT critical reading:	460-580	End year in good standing:	85%
SAT math:	500-610	Return as sophomores:	74%
ACT composite:	20-25	Out-of-state:	1%
Rank in top quarter:	71%	Live on campus:	51%
Rank in top tenth:	26%	International:	3%

Basis for selection. GED not accepted. Admission based on test scores and high school rank. Fourth quarter of high school class must be approved by director of admissions or associate director. SAT or ACT math scores are used for placement of students majoring in architecture, engineering, biology, biochemistry, chemistry, math, physics, and for students in the bachelor's geology or bachelor's psychology program. Interview recommended for academically weak; audition recommended for music; portfolio recommended for art, architecture programs. **Home schooled:** Transcript of courses and grades, letter of recommendation (nonparent) required.

High school preparation. College-preparatory program required. 20 units required. Required and recommended units include English 4, mathematics 3-4, social studies 3-4, science 3, foreign language 2-3 and academic electives 5. 1 computing proficiency, 1 fine arts, 1 music/theater art, 1.5 physical education, .5 health recommended.

2011-2012 Annual costs. Tuition/fees: $8,878; $18,268 out-of-state. Room/board: $7,554. Books/supplies: $908. Personal expenses: $1,528.

2011-2012 Financial aid. **Need-based:** 1,841 full-time freshmen applied for aid; 1,566 were judged to have need; 1,566 of these received aid. Average need met was 77%. Average scholarship/grant was $7,781; average loan $3,205. 50% of total undergraduate aid awarded as scholarships/grants, 50% as loans/jobs. **Non-need-based:** Awarded to 3,367 full-time undergraduates, including 918 freshmen. Scholarships awarded for academics, art, athletics, leadership, music/drama, ROTC. **Additional information:** Free tuition to eligible students whose household income is $65,000 or less through the Maverick Promise program.

Application procedures. **Admission:** Priority date 6/1; no deadline. $50 fee, may be waived for applicants with need. Notified 3-7 days after application completed. **Financial aid:** Priority date 5/15; no closing date. FAFSA required. Applicants notified on a rolling basis starting 4/1; must reply within 3 week(s) of notification.

Academics. **Special study options:** Combined bachelor's/graduate degree, cross-registration, distance learning, double major, dual enrollment of high school students, honors, independent study, internships, student-designed major, study abroad, teacher certification program. **Credit/placement by examination:** AP, CLEP, IB, institutional tests. Credit by exam does not count as credit earned in residence. **Support services:** Learning center, reduced course load, remedial instruction, study skills assistance, tutoring, writing center.

Majors. **Architecture:** Architecture, interior. **Biology:** General, biochemistry, microbiology. **Business:** Accounting, banking/financial services, business admin, international, management information systems, managerial economics, marketing, real estate. **Communications:** Advertising, digital media, journalism, public relations, radio/TV. **Computer sciences:** Computer science. **Engineering:** Aerospace, biomedical, civil, computer, electrical, industrial, mechanical, software. **English:** English lit, rhetoric/composition. **Foreign languages:** General, French, German, linguistics, Russian, Spanish. **Health services:** Athletic training, clinical lab science, nursing (RN). **History:** General. **Human services:** Social work. **Math:** General. **Parks/recreation:** Exercise sciences. **Philosophy/religion:** Philosophy. **Physical sciences:** Chemistry, geology, physics. **Protective services:** Criminal justice. **Psychology:** General. **Social sciences:** Anthropology, economics, political science, sociology. **Visual/performing arts:** Art, art history/conservation, dramatic, music, music performance, studio arts. **Work/family studies:** Child development.

Most popular majors. Biology 7%, business/marketing 18%, health sciences 21%, interdisciplinary studies 10%.

Computing on campus. 500 workstations in dormitories, library. Dormitories wired for high-speed internet access and linked to campus network. Commuter students can connect to campus network. Online course registration, online library, helpline, student web hosting, wireless network available.

Student life. **Freshman orientation:** Mandatory. Preregistration for classes offered. One-and-a-half-day sessions held in June, July, August. Students stay in residence halls. **Housing:** Coed dorms, single-sex dorms, apartments, fraternity/sorority housing available. $150 nonrefundable deposit. Priority given to students with dependent children. **Activities:** Bands, campus ministries, choral groups, dance, drama, film society, international student organizations, literary magazine, music ensembles, opera, radio station, student government, student newspaper, symphony orchestra, University Democrats, association of Mexican American students, Vietnamese student association, Wesley Foundation, Mavericks for Christ, Business Beta Gamma Sigma, College Republicans, Business Delta Sigma Pi.

Athletics. NCAA. **Intercollegiate:** Baseball M, basketball, golf M, softball W, tennis, track and field, volleyball W. **Intramural:** Badminton, basketball, bowling, golf M, racquetball, soccer, softball, table tennis, tennis, track and field, volleyball. **Team name:** Mavericks.

Student services. Alcohol/substance abuse counseling, chaplain/spiritual director, career counseling, services for economically disadvantaged, student employment services, financial aid counseling, health services, legal services, minority student services, on-campus daycare, personal counseling, placement for graduates, veterans' counselor. **Physically disabled:** Services for visually, hearing impaired.

Contact. E-mail: admissions@uta.edu
Phone: (817) 272-6287 Fax: (817) 272-3435
Hans Gatterdam, Executive Director of Admissions, Records and Registration, University of Texas at Arlington, UTA Box 19088, Arlington, TX 76019

University of Texas at Austin
Austin, Texas
www.utexas.edu

CB member
CB code: 6882

- Public 4-year university
- Commuter campus in very large city
- 37,725 degree-seeking undergraduates: 6% part-time, 51% women, 5% African American, 18% Asian American, 20% Hispanic American, 5% international
- 12,672 degree-seeking graduate students
- 47% of applicants admitted
- SAT or ACT with writing, application essay required
- 81% graduate within 6 years

General. Founded in 1883. Regionally accredited. **Degrees:** 9,054 bachelor's awarded; master's, professional, doctoral offered. **ROTC:** Army, Naval, Air Force. **Location:** 70 miles from San Antonio, 163 miles from Houston. **Calendar:** Semester, extensive summer session. **Full-time faculty:** 2,688 total; 90% have terminal degrees, 21% minority, 38% women. **Part-time faculty:** 276 total; 68% have terminal degrees, 19% minority, 42% women. **Class size:** 34% < 20, 35% 20-39, 7% 40-49, 15% 50-99, 10% >100. **Special facilities:** Humanities and scientific research centers, observatory, marine science institute, fusion reactor, presidential library and museum, performing arts center, museum of natural history, museum of art.

Freshman class profile. 32,589 applied, 15,172 admitted, 7,149 enrolled.

Mid 50% test scores		Return as sophomores:	92%
SAT critical reading:	540-670	Out-of-state:	9%
SAT math:	580-710	Live on campus:	66%
SAT writing:	540-680	International:	4%
ACT composite:	25-31	Fraternities:	13%
Rank in top quarter:	91%	Sororities:	18%
Rank in top tenth:	73%		

Basis for selection. Applicants from top 10% of class from accredited Texas high school automatically admitted with completed application, but available seats limited to 75% of first-time in college cohort. Off-campus coordinated admission program for Texans who complete all required high school units and apply immediately upon high school graduation, but are not otherwise eligible for regular admission. Audition required, interview recommended for music program; interview recommended for art, liberal arts honors program.

High school preparation. College-preparatory program required. 26 units required. Required units include English 4, mathematics 4, social studies 3.5, science 4, foreign language 2 and academic electives 6. Economics (0.5), physical education (1), fine arts (1), speech (0.5), may count as elective.

2011-2012 Annual costs. Tuition/fees: $9,792; $32,379 out-of-state. Room/board: $10,422. Books/supplies: $874. Personal expenses: $2,424.

2011-2012 Financial aid. Need-based: 5,334 full-time freshmen applied for aid; 3,449 were judged to have need; 3,444 of these received aid. Average need met was 75%. Average scholarship/grant was $8,319; average loan $3,540. 56% of total undergraduate aid awarded as scholarships/grants, 44% as loans/jobs. **Non-need-based:** Awarded to 4,576 full-time undergraduates, including 1,686 freshmen. Scholarships awarded for academics, art, athletics, leadership, music/drama, ROTC, state residency.

Application procedures. Admission: Closing date 12/1 (receipt date). $75 fee, may be waived for applicants with need. Admission notification by 4/1. Admission notification on a rolling basis. Must reply by May 1 or within 2 week(s) if notified thereafter. **Financial aid:** Priority date 3/31; no closing date. FAFSA, institutional form required. Applicants notified on a rolling basis starting 3/15; must reply by 5/1 or within 3 week(s) of notification.

Academics. Special study options: Accelerated study, combined bachelor's/graduate degree, cooperative education, distance learning, double major, dual enrollment of high school students, ESL, honors, independent study, internships, liberal arts/career combination, student-designed major, study abroad, teacher certification program, Washington semester. **Credit/placement by examination:** AP, CLEP, IB, institutional tests. **Support services:** Learning center, reduced course load, remedial instruction, study skills assistance, tutoring, writing center.

Majors. Architecture: Architecture. **Area/ethnic studies:** General, African-American, American, Asian, European, Latin American, Near/Middle Eastern, Russian/Slavic, women's. **Biology:** General, biochemistry. **Business:** General, accounting, business admin, finance, logistics, management information systems, marketing. **Communications:** Advertising, communications/speech/rhetoric, journalism, public relations, radio/TV. **Computer sciences:** General. **Engineering:** Aerospace, architectural, biomedical, chemical, civil, electrical, mechanical, petroleum. **English:** English lit, writing. **Foreign languages:** Classics, East Asian, French, German, Italian, Latin, linguistics, Portuguese, Scandinavian, Semitic, Spanish. **Health services:** Athletic training, clinical lab science, communication disorders, nursing (RN). **History:** General. **Human services:** Social work. **Liberal arts:** Arts/sciences, humanities. **Math:** General. **Parks/recreation:** Exercise sciences, health/fitness, sports admin. **Philosophy/religion:** Islamic, Judaic, philosophy, religion. **Physical sciences:** Astronomy, chemistry, geology, geophysics, hydrology, physics. **Psychology:** General. **Social sciences:** Anthropology, archaeology, economics, geography, political science, sociology, urban studies. **Visual/performing arts:** General, art, art history/conservation, dance, design, dramatic, interior design, jazz, music, music performance, music theory/composition, studio arts. **Work/family studies:** General, clothing/textiles, family studies, food/nutrition.

Most popular majors. Biology 9%, business/marketing 12%, communications/journalism 13%, engineering/engineering technologies 11%, social sciences 13%.

Computing on campus. 500 workstations in dormitories, library, computer center, student center. Dormitories wired for high-speed internet access and linked to campus network. Commuter students can connect to campus network. Online course registration, online library, helpline, repair service, student web hosting, wireless network available.

Student life. Freshman orientation: Available, $125 fee. Preregistration for classes offered. **Housing:** Coed dorms, single-sex dorms, apartments available. $300 fully refundable deposit. Honors residence, living learning centers. **Activities:** Bands, campus ministries, choral groups, dance, drama, film society, international student organizations, literary magazine, music ensembles, musical theater, radio station, student government, student newspaper, TV station, variety of religious, political, ethnic, and social service organizations.

Athletics. NCAA. **Intercollegiate:** Baseball M, basketball, cross-country, diving, football (tackle) M, golf, rowing (crew) W, soccer W, softball W, swimming, tennis, track and field, volleyball W. **Intramural:** Badminton, basketball, football (non-tackle), golf, handball, racquetball, soccer, softball, swimming, table tennis, tennis, track and field, volleyball. **Team name:** Longhorns.

Student services. Adult student services, alcohol/substance abuse counseling, career counseling, services for economically disadvantaged, student employment services, financial aid counseling, health services, legal services, minority student services, on-campus daycare, personal counseling, placement for graduates, veterans' counselor, women's services. **Physically disabled:** Services for visually, speech, hearing impaired.

Contact. Phone: (512) 475-7399 Fax: (512) 475-7478
Kedra Ishop, Vice Provost and Director of Admissions, University of Texas at Austin, PO Box 8058, Austin, TX 78713-8058

University of Texas at Brownsville - Texas Southmost College

Brownsville, Texas · **CB member**
www.utb.edu · **CB code: 6825**

- Public 4-year university and community college
- Commuter campus in small city
- 15,403 degree-seeking undergraduates
- 1,116 graduate students

General. Founded in 1977. Regionally accredited. **Degrees:** 1,063 bachelor's, 823 associate awarded; master's, doctoral offered. **ROTC:** Army. **Location:** 150 miles from Corpus Christi. **Calendar:** Semester, extensive summer session. **Full-time faculty:** 408 total. **Part-time faculty:** 328 total. **Class size:** 64% < 20, 30% 20-39, 2% 40-49, 4% 50-99, less than 1% >100.

Freshman class profile.

GPA 3.75 or higher:	11%	Rank in top quarter:	27%
GPA 3.50-3.74:	6%	Rank in top tenth:	10%
GPA 3.0-3.49:	17%	Out-of-state:	1%
GPA 2.0-2.99:	45%	Live on campus:	1%

Basis for selection. Open admission, but selective for some programs. Special requirements for nursing and allied health programs.

High school preparation. College-preparatory program recommended.

2011-2012 Annual costs. Tuition/fees: $5,994; $15,384 out-of-state. Books/supplies: $646. Personal expenses: $2,651.

Financial aid. Non-need-based: Scholarships awarded for academics, alumni affiliation, art, athletics, minority status, music/drama, state residency.

Application procedures. Admission: Priority date 3/1; deadline 7/1 (receipt date). No application fee. Admission notification on a rolling basis. **Financial aid:** Priority date 3/1, closing date 8/15. FAFSA required. Applicants notified on a rolling basis; must reply by 7/1 or within 12 week(s) of notification.

Academics. Special study options: Cooperative education, cross-registration, distance learning, double major, dual enrollment of high school students, ESL, independent study, internships, liberal arts/career combination, study abroad, teacher certification program. **Credit/placement by examination:** AP, CLEP, IB, institutional tests. **Support services:** Learning center, pre-admission summer program, reduced course load, remedial instruction, study skills assistance, tutoring, writing center.

Majors. Biology: General. **Business:** General, accounting, business admin, entrepreneurial studies, finance, international, marketing. **Communications:** Communications/speech/rhetoric. **Computer sciences:** General, information systems. **Conservation:** Environmental science. **Engineering:** Applied physics. **English:** English lit. **Foreign languages:** Spanish, translation. **Health services:** Nursing (RN). **History:** General. **Human services:** General. **Liberal arts:** Arts/sciences. **Math:** General. **Parks/recreation:** Health/fitness. **Physical sciences:** Chemistry, physics. **Protective services:** Corrections, criminal justice, law enforcement admin. **Psychology:** General. **Social sciences:** Political science, sociology. **Visual/performing arts:** Art, music.

Most popular majors. Biology 6%, business/marketing 16%, interdisciplinary studies 27%, parks/recreation 6%, security/protective services 9%.

Computing on campus. 650 workstations in dormitories, library, computer center. Dormitories wired for high-speed internet access and linked to campus network. Commuter students can connect to campus network. Online course registration, online library, helpline, repair service, student web hosting, wireless network available.

Student life. Freshman orientation: Mandatory, $50 fee. Preregistration for classes offered. **Housing:** Coed dorms, wellness housing available. **Activities:** Jazz band, campus ministries, choral groups, dance, international student organizations, music ensembles, student government, student newspaper.

Athletics. NAIA. **Intercollegiate:** Baseball M, golf, soccer, volleyball W. **Team name:** Scorpions.

Student services. Adult student services, career counseling, services for economically disadvantaged, student employment services, financial aid counseling, health services, minority student services, on-campus daycare, personal counseling, placement for graduates, veterans' counselor. **Physically disabled:** Services for visually, speech, hearing impaired.

Contact. E-mail: admissions@utb.edu
Phone: (956) 882-8295 Toll-free number: (800) 850-0160
Fax: (956) 882-7810
Rene Villarreal, Director of Admissions, University of Texas at Brownsville - Texas Southmost College, 80 Fort Brown, Brownsville, TX 78520

University of Texas at Dallas
Richardson, Texas
www.utdallas.edu

CB member
CB code: 6897

- Public 4-year university
- Commuter campus in very large city
- 11,410 degree-seeking undergraduates: 21% part-time, 44% women, 6% African American, 23% Asian American, 15% Hispanic American, 5% international
- 6,698 degree-seeking graduate students
- 53% of applicants admitted
- SAT or ACT (ACT writing optional) required
- 61% graduate within 6 years

General. Founded in 1969. Regionally accredited. Established internships in industrial practice positions with over 200 advanced technology firms located near the university. **Degrees:** 2,354 bachelor's awarded; master's, professional, doctoral offered. **ROTC:** Army, Air Force. **Location:** 18 miles from downtown Dallas. **Calendar:** Semester, extensive summer session. **Full-time faculty:** 621 total; 93% have terminal degrees, 27% minority, 27% women. **Part-time faculty:** 303 total; 52% women. **Class size:** 22% < 20, 37% 20-39, 10% 40-49, 23% 50-99, 8% >100. **Special facilities:** Geological information library, history of aviation library, motion capture lab, rare book library, philatelic research library, center for communications disorders, Holocaust collection, translation library.

Freshman class profile. 6,881 applied, 3,672 admitted, 1,789 enrolled.

Mid 50% test scores		Rank in top quarter:	75%
SAT critical reading:	540-660	Rank in top tenth:	39%
SAT math:	600-700	End year in good standing:	85%
SAT writing:	520-650	Return as sophomores:	83%
ACT composite:	25-30	Out-of-state:	6%
GPA 3.75 or higher:	61%	Live on campus:	50%
GPA 3.50-3.74:	20%	International:	6%
GPA 3.0-3.49:	17%	Fraternities:	4%
GPA 2.0-2.99:	2%	Sororities:	3%

Basis for selection. In-state high school students in top 10% of class automatically admitted to state public universities. Assured admission at UTD for applicants who score 1200 SAT (Critical Reading and Math) or 26 ACT, OR who rank in top 15% of class. Completion of required high school course work required. All others reviewed for admission. Texas Higher Education Assessment test required for some based on high school performance. International students must take TOEFL (minimum score 550 on paper-based or 80 on Internet-based), IELTS Academic (minimum score 6.5) or PTE Academic (minimum score 67).

High school preparation. College-preparatory program required. 18 units required; 24 recommended. Required and recommended units include English 4, mathematics 4, social studies 3-4, science 3 (laboratory 3), foreign language 2-3, computer science 1, visual/performing arts .5-1, academic electives 1.5-2.5. 0.5 health, 1.5 physical education recommended.

2011-2012 Annual costs. Tuition/fees: $11,168; $28,194 out-of-state. Tuition and fees reflect the Guaranteed Tuition rate for incoming students enrolled for the first time during the Fall 2011 or Spring 2012 term. Room/board: $8,364. Books/supplies: $1,200. Personal expenses: $1,930.

2010-2011 Financial aid. Need-based: 915 full-time freshmen applied for aid; 698 were judged to have need; 684 of these received aid. Average need met was 79%. Average scholarship/grant was $11,183; average loan $3,239. 56% of total undergraduate aid awarded as scholarships/grants, 44% as loans/jobs. **Non-need-based:** Awarded to 583 full-time undergraduates, including 305 freshmen. Scholarships awarded for academics.

Application procedures. Admission: Closing date 7/1 (postmark date). $50 fee, may be waived for applicants with need. Admission notification on a rolling basis. **Financial aid:** Priority date 3/31, closing date 4/12. FAFSA required. Applicants notified on a rolling basis starting 3/1; must reply within 2 week(s) of notification.

Academics. Special study options: Accelerated study, combined bachelor's/graduate degree, cooperative education, cross-registration, distance learning, double major, dual enrollment of high school students, ESL, honors, independent study, internships, liberal arts/career combination, student-designed major, study abroad, teacher certification program, Washington semester, weekend college. 3-2 engineering and 2-2 transfer programs. **Credit/placement by examination:** AP, CLEP, IB, institutional tests. 30 credit hours maximum toward bachelor's degree. No limit on lower-level courses, 6 hours limit on upper-level courses. SAT Subject Tests in Math Levels I and II accepted for advanced placement. **Support services:** Learning center, pre-admission summer program, reduced course load, remedial instruction, study skills assistance, tutoring, writing center.

Majors. Area/ethnic studies: American. **Biology:** General, biochemistry, molecular, neuroscience. **Business:** General, accounting, actuarial science, finance, international, management information systems, marketing. **Communications:** Digital media. **Computer sciences:** General. **Engineering:** Biomedical, computer, electrical, mechanical, software, telecommunications. **Foreign languages:** Comparative lit. **Health services:** Audiology/speech pathology. **History:** General. **Human services:** General, public policy. **Liberal arts:** Arts/sciences. **Math:** General. **Physical sciences:** Chemistry, geology, physics. **Psychology:** General, developmental. **Social sciences:** Criminology, economics, GIS/cartography, political science, sociology. **Visual/performing arts:** General, game design.

Most popular majors. Biology 10%, business/marketing 32%, engineering/engineering technologies 7%, interdisciplinary studies 9%, psychology 9%, social sciences 9%, visual/performing arts 7%.

Computing on campus. 650 workstations in library, computer center, student center. Dormitories wired for high-speed internet access and linked to campus network. Commuter students can connect to campus network. Online course registration, online library, helpline, wireless network available.

Student life. Freshman orientation: Mandatory, $100 fee. Preregistration for classes offered. Family 1-day sessions and student 2-day sessions held in April, July and August. **Housing:** Coed dorms, apartments available. $100 partly refundable deposit, deadline 6/30. Pets allowed in dorm rooms. Living-learning communities for freshmen. **Activities:** Bands, choral groups, dance, drama, film society, international student organizations, literary magazine, music ensembles, Model UN, musical theater, radio station, student government, student newspaper, symphony orchestra, TV station, College Republicans, University Democrats, black student alliance, Friendship Association of Chinese Students and Scholars, LULAC, Christians on Campus, Muslim student association, Habitat for Humanity, world aid organization, Alpha Phi Omega (service fraternity).

Athletics. NCAA. **Intercollegiate:** Baseball M, basketball, cross-country, golf, soccer, softball W, tennis, volleyball W. **Intramural:** Basketball, cheerleading, football (non-tackle), soccer, volleyball, water polo. **Team name:** Comets.

Student services. Alcohol/substance abuse counseling, career counseling, student employment services, financial aid counseling, health services, legal services, minority student services, on-campus daycare, personal counseling, placement for graduates, veterans' counselor, women's services. **Physically disabled:** Services for visually, speech, hearing impaired.

Contact. E-mail: interest@utdallas.edu
Phone: (972) 883-2270 Toll-free number: (800) 889-2443
Fax: (972) 883-2599
Curt Eley, VP of Enrollment Management, University of Texas at Dallas, Office of Admissions, Richardson, TX 75080-3021

University of Texas at El Paso
El Paso, Texas
www.utep.edu

CB member
CB code: 6829

- Public 4-year university
- Commuter campus in very large city

▶ 18,503 degree-seeking undergraduates
▶ 3,607 graduate students

General. Founded in 1913. Regionally accredited. Bilingual community, programs, and student body; located within 100 yards of Mexico. **Degrees:** 3,059 bachelor's awarded; master's, professional, doctoral offered. **ROTC:** Army, Air Force. **Calendar:** Semester, extensive summer session. **Full-time faculty:** 676 total. **Part-time faculty:** 288 total. **Class size:** 35% < 20, 47% 20-39, 7% 40-49, 8% 50-99, 3% >100. **Special facilities:** Solar energy facility.

Freshman class profile.

GPA 3.75 or higher:	8%	Rank in top quarter:	42%
GPA 3.50-3.74:	15%	Rank in top tenth:	18%
GPA 3.0-3.49:	47%	Out-of-state:	2%
GPA 2.0-2.99:	27%		

Basis for selection. Minimum GED score of 45, or top half of high school class with 20 ACT or 920 SAT (exclusive of Writing). Provisional admission for in-state residents not meeting these criteria. For students in top quarter of high school class, any score acceptable. SAT or ACT, when required, may be used for counseling. Credit may be given for selected SAT Subject Tests.

High school preparation. College-preparatory program required. 21 units recommended. Recommended units include English 4, mathematics 3, social studies 2, history 2, science 3 and foreign language 2. 1 additional math for science and engineering majors.

2011-2012 Annual costs. Tuition/fees: $6,869; $16,259 out-of-state. Reported room-only cost based on double-occupancy apartment at $525 per month for nine months. Optional a la carte meal plan. Room only: $4,725.

Financial aid. Non-need-based: Scholarships awarded for academics, alumni affiliation, art, athletics, job skills, leadership, minority status, music/drama, religious affiliation, ROTC, state residency. **Additional information:** Emergency loans available.

Application procedures. Admission: Priority date 5/1; deadline 7/31 (postmark date). No application fee. Admission notification on a rolling basis. Notification of early action applicants when admission file is complete. **Financial aid:** Closing date 3/15. FAFSA, institutional form required. Applicants notified by 6/30; must reply within 2 week(s) of notification.

Academics. Special study options: Accelerated study, combined bachelor's/graduate degree, cooperative education, cross-registration, distance learning, double major, dual enrollment of high school students, ESL, exchange student, honors, independent study, internships, study abroad, teacher certification program, weekend college. **Credit/placement by examination:** AP, CLEP, IB, institutional tests. **Support services:** Learning center, pre-admission summer program, reduced course load, remedial instruction, study skills assistance, tutoring, writing center.

Majors. Area/ethnic studies: Chicano/Hispanic-American/Latino, Latin American. **Biology:** General, microbiology, molecular biochemistry. **Business:** General, accounting, business admin, finance, management information systems, managerial economics, marketing, operations. **Communications:** General, advertising, communications/speech/rhetoric, digital media, organizational. **Computer sciences:** General. **Conservation:** Environmental science. **Engineering:** Civil, electrical, industrial, mechanical, metallurgical. **English:** Creative writing, English lit. **Foreign languages:** French, linguistics, Spanish. **Health services:** Clinical lab science, nursing (RN), public health ed. **History:** General. **Human services:** Social work. **Math:** General, applied. **Parks/recreation:** Health/fitness. **Philosophy/religion:** Philosophy. **Physical sciences:** Chemistry, geology, geophysics, physics. **Protective services:** Criminal justice. **Psychology:** General. **Social sciences:** Anthropology, political science, sociology. **Visual/performing arts:** Art, art history/conservation, ceramics, dance, dramatic, drawing, graphic design, metal/jewelry, music, music management, music performance, music theory/composition, musical theater, painting, piano/keyboard, printmaking, sculpture, studio arts, theater arts management, voice/opera.

Most popular majors. Biology 7%, business/marketing 17%, education 14%, engineering/engineering technologies 9%, health sciences 12%, interdisciplinary studies 7%.

Computing on campus. 2,500 workstations in library, computer center, student center. Dormitories wired for high-speed internet access. Commuter students can connect to campus network. Online course registration, online library, helpline, repair service, student web hosting, wireless network available.

Student life. Freshman orientation: Available. Preregistration for classes offered. 3-5 day program. **Housing:** Special housing for disabled, apartments available. **Activities:** Bands, choral groups, dance, drama, film society, literary magazine, music ensembles, musical theater, opera, radio station, student government, student newspaper, symphony orchestra, black student coalition, Mexican student organizations, Society of Hispanic Professional Engineers.

Athletics. NCAA. **Intercollegiate:** Basketball, cross-country, football (tackle) M, golf, rifle, soccer W, softball W, tennis, track and field, volleyball W. **Intramural:** Badminton, baseball M, basketball, bowling, fencing, football (tackle) M, golf, gymnastics, handball, racquetball, skiing, soccer, softball, squash, swimming, table tennis, tennis, track and field, volleyball, water polo, wrestling M. **Team name:** Miners.

Student services. Alcohol/substance abuse counseling, chaplain/spiritual director, career counseling, student employment services, financial aid counseling, health services, on-campus daycare, personal counseling, placement for graduates, veterans' counselor, women's services. **Physically disabled:** Services for visually, speech, hearing impaired.

Contact. E-mail: futureminer@utep.edu
Phone: (915) 747-5890 Fax: (915) 747-8893
Luisa Havens, Director of Admissions, University of Texas at El Paso, 500 West University Avenue, El Paso, TX 79968-0510

University of Texas at San Antonio
San Antonio, Texas — CB member
www.utsa.edu — CB code: 6919

▶ Public 4-year university
▶ Commuter campus in very large city
▶ 25,830 degree-seeking undergraduates: 18% part-time, 48% women, 9% African American, 5% Asian American, 46% Hispanic American, 3% international
▶ 4,665 degree-seeking graduate students
▶ 79% of applicants admitted

General. Founded in 1969. Regionally accredited. Additional downtown and Hemisfair Park campuses. **Degrees:** 4,137 bachelor's awarded; master's, doctoral offered. **ROTC:** Army, Air Force. **Location:** 15 miles from downtown. **Calendar:** Semester, limited summer session. **Full-time faculty:** 985 total; 74% have terminal degrees, 37% minority, 42% women. **Part-time faculty:** 265 total; 49% have terminal degrees, 29% minority, 43% women. **Class size:** 24% < 20, 43% 20-39, 11% 40-49, 13% 50-99, 9% >100. **Special facilities:** Institute of Texan cultures, center for archaeological research, neuroscience research center, center for water research, center for lasers and materials science, center for economic development, culture and policy institute, institute for music research, center for professional excellence.

Freshman class profile. 14,438 applied, 11,450 admitted, 4,974 enrolled.

Mid 50% test scores			
SAT critical reading:	450-560	Return as sophomores:	62%
SAT math:	480-580	Out-of-state:	2%
SAT writing:	430-540	Live on campus:	43%
ACT composite:	20-24	International:	5%
Rank in top quarter:	40%	Fraternities:	4%
Rank in top tenth:	13%	Sororities:	6%

Basis for selection. Texas residents who graduate in top 10% of high school graduating class admitted, regardless of ACT or SAT scores. Those not in top 10% must meet appropriate ACT or SAT scores based on class rank. If test score/rank criteria not met, additional factors may be taken into consideration. Out-of-state applicants must graduate in top half of graduating class in addition to meeting corresponding ACT or SAT score requirements. **Home schooled:** Conditional admissions decision based on SAT score over 1020 (exclusive of Writing) plus high school educational record (courses taken and grades earned) signed and dated by person responsible for conducting educational program. Upon high school graduation, final high school record indicating graduation date signed and dated by responsible educator must be submitted.

High school preparation. College-preparatory program required. 26 units required. Required units include English 4, mathematics 4, social studies 2, history 2, science 4, foreign language 2, visual/performing arts 1, academic electives 5.5. 1.5 for physical education and speech.

2011-2012 Annual costs. Tuition/fees: $8,783; $18,173 out-of-state. Reported room cost is for college-operated suite-style apartments. Independently operated double-occupancy dorms available. Room/board: $9,177. Books/supplies: $1,000. Personal expenses: $1,785.

2011-2012 Financial aid. Need-based: 3,870 full-time freshmen applied for aid; 3,118 were judged to have need; 3,067 of these received aid. Average need met was 68%. Average scholarship/grant was $9,330; average loan $3,110. 59% of total undergraduate aid awarded as scholarships/grants, 41% as loans/jobs. **Non-need-based:** Awarded to 3,448 full-time undergraduates, including 1,230 freshmen. Scholarships awarded for academics, alumni affiliation, art, athletics, job skills, leadership, music/drama, ROTC, state residency.

Application procedures. Admission: Priority date 3/1; deadline 6/1 (receipt date). $40 fee, may be waived for applicants with need. Admission notification by 9/1. Admission notification on a rolling basis. **Financial aid:** Priority date 3/15; no closing date. FAFSA, institutional form required. Applicants notified on a rolling basis starting 4/1; must reply within 4 week(s) of notification.

Academics. Freshman Initiative includes learning communities and freshman seminar program, enhancing academic services for new students in order to increase retention and success in college. **Special study options:** Accelerated study, cooperative education, distance learning, double major, dual enrollment of high school students, ESL, exchange student, honors, independent study, internships, study abroad, teacher certification program. 2-2 programs with Alamo Community College District, Southwest Texas Junior College, Laredo Junior College, Victoria College, Del Mar College, Coastal Bend Community College, Austin Community College; telecampus agreement with UT System. **Credit/placement by examination:** AP, CLEP, institutional tests. Some departments have limits on number of credits earned by examination. **Support services:** Learning center, pre-admission summer program, remedial instruction, study skills assistance, tutoring, writing center.

Majors. Architecture: Architecture, interior. **Area/ethnic studies:** American, Chicano/Hispanic-American/Latino, women's. **Biology:** General. **Business:** General, accounting, actuarial science, business admin, entrepreneurial studies, finance, human resources, international, management information systems, management science, managerial economics, marketing, real estate, tourism/travel. **Communications:** Communications/speech/rhetoric, public relations. **Computer sciences:** General, security. **Conservation:** Environmental science. **Engineering:** Civil, electrical, mechanical. **English:** English lit, technical writing. **Foreign languages:** General, Spanish. **Health services:** General. **History:** General. **Human services:** General. **Liberal arts:** Humanities. **Math:** General, statistics. **Philosophy/religion:** Philosophy. **Physical sciences:** Chemistry, geology, physics. **Protective services:** Criminal justice. **Psychology:** General. **Social sciences:** Anthropology, geography, political science, sociology. **Visual/performing arts:** Art, art history/conservation, music, studio arts.

Most popular majors. Biology 8%, business/marketing 24%, interdisciplinary studies 11%, psychology 8%, social sciences 7%.

Computing on campus. 550 workstations in dormitories, library, computer center, student center. Dormitories wired for high-speed internet access and linked to campus network. Commuter students can connect to campus network. Online course registration, online library, helpline, repair service, student web hosting, wireless network available.

Student life. Freshman orientation: Mandatory, $60 fee. Preregistration for classes offered. One-day sessions held throughout the year; optional 2-day camp held in August. **Housing:** Coed dorms, special housing for disabled, apartments available. $200 nonrefundable deposit. **Activities:** Bands, campus ministries, choral groups, dance, drama, international student organizations, literary magazine, music ensembles, student government, student newspaper, symphony orchestra, IDS student association, pre-med society, Golden Key national honor society, Intervarsity Christian Fellowship, S/B Alpha Chi national honor society, Catholic student association, Mortar Board national college senior honor society, Texas Association of Chicanos in Higher Education.

Athletics. NCAA. **Intercollegiate:** Baseball M, basketball, cross-country, football (tackle) M, golf, soccer W, softball W, tennis, track and field, volleyball W. **Intramural:** Badminton, basketball, bowling, football (non-tackle), golf, racquetball, soccer, softball, table tennis, tennis, volleyball, weight lifting. **Team name:** Roadrunners.

Student services. Career counseling, student employment services, financial aid counseling, health services, personal counseling, placement for graduates, veterans' counselor. **Physically disabled:** Services for visually, speech, hearing impaired.

Contact. E-mail: prospects@utsa.edu
Phone: (210) 458-4011 Toll-free number: (800) 669-0919
Fax: (210) 458-2001
George Norton, Associate Vice President, University of Texas at San Antonio, One UTSA Circle, San Antonio, TX 78249-0617

University of Texas at Tyler
Tyler, Texas   **CB member**
www.uttyler.edu   **CB code: 0389**

▶ Public 4-year university
▶ Commuter campus in small city

▶ 5,111 degree-seeking undergraduates: 24% part-time, 57% women, 9% African American, 2% Asian American, 12% Hispanic American, 1% international
▶ 1,372 degree-seeking graduate students
▶ 69% of applicants admitted
▶ SAT or ACT (ACT writing recommended) required
▶ 38% graduate within 6 years

General. Founded in 1971. Regionally accredited. Off-campus sites at Palestine and Longview. Internet courses and telecampus available. **Degrees:** 1,180 bachelor's awarded; master's, doctoral offered. **Location:** 80 miles from Dallas. **Calendar:** Semester, limited summer session. **Full-time faculty:** 268 total; 73% have terminal degrees, 14% minority, 55% women. **Part-time faculty:** 112 total; 30% have terminal degrees, 9% minority, 54% women. **Class size:** 35% < 20, 44% 20-39, 10% 40-49, 9% 50-99, 2% >100. **Special facilities:** Desktop manufacturing lab, computer-based virtual lab instruments.

Freshman class profile. 1,839 applied, 1,270 admitted, 642 enrolled.

Mid 50% test scores			
SAT critical reading:	470-580	GPA 2.0-2.99:	15%
SAT math:	490-580	Rank in top quarter:	46%
SAT writing:	460-560	Rank in top tenth:	18%
ACT composite:	20-25	Return as sophomores:	64%
GPA 3.75 or higher:	21%	Out-of-state:	3%
GPA 3.50-3.74:	26%	Live on campus:	63%
GPA 3.0-3.49:	38%	Fraternities:	9%
		Sororities:	8%

Basis for selection. Top 10% accepted automatically, others admitted based on ACT/SAT scores and high school preparation. **Home schooled:** Transcript of courses and grades required.

High school preparation. College-preparatory program recommended. Required and recommended units include English 4, mathematics 4, social studies 1.5, history 2, science 4 (laboratory 3), foreign language 2, computer science 1, visual/performing arts 1 and academic electives 6. Math requirement must be algebra I and higher. 4 mathematics recommended for science, engineering, and other technical fields.

2011-2012 Annual costs. Tuition/fees: $6,592; $15,982 out-of-state. Room/board: $8,527. Books/supplies: $1,301. Personal expenses: $1,224.

2010-2011 Financial aid. Need-based: 396 full-time freshmen applied for aid; 316 were judged to have need; 315 of these received aid. Average need met was 53%. Average scholarship/grant was $8,497; average loan $3,317. 51% of total undergraduate aid awarded as scholarships/grants, 49% as loans/jobs. **Non-need-based:** Awarded to 446 full-time undergraduates, including 55 freshmen. Scholarships awarded for academics, art, music/drama. **Additional information:** Apply early for all programs.

Application procedures. Admission: No deadline. $25 fee, may be waived for applicants with need. Application must be submitted online. Admission notification on a rolling basis. Must reply by May 1 or within 4 week(s) if notified thereafter. **Financial aid:** Priority date 4/1; no closing date. FAFSA, institutional form required. Applicants notified on a rolling basis starting 4/15; must reply within 2 week(s) of notification.

Academics. Special study options: Cooperative education, distance learning, double major, honors, independent study, internships, student-designed major, study abroad, teacher certification program. **Credit/placement by examination:** AP, CLEP, IB, SAT, ACT, institutional tests. AP, CLEP and International Baccalaureate awarded transfer credit with no maximum limit. **Support services:** Learning center, remedial instruction, study skills assistance, tutoring, writing center.

Honors college/program. Admission Committee typically looks at students with minimum 28 ACT composite score or minimum 1860 SAT combined score, and 3.5 or higher high school GPA.

Majors. Biology: General. **Business:** Accounting, business admin, construction management, finance, managerial economics, marketing, training/development. **Communications:** Journalism. **Computer sciences:** General. **Engineering:** Civil, electrical, mechanical. **English:** English lit, rhetoric/composition. **Foreign languages:** General, Spanish. **Health services:** General, clinical lab science, community health services, nursing (RN). **History:** General. **Math:** General. **Parks/recreation:** Health/fitness. **Philosophy/religion:** Religion. **Physical sciences:** Chemistry. **Protective services:** Criminal justice. **Psychology:** General. **Social sciences:** Political science, sociology. **Visual/performing arts:** Art, music.

Most popular majors. Business/marketing 24%, engineering/engineering technologies 9%, health sciences 20%, interdisciplinary studies 14%, psychology 6%.

Computing on campus. Dormitories wired for high-speed internet access and linked to campus network. Commuter students can connect to campus network. Online course registration, online library, wireless network available.

Student life. Freshman orientation: Mandatory, $75 fee. Preregistration for classes offered. One-day orientation in summer for students and parents. **Housing:** Coed dorms available. **Activities:** Bands, choral groups, international student organizations, music ensembles, Model UN, student government, student newspaper, Bible study fellowship, University Democrats, Nurses Christian Fellowship, Wesley Foundation Student Fellowship, Baptist student ministry, Patriots Special Olympics Texas Volunteers (Patriots SOTX), University Mothers Against Drunk Driving (UMADD), Indian student association.

Athletics. NCAA. **Intercollegiate:** Baseball M, basketball, cheerleading, cross-country, golf, soccer, softball W, tennis, track and field, volleyball W. **Intramural:** Baseball M, basketball, bowling, football (non-tackle), football (tackle), golf, racquetball, soccer, softball, table tennis, tennis, volleyball. **Team name:** Patriots.

Student services. Adult student services, alcohol/substance abuse counseling, career counseling, student employment services, financial aid counseling, health services, personal counseling, veterans' counselor. **Physically disabled:** Services for visually, speech, hearing impaired.

Contact. E-mail: admrequest@uttyler.edu
Phone: (903) 566-7202 Toll-free number: (800) 888-9537
Fax: (903) 566-7068
Sarah Bowdin, Director of Admissions, University of Texas at Tyler, 3900 University Boulevard, Tyler, TX 75799

University of Texas Health Science Center at Houston
Houston, Texas
www.uth.tmc.edu   **CB code: 6906**

▶ Public two-year upper-division university and health science college
▶ Commuter campus in very large city
▶ Interview required

General. Founded in 1972. Regionally accredited. Located in the Texas Medical Center. **Degrees:** 335 bachelor's awarded; master's, professional, doctoral offered. **Location:** 5 miles from downtown. **Calendar:** Semester, limited summer session. **Full-time faculty:** 925 total. **Part-time faculty:** 275 total.

Student profile. 593 degree-seeking undergraduates, 4,007 graduate students. 70% entered as juniors.

Basis for selection. College transcript, interview required. Applicants must submit official transcript from all previous institutions. Application closing dates, admissions policies vary by program. Dental hygiene application closing date: December 31. Minimum number of credits: 28. Nursing application closing date: January 1. Minimum number of credits: 60. Transfer accepted as sophomores, juniors.

2011-2012 Annual costs. Tuition/fees: $6,985; $22,855 out-of-state. Costs may vary by program. Books/supplies: $1,050.

Application procedures. Admission: Deadline 12/31. $30 fee. **Financial aid:** FAFSA, institutional form required.

Academics. Upper division bachelor's program for nursing, with accelerated RN-master's program. **Special study options:** Accelerated study, combined bachelor's/graduate degree, distance learning. **Credit/placement by examination:** AP, CLEP. All CLEP must appear on college transcript with credit hours and grade.

Majors. Health services: Dental hygiene, nursing (RN).

Computing on campus. PC or laptop required. Helpline available.

Student life. Housing: Apartments available. University operates apartment complex as only student housing available. Complex located approximately 1 mile from campus. **Activities:** Student government.

Student services. Adult student services, alcohol/substance abuse counseling, financial aid counseling, health services, on-campus daycare, personal counseling. **Physically disabled:** Services for visually, hearing impaired.

Contact. E-mail: admissions@uth.tmc.edu
Phone: (713) 500-3361 Fax: (713) 500-3356
Robert Jenkins, Registrar, University of Texas Health Science Center at Houston, Box 20036, Houston, TX 77225

University of Texas Health Science Center at San Antonio
San Antonio, Texas
www.uthscsa.edu   **CB code: 6908**

▶ Public two-year upper-division university and health science college
▶ Commuter campus in very large city

General. Founded in 1969. Regionally accredited. Located in South Texas Medical Center. **Degrees:** 217 bachelor's awarded; master's, professional, doctoral offered. **Location:** 10 miles from downtown. **Calendar:** Semester, limited summer session. **Full-time faculty:** 1,345 total; 42% women. **Part-time faculty:** 534 total; 40% women.

Student profile. 835 degree-seeking undergraduates, 2,217 degree-seeking graduate students. 99% entered as juniors, 1% entered as seniors.

Women:	80%	International:	1%
African American:	4%	Part-time:	15%
Asian American:	7%	Out-of-state:	13%
Hispanic American:	36%		

Basis for selection. High school transcript, college transcript required. Admission varies with each program. In many cases, academic records and interview required. Application closing and priority dates vary with each program. Transfer accepted as juniors.

2011-2012 Annual costs. Tuition/fees: $7,186; $18,766 out-of-state. Tuition and fees vary by program. Books/supplies: $1,545. Personal expenses: $2,130.

Financial aid. Non-need-based: Scholarships awarded for academics, leadership. **Additional information:** Students strongly advised to provide parental information on need analysis form regardless of dependency status.

Application procedures. Admission: $45 fee. Application must be submitted online. Application fees vary from $10 to $55 depending on program. **Financial aid:** No deadline. Applicants notified on a rolling basis starting 4/15. FAFSA required.

Academics. Special study options: Accelerated study, combined bachelor's/graduate degree, cross-registration, distance learning, dual enrollment of high school students, internships. PharmD program with University of Texas-Austin; joint degree Health Professions program with University of Texas-San Antonio. **Credit/placement by examination:** AP, CLEP, institutional tests.

Majors. Health services: Clinical lab science, cytogenetics, dental hygiene, dietetics, EMT paramedic, nursing (RN), respiratory therapy technology.

Computing on campus. PC or laptop required. 50 workstations in library. Commuter students can connect to campus network. Helpline, wireless network available.

Student life. Activities: International student organizations, literary magazine, student government, student newspaper, Asian Pacific American Medical Student Association, Christian Medical and Dental Association, Ethiopia Outreach, Frontera De Salud, International Nursing Student Association, JewTHSCA, Pride, Project Hispaniola, Students Going Global, Vamos Guatemala, Texas Association of Mexican-American Medical Students, Latin-American Nursing Student Association, Diversified Dental Students.

Athletics. Intramural: Basketball, football (non-tackle), soccer, softball, swimming, table tennis, tennis, volleyball, weight lifting.

Student services. Adult student services, alcohol/substance abuse counseling, career counseling, financial aid counseling, health services, personal counseling, veterans' counselor.

Contact. E-mail: AppCenter@uthscsa.edu
Phone: (210) 567-2622 Fax: (210) 567-2685
Jackson Jeff, Student Activities and Application Center Director, University of Texas Health Science Center at San Antonio, 7703 Floyd Curl Drive, San Antonio, TX 78229-3900

University of Texas Medical Branch at Galveston
Galveston, Texas
www.utmb.edu   CB code: 6887

▶ Public two-year upper-division health science and nursing college
▶ Commuter campus in large town

General. Founded in 1881. Regionally accredited. **Degrees:** 3,328 bachelor's awarded; master's, professional, doctoral offered. **Location:** 50 miles from Houston. **Calendar:** Semester, limited summer session.

Student profile. 651 degree-seeking undergraduates, 2,136 degree-seeking graduate students.

Women:	78%	Part-time:	23%
African American:	14%	Out-of-state:	1%
Asian American:	14%	25 or older:	59%
Hispanic American:	12%		

Basis for selection. College transcript required. Students with 60 hours from accredited college or university considered. Nonresident enrollment limited by legislature to not more than 10% of any class. Transfer decisions based on competitive comparison of transcripts, allied health experience, departmental testing, and personal interviews. Specific prerequisites and application closing dates vary by program. Transfer accepted as juniors, seniors.

2011-2012 Annual costs. Tuition/fees: $6,052; $15,442 out-of-state. Costs reported are for undergraduate Allied Health Sciences program. Tuition and fees vary for other programs.

Financial aid. Non-need-based: Scholarships awarded for academics, minority status, state residency.

Application procedures. Admission: $50 fee. Application must be submitted online. **Financial aid:** FAFSA required.

Academics. Special study options: Distance learning, independent study, internships. **Credit/placement by examination:** AP, CLEP, IB. 30 credit hours maximum toward bachelor's degree.

Majors. Health services: Clinical lab science, nursing (RN), respiratory therapy technology.

Computing on campus. Dormitories wired for high-speed internet access and linked to campus network. Commuter students can connect to campus network. Online library, helpline, repair service, wireless network available.

Student life. Housing: Coed dorms, apartments, fraternity/sorority housing available. $200 fully refundable deposit. **Activities:** Campus ministries, international student organizations, student government, Wesley Foundation, Newman Center, sports clubs, Christian Medical and Dental Society, Jewish student and faculty organization, multicultural awareness council, student national medical association, Texas Association of Latin American Medical Students.

Athletics. Intramural: Basketball, football (non-tackle), soccer, softball, volleyball.

Student services. Alcohol/substance abuse counseling, chaplain/spiritual director, career counseling, student employment services, financial aid counseling, health services, legal services, on-campus daycare, personal counseling, veterans' counselor, women's services. **Physically disabled:** Services for visually, speech, hearing impaired.

Contact. E-mail: enrollment.services@utmb.edu
Phone: (409) 772-1215 Fax: (409) 772-4466
University of Texas Medical Branch at Galveston, 301 University Boulevard, Galveston, TX 77555-1305

University of Texas of the Permian Basin
Odessa, Texas   CB member
www.utpb.edu   CB code: 0448

▶ Public 4-year university
▶ Commuter campus in small city
▶ 2,674 degree-seeking undergraduates: 25% part-time, 59% women, 5% African American, 2% Asian American, 44% Hispanic American, 1% Native American
▶ 642 degree-seeking graduate students

▶ 82% of applicants admitted
▶ SAT or ACT (ACT writing optional) required
▶ 32% graduate within 6 years

General. Founded in 1969. Regionally accredited. **Degrees:** 545 bachelor's awarded; master's offered. **Location:** 150 miles from Lubbock, 350 miles from Dallas. **Calendar:** Semester, extensive summer session. **Full-time faculty:** 119 total; 85% have terminal degrees, 19% minority, 47% women. **Part-time faculty:** 63 total; 25% have terminal degrees, 14% minority, 44% women. **Class size:** 35% < 20, 48% 20-39, 6% 40-49, 10% 50-99, less than 1% >100.

Freshman class profile. 954 applied, 781 admitted, 359 enrolled.

Mid 50% test scores			
SAT critical reading:	430-530	**Rank in top tenth:**	24%
SAT math:	460-550	**Return as sophomores:**	59%
ACT composite:	19-23	**Out-of-state:**	4%
Rank in top quarter:	57%	**Live on campus:**	41%

Basis for selection. Secondary school record, class rank, test scores important. Foreign students whose native language is not English must take TOEFL. Requirement may be waived for non-English speakers transferring from a U.S. college or high school. Essay not required but considered if provided. **Home schooled:** No additional requirements. Home-schooled students reviewed on an individual basis. **Learning Disabled:** No special requirements but must meet minimum admission standards.

High school preparation. College-preparatory program recommended. 26 units required. Required units include English 4, mathematics 4, social studies 3.5, science 4 (laboratory 3), foreign language 2, computer science 1, visual/performing arts 1, academic electives 3.5. Economics, 0.5; physical education, 1.5; health education, 0.5; speech (communications applications), 0.5.

2011-2012 Annual costs. Tuition/fees: $6,302; $15,692 out-of-state. Books/supplies: $915. Personal expenses: $1,834.

2010-2011 Financial aid. Need-based: 275 full-time freshmen applied for aid; 230 were judged to have need; 230 of these received aid. Average need met was 54%. Average scholarship/grant was $7,349; average loan $2,441. 62% of total undergraduate aid awarded as scholarships/grants, 38% as loans/jobs. **Non-need-based:** Awarded to 1,389 full-time undergraduates, including 309 freshmen. Scholarships awarded for academics, art, athletics, leadership, music/drama.

Application procedures. Admission: Closing date 7/15 (postmark date). No application fee. Admission notification on a rolling basis. **Financial aid:** Priority date 3/1; no closing date. FAFSA required. Applicants notified on a rolling basis starting 3/15.

Academics. Special study options: Accelerated study, combined bachelor's/graduate degree, distance learning, double major, dual enrollment of high school students, honors, independent study, internships, teacher certification program. **Credit/placement by examination:** AP, CLEP, SAT, ACT, institutional tests. 28 credit hours maximum toward bachelor's degree. Credit/placement awarded on AP or CLEP exams, special exams administered by School of Business. **Support services:** Learning center, remedial instruction, study skills assistance, tutoring, writing center.

Majors. Biology: General. **Business:** Accounting, business admin, finance, managerial economics, marketing. **Communications:** Communications/speech/rhetoric. **Computer sciences:** General, information systems. **Conservation:** Environmental science. **Engineering:** Mechanical. **English:** English lit. **Foreign languages:** Spanish. **Health services:** Athletic training. **History:** General. **Human services:** Social work. **Liberal arts:** Humanities. **Math:** General. **Parks/recreation:** Exercise sciences. **Physical sciences:** Chemistry, geology. **Protective services:** Criminal justice. **Psychology:** General. **Social sciences:** Criminology, political science, sociology. **Visual/performing arts:** Art. **Work/family studies:** Family studies.

Most popular majors. Business/marketing 25%, communications/journalism 6%, family/consumer sciences 11%, psychology 7%, social sciences 9%.

Computing on campus. 170 workstations in dormitories, library, computer center. Dormitories wired for high-speed internet access and linked to campus network. Commuter students can connect to campus network. Online course registration, online library, helpline, wireless network available.

Student life. Freshman orientation: Mandatory, $75 fee. Preregistration for classes offered. Choice of three separate 3-day sessions in June, July, August, includes some meals and lodging for out-of-town students. **Housing:** Coed dorms, apartments available. $200 fully refundable deposit, deadline 7/15. Family housing units. **Activities:** Bands, campus ministries, choral groups, dance, drama, international student organizations, literary magazine, music ensembles, student government, student newspaper, symphony orchestra, black leadership council, Catholic student association, Falcons for Christ,

Campus Crusade for Christ, College Republicans, black student organization, Christians on Campus, Young Democrats.

Athletics. NCAA. **Intercollegiate:** Baseball M, basketball, cheerleading, cross-country, soccer, softball W, swimming, tennis, volleyball W. **Intramural:** Basketball, football (non-tackle), racquetball, tennis, volleyball, water polo. **Team name:** Falcons.

Student services. Adult student services, alcohol/substance abuse counseling, career counseling, services for economically disadvantaged, student employment services, financial aid counseling, health services, minority student services, on-campus daycare, personal counseling, placement for graduates. **Physically disabled:** Services for visually, speech, hearing impaired.

Contact. E-mail: admissions@utpb.edu
Phone: (432) 552-2605 Toll-free number: (866) 552-8872
Fax: (432) 552-3605
Scott Smiley, Director of Admissions, University of Texas of the Permian Basin, 4901 East University, Odessa, TX 79762

University of Texas-Pan American
Edinburg, Texas   **CB member**
www.utpa.edu   **CB code: 6570**

- Public 4-year university
- Commuter campus in small city
- 16,346 degree-seeking undergraduates: 26% part-time, 55% women, 1% African American, 1% Asian American, 91% Hispanic American, 2% international
- 2,351 degree-seeking graduate students
- 68% of applicants admitted
- SAT or ACT (ACT writing optional) required
- 42% graduate within 6 years

General. Founded in 1927. Regionally accredited. Hispanic-serving institution. **Degrees:** 2,683 bachelor's awarded; master's, doctoral offered. **ROTC:** Army. **Location:** 250 miles from San Antonio, 300 miles from Austin. **Calendar:** Semester, extensive summer session. **Full-time faculty:** 633 total; 82% have terminal degrees, 46% minority, 38% women. **Part-time faculty:** 128 total; 48% have terminal degrees, 55% minority, 47% women. **Class size:** 16% < 20, 53% 20-39, 9% 40-49, 19% 50-99, 3% >100. **Special facilities:** Coastal studies laboratory at South Padre Island, planetarium.

Freshman class profile. 8,778 applied, 6,004 admitted, 3,146 enrolled.

Mid 50% test scores			
SAT critical reading:	420-520	Rank in top tenth:	21%
SAT math:	450-550	Return as sophomores:	74%
SAT writing:	410-500	Out-of-state:	1%
ACT composite:	18-22	Live on campus:	11%
Rank in top quarter:	51%	International:	2%

Basis for selection. For regular admission, rank in top quartile of class or acceptable ACT/SAT scores required. Students who do not meet criteria for admission placed in PEP (Provisional Enrollment Program). **Home schooled:** Students graduating from a private or home school required to file completed Texas Private High School Certification with transcript.

High school preparation. 24 units required. Required units include English 4, mathematics 4, social studies 3.5, science 4, foreign language 2, academic electives 3.5. .5 economics, 1 fine arts, 1 physical education, .5 speech. Algebra 2 required of business and engineering majors. Geometry, trigonometry, chemistry, and physics required of engineering majors.

2011-2012 Annual costs. Tuition/fees: $5,978; $15,367 out-of-state. Mexican citizens may be eligible for in-state tuition rates. Room/board: $5,614. Books/supplies: $1,000. Personal expenses: $1,847.

2010-2011 Financial aid. **Need-based:** 2,415 full-time freshmen applied for aid; 2,309 were judged to have need; 2,309 of these received aid. Average need met was 82%. Average scholarship/grant was $12,094; average loan $2,197. 76% of total undergraduate aid awarded as scholarships/grants, 24% as loans/jobs. **Non-need-based:** Awarded to 450 full-time undergraduates, including 142 freshmen. Scholarships awarded for academics, alumni affiliation, art, athletics, leadership.

Application procedures. **Admission:** Priority date 2/1; deadline 8/11 (receipt date). No application fee. Admission notification on a rolling basis. **Financial aid:** Priority date 4/1; no closing date. FAFSA required. Applicants notified on a rolling basis starting 3/15; must reply within 2 week(s) of notification.

Academics. **Special study options:** Accelerated study, combined bachelor's/graduate degree, cooperative education, distance learning, double major, dual enrollment of high school students, ESL, exchange student, honors, independent study, internships, study abroad, teacher certification program, weekend college. **Credit/placement by examination:** AP, CLEP, IB, institutional tests. 45 credit hours maximum toward bachelor's degree. **Support services:** Learning center, pre-admission summer program, remedial instruction, study skills assistance, tutoring, writing center.

Majors. **Area/ethnic studies:** American, Chicano/Hispanic-American/Latino. **Biology:** General. **Business:** Accounting, business admin, finance, international, management information systems, marketing. **Communications:** Communications/speech/rhetoric, journalism, media studies. **Computer sciences:** General, computer science. **Conservation:** Environmental science. **Engineering:** Civil, computer, electrical, industrial, manufacturing, mechanical. **English:** English lit. **Foreign languages:** French, Spanish. **Health services:** General, audiology/speech pathology, clinical lab science, dietetics, nursing (RN), rehabilitation science, substance abuse counseling. **History:** General. **Human services:** Social work. **Math:** General. **Parks/recreation:** Exercise sciences. **Philosophy/religion:** Philosophy. **Physical sciences:** Chemistry, physics. **Protective services:** Law enforcement admin. **Psychology:** General. **Social sciences:** General, anthropology, economics, political science, sociology. **Visual/performing arts:** Dance, dramatic, music, music performance, studio arts.

Most popular majors. Biology 8%, business/marketing 17%, English 6%, health sciences 13%, interdisciplinary studies 11%, psychology 7%, security/protective services 7%.

Computing on campus. 900 workstations in dormitories, library, computer center. Dormitories wired for high-speed internet access and linked to campus network. Commuter students can connect to campus network. Online course registration, online library, helpline, student web hosting, wireless network available.

Student life. **Freshman orientation:** Mandatory, $15 fee. Preregistration for classes offered. Several 1-day sessions held prior to beginning of semester. **Housing:** Coed dorms, single-sex dorms, apartments available. $75 fully refundable deposit, deadline 7/1. **Activities:** Bands, campus ministries, choral groups, dance, drama, international student organizations, music ensembles, musical theater, student government, student newspaper, symphony orchestra, Episcopal Canterbury Association, Latter-day Saints student association, Baha'i association, Baptist student union, Campus Crusade for Christ, Fellowship of Christian Athletes, Asian American students association, Society of Hispanic Professional Engineers.

Athletics. NCAA. **Intercollegiate:** Baseball M, basketball, cross-country, golf, tennis, track and field, volleyball W. **Intramural:** Badminton, basketball, bowling, cheerleading, football (non-tackle), golf, racquetball, soccer, softball, tennis, volleyball. **Team name:** Broncs/Lady Broncs.

Student services. Alcohol/substance abuse counseling, career counseling, services for economically disadvantaged, student employment services, financial aid counseling, health services, on-campus daycare, personal counseling, placement for graduates, veterans' counselor, women's services. **Physically disabled:** Services for visually, speech, hearing impaired.

Contact. E-mail: admissions@utpa.edu
Phone: (956) 665-2999 Toll-free number: (866) 441-8872
Fax: (956) 665-2212
Magdalena Hinojosa, Dean of Admissions & Enrollment Services, University of Texas-Pan American, 1201 West University Drive, Edinburg, TX 78539-2999

University of the Incarnate Word
San Antonio, Texas   **CB member**
www.uiw.edu   **CB code: 6303**

- Private 4-year university affiliated with Roman Catholic Church
- Commuter campus in very large city
- 5,863 degree-seeking undergraduates: 31% part-time, 63% women, 7% African American, 2% Asian American, 58% Hispanic American, 3% international
- 1,811 degree-seeking graduate students
- 95% of applicants admitted
- SAT or ACT (ACT writing optional) required
- 43% graduate within 6 years

General. Founded in 1881. Regionally accredited. Seven Adult Degree Completion program sites including one in Corpus Christi. UIW also has a Virtual campus. International campuses in Mexico City and in Guangzhou, China. **Degrees:** 998 bachelor's, 6 associate awarded; master's, professional,

doctoral offered. **ROTC:** Army, Air Force. **Location:** 5 miles from San Antonio. **Calendar:** Semester, extensive summer session. **Full-time faculty:** 257 total; 79% have terminal degrees, 31% minority, 55% women. **Part-time faculty:** 242 total; 34% have terminal degrees, 29% minority, 55% women. **Class size:** 54% < 20, 42% 20-39, 2% 40-49, 1% 50-99, less than 1% >100. **Special facilities:** Semmes Gallery.

Freshman class profile. 3,595 applied, 3,401 admitted, 1,050 enrolled.

Mid 50% test scores			
SAT critical reading:	420-530	Rank in top quarter:	48%
SAT math:	440-550	Rank in top tenth:	18%
SAT writing:	420-520	Return as sophomores:	78%
ACT composite:	17-23	Out-of-state:	2%
GPA 3.75 or higher:	27%	Live on campus:	46%
GPA 3.50-3.74:	29%	International:	3%
GPA 3.0-3.49:	37%	Fraternities:	1%
GPA 2.0-2.99:	6%	Sororities:	2%

Basis for selection. Test scores and school achievement record most important. Extracurricular activities and positions of leadership held by the student also taken into consideration. Letters of recommendation from people familiar with the student's character and student essays explaining extenuating circumstances not required but are encouraged and will be reviewed if submitted. Rolling policy for submission of test scores. Personal statement and interview with the Dean of Admissions recommended for students whose academic record is considered to be below average. **Home schooled:** Statement describing home school structure and mission, transcript of courses and grades required. Required to submit official copy of SAT or ACT exam scores. Interview, letters of recommendation, assessment testing may be required.

High school preparation. College-preparatory program required. 16 units required; 18 recommended. Required and recommended units include English 4, mathematics 3-4, social studies 3-4, science 3, foreign language 2 and visual/performing arts 1.

2012-2013 Annual costs. Tuition/fees (projected): $22,790. Room/board: $9,658. Books/supplies: $1,200. Personal expenses: $1,620.

2010-2011 Financial aid. **Need-based:** 782 full-time freshmen applied for aid; 707 were judged to have need; 707 of these received aid. Average need met was 75%. Average scholarship/grant was $15,448; average loan $3,198. 58% of total undergraduate aid awarded as scholarships/grants, 42% as loans/jobs. **Non-need-based:** Awarded to 2,876 full-time undergraduates, including 787 freshmen. Scholarships awarded for academics, alumni affiliation, art, athletics, leadership, music/drama, religious affiliation, ROTC, state residency. **Additional information:** Students encouraged to pursue outside scholarship programs.

Application procedures. **Admission:** Priority date 2/1; no deadline. $20 fee, may be waived for applicants with need. Admission notification on a rolling basis. Must reply by May 1 or within 4 week(s) if notified thereafter. Notification approximately 2 weeks following submission. **Financial aid:** Priority date 4/1; no closing date. FAFSA required. Applicants notified on a rolling basis starting 2/15; must reply within 2 week(s) of notification.

Academics. Combined baccalaureate/master's in communication arts. **Special study options:** Accelerated study, combined bachelor's/graduate degree, cross-registration, distance learning, double major, dual enrollment of high school students, ESL, honors, independent study, internships, student-designed major, study abroad, teacher certification program, weekend college. **Credit/placement by examination:** AP, CLEP, IB, SAT, ACT, institutional tests. 30 credit hours maximum toward bachelor's degree. **Support services:** Learning center, reduced course load, remedial instruction, study skills assistance, tutoring, writing center.

Honors college/program. Incoming freshmen should submit an application, have a minimum high school GPA of 3.5, and combined SAT score (Verbal, Math and Writing) of 1800 and/or a 27 composite ACT score. Applicants also need an essay, teacher recommendation, and interview. Students enroll in advanced courses, participate in one mission trip, a travel or study abroad experience, additional professional development experiences, and complete a senior project.

Majors. Biology: General, biochemistry, vision science. **Business:** Accounting, banking/financial services, business admin, human resources, international, management information systems, managerial economics, marketing, organizational behavior, sales/distribution. **Communications:** Communications/speech/rhetoric, journalism, media studies, radio/TV. **Communications technology:** Animation/special effects. **Computer sciences:** Networking. **Conservation:** Environmental science. **Education:** Elementary, music, physical. **English:** English lit. **Foreign languages:** Spanish. **Health services:** Athletic training, music therapy, nuclear medical technology, nursing (RN). **History:** General. **Liberal arts:** Arts/sciences. **Math:** General. **Parks/recreation:** Exercise sciences, sports admin. **Philosophy/religion:**

Philosophy, religion. **Physical sciences:** Chemistry, meteorology. **Psychology:** General. **Social sciences:** International relations, political science, sociology. **Visual/performing arts:** Art, art history/conservation, dramatic, fashion design, graphic design, interior design, music, music management. **Work/family studies:** Apparel marketing, child development.

Most popular majors. Biology 8%, business/marketing 43%, education 7%, health sciences 9%, visual/performing arts 7%.

Computing on campus. PC or laptop required. 180 workstations in library, computer center. Dormitories wired for high-speed internet access and linked to campus network. Commuter students can connect to campus network. Online course registration, online library, helpline, repair service, wireless network available.

Student life. Freshman orientation: Mandatory. Preregistration for classes offered. 1-day sessions offered for freshmen and transfer students, usually beginning in mid-May for the Fall semesters and mid-November for Spring semesters. Parents encouraged to participate. **Housing:** Coed dorms, single-sex dorms, special housing for disabled, apartments available. $225 fully refundable deposit, deadline 5/1. **Activities:** Bands, campus ministries, choral groups, dance, drama, international student organizations, literary magazine, music ensembles, musical theater, radio station, student government, student newspaper, symphony orchestra, TV station, Society of Leadership and Success, pre-pharmacy association, Alpha Sigma Alpha, Lambda Chi Alpha, Hispanic student association, Alpha Phi Omega, ethics club, Christian Pharmacy Fellowship International.

Athletics. NCAA. **Intercollegiate:** Baseball M, basketball, cross-country, diving, football (tackle) M, golf, soccer, softball W, swimming, synchronized swimming W, tennis, track and field, volleyball W. **Intramural:** Basketball, football (non-tackle), racquetball, soccer, softball, tennis, volleyball, water polo. **Team name:** Cardinals.

Student services. Adult student services, alcohol/substance abuse counseling, chaplain/spiritual director, career counseling, services for economically disadvantaged, student employment services, financial aid counseling, health services, personal counseling, veterans' counselor. **Physically disabled:** Services for visually, speech, hearing impaired.

Contact. E-mail: admis@uiwtx.edu
Phone: (210) 829-6005 Toll-free number: (800) 749-9673
Fax: (210) 829-3921
Andrea Cyterski-Acosta, Dean of Enrollment, University of the Incarnate Word, 4301 Broadway, San Antonio, TX 78209-6397

Wayland Baptist University
Plainview, Texas   **CB member**
www.wbu.edu   **CB code: 6930**

- Private 4-year university and liberal arts college affiliated with Southern Baptist Convention
- Residential campus in large town
- 1,213 degree-seeking undergraduates: 19% part-time, 45% women, 13% African American, 1% Asian American, 28% Hispanic American, 1% Native American, 3% international
- 375 degree-seeking graduate students
- 99% of applicants admitted
- SAT or ACT (ACT writing optional) required
- 41% graduate within 6 years

General. Founded in 1908. Regionally accredited. Off-campus sites in Amarillo, Lubbock, San Antonio, Wichita Falls, Alaska, Arizona, Hawaii, Oklahoma, New Mexico. **Degrees:** 138 bachelor's, 2 associate awarded; master's offered. **ROTC:** Army, Air Force. **Location:** 50 miles from Lubbock, 70 miles from Amarillo. **Calendar:** Semester, limited summer session. **Full-time faculty:** 90 total; 77% have terminal degrees, 6% minority, 31% women. **Part-time faculty:** 55 total; 16% have terminal degrees, 2% minority, 40% women. **Class size:** 70% < 20, 29% 20-39, less than 1% 40-49, less than 1% 50-99. **Special facilities:** Museum of the Llano Estacado.

Freshman class profile. 563 applied, 556 admitted, 377 enrolled.

Mid 50% test scores			
SAT critical reading:	380-490	Rank in top quarter:	24%
SAT math:	400-500	Rank in top tenth:	8%
SAT writing:	370-460	Return as sophomores:	53%
ACT composite:	16-22	Out-of-state:	10%
GPA 3.75 or higher:	15%	Live on campus:	68%
GPA 3.50-3.74:	14%	International:	3%
GPA 3.0-3.49:	37%	Fraternities:	2%
GPA 2.0-2.99:	32%	Sororities:	1%

Basis for selection. Regular freshman admission based on combination of class rank and on either the ACT composite or SAT score. Interview, audition recommended for music and theater.

High school preparation. 9 units required. Required and recommended units include English 3, mathematics 2-3, social studies 2 and science 2-3.

2011-2012 Annual costs. Tuition/fees: $13,940. Room/board: $4,476. Books/supplies: $1,300. Personal expenses: $3,074.

2011-2012 Financial aid. Need-based: 297 full-time freshmen applied for aid; 253 were judged to have need; 252 of these received aid. Average need met was 62%. Average scholarship/grant was $8,685; average loan $3,146. 51% of total undergraduate aid awarded as scholarships/grants, 49% as loans/jobs. **Non-need-based:** Awarded to 321 full-time undergraduates, including 110 freshmen. Scholarships awarded for academics, alumni affiliation, art, athletics, leadership, music/drama.

Application procedures. Admission: Priority date 8/1; no deadline. $35 fee. Admission notification on a rolling basis beginning on or about 3/1. **Financial aid:** Priority date 5/1; no closing date. FAFSA, institutional form required. Applicants notified on a rolling basis starting 2/15; must reply within 3 week(s) of notification.

Academics. Special study options: Accelerated study, distance learning, double major, dual enrollment of high school students, external degree, honors, internships, study abroad, teacher certification program. **Credit/placement by examination:** AP, CLEP, IB, SAT, ACT, institutional tests. 30 credit hours maximum toward bachelor's degree. **Support services:** Learning center, reduced course load, remedial instruction, study skills assistance, tutoring, writing center.

Majors. Biology: General, molecular. **Business:** Business admin. **Communications:** Communications/speech/rhetoric, media studies. **Conservation:** Environmental science, environmental studies. **Education:** Business, early childhood, elementary, English, middle, multi-level teacher, music, physical, science, social studies, technology/industrial arts, trade/industrial. **English:** English lit. **Foreign languages:** Spanish. **Health services:** Nursing (RN). **History:** General. **Math:** General. **Parks/recreation:** Facilities management, sports admin. **Philosophy/religion:** Christian. **Physical sciences:** Chemistry, geology. **Protective services:** Law enforcement admin. **Psychology:** General. **Social sciences:** Sociology, U.S. government. **Theology:** Religious ed, sacred music. **Visual/performing arts:** Art, dramatic, graphic design, music, music performance.

Most popular majors. Biology 8%, business/marketing 23%, education 25%, philosophy/religious studies 6%, psychology 6%, security/protective services 6%, visual/performing arts 10%.

Computing on campus. 231 workstations in library, computer center. Dormitories wired for high-speed internet access and linked to campus network. Commuter students can connect to campus network. Online library, helpline, wireless network available.

Student life. Freshman orientation: Mandatory, $15 fee. Preregistration for classes offered. Entry seminar course designed to help students succeed academically, socially, and spiritually. Taken during initial term of enrollment. **Policies:** Religious observance required. **Housing:** Guaranteed on-campus for freshmen. Single-sex dorms, apartments available. $100 fully refundable deposit. **Activities:** Bands, campus ministries, choral groups, drama, music ensembles, musical theater, radio station, student government, student newspaper, TV station, Over 20 religious, service, and special interest organizations available.

Athletics. NAIA. **Intercollegiate:** Baseball M, basketball, cheerleading, cross-country, golf, soccer, track and field, volleyball W, wrestling. **Intramural:** Basketball, football (non-tackle), softball, volleyball. **Team name:** Pioneers, Flying Queens.

Student services. Chaplain/spiritual director, career counseling, student employment services, financial aid counseling, health services, personal counseling, placement for graduates.

Contact. E-mail: admityou@wbu.edu
Phone: (806) 291-3500 Toll-free number: (800) 588-1928
Fax: (806) 291-1960
Debbie Stennett, Director of Admissions, Wayland Baptist University, 1900 West Seventh Street, CMB #712, Plainview, TX 79072

West Texas A&M University
Canyon, Texas

CB member
CB code: 6938

www.wtamu.edu

- Public 4-year university
- Commuter campus in large town

- 6,460 degree-seeking undergraduates: 20% part-time, 54% women, 5% African American, 1% Asian American, 22% Hispanic American, 1% Native American, 1% international
- 1,312 degree-seeking graduate students
- 69% of applicants admitted
- SAT or ACT (ACT writing optional) required
- 41% graduate within 6 years

General. Founded in 1909. Regionally accredited. **Degrees:** 1,259 bachelor's awarded; master's, doctoral offered. **Location:** 17 miles from Amarillo. **Calendar:** Semester, limited summer session. **Full-time faculty:** 255 total; 74% have terminal degrees, 12% minority, 43% women. **Part-time faculty:** 112 total; 23% have terminal degrees, 8% minority, 55% women. **Class size:** 42% < 20, 45% 20-39, 5% 40-49, 7% 50-99, less than 1% >100. **Special facilities:** 24,000-acre farm and ranch, alternative energy institute, historical museum, event center.

Freshman class profile. 4,096 applied, 2,833 admitted, 1,214 enrolled.

Mid 50% test scores		Out-of-state:	10%
SAT critical reading:	420-540	Live on campus:	82%
SAT math:	450-550	International:	2%
Rank in top quarter:	41%	Fraternities:	7%
Rank in top tenth:	17%	Sororities:	12%
Return as sophomores:	65%		

Basis for selection. Freshman applicants must be in top half of graduating class, have minimum 950 SAT (exclusive of Writing) or 20 ACT, or attend a summer provisional term. Texas Success Initiative Testing required of all incoming students before entrance. Audition required for music program; portfolio recommended for art, theater programs.

High school preparation. College-preparatory program required. 26 units required. Required units include English 4, mathematics 4, social studies 4, science 4, foreign language 2, visual/performing arts 1, academic electives 5.5. Physical education 1, speech .5.

2012-2013 Annual costs. Tuition/fees (projected): $6,282; $15,582 out-of-state. Room/board: $6,600. Books/supplies: $1,000. Personal expenses: $2,000.

2010-2011 Financial aid. Need-based: 1,028 full-time freshmen applied for aid; 850 were judged to have need; 782 of these received aid. Average need met was 58%. Average scholarship/grant was $7,293; average loan $3,004. 57% of total undergraduate aid awarded as scholarships/grants, 43% as loans/jobs. **Non-need-based:** Awarded to 909 full-time undergraduates, including 460 freshmen. Scholarships awarded for academics, art, athletics, leadership, music/drama. **Additional information:** Scholarship deadline February 1.

Application procedures. Admission: Priority date 7/20; no deadline. $25 fee, may be waived for applicants with need. Admission notification on a rolling basis beginning on or about 9/1. **Financial aid:** Priority date 4/15; no closing date. FAFSA required. Applicants notified on a rolling basis starting 3/1; must reply within 2 week(s) of notification.

Academics. Special study options: Combined bachelor's/graduate degree, cooperative education, distance learning, double major, ESL, honors, independent study, internships, liberal arts/career combination, study abroad, teacher certification program, Washington semester. **Credit/placement by examination:** AP, CLEP, IB, institutional tests. Only 6 of a student's last 30 hours can come from CLEP. **Support services:** Learning center, remedial instruction, study skills assistance, tutoring, writing center.

Majors. Biology: General, biotechnology, wildlife. **Business:** General, accounting, business admin, finance, management information systems, managerial economics, marketing. **Communications:** Advertising, broadcast journalism, communications/speech/rhetoric, journalism. **Computer sciences:** General, computer science. **Conservation:** Environmental science. **Engineering:** Civil, mechanical, pre-engineering. **English:** English lit. **Foreign languages:** Spanish. **General:** Agribusiness operations, agronomy, animal sciences, business, communications, equestrian studies. **Health services:** Athletic training, clinical lab science, communication disorders, music therapy, nursing (RN). **History:** General. **Human services:** General, social work. **Math:** General. **Parks/recreation:** Exercise sciences. **Physical sciences:** Chemistry, geology, physics. **Protective services:** Law enforcement admin. **Psychology:** General. **Social sciences:** General, economics, geography, political science, sociology. **Visual/performing arts:** Art, dance, dramatic, graphic design, music, music theory/composition, musical theater, studio arts.

Most popular majors. Agriculture 7%, business/marketing 13%, health sciences 10%, interdisciplinary studies 17%, liberal arts 13%, visual/performing arts 6%.

Computing on campus. 1,800 workstations in dormitories, library, computer center, student center. Dormitories wired for high-speed internet access

and linked to campus network. Commuter students can connect to campus network. Online course registration, online library, helpline, student web hosting, wireless network available.

Student life. Freshman orientation: Available, $50 fee. Preregistration for classes offered. 2-day summer orientation and preregistration and 3-day orientation before school starts. **Policies:** Students with fewer than 60 semester hours accumulated, enrolled in 9 or more semester hours, and under 21 on first day of class each semester required to live in university residence halls. **Housing:** Guaranteed on-campus for all undergraduates. Coed dorms, single-sex dorms, special housing for disabled, fraternity/sorority housing available. $100 fully refundable deposit, deadline 5/1. Honors hall available. **Activities:** Bands, campus ministries, choral groups, dance, drama, international student organizations, literary magazine, music ensembles, musical theater, opera, radio station, student government, student newspaper, symphony orchestra, Chinese student association, Hispanic association, agriculture organizations, Students in Free Enterprise, pre-professional organizations, Black students association, College Republicans, Catholic student association.

Athletics. NCAA. **Intercollegiate:** Baseball M, basketball, cross-country, equestrian W, football (tackle) M, golf, soccer, softball W, volleyball W. **Intramural:** Archery, badminton, basketball, bowling, football (non-tackle), golf, racquetball, rodeo, soccer, softball, swimming, table tennis, tennis, volleyball. **Team name:** Buffaloes.

Student services. Alcohol/substance abuse counseling, career counseling, services for economically disadvantaged, student employment services, financial aid counseling, health services, on-campus daycare, personal counseling, placement for graduates, veterans' counselor. **Physically disabled:** Services for visually, speech, hearing impaired.

Contact. E-mail: admissions@wtamu.edu
Phone: (806) 651-2020 Toll-free number: (800) 999-8268
Fax: (806) 651-5268
Shawn Thomas, Director of Admissions, West Texas A&M University, 2501 Fourth Avenue, WTAMU Box 60907, Canyon, TX 79016-0001

Wiley College
Marshall, Texas
www.wileyc.edu

CB member
CB code: 6940

- Private 4-year liberal arts college affiliated with United Methodist Church
- Residential campus in large town
- 1,345 degree-seeking undergraduates

General. Founded in 1873. Regionally accredited. **Degrees:** 198 bachelor's awarded. **Location:** 40 miles from Shreveport, Louisiana, 150 miles from Dallas. **Calendar:** Semester, extensive summer session. **Full-time faculty:** 63 total. **Part-time faculty:** 57 total. **Class size:** 60% < 20, 35% 20-39, 3% 40-49, 2% 50-99. **Special facilities:** Nature trail.

Freshman class profile.

Rank in top quarter:	15%	Out-of-state:	38%
Rank in top tenth:	3%	Live on campus:	90%

Basis for selection. Open admission, but selective for some programs.

High school preparation. 16 units recommended. Recommended units include English 4, mathematics 2, social studies 2, science 2 and academic electives 6.

2011-2012 Annual costs. Tuition/fees: $11,050. Reported tuition includes cost of books. Room/board: $6,136. Personal expenses: $1,002.

Financial aid. All financial aid based on need.

Application procedures. Admission: No deadline. $25 fee. Admission notification on a rolling basis. $40 application fee for non-traditional students. **Financial aid:** No deadline. FAFSA, institutional form required. Applicants notified on a rolling basis.

Academics. Special study options: Accelerated study, cross-registration, distance learning, double major, dual enrollment of high school students, honors, independent study, internships, liberal arts/career combination, study abroad, teacher certification program, weekend college. **Credit/placement by examination:** AP, CLEP, institutional tests. **Support services:** Learning center, reduced course load, remedial instruction, study skills assistance, tutoring.

Majors. Biology: General. **Business:** Accounting, business admin, operations. **Communications:** Journalism. **Computer sciences:** Computer science. **Education:** Elementary, physical, secondary. **English:** English lit. **History:**

General. **Math:** General. **Physical sciences:** Chemistry. **Protective services:** Law enforcement admin. **Social sciences:** Sociology. **Visual/performing arts:** Music.

Most popular majors. Business/marketing 66%, education 6%.

Computing on campus. 177 workstations in dormitories, library, computer center. Dormitories wired for high-speed internet access and linked to campus network. Commuter students can connect to campus network. Online course registration, online library, helpline, wireless network available.

Student life. Freshman orientation: Mandatory. Preregistration for classes offered. **Policies:** Religious observance required. **Housing:** Single-sex dorms, wellness housing available. $50 deposit. **Activities:** Choral groups, drama, music ensembles, radio station, student government, student newspaper, national service fraternity, interdenominational student movement, religion majors club.

Athletics. NAIA. **Intercollegiate:** Baseball M, basketball, cross-country, softball W, track and field, volleyball W. **Intramural:** Baseball M, basketball, cheerleading, softball, table tennis, tennis, track and field, volleyball, weight lifting M. **Team name:** Wildcats.

Student services. Adult student services, chaplain/spiritual director, career counseling, services for economically disadvantaged, student employment services, financial aid counseling, health services, personal counseling, placement for graduates, veterans' counselor.

Contact. E-mail: admissions@wileyc.edu
Phone: (903) 927-3311 Toll-free number: (800) 658-6889
Fax: (903) 927-3366
Ashley Bennett, Director of Admissions, Wiley College, 711 Wiley Avenue, Marshall, TX 75670

Utah

Argosy University: Salt Lake City
Draper, Utah
www.argosy.edu

CB code: 6238

▶ For-profit 4-year university
▶ Commuter campus in small city
▶ 159 degree-seeking undergraduates

General. Degrees: 8 bachelor's awarded; master's, doctoral offered. **Calendar:** Differs by program. **Full-time faculty:** 1 total. **Part-time faculty:** 60 total.

Basis for selection. Open admission.

2011-2012 Annual costs. Tuition/fees: $17,962.

Application procedures. Admission: Closing date 9/12. $50 fee. **Financial aid:** No deadline.

Academics. Credit/placement by examination: AP, CLEP.

Majors. Business: Business admin. **Liberal arts:** Arts/sciences. **Protective services:** Law enforcement admin. **Psychology:** General.

Contact. Phone: (601) 601-5000 Toll-free number: (888) 639-4756 Todd Harrison, Senior Director of Admissions, Argosy University: Salt Lake City, 121 Election Road, Suite 300, Draper, UT 84020

Brigham Young University
Provo, Utah
www.byu.edu

CB member
CB code: 4019

▶ Private 4-year university affiliated with Church of Jesus Christ of Latter-day Saints
▶ Residential campus in small city
▶ 30,684 degree-seeking undergraduates: 9% part-time, 49% women
▶ 3,417 degree-seeking graduate students
▶ 63% of applicants admitted
▶ SAT or ACT (ACT writing recommended), application essay, interview required
▶ 78% graduate within 6 years

General. Founded in 1875. Regionally accredited. Additional educational center in Salt Lake City. **Degrees:** 6,742 bachelor's awarded; master's, professional, doctoral offered. **ROTC:** Army, Air Force. **Location:** 45 miles from Salt Lake City. **Calendar:** Semester, limited summer session. **Full-time faculty:** 1,216 total; 93% have terminal degrees, 4% minority, 21% women. **Part-time faculty:** 483 total; 39% have terminal degrees, 6% minority, 63% women. **Class size:** 47% < 20, 36% 20-39, 6% 40-49, 8% 50-99, 3% >100. **Special facilities:** Aquatic ecology laboratory, science and anthropological museums, veterinary pathology laboratory, fine arts museum, reading and writing laboratories, math and language computer laboratories, supercomputer.

Freshman class profile. 11,238 applied, 7,055 admitted, 5,624 enrolled.

Mid 50% test scores		GPA 2.0-2.99:	1%
SAT critical reading:	570-680	Rank in top quarter:	84%
SAT math:	580-680	Rank in top tenth:	53%
SAT writing:	540-650	Return as sophomores:	87%
ACT composite:	26-30	Out-of-state:	67%
GPA 3.75 or higher:	66%	Live on campus:	79%
GPA 3.50-3.74:	23%	International:	1%
GPA 3.0-3.49:	10%		

Basis for selection. GED not accepted. School achievement record, test scores, endorsements and recommendations important. Students must maintain ideals and standards in harmony with The Church of Jesus Christ of Latter-Day Saints. Interview is ecclesiastical. **Learning Disabled:** Untimed ACT accepted.

High school preparation. College-preparatory program recommended. Required and recommended units include English 4, mathematics 3-4, history 2, science 2-3 (laboratory 2-3), foreign language 2-4, computer science 1 and visual/performing arts 1. 2 units of literature/writing required.

2011-2012 Annual costs. Tuition/fees: $4,560. Tuition is $9,120 for non-members of The Church of Jesus Christ of Latter-day Saints. Undergraduate per-credit-hour charge $468 for nonmembers. Room/board: $7,228. Books/supplies: $900. Personal expenses: $1,720.

2010-2011 Financial aid. Need-based: 2,280 full-time freshmen applied for aid; 1,727 were judged to have need; 1,514 of these received aid. Average need met was 28%. Average scholarship/grant was $4,140; average loan $3,105. 76% of total undergraduate aid awarded as scholarships/grants, 24% as loans/jobs. **Non-need-based:** Awarded to 14,333 full-time undergraduates, including 3,037 freshmen. Scholarships awarded for academics, art, athletics, leadership, minority status, music/drama, religious affiliation, ROTC, state residency. **Additional information:** Students notified of scholarships on or about April 20.

Application procedures. Admission: Priority date 12/1; deadline 2/1 (receipt date). $35 fee. Admission notification by 2/28. Admission notification on a rolling basis. Must reply by 5/1. **Financial aid:** Priority date 4/15; no closing date. FAFSA required. Applicants notified on a rolling basis starting 4/1.

Academics. Special study options: Accelerated study, combined bachelor's/graduate degree, cooperative education, cross-registration, distance learning, double major, ESL, external degree, honors, independent study, internships, liberal arts/career combination, study abroad, teacher certification program, Washington semester. **Credit/placement by examination:** AP, CLEP, IB, SAT, ACT, institutional tests. **Support services:** Learning center, pre-admission summer program, reduced course load, remedial instruction, study skills assistance, tutoring, writing center.

Majors. Area/ethnic studies: American, Asian, European, French, German, Latin American, Russian/Eastern European/Eurasian. **Biology:** Biochemistry, bioinformatics, biophysics, biostatistics, biotechnology, conservation, exercise physiology, microbiology, molecular, neuroscience, physiology, wildlife. **Business:** General, accounting, actuarial science, business admin, construction management, entrepreneurial studies, finance, information resources management, logistics, management information systems, managerial economics, marketing, organizational behavior, statistics. **Communications:** Advertising, journalism, public relations. **Communications technology:** Animation/special effects, recording arts. **Computer sciences:** Computer graphics, computer science, information technology. **Conservation:** Environmental science. **Education:** Biology, chemistry, drama/dance, early childhood, elementary, English, family/consumer sciences, French, German, health, history, Latin, mathematics, music, physical, physics, science, social science, Spanish, special ed. **Engineering:** Chemical, civil, computer, electrical, manufacturing, mechanical. **English:** English lit. **Foreign languages:** General, ancient Greek, Arabic, Biblical, Chinese, classics, comparative lit, French, German, Germanic, Japanese, Korean, Latin, linguistics, Portuguese, Russian, Spanish, translation. **General:** Food science, landscaping. **Health services:** Athletic training, audiology/speech pathology, clinical lab science, dietetics, nursing (RN), recreational therapy. **History:** General. **Liberal arts:** Humanities. **Math:** General, statistics. **Parks/recreation:** General, health/fitness. **Philosophy/religion:** Philosophy. **Physical sciences:** Astronomy, chemistry, geology, hydrology, physics. **Psychology:** General. **Social sciences:** Anthropology, archaeology, economics, geography, GIS/cartography, international relations, political science, sociology. **Visual/performing arts:** Acting, art, art history/conservation, ballet, dance, design, dramatic, film/cinema/video, graphic design, illustration, industrial design, jazz, music, music history, music performance, music theory/composition, musical theater, photography, piano/keyboard, stringed instruments, studio arts, theater history, voice/opera. **Work/family studies:** General, facilities/event planning, family studies, family systems.

Most popular majors. Biology 11%, business/marketing 12%, education 10%, engineering/engineering technologies 6%, family/consumer sciences 6%, foreign language 6%, social sciences 11%, visual/performing arts 6%.

Computing on campus. 2,000 workstations in dormitories, library, computer center, student center. Dormitories wired for high-speed internet access and linked to campus network. Commuter students can connect to campus network. Online course registration, online library, helpline, repair service, student web hosting, wireless network available.

Student life. Freshman orientation: Available. Preregistration for classes offered. **Policies:** Honor code enforced. Religious observance required. **Housing:** Single-sex dorms, special housing for disabled, apartments available. $150 partly refundable deposit. Foreign language houses available. **Activities:** Bands, choral groups, dance, drama, film society, literary magazine, music ensembles, musical theater, opera, radio station, student government, student newspaper, symphony orchestra, TV station, College Republicans, College Democrats, African American club, black student union, Latin American

student association, international student association, Intercollegiate Knights, Circle-K International, Southeast Asian club, Baptist student union.

Athletics. NCAA. **Intercollegiate:** Baseball M, basketball, cheerleading, cross-country, diving, football (tackle) M, golf, gymnastics W, soccer W, softball W, swimming, tennis, track and field, volleyball. **Intramural:** Badminton, basketball, football (non-tackle), football (tackle), golf, racquetball, soccer, softball, tennis, volleyball, water polo, wrestling M. **Team name:** Cougars.

Student services. Chaplain/spiritual director, career counseling, services for economically disadvantaged, student employment services, financial aid counseling, health services, minority student services, personal counseling, placement for graduates, veterans' counselor, women's services. **Physically disabled:** Services for visually, speech, hearing impaired.

Contact. E-mail: admissions@byu.edu
Phone: (801) 422-2507 Fax: (801) 422-0005
Tom Gourley, Director of Admissions, Brigham Young University, A-41ASB, BYU, Provo, UT 84602

Broadview University: Orem
Orem, Utah
www.broadviewuniversity.edu

⬧ For-profit 4-year career college
⬧ Large city
⬧ 226 degree-seeking undergraduates

General. Regionally accredited; also accredited by ACICS. **Degrees:** 2 bachelor's, 17 associate awarded; master's offered. **Calendar:** Quarter. **Full-time faculty:** 9 total. **Part-time faculty:** 17 total.

Basis for selection. Open admission.

2011-2012 Annual costs. Tuition/fees: $18,450. Nursing: $565 per quarter hour.

Application procedures. **Admission:** No deadline. $50 fee. **Financial aid:** No deadline.

Academics. Credit/placement by examination: AP, CLEP.

Majors. **Business:** Accounting, business admin. **Computer sciences:** Information technology. **Health services:** Health care admin. **Protective services:** Police science.

Contact. E-mail: mmoon@broadviewuniversity.edu
Phone: (801) 822-5800
Matt Moon, Director of Admissions, Broadview University: Orem, 898 North 1200 West, Orem, UT 84057

Dixie State College
St. George, Utah
www.dixie.edu   CB code: 4283

⬧ Public 4-year liberal arts college
⬧ Commuter campus in small city
⬧ 7,877 degree-seeking undergraduates: 32% part-time, 52% women, 2% African American, 1% Asian American, 7% Hispanic American, 1% Native American, 1% international
⬧ 32% graduate within 6 years

General. Founded in 1911. Regionally accredited. **Degrees:** 382 bachelor's, 1,080 associate awarded. **ROTC:** Army. **Location:** 305 miles from Salt Lake City, 121 miles from Las Vegas. **Calendar:** Semester, limited summer session. **Full-time faculty:** 147 total. **Part-time faculty:** 285 total.

Freshman class profile. 4,894 applied, 3,088 admitted, 1,957 enrolled.

Mid 50% test scores			
SAT critical reading:	390-510	GPA 3.0-3.49:	30%
SAT math:	390-500	GPA 2.0-2.99:	33%
SAT writing:	380-490	Rank in top quarter:	27%
ACT composite:	18-23	Rank in top tenth:	8%
GPA 3.75 or higher:	18%	Return as sophomores:	57%
GPA 3.50-3.74:	16%	Out-of-state:	16%
		International:	1%

Basis for selection. Open admission, but selective for some programs. Some health occupation programs have prerequisites. Applicants for bachelor's degrees in elementary education, business administration, and nursing

must have associate degree or advance standing. **Home schooled:** Letter of recommendation (nonparent) required. Copy of formal letter of release from high school counselor or secondary school district that states the student is no longer required to attend secondary school required. Statement from student certifying that they have completed the equivalent of a high school diploma required.

High school preparation. College-preparatory program recommended. 16 units recommended. Recommended units include English 4, mathematics 4, history 3, science 2 (laboratory 1) and foreign language 2. One computer literacy unit recommended.

2011-2012 Annual costs. Tuition/fees: $3,888; $13,536 out-of-state. Room/board: $4,348.

2010-2011 Financial aid. **Need-based:** 62% of total undergraduate aid awarded as scholarships/grants, 38% as loans/jobs. **Non-need-based:** Scholarships awarded for academics, alumni affiliation, art, athletics, leadership, minority status, music/drama, religious affiliation.

Application procedures. **Admission:** Closing date 8/15 (receipt date). $35 fee. Admission notification on a rolling basis. Students who have received approval for early release from high school must provide copy of formal letter or release from high school counselor, as well as written authorization from parent or legal guardian; submit application and pay non-refundable application fee, and demonstrate college readiness by submitting ACT, SAT, or Accuplacer scores equivalent to the following ACT minimums for early enrollment students: Reading 17 or higher; English 19 or higher; Math 18 or higher. **Financial aid:** No deadline. FAFSA required. Applicants notified on a rolling basis starting 2/1; must reply within 2 week(s) of notification.

Academics. Bachelor's and master's degree course work from Utah's 4-year universities presented over distance-learning media and on-campus instruction. Four-year programs in accounting, biology, business administration, computer technology, communication, elementary education, English, nursing, dental hygiene, integrated studies, mathematics, music, psychology, and theater offered on campus. **Special study options:** Accelerated study, cooperative education, distance learning, double major, dual enrollment of high school students, ESL, honors, independent study, internships, student-designed major, study abroad, teacher certification program. **Credit/placement by examination:** AP, CLEP. 30 credit hours maximum toward associate degree, 30 toward bachelor's. **Support services:** Learning center, remedial instruction, study skills assistance, tutoring, writing center.

Majors. **Biology:** General. **Business:** Accounting, business admin. **Communications:** Communications/speech/rhetoric. **Computer sciences:** General. **Education:** Biology, elementary, English, mathematics, music, science. **English:** English lit. **Health services:** Dental hygiene, nursing (RN). **Math:** General. **Psychology:** General. **Visual/performing arts:** Music, theater design.

Most popular majors. Business/marketing 26%, communications/journalism 12%, computer/information sciences 7%, education 14%, health sciences 9%, interdisciplinary studies 13%.

Computing on campus. 400 workstations in dormitories, library, computer center, student center. Dormitories wired for high-speed internet access and linked to campus network. Commuter students can connect to campus network. Online course registration, online library, helpline, repair service, wireless network available.

Student life. **Freshman orientation:** Mandatory. Preregistration for classes offered. All-day sessions offered on Mondays and Tuesdays from the 2nd week of June to the 1st week of August. **Policies:** Stringent drug and alcohol policies. **Housing:** Coed dorms, single-sex dorms, apartments, wellness housing available. $75 fully refundable deposit. **Activities:** Bands, campus ministries, choral groups, dance, drama, international student organizations, literary magazine, music ensembles, musical theater, radio station, student government, student newspaper, symphony orchestra, TV station, Native American student association, Polynesian cultural club, Black student association, Hispanic student association, diversity club, Latter-Day Saints student association, campus Christian connection, Phi Beta Lambda, College Democrats, College Republicans.

Athletics. NCAA. **Intercollegiate:** Baseball M, basketball, cross-country, football (tackle) M, golf, soccer, softball W, tennis W, volleyball W. **Intramural:** Basketball, football (non-tackle), table tennis, tennis. **Team name:** Red Storm.

Student services. Adult student services, alcohol/substance abuse counseling, career counseling, services for economically disadvantaged, student employment services, financial aid counseling, health services, minority student services, personal counseling, placement for graduates, veterans' counselor. **Physically disabled:** Services for visually, speech, hearing impaired.

Contact. E-mail: admissions@dixie.edu
Phone: (435) 652-7777 Fax: (435) 656-4015
Laralee Davenport, Assistant Director of Admissions, Dixie State College, 225 South 700 East, St. George, UT 84770-3876

Independence University
Murray, Utah
www.independence.edu

- For-profit 4-year health science college
- Commuter campus in small city
- 952 full-time, degree-seeking undergraduates

General. Founded in 1975. Regionally accredited; also accredited by ACCSC. Primarily serves home-study students. **Degrees:** 49 bachelor's, 180 associate awarded; master's offered. **Calendar:** Differs by program. **Full-time faculty:** 10 total. **Part-time faculty:** 100 total.

Basis for selection. Open admission.

2012-2013 Annual costs. Cost of associate degree programs range from $22,500 - $47,615; bachelor's degree programs: $49,500; bachelor's completion programs: $25,000.

Financial aid. Additional information: Financial aid available for resident students only, not correspondence students.

Application procedures. Admission: No deadline. No application fee. Admission notification on a rolling basis. **Financial aid:** Closing date 7/23. FAFSA required.

Academics. Special study options: Liberal arts/career combination. **Credit/placement by examination:** AP, CLEP. 30 credit hours maximum toward associate degree, 30 toward bachelor's. **Support services:** Tutoring.

Majors. Business: General. **Health services:** Health care admin.

Most popular majors. Business/marketing 11%, health sciences 89%.

Student life. Activities: Student newspaper.

Contact. E-mail: admissns@cchs.edu
Phone: (800) 972-5149 Toll-free number: (800) 972-5149
Independence University, 4021 South 700 East, Suite 400, Murray, UT 84107

ITT Technical Institute: Murray
Murray, Utah
www.itt-tech.edu   **CB code: 3601**

- For-profit 4-year technical college
- Commuter campus in small city
- 868 undergraduates
- Interview required

General. Founded in 1984. Accredited by ACICS. **Degrees:** 70 bachelor's, 187 associate awarded. **Location:** 10 miles from Salt Lake City. **Calendar:** Quarter, extensive summer session. **Full-time faculty:** 11 total. **Part-time faculty:** 65 total.

Basis for selection. Satisfactory scores from on-site tests in English and math required.

2011-2012 Annual costs. Estimated costs as of June 2011: per-credit-hour charge, $493, depending upon level and course of study; academic fee, $300. Certain programs of study require purchase of tools, which could cost an additional $100 to $500. All costs are subject to change.

Application procedures. Admission: No deadline. No application fee. Admission notification on a rolling basis. **Financial aid:** No deadline. FAFSA, institutional form required. Applicants notified on a rolling basis.

Academics. Credit/placement by examination: AP, CLEP. **Support services:** Learning center, tutoring.

Majors. Business: Business admin, construction management, project management. **Communications technology:** Animation/special effects. **Computer sciences:** Security. **Protective services:** Law enforcement admin. **Visual/performing arts:** Graphic design.

Computing on campus. Online library available.

Student life. Freshman orientation: Available. Preregistration for classes offered.

Student services. Career counseling, student employment services, placement for graduates.

Contact. Phone: (801) 263-3313 Toll-free number: (800) 365-2136
Fax: (801) 263-3497
Gary Wood, Director of Recruitment, ITT Technical Institute: Murray, 920 West LeVoy Drive, Murray, UT 84123

Neumont University
South Jordan, Utah
www.neumont.edu   **CB code: 4516**

- For-profit 4-year engineering and technical college
- Residential campus in very large city
- 346 degree-seeking undergraduates: 9% women
- 85% of applicants admitted
- Application essay required

General. Regionally accredited; also accredited by ACICS. **Degrees:** 51 bachelor's awarded; master's offered. **Location:** 20 miles from Salt Lake City. **Calendar:** Quarter, extensive summer session. **Full-time faculty:** 14 total; 21% women. **Part-time faculty:** 19 total; 21% women. **Special facilities:** Evolution Chamber gaming lab.

Freshman class profile. 530 applied, 452 admitted, 223 enrolled.

GPA 3.75 or higher:	22%	Return as sophomores:	83%
GPA 3.50-3.74:	12%	Out-of-state:	82%
GPA 3.0-3.49:	30%	Live on campus:	81%
GPA 2.0-2.99:	36%		

Basis for selection. Strong work ethic, accomplishments, and aptitude most important. SAT or ACT recommended. **Home schooled:** State high school equivalency certificate required.

2012-2013 Annual costs. Tuition/fees (projected): $23,100. One time laptop cost of $2,000. Room only: $4,230. Books/supplies: $1,080.

Application procedures. Admission: No deadline. $35 fee, may be waived for applicants with need. Application must be submitted online. Admission notification on a rolling basis. **Financial aid:** No deadline. FAFSA, institutional form required.

Academics. Special study options: Accelerated study, cooperative education, internships. **Credit/placement by examination:** AP, CLEP. **Support services:** Remedial instruction, study skills assistance, tutoring.

Majors. Business: Management information systems. **Computer sciences:** Computer science, information technology, web page design, webmaster. **Visual/performing arts:** Game design.

Computing on campus. PC or laptop required. Dormitories wired for high-speed internet access and linked to campus network. Commuter students can connect to campus network. Online course registration, online library, helpline, repair service, student web hosting, wireless network available.

Student life. Freshman orientation: Mandatory. Preregistration for classes offered. **Housing:** Guaranteed on-campus for all undergraduates. Single-sex dorms, apartments available. $350 nonrefundable deposit, deadline 8/1. **Activities:** Student government.

Student services. Career counseling, financial aid counseling, placement for graduates.

Contact. E-mail: admissions@neumont.edu
Phone: (801) 302-2800 Toll-free number: (888) 638-6668
Fax: (801) 302-2880
Karick Heaton, Director of Admissions, Neumont University, 10701 South River Front Parkway, Suite 300, South Jordan, UT 84095

Southern Utah University
Cedar City, Utah   **CB member**
www.suu.edu   **CB code: 4092**

- Public 4-year university
- Residential campus in large town

- 5,774 degree-seeking undergraduates: 11% part-time, 55% women, 2% African American, 1% Asian American, 4% Hispanic American, 2% Native American, 4% international
- 575 degree-seeking graduate students
- 72% of applicants admitted
- SAT or ACT (ACT writing optional) required
- 38% graduate within 6 years

General. Founded in 1897. Regionally accredited. **Degrees:** 938 bachelor's, 359 associate awarded; master's offered. **ROTC:** Army. **Location:** 265 miles from Salt Lake City, 160 miles from Las Vegas. **Calendar:** Semester, limited summer session. **Full-time faculty:** 246 total; 74% have terminal degrees, 9% minority, 33% women. **Part-time faculty:** 173 total; 13% have terminal degrees, 5% minority, 44% women. **Class size:** 37% < 20, 45% 20-39, 8% 40-49, 9% 50-99, less than 1% >100. **Special facilities:** Natural life museum, observatory, Shakespearean theater, fine arts gallery.

Freshman class profile. 4,249 applied, 3,071 admitted, 1,249 enrolled.

Mid 50% test scores			
SAT critical reading:	460-580	GPA 2.0-2.99:	7%
SAT math:	450-580	Rank in top quarter:	45%
SAT writing:	450-560	Rank in top tenth:	19%
ACT composite:	20-25	Return as sophomores:	66%
GPA 3.75 or higher:	48%	Out-of-state:	18%
GPA 3.50-3.74:	18%	Live on campus:	43%
GPA 3.0-3.49:	27%	International:	5%

Basis for selection. Admission based on GPA and ACT/SAT scores. **Home schooled:** Transcript of courses and grades required.

High school preparation. College-preparatory program recommended. Recommended units include English 4, mathematics 3, social studies 3, science 3 (laboratory 1) and foreign language 2. 1 unit of social studies should be U.S. history and government; 2 math units should be elementary algebra or above; English units should have a composition and literature emphasis.

2011-2012 Annual costs. Tuition/fees: $5,198; $15,910 out-of-state. Room/board: $5,496. Books/supplies: $1,600. Personal expenses: $2,400.

2010-2011 Financial aid. **Need-based:** 1,015 full-time freshmen applied for aid; 839 were judged to have need; 830 of these received aid. Average need met was 54%. Average scholarship/grant was $8,174; average loan $3,438. 55% of total undergraduate aid awarded as scholarships/grants, 45% as loans/jobs. **Non-need-based:** Awarded to 1,689 full-time undergraduates, including 642 freshmen. Scholarships awarded for academics, alumni affiliation, art, athletics, job skills, leadership, minority status, music/drama, ROTC, state residency.

Application procedures. **Admission:** Priority date 12/1; deadline 5/1. $45 fee. Admission notification on a rolling basis. Commitment fee requested by May 1st. **Financial aid:** Priority date 12/1; no closing date. FAFSA required. Applicants notified on a rolling basis starting 11/1; must reply within 4 week(s) of notification.

Academics. **Special study options:** Combined bachelor's/graduate degree, cooperative education, distance learning, double major, dual enrollment of high school students, ESL, exchange student, honors, independent study, internships, liberal arts/career combination, student-designed major, study abroad, teacher certification program, weekend college. **Credit/placement by examination:** AP, CLEP, SAT, ACT, institutional tests. **Support services:** Learning center, pre-admission summer program, reduced course load, remedial instruction, study skills assistance, tutoring, writing center.

Most popular majors. Biology 7%, business/marketing 15%, communications/journalism 6%, education 24%, health sciences 8%, psychology 7%, visual/performing arts 6%.

Computing on campus. 300 workstations in dormitories, library, computer center, student center. Dormitories wired for high-speed internet access and linked to campus network. Commuter students can connect to campus network. Online course registration, online library, helpline, student web hosting, wireless network available.

Student life. **Freshman orientation:** Mandatory. Preregistration for classes offered. One-day program held throughout summer. Parents welcome and encouraged to attend. **Housing:** Coed dorms, special housing for disabled, apartments available. $100 fully refundable deposit. **Activities:** Bands, choral groups, dance, drama, international student organizations, literary magazine, music ensembles, musical theater, opera, radio station, student government, student newspaper, symphony orchestra, TV station, Latter-day Saint student association, Newman Club, Campus Christian Fellowship, Arabic club, multicultural club, Queer Straight Alliance, Young Democrats of Utah, College Republicans, Student Alliance of Interfaith Leaders.

Athletics. NAIA, NCAA. **Intercollegiate:** Baseball M, basketball, cross-country, football (tackle) M, golf M, gymnastics W, soccer W, softball W, tennis W, track and field. **Intramural:** Basketball, golf, soccer, tennis, volleyball. **Team name:** Thunderbirds.

Student services. Career counseling, services for economically disadvantaged, student employment services, financial aid counseling, minority student services, personal counseling, placement for graduates, veterans' counselor, women's services. **Physically disabled:** Services for visually, speech, hearing impaired.

Contact. E-mail: adminfo@suu.edu
Phone: (435) 586-7740 Fax: (435) 865-8223
Stephen Allen, Associate Vice President for Enrollment Management, Southern Utah University, 351 West University Blvd, Cedar City, UT 84720

Stevens-Henager College: Logan
Logan, Utah
www.stevenshenager.edu

- For-profit 4-year business, health science and technical college
- Large town
- 180 full-time, degree-seeking undergraduates

General. Accredited by ACCSC. **Degrees:** 27 bachelor's, 38 associate awarded. **Calendar:** Differs by program. **Full-time faculty:** 3 total; 33% have terminal degrees. **Part-time faculty:** 14 total; 43% women.

Basis for selection. Open admission. **Home schooled:** State high school equivalency certificate required.

2011-2012 Annual costs. Tuition/fees: $16,356. Cost shown is for associates degree program. Academic year cost of bachelor's degree program is $16,016. All costs inclusive of books, fees, and supplies.

Application procedures. **Admission:** No deadline. Admission notification on a rolling basis.

Academics. **Special study options:** Accelerated study, distance learning, internships. **Credit/placement by examination:** AP, CLEP.

Majors. **Business:** Accounting, business admin. **Computer sciences:** Computer science. **Health services:** Health care admin.

Most popular majors. Business/marketing 46%, computer/information sciences 36%, health sciences 18%.

Student life. **Freshman orientation:** Mandatory. Preregistration for classes offered.

Student services. Career counseling, student employment services, financial aid counseling, personal counseling, placement for graduates, veterans' counselor.

Contact. E-mail: clay.buttars@stevenshenager.edu
Phone: (435) 792-6970 ext. 5002 Fax: (435) 755-7611
Clay Buttars, Director of Admissions, Stevens-Henager College: Logan, 755 South Main, Logan, UT 84321

Stevens-Henager College: Murray
Salt Lake City, Utah
www.stevenshenager.edu

- For-profit 4-year business and health science college
- Commuter campus in large town

General. Accredited by ACCSCT. **Location:** 5 Miles from Salt Lake City. **Calendar:** Differs by program.

Annual costs/financial aid. Tuition/fees (2011-2012): $16,356. Cost shown is for associates degree program. Academic year cost of bachelor's degree program is $16,016. All costs inclusive of books, fees, and supplies.

Contact. Phone: (800) 622-2640
Admissions Director, 383 West Vine Street, Salt Lake City, UT 84123

Stevens-Henager College: Ogden
Ogden, Utah
www.stevenshenager.edu   CB code: 4751

- For-profit 4-year liberal arts college
- Commuter campus in small city

General. Accredited by ACCSCT. **Location:** 35 miles from Salt Lake City. **Calendar:** Differs by program.

Annual costs/financial aid. Tuition/fees (2011-2012): $16,356. Cost shown is for associates degree program. Academic year cost of bachelor's degree program is $16,016. All costs inclusive of books, fees, and supplies. Personal expenses: $4,000.

Contact. Phone: (801) 394-7791
Director of Admissions, 1890 South 1350 West, Ogden, UT 84401

Stevens-Henager College: Orem
Orem, Utah
www.stevenshenager.edu

- For-profit 4-year health science and career college
- Large city

General. Founded in 1891. Accredited by ACCSCT. **Location:** 35 miles from Salt Lake City. **Calendar:** Differs by program.

Annual costs/financial aid. Tuition/fees (2011-2012): $16,356. Cost shown is for associates degree program. Academic year cost of bachelor's degree program is $16,016. All costs inclusive of books, fees, and supplies. Personal expenses: $2,123.

Contact. Phone: (801) 418-6636
Director of Admissions, 1476 South Sand Hill Road, Orem, UT 84058

University of Phoenix: Utah
Salt Lake City, Utah
www.phoenix.edu

- For-profit 4-year university
- Commuter campus in small city
- 1,426 degree-seeking undergraduates

General. Regionally accredited. **Degrees:** 444 bachelor's awarded; master's offered. **Calendar:** Differs by program. **Full-time faculty:** 28 total. **Part-time faculty:** 247 total.

Basis for selection. Open admission.

2011-2012 Annual costs. Estimated costs as of August 2011: per-credit-hour charge, $405 to $420, depending upon level and course of study; electronic course materials fee, $95, if applicable. Book and material charges may vary by course and program. All fees are subject to change.

Application procedures. Admission: No deadline. No application fee. **Financial aid:** No deadline.

Academics. Credit/placement by examination: AP, CLEP.

Majors. Business: Accounting, business admin, marketing. **Computer sciences:** General, information technology, security, web page design. **Education:** Elementary. **Health services:** Facilities admin, health care admin. **Protective services:** Law enforcement admin. **Psychology:** General.

Most popular majors. Business/marketing 72%, computer/information sciences 11%, education 6%.

Contact. Toll-free number: (866) 766-0766
Marc Booker, Director of Admission and Evaluation, University of Phoenix: Utah, 5373 South Green Street, Salt Lake City, UT 84123-4642

University of Utah
Salt Lake City, Utah   CB member
www.utah.edu   CB code: 4853

- Public 4-year university
- Commuter campus in very large city

- 23,275 degree-seeking undergraduates: 28% part-time, 44% women, 1% African American, 5% Asian American, 8% Hispanic American, 1% Native American, 5% international
- 7,363 degree-seeking graduate students
- 83% of applicants admitted
- SAT or ACT (ACT writing optional) required
- 60% graduate within 6 years

General. Founded in 1850. Regionally accredited. **Degrees:** 4,801 bachelor's awarded; master's, professional, doctoral offered. **ROTC:** Army, Naval, Air Force. **Location:** 2 miles from downtown. **Calendar:** Semester, limited summer session. **Full-time faculty:** 1,301 total; 82% have terminal degrees, 10% minority, 41% women. **Part-time faculty:** 632 total; 27% have terminal degrees, 6% minority, 44% women. **Class size:** 42% < 20, 35% 20-39, 6% 40-49, 12% 50-99, 5% >100. **Special facilities:** Arboretum, fine arts museum, natural history museum, architecture exhibition hall, Olympic Cauldron Park, cancer research institute.

Freshman class profile. 9,545 applied, 7,941 admitted, 3,268 enrolled.

Mid 50% test scores			
SAT critical reading:	490-630	Rank in top quarter:	48%
SAT math:	510-650	Rank in top tenth:	21%
SAT writing:	490-610	End year in good standing:	93%
ACT composite:	21-27	Return as sophomores:	88%
GPA 3.75 or higher:	39%	Out-of-state:	20%
GPA 3.50-3.74:	21%	Live on campus:	35%
GPA 3.0-3.49:	30%	International:	7%
GPA 2.0-2.99:	10%	Fraternities:	4%
		Sororities:	4%

Basis for selection. High school course requirements, admissions index using high school GPA and test scores important. Recommendations and extracurricular activities considered. Audition required for dance, drama, music programs; portfolio required for art program. **Home schooled:** Transcript of courses and grades, state high school equivalency certificate required. 23 ACT or 1060 SAT (exclusive of Writing), score of 550 on each of the sub-sections of the GED required. Students who graduate from non-accredited high school with test score in upper quartile (25 ACT, 1140 SAT), with no individual score below freshman class average, will not be required to take GED. **Learning Disabled:** Disclosure of learning disabilities not required; Center for Disability Services assists students with disabilities in the admission process.

High school preparation. College-preparatory program required. 16 units required. Required units include English 4, mathematics 2, history 1, science 3 (laboratory 1), foreign language 2 and academic electives 4. 4 units from at least 2 of the following: history, English, math beyond algebra, laboratory science, foreign language, social science, fine arts.

2011-2012 Annual costs. Tuition/fees: $6,763; $21,389 out-of-state. Room/board: $6,699. Books/supplies: $1,090. Personal expenses: $4,500.

2011-2012 Financial aid. Need-based: 1,801 full-time freshmen applied for aid; 1,315 were judged to have need; 1,252 of these received aid. Average need met was 61%. Average scholarship/grant was $6,935; average loan $3,339. 53% of total undergraduate aid awarded as scholarships/grants, 47% as loans/jobs. **Non-need-based:** Awarded to 943 full-time undergraduates, including 171 freshmen. Scholarships awarded for academics, alumni affiliation, art, athletics, leadership, minority status, music/drama, ROTC, state residency.

Application procedures. Admission: Priority date 12/15; deadline 4/1 (postmark date). $45 fee, may be waived for applicants with need. Admission notification on a rolling basis. **Financial aid:** Priority date 4/1; no closing date. FAFSA, institutional form required. Applicants notified on a rolling basis starting 4/15; must reply within 6 week(s) of notification.

Academics. Special study options: Accelerated study, combined bachelor's/graduate degree, distance learning, double major, dual enrollment of high school students, ESL, exchange student, honors, independent study, internships, student-designed major, study abroad, teacher certification program, Washington semester. **Credit/placement by examination:** AP, CLEP, IB, SAT, ACT, institutional tests. 32 credit hours maximum toward bachelor's degree. **Support services:** Learning center, pre-admission summer program, reduced course load, remedial instruction, study skills assistance, tutoring, writing center.

Honors college/program. Entering freshmen accepted based on 120 admissions index and 3.5 GPA.

Majors. Architecture: Architecture. **Area/ethnic studies:** Asian, Latin American, Near/Middle Eastern, women's. **Biology:** General, cell/histology. **Business:** General, accounting, business admin, entrepreneurial studies,

finance, management information systems, marketing, operations. **Communications:** Communications/speech/rhetoric, media studies. **Computer sciences:** Computer science. **Conservation:** Environmental science, environmental studies. **Education:** General, elementary, social science, special ed. **Engineering:** General, biomedical, chemical, civil, computer, electrical, geological, materials, mechanical, metallurgical, mining. **English:** English lit. **Foreign languages:** Arabic, Chinese, classics, comparative lit, French, German, Hebrew, Iranian, Japanese, linguistics, Russian, Spanish, Turkish. **Health services:** Athletic training, audiology/speech pathology, clinical lab science, nursing (RN), occupational therapy, physical therapy, predental, premedicine, prenursing, prepharmacy, public health ed. **History:** General. **Human services:** Social work. **Liberal arts:** Humanities. **Math:** General, applied. **Parks/recreation:** General, exercise sciences, health/fitness. **Philosophy/religion:** Philosophy. **Physical sciences:** General, atmospheric science, chemistry, geology, geophysics, meteorology, physics. **Psychology:** General. **Social sciences:** General, anthropology, economics, geography, political science, sociology, urban studies. **Visual/performing arts:** General, art, art history/conservation, ballet, dance, dramatic, film/cinema/video, music. **Work/family studies:** Consumer economics, family studies.

Most popular majors. Business/marketing 13%, communications/journalism 9%, engineering/engineering technologies 7%, health sciences 8%, social sciences 17%, visual/performing arts 6%.

Computing on campus. 8,800 workstations in dormitories, library, computer center, student center. Dormitories wired for high-speed internet access and linked to campus network. Commuter students can connect to campus network. Online course registration, online library, helpline, repair service, student web hosting, wireless network available.

Student life. Freshman orientation: Mandatory. Preregistration for classes offered. One-day, 2-day, and 4-day programs offered before fall semester. Late orientations offered in August and mini-orientations held the first day of class. Some orientation options have fees. **Housing:** Coed dorms, single-sex dorms, special housing for disabled, apartments, fraternity/sorority housing available. $200 partly refundable deposit. Limited visitation, 24-hour quiet housing available. **Activities:** Bands, campus ministries, choral groups, dance, drama, film society, international student organizations, literary magazine, music ensembles, Model UN, musical theater, opera, radio station, student government, student newspaper, symphony orchestra, TV station, Intervarsity Christian Fellowship, Jewish student association, Latter Day Saint student association, Hinckley Institute student alliance, foreign policy studies club, cross culture club, Asian American student association, black student union, Operation Smile student association, tech club.

Athletics. NCAA. **Intercollegiate:** Baseball M, basketball, cheerleading, cross-country W, diving, football (tackle) M, golf M, gymnastics W, skiing, soccer W, softball W, swimming, tennis, track and field W, volleyball W. **Intramural:** Badminton, basketball, bowling, field hockey, football (non-tackle) M, racquetball, soccer, softball, squash, tennis, volleyball. **Team name:** Utes.

Student services. Adult student services, alcohol/substance abuse counseling, chaplain/spiritual director, career counseling, student employment services, financial aid counseling, health services, minority student services, on-campus daycare, personal counseling, placement for graduates, veterans' counselor, women's services. **Physically disabled:** Services for visually, speech, hearing impaired.

Contact. E-mail: admissions@sa.utah.edu
Phone: (801) 581-7281 Fax: (801) 585-7864
Barbara Forlin, Director of Admissions, University of Utah, 201 South 1460 East, Room 250 S, Salt Lake City, UT 84112-9057

Utah State University
Logan, Utah
www.usu.edu

CB member
CB code: 4857

- Public 4-year university
- Residential campus in small city
- 19,460 degree-seeking undergraduates: 26% part-time, 54% women, 1% African American, 1% Asian American, 5% Hispanic American, 2% Native American, 2% international
- 2,674 degree-seeking graduate students
- 97% of applicants admitted
- SAT or ACT (ACT writing optional) required
- 56% graduate within 6 years

General. Founded in 1888. Regionally accredited. **Degrees:** 3,232 bachelor's, 505 associate awarded; master's, professional, doctoral offered. **ROTC:**

Army, Air Force. **Location:** 80 miles from Salt Lake City. **Calendar:** Semester, extensive summer session. **Full-time faculty:** 702 total; 85% have terminal degrees, 7% minority, 32% women. **Part-time faculty:** 177 total; 6% minority, 48% women. **Class size:** 32% < 20, 42% 20-39, 8% 40-49, 11% 50-99, 7% >100. **Special facilities:** Agricultural experiment stations, water research laboratory, space shuttle experiments, forestry research facility, botanical gardens, teaching greenhouse, research park, laboratory school, off-campus theater performance lab, anthropology museum.

Freshman class profile. 8,657 applied, 8,414 admitted, 3,936 enrolled.

Mid 50% test scores			
SAT critical reading:	470-620	GPA 2.0-2.99:	16%
SAT math:	490-610	Rank in top quarter:	46%
ACT composite:	20-26	Rank in top tenth:	20%
GPA 3.75 or higher:	37%	Out-of-state:	24%
GPA 3.50-3.74:	20%	International:	1%
GPA 3.0-3.49:	26%	Fraternities:	2%
		Sororities:	2%

Basis for selection. High school record, test scores most important. Audition required for music; portfolio required for art. **Home schooled:** Early entry policy applies: junior equivalent, letters of approval. **Learning Disabled:** Recent documentation/diagnosis required for special consideration.

High school preparation. College-preparatory program required. Required and recommended units include English 4, mathematics 3, history 1, science 3 (laboratory 1), foreign language 2 and academic electives 4. Some social studies electives required.

2011-2012 Annual costs. Tuition/fees: $5,563; $16,079 out-of-state. Room/board: $5,280.

Financial aid. Non-need-based: Scholarships awarded for academics, alumni affiliation, art, athletics, leadership, minority status, music/drama, religious affiliation, ROTC.

Application procedures. Admission: Priority date 4/1; no deadline. $40 fee. Admission notification on a rolling basis. **Financial aid:** No deadline. FAFSA required. Applicants notified on a rolling basis starting 4/1; must reply within 4 week(s) of notification.

Academics. Special study options: Accelerated study, cooperative education, cross-registration, distance learning, double major, dual enrollment of high school students, ESL, exchange student, honors, independent study, internships, liberal arts/career combination, student-designed major, study abroad, teacher certification program, weekend college. **Credit/placement by examination:** AP, CLEP, IB, SAT, ACT, institutional tests. 30 credit hours maximum toward bachelor's degree. 16 credits of lower division course work per language. **Support services:** Learning center, pre-admission summer program, reduced course load, remedial instruction, study skills assistance, tutoring, writing center.

Majors. Architecture: Environmental design, landscape. **Area/ethnic studies:** American, Asian. **Biology:** General, biochemistry, conservation, wildlife. **Business:** Accounting, business admin, entrepreneurial studies, finance, human resources, international, marketing, operations. **Communications:** Intercultural, journalism. **Computer sciences:** General, information systems. **Conservation:** Environmental studies, fisheries, forestry, wildlife/wilderness. **Education:** Agricultural, biology, chemistry, early childhood, early childhood special, elementary, English, family/consumer sciences, French, geography, German, health, mathematics, physical, physics, psychology, science, secondary, social studies, Spanish, special ed, technology/industrial arts. **Engineering:** Agricultural, civil, computer, electrical, environmental, mechanical. **English:** English lit, rhetoric/composition. **Foreign languages:** French, German, Spanish. **General:** Animal sciences, business, communications, economics, international, plant sciences, production, range science. **Health services:** Clinical lab science, communication disorders, music therapy. **History:** General. **Human services:** Social work. **Liberal arts:** Arts/sciences. **Math:** General, statistics. **Parks/recreation:** General. **Philosophy/religion:** Philosophy, religion. **Physical sciences:** Chemistry, geology, physics. **Psychology:** General. **Social sciences:** Anthropology, economics, geography, political science, sociology. **Visual/performing arts:** Art, dramatic, interior design, music. **Work/family studies:** General, clothing/textiles, family studies, food/nutrition.

Most popular majors. Business/marketing 17%, education 13%, engineering/engineering technologies 6%, health sciences 6%, social sciences 14%.

Computing on campus. 910 workstations in dormitories, library, computer center, student center. Dormitories wired for high-speed internet access and linked to campus network. Commuter students can connect to campus network. Online course registration, helpline, repair service, student web hosting, wireless network available.

Student life. Freshman orientation: Mandatory, $25 fee. Preregistration for classes offered. Sessions ranging from half-day to 4-days available in June and July. **Housing:** Coed dorms, single-sex dorms, special housing

for disabled, apartments, fraternity/sorority housing available. $150 partly refundable deposit, deadline 3/15. **Activities:** Bands, campus ministries, choral groups, dance, drama, film society, international student organizations, music ensembles, musical theater, opera, radio station, student government, student newspaper, symphony orchestra, TV station, Latter-Day Saints student organization, Catholic student organization, Lutheran student organization, Baptist student organization, Christian Fellowship, Black student union, Hispanic student union, Native American student union, Polynesian student union, Asian American student union.

Athletics. NCAA. **Intercollegiate:** Basketball, cross-country, football (tackle) M, golf M, gymnastics W, soccer W, softball W, tennis, track and field, volleyball W. **Intramural:** Badminton, basketball, cross-country, football (non-tackle), golf, racquetball, soccer, softball, table tennis, tennis, triathlon, volleyball. **Team name:** Aggies.

Student services. Adult student services, alcohol/substance abuse counseling, career counseling, student employment services, financial aid counseling, health services, minority student services, on-campus daycare, personal counseling, placement for graduates, veterans' counselor, women's services. **Physically disabled:** Services for visually, speech, hearing impaired.

Contact. E-mail: admit@usu.edu
Phone: (435) 797-1079 Toll-free number: (800) 488-8108
Fax: (435) 797-3708
Jeff Sorensen, Associate Director of Admissions, Utah State University, 0160 Old Main Hill, Logan, UT 84322-0160

Utah Valley University
Orem, Utah
www.uvu.edu

CB member
CB code: 4870

- Public 4-year university and technical college
- Commuter campus in small city
- 26,917 degree-seeking undergraduates: 39% part-time, 43% women, 1% African American, 1% Asian American, 9% Hispanic American, 1% Native American, 1% international
- 149 degree-seeking graduate students

General. Founded in 1941. Regionally accredited. **Degrees:** 2,276 bachelor's, 1,814 associate awarded; master's offered. **ROTC:** Army, Air Force. **Location:** 45 miles from Salt Lake City. **Calendar:** Semester, limited summer session. **Full-time faculty:** 553 total; 65% have terminal degrees, 12% minority, 34% women. **Part-time faculty:** 1,056 total; 5% have terminal degrees, 8% minority, 36% women. **Class size:** 38% < 20, 51% 20-39, 6% 40-49, 4% 50-99, less than 1% >100. **Special facilities:** Provo airport campus.

Freshman class profile. 6,078 applied, 6,078 admitted, 4,265 enrolled.

Mid 50% test scores			
ACT composite:	18-24	GPA 2.0-2.99:	27%
GPA 3.75 or higher:	22%	Rank in top quarter:	25%
GPA 3.50-3.74:	19%	Rank in top tenth:	8%
GPA 3.0-3.49:	28%	Out-of-state:	11%
		International:	1%

Basis for selection. Open admission. Students under 21 years of age must complete ACT/SAT prior to registration for placement purposes only. New Student Assessment may be required for some. **Home schooled:** State high school equivalency certificate required. **Learning Disabled:** Students with learning disabilities may apply for reasonable accommodations and assistance through the Accessibility Services Department.

2011-2012 Annual costs. Tuition/fees: $4,584; $12,940 out-of-state. Books/supplies: $1,371. Personal expenses: $1,703.

2011-2012 Financial aid. **Need-based:** 2,482 full-time freshmen applied for aid; 1,799 were judged to have need; 1,718 of these received aid. Average need met was 56%. Average scholarship/grant was $5,099; average loan $419. 39% of total undergraduate aid awarded as scholarships/grants, 61% as loans/jobs. **Non-need-based:** Awarded to 1,529 full-time undergraduates, including 562 freshmen. Scholarships awarded for academics, alumni affiliation, art, athletics, job skills, leadership, minority status, music/drama, religious affiliation, ROTC, state residency.

Application procedures. **Admission:** Closing date 8/15. $35 fee, may be waived for applicants with need. Admission notification on a rolling basis beginning on or about 1/1. **Financial aid:** Priority date 5/1; no closing date. FAFSA, institutional form required. Applicants notified on a rolling basis starting 5/15; must reply within 2 week(s) of notification.

Academics. **Special study options:** Cooperative education, distance learning, double major, dual enrollment of high school students, ESL, honors, independent study, internships, student-designed major, study abroad, teacher certification program, weekend college. Evening school, internet programs.

Credit/placement by examination: AP, CLEP, IB, institutional tests. 16 credit hours maximum toward associate degree, 16 toward bachelor's. No more than 25% of credits applied toward associate degree, diploma, or certificate may be awarded through challenge credit. **Support services:** Learning center, reduced course load, remedial instruction, study skills assistance, tutoring, writing center.

Majors. Biology: General, biotechnology. **Business:** Accounting, business admin, hospitality admin, operations. **Communications:** Communications/speech/rhetoric. **Computer sciences:** General, computer science, data processing, web page design. **Education:** Biology, business, chemistry, drama/dance, elementary, English, health, history, kindergarten/preschool, mathematics, music, physical, science, Spanish. **English:** English lit. **Foreign languages:** American Sign Language, Spanish. **Health services:** Community health, nursing (RN). **History:** General. **Math:** General. **Parks/recreation:** Health/fitness. **Philosophy/religion:** Philosophy. **Physical sciences:** Chemistry, physics. **Protective services:** Fire services admin, forensics, law enforcement admin. **Psychology:** General. **Social sciences:** Economics, political science. **Visual/performing arts:** Dance, design, dramatic, music.

Most popular majors. Business/marketing 24%, computer/information sciences 6%, education 12%, psychology 11%, trade and industry 9%.

Computing on campus. 1,000 workstations in library, computer center, student center. Commuter students can connect to campus network. Online course registration, online library, helpline, repair service, wireless network available.

Student life. Freshman orientation: Mandatory. Preregistration for classes offered. **Activities:** Bands, choral groups, dance, drama, film society, international student organizations, literary magazine, music ensembles, musical theater, student government, student newspaper, symphony orchestra, TV station, Baptist student union, Black student union, German club, international student council, Japan club, Latin American club, Latter-Day Saint student association, multi-cultural voices, Native Sun, Russian club.

Athletics. NCAA. **Intercollegiate:** Baseball M, basketball, cross-country, golf, soccer W, softball W, track and field, volleyball W, wrestling M. **Intramural:** Football (tackle). **Team name:** Wolverines.

Student services. Adult student services, alcohol/substance abuse counseling, career counseling, services for economically disadvantaged, student employment services, financial aid counseling, health services, legal services, minority student services, on-campus daycare, personal counseling, placement for graduates, veterans' counselor, women's services. **Physically disabled:** Services for visually, speech, hearing impaired.

Contact. E-mail: admissions@uvu.edu
Phone: (801) 863-8466 Fax: (801) 225-4677
Ryan Burton, Director of Admissions, Utah Valley University, 800 West University Parkway, Orem, UT 84058-5999

Weber State University
Ogden, Utah
www.weber.edu

CB member
CB code: 4941

- Public 4-year university
- Commuter campus in small city
- 18,461 degree-seeking undergraduates: 39% part-time, 51% women, 2% African American, 2% Asian American, 7% Hispanic American, 1% Native American, 2% international
- 684 degree-seeking graduate students
- 38% graduate within 6 years

General. Founded in 1889. Regionally accredited. **Degrees:** 2,029 bachelor's, 1,798 associate awarded; master's offered. **ROTC:** Army, Naval, Air Force. **Location:** 35 miles from Salt Lake City. **Calendar:** Semester, extensive summer session. **Full-time faculty:** 462 total; 10% minority, 44% women. **Part-time faculty:** 358 total; 5% minority, 47% women. **Class size:** 51% < 20, 40% 20-39, 4% 40-49, 5% 50-99, less than 1% >100. **Special facilities:** Planetarium, natural history museum.

Freshman class profile. 5,346 applied, 5,346 admitted, 2,932 enrolled.

Mid 50% test scores			
ACT composite:	18-24	International:	3%
Return as sophomores:	71%	Fraternities:	21%
Out-of-state:	11%	Sororities:	12%

Basis for selection. Open admission, but selective for some programs. Special requirements for nursing, dental health, health professions. **Home schooled:** Home-schooled applicants without GED must have 25 ACT.

High school preparation. 15 units recommended. Recommended units include English 4, mathematics 2, history 1, science 2 and academic electives 4. 4 additional courses recommended, at least 2 of which should be from the following: history, English, math beyond algebra, laboratory science, fine arts and computer science.

2011-2012 Annual costs. Tuition/fees: $4,540; $12,251 out-of-state. Room only: $4,944. Books/supplies: $1,200. Personal expenses: $2,892.

Financial aid. All financial aid based on need.

Application procedures. Admission: Closing date 8/21 (postmark date). $30 fee. Admission notification on a rolling basis. **Financial aid:** Priority date 3/1; no closing date. FAFSA, institutional form required. Applicants notified on a rolling basis starting 3/15; must reply within 2 week(s) of notification.

Academics. Students apply for upper-division courses in junior year. **Special study options:** Accelerated study, cooperative education, distance learning, double major, dual enrollment of high school students, ESL, exchange student, external degree, honors, independent study, internships, New York semester, semester at sea, student-designed major, study abroad, teacher certification program, United Nations semester, Washington semester. First-year experience. **Credit/placement by examination:** AP, CLEP, IB, institutional tests. 30 credit hours maximum toward bachelor's degree. **Support services:** Learning center, pre-admission summer program, reduced course load, remedial instruction, study skills assistance, tutoring, writing center.

Majors. Area/ethnic studies: African-American, Chicano/Hispanic-American/Latino, Native American. **Biology:** Bacteriology, botany, microbiology, zoology. **Business:** Accounting, administrative services, business admin, finance, human resources, logistics, management information systems, managerial economics, marketing, office management, selling. **Communications:** Broadcast journalism, communications/speech/rhetoric, journalism, persuasive communications, political, public relations. **Computer sciences:** General, computer science, information systems, networking, security. **Education:** Art, bilingual, biology, business, chemistry, drama/dance, early childhood, elementary, English, French, German, history, mathematics, music, physical, physics, science, secondary, social science, social studies, Spanish, special ed. **Engineering:** General. **English:** Creative writing, English lit, technical writing. **Foreign languages:** French, German, Spanish. **Health services:** Athletic training, clinical lab science, dental hygiene, health care admin, long term care admin, medical radiologic technology/radiation therapy, medical records admin, nuclear medical technology, nursing (RN), public health ed, respiratory therapy technology, sonography. **History:** General. **Human services:** Social work. **Liberal arts:** Arts/sciences. **Math:** General, applied. **Parks/recreation:** Exercise sciences, health/fitness. **Philosophy/religion:** Philosophy. **Physical sciences:** Chemistry, geology, physics. **Protective services:** Corrections, criminal justice, forensics, police science. **Psychology:** General. **Social sciences:** Anthropology, econometrics, economics, geography, international economics, political science, sociology. **Visual/performing arts:** General, art, commercial/advertising art, dance, design, dramatic, interior design, multimedia, music, music performance, photography, piano/keyboard, studio arts, voice/opera. **Work/family studies:** Child development, family studies, family systems.

Most popular majors. Business/marketing 19%, education 12%, health sciences 24%.

Computing on campus. 558 workstations in dormitories, library, computer center, student center. Dormitories wired for high-speed internet access and linked to campus network. Commuter students can connect to campus network. Online course registration, online library, helpline, repair service, student web hosting, wireless network available.

Student life. Freshman orientation: Available. Preregistration for classes offered. Student and parent orientations offered by appointment. **Housing:** Single-sex dorms, special housing for disabled, apartments, wellness housing available. $175 partly refundable deposit, deadline 8/1. **Activities:** Bands, choral groups, dance, drama, film society, literary magazine, music ensembles, musical theater, opera, radio station, student government, student newspaper, symphony orchestra, TV station, Latter-day Saint student association, Newman Center, Black Scholars United, international student association, Physically Challenged student association, Youth Impact Partnership Project, NAACP chapter, Amnesty International, international club, College Democrats.

Athletics. NCAA. **Intercollegiate:** Basketball, cross-country, football (tackle) M, golf, soccer W, tennis, track and field, volleyball W. **Intramural:** Baseball M, basketball, bowling, racquetball, soccer, softball, tennis, track and field, volleyball. **Team name:** Wildcats.

Student services. Adult student services, alcohol/substance abuse counseling, chaplain/spiritual director, career counseling, services for economically disadvantaged, student employment services, financial aid counseling, health services, legal services, minority student services, on-campus daycare, personal counseling, placement for graduates, veterans' counselor, women's

services. **Physically disabled:** Services for visually, speech, hearing impaired.

Contact. E-mail: admissions@weber.edu
Phone: (801) 626-6744 Toll-free number: (800) 848-7770
Fax: (801) 626-6747
Scott Teichert, Director of Admissions, Weber State University, 1137 University Circle, Ogden, UT 84408-1137

Western Governors University
Salt Lake City, Utah
www.wgu.edu   **CB code: 3949**

- Private 4-year virtual university
- Very large city
- 25,606 degree-seeking undergraduates: 59% women
- 8,198 degree-seeking graduate students
- Interview required

General. Candidate for regional accreditation; also accredited by DETC. **Degrees:** 2,297 bachelor's awarded; master's offered. **Calendar:** Differs by program, extensive summer session. **Full-time faculty:** 636 total; 18% have terminal degrees, 21% minority, 69% women. **Part-time faculty:** 5 total; 80% women.

Basis for selection. Open admission, but selective for some programs. The following criteria considered: interview, prior college and work experience, results from the mandatory WGU Collegiate Readiness Assessment, time commitment to studies. Other specific admission requirements may also apply for certain degree programs.

High school preparation. College-preparatory program recommended.

2012-2013 Annual costs. Tuition/fees (projected): $5,925. Most programs cost $2,890 per six-month term. Students may complete an unlimited number of credit equivalency units in any term.

2010-2011 Financial aid. All financial aid based on need. 41% of total undergraduate aid awarded as scholarships/grants, 59% as loans/jobs.

Application procedures. Admission: No deadline. $65 fee, may be waived for applicants with need. Application must be submitted online. Admission notification on a rolling basis. **Financial aid:** No deadline. Applicants notified on a rolling basis.

Academics. All students are provided mentoring support through their degree program. Students have access to online communities, textbooks, interactive learning resources, webinars, and academic mentors in their field of study. Students with prior education and experience in their field of study can often accelerate degree completion. **Special study options:** Accelerated study, distance learning, independent study, teacher certification program. **Credit/placement by examination:** AP, CLEP. **Support services:** Learning center, study skills assistance, tutoring, writing center.

Majors. Business: Accounting, business admin, human resources, marketing. **Computer sciences:** Information technology, security, system admin. **Education:** Biology, chemistry, early childhood, elementary, mathematics, physics, science, special ed. **Health services:** Medical informatics, nursing (RN).

Most popular majors. Business/marketing 29%, computer/information sciences 17%, education 31%, health sciences 23%.

Computing on campus. PC or laptop required. Online library, helpline available.

Student life. Freshman orientation: Mandatory. Preregistration for classes offered.

Student services. Adult student services, career counseling, financial aid counseling, personal counseling, veterans' counselor.

Contact. E-mail: info@wgu.edu
Phone: (801) 274-3280 Toll-free number: (866) 225-5948
Fax: (801) 274-3305
Eddie Rios, Director of Enrollment, Western Governors University, 4001 South 700 East, Suite 700, Salt Lake City, UT 84107

Westminster College
Salt Lake City, Utah
www.westminstercollege.edu   CB code: 4948

- Private 4-year liberal arts college
- Commuter campus in very large city
- 2,376 degree-seeking undergraduates: 5% part-time, 55% women
- 798 degree-seeking graduate students
- 68% of applicants admitted
- SAT or ACT (ACT writing recommended), application essay required
- 66% graduate within 6 years

General. Founded in 1875. Regionally accredited. **Degrees:** 461 bachelor's awarded; master's offered. **ROTC:** Army, Naval, Air Force. **Location:** 6 miles from downtown. **Calendar:** 4-1-4, limited summer session. **Full-time faculty:** 145 total; 94% have terminal degrees, 6% minority, 48% women. **Part-time faculty:** 249 total; 20% have terminal degrees, 3% minority, 57% women. **Class size:** 58% < 20, 41% 20-39, 1% 40-49. **Special facilities:** Food science brewery, Meade Lx200 telescope, mass spectrometers, chromatography lab, high performance liquid chromatography, nuclear magnetic resonance instrumentation, polymerase chain reaction machines, DNA sequencer, advanced optics lab, machine shop.

Freshman class profile. 3,414 applied, 2,321 admitted, 513 enrolled.

Mid 50% test scores			
SAT critical reading:	490-620	GPA 2.0-2.99:	14%
SAT math:	500-620	Rank in top quarter:	56%
ACT composite:	22-27	Rank in top tenth:	23%
GPA 3.75 or higher:	36%	Return as sophomores:	80%
GPA 3.50-3.74:	25%	Out-of-state:	53%
GPA 3.0-3.49:	25%	Live on campus:	71%
		International:	5%

Basis for selection. Each application reviewed individually and holistically, taking into consideration quality of academic preparation (which includes both rigor of course work and grades), extracurricular activities, individual talents and character, recommendations, and ACT or SAT scores. Campus visit to meet with admissions counselor recommended. Conditional admission for students who have scored 45 or higher on internet-based TOEFL. Interviews recommended.

High school preparation. College-preparatory program recommended. Required and recommended units include English 4, mathematics 2-3, social studies 2, history 1, science 3, foreign language 2-3 and academic electives 2-3.

2011-2012 Annual costs. Tuition/fees: $27,182. Room/board: $7,584. Books/supplies: $1,000. Personal expenses: $2,304.

2011-2012 Financial aid. Need-based: 426 full-time freshmen applied for aid; 341 were judged to have need; 341 of these received aid. Average need met was 84%. Average scholarship/grant was $17,628; average loan $3,716. 61% of total undergraduate aid awarded as scholarships/grants, 39% as loans/jobs. **Non-need-based:** Awarded to 882 full-time undergraduates, including 178 freshmen. Scholarships awarded for academics, alumni affiliation, art, athletics, music/drama, ROTC.

Application procedures. Admission: Priority date 3/1; deadline 8/27. $50 fee, may be waived for applicants with need. Admission notification on a rolling basis beginning on or about 9/1. Must reply by May 1 or within 3 week(s) if notified thereafter. **Financial aid:** Priority date 4/15; no closing date. FAFSA required. Applicants notified on a rolling basis starting 3/1; must reply within 3 week(s) of notification.

Academics. Curriculum combines professional and liberal arts study. **Special study options:** Accelerated study, combined bachelor's/graduate degree, cooperative education, distance learning, double major, dual enrollment of high school students, ESL, honors, independent study, internships, liberal arts/career combination, semester at sea, student-designed major, study abroad, teacher certification program, weekend college. **Credit/placement by examination:** AP, CLEP, IB, SAT, ACT, institutional tests. 40 credit hours maximum toward bachelor's degree. **Support services:** Pre-admission summer program, reduced course load, remedial instruction, study skills assistance, tutoring, writing center.

Honors college/program. 26 ACT (1760 SAT), strong academic preparation required. Campus visit strongly recommended.

Majors. Area/ethnic studies: Latin American. **Biology:** General, neuroscience. **Business:** General, accounting, business admin, entrepreneurial studies, finance, human resources, information resources management, international, management information systems, management science, managerial economics, marketing. **Communications:** Communications/speech/rhetoric. **Computer sciences:** Computer science. **Conservation:** Environmental studies. **Education:** General, early childhood, elementary, secondary, special ed.

English: English lit. **Health services:** Nursing (RN). **History:** General. **Math:** General. **Philosophy/religion:** Philosophy. **Physical sciences:** Chemistry, physics. **Protective services:** Criminal justice. **Psychology:** General. **Social sciences:** General, economics, political science, sociology. **Visual/performing arts:** Art, dramatic, music, studio arts management.

Most popular majors. Biology 6%, business/marketing 26%, English 7%, health sciences 19%, psychology 7%, social sciences 9%.

Computing on campus. 412 workstations in dormitories, library, computer center, student center. Dormitories wired for high-speed internet access and linked to campus network. Commuter students can connect to campus network. Online course registration, online library, helpline, student web hosting, wireless network available.

Student life. Freshman orientation: Mandatory. Preregistration for classes offered. Held the 4 days before fall semester begins. **Housing:** Guaranteed on-campus for freshmen. Coed dorms, single-sex dorms, special housing for disabled, apartments, cooperative housing available. $200 nonrefundable deposit, deadline 6/1. **Activities:** Jazz band, campus ministries, choral groups, dance, drama, film society, international student organizations, literary magazine, music ensembles, musical theater, student government, student newspaper, symphony orchestra, African American intellectual union, American Sign Language club, Asian/Pacific Islander club, Circle K, Habitat for Humanity, international students association, Latter Day Saints student association, social science club, Students for a Free Tibet, Students for Choice.

Athletics. NAIA. **Intercollegiate:** Basketball, cross-country, golf, lacrosse, skiing, soccer, track and field, volleyball W. **Intramural:** Basketball, football (non-tackle), volleyball. **Team name:** Griffins.

Student services. Alcohol/substance abuse counseling, chaplain/spiritual director, career counseling, student employment services, financial aid counseling, health services, minority student services, personal counseling, placement for graduates, veterans' counselor, women's services. **Physically disabled:** Services for visually, speech, hearing impaired.

Contact. E-mail: admission@westminstercollege.edu
Phone: (801) 832-2200 Toll-free number: (800) 748-4753
Fax: (801) 832-3101
Elizabeth Key, Director of Admissions, Westminster College, 1840 South 1300 East, Salt Lake City, UT 84105

Vermont

Bennington College

Bennington, Vermont
www.bennington.edu

CB member
CB code: 3080

- Private 4-year liberal arts college
- Residential campus in large town
- 686 degree-seeking undergraduates: 66% women, 1% African American, 2% Asian American, 4% Hispanic American, 1% Native American, 6% international
- 136 degree-seeking graduate students
- 72% of applicants admitted
- Application essay required
- 67% graduate within 6 years

General. Founded in 1932. Regionally accredited. **Degrees:** 156 bachelor's awarded; master's offered. **Location:** 40 miles from Albany, New York; 150 miles from Boston. **Calendar:** Semester. **Full-time faculty:** 63 total; 71% have terminal degrees, 13% minority, 48% women. **Part-time faculty:** 19 total; 47% have terminal degrees, 32% minority, 37% women. **Class size:** 79% < 20, 19% 20-39, less than 1% 40-49, less than 1% 50-99. **Special facilities:** Center for the Advancement of Public Action, observatory, digital arts lab, architecture, drawing, painting, printmaking, and sculpture studios; ceramics studio and kilns, photography darkrooms, film and video editing studio, several fully equipped theaters, dance studios and archives, scripts library, costume shop, electronic music and sound recording studios, music practice rooms and music library, greenhouse, 440 acres of forest, ponds, wetlands, and fields for recreation and scientific study.

Freshman class profile. 1,145 applied, 829 admitted, 212 enrolled.

Mid 50% test scores			
SAT critical reading:	620-710	GPA 2.0-2.99:	13%
SAT math:	550-650	Rank in top quarter:	68%
SAT writing:	590-690	Rank in top tenth:	36%
ACT composite:	26-30	End year in good standing:	83%
GPA 3.75 or higher:	37%	Return as sophomores:	85%
GPA 3.50-3.74:	25%	Out-of-state:	96%
GPA 3.0-3.49:	25%	Live on campus:	100%
		International:	4%

Basis for selection. Strength of academic record and extracurricular activities, quality of ideas expressed in application, and recommendations important. Interviews strongly encouraged. Supplemental materials welcome. **Home schooled:** Statement describing home school structure and mission, state high school equivalency certificate, letter of recommendation (nonparent) required. Documentation of academic work, course descriptions, reading list required. SAT/ACT strongly encouraged.

High school preparation. College-preparatory program recommended. 21 units recommended. Recommended units include English 4, mathematics 4, social studies 4, history 4, science 3 and foreign language 2.

2011-2012 Annual costs. Tuition/fees: $42,800. Room/board: $12,160. Books/supplies: $800. Personal expenses: $2,100.

2011-2012 Financial aid. Need-based: 176 full-time freshmen applied for aid; 152 were judged to have need; 152 of these received aid. Average need met was 81%. Average scholarship/grant was $30,109; average loan $2,933. 80% of total undergraduate aid awarded as scholarships/grants, 20% as loans/jobs. **Non-need-based:** Awarded to 172 full-time undergraduates, including 63 freshmen. Scholarships awarded for academics. **Additional information:** All applicants for undergraduate admission considered for scholarships based on quality of overall application.

Application procedures. Admission: Closing date 1/3 (postmark date). $60 fee, may be waived for applicants with need. Admission notification by 4/1. Must reply by May 1 or within 2 week(s) if notified thereafter. **Financial aid:** Priority date 2/1, closing date 2/15. FAFSA, institutional form required. CSS PROFILE required of early decision applicants only. Applicants notified by 4/1; must reply by 5/1 or within 2 week(s) of notification.

Academics. Internships and field work required. **Special study options:** Accelerated study, cross-registration, double major, independent study, internships, student-designed major, study abroad. Annual 7-week winter internship/field work period; Postbaccalaureate program in preparation for medical or allied health school graduate programs. **Credit/placement by examination:** AP, CLEP, IB. **Support services:** Reduced course load, study skills assistance, tutoring, writing center.

Majors. Architecture: Architecture, environmental design. **Area/ethnic studies:** American, Asian, European, gay/lesbian, Latin American, women's. **Biology:** General, botany, cellular/molecular, ecology, environmental, evolutionary, zoology. **Communications:** General, journalism. **Communications technology:** Animation/special effects. **Computer sciences:** General, computer science. **Conservation:** Environmental science, environmental studies. **Education:** General, early childhood, elementary, middle, secondary. **English:** American lit, British lit, creative writing, English lit, writing. **Foreign languages:** General, Chinese, French, Germanic, Italian, Japanese, Spanish. **Health services:** Premedicine. **History:** General, American, European. **Liberal arts:** Arts/sciences, humanities. **Math:** General. **Philosophy/religion:** Judaic, philosophy. **Physical sciences:** General, astronomy, chemistry, physics. **Psychology:** General, social. **Social sciences:** General, anthropology, international relations, political science, sociology, U.S. government. **Visual/performing arts:** General, acting, art history/conservation, ceramics, cinematography, dance, design, directing/producing, dramatic, drawing, fashion design, film/cinema/video, jazz, multimedia, music, music history, music performance, music theory/composition, musicology, painting, photography, piano/keyboard, play/screenwriting, printmaking, sculpture, stringed instruments, studio arts, theater design, theater history, voice/opera. **Work/family studies:** Child development.

Most popular majors. English 11%, foreign language 8%, liberal arts 6%, social sciences 12%, visual/performing arts 39%.

Computing on campus. 100 workstations in library, computer center, student center. Dormitories wired for high-speed internet access and linked to campus network. Commuter students can connect to campus network. Online library, helpline, repair service, student web hosting, wireless network available.

Student life. Freshman orientation: Available. Preregistration for classes offered. Six-day program held prior to start of fall classes. May also participate in pre-orientation service or camping trips run by Outing Club. **Housing:** Guaranteed on-campus for all undergraduates. Coed dorms, cooperative housing available. **Activities:** Choral groups, dance, drama, international student organizations, literary magazine, music ensembles, student newspaper, symphony orchestra, Bennington Asia Initiative, Bennington College SGI-US, Bennington Sustainable Food Project, Community Outreach and Action Program, German club, Interfaith Community, Korean Drumming.

Athletics. Intramural: Archery, badminton, basketball, bowling, cross-country, equestrian, fencing, football (non-tackle), golf, skiing, soccer, softball, swimming, table tennis, tennis, volleyball, weight lifting.

Student services. Alcohol/substance abuse counseling, career counseling, student employment services, financial aid counseling, health services, minority student services, personal counseling, placement for graduates, women's services. **Physically disabled:** Services for hearing impaired.

Contact. E-mail: admissions@bennington.edu
Phone: (802) 440-4312 Toll-free number: (800) 833-6845
Fax: (802) 440-4320
Ken Himmelman, Dean of Admissions and Financial Aid, Bennington College, One College Drive, Bennington, VT 05201-6003

Burlington College

Burlington, Vermont
www.burlington.edu

CB code: 1119

- Private 4-year visual arts and liberal arts college
- Commuter campus in small city
- 178 degree-seeking undergraduates: 20% part-time, 48% women, 1% African American, 1% Asian American, 2% Hispanic American, 1% Native American, 2% international
- 2 degree-seeking graduate students
- 86% of applicants admitted
- Application essay required
- 33% graduate within 6 years; 15% enter graduate study

General. Founded in 1972. Regionally accredited. **Degrees:** 30 bachelor's, 4 associate awarded; master's offered. **Calendar:** Semester, limited summer session. **Full-time faculty:** 5 total; 60% have terminal degrees, 60% women. **Part-time faculty:** 71 total; 34% have terminal degrees, 41% women. **Class size:** 99% < 20, 1% 20-39.

Freshman class profile. 180 applied, 154 admitted, 38 enrolled.

Mid 50% test scores			
SAT critical reading:	440-580	GPA 2.0-2.99:	53%
SAT math:	430-530	Rank in top quarter:	19%
SAT writing:	420-570	Rank in top tenth:	5%
ACT composite:	18-26	End year in good standing:	75%
GPA 3.50-3.74:	17%	Return as sophomores:	40%
GPA 3.0-3.49:	23%	Out-of-state:	62%
		Live on campus:	70%

Basis for selection. Attention given to transcript, GPA, and letters of recommendation; application essay most important. Interviews, portfolios recommended. **Home schooled:** Portfolio style transcripts accepted. **Learning Disabled:** Students diagnosed with disability as defined under federal or state law may request academic adjustments and/or auxiliary aid by notifying Director of Student Services in writing.

High school preparation. College-preparatory program recommended. 24 units recommended. Recommended units include English 4, mathematics 3, social studies 4, history 3, science 2 (laboratory 2), foreign language 2 and academic electives 4.

2011-2012 Annual costs. Tuition/fees: $22,435. Room only: $6,670. Books/supplies: $1,064. Personal expenses: $900.

2011-2012 Financial aid. Need-based: 30 full-time freshmen applied for aid; 27 were judged to have need; 27 of these received aid. Average need met was 49%. Average scholarship/grant was $9,801; average loan $5,129. 47% of total undergraduate aid awarded as scholarships/grants, 53% as loans/jobs. **Non-need-based:** Awarded to 4 full-time undergraduates, including 2 freshmen. Scholarships awarded for academics, leadership.

Application procedures. Admission: Closing date 8/15 (postmark date). $50 fee, may be waived for applicants with need. Admission notification on a rolling basis beginning on or about 11/1. Must reply by May 1 or within 2 week(s) if notified thereafter. **Financial aid:** No deadline. FAFSA required. Applicants notified on a rolling basis starting 2/15.

Academics. Special study options: Cross-registration, distance learning, double major, dual enrollment of high school students, exchange student, external degree, independent study, internships, liberal arts/career combination, student-designed major, study abroad. Self-designed degree programs, independent study option. **Credit/placement by examination:** AP, CLEP, IB, institutional tests. 45 credit hours maximum toward associate degree, 90 toward bachelor's. **Support services:** Reduced course load, study skills assistance, tutoring, writing center.

Majors. Area/ethnic studies: Latin American/Caribbean. **Business:** Hospitality admin. **Visual/performing arts:** Documentaries, film/cinema/video, graphic design, photography, studio arts.

Most popular majors. English 17%, interdisciplinary studies 17%, psychology 20%, visual/performing arts 40%.

Computing on campus. 21 workstations in library, computer center. Dormitories wired for high-speed internet access. Commuter students can connect to campus network. Online library, wireless network available.

Student life. Freshman orientation: Mandatory, $150 fee. Preregistration for classes offered. 4 days at the beginning of each term. **Policies:** On-campus student housing is required for any full-time, first-year college students from outside the greater Burlington area. Waivers are granted by petition in certain circumstances. Assistance procuring off-campus housing is offered through the Director of Student Life. **Housing:** Coed dorms, single-sex dorms, special housing for disabled, apartments, cooperative housing available. $200 nonrefundable deposit. **Activities:** Literary magazine, student government, student newspaper, The Institute for Civic Engagement.

Student services. Career counseling, financial aid counseling, legal services.

Contact. E-mail: admissions@burlington.edu
Phone: (802) 862-9616 ext. 104
Toll-free number: (800) 862-9616 ext. 104 Fax: (802) 660-4331
Gillian Homsted, Admissions Director, Burlington College, 351 North Avenue, Burlington, VT 05401

Castleton State College
Castleton, Vermont
www.castleton.edu

CB member
CB code: 3765

♦ Public 4-year liberal arts college
♦ Residential campus in small town

♦ 1,982 degree-seeking undergraduates: 7% part-time, 52% women, 1% African American, 1% Asian American, 2% Hispanic American, 1% Native American, 1% international

♦ 67 degree-seeking graduate students

♦ 78% of applicants admitted

♦ SAT or ACT with writing, application essay required

♦ 46% graduate within 6 years

General. Founded in 1787. Regionally accredited. **Degrees:** 328 bachelor's, 57 associate awarded; master's offered. **ROTC:** Army. **Location:** 12 miles from Rutland. **Calendar:** Semester, limited summer session. **Full-time faculty:** 92 total; 96% have terminal degrees, 6% minority, 47% women. **Part-time faculty:** 142 total; 25% have terminal degrees, 43% women. **Class size:** 67% < 20, 31% 20-39, less than 1% 40-49, 2% 50-99, less than 1% >100. **Special facilities:** Medical college museum, outdoor classroom.

Freshman class profile. 2,094 applied, 1,623 admitted, 462 enrolled.

Mid 50% test scores			
SAT critical reading:	430-530	GPA 2.0-2.99:	56%
SAT math:	440-530	Rank in top quarter:	12%
SAT writing:	420-510	Rank in top tenth:	3%
ACT composite:	18-22	Return as sophomores:	69%
GPA 3.75 or higher:	5%	Out-of-state:	39%
GPA 3.50-3.74:	8%	Live on campus:	88%
GPA 3.0-3.49:	31%	International:	1%

Basis for selection. School achievement record, test scores, essay, recommendations, class rank very important. Interview recommended for all; audition recommended for music.

High school preparation. College-preparatory program required. 16 units required; 18 recommended. Required and recommended units include English 4, mathematics 3, social studies 3, history 3, science 3 (laboratory 2) and foreign language 2.

2011-2012 Annual costs. Tuition/fees: $9,468; $21,012 out-of-state. New England Board of Higher Education rate for students from other New England states: 150% of Vermont resident tuition. Available to degree candidates in academic areas not offered by educational institutions in their home states. Room/board: $8,446. Books/supplies: $1,000. Personal expenses: $720.

Financial aid. Non-need-based: Scholarships awarded for academics, alumni affiliation, music/drama, state residency.

Application procedures. Admission: Priority date 5/1; no deadline. $40 fee, may be waived for applicants with need. Admission notification on a rolling basis beginning on or about 12/1. **Financial aid:** Priority date 4/1; no closing date. FAFSA required. Applicants notified on a rolling basis starting 2/15; must reply by 5/1 or within 2 week(s) of notification.

Academics. Special study options: Combined bachelor's/graduate degree, cooperative education, cross-registration, double major, dual enrollment of high school students, honors, independent study, internships, liberal arts/career combination, student-designed major, study abroad, teacher certification program. 5-year Master's in Accounting through Castleton; 5-year MBA with Clarkson University; 7-year physical therapy with Sage Graduate School; 6-year occupational therapy with Sage Graduate School. **Credit/placement by examination:** AP, CLEP, SAT, ACT, institutional tests. 30 credit hours maximum toward associate degree, 60 toward bachelor's. **Support services:** Learning center, pre-admission summer program, reduced course load, remedial instruction, study skills assistance, tutoring, writing center.

Majors. Biology: General. **Business:** General, accounting, business admin, management science, marketing. **Communications:** Digital media, journalism, media studies. **Computer sciences:** General. **Conservation:** Environmental science. **Education:** Art, biology, chemistry, drama/dance, elementary, English, foreign languages, history, mathematics, middle, music, physical, physics, science, secondary, social science, social studies, Spanish. **English:** American lit, English lit. **Foreign languages:** Spanish. **Health services:** Athletic training, nursing (RN). **History:** General. **Human services:** Social work. **Math:** General, statistics. **Parks/recreation:** Exercise sciences, health/fitness, sports admin. **Philosophy/religion:** Philosophy. **Physical sciences:** Geology. **Protective services:** Criminal justice. **Psychology:** General. **Social sciences:** General, criminology, sociology. **Visual/performing arts:** General, art, dramatic, music.

Most popular majors. Business/marketing 21%, communications/journalism 9%, health sciences 6%, parks/recreation 10%, psychology 7%, visual/performing arts 9%.

Computing on campus. 225 workstations in dormitories, library, computer center. Dormitories wired for high-speed internet access and linked to campus network. Commuter students can connect to campus network. Repair service, wireless network available.

Student life. Freshman orientation: Mandatory. Preregistration for classes offered. 2 and a half day program. **Housing:** Guaranteed on-campus for freshmen. Coed dorms available. $200 nonrefundable deposit, deadline 5/1. **Activities:** Bands, choral groups, dance, drama, literary magazine, music ensembles, Model UN, musical theater, radio station, student government, student newspaper, TV station, Christian fellowships, political discussion group, Spanish club, social issues club, community service club, women's issues group.

Athletics. NCAA. **Intercollegiate:** Baseball M, basketball, cross-country, field hockey W, football (tackle) M, golf M, ice hockey, lacrosse, skiing, soccer, softball W, tennis, volleyball W. **Intramural:** Basketball, football (non-tackle), racquetball, soccer M, softball, swimming, table tennis, tennis, volleyball, water polo. **Team name:** Spartans.

Student services. Adult student services, alcohol/substance abuse counseling, career counseling, services for economically disadvantaged, student employment services, financial aid counseling, health services, personal counseling, placement for graduates, women's services.

Contact. E-mail: info@castleton.edu
Phone: (802) 468-1213 Toll-free number: (800) 639-8521
Fax: (802) 468-1476
Maurice Ouimet, Dean of Enrollment, Castleton State College, Seminary Street, Castleton, VT 05735

Champlain College
Burlington, Vermont
www.champlain.edu

CB member
CB code: 3291

- Private 4-year liberal arts and career college
- Residential campus in small city
- 2,011 degree-seeking undergraduates: 1% part-time, 38% women, 2% African American, 1% Asian American, 3% Hispanic American
- 407 degree-seeking graduate students
- 85% of applicants admitted
- SAT or ACT (ACT writing optional), application essay required
- 61% graduate within 6 years; 6% enter graduate study

General. Founded in 1878. Regionally accredited. **Degrees:** 474 bachelor's awarded; master's offered. **ROTC:** Army. **Location:** 200 miles from Boston, 90 miles from Montreal. **Calendar:** Semester, extensive summer session. **Full-time faculty:** 101 total; 58% have terminal degrees, 10% minority, 32% women. **Part-time faculty:** 247 total; 24% have terminal degrees, 4% minority, 47% women. **Class size:** 58% < 20, 42% 20-39, less than 1% 50-99. **Special facilities:** Center for digital investigation, emergent media center.

Freshman class profile. 2,587 applied, 2,188 admitted, 488 enrolled.

Mid 50% test scores			
SAT critical reading:	480-600	**GPA 2.0-2.99:**	64%
SAT math:	490-590	**Rank in top quarter:**	29%
ACT composite:	21-27	**Rank in top tenth:**	10%
GPA 3.75 or higher:	4%	**End year in good standing:**	88%
GPA 3.50-3.74:	4%	**Return as sophomores:**	76%
GPA 3.0-3.49:	20%	**Out-of-state:**	72%
		Live on campus:	89%

Basis for selection. GPA, level of difficulty of high school curriculum, essay, SAT/ACT and counselor recommendations most important. Waiting list for the Radiography program. Portfolios required for certain majors. Interviews may be requested by applicant once full application is submitted, but not required. **Home schooled:** Transcript of courses and grades, state high school equivalency certificate, letter of recommendation (nonparent) required. GED or 2 SAT Subject Tests required. **Learning Disabled:** Interview.

High school preparation. College-preparatory program required. 20 units required. Required and recommended units include English 4, mathematics 3-4, social studies 2, history 4, science 3-4 (laboratory 2-3), foreign language 2 and academic electives 4.

2011-2012 Annual costs. Tuition/fees: $28,490. Room/board: $12,520. Books/supplies: $600. Personal expenses: $600.

2010-2011 Financial aid. Need-based: 517 full-time freshmen applied for aid; 409 were judged to have need; 409 of these received aid. Average need met was 71%. Average scholarship/grant was $13,732; average loan $3,394. 43% of total undergraduate aid awarded as scholarships/grants, 57% as loans/jobs. **Non-need-based:** Awarded to 947 full-time undergraduates, including 256 freshmen. Scholarships awarded for academics, leadership.

Application procedures. Admission: Closing date 2/1 (postmark date). $50 fee, may be waived for applicants with need, free for online applicants.

Admission notification on a rolling basis beginning on or about 12/15. Must reply by 5/1. Students eligible to defer admission once tuition deposit and housing deposit (if required) are received. **Financial aid:** Closing date 3/1. FAFSA required. Applicants notified by 3/19; must reply by 5/1 or within 2 week(s) of notification.

Academics. 96% of majors include required internship. **Special study options:** Cooperative education, cross-registration, distance learning, double major, independent study, internships, liberal arts/career combination, study abroad, teacher certification program. Clinical internships at Fletcher Allen Medical Center. **Credit/placement by examination:** AP, CLEP, IB, institutional tests. 75 credit hours maximum toward bachelor's degree. **Support services:** Reduced course load, study skills assistance, tutoring, writing center.

Majors. Business: General, accounting, business admin, hospitality admin, international, marketing. **Communications:** Communications/speech/rhetoric, public relations. **Communications technology:** Animation/special effects, graphics. **Computer sciences:** Applications programming, computer graphics, computer science, networking, programming, system admin, web page design, webmaster. **Conservation:** Environmental studies. **Education:** Early childhood, elementary, middle, secondary. **Engineering:** Software. **English:** Writing. **Health services:** Facilities admin, medical informatics. **Human services:** Social work. **Liberal arts:** Arts/sciences. **Protective services:** Computer forensics, criminal justice, financial forensics. **Visual/performing arts:** General, arts management, film/cinema/video, game design, multimedia.

Most popular majors. Business/marketing 32%, computer/information sciences 26%, education 8%, visual/performing arts 11%.

Computing on campus. 260 workstations in library, computer center, student center. Dormitories wired for high-speed internet access and linked to campus network. Commuter students can connect to campus network. Online course registration, online library, helpline, wireless network available.

Student life. Freshman orientation: Available, $60 fee. Preregistration for classes offered. Three-day program. **Policies:** No alcohol permitted on campus. Freshmen not permitted cars on campus. **Housing:** Guaranteed on-campus for freshmen. Coed dorms, special housing for disabled, apartments, wellness housing available. $400 nonrefundable deposit, deadline 5/1. **Activities:** Choral groups, dance, drama, international student organizations, literary magazine, musical theater, radio station, student government, student newspaper, cultural diversity committee, community service, wilderness club, heritage society, reader's exchange, flash animation club, intercollegiate writers exchange, anime club.

Athletics. Intramural: Basketball, bowling, field hockey W, football (non-tackle), golf, ice hockey, skiing, soccer, volleyball.

Student services. Adult student services, alcohol/substance abuse counseling, career counseling, student employment services, financial aid counseling, health services, minority student services, personal counseling, placement for graduates. **Physically disabled:** Services for visually, hearing impaired.

Contact. E-mail: admission@champlain.edu
Phone: (802) 860-2727 Toll-free number: (800) 570-5858
Fax: (802) 860-2767
Ian Mortimer, Assistant Vice President for Admission, Champlain College, 163 South Willard Street, Burlington, VT 05402-0670

College of St. Joseph in Vermont
Rutland, Vermont
www.csj.edu

CB member
CB code: 3297

- Private 4-year liberal arts and teachers college affiliated with Roman Catholic Church
- Residential campus in large town
- 205 degree-seeking undergraduates: 20% part-time, 63% women, 10% African American, 1% Native American
- 126 degree-seeking graduate students
- 69% of applicants admitted
- SAT or ACT (ACT writing optional), application essay required
- 47% graduate within 6 years

General. Founded in 1950. Regionally accredited. **Degrees:** 35 bachelor's, 9 associate awarded; master's offered. **Location:** 70 miles from Burlington; 100 miles from Albany, NY. **Calendar:** Semester, extensive summer session. **Full-time faculty:** 12 total; 75% have terminal degrees, 8% minority, 33% women. **Part-time faculty:** 46 total; 17% have terminal degrees, 4% minority, 37% women. **Class size:** 95% < 20, 5% 20-39.

Freshman class profile. 146 applied, 101 admitted, 44 enrolled.

Mid 50% test scores		
SAT critical reading:	420-450	
SAT math:	400-440	
SAT writing:	400-430	
ACT composite:	17-21	
GPA 3.75 or higher:	5%	
GPA 3.50-3.74:	4%	
GPA 3.0-3.49:		36%
GPA 2.0-2.99:		54%
Rank in top quarter:		20%
End year in good standing:		49%
Return as sophomores:		53%
Out-of-state:		35%
Live on campus:		79%

Basis for selection. Course selection, GPA in college preparatory courses, 2 academic letters of recommendation, personal statement/essay, ACT or SAT scores most important. Extracurricular activities and evidence of leadership skills considered. Although not required, interviews are available. **Home schooled:** Statement describing home school structure and mission, transcript of courses and grades, interview, letter of recommendation (nonparent) required. Successful completion of GED.

High school preparation. College-preparatory program recommended. 16 units recommended. Recommended units include English 4, mathematics 3, social studies 2, science 2 (laboratory 2) and academic electives 5.

2011-2012 Annual costs. Tuition/fees: $19,465. Room/board: $9,200. Books/supplies: $1,200. Personal expenses: $1,350.

2010-2011 Financial aid. **Need-based:** 46 full-time freshmen applied for aid; 46 were judged to have need; 46 of these received aid. Average need met was 83%. Average scholarship/grant was $12,892; average loan $2,958. 57% of total undergraduate aid awarded as scholarships/grants, 43% as loans/jobs. **Non-need-based:** Scholarships awarded for academics, alumni affiliation.

Application procedures. **Admission:** Priority date 3/1; no deadline. $25 fee, may be waived for applicants with need. Admission notification on a rolling basis beginning on or about 11/15. Must reply by May 1 or within 2 week(s) if notified thereafter. **Financial aid:** Priority date 3/1; no closing date. FAFSA, institutional form required. Applicants notified on a rolling basis starting 3/1.

Academics. Experiential educational options including internships available. **Special study options:** Accelerated study, combined bachelor's/graduate degree, double major, dual enrollment of high school students, independent study, internships, liberal arts/career combination, teacher certification program. **Credit/placement by examination:** AP, CLEP, IB, SAT, ACT, institutional tests. 12 credit hours maximum toward associate degree, 12 toward bachelor's. **Support services:** Learning center, reduced course load, remedial instruction, study skills assistance, tutoring, writing center.

Majors. **Business:** Accounting, business admin, operations. **Education:** Elementary, English, history, multi-level teacher, secondary, social studies. **English:** English lit. **Health services:** Radiologic technology/medical imaging, substance abuse counseling. **History:** General. **Liberal arts:** Arts/sciences. **Parks/recreation:** Sports admin. **Protective services:** Law enforcement admin. **Psychology:** General.

Most popular majors. Business/marketing 54%, education 15%, liberal arts 7%, psychology 20%.

Computing on campus. 45 workstations in library, computer center, student center. Dormitories wired for high-speed internet access and linked to campus network. Commuter students can connect to campus network. Online library, helpline, repair service, wireless network available.

Student life. **Freshman orientation:** Mandatory, $125 fee. Preregistration for classes offered. 5-day orientation before upperclassmen move into dorms. **Housing:** Guaranteed on-campus for all undergraduates. Single-sex dorms available. $200 nonrefundable deposit, deadline 5/1. Some single rooms available and graduate housing available. **Activities:** Campus ministries, choral groups, dance, literary magazine, student government, student ambassadors, human services club, education club, honor societies.

Athletics. NAIA. **Intercollegiate:** Basketball, cross-country, soccer. **Intramural:** Baseball M, basketball, soccer, softball. **Team name:** Fighting Saints.

Student services. Adult student services, alcohol/substance abuse counseling, chaplain/spiritual director, career counseling, services for economically disadvantaged, student employment services, financial aid counseling, personal counseling, placement for graduates, veterans' counselor. **Physically disabled:** Services for visually, speech, hearing impaired.

Contact. E-mail: admissions@csj.edu
Phone: (802) 773-5900 ext. 3286 Toll-free number: (877) 270-9998
Fax: (802) 776-5258
Alan Young, Dean of Admissions, College of St. Joseph in Vermont, 71 Clement Road, Rutland, VT 05701-3899

Goddard College
Plainfield, Vermont
www.goddard.edu   CB code: 3416

- Private 4-year liberal arts college
- Commuter campus in rural community
- 240 degree-seeking undergraduates: 68% women
- 498 degree-seeking graduate students
- Application essay, interview required

General. Founded in 1938. Regionally accredited. All programs operate exclusively on a low-residency model entailing eight days on campus at the start of each semester; then from home the rest of the term. **Degrees:** 98 bachelor's awarded; master's offered. **Location:** 10 miles from Montpelier, 45 miles from Burlington. **Calendar:** Semester. **Full-time faculty:** 14 total; 64% have terminal degrees, 71% women. **Part-time faculty:** 97 total; 79% have terminal degrees, 74% women. **Special facilities:** Radio station.

Basis for selection. Academic potential, maturity, ability to work independently, personal statement, interview most important; additional writing sample may be needed. Portfolios required for creative writing program. **Home schooled:** State high school equivalency certificate required. GED recommended.

High school preparation. College-preparatory program recommended.

2011-2012 Annual costs. Annualized tuition for Individualized Bachelor of Arts, Education BA non-licensure, Sustainability BA, and Health Arts and Sciences BA is $13,496. Education BA with licensure and the Bachelor of Fine Arts in Creative Writing, $14,630. Required fees are $174, Room and board $1312. Books/supplies: $600.

Financial aid. **Non-need-based:** Scholarships awarded for academics, art, job skills, leadership, music/drama, state residency.

Application procedures. **Admission:** $40 fee, may be waived for applicants with need. Admission notification on a rolling basis. Application closing dates and reply dates vary by program. **Financial aid:** No deadline. FAFSA required. Applicants notified on a rolling basis starting 4/15; must reply within 4 week(s) of notification.

Academics. Written evaluations replace grades. Individually designed majors at bachelor's and master's levels. Students design programs of study in collaboration with faculty mentor. Students on campus for 8 days at beginning of each semester and then work from home following study plan designed in collaboration with advisor. **Special study options:** Distance learning, external degree, independent study, internships, student-designed major, study abroad, teacher certification program. Guided-independent study programs convenient for working adults. MFA in Creative Writing and MFA in Interdisciplinary Arts also offered in Port Townsend, WA. **Credit/placement by examination:** AP, CLEP, IB. 30 credit hours maximum toward bachelor's degree. **Support services:** Study skills assistance.

Majors. **Area/ethnic studies:** General, African-American, American, European, gay/lesbian, Latin American, Native American, Near/Middle Eastern, women's. **Business:** Business admin. **Conservation:** Environmental studies. **Education:** General, art, early childhood, elementary, English, foundations, history, middle, secondary, social studies. **English:** Creative writing, English lit. **Health services:** Aromatherapy, community health, community health services, environmental health, herbalism, movement therapy, polarity therapy, public health ed, Reiki, somatic bodywork. **History:** General. **Liberal arts:** Arts/sciences, humanities.

Computing on campus. PC or laptop required. 100 workstations in library, computer center, student center. Dormitories wired for high-speed internet access and linked to campus network. Commuter students can connect to campus network. Online library, helpline, wireless network available.

Student life. **Freshman orientation:** Mandatory, $125 fee. Preregistration for classes offered. Held day before registration. **Policies:** Dogs are not allowed on campus, with the exception of service dogs. **Housing:** Coed dorms, wellness housing available. $250 nonrefundable deposit. Housing available 8 days per semester. **Activities:** Literary magazine, radio station, student government.

Student services. Financial aid counseling.

Contact. E-mail: admissions@goddard.edu
Phone: (802) 454-8311 ext. 243 Toll-free number: (800) 906-8312
Fax: (802) 454-1029
Josh Castle, Associate Academic Dean and Registrar, Goddard College, 123 Pitkin Road, Plainfield, VT 05667

Green Mountain College

Poultney, Vermont
www.greenmtn.edu

CB member
CB code: 3418

- Private 4-year liberal arts college affiliated with United Methodist Church
- Residential campus in small town
- 626 degree-seeking undergraduates: 3% part-time, 55% women, 4% African American, 2% Asian American, 1% Hispanic American, 3% international
- 70 degree-seeking graduate students
- 67% of applicants admitted
- Application essay required
- 43% graduate within 6 years; 14% enter graduate study

General. Founded in 1834. Regionally accredited. **Degrees:** 155 bachelor's awarded; master's offered. **Location:** 20 miles from Rutland, 35 miles from Killington. **Calendar:** Continuous, limited summer session. **Full-time faculty:** 46 total; 98% have terminal degrees, 4% minority, 33% women. **Part-time faculty:** 30 total; 17% have terminal degrees, 3% minority, 33% women. **Class size:** 49% < 20, 51% 20-39. **Special facilities:** Student-operated organically managed farm, ropes course, 80-acre nature preserve, collection of Welsh artifacts and literature, collection of early American decoration, art collection.

Freshman class profile. 1,302 applied, 872 admitted, 140 enrolled.

Mid 50% test scores			
SAT critical reading:	480-610	End year in good standing:	77%
SAT math:	460-570	Return as sophomores:	63%
SAT writing:	450-580	Out-of-state:	89%
ACT composite:	20-25	Live on campus:	97%
		International:	8%

Basis for selection. Academic achievement, recommendations, interview, essay, test scores or Insight portfolio submission, personal statement, school and community activities important. SAT/ACT required for students with GED and students attending high schools outside of the US. Interview recommended; audition recommended for theater or music; portfolio recommended for art. **Home schooled:** Statement describing home school structure and mission, transcript of courses and grades, state high school equivalency certificate, letter of recommendation (nonparent) required. Applicants advised to develop thorough portfolio of all work completed; on-campus interview highly encouraged. SAT/ACT required.

High school preparation. College-preparatory program recommended. 21 units required. Required and recommended units include English 4, mathematics 3-4, social studies 3, history 1-2, science 3-4 (laboratory 2), foreign language 2-3 and academic electives 5.

2011-2012 Annual costs. Tuition/fees: $29,316. Room/board: $10,640. Books/supplies: $1,300. Personal expenses: $590.

2011-2012 Financial aid. Need-based: 112 full-time freshmen applied for aid; 108 were judged to have need; 108 of these received aid. Average need met was 69%. Average scholarship/grant was $19,682; average loan $3,496. 68% of total undergraduate aid awarded as scholarships/grants, 32% as loans/jobs. **Non-need-based:** Awarded to 149 full-time undergraduates, including 29 freshmen. Scholarships awarded for academics, alumni affiliation, art, leadership, music/drama, religious affiliation, state residency. **Additional information:** Service/recognition awards available to all students, determined by their admission application and supplemental documentation.

Application procedures. Admission: Priority date 3/1; no deadline. $30 fee, may be waived for applicants with need, free for online applicants. Admission notification on a rolling basis beginning on or about 9/1. Must reply by May 1 or within 2 week(s) if notified thereafter. **Financial aid:** Priority date 3/1; no closing date. FAFSA required. CSS PROFILE is recommended to receive an earlier financial aid package. Applicants notified on a rolling basis starting 11/1; must reply by 5/1 or within 3 week(s) of notification.

Academics. Special study options: Accelerated study, double major, ESL, exchange student, honors, independent study, internships, liberal arts/career combination, student-designed major, study abroad, teacher certification program. Exchange programs at Aberystwyth University (Wales), Hannam University (Korea), Nogoya University (Japan). Credit granted for programs of National Outdoor Leadership School. Member of Eco-League Consortium; students can spend up to 2 semesters at one of 4 other schools: Alaska Pacific University, College of the Atlantic, Northand College, Prescott College. **Credit/placement by examination:** AP, CLEP, IB, SAT, ACT, institutional tests. **Support services:** Learning center, reduced course load, remedial instruction, study skills assistance, tutoring, writing center.

Majors. Biology: General. **Business:** Hospitality/recreation, managerial economics, resort management. **Communications:** Media studies. **Conservation:** General, environmental studies. **Education:** Art, biology, elementary, English, secondary, social studies, special ed. **English:** Creative writing, English lit. **History:** General. **Liberal arts:** Arts/sciences. **Parks/recreation:** General. **Philosophy/religion:** Philosophy. **Psychology:** General. **Social sciences:** Sociology. **Visual/performing arts:** Art, studio arts.

Most popular majors. Biology 6%, business/marketing 8%, education 7%, English 8%, liberal arts 8%, natural resources/environmental science 28%, parks/recreation 8%, visual/performing arts 8%.

Computing on campus. 99 workstations in library, computer center, student center. Dormitories wired for high-speed internet access and linked to campus network. Commuter students can connect to campus network. Online course registration, online library, helpline, wireless network available.

Student life. Freshman orientation: Mandatory, $250 fee. Preregistration for classes offered. Held week before classes begin in August and January. Students may opt to come to campus earlier in the summer for wilderness trips. **Housing:** Guaranteed on-campus for all undergraduates. Coed dorms, wellness housing available. **Activities:** Bands, choral groups, drama, film society, international student organizations, literary magazine, music ensembles, radio station, student government, student newspaper, outdoor adventure programs, Poultney Partners Mentoring Program, environmental volunteer and research groups, African American Culture Club, diversity club, UNICEF.

Athletics. NCAA. **Intercollegiate:** Basketball, cross-country, golf W, lacrosse, soccer, softball W, tennis, volleyball W. **Team name:** Eagles.

Student services. Chaplain/spiritual director, career counseling, student employment services, financial aid counseling, health services, personal counseling, placement for graduates.

Contact. E-mail: admiss@greenmtn.edu
Phone: (802) 287-8207 Toll-free number: (800) 776-6675
Fax: (802) 287-8099
Robert Gould, Vice President of Enrollment Management, Green Mountain College, One Brennan Circle, Poultney, VT 05764

Johnson State College

Johnson, Vermont
www.jsc.edu

CB member
CB code: 3766

- Public 4-year liberal arts college
- Residential campus in small town
- 1,640 degree-seeking undergraduates: 31% part-time, 62% women, 3% African American, 1% Asian American, 1% Hispanic American, 1% Native American
- 186 degree-seeking graduate students
- 87% of applicants admitted
- SAT or ACT (ACT writing optional), application essay required

General. Founded in 1828. Regionally accredited. Special tuition rate for New England residents who apply to selected fields of study. **Degrees:** 340 bachelor's, 11 associate awarded; master's offered. **ROTC:** Army. **Location:** 50 miles from Burlington, 90 miles from Montreal. **Calendar:** Semester, limited summer session. **Full-time faculty:** 50 total; 98% have terminal degrees, 4% minority, 36% women. **Part-time faculty:** 87 total; 25% have terminal degrees, 2% minority, 56% women. **Class size:** 74% < 20, 26% 20-39. **Special facilities:** 1,000-acre nature preserve, visual arts center, human performance laboratory, interactive multimedia math, science laboratory, recording studio, community service learning center, Vermont interactive television site, snowboard park.

Freshman class profile. 973 applied, 843 admitted, 290 enrolled.

Mid 50% test scores			
SAT critical reading:	430-550	Return as sophomores:	64%
SAT math:	430-550	Out-of-state:	29%
ACT composite:	20-28	Live on campus:	80%

Basis for selection. High school transcript, GPA, SAT/ACT, class rank, recommendations, and essay important. Tests not required with GED. Interview recommended. **Home schooled:** Transcript of courses and grades, state high school equivalency certificate, letter of recommendation (nonparent) required. Applicants encouraged to complete GED or other state certified achievement test to demonstrate aptitude.

High school preparation. 9 units required; 15 recommended. Required and recommended units include English 4, mathematics 3-4, social studies 2, history 2, science 2-3 (laboratory 1-2) and foreign language 1. Math units must include algebra I, geometry and algebra II.

2011-2012 Annual costs. Tuition/fees: $9,468; $19,908 out-of-state. New England Board of Higher Education rate for students from other New England states: 150% of Vermont resident tuition. Available to degree candidates in academic areas not offered by educational institutions in their home states. Room/board: $8,446. Books/supplies: $1,000. Personal expenses: $850.

Financial aid. Non-need-based: Scholarships awarded for academics, alumni affiliation, art, leadership, music/drama, state residency.

Application procedures. Admission: Priority date 3/1; no deadline. $40 fee, may be waived for applicants with need. Admission notification on a rolling basis beginning on or about 12/1. Must reply by May 1 or within 2 week(s) if notified thereafter. **Financial aid:** Priority date 3/1; no closing date. FAFSA required. Applicants notified on a rolling basis starting 4/1; must reply within 3 week(s) of notification.

Academics. Transition program for students who show potential academic success but may be unprepared academically and/or socially. **Special study options:** Cross-registration, distance learning, double major, dual enrollment of high school students, ESL, exchange student, external degree, independent study, internships, study abroad, teacher certification program. **Credit/placement by examination:** AP, CLEP, IB, institutional tests. **Support services:** Learning center, pre-admission summer program, reduced course load, remedial instruction, study skills assistance, tutoring, writing center.

Majors. Biology: General, cell/histology, molecular. **Business:** General, business admin, hospitality admin, tourism/travel. **Communications:** Journalism. **Conservation:** General, environmental studies, management/policy. **Education:** General, art, biology, drama/dance, elementary, English, history, mathematics, middle, multi-level teacher, music, physical, science, secondary, social science, social studies. **English:** English lit. **Foreign languages:** Comparative lit. **Health services:** Athletic training, premedicine. **History:** General. **Liberal arts:** Arts/sciences. **Math:** General. **Parks/recreation:** General, exercise sciences, health/fitness, sports admin. **Psychology:** General. **Social sciences:** General, anthropology, political science, sociology. **Visual/performing arts:** General, art, dance, dramatic, jazz, music, music history, music performance, music theory/composition, musical theater, piano/keyboard, studio arts, theater design, voice/opera.

Most popular majors. Business/marketing 19%, education 8%, liberal arts 22%, science technologies 16%, visual/performing arts 12%.

Computing on campus. 131 workstations in library, computer center, student center. Dormitories wired for high-speed internet access and linked to campus network. Commuter students can connect to campus network. Online course registration, online library, helpline, wireless network available.

Student life. Freshman orientation: Mandatory, $189 fee. Preregistration for classes offered. Held prior to start of semester. **Policies:** Campus housing required for first four semesters of college. **Housing:** Guaranteed on-campus for freshmen. Coed dorms, apartments, wellness housing available. $100 nonrefundable deposit, deadline 5/1. **Activities:** Bands, choral groups, dance, drama, film society, international student organizations, literary magazine, music ensembles, musical theater, radio station, student government, student newspaper, behavioral science club, Christian fellowship club, diversity committee, political awareness club, Little Brother/Little Sister, Habitat for Humanity, Native American club, Students Enriching and Responding Through Volunteer Efforts, Earth awareness club.

Athletics. NCAA. **Intercollegiate:** Basketball, cross-country, golf M, lacrosse M, soccer, softball W, tennis, volleyball W. **Intramural:** Archery, badminton, baseball, basketball, bowling, golf, lacrosse, racquetball, rugby, soccer, softball, swimming, table tennis, tennis, volleyball, water polo, weight lifting. **Team name:** Badgers.

Student services. Adult student services, alcohol/substance abuse counseling, career counseling, services for economically disadvantaged, student employment services, financial aid counseling, health services, minority student services, personal counseling, placement for graduates, women's services. **Physically disabled:** Services for visually, hearing impaired.

Contact. E-mail: jscadmissions@jsc.edu
Phone: (802) 635-1219 Toll-free number: (800) 635-2356
Fax: (802) 635-1230
Penny Howrigan, Associate Dean of Enrollment Services, Johnson State College, 337 College Hill, Johnson, VT 05656

Lyndon State College
Lyndonville, Vermont
www.lyndonstate.edu   CB code: 3767

- Public 4-year liberal arts and teachers college
- Residential campus in small town

- 1,400 degree-seeking undergraduates: 7% African American, 1% Hispanic American, 1% international
- 15 graduate students
- 99% of applicants admitted
- SAT or ACT with writing, application essay, interview required
- 38% graduate within 6 years; 5% enter graduate study

General. Founded in 1911. Regionally accredited. **Degrees:** 230 bachelor's, 18 associate awarded; master's offered. **ROTC:** Air Force. **Location:** 10 miles from St. Johnsbury, 75 miles from Burlington. **Calendar:** Semester, limited summer session. **Full-time faculty:** 58 total; 93% have terminal degrees, 40% women. **Part-time faculty:** 93 total; 43% have terminal degrees, 2% minority, 46% women. **Class size:** 75% < 20, 25% 20-39, less than 1% 40-49. **Special facilities:** Meteorology laboratory and observation deck, ropes course, rock climbing wall, ski resorts, force plate, music production studio, television studio.

Freshman class profile. 1,115 applied, 1,104 admitted, 397 enrolled.

Mid 50% test scores		End year in good standing:	94%
SAT critical reading:	410-510	Return as sophomores:	62%
SAT math:	420-530	Out-of-state:	43%
SAT writing:	400-510	Live on campus:	50%
ACT composite:	15-21		

Basis for selection. School record, GPA, recommendations and optional test scores most important. **Home schooled:** Transcript of courses and grades, interview, letter of recommendation (nonparent) required. **Learning Disabled:** Students must meet with learning specialist and provide documentation of disability.

High school preparation. College-preparatory program recommended. Required and recommended units include English 4, mathematics 3-4, social studies 2, history 1, science 2-4 (laboratory 2) and foreign language 2. Physics and pre-calc for meteorology and computer science recommended.

2011-2012 Annual costs. Tuition/fees: $9,468; $19,356 out-of-state. New England Board of Higher Education rate for students from other New England states: 150% of Vermont resident tuition. Available to degree candidates in academic areas not offered by educational institutions in their home states. Room/board: $8,446. Books/supplies: $600. Personal expenses: $900.

Financial aid. Non-need-based: Scholarships awarded for academics, leadership.

Application procedures. Admission: Priority date 5/1; no deadline. $40 fee, may be waived for applicants with need. Admission notification on a rolling basis beginning on or about 11/1. Must reply by May 1 or within 2 week(s) if notified thereafter. **Financial aid:** Priority date 2/1; no closing date. FAFSA required. Applicants notified on a rolling basis starting 4/1; must reply within 2 week(s) of notification.

Academics. Special study options: Combined bachelor's/graduate degree, cooperative education, distance learning, double major, dual enrollment of high school students, ESL, internships, liberal arts/career combination, student-designed major, study abroad, teacher certification program. **Credit/placement by examination:** AP, CLEP, IB, SAT, ACT, institutional tests. 60 credit hours maximum toward bachelor's degree. **Support services:** Learning center, reduced course load, remedial instruction, study skills assistance, tutoring, writing center.

Majors. Business: Accounting, accounting/business management, accounting/finance, business admin, entrepreneurial studies, finance, marketing, resort management, small business admin. **Communications:** Broadcast journalism, communications/speech/rhetoric, journalism, media studies, photojournalism, radio/TV. **Communications technology:** General. **Computer sciences:** General. **Conservation:** Environmental science. **Education:** General, early childhood, elementary, English, physical, science, social science, special ed. **English:** English lit. **Health services:** Athletic training, prenursing. **Liberal arts:** Arts/sciences. **Math:** General. **Parks/recreation:** Exercise sciences, facilities management, health/fitness, sports admin. **Philosophy/religion:** Philosophy. **Physical sciences:** Atmospheric science, meteorology. **Protective services:** Criminal justice. **Psychology:** General. **Social sciences:** General. **Visual/performing arts:** General, commercial/advertising art, design, digital arts, graphic design, illustration, music management, music performance.

Most popular majors. Business/marketing 13%, communications/journalism 7%, communication technologies 11%, parks/recreation 13%, physical sciences 10%, psychology 7%, public administration/social services 14%, visual/performing arts 7%.

Computing on campus. 280 workstations in library, computer center, student center. Dormitories wired for high-speed internet access and linked to campus network. Commuter students can connect to campus network.

Online course registration, online library, helpline, repair service, wireless network available.

Student life. Freshman orientation: Mandatory. Preregistration for classes offered. **Policies:** Unmarried students under 23 must live on-campus for 2 consecutive years (1 year requirement for sophomore-level transfers) unless residing with parents within 45-mile commuting distance. Exceptions made on case-by-case basis. **Housing:** Guaranteed on-campus for freshmen. Coed dorms, special housing for disabled, apartments, wellness housing available. $100 deposit, deadline 5/1. **Activities:** Concert band, choral groups, dance, drama, international student organizations, literary magazine, music ensembles, Model UN, musical theater, radio station, student government, student newspaper, TV station, American Meteorological Society (student chapter), community service learning group, alternative spring break.

Athletics. NAIA, NCAA. **Intercollegiate:** Baseball M, basketball, cross-country, ice hockey, lacrosse M, soccer, softball W, tennis. **Intramural:** Basketball, cross-country, handball, ice hockey, racquetball, rugby, soccer, softball, squash, swimming, table tennis, tennis, track and field, volleyball, water polo M, weight lifting. **Team name:** Hornets.

Student services. Alcohol/substance abuse counseling, career counseling, student employment services, financial aid counseling, health services, personal counseling, placement for graduates, veterans' counselor. **Physically disabled:** Services for visually, hearing impaired.

Contact. E-mail: admissions@lyndonstate.edu
Phone: (802) 626-6413 Toll-free number: (800) 225-1998
Fax: (802) 626-6335
Vincent Maloney, Director of Admissions, Lyndon State College, 1001 College Road, Lyndonville, VT 05851

Marlboro College
Marlboro, Vermont
www.marlboro.edu

CB member
CB code: 3509

- Private 4-year liberal arts college
- Residential campus in rural community
- 262 degree-seeking undergraduates: 1% part-time, 51% women, 1% African American, 3% Asian American, 2% Hispanic American, 1% Native American
- 75% of applicants admitted
- Application essay required
- 64% graduate within 6 years

General. Founded in 1946. Regionally accredited. **Degrees:** 69 bachelor's awarded; master's offered. **Location:** 12 miles from Brattleboro; 70 miles from Albany, NY. **Calendar:** Semester. **Full-time faculty:** 42 total; 79% have terminal degrees, 12% minority, 43% women. **Part-time faculty:** 9 total; 78% have terminal degrees, 44% women. **Class size:** 97% < 20, 3% 20-39. **Special facilities:** Aviary, observatory, darkroom, theater 3/4 round, robotics lab, DNA lab, nature preserve, organic campus farm.

Freshman class profile. 279 applied, 209 admitted, 61 enrolled.

Mid 50% test scores			
SAT critical reading:	590-690	GPA 3.50-3.74:	20%
SAT math:	510-640	GPA 3.0-3.49:	32%
SAT writing:	550-660	GPA 2.0-2.99:	32%
ACT composite:	24-32	Return as sophomores:	80%
GPA 3.75 or higher:	16%	Out-of-state:	88%
		Live on campus:	100%

Basis for selection. Academic ability, intellectual potential, writing skills, demonstrated leadership qualities, and potential to offer contribution to college community most important. Interview may be required at discretion of admission committee. **Home schooled:** Statement describing home school structure and mission, letter of recommendation (nonparent) required. Provide documentation of home school curriculum and projects. List of textbooks preferred. Writing sample required. **Learning Disabled:** Additional documentation may be required.

High school preparation. College-preparatory program recommended. 23 units recommended. Recommended units include English 4, mathematics 3, social studies 3, history 3, science 3 (laboratory 1), foreign language 3 and academic electives 3. Advanced electives in area of interest and in performing and/or visual arts also recommended.

2011-2012 Annual costs. Tuition/fees: $36,560. Room/board: $9,640. Books/supplies: $1,200.

2011-2012 Financial aid. Need-based: 49 full-time freshmen applied for aid; 48 were judged to have need; 48 of these received aid. Average need met was 75%. Average scholarship/grant was $24,038; average loan $3,500.

71% of total undergraduate aid awarded as scholarships/grants, 29% as loans/jobs. **Non-need-based:** Awarded to 65 full-time undergraduates, including 15 freshmen. Scholarships awarded for academics, leadership.

Application procedures. Admission: Priority date 3/1; no deadline. $50 fee, may be waived for applicants with need. Admission notification on a rolling basis beginning on or about 12/1. Must reply by May 1 or within 2 week(s) if notified thereafter. **Financial aid:** Closing date 3/1. FAFSA required. Applicants notified on a rolling basis starting 3/15; must reply by 5/1 or within 2 week(s) of notification.

Academics. Students self-design field of study, often interdisciplinary in nature. They work closely with faculty to determine concentration and have formal review in senior year by internal and external faculty. **Special study options:** Double major, dual enrollment of high school students, independent study, internships, student-designed major, study abroad. World Studies Program: opportunity to integrate study-abroad experience and/or internship in undergraduate course of study. **Credit/placement by examination:** AP, CLEP, IB, institutional tests. **Support services:** Learning center, reduced course load, study skills assistance, tutoring, writing center.

Majors. Area/ethnic studies: American, Asian, East Asian, European, Latin American, Near/Middle Eastern, Russian/Eastern European/Eurasian, Russian/Slavic, South Asian, Southeast Asian, Western European. **Biology:** General, biochemistry, botany, cell/histology, ecology, genetics, molecular, plant physiology. **Computer sciences:** General, computer science. **Conservation:** General, environmental studies. **English:** American lit, British lit, creative writing, English lit, writing. **Foreign languages:** General, comparative lit, linguistics, Spanish, translation. **History:** General. **Liberal arts:** Arts/sciences. **Math:** General. **Philosophy/religion:** Philosophy, religion. **Physical sciences:** Astronomy, chemistry, organic chemistry, physics, theoretical physics. **Psychology:** General. **Social sciences:** General, anthropology, economics, political science, sociology. **Visual/performing arts:** General, art, art history/conservation, ceramics, cinematography, dance, dramatic, drawing, film/cinema/video, music, music history, painting, photography, play/screenwriting, sculpture, studio arts, theater design, theater history.

Most popular majors. English 15%, philosophy/religious studies 12%, psychology 7%, social sciences 17%, visual/performing arts 31%.

Computing on campus. 45 workstations in dormitories, library, computer center. Dormitories wired for high-speed internet access and linked to campus network. Commuter students can connect to campus network. Online course registration, online library, helpline, student web hosting, wireless network available.

Student life. Freshman orientation: Mandatory. Preregistration for classes offered. 5-day program in late August; pre-orientation outdoor trips held the week prior to on-campus orientation and student enrollment. **Policies:** Self-governing community based on old-fashioned, historical New England-style town meeting. Students, faculty, and staff have equal vote. Elected community court enforces bylaws. **Housing:** Guaranteed on-campus for freshmen. Coed dorms, single-sex dorms, apartments, wellness housing available. $400 nonrefundable deposit, deadline 5/1. **Activities:** Dance, drama, film society, literary magazine, music ensembles, musical theater, radio station, student government, student newspaper, Amnesty International, animal rights, gay/lesbian and bisexual group, committee on environmental quality, fire and safety commission.

Athletics. Intercollegiate: Soccer. **Intramural:** Basketball, fencing, soccer, volleyball.

Student services. Alcohol/substance abuse counseling, career counseling, student employment services, financial aid counseling, health services, personal counseling, placement for graduates. **Physically disabled:** Services for visually, speech, hearing impaired.

Contact. E-mail: admissions@marlboro.edu
Phone: (802) 258-9236 Toll-free number: (800) 343-0049
Fax: (802) 451-7555
Nicole Curvin, Dean of Admission, Marlboro College, PO Box A, Marlboro, VT 05344-0300

Middlebury College
Middlebury, Vermont
www.middlebury.edu

CB member
CB code: 3526

- Private 4-year liberal arts college
- Residential campus in small town
- 2,474 degree-seeking undergraduates: 1% part-time, 51% women, 2% African American, 6% Asian American, 6% Hispanic American, 10% international
- 18% of applicants admitted

◆ SAT or ACT (ACT writing optional), application essay required

◆ 90% graduate within 6 years

General. Founded in 1800. Regionally accredited. Affiliated with Monterey Institute of International Studies. **Degrees:** 689 bachelor's awarded; master's, doctoral offered. **ROTC:** Army. **Location:** 200 miles from Boston, 250 miles from New York City. **Calendar:** 4-1-4, limited summer session. **Full-time faculty:** 263 total; 95% have terminal degrees, 10% minority, 42% women. **Part-time faculty:** 60 total; 60% have terminal degrees, 2% minority, 45% women. **Class size:** 68% < 20, 25% 20-39, 5% 40-49, 1% 50-99. **Special facilities:** Observatory, fine arts center, downhill and cross country ski areas, interactive language laboratories, 18-hole golf course.

Freshman class profile. 8,533 applied, 1,563 admitted, 602 enrolled.

Mid 50% test scores		Return as sophomores:	95%
SAT critical reading:	640-740	Out-of-state:	96%
SAT math:	650-740	Live on campus:	100%
SAT writing:	650-760	International:	9%
ACT composite:	30-33		

Basis for selection. School record most important (including course selection and course load), followed by class rank, extracurricular activities, letters of recommendation, and test scores. ACT or SAT or 3 SAT Subject Tests required.

High school preparation. College-preparatory program recommended. Recommended units include English 4, mathematics 4, social studies 3, science 3 (laboratory 3) and foreign language 4. Music, art, or drama recommended.

2011-2012 Annual costs. Comprehensive fee: $53,800. Books/supplies: $750. Personal expenses: $1,000.

2010-2011 Financial aid. All financial aid based on need. 270 full-time freshmen applied for aid; 211 were judged to have need; 211 of these received aid. Average need met was 100%. Average scholarship/grant was $32,638; average loan $2,393. 88% of total undergraduate aid awarded as scholarships/grants, 12% as loans/jobs. **Additional information:** College maintains need-blind admissions policy and meets full demonstrated financial need of students who qualify for admission, to degree resources permit.

Application procedures. Admission: Closing date 1/1 (postmark date). $65 fee, may be waived for applicants with need. Admission notification by 4/1. Must reply by 5/1. **Financial aid:** Priority date 11/15, closing date 2/1. FAFSA, CSS PROFILE required. Applicants notified by 4/1; must reply by 5/1.

Academics. Special study options: Accelerated study, double major, exchange student, honors, independent study, internships, semester at sea, student-designed major, study abroad, teacher certification program, Washington semester. Williams College-Mystic Seaport Program in American Maritime Studies, Oxford University summer program, independent scholar program, exchange programs with Berea College and Swarthmore College, 3-year international major. **Credit/placement by examination:** AP, CLEP, IB, institutional tests. **Support services:** Learning center, pre-admission summer program, reduced course load, study skills assistance, tutoring, writing center.

Majors. Area/ethnic studies: African, American, East Asian, European, Latin American, Near/Middle Eastern, Russian/Eastern European/Eurasian, Russian/Slavic, Southeast Asian, women's. **Biology:** General, biochemistry, molecular, neuroscience. **Computer sciences:** Computer science. **Conservation:** Environmental studies. **English:** American lit, English lit. **Foreign languages:** Chinese, classics, French, German, Italian, Japanese, Russian, Spanish. **History:** General. **Liberal arts:** Arts/sciences. **Math:** General. **Philosophy/religion:** Philosophy, religion. **Physical sciences:** Chemistry, geology, physics. **Psychology:** General. **Social sciences:** Economics, geography, international relations, political science, sociology. **Visual/performing arts:** Art history/conservation, dance, dramatic, music, studio arts.

Most popular majors. Area/ethnic studies 9%, biology 9%, English 8%, foreign language 9%, natural resources/environmental science 6%, psychology 7%, social sciences 30%, visual/performing arts 7%.

Computing on campus. 494 workstations in dormitories, library, computer center, student center. Dormitories wired for high-speed internet access and linked to campus network. Commuter students can connect to campus network. Online course registration, online library, helpline, repair service, student web hosting, wireless network available.

Student life. Freshman orientation: Mandatory. Preregistration for classes offered. Elective portion of orientation carries cost of $150. **Housing:** Guaranteed on-campus for all undergraduates. Coed dorms, special housing for disabled, apartments, wellness housing available. $200 deposit, deadline 5/1. Multicultural, environmental, foreign language, and 5 social houses available. Commons System organizes residence halls into 5 groups, each

with own budget, government, faculty, and staff associates. **Activities:** Jazz band, choral groups, dance, drama, film society, international student organizations, literary magazine, music ensembles, musical theater, radio station, student government, student newspaper, symphony orchestra, African-American Alliance, Alianza Latinoamerica y Caribena, Asian students organization, environmental quality, Hillel, gay/lesbian/bisexual alliance, mountain club, volunteer service program, women's organization.

Athletics. NCAA. **Intercollegiate:** Baseball M, basketball, cross-country, diving, field hockey W, football (tackle) M, golf, ice hockey, lacrosse, skiing, soccer, softball W, squash W, swimming, tennis, track and field, volleyball W. **Intramural:** Badminton, basketball, cross-country, diving, football (non-tackle), golf, ice hockey, lacrosse, skiing, soccer, softball, squash W, swimming, table tennis, tennis, triathlon, volleyball. **Team name:** Panthers.

Student services. Alcohol/substance abuse counseling, chaplain/spiritual director, career counseling, student employment services, financial aid counseling, health services, minority student services, personal counseling, placement for graduates, women's services. **Physically disabled:** Services for visually, speech, hearing impaired.

Contact. E-mail: admissions@middlebury.edu
Phone: (802) 443-3000 Fax: (802) 443-0258
Greg Buckles, Dean of Admissions, Middlebury College, The Emma Willard House, Middlebury, VT 05753-6002

Norwich University
Northfield, Vermont   **CB member**
www.norwich.edu   **CB code: 3669**

◆ Private 4-year university and military college

◆ Residential campus in small town

◆ 2,201 degree-seeking undergraduates: 2% part-time, 26% women, 3% African American, 2% Asian American, 4% Hispanic American, 1% Native American, 2% international

◆ 1,054 degree-seeking graduate students

◆ 56% of applicants admitted

◆ SAT or ACT (ACT writing optional) required

◆ 55% graduate within 6 years

General. Founded in 1819. Regionally accredited. **Degrees:** 378 bachelor's awarded; master's offered. **ROTC:** Army, Naval, Air Force. **Location:** 50 miles from Burlington, 180 miles from Boston. **Calendar:** Semester, limited summer session. **Full-time faculty:** 140 total; 9% minority, 36% women. **Part-time faculty:** 65 total; 9% minority, 43% women. **Class size:** 50% < 20, 48% 20-39, 2% 40-49, less than 1% 50-99.

Freshman class profile. 3,131 applied, 1,769 admitted, 633 enrolled.

Mid 50% test scores		GPA 3.0-3.49:	40%
SAT critical reading:	480-580	GPA 2.0-2.99:	38%
SAT math:	500-640	Rank in top quarter:	37%
SAT writing:	460-620	Rank in top tenth:	11%
ACT composite:	21-26	Out-of-state:	91%
GPA 3.75 or higher:	7%	Live on campus:	94%
GPA 3.50-3.74:	14%	International:	2%

Basis for selection. High school record, recommendations, activities, honors, awards, test scores important. Class rank considered and is criterion for financial aid.

High school preparation. Recommended units include English 4, mathematics 4, social studies 3, science 4 (laboratory 3) and foreign language 2.

2012-2013 Annual costs. Tuition/fees: $31,782. Corps of Cadets freshmen students are charged $1956 for Rooks Uniform for first two years. Room/board: $10,976. Books/supplies: $1,000. Personal expenses: $1,500.

2010-2011 Financial aid. Need-based: 633 full-time freshmen applied for aid; 573 were judged to have need; 573 of these received aid. Average need met was 82%. Average scholarship/grant was $22,368; average loan $4,237. 75% of total undergraduate aid awarded as scholarships/grants, 25% as loans/jobs. **Non-need-based:** Awarded to 755 full-time undergraduates, including 220 freshmen. Scholarships awarded for academics, ROTC. **Additional information:** Winners of ROTC scholarships receive full room and board; must maintain 2.75 GPA. Renewable up to 4 years.

Application procedures. Admission: Priority date 2/1; no deadline. $35 fee, may be waived for applicants with need. Admission notification on a rolling basis beginning on or about 9/1. Must reply by May 1 or within 3 week(s) if notified thereafter. **Financial aid:** Priority date 3/1; no closing date. FAFSA required. Applicants notified on a rolling basis starting 12/15.

Academics. Special study options: Combined bachelor's/graduate degree, double major, dual enrollment of high school students, ESL, exchange student, honors, internships, study abroad, teacher certification program. **Credit/ placement by examination:** AP, CLEP, IB, institutional tests. 12 credit hours maximum toward bachelor's degree. **Support services:** Learning center, pre-admission summer program, reduced course load, remedial instruction, tutoring.

Majors. Architecture: Architecture. **Biology:** General, biochemistry. **Business:** Accounting, business admin. **Communications:** Media studies. **Computer sciences:** Computer science, security. **Conservation:** Environmental science. **Education:** Physical. **Engineering:** Civil, electrical, environmental, mechanical. **English:** English lit. **Foreign languages:** Spanish. **Health services:** Athletic training, nursing (RN). **History:** General. **Math:** General. **Parks/recreation:** Health/fitness, sports admin. **Physical sciences:** Chemistry, geology, physics. **Protective services:** Criminal justice. **Psychology:** General. **Social sciences:** Economics, international relations, political science.

Most popular majors. Architecture 6%, business/marketing 11%, engineering/engineering technologies 9%, health sciences 11%, security/protective services 19%, social sciences 6%.

Computing on campus. 150 workstations in library, computer center. Dormitories linked to campus network. Commuter students can connect to campus network. Online library, helpline, repair service, wireless network available.

Student life. Freshman orientation: Available, $10 fee. Preregistration for classes offered. Held Wednesday-Sunday; includes 1-day cruise dinner. **Policies:** ROTC participants must live in dormitories. **Housing:** Guaranteed on-campus for freshmen. Coed dorms available. $250 deposit, deadline 5/1. **Activities:** Marching band, campus ministries, dance, international student organizations, Model UN, radio station, student government, student newspaper, Arnold Air Society, Special Operations Company Association of the United States Army, volunteer organization, Christian Fellowship, ambulance rescue squad, Young Republicans, Square and Compass.

Athletics. NCAA. **Intercollegiate:** Baseball M, basketball, cross-country, diving, football (tackle) M, golf, ice hockey, lacrosse, rifle, rugby, soccer, softball W, swimming, wrestling M. **Intramural:** Basketball, cross-country, fencing, football (tackle) M, ice hockey, lacrosse M, racquetball, skiing, soccer, softball, tennis, track and field, volleyball. **Team name:** Cadets.

Student services. Adult student services, chaplain/spiritual director, career counseling, student employment services, financial aid counseling, health services, personal counseling, placement for graduates, veterans' counselor.

Contact. E-mail: nuadm@norwich.edu
Phone: (802) 485-2002 Toll-free number: (800) 468-6679
Fax: (802) 485-2032
Karen McGrath, Dean of Enrollment, Norwich University, 158 Harmon Drive, Northfield, VT 05663

Southern Vermont College
Bennington, Vermont   **CB member**
www.svc.edu   **CB code: 3796**

- Private 4-year liberal arts college
- Residential campus in large town
- 530 degree-seeking undergraduates: 12% part-time, 65% women
- 75% of applicants admitted
- SAT or ACT (ACT writing recommended), application essay required
- 42% graduate within 6 years; 50% enter graduate study

General. Founded in 1926. Regionally accredited. **Degrees:** 67 bachelor's, 48 associate awarded. **Location:** 40 miles from Albany, NY; 90 miles from Springfield, MA. **Calendar:** Semester, limited summer session. **Full-time faculty:** 26 total; 42% have terminal degrees, 62% women. **Part-time faculty:** 28 total; 14% have terminal degrees, 68% women. **Class size:** 71% < 20, 29% 20-39. **Special facilities:** 25 miles of trails, 2 natural ponds, 27-room Edwardian mansion, 371 acre campus.

Freshman class profile. 463 applied, 349 admitted, 154 enrolled.

Mid 50% test scores			
SAT critical reading:	390-490	Rank in top quarter:	4%
SAT math:	400-500	Return as sophomores:	53%
ACT composite:	15-21	Out-of-state:	75%
		Live on campus:	91%

Basis for selection. Potential for academic achievement most important. Test scores, interview, personal references also important. Admissions criteria not intended as absolute cut-offs, but students failing to meet these standards must demonstrate potential for academic success in other ways. SAT or

---

ACT required for first year students only. Interviews recommended. **Home schooled:** Statement describing home school structure and mission, transcript of courses and grades required. **Learning Disabled:** Documentation of learning disabilities to Learning Differences Office required.

High school preparation. College-preparatory program recommended. Required and recommended units include English 4, mathematics 3, social studies 4, history 4, science 3, foreign language 2 and academic electives 4.

2011-2012 Annual costs. Tuition/fees: $21,180. Room/board: $9,560.

Financial aid. Non-need-based: Scholarships awarded for academics, leadership.

Application procedures. Admission: Priority date 5/1; no deadline. $30 fee, may be waived for applicants with need, free for online applicants. Admission notification on a rolling basis beginning on or about 9/1. Must reply by May 1 or within 2 week(s) if notified thereafter. **Financial aid:** No deadline. FAFSA required. Applicants notified on a rolling basis.

Academics. Students receive free walk-in tutoring, individualized tutoring, study group sessions, workshops for skill review, proofreading, and notetaking. Disabilities Support Program available. **Special study options:** Combined bachelor's/graduate degree, cross-registration, double major, dual enrollment of high school students, independent study, internships, liberal arts/career combination, student-designed major, study abroad. **Credit/placement by examination:** AP, CLEP, SAT, ACT. **Support services:** Learning center, reduced course load, remedial instruction, study skills assistance, tutoring, writing center.

Majors. Business: Business admin, entrepreneurial studies. **Communications:** General. **English:** Creative writing, English lit. **Health services:** Health care admin, nursing (RN), radiologic technology/medical imaging. **Liberal arts:** Arts/sciences. **Parks/recreation:** Sports admin. **Protective services:** Police science. **Psychology:** General.

Most popular majors. Business/marketing 41%, communications/journalism 8%, English 8%, health sciences 13%, legal studies 6%, liberal arts 6%, psychology 10%, security/protective services 8%.

Computing on campus. 50 workstations in dormitories, library, computer center. Dormitories wired for high-speed internet access and linked to campus network. Commuter students can connect to campus network. Online course registration, online library, repair service, student web hosting, wireless network available.

Student life. Freshman orientation: Mandatory. Preregistration for classes offered. **Housing:** Guaranteed on-campus for freshmen. Coed dorms, wellness housing available. $200 nonrefundable deposit. **Activities:** Drama, music ensembles, student government, Diversity Advisory Committee, Gay-Straight Alliance, drama club, mountaineer events board, community service club.

Athletics. NCAA. **Intercollegiate:** Baseball M, basketball, cross-country, soccer, softball W, volleyball. **Intramural:** Basketball, soccer, volleyball. **Team name:** Mountaineers.

Student services. Adult student services, alcohol/substance abuse counseling, career counseling, student employment services, financial aid counseling, health services, personal counseling, placement for graduates, veterans' counselor. **Physically disabled:** Services for visually, speech, hearing impaired.

Contact. E-mail: admissions@svc.edu
Phone: (802) 447-6300 Fax: (802) 681-2868
Jeremy Gibbons, Director of Admissions, Southern Vermont College, 982 Mansion Drive, Bennington, VT 05201-6002

St. Michael's College
Colchester, Vermont   **CB member**
www.smcvt.edu   **CB code: 3757**

- Private 4-year liberal arts college affiliated with Roman Catholic Church
- Residential campus in small city
- 1,948 degree-seeking undergraduates: 52% women, 1% African American, 1% Asian American, 3% Hispanic American, 2% international
- 232 degree-seeking graduate students
- 78% of applicants admitted
- Application essay required
- 82% graduate within 6 years; 19% enter graduate study

General. Founded in 1904. Regionally accredited. **Degrees:** 437 bachelor's awarded; master's offered. **ROTC:** Army, Air Force. **Location:** 3 miles from

Burlington; 95 miles from Montreal, Canada. **Calendar:** Semester, limited summer session. **Full-time faculty:** 150 total; 86% have terminal degrees, 7% minority, 43% women. **Part-time faculty:** 58 total; 45% have terminal degrees, 5% minority, 55% women. **Class size:** 57% < 20, 41% 20-39, 1% 50-99. **Special facilities:** Observatory, art gallery.

Freshman class profile. 4,474 applied, 3,493 admitted, 543 enrolled.

Mid 50% test scores		GPA 2.0-2.99:	19%
SAT critical reading:	530-630	Rank in top quarter:	59%
SAT math:	530-610	Rank in top tenth:	27%
SAT writing:	530-620	End year in good standing:	95%
ACT composite:	23-27	Return as sophomores:	87%
GPA 3.75 or higher:	39%	Out-of-state:	83%
GPA 3.50-3.74:	19%	Live on campus:	99%
GPA 3.0-3.49:	23%	International:	4%

Basis for selection. Overall high school record and strength of college preparatory curriculum, high school rank in class, standardized test scores (if submitted), application essay, letters of recommendation, extracurricular interests, campus visit considered. SAT/ACT optional. SAT Subject Tests may be used for language placement. Campus visit strongly encouraged for applicants. **Home schooled:** Statement describing home school structure and mission, transcript of courses and grades, state high school equivalency certificate required. SAT/ACT take on additional emphasis.

High school preparation. College-preparatory program required. 16 units required; 20 recommended. Required and recommended units include English 4, mathematics 3-4, social studies 3-4, science 3-4 (laboratory 2-3) and foreign language 3-4. Physics, math, chemistry, biology emphasized for science applicants. History courses fulfill social studies requirement.

2011-2012 Annual costs. Tuition/fees: $36,240. Room/board: $9,030. Books/supplies: $1,200. Personal expenses: $450.

2011-2012 Financial aid. **Need-based:** 446 full-time freshmen applied for aid; 377 were judged to have need; 377 of these received aid. Average need met was 78%. Average scholarship/grant was $19,208; average loan $4,955. 71% of total undergraduate aid awarded as scholarships/grants, 29% as loans/jobs. **Non-need-based:** Awarded to 818 full-time undergraduates, including 228 freshmen. Scholarships awarded for academics, art, athletics, ROTC.

Application procedures. **Admission:** Priority date 11/1; deadline 2/1 (postmark date). $50 fee, may be waived for applicants with need. Admission notification by 4/1. Must reply by May 1 or within 2 week(s) if notified thereafter. **Financial aid:** Closing date 2/15. FAFSA required. Applicants notified on a rolling basis starting 1/15; must reply by 5/1 or within 2 week(s) of notification.

Academics. All students required to achieve low-intermediate level of a second language in order to graduate. **Special study options:** Combined bachelor's/graduate degree, cross-registration, distance learning, double major, dual enrollment of high school students, ESL, honors, independent study, internships, liberal arts/career combination, semester at sea, student-designed major, study abroad, teacher certification program, Washington semester. 3-2 engineering with University of Vermont and Clarkson University, 4-1 MBA with Clarkson University, International exchange student program (Thailand, Japan, Korea), Pre-Pharmacy Duel Degree (BS, D.Pharm.) with Albany College of Pharmacy and Health Sciences, Burlington, Vermont Area Independent College Consortium. **Credit/placement by examination:** AP, CLEP, IB, institutional tests. 30 credit hours maximum toward bachelor's degree. **Support services:** Learning center, reduced course load, study skills assistance, tutoring, writing center.

Majors. **Area/ethnic studies:** American. **Biology:** General, biochemistry. **Business:** Accounting, business admin. **Communications:** Media studies. **Computer sciences:** Computer science, information systems. **Conservation:** Environmental studies. **Education:** Art, elementary, secondary. **Engineering:** General. **English:** English lit. **Foreign languages:** General, classics, French, Latin, Spanish. **Health services:** Prepharmacy. **History:** General. **Math:** General. **Philosophy/religion:** Philosophy, religion. **Physical sciences:** General, chemistry, physics. **Psychology:** General. **Social sciences:** Anthropology, economics, political science, sociology. **Visual/performing arts:** Art, dramatic, music, studio arts.

Most popular majors. Biology 9%, business/marketing 23%, education 6%, English 6%, history 6%, psychology 12%, social sciences 15%.

Computing on campus. 390 workstations in dormitories, library, computer center, student center. Dormitories wired for high-speed internet access and linked to campus network. Commuter students can connect to campus network. Online course registration, online library, helpline, repair service, student web hosting, wireless network available.

Student life. **Freshman orientation:** Mandatory. Preregistration for classes offered. One-day session held in July. Off-campus weekend experience during summer offered. **Policies:** Limited number of parking permits

available for first-time, first-year students during spring semester. **Housing:** Guaranteed on-campus for all undergraduates. Coed dorms, single-sex dorms, special housing for disabled, apartments, wellness housing available. $500 nonrefundable deposit, deadline 5/1. Ambassador housing program allows American students to live with international students. Honors housing available. **Activities:** Bands, campus ministries, choral groups, dance, drama, literary magazine, music ensembles, musical theater, radio station, student government, student newspaper, fire and rescue squad, mobilization of volunteer efforts, Martin Luther King society, diversity coalition, environmental club, Alianza Society, student global AIDS campaign, peace and justice club, Common Ground, Founders Society.

Athletics. NCAA. **Intercollegiate:** Baseball M, basketball, cross-country, diving, field hockey W, golf M, ice hockey, lacrosse, skiing, soccer, softball W, swimming, tennis, volleyball W. **Intramural:** Basketball, football (non-tackle), ice hockey, racquetball, soccer, softball, squash, table tennis, volleyball. **Team name:** Purple Knights.

Student services. Alcohol/substance abuse counseling, chaplain/spiritual director, career counseling, student employment services, financial aid counseling, health services, minority student services, on-campus daycare, personal counseling, placement for graduates, veterans' counselor, women's services. **Physically disabled:** Services for visually, speech, hearing impaired.

Contact. E-mail: admission@smcvt.edu
Phone: (802) 654-3000 Toll-free number: (800) 762-8000
Fax: (802) 654-2906
Jacqueline Murphy, Director of Admissions, St. Michael's College, One Winooski Park, Colchester, VT 05439

Sterling College
Craftsbury Common, Vermont
www.sterlingcollege.edu

CB member
CB code: 3752

- Private 4-year liberal arts college
- Residential campus in rural community
- 98 degree-seeking undergraduates: 4% part-time, 48% women, 1% African American, 1% Asian American, 3% Hispanic American
- 89% of applicants admitted
- Application essay required
- 47% graduate within 6 years

General. Founded in 1958. Regionally accredited. Member of National Work Colleges Consortium. Special accreditation through Association of Experiential Educators. **Degrees:** 20 bachelor's awarded. **Location:** 40 miles from Montpelier, 70 miles from Burlington. **Calendar:** Differs by program, extensive summer session. **Full-time faculty:** 10 total; 80% have terminal degrees, 60% women. **Part-time faculty:** 19 total; 10% have terminal degrees, 42% women. **Class size:** 100% < 20. **Special facilities:** Managed woodlots, livestock farm, cross-country ski trails, back-country recreation, solar and wind powered barns, organic gardens, greenhouse, 32-foot climbing wall, low and high ropes challenge course, sugar house, 300-acre educational swamp (boreal forest and muskeg).

Freshman class profile. 53 applied, 47 admitted, 21 enrolled.

Return as sophomores:	75%	Live on campus:	92%

Basis for selection. Demonstrated interest in programs via activities and essay, motivation, interview/campus visit, academic record, letters of recommendation. Admissions interview/campus visit strongly recommended. **Home schooled:** Transcript of courses and grades required. Portfolio of educational and life experience may be submitted in lieu of diploma or equivalency. Students must meet homeschool requirements for their particular state of residence.

High school preparation. College-preparatory program recommended. Required and recommended units include English 4, mathematics 3-4, social studies 2, history 2, science 2-3 (laboratory 2-3) and foreign language 2.

2012-2013 Annual costs. Tuition/fees: $28,760. Room/board: $8,332. Books/supplies: $1,500. Personal expenses: $1,000.

2010-2011 Financial aid. **Need-based:** 15 full-time freshmen applied for aid; 14 were judged to have need; 14 of these received aid. Average need met was 88%. Average scholarship/grant was $18,463; average loan $3,026. 68% of total undergraduate aid awarded as scholarships/grants, 32% as loans/jobs. **Non-need-based:** Awarded to 13 full-time undergraduates, including 2 freshmen. Scholarships awarded for academics, leadership, state residency.

Application procedures. **Admission:** Priority date 2/15; no deadline. $35 fee, may be waived for applicants with need. Admission notification on a rolling basis. Must reply by May 1 or within 3 week(s) if notified thereafter.

Exceptions made to early admission of high school students, on a case by case basis. **Financial aid:** Priority date 3/15; no closing date. FAFSA, institutional form required. Applicants notified on a rolling basis starting 2/1; must reply by 5/1 or within 3 week(s) of notification.

Academics. **Special study options:** Double major, dual enrollment of high school students, exchange student, independent study, internships, student-designed major, study abroad. 2-week and 5-week Global Field Studies. **Credit/placement by examination:** AP, CLEP, IB, institutional tests. Credit for life experience and credit by exam evaluated on a case-by-case basis. **Support services:** Learning center, reduced course load, remedial instruction, study skills assistance, tutoring, writing center.

Majors. **Biology:** Conservation, ecology, environmental, wildlife. **Conservation:** General, environmental studies, water/wetlands/marine, wildlife/wilderness. **Education:** Curriculum. **General:** Sustainable agriculture. **Liberal arts:** Arts/sciences. **Parks/recreation:** General.

Most popular majors. Agriculture 15%, natural resources/environmental science 30%.

Computing on campus. 20 workstations in library, computer center. Dormitories wired for high-speed internet access and linked to campus network. Commuter students can connect to campus network. Online library, helpline, repair service, wireless network available.

Student life. **Freshman orientation:** Mandatory. Preregistration for classes offered. **Housing:** Guaranteed on-campus for all undergraduates. Coed dorms, wellness housing available. $200 deposit. **Activities:** Choral groups, drama, film society, music ensembles, student government, service learning; all-college work days.

Student services. Adult student services, alcohol/substance abuse counseling, career counseling, financial aid counseling, health services, personal counseling, veterans' counselor.

Contact. E-mail: admissions@sterlingcollege.edu
Phone: (802) 586-7711 ext. 100
Toll-free number: (800) 648-3591 ext. 100 Fax: (802) 586-2596
Lynne Birdsall, Director of Admissions, Sterling College, PO Box 72, Craftsbury Common, VT 05827-0072

University of Vermont
Burlington, Vermont
www.uvm.edu

CB member
CB code: 3920

- Public 4-year university
- Residential campus in large town
- 10,459 degree-seeking undergraduates: 4% part-time, 56% women, 1% African American, 2% Asian American, 4% Hispanic American, 1% international
- 1,979 degree-seeking graduate students
- 75% of applicants admitted
- SAT or ACT with writing, application essay required
- 72% graduate within 6 years; 22% enter graduate study

General. Founded in 1791. Regionally accredited. **Degrees:** 2,422 bachelor's awarded; master's, professional, doctoral offered. **ROTC:** Army. **Location:** 225 miles from Boston, 100 miles from Montreal. **Calendar:** Semester, extensive summer session. **Full-time faculty:** 594 total; 87% have terminal degrees, 16% minority, 46% women. **Part-time faculty:** 149 total; 41% have terminal degrees, 3% minority, 58% women. **Class size:** 47% < 20, 34% 20-39, 5% 40-49, 8% 50-99, 6% >100. **Special facilities:** Horse farm, dairy farm, geology museum, natural areas, science center, research vessel on Lake Champlain, ecosystem science laboratory on Lake Champlain, art and anthropology museum, maple research facility.

Freshman class profile. 22,341 applied, 16,841 admitted, 2,423 enrolled.

Mid 50% test scores			
SAT critical reading:	540-640	Rank in top tenth:	28%
SAT math:	550-640	End year in good standing:	89%
SAT writing:	540-640	Return as sophomores:	85%
ACT composite:	24-29	Out-of-state:	73%
Rank in top quarter:	68%	Live on campus:	97%
		International:	1%

Basis for selection. School achievement record of primary importance; test scores also important. Essay, extracurricular activities considered. Letter of recommendation required. Special consideration to Vermont residents, children of alumni, minority students, and foreign students. Informational interview recommended. Music applicants must present audition tape or CD. **Home schooled:** Transcript of courses and grades, state high school

equivalency certificate, letter of recommendation (nonparent) required. Applicants must provide proof of completion of minimum entrance requirements and completion of GED.

High school preparation. College-preparatory program required. 16 units required. Required units include English 4, mathematics 3, social studies 3, science 2 (laboratory 1) and foreign language 2. Additional mathematics and/or science units required in engineering, business, health science programs.

2011-2012 Annual costs. Tuition/fees: $14,784; $34,424 out-of-state. Room/board: $9,708. Books/supplies: $1,200. Personal expenses: $1,866.

2010-2011 Financial aid. **Need-based:** 1,916 full-time freshmen applied for aid; 1,534 were judged to have need; 1,522 of these received aid. Average need met was 72%. Average scholarship/grant was $16,707; average loan $3,443. 80% of total undergraduate aid awarded as scholarships/grants, 20% as loans/jobs. **Non-need-based:** Awarded to 2,133 full-time undergraduates, including 714 freshmen. Scholarships awarded for academics, art, athletics, ROTC.

Application procedures. **Admission:** Closing date 1/15 (postmark date). $55 fee, may be waived for applicants with need. Application must be submitted online. Admission notification by 3/31. Must reply by May 1 or within 3 week(s) if notified thereafter. Waitlist admits have 2 days to reply. Early action candidates may have final decision deferred until completion of fall semester review. **Financial aid:** Priority date 2/10; no closing date. FAFSA required. Applicants notified on a rolling basis starting 3/15; must reply within 4 week(s) of notification.

Academics. **Special study options:** Combined bachelor's/graduate degree, cooperative education, cross-registration, distance learning, double major, dual enrollment of high school students, exchange student, honors, independent study, internships, liberal arts/career combination, student-designed major, study abroad, teacher certification program, Washington semester. Evening university option available in several programs, limited ESL available. **Credit/placement by examination:** AP, CLEP, IB, institutional tests. Half of major and half of minor requirements must be completed in residence. **Support services:** Learning center, pre-admission summer program, reduced course load, study skills assistance, tutoring, writing center.

Honors college/program. Admissions based on excellent SAT and/or ACT scores, class rank, challenging course work, and ability to overcome obstacles; about 100 admitted each year.

Majors. **Area/ethnic studies:** Asian, Canadian, European, Italian, Latin American/Caribbean, Russian/Slavic, women's. **Biology:** General, biochemistry, botany, microbiology, molecular, neuroscience, wildlife, zoology. **Business:** Business admin, entrepreneurial studies. **Communications:** Public relations. **Computer sciences:** Computer science, systems analysis. **Conservation:** General, environmental science, environmental studies, forestry, nature tourism. **Education:** General, art, early childhood, early childhood special, elementary, English, foreign languages, mathematics, middle, music, physical, science, secondary, social studies. **Engineering:** General, civil, electrical, environmental, industrial, mechanical. **English:** English lit. **Foreign languages:** Ancient Greek, Chinese, classics, French, German, Japanese, Latin, linguistics, Russian, Spanish. **General:** Agronomy, animal sciences, horticultural science. **Health services:** Athletic training, clinical lab science, communication disorders, dietetics, medical radiologic technology/radiation therapy, nuclear medical technology, nursing (RN). **History:** General. **Human services:** Social work. **Liberal arts:** Arts/sciences. **Math:** General, statistics. **Parks/recreation:** Exercise sciences. **Philosophy/religion:** Philosophy, religion. **Physical sciences:** Chemistry, geology, physics. **Psychology:** General. **Social sciences:** Anthropology, economics, geography, international economic development, political science, sociology. **Visual/performing arts:** Art history/conservation, dramatic, film/cinema/video, music, music performance, studio arts. **Work/family studies:** Family studies.

Most popular majors. Biology 6%, business/marketing 10%, education 6%, engineering/engineering technologies 7%, English 6%, health sciences 8%, natural resources/environmental science 9%, psychology 7%, social sciences 15%.

Computing on campus. 855 workstations in dormitories, library, computer center, student center. Dormitories wired for high-speed internet access and linked to campus network. Commuter students can connect to campus network. Online course registration, online library, helpline, repair service, student web hosting, wireless network available.

Student life. **Freshman orientation:** Mandatory. Preregistration for classes offered. 2-day sessions held at various times in June; additional session held prior to start of term in August. **Policies:** Student code of conduct. Freshmen not permitted cars on campus. **Housing:** Guaranteed on-campus for freshmen. Coed dorms, apartments, fraternity/sorority housing, wellness housing available. **Activities:** Bands, campus ministries, choral

groups, dance, drama, film society, international student organizations, literary magazine, music ensembles, musical theater, radio station, student government, student newspaper, symphony orchestra, TV station, Hillel, black student union, Asian American student union, gay/lesbian/bisexual/transgender alliance, Alianza Latina, Catholic center, Volunteers in Action, Vermont student environmental program, ALANA Coalition.

Athletics. NCAA. **Intercollegiate:** Basketball, cross-country, diving W, field hockey W, ice hockey, lacrosse, skiing, soccer, swimming W, track and field. **Intramural:** Badminton, basketball, football (non-tackle), ice hockey, racquetball, soccer, softball, table tennis, tennis, volleyball. **Team name:** Catamounts.

Student services. Alcohol/substance abuse counseling, chaplain/spiritual director, career counseling, services for economically disadvantaged, student employment services, financial aid counseling, health services, minority student services, on-campus daycare, personal counseling, placement for graduates, veterans' counselor, women's services. **Physically disabled:** Services for visually, speech, hearing impaired.

Contact. E-mail: admissions@uvm.edu
Phone: (802) 656-3370 Fax: (802) 656-8611
Beth Wiser, Director of Admissions, University of Vermont, 194 South Prospect Street, Burlington, VT 05401-3596

Vermont Technical College

Randolph Center, Vermont	CB member
www.vtc.edu	CB code: 3941

- Public 4-year nursing and technical college
- Residential campus in small town
- 1,507 degree-seeking undergraduates: 18% part-time, 42% women, 2% African American, 1% Asian American, 1% Hispanic American, 1% Native American
- 63% of applicants admitted
- 33% graduate within 6 years

General. Founded in 1866. Regionally accredited. **Degrees:** 127 bachelor's, 343 associate awarded. **ROTC:** Army. **Location:** 25 miles from Montpelier, 60 miles from Burlington. **Calendar:** Semester, limited summer session. **Full-time faculty:** 81 total; 17% have terminal degrees, 2% minority, 47% women. **Part-time faculty:** 101 total; 11% have terminal degrees, 1% minority, 62% women. **Class size:** 65% < 20, 34% 20-39, less than 1% 40-49, less than 1% 50-99. **Special facilities:** 500-acre farmstead and orchard, lighted ski hill.

Freshman class profile. 810 applied, 509 admitted, 292 enrolled.

Mid 50% test scores		GPA 3.0-3.49:	34%
SAT critical reading:	410-520	GPA 2.0-2.99:	39%
SAT math:	430-540	Rank in top quarter:	29%
SAT writing:	400-500	Rank in top tenth:	10%
ACT composite:	17-22	End year in good standing:	63%
GPA 3.75 or higher:	9%	Return as sophomores:	69%
GPA 3.50-3.74:	15%	Out-of-state:	22%

Basis for selection. School achievement record most important, followed by test scores, recommendations, and recommended interview. Veterinary technology, dental hygiene, and nursing programs highly selective. Entrance exam required for nursing applicants. SAT or ACT not required of nursing applicants or non-traditional students. Accuplacer may be used in place of SAT/ACT. Interview and essay required for VAST applicants. **Home schooled:** Statement describing home school structure and mission required. Students may attend Vermont Academy of Science and Technology to obtain diploma and first year of college simultaneously.

High school preparation. 16 units required. Required and recommended units include English 4, mathematics 3-4, social studies 2, history 2, science 2-3 (laboratory 1-2), foreign language 2 and academic electives 2.

2011-2012 Annual costs. Tuition/fees: $11,556; $21,276 out-of-state. New England Board of Higher Education rate for students from other New England states: 150% of Vermont resident tuition. Available to degree candidates in academic areas not offered by educational institutions in their home states. Room/board: $8,446. Books/supplies: $1,200. Personal expenses: $650.

Financial aid. **Non-need-based:** Scholarships awarded for academics.

Application procedures. **Admission:** Priority date 3/1; no deadline. $40 fee, may be waived for applicants with need. Admission notification on a rolling basis beginning on or about 12/15. Must reply by May 1 or within 4 week(s) if notified thereafter. Nursing, dental hygiene, respiratory therapy

and veterinary technology applicants may not defer acceptance. **Financial aid:** Priority date 3/1; no closing date. FAFSA required. Applicants notified on a rolling basis starting 3/15; must reply within 2 week(s) of notification.

Academics. 3-year preparatory program options for students planning engineering programs. **Special study options:** Distance learning, double major, dual enrollment of high school students, ESL, honors, independent study, internships. Vermont Academy of Science and Technology program combines senior year of high school and first year of college. **Credit/placement by examination:** AP, CLEP, institutional tests. 30 credit hours maximum toward associate degree, 60 toward bachelor's. No more than 50% of the degree requirements may be counted toward any degree. **Support services:** Learning center, pre-admission summer program, reduced course load, remedial instruction, study skills assistance, tutoring, writing center.

Majors. **Business:** General, business admin. **Computer sciences:** General, information technology, programming. **General:** Dairy husbandry, equestrian studies, equine science. **Health services:** Dental hygiene.

Most popular majors. Business/marketing 30%, computer/information sciences 12%, engineering/engineering technologies 40%, trade and industry 9%.

Computing on campus. 250 workstations in dormitories, library, computer center. Dormitories wired for high-speed internet access and linked to campus network. Commuter students can connect to campus network. Online library, helpline, repair service, student web hosting, wireless network available.

Student life. **Freshman orientation:** Mandatory, $100 fee. Preregistration for classes offered. Held 2 days prior to start of classes. **Housing:** Coed dorms, special housing for disabled, wellness housing available. $100 deposit, deadline 6/1. Williston Campus has townhouse style residence halls. **Activities:** Campus ministries, international student organizations, music ensembles, radio station, student government, TV station, American Institute of Architects, American Society of Civil Engineers, Institute of Electrical and Electronic Engineers, Society of Manufacturing Engineers, Society of Women Engineers, National Association of Veterinary Technicians, Women Issues Christian Fellowship, Phi Theta Kappa, Tau Alpha Pi.

Athletics. NAIA, USCAA. **Intercollegiate:** Baseball M, basketball, cross-country, golf, soccer, softball W. **Intramural:** Basketball, football (non-tackle), golf, skiing, soccer, softball, swimming, table tennis, tennis, volleyball, water polo. **Team name:** Knights.

Student services. Alcohol/substance abuse counseling, career counseling, services for economically disadvantaged, student employment services, financial aid counseling, health services, minority student services, personal counseling, placement for graduates, veterans' counselor, women's services. **Physically disabled:** Services for visually, hearing impaired.

Contact. E-mail: admissions@vtc.edu
Phone: (802) 728-1244 Toll-free number: (800) 442-8821
Fax: (802) 728-1390
Dwight Cross, Assistant Dean of Enrollment, Vermont Technical College, PO Box 500, Randolph Center, VT 05061-0500

Virginia

Argosy University: Washington D.C.
Arlington, Virginia
www.argosy.edu/washingtondc

- For-profit 4-year university
- Very large city
- 96 degree-seeking undergraduates

General. Regionally accredited. **Degrees:** 14 bachelor's awarded; master's, professional, doctoral offered. **Calendar:** Differs by program. **Full-time faculty:** 30 total. **Part-time faculty:** 109 total.

Basis for selection. Open admission.

2011-2012 Annual costs. Tuition/fees: $17,962.

Application procedures. Admission: Closing date 9/13. $50 fee.

Academics. Credit/placement by examination: AP, CLEP.

Majors. Business: Business admin. **Liberal arts:** Arts/sciences. **Protective services:** Police science. **Psychology:** General.

Contact. E-mail: auwadmissions@argosy.edu
Phone: (703) 526-5800 Toll-free number: (866) 703-2777
Frank Marranzini, Senior Director of Admissions, Argosy University: Washington D.C., 1550 Wilson Boulevard, Suite 600, Arlington, VA 22209

Art Institute of Washington
Arlington, Virginia
www.aiw.artinstitutes.edu   **CB code: 3836**

- For-profit 4-year culinary school and visual arts college
- Commuter campus in small city

General. Regionally accredited. **Location:** One mile from Washington, DC. **Calendar:** Quarter.

Annual costs/financial aid. Tuition/fees (2011-2012): $23,328. Room: $10,398. Need-based financial aid available to part-time students.

Contact. Phone: (703) 358-9550
Director of Admissions, 1820 North Fort Myer Drive, Arlington, VA 22209-1802

Averett University
Danville, Virginia
www.averett.edu   **CB code: 5017**

- Private 4-year university and liberal arts college affiliated with Baptist General Association of Virginia (BGAV)
- Residential campus in small city
- 859 degree-seeking undergraduates: 3% part-time, 49% women, 25% African American, 1% Asian American, 3% Hispanic American, 1% Native American, 8% international
- 18 degree-seeking graduate students
- 54% of applicants admitted
- SAT or ACT (ACT writing optional) required
- 42% graduate within 6 years

General. Founded in 1859. Regionally accredited. **Degrees:** 134 bachelor's awarded; master's offered. **Location:** 45 miles from Greensboro, NC;150 miles from Richmond. **Calendar:** Semester, limited summer session. **Full-time faculty:** 59 total; 73% have terminal degrees, 5% minority, 51% women. **Part-time faculty:** 66 total; 21% have terminal degrees, 8% minority, 44% women. **Class size:** 74% < 20, 26% 20-39. **Special facilities:** 121-acre equestrian center, flight center.

Freshman class profile. 2,315 applied, 1,254 admitted, 255 enrolled.

Mid 50% test scores			
SAT critical reading:	410-520	GPA 2.0-2.99:	36%
SAT math:	420-530	Rank in top quarter:	21%
ACT composite:	17-23	Rank in top tenth:	8%
GPA 3.75 or higher:	17%	Return as sophomores:	67%
GPA 3.50-3.74:	12%	Out-of-state:	41%
GPA 3.0-3.49:	34%	Live on campus:	80%
		International:	7%

Basis for selection. Rigor of secondary school record and GPA very important; standardized test scores important. Recommendations, essay, interview, extracurricular activities, talent/ability/alumni/ae relation, volunteer work, work experience and level of interest all considered. Auditions required for music program; portfolios for art recommended. Essay recommended. **Home schooled:** Transcript of courses and grades, state high school equivalency certificate required. **Learning Disabled:** Documentation of neuropsychological or comprehensive psychoeducational evaluation required for access to learning disabled services. Minimum SAT requirements may be waived.

High school preparation. College-preparatory program required. 16 units required; 25 recommended. Required and recommended units include English 4, mathematics 3-4, social studies 3-4, history 3, science 3-4 (laboratory 3), foreign language 3, computer science 2, visual/performing arts 1 and academic electives 3.

2011-2012 Annual costs. Tuition/fees: $24,480. Room/board: $8,220. Books/supplies: $900. Personal expenses: $1,400.

2011-2012 Financial aid. Need-based: 228 full-time freshmen applied for aid; 213 were judged to have need; 212 of these received aid. Average need met was 72%. Average scholarship/grant was $15,873; average loan $3,595. 71% of total undergraduate aid awarded as scholarships/grants, 29% as loans/jobs. **Non-need-based:** Awarded to 245 full-time undergraduates, including 71 freshmen. Scholarships awarded for academics, alumni affiliation, art, job skills, leadership, minority status, religious affiliation, state residency.

Application procedures. Admission: Priority date 5/1; deadline 7/15 (receipt date). No application fee. Admission notification on a rolling basis. Must reply by May 1 or within 2 week(s) if notified thereafter. Deferred admission is up to 1 year. **Financial aid:** Priority date 4/1; no closing date. FAFSA required. Applicants notified on a rolling basis starting 2/15; must reply within 2 week(s) of notification.

Academics. Special study options: Accelerated study, cooperative education, cross-registration, distance learning, double major, dual enrollment of high school students, exchange student, honors, independent study, internships, study abroad, teacher certification program, Washington semester. Undergraduates may take graduate level classes. **Credit/placement by examination:** AP, CLEP, SAT, ACT, institutional tests. 27 credit hours maximum toward associate degree, 90 toward bachelor's. **Support services:** Reduced course load, remedial instruction, study skills assistance, tutoring, writing center.

Majors. Biology: General, ecology. **Business:** Accounting, business admin, finance, management science, marketing. **Communications:** Journalism. **Computer sciences:** Information systems. **Conservation:** Environmental science. **Education:** Art, biology, chemistry, English, health, mathematics, multi-level teacher, social studies. **English:** English lit. **Foreign languages:** General. **General:** Equestrian studies. **Health services:** Athletic training, clinical lab science, medical radiologic technology/radiation therapy, premedicine. **History:** General. **Liberal arts:** Arts/sciences. **Math:** General. **Parks/recreation:** Health/fitness, sports admin. **Philosophy/religion:** Religion. **Physical sciences:** Chemistry. **Protective services:** Law enforcement admin. **Psychology:** Clinical, cognitive, industrial, psychobiology. **Social sciences:** Political science, sociology. **Visual/performing arts:** Art, dramatic, music, theater history.

Computing on campus. 150 workstations in library, computer center, student center. Dormitories wired for high-speed internet access. Online course registration, online library, wireless network available.

Student life. Freshman orientation: Mandatory, $50 fee. Preregistration for classes offered. **Housing:** Guaranteed on-campus for all undergraduates. Coed dorms, single-sex dorms, apartments available. $400 deposit, deadline 5/1. Coed housing by floor or suite available. **Activities:** Pep band, campus ministries, choral groups, drama, international student organizations, literary magazine, musical theater, student government, student newspaper, Alpha Chi, Alpha Kappa Delta, Alpha Psi Omega, equestrian club, gospel choir, psychology club, campus activities board, Catholic Campus Ministries, The Chanticleer, Christian Student Union.

Athletics. NCAA. **Intercollegiate:** Baseball M, basketball, cross-country, equestrian, football (tackle) M, golf M, soccer, softball W, tennis, volleyball W. **Intramural:** Basketball, cheerleading, football (non-tackle) M, soccer, softball. **Team name:** Cougars.

Student services. Adult student services, alcohol/substance abuse counseling, chaplain/spiritual director, career counseling, student employment services, financial aid counseling, personal counseling, placement for graduates, veterans' counselor.

Contact. E-mail: admit@averett.edu
Phone: (434) 791-4996 Toll-free number: (800) 283-7388
Fax: (434) 797-2784
Joel Nester, Director of Admissions, Averett University, 420 West Main Street, Danville, VA 24541

Bluefield College
Bluefield, Virginia
www.bluefield.edu
CB code: 5063

- Private 4-year liberal arts and teachers college affiliated with Baptist faith
- Residential campus in small town
- 679 degree-seeking undergraduates: 13% part-time, 52% women
- 49% of applicants admitted
- SAT or ACT (ACT writing optional) required

General. Founded in 1920. Regionally accredited. **Degrees:** 237 bachelor's awarded. **Location:** 90 miles from Roanoke. **Calendar:** Semester, limited summer session. **Full-time faculty:** 38 total; 66% have terminal degrees, 3% minority, 34% women. **Part-time faculty:** 66 total; 29% have terminal degrees, 2% minority, 50% women. **Class size:** 72% < 20, 27% 20-39, less than 1% 40-49.

Freshman class profile. 1,171 applied, 572 admitted, 153 enrolled.

Mid 50% test scores		Rank in top quarter:	29%
SAT critical reading:	400-510	Rank in top tenth:	10%
SAT math:	410-490	End year in good standing:	32%
ACT composite:	16-21	Return as sophomores:	56%
GPA 3.75 or higher:	13%	Out-of-state:	31%
GPA 3.50-3.74:	12%	Live on campus:	85%
GPA 3.0-3.49:	22%	Fraternities:	2%
GPA 2.0-2.99:	51%	Sororities:	4%

Basis for selection. Students must have minimum 2.0 GPA, 18 ACT or 860 (Critical Reading + Math) SAT, and be in the top half of their class. **Home schooled:** Must supply written description and transcript of curriculum.

High school preparation. College-preparatory program recommended. 22 units recommended. Recommended units include English 4, mathematics 3, social studies 3, science 3, visual/performing arts 1 and academic electives 6. 2 units of health and physical education.

2012-2013 Annual costs. Tuition/fees (projected): $21,060. Room/board: $7,800. Books/supplies: $1,200. Personal expenses: $1,500.

2010-2011 Financial aid. **Need-based:** 103 full-time freshmen applied for aid; 91 were judged to have need; 91 of these received aid. Average need met was 69%. Average scholarship/grant was $10,692; average loan $3,296. 51% of total undergraduate aid awarded as scholarships/grants, 49% as loans/jobs. **Non-need-based:** Awarded to 180 full-time undergraduates, including 49 freshmen. Scholarships awarded for academics, art, athletics, music/drama.

Application procedures. **Admission:** Closing date 8/31 (receipt date). $30 fee, may be waived for applicants with need, free for online applicants. Admission notification by 8/31. Admission notification on a rolling basis beginning on or about 9/1. **Financial aid:** Priority date 3/15; no closing date. FAFSA required. Applicants notified on a rolling basis starting 3/1; must reply within 3 week(s) of notification.

Academics. **Special study options:** Accelerated study, combined bachelor's/graduate degree, distance learning, double major, dual enrollment of high school students, honors, independent study, internships, study abroad, teacher certification program. **Credit/placement by examination:** AP, CLEP, IB, institutional tests. 30 credit hours maximum toward bachelor's degree. **Support services:** Learning center, reduced course load, remedial instruction, study skills assistance, tutoring, writing center.

Majors. **Biology:** General, exercise physiology. **Business:** Business admin. **Communications:** General, journalism. **Communications technology:** Graphics. **Computer sciences:** Information technology. **Education:** General, art, biology, business, chemistry, elementary, English, health, history, mathematics, middle, multi-level teacher, music, physical, reading, secondary, social studies. **English:** English lit, general lit, writing. **Health services:** Predental, premedicine, prepharmacy, prephysical therapy, preveterinary. **History:** General. **Math:** General. **Parks/recreation:** Facilities management,

health/fitness, sports admin. **Philosophy/religion:** Christian. **Physical sciences:** Chemistry. **Protective services:** Corrections, forensics, law enforcement admin, police science. **Psychology:** General. **Theology:** Bible, preministerial, sacred music, theology, youth ministry. **Visual/performing arts:** Art, dramatic, graphic design, music, music performance, music theory/composition.

Most popular majors. Biology 9%, business/marketing 23%, communications/journalism 7%, interdisciplinary studies 14%, parks/recreation 7%, philosophy/religious studies 7%, psychology 23%, security/protective services 12%.

Computing on campus. 105 workstations in dormitories, library, computer center, student center. Dormitories wired for high-speed internet access and linked to campus network. Commuter students can connect to campus network. Online library, wireless network available.

Student life. **Freshman orientation:** Mandatory. Preregistration for classes offered. **Policies:** Weekly convocation attendance required. Limited visitation hours in dormitories. Religious observance required. **Housing:** Single-sex dorms, special housing for disabled, apartments, wellness housing available. $125 fully refundable deposit. **Activities:** Bands, campus ministries, choral groups, drama, literary magazine, music ensembles, musical theater, student government, student newspaper, Fellowship of Christian Athletes, Alpha Delta, Phi Mu Delta, Kappa Psi Omicron, Sigma Alpha Alpha, Bonner Leaders.

Athletics. NAIA, NCCAA. **Intercollegiate:** Baseball M, basketball, cross-country, football (tackle) M, golf M, soccer, softball W, tennis, volleyball W. **Intramural:** Basketball, football (non-tackle), golf, racquetball, softball, swimming, table tennis, tennis, volleyball. **Team name:** Rams.

Student services. Chaplain/spiritual director, career counseling, financial aid counseling, health services, personal counseling, veterans' counselor.

Contact. E-mail: admissions@bluefield.edu
Phone: (276) 326-4231 Toll-free number: (800) 872-0175
Fax: (276) 326-4395
Mark Hipes, Director of Traditional Admissions, Bluefield College, 3000 College Drive, Bluefield, VA 24605

Bridgewater College
Bridgewater, Virginia
CB member
www.bridgewater.edu
CB code: 5069

- Private 4-year liberal arts college affiliated with Church of the Brethren
- Residential campus in small town
- 1,638 degree-seeking undergraduates: 1% part-time, 59% women, 8% African American, 1% Asian American, 3% Hispanic American
- 52% of applicants admitted
- SAT or ACT (ACT writing optional) required
- 59% graduate within 6 years

General. Founded in 1880. Regionally accredited. **Degrees:** 324 bachelor's awarded. **Location:** 8 miles from Harrisonburg, 130 miles from Washington, DC. **Calendar:** 4-1-4, limited summer session. **Full-time faculty:** 107 total; 82% have terminal degrees, 5% minority, 39% women. **Part-time faculty:** 35 total; 34% have terminal degrees, 6% minority, 54% women. **Class size:** 54% < 20, 43% 20-39, 3% 40-49. **Special facilities:** Museum of the Shenandoah Valley and Church of the Brethren; 75-acre equestrian center for equestrian competitions and boarding of College- and student-owned horses.

Freshman class profile. 6,459 applied, 3,327 admitted, 471 enrolled.

Mid 50% test scores		GPA 3.0-3.49:	35%
SAT critical reading:	450-570	GPA 2.0-2.99:	16%
SAT math:	470-560	Rank in top quarter:	48%
SAT writing:	450-540	Rank in top tenth:	17%
ACT composite:	20-24	Return as sophomores:	76%
GPA 3.75 or higher:	28%	Out-of-state:	25%
GPA 3.50-3.74:	21%	Live on campus:	94%

Basis for selection. High school GPA most important, followed by test scores and letters of recommendation. Prefer applicants in top half of high school class. Consider those in bottom half with strong compensating qualities. Interview required for some, recommended for all. **Home schooled:** GED required for students applying for Title IV financial aid.

High school preparation. College-preparatory program recommended. 15 units required; 22 recommended. Required and recommended units include English 4, mathematics 3-4, science 2-4 (laboratory 2), foreign language 3 and academic electives 4. Social studies and history: 2 required, 3 recommended.

2011-2012 Annual costs. Tuition/fees: $26,750. Room/board: $10,350. Books/supplies: $1,100. Personal expenses: $1,080.

2011-2012 Financial aid. Need-based: 448 full-time freshmen applied for aid; 409 were judged to have need; 409 of these received aid. Average need met was 80%. Average scholarship/grant was $19,653; average loan $3,831. 76% of total undergraduate aid awarded as scholarships/grants, 24% as loans/jobs. **Non-need-based:** Awarded to 1,551 full-time undergraduates, including 446 freshmen. Scholarships awarded for academics, minority status, music/drama, religious affiliation.

Application procedures. Admission: No deadline. $30 fee, may be waived for applicants with need. Application must be submitted online. Admission notification on a rolling basis beginning on or about 9/1. Must reply by May 1 or within 2 week(s) if notified thereafter. **Financial aid:** Priority date 3/1; no closing date. FAFSA required. Applicants notified on a rolling basis starting 3/16; must reply within 2 week(s) of notification.

Academics. Special study options: Combined bachelor's/graduate degree, double major, honors, independent study, internships, liberal arts/career combination, study abroad, teacher certification program, Washington semester. 3-2 engineering with George Washington University (BA/BA) and 3-2 engineering with Virginia Tech (BA/BA), 3-2 nursing with Vanderbilt University (BA/MN), 3-4 physical therapy with Shenandoah University (BA/DPT). **Credit/placement by examination:** AP, CLEP, IB, institutional tests. **Support services:** Learning center, reduced course load, study skills assistance, tutoring, writing center.

Majors. Biology: General. **Business:** Business admin, management information systems. **Communications:** Media studies. **Computer sciences:** Computer science. **Conservation:** Environmental science. **Education:** Family/consumer sciences, physical. **English:** English lit. **Foreign languages:** French, Spanish. **Health services:** Athletic training. **History:** General. **Liberal arts:** Arts/sciences. **Math:** General. **Parks/recreation:** Health/fitness. **Physical sciences:** Chemistry, physics. **Psychology:** General. **Social sciences:** Economics, international relations, political science, sociology. **Visual/performing arts:** Music history, studio arts. **Work/family studies:** General, food/nutrition.

Most popular majors. Biology 9%, business/marketing 17%, communications/journalism 8%, family/consumer sciences 8%, liberal arts 8%, parks/recreation 13%, psychology 7%, social sciences 8%.

Computing on campus. 197 workstations in library. Dormitories wired for high-speed internet access and linked to campus network. Commuter students can connect to campus network. Online course registration, online library, helpline, repair service, student web hosting, wireless network available.

Student life. Freshman orientation: Mandatory. Preregistration for classes offered. 2 spring 2-day sessions. One-day, summer program offered for students unable to attend a spring session. Further orientation activities 2 days preceding classes. Parents included in spring and summer orientations. **Policies:** Alcoholic beverages not permitted on campus. Co-ed visitation hours. Smoking and other tobacco products permitted only in designated areas. With some exceptions, all full-time students live on campus. **Housing:** Coed dorms, single-sex dorms, special housing for disabled, apartments, wellness housing available. Honor Housing available. **Activities:** Bands, campus ministries, choral groups, dance, drama, international student organizations, literary magazine, music ensembles, musical theater, radio station, student government, student newspaper, Believers Strongly United, Brethren Student Movement, Campus Crusade for Christ, Catholic Campus Ministry, Black Student Association, Fellowship of Christian Athletes, Habitat for Humanity, Student Anti-Genocide Coalition, New Community Project, Multicultural Leadership Program.

Athletics. NCAA. **Intercollegiate:** Baseball M, basketball, cross-country, equestrian, field hockey W, football (tackle) M, golf, lacrosse, soccer, softball W, swimming W, tennis, track and field, volleyball W. **Intramural:** Badminton, basketball, bowling, football (non-tackle), golf, racquetball, soccer, softball, table tennis, tennis, volleyball. **Team name:** Eagles.

Student services. Alcohol/substance abuse counseling, chaplain/spiritual director, career counseling, student employment services, financial aid counseling, health services, minority student services, personal counseling, placement for graduates. **Physically disabled:** Services for visually impaired.

Contact. E-mail: admissions@bridgewater.edu
Phone: (540) 828-5375 Toll-free number: (800) 759-8328
Fax: (540) 828-5481
Jarret Smith, Director of Admissions, Bridgewater College, 402 East College Street, Bridgewater, VA 22812-1599

Catholic Distance University
Hamilton, Virginia
www.cdu.edu

▶ Private two-year upper-division virtual university affiliated with Roman Catholic Church
▶ Residential campus in rural community

General. Accredited by DETC. The university is a Catholic school of theology offering an MA in Theology degree, BA in Theology degree completion program, noncredit courses and seminars, and a new AA in Catholic studies. **Degrees:** 10 bachelor's awarded; master's offered. **Location:** Online. **Calendar:** Trimester, limited summer session. **Part-time faculty:** 42 total; 71% have terminal degrees, 19% women.

Student profile. 99 degree-seeking undergraduates, 150 degree-seeking graduate students.

Women:	51%	Part-time:	100%

Basis for selection. Open admission.

2011-2012 Annual costs. Tuition/fees: $8,265. Books/supplies: $300.

Application procedures. Admission: $100 fee.

Academics. Online student center available for academic support and techincal support. **Special study options:** Distance learning. **Credit/placement by examination:** AP, CLEP.

Majors. Theology: Religious ed, theology.

Contact. E-mail: admissions@cdu.edu
Phone: (540) 338-2700 ext. 710
Toll-free number: (888) 254-4238 ext. 710 Fax: (540) 338-4788
Carol Ciullo, Director of Admissions, Catholic Distance University, 120 East Colonial Highway, Hamilton, VA 20158-9012

Christendom College
Front Royal, Virginia
www.christendom.edu   CB code: 5691

▶ Private 4-year liberal arts college affiliated with Roman Catholic Church
▶ Residential campus in large town
▶ 407 degree-seeking undergraduates: 1% part-time, 55% women, 2% international
▶ 55 degree-seeking graduate students
▶ 83% of applicants admitted
▶ SAT or ACT (ACT writing optional), application essay required
▶ 69% graduate within 6 years

General. Founded in 1977. Regionally accredited. **Degrees:** 80 bachelor's, 1 associate awarded; master's offered. **Location:** 70 miles from Washington, DC. **Calendar:** Semester, limited summer session. **Full-time faculty:** 18 total; 72% have terminal degrees, 11% women. **Part-time faculty:** 20 total; 50% have terminal degrees, 30% women. **Class size:** 51% < 20, 47% 20-39, 2% 40-49.

Freshman class profile. 288 applied, 239 admitted, 111 enrolled.

Mid 50% test scores		GPA 2.0-2.99:	13%
SAT critical reading:	580-690	Rank in top quarter:	65%
SAT math:	520-610	Rank in top tenth:	45%
SAT writing:	570-680	End year in good standing:	95%
ACT composite:	24-28	Return as sophomores:	80%
GPA 3.75 or higher:	50%	Out-of-state:	75%
GPA 3.50-3.74:	20%	Live on campus:	98%
GPA 3.0-3.49:	17%		

Basis for selection. Secondary school record, essay, test scores, class rank, GPA, recommendations important. Applicants can present additional material and explain scores, evaluations, etc. which they believe do not adequately reflect their abilities. Interview recommended. **Home schooled:** Transcript forms required (available from college).

High school preparation. 14 units recommended. Recommended units include English 4, mathematics 2, social studies 1, history 2, science 2, foreign language 2 and academic electives 1.

2011-2012 Annual costs. Tuition/fees: $20,434. Room/board: $7,656. Books/supplies: $500. Personal expenses: $300.

2011-2012 Financial aid. Need-based: 76 full-time freshmen applied for aid; 60 were judged to have need; 60 of these received aid. Average need met was 90%. Average scholarship/grant was $5,500; average loan $6,595. 48% of total undergraduate aid awarded as scholarships/grants, 52% as loans/jobs. **Non-need-based:** Awarded to 168 full-time undergraduates, including 54 freshmen. Scholarships awarded for academics, alumni affiliation. **Additional information:** Christendom accepts no direct federal aid, nor does it participate in indirect programs of federal aid.

Application procedures. Admission: Priority date 3/1; no deadline. $25 fee. Admission notification on a rolling basis. **Financial aid:** Priority date 4/1, closing date 6/1. Institutional form required. Applicants notified on a rolling basis starting 2/1; must reply within 4 week(s) of notification.

Academics. Special study options: Double major, honors, independent study, internships, liberal arts/career combination, study abroad. Junior semester in Rome. **Credit/placement by examination:** AP, CLEP, institutional tests. **Support services:** Pre-admission summer program, reduced course load, study skills assistance, writing center.

Majors. English: English lit. **Foreign languages:** Classics. **History:** General. **Philosophy/religion:** Philosophy. **Social sciences:** Political science.

Most popular majors. English 15%, foreign language 8%, history 29%, philosophy/religious studies 23%, social sciences 14%, theological studies 11%.

Computing on campus. 70 workstations in library, computer center. Online course registration, online library, wireless network available.

Student life. Freshman orientation: Mandatory. Preregistration for classes offered. Orientation held weekend before school starts. **Policies:** Although no student is required to participate, college encourages religious activities. **Housing:** Guaranteed on-campus for all undergraduates. Single-sex dorms, wellness housing available. $250 deposit, deadline 3/15. **Activities:** Campus ministries, choral groups, dance, drama, film society, musical theater, student government, student newspaper, Legion of Mary, Shield of Roses, St. Genesius Society, Holy Rood Guild, College Republicans, works of mercy group.

Athletics. USCAA. **Intercollegiate:** Baseball M, basketball, rugby M, soccer, volleyball W. **Intramural:** Basketball, boxing M, cross-country, fencing, football (non-tackle), handball, racquetball, skiing, soccer, softball, table tennis, tennis, volleyball. **Team name:** Crusaders.

Student services. Chaplain/spiritual director, career counseling, financial aid counseling, health services, personal counseling, placement for graduates.

Contact. E-mail: admissions@christendom.edu
Phone: (540) 636-2900 Toll-free number: (800) 877-5456
Fax: (540) 636-1655
Thomas McFadden, Director of Admissions, Christendom College, 134 Christendom Drive, Front Royal, VA 22630

Christopher Newport University

Newport News, Virginia **CB member**
www.cnu.edu **CB code: 5128**

- Public 4-year university and liberal arts college
- Residential campus in small city
- 4,829 degree-seeking undergraduates: 3% part-time, 57% women, 8% African American, 2% Asian American, 5% Hispanic American
- 137 degree-seeking graduate students
- 59% of applicants admitted
- 63% graduate within 6 years

General. Founded in 1960. Regionally accredited. **Degrees:** 994 bachelor's awarded; master's offered. **ROTC:** Army. **Location:** 20 miles from Norfolk, 70 miles from Richmond, 170 miles from Washington, DC. **Calendar:** Semester, extensive summer session. **Full-time faculty:** 246 total; 87% have terminal degrees, 11% minority, 45% women. **Part-time faculty:** 142 total; 32% have terminal degrees, 16% minority, 49% women. **Class size:** 54% < 20, 35% 20-39, 7% 40-49, less than 1% 50-99, 3% >100. **Special facilities:** Center for the arts, mariner's museum library collection.

Freshman class profile. 7,351 applied, 4,307 admitted, 1,243 enrolled.

Mid 50% test scores			
SAT critical reading:	520-630	GPA 2.0-2.99:	2%
SAT math:	520-610	Rank in top quarter:	54%
ACT composite:	22-26	Rank in top tenth:	19%
GPA 3.75 or higher:	41%	End year in good standing:	88%
GPA 3.50-3.74:	32%	Return as sophomores:	84%
GPA 3.0-3.49:	25%	Out-of-state:	6%
		Live on campus:	97%

Basis for selection. Minimum 3.0 GPA, rank in top half of class. Type of diploma and difficulty of classes taken and application essays are considered. Freshman applicants who have achieved a 3.50 GPA (on a 4.00 scale) and have pursued a rigorous curriculum, may apply to the University without submitting a standardized test score (ACT or SAT). Test optional applicants will be reviewed for the strength of the curriculum and recommendations. SAT or ACT recommended. Students with cumulative high school GPA of 3.5 or higher from a rigorous curriculum do not need to submit SAT or ACT scores. Audition required for music; interview recommended for marginal; portfolio recommended for art. **Home schooled:** Applicants should submit copy of high school transcript and descriptions, along with ACT or SAT score.

High school preparation. College-preparatory program required. Recommended units include English 4, mathematics 4, social studies 4, science 4 (laboratory 3) and foreign language 3.

2011-2012 Annual costs. Tuition/fees: $10,084; $19,306 out-of-state. Residential students pay annual $200 telecommunication fee. Out-of-state students pay annual $240 capital fee. Room/board: $9,528.

2011-2012 Financial aid. Need-based: 944 full-time freshmen applied for aid; 586 were judged to have need; 580 of these received aid. Average need met was 69%. Average scholarship/grant was $5,277; average loan $3,264. 51% of total undergraduate aid awarded as scholarships/grants, 49% as loans/jobs. **Non-need-based:** Awarded to 1,156 full-time undergraduates, including 481 freshmen. Scholarships awarded for academics, art, leadership, music/drama, ROTC, state residency.

Application procedures. Admission: Priority date 12/1; deadline 2/1 (receipt date). $50 fee, may be waived for applicants with need. Admission notification on a rolling basis. **Financial aid:** Priority date 3/1; no closing date. FAFSA required. Applicants notified on a rolling basis starting 2/21; must reply within 3 week(s) of notification.

Academics. Special programs for leadership, honors, service/learning and freshman learning communities. **Special study options:** Cross-registration, double major, dual enrollment of high school students, honors, independent study, internships, student-designed major, study abroad. Member of Virginia Tidewater Consortium, Freshman Learning Communities, Service Learning Opportunities. **Credit/placement by examination:** AP, CLEP, IB, institutional tests. **Support services:** Study skills assistance, tutoring, writing center.

Majors. Area/ethnic studies: American. **Biology:** General, cellular/molecular, environmental. **Business:** Accounting, business admin, finance, marketing. **Communications:** Communications/speech/rhetoric. **Computer sciences:** Computer science, information systems. **Engineering:** Computer. **English:** English lit. **Foreign languages:** Classics, French, German, Spanish. **History:** General. **Human services:** Social work. **Math:** General. **Philosophy/religion:** Philosophy. **Physical sciences:** Chemistry. **Psychology:** General. **Social sciences:** Economics, political science, sociology. **Visual/performing arts:** Dramatic, music performance, studio arts.

Most popular majors. Biology 12%, business/marketing 12%, communications/journalism 13%, English 6%, history 9%, psychology 11%, social sciences 16%, visual/performing arts 7%.

Computing on campus. Dormitories wired for high-speed internet access and linked to campus network. Commuter students can connect to campus network. Online course registration, online library, helpline, student web hosting, wireless network available.

Student life. Freshman orientation: Mandatory, $250 fee. Preregistration for classes offered. 2 programs required: 1.5-day program with overnight stay in residence halls, offered June-July, and welcome week program prior to start of classes in fall. **Policies:** 1st, 2nd, and 3rd year students required to live on campus unless they reside with their parents or legal guardians in Newport News, Hampton, Poquoson, Yorktown, Seaford, Grafton, or Tabb. (This policy does not apply to transfer students.). **Housing:** Guaranteed on-campus for freshmen. Coed dorms, apartments, fraternity/sorority housing available. $250 partly refundable deposit. Learning communities available. **Activities:** Bands, campus ministries, choral groups, dance, drama, international student organizations, literary magazine, music ensembles, Model UN, musical theater, radio station, student government, student newspaper, symphony orchestra, Baptist Student Union, Intervarsity Christian Fellowship, Lutheran student association, honor societies, Young Life.

Athletics. NCAA. **Intercollegiate:** Baseball M, basketball, cheerleading, cross-country, field hockey W, football (tackle) M, golf M, lacrosse, sailing, soccer, softball W, tennis, track and field, volleyball W. **Intramural:** Badminton, basketball, football (non-tackle), soccer, softball, volleyball. **Team name:** Captains.

Student services. Chaplain/spiritual director, career counseling, student employment services, financial aid counseling, health services, minority student services, personal counseling, placement for graduates, veterans' counselor. **Physically disabled:** Services for visually, speech, hearing impaired.

Contact. E-mail: admit@cnu.edu
Phone: (757) 594-7015 Toll-free number: (800) 333-4268
Fax: (757) 594-7333
Rob Lange, Dean of Admissions, Christopher Newport University, 1
University Place, Newport News, VA 23606-2998

College of William and Mary
Williamsburg, Virginia
www.wm.edu

CB member
CB code: 5115

- Public 4-year university
- Residential campus in large town
- 6,020 degree-seeking undergraduates: 1% part-time, 55% women, 7% African American, 7% Asian American, 8% Hispanic American, 3% international
- 2,070 degree-seeking graduate students
- 35% of applicants admitted
- SAT or ACT (ACT writing optional), application essay required
- 90% graduate within 6 years

General. Founded in 1693. Regionally accredited. **Degrees:** 1,497 bachelor's awarded; master's, professional, doctoral offered. **ROTC:** Army. **Location:** 50 miles from Richmond, 50 miles from Norfolk. **Calendar:** Semester, limited summer session. **Full-time faculty:** 591 total. **Part-time faculty:** 229 total. **Special facilities:** Observatory, continuous beam accelerator, 3 interdisciplinary centers (humanities, international studies, writing resources), marine science institute, materials processes research center, public policy research center, health policy research center, center for geospatial analysis, center for archeological research, Institute for the Theory and Practice of International Relations, environmental field laboratory.

Freshman class profile. 12,825 applied, 4,443 admitted, 1,485 enrolled.

Mid 50% test scores			
SAT critical reading:	620-730	Rank in top quarter:	96%
SAT math:	620-720	Rank in top tenth:	79%
SAT writing:	620-720	Return as sophomores:	95%
ACT composite:	28-32	Out-of-state:	35%
GPA 3.75 or higher:	86%	Live on campus:	100%
GPA 3.50-3.74:	9%	International:	5%
GPA 3.0-3.49:	5%	Fraternities:	15%
		Sororities:	18%

Basis for selection. Primary importance is placed on the academic record, including in-class achievement, rigor of curriculum and standardized testing. Extracurricular involvements, writing samples, recommendations, talents and abilities also receive consideration. Preference is given to Virginia residents. Children of alumni receive special consideration.

High school preparation. College-preparatory program recommended. Recommended units include English 4, mathematics 4, social studies 4, science 4 (laboratory 3) and foreign language 4.

2011-2012 Annual costs. Tuition/fees: $13,132; $35,409 out-of-state. Room/board: $8,772.

Financial aid. Non-need-based: Scholarships awarded for academics, art, athletics, leadership, music/drama, ROTC, state residency.

Application procedures. Admission: Closing date 1/1 (postmark date). $60 fee, may be waived for applicants with need. Admission notification by 4/1. Must reply by 5/1. **Financial aid:** Closing date 3/15. FAFSA, CSS PROFILE required. Applicants notified on a rolling basis starting 4/1; must reply by 5/1 or within 2 week(s) of notification.

Academics. Special study options: Accelerated study, combined bachelor's/graduate degree, double major, dual enrollment of high school students, honors, independent study, internships, student-designed major, study abroad, teacher certification program, Washington semester. Joint degree program with University of St Andrews. **Credit/placement by examination:** AP, CLEP, IB, institutional tests. **Support services:** Pre-admission summer program, reduced course load, study skills assistance, tutoring, writing center.

Majors. Area/ethnic studies: General, African-American, American, women's. **Biology:** General, neuroscience. **Business:** Business admin. **Computer sciences:** General. **Conservation:** Environmental studies. **English:** English lit. **Foreign languages:** Chinese, classics, French, German, linguistics, Spanish. **History:** General. **Human services:** Public policy. **Math:** General. **Parks/recreation:** Exercise sciences. **Philosophy/religion:** Philosophy, religion. **Physical sciences:** Chemistry, geology, physics. **Psychology:** General. **Social sciences:** Anthropology, economics, international relations, political science, sociology. **Visual/performing arts:** Art, dramatic, music.

Most popular majors. Business/marketing 11%, English 8%, history 8%, interdisciplinary studies 10%, psychology 7%, social sciences 24%.

Computing on campus. PC or laptop required. 350 workstations in library, computer center, student center. Dormitories wired for high-speed internet access and linked to campus network. Commuter students can connect to campus network. Online course registration, online library, helpline, repair service, student web hosting, wireless network available.

Student life. Freshman orientation: Mandatory, $154 fee. Preregistration for classes offered. 5-day program immediately preceding fall semester. **Policies:** All students pledge to uphold the Honor Code. Freshman students are required to live on campus. Freshmen not permitted cars on campus. **Housing:** Guaranteed on-campus for freshmen. Coed dorms, special housing for disabled, apartments, fraternity/sorority housing, wellness housing available. $200 nonrefundable deposit, deadline 5/1. International Studies Hall, Eco-House, Community Scholars House, Africana House, Multicultural Unit, 8 Language Houses (Arabic, Chinese, French, German, Italian, Japanese, Russian, Spanish) available. **Activities:** Bands, campus ministries, choral groups, dance, drama, film society, international student organizations, literary magazine, music ensembles, Model UN, musical theater, opera, radio station, student government, student newspaper, symphony orchestra, TV station, AIDS Tanzania, Asian Student Council, Black Student Organization, College Partnership for Kids, College Republicans, Global Village Project, Hispanic Cultural Organization, Student Environmental Action Coalition, I-Faith, Young Democrats.

Athletics. NCAA. **Intercollegiate:** Baseball M, basketball, cross-country, diving, field hockey W, football (tackle) M, golf, gymnastics, lacrosse W, soccer, swimming, tennis, track and field, volleyball W. **Intramural:** Basketball, bowling, football (non-tackle), golf, racquetball, soccer, softball, table tennis, tennis, volleyball, weight lifting. **Team name:** Tribe.

Student services. Alcohol/substance abuse counseling, career counseling, student employment services, financial aid counseling, health services, legal services, minority student services, on-campus daycare, personal counseling, placement for graduates. **Physically disabled:** Services for visually, hearing impaired.

Contact. E-mail: admission@wm.edu
Phone: (757) 221-4223 Fax: (757) 221-1242
Henry Broaddus, Dean of Admission, College of William and Mary, PO Box 8795, Williamsburg, VA 23187-8795

DeVry University: Arlington
Arlington, Virginia
www.devry.edu

CB code: 3813

- For-profit 4-year university
- Commuter campus in very large city
- Interview required

General. Additional locations: Manassas, Norfolk; Bethesda (MD); Charlotte, Raleigh-Durham (NC). **Degrees:** 96 bachelor's, 14 associate awarded; master's offered. **Calendar:** Semester, extensive summer session. **Full-time faculty:** 16 total. **Part-time faculty:** 123 total.

Basis for selection. Applicant must have high school diploma or equivalent, degree from an accredited postsecondary institution, or submit acceptable test scores and be at least 17 years of age. CPT also accepted.

High school preparation. Required units include mathematics 1. Math unit must be algebra or higher.

2011-2012 Annual costs. Tuition/fees: $15,294. Books/supplies: $1,300. Personal expenses: $3,152.

Financial aid. All financial aid based on need.

Application procedures. Admission: No deadline. $50 fee. Admission notification on a rolling basis. **Financial aid:** No deadline. FAFSA required. Applicants notified on a rolling basis.

Academics. Special study options: Accelerated study, cooperative education, distance learning. **Credit/placement by examination:** AP, CLEP. **Support services:** Learning center, remedial instruction, tutoring.

Majors. Business: Business admin. **Computer sciences:** Networking, systems analysis, web page design. **Engineering:** Software.

Most popular majors. Business/marketing 53%, computer/information sciences 16%, engineering/engineering technologies 31%.

Computing on campus. Online course registration, online library, helpline available.

Student life. Freshman orientation: Mandatory. Preregistration for classes offered. **Activities:** Linux users' group.

Athletics. Intramural: Basketball, volleyball.

Student services. Career counseling, student employment services, financial aid counseling, placement for graduates, veterans' counselor. **Physically disabled:** Services for visually, hearing impaired.

Contact. E-mail: admissions@crys.devry.edu
Phone: (703) 414-4100 Toll-free number: (866) 338-7932
Fax: (703) 414-4040
Bob Pavlovics, Director of Admissions, DeVry University: Arlington, 2450 Crystal Drive, Arlington, VA 22202

Eastern Mennonite University
Harrisonburg, Virginia   **CB member**
www.emu.edu   **CB code: 5181**

- Private 4-year university and liberal arts college affiliated with Mennonite Church
- Residential campus in large town
- 1,017 degree-seeking undergraduates: 1% part-time, 64% women, 6% African American, 1% Asian American, 6% Hispanic American, 3% international
- 272 degree-seeking graduate students
- 68% of applicants admitted
- SAT or ACT with writing required
- 66% graduate within 6 years

General. Founded in 1917. Regionally accredited. Cross-cultural study (usually a semester in another country) and community service required of all students. **Degrees:** 334 bachelor's awarded; master's offered. **Location:** 110 miles from Richmond, 110 miles from Washington, DC. **Calendar:** Semester, limited summer session. **Full-time faculty:** 104 total; 77% have terminal degrees, 3% minority, 51% women. **Part-time faculty:** 101 total; 12% minority, 54% women. **Class size:** 66% < 20, 30% 20-39, 2% 40-49, 2% 50-99. **Special facilities:** Museum of natural history, arboretum, campus garden, student-run coffee shop.

Freshman class profile. 845 applied, 578 admitted, 234 enrolled.

Mid 50% test scores			
SAT critical reading:	450-610	GPA 2.0-2.99:	15%
SAT math:	460-590	Rank in top quarter:	47%
SAT writing:	450-590	Rank in top tenth:	20%
ACT composite:	21-28	End year in good standing:	84%
GPA 3.75 or higher:	41%	Return as sophomores:	78%
GPA 3.50-3.74:	16%	Out-of-state:	44%
GPA 3.0-3.49:	28%	Live on campus:	90%
		International:	2%

Basis for selection. 2.2 high school GPA required. SAT score of 920 (exclusive of Writing) or ACT minimum composite score of 20 required. Conditional admission possible for motivated applicants who fail to reach minimum admissions requirements. Interviews recommended. **Home schooled:** Detailed record of coursework completed for grades 9-12, SAT or ACT required. **Learning Disabled:** Interview recommended for learning disabled; meet with academic support center personnel.

High school preparation. College-preparatory program recommended. 21 units recommended. Recommended units include English 4, mathematics 3, social studies 3, science 3 (laboratory 3), foreign language 2 and academic electives 6.

2011-2012 Annual costs. Tuition/fees: $26,400. Room/board: $8,520. Books/supplies: $1,000. Personal expenses: $1,000.

Financial aid. Non-need-based: Scholarships awarded for academics, alumni affiliation, art, leadership, religious affiliation, state residency.

Application procedures. Admission: No deadline. $25 fee, may be waived for applicants with need. Admission notification on a rolling basis. **Financial aid:** Priority date 3/1; no closing date. FAFSA required. Applicants notified on a rolling basis starting 3/1; must reply within 4 week(s) of notification.

Academics. Cross-cultural education component required in 3-week or 3-month program to locations around the world. **Special study options:** Distance learning, double major, ESL, honors, independent study, internships, liberal arts/career combination, study abroad, teacher certification program,

Washington semester. Adult degree completion programs in nursing and management. **Credit/placement by examination:** AP, CLEP, IB, SAT, ACT, institutional tests. 30 credit hours maximum toward bachelor's degree. **Support services:** Learning center, reduced course load, study skills assistance, tutoring, writing center.

Majors. Biology: General, biochemistry. **Business:** Accounting, business admin, international, organizational behavior. **Communications:** General, digital media. **Computer sciences:** Computer science. **Conservation:** Environmental studies. **Education:** Physical. **English:** English lit. **Foreign languages:** Spanish. **Health services:** Clinical lab science, nursing (RN). **History:** General. **Human services:** Social work. **Liberal arts:** Arts/sciences. **Math:** General. **Parks/recreation:** Sports admin. **Physical sciences:** Chemistry. **Psychology:** General. **Social sciences:** General, economics, international economic development. **Theology:** Bible, preministerial. **Visual/performing arts:** Art, dramatic, music, photography.

Most popular majors. Biology 7%, business/marketing 10%, health sciences 16%, interdisciplinary studies 7%, liberal arts 15%, visual/performing arts 9%.

Computing on campus. 100 workstations in library, computer center, student center. Dormitories wired for high-speed internet access and linked to campus network. Commuter students can connect to campus network. Online library, helpline, student web hosting, wireless network available.

Student life. Freshman orientation: Mandatory. Preregistration for classes offered. 5 days before start of fall semester for 5 days. **Policies:** Alcohol and drug use by students prohibited. Chapel attendance expected. Students must sign and adhere to Community Lifestyle Commitment. Emphasis on justice and peacebuilding. **Housing:** Guaranteed on-campus for freshmen. Coed dorms, single-sex dorms, special housing for disabled, apartments, wellness housing available. International communities available. **Activities:** Jazz band, campus ministries, choral groups, dance, drama, film society, international student organizations, literary magazine, music ensembles, musical theater, student government, student newspaper, symphony orchestra, Young People's Christian Association, Peace Fellowship, Black student union, Latino Student Alliance, Earth Keepers, Social Work is People, A Safe Place, Alpha Omega Steppers for Christ.

Athletics. NCAA. **Intercollegiate:** Baseball M, basketball, cross-country, field hockey W, soccer, softball W, track and field, volleyball. **Intramural:** Basketball, football (non-tackle), golf, soccer, softball, table tennis, tennis, volleyball. **Team name:** Royals.

Student services. Adult student services, alcohol/substance abuse counseling, chaplain/spiritual director, career counseling, student employment services, financial aid counseling, health services, minority student services, personal counseling, placement for graduates. **Physically disabled:** Services for visually, speech, hearing impaired.

Contact. E-mail: admiss@emu.edu
Phone: (540) 432-4118 Toll-free number: (800) 368-2665
Fax: (540) 432-4444
Stephanie Shafer, Director of Admissions, Eastern Mennonite University, 1200 Park Road, Harrisonburg, VA 22802-2462

ECPI University
Virginia Beach, Virginia
www.ecpi.edu   **CB code: 7140**

- For-profit 4-year health science and technical college
- Commuter campus in very large city

General. Founded in 1966. Regionally accredited. **Calendar:** Differs by program.

Annual costs/financial aid. Need-based financial aid available to full-time and part-time students.

Contact. Phone: (757) 490-9090
Director of Admissions, 5555 Greenwich Road, Suite 300, Virginia Beach, VA 23462-6542

Emory & Henry College
Emory, Virginia   **CB member**
www.ehc.edu   **CB code: 5185**

- Private 4-year liberal arts college affiliated with United Methodist Church
- Residential campus in rural community
- 911 degree-seeking undergraduates: 1% part-time, 48% women

- 43 degree-seeking graduate students
- 71% of applicants admitted
- SAT or ACT (ACT writing recommended) required
- 48% graduate within 6 years

General. Founded in 1836. Regionally accredited. **Degrees:** 205 bachelor's awarded; master's offered. **Location:** 25 miles from Bristol, VA. **Calendar:** Semester, limited summer session. **Full-time faculty:** 70 total; 86% have terminal degrees, 6% minority, 44% women. **Part-time faculty:** 57 total; 30% have terminal degrees, 39% women. **Class size:** 83% < 20, 17% 20-39. **Special facilities:** Observatory, 1912 art depot, outdoor leadership center, disc golf course, golf course.

Freshman class profile. 1,367 applied, 971 admitted, 277 enrolled.

Mid 50% test scores			
SAT critical reading:	440-560	GPA 3.0-3.49:	34%
SAT math:	430-560	GPA 2.0-2.99:	19%
SAT writing:	420-560	Rank in top quarter:	45%
ACT composite:	21-26	Rank in top tenth:	20%
GPA 3.75 or higher:	32%	Out-of-state:	42%
GPA 3.50-3.74:	14%	Live on campus:	93%
		International:	1%

Basis for selection. School achievement record, test scores, involvement in extracurricular and community activities, class rank, recommendations used. Audition required for preprofessional degrees in acting, directing, musical theater, and design/production. Auditions required for performance and teacher preparation tracks within music program. Portfolio recommended for art program.

High school preparation. College-preparatory program required. 15 units required. Required and recommended units include English 4, mathematics 3, social studies 2, science 2 (laboratory 2), foreign language 2 and visual/performing arts 1. 1 fine arts recommended.

2011-2012 Annual costs. Tuition/fees: $27,040. Room/board: $9,064. Books/supplies: $1,000. Personal expenses: $1,050.

2011-2012 Financial aid. Need-based: 263 full-time freshmen applied for aid; 236 were judged to have need; 236 of these received aid. Average need met was 87%. Average scholarship/grant was $21,507; average loan $3,488. 78% of total undergraduate aid awarded as scholarships/grants, 22% as loans/jobs. **Non-need-based:** Awarded to 217 full-time undergraduates, including 67 freshmen. Scholarships awarded for academics, art, music/drama, religious affiliation, state residency. **Additional information:** Virginia residents eligible for additional in-state tuition grants.

Application procedures. Admission: Priority date 3/1; no deadline. No application fee. Admission notification on a rolling basis beginning on or about 1/1. Must reply by May 1 or within 4 week(s) if notified thereafter. **Financial aid:** Priority date 4/1; no closing date. FAFSA required. Applicants notified on a rolling basis starting 3/1; must reply by 6/15.

Academics. Special study options: Combined bachelor's/graduate degree, cooperative education, distance learning, double major, dual enrollment of high school students, honors, independent study, internships, liberal arts/career combination, student-designed major, study abroad, teacher certification program. **Credit/placement by examination:** AP, CLEP, IB, SAT, ACT, institutional tests. **Support services:** Learning center, pre-admission summer program, reduced course load, study skills assistance, tutoring, writing center.

Majors. Area/ethnic studies: East Asian, European, French, Near/Middle Eastern, Spanish/Iberian. **Biology:** General. **Business:** Accounting, business admin, international. **Communications:** Media studies. **Computer sciences:** General, computer science. **Conservation:** Environmental science, environmental studies. **Education:** Art, biology, business, chemistry, English, French, mathematics, music, physical, Spanish. **English:** Creative writing, English lit. **Foreign languages:** French, Spanish. **Health services:** Athletic training, prepharmacy, preveterinary. **History:** General, applied. **Human services:** Community org/advocacy. **Math:** General. **Parks/recreation:** Health/fitness, sports admin. **Philosophy/religion:** Philosophy, religion. **Physical sciences:** Chemistry, physics. **Psychology:** General. **Social sciences:** Anthropology, economics, geography, political science, sociology, U.S. government. **Visual/performing arts:** Acting, art, directing/producing, dramatic, graphic design, music, music performance, musical theater.

Most popular majors. Biology 6%, business/marketing 9%, education 19%, parks/recreation 8%, physical sciences 7%, social sciences 12%.

Computing on campus. 250 workstations in dormitories, library, computer center, student center. Dormitories wired for high-speed internet access and linked to campus network. Commuter students can connect to campus network. Online library, helpline, wireless network available.

Student life. Freshman orientation: Mandatory. Preregistration for classes offered. Orientation occurs before registration. Students participate in community service activity and attend fine arts event following weekend as part of extended orientation. **Housing:** Guaranteed on-campus for all undergraduates. Coed dorms, single-sex dorms, special housing for disabled, wellness housing available. $400 fully refundable deposit, deadline 8/1. Small houses available. **Activities:** Pep band, campus ministries, choral groups, dance, drama, international student organizations, literary magazine, music ensembles, musical theater, radio station, student government, student newspaper, TV station, Young Democrats, Young Republicans, Libertarians, Alpha Phi Omega, Fellowship of Christian Athletes, outdoor leadership program, Habitat for Humanity, Campus Christian Fellowship, multicultural student association.

Athletics. NCAA. **Intercollegiate:** Baseball M, basketball, cheerleading, cross-country, football (tackle) M, golf M, soccer, softball W, swimming W, tennis, volleyball W. **Intramural:** Badminton, basketball, football (non-tackle), golf, racquetball, soccer, softball, swimming, table tennis, tennis, volleyball. **Team name:** Wasps.

Student services. Alcohol/substance abuse counseling, chaplain/spiritual director, career counseling, student employment services, financial aid counseling, health services, on-campus daycare, personal counseling, placement for graduates, veterans' counselor. **Physically disabled:** Services for visually, hearing impaired.

Contact. E-mail: ehadmiss@ehc.edu
Phone: (276) 944-6133 Toll-free number: (800) 848-5494
David Hawsey, Vice President of Enrollment Management, Emory & Henry College, Box 10, Emory, VA 24327

Ferrum College
Ferrum, Virginia
www.ferrum.edu

CB member
CB code: 5213

- Private 4-year liberal arts college affiliated with United Methodist Church
- Residential campus in rural community
- 1,510 degree-seeking undergraduates: 1% part-time, 47% women
- SAT or ACT (ACT writing optional) required
- 31% graduate within 6 years

General. Founded in 1913. Regionally accredited. **Degrees:** 192 bachelor's awarded. **Location:** 35 miles from Roanoke, 65 miles from Greensboro, North Carolina. **Calendar:** Semester, limited summer session. **Full-time faculty:** 72 total; 74% have terminal degrees, 44% women. **Part-time faculty:** 51 total; 35% have terminal degrees, 45% women. **Class size:** 48% < 20, 51% 20-39, 1% 40-49, less than 1% 50-99. **Special facilities:** Farm museum, state center for Blue Ridge folklore, forest and agricultural acreage used as outdoor labs in science, high and low ropes courses, dinner theater.

Freshman class profile.

Mid 50% test scores			
SAT critical reading:	390-490	GPA 2.0-2.99:	62%
SAT math:	390-490	Rank in top quarter:	14%
ACT composite:	16-21	Rank in top tenth:	3%
GPA 3.75 or higher:	5%	Return as sophomores:	55%
GPA 3.50-3.74:	7%	Out-of-state:	20%
GPA 3.0-3.49:	23%	Live on campus:	99%
		International:	1%

Basis for selection. High school record most important, followed by test scores, counselor recommendations, areas of intended college study, and extracurricular activities. Essay and interview recommended. **Home schooled:** Transcript of courses and grades required. **Learning Disabled:** Submit current disability documentation to Director of Disability Services.

High school preparation. 22 units required; 24 recommended. Required and recommended units include English 4, mathematics 3, social studies 1, history 2, science 2 (laboratory 1), foreign language 2 and visual/performing arts 1.

2011-2012 Annual costs. Tuition/fees: $26,375. Room/board: $8,530. Books/supplies: $800. Personal expenses: $1,300.

Financial aid. Non-need-based: Scholarships awarded for academics, leadership, religious affiliation, state residency.

Application procedures. Admission: $25 fee, may be waived for applicants with need. Admission notification on a rolling basis beginning on or about 9/16. Must reply by May 1 or within 4 week(s) if notified thereafter. Must reply no later than 30 days after receiving official acceptance letter. **Financial aid:** Priority date 3/1; no closing date. FAFSA required. Applicants notified on a rolling basis starting 1/10.

Academics. Field experiences and internships emphasized. Academic services/support available fall and spring academic semesters. **Special study**

options: Double major, dual enrollment of high school students, exchange student, honors, independent study, internships, liberal arts/career combination, student-designed major, study abroad, teacher certification program. **Credit/placement by examination:** AP, CLEP, IB, institutional tests. 12 credit hours maximum toward bachelor's degree. **Support services:** Learning center, pre-admission summer program, reduced course load, remedial instruction, study skills assistance, tutoring, writing center.

Majors. Biology: General. **Business:** Accounting, business admin, finance, management information systems, marketing. **Computer sciences:** Information systems. **Conservation:** Environmental science. **Education:** General. **English:** English lit. **Foreign languages:** Russian, Spanish. **General:** Business, horticultural science. **Health services:** Clinical lab science. **History:** General. **Human services:** Social work. **Liberal arts:** Arts/sciences. **Math:** General. **Parks/recreation:** General, health/fitness, sports admin. **Philosophy/religion:** Philosophy, religion. **Physical sciences:** Chemistry. **Protective services:** Criminal justice. **Psychology:** General. **Social sciences:** General, international relations, political science. **Visual/performing arts:** General, art, dramatic.

Most popular majors. Agriculture 7%, business/marketing 24%, health sciences 12%, liberal arts 7%, natural resources/environmental science 6%, parks/recreation 7%, security/protective services 12%.

Computing on campus. PC or laptop required. 600 workstations in dormitories, library, computer center, student center. Dormitories wired for high-speed internet access and linked to campus network. Commuter students can connect to campus network. Online course registration, online library, helpline, repair service, student web hosting, wireless network available.

Student life. Freshman orientation: Mandatory. Preregistration for classes offered. 2-day student orientation held immediately prior to fall semester. **Policies:** All housing substance-free; no alcohol or tobacco products allowed. **Housing:** Guaranteed on-campus for all undergraduates. Coed dorms, single-sex dorms, special housing for disabled, apartments, wellness housing available. **Activities:** Bands, campus ministries, choral groups, dance, drama, international student organizations, literary magazine, music ensembles, Model UN, musical theater, radio station, student government, student newspaper, Environmental Action Coalition, Big Buddy/Little Buddy, African American student association, Bonner Scholars, Student Christian Fellowship, Kappa Delta Chi, Habitat for Humanity, Colleges Against Cancer, Alpha Phi Omega.

Athletics. NCAA. **Intercollegiate:** Baseball M, basketball, cheerleading, cross-country, football (tackle) M, golf M, lacrosse W, soccer, softball W, tennis, volleyball W. **Intramural:** Basketball, bowling, football (non-tackle), racquetball, soccer, softball, swimming, table tennis, tennis, volleyball. **Team name:** Panthers.

Student services. Adult student services, alcohol/substance abuse counseling, chaplain/spiritual director, career counseling, student employment services, financial aid counseling, health services, minority student services, personal counseling, placement for graduates, veterans' counselor.

Contact. E-mail: admissions@ferrum.edu
Phone: (540) 365-4290 Toll-free number: (800) 868-9797
Fax: (540) 365-4266
Gilda Woods, Associate Vice President and Dean of Admissions, Ferrum College, Spilman-Daniel House, 40 Stratton Lane, Ferrum, VA 24088

George Mason University
Fairfax, Virginia
www.gmu.edu

CB member
CB code: 5827

- Public 4-year university
- Residential campus in large town
- 20,194 degree-seeking undergraduates: 20% part-time, 52% women, 9% African American, 17% Asian American, 10% Hispanic American, 3% international
- 10,848 degree-seeking graduate students
- 53% of applicants admitted
- Application essay required
- 64% graduate within 6 years

General. Founded in 1972. Regionally accredited. **Degrees:** 4,255 bachelor's awarded; master's, professional, doctoral offered. **ROTC:** Army, Air Force. **Location:** 21 miles from Washington, DC. **Calendar:** Semester, extensive summer session. **Full-time faculty:** 1,155 total; 91% have terminal degrees, 16% minority, 41% women. **Part-time faculty:** 1,220 total; 15% minority, 52% women. **Class size:** 28% < 20, 46% 20-39, 11% 40-49, 12% 50-99, 3% >100. **Special facilities:** Center for the arts, astronomy observatory,

Smithsonian conservation and research center, library of congress federal theater project collection.

Freshman class profile. 17,548 applied, 9,263 admitted, 2,665 enrolled.

Mid 50% test scores			
SAT critical reading:	520-620	Rank in top tenth:	23%
SAT math:	530-630	End year in good standing:	85%
ACT composite:	23-28	Return as sophomores:	87%
GPA 3.75 or higher:	37%	Out-of-state:	23%
GPA 3.50-3.74:	30%	Live on campus:	73%
GPA 3.0-3.49:	32%	International:	3%
GPA 2.0-2.99:	1%	Fraternities:	13%
Rank in top quarter:	60%	Sororities:	18%

Basis for selection. Test scores, class rank, academic record with emphasis on courses taken, and GPA (minimum 3.5) are most important. Special talents and abilities and counselor recommendations are also important. SAT and SAT Subject Tests or ACT recommended. Writing tests are not used in admissions process. Recommended students submit standardized test scores (SAT or ACT), however, option available for admission without submitting test scores. Audition required for Dance and Music; portfolio required for Art and Visual Technology BFA and Computer Game Design. Interview and audition or portfolio required for Theater. **Home schooled:** Transcript of courses and grades, letter of recommendation (nonparent) required.

High school preparation. College-preparatory program required. 17 units required; 23 recommended. Required and recommended units include English 4, mathematics 3-4, social studies 3-4, (laboratory 2-3), foreign language 2-3 and academic electives 3-5. Additional mathematics and science units required for applicants who intend to major in pre-business, chemistry, computer science, engineering, geology, mathematics, and physics.

2011-2012 Annual costs. Tuition/fees: $9,266; $25,748 out-of-state. Room/board: $9,050. Books/supplies: $900. Personal expenses: $1,440.

2010-2011 Financial aid. **Need-based:** 2,012 full-time freshmen applied for aid; 1,295 were judged to have need; 1,218 of these received aid. Average need met was 73%. Average scholarship/grant was $7,222; average loan $3,325. 58% of total undergraduate aid awarded as scholarships/grants, 42% as loans/jobs. **Non-need-based:** Awarded to 1,976 full-time undergraduates, including 526 freshmen. Scholarships awarded for academics, athletics, minority status, music/drama, ROTC, state residency.

Application procedures. **Admission:** Priority date 12/1; deadline 1/15 (postmark date). $60 fee, may be waived for applicants with need. Admission notification by 4/1. Must reply by May 1 or within 3 week(s) if notified thereafter. **Financial aid:** Priority date 3/1; no closing date. FAFSA required. Applicants notified on a rolling basis starting 4/1; must reply within 3 week(s) of notification.

Academics. Special study options: Accelerated study, combined bachelor's/graduate degree, cooperative education, cross-registration, distance learning, double major, dual enrollment of high school students, ESL, exchange student, external degree, honors, independent study, internships, liberal arts/career combination, student-designed major, study abroad, teacher certification program. **Credit/placement by examination:** AP, CLEP, IB, institutional tests. **Support services:** Learning center, reduced course load, study skills assistance, tutoring, writing center.

Majors. Area/ethnic studies: Latin American, Russian/Slavic. **Biology:** General, neuroscience. **Business:** Accounting, business admin, finance, marketing, tourism/travel. **Communications:** Communications/speech/rhetoric. **Communications technology:** Animation/special effects. **Computer sciences:** General, computer science, information technology. **Conservation:** Environmental science. **Education:** Health, physical. **Engineering:** General, biomedical, civil, computer, electrical, systems. **English:** English lit, rhetoric/composition. **Foreign languages:** General. **Health services:** Athletic training, clinical lab science, community health, health care admin, nursing (RN). **History:** General. **Human services:** General, social work. **Liberal arts:** Arts/sciences. **Math:** General. **Philosophy/religion:** Philosophy, religion. **Physical sciences:** Astronomy, chemistry, geology, physics. **Protective services:** Forensics, police science. **Psychology:** General. **Social sciences:** Anthropology, economics, geography, international relations, sociology. **Visual/performing arts:** General, art history/conservation, cinematography, dance, dramatic, music performance.

Most popular majors. Biology 6%, business/marketing 21%, computer/information sciences 6%, English 10%, health sciences 7%, psychology 7%, social sciences 14%, visual/performing arts 6%.

Computing on campus. 628 workstations in library, computer center. Dormitories wired for high-speed internet access and linked to campus network. Commuter students can connect to campus network. Online course registration, online library, helpline, repair service, student web hosting, wireless network available.

Student life. Freshman orientation: Mandatory, $180 fee. Preregistration for classes offered. 2-day comprehensive overnight program. Transfer orientation occurs from June through July and students are given a half or full day option. **Housing:** Guaranteed on-campus for freshmen. Coed dorms, special housing for disabled, apartments, wellness housing available. $300 nonrefundable deposit, deadline 5/1. Housing for faculty, staff, and graduate students; townhouses available. **Activities:** Bands, campus ministries, choral groups, dance, drama, film society, international student organizations, literary magazine, music ensembles, Model UN, musical theater, opera, radio station, student government, student newspaper, symphony orchestra, TV station, Campus Crusade for Christ, Pakistani student association, Invisible Children GMU, UNICEF Campus Initiative, Students for Democracy, Hispanic student association, environmental action group, Alpha Phi Omega, Muslim student association, Hellenic Society.

Athletics. NCAA. **Intercollegiate:** Baseball M, basketball, cheerleading, cross-country, diving, golf M, lacrosse W, rowing (crew) W, soccer, softball W, swimming, tennis, track and field, volleyball, wrestling M. **Intramural:** Basketball, cricket, football (non-tackle), golf, soccer, softball, swimming, table tennis, tennis, track and field, volleyball. **Team name:** Patriots.

Student services. Adult student services, alcohol/substance abuse counseling, chaplain/spiritual director, career counseling, services for economically disadvantaged, student employment services, financial aid counseling, health services, minority student services, on-campus daycare, personal counseling, placement for graduates, veterans' counselor, women's services. **Physically disabled:** Services for visually, speech, hearing impaired.

Contact. E-mail: admissions@gmu.edu
Phone: (703) 993-2400 Fax: (703) 993-4622
Daniel Robb, Assistant Vice President, Enrollment Development/Associate Dean, George Mason University, 4400 University Drive, MSN 3A4, Fairfax, VA 22030-4444

Hampden-Sydney College
Hampden-Sydney, Virginia
www.hsc.edu

CB member
CB code: 5291

- Private 4-year liberal arts college for men affiliated with Presbyterian Church (USA)
- Residential campus in rural community
- 1,057 degree-seeking undergraduates: 8% African American, 1% Asian American, 2% Hispanic American, 1% Native American, 1% international
- 55% of applicants admitted
- SAT or ACT (ACT writing optional), application essay required
- 66% graduate within 6 years; 19% enter graduate study

General. Founded in 1776. Regionally accredited. **Degrees:** 241 bachelor's awarded. **ROTC:** Army. **Location:** 60 miles from Richmond. **Calendar:** Semester, limited summer session. **Full-time faculty:** 100 total; 89% have terminal degrees, 6% minority, 35% women. **Part-time faculty:** 14 total; 57% have terminal degrees, 7% minority, 21% women. **Class size:** 74% < 20, 26% 20-39, less than 1% 40-49. **Special facilities:** International communications center, observatory, college operated museum, Athlete Hall of Fame museum, hiking trails, center for leadership.

Freshman class profile. 2,484 applied, 1,361 admitted, 320 enrolled.

Mid 50% test scores		GPA 2.0-2.99:	25%
SAT critical reading:	490-600	Rank in top quarter:	19%
SAT math:	510-610	Rank in top tenth:	10%
SAT writing:	470-580	End year in good standing:	96%
ACT composite:	21-27	Return as sophomores:	80%
GPA 3.75 or higher:	20%	Out-of-state:	31%
GPA 3.50-3.74:	17%	Live on campus:	100%
GPA 3.0-3.49:	38%	Fraternities:	34%

Basis for selection. High school academic record, recommendations, test scores, extracurricular activities, essay most important. SAT Subject Tests recommended. SAT Subject Test in Math Level 1 recommended. Interview recommended. **Home schooled:** Letter of recommendation (nonparent) required. Curriculum statement required.

High school preparation. College-preparatory program recommended. 16 units required. Required and recommended units include English 4, mathematics 3-4, social studies 1, history 1, science 2-3 (laboratory 1), foreign language 2-3 and academic electives 3.

2011-2012 Annual costs. Tuition/fees: $34,219. Room/board: $10,632. Books/supplies: $1,236. Personal expenses: $1,178.

2011-2012 Financial aid. Need-based: 240 full-time freshmen applied for aid; 189 were judged to have need; 189 of these received aid. Average need met was 82%. Average scholarship/grant was $22,313; average loan $4,003. 77% of total undergraduate aid awarded as scholarships/grants, 23% as loans/jobs. **Non-need-based:** Awarded to 524 full-time undergraduates, including 161 freshmen. Scholarships awarded for academics, leadership, minority status, music/drama, religious affiliation, ROTC, state residency.

Application procedures. Admission: Closing date 3/1 (postmark date). $30 fee, may be waived for applicants with need, free for online applicants. Admission notification by 4/15. Must reply by 5/1. **Financial aid:** Priority date 3/1, closing date 5/1. FAFSA required. Applicants notified by 3/15; must reply by 5/1 or within 2 week(s) of notification.

Academics. Public service concentration for men interested in government involves classwork and internship followed by paper presented and defended publicly. **Special study options:** Combined bachelor's/graduate degree, cooperative education, cross-registration, double major, dual enrollment of high school students, exchange student, honors, independent study, internships, semester at sea, study abroad, Washington semester. Appalachian semester, junior year exchange program with members of Virginia consortium. **Credit/placement by examination:** AP, CLEP, IB, SAT, ACT, institutional tests. **Support services:** Reduced course load, study skills assistance, tutoring, writing center.

Majors. Biology: General, biochemistry, biophysics. **Business:** Managerial economics. **Computer sciences:** Computer science. **English:** English lit. **Foreign languages:** Ancient Greek, classics, French, German, Latin, Spanish. **History:** General. **Liberal arts:** Humanities. **Math:** General, applied. **Philosophy/religion:** Philosophy, religion. **Physical sciences:** Chemistry, physics. **Psychology:** General. **Social sciences:** Econometrics, economics, international relations, political science. **Visual/performing arts:** Studio arts.

Most popular majors. Biology 7%, business/marketing 11%, history 16%, social sciences 36%.

Computing on campus. 98 workstations in dormitories, library, computer center. Dormitories wired for high-speed internet access and linked to campus network. Commuter students can connect to campus network. Online course registration, online library, helpline, repair service, wireless network available.

Student life. Freshman orientation: Mandatory, $325 fee. Preregistration for classes offered. 4-day program before start of classes. **Policies:** All entering freshman participate in a presentation and discussion regarding the H-SC Honor Code. **Housing:** Guaranteed on-campus for all undergraduates. Apartments, fraternity/sorority housing available. **Activities:** Pep band, campus ministries, choral groups, drama, international student organizations, literary magazine, music ensembles, radio station, student government, student newspaper, Inter-Varsity Christian Fellowship, Republican Society, volunteer fire department, Good Men and Good Citizens, Student Environmental Action Coalition, museum board, Fellowship of Christian Athletes, Minority Student Union, Young Democrats.

Athletics. NCAA. **Intercollegiate:** Baseball M, basketball M, cross-country M, football (tackle) M, golf M, lacrosse M, soccer M, swimming M, tennis M. **Intramural:** Basketball M, racquetball M, rugby M, soccer M, softball M, volleyball M. **Team name:** Tigers.

Student services. Alcohol/substance abuse counseling, chaplain/spiritual director, career counseling, student employment services, financial aid counseling, health services, minority student services, personal counseling, placement for graduates.

Contact. E-mail: hsapp@hsc.edu
Phone: (434) 223-6120 Toll-free number: (800) 755-0733
Fax: (434) 223-6346
Jason Ferguson, Director of Admissions, Hampden-Sydney College, Box 667, Hampden-Sydney, VA 23943

Hampton University
Hampton, Virginia
www.hamptonu.edu

CB member
CB code: 5292

- Private 4-year university
- Residential campus in small city
- 4,110 degree-seeking undergraduates
- 37% of applicants admitted
- SAT or ACT (ACT writing optional), application essay required

General. Founded in 1868. Regionally accredited. **Degrees:** 832 bachelor's awarded; master's, professional, doctoral offered. **ROTC:** Army, Naval. **Location:** 10 miles from Norfolk. **Calendar:** Semester, extensive summer

session. **Full-time faculty:** 370 total. **Part-time faculty:** 109 total. **Class size:** 51% < 20, 38% 20-39, 7% 40-49, 4% 50-99, less than 1% >100. **Special facilities:** African American literature and history collection, university archives, North American Indian, African, Oceanic and Black American art collections, proton therapy institute; medical research, atmospheric sciences with satellites in earth's orbit.

Freshman class profile. 10,569 applied, 3,911 admitted, 939 enrolled.

Mid 50% test scores			
SAT critical reading:	480-540	GPA 3.0-3.49:	47%
SAT math:	480-530	GPA 2.0-2.99:	27%
ACT composite:	21-25	Out-of-state:	68%
GPA 3.75 or higher:	10%	Live on campus:	71%
GPA 3.50-3.74:	15%	Fraternities:	5%
		Sororities:	4%

Basis for selection. Academic record, rank in top half of graduating class, personal references, intended major, test scores and personal statement important. Extracurricular activities, essay, school recommendation considered. Audition required for music. **Home schooled:** Transcript of courses and grades required. Must present secondary school record if it exists, GED test scores, verification by state/regional official, SAT or ACT results.

High school preparation. College-preparatory program recommended. 17 units required. Required and recommended units include English 4, mathematics 3, social studies 2, science 2 (laboratory 2), foreign language 2 and academic electives 6. One chemistry, biology with lab, algebra I and II, geometry required.

2011-2012 Annual costs. Tuition/fees: $18,798. Room/board: $8,370. Books/supplies: $1,025. Personal expenses: $1,423.

Financial aid. **Non-need-based:** Scholarships awarded for academics, athletics, leadership, music/drama, ROTC.

Application procedures. Admission: Priority date 12/1; deadline 3/1 (postmark date). $35 fee. Admission notification on a rolling basis beginning on or about 12/15. Must reply by 5/1. **Financial aid:** Priority date 3/1; no closing date. FAFSA required. Applicants notified on a rolling basis starting 3/1; must reply within 2 week(s) of notification.

Academics. Students who have completed one semester with minimum 3.2 GPA may apply to honors program. Academic skills workshops held throughout year available for all students. Students may take courses at other Tidewater consortium schools. **Special study options:** Accelerated study, combined bachelor's/graduate degree, cooperative education, cross-registration, distance learning, double major, dual enrollment of high school students, honors, independent study, internships, study abroad, teacher certification program. Grad level programs for undergraduates, coop programs in arts, business, education, engineering, social/behavioral science. **Credit/placement by examination:** AP, CLEP, IB, SAT, ACT, institutional tests. 30 credit hours maximum toward bachelor's degree. **Support services:** Learning center, pre-admission summer program, reduced course load, remedial instruction, study skills assistance, tutoring, writing center.

Majors. Architecture: Architecture. **Biology:** General, marine, molecular. **Business:** Accounting, banking/financial services, business admin, finance, management information systems, managerial economics, marketing. **Communications:** Advertising, broadcast journalism, journalism, media studies, public relations. **Computer sciences:** General, computer science, networking. **Conservation:** Environmental science. **Education:** General, health, physical, special ed. **Engineering:** General, chemical, computer, electrical. **English:** English lit, rhetoric/composition. **Foreign languages:** Spanish. **Health services:** Audiology/speech pathology, communication disorders, nursing (RN). **History:** General. **Liberal arts:** Arts/sciences. **Math:** General. **Parks/recreation:** General, facilities management, sports admin. **Physical sciences:** Chemistry, physics. **Protective services:** Fire services admin, law enforcement admin. **Psychology:** General. **Social sciences:** Political science, sociology. **Theology:** Theology. **Visual/performing arts:** Art, commercial/advertising art, dramatic, music, music performance.

Most popular majors. Biology 6%, business/marketing 27%, communications/journalism 10%, health sciences 18%, psychology 13%, social sciences 6%.

Computing on campus. 1,500 workstations in dormitories, library, computer center, student center. Dormitories wired for high-speed internet access and linked to campus network. Commuter students can connect to campus network. Online course registration, online library, helpline, repair service, student web hosting, wireless network available.

Student life. Freshman orientation: Mandatory. Preregistration for classes offered. One-week orientation held in August. **Housing:** Guaranteed on-campus for freshmen. Coed dorms, single-sex dorms, apartments, wellness housing available. $500 deposit, deadline 5/1. **Activities:** Bands, campus ministries, choral groups, dance, drama, international student organizations, music ensembles, musical theater, opera, radio station, student government,

student newspaper, symphony orchestra, TV station, Christian student association, Big Brothers/Big Sisters, political science/pre-law club, Women in Communications, Muslim student fellowship, service learning and leadership organizations, National Leadership of Black Journalists.

Athletics. NCAA. **Intercollegiate:** Basketball, bowling W, cheerleading M, cross-country, football (tackle) M, golf, sailing, softball W, tennis, track and field, volleyball W. **Intramural:** Basketball, bowling W, softball W, swimming. **Team name:** Pirates.

Student services. Adult student services, alcohol/substance abuse counseling, chaplain/spiritual director, career counseling, services for economically disadvantaged, student employment services, financial aid counseling, health services, minority student services, on-campus daycare, personal counseling, placement for graduates, veterans' counselor, women's services. **Physically disabled:** Services for visually, speech, hearing impaired.

Contact. E-mail: admit@hamptonu.edu
Phone: (757) 727-5328 Toll-free number: (800) 624-3328
Fax: (757) 727-5095
Angela Boyd, Director of Admissions, Hampton University, Office of Admissions, Hampton, VA 23668

Hollins University
Roanoke, Virginia
www.hollins.edu

CB member
CB code: 5294

- Private 4-year university and liberal arts college for women
- Residential campus in small city
- 716 degree-seeking undergraduates: 3% part-time, 100% women, 11% African American, 2% Asian American, 5% Hispanic American, 5% international
- 204 degree-seeking graduate students
- 83% of applicants admitted
- SAT or ACT (ACT writing optional), application essay required
- 63% graduate within 6 years

General. Founded in 1842. Regionally accredited. **Degrees:** 172 bachelor's awarded; master's offered. **Location:** 175 miles from Richmond, 250 miles from Washington, DC. **Calendar:** 4-1-4, limited summer session. **Full-time faculty:** 68 total; 100% have terminal degrees, 12% minority, 53% women. **Part-time faculty:** 37 total; 57% have terminal degrees, 16% minority, 68% women. **Class size:** 85% < 20, 13% 20-39, less than 1% 40-49, less than 1% 50-99. **Special facilities:** EEG and biofeedback equipment, research facilities for chromatography, spectrophotometry, electrochemistry, and gas kinetics.

Freshman class profile. 813 applied, 672 admitted, 182 enrolled.

Mid 50% test scores			
SAT critical reading:	460-620	GPA 2.0-2.99:	16%
SAT math:	450-580	Rank in top quarter:	56%
SAT writing:	450-610	Rank in top tenth:	25%
ACT composite:	21-28	Return as sophomores:	67%
GPA 3.75 or higher:	36%	Out-of-state:	58%
GPA 3.50-3.74:	18%	Live on campus:	92%
GPA 3.0-3.49:	30%	International:	9%

Basis for selection. School achievement record, school recommendation, and test scores very important. Essay, talent/ability important. Interview, class rank, character, alumni relation, extracurricular activities, volunteer work, work experience considered. Interview recommended. **Home schooled:** Applicants encouraged to take 3 SAT Subject Tests.

High school preparation. College-preparatory program recommended. 16 units required. Required units include English 4, mathematics 3, social studies 3, science 3 and foreign language 3.

2011-2012 Annual costs. Tuition/fees: $30,795. Room/board: $10,670.

2011-2012 Financial aid. Need-based: 159 full-time freshmen applied for aid; 142 were judged to have need; 142 of these received aid. Average need met was 76%. Average scholarship/grant was $23,704; average loan $3,693. 68% of total undergraduate aid awarded as scholarships/grants, 32% as loans/jobs. **Non-need-based:** Awarded to 669 full-time undergraduates, including 182 freshmen. Scholarships awarded for academics, alumni affiliation, art, leadership, music/drama, state residency.

Application procedures. Admission: Priority date 2/1; no deadline. $40 fee, may be waived for applicants with need. Admission notification on a rolling basis beginning on or about 12/15. Must reply by May 1 or within 2 week(s) if notified thereafter. **Financial aid:** Priority date 2/15; no closing

date. FAFSA required. Applicants notified on a rolling basis starting 3/1; must reply by 5/1.

Academics. Special study options: Accelerated study, combined bachelor's/graduate degree, cross-registration, double major, dual enrollment of high school students, exchange student, independent study, internships, student-designed major, study abroad, teacher certification program, Washington semester. **Credit/placement by examination:** AP, CLEP, IB, institutional tests. **Support services:** Tutoring, writing center.

Majors. Area/ethnic studies: Women's. **Biology:** General, environmental. **Business:** General. **Communications:** Communications/speech/rhetoric. **Conservation:** Environmental studies. **English:** Creative writing, English lit. **Foreign languages:** Classics, French, Spanish. **History:** General. **Math:** General. **Philosophy/religion:** Philosophy, religion. **Physical sciences:** Chemistry, physics. **Psychology:** General. **Social sciences:** Economics, political science, sociology. **Visual/performing arts:** Art history/conservation, dance, dramatic, film/cinema/video, music, studio arts.

Most popular majors. Business/marketing 6%, English 23%, foreign language 6%, psychology 12%, social sciences 10%, visual/performing arts 19%.

Computing on campus. 100 workstations in dormitories, library, computer center, student center. Dormitories wired for high-speed internet access and linked to campus network. Commuter students can connect to campus network. Online course registration, online library, helpline, repair service, student web hosting, wireless network available.

Student life. Freshman orientation: Mandatory, $200 fee. Preregistration for classes offered. 5-day program including mini-classes and community service held week before start of fall term. **Housing:** Guaranteed on-campus for all undergraduates. Special housing for disabled, apartments, wellness housing available. $400 nonrefundable deposit. **Activities:** Campus ministries, choral groups, dance, drama, international student organizations, literary magazine, music ensembles, Model UN, musical theater, student government, student newspaper, TV station, Black Student Alliance, College Democrats, community garden, Global Interest Association, OUTloud, spirit squad, spiritual and religious life association, Students Helping Achieve Rewarding Experiences , University Republicans, wilderness adventure club.

Athletics. NCAA. **Intercollegiate:** Basketball W, equestrian W, golf W, lacrosse W, soccer W, swimming W, tennis W, volleyball W.

Student services. Adult student services, alcohol/substance abuse counseling, chaplain/spiritual director, career counseling, student employment services, financial aid counseling, health services, minority student services, personal counseling, placement for graduates, women's services. **Physically disabled:** Services for visually, hearing impaired.

Contact. E-mail: huadm@hollins.edu
Phone: (540) 362-6401 Toll-free number: (800) 456-9595
Fax: (540) 362-6218
Stephanie Niles, Vice President of Enrollment, Hollins University, PO Box 9707, Roanoke, VA 24020-1707

ITT Technical Institute: Chantilly
Chantilly, Virginia
www.itt-tech.edu   **CB code: 4086**

- For-profit 4-year technical college
- Commuter campus in large town
- 715 degree-seeking undergraduates

General. Accredited by ACICS. **Degrees:** 42 bachelor's, 180 associate awarded. **Calendar:** Quarter. **Full-time faculty:** 10 total. **Part-time faculty:** 43 total.

Basis for selection. Additional requirements for some programs.

2011-2012 Annual costs. Estimated costs as of June 2011: per-credit-hour charge, $493, depending upon level and course of study; academic fee, $200. Certain programs of study require purchase of tools, which could cost an additional $100 to $500. All costs are subject to change.

Application procedures. Admission: No deadline.

Academics. Credit/placement by examination: AP, CLEP.

Majors. Business: Business admin, construction management. **Computer sciences:** Security. **Protective services:** Law enforcement admin.

Contact. Phone: (703) 263-2541 Toll-free number: (888) 895-8324
Fax: (703) 263-0846
Steve Anderson, Director of Recruitment, ITT Technical Institute: Chantilly, 14420 Albemarle Point Place, Chantilly, VA 20151

ITT Technical Institute: Norfolk
Norfolk, Virginia
www.itt-tech.edu   **CB code: 2737**

- For-profit 4-year technical college
- Commuter campus in large city
- 1,231 degree-seeking undergraduates
- Interview required

General. Accredited by ACICS. **Degrees:** 76 bachelor's, 229 associate awarded. **Location:** 81 miles from Richmond, 145 miles from Washington, DC. **Calendar:** Quarter, extensive summer session. **Full-time faculty:** 17 total. **Part-time faculty:** 67 total.

Basis for selection. Satisfactory scores from on-site tests in English and mathematics required.

2011-2012 Annual costs. Estimated costs as of June 2011: per-credit-hour charge, $493, depending upon level and course of study; academic fee, $200. Certain programs of study require purchase of tools, which could cost an additional $100 to $500. All costs are subject to change.

Application procedures. Admission: No deadline. No application fee. Admission notification on a rolling basis. **Financial aid:** No deadline. FAFSA, institutional form required. Applicants notified on a rolling basis.

Academics. Credit/placement by examination: AP, CLEP. **Support services:** Learning center, tutoring.

Majors. Business: Business admin, construction management, e-commerce. **Communications technology:** Animation/special effects. **Computer sciences:** Programming, security. **Protective services:** Law enforcement admin.

Computing on campus. Online library available.

Student life. Freshman orientation: Available. Preregistration for classes offered.

Student services. Career counseling, student employment services, placement for graduates.

Contact. Phone: (757) 466-1260 Toll-free number: (888) 253-8324
Fax: (757) 466-7630
Jack Keesee, Director of Recruitment, ITT Technical Institute: Norfolk, 863 Glenrock Road, Suite 100, Norfolk, VA 23502

ITT Technical Institute: Richmond
Richmond, Virginia
www.itt-tech.edu   **CB code: 2748**

- For-profit 4-year technical college
- Commuter campus in small city
- 866 degree-seeking undergraduates
- Interview required

General. Accredited by ACICS. **Degrees:** 42 bachelor's, 184 associate awarded. **Location:** 98 miles from Washington, DC. **Calendar:** Quarter, extensive summer session. **Full-time faculty:** 10 total. **Part-time faculty:** 41 total.

Basis for selection. Satisfactory scores from on-site tests in English and mathematics required.

2011-2012 Annual costs. Estimated costs as of June 2011: per-credit-hour charge, $493, depending upon level and course of study; academic fee, $200. Certain programs of study require purchase of tools, which could cost an additional $100 to $500. All costs are subject to change.

Application procedures. Admission: No deadline. No application fee. Admission notification on a rolling basis. **Financial aid:** No deadline. FAFSA, institutional form required. Applicants notified on a rolling basis.

Academics. Credit/placement by examination: AP, CLEP. **Support services:** Learning center, tutoring.

Majors. Business: Business admin, construction management. **Communications technology:** Animation/special effects. **Computer sciences:** Programming, security. **Protective services:** Law enforcement admin.

Computing on campus. Online library available.

Student life. Freshman orientation: Available. Preregistration for classes offered.

Student services. Career counseling, student employment services, placement for graduates.

Contact. Phone: (804) 330-4992 Toll-free number: (888) 330-4888
Fax: (804) 330-4993
Elaine Bartoli, Director of Recruitment, ITT Technical Institute: Richmond, 300 Gateway Centre Parkway, Richmond, VA 23235

ITT Technical Institute: Springfield
Springfield, Virginia
www.itt-tech.edu   CB code: 5149

▶ For-profit 4-year technical college
▶ Commuter campus in large town

General. Accredited by ACICS. **Degrees:** 70 bachelor's, 230 associate awarded. **Calendar:** Quarter. **Full-time faculty:** 9 total. **Part-time faculty:** 64 total.

Basis for selection. Additional requirements for some programs.

2011-2012 Annual costs. Estimated costs as of June 2011: per-credit-hour charge, $493, depending upon level and course of study; academic fee, $200. Certain programs of study require purchase of tools, which could cost an additional $100 to $500. All costs are subject to change.

Academics. Credit/placement by examination: AP, CLEP.

Majors. Business: Business admin, construction management. **Computer sciences:** Programming, security. **Protective services:** Law enforcement admin.

Contact. Phone: (703) 440-9535 Toll-free number: (866) 817-8324
Fax: (703) 440-9561
Paul Ochoa, Director of Recruitment, ITT Technical Institute: Springfield, 7300 Boston Boulevard, Springfield, VA 22153

James Madison University
Harrisonburg, Virginia   CB member
www.jmu.edu   CB code: 5392

▶ Public 4-year university
▶ Residential campus in large town
▶ 17,575 degree-seeking undergraduates: 3% part-time, 59% women, 4% African American, 5% Asian American, 4% Hispanic American, 1% international
▶ 1,513 degree-seeking graduate students
▶ 60% of applicants admitted
▶ SAT or ACT (ACT writing optional) required
▶ 82% graduate within 6 years

General. Founded in 1908. Regionally accredited. **Degrees:** 3,877 bachelor's awarded; master's, professional, doctoral offered. **ROTC:** Army, Air Force. **Location:** 123 miles from Washington, DC. **Calendar:** Semester, extensive summer session. **Full-time faculty:** 924 total; 79% have terminal degrees, 8% minority, 46% women. **Part-time faculty:** 476 total; 27% have terminal degrees, 4% minority, 52% women. **Class size:** 31% < 20, 48% 20-39, 8% 40-49, 9% 50-99, 4% >100. **Special facilities:** Arboretum, observatory, planetarium, mineral museum, science on a sphere (SOS), performing arts center.

Freshman class profile. 22,864 applied, 13,705 admitted, 4,028 enrolled.

Mid 50% test scores			
SAT critical reading:	520-620	Rank in top quarter:	70%
SAT math:	530-620	Rank in top tenth:	26%
SAT writing:	520-610	Return as sophomores:	91%
ACT composite:	23-27	Out-of-state:	29%
GPA 3.75 or higher:	56%	Live on campus:	99%
GPA 3.50-3.74:	29%	International:	1%
GPA 3.0-3.49:	14%	Fraternities:	6%
GPA 2.0-2.99:	1%	Sororities:	6%

Basis for selection. Rigor of high school curriculum, as shown by the quantity and quality of courses, most important. Class rank or GPA, test scores, extracurricular activities, special skills or talents important. Counselor recommendation considered. Applicants with solid achievement in 5 or more academic courses in each of 4 years of high school have decided advantage in admissions process. Audition required for dance, music, theater programs; portfolio and interview required for art. Nursing, justice studies, media arts and design, political science, psychology, and social work students must apply to their applicable departments in addition to applying for undergraduate admission. **Home schooled:** Statement describing home school structure and mission required. **Learning Disabled:** Admission decisions are made without regard to disabilities.

High school preparation. College-preparatory program required. Required units include English 4, mathematics 4, social studies 3, science 3 (laboratory 3) and foreign language 2. 3 of same foreign language recommended, or 2 of one language and 2 of another. Social studies may include units in history. History and social studies "units required" and "units recommended" are combined for the two subjects.

2011-2012 Annual costs. Tuition/fees: $8,448; $21,738 out-of-state. Room/board: $8,340. Books/supplies: $876. Personal expenses: $1,854.

2011-2012 Financial aid. Need-based: 3,382 full-time freshmen applied for aid; 1,900 were judged to have need; 1,557 of these received aid. Average need met was 41%. Average scholarship/grant was $7,155; average loan $3,578. 55% of total undergraduate aid awarded as scholarships/grants, 45% as loans/jobs. **Non-need-based:** Awarded to 1,219 full-time undergraduates, including 402 freshmen. Scholarships awarded for academics, alumni affiliation, art, athletics, leadership, minority status, music/drama, state residency.

Application procedures. Admission: Priority date 11/1; deadline 1/15 (postmark date). $50 fee, may be waived for applicants with need. Admission notification by 4/1. Must reply by 5/1. **Financial aid:** Priority date 3/1; no closing date. FAFSA required. Applicants notified on a rolling basis starting 4/1; must reply within 4 week(s) of notification.

Academics. Special study options: Accelerated study, combined bachelor's/graduate degree, distance learning, double major, dual enrollment of high school students, ESL, honors, independent study, internships, study abroad, teacher certification program, Washington semester. Continuing education programs offered on campus. **Credit/placement by examination:** AP, CLEP, IB, institutional tests. Students enrolled in the BIS program earn up to 30 credits toward their bachelor's degrees through non-traditional means, such as prior learning experience and CLEP exams. Eight non-traditional credits, considered earned credits, the remainder treated as transfer credits when calculating the minimum credits earned at the university in order to obtain a degree from JMU. **Support services:** Learning center, study skills assistance, tutoring, writing center.

Majors. Biology: General, biotechnology. **Business:** Accounting, business admin, finance, hospitality admin, international, managerial economics, marketing. **Communications:** Communications/speech/rhetoric. **Computer sciences:** General, information systems. **Engineering:** General. **English:** English lit, technical writing. **Foreign languages:** General. **Health services:** Athletic training, community health services, health care admin, nursing (RN), speech pathology. **History:** General. **Human services:** General, social work. **Liberal arts:** Arts/sciences. **Math:** General. **Parks/recreation:** Health/fitness. **Physical sciences:** Chemistry, geology, physics. **Psychology:** General. **Social sciences:** General, anthropology, economics, geography, international relations, political science, sociology. **Visual/performing arts:** Art, art history/conservation, dramatic, music performance. **Work/family studies:** Food/nutrition.

Most popular majors. Business/marketing 16%, communications/journalism 10%, health sciences 14%, liberal arts 6%, parks/recreation 6%, social sciences 9%, visual/performing arts 6%.

Computing on campus. 1,583 workstations in dormitories, library, computer center, student center. Dormitories wired for high-speed internet access and linked to campus network. Commuter students can connect to campus network. Online course registration, online library, helpline, repair service, student web hosting, wireless network available.

Student life. Freshman orientation: Mandatory, $175 fee. Preregistration for classes offered. One-day orientation in June or July, plus 5-day program in August prior to the beginning of classes. **Housing:** Guaranteed on-campus for freshmen. Coed dorms, special housing for disabled, apartments, fraternity/sorority housing, wellness housing available. Fraternities located off campus. **Activities:** Bands, campus ministries, choral groups, dance, drama, film society, international student organizations, literary magazine, music ensembles, musical theater, opera, radio station, student government, student newspaper, symphony orchestra, 284 student organizations and clubs.

Athletics. NCAA. **Intercollegiate:** Baseball M, basketball, cheerleading, cross-country W, diving W, field hockey W, football (tackle) M, golf, lacrosse W, soccer, softball W, swimming W, tennis, track and field W, volleyball

W. **Intramural:** Basketball, bowling, football (non-tackle), golf, racquetball, soccer, softball, table tennis, tennis, volleyball. **Team name:** Dukes.

Student services. Adult student services, alcohol/substance abuse counseling, chaplain/spiritual director, career counseling, student employment services, financial aid counseling, health services, minority student services, personal counseling, placement for graduates. **Physically disabled:** Services for visually, speech, hearing impaired.

Contact. E-mail: admissions@jmu.edu
Phone: (540) 568-5681 Fax: (540) 568-3332
Michael Walsh, Director of Admissions, James Madison University, Sonner Hall, MSC 0101, Harrisonburg, VA 22807

Jefferson College of Health Sciences
Roanoke, Virginia
www.jchs.edu   **CB code: 5099**

- Private 4-year health science and nursing college
- Commuter campus in small city
- 853 degree-seeking undergraduates: 18% part-time, 81% women
- 195 degree-seeking graduate students
- 45% of applicants admitted
- SAT or ACT (ACT writing optional) required

General. Founded in 1982. Regionally accredited. Part of academic medical center including Carilion Clinic and Virginia Tech Carilion School of Medicine. Ongoing initiatives on Interprofessional Education at the undergraduate and graduate level. **Degrees:** 109 bachelor's, 70 associate awarded; master's offered. **Location:** 164 miles from Richmond, 100 miles from Greensboro, NC. **Calendar:** Semester, limited summer session. **Full-time faculty:** 68 total. **Part-time faculty:** 90 total. **Class size:** 57% < 20, 43% 20-39.

Freshman class profile. 447 applied, 201 admitted, 72 enrolled.

Mid 50% test scores			
SAT critical reading:	420-500	GPA 3.50-3.74:	27%
SAT math:	430-470	GPA 3.0-3.49:	42%
SAT writing:	420-490	GPA 2.0-2.99:	21%
ACT composite:	17-21	Out-of-state:	4%
GPA 3.75 or higher:	10%	Live on campus:	28%

Basis for selection. Certification required for some programs. SAT/ACT test scores are not required if applicant has been out of high school for three years or more. **Home schooled:** State high school equivalency certificate required. Must meet criteria in curriculum, covering 4 years of english, 3 years of mathematics, and 3 years of science instruction.

High school preparation. College-preparatory program recommended. 16 units required. Required and recommended units include English 4, mathematics 2-3 and science 2-4.

2011-2012 Annual costs. Tuition/fees: $19,750. Room only: $5,200. Books/supplies: $1,200. Personal expenses: $2,576.

Financial aid. Non-need-based: Scholarships awarded for academics.

Application procedures. Admission: No deadline. $35 fee, may be waived for applicants with need, free for online applicants. Admission notification on a rolling basis. Must reply by May 1 or within 2 week(s) if notified thereafter. **Financial aid:** No deadline. FAFSA, institutional form required. Applicants notified on a rolling basis; must reply within 2 week(s) of notification.

Academics. Special study options: Accelerated study, cross-registration, distance learning, double major, dual enrollment of high school students, independent study, internships, liberal arts/career combination. **Credit/placement by examination:** AP, CLEP, IB, SAT, ACT, institutional tests. Maximum of 18 credit hours may be satisfied by CLEP/DANTES examinations. **Support services:** Learning center, pre-admission summer program, study skills assistance, tutoring, writing center.

Majors. Biology: Biomedical sciences. **Health services:** Athletic training, EMT paramedic, health care admin, nursing (RN), premedicine, prepharmacy. **Parks/recreation:** Exercise sciences. **Protective services:** Firefighting. **Psychology:** Medical.

Most popular majors. Biology 7%, health sciences 88%.

Computing on campus. 60 workstations in library, computer center. Dormitories wired for high-speed internet access and linked to campus network. Online course registration, online library, helpline, wireless network available.

Student life. Freshman orientation: Mandatory. Preregistration for classes offered. One-day orientation held multiple times during summer. **Housing:** Coed dorms available. $250 nonrefundable deposit. **Activities:** Student government, student newspaper, student nurse association, student occupational therapy association, student physical therapy assistant assembly, AMSA, PA Society, Hands of Healing.

Athletics. Team name: Blue Healers.

Student services. Adult student services, career counseling, student employment services, financial aid counseling, personal counseling. **Physically disabled:** Services for visually impaired.

Contact. E-mail: admissions@jchs.edu
Phone: (540) 985-8483 Toll-free number: (888) 985-8483
Fax: (540) 985-9773
Judith McKeon, Director of Admissions, Jefferson College of Health Sciences, 101 Elm Avenue, SE, Roanoke, VA 24013-2222

Liberty University
Lynchburg, Virginia   **CB member**
www.liberty.edu   **CB code: 5385**

- Private 4-year university affiliated with Baptist faith
- Residential campus in small city
- 11,457 degree-seeking undergraduates: 3% part-time, 52% women, 7% African American, 1% Asian American, 4% Hispanic American, 7% international
- 1,021 degree-seeking graduate students
- SAT or ACT (ACT writing optional), application essay required
- 54% graduate within 6 years

General. Founded in 1971. Regionally accredited. **Degrees:** 1,696 bachelor's, 7 associate awarded; master's, professional, doctoral offered. **ROTC:** Army, Air Force. **Location:** 120 miles from Richmond, 150 miles from Raleigh, NC. **Calendar:** Semester, limited summer session. **Full-time faculty:** 634 total. **Part-time faculty:** 1,254 total. **Class size:** 41% < 20, 43% 20-39, 4% 40-49, 6% 50-99, 5% >100. **Special facilities:** Snowflex ski slope, ice rink, running and hiking trails, paintball fields, indoor soccer complex.

Freshman class profile.

Mid 50% test scores			
SAT critical reading:	470-590	GPA 2.0-2.99:	23%
SAT math:	450-570	Rank in top quarter:	44%
SAT writing:	450-570	Rank in top tenth:	19%
ACT composite:	20-25	Return as sophomores:	78%
GPA 3.75 or higher:	27%	Out-of-state:	65%
GPA 3.50-3.74:	18%	Live on campus:	91%
GPA 3.0-3.49:	32%	International:	6%

Basis for selection. Secondary school record, standardized test scores, and essay most important. Applicants who fail to meet the minimum required GPA may be admitted on academic warning status and will be limited to 13 semester hours of coursework. TOEFL required for international students. **Home schooled:** Transcript of courses and grades required.

High school preparation. College-preparatory program recommended. 17 units recommended. Recommended units include English 4, mathematics 3, social studies 2, science 2 (laboratory 2), foreign language 2 and academic electives 4.

2012-2013 Annual costs. Tuition/fees (projected): $19,968. Room/board: $7,050. Books/supplies: $1,400. Personal expenses: $1,000.

Financial aid. Non-need-based: Scholarships awarded for academics, alumni affiliation, athletics, leadership, music/drama, religious affiliation, ROTC, state residency.

Application procedures. Admission: Priority date 1/31; no deadline. $40 fee, may be waived for applicants with need. Admission notification on a rolling basis. Must reply by May 1 or within 2 week(s) if notified thereafter. **Financial aid:** Closing date 3/1. FAFSA required. Applicants notified on a rolling basis starting 3/15; must reply within 3 week(s) of notification.

Academics. Special study options: Accelerated study, cooperative education, distance learning, double major, dual enrollment of high school students, ESL, external degree, honors, independent study, internships, student-designed major, study abroad, teacher certification program, Washington semester, weekend college. Associate school of the Institute of Holy Land Studies in Jerusalem. **Credit/placement by examination:** AP, CLEP, IB, SAT, ACT, institutional tests. 30 credit hours maximum toward bachelor's

degree. **Support services:** Learning center, reduced course load, remedial instruction, study skills assistance, tutoring, writing center.

Majors. Biology: General, biochemistry. **Business:** General, accounting, business admin, management information systems. **Communications:** Communications/speech/rhetoric. **Computer sciences:** General, information technology. **Education:** ESL. **Engineering:** Computer, electrical, industrial, software, systems. **English:** English lit. **Foreign languages:** Spanish. **Health services:** Athletic training, nursing (RN), public health ed. **History:** General. **Liberal arts:** Arts/sciences. **Math:** General. **Parks/recreation:** Exercise sciences, health/fitness, sports admin. **Philosophy/religion:** Philosophy, religion. **Protective services:** Criminal justice. **Psychology:** General. **Social sciences:** General, political science. **Theology:** Bible, missionary, pastoral counseling, sacred music, youth ministry. **Visual/performing arts:** Dramatic, graphic design, music. **Work/family studies:** General, clothing/textiles, family studies.

Most popular majors. Business/marketing 10%, communications/journalism 7%, health sciences 12%, parks/recreation 7%, philosophy/religious studies 11%, psychology 10%, social sciences 6%, visual/performing arts 7%.

Computing on campus. 800 workstations in library, computer center, student center. Dormitories wired for high-speed internet access and linked to campus network. Commuter students can connect to campus network. Online course registration, online library, helpline, repair service, wireless network available.

Student life. Freshman orientation: Mandatory. Preregistration for classes offered. **Policies:** All students involved in Christian or community service. **Housing:** Guaranteed on-campus for all undergraduates. Single-sex dorms, special housing for disabled, apartments, wellness housing available. $250 nonrefundable deposit. Students required to live on campus unless living with parents, over age 21, or married. **Activities:** Bands, campus ministries, choral groups, drama, literary magazine, music ensembles, musical theater, radio station, student government, student newspaper, symphony orchestra, TV station, Circle K, Youthquest, Light Ministries, Fellowship of Christian Athletes, Students Teaching Elementary School, College Republicans, Campus SERVE.

Athletics. NCAA. **Intercollegiate:** Baseball M, basketball, cheerleading, cross-country, football (tackle) M, golf M, soccer, softball W, tennis, track and field, volleyball W. **Intramural:** Basketball, football (non-tackle), soccer, softball, table tennis, tennis, volleyball. **Team name:** Flames.

Student services. Chaplain/spiritual director, career counseling, student employment services, financial aid counseling, health services, minority student services, personal counseling, placement for graduates, veterans' counselor, women's services. **Physically disabled:** Services for hearing impaired.

Contact. E-mail: admissions@liberty.edu
Phone: (434) 582-5985 Toll-free number: (800) 543-5317
Fax: (800) 542-2311
Terrell Elam, Director of Residential Admissions, Liberty University, 1971 University Boulevard, Lynchburg, VA 24502

Longwood University
Farmville, Virginia
www.longwood.edu

CB member
CB code: 5368

- Public 4-year university
- Residential campus in small town
- 4,160 degree-seeking undergraduates: 4% part-time, 66% women, 6% African American, 1% Asian American, 3% Hispanic American
- 353 degree-seeking graduate students
- 75% of applicants admitted
- SAT or ACT (ACT writing optional), application essay required
- 60% graduate within 6 years

General. Founded in 1839. Regionally accredited. **Degrees:** 820 bachelor's awarded; master's offered. **ROTC:** Army. **Location:** 65 miles from Richmond, 60 miles from Charlottesville. **Calendar:** Semester, limited summer session. **Full-time faculty:** 222 total; 85% have terminal degrees, 8% minority, 48% women. **Part-time faculty:** 78 total; 22% have terminal degrees, 6% minority, 60% women. **Class size:** 47% < 20, 47% 20-39, 5% 40-49, 1% 50-99. **Special facilities:** Golf course, rock climbing wall, flora collection, visual arts center, greenhouse, fitness center.

Freshman class profile. 4,080 applied, 3,044 admitted, 1,074 enrolled.

Mid 50% test scores			
SAT critical reading:	470-560	GPA 2.0-2.99:	15%
SAT math:	470-550	Rank in top quarter:	38%
ACT composite:	20-24	Rank in top tenth:	12%
GPA 3.75 or higher:	20%	Return as sophomores:	78%
GPA 3.50-3.74:	18%	Out-of-state:	3%
GPA 3.0-3.49:	47%	Live on campus:	98%

Basis for selection. Rank in top half of class, combined SAT score (exclusive of Writing) of 1000 minimum and GPA of 2.7 minimum in college preparatory courses required. Extracurricular activities and recommendations also considered. Early Action consideration, applicants must have 3.0 GPA and 1000 on SAT (exclusive of Writing). Audition required for music. **Home schooled:** Statement describing home school structure and mission, letter of recommendation (nonparent) required. Applications reviewed on case-by-case basis.

High school preparation. College-preparatory program required. 24 units required. Required and recommended units include English 4, mathematics 3-4, social studies 2, history 2, science 3-4 (laboratory 2-3), foreign language 2-4 and visual/performing arts 1. 2 physical education.

2011-2012 Annual costs. Tuition/fees: $10,530; $21,720 out-of-state. Room/board: $8,760. Books/supplies: $1,000. Personal expenses: $1,500.

2010-2011 Financial aid. Need-based: 767 full-time freshmen applied for aid; 547 were judged to have need; 528 of these received aid. Average need met was 78%. Average scholarship/grant was $5,802; average loan $6,790. 43% of total undergraduate aid awarded as scholarships/grants, 57% as loans/jobs. **Non-need-based:** Awarded to 398 full-time undergraduates, including 79 freshmen. Scholarships awarded for academics, alumni affiliation, art, athletics, leadership, music/drama, ROTC, state residency.

Application procedures. Admission: Priority date 3/1; no deadline. $50 fee, may be waived for applicants with need. Admission notification on a rolling basis beginning on or about 1/15. Must reply by May 1 or within 1 week(s) if notified thereafter. **Financial aid:** Priority date 3/1; no closing date. FAFSA required. Applicants notified on a rolling basis starting 4/1; must reply within 4 week(s) of notification.

Academics. Special study options: Accelerated study, combined bachelor's/graduate degree, cross-registration, distance learning, double major, dual enrollment of high school students, honors, independent study, internships, study abroad, teacher certification program. Summer field programs in archaeology and botany. **Credit/placement by examination:** AP, CLEP, IB, institutional tests. **Support services:** Learning center, reduced course load, study skills assistance, tutoring, writing center.

Honors college/program. Students must have at least a 1200 on the SAT (combined Critical Reading and Math only) and at least a 3.5 GPA to be considered for the Cormier Honors College. About 40-50 freshman admitted each year.

Majors. Biology: General. **Business:** Business admin. **Communications:** Communications/speech/rhetoric. **Computer sciences:** Computer science. **English:** English lit. **Foreign languages:** General. **Health services:** Athletic training, audiology/speech pathology, community health services, recreational therapy. **History:** General. **Human services:** Social work. **Liberal arts:** Arts/sciences. **Math:** General. **Parks/recreation:** Health/fitness. **Physical sciences:** Chemistry, physics. **Protective services:** Criminal justice. **Psychology:** General. **Social sciences:** Anthropology, economics, political science, sociology. **Visual/performing arts:** General.

Most popular majors. Biology 6%, business/marketing 20%, communications/journalism 7%, liberal arts 18%, psychology 7%, security/protective services 6%, visual/performing arts 7%.

Computing on campus. PC or laptop required. 197 workstations in dormitories, library, computer center, student center. Dormitories wired for high-speed internet access and linked to campus network. Commuter students can connect to campus network. Online course registration, online library, helpline, repair service, student web hosting, wireless network available.

Student life. Freshman orientation: Mandatory, $150 fee. Preregistration for classes offered. One-day orientation held during spring and summer. **Policies:** Freshmen not permitted cars on campus. **Housing:** Guaranteed on-campus for freshmen. Coed dorms, single-sex dorms, special housing for disabled, apartments, fraternity/sorority housing, wellness housing available. $400 nonrefundable deposit, deadline 5/1. **Activities:** Bands, campus ministries, choral groups, dance, drama, music ensembles, radio station, student government, student newspaper, College Democrats, unity alliance, interfraternity council, Habitat for Humanity, Alpha Phi Omega, Students Educating for Active Leadership, College Republicans, Peer Helpers, Big Sibling Program.

Athletics. NCAA. **Intercollegiate:** Baseball M, basketball, cheerleading, cross-country, field hockey W, golf, soccer, softball W, tennis. **Intramural:** Basketball, bowling, football (non-tackle), soccer, softball, tennis, volleyball. **Team name:** Lancers.

Student services. Alcohol/substance abuse counseling, career counseling, student employment services, financial aid counseling, health services, minority student services, personal counseling, placement for graduates, women's services. **Physically disabled:** Services for visually, speech, hearing impaired.

Contact. E-mail: admissions@longwood.edu
Phone: (434) 395-2060 Toll-free number: (800) 281-4677 ext. 2
Fax: (434) 395-2332
Sallie McMullin, Dean of Admissions, Longwood University, 201 High Street, Farmville, VA 23909-1898

Lynchburg College
Lynchburg, Virginia
www.lynchburg.edu

CB member
CB code: 5372

- Private 4-year liberal arts college affiliated with Christian Church (Disciples of Christ)
- Residential campus in small city
- 2,208 degree-seeking undergraduates: 3% part-time, 59% women, 10% African American, 1% Asian American, 3% Hispanic American
- 417 degree-seeking graduate students
- 68% of applicants admitted
- SAT or ACT (ACT writing optional) required
- 52% graduate within 6 years

General. Founded in 1903. Regionally accredited. **Degrees:** 437 bachelor's awarded; master's, professional, doctoral offered. **Location:** 180 miles from Washington, DC, 120 miles from Richmond, 50 miles from Roanoke. **Calendar:** Semester, extensive summer session. **Full-time faculty:** 176 total; 76% have terminal degrees, 6% minority, 51% women. **Part-time faculty:** 118 total; 31% have terminal degrees, 3% minority, 55% women. **Class size:** 61% < 20, 37% 20-39, less than 1% 40-49, less than 1% 50-99. **Special facilities:** Nature study center, center for media development, forensic cadaver lab, astronomical observatory, fine arts gallery.

Freshman class profile. 4,617 applied, 3,151 admitted, 609 enrolled.

Mid 50% test scores		GPA 2.0-2.99:	35%
SAT critical reading:	440-560	Rank in top quarter:	42%
SAT math:	450-550	Rank in top tenth:	16%
SAT writing:	440-540	Return as sophomores:	73%
ACT composite:	19-24	Out-of-state:	34%
GPA 3.75 or higher:	18%	Live on campus:	91%
GPA 3.50-3.74:	15%	International:	1%
GPA 3.0-3.49:	32%		

Basis for selection. School record, test scores, school and community involvement, recommendation, academic quality of secondary school attended, essay, interview important. Audition recommended for music, theater arts programs; portfolio recommended for studio art. Essay or personal statement strongly encouraged, but not formally required. **Learning Disabled:** Documentation must be received no later than 45 days prior to the first day of class.

High school preparation. College-preparatory program required. 16 units required; 20 recommended. Required and recommended units include English 4, mathematics 3-4, social studies 2, history 2, science 3-4 (laboratory 2), foreign language 2-3 and academic electives 1.

2011-2012 Annual costs. Tuition/fees: $30,805. Room/board: $8,380. Books/supplies: $1,000. Personal expenses: $900.

2011-2012 Financial aid. Need-based: 565 full-time freshmen applied for aid; 488 were judged to have need; 488 of these received aid. Average need met was 82%. Average scholarship/grant was $20,421; average loan $3,153. 76% of total undergraduate aid awarded as scholarships/grants, 24% as loans/jobs. **Non-need-based:** Awarded to 651 full-time undergraduates, including 176 freshmen. Scholarships awarded for academics, leadership, music/drama, religious affiliation.

Application procedures. Admission: No deadline. $30 fee, may be waived for applicants with need, free for online applicants. Admission notification on a rolling basis beginning on or about 9/1. Must reply by May 1 or within 2 week(s) if notified thereafter. **Financial aid:** Priority date 3/1; no closing date. FAFSA required. Applicants notified on a rolling basis starting 3/5; must reply by 5/1 or within 2 week(s) of notification.

Academics. Special study options: Accelerated study, combined bachelor's/graduate degree, cross-registration, distance learning, double major, honors, independent study, internships, study abroad, teacher certification program. **Credit/placement by examination:** AP, CLEP, IB, institutional tests. **Support services:** Study skills assistance, tutoring, writing center.

Majors. Biology: General, biomedical sciences, exercise physiology. **Business:** Accounting, business admin, human resources, management science, marketing. **Communications:** General. **Computer sciences:** General. **Conservation:** Environmental science, environmental studies. **Education:** Elementary, secondary. **English:** English lit. **Foreign languages:** French, Spanish. **Health services:** Athletic training, nursing (RN), public health ed. **History:** General. **Parks/recreation:** General. **Philosophy/religion:** Philosophy, religion. **Physical sciences:** Chemistry, physics. **Psychology:** General. **Social sciences:** Criminology, economics, international relations, political science, sociology. **Visual/performing arts:** Art, dramatic, music.

Most popular majors. Business/marketing 11%, communications/journalism 8%, education 10%, English 6%, health sciences 15%, parks/recreation 6%, social sciences 12%, visual/performing arts 6%.

Computing on campus. Dormitories wired for high-speed internet access and linked to campus network. Online library, repair service, wireless network available.

Student life. Freshman orientation: Mandatory. Preregistration for classes offered. Held during summer for fall semester students and in January for spring semester students. Separate but concurrent orientation programs available to parents and other guests of new students. **Policies:** We promote and adhere to our Honor System. **Housing:** Guaranteed on-campus for all undergraduates. Coed dorms, single-sex dorms, special housing for disabled, apartments, fraternity/sorority housing, wellness housing available. $200 non-refundable deposit, deadline 5/1. College-owned townhomes, houses, and special interest houses available. **Activities:** Bands, campus ministries, choral groups, dance, drama, film society, international student organizations, literary magazine, music ensembles, Model UN, musical theater, student government, student newspaper, symphony orchestra, over 100 clubs and organizations.

Athletics. NCAA. **Intercollegiate:** Baseball M, basketball, cheerleading M, cross-country, equestrian, field hockey W, golf M, lacrosse, soccer, softball W, tennis, track and field, volleyball W. **Intramural:** Basketball, football (non-tackle), lacrosse M, soccer, softball, tennis, volleyball. **Team name:** Hornets.

Student services. Adult student services, chaplain/spiritual director, career counseling, student employment services, financial aid counseling, health services, minority student services, personal counseling, veterans' counselor. **Physically disabled:** Services for visually, hearing impaired.

Contact. E-mail: admissions@lynchburg.edu
Phone: (434) 544-8300 Toll-free number: (800) 426-8101 ext. 8300
Fax: (434) 544-8653
Sharon Walters-Bower, Director of Admissions, Lynchburg College, 1501 Lakeside Drive, Lynchburg, VA 24501-3199

Mary Baldwin College
Staunton, Virginia
www.mbc.edu

CB member
CB code: 5397

- Private 4-year liberal arts college for women affiliated with Presbyterian Church (USA)
- Residential campus in large town
- 1,385 degree-seeking undergraduates: 24% part-time, 96% women
- 261 graduate students
- 44% of applicants admitted
- SAT or ACT (ACT writing optional), interview required
- 47% graduate within 6 years; 25% enter graduate study

General. Founded in 1842. Regionally accredited. Bachelor's degree available for younger women (13-15) in program for exceptionally gifted. Adult degree program available on main campus and at several satellite campuses throughout Virginia. Men admitted to adult program. The Virginia Women's Institute for Leadership program. **Degrees:** 235 bachelor's awarded; master's offered. **ROTC:** Army, Naval, Air Force. **Location:** 100 miles from Richmond, 150 miles from Washington, DC. **Calendar:** 4-1-4, limited summer session. **Full-time faculty:** 80 total; 98% have terminal degrees, 12% minority, 58% women. **Part-time faculty:** 56 total; 29% minority, 70% women. **Class size:** 68% < 20, 30% 20-39, less than 1% 40-49, less than 1% 50-99. **Special facilities:** Electron microscope, gas chromatoscope.

Four-Year Colleges

Freshman class profile. 5,426 applied, 2,398 admitted, 289 enrolled.

Mid 50% test scores			
SAT critical reading:	440-570	GPA 3.0-3.49:	28%
SAT math:	420-500	GPA 2.0-2.99:	32%
SAT writing:	430-540	Rank in top quarter:	49%
ACT composite:	18-24	Rank in top tenth:	20%
GPA 3.75 or higher:	26%	Out-of-state:	47%
GPA 3.50-3.74:	13%	Live on campus:	94%

Basis for selection. School achievement record most important; test scores, involvement in school or civic groups also important; recommendations considered; 3.0 GPA recommended. Portfolio recommended for art majors.

High school preparation. Required and recommended units include English 4, mathematics 3, social studies 3, science 2 (laboratory 1), foreign language 2-3 and academic electives 2. Higher requirements for Virginia Women's Institute for Leadership.

2011-2012 Annual costs. Tuition/fees: $26,960. Room/board: $7,790. Books/supplies: $900. Personal expenses: $1,000.

Financial aid. Non-need-based: Scholarships awarded for academics, leadership, state residency.

Application procedures. Admission: No deadline. $35 fee, may be waived for applicants with need. Admission notification on a rolling basis beginning on or about 9/1. Regular admission notification within 48 hours of receipt of all necessary materials. It is recommended for International Students to get applications in by June 1 to allow time to get a visa. **Financial aid:** Priority date 3/1; no closing date. FAFSA required. Applicants notified on a rolling basis starting 2/27; must reply by 5/1.

Academics. Students complete requirements in experiential education, international education, women's studies. May term offers opportunity for individualized programming, externships, study abroad. Institute combines academics, physical training and leadership development in rigorous 4-year bachelor's program. **Special study options:** Accelerated study, combined bachelor's/graduate degree, cooperative education, cross-registration, distance learning, double major, dual enrollment of high school students, ESL, exchange student, external degree, honors, independent study, internships, liberal arts/career combination, semester at sea, student-designed major, study abroad, teacher certification program. Summer exchange program with Doshisha Women's College in Kyoto, Japan. **Credit/placement by examination:** AP, CLEP, IB, institutional tests. 25% of required credits may be counted toward bachelor's degree. **Support services:** Learning center, reduced course load, study skills assistance, tutoring, writing center.

Honors college/program. Minimum SAT score of 1150 (exclusive of Writing) or ACT score of 25, minimum 3.5 high school GPA, essay, interview required for admission. About 36 freshmen admitted.

Majors. Area/ethnic studies: Asian. **Biology:** General. **Business:** Business admin. **Communications:** Communications/speech/rhetoric. **Computer sciences:** General. **English:** English lit. **Foreign languages:** French, Spanish. **Health services:** Clinical lab science, health care admin. **History:** General. **Math:** General, applied. **Philosophy/religion:** Philosophy, religion. **Physical sciences:** Chemistry, physics. **Psychology:** General. **Social sciences:** Anthropology, economics, international relations, political science, sociology. **Visual/performing arts:** Art, dramatic, music, studio arts management.

Most popular majors. Business/marketing 11%, communications/journalism 6%, history 16%, psychology 18%, social sciences 20%, visual/performing arts 11%.

Computing on campus. 244 workstations in dormitories, library, computer center. Dormitories wired for high-speed internet access and linked to campus network. Commuter students can connect to campus network. Online course registration, online library, helpline, repair service, wireless network available.

Student life. Freshman orientation: Mandatory. Preregistration for classes offered. **Policies:** College prohibits drinking under age 21. Honor code observed. Working dogs (to aid the handicaped) are allowed in dorm rooms. **Housing:** Guaranteed on-campus for all undergraduates. Apartments, wellness housing available. $300 partly refundable deposit. **Activities:** Marching band, choral groups, dance, drama, film society, literary magazine, music ensembles, musical theater, radio station, student government, student newspaper, TV station, Circle K, Habitat for Humanity, College Republicans, College Democrats, Black Student Alliance, Latinas Unidas, Christian Student Union, Campus Crusade for Christ, Anointed Voices of Praise Gospel Choir.

Athletics. NCAA. **Intercollegiate:** Basketball W, cross-country W, field hockey W, soccer W, softball W, swimming W, tennis W, volleyball W. **Team name:** Squirrels.

Student services. Adult student services, chaplain/spiritual director, career counseling, student employment services, health services, minority student services, personal counseling, placement for graduates, women's services. **Physically disabled:** Services for visually, hearing impaired.

Contact. E-mail: admit@mbc.edu
Phone: (540) 887-7019 Toll-free number: (800) 468-2262
Fax: (540) 887-7279
Andrew Modlin, Executive Director of Enrollment Management, Mary Baldwin College, Office of Admissions, Staunton, VA 24401

Marymount University
Arlington, Virginia
www.marymount.edu
CB member
CB code: 5405

- Private 4-year university affiliated with Roman Catholic Church
- Residential campus in small city
- 2,350 degree-seeking undergraduates: 11% part-time, 70% women
- 1,216 degree-seeking graduate students
- 78% of applicants admitted
- SAT or ACT (ACT writing optional) required
- 57% graduate within 6 years

General. Founded in 1950. Regionally accredited. Courses taught in three sites: Marymount's main campus, the Ballston Center in Arlington, VA, and Reston Center in Reston, VA. **Degrees:** 583 bachelor's awarded; master's, doctoral offered. **ROTC:** Army. **Location:** 7 miles from Washington, DC. **Calendar:** Semester, extensive summer session. **Full-time faculty:** 146 total; 87% have terminal degrees, 7% minority, 71% women. **Part-time faculty:** 200 total; 46% have terminal degrees, 10% minority, 56% women. **Class size:** 50% < 20, 49% 20-39, less than 1% 40-49, less than 1% 50-99.

Freshman class profile. 2,024 applied, 1,574 admitted, 409 enrolled.

Mid 50% test scores			
SAT critical reading:	440-560	GPA 2.0-2.99:	40%
SAT math:	430-540	Rank in top quarter:	31%
SAT writing:	430-550	Rank in top tenth:	12%
ACT composite:	19-23	Return as sophomores:	70%
GPA 3.75 or higher:	11%	Out-of-state:	50%
GPA 3.50-3.74:	13%	Live on campus:	56%
GPA 3.0-3.49:	35%	International:	6%

Basis for selection. GPA in academic courses and test scores most important. Class rank, recommendations from guidance counselors and teachers also important. Essay, interview recommended.

High school preparation. College-preparatory program required. 15 units required. Required and recommended units include English 4, mathematics 3, social studies 3, science 2 and foreign language 3.

2011-2012 Annual costs. Tuition/fees: $23,972. Room/board: $10,580. Books/supplies: $1,000. Personal expenses: $1,300.

2010-2011 Financial aid. Non-need-based: Scholarships awarded for academics, alumni affiliation, leadership, ROTC, state residency.

Application procedures. Admission: Priority date 4/1; no deadline. $40 fee, may be waived for applicants with need. Notified within 3-4 weeks after application received. Must reply by May 1 or within 3 week(s) if notified thereafter. **Financial aid:** Priority date 3/1; no closing date. FAFSA required. Applicants notified on a rolling basis starting 3/15; must reply within 2 week(s) of notification.

Academics. All undergraduates complete internship before graduation. **Special study options:** Accelerated study, combined bachelor's/graduate degree, cross-registration, distance learning, double major, ESL, honors, independent study, internships, student-designed major, study abroad, teacher certification program. Member of the Consortium of Universities of the Washington Metropolitan Area. **Credit/placement by examination:** AP, CLEP, IB, institutional tests. 30 credit hours maximum toward bachelor's degree. Credit for prior work/life experience available through Portfolio Assessment and Credit by Examination program. **Support services:** Learning center, reduced course load, tutoring.

Honors college/program. Admission competitive and limited to 20 students each year. Minimum high school or college GPA of 3.5, minimum composite SAT score of 1200 (exclusive of Writing) or ACT score of 26, minimum TOEFL score of 617 (paper), 260 (computer), or 105 (internet) for international students, and strong background in English composition and literature.

Majors. Biology: General, cellular/molecular. **Business:** Business admin, fashion, human resources. **Communications:** General. **Computer sciences:**

Information technology. **English:** English lit. **Health services:** Medical records admin, nursing (RN). **History:** General. **Liberal arts:** Arts/sciences. **Math:** General. **Philosophy/religion:** Philosophy, religion. **Protective services:** Forensics, law enforcement admin. **Psychology:** General. **Social sciences:** Criminology, economics, political science, sociology. **Visual/performing arts:** Fashion design, graphic design, interior design, studio arts.

Most popular majors. Business/marketing 19%, health sciences 29%, visual/performing arts 15%.

Computing on campus. 270 workstations in dormitories, library, computer center. Dormitories wired for high-speed internet access and linked to campus network. Commuter students can connect to campus network. Online course registration, online library, helpline, wireless network available.

Student life. Freshman orientation: Mandatory. Preregistration for classes offered. 3 weekend sessions in summer. **Housing:** Guaranteed on-campus for freshmen. Coed dorms, single-sex dorms available. $300 nonrefundable deposit, deadline 5/1. **Activities:** Campus ministries, choral groups, dance, drama, international student organizations, literary magazine, student government, student newspaper, African Caribbean student association, Black Student Alliance, College Democrats, College Republicans, Circle K, Global Charity Project, Latino student association, Muslim student association, Students in Free Enterprise.

Athletics. NCAA. **Intercollegiate:** Basketball, cross-country, golf M, lacrosse, soccer, swimming, volleyball W. **Intramural:** Basketball, football (non-tackle), golf M, soccer, softball, swimming, volleyball, water polo, weight lifting. **Team name:** Saints.

Student services. Alcohol/substance abuse counseling, chaplain/spiritual director, career counseling, student employment services, financial aid counseling, health services, personal counseling. **Physically disabled:** Services for visually, speech, hearing impaired.

Contact. E-mail: admissions@marymount.edu
Phone: (703) 284-1500 Toll-free number: (800) 548-7638
Fax: (703) 522-0349
Michael Canfield, Director, Undergraduate Admissions, Marymount University, 2807 North Glebe Road, Arlington, VA 22207-4299

National College: Salem
Roanoke, Virginia
www.national-college.edu   **CB code: 5502**

- For-profit 4-year business college
- Commuter campus in large city
- 415 degree-seeking undergraduates
- Interview required

General. Founded in 1886. Accredited by ACICS. **Degrees:** 23 bachelor's, 102 associate awarded; master's offered. **Calendar:** Quarter, limited summer session. **Full-time faculty:** 15 total. **Part-time faculty:** 55 total.

Basis for selection. Open admission.

2011-2012 Annual costs. Tuition/fees: $13,770.

Financial aid. All financial aid based on need.

Application procedures. Admission: Closing date 9/1 (receipt date). $50 fee, may be waived for applicants with need. Admission notification on a rolling basis. **Financial aid:** No deadline. FAFSA required. Applicants notified on a rolling basis.

Academics. Special study options: Double major, internships. **Credit/placement by examination:** AP, CLEP, institutional tests. **Support services:** Tutoring.

Majors. Business: Accounting, business admin.

Computing on campus. 35 workstations in library, computer center.

Student life. Freshman orientation: Mandatory. Preregistration for classes offered. **Housing:** Coed dorms available. Hotel accommodations available. **Activities:** Student government.

Student services. Career counseling, financial aid counseling, placement for graduates.

Contact. Phone: (540) 986-1800 Fax: (540) 444-4198
Ron Smith, Director of Admissions & International Programs, National College: Salem, PO Box 6400, Roanoke, VA 24017-0400

Norfolk State University
Norfolk, Virginia   **CB member**
www.nsu.edu   **CB code: 5864**

- Public 4-year university
- Commuter campus in small city
- 6,222 degree-seeking undergraduates: 20% part-time, 65% women, 89% African American, 1% Asian American, 1% Hispanic American
- 799 degree-seeking graduate students
- 65% of applicants admitted
- SAT or ACT (ACT writing optional) required
- 34% graduate within 6 years

General. Founded in 1935. Regionally accredited. **Degrees:** 728 bachelor's, 79 associate awarded; master's, doctoral offered. **ROTC:** Army, Naval. **Location:** 5 miles from downtown. **Calendar:** Semester, extensive summer session. **Full-time faculty:** 270 total. **Part-time faculty:** 105 total. **Special facilities:** Planetarium, crystal laboratory, laser laboratory, nuclear magnetic resonance laboratory, institute for service learning, literacy center for entrepreneurial studies, center for materials research, institute for minorities in applied sciences, assistive technology laboratory.

Freshman class profile. 4,125 applied, 2,692 admitted, 923 enrolled.

Mid 50% test scores			
SAT critical reading:	400-480	Rank in top quarter:	17%
SAT math:	390-470	Rank in top tenth:	10%
ACT composite:	17-20	Return as sophomores:	73%
GPA 3.75 or higher:	4%	Out-of-state:	21%
GPA 3.50-3.74:	5%	Live on campus:	81%
GPA 3.0-3.49:	26%		
GPA 2.0-2.99:	65%		

Basis for selection. Combination of academic preparation, aptitude, achievements, and motivation predict a reasonable probability of success are most important. Interview recommended for electronics, engineering, nursing programs; audition recommended for music; portfolio recommended for art. **Home schooled:** Transcript of courses and grades required.

High school preparation. 22 units required. Required units include English 4, mathematics 3, history 3, science 3 and academic electives 9. 2 science required for nursing applicants: 1 chemistry, 1 biology, 2 high school math (1 algebra), 2 science required for business applicants. 1 geometry, 2 algebra recommended for mathematics applicants. 2 mathematics must include algebra for computer science applicants.

2011-2012 Annual costs. Tuition/fees: $6,700; $21,478 out-of-state. Room/board: $7,927. Books/supplies: $1,125. Personal expenses: $1,819.

Financial aid. Non-need-based: Scholarships awarded for academics, alumni affiliation, athletics, leadership, music/drama, ROTC, state residency.

Application procedures. Admission: Closing date 5/31 (postmark date). $35 fee, may be waived for applicants with need. Admission notification on a rolling basis. Must reply by May 1 or within 2 week(s) if notified thereafter. **Financial aid:** Priority date 5/31; no closing date. FAFSA required. Applicants notified on a rolling basis starting 4/1; must reply within 2 week(s) of notification.

Academics. Special study options: Combined bachelor's/graduate degree, cooperative education, cross-registration, distance learning, double major, dual enrollment of high school students, ESL, honors, independent study, internships, liberal arts/career combination, teacher certification program. **Credit/placement by examination:** AP, CLEP, SAT, ACT, institutional tests. No limit on number of credits university will accept, as long as student passes exam and has departmental approval. **Support services:** Learning center, reduced course load, study skills assistance, tutoring, writing center.

Majors. Biology: General. **Business:** General, accounting, hospitality admin. **Communications:** Journalism, media studies. **Computer sciences:** General. **Education:** Business, kindergarten/preschool, special ed, trade/industrial. **Engineering:** Electrical. **English:** English lit. **Health services:** Clinical lab science, health care admin, medical records admin, nursing (RN). **History:** General. **Human services:** Social work. **Math:** General. **Parks/recreation:** Exercise sciences. **Physical sciences:** Chemistry, optics, physics. **Psychology:** General. **Social sciences:** Political science, sociology. **Visual/performing arts:** Art, music.

Most popular majors. Business/marketing 17%, communications/journalism 6%, health sciences 13%, interdisciplinary studies 12%, psychology 8%, social sciences 7%.

Computing on campus. 1,010 workstations in dormitories, library, computer center. Dormitories linked to campus network. Online library, helpline available.

Student life. Freshman orientation: Mandatory. Preregistration for classes offered. Held during June, July and August. **Housing:** Single-sex dorms, special housing for disabled, wellness housing available. $300 nonrefundable deposit, deadline 5/31. **Activities:** Bands, choral groups, dance, drama, music ensembles, radio station, student government, student newspaper, symphony orchestra, TV station, Beta Psi Club, Omega Psi Phi, Alpha Kappa Alpha, Delta Sigma Theta, Alpha Delta Mu, Young Democrats, Young Republicans, Alpha Phi Alpha, Kappa Alpha Psi.

Athletics. NCAA. **Intercollegiate:** Baseball M, basketball, bowling W, cross-country, football (tackle) M, softball W, tennis, track and field, volleyball W. **Intramural:** Basketball, bowling, cheerleading, football (non-tackle) M, soccer M, softball, swimming, table tennis, tennis, volleyball. **Team name:** Spartans.

Student services. Adult student services, alcohol/substance abuse counseling, chaplain/spiritual director, career counseling, student employment services, financial aid counseling, health services, on-campus daycare, personal counseling, placement for graduates, veterans' counselor, women's services. **Physically disabled:** Services for visually, speech, hearing impaired.

Contact. E-mail: admissions@nsu.edu
Phone: (757) 823-8396 Fax: (757) 823-2078
Lakeisha Mayes, Director of Admissions, Norfolk State University, 700 Park Avenue, Norfolk, VA 23504

Old Dominion University
Norfolk, Virginia
CB member
www.odu.edu
CB code: 5126

- Public 4-year university
- Residential campus in small city
- 18,881 degree-seeking undergraduates: 23% part-time, 54% women, 23% African American, 4% Asian American, 5% Hispanic American, 1% international
- 4,112 degree-seeking graduate students
- 75% of applicants admitted
- SAT or ACT (ACT writing recommended) required
- 50% graduate within 6 years

General. Founded in 1930. Regionally accredited. Classes also offered at three regional Centers of Higher Education, and at 40 locations, including community colleges, military installations, and hospitals, across Virginia, Arizona, and Washington. Courses are offered via satellite broadcast network, 2-way video, video streaming, web-based, hybrid and portable media and devices. **Degrees:** 3,180 bachelor's awarded; master's, professional, doctoral offered. **ROTC:** Army, Naval. **Location:** 2 miles from downtown, 200 miles from Washington, DC. **Calendar:** Semester, extensive summer session. **Full-time faculty:** 746 total; 79% have terminal degrees, 19% minority, 42% women. **Part-time faculty:** 500 total; 25% have terminal degrees, 13% minority, 57% women. **Class size:** 34% < 20, 45% 20-39, 10% 40-49, 7% 50-99, 4% >100. **Special facilities:** Student art gallery, centers for urban research/service, economic education and child study centers, laser optics lab, planetarium, robotics lab, sub-/super-sonic wind tunnels, marine science research vessel, random wave pool.

Freshman class profile. 10,276 applied, 7,746 admitted, 2,738 enrolled.

Mid 50% test scores			
SAT critical reading:	460-560	Rank in top quarter:	35%
SAT math:	460-560	Rank in top tenth:	10%
SAT writing:	440-540	End year in good standing:	76%
ACT composite:	19-24	Return as sophomores:	80%
GPA 3.75 or higher:	12%	Out-of-state:	9%
GPA 3.50-3.74:	14%	Live on campus:	74%
GPA 3.0-3.49:	45%	International:	1%
GPA 2.0-2.99:	29%	Fraternities:	8%
		Sororities:	11%

Basis for selection. Students who submit acceptable GPA and SAT/ACT scores are admitted. Those who do not meet acceptable GPA or SAT scores are reviewed by admissions committee. Committee looks at grades in core curriculum courses, student essay, student activity, resume/letters of recommendation, high school attended, IB and AP courses taken, etc. Audition required for music. **Home schooled:** Transcript of courses and grades required. Scores from SAT or ACT must be submitted. GED not required. Students not attending program that requires regular curriculum review and submission of test scores to local school board must submit Stanford 9 results. **Learning Disabled:** Documentation of disabilities must be submitted before receiving services from Office of Educational Accessibility.

High school preparation. College-preparatory program recommended. 16 units required. Required units include English 4, mathematics 3, social studies 3, science 3 and foreign language 3.

2011-2012 Annual costs. Tuition/fees: $8,144; $22,484 out-of-state. Room/board: $8,796. Books/supplies: $1,000. Personal expenses: $1,875.

2011-2012 Financial aid. Need-based: 2,307 full-time freshmen applied for aid; 1,969 were judged to have need; 1,708 of these received aid. Average need met was 74%. Average scholarship/grant was $5,977; average loan $3,478. 49% of total undergraduate aid awarded as scholarships/grants, 51% as loans/jobs. **Non-need-based:** Awarded to 2,837 full-time undergraduates, including 922 freshmen. Scholarships awarded for academics, alumni affiliation, art, athletics, leadership, music/drama, ROTC, state residency.

Application procedures. Admission: Priority date 12/1; deadline 2/1 (receipt date). $50 fee, may be waived for applicants with need. Admission notification on a rolling basis beginning on or about 1/15. Must reply by May 1 or within 2 week(s) if notified thereafter. Students are required to submit following: $50 application fee, high school transcripts, application, SAT or ACT scores, 1-3 letters of recommendation, one essay, one student activity resume. **Financial aid:** Priority date 2/15, closing date 3/15. FAFSA required. Applicants notified on a rolling basis starting 2/1; must reply within 2 week(s) of notification.

Academics. Guaranteed work or internship experience for credit in all fields of study. **Special study options:** Accelerated study, combined bachelor's/graduate degree, cooperative education, cross-registration, distance learning, double major, dual enrollment of high school students, ESL, exchange student, honors, independent study, internships, liberal arts/career combination, student-designed major, study abroad, teacher certification program. Experiential learning. **Credit/placement by examination:** AP, CLEP, IB, institutional tests. 60 credit hours maximum toward bachelor's degree. Credit hours earned for assessment of prior learning outside of the college classroom not to exceed 60. Work life credits awarded through certification or department evaluations. Essay required to receive CLEP credit in Analysis and Interpretation of Literature. **Support services:** Learning center, reduced course load, study skills assistance, tutoring, writing center.

Honors college/program. Must have minimum GPA of 3.40; minimum total SAT of 1200. All honor students receive an annual stipend. Honors College requires a separate application to apply.

Majors. Area/ethnic studies: African-American, Asian, women's. **Biology:** General, biochemistry. **Business:** Accounting, business admin, finance, management information systems, managerial economics, marketing. **Computer sciences:** General. **Education:** Physical. **Engineering:** General, civil, computer, electrical, environmental, mechanical. **English:** English lit, rhetoric/composition. **Foreign languages:** General. **Health services:** Audiology/speech pathology, clinical lab science, dental hygiene, nuclear medical technology, nursing (RN). **History:** General. **Math:** General. **Parks/recreation:** Facilities management. **Philosophy/religion:** Philosophy. **Physical sciences:** Chemistry, physics. **Psychology:** General. **Social sciences:** Criminology, economics, geography, international relations, political science, sociology. **Visual/performing arts:** Acting, art, art history/conservation, dramatic, music performance.

Most popular majors. Business/marketing 19%, education 7%, engineering/engineering technologies 10%, English 8%, health sciences 15%, interdisciplinary studies 7%, psychology 7%, social sciences 12%.

Computing on campus. 1,130 workstations in dormitories, library, computer center, student center. Dormitories wired for high-speed internet access and linked to campus network. Commuter students can connect to campus network. Online course registration, online library, helpline, repair service, wireless network available.

Student life. Freshman orientation: Mandatory, $110 fee. Preregistration for classes offered. One-day event held on various days throughout the summer. **Policies:** All student sponsored dances are restricted to ODU students only. Students must agree to hazing policy and can agree to FERPA when they sign up on-line for their organizations. Freshmen not permitted cars on campus. **Housing:** Coed dorms, special housing for disabled, apartments available. $250 partly refundable deposit, deadline 5/15. **Activities:** Bands, campus ministries, choral groups, dance, drama, international student organizations, music ensembles, Model UN, musical theater, radio station, student government, student newspaper, College Democrats, College Republicans, Baptist Student Union, Black Student Alliance, African Caribbean Association, Catholic Campus Ministry, Latino Student Alliance, Colleges Against Cancer, ODU Out, Circle K.

Athletics. NCAA. **Intercollegiate:** Baseball M, basketball, cheerleading M, diving, field hockey W, football (tackle) M, golf, lacrosse W, rowing (crew) W, sailing, soccer, tennis, wrestling M. **Intramural:** Badminton, basketball, cross-country, football (non-tackle), golf, racquetball, sailing, soccer, softball, table tennis, tennis, volleyball. **Team name:** Monarchs.

Student services. Adult student services, alcohol/substance abuse counseling, chaplain/spiritual director, career counseling, services for economically disadvantaged, student employment services, financial aid counseling,

health services, minority student services, on-campus daycare, personal counseling, placement for graduates, veterans' counselor, women's services. **Physically disabled:** Services for visually, speech, hearing impaired.

Contact. E-mail: admissions@odu.edu
Phone: (757) 683-3685 Toll-free number: (800) 348-7926
Fax: (757) 683-3255
Nechell Bonds, Director of Admissions, Old Dominion University, 108 Rollins Hall, 5215 Hampton Boulevard, Norfolk, VA 23529

Patrick Henry College
Purcellville, Virginia
www.phc.edu   CB code: 2804

- Private 4-year liberal arts college affiliated with Christian Church
- Residential campus in small town
- 327 degree-seeking undergraduates: 4% part-time, 46% women
- 86% of applicants admitted
- SAT or ACT (ACT writing optional), application essay, interview required
- 66% graduate within 6 years; 37% enter graduate study

General. Regionally accredited; also accredited by TRACS. **Degrees:** 61 bachelor's awarded. **Location:** 50 miles from Washington, DC. **Calendar:** Semester, limited summer session. **Full-time faculty:** 22 total; 91% have terminal degrees, 14% women. **Part-time faculty:** 28 total; 46% have terminal degrees, 39% women. **Class size:** 62% < 20, 38% 20-39.

Freshman class profile. 213 applied, 184 admitted, 110 enrolled.

Mid 50% test scores			
SAT critical reading:	640-750	GPA 3.50-3.74:	6%
SAT math:	560-660	GPA 3.0-3.49:	8%
SAT writing:	600-690	Return as sophomores:	93%
ACT composite:	26-31	Out-of-state:	88%
GPA 3.75 or higher:	86%	Live on campus:	98%

Basis for selection. School record, GPA, recommendations, test scores, essay, interview, character, and religious commitment very important. Reading List.

High school preparation. College-preparatory program required. 18 units required. Required and recommended units include English 4, mathematics 3, social studies 1, history 2, science 2 (laboratory 2), foreign language 1 and academic electives 5. Social Studies unit is expected to be fulfilled with Government.

2011-2012 Annual costs. Tuition/fees: $22,758. Room/board: $9,128. Books/supplies: $1,000. Personal expenses: $1,000.

2010-2011 Financial aid. **Need-based:** 70% of total undergraduate aid awarded as scholarships/grants, 30% as loans/jobs. **Non-need-based:** Scholarships awarded for academics, leadership, music/drama.

Application procedures. **Admission:** $20 fee. Admission notification on a rolling basis beginning on or about 11/1. **Financial aid:** Priority date 3/15, closing date 6/15. Required for students seeking need-based aid. Applicants notified on a rolling basis starting 3/1; must reply within 4 week(s) of notification.

Academics. **Special study options:** Accelerated study, distance learning, independent study, internships. **Credit/placement by examination:** AP, CLEP, IB, institutional tests. Credits from the Program on Non-Collegiate Sponsored Instruction, Dantes Subject Standardized Tests, and International Baccalaureate are evaluated on a case by case basis. **Support services:** Reduced course load, tutoring.

Majors. **Communications:** Journalism. **English:** English lit. **History:** General. **Liberal arts:** Arts/sciences. **Social sciences:** Political science.

Most popular majors. Communications/journalism 11%, English 15%, history 7%, liberal arts 8%, social sciences 59%.

Computing on campus. PC or laptop required. 6 workstations in library. Dormitories wired for high-speed internet access and linked to campus network. Commuter students can connect to campus network. Online course registration, online library, helpline, repair service, student web hosting, wireless network available.

Student life. Freshman orientation: Mandatory. Preregistration for classes offered. Held for 4 days prior to beginning of fall classes. **Policies:** Students are accountable to public legal standards, to Biblical standards, and to the College's community standards. We have a redemptive approach to

discipline. Religious observance required. **Housing:** Guaranteed on-campus for freshmen. Single-sex dorms available. $275 fully refundable deposit, deadline 7/1. **Activities:** Choral groups, drama, film society, literary magazine, music ensembles, Model UN, student government, student newspaper, Streaming Media Film, College Republicans, College Democrats, Alexis de Tocqueville Society, Sans Frontieres, Libertas Society, Titan Society, IJM, All girls allowed.

Athletics. Intercollegiate: Basketball, soccer. **Intramural:** Football (non-tackle) M, softball M, tennis, volleyball. **Team name:** The Sentinels.

Student services. Chaplain/spiritual director, career counseling, student employment services, financial aid counseling, personal counseling. **Physically disabled:** Services for visually impaired.

Contact. E-mail: admissions@phc.edu
Phone: (540) 441-8110 Toll-free number: (888) 338-1776 ext. 8881
Fax: (540) 441-8119
William Kellaris, Assistant Vice President for Enrollment Management, Patrick Henry College, 10 Patrick Henry Circle, Purcellville, VA 20132-3197

Potomac College
Herndon, Virginia
www.potomac.edu   CB code: 2604

- For-profit 4-year business college
- Commuter campus in large town
- 31 degree-seeking undergraduates

General. **Degrees:** 16 bachelor's, 4 associate awarded. **Location:** 30 miles from Washington, DC. **Calendar:** Differs by program, extensive summer session. **Full-time faculty:** 2 total. **Part-time faculty:** 20 total.

Basis for selection. Open admission.

2011-2012 Annual costs. Books/supplies: $630.

Application procedures. Admission: No deadline. No application fee. Admission notification on a rolling basis. **Financial aid:** No deadline. FAFSA, institutional form required. Applicants notified on a rolling basis.

Academics. Credit earned for work related research projects. **Special study options:** Accelerated study, distance learning, independent study, weekend college. **Credit/placement by examination:** AP, CLEP, institutional tests. 15 credit hours maximum toward associate degree, 30 toward bachelor's. **Support services:** Learning center, remedial instruction, tutoring.

Majors. Business: Accounting, accounting/business management, business admin, management science, purchasing. **Computer sciences:** General, LAN/WAN management, security.

Most popular majors. Business/marketing 73%, computer/information sciences 27%.

Computing on campus. 16 workstations in library, computer center, student center. Online library, wireless network available.

Student life. Freshman orientation: Mandatory. Preregistration for classes offered. **Activities:** Student government.

Student services. Adult student services, financial aid counseling.

Contact. E-mail: admissions@potomac.edu
Phone: (703) 709-5875 Fax: (703) 709-8972
Angeliqua Wesley, Admissions Director, Potomac College, 1029 Herndon Parkway, Herndon, VA 20170

Radford University
Radford, Virginia   CB member
www.radford.edu   CB code: 5565

- Public 4-year university
- Residential campus in large town
- 8,319 degree-seeking undergraduates: 4% part-time, 56% women, 7% African American, 2% Asian American, 3% Hispanic American, 1% international
- 969 degree-seeking graduate students
- 80% of applicants admitted

◆ SAT or ACT (ACT writing optional) required
◆ 76% graduate within 6 years; 17% enter graduate study

General. Founded in 1910. Regionally accredited. **Degrees:** 1,725 bachelor's awarded; master's, doctoral offered. **ROTC:** Army. **Location:** 45 miles from Roanoke. **Calendar:** Semester, limited summer session. **Full-time faculty:** 406 total; 84% have terminal degrees, 11% minority, 48% women. **Part-time faculty:** 217 total; 26% have terminal degrees, 5% minority, 63% women. **Class size:** 33% < 20, 53% 20-39, 9% 40-49, 5% 50-99, less than 1% >100. **Special facilities:** Center for visual and performing arts, observatory, planetarium, nature conservancy, motion analysis lab, clinical simulation center, cadaver lab, speech-language-hearing center, earth sciences museum, GIS center; games, animation, modeling and simulation lab.

Freshman class profile. 7,596 applied, 6,095 admitted, 2,035 enrolled.

Mid 50% test scores			
SAT critical reading:	460-560	GPA 3.0-3.49:	38%
SAT math:	460-550	GPA 2.0-2.99:	40%
SAT writing:	440-530	Rank in top quarter:	22%
ACT composite:	17-21	Rank in top tenth:	6%
GPA 3.75 or higher:	10%	Out-of-state:	7%
GPA 3.50-3.74:	12%	Live on campus:	97%

Basis for selection. High school records, including grades, strength of academic program, and performance trend: standardized test scores, optional student essay, and evidence of interest and motivation as indicated in supplied materials. Informal interviews are available and written statements will be considered if submitted. **Home schooled:** SAT subject tests in Math and English recommended. If curriculum is not supported by a recognized home school organization, the student may need to supply course descriptions (including text book information, where appropriate.).

High school preparation. College-preparatory program recommended. 24 units recommended. Recommended units include English 4, mathematics 4, social studies 2, history 2, science 4 (laboratory 3), foreign language 3 and academic electives 5. Pre-nursing students should complete units in both biology and chemistry.

2011-2012 Annual costs. Tuition/fees: $8,320; $19,478 out-of-state. Room/board: $7,589. Books/supplies: $1,100. Personal expenses: $1,900.

2011-2012 Financial aid. **Need-based:** 1,646 full-time freshmen applied for aid; 1,084 were judged to have need; 1,010 of these received aid. Average need met was 81%. Average scholarship/grant was $7,622; average loan $3,290. 42% of total undergraduate aid awarded as scholarships/grants, 58% as loans/jobs. **Non-need-based:** Awarded to 1,268 full-time undergraduates, including 412 freshmen. Scholarships awarded for academics, alumni affiliation, art, athletics, leadership, music/drama, ROTC. **Additional information:** Student's need and grades considered. Top consideration given to those with greatest need and who apply by deadline.

Application procedures. **Admission:** Closing date 2/1 (postmark date). $50 fee, may be waived for applicants with need. Admission notification by 4/1. Must reply by 5/1. **Financial aid:** Priority date 2/15; no closing date. FAFSA required. Applicants notified on a rolling basis starting 4/15; must reply within 2 week(s) of notification.

Academics. Students have opportunity to participate in research collaboration with faculty. **Special study options:** Accelerated study, cross-registration, distance learning, double major, dual enrollment of high school students, honors, independent study, internships, student-designed major, study abroad, teacher certification program. **Credit/placement by examination:** AP, CLEP, IB. **Support services:** Learning center, study skills assistance, tutoring, writing center.

Honors college/program. Students must meet two of the following: 1100 SAT/24 ACT, 3.5 GPA, top 20% of high school class. Number of freshmen admitted each fall averages 146.

Majors. **Biology:** General. **Business:** Accounting, business admin, finance, marketing. **Communications:** Communications/speech/rhetoric, journalism. **Computer sciences:** Computer science, information systems. **Education:** Physical. **English:** English lit. **Foreign languages:** General. **Health services:** Athletic training, communication disorders, nursing (RN). **History:** General. **Human services:** Social work. **Math:** General. **Parks/recreation:** General. **Physical sciences:** Chemistry, geology, physics. **Protective services:** Criminal justice. **Psychology:** General. **Social sciences:** General, anthropology, economics, geography, GIS/cartography, political science, sociology. **Visual/performing arts:** Art, dance, design, dramatic, music. **Work/family studies:** Food/nutrition.

Most popular majors. Business/marketing 20%, communications/journalism 10%, education 6%, health services 9%, interdisciplinary studies 9%, security/protective services 7%, social sciences 6%, visual/performing arts 8%.

Computing on campus. 772 workstations in dormitories, library, computer center, student center. Dormitories wired for high-speed internet access and linked to campus network. Commuter students can connect to campus network. Online course registration, online library, helpline, repair service, student web hosting, wireless network available.

Student life. **Freshman orientation:** Available, $275 fee. Preregistration for classes offered. 5, 2-day sessions in June and a one-day session in January and August for freshmen and one-day sessions in July for transfers. **Policies:** In accepting admission, each student makes a commitment to support and uphold the Honor Code without compromise or exception. **Housing:** Guaranteed on-campus for freshmen. Coed dorms, special housing for disabled, apartments, wellness housing available. $200 nonrefundable deposit, deadline 5/1. **Activities:** Bands, campus ministries, choral groups, dance, drama, international student organizations, literary magazine, music ensembles, musical theater, opera, radio station, student government, student newspaper, TV station, Crossroads Presbyterian Fellowship, Baptist Collegiate Ministry, Deliverance Gospel Choir, Young Democrats, College Republicans, Gay-Straight Alliance, La Sociedad Hispanica, Students Helping Honduras, Alpha Phi Omega Co-Ed Service Fraternity, Highlander Helpers Backpack Program.

Athletics. NCAA. **Intercollegiate:** Baseball M, basketball, cross-country, diving W, field hockey W, golf, soccer, softball W, swimming W, tennis, track and field, volleyball W. **Intramural:** Basketball, bowling, cross-country, football (non-tackle), racquetball, soccer, softball, table tennis, tennis, volleyball, weight lifting. **Team name:** Highlanders.

Student services. Adult student services, alcohol/substance abuse counseling, chaplain/spiritual director, career counseling, services for economically disadvantaged, student employment services, financial aid counseling, health services, minority student services, personal counseling, placement for graduates, veterans' counselor, women's services. **Physically disabled:** Services for visually, speech, hearing impaired.

Contact. E-mail: admissions@radford.edu
Phone: (540) 831-5371 Fax: (540) 831-5038
James Pennix, Dean of Admissions, Radford University, 115 Martin Hall, Radford, VA 24142

Randolph College
Lynchburg, Virginia
www.randolphcollege.edu

CB member
CB code: 5567

◆ Private 4-year liberal arts college affiliated with United Methodist Church
◆ Residential campus in small city
◆ 555 degree-seeking undergraduates: 2% part-time, 66% women, 9% African American, 2% Asian American, 6% Hispanic American, 12% international
◆ 5 degree-seeking graduate students
◆ 71% of applicants admitted
◆ SAT or ACT (ACT writing optional), application essay required
◆ 64% graduate within 6 years

General. Founded in 1891. Regionally accredited. **Degrees:** 113 bachelor's awarded; master's offered. **Location:** 60 miles from Roanoke and Charlottesville. **Calendar:** Semester, limited summer session. **Full-time faculty:** 68 total; 94% have terminal degrees, 15% minority, 54% women. **Part-time faculty:** 6 total; 50% have terminal degrees, 67% women. **Class size:** 89% < 20, 10% 20-39, less than 1% 40-49. **Special facilities:** Observatory, 3 nature preserves, botanical garden, 100-acre equestrian center, museum of American art, science and mathematics resource center, learning resources center, writing lab, artificial turf field and track facility, organic garden.

Freshman class profile. 979 applied, 696 admitted, 177 enrolled.

Mid 50% test scores			
SAT critical reading:	490-620	GPA 2.0-2.99:	21%
SAT math:	480-620	Rank in top quarter:	55%
SAT writing:	470-610	Rank in top tenth:	27%
ACT composite:	20-25	Return as sophomores:	75%
GPA 3.75 or higher:	29%	Out-of-state:	48%
GPA 3.50-3.74:	23%	Live on campus:	97%
GPA 3.0-3.49:	27%	International:	13%

Basis for selection. Rigor of high school curriculum and achievement most important, followed by teacher and counselor recommendations, test scores, activities, personal achievement. International students may submit SAT or ACT in lieu of TOEFL. Interview recommended. Essay submission may be essay written on topic of applicant's choice, copy of graded essay written by applicant in 11th or 12th grade, or SAT/ACT writing component. **Learning Disabled:** Submit documentation to Director of the Learning Resources Center, who will work in consultation with Office of the Dean

of the College and faculty to determine reasonable and appropriate accommodations.

High school preparation. College-preparatory program required. 16 units required. Required and recommended units include English 4, mathematics 3-4, history 2, science 3 (laboratory 2), foreign language 3 and academic electives 1-3.

2011-2012 Annual costs. Tuition/fees: $30,376. Room/board: $10,386. Books/supplies: $100. Personal expenses: $1,200.

2011-2012 Financial aid. Need-based: 142 full-time freshmen applied for aid; 121 were judged to have need; 121 of these received aid. Average need met was 79%. Average scholarship/grant was $19,871; average loan $4,599. 72% of total undergraduate aid awarded as scholarships/grants, 28% as loans/jobs. **Non-need-based:** Awarded to 107 full-time undergraduates, including 43 freshmen. Scholarships awarded for academics, alumni affiliation, art, leadership, minority status, music/drama, religious affiliation, state residency.

Application procedures. Admission: Priority date 12/1; deadline 3/1 (postmark date). $35 fee, may be waived for applicants with need. Admission notification by 4/1. Admission notification on a rolling basis beginning on or about 12/15. Must reply by May 1 or within 2 week(s) if notified thereafter. **Financial aid:** Priority date 3/1; no closing date. FAFSA required. Applicants notified on a rolling basis starting 3/1; must reply by 5/1 or within 2 week(s) of notification.

Academics. Honor system includes self-scheduled examinations. **Special study options:** Accelerated study, combined bachelor's/graduate degree, cross-registration, double major, dual enrollment of high school students, exchange student, honors, independent study, internships, liberal arts/career combination, student-designed major, study abroad, teacher certification program, Washington semester. **Credit/placement by examination:** AP, CLEP, IB, SAT, ACT, institutional tests. Applicants with scores at or above 50th percentile awarded credit for CLEP subject examinations in subject areas offered by college. However, subject tests in foreign languages granted credit only if they represent achievement beyond that of previous high school or college preparation. **Support services:** Learning center, reduced course load, study skills assistance, tutoring, writing center.

Majors. Biology: General. **Business:** General. **Communications:** Communications/speech/rhetoric. **Conservation:** Environmental studies. **Engineering:** Applied physics. **English:** British lit, creative writing, English lit. **Foreign languages:** Ancient Greek, classics, French, Latin, Spanish. **History:** General. **Math:** General. **Philosophy/religion:** Philosophy, religion. **Physical sciences:** Chemistry, physics. **Psychology:** General. **Social sciences:** Economics, political science, sociology. **Visual/performing arts:** Art history/conservation, dance, dramatic, music history, music performance, music theory/composition, studio arts.

Most popular majors. Biology 9%, business/marketing 6%, communications/journalism 6%, English 8%, history 10%, psychology 7%, social sciences 23%, visual/performing arts 6%.

Computing on campus. 155 workstations in dormitories, library, computer center, student center. Dormitories wired for high-speed internet access and linked to campus network. Commuter students can connect to campus network. Online course registration, online library, helpline, student web hosting, wireless network available.

Student life. Freshman orientation: Mandatory, $150 fee. Preregistration for classes offered. 2-day summer sessions as well as program prior to the start of fall and spring classes. Sessions include advising, and activities designed to acquaint students with the campus, the community, and each other. **Policies:** The Honor code is fundamental to the conduct and governance of the College. **Housing:** Guaranteed on-campus for all undergraduates. Coed dorms, single-sex dorms, wellness housing available. $300 nonrefundable deposit, deadline 5/1. **Activities:** Pep band, campus ministries, choral groups, dance, drama, film society, international student organizations, literary magazine, music ensembles, Model UN, radio station, student government, student newspaper, Young Democrats, College Republicans, Amnesty International, Club Asia, Catholic Students Association, Black Students Alliance, Circle K, Pan World Club.

Athletics. NCAA. **Intercollegiate:** Basketball, cross-country, equestrian, lacrosse, soccer, softball W, tennis, volleyball W. **Intramural:** Basketball, softball, table tennis, tennis, volleyball. **Team name:** Wildcats.

Student services. Adult student services, alcohol/substance abuse counseling, chaplain/spiritual director, career counseling, student employment services, financial aid counseling, health services, minority student services, personal counseling, placement for graduates, women's services. **Physically disabled:** Services for visually, hearing impaired.

Contact. E-mail: admissions@randolphcollege.edu
Phone: (434) 947-8100 Toll-free number: (800) 745-7692
Fax: (434) 947-8996
Margaret Blount, Director of Admissions, Randolph College, 2500 Rivermont Avenue, Lynchburg, VA 24503-1555

Randolph-Macon College
Ashland, Virginia
www.rmc.edu

CB member
CB code: 5566

- Private 4-year liberal arts college affiliated with United Methodist Church
- Residential campus in small town
- 1,241 degree-seeking undergraduates: 1% part-time, 53% women, 13% African American, 2% Asian American, 4% Hispanic American, 1% international
- 56% of applicants admitted
- SAT or ACT (ACT writing recommended), application essay required
- 62% graduate within 6 years

General. Founded in 1830. Regionally accredited. **Degrees:** 273 bachelor's awarded. **ROTC:** Army. **Location:** 15 miles from Richmond, 90 miles from Washington, DC. **Calendar:** 4-1-4, limited summer session. **Full-time faculty:** 93 total; 97% have terminal degrees, 6% minority, 43% women. **Part-time faculty:** 57 total; 21% have terminal degrees, 7% minority, 56% women. **Class size:** 71% < 20, 29% 20-39. **Special facilities:** Observatory with 12-inch reflecting telescope and 3-meter radio telescope, 6 historic buildings, greenhouse.

Freshman class profile. 4,249 applied, 2,369 admitted, 410 enrolled.

Mid 50% test scores		GPA 2.0-2.99:	26%
SAT critical reading:	490-580	Rank in top quarter:	49%
SAT math:	490-580	Rank in top tenth:	20%
SAT writing:	470-570	Return as sophomores:	80%
GPA 3.75 or higher:	25%	Out-of-state:	21%
GPA 3.50-3.74:	20%	Live on campus:	91%
GPA 3.0-3.49:	29%	International:	2%

Basis for selection. High school academic record and course schedule is most important, meeting with an admissions counselor recommended but not required. Interview recommended. **Home schooled:** Statement describing home school structure and mission, transcript of courses and grades, letter of recommendation (nonparent) required. **Learning Disabled:** Students with learning disabilities encouraged to meet with director of disability support services.

High school preparation. College-preparatory program required. 16 units required; 22 recommended. Required and recommended units include English 4, mathematics 3-4, social studies 2-3, history 1-3, science 3-4 (laboratory 2-4), foreign language 2-4 and academic electives 1-2.

2011-2012 Annual costs. Tuition/fees: $32,265. Room/board: $9,575. Books/supplies: $1,000. Personal expenses: $720.

2011-2012 Financial aid. Need-based: 75% of total undergraduate aid awarded as scholarships/grants, 25% as loans/jobs. **Non-need-based:** Scholarships awarded for academics, alumni affiliation, minority status, religious affiliation, state residency.

Application procedures. Admission: Priority date 2/1; deadline 3/1 (postmark date). $30 fee, may be waived for applicants with need, free for online applicants. Admission notification by 4/1. Must reply by May 1 or within 2 week(s) if notified thereafter. Applications accepted after March 1 on space-available basis. **Financial aid:** Priority date 3/1, closing date 2/15. FAFSA required. Applicants notified by 3/15; must reply by 5/1 or within 2 week(s) of notification.

Academics. Comprehensive liberal arts core curriculum. All students must complete an internship, study abroad, or original research project for graduation. Interdisciplinary First-Year Experience for all freshmen. **Special study options:** Accelerated study, combined bachelor's/graduate degree, cross-registration, double major, dual enrollment of high school students, exchange student, honors, independent study, internships, liberal arts/career combination, study abroad, teacher certification program, United Nations semester, Washington semester. Member of Seven College consortium, 3-2 program in engineering with Columbia University and University of Virginia, 3-2 in forestry with Duke University, 4-1 in accounting with Virginia Commonwealth University. **Credit/placement by examination:** AP, CLEP, IB, institutional tests. 75 credit hours maximum toward bachelor's degree. At least one-half major course of study must be completed at Randolph-Macon College. **Support services:** Learning center, reduced course load, study skills assistance, tutoring, writing center.

Majors. **Area/ethnic studies:** Asian, women's. **Biology:** General. **Business:** Accounting, managerial economics. **Communications:** General. **Computer sciences:** General. **Conservation:** Environmental studies. **English:** English lit. **Foreign languages:** Ancient Greek, classics, French, German, Latin, Spanish. **History:** General. **Math:** General. **Philosophy/religion:** Philosophy, religion. **Physical sciences:** Chemistry, physics. **Psychology:** General. **Social sciences:** Economics, political science, sociology. **Visual/performing arts:** Art history/conservation, dramatic, music, studio arts, studio arts management.

Most popular majors. Biology 9%, business/marketing 7%, English 9%, history 10%, psychology 10%, social sciences 30%, visual/performing arts 6%.

Computing on campus. 350 workstations in library, computer center, student center. Dormitories wired for high-speed internet access and linked to campus network. Commuter students can connect to campus network. Online course registration, online library, helpline, repair service, student web hosting, wireless network available.

Student life. **Freshman orientation:** Mandatory, $100 fee. Preregistration for classes offered. 4-day program held for students and parents prior to start of fall classes. **Housing:** Guaranteed on-campus for all undergraduates. Coed dorms, single-sex dorms, special housing for disabled, apartments, fraternity/sorority housing, wellness housing available. Honors house, special interest housing available. **Activities:** Bands, campus ministries, choral groups, dance, drama, film society, international student organizations, literary magazine, music ensembles, musical theater, radio station, student government, student newspaper, TV station, over 100 clubs and organizations.

Athletics. NCAA. **Intercollegiate:** Baseball M, basketball, field hockey W, football (tackle) M, golf M, lacrosse, soccer, softball W, swimming, tennis, volleyball W. **Intramural:** Basketball, football (non-tackle), lacrosse, racquetball, rugby, soccer, softball, table tennis, tennis, volleyball. **Team name:** Yellow Jackets.

Student services. Alcohol/substance abuse counseling, chaplain/spiritual director, career counseling, student employment services, financial aid counseling, health services, minority student services, personal counseling, placement for graduates, women's services. **Physically disabled:** Services for visually, speech, hearing impaired.

Contact. E-mail: admissions@rmc.edu
Phone: (804) 752-7305 Toll-free number: (800) 888-1762
Fax: (804) 752-4707
David Lesesne, Dean of Admissions and Financial Aid, Randolph-Macon College, PO Box 5005, Ashland, VA 23005-5505

Regent University
Virginia Beach, Virginia
www.regent.edu
CB code: 4452

- Private 4-year university affiliated with interdenominational tradition
- Residential campus in large city
- 2,259 degree-seeking undergraduates: 40% part-time, 63% women, 23% African American, 2% Asian American, 6% Hispanic American, 1% Native American, 2% international
- 3,287 degree-seeking graduate students
- 84% of applicants admitted
- SAT or ACT (ACT writing optional), application essay required

General. Founded in 1977. Regionally accredited. **Degrees:** 301 bachelor's, 10 associate awarded; master's, professional, doctoral offered. **ROTC:** Army. **Location:** 8 miles from Norfolk. **Calendar:** Semester, extensive summer session. **Full-time faculty:** 196 total; 84% have terminal degrees, 21% minority, 34% women. **Part-time faculty:** 341 total; 72% have terminal degrees, 15% minority, 40% women. **Class size:** 61% < 20, 38% 20-39, less than 1% 40-49. **Special facilities:** Communication and performing arts center, The Founders Inn and Spa.

Freshman class profile. 1,450 applied, 1,216 admitted, 382 enrolled.

Mid 50% test scores			
SAT critical reading:	480-600	GPA 3.0-3.49:	43%
SAT math:	450-570	GPA 2.0-2.99:	14%
SAT writing:	470-590	End year in good standing:	71%
ACT composite:	20-24	Return as sophomores:	72%
GPA 3.75 or higher:	36%	Out-of-state:	57%
GPA 3.50-3.74:	7%	Live on campus:	56%
		International:	3%

Basis for selection. GPA, test scores, response to an essay question all required along with application. **Home schooled:** Transcript of courses and grades required.

High school preparation. Recommended units include English 4, mathematics 3, social studies 3, science 3 and foreign language 3.

2011-2012 Annual costs. Tuition/fees: $15,308. Room only: $3,900. Books/supplies: $780. Personal expenses: $6,100.

2011-2012 Financial aid. **Need-based:** 276 full-time freshmen applied for aid; 251 were judged to have need; 250 of these received aid. Average need met was 57%. Average scholarship/grant was $8,274; average loan $3,323. 64% of total undergraduate aid awarded as scholarships/grants, 36% as loans/jobs. **Non-need-based:** Scholarships awarded for academics, alumni affiliation, leadership, ROTC.

Application procedures. **Admission:** Closing date 5/1 (receipt date). $50 fee. Admission notification on a rolling basis. Must reply by 5/1. **Financial aid:** Priority date 3/15; no closing date. FAFSA, institutional form required. Applicants notified on a rolling basis starting 3/1; must reply within 2 week(s) of notification.

Academics. **Special study options:** Combined bachelor's/graduate degree, distance learning, double major, dual enrollment of high school students, internships, study abroad, teacher certification program, Washington semester. **Credit/placement by examination:** AP, CLEP, IB. 30 credit hours maximum toward bachelor's degree. **Support services:** Remedial instruction, study skills assistance, tutoring, writing center.

Majors. **Business:** Accounting, business admin, international, organizational behavior. **Communications:** Communications/speech/rhetoric. **Communications technology:** Animation/special effects. **Computer sciences:** Information technology. **Education:** General. **English:** English lit. **History:** General. **Human services:** Public policy. **Math:** General. **Philosophy/religion:** Religion. **Protective services:** Law enforcement admin. **Psychology:** General. **Social sciences:** Political science. **Theology:** Bible, theology. **Visual/performing arts:** Cinematography, theater arts management.

Most popular majors. Business/marketing 24%, communications/journalism 10%, English 12%, interdisciplinary studies 6%, philosophy/religious studies 15%, psychology 29%.

Computing on campus. 130 workstations in library, computer center, student center. Dormitories wired for high-speed internet access and linked to campus network. Online course registration, online library, helpline, wireless network available.

Student life. **Freshman orientation:** Mandatory. Preregistration for classes offered. **Housing:** Guaranteed on-campus for freshmen. Apartments available. $350 deposit, deadline 5/1. Pets allowed in dorm rooms. **Activities:** Concert band, campus ministries, choral groups, dance, drama, international student organizations, student government, student newspaper, Association of Black Psychologists, College Republicans, Undergraduate Student Advisory Council, Newman Club, Regent Students for Life, Students in Free Enterprise, Student Alumni Association, Student Advisory Leadership Team.

Athletics. **Intramural:** Basketball, soccer, volleyball.

Student services. Chaplain/spiritual director, career counseling, financial aid counseling, veterans' counselor.

Contact. E-mail: admissions@regent.edu
Phone: (757) 352-4127 Toll-free number: (800) 373-5504
Fax: (757) 352-4381
Ken Baker, Director of Admissions, Regent University, 1000 Regent University Drive, Virginia Beach, VA 23464-9800

Roanoke College
Salem, Virginia
www.roanoke.edu
CB member
CB code: 5571

- Private 4-year liberal arts college affiliated with Evangelical Lutheran Church in America
- Residential campus in large town
- 1,997 degree-seeking undergraduates: 2% part-time, 56% women, 4% African American, 1% Asian American, 3% Hispanic American, 1% international
- 70% of applicants admitted
- SAT or ACT (ACT writing optional) required
- 69% graduate within 6 years; 32% enter graduate study

General. Founded in 1842. Regionally accredited. **Degrees:** 444 bachelor's awarded. **Location:** 7 miles from Roanoke. **Calendar:** Semester, extensive summer session. **Full-time faculty:** 167 total; 86% have terminal degrees, 10% minority, 47% women. **Part-time faculty:** 49 total; 16% have terminal

degrees, 12% minority, 53% women. **Class size:** 56% < 20, 43% 20-39, less than 1% 40-49. **Special facilities:** Nuclear magnetic resonance equipment, center for community research, center for church and society, center for learning and teaching, writing center.

Freshman class profile. 4,184 applied, 2,910 admitted, 533 enrolled.

Mid 50% test scores			
SAT critical reading:	500-590	Rank in top quarter:	55%
SAT math:	490-590	Rank in top tenth:	22%
SAT writing:	490-590	Return as sophomores:	77%
ACT composite:	21-26	Out-of-state:	51%
GPA 3.75 or higher:	31%	Live on campus:	90%
GPA 3.50-3.74:	16%	International:	1%
GPA 3.0-3.49:	28%	Fraternities:	12%
GPA 2.0-2.99:	25%	Sororities:	16%

Basis for selection. Rigor of secondary school record and academic GPA are most important. IB exams area also used for placement. Students who rank in the top 20% of their class and who have at least a 3.25 academic GPA may submit two graded writing samples in lieu of SAT or ACT test scores. Essay, interview recommended for all; audition recommended for music; portfolio recommended for graphic arts. **Home schooled:** Transcript of courses and grades required. **Learning Disabled:** Documentation of learning disability needed for special services after enrollment.

High school preparation. College-preparatory program recommended. 16 units required. Required and recommended units include English 4, mathematics 3, social studies 2, science 2 (laboratory 2), foreign language 4 and academic electives 5. Mathematics must include Algebra II.

2012-2013 Annual costs. Tuition/fees: $34,496. Room/board: $11,142. Books/supplies: $1,000. Personal expenses: $1,000.

2011-2012 Financial aid. Need-based: 470 full-time freshmen applied for aid; 429 were judged to have need; 429 of these received aid. Average need met was 77%. Average scholarship/grant was $21,842; average loan $4,095. 69% of total undergraduate aid awarded as scholarships/grants, 31% as loans/jobs. **Non-need-based:** Awarded to 1,894 full-time undergraduates, including 506 freshmen. Scholarships awarded for academics, minority status, music/drama, religious affiliation, state residency.

Application procedures. Admission: Closing date 3/15 (postmark date). $30 fee, may be waived for applicants with need, free for online applicants. Admission notification by 4/1. Admission notification on a rolling basis beginning on or about 10/1. Must reply by May 1 or within 2 week(s) if notified thereafter. **Financial aid:** Priority date 3/1; no closing date. FAFSA required. Applicants notified on a rolling basis starting 11/1; must reply within 2 week(s) of notification.

Academics. Special study options: Accelerated study, combined bachelor's/graduate degree, cross-registration, double major, dual enrollment of high school students, ESL, honors, independent study, internships, liberal arts/career combination, study abroad, teacher certification program, Washington semester. **Credit/placement by examination:** AP, CLEP, IB, institutional tests. 32 credit hours maximum toward bachelor's degree. **Support services:** Learning center, reduced course load, study skills assistance, tutoring, writing center.

Majors. Biology: General, biochemistry. **Business:** Business admin. **Communications:** General. **Computer sciences:** General, computer science. **Conservation:** Environmental studies, management/policy. **Education:** Physical. **English:** Creative writing, English lit. **Foreign languages:** French, Spanish. **Health services:** Athletic training. **History:** General. **Math:** General. **Parks/recreation:** Exercise sciences, sports admin. **Philosophy/religion:** Christian, philosophy, religion. **Physical sciences:** Chemistry, physics. **Protective services:** Criminal justice. **Psychology:** General. **Social sciences:** Economics, international relations, political science, sociology. **Visual/performing arts:** Art, art history/conservation, dramatic, music.

Most popular majors. Biology 6%, business/marketing 25%, English 6%, history 9%, psychology 10%, social sciences 16%, visual/performing arts 7%.

Computing on campus. 202 workstations in library, computer center, student center. Dormitories wired for high-speed internet access and linked to campus network. Commuter students can connect to campus network. Online course registration, online library, helpline, repair service, student web hosting, wireless network available.

Student life. Freshman orientation: Mandatory, $125 fee. Preregistration for classes offered. Spring/Summer orientation program in June, one full day on campus. Includes general orientation, advising and registration for fall courses, placement testing, and student activities. **Housing:** Guaranteed on-campus for freshmen. Coed dorms, single-sex dorms, special housing for disabled, apartments, fraternity/sorority housing available. $300 fully refundable deposit, deadline 5/1. **Activities:** Bands, campus ministries, choral groups, dance, drama, film society, international student organizations, literary magazine, music ensembles, Model UN, musical theater, radio station,

student government, student newspaper, Alpha Phi Omega, Earthbound, Fellowship of Christian Athletes, Habitat for Humanity, Lutheran Student Movement, Baptist Student Union, Shades of Maroon, InterVarsity.

Athletics. NCAA. Intercollegiate: Baseball M, basketball, cross-country, field hockey W, golf M, lacrosse, soccer, softball W, tennis, track and field, volleyball W. **Intramural:** Badminton, basketball, football (non-tackle), golf W, racquetball, soccer, softball, table tennis, tennis, volleyball. **Team name:** Maroons.

Student services. Adult student services, alcohol/substance abuse counseling, chaplain/spiritual director, career counseling, student employment services, financial aid counseling, health services, minority student services, personal counseling, placement for graduates.

Contact. E-mail: admissions@roanoke.edu
Phone: (540) 375-2270 Toll-free number: (800) 388-2276
Fax: (540) 375-2267
Brenda Poggendorf, Vice President of Enrollment Management, Roanoke College, 221 College Lane, Salem, VA 24153-3794

Sanford-Brown College: Vienna
McLean, Virginia
www.sbcvienna.com   **CB code: 5655**

▶ For-profit 4-year business and technical college
▶ Large city

General. Accredited by ACICS. **Calendar:** Quarter.

Contact. Phone: (703) 556-8888
1761 Old Meadow Road, McLean, VA 22102

Shenandoah University
Winchester, Virginia   **CB member**
www.su.edu   **CB code: 5613**

▶ Private 4-year university affiliated with United Methodist Church
▶ Residential campus in large town
▶ 1,812 degree-seeking undergraduates: 3% part-time, 59% women, 13% African American, 3% Asian American, 3% Hispanic American, 1% Native American, 3% international
▶ 1,627 degree-seeking graduate students
▶ 77% of applicants admitted
▶ SAT or ACT (ACT writing optional) required
▶ 47% graduate within 6 years

General. Founded in 1875. Regionally accredited. **Degrees:** 427 bachelor's awarded; master's, professional, doctoral offered. **Location:** 96 miles from Baltimore, 75 miles from Washington, DC. **Calendar:** Semester, limited summer session. **Full-time faculty:** 214 total; 86% have terminal degrees, 10% minority, 52% women. **Part-time faculty:** 214 total; 29% have terminal degrees, 8% minority, 69% women. **Class size:** 75% < 20, 23% 20-39, 1% 40-49, less than 1% 50-99, less than 1% >100. **Special facilities:** Arts and media centers, conservatory, recording studio, Feltner museum, environmental studies green rooftop.

Freshman class profile. 1,397 applied, 1,070 admitted, 343 enrolled.

Mid 50% test scores			
SAT critical reading:	440-560	GPA 3.0-3.49:	25%
SAT math:	460-560	GPA 2.0-2.99:	24%
SAT writing:	440-560	Return as sophomores:	76%
ACT composite:	19-27	Out-of-state:	44%
GPA 3.75 or higher:	34%	Live on campus:	91%
GPA 3.50-3.74:	17%	International:	2%

Basis for selection. Applicants evaluated on basis of GPA and standardized test scores along with recommendation. Audition required for Conservatory applicants for dance, music, and theater programs. Nursing applicants must take ATI Test of Essential Academic Skills. In-house English proficiency tests administered. Interview recommended for all; audition required for dance, music, and theater programs. **Home schooled:** Transcript of courses and grades, letter of recommendation (nonparent) required. May request GED score. Applicants must submit written documentation of local school district approval of the home school arrangement if available.

High school preparation. College-preparatory program recommended. 15 units required. Required units include English 4, mathematics 3, social studies 2, science 2 (laboratory 1) and foreign language 2.

2011-2012 Annual costs. Tuition/fees: $27,940. Room/board: $8,950. Books/supplies: $1,500. Personal expenses: $2,000.

2011-2012 Financial aid. Need-based: 292 full-time freshmen applied for aid; 254 were judged to have need; 254 of these received aid. Average need met was 71%. Average scholarship/grant was $8,500; average loan $3,500. 80% of total undergraduate aid awarded as scholarships/grants, 20% as loans/jobs. **Non-need-based:** Awarded to 1,073 full-time undergraduates, including 254 freshmen. Scholarships awarded for academics, music/drama, religious affiliation, state residency. **Additional information:** Emergency Grant Fund available for books, meals, tuition and fees.

Application procedures. Admission: Priority date 3/1; deadline 8/20 (receipt date). $30 fee, may be waived for applicants with need. Admission notification on a rolling basis beginning on or about 10/1. Must reply by May 1 or within 2 week(s) if notified thereafter. **Financial aid:** No deadline. FAFSA required. Applicants notified on a rolling basis starting 3/15; must reply within 4 week(s) of notification.

Academics. Special study options: Accelerated study, combined bachelor's/graduate degree, distance learning, double major, dual enrollment of high school students, ESL, independent study, internships, student-designed major, study abroad, teacher certification program, weekend college. **Credit/placement by examination:** AP, CLEP, IB, SAT, ACT, institutional tests. AP placement grade may be higher for exams taken in student's major. CEEB, CLEP, academic department exams used. **Support services:** Learning center, reduced course load, remedial instruction, study skills assistance, tutoring, writing center.

Majors. Biology: General. **Business:** Business admin. **Communications:** Communications/speech/rhetoric. **Conservation:** Environmental studies. **Education:** Drama/dance, music, physical. **English:** English lit. **Foreign languages:** Spanish. **Health services:** Music therapy, nursing (RN), respiratory therapy technology. **History:** General. **Human services:** General. **Liberal arts:** Arts/sciences. **Math:** General. **Philosophy/religion:** Religion. **Physical sciences:** Chemistry. **Protective services:** Law enforcement admin. **Psychology:** General. **Social sciences:** Sociology. **Theology:** Sacred music. **Visual/performing arts:** General, acting, arts management, costume design, dance, dramatic, jazz, music, music performance, music technology, music theory/composition, musical theater, piano/keyboard, theater design.

Most popular majors. Business/marketing 10%, education 12%, health sciences 37%, visual/performing arts 18%.

Computing on campus. 60 workstations in library. Dormitories wired for high-speed internet access and linked to campus network. Commuter students can connect to campus network. Online course registration, online library, helpline, repair service, wireless network available.

Student life. Freshman orientation: Mandatory. Preregistration for classes offered. One week; the week before start of classes. Also, one-day student/family Summer Freshman Orientation sessions offered four times in June/July. **Policies:** Strongly encouraged and recommended that all first and second year undergraduate students live in on-campus housing. Students are allowed to have fish only as "pets" in dorm rooms. **Housing:** Guaranteed on-campus for freshmen. Coed dorms, special housing for disabled available. $100 nonrefundable deposit, deadline 4/15. Honors housing available. **Activities:** Bands, campus ministries, choral groups, dance, drama, international student organizations, literary magazine, music ensembles, musical theater, opera, radio station, student government, student newspaper, symphony orchestra, TV station, Circle K, Alpha Chi Honor Society, Alpha Lambda Delta Freshman Honor Society, health professions organization, Christian Pharmacists Fellowship International, College Democrats, Kappa Kappa Psi Musicianship Fraternity, Catholic campus ministry, Muslim student association, Political Science society.

Athletics. NCAA. **Intercollegiate:** Baseball M, basketball, cross-country, field hockey W, football (tackle) M, golf M, lacrosse, soccer, softball W, tennis, track and field, volleyball W. **Intramural:** Basketball, football (non-tackle), soccer, softball, volleyball. **Team name:** Hornets.

Student services. Adult student services, alcohol/substance abuse counseling, chaplain/spiritual director, career counseling, student employment services, financial aid counseling, health services, minority student services, personal counseling, placement for graduates, veterans' counselor. **Physically disabled:** Services for visually, speech, hearing impaired.

Contact. E-mail: admit@su.edu
Phone: (540) 665-4581 Toll-free number: (800) 432-2266
Fax: (540) 665-4627
David Anthony, Dean of Admissions, Shenandoah University, 1460 University Drive, Winchester, VA 22601-5195

Southern Virginia University
Buena Vista, Virginia
www.svu.edu

CB member
CB code: 5625

- Private 4-year liberal arts college affiliated with Church of Jesus Christ of Latter-day Saints
- Residential campus in small town
- 794 degree-seeking undergraduates: 4% part-time, 50% women, 4% African American, 1% Asian American, 2% Hispanic American, 1% Native American, 1% international
- 99% of applicants admitted
- SAT or ACT (ACT writing optional) required

General. Degrees: 93 bachelor's awarded. **ROTC:** Army. **Location:** 60 miles from Roanoke, 60 miles from Charlottesville. **Calendar:** Semester, extensive summer session. **Full-time faculty:** 38 total; 68% have terminal degrees, 10% minority, 40% women. **Part-time faculty:** 28 total; 14% have terminal degrees, 46% women. **Class size:** 59% < 20, 40% 20-39, 1% 40-49.

Freshman class profile. 1,065 applied, 1,054 admitted, 293 enrolled.

Mid 50% test scores			
SAT critical reading:	460-600	GPA 2.0-2.99:	30%
SAT math:	450-580	Rank in top quarter:	38%
SAT writing:	450-570	Rank in top tenth:	15%
ACT composite:	20-27	Return as sophomores:	42%
GPA 3.75 or higher:	22%	Out-of-state:	86%
GPA 3.50-3.74:	13%	Live on campus:	94%
GPA 3.0-3.49:	33%	International:	1%

Basis for selection. GPA, test scores, interview, religious affiliation or commitment all important. **Home schooled:** Transcript of courses and grades required.

High school preparation. College-preparatory program recommended. Recommended units include English 4, mathematics 3, social studies 2, history 2, science 3 (laboratory 2), foreign language 2, computer science 1, visual/performing arts 1 and academic electives 1.

2011-2012 Annual costs. Tuition/fees: $18,300. Room/board: $6,400. Books/supplies: $1,200. Personal expenses: $1,500.

2010-2011 Financial aid. Need-based: 236 full-time freshmen applied for aid; 199 were judged to have need; 199 of these received aid. Average need met was 60%. Average scholarship/grant was $9,378; average loan $2,946. 68% of total undergraduate aid awarded as scholarships/grants, 32% as loans/jobs. **Non-need-based:** Awarded to 268 full-time undergraduates, including 123 freshmen. Scholarships awarded for academics, art, athletics, leadership, music/drama, ROTC.

Application procedures. Admission: No deadline. $35 fee, may be waived for applicants with need. Admission notification on a rolling basis beginning on or about 11/1. **Financial aid:** Priority date 5/1; no closing date. FAFSA required. Applicants notified on a rolling basis starting 3/1; must reply by 5/1 or within 3 week(s) of notification.

Academics. Special study options: Cross-registration, double major, independent study, internships, study abroad. **Credit/placement by examination:** AP, CLEP, IB, SAT, ACT, institutional tests. **Support services:** Learning center, remedial instruction, study skills assistance, tutoring, writing center.

Majors. Biology: General. **Business:** Business admin. **Computer sciences:** General. **English:** English lit. **Foreign languages:** Spanish. **History:** General. **Liberal arts:** Arts/sciences. **Philosophy/religion:** Philosophy. **Visual/performing arts:** Art, dramatic, music. **Work/family studies:** Family systems.

Most popular majors. Biology 9%, business/marketing 21%, English 13%, family/consumer sciences 13%, liberal arts 14%, visual/performing arts 12%.

Computing on campus. 48 workstations in library, computer center. Dormitories wired for high-speed internet access and linked to campus network. Commuter students can connect to campus network. Online course registration, online library, helpline, repair service, wireless network available.

Student life. Freshman orientation: Mandatory. Preregistration for classes offered. **Policies:** Must abide by the honor code, the dress and grooming standards, and the residential living policies. Most housing is wheelchair accessible. **Housing:** Guaranteed on-campus for freshmen. Single-sex dorms, special housing for disabled, apartments available. $250 partly refundable deposit. **Activities:** Bands, campus ministries, choral groups, dance, drama, international student organizations, literary magazine, music ensembles,

musical theater, opera, student government, student newspaper, symphony orchestra.

Athletics. NAIA, USCAA. **Intercollegiate:** Baseball M, basketball, cheerleading, cross-country, football (tackle) M, soccer, softball W, tennis, volleyball W, wrestling M. **Team name:** Knights.

Student services. Chaplain/spiritual director, career counseling, financial aid counseling, health services, personal counseling.

Contact. E-mail: admissions@svu.edu
Phone: (540) 261-2756 Toll-free number: (800) 229-8420
Fax: (540) 264-8559
Brett Garcia, Dean of Admissions, Southern Virginia University, One University Hill Drive, Buena Vista, VA 24416-3097

St. Paul's College
Lawrenceville, Virginia
www.saintpauls.edu
CB member
CB code: 5604

- Private 4-year liberal arts college affiliated with Episcopal Church
- Residential campus in small town
- 400 degree-seeking undergraduates
- 100% of applicants admitted
- SAT or ACT (ACT writing optional), application essay required

General. Founded in 1888. Regionally accredited. **Degrees:** 129 bachelor's awarded. **ROTC:** Army. **Location:** 80 miles from Richmond. **Calendar:** Semester, limited summer session. **Full-time faculty:** 25 total. **Part-time faculty:** 25 total. **Class size:** 73% < 20, 20% 20-39, 6% 40-49, less than 1% 50-99, less than 1% >100.

Freshman class profile. 803 applied, 803 admitted, 185 enrolled.

Mid 50% test scores			
SAT critical reading:	330-400	GPA 3.50-3.74:	1%
SAT math:	300-400	GPA 3.0-3.49:	9%
SAT writing:	300-390	GPA 2.0-2.99:	49%
ACT composite:	12-17	Out-of-state:	34%
		Live on campus:	90%

Basis for selection. School achievement record most important. School recommendations considered. Rank in top half of class important. 3.0 GPA recommended. Interview recommended.

High school preparation. Required units include English 4, mathematics 2, social studies 2, science 2 and foreign language 1.

2011-2012 Annual costs. Tuition/fees: $13,210. Room/board: $6,640. Books/supplies: $1,500. Personal expenses: $1,400.

Financial aid. Non-need-based: Scholarships awarded for academics, alumni affiliation, athletics.

Application procedures. Admission: No deadline. $20 fee, may be waived for applicants with need. Must reply by May 1 or within 2 week(s) if notified thereafter. **Financial aid:** No deadline. FAFSA required. Applicants notified on a rolling basis starting 1/15; must reply by 7/1 or within 4 week(s) of notification.

Academics. Special study options: Accelerated study, double major, honors, independent study, internships, liberal arts/career combination, teacher certification program. Organizational Management Program for adults 25 and older. **Credit/placement by examination:** AP, CLEP, institutional tests. 24 credit hours maximum toward bachelor's degree. **Support services:** Learning center, pre-admission summer program, reduced course load, remedial instruction, tutoring.

Majors. Biology: General, marine. **Business:** Accounting, administrative services, business admin, management information systems, operations. **Computer sciences:** General. **Conservation:** General. **Education:** Business. **English:** English lit. **Math:** General. **Philosophy/religion:** Philosophy, religion. **Protective services:** Criminal justice. **Social sciences:** General, political science, sociology.

Most popular majors. Business/marketing 65%, liberal arts 12%, security/protective services 8%.

Computing on campus. 100 workstations in dormitories, library, computer center, student center. Dormitories wired for high-speed internet access and linked to campus network. Commuter students can connect to campus network. Helpline, repair service, wireless network available.

Student life. Freshman orientation: Mandatory. Preregistration for classes offered. **Housing:** Single-sex dorms available. $50 nonrefundable

deposit. **Activities:** Pep band, campus ministries, choral groups, dance, student government, Altar Guild, veterans club, Canterbury club, NAACP, single parent support system.

Athletics. NCAA. **Intramural:** Basketball, softball, volleyball. **Team name:** Tigers.

Student services. Adult student services, career counseling, student employment services, financial aid counseling, health services, on-campus daycare, personal counseling, placement for graduates, veterans' counselor.

Contact. E-mail: admissions@saintpauls.edu
Phone: (434) 848-3111 Toll-free number: (800) 678-7071
Fax: (434) 848-1846
William Herrington, Director of Admissions, St. Paul's College, 115 College Drive, Lawrenceville, VA 23868

Stratford University: Falls Church
Falls Church, Virginia
www.stratford.edu
CB code: 3778

- For-profit 4-year university and career college
- Commuter campus in small city
- 666 degree-seeking undergraduates
- Interview required

General. Accredited by ACICS. **Degrees:** 46 bachelor's, 74 associate awarded; master's offered. **Location:** 12 Miles from the District of Columbia. **Calendar:** Quarter, extensive summer session. **Full-time faculty:** 13 total. **Part-time faculty:** 96 total. **Special facilities:** Complete kitchen laboratory facilities.

Basis for selection. Open admission. **Home schooled:** Transcript of courses and grades, state high school equivalency certificate, interview required.

2011-2012 Annual costs. Tuition/fees: $16,650.

Application procedures. Admission: No deadline. $50 fee. Admission notification on a rolling basis.

Academics. Special study options: Accelerated study, distance learning, external degree, independent study, internships. **Credit/placement by examination:** AP, CLEP. **Support services:** Remedial instruction, study skills assistance, tutoring.

Majors. Business: General, business admin, hospitality admin, management information systems. **Computer sciences:** General, computer graphics, information technology, networking.

Most popular majors. Business/marketing 17%, computer/information sciences 83%.

Computing on campus. Online course registration, online library available.

Student life. Freshman orientation: Mandatory. Preregistration for classes offered. **Activities:** Student newspaper.

Student services. Adult student services, placement for graduates, veterans' counselor.

Contact. E-mail: admissions@stratford.edu
Phone: (703) 821-8570 Toll-free number: (800) 444-0804
James Ray, Director of Admissions, Stratford University: Falls Church, 7777 Leesburg Pike, Falls Church, VA 22043

Stratford University: Woodbridge
Woodbridge, Virginia
www.stratford.edu

- For-profit 4-year university and branch campus college
- Large town
- 691 degree-seeking undergraduates

General. Accredited by ACICS. **Degrees:** 39 bachelor's, 68 associate awarded; master's offered. **Calendar:** Quarter, extensive summer session. **Full-time faculty:** 30 total. **Part-time faculty:** 150 total.

Basis for selection. Open admission.

2011-2012 Annual costs. Tuition/fees: $16,650.

Application procedures. Admission: No deadline. $50 fee, may be waived for applicants with need. Admission notification on a rolling basis. **Financial aid:** FAFSA required.

Academics. Special study options: Accelerated study, distance learning, ESL, independent study, internships. **Credit/placement by examination:** AP, CLEP. **Support services:** Remedial instruction, tutoring, writing center.

Majors. Business: Accounting, business admin. **Computer sciences:** Information systems.

Student life. Freshman orientation: Available. Preregistration for classes offered.

Contact. E-mail: admissions@stratford.edu
Phone: (703) 897-1982 Toll-free number: (888) 546-1250
Halima Griffin, Director of Admissions, Stratford University: Woodbridge, 14349 Gideon Drive, Woodbridge, VA 22192

Sweet Briar College
Sweet Briar, Virginia
www.sbc.edu

CB member
CB code: 5634

- Private 4-year liberal arts college for women
- Residential campus in rural community
- 610 degree-seeking undergraduates: 1% part-time, 100% women, 7% African American, 2% Asian American, 6% Hispanic American, 1% Native American, 2% international
- 12 degree-seeking graduate students
- 80% of applicants admitted
- SAT or ACT (ACT writing optional), application essay required
- 70% graduate within 6 years

General. Founded in 1901. Regionally accredited. **Degrees:** 139 bachelor's awarded; master's offered. **Location:** 12 miles from Lynchburg, 166 miles from Washington, DC. **Calendar:** Semester, limited summer session. **Full-time faculty:** 75 total. **Part-time faculty:** 30 total. **Special facilities:** Indoor and outdoor riding facilities, three nature sanctuaries, art barn, college-run nursery school and kindergarten for student teaching, observatory, environmental education and nature center.

Freshman class profile. 688 applied, 547 admitted, 194 enrolled.

Mid 50% test scores			
SAT critical reading:	480-610	GPA 2.0-2.99:	23%
SAT math:	430-580	Rank in top quarter:	50%
SAT writing:	470-600	Rank in top tenth:	20%
ACT composite:	22-28	Return as sophomores:	78%
GPA 3.75 or higher:	31%	Out-of-state:	47%
GPA 3.50-3.74:	17%	Live on campus:	98%
GPA 3.0-3.49:	29%	International:	1%

Basis for selection. High school curriculum and grades are of primary importance, followed by school and teacher recommendations, test scores, and writing ability as demonstrated by essay or personal statement. Interview, extracurricular activities, and personal characteristics are also considered. **Learning Disabled:** Applicant must submit written request for accommodated admissions review to Office of Admissions and enclose appropriate documentation with request.

High school preparation. College-preparatory program required. 16 units required; 20 recommended. Required and recommended units include English 4, mathematics 3-4, social studies 3-4, science 3-4 (laboratory 2-3) and foreign language 2-4. Math prep must be at least through Algebra II; must have at least two consecutive years of the same foreign language.

2011-2012 Annual costs. Tuition/fees: $31,095. Room/board: $11,100. Books/supplies: $1,100. Personal expenses: $1,150.

2010-2011 Financial aid. Non-need-based: Scholarships awarded for academics, art, leadership, music/drama, state residency.

Application procedures. Admission: Closing date 2/1 (postmark date). $40 fee, may be waived for applicants with need. Admission notification on a rolling basis. Must reply by 5/1. **Financial aid:** Priority date 2/15; no closing date. FAFSA required. Applicants notified on a rolling basis starting 3/1; must reply by 5/1.

Academics. General Education Program: students complete requirements that involve communication and quantitative reasoning skills; rationale for broad liberal arts background; emphasis on internships; regular progress self-assessments. Summer research program provides opportunities for high-level work with faculty. **Special study options:** Accelerated study, combined bachelor's/graduate degree, cross-registration, double major, dual enrollment of high school students, exchange student, honors, independent study, internships, liberal arts/career combination, student-designed major, study abroad, teacher certification program, Washington semester. **Credit/placement by examination:** AP, CLEP, IB, institutional tests. Exemption from 1 or more of degree requirements and/or admission to advanced courses may be granted on basis of Advanced Placement Exams, International Baccalaureate Program, transfer credit, or, in some cases, placement tests taken at college. **Support services:** Learning center, study skills assistance, tutoring, writing center.

Majors. Area/ethnic studies: German. **Biology:** General, Biochemistry/molecular biology. **Business:** General. **Conservation:** Environmental science, environmental studies. **Engineering:** Engineering science. **English:** Creative writing, English lit. **Foreign languages:** General, classics, French, German, Spanish. **History:** General. **Liberal arts:** Arts/sciences. **Math:** General. **Philosophy/religion:** Philosophy, religion. **Physical sciences:** Chemistry, physics, theoretical physics. **Psychology:** General. **Social sciences:** Anthropology, archaeology, economics, international relations, political science, sociology. **Visual/performing arts:** Art history/conservation, dance, dramatic, music, studio arts.

Most popular majors. Biology 13%, business/marketing 13%, engineering/engineering technologies 6%, psychology 9%, social sciences 15%, visual/performing arts 14%.

Computing on campus. 117 workstations in library, computer center. Dormitories wired for high-speed internet access and linked to campus network. Commuter students can connect to campus network. Online course registration, online library, helpline, repair service, student web hosting, wireless network available.

Student life. Freshman orientation: Mandatory. Preregistration for classes offered. Begins on a Saturday in August through the following Thursday, which is the official beginning of classes. **Policies:** Self-governing student body; honor system observed. **Housing:** Guaranteed on-campus for all undergraduates. Wellness housing available. **Activities:** Campus ministries, choral groups, dance, drama, film society, literary magazine, music ensembles, musical theater, radio station, student government, student newspaper, symphony orchestra, TV station, Campus Christian Fellowship, campus spirituality coalition, College Republicans, College Democrats, Circle K, Habitat for Humanity, student environmental organization, Vixen PAWS, Newman Club.

Athletics. NCAA. **Intercollegiate:** Field hockey W, lacrosse W, soccer W, softball W, swimming W, tennis W. **Team name:** Vixens.

Student services. Alcohol/substance abuse counseling, chaplain/spiritual director, career counseling, student employment services, financial aid counseling, health services, personal counseling, placement for graduates, women's services. **Physically disabled:** Services for hearing impaired.

Contact. E-mail: admissions@sbc.edu
Phone: (434) 381-6142 Toll-free number: (800) 381-6142
Fax: (434) 381-6152
Ken Huus, Dean of Admissions, Sweet Briar College, PO Box 1052, Sweet Briar, VA 24595-1502

University of Management and Technology
Arlington, Virginia
www.umtweb.edu

- For-profit 4-year university
- Very large city
- 2,880 degree-seeking undergraduates

General. Accredited by DETC. **Degrees:** 396 bachelor's, 135 associate awarded; master's, doctoral offered. **Location:** 0.1 mile from District of Columbia. **Calendar:** Differs by program, extensive summer session. **Full-time faculty:** 26 total. **Part-time faculty:** 94 total.

Basis for selection. Open admission, but selective for some programs.

Application procedures. Admission: $30 fee, may be waived for applicants with need. Application must be submitted online. Admission notification on a rolling basis.

Academics. Special study options: Accelerated study, combined bachelor's/graduate degree, distance learning, independent study. **Credit/placement by examination:** AP, CLEP. 45 credit hours maximum toward associate degree, 90 toward bachelor's.

Majors. Business: General, business admin, international marketing, market research, marketing. **Computer sciences:** General, computer science, information systems, information technology, LAN/WAN management, networking, security, systems analysis, web page design, webmaster. **Protective services:** Homeland security.

Computing on campus. PC or laptop required.

Contact. E-mail: admissions@umtweb.edu
Phone: (703) 516-0035 Fax: (703) 516-0985
University of Management and Technology, 1901 Fort Myer Drive, Suite 700, Arlington, VA 22209-1609

University of Mary Washington
Fredericksburg, Virginia CB member
www.umw.edu CB code: 5398

- Public 4-year university and teachers college
- Residential campus in small city
- 4,312 degree-seeking undergraduates: 12% part-time, 64% women, 6% African American, 5% Asian American, 6% Hispanic American
- 612 degree-seeking graduate students
- 76% of applicants admitted
- SAT or ACT (ACT writing optional), application essay required
- 70% graduate within 6 years; 36% enter graduate study

General. Founded in 1908. Regionally accredited. Stafford location offering bachelor's degree-completion program and master's degrees. **Degrees:** 1,046 bachelor's awarded; master's offered. **ROTC:** Army. **Location:** 50 miles from Richmond, 50 miles from Washington, DC. **Calendar:** Semester, limited summer session. **Full-time faculty:** 246 total; 76% have terminal degrees, 15% minority, 48% women. **Part-time faculty:** 131 total; 38% have terminal degrees, 11% minority, 50% women. **Class size:** 42% < 20, 51% 20-39, 3% 40-49, 4% 50-99. **Special facilities:** Center for Historic Preservation, James Monroe Museum and Memorial Library, Gari Melchers Home and Studio, Center for Asian Studies, James Farmer Multicultural Center.

Freshman class profile. 4,807 applied, 3,638 admitted, 982 enrolled.

Mid 50% test scores			
SAT critical reading:	530-640	GPA 3.0-3.49:	34%
SAT math:	500-610	GPA 2.0-2.99:	7%
SAT writing:	520-620	End year in good standing:	82%
ACT composite:	22-27	Return as sophomores:	84%
GPA 3.75 or higher:	33%	Out-of-state:	16%
GPA 3.50-3.74:	26%	Live on campus:	93%

Basis for selection. Rigor of high school program most important, followed by GPA, standardized test scores, activities, essays, recommendations. Music majors encouraged to audition. **Home schooled:** Transcript of courses and grades required. Students are advised to take 3 SAT Subject Tests to demonstrate abilities in core curriculum.

High school preparation. College-preparatory program recommended. 15 units required; 20 recommended. Required and recommended units include English 4, mathematics 3-4, social studies 2, history 1-2, science 3-4 (laboratory 3-4) and foreign language 2-4.

2011-2012 Annual costs. Tuition/fees: $8,806; $20,534 out-of-state. Room/board: $9,840. Books/supplies: $1,000. Personal expenses: $1,500.

2010-2011 Financial aid. Need-based: 706 full-time freshmen applied for aid; 387 were judged to have need; 338 of these received aid. Average need met was 52%. Average scholarship/grant was $7,900; average loan $3,400. 51% of total undergraduate aid awarded as scholarships/grants, 49% as loans/jobs. **Non-need-based:** Awarded to 721 full-time undergraduates, including 280 freshmen. Scholarships awarded for academics, alumni affiliation, art, leadership, music/drama, state residency.

Application procedures. Admission: Priority date 11/15; deadline 2/1 (postmark date). $50 fee, may be waived for applicants with need. Admission notification by 4/1. Must reply by 5/1. **Financial aid:** Priority date 3/1, closing date 5/15. FAFSA required. Applicants notified by 4/5; Applicants notified on a rolling basis starting 4/5; must reply by 5/1 or within 2 week(s) of notification.

Academics. College provides grants for undergraduate research program enabling students to work individually with faculty members. **Special study options:** Accelerated study, combined bachelor's/graduate degree, distance learning, double major, independent study, internships, semester at sea, student-designed major, study abroad, teacher certification program, Washington semester. **Credit/placement by examination:** AP, CLEP, IB, institutional tests. Credit from CLEP scores applicable to adult degree; limited to

BA/BS degree program. **Support services:** Pre-admission summer program, study skills assistance, tutoring, writing center.

Majors. Area/ethnic studies: American, women's. **Biology:** General. **Business:** Business admin. **Computer sciences:** General. **English:** English lit. **Foreign languages:** General, classics, French, German, Latin, Spanish. **History:** General. **Liberal arts:** Arts/sciences. **Math:** General. **Philosophy/religion:** Philosophy, religion. **Physical sciences:** Chemistry, physics. **Psychology:** General. **Social sciences:** Anthropology, economics, geography, international relations, political science, sociology. **Visual/performing arts:** General, art history/conservation, music.

Most popular majors. Biology 7%, business/marketing 12%, English 11%, interdisciplinary studies 11%, physical sciences 6%, psychology 8%, social sciences 19%.

Computing on campus. 350 workstations in library, computer center, student center. Dormitories wired for high-speed internet access and linked to campus network. Commuter students can connect to campus network. Online course registration, online library, helpline, repair service, wireless network available.

Student life. Freshman orientation: Mandatory. Preregistration for classes offered. 5-day freshmen/transfer orientation held in August prior to start of classes. **Policies:** Honor System. Freshmen not permitted cars on campus. **Housing:** Guaranteed on-campus for freshmen. Coed dorms, single-sex dorms, special housing for disabled, apartments, wellness housing available. $250 nonrefundable deposit, deadline 5/1. Gender neutral housing, year-round housing available. **Activities:** Bands, campus ministries, choral groups, dance, drama, film society, international student organizations, literary magazine, music ensembles, Model UN, musical theater, opera, radio station, student government, student newspaper, symphony orchestra, Amnesty International, Baptist Student Union, Catholic Student Union, Hispanic student association, Asian student association, Young Democrats, Campus Christian Community, College Republicans, PRISM, BOND.

Athletics. NCAA. **Intercollegiate:** Baseball M, basketball, cross-country, equestrian, field hockey W, lacrosse, rowing (crew), soccer, softball W, swimming, tennis, track and field, volleyball W. **Intramural:** Badminton, basketball, bowling, football (non-tackle), soccer, softball, volleyball, water polo. **Team name:** Eagles.

Student services. Adult student services, alcohol/substance abuse counseling, chaplain/spiritual director, career counseling, services for economically disadvantaged, student employment services, financial aid counseling, health services, minority student services, personal counseling, placement for graduates, veterans' counselor, women's services. **Physically disabled:** Services for visually, speech, hearing impaired.

Contact. E-mail: admit@umw.edu
Phone: (540) 654-2000 Toll-free number: (800) 468-5614
Fax: (540) 654-1857
Kim Johnston, Dean of Admissions, University of Mary Washington, 1301 College Avenue, Fredericksburg, VA 22401-5300

University of Phoenix: Northern Virginia
Reston, Virginia
www.phoenix.edu

- For-profit 4-year university
- Small city
- 719 degree-seeking undergraduates

General. Regionally accredited. **Degrees:** 64 bachelor's awarded; master's offered. **Calendar:** Differs by program. **Full-time faculty:** 9 total. **Part-time faculty:** 103 total.

Basis for selection. Open admission, but selective for some programs.

2011-2012 Annual costs. Estimated costs as of August 2011: per-credit-hour charge, $380 to $480, depending upon level and course of study; electronic course materials fee, $95, if applicable. Book and material charges may vary by course and program. All fees are subject to change.

Application procedures. Admission: No deadline. No application fee. **Financial aid:** No deadline.

Academics. Credit/placement by examination: AP, CLEP.

Majors. Business: Accounting, apparel, business admin, human resources, management information systems, marketing. **Computer sciences:** General, security, webmaster. **Health services:** Health care admin. **Protective services:** Security services.

Contact. Marc Booker, Director of Admission and Evaluation, University of Phoenix: Northern Virginia, 11730 Plaza America Drive, Suite 200, Reston, VA 20190-4750

University of Phoenix: Richmond
Richmond, Virginia
www.phoenix.edu

▶ For-profit 4-year university
▶ Small city
▶ 545 degree-seeking undergraduates

General. Regionally accredited. **Degrees:** 19 bachelor's awarded; master's offered. **Calendar:** Differs by program. **Full-time faculty:** 13 total. **Part-time faculty:** 84 total.

Basis for selection. Open admission, but selective for some programs.

2011-2012 Annual costs. Estimated costs as of August 2011: per-credit-hour charge, $380 to $480, depending upon level and course of study; electronic course materials fee, $95, if applicable. Book and material charges may vary by course and program. All fees are subject to change.

Application procedures. Admission: No deadline. No application fee. **Financial aid:** No deadline.

Academics. Credit/placement by examination: AP, CLEP.

Majors. Business: Accounting/business management, business admin. **Computer sciences:** Webmaster. **Protective services:** Law enforcement admin.

Contact. Marc Booker, Director of Admission and Evaluation, University of Phoenix: Richmond, 6600 West Broad Street, Richmond, VA 23230-1709

University of Richmond
University of Richmond, Virginia
www.richmond.edu

CB member
CB code: 5569

▶ Private 4-year university and liberal arts college
▶ Residential campus in small city
▶ 2,886 degree-seeking undergraduates: 54% women, 7% African American, 5% Asian American, 6% Hispanic American, 7% international
▶ 547 degree-seeking graduate students
▶ 33% of applicants admitted
▶ SAT or ACT (ACT writing optional), application essay required
▶ 83% graduate within 6 years; 25% enter graduate study

General. Founded in 1830. Regionally accredited. **Degrees:** 778 bachelor's awarded; master's, professional offered. **ROTC:** Army. **Location:** 6 miles from downtown; 90 miles from Washington, DC. **Calendar:** Semester, limited summer session. **Full-time faculty:** 325 total; 88% have terminal degrees, 11% minority, 42% women. **Part-time faculty:** 102 total; 59% have terminal degrees, 5% minority, 41% women. **Class size:** 67% < 20, 33% 20-39. **Special facilities:** Museum of art and print study center, greenhouse, electron microscope, radionuclide complex, neuroscience research laboratory, music technology laboratory, art technology laboratory, foundry, herbarium, computer connection to the Jefferson Lab's particle accelerator.

Freshman class profile. 9,431 applied, 3,085 admitted, 781 enrolled.

Mid 50% test scores			
SAT critical reading:	580-690	Rank in top tenth:	59%
SAT math:	610-700	Return as sophomores:	94%
SAT writing:	580-690	Out-of-state:	82%
ACT composite:	28-31	Live on campus:	100%
Rank in top quarter:	85%	International:	9%

Basis for selection. Admission based on character, service, special talents, creativity, life experience, as well as grades, rigor of curriculum, test scores, and recommendations. Campus visits are highly recommended. SAT Subject Tests in foreign languages may be used for placement, but not required. January SAT and SAT Subject Test date and February ACT test date are last acceptable testing dates for fall admission. Character statement required. **Home schooled:** Statement describing home school structure and mission, transcript of courses and grades, interview, letter of recommendation (nonparent) required. Must submit narrative description of home schooling environment. SAT Subject Tests in history, a foreign language and natural science are strongly recommended.

High school preparation. College-preparatory program recommended. 15 units required; 24 recommended. Required and recommended units include English 4, mathematics 3-4, history 2-4, science 2-4 (laboratory 2-4) and foreign language 2-4.

2012-2013 Annual costs. Tuition/fees: $44,210. Room/board: $9,760. Books/supplies: $1,050. Personal expenses: $1,050.

2011-2012 Financial aid. Need-based: 465 full-time freshmen applied for aid; 314 were judged to have need; 314 of these received aid. Average need met was 100%. Average scholarship/grant was $34,155; average loan $2,952. 92% of total undergraduate aid awarded as scholarships/grants, 8% as loans/jobs. **Non-need-based:** Scholarships awarded for academics, art, athletics, leadership, minority status, music/drama, ROTC. **Additional information:** VA residents whose family income is $40,000 or less and who qualify for need-based aid will receive grant assistance equal to full tuition, room and board. Early decision: Financial aid package estimated using historical data; applicant still required to submit all financial aid forms.

Application procedures. Admission: Closing date 1/15 (postmark date). $50 fee, may be waived for applicants with need. Admission notification by 4/1. Must reply by May 1 or within 2 week(s) if notified thereafter. **Financial aid:** Closing date 2/15. FAFSA required. Prior year federal tax return. Applicants notified by 4/1; must reply within 4 week(s) of notification.

Academics. Special study options: Cross-registration, double major, ESL, exchange student, honors, independent study, internships, student-designed major, study abroad, teacher certification program, Washington semester. **Credit/placement by examination:** AP, CLEP, IB, institutional tests. 7 credit hours maximum toward bachelor's degree. Seven unit hours of credit examination may be counted toward a bachelor's degree. **Support services:** Learning center, study skills assistance, tutoring, writing center.

Majors. Area/ethnic studies: American, German, Italian, Latin American, Russian/Slavic, women's. **Biology:** General. **Business:** Accounting, business admin. **Communications:** Journalism. **Computer sciences:** Computer science. **Conservation:** Environmental studies. **English:** English lit, rhetoric/composition. **Foreign languages:** Ancient Greek, Chinese, French, Latin, Spanish. **History:** General. **Math:** General. **Philosophy/religion:** Philosophy, religion. **Physical sciences:** Chemistry, physics. **Protective services:** Criminal justice. **Psychology:** General. **Social sciences:** Anthropology, economics, political science, sociology. **Visual/performing arts:** Art history/conservation, dance, film/cinema/video, music, studio arts, theater arts management.

Most popular majors. Business/marketing 33%, English 8%, foreign language 6%, social sciences 19%.

Computing on campus. 1,018 workstations in dormitories, library, computer center, student center. Dormitories wired for high-speed internet access and linked to campus network. Commuter students can connect to campus network. Online course registration, online library, helpline, repair service, student web hosting, wireless network available.

Student life. Freshman orientation: Mandatory. Preregistration for classes offered. Held the week before classes begin, from Wednesday through Sunday. **Housing:** Guaranteed on-campus for freshmen. Coed dorms, single-sex dorms, apartments available. $300 nonrefundable deposit, deadline 5/1. **Activities:** Bands, campus ministries, choral groups, dance, drama, film society, international student organizations, literary magazine, music ensembles, Model UN, musical theater, radio station, student government, student newspaper, symphony orchestra, Alpha Phi Omega, Amnesty International, Black Student Alliance, Global Health and Human Rights Club, Habitat for Humanity, Multicultural Student Union, Omicron Delta Kappa, Safe Zone, Student Alliance for Sexual Diversity.

Athletics. NCAA. **Intercollegiate:** Baseball M, basketball, cross-country, diving W, field hockey W, football (tackle) M, golf, lacrosse W, soccer, swimming W, tennis, track and field. **Intramural:** Basketball, football (tackle) M, golf, handball, racquetball, soccer, softball, squash, swimming, synchronized swimming W, tennis, volleyball, water polo M, wrestling M. **Team name:** Spiders.

Student services. Alcohol/substance abuse counseling, chaplain/spiritual director, career counseling, student employment services, financial aid counseling, health services, minority student services, personal counseling, placement for graduates, veterans' counselor, women's services. **Physically disabled:** Services for visually, speech, hearing impaired.

Contact. E-mail: admissions@richmond.edu
Phone: (804) 289-8640 Toll-free number: (800) 700-1662
Fax: (804) 287-6003
Gil Villanueva, Dean of Admissions, University of Richmond, Brunet Memorial Hall: 28 Westhampton Way, University of Richmond, VA 23173

University of Virginia
Charlottesville, Virginia
www.virginia.edu

CB member
CB code: 5820

- Public 4-year university
- Residential campus in small city
- 14,539 degree-seeking undergraduates: 3% part-time, 55% women, 7% African American, 12% Asian American, 5% Hispanic American, 6% international
- 6,668 degree-seeking graduate students
- 33% of applicants admitted
- SAT or ACT with writing, application essay required
- 93% graduate within 6 years

General. Founded in 1819. Regionally accredited. **Degrees:** 3,637 bachelor's awarded; master's, professional, doctoral offered. **ROTC:** Army, Naval, Air Force. **Location:** 70 miles from Richmond, 120 miles from Washington, DC. **Calendar:** Semester, extensive summer session. **Full-time faculty:** 1,232 total; 92% have terminal degrees, 13% minority, 32% women. **Part-time faculty:** 64 total; 66% have terminal degrees, 2% minority, 55% women. **Class size:** 53% < 20, 26% 20-39, 6% 40-49, 9% 50-99, 7% >100. **Special facilities:** Observatory, center for biological timing, experimental farm, art museum.

Freshman class profile. 23,587 applied, 7,851 admitted, 3,434 enrolled.

Mid 50% test scores			
SAT critical reading:	610-720	Rank in top quarter:	98%
SAT math:	630-740	Rank in top tenth:	91%
SAT writing:	620-720	End year in good standing:	97%
ACT composite:	28-32	Return as sophomores:	97%
GPA 3.75 or higher:	92%	Out-of-state:	29%
GPA 3.50-3.74:	5%	Live on campus:	100%
GPA 3.0-3.49:	3%	International:	6%

Basis for selection. School achievement record, class rank, test scores most important. Extracurricular activities and interests, quality of writing, recommendation also important. Special consideration for minorities, children of alumni, and in-state students. School diploma may be waived for especially qualified applicants. Following international tests accepted: International Baccalaureate, German Abitur, British AICE, French Baccalaureate, Swiss Federal Maturity Certificate. SAT Subject Tests recommended. Two SAT subject tests of the student's choosing are strongly recommended.

High school preparation. College-preparatory program required. 16 units required. Required and recommended units include English 4, mathematics 4-5, social studies 1-4, science 2-4 and foreign language 2-5. 3 units of science (1 chemistry, 1 physics) required if applying to the School of Engineering and Applied Science.

2011-2012 Annual costs. Tuition/fees: $11,576; $35,898 out-of-state. Room/board: $9,240.

2011-2012 Financial aid. Need-based: 2,501 full-time freshmen applied for aid; 1,181 were judged to have need; 1,181 of these received aid. Average need met was 100%. Average scholarship/grant was $16,781; average loan $5,652. 78% of total undergraduate aid awarded as scholarships/grants, 22% as loans/jobs. **Non-need-based:** Awarded to 2,287 full-time undergraduates, including 625 freshmen. Scholarships awarded for academics, athletics, leadership, minority status, music/drama, state residency.

Application procedures. Admission: Closing date 1/1 (receipt date). $60 fee, may be waived for applicants with need. Application must be submitted online. Admission notification by 4/1. Must reply by May 1 or within 2 week(s) if notified thereafter. Deferred admission maximum postponement is one year. **Financial aid:** Priority date 3/1; no closing date. FAFSA, institutional form required. Must reply by 5/1.

Academics. Special study options: Accelerated study, combined bachelor's/graduate degree, cooperative education, double major, ESL, exchange student, honors, independent study, internships, liberal arts/career combination, semester at sea, student-designed major, study abroad, teacher certification program. Jefferson, Echols, Rodman, and College Science Scholar programs for highest-achieving high school students. January Term. **Credit/placement by examination:** AP, CLEP, IB, institutional tests. 60 credit hours maximum toward bachelor's degree. **Support services:** Learning center, pre-admission summer program, reduced course load, study skills assistance, tutoring, writing center.

Majors. Architecture: Architecture, history/criticism, urban/community planning. **Area/ethnic studies:** African-American, Latin American. **Biology:** General. **Business:** General. **Computer sciences:** General. **Conservation:** Environmental science. **Engineering:** General, aerospace, biomedical, chemical, civil, computer, electrical, mechanical, systems. **English:** English lit.

Foreign languages: Classics, comparative lit, French, German, Italian, Slavic, Spanish. **Health services:** Audiology/speech pathology, nursing (RN). **History:** General. **Liberal arts:** Arts/sciences. **Math:** General. **Parks/recreation:** Exercise sciences. **Philosophy/religion:** Philosophy, religion. **Physical sciences:** Astronomy, chemistry, physics. **Psychology:** General. **Social sciences:** Anthropology, economics, international relations, political science, sociology. **Visual/performing arts:** Art, dramatic, music.

Most popular majors. Biology 7%, business/marketing 9%, engineering/engineering technologies 12%, history 6%, liberal arts 7%, psychology 8%, social sciences 20%.

Computing on campus. Dormitories wired for high-speed internet access and linked to campus network. Commuter students can connect to campus network. Online course registration, online library, helpline, repair service, student web hosting, wireless network available.

Student life. Freshman orientation: Mandatory, $210 fee. Preregistration for classes offered. 2-day program held in July; August session held for international students. **Housing:** Guaranteed on-campus for freshmen. Coed dorms, apartments, fraternity/sorority housing available. Three residential colleges available. **Activities:** Bands, campus ministries, choral groups, dance, drama, film society, international student organizations, literary magazine, music ensembles, Model UN, musical theater, opera, radio station, student government, student newspaper, symphony orchestra, TV station, community service group, Black Student Alliance, general clubs and religious organizations, political organizations, service fraternities and sororities, debating union.

Athletics. NCAA. **Intercollegiate:** Baseball M, basketball, cross-country, diving, field hockey W, football (tackle) M, golf, lacrosse, rowing (crew) W, soccer, softball W, swimming, tennis, track and field, volleyball W, wrestling M. **Intramural:** Badminton, basketball, football (non-tackle), golf, racquetball, soccer, softball, table tennis, tennis, volleyball, water polo, wrestling. **Team name:** Cavaliers.

Student services. Alcohol/substance abuse counseling, career counseling, student employment services, financial aid counseling, health services, legal services, minority student services, on-campus daycare, personal counseling, placement for graduates, veterans' counselor, women's services. **Physically disabled:** Services for visually, speech, hearing impaired.

Contact. E-mail: undergradadmission@virginia.edu
Phone: (434) 982-3200 Fax: (434) 924-3587
Gregory Roberts, Dean of Admission, University of Virginia, Box 400160, Charlottesville, VA 22904-4160

University of Virginia's College at Wise
Wise, Virginia
www.uvawise.edu

CB member
CB code: 5124

- Public 4-year liberal arts college
- Commuter campus in small town
- 1,608 degree-seeking undergraduates: 7% part-time, 49% women, 11% African American, 1% Asian American, 2% Hispanic American
- 77% of applicants admitted
- SAT or ACT (ACT writing recommended) required
- 38% graduate within 6 years

General. Founded in 1954. Regionally accredited. **Degrees:** 265 bachelor's awarded. **ROTC:** Army. **Location:** 60 miles from Bristol. **Calendar:** Semester, limited summer session. **Full-time faculty:** 87 total; 68% have terminal degrees, 7% minority, 42% women. **Part-time faculty:** 88 total; 12% have terminal degrees, 2% minority, 54% women. **Class size:** 69% < 20, 28% 20-39, 2% 40-49, less than 1% 50-99. **Special facilities:** Observatory, scanning electron microscope, oral communication center, nursing assessment stations.

Freshman class profile. 1,121 applied, 865 admitted, 356 enrolled.

Mid 50% test scores			
SAT critical reading:	420-540	Rank in top quarter:	39%
SAT math:	420-530	Rank in top tenth:	16%
SAT writing:	410-510	End year in good standing:	74%
ACT composite:	17-22	Return as sophomores:	62%
GPA 3.75 or higher:	27%	Out-of-state:	8%
GPA 3.50-3.74:	15%	Live on campus:	73%
GPA 3.0-3.49:	29%	Fraternities:	8%
GPA 2.0-2.99:	29%	Sororities:	7%

Basis for selection. Applications reviewed on rolling basis. Emphasis given to academic courses and grades earned in those courses. Interview required for marginal applicants.

High school preparation. 18 units required. Required units include English 4, mathematics 3, social studies 1, history 1, science 2 (laboratory 2), foreign language 2 and academic electives 5. 1 American history, 1 world history required.

2011-2012 Annual costs. Tuition/fees: $7,721; $20,804 out-of-state. Room/board: $8,890. Books/supplies: $830. Personal expenses: $1,300.

Financial aid. Non-need-based: Scholarships awarded for academics, alumni affiliation, art, athletics, job skills, leadership, music/drama, religious affiliation, state residency.

Application procedures. Admission: Priority date 12/1; deadline 8/15 (postmark date). $25 fee, may be waived for applicants with need. Admission notification by 8/20. Admission notification on a rolling basis. Must reply by May 1 or within 2 week(s) if notified thereafter. Early action notification on a rolling basis. **Financial aid:** Priority date 4/1; no closing date. FAFSA required. Applicants notified on a rolling basis starting 2/15; must reply within 4 week(s) of notification.

Academics. Special study options: Accelerated study, cooperative education, distance learning, double major, dual enrollment of high school students, honors, independent study, internships, liberal arts/career combination, student-designed major, study abroad, teacher certification program. **Credit/placement by examination:** AP, CLEP, IB, institutional tests. **Support services:** Learning center, reduced course load, remedial instruction, study skills assistance, tutoring, writing center.

Majors. Biology: General. **Business:** Accounting, business admin, management information systems. **Communications:** Communications/speech/rhetoric. **Computer sciences:** Computer science. **Conservation:** Environmental studies. **English:** English lit. **Foreign languages:** General, French, Spanish. **Health services:** Clinical lab science, nursing (RN). **History:** General. **Human services:** General. **Liberal arts:** Arts/sciences. **Math:** General. **Physical sciences:** Chemistry. **Protective services:** Criminal justice. **Psychology:** General. **Social sciences:** Economics, political science, sociology. **Visual/performing arts:** Art, dramatic.

Most popular majors. Biology 6%, business/marketing 17%, education 17%, health sciences 6%, history 7%, psychology 8%, social sciences 20%.

Computing on campus. 300 workstations in dormitories, library, computer center. Dormitories wired for high-speed internet access and linked to campus network. Commuter students can connect to campus network. Helpline, repair service, student web hosting available.

Student life. Freshman orientation: Mandatory, $45 fee. Preregistration for classes offered. 2-day program held for students and parents. Dormitory space available (free for students, $35 per night for parents). **Housing:** Coed dorms, single-sex dorms, special housing for disabled, apartments available. $150 deposit, deadline 5/1. **Activities:** Concert band, choral groups, dance, drama, international student organizations, literary magazine, music ensembles, musical theater, radio station, student government, student newspaper, TV station, Young Republicans, Young Democrats, multicultural alliance, honors societies, professional organizations, student activities board, Baptist Student Union, Wesley Foundation.

Athletics. NAIA. **Intercollegiate:** Baseball M, basketball, cross-country, football (tackle) M, golf M, softball W, tennis, track and field, volleyball W. **Intramural:** Badminton, basketball, football (non-tackle), racquetball, soccer, softball, table tennis, tennis, volleyball, water polo. **Team name:** Cavaliers.

Student services. Alcohol/substance abuse counseling, chaplain/spiritual director, career counseling, services for economically disadvantaged, student employment services, financial aid counseling, health services, minority student services, personal counseling, placement for graduates. **Physically disabled:** Services for visually, speech, hearing impaired.

Contact. E-mail: admissions@uvawise.edu
Phone: (276) 328-0102 Toll-free number: (888) 282-9324
Fax: (276) 328-0251
Russell Necessary, Vice Chancellor of Enrollment Management, University of Virginia's College at Wise, 1 College Avenue, Wise, VA 24293-4412

Virginia Baptist College
Fredericksburg, Virginia
www.vbc.edu   CB code: 4230

- Private 4-year Bible college
- Large city
- 93 degree-seeking undergraduates
- Application essay required

General. Regionally accredited; also accredited by TRACS. **Degrees:** 4 bachelor's, 3 associate awarded; master's offered. **Location:** 50 miles from Washington, DC. **Calendar:** Semester, limited summer session. **Full-time faculty:** 2 total. **Part-time faculty:** 23 total.

Basis for selection. Application reviewed by admissions to determine acceptance.

2011-2012 Annual costs. Tuition/fees: $4,020. Books/supplies: $400.

Application procedures. Admission: No deadline. $25 fee, may be waived for applicants with need.

Academics. Credit/placement by examination: AP, CLEP, institutional tests. **Support services:** Reduced course load, remedial instruction, tutoring.

Computing on campus. Online library, wireless network available.

Contact. E-mail: office@vbc.edu
Phone: (540) 785-5440
Wayne Scott, Director of Admissions, Virginia Baptist College, 4105 Plank Road, Fredericksburg, VA 22407

Virginia Commonwealth University
Richmond, Virginia   CB member
www.vcu.edu   CB code: 5570

- Public 4-year university
- Commuter campus in small city
- 22,202 degree-seeking undergraduates: 12% part-time, 57% women, 19% African American, 12% Asian American, 6% Hispanic American, 3% international
- 7,056 degree-seeking graduate students
- 66% of applicants admitted
- SAT or ACT (ACT writing optional) required
- 53% graduate within 6 years

General. Founded in 1838. Regionally accredited. **Degrees:** 4,379 bachelor's awarded; master's, professional, doctoral offered. **ROTC:** Army. **Location:** 100 miles from Washington, DC. **Calendar:** Semester, extensive summer session. **Full-time faculty:** 2,032 total; 23% minority, 43% women. **Part-time faculty:** 1,178 total; 18% minority, 52% women. **Class size:** 35% < 20, 41% 20-39, 8% 40-49, 9% 50-99, 8% >100.

Freshman class profile. 14,336 applied, 9,412 admitted, 3,803 enrolled.

Mid 50% test scores			
SAT critical reading:	490-600	Rank in top quarter:	48%
SAT math:	490-590	Rank in top tenth:	18%
SAT writing:	470-590	Return as sophomores:	86%
ACT composite:	20-26	Out-of-state:	12%
GPA 3.75 or higher:	29%	Live on campus:	79%
GPA 3.50-3.74:	18%	International:	3%
GPA 3.0-3.49:	42%	Fraternities:	7%
GPA 2.0-2.99:	11%	Sororities:	7%

Basis for selection. The strength of high school transcripts, grades and test scores are important. Art portfolios or auditions required for some programs. **Home schooled:** Transcript of courses and grades required.

High school preparation. College-preparatory program recommended. 20 units required; 24 recommended. Required and recommended units include English 4, mathematics 3-4, social studies 1, history 2-3, science 3-4 (laboratory 1), foreign language 2-3 and visual/performing arts 1.

2011-2012 Annual costs. Tuition/fees: $9,517; $22,949 out-of-state. Room/board: $8,646.

2010-2011 Financial aid. Need-based: 2,828 full-time freshmen applied for aid; 2,192 were judged to have need; 2,111 of these received aid. Average need met was 59%. Average scholarship/grant was $7,310; average loan $3,501. 43% of total undergraduate aid awarded as scholarships/grants, 57% as loans/jobs. **Non-need-based:** Awarded to 5,781 full-time undergraduates, including 1,357 freshmen. Scholarships awarded for academics, alumni affiliation, art, athletics, leadership, music/drama.

Application procedures. Admission: $40 fee, may be waived for applicants with need. Admission notification on a rolling basis beginning on or about 11/1. Must reply by May 1 or within 2 week(s) if notified thereafter. **Financial aid:** Priority date 3/1; no closing date. FAFSA required. Applicants notified on a rolling basis starting 4/1; must reply within 2 week(s) of notification.

Academics. Special study options: Accelerated study, combined bachelor's/graduate degree, cooperative education, distance learning, double major, dual enrollment of high school students, ESL, honors, independent study, internships, student-designed major, study abroad, teacher certification program. **Credit/placement by examination:** AP, CLEP, IB, institutional tests. **Support services:** Learning center, reduced course load, study skills assistance, tutoring, writing center.

Honors college/program. Entering students with combined SAT scores of at least 1910, rank in the upper 15 percent of graduating class and 3.5 or higher unweighted high school GPA (on a 4-point scale) or recipients of a VCU Presidential Scholarship are eligible for admission. Transfer students with at least a 3.5 cumulative GPA in 12 to 30 semester credit hours of study from transfer institution must complete an Honors College application and present a personal education essay. Continuing students with more than 30 credits and less than 76 credits and a minimum 3.5 cumulative GPA are eligible for admission upon application.

Majors. Area/ethnic studies: African-American, women's. **Biology:** General, bioinformatics. **Business:** General, accounting, managerial economics, marketing, real estate. **Communications:** Media studies. **Computer sciences:** General, information systems. **Conservation:** Environmental studies. **Education:** Art, health. **Engineering:** Biomedical, chemical, computer, electrical, mechanical. **English:** English lit. **Foreign languages:** General. **Health services:** Clinical lab science, dental hygiene, nursing (RN), radiologic technology/medical imaging. **History:** General. **Human services:** Social work. **Math:** General. **Parks/recreation:** General. **Philosophy/religion:** Philosophy, religion. **Physical sciences:** Chemistry, physics. **Protective services:** Forensics, law enforcement admin. **Psychology:** General. **Social sciences:** Anthropology, political science, sociology, urban studies. **Visual/performing arts:** Art history/conservation, cinematography, crafts, dance, dramatic, fashion design, graphic design, illustration, interior design, music performance, painting, photography, sculpture.

Most popular majors. Biology 6%, business/marketing 15%, communications/journalism 6%, health sciences 9%, psychology 8%, security/protective services 8%, visual/performing arts 14%.

Computing on campus. PC or laptop required. 1,400 workstations in dormitories, library, computer center, student center. Dormitories wired for high-speed internet access and linked to campus network. Commuter students can connect to campus network. Online course registration, online library, helpline, repair service, student web hosting, wireless network available.

Student life. Freshman orientation: Mandatory, $45 fee. Preregistration for classes offered. Two-day program. **Housing:** Coed dorms, single-sex dorms available. $250 fully refundable deposit, deadline 6/1. **Activities:** Pep band, campus ministries, choral groups, dance, drama, film society, international student organizations, literary magazine, music ensembles, Model UN, musical theater, radio station, student government, student newspaper, TV station, Chi Alpha Christian Fellowship, Christians on Campus, Eternity, Young Americans for Liberty, African Student Union, German club, intercultural dialogue club, Change for Change, Circle K, Engineers Without Borders Habitat for Humanity.

Athletics. NCAA. **Intercollegiate:** Baseball M, basketball, cross-country, field hockey W, golf M, soccer, tennis, track and field, volleyball W. **Intramural:** Badminton, basketball, football (non-tackle), racquetball, soccer, softball, table tennis, tennis, volleyball. **Team name:** Rams.

Student services. Adult student services, alcohol/substance abuse counseling, career counseling, student employment services, financial aid counseling, health services, minority student services, on-campus daycare, personal counseling, placement for graduates, veterans' counselor. **Physically disabled:** Services for visually, speech, hearing impaired.

Contact. E-mail: ugrad@vcu.edu
Phone: (804) 828-1222 Toll-free number: (800) 841-3638
Fax: (804) 828-1899
Sybil Halloran, Director of Admissions, Virginia Commonwealth University, Box 842526, Richmond, VA 23284-2526

Virginia Intermont College
Bristol, Virginia
www.vic.edu

CB member
CB code: 5857

- Private 4-year liberal arts and teachers college affiliated with Baptist faith
- Residential campus in small city
- 519 degree-seeking undergraduates: 8% part-time, 70% women, 8% African American, 1% Asian American, 2% Hispanic American, 1% Native American, 1% international
- 97% of applicants admitted

- SAT or ACT (ACT writing optional) required
- 31% graduate within 6 years

General. Founded in 1884. Regionally accredited. Evening and weekend college available for working adults; limited majors available. **Degrees:** 97 bachelor's awarded. **Location:** 144 miles from Roanoke, 114 miles from Knoxville, Tennessee. **Calendar:** Semester, limited summer session. **Full-time faculty:** 40 total; 65% have terminal degrees, 52% women. **Part-time faculty:** 98 total; 48% have terminal degrees, 56% women. **Class size:** 95% < 20, 5% 20-39, less than 1% 50-99. **Special facilities:** 120-acre riding center with 2 indoor riding arenas.

Freshman class profile. 370 applied, 359 admitted, 109 enrolled.

Mid 50% test scores			
SAT critical reading:	440-530	GPA 2.0-2.99:	36%
SAT math:	420-520	Rank in top quarter:	30%
SAT writing:	440-520	Rank in top tenth:	11%
ACT composite:	18-24	Return as sophomores:	59%
GPA 3.75 or higher:	20%	Out-of-state:	56%
GPA 3.50-3.74:	13%	Live on campus:	68%
GPA 3.0-3.49:	30%	International:	3%

Basis for selection. School achievement record, SAT or ACT scores, school and community activities important. Essay, interview recommended for all; audition recommended for equine studies; performing arts: portfolio recommended for art, photography. **Home schooled:** Statement describing home school structure and mission, transcript of courses and grades, state high school equivalency certificate required. **Learning Disabled:** Students admitted conditionally, restricted to 12 credit hours in first semester.

High school preparation. College-preparatory program recommended. 16 units required. Required and recommended units include English 4, mathematics 2, social studies 2, science 2 (laboratory 1), foreign language 2 and academic electives 5-8.

2011-2012 Annual costs. Tuition/fees: $24,542. Room/board: $7,690. Books/supplies: $1,200. Personal expenses: $3,000.

2010-2011 Financial aid. Need-based: 107 full-time freshmen applied for aid; 95 were judged to have need; 95 of these received aid. Average need met was 70%. Average scholarship/grant was $17,783; average loan $3,092. 58% of total undergraduate aid awarded as scholarships/grants, 42% as loans/jobs. **Non-need-based:** Awarded to 208 full-time undergraduates, including 68 freshmen. Scholarships awarded for art, athletics, music/drama, religious affiliation, state residency.

Application procedures. Admission: No deadline. $25 fee, may be waived for applicants with need. Admission notification on a rolling basis. **Financial aid:** Priority date 3/1, closing date 6/1. FAFSA required. Applicants notified on a rolling basis starting 2/15; must reply within 3 week(s) of notification.

Academics. Special study options: Accelerated study, cross-registration, distance learning, double major, dual enrollment of high school students, honors, independent study, internships, teacher certification program. **Credit/placement by examination:** AP, CLEP, IB, institutional tests. No maximums for prior work or credit by examination; no cumulative restrictions imposed upon hours earned toward elective credits. Students must complete at least one half of major and take minimum of 25% of classes at school to meet minimum residency requirement. **Support services:** Learning center, reduced course load, study skills assistance, tutoring, writing center.

Majors. Biology: General. **Business:** Business admin, international, marketing. **Conservation:** Environmental studies. **Education:** General, art, biology, elementary, English, physical, secondary, social studies, special ed. **English:** English lit. **General:** Equestrian studies. **Health services:** Premedicine, preveterinary. **History:** General. **Human services:** Social work. **Parks/recreation:** Health/fitness, sports admin. **Philosophy/religion:** Religion. **Protective services:** Law enforcement admin. **Psychology:** General. **Social sciences:** Political science. **Visual/performing arts:** Art, dance, dramatic, music, photography.

Most popular majors. Agriculture 15%, business/marketing 15%, interdisciplinary studies 31%, parks/recreation 7%, public administration/social services 7%, visual/performing arts 13%.

Computing on campus. 100 workstations in dormitories, library, computer center, student center. Dormitories wired for high-speed internet access and linked to campus network. Commuter students can connect to campus network. Online course registration, online library, helpline, wireless network available.

Student life. Freshman orientation: Mandatory. Preregistration for classes offered. **Policies:** Alcohol and tobacco use prohibited on campus. No open flame items or cooking appliances other than microwave ovens. (Juniors and seniors may live off campus, but all other students under 21 years of

age not living with parents must live on campus.). **Housing:** Guaranteed on-campus for all undergraduates. Coed dorms, single-sex dorms, apartments, wellness housing available. $200 partly refundable deposit. **Activities:** Campus ministries, choral groups, drama, international student organizations, music ensembles, musical theater, student government, student newspaper, Christian student union, Cardinal Key, social work action group, Fellowship of Christian Athletes, Alpha Phi Omega.

Athletics. NAIA. **Intercollegiate:** Baseball M, basketball, cheerleading M, equestrian, golf M, soccer M, softball W, volleyball W. **Intramural:** Basketball, bowling, football (non-tackle), golf, softball, table tennis, volleyball. **Team name:** Cobras.

Student services. Adult student services, alcohol/substance abuse counseling, chaplain/spiritual director, career counseling, student employment services, financial aid counseling, health services, minority student services, personal counseling, placement for graduates. **Physically disabled:** Services for visually, hearing impaired.

Contact. E-mail: viadmit@vic.edu
Phone: (276) 466-7856 Toll-free number: (800) 451-1842
Fax: (276) 466-7855
Robin Brooks, Director of Admissions, Virginia Intermont College, 1013 Moore Street, Bristol, VA 24201

Virginia Military Institute
Lexington, Virginia CB member
www.vmi.edu CB code: 5858

- Public 4-year liberal arts and military college
- Residential campus in small town
- 1,605 degree-seeking undergraduates: 10% women, 5% African American, 5% Asian American, 4% Hispanic American, 1% international
- 46% of applicants admitted
- SAT or ACT (ACT writing optional) required
- 70% graduate within 6 years

General. Founded in 1839. Regionally accredited. Mandatory ROTC classes and optional commissioning in the Army, Air Force, Navy, or Marines. **Degrees:** 324 bachelor's awarded. **ROTC:** Army, Naval, Air Force. **Location:** 55 miles from Roanoke, 140 miles from Richmond. **Calendar:** Semester, limited summer session. **Full-time faculty:** 119 total; 97% have terminal degrees, 7% minority, 19% women. **Part-time faculty:** 63 total; 38% have terminal degrees, 8% minority, 35% women. **Class size:** 67% < 20, 33% 20-39. **Special facilities:** Historical museums, research library, observatory, particle accelerator.

Freshman class profile. 2,095 applied, 969 admitted, 480 enrolled.

Mid 50% test scores			
SAT critical reading:	510-620	GPA 3.0-3.49:	41%
SAT math:	530-610	GPA 2.0-2.99:	10%
SAT writing:	480-580	Rank in top quarter:	47%
ACT composite:	22-27	Rank in top tenth:	15%
GPA 3.75 or higher:	29%	Return as sophomores:	87%
GPA 3.50-3.74:	20%	Out-of-state:	42%
		Live on campus:	100%

Basis for selection. GED not accepted. Admissions based on secondary school record, class rank, standardized test scores, character, and personal qualities. Interview, extracurricular activities, state residency, minority status, and volunteer work also important. **Home schooled:** Require transcript with list of texts used or group affiliation.

High school preparation. College-preparatory program required. 16 units required; 19 recommended. Required and recommended units include English 4, mathematics 3-4, social studies 2, history 1, science 3-4 (laboratory 3-4) and foreign language 3-4.

2011-2012 Annual costs. Tuition/fees: $13,184; $32,164 out-of-state. Room/board: $7,446. Books/supplies: $775.

2010-2011 Financial aid. Need-based: 346 full-time freshmen applied for aid; 245 were judged to have need; 243 of these received aid. Average need met was 90%. Average scholarship/grant was $11,709; average loan $3,213. 80% of total undergraduate aid awarded as scholarships/grants, 20% as loans/jobs. **Non-need-based:** Awarded to 776 full-time undergraduates, including 190 freshmen. Scholarships awarded for academics, alumni affiliation, athletics, leadership, music/drama, ROTC.

Application procedures. Admission: Closing date 2/1 (postmark date). $40 fee, may be waived for applicants with need. Admission notification on a rolling basis beginning on or about 1/1. Must reply by May 1 or within 2 week(s) if notified thereafter. **Financial aid:** Closing date 3/1. FAFSA,

institutional form required. Applicants notified on a rolling basis starting 3/1; must reply by 5/1.

Academics. Special study options: Double major, exchange student, honors, independent study, internships, study abroad, teacher certification program. Summer Transition program: Optional for incoming freshmen. **Credit/placement by examination:** AP, CLEP, IB, institutional tests. No policy, but it is unlikely any student would receive more than 36 hours credit. **Support services:** Learning center, pre-admission summer program, study skills assistance, tutoring, writing center.

Majors. Biology: General. **Computer sciences:** Computer science. **Engineering:** Civil, electrical, mechanical. **English:** English lit. **Foreign languages:** General. **History:** General. **Math:** General. **Physical sciences:** Chemistry, physics. **Psychology:** General. **Social sciences:** Economics.

Most popular majors. Biology 6%, engineering/engineering technologies 25%, history 15%, psychology 12%, social sciences 30%.

Computing on campus. PC or laptop required. 200 workstations in library, computer center. Dormitories wired for high-speed internet access and linked to campus network. Online course registration, online library, helpline, repair service, wireless network available.

Student life. Freshman orientation: Mandatory. Preregistration for classes offered. 8 days before beginning of fall classes. Optional month-long summer orientation program coincides with summer academic session, and participants can complete 1 freshman course. **Policies:** Student-run honor system integral part of institution. **Housing:** Guaranteed on-campus for all undergraduates. Coed dorms available. Barracks houses 3-5 students per room. **Activities:** Bands, choral groups, drama, international student organizations, literary magazine, music ensembles, musical theater, student government, student newspaper, more than 50 clubs and student organizations available.

Athletics. NCAA. **Intercollegiate:** Baseball M, basketball M, cross-country, diving M, football (tackle) M, golf M, lacrosse M, rifle M, soccer, swimming, tennis M, track and field, wrestling M. **Intramural:** Basketball, football (non-tackle), soccer, softball. **Team name:** Keydets.

Student services. Alcohol/substance abuse counseling, chaplain/spiritual director, career counseling, student employment services, financial aid counseling, health services, personal counseling, placement for graduates.

Contact. E-mail: admissions@vmi.edu
Phone: (540) 464-7211 Toll-free number: (800) 767-4207
Fax: (540) 464-7746
Col. Vernon Beitzel, Director of Admissions, Virginia Military Institute, VMI Office of Admissions, Lexington, VA 24450-9967

Virginia Polytechnic Institute and State University
Blacksburg, Virginia CB member
www.vt.edu CB code: 5859

- Public 4-year university
- Residential campus in large town
- 23,589 degree-seeking undergraduates: 2% part-time, 42% women, 4% African American, 8% Asian American, 4% Hispanic American, 2% international
- 7,236 degree-seeking graduate students
- 67% of applicants admitted
- SAT or ACT with writing required
- 82% graduate within 6 years

General. Founded in 1872. Regionally accredited. Option of enrolling as member of cadet corps. **Degrees:** 5,705 bachelor's, 43 associate awarded; master's, professional, doctoral offered. **ROTC:** Army, Naval, Air Force. **Location:** 38 miles from Roanoke. **Calendar:** Semester, limited summer session. **Full-time faculty:** 1,368 total; 89% have terminal degrees, 17% minority, 32% women. **Part-time faculty:** 281 total; 12% minority, 47% women. **Class size:** 28% < 20, 41% 20-39, 10% 40-49, 12% 50-99, 8% >100. **Special facilities:** Natural history, geology and art museums, observatory, wind tunnel, Black cultural center, digital music center, robotics laboratory, multimedia laboratory, media center, women's center, math emporium, experimental theater, advanced communications/information technology center, teaching forest.

Freshman class profile. 20,828 applied, 13,860 admitted, 5,221 enrolled.

Mid 50% test scores		GPA 2.0-2.99:	1%
SAT critical reading:	540-640	Rank in top quarter:	85%
SAT math:	570-670	Rank in top tenth:	43%
SAT writing:	540-630	Return as sophomores:	91%
GPA 3.75 or higher:	72%	Out-of-state:	29%
GPA 3.50-3.74:	19%	Live on campus:	98%
GPA 3.0-3.49:	8%	International:	2%

Basis for selection. High school course work, grades, and test scores most important. Prospective students are encouraged to pursue rigorous preparatory course of study through senior year. Audition required for music. **Home schooled:** Transcript of courses and grades required. Must submit standardized test scores; statement describing home school structure and mission recommended but not required.

High school preparation. 18 units required. Required and recommended units include English 4, mathematics 3-4, social studies 1, history 1, science 2-3 (laboratory 2), foreign language 3 and academic electives 4. Preference given to applicants with mathematics beyond algebra II. 4 mathematics units required for general engineering, biochemistry, chemistry, computer science, math, physics and statistics. 3 units of science including physics required for engineering and recommended for all science-related majors.

2011-2012 Annual costs. Tuition/fees: $10,509; $24,480 out-of-state. Funds for the Future program provides tuition increase protection varying levels of protection based on family income for both VA residents and non-VA residents. Room/board: $6,856. Books/supplies: $1,080. Personal expenses: $1,160.

2010-2011 Financial aid. Need-based: 3,949 full-time freshmen applied for aid; 2,498 were judged to have need; 2,261 of these received aid. Average need met was 62%. Average scholarship/grant was $7,931; average loan $4,159. 52% of total undergraduate aid awarded as scholarships/grants, 48% as loans/jobs. **Non-need-based:** Awarded to 10,925 full-time undergraduates, including 2,554 freshmen. Scholarships awarded for academics, art, athletics, leadership, minority status, music/drama, ROTC, state residency. **Additional information:** Funds for the future (FFF) program provides tuition increase protection with varying levels of protection based on family income for both VA residents and non VA residents. A three year renewable need-based program.

Application procedures. Admission: Closing date 1/15 (postmark date). $60 fee, may be waived for applicants with need. Admission notification by 4/1. Must reply by 5/1. $400 fee is required of all freshmen and transfer students at the time they accept the offer of admission. To request refund of $400 matriculation deposit, mail written request to the Office of Undergraduate Admissions, postmarked no later than May 1, 2012. **Financial aid:** Priority date 3/1; no closing date. FAFSA required. Applicants notified by 4/1; must reply by 5/1 or within 4 week(s) of notification.

Academics. Special study options: Accelerated study, combined bachelor's/graduate degree, cooperative education, distance learning, double major, ESL, honors, independent study, internships, liberal arts/career combination, semester at sea, study abroad, teacher certification program, Washington semester. **Credit/placement by examination:** AP, CLEP, IB, institutional tests. 12 credit hours maximum toward bachelor's degree. **Support services:** Learning center, study skills assistance, tutoring, writing center.

Honors college/program. 1350 minimum SAT math and critical reading, 3.7 unweighted GPA, application, letters of recommendation, and personal statement.

Majors. Architecture: Architecture, landscape. **Biology:** General, biochemistry. **Business:** Accounting, business admin, construction management, finance, hospitality admin, management science, managerial economics, marketing. **Communications:** Communications/speech/rhetoric. **Computer sciences:** General. **Conservation:** Environmental science, environmental studies, forestry. **Education:** Secondary. **Engineering:** Aerospace, agricultural, chemical, civil, computer, construction, electrical, engineering mechanics, industrial, materials, mechanical, mining. **English:** English lit. **Foreign languages:** General. **General:** Agribusiness operations, agronomy, animal sciences, dairy, food science, horticultural science. **History:** General. **Human services:** Public policy. **Liberal arts:** Arts/sciences. **Math:** General, statistics. **Philosophy/religion:** Philosophy. **Physical sciences:** Chemistry, geology, meteorology, physics. **Psychology:** General. **Social sciences:** Applied economics, economics, geography, international relations, political science, sociology. **Visual/performing arts:** Art, dramatic, industrial design, interior design, music. **Work/family studies:** Business, family studies, food/nutrition.

Most popular majors. Biology 8%, business/marketing 20%, engineering/engineering technologies 20%, family/consumer sciences 7%, social sciences 8%.

Computing on campus. PC or laptop required. 331 workstations in dormitories, library, computer center, student center. Dormitories wired for high-speed internet access and linked to campus network. Commuter students can connect to campus network. Online course registration, online library, helpline, repair service, student web hosting, wireless network available.

Student life. Freshman orientation: Available, $140 fee. Preregistration for classes offered. Day and a half long program held in July. **Policies:** Freshmen required to live on campus, unless living with parents or close relatives, married, veteran, or at least 21 years old. Honor system is enforced. **Housing:** Guaranteed on-campus for freshmen. Coed dorms, single-sex dorms, special housing for disabled, fraternity/sorority housing, wellness housing available. Cadets live in cadet residence halls. **Activities:** Bands, campus ministries, choral groups, dance, drama, international student organizations, literary magazine, music ensembles, musical theater, radio station, student government, student newspaper, over 600 clubs and organizations available.

Athletics. NCAA. **Intercollegiate:** Baseball M, basketball, cheerleading, cross-country, diving, football (tackle) M, golf M, lacrosse W, soccer, softball W, swimming, tennis, track and field, volleyball W, wrestling M. **Intramural:** Basketball, bowling, football (non-tackle), racquetball, soccer, softball, swimming, table tennis, tennis, volleyball. **Team name:** Hokies.

Student services. Alcohol/substance abuse counseling, chaplain/spiritual director, career counseling, student employment services, financial aid counseling, health services, legal services, minority student services, personal counseling, placement for graduates, veterans' counselor, women's services. **Physically disabled:** Services for visually, hearing impaired.

Contact. E-mail: vtadmiss@vt.edu
Phone: (540) 231-6267 Fax: (540) 231-3242
Mildred Johnson, Director of Undergraduate Admissions, Virginia Polytechnic Institute and State University, 965 Prices Fork Road, Blacksburg, VA 24061-0202

Virginia State University
Petersburg, Virginia
www.vsu.edu

CB member
CB code: 5860

- Public 4-year university
- Residential campus in large town
- 5,181 degree-seeking undergraduates: 4% part-time, 60% women, 85% African American, 2% Hispanic American
- 554 degree-seeking graduate students
- 71% of applicants admitted
- SAT or ACT (ACT writing optional) required
- 40% graduate within 6 years

General. Founded in 1882. Regionally accredited. **Degrees:** 712 bachelor's, 11 associate awarded; master's, doctoral offered. **ROTC:** Army. **Location:** 25 miles from Richmond. **Calendar:** Semester, limited summer session. **Full-time faculty:** 280 total; 67% minority, 43% women. **Part-time faculty:** 219 total; 71% minority, 51% women. **Class size:** 33% < 20, 50% 20-39, 9% 40-49, 8% 50-99, less than 1% >100.

Freshman class profile. 6,515 applied, 4,606 admitted, 1,228 enrolled.

Mid 50% test scores		GPA 3.0-3.49:	22%
SAT critical reading:	390-460	GPA 2.0-2.99:	73%
SAT math:	390-460	Rank in top quarter:	7%
SAT writing:	380-450	Rank in top tenth:	1%
ACT composite:	15-19	Out-of-state:	38%
GPA 3.75 or higher:	2%	Live on campus:	94%
GPA 3.50-3.74:	3%		

Basis for selection. School achievement record most important; recommendation required. Essay recommended for all; audition required for music; portfolio recommended for art.

High school preparation. 11 units required. Required and recommended units include English 4, mathematics 3, social studies 2, science 2 (laboratory 1) and foreign language 2. Mathematics requirement must include algebra I.

2011-2012 Annual costs. Tuition/fees: $7,090; $15,458 out-of-state. Out-of-state students pay an additional required fee of $530. Room/board: $8,880. Books/supplies: $1,300. Personal expenses: $675.

Financial aid. Non-need-based: Scholarships awarded for academics, alumni affiliation, art, athletics, job skills, leadership, music/drama, religious affiliation, ROTC. **Additional information:** Strongly recommend that students apply for scholarship assistance through federal, state, local and private agencies.

Application procedures. Admission: Priority date 3/31; deadline 5/1 (postmark date). $25 fee, may be waived for applicants with need. Admission

notification on a rolling basis. Must reply by May 1 or within 2 week(s) if notified thereafter. **Financial aid:** Priority date 3/31, closing date 5/1. FAFSA, institutional form required. Applicants notified on a rolling basis starting 5/1; must reply within 2 week(s) of notification.

Academics. **Special study options:** Cooperative education, double major, dual enrollment of high school students, exchange student, honors, independent study, internships, teacher certification program. **Credit/placement by examination:** AP, CLEP, institutional tests. 12 credit hours maximum toward bachelor's degree. **Support services:** Study skills assistance, tutoring, writing center.

Majors. **Biology:** General. **Business:** Accounting, business admin, hospitality admin, managerial economics, marketing. **Communications:** Media studies. **Computer sciences:** Computer science, information technology. **Education:** Business, physical, trade/industrial. **Engineering:** Computer, manufacturing. **English:** English lit. **History:** General. **Human services:** General, social work. **Liberal arts:** Arts/sciences. **Math:** General. **Physical sciences:** Chemistry, physics. **Protective services:** Criminal justice. **Psychology:** General. **Social sciences:** Political science, sociology. **Visual/performing arts:** General, music performance. **Work/family studies:** Communication.

Most popular majors. Business/marketing 18%, communications/journalism 7%, education 14%, interdisciplinary studies 8%, psychology 8%, security/protective services 9%.

Computing on campus. 1,461 workstations in dormitories, library, student center. Dormitories wired for high-speed internet access and linked to campus network. Commuter students can connect to campus network. Online course registration, online library, helpline, repair service available.

Student life. **Freshman orientation:** Mandatory, $75 fee. Preregistration for classes offered. Two-day orientation held at various times in the summer. **Housing:** Guaranteed on-campus for freshmen. Coed dorms, single-sex dorms, apartments, wellness housing available. $150 nonrefundable deposit. **Activities:** Bands, campus ministries, choral groups, dance, drama, literary magazine, music ensembles, radio station, student government, student newspaper, TV station, NAACP, Black Students Against Drugs, Muslim student organization, peer mediators, Betterment of Brothers and Sisters, Caribbean students association, Institute for Leadership Development.

Athletics. NCAA. **Intercollegiate:** Baseball M, basketball, bowling W, cheerleading, cross-country, football (tackle) M, golf, softball W, tennis, track and field, volleyball W. **Intramural:** Basketball, football (tackle) M, swimming, table tennis, tennis, track and field, volleyball W. **Team name:** Trojans.

Student services. Alcohol/substance abuse counseling, chaplain/spiritual director, career counseling, services for economically disadvantaged, student employment services, financial aid counseling, health services, personal counseling, placement for graduates, veterans' counselor. **Physically disabled:** Services for visually, hearing impaired.

Contact. E-mail: admiss@vsu.edu
Phone: (804) 524-5902 Toll-free number: (800) 871-7611
Fax: (804) 524-5055
Irene Logan, Director of Admissions, Virginia State University, 1 Hayden Drive, Petersburg, VA 23806

Virginia Union University
Richmond, Virginia
www.vuu.edu
CB member
CB code: 5862

- Private 4-year university and liberal arts college affiliated with Baptist faith
- Residential campus in small city
- 1,333 degree-seeking undergraduates
- 75% of applicants admitted
- SAT or ACT (ACT writing recommended) required

General. Founded in 1865. Regionally accredited. **Degrees:** 154 bachelor's awarded; master's, professional offered. **ROTC:** Army. **Location:** 90 miles from Norfolk, 100 miles from Washington, DC. **Calendar:** Semester, limited summer session. **Full-time faculty:** 77 total. **Part-time faculty:** 9 total. **Special facilities:** Police academy, learning resource center.

Freshman class profile. 8,327 applied, 6,245 admitted, 503 enrolled.

Mid 50% test scores			
SAT critical reading:	350-430	GPA 3.0-3.49:	8%
SAT math:	340-440	GPA 2.0-2.99:	70%
ACT composite:	13-17	Rank in top quarter:	12%
GPA 3.75 or higher:	2%	Rank in top tenth:	4%
GPA 3.50-3.74:	2%	Out-of-state:	54%
		Live on campus:	64%

Basis for selection. Secondary school record, test scores, extracurricular activities most important. Essay, interview, and talent or ability also important. Essay recommended for all. Interview recommended for academically weak. Audition required for band, choir, music, university players.

High school preparation. 16 units required. Required units include English 4, mathematics 3, social studies 2, science 2, foreign language 2 and academic electives 3.

2011-2012 Annual costs. Tuition/fees: $14,630. Room/board: $7,174. Books/supplies: $1,080. Personal expenses: $1,750.

Financial aid. **Non-need-based:** Scholarships awarded for academics, athletics, ROTC, state residency.

Application procedures. **Admission:** Priority date 6/30; no deadline. $25 fee, may be waived for applicants with need. Admission notification on a rolling basis. **Financial aid:** Priority date 4/27; no closing date. FAFSA required. Applicants notified on a rolling basis starting 5/1; must reply within 2 week(s) of notification.

Academics. **Special study options:** Cooperative education, double major, honors, independent study, internships, liberal arts/career combination, study abroad, teacher certification program, weekend college. **Credit/placement by examination:** AP, CLEP, IB, institutional tests. 18 credit hours maximum toward bachelor's degree. **Support services:** Learning center, reduced course load, remedial instruction, tutoring, writing center.

Majors. **Biology:** General. **Business:** Accounting, business admin, finance, management information systems, sales/distribution. **Communications:** Journalism, media studies. **Computer sciences:** General. **Education:** Multi-level teacher. **English:** English lit. **History:** General. **Human services:** General, social work. **Math:** General. **Philosophy/religion:** Religion. **Physical sciences:** Chemistry. **Psychology:** General. **Social sciences:** Criminology, political science. **Visual/performing arts:** Art.

Most popular majors. Business/marketing 14%, education 9%, psychology 8%, social sciences 11%, theological studies 42%.

Computing on campus. PC or laptop required. 148 workstations in library, computer center. Dormitories linked to campus network. Online course registration, wireless network available.

Student life. **Freshman orientation:** Mandatory. Preregistration for classes offered. **Housing:** Coed dorms, single-sex dorms available. $250 deposit, deadline 7/1. **Activities:** Bands, campus ministries, choral groups, dance, drama, music ensembles, musical theater, opera, student government, student newspaper, social work club, sociology club, student education association, Ministers Alliance.

Athletics. NCAA. **Intercollegiate:** Basketball, bowling W, cross-country, football (tackle) M, golf, softball W, tennis, track and field, volleyball W. **Intramural:** Basketball, football (non-tackle) M, softball, table tennis. **Team name:** Panthers.

Student services. Career counseling, student employment services, health services, personal counseling, placement for graduates.

Contact. E-mail: admissions@vuu.edu
Phone: (804) 342-3570 Toll-free number: (800) 368-3227
Fax: (804) 342-3511
James Edwards, Office of Enrollment, Virginia Union University, 1500 North Lombardy Street, Richmond, VA 23220

Virginia University of Lynchburg
Lynchburg, Virginia
www.vul.edu

- Private 4-year liberal arts and seminary college
- Commuter campus in small city
- 639 degree-seeking undergraduates: 35% part-time, 37% women
- 77 degree-seeking graduate students

General. Regionally accredited; also accredited by TRACS. **Degrees:** 15 bachelor's, 3 associate awarded; master's, doctoral offered. **Location:** 63 miles from Charlottesville. **Calendar:** Semester, limited summer session. **Full-time faculty:** 12 total. **Part-time faculty:** 76 total.

Basis for selection. Open admission. **Home schooled:** Transcript of courses and grades, state high school equivalency certificate required.

2012-2013 Annual costs. Tuition/fees (projected): $7,880. Room/board: $8,520. Books/supplies: $650.

Application procedures. Admission: No deadline. $25 fee, may be waived for applicants with need. Application must be submitted on paper. Admission notification on a rolling basis.

Academics. Special study options: Distance learning, external degree. **Credit/placement by examination:** AP, CLEP, IB, institutional tests. **Support services:** Learning center, reduced course load, remedial instruction, study skills assistance, tutoring, writing center.

Majors. Business: Business admin, management science. **Philosophy/religion:** Religion. **Social sciences:** Sociology.

Computing on campus. 10 workstations in library, computer center. Dormitories wired for high-speed internet access and linked to campus network. Commuter students can connect to campus network. Online course registration, online library, helpline, wireless network available.

Student life. Freshman orientation: Mandatory. Preregistration for classes offered. **Housing:** Coed dorms available. $100 partly refundable deposit. **Activities:** Campus ministries, choral groups, student government.

Athletics. USCAA. **Intramural:** Basketball, football (tackle), track and field. **Team name:** Dragons.

Student services. Adult student services, chaplain/spiritual director, career counseling, financial aid counseling, health services, personal counseling, veterans' counselor.

Contact. E-mail: yburns@vul.edu
Phone: (434) 528-5276 ext. 1150 Fax: (434) 528-4257
Yolanda Burns, Director of Admissions, Virginia University of Lynchburg, 2058 Garfield Avenue, Lynchburg, VA 24501-6417

Virginia Wesleyan College
Norfolk, Virginia
www.vwc.edu
CB member
CB code: 5867

- Private 4-year liberal arts college affiliated with United Methodist Church
- Residential campus in large city
- 1,367 degree-seeking undergraduates: 9% part-time, 63% women, 23% African American, 1% Asian American, 6% Hispanic American
- 86% of applicants admitted
- Application essay required
- 48% graduate within 6 years; 32% enter graduate study

General. Founded in 1961. Regionally accredited. **Degrees:** 250 bachelor's awarded. **ROTC:** Army. **Location:** 8 miles from downtown. **Calendar:** 4-1-4, limited summer session. **Full-time faculty:** 87 total; 90% have terminal degrees, 10% minority, 47% women. **Part-time faculty:** 44 total; 23% have terminal degrees, 23% minority, 50% women. **Class size:** 80% < 20, 20% 20-39. **Special facilities:** Research vessel, Center for Sacred Music, greenhouse, Center for the Study of Religious Freedom, rock climbing wall.

Freshman class profile. 3,174 applied, 2,730 admitted, 439 enrolled.

Mid 50% test scores			
SAT critical reading:	440-540	Rank in top quarter:	40%
SAT math:	430-540	Rank in top tenth:	14%
SAT writing:	430-520	End year in good standing:	90%
ACT composite:	19-23	Return as sophomores:	64%
GPA 3.75 or higher:	15%	Out-of-state:	33%
GPA 3.50-3.74:	19%	Live on campus:	85%
GPA 3.0-3.49:	32%		
GPA 2.0-2.99:	33%		

Basis for selection. Above average grades in solid college-preparatory curriculum, SAT scores, campus interview, personal statement, extracurricular activities important. SAT/ACT tests may be optional to prospective freshmen who present a 3.5 GPA on a 4.0 scale and who have taken a strong, college preparatory curriculum in high school. **Home schooled:** Transcript of courses and grades required. **Learning Disabled:** Interview with student disabilities coordinator, appropriate documentation dated within past 3-5 years.

High school preparation. College-preparatory program recommended. 12 units required; 16 recommended. Required and recommended units include English 4, mathematics 3, history 1, science 2 (laboratory 2), foreign language 2, computer science 1 and academic electives 4.

2011-2012 Annual costs. Tuition/fees: $29,680. Room/board: $7,988. Books/supplies: $1,000. Personal expenses: $1,800.

2010-2011 Financial aid. Need-based: 294 full-time freshmen applied for aid; 251 were judged to have need; 249 of these received aid. Average

need met was 63%. Average scholarship/grant was $16,171; average loan $5,885. 67% of total undergraduate aid awarded as scholarships/grants, 33% as loans/jobs. **Non-need-based:** Awarded to 294 full-time undergraduates, including 65 freshmen. Scholarships awarded for academics, alumni affiliation, leadership, religious affiliation, ROTC, state residency.

Application procedures. Admission: Priority date 3/1; no deadline. $40 fee, may be waived for applicants with need. Admission notification on a rolling basis beginning on or about 9/15. Must reply by May 1 or within 2 week(s) if notified thereafter. **Financial aid:** Priority date 3/1; no closing date. FAFSA required. Applicants notified on a rolling basis starting 2/15; must reply by 5/1 or within 2 week(s) of notification.

Academics. Special study options: Cross-registration, double major, honors, independent study, internships, liberal arts/career combination, student-designed major, study abroad, teacher certification program. Alternative teacher certification program; living and learning communities; distance learning/hybrid courses offerings. **Credit/placement by examination:** AP, CLEP, IB, institutional tests. 30 credit hours maximum toward bachelor's degree. **Support services:** Learning center, reduced course load, remedial instruction, study skills assistance, tutoring, writing center.

Majors. Area/ethnic studies: Women's. **Biology:** General. **Business:** Business admin. **Communications:** Communications/speech/rhetoric. **Computer sciences:** Computer science. **Conservation:** Environmental studies. **Education:** General, art, elementary, learning disabled, middle, secondary. **English:** English lit. **Foreign languages:** General, French, German, Spanish. **Health services:** Predental, premedicine, prepharmacy, preveterinary. **History:** General. **Math:** General. **Parks/recreation:** General. **Philosophy/religion:** Philosophy, religion. **Physical sciences:** Chemistry. **Protective services:** Criminal justice. **Psychology:** General. **Social sciences:** General, international relations, political science, sociology. **Visual/performing arts:** Art, dramatic, music, theater history.

Most popular majors. Business/marketing 17%, communications/journalism 10%, education 9%, interdisciplinary studies 6%, parks/recreation 7%, security/protective services 9%, social sciences 13%.

Computing on campus. 99 workstations in library, computer center, student center. Dormitories wired for high-speed internet access and linked to campus network. Online course registration, online library, helpline, repair service, student web hosting, wireless network available.

Student life. Freshman orientation: Mandatory, $225 fee. Preregistration for classes offered. One-day event scheduled twice during the months of June and July; multi-day academic-related orientation in August. **Policies:** Virginia State Alcohol and Drug Laws enforced. **Housing:** Guaranteed on-campus for freshmen. Coed dorms, single-sex dorms, special housing for disabled, apartments, fraternity/sorority housing, wellness housing available. $300 nonrefundable deposit, deadline 5/1. If campus housing is full and student cannot commute, Residential Life will locate nearby off-campus housing. **Activities:** Campus ministries, choral groups, dance, drama, international student organizations, literary magazine, music ensembles, Model UN, musical theater, radio station, student government, student newspaper, political science association, Habitat for Humanity, black student union, Holy Fire, Honors & Scholars, Campus Kaleidoscope, SALSA, activities council.

Athletics. NCAA. **Intercollegiate:** Baseball M, basketball, cheerleading, cross-country, field hockey W, golf M, lacrosse, soccer, softball W, tennis, track and field, volleyball W. **Intramural:** Basketball, field hockey W, football (non-tackle), racquetball, soccer, table tennis, volleyball. **Team name:** Marlins.

Student services. Adult student services, alcohol/substance abuse counseling, chaplain/spiritual director, career counseling, student employment services, financial aid counseling, health services, minority student services, personal counseling, veterans' counselor, women's services. **Physically disabled:** Services for visually, hearing impaired.

Contact. E-mail: admissions@vwc.edu
Phone: (757) 455-3208 Toll-free number: (800) 737-8684
Fax: (757) 461-5238
Patricia Patten, Dean of Admissions, Virginia Wesleyan College, 1584 Wesleyan Drive, Norfolk, VA 23502-5599

Washington and Lee University
Lexington, Virginia
www.wlu.edu
CB member
CB code: 5887

- Private 4-year university and liberal arts college
- Residential campus in small town
- 1,788 degree-seeking undergraduates: 49% women, 3% African American, 3% Asian American, 3% Hispanic American, 4% international

♦ 396 degree-seeking graduate students
♦ 18% of applicants admitted
♦ SAT or ACT with writing, application essay required
♦ 91% graduate within 6 years; 27% enter graduate study

General. Founded in 1749. Regionally accredited. **Degrees:** 423 bachelor's awarded; master's, professional offered. **ROTC:** Army. **Location:** 50 miles from Roanoke, 60 miles from Charlottesville. **Calendar:** 4-4-1. **Full-time faculty:** 217 total. **Part-time faculty:** 17 total. **Class size:** 74% < 20, 26% 20-39, less than 1% 40-49, less than 1% 50-99. **Special facilities:** Japanese Tea Room, university special collections, multimedia center, archaeology museum.

Freshman class profile. 6,487 applied, 1,182 admitted, 495 enrolled.

Mid 50% test scores		End year in good standing:	96%
SAT critical reading:	650-740	Return as sophomores:	93%
SAT math:	660-740	Out-of-state:	88%
SAT writing:	650-730	Live on campus:	100%
ACT composite:	29-32	International:	3%
Rank in top quarter:	98%	Fraternities:	85%
Rank in top tenth:	81%	Sororities:	78%

Basis for selection. School achievement record most important, followed closely by test scores, school and community activities, recommendations and personal qualities. Special consideration given to children of alumni and applicants from minorities and low-income families. SAT Subject Tests recommended. 2 unrelated SAT Subject Tests recommended, not required. Interview recommended. **Home schooled:** Transcript of courses and grades, letter of recommendation (nonparent) required. Recommend taking 5 SAT Subject Tests in unrelated fields, interview with admissions officer. Require documentation of reading lists and syllabi.

High school preparation. College-preparatory program recommended. 17 units required. Required and recommended units include English 4, mathematics 3-4, social studies 1-2, history 1-2, science 1-4 (laboratory 1), foreign language 3-4 and academic electives 4.

2011-2012 Annual costs. Tuition/fees: $41,927. Room/board: $10,687.

2011-2012 Financial aid. Need-based: 284 full-time freshmen applied for aid; 231 were judged to have need; 231 of these received aid. Average need met was 100%. Average scholarship/grant was $36,962; average loan $2,440. 93% of total undergraduate aid awarded as scholarships/grants, 7% as loans/jobs. **Non-need-based:** Awarded to 417 full-time undergraduates, including 89 freshmen. Scholarships awarded for academics.

Application procedures. Admission: Priority date 11/15; deadline 1/2 (postmark date). $50 fee, may be waived for applicants with need. Admission notification by 4/1. Must reply by 5/1. **Financial aid:** Closing date 2/15. FAFSA, CSS PROFILE required. Applicants notified by 4/1; must reply by 5/1.

Academics. Special study options: Cross-registration, double major, exchange student, honors, independent study, internships, liberal arts/career combination, New York semester, student-designed major, study abroad, teacher certification program, Washington semester. Member Seven College Consortium, professional ethics seminars in business, law, medicine, journalism. **Credit/placement by examination:** AP, CLEP, IB, institutional tests. **Support services:** Study skills assistance, tutoring, writing center.

Majors. Area/ethnic studies: East Asian, Russian/Slavic. **Biology:** General, biochemistry, neuroscience. **Business:** Accounting, accounting/business management, business admin. **Communications:** Journalism. **Computer sciences:** Computer science. **Conservation:** Environmental studies. **Engineering:** Applied physics, chemical. **English:** English lit. **Foreign languages:** Classics, East Asian, French, German, Romance, Spanish. **History:** General. **Math:** General. **Philosophy/religion:** Philosophy, religion. **Physical sciences:** Chemistry, geology, physics. **Psychology:** General. **Social sciences:** Anthropology, economics, political science, sociology. **Visual/performing arts:** Art history/conservation, dramatic, music, studio arts.

Most popular majors. Biology 6%, business/marketing 18%, English 7%, foreign language 9%, history 7%, social sciences 20%, visual/performing arts 6%.

Computing on campus. 190 workstations in dormitories, library, computer center, student center. Dormitories wired for high-speed internet access and linked to campus network. Commuter students can connect to campus network. Online course registration, online library, helpline, repair service, student web hosting, wireless network available.

Student life. Freshman orientation: Mandatory. Preregistration for classes offered. 4 days prior to beginning of fall term. **Policies:** Student-run honor system, observed with single sanction. **Housing:** Guaranteed on-campus for freshmen. Coed dorms, special housing for disabled, apartments, fraternity/sorority housing, wellness housing available. $150 nonrefundable

deposit, deadline 5/1. Outing Club House, Spanish House, Chavis House available, substance-free halls. **Activities:** Bands, campus ministries, choral groups, dance, drama, film society, international student organizations, literary magazine, music ensembles, Model UN, radio station, student government, student newspaper, symphony orchestra, TV station, Alpha Phi Omega, Young Life, Generals Fellowship, Multicultural Student Association, Hillel, Habitat for Humanity, Americans for Informed Democracy, Baptist Student Union, Catholic Campus Ministry, Campus Kitchen.

Athletics. NCAA. **Intercollegiate:** Baseball M, basketball, cross-country, equestrian W, field hockey W, football (tackle) M, golf, lacrosse, soccer, swimming, tennis, track and field, volleyball W, wrestling M. **Intramural:** Badminton, basketball, football (non-tackle), soccer, softball, swimming, table tennis, tennis, volleyball, water polo, wrestling M. **Team name:** Generals.

Student services. Alcohol/substance abuse counseling, chaplain/spiritual director, career counseling, student employment services, financial aid counseling, health services, minority student services, personal counseling, placement for graduates. **Physically disabled:** Services for visually, hearing impaired.

Contact. E-mail: admissions@wlu.edu
Phone: (540) 458-8710 Fax: (540) 458-8062
William Hartog, Dean of Admissions and Financial Aid, Washington and Lee University, 204 West Washington Street, Lexington, VA 24450-2116

Westwood College: Annandale
Annandale, Virginia
www.westwood.edu

♦ For-profit 3-year career college
♦ Very large city

General. Regionally accredited. **Calendar:** Quarter.

Annual costs/financial aid. Tuition/fees (2011-2012): $15,020. Books/supplies: $1,106.

Contact. Phone: (703) 642-3770
Director of Admissions, 7619 Little River Turnpike, Suite 500, Annandale, VA 22003

Westwood College: Arlington Ballston
Arlington, Virginia
www.westwood.edu

♦ For-profit 3-year career college
♦ Very large city

General. Regionally accredited. **Calendar:** Quarter.

Annual costs/financial aid. Tuition/fees (2011-2012): $15,020. Books/supplies: $1,106.

Contact. Phone: (703) 243-3900
Director of Admissions, 7619 Litlle River Turnpike, Suite 500, Arlington, VA 22203

World College
Virginia Beach, Virginia
www.worldcollege.edu
CB code: 3970

♦ For-profit 4-year technical college
♦ Large city
♦ 521 degree-seeking undergraduates

General. Accredited by DETC. Affiliated with Cleveland Institute of Electronics. **Degrees:** 26 bachelor's awarded. **Calendar:** Differs by program. **Full-time faculty:** 3 total. **Part-time faculty:** 75 total.

Basis for selection. Open admission, but selective for some programs.

Application procedures. Admission: No deadline. No application fee. Admission notification on a rolling basis.

Academics. Special study options: Accelerated study, distance learning, independent study. **Credit/placement by examination:** AP, CLEP.

Majors. Computer sciences: Security.

Computing on campus. PC or laptop required.

Contact. E-mail: instruct@cie-wc.edu
Phone: (800) 696-7532 Toll-free number: (800) 696-7532
World College, Lake Shore Plaza, 5193 Shore Drive, Virginia Beach, VA
23455-2500

Washington

Antioch University Seattle
Seattle, Washington
www.antiochseattle.edu

CB code: 3070

- Private two-year upper-division university and liberal arts college
- Commuter campus in very large city

General. Founded in 1976. Regionally accredited. **Location:** Less than 1 mile north of the city center in Downtown Seattle. **Calendar:** Quarter.

Annual costs/financial aid. Tuition/fees (2011-2012): $24,030. Books/supplies: $972. Personal expenses: $555. Need-based financial aid available to full-time and part-time students.

Contact. Phone: (206) 268-4202
Acting Director of Admissions, 2326 Sixth Avenue, Seattle, WA 98121-1814

Argosy University: Seattle
Seattle, Washington
www.argosy.edu/seattle

- For-profit 4-year university
- Commuter campus in very large city
- 99 degree-seeking undergraduates

General. Regionally accredited. **Degrees:** 14 bachelor's awarded; master's, professional, doctoral offered. **Calendar:** Differs by program. **Full-time faculty:** 15 total. **Part-time faculty:** 46 total.

Basis for selection. Open admission.

2011-2012 Annual costs. Tuition/fees: $17,962.

Application procedures. Admission: Closing date 9/14. $50 fee. **Financial aid:** No deadline.

Academics. Credit/placement by examination: AP, CLEP.

Majors. Business: Business admin. **Liberal arts:** Arts/sciences. **Protective services:** Police science. **Psychology:** General.

Contact. E-mail: ausadmissions@argosy.edu
Phone: (206) 393-3516 Toll-free number: (888) 283-2777
Tina Jacobs, Senior Director of Admissions, Argosy University: Seattle, 2601-A Elliott Avenue, Seattle, WA 98121

Art Institute of Seattle
Seattle, Washington
www.ais.edu

CB code: 4805

- For-profit 4-year culinary school and visual arts college
- Commuter campus in very large city
- 1,956 degree-seeking undergraduates: 35% part-time, 49% women, 2% African American, 4% Asian American, 8% Hispanic American, 1% Native American, 7% international
- Application essay, interview required

General. Founded in 1982. Regionally accredited. We also offer diplomas in the following areas: Baking and Pastry, Art of Cooking, Digital Design, Digital Image Management, Residential Design, Web Design and Development, and Web Design and Interactive Communication. **Degrees:** 168 bachelor's, 204 associate awarded. **Calendar:** Quarter, extensive summer session. **Full-time faculty:** 61 total; 8% minority, 34% women. **Part-time faculty:** 75 total; 12% minority, 37% women. **Class size:** 13% < 20, 87% 20-39, less than 1% 40-49. **Special facilities:** Gallery with rotating art/design shows.

Basis for selection. Open admission, but selective for some programs. Secondary school record, essay, interview most important; recommendations,

academic records, test scores required. Some programs require a portfolio. **Learning Disabled:** Admissions notifies counselors of students who disclose learning disabilities and special needs. Counselor determines eligibility.

Financial aid. Non-need-based: Scholarships awarded for academics, art.

Application procedures. Admission: No deadline. $50 fee. Admission notification on a rolling basis. **Financial aid:** No deadline. FAFSA required. Applicants notified on a rolling basis.

Academics. Special study options: Distance learning, independent study, internships. **Credit/placement by examination:** AP, CLEP, IB, institutional tests. Course waived by proficiency exam; credit does not count toward degree. **Support services:** Learning center, reduced course load, remedial instruction, study skills assistance, tutoring.

Majors. Business: Apparel. **Communications technology:** Recording arts. **Computer sciences:** Computer graphics, web page design. **Visual/performing arts:** Cinematography, commercial photography, fashion design, game design, graphic design, industrial design, interior design.

Most popular majors. Business/marketing 13%, computer/information sciences 18%, visual/performing arts 66%.

Computing on campus. 480 workstations in library, computer center, student center. Dormitories wired for high-speed internet access. Online course registration, online library, helpline, student web hosting, wireless network available.

Student life. Freshman orientation: Available. Preregistration for classes offered. 1-day program held 1 week before start of the quarter. **Housing:** Guaranteed on-campus for all undergraduates. Coed dorms available. $250 deposit. AIS housing located 1 mile from campus. Students share 1 bedroom and studio apartments in secured apartment complexes. **Activities:** Student government, student newspaper.

Athletics. Intramural: Soccer, softball.

Student services. Adult student services, career counseling, student employment services, financial aid counseling, personal counseling, placement for graduates, veterans' counselor. **Physically disabled:** Services for visually, speech, hearing impaired.

Contact. E-mail: aisadm@edmc.edu
Phone: (206) 448-6600 Toll-free number: (800) 275-2471
Fax: (206) 269-0275
Liane Soohoo, Director of Admissions, Art Institute of Seattle, 2323 Elliott Avenue, Seattle, WA 98121-1622

Bastyr University
Kenmore, Washington
www.bastyr.edu

CB code: 0181

- Private two-year upper-division university and health science college
- Commuter campus in small city
- Application essay required

General. Founded in 1978. Regionally accredited. **Degrees:** 76 bachelor's awarded; master's, professional offered. **Location:** 6 miles from Seattle. **Calendar:** Quarter, limited summer session. **Full-time faculty:** 39 total; 95% have terminal degrees, 59% women. **Part-time faculty:** 69 total; 55% have terminal degrees, 10% minority, 71% women. **Class size:** 78% < 20, 16% 20-39, 1% 40-49, 4% 50-99. **Special facilities:** Whole-food dining commons, research institute and laboratory, natural health sciences library and bookstore, medicinal herb and culinary garden, reflexology path, LEED-platinum student village.

Student profile. 206 degree-seeking undergraduates, 754 degree-seeking graduate students. 98 applied as first time-transfer students. 100% entered as juniors. 75% transferred from two-year, 25% transferred from four-year institutions.

Women:	83%	Live on campus:	8%
Part-time:	13%	25 or older:	85%
Out-of-state:	52%		

Basis for selection. High school transcript, college transcript, application essay required. Transfer accepted as juniors, seniors.

2011-2012 Annual costs. Tuition/fees: $21,000. Room only: $7,050. Books/supplies: $1,150. Personal expenses: $2,940.

Financial aid. Need-based: 167 applied for aid; 162 were judged to have need; 162 of these received aid. Average need met was 31%. 38% of total

undergraduate aid awarded as scholarships/grants, 62% as loans/jobs. **Non-need-based:** Scholarships awarded for academics, alumni affiliation, job skills, leadership.

Application procedures. Admission: Priority date 3/15. $60 fee. **Financial aid:** No deadline. Applicants notified on a rolling basis; must reply within 3 weeks of notification. FAFSA, institutional form required.

Academics. Special study options: Double major, independent study, internships, study abroad, weekend college. Combined BS/MS programs. **Credit/placement by examination:** AP, CLEP.

Majors. Health services: Acupuncture, Chinese medicine/herbology, herbalism, midwifery. **Parks/recreation:** Exercise sciences. **Psychology:** General. **Work/family studies:** Food/nutrition.

Most popular majors. Family/consumer sciences 16%, health sciences 57%, personal/culinary services 17%, psychology 11%.

Computing on campus. 72 workstations in library, computer center. Dormitories wired for high-speed internet access and linked to campus network. Online library, helpline, wireless network available.

Student life. Housing: Coed dorms, special housing for disabled, apartments available. Eco-friendly LEED-platinum-certified Student Village on campus. **Activities:** Campus ministries, choral groups, dance, international student organizations, music ensembles, student government, Student Physicians for Social Responsibility, Herbal Ways club, intuition club, nature cure club, Ayurvedic club, karate club, Bastyr Supernaturals soccer club, Bach Flower Remedies club, Christian Fellowship, pediatrics club, student nutrition association, sports medicine club.

Athletics. Intramural: Basketball.

Student services. Career counseling, financial aid counseling, health services, personal counseling. **Physically disabled:** Services for visually impaired.

Contact. E-mail: admissions@bastyr.edu
Phone: (425) 602-3330 Fax: (425) 602-3090
Chris Masterson, Assistant Vice President for Recruitment and Retention, Bastyr University, 14500 Juanita Drive, NE, Kenmore, WA 98028

Central Washington University
Ellensburg, Washington
www.cwu.edu
CB member
CB code: 4044

◆ Public 4-year university
◆ Residential campus in large town

General. Founded in 1890. Regionally accredited. **Location:** 105 miles from Seattle. **Calendar:** Quarter.

Annual costs/financial aid. Tuition/fees (2011-2012): $7,962; $18,633 out-of-state. Room/board: $9,000. Books/supplies: $972. Personal expenses: $1,704. Need-based financial aid available to full-time and part-time students.

Contact. Phone: (509) 963-1211
Director of Admissions, 400 East University Way, Ellensburg, WA 98926-7463

City University of Seattle
Bellevue, Washington
www.cityu.edu
CB code: 4042

◆ Private two-year upper-division university
◆ Commuter campus in very large city

General. Founded in 1973. Regionally accredited. University maintains satellite sites in Renton, Everett, North Seattle, Tacoma, and Vancouver, Washington; Victoria, Vancouver, Edmonton, and Calgary, Canada; Trencin and Bratislava, Slovakia; Prague, Czech Republic; Sofia and Pratvetz, Bulgaria; Athens, Greece; Zurich, Switzerland; and Beijing, China; partnership in Queensland, Australia. **Degrees:** 704 bachelor's, 36 associate awarded; master's, professional offered. **Location:** 12 miles from Seattle. **Calendar:** Quarter, extensive summer session. **Full-time faculty:** 29 total; 38% have terminal degrees, 10% minority, 45% women. **Part-time faculty:** 588 total; 20% have terminal degrees, 11% minority, 42% women. **Class size:** 94% < 20, 6% 20-39, less than 1% 50-99.

Student profile. 1,009 degree-seeking undergraduates, 1,241 degree-seeking graduate students. 219 applied as first time-transfer students.

Women:	59%	International:	8%
African American:	7%	Part-time:	40%
Asian American:	4%	25 or older:	79%
Hispanic American:	3%		

Basis for selection. Open admission. College transcript required. Based on course content equivalency and grade point average. Transfer accepted as sophomores, juniors, seniors.

2011-2012 Annual costs. Tuition/fees: $17,190. Books/supplies: $1,000.

Financial aid. Non-need-based: Scholarships awarded for academics. **Additional information:** All degree programs approved for veteran's administration education benefits.

Application procedures. Admission: Rolling admission. $50 fee. **Financial aid:** FAFSA, institutional form required.

Academics. Online tutoring service available to all registered students at all times. **Special study options:** Accelerated study, cooperative education, distance learning, double major, dual enrollment of high school students, ESL, exchange student, external degree, independent study, internships, study abroad, teacher certification program, weekend college. **Credit/placement by examination:** AP, CLEP, IB. 45 credit hours maximum toward associate degree, 90 toward bachelor's. **Support services:** Reduced course load, tutoring.

Majors. Business: Accounting, business admin, international, management information systems, marketing. **Communications:** Communications/speech/rhetoric. **Computer sciences:** Programming. **Education:** Elementary, middle, special ed. **Liberal arts:** Arts/sciences. **Psychology:** General.

Most popular majors. Business/marketing 65%, computer/information sciences 6%, education 23%.

Computing on campus. PC or laptop required. 150 workstations in library, computer center. Commuter students can connect to campus network. Online course registration, online library, helpline, wireless network available.

Student life. Activities: International student organizations, student government.

Student services. Adult student services, career counseling, financial aid counseling, personal counseling, veterans' counselor. **Physically disabled:** Services for visually, hearing impaired.

Contact. E-mail: info@cityu.edu
Phone: (425) 637-1010 Toll-free number: (888) 422-4898
Fax: (425) 709-5361
Melissa Mecham, Vice President Admissions/Student Affairs, City University of Seattle, 11900 NE First Street, Bellevue, WA 98005

Cornish College of the Arts
Seattle, Washington
www.cornish.edu
CB code: 0058

◆ Private 4-year visual arts and performing arts college
◆ Residential campus in very large city
◆ 833 degree-seeking undergraduates: 66% women, 3% African American, 6% Asian American, 7% Hispanic American, 1% Native American, 2% international
◆ 57% of applicants admitted
◆ Application essay required
◆ 45% graduate within 6 years

General. Founded in 1914. Regionally accredited. **Degrees:** 160 bachelor's awarded. **Calendar:** Semester, limited summer session. **Full-time faculty:** 60 total; 13% minority, 53% women. **Part-time faculty:** 116 total; 15% minority, 58% women. **Special facilities:** Electronic music laboratory, experimental books laboratory, music listening center, costumemaking facilities, video editing facilities.

Freshman class profile. 1,076 applied, 616 admitted, 213 enrolled.

GPA 3.75 or higher:	11%	Out-of-state:	52%
GPA 3.50-3.74:	22%	Live on campus:	87%
GPA 3.0-3.49:	31%	International:	1%
GPA 2.0-2.99:	34%		

Basis for selection. Portfolio (for visual artists) or audition (for performing artists), academic achievement history, creative ability, and artistic

goals considered. SAT or ACT recommended. Interview recommended for all; audition required for dance, music, theater; portfolio required for art, design, performance production. Alternative audition and portfolio arrangements for long-distance applicants. **Home schooled:** Transcript of courses and grades, state high school equivalency certificate required.

High school preparation. Required and recommended units include English 4, mathematics 2-4, social studies 3, science 2-4 (laboratory 1) and foreign language 2.

2011-2012 Annual costs. Tuition/fees: $31,055. Room/board: $8,300. Books/supplies: $1,800. Personal expenses: $2,000.

Financial aid. **Non-need-based:** Scholarships awarded for academics, art, music/drama, state residency.

Application procedures. **Admission:** Priority date 3/1; deadline 8/15 (receipt date). $40 fee, may be waived for applicants with need. Admission notification on a rolling basis beginning on or about 1/1. Must reply by May 1 or within 2 week(s) if notified thereafter. **Financial aid:** Priority date 3/1; no closing date. FAFSA required. Applicants notified on a rolling basis starting 3/15; must reply by 5/1 or within 2 week(s) of notification.

Academics. **Special study options:** Cooperative education, independent study, internships, study abroad. **Credit/placement by examination:** AP, CLEP, institutional tests. 30 credit hours maximum toward bachelor's degree. A total of 30 credits through a combination of prior work experience and credit by exam allowed. **Support services:** Remedial instruction, study skills assistance, tutoring, writing center.

Majors. **Visual/performing arts:** General, acting, art, cinematography, commercial/advertising art, dance, design, directing/producing, dramatic, drawing, graphic design, illustration, interior design, jazz, music performance, music theory/composition, painting, photography, piano/keyboard, play/screenwriting, printmaking, sculpture, stringed instruments, studio arts, theater design, voice/opera.

Computing on campus. 91 workstations in library, computer center, student center. Dormitories wired for high-speed internet access and linked to campus network. Online course registration, online library, helpline, wireless network available.

Student life. **Freshman orientation:** Mandatory, $175 fee. Preregistration for classes offered. Begins one week before class starts each fall. Students will meet the Chair of their department and register for classes. **Housing:** Guaranteed on-campus for freshmen. Coed dorms available. $300 deposit, deadline 7/25. **Activities:** Bands, choral groups, dance, drama, film society, literary magazine, music ensembles, musical theater, opera, student government, student newspaper, art history club, Birds and Whistles, Black student alliance, bowling club, digital illustration club, Inform the Misinformed Campaign/Corporate Watchdogs, movie club, Salt and Light (Bible study), sports/intramural club.

Student services. Adult student services, alcohol/substance abuse counseling, career counseling, student employment services, financial aid counseling, personal counseling, placement for graduates. **Physically disabled:** Services for visually impaired.

Contact. E-mail: admission@cornish.edu
Phone: (206) 726-5016 Toll-free number: (800) 726-2787
Fax: (206) 720-1011
Sharron Starling, Director of Admission, Cornish College of the Arts, 1000 Lenora Street, Seattle, WA 98121

DeVry University: Federal Way
Federal Way, Washington
www.devry.edu   CB code: 3696

- For-profit 4-year university
- Commuter campus in large city
- 635 degree-seeking undergraduates
- Interview required

General. Additional locations: Seattle Bellevue; Portland (OR). **Degrees:** 101 bachelor's, 15 associate awarded; master's offered. **ROTC:** Army. **Calendar:** Semester, extensive summer session. **Full-time faculty:** 18 total. **Part-time faculty:** 61 total.

Basis for selection. Applicants must have high school diploma or equivalent, or a degree from an accredited postsecondary institution. Must demonstrate proficiency in basic college level skills through test scores and/or institutionally-administered placement exams, and be at least 17 years of age on the first day of classes. New students may enter at the beginning of any semester. CPT also accepted.

High school preparation. College-preparatory program recommended. Required units include mathematics 1. Math unit must be algebra or higher.

2011-2012 Annual costs. Tuition/fees: $15,294. Books/supplies: $1,310. Personal expenses: $3,574.

Financial aid. All financial aid based on need.

Application procedures. **Admission:** No deadline. $50 fee. Admission notification on a rolling basis. **Financial aid:** No deadline. FAFSA required. Applicants notified on a rolling basis.

Academics. **Special study options:** Accelerated study, distance learning. **Credit/placement by examination:** AP, CLEP. **Support services:** Learning center, remedial instruction, tutoring.

Majors. **Business:** General, business admin. **Computer sciences:** Information technology, networking, security, systems analysis, web page design. **Engineering:** Software. **Visual/performing arts:** Game design.

Most popular majors. Business/marketing 45%, computer/information sciences 24%, engineering/engineering technologies 31%.

Computing on campus. 335 workstations in library, computer center. Online course registration, online library, helpline available.

Student life. **Freshman orientation:** Mandatory. Preregistration for classes offered. **Housing:** Private apartments, student-plan housing, private rooms. **Activities:** Student government, student newspaper, alternative sports, business & technology club, gaming, robotics, Institution of Electrical and Electronic Engineers, network gaming.

Student services. Career counseling, student employment services, financial aid counseling, placement for graduates, veterans' counselor. **Physically disabled:** Services for visually, hearing impaired.

Contact. E-mail: admissions@sea.devry.edu
Phone: (253) 943-2810 Toll-free number: (877) 923-3879
Fax: (253) 943-3291
Fred Pressel, Director of Admissions, DeVry University: Federal Way, 3600 South 344th Way, Federal Way, WA 98001-9558

DigiPen Institute of Technology
Redmond, Washington
www.digipen.edu   CB code: 4138

- For-profit 4-year visual arts and engineering college
- Residential campus in large town
- 913 degree-seeking undergraduates: 7% Asian American, 6% Hispanic American, 10% international
- 63 graduate students
- 46% of applicants admitted
- Application essay required
- 72% graduate within 6 years

General. Accredited by ACCSC. Located near more than 150 game and game-related companies, granting students access to internships, jobs, and networking opportunities. Branch campuses in Singapore and Spain. **Degrees:** 151 bachelor's awarded; master's offered. **Location:** 20 miles from downtown Seattle. **Calendar:** Semester, limited summer session. **Full-time faculty:** 47 total; 36% have terminal degrees, 11% minority, 21% women. **Part-time faculty:** 35 total; 31% have terminal degrees, 9% minority, 14% women. **Class size:** 54% < 20, 32% 20-39, 7% 40-49, 5% 50-99, 2% >100. **Special facilities:** Computer labs with variety of professional software development kits (SDKs), including those for Nintendo Wii, Nintendo DS, and Microsoft Kinect; computer engineering lab; game production and testing lab; sound lab; library specialized in gaming, simulation, computer engineering, and animation.

Freshman class profile. 377 applied, 172 admitted, 128 enrolled.

Mid 50% test scores			
		SAT writing:	490-610
SAT critical reading:	520-660	ACT composite:	23-29
SAT math:	540-670	Out-of-state:	43%

Basis for selection. Applicants to bachelor of science programs must have completed math through pre-calculus before attending DigiPen; however, an applicant may be enrolled in a pre-calculus class at the time of application. Animation program applicants must submit official transcripts, test scores, recommendation letters, a personal statement, and an art portfolio when applying. Applicants to game design programs should pay particular attention to their essay responses. Non-native English speakers must provide a minimum TOEFL iBT score of 80 or other pre-approved proof of having English

proficiency. Portfolios of 15-20 pieces of artwork required for MFA/BFA program applicants. Supplemental pieces required for Game Design degrees. **Home schooled:** Transcript of courses and grades, state high school equivalency certificate required. In addition to standard application materials, in-state applicants should submit detailed transcript that provides course titles, brief description of each course's content, grade or performance assessment for each course, details concerning duration of study, and expected graduation date. Out-of-state applicants should submit transcript from nationally recognized home school program or detailed transcript (as described above for Washington residents) and passing GED scores. Other proof of high school equivalence will be considered on a case-by-case basis by admissions office. **Learning Disabled:** Students desiring special needs should contact the Disability Support Services Coordinator to self-identify and arrange for appropriate accommodations.

High school preparation. College-preparatory program recommended. Recommended units include English 4, mathematics 4, science 4, computer science 1 and visual/performing arts 1. Applicants for the BFA program are recommended to take as many art classes as possible; BS applicants encouraged to take classes in computer science and physics.

2012-2013 Annual costs. Tuition/fees: $24,910. In order to complete the degree program in four years, students must take an average of 16-22 credits per semester. The cost for students taking 16-22 credits is $12,800 per semester or $25,600 a year (U.S. citizens and residents). The cost of 16-22 credits for international students is $14,080 per semester or $28,160 annually.

2010-2011 Financial aid. Need-based: 45% of total undergraduate aid awarded as scholarships/grants, 55% as loans/jobs. **Non-need-based:** Scholarships awarded for art, job skills, leadership, minority status. **Additional information:** Many aid programs are on a first-come, first-served basis.

Application procedures. Admission: Priority date 2/1; no deadline. $35 fee, may be waived for applicants with need. Admission notification on a rolling basis. Applicants must respond by the date listed on their individual acceptance letters. Enrollment happens once a year in the fall and admission is on a rolling basis. Qualified new students are accepted and enrolled into programs beginning in September for the following year until all spaces are filled. **Financial aid:** Priority date 4/15; no closing date. FAFSA, institutional form required. Applicants notified on a rolling basis starting 1/1; must reply within 4 week(s) of notification.

Academics. College 101 courses available to help first-year students successfully transition to college life. Short-term individual counseling services offered to students through Counseling Center, and strives to ensure all students are provided with equal opportunity to participate in college's programs, courses, and activities through Disability Support Services department. **Special study options:** Accelerated study, double major, independent study, internships, study abroad. Branch campuses in Singapore and Spain; students in some of the programs may take advantage of study abroad opportunities at either of those campuses. **Credit/placement by examination:** AP, CLEP, IB, institutional tests. **Support services:** Learning center, pre-admission summer program, reduced course load, study skills assistance, tutoring.

Majors. Communications technology: Animation/special effects. **Computer sciences:** Modeling/simulation. **Engineering:** Computer. **Visual/performing arts:** Game design.

Most popular majors. Communication technologies 30%, computer/information sciences 69%.

Computing on campus. Online course registration, online library, helpline, student web hosting, wireless network available.

Student life. Freshman orientation: Mandatory. Preregistration for classes offered. 3-4 day orientation held the week before classes begin. **Activities:** International student organizations, music ensembles, student government.

Student services. Career counseling, student employment services, financial aid counseling, personal counseling, veterans' counselor. **Physically disabled:** Services for hearing impaired.

Contact. E-mail: admissions@digipen.edu
Phone: (425) 629-5001 Toll-free number: (866) 478-5236
Fax: (425) 558-0378
Angela Kugler, Director of Admissions, DigiPen Institute of Technology, 9931 Willows Road NE, Redmond, WA 98052

Eastern Washington University
Cheney, Washington
www.ewu.edu   CB code: 4301

▸ Public 4-year university
▸ Commuter campus in large town

▸ 10,885 degree-seeking undergraduates: 15% part-time, 55% women, 4% African American, 3% Asian American, 10% Hispanic American, 1% Native American, 2% international
▸ 1,227 degree-seeking graduate students
▸ 79% of applicants admitted
▸ SAT or ACT (ACT writing optional) required
▸ 46% graduate within 6 years

General. Founded in 1882. Regionally accredited. Programs available in Bellevue, Everett, Kent, Seattle, Shoreline, Spokane, Tacoma, Vancouver and Yakima WA. **Degrees:** 2,059 bachelor's awarded; master's, doctoral offered. **ROTC:** Army. **Location:** 17 miles from Spokane, 200 miles from Seattle. **Calendar:** Quarter, extensive summer session. **Full-time faculty:** 411 total; 98% have terminal degrees, 13% minority, 44% women. **Part-time faculty:** 236 total; 10% minority, 53% women. **Class size:** 34% < 20, 44% 20-39, 10% 40-49, 12% 50-99, less than 1% >100. **Special facilities:** Planetarium, 17,000-acre national wildlife refuge, anthropology museum, laboratory for ecological studies, art, photography and print gallery, children's center, English Language Institute, state crime lab, Washington State digital archives building, GIS and computer-mapping laboratory and map library, Spokane Intercollegiate Research and Technology Institute, health sciences building in Spokane, Roos Field Red Turf.

Freshman class profile. 4,525 applied, 3,575 admitted, 1,506 enrolled.

Mid 50% test scores			
SAT critical reading:	420-530	GPA 3.0-3.49:	38%
SAT math:	440-540	GPA 2.0-2.99:	29%
SAT writing:	410-520	Return as sophomores:	75%
ACT composite:	18-24	Out-of-state:	8%
GPA 3.75 or higher:	16%	Live on campus:	63%
GPA 3.50-3.74:	17%	International:	3%

Basis for selection. Admission based on index combining GPA, test scores and requisite high school core curriculum. Essay and special review considered for applicants who do not meet these standards. Limited number enrolled below index and core requirements. Letters of recommendation from teachers and/or counselors encouraged. Interview or essay required for returning adult applicants and high school students below admission index. **Home schooled:** Must show evidence of completing required core courses.

High school preparation. College-preparatory program required. 15 units required. Required units include English 4, mathematics 3, social studies 3, science 2 (laboratory 2), foreign language 2 and visual/performing arts 1. Math requirement includes algebra, geometry, and trigonometry or advanced algebra. Quantitative Reasoning required in the Senior year. One year fine arts or core elective required. Foreign language requirement includes 2 years in one foreign language (American Sign Language accepted).

2011-2012 Annual costs. Tuition/fees: $7,240; $16,919 out-of-state. Room/board: $7,852. Books/supplies: $1,050. Personal expenses: $2,100.

2010-2011 Financial aid. Need-based: 1,311 full-time freshmen applied for aid; 1,000 were judged to have need; 990 of these received aid. Average need met was 91%. Average scholarship/grant was $7,169; average loan $3,083. 49% of total undergraduate aid awarded as scholarships/grants, 51% as loans/jobs. **Non-need-based:** Awarded to 1,493 full-time undergraduates, including 481 freshmen. Scholarships awarded for academics, alumni affiliation, art, athletics, job skills, music/drama, state residency. **Additional information:** The High Demand Scholarship program helps low income students pursue "high demand" careers.

Application procedures. Admission: Priority date 2/15; deadline 5/15. $50 fee, may be waived for applicants with need. Admission notification on a rolling basis beginning on or about 11/1. Must reply by May 1 or within 4 week(s) if notified thereafter. **Financial aid:** Priority date 2/15; no closing date. FAFSA required. Applicants notified on a rolling basis starting 4/1; must reply within 4 week(s) of notification.

Academics. Extensive internship opportunities available. **Special study options:** Combined bachelor's/graduate degree, distance learning, double major, dual enrollment of high school students, ESL, honors, independent study, internships, student-designed major, study abroad, teacher certification program. Nursing consortium with Washington State University, Whitworth College, Gonzaga University. Dual degree program: Master's of Social Work (EWU) and Law (Gonzaga). **Credit/placement by examination:** AP, CLEP, IB, institutional tests. 45 credit hours maximum toward bachelor's degree. **Support services:** Learning center, pre-admission summer program, remedial instruction, study skills assistance, tutoring, writing center.

Majors. Architecture: Urban/community planning. **Area/ethnic studies:** Women's. **Biology:** General. **Business:** Accounting, business admin, finance, human resources, management information systems, managerial economics, marketing. **Communications:** Communications/speech/rhetoric, journalism.

Communications technology: Graphics. **Computer sciences:** General. **Conservation:** Environmental science. **Education:** Art, biology, business, chemistry, early childhood, early childhood special, English, French, health, mathematics, music, physics, reading, science, social studies, Spanish, special ed. **Engineering:** Electrical, mechanical. **English:** English lit, technical writing. **Foreign languages:** French, Spanish. **Health services:** Athletic training, community health services, dental hygiene, health care admin, nursing (RN), recreational therapy, speech pathology. **History:** General. **Human services:** Social work. **Liberal arts:** Humanities. **Math:** General. **Parks/recreation:** General, exercise sciences, facilities management. **Philosophy/religion:** Philosophy. **Physical sciences:** Chemistry, geology, physics. **Psychology:** General, developmental. **Social sciences:** Anthropology, criminology, economics, geography, international relations, political science, sociology. **Visual/performing arts:** Art history/conservation, dramatic, film/cinema/video, music, studio arts. **Work/family studies:** Child development.

Most popular majors. Business/marketing 19%, education 11%, health sciences 10%, interdisciplinary studies 8%, psychology 7%, social sciences 8%.

Computing on campus. 812 workstations in dormitories, library, computer center, student center. Dormitories wired for high-speed internet access and linked to campus network. Commuter students can connect to campus network. Online course registration, online library, helpline, student web hosting, wireless network available.

Student life. Freshman orientation: Available. Preregistration for classes offered. One-day sessions in summer plus a 3-day program prior to start of classes with advising, student activities, enrollment services. **Policies:** Student conduct code, academic integrity policy, alcohol/substance use and abuse policy. **Housing:** Coed dorms, special housing for disabled, apartments, fraternity/sorority housing, wellness housing available. $250 nonrefundable deposit, deadline 5/1. **Activities:** Bands, campus ministries, choral groups, dance, drama, film society, international student organizations, literary magazine, music ensembles, Model UN, musical theater, radio station, student government, student newspaper, symphony orchestra, Native American student association, Black Student Union, M.E.Ch.A. (Movimiento Estudiantil Chicana/o de Aztlan), United Ministries, international affairs club; Mind, Body, and Soul; Eastern Environmental, debate club, Student Network for Organizing and Rebuilding Communities, Scary Feminist (WAFER), ROTC Fighting Eagles.

Athletics. NCAA. **Intercollegiate:** Basketball, cross-country, football (tackle) M, golf W, soccer W, tennis, track and field, volleyball W. **Intramural:** Baseball, basketball, bowling, cross-country, football (tackle), golf W, racquetball, soccer, softball, tennis, track and field, volleyball. **Team name:** Eagles.

Student services. Adult student services, alcohol/substance abuse counseling, career counseling, services for economically disadvantaged, student employment services, financial aid counseling, health services, minority student services, on-campus daycare, personal counseling, placement for graduates, veterans' counselor, women's services. **Physically disabled:** Services for visually, speech, hearing impaired.

Contact. E-mail: admissions@ewu.edu
Phone: (509) 359-2397 Fax: (509) 359-6692
Shannon Carr, Director of Admissions, Eastern Washington University, 101 Sutton Hall, Cheney, WA 99004-2447

Evergreen State College
Olympia, Washington **CB member**
www.evergreen.edu **CB code: 4292**

- Public 4-year liberal arts college
- Commuter campus in small city
- 4,371 degree-seeking undergraduates: 7% part-time, 54% women, 5% African American, 2% Asian American, 6% Hispanic American, 2% Native American, 1% international
- 324 degree-seeking graduate students
- 96% of applicants admitted
- SAT or ACT (ACT writing optional) required
- 52% graduate within 6 years; 24% enter graduate study

General. Founded in 1967. Regionally accredited. **Degrees:** 1,249 bachelor's awarded; master's offered. **Location:** 6 miles from downtown, 60 miles from Seattle. **Calendar:** Quarter, limited summer session. **Full-time faculty:** 175 total; 86% have terminal degrees, 23% minority, 50% women. **Part-time faculty:** 72 total; 49% have terminal degrees, 21% minority, 51% women. **Class size:** 40% < 20, 34% 20-39, 17% 40-49, 9% 50-99. **Special facilities:** Center for Creative and Applied Media, sustainable agriculture lab building, organic farm and community gardens, Longhouse Education

---

and Cultural Center, animation and design studio, ceramics studio, metal shop, wood shop, photography studios and darkrooms, 3,000 feet of waterfront property on Puget Sound.

Freshman class profile. 1,725 applied, 1,651 admitted, 542 enrolled.

Mid 50% test scores			
SAT critical reading:	510-640	GPA 2.0-2.99:	40%
SAT math:	460-580	Rank in top quarter:	28%
SAT writing:	470-610	Rank in top tenth:	11%
ACT composite:	21-26	Return as sophomores:	71%
GPA 3.75 or higher:	7%	Out-of-state:	47%
GPA 3.50-3.74:	13%	Live on campus:	78%
GPA 3.0-3.49:	39%	International:	1%

Basis for selection. School achievement record, test scores, strength of curriculum taken in high school, personal statement, and understanding of interdisciplinary study. Official TOEFL test scores are required for most students whose native language is not English. Essay or personal statement required for international and home-schooled applicants, recommended for all other applicants. Interviews optional (by appointment for non-residents). **Home schooled:** Transcript of courses and grades required. Personal statement required.

High school preparation. College-preparatory program recommended. 15 units required. Required units include English 4, mathematics 3, social studies 3, science 2 (laboratory 2), foreign language 2 and academic electives 1. One fine, visual, or performing arts elective or college prep elective from the areas above required.

2011-2012 Annual costs. Tuition/fees: $7,486; $18,667 out-of-state. Entering freshmen living in campus housing are required to choose a mandatory dining plan. Room/board: $9,000. Books/supplies: $972. Personal expenses: $1,830.

2010-2011 Financial aid. Need-based: 475 full-time freshmen applied for aid; 373 were judged to have need; 354 of these received aid. Average need met was 75%. Average scholarship/grant was $8,031; average loan $3,178. 53% of total undergraduate aid awarded as scholarships/grants, 47% as loans/jobs. **Non-need-based:** Awarded to 490 full-time undergraduates, including 233 freshmen. Scholarships awarded for academics, art, athletics, state residency. **Additional information:** Application packets for all scholarships and tuition awards EXCEPT the Merit Award (due by May 2) must be received by February 1. To meet priority deadline for required financial aid forms, official results of FAFSA must be received by March 1.

Application procedures. Admission: Priority date 3/1; no deadline. $50 fee, may be waived for applicants with need. Admission notification on a rolling basis beginning on or about 11/1. Must reply by May 1 or within 4 week(s) if notified thereafter. **Financial aid:** Priority date 3/1; no closing date. FAFSA, institutional form required. Applicants notified on a rolling basis starting 4/1; must reply within 6 week(s) of notification.

Academics. Special study options: Accelerated study, double major, exchange student, independent study, internships, semester at sea, student-designed major, study abroad, teacher certification program, weekend college. **Credit/placement by examination:** AP, CLEP, IB. 135 credit hours maximum toward bachelor's degree. **Support services:** Learning center, reduced course load, study skills assistance, tutoring, writing center.

Majors. Area/ethnic studies: Native American. **Biology:** General. **Business:** Business admin. **Communications:** Communications/speech/rhetoric, journalism. **Computer sciences:** General. **Conservation:** General, environmental science, environmental studies. **Education:** General. **English:** English lit. **Foreign languages:** General, classics, linguistics. **General:** Sustainable agriculture. **Human services:** General. **Liberal arts:** Arts/sciences, humanities. **Math:** Mathematics/statistics. **Philosophy/religion:** Philosophy, religion. **Physical sciences:** General. **Psychology:** General. **Social sciences:** General, political economy, political science, sociology. **Visual/performing arts:** General, art, cinematography, dramatic, film/cinema/video, multimedia, studio arts.

Most popular majors. Interdisciplinary studies 17%, liberal arts 83%.

Computing on campus. 470 workstations in dormitories, library, computer center, student center. Dormitories wired for high-speed internet access and linked to campus network. Commuter students can connect to campus network. Online course registration, online library, helpline, student web hosting, wireless network available.

Student life. Freshman orientation: Mandatory. Preregistration for classes offered. Week-long orientation offers academic and social events to familiarize students with teaching, learning, and resources at campus. **Policies:** The Evergreen Social Contract: an agreement; a guide for civility and tolerance toward others; a reminder that respecting others and remaining open to others and their ideas provides a powerful framework for teaching and learning. Also have Student Rights and Responsibilities and Residential and Dining Services Policies. **Housing:** Guaranteed on-campus for freshmen.

Coed dorms, special housing for disabled, apartments, wellness housing available. $250 fully refundable deposit, deadline 7/15. Freshman Halls, Freshman Quiet, apartment-style (quiet, substance free, sustainability, rainbow fort, no theme). **Activities:** Pep band, choral groups, dance, drama, film society, literary magazine, music ensembles, Model UN, radio station, student government, student newspaper, TV station, Developing Ecological Agricultural Practices (DEAP), Common Bread, Queer People of Color (QPOC), Student Veterans Organization, Native Student Alliance, Movimento Estudiantil Chicano(a) de Aztlan (MEChA), Asian Pacific Islander Coalition (APIC), Black Student Union, Women's Resource Center, Coalition Against Sexual Violence, Greener Community Support Group, Geoduck Student Union.

Athletics. NAIA. **Intercollegiate:** Basketball, cross-country, soccer, track and field, volleyball W. **Intramural:** Basketball, soccer, volleyball, wrestling. **Team name:** Geoducks.

Student services. Adult student services, alcohol/substance abuse counseling, career counseling, services for economically disadvantaged, student employment services, financial aid counseling, health services, minority student services, on-campus daycare, personal counseling, placement for graduates, veterans' counselor, women's services. **Physically disabled:** Services for visually, speech, hearing impaired.

Contact. E-mail: admissions@evergreen.edu
Phone: (360) 867-6170 Fax: (360) 867-5114
Bryan Gould, Director of Admissions, Evergreen State College, 2700 Evergreen Parkway NW, Olympia, WA 98505

Faith Evangelical Seminary
Tacoma, Washington
www.faithseminary.edu

▸ Private 4-year Bible and seminary college affiliated with Christian Church
▸ Large city

General. Regionally accredited. **Location:** 30 Miles from Seattle, WA. **Calendar:** Quarter.

Annual costs/financial aid. Tuition/fees (2011-2012): $7,560. Books/supplies: $525. Personal expenses: $2,052.

Contact. Phone: (253) 752-2020 ext. 21
Dean of Students, Faith Evangelical College & Seminary, Tacoma, WA 98407

Gonzaga University
Spokane, Washington   CB member
www.gonzaga.edu   CB code: 4330

▸ Private 4-year university and liberal arts college affiliated with Roman Catholic Church
▸ Residential campus in large city
▸ 4,796 degree-seeking undergraduates: 1% part-time, 53% women, 1% African American, 4% Asian American, 7% Hispanic American, 1% Native American, 2% international
▸ 2,780 degree-seeking graduate students
▸ 62% of applicants admitted
▸ SAT or ACT (ACT writing optional), application essay required
▸ 83% graduate within 6 years

General. Founded in 1887. Regionally accredited. **Degrees:** 1,065 bachelor's awarded; master's, professional, doctoral offered. **ROTC:** Army. **Location:** 300 miles from Seattle. **Calendar:** Semester, extensive summer session. **Full-time faculty:** 403 total; 85% have terminal degrees, 8% minority, 40% women. **Part-time faculty:** 317 total; 4% have terminal degrees, less than 1% minority, 45% women. **Class size:** 42% < 20, 53% 20-39, 4% 40-49, 2% 50-99. **Special facilities:** 2 electron microscopes.

Freshman class profile. 6,851 applied, 4,217 admitted, 1,131 enrolled.

Mid 50% test scores			
SAT critical reading:	550-700	Rank in top quarter:	72%
SAT math:	560-690	Rank in top tenth:	41%
ACT composite:	24-28	End year in good standing:	97%
GPA 3.75 or higher:	54%	Return as sophomores:	91%
GPA 3.50-3.74:	26%	Out-of-state:	52%
GPA 3.0-3.49:	19%	Live on campus:	98%
GPA 2.0-2.99:	1%	International:	2%

Basis for selection. GED not accepted. Academic achievement, scholastic aptitude, personal characteristics important. GPA below 3.0 reevaluated to include only grades in academic subjects. Course content and test scores important. Gonzaga recommends interviews for borderline applicants, but they are not required. **Home schooled:** Letter of recommendation (nonparent) required. Students must complete the Common Application and the Common Application Home School Supplement. One letter of recommendation, by someone other than a parent, addressing academic accomplishments. The Common Application School Report, which can be filled out by a parent/guardian.

High school preparation. College-preparatory program recommended. Required and recommended units include English 4, mathematics 3-4, social studies 2-3, history 2-3, science 3-4 (laboratory 3-4), foreign language 3-4 and academic electives 3. Algebra, geometry, trigonometry required of engineering applicants. Of 6 additional electives 4 must be from subjects mentioned and the arts.

2011-2012 Annual costs. Tuition/fees: $32,215. Room/board: $8,540. Books/supplies: $1,000. Personal expenses: $1,700.

2010-2011 Financial aid. Need-based: 925 full-time freshmen applied for aid; 680 were judged to have need; 680 of these received aid. Average need met was 85%. Average scholarship/grant was $18,150; average loan $4,383. 62% of total undergraduate aid awarded as scholarships/grants, 38% as loans/jobs. **Non-need-based:** Awarded to 2,358 full-time undergraduates, including 616 freshmen. Scholarships awarded for academics, alumni affiliation, athletics, leadership, minority status, music/drama, ROTC.

Application procedures. Admission: Priority date 11/15; deadline 2/1 (postmark date). $50 fee, may be waived for applicants with need. Admission notification by 3/15. Must reply by 5/1. **Financial aid:** Priority date 2/1, closing date 6/30. FAFSA required. Applicants notified on a rolling basis starting 3/1; must reply by 5/1 or within 3 week(s) of notification.

Academics. Special study options: Combined bachelor's/graduate degree, cross-registration, double major, dual enrollment of high school students, ESL, exchange student, honors, independent study, internships, semester at sea, study abroad, teacher certification program, Washington semester. **Credit/placement by examination:** AP, CLEP, IB, SAT, ACT. 32 credit hours maximum toward bachelor's degree. **Support services:** Pre-admission summer program, study skills assistance, writing center.

Majors. Area/ethnic studies: Asian, European, Latin American, women's. **Biology:** General, biochemistry. **Business:** Accounting, banking/financial services, business admin, international, management information systems, managerial economics. **Communications:** Broadcast journalism, journalism, public relations. **Computer sciences:** Computer science. **Education:** Music, physical, special ed. **Engineering:** General, civil, computer, electrical, mechanical. **English:** English lit, rhetoric/composition. **Foreign languages:** Comparative lit, French, Italian, Spanish. **Health services:** Preop/surgical nursing. **History:** General. **Liberal arts:** Arts/sciences. **Math:** General. **Parks/recreation:** Sports admin. **Philosophy/religion:** Philosophy, religion. **Physical sciences:** Chemistry, physics. **Protective services:** Criminal justice. **Psychology:** General. **Social sciences:** Economics, international relations, political science, sociology. **Visual/performing arts:** Dramatic, music performance, studio arts.

Most popular majors. Biology 6%, business/marketing 29%, communications/journalism 8%, engineering/engineering technologies 11%, psychology 6%, social sciences 11%.

Computing on campus. 900 workstations in library, computer center. Dormitories wired for high-speed internet access and linked to campus network. Commuter students can connect to campus network. Online course registration, online library, helpline, repair service, student web hosting, wireless network available.

Student life. Freshman orientation: Mandatory, $60 fee. Preregistration for classes offered. **Housing:** Guaranteed on-campus for freshmen. Coed dorms, single-sex dorms, special housing for disabled, apartments, wellness housing available. $200 fully refundable deposit, deadline 5/1. International students, freshmen and sophomores under 21 must live on campus, unless living at home. **Activities:** Bands, campus ministries, choral groups, dance, drama, international student organizations, literary magazine, music ensembles, musical theater, radio station, student government, student newspaper, symphony orchestra, TV station, 108 student clubs and service organizations.

Athletics. NCAA. **Intercollegiate:** Baseball M, basketball, cross-country, golf, rowing (crew), soccer, tennis, track and field, volleyball W. **Intramural:** Badminton, basketball, racquetball, soccer, softball, tennis, volleyball, weight lifting, wrestling M. **Team name:** Bulldogs.

Student services. Adult student services, alcohol/substance abuse counseling, chaplain/spiritual director, career counseling, student employment services, financial aid counseling, health services, minority student services,

personal counseling, veterans' counselor. **Physically disabled:** Services for visually, speech, hearing impaired.

Contact. E-mail: mcculloh@gu.gonzaga.edu
Phone: (509) 313-6572 Toll-free number: (800) 322-2584
Fax: (509) 313-5780
Julie McCulloh, Dean of Admissions, Gonzaga University, 502 East Boone Avenue, Spokane, WA 99258-0001

Heritage University
Toppenish, Washington
www.heritage.edu   CB code: 4344

- Private 4-year liberal arts and teachers college affiliated with interdenominational tradition
- Commuter campus in small town

General. Founded in 1982. Regionally accredited. **Location:** 165 miles from Seattle, 20 miles from Yakima. **Calendar:** Semester.

Annual costs/financial aid. Tuition/fees (2011-2012): $15,550. Books/supplies: $1,155. Personal expenses: $2,984. Need-based financial aid available to full-time and part-time students.

Contact. Phone: (509) 865-8508
Director of Admissions, 3240 Fort Road, Toppenish, WA 98948-9599

International Academy of Design and Technology: Seattle
Seattle, Washington
www.iadt.edu/seattle

- For-profit 4-year career college
- Very large city
- 436 degree-seeking undergraduates

General. Accredited by ACICS. **Degrees:** 69 bachelor's, 27 associate awarded. **Calendar:** Quarter. **Full-time faculty:** 7 total. **Part-time faculty:** 44 total.

Basis for selection. SAT or ACT, and Wonderlic entrance assessment required; specific scores determine eligibility to specific programs. Applicants for certain programs are required to submit to a background check. Portfolio required for Fashion Design program.

2011-2012 Annual costs. Books/supplies: $1,400.

Application procedures. Admission: No deadline. $50 fee. **Financial aid:** No deadline.

Academics. Special study options: Study abroad, weekend college. **Credit/placement by examination:** AP, CLEP.

Majors. Business: Fashion. **Visual/performing arts:** Fashion design, graphic design, interior design.

Most popular majors. Business/marketing 10%, visual/performing arts 90%.

Contact. Phone: (206) 575-1865 Toll-free number: (866) 903-4238
Fax: (206) 575-1724
Melissa Maxwell, Director of Admissions, International Academy of Design and Technology: Seattle, 645 Andover Park West, Seattle, WA 98188

ITT Technical Institute: Everett
Everett, Washington
www.itt-tech.edu   CB code: 2697

- For-profit 4-year technical college
- Commuter campus in large town
- 549 undergraduates
- Interview required

General. Accredited by ACICS. **Degrees:** 25 bachelor's, 101 associate awarded. **Calendar:** Quarter, extensive summer session. **Full-time faculty:** 11 total. **Part-time faculty:** 29 total.

Basis for selection. Satisfactory scores from on-site tests in English and mathematics required.

2011-2012 Annual costs. Estimated costs as of August 2011: per-credit-hour charge, $493, depending upon level and course of study; academic fee, $200. Certain programs of study require purchase of tools, which could cost an additional $100 to $500. All costs are subject to change.

Application procedures. Admission: No application fee. Admission notification on a rolling basis. **Financial aid:** No deadline. FAFSA, institutional form required. Applicants notified on a rolling basis.

Academics. Credit/placement by examination: AP, CLEP. **Support services:** Learning center, tutoring.

Majors. Business: Business admin, construction management, e-commerce, project management. **Communications technology:** Animation/special effects. **Computer sciences:** Programming, security. **Protective services:** Law enforcement admin.

Computing on campus. Online library available.

Student life. Freshman orientation: Available. Preregistration for classes offered.

Student services. Career counseling, student employment services, placement for graduates.

Contact. Phone: (425) 485-0303 Toll-free number: (800) 272-3791
Fax: (425) 485-3438
Jon Scherrer, Director of Recruitment, ITT Technical Institute: Everett, 1615 75th Street S.W., Suite 220, Everett, WA 98203

ITT Technical Institute: Seattle
Seattle, Washington
www.itt-tech.edu   CB code: 3599

- For-profit 4-year technical college
- Commuter campus in very large city
- 755 undergraduates
- Interview required

General. Founded in 1932. Accredited by ACICS. **Degrees:** 50 bachelor's, 147 associate awarded. **Location:** 12 miles from downtown. **Calendar:** Quarter, extensive summer session. **Full-time faculty:** 11 total. **Part-time faculty:** 54 total.

Basis for selection. Satisfactory scores from on-site tests in English and mathematics required.

2011-2012 Annual costs. Estimated costs as of June 2011: per-credit-hour charge, $493, depending upon level and course of study; academic fee, $200. Certain programs of study require purchase of tools, which could cost an additional $100 to $500. All costs are subject to change.

Application procedures. Admission: No deadline. No application fee. Admission notification on a rolling basis. **Financial aid:** No deadline. FAFSA, institutional form required. Applicants notified on a rolling basis.

Academics. Credit/placement by examination: AP, CLEP. **Support services:** Learning center, tutoring.

Majors. Business: Business admin, construction management, project management. **Communications technology:** Animation/special effects. **Computer sciences:** Programming, security. **Protective services:** Law enforcement admin.

Most popular majors. Business/marketing 7%, communication technologies 25%, computer/information sciences 18%, engineering/engineering technologies 30%, security/protective services 20%.

Computing on campus. Online library available.

Student life. Freshman orientation: Available. Preregistration for classes offered.

Student services. Career counseling, student employment services, placement for graduates.

Contact. Phone: (206) 244-3300 Toll-free number: (800) 422-2029
Fax: (206) 246-7635
Jose Luis Saez, Director of Recruitment, ITT Technical Institute: Seattle, 12720 Gateway Drive, Suite 100, Seattle, WA 98168

ITT Technical Institute: Spokane
Spokane Valley, Washington
www.itt-tech.edu   CB code: 7027

- For-profit 4-year technical college
- Commuter campus in large town
- 494 undergraduates
- Interview required

General. Accredited by ACICS. **Degrees:** 50 bachelor's, 108 associate awarded. **Location:** 5 miles from downtown. **Calendar:** Quarter, extensive summer session. **Full-time faculty:** 9 total. **Part-time faculty:** 61 total.

Basis for selection. Satisfactory scores from on-site test in English and mathematics required.

2011-2012 Annual costs. Estimated costs as of June 2011: per-credit-hour charge, $493, depending upon level and course of study; academic fee, $200. Certain programs of study require purchase of tools, which could cost an additional $100 to $500. All costs are subject to change.

Application procedures. Admission: No deadline. No application fee. Admission notification on a rolling basis. **Financial aid:** No deadline. FAFSA, institutional form required. Applicants notified on a rolling basis.

Academics. Credit/placement by examination: AP, CLEP. **Support services:** Learning center, tutoring.

Majors. Business: Business admin, construction management, project management. **Communications technology:** Animation/special effects. **Computer sciences:** Networking, security. **Protective services:** Law enforcement admin.

Most popular majors. Communication technologies 23%, computer/information sciences 37%, security/protective services 40%.

Computing on campus. 50 workstations in computer center. Online library available.

Student life. Freshman orientation: Available. Preregistration for classes offered.

Student services. Career counseling, student employment services, placement for graduates.

Contact. Phone: (509) 926-2900 Toll-free number: (800) 777-8324
Fax: (509) 926-2908
Gregory Alexander, Director of Recruitment, ITT Technical Institute: Spokane, 13518 East Indiana Avenue, Spokane Valley, WA 99216

Northwest College of Art
Poulsbo, Washington
www.ncad.edu   CB code: 2432

- For-profit 4-year visual arts college
- Commuter campus in small town
- 83 degree-seeking undergraduates: 66% women
- Application essay, interview required

General. Founded in 1982. Accredited by ACCSC. **Degrees:** 13 bachelor's awarded. **Location:** 30 miles from Seattle, 60 miles from Tacoma. **Calendar:** Semester, extensive summer session. **Part-time faculty:** 15 total.

Basis for selection. Requirements include minimum 2.5 GPA, interview, 2-3 page typed essay, portfolio. TOEFL test required for international students from non-English speaking countries. SAT required for students with a GED. **Home schooled:** GED required except when home school programs show proof of school or program accreditation.

2011-2012 Annual costs. Tuition/fees: $18,815.

Financial aid. Non-need-based: Scholarships awarded for academics, art, state residency.

Application procedures. Admission: No deadline. $50 fee. Admission notification on a rolling basis. **Financial aid:** Priority date 3/1, closing date 6/1. FAFSA required. Applicants notified on a rolling basis.

Academics. Special study options: Accelerated study, double major, internships. **Credit/placement by examination:** AP, CLEP.

Majors. Visual/performing arts: Design.

Computing on campus. PC or laptop required. Wireless network available.

Student life. Freshman orientation: Mandatory, $15 fee. Preregistration for classes offered.

Student services. Adult student services, career counseling, student employment services, financial aid counseling, placement for graduates.

Contact. E-mail: admissions@ncad.edu
Phone: (360) 779-9993 Toll-free number: (800) 769-2787
Fax: (360) 779-9933
Kim Perigard, Northwest College of Art & Design, Northwest College of Art, 16301 Creative Drive NE, Poulsbo, WA 98370-8651

Northwest University
Kirkland, Washington   **CB member**
www.northwestu.edu   **CB code: 4541**

- Private 4-year university and liberal arts college affiliated with Assemblies of God
- Residential campus in small city
- 1,213 degree-seeking undergraduates: 10% part-time, 60% women, 6% African American, 5% Asian American, 7% Hispanic American, 1% Native American, 2% international
- 260 degree-seeking graduate students
- 62% of applicants admitted
- SAT or ACT (ACT writing optional), application essay required
- 50% graduate within 6 years

General. Founded in 1934. Regionally accredited. **Degrees:** 212 bachelor's, 3 associate awarded; master's, professional offered. **ROTC:** Army. **Location:** 10 miles from Seattle. **Calendar:** Semester, limited summer session. **Full-time faculty:** 66 total; 61% have terminal degrees, 8% minority, 38% women. **Part-time faculty:** 63 total; 6% have terminal degrees, 49% women. **Class size:** 61% < 20, 30% 20-39, 5% 40-49, 4% 50-99.

Freshman class profile. 702 applied, 432 admitted, 163 enrolled.

Mid 50% test scores			
SAT critical reading:	450-590	GPA 3.0-3.49:	28%
SAT math:	450-570	GPA 2.0-2.99:	14%
SAT writing:	440-560	End year in good standing:	92%
ACT composite:	19-26	Return as sophomores:	77%
GPA 3.75 or higher:	29%	Out-of-state:	32%
GPA 3.50-3.74:	29%	Live on campus:	61%
		International:	3%

Basis for selection. Entire application reviewed: includes essay, references, transcript, SAT or ACT. GPA of 2.3 required: those with GPA below 2.3 but greater than 2.0 admitted on academic probation if space available. TOEFL (minimum score 500) required for non-native speakers of English. Audition recommended for music and drama scholarships. **Home schooled:** Transcript of courses and grades, letter of recommendation (nonparent) required. **Learning Disabled:** Interview with Director of Student Success.

High school preparation. College-preparatory program recommended. 16 units recommended. Recommended units include English 4, mathematics 3, social studies 2, history 2, science 2, foreign language 2 and academic electives 3.

2012-2013 Annual costs. Tuition/fees: $24,766. Room/board: $7,060. Books/supplies: $1,000. Personal expenses: $1,650.

2011-2012 Financial aid. Need-based: 160 full-time freshmen applied for aid; 130 were judged to have need; 130 of these received aid. Average need met was 59%. Average scholarship/grant was $14,879; average loan $3,173. 64% of total undergraduate aid awarded as scholarships/grants, 36% as loans/jobs. **Non-need-based:** Awarded to 285 full-time undergraduates, including 53 freshmen. Scholarships awarded for academics, art, athletics, leadership, music/drama, religious affiliation.

Application procedures. Admission: Priority date 3/1; deadline 8/1 (postmark date). $30 fee, may be waived for applicants with need. Admission notification on a rolling basis beginning on or about 10/1. **Financial aid:** Priority date 2/15, closing date 8/1. FAFSA, institutional form required. Applicants notified on a rolling basis starting 3/3; must reply within 4 week(s) of notification.

Academics. Special study options: Accelerated study, combined bachelor's/graduate degree, distance learning, double major, dual enrollment of high school students, ESL, independent study, internships, student-designed major, study abroad, teacher certification program, Washington semester. **Credit/placement by examination:** AP, CLEP, IB, SAT, ACT, institutional

tests. 30 credit hours maximum toward associate degree, 30 toward bachelor's. **Support services:** Learning center, reduced course load, remedial instruction, study skills assistance, tutoring, writing center.

Majors. Biology: General. **Business:** Business admin. **Communications:** Communications/speech/rhetoric, media studies, organizational. **Conservation:** Environmental science. **Education:** Elementary, middle, secondary. **English:** English lit. **Health services:** Nursing (RN), premedicine. **History:** General. **Math:** General. **Philosophy/religion:** Philosophy. **Psychology:** General. **Social sciences:** Political science. **Theology:** Bible, missionary, pastoral counseling, sacred music, theology, youth ministry. **Visual/performing arts:** Music.

Most popular majors. Business/marketing 17%, communications/journalism 10%, education 9%, health sciences 11%, psychology 9%, theological studies 24%.

Computing on campus. 135 workstations in dormitories, library, computer center, student center. Dormitories wired for high-speed internet access and linked to campus network. Commuter students can connect to campus network. Online course registration, online library, helpline, repair service, student web hosting, wireless network available.

Student life. Freshman orientation: Mandatory. Preregistration for classes offered. Held in August the week before classes begin. **Policies:** Religious observance required. **Housing:** Guaranteed on-campus for all undergraduates. Single-sex dorms, apartments available. $300 fully refundable deposit, deadline 5/1. **Activities:** Bands, campus ministries, choral groups, drama, music ensembles, musical theater, radio station, student government, student newspaper, community outreach groups, Psi Chi Honor Society (psychology), Association of International Students, Environmental Stewardship Club, Students in Free Enterprise.

Athletics. NAIA, NCCAA. **Intercollegiate:** Basketball, cross-country, soccer, track and field, volleyball W. **Intramural:** Football (non-tackle). **Team name:** Eagles.

Student services. Adult student services, alcohol/substance abuse counseling, chaplain/spiritual director, financial aid counseling, health services, personal counseling, veterans' counselor. **Physically disabled:** Services for visually impaired.

Contact. E-mail: admissions@northwestu.edu
Phone: (425) 889-5231 Toll-free number: (800) 669-3781
Fax: (425) 889-5224
Jessica Velasco, Director of Admissions, Northwest University, 5520 108th Ave NE, Kirkland, WA 98083-0579

Pacific Lutheran University

Tacoma, Washington
www.plu.edu

CB member
CB code: 4597

- Private 4-year university affiliated with Evangelical Lutheran Church in America
- Residential campus in large city
- 3,133 degree-seeking undergraduates: 3% part-time, 62% women, 3% African American, 6% Asian American, 6% Hispanic American, 1% Native American, 4% international
- 257 degree-seeking graduate students
- 77% of applicants admitted
- SAT or ACT (ACT writing optional), application essay required
- 66% graduate within 6 years

General. Founded in 1890. Regionally accredited. **Degrees:** 835 bachelor's awarded; master's offered. **ROTC:** Army. **Location:** 7 miles from Tacoma, 30 miles from Seattle. **Calendar:** 4-1-4, extensive summer session. **Full-time faculty:** 203 total; 11% minority, 52% women. **Part-time faculty:** 45 total; 11% minority, 64% women. **Class size:** 49% < 20, 44% 20-39, 4% 40-49, 2% 50-99, less than 1% >100. **Special facilities:** Herbarium, invertebrate and vertebrate museums, greenhouse, field station and boat equipped for studies of Puget Sound, Scandinavian cultural center, observatory, performing arts center.

Freshman class profile. 3,289 applied, 2,520 admitted, 731 enrolled.

Mid 50% test scores			
SAT critical reading:	490-620	GPA 3.0-3.49:	22%
SAT math:	480-600	GPA 2.0-2.99:	8%
SAT writing:	480-600	Rank in top quarter:	67%
ACT composite:	21-27	Rank in top tenth:	33%
GPA 3.75 or higher:	46%	Return as sophomores:	82%
GPA 3.50-3.74:	24%	Out-of-state:	28%
		Live on campus:	88%

Basis for selection. Grades, test scores, essay, recommendations, service, leadership. Admission on rolling basis until class is full. Interview recommended for borderline, exceptional; audition required for music, forensics, theater; portfolio recommended for art. **Home schooled:** Must provide proof of high-school equivalency.

High school preparation. College-preparatory program required. 17 units recommended. Required and recommended units include English 4, mathematics 2-3, social studies 2, science 2 (laboratory 2), foreign language 2, visual/performing arts 1 and academic electives 3. Computer science, speech, debate, music also recommended. 2 years visual or performing arts recommended.

2011-2012 Annual costs. Tuition/fees: $30,950. Room/board: $9,350. Books/supplies: $924. Personal expenses: $2,094.

2011-2012 Financial aid. Need-based: 683 full-time freshmen applied for aid; 587 were judged to have need; 587 of these received aid. Average need met was 90%. Average scholarship/grant was $19,337; average loan $6,862. 71% of total undergraduate aid awarded as scholarships/grants, 29% as loans/jobs. **Non-need-based:** Awarded to 2,470 full-time undergraduates, including 597 freshmen. Scholarships awarded for academics, alumni affiliation, art, leadership, music/drama, religious affiliation, ROTC.

Application procedures. Admission: Priority date 2/1; no deadline. $40 fee, may be waived for applicants with need, free for online applicants. Admission notification on a rolling basis beginning on or about 10/1. Must reply by May 1 or within 2 week(s) if notified thereafter. Housing deposit is refundable only through May 1. **Financial aid:** Priority date 1/15; no closing date. FAFSA required. Applicants notified on a rolling basis starting 3/15; must reply by 5/1 or within 3 week(s) of notification.

Academics. Freshman year program includes topic-oriented writing and critical conversation classes. **Special study options:** Combined bachelor's/graduate degree, cooperative education, cross-registration, double major, dual enrollment of high school students, ESL, exchange student, honors, independent study, internships, liberal arts/career combination, student-designed major, study abroad, teacher certification program. **Credit/placement by examination:** AP, CLEP, IB, institutional tests. 30 credit hours maximum toward bachelor's degree. **Support services:** Pre-admission summer program, reduced course load, study skills assistance, tutoring, writing center.

Majors. Area/ethnic studies: Scandinavian, women's. **Biology:** General. **Business:** Business admin. **Communications:** Communications/speech/rhetoric. **Computer sciences:** Computer science. **Conservation:** Environmental science. **Education:** Elementary, secondary. **Engineering:** Computer, engineering science. **English:** English lit. **Foreign languages:** Chinese, classics, French, German, Norwegian, Spanish. **Health services:** Nursing (RN). **History:** General. **Human services:** Social work. **Math:** General. **Parks/recreation:** General, health/fitness. **Philosophy/religion:** Philosophy, religion. **Physical sciences:** Chemistry, geology, physics. **Psychology:** General. **Social sciences:** Anthropology, economics, political science, sociology. **Visual/performing arts:** Art, music, studio arts, theater arts management.

Most popular majors. Business/marketing 14%, communications/journalism 7%, education 6%, health sciences 8%, psychology 6%, social sciences 12%, visual/performing arts 6%.

Computing on campus. 250 workstations in library, student center. Dormitories wired for high-speed internet access and linked to campus network. Commuter students can connect to campus network. Helpline, student web hosting, wireless network available.

Student life. Freshman orientation: Available. Preregistration for classes offered. **Policies:** All single, full-time students must live in university housing, unless student lives at home with parent or legal guardian, is 20 years of age or older on or before a specific college-designated date, or has achieved junior status. **Housing:** Guaranteed on-campus for all undergraduates. Coed dorms, single-sex dorms, special housing for disabled, apartments available. $200 nonrefundable deposit, deadline 5/1. **Activities:** Bands, campus ministries, choral groups, dance, drama, film society, international student organizations, literary magazine, music ensembles, musical theater, opera, radio station, student government, student newspaper, symphony orchestra, TV station, Intervarsity Christian Fellowship, Advocates for Social Justice, Asian & Pacific Islanders club, B.L.A.C.K. at PLU, environmental action, Puentes, social work organization, Amnesty International, Habitat for Humanity, Young Life.

Athletics. NCAA. **Intercollegiate:** Baseball M, basketball, cheerleading, cross-country, football (tackle) M, golf, rowing (crew), soccer, softball W, swimming, tennis, track and field, volleyball W. **Intramural:** Badminton, basketball, bowling, cross-country, football (non-tackle), golf, handball, racquetball, soccer, softball, squash, table tennis, tennis, track and field, volleyball. **Team name:** Lutes.

Student services. Adult student services, chaplain/spiritual director, career counseling, student employment services, financial aid counseling,

health services, minority student services, personal counseling, placement for graduates, veterans' counselor, women's services. **Physically disabled:** Services for visually, speech, hearing impaired.

Contact. E-mail: admission@plu.edu
Phone: (253) 535-7151 Toll-free number: (800) 274-6758
Fax: (253) 536-5136
Karl Stumo, Vice President of Admission & Enrollment Services, Pacific Lutheran University, 1010 South 122nd Street, Tacoma, WA 98447-0003

Saint Martin's University
Lacey, Washington
www.stmartin.edu

CB member
CB code: 4674

- Private 4-year university affiliated with Roman Catholic Church
- Residential campus in large town
- 1,342 degree-seeking undergraduates: 16% part-time, 52% women, 8% African American, 5% Asian American, 10% Hispanic American, 1% Native American, 5% international
- 374 degree-seeking graduate students
- 74% of applicants admitted
- SAT or ACT with writing, application essay required
- 48% graduate within 6 years

General. Founded in 1895. Regionally accredited. Saint Martin's Abbey, located on campus, is the home of the Benedictine monks. **Degrees:** 345 bachelor's awarded; master's offered. **ROTC:** Army, Air Force. **Location:** 3 miles from Olympia, 60 miles from Seattle. **Calendar:** Semester, limited summer session. **Full-time faculty:** 77 total; 75% have terminal degrees, 12% minority, 38% women. **Part-time faculty:** 125 total; 26% have terminal degrees, 6% minority, 49% women. **Class size:** 63% < 20, 25% 20-39, 5% 40-49, 6% 50-99, 1% >100.

Freshman class profile. 728 applied, 542 admitted, 235 enrolled.

Mid 50% test scores			
SAT critical reading:	440-560	GPA 3.0-3.49:	36%
SAT math:	450-560	GPA 2.0-2.99:	29%
SAT writing:	440-540	Rank in top quarter:	41%
ACT composite:	19-25	Rank in top tenth:	19%
GPA 3.75 or higher:	20%	Return as sophomores:	73%
GPA 3.50-3.74:	14%	Out-of-state:	18%
		Live on campus:	77%

Basis for selection. School achievement record most important. Test scores important. 3.0 GPA required for regular admittance. Interview recommended. **Home schooled:** Statement describing home school structure and mission, transcript of courses and grades required. **Learning Disabled:** Students with disabilities should initiate contact with the Office of Disability Support Services.

High school preparation. College-preparatory program recommended. 17 units recommended. Recommended units include English 4, mathematics 3, social studies 2, science 3 (laboratory 1), foreign language 2 and academic electives 3.

2011-2012 Annual costs. Tuition/fees: $27,622. Room/board: $8,960. Books/supplies: $1,000. Personal expenses: $1,000.

2010-2011 Financial aid. Need-based: 191 full-time freshmen applied for aid; 169 were judged to have need; 169 of these received aid. Average need met was 81%. Average scholarship/grant was $18,988; average loan $2,967. 63% of total undergraduate aid awarded as scholarships/grants, 37% as loans/jobs. **Non-need-based:** Awarded to 268 full-time undergraduates, including 65 freshmen. Scholarships awarded for academics, alumni affiliation, art, athletics, leadership, minority status, music/drama, religious affiliation, ROTC, state residency.

Application procedures. Admission: Priority date 3/1; no deadline. $35 fee, may be waived for applicants with need. Admission notification on a rolling basis beginning on or about 10/1. Must reply by May 1 or within 3 week(s) if notified thereafter. **Financial aid:** Priority date 4/15; no closing date. FAFSA required. Applicants notified on a rolling basis starting 2/15; must reply within 3 week(s) of notification.

Academics. Special study options: Combined bachelor's/graduate degree, distance learning, double major, ESL, exchange student, independent study, internships, study abroad, teacher certification program, Washington semester. **Credit/placement by examination:** AP, CLEP, IB, institutional tests. 32 credit hours maximum toward bachelor's degree. **Support services:** Learning center, pre-admission summer program, reduced course load, remedial instruction, study skills assistance, tutoring, writing center.

Majors. Biology: General. **Business:** Accounting, business admin. **Computer sciences:** Computer science. **Education:** Adult/continuing, elementary, special ed. **Engineering:** Civil, mechanical. **English:** English lit. **History:** General. **Human services:** Community org/advocacy. **Math:** General. **Philosophy/religion:** Philosophy, religion. **Physical sciences:** Chemistry. **Protective services:** Criminal justice. **Psychology:** General. **Social sciences:** Anthropology, political science. **Visual/performing arts:** Dramatic, music.

Most popular majors. Biology 8%, business/marketing 28%, education 7%, engineering/engineering technologies 13%, psychology 16%, security/protective services 7%, social sciences 6%.

Computing on campus. 80 workstations in library, computer center. Dormitories wired for high-speed internet access and linked to campus network. Commuter students can connect to campus network. Online library, helpline, repair service, student web hosting, wireless network available.

Student life. Freshman orientation: Mandatory, $275 fee. Preregistration for classes offered. Freshmen orientation program begins on the Thursday before school starts in the fall. **Policies:** Alcohol possession, consumption, possession by means of consumption (if under the age of 21) and the sale of alcoholic beverages is prohibited in or around University-owned or University-controlled property. **Housing:** Guaranteed on-campus for freshmen. Coed dorms, special housing for disabled, apartments available. $200 fully refundable deposit, deadline 7/1. **Activities:** Bands, campus ministries, choral groups, dance, drama, international student organizations, Model UN, musical theater, student government, student newspaper, Circle K, Hawaiian club, international club, non-traditional students group, social action club, College Republicans, Gay/Straight Alliance, Young Democrats, Saint for Life.

Athletics. NCAA. **Intercollegiate:** Baseball M, basketball, cross-country, golf, soccer, softball W, track and field, volleyball W. **Intramural:** Basketball, bowling, football (non-tackle), soccer, softball, tennis, volleyball. **Team name:** Saints.

Student services. Adult student services, alcohol/substance abuse counseling, chaplain/spiritual director, career counseling, financial aid counseling, health services, personal counseling, veterans' counselor. **Physically disabled:** Services for visually, hearing impaired.

Contact. E-mail: admissions@stmartin.edu
Phone: (360) 438-4596 Toll-free number: (800) 368-8803
Fax: (360) 412-6189
Scott Schulz, Director of Admissions, Saint Martin's University, 5000 Abbey Way SE, Lacey, WA 98503-7500

Seattle Pacific University
Seattle, Washington
www.spu.edu

CB member
CB code: 4694

- Private 4-year university affiliated with Free Methodist Church of North America
- Residential campus in very large city
- 3,176 degree-seeking undergraduates: 3% part-time, 67% women, 4% African American, 9% Asian American, 7% Hispanic American, 1% international
- 946 degree-seeking graduate students
- 80% of applicants admitted
- SAT or ACT (ACT writing optional), application essay required
- 76% graduate within 6 years

General. Founded in 1891. Regionally accredited. **Degrees:** 729 bachelor's awarded; master's, doctoral offered. **ROTC:** Army, Naval, Air Force. **Location:** 3 miles from downtown. **Calendar:** Quarter, limited summer session. **Full-time faculty:** 204 total; 89% have terminal degrees, 10% minority, 43% women. **Part-time faculty:** 159 total; 7% have terminal degrees, 6% minority, 58% women. **Class size:** 48% < 20, 38% 20-39, 7% 40-49, 6% 50-99, less than 1% >100. **Special facilities:** 2 island campuses used for biological studies.

Freshman class profile. 4,211 applied, 3,362 admitted, 760 enrolled.

Mid 50% test scores			
SAT critical reading:	520-630	GPA 2.0-2.99:	4%
SAT math:	520-630	Rank in top quarter:	60%
SAT writing:	510-620	Rank in top tenth:	32%
ACT composite:	22-28	Return as sophomores:	85%
GPA 3.75 or higher:	38%	Out-of-state:	48%
GPA 3.50-3.74:	27%	Live on campus:	96%
GPA 3.0-3.49:	31%	International:	1%

Basis for selection. Admission decisions based primarily based on grades, grade trend, test scores, essays, letters of recommendation and extracurricular

activities. Audition required for music, performing art workshop; portfolio required for fine art scholarship. **Home schooled:** Copy of reading list and information regarding the curriculum used in homeschool program. **Learning Disabled:** Contact Disability Support Services in the Center for Learning to make arrangements for an interview to determine the level of assistance needed. Students required to provide documentation of the nature of the disability.

High school preparation. College-preparatory program recommended. Recommended units include English 4, mathematics 3, history 2, science 3 and foreign language 3.

2011-2012 Annual costs. Tuition/fees: $30,339. Room/board: $9,081. Books/supplies: $942. Personal expenses: $1,785.

2011-2012 Financial aid. Need-based: 682 full-time freshmen applied for aid; 575 were judged to have need; 573 of these received aid. Average need met was 81%. Average scholarship/grant was $21,419; average loan $5,003. 64% of total undergraduate aid awarded as scholarships/grants, 36% as loans/jobs. **Non-need-based:** Awarded to 734 full-time undergraduates, including 161 freshmen. Scholarships awarded for academics, alumni affiliation, art, athletics, leadership, minority status, music/drama, religious affiliation, ROTC.

Application procedures. Admission: Closing date 2/1 (postmark date). $50 fee, may be waived for applicants with need. Admission notification by 3/1. Admission notification on a rolling basis. Must reply by May 1 or within 2 week(s) if notified thereafter. **Financial aid:** Priority date 2/1; no closing date. FAFSA required. Applicants notified on a rolling basis starting 3/15; must reply by 5/1 or within 30 week(s) of notification.

Academics. Special study options: Distance learning, double major, exchange student, external degree, honors, independent study, internships, liberal arts/career combination, student-designed major, study abroad, teacher certification program, Washington semester. **Credit/placement by examination:** AP, CLEP, IB, SAT, ACT, institutional tests. 45 credit hours maximum toward bachelor's degree. **Support services:** Learning center, reduced course load, remedial instruction, study skills assistance, tutoring, writing center.

Majors. Area/ethnic studies: European, Latin American. **Biology:** General, biochemistry. **Business:** Accounting. **Communications:** Communications/speech/rhetoric. **Computer sciences:** Computer science. **Education:** Art, English, mathematics, music, science, social science, special ed. **Engineering:** Computer, electrical, engineering science. **English:** English lit. **Foreign languages:** Classics, French, German, Latin, Russian, Spanish. **Health services:** Nursing (RN). **History:** General. **Liberal arts:** Arts/sciences. **Math:** General, computational. **Parks/recreation:** Exercise sciences. **Philosophy/religion:** Philosophy. **Physical sciences:** Chemistry, physics. **Psychology:** General. **Social sciences:** Economics, political science, sociology. **Theology:** Religious ed. **Visual/performing arts:** General, art, dramatic, interior design, music. **Work/family studies:** Clothing/textiles, food/nutrition.

Most popular majors. Biology 7%, business/marketing 13%, communications/journalism 7%, English 6%, family/consumer sciences 7%, health sciences 9%, psychology 8%, social sciences 11%, visual/performing arts 11%.

Computing on campus. 475 workstations in dormitories, library, computer center, student center. Dormitories wired for high-speed internet access and linked to campus network. Commuter students can connect to campus network. Online course registration, online library, helpline, repair service, wireless network available.

Student life. Freshman orientation: Mandatory. Preregistration for classes offered. **Policies:** Religious observance required. **Housing:** Coed dorms, special housing for disabled, apartments available. $300 fully refundable deposit, deadline 6/1. **Activities:** Bands, campus ministries, choral groups, drama, literary magazine, music ensembles, musical theater, radio station, student government, student newspaper, symphony orchestra, more than 25 clubs and organizations.

Athletics. NCAA. **Intercollegiate:** Basketball, cross-country, gymnastics W, rowing (crew), soccer, track and field, volleyball W. **Intramural:** Archery, basketball, bowling, cross-country, football (non-tackle), softball, tennis, volleyball, weight lifting. **Team name:** Falcons.

Student services. Adult student services, chaplain/spiritual director, career counseling, student employment services, financial aid counseling, health services, minority student services, personal counseling, placement for graduates, veterans' counselor. **Physically disabled:** Services for visually, hearing impaired.

Contact. E-mail: admissions@spu.edu
Phone: (206) 281-2021 Toll-free number: (800) 366-3344
Fax: (206) 281-2544
Jobe Korb-Nice, Director of Undergraduate Admissions, Seattle Pacific University, 3307 Third Avenue West, Suite 115, Seattle, WA 98119-1997

Seattle University
Seattle, Washington
www.seattleu.edu

CB member
CB code: 4695

- Private 4-year university affiliated with Roman Catholic Church
- Residential campus in very large city
- 4,593 degree-seeking undergraduates: 4% part-time, 60% women, 4% African American, 16% Asian American, 8% Hispanic American, 1% Native American, 9% international
- 3,102 degree-seeking graduate students
- 71% of applicants admitted
- SAT or ACT (ACT writing optional) required
- 71% graduate within 6 years

General. Founded in 1891. Regionally accredited. Courses also offered at Bellevue Campus. **Degrees:** 1,131 bachelor's awarded; master's, professional, doctoral offered. **ROTC:** Army, Naval, Air Force. **Location:** One mile from downtown. **Calendar:** Quarter, extensive summer session. **Full-time faculty:** 464 total; 76% have terminal degrees, 16% minority, 49% women. **Part-time faculty:** 255 total; 22% have terminal degrees, 10% minority, 53% women. **Class size:** 49% < 20, 47% 20-39, 3% 40-49, less than 1% 50-99. **Special facilities:** Design center (where engineering students work with major companies in the area), observatory.

Freshman class profile. 6,317 applied, 4,456 admitted, 870 enrolled.

Mid 50% test scores			
SAT critical reading:	520-630	GPA 2.0-2.99:	4%
SAT math:	530-630	Rank in top quarter:	60%
SAT writing:	530-630	Rank in top tenth:	29%
ACT composite:	24-28	Return as sophomores:	86%
GPA 3.75 or higher:	37%	Out-of-state:	59%
GPA 3.50-3.74:	24%	Live on campus:	94%
GPA 3.0-3.49:	35%	International:	3%

Basis for selection. 2.75 GPA minimum, higher for some programs. Secondary school record, recommendations, test scores most important. Essay, school, community activities also important. Applicants must submit one test with writing component. ACT writing component is required if applicant does not submit SAT Reasoning scores. **Home schooled:** Transcript of courses and grades, letter of recommendation (nonparent) required. SAT II, ACT subject tests, AP tests, IB tests and/or transcript(s) of courses taken at college(s).

High school preparation. College-preparatory program required. 16 units required. Required units include English 4, mathematics 3, social studies 3, history 1, science 2 (laboratory 2), foreign language 2 and academic electives 2.

2011-2012 Annual costs. Tuition/fees: $32,700. Room/board: $9,855.

2011-2012 Financial aid. Need-based: 737 full-time freshmen applied for aid; 562 were judged to have need; 562 of these received aid. Average need met was 65%. Average scholarship/grant was $13,192; average loan $3,937. 72% of total undergraduate aid awarded as scholarships/grants, 28% as loans/jobs. **Non-need-based:** Awarded to 1,475 full-time undergraduates, including 427 freshmen. Scholarships awarded for academics, alumni affiliation, athletics, leadership, minority status, music/drama, ROTC, state residency.

Application procedures. Admission: Priority date 1/15; no deadline. $50 fee, may be waived for applicants with need. Admission notification on a rolling basis beginning on or about 3/1. Must reply by May 1 or within 4 week(s) if notified thereafter. **Financial aid:** Priority date 2/1; no closing date. FAFSA required. Applicants notified on a rolling basis starting 3/1; must reply by 5/1 or within 2 week(s) of notification.

Academics. Special study options: Cooperative education, cross-registration, double major, honors, independent study, internships, liberal arts/career combination, student-designed major, study abroad. **Credit/placement by examination:** AP, CLEP, IB, institutional tests. 45 credit hours maximum toward bachelor's degree. Special arrangements for nursing majors who take NLN exams. 50 credits maximum. **Support services:** Learning center, pre-admission summer program, reduced course load, study skills assistance, tutoring, writing center.

Majors. Area/ethnic studies: Asian, women's. **Biology:** General, biochemistry. **Business:** General, accounting, business admin, e-commerce, finance, international, managerial economics, marketing. **Communications:** Journalism, media studies, public relations. **Computer sciences:** Computer science. **Conservation:** General. **Engineering:** Civil, electrical, mechanical. **English:** Creative writing, English lit. **Foreign languages:** General, French, Spanish. **Health services:** Clinical lab science, nursing (RN), sonography. **History:** General. **Human services:** General, social work. **Liberal arts:** Arts/sciences,

humanities. **Math:** General. **Parks/recreation:** Exercise sciences. **Philosophy/religion:** Philosophy, religion. **Physical sciences:** General, chemistry, physics. **Protective services:** Criminal justice, criminalistics. **Psychology:** General. **Social sciences:** Economics, political science, sociology. **Visual/performing arts:** General, art history/conservation, dramatic, music.

Most popular majors. Business/marketing 25%, health sciences 14%, social sciences 8%.

Computing on campus. 467 workstations in dormitories, library, computer center, student center. Dormitories wired for high-speed internet access and linked to campus network. Commuter students can connect to campus network. Online course registration, helpline, student web hosting, wireless network available.

Student life. Freshman orientation: Mandatory. Preregistration for classes offered. 3 days prior to start of classes. **Housing:** Guaranteed on-campus for freshmen. Coed dorms, special housing for disabled, apartments, wellness housing available. $300 nonrefundable deposit, deadline 5/1. Single-gender floors available. **Activities:** Bands, campus ministries, choral groups, dance, drama, international student organizations, literary magazine, music ensembles, Model UN, radio station, student government, student newspaper, 65 clubs available.

Athletics. NCAA. Intercollegiate: Baseball M, basketball, cross-country, golf, soccer, softball W, swimming, tennis, track and field, volleyball W. **Intramural:** Basketball, football (non-tackle), soccer, softball, tennis, volleyball. **Team name:** Redhawks.

Student services. Adult student services, alcohol/substance abuse counseling, chaplain/spiritual director, career counseling, student employment services, financial aid counseling, health services, minority student services, personal counseling, placement for graduates, veterans' counselor, women's services. **Physically disabled:** Services for visually, speech, hearing impaired.

Contact. E-mail: admissions@seattleu.edu
Phone: (206) 296-2000 Toll-free number: (800) 426-7123
Fax: (206) 296-5656
Melore Nielsen, Dean of Admissions, Seattle University, 901 12th Avenue, Seattle, WA 98122-4340

Trinity Lutheran College
Everett, Washington
www.tlc.edu
CB code: 4408

- Private 4-year Bible and liberal arts college affiliated with Lutheran Church
- Residential campus in small city
- 160 degree-seeking undergraduates
- 73% of applicants admitted
- SAT or ACT (ACT writing optional) required

General. Founded in 1944. Regionally accredited. All students participate in off-campus service learning practicums. **Degrees:** 44 bachelor's awarded. **Location:** 30 miles from Seattle. **Calendar:** 4-1-4. **Full-time faculty:** 13 total. **Part-time faculty:** 24 total. **Class size:** 89% < 20, 10% 20-39, 1% 40-49. **Special facilities:** Children, youth and family resource center; preschool and Christian school.

Freshman class profile. 253 applied, 185 admitted, 28 enrolled.

Basis for selection. High school GPA, test scores, one recommendation. Interview considered. **Home schooled:** Statement describing home school structure and mission, transcript of courses and grades, letter of recommendation (nonparent) required.

High school preparation. Recommended units include English 3, mathematics 2, history 2, science 2 and foreign language 1.

2011-2012 Annual costs. Tuition/fees: $22,260. Lunch-only meal plan (5 days per week) for academic year, $1,000. Room only: $6,883. Books/supplies: $924. Personal expenses: $1,818.

Financial aid. Non-need-based: Scholarships awarded for academics, alumni affiliation, art, athletics, leadership, music/drama.

Application procedures. Admission: $30 fee, may be waived for applicants with need, free for online applicants. Admission notification on a rolling basis beginning on or about 10/1. Must reply by May 1 or within 2 week(s) if notified thereafter. **Financial aid:** Closing date 3/1. FAFSA, institutional form required. Applicants notified on a rolling basis starting 3/15; must reply within 2 week(s) of notification.

Academics. Special study options: Combined bachelor's/graduate degree, cooperative education, distance learning, dual enrollment of high school students, independent study, internships, liberal arts/career combination, student-designed major, study abroad, urban semester. Study trips to Holy Lands, Italy, Greece, Africa, India, South America. **Credit/placement by examination:** AP, CLEP, IB, institutional tests. 8 credit hours maximum toward associate degree, 8 toward bachelor's. **Support services:** Reduced course load, remedial instruction, study skills assistance, tutoring, writing center.

Majors. Business: Business admin, nonprofit/public. **Communications:** Media studies. **Education:** Early childhood. **Philosophy/religion:** Christian, religion. **Psychology:** General. **Theology:** Bible, missionary, sacred music, theology, youth ministry.

Most popular majors. Area/ethnic studies 11%, business/marketing 11%, communications/journalism 11%, education 6%, philosophy/religious studies 17%, public administration/social services 11%, theological studies 33%.

Computing on campus. 15 workstations in dormitories, library, computer center, student center. Dormitories wired for high-speed internet access and linked to campus network. Commuter students can connect to campus network. Online library, helpline, wireless network available.

Student life. Freshman orientation: Mandatory. Preregistration for classes offered. 3-day session held before classes begin. **Housing:** Guaranteed on-campus for all undergraduates. Coed dorms, single-sex dorms, special housing for disabled, apartments, wellness housing available. $75 partly refundable deposit, deadline 5/1. **Activities:** Choral groups, drama, music ensembles, musical theater, student government, student newspaper, Student learning practicums, Global Concerns Mission, Worship Commission, Environmental Commission.

Athletics. NCCAA. Intercollegiate: Soccer. **Intramural:** Basketball, football (non-tackle), soccer, softball, table tennis, tennis, volleyball. **Team name:** Eagles.

Student services. Adult student services, alcohol/substance abuse counseling, chaplain/spiritual director, career counseling, student employment services, financial aid counseling, health services, on-campus daycare, personal counseling, placement for graduates, veterans' counselor. **Physically disabled:** Services for visually impaired.

Contact. E-mail: admissions@tlc.edu
Phone: (425) 249-4800 Toll-free number: (800) 843-5659
Fax: (425) 249-4801
Director of Admissions, Trinity Lutheran College, 2802 Wetmore Avenue, Everett, WA 98201

University of Phoenix: Western Washington
Tukwila, Washington
www.phoenix.edu

- For-profit 4-year university
- Commuter campus in large city
- 729 degree-seeking undergraduates

General. Regionally accredited. **Degrees:** 133 bachelor's awarded; master's offered. **Calendar:** Differs by program. **Full-time faculty:** 8 total. **Part-time faculty:** 103 total.

Basis for selection. Open admission.

2011-2012 Annual costs. Estimated costs as of August 2011: per-credit-hour charge, $435 to $480, depending upon level and course of study; electronic course materials fee, $95 plus sales tax, if applicable. Book and material charges may vary by course and program. All fees are subject to change.

Application procedures. Admission: No deadline. No application fee. **Financial aid:** No deadline.

Academics. Credit/placement by examination: AP, CLEP.

Majors. Business: Accounting, business admin, credit management, e-commerce, entrepreneurial studies, human resources, marketing, operations. **Computer sciences:** General, networking, programming, security, systems analysis, web page design, webmaster. **Health services:** Facilities admin. **Human services:** General. **Protective services:** Law enforcement admin. **Psychology:** General.

Most popular majors. Business/marketing 80%, computer/information sciences 8%, public administration/social services 11%.

Contact. Toll-free number: (866) 766-0766
Marc Booker, Director of Admission and Evaluation, University of
Phoenix: Western Washington, 7100 Fort Dent Way, Tukwila, WA
98188-8553

University of Puget Sound
Tacoma, Washington
www.pugetsound.edu

CB member
CB code: 4067

- Private 4-year liberal arts college
- Residential campus in small city
- 2,645 degree-seeking undergraduates: 1% part-time, 57% women
- 270 degree-seeking graduate students
- 52% of applicants admitted
- SAT or ACT (ACT writing recommended), application essay required
- 73% graduate within 6 years; 13% enter graduate study

General. Founded in 1888. Regionally accredited. **Degrees:** 563 bachelor's
awarded; master's, professional offered. **ROTC:** Army. **Location:** 35 miles
from Seattle, 28 miles from Olympia. **Calendar:** Semester, limited summer
session. **Full-time faculty:** 230 total; 86% have terminal degrees, 7% minority, 45% women. **Part-time faculty:** 53 total; 43% have terminal degrees,
4% minority, 51% women. **Class size:** 50% < 20, 49% 20-39, less than 1%
40-49, less than 1% 50-99. **Special facilities:** Sculpture building, natural
history museum, theaters, greenhouse, transmission and scanning electron
microscopes, confocal microscope, DNA sequencer, NMR, X-ray diffractometer, microcomputer labs, sedimentology lab, stereoscopic and petrographic
microscopes, computerized plotting/digitizing board and image analysis system, portable seismograph, gravimeter, proton precession magnetometer, ICP,
GPS GIS lab, observatory, concert hall, exercise science labs, physiology
labs, rock and mineral collection, arboretum.

Freshman class profile. 7,194 applied, 3,729 admitted, 686 enrolled.

Mid 50% test scores		GPA 2.0-2.99:	8%
SAT critical reading:	570-680	Rank in top quarter:	69%
SAT math:	560-660	Rank in top tenth:	32%
SAT writing:	570-670	End year in good standing:	94%
ACT composite:	26-30	Return as sophomores:	88%
GPA 3.75 or higher:	31%	Out-of-state:	81%
GPA 3.50-3.74:	25%	Live on campus:	98%
GPA 3.0-3.49:	36%		

Basis for selection. All applications evaluated through a wholistic process. High school record most important followed by academic GPA. Writing
ability as demonstrated through the essay and short answer questions. Recommendations and activities important. If applicants have taken both SAT and
ACT, they should submit all scores. Interview recommended for all; audition
required for music; portfolio recommended for art; audition recommended
for theater.

High school preparation. College-preparatory program recommended.
19 units recommended. Recommended units include English 4, mathematics
4, social studies 3, history 3, science 4 (laboratory 4), foreign language 3 and
visual/performing arts 1. One fine, visual, or performing art recommended.

2011-2012 Annual costs. Tuition/fees: $38,720. Students are charged an
annual fee of $165 for a Student Health Insurance Plan, but they may request
a waiver of that fee if they can demonstrate that they are covered under a
health insurance plan that is valid for treatment in the Tacoma area. Room/
board: $10,020. Books/supplies: $1,000. Personal expenses: $1,800.

2011-2012 Financial aid. **Need-based:** 553 full-time freshmen applied
for aid; 467 were judged to have need; 467 of these received aid. Average
need met was 73%. Average scholarship/grant was $22,157; average loan
$4,333. 72% of total undergraduate aid awarded as scholarships/grants, 28%
as loans/jobs. **Non-need-based:** Awarded to 799 full-time undergraduates,
including 252 freshmen. Scholarships awarded for academics, alumni affiliation, art, leadership, music/drama, religious affiliation. **Additional information:** Cooperative education allows qualified upperclassmen to alternate
semesters of full-time study and full-time work.

Application procedures. **Admission:** Closing date 1/15 (postmark date).
$50 fee, may be waived for applicants with need. Admission notification by
4/1. Must reply by May 1 or within 2 week(s) if notified thereafter. **Financial
aid:** Priority date 2/1; no closing date. FAFSA required. Students applying
for Early Decision must complete the CSS PROFILE for notification of need-
based financial aid eligibility. Applicants notified on a rolling basis starting
3/15; must reply by 5/1 or within 2 week(s) of notification.

Academics. All students complete core curriculum, including courses in
writing and rhetoric, scholarly and creative inquiry, fine arts, humanistic,

mathematical, natural scientific and social scientific approaches, and a connections course intended to develop an understanding of the interrelationship
of fields of knowledge. **Special study options:** Cooperative education, double
major, honors, independent study, internships, student-designed major, study
abroad, teacher certification program. Institution offers year of study in Asia,
3-2 engineering program, business leadership program. **Credit/placement by
examination:** AP, CLEP, IB, institutional tests. **Support services:** Learning
center, reduced course load, study skills assistance, tutoring, writing center.

Majors. **Area/ethnic studies:** Asian. **Biology:** General, biochemistry, cellu-
lar/molecular. **Business:** Business admin, management information systems.
Communications: Communications/speech/rhetoric. **Computer sciences:**
Computer science. **Education:** Music. **English:** English lit. **Foreign languages:** General, Chinese, classics, East Asian, French, German, Japanese,
Spanish. **History:** General. **Math:** General. **Parks/recreation:** Exercise sciences. **Philosophy/religion:** Philosophy, religion. **Physical sciences:** Chemistry, geology, physics. **Psychology:** General. **Social sciences:** Economics,
international economics, political science, sociology. **Visual/performing
arts:** Art, dramatic, music, music management, music performance.

Most popular majors. Biology 9%, business/marketing 11%, English 9%,
foreign language 8%, interdisciplinary studies 6%, psychology 8%, social
sciences 21%, visual/performing arts 9%.

Computing on campus. 600 workstations in dormitories, library, computer center, student center. Dormitories wired for high-speed internet access
and linked to campus network. Commuter students can connect to campus
network. Online course registration, online library, helpline, repair service,
student web hosting, wireless network available.

Student life. **Freshman orientation:** Available. Preregistration for classes
offered. 9-day introduction to academic life and campus community. **Housing:** Guaranteed on-campus for freshmen. Coed dorms, single-sex dorms,
special housing for disabled, fraternity/sorority housing, wellness housing
available. $200 nonrefundable deposit, deadline 5/1. Coed by floor, coed by
door, academically-themed programs, 56 university-owned homes on campus.
Activities: Bands, campus ministries, choral groups, dance, drama, film
society, international student organizations, literary magazine, music ensembles, Model UN, musical theater, opera, radio station, student government,
student newspaper, symphony orchestra, Black Student Union, Hui-o-Hawaii,
Circle K, Jewish Student Organization; Bisexuals, Gays, Lesbians, and Allies
for Diversity, Pacific American Student Union, Students for Peace and Justice,
First Nations, Habitat for Humanity, Film and Theatre Society.

Athletics. NCAA. **Intercollegiate:** Baseball M, basketball, cheerleading,
cross-country, football (tackle) M, golf, lacrosse W, rowing (crew), soccer,
softball W, swimming, tennis, track and field, volleyball W. **Intramural:**
Basketball, football (non-tackle), soccer, softball, table tennis, tennis, volleyball. **Team name:** Loggers.

Student services. Alcohol/substance abuse counseling, chaplain/spiritual
director, career counseling, student employment services, financial aid counseling, health services, legal services, minority student services, personal
counseling, placement for graduates. **Physically disabled:** Services for visually, speech, hearing impaired.

Contact. E-mail: admission@pugetsound.edu
Phone: (253) 879-3211 Toll-free number: (800) 396-7191
Fax: (253) 879-3993
George Mills, Vice President for Enrollment, University of Puget Sound,
1500 North Warner Street, Tacoma, WA 98416-1062

University of Washington
Seattle, Washington
www.washington.edu

CB member
CB code: 4854

- Public 4-year university
- Residential campus in very large city
- 27,867 degree-seeking undergraduates: 7% part-time, 52% women
- 13,081 degree-seeking graduate students
- 58% of applicants admitted
- SAT or ACT with writing, application essay required
- 80% graduate within 6 years

General. Founded in 1861. Regionally accredited. **Degrees:** 7,610 bachelor's awarded; master's, professional, doctoral offered. **ROTC:** Army, Naval,
Air Force. **Location:** 5 miles from downtown Seattle. **Calendar:** Quarter,
extensive summer session. **Full-time faculty:** 2,818 total; 87% have terminal
degrees, 20% minority, 38% women. **Part-time faculty:** 784 total; 66% have
terminal degrees, 15% minority, 52% women. **Class size:** 34% < 20, 36%
20-39, 9% 40-49, 12% 50-99, 8% >100. **Special facilities:** Arboretum, observatory, anthropological museum, applied physics laboratory, planetarium.

Freshman class profile. 24,540 applied, 14,340 admitted, 5,788 enrolled.

Mid 50% test scores			
SAT critical reading:	510-650	Rank in top quarter:	98%
SAT math:	570-700	Rank in top tenth:	92%
SAT writing:	520-640	Return as sophomores:	93%
ACT composite:	24-30	Out-of-state:	20%
GPA 3.75 or higher:	59%	Live on campus:	67%
GPA 3.50-3.74:	28%	Fraternities:	10%
GPA 3.0-3.49:	12%	Sororities:	9%

Basis for selection. Applicants holistically reviewed on the basis of completion of core subject requirements, grades and test scores and supplemental factors including personal statement, completion of substantial number of courses beyond minimum, grades in college-preparatory courses, enrollment in AP or honors courses, cultural diversity and documented evidence of exceptional artistic talent. Auditions required for admission to performing arts programs. Application interviews not available, only informational appointments. **Home schooled:** Transcript of courses and grades required. Each applicant is reviewed case-by-case. To confirm successful completion of certain core subject requirements or levels, applicants may be asked to provide additional documentation or placement testing information. **Learning Disabled:** Applicants with documented disabilities not expected to disclose them at time of application, but welcome do so in the applicant's own written materials, or via relevant documentation or letters. Students encouraged to first speak with an admissions counselor.

High school preparation. College-preparatory program required. 15 units required; 21 recommended. Required and recommended units include English 4, mathematics 3-4, social studies 3-4, history 1, science 2-4 (laboratory 2-3), foreign language 2-3, computer science 1, visual/performing arts .5-1, academic electives 0.5. One semester (.5) elective from required subjects list and .5 fine arts course.

2011-2012 Annual costs. Tuition/fees: $10,826; $28,310 out-of-state. Room/board: $9,000. Books/supplies: $1,035. Personal expenses: $2,265.

2011-2012 Financial aid. **Need-based:** 3,831 full-time freshmen applied for aid; 2,499 were judged to have need; 2,223 of these received aid. Average need met was 82%. Average scholarship/grant was $12,500; average loan $6,000. 64% of total undergraduate aid awarded as scholarships/grants, 36% as loans/jobs. **Non-need-based:** Awarded to 1,218 full-time undergraduates, including 342 freshmen. Scholarships awarded for academics, alumni affiliation, art, athletics, leadership, music/drama, ROTC. **Additional information:** Tuition not due until third week of term.

Application procedures. **Admission:** Closing date 12/1 (postmark date). $60 fee, may be waived for applicants with need. Admission notification by 3/31. Admission notification on a rolling basis beginning on or about 3/15. Must reply by 5/1. **Financial aid:** Priority date 2/28; no closing date. FAFSA required. Applicants notified by 4/1; must reply within 3 week(s) of notification.

Academics. **Special study options:** Combined bachelor's/graduate degree, cooperative education, distance learning, double major, ESL, exchange student, honors, independent study, internships, student-designed major, study abroad, teacher certification program, Washington semester. Quarter at Friday Harbor Laboratories, San Juan Islands. **Credit/placement by examination:** AP, CLEP, IB, institutional tests. 90 credit hours maximum toward bachelor's degree. **Support services:** Learning center, pre-admission summer program, reduced course load, remedial instruction, study skills assistance, tutoring, writing center.

Majors. **Architecture:** Architecture, landscape, urban/community planning. **Area/ethnic studies:** African, African-American, Asian, Asian-American, Canadian, Chicano/Hispanic-American/Latino, Chinese, European, French, German, Italian, Japanese, Korean, Latin American, Native American, Near/Middle Eastern, Russian/Eastern European/Eurasian, Russian/Slavic, Scandinavian, Slavic, South Asian, Southeast Asian, women's. **Biology:** General, bacteriology, biochemistry, botany, ecology, marine, microbiology, zoology. **Business:** Accounting, business admin, construction management, finance, human resources, international, management information systems, organizational behavior. **Communications:** Communications/speech/rhetoric. **Computer sciences:** General, computer science, information systems, information technology. **Conservation:** General, fisheries, forest resources, forestry, wildlife/wilderness. **Education:** Music. **Engineering:** General, aerospace, biomedical, ceramic, chemical, civil, computer, electrical, environmental, forest, industrial, materials, mechanical, metallurgical. **English:** English lit, rhetoric/composition, technical writing. **Foreign languages:** Ancient Greek, Arabic, Chinese, classics, comparative lit, Danish, East Asian, French, German, Germanic, Hebrew, Italian, Japanese, Korean, Latin, linguistics, Norwegian, Russian, Scandinavian, South Asian, Southeast Asian, Spanish, Swedish, Turkish, Ukrainian. **Health services:** Audiology/speech pathology, clinical lab science, dental hygiene, environmental health, nursing (RN), orthotics/prosthetics, physician assistant. **History:** General. **Human services:** Social work. **Liberal arts:** Arts/sciences. **Math:** General, applied. **Philosophy/**

religion: Judaic, philosophy, religion. **Physical sciences:** Astronomy, astrophysics, atmospheric science, chemistry, geology, materials science, oceanography, physics, planetary. **Psychology:** General. **Social sciences:** General, anthropology, economics, geography, international relations, political science, sociology. **Visual/performing arts:** Art, art history/conservation, ceramics, commercial/advertising art, dance, dramatic, fiber arts, industrial design, metal/jewelry, music, music history, music performance, music theory/composition, musicology, painting, photography, piano/keyboard, printmaking, sculpture, stringed instruments, voice/opera.

Most popular majors. Biology 10%, business/marketing 11%, engineering/engineering technologies 8%, social sciences 19%, visual/performing arts 9%.

Computing on campus. 2,000 workstations in dormitories, library, computer center, student center. Dormitories wired for high-speed internet access and linked to campus network. Commuter students can connect to campus network. Online course registration, online library, helpline, repair service, student web hosting, wireless network available.

Student life. **Freshman orientation:** Mandatory, $272 fee. Preregistration for classes offered. Advising and registration throughout the summer. **Housing:** Coed dorms, special housing for disabled, apartments, fraternity/sorority housing, wellness housing available. $500 nonrefundable deposit, deadline 6/1. Special interest houses available. **Activities:** Bands, campus ministries, choral groups, dance, drama, film society, international student organizations, literary magazine, music ensembles, Model UN, musical theater, opera, radio station, student government, student newspaper, symphony orchestra, TV station, over 500 student organizations.

Athletics. NCAA. **Intercollegiate:** Baseball M, basketball, cheerleading, cross-country, football (tackle) M, golf, gymnastics W, rowing (crew), soccer, softball W, tennis, track and field, volleyball W. **Intramural:** Basketball, football (non-tackle), racquetball, rowing (crew), soccer, softball, swimming, tennis, volleyball. **Team name:** Huskies.

Student services. Alcohol/substance abuse counseling, career counseling, services for economically disadvantaged, student employment services, financial aid counseling, health services, legal services, minority student services, on-campus daycare, personal counseling, placement for graduates, veterans' counselor, women's services. **Physically disabled:** Services for visually, speech, hearing impaired.

Contact. Phone: (206) 543-9686 Fax: (206) 685-3655
Philip Ballinger, Director of Admissions, University of Washington, 1410 Northeast Campus Parkway, Box 355852, Seattle, WA 98195-5852

University of Washington Bothell
Bothell, Washington
www.uwb.edu **CB code: 4467**

- Public 4-year university
- Residential campus in large town
- 3,217 degree-seeking undergraduates: 18% part-time, 52% women
- 488 degree-seeking graduate students
- 74% of applicants admitted
- SAT or ACT (ACT writing recommended), application essay required

General. **Degrees:** 804 bachelor's awarded; master's offered. **ROTC:** Army, Naval, Air Force. **Location:** 20 miles from Seattle. **Calendar:** Quarter, limited summer session. **Full-time faculty:** 133 total; 89% have terminal degrees, 21% minority, 47% women. **Part-time faculty:** 88 total; 42% have terminal degrees, 14% minority, 64% women. **Class size:** 20% < 20, 50% 20-39, 27% 40-49, 3% 50-99. **Special facilities:** 58 acres of wetlands.

Freshman class profile. 2,075 applied, 1,529 admitted, 529 enrolled.

Mid 50% test scores			
SAT critical reading:	440-570	GPA 3.50-3.74:	23%
SAT math:	470-580	GPA 3.0-3.49:	47%
SAT writing:	420-540	GPA 2.0-2.99:	20%
ACT composite:	19-25	Return as sophomores:	85%
GPA 3.75 or higher:	10%	Out-of-state:	4%
		Live on campus:	28%

Basis for selection. GPA, test scores, academic rigor, and essays/personal statement are very important. Non-resident alien applicants must report scores from TOEFL or the International English Language Testing System (IELTS). SAT essay component used for admission for the Business program only. **Home schooled:** Transcript of courses and grades required.

High school preparation. College-preparatory program required. Required and recommended units include English 4, mathematics 3-4, social

studies 3-4, science 2-4 (laboratory 2-3), foreign language 2-4, visual/performing arts .5-1, academic electives 0.5. One semester (.5) elective from required subject lists and .5 fine arts course.

2011-2012 Annual costs. Tuition/fees: $10,241; $27,725 out-of-state. Books/supplies: $1,035. Personal expenses: $2,265.

2011-2012 Financial aid. Need-based: 411 full-time freshmen applied for aid; 322 were judged to have need; 305 of these received aid. Average need met was 79%. Average scholarship/grant was $10,700; average loan $5,000. 61% of total undergraduate aid awarded as scholarships/grants, 39% as loans/jobs. **Non-need-based:** Awarded to 32 full-time undergraduates, including 20 freshmen. Scholarships awarded for academics.

Application procedures. Admission: Priority date 1/15; no deadline. $60 fee, may be waived for applicants with need. Application must be submitted online. Admission notification on a rolling basis beginning on or about 9/1. Must reply by May 1 or within 3 week(s) if notified thereafter. **Financial aid:** Priority date 2/28; no closing date. FAFSA required. Applicants notified by 4/1; must reply within 3 week(s) of notification.

Academics. Special study options: Combined bachelor's/graduate degree, cross-registration, double major, dual enrollment of high school students, ESL, independent study, internships, student-designed major, study abroad, teacher certification program. **Credit/placement by examination:** AP, CLEP, IB, institutional tests. **Support services:** Learning center, pre-admission summer program, reduced course load, study skills assistance, writing center.

Majors. Area/ethnic studies: American. **Biology:** General. **Business:** Accounting, business admin. **Communications:** Media studies. **Computer sciences:** General, applications programming, information systems, systems analysis. **Conservation:** Environmental science, environmental studies. **Education:** General. **Engineering:** Electrical. **Health services:** Nursing (RN). **Liberal arts:** Humanities. **Philosophy/religion:** Ethics. **Psychology:** Community. **Visual/performing arts:** Art.

Most popular majors. Business/marketing 35%, computer/information sciences 8%, health sciences 18%, interdisciplinary studies 15%, philosophy/religious studies 9%, psychology 6%.

Computing on campus. 850 workstations in library, computer center. Dormitories wired for high-speed internet access. Commuter students can connect to campus network. Online course registration, online library, helpline, student web hosting, wireless network available.

Student life. Freshman orientation: Mandatory, $250 fee. Preregistration for classes offered. **Housing:** Coed dorms, special housing for disabled, apartments available. $50 nonrefundable deposit. **Activities:** Campus ministries, literary magazine, Model UN, student government, student newspaper, African American student union, Chinese culture club, Christians in Action, entrepreneur's network, Gay/Straight Alliance, Human Equality and Rights Everywhere, intercultural club, Policy Information and Networking Group, Still I Rise Organization, Woman and Leadership Development.

Athletics. Intramural: Basketball, football (non-tackle), soccer, softball, tennis, volleyball. **Team name:** Huskies.

Student services. Career counseling, student employment services, financial aid counseling, personal counseling, veterans' counselor. **Physically disabled:** Services for visually, speech, hearing impaired.

Contact. E-mail: admissions@uwb.edu
Phone: (425) 352-5000 Toll-free number: (800) 736-6650
Fax: (425) 352-5455
Jill Orcutt, Director of Admission, University of Washington Bothell, 18115 Campus Way NE, Bothell, WA 98011-8246

University of Washington Tacoma
Tacoma, Washington   **CB member**
www.tacoma.uw.edu   **CB code: 4445**

- Public 4-year university and branch campus college
- Commuter campus in small city
- 3,081 degree-seeking undergraduates: 19% part-time, 56% women
- 544 degree-seeking graduate students
- 77% of applicants admitted
- SAT or ACT with writing, application essay required

General. Regionally accredited. Campus set in the historic Warehouse District of downtown Tacoma. The university has earned architectural awards for transforming the buildings into modern classrooms. **Degrees:** 804 bachelor's awarded; master's offered. **ROTC:** Army, Naval, Air Force. **Location:** 30 miles from Seattle. **Calendar:** Quarter, limited summer session. **Full-time faculty:** 153 total; 82% have terminal degrees, 23% minority, 55% women. **Part-time faculty:** 58 total; 45% have terminal degrees, 16% minority, 52% women. **Class size:** 21% <20, 58% 20-39, 19% 40-49, 2% 50-99. **Special facilities:** Center for Urban Waters: a collective for scientists, analysts, engineers and policy makers seeking creative and sustainable solutions to the restoration and protection of urban waterways; access to the environmental and oceanic labs at Friday Harbor; experimental forest lands and gardens; museums.

Freshman class profile. 854 applied, 658 admitted, 252 enrolled.

Mid 50% test scores			
SAT critical reading:	440-560	GPA 3.0-3.49:	46%
SAT math:	460-570	GPA 2.0-2.99:	21%
SAT writing:	420-540	Rank in top quarter:	30%
ACT composite:	18-23	Rank in top tenth:	9%
GPA 3.75 or higher:	12%	Return as sophomores:	85%
GPA 3.50-3.74:	21%	Out-of-state:	2%

Basis for selection. Admissions based on school achievement record, including quality of test scores, fullness of application including essay and involvement. **Home schooled:** Transcript of courses and grades required.

High school preparation. College-preparatory program required. 15 units required. Required units include English 4, mathematics 3, social studies 3, science 2 (laboratory 1), foreign language 2, visual/performing arts .5, academic electives 0.5.

2011-2012 Annual costs. Tuition/fees: $10,910; $28,394 out-of-state. Books/supplies: $1,035. Personal expenses: $2,265.

2011-2012 Financial aid. Need-based: 207 full-time freshmen applied for aid; 168 were judged to have need; 144 of these received aid. Average need met was 78%. Average scholarship/grant was $11,700; average loan $5,000. 61% of total undergraduate aid awarded as scholarships/grants, 39% as loans/jobs. **Non-need-based:** Awarded to 182 full-time undergraduates, including 33 freshmen. Scholarships awarded for academics, state residency.

Application procedures. Admission: Priority date 3/1; deadline 6/1 (receipt date). $60 fee, may be waived for applicants with need. Application must be submitted online. Admission notification on a rolling basis beginning on or about 11/1. Must reply by May 1 or within 2 week(s) if notified thereafter. **Financial aid:** Priority date 2/28; no closing date. FAFSA required. Applicants notified on a rolling basis starting 4/1; must reply within 3 week(s) of notification.

Academics. Special study options: Cross-registration, distance learning, double major, honors, independent study, internships, semester at sea, student-designed major, study abroad, teacher certification program. **Credit/placement by examination:** AP, CLEP, IB, SAT, institutional tests. 90 credit hours maximum toward bachelor's degree. **Support services:** Learning center, pre-admission summer program, remedial instruction, study skills assistance, tutoring, writing center.

Majors. Area/ethnic studies: American, Asian, Chicano/Hispanic-American/Latino. **Business:** General, accounting, business admin, finance, management science, marketing. **Communications:** Communications/speech/rhetoric. **Computer sciences:** General, information technology, security, systems analysis. **Conservation:** Environmental science, environmental studies. **Health services:** Nursing (RN). **Human services:** Social work. **Liberal arts:** Arts/sciences, humanities. **Protective services:** Police science. **Psychology:** General. **Social sciences:** International relations, political science, urban studies.

Most popular majors. Business/marketing 22%, computer/information sciences 10%, health sciences 8%, liberal arts 11%, psychology 8%, social sciences 20%.

Computing on campus. 138 workstations in library, computer center, student center. Dormitories wired for high-speed internet access. Commuter students can connect to campus network. Online course registration, online library, helpline, student web hosting, wireless network available.

Student life. Freshman orientation: Mandatory. Preregistration for classes offered. **Housing:** Special housing for disabled, apartments available. $250 partly refundable deposit, deadline 6/1. On-campus housing program houses a small number of students in apartments. Off-campus housing listings as well as resources to obtain off-campus living options available. **Activities:** Campus ministries, dance, international student organizations, literary magazine, student government, student newspaper, accounting student association, Asian Pacific Islander, black student union, Civitas, game developers club, global business society, Grey Hat Group, Hip-Hop Dance Crew, international student association, Korean American international student team, Latino student organization, Marketing Society, Minority Association of Pre-Med Students, Native American student organization, Women in Computer Science.

Athletics. Team name: Huskies.

Student services. Alcohol/substance abuse counseling, career counseling, student employment services, financial aid counseling, health services, minority student services, personal counseling, veterans' counselor, women's services. **Physically disabled:** Services for visually, speech, hearing impaired.

Contact. E-mail: uwtinfo@u.washington.edu
Phone: (253) 692-4742 Toll-free number: (800) 736-7750
Fax: (253) 692-4414
Lisa Garcia-Hanson, Director of Admissions, University of Washington Tacoma, Campus Box 358430, Tacoma, WA 98402-3100

Walla Walla University
College Place, Washington
www.wallawalla.edu   **CB code: 4940**

- Private 4-year university and liberal arts college affiliated with Seventh-day Adventists
- Residential campus in large town
- 1,602 degree-seeking undergraduates
- SAT or ACT (ACT writing optional) required

General. Founded in 1892. Regionally accredited. Branch campus in Portland, Oregon for students in the final two years of the nursing program. Summer biology courses offered at school's marine research facility near Anacortes, Washington. Graduate social work program with course offerings in Billings and Missoula, Montana. **Degrees:** 274 bachelor's, 11 associate awarded; master's offered. **ROTC:** Army. **Location:** 270 miles from Seattle and 250 miles from Portland, Oregon. **Calendar:** Quarter, extensive summer session. **Full-time faculty:** 112 total; 69% have terminal degrees, 6% minority, 39% women. **Part-time faculty:** 95 total; 30% have terminal degrees, 3% minority, 57% women. **Class size:** 62% < 20, 28% 20-39, 5% 40-49, 5% 50-99, less than 1% >100. **Special facilities:** Marine biological research facility, observatory.

Freshman class profile.

GPA 3.75 or higher:	35%	GPA 3.0-3.49:	27%
GPA 3.50-3.74:	21%	GPA 2.0-2.99:	17%

Basis for selection. Must have combined 2.0 high school GPA. If entering with GED must have average score of 500 or higher and each test must be 450 or higher. Official TOEFL scores required for prospective students whose first language is not English. ACT recommended. Audition recommended. **Home schooled:** May be admitted by acceptable score on ACT test, GED test, or transcript from accredited home school organization.

High school preparation. College-preparatory program recommended. 11 units required; 16 recommended. Required and recommended units include English 4, mathematics 3-4, social studies 1, history 2, science 2-3 (laboratory 2) and foreign language 2. Mathematics units must be algebra and geometry. 2 laboratory units recommended.

2011-2012 Annual costs. Tuition/fees: $24,198. Room/board: $5,655. Books/supplies: $1,101. Personal expenses: $1,725.

2010-2011 Financial aid. Need-based: 284 full-time freshmen applied for aid; 209 were judged to have need; 209 of these received aid. Average need met was 90%. Average scholarship/grant was $7,116; average loan $6,676. 53% of total undergraduate aid awarded as scholarships/grants, 47% as loans/jobs. **Non-need-based:** Awarded to 1,045 full-time undergraduates, including 279 freshmen. Scholarships awarded for academics, leadership, music/drama.

Application procedures. Admission: No deadline. $40 fee, may be waived for applicants with need. Admission notification on a rolling basis beginning on or about 9/26. **Financial aid:** Priority date 4/30; no closing date. FAFSA, institutional form required. Applicants notified on a rolling basis starting 3/15.

Academics. Special study options: Combined bachelor's/graduate degree, cooperative education, distance learning, double major, honors, independent study, internships, liberal arts/career combination, study abroad, teacher certification program. **Credit/placement by examination:** AP, CLEP, IB, SAT, ACT, institutional tests. 12 credit hours maximum toward associate degree, 24 toward bachelor's. **Support services:** Learning center, pre-admission summer program, reduced course load, remedial instruction, study skills assistance, tutoring, writing center.

Majors. Biology: General, biochemistry, biophysics. **Business:** Accounting, business admin, finance, human resources, international, management science. **Communications:** Communications/speech/rhetoric, journalism, media studies. **Communications technology:** Graphic/printing. **Computer sciences:** General, computer graphics, computer science, data processing,

information systems. **Education:** General, business, elementary, music, physical, special ed, voc/tech. **Engineering:** General, biomedical, civil, computer, electrical, mechanical. **English:** English lit. **Foreign languages:** French, German, Spanish. **Health services:** Nursing (RN). **History:** General. **Human services:** Social work. **Liberal arts:** Arts/sciences. **Math:** General. **Philosophy/religion:** Religion. **Physical sciences:** Chemistry, physics. **Psychology:** General. **Social sciences:** Sociology. **Theology:** Theology. **Visual/performing arts:** Art, music, music performance.

Most popular majors. Biology 6%, business/marketing 13%, education 6%, engineering/engineering technologies 13%, foreign language 6%, health sciences 21%.

Computing on campus. 105 workstations in dormitories, library, computer center. Dormitories wired for high-speed internet access and linked to campus network. Commuter students can connect to campus network. Online course registration, online library, helpline, repair service, student web hosting, wireless network available.

Student life. Freshman orientation: Mandatory. Preregistration for classes offered. Held during week before classes begin. **Policies:** Chapel requirement once a week; worship policy for resident students. Religious observance required. **Housing:** Guaranteed on-campus for all undergraduates. Single-sex dorms, special housing for disabled, apartments, wellness housing available. **Activities:** Bands, campus ministries, choral groups, drama, international student organizations, literary magazine, music ensembles, radio station, student government, student newspaper, symphony orchestra, TV station, student entrepreneur group, student missionary groups, drama, foreign student organizations, academic department clubs, service clubs, music groups.

Athletics. NCCAA. **Intercollegiate:** Basketball, golf, ice hockey M, soccer M, softball W, volleyball. **Intramural:** Badminton, basketball, football (non-tackle), racquetball, soccer, softball, table tennis, tennis, volleyball. **Team name:** Wolves.

Student services. Chaplain/spiritual director, career counseling, student employment services, financial aid counseling, health services, minority student services, on-campus daycare, personal counseling, placement for graduates, veterans' counselor. **Physically disabled:** Services for visually, speech, hearing impaired.

Contact. E-mail: info@wallawalla.edu
Phone: (509) 527-2615 Toll-free number: (800) 541-8900
Fax: (509) 527-2397
Dallas Weis, Director for Admissions/International Student Advisor, Walla Walla University, 204 South College Avenue, College Place, WA 99324-3000

Washington State University
Pullman, Washington   **CB member**
www.wsu.edu   **CB code: 4705**

- Public 4-year university
- Residential campus in large town
- 22,403 degree-seeking undergraduates: 12% part-time, 51% women, 3% African American, 5% Asian American, 8% Hispanic American, 1% Native American, 4% international
- 4,410 degree-seeking graduate students
- 82% of applicants admitted
- SAT or ACT (ACT writing optional) required
- 67% graduate within 6 years; 38% enter graduate study

General. Founded in 1890. Regionally accredited. Regional campuses in Spokane, Tri-Cities, Vancouver, and online degree programs. **Degrees:** 5,221 bachelor's awarded; master's, professional, doctoral offered. **ROTC:** Army, Naval, Air Force. **Location:** 80 miles from Spokane. **Calendar:** Semester, extensive summer session. **Full-time faculty:** 1,178 total; 90% have terminal degrees, 15% minority, 38% women. **Part-time faculty:** 472 total; 48% have terminal degrees, 10% minority, 54% women. **Class size:** 35% < 20, 35% 20-39, 6% 40-49, 14% 50-99, 10% >100. **Special facilities:** Agronomic research farms, child development lab, culinary lab and teaching kitchen, dairy center, ecological reserves, entomological collection, feed preparation lab, food sensory evaluation lab, genomics and gene sequencing lab, greenhouses, herbaria, hydraulics lab, horticultural orchard, organic teaching farm, biomolecular x-ray crystallography center, cadaver anatomy lab, electron microscopy center, geoanalytical lab, geological collections, biotechnology and bioanalysis lab, mass spectrometry and proteomics lab, nuclear research reactor, oil and gas processing lab, observatory, planetarium, clean room, composite materials and engineering center, electromagnetics and renewable energy lab, atmospheric research lab, semiconductor lab, virtual reality lab, veterinary teaching hospital, simulation and nursing practice lab, clinical

exam practice rooms, speech and hearing clinic, audio labs, electronic piano/music computer lab, historic textiles and costume collection, behavioral business research cener, business information systems classroom, electronic trading room, social and economic sciences research center, K-12 classrooms for teacher education in art and science, writing center; museums of natural history, vertebrate zoology, veterinary anatomy, anthropology, art.

Freshman class profile. 14,071 applied, 11,601 admitted, 4,473 enrolled.

Mid 50% test scores			
SAT critical reading:	470-580	Rank in top quarter:	46%
SAT math:	480-600	Rank in top tenth:	26%
SAT writing:	460-560	End year in good standing:	85%
ACT composite:	20-26	Return as sophomores:	84%
GPA 3.75 or higher:	19%	Out-of-state:	12%
GPA 3.50-3.74:	22%	Live on campus:	94%
GPA 3.0-3.49:	39%	International:	3%
GPA 2.0-2.99:	20%	Fraternities:	29%
		Sororities:	28%

Basis for selection. Combination of high school GPA and SAT or ACT scores, completion of required course work, and personal statement. Special circumstances and recommendations considered in some cases. Assured admission for U.S. high school students ranked in top 10% of high school class or with minimum 3.5 GPA. Updated admission requirements for English proficiency for nonnative speakers: MELAB minimum score of 77, IELTS minimum score of 6.5. Minimum scores for TOEFL: 550 paper-based, 79 internet-based, and 213 computer based. An appeal process is available for those denied admission. **Home schooled:** Transcript of courses and grades required. An academic resume (homeschool transcript) should provide documentation of all subjects studied, and detailed proof that home-based instruction fulfills core requirements. Resume must include signature of parent or guardian responsible for the student's curriculum. **Learning Disabled:** Upon acceptance a student can opt to notify Access Center of desire to have assistance with disability.

High school preparation. College-preparatory program required. 16 units required; 17 recommended. Required and recommended units include English 4, mathematics 3-4, social studies 3, science 2, foreign language 2 and visual/performing arts 1. English: 4 credits, including 3 credits of composition and literature. Math credits must include algebra, geometry, and senior year math based. Science: 2 credits of lab science, including 1 credit of algebra-based biology, chemistry, or physics. World Language: 2 credits of the same world language, Native American language, or American Sign Language. 1 credit of fine, visual, or performing arts, or 1 additional credit of academic elective from required subjects.

2011-2012 Annual costs. Tuition/fees: $10,799; $22,077 out-of-state. Room/board: $9,662. Books/supplies: $936. Personal expenses: $2,108.

Financial aid. Non-need-based: Scholarships awarded for academics, alumni affiliation, art, athletics, job skills, leadership, minority status, music/drama, ROTC, state residency.

Application procedures. Admission: Priority date 1/31; no deadline. $50 fee, may be waived for applicants with need. Admission notification on a rolling basis beginning on or about 11/1. Must reply by May 1 or within 2 week(s) if notified thereafter. **Financial aid:** Priority date 2/15; no closing date. FAFSA required. Applicants notified on a rolling basis starting 4/15.

Academics. Special study options: Accelerated study, combined bachelor's/graduate degree, cooperative education, cross-registration, distance learning, double major, dual enrollment of high school students, ESL, exchange student, external degree, honors, independent study, internships, liberal arts/career combination, semester at sea, student-designed major, study abroad, teacher certification program. **Credit/placement by examination:** AP, CLEP, IB, SAT, ACT, institutional tests. **Support services:** Learning center, pre-admission summer program, reduced course load, study skills assistance, tutoring, writing center.

Honors college/program. Acceptance into the Honors College is competitive; spaces are limited. No separate application but selection based on GPA, SAT/ACT scores, essay responses, strength of high school or college coursework, Running Start credits, AP/IB programs, honors courses, and evidence of overall motivation, organizational skills, and a desire for challenge.

Majors. Architecture: Architecture, landscape. **Area/ethnic studies:** Asian, women's. **Biology:** General, biochemistry, biomedical sciences, genetics, microbiology, molecular genetics, neuroscience, zoology. **Business:** General, accounting, business admin, construction management, entrepreneurial studies, finance, hospitality admin, international, management information systems, marketing, operations, real estate. **Communications:** Digital media, media studies. **Computer sciences:** General, computer science. **Conservation:** General, environmental science, wildlife/wilderness. **Education:** General, agricultural, bilingual, biology, chemistry, early childhood, elementary, English, ESL, family/consumer sciences, foreign languages, French, German, health, history, kindergarten/preschool, mathematics, multi-level teacher, music, physical, physics, reading, science, secondary, social studies, Spanish,

special ed. **Engineering:** Biomedical, chemical, civil, computer, electrical, manufacturing, materials, mechanical. **English:** English lit. **Foreign languages:** General, French, linguistics, Spanish. **General:** Agronomy, animal sciences, business, business technology, communications, crop production, economics, food science, horticultural science, mechanization, plant protection, plant sciences, products processing, soil science. **Health services:** Athletic training, audiology/speech pathology, nursing (RN), premedicine. **History:** General. **Human services:** Public policy. **Liberal arts:** Arts/sciences, humanities. **Math:** General, applied. **Parks/recreation:** Exercise sciences, sports admin. **Philosophy/religion:** Philosophy, religion. **Physical sciences:** General, chemistry, geology, physics. **Protective services:** Law enforcement admin. **Psychology:** General. **Social sciences:** General, anthropology, economics, political science, sociology. **Visual/performing arts:** Interior design, music, music performance, music theory/composition, studio arts. **Work/family studies:** General, clothing/textiles, family studies, food/nutrition, human nutrition.

Most popular majors. Business/marketing 17%, communications/journalism 6%, education 6%, engineering/engineering technologies 9%, health sciences 12%, social sciences 14%.

Computing on campus. 2,500 workstations in dormitories, library, computer center, student center. Dormitories wired for high-speed internet access and linked to campus network. Commuter students can connect to campus network. Online course registration, online library, helpline, student web hosting, wireless network available.

Student life. Freshman orientation: Mandatory, $230 fee. Preregistration for classes offered. Two-day orientation for students and their families throughout the year, depending on enrolled semester start date. **Policies:** Washington State Law requires single undergraduate freshmen under 20 years of age to live in organized living groups recognized by the university (residence halls, fraternities and sororities), for one academic year. **Housing:** Guaranteed on-campus for freshmen. Coed dorms, single-sex dorms, special housing for disabled, apartments, fraternity/sorority housing, wellness housing available. $550 partly refundable deposit, deadline 6/1. Freshman Focus living/learning communities. **Activities:** Bands, campus ministries, choral groups, dance, drama, film society, international student organizations, literary magazine, music ensembles, Model UN, musical theater, opera, radio station, student government, student newspaper, symphony orchestra, TV station, over 350 clubs and special interest groups.

Athletics. NCAA. **Intercollegiate:** Baseball M, basketball, cheerleading, cross-country, football (tackle) M, golf, rowing (crew) W, soccer W, swimming W, tennis W, track and field, volleyball W. **Intramural:** Badminton, basketball, football (non-tackle), golf, racquetball, soccer, softball, table tennis, tennis, triathlon, volleyball. **Team name:** Cougars.

Student services. Adult student services, alcohol/substance abuse counseling, career counseling, services for economically disadvantaged, student employment services, financial aid counseling, health services, legal services, minority student services, on-campus daycare, personal counseling, placement for graduates, veterans' counselor, women's services. **Physically disabled:** Services for visually, speech, hearing impaired.

Contact. E-mail: admissions@wsu.edu
Phone: (509) 335-5586 Toll-free number: (888) 468-6978
Fax: (509) 335-4902
Wendy Peterson, Director of Admissions, Washington State University, 370 Lighty Student Services Bldg, Pullman, WA 99164-1067

Western Washington University
Bellingham, Washington — **CB member**
www.wwu.edu — **CB code: 4947**

- Public 4-year university
- Residential campus in small city
- 13,685 degree-seeking undergraduates: 7% part-time, 56% women, 2% African American, 6% Asian American, 6% Hispanic American, 1% Native American, 1% international
- 1,059 graduate students
- 78% of applicants admitted
- SAT or ACT (ACT writing recommended), application essay required
- 73% graduate within 6 years

General. Founded in 1893. Regionally accredited. **Degrees:** 2,995 bachelor's awarded; master's offered. **Location:** 90 miles from Seattle. **Calendar:** Quarter, extensive summer session. **Full-time faculty:** 501 total; 80% have terminal degrees, 13% minority, 46% women. **Part-time faculty:** 286 total; 35% have terminal degrees, 11% minority, 54% women. **Class size:** 33% < 20, 44% 20-39, 6% 40-49, 12% 50-99, 4% >100. **Special facilities:** Wind tunnel, electron microscope, neutron generator laboratory, planetarium, air

pollution laboratory, motor vehicle research laboratory, electronic music studio, 11-acre recreational park on lake, marine laboratory, integrated laboratory network.

Freshman class profile. 9,083 applied, 7,113 admitted, 2,694 enrolled.

Mid 50% test scores			
SAT critical reading:	500-620	GPA 2.0-2.99:	7%
SAT math:	500-610	Rank in top quarter:	52%
SAT writing:	490-600	Rank in top tenth:	20%
ACT composite:	22-27	End year in good standing:	85%
GPA 3.75 or higher:	21%	Return as sophomores:	84%
GPA 3.50-3.74:	27%	Out-of-state:	9%
GPA 3.0-3.49:	45%	Live on campus:	92%

Basis for selection. Academic achievement most significant factor. Curriculum rigor (level and difficulty of courses), grade trends, school, community activities, special talent, multicultural experience, personal circumstances considered. All students encouraged to take courses beyond minimums. Consideration given to motivation, achievements outside of classroom, multicultural experience, and attributes that will enhance institution's learning community. Audition recommended for music; portfolio required for art.

High school preparation. College-preparatory program required. 16 units required. Required units include English 4, mathematics 3, social studies 3, science 2 (laboratory 1), foreign language 2, visual/performing arts .5, academic electives 0.5. Mathematics requirement includes 1 geometry and 2 algebra. Sciences include 1 algebra-based chemistry or physics. Foreign language should be in 1 language. .5 fine arts and .5 academic elective required.

2011-2012 Annual costs. Tuition/fees: $7,758; $18,105 out-of-state. Room/board: $8,755. Books/supplies: $1,020. Personal expenses: $1,713.

2011-2012 Financial aid. Need-based: 2,124 full-time freshmen applied for aid; 1,325 were judged to have need; 1,266 of these received aid. Average need met was 85%. Average scholarship/grant was $7,683; average loan $3,713. 49% of total undergraduate aid awarded as scholarships/grants, 51% as loans/jobs. **Non-need-based:** Awarded to 531 full-time undergraduates, including 159 freshmen. Scholarships awarded for academics, alumni affiliation, art, athletics, job skills, leadership, minority status, music/drama, state residency. **Additional information:** Short-term student loans ranging from $100 to $1,000 available on a quarterly basis.

Application procedures. Admission: Closing date 1/31 (postmark date). $55 fee, may be waived for applicants with need. Admission notification on a rolling basis beginning on or about 11/1. Must reply by May 1 or within 2 week(s) if notified thereafter. **Financial aid:** Priority date 2/15; no closing date. FAFSA required. Applicants notified on a rolling basis starting 3/20; must reply within 3 week(s) of notification.

Academics. Special study options: Distance learning, double major, ESL, exchange student, honors, independent study, internships, student-designed major, study abroad, teacher certification program. **Credit/placement by examination:** AP, CLEP, IB, institutional tests. 135 credit hours maximum toward bachelor's degree. **Support services:** Learning center, study skills assistance, tutoring, writing center.

Majors. Area/ethnic studies: American, Canadian, East Asian. **Biology:** General, biochemistry, botany, cell/histology, cellular/molecular, ecology, evolutionary, marine, zoology. **Business:** Accounting, business admin, finance, human resources, international, management information systems, marketing, operations. **Communications:** Communications/speech/rhetoric, journalism. **Computer sciences:** General. **Conservation:** Environmental science, environmental studies. **Education:** Art, biology, chemistry, drama/dance, elementary, English, German, history, mathematics, music, physical, science, social science, social studies, Spanish, special ed, speech, technology/industrial arts. **English:** Creative writing, English lit. **Foreign languages:** General, French, German, Japanese, linguistics, Spanish. **Health services:** Audiology/speech pathology, community health services. **History:** General. **Liberal arts:** Humanities. **Math:** General, applied. **Parks/recreation:** General, health/fitness. **Philosophy/religion:** Philosophy. **Physical sciences:** Chemistry, geology, geophysics, physics. **Psychology:** General, developmental. **Social sciences:** Anthropology, archaeology, economics, geography, political science, sociology. **Visual/performing arts:** General, art, art history/conservation, ceramics, commercial/advertising art, dance, design, dramatic, drawing, fiber arts, graphic design, industrial design, multimedia, music, music history, music performance, music theory/composition, painting, photography, printmaking, sculpture. **Work/family studies:** Child development.

Most popular majors. Business/marketing 13%, education 6%, English 8%, psychology 6%, social sciences 13%, visual/performing arts 6%.

Computing on campus. 2,479 workstations in dormitories, library, computer center, student center. Dormitories wired for high-speed internet access and linked to campus network. Commuter students can connect to campus network. Online course registration, online library, helpline, repair service, student web hosting, wireless network available.

Student life. Freshman orientation: Available. Preregistration for classes offered. 6 programs offered for students and family members, early-mid August. Program 1-2 days, based on housing needs. **Housing:** Coed dorms, special housing for disabled, apartments, wellness housing available. $200 partly refundable deposit, deadline 6/15. Multicultural floors, honors, quiet floors, freshman interest groups available. **Activities:** Bands, campus ministries, choral groups, dance, drama, film society, international student organizations, literary magazine, music ensembles, musical theater, opera, radio station, student government, student newspaper, symphony orchestra, TV station, Campus Christian Fellowship, veteran's outreach center, volunteer services and resources, international student club, The Inn (nondenominational), ethnic student center, Mecha, Circle K, American Red Cross chapter.

Athletics. NCAA. **Intercollegiate:** Basketball, cross-country, golf, rowing (crew), soccer, softball W, track and field, volleyball W. **Intramural:** Basketball, football (non-tackle), golf, racquetball, soccer, softball, table tennis, tennis, volleyball. **Team name:** Vikings.

Student services. Adult student services, alcohol/substance abuse counseling, chaplain/spiritual director, career counseling, student employment services, financial aid counseling, health services, minority student services, on-campus daycare, personal counseling, placement for graduates, veterans' counselor. **Physically disabled:** Services for visually, speech, hearing impaired.

Contact. E-mail: admit@wwu.edu
Phone: (360) 650-3440 Fax: (360) 650-7369
Clara Capron, Director of Admissions and Enrollment Planning, Western Washington University, 516 High Street, Bellingham, WA 98225-9009

Whitman College
Walla Walla, Washington
www.whitman.edu

CB member
CB code: 4951

- Private 4-year liberal arts college
- Residential campus in large town
- 1,580 degree-seeking undergraduates: 1% part-time, 58% women, 2% African American, 8% Asian American, 6% Hispanic American, 1% Native American, 2% international
- 54% of applicants admitted
- SAT or ACT with writing, application essay required
- 85% graduate within 6 years

General. Founded in 1883. Regionally accredited. **Degrees:** 378 bachelor's awarded. **Location:** 235 miles from Portland, Oregon; 260 miles from Seattle. **Calendar:** Semester. **Full-time faculty:** 134 total; 93% have terminal degrees, 14% minority, 44% women. **Part-time faculty:** 66 total; 64% have terminal degrees, 6% minority, 53% women. **Class size:** 62% < 20, 32% 20-39, 5% 40-49, less than 1% 50-99. **Special facilities:** Asian art collection, natural history museum, planetarium, 2 electron microscopes, outdoor observatory, rock-climbing walls, outdoor sculpture walk, organic garden.

Freshman class profile. 3,086 applied, 1,654 admitted, 399 enrolled.

Mid 50% test scores			
SAT critical reading:	630-730	Rank in top tenth:	68%
SAT math:	620-710	End year in good standing:	98%
SAT writing:	630-710	Return as sophomores:	95%
ACT composite:	27-31	Out-of-state:	67%
GPA 3.75 or higher:	69%	Live on campus:	100%
GPA 3.50-3.74:	23%	International:	2%
GPA 3.0-3.49:	8%	Fraternities:	42%
Rank in top quarter:	92%	Sororities:	25%

Basis for selection. Scholastic record, quality of written expression, level of motivation very important. Evidence of talent, imagination, creativity, leadership, responsibility, maturity also considered. Writing for all students. TOEFL, ELPT, or APIEL accepted as language proficiency exams. Interview recommended.

High school preparation. College-preparatory program recommended. 16 units recommended. Recommended units include English 4, mathematics 4, social studies 2, history 2, science 3 (laboratory 2), foreign language 2 and visual/performing arts 1.

2011-2012 Annual costs. Tuition/fees: $40,496. Room/board: $10,160. Books/supplies: $1,400.

2011-2012 Financial aid. Need-based: 273 full-time freshmen applied for aid; 194 were judged to have need; 194 of these received aid. Average need met was 91%. Average scholarship/grant was $22,139; average loan $4,322. 83% of total undergraduate aid awarded as scholarships/grants, 17% as loans/jobs. **Non-need-based:** Awarded to 642 full-time undergraduates,

including 202 freshmen. Scholarships awarded for academics, art, leadership, minority status, music/drama.

Application procedures. Admission: Priority date 11/15; deadline 1/15 (postmark date). $50 fee, may be waived for applicants with need. Admission notification by 4/1. Must reply by 5/1. **Financial aid:** Closing date 2/1. FAFSA, CSS PROFILE required. Applicants notified by 3/26; must reply by 5/1.

Academics. Special study options: Accelerated study, combined bachelor's/graduate degree, cooperative education, cross-registration, double major, dual enrollment of high school students, exchange student, honors, independent study, liberal arts/career combination, student-designed major, study abroad, urban semester, Washington semester. Study abroad opportunities in over 20 countries; Whitman-In-China allows recent graduates to spend a year teaching English in one of 3 Chinese universities; 3-2 engineering and computer science programs with California Institute of Technology, Columbia University (NY), Duke University (NC), Washington University (MO) and University of Washington; 3-2 oceanography and biology or geology program with University of Washington; 3-3 law program with Columbia University; 3-2 program with Monterey Institute of International Studies; 4-1 program with Bank Street College of Education; undergraduate research conference; semester in the West field study. **Credit/placement by examination:** AP, CLEP, IB, institutional tests. 30 credit hours maximum toward bachelor's degree. **Support services:** Learning center, reduced course load, study skills assistance, tutoring, writing center.

Majors. Area/ethnic studies: Asian, Latin American. **Biology:** General, Biochemistry/molecular biology. **Communications:** Communications/speech/rhetoric. **Conservation:** Environmental studies. **Engineering:** General. **English:** English lit. **Foreign languages:** Classics, French, German, Spanish. **History:** General. **Math:** General. **Philosophy/religion:** Philosophy, religion. **Physical sciences:** Astronomy, chemistry, geology, physics. **Psychology:** General. **Social sciences:** Anthropology, economics, political science, sociology. **Visual/performing arts:** Art history/conservation, dramatic, film/cinema/video, music, studio arts.

Most popular majors. Biology 15%, English 7%, physical sciences 10%, psychology 8%, social sciences 26%, visual/performing arts 11%.

Computing on campus. 410 workstations in library, computer center, student center. Dormitories wired for high-speed internet access and linked to campus network. Commuter students can connect to campus network. Online course registration, online library, helpline, repair service, student web hosting, wireless network available.

Student life. Freshman orientation: Available. Preregistration for classes offered. **Housing:** Guaranteed on-campus for freshmen. Coed dorms, single-sex dorms, fraternity/sorority housing available. $300 nonrefundable deposit, deadline 5/1. German, French, Spanish, Japanese language houses. Asian Studies, multi-ethnic, environmental, fine arts, community service, writing, global awareness houses available, college-owned rentals. **Activities:** Bands, campus ministries, choral groups, dance, drama, film society, international student organizations, literary magazine, music ensembles, Model UN, musical theater, radio station, student government, student newspaper, symphony orchestra, multi-ethnic cultural association, many religious groups, community service, political organizations, environmental groups.

Athletics. NCAA. **Intercollegiate:** Baseball M, basketball, cross-country, golf, soccer, swimming, tennis, volleyball W. **Intramural:** Basketball, bowling, football (non-tackle), soccer, softball, tennis, triathlon, volleyball. **Team name:** Missionaries.

Student services. Alcohol/substance abuse counseling, chaplain/spiritual director, career counseling, student employment services, financial aid counseling, health services, minority student services, on-campus daycare, personal counseling, placement for graduates, veterans' counselor, women's services. **Physically disabled:** Services for visually, speech, hearing impaired.

Contact. E-mail: admission@whitman.edu
Phone: (509) 527-5176 Toll-free number: (877) 462-9448
Fax: (509) 527-4967
Tony Cabasco, Dean of Admission and Financial Aid, Whitman College, 345 Boyer Avenue, Walla Walla, WA 99362-2046

Whitworth University
Spokane, Washington
www.whitworth.edu

CB member
CB code: 4953

- Private 4-year liberal arts college affiliated with Presbyterian Church (USA)
- Residential campus in large city

- 2,229 degree-seeking undergraduates: 1% part-time, 57% women, 1% African American, 3% Asian American, 6% Hispanic American, 2% international
- 213 degree-seeking graduate students
- 48% of applicants admitted
- Application essay required

General. Founded in 1890. Regionally accredited. **Degrees:** 503 bachelor's awarded; master's offered. **ROTC:** Army. **Location:** 6 miles from downtown, 280 miles from Seattle. **Calendar:** 4-1-4, limited summer session. **Full-time faculty:** 168 total; 71% have terminal degrees, 9% minority, 47% women. **Part-time faculty:** 161 total; 11% minority, 47% women. **Class size:** 55% < 20, 39% 20-39, 2% 40-49, 3% 50-99, less than 1% >100.

Freshman class profile. 7,040 applied, 3,356 admitted, 523 enrolled.

GPA 3.75 or higher:	52%	Out-of-state:	42%
GPA 3.50-3.74:	24%	Live on campus:	95%
GPA 3.0-3.49:	19%	International:	2%
GPA 2.0-2.99:	5%		

Basis for selection. School achievement, extracurricular activities, recommendations most important. SAT or ACT recommended. Interview recommended.

High school preparation. College-preparatory program recommended. 18 units recommended. Recommended units include English 4, mathematics 3, social studies 3, history 3, science 3 (laboratory 2) and foreign language 2.

2011-2012 Annual costs. Tuition/fees: $32,144. Room/board: $8,918. Books/supplies: $860. Personal expenses: $1,036.

2011-2012 Financial aid. Need-based: 461 full-time freshmen applied for aid; 398 were judged to have need; 398 of these received aid. Average need met was 80%. Average scholarship/grant was $19,392; average loan $4,121. 73% of total undergraduate aid awarded as scholarships/grants, 27% as loans/jobs. **Non-need-based:** Awarded to 670 full-time undergraduates, including 154 freshmen. Scholarships awarded for academics, art, minority status, music/drama, ROTC.

Application procedures. Admission: Closing date 3/1 (postmark date). No application fee. Admission notification on a rolling basis beginning on or about 12/20. Must reply by 5/1. **Financial aid:** Priority date 3/1; no closing date. FAFSA required. Applicants notified on a rolling basis starting 3/1; must reply by 5/1 or within 4 week(s) of notification.

Academics. Special study options: Accelerated study, distance learning, double major, dual enrollment of high school students, ESL, exchange student, independent study, internships, student-designed major, study abroad, teacher certification program, Washington semester. 3-2 engineering programs. **Credit/placement by examination:** AP, CLEP, IB, SAT, ACT, institutional tests. 32 credit hours maximum toward bachelor's degree. **Support services:** Learning center, reduced course load, study skills assistance, tutoring, writing center.

Majors. Area/ethnic studies: American. **Biology:** General, biophysics. **Business:** Accounting, business admin, international, marketing. **Communications:** Communications/speech/rhetoric, journalism. **Computer sciences:** General, computer science. **Education:** General, biology, chemistry, elementary, ESL, French, history, mathematics, middle, multi-level teacher, music, physical, physics, secondary, Spanish, special ed, speech. **Engineering:** General, applied physics. **English:** English lit. **Foreign languages:** French, Spanish. **Health services:** Athletic training, nursing (RN). **History:** General. **Liberal arts:** Arts/sciences. **Math:** General, applied. **Parks/recreation:** Health/fitness. **Philosophy/religion:** Philosophy. **Physical sciences:** Chemistry, nuclear physics, physics. **Psychology:** General. **Social sciences:** General, economics, international relations, political science, sociology. **Theology:** Theology. **Visual/performing arts:** General, art, jazz, music, music performance, piano/keyboard, theater history, voice/opera.

Most popular majors. Business/marketing 16%, education 10%, English 6%, foreign language 6%, health sciences 8%, physical sciences 6%, social sciences 9%, visual/performing arts 6%.

Computing on campus. 175 workstations in library, computer center, student center. Dormitories wired for high-speed internet access and linked to campus network. Commuter students can connect to campus network. Online course registration, online library, helpline, repair service available.

Student life. Freshman orientation: Mandatory. Preregistration for classes offered. **Housing:** Guaranteed on-campus for freshmen. Coed dorms, single-sex dorms, special housing for disabled, apartments available. $100 partly refundable deposit, deadline 5/1. **Activities:** Bands, campus ministries, choral groups, dance, drama, international student organizations, music ensembles, musical theater, radio station, student government, student newspaper, symphony orchestra, Black Student Union, Fellowship of Christian

Athletes, international club, Hawaiian club, political activist club, Native American club, Amnesty International, Habitat for Humanity, Asian American club, Circle-K International.

Athletics. NCAA. **Intercollegiate:** Baseball M, basketball, cross-country, football (tackle) M, golf, soccer, softball W, swimming, tennis, track and field, volleyball W. **Intramural:** Basketball, soccer, softball, table tennis, tennis, volleyball. **Team name:** Pirates.

Student services. Adult student services, chaplain/spiritual director, career counseling, student employment services, financial aid counseling, health services, minority student services, personal counseling, placement for graduates, veterans' counselor. **Physically disabled:** Services for visually, speech, hearing impaired.

Contact. E-mail: admissions@whitworth.edu
Phone: (509) 777-4786 Toll-free number: (800) 533-4668
Fax: (509) 777-3758
Fred Pfursich, Vice President, Admissions and Financial Aid, Whitworth University, 300 West Hawthorne Road, Spokane, WA 99251-0002

West Virginia

Alderson-Broaddus College
Philippi, West Virginia
www.ab.edu

CB member
CB code: 5005

▶ Private 4-year liberal arts college affiliated with American Baptist Churches in the USA
▶ Residential campus in small town
▶ 541 degree-seeking undergraduates: 4% part-time, 68% women
▶ 60 degree-seeking graduate students
▶ 70% of applicants admitted
▶ SAT and SAT Subject Tests or ACT (ACT writing optional) required

General. Founded in 1871. Regionally accredited. **Degrees:** 127 bachelor's, 24 associate awarded; master's offered. **Location:** 100 miles from Charleston, 125 miles from Pittsburgh. **Calendar:** Semester, limited summer session. **Full-time faculty:** 57 total; 44% have terminal degrees, 12% minority, 56% women. **Part-time faculty:** 26 total; 23% have terminal degrees, 4% minority, 35% women. **Class size:** 82% < 20, 15% 20-39, 1% 40-49, 1% 50-99. **Special facilities:** Gross anatomy laboratory, hydro-therapy pool, simulation lab.

Freshman class profile. 836 applied, 585 admitted, 140 enrolled.

Mid 50% test scores			
SAT critical reading:	470-560	GPA 3.0-3.49:	30%
SAT math:	460-580	GPA 2.0-2.99:	24%
SAT writing:	460-540	Rank in top quarter:	44%
ACT composite:	19-24	Rank in top tenth:	25%
GPA 3.75 or higher:	31%	Return as sophomores:	67%
GPA 3.50-3.74:	14%	Out-of-state:	27%
		Live on campus:	87%

Basis for selection. High school record, rank in top half of class, test scores, interview very important. Physician's assistant and nursing applicants should have strong background in science. Interview required for physician's assistant applicants, recommended for all others. Audition required for music.

High school preparation. College-preparatory program recommended. 11 units required; 14 recommended. Required and recommended units include English 4, mathematics 3, social studies 1-3, science 3 (laboratory 1-3) and foreign language 1.

2011-2012 Annual costs. Tuition/fees: $22,740. Room/board: $7,236. Books/supplies: $800. Personal expenses: $1,500.

Financial aid. Non-need-based: Scholarships awarded for academics, athletics, music/drama.

Application procedures. Admission: No deadline. $25 fee, may be waived for applicants with need. Admission notification on a rolling basis. **Financial aid:** Priority date 3/1; no closing date. FAFSA required. Applicants notified on a rolling basis starting 3/1; must reply within 2 week(s) of notification.

Academics. Special study options: Accelerated study, double major, honors, independent study, internships, liberal arts/career combination, study abroad, teacher certification program. Business department offers on-line certificate program. **Credit/placement by examination:** AP, CLEP, SAT, ACT, institutional tests. 40 credit hours maximum toward associate degree, 60 toward bachelor's. **Support services:** Learning center, reduced course load, remedial instruction, study skills assistance, tutoring.

Majors. Biology: General. **Business:** Accounting, business admin, human resources, marketing, nonprofit/public. **Communications:** Communications/speech/rhetoric. **Computer sciences:** Computer science. **Conservation:** Environmental science. **Education:** Elementary, music, physical, secondary. **English:** Creative writing, English lit. **Health services:** Athletic training, medical radiologic technology/radiation therapy, nursing (RN), recreational therapy. **History:** General. **Liberal arts:** Arts/sciences. **Math:** Applied. **Parks/recreation:** Facilities management, sports admin. **Philosophy/religion:** Christian. **Physical sciences:** Chemistry. **Psychology:** General. **Social sciences:** Criminology, political science. **Visual/performing arts:** Music, music performance, studio arts. **Work/family studies:** Family systems.

Most popular majors. Biology 7%, business/marketing 9%, health sciences 37%, parks/recreation 11%, visual/performing arts 6%.

Computing on campus. 100 workstations in dormitories, library, student center. Dormitories wired for high-speed internet access and linked to campus network. Commuter students can connect to campus network. Online library, helpline, student web hosting, wireless network available.

Student life. Freshman orientation: Available. Preregistration for classes offered. Held Saturday prior to start of fall classes. **Policies:** Participation in campus activities stressed. Voluntary weekly chapel service offered. **Housing:** Guaranteed on-campus for all undergraduates. Coed dorms, single-sex dorms, special housing for disabled, apartments, wellness housing available. $100 fully refundable deposit. **Activities:** Bands, campus ministries, choral groups, drama, literary magazine, music ensembles, musical theater, radio station, student government, student newspaper, TV station, Collegiate 4-H, ambassadors club, College Players, Baptist campus ministries, Students in Free Enterprise, Students Learning in Community Education, mission team, outdoor club.

Athletics. NCAA. Intercollegiate: Baseball M, basketball, cross-country, soccer, softball W, track and field, volleyball W. **Intramural:** Basketball, bowling, football (non-tackle), golf, racquetball, soccer, softball W, table tennis, tennis, volleyball. **Team name:** Battlers.

Student services. Adult student services, alcohol/substance abuse counseling, chaplain/spiritual director, career counseling, financial aid counseling, health services, personal counseling, placement for graduates, veterans' counselor. **Physically disabled:** Services for visually, hearing impaired.

Contact. E-mail: admissions@ab.edu
Phone: (304) 457-6256 Toll-free number: (800) 263-1549
Fax: (304) 457-6239
Kimberly Klaus, Dean of Enrollment Management, Alderson-Broaddus College, 101 College Hill Drive, Philippi, WV 26416

American Public University System
Charles Town, West Virginia
www.apus.edu

▶ For-profit 4-year virtual university
▶ Small town
▶ 68,845 degree-seeking undergraduates
▶ 19,204 graduate students

General. Accredited by DETC. Regionally and nationally accredited online institution serving military and public service communities through American Military University and American Public University. **Degrees:** 2,491 bachelor's, 681 associate awarded; master's offered. **Location:** Online university. **Calendar:** Differs by program, extensive summer session. **Full-time faculty:** 323 total. **Part-time faculty:** 1,388 total.

Basis for selection. Open admission.

2012-2013 Annual costs. Tuition/fees: $7,500. Personal expenses: $1,920.

2010-2011 Financial aid. Additional information: Students should complete a Federal Student Aid Intent Form and register for classes at least 37 days prior to start to allow sufficient time for financial aid process.

Application procedures. Admission: No deadline. No application fee. Application must be submitted online. Admission notification on a rolling basis. **Financial aid:** No deadline. FAFSA, institutional form required. Applicants notified on a rolling basis; must reply within 14 week(s) of notification.

Academics. Special study options: Distance learning, internships, teacher certification program. **Credit/placement by examination:** AP, CLEP, IB, institutional tests. 15 credit hours maximum toward associate degree, 30 toward bachelor's. **Support services:** Remedial instruction, study skills assistance, tutoring.

Majors. Business: Accounting, business admin, hospitality admin, logistics, marketing, retailing. **Computer sciences:** Information technology, security, webmaster. **Conservation:** Environmental science. **English:** English lit. **Health services:** Nursing (RN). **History:** General, military. **Parks/recreation:** Exercise sciences. **Philosophy/religion:** Philosophy, religion. **Protective services:** Disaster management, fire services admin, forensics, homeland security, law enforcement admin, security management. **Psychology:** General. **Social sciences:** International relations, political science, sociology. **Work/family studies:** Child care management.

Most popular majors. Business/marketing 20%, computer/information sciences 8%, interdisciplinary studies 14%, security/protective services 30%, social sciences 7%.

Computing on campus. PC or laptop required. Online library available.

Student life. Freshman orientation: Mandatory. Preregistration for classes offered.

Contact. E-mail: info@apus.edu
Phone: (877) 777-9081 Toll-free number: (877) 777-9081
Terry Grant, Associate Vice President, Enrollment Management, American Public University System, 111 West Congress Street, Charles Town, WV 25414

Appalachian Bible College
Mount Hope, West Virginia
www.abc.edu
CB code: 7305

- Private 4-year Bible college affiliated with nondenominational tradition
- Residential campus in large town
- 189 degree-seeking undergraduates
- 66% of applicants admitted
- SAT or ACT (ACT writing optional), application essay required

General. Founded in 1950. Regionally accredited; also accredited by ABHE. Accreditation by both the Higher Learning Commision and The Association for Biblical Higher Education. **Degrees:** 64 bachelor's, 15 associate awarded; master's offered. **Location:** 1/2 mile from North Beckley. **Calendar:** Semester, limited summer session. **Full-time faculty:** 22 total. **Part-time faculty:** 7 total.

Freshman class profile. 96 applied, 63 admitted, 45 enrolled.

Mid 50% test scores			
SAT critical reading:	530-620	ACT composite:	18-26
SAT math:	460-540	Out-of-state:	64%
		Live on campus:	89%

Basis for selection. Profession of Jesus Christ as Savior, essential agreement with doctrinal statement of college, approved character very important. Minimum 2.0 GPA, test scores, achievement and potential in English also considered. Interview recommended. **Home schooled:** Must provide accurate record of curriculum used, subjects studied, grades earned for grade levels 9-12.

High school preparation. College-preparatory program recommended. Recommended units include English 4, mathematics 3, social studies 3, history 3, science 3, foreign language 1 and academic electives 4.

2011-2012 Annual costs. Tuition/fees: $11,782. Room/board: $6,200. Books/supplies: $900. Personal expenses: $1,208.

Financial aid. All financial aid based on need.

Application procedures. Admission: Priority date 4/1; no deadline. $35 fee, may be waived for applicants with need. Admission notification on a rolling basis. **Financial aid:** Closing date 6/15. FAFSA, institutional form required. Applicants notified on a rolling basis starting 6/15; must reply by 8/1 or within 4 week(s) of notification.

Academics. Special study options: Combined bachelor's/graduate degree, cooperative education, dual enrollment of high school students, independent study, internships, teacher certification program. **Credit/placement by examination:** AP, CLEP, SAT, ACT, institutional tests. 29 credit hours maximum toward bachelor's degree. **Support services:** Reduced course load, remedial instruction, study skills assistance, tutoring.

Majors. Theology: Bible.

Computing on campus. 30 workstations in dormitories, library, computer center, student center. Dormitories wired for high-speed internet access and linked to campus network. Commuter students can connect to campus network. Online library, helpline, repair service, student web hosting, wireless network available.

Student life. Freshman orientation: Mandatory. Preregistration for classes offered. Held for 3 days immediately prior to beginning of semester. **Policies:** Chapel held three times a week. Annual Spiritual Life Conference, Distinguished Christian Lecture Series, Bible and missions conferences. Religious observance required. **Housing:** Single-sex dorms, apartments, wellness housing available. $25 nonrefundable deposit. **Activities:** Choral groups, drama, music ensembles, student government, student newspaper.

Athletics. NCCAA. **Intercollegiate:** Basketball, soccer M, volleyball W. **Intramural:** Basketball, soccer M, table tennis, tennis, volleyball. **Team name:** Warriors.

Student services. Chaplain/spiritual director, career counseling, financial aid counseling, health services, personal counseling, placement for graduates, veterans' counselor.

Contact. E-mail: admissions@abc.edu
Phone: (304) 877-6428 Toll-free number: (800) 678-9222
Fax: (304) 877-5082
Scott Ross, Director of Admissions, Appalachian Bible College, Director of Admissions, Mount Hope, WV 25880

Bethany College
Bethany, West Virginia
www.bethanywv.edu
CB member
CB code: 5060

- Private 4-year liberal arts college affiliated with Christian Church (Disciples of Christ)
- Residential campus in rural community
- 780 degree-seeking undergraduates: 1% part-time, 45% women, 15% African American, 1% Native American, 1% international
- 21 graduate students
- 59% of applicants admitted
- SAT or ACT (ACT writing optional), application essay required
- 48% graduate within 6 years; 45% enter graduate study

General. Founded in 1840. Regionally accredited. **Degrees:** 135 bachelor's awarded; master's offered. **Location:** 14 miles from Wheeling, 40 miles from Pittsburgh. **Calendar:** 4-1-4. **Full-time faculty:** 47 total; 83% have terminal degrees, 4% minority, 36% women. **Part-time faculty:** 30 total; 13% have terminal degrees, 3% minority, 63% women. **Class size:** 79% < 20, 18% 20-39, 2% 40-49, less than 1% 50-99, less than 1% >100. **Special facilities:** Alexander Campbell Mansion and archives, forest.

Freshman class profile. 1,463 applied, 865 admitted, 214 enrolled.

Mid 50% test scores			
SAT critical reading:	390-520	Rank in top quarter:	14%
SAT math:	380-510	Rank in top tenth:	7%
SAT writing:	380-510	End year in good standing:	59%
ACT composite:	17-24	Return as sophomores:	59%
GPA 3.75 or higher:	13%	Out-of-state:	83%
GPA 3.50-3.74:	9%	Live on campus:	95%
GPA 3.0-3.49:	26%	Fraternities:	24%
GPA 2.0-2.99:	39%	Sororities:	52%

Basis for selection. Rank in top half of graduating class, test scores, interview, activities, and recommendations important. Interviews strongly recommended. **Home schooled:** Statement describing home school structure and mission required. **Learning Disabled:** Students with learning disabilities must apply by February 15 for priority consideration in limited-enrollment learning disabled program. Students should submit official diagnosis of learning disability after acceptance.

High school preparation. College-preparatory program recommended. 15 units required. Required units include English 4, mathematics 3, social studies 3, science 3 and foreign language 2.

2011-2012 Annual costs. Tuition/fees: $23,854. Room/board: $9,546. Books/supplies: $1,300. Personal expenses: $1,300.

2010-2011 Financial aid. Additional information: Scholarships available for travel program.

Application procedures. Admission: Priority date 4/1; no deadline. No application fee. Admission notification on a rolling basis beginning on or about 9/1. Maximum postponement for deferred admission is one year. **Financial aid:** Priority date 3/1; no closing date. FAFSA required. Applicants notified on a rolling basis starting 3/1; must reply within 2 week(s) of notification.

Academics. Special study options: Accelerated study, combined bachelor's/graduate degree, distance learning, double major, dual enrollment of high school students, ESL, independent study, internships, liberal arts/career combination, student-designed major, study abroad, teacher certification program, United Nations semester, urban semester, Washington semester. **Credit/placement by examination:** AP, CLEP, IB, SAT, ACT, institutional tests. 80 credit hours maximum toward bachelor's degree. **Support services:** Learning center, pre-admission summer program, remedial instruction, study skills assistance, tutoring, writing center.

Majors. Biology: General, biochemistry. **Business:** General, accounting, finance, international, international finance. **Communications:** Advertising, broadcast journalism, communications/speech/rhetoric, journalism, public relations, radio/TV. **Communications technology:** Graphics. **Computer sciences:** General, computer science. **Conservation:** Environmental studies. **Education:** General, art, biology, chemistry, elementary, English, foreign

languages, French, German, history, learning disabled, mathematics, multi-level teacher, multiple handicapped, physical, secondary, social studies, Spanish, special ed. **English:** English lit. **Foreign languages:** Spanish. **General:** Equestrian studies. **History:** General. **Human services:** Social work. **Math:** General. **Parks/recreation:** Health/fitness, sports admin. **Philosophy/religion:** Religion. **Physical sciences:** Chemistry. **Psychology:** General. **Social sciences:** Economics, international relations, political science. **Visual/performing arts:** General, art, design, dramatic, music, studio arts.

Most popular majors. Communications/journalism 11%, education 16%, interdisciplinary studies 6%, psychology 14%, public administration/social services 9%, social sciences 11%, visual/performing arts 8%.

Computing on campus. 145 workstations in dormitories, library, computer center, student center. Dormitories wired for high-speed internet access and linked to campus network. Commuter students can connect to campus network. Online library, helpline, repair service, student web hosting, wireless network available.

Student life. Freshman orientation: Mandatory, $125 fee. Preregistration for classes offered. Held prior to start of fall classes. **Housing:** Guaranteed on-campus for all undergraduates. Coed dorms, single-sex dorms, special housing for disabled, apartments, fraternity/sorority housing available. $150 fully refundable deposit, deadline 8/20. **Activities:** Bands, campus ministries, choral groups, dance, drama, film society, international student organizations, literary magazine, music ensembles, Model UN, musical theater, radio station, student government, student newspaper, TV station, community service organization, ecumenical religious organization, multicultural students club, advertising club, social work club, Amnesty International, Coalition for Christian Outreach, Circle K, equestrian club.

Athletics. NCAA. **Intercollegiate:** Baseball M, basketball, cross-country, diving, football (tackle) M, golf, lacrosse M, soccer, softball W, swimming, tennis, track and field, volleyball W. **Intramural:** Basketball, football (non-tackle) M, handball, racquetball, soccer, softball, swimming, tennis, volleyball. **Team name:** Bison.

Student services. Alcohol/substance abuse counseling, chaplain/spiritual director, career counseling, student employment services, financial aid counseling, health services, minority student services, personal counseling, placement for graduates, veterans' counselor, women's services. **Physically disabled:** Services for visually, speech, hearing impaired.

Contact. E-mail: rzitzelsberger@bethanywv.edu
Phone: (304) 829-7611 Toll-free number: (800) 922-7611
Fax: (304) 829-7142
RJ Zitzelberger, Director of Admission, Bethany College, Office of Admission, Bethany, WV 26032-0428

Bluefield State College
Bluefield, West Virginia
www.bluefieldstate.edu
CB code: 5064

- Public 4-year liberal arts and technical college
- Commuter campus in large town
- 1,929 degree-seeking undergraduates: 21% part-time, 64% women
- 40% of applicants admitted
- SAT or ACT (ACT writing optional) required

General. Founded in 1895. Regionally accredited. Off-campus locations in Lewisburg, Welch, and Beckley. **Degrees:** 242 bachelor's, 82 associate awarded. **Location:** 100 miles from Charleston; 100 miles from Roanoke, Virginia. **Calendar:** Semester, limited summer session. **Full-time faculty:** 75 total; 53% have terminal degrees, 11% minority, 44% women. **Part-time faculty:** 70 total; 13% have terminal degrees, 3% minority, 59% women. **Class size:** 52% < 20, 40% 20-39, 6% 40-49, 2% 50-99. **Special facilities:** Instructional technology center.

Freshman class profile. 980 applied, 388 admitted, 262 enrolled.

Mid 50% test scores			
SAT critical reading:	410-500	Return as sophomores:	56%
SAT math:	420-520	Out-of-state:	9%
ACT composite:	17-21	International:	1%
GPA 3.75 or higher:	29%	Fraternities:	1%
GPA 3.50-3.74:	16%	Sororities:	1%
GPA 3.0-3.49:	29%		
GPA 2.0-2.99:	25%		

Basis for selection. 2.5 GPA, college preparatory program, test scores required for applicants to health, teacher education, humanities, social science and business administration programs. High school requirements not necessary for associate's program.

High school preparation. College-preparatory program recommended. 17 units required. Required units include English 4, mathematics 4, social studies 3, science 3 (laboratory 3), foreign language 2 and visual/performing arts 1.

2011-2012 Annual costs. Tuition/fees: $4,908; $9,456 out-of-state. Tuition for students residing in border counties is $7,176. Books/supplies: $1,600. Personal expenses: $1,100.

2011-2012 Financial aid. Need-based: Average need met was 70%. Average scholarship/grant was $3,500; average loan $3,600. 57% of total undergraduate aid awarded as scholarships/grants, 43% as loans/jobs. **Non-need-based:** Scholarships awarded for academics, alumni affiliation, art, athletics, job skills, leadership, minority status, state residency.

Application procedures. Admission: No deadline. No application fee. Admission notification on a rolling basis beginning on or about 8/1. **Financial aid:** Priority date 3/1; no closing date. FAFSA, institutional form required. Applicants notified on a rolling basis starting 5/1.

Academics. Special study options: Distance learning, double major, dual enrollment of high school students, honors, independent study, internships, teacher certification program. **Credit/placement by examination:** AP, CLEP, IB, ACT, institutional tests. **Support services:** Learning center, pre-admission summer program, reduced course load, remedial instruction, study skills assistance, tutoring, writing center.

Majors. Business: Accounting, business admin. **Computer sciences:** General. **Education:** Elementary. **Health services:** Nursing (RN), radiologic technology/medical imaging. **Liberal arts:** Arts/sciences, humanities. **Protective services:** Criminal justice. **Social sciences:** General.

Most popular majors. Business/marketing 21%, computer/information sciences 7%, education 12%, engineering/engineering technologies 15%, health sciences 7%, liberal arts 22%, social sciences 9%.

Computing on campus. 370 workstations in library, computer center. Online library, helpline, student web hosting, wireless network available.

Student life. Freshman orientation: Available. Preregistration for classes offered. One day in July or August. **Activities:** Choral groups, drama, international student organizations, Model UN, radio station, student government, student newspaper, Minorities on the Move, student nurses association.

Athletics. NCAA. **Intercollegiate:** Baseball M, basketball, cheerleading, cross-country, golf M, softball W, tennis, volleyball W. **Intramural:** Badminton, basketball, bowling, football (non-tackle) M, golf, racquetball, softball, swimming, table tennis, tennis, volleyball. **Team name:** Big Blues.

Student services. Career counseling, student employment services, financial aid counseling, health services, minority student services, personal counseling, placement for graduates, veterans' counselor. **Physically disabled:** Services for visually, speech, hearing impaired.

Contact. E-mail: bscadmit@bluefieldstate.edu
Phone: (304) 327-4065 Toll-free number: (800) 654-7798
Fax: (304) 325-7747
Kenny Mandeville, Director of Admissions, Bluefield State College, 219 Rock Street, Bluefield, WV 24701

Concord University
Athens, West Virginia
www.concord.edu
CB member
CB code: 5120

- Public 4-year university and liberal arts college
- Residential campus in small town
- 2,616 degree-seeking undergraduates: 9% part-time, 57% women, 6% African American, 2% Asian American, 1% Hispanic American
- 181 degree-seeking graduate students
- 61% of applicants admitted
- SAT or ACT (ACT writing optional) required
- 31% graduate within 6 years

General. Founded in 1872. Regionally accredited. **Degrees:** 401 bachelor's awarded; master's offered. **Location:** 5 miles from Princeton, 80 miles from Charleston. **Calendar:** Semester, extensive summer session. **Full-time faculty:** 121 total; 3% minority, 44% women. **Part-time faculty:** 86 total; 5% minority, 58% women. **Class size:** 60% < 20, 32% 20-39, 5% 40-49, 3% 50-99, less than 1% >100. **Special facilities:** Southern West Virginia technology center.

Freshman class profile. 2,351 applied, 1,431 admitted, 645 enrolled.

Mid 50% test scores			
SAT critical reading:	420-540	Rank in top quarter:	43%
SAT math:	420-530	Rank in top tenth:	18%
SAT writing:	390-510	End year in good standing:	89%
ACT composite:	18-23	Return as sophomores:	61%
GPA 3.75 or higher:	21%	Out-of-state:	24%
GPA 3.50-3.74:	15%	Live on campus:	59%
GPA 3.0-3.49:	29%	Fraternities:	20%
GPA 2.0-2.99:	32%	Sororities:	25%

Basis for selection. 2.0 GPA and 870 SAT (exclusive of Writing) or 18 ACT required. **Home schooled:** Statement describing home school structure and mission, transcript of courses and grades required.

High school preparation. Required units include English 4, mathematics 3, social studies 2, history 1, science 1 (laboratory 2). Math courses must include algebra I and another higher level course. Social science requirement includes 1 US history.

2011-2012 Annual costs. Tuition/fees: $5,446; $12,100 out-of-state. Room/board: $7,240. Books/supplies: $1,500. Personal expenses: $2,169.

Financial aid. **Non-need-based:** Scholarships awarded for academics, alumni affiliation, art, athletics, job skills, leadership, minority status, music/drama, state residency. **Additional information:** March 1 priority deadline for state forms. April 15 priority deadline for FAFSA.

Application procedures. **Admission:** No deadline. No application fee. Admission notification on a rolling basis beginning on or about 9/1. **Financial aid:** Closing date 4/15. FAFSA, institutional form required. Applicants notified on a rolling basis starting 3/1; must reply within 2 week(s) of notification.

Academics. **Special study options:** Cooperative education, distance learning, double major, dual enrollment of high school students, ESL, honors, internships, liberal arts/career combination, student-designed major, study abroad, teacher certification program. English as a second language program for foreign students, mentoring programs for pre-law and pre-med students. **Credit/placement by examination:** AP, CLEP, SAT, ACT, institutional tests. **Support services:** Learning center, reduced course load, remedial instruction, study skills assistance, tutoring, writing center.

Majors. **Biology:** General, genetics. **Business:** General, accounting, business admin, finance, hospitality admin, hospitality/recreation, hotel/motel admin, human resources, managerial economics, marketing, resort management, restaurant/food services, tourism promotion, tourism/travel. **Communications:** Advertising, broadcast journalism, communications/speech/rhetoric, journalism, public relations. **Computer sciences:** General, computer science. **Education:** General, art, biology, business, chemistry, early childhood, elementary, English, health, learning disabled, mathematics, mentally handicapped, music, physical, science, social studies, speech. **English:** British lit, English lit, writing. **Health services:** Athletic training, clinical lab science, predental, premedicine, prepharmacy, preveterinary. **History:** General. **Human services:** General, social work. **Liberal arts:** Arts/sciences, library science. **Math:** General. **Parks/recreation:** General, facilities management, health/fitness, sports admin. **Physical sciences:** Chemistry, geology. **Psychology:** General. **Social sciences:** Geography, political science, sociology. **Visual/performing arts:** Art, commercial/advertising art, dramatic, graphic design, music, studio arts.

Most popular majors. Biology 9%, business/marketing 21%, education 19%, liberal arts 7%, public administration/social services 6%, social sciences 8%.

Computing on campus. 250 workstations in dormitories, library, computer center, student center. Dormitories wired for high-speed internet access and linked to campus network. Commuter students can connect to campus network. Online course registration, online library, helpline, wireless network available.

Student life. **Freshman orientation:** Mandatory, $85 fee. Preregistration for classes offered. **Housing:** Guaranteed on-campus for freshmen. Coed dorms, single-sex dorms, special housing for disabled, apartments, fraternity/sorority housing, wellness housing available. $50 deposit. **Activities:** Bands, campus ministries, choral groups, dance, drama, film society, international student organizations, literary magazine, music ensembles, radio station, student government, student newspaper, TV station, over 50 clubs and organizations.

Athletics. NCAA. **Intercollegiate:** Baseball M, basketball, cross-country, football (tackle) M, golf, soccer, softball W, tennis, track and field, volleyball W. **Intramural:** Archery, badminton, basketball, bowling, football (tackle) M, golf, handball, racquetball, soccer W, softball, swimming, tennis, track and field, volleyball, water polo. **Team name:** Mountain Lions.

Student services. Career counseling, student employment services, financial aid counseling, health services, on-campus daycare, personal counseling, placement for graduates, veterans' counselor.

Contact. E-mail: admissions@concord.edu
Phone: (304) 384-5248 Toll-free number: (888) 384-5249
Fax: (304) 384-3218
Kent Gamble, Director of Enrollment, Concord University, PO Box 1000, Athens, WV 24712-1000

Davis and Elkins College
Elkins, West Virginia
www.dewv.edu

CB member
CB code: 5151

- Private 4-year liberal arts college affiliated with Presbyterian Church (USA)
- Residential campus in small town
- 760 degree-seeking undergraduates: 2% part-time, 56% women, 2% African American, 10% international
- 53% of applicants admitted
- SAT or ACT (ACT writing optional) required
- 36% graduate within 6 years; 13% enter graduate study

General. Founded in 1904. Regionally accredited. **Degrees:** 67 bachelor's, 42 associate awarded. **Location:** 130 miles from Pittsburgh; 200 miles from Washington, DC. **Calendar:** 4-1-4, extensive summer session. **Full-time faculty:** 48 total; 67% have terminal degrees, 8% minority, 54% women. **Part-time faculty:** 38 total; 13% have terminal degrees, 37% women. **Class size:** 66% < 20, 32% 20-39, less than 1% 40-49, less than 1% 50-99. **Special facilities:** Pearl S. Buck collection, observatory, greenhouse, planetarium, 8 buildings on the national historic registry.

Freshman class profile. 2,011 applied, 1,065 admitted, 231 enrolled.

Mid 50% test scores			
SAT critical reading:	410-510	Rank in top quarter:	21%
SAT math:	420-530	Rank in top tenth:	5%
SAT writing:	380-500	End year in good standing:	84%
ACT composite:	17-22	Return as sophomores:	62%
GPA 3.75 or higher:	14%	Out-of-state:	30%
GPA 3.50-3.74:	12%	Live on campus:	65%
GPA 3.0-3.49:	26%	International:	13%
GPA 2.0-2.99:	46%	Fraternities:	1%

Basis for selection. Admission based on school achievement record, 2.0 GPA, test scores, and extracurricular activities. Recommended interview also important. Essay, academic/personal recommendations recommended for all applicants; audition required for musicians and theater students; portfolio required for art students. **Home schooled:** Transcript of courses and grades required. **Learning Disabled:** Must complete a separate application for the Supported Learning Program.

High school preparation. College-preparatory program recommended. 15 units required. Required and recommended units include English 4, mathematics 3-4, social studies 3-4, science 3-4 (laboratory 1-2), foreign language 1-2 and academic electives 4. Math units must include algebra I or algebra II, and geometry.

2011-2012 Annual costs. Tuition/fees: $22,320. Reduced tuition for qualified students in 7 surrounding counties through Highland Scholars Program. Room/board: $7,950. Books/supplies: $1,200. Personal expenses: $1,500.

2011-2012 Financial aid. **Need-based:** 178 full-time freshmen applied for aid; 166 were judged to have need; 166 of these received aid. Average need met was 82%. Average scholarship/grant was $17,061; average loan $3,385. 70% of total undergraduate aid awarded as scholarships/grants, 30% as loans/jobs. **Non-need-based:** Awarded to 341 full-time undergraduates, including 98 freshmen. Scholarships awarded for academics, alumni affiliation, art, athletics, leadership, music/drama, religious affiliation, state residency.

Application procedures. **Admission:** Priority date 5/1; no deadline. No application fee. Admission notification on a rolling basis beginning on or about 9/30. **Financial aid:** Priority date 3/1; no closing date. Applicants notified on a rolling basis starting 9/28; must reply by 8/30.

Academics. **Special study options:** Combined bachelor's/graduate degree, cooperative education, cross-registration, distance learning, double major, dual enrollment of high school students, external degree, honors, independent study, internships, liberal arts/career combination, student-designed major, study abroad, teacher certification program, Washington semester. **Credit/placement by examination:** AP, CLEP, IB, institutional tests. **Support**

services: Learning center, reduced course load, remedial instruction, study skills assistance, tutoring, writing center.

Majors. Biology: General. **Business:** Accounting, business admin, finance, hospitality admin, international, international marketing, management information systems, marketing. **Computer sciences:** Computer science. **Conservation:** Environmental science. **Education:** Business, drama/dance, elementary, mathematics, physical. **English:** English lit. **Foreign languages:** Spanish. **History:** General. **Math:** General. **Parks/recreation:** General, exercise sciences, sports admin. **Philosophy/religion:** Religion. **Physical sciences:** Chemistry. **Psychology:** General. **Social sciences:** Criminology, economics, political science, sociology. **Theology:** Religious ed. **Visual/performing arts:** Dramatic, painting, theater design.

Most popular majors. Biology 6%, business/marketing 30%, education 12%, parks/recreation 19%, social sciences 9%, visual/performing arts 8%.

Computing on campus. 87 workstations in library. Dormitories wired for high-speed internet access and linked to campus network. Helpline, repair service, wireless network available.

Student life. Freshman orientation: Mandatory. Preregistration for classes offered. **Housing:** Guaranteed on-campus for all undergraduates. Coed dorms, single-sex dorms, fraternity/sorority housing, wellness housing available. **Activities:** Bands, choral groups, drama, international student organizations, literary magazine, music ensembles, musical theater, radio station, student government, student newspaper, Alpha Phi Omega, Appalachian music and dance, Green Works.

Athletics. NCAA. **Intercollegiate:** Baseball M, basketball, cross-country, golf M, skiing, soccer, softball W, swimming, tennis, volleyball W. **Intramural:** Basketball, soccer, volleyball. **Team name:** Senators.

Student services. Alcohol/substance abuse counseling, chaplain/spiritual director, career counseling, student employment services, financial aid counseling, health services, personal counseling, placement for graduates, veterans' counselor.

Contact. E-mail: admiss@dewv.edu
Phone: (304) 637-1230 Toll-free number: (800) 624-3157 ext. 1230
Fax: (304) 637-1800
Kevin Wilson, Executive Vice President/Chief Operating Officer, Davis and Elkins College, 100 Campus Drive, Elkins, WV 26241-3996

Fairmont State University
Fairmont, West Virginia
www.fairmontstate.edu   **CB code: 5211**

- Public 4-year university
- Commuter campus in large town
- 4,178 degree-seeking undergraduates: 12% part-time, 56% women, 4% African American, 2% Hispanic American, 2% international
- 328 degree-seeking graduate students
- 55% of applicants admitted
- SAT or ACT (ACT writing recommended) required
- 31% graduate within 6 years

General. Founded in 1865. Regionally accredited. **Degrees:** 559 bachelor's, 113 associate awarded; master's offered. **ROTC:** Army, Air Force. **Location:** 90 miles from Pittsburgh. **Calendar:** Semester, limited summer session. **Full-time faculty:** 178 total; 71% have terminal degrees, 8% minority, 48% women. **Part-time faculty:** 139 total; 32% have terminal degrees, 16% minority, 53% women. **Class size:** 35% < 20, 50% 20-39, 5% 40-49, 9% 50-99, less than 1% >100. **Special facilities:** West Virginia folklife center.

Freshman class profile. 3,461 applied, 1,899 admitted, 751 enrolled.

Mid 50% test scores		Rank in top quarter:	34%
SAT critical reading:	410-510	Rank in top tenth:	12%
SAT math:	420-520	Return as sophomores:	66%
ACT composite:	18-23	Out-of-state:	14%
GPA 3.75 or higher:	14%	Live on campus:	47%
GPA 3.50-3.74:	14%	International:	1%
GPA 3.0-3.49:	37%	Fraternities:	3%
GPA 2.0-2.99:	35%	Sororities:	2%

Basis for selection. 2.5 GPA and 17 ACT or 830 SAT (exclusive of Writing) required for bachelor's programs. For associate degree programs, SAT or ACT required for placement only. **Home schooled:** GED required.

High school preparation. College-preparatory program recommended. 26 units required. Required units include English 4, mathematics 4, social studies 2, history 1, science 3 (laboratory 2), foreign language 2 and academic electives 8. 1 unit U.S. history required. Math must include algebra and at least 1 higher unit. 2 units lab science required for biology, chemistry, and physics majors.

2011-2012 Annual costs. Tuition/fees: $5,326; $11,230 out-of-state. Room/board: $7,086. Books/supplies: $1,000. Personal expenses: $2,078.

2010-2011 Financial aid. All financial aid based on need. 714 full-time freshmen applied for aid; 570 were judged to have need; 559 of these received aid. Average need met was 70%. Average scholarship/grant was $6,538; average loan $2,991. 64% of total undergraduate aid awarded as scholarships/grants, 36% as loans/jobs.

Application procedures. Admission: Priority date 3/1; deadline 8/15 (postmark date). No application fee. Admission notification on a rolling basis beginning on or about 10/1. **Financial aid:** Closing date 3/1. FAFSA required. Applicants notified on a rolling basis starting 4/1; must reply within 2 week(s) of notification.

Academics. Special study options: Accelerated study, cooperative education, cross-registration, distance learning, double major, ESL, honors, independent study, internships, liberal arts/career combination, study abroad, teacher certification program, Washington semester, weekend college. **Credit/placement by examination:** AP, CLEP, IB, SAT, ACT, institutional tests. 28 credit hours maximum toward bachelor's degree. **Support services:** Learning center, reduced course load, remedial instruction, study skills assistance, tutoring.

Majors. Biology: General. **Business:** General, accounting, banking/financial services, business admin, management information systems, management science, office management. **Communications:** Communications/speech/rhetoric. **Communications technology:** Graphic/printing. **Computer sciences:** General, computer science. **Education:** General, art, biology, business, chemistry, early childhood, elementary, emotionally handicapped, English, family/consumer sciences, gifted/talented, history, mathematics, mentally handicapped, middle, music, physical, physics, science, secondary, social studies, speech, technology/industrial arts, trade/industrial. **English:** English lit. **Foreign languages:** French, Spanish. **Health services:** Health care admin, nursing (RN). **History:** General. **Math:** General. **Parks/recreation:** Exercise sciences, health/fitness. **Physical sciences:** Chemistry. **Protective services:** Criminal justice, forensics, law enforcement admin. **Psychology:** General. **Social sciences:** Political science, sociology. **Visual/performing arts:** Commercial/advertising art, dramatic. **Work/family studies:** General.

Most popular majors. Business/marketing 24%, education 10%, engineering/engineering technologies 10%, health sciences 11%, liberal arts 9%, psychology 7%, security/protective services 10%, social sciences 7%.

Computing on campus. 950 workstations in dormitories, library, computer center, student center. Dormitories wired for high-speed internet access and linked to campus network. Commuter students can connect to campus network. Online library, helpline, student web hosting, wireless network available.

Student life. Freshman orientation: Available. Preregistration for classes offered. Held 2 days in fall, one day in spring. **Policies:** Alcohol not allowed. **Housing:** Guaranteed on-campus for freshmen. Coed dorms, single-sex dorms, apartments available. $200 fully refundable deposit, deadline 7/18. **Activities:** Bands, campus ministries, choral groups, dance, drama, international student organizations, literary magazine, music ensembles, musical theater, student government, student newspaper, symphony orchestra, black student union, Circle K, disabled students society, society of nontraditional students.

Athletics. NCAA. **Intercollegiate:** Baseball M, basketball, cheerleading M, cross-country, football (tackle) M, golf, softball W, swimming, tennis, volleyball W. **Intramural:** Archery, badminton W, basketball, bowling, cross-country, field hockey W, football (tackle) M, golf, gymnastics, racquetball, softball, swimming, table tennis, tennis, track and field, volleyball, wrestling M. **Team name:** Falcons.

Student services. Adult student services, career counseling, student employment services, financial aid counseling, health services, on-campus daycare, personal counseling, placement for graduates, veterans' counselor. **Physically disabled:** Services for visually, hearing impaired.

Contact. E-mail: admit@fairmontstate.edu
Phone: (304) 367-4892 Toll-free number: (800) 641-5678
Fax: (304) 367-4789
Lori Schoonmaker, Associate Director of Admissions and Recruitment, Fairmont State University, Office of Admissions, Fairmont, WV 26554-2470

Glenville State College

Glenville, West Virginia
www.glenville.edu

CB member
CB code: 5254

- Public 4-year liberal arts and teachers college
- Commuter campus in rural community
- 1,549 degree-seeking undergraduates: 23% part-time, 41% women, 19% African American, 2% Hispanic American
- 82% of applicants admitted
- SAT or ACT (ACT writing optional) required

General. Founded in 1872. Regionally accredited. **Degrees:** 161 bachelor's, 36 associate awarded. **ROTC:** Army. **Location:** 87 miles from Charleston, 86 miles from Morgantown. **Calendar:** Semester, limited summer session. **Full-time faculty:** 67 total; 48% have terminal degrees, 6% minority, 36% women. **Part-time faculty:** 38 total; 3% have terminal degrees, 3% minority, 71% women. **Class size:** 58% < 20, 38% 20-39, 3% 40-49, 2% 50-99.

Freshman class profile. 1,246 applied, 1,023 admitted, 355 enrolled.

Mid 50% test scores			
SAT critical reading:	350-440	GPA 2.0-2.99:	42%
SAT math:	350-440	Rank in top quarter:	20%
ACT composite:	16-21	Rank in top tenth:	12%
GPA 3.75 or higher:	8%	End year in good standing:	81%
GPA 3.50-3.74:	8%	Return as sophomores:	70%
GPA 3.0-3.49:	29%	Out-of-state:	11%
		Live on campus:	69%

Basis for selection. Students must have graduated from accredited high school with 2.0 GPA or 18 ACT/860 SAT (exclusive of Writing). Associate degree programs open to all students who have graduated from high school or hold a GED. Students who want to pursue bachelor's degree, but do not meet the requirements may enter 2-year program and later transfer into bachelor's degree program. Audition required for music. **Home schooled:** GED required. Case by case evaluation. **Learning Disabled:** Students must provide documentation of their disability to the disabilities coordinator to receive services.

High school preparation. College-preparatory program recommended. 28 units required. Required units include English 4, mathematics 4, social studies 3, science 3 (laboratory 3), foreign language 2, visual/performing arts 1 and academic electives 15. 3 math units must be algebra I or higher. Social studies should include US history. English should include courses in grammar, composition, and literature.

2011-2012 Annual costs. Tuition/fees: $5,352; $12,720 out-of-state. Tuition for students residing in border counties is $8,232. Room/board: $7,900. Books/supplies: $1,200. Personal expenses: $2,373.

Financial aid. Non-need-based: Scholarships awarded for academics, athletics, music/drama, state residency.

Application procedures. Admission: No deadline. $20 fee, may be waived for applicants with need. Admission notification on a rolling basis. **Financial aid:** Priority date 2/1; no closing date. FAFSA required. Applicants notified on a rolling basis starting 3/1; must reply within 3 week(s) of notification.

Academics. Students can receive credit for employment, military, and/or life experience in Regents Bachelor of Arts program (designed for nontraditional students). **Special study options:** Combined bachelor's/graduate degree, distance learning, double major, dual enrollment of high school students, internships, student-designed major, study abroad, teacher certification program, Washington semester. **Credit/placement by examination:** AP, CLEP, SAT, ACT, institutional tests. Unlimited number of hours of credit may be counted for degree. **Support services:** Remedial instruction, study skills assistance, tutoring, writing center.

Majors. Biology: General. **Business:** General, business admin. **Conservation:** Management/policy. **Education:** Elementary, kindergarten/preschool, secondary, special ed. **English:** English lit. **History:** General. **Physical sciences:** Chemistry. **Social sciences:** General. **Visual/performing arts:** Music performance.

Most popular majors. Business/marketing 12%, education 28%, liberal arts 15%, natural resources/environmental science 11%, social sciences 22%.

Computing on campus. 194 workstations in library, computer center, student center. Dormitories wired for high-speed internet access and linked to campus network. Commuter students can connect to campus network. Online course registration, online library, wireless network available.

Student life. Freshman orientation: Mandatory, $100 fee. Preregistration for classes offered. **Policies:** All unmarried students who have earned less than 58 credit hours required to reside on campus. Alcoholic beverages and controlled substances not permitted on campus. All students required to adhere to Student Code of Conduct. Community service required of student organizations. **Housing:** Guaranteed on-campus for freshmen. Single-sex dorms, special housing for disabled, apartments, wellness housing available. $100 partly refundable deposit, deadline 4/1. **Activities:** Bands, campus ministries, choral groups, drama, literary magazine, music ensembles, student government, student newspaper, Fellowship of Christian Athletes, environmental organization, students in free enterprise, Student National Education Association, student athlete advisory committee, student awareness organization, Music Educators National Conference, Kappa Delta Pi.

Athletics. NCAA. **Intercollegiate:** Baseball M, basketball, cross-country, football (tackle) M, golf, softball W, track and field, volleyball W. **Intramural:** Badminton, basketball, football (non-tackle), softball, table tennis, tennis, volleyball, weight lifting. **Team name:** Pioneers.

Student services. Adult student services, alcohol/substance abuse counseling, chaplain/spiritual director, career counseling, services for economically disadvantaged, student employment services, financial aid counseling, health services, minority student services, personal counseling, placement for graduates, veterans' counselor. **Physically disabled:** Services for visually, speech, hearing impaired.

Contact. E-mail: admissions@glenville.edu
Phone: (304) 462-4128 Toll-free number: (800) 924-2010
Fax: (304) 462-8619
Donald Chapman, Vice President for Enrollment Services, Glenville State College, 200 High Street, Glenville, WV 26351-1292

Marshall University

Huntington, West Virginia
www.marshall.edu

CB member
CB code: 5396

- Public 4-year university
- Commuter campus in small city
- 9,506 degree-seeking undergraduates: 10% part-time, 56% women, 6% African American, 1% Asian American, 2% Hispanic American, 1% international
- 3,086 degree-seeking graduate students
- 81% of applicants admitted
- SAT or ACT (ACT writing optional) required
- 46% graduate within 6 years

General. Founded in 1837. Regionally accredited. **Degrees:** 1,395 bachelor's, 91 associate awarded; master's, professional, doctoral offered. **ROTC:** Army. **Location:** 126 miles from Lexington, KY; 160 miles from Columbus, OH. **Calendar:** Semester, limited summer session. **Full-time faculty:** 506 total; 78% have terminal degrees, 13% minority, 42% women. **Part-time faculty:** 254 total; 9% have terminal degrees, 3% minority, 48% women. **Class size:** 39% < 20, 50% 20-39, 6% 40-49, 4% 50-99, less than 1% >100. **Special facilities:** Confederate history collection, superconducting nuclear magnetic resonance spectrometer.

Freshman class profile. 2,912 applied, 2,368 admitted, 2,002 enrolled.

Mid 50% test scores			
SAT critical reading:	450-560	GPA 3.0-3.49:	27%
SAT math:	440-560	GPA 2.0-2.99:	25%
ACT composite:	19-24	Return as sophomores:	70%
GPA 3.75 or higher:	30%	Out-of-state:	28%
GPA 3.50-3.74:	17%	International:	1%

Basis for selection. Full admission requires 2.0 GPA and 19 ACT/910 SAT (exclusive of Writing). Conditional admission granted with below 2.0 GPA or the above scores, on a limited, first-come, first-served basis. Programs and colleges may have different requirements for admissions. Audition required for music majors; interview recommended for academically weak, learning disabled; portfolio recommended. **Home schooled:** Applicants should apply early and have home schooling well documented.

High school preparation. College-preparatory program required. 20 units required. Required units include English 4, mathematics 4, social studies 3, science 3 (laboratory 3), foreign language 2 and visual/performing arts 1.

2011-2012 Annual costs. Tuition/fees: $5,648; $13,480 out-of-state. Room/board: $8,094. Books/supplies: $1,100. Personal expenses: $2,232.

2011-2012 Financial aid. Need-based: 1,400 full-time freshmen applied for aid; 1,076 were judged to have need; 1,061 of these received aid. Average need met was 51%. Average scholarship/grant was $6,158; average loan $5,749. 40% of total undergraduate aid awarded as scholarships/grants, 60% as loans/jobs. **Non-need-based:** Awarded to 3,771 full-time undergraduates,

including 965 freshmen. Scholarships awarded for academics, art, athletics, minority status, music/drama, ROTC, state residency.

Application procedures. Admission: No deadline. $30 fee, may be waived for applicants with need. Admission notification on a rolling basis beginning on or about 9/1. **Financial aid:** Priority date 3/1; no closing date. FAFSA required. Applicants notified on a rolling basis starting 5/1.

Academics. Special study options: Accelerated study, combined bachelor's/graduate degree, cooperative education, cross-registration, distance learning, double major, dual enrollment of high school students, ESL, exchange student, honors, independent study, internships, study abroad, teacher certification program, Washington semester. **Credit/placement by examination:** AP, CLEP, IB, SAT, ACT, institutional tests. **Support services:** Learning center, pre-admission summer program, reduced course load, remedial instruction, study skills assistance, tutoring, writing center.

Majors. Biology: General. **Business:** Accounting, business admin, finance, international, management information systems, managerial economics, marketing. **Communications:** Journalism. **Computer sciences:** General. **Conservation:** Environmental science. **Education:** Elementary, kindergarten/preschool, physical, school counseling, secondary. **Engineering:** General. **English:** English lit, rhetoric/composition. **Foreign languages:** General. **Health services:** Athletic training, clinical lab science, cytotechnology, dietetics, nursing (RN), radiologic technology/medical imaging, respiratory therapy technology, speech pathology. **History:** General. **Human services:** Social work. **Liberal arts:** Humanities. **Math:** General. **Parks/recreation:** Exercise sciences, facilities management. **Physical sciences:** Chemistry, geology, physics. **Protective services:** Criminal justice. **Psychology:** General. **Social sciences:** Economics, geography, international relations, political science, sociology. **Visual/performing arts:** Art. **Work/family studies:** General.

Most popular majors. Biology 8%, business/marketing 16%, education 13%, health sciences 11%, liberal arts 17%, psychology 6%.

Computing on campus. 1,461 workstations in dormitories, library, computer center, student center. Dormitories wired for high-speed internet access and linked to campus network. Commuter students can connect to campus network. Online course registration, online library, helpline, student web hosting, wireless network available.

Student life. Freshman orientation: Available. Preregistration for classes offered. One-day programs in June, July, August. **Housing:** Guaranteed on-campus for freshmen. Coed dorms, single-sex dorms, special housing for disabled available. $200 deposit, deadline 5/15. **Activities:** Bands, campus ministries, choral groups, dance, drama, international student organizations, literary magazine, music ensembles, Model UN, musical theater, opera, radio station, student government, student newspaper, symphony orchestra, TV station, Black United Students, College Republicans, Lambda Society, Habitat for Humanity, student organization for alumni relations.

Athletics. NCAA. **Intercollegiate:** Baseball M, basketball, cross-country, football (tackle) M, golf, soccer, softball W, swimming W, tennis W, track and field, volleyball W. **Intramural:** Basketball, bowling, football (tackle), golf, racquetball, soccer, softball, swimming, tennis, track and field, volleyball. **Team name:** Thundering Herd.

Student services. Adult student services, alcohol/substance abuse counseling, chaplain/spiritual director, career counseling, student employment services, health services, minority student services, on-campus daycare, personal counseling, placement for graduates, veterans' counselor, women's services. **Physically disabled:** Services for visually, speech, hearing impaired.

Contact. E-mail: admissions@marshall.edu
Phone: (304) 696-3160 Toll-free number: (800) 642-3499
Fax: (304) 696-3135
Tammy Johnson, Director of Admissions, Marshall University, One John Marshall Drive, Huntington, WV 25755

Mountain State University
Beckley, West Virginia
www.mountainstate.edu

CB member
CB code: 5054

- Private 4-year university and health science college
- Commuter campus in large town
- 4,102 degree-seeking undergraduates: 37% part-time, 64% women, 20% African American, 1% Asian American, 3% Hispanic American, 1% Native American, 3% international
- 534 degree-seeking graduate students

General. Founded in 1933. Regionally accredited. **Degrees:** 754 bachelor's, 191 associate awarded; master's, doctoral offered. **Location:** 55 miles from Charleston; 125 miles from Roanoke, Virginia. **Calendar:** Semester, limited summer session. **Full-time faculty:** 91 total; 30% have terminal degrees, 90% minority, 72% women. **Part-time faculty:** 305 total; 21% have terminal degrees, 66% minority, 48% women. **Class size:** 86% < 20, 13% 20-39, less than 1% 40-49, less than 1% 50-99. **Special facilities:** YMCA, medicinal botanical garden, greenhouse.

Freshman class profile. 1,611 applied, 1,611 admitted, 508 enrolled.

GPA 3.75 or higher:	5%	Rank in top tenth:	3%
GPA 3.50-3.74:	7%	Return as sophomores:	45%
GPA 3.0-3.49:	25%	Out-of-state:	47%
GPA 2.0-2.99:	43%	Live on campus:	41%
Rank in top quarter:	11%	International:	2%

Basis for selection. Open admission, but selective for some programs. Special requirements for health science programs. ACT/SAT scores required for nursing and physician's assistant programs. **Home schooled:** State high school equivalency certificate required. Official academic records required. **Learning Disabled:** Students requesting accommodations must submit documentation of disability which consists of evaluation by appropriate professional and describes current impact of disability as it relates to accommodation request.

High school preparation. College-preparatory program recommended. 15 units recommended. Recommended units include English 4, mathematics 2, social studies 3, history 2, science 2 (laboratory 2).

2011-2012 Annual costs. Tuition/fees: $9,600. Higher costs may apply, depending on program. Room/board: $6,650. Books/supplies: $2,000. Personal expenses: $2,000.

2010-2011 Financial aid. Need-based: 311 full-time freshmen applied for aid; 291 were judged to have need; 291 of these received aid. Average need met was 71%. Average scholarship/grant was $4,884. 47% of total undergraduate aid awarded as scholarships/grants, 53% as loans/jobs. **Non-need-based:** Scholarships awarded for academics, alumni affiliation, athletics, leadership, minority status, state residency. **Additional information:** Military discount available to active duty, Reserve, and National Guard members, spouses, and dependents in select degree programs.

Application procedures. Admission: No deadline. $25 fee, may be waived for applicants with need. Admission notification on a rolling basis. **Financial aid:** Priority date 3/1; no closing date. FAFSA, institutional form required. Applicants notified on a rolling basis starting 4/1.

Academics. Special study options: Accelerated study, combined bachelor's/graduate degree, cooperative education, cross-registration, distance learning, double major, dual enrollment of high school students, ESL, honors, independent study, internships, liberal arts/career combination, student-designed major, weekend college. Degree completion program, credit for prior learning (challenge exam and portfolio assessment). **Credit/placement by examination:** AP, CLEP, IB, institutional tests. 30 credit hours maximum toward associate degree, 60 toward bachelor's. CLEP, DSST, DANTES and Challenge exams available. **Support services:** Learning center, reduced course load, remedial instruction, study skills assistance, tutoring, writing center.

Majors. Biology: General. **Business:** Accounting, business admin, nonprofit/public, organizational leadership. **Computer sciences:** Computer science, information technology, LAN/WAN management. **Health services:** Nursing (RN), sonography. **Human services:** Social work. **Philosophy/religion:** Religion. **Protective services:** Criminal justice, forensics, law enforcement admin. **Psychology:** General. **Visual/performing arts:** Graphic design.

Most popular majors. Business/marketing 35%, health sciences 47%, security/protective services 11%.

Computing on campus. Dormitories wired for high-speed internet access and linked to campus network. Commuter students can connect to campus network. Online course registration, online library, helpline, student web hosting, wireless network available.

Student life. Policies: All policies, regulations and requirements are in the student handbook online. **Housing:** Guaranteed on-campus for freshmen. Coed dorms, special housing for disabled, apartments, wellness housing available. $200 nonrefundable deposit. Off-campus housing for athletes. **Activities:** Pep band, campus ministries, choral groups, drama, international student organizations, literary magazine, music ensembles, student government, Christian volunteers, criminal justice club, forensic investigation association, student nurses association, Student in Free Enterprise, student social work organization, Campus Crusade for Christ, culinary club, student radiologic technologist association.

Athletics. NAIA. **Intercollegiate:** Basketball M, cheerleading, cross-country, soccer, track and field, volleyball W. **Intramural:** Basketball, bowling, football (non-tackle), soccer, volleyball W. **Team name:** Cougars.

Student services. Adult student services, alcohol/substance abuse counseling, chaplain/spiritual director, career counseling, student employment services, financial aid counseling, personal counseling, placement for graduates, veterans' counselor. **Physically disabled:** Services for visually, hearing impaired.

Contact. E-mail: gomsu@mountainstate.edu
Phone: (304) 929-1433 Toll-free number: (800) 766-6067
Fax: (304) 253-3463
Tammy Toney, Director of the Admissions Process, Mountain State University, 410 Neville Street, Beckley, WV 25801

Ohio Valley University
Vienna, West Virginia
www.ovu.edu   **CB code: 5519**

- Private 4-year university and liberal arts college affiliated with Church of Christ
- Residential campus in small city
- 462 degree-seeking undergraduates: 5% part-time, 45% women, 6% African American, 3% Hispanic American, 5% international
- 39 degree-seeking graduate students
- 46% of applicants admitted
- SAT or ACT (ACT writing optional) required

General. Founded in 1960. Regionally accredited. **Degrees:** 88 bachelor's, 32 associate awarded; master's offered. **Location:** 95 miles from Columbus, 120 miles from Pittsburgh. **Calendar:** Semester, limited summer session. **Full-time faculty:** 22 total; 68% have terminal degrees, 4% minority, 32% women. **Part-time faculty:** 53 total; 28% have terminal degrees, 51% women. **Class size:** 87% < 20, 13% 20-39.

Freshman class profile. 870 applied, 397 admitted, 147 enrolled.

Mid 50% test scores			
SAT critical reading:	430-590	GPA 2.0-2.99:	35%
SAT math:	430-540	Rank in top quarter:	15%
SAT writing:	420-560	Rank in top tenth:	8%
ACT composite:	18-24	Return as sophomores:	67%
GPA 3.75 or higher:	9%	Out-of-state:	58%
GPA 3.50-3.74:	13%	Live on campus:	86%
GPA 3.0-3.49:	34%	International:	3%

Basis for selection. School achievement record, test scores and reference considered. Essay, interview recommended.

High school preparation. 12 units recommended. Recommended units include English 3, mathematics 3, social studies 2, history 1, science 3 (laboratory 1).

2011-2012 Annual costs. Tuition/fees: $16,960. Room/board: $6,886. Books/supplies: $1,000. Personal expenses: $800.

Financial aid. Non-need-based: Scholarships awarded for academics, alumni affiliation, athletics, job skills, leadership, music/drama.

Application procedures. Admission: No deadline. $20 fee, may be waived for applicants with need. Admission notification on a rolling basis. **Financial aid:** Priority date 2/15; no closing date. FAFSA required. Applicants notified on a rolling basis starting 3/15; must reply within 4 week(s) of notification.

Academics. Bible course required of full-time students each semester. **Special study options:** Cooperative education, double major, dual enrollment of high school students, ESL, honors, independent study, internships, student-designed major, study abroad, teacher certification program, Washington semester, weekend college. Degree completion programs and special certifications. **Credit/placement by examination:** AP, CLEP, IB, SAT, ACT, institutional tests. 30 credit hours maximum toward associate degree, 30 toward bachelor's. Challenge course testing. **Support services:** Learning center, pre-admission summer program, reduced course load, remedial instruction, study skills assistance, tutoring.

Majors. Business: Accounting, business admin, human resources, non-profit/public. **Computer sciences:** Information technology. **Education:** General, elementary, English, mathematics, multi-level teacher, physical, science, secondary, social studies. **Liberal arts:** Arts/sciences. **Philosophy/religion:** Religion. **Psychology:** General. **Theology:** Bible.

Most popular majors. Business/marketing 48%, education 21%, liberal arts 9%, theological studies 11%.

Computing on campus. 44 workstations in dormitories, library, computer center. Dormitories wired for high-speed internet access and linked to campus network. Commuter students can connect to campus network. Online library, repair service, wireless network available.

Student life. Freshman orientation: Mandatory. Preregistration for classes offered. One-week session held in late August. **Policies:** Chapel/assembly attendance required 3 times a week. Religious observance required. **Housing:** Guaranteed on-campus for all undergraduates. Single-sex dorms, apartments, wellness housing available. $150 deposit, deadline 8/20. **Activities:** Bands, choral groups, drama, literary magazine, music ensembles, musical theater, student government, student newspaper, symphony orchestra, prospective ministers and prospective missionaries clubs, women's club, Diversity at the University club, ACEPP.

Athletics. NCAA. **Intercollegiate:** Baseball M, basketball, cross-country, golf, lacrosse M, soccer, softball W, volleyball W, wrestling M. **Intramural:** Basketball, bowling, cross-country, football (non-tackle), soccer, softball, table tennis, track and field, volleyball. **Team name:** Fighting Scots.

Student services. Adult student services, alcohol/substance abuse counseling, chaplain/spiritual director, career counseling, student employment services, financial aid counseling, health services, minority student services, personal counseling, placement for graduates.

Contact. E-mail: admissions@ovu.edu
Phone: (304) 865-6200 Toll-free number: (877) 446-8668
Fax: (304) 865-6175
Larry Lyons, Director of Admissions, Ohio Valley University, One Campus View Drive, Vienna, WV 26105

Salem International University
Salem, West Virginia
www.salemu.edu   **CB code: 5608**

- For-profit 4-year university and liberal arts college
- Residential campus in rural community
- 568 degree-seeking undergraduates

General. Founded in 1888. Regionally accredited. Established in 1888 as Salem College, Salem International University has a strong tradition of academic excellence and innovation. Our beautiful 100-acre campus is nestled in the Appalachian mountains of West Virginia. **Degrees:** 29 bachelor's, 13 associate awarded; master's offered. **Location:** 12 miles from Clarksburg, 125 miles from Pittsburgh. **Calendar:** Semester, limited summer session. **Full-time faculty:** 20 total. **Part-time faculty:** 28 total. **Class size:** 77% < 20, 17% 20-39, 6% 40-49.

Freshman class profile.

Out-of-state:	46%	Fraternities:	5%
Live on campus:	90%	Sororities:	8%

Basis for selection. School achievement record, test scores, counselor recommendations most important. Essay, interview recommended. **Home schooled:** State high school equivalency certificate required.

High school preparation. 16 units recommended. Recommended units include English 4, mathematics 2, social studies 3, science 2 and foreign language 2.

2011-2012 Annual costs. Tuition/fees: $14,100. Room/board: $6,600. Books/supplies: $660. Personal expenses: $320.

Financial aid. Non-need-based: Scholarships awarded for academics.

Application procedures. Admission: No deadline. $20 fee, may be waived for applicants with need. Admission notification on a rolling basis. **Financial aid:** Priority date 4/15; no closing date. FAFSA required. Applicants notified on a rolling basis starting 2/15; must reply within 4 week(s) of notification.

Academics. In keeping with college's mission to foster global awareness, all students required to complete international core curriculum. **Special study options:** Accelerated study, distance learning, double major, independent study, internships, student-designed major, study abroad, teacher certification program. **Credit/placement by examination:** AP, CLEP, IB, institutional tests. 24 credit hours maximum toward bachelor's degree. **Support services:** Learning center, remedial instruction, study skills assistance, tutoring, writing center.

Majors. Biology: General. **Business:** Business admin. **Computer sciences:** General, computer science. **Education:** General, multi-level teacher, secondary. **Liberal arts:** Arts/sciences. **Protective services:** Criminal justice.

Most popular majors. Business/marketing 44%, computer/information sciences 26%, liberal arts 13%.

Computing on campus. 50 workstations in library, computer center. Dormitories wired for high-speed internet access and linked to campus network. Commuter students can connect to campus network. Online library, helpline, wireless network available.

Student life. Freshman orientation: Available, $30 fee. Preregistration for classes offered. Program includes introduction to international aspects of college. Special orientation for international students with U.S. life-skills training. **Policies:** Unless local resident, freshmen and sophomores required to live on-campus. **Housing:** Guaranteed on-campus for all undergraduates. Coed dorms, single-sex dorms, wellness housing available. $50 fully refundable deposit. Private rooms subject to availability. **Activities:** Choral groups, international student organizations, student government, student newspaper, Gamma Beta Phi honor society, Alpha Phi Omega fraternity service organization, Campus Crusade for Christ, Rainbow Alliance, international woman's alliance, Christian Student Fellowship, Indian student association, Chinese student association.

Athletics. NCAA. **Intercollegiate:** Baseball M, basketball, golf, soccer, softball W, tennis M, volleyball W, water polo. **Intramural:** Basketball, football (non-tackle), racquetball, skiing M, soccer, swimming, table tennis, tennis, volleyball. **Team name:** Tigers.

Student services. Services for economically disadvantaged, financial aid counseling.

Contact. E-mail: admissions@salemu.edu
Phone: (888) 235-5024 Toll-free number: (888) 235-5024
Fax: (304) 326-1592
Andrew Anderson, Vice President, Recruiting and Marketing, Salem International University, 223 West Main Street, Salem, WV 26426

Shepherd University
Shepherdstown, West Virginia
www.shepherd.edu

CB member
CB code: 5615

- Public 4-year university
- Commuter campus in small town
- 3,836 degree-seeking undergraduates: 9% part-time, 58% women, 7% African American, 2% Asian American, 3% Hispanic American, 1% Native American
- 153 degree-seeking graduate students
- 87% of applicants admitted
- SAT or ACT (ACT writing optional) required
- 46% graduate within 6 years; 33% enter graduate study

General. Founded in 1871. Regionally accredited. **Degrees:** 648 bachelor's awarded; master's offered. **ROTC:** Air Force. **Location:** 8 miles from Martinsburg; 70 miles from Washington, DC. **Calendar:** Semester, extensive summer session. **Full-time faculty:** 134 total; 87% have terminal degrees, 13% minority, 42% women. **Part-time faculty:** 213 total; 27% have terminal degrees, 7% minority, 51% women. **Class size:** 51% < 20, 46% 20-39, 2% 40-49, less than 1% 50-99. **Special facilities:** Computer-controlled theater, recital hall with concert grand piano, recording studio, nursery school, 3 theaters, Civil War center, observatory, legislative studies center, nursing building, center for contemporary arts.

Freshman class profile. 2,056 applied, 1,798 admitted, 794 enrolled.

Mid 50% test scores			
SAT critical reading:	450-560	GPA 3.0-3.49:	33%
SAT math:	450-550	GPA 2.0-2.99:	31%
ACT composite:	19-24	End year in good standing:	70%
GPA 3.75 or higher:	21%	Return as sophomores:	68%
GPA 3.50-3.74:	14%	Out-of-state:	59%
		Live on campus:	39%

Basis for selection. 2.0 GPA and 19 ACT/910 SAT (exclusive of Writing) required. Essays and recommendations optional but important. Interview required for honors program and nursing applicants; recommended for others. Audition required for music; portfolio required for art majors. **Home schooled:** Transcript of courses and grades required. Portfolio of completed work required.

High school preparation. College-preparatory program recommended. 21 units required. Required units include English 4, mathematics 4, social studies 2, history 1, science 3 (laboratory 3), foreign language 2, visual/performing arts 1 and academic electives 6. History unit must include US history; science unit must include biology. All science courses must be college preparatory laboratory sciences.

2011-2012 Annual costs. Tuition/fees: $5,554; $14,418 out-of-state. Room/board: $8,130. Books/supplies: $1,100. Personal expenses: $1,000.

2011-2012 Financial aid. Need-based: 750 full-time freshmen applied for aid; 462 were judged to have need; 450 of these received aid. Average need met was 78%. Average scholarship/grant was $5,362; average loan $3,330. 53% of total undergraduate aid awarded as scholarships/grants, 47% as loans/jobs. **Non-need-based:** Awarded to 1,407 full-time undergraduates, including 453 freshmen. Scholarships awarded for academics, art, athletics, job skills, leadership, minority status, music/drama, state residency.

Application procedures. Admission: Priority date 2/1; no deadline. $45 fee, may be waived for applicants with need. Admission notification on a rolling basis beginning on or about 9/1. Must reply by May 1 or within 3 week(s) if notified thereafter. **Financial aid:** Priority date 3/1; no closing date. FAFSA required. Applicants notified on a rolling basis starting 3/15; must reply within 3 week(s) of notification.

Academics. Special study options: Cooperative education, double major, honors, independent study, internships, liberal arts/career combination, study abroad, teacher certification program, Washington semester. **Credit/placement by examination:** AP, CLEP, IB, SAT, ACT, institutional tests. 32 credit hours maximum toward bachelor's degree. No limit for students pursuing Regents' Bachelor of Arts degree. **Support services:** Learning center, remedial instruction, study skills assistance, tutoring.

Majors. Biology: General. **Business:** Accounting, business admin. **Communications:** Communications/speech/rhetoric. **Computer sciences:** General, applications programming. **Conservation:** General, environmental studies. **Education:** Elementary, secondary. **English:** English lit. **Foreign languages:** Spanish. **Health services:** Nursing (RN). **History:** General. **Human services:** Social work. **Math:** General. **Parks/recreation:** General. **Physical sciences:** Chemistry. **Psychology:** General. **Social sciences:** Economics, political science, sociology. **Visual/performing arts:** Art, music. **Work/family studies:** General.

Most popular majors. Business/marketing 18%, education 13%, health sciences 7%, liberal arts 14%, parks/recreation 7%, social sciences 6%, visual/performing arts 7%.

Computing on campus. 370 workstations in library, computer center, student center. Dormitories wired for high-speed internet access and linked to campus network. Commuter students can connect to campus network. Online course registration, helpline, student web hosting, wireless network available.

Student life. Freshman orientation: Mandatory, $75 fee. Preregistration for classes offered. 2 day sessions held in June and July for students and parents. August orientation conducted on Thursday and/or Friday and Saturday prior to first day of classes. **Housing:** Guaranteed on-campus for all undergraduates. Coed dorms, apartments, wellness housing available. $200 partly refundable deposit, deadline 6/1. Honors housing available. **Activities:** Bands, campus ministries, choral groups, dance, drama, international student organizations, literary magazine, music ensembles, musical theater, radio station, student government, student newspaper, symphony orchestra, College Republicans, College Democrats, United Brothers, Allies, Sistaz, Rotoract, Habitat for Humanity, Alpha Phi Omega, Fellowship of Christian Athletes, Common Ground.

Athletics. NCAA. **Intercollegiate:** Baseball M, basketball, football (tackle) M, golf M, lacrosse W, soccer, softball W, tennis, volleyball W. **Intramural:** Basketball, bowling, football (non-tackle), racquetball, soccer, softball, swimming, table tennis, tennis, volleyball, water polo, weight lifting, wrestling. **Team name:** Rams.

Student services. Adult student services, alcohol/substance abuse counseling, career counseling, services for economically disadvantaged, student employment services, financial aid counseling, health services, minority student services, personal counseling, placement for graduates, veterans' counselor. **Physically disabled:** Services for visually, speech, hearing impaired.

Contact. E-mail: admissions@shepherd.edu
Phone: (304) 876-5212 Toll-free number: (800) 344-5231 ext. 5212
Fax: (304) 876-5165
Randall Friend, Director of Admissions, Shepherd University, PO Box 5000, Shepherdstown, WV 25443-5000

University of Charleston
Charleston, West Virginia
www.ucwv.edu

CB member
CB code: 5419

- Private 4-year university and liberal arts college
- Residential campus in small city

- 999 degree-seeking undergraduates: 2% part-time, 60% women, 12% African American, 1% Asian American, 2% Hispanic American, 10% international
- 366 degree-seeking graduate students
- 57% of applicants admitted
- SAT or ACT (ACT writing recommended) required
- 52% graduate within 6 years

General. Founded in 1888. Regionally accredited. **Degrees:** 198 bachelor's, 21 associate awarded; master's, professional offered. **ROTC:** Army. **Location:** 200 miles from Pittsburgh, 200 miles from Charlotte, NC. **Calendar:** Semester, limited summer session. **Full-time faculty:** 79 total. **Part-time faculty:** 51 total. **Special facilities:** Sports medicine clinic, clinics at nearby hospital, entrepreneurship center.

Freshman class profile. 1,702 applied, 967 admitted, 245 enrolled.

Mid 50% test scores			
SAT critical reading:	440-540	Rank in top quarter:	46%
SAT math:	450-560	Rank in top tenth:	24%
ACT composite:	20-25	Return as sophomores:	61%
GPA 3.75 or higher:	34%	Out-of-state:	47%
GPA 3.50-3.74:	11%	Live on campus:	77%
GPA 3.0-3.49:	26%		
GPA 2.0-2.99:	28%		

Basis for selection. School achievement record and courses taken most important. Test scores, school recommendation, school and community activities, class rank, and interview also considered. GPA recomputed to reflect performance in academic subjects only. Essay, interview, portfolio recommended for all; audition required for music. **Home schooled:** If part of diploma-granting organization, list of coursework completed and level of performance required. Otherwise, detailed portfolio required and essay, 3 letters of reference, on-campus interview recommended. **Learning Disabled:** Documentation from professional within last 2 years required.

High school preparation. College-preparatory program recommended. 16 units recommended. Recommended units include English 4, mathematics 3, social studies 3, history 2, science 3 and foreign language 1. Algebra required for 4-year nursing program.

2011-2012 Annual costs. Tuition/fees: $25,000. Room/board: $9,000. Books/supplies: $1,500. Personal expenses: $250.

Financial aid. Non-need-based: Scholarships awarded for academics, alumni affiliation, art, athletics, leadership, music/drama, ROTC.

Application procedures. Admission: No deadline. $25 fee, may be waived for applicants with need, free for online applicants. Admission notification on a rolling basis beginning on or about 10/1. For most health science programs, application deadline is January 15, early decision recommended. **Financial aid:** Priority date 3/1; no closing date. FAFSA, institutional form required. Applicants notified on a rolling basis starting 3/1; must reply by 5/1 or within 4 week(s) of notification.

Academics. Students can fulfill course requirements at their own pace. **Special study options:** Combined bachelor's/graduate degree, double major, ESL, independent study, internships, liberal arts/career combination, student-designed major, study abroad, teacher certification program. **Credit/placement by examination:** AP, CLEP, IB, SAT, ACT, institutional tests. 30 credit hours maximum toward associate degree, 60 toward bachelor's. **Support services:** Learning center, reduced course load, remedial instruction, study skills assistance, tutoring, writing center.

Majors. Biology: General, biochemistry. **Business:** Accounting, business admin, finance. **Communications:** Media studies. **Education:** General, biology, elementary, English, health, physical, science, secondary, social studies, special ed. **Health services:** Athletic training, nursing (RN), predental, premedicine, prepharmacy, preveterinary, radiologic technology/medical imaging. **History:** General. **Human services:** Public policy. **Parks/recreation:** Sports admin. **Physical sciences:** Chemistry. **Psychology:** General. **Social sciences:** Political science. **Visual/performing arts:** Art, interior design.

Most popular majors. Biology 16%, business/marketing 26%, education 11%, health sciences 20%.

Computing on campus. Dormitories wired for high-speed internet access and linked to campus network. Commuter students can connect to campus network. Online library, helpline, student web hosting, wireless network available.

Student life. Freshman orientation: Mandatory. Preregistration for classes offered. **Policies:** On-campus housing required for dependent freshmen and sophomores not living with parents or legal guardian in local area. **Housing:** Guaranteed on-campus for freshmen. Coed dorms, special housing for disabled, apartments available. $100 fully refundable deposit,

deadline 5/1. Single rooms and suites available. **Activities:** Pep band, campus ministries, choral groups, dance, drama, international student organizations, music ensembles, Model UN, student government, student newspaper, honorary fraternities, Fellowship Christian Athletes, Young Republicans, College Democrats.

Athletics. NCAA. **Intercollegiate:** Baseball M, basketball, cheerleading, cross-country, football (tackle) M, golf M, rowing (crew) W, soccer, softball W, tennis, track and field W, volleyball W. **Intramural:** Basketball, bowling, football (non-tackle) M, tennis, volleyball. **Team name:** Golden Eagles.

Student services. Alcohol/substance abuse counseling, career counseling, student employment services, financial aid counseling, health services, legal services, personal counseling, placement for graduates.

Contact. E-mail: admissions@ucwv.edu
Phone: (304) 357-4750 Toll-free number: (800) 995-4682
Fax: (304) 357-4781
Joan Clark, Vice President for Admissions, University of Charleston, 2300 MacCorkle Avenue, SE, Charleston, WV 25304

West Liberty University
West Liberty, West Virginia
www.westliberty.edu   CB code: 5901

- Public 4-year university
- Residential campus in rural community
- 2,490 degree-seeking undergraduates: 8% part-time, 56% women
- 59 graduate students
- SAT or ACT with writing required

General. Founded in 1837. Regionally accredited. **Degrees:** 416 bachelor's, 34 associate awarded; master's offered. **Location:** 10 miles from Wheeling, 50 miles from Pittsburgh. **Calendar:** Semester, limited summer session. **Full-time faculty:** 134 total; 58% have terminal degrees, 7% minority, 42% women. **Part-time faculty:** 90 total; 22% have terminal degrees, 54% women. **Class size:** 55% < 20, 39% 20-39, 5% 40-49, less than 1% 50-99. **Special facilities:** Media arts center, rare book room, rare sheet music collection.

Freshman class profile.

Mid 50% test scores			
SAT critical reading:	420-530	Rank in top quarter:	33%
SAT math:	410-510	Rank in top tenth:	11%
SAT writing:	390-500	Return as sophomores:	66%
ACT composite:	18-23	Out-of-state:	29%
GPA 3.75 or higher:	25%	Live on campus:	79%
GPA 3.50-3.74:	15%	International:	1%
GPA 3.0-3.49:	30%	Fraternities:	2%
GPA 2.0-2.99:	30%	Sororities:	2%

Basis for selection. 2.0 GPA or 17 ACT or 810 SAT (exclusive of Writing) required. Audition required for music education; portfolio recommended for art.

High school preparation. College-preparatory program required. 17 units required. Required units include English 4, mathematics 4, social studies 2, history 1, (laboratory 3), foreign language 2 and academic electives 1. Math must be algebra I and higher. Social science must include American history.

2011-2012 Annual costs. Tuition/fees: $5,266; $13,140 out-of-state. Room/board: $7,440. Books/supplies: $1,420. Personal expenses: $1,682.

2010-2011 Financial aid. Need-based: 494 full-time freshmen applied for aid; 401 were judged to have need; 383 of these received aid. Average need met was 73%. Average scholarship/grant was $5,503; average loan $3,080. 54% of total undergraduate aid awarded as scholarships/grants, 46% as loans/jobs. **Non-need-based:** Awarded to 849 full-time undergraduates, including 272 freshmen. Scholarships awarded for academics, alumni affiliation, art, athletics, music/drama, state residency. **Additional information:** Non-need based student employment available at food service, college union, bookstore, and tutoring office. Resident assistant and campus security jobs also available.

Application procedures. Admission: No deadline. No application fee. Admission notification on a rolling basis beginning on or about 9/1. **Financial aid:** Priority date 3/1; no closing date. FAFSA required. Applicants notified on a rolling basis starting 3/1; must reply within 2 week(s) of notification.

Academics. Freshman experience course available. **Special study options:** Accelerated study, distance learning, double major, dual enrollment of high school students, external degree, honors, independent study, internships, liberal arts/career combination, student-designed major, study abroad, teacher

certification program, Washington semester. **Credit/placement by examination:** AP, CLEP, SAT, ACT, institutional tests. **Support services:** Reduced course load, remedial instruction, tutoring.

Majors. Biology: General, bacteriology, biotechnology. **Business:** General, accounting, banking/financial services, business admin, managerial economics, tourism promotion, tourism/travel. **Communications:** Communications/speech/rhetoric. **Computer sciences:** Information systems. **Education:** Art, biology, chemistry, early childhood, elementary, English, health, mathematics, mentally handicapped, music, physical, science, secondary, social science, special ed. **English:** English lit. **Health services:** Clinical lab science, dental hygiene. **History:** General. **Liberal arts:** General. **Math:** General. **Parks/recreation:** Exercise sciences. **Physical sciences:** Chemistry. **Protective services:** Criminal justice. **Psychology:** General. **Social sciences:** General, political science, sociology. **Visual/performing arts:** Commercial/advertising art.

Most popular majors. Business/marketing 24%, education 20%, health sciences 13%, liberal arts 11%, security/protective services 7%.

Computing on campus. 300 workstations in dormitories, library, computer center, student center. Dormitories wired for high-speed internet access and linked to campus network. Commuter students can connect to campus network. Online course registration, helpline, repair service available.

Student life. Freshman orientation: Mandatory, $30 fee. Preregistration for classes offered. Held Friday through Sunday before first day of classes. **Housing:** Guaranteed on-campus for all undergraduates. Coed dorms, single-sex dorms, special housing for disabled, apartments, fraternity/sorority housing available. $100 fully refundable deposit, deadline 6/1. Honors residence for students who meet criteria. **Activities:** Bands, campus ministries, choral groups, dance, drama, international student organizations, literary magazine, music ensembles, musical theater, radio station, student government, student newspaper, TV station, Amnesty International, Students for Life, B-Pride, Electric Square, non-traditional student support group, Students in Free Enterprise, Students for Unity and Understanding.

Athletics. NCAA. **Intercollegiate:** Baseball M, basketball, cross-country, football (tackle) M, golf, softball W, tennis, track and field, volleyball W, wrestling M. **Intramural:** Basketball, golf, handball M, racquetball, softball, table tennis, tennis, volleyball. **Team name:** Hilltoppers.

Student services. Alcohol/substance abuse counseling, chaplain/spiritual director, career counseling, student employment services, financial aid counseling, health services, minority student services, personal counseling, placement for graduates, veterans' counselor. **Physically disabled:** Services for visually, hearing impaired.

Contact. E-mail: admissions@westliberty.edu
Phone: (304) 336-8076 Toll-free number: (800) 732-6204
Fax: (304) 336-8403
Brenda King, Director of Admissions and Recruitment, West Liberty University, 208 University Drive, West Liberty, WV 26074

West Virginia State University
Institute, West Virginia
www.wvstateu.edu
CB member
CB code: 5903

- Public 4-year liberal arts and teachers college
- Commuter campus in small town
- 1,955 full-time, degree-seeking undergraduates
- 55 graduate students
- 80% of applicants admitted
- SAT or ACT with writing required

General. Founded in 1891. Regionally accredited. **Degrees:** 379 bachelor's awarded; master's offered. **ROTC:** Army. **Location:** 8 miles from Charleston. **Calendar:** Semester, limited summer session. **Full-time faculty:** 120 total; 79% have terminal degrees, 27% minority, 38% women. **Part-time faculty:** 72 total; 11% minority, 50% women.

Freshman class profile. 1,672 applied, 1,330 admitted, 309 enrolled.

Basis for selection. School achievement record and test scores considered. Interview recommended for academically weak applicants to regents bachelor of arts programs. **Home schooled:** Applicants must provide detailed description of home school curriculum.

High school preparation. 14 units required. Required units include English 4, mathematics 2, social studies 3, science 3 (laboratory 2) and foreign language 2.

2011-2012 Annual costs. Tuition/fees: $5,038; $11,778 out-of-state. Tuition for students residing in border counties is $9,192. Room/board: $6,302. Books/supplies: $948. Personal expenses: $2,951.

Financial aid. Non-need-based: Scholarships awarded for academics, athletics, ROTC, state residency.

Application procedures. Admission: No deadline. $20 fee. Admission notification on a rolling basis. **Financial aid:** Priority date 3/1, closing date 6/15. FAFSA required. Applicants notified on a rolling basis starting 2/15; must reply within 2 week(s) of notification.

Academics. Special study options: Cooperative education, cross-registration, distance learning, double major, dual enrollment of high school students, external degree, honors, internships, teacher certification program, weekend college. Nontraditional life experience degree program. **Credit/placement by examination:** AP, CLEP, IB, institutional tests. **Support services:** Learning center, reduced course load, remedial instruction, study skills assistance, tutoring.

Majors. Biology: General. **Business:** General, accounting, banking/financial services, business admin. **Communications:** Communications/speech/rhetoric. **Computer sciences:** Computer science. **Education:** General, art, early childhood, elementary, English, gifted/talented, health, mathematics, mentally handicapped, middle, music, physical, science, secondary, social studies, special ed. **English:** English lit, technical writing. **Health services:** Recreational therapy. **History:** General. **Human services:** Social work. **Liberal arts:** Arts/sciences. **Math:** General, applied. **Parks/recreation:** Facilities management. **Physical sciences:** Chemistry, physics. **Protective services:** Criminal justice, police science. **Psychology:** General. **Social sciences:** Economics, political science, sociology. **Visual/performing arts:** Ceramics, commercial/advertising art, drawing, fiber arts, music, painting, photography, printmaking, sculpture, studio arts.

Most popular majors. Business/marketing 18%, communications/journalism 9%, education 10%, health sciences 6%, liberal arts 22%, psychology 7%, security/protective services 8%.

Computing on campus. 200 workstations in dormitories, library, computer center, student center. Dormitories linked to campus network. Commuter students can connect to campus network. Helpline available.

Student life. Freshman orientation: Mandatory. Preregistration for classes offered. **Housing:** Guaranteed on-campus for freshmen. Single-sex dorms, apartments available. **Activities:** Bands, choral groups, drama, film society, literary magazine, music ensembles, radio station, student government, student newspaper, TV station, DNA science club, pre-alumni club, College Students for Christ, NAACP, access awareness council, Fellowship for Christian Athletes, poetry workshop.

Athletics. NCAA. **Intercollegiate:** Baseball M, basketball, football (tackle) M, golf, softball W, tennis, track and field, volleyball W. **Intramural:** Basketball, bowling, football (tackle) M, softball, swimming, tennis, volleyball. **Team name:** Yellow Jackets.

Student services. Career counseling, student employment services, health services, on-campus daycare, personal counseling, placement for graduates, veterans' counselor. **Physically disabled:** Services for visually, speech, hearing impaired.

Contact. E-mail: admissions@wvstateu.edu
Phone: (304) 766-3221 Toll-free number: (800) 987-2112
Fax: (304) 766-4104
Trina Sweeney, Director, West Virginia State University, Campus Box 197, Institute, WV 25112-1000

West Virginia University
Morgantown, West Virginia
www.wvu.edu
CB member
CB code: 5904

- Public 4-year university
- Residential campus in small city
- 22,189 degree-seeking undergraduates: 5% part-time, 45% women, 4% African American, 2% Asian American, 3% Hispanic American, 3% international
- 6,906 degree-seeking graduate students
- 85% of applicants admitted
- SAT or ACT with writing required
- 59% graduate within 6 years

General. Founded in 1867. Regionally accredited. Regional centers at Charleston, Clarksburg, Potomac State College in Keyser, Shepherdstown,

WVU Institute of Technology, and West Liberty. Health Sciences Center operates division in Charleston. **Degrees:** 4,060 bachelor's awarded; master's, professional, doctoral offered. **ROTC:** Army, Air Force. **Location:** 70 miles from Pittsburgh, 200 miles from Baltimore. **Calendar:** Semester, extensive summer session. **Full-time faculty:** 976 total; 89% have terminal degrees, 13% minority, 41% women. **Part-time faculty:** 348 total; 36% have terminal degrees, 6% minority, 51% women. **Class size:** 33% < 20, 38% 20-39, 11% 40-49, 11% 50-99, 8% >100. **Special facilities:** Personal rapid transit system, arboretum, planetarium, herbarium, pharmacy museum, 2 art galleries, art museum, 7 experimental farms, 3 forests, software development center, mineral and energy resources museum, black culture and research center.

Freshman class profile. 15,815 applied, 13,415 admitted, 5,022 enrolled.

Mid 50% test scores		Rank in top quarter:	45%
SAT critical reading:	490-570	Rank in top tenth:	20%
SAT math:	480-590	Return as sophomores:	78%
ACT composite:	21-26	Out-of-state:	54%
GPA 3.75 or higher:	29%	Live on campus:	84%
GPA 3.50-3.74:	16%	International:	2%
GPA 3.0-3.49:	30%	Fraternities:	7%
GPA 2.0-2.99:	25%	Sororities:	7%

Basis for selection. GPA and SAT/ACT scores most important. 2.0 GPA and 910 SAT (exclusive of Writing) or 19 ACT required of state residents. 2.5 GPA and 990 SAT or 21 ACT required of nonresidents. Applicants with high GPA, high test scores, or special talents (athletics or the arts) who do not meet all admissions criteria may be considered on individual basis. Up to 5% of each incoming class may be admitted under this special policy. Interview required for dental hygiene; audition required for drama, music; portfolio required for art. Essay required for some programs. **Home schooled:** Typed manuscript of completed courses required, including content of courses, measurement of student assessment, grades, and number of credits earned for each course. Description should be separated by year of study and be signed by the person who administrated the curriculum. West Virginia homeschooled students who are applying for West Virginia PROMISE Scholarship or West Virginia Higher Education Grant must take GED.

High school preparation. College-preparatory program recommended. 17 units required. Required units include English 4, mathematics 4, social studies 3, science 3 (laboratory 3), foreign language 2 and visual/performing arts 1.

2011-2012 Annual costs. Tuition/fees: $5,674; $17,844 out-of-state. Room/board: $8,404. Books/supplies: $1,140. Personal expenses: $972.

2011-2012 Financial aid. **Need-based:** 4,153 full-time freshmen applied for aid; 3,530 were judged to have need; 3,425 of these received aid. Average need met was 72%. Average scholarship/grant was $4,876; average loan $3,385. 51% of total undergraduate aid awarded as scholarships/grants, 49% as loans/jobs. **Non-need-based:** Awarded to 12,584 full-time undergraduates, including 4,516 freshmen. Scholarships awarded for academics, alumni affiliation, art, athletics, leadership, minority status, music/drama, state residency.

Application procedures. **Admission:** Priority date 3/1; deadline 8/1. $25 fee ($45 out-of-state), may be waived for applicants with need. Admission notification on a rolling basis. **Financial aid:** Closing date 3/1. FAFSA required. Applicants notified on a rolling basis starting 4/15; must reply within 4 week(s) of notification.

Academics. **Special study options:** Accelerated study, combined bachelor's/graduate degree, cooperative education, distance learning, double major, ESL, exchange student, external degree, honors, independent study, internships, semester at sea, student-designed major, study abroad, teacher certification program, Washington semester. **Credit/placement by examination:** AP, CLEP, IB, SAT, ACT, institutional tests. 38 credit hours maximum toward bachelor's degree. **Support services:** Learning center, pre-admission summer program, reduced course load, remedial instruction, study skills assistance, tutoring, writing center.

Majors. **Architecture:** Landscape. **Biology:** General, exercise physiology. **Business:** Accounting, business admin, finance, management information systems, managerial economics, marketing. **Communications:** Advertising, broadcast journalism, communications/speech/rhetoric, journalism, media studies, public relations. **Computer sciences:** Computer science. **Conservation:** Forest management, wildlife/wilderness, wood science. **Education:** Agricultural, elementary, physical. **Engineering:** Aerospace, chemical, civil, computer, electrical, industrial, mechanical, mining, petroleum. **English:** English lit. **Foreign languages:** General. **General:** Agronomy, animal sciences, business, economics, horticultural science, plant sciences, soil science. **Health services:** Athletic training, audiology/speech pathology, clinical lab science, dental hygiene, nursing (RN), prenursing, prepharmacy. **History:** General. **Human services:** Social work. **Liberal arts:** Arts/sciences. **Math:** General. **Parks/recreation:** Exercise sciences, facilities management, health/fitness. **Philosophy/religion:** Philosophy. **Physical sciences:** Chemistry, geology, physics. **Protective services:** Criminalistics, forensics. **Psychology:** General. **Social sciences:** Economics, geography, political science, sociology.

Visual/performing arts: General, art, art history/conservation, design, dramatic, music, theater history. **Work/family studies:** Child development, food/nutrition.

Most popular majors. Biology 7%, business/marketing 12%, communications/journalism 8%, engineering/engineering technologies 11%, health sciences 8%, interdisciplinary studies 10%, liberal arts 6%, social sciences 8%.

Computing on campus. 3,000 workstations in dormitories, library, computer center, student center. Dormitories wired for high-speed internet access and linked to campus network. Commuter students can connect to campus network. Online course registration, online library, helpline, repair service, student web hosting, wireless network available.

Student life. **Freshman orientation:** Available, $57 fee. Preregistration for classes offered. Held during summer; several options ranging in length and fees. **Policies:** Anti-hazing, affirmative action and nondiscrimination policies. Mandatory freshmen housing program places faculty residence hall leaders adjacent to residence halls. Freshmen not permitted cars on campus. **Housing:** Guaranteed on-campus for freshmen. Coed dorms, single-sex dorms, special housing for disabled, apartments, fraternity/sorority housing, wellness housing available. $225 partly refundable deposit, deadline 5/1. Special interest floors available. **Activities:** Bands, campus ministries, choral groups, dance, drama, international student organizations, literary magazine, music ensembles, musical theater, radio station, student government, student newspaper, symphony orchestra, TV station, WVU Habitat for Humanity, Sierra Student Coalition, Hillel House, Zeta Delat Phi, Circle K, Campus Crusade for Christ, College Republicans, Muslim Student Association, Newman Club, Baptist Campus Ministry.

Athletics. NCAA. **Intercollegiate:** Baseball M, basketball, cross-country W, diving, football (tackle) M, gymnastics W, rifle, rowing (crew) W, soccer, swimming, tennis W, track and field W, volleyball W, wrestling M. **Intramural:** Badminton, basketball, bowling, football (non-tackle), racquetball, soccer, tennis W, volleyball. **Team name:** Mountaineers.

Student services. Adult student services, alcohol/substance abuse counseling, chaplain/spiritual director, career counseling, services for economically disadvantaged, student employment services, financial aid counseling, health services, legal services, minority student services, on-campus daycare, personal counseling, placement for graduates, veterans' counselor, women's services. **Physically disabled:** Services for visually, speech, hearing impaired.

Contact. E-mail: go2wvu@mail.wvu.edu
Phone: (304) 293-2121 Toll-free number: (800) 344-9881
Fax: (304) 293-3080
Marlynn Potts, Director of Admissions and Records, West Virginia University, Admissions and Records Office, Morgantown, WV 26506-6009

West Virginia University Institute of Technology
Montgomery, West Virginia
www.wvutech.edu — CB code: 5902

- Public 4-year engineering and liberal arts college
- Commuter campus in small town
- 1,160 degree-seeking undergraduates
- 28% of applicants admitted
- SAT or ACT with writing required

General. Founded in 1895. Regionally accredited. **Degrees:** 143 bachelor's awarded. **ROTC:** Army. **Location:** 30 miles from Charleston. **Calendar:** Semester, limited summer session. **Full-time faculty:** 98 total. **Part-time faculty:** 35 total. **Class size:** 64% < 20, 31% 20-39, 3% 40-49, 2% 50-99, less than 1% >100. **Special facilities:** Hiking trail.

Freshman class profile. 1,432 applied, 408 admitted, 263 enrolled.

Basis for selection. 20 GPA and 18 ACT or 870 SAT (exclusive of Writing) required. Engineering applicants must have 19 ACT math. Interview recommended for engineering. **Home schooled:** Students may be required to take GED exam.

High school preparation. College-preparatory program recommended. 17 units required. Required and recommended units include English 4, mathematics 4, social studies 3, history 3, science 3 (laboratory 3). 2 algebra, 1 plane geometry, 1 advanced math required of engineering majors. 1 algebra, 1 chemistry, 1 biology required of dental hygiene majors. 2 laboratory sciences, including chemistry, 2 higher mathematics required for nursing program.

2011-2012 Annual costs. Tuition/fees: $5,344; $13,444 out-of-state. Room/board: $8,130. Books/supplies: $1,140. Personal expenses: $972.

Financial aid. Additional information: Room and board may be deferred for up to 60 days. First 50% due in 30 days.

Application procedures. Admission: No deadline. No application fee. Admission notification on a rolling basis. Must reply by May 1 or within 2 week(s) if notified thereafter. **Financial aid:** Closing date 3/1. FAFSA required. Applicants notified on a rolling basis; must reply within 3 week(s) of notification.

Academics. Special study options: Combined bachelor's/graduate degree, cooperative education, distance learning, double major, dual enrollment of high school students, external degree, independent study, internships, liberal arts/career combination, student-designed major. Cooperative programs in engineering and business. **Credit/placement by examination:** AP, CLEP, SAT, ACT, institutional tests. 90 credit hours maximum toward bachelor's degree. **Support services:** Learning center, pre-admission summer program, reduced course load, remedial instruction, study skills assistance, tutoring.

Majors. Biology: General. **Business:** Business admin. **Computer sciences:** General, computer science, programming. **Education:** Physical. **Engineering:** Chemical, civil, electrical, mechanical. **History:** General. **Math:** General. **Physical sciences:** Chemistry.

Computing on campus. 400 workstations in library, computer center, student center. Dormitories wired for high-speed internet access and linked to campus network. Online course registration, online library, helpline, wireless network available.

Student life. Freshman orientation: Available. Preregistration for classes offered. **Housing:** Guaranteed on-campus for all undergraduates. Coed dorms, single-sex dorms, fraternity/sorority housing available. $200 deposit. **Activities:** Marching band, campus ministries, drama, music ensembles, student government, student newspaper, Christian student union, Alpha Phi Omega service fraternity.

Athletics. NAIA. **Intercollegiate:** Baseball M, basketball, football (tackle) M, golf M, soccer, softball W, swimming, volleyball W, wrestling M. **Intramural:** Basketball, cross-country, softball, swimming, volleyball. **Team name:** Golden Bears.

Student services. Adult student services, career counseling, student employment services, financial aid counseling, health services, personal counseling, placement for graduates, veterans' counselor. **Physically disabled:** Services for speech impaired.

Contact. E-mail: admissions@wvutech.edu
Phone: (304) 442-3167 Toll-free number: (888) 554-8324
Fax: (304) 442-3067
Reeta Piirala-Skoglund, Director of Admissions, West Virginia University Institute of Technology, 405 Fayette Pike, Montgomery, WV 25136-2436

West Virginia Wesleyan College
Buckhannon, West Virginia
www.wvwc.edu   CB code: 5905

- Private 4-year liberal arts college affiliated with United Methodist Church
- Residential campus in small town
- 1,349 degree-seeking undergraduates: 1% part-time, 53% women, 10% African American, 1% Asian American, 2% Hispanic American, 5% international
- 91 degree-seeking graduate students
- 78% of applicants admitted
- SAT or ACT (ACT writing optional) required
- 52% graduate within 6 years; 26% enter graduate study

General. Founded in 1890. Regionally accredited. **Degrees:** 272 bachelor's awarded; master's offered. **Location:** 115 miles from Charleston, 135 miles from Pittsburgh. **Calendar:** Semester, limited summer session. **Full-time faculty:** 78 total. **Class size:** 54% < 20, 42% 20-39, 3% 40-49, less than 1% 50-99. **Special facilities:** Planetarium, botany museum, herbarium, greenhouse, performing arts center, research center.

Freshman class profile. 1,743 applied, 1,361 admitted, 407 enrolled.

Mid 50% test scores			
SAT critical reading:	410-520	GPA 2.0-2.99:	23%
SAT math:	440-550	Rank in top quarter:	49%
SAT writing:	390-520	Rank in top tenth:	22%
ACT composite:	20-26	Return as sophomores:	67%
GPA 3.75 or higher:	31%	Out-of-state:	40%
GPA 3.50-3.74:	17%	Live on campus:	95%
GPA 3.0-3.49:	28%	International:	6%

Basis for selection. School achievement record and test scores required. Essay, interview recommended for all; audition recommended for drama, music; portfolio recommended for art. **Home schooled:** Transcript of courses and grades, state high school equivalency certificate required.

High school preparation. College-preparatory program recommended. 15 units recommended. Recommended units include English 4, mathematics 2, social studies 2, history 2, science 2 (laboratory 2), foreign language 1, computer science 1 and visual/performing arts 1.

2011-2012 Annual costs. Tuition/fees: $24,964. Room/board: $7,390. Books/supplies: $2,500. Personal expenses: $2,500.

2011-2012 Financial aid. Non-need-based: Scholarships awarded for academics, alumni affiliation, art, athletics, leadership, music/drama, religious affiliation.

Application procedures. Admission: Priority date 3/1; no deadline. $35 fee, may be waived for applicants with need, free for online applicants. Admission notification on a rolling basis beginning on or about 9/15. Must reply by May 1 or within 4 week(s) if notified thereafter. **Financial aid:** Priority date 2/15; no closing date. FAFSA required. Applicants notified on a rolling basis starting 3/1; must reply within 4 week(s) of notification.

Academics. Special study options: Combined bachelor's/graduate degree, double major, ESL, exchange student, honors, independent study, internships, liberal arts/career combination, New York semester, student-designed major, study abroad, teacher certification program, Washington semester. **Credit/placement by examination:** AP, CLEP, IB, SAT, ACT, institutional tests. **Support services:** Learning center, reduced course load, remedial instruction, study skills assistance, tutoring, writing center.

Majors. Biology: General. **Business:** Accounting, business admin, international, managerial economics, marketing. **Communications:** Communications/speech/rhetoric, public relations. **Computer sciences:** General, computer science, information systems. **Conservation:** Environmental science. **Education:** General, art, biology, chemistry, elementary, English, health, history, kindergarten/preschool, learning disabled, mathematics, music, physical, science, secondary, social studies, special ed. **Engineering:** Pre-engineering. **English:** Creative writing, English lit. **Health services:** Athletic training, nursing (RN), predental, premedicine, prepharmacy, preveterinary. **History:** General. **Math:** General. **Parks/recreation:** Exercise sciences, health/fitness. **Philosophy/religion:** Philosophy, religion. **Physical sciences:** Chemistry, physics. **Protective services:** Law enforcement admin. **Psychology:** General. **Social sciences:** Economics, international relations, political science, sociology. **Theology:** Religious ed. **Visual/performing arts:** Art, ceramics, dramatic, drawing, graphic design, music, painting, photography, studio arts, studio arts management, theater arts management.

Most popular majors. Business/marketing 22%, education 9%, health sciences 7%, parks/recreation 10%, physical sciences 6%, psychology 8%, visual/performing arts 7%.

Computing on campus. PC or laptop required. Dormitories wired for high-speed internet access and linked to campus network. Commuter students can connect to campus network. Online library, helpline, repair service, wireless network available.

Student life. Freshman orientation: Mandatory, $200 fee. Preregistration for classes offered. Held weekend before fall class registration; provides programs for new students and parents. **Policies:** Full-time students required to live on campus unless married, living with parents, or have received written permission from the Housing Committee to live off campus. **Housing:** Guaranteed on-campus for all undergraduates. Coed dorms, single-sex dorms, special housing for disabled, apartments, fraternity/sorority housing available. $200 deposit. **Activities:** Bands, campus ministries, choral groups, dance, drama, international student organizations, literary magazine, music ensembles, musical theater, opera, radio station, student government, student newspaper, TV station, Christian life council, Fellowship of Christian Athletes, Alpha Phi Omega service fraternity, black student union, College Republicans, Young Democrats, green club, Wesleyan service corps.

Athletics. NCAA. **Intercollegiate:** Baseball M, basketball, cross-country, football (tackle) M, golf, soccer, softball W, swimming, tennis, track and field, volleyball W. **Intramural:** Basketball, football (non-tackle), racquetball, softball, table tennis, volleyball, water polo M. **Team name:** Bobcats.

Student services. Alcohol/substance abuse counseling, chaplain/spiritual director, career counseling, financial aid counseling, health services, minority student services, personal counseling, placement for graduates. **Physically disabled:** Services for visually, speech, hearing impaired.

Contact. E-mail: admission@wvwc.edu
Phone: (304) 473-8510 Toll-free number: (800) 722-9933
Fax: (304) 473-8108
John Waltz, Director of Admission, West Virginia Wesleyan College, 59 College Avenue, Buckhannon, WV 26201-2998

Wheeling Jesuit University

Wheeling, West Virginia

CB member

www.wju.edu

CB code: 5906

- Private 4-year university and liberal arts college affiliated with Roman Catholic Church
- Residential campus in small city
- 935 degree-seeking undergraduates: 10% part-time, 57% women, 3% African American, 1% Asian American, 1% Hispanic American, 4% international
- 357 degree-seeking graduate students
- 66% of applicants admitted
- SAT or ACT (ACT writing optional) required
- 58% graduate within 6 years; 26% enter graduate study

General. Founded in 1954. Regionally accredited. **Degrees:** 215 bachelor's awarded; master's, professional offered. **Location:** 55 miles from Pittsburgh; 125 miles from Columbus, OH. **Calendar:** Semester, limited summer session. **Full-time faculty:** 87 total; 67% have terminal degrees, 6% minority, 48% women. **Part-time faculty:** 67 total; 30% have terminal degrees, 34% women. **Class size:** 73% < 20, 27% 20-39.

Freshman class profile. 1,237 applied, 819 admitted, 195 enrolled.

Mid 50% test scores			
SAT critical reading:	450-540	**GPA 2.0-2.99:**	10%
SAT math:	460-580	**Rank in top quarter:**	48%
SAT writing:	450-550	**Rank in top tenth:**	18%
ACT composite:	21-26	**End year in good standing:**	71%
GPA 3.75 or higher:	37%	**Return as sophomores:**	71%
GPA 3.50-3.74:	25%	**Out-of-state:**	61%
GPA 3.0-3.49:	28%	**Live on campus:**	84%
		International:	5%

Basis for selection. High school GPA, quality of courses taken, and test scores most important. Some exception made to minimum when warranted by high school record. Personal recommendations and extracurricular activities important. In-state and out-of-state applicants treated equally. Interview, essay recommended. **Learning Disabled:** Students need to submit written documentation of disability.

High school preparation. College-preparatory program recommended. 15 units required. Required and recommended units include English 4, mathematics 2, social studies 2, history 2, science 1 (laboratory 1), foreign language 2 and academic electives 6. Applicants for programs in natural sciences should have 1 biology and 1 chemistry. Applicants preparing for future study in physical therapy doctorate program should have 3 years of college preparatory math and 3 years of lab science, including physics.

2012-2013 Annual costs. Tuition/fees (projected): $25,640. There will be no increase in tuition in 2012-2013. Freshmen will pay $5,000 for room and board in 2012-2013, a reduction of $4,028, on average, from 2011-2012. Room/board: $5,000. Books/supplies: $1,300. Personal expenses: $800.

2011-2012 Financial aid. Need-based: 183 full-time freshmen applied for aid; 154 were judged to have need; 154 of these received aid. Average need met was 76%. Average scholarship/grant was $6,480; average loan $4,685. 48% of total undergraduate aid awarded as scholarships/grants, 52% as loans/jobs. **Non-need-based:** Awarded to 830 full-time undergraduates, including 213 freshmen. Scholarships awarded for academics, alumni affiliation, athletics, music/drama.

Application procedures. Admission: No deadline. $25 fee, may be waived for applicants with need, free for online applicants. Admission notification on a rolling basis beginning on or about 9/1. Must reply by May 1 or within 2 week(s) if notified thereafter. **Financial aid:** No deadline. FAFSA required. Applicants notified on a rolling basis starting 3/15; must reply within 2 week(s) of notification.

Academics. Special study options: Combined bachelor's/graduate degree, cooperative education, distance learning, double major, dual enrollment of high school students, ESL, exchange student, honors, independent study, internships, liberal arts/career combination, semester at sea, student-designed major, study abroad, teacher certification program, United Nations semester, Washington semester. **Credit/placement by examination:** AP, CLEP, IB, SAT, ACT, institutional tests. 30 credit hours maximum toward bachelor's degree. **Support services:** Learning center, remedial instruction, study skills assistance, tutoring, writing center.

Majors. Biology: General. **Business:** Accounting, business admin, international, management science, marketing, organizational leadership. **Communications:** General, digital media, media studies, persuasive communications, public relations. **Computer sciences:** Computer science. **Education:** General, biology, business, chemistry, computer, early childhood, elementary, English, foreign languages, French, history, mathematics, middle, multilevel teacher, physics, psychology, science, secondary, social science, social studies, Spanish, special ed. **English:** British lit, creative writing, English lit. **Foreign languages:** French, Spanish. **Health services:** Health care admin, nuclear medical technology, nursing (RN), respiratory therapy technology. **History:** General. **Liberal arts:** Arts/sciences. **Math:** General. **Philosophy/religion:** Philosophy. **Physical sciences:** Chemistry, physics. **Protective services:** Criminal justice. **Psychology:** General. **Social sciences:** International relations, political science. **Theology:** Theology. **Visual/performing arts:** Cinematography, dramatic, music, studio arts.

Most popular majors. Business/marketing 22%, health sciences 34%, psychology 10%, social sciences 9%.

Computing on campus. 274 workstations in dormitories, library, computer center, student center. Dormitories wired for high-speed internet access and linked to campus network. Commuter students can connect to campus network. Online course registration, online library, helpline, wireless network available.

Student life. Freshman orientation: Mandatory, $250 fee. Preregistration for classes offered. 1.5-day session held in summer; 3-day session held prior to beginning of fall semester. **Housing:** Guaranteed on-campus for all undergraduates. Coed dorms, single-sex dorms, special housing for disabled, apartments, cooperative housing, wellness housing available. $100 fully refundable deposit. **Activities:** Bands, campus ministries, choral groups, dance, drama, film society, international student organizations, literary magazine, musical theater, student government, student newspaper, TV station, Appalachian Experience Club, Circle K International, Justice and Peace in Our Times, political science club, Students for Life, Mother Jones House, music ministry, liturgical ministry, praise and worship, small prayer groups.

Athletics. NCAA. **Intercollegiate:** Baseball M, basketball, cross-country, golf, lacrosse, soccer, softball W, swimming, track and field, volleyball W. **Intramural:** Basketball, soccer, softball, tennis, volleyball. **Team name:** Cardinals.

Student services. Adult student services, alcohol/substance abuse counseling, chaplain/spiritual director, career counseling, student employment services, financial aid counseling, health services, personal counseling, placement for graduates. **Physically disabled:** Services for visually, hearing impaired.

Contact. E-mail: admiss@wju.edu
Phone: (304) 243-2359 Toll-free number: (800) 624-6992
Fax: (304) 243-2397
Kimberly Klaus, Director of Undergraduate Enrollment, Wheeling Jesuit University, 316 Washington Avenue, Wheeling, WV 26003-6295

Wisconsin

Alverno College
Milwaukee, Wisconsin
www.alverno.edu

CB member
CB code: 1012

◆ Private 4-year liberal arts college for women affiliated with Roman Catholic Church

◆ Commuter campus in very large city

◆ 2,046 degree-seeking undergraduates: 28% part-time, 100% women, 18% African American, 5% Asian American, 16% Hispanic American, 1% Native American, 1% international

◆ 350 degree-seeking graduate students

◆ 82% of applicants admitted

◆ SAT or ACT (ACT writing optional), application essay required

◆ 40% graduate within 6 years; 15% enter graduate study

General. Founded in 1887. Regionally accredited. **Degrees:** 395 bachelor's, 3 associate awarded; master's offered. **ROTC:** Army, Air Force. **Location:** 5 miles from downtown. **Calendar:** Semester, limited summer session. **Full-time faculty:** 120 total; 92% have terminal degrees, 8% minority, 78% women. **Part-time faculty:** 135 total; 67% have terminal degrees, 9% minority, 82% women. **Class size:** 68% < 20, 32% 20-39. **Special facilities:** Multimedia productions facility, independent science research areas, native prairie, clinical nursing resource center.

Freshman class profile. 529 applied, 433 admitted, 199 enrolled.

Mid 50% test scores			
ACT composite:	16-21	GPA 2.0-2.99:	53%
GPA 3.75 or higher:	9%	Return as sophomores:	70%
GPA 3.50-3.74:	6%	Out-of-state:	9%
GPA 3.0-3.49:	26%	Live on campus:	30%
		Sororities:	1%

Basis for selection. Admissions based on review of transcripts, GPA, academic units, standardized tests, essay, and Communication Placement Assessment results. Audition required for music therapy; portfolio required for studio art. **Home schooled:** Letter of recommendation (nonparent) required. Portfolio of work required.

High school preparation. College-preparatory program required. 17 units required. Required and recommended units include English 4, mathematics 3, social studies 3, science 3, foreign language 2 and academic electives 4.

2011-2012 Annual costs. Tuition/fees: $21,063. Room/board: $6,966. Books/supplies: $1,050. Personal expenses: $1,760.

2011-2012 Financial aid. Need-based: 187 full-time freshmen applied for aid; 184 were judged to have need; 184 of these received aid. Average scholarship/grant was $14,508; average loan $2,856. 73% of total undergraduate aid awarded as scholarships/grants, 27% as loans/jobs. **Non-need-based:** Awarded to 1,214 full-time undergraduates, including 186 freshmen. Scholarships awarded for academics, alumni affiliation.

Application procedures. Admission: No deadline. $20 fee, may be waived for applicants with need, free for online applicants. Admission notification on a rolling basis beginning on or about 9/1. Must reply by May 1 or within 2 week(s) if notified thereafter. **Financial aid:** Priority date 3/15; no closing date. FAFSA, institutional form required. Applicants notified on a rolling basis starting 3/15; must reply within 2 week(s) of notification.

Academics. Required internships in all majors provide research opportunities through federal government, local organizations and businesses. Students in every major area spend from 8 to 12 hours per week for one semester in field internship. Students also have opportunities to do service learning through individual courses. Degrees with honor awarded based on outstanding achievement and application of learning in service to others. **Special study options:** Double major, independent study, internships, semester at sea, student-designed major, study abroad, teacher certification program, Washington semester, weekend college. **Credit/placement by examination:** AP, CLEP, IB, institutional tests. Each student's background and experience are looked at on an individual basis by the department faculty. **Support services:** Learning center, pre-admission summer program, reduced course load, remedial instruction, study skills assistance, tutoring, writing center.

Majors. Area/ethnic studies: Women's. **Biology:** General, molecular. **Business:** Business admin, international. **Communications:** Communications/speech/rhetoric. **Computer sciences:** General. **Conservation:** Environmental science. **Education:** General, art, elementary, English, middle, music, science, social studies. **English:** English lit. **Health services:** Art therapy, music therapy. **History:** General. **Human services:** Community org/advocacy. **Liberal arts:** Arts/sciences. **Math:** General. **Philosophy/religion:** Philosophy, religion. **Physical sciences:** Chemistry. **Psychology:** General. **Social sciences:** General, international relations, political science, sociology. **Visual/performing arts:** Art, music.

Most popular majors. Business/marketing 19%, communications/journalism 6%, education 6%, health sciences 41%.

Computing on campus. 610 workstations in dormitories, library, computer center. Dormitories wired for high-speed internet access and linked to campus network. Commuter students can connect to campus network. Online course registration, online library, student web hosting, wireless network available.

Student life. Freshman orientation: Mandatory. Preregistration for classes offered. Overnight program held during the summer. **Housing:** $100 nonrefundable deposit. All housing smoke-free. Semi-apartment living within residence halls available to older students. **Activities:** Campus ministries, choral groups, dance, drama, international student organizations, literary magazine, music ensembles, Model UN, radio station, student government, student newspaper, Circle K, Co-Exist, Black Students United, Hispanic Women of Alverno, Muslim student association, Women of Asian Ethnicity, Alverno Student Education Organization, Student Nurses Association, Students in Free Enterprise, global studies club.

Athletics. NCAA. **Intercollegiate:** Basketball W, cross-country W, soccer W, softball W, tennis W, volleyball W. **Intramural:** Basketball W, volleyball W. **Team name:** Alverno Inferno.

Student services. Adult student services, chaplain/spiritual director, career counseling, financial aid counseling, health services, on-campus daycare, personal counseling. **Physically disabled:** Services for visually, speech, hearing impaired.

Contact. E-mail: admissions@alverno.edu
Phone: (414) 382-6101 Toll-free number: (800) 933-3401
Fax: (414) 382-6055
Dianna Gaebler, Executive Director of Admissions, Alverno College, 3400 South 43rd Street, Milwaukee, WI 53234-3922

Bellin College
Green Bay, Wisconsin
www.bellincollege.edu

CB code: 1046

◆ Private 4-year nursing college
◆ Commuter campus in small city

General. Founded in 1909. Regionally accredited. **Location:** 120 miles from Milwaukee. **Calendar:** Semester.

Annual costs/financial aid. Tuition/fees (2011-2012): $20,454. Reported costs are for bachelor's program in nursing. Books/supplies: $1,517. Personal expenses: $665. Need-based financial aid available to full-time and part-time students.

Contact. Phone: (920) 433-6650
Director of Admissions, 3201 Eaton Road, Green Bay, WI

Beloit College
Beloit, Wisconsin
www.beloit.edu

CB member
CB code: 1059

◆ Private 4-year liberal arts college
◆ Residential campus in large town
◆ 1,293 degree-seeking undergraduates: 1% part-time, 58% women, 3% African American, 2% Asian American, 8% Hispanic American, 9% international
◆ 71% of applicants admitted
◆ SAT or ACT (ACT writing optional), application essay required
◆ 76% graduate within 6 years

General. Founded in 1846. Regionally accredited. **Degrees:** 300 bachelor's awarded. **Location:** 60 miles from Madison, 90 miles from Chicago. **Calendar:** Semester, limited summer session. **Full-time faculty:** 114 total; 96% have terminal degrees, 14% minority, 52% women. **Part-time faculty:** 13 total; 46% have terminal degrees, 8% minority, 46% women. **Class size:**

70% < 20, 30% 20-39, less than 1% 50-99. **Special facilities:** LEED-certified science center, anthropology museum, art museum, observatory, 2 nature preserves, social science research laboratory, immunology laboratory, 2 electron microscopes, superconducting NMR, ICAP spectrometer, marketing research center, center for entrepreneurial leadership.

Freshman class profile. 2,107 applied, 1,487 admitted, 315 enrolled.

Mid 50% test scores			
SAT critical reading:	560-690	GPA 2.0-2.99:	9%
SAT math:	550-660	Rank in top quarter:	53%
ACT composite:	25-32	Rank in top tenth:	36%
GPA 3.75 or higher:	26%	Return as sophomores:	86%
GPA 3.50-3.74:	25%	Out-of-state:	81%
GPA 3.0-3.49:	40%	Live on campus:	100%
		International:	9%

Basis for selection. Rigor of high school curriculum and high school record most important. Test scores, recommendations, essays, interviews, and extracurricular activities also very important. Interview recommended. **Home schooled:** Letter of recommendation (nonparent) required.

High school preparation. College-preparatory program required. Recommended units include English 4, mathematics 4, social studies 4, science 3 and foreign language 2.

2011-2012 Annual costs. Tuition/fees: $36,674. Room/board: $7,502. Books/supplies: $600. Personal expenses: $900.

2011-2012 Financial aid. **Need-based:** 268 full-time freshmen applied for aid; 224 were judged to have need; 223 of these received aid. Average need met was 92%. Average scholarship/grant was $25,516; average loan $5,549. 72% of total undergraduate aid awarded as scholarships/grants, 28% as loans/jobs. **Non-need-based:** Awarded to 341 full-time undergraduates, including 81 freshmen. Scholarships awarded for academics, leadership, minority status, music/drama.

Application procedures. **Admission:** Priority date 1/15; no deadline. $35 fee, may be waived for applicants with need. Admission notification on a rolling basis beginning on or about 2/15. Must reply by May 1 or within 2 week(s) if notified thereafter. **Financial aid:** Closing date 3/1. FAFSA, institutional form required. Applicants notified on a rolling basis starting 4/1; must reply by 5/1 or within 2 week(s) of notification.

Academics. Heavy emphasis placed on international education, interdisciplinary study, and experiential learning. **Special study options:** Combined bachelor's/graduate degree, double major, ESL, exchange student, independent study, internships, liberal arts/career combination, student-designed major, study abroad, teacher certification program, urban semester, Washington semester. Field schools in archeology and geology, Center for Language Studies, intensive summer foreign language program, reserved admission to Medical College of Wisconsin. 3-2 programs in engineering, nursing, and forestry. **Credit/placement by examination:** AP, CLEP, IB. 32 credit hours maximum toward bachelor's degree. **Support services:** Learning center, study skills assistance, tutoring, writing center.

Majors. **Area/ethnic studies:** Women's. **Biology:** General, biochemistry, cellular/molecular, environmental, molecular. **Business:** Business admin, managerial economics. **Computer sciences:** Computer science. **Conservation:** Environmental science, forestry. **Education:** General, art, science. **Engineering:** General. **English:** Creative writing, English lit, rhetoric/composition. **Foreign languages:** General, classics, comparative lit, East Asian, French, German, Russian, Spanish. **Health services:** Nursing (RN). **History:** General. **Liberal arts:** Arts/sciences. **Math:** General. **Philosophy/religion:** Philosophy, religion. **Physical sciences:** Chemistry, geology, physics. **Psychology:** General. **Social sciences:** Anthropology, economics, international relations, political science, sociology. **Visual/performing arts:** Art history/conservation, dance, dramatic, music.

Most popular majors. Biology 7%, English 7%, foreign language 12%, physical sciences 6%, psychology 6%, social sciences 33%, visual/performing arts 7%.

Computing on campus. 300 workstations in dormitories, library, computer center, student center. Dormitories wired for high-speed internet access and linked to campus network. Commuter students can connect to campus network. Helpline, student web hosting, wireless network available.

Student life. **Freshman orientation:** Mandatory. Preregistration for classes offered. Held 10 days prior to fall semester. **Policies:** Residence hall system is student managed. **Housing:** Guaranteed on-campus for all undergraduates. Coed dorms, single-sex dorms, apartments, cooperative housing, fraternity/sorority housing, wellness housing available. Special-interest housing available to students that have completed at least one semester. **Activities:** Jazz band, choral groups, dance, drama, film society, international student organizations, literary magazine, music ensembles, musical theater, radio station, student government, student newspaper, symphony orchestra, TV station, volunteer community tutoring service, women's center program,

Gay Alliance, Young Republicans, Young Democrats, science fiction and fantasy association, Voces Latinas, Black Students United.

Athletics. NCAA. **Intercollegiate:** Baseball M, basketball, cross-country, diving, football (tackle) M, lacrosse M, soccer, softball W, swimming, tennis, track and field, volleyball W. **Intramural:** Basketball, fencing, handball, ice hockey M, racquetball, rugby M, sailing, soccer, softball, swimming, tennis, volleyball, water polo. **Team name:** Bucs.

Student services. Chaplain/spiritual director, career counseling, services for economically disadvantaged, student employment services, financial aid counseling, health services, minority student services, on-campus daycare, personal counseling, placement for graduates, women's services. **Physically disabled:** Services for visually, hearing impaired.

Contact. E-mail: admiss@beloit.edu
Phone: (608) 363-2500 Toll-free number: (800) 923-5648
Fax: (608) 363-2075
Nancy Benedict, Vice President of Enrollment Services, Beloit College, 700 College Street, Beloit, WI 53511-5595

Cardinal Stritch University
Milwaukee, Wisconsin
www.stritch.edu   **CB code: 1100**

▶ Private 4-year university affiliated with Roman Catholic Church
▶ Commuter campus in very large city
▶ 2,795 degree-seeking undergraduates
▶ 1,945 graduate students
▶ 48% of applicants admitted
▶ SAT or ACT (ACT writing optional), application essay required

General. Founded in 1937. Regionally accredited. **Degrees:** 540 bachelor's, 200 associate awarded; master's, doctoral offered. **Location:** 7 miles from downtown, 85 miles from Chicago. **Calendar:** Semester, limited summer session. **Full-time faculty:** 103 total. **Part-time faculty:** 350 total. **Class size:** 91% < 20, 8% 20-39, less than 1% 40-49, less than 1% 50-99.

Freshman class profile. 955 applied, 455 admitted, 197 enrolled.

Mid 50% test scores			
		ACT composite:	19-24
SAT critical reading:	470-570	Out-of-state:	20%
SAT math:	460-700	Live on campus:	63%

Basis for selection. Admissions based on 2.0 GPA, 20 ACT or 840 SAT (exclusive of Writing). Interview, activities, and recommendations considered. Conditional admission available to applicants not meeting all admissions criteria. Institutional tests used for admission of academically weak students. Interview recommended for all; portfolio recommended for art; audition recommended for music and theatre.

High school preparation. College-preparatory program recommended. 16 units required; 18 recommended. Required and recommended units include English 4, mathematics 2-3, social studies 1, history 1, science 2-3, foreign language 2 and academic electives 4.

2011-2012 Annual costs. Tuition/fees: $23,330. Room/board: $6,895. Books/supplies: $700. Personal expenses: $1,200.

2010-2011 Financial aid. **Need-based:** 63% of total undergraduate aid awarded as scholarships/grants, 37% as loans/jobs. **Non-need-based:** Scholarships awarded for academics, art, athletics, music/drama.

Application procedures. **Admission:** Closing date 8/1. No application fee. **Financial aid:** Priority date 4/15; no closing date. FAFSA, institutional form required. Applicants notified on a rolling basis starting 3/1; must reply within 3 week(s) of notification.

Academics. **Special study options:** Accelerated study, distance learning, double major, exchange student, honors, independent study, internships, study abroad, teacher certification program. **Credit/placement by examination:** AP, CLEP, IB, institutional tests. 30 credit hours maximum toward associate degree, 60 toward bachelor's. **Support services:** Learning center, reduced course load, remedial instruction, study skills assistance, tutoring, writing center.

Majors. **Biology:** General. **Business:** General, accounting, business admin, international, management information systems. **Communications:** Communications/speech/rhetoric. **Computer sciences:** Computer science. **Education:** General, special ed. **English:** Creative writing, English lit. **Foreign languages:** Spanish. **Health services:** Nursing (RN). **History:** General. **Math:** General. **Parks/recreation:** Sports admin. **Philosophy/religion:** Religion. **Physical sciences:** Chemistry. **Psychology:** General. **Social sciences:** General, political science, sociology. **Theology:** Pastoral counseling, youth

ministry. **Visual/performing arts:** Art, commercial/advertising art, dramatic, music performance, photography, studio arts.

Most popular majors. Business/marketing 77%, education 6%.

Computing on campus. 236 workstations in dormitories, library, computer center, student center. Dormitories wired for high-speed internet access and linked to campus network. Commuter students can connect to campus network. Online library, helpline, wireless network available.

Student life. Freshman orientation: Mandatory. Preregistration for classes offered. Week-long program held prior to start of classes. **Housing:** Coed dorms available. **Activities:** Bands, campus ministries, choral groups, dance, drama, literary magazine, music ensembles, Model UN, musical theater, radio station, student government, student newspaper, students for political awareness, multicultural committee, Asian club, black student union, united Latino organization, Fellowship of Christian Students, service corps, peer helpers.

Athletics. NAIA. **Intercollegiate:** Baseball M, basketball, cross-country, soccer, softball W, volleyball. **Intramural:** Basketball, volleyball. **Team name:** Wolves.

Student services. Adult student services, alcohol/substance abuse counseling, chaplain/spiritual director, career counseling, student employment services, financial aid counseling, health services, personal counseling, placement for graduates, veterans' counselor. **Physically disabled:** Services for hearing impaired.

Contact. E-mail: admityou@stritch.edu
Phone: (414) 410-4040 Toll-free number: (800) 347-8822 ext. 4040
Fax: (414) 410-4058
Kirk Messer, Director of Admission, Cardinal Stritch University, 6801 North Yates Road, Box 516, Milwaukee, WI 53217-7516

Carroll University
Waukesha, Wisconsin
www.carrollu.edu   CB code: 1101

- Private 4-year university and liberal arts college affiliated with Presbyterian Church (USA)
- Residential campus in small city
- 3,142 degree-seeking undergraduates: 11% part-time, 64% women
- 266 graduate students
- 81% of applicants admitted
- SAT or ACT (ACT writing optional) required
- 59% graduate within 6 years

General. Founded in 1846. Regionally accredited. **Degrees:** 563 bachelor's awarded; master's, professional offered. **ROTC:** Army, Air Force. **Location:** 15 miles from Milwaukee. **Calendar:** Semester, extensive summer session. **Full-time faculty:** 127 total; 68% have terminal degrees, 4% minority, 51% women. **Part-time faculty:** 203 total; 14% have terminal degrees, 65% women. **Class size:** 57% < 20, 39% 20-39, 1% 40-49, 3% 50-99, less than 1% >100. **Special facilities:** Scientific study and conservancy, class 1 trout stream, wetland and upland habitats.

Freshman class profile. 2,657 applied, 2,156 admitted, 809 enrolled.

Mid 50% test scores			
ACT composite:	20-26	Return as sophomores:	78%
GPA 3.75 or higher:	27%	Out-of-state:	24%
GPA 3.50-3.74:	25%	Live on campus:	86%
GPA 3.0-3.49:	31%	International:	1%
GPA 2.0-2.99:	17%	Fraternities:	4%
Rank in top quarter:	53%	Sororities:	9%

Mid 50% test scores · Rank in top tenth: 25%

Basis for selection. School achievement record most important, followed by test scores. Recommendations, essay, interview considered. Essay, interview recommended for all; audition recommended for music, theater; portfolio recommended for art. **Home schooled:** Transcript of courses and grades required.

High school preparation. College-preparatory program recommended. 17 units recommended. Recommended units include English 4, mathematics 4, social studies 3, history 3, science 3 (laboratory 2).

2011-2012 Annual costs. Tuition/fees: $25,247. Room/board: $7,736. Books/supplies: $1,060. Personal expenses: $1,363.

2011-2012 Financial aid. Need-based: 783 full-time freshmen applied for aid; 693 were judged to have need; 693 of these received aid. Average need met was 100%. Average scholarship/grant was $15,412; average loan

$3,485. 75% of total undergraduate aid awarded as scholarships/grants, 25% as loans/jobs. **Non-need-based:** Awarded to 2,636 full-time undergraduates, including 775 freshmen. Scholarships awarded for academics, alumni affiliation, art, leadership, music/drama, ROTC.

Application procedures. Admission: Priority date 3/15; no deadline. No application fee. Admission notification on a rolling basis beginning on or about 8/1. **Financial aid:** No deadline. FAFSA required. Applicants notified on a rolling basis starting 2/15; must reply by 5/1 or within 2 week(s) of notification.

Academics. Education majors must maintain 2.75 GPA in major and teaching minors. Nursing students must maintain 2.75 GPA. Six majors available for pre-physical therapy programs. **Special study options:** Combined bachelor's/graduate degree, distance learning, double major, dual enrollment of high school students, ESL, exchange student, honors, independent study, internships, liberal arts/career combination, semester at sea, student-designed major, study abroad, teacher certification program, United Nations semester, Washington semester. **Credit/placement by examination:** AP, CLEP, IB, institutional tests. 24 credit hours maximum toward bachelor's degree. **Support services:** Learning center, pre-admission summer program, reduced course load, remedial instruction, study skills assistance, tutoring, writing center.

Majors. Area/ethnic studies: European. **Biology:** General, animal behavior, biochemistry. **Business:** Accounting, actuarial science, business admin, finance, human resources, management information systems, marketing, organizational behavior, small business admin. **Communications:** Communications/speech/rhetoric, journalism, organizational, public relations. **Communications technology:** Graphics, printing management. **Computer sciences:** General, information systems. **Conservation:** General, environmental science. **Education:** General, art, biology, chemistry, early childhood, elementary, English, foreign languages, geography, health, history, mathematics, middle, music, physical, psychology, science, social science, social studies, Spanish. **Engineering:** Applied physics, software. **English:** Creative writing, English lit. **Foreign languages:** Spanish. **Health services:** Athletic training, clinical lab science, nursing (RN), predental, premedicine, prepharmacy, preveterinary, public health ed, radiologic technology/medical imaging. **History:** General, European. **Math:** General, applied. **Parks/recreation:** Exercise sciences, facilities management, health/fitness. **Philosophy/religion:** Religion. **Physical sciences:** Chemistry. **Protective services:** Criminal justice, forensics. **Psychology:** General. **Social sciences:** Political science, sociology. **Visual/performing arts:** Art, commercial/advertising art, dramatic, music, photography, studio arts.

Most popular majors. Business/marketing 17%, education 12%, health sciences 9%, parks/recreation 12%, psychology 8%.

Computing on campus. 250 workstations in dormitories, library, computer center, student center. Dormitories wired for high-speed internet access and linked to campus network. Commuter students can connect to campus network. Online course registration, online library, helpline, student web hosting, wireless network available.

Student life. Freshman orientation: Mandatory, $250 fee. Preregistration for classes offered. **Policies:** Freshmen not permitted cars on campus. **Housing:** Guaranteed on-campus for freshmen. Coed dorms, single-sex dorms, apartments available. $100 nonrefundable deposit. **Activities:** Bands, campus ministries, choral groups, dance, drama, international student organizations, literary magazine, music ensembles, radio station, student government, student newspaper, Bible study group, Intervarsity Christian Fellowship, Fellowship of Christian Athletes, black student union, Queers & Allies, Questions & Answers, international experience club, Latin American student organization, University Republicans, College Democrats.

Athletics. NCAA. **Intercollegiate:** Baseball M, basketball, cross-country, football (tackle) M, golf, soccer, swimming, tennis, track and field, volleyball W. **Intramural:** Basketball, bowling, cheerleading, football (non-tackle), soccer, tennis, volleyball. **Team name:** Pioneers.

Student services. Adult student services, alcohol/substance abuse counseling, chaplain/spiritual director, career counseling, student employment services, financial aid counseling, health services, minority student services, personal counseling, placement for graduates. **Physically disabled:** Services for visually, hearing impaired.

Contact. E-mail: info@carrollu.edu
Phone: (262) 524-7220 Toll-free number: (800) 227-7655
Fax: (262) 951-3037
Jim Wiseman, Vice President for Enrollment, Carroll University, 100 North East Avenue, Waukesha, WI 53186-9988

Carthage College
Kenosha, Wisconsin
www.carthage.edu

CB member
CB code: 1103

- Private 4-year liberal arts college affiliated with Evangelical Lutheran Church in America
- Residential campus in small city
- 2,924 degree-seeking undergraduates: 13% part-time, 54% women, 4% African American, 2% Asian American, 5% Hispanic American, 1% Native American
- 86 degree-seeking graduate students
- 69% of applicants admitted
- SAT or ACT (ACT writing optional) required
- 59% graduate within 6 years

General. Founded in 1847. Regionally accredited. **Degrees:** 584 bachelor's awarded; master's offered. **ROTC:** Army, Air Force. **Location:** 60 miles from Chicago, 30 miles from Milwaukee. **Calendar:** 4-1-4, limited summer session. **Full-time faculty:** 150 total. **Part-time faculty:** 96 total. **Class size:** 54% < 20, 45% 20-39, 1% 40-49. **Special facilities:** Planetarium, paleontology institute, center for children's literature, undergraduate science research laboratory, computer/mathematics research laboratory, greenhouse, arboretum, Audubon sanctuary, geographic information systems (GIS) lab, 24-hour cyber-cafe.

Freshman class profile. 6,919 applied, 4,774 admitted, 668 enrolled.

Mid 50% test scores		GPA 3.0-3.49:	29%
ACT composite:	22-27	GPA 2.0-2.99:	31%
GPA 3.75 or higher:	22%	Return as sophomores:	77%
GPA 3.50-3.74:	18%	Out-of-state:	72%

Basis for selection. High school GPA (calculated based on academic courses) and test scores most important. Interview recommended; audition recommended for music and theater. **Home schooled:** Transcript of courses and grades required.

High school preparation. 18 units recommended. Recommended units include English 4, mathematics 3, social studies 3, science 3 (laboratory 2), foreign language 2 and academic electives 3.

2011-2012 Annual costs. Tuition/fees: $31,300. Room/board: $8,600. Books/supplies: $1,600. Personal expenses: $1,500.

Financial aid. Non-need-based: Scholarships awarded for academics, alumni affiliation, art, leadership, minority status, music/drama, religious affiliation.

Application procedures. Admission: Priority date 12/11; no deadline. $35 fee, may be waived for applicants with need. Admission notification on a rolling basis. Must reply by May 1 or within 2 week(s) if notified thereafter. **Financial aid:** Priority date 2/15; no closing date. FAFSA required. Applicants notified on a rolling basis starting 3/1.

Academics. All students take 2-course combination of oral and written communication skills and cross-cultural studies. Students must also complete symposium and senior thesis. **Special study options:** Accelerated study, combined bachelor's/graduate degree, cross-registration, double major, dual enrollment of high school students, honors, independent study, internships, liberal arts/career combination, student-designed major, study abroad, teacher certification program, Washington semester. **Credit/placement by examination:** AP, CLEP, IB, institutional tests. 32 credit hours maximum toward bachelor's degree. **Support services:** Pre-admission summer program, reduced course load, study skills assistance, tutoring, writing center.

Majors. Area/ethnic studies: Asian. **Biology:** General, neuroscience. **Business:** Accounting, business admin, entrepreneurial studies, finance, marketing. **Communications:** Public relations. **Communications technology:** Graphics. **Computer sciences:** Computer science. **Conservation:** Environmental science. **Education:** Elementary, physical, special ed. **English:** English lit. **Foreign languages:** Chinese, classics, French, German, Japanese, Spanish. **Health services:** Athletic training. **History:** General. **Human services:** Social work. **Math:** General. **Parks/recreation:** Exercise sciences. **Philosophy/religion:** Philosophy, religion. **Physical sciences:** Chemistry, physics. **Protective services:** Police science. **Psychology:** General. **Social sciences:** General, economics, geography, international economics, political science, sociology. **Visual/performing arts:** Art history/conservation, dramatic, music, studio arts, theater design.

Most popular majors. Biology 6%, business/marketing 28%, communications/journalism 7%, education 10%, social sciences 8%, visual/performing arts 7%.

Computing on campus. 275 workstations in dormitories, library, computer center, student center. Dormitories wired for high-speed internet access and linked to campus network. Commuter students can connect to campus network. Online library, helpline, repair service, student web hosting, wireless network available.

Student life. Freshman orientation: Mandatory. Preregistration for classes offered. Held a few days immediately prior to start of classes. **Housing:** Guaranteed on-campus for freshmen. Coed dorms, single-sex dorms, apartments, fraternity/sorority housing, wellness housing available. $300 deposit, deadline 5/1. **Activities:** Bands, campus ministries, choral groups, dance, drama, film society, international student organizations, literary magazine, music ensembles, Model UN, musical theater, opera, radio station, student government, student newspaper, symphony orchestra, black student union, international friendship society, United Women of Color, Christian Fellowship, Latinos Unidos, Circle K International, College Republicans, Young Democrats.

Athletics. NCAA. **Intercollegiate:** Baseball M, basketball, cross-country, football (tackle) M, golf, lacrosse, soccer, softball W, swimming, tennis, track and field, volleyball, water polo W. **Intramural:** Basketball, football (non-tackle), racquetball, soccer, softball, volleyball. **Team name:** Red Men, Lady Reds.

Student services. Adult student services, alcohol/substance abuse counseling, chaplain/spiritual director, career counseling, student employment services, financial aid counseling, health services, personal counseling, placement for graduates, veterans' counselor.

Contact. E-mail: admissions@carthage.edu
Phone: (262) 551-6000 Toll-free number: (800) 351-4058
Fax: (262) 551-5762
Dean Clark, Admissions Director, Carthage College, 2001 Alford Park Drive, Kenosha, WI 53140-1994

Columbia College of Nursing
Glendale, Wisconsin
www.ccon.edu

CB code: 3409

- Private 4-year nursing college
- Commuter campus in very large city
- 155 degree-seeking undergraduates: 11% part-time, 92% women, 13% African American, 1% Asian American, 1% Hispanic American

General. Founded in 1901. Regionally accredited. **Degrees:** 57 bachelor's awarded. **Location:** 90 miles from Chicago, 70 miles from Madison. **Calendar:** Semester, limited summer session. **Full-time faculty:** 17 total; 24% have terminal degrees, 94% women. **Part-time faculty:** 3 total; 100% women. **Class size:** 64% < 20, 15% 20-39, 21% 40-49.

Basis for selection. Students are admitted as first semester juniors. They transfer 62 credits from another accredited institution of higher learning. Admission to nursing major requires 2.8 GPA and all prerequisites successfully completed with grade of C or better.

High school preparation. Required and recommended units include English 4, mathematics 1-2, science 2-3 and foreign language 2. Algebra required. Chemistry, biology required as science units.

2011-2012 Annual costs. Tuition/fees: $23,640. Books/supplies: $1,400. Personal expenses: $2,650.

2011-2012 Financial aid. Need-based: 45% of total undergraduate aid awarded as scholarships/grants, 55% as loans/jobs. **Non-need-based:** Scholarships awarded for academics.

Application procedures. Admission: Closing date 3/1 (receipt date). $25 fee, may be waived for applicants with need. Application must be submitted online. Admission notification on a rolling basis. **Financial aid:** No deadline.

Academics. Students complete their first 62 credits at another institution of higher learning and their last 62 credits at institution. **Special study options:** Independent study, study abroad. Cultural immersion options. **Credit/placement by examination:** AP, CLEP. **Support services:** Learning center, remedial instruction, study skills assistance, tutoring, writing center.

Majors. Health services: Nursing (RN).

Computing on campus. 45 workstations in library, computer center. Online library, wireless network available.

Student life. Activities: Student government, student newspaper, student nursing organization, nursing honor society.

Student services. Career counseling, financial aid counseling, health services, minority student services, personal counseling, placement for graduates.

Contact. E-mail: joua.xiong@ccon.edu
Phone: (414) 326-2334 Toll-free number: (800) Fax: (414) 326-2331
Youa Xiong, Registrar, Columbia College of Nursing, 4425 North Port
Washington Road, Glendale, WI 53212-1099

Concordia University Wisconsin
Mequon, Wisconsin
www.cuw.edu   **CB code: 1139**

- Private 4-year university and liberal arts college affiliated with Lutheran Church - Missouri Synod
- Residential campus in large town
- 4,177 degree-seeking undergraduates: 40% part-time, 66% women, 18% African American, 1% Asian American, 2% Hispanic American, 1% Native American, 1% international
- 3,051 degree-seeking graduate students
- 66% of applicants admitted
- ACT (writing optional) required
- 60% graduate within 6 years

General. Founded in 1881. Regionally accredited. **Degrees:** 659 bachelor's, 42 associate awarded; master's, professional, doctoral offered. **Location:** 15 miles from Milwaukee. **Calendar:** 4-1-4, limited summer session. **Full-time faculty:** 151 total; 74% have terminal degrees, 5% minority, 47% women. **Part-time faculty:** 244 total; 15% have terminal degrees, 6% minority, 68% women. **Class size:** 51% < 20, 45% 20-39, 1% 40-49, 2% 50-99, less than 1% >100. **Special facilities:** Access to Lake Michigan, Center for Environmental Studies.

Freshman class profile. 2,639 applied, 1,735 admitted, 560 enrolled.

Mid 50% test scores			
SAT critical reading:	420-560	GPA 2.0-2.99:	26%
SAT math:	450-550	Rank in top quarter:	43%
SAT writing:	440-530	Rank in top tenth:	17%
ACT composite:	20-26	Return as sophomores:	75%
GPA 3.75 or higher:	22%	Out-of-state:	35%
GPA 3.50-3.74:	15%	Live on campus:	90%
GPA 3.0-3.49:	36%	International:	2%

Basis for selection. School achievement record and test scores important. Essay, interview recommended; audition recommended for music.

High school preparation. College-preparatory program recommended. 16 units required. Required and recommended units include English 3-4, mathematics 2-3, social studies 2, science 2, foreign language 2 and academic electives 5. Two liberal arts required.

2011-2012 Annual costs. Tuition/fees: $23,140. Room/board: $8,700. Books/supplies: $1,100. Personal expenses: $1,950.

2011-2012 Financial aid. Need-based: 531 full-time freshmen applied for aid; 454 were judged to have need; 454 of these received aid. Average need met was 83%. Average scholarship/grant was $14,112; average loan $5,791. 63% of total undergraduate aid awarded as scholarships/grants, 37% as loans/jobs. **Non-need-based:** Scholarships awarded for academics, minority status, religious affiliation.

Application procedures. Admission: Priority date 5/1; deadline 8/15. $35 fee, may be waived for applicants with need, free for online applicants. Admission notification on a rolling basis beginning on or about 10/15. **Financial aid:** Priority date 3/15; no closing date. FAFSA required. Applicants notified on a rolling basis starting 2/1; must reply within 3 week(s) of notification.

Academics. Special study options: Accelerated study, combined bachelor's/graduate degree, cross-registration, distance learning, double major, dual enrollment of high school students, ESL, exchange student, independent study, internships, liberal arts/career combination, student-designed major, study abroad, teacher certification program, weekend college. Cooperative programs with Cardinal Stritch University, Marquette University, and Milwaukee Institute of Art and Design. **Credit/placement by examination:** AP, CLEP, IB, ACT, institutional tests. 15 credit hours maximum toward associate degree, 30 toward bachelor's. **Support services:** Learning center, reduced course load, remedial instruction, tutoring, writing center.

Majors. Biology: General, exercise physiology. **Business:** General, accounting, actuarial science, business admin, finance, international finance, marketing. **Communications:** Broadcast journalism, communications/speech/rhetoric, digital media, media studies. **Computer sciences:** General.

Conservation: Environmental studies. **Education:** General, art, biology, business, early childhood, elementary, English, health, history, kindergarten/preschool, mathematics, middle, multi-level teacher, music, physical, science, secondary, social science, social studies, Spanish. **English:** English lit. **Foreign languages:** Biblical, German, Spanish. **Health services:** Athletic training, clinical/medical social work, medical radiologic technology/radiation therapy, nursing (RN). **History:** General. **Human services:** Social work. **Liberal arts:** Arts/sciences, humanities. **Math:** General. **Philosophy/religion:** Religion. **Protective services:** Criminal justice. **Psychology:** General. **Social sciences:** Economics. **Theology:** Bible, missionary, pastoral counseling, preministerial, religious ed, sacred music, theology, youth ministry. **Visual/performing arts:** Art, commercial/advertising art, graphic design, illustration, interior design, music performance, photography, piano/keyboard.

Most popular majors. Business/marketing 40%, education 12%, health sciences 21%.

Computing on campus. 200 workstations in dormitories, library, computer center, student center. Dormitories wired for high-speed internet access and linked to campus network. Commuter students can connect to campus network. Online library, helpline, repair service available.

Student life. Freshman orientation: Available. Preregistration for classes offered. Held before start of fall semester, includes sessions for parents. **Policies:** Lutheran church services available every Sunday. Chapel services held daily. **Housing:** Single-sex dorms, wellness housing available. $160 deposit, deadline 4/15. **Activities:** Bands, campus ministries, choral groups, dance, drama, international student organizations, music ensembles, musical theater, radio station, student government, student newspaper, Jeremiah Project, Servant Events.

Athletics. NCAA. **Intercollegiate:** Baseball M, basketball, cross-country, football (tackle) M, golf, lacrosse M, soccer, softball W, tennis, track and field, volleyball, wrestling M. **Intramural:** Basketball, soccer, softball, table tennis, tennis, volleyball. **Team name:** Falcons.

Student services. Adult student services, alcohol/substance abuse counseling, chaplain/spiritual director, career counseling, student employment services, financial aid counseling, health services, minority student services, personal counseling, placement for graduates, veterans' counselor. **Physically disabled:** Services for hearing impaired.

Contact. E-mail: admission@cuw.edu
Phone: (262) 243-5700 Toll-free number: (888) 628-9472
Fax: (262) 243-4545
Kenneth Gaschk, Vice President of Enrollment Services, Concordia University Wisconsin, 12800 North Lake Shore Drive, Mequon, WI 53097

Edgewood College
Madison, Wisconsin   **CB member**
www.edgewood.edu   **CB code: 1202**

- Private 4-year liberal arts college affiliated with Roman Catholic Church
- Commuter campus in small city
- 1,867 degree-seeking undergraduates: 16% part-time, 71% women, 3% African American, 2% Asian American, 6% Hispanic American, 2% international
- 547 degree-seeking graduate students
- 72% of applicants admitted
- SAT or ACT (ACT writing optional) required
- 51% graduate within 6 years

General. Founded in 1927. Regionally accredited. **Degrees:** 397 bachelor's awarded; master's, doctoral offered. **ROTC:** Army. **Location:** 82 miles from Milwaukee, 140 miles from Chicago. **Calendar:** Semester, limited summer session. **Full-time faculty:** 111 total; 80% have terminal degrees, 13% minority, 52% women. **Part-time faculty:** 193 total; 19% have terminal degrees, 8% minority, 65% women. **Class size:** 81% < 20, 17% 20-39, 1% 40-49, less than 1% 50-99. **Special facilities:** Science center, biological research station, nursery school.

Freshman class profile. 1,292 applied, 929 admitted, 297 enrolled.

Mid 50% test scores			
ACT composite:	20-25	Rank in top quarter:	33%
GPA 3.75 or higher:	16%	Rank in top tenth:	9%
GPA 3.50-3.74:	18%	Return as sophomores:	80%
GPA 3.0-3.49:	40%	Out-of-state:	8.6%
GPA 2.0-2.99:	26%	Live on campus:	89%
		International:	2%

Basis for selection. Students must meet 2 of the following: 2.5 GPA, rank in top 50% of graduating class, 18 ACT (or equivalent SAT). **Home schooled:** Statement describing home school structure and mission, transcript of courses and grades required.

High school preparation. College-preparatory program recommended. Required units include English 4, mathematics 2, social studies 2, history 1, science 2 (laboratory 1) and foreign language 2.

2011-2012 Annual costs. Tuition/fees: $22,850. Room/board: $8,113.

2010-2011 Financial aid. Need-based: 298 full-time freshmen applied for aid; 270 were judged to have need; 270 of these received aid. Average need met was 79%. Average scholarship/grant was $12,226; average loan $3,622. 52% of total undergraduate aid awarded as scholarships/grants, 48% as loans/jobs. **Non-need-based:** Awarded to 280 full-time undergraduates, including 60 freshmen. Scholarships awarded for academics, alumni affiliation, art, leadership, music/drama, religious affiliation. **Additional information:** Auditions required for music scholarships, portfolios required for fine arts scholarships, essays required for a number of specialty institutional scholarships.

Application procedures. Admission: Priority date 3/1; deadline 8/14 (receipt date). $25 fee, may be waived for applicants with need. Admission notification on a rolling basis beginning on or about 9/15. **Financial aid:** Priority date 3/1; no closing date. FAFSA required. Applicants notified on a rolling basis starting 3/15.

Academics. Special study options: Accelerated study, cross-registration, distance learning, double major, dual enrollment of high school students, honors, independent study, internships, liberal arts/career combination, student-designed major, study abroad, teacher certification program. **Credit/placement by examination:** AP, CLEP, IB, ACT, institutional tests. 60 credit hours maximum toward bachelor's degree. **Support services:** Learning center, reduced course load, remedial instruction, study skills assistance, tutoring, writing center.

Majors. Biology: General. **Business:** General, accounting, business admin, management information systems, organizational behavior. **Communications:** General. **Computer sciences:** General. **Education:** Art, biology, business, chemistry, computer, drama/dance, early childhood, early childhood special, elementary, English, French, mathematics, music, science, Spanish. **English:** English lit. **Foreign languages:** French, Spanish. **Health services:** Art therapy, cytotechnology, nursing (RN). **History:** General. **Math:** General. **Philosophy/religion:** Religion. **Physical sciences:** Chemistry. **Protective services:** Criminal justice. **Psychology:** General. **Social sciences:** General, economics, international relations, political science, sociology. **Theology:** Religious ed. **Visual/performing arts:** Art, dramatic, graphic design, music.

Most popular majors. Business/marketing 23%, communications/journalism 6%, education 15%, health sciences 25%, psychology 6%, visual/performing arts 6%.

Computing on campus. 100 workstations in dormitories, library, computer center, student center. Dormitories wired for high-speed internet access and linked to campus network. Commuter students can connect to campus network. Online course registration, online library, helpline, wireless network available.

Student life. Freshman orientation: Available. Preregistration for classes offered. Three-day program held in fall. **Policies:** Freshmen not permitted cars on campus. **Housing:** Coed dorms, single-sex dorms, special housing for disabled, apartments available. $150 fully refundable deposit. **Activities:** Bands, campus ministries, choral groups, dance, drama, international student organizations, literary magazine, music ensembles, musical theater, student government, student newspaper, symphony orchestra, Student Nurse Association, Habitat for Humanity, Association of Latino(a) Students (ALAS), Black Student Union (BSU), international club, student government association, ethnic studies club, peace group, student education association, cultural studies group.

Athletics. NCAA. **Intercollegiate:** Baseball M, basketball, cross-country, golf, soccer, softball W, tennis, track and field, volleyball W. **Intramural:** Basketball, soccer, swimming, volleyball. **Team name:** Eagles.

Student services. Chaplain/spiritual director, career counseling, student employment services, financial aid counseling, health services, minority student services, personal counseling, placement for graduates, veterans' counselor. **Physically disabled:** Services for visually, speech, hearing impaired.

Contact. E-mail: admissions@edgewood.edu
Phone: (608) 663-2294 Toll-free number: (800) 444-4861 ext. 2294
Fax: (608) 663-2214
Christine Benedict, Director of Undergraduate Admissions, Edgewood College, 1000 Edgewood College Drive, Madison, WI 53711-1997

Globe University: Green Bay
Green Bay, Wisconsin
www.globeuniversity.edu

▶ For-profit 4-year career college
▶ Small city
▶ 285 degree-seeking undergraduates

General. Regionally accredited; also accredited by ACICS. **Calendar:** Quarter. **Full-time faculty:** 9 total. **Part-time faculty:** 30 total.

Basis for selection. Open admission.

Application procedures. Admission: $50 fee.

Academics. Credit/placement by examination: AP, CLEP.

Majors. Business: Accounting, business admin. **Computer sciences:** Information technology. **Protective services:** Law enforcement admin.

Contact. E-mail: cheltsley@globeuniversity.edu
Phone: (920) 264-1600
Beth Francour, Director of Admissions, Globe University: Green Bay, 2620 Development Drive, Green Bay, WI 54311

Herzing University: Brookfield
Brookfield, Wisconsin
www.herzing.edu

▶ For-profit 4-year business and technical college
▶ Large town
▶ 178 degree-seeking undergraduates

General. Regionally accredited. **Calendar:** Semester. **Full-time faculty:** 2 total. **Part-time faculty:** 1 total.

Basis for selection. Wonderlic exam required for some programs.

2011-2012 Annual costs. Tuition/fees: $11,040. Reported annual tuition is representative. Actual costs vary by program with nursing programs somewhat more expensive.

Academics. Credit/placement by examination: AP, CLEP.

Majors. Business: Business admin, entrepreneurial studies, human resources, international. **Computer sciences:** Networking. **Health services:** Health care admin, medical records admin. **Protective services:** Criminal justice. **Visual/performing arts:** Graphic design.

Contact. E-mail: info@brk.herzing.edu
Monica Beere, Director of Admissions, Herzing University: Brookfield, 555 South Executive Drive, Brookfield, WI 53005

Herzing University: Kenosha
Kenosha, Wisconsin
www.herzing.edu

▶ For-profit 4-year business and technical college
▶ Small city
▶ 337 degree-seeking undergraduates

General. Regionally accredited. **Degrees:** 1 bachelor's, 10 associate awarded. **Calendar:** Semester. **Full-time faculty:** 11 total. **Part-time faculty:** 5 total.

Basis for selection. Wonderlic exam required for some programs.

2011-2012 Annual costs. Tuition/fees: $11,040. Reported annual tuition is representative. Actual costs vary by program with nursing programs somewhat more expensive.

Academics. Credit/placement by examination: AP, CLEP.

Majors. Business: Accounting, business admin, entrepreneurial studies, human resources, international, marketing. **Computer sciences:** Networking. **Health services:** Nursing (RN). **Protective services:** Criminal justice. **Visual/performing arts:** Graphic design.

Contact. E-mail: info@ken.herzing.edu
Monica Beere, Director of Admissions, Herzing University: Kenosha, 4006 Washington Road, Kenosha, WI 53144

Herzing University: Madison
Madison, Wisconsin
www.herzing.edu/madison   **CB code: 0388**

- For-profit 3-year business and career college
- Commuter campus in small city
- 874 degree-seeking undergraduates
- Interview required

General. Founded in 1948. Regionally accredited. **Degrees:** 122 bachelor's, 109 associate awarded. **Location:** 90 miles from Milwaukee, 150 miles from Chicago. **Calendar:** Differs by program, extensive summer session. **Full-time faculty:** 31 total. **Part-time faculty:** 29 total.

Basis for selection. Open admission, but selective for some programs. Interview and placement test required prior to acceptance. Application process varies by program. **Home schooled:** State high school equivalency certificate required. **Learning Disabled:** Must provide documentation to admissions advisor prior to starting classes.

2011-2012 Annual costs. Tuition/fees: $11,040. Reported annual tuition is representative. Actual costs vary by program with nursing programs somewhat more expensive. Personal expenses: $3,213.

Application procedures. Admission: No deadline. No application fee. Application must be submitted on paper. Admission notification on a rolling basis. **Financial aid:** No deadline. FAFSA, institutional form required. Applicants notified on a rolling basis.

Academics. Bachelors degree may be acquired in 3 years, associate degree in 1 year, 8 months. **Special study options:** Combined bachelor's/graduate degree, cooperative education, distance learning, honors, independent study, internships, liberal arts/career combination, study abroad, weekend college. **Credit/placement by examination:** AP, CLEP, institutional tests. **Support services:** Learning center, reduced course load, remedial instruction, study skills assistance, tutoring, writing center.

Majors. BACHELOR'S. Business: Accounting, accounting/business management, accounting/finance, business admin, finance, human resources, office management, office technology, office/clerical. **Communications technology:** Animation/special effects. **Computer sciences:** General, applications programming, computer graphics, computer science, information systems, information technology, LAN/WAN management, networking, programming. **Engineering:** Software. **Health services:** Facilities admin, health care admin, medical records admin, medical records technology, office admin, ward supervisor. **Protective services:** Homeland security. **Visual/performing arts:** Game design, graphic design. **ASSOCIATE. Business:** Accounting/business management, business admin, office management, office technology, office/clerical. **Communications technology:** Animation/special effects. **Computer sciences:** General, applications programming, computer graphics, computer science, information systems, information technology, LAN/WAN management, networking, programming. **Engineering:** Software. **Health services:** Insurance coding, insurance specialist, medical records admin, nursing (RN), office admin, office assistant, office computer specialist, receptionist. **Visual/performing arts:** Graphic design.

Computing on campus. 450 workstations in library, computer center, student center. Commuter students can connect to campus network. Online library, helpline, repair service, wireless network available.

Student life. Freshman orientation: Mandatory. Preregistration for classes offered. **Activities:** Student government, student newspaper.

Student services. Adult student services, career counseling, student employment services, financial aid counseling, personal counseling, placement for graduates. **Physically disabled:** Services for visually, speech, hearing impaired.

Contact. E-mail: info@msn.herzing.edu
Phone: (608) 249-6611 Toll-free number: (800) 582-1227
Fax: (608) 249-8593
Matthew Schneider, Director of Admissions, Herzing University: Madison, 5218 East Terrace Drive, Madison, WI 53718

ITT Technical Institute: Green Bay
Green Bay, Wisconsin
www.itt-tech.edu

- For-profit 4-year technical college
- Small city
- 924 undergraduates

General. Accredited by ACICS. **Degrees:** 103 bachelor's, 193 associate awarded. **Calendar:** Trimester. **Full-time faculty:** 14 total. **Part-time faculty:** 50 total.

Basis for selection. Satisfactory scores from on-site tests in English and mathematics required.

2011-2012 Annual costs. Estimated costs as of June 2011: per-credit-hour charge, $493, depending upon level and course of study; academic fee, $200. Certain programs of study require purchase of tools, which could cost an additional $100 to $500. All costs are subject to change.

Academics. Credit/placement by examination: AP, CLEP.

Majors. Business: Accounting/business management, business admin, construction management, e-commerce. **Communications technology:** Animation/special effects. **Computer sciences:** Security. **Protective services:** Criminal justice.

Computing on campus. Online library available.

Student life. Freshman orientation: Available. Preregistration for classes offered.

Contact. Phone: (920) 662-9000 Toll-free number: (888) 884-3626
Fax: (920) 662-9384
Raymond Sweetman, Director of Recruitment, ITT Technical Institute: Green Bay, 470 Security Boulevard, Green Bay, WI 54313

ITT Technical Institute: Greenfield
Greenfield, Wisconsin
www.itt-tech.edu   **CB code: 2706**

- For-profit 4-year technical college
- Commuter campus in large town
- 1,264 undergraduates
- Interview required

General. Accredited by ACICS. **Degrees:** 75 bachelor's, 333 associate awarded. **Calendar:** Quarter, extensive summer session. **Full-time faculty:** 16 total. **Part-time faculty:** 91 total.

Basis for selection. Satisfactory scores from on-site tests in English and mathematics required.

2011-2012 Annual costs. Estimated costs as of June 2011: per-credit-hour charge, $493, depending upon level and course of study; academic fee, $200. Certain programs of study require purchase of tools, which could cost an additional $100 to $500. All costs are subject to change.

Application procedures. Admission: No application fee. Admission notification on a rolling basis. **Financial aid:** No deadline. FAFSA, institutional form required. Applicants notified on a rolling basis.

Academics. Credit/placement by examination: AP, CLEP. **Support services:** Learning center, tutoring.

Majors. Business: Accounting/business management, business admin, construction management, e-commerce. **Communications technology:** Animation/special effects. **Computer sciences:** Networking, security. **Protective services:** Law enforcement admin. **Visual/performing arts:** Game design.

Computing on campus. Online library available.

Student life. Freshman orientation: Available. Preregistration for classes offered.

Student services. Career counseling, student employment services, placement for graduates.

Contact. Phone: (414) 282-9494 Fax: (414) 282-9698
Brian Guenther, Director of Recruitment, ITT Technical Institute: Greenfield, 6300 West Layton Avenue, Greenfield, WI 53220-4612

Lakeland College
Sheboygan, Wisconsin
www.lakeland.edu
CB code: 1393

- Private 4-year liberal arts college affiliated with United Church of Christ
- Residential campus in small city
- 2,587 degree-seeking undergraduates
- 82% of applicants admitted
- SAT or ACT (ACT writing recommended) required

General. Founded in 1862. Regionally accredited. Evening, online, and graduate classes offered for nontraditional students at 7 in-state sites. Associate program available at Tokyo, Japan campus. **Degrees:** 545 bachelor's awarded; master's offered. **Location:** 60 miles from Milwaukee, 60 miles from Green Bay. **Calendar:** 4-4-1. Limited summer session. **Full-time faculty:** 60 total. **Part-time faculty:** 366 total. **Class size:** 69% < 20, 30% 20-39, 1% 40-49.

Freshman class profile. 621 applied, 509 admitted, 209 enrolled.

Mid 50% test scores			
SAT math:	420-560	Rank in top quarter:	24%
ACT composite:	19-24	Rank in top tenth:	8%
GPA 3.75 or higher:	10%	Out-of-state:	15%
GPA 3.50-3.74:	9%	Live on campus:	90%
GPA 3.0-3.49:	29%	Fraternities:	3%
GPA 2.0-2.99:	49%	Sororities:	3%

Basis for selection. Applicants with 19 ACT, 2.0 GPA and rank in the top half of class admitted. Essays are recommended. **Home schooled:** Transcript of courses and grades, state high school equivalency certificate required.

High school preparation. Recommended units include English 4, mathematics 2, social studies 2, history 2, science 2, foreign language 2 and academic electives 2.

2011-2012 Annual costs. Tuition/fees: $20,230. Room/board: $7,360. Books/supplies: $900. Personal expenses: $750.

Financial aid. **Non-need-based:** Scholarships awarded for academics.

Application procedures. **Admission:** No deadline. $20 fee, may be waived for applicants with need. Admission notification on a rolling basis. **Financial aid:** Priority date 3/31, closing date 7/1. FAFSA, institutional form required. Applicants notified on a rolling basis starting 2/1; must reply within 2 week(s) of notification.

Academics. Applicants whose test scores reflect weakness in basic skills must take basic skills courses in freshman year. **Special study options:** Combined bachelor's/graduate degree, cooperative education, distance learning, double major, dual enrollment of high school students, ESL, honors, independent study, internships, liberal arts/career combination, study abroad, teacher certification program. Engineering program with University of Wisconsin-Madison, nursing program with Bellin College of Nursing. **Credit/placement by examination:** AP, CLEP, IB, institutional tests. 30 credit hours maximum toward bachelor's degree. **Support services:** Learning center, reduced course load, remedial instruction, study skills assistance, tutoring, writing center.

Majors. **Biology:** General, biochemistry. **Business:** Accounting, business admin, international, marketing, nonprofit/public, resort management. **Computer sciences:** Computer science. **Education:** Elementary, kindergarten/preschool, middle, secondary. **English:** English lit, writing. **Foreign languages:** German, Spanish. **History:** General. **Math:** General. **Philosophy/religion:** Religion. **Physical sciences:** Chemistry. **Protective services:** Law enforcement admin. **Psychology:** General. **Social sciences:** Sociology. **Visual/performing arts:** Art, music.

Most popular majors. Business/marketing 68%, computer/information sciences 19%, education 11%.

Computing on campus. 218 workstations in dormitories, library, computer center, student center. Dormitories wired for high-speed internet access and linked to campus network. Commuter students can connect to campus network. Online course registration, online library, helpline, wireless network available.

Student life. **Freshman orientation:** Mandatory. Preregistration for classes offered. **Housing:** Guaranteed on-campus for freshmen. Coed dorms, single-sex dorms, special housing for disabled, apartments available. $50 deposit. Honor apartments and apartments for students with senior standing available. **Activities:** Concert band, choral groups, drama, international student organizations, music ensembles, student government, student newspaper, campus activities board, black student union, Mortar Board, global students association, business fraternity, Inter-Greek Council.

Athletics. NCAA. **Intercollegiate:** Baseball M, basketball, cross-country, football (tackle) M, golf, soccer, softball W, tennis, track and field, volleyball W, wrestling M. **Team name:** Muskies.

Student services. Alcohol/substance abuse counseling, chaplain/spiritual director, career counseling, services for economically disadvantaged, student employment services, financial aid counseling, health services, on-campus daycare, personal counseling, placement for graduates, veterans' counselor. **Physically disabled:** Services for visually impaired.

Contact. E-mail: admissions@lakeland.edu
Phone: (920) 565-1217 Toll-free number: (800) 242-3347
Fax: (920) 565-1206
Nick Spaeth, Director of Admissions, Lakeland College, Box 359, Sheboygan, WI 53082-0359

Lawrence University
Appleton, Wisconsin
CB member
www.lawrence.edu
CB code: 1398

- Private 4-year music and liberal arts college
- Residential campus in small city
- 1,445 degree-seeking undergraduates: 2% part-time, 54% women, 3% African American, 3% Asian American, 4% Hispanic American, 7% international
- 53% of applicants admitted
- Application essay required
- 76% graduate within 6 years

General. Founded in 1847. Regionally accredited. **Degrees:** 364 bachelor's awarded. **Location:** 100 miles from Milwaukee, 30 miles from Green Bay. **Calendar:** Trimester. **Full-time faculty:** 163 total; 96% have terminal degrees, 13% minority, 39% women. **Part-time faculty:** 38 total; 18% have terminal degrees, 10% minority, 40% women. **Class size:** 75% < 20, 20% 20-39, 3% 40-49, 2% 50-99. **Special facilities:** Laser physics laboratory, 250 MHz nuclear magnetic resonance spectrometer, physics/computational graphics laboratory, lakefront retreat center.

Freshman class profile. 2,666 applied, 1,405 admitted, 326 enrolled.

Mid 50% test scores			
SAT critical reading:	600-710	GPA 2.0-2.99:	5%
SAT math:	580-690	Rank in top quarter:	81%
SAT writing:	570-690	Rank in top tenth:	46%
ACT composite:	27-31	End year in good standing:	92%
GPA 3.75 or higher:	50%	Return as sophomores:	89%
GPA 3.50-3.74:	23%	Out-of-state:	68%
GPA 3.0-3.49:	22%	Live on campus:	98%
		International:	6%

Basis for selection. Strength of curriculum, school achievement record most important. Recommendations, out-of-class activities, test scores considered. Music applicants judged on musicianship, teacher's recommendations and academic ability. Interview recommended for all; portfolio recommended for studio art; audition required for conservatory of music study. **Home schooled:** Require evidence of coursework completed and level of performance, letters of recommendation and GED if applicable. Recommend standardized test results.

High school preparation. College-preparatory program recommended. 16 units recommended. Recommended units include English 4, mathematics 3, social studies 2, history 2, science 3 and foreign language 2. Strong musical preparation required of music applicants.

2011-2012 Annual costs. Tuition/fees: $38,481. Room/board: $7,890. Books/supplies: $900. Personal expenses: $900.

2011-2012 Financial aid. **Need-based:** 254 full-time freshmen applied for aid; 208 were judged to have need; 208 of these received aid. Average need met was 89%. Average scholarship/grant was $24,896; average loan $4,750. 79% of total undergraduate aid awarded as scholarships/grants, 21% as loans/jobs. **Non-need-based:** Awarded to 499 full-time undergraduates, including 104 freshmen. Scholarships awarded for academics, alumni affiliation, leadership, minority status, music/drama. **Additional information:** The first $1,000 (aggregate) of independently-sponsored scholarships received by a needy student will reduce student's loan or work-study commitment. Half of scholarships in excess of $1,000 will offset loan or work-study and the other half will reduce institutional need-based grant funding.

Application procedures. **Admission:** Closing date 1/15 (postmark date). $40 fee, may be waived for applicants with need. Admission notification by 4/1. Must reply by May 1 or within 2 week(s) if notified thereafter. **Financial aid:** Priority date 3/1; no closing date. FAFSA, institutional form required.

Applicants notified on a rolling basis starting 3/1; must reply by 5/1 or within 2 week(s) of notification.

Academics. As an adjunct to a major, students may pursue 1 interdisciplinary area of study: biomedical ethics, international studies, neuroscience or cognitive science. **Special study options:** Combined bachelor's/graduate degree, double major, independent study, internships, semester at sea, student-designed major, study abroad, teacher certification program, urban semester, Washington semester. Study abroad programs in 27 countries; marine biology term, Oak Ridge science semester; urban semester in Chicago; Newberry Library Program in humanities; environmental studies and forestry programs with Duke University; occupational therapy program with Washington University, St. Louis. **Credit/placement by examination:** AP, CLEP, IB, institutional tests. 30 credit hours maximum toward bachelor's degree. Course credit awarded for scores of at least 5 on International Baccalaureate examinations. **Support services:** Learning center, reduced course load, study skills assistance, tutoring, writing center.

Majors. Area/ethnic studies: Chinese, East Asian, Japanese, Russian/Slavic. **Biology:** General, biochemistry, neuroscience. **Computer sciences:** General. **Conservation:** Environmental studies. **Education:** Music. **English:** English lit. **Foreign languages:** Ancient Greek, Chinese, classics, East Asian, French, German, Japanese, Latin, linguistics, Russian, Spanish. **History:** General. **Math:** General. **Philosophy/religion:** Philosophy, religion. **Physical sciences:** Chemistry, geology, physics. **Psychology:** General. **Social sciences:** Anthropology, economics, political science. **Visual/performing arts:** Art, art history/conservation, dramatic, music, music performance, music theory/composition, studio arts.

Most popular majors. Biology 9%, English 6%, foreign language 8%, physical sciences 7%, psychology 8%, social sciences 12%, visual/performing arts 26%.

Computing on campus. 354 workstations in dormitories, library, computer center, student center. Dormitories wired for high-speed internet access and linked to campus network. Commuter students can connect to campus network. Online course registration, online library, helpline, repair service, wireless network available.

Student life. Freshman orientation: Mandatory. Preregistration for classes offered. Held 5 days prior to start of fall classes. **Policies:** Honor code in effect. **Housing:** Guaranteed on-campus for all undergraduates. Coed dorms, single-sex dorms, special housing for disabled, apartments, cooperative housing, wellness housing available. Apartment-style units available to upperclass students. All single students required to live on-campus for 4 years. **Activities:** Bands, campus ministries, choral groups, dance, drama, film society, international student organizations, music ensembles, Model UN, musical theater, opera, radio station, student government, student newspaper, symphony orchestra, Chavurah, Christian fellowship, black organization of students, Latin American student organization, social service groups, political and academic clubs, professional sororities and fraternities.

Athletics. NCAA. **Intercollegiate:** Baseball M, basketball, cross-country, diving, fencing, football (tackle) M, golf M, ice hockey M, soccer, softball W, swimming, tennis, track and field, volleyball W. **Intramural:** Badminton, basketball, bowling, fencing, football (non-tackle), golf, handball, racquetball, soccer, softball, squash, table tennis, tennis, volleyball, water polo. **Team name:** Vikings.

Student services. Alcohol/substance abuse counseling, career counseling, student employment services, financial aid counseling, health services, minority student services, personal counseling, placement for graduates. **Physically disabled:** Services for visually, speech, hearing impaired.

Contact. E-mail: excel@lawrence.edu
Phone: (920) 832-6500 Toll-free number: (800) 227-0982
Fax: (920) 832-6782
Ken Anselment, Dean of Admissions and Financial Aid, Lawrence University, 711 East Boldt Way SPC 29, Appleton, WI 54911-5699

Maranatha Baptist Bible College
Watertown, Wisconsin
www.mbbc.edu   CB code: 2732

- Private 4-year Bible and liberal arts college affiliated with Baptist faith
- Residential campus in large town
- 817 degree-seeking undergraduates: 6% part-time, 53% women, 1% Asian American, 1% Hispanic American
- 72 degree-seeking graduate students
- 75% of applicants admitted
- SAT or ACT (ACT writing optional), application essay required
- 51% graduate within 6 years; 20% enter graduate study

General. Founded in 1968. Regionally accredited. **Degrees:** 133 bachelor's, 12 associate awarded; master's offered. **ROTC:** Army, Air Force. **Location:** 45 miles from Milwaukee, 38 miles from Madison. **Calendar:** Semester, limited summer session. **Full-time faculty:** 44 total; 32% have terminal degrees, 7% minority, 32% women. **Part-time faculty:** 32 total; 12% have terminal degrees, 3% minority, 47% women. **Class size:** 63% < 20, 26% 20-39, 4% 40-49, 6% 50-99, less than 1% >100.

Freshman class profile. 426 applied, 321 admitted, 215 enrolled.

Mid 50% test scores		End year in good standing:	92%
SAT critical reading:	450-570	Return as sophomores:	76%
SAT math:	410-530	Out-of-state:	75%
SAT writing:	410-600	Live on campus:	79%
ACT composite:	19-24		

Basis for selection. Recommendations, religious commitment most important. Secondary school record, test scores, character also important. Class rank, essay considered. At-risk students placed on admissions probation. Audition required for fine arts.

High school preparation. College-preparatory program recommended. 18 units recommended. Recommended units include English 4, mathematics 3, social studies 3, history 3, science 3 and foreign language 2. Two units of physical education and one unit of word processing recommended.

2011-2012 Annual costs. Tuition/fees: $12,260. Room/board: $6,290. Books/supplies: $1,010. Personal expenses: $2,780.

Financial aid. Non-need-based: Scholarships awarded for academics.

Application procedures. Admission: No deadline. $50 fee. Admission notification on a rolling basis. **Financial aid:** Priority date 3/1; no closing date. FAFSA required. Applicants notified on a rolling basis starting 2/1; must reply within 2 week(s) of notification.

Academics. Hands-on ministerial work available. **Special study options:** Distance learning, double major, independent study, internships, liberal arts/career combination, study abroad, teacher certification program. **Credit/placement by examination:** AP, CLEP, SAT, ACT, institutional tests. 30 credit hours maximum toward associate degree, 30 toward bachelor's. Only 12 credits may be counted in any one field of study. **Support services:** Reduced course load, remedial instruction, study skills assistance, tutoring, writing center.

Majors. Biology: General. **Business:** Accounting, accounting/business management, business admin, marketing, office management. **Education:** Biology, business, early childhood, elementary, English, history, mathematics, music, physical, science, social studies. **English:** English lit. **Health services:** Nursing (RN). **Liberal arts:** Humanities. **Parks/recreation:** Sports admin. **Theology:** Bible, missionary, pastoral counseling, sacred music, youth ministry. **Visual/performing arts:** Music pedagogy, music performance.

Most popular majors. Business/marketing 17%, education 26%, health sciences 11%, liberal arts 24%, theological studies 15%.

Computing on campus. 120 workstations in dormitories, library, computer center. Dormitories wired for high-speed internet access and linked to campus network. Commuter students can connect to campus network. Online library, repair service, student web hosting, wireless network available.

Student life. Freshman orientation: Mandatory. Preregistration for classes offered. Held Saturday through Monday before classes begin. **Policies:** Religious observance required. **Housing:** Guaranteed on-campus for all undergraduates. Single-sex dorms, wellness housing available. $175 nonrefundable deposit. **Activities:** Bands, campus ministries, choral groups, drama, music ensembles, musical theater, student government, symphony orchestra.

Athletics. NCAA, NCCAA. **Intercollegiate:** Baseball M, basketball, cross-country, football (tackle) M, soccer, softball W, volleyball W, wrestling M. **Intramural:** Basketball, soccer W, volleyball. **Team name:** Crusaders.

Student services. Chaplain/spiritual director, career counseling, financial aid counseling, health services, on-campus daycare, personal counseling, placement for graduates, veterans' counselor.

Contact. E-mail: admissions@mbbc.edu
Phone: (920) 261-9300 Toll-free number: (800) 611-1947
Fax: (920) 261-9109
James Harrison, Director of Admissions, Maranatha Baptist Bible College, 745 West Main Street, Watertown, WI 53094

Marian University
Fond du Lac, Wisconsin
www.marianuniversity.edu

CB member
CB code: 1443

- Private 4-year university and liberal arts college affiliated with Roman Catholic Church
- Residential campus in large town
- 1,879 degree-seeking undergraduates: 20% part-time, 73% women, 5% African American, 2% Asian American, 5% Hispanic American, 1% Native American, 1% international
- 619 degree-seeking graduate students
- 82% of applicants admitted
- SAT or ACT (ACT writing optional) required
- 52% graduate within 6 years

General. Founded in 1936. Regionally accredited. **Degrees:** 415 bachelor's awarded; master's, doctoral offered. **Location:** 60 miles from Milwaukee, 65 miles from Green Bay. **Calendar:** Semester, extensive summer session. **Full-time faculty:** 90 total; 54% have terminal degrees, 6% minority, 57% women. **Part-time faculty:** 187 total; 9% have terminal degrees, 6% minority, 46% women. **Class size:** 75% < 20, 21% 20-39, 3% 40-49, less than 1% 50-99.

Freshman class profile. 1,057 applied, 866 admitted, 321 enrolled.

Mid 50% test scores			
ACT composite:	18-23	Rank in top tenth:	11%
GPA 3.75 or higher:	13%	Return as sophomores:	67%
GPA 3.50-3.74:	12%	Out-of-state:	16%
GPA 3.0-3.49:	28%	Live on campus:	81%
GPA 2.0-2.99:	44%	International:	2%
Rank in top quarter:	29%	Fraternities:	2%
		Sororities:	8%

Basis for selection. School achievement record most important, followed by test scores. Applicants must meet 2 of following 3 criteria: 2.0 GPA, top half of class, 18 ACT. Special admissions procedures required for nursing and education divisions. If admission criteria not met, students may be admitted on provisional basis. Interview, audition recommended. **Home schooled:** Transcript of courses and grades required. **Learning Disabled:** Copies of paperwork needed to qualify for supportive services.

High school preparation. College-preparatory program required. 20 units required. Required and recommended units include English 4, mathematics 2-3, social studies 2, history 1, science 2 (laboratory 1), foreign language 2, computer science 1, visual/performing arts 1 and academic electives 2. Biology and chemistry prerequisite for nursing program.

2011-2012 Annual costs. Tuition/fees: $22,440. Room/board: $5,900. Books/supplies: $700. Personal expenses: $1,420.

2010-2011 Financial aid. Need-based: 307 full-time freshmen applied for aid; 290 were judged to have need; 290 of these received aid. Average need met was 82%. Average scholarship/grant was $11,868. 60% of total undergraduate aid awarded as scholarships/grants, 40% as loans/jobs. **Non-need-based:** Awarded to 1,164 full-time undergraduates, including 269 freshmen. Scholarships awarded for academics.

Application procedures. Admission: Priority date 4/1; no deadline. $20 fee, may be waived for applicants with need. Admission notification on a rolling basis. Must reply by May 1 or within 4 week(s) if notified thereafter. **Financial aid:** Priority date 3/1; no closing date. FAFSA, institutional form required. Applicants notified on a rolling basis starting 3/1; must reply within 4 week(s) of notification.

Academics. Special study options: Accelerated study, combined bachelor's/graduate degree, cooperative education, distance learning, double major, dual enrollment of high school students, honors, independent study, internships, liberal arts/career combination, student-designed major, study abroad, teacher certification program. Accelerated programs for adults in business, nursing, operation management, radiologic technology, organizational communication, administration of justice. **Credit/placement by examination:** AP, CLEP, IB, institutional tests. 30 credit hours maximum toward bachelor's degree. Writing sample required for placement and counseling. **Support services:** Learning center, pre-admission summer program, reduced course load, remedial instruction, study skills assistance, tutoring, writing center.

Honors college/program. Unrestricted admissions with 25 ACT, 3.5 GPA, positive recommendation, application essay.

Majors. Biology: General. **Business:** Accounting, business admin, finance, human resources, marketing, operations. **Communications:** Communications/speech/rhetoric, organizational. **Computer sciences:** Information technology. **Education:** Art, early childhood, elementary, English, music, science, secondary, social studies, Spanish. **English:** British lit, English lit, writing.

Foreign languages: Spanish. **Health services:** Cytotechnology, health care admin, nursing (RN), radiologic technology/medical imaging. **History:** General. **Human services:** Social work. **Liberal arts:** Arts/sciences. **Math:** General. **Parks/recreation:** Sports admin. **Philosophy/religion:** Religion. **Physical sciences:** Chemistry. **Protective services:** Forensics, homeland security, police science. **Psychology:** General. **Visual/performing arts:** Graphic design, music, music management, studio arts.

Most popular majors. Business/marketing 28%, health sciences 36%, security/protective services 13%.

Computing on campus. 500 workstations in library, computer center, student center. Dormitories wired for high-speed internet access and linked to campus network. Commuter students can connect to campus network. Online course registration, online library, helpline, repair service, wireless network available.

Student life. Freshman orientation: Mandatory. Preregistration for classes offered. **Policies:** Emphasis on community volunteer activity. Service transcript available for graduates. **Housing:** Guaranteed on-campus for all undergraduates. Coed dorms, special housing for disabled, apartments, fraternity/sorority housing, wellness housing available. $100 nonrefundable deposit. Townhouses, penthouses and residential suites available. **Activities:** Bands, campus ministries, choral groups, dance, international student organizations, music ensembles, Model UN, student government, student newspaper, symphony orchestra, environmental club, social justice committee, African American student union, Association Latina, math and science association.

Athletics. NCAA. **Intercollegiate:** Baseball M, basketball, cross-country, golf, ice hockey, soccer, softball W, tennis, volleyball W. **Intramural:** Badminton, basketball, bowling, football (non-tackle) M, skiing, softball M, tennis, volleyball. **Team name:** Sabres.

Student services. Adult student services, alcohol/substance abuse counseling, chaplain/spiritual director, career counseling, services for economically disadvantaged, student employment services, financial aid counseling, health services, minority student services, on-campus daycare, personal counseling, placement for graduates, women's services. **Physically disabled:** Services for visually, speech, hearing impaired.

Contact. E-mail: admissions@marianuniversity.edu
Phone: (920) 923-7650 Toll-free number: (800) 262-7426
Fax: (920) 923-8755
Shannon LaLuzerne, Senior Director of Admissions, Marian University, 45 South National Avenue, Fond du Lac, WI 54935-4699

Marquette University
Milwaukee, Wisconsin
www.marquette.edu

CB member
CB code: 1448

- Private 4-year university affiliated with Roman Catholic Church
- Residential campus in very large city
- 8,195 degree-seeking undergraduates: 3% part-time, 52% women, 5% African American, 4% Asian American, 7% Hispanic American, 3% international
- 3,536 degree-seeking graduate students
- 57% of applicants admitted
- SAT or ACT (ACT writing recommended), application essay required
- 81% graduate within 6 years; 27% enter graduate study

General. Founded in 1881. Regionally accredited. **Degrees:** 1,722 bachelor's awarded; master's, professional, doctoral offered. **ROTC:** Army, Naval, Air Force. **Location:** Downtown. **Calendar:** Semester, extensive summer session. **Full-time faculty:** 631 total; 85% have terminal degrees, 15% minority, 40% women. **Part-time faculty:** 497 total; 22% have terminal degrees, 9% minority, 45% women. **Class size:** 39% < 20, 42% 20-39, 8% 40-49, 8% 50-99, 4% >100. **Special facilities:** 15th century St. Joan of Arc chapel.

Freshman class profile. 22,354 applied, 12,707 admitted, 2,068 enrolled.

Mid 50% test scores			
SAT critical reading:	520-630	Rank in top tenth:	33%
SAT math:	530-650	End year in good standing:	93%
SAT writing:	520-630	Return as sophomores:	90%
ACT composite:	24-29	Out-of-state:	64%
Rank in top quarter:	63%	Live on campus:	92%
		International:	3%

Basis for selection. High school course selection, trend of performance, test scores and class rank most important. Essay, leadership, community service and extracurricular activities considered. **Home schooled:** Provide detailed list of curriculum and bibliography. Personal interview may be required.

High school preparation. College-preparatory program required. 16 units required; 22 recommended. Required and recommended units include English 4, mathematics 2-4, social studies 2-3, science 2-3 (laboratory 2-3), foreign language 2 and academic electives 2-5. Algebra, geometry, and intermediate algebra required for arts & sciences, business administration and health sciences. Algebra and geometry required for nursing. 3 years of science recommended for premedical, predental and science majors. Students interested in international business strongly urged to complete 4 units of single foreign language.

2011-2012 Annual costs. Tuition/fees: $31,822. Antivirus software supplied to all students at no additional charge. Room/board: $10,340.

2011-2012 Financial aid. **Need-based:** 1,672 full-time freshmen applied for aid; 1,279 were judged to have need; 1,279 of these received aid. Average need met was 74%. Average scholarship/grant was $16,674; average loan $4,157. 63% of total undergraduate aid awarded as scholarships/grants, 37% as loans/jobs. **Non-need-based:** Awarded to 3,095 full-time undergraduates, including 928 freshmen. Scholarships awarded for academics, athletics, leadership, music/drama, ROTC.

Application procedures. **Admission:** Closing date 12/1 (postmark date). $30 fee, may be waived for applicants with need, free for online applicants. Admission notification by 1/31. Admission notification on a rolling basis. Must reply by May 1 or within 2 week(s) if notified thereafter. **Financial aid:** Priority date 2/1; no closing date. FAFSA required. Applicants notified on a rolling basis starting 3/20; must reply by 5/1 or within 3 week(s) of notification.

Academics. **Special study options:** Accelerated study, combined bachelor's/graduate degree, cooperative education, cross-registration, distance learning, double major, dual enrollment of high school students, ESL, honors, independent study, internships, student-designed major, study abroad, teacher certification program, Washington semester, weekend college. **Credit/placement by examination:** AP, CLEP, IB, institutional tests. 30 credit hours maximum toward bachelor's degree. **Support services:** Learning center, pre-admission summer program, reduced course load, study skills assistance, tutoring, writing center.

Majors. **Biology:** General, Biochemistry/molecular biology, biomedical sciences, physiology. **Business:** Accounting, business admin, entrepreneurial studies, finance, human resources, managerial economics, marketing, organizational leadership, real estate. **Communications:** Advertising, journalism, public relations. **Computer sciences:** General, information technology. **Education:** Drama/dance, elementary, mathematics, secondary. **Engineering:** Biomedical, civil, computer, construction, electrical, environmental, mechanical. **English:** English lit, writing. **Foreign languages:** Classics, French, German, Spanish. **Health services:** Athletic training, audiology/speech pathology, clinical lab science, nursing (RN). **History:** General. **Math:** General, computational. **Philosophy/religion:** Philosophy. **Physical sciences:** Chemistry, physics. **Psychology:** General. **Social sciences:** Anthropology, criminology, economics, political science, sociology. **Theology:** Theology. **Visual/performing arts:** Dramatic.

Most popular majors. Biology 8%, business/marketing 27%, communications/journalism 10%, engineering/engineering technologies 9%, health sciences 9%, social sciences 8%.

Computing on campus. 1,129 workstations in dormitories, library, computer center, student center. Dormitories wired for high-speed internet access and linked to campus network. Commuter students can connect to campus network. Online course registration, online library, helpline, student web hosting, wireless network available.

Student life. **Freshman orientation:** Available. Preregistration for classes offered. 4-day session held week before classes begin; June program also available. **Policies:** Written policies in effect concerning racial and sexual harassment, alcohol, drugs and safety. **Housing:** Guaranteed on-campus for freshmen. Coed dorms, single-sex dorms, special housing for disabled, apartments, cooperative housing, fraternity/sorority housing, wellness housing available. $300 nonrefundable deposit, deadline 5/1. Special housing for engineering, nursing, and honor students. **Activities:** Bands, campus ministries, choral groups, dance, drama, international student organizations, literary magazine, music ensembles, Model UN, musical theater, opera, radio station, student government, student newspaper, symphony orchestra, TV station, JUSTICE, College Republicans, College Democrats, Campus Crusade for Christ, Intervarsity, Latin American student organization.

Athletics. NCAA. **Intercollegiate:** Basketball, cheerleading, cross-country, golf M, lacrosse, soccer, tennis, track and field, volleyball W. **Intramural:** Badminton, basketball, football (non-tackle), racquetball, soccer, softball, tennis, track and field, volleyball, water polo, weight lifting. **Team name:** Golden Eagles.

Student services. Adult student services, alcohol/substance abuse counseling, chaplain/spiritual director, career counseling, services for economically disadvantaged, student employment services, financial aid counseling, health services, minority student services, on-campus daycare, personal counseling, placement for graduates. **Physically disabled:** Services for visually, speech, hearing impaired.

Contact. E-mail: admissions@marquette.edu
Phone: (414) 288-7302 Toll-free number: (800) 222-6544
Fax: (414) 288-3764
Robert Blust, Dean of Undergraduate Admissions, Marquette University, PO Box 1881, Milwaukee, WI 53201-1881

Milwaukee Institute of Art & Design
Milwaukee, Wisconsin
www.miad.edu   CB code: 1506

- Private 4-year visual arts college
- Commuter campus in very large city
- 724 degree-seeking undergraduates: 2% part-time, 62% women, 5% African American, 3% Asian American, 9% Hispanic American, 1% international
- 61% of applicants admitted
- Interview required
- 57% graduate within 6 years

General. Founded in 1974. Regionally accredited. **Degrees:** 124 bachelor's awarded. **Location:** 90 miles from Chicago. **Calendar:** Semester, limited summer session. **Full-time faculty:** 41 total; 76% have terminal degrees, 12% minority, 46% women. **Part-time faculty:** 83 total; 35% have terminal degrees, 2% minority, 39% women. **Class size:** 93% < 20, 6% 20-39, less than 1% 50-99. **Special facilities:** Gallery of industrial design, public art project, 6 art galleries, foundry, 3-D lab.

Freshman class profile. 580 applied, 354 admitted, 176 enrolled.

GPA 3.75 or higher:	10%	Rank in top tenth:	10%
GPA 3.50-3.74:	13%	Return as sophomores:	77%
GPA 3.0-3.49:	26%	Out-of-state:	43%
GPA 2.0-2.99:	47%	Live on campus:	77%
Rank in top quarter:	29%	International:	1%

Basis for selection. Portfolio and interview most important. 3.0 GPA in art curriculum recommended. Portfolio of 15-20 pieces of artwork required. SAT or ACT recommended. **Home schooled:** Transcript of courses and grades required.

High school preparation. Recommended units include visual/performing arts 4. 4 years high school visual art study highly recommended.

2011-2012 Annual costs. Tuition/fees: $28,654. Room/board: $8,416. Books/supplies: $1,580. Personal expenses: $1,918.

2010-2011 Financial aid. **Need-based:** 166 full-time freshmen applied for aid; 157 were judged to have need; 157 of these received aid. Average need met was 62%. Average scholarship/grant was $15,160; average loan $4,404. 62% of total undergraduate aid awarded as scholarships/grants, 38% as loans/jobs. **Non-need-based:** Awarded to 101 full-time undergraduates, including 24 freshmen. Scholarships awarded for academics, art.

Application procedures. **Admission:** Priority date 2/15; no deadline. $25 fee, may be waived for applicants with need, free for online applicants. Admission notification on a rolling basis beginning on or about 9/1. Must reply by May 1 or within 2 week(s) if notified thereafter. **Financial aid:** Priority date 2/15; no closing date. FAFSA required. Applicants notified on a rolling basis starting 3/1; must reply by 5/1 or within 4 week(s) of notification.

Academics. **Special study options:** Cross-registration, double major, exchange student, independent study, internships, New York semester, semester at sea, study abroad. **Credit/placement by examination:** AP, CLEP. **Support services:** Learning center, reduced course load, remedial instruction, study skills assistance, tutoring, writing center.

Majors. **Visual/performing arts:** Drawing, graphic design, illustration, industrial design, interior design, painting, photography, printmaking, sculpture, studio arts.

Computing on campus. PC or laptop required. 90 workstations in library, computer center. Dormitories wired for high-speed internet access. Commuter students can connect to campus network. Online course registration, helpline, wireless network available.

Student life. **Freshman orientation:** Mandatory. Preregistration for classes offered. Four-day program held prior to fall semester. **Housing:** Coed dorms available. **Activities:** Drama, student government, Interior Design

Society of America, National Industrial Design Society, student activities committee, AIGA Student Chapter.

Student services. Alcohol/substance abuse counseling, career counseling, student employment services, financial aid counseling, health services, minority student services, personal counseling, placement for graduates, veterans' counselor.

Contact. E-mail: admissions@miad.edu
Phone: (414) 291-8070 Toll-free number: (888) 749-6423
Fax: (414) 291-8077
Stacey Steinberg, Director of Admissions, Milwaukee Institute of Art & Design, 273 East Erie Street, Milwaukee, WI 53202

Milwaukee School of Engineering
Milwaukee, Wisconsin
www.msoe.edu

CB member
CB code: 1476

- Private 4-year university
- Residential campus in very large city
- 2,310 degree-seeking undergraduates: 8% part-time, 21% women
- 176 degree-seeking graduate students
- 64% of applicants admitted
- SAT or ACT (ACT writing optional) required
- 57% graduate within 6 years; 10% enter graduate study

General. Founded in 1903. Regionally accredited. **Degrees:** 485 bachelor's awarded; master's offered. **ROTC:** Army, Naval, Air Force. **Location:** 90 miles from Chicago. **Calendar:** Quarter, limited summer session. **Full-time faculty:** 133 total; 74% have terminal degrees, 10% minority, 26% women. **Part-time faculty:** 110 total; 27% have terminal degrees, 13% minority, 38% women. **Class size:** 48% < 20, 52% 20-39. **Special facilities:** Museum, teaching and research laboratories for fluid power motion control, construction management, energy systems, renewable energy, rapid prototyping, software development, health and wellness fitness facility, indoor ice hockey arena.

Freshman class profile. 2,199 applied, 1,407 admitted, 448 enrolled.

Mid 50% test scores			
SAT critical reading:	530-670	End year in good standing:	81%
SAT math:	620-710	Return as sophomores:	76%
ACT composite:	24-29	Out-of-state:	33%
GPA 3.75 or higher:	43%	Live on campus:	80%
GPA 3.50-3.74:	23%	International:	4%
GPA 3.0-3.49:	32%	Fraternities:	1%
GPA 2.0-2.99:	2%	Sororities:	6%

Basis for selection. Admissions based on secondary school record and standardized test scores. **Home schooled:** Transcript of courses and grades required. **Learning Disabled:** Untimed standardized tests required.

High school preparation. College-preparatory program recommended. 10 units required. Required and recommended units include English 4, mathematics 4, science 2 (laboratory 2). For business and technical communication, math units should include 1 algebra. For biomedical engineering, science units should include 1 biological science.

2012-2013 Annual costs. Tuition/fees (projected): $31,920. Room/board: $8,028. Books/supplies: $1,500. Personal expenses: $1,500.

2010-2011 Financial aid. Need-based: 446 full-time freshmen applied for aid; 402 were judged to have need; 401 of these received aid. Average need met was 73%. Average scholarship/grant was $19,087; average loan $2,589. 71% of total undergraduate aid awarded as scholarships/grants, 29% as loans/jobs. **Non-need-based:** Awarded to 442 full-time undergraduates, including 113 freshmen. Scholarships awarded for academics, ROTC.

Application procedures. Admission: Priority date 2/1; no deadline. No application fee. Admission notification on a rolling basis beginning on or about 10/1. **Financial aid:** Priority date 3/15; no closing date. FAFSA required. Applicants notified on a rolling basis starting 3/1; must reply within 2 week(s) of notification.

Academics. Students receive an average of 600 hours of laboratory experience. **Special study options:** Accelerated study, combined bachelor's/graduate degree, distance learning, double major, dual enrollment of high school students, ESL, internships, study abroad. Bachelor of Science in business, mechanical engineering, and in electrical engineering with Lubeck University of Applied Sciences, Germany; exchange program with Czech Technical University, bachelor's or master's option in an engineering discipline. **Credit/placement by examination:** AP, CLEP, IB, SAT, ACT. **Support services:**

Learning center, pre-admission summer program, reduced course load, study skills assistance, tutoring, writing center.

Majors. Business: General, business admin, construction management, international, management information systems. **Communications:** Communications/speech/rhetoric. **Engineering:** General, architectural, biomedical, biomolecular, civil, computer, electrical, industrial, mechanical, software. **Health services:** Nursing (RN).

Most popular majors. Business/marketing 13%, engineering/engineering technologies 71%, health sciences 9%, trade and industry 6%.

Computing on campus. PC or laptop required. 150 workstations in dormitories, library, computer center, student center. Dormitories wired for high-speed internet access and linked to campus network. Commuter students can connect to campus network. Online course registration, online library, helpline, repair service, student web hosting, wireless network available.

Student life. Freshman orientation: Mandatory. Preregistration for classes offered. Held the week before classes begin. **Policies:** Smoke-free campus and residential facilities. **Housing:** Guaranteed on-campus for all undergraduates. Coed dorms, special housing for disabled, wellness housing available. $75 fully refundable deposit, deadline 6/1. **Activities:** Bands, campus ministries, dance, drama, international student organizations, literary magazine, radio station, student government, symphony orchestra, Residence Hall Association, Circle-K, Society of Hispanic Professional Engineers, National Society of Black Engineers, Student Nurses Association, Campus Volunteer Services, Healthcare Without Borders, Engineers Without Borders, Future Business Leaders of America.

Athletics. NCAA. **Intercollegiate:** Baseball M, basketball, cheerleading, cross-country, golf, ice hockey M, lacrosse M, rowing (crew) M, soccer, softball W, tennis, track and field, volleyball, wrestling M. **Intramural:** Basketball, football (non-tackle), soccer, softball, volleyball. **Team name:** Raiders.

Student services. Alcohol/substance abuse counseling, career counseling, services for economically disadvantaged, student employment services, financial aid counseling, health services, personal counseling, placement for graduates, veterans' counselor, women's services. **Physically disabled:** Services for visually, speech, hearing impaired.

Contact. E-mail: explore@msoe.edu
Phone: (414) 277-6763 Toll-free number: (800) 332-6763
Fax: (414) 277-7475
Dana Grennier, Director, Admission, Milwaukee School of Engineering, 1025 North Broadway, Milwaukee, WI 53202-3109

Mount Mary College
Milwaukee, Wisconsin
www.mtmary.edu

CB code: 1490

- Private 4-year liberal arts college for women affiliated with Roman Catholic Church
- Commuter campus in very large city
- 1,049 degree-seeking undergraduates: 23% part-time, 99% women, 23% African American, 5% Asian American, 11% Hispanic American, 1% international
- 498 degree-seeking graduate students
- 53% of applicants admitted
- SAT or ACT (ACT writing optional) required
- 46% graduate within 6 years

General. Founded in 1913. Regionally accredited. Open to all faiths. Small number of men admitted as part-time non-degree-seeking students, as joint nursing students with Columbia College of Nursing, and in graduate programs. **Degrees:** 204 bachelor's awarded; master's, professional offered. **ROTC:** Army, Naval. **Location:** 7 miles from downtown. **Calendar:** Semester, limited summer session. **Full-time faculty:** 62 total; 66% have terminal degrees, 84% women. **Part-time faculty:** 152 total; 22% have terminal degrees, 72% women. **Class size:** 82% < 20, 17% 20-39, less than 1% 40-49, less than 1% 50-99. **Special facilities:** Historic costume collection, labyrinth.

Freshman class profile. 423 applied, 226 admitted, 116 enrolled.

Mid 50% test scores			
ACT composite:	17-25	Rank in top quarter:	38%
GPA 3.75 or higher:	6%	Rank in top tenth:	13%
GPA 3.50-3.74:	11%	Return as sophomores:	65%
GPA 3.0-3.49:	32%	Out-of-state:	2%
GPA 2.0-2.99:	49%	Live on campus:	32%

Basis for selection. Academic record, test scores and supplemental information reviewed. Class rank, core curriculum, test scores and GPA important. Interview recommended and essay required for students who do not meet direct admission requirements. **Home schooled:** Transcript of courses and grades required. ACT or MMC assessment testing. **Learning Disabled:** Students encouraged to talk with Disabilities Coordinator at least one semester prior to enrollment to determine if reasonable accommodations can be made.

High school preparation. College-preparatory program recommended. 16 units required. Required and recommended units include English 4, mathematics 2-3, social studies 2, history 2, science 2 (laboratory 2), foreign language 2 and academic electives 2.

2011-2012 Annual costs. Tuition/fees: $23,000. Room/board: $7,550. Books/supplies: $1,260.

Financial aid. Non-need-based: Scholarships awarded for academics, alumni affiliation, art, leadership, music/drama.

Application procedures. Admission: No deadline. No application fee. Admission notification on a rolling basis beginning on or about 9/15. **Financial aid:** Priority date 3/1; no closing date. FAFSA required. Applicants notified on a rolling basis starting 3/1; must reply within 2 week(s) of notification.

Academics. Special study options: Accelerated study, combined bachelor's/graduate degree, double major, honors, independent study, internships, liberal arts/career combination, student-designed major, study abroad, teacher certification program. **Credit/placement by examination:** AP, CLEP, IB, ACT, institutional tests. Maximum of 24 credits earned through a combination of credit exams, credit from life experience, directed and independent study. **Support services:** Learning center, reduced course load, remedial instruction, study skills assistance, tutoring.

Majors. Biology: General. **Business:** Accounting, business admin, fashion, marketing. **Communications:** Communications/speech/rhetoric, public relations. **Education:** General, art, biology, business, chemistry, early childhood, elementary, English, foreign languages, history, mathematics, music, science, secondary, social studies, Spanish. **English:** English lit, technical writing. **Foreign languages:** Spanish. **Health services:** Art therapy, dietetics, medical radiologic technology/radiation therapy, nursing (RN), predental, premedicine, preveterinary, sonography. **History:** General. **Human services:** Social work. **Math:** General. **Philosophy/religion:** Philosophy, religion. **Physical sciences:** Chemistry. **Protective services:** Criminal justice. **Psychology:** General. **Social sciences:** General, international relations. **Theology:** Religious ed. **Visual/performing arts:** Art, commercial/advertising art, fashion design, interior design.

Most popular majors. Business/marketing 11%, health sciences 46%, psychology 8%, visual/performing arts 19%.

Computing on campus. 320 workstations in dormitories, library, computer center, student center. Dormitories wired for high-speed internet access and linked to campus network. Commuter students can connect to campus network. Online course registration, online library, helpline, wireless network available.

Student life. Freshman orientation: Mandatory. Preregistration for classes offered. **Housing:** Guaranteed on-campus for freshmen. $100 nonrefundable deposit, deadline 5/1. **Activities:** Campus ministries, choral groups, dance, international student organizations, literary magazine, music ensembles, Model UN, student government, student newspaper, commuter council, hall council, gospel choir, programming and activities council, department-affiliated clubs.

Athletics. NCAA. **Intercollegiate:** Basketball W, cross-country W, soccer W, softball W, tennis W, volleyball W. **Intramural:** Basketball W, bowling W, cross-country W, golf W, skiing W, soccer W, swimming W, tennis W, track and field W, volleyball W. **Team name:** Blue Angels.

Student services. Adult student services, chaplain/spiritual director, career counseling, services for economically disadvantaged, student employment services, financial aid counseling, minority student services, on-campus daycare, personal counseling. **Physically disabled:** Services for visually, hearing impaired.

Contact. E-mail: admiss@mtmary.edu
Phone: (414) 256-1219 Toll-free number: (800) 321-6265
Fax: (414) 256-0180
David Wegener, Vice President for Enrollment Services, Mount Mary College, 2900 North Menomonee River Parkway, Milwaukee, WI 53222-4597

Northland College
Ashland, Wisconsin   **CB member**
www.northland.edu   **CB code: 1561**

- Private 4-year liberal arts college affiliated with United Church of Christ
- Residential campus in small town
- 519 degree-seeking undergraduates: 3% part-time, 52% women
- 20 graduate students
- 73% of applicants admitted
- SAT or ACT (ACT writing optional), application essay required
- 48% graduate within 6 years

General. Founded in 1892. Regionally accredited. **Degrees:** 133 bachelor's awarded. **Location:** 65 miles from Duluth, MN. **Calendar:** 4-1-4, limited summer session. **Full-time faculty:** 46 total; 91% have terminal degrees, 4% minority, 39% women. **Part-time faculty:** 15 total; 20% have terminal degrees, 20% minority, 47% women. **Class size:** 74% < 20, 26% 20-39. **Special facilities:** Field stations for natural science courses, atmospheric and environmental satellite links.

Freshman class profile. 644 applied, 469 admitted, 146 enrolled.

Mid 50% test scores			
SAT critical reading:	440-580	GPA 2.0-2.99:	28%
SAT math:	420-570	Rank in top quarter:	41%
SAT writing:	440-580	Rank in top tenth:	12%
ACT composite:	20-27	Return as sophomores:	63%
GPA 3.75 or higher:	17%	Out-of-state:	57%
GPA 3.50-3.74:	19%	Live on campus:	92%
GPA 3.0-3.49:	36%	International:	3%

Basis for selection. High school curriculum evaluation, class rank, guidance counselor recommendation, GPA, and test scores considered. **Learning Disabled:** Strongly recommend students contact disabilities coordinator.

High school preparation. College-preparatory program recommended. 18 units required; 21 recommended. Required and recommended units include English 4, mathematics 3, social studies 3, science 3 (laboratory 2), foreign language 2 and academic electives 3-4.

2011-2012 Annual costs. Tuition/fees: $26,566. Room/board: $7,210. Books/supplies: $800. Personal expenses: $1,650.

2011-2012 Financial aid. Need-based: 140 full-time freshmen applied for aid; 132 were judged to have need; 132 of these received aid. Average need met was 87%. Average scholarship/grant was $19,954; average loan $3,731. 66% of total undergraduate aid awarded as scholarships/grants, 34% as loans/jobs. **Non-need-based:** Awarded to 133 full-time undergraduates, including 52 freshmen. Scholarships awarded for academics, alumni affiliation, art, job skills, leadership, minority status, music/drama, religious affiliation, state residency.

Application procedures. Admission: Priority date 12/1; no deadline. No application fee. Admission notification on a rolling basis beginning on or about 9/1. Must reply by May 1 or within 2 week(s) if notified thereafter. **Financial aid:** Priority date 3/15; no closing date. FAFSA required. Applicants notified on a rolling basis starting 3/1; must reply by 5/1 or within 4 week(s) of notification.

Academics. Special study options: Double major, dual enrollment of high school students, exchange student, independent study, internships, student-designed major, study abroad, teacher certification program. 3-2 cooperative degree programs in engineering with Michigan Technological University and Washington University. Member of the Ecoleague exchange consortium with Alaska Pacific University, Green Mountain College, Prescott College, and College of the Atlantic. **Credit/placement by examination:** AP, CLEP, IB, SAT, ACT, institutional tests. 30 credit hours maximum toward bachelor's degree. **Support services:** Remedial instruction, tutoring.

Majors. Area/ethnic studies: Native American. **Biology:** General. **Business:** Business admin. **Conservation:** General, environmental studies. **Education:** Multi-level teacher, science, secondary, social studies. **Engineering:** General. **English:** Creative writing. **Human services:** Community org/advocacy. **Liberal arts:** Humanities. **Math:** General. **Parks/recreation:** Outdoor education. **Physical sciences:** Environmental chemistry. **Social sciences:** Sociology. **Visual/performing arts:** Art.

Most popular majors. Biology 21%, business/marketing 9%, education 14%, natural resources/environmental science 24%, parks/recreation 6%, physical sciences 8%, social sciences 7%.

Computing on campus. 125 workstations in dormitories, library, computer center, student center. Dormitories wired for high-speed internet access and linked to campus network. Commuter students can connect to campus

network. Online course registration, online library, repair service, wireless network available.

Student life. Freshman orientation: Mandatory. Preregistration for classes offered. Outdoor program held for 5 days. **Housing:** Guaranteed on-campus for freshmen. Coed dorms, single-sex dorms, special housing for disabled, apartments, cooperative housing, wellness housing available. $100 fully refundable deposit, deadline 5/1. **Activities:** Bands, campus ministries, choral groups, dance, drama, international student organizations, literary magazine, music ensembles, radio station, student government, student newspaper, symphony orchestra, environmental institute, communications commission, volunteer program, environmental council, Native American student association, eco-visionary program, community bike shop, LGBT Alliance, community gardens.

Athletics. NCAA. **Intercollegiate:** Baseball M, basketball, cross-country, ice hockey M, soccer, softball W, volleyball W. **Intramural:** Archery, badminton, basketball, football (non-tackle), skiing W, soccer, softball, table tennis, volleyball. **Team name:** Lumberjacks, Lumberjills.

Student services. Alcohol/substance abuse counseling, chaplain/spiritual director, career counseling, services for economically disadvantaged, student employment services, financial aid counseling, health services, minority student services, personal counseling, placement for graduates, women's services. **Physically disabled:** Services for visually, hearing impaired.

Contact. E-mail: admit@northland.edu
Phone: (715) 682-1224 Toll-free number: (800) 753-1840
Fax: (715) 682-1258
Rick Smith, Vice President of Enrollment Management, Northland College, 1411 Ellis Avenue, Ashland, WI 54806-3999

Northland International University
Dunbar, Wisconsin
www.ni.edu   **CB code: 1787**

- Private 4-year university and Bible college affiliated with Baptist faith
- Residential campus in rural community
- 413 degree-seeking undergraduates: 8% part-time, 54% women, 1% Asian American, 1% Native American
- 82 degree-seeking graduate students

General. Regionally accredited; also accredited by TRACS. **Degrees:** 111 bachelor's, 9 associate awarded; master's, doctoral offered. **Location:** 82 miles from Green Bay. **Calendar:** Semester, limited summer session. **Full-time faculty:** 26 total. **Part-time faculty:** 14 total.

Basis for selection. Open admission.

High school preparation. College-preparatory program recommended.

2011-2012 Annual costs. Tuition/fees: $12,880. Room/board: $5,400. Books/supplies: $650. Personal expenses: $2,500.

2011-2012 Financial aid. Need-based: Average need met was 45%. Average scholarship/grant was $8,153; average loan $3,385. 81% of total undergraduate aid awarded as scholarships/grants, 19% as loans/jobs. **Non-need-based:** Scholarships awarded for academics, job skills, state residency.

Application procedures. Admission: No deadline. $50 fee, may be waived for applicants with need. Admission notification on a rolling basis. **Financial aid:** Priority date 6/1, closing date 12/1. FAFSA, institutional form required. Applicants notified by 1/1; Applicants notified on a rolling basis starting 1/1; must reply by 8/1.

Academics. Special study options: Distance learning, double major, dual enrollment of high school students, ESL, study abroad. **Credit/placement by examination:** AP, CLEP, institutional tests. **Support services:** Tutoring.

Majors. Education: Elementary, mathematics, speech. **English:** English lit. **History:** General. **Theology:** Bible. **Visual/performing arts:** Music.

Computing on campus. Dormitories wired for high-speed internet access and linked to campus network. Online course registration, online library, helpline, wireless network available.

Student life. Freshman orientation: Mandatory. Preregistration for classes offered. Four-day program held the week before start of classes. **Policies:** Religious observance required. **Housing:** Guaranteed on-campus for all undergraduates. Single-sex dorms, apartments available. **Activities:** Concert band, campus ministries, choral groups, drama, international student organizations, music ensembles, student government.

Athletics. NCCAA. **Intercollegiate:** Basketball, soccer, volleyball W. **Team name:** Pioneers.

Student services. Chaplain/spiritual director, financial aid counseling, health services, personal counseling.

Contact. E-mail: admissions@ni.edu
Phone: (715) 324-6900 ext. 3100 Toll-free number: (888) 466-7845
Fax: (715) 324-6133
Trevor Gearhart, Director of Admissions, Northland International University, W10085 Pike Plains Road, Dunbar, WI 54119

Rasmussen College: Appleton
Appleton, Wisconsin
www.rasmussen.edu

- For-profit 4-year branch campus and career college
- Small city

General. Regionally accredited. **Calendar:** Quarter.

Basis for selection. Open admission, but selective for some programs.

Application procedures. Admission: No deadline. $40 fee.

Academics. Credit/placement by examination: AP, CLEP.

Contact. Phone: (920) 750-5900
Susan Hammerstrom, Director of Admissions, Rasmussen College: Appleton, 3500 East Destination Drive, Appleton, WI 54915

Ripon College
Ripon, Wisconsin   **CB member**
www.ripon.edu   **CB code: 1664**

- Private 4-year liberal arts college
- Residential campus in small town
- 968 degree-seeking undergraduates: 51% women, 2% African American, 1% Asian American, 4% Hispanic American, 1% Native American, 3% international
- 75% of applicants admitted
- SAT or ACT (ACT writing optional), application essay required
- 70% graduate within 6 years; 32% enter graduate study

General. Founded in 1851. Regionally accredited. **Degrees:** 225 bachelor's awarded. **ROTC:** Army. **Location:** 80 miles from Milwaukee, 80 miles from Madison. **Calendar:** Semester. **Full-time faculty:** 67 total; 96% have terminal degrees, 10% minority, 39% women. **Part-time faculty:** 36 total; 42% have terminal degrees, 3% minority, 44% women. **Class size:** 66% < 20, 31% 20-39, 1% 40-49, 2% 50-99. **Special facilities:** Woodland preservation area with outdoor classroom.

Freshman class profile. 1,115 applied, 837 admitted, 227 enrolled.

Mid 50% test scores		Rank in top tenth:	23%
SAT critical reading:	500-650	End year in good standing:	89%
SAT math:	490-580	Return as sophomores:	81%
ACT composite:	22-27	Out-of-state:	29%
GPA 3.75 or higher:	27%	Live on campus:	98%
GPA 3.50-3.74:	18%	International:	2%
GPA 3.0-3.49:	36%	Fraternities:	44%
GPA 2.0-2.99:	19%	Sororities:	24%
Rank in top quarter:	54%		

Basis for selection. School achievement record, interview, class rank, test scores, recommendations, extracurricular or community activities important. **Home schooled:** Transcript of courses and grades required.

High school preparation. College-preparatory program recommended. 17 units required. Required and recommended units include English 4, mathematics 2-4, social studies 2-4, science 2-4 and foreign language 2. Math must include 1 algebra and geometry. 7 units chosen from additional units in math, science, social science, foreign language.

2011-2012 Annual costs. Tuition/fees: $28,689. Room/board: $8,270. Books/supplies: $1,000. Personal expenses: $800.

2011-2012 Financial aid. Need-based: 216 full-time freshmen applied for aid; 195 were judged to have need; 195 of these received aid. Average need met was 87%. Average scholarship/grant was $21,250; average loan

$4,413. 72% of total undergraduate aid awarded as scholarships/grants, 28% as loans/jobs. **Non-need-based:** Awarded to 215 full-time undergraduates, including 48 freshmen. Scholarships awarded for academics, alumni affiliation, art, leadership, minority status, music/drama, religious affiliation, ROTC, state residency.

Application procedures. Admission: Priority date 3/15; no deadline. $30 fee, may be waived for applicants with need. Admission notification on a rolling basis beginning on or about 1/15. Must reply by May 1 or within 2 week(s) if notified thereafter. **Financial aid:** Priority date 3/1, closing date 6/15. FAFSA required. Applicants notified on a rolling basis starting 3/1; must reply within 2 week(s) of notification.

Academics. Special study options: Accelerated study, combined bachelor's/graduate degree, double major, exchange student, internships, student-designed major, study abroad, teacher certification program, urban semester, Washington semester. Domestic and international off-campus study programs. **Credit/placement by examination:** AP, CLEP, IB. Amount of credit and placement for AP exams subject to departmental approval. **Support services:** Learning center, study skills assistance, tutoring.

Majors. Area/ethnic studies: Latin American, women's. **Biology:** General, biochemistry. **Business:** Business admin. **Communications:** Communications/speech/rhetoric. **Computer sciences:** Computer science. **Conservation:** Environmental studies. **Education:** General. **English:** English lit. **Foreign languages:** General, classics, French, German, Spanish. **Health services:** Predental, premedicine, prenursing, prepharmacy, preveterinary. **History:** General. **Math:** General. **Parks/recreation:** Exercise sciences. **Philosophy/religion:** Philosophy, religion. **Physical sciences:** General, chemistry, physics. **Psychology:** General. **Social sciences:** Anthropology, economics, political science, sociology. **Visual/performing arts:** Art, art history/conservation, dramatic, music.

Most popular majors. Biology 8%, business/marketing 12%, English 7%, history 9%, parks/recreation 12%, psychology 8%, social sciences 14%, theological studies 6%.

Computing on campus. 150 workstations in dormitories, library, computer center. Dormitories wired for high-speed internet access and linked to campus network. Commuter students can connect to campus network. Helpline, student web hosting available.

Student life. Freshman orientation: Available, $45 fee. Preregistration for classes offered. 2-day overnight orientation held in late June for students and family. **Housing:** Guaranteed on-campus for all undergraduates. Coed dorms, single-sex dorms, fraternity/sorority housing, wellness housing available. $200 nonrefundable deposit, deadline 8/15. **Activities:** Bands, campus ministries, choral groups, dance, drama, film society, international student organizations, literary magazine, music ensembles, musical theater, radio station, student government, student newspaper, symphony orchestra, Christian Fellowship, Big Brother/Big Sister, multicultural club, romance language club, environmental group, Feminists for Equality, College Democrats, College Republicans.

Athletics. NCAA. **Intercollegiate:** Baseball M, basketball, cross-country, diving, football (tackle) M, golf, soccer, softball W, swimming, tennis, track and field, volleyball W. **Intramural:** Basketball, bowling, fencing, football (non-tackle), golf, racquetball, soccer, softball, table tennis, tennis, volleyball, water polo. **Team name:** Red Hawks.

Student services. Career counseling, student employment services, financial aid counseling, health services, personal counseling, placement for graduates.

Contact. E-mail: adminfo@ripon.edu
Phone: (920) 748-8337 Toll-free number: (800) 947-4766
Fax: (920) 748-8335
Leigh Mlodzik, Dean of Admission, Ripon College, 300 Seward Street, Ripon, WI 54971-0248

Sanford-Brown College: Milwaukee
West Allis, Wisconsin
www.sbcmilwaukee.com   CB code: 5702

- For-profit 4-year business and health science college
- Commuter campus in small city

General. Accredited by ACICS. **Calendar:** Differs by program.

Contact. Phone: (414) 771-2200
6737 West Washington Street, Suite 2355, West Allis, WI 53214

Silver Lake College of the Holy Family
Manitowoc, Wisconsin
www.sl.edu   CB code: 1300

- Private 4-year liberal arts college affiliated with Roman Catholic Church
- Commuter campus in large town
- 316 degree-seeking undergraduates: 43% part-time, 74% women, 5% African American, 1% Asian American, 4% Hispanic American, 2% Native American, 2% international
- 118 degree-seeking graduate students
- 60% of applicants admitted
- SAT or ACT (ACT writing optional) required
- 42% graduate within 6 years

General. Founded in 1935. Regionally accredited. **Degrees:** 91 bachelor's awarded; master's offered. **Location:** 80 miles from Milwaukee, 30 miles from Green Bay. **Calendar:** Semester, limited summer session. **Full-time faculty:** 37 total; 43% have terminal degrees, 5% minority, 81% women. **Part-time faculty:** 3 total; 33% women. **Class size:** 96% < 20, 4% 20-39. **Special facilities:** Nature preserve.

Freshman class profile. 176 applied, 105 admitted, 46 enrolled.

Mid 50% test scores			
SAT critical reading:	370-410	Rank in top quarter:	15%
ACT composite:	16-22	Rank in top tenth:	6%
GPA 3.75 or higher:	11%	End year in good standing:	76%
GPA 3.50-3.74:	11%	Return as sophomores:	63%
GPA 3.0-3.49:	28%	Out-of-state:	4%
GPA 2.0-2.99:	50%	Live on campus:	80%
		International:	2%

Basis for selection. Admission based on formula of GPA x ACT x 10. Those below 300 will be denied admission, 301-449 granted provisional admission, and 450 and above accepted. Audition and interview recommended for music; portfolio and interview recommended for art. **Home schooled:** Transcript of courses and grades required. **Learning Disabled:** IEP should be submitted to Director of Learning Resources.

High school preparation. College-preparatory program recommended. 16 units required. Required units include English 4, mathematics 3, social studies 2, history 1, science 3 (laboratory 1) and foreign language 1. 1 unit of fine arts may be substituted for foreign language requirement.

2011-2012 Annual costs. Tuition/fees: $21,820. Room/board: $8,500. Books/supplies: $1,050. Personal expenses: $1,500.

2011-2012 Financial aid. Need-based: 40 full-time freshmen applied for aid; 39 were judged to have need; 39 of these received aid. Average need met was 85%. Average scholarship/grant was $17,775; average loan $3,316. 49% of total undergraduate aid awarded as scholarships/grants, 51% as loans/jobs. **Non-need-based:** Awarded to 171 full-time undergraduates, including 51 freshmen. Scholarships awarded for academics, art, athletics, leadership, music/drama, state residency.

Application procedures. Admission: Priority date 8/1; no deadline. $50 fee, may be waived for applicants with need. Admission notification on a rolling basis beginning on or about 9/1. **Financial aid:** Priority date 3/15; no closing date. FAFSA required. Applicants notified on a rolling basis starting 3/15.

Academics. Special study options: Accelerated study, distance learning, double major, dual enrollment of high school students, independent study, internships, liberal arts/career combination, student-designed major, teacher certification program. **Credit/placement by examination:** AP, CLEP, IB, SAT, ACT, institutional tests. 30 credit hours maximum toward associate degree, 60 toward bachelor's. **Support services:** Learning center, reduced course load, remedial instruction, study skills assistance, tutoring.

Majors. Biology: General. **Business:** Accounting, business admin, human resources. **Computer sciences:** Computer science, information systems. **Education:** Art, early childhood, early childhood special, elementary, learning disabled, mentally handicapped, music. **English:** English lit. **Health services:** Nursing (RN). **History:** General. **Math:** General. **Psychology:** General. **Theology:** Theology. **Visual/performing arts:** Art, music.

Most popular majors. Business/marketing 44%, education 15%, English 7%, psychology 10%, visual/performing arts 8%.

Computing on campus. 78 workstations in dormitories, library, computer center, student center. Dormitories wired for high-speed internet access and linked to campus network. Commuter students can connect to campus network. Online course registration, online library, wireless network available.

Student life. Freshman orientation: Mandatory. Preregistration for classes offered. **Housing:** Guaranteed on-campus for all undergraduates. Coed dorms, special housing for disabled, wellness housing available. $100 nonrefundable deposit, deadline 8/1. **Activities:** Bands, campus ministries, choral groups, dance, literary magazine, music ensembles, student government, student newspaper, Wisconsin Art Education Association, National Art Education Association student chapter, student education association, Student Council for Exceptional Children, early childhood association, human resource management association, psychology student organization, Young Democrats and Republicans.

Athletics. USCAA. **Intercollegiate:** Basketball, cross-country, golf. **Intramural:** Football (non-tackle), table tennis, volleyball. **Team name:** Lakers.

Student services. Adult student services, alcohol/substance abuse counseling, chaplain/spiritual director, career counseling, student employment services, financial aid counseling, health services, personal counseling, placement for graduates.

Contact. E-mail: admslc@sl.edu
Phone: (920) 686-6175 Toll-free number: (800) 236-4752 ext. 175
Fax: (920) 686-6322
Cynthia St. John, Director of Admissions, Silver Lake College of the Holy Family, 2406 South Alverno Road, Manitowoc, WI 54220-9319

St. Norbert College
De Pere, Wisconsin
www.snc.edu
CB member
CB code: 1706

- Private 4-year liberal arts college affiliated with Roman Catholic Church
- Residential campus in large town
- 2,128 degree-seeking undergraduates: 2% part-time, 58% women, 1% African American, 1% Asian American, 2% Hispanic American, 1% Native American, 5% international
- 31 degree-seeking graduate students
- 80% of applicants admitted
- SAT or ACT (ACT writing optional) required
- 71% graduate within 6 years; 23% enter graduate study

General. Founded in 1898. Regionally accredited. **Degrees:** 492 bachelor's awarded; master's offered. **ROTC:** Army. **Location:** 5 miles from Green Bay. **Calendar:** Semester, limited summer session. **Full-time faculty:** 139 total; 87% have terminal degrees, 7% minority, 43% women. **Part-time faculty:** 58 total; 28% have terminal degrees, 3% minority, 52% women. **Class size:** 45% < 20, 53% 20-39, 2% 40-49. **Special facilities:** Marina, on-campus hotel and conference center, fine and performing arts centers, center for international education, peace and justice center, center for leadership and service, children's center, women's center, Strategic Research Institute, center for Norbertine studies.

Freshman class profile. 2,382 applied, 1,917 admitted, 594 enrolled.

Mid 50% test scores		End year in good standing:	91%
ACT composite:	22-27	Return as sophomores:	82%
GPA 3.75 or higher:	30%	Out-of-state:	28%
GPA 3.50-3.74:	21%	Live on campus:	96%
GPA 3.0-3.49:	33%	International:	3%
GPA 2.0-2.99:	16%	Fraternities:	6%
Rank in top quarter:	53%	Sororities:	10%
Rank in top tenth:	26%		

Basis for selection. High school record, rigor of courses, and grades earned important. Preference given to students successfully completing challenging courses. Counselor and teacher recommendations, community service considered. Students not in college preparatory programs may be offered admission if test results, class rank, and grades demonstrate aptitude for college work. Essay, interview recommended for all; audition recommended for music. **Learning Disabled:** Students should submit documentation of specific disability to receive proper level of support from institution.

High school preparation. College-preparatory program recommended. 16 units recommended. Recommended units include English 4, mathematics 3, social studies 2, history 2, science 3 (laboratory 3) and foreign language 2. As many college-prep elective units as possible.

2011-2012 Annual costs. Tuition/fees: $29,398. Room/board: $7,513. Books/supplies: $950. Personal expenses: $750.

2010-2011 Financial aid. Need-based: 529 full-time freshmen applied for aid; 457 were judged to have need; 457 of these received aid. Average need met was 84%. Average scholarship/grant was $17,922; average loan $3,756. 61% of total undergraduate aid awarded as scholarships/grants, 39% as loans/jobs. **Non-need-based:** Awarded to 594 full-time undergraduates, including 147 freshmen. Scholarships awarded for academics, art, leadership, minority status, music/drama, ROTC, state residency.

Application procedures. Admission: Priority date 4/1; no deadline. $25 fee, may be waived for applicants with need. Admission notification on a rolling basis beginning on or about 10/1. Must reply by May 1 or within 3 week(s) if notified thereafter. **Financial aid:** Priority date 3/1; no closing date. FAFSA required. Applicants notified on a rolling basis starting 3/15; must reply within 2 week(s) of notification.

Academics. Study abroad strongly supported, and students are allowed to apply all of their financial aid to their study abroad program costs; student/faculty collaborative research. **Special study options:** Distance learning, double major, ESL, honors, independent study, internships, student-designed major, study abroad, teacher certification program, Washington semester. Foundation for International Education (London) Internship. **Credit/placement by examination:** AP, CLEP, IB, institutional tests. **Support services:** Learning center, reduced course load, remedial instruction, study skills assistance, tutoring, writing center.

Majors. Biology: General, biochemistry. **Business:** General, accounting, business admin, finance, human resources, international, management information systems, marketing. **Communications:** Communications/speech/rhetoric, media studies. **Computer sciences:** Computer graphics, computer science. **Conservation:** Environmental science. **Education:** Early childhood, elementary, music. **English:** Creative writing, English lit. **Foreign languages:** French, German, Spanish. **Health services:** Predental, premedicine, prenursing, prepharmacy, preveterinary. **History:** General. **Liberal arts:** Humanities. **Math:** General. **Philosophy/religion:** Philosophy, religion. **Physical sciences:** Chemistry, geology, physics. **Psychology:** General. **Social sciences:** Anthropology, economics, international relations, political science, sociology. **Theology:** Religious ed. **Visual/performing arts:** Art, commercial/advertising art, dramatic, graphic design, music.

Most popular majors. Biology 7%, business/marketing 27%, communications/journalism 10%, education 15%, social sciences 8%.

Computing on campus. 247 workstations in dormitories, library, computer center, student center. Dormitories wired for high-speed internet access and linked to campus network. Commuter students can connect to campus network. Online course registration, online library, helpline, repair service, wireless network available.

Student life. Freshman orientation: Mandatory. Preregistration for classes offered. 2-day summer program for students and parents. **Housing:** Guaranteed on-campus for all undergraduates. Coed dorms, single-sex dorms, special housing for disabled, apartments, wellness housing available. $100 nonrefundable deposit, deadline 5/1. Townhouses and college-owned houses near campus available. **Activities:** Bands, campus ministries, choral groups, drama, film society, international student organizations, literary magazine, music ensembles, musical theater, radio station, student government, student newspaper, TV station, Campus Crusade for Christ, College Republicans, College Democrats, Japan club, Spanish club, Beyond Borders, Discoveries International, Circle K, Optimist Club.

Athletics. NCAA. **Intercollegiate:** Baseball M, basketball, cross-country, football (tackle) M, golf, ice hockey, soccer, softball W, tennis, track and field, volleyball W. **Intramural:** Basketball, football (non-tackle), softball, volleyball. **Team name:** Green Knights.

Student services. Alcohol/substance abuse counseling, chaplain/spiritual director, career counseling, student employment services, financial aid counseling, health services, minority student services, on-campus daycare, personal counseling, placement for graduates, veterans' counselor, women's services. **Physically disabled:** Services for visually, speech, hearing impaired.

Contact. E-mail: admit@snc.edu
Phone: (920) 403-3005 Toll-free number: (800) 236-4878
Fax: (920) 403-4072
Ed Lamm, Executive Director of Enrollment Management and Marketing, St. Norbert College, 100 Grant Street, De Pere, WI 54115-2099

University of Phoenix: Madison
Madison, Wisconsin
www.phoenix.edu

- For-profit 4-year university
- Small city
- 187 degree-seeking undergraduates

General. Regionally accredited. **Degrees:** 7 bachelor's awarded; master's offered. **Calendar:** Differs by program. **Full-time faculty:** 4 total. **Part-time faculty:** 66 total.

Basis for selection. Open admission, but selective for some programs.

2011-2012 Annual costs. Estimated costs as of August 2011: per-credit-hour charge, $380 to $450, depending upon level and course of study; electronic course materials fee, $95, if applicable. Book and material charges may vary by course and program. All fees are subject to change.

Application procedures. Admission: No deadline. No application fee. **Financial aid:** No deadline.

Academics. Credit/placement by examination: AP, CLEP.

Majors. Business: Business admin. **Communications:** General.

Contact. Toll-free number: (866) 766-0766
Marc Booker, Director of Admission and Evaluation, University of Phoenix: Madison, 2310 Crossroads Drive, Madison, WI 53718-2416

University of Phoenix: Milwaukee
Brookfield, Wisconsin
www.phoenix.edu

- For-profit 4-year university
- Large city
- 438 degree-seeking undergraduates

General. Regionally accredited. **Degrees:** 73 bachelor's awarded; master's offered. **Calendar:** Differs by program. **Full-time faculty:** 16 total. **Part-time faculty:** 151 total.

Basis for selection. Open admission, but selective for some programs.

2011-2012 Annual costs. Estimated costs as of August 2011: per-credit-hour charge, $420 to $450, depending upon level and course of study; electronic course materials fee, $95, if applicable. Book and material charges may vary by course and program. All fees are subject to change.

Application procedures. Admission: No deadline. No application fee. **Financial aid:** No deadline.

Academics. Credit/placement by examination: AP, CLEP.

Majors. Business: Business admin. **Communications technology:** General. **Computer sciences:** Information technology.

Contact. Marc Booker, Director of Admission and Evaluation, University of Phoenix: Milwaukee, 20075 Watertower Road, Brookfield, WI 53045-3573

University of Wisconsin-Eau Claire
Eau Claire, Wisconsin
www.uwec.edu   **CB code: 1913**

- Public 4-year university
- Residential campus in small city
- 10,382 degree-seeking undergraduates: 7% part-time, 58% women, 1% African American, 3% Asian American, 2% Hispanic American, 2% international
- 517 degree-seeking graduate students
- 77% of applicants admitted
- SAT or ACT (ACT writing optional) required
- 65% graduate within 6 years; 10% enter graduate study

General. Founded in 1916. Regionally accredited. **Degrees:** 2,020 bachelor's, 7 associate awarded; master's, professional offered. **ROTC:** Army. **Location:** 90 miles from Minneapolis-St. Paul. **Calendar:** Semester, extensive summer session. **Full-time faculty:** 425 total; 78% have terminal degrees, 13% minority, 47% women. **Part-time faculty:** 104 total; 30% have terminal degrees, 6% minority, 71% women. **Class size:** 29% < 20, 53% 20-39, 7% 40-49, 9% 50-99, 2% >100. **Special facilities:** Bird museum, human development center, planetarium, natural preserve, ropes course, material sciences center, clinical simulation skills lab, 200 kev transmission electron microscope, x-ray photoelectron spectroscopy system, scanning tunneling microscope, scanning electron microscope with energy dispersive x-ray microanalysis, x-ray fluorescence spectrometer, x-ray diffractometer, high resolution inductively coupled plasma mass spectrometer.

Freshman class profile. 6,503 applied, 4,980 admitted, 1,948 enrolled.

Mid 50% test scores		
SAT critical reading:	510-670	
SAT math:	510-660	
ACT composite:	22-26	
Rank in top quarter:	54%	
Rank in top tenth:	20%	

End year in good standing:	85%
Return as sophomores:	84%
Out-of-state:	28%
Live on campus:	92%
International:	1%

Basis for selection. Applicants must present required combination of rank and test scores. Special consideration given to disadvantaged, veterans, and minority applicants. Applicants with rank in top 50% or 23 ACT given first priority. Some applicants not admitted to fall semester may be considered for following spring semester. Wisconsin residents required to take ACT; non-residents may submit SAT. Audition required for music programs.

High school preparation. College-preparatory program required. 17 units required. Required units include English 4, mathematics 3, social studies 3, science 3, foreign language 2 and academic electives 2.

2011-2012 Annual costs. Tuition/fees: $8,025; $15,598 out-of-state. Minnesota reciprocity tuition: $281 per-credit-hour. Room/board: $5,950. Books/supplies: $460. Personal expenses: $1,900.

2010-2011 Financial aid. Need-based: 1,683 full-time freshmen applied for aid; 1,095 were judged to have need; 1,073 of these received aid. Average need met was 88%. Average scholarship/grant was $5,658; average loan $3,714. 43% of total undergraduate aid awarded as scholarships/grants, 57% as loans/jobs. **Non-need-based:** Awarded to 565 full-time undergraduates, including 151 freshmen. Scholarships awarded for academics, art, leadership, minority status, music/drama, state residency.

Application procedures. Admission: Priority date 12/1; no deadline. $44 fee, may be waived for applicants with need. Admission notification on a rolling basis beginning on or about 9/15. Closing and priority dates may vary by program. **Financial aid:** Priority date 4/15; no closing date. FAFSA required. Applicants notified on a rolling basis starting 4/15.

Academics. Baccalaureate degree includes service-learning requirement, freshman seminars, capstone courses, internships in most majors, and opportunities for students to collaborate with faculty on research and scholarly projects. **Special study options:** Accelerated study, cooperative education, cross-registration, distance learning, double major, dual enrollment of high school students, ESL, exchange student, external degree, honors, independent study, internships, student-designed major, study abroad, teacher certification program. Program with University of Wisconsin-Stout in early childhood education. **Credit/placement by examination:** AP, CLEP, IB, ACT, institutional tests. 15 credit hours maximum toward associate degree, 30 toward bachelor's. **Support services:** Learning center, pre-admission summer program, reduced course load, remedial instruction, study skills assistance, tutoring, writing center.

Majors. Area/ethnic studies: Latin American, Native American, women's. **Biology:** General, molecular. **Business:** Accounting, business admin, finance, information resources management, international, marketing, organizational leadership. **Communications:** Communications/speech/rhetoric, journalism, media studies. **Computer sciences:** General. **Education:** Elementary, science, social studies, special ed. **English:** English lit. **Foreign languages:** French, Germanic, Spanish. **Health services:** Athletic training, communication disorders, community health, health care admin, nursing (RN). **History:** General. **Human services:** Social work. **Liberal arts:** Arts/sciences. **Math:** General. **Parks/recreation:** Exercise sciences. **Philosophy/religion:** Philosophy, religion. **Physical sciences:** Chemistry, geology, physics. **Protective services:** Criminal justice. **Psychology:** General. **Social sciences:** Economics, geography, political science, sociology. **Visual/performing arts:** Art, dramatic, music.

Most popular majors. Biology 6%, business/marketing 23%, communications/journalism 6%, education 8%, health sciences 14%, parks/recreation 6%, social sciences 6%, visual/performing arts 6%.

Computing on campus. 900 workstations in dormitories, library, computer center, student center. Dormitories wired for high-speed internet access and linked to campus network. Commuter students can connect to campus network. Online course registration, online library, helpline, wireless network available.

Student life. Freshman orientation: Mandatory, $100 fee. Preregistration for classes offered. One-day session. **Housing:** Guaranteed on-campus for freshmen. Coed dorms, single-sex dorms, apartments, wellness housing available. $75 fully refundable deposit. **Activities:** Bands, campus ministries, choral groups, dance, drama, film society, international student organizations, literary magazine, music ensembles, Model UN, musical theater, opera, radio station, student government, student newspaper, symphony orchestra, TV station, College Republicans, College Democrats, Newman Student Association, ecumenical religious center student association, Alpha Phi Omega service fraternity, Mortar Board, black student organization, Native American student organization, Hmong student association.

Athletics. NCAA. **Intercollegiate:** Basketball, cross-country, diving, football (tackle) M, golf, gymnastics W, ice hockey, soccer W, softball W, swimming, tennis, track and field, volleyball W, wrestling M. **Intramural:** Basketball, football (non-tackle), racquetball, soccer, softball, tennis, volleyball. **Team name:** Blugolds.

Student services. Adult student services, alcohol/substance abuse counseling, chaplain/spiritual director, career counseling, services for economically disadvantaged, student employment services, financial aid counseling, health services, legal services, minority student services, on-campus daycare, personal counseling, placement for graduates, veterans' counselor, women's services. **Physically disabled:** Services for visually, speech, hearing impaired.

Contact. E-mail: admissions@uwec.edu
Phone: (715) 836-5415 Fax: (715) 836-2409
Kristina Anderson, Executive Director, Enrollment Services & Admissions, University of Wisconsin-Eau Claire, 111 Schofield Hall, Eau Claire, WI 54701

University of Wisconsin-Green Bay

Green Bay, Wisconsin — **CB member**
www.uwgb.edu — **CB code: 1859**

- Public 4-year university and liberal arts college
- Residential campus in small city
- 6,094 degree-seeking undergraduates: 24% part-time, 64% women
- 124 degree-seeking graduate students
- 65% of applicants admitted
- SAT or ACT (ACT writing optional) required
- 54% graduate within 6 years; 15% enter graduate study

General. Founded in 1965. Regionally accredited. **Degrees:** 1,127 bachelor's, 10 associate awarded; master's offered. **ROTC:** Army. **Location:** 80 miles from Milwaukee. **Calendar:** Semester, limited summer session. **Full-time faculty:** 181 total; 88% have terminal degrees, 18% minority, 44% women. **Part-time faculty:** 163 total; 58% women. **Class size:** 24% < 20, 47% 20-39, 16% 40-49, 10% 50-99, 3% >100. **Special facilities:** Natural history museum, herbarium, 290-acre arboretum, performing arts center.

Freshman class profile. 3,471 applied, 2,249 admitted, 910 enrolled.

Mid 50% test scores		**GPA 2.0-2.99:**	23%
SAT critical reading:	500-590	**End year in good standing:**	80%
SAT math:	450-560	**Return as sophomores:**	73%
SAT writing:	490-590	**Out-of-state:**	5%
ACT composite:	21-25	**Live on campus:**	78%
GPA 3.75 or higher:	19%	**International:**	1%
GPA 3.50-3.74:	19%	**Fraternities:**	1%
GPA 3.0-3.49:	39%	**Sororities:**	1%

Basis for selection. 17 ACT, 2.25 GPA and extracurricular or community involvement important. Priority given to students with 23 ACT or 3.25 GPA. Students not meeting standard admission requirements may be considered on individual basis. Interview may be requested of borderline applicants; audition required for music. **Home schooled:** Transcript of courses and grades required.

High school preparation. College-preparatory program required. 17 units required; 19 recommended. Required and recommended units include English 4, mathematics 3, social studies 3, science 3 (laboratory 1), foreign language 2 and academic electives 4. Math must include algebra or more advanced course. 2 of the 4 required academic electives must be from English, math, science, social studies, or foreign language.

2011-2012 Annual costs. Tuition/fees: $7,282; $14,855 out-of-state. Minnesota reciprocity tuition: $270 per-credit-hour. Room/board: $5,700. Books/supplies: $800. Personal expenses: $2,000.

2011-2012 Financial aid. Need-based: 801 full-time freshmen applied for aid; 620 were judged to have need; 599 of these received aid. Average need met was 82%. Average scholarship/grant was $5,230; average loan $4,525. 44% of total undergraduate aid awarded as scholarships/grants, 56% as loans/jobs. **Non-need-based:** Awarded to 1,309 full-time undergraduates, including 320 freshmen. Scholarships awarded for academics, art, athletics, leadership, minority status, music/drama. **Additional information:** Auditions required for music and theater scholarships. Tuition waived for veterans and for children of Wisconsin soldiers or policemen who were slain in the line of duty.

Application procedures. Admission: Priority date 4/15; no deadline. $44 fee, may be waived for applicants with need. Admission notification on a rolling basis beginning on or about 9/15. **Financial aid:** Priority date 4/1; no closing date. FAFSA required. Applicants notified on a rolling basis starting 1/1; must reply within 3 week(s) of notification.

Academics. Teacher certification available in conjunction with bachelor's degree. **Special study options:** Combined bachelor's/graduate degree, distance learning, double major, dual enrollment of high school students, exchange student, external degree, independent study, internships, liberal arts/career combination, student-designed major, study abroad, teacher certification program. **Credit/placement by examination:** AP, CLEP, IB, ACT, institutional tests. 47 credit hours maximum toward associate degree, 93 toward bachelor's. **Support services:** Pre-admission summer program, reduced course load, remedial instruction, study skills assistance, tutoring, writing center.

Majors. Area/ethnic studies: Native American, women's. **Biology:** General. **Business:** Accounting, business admin. **Communications:** Communications/speech/rhetoric. **Computer sciences:** Computer science, information systems. **Conservation:** Environmental science, environmental studies. **Education:** Elementary, music. **English:** English lit. **Foreign languages:** French, German, Spanish. **Health services:** Nursing (RN). **History:** General. **Human services:** General, social work. **Liberal arts:** Arts/sciences, humanities. **Math:** General. **Philosophy/religion:** Philosophy. **Physical sciences:** Chemistry, physics. **Psychology:** General. **Social sciences:** Economics, political science, sociology, urban studies. **Visual/performing arts:** General, art, arts management, dramatic, music, music performance.

Most popular majors. Business/marketing 16%, education 6%, health sciences 6%, interdisciplinary studies 15%, liberal arts 9%, psychology 8%, social sciences 6%, visual/performing arts 7%.

Computing on campus. 600 workstations in dormitories, library, computer center, student center. Dormitories wired for high-speed internet access and linked to campus network. Commuter students can connect to campus network. Online course registration, online library, helpline, repair service, wireless network available.

Student life. Freshman orientation: Available, $200 fee. Preregistration for classes offered. Held the week before fall classes begin. **Housing:** Coed dorms, apartments, wellness housing available. $225 fully refundable deposit. Suite-style apartments with private bathrooms available. **Activities:** Bands, choral groups, dance, drama, film society, international student organizations, literary magazine, music ensembles, Model UN, musical theater, radio station, student government, student newspaper, TV station, College Republicans, College Democrats, Habitat for Humanity, Circle K, Ten Percent Society, Athletes in Action, American Marketing Association, psychology and human development club, Wisconsin Education Association Council.

Athletics. NCAA. **Intercollegiate:** Basketball, cheerleading, cross-country, diving, golf, skiing, soccer, softball W, swimming, tennis, volleyball W. **Intramural:** Basketball, football (non-tackle), golf, racquetball, soccer, softball, tennis, volleyball. **Team name:** Phoenix.

Student services. Adult student services, alcohol/substance abuse counseling, career counseling, student employment services, financial aid counseling, health services, minority student services, personal counseling, placement for graduates, veterans' counselor. **Physically disabled:** Services for visually, hearing impaired.

Contact. E-mail: admissions@uwgb.edu
Phone: (920) 465-2111 Toll-free number: (800) 621-2313
Fax: (920) 465-5754
Pam Harvey-Jacobs, Director of Admissions, University of Wisconsin-Green Bay, 2420 Nicolet Drive, Green Bay, WI 54311-7001

University of Wisconsin-La Crosse

La Crosse, Wisconsin — **CB member**
www.uwlax.edu — **CB code: 1914**

- Public 4-year university
- Residential campus in small city
- 8,878 degree-seeking undergraduates: 3% part-time, 58% women, 1% African American, 3% Asian American, 2% Hispanic American, 3% international
- 866 degree-seeking graduate students
- 76% of applicants admitted
- SAT or ACT (ACT writing optional) required
- 69% graduate within 6 years

General. Founded in 1909. Regionally accredited. **Degrees:** 1,654 bachelor's, 4 associate awarded; master's, doctoral offered. **ROTC:** Army. **Location:** 140 miles from Madison, 160 miles from Minneapolis-St. Paul. **Calendar:** Semester, limited summer session. **Full-time faculty:** 419 total; 76%

have terminal degrees, 15% minority, 48% women. **Part-time faculty:** 132 total; 6% have terminal degrees, 4% minority, 48% women. **Class size:** 31% < 20, 54% 20-39, 6% 40-49, 8% 50-99, 1% >100. **Special facilities:** Greenhouse, planetarium, nuclear radiation laboratory, river studies center, archaeology center.

Freshman class profile. 6,438 applied, 4,866 admitted, 1,978 enrolled.

Mid 50% test scores		Out-of-state:	17%
ACT composite:	23-27	Live on campus:	96%
Rank in top quarter:	70%	International:	1%
Rank in top tenth:	24%	Fraternities:	1%
Return as sophomores:	85%	Sororities:	1%

Basis for selection. Academic preparation (rigor of courses, class rank, GPA, test scores) very important. Demonstrated leadership, extracurricular involvement, special talent, personal statement, recommendations, and ability to add diversity to campus community considered. Interviews optional but may be considered. Auditions may be required for some scholarships. Portfolios and essays optional but will be considered. **Home schooled:** Interview may be required. **Learning Disabled:** Information regarding learning disability may be considered in admission decision.

High school preparation. College-preparatory program required. 17 units required; 23 recommended. Required and recommended units include English 4, mathematics 3-4, social studies 3-4, science 3-4 (laboratory 2-3), foreign language 3 and academic electives 4.

2011-2012 Annual costs. Tuition/fees: $8,329; $15,902 out-of-state. Minnesota reciprocity tuition: $300 per-credit-hour. Room/board: $5,930.

2010-2011 Financial aid. **Need-based:** 1,466 full-time freshmen applied for aid; 966 were judged to have need; 952 of these received aid. Average need met was 77%. Average scholarship/grant was $5,891; average loan $3,274. 42% of total undergraduate aid awarded as scholarships/grants, 58% as loans/jobs. **Non-need-based:** Awarded to 1,355 full-time undergraduates, including 475 freshmen. Scholarships awarded for academics, alumni affiliation, art, leadership, minority status, music/drama, ROTC.

Application procedures. **Admission:** Priority date 2/1; no deadline. $44 fee, may be waived for applicants with need. Admission notification on a rolling basis beginning on or about 9/15. **Financial aid:** Priority date 3/15; no closing date. FAFSA required. Applicants notified on a rolling basis starting 4/1.

Academics. **Special study options:** Combined bachelor's/graduate degree, cooperative education, cross-registration, distance learning, double major, dual enrollment of high school students, ESL, exchange student, independent study, internships, liberal arts/career combination, study abroad, teacher certification program. **Credit/placement by examination:** AP, CLEP, IB, SAT, ACT, institutional tests. 16 credit hours maximum toward associate degree, 32 toward bachelor's. **Support services:** Learning center, pre-admission summer program, reduced course load, remedial instruction, study skills assistance, tutoring, writing center.

Majors. **Biology:** General, biochemistry, microbiology. **Business:** Accounting, business admin, finance, international, management information systems, marketing. **Communications:** Communications/speech/rhetoric. **Computer sciences:** General. **Education:** Elementary, health, science, social studies. **English:** English lit. **Foreign languages:** French, German, Spanish. **Health services:** General, athletic training, clinical lab science, community health, medical radiologic technology/radiation therapy, nuclear medical technology, recreational therapy. **History:** General. **Math:** General. **Parks/recreation:** Exercise sciences, facilities management. **Philosophy/religion:** Philosophy. **Physical sciences:** Chemistry, physics. **Psychology:** General. **Social sciences:** Archaeology, economics, geography, political science, sociology. **Visual/performing arts:** Art, dramatic, music.

Most popular majors. Biology 12%, business/marketing 22%, education 11%, health sciences 11%, parks/recreation 7%, psychology 8%, social sciences 10%.

Computing on campus. 550 workstations in dormitories, library, computer center, student center. Dormitories wired for high-speed internet access and linked to campus network. Commuter students can connect to campus network. Online course registration, online library, helpline, wireless network available.

Student life. **Freshman orientation:** Available, $140 fee. Preregistration for classes offered. One-day program held in June and prior to start of fall term. **Housing:** Coed dorms, special housing for disabled, apartments available. $75 fully refundable deposit, deadline 5/1. First Year Experience housing available. **Activities:** Bands, campus ministries, choral groups, dance, drama, international student organizations, literary magazine, music ensembles, musical theater, radio station, student government, student newspaper, symphony orchestra, TV station, Black Students Unity, Native American Council, Hispanic student organization, Asian association, Amnesty International, Newman Club, hall councils, Intervarsity Christian Fellowship, Cru.

Athletics. NAIA, NCAA. **Intercollegiate:** Baseball M, basketball, cross-country, diving, football (tackle) M, gymnastics W, soccer W, softball W, swimming, tennis, track and field, volleyball W, wrestling M. **Intramural:** Badminton, basketball, cheerleading, football (non-tackle), golf, racquetball, soccer, softball, table tennis, tennis, volleyball, weight lifting. **Team name:** Eagles.

Student services. Adult student services, alcohol/substance abuse counseling, chaplain/spiritual director, career counseling, services for economically disadvantaged, student employment services, financial aid counseling, health services, legal services, minority student services, on-campus daycare, personal counseling, placement for graduates, veterans' counselor, women's services. **Physically disabled:** Services for visually, speech, hearing impaired.

Contact. E-mail: admissions@uwlax.edu
Phone: (608) 785-8939 Fax: (608) 785-8940
Kathryn Kiefer, Director of Admissions, University of Wisconsin-La Crosse, 1725 State Street, Cleary Center, La Crosse, WI 54601

University of Wisconsin-Madison

Madison, Wisconsin
www.wisc.edu

CB member
CB code: 1846

- ▶ Public 4-year university
- ▶ Residential campus in small city
- ▶ 28,737 degree-seeking undergraduates: 4% part-time, 52% women, 2% African American, 5% Asian American, 4% Hispanic American, 6% international
- ▶ 12,074 degree-seeking graduate students
- ▶ 50% of applicants admitted
- ▶ SAT or ACT with writing, application essay required
- ▶ 83% graduate within 6 years

General. Founded in 1849. Regionally accredited. **Degrees:** 6,650 bachelor's awarded; master's, professional, doctoral offered. **ROTC:** Army, Naval, Air Force. **Location:** 90 miles from Milwaukee, 150 miles from Chicago. **Calendar:** Semester, extensive summer session. **Full-time faculty:** 2,350 total; 91% have terminal degrees, 17% minority, 36% women. **Part-time faculty:** 506 total; 70% have terminal degrees, 8% minority, 46% women. **Class size:** 44% < 20, 31% 20-39, 5% 40-49, 10% 50-99, 9% >100. **Special facilities:** Teaching nuclear reactor, observatory, botanical gardens, arboretum, museums.

Freshman class profile. 28,983 applied, 14,627 admitted, 5,828 enrolled.

Mid 50% test scores		Rank in top quarter:	94%
SAT critical reading:	550-670	Rank in top tenth:	58%
SAT math:	620-740	Return as sophomores:	94%
SAT writing:	590-680	Out-of-state:	38%
ACT composite:	26-30	Live on campus:	90%
GPA 3.75 or higher:	57%	International:	4%
GPA 3.50-3.74:	25%	Fraternities:	9%
GPA 3.0-3.49:	16%	Sororities:	8%
GPA 2.0-2.99:	2%		

Basis for selection. Secondary school record including level of challenge relative to high school offerings, evidence of either increasing or consistent level of academic challenge and performance, course grades, class rank, ACT or SAT test scores important. Application statement/essay, recommendations, extracurricular activities and personal characteristics also considered. Audition required for music; portfolio recommended for fine arts.

High school preparation. College-preparatory program required. 17 units required; 22 recommended. Required and recommended units include English 4, mathematics 3-4, social studies 3-4, science 3-4, foreign language 2-4 and academic electives 2-4. Math units must include 1 each algebra and geometry, plus 1 year advanced math. Computer science or statistics will not fulfill math requirement. Applicants strongly advised to present academic credentials well in excess of minimum units.

2011-2012 Annual costs. Tuition/fees: $9,671; $25,421 out-of-state. Room/board: $7,780. Books/supplies: $1,140. Personal expenses: $3,180.

2010-2011 Financial aid. **Need-based:** 3,943 full-time freshmen applied for aid; 2,506 were judged to have need; 2,425 of these received aid. Average need met was 71%. Average scholarship/grant was $6,456; average loan $3,917. 47% of total undergraduate aid awarded as scholarships/grants, 53% as loans/jobs. **Non-need-based:** Awarded to 10,888 full-time undergraduates, including 2,571 freshmen. Scholarships awarded for academics, alumni affiliation, art, athletics, job skills, leadership, minority status, music/drama, ROTC, state residency.

Application procedures. Admission: Closing date 2/1 (receipt date). $44 fee, may be waived for applicants with need. Admission notification on a rolling basis beginning on or about 11/1. Must reply by 5/1. **Financial aid:** No deadline. FAFSA, institutional form required. Applicants notified on a rolling basis starting 4/1; must reply within 9 week(s) of notification.

Academics. Special study options: Accelerated study, combined bachelor's/graduate degree, cooperative education, distance learning, double major, dual enrollment of high school students, ESL, exchange student, honors, independent study, internships, liberal arts/career combination, student-designed major, study abroad, teacher certification program. **Credit/placement by examination:** AP, CLEP, IB, institutional tests. **Support services:** Learning center, pre-admission summer program, reduced course load, remedial instruction, study skills assistance, tutoring, writing center.

Majors. Architecture: Landscape. **Area/ethnic studies:** African-American, Asian, Latin American/Caribbean, Scandinavian, South Asian, women's. **Biology:** General, biochemistry, botany, conservation, entomology, genetics, microbiology, microbiology/immunology, molecular, pharmacology/toxicology, plant pathology, zoology. **Business:** General, accounting, actuarial science, business admin, finance, financial planning, insurance, international, management information systems, marketing, operations, real estate, retailing. **Communications:** Communications/speech/rhetoric, journalism. **Computer sciences:** General. **Conservation:** Forest sciences, wildlife/wilderness. **Education:** Agricultural, art, earth science, elementary, family/consumer sciences, music, science, social studies, special ed. **Engineering:** Agricultural, applied physics, biomedical, chemical, civil, computer, electrical, engineering mechanics, geological, industrial, marine, materials, mechanical, nuclear. **English:** English lit. **Foreign languages:** African, Chinese, classics, comparative lit, French, Germanic, Hebrew, Italian, Japanese, Latin, linguistics, Polish, Portuguese, Russian, Spanish. **General:** Agronomy, animal sciences, business, communications, dairy, economics, food science, horticultural science, poultry, soil science. **Health services:** Audiology/speech pathology, nursing (RN), premedicine, vocational rehab counseling. **History:** General, science/technology. **Human services:** Social work. **Math:** General, applied, statistics. **Parks/recreation:** Exercise sciences, facilities management. **Philosophy/religion:** Judaic, philosophy, religion. **Physical sciences:** Astrophysics, atmospheric science, chemistry, geology, physics. **Psychology:** General. **Social sciences:** Anthropology, economics, geography, GIS/cartography, political science, rural sociology, sociology. **Visual/performing arts:** Art, art history/conservation, dance, dramatic, interior design, music, music performance. **Work/family studies:** General, clothing/textiles, consumer economics, family studies, family/community services.

Most popular majors. Biology 13%, business/marketing 9%, communications/journalism 6%, engineering/engineering technologies 10%, social sciences 14%.

Computing on campus. 3,350 workstations in dormitories, library, computer center, student center. Dormitories wired for high-speed internet access and linked to campus network. Commuter students can connect to campus network. Online course registration, online library, helpline, repair service, student web hosting, wireless network available.

Student life. Freshman orientation: Mandatory, $200 fee. Preregistration for classes offered. Held in the summer. **Policies:** Freshmen not permitted cars on campus. **Housing:** Coed dorms, single-sex dorms, cooperative housing, fraternity/sorority housing, wellness housing available. $300 partly refundable deposit, deadline 5/2. Residential learning communities available, apartments for student families. **Activities:** Bands, choral groups, dance, drama, film society, international student organizations, literary magazine, music ensembles, musical theater, opera, radio station, student government, student newspaper, symphony orchestra, TV station.

Athletics. NCAA. **Intercollegiate:** Basketball, cheerleading, cross-country, football (tackle) M, golf, ice hockey, rowing (crew), soccer, softball W, swimming, tennis, track and field, volleyball W, wrestling M. **Intramural:** Basketball, field hockey, football (non-tackle), ice hockey, soccer, tennis, volleyball. **Team name:** Badgers.

Student services. Adult student services, alcohol/substance abuse counseling, career counseling, services for economically disadvantaged, student employment services, financial aid counseling, health services, minority student services, personal counseling, placement for graduates, veterans' counselor, women's services. **Physically disabled:** Services for visually, speech, hearing impaired.

Contact. E-mail: onwisconsin@admissions.wisc.edu
Phone: (608) 262-3961 Fax: (608) 262-7706
Adele Brumfield, Director of Undergraduate Admissions and Recruitment, University of Wisconsin-Madison, 702 West Johnson Street, Suite 1101, Madison, WI 53715-1007

University of Wisconsin-Milwaukee
Milwaukee, Wisconsin
www.uwm.edu

CB member
CB code: 1473

▸ Public 4-year university
▸ Residential campus in very large city
▸ 23,164 degree-seeking undergraduates: 13% part-time, 50% women, 8% African American, 6% Asian American, 6% Hispanic American, 2% international
▸ 4,699 degree-seeking graduate students
▸ 71% of applicants admitted
▸ SAT or ACT (ACT writing optional) required
▸ 43% graduate within 6 years

General. Founded in 1956. Regionally accredited. **Degrees:** 3,701 bachelor's awarded; master's, professional, doctoral offered. **ROTC:** Army, Naval, Air Force. **Location:** 90 miles from Chicago. **Calendar:** Semester, extensive summer session. **Class size:** 41% < 20, 44% 20-39, 6% 40-49, 6% 50-99, 4% >100. **Special facilities:** Planetarium, geological museum, American Geological Society Collection.

Freshman class profile. 11,622 applied, 8,246 admitted, 3,677 enrolled.

Mid 50% test scores			
ACT composite:	19-24	Rank in top quarter:	28%
GPA 3.75 or higher:	8%	Rank in top tenth:	8%
GPA 3.50-3.74:	12%	End year in good standing:	71%
GPA 3.0-3.49:	35%	Out-of-state:	3%
GPA 2.0-2.99:	44%	Live on campus:	68%
		International:	2%

Basis for selection. Academic record and class rank in top half important. If applicant ranks in lower half of class, 21 ACT required. Additional requirements for architecture. Students who do not meet standard admission requirements may apply through Academic Opportunity Program Office. Some applicants must take placement tests in chemistry and/or foreign language. Audition required for dance, music, theater.

High school preparation. College-preparatory program required. 17 units required; 20 recommended. Required and recommended units include English 4, mathematics 3-4, social studies 3, science 3 (laboratory 1), foreign language 2 and academic electives 2. Math includes algebra, geometry, and beyond. 3 social studies or history required.

2011-2012 Annual costs. Tuition/fees: $8,675; $18,404 out-of-state. Minnesota reciprocity tuition: $472 per-credit-hour. Room/board: $8,182. Books/supplies: $1,000. Personal expenses: $1,600.

2011-2012 Financial aid. Need-based: 3,045 full-time freshmen applied for aid; 2,571 were judged to have need; 2,450 of these received aid. Average need met was 42%. Average scholarship/grant was $6,630; average loan $3,646. 48% of total undergraduate aid awarded as scholarships/grants, 52% as loans/jobs. **Non-need-based:** Awarded to 3,703 full-time undergraduates, including 545 freshmen. Scholarships awarded for academics, art, athletics, music/drama.

Application procedures. Admission: Closing date 7/1. $44 fee, may be waived for applicants with need. Admission notification on a rolling basis beginning on or about 9/15. **Financial aid:** No deadline. FAFSA required. Applicants notified on a rolling basis starting 3/10; must reply within 2 week(s) of notification.

Academics. Special study options: Accelerated study, cooperative education, cross-registration, distance learning, double major, dual enrollment of high school students, ESL, external degree, honors, independent study, internships, liberal arts/career combination, student-designed major, study abroad, teacher certification program. **Credit/placement by examination:** AP, CLEP, IB, institutional tests. **Support services:** Learning center, pre-admission summer program, reduced course load, remedial instruction, study skills assistance, tutoring, writing center.

Majors. Architecture: Architecture. **Area/ethnic studies:** African-American, Latin American/Caribbean, women's. **Biology:** General, biochemistry, microbiology. **Business:** General, accounting, actuarial science, finance, management information systems, marketing, operations, training/development. **Communications:** Communications/speech/rhetoric. **Computer sciences:** Computer science, information systems. **Conservation:** Environmental science, forestry. **Education:** General, art, ESL, music, special ed, urban. **Engineering:** General, civil, computer, electrical, engineering science, industrial, materials, mechanical. **English:** English lit. **Foreign languages:** Classics, comparative lit, French, Germanic, Hebrew, Italian, linguistics, Russian, Spanish. **Health services:** Audiology/speech pathology, clinical lab science, facilities admin, nursing (RN), occupational therapy, premedicine, recreational therapy. **History:** General. **Human services:** Social work. **Liberal arts:** Arts/sciences. **Math:** General, applied. **Parks/recreation:** Exercise

sciences. **Philosophy/religion:** Philosophy, religion. **Physical sciences:** Chemistry, geology, meteorology, physics. **Protective services:** Criminal justice. **Psychology:** General. **Social sciences:** Anthropology, economics, geography, sociology. **Visual/performing arts:** Art, art history/conservation, dance, dramatic, film/cinema/video, music.

Most popular majors. Business/marketing 27%, communications/journalism 7%, education 7%, health sciences 10%, social sciences 7%, visual/performing arts 7%.

Computing on campus. 582 workstations in dormitories, library, computer center, student center. Dormitories wired for high-speed internet access and linked to campus network. Commuter students can connect to campus network. Online course registration, online library, helpline, repair service, student web hosting, wireless network available.

Student life. Freshman orientation: Available. Preregistration for classes offered. **Housing:** Coed dorms, special housing for disabled, apartments available. $300 partly refundable deposit. Living Learning communities available. **Activities:** Bands, campus ministries, choral groups, dance, drama, film society, international student organizations, literary magazine, music ensembles, Model UN, musical theater, radio station, student government, student newspaper, symphony orchestra.

Athletics. NCAA. **Intercollegiate:** Baseball M, basketball, cross-country, diving, soccer, swimming, tennis W, track and field, volleyball W. **Intramural:** Badminton, basketball, football (non-tackle), football (tackle), racquetball, soccer, softball, volleyball. **Team name:** Panthers.

Student services. Adult student services, alcohol/substance abuse counseling, career counseling, student employment services, financial aid counseling, health services, legal services, minority student services, on-campus daycare, personal counseling, placement for graduates, veterans' counselor, women's services. **Physically disabled:** Services for visually, speech, hearing impaired.

Contact. E-mail: uwmlook@uwm.edu
Phone: (414) 229-2222 Fax: (414) 229-6940
Beth Weckmueller, Executive Director of Enrollment Services and Registrar, University of Wisconsin-Milwaukee, Box 749, Milwaukee, WI 53201

University of Wisconsin-Oshkosh
Oshkosh, Wisconsin
www.uwosh.edu

CB member
CB code: 1916

- Public 4-year university
- Residential campus in small city
- 10,802 degree-seeking undergraduates: 13% part-time, 57% women, 2% African American, 4% Asian American, 2% Hispanic American, 1% Native American, 1% international
- 964 degree-seeking graduate students
- ACT (writing optional) required
- 50% graduate within 6 years

General. Founded in 1871. Regionally accredited. **Degrees:** 1,890 bachelor's awarded; master's offered. **ROTC:** Army. **Location:** 90 miles from Milwaukee. **Calendar:** Semester, limited summer session. **Full-time faculty:** 425 total; 80% have terminal degrees, 9% minority, 47% women. **Part-time faculty:** 220 total; 26% have terminal degrees, 4% minority, 67% women. **Class size:** 38% < 20, 49% 20-39, 4% 40-49, 6% 50-99, 3% >100. **Special facilities:** Planetarium.

Freshman class profile. 1,870 enrolled.

Mid 50% test scores		Rank in top quarter:	38%
ACT composite:	20-24	Rank in top tenth:	12%
GPA 3.75 or higher:	15%	Return as sophomores:	74%
GPA 3.50-3.74:	19%	Out-of-state:	4%
GPA 3.0-3.49:	41%	Live on campus:	87%
GPA 2.0-2.99:	25%	International:	1%

Basis for selection. Students must rank in top half of high school class or have 22 ACT if rank is in third quartile. Out-of-state applicants may submit SAT scores. Interview recommended for all; audition required for music.

High school preparation. College-preparatory program required. 17 units required. Required and recommended units include English 4, mathematics 3-4, social studies 3, science 3-4 (laboratory 3-4), foreign language 2 and academic electives 4. Social studies must include 1 history.

2011-2012 Annual costs. Tuition/fees: $6,995; $14,568 out-of-state. Minnesota reciprocity tuition: $270 per-credit-hour. Room/board: $6,128. Books/supplies: $1,000. Personal expenses: $500.

2011-2012 Financial aid. Need-based: 1,162 full-time freshmen applied for aid; 890 were judged to have need; 400 of these received aid. Average need met was 33%. Average scholarship/grant was $2,200; average loan $3,750. 46% of total undergraduate aid awarded as scholarships/grants, 54% as loans/jobs. **Non-need-based:** Awarded to 1,501 full-time undergraduates, including 525 freshmen. Scholarships awarded for academics, art, job skills, leadership, minority status, music/drama, ROTC, state residency.

Application procedures. Admission: No deadline. $44 fee, may be waived for applicants with need. Admission notification on a rolling basis. **Financial aid:** Priority date 3/15; no closing date. FAFSA required. Applicants notified on a rolling basis starting 4/15; must reply within 2 week(s) of notification.

Academics. Special study options: Accelerated study, cooperative education, cross-registration, distance learning, double major, dual enrollment of high school students, ESL, exchange student, honors, independent study, internships, liberal arts/career combination, student-designed major, study abroad, teacher certification program, weekend college. **Credit/placement by examination:** AP, CLEP, IB, institutional tests. 32 credit hours maximum toward bachelor's degree. **Support services:** Learning center, pre-admission summer program, reduced course load, study skills assistance, tutoring, writing center.

Majors. Biology: General, bacteriology. **Business:** Accounting, finance, human resources, management information systems, operations. **Communications:** Broadcast journalism, communications/speech/rhetoric, journalism. **Computer sciences:** Computer science. **Education:** Elementary, emotionally handicapped, learning disabled, mentally handicapped, music, physical, science, secondary, social science, special ed. **English:** English lit. **Foreign languages:** French, German, Spanish. **Health services:** Clinical lab technology, nursing (RN), predental, premedicine, prepharmacy, preveterinary. **History:** General. **Human services:** Social work. **Liberal arts:** Arts/sciences. **Math:** General. **Philosophy/religion:** Philosophy, religion. **Physical sciences:** Chemistry, geology, physics. **Psychology:** General. **Social sciences:** Anthropology, economics, geography, political science, sociology, urban studies. **Visual/performing arts:** Art, cinematography, dramatic, music, studio arts.

Most popular majors. Business/marketing 18%, communications/journalism 7%, education 15%, health sciences 12%, public administration/social services 6%, social sciences 7%.

Computing on campus. 475 workstations in dormitories, library, computer center, student center. Dormitories wired for high-speed internet access and linked to campus network. Commuter students can connect to campus network. Online course registration, helpline, wireless network available.

Student life. Freshman orientation: Available. Preregistration for classes offered. **Housing:** Guaranteed on-campus for freshmen. Coed dorms, single-sex dorms, fraternity/sorority housing, wellness housing available. $125 deposit, deadline 6/15. Select group of freshmen take part in residential college experience with more individualized instruction. **Activities:** Bands, campus ministries, choral groups, dance, drama, film society, international student organizations, Model UN, radio station, student government, student newspaper, symphony orchestra, TV station, black student union, Asian student association, American Indian student association, Hispanic Cultures United, InterVarsity Christian Fellowship, Athletes in Action, community involvement program, Habitat for Humanity.

Athletics. NCAA. **Intercollegiate:** Baseball M, basketball, cross-country, diving, football (tackle) M, golf W, gymnastics W, rifle, soccer, softball W, swimming, tennis, track and field, volleyball W, wrestling M. **Intramural:** Basketball, racquetball, skiing, soccer, softball, volleyball. **Team name:** Titans.

Student services. Adult student services, alcohol/substance abuse counseling, career counseling, services for economically disadvantaged, student employment services, financial aid counseling, health services, minority student services, on-campus daycare, personal counseling, placement for graduates, veterans' counselor, women's services. **Physically disabled:** Services for visually, speech, hearing impaired.

Contact. E-mail: oshadmuw@uwosh.edu
Phone: (920) 424-0202 Fax: (920) 424-1098
Jill Endries, Director of Admissions, University of Wisconsin-Oshkosh, 800 Algoma Boulevard, Oshkosh, WI 54901-8602

University of Wisconsin-Parkside
Kenosha, Wisconsin
www.uwp.edu

CB member
CB code: 1860

- Public 4-year university
- Commuter campus in small city
- 4,508 degree-seeking undergraduates: 25% part-time, 52% women, 11% African American, 2% Asian American, 10% Hispanic American, 2% international
- 114 degree-seeking graduate students
- 67% of applicants admitted

General. Founded in 1968. Regionally accredited. **Degrees:** 703 bachelor's awarded; master's offered. **ROTC:** Army. **Location:** 30 miles from Milwaukee, 60 miles from Chicago. **Calendar:** Semester, extensive summer session. **Full-time faculty:** 182 total; 58% have terminal degrees, 24% minority, 50% women. **Part-time faculty:** 114 total; 5% have terminal degrees, 12% minority, 56% women. **Class size:** 49% < 20, 37% 20-39, 7% 40-49, 7% 50-99, less than 1% >100. **Special facilities:** Communication arts building.

Freshman class profile. 1,987 applied, 1,337 admitted, 766 enrolled.

Mid 50% test scores			
ACT composite:	18-23	Out-of-state:	11%
Rank in top quarter:	30%	Live on campus:	40%
Rank in top tenth:	9%	International:	3%

Basis for selection. Rank in top half of class with specified distribution of high school units required for standard admission. Conditional admissions may be granted to applicants in top 65% of class or with 18 ACT. Test scores also used for placement in English and math courses. Audition required for theater, recommended for music; portfolio recommended for art.

High school preparation. College-preparatory program required. 17 units required; 20 recommended. Required and recommended units include English 4, mathematics 3-4, social studies 3-4, science 3-4 (laboratory 1-2), foreign language 2 and academic electives 4-7.

2011-2012 Annual costs. Tuition/fees: $6,930; $14,503 out-of-state. Minnesota reciprocity tuition: $270 per-credit-hour. Room/board: $6,192. Books/supplies: $904. Personal expenses: $1,670.

2010-2011 Financial aid. Need-based: 599 full-time freshmen applied for aid; 490 were judged to have need; 466 of these received aid. Average scholarship/grant was $6,304. 59% of total undergraduate aid awarded as scholarships/grants, 41% as loans/jobs. **Non-need-based:** Awarded to 475 full-time undergraduates, including 118 freshmen. Scholarships awarded for academics, art, athletics, minority status, music/drama, state residency.

Application procedures. Admission: Priority date 3/1; deadline 7/15 (postmark date). $44 fee, may be waived for applicants with need. Admission notification on a rolling basis beginning on or about 9/15. **Financial aid:** Priority date 3/15; no closing date. FAFSA required. Applicants notified on a rolling basis starting 4/1; must reply within 2 week(s) of notification.

Academics. Special study options: Accelerated study, combined bachelor's/graduate degree, distance learning, double major, dual enrollment of high school students, exchange student, honors, independent study, internships, liberal arts/career combination, study abroad, teacher certification program, weekend college. Cooperative nursing program with University of Wisconsin-Milwaukee. **Credit/placement by examination:** AP, CLEP, IB, SAT, ACT, institutional tests. 30 credit hours maximum toward bachelor's degree. Retroactive credit policy for foreign language study. **Support services:** Learning center, reduced course load, remedial instruction, study skills assistance, tutoring, writing center.

Majors. Area/ethnic studies: French, German. **Biology:** General, molecular. **Business:** General, accounting, business admin, finance, human resources, management information systems. **Communications:** Communications/speech/rhetoric. **Computer sciences:** Computer science. **English:** English lit. **Foreign languages:** French, German, Spanish. **Health services:** Predental, premedicine, preveterinary. **History:** General. **Liberal arts:** Arts/sciences. **Math:** General. **Parks/recreation:** Sports admin. **Philosophy/religion:** Philosophy. **Physical sciences:** Chemistry, geology, physics. **Protective services:** Criminal justice. **Psychology:** General. **Social sciences:** Economics, geography, political science, sociology. **Visual/performing arts:** Art, dramatic, music.

Most popular majors. Biology 8%, business/marketing 20%, parks/recreation 6%, security/protective services 13%, social sciences 10%, visual/performing arts 9%.

Computing on campus. 225 workstations in dormitories, library, computer center, student center. Dormitories wired for high-speed internet access and linked to campus network. Commuter students can connect to campus network. Online course registration, online library, helpline, student web hosting, wireless network available.

Student life. Freshman orientation: Mandatory, $52 fee. Preregistration for classes offered. Day-long session offered several times throughout summer. **Housing:** Coed dorms, special housing for disabled, apartments, wellness housing available. $50 fully refundable deposit. **Activities:** Bands, choral groups, dance, drama, literary magazine, music ensembles, musical theater, radio station, student government, student newspaper, symphony orchestra, Campus Crusade for Christ, Intervarsity Christian Fellowship, ethnic organization, Amnesty International, black student union, activities board.

Athletics. NCAA. **Intercollegiate:** Baseball M, basketball, cross-country, golf M, soccer, softball W, track and field, volleyball W, wrestling M. **Intramural:** Basketball, racquetball, soccer, softball, table tennis, tennis, volleyball. **Team name:** Rangers.

Student services. Adult student services, alcohol/substance abuse counseling, career counseling, services for economically disadvantaged, student employment services, financial aid counseling, health services, minority student services, on-campus daycare, personal counseling, placement for graduates, veterans' counselor, women's services. **Physically disabled:** Services for visually, speech, hearing impaired.

Contact. E-mail: admissions@uwp.edu
Phone: (262) 595-2355 Fax: (262) 595-2008
DeAnn Possehl, Executive Director of Enrollment Management, University of Wisconsin-Parkside, PO Box 2000, Kenosha, WI 53141-2000

University of Wisconsin-Platteville
Platteville, Wisconsin
www.uwplatt.edu

CB member
CB code: 1917

- Public 4-year university
- Residential campus in large town
- 7,293 degree-seeking undergraduates: 9% part-time, 35% women, 2% African American, 1% Asian American, 2% Hispanic American, 1% Native American, 1% international
- 679 degree-seeking graduate students
- 80% of applicants admitted
- SAT or ACT (ACT writing optional) required
- 52% graduate within 6 years

General. Founded in 1866. Regionally accredited. **Degrees:** 1,143 bachelor's, 1 associate awarded; master's offered. **ROTC:** Army. **Location:** 25 miles from Dubuque, IA; 75 miles from Madison. **Calendar:** Semester, limited summer session. **Full-time faculty:** 237 total; 89% have terminal degrees, 21% minority, 32% women. **Part-time faculty:** 6 total; 67% have terminal degrees, 17% minority, 33% women. **Class size:** 27% < 20, 61% 20-39, 6% 40-49, 5% 50-99, 1% >100. **Special facilities:** Pioneer farm, nature trail, disc golf course, cadaver lab, forensic crime scene house.

Freshman class profile. 4,007 applied, 3,195 admitted, 1,603 enrolled.

Mid 50% test scores			
		Return as sophomores:	74%
ACT composite:	20-26	Out-of-state:	23%
Rank in top quarter:	32%	Live on campus:	92%
Rank in top tenth:	11%	International:	1%

Basis for selection. Class rank, test scores, and high school transcripts are most important. Audition required for music scholarships. **Home schooled:** Transcript of courses and grades required.

High school preparation. College-preparatory program recommended. 17 units required. Required units include English 4, mathematics 3, social studies 3, science 3 (laboratory 2) and academic electives 4. 3 units natural science (2 from biology, chemistry, or physics); 3 units of math must be Algebra 1 or higher.

2011-2012 Annual costs. Tuition/fees: $7,113; $14,685 out-of-state. Minnesota reciprocity tuition: $270 per-credit-hour. Tri-State Initiative offers Illinois and Iowa students discounted out-of-state rate for select majors. Room/board: $6,042. Books/supplies: $300. Personal expenses: $1,170.

Financial aid. All financial aid based on need.

Application procedures. Admission: No deadline. $44 fee, may be waived for applicants with need. Admission notification on a rolling basis. **Financial aid:** Priority date 3/15; no closing date. FAFSA required. Applicants notified on a rolling basis starting 6/1; must reply within 2 week(s) of notification.

Academics. Special study options: Combined bachelor's/graduate degree, cooperative education, distance learning, double major, dual enrollment of high school students, exchange student, external degree, independent study, internships, student-designed major, study abroad, teacher certification program. **Credit/placement by examination:** AP, CLEP, institutional tests. 30 credit hours maximum toward bachelor's degree. **Support services:** Learning center, study skills assistance, tutoring, writing center.

Majors. Biology: General. **Business:** General, accounting, business admin, entrepreneurial studies, finance, human resources, investments/securities, organizational behavior. **Communications:** Communications/speech/rhetoric. **Computer sciences:** Computer science. **Conservation:** General. **Education:** Agricultural, art, biology, chemistry, early childhood, elementary, English, German, history, mathematics, science, social science, social studies, Spanish, speech, technology/industrial arts, voc/tech. **Engineering:** Applied physics, civil, electrical, mechanical. **English:** English lit. **Foreign languages:** German, Spanish. **General:** Agribusiness operations, agronomy, animal sciences, economics. **History:** General. **Liberal arts:** Arts/sciences. **Math:** General. **Parks/recreation:** Health/fitness. **Philosophy/religion:** Philosophy. **Physical sciences:** Chemistry. **Protective services:** Law enforcement admin. **Psychology:** General. **Social sciences:** General, economics, geography, political science, sociology. **Visual/performing arts:** Art, commercial/advertising art, dramatic, music.

Most popular majors. Agriculture 11%, biology 6%, business/marketing 16%, education 10%, engineering/engineering technologies 29%, security/protective services 10%.

Computing on campus. Dormitories wired for high-speed internet access and linked to campus network. Commuter students can connect to campus network. Online course registration, online library, helpline, repair service, student web hosting available.

Student life. Freshman orientation: Available. Preregistration for classes offered. **Policies:** Student governance is given authority under Wisconsin state statute. **Housing:** Guaranteed on-campus for freshmen. Coed dorms, single-sex dorms, special housing for disabled, apartments, wellness housing available. $100 partly refundable deposit. **Activities:** Bands, campus ministries, choral groups, dance, drama, international student organizations, literary magazine, music ensembles, musical theater, radio station, student government, student newspaper, symphony orchestra, TV station, black student union, ASIA student group, Hmong club, inter-tribal council, Young Democrats, College Republicans, Circle K, InterVarsity, Campus Crusade.

Athletics. NCAA. **Intercollegiate:** Baseball M, basketball, cross-country, football (tackle) M, golf W, soccer, softball W, track and field, volleyball W, wrestling M. **Intramural:** Badminton, basketball, bowling, football (non-tackle), racquetball, soccer, softball, tennis, volleyball, water polo. **Team name:** Pioneers.

Student services. Adult student services, alcohol/substance abuse counseling, career counseling, services for economically disadvantaged, student employment services, financial aid counseling, health services, minority student services, on-campus daycare, personal counseling, placement for graduates, veterans' counselor, women's services. **Physically disabled:** Services for visually, speech, hearing impaired.

Contact. E-mail: admit@uwplatt.edu
Phone: (608) 342-1125 Toll-free number: (800) 362-5515
Fax: (608) 342-1122
Angela Udelhofen, Dean of Admissions and Enrollment Management, University of Wisconsin-Platteville, One University Plaza, Platteville, WI 53818

University of Wisconsin-River Falls
River Falls, Wisconsin
www.uwrf.edu   **CB code: 1918**

▶ Public 4-year university and liberal arts college
▶ Residential campus in large town
▶ 6,324 degree-seeking undergraduates
▶ SAT or ACT (ACT writing optional), application essay required

General. Founded in 1874. Regionally accredited. **Degrees:** 1,039 bachelor's awarded; master's offered. **ROTC:** Army. **Location:** 30 miles from Minneapolis-St. Paul. **Calendar:** Semester, limited summer session. **Full-time faculty:** 277 total. **Part-time faculty:** 83 total. **Class size:** 26% < 20, 57% 20-39, 10% 40-49, 6% 50-99, less than 1% >100. **Special facilities:** 2 laboratory farms, 20-inch reflecting telescope, USDA-approved food science laboratory, computerized greenhouse, 42-foot rapelling and climbing wall, indoor track and field house, ice arena, electron microscope, observatory, education regional archive collection.

Freshman class profile.

GPA 3.75 or higher:	17%	Rank in top tenth:	12%
GPA 3.50-3.74:	18%	Out-of-state:	48%
GPA 3.0-3.49:	41%	Live on campus:	75%
GPA 2.0-2.99:	23%	Fraternities:	5%
Rank in top quarter:	35%	Sororities:	3%

Basis for selection. Rank in top 40% of class with 18 ACT, or rank in top 60% with 22 ACT required. Minority student applications given special consideration. Elementary Education and Animal Science applicants must rank in the top 40% of class with 24 ACT. ACT recommended.

High school preparation. College-preparatory program required. 17 units required; 22 recommended. Required and recommended units include English 4, mathematics 3-4, social studies 3-4, science 3-4 (laboratory 1), foreign language 2 and academic electives 4. Vocational agriculture units also recommended for applicants to College of Agriculture. Wisconsin residents who receive GED must also complete Wisconsin high school equivalency diploma.

2011-2012 Annual costs. Tuition/fees: $7,277; $14,850 out-of-state. Minnesota reciprocity tuition: $270 per-credit-hour. Room/board: $5,715. Books/supplies: $330. Personal expenses: $1,900.

Financial aid. All financial aid based on need.

Application procedures. Admission: Priority date 2/1; no deadline. $44 fee, may be waived for applicants with need. Admission notification on a rolling basis beginning on or about 9/15. **Financial aid:** Priority date 3/15; no closing date. FAFSA required. Applicants notified on a rolling basis starting 4/15.

Academics. Special study options: Combined bachelor's/graduate degree, cross-registration, distance learning, double major, dual enrollment of high school students, ESL, exchange student, external degree, honors, independent study, internships, liberal arts/career combination, study abroad, teacher certification program. **Credit/placement by examination:** AP, CLEP, IB, institutional tests. 27 credit hours maximum toward bachelor's degree. Placement in English, foreign languages, and math based on university system placement exams. **Support services:** Learning center, reduced course load, remedial instruction, study skills assistance, tutoring, writing center.

Majors. Biology: General, biochemistry, biotechnology. **Business:** Accounting, business admin. **Communications:** Communications/speech/rhetoric, journalism. **Computer sciences:** General. **Conservation:** General, environmental science, management/policy. **Education:** Agricultural, art, elementary, ESL, music, physical, speech impaired. **English:** English lit, rhetoric/composition. **Foreign languages:** French, German, Spanish. **General:** Agronomy, animal sciences, business, crop production, dairy, dairy husbandry, equestrian studies, equine science, equipment technology, food science, greenhouse operations, horticultural science, horticulture, landscaping, products processing, soil science. **Health services:** Communication disorders. **History:** General. **Human services:** Social work. **Math:** General. **Physical sciences:** Chemistry, geology, organic chemistry, physics, planetary, polymer chemistry. **Psychology:** General. **Social sciences:** General, economics, geography, political science, sociology. **Visual/performing arts:** Art, music, studio arts.

Most popular majors. Agriculture 14%, biology 7%, business/marketing 16%, communications/journalism 10%, education 12%, social sciences 9%.

Computing on campus. 700 workstations in dormitories, library, computer center, student center. Dormitories wired for high-speed internet access and linked to campus network. Commuter students can connect to campus network. Online course registration, online library, helpline, repair service, student web hosting, wireless network available.

Student life. Freshman orientation: Mandatory. Preregistration for classes offered. Held weekend prior to classes starting. **Policies:** Freshmen and sophomores must live in residence halls unless they reside with parents. **Housing:** Guaranteed on-campus for freshmen. Coed dorms, single-sex dorms, special housing for disabled available. $175 partly refundable deposit, deadline 6/1. **Activities:** Bands, campus ministries, choral groups, dance, drama, international student organizations, literary magazine, music ensembles, Model UN, musical theater, radio station, student government, student newspaper, symphony orchestra, TV station, African American Alliance, Hispanic Student Coalition, Native American Council, Hmong student association, Habitat for Humanity, Fellowship of Christian Athletes, Young Democrats, Young Republicans, Young Life, Intervarsity Christian Fellowship.

Athletics. NCAA. **Intercollegiate:** Basketball, cross-country, diving, football (tackle) M, golf W, ice hockey, soccer W, softball W, swimming, tennis W, track and field, volleyball W. **Intramural:** Basketball, football (non-tackle), softball, volleyball. **Team name:** Falcons.

Student services. Adult student services, alcohol/substance abuse counseling, chaplain/spiritual director, career counseling, services for economically disadvantaged, student employment services, financial aid counseling,

health services, minority student services, on-campus daycare, personal counseling, placement for graduates, veterans' counselor, women's services. **Physically disabled:** Services for visually, speech, hearing impaired.

Contact. E-mail: admit@uwrf.edu
Phone: (715) 425-3500 Fax: (715) 425-0676
Mark Meydam, Director of Admission, University of Wisconsin-River Falls, 410 South 3rd Street, River Falls, WI 54022-5001

University of Wisconsin-Stevens Point

Stevens Point, Wisconsin — CB member
www.uwsp.edu — CB code: 1919

- Public 4-year university
- Residential campus in large town
- 8,943 degree-seeking undergraduates: 5% part-time, 53% women, 1% African American, 1% Asian American, 2% Hispanic American, 2% international
- 262 degree-seeking graduate students
- 69% of applicants admitted
- SAT or ACT (ACT writing optional) required
- 61% graduate within 6 years; 13% enter graduate study

General. Founded in 1894. Regionally accredited. **Degrees:** 1,657 bachelor's, 20 associate awarded; master's, doctoral offered. **ROTC:** Army. **Location:** 110 miles from Madison, 240 miles from Chicago. **Calendar:** Semester, extensive summer session. **Full-time faculty:** 391 total; 84% have terminal degrees, 7% minority, 43% women. **Part-time faculty:** 62 total; 37% have terminal degrees, 3% minority, 66% women. **Class size:** 25% < 20, 55% 20-39, 7% 40-49, 10% 50-99, 3% >100. **Special facilities:** Natural history museum, planetarium and observatory, nature preserve, Foucault pendulum, electron microscope, 1,000-acre natural resources summer camp, fire science center, multicultural center.

Freshman class profile. 5,571 applied, 3,851 admitted, 1,606 enrolled.

Mid 50% test scores		Rank in top quarter:	50%
ACT composite:	21-25	Rank in top tenth:	17%
GPA 3.75 or higher:	26%	Return as sophomores:	81%
GPA 3.50-3.74:	22%	Out-of-state:	9%
GPA 3.0-3.49:	43%	Live on campus:	91%
GPA 2.0-2.99:	9%	International:	1%

Basis for selection. Applicants must rank in top 25% of class, or have 21 ACT/990 SAT (exclusive of Writing) and rank in top 50% of class, or have 3.25 GPA. Campus visit recommended. Students interested in dance, drama, music, and musical theater required to complete on-campus performance audition and/or interview.

High school preparation. College-preparatory program required. 17 units required; 22 recommended. Required and recommended units include English 4, mathematics 3-4, social studies 3-4, science 3-4 and foreign language 4. Additional 2 units from English, math, social sciences, sciences, or foreign language and 2 units from above areas or fine arts, computer science, or other academic areas.

2011-2012 Annual costs. Tuition/fees: $7,152; $14,725 out-of-state. Minnesota reciprocity tuition: $270 per-credit-hour. Room/board: $6,002. Books/supplies: $500. Personal expenses: $1,867.

2010-2011 Financial aid. Need-based: 1,356 full-time freshmen applied for aid; 963 were judged to have need; 900 of these received aid. Average need met was 75%. Average scholarship/grant was $6,245; average loan $3,863. 38% of total undergraduate aid awarded as scholarships/grants, 62% as loans/jobs. **Non-need-based:** Awarded to 3,109 full-time undergraduates, including 140 freshmen. Scholarships awarded for academics, alumni affiliation, art, music/drama, ROTC. **Additional information:** Tuition discounts offered to qualified residents from other states. Tuition waiver for state veterans.

Application procedures. Admission: No deadline. $44 fee, may be waived for applicants with need. Admission notification on a rolling basis beginning on or about 9/15. **Financial aid:** Priority date 3/15, closing date 5/1. FAFSA required. Applicants notified on a rolling basis starting 3/1; must reply within 4 week(s) of notification.

Academics. Special study options: Accelerated study, distance learning, double major, dual enrollment of high school students, ESL, independent study, internships, student-designed major, study abroad, teacher certification program. Cooperative program with University of Wisconsin: Eau Claire and St. Joseph's Hospital; collaborative degree program with University of Wisconsin-Marshfield, University of Wisconsin-Marathon and University of Wisconsin-Marinette. **Credit/placement by examination:** AP, CLEP, IB,

institutional tests. 16 credit hours maximum toward associate degree, 32 toward bachelor's. **Support services:** Learning center, pre-admission summer program, reduced course load, remedial instruction, study skills assistance, tutoring, writing center.

Majors. Architecture: Interior. **Biology:** General, biochemistry. **Business:** Accounting, business admin. **Communications:** Communications/speech/rhetoric. **Computer sciences:** General, web page design. **Conservation:** General, fisheries, forestry, water/wetlands/marine, wildlife/wilderness, wood science. **Education:** Early childhood, elementary, family/consumer sciences, music, physical, secondary. **English:** English lit. **Foreign languages:** French, German, Spanish. **General:** Soil science. **Health services:** General, athletic training, audiology/speech pathology, clinical lab science. **History:** General. **Human services:** General, social work. **Liberal arts:** Arts/sciences. **Math:** General. **Parks/recreation:** Health/fitness. **Philosophy/religion:** Philosophy. **Physical sciences:** Chemistry, geology, physics. **Psychology:** General. **Social sciences:** General, economics, geography, political science, sociology. **Visual/performing arts:** General, art, dance, dramatic, interior design, music, music history, music performance, studio arts management.

Most popular majors. Biology 7%, business/marketing 9%, education 12%, health sciences 6%, natural resources/environmental science 13%, social sciences 11%, visual/performing arts 7%.

Computing on campus. 634 workstations in dormitories, library, computer center, student center. Dormitories wired for high-speed internet access and linked to campus network. Commuter students can connect to campus network. Online course registration, online library, helpline, repair service, student web hosting, wireless network available.

Student life. Freshman orientation: Mandatory, $45 fee. Preregistration for classes offered. **Policies:** Non-smoking policy for all campus buildings. **Housing:** Coed dorms, single-sex dorms, wellness housing available. $125 partly refundable deposit. Freshman interest-group housing available. **Activities:** Bands, campus ministries, choral groups, dance, drama, film society, international student organizations, literary magazine, music ensembles, Model UN, musical theater, opera, radio station, student government, student newspaper, symphony orchestra, TV station, American Indians Reaching for Opportunities, black student union, College Republicans, College Democrats, Lutheran Collegians, Association for Community Tasks, Newman Catholic student association, Habitat for Humanity, Gay-Straight Alliance, Hmong and Southeast Asian American Club.

Athletics. NCAA. **Intercollegiate:** Baseball M, basketball, cross-country, diving, football (tackle) M, golf W, ice hockey, soccer W, softball W, swimming, tennis W, track and field, volleyball W, wrestling M. **Intramural:** Badminton, basketball, football (non-tackle), football (tackle) M, golf, ice hockey, racquetball, soccer, softball, table tennis, tennis, volleyball. **Team name:** Pointers.

Student services. Adult student services, alcohol/substance abuse counseling, career counseling, services for economically disadvantaged, student employment services, financial aid counseling, health services, minority student services, on-campus daycare, personal counseling, placement for graduates, veterans' counselor, women's services. **Physically disabled:** Services for visually, speech, hearing impaired.

Contact. E-mail: admiss@uwsp.edu
Phone: (715) 346-2441 Fax: (715) 346-3296
Bill Jordan, Director of Admissions, University of Wisconsin-Stevens Point, Student Services Center, Stevens Point, WI 54481

University of Wisconsin-Stout

Menomonie, Wisconsin
www.uwstout.edu — CB code: 1740

- Public 4-year university
- Residential campus in large town
- 8,171 degree-seeking undergraduates: 16% part-time, 48% women, 1% African American, 1% Hispanic American, 3% Native American, 1% international
- 727 degree-seeking graduate students
- 78% of applicants admitted
- SAT or ACT (ACT writing optional) required
- 53% graduate within 6 years

General. Founded in 1891. Regionally accredited. **Degrees:** 1,562 bachelor's awarded; master's offered. **ROTC:** Army, Air Force. **Location:** 60 miles from Minneapolis-St. Paul. **Calendar:** 4-1-4, limited summer session. **Full-time faculty:** 387 total; 72% have terminal degrees, 11% minority, 42% women. **Part-time faculty:** 90 total; 36% have terminal degrees, 1% minority, 61% women. **Class size:** 31% < 20, 62% 20-39, 4% 40-49, 2% 50-99, less

than 1% >100. **Special facilities:** Teleproduction center, technology transfer institute, vocational rehabilitation institute.

Freshman class profile. 3,658 applied, 2,855 admitted, 1,476 enrolled.

Mid 50% test scores		Rank in top tenth:	8%
ACT composite:	20-24	Return as sophomores:	71%
GPA 3.75 or higher:	12%	Out-of-state:	35%
GPA 3.50-3.74:	15%	Live on campus:	95%
GPA 3.0-3.49:	42%	International:	1%
GPA 2.0-2.99:	31%	Fraternities:	5%
Rank in top quarter:	29%	Sororities:	12%

Basis for selection. Rank in top half of class or 22 ACT required. Limited enrollment in all programs. Applied science and manufacturing engineering require upper 40% of class or 22 ACT along with 22 ACT math. **Learning Disabled:** Current IEP may be submitted with application.

High school preparation. College-preparatory program required. Required and recommended units include English 4, mathematics 3, social studies 3, science 3, foreign language 2 and academic electives 4. Electives in English, math, social sciences, and sciences, technology business, fine art, family & consumer education, sciences.

2011-2012 Annual costs. Tuition/fees: $8,542; $16,287 out-of-state. Laptop computer included in the cost of tuition. Minnesota reciprocity tuition: $226 per-credit-hour. Room/board: $5,844. Books/supplies: $372. Personal expenses: $1,954.

2011-2012 Financial aid. Need-based: 1,258 full-time freshmen applied for aid; 916 were judged to have need; 907 of these received aid. Average need met was 83%. Average scholarship/grant was $2,331; average loan $3,574. 36% of total undergraduate aid awarded as scholarships/grants, 64% as loans/jobs. **Non-need-based:** Awarded to 672 full-time undergraduates, including 441 freshmen. Scholarships awarded for academics.

Application procedures. Admission: Priority date 1/1; no deadline. $44 fee, may be waived for applicants with need. Admission notification on a rolling basis beginning on or about 9/15. Early application recommended. Art-graphic design deadline of 11/1; not all qualified applicants will be admitted. **Financial aid:** Priority date 3/15; no closing date. FAFSA required. Applicants notified on a rolling basis starting 4/1; must reply within 4 week(s) of notification.

Academics. Special study options: Accelerated study, cooperative education, cross-registration, distance learning, double major, dual enrollment of high school students, exchange student, external degree, honors, independent study, internships, study abroad, teacher certification program. **Credit/placement by examination:** AP, CLEP, IB, ACT, institutional tests. **Support services:** Learning center, pre-admission summer program, reduced course load, remedial instruction, study skills assistance, tutoring, writing center.

Majors. Business: Business admin, construction management, hospitality admin, logistics, operations, real estate, sales/distribution. **Computer sciences:** Information technology, networking. **Education:** Art, early childhood, family/consumer sciences, sales/marketing, science, special ed, technology/industrial arts, voc/tech. **Engineering:** Computer, manufacturing, polymer. **English:** Technical writing. **Health services:** Dietetics, vocational rehab counseling. **Math:** Applied. **Parks/recreation:** Golf management. **Psychology:** General. **Social sciences:** General. **Work/family studies:** Clothing/textiles, family studies, institutional food production.

Most popular majors. Business/marketing 43%, education 10%, engineering/engineering technologies 9%, family/consumer sciences 7%, health sciences 6%, visual/performing arts 13%.

Computing on campus. PC or laptop required. 590 workstations in dormitories, library, computer center, student center. Dormitories wired for high-speed internet access and linked to campus network. Commuter students can connect to campus network. Online course registration, online library, helpline, repair service, student web hosting, wireless network available.

Student life. Freshman orientation: Available. Preregistration for classes offered. 1-day program with additional activities held the week before classes begin. **Housing:** Guaranteed on-campus for freshmen. Coed dorms, special housing for disabled, apartments, wellness housing available. $125 partly refundable deposit. **Activities:** Bands, campus ministries, choral groups, dance, drama, film society, international student organizations, literary magazine, music ensembles, Model UN, musical theater, radio station, student government, student newspaper, black student union, Hmong student organization, Lutheran student fellowship, College Democrats, College Republicans, Chi Alpha Christians in Action, single parent association, Club Los Hispanos.

Athletics. NCAA. **Intercollegiate:** Baseball M, basketball, cross-country, football (tackle) M, gymnastics W, ice hockey M, soccer W, softball W, tennis W, track and field, volleyball W. **Intramural:** Baseball M, basketball,

golf, ice hockey, racquetball, soccer, softball, volleyball. **Team name:** Blue Devils.

Student services. Chaplain/spiritual director, career counseling, student employment services, health services, on-campus daycare, personal counseling, placement for graduates, veterans' counselor. **Physically disabled:** Services for visually, speech, hearing impaired.

Contact. E-mail: admissions@uwstout.edu
Phone: (715) 232-1411 Toll-free number: (800) 447-8688
Fax: (715) 232-1667
Pam Holsinger-Fuchs, Executive Director of Enrollment Services, University of Wisconsin-Stout, 1 Clocktower Plaza, Menomonie, WI 54751

University of Wisconsin-Superior
Superior, Wisconsin
www.uwsuper.edu   **CB code: 1920**

- Public 4-year university and liberal arts college
- Commuter campus in small city
- 2,558 degree-seeking undergraduates: 18% part-time, 56% women, 1% African American, 1% Asian American, 1% Hispanic American, 2% Native American, 6% international
- 162 degree-seeking graduate students
- 70% of applicants admitted
- SAT or ACT (ACT writing optional) required
- 44% graduate within 6 years; 15% enter graduate study

General. Founded in 1893. Regionally accredited. **Degrees:** 389 bachelor's, 13 associate awarded; master's offered. **ROTC:** Air Force. **Location:** 2 miles from Duluth, Minnesota; 150 miles from Minneapolis-St. Paul. **Calendar:** Semester, limited summer session. **Full-time faculty:** 113 total; 80% have terminal degrees, 11% minority. **Part-time faculty:** 110 total; 19% have terminal degrees, 2% minority. **Class size:** 52% < 20, 40% 20-39, 5% 40-49, 2% 50-99, less than 1% >100. **Special facilities:** Observatory, Lake Superior National Estuarine Research Reserve, research vessel on Lake Superior.

Freshman class profile. 991 applied, 697 admitted, 352 enrolled.

Mid 50% test scores		Out-of-state:	43%
ACT composite:	20-24	Live on campus:	72%
Rank in top quarter:	36%	International:	6%
Rank in top tenth:	10%	Sororities:	5%
Return as sophomores:	68%		

Basis for selection. Admissions based on secondary school record and class rank. Standardized test scores also important. Essay, audition, portfolio, interview recommended. **Home schooled:** Statement describing home school structure and mission, transcript of courses and grades required.

High school preparation. College-preparatory program required. 17 units required. Required and recommended units include English 4, mathematics 3-4, social studies 3-4, science 3-4, foreign language 2 and academic electives 4.

2011-2012 Annual costs. Tuition/fees: $7,536; $15,109 out-of-state. Minnesota reciprocity tuition: $270 per-credit-hour. Room/board: $5,420. Books/supplies: $820. Personal expenses: $2,100.

Financial aid. Non-need-based: Scholarships awarded for academics, alumni affiliation, art, leadership, minority status, music/drama, ROTC, state residency. **Additional information:** Tuition Assistance Program (TAP) available to non-resident students on limited basis.

Application procedures. Admission: Priority date 4/1; deadline 8/1 (postmark date). $44 fee, may be waived for applicants with need. Admission notification on a rolling basis beginning on or about 10/1. Must reply by May 1 or within 4 week(s) if notified thereafter. **Financial aid:** Priority date 4/1; no closing date. FAFSA required. Applicants notified on a rolling basis starting 3/15; must reply by 5/1 or within 4 week(s) of notification.

Academics. Post-bachelor's certificates offered in early childhood education, counseling, and secondary education. Post-master's certificate offered in library science. **Special study options:** Combined bachelor's/graduate degree, cooperative education, cross-registration, distance learning, double major, dual enrollment of high school students, ESL, exchange student, external degree, independent study, internships, liberal arts/career combination, student-designed major, study abroad, teacher certification program. Engineering with University of Wisconsin-Madison and Michigan Technological University, Forestry with Michigan Technological University. **Credit/placement by examination:** AP, CLEP, IB, ACT, institutional tests. 32 credit hours maximum toward associate degree, 32 toward bachelor's. **Support

services: Learning center, pre-admission summer program, reduced course load, remedial instruction, study skills assistance, tutoring, writing center.

Majors. Biology: General, aquatic, botany, cell/histology, ecology, environmental, molecular. **Business:** General, accounting, business admin, finance, international, management information systems, marketing. **Communications:** Broadcast journalism, communications/speech/rhetoric, journalism, media studies. **Computer sciences:** Computer science. **Education:** Art, biology, chemistry, elementary, English, history, mathematics, multi-level teacher, music, physical, science, social science, social studies. **English:** English lit, rhetoric/composition. **Health services:** General, art therapy. **History:** General. **Human services:** General, public policy, social work. **Liberal arts:** Arts/sciences. **Math:** General. **Physical sciences:** Chemistry. **Protective services:** Criminal justice, police science. **Psychology:** General. **Social sciences:** General, economics, political science, sociology. **Visual/performing arts:** General, art, art history/conservation, dramatic, music, music performance, studio arts.

Most popular majors. Business/marketing 18%, communications/journalism 13%, education 19%, interdisciplinary studies 10%, social sciences 7%.

Computing on campus. 345 workstations in dormitories, library, computer center, student center. Dormitories wired for high-speed internet access and linked to campus network. Commuter students can connect to campus network. Online course registration, online library, helpline, repair service, student web hosting, wireless network available.

Student life. Freshman orientation: Mandatory, $105 fee. Preregistration for classes offered. Sessions held in spring and summer; 2 1/2 day program just prior to classes beginning. **Housing:** Guaranteed on-campus for freshmen. Coed dorms, special housing for disabled, apartments, wellness housing available. $200 partly refundable deposit, deadline 7/1. Suites available in nontraditional residence halls for married students. Single parents have access to student residences. **Activities:** Bands, campus ministries, choral groups, dance, drama, international student organizations, literary magazine, music ensembles, musical theater, radio station, student government, student newspaper, symphony orchestra, criminal justice association, black student union, College Democrats, social work student association, College Republicans, intervarsity Christian fellowship, World Student Association.

Athletics. NCAA. **Intercollegiate:** Baseball M, basketball, cross-country, golf W, ice hockey, soccer, softball W, track and field, volleyball W. **Intramural:** Badminton, basketball, bowling, cheerleading, football (non-tackle), golf, ice hockey, racquetball, rifle, skiing, soccer, softball, swimming, table tennis, tennis, volleyball. **Team name:** Yellowjackets.

Student services. Adult student services, alcohol/substance abuse counseling, chaplain/spiritual director, career counseling, services for economically disadvantaged, student employment services, financial aid counseling, health services, minority student services, on-campus daycare, personal counseling, placement for graduates, veterans' counselor, women's services. **Physically disabled:** Services for visually, hearing impaired.

Contact. E-mail: admissions@uwsuper.edu
Phone: (715) 394-8230 Fax: (715) 394-8407
Tonya Roth, Director of Admission, University of Wisconsin-Superior, Belknap and Catlin, PO Box 2000, Superior, WI 54880

University of Wisconsin-Whitewater
Whitewater, Wisconsin
www.uww.edu   CB code: 1921

- Public 4-year university
- Residential campus in large town
- 10,019 degree-seeking undergraduates

General. Founded in 1868. Regionally accredited. **Degrees:** 1,805 bachelor's, 16 associate awarded; master's offered. **ROTC:** Army, Air Force. **Location:** 40 miles from Madison, 50 miles from Milwaukee. **Calendar:** Semester, extensive summer session. **Full-time faculty:** 408 total. **Part-time faculty:** 124 total. **Class size:** 42% < 20, 45% 20-39, 7% 40-49, 5% 50-99, less than 1% >100. **Special facilities:** Observatory, nature preserve and recreation area, weather station.

Freshman class profile.

GPA 3.75 or higher:	11%	Rank in top tenth:	9%
GPA 3.50-3.74:	15%	Out-of-state:	7%
GPA 3.0-3.49:	44%	Live on campus:	90%
GPA 2.0-2.99:	30%	Fraternities:	7%
Rank in top quarter:	31%	Sororities:	6%

Basis for selection. College prep curriculum and rank in top 40% of high school class important. SAT or ACT recommended. Audition required for music; portfolio recommended for art. **Home schooled:** Transcript of courses and grades required. **Learning Disabled:** Disability should be referenced in essay and include review by Center for Students with Disabilities. Medical documentation may be requested.

High school preparation. 17 units required; 20 recommended. Required and recommended units include English 4, mathematics 3-4, social studies 3-4, science 3-4 (laboratory 1), foreign language 2 and academic electives 4.

2011-2012 Annual costs. Tuition/fees: $7,195; $14,768 out-of-state. Minnesota reciprocity tuition: $252 per-credit-hour. Room/board: $5,500. Books/supplies: $170. Personal expenses: $400.

Financial aid. Non-need-based: Scholarships awarded for academics, alumni affiliation, art, leadership, minority status, music/drama, ROTC, state residency.

Application procedures. Admission: Priority date 12/1; deadline 5/1 (postmark date). $44 fee, may be waived for applicants with need. Admission notification on a rolling basis beginning on or about 9/15. **Financial aid:** Priority date 3/15; no closing date. FAFSA required. Applicants notified on a rolling basis starting 4/1; must reply within 3 week(s) of notification.

Academics. Special study options: Accelerated study, combined bachelor's/graduate degree, cooperative education, cross-registration, distance learning, double major, dual enrollment of high school students, ESL, exchange student, external degree, honors, independent study, internships, liberal arts/career combination, student-designed major, study abroad, teacher certification program, weekend college. **Credit/placement by examination:** AP, CLEP, IB, SAT, ACT, institutional tests. 30 credit hours maximum toward associate degree, 60 toward bachelor's. **Support services:** Learning center, pre-admission summer program, reduced course load, remedial instruction, study skills assistance, tutoring, writing center.

Majors. Area/ethnic studies: Women's. **Biology:** General. **Business:** General, accounting, business admin, finance, human resources, managerial economics, marketing, nonprofit/public, office/clerical, operations. **Communications:** Broadcast journalism, communications/speech/rhetoric, journalism. **Computer sciences:** General, information technology, systems analysis, web page design. **Education:** General, art, biology, business, chemistry, computer, drama/dance, early childhood, elementary, English, French, German, history, learning disabled, mathematics, music, physical, sales/marketing, science, secondary, social science, social studies, Spanish, special ed, speech. **English:** Creative writing, English lit, rhetoric/composition. **Foreign languages:** French, German, Spanish. **Health services:** Speech pathology. **History:** General. **Human services:** General, public policy, social work. **Liberal arts:** Arts/sciences. **Math:** General. **Physical sciences:** Chemistry, physics. **Psychology:** General. **Social sciences:** General, economics, geography, political science, sociology. **Visual/performing arts:** Art, art history/conservation, dance, dramatic, music, music theory/composition, theater arts management, theater history.

Most popular majors. Business/marketing 28%, communications/journalism 10%, education 17%, public administration/social services 6%, social sciences 9%.

Computing on campus. 1,373 workstations in dormitories, library, computer center, student center. Dormitories wired for high-speed internet access and linked to campus network. Commuter students can connect to campus network. Online course registration, online library, helpline, repair service, student web hosting, wireless network available.

Student life. Freshman orientation: Mandatory, $75 fee. Preregistration for classes offered. Full-day program held in summer. **Housing:** Guaranteed on-campus for freshmen. Coed dorms, single-sex dorms, special housing for disabled, wellness housing available. $125 fully refundable deposit. **Activities:** Bands, choral groups, dance, drama, literary magazine, music ensembles, musical theater, opera, radio station, student government, student newspaper, symphony orchestra, TV station, Campus Crusade for Christ, Diamond Way Buddhist, College Democrats, College Republicans, Arabic club, black student union, Adopt-A-School Program, America Reads.

Athletics. NCAA. **Intercollegiate:** Baseball M, basketball, bowling W, cross-country, diving, football (tackle) M, golf W, gymnastics W, soccer, softball W, swimming, tennis, track and field, volleyball W, wrestling M. **Intramural:** Badminton, basketball, bowling, football (non-tackle), golf, racquetball, soccer, softball, table tennis, tennis, volleyball. **Team name:** Warhawks.

Student services. Adult student services, alcohol/substance abuse counseling, chaplain/spiritual director, career counseling, services for economically disadvantaged, student employment services, financial aid counseling, health services, legal services, minority student services, on-campus daycare, personal counseling, placement for graduates, veterans' counselor, women's services. **Physically disabled:** Services for visually, speech, hearing impaired.

Contact. E-mail: uwwadmit@uww.edu
Phone: (262) 472-1440 Fax: (262) 472-1515
Jodi Hare, Director of Admissions, University of Wisconsin-Whitewater, 800 West Main Street, Whitewater, WI 53190-1790

Viterbo University
La Crosse, Wisconsin
www.viterbo.edu
CB member
CB code: 1878

- Private 4-year university and liberal arts college affiliated with Roman Catholic Church
- Residential campus in small city
- 2,153 degree-seeking undergraduates
- 78% of applicants admitted
- ACT (writing optional) required

General. Founded in 1890. Regionally accredited. **Degrees:** 438 bachelor's, 22 associate awarded; master's offered. **ROTC:** Army. **Location:** 150 miles from Minneapolis-St. Paul, 150 miles from Madison. **Calendar:** Semester, limited summer session. **Full-time faculty:** 119 total; 55% have terminal degrees, 4% minority, 56% women. **Part-time faculty:** 259 total. **Class size:** 66% < 20, 30% 20-39, less than 1% 40-49, 3% 50-99. **Special facilities:** Center for ethics, science and technology; fine arts center; center for recreation and education in conjunction with Boys and Girls Club of America.

Freshman class profile. 1,610 applied, 1,256 admitted, 364 enrolled.

Mid 50% test scores		GPA 2.0-2.99:	27%
ACT composite:	21-26	Rank in top quarter:	40%
GPA 3.75 or higher:	24%	Rank in top tenth:	16%
GPA 3.50-3.74:	17%	Out-of-state:	33%
GPA 3.0-3.49:	30%	Live on campus:	82%

Basis for selection. High school GPA and ACT score most important, then placement testing. Auditions and portfolio reviews required for students applying to School of Fine Arts (music, theater, art, dance). Interview required for students not meeting admission requirements. **Home schooled:** Transcript of courses and grades required. **Learning Disabled:** All students encouraged to file ADA petition for reasonable accommodations, preferably 8 weeks prior to start of classes.

High school preparation. College-preparatory program recommended. 16 units required; 19 recommended. Required and recommended units include English 3-4, mathematics 2, social studies 2, history 2, science 2 (laboratory 2), foreign language 2 and academic electives 5. Chemistry required for nursing, dietetics, natural sciences, allied health preprofessional students. Portfolios or auditions required for fine arts students.

2011-2012 Annual costs. Tuition/fees: $21,870. Room/board: $7,180. Books/supplies: $850. Personal expenses: $1,800.

Financial aid. Non-need-based: Scholarships awarded for academics, alumni affiliation, art, athletics, leadership, minority status, music/drama, ROTC.

Application procedures. Admission: Closing date 8/15 (receipt date). $25 fee, may be waived for applicants with need, free for online applicants. Admission notification on a rolling basis. Must reply by May 1 or within 2 week(s) if notified thereafter. **Financial aid:** Priority date 3/15; no closing date. FAFSA, institutional form required. Applicants notified on a rolling basis starting 4/1; must reply within 3 week(s) of notification.

Academics. Learning Center offers individual and small group tutoring in all subject areas daily. Library services available daily, on weekends and evenings. **Special study options:** Accelerated study, combined bachelor's/graduate degree, cross-registration, distance learning, double major, dual enrollment of high school students, honors, independent study, internships, liberal arts/career combination, student-designed major, study abroad, teacher certification program, urban semester, Washington semester, weekend college. Weekend college is primarily for students at master's level. **Credit/placement by examination:** AP, CLEP, IB, SAT, ACT, institutional tests. 30 credit hours maximum toward bachelor's degree. 16 hours awarded for military services. **Support services:** Learning center, reduced course load, remedial instruction, study skills assistance, tutoring, writing center.

Majors. Biology: General, biochemistry. **Business:** Accounting, business admin, management information systems, marketing. **Communications:** Organizational. **Computer sciences:** General. **Education:** Art, biology, business, chemistry, drama/dance, elementary, English, mathematics, music, science, secondary, social studies, Spanish, technology/industrial arts. **English:** English lit. **Foreign languages:** Spanish. **Health services:** Clinical lab technology, dietetics, nursing (RN). **Human services:** Social work. **Liberal arts:** Arts/sciences. **Math:** General. **Parks/recreation:** Exercise sciences, sports admin. **Philosophy/religion:** Philosophy, religion. **Physical sciences:** Chemistry. **Protective services:** Criminal justice. **Psychology:** General. **Social sciences:** General, sociology. **Visual/performing arts:** General, art, design, dramatic, graphic design, music, music pedagogy, music performance, studio arts, studio arts management.

Most popular majors. Business/marketing 20%, education 8%, health sciences 36%, interdisciplinary studies 11%, visual/performing arts 7%.

Computing on campus. 396 workstations in dormitories, library, computer center, student center. Dormitories wired for high-speed internet access and linked to campus network. Commuter students can connect to campus network. Online course registration, online library, helpline, wireless network available.

Student life. Freshman orientation: Mandatory. Preregistration for classes offered. One-day program offered 4 times in the summer for incoming freshmen and parents. **Policies:** Standards of conduct, sexual harassment code, anti-hazing initiation policy, academic honesty policy, academic due process, campus security policy, residence hall terms and conditions, alcohol and drug policy, student event policies. **Housing:** Guaranteed on-campus for freshmen. Single-sex dorms, apartments available. $100 fully refundable deposit, deadline 5/1. **Activities:** Pep band, campus ministries, choral groups, dance, drama, international student organizations, literary magazine, music ensembles, musical theater, student government, student newspaper, Connect, Students in Free Enterprise, Circle K, student nurses association, education club, Sigma Pi Delta, CREW, Global Rhythms, psychology club.

Athletics. NAIA. **Intercollegiate:** Baseball M, basketball, bowling, cross-country, golf, soccer, softball W, volleyball W. **Intramural:** Badminton, basketball, bowling, cross-country, football (non-tackle), golf, handball, racquetball, rugby M, skiing, soccer, softball, table tennis, tennis, volleyball. **Team name:** V-Hawks.

Student services. Adult student services, alcohol/substance abuse counseling, chaplain/spiritual director, career counseling, services for economically disadvantaged, student employment services, financial aid counseling, health services, personal counseling, placement for graduates, veterans' counselor, women's services. **Physically disabled:** Services for visually, hearing impaired.

Contact. E-mail: admission@viterbo.edu
Phone: (608) 796-3010 Toll-free number: (800) 848-3726
Fax: (608) 796-3020
Robert Forget, Dean of Admission, Viterbo University, 900 Viterbo Drive, La Crosse, WI 54601-8804

Wisconsin Lutheran College
Milwaukee, Wisconsin
www.wlc.edu
CB code: 1513

- Private 4-year liberal arts college affiliated with Wisconsin Evangelical Lutheran Synod
- Residential campus in very large city
- 979 degree-seeking undergraduates
- 65% of applicants admitted
- SAT or ACT (ACT writing optional) required

General. Founded in 1973. Regionally accredited. **Degrees:** 141 bachelor's awarded. **ROTC:** Army, Naval, Air Force. **Calendar:** Semester, limited summer session. **Full-time faculty:** 64 total. **Part-time faculty:** 52 total. **Class size:** 73% < 20, 25% 20-39, less than 1% 40-49, less than 1% 50-99.

Freshman class profile. 802 applied, 521 admitted, 261 enrolled.

Mid 50% test scores		GPA 3.0-3.49:	38%
SAT critical reading:	400-520	GPA 2.0-2.99:	21%
SAT math:	430-570	Rank in top quarter:	43%
ACT composite:	21-27	Rank in top tenth:	18%
GPA 3.75 or higher:	25%	Out-of-state:	25%
GPA 3.50-3.74:	16%	Live on campus:	92%

Basis for selection. ACT, GPA, high school rank considered. Interview recommended for some; audition required for music scholarships.

High school preparation. College-preparatory program recommended. 16 units required; 20 recommended. Required and recommended units include English 4, mathematics 3-4, history 2, science 2-3 (laboratory 1-2), foreign language 2-4 and academic electives 3. Mathematics or science majors should complete 4 units of mathematics and 3-4 units of appropriate science courses.

2011-2012 Annual costs. Tuition/fees: $22,830. Room/board: $8,240. Books/supplies: $700. Personal expenses: $1,530.

Financial aid. Non-need-based: Scholarships awarded for academics, art, leadership, music/drama.

Application procedures. Admission: Priority date 3/1; no deadline. $20 fee, may be waived for applicants with need, free for online applicants. Admission notification on a rolling basis beginning on or about 9/1. Must reply by May 1 or within 2 week(s) if notified thereafter. **Financial aid:** Priority date 3/1; no closing date. FAFSA, institutional form required. Applicants notified on a rolling basis starting 3/15; must reply within 2 week(s) of notification.

Academics. Special graduation requirements include freshman seminar. **Special study options:** Double major, dual enrollment of high school students, ESL, independent study, internships, student-designed major, study abroad, teacher certification program. **Credit/placement by examination:** AP, CLEP, SAT, ACT, institutional tests. **Support services:** Learning center, reduced course load, study skills assistance, tutoring, writing center.

Majors. Area/ethnic studies: Chinese. **Biology:** General, biochemistry. **Business:** Business admin. **Communications:** Communications/speech/rhetoric. **Conservation:** Environmental science, environmental studies. **Education:** General, early childhood, elementary, secondary. **English:** English lit. **Foreign languages:** German, Spanish. **Health services:** Nursing (RN). **History:** General. **Math:** General. **Parks/recreation:** Exercise sciences. **Philosophy/religion:** Philosophy. **Physical sciences:** Chemistry. **Psychology:** General. **Social sciences:** General. **Theology:** Theology. **Visual/performing arts:** Art, dramatic, graphic design, music.

Most popular majors. Biology 8%, business/marketing 12%, communications/journalism 23%, education 11%, psychology 13%, visual/performing arts 13%.

Computing on campus. 100 workstations in dormitories, library, computer center, student center. Dormitories wired for high-speed internet access and linked to campus network. Commuter students can connect to campus network. Online course registration, online library, helpline, repair service, wireless network available.

Student life. Freshman orientation: Mandatory. Preregistration for classes offered. 2-day program held over the weekend before start of fall semester. **Policies:** Drug-free, alcohol-free campus. Smoking permitted ouside only. **Housing:** Guaranteed on-campus for all undergraduates. Single-sex dorms, apartments available. $100 fully refundable deposit, deadline 5/1. All traditional age, unmarried students less than 5 years out of high school must live in college housing. Upperclassmen eligible for college apartments. **Activities:** Bands, campus ministries, choral groups, dance, drama, international student organizations, music ensembles, student government, student newspaper.

Athletics. NCAA. **Intercollegiate:** Baseball M, basketball, cross-country, football (tackle) M, golf, soccer, softball W, tennis, track and field, volleyball W. **Intramural:** Volleyball. **Team name:** Warriors.

Student services. Adult student services, chaplain/spiritual director, career counseling, student employment services, financial aid counseling, health services, minority student services, personal counseling, placement for graduates. **Physically disabled:** Services for visually, hearing impaired.

Contact. E-mail: admissions@wlc.edu
Phone: (414) 443-8811 Fax: (414) 443-8547
Jeff Weber, Director of Admissions, Wisconsin Lutheran College, 8800 West Bluemound Road, Milwaukee, WI 53226-4699

Wyoming

University of Phoenix: Cheyenne
Cheyenne, Wyoming
www.phoenix.edu

- For-profit 4-year university
- Small city
- 36 degree-seeking undergraduates

General. Regionally accredited. **Degrees:** 3 bachelor's awarded; master's offered. **Calendar:** Differs by program.

Basis for selection. Admission requirements vary by program.

Application procedures. Admission: No deadline. No application fee.

Academics. Credit/placement by examination: AP, CLEP.

Majors. Business: Business admin, office management.

Contact. Marc Booker, Director of Admission and Evaluation, University of Phoenix: Cheyenne, 6900 Yellowtail Road, Cheyenne, WY 82009-6112

University of Wyoming
Laramie, Wyoming   **CB member**
www.uwyo.edu   **CB code: 4855**

- Public 4-year university
- Residential campus in large town
- 9,993 degree-seeking undergraduates: 16% part-time, 52% women, 1% African American, 1% Asian American, 5% Hispanic American, 1% Native American, 3% international
- 2,516 degree-seeking graduate students
- 96% of applicants admitted
- SAT or ACT (ACT writing optional) required
- 53% graduate within 6 years

General. Founded in 1886. Regionally accredited. Undergraduate and graduate degree programs offered in Casper. Extension classes available in off-campus locations throughout the state. Online classes offered nationally. **Degrees:** 1,853 bachelor's awarded; master's, professional, doctoral offered. **ROTC:** Army, Air Force. **Location:** 45 miles from Cheyenne, 130 miles from Denver. **Calendar:** Semester, extensive summer session. **Full-time faculty:** 749 total; 85% have terminal degrees, 9% minority, 38% women. **Part-time faculty:** 62 total; 39% have terminal degrees, 6% minority, 50% women. **Class size:** 42% < 20, 42% 20-39, 5% 40-49, 7% 50-99, 4% >100. **Special facilities:** Museums (art, geological, anthropology, entomology, law), herbariums, spatial data and visualization center, botany conservatory, zoological center, learning resource center, meteorological station, Grand Teton National Park research center, planetarium, veterinary laboratory, materials characterization laboratory, biological research facility, on-site elementary school, infrared telescope observatory, institute of environment/natural resources, fishery and wildlife research unit, American heritage center, insect galleries.

Freshman class profile. 3,883 applied, 3,728 admitted, 1,536 enrolled.

Mid 50% test scores			
SAT critical reading:	490-600	**Rank in top tenth:**	21%
SAT math:	490-630	**End year in good standing:**	74%
ACT composite:	22-27	**Return as sophomores:**	73%
GPA 3.75 or higher:	35%	**Out-of-state:**	46%
GPA 3.50-3.74:	20%	**Live on campus:**	88%
GPA 3.0-3.49:	29%	**International:**	2%
GPA 2.0-2.99:	16%	**Fraternities:**	9%
Rank in top quarter:	51%	**Sororities:**	8%

Basis for selection. For assured admission, required to submit high school GPA, ACT or SAT score, and complete 13 required units in a pre-college curriculum. Test scores are not required for non-degree-seeking students or for students over the age of 21. **Home schooled:** A home school credit evaluation form must be submitted. **Learning Disabled:** Must formally apply to University Disability Support Services for accommodations and provide documentation of disability.

High school preparation. College-preparatory program required. 13 units required; 19 recommended. Required and recommended units include English 4, mathematics 3-4, science 3-4 (laboratory 3) and foreign language 2. 3 cultural context electives are required. These can be from any combination of behavioral or social sciences, visual or performing arts, humanities, or foreign languages.

2012-2013 Annual costs. Tuition/fees (projected): $4,125; $12,855 out-of-state. Room/board: $8,759. Books/supplies: $1,200. Personal expenses: $2,200.

2010-2011 Financial aid. Need-based: 1,114 full-time freshmen applied for aid; 701 were judged to have need; 689 of these received aid. Average need met was 40%. Average scholarship/grant was $1,292; average loan $1,513. 60% of total undergraduate aid awarded as scholarships/grants, 40% as loans/jobs. **Non-need-based:** Awarded to 4,627 full-time undergraduates, including 889 freshmen. Scholarships awarded for academics, alumni affiliation, art, athletics, leadership, minority status, music/drama, ROTC, state residency.

Application procedures. Admission: Priority date 3/1; deadline 8/10 (postmark date). $40 fee, may be waived for applicants with need. Within 2 weeks of receipt of required materials. Must reply by May 1 or within 3 week(s) if notified thereafter. Early application recommended for students seeking financial aid and university housing preferences. **Financial aid:** Priority date 3/1; no closing date. FAFSA required. Applicants notified on a rolling basis starting 4/1; must reply within 3 week(s) of notification.

Academics. Remedial instruction offered on campus through Laramie County Community College. **Special study options:** Accelerated study, distance learning, double major, exchange student, external degree, honors, independent study, internships, student-designed major, study abroad, Washington semester. **Credit/placement by examination:** AP, CLEP, IB, SAT, ACT, institutional tests. Unlimited hours of credit by examination counted toward bachelor's degree, as long as course requirements are still met. Individual departments may allow additional tests on a case-by-case basis. **Support services:** Learning center, pre-admission summer program, reduced course load, study skills assistance, tutoring, writing center.

Majors. Area/ethnic studies: American, Native American, women's. **Biology:** General, botany, microbiology, molecular, physiology, wildlife, zoology. **Business:** Accounting, business admin, finance, management science, managerial economics, marketing. **Communications:** Communications/speech/rhetoric, journalism. **Computer sciences:** Computer science. **Conservation:** Environmental studies. **Education:** Agricultural, elementary, elementary special ed, music, physical, secondary, special ed, technology/industrial arts, trade/industrial. **Engineering:** Architectural, chemical, civil, computer, electrical, mechanical, petroleum, systems. **English:** English lit. **Foreign languages:** French, German, Russian, Spanish. **General:** Agribusiness operations, animal sciences, communications, range science, sustainable agriculture. **Health services:** Audiology/speech pathology, dental hygiene, nursing (RN). **History:** General. **Human services:** Social work. **Liberal arts:** Humanities. **Math:** General, statistics. **Parks/recreation:** Exercise sciences. **Philosophy/religion:** Philosophy, religion. **Physical sciences:** General, astronomy, astrophysics, chemistry, geology, physics. **Protective services:** Criminal justice. **Psychology:** General. **Social sciences:** General, anthropology, geography, political science, sociology. **Visual/performing arts:** Art, dramatic, music, music performance. **Work/family studies:** General.

Most popular majors. Agriculture 6%, biology 7%, business/marketing 13%, education 13%, engineering/engineering technologies 13%, health sciences 10%, psychology 6%, social sciences 7%.

Computing on campus. 1,413 workstations in dormitories, library, computer center, student center. Dormitories wired for high-speed internet access and linked to campus network. Commuter students can connect to campus network. Online course registration, online library, helpline, student web hosting, wireless network available.

Student life. Freshman orientation: Available, $60 fee. Preregistration for classes offered. 10 2-day sessions offered in June. **Policies:** New freshmen subject to live-in policy. **Housing:** Guaranteed on-campus for freshmen. Coed dorms, single-sex dorms, special housing for disabled, apartments, fraternity/sorority housing available. $100 nonrefundable deposit. **Activities:** Bands, campus ministries, choral groups, dance, drama, film society, international student organizations, literary magazine, music ensembles, Model UN, musical theater, opera, student government, student newspaper, symphony orchestra, TV station, black student leaders, local church organizations, College Republicans, Rocky Mountain Democrats, Fellowship of Christian Athletes, Amnesty International, lesbian/gay/bisexual/transgendered association, Movimiento Estudiantil Chicanos de Atzlan, student health advisory council.

Athletics. NCAA. **Intercollegiate:** Basketball, cross-country, diving, football (tackle) M, golf, soccer W, swimming, tennis W, track and field, volleyball W, wrestling M. **Intramural:** Badminton, basketball, bowling, cross-country, football (non-tackle), golf, racquetball, soccer, softball, swimming, table tennis, tennis, track and field, volleyball, water polo, wrestling M. **Team name:** Cowboys, Cowgirls.

Student services. Adult student services, alcohol/substance abuse counseling, career counseling, services for economically disadvantaged, student employment services, financial aid counseling, health services, legal services, minority student services, on-campus daycare, personal counseling, placement for graduates, veterans' counselor, women's services. **Physically disabled:** Services for visually, speech, hearing impaired.

Contact. E-mail: admissions@uwyo.edu
Phone: (307) 766-5160 Toll-free number: (800) 342-5996
Fax: (307) 766-4042
Shelley Dodd, Director of Admissions, University of Wyoming, Dept 3435, Laramie, WY 82071

Guam

University of Guam
Mangilao, Guam
www.uog.edu   CB code: 0959

- Public 4-year university
- Commuter campus in large town
- 3,317 degree-seeking undergraduates: 25% part-time, 60% women, 1% African American, 42% Asian American, 1% international
- 321 degree-seeking graduate students

General. Founded in 1952. Regionally accredited. Academic programs offered by two colleges and three schools: College of Liberal Arts and Sciences, College of Natural and Applied Sciences, School of Business and Public Administration, School of Education, and School of Nursing and Health Sciences. **Degrees:** 365 bachelor's, 6 associate awarded; master's offered. **ROTC:** Army. **Calendar:** Semester, limited summer session. **Full-time faculty:** 182 total; 50% minority, 42% women. **Part-time faculty:** 76 total; 83% minority, 67% women. **Class size:** 52% < 20, 43% 20-39, 3% 40-49, 2% 50-99, less than 1% >100. **Special facilities:** Planetarium, marine lab, Pacific and Micronesian library resources, art gallery, shrimp hatchery.

Freshman class profile. 672 applied, 572 admitted, 359 enrolled.

GPA 3.75 or higher:	25%	End year in good standing:	77%
GPA 3.50-3.74:	10%	Return as sophomores:	65%
GPA 3.0-3.49:	24%	Out-of-state:	1%
GPA 2.0-2.99:	32%	Live on campus:	3%
Rank in top quarter:	47%	International:	1%
Rank in top tenth:	23%		

Basis for selection. Open admission, but selective for some programs. Nursing students required to complete certain science, math, and English high school courses. **Home schooled:** Transcript of courses and grades, state high school equivalency certificate required. **Learning Disabled:** UOG will reasonably accommodate individuals with disabilities. Students expected to make timely requests for special accommodation.

2011-2012 Annual costs. Tuition/fees: $6,198; $17,448 out-of-state. Room only: $1,880. Books/supplies: $4,570. Personal expenses: $5,540.

Financial aid. Non-need-based: Scholarships awarded for state residency.

Application procedures. Admission: Priority date 6/1; deadline 8/20 (receipt date). $49 fee. Admission notification on a rolling basis. **Financial aid:** Priority date 4/15; no closing date. FAFSA, institutional form required. Applicants notified on a rolling basis starting 6/1; must reply within 2 week(s) of notification.

Academics. Special study options: Accelerated study, distance learning, double major, dual enrollment of high school students, ESL, exchange student, honors, internships, study abroad, teacher certification program. **Credit/placement by examination:** AP, CLEP, IB, institutional tests. **Support services:** Pre-admission summer program, reduced course load, remedial instruction, study skills assistance, tutoring, writing center.

Majors. Area/ethnic studies: East Asian, Japanese. **Biology:** General. **Business:** Accounting, business admin. **Communications:** Communications/speech/rhetoric. **Computer sciences:** General, computer science. **Education:** Bilingual, biology, chemistry, early childhood, elementary, English, mathematics, physical, secondary, social studies, special ed. **English:** English lit. **Health services:** Nursing (RN). **History:** General. **Human services:** General, social work. **Math:** General. **Parks/recreation:** General, health/fitness. **Philosophy/religion:** Philosophy. **Physical sciences:** Chemistry. **Protective services:** Criminal justice. **Psychology:** General. **Social sciences:** Anthropology, political science, sociology. **Visual/performing arts:** Art. **Work/family studies:** General.

Most popular majors. Business/marketing 27%, education 27%, health sciences 6%.

Computing on campus. 545 workstations in dormitories, library, computer center, student center. Dormitories wired for high-speed internet access and linked to campus network. Commuter students can connect to campus network. Online library, wireless network available.

Student life. Freshman orientation: Available. Preregistration for classes offered. Held one week before semester begins and includes campus tour; students receive results of English and math placement tests, academic advising, and orientation of support services. **Housing:** Coed dorms available. $100 partly refundable deposit, deadline 8/7. **Activities:** Concert band, campus ministries, choral groups, dance, drama, musical theater, student government, student newspaper.

Athletics. Intramural: Basketball M, softball, table tennis, volleyball. **Team name:** Tritons.

Student services. Alcohol/substance abuse counseling, career counseling, services for economically disadvantaged, student employment services, financial aid counseling, health services, personal counseling, placement for graduates, veterans' counselor. **Physically disabled:** Services for visually, speech, hearing impaired.

Contact. E-mail: admitme@uguam.uog.edu
Phone: (671) 735-2201 Fax: (671) 735-2203
Remedios Cristobal, Registrar, University of Guam, UOG Station, Mangilao, GU 96923

Virgin Islands

University of the Virgin Islands
St. Thomas, Virgin Islands   CB member
www.uvi.edu   CB code: 0879

- Public 4-year university
- Commuter campus in small city
- 2,299 degree-seeking undergraduates: 37% part-time, 71% women, 74% African American, 7% Hispanic American, 5% international
- 210 degree-seeking graduate students
- 95% of applicants admitted
- SAT or ACT (ACT writing recommended) required
- 31% graduate within 6 years

General. Founded in 1962. Regionally accredited. Additional campus on St. Croix, St. John Academic Center. **Degrees:** 228 bachelor's, 74 associate awarded; master's offered. **ROTC:** Army. **Location:** 45 miles from San Juan, Puerto Rico. **Calendar:** Semester, limited summer session. **Full-time faculty:** 108 total; 73% have terminal degrees, 53% minority, 45% women. **Part-time faculty:** 133 total; 26% have terminal degrees, 81% minority, 57% women. **Class size:** 58% < 20, 21% 20-39, 4% 40-49, 9% 50-99, 8% >100. **Special facilities:** Amphitheater, Caribbean collection, African art collection.

Freshman class profile. 795 applied, 758 admitted, 453 enrolled.

Mid 50% test scores			
SAT critical reading:	340-460	GPA 2.0-2.99:	69%
SAT math:	310-430	Rank in top quarter:	33%
SAT writing:	350-450	Rank in top tenth:	8%
ACT composite:	13-21	End year in good standing:	67%
GPA 3.75 or higher:	2%	Return as sophomores:	72%
GPA 3.50-3.74:	7%	Out-of-state:	2%
GPA 3.0-3.49:	18%	International:	3%

Basis for selection. Secondary school record important in admission decisions. Students must have a minimum 2.0 GPA.

High school preparation. College-preparatory program recommended. 14 units required. Required units include English 4, mathematics 3, social studies 3, science 3 and foreign language 2.

2012-2013 Annual costs. Tuition/fees (projected): $4,594; $12,574 out-of-state. Room/board: $9,386. Books/supplies: $1,750. Personal expenses: $2,040.

2011-2012 Financial aid. Non-need-based: Scholarships awarded for academics, art, athletics.

Application procedures. Admission: Priority date 2/1; deadline 4/30 (postmark date). $25 fee, may be waived for applicants with need. Admission notification on a rolling basis. Must reply by 6/30. **Financial aid:** Closing date 3/1. FAFSA required. Applicants notified on a rolling basis starting 4/1; must reply within 2 week(s) of notification.

Academics. **Special study options:** Combined bachelor's/graduate degree, distance learning, double major, exchange student, external degree, honors, independent study, internships. **Credit/placement by examination:** AP, CLEP, SAT, ACT, institutional tests. **Support services:** Learning center, pre-admission summer program, reduced course load, remedial instruction, study skills assistance, tutoring, writing center.

Majors. **Biology:** General, marine. **Business:** Accounting, business admin, hotel/motel admin. **Communications:** Communications/speech/rhetoric. **Computer sciences:** Computer science. **Conservation:** Water/wetlands/ marine. **Education:** Early childhood, elementary, music. **English:** English lit. **Health services:** Nursing (RN). **Liberal arts:** Arts/sciences. **Math:** General. **Physical sciences:** Chemistry. **Protective services:** Police science. **Psychology:** General. **Social sciences:** General.

Most popular majors. Biology 8%, business/marketing 50%, health sciences 7%, mathematics 14%, psychology 9%.

Computing on campus. 300 workstations in library, computer center, student center. Dormitories wired for high-speed internet access and linked to campus network. Commuter students can connect to campus network. Online course registration, online library, helpline, wireless network available.

Student life. **Freshman orientation:** Mandatory, $90 fee. Preregistration for classes offered. One-week orientation activities held on both campuses. **Policies:** Drug and alcohol policy, code of student conduct policy, student government association, sexual harassment policy. **Housing:** Single-sex dorms, wellness housing available. $100 partly refundable deposit, deadline 6/1. **Activities:** Bands, choral groups, dance, drama, literary magazine, music ensembles, student government, student newspaper, political clubs, Future Business Leaders of America, Virgin Islands student association, British Virgin Islands Student Association, Environment Association, health educators, Golden Key International Honor Society, Accounting Association, ROTARACT, St. Kitts/Nevis Association.

Athletics. **Intercollegiate:** Basketball, cheerleading M, cross-country, soccer M, swimming, tennis, track and field, volleyball. **Intramural:** Archery, badminton, basketball, fencing, golf, gymnastics, racquetball, softball, swimming, table tennis, tennis, track and field, volleyball. **Team name:** Bucs.

Student services. Career counseling, student employment services, financial aid counseling, health services, personal counseling, placement for graduates. **Physically disabled:** Services for visually, speech, hearing impaired.

Contact. E-mail: admissions@uvi.edu
Phone: (340) 693-1150 Fax: (340) 693-1155
Xuri Allen, Director of Admissions and Recruitment, University of the Virgin Islands, No. 2 John Brewers Bay, St. Thomas, VI 00802-9990

Commonwealth of The Marianas

Northern Marianas College
Saipan, Commonwealth of The Marianas
www.nmcnet.edu   **CB code: 0781**

◗ Public two-year upper-division community and liberal arts college
◗ Commuter campus in large town

General. Founded in 1981. Regionally accredited. **Location:** 150 miles from Guam, 3,000 miles from Hawaii. **Calendar:** Semester.

Annual costs/financial aid. Personal expenses: $900.

Contact. Phone: (670) 234-3690 ext. 1528
Director of Admissions, PO Box 501250, Saipan, MP 96950

Canada

McGill University
Montreal, Canada   **CB member**
www.mcgill.ca   **CB code: 0935**

◗ Public 4-year university
◗ Commuter campus in very large city

General. Founded in 1821. **Location:** Main campus located at the foot of Mount Royal, in the heart of downtown Montreal. The Macdonald campus is situated on the western tip of the island of Montreal, in Saint Anne de Bellevue. **Calendar:** Semester.

Annual costs/financial aid. Need-based financial aid available for full-time students.

Contact. Phone: (514) 398-3910
Director, Admissions and Recruitment, 845 Sherbrooke Street West, Montreal, CC H3A-2T5

Memorial University of Newfoundland
St. John's, Canada   **CB member**
www.mun.ca   **CB code: 0885**

◗ Public 4-year university
◗ Commuter campus in small city

General. Founded in 1925. **Location:** Located in St. John's. **Calendar:** Trimester.

Annual costs/financial aid. Books/supplies: $700. Need-based financial aid available for full-time students.

Contact. Phone: (709) 737-4431
Registrar, Memorial University of Newfoundland, Admissions Office-Arts and Admin. Bldg, St. John's, Newfoundland, Canada, CC A1C-S7

Queen's University
Kingston, Canada   **CB member**
www.queensu.ca   **CB code: 0949**

◗ Public 4-year university
◗ Residential campus in small city
◗ 13,862 undergraduates
◗ 4,417 graduate students
◗ Application essay required

General. **Calendar:** Semester, limited summer session. **Full-time faculty:** 833 total.

Freshman class profile.

Return as sophomores:	95%	**Live on campus:**	86%

Basis for selection. GED not accepted. GPA, application essay, level of applicant's interest most important. **Home schooled:** Statement describing home school structure and mission, transcript of courses and grades, state high school equivalency certificate required.

2012-2013 Annual costs. Tuition ranges from $5,461 to $13,093 for domestic students and $18,730 to $26,505 for international students.

Application procedures. **Admission:** Closing date 2/15 (receipt date). Application must be submitted online. Admission notification on a rolling basis beginning on or about 12/1. Must reply by 5/1. Separate application for a place in residence is due by June 7.

Academics. **Special study options:** Combined bachelor's/graduate degree, distance learning, double major, ESL, exchange student, honors, internships,

study abroad, teacher certification program. **Credit/placement by examination:** AP, CLEP, IB, SAT, ACT. **Support services:** Learning center, preadmission summer program, reduced course load, remedial instruction, study skills assistance, tutoring, writing center.

Majors. Computer sciences: General. **Education:** General. **Engineering:** General. **Parks/recreation:** Exercise sciences, health/fitness. **Physical sciences:** General. **Visual/performing arts:** General, music, studio arts.

Computing on campus. Dormitories wired for high-speed internet access and linked to campus network. Online course registration, online library, helpline, repair service, wireless network available.

Student life. Freshman orientation: Available. Preregistration for classes offered. Held the week before classes begin in September; covers residence events and information on academic endeavors, student life. **Housing:** Guaranteed on-campus for freshmen. Coed dorms, single-sex dorms, cooperative housing, wellness housing available. $525 partly refundable deposit, deadline 6/7. **Activities:** Bands, choral groups, dance, drama, film society, international student organizations, literary magazine, music ensembles, Model UN, musical theater, radio station, student government, student newspaper, TV station, Asian cooking club, Campus for Christ, Indian students association, Israel on Campus, Journalists for Human Rights, Japanese Relations at Queen's, New Democrat Party, Interfaith Council, Project on International Development, African Caribbean students association.

Athletics. Intercollegiate: Basketball, cross-country, football (tackle) M, ice hockey, rowing (crew), rugby, soccer, volleyball. **Intramural:** Basketball, football (non-tackle) M, ice hockey, soccer, volleyball, water polo. **Team name:** Gaels.

Student services. Adult student services, alcohol/substance abuse counseling, chaplain/spiritual director, career counseling, services for economically disadvantaged, student employment services, financial aid counseling, health services, legal services, on-campus daycare, personal counseling, women's services. **Physically disabled:** Services for visually, speech, hearing impaired.

Contact. E-mail: admission@queensu.ca
Phone: (613) 533-2218 Fax: (613) 533-6810
Andrea MacIntyre, Admission Manager, Queen's University, 74 Union Street, Kingston, CC

Simon Fraser University
Burnaby, Canada
www.sfu.ca

CB member
CB code: 0999

- Public 4-year university
- Commuter campus in very large city
- 23,883 degree-seeking undergraduates: 46% part-time, 53% women
- 3,785 degree-seeking graduate students
- 69% of applicants admitted
- 67% graduate within 6 years

General. Founded in 1965. Regionally accredited. Harbour Centre campus in downtown Vancouver; Surrey campus in Surrey, British Columbia. **Degrees:** 4,472 bachelor's awarded; master's, doctoral offered. **Location:** 9 miles from Vancouver, British Columbia; 130 miles from Seattle, Washington. **Calendar:** Trimester, extensive summer session. **Full-time faculty:** 932 total; 89% have terminal degrees, 34% women. **Part-time faculty:** 13 total; 77% have terminal degrees, 62% women. **Class size:** 22% < 20, 36% 20-39, 5% 40-49, 20% 50-99, 17% >100. **Special facilities:** Art gallery, child care facility, hyperbaric chamber, underwater laboratory, combative room, apiary, archaeology museum.

Freshman class profile. 10,654 applied, 7,392 admitted, 3,028 enrolled.

GPA 3.75 or higher:	5%	GPA 2.0-2.99:	4%
GPA 3.50-3.74:	22%	Return as sophomores:	85%
GPA 3.0-3.49:	69%	Out-of-state:	8%

Basis for selection. GED not accepted. Senior academic courses, test scores, and advanced academic course work (IB, AP, honors, etc.). Successful applicants normally have 2.8 GPA (3.0 for programs in Business Administration) and 1550 SAT (22 ACT). Academic background, GPA, and test scores most important. Canadian residents not required to submit SAT or ACT. Audition/interview may be required for school of contemporary arts. Applicants may submit personal information profile and at least 1 letter of reference. **Home schooled:** Transcript of courses and grades required. Applicants must meet state high school graduation requirements.

High school preparation. 13 units required. Required units include English 4, mathematics 3, social studies 1, history 1, science 2 (laboratory 1), foreign language 2 and academic electives 3.

2010-2011 Financial aid. Need-based: 19% of total undergraduate aid awarded as scholarships/grants, 81% as loans/jobs. **Non-need-based:** Scholarships awarded for academics, alumni affiliation, art, athletics, leadership, music/drama, state residency.

Application procedures. Admission: Priority date 2/28; deadline 4/30 (receipt date). $100 fee. Application must be submitted online. Admission notification by 6/30. Admission notification on a rolling basis beginning on or about 1/15. Application fee of $100 (Canadian) if academic records originate outside of Canada. **Financial aid:** Priority date 6/1, closing date 11/15. FAFSA, institutional form required. Applicants notified on a rolling basis.

Academics. Special study options: Cooperative education, distance learning, double major, exchange student, honors, independent study, internships, study abroad, teacher certification program. Dual degree program with Zhejiang University in China. **Credit/placement by examination:** AP, CLEP, IB, SAT, ACT. 60 credit hours maximum toward bachelor's degree. **Support services:** Learning center, study skills assistance, writing center.

Majors. Area/ethnic studies: Women's. **Biology:** General, biochemistry, molecular. **Business:** Accounting/business management, actuarial science, business admin, entrepreneurial studies, finance, management information systems, management science, marketing. **Communications:** Communications/speech/rhetoric, digital media. **Computer sciences:** General, information systems, programming. **Conservation:** General, environmental science, environmental studies. **Education:** General. **Engineering:** Engineering science. **English:** English lit. **Foreign languages:** French, linguistics. **Health services:** International public health. **History:** General. **Liberal arts:** Arts/sciences. **Math:** General, applied, statistics. **Parks/recreation:** Exercise sciences. **Philosophy/religion:** Philosophy. **Physical sciences:** Chemical physics, chemistry, geology, physics, planetary, theoretical physics. **Protective services:** Police science. **Psychology:** General. **Social sciences:** Anthropology, archaeology, criminology, economics, geography, political science, sociology. **Visual/performing arts:** General, cinematography, dance, design, dramatic, music.

Most popular majors. Business/marketing 15%, communications/journalism 6%, education 10%, social sciences 19%.

Computing on campus. 900 workstations in library, computer center, student center. Dormitories wired for high-speed internet access. Commuter students can connect to campus network. Online course registration, online library, helpline, repair service, student web hosting, wireless network available.

Student life. Freshman orientation: Available, $30 fee. Preregistration for classes offered. Depending on type of program, 1 or 2 days immediately preceding the start of classes for a particular term. **Housing:** Coed dorms, single-sex dorms, special housing for disabled, apartments available. $450 nonrefundable deposit. **Activities:** Dance, drama, film society, international student organizations, radio station, student government, student newspaper, First Nations student center, center for students with disabilities, crisis line, public interest research group, women's center, interfaith center, harassment resolution office, student society.

Athletics. NCAA. Intercollegiate: Basketball, cross-country, diving, field hockey W, football (tackle) M, golf M, soccer, softball W, swimming, track and field, volleyball W, wrestling. **Intramural:** Badminton, basketball, football (non-tackle), soccer, softball, tennis, volleyball. **Team name:** The Clan.

Student services. Alcohol/substance abuse counseling, chaplain/spiritual director, career counseling, financial aid counseling, health services, legal services, minority student services, on-campus daycare, personal counseling, women's services. **Physically disabled:** Services for visually, speech, hearing impaired.

Contact. E-mail: undergraduate-admissions@sfu.ca
Phone: (778) 782-3397 Fax: (778) 782-4969
Louise Legris, Director of Admission, Simon Fraser University, 8888 University Drive, Burnaby, CC

University of Alberta
Edmonton, Canada
www.ualberta.ca

CB member
CB code: 0963

- Public 4-year university
- Commuter campus in very large city
- 31,309 degree-seeking undergraduates
- 7,475 graduate students

General. Founded in 1906. Regionally accredited. Campus Saint-Jean is the French-speaking element within the university and offers degree programs in education, science, and the arts, with graduate programs in education (MEd) and Canadian Studies (MA). **Degrees:** 7,227 bachelor's awarded;

master's, professional, doctoral offered. **Location:** 180 miles from Calgary. **Calendar:** Semester, extensive summer session. **Full-time faculty:** 3,787 total. **Special facilities:** Center for the arts, museums, research library system, botanical gardens, research farm, agricultural research stations, professional development center, nanotechnology institute, heart institute, diabetes institute.

Basis for selection. Most undergraduate admission is based on completion of 5 appropriate Grade 12 subjects (program specific), including English. Must present at least 70% to apply and must present a competitive average for admission, with minimum grade of 50% in each subject (based on 50% passing grade). Competitive averages range from 70-85%. SAT or ACT, SAT Subject Tests recommended. Auditions, portfolios, letters of intent/ essays, or interviews required for several programs.

High school preparation. Required and recommended units include English 3, mathematics 3, social studies 3, history 3, science 3 (laboratory 3), foreign language 3 and academic electives 3. Specific course requirements vary by program.

2011-2012 Annual costs. Full-time undergraduate tuition and required fees (most degree programs): Canadian citizens and permanent residents, $6,688; non-Canadian citizens, $19,552; standard double-occupancy on-campus room, $2,752 ; board (19 meals per week), $3,393. Figures, which cover the academic year (2 terms at 15 credits per term), are in Canadian dollars. Books/supplies: $1,000. Personal expenses: $2,200.

Financial aid. **Additional information:** American students may apply U.S. federal aid and student loans toward university tuition, but must apply for that aid in U.S. prior to attending university.

Application procedures. **Admission:** Closing date 5/1 (postmark date). $115 fee. Admission notification on a rolling basis beginning on or about 12/1. Must reply by 8/15. Early Admission contingent upon completion of admission criteria and maintaining competitive average. **Financial aid:** Closing date 5/1. FAFSA, institutional form required. Applicants notified on a rolling basis; must reply by 8/15.

Academics. **Special study options:** Accelerated study, combined bachelor's/graduate degree, cooperative education, distance learning, double major, dual enrollment of high school students, ESL, exchange student, honors, independent study, internships, student-designed major, study abroad, teacher certification program. **Credit/placement by examination:** AP, CLEP, IB. **Support services:** Learning center, pre-admission summer program, reduced course load, remedial instruction, study skills assistance, tutoring, writing center.

Majors. **Area/ethnic studies:** African, East Asian, Latin American, Near/ Middle Eastern, Russian/Eastern European/Eurasian, Scandinavian, Southeast Asian, women's. **Biology:** General, animal physiology, biochemistry, bioinformatics, botany, cell/histology, environmental, microbiology, molecular genetics, neurobiology/anatomy, pharmacology, physiology, plant molecular, zoology. **Business:** General, accounting, actuarial science, business admin, communications, entrepreneurial studies, finance, human resources, international, international finance, management information systems, marketing, operations, organizational behavior, retailing, sales/distribution. **Computer sciences:** General, computer science, programming. **Conservation:** General, forestry, wildlife/wilderness. **Education:** Agricultural, art, biology, comparative, computer, drama/dance, early childhood, elementary, English, ESL, foreign languages, French, mathematics, middle, music, physical, physics, science, secondary, social studies, special ed, trade/industrial. **Engineering:** General, applied physics, chemical, civil, computer, electrical, engineering mechanics, materials, mechanical, mining, petroleum, software. **English:** English lit. **Foreign languages:** General, Chinese, classics, French, German, Italian, Japanese, Latin, linguistics, modern Greek, Romance, Scandinavian, Spanish. **General:** Animal sciences, business, crop production, economics, food science, horticultural science. **Health services:** Athletic training, clinical lab technology, dental hygiene, nursing (RN), occupational therapy assistant, predental, premedicine, preop/surgical nursing, prepharmacy, preveterinary. **History:** General. **Math:** General, computational, statistics. **Parks/recreation:** General, exercise sciences, sports admin. **Philosophy/ religion:** Philosophy, religion. **Physical sciences:** Atmospheric science, chemistry, physics. **Protective services:** Criminal justice. **Psychology:** General. **Social sciences:** Anthropology, criminology, economics, geography, international relations, political science, sociology. **Visual/performing arts:** Dramatic, film/cinema/video, metal/jewelry, music, music history, music theory/composition, printmaking, studio arts, theater design. **Work/family studies:** Clothing/textiles, family/community services, food/nutrition.

Computing on campus. 1,300 workstations in dormitories, library, computer center, student center. Dormitories wired for high-speed internet access and linked to campus network. Commuter students can connect to campus network. Online course registration, online library, helpline, student web hosting, wireless network available.

Student life. **Freshman orientation:** Available. Preregistration for classes offered. Two-day program includes peer advice presentations and campus

tour. **Housing:** Guaranteed on-campus for freshmen. Coed dorms, single-sex dorms, special housing for disabled, apartments, fraternity/sorority housing available. $175 nonrefundable deposit. **Activities:** Bands, campus ministries, choral groups, dance, drama, film society, international student organizations, literary magazine, music ensembles, Model UN, musical theater, opera, radio station, student government, student newspaper, symphony orchestra, more than 300 clubs available.

Athletics. **Intercollegiate:** Basketball, cross-country, field hockey W, football (tackle) M, golf, gymnastics, ice hockey, rugby W, soccer, swimming, tennis, track and field, volleyball, wrestling. **Intramural:** Archery M, badminton, baseball, basketball, bowling, cross-country, diving, football (nontackle) M, football (tackle) M, golf, gymnastics, ice hockey, judo, racquetball, rugby, skiing, soccer, softball, squash, swimming, table tennis, tennis, track and field, triathlon, volleyball, water polo, wrestling. **Team name:** Golden Bears, Pandas.

Student services. Adult student services, alcohol/substance abuse counseling, chaplain/spiritual director, career counseling, services for economically disadvantaged, student employment services, financial aid counseling, health services, legal services, minority student services, on-campus daycare, personal counseling, placement for graduates, women's services. **Physically disabled:** Services for visually, speech, hearing impaired.

Contact. E-mail: admissions.international@ualberta.ca
Phone: (780) 492-3113 Fax: (780) 492-7172
Pat Dalton, Associate Registrar and Director of Enrollment Management, University of Alberta, Administration Building, Edmonton, CC T6G 2-M7

University of British Columbia
Vancouver, Canada   **CB member**
www.ubc.ca   **CB code: 0965**

- Public 4-year university
- Commuter campus in very large city
- 29,717 degree-seeking undergraduates: 26% part-time, 54% women
- 15,675 graduate students
- 49% of applicants admitted
- 76% graduate within 6 years

General. Founded in 1915. UBC comprises 18 faculties, 14 schools and 3 colleges across two major campuses (Vancouver & Okanagan) and two satellite campuses. **Degrees:** 6,559 bachelor's awarded; master's, professional, doctoral offered. **Location:** 6 miles from downtown Vancouver (Vancouver campus), 5 miles from downtown Kelowna (Okanagan campus). **Calendar:** Semester, extensive summer session. **Full-time faculty:** 2,722 total; 99% have terminal degrees, 10% minority, 36% women. **Class size:** 23% < 20, 34% 20-39, 10% 40-49, 18% 50-99, 15% >100. **Special facilities:** Museum of anthropology, museum of biodiversity, museum of geological sciences, botany collection and herbarium, botanical garden, Japanese garden, astronomical observatories, performing arts center, opera theater, drama theater, global issues center, winter sports center, particle accelerator, forests, model farm.

Freshman class profile. 27,134 applied, 13,166 admitted, 6,365 enrolled.

Basis for selection. GED not accepted. Academic averages most important. Minimum requirement is strong B+ average; for science and engineering-based programs, strong A average likely to be required. Evaluation of those from US curriculum made on best 8 academic courses from junior and senior years. US curriculum students must also submit SAT or ACT scores (including Writing component). All applicants, regardless of citizenship and schooling, must meet the university's English language admission standard. Applicants schooled outside Canada encouraged to complete the application section regarding academic and extracurricular achievements. Applicants must also meet specific program requirements. Applications encouraged from students completing enriched secondary school programs such as International Baccalaureate (IB), Advanced Placement (AP), General Certificate of Education (GCE), and French Baccalaureate. Generous first-year credit offered to students with high academic achievement in these programs. Standardized achievement test results must be submitted by applicants following US curriculum. (Exceptions may be granted for countries where tests are not available.) Minimum competitive score for SAT is 1500. Minimum competitive score for ACT is 24 + 8 writing. Interviews generally not required. At Vancouver, application to School of Music requires interview, audition, and/or portfolio. At Okanagan, application to Fine Arts programs requires portfolio and letter of intent. For most UBC programs, a section (which may be either compulsory or optional but strongly encouraged) calling for brief essay and/or statements on academic or personal achievement is included in the online application form.

High school preparation. College-preparatory program required. 19 units required. Required units include English 4, mathematics 3 and academic electives 12.

2011-2012 Annual costs. Tuition and fees for international students will be assessed at fixed rates of increase each year. Books/supplies: $2,200. Personal expenses: $3,500.

Financial aid. Non-need-based: Scholarships awarded for academics, athletics. **Additional information:** Need-based financial aid from public funds available only to Canadian citizens or permanent residents. Limited need-based financial aid for international students; however, outstanding international students may be nominated for need-based aid.

Application procedures. Admission: Closing date 1/31 (receipt date). $61.2 fee ($102 out-of-state). Application must be submitted online. Admission notification on a rolling basis beginning on or about 1/30. Must reply by 6/1. To accept an offer, students must pay a deposit ($100 Canadian students, $500 international students) credited to tuition fees. Students applying for on-campus student housing must accept offer of academic admission by June 1 in order to retain offer of housing placement. Housing deposit ($700 Canadian) is due at time of accepting housing offer. Students must normally accept admission offers by June 1. Supporting documents should be submitted as soon as possible, in order to secure a timely admissions decision. Admitted students may request deferment of offer of admission for up to one year. Requests for deferment must be received by July 15, or within 30 days of offer, whichever is later. **Financial aid:** Closing date 1/31. Institutional form required. Applicants notified by 4/1; must reply by 4/30.

Academics. Several cross-disciplinary options available in first-year study. Undergraduate students encouraged to engage in research projects supported by annual Undergraduate Research Conference. **Special study options:** Combined bachelor's/graduate degree, cooperative education, cross-registration, distance learning, double major, dual enrollment of high school students, ESL, exchange student, honors, internships, student-designed major, study abroad, teacher certification program. Undergraduate students may study abroad at any one of 167 partner institutions in 37 countries. **Credit/placement by examination:** AP, CLEP, IB. UBC offers credits to students entering from enriched programs, including Advanced Placement, International Baccalaureate, British patterned Advanced Levels, or French Baccalaureate. Exact credits offered depend on degree program and will be determined in each case by Faculty at time of entry. **Support services:** Learning center, preadmission summer program, reduced course load, study skills assistance, tutoring, writing center.

Majors. Architecture: Environmental design. **Area/ethnic studies:** Asian, Canadian, Chicano/Hispanic-American/Latino, East Asian, European, German, Italian, Latin American, Russian/Eastern European/Eurasian, Russian/Slavic, Slavic, South Asian, Southeast Asian, Western European, women's. **Biology:** General, anatomy, animal physiology, bacteriology, biochemistry, biophysics, biotechnology, cell/histology, conservation, ecology, environmental, epidemiology, evolutionary, genetics, molecular, molecular biochemistry, neuroscience, pathology, pharmacology/toxicology, physiology, reproductive, zoology. **Business:** General, accounting, business admin, finance, human resources, international, international finance, international marketing, investments/securities, labor relations, management information systems, management science, managerial economics, marketing, operations, real estate, transportation. **Computer sciences:** General, artificial intelligence, computer science. **Conservation:** General, economics, environmental science, environmental studies, forest management, forest resources, forest sciences, forestry, management/policy, wood science. **Education:** General, elementary, middle, multi-level teacher, Native American, physical, secondary. **Engineering:** General, applied physics, biomedical, chemical, civil, computer, electrical, engineering mechanics, environmental, forest, geological, materials, mechanical, metallurgical, mining, operations research, software. **English:** British lit, Canadian lit, creative writing, English lit. **Foreign languages:** Chinese, classics, French, German, Germanic, Italian, Japanese, Korean, Latin, linguistics, Native American, Portuguese, Romance, Slavic, South Asian, Spanish, Urdu. **General:** Agronomy, animal sciences, aquaculture, economics, food processing, food science, horticultural science, plant sciences, soil science. **Health services:** Athletic training, clinical lab assistant, community health, dental hygiene, nurse midwife, nursing (RN), occupational health, preveterinary. **History:** General. **Human services:** Social work. **Math:** General, applied, statistics. **Parks/recreation:** Exercise sciences, facilities management, health/fitness, sports admin. **Philosophy/religion:** Philosophy, religion. **Physical sciences:** Astronomy, atmospheric science, chemistry, geology, geophysics, materials science, oceanography, physics, planetary, theoretical physics. **Psychology:** General. **Social sciences:** Anthropology, archaeology, Canadian government, economics, geography, international relations, political science, sociology. **Visual/performing arts:** General, art, art history/conservation, cinematography, conducting, dramatic, film/cinema/video, music, music history, music performance, music theory/composition, musicology, piano/keyboard, stringed instruments, theater arts management, theater design, voice/opera. **Work/family studies:** General, family/community services, food/nutrition, human nutrition.

Computing on campus. Dormitories wired for high-speed internet access and linked to campus network. Commuter students can connect to campus network. Online course registration, online library, helpline, repair service, student web hosting, wireless network available.

Student life. Freshman orientation: Available. Preregistration for classes offered. Four orientation programs: JUMP START (full week program before school start, offering academic preparation for students new to North America); GALA International Orientation (3-day event held during week before start of winter term); Parents Orientation (on Sunday before start of term); IMAGINE UBC (Vancouver) and CREATE (UBC Okanagan), official welcome and orientation experience on first day of winter term. **Housing:** Guaranteed on-campus for freshmen. Coed dorms, single-sex dorms, apartments, fraternity/sorority housing available. $700 partly refundable deposit. Cultural houses in partnership with universities in Japan, Korea, and Mexico available. **Activities:** Bands, choral groups, dance, drama, film society, international student organizations, literary magazine, music ensembles, Model UN, musical theater, opera, radio station, student government, student newspaper, symphony orchestra, TV station, over 250 clubs, societies, and other groups.

Athletics. NAIA. **Intercollegiate:** Baseball M, basketball, cross-country, equestrian, field hockey, football (tackle) M, golf, ice hockey, rowing (crew), rugby, skiing, soccer, softball W, swimming, track and field, volleyball. **Intramural:** Badminton, basketball, cheerleading, cross-country, football (non-tackle), ice hockey, judo, racquetball, skiing, soccer, softball W, squash, swimming, tennis, triathlon, volleyball, water polo, wrestling M. **Team name:** Thunderbirds.

Student services. Alcohol/substance abuse counseling, career counseling, student employment services, financial aid counseling, health services, minority student services, on-campus daycare, personal counseling, placement for graduates, women's services. **Physically disabled:** Services for visually, speech, hearing impaired.

Contact. Phone: (604) 822-8999 Toll-free number: (877) 272-1422 Fax: (604) 822-9858
Michael Bluhm, Associate Director, Undergraduate Admissions, University of British Columbia, 2016 - 1874 East Mall, Vancouver, CC

University of Manitoba
Winnipeg, Canada
www.umanitoba.ca

CB member
CB code: 0973

- Public 4-year university
- Commuter campus in very large city

General. Founded in 1877. **Location:** 10 miles from downtown Winnipeg. **Calendar:** Semester.

Contact. Phone: (204) 474-8808
Director of Admissions, 424 University Centre, Winnipeg, CC R3T 2-N2

University of Toronto
Toronto, Canada
www.utoronto.ca

CB member
CB code: 0982

- Public 4-year university
- Commuter campus in very large city
- 64,962 degree-seeking undergraduates: 11% part-time, 56% women
- 15,303 degree-seeking graduate students
- 69% of applicants admitted
- SAT or ACT with writing, SAT Subject Tests, application essay required
- 82% graduate within 6 years

General. Degrees: 11,344 bachelor's awarded; master's, professional, doctoral offered. **Location:** 95 miles from Buffalo, NY. **Calendar:** Semester, extensive summer session. **Full-time faculty:** 5,381 total. **Part-time faculty:** 5,269 total. **Special facilities:** Greenhouses, observatory, university-operated art galleries and theaters, teaching hospitals, 150-acre farm.

Freshman class profile. 67,955 applied, 46,709 admitted, 8,243 enrolled.

Basis for selection. Typically, applicants who are competitive for admission to the University of Toronto are in the top third of their class. Only those applicants who have attained a high level of academic achievement and who present credits to satisfy any prerequisites of specific courses or programs in which they intend to enroll will be admitted. The Faculty of Arts and Science St. George campus, University of Toronto Mississauga, University of Toronto Scarborough, the Faculty of Music, and the Faculty

of Physical Education and Health/Kinesiology will consider applications from students in the USA and other countries who have completed or who are completing 12th grade in an accredited high school; such applicants must present high scores in SAT Reasoning or ACT examinations including the Writing Test component and at least three SAT Subject Tests or AP/IB subjects appropriate to their proposed area of study. Scores below 500 in any part of the SAT Reasoning or SAT Subject Tests are not acceptable. Many programs require higher scores. Students seeking admission to science or business/commerce programs are strongly advised to complete AP Calculus (AB or BC) or IB Mathematics (HL or SL or Math Methods with Calculus option). Student profiles required for some programs. **Home schooled:** Statement describing home school structure and mission, transcript of courses and grades required. Application should include course outlines, textbooks and method of evaluation used, samples of written work, relevant details of any independent evaluations or assessments; results of standardized tests may also be considered. **Learning Disabled:** Students can send a letter with supporting documentation.

2011-2012 Annual costs. Tuition/fees: $6,818. Room/board: $12,000. Books/supplies: $1,000.

Financial aid. All financial aid based on need.

Application procedures. Admission: Closing date 3/1 (receipt date). $120 fee. Admission notification by 5/1. Admission notification on a rolling basis. Must reply by 5/28. Application deadlines vary by program.

Academics. Special study options: Combined bachelor's/graduate degree, cooperative education, double major, ESL, exchange student, honors, independent study, internships, student-designed major, study abroad, teacher certification program. **Credit/placement by examination:** AP, CLEP, IB, SAT, ACT, institutional tests. **Support services:** Learning center, reduced course load, study skills assistance, tutoring, writing center.

Majors. Architecture: Architecture, environmental design, history/criticism, urban/community planning. **Area/ethnic studies:** African, African-American, American, Asian, Canadian, Caribbean, Chinese, East Asian, European, French, gay/lesbian, German, Italian, Latin American, Native American, Near/Middle Eastern, Polish, Russian/Eastern European/Eurasian, Russian/Slavic, Slavic, Spanish/Iberian, Ukraine, women's. **Biology:** General, animal physiology, biochemistry, Biochemistry/molecular biology, bioinformatics, biophysics, biotechnology, botany, cellular/anatomical, conservation, ecology, environmental, genetics, molecular, molecular biochemistry, molecular biophysics, molecular pharmacology, neuroscience, pharmacology, pharmacology/toxicology, toxicology, zoology. **Business:** General. **Communications:** Communications/speech/rhetoric, digital media, health, journalism, media studies. **Communications technology:** General. **Computer sciences:** General, artificial intelligence, computer science, information systems, information technology, programming, systems analysis. **Conservation:** General, environmental science, environmental studies, forestry. **Education:** General, elementary, middle, multi-level teacher, secondary. **Engineering:** General, aerospace, agricultural, applied physics, biomedical, chemical, civil, computer, engineering science, environmental, industrial, materials, mechanical. **English:** Creative writing, English lit. **Foreign languages:** Ancient Greek, Biblical, Bosnian/Serbo/Croatian, Celtic, classics, Czech, French, German, Germanic, Hebrew, Italian, Latin, linguistics, Polish, Portuguese, Russian, Slavic, Slovak, South Asian, Southeast Asian, Spanish, Ukrainian. **Health services:** EMT paramedic, ethics, pharmaceutical sciences, predental, premedicine, prepharmacy. **History:** General, European, science/technology. **Liberal arts:** Arts/sciences, humanities. **Math:** General, probability, statistics. **Parks/recreation:** Exercise sciences, health/fitness. **Philosophy/religion:** Buddhist, Christian, ethics, Judaic, logic, philosophy, religion. **Physical sciences:** General, astronomy, astrophysics, chemistry, forensic chemistry, paleontology, physics, planetary. **Psychology:** General, forensic. **Social sciences:** Anthropology, archaeology, Canadian government, criminology, economics, geography, international economic development, international economics, international relations, physical anthropology, political science, sociology, U.S. government, urban studies. **Theology:** Religious ed, theology. **Visual/performing arts:** General, art, art history/conservation, dramatic, film/cinema/video, jazz, music, music history, music performance, music theory/composition, stringed instruments, studio arts, voice/opera.

Computing on campus. Dormitories wired for high-speed internet access and linked to campus network. Commuter students can connect to campus network. Online course registration, online library, helpline, repair service, student web hosting, wireless network available.

Student life. Freshman orientation: Available. Preregistration for classes offered. Usually held the week before classes begin. **Policies:** Code of Student Conduct. **Housing:** Guaranteed on-campus for freshmen. Coed dorms, single-sex dorms, special housing for disabled, apartments, cooperative housing, wellness housing available. $600 nonrefundable deposit, deadline 6/15. **Activities:** Bands, campus ministries, choral groups, dance, drama, film society, international student organizations, literary magazine, music ensembles, Model UN, musical theater, opera, radio station, student government, student newspaper, symphony orchestra, TV station.

Athletics. Intercollegiate: Badminton, baseball M, basketball, cross-country, fencing, field hockey W, football (non-tackle) M, football (tackle) M, golf, ice hockey, lacrosse, rowing (crew), rugby M, skiing, soccer, softball W, swimming, synchronized swimming W, tennis, track and field, volleyball, water polo, wrestling M. **Intramural:** Badminton, baseball M, basketball, cross-country, fencing, field hockey W, football (non-tackle) M, football (tackle) M, golf, ice hockey, lacrosse, rowing (crew) M, rugby M, skiing, soccer, softball W, swimming, tennis, track and field, volleyball, water polo, wrestling M. **Team name:** Varsity Blues.

Student services. Adult student services, alcohol/substance abuse counseling, chaplain/spiritual director, career counseling, services for economically disadvantaged, student employment services, financial aid counseling, health services, legal services, minority student services, on-campus daycare, personal counseling, placement for graduates, women's services. **Physically disabled:** Services for visually, speech, hearing impaired.

Contact. E-mail: admissions.help@utoronto.ca
Phone: (416) 978-2190 Fax: (416) 978-7022
Merike Remmel, Director of Admissions, University of Toronto, 172 St. George Street, Toronto, CC

University of Waterloo
Waterloo, Canada — **CB member**
www.uwaterloo.ca — **CB code: 0996**

- Public 4-year university
- Residential campus in large city
- 26,987 degree-seeking undergraduates
- 63% of applicants admitted
- SAT or ACT (ACT writing optional), application essay, interview required

General. Regionally accredited. Four affiliated university colleges: Conrad Grebel College (Mennonite), St. Jerome's University (Catholic), St. Paul's University (United), and Renison University College (Anglican). Each college is coed and open to students of all religious/non-religious backgrounds. **Degrees:** 4,365 bachelor's awarded; master's, doctoral offered. **Location:** 62 miles from Toronto. **Calendar:** Trimester, limited summer session. **Full-time faculty:** 951 total; 93% have terminal degrees, 25% women. **Part-time faculty:** 694 total; 24% women. **Special facilities:** Dinosaur museum, observatory, greenhouses, optometry clinic, museum of vision science, real-time programming lab, center for education in mathematics and computing, ecology lab, living wetland lab, digital media lab.

Freshman class profile. 42,793 applied, 26,753 admitted, 6,594 enrolled.

Out-of-state:	7%	Live on campus:	71%

Basis for selection. GED not accepted. All applicants encouraged to complete Admission Information Form (AIF) to augment their application and to explain any extenuating circumstances that may have affected past academic performance. 1100 SAT normally required (exclusive of Writing). SAT Writing evaluated on individual basis. Faculty of Arts and Faculty of Environment require 600 SAT Critical Reading. 26 ACT normally required. Faculty of Arts and Faculty of Environment require 26 ACT English. Selected accounting and financial management applicants will be invited to write the Accounting and Financial Management Admission Assessment. Selected architecture applicants will be invited for interview, writing exercise, and discussion of their portfolios. Social work applicants will need letter of reference and personal statement that confirm sufficient practical experience and personal suitability. **Home schooled:** Transcript of courses and grades, state high school equivalency certificate required. Admissions office prefers that applicants complete final year of pre-university studies at traditional (accredited) high school. **Learning Disabled:** Contact Office of Persons with Disabilities.

2011-2012 Annual costs. Tuition for international students (not Canadian citizens or permanent residents), $1,865 per credit for most undergraduate programs. Full-time tuition ranges from $18,700 for arts-related programs to $26,000 for engineering programs. Tuition for Canadian citizens, $611 per credit for most programs. Student fees, including universal transit pass, $1,600. Fees do not include extended health or dental insurance. On-campus room and board ranges from $6,200 to $10,000. Books and supplies average $2,000. Figures, which cover expenses for two terms (academic year), are in Canadian dollars. Books/supplies: $2,000. Personal expenses: $2,900.

Financial aid. All financial aid based on need. **Additional information:** Students who are not residents of the Province of Ontario (Canada) as defined by the Ontario Student Assistance Program (OSAP) should apply for financial aid in home states/countries.

Application procedures. Admission: Closing date 3/30 (postmark date). $140 fee. Admission notification by 5/28. Admission notification on a rolling

basis beginning on or about 12/15. Must reply by 6/1. **Financial aid:** Closing date 6/15. Institutional form required.

Academics. Special study options: Combined bachelor's/graduate degree, cooperative education, cross-registration, distance learning, double major, ESL, exchange student, honors, independent study, student-designed major, study abroad. **Credit/placement by examination:** AP, CLEP, IB, SAT, ACT. **Support services:** Pre-admission summer program, study skills assistance, tutoring, writing center.

Majors. Architecture: Architecture, urban/community planning. **Area/ethnic studies:** East Asian, French, Italian, Latin American, Russian/Eastern European/Eurasian, Russian/Slavic, women's. **Biology:** General, biochemistry, bioinformatics, biomedical sciences, biotechnology. **Business:** General, accounting, actuarial science, business admin, finance, human resources, information resources management, international, investments/securities, tourism/travel. **Communications:** Communications/speech/rhetoric, digital media. **Computer sciences:** Computer science. **Conservation:** Environmental science, environmental studies, management/policy. **Education:** French, mathematics. **Engineering:** General, chemical, civil, computer, electrical, environmental, geological, mechanical, operations research, robotics, software, systems. **English:** English lit, rhetoric/composition. **Foreign languages:** German. **Health services:** Premedicine, prepharmacy, recreational therapy. **History:** General. **Human services:** Social work. **Liberal arts:** Arts/sciences. **Math:** General, applied, computational, statistics. **Parks/recreation:** General, exercise sciences. **Philosophy/religion:** Islamic, Judaic, philosophy, religion. **Physical sciences:** General, chemistry, geology, physics, theoretical physics. **Psychology:** General. **Social sciences:** Anthropology, criminology, economics, geography, international economic development, political science, sociology. **Theology:** Sacred music. **Visual/performing arts:** General, dramatic, music, studio arts.

Most popular majors. Mathematics 8%.

Computing on campus. Dormitories wired for high-speed internet access and linked to campus network. Commuter students can connect to campus network. Online course registration, online library, helpline, repair service, wireless network available.

Student life. Freshman orientation: Available, $101 fee. Preregistration for classes offered. 3 to 5-day academic and social program. **Housing:** Guaranteed on-campus housing for freshmen. Coed dorms, special housing for disabled, apartments available. $500 nonrefundable deposit, deadline 6/1. Living-learning communities allow students to live in small groups, with all students in a given community enrolled in the same academic program. **Activities:** Bands, campus ministries, choral groups, dance, drama, film society, international student organizations, literary magazine, music ensembles, Model UN, musical theater, opera, radio station, student government, student newspaper, symphony orchestra, Aboriginal students association, Caribbean students association, University Association of New Democrats, Chinese drama club, Hindu students association, Konnichiwa Japan, Latin American student association, Polish students association, World Vision club, International Health Development Association.

Athletics. Intercollegiate: Badminton, baseball M, basketball, cheerleading, cross-country, field hockey W, football (tackle) M, golf, ice hockey, rugby, skiing, soccer, squash M, swimming, tennis, track and field, volleyball. **Intramural:** Badminton, baseball, basketball, cricket, football (non-tackle), ice hockey, soccer, softball, squash, volleyball. **Team name:** Warriors.

Student services. Alcohol/substance abuse counseling, chaplain/spiritual director, career counseling, student employment services, financial aid counseling, health services, legal services, on-campus daycare, personal counseling. **Physically disabled:** Services for visually, speech, hearing impaired.

Contact. E-mail: myapplication@uwaterloo.ca
Phone: (519) 888-4567 ext. 33106
Toll-free number: (519) 888-4567 ext. 33107 Fax: (519) 746-2882
Nancy Weiner, Associate Registrar, University of Waterloo, Ontario Universities Application Centre, Guelph, CC

Egypt

American University in Cairo
Cairo, Egypt — CB member
www.aucegypt.edu — CB code: 0903

▸ Private 4-year university
▸ Commuter campus in very large city

▸ 5,244 degree-seeking undergraduates: 9% part-time, 51% women
▸ 1,259 degree-seeking graduate students
▸ 56% of applicants admitted
▸ Application essay required
▸ 82% graduate within 6 years

General. Founded in 1919. Regionally accredited. Language of instruction is English; 75% of degree-seeking students must be of Egyptian nationality. **Degrees:** 847 bachelor's awarded; master's, doctoral offered. **Location:** 40 kilometers from downtown. **Calendar:** Semester, extensive summer session. **Full-time faculty:** 447 total; 72% have terminal degrees, 47% women. **Part-time faculty:** 358 total; 62% have terminal degrees, 49% women. **Class size:** 52% < 20, 41% 20-39, 7% 40-49, less than 1% 50-99.

Freshman class profile. 2,891 applied, 1,618 admitted, 1,240 enrolled.

Mid 50% test scores			
SAT critical reading:	410-520	GPA 3.0-3.49:	32%
SAT math:	520-640	GPA 2.0-2.99:	43%
SAT writing:	500-600	Return as sophomores:	89%
GPA 3.75 or higher:	11%	Out-of-state:	42%
GPA 3.50-3.74:	14%	Live on campus:	8%

Basis for selection. Applicants from the United States expected to have completed college preparatory (academic) high school program and to submit minimum SAT score of 1350. Arab students must take Thanawiya 'Amma, with minimum score of 75% required. CE/GCSE/IGCSE certificates will also be considered for admission. SAT Subject Tests required for applicants who have graduated from American-style high schools with less than 3 semesters in residence. TOEFL/English placements are required for all students. **Home schooled:** Transcript of courses and grades, state high school equivalency certificate required.

High school preparation. Recommended units include English 3, mathematics 3, social studies 3, science 2 and foreign language 2. One unit fine arts recommended.

2011-2012 Annual costs. Tuition/fees: $16,064. On-campus housing (no meals included) ranges from $1,965 (double room) to $2,200 (single room); off-campus housing through AUC (no meals included) ranges from $2,080 (double room) to $3,300 (single room). All housing figures are reported on a per-semester basis.

Financial aid. Non-need-based: Scholarships awarded for academics, art, athletics, leadership, music/drama, state residency.

Application procedures. Admission: Priority date 3/2; deadline 5/15 (receipt date). $50 fee. Admission notification on a rolling basis beginning on or about 7/20. **Financial aid:** Closing date 5/15. Institutional form required. Applicants notified by 8/15.

Academics. Special study options: Double major, ESL, independent study, internships, liberal arts/career combination, study abroad. **Credit/placement by examination:** AP, CLEP, IB, SAT, institutional tests. **Support services:** Learning center, reduced course load, remedial instruction, study skills assistance, tutoring, writing center.

Majors. Area/ethnic studies: Near/Middle Eastern. **Biology:** General. **Business:** Accounting, actuarial science, business admin. **Communications:** Journalism, media studies. **Computer sciences:** General. **Engineering:** Architectural, computer, construction, electrical, mechanical, petroleum. **English:** English lit. **Foreign languages:** Arabic, comparative lit. **History:** General, Asian. **Math:** General. **Philosophy/religion:** Philosophy. **Physical sciences:** Chemistry, physics. **Psychology:** General. **Social sciences:** Anthropology, archaeology, economics, political science, sociology. **Visual/performing arts:** Art, dramatic.

Most popular majors. Business/marketing 33%, communications/journalism 25%, engineering/engineering technologies 19%, social sciences 10%.

Computing on campus. 935 workstations in dormitories, library, computer center. Dormitories wired for high-speed internet access and linked to campus network. Commuter students can connect to campus network. Online course registration, online library, helpline, repair service, wireless network available.

Student life. Freshman orientation: Available. Preregistration for classes offered. Held in August for 3 days. **Policies:** Non-smoking campus. **Housing:** Single-sex dorms, special housing for disabled, apartments available. $300 nonrefundable deposit. **Activities:** Concert band, choral groups, dance, drama, film society, international student organizations, literary magazine, music ensembles, Model UN, radio station, student government, student newspaper, African students association, community service society, Model Arab League.

Athletics. Intercollegiate: Basketball, boxing M, fencing, football (tackle), gymnastics, handball, judo, rowing (crew), rugby M, soccer, squash, swimming, table tennis, tennis, track and field, volleyball, water polo M, wrestling

M. **Intramural:** Basketball, football (tackle), soccer, squash, swimming, table tennis, tennis, track and field, volleyball, weight lifting M.

Student services. Adult student services, career counseling, student employment services, financial aid counseling, health services, on-campus daycare, personal counseling, placement for graduates. **Physically disabled:** Services for visually, hearing impaired.

Contact. E-mail: aucegypt@aucnyo.edu
Phone: (212) 730-8800 ext. 223 Fax: (212) 730-1600
Ghada Hazem, Director of Admissions, American University in Cairo, 420 Fifth Avenue, Third Floor, New York, NY 10018-2729

France

American University of Paris
Paris, France — CB member
www.aup.edu — CB code: 0866

- Private 4-year university and liberal arts college
- Commuter campus in very large city
- 639 degree-seeking undergraduates: 9% part-time, 69% women
- 201 degree-seeking graduate students
- 80% of applicants admitted
- Application essay required

General. Founded in 1962. Regionally accredited. Founded as a liberal arts institution in the 1960s, AUP is an independent university that provides American undergraduate and graduate programs to students from all national, linguistic, and educational backgrounds. **Degrees:** 176 bachelor's awarded; master's offered. **Calendar:** Semester, extensive summer session. **Full-time faculty:** 70 total; 79% have terminal degrees, 40% women. **Part-time faculty:** 57 total; 39% have terminal degrees, 37% women. **Class size:** 80% < 20, 20% 20-39.

Freshman class profile. 586 applied, 469 admitted, 202 enrolled.

Basis for selection. Applicants evaluated on basis of academic performance. Most important sources of information about academic achievements include academic transcripts of all secondary and/or university-level coursework, as well as applicable test scores such as SAT, ACT, and national exams. AUP's admissions based upon evaluation of applicant's potential as manifested in application and supporting materials. New, visiting, and transfer students may apply to enter university either in September or January. Candidates for admission to undergraduate programs should have attended or be attending a high school recognized or accredited by their state/regional/national education certifying agency. Candidates for admission to graduate programs must hold or be in the course of finishing successfully an accredited university-level degree. Non-English speakers are required to take TOEFL, TOEIC, IELTS, or the university's internal English test. Interviews recommended. **Home schooled:** Statement describing home school structure and mission, transcript of courses and grades, state high school equivalency certificate, interview, letter of recommendation (nonparent) required.

High school preparation. 18 units recommended. Recommended units include English 4, mathematics 3, social studies 3, history 2, science 2 (laboratory 1) and foreign language 3.

2011-2012 Annual costs. Tuition/fees: $35,400. Estimated living expenses for academic year: room and board, $11,650; local transportation, $420; utilities (including phone), $1,100; books and supplies, $1,360; miscellaneous personal expenses, $3,065. All amounts shown are in US dollars, although payment must be made in euros.

2010-2011 Financial aid. **Need-based:** 63 full-time freshmen applied for aid; 60 were judged to have need; 60 of these received aid. Average need met was 39%. Average scholarship/grant was $11,579. **Non-need-based:** Awarded to 27 full-time undergraduates, including 20 freshmen. Scholarships awarded for academics.

Application procedures. Admission: No deadline. $65 fee, may be waived for applicants with need. Admission notification on a rolling basis. Must reply by May 1 or within 2 week(s) if notified thereafter. **Financial aid:** No deadline. FAFSA, institutional form required. Applicants notified on a rolling basis; must reply within 4 week(s) of notification.

Academics. Special study options: Cooperative education, cross-registration, double major, exchange student, honors, independent study, internships, student-designed major, study abroad. **Credit/placement by examination:** AP, CLEP, IB, institutional tests. Advanced academic standing can never exceed 30 credits, in the event of multiple secondary school examinations. **Support services:** Pre-admission summer program, reduced course load, study skills assistance, tutoring, writing center.

Majors. Area/ethnic studies: European, French. **Business:** Entrepreneurial studies, international, international finance. **Communications:** Intercultural. **Computer sciences:** Information technology. **Foreign languages:** Comparative lit. **History:** General. **Psychology:** General. **Social sciences:** International economics, urban studies. **Visual/performing arts:** Art history/conservation, film/cinema/video.

Most popular majors. Business/marketing 20%, communications/journalism 28%, history 6%, social sciences 15%, visual/performing arts 7%.

Computing on campus. 120 workstations in library, computer center, student center. Commuter students can connect to campus network. Online course registration, online library, helpline, student web hosting, wireless network available.

Student life. Freshman orientation: Mandatory, $700 fee. Preregistration for classes offered. Orientation, held the week before classes begin, consists of assistance with housing and academic advising, as well as workshops devoted to life in Paris and academic life in a multicultural environment. **Housing:** AUP housing office assists students in finding affordable accommodations within easy commuting distance from school. Most students are situated during the first three days of orientation, after they meet with housing advisor who takes into consideration their personal requirements, interests, and budget. Students live in various neighborhoods of Paris, in independent rooms or with French families or landlords. **Activities:** Choral groups, dance, drama, film society, international student organizations, literary magazine, music ensembles, musical theater, radio station, student government, student newspaper, TV station.

Student services. Career counseling, student employment services, financial aid counseling, health services, personal counseling.

Contact. E-mail: admissions@aup.edu
Phone: (331) 406-20720 Fax: (331) 470-53532
Brad Walp, Director Enrollment Management, American University of Paris, 6, rue du Colonel Combes, Paris, FR

Institut D'Etudes Politiques de Paris
Paris, France — CB member
www.sciencespo.fr

- Public 3-year university
- Commuter campus in very large city
- 4,112 degree-seeking undergraduates
- 5,066 graduate students
- SAT or ACT with writing, application essay, interview required

General. Degrees: 1 bachelor's awarded; master's, doctoral offered. **Calendar:** Semester. **Full-time faculty:** 60 total. **Part-time faculty:** 2,700 total.

Basis for selection. Admission based on comprehensive application form and an oral interview in which applicants present their international background, knowledge of foreign languages, extracurricular activities as well as future career plans. All of the above considered in addition to candidates' academic qualities, allowing selection of candidates with different backgrounds and experiences. In order to attract students with a truly international profile, Sciences Po introduced an international admissions procedure, as part of which interviews are held in 70 cities across the world. Applicants must have completed and submitted their application, including all the required documents, at least four weeks prior the proposed interview date. For further information about admission deadlines please refer to the undergraduate admissions calendar on our web site. SAT Subject Tests recommended. SAT Subject test optional; if candidates have taken Advanced Placement exam(s), they must include the results in their application, along with school profile and reference letter from school counselor.

2012-2013 Annual costs. Tuition/fees (projected): $12,965. Full-time tuition for students whose tax residence is not in European Union: 9,300 euros; housing rates vary, and all accommodations are off-campus. Typically, students should expect to spend 4,500 - 9,000 euros for living expenses. Costs cover academic year. Students whose tax residence is in the European Union pay fees according to a sliding scale, the amount depends on income and household size. Books/supplies: $160.

2010-2011 Financial aid. Non-need-based: Scholarships awarded for academics.

Application procedures. Admission: Closing date 5/2. $120 fee. Application must be submitted online. Admission notification on a rolling basis. Reply policy dependent on program. **Financial aid:** Closing date 5/2. Institutional form required.

Academics. Most undergraduates complete bachelor's degree programs in 3 academic years. Students come from 130 countries, and 40% are non-French citizens. All undergraduates take core curriculum featuring political science, economics, history, international relations, law, and sociology. Joint programs with other schools and colleges available. **Special study options:** Combined bachelor's/graduate degree, double major, dual enrollment of high school students, internships, study abroad. Dual degree conventions with several major universities throughout the world; dual BA, MA, PhD with Columbia University; dual MA with Georgetown University; dual MA with University of Pennsylvania. **Credit/placement by examination:** AP, CLEP. **Support services:** Pre-admission summer program, tutoring.

Majors. Social sciences: General.

Computing on campus. Online course registration, online library, helpline, wireless network available.

Student life. Freshman orientation: Available, $330 fee. Preregistration for classes offered. Orientation for international students organized at the beginning of each semester. **Housing:** Single-sex dorms, apartments available. **Activities:** Concert band, choral groups, dance, drama, film society, international student organizations, literary magazine, music ensembles, Model UN, radio station, student newspaper.

Student services. Career counseling, financial aid counseling, health services, personal counseling, placement for graduates. **Physically disabled:** Services for visually, speech, hearing impaired.

Contact. E-mail: admissions@sciences-po.fr
Phone: (33) 014-5495082 Fax: (33) 014-5484749
Diana Buciamas, Admissions Officer, Institut D'Etudes Politiques de Paris, Service des Admissions, Paris, FR

Parsons Paris School of Design
Paris, France
www.parsons-paris.com

CB member
CB code: 4627

- Private 4-year visual arts and business college
- Commuter campus in very large city
- 160 degree-seeking undergraduates
- 48% of applicants admitted
- Application essay, interview required

General. Calendar: Semester, limited summer session. **Full-time faculty:** 1 total. **Part-time faculty:** 94 total.

Freshman class profile. 188 applied, 90 admitted, 45 enrolled.

Out-of-state: 100%   **Live on campus:** 6%

Basis for selection. A large part of the Admissions Committee's decision is based upon evaluation of the portfolio and home exam. A prospective student's potential for artistic achievement is one of the most important criteria in evaluating candidates for admission. Portfolio of art work and home assignment.

2011-2012 Annual costs. Tuition/fees: $35,800. **Books/supplies:** $1,900.

Financial aid. Non-need-based: Scholarships awarded for art.

Application procedures. Admission: Priority date 3/1; deadline 7/1. $68 fee. Application must be submitted online. Admission notification on a rolling basis. Must reply by May 1 or within 2 week(s) if notified thereafter. **Financial aid:** Priority date 3/1, closing date 5/1. Institutional form required. Applicants notified on a rolling basis starting 3/1.

Academics. Special study options: Accelerated study, ESL, independent study, internships, study abroad. **Credit/placement by examination:** AP, CLEP, IB. 18 credit hours maximum toward bachelor's degree. **Support services:** Pre-admission summer program, writing center.

Majors. Visual/performing arts: Design, fashion design, illustration, photography, studio arts.

Computing on campus. PC or laptop required. 40 workstations in computer center. Wireless network available.

Student life. Freshman orientation: Mandatory. Preregistration for classes offered. Held during the 5 days before the first day of classes. **Housing:** Coed dorms available.

Student services. Career counseling, personal counseling.

Contact. E-mail: admissions@parsons-paris.com
Phone: (33) 145-771999
Matthew Gallagher, Director of Admissions, Parsons Paris School of Design, 14 rue Letellier, Paris, FR

Germany

University of Karlsruhe
Karlsruhe, Germany
www.university-karlsruhe.de

CB member
CB code: 3592

- Public 3-year university
- Small city

General. Calendar: Semester.

Annual costs/financial aid. Undergraduate expenses in euros, academic year: tuition, 14,500; on-campus room, 7,000; health insurance, 900; books and supplies, 500; transportation and miscellaneous expenses, 400.

Contact. Phone: (721) 608-7880
Admissions Director, Schlossplatz 19, Karlsruhe, GE

Guatemala

Universidad del Valle de Guatemala
Guatemala City, Guatemala
www.uvg.edu.gt

CB member
CB code: 3875

- Private 5-year university
- Commuter campus in very large city

General. Calendar: Semester.

Annual costs/financial aid. Need-based financial aid available to full-time and part-time students.

Contact. Phone: (2) 364-0336 ext. 451
Secretaria General, 18 Avenida 11-95 zona 15, Vista Hermosa III, Guatemala City, GT

Italy

The American University of Rome
Rome, Italy
www.aur.edu/american-university-rome

CB member
CB code: 0262

- Private 4-year university and liberal arts college
- Very large city
- 153 degree-seeking undergraduates

General. **Calendar:** Semester. **Full-time faculty:** 13 total. **Part-time faculty:** 50 total.

Freshman class profile. 33 enrolled.

Basis for selection. Minimum high school GPA of 2.5 and a combined SAT total score of 1500 or 21 on ACT. However, each applicant is reviewed individually. Leadership, motivation, academic improvement, level of high school program's difficulty, activities and potential for growth important considerations .

Application procedures. **Admission:** No deadline. Admission notification on a rolling basis. **Financial aid:** Closing date 5/1.

Academics. **Credit/placement by examination:** AP, CLEP.

Majors. **Area/ethnic studies:** Italian. **Business:** Business admin. **Communications:** General. **Social sciences:** Archaeology, international relations. **Visual/performing arts:** Art history/conservation, digital arts.

Contact. E-mail: admissions@aur.edu
Phone: (888) 791-8327
Hanna Suni, Enrollment Specialist, The American University of Rome, Via Pietro Roselli, 4, Rome, IT

John Cabot University
Rome, Italy
www.johncabot.edu/
CB member
CB code: 2795

- Private 4-year liberal arts college
- Very large city
- 1,100 undergraduates
- SAT or ACT, application essay required

General. Regionally accredited. **Degrees:** 50 bachelor's awarded. **Calendar:** Semester. **Full-time faculty:** 108 total.

Basis for selection. Admission based on personal essay, test scores, GPA, and letters of recommendation. **Home schooled:** Statement describing home school structure and mission, transcript of courses and grades, state high school equivalency certificate, interview required.

2012-2013 Annual costs. Tuition/fees (projected): $21,800. Room/board: $11,400. Books/supplies: $700. Personal expenses: $4,000.

Application procedures. **Admission:** Closing date 6/1. $50 fee.

Academics. **Special study options:** Study abroad. **Credit/placement by examination:** AP, CLEP.

Majors. **Area/ethnic studies:** Italian. **Business:** Business admin, marketing. **Communications:** Communications/speech/rhetoric. **English:** English lit. **History:** General. **Liberal arts:** Humanities. **Social sciences:** Economics, international relations, political science. **Visual/performing arts:** Art history/conservation.

Student life. **Housing:** Apartments available. **Activities:** Student newspaper.

Athletics. **Team name:** Gladiators.

Contact. E-mail: admissions@johncabot.edu
Phone: (06) 681-91245
Luke Kasim, Director of Admissions, John Cabot University, Via della Lungara, 233, Rome, IT

Korea

Yonsei University
Seoul, Korea
www.yonsei.ac.kr/eng/
CB member
CB code: 9893

- Private 4-year university
- Commuter campus in very large city

General. **Calendar:** Semester.

Annual costs/financial aid. Books/supplies: $2,000.

Contact. Phone: (822) 212-34131
Admissions Officer, 262 Seongsanno, Seodaemun-gu, Seoul, KR

Kuwait

American University of Kuwait
Safat, Kuwait
www.auk.edu.kw
CB member
CB code: 4185

- For-profit 4-year university and liberal arts college
- Commuter campus in very large city
- 1,978 degree-seeking undergraduates: 14% part-time, 55% women
- 89% of applicants admitted
- 69% graduate within 6 years

General. **Degrees:** 487 bachelor's awarded. **Calendar:** Semester, limited summer session. **Full-time faculty:** 89 total; 83% have terminal degrees, 38% women. **Part-time faculty:** 29 total; 28% have terminal degrees, 59% women. **Class size:** 36% < 20, 61% 20-39, 2% 40-49, less than 1% 50-99, less than 1% >100.

Freshman class profile. 364 applied, 324 admitted, 237 enrolled.

GPA 3.75 or higher:	6%	GPA 2.0-2.99:	56%
GPA 3.50-3.74:	7%	End year in good standing:	86%
GPA 3.0-3.49:	26%	Return as sophomores:	86%

Basis for selection. Admissions is open to those that meet our minimum standards. Secondary school record and GPA most important. **Learning Disabled:** Students are evaluated to determine if the student is capable of success at AUK. Evaluation also conducted to determine if AUK has resources to assist in special needs based on this evaluation and academic history.

High school preparation. College-preparatory program recommended.

2011-2012 Annual costs. All costs reported in Kuwaiti dinars. Undergraduate tuition, 175 per credit hour; required fees, 115 per semester.

Application procedures. **Admission:** Priority date 2/21; deadline 9/6. $126 fee. Notified 3 days after receiving a complete application.

Academics. **Special study options:** Accelerated study, double major, ESL. **Credit/placement by examination:** AP, CLEP, IB, institutional tests. **Support services:** Pre-admission summer program, remedial instruction, study skills assistance, tutoring, writing center.

Majors. **Business:** Accounting, business admin, finance, marketing. **Communications:** Communications/speech/rhetoric. **Computer sciences:** General. **Engineering:** Computer. **English:** English lit. **Social sciences:** General, economics. **Visual/performing arts:** Graphic design.

Most popular majors. Business/marketing 44%, communications/journalism 21%, computer/information sciences 8%, English 8%, visual/performing arts 13%.

Computing on campus. 122 workstations in library, computer center. Commuter students can connect to campus network. Online course registration, online library, helpline, repair service, wireless network available.

Student life. **Freshman orientation:** Mandatory. Preregistration for classes offered. **Policies:** Religious observance required. **Activities:** Drama, international student organizations, literary magazine, student government, student newspaper, community service club, human rights club, Al-Akhdar environmental club, Hope club, Arabic literature club, cooperation club, international club, Armenian club, Lebanese "Culture Club", patriots club.

Athletics. **Intercollegiate:** Badminton, basketball, soccer, table tennis, tennis, volleyball. **Intramural:** Badminton, basketball, soccer, volleyball. **Team name:** Wolfpack.

Student services. Career counseling, student employment services, health services, personal counseling, placement for graduates.

Contact. E-mail: admissions@auk.edu.kw
Phone: (965) 222-48399 ext. 206
Maher Dabbouseh, Director of Admissions, American University of
Kuwait, P.O. Box 3323, Safat, KW

Lebanon

American University of Beirut
Beirut, Lebanon — **CB member**
www.aub.edu.lb — **CB code: 0902**

- Private 4-year university
- Commuter campus in very large city
- 6,148 degree-seeking undergraduates: 4% part-time, 48% women
- 1,571 degree-seeking graduate students
- 67% of applicants admitted
- SAT required
- 81% graduate within 6 years; 17% enter graduate study

General. Regionally accredited. Most students are from the Arab world.
Degrees: 1,439 bachelor's awarded; master's, professional, doctoral offered.
Location: In Beirut City. **Calendar:** Semester, extensive summer session.
Full-time faculty: 531 total; 75% have terminal degrees, 38% women. **Part-time faculty:** 286 total; 32% have terminal degrees, 44% women. **Class size:** 38% < 20, 53% 20-39, 3% 40-49, 4% 50-99, 3% >100. **Special facilities:** Archaeological museum, geological museum, rare biological collection.

Freshman class profile. 3,952 applied, 2,650 admitted, 1,439 enrolled.

Mid 50% test scores			
SAT critical reading:	440-540	GPA 2.0-2.99:	37%
SAT math:	600-700	Rank in top quarter:	60%
SAT writing:	470-580	Rank in top tenth:	35%
GPA 3.75 or higher:	8%	End year in good standing:	94%
GPA 3.50-3.74:	16%	Return as sophomores:	92%
GPA 3.0-3.49:	33%	Live on campus:	22%

Basis for selection. Admission based on composite scores: 50% SAT (25% verbal, 25% math) and 50% standardized school grades. Holders of Lebanese, French, and International Baccalaureate, among other regional governmental secondary diplomas, will be admitted directly into the sophomore class. SAT must be taken before January of the year preceding admissions. **Home schooled:** State high school equivalency certificate required. Most applicants must take 3 SAT Subject Tests.

2010-2011 Financial aid. **Need-based:** 87 full-time freshmen applied for aid; 78 were judged to have need; 74 of these received aid. Average scholarship/grant was $3,717. 84% of total undergraduate aid awarded as scholarships/grants, 16% as loans/jobs. **Non-need-based:** Awarded to 74 full-time undergraduates, including 8 freshmen. Scholarships awarded for academics.

Application procedures. **Admission:** Priority date 11/30; deadline 2/1 (receipt date). $50 fee. Admission notification by 4/30. Must reply by 6/30. Early action applicants must have a minimum SAT and must have been in top 25th percentile of their class for the past two years. **Financial aid:** Priority date 9/1, closing date 2/2. FAFSA, institutional form required. Applicants notified by 6/15; must reply by 6/30.

Academics. **Special study options:** Cross-registration, double major, ESL, exchange student, honors, independent study, internships, liberal arts/career combination, study abroad, teacher certification program. **Credit/placement by examination:** AP, CLEP, IB, SAT, institutional tests. **Support services:** Learning center, remedial instruction, study skills assistance, tutoring, writing center.

Majors. **Architecture:** Architecture. **Biology:** General. **Business:** Business admin. **Computer sciences:** Computer science. **Education:** Elementary. **Engineering:** Chemical, civil, construction, mechanical. **English:** English lit. **Foreign languages:** Arabic. **General:** Agribusiness operations, landscaping, mechanization. **Health services:** Environmental health, nursing (RN). **History:** General. **Human services:** General. **Math:** General, applied, statistics. **Philosophy/religion:** Philosophy. **Physical sciences:** Chemistry, geology, physics. **Psychology:** General. **Social sciences:** Archaeology, economics, political science. **Visual/performing arts:** Art history/conservation, graphic design, studio arts.

Most popular majors. Biology 10%, business/marketing 23%, engineering/engineering technologies 18%, history 10%.

Computing on campus. 1,229 workstations in dormitories, library, computer center, student center. Dormitories wired for high-speed internet access and linked to campus network. Commuter students can connect to campus network. Online course registration, online library, helpline, repair service, student web hosting, wireless network available.

Student life. Freshman orientation: Mandatory. Preregistration for classes offered. Week-long program held in September, one week before classes begin. **Policies:** Student code of conduct; violations may be of an academic or non-academic nature. Designated smoking areas. **Housing:** Guaranteed on-campus for freshmen. Single-sex dorms, wellness housing available. $200 fully refundable deposit, deadline 7/29. **Activities:** Choral groups, dance, drama, film society, international student organizations, music ensembles, Model UN, student government, student newspaper, Palestinian cultural club, Syrian cultural club, Jordanian cultural club, Saudi cultural club, Lebanese Armenian heritage club, Lebanese Red Cross club, human rights and peace club, UNESCO club, drama club.

Athletics. Intercollegiate: Basketball, cross-country, football (tackle) M, gymnastics M, handball, judo, rugby M, skiing, soccer, squash, swimming, table tennis, tennis, track and field, triathlon, volleyball, water polo M. **Intramural:** Basketball, cross-country, diving, gymnastics M, handball, lacrosse, racquetball, soccer, squash, swimming, table tennis, tennis, volleyball, weight lifting.

Student services. Alcohol/substance abuse counseling, career counseling, student employment services, financial aid counseling, health services, personal counseling, placement for graduates. **Physically disabled:** Services for visually, hearing impaired.

Contact. E-mail: admissions@aub.edu.lb
Phone: (961) 137-4374 ext. 2590 Fax: (961) 175-0775
Salim Kanaan, Director of Admissions, American University of Beirut,
PO Box 11-0236, Beirut, LB

Notre Dame University: Louaize
Zouk Mosbeh, Lebanon — **CB member**
www.ndu.edu.lb — **CB code: 7696**

- Private 4-year university and liberal arts college
- Residential campus in small town
- 6,529 degree-seeking undergraduates

General. **Degrees:** 73 bachelor's awarded; master's, doctoral offered. **Calendar:** Semester, limited summer session. **Full-time faculty:** 152 total. **Part-time faculty:** 404 total. **Special facilities:** Museum, engineering and science laboratories, hotel management laboratories, science labs.

Basis for selection. Open admission, but selective for some programs. SAT I or our entrance exams required. **Learning Disabled:** Special exams required.

2011-2012 Annual costs. Tuition/fees: $7,613. Engineering and architecture majors pay $290 per credit hour. Room/board: $1,750. Books/supplies: $300.

Financial aid. All financial aid based on need.

Application procedures. **Admission:** Priority date 5/2; deadline 7/31. $250 fee. Application must be submitted on paper. **Financial aid:** Priority date 4/26, closing date 6/10.

Academics. **Special study options:** Combined bachelor's/graduate degree, cross-registration, exchange student, internships, teacher certification program. **Credit/placement by examination:** AP, CLEP. 106 credit hours maximum toward bachelor's degree. **Support services:** Learning center, writing center.

Majors. **Architecture:** Architecture. **Business:** Actuarial science, business admin, customer service support, hotel/motel admin, office technology, tourism/travel. **Computer sciences:** General. **Conservation:** Environmental studies. **Education:** General. **Engineering:** Civil, computer, electrical, mechanical. **Foreign languages:** General, translation. **Health services:** Nursing (RN). **Human services:** General. **Liberal arts:** Humanities. **Math:** General, statistics. **Physical sciences:** Chemistry, physics. **Psychology:** General. **Social sciences:** GIS/cartography, international relations, political science. **Visual/performing arts:** General, design, music, photography.

Computing on campus. Dormitories wired for high-speed internet access and linked to campus network. Commuter students can connect to campus

network. Online course registration, online library, helpline, repair service, student web hosting, wireless network available.

Student life. Freshman orientation: Mandatory. Preregistration for classes offered. **Housing:** Guaranteed on-campus for all undergraduates. Single-sex dorms available. $1,700 deposit. **Activities:** Choral groups, drama, international student organizations, musical theater.

Student services. Alcohol/substance abuse counseling, chaplain/spiritual director, career counseling, student employment services, financial aid counseling, health services, personal counseling, placement for graduates. **Physically disabled:** Services for visually, hearing impaired.

Contact. E-mail: admission@ndu.edu.lb
Phone: (961) 922-5164
Viviane Naimy, Director of Admissions, Notre Dame University: Louaize, PO Box 72 Zouk Mikhael, Zouk Mosbeh, LB

Mexico

Instituto Tecnologico Autonomo de Mexico
Mexico City, Mexico   **CB member**
www.itam.mx   **CB code: 7144**

- Private 4-year business and engineering college
- Residential campus in very large city
- 4,550 undergraduates

General. Calendar: Semester, limited summer session. **Full-time faculty:** 476 total. **Part-time faculty:** 454 total.

Basis for selection. High school records and admission test mandatory. **Home schooled:** Complete high school diploma, minimum GPA, and admission test.

Application procedures. Admission: No deadline. $54 fee, may be waived for applicants with need. Application must be submitted on paper. Admission notification on a rolling basis.

Academics. Special study options: Combined bachelor's/graduate degree, double major, ESL, exchange student, liberal arts/career combination, study abroad. **Credit/placement by examination:** AP, CLEP, IB, institutional tests. **Support services:** Study skills assistance, tutoring, writing center.

Majors. Business: Accounting, accounting/business management, actuarial science, business admin. **Communications:** Digital media. **Communications technology:** Computer typography. **Computer sciences:** General. **Engineering:** Computer. **Math:** Applied. **Social sciences:** Economics, international relations, political science.

Computing on campus. 140 workstations in library, computer center. Commuter students can connect to campus network. Online library, wireless network available.

Student life. Freshman orientation: Available. Preregistration for classes offered. **Activities:** Concert band, choral groups, dance, drama, international student organizations, literary magazine, music ensembles, Model UN, radio station, student government, student newspaper.

Athletics. Intercollegiate: Baseball M, basketball, soccer, volleyball. **Team name:** Dragones.

Student services. Student employment services, health services, legal services.

Contact. E-mail: admisiones@itam.mx
Phone: (5) 556-284156 Toll-free number: (55) 018-00000 ext. 4826
Fax: (5) 554-904655
Gisela Carmona, Director of Admissions, Instituto Tecnologico Autonomo de Mexico, Rio Hondo 1, Colonia Progreso Tizapan, Mexico City, MX

Instituto Tecnologico y de Estudios Superiores de Occidente
Tlaquepaque, Mexico   **CB member**
www.iteso.mx   **CB code: 7145**

- Private 4-year business and engineering college affiliated with Roman Catholic Church
- Commuter campus in very large city
- 8,634 full-time, degree-seeking undergraduates

General. Degrees: 1,308 bachelor's awarded; master's, doctoral offered. **Location:** In metropolitan Guadalajara. **Calendar:** Semester, extensive summer session.

Basis for selection. Open admission, but selective for some programs.

2012-2013 Annual costs. Cost per semester is about 62,300 MXN pesos. Includes parent's life insurance.

Academics. Special study options: Combined bachelor's/graduate degree, ESL, exchange student, liberal arts/career combination, study abroad. **Credit/placement by examination:** AP, CLEP.

Majors. Architecture: Architecture. **Business:** Accounting, business admin, international, labor relations, marketing. **Communications:** Digital media, media studies, organizational, radio/TV. **Computer sciences:** Information technology. **Education:** General, multicultural, statistics. **Human services:** General. **Philosophy/religion:** Philosophy. **Psychology:** General. **Visual/performing arts:** Design, fashion design, graphic design, industrial design, interior design.

Computing on campus. Repair service, wireless network available.

Student life. Activities: Choral groups, dance, drama, literary magazine, music ensembles, student newspaper.

Contact. E-mail: admision@iteso.mx
Phone: (52) 333-6693535 Toll-free number: (01) 800-7149092
Fax: (52) 333-1342956
Alfonso Aldrete Saldívar, Chief of the Admissions Office, Instituto Tecnologico y de Estudios Superiores de Occidente, AP 31-175, Zapopan, MX 45090

Universidad Anahuac
Huixquilucan, Mexico   **CB member**
www.anahuac.mx   **CB code: 7146**

- Private 6-year university and career college affiliated with Roman Catholic Church
- Commuter campus in small city
- 8,486 degree-seeking undergraduates: 54% women
- Application essay, interview required

General. Founded in 1964. **Location:** 4 miles from Mexico City. **Calendar:** Semester, limited summer session. **Full-time faculty:** 1,131 total; 13% have terminal degrees, 37% women. **Part-time faculty:** 1,087 total; 20% have terminal degrees, 41% women.

Basis for selection. GED not accepted. Admission decisions based on careful consideration of all factors, not on numerical factors alone. The exam used is de PAA, not the SAT.

High school preparation. 13 units required. Required units include English 2, mathematics 2, social studies 1, history 2, science 2, foreign language 3 and academic electives 1.

2012-2013 Annual costs. Undergraduates pay $130 per credit; most students take 48 credits per semester. In addition, students pay registration fee of $2,200 per semester. Total cost per academic year, not including room and board, $16,880 (U.S. dollars). Books/supplies: $400. Personal expenses: $550.

Financial aid. All financial aid based on need.

Application procedures. Admission: Closing date 7/31 (receipt date). $100 fee. Application must be submitted on paper. Must reply by 7/31. **Financial aid:** Priority date 7/20; no closing date. Institutional form required. Applicants notified on a rolling basis starting 8/13; must reply within 2 week(s) of notification.

Academics. Special study options: Cooperative education, double major, dual enrollment of high school students, ESL, exchange student, study abroad,

teacher certification program. **Credit/placement by examination:** AP, CLEP, institutional tests. **Support services:** Learning center, pre-admission summer program, reduced course load, remedial instruction, study skills assistance, tutoring.

Majors. Architecture: Architecture. **Business:** General, accounting, actuarial science, business admin, international, management information systems, market research, tourism/travel. **Communications:** Advertising, communications/speech/rhetoric, public relations. **Communications technology:** General. **Computer sciences:** Data processing, information systems. **Education:** General. **Engineering:** Biomedical, civil, electrical, engineering mechanics, systems. **Health services:** Medical secretary. **Human services:** General. **Math:** Applied. **Psychology:** General, school. **Social sciences:** Economics, international relations, political science. **Visual/performing arts:** General, design, digital arts, dramatic, graphic design, industrial design. **Work/family studies:** General.

Most popular majors. Business/marketing 15%, engineering/engineering technologies 8%, health sciences 15%, legal studies 6%, mathematics 8%, psychology 12%, public administration/social services 13%.

Computing on campus. 500 workstations in library, computer center, student center. Online course registration, online library, helpline, wireless network available.

Student life. Freshman orientation: Mandatory. Preregistration for classes offered. Orientation mandatory for some students. **Housing:** Host families provide housing for international and out-of-state students. **Activities:** Bands, campus ministries, choral groups, dance, drama, music ensembles, musical theater, opera, radio station, student government, student newspaper, Anahuac Challenge, Anahuac for Mexico, Anahuac Social Action, Anahuac Social Foundation, Center for Integral Community Development, Perpetual Adoration Society, Red Cross, Youth Weekend Mission Program.

Athletics. Intercollegiate: Baseball M, basketball M, cheerleading M, diving, football (tackle), judo, soccer, swimming, tennis, volleyball. **Intramural:** Cheerleading W, diving, judo, soccer, swimming, tennis, volleyball. **Team name:** Leones.

Student services. Chaplain/spiritual director, career counseling, financial aid counseling, health services, personal counseling, placement for graduates.

Contact. E-mail: pbertha@anahuac.mx
Phone: (555) 627-0210 ext. 8458 Toll-free number: (800) 508-9800
Fax: (555) 596-1938
Bertha Perez Vera, Chief of Admissions, Universidad Anahuac, Av. Lomas Anahuac #46., Huixquilucan, MX

Universidad Autonoma de Coahuila

Saltillo, Mexico	**CB member**
www.uadec.mx	**CB code: 7148**

- Public 4-year university
- Commuter campus in very large city

General. Location: 55 miles from Monterrey. **Calendar:** Semester.

Annual costs/financial aid. Books/supplies: $80. Need-based financial aid available for full-time students.

Contact. Phone: (844) 438-1651 ext. 1655
Director of Admissions, Blvd. V. Carranza y Gonzalez Lobo, Saltillo, MX

Morocco

Al Akhawayn University

Ifrane, Morocco	**CB member**
www.aui.ma	**CB code: 6596**

- Public 4-year university and liberal arts college
- Residential campus in small town
- 1,461 degree-seeking undergraduates: 52% women
- 212 degree-seeking graduate students
- 52% of applicants admitted

General. Degrees: 210 bachelor's awarded; master's offered. **Location:** 40 miles from Fez. **Calendar:** Semester, extensive summer session. **Full-time faculty:** 126 total; 66% have terminal degrees, 26% women. **Part-time faculty:** 10 total; 70% have terminal degrees, 10% women. **Class size:** 59% < 20, 39% 20-39, 2% 40-49, less than 1% 50-99.

Freshman class profile. 1,192 applied, 624 admitted, 235 enrolled.

GPA 3.75 or higher:	1%	Rank in top quarter:	77%
GPA 3.50-3.74:	11%	Rank in top tenth:	58%
GPA 3.0-3.49:	71%	Live on campus:	98%
GPA 2.0-2.99:	17%		

Basis for selection. GED not accepted. Due to competitive nature of selection process, only candidates with promising academic backgrounds are admitted. SAT quantitative, 500 minimum; Verbal and Writing average should be 500 minimum. An 80 point allowance is made for non-native speakers of English, who must take TOEFL for English placement. SAT required of US high school graduates. Other high school graduates take General Admission Test, an institutional test devoted to three areas: general knowledge, verbal skills (sentence completion, critical reading, writing) and quantitative skills (both numerical and spatial). Most domestic applicants are invited to an interview, which allows for evaluation of personality, motivation, communicative force, and general cognitive ability.

2011-2012 Annual costs. Full-time tuition, $6,352 for residents, $9,529 for non-resident aliens; required fees, $964. On-campus room and board, $3,035. Annual insurance fee, $179. All amounts indicated in US dollars, payable in Moroccan dirhams. Books/supplies: $847.

2010-2011 Financial aid. Need-based: 62% of total undergraduate aid awarded as scholarships/grants, 38% as loans/jobs. **Non-need-based:** Scholarships awarded for academics, athletics.

Application procedures. Admission: Priority date 3/31; deadline 5/31 (postmark date). $35 fee. Application must be submitted online. Admission notification by 7/15. Two weeks after notification. **Financial aid:** Priority date 1/15, closing date 5/31. Institutional form required. Applicants notified by 7/15.

Academics. Special study options: Combined bachelor's/graduate degree, ESL, external degree, honors, independent study, internships, study abroad. **Credit/placement by examination:** AP, CLEP, institutional tests. 6 credit hours maximum toward bachelor's degree. **Support services:** Reduced course load, study skills assistance, tutoring, writing center.

Majors. Business: Business admin, training/development. **Communications:** Communications/speech/rhetoric. **Engineering:** General.

Most popular majors. Business/marketing 57%, computer/information sciences 9%, engineering/engineering technologies 8%.

Computing on campus. 150 workstations in dormitories, library, computer center. Dormitories wired for high-speed internet access and linked to campus network. Commuter students can connect to campus network. Online library, helpline, repair service, student web hosting, wireless network available.

Student life. Freshman orientation: Mandatory. Preregistration for classes offered. Orientation held during registration, which takes place immediately prior to first day of classes. **Housing:** Single-sex dorms available. $1,205 partly refundable deposit, deadline 7/2. **Activities:** Concert band, choral groups, dance, drama, film society, international student organizations, Model UN, radio station, student government, student newspaper, TV station.

Athletics. Intercollegiate: Basketball, soccer, tennis, volleyball. **Intramural:** Basketball, soccer, volleyball. **Team name:** AUI Lions.

Student services. Chaplain/spiritual director, financial aid counseling, health services, personal counseling.

Contact. E-mail: admissions@aui.ma
Phone: (535) 862-086 Fax: (535) 862-177
Latifa Ouanaim, Director of Admissions, Al Akhawayn University, PO Box 104, Ifrane, MK

Pakistan

Forman Christian College
Lahore, Pakistan
www.fccollege.edu.pk

CB member

- Private 4-year university and liberal arts college affiliated with Presbyterian Church (USA)
- Commuter campus in very large city
- 2,959 degree-seeking undergraduates: 32% women
- 183 degree-seeking graduate students
- 62% of applicants admitted
- 57% graduate within 6 years; 47% enter graduate study

General. Chapel and mosques on campus. **Degrees:** 408 bachelor's, 4 associate awarded; master's offered. **Calendar:** Semester, limited summer session. **Full-time faculty:** 189 total; 47% have terminal degrees, 20% minority, 39% women. **Class size:** 25% < 20, 65% 20-39, 7% 40-49, 2% 50-99, less than 1% >100. **Special facilities:** Museum.

Freshman class profile. 2,163 applied, 1,337 admitted, 831 enrolled.

Basis for selection. Students are admitted based scores earned on annual exams taken after the 11th and 12th grades, and scores on ACCUPLACER (ESL Language Use, ESL Reading Skills, Arithmetic). ACCUPLACER used for course placement.

2011-2012 Annual costs. Tuition/fees: $1,104. Room/board: $1,100. Books/supplies: $400.

2010-2011 Financial aid. All financial aid based on need. 400 full-time freshmen applied for aid; 279 were judged to have need; 279 of these received aid. Average need met was 55%. Average scholarship/grant was $482. 98% of total undergraduate aid awarded as scholarships/grants, 2% as loans/jobs.

Application procedures. Admission: Closing date 6/30 (receipt date). $7 fee. **Financial aid:** Closing date 10/18. Institutional form required. Applicants notified on a rolling basis.

Academics. Special study options: Double major, ESL, internships, teacher certification program. **Credit/placement by examination:** AP, CLEP, institutional tests. **Support services:** Remedial instruction.

Majors. Biology: General. **Business:** Business admin. **Communications:** Media studies. **Computer sciences:** General, information technology. **Conservation:** Environmental science. **Education:** General. **Engineering:** Software. **English:** English lit. **Foreign languages:** Urdu. **History:** General. **Math:** General, statistics. **Philosophy/religion:** Christian, Islamic, philosophy. **Physical sciences:** Chemistry, physics. **Psychology:** General. **Social sciences:** Economics, geography, political science, sociology.

Most popular majors. Business/marketing 15%, communications/journalism 15%, computer/information sciences 7%, physical sciences 10%, social sciences 37%.

Computing on campus. 350 workstations in library, computer center. Dormitories wired for high-speed internet access. Online library, helpline, wireless network available.

Student life. Freshman orientation: Mandatory. Preregistration for classes offered. **Housing:** Single-sex dorms available. **Activities:** Campus ministries, choral groups, drama, film society, literary magazine, music ensembles, Model UN, student government, Islamic Society, Christian Life Program, Political Science Society, Red Crescent Society, Forman Sociological Association, Earth Watch.

Athletics. Intercollegiate: Badminton M, basketball, cricket M, field hockey M, soccer M, swimming M, table tennis M, tennis M, track and field, volleyball M, weight lifting M. **Intramural:** Badminton, basketball M, cricket M, field hockey M, soccer M, swimming M, table tennis M, tennis M, track and field, volleyball M. **Team name:** Formanites.

Student services. Alcohol/substance abuse counseling, chaplain/spiritual director, career counseling, services for economically disadvantaged, student employment services, financial aid counseling, health services, minority student services, personal counseling, placement for graduates, women's services.

Contact. E-mail: ambermall@fccollege.edu.pk
Amber Mall, Director of Admissions, Forman Christian College, Ferozepur Road, Lahore, PK

Poland

Warsaw University of Technology
Warsaw, Poland
www.pw.edu.pl

CB member

- Public 3-year engineering and technical college
- Residential campus in very large city

General. Calendar: Semester.

Contact. Phone: (48) 222-34 ext. 5091
Admissions Director, Plac Politechniki 1, Warsaw, PL

Singapore

Singapore Management University
Singapore, Singapore
www.smu.edu.sg/admissions

CB member
CB code: 2861

- Private 4-year university
- Commuter campus in small city
- 6,853 degree-seeking undergraduates
- 680 graduate students
- SAT or ACT with writing required

General. Degrees: 1,504 bachelor's awarded; master's, doctoral offered. **Calendar:** Semester, limited summer session. **Full-time faculty:** 233 total. **Part-time faculty:** 262 total.

Basis for selection. GED not accepted. Holistic selection approach based on academic record, co-curricular activities, SAT scores, and admissions interview for shortlisted applicants; application fee is $15 (Singapore dollars). **Home schooled:** Statement describing home school structure and mission, transcript of courses and grades, state high school equivalency certificate, interview, letter of recommendation (nonparent) required.

Application procedures. Admission: Closing date 4/1. $15 fee. Admission notification by 7/1. **Financial aid:** No deadline.

Academics. Special study options: Combined bachelor's/graduate degree, double major, exchange student, honors, internships, study abroad. **Credit/placement by examination:** AP, CLEP, SAT, ACT.

Majors. Business: Accounting, business admin, communications, finance, marketing, operations, organizational behavior. **Computer sciences:** Information systems. **Psychology:** General. **Social sciences:** General, economics, political science, sociology.

Computing on campus. PC or laptop required.

Student life. Freshman orientation: Mandatory. Preregistration for classes offered. **Housing:** Coed dorms available. **Activities:** Bands, choral groups, dance, drama, international student organizations, literary magazine, music ensembles, musical theater, radio station, student newspaper, symphony orchestra.

Athletics. Intramural: Archery, badminton, basketball, bowling, cricket, cross-country, fencing, football (non-tackle), football (tackle) M, golf, handball, judo, rifle, rugby, sailing, soccer M, squash, swimming, table tennis, tennis, track and field, volleyball, water polo.

Student services. Career counseling, student employment services, financial aid counseling, health services, personal counseling. **Physically disabled:** Services for visually, speech, hearing impaired.

Contact. E-mail: admissions@smu.edu.sg
Phone: (65) 682-80305 Fax: (65) 682-80303
Singapore Management University, 81 Victoria Street, Singapore, SG 25975

Spain

Saint Louis University: Madrid
Madrid, Spain
CB member
spain.slu.edu
CB code: 2586

- Private 4-year university affiliated with Roman Catholic Church
- Very large city
- 379 degree-seeking undergraduates
- 43 graduate students
- Application essay required

General. Regionally accredited. Students, faculty, and staff representing more than 65 nationalities. **Degrees:** 64 bachelor's awarded; master's offered. **Calendar:** Semester, limited summer session.

Basis for selection. As student applications are received from all over the world, SLU-Madrid's admission requirements are flexible enough to account for differences in secondary school educational systems. All students are required to have completed the university entry requirements of the country where they have completed their secondary education.

2011-2012 Annual costs. Full-time tuition and required fees, 16280 euros. Students may choose to live with host families and pay according to one of two plans: room and board (breakfast and evening meal), 6360 euros; room and kitchen privileges (with student being responsible for purchase and preparation of all meals), 4790 euros. All costs are for academic year only.

Application procedures. Admission: No application fee. Application must be submitted online. Admission notification on a rolling basis. **Financial aid:** Priority date 3/1; no closing date.

Academics. Special study options: Distance learning, double major, ESL, honors, independent study, internships, study abroad. **Credit/placement by examination:** AP, CLEP, IB. **Support services:** Tutoring, writing center.

Majors. Business: International. **Communications:** Communications/speech/rhetoric. **English:** English lit. **Foreign languages:** Spanish. **Social sciences:** Economics, international relations.

Computing on campus. Online course registration, helpline, wireless network available.

Student life. Freshman orientation: Mandatory. Preregistration for classes offered. **Housing:** "Host family" housing available. **Activities:** Campus ministries, choral groups, dance, drama, literary magazine, student government, student newspaper.

Athletics. Intramural: Soccer. **Team name:** Billikens.

Student services. Chaplain/spiritual director, career counseling, financial aid counseling, personal counseling.

Contact. E-mail: admissions-madrid@slu.edu
Phone: (34) 915-545858 Fax: (91) 554-6202
Maria Morell, Director of Enrollment Management, Saint Louis University: Madrid, Avenida del Valle, 34, Madrid, ES

Switzerland

Ecole Hoteliere de Lausanne
Lausanne, Switzerland
CB member
www.ehl.edu
CB code: 4102

- Private 4-year university and business college
- Residential campus in small city
- 1,662 degree-seeking undergraduates: 56% women
- 27 degree-seeking graduate students
- 35% of applicants admitted
- Application essay, interview required
- 88% graduate within 6 years; 9% enter graduate study

General. EHL is both a school (fully equipped to provide the best possible learning experience for its students) and a hotel (complete with restaurants, accommodations, conference and banqueting facilities); students, employees, and visitors benefit from the full range of hospitality experiences. **Degrees:** 546 bachelor's, 61 associate awarded; master's offered. **Location:** 4 miles from Lausanne, 35 miles from Geneva. **Calendar:** Continuous. **Full-time faculty:** 52 total; 21% have terminal degrees, 36% women. **Part-time faculty:** 54 total; 22% have terminal degrees, 37% women. **Class size:** 33% < 20, 46% 20-39, 9% 40-49, 5% 50-99, 6% >100. **Special facilities:** Onsite restaurants and bars that function as classrooms include a fine-dining training restaurant, "Le Berceau des Sens" (The Cradle of the Senses).

Freshman class profile. 1,360 applied, 470 admitted, 384 enrolled.

GPA 3.75 or higher:	37%	End year in good standing:	92%
GPA 3.50-3.74:	26%	Return as sophomores:	95%
GPA 3.0-3.49:	32%	Live on campus:	99%
GPA 2.0-2.99:	5%		

Basis for selection. GED not accepted. Candidates who meet minimum requirements invited for Selection Day at EHL or abroad, which includes quantitative and analytical aptitude test (computer-based), hospitality aptitude test (computer-based), role play exercise, and interview. Students selected on basis of overall quality of application and Selection Day scores. SAT only required for students enrolled in American high school curriculum; evidence of higher achievement (3 AP exams, SAT II subject tests or IB Higher Level certificates) also required. **Home schooled:** Transcript of courses and grades, state high school equivalency certificate required.

High school preparation. College-preparatory program required.

2011-2012 Annual costs. Expenses for first-year undergraduate students: full-time tuition, $15,000; required fees, $6,080; prepaid food and beverage account, $3,500; on-campus housing, $5,381. Swiss students and permanent residents, in their junior and senior years, are eligible for partial tuition reimbursement by Swiss Government. All amounts in Swiss francs. Books/supplies: $1,000. Personal expenses: $5,400.

2011-2012 Financial aid. All financial aid based on need. Average scholarship/grant was $17,916; average loan $9,752. 81% of total undergraduate aid awarded as scholarships/grants, 19% as loans/jobs. **Additional information:** EHL is eligible to participate in Title IV financial aid programs (Direct Loans).

Application procedures. Admission: Priority date 12/1; deadline 2/1 (receipt date). $300 fee. Application must be submitted online. Admission notification by 4/19. Admission notification on a rolling basis beginning on or about 2/15. Must reply by May 1 or within 2 week(s) if notified thereafter. **Financial aid:** Closing date 2/1. FAFSA, institutional form required. Applicants notified by 6/15; must reply within 2 week(s) of notification.

Academics. Special study options: Internships, study abroad. **Credit/placement by examination:** AP, CLEP, institutional tests. **Support services:** Study skills assistance, tutoring, writing center.

Majors. Business: Hospitality admin.

Computing on campus. PC or laptop required. Dormitories wired for high-speed internet access and linked to campus network. Commuter students can connect to campus network. Online course registration, online library, repair service, student web hosting, wireless network available.

Student life. Freshman orientation: Mandatory. Preregistration for classes offered. Held 2 weeks before classes begin. **Housing:** Guaranteed

on-campus for freshmen. Single-sex dorms, apartments available. **Activities:** Concert band, dance, drama, international student organizations, student government, student newspaper.

Athletics. Intramural: Badminton, basketball, cricket, equestrian, field hockey, golf, ice hockey, rugby, sailing, soccer, squash, tennis, volleyball.

Student services. Alcohol/substance abuse counseling, chaplain/spiritual director, career counseling, student employment services, financial aid counseling, health services, personal counseling, placement for graduates.

Contact. E-mail: admissions@ehl.ch
Phone: (41) 217-851121 Fax: (41) 217-851376
Lucila Perez Mollo, Director of Admissions, Ecole Hoteliere de Lausanne, Le Chalet-a-Gobet, Lausanne 25, CH

Franklin College Switzerland
Sorengo (Lugano), Switzerland   **CB member**
www.fc.edu   **CB code: 0922**

- Private 4-year liberal arts college
- Residential campus in small city
- 420 degree-seeking undergraduates: 65% women
- 63% of applicants admitted
- SAT or ACT with writing, application essay required
- 52% graduate within 6 years

General. Founded in 1969. Regionally accredited. Undergraduate degree programs accredited in United States and Switzerland. Classes taught in English. Students from 60 nations. **Degrees:** 110 bachelor's, 1 associate awarded. **Location:** 60 miles from Milan, Italy; 80 miles from Zurich. **Calendar:** Semester, extensive summer session. **Full-time faculty:** 25 total; 88% have terminal degrees, 44% women. **Part-time faculty:** 29 total; 48% have terminal degrees, 55% women. **Class size:** 68% < 20, 32% 20-39.

Freshman class profile. 616 applied, 390 admitted, 133 enrolled.

Mid 50% test scores			
SAT critical reading:	560-670	GPA 3.50-3.74:	21%
SAT math:	520-610	GPA 3.0-3.49:	32%
SAT writing:	550-640	GPA 2.0-2.99:	39%
ACT composite:	24-28	End year in good standing:	97%
GPA 3.75 or higher:	8%	Return as sophomores:	80%
		Live on campus:	97%

Basis for selection. High school academic record, recommendations, extracurricular participation most important. Essay, test scores, interview also important. TOEFL or IELTS required for students whose first language is not English. SAT Subject Tests recommended. Essay and personal statement required. Interview recommended for all. **Home schooled:** Statement describing home school structure and mission, letter of recommendation (nonparent) required.

High school preparation. College-preparatory program required. 19 units recommended. Recommended units include English 4, mathematics 3, social studies 1, history 3, science 3, foreign language 3 and academic electives 2. Electives include computer science, art, music.

2011-2012 Annual costs. Tuition/fees: $37,420. Cost of 10-meals-per-week plan, $3,200, for academic year. Freshman students may apply for exemption from Swiss health insurance plan, if they provide proof of comparable coverage by U.S. insurance companies. Otherwise, first-year students pay $1,770 for Swiss health insurance premium. Room only: $8,000. Books/supplies: $1,600. Personal expenses: $1,400.

2010-2011 Financial aid. All financial aid based on need. 82 full-time freshmen applied for aid; 63 were judged to have need; 63 of these received aid. Average need met was 80%. Average scholarship/grant was $19,511; average loan $2,231. 64% of total undergraduate aid awarded as scholarships/grants, 36% as loans/jobs.

Application procedures. Admission: Priority date 3/15; no deadline. $90 fee. Admission notification on a rolling basis beginning on or about 12/15. Must reply by May 1 or within 2 week(s) if notified thereafter. **Financial aid:** Priority date 2/15, closing date 4/15. FAFSA, institutional form, CSS PROFILE required. Applicants notified on a rolling basis starting 3/10; must reply by 5/1 or within 3 week(s) of notification.

Academics. 2-week credit-bearing academic travel program required each semester. **Special study options:** Double major, ESL, honors, independent study, internships, semester at sea, study abroad, Washington semester. Sophomore and junior year abroad programs with cooperating colleges/universities. **Credit/placement by examination:** AP, CLEP, IB, institutional tests. 15 credit hours maximum toward associate degree, 27 toward bachelor's.

Support services: Learning center, reduced course load, study skills assistance, tutoring, writing center.

Majors. Business: International finance. **Communications:** Media studies. **Conservation:** Environmental science. **Foreign languages:** General, French, Italian. **History:** General. **Social sciences:** International economics, international relations. **Visual/performing arts:** General, art history/conservation.

Most popular majors. Business/marketing 36%, communications/journalism 10%, interdisciplinary studies 10%, liberal arts 8%, natural resources/environmental science 9%, social sciences 16%.

Computing on campus. 140 workstations in library, computer center, student center. Dormitories wired for high-speed internet access and linked to campus network. Commuter students can connect to campus network. Online library, helpline, repair service, student web hosting, wireless network available.

Student life. Freshman orientation: Mandatory, $375 fee. Preregistration for classes offered. **Policies:** All students required to live in on-campus housing their first year. **Housing:** Guaranteed on-campus for all undergraduates. Coed dorms, single-sex dorms, apartments, wellness housing available. $400 partly refundable deposit, deadline 6/15. College-owned and leased apartments on and adjacent to campus and in Lugano; freshmen and sophomores must live in college housing. **Activities:** Dance, drama, literary magazine, Model UN, student government, student newspaper, Baobab Initiative (student-run enterprise formed to help a small village in Zambia), language clubs, cultural and ethnic clubs, literary society, honor society, drama society, creative arts club, Christian Fellowship, Environmental Action Alliance.

Athletics. Intramural: Basketball, soccer, tennis, volleyball. **Team name:** Falcons.

Student services. Alcohol/substance abuse counseling, career counseling, student employment services, financial aid counseling, health services, personal counseling, placement for graduates, women's services.

Contact. E-mail: info@fc.edu
Phone: (091) 986-3613 Fax: (091) 993-3906
Karen Ballard, Dean of Admissions, Franklin College Switzerland, U.S. Admissions: The Graybar Building, Suite 2746, New York, NY 10170

United Arab Emirates

American University in Dubai
Dubai, United Arab Emirates   **CB member**
www.aud.edu   **CB code: 2688**

- Private 4-year university
- Commuter campus in very large city
- 2,357 degree-seeking undergraduates: 47% women
- 112 degree-seeking graduate students
- 88% of applicants admitted
- Application essay required

General. Regionally accredited. **Degrees:** 125 bachelor's awarded; master's offered. **Calendar:** Semester, extensive summer session. **Full-time faculty:** 106 total. **Part-time faculty:** 61 total.

Freshman class profile. 1,062 applied, 930 admitted, 563 enrolled.

Basis for selection. GED not accepted. Well-rounded students who demonstrate a probability for success in the institution's programs of study sought. Such factors as high school completion, recommendations from school personnel familiar with the potential of applicants, leadership and student activity records, scholastic achievement test scores, evidence of school and community service, student work or employment records, and distinctive talents or abilities considered. Students can take math placement test or submit acceptable SAT score. All engineering applicants must take SAT; combined score of 1090 (exclusive of Writing) required for admission to the program. **Learning Disabled:** Student should declare disability upon applying. Student services provides support on a case by case basis.

2011-2012 Annual costs. Books/supplies: $600.

Financial aid. Non-need-based: Scholarships awarded for academics, athletics.

Application procedures. Admission: Closing date 8/20. $56 fee. Application must be submitted on paper. Admission notification on a rolling basis. Applications reviewed on a rolling basis. Students will be notified of their admissions status within two weeks after applying.

Academics. Special study options: Combined bachelor's/graduate degree, double major, ESL, internships, study abroad. **Credit/placement by examination:** AP, CLEP, IB, SAT, institutional tests. **Support services:** Pre-admission summer program, reduced course load, remedial instruction, study skills assistance, tutoring, writing center.

Majors. Architecture: Architecture. **Business:** General, accounting, banking/financial services, e-commerce, management science, marketing. **Communications:** Media studies. **Communications technology:** Graphics. **Computer sciences:** Information technology. **Engineering:** Civil, computer, electrical, mechanical. **Visual/performing arts:** Commercial/advertising art, graphic design, illustration, interior design, photography.

Computing on campus. 936 workstations in library, computer center. Dormitories wired for high-speed internet access. Commuter students can connect to campus network. Online library, helpline, repair service, wireless network available.

Student life. Freshman orientation: Mandatory. Preregistration for classes offered. **Policies:** Dress code; no alcohol and no drugs on campus. **Housing:** Single-sex dorms, special housing for disabled, wellness housing available. $685 nonrefundable deposit, deadline 6/2. **Activities:** Dance, drama, international student organizations, Model UN, student government, student newspaper, African cultural club, Egyptian cultural club, Indian cultural club, Khaleej student association, Lebanese student association, Palestinian student association, Pakistani student association, Syrian and Islamic awareness club.

Athletics. Intercollegiate: Basketball, cricket M, soccer, swimming, tennis, volleyball. **Intramural:** Basketball, football (tackle), soccer, table tennis, tennis, track and field, volleyball, water polo. **Team name:** Knights.

Student services. Alcohol/substance abuse counseling, career counseling, student employment services, health services, on-campus daycare, personal counseling, placement for graduates. **Physically disabled:** Services for visually, speech, hearing impaired.

Contact. E-mail: admissions@aud.edu
Phone: (4) 399-9000 ext. 171 Fax: (4) 399-8899
Zeina Tannir, Director of Admissions, American University in Dubai, PO Box 28282, Dubai, AE

United Kingdom

King's College London
London, United Kingdom   CB member
www.kcl.ac.uk   CB code: 7884

▸ Public 3-year university
▸ Residential campus in very large city
▸ 14,493 undergraduates
▸ 8,879 graduate students
▸ SAT or ACT, SAT Subject Tests, application essay required

General. Location: Downtown. **Calendar:** Semester, limited summer session. **Full-time faculty:** 1,060 total. **Part-time faculty:** 130 total.

Basis for selection. Because entry requirements vary according to program of study, it is important that prospective students refer to online descriptions of undergraduate programs before submitting application for admission. 1800 SAT (minimum of 600 in each of the three sections) or 27 ACT required, in addition to three SAT subject tests (minimum score of 600 on each).

Financial aid. All financial aid based on need.

Application procedures. Admission: Closing date 1/15 (receipt date). $35 fee. Admission notification on a rolling basis. **Financial aid:** No deadline. FAFSA required.

Academics. Special study options: Double major, ESL, exchange student, internships, New York semester, study abroad, Washington semester. **Credit/**

placement by examination: AP, CLEP. **Support services:** Learning center, study skills assistance, tutoring, writing center.

Majors. Area/ethnic studies: European, French, German, Spanish/Iberian, Western European. **Business:** Business admin. **Communications:** Advertising. **Computer sciences:** Computer science, programming, security. **English:** English lit. **Foreign languages:** French, German, Spanish. **History:** General, European. **Math:** General. **Philosophy/religion:** Philosophy. **Physical sciences:** Physics. **Theology:** Theology. **Visual/performing arts:** Music.

Computing on campus. Dormitories wired for high-speed internet access and linked to campus network. Online library, helpline, repair service, wireless network available.

Student life. Freshman orientation: Available. Preregistration for classes offered. **Policies:** Freshmen not permitted cars on campus. **Housing:** Coed dorms, apartments available. **Activities:** Bands, campus ministries, choral groups, dance, drama, film society, international student organizations, music ensembles, radio station, student government, student newspaper, symphony orchestra.

Athletics. Team name: King's.

Student services. Alcohol/substance abuse counseling, chaplain/spiritual director, career counseling, student employment services, financial aid counseling, health services, personal counseling, placement for graduates. **Physically disabled:** Services for visually, speech, hearing impaired.

Contact. E-mail: paul.teulon@kcl.ac.uk
Phone: (020) 783-65454
Paul Teulon, Head of Student Admissions & Records Development and Policy, King's College London, Centre for Arts and Sciences Admissions, London, GB

Richmond, The American International University in London
Richmond-upon-Thames, United Kingdom   CB member
www.richmond.ac.uk   CB code: 0823

▸ Private 4-year university and liberal arts college
▸ Residential campus in very large city
▸ 854 degree-seeking undergraduates
▸ Application essay required

General. Founded in 1972. Regionally accredited. International student body with over 100 countries represented. Students spend their first two years on the Richmond Hill campus and the second two on the Kensington campus in London. Richmond also has study centers in Florence and Rome. Richmond degrees are accredited in both the US and the UK. **Degrees:** 171 bachelor's awarded; master's offered. **Location:** Richmond upon Thames campus on the outskirts of London; Kensington campus in central London. **Calendar:** Semester, limited summer session. **Full-time faculty:** 44 total. **Part-time faculty:** 54 total. **Class size:** 68% < 20, 32% 20-39, less than 1% 40-49.

Freshman class profile.

Out-of-state:	100%	Live on campus:	86%

Basis for selection. School achievement record most important. Letters of recommendation and personal statement considered. SAT/ACT considered but not required.

High school preparation. 19 units required. Required and recommended units include English 4, mathematics 3-4, social studies 1, history 1, science 3-4 (laboratory 1), foreign language 2-3, computer science 1, visual/performing arts 1 and academic electives 2-4.

2012-2013 Annual costs. Tuition/fees (projected): $27,000. Room/board: $13,100. Books/supplies: $605. Personal expenses: $9,012.

Financial aid. Non-need-based: Scholarships awarded for academics. **Additional information:** U.S. government loan programs available for eligible U.S. citizens/students.

Application procedures. Admission: Priority date 3/1; no deadline. $50 fee, may be waived for applicants with need. Admission notification on a rolling basis. Must reply by May 1 or within 4 week(s) if notified thereafter. **Financial aid:** Priority date 3/15, closing date 8/1. FAFSA required. Applicants notified on a rolling basis starting 3/1; must reply by 5/1 or within 4 week(s) of notification.

Academics. English language development programs for non-native English speakers. **Special study options:** Combined bachelor's/graduate

degree, cross-registration, double major, ESL, independent study, internships, liberal arts/career combination, study abroad. **Credit/placement by examination:** AP, CLEP, IB, institutional tests. **Support services:** Reduced course load, remedial instruction, study skills assistance, tutoring, writing center.

Majors. Business: Finance, international, marketing. **Communications:** Journalism, media studies. **History:** General. **Psychology:** General. **Social sciences:** Economics, international relations, political science, sociology. **Visual/performing arts:** Design, studio arts.

Most popular majors. Business/marketing 35%, communications/journalism 20%, computer/information sciences 9%, psychology 6%, social sciences 18%, visual/performing arts 6%.

Computing on campus. 140 workstations in dormitories, library, computer center, student center. Dormitories wired for high-speed internet access and linked to campus network. Commuter students can connect to campus network. Online library, helpline, student web hosting, wireless network available.

Student life. Freshman orientation: Mandatory. Preregistration for classes offered. Orientation held Tuesday-Sunday prior to the beginning of semester. **Housing:** Guaranteed on-campus for freshmen. Coed dorms, single-sex dorms, special housing for disabled, apartments, wellness housing available. $500 nonrefundable deposit, deadline 5/1. **Activities:** Bands, choral groups, dance, drama, film society, international student organizations, literary magazine, music ensembles, Model UN, musical theater, student government, student newspaper, community outreach club, Amnesty International, Pan-African club, Middle Eastern Society, Literary Society, International Night, Student Ambassadors, Kuwaiti United, history/politics society, Royal United Services Institute for Defense and Security Studies (RUSI for Richmond University).

Athletics. Team name: Roebucks.

Student services. Alcohol/substance abuse counseling, career counseling, student employment services, financial aid counseling, health services, minority student services, personal counseling, placement for graduates.

Contact. E-mail: usadmissions@richmond.ac.uk
Phone: (617) 450-5617 Fax: (617) 450-5601
Nicholas Atkinson, Director of U.S. Admissions, Richmond, The American International University in London, 343 Congress Street, Suite 3100, Boston, MA 02210-1214

Two-year colleges

Alabama

Alabama Southern Community College
Monroeville, Alabama
www.ascc.edu   **CB code: 1644**

▶ Public 2-year community and junior college
▶ Commuter campus in small town

General. Founded in 1965. Regionally accredited. Institution has 3 campuses and 3 centers. **Enrollment:** 1,432 degree-seeking undergraduates. **Degrees:** 184 associate awarded. **Location:** 85 miles from Mobile. **Calendar:** Semester, extensive summer session. **Full-time faculty:** 45 total. **Part-time faculty:** 70 total. **Special facilities:** Nature trail.

Basis for selection. Open admission.

2011-2012 Annual costs. Tuition/fees: $4,080; $7,290 out-of-state. Per-credit charge: $107 in-state; $214 out-of-state. Books/supplies: $1,500. Personal expenses: $1,500.

Financial aid. Need-based: Work-study available nights, weekends and for part-time students.

Application procedures. Admission: No deadline. No application fee. Admission notification on a rolling basis. **Financial aid:** Priority date 7/15; no closing date. FAFSA required. Applicants notified on a rolling basis; must reply within 4 week(s) of notification.

Academics. Special study options: Accelerated study, dual enrollment of high school students, honors, independent study. Degrees in allied health available through University of Alabama at Birmingham, registered nurse program through Jefferson Davis State Junior College. **Credit/placement by examination:** AP, CLEP, institutional tests. 30 credit hours maximum toward associate degree. **Support services:** GED preparation and test center, learning center, pre-admission summer program, reduced course load, remedial instruction, tutoring.

Majors. Business: General, administrative services. **Computer sciences:** General. **Engineering:** Electrical. **Health services:** Licensed practical nurse, nursing (RN), nursing assistant. **Liberal arts:** Arts/sciences. **Protective services:** Firefighting.

Computing on campus. 9 workstations in library, computer center.

Student life. Freshman orientation: Mandatory. Preregistration for classes offered. **Activities:** Bands, choral groups, student government, student newspaper, Baptist student union, Circle K, ethnic student society, Phi Theta Kappa, Phi Beta Lambda, Baptist campus ministry, Students in Free Enterprise.

Athletics. NJCAA. **Intercollegiate:** Baseball M, basketball M. **Intramural:** Basketball M, softball, table tennis, tennis, volleyball. **Team name:** Eagles.

Student services. Adult student services, career counseling, personal counseling, placement for graduates, veterans' counselor.

Contact. Phone: (251) 575-3156 Fax: (251) 575-5238
Jana Horton, Director of Enrollment Management, Alabama Southern Community College, Box 2000, Monroeville, AL 36461

Bevill State Community College
Jasper, Alabama
www.bscc.edu   **CB code: 0723**

▶ Public 2-year community college
▶ Commuter campus in small town

General. Founded in 1969. Regionally accredited. Additional campuses in Fayette, Hamilton, and Sumiton. Learning sites in Carrollton and Mt. Olive. **Enrollment:** 4,073 undergraduates. **Degrees:** 422 associate awarded. **Location:** 25 miles from Birmingham. **Calendar:** Semester, limited summer session. **Full-time faculty:** 121 total. **Part-time faculty:** 182 total. **Special facilities:** Observatory, simulated underground mine, mining museum, small business incubator. **Partnerships:** Formal partnerships with 3M, Alabama Power, McWane Cast Iron Pipe Co.

Transfer out. Colleges most students transferred to 2011: University of Alabama, Auburn University, University of North Alabama, University of Alabama Birmingham, University of Montevallo.

Basis for selection. Open admission, but selective for some programs. Admission to nursing programs competitive and limited. High school diploma not required in some technical programs. COMPASS required for placement unless applicant has 480 SAT verbal and 526 SAT math, or 20 ACT. **Adult students:** COMPASS placement testing required unless student is senior citizen or non-award seeking major taking classes for vocational reasons. **Home schooled:** Transcript of courses and grades required. 16 ACT required.

2011-2012 Annual costs. Tuition/fees: $4,080; $7,290 out-of-state. Per-credit charge: $107 in-state; $214 out-of-state. Room only: $1,450. Books/supplies: $1,200. Personal expenses: $6,450.

Financial aid. Need-based: Need-based aid available for part-time students. Work-study available nights, weekends and for part-time students. **Non-need-based:** Scholarships awarded for academics, athletics, leadership, music/drama.

Application procedures. Admission: No deadline. No application fee. Admission notification on a rolling basis beginning on or about 7/1. **Financial aid:** Priority date 5/1; no closing date. FAFSA required. Applicants notified on a rolling basis starting 7/1.

Academics. Special study options: Accelerated study, cooperative education, distance learning, dual enrollment of high school students, ESL, honors, weekend college. License preparation in nursing, paramedic, physical therapy, real estate. **Credit/placement by examination:** AP, CLEP, institutional tests. Only 25% of program credits can be awarded through nontraditional means. **Support services:** GED preparation and test center, learning center, reduced course load, remedial instruction, tutoring, writing center.

Majors. Business: Administrative services. **Computer sciences:** General, computer science. **Health services:** EMT paramedic, nursing (RN). **Liberal arts:** Arts/sciences. **Work/family studies:** Child care management.

Computing on campus. 1,200 workstations in library, computer center, student center. Commuter students can connect to campus network. Online course registration, online library, helpline, wireless network available.

Student life. Freshman orientation: Mandatory, $30 fee. Preregistration for classes offered. **Housing:** Coed dorms, wellness housing available. Housing for student athletes available. **Activities:** Bands, campus ministries, choral groups, dance, drama, music ensembles, student government, student newspaper, Cross Seekers, Circle K, College Democrats, College Republicans, Phi Theta Kappa.

Athletics. NJCAA. **Intercollegiate:** Baseball M, basketball, cheerleading, cross-country W, softball W, volleyball W. **Intramural:** Basketball, bowling, boxing, football (non-tackle), softball, table tennis. **Team name:** Bears.

Student services. Chaplain/spiritual director, career counseling, services for economically disadvantaged, student employment services, financial aid counseling, on-campus daycare, placement for graduates. **Physically disabled:** Services for visually, speech, hearing impaired. **Transfer:** Transfer

adviser, college fairs on campus for students transferring to 4-year colleges.

Contact. Phone: (205) 387-0511 ext. 5726
Toll-free number: (800) 648-3271 ext. 5400 Fax: (205) 648-3311
Melissa Stowe, Assistant to the Dean of Student Services, Bevill State
Community College, 1411 Indiana Avenue, Jasper, AL 35501

Bishop State Community College
Mobile, Alabama
www.bishop.edu
CB code: 1517

▶ Public 2-year community college
▶ Commuter campus in small city

General. Founded in 1963. Regionally accredited. **Enrollment:** 3,397
degree-seeking undergraduates. **Degrees:** 240 associate awarded. **ROTC:**
Army, Air Force. **Calendar:** Semester, limited summer session. **Full-time
faculty:** 93 total. **Part-time faculty:** 108 total.

Basis for selection. Open admission. **Home schooled:** GED or 16
ACT required.

2011-2012 Annual costs. Tuition/fees: $4,080; $7,290 out-of-state. Per-
credit charge: $107 in-state; $214 out-of-state. Books/supplies: $700. Personal
expenses: $1,033.

Financial aid. Need-based: Work-study available nights, weekends and
for part-time students. **Non-need-based:** Scholarships awarded for academics, athletics.

Application procedures. Admission: No deadline. No application fee.
Admission notification on a rolling basis. **Financial aid:** Priority date 4/1;
no closing date. FAFSA, institutional form required. Applicants notified on
a rolling basis; must reply within 2 week(s) of notification.

Academics. Special study options: Accelerated study, cooperative education, distance learning, dual enrollment of high school students, weekend
college. Degree programs available in allied health through University of
Alabama at Birmingham. License preparation in nursing. **Credit/placement
by examination:** AP, CLEP. **Support services:** GED preparation and test
center, learning center, reduced course load, remedial instruction, tutoring.

Majors. Business: Accounting, administrative services, business admin.
Communications technology: Graphic/printing. **Computer sciences:** General. **Education:** General, early childhood. **Health services:** EMT paramedic,
medical records technology, nursing (RN), physical therapy assistant. **Liberal
arts:** Arts/sciences. **Protective services:** Law enforcement admin.

Computing on campus. 71 workstations in library, computer center.
Commuter students can connect to campus network. Online course registration, helpline, wireless network available.

Student life. Freshman orientation: Available. Preregistration for classes
offered. **Activities:** Bands, campus ministries, choral groups, dance, international student organizations, music ensembles, student government.

Athletics. NJCAA. **Intercollegiate:** Baseball M, basketball, cheerleading
M, softball W. **Team name:** Wildcats.

Student services. Career counseling, services for economically disadvantaged, student employment services, financial aid counseling, on-campus
daycare, personal counseling, placement for graduates, veterans' counselor.
Physically disabled: Services for visually, speech, hearing impaired. **Transfer:** Transfer adviser for students transferring to 4-year colleges.

Contact. E-mail: admiss@bishop.edu
Phone: (251) 405-7000 Fax: (251) 690-6998
Wanda Daniels, Director of Admissions, Bishop State Community
College, 351 North Broad Street, Mobile, AL 36603-5898

Calhoun Community College
Decatur, Alabama
www.calhoun.edu
CB member
CB code: 1356

▶ Public 2-year community and junior college
▶ Commuter campus in small city

General. Founded in 1963. Regionally accredited. Satellite campus at
Research Park in Huntsville. **Enrollment:** 12,300 degree-seeking undergrad-
uates. **Degrees:** 964 associate awarded. **Location:** 20 miles from Huntsville.
Calendar: Semester, limited summer session. **Full-time faculty:** 129 total.

Part-time faculty: 289 total. **Partnerships:** Formal partnership with Boeing.

Transfer out. Colleges most students transferred to 2011: Athens State
University, University of North Alabama, Auburn University, University of
Alabama, University of Alabama at Huntsville.

Basis for selection. Open admission, but selective for some programs.
SAT/ACT used for placement. Students from unaccredited high schools
required to have 16 ACT or 790 SAT (exclusive of Writing). Selective
admission to nursing program. Portfolio recommended for art majors. **Home
schooled:** Transcript of courses and grades required. 16 ACT/790 SAT (exclusive of Writing), successful completion of GED or high school graduation
examination required.

High school preparation. 26 units recommended. Recommended units
include English 4, mathematics 4, social studies 4, science 4, foreign language
2 and academic electives 10. In-state high school graduates must pass state
high school competency examination.

2011-2012 Annual costs. Tuition/fees: $3,930; $7,140 out-of-state. Per-
credit charge: $107 in-state; $214 out-of-state. Books/supplies: $1,500. Per-
sonal expenses: $1,000.

Financial aid. Need-based: Work-study available nights, weekends and for
part-time students. **Non-need-based:** Scholarships awarded for academics.

Application procedures. Admission: No deadline. No application fee.
Admission notification on a rolling basis. **Financial aid:** Priority date 5/1;
no closing date. FAFSA, institutional form required. Applicants notified on
a rolling basis starting 7/1; must reply within 2 week(s) of notification.

Academics. Numerous courses available online. **Special study options:**
Accelerated study, distance learning, dual enrollment of high school students,
liberal arts/career combination, weekend college. License preparation in dental hygiene, nursing, paramedic, real estate. **Credit/placement by examination:** AP, CLEP, IB, institutional tests. 30 credit hours maximum toward
associate degree. AP Exam credit limited to 18 semester hours. **Support
services:** GED preparation and test center, reduced course load, remedial
instruction, tutoring, writing center.

Majors. Biology: General. **Business:** Accounting, business admin. **Communications technology:** General, photo/film/video. **Computer sciences:**
General, applications programming, computer graphics, programming. **Education:** General, secondary. **English:** English lit. **Health services:** Cytogenetics, dental assistant, EMT paramedic, nursing (RN), predental, premedicine,
prenursing, prepharmacy, preveterinary. **History:** General. **Liberal arts:**
Arts/sciences. **Math:** General. **Parks/recreation:** Health/fitness. **Physical
sciences:** Chemistry. **Social sciences:** General. **Visual/performing arts:**
Commercial/advertising art, music, photography, theater arts management.
Work/family studies: Child care management, child development.

Most popular majors. Business/marketing 20%, health sciences 43%,
legal studies 9%, liberal arts 13%.

Computing on campus. 166 workstations in library, student center. Commuter students can connect to campus network. Online course registration,
online library, helpline, wireless network available.

Student life. Freshman orientation: Mandatory. Preregistration for
classes offered. **Activities:** Jazz band, campus ministries, choral groups,
drama, music ensembles, student government, student newspaper, TV station,
BACCHUS/SADD, black students alliance, criminal justice club, Native
American club, Phi Theta Kappa, allied health students association, The Cent-
urians.

Athletics. NJCAA. **Intercollegiate:** Baseball M, softball W. **Team
name:** Warhawks.

Student services. Career counseling, financial aid counseling, minority
student services, on-campus daycare, veterans' counselor. **Transfer:** Transfer
adviser, college fairs on campus for students transferring to 4-year colleges.

Contact. E-mail: admissions@calhoun.edu
Phone: (256) 306-2593 Toll-free number: (855) 501-0860
Fax: (256) 306-2941
Dan Opalewski, Associate Dean of Enrollment Management and
Registrar, Calhoun Community College, Box 2216, Decatur, AL
35609-2216

Central Alabama Community College
Childersburg, Alabama
www.cacc.cc.al.us
CB code: 0715

▶ Public 2-year community college
▶ Commuter campus in large town

General. Founded in 1965. Regionally accredited. 2 campuses: Childersburg, predominantly for technical courses, and Alexander City, predominantly for transfer courses. 1 instructional site in Talladega. **Enrollment:** 2,232 degree-seeking undergraduates. **Degrees:** 249 associate awarded. **Calendar:** Semester, extensive summer session. **Full-time faculty:** 53 total. **Part-time faculty:** 63 total. **Class size:** 59% < 20, 37% 20-39, 3% 40-49, 1% 50-99, less than 1% >100. **Special facilities:** Wildlife museum, wellness center, pioneer village.

Student profile.

Out-of-state:	1%	25 or older:	39%

Basis for selection. Open admission, but selective for some programs. Graduates of non-accredited high schools and certain nursing applicants may be required to take SAT or ACT. Admission to nursing program based on a point system.

2011-2012 Annual costs. Tuition/fees: $4,350; $7,560 out-of-state. Per-credit charge: $126 in-state; $233 out-of-state. Books/supplies: $800. Personal expenses: $500.

2010-2011 Financial aid. Need-based: Work-study available nights, weekends and for part-time students. **Non-need-based:** Scholarships awarded for academics, athletics, state residency.

Application procedures. Admission: No deadline. No application fee. Admission notification on a rolling basis. **Financial aid:** Priority date 7/15; no closing date. FAFSA, institutional form required. Applicants notified on a rolling basis.

Academics. Special study options: Cooperative education, dual enrollment of high school students, independent study. Bachelor's degree programs available on campus. **Credit/placement by examination:** AP, CLEP, institutional tests. 48 credit hours maximum toward associate degree. **Support services:** GED preparation and test center, learning center, remedial instruction, study skills assistance, tutoring.

Majors. Business: General, administrative services, business admin, management information systems. **Computer sciences:** General, computer science. **Education:** General. **Engineering:** General. **General:** Business. **Health services:** Clinical lab science, EMT paramedic, medical assistant, medical radiologic technology/radiation therapy, medical records technology, occupational therapy assistant, physical therapy assistant, respiratory therapy technology. **Liberal arts:** Arts/sciences. **Protective services:** Criminal justice, firefighting, police science.

Computing on campus. 45 workstations in library, computer center, student center. Online course registration available.

Student life. Freshman orientation: Mandatory. Preregistration for classes offered. **Activities:** Jazz band, choral groups, dance, drama, radio station, student government.

Athletics. NJCAA. **Intercollegiate:** Baseball M, golf M, softball W, tennis, volleyball W. **Team name:** Trojans.

Student services. Career counseling, financial aid counseling, personal counseling, veterans' counselor. **Transfer:** Pre-admission transcript evaluation for new students. Transfer adviser, college fairs on campus for students transferring to 4-year colleges.

Contact. Phone: (256) 215-4255 Toll-free number: (800) 643-2657 Donna Whaley, Director of Admissions, Central Alabama Community College, 34091 US Highway 280 South, Childersburg, AL 35044

Chattahoochee Valley Community College
Phenix City, Alabama
www.cv.edu   CB code: 1187

▶ Public 2-year community college
▶ Commuter campus in small city

General. Founded in 1974. Regionally accredited. **Enrollment:** 1,553 degree-seeking undergraduates. **Degrees:** 173 associate awarded. **ROTC:** Army. **Location:** 5 miles from Columbus, GA. **Calendar:** Semester, extensive summer session. **Full-time faculty:** 35 total; 23% have terminal degrees, 20% minority, 66% women. **Part-time faculty:** 89 total; 9% have terminal degrees, 33% minority, 63% women.

Student profile. Among degree-seeking undergraduates, 353 enrolled as first-time, first-year students, 648 transferred in from other institutions.

Part-time:	39%	Women:	65%

Transfer out. Colleges most students transferred to 2011: Columbus State University, Auburn University, Columbus Technical College, Southern Union State Community College, Troy State University.

Basis for selection. Open admission, but selective for some programs. COMPASS placement exam waived for students submitting appropriate ACT/SAT scores. Additional requirements for health occupation programs. **Home schooled:** State high school equivalency certificate required. Program must be accredited by state or federal department of education.

2011-2012 Annual costs. Tuition/fees: $4,140; $7,350 out-of-state. Per-credit charge: $107 in-state; $214 out-of-state. Books/supplies: $1,000. Personal expenses: $750.

2010-2011 Financial aid. Need-based: 98% of total undergraduate aid awarded as scholarships/grants, 2% as loans/jobs. Need-based aid available for part-time students. Work-study available nights, weekends and for part-time students. **Non-need-based:** Scholarships awarded for academics, art, athletics, leadership, music/drama.

Application procedures. Admission: Priority date 7/15; no deadline. No application fee. Application must be submitted on paper. Admission notification on a rolling basis. **Financial aid:** Priority date 7/1; no closing date. FAFSA required. Applicants notified on a rolling basis; must reply within 1 week(s) of notification.

Academics. Special study options: Accelerated study, distance learning, dual enrollment of high school students, ESL, honors, independent study, liberal arts/career combination. License preparation in nursing, paramedic. **Credit/placement by examination:** AP, CLEP, institutional tests. 18 credit hours maximum toward associate degree. **Support services:** GED preparation and test center, learning center, reduced course load, remedial instruction, tutoring, writing center.

Majors. Biology: General. **Business:** Accounting, administrative services, business admin. **Computer sciences:** General, data processing. **Education:** Business, elementary, physical, secondary. **Engineering:** General. **Health services:** Medical records technology, nursing (RN). **Liberal arts:** Arts/sciences. **Math:** General. **Parks/recreation:** Health/fitness. **Physical sciences:** Chemistry, physics. **Protective services:** Criminal justice, firefighting. **Visual/performing arts:** Art history/conservation, dramatic, music.

Most popular majors. Business/marketing 13%, health sciences 26%, liberal arts 50%.

Computing on campus. 150 workstations in library, computer center. Online library, wireless network available.

Student life. Freshman orientation: Available. Preregistration for classes offered. **Activities:** Choral groups, drama, music ensembles, musical theater, student government, student newspaper.

Athletics. NJCAA. **Intercollegiate:** Baseball M, basketball, softball W. **Team name:** Pirates.

Student services. Adult student services, career counseling, financial aid counseling, personal counseling, placement for graduates, veterans' counselor. **Physically disabled:** Services for visually, hearing impaired.

Contact. E-mail: admissions@cv.edu
Phone: (334) 291-4900 ext. 4929 Fax: (334) 291-4994
David Hodge, Dean of Student and Administrative Services, Chattahoochee Valley Community College, 2602 College Drive, Phenix City, AL 36869

Community College of the Air Force
Maxwell-Gunter AFB, Alabama   CB member
www.au.af.mil/au/ccaf   CB code: 1175

▶ Public 2-year community and technical college
▶ Commuter campus in small city
▶ Interview required

General. Founded in 1972. Regionally accredited. Multicampus, worldwide, for United States Air Force enlisted personnel. Administrative offices at Maxwell Air Force Base. Primary campuses are technical training centers located at 5 Air Force bases in 3 states. Other campuses include USAF PME Centers, USAF Command Sponsored Schools, and Field Training Detachments. **Enrollment:** 317,356 degree-seeking undergraduates. **Degrees:** 18,494 associate awarded. **Location:** 160 miles from Atlanta, 90 miles from Birmingham. **Calendar:** Differs by program, extensive summer session. **Full-time faculty:** 6,274 total.

Basis for selection. Admission to CCAF is restricted to enlisted members of the U.S. Air Force, Air National Guard, Air Force Reserve Command, and other-service instructors serving as CCAS affiliated school faculty. All eligible students are automatically enrolled into the degree program for their occupational specialty upon completion of Basic Military Training. All USAF enlisted personnel automatically registered upon completion of basic military training and assignment to an Air Force career field. All applicants must take the Armed Services Vocational Aptitude Battery.

High school preparation. 16 units recommended. Recommended units include English 4, mathematics 3, social studies 3, science 2 and foreign language 2.

2011-2012 Annual costs. Students pay no tuition or fees.

Financial aid. Need-based: Work-study available nights, weekends and for part-time students. **Additional information:** Air Force Tuition Assistance program available for general and technical education courses taken at civilian colleges and universities. Pays 75% of tuition costs.

Application procedures. Admission: No deadline. No application fee. Admission notification on a rolling basis. **Financial aid:** No deadline.

Academics. Special study options: Accelerated study, distance learning, independent study, internships, liberal arts/career combination. License preparation in aviation, physical therapy, radiology. **Credit/placement by examination:** AP, CLEP, institutional tests. 30 credit hours maximum toward associate degree. **Support services:** Reduced course load, remedial instruction, tutoring.

Majors. Business: Human resources, management information systems, office management, operations, purchasing. **Communications:** Public relations. **Communications technology:** General. **Computer sciences:** General, networking. **Education:** Technology/industrial arts. **Health services:** Cardiovascular technology, dental assistant, dental lab technology, health care admin, histologic assistant, medical assistant, nuclear medical technology, ophthalmic lab technology, pharmacy assistant, physical therapy assistant, radiologic technology/medical imaging, sonography, surgical technology. **History:** General. **Human services:** Social work. **Parks/recreation:** General. **Physical sciences:** Atmospheric science. **Protective services:** Criminal justice, fire safety technology. **Visual/performing arts:** Music.

Student life. Policies: Air Force bases provide housing, student services, activities, and athletics. **Housing:** Coed dorms, single-sex dorms, apartments available.

Athletics. Intramural: Badminton, baseball M, basketball, bowling, boxing M, cross-country, golf, handball, racquetball, rifle, soccer M, softball, squash, swimming, table tennis, tennis, track and field, volleyball, weight lifting.

Student services. Adult student services, alcohol/substance abuse counseling, career counseling, financial aid counseling, health services, legal services, on-campus daycare, personal counseling, veterans' counselor. **Transfer:** Transfer center, transfer adviser, college fairs on campus for students transferring to 4-year colleges.

Contact. E-mail: registrar.ccat@maxwell.af.mil
Phone: (334) 953-2794 Fax: (334) 953-5231
Terri Amatuzzi, Director of Enrollment Management, Community College of the Air Force, 100 South Turner Boulevard, Maxwell-Gunter AFB, AL 36114-3011

Enterprise State Community College
Enterprise, Alabama
www.escc.edu   **CB code: 1213**

- Public 2-year community college
- Commuter campus in large town

General. Founded in 1963. Regionally accredited. Courses offered at Enterprise, Ozark, Fort Rucker, Mobile, Andalusia, Albertville and Decatur. **Enrollment:** 2,489 degree-seeking undergraduates. **Degrees:** 262 associate awarded. **Location:** 25 miles from Dothan, 85 miles from Montgomery. **Calendar:** Semester, limited summer session. **Full-time faculty:** 67 total; 33% women. **Part-time faculty:** 78 total; 31% women.

Transfer out. Colleges most students transferred to 2011: Troy University, Auburn University, University of Alabama.

Basis for selection. Open admission. **Home schooled:** If sponsoring organization is not accredited, the student must either take Alabama High School Exit Exam and pass all five parts or submit 16 ACT.

High school preparation. 28 units recommended. Recommended units include English 4, mathematics 4, social studies 4 and science 4.

2011-2012 Annual costs. Tuition/fees: $3,930; $7,140 out-of-state. Per-credit charge: $107 in-state; $204 out-of-state. Books/supplies: $1,000. Personal expenses: $750.

Financial aid. Need-based: Work-study available nights, weekends and for part-time students. **Non-need-based:** Scholarships awarded for academics, art, athletics, leadership, music/drama, state residency.

Application procedures. Admission: No deadline. No application fee. Admission notification on a rolling basis. **Financial aid:** Priority date 6/15; no closing date. FAFSA, institutional form required. Applicants notified on a rolling basis starting 7/1; must reply within 2 week(s) of notification.

Academics. Federal Aviation Administration certified Aviation Maintenance Technology program. **Special study options:** Distance learning, dual enrollment of high school students, ESL, honors, internships, weekend college. Bachelor's degree programs available on campus. License preparation in aviation, paramedic. **Credit/placement by examination:** AP, CLEP, institutional tests. 30 credit hours maximum toward associate degree. **Support services:** GED preparation and test center, learning center, remedial instruction, tutoring.

Majors. Business: Administrative services, business admin, management information systems, office management. **Computer sciences:** General. **Health services:** EMT paramedic, medical assistant, medical records technology. **Liberal arts:** Arts/sciences.

Computing on campus. Commuter students can connect to campus network. Online course registration, helpline, wireless network available.

Student life. Freshman orientation: Mandatory. Preregistration for classes offered. **Activities:** Concert band, campus ministries, choral groups, dance, drama, music ensembles, student government, student newspaper, community band, concert choir.

Athletics. NJCAA. **Intercollegiate:** Baseball M, basketball, softball W. **Team name:** Boll Weevils.

Student services. Adult student services, career counseling, services for economically disadvantaged, student employment services, financial aid counseling, personal counseling, placement for graduates, veterans' counselor, women's services. **Physically disabled:** Services for visually, speech, hearing impaired. **Transfer:** Transfer adviser, college fairs on campus for students transferring to 4-year colleges.

Contact. E-mail: gdeas@escc.edu
Phone: (334) 347-2623 ext. 2234 Fax: (334) 347-5569
M. Gary Deas, Associate Dean of Students for Enrollment Management, Enterprise State Community College, Box 1300, Enterprise, AL 36331

Faulkner State Community College
Bay Minette, Alabama
www.faulknerstate.edu   **CB code: 1939**

- Public 2-year community college
- Commuter campus in large town

General. Founded in 1965. Regionally accredited. Branch campuses in Fairhope and Gulf Shores. **Enrollment:** 4,258 degree-seeking undergraduates; 157 non-degree-seeking students. **Degrees:** 378 associate awarded. **Location:** 35 miles from Mobile. **Calendar:** Semester, extensive summer session. **Full-time faculty:** 76 total; 46% minority. **Part-time faculty:** 182 total; 29% minority, 62% women.

Student profile. Among degree-seeking undergraduates, 1,148 enrolled as first-time, first-year students.

Part-time:	42%	25 or older:	31%
Women:	63%	Live on campus:	10%

Transfer out. Colleges most students transferred to 2011: University of Alabama, Auburn University, University of South Alabama, Troy University, Alabama State University.

Basis for selection. Open admission, but selective for some programs. Special requirements for nursing and surgical technology programs. Audition recommended for music majors, portfolio for art majors. **Home schooled:** If school is non-accredited, 16 ACT or GED required.

2011-2012 Annual costs. Tuition/fees: $4,080; $7,290 out-of-state. Per-credit charge: $107 in-state; $214 out-of-state. Room/board: $5,400. Books/supplies: $1,400. Personal expenses: $800.

Financial aid. Need-based: Work-study available nights, weekends and for part-time students. **Non-need-based:** Scholarships awarded for academics, art, athletics, leadership, music/drama.

Application procedures. Admission: No deadline. No application fee. Application must be submitted on paper. Admission notification on a rolling basis. **Financial aid:** Priority date 7/1; no closing date. FAFSA, institutional form required. Applicants notified on a rolling basis starting 8/1.

Academics. Special study options: Accelerated study, cooperative education, distance learning, double major, dual enrollment of high school students, honors, independent study, internships. License preparation in nursing, paramedic. **Credit/placement by examination:** AP, CLEP. 20 credit hours maximum toward associate degree. **Support services:** GED preparation and test center, learning center, remedial instruction, tutoring.

Majors. Biology: General. **Business:** Administrative services, business admin, finance, hospitality admin, office technology. **Communications:** Journalism. **Computer sciences:** General, computer graphics, systems analysis. **Conservation:** Forestry. **Education:** Business, early childhood, elementary, physical. **English:** English lit. **General:** Business, landscaping. **Health services:** Clinical lab science, clinical lab technology, dental assistant, EMT paramedic, medical secretary, predental, premedicine, prenursing, prepharmacy, preveterinary. **Liberal arts:** Arts/sciences. **Math:** General. **Parks/recreation:** Facilities management. **Physical sciences:** Chemistry. **Social sciences:** General. **Visual/performing arts:** General, art, commercial/advertising art, music, studio arts. **Work/family studies:** General.

Computing on campus. 66 workstations in dormitories, library, computer center. Dormitories wired for high-speed internet access and linked to campus network. Commuter students can connect to campus network. Online course registration, online library, helpline, wireless network available.

Student life. Freshman orientation: Available. Preregistration for classes offered. **Housing:** Coed dorms, single-sex dorms available. $50 nonrefundable deposit. **Activities:** Bands, campus ministries, choral groups, drama, music ensembles, student government, student newspaper, pow-wow leadership, Phi Beta Lambda, Baptist campus ministries, Phi Theta Kappa, Psi Beta, association of computational machinery, engineering club, Fusion, National Student Nurses' Association, scholars' bowl.

Athletics. NJCAA. **Intercollegiate:** Baseball M, basketball, cheerleading, golf, softball W, tennis, volleyball W. **Intramural:** Basketball M, bowling, racquetball, softball, volleyball W. **Team name:** Sun Chiefs.

Student services. Career counseling, student employment services, financial aid counseling, personal counseling, placement for graduates, veterans' counselor. **Physically disabled:** Services for visually impaired. **Transfer:** Transfer adviser, college fairs on campus for students transferring to 4-year colleges.

Contact. E-mail: admissions@faulknerstate.edu
Phone: (251) 580-2111 Toll-free number: (800) 231-3752
Fax: (251) 580-2285
Michael Nikolakis, Dean of Student Services, Faulkner State Community College, 1900 Highway 31 South, Bay Minette, AL 36507

Gadsden State Community College
Gadsden, Alabama
www.gadsdenstate.edu   CB code: 1262

▶ Public 2-year community and technical college
▶ Commuter campus in small city

General. Founded in 1985. Regionally accredited. Off-campus sites include Ayers Campus, McClellan Campus, Gadsden State Cherokee and Valley Street Campus (HBCU). **Enrollment:** 6,426 degree-seeking undergraduates; 309 non-degree-seeking students. **Degrees:** 609 associate awarded. **ROTC:** Army. **Location:** 60 miles from Birmingham. **Calendar:** Semester, extensive summer session. **Full-time faculty:** 153 total; 7% minority, 56% women. **Part-time faculty:** 207 total; 7% minority, 65% women. **Special facilities:** Advanced technology center, language institute, aquaculture education, cadaver lab.

Student profile. Among degree-seeking undergraduates, 61% enrolled in a transfer program, 39% enrolled in a vocational program, 4,221 enrolled as first-time, first-year students.

Part-time:	40%	Asian American:	1%
Out-of-state:	1%	Hispanic American:	3%
Women:	63%	25 or older:	30%
African American:	22%	Live on campus:	1%

Transfer out. 18% of students enrolled in the transfer program go on to 4-year colleges. **Colleges most students transferred to 2011:** Jacksonville

State University, Auburn University, University of Alabama, University of Alabama at Birmingham, University of Alabama at Huntsville.

Basis for selection. Open admission, but selective for some programs. Special requirements for health-related programs. Career Program Assessment Test required for some programs. Interview recommended for computer technology, court reporting, and most health science majors. **Home schooled:** Transcript of courses and grades required. 16 ACT or 790 SAT required. **Learning Disabled:** Accommodations must be requested for each school term. Students are responsible for providing adequate documentation of disability, requesting accommodation through appropriate campus officer, maintaining contact with that person, and notifying the officer of any changes in accommodations needed and of new courses for which accommodations are required each semester.

High school preparation. 27 units recommended. Recommended units include English 4, mathematics 4, social studies 4, science 4 (laboratory 2) and academic electives 9. Electives must include .5 unit computer, .5 unit of fine arts.

2011-2012 Annual costs. Tuition/fees: $4,350; $7,560 out-of-state. Per-credit charge: $126 in-state; $233 out-of-state. Room/board: $3,200. Books/supplies: $1,000. Personal expenses: $825.

2010-2011 Financial aid. Need-based: 97% of total undergraduate aid awarded as scholarships/grants, 3% as loans/jobs. Need-based aid available for part-time students. Work-study available nights, weekends and for part-time students. **Non-need-based:** Scholarships awarded for academics, alumni affiliation, art, athletics, job skills, leadership, minority status, music/drama, state residency.

Application procedures. Admission: No deadline. No application fee. Admission notification on a rolling basis. **Financial aid:** Priority date 4/15; no closing date. FAFSA, institutional form required. Applicants notified on a rolling basis starting 6/10.

Academics. Special study options: Accelerated study, cooperative education, cross-registration, distance learning, dual enrollment of high school students, ESL, honors, independent study, internships, weekend college. License preparation in nursing, paramedic, radiology. **Credit/placement by examination:** AP, CLEP, institutional tests. 20 credit hours maximum toward associate degree. **Support services:** GED preparation and test center, remedial instruction, study skills assistance, tutoring, writing center.

Majors. Area/ethnic studies: American. **Biology:** General. **Business:** Accounting technology, administrative services, business admin, sales/distribution. **Communications:** Communications/speech/rhetoric. **Communications technology:** General, graphics. **Computer sciences:** General, computer science, information systems, information technology, LAN/WAN management, networking, programming. **Conservation:** Forestry. **Education:** General, early childhood, elementary, kindergarten/preschool, mathematics. **Engineering:** General. **English:** English lit. **Health services:** Clinical lab assistant, clinical lab technology, EMT paramedic, medical radiologic technology/radiation therapy, medical records technology, nursing (RN), predental, premedicine, prenursing, prepharmacy, preveterinary, substance abuse counseling. **History:** General. **Liberal arts:** Arts/sciences. **Math:** General. **Parks/recreation:** Health/fitness. **Philosophy/religion:** Religion. **Physical sciences:** Chemistry. **Protective services:** Law enforcement admin. **Psychology:** General. **Social sciences:** Sociology. **Visual/performing arts:** Art, music. **Work/family studies:** Child development.

Most popular majors. Business/marketing 14%, engineering/engineering technologies 15%, health sciences 23%, liberal arts 29%, trade and industry 9%.

Computing on campus. 250 workstations in dormitories, library, computer center, student center. Dormitories wired for high-speed internet access. Online course registration, online library available.

Student life. Freshman orientation: Mandatory, $126 fee. Preregistration for classes offered. **Housing:** Coed dorms, wellness housing available. $200 fully refundable deposit. **Activities:** Bands, campus ministries, choral groups, dance, drama, international student organizations, music ensembles, student government, Circle-K, international club, Baptist student union, Phi Beta Lambda.

Athletics. NJCAA. **Intercollegiate:** Baseball M, basketball, cross-country W, softball W, tennis M, volleyball W. **Team name:** Cardinals.

Student services. Adult student services, career counseling, services for economically disadvantaged, student employment services, financial aid counseling, personal counseling, placement for graduates, veterans' counselor. **Physically disabled:** Services for visually, speech, hearing impaired. **Transfer:** Pre-admission transcript evaluation for new students. Transfer adviser, college fairs on campus for students transferring to 4-year colleges.

Contact. Phone: (256) 549-8210 Toll-free number: (800) 226-5563 Fax: (256) 549-8205
Jennie Dobson, Assistant to the President/Registrar, Gadsden State Community College, 1001 George Wallace Drive, Gadsden, AL 35902-0227

George C. Wallace Community College at Dothan
Dothan, Alabama
www.wallace.edu   CB code: 1264

▶ Public 2-year community college
▶ Commuter campus in small city

General. Founded in 1949. Regionally accredited. Additional campuses in Eufaula and Ft. Rucker. **Enrollment:** 4,667 degree-seeking undergraduates. **Degrees:** 470 associate awarded. **Calendar:** Semester, extensive summer session. **Full-time faculty:** 130 total. **Part-time faculty:** 122 total.

Student profile.

Out-of-state: 4%   25 or older: 43%

Transfer out. Colleges most students transferred to 2011: University of Alabama, Auburn University, University of Alabama at Birmingham.

Basis for selection. Open admission, but selective for some programs. Additional requirements for allied health. National League for Nursing exam and interview required for nursing applicants.

2011-2012 Annual costs. Tuition/fees: $3,780; $6,990 out-of-state. Per-credit charge: $107 in-state; $214 out-of-state. Books/supplies: $1,900. Personal expenses: $666.

Financial aid. Need-based: Work-study available nights, weekends and for part-time students. **Non-need-based:** Scholarships awarded for academics, athletics, leadership.

Application procedures. Admission: No deadline. No application fee. Admission notification on a rolling basis. **Financial aid:** Priority date 5/1; no closing date. FAFSA required. Applicants notified on a rolling basis.

Academics. Special study options: Accelerated study, cooperative education, cross-registration, distance learning, dual enrollment of high school students, ESL, honors. License preparation in nursing, paramedic, physical therapy, radiology. **Credit/placement by examination:** AP, CLEP, institutional tests. 48 credit hours maximum toward associate degree. **Support services:** GED preparation and test center, learning center, pre-admission summer program, remedial instruction, study skills assistance, tutoring.

Majors. Business: Administrative services. **Computer sciences:** General. **Health services:** EMT paramedic, medical assistant, medical radiologic technology/radiation therapy, respiratory therapy technology. **Liberal arts:** Arts/sciences.

Student life. Freshman orientation: Mandatory. Preregistration for classes offered. **Activities:** Jazz band, choral groups, drama, music ensembles, student government, student newspaper, Association of Student Practical Nursing, Diplomats, Elite club, National Vocational-Technical Honor Society, Phi Theta Kappa, Phi Beta Lambda, Respiratory Therapy Association for Better Breathing.

Athletics. NJCAA. **Intercollegiate:** Baseball M, softball W. **Team name:** Govs (M), Lady Govs (W).

Student services. Adult student services, career counseling, services for economically disadvantaged, student employment services, financial aid counseling, personal counseling, placement for graduates, veterans' counselor. **Transfer:** Transfer adviser, college fairs on campus for students transferring to 4-year colleges.

Contact. Phone: (334) 983-3521 Toll-free number: (800) 543-2426 Fax: (334) 983-6066
Keith Saulsberry, Admissions Director, George C. Wallace Community College at Dothan, 1141 Wallace Drive, Dothan, AL 36303-0943

George C. Wallace State Community College at Selma
Selma, Alabama
www.wccs.edu   CB code: 3146

▶ Public 2-year community and technical college
▶ Commuter campus in large town

General. Founded in 1963. Regionally accredited. **Enrollment:** 2,066 degree-seeking undergraduates. **Degrees:** 379 associate awarded. **Location:** 50 miles from Montgomery, 90 miles from Birmingham. **Calendar:** Semester, extensive summer session. **Full-time faculty:** 50 total. **Part-time faculty:** 56 total.

Basis for selection. Open admission, but selective for some programs. Generic/mobility (RN) nursing candidates need 20 ACT. Practical (LPN) nursing candidates need 18 ACT, or 41 on the Nursing Entrance Test.

2011-2012 Annual costs. Tuition/fees: $3,780; $6,990 out-of-state. Per-credit charge: $107 in-state; $214 out-of-state. Books/supplies: $690. Personal expenses: $976.

Financial aid. Need-based: Work-study available nights, weekends and for part-time students. **Non-need-based:** Scholarships awarded for academics, athletics.

Application procedures. Admission: Priority date 8/21; no deadline. No application fee. Admission notification on a rolling basis. **Financial aid:** Priority date 6/1; no closing date. FAFSA required. Applicants notified on a rolling basis starting 6/15.

Academics. Special study options: Accelerated study, double major, dual enrollment of high school students. **Credit/placement by examination:** AP, CLEP, institutional tests. 30 credit hours maximum toward associate degree. **Support services:** GED preparation and test center, learning center, reduced course load, remedial instruction, study skills assistance, tutoring.

Majors. Business: Administrative services, business admin. **Computer sciences:** General. **Health services:** Nursing (RN). **Liberal arts:** Arts/sciences.

Student life. Freshman orientation: Available. Preregistration for classes offered. **Activities:** Student government, Baptist student union, Phi Theta Kappa, Fellowship of Christian Athletes.

Athletics. NJCAA. **Intercollegiate:** Baseball M, basketball, softball W. **Intramural:** Baseball M, basketball, softball. **Team name:** Patriots.

Student services. Career counseling, student employment services, personal counseling, placement for graduates, veterans' counselor. **Physically disabled:** Services for visually, speech, hearing impaired. **Transfer:** Transfer adviser, college fairs on campus for students transferring to 4-year colleges.

Contact. Phone: (334) 876-9295 Fax: (334) 876-9300
Lonzy Clifton, Director of Admissions and Records, George C. Wallace State Community College at Selma, PO Box 2530, Selma, AL 36702-2530

Jefferson Davis Community College
Brewton, Alabama
www.jdcc.edu   CB code: 1355

▶ Public 2-year nursing and community college
▶ Commuter campus in small town

General. Founded in 1965. Regionally accredited. **Enrollment:** 1,190 degree-seeking undergraduates; 62 non-degree-seeking students. **Degrees:** 142 associate awarded. **Location:** 60 miles from Pensacola, FL. **Calendar:** Semester, limited summer session. **Full-time faculty:** 33 total. **Part-time faculty:** 35 total. **Class size:** 63% < 20, 37% 20-39. **Special facilities:** Museum, golf course, telecommunications center.

Student profile. Among degree-seeking undergraduates, 58% enrolled in a transfer program, 37% enrolled in a vocational program, 365 enrolled as first-time, first-year students, 337 transferred in from other institutions.

Part-time:	47%	Hispanic American:	1%
Out-of-state:	8%	Native American:	4%
Women:	55%	25 or older:	48%
African American:	32%	Live on campus:	6%
Asian American:	2%		

Basis for selection. Open admission, but selective for some programs. Special admissions requirements for nursing program. **Home schooled:** 16 ACT required.

High school preparation. 24 units recommended. Recommended units include English 4, mathematics 4, social studies 4, science 4 and academic electives 8.

2011-2012 Annual costs. Tuition/fees: $3,780; $6,990 out-of-state. Per-credit charge: $107 in-state; $214 out-of-state. Room only: $2,000. Books/supplies: $800. Personal expenses: $400.

Financial aid. Need-based: Need-based aid available for part-time students. Work-study available nights, weekends and for part-time students. **Non-need-based:** Scholarships awarded for academics, athletics, leadership.

Application procedures. Admission: No deadline. No application fee. Admission notification on a rolling basis. **Financial aid:** No deadline. FAFSA required. Applicants notified on a rolling basis; must reply within 2 week(s) of notification.

Academics. Special study options: Cooperative education, distance learning, dual enrollment of high school students, ESL, honors, independent study. Bachelor's degree programs available on campus. License preparation in nursing, paramedic. **Credit/placement by examination:** AP, CLEP. **Support services:** GED preparation and test center, learning center, remedial instruction, study skills assistance, tutoring.

Majors. Business: Administrative services. **Health services:** Nursing (RN). **Liberal arts:** Arts/sciences.

Most popular majors. Health sciences 34%, liberal arts 60%.

Computing on campus. 420 workstations in library, computer center. Dormitories wired for high-speed internet access. Online course registration, helpline, wireless network available.

Student life. Freshman orientation: Mandatory, $126 fee. Preregistration for classes offered. **Housing:** Coed dorms, wellness housing available. $150 partly refundable deposit. **Activities:** Campus ministries, student government, student newspaper, Baptist student union, Phi Theta Kappa, Phi Beta Lambda, Psi Beta.

Athletics. NJCAA. **Intercollegiate:** Baseball M, basketball M, softball W, volleyball W. **Team name:** Warhawks.

Student services. Adult student services, chaplain/spiritual director, career counseling, services for economically disadvantaged, financial aid counseling, personal counseling, veterans' counselor. **Physically disabled:** Services for visually impaired. **Transfer:** Pre-admission transcript evaluation for new students. Transfer adviser, college fairs on campus for students transferring to 4-year colleges.

Contact. Phone: (251) 809-1594 Fax: (251) 809-1593
Robin Sessions, Registrar, Jefferson Davis Community College, PO Box 958, Brewton, AL 36427

Jefferson State Community College
Birmingham, Alabama
www.jeffstateonline.com
CB code: 1352

- Public 2-year community college
- Commuter campus in large city

General. Founded in 1963. Regionally accredited. **Enrollment:** 8,444 degree-seeking undergraduates; 1,016 non-degree-seeking students. **Degrees:** 764 associate awarded. **ROTC:** Army, Air Force. **Location:** 12 miles from downtown. **Calendar:** Semester, extensive summer session. **Full-time faculty:** 128 total; 19% have terminal degrees, 16% minority, 66% women. **Part-time faculty:** 277 total; 12% have terminal degrees, 18% minority, 60% women. **Class size:** 38% < 20, 51% 20-39, 10% 40-49, 1% 50-99, less than 1% >100. **Special facilities:** Learning success center, bistro.

Student profile. Among degree-seeking undergraduates, 54% enrolled in a transfer program, 46% enrolled in a vocational program, 1,860 enrolled as first-time, first-year students, 927 transferred in from other institutions.

Part-time:	59%	Asian American:	2%
Out-of-state:	2%	Hispanic American:	3%
Women:	60%	International:	1%
African American:	23%	25 or older:	41%

Transfer out. Colleges most students transferred to 2011: University of Alabama at Birmingham, University of Alabama, Auburn University.

Basis for selection. Open admission, but selective for some programs. Students registering for 5 or more hours of credit must take ACT ASSET or ACT COMPASS for placement. Exemptions given for students who have completed college level math or English courses, or students who have equivalent ACT scores. Applicants from non-accredited high schools admitted with high school diploma and 16 ACT or equivalent SAT. **Home schooled:** Must have 16 ACT or pass Alabama Public High School Graduation Exam.

2011-2012 Annual costs. Tuition/fees: $4,140; $7,350 out-of-state. Per-credit charge: $107 in-state; $214 out-of-state. Books/supplies: $1,834. Personal expenses: $1,434.

Financial aid. Need-based: Need-based aid available for part-time students. Work-study available nights, weekends and for part-time students. **Non-need-based:** Scholarships awarded for academics, art, leadership, music/drama. **Additional information:** Any Alabama resident over age 60 may attend classes tuition free, on a space available basis.

Application procedures. Admission: No deadline. No application fee. Admission notification on a rolling basis. **Financial aid:** Priority date 5/1; no closing date. FAFSA, institutional form required. Applicants notified on a rolling basis starting 6/1.

Academics. Special study options: Accelerated study, distance learning, dual enrollment of high school students, ESL, honors, independent study, internships. Bachelor's degree programs available on campus. License preparation in nursing, paramedic, radiology, real estate. **Credit/placement by examination:** AP, CLEP, IB, institutional tests. 20 credit hours maximum toward associate degree. **Support services:** GED preparation and test center, learning center, reduced course load, remedial instruction, study skills assistance.

Majors. Business: Accounting technology, administrative services, hospitality admin, office management. **Computer sciences:** General. **Health services:** Clinical lab technology, EMT paramedic, nursing (RN), physical therapy assistant, radiologic technology/medical imaging, veterinary technology/assistant. **Liberal arts:** Arts/sciences. **Protective services:** Fire services admin, police science. **Work/family studies:** Child care management.

Most popular majors. Business/marketing 14%, health sciences 35%, liberal arts 34%.

Computing on campus. 295 workstations in library, computer center. Commuter students can connect to campus network. Online course registration, online library, helpline available.

Student life. Freshman orientation: Available. Preregistration for classes offered. **Activities:** Campus ministries, choral groups, drama, literary magazine, music ensembles, musical theater, student government, senior adult student club, BACCHUS, Students in Free Enterprise, Ambassadors, speech team, PTK, nursing club, chess club, SKD.

Student services. Adult student services, career counseling, student employment services, financial aid counseling, placement for graduates, veterans' counselor, women's services. **Physically disabled:** Services for visually, speech, hearing impaired. **Transfer:** Transfer adviser, college fairs on campus for students transferring to 4-year colleges.

Contact. E-mail: admissions@jeffstateonline.com
Phone: (205) 856-7704 Toll-free number: (800) 239-5900 ext. 7704
Fax: (205) 856-6070
Lillian Owens, Director, Admissions & Retention, Jefferson State Community College, 2601 Carson Road, Birmingham, AL 35215-3098

Lawson State Community College
Birmingham, Alabama
www.lawsonstate.edu
CB code: 1933

- Public 2-year community college
- Commuter campus in small city

General. Founded in 1949. Regionally accredited. **Enrollment:** 4,079 degree-seeking undergraduates; 79 non-degree-seeking students. **Degrees:** 244 associate awarded. **Calendar:** Semester, limited summer session. **Full-time faculty:** 96 total. **Part-time faculty:** 125 total. **Class size:** 100% >100.

Student profile. Among degree-seeking undergraduates, 1,083 enrolled as first-time, first-year students, 215 transferred in from other institutions.

Part-time:	37%	African American:	77%
Out-of-state:	1%	Hispanic American:	1%
Women:	60%	Live on campus:	2%

Transfer out. Colleges most students transferred to 2011: Miles College, University of Alabama at Birmingham, Alabama A&M University, Alabama State University, Jefferson State Community College.

Basis for selection. Open admission, but selective for some programs. Advanced placement option for licensed practical nurses (LPN) and nursing education. Nursing students must pass nursing entrance exam or have 20 ACT or comparable SAT.

2011-2012 Annual costs. Tuition/fees: $4,080; $7,290 out-of-state. Per-credit charge: $107 in-state; $214 out-of-state. Room/board: $4,000. Books/supplies: $1,200. Personal expenses: $400.

2011-2012 Financial aid. All financial aid based on need. 98% of total undergraduate aid awarded as scholarships/grants, 2% as loans/jobs. Need-based aid available for part-time students. Work-study available nights, weekends and for part-time students.

Application procedures. Admission: No deadline. No application fee. Admission notification on a rolling basis. **Financial aid:** Priority date 6/1; no closing date. FAFSA required. Applicants notified on a rolling basis starting 8/1; must reply within 2 week(s) of notification.

Academics. Special study options: Accelerated study, double major, dual enrollment of high school students, internships, liberal arts/career combination, student-designed major. License preparation in dental hygiene, nursing, real estate. **Credit/placement by examination:** AP, CLEP, institutional tests. **Support services:** GED preparation and test center, learning center, reduced course load, remedial instruction, tutoring, writing center.

Majors. Business: Accounting, administrative services, business admin, office management, office technology, operations. **Computer sciences:** Computer science. **Engineering:** Electrical. **Health services:** Medical secretary, nursing (RN). **Human services:** Social work. **Liberal arts:** Arts/sciences. **Protective services:** Criminal justice.

Most popular majors. Business/marketing 20%, computer/information sciences 9%, engineering/engineering technologies 8%, health sciences 16%, liberal arts 37%.

Computing on campus. 484 workstations in dormitories, library, computer center, student center. Dormitories linked to campus network. Online course registration, online library, wireless network available.

Student life. Freshman orientation: Mandatory. Preregistration for classes offered. **Housing:** Coed dorms available. **Activities:** Jazz band, choral groups, dance, drama, music ensembles, student government, scholars bowl team, Sophist club.

Athletics. NJCAA. **Intercollegiate:** Baseball M, basketball, volleyball W. **Intramural:** Baseball M, basketball. **Team name:** Cougars.

Student services. Adult student services, career counseling, services for economically disadvantaged, student employment services, financial aid counseling, health services, on-campus daycare, personal counseling, placement for graduates, veterans' counselor. **Physically disabled:** Services for hearing impaired. **Transfer:** College fairs on campus for students transferring to 4-year colleges.

Contact. E-mail: jshelley@lawsonstate.edu
Phone: (205) 929-6309 Fax: (205) 923-7106
Jeff Shelley, Director of Admissions, Lawson State Community College, 3060 Wilson Road SW, Birmingham, AL 35221-1717

studies 4, science 4, computer science .5, visual/performing arts .5, academic electives 5.5.

2011-2012 Annual costs. Tuition/fees: $4,080; $7,290 out-of-state. Per-credit charge: $107 in-state; $214 out-of-state. Books/supplies: $1,192. Personal expenses: $3,825.

Financial aid. Need-based: Work-study available nights, weekends and for part-time students.

Application procedures. Admission: No deadline. No application fee. Application must be submitted on paper. Admission notification on a rolling basis. **Financial aid:** Priority date 5/1; no closing date. Applicants notified on a rolling basis starting 7/1; must reply within 2 week(s) of notification.

Academics. Special study options: Accelerated study, cooperative education, distance learning, dual enrollment of high school students, honors. License preparation in nursing, paramedic. **Credit/placement by examination:** AP, CLEP, institutional tests. **Support services:** GED preparation and test center, learning center, reduced course load, remedial instruction, tutoring.

Majors. Business: Administrative services. **Computer sciences:** General. **Conservation:** Forest resources. **Health services:** EMT paramedic, nursing (RN). **Liberal arts:** Arts/sciences. **Work/family studies:** Child care management.

Most popular majors. Business/marketing 6%, health sciences 16%, liberal arts 61%.

Computing on campus. 50 workstations in library, computer center, student center. Online library, wireless network available.

Student life. Freshman orientation: Mandatory, $10 fee. Preregistration for classes offered. Offered as a hybrid course: half on-campus activities; half on-line. Students meet with advisers and register for classes. **Activities:** Jazz band, choral groups, drama, music ensembles, musical theater, student government, Collegiate Civitan club, adult re-entry club.

Athletics. NJCAA. **Intercollegiate:** Baseball M, basketball, softball W. **Team name:** Saints.

Student services. Career counseling, services for economically disadvantaged, student employment services, personal counseling, placement for graduates, veterans' counselor. **Transfer:** Transfer adviser for students transferring to 4-year colleges.

Contact. E-mail: jriley@lbwcc.edu
Phone: (334) 222-6591 ext. 273 Fax: (334) 881-2201
Jan Riley, Director of Admissions, Lurleen B. Wallace Community College, Box 1418, Andalusia, AL 36420-1418

Lurleen B. Wallace Community College
Andalusia, Alabama
www.lbwcc.edu   CB code: 1429

- Public 2-year community college
- Commuter campus in small town

General. Founded in 1969. Regionally accredited. Additional campuses in Opp, Greenville, Luverne. **Enrollment:** 1,581 degree-seeking undergraduates; 198 non-degree-seeking students. **Degrees:** 238 associate awarded. **Location:** 90 miles from Montgomery. **Calendar:** Semester, limited summer session. **Full-time faculty:** 55 total; 11% have terminal degrees, 16% minority, 71% women. **Part-time faculty:** 65 total; 11% minority, 77% women. **Class size:** 75% < 20, 23% 20-39, less than 1% 40-49, less than 1% 50-99, less than 1% >100. **Special facilities:** Nature trail, tennis courts, 9-hole golf course, children's playground.

Student profile. Among degree-seeking undergraduates, 437 enrolled as first-time, first-year students.

Part-time:	34%	Women:	67%
Out-of-state:	3%		

Transfer out. Colleges most students transferred to 2011: Troy University, Auburn University, Auburn University in Montgomery, University of Alabama.

Basis for selection. Open admission. COMPASS required for placement unless student scores 20 ACT math and English. **Home schooled:** 16 ACT required. **Learning Disabled:** Students with disabilities encouraged to meet with ADA coordinator.

High school preparation. College-preparatory program recommended. 24 units required. Required units include English 4, mathematics 4, social

---

Marion Military Institute
Marion, Alabama
www.marionmilitary.edu   CB code: 1447

- Public 2-year junior and military college
- Residential campus in small town
- SAT or ACT (ACT writing optional) required

General. Founded in 1842. Regionally accredited. One of 5 military junior colleges that provides academic prep for the U.S. Service Academies. **Enrollment:** 406 degree-seeking undergraduates; 3 non-degree-seeking students. **Degrees:** 93 associate awarded. **ROTC:** Army, Air Force. **Location:** 70 miles from Birmingham, 52 miles from Tuscaloosa. **Calendar:** Semester. **Full-time faculty:** 19 total; 47% have terminal degrees, 10% minority, 26% women. **Part-time faculty:** 11 total; 27% have terminal degrees, 27% women. **Class size:** 49% < 20, 49% 20-39, less than 1% 50-99, 1% >100. **Special facilities:** Alabama Military Hall of Honor, golf course. **Partnerships:** Formal partnership with Sanders Flight Training Center, Inc. to preclude U.S. Air Force and Navy Initial Flight Screening (IFS) requirements by achievement of a private pilot's certificate to significantly enhance candidacy for selection to military aviation training.

Student profile. Among degree-seeking undergraduates, 100% enrolled in a transfer program, 272 enrolled as first-time, first-year students, 18 transferred in from other institutions.

Out-of-state:	16%	Hispanic American:	10%
Women:	17%	25 or older:	2%
African American:	23%	Live on campus:	100%
Asian American:	4%		

Basis for selection. 16 ACT (or SAT equivalent) required for general admissions. Additional criteria for applicants to early commissioning program

or service academy preparatory program. Interview recommended. **Home schooled:** Applicants must have been enrolled in approved programs.

High school preparation. College-preparatory program required. 25 units required. Required and recommended units include English 4, mathematics 4, social studies 1, history 3, science 4, foreign language 2 and academic electives 8.

2011-2012 Annual costs. Tuition/fees: $8,570; $14,570 out-of-state. Per-credit charge: $200 in-state; $400 out-of-state. Required fees include one-time uniform fee of $1,850 and accident insurance of $150 per academic year. Room/board: $3,950. Books/supplies: $1,200. Personal expenses: $2,800.

Financial aid. Need-based: Need-based aid available for part-time students. Work-study available nights, weekends and for part-time students.

Application procedures. Admission: Priority date 5/1; deadline 8/15 (receipt date). $30 fee, may be waived for applicants with need. Admission notification on a rolling basis. **Financial aid:** No deadline. FAFSA required. Applicants notified on a rolling basis starting 6/15; must reply within 6 week(s) of notification.

Academics. Online tutoring program provides live tutoring 24 hours a day, 7 days a week. **Special study options:** ESL. **Credit/placement by examination:** AP, CLEP, SAT, ACT, institutional tests. **Support services:** Remedial instruction, study skills assistance, tutoring.

Majors. Liberal arts: Arts/sciences.

Computing on campus. 90 workstations in library, computer center. Dormitories wired for high-speed internet access and linked to campus network. Commuter students can connect to campus network. Online course registration, online library, helpline, wireless network available.

Student life. Freshman orientation: Mandatory. Preregistration for classes offered. **Policies:** Structured military school environment. Students must live on campus. **Housing:** Guaranteed on-campus for all undergraduates. Coed dorms, wellness housing available. $200 nonrefundable deposit, deadline 8/15. **Activities:** Bands, campus ministries, choral groups, drama, music ensembles, musical theater, student government, Scabbard & Blade, Normandy society, Christian ministries, Christian athletes, Swamp Fox, Honor Guard, White Knights.

Athletics. NJCAA. **Intercollegiate:** Baseball M, basketball M, softball W, tennis. **Intramural:** Basketball, cross-country, football (non-tackle), golf, rifle, swimming, track and field, volleyball, weight lifting. **Team name:** Tigers.

Student services. Chaplain/spiritual director, financial aid counseling, health services, personal counseling, veterans' counselor. **Transfer:** Transfer center, transfer adviser, college fairs on campus for students transferring to 4-year colleges.

Contact. E-mail: admissions@marionmilitary.edu
Phone: (334) 683-2305 Toll-free number: (800) 664-1842
Fax: (334) 683-2383
Lt. Col. James Lake, Vice President for Enrollment Management, Marion Military Institute, 1101 Washington Street, Marion, AL 36756-0420

Northeast Alabama Community College
Rainsville, Alabama
www.nacc.edu   CB code: 1576

- Public 2-year community college
- Commuter campus in rural community

General. Founded in 1963. Regionally accredited. **Enrollment:** 2,888 degree-seeking undergraduates. **Degrees:** 505 associate awarded. **Location:** 55 miles from Huntsville, 110 miles from Birmingham. **Calendar:** Semester, extensive summer session. **Full-time faculty:** 59 total. **Part-time faculty:** 118 total. **Special facilities:** Community theater, lakeside walking trail.

Transfer out. Colleges most students transferred to 2011: Jacksonville State University, University of Alabama at Huntsville, Athens State University, University of Alabama, Auburn University.

Basis for selection. Open admission. **Home schooled:** Transcript of courses and grades required. 16 ACT required. **Learning Disabled:** Students who may require accommodations encouraged to communicate with Disability Services.

High school preparation. 24 units recommended. Recommended units include English 4, mathematics 4, social studies 2, history 2, science 4

(laboratory 2), foreign language 2, computer science .5, academic electives 3.5.

2011-2012 Annual costs. Tuition/fees: $3,930; $7,140 out-of-state. Per-credit charge: $107 in-state; $214 out-of-state. Personal expenses: $1,500.

Financial aid. Need-based: Need-based aid available for part-time students. Work-study available nights, weekends and for part-time students. **Non-need-based:** Scholarships awarded for academics, art, leadership, minority status, music/drama.

Application procedures. Admission: No deadline. No application fee. Admission notification on a rolling basis. **Financial aid:** No deadline. FAFSA required. Applicants notified on a rolling basis.

Academics. Special study options: Accelerated study, distance learning, dual enrollment of high school students, ESL. 2-year degree programs in allied health available requiring 1 year study at Wallace State Community College at Hanceville. Bachelor's degree programs available on campus. License preparation in dental hygiene, nursing, paramedic. **Credit/placement by examination:** AP, CLEP, institutional tests. 16 credit hours maximum toward associate degree. **Support services:** GED preparation and test center, learning center, remedial instruction, study skills assistance, tutoring, writing center.

Majors. Business: General, administrative services, business admin, office management. **Computer sciences:** General, computer science. **English:** English lit. **Health services:** EMT paramedic, medical assistant, nursing (RN), office admin, office assistant. **Liberal arts:** Arts/sciences. **Protective services:** Law enforcement admin, police science.

Computing on campus. 475 workstations in library, computer center. Commuter students can connect to campus network. Online course registration, online library, helpline, wireless network available.

Student life. Freshman orientation: Mandatory. Preregistration for classes offered. Groups of 100 meet for an afternoon. **Activities:** Bands, campus ministries, choral groups, dance, drama, literary magazine, music ensembles, musical theater, student government.

Athletics. Intramural: Basketball. **Team name:** Mustangs.

Student services. Career counseling, student employment services, financial aid counseling, personal counseling, veterans' counselor. **Physically disabled:** Services for visually, speech, hearing impaired. **Transfer:** Pre-admission transcript evaluation for new students. Transfer adviser, college fairs on campus for students transferring to 4-year colleges.

Contact. E-mail: niblettt@nacc.edu
Phone: (256) 228-6001 ext. 222 Fax: (256) 638-6043
Tonie Niblett, Dean of Student Services, Northeast Alabama Community College, Admissions Office, NACC, Rainsville, AL 35986-0159

Northwest-Shoals Community College
Muscle Shoals, Alabama
www.nwscc.edu   CB code: 0188

- Public 2-year community and technical college
- Commuter campus in large town

General. Founded in 1966. Regionally accredited. Two campuses: Phil Campbell and Muscle Shoals. **Enrollment:** 3,473 degree-seeking undergraduates; 466 non-degree-seeking students. **Degrees:** 295 associate awarded. **Location:** 120 miles from Birmingham; 134 miles from Memphis, Tennessee. **Calendar:** Semester, extensive summer session. **Full-time faculty:** 84 total; 6% have terminal degrees, 10% minority, 50% women. **Part-time faculty:** 149 total; 7% have terminal degrees, 9% minority, 58% women.

Student profile. Among degree-seeking undergraduates, 42% enrolled in a transfer program, 34% enrolled in a vocational program, 894 enrolled as first-time, first-year students, 328 transferred in from other institutions.

Part-time:	40%	African American:	11%
Out-of-state:	1%	Hispanic American:	3%
Women:	58%	25 or older:	30%

Transfer out. 18% of students enrolled in the transfer program go on to 4-year colleges. **Colleges most students transferred to 2011:** University of North Alabama, University of Alabama, Athens State University, University of Alabama at Huntsville.

Basis for selection. Open admission, but selective for some programs. Additional requirements for health occupation programs. **Home schooled:** Equivalent number of required units for graduation and 16 ACT or 790 SAT (exclusive of Writing) required.

High school preparation. 22 units recommended. Recommended units include English 4, mathematics 2, social studies 3 and science 4.

2011-2012 Annual costs. Tuition/fees: $4,020; $7,230 out-of-state. Per-credit charge: $107 in-state; $214 out-of-state. Books/supplies: $1,300. Personal expenses: $1,000.

2010-2011 Financial aid. Need-based: 68% of total undergraduate aid awarded as scholarships/grants, 32% as loans/jobs. Need-based aid available for part-time students. Work-study available nights, weekends and for part-time students. **Non-need-based:** Scholarships awarded for academics, art, leadership, minority status, music/drama.

Application procedures. Admission: No deadline. No application fee. Admission notification on a rolling basis. **Financial aid:** Priority date 4/1, closing date 8/1. FAFSA, institutional form required. Applicants notified on a rolling basis; must reply within 2 week(s) of notification.

Academics. Special study options: Accelerated study, cooperative education, cross-registration, distance learning, dual enrollment of high school students, honors, independent study, internships, liberal arts/career combination. License preparation in nursing, paramedic. **Credit/placement by examination:** AP, CLEP, institutional tests. 30 credit hours maximum toward associate degree. **Support services:** GED preparation and test center, learning center, pre-admission summer program, remedial instruction, tutoring.

Majors. Business: Administrative services. **Computer sciences:** General, applications programming, information systems, information technology, programming. **Health services:** EMT paramedic, nursing (RN). **Liberal arts:** Arts/sciences. **Protective services:** Police science. **Work/family studies:** Child care management.

Most popular majors. Business/marketing 6%, health sciences 29%, interdisciplinary studies 8%, liberal arts 44%.

Computing on campus. 850 workstations in library, computer center. Online course registration, online library, helpline, repair service, wireless network available.

Student life. Freshman orientation: Mandatory, $10 fee. Preregistration for classes offered. Program includes components for developing research skills and good study habits. Occupational students also receive orientation to work ethics and workplace readiness. **Activities:** Bands, campus ministries, choral groups, music ensembles, student government, Phi Theta Kappa, Ambassadors, Music Educators National Conference, College Bowl team, science club, American Society of Heating, Refrigerating and Air Conditioning Engineers, Baptist campus ministries, Patriots for Christ, NW-SCC fishing club, Skills USA.

Athletics. Intramural: Basketball, football (non-tackle), table tennis. **Team name:** Patriots.

Student services. Career counseling, student employment services, financial aid counseling, on-campus daycare, personal counseling, placement for graduates, veterans' counselor. **Physically disabled:** Services for visually, speech, hearing impaired. **Transfer:** Pre-admission transcript evaluation for new students. Transfer adviser, college fairs on campus for students transferring to 4-year colleges.

Contact. Phone: (256) 331-5363 Fax: (256) 331-5366
Karen Berryhill, Vice President for Student Development Services, Northwest-Shoals Community College, PO Box 2545, Muscle Shoals, AL 35662

Prince Institute of Professional Studies
Montgomery, Alabama
www.princeinstitute.edu   CB code: 3450

- For-profit 2-year technical and career college
- Commuter campus in large city
- Interview required

General. Accredited by ACICS. **Enrollment:** 96 undergraduates. **Degrees:** 4 associate awarded. **Calendar:** Quarter, limited summer session. **Full-time faculty:** 15 total. **Part-time faculty:** 5 total.

Basis for selection. Open admission. **Home schooled:** Transcript of courses and grades required.

2011-2012 Annual costs. Tuition/fees: $8,695. Per-credit charge: $234. Books/supplies: $2,000. Personal expenses: $1,674.

Financial aid. All financial aid based on need. Need-based aid available for part-time students. Work-study available nights, weekends and for part-time students.

Application procedures. Admission: No deadline. $125 fee. Applications must be received before class start. **Financial aid:** No deadline. FAFSA required.

Academics. Special study options: Distance learning. **Credit/placement by examination:** AP, CLEP.

Majors. Computer sciences: Information systems. **Health services:** Medical transcription.

Student life. Freshman orientation: Available. Preregistration for classes offered. **Activities:** Student newspaper.

Student services. Transfer: Re-entry adviser, pre-admission transcript evaluation for new students.

Contact. E-mail: shill@princeinstitute.edu
Phone: (334) 271-1670 ext. 209 Toll-free number: (877) 853-5569
Fax: (334) 271-1671
Sherry Hill, Admissions Director, Prince Institute of Professional Studies, 7735 Atlanta Highway, Montgomery, AL 36117-4231

Remington College: Mobile
Mobile, Alabama
www.remingtoncollege.edu   CB code: 3157

- For-profit 2-year career college
- Commuter campus in large city

General. Accredited by ACCSC. **Enrollment:** 623 degree-seeking undergraduates. **Degrees:** 1 bachelor's, 46 associate awarded. **Calendar:** Quarter, extensive summer session. **Full-time faculty:** 20 total. **Part-time faculty:** 28 total.

Basis for selection. Open admission. **Home schooled:** Transcript of courses and grades, state high school equivalency certificate required.

Financial aid. All financial aid based on need. Work-study available nights, weekends and for part-time students.

Application procedures. Admission: No deadline. $50 fee. **Financial aid:** FAFSA required.

Academics. Special study options: Cooperative education, distance learning, honors, liberal arts/career combination. **Credit/placement by examination:** AP, CLEP. **Support services:** Tutoring.

Majors. Computer sciences: System admin. **Protective services:** Law enforcement admin.

Computing on campus. PC or laptop required. Online library, helpline, repair service, wireless network available.

Student life. Freshman orientation: Mandatory. Preregistration for classes offered. Held the week before class for 2 1/2 hours.

Student services. Career counseling, financial aid counseling, placement for graduates. **Transfer:** Pre-admission transcript evaluation for new students.

Contact. E-mail: admissions@remingtoncollege.edu
Phone: (251) 343-8200 Toll-free number: (800) 866-0850
Fax: (251) 343-8200
Brent Malveaux, Director of Admissions, Remington College: Mobile, 828 Downtowner Loop West, Mobile, AL 36609-5404

Shelton State Community College
Tuscaloosa, Alabama
www.sheltonstate.edu   CB code: 3338

- Public 2-year community and technical college
- Commuter campus in small city

General. Founded in 1963. Regionally accredited. Designated as Alabama's Community College of the Fine Arts; includes C.A. Fredd campus, a Historically Black College. **Enrollment:** 5,313 degree-seeking undergraduates. **Degrees:** 386 associate awarded. **ROTC:** Army, Air Force. **Location:** 60 miles from Birmingham. **Calendar:** Semester, extensive summer session.

Full-time faculty: 93 total. **Part-time faculty:** 213 total. **Class size:** 42% < 20, 48% 20-39, 10% 40-49, less than 1% 50-99. **Special facilities:** Observatories, wellness center, community theatre.

Student profile.

Out-of-state: 5%   25 or older: 32%

Transfer out. Colleges most students transferred to 2011: University of Alabama, Auburn University, Stillman College, University of Alabama at Birmingham.

Basis for selection. Open admission. COMPASS test required of all first-time freshmen for placement unless students submit ACT.

2011-2012 Annual costs. Tuition/fees: $4,080; $7,290 out-of-state. Per-credit charge: $107 in-state; $214 out-of-state. Cost of tools and uniforms: $750. Books/supplies: $750. Personal expenses: $200.

Financial aid. All financial aid based on need. Need-based aid available for part-time students. Work-study available nights, weekends and for part-time students.

Application procedures. Admission: No deadline. No application fee. Admission notification on a rolling basis. **Financial aid:** Priority date 6/30; no closing date. FAFSA required. Applicants notified on a rolling basis starting 7/30.

Academics. Special study options: Accelerated study, distance learning, double major, dual enrollment of high school students, honors, liberal arts/career combination. License preparation in nursing, real estate. **Credit/placement by examination:** AP, CLEP, IB, institutional tests. 20 credit hours maximum toward associate degree. **Support services:** GED preparation and test center, learning center, reduced course load, remedial instruction, study skills assistance, tutoring.

Majors. Architecture: Technology. **Business:** Administrative services. **Education:** General, music, secondary. **Engineering:** General. **Health services:** Nursing (RN), respiratory therapy technology. **Human services:** Social work. **Liberal arts:** Arts/sciences. **Math:** General. **Visual/performing arts:** Studio arts.

Most popular majors. Business/marketing 25%, health sciences 26%, liberal arts 33%, trade and industry 11%.

Computing on campus. 300 workstations in library, computer center. Commuter students can connect to campus network. Online course registration, wireless network available.

Student life. Freshman orientation: Mandatory. Preregistration for classes offered. **Activities:** Jazz band, choral groups, dance, drama, music ensembles, musical theater, student government, student newspaper, Phi Theta Kappa, Circle K.

Athletics. NJCAA. **Intercollegiate:** Baseball M, basketball, cheerleading, soccer W, softball W. **Team name:** Buccaneers.

Student services. Career counseling, student employment services, financial aid counseling, personal counseling, placement for graduates, veterans' counselor. **Transfer:** College fairs on campus for students transferring to 4-year colleges.

Contact. E-mail: admissions@sheltonstate.edu
Phone: (205) 391-2214 Fax: (205) 391-3910
Byron Abston, Director of Admissions, Shelton State Community College, 9500 Old Greensboro Road, Tuscaloosa, AL 35405-8522

Snead State Community College
Boaz, Alabama
www.snead.edu
CB code: 1721

- Public 2-year community college
- Commuter campus in small town

General. Founded in 1898. Regionally accredited. Upper-level courses offered on campus through Athens State University and distance learning. **Enrollment:** 2,417 degree-seeking undergraduates. **Degrees:** 345 associate awarded. **Location:** 65 miles from Birmingham. **Calendar:** Semester, extensive summer session. **Full-time faculty:** 34 total. **Part-time faculty:** 88 total. **Special facilities:** Museum, state diagnostic lab. **Partnerships:** Formal partnership with Marshall County Tech Prep Consortium (grant writer and fiscal agent for eight secondary schools).

Student profile.

Out-of-state: 2%   Live on campus: 4%
25 or older: 33%

Transfer out. Colleges most students transferred to 2011: Jacksonville State University, Auburn University, University of Alabama, University of Alabama at Birmingham, University of Alabama in Huntsville.

Basis for selection. Open admission. 16 ACT or equivalent SAT required for high school graduates from non-accredited schools and for those receiving occupational diplomas.

High school preparation. 24 units recommended. Recommended units include English 4, mathematics 4, social studies 4, science 4, foreign language 2 and academic electives 8. Half unit fine arts, 1/2 computer applications, 5 1/2 electives recommended.

2011-2012 Annual costs. Tuition/fees: $4,140; $7,350 out-of-state. Per-credit charge: $107 in-state; $214 out-of-state. Room/board: $3,390. Books/supplies: $1,050. Personal expenses: $1,200.

Financial aid. Need-based: Need-based aid available for part-time students. Work-study available nights, weekends and for part-time students. **Non-need-based:** Scholarships awarded for academics, alumni affiliation, art, athletics, leadership, music/drama.

Application procedures. Admission: Closing date 8/14 (postmark date). No application fee. Application must be submitted on paper. Admission notification on a rolling basis. **Financial aid:** Closing date 4/15. FAFSA required. Applicants notified on a rolling basis starting 4/15.

Academics. Special study options: Accelerated study, distance learning, dual enrollment of high school students, independent study, internships, student-designed major. **Credit/placement by examination:** AP, CLEP, institutional tests. 20 credit hours maximum toward associate degree. **Support services:** GED preparation and test center, learning center, remedial instruction, study skills assistance, tutoring, writing center.

Majors. Business: Administrative services. **Computer sciences:** General. **Engineering:** General. **Health services:** Nursing (RN). **Liberal arts:** Arts/sciences. **Work/family studies:** Child care management.

Computing on campus. 350 workstations in library, computer center, student center. Online course registration, online library available.

Student life. Freshman orientation: Available, $94 fee. Preregistration for classes offered. Orientation offered on 2 consecutive Fridays or Saturdays. **Housing:** Coed dorms available. $25 deposit. **Activities:** Jazz band, choral groups, music ensembles, student government, student newspaper, Baptist campus ministry, Ambassadors, agricultural organization, Phi Beta Lambda, Phi Theta Kappa, College Republicans, Civitans.

Athletics. NJCAA. **Intercollegiate:** Baseball M, basketball, softball W, tennis W. **Intramural:** Basketball, softball, table tennis, volleyball. **Team name:** Parsons.

Student services. Chaplain/spiritual director, career counseling, services for economically disadvantaged, student employment services, financial aid counseling, personal counseling, placement for graduates, veterans' counselor. **Physically disabled:** Services for visually, speech, hearing impaired. **Transfer:** Pre-admission transcript evaluation for new students. Transfer center, transfer adviser, college fairs on campus for students transferring to 4-year colleges.

Contact. E-mail: studentservices@snead.edu
Phone: (256) 593-5120 ext. 207 Fax: (256) 593-7180
Jason Cannon, Admissions and Records Director, Snead State Community College, PO Box 734, Boaz, AL 35957-0734

Southern Union State Community College
Wadley, Alabama
www.suscc.edu
CB code: 1728

- Public 2-year community and technical college
- Commuter campus in small city

General. Founded in 1963. Regionally accredited. Additional campuses in Opelika and Valley. **Enrollment:** 4,852 undergraduates. **Degrees:** 507 associate awarded. **Location:** 90 miles from Atlanta, 90 miles from Birmingham. **Calendar:** Semester, extensive summer session. **Full-time faculty:** 85 total. **Part-time faculty:** 240 total.

Student profile.

Out-of-state:	20%	Live on campus:	4%
25 or older:	25%		

Basis for selection. Open admission, but selective for some programs. Criteria for some health sciences programs include test scores. **Home schooled:** Transcript of courses and grades required.

2011-2012 Annual costs. Tuition/fees: $4,350; $6,990 out-of-state. Per-credit charge: $107 in-state; $214 out-of-state. Room/board: $3,200. Books/supplies: $400. Personal expenses: $1,100.

Financial aid. Need-based: Need-based aid available for part-time students. Work-study available nights, weekends and for part-time students.

Application procedures. Admission: No deadline. No application fee. Admission notification on a rolling basis. **Financial aid:** Priority date 4/1; no closing date. FAFSA required. Applicants notified on a rolling basis.

Academics. Special study options: Accelerated study, distance learning, dual enrollment of high school students. License preparation in nursing, paramedic, radiology. **Credit/placement by examination:** AP, CLEP. **Support services:** GED preparation and test center, remedial instruction, tutoring.

Majors. Biology: General. **Business:** General, accounting, administrative services, office management. **Communications:** Communications/speech/rhetoric. **Computer sciences:** General. **Education:** Physical. **Health services:** EMT paramedic, insurance coding, nursing (RN), radiologic technology/medical imaging. **Physical sciences:** Chemistry. **Social sciences:** General.

Student life. Freshman orientation: Available. Preregistration for classes offered. Held during June and July. **Housing:** Single-sex dorms, wellness housing available. **Activities:** Campus ministries, choral groups, dance, drama, musical theater, student government, student newspaper, association of radiologic students, global environmental organization of students, music club, letterman's club, National Student Nurses' Association, Phi Beta Lambda, Phi Theta Kappa, Southern Union Players.

Athletics. NJCAA. **Intercollegiate:** Baseball M, basketball, cheerleading, cross-country, softball W, volleyball W. **Team name:** Bison.

Student services. Adult student services, career counseling, financial aid counseling.

Contact. E-mail: cstringfellow@suscc.edu
Phone: (256) 395-2211 Fax: (256) 395-2215
Catherine Stringfellow, Registrar, Southern Union State Community College, 750 Roberts Street, Wadley, AL 36276

Virginia College at Mobile
Mobile, Alabama
www.vc.edu/mobile

▶ For-profit 2-year technical and career college
▶ Commuter campus in large city

General. Accredited by ACICS. **Enrollment:** 682 degree-seeking undergraduates. **Degrees:** 101 associate awarded. **Calendar:** Differs by program.

Basis for selection. Open admission, but selective for some programs.

2011-2012 Annual costs. Tuition/fees: $21,900. Tuition is typical for full-time attendance for four quarters and depends on program, hours attempted, and other factors. Tuition includes textbooks and fees.

Financial aid. Need-based: Work-study available nights, weekends and for part-time students.

Application procedures. Admission: No deadline. Admission notification on a rolling basis.

Academics. Special study options: Accelerated study, independent study. **Credit/placement by examination:** AP, CLEP.

Majors. Business: Administrative services, business admin, office management. **Health services:** Medical assistant, nursing (RN), surgical technology.

Contact. Phone: (251) 343-7227 Toll-free number: (888) 208-6932
Fax: (251) 343-7287
April Martin, Director of Admissions, Virginia College at Mobile, 3725 Airport Boulevard, Suite 165, Mobile, AL 36608

Virginia College at Montgomery
Montgomery, Alabama
www.vc.edu

▶ For-profit 2-year health science and career college
▶ Large city

General. Regionally accredited; also accredited by ACICS. **Enrollment:** 815 degree-seeking undergraduates. **Degrees:** 15 associate awarded. **Calendar:** Quarter. **Full-time faculty:** 12 total. **Part-time faculty:** 16 total.

Basis for selection. Selective admissions to certain programs.

2011-2012 Annual costs. Tuition/fees: $21,900. Tuition is typical for full-time attendance for four quarters and depends on program, hours attempted, and other factors. Tuition includes textbooks and fees.

Financial aid. Need-based: Work-study available nights, weekends and for part-time students.

Application procedures. Financial aid: Closing date 9/30.

Academics. Credit/placement by examination: AP, CLEP.

Majors. Business: Administrative services, business admin, office management. **Health services:** Massage therapy, nursing (RN), office admin, surgical technology.

Contact. Phone: (334) 277-3390
Lawrence Brown, Director of Admissions, Virginia College at Montgomery, 6200 Atlanta Highway, Montgomery, AL 36117

Wallace State Community College at Hanceville
Hanceville, Alabama
www.wallacestate.edu   CB code: 0528

▶ Public 2-year health science and community college
▶ Commuter campus in rural community

General. Founded in 1966. Regionally accredited. **Enrollment:** 5,741 degree-seeking undergraduates. **Degrees:** 995 associate awarded. **Location:** 35 miles from Birmingham, 50 miles from Huntsville. **Calendar:** Semester, limited summer session. **Full-time faculty:** 129 total. **Part-time faculty:** 159 total. **Special facilities:** Genealogy collection, recording studio, nature trail, college-operated museum, advanced visualization center (3-D).

Student profile. Among degree-seeking undergraduates, 67% enrolled in a transfer program, 33% enrolled in a vocational program, 2% already have a bachelor's degree or higher, 1,048 enrolled as first-time, first-year students.

Part-time:	43%	Women:	64%

Transfer out. Colleges most students transferred to 2011: Athens State College, University of Alabama, University of Alabama in Huntsville, University of Alabama at Birmingham, Auburn University.

Basis for selection. Open admission, but selective for some programs. ACT required of applicants to certain allied health programs. National League for Nursing, Pre-Nursing and Guidance Examination required for nursing applicants. Interview recommended for health program applicants; auditions recommended for music education majors.

2011-2012 Annual costs. Tuition/fees: $4,080; $7,290 out-of-state. Per-credit charge: $107 in-state; $214 out-of-state. Room only: $1,800. Books/supplies: $700. Personal expenses: $2,650.

Financial aid. All financial aid based on need. Need-based aid available for part-time students. Work-study available nights, weekends and for part-time students.

Application procedures. Admission: No deadline. No application fee. Admission notification on a rolling basis beginning on or about 7/15. **Financial aid:** Priority date 5/1; no closing date. FAFSA required. Applicants notified on a rolling basis starting 7/15; must reply within 2 week(s) of notification.

Academics. Special study options: Accelerated study, cooperative education, distance learning, double major, dual enrollment of high school students, internships, weekend college. Bachelor's degree programs available on campus. License preparation in aviation, dental hygiene, nursing, occupational therapy, paramedic, physical therapy, radiology, real estate. **Credit/placement by examination:** AP, CLEP, institutional tests. 26 credit hours maximum toward associate degree. **Support services:** GED preparation and test

center, learning center, reduced course load, remedial instruction, study skills assistance, tutoring.

Majors. Business: General, accounting, banking/financial services, fashion, insurance, labor relations, office management, office/clerical, sales/distribution. **Computer sciences:** Data processing, programming. **Education:** General. **Engineering:** General, electrical. **General:** Agribusiness operations. **Health services:** Athletic training, clinical lab technology, dental assistant, dental hygiene, EMT paramedic, medical assistant, medical radiologic technology/radiation therapy, medical records technology, nursing (RN), occupational therapy assistant, physical therapy assistant, respiratory therapy technology, sonography, substance abuse counseling. **Liberal arts:** Arts/sciences. **Parks/recreation:** Facilities management. **Protective services:** Police science. **Visual/performing arts:** Art, fashion design, interior design, music. **Work/family studies:** Child care management, food/nutrition, institutional food production.

Most popular majors. Business/marketing 6%, health sciences 61%, liberal arts 17%.

Computing on campus. 65 workstations in library, computer center. Commuter students can connect to campus network. Online course registration, online library, helpline, wireless network available.

Student life. Freshman orientation: Available. Preregistration for classes offered. **Housing:** Single-sex dorms, wellness housing available. $200 deposit. **Activities:** Bands, choral groups, drama, music ensembles, student government, student newspaper, Baptist campus ministry.

Athletics. NJCAA. **Intercollegiate:** Baseball M, basketball, cheerleading, cross-country, golf M, soccer M, softball W, track and field M, volleyball. **Intramural:** Badminton, basketball, softball, tennis, track and field, volleyball. **Team name:** Lions.

Student services. Chaplain/spiritual director, career counseling, student employment services, financial aid counseling, placement for graduates, veterans' counselor. **Physically disabled:** Services for visually, speech, hearing impaired. **Transfer:** Transfer adviser, college fairs on campus for students transferring to 4-year colleges.

Contact. Phone: (256) 352-8236 Toll-free number: (866) 350-9722
Fax: (256) 352-8129
Linda Sperling, Director of Admissions/Registrar, Wallace State Community College at Hanceville, PO Box 2000, Hanceville, AL 35077-2000

Alaska

Ilisagvik College
Barrow, Alaska
www.ilisagvik.edu   CB code: 0469

▶ Public 2-year Tribal community college
▶ Commuter campus in rural community

General. **Enrollment:** 110 degree-seeking undergraduates; 116 non-degree-seeking students. **Degrees:** 11 associate awarded. **Location:** 500 miles from Fairbanks. **Calendar:** Semester, limited summer session. **Full-time faculty:** 12 total. **Part-time faculty:** 19 total.

Student profile. Among degree-seeking undergraduates, 13% enrolled in a transfer program, 1% enrolled in a vocational program, 22 enrolled as first-time, first-year students, 14 transferred in from other institutions.

Part-time:	53%	Asian American:	11%
Women:	73%	Hispanic American:	3%
African American:	2%	Native American:	68%

2011-2012 Annual costs. Tuition/fees: $2,820; $4,020 out-of-state. Per-credit charge: $100 in-state; $150 out-of-state. Room/board: $10,650. Books/supplies: $800. Personal expenses: $2,730.

2010-2011 Financial aid. All financial aid based on need. 10 full-time freshmen applied for aid; 9 were judged to have need; 9 of these received aid. Average need met was 66%. Average scholarship/grant was $7,170. 81% of total undergraduate aid awarded as scholarships/grants, 19% as loans/jobs. Need-based aid available for part-time students. Work-study available nights, weekends and for part-time students.

Application procedures. **Admission:** Closing date 8/9 (receipt date). No application fee. Application must be submitted on paper. Admission notification on a rolling basis. **Financial aid:** Closing date 4/15. FAFSA required. Applicants notified by 4/15; must reply by 4/15.

Academics. Many Inupiat Eskimo traditional courses offered. **Special study options:** Double major, dual enrollment of high school students, ESL, independent study. **Credit/placement by examination:** AP, CLEP. 12 credit hours maximum toward associate degree. **Support services:** GED preparation, remedial instruction, tutoring.

Majors. **Area/ethnic studies:** Native American. **Business:** Accounting, business admin, management science, office management.

Computing on campus. Commuter students can connect to campus network. Helpline, wireless network available.

Student life. **Freshman orientation:** Available. Preregistration for classes offered. **Housing:** Coed dorms, apartments available. **Activities:** Student government.

Student services. Financial aid counseling, personal counseling.

Contact. E-mail: amm.cahoon@ilisagvik.edu
Phone: (907) 852-1763 Toll-free number: (800) 478-7337 ext. 1763
Fax: (907) 852-1784
Dararath Cahoon, Registrar Officer, Ilisagvik College, 100 Stevenson Road, Barrow, AK 99723

Prince William Sound Community College
Valdez, Alaska
www.pwscc.edu   CB code: 4636

▶ Public 2-year community college
▶ Commuter campus in small town

General. Founded in 1978. Regionally accredited. Service area of 44,000 square miles. Full schedule of courses plus live video and audio conferencing for students in remote areas. Off-campus centers at Cordova and Glennallen offer credit-bearing courses. **Enrollment:** 210 degree-seeking undergraduates. **Degrees:** 18 associate awarded. **Location:** 300 miles from Anchorage. **Calendar:** Semester, limited summer session. **Full-time faculty:** 9 total.

Part-time faculty: 50 total. **Class size:** 94% < 20, 5% 20-39, less than 1% 40-49, less than 1% 50-99, less than 1% >100. **Special facilities:** Alaska native museum.

Student profile.

African American:	10%	Hispanic American:	16%
Asian American:	10%	Native American:	9%

Transfer out. Colleges most students transferred to 2011: University of Alaska-Anchorage.

Basis for selection. Open admission. Open admission policy does not apply to international students. **Home schooled:** Statement describing home school structure and mission required.

2011-2012 Annual costs. Tuition/fees: $4,350; $4,350 out-of-state. Per-credit charge: $133. Room only: $5,000. Books/supplies: $800. Personal expenses: $2,206.

Financial aid. **Need-based:** Need-based aid available for part-time students. Work-study available nights, weekends and for part-time students. **Non-need-based:** Scholarships awarded for state residency.

Application procedures. **Admission:** No deadline. $25 fee. **Financial aid:** Priority date 6/30; no closing date. FAFSA required. Applicants notified on a rolling basis.

Academics. **Special study options:** Distance learning, double major, dual enrollment of high school students, ESL, external degree, honors, independent study, internships. Bachelor's degree programs available on campus. **Credit/placement by examination:** AP, CLEP, IB, institutional tests. **Support services:** GED preparation and test center, learning center, reduced course load, remedial instruction, study skills assistance, tutoring.

Majors. **Business:** Office management. **Liberal arts:** Arts/sciences.

Computing on campus. 50 workstations in dormitories, library, computer center. Online library, helpline available.

Student life. **Freshman orientation:** Available. Preregistration for classes offered. **Housing:** Coed dorms, apartments, wellness housing available. $400 fully refundable deposit. **Activities:** Drama, film society, student government.

Student services. Adult student services, career counseling, financial aid counseling, veterans' counselor. **Transfer:** Transfer adviser, college fairs on campus for students transferring to 4-year colleges.

Contact. E-mail: sfoster@pwscc.edu
Phone: (907) 834-1632 Toll-free number: (800) 478-8800
Fax: (907) 834-1635
Shannon Foster, Registrar, Prince William Sound Community College, Box 97, Valdez, AK 99686

Arizona

Anthem College: Phoenix
Phoenix, Arizona
www.anthem.edu

- For-profit 2-year technical college
- Commuter campus in very large city
- Interview required

General. Regionally accredited; also accredited by ACICS. **Enrollment:** 2,646 degree-seeking undergraduates. **Degrees:** 55 bachelor's, 66 associate awarded. **Calendar:** Differs by program, extensive summer session. **Full-time faculty:** 14 total. **Part-time faculty:** 129 total.

Basis for selection. Open admission. **Home schooled:** Transcript of courses and grades, state high school equivalency certificate, interview required.

2011-2012 Annual costs. Personal expenses: $205.

Financial aid. All financial aid based on need. Work-study available nights, weekends and for part-time students.

Application procedures. Admission: No deadline. $20 fee. Application must be submitted on paper. Admission notification on a rolling basis. **Financial aid:** No deadline.

Academics. Special study options: Distance learning. Bachelor's degree programs available on campus. **Credit/placement by examination:** AP, CLEP, institutional tests. **Support services:** GED preparation, study skills assistance, tutoring.

Majors. Business: Business admin. **Computer sciences:** Security, web page design. **Engineering:** General, electrical. **Health services:** Insurance specialist, office computer specialist. **Protective services:** Police science.

Most popular majors. Computer/information sciences 73%, health sciences 27%.

Computing on campus. 2 workstations in library, computer center. Commuter students can connect to campus network. Online course registration, online library, helpline available.

Student life. Freshman orientation: Mandatory. Preregistration for classes offered.

Student services. Financial aid counseling, placement for graduates. **Transfer:** Pre-admission transcript evaluation for new students.

Contact. Phone: (602) 279-9700 Toll-free number: (800) 832-4011 Fax: (602) 279-2999
Teri Garver, Director of Admissions, Anthem College: Phoenix, 1515 East Indian School Road, Phoenix, AZ 85014-4901

Arizona Automotive Institute
Glendale, Arizona
www.aai.edu   **CB code: 3196**

- For-profit 2-year technical college
- Commuter campus in small city

General. Founded in 1967. Accredited by ACCSC. **Enrollment:** 1,059 degree-seeking undergraduates. **Degrees:** 427 associate awarded. **Location:** 2 miles from Phoenix. **Calendar:** Quarter, extensive summer session. **Full-time faculty:** 48 total; 4% women. **Part-time faculty:** 3 total.

Basis for selection. Open admission. GED or high school diploma required. Interview highly recommended. **Home schooled:** Transcript of courses and grades, state high school equivalency certificate required.

2012-2013 Annual costs. Tuition/fees (projected): $28,880.

Financial aid. Need-based: Work-study available nights, weekends and for part-time students.

Application procedures. Admission: No deadline. $100 fee. Admission notification on a rolling basis. **Financial aid:** No deadline. FAFSA, institutional form required. Applicants notified on a rolling basis.

Academics. Credit/placement by examination: AP, CLEP. **Support services:** Tutoring.

Computing on campus. 15 workstations in library.

Student life. Freshman orientation: Available. Preregistration for classes offered. **Housing:** Apartments available.

Athletics. Intramural: Basketball M, bowling, football (tackle) M, softball.

Student services. Career counseling, student employment services, personal counseling, placement for graduates, veterans' counselor.

Contact. E-mail: info@azautoinst.com
Phone: (623) 934-7273 Fax: (623) 937-5000
Deborah Armstrong, Director of Admissions, Arizona Automotive Institute, 6829 North 46th Avenue, Glendale, AZ 85301

Arizona Western College
Yuma, Arizona   **CB member**
www.azwestern.edu   **CB code: 4013**

- Public 2-year community college
- Commuter campus in small city

General. Founded in 1963. Regionally accredited. Satellite sites in Parker, San Luis-Somerton, Wellton. Campus shared with Northern Arizona University, which offers completion of bachelor's, master's and doctoral programs. **Enrollment:** 7,915 degree-seeking undergraduates; 503 non-degree-seeking students. **Degrees:** 678 associate awarded. **Location:** 7 miles from Yuma. **Calendar:** Semester, limited summer session. **Full-time faculty:** 109 total; 19% minority, 45% women. **Part-time faculty:** 325 total; 32% minority, 49% women. **Class size:** 10% <20, 14% 20-39, 13% 40-49, 14% 50-99, 49% >100. **Partnerships:** Formal partnerships with Yuma Educational Consortium, Yuma Regional Medical Center.

Student profile. Among degree-seeking undergraduates, 20% enrolled in a transfer program, 17% enrolled in a vocational program, 2,369 enrolled as first-time, first-year students.

Part-time:	65%	Hispanic American:	61%
Out-of-state:	3%	Native American:	1%
Women:	57%	International:	9%
African American:	3%	25 or older:	37%
Asian American:	1%		

Transfer out. Colleges most students transferred to 2011: Northern Arizona University at Yuma, Arizona State University, University of Arizona, Universtiy of Phoenix.

Basis for selection. Open admission, but selective for some programs. Special requirements for students under age 18, international students, undergraduate exchange program, Colorado River Consortium, nursing program, massage therapy program, radiologic technology program. **Home schooled:** Admissions decision dependent upon one or more of the following: placement test scores, academic history, current course enrollment, instructor approval. **Learning Disabled:** Proof of disability written by specialist must be submitted to Coordinator of Services for Students with Disabilities at least 8 weeks before start of classes to ensure accommodations by the first day of class.

High school preparation. College-preparatory program recommended.

2012-2013 Annual costs. Tuition/fees (projected): $2,300; $7,478 out-of-state. Per-credit charge: $70 in-state; $242 out-of-state. Room/board: $5,610. Books/supplies: $1,404. Personal expenses: $3,276.

Financial aid. Need-based: Need-based aid available for part-time students. Work-study available nights, weekends and for part-time students. **Non-need-based:** Scholarships awarded for academics, art, athletics, leadership, minority status, music/drama.

Application procedures. Admission: No deadline. No application fee. Admission notification on a rolling basis. **Financial aid:** Priority date 4/1; no closing date. FAFSA, institutional form required. Applicants notified on a rolling basis starting 5/1.

Academics. Special study options: Accelerated study, cooperative education, distance learning, dual enrollment of high school students, ESL, honors, independent study, internships, study abroad, teacher certification program,

weekend college. License preparation in nursing, occupational therapy, paramedic, radiology. **Credit/placement by examination:** AP, CLEP, IB, institutional tests. 24 credit hours maximum toward associate degree. **Support services:** GED preparation, learning center, reduced course load, remedial instruction, study skills assistance, tutoring, writing center.

Majors. Biology: General. **Business:** General, business admin, hospitality admin, management science, marketing, office management. **Communications:** Communications/speech/rhetoric, radio/TV. **Communications technology:** Radio/TV. **Computer sciences:** General, computer graphics, data entry. **Conservation:** Environmental science. **Education:** General, secondary. **Engineering:** General. **English:** English lit. **Foreign languages:** Spanish. **General:** Business, crop production, plant sciences. **Health services:** EMT paramedic, massage therapy, nursing (RN), radiologic technology/medical imaging. **History:** General. **Math:** General. **Parks/recreation:** Health/fitness. **Philosophy/religion:** Philosophy. **Physical sciences:** Chemistry, oceanography, physics. **Protective services:** Firefighting, law enforcement admin, police science. **Social sciences:** General, political science. **Visual/performing arts:** Dramatic, multimedia, music, studio arts. **Work/family studies:** General, child development.

Most popular majors. Business/marketing 12%, education 10%, health sciences 17%, liberal arts 32%, security/protective services 8%.

Computing on campus. 270 workstations in dormitories, library, computer center, student center. Dormitories wired for high-speed internet access and linked to campus network. Commuter students can connect to campus network. Online course registration, online library, helpline, repair service, student web hosting, wireless network available.

Student life. Freshman orientation: Available. Preregistration for classes offered. **Housing:** Coed dorms, single-sex dorms, special housing for disabled, wellness housing available. $100 fully refundable deposit. **Activities:** Bands, choral groups, dance, drama, international student organizations, literary magazine, music ensembles, radio station, student government, student newspaper, TV station, AACHE, Phi Theta Kappa, Native American club, Hispanic students club.

Athletics. NJCAA. **Intercollegiate:** Baseball M, basketball, football (tackle) M, soccer M, softball W, volleyball W. **Team name:** Matadors.

Student services. Adult student services, alcohol/substance abuse counseling, career counseling, services for economically disadvantaged, student employment services, financial aid counseling, health services, minority student services, on-campus daycare, personal counseling, placement for graduates, veterans' counselor, women's services. **Physically disabled:** Services for visually, speech, hearing impaired. **Transfer:** Pre-admission transcript evaluation for new students. Transfer center, transfer adviser, college fairs on campus for students transferring to 4-year colleges.

Contact. E-mail: amy.pignatore@azwestern.edu
Phone: (928) 317-6000 Toll-free number: (888) 293-0392
Fax: (928) 344-7543
Amy Pignatore, Director of Admissions/Registrar, Arizona Western College, PO Box 929, Yuma, AZ 85366-0929

Brookline College: Phoenix
Phoenix, Arizona
www.brooklinecollege.edu   CB code: 2188

- For-profit 2-year career college
- Commuter campus in very large city
- Interview required

General. Accredited by ACICS. Additional campuses in Tempe, Tucson, Albuquerque, and Oklahoma City. **Enrollment:** 940 degree-seeking undergraduates. **Degrees:** 11 bachelor's, 115 associate awarded. **Calendar:** Differs by program, extensive summer session. **Full-time faculty:** 60 total. **Part-time faculty:** 25 total.

Basis for selection. Open admission. Must be 18 years of age or 17 years 6 months with parent or legal guardian consent. Must be citizen of the US or eligible non-citizen as classified by Department of Homeland Security. **Home schooled:** Letter of Attestation required.

2011-2012 Annual costs. Personal expenses: $5,880.

Financial aid. All financial aid based on need. Work-study available nights, weekends and for part-time students.

Application procedures. Admission: No deadline. No application fee. Admission notification on a rolling basis. **Financial aid:** No deadline. FAFSA, institutional form required.

Academics. Special study options: Accelerated study, distance learning. Bachelor's degree programs available on campus. License preparation in nursing. **Credit/placement by examination:** AP, CLEP, institutional tests. **Support services:** GED preparation and test center, learning center, tutoring.

Majors. Business: Accounting, business admin. **Health services:** Clinical lab technology, health care admin, medical records technology. **Protective services:** Law enforcement admin.

Most popular majors. Business/marketing 16%, health sciences 63%, legal studies 21%.

Computing on campus. 240 workstations in library, computer center. Commuter students can connect to campus network. Online library available.

Student life. Freshman orientation: Mandatory. Preregistration for classes offered.

Student services. Career counseling, services for economically disadvantaged, financial aid counseling, placement for graduates. **Transfer:** Pre-admission transcript evaluation for new students.

Contact. E-mail: madkins@brooklinecollege.edu
Phone: (602) 242-6265 Toll-free number: (800) 793-2428
Fax: (602) 973-2572
Donna Green, Brookline College: Phoenix, 2445 West Dunlap Avenue, Suite 100, Phoenix, AZ 85021-5820

Brookline College: Tempe
Tempe, Arizona
www.brooklinecollege.edu   CB code: 3455

- For-profit 2-year branch campus and career college
- Commuter campus in very large city
- Interview required

General. Accredited by ACICS. Additional campuses in Phoenix, Tucson, Oklahoma City, and Albuquerque. **Enrollment:** 342 degree-seeking undergraduates. **Degrees:** 19 associate awarded. **Calendar:** Differs by program, extensive summer session. **Full-time faculty:** 15 total; 20% have terminal degrees, 7% minority, 73% women. **Part-time faculty:** 20 total.

Basis for selection. Open admission, but selective for some programs. Must be 18 years of age or 17 years 6 months with parent or legal guardian consent. Must be US citizen or eligible non-citizen as classified by Department of Homeland Security. **Home schooled:** Letter of Attestation required.

2011-2012 Annual costs. Personal expenses: $5,880.

Financial aid. All financial aid based on need. Work-study available nights, weekends and for part-time students.

Application procedures. Admission: No deadline. No application fee. Admission notification on a rolling basis. **Financial aid:** No deadline. FAFSA, institutional form required.

Academics. Special study options: Accelerated study. **Credit/placement by examination:** AP, CLEP. **Support services:** GED preparation and test center, learning center, tutoring.

Majors. Business: Business admin. **Health services:** Clinical lab technology. **Protective services:** Law enforcement admin.

Most popular majors. Business/marketing 55%, health sciences 6%, legal studies 39%.

Computing on campus. 240 workstations in library. Commuter students can connect to campus network. Online library available.

Student life. Freshman orientation: Mandatory. Preregistration for classes offered.

Student services. Career counseling, services for economically disadvantaged, financial aid counseling, placement for graduates. **Transfer:** Pre-admission transcript evaluation for new students.

Contact. E-mail: ckindred@brooklinecollege.edu
Phone: (480) 545-8755 Toll-free number: (888) 886-2428
Fax: (480) 926-1371
Cheryl Kindred, Campus Director, Brookline College: Tempe, 1140-1150 South Priest Drive, Tempe, AZ 85281-5240

Brookline College: Tucson
Tucson, Arizona
www.brooklinecollege.edu   CB code: 3454

- For-profit 2-year branch campus and career college
- Commuter campus in very large city
- Interview required

General. Accredited by ACICS. Additional campuses in Phoenix, Tempe, Albuquerque, and Oklahoma City. **Enrollment:** 458 degree-seeking undergraduates. **Degrees:** 62 associate awarded. **Calendar:** Differs by program, extensive summer session. **Full-time faculty:** 22 total. **Part-time faculty:** 15 total.

Basis for selection. Open admission. Must be 18 years of age or 17 years 6 months with parent or legal guardian consent. Must be US citizen or eligible non-citizen as classified by Department of Homeland Security. **Home schooled:** Letter of Attestation required.

2011-2012 Annual costs. Personal expenses: $5,880.

Financial aid. All financial aid based on need. Need-based aid available for part-time students. Work-study available nights, weekends and for part-time students.

Application procedures. Admission: No deadline. No application fee. Admission notification on a rolling basis. **Financial aid:** No deadline. FAFSA, institutional form required.

Academics. Special study options: Accelerated study. **Credit/placement by examination:** AP, CLEP, institutional tests. **Support services:** GED preparation and test center, learning center, tutoring.

Majors. Business: Business admin. **Health services:** Clinical lab technology. **Protective services:** Law enforcement admin.

Most popular majors. Business/marketing 34%, health sciences 6%, legal studies 60%.

Computing on campus. 240 workstations in library, computer center. Commuter students can connect to campus network. Online library available.

Student life. Freshman orientation: Mandatory. Preregistration for classes offered.

Student services. Career counseling, services for economically disadvantaged, financial aid counseling, placement for graduates. **Transfer:** Pre-admission transcript evaluation for new students.

Contact. E-mail: lpechota@brooklinecollege.edu
Phone: (520) 748-9799 Toll-free number: (888) 292-2428
Fax: (520) 748-9355
Leigh Pechota, Campus Director, Brookline College: Tucson, 5441 East 22nd Street, Suite 125, Tucson, AZ 85711-5444

Bryman School of Arizona
Phoenix, Arizona
www.brymanschool.edu   CB code: 3040

- For-profit 2-year health science college
- Very large city

General. Regionally accredited; also accredited by ACICS, ACCSC. **Enrollment:** 800 degree-seeking undergraduates. **Degrees:** 13 associate awarded. **Calendar:** Differs by program. **Full-time faculty:** 60 total.

Basis for selection. Open admission.

2011-2012 Annual costs. Books/supplies: $642. Personal expenses: $3,360.

Financial aid. Need-based: Work-study available nights, weekends and for part-time students.

Application procedures. Admission: No deadline. $20 fee. Admission notification on a rolling basis.

Academics. Credit/placement by examination: AP, CLEP.

Majors. Health services: Insurance coding, insurance specialist.

Student life. Freshman orientation: Mandatory. Preregistration for classes offered.

Contact. Phone: (602) 274-4300 Toll-free number: (800) 987-0110
Cecilia Gomez, Director of Admissions, Bryman School of Arizona, 2250 West Peoria Avenue, Phoenix, AZ 85029-4919

Carrington College: Mesa
Mesa, Arizona
www.carrington.edu

- For-profit 2-year career college
- Very large city

General. Regionally accredited; also accredited by ACICS. **Enrollment:** 853 degree-seeking undergraduates. **Degrees:** 88 associate awarded. **Calendar:** Differs by program. **Full-time faculty:** 23 total. **Part-time faculty:** 32 total.

Basis for selection. Open admission.

2011-2012 Annual costs. Tuition/fees: $13,700. Program cost $13,700 (40 weeks). Costs are provided for the largest program. Other programs may vary.

Financial aid. Need-based: Work-study available nights, weekends and for part-time students.

Application procedures. Admission: No deadline. No application fee. Admission notification on a rolling basis.

Academics. Credit/placement by examination: AP, CLEP.

Majors. Health services: Dental hygiene, office admin, physical therapy assistant, respiratory therapy technology.

Contact. Phone: (888) 720-5014
Baxter Papik, Director of Admissions, Carrington College: Mesa, 630 West Southern Avenue, Mesa, AZ 85210

Carrington College: Phoenix
Phoenix, Arizona
www.carrington.edu

- For-profit 2-year career college
- Very large city

General. Regionally accredited; also accredited by ACICS. **Enrollment:** 785 degree-seeking undergraduates. **Degrees:** 5 associate awarded. **Calendar:** Differs by program. **Full-time faculty:** 16 total. **Part-time faculty:** 14 total.

Basis for selection. Open admission.

2011-2012 Annual costs. Tuition/fees: $14,200. Program cost $14,200 (39 weeks). Costs are provided for the largest program. Other programs may vary.

Financial aid. Need-based: Work-study available nights, weekends and for part-time students.

Application procedures. Admission: No deadline. No application fee. Admission notification on a rolling basis.

Academics. Credit/placement by examination: AP, CLEP.

Majors. Health services: Nursing (RN), office admin, physical therapy assistant.

Contact. Phone: (888) 720-5014
Tim Sheahan, Director of Admissions, Carrington College: Phoenix, 8503 North 27th Avenue, Phoenix, AZ 85051-4063

Carrington College: Phoenix Westside
Phoenix, Arizona
www.carrington.edu

- For-profit 2-year career college
- Very large city

General. Regionally accredited; also accredited by ACICS. **Enrollment:** 600 degree-seeking undergraduates. **Degrees:** 172 associate awarded. **Calendar:** Differs by program. **Full-time faculty:** 20 total. **Part-time faculty:** 27 total.

Basis for selection. Open admission.

2011-2012 Annual costs. Tuition/fees: $13,419. Program cost $46,715 (96 weeks). Costs are provided for the largest program. Other programs may vary.

Financial aid. Need-based: Work-study available nights, weekends and for part-time students.

Application procedures. Admission: No deadline. No application fee. Admission notification on a rolling basis.

Academics. Credit/placement by examination: AP, CLEP.

Majors. Health services: Clinical lab technology, medical radiologic technology/radiation therapy, nursing (RN).

Contact. Phone: (888) 720-5014
Monica Ferguson, Director of Admissions, Carrington College: Phoenix Westside, 2701 West Bethany Home Road, Phoenix, AZ 85017-5885

Carrington College: Tucson
Tucson, Arizona
www.carrington.edu

- For-profit 2-year career college
- Very large city

General. Regionally accredited; also accredited by ACICS. **Enrollment:** 592 degree-seeking undergraduates. **Degrees:** 17 associate awarded. **Calendar:** Differs by program. **Full-time faculty:** 11 total. **Part-time faculty:** 13 total.

Basis for selection. Open admission.

2011-2012 Annual costs. Tuition/fees: $14,200. Program cost $14,200 (39 weeks). Costs are provided for the largest program. Other programs may vary.

Financial aid. Need-based: Work-study available nights, weekends and for part-time students.

Application procedures. Admission: No deadline. No application fee. Admission notification on a rolling basis.

Academics. Credit/placement by examination: AP, CLEP.

Majors. Health services: Clinical lab technology, office admin.

Contact. Phone: (888) 720-5014
Rodney Fitzsimmons, Director of Admissions, Carrington College: Tucson, 3550 North Oracle Road, Tucson, AZ 85705-5885

Central Arizona College
Coolidge, Arizona
www.centralaz.edu   CB code: 4122

- Public 2-year community college
- Commuter campus in large town

General. Founded in 1962. Regionally accredited. **Enrollment:** 6,240 degree-seeking undergraduates. **Degrees:** 440 associate awarded. **Location:** 45 miles from Phoenix, 60 miles from Tucson. **Calendar:** Semester, limited summer session. **Full-time faculty:** 91 total. **Part-time faculty:** 361 total. **Special facilities:** Observatory, 2 recording studios, digital audio Mac labs, burn training facility, safety vehicle training track and firing range for law enforcement training, theater. **Partnerships:** Formal partnership with CAVIT.

Student profile.

Out-of-state: 4%   25 or older: 14%

Transfer out. Colleges most students transferred to 2011: Arizona State University, Northern Arizona University, University of Arizona.

Basis for selection. Open admission, but selective for some programs. Special requirement for nursing and radiology technology programs. **Learning Disabled:** Student must register disability and present appropriate documentation.

High school preparation. College-preparatory program recommended.

2011-2012 Annual costs. Tuition/fees: $2,100; $9,360 out-of-state. Per-credit charge: $70 in-state; $140 out-of-state. Room/board: $5,030. Books/supplies: $1,300. Personal expenses: $3,000.

Financial aid. Need-based: Need-based aid available for part-time students. Work-study available nights, weekends and for part-time students.

Application procedures. Admission: No deadline. No application fee. Admission notification on a rolling basis. **Financial aid:** Priority date 5/1, closing date 7/15. FAFSA required. Must reply within 3 week(s) of notification.

Academics. Special study options: Distance learning, dual enrollment of high school students, ESL, honors, independent study, internships, liberal arts/career combination, teacher certification program, weekend college. Bachelor's degree programs available on campus. License preparation in nursing, paramedic, radiology, real estate. **Credit/placement by examination:** AP, CLEP, institutional tests. 30 credit hours maximum toward associate degree. **Support services:** GED preparation and test center, learning center, pre-admission summer program, reduced course load, remedial instruction, study skills assistance, tutoring, writing center.

Majors. Biology: General. **Business:** General, accounting, accounting technology, administrative services, business admin, hospitality/recreation, hotel/motel/restaurant management, marketing, office technology. **Communications:** Journalism, sports. **Communications technology:** Desktop publishing. **Computer sciences:** General, applications programming, data processing, programming. **Education:** General, early childhood, elementary, special ed. **English:** English lit, writing. **General:** Business. **Health services:** Clinical nutrition, dietetic technician, EMT paramedic, health care admin, massage therapy, medical assistant, medical records admin, medical secretary, medical transcription, nursing (RN), nursing assistant, pharmacy assistant, preveterinary, radiologic technology/medical imaging. **Human services:** General, social work. **Liberal arts:** Arts/sciences, humanities. **Math:** General. **Parks/recreation:** Exercise sciences. **Physical sciences:** Chemistry. **Protective services:** Corrections, criminal justice, fire safety technology, firefighting, police science. **Psychology:** General. **Social sciences:** General, criminology. **Visual/performing arts:** General, art, dramatic, music. **Work/family studies:** Child care service, child development, family studies.

Computing on campus. 500 workstations in dormitories, library, computer center. Dormitories wired for high-speed internet access and linked to campus network. Commuter students can connect to campus network. Online course registration, online library, helpline, wireless network available.

Student life. Freshman orientation: Available. Preregistration for classes offered. **Policies:** Student code of conduct must be followed. **Housing:** Coed dorms, special housing for disabled, wellness housing available. $100 fully refundable deposit. **Activities:** Bands, choral groups, drama, international student organizations, music ensembles, student government, student newspaper, Phi Theta, Kappa/Lamba, art club, Playmasters, Campus Crusade For Christ, Native American club, rodeo club, Student Nurses Association of Arizona.

Athletics. NJCAA. **Intercollegiate:** Baseball M, basketball, cross-country, rodeo, softball W, track and field, volleyball W. **Team name:** Vaqueros.

Student services. Adult student services, alcohol/substance abuse counseling, career counseling, student employment services, financial aid counseling, on-campus daycare, personal counseling. **Physically disabled:** Services for visually, hearing impaired. **Transfer:** Re-entry adviser, pre-admission transcript evaluation for new students. Transfer center, transfer adviser, college fairs on campus for students transferring to 4-year colleges.

Contact. E-mail: Admissions@centralaz.edu
Phone: (520) 494-5260 Toll-free number: (800) 237-9814
Fax: (520) 494-5083
Luis Sanchez, Director of Admission and Records, Central Arizona College, Admissions Office, Coolidge, AZ 85128-9030

Chandler-Gilbert Community College
Chandler, Arizona
www.cgc.maricopa.edu   CB code: 0535

- Public 2-year community college
- Commuter campus in small city

General. Regionally accredited. Additional campuses in Sun Lakes and Williams. **Enrollment:** 11,919 degree-seeking undergraduates. **Degrees:** 606 associate awarded. **Location:** 20 miles from Phoenix. **Calendar:** Semester, limited summer session. **Full-time faculty:** 129 total. **Part-time faculty:** 516 total. **Class size:** 44% < 20, 47% 20-39, 9% 40-49, less than 1% 50-99.

Student profile.

Out-of-state:	5%	Live on campus:	2%
25 or older:	28%		

Transfer out. Colleges most students transferred to 2011: Arziona State University, Northern Arizona University, University of Arizona.

Basis for selection. Open admission, but selective for some programs. Special requirements for nursing and aviation.

2011-2012 Annual costs. Tuition/fees: $2,295; $9,525 out-of-state. Per-credit charge: $76 in-state; $317 out-of-state. Books/supplies: $1,064. Personal expenses: $4,878.

Financial aid. Need-based: Work-study available nights, weekends and for part-time students.

Application procedures. Admission: No deadline. No application fee.

Academics. Special study options: Distance learning, dual enrollment of high school students, ESL, honors, independent study, teacher certification program, weekend college. License preparation in aviation, nursing. **Credit/placement by examination:** AP, CLEP, IB, institutional tests. 30 credit hours maximum toward associate degree. **Support services:** Learning center, reduced course load, remedial instruction, study skills assistance, tutoring, writing center.

Majors. Business: General, accounting, nonprofit/public, office technology, retailing. **Computer sciences:** General, computer science, data entry, information technology, networking, system admin, vendor certification. **Education:** Elementary. **Health services:** Clinical nutrition, dietetic technician, massage therapy, nursing assistant. **Visual/performing arts:** Music management.

Most popular majors. Computer/information sciences 7%, education 10%, history 7%, liberal arts 63%, physical sciences 9%.

Computing on campus. 150 workstations in library, computer center. Commuter students can connect to campus network. Online course registration, online library, wireless network available.

Student life. Freshman orientation: Mandatory. Preregistration for classes offered. One-day sessions held at beginning of term; choice of weekend day and weeknight evening. **Housing:** Coed dorms available. Student housing for CGCC students available on-campus only at Williams campus in cooperation with Arizona State University Polytechnic. CGCC students attending any of the college's campuses can apply for student housing at the Williams campus. **Activities:** Bands, choral groups, dance, drama, music ensembles, musical theater, student government, political science organization, Christians in Action, Latter Day Saints student association, intercultural exchange club, Wall Street club, Phi Theta Kappa, black student union, Hispanic student organization.

Athletics. NJCAA. **Intercollegiate:** Baseball M, basketball, golf, soccer, softball W, volleyball W. **Team name:** Coyotes.

Student services. Adult student services, alcohol/substance abuse counseling, career counseling, services for economically disadvantaged, student employment services, financial aid counseling, personal counseling, placement for graduates, veterans' counselor. **Physically disabled:** Services for visually, speech, hearing impaired. **Transfer:** Pre-admission transcript evaluation for new students. Transfer center, transfer adviser, college fairs on campus for students transferring to 4-year colleges.

Contact. Phone: (480) 732-7320
Linda Shaw, Director of Admissions, Chandler-Gilbert Community College, 2626 East Pecos Road, Chandler, AZ 85225

Cochise College
Douglas, Arizona
www.cochise.edu

CB member
CB code: 4097

▸ Public 2-year community college
▸ Commuter campus in large town

General. Founded in 1962. Regionally accredited. Courses offered at 2 campuses; 4 extended learning centers located in 2 counties and online. **Enrollment:** 3,506 degree-seeking undergraduates; 782 non-degree-seeking students. **Degrees:** 1,198 associate awarded. **Location:** 120 miles from Tucson. **Calendar:** Semester, limited summer session. **Full-time faculty:** 92 total; 27% minority, 48% women. **Part-time faculty:** 313 total; 31% minority, 50% women. **Class size:** 85% < 20, 14% 20-39, less than 1% 40-49. **Special facilities:** Asian art collection, college airport. **Partnerships:** Formal partnerships with Sierra Vista Public Schools, City of Sierra Vista, AEPCO, SSVEC, SW Gas, Sierra Vista Herald, Mantech, JITC, General Dynamics, STG, Office of Congresswoman Gabriella Gifford, Fort Huachuca Public Affairs, Fort Huachuca Biometrics/Forensic Unit, Fort Huachuca Accomodation Schools, Fort Huachuca STEP Program, Desert Automotive, Sierra Vista Fire Department, Disney Inc., Child and Family Resources, NAMI, Cochise County Workforce Development, Cochise County Court System, City of Douglas, Bisbee Fire Department, Sierra Vista Chamber of Commerce, Douglas Public Schools, Naco Public School, Cochise County, UPS, Ginger's Auto Title Service, E.F. Edwards Financial Inc., State Farm, Bayada Nurse, Legacy Home Support, Visiting Angels.

Student profile. Among degree-seeking undergraduates, 34% enrolled in a transfer program, 66% enrolled in a vocational program, 1% already have a bachelor's degree or higher, 785 enrolled as first-time, first-year students, 105 transferred in from other institutions.

Part-time:	72%	Hispanic American:	45%
Out-of-state:	4%	Native American:	1%
Women:	53%	25 or older:	48%
African American:	5%	Live on campus:	1%
Asian American:	2%		

Transfer out. Colleges most students transferred to 2011: Pima Community College, University of Arizona, Univeristy of Phoenix, Arizona State University, Northern Arizona University.

Basis for selection. Open admission, but selective for some programs. Nursing program requires additional application and satisfactory score on HESI Entrance Exam. Aviation students must be TSA approved and must have airman medical exam class 2 or 3 to start training. **Learning Disabled:** Students with learning disabilities need to provide documentation regarding their disability.

2011-2012 Annual costs. Tuition/fees: $1,970; $8,780 out-of-state. Per-credit charge: $63 in-state; $290 out-of-state. Room/board: $4,850. Books/supplies: $1,000. Personal expenses: $1,350.

2010-2011 Financial aid. Need-based: 395 full-time freshmen applied for aid; 339 were judged to have need; 330 of these received aid. Average scholarship/grant was $3,836; average loan $3,149. 87% of total undergraduate aid awarded as scholarships/grants, 13% as loans/jobs. Need-based aid available for part-time students. Work-study available nights, weekends and for part-time students. **Non-need-based:** Awarded to 307 full-time undergraduates, including 139 freshmen. Scholarships awarded for academics, athletics.

Application procedures. Admission: No deadline. No application fee. Admission notification on a rolling basis. **Financial aid:** Closing date 4/15. FAFSA, institutional form required. Applicants notified on a rolling basis starting 6/1; must reply within 2 week(s) of notification.

Academics. Special study options: Distance learning, dual enrollment of high school students, ESL, honors, independent study, internships. License preparation in aviation, nursing, paramedic. **Credit/placement by examination:** AP, CLEP, IB, institutional tests. 30 credit hours maximum toward associate degree. **Support services:** GED preparation and test center, learning center, pre-admission summer program, reduced course load, remedial instruction, study skills assistance, tutoring, writing center.

Majors. Biology: General. **Business:** Administrative services, business admin, logistics. **Communications:** Communications/speech/rhetoric, journalism. **Computer sciences:** Computer science, data processing, information systems, networking, programming, security. **Education:** Art, early childhood, elementary, English, foreign languages, history, mathematics. **Engineering:** General. **English:** English lit. **Foreign languages:** General. **General:** Business. **Health services:** EMT paramedic, nursing (RN). **History:** General. **Human services:** Social work. **Liberal arts:** Humanities. **Math:** General. **Military:** "intel, generally", aerospace ground equipment. **Parks/recreation:** Health/fitness. **Philosophy/religion:** Philosophy. **Physical sciences:** Chemistry, physics. **Protective services:** Firefighting, police science. **Psychology:** General. **Social sciences:** Anthropology, economics, political science, sociology. **Visual/performing arts:** Art, dramatic, game design, music.

Most popular majors. Liberal arts 13%, military 62%.

Computing on campus. 706 workstations in dormitories, library, computer center, student center. Dormitories wired for high-speed internet access and linked to campus network. Commuter students can connect to campus network. Online course registration, online library, helpline, repair service, wireless network available.

Student life. **Freshman orientation:** Available. Preregistration for classes offered. 30-minute program available on-line at all times. **Housing:** Coed dorms, special housing for disabled, apartments available. $100 partly refundable deposit. **Activities:** Dance, drama, literary magazine, music ensembles, student government, student newspaper, American Sign Language club, Circle K International, geology club, Literary Guild, math and computer sciences club, Phi Theta Kappa, pre-pharmacy club, psychology club, Student Nurses, technology club.

Athletics. NJCAA. **Intercollegiate:** Baseball M, basketball, rodeo, soccer W. **Team name:** Apaches.

Student services. Career counseling, services for economically disadvantaged, student employment services, financial aid counseling, personal counseling, placement for graduates, veterans' counselor. **Physically disabled:** Services for visually, speech, hearing impaired. **Transfer:** Pre-admission transcript evaluation for new students. Transfer adviser, college fairs on campus for students transferring to 4-year colleges.

Contact. E-mail: admissions@cochise.edu
Phone: (520) 515-5336 Toll-free number: (800) 593-9567
Fax: (520) 515-5452
Debbie Quick, Director of Admissions, Cochise College, 901 North Colombo Avenue, Sierra Vista, AZ 85635

Coconino County Community College
Flagstaff, Arizona
www.coconino.edu   **CB code: 1712**

‣ Public 2-year community college
‣ Commuter campus in small city

General. Regionally accredited. **Enrollment:** 1,406 full-time, degree-seeking students. **Degrees:** 236 associate awarded. **ROTC:** Army, Air Force. **Location:** 140 miles from Phoenix. **Calendar:** Semester, limited summer session. **Full-time faculty:** 41 total. **Part-time faculty:** 159 total. **Special facilities:** Community garden, wind turbine, green building, telescope.

Student profile.

Out-of-state: 7%   25 or older: 42%

Transfer out. **Colleges most students transferred to 2011:** Northern Arizona University, Arizona State University, University of Arizona.

Basis for selection. Open admission, but selective for some programs. Special requirements for nursing program.

2011-2012 Annual costs. Tuition/fees: $2,640; $8,865 out-of-state. Per-credit charge: $83 in-state; $291 out-of-state. Books/supplies: $1,268. Personal expenses: $1,404.

Financial aid. **Need-based:** Work-study available nights, weekends and for part-time students.

Application procedures. **Admission:** No deadline. No application fee. Application must be submitted on paper. Admission notification on a rolling basis. **Financial aid:** Priority date 4/15, closing date 6/30.

Academics. Writing center, learning center and tutoring available. **Special study options:** Distance learning, dual enrollment of high school students, honors, internships. License preparation in nursing, paramedic, real estate. **Credit/placement by examination:** AP, CLEP. **Support services:** GED preparation and test center, learning center, remedial instruction, study skills assistance, tutoring, writing center.

Majors. **Architecture:** Technology. **Business:** General, accounting, business admin, construction management, finance, hospitality admin, marketing. **Computer sciences:** System admin. **Conservation:** Environmental science. **Education:** General, early childhood, elementary. **Engineering:** General. **Health services:** Medical secretary, nursing assistant. **Human services:** Social work. **Protective services:** Criminal justice, firefighting. **Psychology:** General. **Social sciences:** Anthropology, sociology. **Visual/performing arts:** Art.

Most popular majors. Education 6%, health sciences 8%, liberal arts 60%, security/protective services 8%.

Computing on campus. 100 workstations in library, computer center, student center. Online course registration, online library, helpline available.

Student life. **Freshman orientation:** Available. Preregistration for classes offered. **Activities:** Dance, literary magazine, music ensembles, symphony orchestra.

Athletics. **Team name:** Comets.

Student services. Adult student services, career counseling, financial aid counseling, on-campus daycare, veterans' counselor. **Physically disabled:** Services for visually, speech, hearing impaired. **Transfer:** Pre-admission transcript evaluation for new students. Transfer adviser, college fairs on campus for students transferring to 4-year colleges.

Contact. E-mail: admissions&registration@coconino.edu
Phone: (928) 527-1222 ext. 4299
Toll-free number: (800) 350-7122 ext. 4299 Fax: (928) 226-4110
Liz Gallegos, Registrar/Director for Admissions, Coconino County Community College, 2800 South Lone Tree Road, Flagstaff, AZ 86001

Dine College
Tsaile, Arizona   **CB member**
www.dinecollege.edu   **CB code: 4550**

‣ Public 2-year community college
‣ Residential campus in rural community

General. Founded in 1968. Regionally accredited. The first tribally controlled community college in the United States; chartered by the Navajo Nation. **Enrollment:** 1,969 degree-seeking undergraduates. **Degrees:** 5 bachelor's, 198 associate awarded. **Location:** 55 miles from Window Rock. **Calendar:** Semester, limited summer session. **Full-time faculty:** 62 total. **Part-time faculty:** 90 total. **Special facilities:** Museum.

Student profile.

Out-of-state: 15%   **Live on campus:**   20%
25 or older: 49%

Transfer out. **Colleges most students transferred to 2011:** Northern Arizona University, Arizona State University, Fort Lewis College, University of Arizona, University of New Mexico.

Basis for selection. Open admission. **Home schooled:** Statement describing home school structure and mission, transcript of courses and grades, state high school equivalency certificate required.

2011-2012 Annual costs. Tuition/fees: $850; $850 out-of-state. Room/board: $3,720. Books/supplies: $1,400. Personal expenses: $2,500.

2010-2011 Financial aid. All financial aid based on need. 99% of total undergraduate aid awarded as scholarships/grants, 1% as loans/jobs. Need-based aid available for part-time students. Work-study available nights, weekends and for part-time students.

Application procedures. **Admission:** No deadline. $20 fee. Application must be submitted on paper. Admission notification on a rolling basis. **Financial aid:** Priority date 4/15; no closing date. FAFSA, institutional form required. Applicants notified on a rolling basis starting 5/1; must reply within 4 week(s) of notification.

Academics. **Special study options:** Cooperative education, distance learning, double major, independent study. Bachelor's degree programs available on campus. **Credit/placement by examination:** AP, CLEP, institutional tests. 12 credit hours maximum toward associate degree. **Support services:** Learning center, pre-admission summer program, remedial instruction, tutoring.

Majors. **Area/ethnic studies:** Native American. **Biology:** General. **Business:** Administrative services, business admin, office/clerical. **Computer sciences:** General, computer science. **Conservation:** Environmental science. **Education:** General, early childhood, elementary. **Engineering:** Pre-engineering. **Foreign languages:** Native American. **Health services:** Public health ed. **Liberal arts:** Arts/sciences. **Psychology:** General. **Social sciences:** General. **Visual/performing arts:** Studio arts.

Computing on campus. 104 workstations in dormitories, library, computer center, student center. Dormitories wired for high-speed internet access and linked to campus network. Online library, helpline, repair service, wireless network available.

Student life. **Freshman orientation:** Available. Preregistration for classes offered. **Housing:** Coed dorms, single-sex dorms, wellness housing available. **Activities:** Student government, Red Dawn Indian club.

Athletics. NJCAA. **Intercollegiate:** Archery, cross-country, rodeo. **Intramural:** Archery, cross-country, rodeo. **Team name:** Warrior.

Student services. Alcohol/substance abuse counseling, career counseling, personal counseling, veterans' counselor. **Transfer:** Pre-admission transcript

evaluation for new students. Transfer adviser, college fairs on campus for students transferring to 4-year colleges.

Contact. Phone: (928) 724-6630 Fax: (928) 724-3349
Louise Litzin, Registrar, Dine College, Box 67, Tsaile, AZ 86556

Eastern Arizona College
Thatcher, Arizona
www.eac.edu   **CB code: 4297**

- Public 2-year community college
- Commuter campus in large town

General. Founded in 1888. Regionally accredited. Near archaeological sites. Several continuing education centers within 165 miles of campus. **Enrollment:** 5,123 degree-seeking undergraduates. **Degrees:** 298 associate awarded. **Location:** 160 miles from Phoenix, 130 miles from Tucson. **Calendar:** Semester, limited summer session. **Full-time faculty:** 88 total; 16% have terminal degrees, 12% minority, 32% women. **Part-time faculty:** 188 total; 7% have terminal degrees, 13% minority, 55% women. **Class size:** 82% <20, 14% 20-39, 1% 40-49, 2% 50-99, less than 1% >100. **Special facilities:** Observatory, golf course, wilderness area. **Partnerships:** Formal partnerships with local high schools allow high school students to obtain degrees in areas such as office technology and drafting.

Student profile. Among degree-seeking undergraduates, 68% enrolled in a transfer program, 32% enrolled in a vocational program, 1,508 enrolled as first-time, first-year students, 590 transferred in from other institutions.

Part-time:	59%	Hispanic American:	21%
Out-of-state:	5%	Native American:	8%
Women:	51%	International:	1%
African American:	5%	25 or older:	54%
Asian American:	1%	Live on campus:	6%

Basis for selection. Open admission, but selective for some programs. Special requirements for nursing and several paramedical programs.

High school preparation. 15 units recommended. Recommended units include English 4, mathematics 4, social studies 1, history 1, science 3 (laboratory 3) and foreign language 2.

2011-2012 Annual costs. Tuition/fees: $1,600; $8,200 out-of-state. Per-credit charge: $65 in-state; $140 out-of-state. Room/board: $5,130. Books/supplies: $800. Personal expenses: $1,722.

2010-2011 Financial aid. Need-based: 478 full-time freshmen applied for aid; 417 were judged to have need; 404 of these received aid. Average need met was 64%. Average scholarship/grant was $5,457. 85% of total undergraduate aid awarded as scholarships/grants, 15% as loans/jobs. Need-based aid available for part-time students. Work-study available nights, weekends and for part-time students. **Non-need-based:** Awarded to 216 full-time undergraduates, including 89 freshmen. Scholarships awarded for academics, art, athletics, leadership, music/drama, state residency. **Additional information:** Limited number of tuition waivers for New Mexico residents. Unlimited number of waivers for those meeting WUE requirements.

Application procedures. Admission: No deadline. No application fee. Admission notification on a rolling basis. **Financial aid:** Priority date 3/1; no closing date. FAFSA, institutional form required. Applicants notified on a rolling basis starting 3/15.

Academics. Special study options: Cooperative education, distance learning, double major, dual enrollment of high school students, independent study. Bachelor's degree programs available on campus. License preparation in nursing, paramedic. **Credit/placement by examination:** AP, CLEP, IB, institutional tests. 48 credit hours maximum toward associate degree. **Support services:** GED preparation and test center, learning center, reduced course load, remedial instruction, study skills assistance, tutoring, writing center.

Majors. Biology: General, environmental, wildlife. **Business:** Administrative services, business admin, entrepreneurial studies, office technology. **Computer sciences:** Information systems, system admin. **Conservation:** Forestry. **Education:** Art, business, elementary, secondary, technology/industrial arts. **English:** English lit. **Foreign languages:** General. **General:** Agribusiness operations. **Health services:** EMT paramedic, nursing (RN), pharmacy assistant, premedicine, prepharmacy. **History:** General. **Liberal arts:** Arts/sciences. **Math:** General. **Parks/recreation:** Health/fitness. **Physical sciences:** Chemistry, geology, physics. **Protective services:** Law enforcement admin, police science. **Psychology:** General. **Social sciences:** Anthropology, political science, sociology. **Visual/performing arts:** Art, commercial/advertising art, dramatic, music, studio arts.

Most popular majors. Business/marketing 11%, health sciences 30%, liberal arts 38%.

Computing on campus. 564 workstations in library, computer center. Dormitories wired for high-speed internet access and linked to campus network. Online course registration, online library, wireless network available.

Student life. Freshman orientation: Available. Preregistration for classes offered. Half-day session given the week prior to beginning of classes each semester and weekly during summer months. **Housing:** Single-sex dorms, wellness housing available. $150 fully refundable deposit. **Activities:** Bands, choral groups, dance, drama, literary magazine, music ensembles, musical theater, student government, symphony orchestra, Latter Day Saints student association, Newman club, drama club, Hispanic leaders, intertribal club, Phi Theta Kappa, Spanish club, Gila Force, Rowdy Reptiles.

Athletics. NJCAA. **Intercollegiate:** Baseball M, basketball, football (tackle) M, golf M, softball W, tennis W, volleyball W. **Intramural:** Basketball, soccer, swimming, tennis, volleyball. **Team name:** Gila Monsters.

Student services. Adult student services, alcohol/substance abuse counseling, career counseling, services for economically disadvantaged, student employment services, financial aid counseling, minority student services, personal counseling, placement for graduates, veterans' counselor, women's services. **Physically disabled:** Services for visually, speech, hearing impaired. **Transfer:** Re-entry adviser, pre-admission transcript evaluation for new students. Transfer adviser, college fairs on campus for students transferring to 4-year colleges.

Contact. E-mail: admissions@eac.edu
Phone: (928) 428-8272 Toll-free number: (800) 678-3808 ext. 8272
Fax: (928) 428-2578
Erik Lehmann, Admissions Counselor, Eastern Arizona College, 615 North Stadium Avenue, Thatcher, AZ 85552-0769

Estrella Mountain Community College
Avondale, Arizona
www.estrellamountain.edu   **CB code: 3810**

- Public 2-year community college
- Commuter campus in small city

General. Regionally accredited. **Enrollment:** 5,800 degree-seeking undergraduates. **Degrees:** 649 associate awarded. **ROTC:** Air Force. **Location:** 15 miles from Phoenix. **Calendar:** Semester, limited summer session. **Full-time faculty:** 76 total. **Part-time faculty:** 391 total.

Transfer out. Colleges most students transferred to 2011: Arizona State University.

Basis for selection. Open admission.

2011-2012 Annual costs. Tuition/fees: $2,295; $9,375 out-of-state. Per-credit charge: $71 in-state; $312 out-of-state. Books/supplies: $1,104. Personal expenses: $2,718.

Financial aid. Need-based: Need-based aid available for part-time students. Work-study available nights, weekends and for part-time students. **Non-need-based:** Scholarships awarded for leadership.

Application procedures. Admission: No deadline. No application fee. **Financial aid:** Priority date 4/1; no closing date. Applicants notified on a rolling basis starting 4/15.

Academics. Special study options: Accelerated study, distance learning, dual enrollment of high school students, ESL, honors, independent study, internships, teacher certification program, weekend college. License preparation in nursing, paramedic. **Credit/placement by examination:** AP, CLEP, IB. 30 credit hours maximum toward associate degree. **Support services:** GED test center, learning center, pre-admission summer program, reduced course load, remedial instruction, study skills assistance, tutoring, writing center.

Majors. Business: Business admin, hotel/motel admin, organizational behavior. **Computer sciences:** Applications programming, data entry, LAN/WAN management, vendor certification. **Education:** General, secondary, teacher assistance. **Health services:** Speech-language pathology assistant. **Human services:** Social work. **Liberal arts:** Arts/sciences. **Protective services:** Criminal justice. **Psychology:** General.

Computing on campus. 198 workstations in library, computer center, student center. Online course registration, online library, helpline, wireless network available.

Student life. Freshman orientation: Available. Preregistration for classes offered. **Activities:** Student government.

Athletics. Team name: Mountain Lions.

Student services. Adult student services, alcohol/substance abuse counseling, career counseling, financial aid counseling, personal counseling, veterans' counselor. **Physically disabled:** Services for visually, speech, hearing impaired. **Transfer:** Pre-admission transcript evaluation for new students. College fairs on campus for students transferring to 4-year colleges.

Contact. E-mail: frank.amparo@estrellamountain.edu
Phone: (623) 935-8888 Fax: (623) 935-8870
Frank Amparo, Director of Admission and Records, Estrella Mountain Community College, 3000 North Dysart Road, Avondale, AZ 85392

GateWay Community College
Phoenix, Arizona
www.gatewaycc.edu   **CB code: 0455**

▶ Public 2-year community and technical college
▶ Commuter campus in very large city

General. Founded in 1968. Regionally accredited. **Enrollment:** 6,531 degree-seeking undergraduates. **Degrees:** 566 associate awarded. **ROTC:** Army, Naval, Air Force. **Calendar:** Semester, extensive summer session. **Full-time faculty:** 99 total; 16% minority. **Part-time faculty:** 391 total; 17% minority, 59% women. **Partnerships:** Formal partnerships with Johnson Control, Toyota, Honda, Nissan, Banner Health.

Student profile. Among degree-seeking undergraduates, 6% enrolled in a transfer program, 58% enrolled in a vocational program, 9% already have a bachelor's degree or higher, 716 enrolled as first-time, first-year students.

Out-of-state: 5%   **25 or older:**   62%

Transfer out. Colleges most students transferred to 2011: Arizona State Unversity, Northern Arizona University, University of Arizona.

Basis for selection. Open admission, but selective for some programs. Special requirements for nursing and some allied health programs. General Aptitude Test Battery required of health science applicants.

2011-2012 Annual costs. Tuition/fees: $2,295; $9,525 out-of-state. Per-credit charge: $76 in-state; $317 out-of-state. Books/supplies: $1,200. Personal expenses: $484.

2011-2012 Financial aid. Need-based: 37% of total undergraduate aid awarded as scholarships/grants, 63% as loans/jobs. Need-based aid available for part-time students. Work-study available nights, weekends and for part-time students. **Non-need-based:** Scholarships awarded for athletics.

Application procedures. Admission: No deadline. No application fee. Admission notification on a rolling basis. **Financial aid:** Priority date 4/15; no closing date. FAFSA, institutional form required. Applicants notified on a rolling basis; must reply within 4 week(s) of notification.

Academics. Special study options: Accelerated study, cooperative education, cross-registration, distance learning, double major, dual enrollment of high school students, ESL, external degree, honors, independent study, internships, liberal arts/career combination, study abroad. License preparation in nursing, physical therapy, radiology. **Credit/placement by examination:** AP, CLEP, IB, institutional tests. 30 credit hours maximum toward associate degree. **Support services:** Learning center, reduced course load, remedial instruction, study skills assistance, tutoring, writing center.

Majors. Business: General, accounting, administrative services, banking/financial services, international, office management. **Computer sciences:** General, information systems, LAN/WAN management, networking, system admin, systems analysis. **Engineering:** General. **Health services:** Health care admin, medical radiologic technology/radiation therapy, medical transcription, nuclear medical technology, nursing (RN), physical therapy assistant, respiratory therapy technology, sonography, surgical technology. **Liberal arts:** Arts/sciences. **Social sciences:** Sociology.

Most popular majors. Health sciences 67%, liberal arts 23%, trade and industry 6%.

Computing on campus. 100 workstations in library, computer center, student center. Commuter students can connect to campus network. Online course registration, online library, helpline, wireless network available.

Student life. Freshman orientation: Mandatory. Preregistration for classes offered. **Activities:** Film society, student government, student newspaper, MEHCA, Indian Tribal club, single parents association, women's club, health sciences club, business club.

Athletics. NJCAA. Intercollegiate: Cross-country, golf, soccer M, softball W, tennis. **Team name:** Geckos.

Student services. Adult student services, alcohol/substance abuse counseling, career counseling, services for economically disadvantaged, student employment services, financial aid counseling, minority student services, on-campus daycare, personal counseling, placement for graduates, veterans' counselor, women's services. **Physically disabled:** Services for visually, speech, hearing impaired. **Transfer:** Re-entry adviser, pre-admission transcript evaluation for new students. Transfer center, transfer adviser, college fairs on campus for students transferring to 4-year colleges.

Contact. E-mail: brenda.starck@gwmail.maricopa.edu
Phone: (602) 286-8200 Fax: (602) 286-8072
Brenda Starck, Supervisor Registration and Records, GateWay Community College, 108 North 40th Street, Phoenix, AZ 85034

Glendale Community College
Glendale, Arizona
www.gccaz.edu   **CB code: 4338**

▶ Public 2-year community college
▶ Commuter campus in small city

General. Founded in 1965. Regionally accredited. Additional campus in Peoria. **Enrollment:** 14,449 degree-seeking undergraduates; 6,924 non-degree-seeking students. **Degrees:** 1,251 associate awarded. **Location:** 17 miles from Phoenix. **Calendar:** Semester, extensive summer session. **Full-time faculty:** 255 total; 19% minority, 50% women. **Part-time faculty:** 933 total; 20% minority, 49% women. **Class size:** 31% < 20, 64% 20-39, 3% 40-49, 1% 50-99, less than 1% >100. **Special facilities:** Performing arts center, high-technology centers, international student center, public safety sciences building, Veterans service center. **Partnerships:** Formal partnerships with General Motors, Ford, Chrysler, Best Western, and John Deere.

Student profile. Among degree-seeking undergraduates, 3,810 enrolled as first-time, first-year students.

Part-time:	58%	**Hispanic American:**	27%
Out-of-state:	5%	**Native American:**	2%
Women:	53%	**International:**	1%
African American:	8%	**25 or older:**	32%
Asian American:	4%		

Transfer out. Colleges most students transferred to 2011: Arizona State University, Arizona State University West, University of Arizona, Grand Canyon University.

Basis for selection. Open admission, but selective for some programs. Special requirements for nursing, basic emergency medical technology, General Motors and Ford automotive programs, international students. **Home schooled:** If under 18, special admissions required.

2012-2013 Annual costs. Tuition/fees (projected): $2,310; $9,540 out-of-state. Books/supplies: $1,200. Personal expenses: $2,484.

Financial aid. Need-based: Need-based aid available for part-time students. Work-study available nights, weekends and for part-time students. **Non-need-based:** Scholarships awarded for art, athletics, music/drama.

Application procedures. Admission: No deadline. No application fee. Admission notification on a rolling basis. **Financial aid:** Priority date 4/30; no closing date. FAFSA required. Applicants notified on a rolling basis starting 5/1.

Academics. Special study options: Cooperative education, distance learning, dual enrollment of high school students, ESL, honors, independent study, internships, study abroad, weekend college. ACE Plus (Achieving College Education), high school bridge program, intensive English program. License preparation in nursing, paramedic. **Credit/placement by examination:** AP, CLEP, IB, institutional tests. 30 credit hours maximum toward associate degree. **Support services:** GED preparation and test center, learning center, remedial instruction, study skills assistance, tutoring, writing center.

Majors. Biology: Biotechnology. **Business:** General, accounting technology, administrative services, business admin, marketing. **Communications:** Public relations. **Communications technology:** Recording arts. **Computer sciences:** General, data entry, networking, security, systems analysis, web page design. **Education:** Early childhood, elementary, leadership. **Health services:** EMT paramedic, nursing (RN). **Liberal arts:** Arts/sciences. **Parks/recreation:** Exercise sciences. **Physical sciences:** General. **Protective services:** Criminal justice, disaster management, firefighting. **Visual/performing arts:** General, art, cinematography, dramatic, graphic design, music management, studio arts. **Work/family studies:** Family/community services.

Most popular majors. Business/marketing 8%, health sciences 11%, liberal arts 57%, physical sciences 9%.

Computing on campus. 1,500 workstations in library, computer center, student center. Commuter students can connect to campus network. Online course registration, online library, helpline, student web hosting, wireless network available.

Student life. Freshman orientation: Available. Preregistration for classes offered. **Activities:** Bands, choral groups, dance, drama, international student organizations, literary magazine, music ensembles, musical theater, opera, student government, student newspaper, black student union, Christian Challenge, MECHa, Unification of Africa, Native American club, Amnesty International, environmental club, Young Life, Fellowship of College Christians, Students for Life.

Athletics. NJCAA. **Intercollegiate:** Baseball M, basketball, cheerleading, cross-country, football (tackle) M, golf M, soccer, softball W, tennis, track and field, volleyball W. **Team name:** Gauchos.

Student services. Adult student services, career counseling, student employment services, financial aid counseling, minority student services, on-campus daycare, personal counseling, veterans' counselor. **Physically disabled:** Services for visually, speech, hearing impaired. **Transfer:** Transfer adviser, college fairs on campus for students transferring to 4-year colleges.

Contact. E-mail: admissions.recruitment@gcmail.maricopa.edu
Phone: (623) 845-3333 Fax: (623) 845-3060
Mary Blackwell, Dean, Enrollment Services, Glendale Community College, 6000 West Olive Avenue, Glendale, AZ 85302

Golf Academy of America: Phoenix
Chandler, Arizona
www.golfacademy.edu
CB code: 3460

‣ For-profit 2-year college of golf course management
‣ Small city

General. Accredited by ACICS. **Enrollment:** 225 degree-seeking undergraduates. **Degrees:** 146 associate awarded. **Calendar:** Semester. **Full-time faculty:** 5 total. **Part-time faculty:** 11 total.

Basis for selection. Golf Program requires playing ability experience.

2011-2012 Annual costs. Tuition/fees: $16,443. Cost for three semesters, $24,650, covers tuition, fees, and textbooks. Typically, students enroll for the calendar year and attend classes for three semesters consecutively. Books/supplies: $700. Personal expenses: $2,862.

Financial aid. Need-based: Work-study available nights, weekends and for part-time students.

Application procedures. Admission: $50 fee.

Academics. Credit/placement by examination: AP, CLEP.

Majors. Business: Business admin. **Parks/recreation:** Facilities management.

Student life. Freshman orientation: Mandatory. Preregistration for classes offered.

Contact. E-mail: phoenix.info@golfacademy.edu
Phone: (480) 905-9288 Toll-free number: (800) 342-7342
Fax: (480) 905-8705
Mark Shabaker, Director of Admissions, Golf Academy of America: Phoenix, 2031 North Arizona Avenue, Suite 2, Chandler, AZ 85225

Kaplan College: Phoenix
Phoenix, Arizona
www.kc-phoenix.com
CB code: 3052

‣ For-profit 2-year technical college
‣ Residential campus in very large city
‣ Interview required

General. Regionally accredited; also accredited by ACCSC. **Enrollment:** 644 undergraduates. **Degrees:** 137 associate awarded. **Calendar:** Differs by program. **Full-time faculty:** 12 total. **Part-time faculty:** 28 total.

Basis for selection. Open admission, but selective for some programs. Wonderlic entrance exam required for placement.

Financial aid. Need-based: Work-study available nights, weekends and for part-time students.

Application procedures. Admission: No deadline. $10 fee. **Financial aid:** No deadline.

Academics. Credit/placement by examination: AP, CLEP. **Support services:** Learning center, tutoring.

Majors. Health services: Respiratory therapy technology.

Student life. Freshman orientation: Mandatory, $20 fee. Preregistration for classes offered.

Contact. E-mail: mcrance@kaplan.edu
Phone: (602) 548-1955 ext. 1366
Toll-free number: (877) 548-1955 ext. 1366 Fax: (602) 548-1956
Danelle Morrell, Director of Admissions, Kaplan College: Phoenix, 13610 North Black Canyon Highway, Suite 104, Phoenix, AZ 85029

Le Cordon Bleu College of Culinary Arts: Scottsdale
Scottsdale, Arizona
www.scichefs.com
CB code: 3028

‣ For-profit 2-year culinary school and technical college
‣ Commuter campus in large city
‣ Application essay, interview required

General. Regionally accredited; also accredited by ACCSC. **Enrollment:** 1,820 degree-seeking undergraduates. **Degrees:** 191 bachelor's, 304 associate awarded. **Location:** 2 miles from downtown. **Calendar:** Differs by program. **Full-time faculty:** 49 total. **Part-time faculty:** 7 total.

Student profile.

Out-of-state:	55%	25 or older:	60%

Basis for selection. Open admission.

2011-2012 Annual costs. Personal expenses: $2,275.

Financial aid. Need-based: Work-study available nights, weekends and for part-time students.

Application procedures. Admission: No deadline. $50 fee. Admission notification on a rolling basis.

Academics. Special study options: Distance learning, internships. **Credit/placement by examination:** AP, CLEP. **Support services:** Learning center, remedial instruction, tutoring.

Student life. Freshman orientation: Mandatory. Preregistration for classes offered.

Student services. Alcohol/substance abuse counseling, career counseling, financial aid counseling, placement for graduates.

Contact. E-mail: sciadmissions@scichefs.com
Phone: (480) 990-3773 Toll-free number: (800) 848-2433
Fax: (480) 990-0351
Vice President of Admissions, Le Cordon Bleu College of Culinary Arts: Scottsdale, 8100 East Camelback Road, Suite 1001, Scottsdale, AZ 85251

Mesa Community College
Mesa, Arizona
www.mesacc.edu
CB member
CB code: 4513

‣ Public 2-year community college
‣ Commuter campus in very large city

General. Founded in 1965. Regionally accredited. **Enrollment:** 21,582 degree-seeking undergraduates. **Degrees:** 1,934 associate awarded. **ROTC:** Army, Naval, Air Force. **Location:** 12 miles from Phoenix. **Calendar:** Semester, extensive summer session. **Class size:** 44% < 20, 52% 20-39, 2% 40-49, 1% 50-99.

Student profile.

Out-of-state:	1%	25 or older:	41%

Transfer out. Colleges most students transferred to 2011: Arizona State University, Northern Arizona University, University of Arizona.

Basis for selection. Open admission, but selective for some programs. General education requirements and 2.5 GPA required for nursing, mortuary science, and fire academy programs.

2011-2012 Annual costs. Tuition/fees: $2,295; $9,525 out-of-state. Per-credit charge: $76 in-state; $317 out-of-state. Books/supplies: $1,200. Personal expenses: $2,484.

Financial aid. Need-based: Need-based aid available for part-time students. Work-study available nights, weekends and for part-time students. **Non-need-based:** Scholarships awarded for academics, athletics. **Additional information:** Awards available for Maricopa County residents.

Application procedures. Admission: No deadline. No application fee. Admission notification on a rolling basis. **Financial aid:** Priority date 5/1; no closing date. FAFSA, institutional form required. Applicants notified on a rolling basis starting 7/1.

Academics. Associate of General Studies degree allows students to take half of credits in required courses, and dictate own program of electives. **Special study options:** Cooperative education, cross-registration, distance learning, dual enrollment of high school students, ESL, exchange student, honors, independent study, internships, liberal arts/career combination, student-designed major, study abroad, teacher certification program, weekend college. License preparation in dental hygiene, nursing, real estate. **Credit/placement by examination:** AP, CLEP, IB, institutional tests. 30 credit hours maximum toward associate degree. **Support services:** GED preparation and test center, learning center, remedial instruction, study skills assistance, tutoring, writing center.

Honors college/program. 3.5 GPA required.

Majors. Biology: Biotechnology. **Business:** General, accounting, business admin, fashion, marketing, organizational behavior, real estate. **Communications:** Journalism, public relations. **Communications technology:** Recording arts. **Computer sciences:** General, applications programming, computer science, networking, systems analysis, web page design. **Education:** Early childhood, elementary, ESL, teacher assistance. **Engineering:** Manufacturing. **English:** Creative writing. **General:** Agribusiness operations, horticulture, landscaping. **Health services:** Dental hygiene, EMT paramedic, nursing (RN), veterinary technology/assistant. **Human services:** Social work. **Liberal arts:** Arts/sciences, library assistant. **Parks/recreation:** General, exercise sciences. **Physical sciences:** General. **Protective services:** Criminal justice, firefighting, police science. **Psychology:** General. **Social sciences:** Geography. **Visual/performing arts:** General, commercial/advertising art, design, dramatic, interior design, music management, music theory/composition, studio arts. **Work/family studies:** Child development, institutional food production.

Most popular majors. Business/marketing 6%, health sciences 15%, liberal arts 54%, physical sciences 7%, security/protective services 6%.

Computing on campus. 1,000 workstations in library, computer center, student center. Commuter students can connect to campus network. Online course registration, online library, helpline, repair service, student web hosting, wireless network available.

Student life. Freshman orientation: Available. Preregistration for classes offered. Students may attend orientation at either campus location. **Activities:** Jazz band, choral groups, dance, drama, international student organizations, music ensembles, Model UN, musical theater, opera, student government, student newspaper.

Athletics. NJCAA. **Intercollegiate:** Baseball M, basketball, cheerleading, cross-country, football (tackle) M, golf, soccer, softball W, tennis, track and field, volleyball W, wrestling M. **Team name:** Thunderbirds.

Student services. Adult student services, alcohol/substance abuse counseling, career counseling, services for economically disadvantaged, student employment services, financial aid counseling, legal services, minority student services, on-campus daycare, personal counseling, placement for graduates, veterans' counselor. **Physically disabled:** Services for visually, speech, hearing impaired. **Transfer:** Re-entry adviser, pre-admission transcript evaluation for new students. Transfer adviser, college fairs on campus for students transferring to 4-year colleges.

Contact. E-mail: admissions@mesacc.edu
Phone: (480) 461-7000 Fax: (480) 461-7805
Gerri Silva, Coordinator of Student Services, Mesa Community College, 1833 West Southern Avenue, Mesa, AZ 85202

Mohave Community College
Kingman, Arizona
www.mohave.edu   CB code: 0443

- Public 2-year community college
- Commuter campus in small city

General. Founded in 1971. Regionally accredited. **Enrollment:** 6,050 degree-seeking undergraduates. **Degrees:** 399 associate awarded. **Location:** 200 miles from Phoenix, 100 miles from Las Vegas. **Calendar:** Semester, limited summer session. **Full-time faculty:** 76 total. **Part-time faculty:** 361 total.

Transfer out. Colleges most students transferred to 2011: Northern Arizona University, University of Arizona, Arizona State University.

Basis for selection. Open admission, but selective for some programs. Special requirements for nursing, dental hygiene and EMT/paramedic programs.

2011-2012 Annual costs. Tuition/fees: $2,516; $9,176 out-of-state. Per-credit charge: $74 in-state; $296 out-of-state. Books/supplies: $1,000.

Financial aid. Need-based: Need-based aid available for part-time students. Work-study available nights, weekends and for part-time students.

Application procedures. Admission: No deadline. No application fee. **Financial aid:** Priority date 4/15, closing date 7/15. FAFSA, institutional form required. Applicants notified on a rolling basis starting 5/1; must reply within 2 week(s) of notification.

Academics. Special study options: Distance learning, dual enrollment of high school students, ESL, independent study, internships, liberal arts/career combination, student-designed major. License preparation in dental hygiene, nursing, paramedic, physical therapy. **Credit/placement by examination:** AP, CLEP, IB, institutional tests. 20 credit hours maximum toward associate degree. **Support services:** GED preparation, learning center, reduced course load, remedial instruction, study skills assistance, tutoring.

Majors. Business: Accounting, administrative services, business admin, finance. **Computer sciences:** General. **Education:** General. **English:** English lit. **Health services:** Dental hygiene, nursing (RN), pharmacy assistant, physical therapy assistant, surgical technology. **Liberal arts:** Arts/sciences. **Protective services:** Firefighting, police science.

Computing on campus. 300 workstations in library, computer center. Commuter students can connect to campus network. Online course registration, online library, helpline, wireless network available.

Student life. Freshman orientation: Mandatory. Preregistration for classes offered. **Activities:** Dance, drama, music ensembles, musical theater, student government.

Student services. Adult student services, career counseling, student employment services, financial aid counseling, veterans' counselor. **Physically disabled:** Services for visually, speech, hearing impaired.

Contact. E-mail: johwil@mohave.edu
Phone: (928) 757-0847 Toll-free number: (866) 664-2832
Fax: (928) 757-0808
John Wilson, Registrar, Mohave Community College, 1971 Jagerson Avenue, Kingman, AZ 86409

Northland Pioneer College
Holbrook, Arizona
www.npc.edu   CB code: 0325

- Public 2-year community and technical college
- Commuter campus in small town

General. Founded in 1973. Regionally accredited. 10 locations in Navajo and Apache Counties. **Enrollment:** 1,500 degree-seeking undergraduates. **Degrees:** 143 associate awarded. **Location:** 200 miles from Phoenix, 90 miles from Flagstaff. **Calendar:** Semester, limited summer session. **Full-time faculty:** 85 total; 12% have terminal degrees. **Part-time faculty:** 260 total.

Student profile.

Out-of-state:	1%	25 or older:	69%

Transfer out. Colleges most students transferred to 2011: Northern Arizona University, University of Arizona, Arizona State University, Western New Mexico University, Brigham Young University.

Basis for selection. Open admission, but selective for some programs. Students under 18 must have satisfactory placement test score. Special requirements for nursing and cosmetology.

2011-2012 Annual costs. Tuition/fees: $1,870; $8,920 out-of-state. Per-credit charge: $60 in-state; $95 out-of-state. Books/supplies: $1,400. Personal expenses: $3,292.

Financial aid. Need-based: Need-based aid available for part-time students. Work-study available nights, weekends and for part-time students. **Non-need-based:** Scholarships awarded for academics, art, job skills, leadership, minority status, music/drama, state residency.

Application procedures. Admission: No deadline. No application fee. Admission notification on a rolling basis. **Financial aid:** Priority date 6/1; no closing date. FAFSA, institutional form required. Applicants notified on a rolling basis starting 5/15; must reply within 2 week(s) of notification.

Academics. Special study options: Cooperative education, distance learning, dual enrollment of high school students, honors, independent study, internships, liberal arts/career combination. License preparation in nursing, paramedic, real estate. **Credit/placement by examination:** AP, CLEP, IB, institutional tests. 52 credit hours maximum toward associate degree. **Support services:** GED preparation and test center, learning center, remedial instruction, study skills assistance, tutoring, writing center.

Majors. Business: General, accounting, administrative services, business admin. **Communications technology:** General. **Computer sciences:** General, computer graphics, data processing, networking. **Education:** General, early childhood, elementary. **General:** Turf management. **Health services:** EMT paramedic, medical assistant, medical transcription, nursing (RN). **Liberal arts:** Arts/sciences, library assistant. **Parks/recreation:** General. **Protective services:** Criminal justice, firefighting. **Work/family studies:** Child care management.

Most popular majors. Business/marketing 13%, education 9%, health sciences 22%.

Computing on campus. 140 workstations in library, computer center. Commuter students can connect to campus network. Online course registration, online library, helpline, wireless network available.

Student life. Freshman orientation: Available. Preregistration for classes offered. **Activities:** Jazz band, choral groups, dance, drama, literary magazine, music ensembles, musical theater, student government, symphony orchestra, National Honor Society, Phi Theta Kappa.

Student services. Adult student services, career counseling, services for economically disadvantaged, student employment services, financial aid counseling, placement for graduates, veterans' counselor. **Physically disabled:** Services for visually, hearing impaired. **Transfer:** Pre-admission transcript evaluation for new students. Transfer adviser, college fairs on campus for students transferring to 4-year colleges.

Contact. E-mail: admissions@npc.edu
Phone: (928) 536-6257 Toll-free number: (800) 266-7845
Fax: (928) 524-7612
Jake Hinton-Rivera, Director of Enrollment Services, Northland Pioneer College, PO Box 610, Holbrook, AZ 86025-0610

Paradise Valley Community College
Phoenix, Arizona   **CB member**
www.pvc.maricopa.edu   **CB code: 2179**

- Public 2-year community college
- Commuter campus in very large city

General. Founded in 1985. Regionally accredited. **Enrollment:** 3,038 full-time, degree-seeking students. **Degrees:** 637 associate awarded. **ROTC:** Army. **Calendar:** Semester, limited summer session. **Full-time faculty:** 101 total. **Part-time faculty:** 436 total. **Special facilities:** Studio theater, performing arts center.

Student profile.

Out-of-state:	3%	25 or older:	50%

Transfer out. Colleges most students transferred to 2011: Arizona State University, Arizona State University West, Northern Arizona University, University of Arizona.

Basis for selection. Open admission.

2011-2012 Annual costs. Tuition/fees: $2,310; $9,540 out-of-state. Per-credit charge: $76 in-state; $317 out-of-state. Books/supplies: $1,200. Personal expenses: $2,805.

Financial aid. Need-based: Need-based aid available for part-time students. Work-study available nights, weekends and for part-time students.

Application procedures. Admission: No deadline. No application fee. Admission notification on a rolling basis. **Financial aid:** No deadline. FAFSA required. Applicants notified on a rolling basis starting 6/1.

Academics. Special study options: Accelerated study, cooperative education, cross-registration, distance learning, dual enrollment of high school students, ESL, honors, independent study, internships, teacher certification program, weekend college. License preparation in nursing, paramedic. **Credit/placement by examination:** AP, CLEP, institutional tests. 30 credit hours maximum toward associate degree. **Support services:** Learning center, remedial instruction, study skills assistance, tutoring, writing center.

Majors. Business: General, accounting, administrative services, customer service support, international, office technology, office/clerical, organizational behavior. **Computer sciences:** General, word processing. **Education:** Educational technology. **Liberal arts:** Arts/sciences.

Computing on campus. 600 workstations in library, computer center, student center. Commuter students can connect to campus network. Online course registration, helpline, wireless network available.

Student life. Freshman orientation: Mandatory. Preregistration for classes offered. **Activities:** Jazz band, choral groups, dance, drama, international student organizations, literary magazine, music ensembles, musical theater, opera, student government, student newspaper, Phi Theta Kappa, student Christian association, human service club, Returning Adults to Education, environmental club, Latter Day Saints student association, recreational outdoor club.

Athletics. NJCAA. **Intercollegiate:** Baseball M, cross-country, golf, soccer, softball W, tennis, track and field. **Team name:** Pumas.

Student services. Adult student services, alcohol/substance abuse counseling, career counseling, student employment services, financial aid counseling, minority student services, on-campus daycare, personal counseling, placement for graduates, veterans' counselor, women's services. **Physically disabled:** Services for visually, speech, hearing impaired. **Transfer:** Transfer adviser, college fairs on campus for students transferring to 4-year colleges.

Contact. Phone: (602) 787-7020 Fax: (602) 787-6625
Shirley Green, Associate Dean Student Services, Paradise Valley Community College, 18401 North 32nd Street, Phoenix, AZ 85032

Paralegal Institute
Scottsdale, Arizona
www.theparalegalinstitute.edu   **CB code: 3888**

- For-profit 2-year virtual career college
- Very large city

General. Accredited by DETC. **Enrollment:** 330 degree-seeking undergraduates. **Degrees:** 15 associate awarded. **Calendar:** Differs by program, extensive summer session. **Full-time faculty:** 2 total. **Part-time faculty:** 3 total.

Basis for selection. Open admission.

2011-2012 Annual costs. Per-credit charge: $150. Diploma programs are $4,600; associate degree programs are $9,000.

Financial aid. Need-based: Work-study available nights, weekends and for part-time students.

Application procedures. Admission: No deadline. No application fee. Application must be submitted on paper.

Academics. Special study options: Distance learning. **Credit/placement by examination:** AP, CLEP.

Student life. Freshman orientation: Available. Preregistration for classes offered.

Student services. Transfer: Pre-admission transcript evaluation for new students.

Contact. E-mail: blaing@theparalegalinstitute.edu
Phone: (602) 212-0501 Toll-free number: (800) 354-1254
Fax: (602) 212-0502
Keith Scheib, Director of Admissions, Paralegal Institute, 7332 East
Butherus Drive, Suite 102, Scottsdale, AZ 85260

Penn Foster College
Scottsdale, Arizona
www.pennfostercollege.edu

- For-profit 2-year virtual college
- Commuter campus in small city

General. Founded in 1975. Accredited by DETC. All courses offered via
distance learning. **Enrollment:** 33,000 undergraduates. **Degrees:** 210 associate awarded. **Calendar:** Differs by program. **Full-time faculty:** 21 total.
Part-time faculty: 58 total.

Basis for selection. Open admission. **Home schooled:** Copy of completion document from a school or copy of standardized tests required. **Learning
Disabled:** Evidence of disability recommended so that accommodations can
be made.

2011-2012 Annual costs. Tuition is $65.00 per-credit-hour for first
semester, $90.00 per-credit-hour for subsequent semesters. Registration
fee: $200.

Financial aid. Need-based: Work-study available nights, weekends and
for part-time students.

Application procedures. Admission: No deadline. $75 fee. Admission
notification on a rolling basis.

Academics. Students allowed 12 months to complete semester (15-20
credit hours). **Special study options:** Distance learning, external degree,
independent study. Bachelor's degree programs available on campus. **Credit/
placement by examination:** AP, CLEP. **Support services:** Remedial instruction, tutoring.

Majors. Business: General, accounting, finance, hospitality admin, marketing. **Computer sciences:** General. **Education:** Early childhood. **Health services:** Medical records technology. **Protective services:** Police science.

Student life. Freshman orientation: Mandatory. Preregistration for
classes offered.

Student services. Veterans' counselor. **Transfer:** Pre-admission transcript evaluation for new students.

Contact. E-mail: info@pennfoster.edu
Phone: (800) 275-4410 Toll-free number: (800) 275-4410
Linda Smith, Manager, DP Services, Penn Foster College, 14300 North
Northsight Boulevard, Suite 120, Scottsdale, AZ 85260

Phoenix College
Phoenix, Arizona
www.pc.maricopa.edu   CB code: 4606

- Public 2-year community college
- Commuter campus in very large city

General. Founded in 1920. Regionally accredited. **Enrollment:** 9,325
degree-seeking undergraduates; 3,675 non-degree-seeking students. **Degrees:**
870 associate awarded. **ROTC:** Army, Air Force. **Calendar:** Semester, limited summer session. **Full-time faculty:** 157 total; 63% women. **Part-time
faculty:** 508 total. **Class size:** 54% < 20, 44% 20-39, 2% 40-49, less than
1% 50-99, less than 1% >100.

Student profile. Among degree-seeking undergraduates, 1,912 enrolled as
first-time, first-year students, 1,496 transferred in from other institutions.

Part-time:	70%	Women:	63%
Out-of-state:	5%	25 or older:	51%

Basis for selection. Open admission, but selective for some programs.
ASSET, COMPASS, ACCUPLACER and Celsa test scores used for placement.

2011-2012 Annual costs. Tuition/fees: $2,340; $9,570 out-of-state. Per-
credit charge: $76 in-state; $317 out-of-state. Books/supplies: $1,200. Per-
sonal expenses: $5,544.

Financial aid. Need-based: Work-study available nights, weekends and
for part-time students.

Application procedures. Admission: No deadline. No application fee.
Admission notification on a rolling basis. **Financial aid:** Priority date 6/30;
no closing date. FAFSA required. Applicants notified on a rolling basis.

Academics. Special study options: Cooperative education, cross-
registration, distance learning, dual enrollment of high school students, ESL,
honors, independent study, internships, liberal arts/career combination, study
abroad. License preparation in nursing. **Credit/placement by examination:**
AP, CLEP, IB, institutional tests. 30 credit hours maximum toward associate
degree. **Support services:** GED test center, learning center, reduced course
load, remedial instruction, study skills assistance, tutoring, writing center.

Honors college/program. Requires 3.0 GPA.

Majors. Business: General, accounting, administrative services, banking/
financial services, business admin, construction management, fashion, management information systems, management science, marketing. **Communications:** Communications/speech/rhetoric. **Communications technology:**
Recording arts. **Computer sciences:** General, computer graphics, systems
analysis, web page design. **Education:** General, family/consumer sciences.
Engineering: General, software. **Foreign languages:** Sign language interpretation. **Health services:** Clinical lab technology, dental assistant, dental
hygiene, EMT paramedic, histologic technology, massage therapy, medical
assistant, medical records technology, medical transcription, nursing (RN),
office admin, premedicine. **Liberal arts:** Arts/sciences. **Parks/recreation:**
General. **Physical sciences:** General. **Protective services:** Criminal justice,
firefighting, forensics. **Visual/performing arts:** General, art, commercial
photography, commercial/advertising art, dramatic, fashion design, graphic
design, interior design, music management, studio arts. **Work/family studies:**
General, child care management, family/community services, institutional
food production.

Computing on campus. 230 workstations in library, computer center.
Online course registration, online library, helpline, wireless network available.

Student life. Freshman orientation: Available. Preregistration for classes
offered. **Activities:** Bands, choral groups, dance, drama, music ensembles,
musical theater, opera, student newspaper, symphony orchestra, TV station.

Athletics. NJCAA. **Intercollegiate:** Baseball M, basketball, cross-country,
football (tackle) M, golf M, soccer, softball W, volleyball W. **Team name:**
PC Bears.

Student services. Adult student services, career counseling, services for
economically disadvantaged, student employment services, financial aid
counseling, legal services, on-campus daycare, personal counseling, placement for graduates, veterans' counselor. **Physically disabled:** Services for
visually, speech, hearing impaired. **Transfer:** Re-entry adviser, pre-admission
transcript evaluation for new students. Transfer adviser, college fairs on
campus for students transferring to 4-year colleges.

Contact. E-mail: info@pcmail.maricopa.edu
Phone: (602) 285-7502 Fax: (602) 285-7813
Kathy French, Director of Admissions and Records, Phoenix College,
1202 West Thomas Road, Phoenix, AZ 85013

Pima Community College
Tucson, Arizona   CB member
www.pima.edu   CB code: 4623

- Public 2-year community and technical college
- Commuter campus in very large city

General. Founded in 1966. Regionally accredited. 6 campuses, distance
education/online courses available. **Enrollment:** 32,624 degree-seeking
undergraduates. **Degrees:** 2,283 associate awarded. **ROTC:** Army, Naval,
Air Force. **Location:** 120 miles from Phoenix. **Calendar:** Semester, extensive
summer session. **Full-time faculty:** 320 total; 61% women. **Part-time faculty:** 1,223 total. **Special facilities:** Performing arts center, arts center, public
safety institute.

Student profile. Of all enrolled students, 7% already have a bachelor's
degree or higher.

Transfer out. 33% of students enrolled in the transfer program go on to
4-year colleges. **Colleges most students transferred to 2011:** University of
Arizona, Arizona State University, Northern Arizona University, University
of Phoenix, Eastern New Mexico University.

Basis for selection. Open admission, but selective for some programs. Special requirements for programs in the health related professions, such as nursing.

2011-2012 Annual costs. Tuition/fees: $1,910; $8,975 out-of-state. Per-credit charge: $58. Books/supplies: $1,600. Personal expenses: $1,300.

Financial aid. Need-based: Need-based aid available for part-time students. Work-study available nights, weekends and for part-time students. **Non-need-based:** Scholarships awarded for academics, alumni affiliation, art, athletics, minority status, music/drama.

Application procedures. Admission: No deadline. No application fee. Admission notification on a rolling basis. **Financial aid:** Priority date 4/1; no closing date. FAFSA required. Applicants notified on a rolling basis starting 5/1; must reply within 2 week(s) of notification.

Academics. Upward Bound and Talent Search programs available. **Special study options:** Accelerated study, distance learning, dual enrollment of high school students, ESL, honors, independent study, internships, student-designed major, teacher certification program, weekend college. Bachelor's degree programs available on campus. License preparation in aviation, nursing, radiology, real estate. **Credit/placement by examination:** AP, CLEP, IB, institutional tests. 45 credit hours maximum toward associate degree. **Support services:** GED preparation and test center, learning center, pre-admission summer program, reduced course load, remedial instruction, study skills assistance, tutoring, writing center.

Majors. Area/ethnic studies: Native American. **Business:** General, accounting, administrative services, fashion, hospitality admin, logistics. **Communications:** Digital media. **Computer sciences:** General, networking, systems analysis. **Education:** General, early childhood. **Foreign languages:** Sign language interpretation, translation. **Health services:** Clinical lab assistant, clinical lab technology, clinical/medical social work, dental hygiene, dental lab technology, EMT paramedic, histologic assistant, massage therapy, medical records technology, nursing (RN), pharmacy assistant, radiologic technology/medical imaging, respiratory therapy technology, veterinary technology/assistant. **Liberal arts:** Arts/sciences. **Protective services:** Criminal justice, firefighting, police science. **Social sciences:** Anthropology, political science, sociology. **Visual/performing arts:** General, cinematography, design, game design. **Work/family studies:** Child development.

Most popular majors. Business/marketing 12%, health sciences 16%, liberal arts 55%.

Computing on campus. 3,912 workstations in library, computer center. Commuter students can connect to campus network. Online course registration, online library, helpline, wireless network available.

Student life. Freshman orientation: Available. Preregistration for classes offered. Orientation programs based on majors. **Activities:** Bands, choral groups, dance, drama, international student organizations, literary magazine, music ensembles, musical theater, student government, student newspaper, symphony orchestra, TV station.

Athletics. NJCAA. **Intercollegiate:** Baseball M, basketball, cross-country, football (tackle) M, golf, soccer, softball W, track and field. **Team name:** Aztecs.

Student services. Alcohol/substance abuse counseling, career counseling, services for economically disadvantaged, financial aid counseling, health services, minority student services, personal counseling, veterans' counselor, women's services. **Physically disabled:** Services for visually, speech, hearing impaired. **Transfer:** Pre-admission transcript evaluation for new students. Transfer adviser, college fairs on campus for students transferring to 4-year colleges.

Contact. E-mail: coadmissions@pima.edu
Phone: (520) 206-4640 Toll-free number: (800) 860-7462
Fax: (520) 206-4790
Michael Tulino, Director and Registrar, Pima Community College, 4905B East Broadway, Tucson, AZ 85709-1120

Refrigeration School
Phoenix, Arizona
www.rsiaz.edu   **CB code: 2888**

- For-profit 2-year technical college
- Commuter campus in very large city
- Interview required

General. Accredited by ACCSC. **Enrollment:** 505 degree-seeking undergraduates. **Degrees:** 40 associate awarded. **Calendar:** Differs by program. **Full-time faculty:** 12 total. **Part-time faculty:** 14 total.

Basis for selection. Open admission, but selective for some programs. **Home schooled:** State high school equivalency certificate required.

2011-2012 Annual costs. Costs for diplomas and associates degree programs range from $7,855 to 29,420; includes books, fees and supplies.

Financial aid. Need-based: Work-study available nights, weekends and for part-time students.

Application procedures. Admission: No deadline. No application fee. Admission notification on a rolling basis.

Academics. Special study options: Weekend college. **Credit/placement by examination:** AP, CLEP. **Support services:** Tutoring.

Computing on campus. 4 workstations in library, computer center. Student web hosting available.

Student services. Career counseling, student employment services, financial aid counseling, placement for graduates. **Physically disabled:** Services for hearing impaired.

Contact. Phone: (602) 275-7133 Toll-free number: (877) 477-4669
Fax: (602) 267-4805
Melissa cairns, Director of Admissions, Refrigeration School, 4210 East Washington Street, Phoenix, AZ 85034-1816

Rio Salado College
Tempe, Arizona   **CB member**
www.riosalado.edu   **CB code: 0997**

- Public 2-year community college
- Commuter campus in very large city

General. Founded in 1978. Regionally accredited. Access to libraries at Arizona State University and 10 Maricopa County community colleges. **Enrollment:** 12,704 degree-seeking undergraduates; 11,937 non-degree-seeking students. **Degrees:** 484 associate awarded. **Location:** 120 miles from Tucson, 10 miles from Phoenix. **Calendar:** Semester, extensive summer session. **Full-time faculty:** 24 total; 12% minority, 75% women. **Part-time faculty:** 962 total; 12% minority, 69% women. **Class size:** 83% < 20, 14% 20-39, 3% 40-49. **Special facilities:** Public radio stations.

Student profile. Among degree-seeking undergraduates, 49% enrolled in a transfer program, 54% enrolled in a vocational program, 8% already have a bachelor's degree or higher, 2,408 enrolled as first-time, first-year students, 154 transferred in from other institutions.

Part-time:	78%	Asian American:	2%
Out-of-state:	5%	Hispanic American:	16%
Women:	66%	Native American:	2%
African American:	20%	25 or older:	71%

Transfer out. Colleges most students transferred to 2011: Arizona State University, University of Arizona, Northern Arizona University.

Basis for selection. Open admission, but selective for some programs. Dental hygiene program has GPA requirements.

2012-2013 Annual costs. Tuition/fees (projected): $2,310; $9,540 out-of-state. Per-credit charge: $76 in-state; $317 out-of-state. Books/supplies: $1,000. Personal expenses: $2,988.

Financial aid. All financial aid based on need. Need-based aid available for part-time students. Work-study available nights, weekends and for part-time students.

Application procedures. Admission: No deadline. No application fee. Admission notification on a rolling basis. **Financial aid:** Priority date 6/30; no closing date. FAFSA, institutional form required. Applicants notified on a rolling basis starting 6/30.

Academics. Agreement with Army allows military personnel to take Internet courses. Online clinical dental assisting program offered. **Special study options:** Accelerated study, cooperative education, cross-registration, distance learning, double major, dual enrollment of high school students, ESL, honors, independent study, internships, liberal arts/career combination, teacher certification program, weekend college. License preparation in dental hygiene, nursing. **Credit/placement by examination:** AP, CLEP, institutional tests. 30 credit hours maximum toward associate degree. **Support services:** GED preparation, learning center, remedial instruction, study skills assistance, tutoring, writing center.

Majors. Business: General, accounting, banking/financial services, business admin, international, office management. **Computer sciences:** General.

Health services: Dental hygiene, nursing assistant, substance abuse counseling. **Human services:** General. **Protective services:** Law enforcement admin.

Computing on campus. 500 workstations in library, computer center. Commuter students can connect to campus network. Online course registration, online library, helpline, wireless network available.

Student life. Freshman orientation: Available. Preregistration for classes offered. Online orientation materials available. **Activities:** Radio station, TV station, Phi Theta Kappa.

Student services. Adult student services, career counseling, student employment services, financial aid counseling, personal counseling, veterans' counselor. **Physically disabled:** Services for visually, speech, hearing impaired. **Transfer:** Re-entry adviser, pre-admission transcript evaluation for new students. Transfer adviser for students transferring to 4-year colleges.

Contact. E-mail: admissions@email.rio.maricopa.edu
Phone: (480) 517-8150 Toll-free number: (800) 729-1197
Fax: (480) 517-8199
Ruby Miller, Associate Dean, Student Enrollment Services, Rio Salado College, 2323 West 14th Street, Tempe, AZ 85281

Scottsdale Community College
Scottsdale, Arizona
www.scottsdalecc.edu CB code: 4755

- Public 2-year community college
- Commuter campus in small city

General. Founded in 1969. Regionally accredited. **Enrollment:** 2,415 degree-seeking undergraduates; 8,930 non-degree-seeking students. **Degrees:** 878 associate awarded. **Location:** 10 miles from Tempe. **Calendar:** Semester, limited summer session. **Full-time faculty:** 157 total; 29% have terminal degrees, 11% minority, 46% women. **Part-time faculty:** 619 total; 6% have terminal degrees, 12% minority, 52% women. **Class size:** 52% < 20, 45% 20-39, 1% 40-49, less than 1% 50-99. **Special facilities:** Student-operated restaurant associated with school of culinary arts.

Student profile. Among degree-seeking undergraduates, 663 enrolled as first-time, first-year students.

Part-time:	61%	Women:	49%
Out-of-state:	5%	25 or older:	39%

Basis for selection. Open admission.

High school preparation. 16 units recommended. Recommended units include English 4, mathematics 4, social studies 2, history 1, science 3 and foreign language 2.

2011-2012 Annual costs. Tuition/fees: $2,310; $9,540 out-of-state. Per-credit charge: $76 in-state; $317 out-of-state. Books/supplies: $1,200. Personal expenses: $5,544.

Financial aid. Need-based: Work-study available nights, weekends and for part-time students. **Non-need-based:** Scholarships awarded for academics, athletics. **Additional information:** Athletic scholarships offered in rodeo. All athletic scholarships limited to county residents.

Application procedures. Admission: No deadline. No application fee. Admission notification on a rolling basis. **Financial aid:** Priority date 6/30; no closing date. FAFSA, institutional form required. Applicants notified on a rolling basis starting 4/1; must reply by 7/15 or within 3 week(s) of notification.

Academics. Special study options: Cooperative education, cross-registration, distance learning, dual enrollment of high school students, ESL, honors, internships, study abroad, teacher certification program. **Credit/placement by examination:** AP, CLEP, institutional tests. 52 credit hours maximum toward associate degree. **Support services:** Learning center, remedial instruction, tutoring, writing center.

Majors. Architecture: Environmental design. **Area/ethnic studies:** Native American. **Business:** General, accounting, administrative services, fashion, hospitality admin, international, management information systems, retailing. **Communications:** Public relations. **Communications technology:** Radio/TV. **Computer sciences:** General, information systems. **Education:** Early childhood. **General:** Equestrian studies. **Health services:** EMT paramedic, medical radiologic technology/radiation therapy, nursing (RN). **Liberal arts:** Arts/sciences. **Parks/recreation:** General. **Physical sciences:** General. **Protective services:** Criminal justice, firefighting, law enforcement admin. **Visual/performing arts:** General, cinematography, dance, dramatic, interior design, music, studio arts. **Work/family studies:** Child care management.

Most popular majors. Business/marketing 13%, health sciences 15%, liberal arts 44%, visual/performing arts 11%.

Computing on campus. 998 workstations in library, computer center, student center. Commuter students can connect to campus network. Online course registration, online library, helpline, repair service, wireless network available.

Student life. Freshman orientation: Available. Preregistration for classes offered. **Activities:** Bands, choral groups, dance, drama, international student organizations, music ensembles, student government, student newspaper, symphony orchestra, TV station, American Indian honor society, black student union, Latino student association, green club, GLBT-straight alliance, Rotoract, advocacy group, student leadership club.

Athletics. NAIA, NJCAA. **Intercollegiate:** Baseball M, basketball, cross-country, football (tackle) M, golf M, soccer M, softball W, tennis, track and field, volleyball W. **Intramural:** Baseball M. **Team name:** Artichokes.

Student services. Alcohol/substance abuse counseling, career counseling, student employment services, financial aid counseling, personal counseling, veterans' counselor. **Physically disabled:** Services for visually, speech, hearing impaired. **Transfer:** Transfer adviser, college fairs on campus for students transferring to 4-year colleges.

Contact. E-mail: admissions@sccmail.maricopa.edu
Phone: (480) 423-6100 Fax: (480) 423-6200
Fran Watkins, Director of Admissions and Records, Scottsdale Community College, 9000 East Chaparral Road, Scottsdale, AZ 85256-2626

Sessions College for Professional Design
Tempe, Arizona
www.sessions.edu CB code: 6356

- Private 2-year virtual visual arts college
- Very large city
- Application essay required

General. Regionally accredited; also accredited by DETC. Fully online certificate and degree programs in visual arts and design. **Enrollment:** 35 degree-seeking undergraduates. **Calendar:** Continuous, extensive summer session. **Part-time faculty:** 35 total.

Basis for selection. Open admission, but selective for some programs. Certificate programs are open enrollment with high school diploma/GED requirement. Degree programs are selective, requiring review of art/design portfolio, letters of recommendation, essay, and prior transcripts. Degree program applicants must provide a portfolio of 5-10 art/design samples. **Home schooled:** Transcript of courses and grades, state high school equivalency certificate required.

Financial aid. Need-based: Work-study available nights, weekends and for part-time students.

Application procedures. Admission: No deadline. $50 fee. Application must be submitted online. Admission notification on a rolling basis.

Academics. Special study options: Distance learning. **Credit/placement by examination:** AP, CLEP.

Majors. Computer sciences: Web page design. **Visual/performing arts:** Graphic design.

Computing on campus. PC or laptop required. Online library available.

Student life. Freshman orientation: Mandatory. Preregistration for classes offered.

Contact. E-mail: admissions@sessions.edu
Phone: (480) 212-1704 Toll-free number: (800) 258-4115
Jonathan Price, Director of Admissions, Sessions College for Professional Design, 398 South Mill Avenue, Suite 300, Tempe, AZ 85281

South Mountain Community College
Phoenix, Arizona
CB member
www.southmountaincc.edu CB code: 4734

- Public 2-year community college
- Commuter campus in very large city

General. Founded in 1979. Regionally accredited. Learning Center in Guadalupe. Arizona Agribusiness Equine Charter school located on campus. **Enrollment:** 1,480 full-time, degree-seeking students. **Degrees:** 369 associate awarded. **Location:** 8 miles from downtown. **Calendar:** Semester, limited summer session. **Full-time faculty:** 66 total. **Part-time faculty:** 194 total. **Partnerships:** Formal partnership with Arizona Agribusiness Equine Charter School.

Student profile.

Out-of-state:	2%	25 or older:	45%

Basis for selection. Open admission.

2011-2012 Annual costs. Tuition/fees: $2,310; $9,540 out-of-state. Per-credit charge: $76 in-state; $317 out-of-state. Books/supplies: $760. Personal expenses: $1,250.

Financial aid. Need-based: Need-based aid available for part-time students. Work-study available nights, weekends and for part-time students. **Non-need-based:** Scholarships awarded for academics, athletics, minority status, music/drama.

Application procedures. Admission: No deadline. $15 fee. Admission notification on a rolling basis. **Financial aid:** Priority date 5/1; no closing date. FAFSA required. Applicants notified on a rolling basis starting 5/15; must reply within 3 week(s) of notification.

Academics. Special study options: Cooperative education, cross-registration, dual enrollment of high school students, ESL, honors, independent study. **Credit/placement by examination:** AP, CLEP, IB, institutional tests. 30 credit hours maximum toward associate degree. **Support services:** GED preparation and test center, learning center, remedial instruction, tutoring.

Majors. Biology: General. **Business:** Administrative services, business admin, customer service support, international, logistics, office technology. **Computer sciences:** General, information systems, security, system admin, systems analysis. **Education:** General, early childhood, music, physical. **English:** English lit. **History:** General. **Liberal arts:** Arts/sciences. **Math:** General. **Physical sciences:** General, chemistry, physics. **Psychology:** General. **Social sciences:** Political science, sociology. **Visual/performing arts:** Art, music. **Work/family studies:** General.

Most popular majors. Computer/information sciences 6%, liberal arts 83%.

Computing on campus. 125 workstations in library, computer center.

Student life. Freshman orientation: Available. Preregistration for classes offered. **Activities:** Concert band, choral groups, dance, drama, music ensembles, student government, student newspaper, African-American unity coalition, Society of Hispanic Engineers and Scientists, Christian student club, Native American club, forensic club, music club, volunteers program, Phi Theta Kappa.

Athletics. NJCAA. **Intercollegiate:** Baseball M, basketball, golf, soccer M, softball W, tennis, volleyball W. **Team name:** Cougars.

Student services. Career counseling, student employment services, on-campus daycare, personal counseling, veterans' counselor. **Transfer:** Re-entry adviser, pre-admission transcript evaluation for new students. Transfer adviser, college fairs on campus for students transferring to 4-year colleges.

Contact. Phone: (602) 243-8124 Fax: (602) 243-8199
Gia Garcia-Taylor, Associate Dean of Student Services, South Mountain Community College, 7050 South 24th Street, Phoenix, AZ 85042

Tohono O'odham Community College
Sells, Arizona
www.tocc.cc.az.us

- Public 2-year community college
- Commuter campus in rural community

General. Enrollment: 172 degree-seeking undergraduates; 123 non-degree-seeking students. **Degrees:** 6 associate awarded. **Location:** 60 miles from Tucson. **Calendar:** Semester, limited summer session. **Full-time faculty:** 14 total; 21% have terminal degrees. **Part-time faculty:** 15 total. **Class size:** 98% < 20, 2% 20-39.

Student profile. Among degree-seeking undergraduates, 55% enrolled in a transfer program, 15% enrolled in a vocational program, 7% already have a bachelor's degree or higher, 37 enrolled as first-time, first-year students.

Part-time:	72%	Hispanic American:	5%
Women:	55%	Native American:	90%
African American:	2%	25 or older:	81%

Basis for selection. Open admission. **Home schooled:** Transcript of courses and grades, state high school equivalency certificate required.

2011-2012 Annual costs. Books/supplies: $750.

Financial aid. All financial aid based on need. Need-based aid available for part-time students. Work-study available nights, weekends and for part-time students.

Application procedures. Admission: No deadline. No application fee. **Financial aid:** No deadline. FAFSA, institutional form required. Applicants notified on a rolling basis.

Academics. Special study options: Distance learning, dual enrollment of high school students, independent study. **Credit/placement by examination:** AP, CLEP. **Support services:** GED preparation, learning center, remedial instruction, study skills assistance, tutoring, writing center.

Majors. Business: Business admin. **Computer sciences:** System admin. **Education:** Early childhood special, elementary. **General:** Production. **Liberal arts:** Arts/sciences. **Social sciences:** General.

Most popular majors. Business/marketing 17%, education 33%, interdisciplinary studies 33%, public administration/social services 17%.

Student life. Freshman orientation: Mandatory. Preregistration for classes offered. Orientation class offers information on student services and academic support services. **Activities:** Student government.

Athletics. Team name: Jegos.

Student services. Adult student services, career counseling, student employment services, financial aid counseling, personal counseling, placement for graduates. **Transfer:** Re-entry adviser, pre-admission transcript evaluation for new students. College fairs on campus for students transferring to 4-year colleges.

Contact. E-mail: lluna@tocc.edu
Phone: (520) 383-8401 ext. 35 Fax: (520) 383-0029
Leslie Luna, Registrar, Tohono O'odham Community College, PO Box 3129, Sells, AZ 85634-3129

Universal Technical Institute
Avondale, Arizona
www.uti.edu   CB code: 2504

- For-profit 2-year technical college
- Commuter campus in small city

General. Founded in 1965. Accredited by ACCSC. **Enrollment:** 3,223 full-time, degree-seeking students. **Degrees:** 1,589 associate awarded. **Location:** 17 miles from Phoenix, 11 miles from Glendale. **Calendar:** Differs by program, extensive summer session. **Full-time faculty:** 96 total.

Basis for selection. Open admission. **Home schooled:** Must pass Wonderlic Scholastic Level Exam. **Learning Disabled:** Students seeking accommodations must provide copy of IEP from high school and/or medical documentation. They must also complete paperwork requesting accommodation and meet with School Counselor or Student Services Director prior to starting school.

Financial aid. Need-based: Work-study available nights, weekends and for part-time students.

Application procedures. Admission: No deadline. No application fee. Admission notification on a rolling basis. **Financial aid:** No deadline. FAFSA required.

Academics. Special study options: Accelerated study. **Credit/placement by examination:** AP, CLEP. **Support services:** Tutoring.

Computing on campus. 9 workstations in library.

Student life. Freshman orientation: Mandatory. Preregistration for classes offered. **Activities:** Student government.

Student services. Career counseling, services for economically disadvantaged, student employment services, financial aid counseling, veterans' counselor. **Physically disabled:** Services for hearing impaired.

Contact. E-mail: info@uticorp.com
Phone: (623) 245-4600 Toll-free number: (800) 859-1202
Fax: (623) 245-4605
Admissions Director, Universal Technical Institute, 10695 West Pierce Street, Avondale, AZ 85323

Yavapai College
Prescott, Arizona
www.yc.edu   CB code: 4996

- Public 2-year community college
- Commuter campus in large town

General. Founded in 1966. Regionally accredited. Classes offered at branch campus in Clarkdale and several locations in Yavapai County. **Enrollment:** 7,837 degree-seeking undergraduates. **Degrees:** 457 associate awarded. **ROTC:** Army, Air Force. **Location:** 100 miles from Phoenix. **Calendar:** Semester, limited summer session. **Full-time faculty:** 98 total; 9% minority, 45% women. **Part-time faculty:** 309 total; 16% minority, 52% women. **Special facilities:** Solar laboratory, solar greenhouse, performance hall, career technical educational center.

Student profile.

Out-of-state:	6%	Native American:	3%
African American:	1%	25 or older:	24%
Asian American:	1%	Live on campus:	10%
Hispanic American:	9%		

Transfer out. **Colleges most students transferred to 2011:** Arizona State University, Northern Arizona University, University of Arizona, Old Dominion University.

Basis for selection. Open admission, but selective for some programs. Limited admission for registered nursing, gunsmithing, and independent filmmaking. Interview required of nursing majors. Essay for independent filmmaking.

2011-2012 Annual costs. Tuition/fees: $2,010; $8,802 out-of-state. Per-credit charge: $67 in-state; $350 out-of-state. Room/board: $6,528. Books/supplies: $1,000. Personal expenses: $1,900.

Financial aid. **Need-based:** Need-based aid available for part-time students. Work-study available nights, weekends and for part-time students. **Non-need-based:** Scholarships awarded for academics, athletics.

Application procedures. **Admission:** No deadline. No application fee. Admission notification on a rolling basis. **Financial aid:** Priority date 4/1; no closing date. FAFSA required. Applicants notified on a rolling basis.

Academics. **Special study options:** Accelerated study, distance learning, dual enrollment of high school students, ESL, honors, independent study, internships, liberal arts/career combination, teacher certification program, weekend college. 2-2 program with Northern Arizona University for bachelor degree in education and business, program with Old Dominion University offering bachelor degree completion. Bachelor's degree programs available on campus. License preparation in nursing, paramedic, real estate. **Credit/placement by examination:** AP, CLEP, IB, institutional tests. 30 credit hours maximum toward associate degree. **Support services:** GED preparation and test center, learning center, pre-admission summer program, reduced course load, remedial instruction, study skills assistance, tutoring, writing center.

Majors. **Architecture:** Environmental design. **Business:** Accounting, administrative services, business admin, office management, office technology. **Computer sciences:** General. **Education:** Early childhood. **General:** Business. **Health services:** Medical secretary, nursing (RN). **Liberal arts:** Arts/sciences. **Protective services:** Firefighting, law enforcement admin. **Visual/performing arts:** Commercial/advertising art, industrial design.

Computing on campus. 1,609 workstations in dormitories, library, computer center. Dormitories wired for high-speed internet access and linked to campus network. Commuter students can connect to campus network. Online course registration, online library, wireless network available.

Student life. **Freshman orientation:** Available. Preregistration for classes offered. **Housing:** Coed dorms, special housing for disabled, wellness housing available. $150 deposit. **Activities:** Bands, choral groups, dance, drama, literary magazine, music ensembles, musical theater, student government, student newspaper, nursing association, Native American club, international

student club, Hispanic club, Campus Crusade for Christ, Bahai club, PTK, Veterans' club.

Athletics. NJCAA. **Intercollegiate:** Baseball M, basketball, soccer M, volleyball W. **Team name:** Roughriders.

Student services. Adult student services, career counseling, student employment services, financial aid counseling, health services, personal counseling, placement for graduates, veterans' counselor. **Physically disabled:** Services for visually, hearing impaired. **Transfer:** College fairs on campus for students transferring to 4-year colleges.

Contact. E-mail: registration@yc.edu
Phone: (928) 445-7300 ext. 2148 Toll-free number: (800) 922-6787
Fax: (928) 776-2151
Sheila Jarrell, Registrar, Yavapai College, 1100 East Sheldon Street, Prescott, AZ 86301

Arkansas

Arkansas Northeastern College
Blytheville, Arkansas
www.anc.edu   CB code: 1267

▶ Public 2-year community college
▶ Commuter campus in small town

General. Founded in 1974. Regionally accredited. **Enrollment:** 2,000 undergraduates. **Degrees:** 283 associate awarded. **Location:** 65 miles from Memphis, TN. **Calendar:** Semester, limited summer session. **Full-time faculty:** 79 total. **Part-time faculty:** 69 total. **Class size:** 66% < 20, 32% 20-39, less than 1% 40-49, 1% 50-99.

Student profile.

Out-of-state: 18%   25 or older: 50%

Transfer out. Colleges most students transferred to 2011: Arkansas State University, Southeast Missouri State University.

Basis for selection. Open admission, but selective for some programs. Entrance exam required for both the LPN and RN programs.

High school preparation. College-preparatory program recommended.

2011-2012 Annual costs. Tuition/fees: $1,880; $2,180 out-of-district; $3,680 out-of-state. Per-credit charge: $55 in-district; $65 out-of-district; $115 out-of-state. Books/supplies: $1,446. Personal expenses: $5,387.

Financial aid. Need-based: Need-based aid available for part-time students. Work-study available nights, weekends and for part-time students. **Non-need-based:** Scholarships awarded for academics, art, minority status, music/drama, state residency.

Application procedures. Admission: No deadline. No application fee. Admission notification on a rolling basis. **Financial aid:** Priority date 4/15; no closing date. FAFSA, institutional form required. Applicants notified on a rolling basis starting 5/1; must reply within 2 week(s) of notification.

Academics. Special study options: Accelerated study, distance learning, double major, dual enrollment of high school students. Bachelor's degree programs available on campus. License preparation in aviation, dental hygiene, nursing, paramedic. **Credit/placement by examination:** AP, CLEP, institutional tests. 15 credit hours maximum toward associate degree. Placement tests required for algebra and English composition. **Support services:** GED preparation and test center, learning center, reduced course load, remedial instruction, study skills assistance, tutoring, writing center.

Majors. Business: General, administrative services, management information systems. **Education:** Middle. **General:** Food science, horticulture. **Health services:** Nursing (RN). **Liberal arts:** Arts/sciences. **Protective services:** Police science. **Work/family studies:** Child care service.

Most popular majors. Business/marketing 12%, education 8%, health sciences 12%, liberal arts 58%.

Computing on campus. 400 workstations in library, computer center. Commuter students can connect to campus network. Online course registration, online library, wireless network available.

Student life. Freshman orientation: Available. Preregistration for classes offered. **Activities:** Choral groups, music ensembles, cultural diversity association, Baptist college ministry, adult student association.

Student services. Adult student services, career counseling, services for economically disadvantaged, student employment services, financial aid counseling, on-campus daycare, personal counseling, placement for graduates, veterans' counselor. **Physically disabled:** Services for visually, speech, hearing impaired. **Transfer:** Pre-admission transcript evaluation for new students. Transfer adviser, college fairs on campus for students transferring to 4-year colleges.

Contact. Phone: (870) 762-1020 ext. 1103 Fax: (870) 763-1654
Laura Yarbrough, Registrar, Arkansas Northeastern College, PO Box 1109, Blytheville, AR 72316-1109

Arkansas State University: Beebe
Beebe, Arkansas
www.asub.edu   CB code: 0782

▶ Public 2-year community college
▶ Commuter campus in small town

General. Founded in 1927. Regionally accredited. Approved as Serviceman's Opportunity College. **Enrollment:** 3,682 degree-seeking undergraduates; 1,007 non-degree-seeking students. **Degrees:** 554 associate awarded. **ROTC:** Army. **Location:** 35 miles from Little Rock. **Calendar:** Semester, extensive summer session. **Class size:** 56% < 20, 43% 20-39, 1% 40-49.

Student profile. Among degree-seeking undergraduates, 986 enrolled as first-time, first-year students.

Part-time: 34%   Women: 60%

Basis for selection. Open admission, but selective for some programs.

High school preparation. College-preparatory program recommended. 15 units recommended. Recommended units include English 3, mathematics 1, social studies 2 and science 2.

2011-2012 Annual costs. Tuition/fees: $2,850; $4,650 out-of-state. Per-credit charge: $83 in-state; $143 out-of-state. Room/board: $4,570. Books/supplies: $1,242. Personal expenses: $2,655.

Financial aid. Need-based: Need-based aid available for part-time students. Work-study available nights, weekends and for part-time students. **Non-need-based:** Scholarships awarded for academics, leadership, music/drama.

Application procedures. Admission: No deadline. No application fee. Admission notification on a rolling basis. **Financial aid:** Priority date 6/1; no closing date. FAFSA, institutional form required. Applicants notified on a rolling basis starting 6/1; must reply within 2 week(s) of notification.

Academics. Special study options: Accelerated study, distance learning, double major, dual enrollment of high school students, external degree, honors, independent study, internships. Bachelor's degree programs available on campus. License preparation in nursing, paramedic. **Credit/placement by examination:** AP, CLEP. 30 credit hours maximum toward associate degree. **Support services:** Learning center, reduced course load, remedial instruction, tutoring.

Majors. Business: General, hospitality admin, management information systems. **Education:** Early childhood, multi-level teacher. **General:** Agribusiness operations. **Health services:** Clinical lab technology, EMT paramedic, pharmacy assistant, veterinary technology/assistant. **Liberal arts:** Arts/sciences. **Protective services:** Criminal justice, forensics, law enforcement admin, police science. **Visual/performing arts:** Music.

Most popular majors. Education 7%, engineering/engineering technologies 6%, health sciences 16%, liberal arts 59%, security/protective services 6%, trade and industry 6%.

Computing on campus. Dormitories linked to campus network. Online course registration, online library, repair service, wireless network available.

Student life. Freshman orientation: Mandatory. Preregistration for classes offered. **Housing:** Coed dorms available. $150 partly refundable deposit. **Activities:** Bands, campus ministries, choral groups, drama, international student organizations, music ensembles, student government, Gamma Beta Phi, Phi Beta Lambda, Student Advisory Board, Leadership Council.

Athletics. Intramural: Archery, badminton, basketball, bowling, football (non-tackle), golf, racquetball, softball, table tennis, tennis, track and field, volleyball.

Student services. Career counseling, services for economically disadvantaged, financial aid counseling, personal counseling, placement for graduates, veterans' counselor. **Transfer:** Transfer adviser, college fairs on campus for students transferring to 4-year colleges.

Contact. E-mail: rahayes@asub.edu
Phone: (501) 882-8860 Toll-free number: (800) 632-9985
Fax: (501) 882-8895
Robin Hayes, Director of Admissions, Arkansas State University: Beebe, PO Box 1000, Beebe, AR 72012-1000

Arkansas State University: Mountain Home
Mountain Home, Arkansas
www.asumh.edu   CB code: 6057

▶ Public 2-year community and technical college
▶ Commuter campus in large town

General. Enrollment: 1,263 degree-seeking undergraduates. **Degrees:** 244 associate awarded. **Location:** 130 miles from Little Rock. **Calendar:** Semester, limited summer session. **Full-time faculty:** 48 total; 21% have terminal degrees, 6% minority, 62% women. **Part-time faculty:** 21 total; 14% have terminal degrees, 43% women. **Class size:** 62% < 20, 37% 20-39, less than 1% 40-49, less than 1% 50-99.

Student profile. Among degree-seeking undergraduates, 23% enrolled in a transfer program, 3% enrolled in a vocational program, 1% already have a bachelor's degree or higher, 316 enrolled as first-time, first-year students, 119 transferred in from other institutions.

Part-time:	30%	Women:	65%
Out-of-state:	1%	25 or older:	36%

Transfer out. Colleges most students transferred to 2011: Arkansas State University-Jonesboro, University of Central Arkansas-Conway, University of Arkansas-Fayetteville.

Basis for selection. Open admission, but selective for some programs. Additional requirements for practical nursing, respiratory care, and phlebotomy programs. **Home schooled:** Statement describing home school structure and mission, transcript of courses and grades, state high school equivalency certificate required. **Learning Disabled:** Students with learning disabilities must document them with disability coordinator.

High school preparation. College-preparatory program recommended. Recommended units include English 4, mathematics 4, social studies 3 and science 4.

2011-2012 Annual costs. Tuition/fees: $3,030; $4,770 out-of-state. Per-credit charge: $84 in-state; $142 out-of-state. Books/supplies: $1,250. Personal expenses: $3,055.

2011-2012 Financial aid. Need-based: Average need met was 95%. Average scholarship/grant was $5,076; average loan $3,151. 73% of total undergraduate aid awarded as scholarships/grants, 27% as loans/jobs. Need-based aid available for part-time students. Work-study available nights, weekends and for part-time students. **Non-need-based:** Scholarships awarded for academics, alumni affiliation, leadership, state residency. **Additional information:** Satisfactory academic progress policy for Title IV aid.

Application procedures. Admission: Closing date 8/15 (receipt date). No application fee. Admission notification on a rolling basis. **Financial aid:** Priority date 7/1; no closing date. FAFSA, institutional form required. Applicants notified on a rolling basis starting 5/1; must reply within 2 week(s) of notification.

Academics. Special study options: Cooperative education, distance learning, dual enrollment of high school students, ESL, honors, independent study, liberal arts/career combination. License preparation in funeral sciences, practical nursing, respiratory care, and paramedic tech. Bachelor's degree programs available on campus. License preparation in nursing, paramedic. **Credit/placement by examination:** AP, CLEP. 15 credit hours maximum toward associate degree, 15 toward bachelor's. **Support services:** GED preparation and test center, learning center, remedial instruction, study skills assistance, tutoring, writing center.

Majors. Business: General, administrative services. **Computer sciences:** Information systems. **Education:** Early childhood, multi-level teacher. **Health services:** EMT paramedic, respiratory therapy technology. **Liberal arts:** Arts/sciences. **Protective services:** Law enforcement admin.

Most popular majors. Business/marketing 11%, education 15%, liberal arts 55%, personal/culinary services 6%.

Computing on campus. 100 workstations in library, computer center, student center. Commuter students can connect to campus network. Online course registration, online library, helpline, wireless network available.

Student life. Freshman orientation: Available. Preregistration for classes offered. **Activities:** Campus ministries, drama, literary magazine, student government, Circle K, criminal justice club, mortuary science club, student ambassadors, student practical nurses association, Phi Beta Lambda, Phi Delta Kappa, Phi Theta Kappa, Rotaract.

Student services. Adult student services, career counseling, student employment services, financial aid counseling, placement for graduates, veterans' counselor. **Physically disabled:** Services for visually, hearing impaired.

Transfer: Pre-admission transcript evaluation for new students. College fairs on campus for students transferring to 4-year colleges.

Contact. E-mail: rblagg@asumh.edu
Phone: (870) 508-6100 ext. 104 Fax: (870) 508-6287
Rosalyn Blagg, Assistant Vice Chancellor for Enrollment, Arkansas State University: Mountain Home, 1600 South College Street, Mountain Home, AR 72653

Arkansas State University: Newport
Newport, Arkansas
www.asun.edu

▶ Public 2-year community and liberal arts college
▶ Commuter campus in small town

General. Enrollment: 885 full-time, degree-seeking students. **Degrees:** 137 associate awarded. **Location:** 100 miles from Little Rock, 45 miles from Jonesboro. **Calendar:** Semester, limited summer session. **Full-time faculty:** 73 total. **Part-time faculty:** 30 total.

Student profile. Among full-time, degree-seeking students, 30% enrolled in a transfer program, 40% enrolled in a vocational program, 1% already have a bachelor's degree or higher.

Transfer out. Colleges most students transferred to 2011: University of Central Arkansas, Arkansas State University: Jonesboro, University of Arkansas, Arkansas Tech University.

Basis for selection. Students may be required to remove deficiencies before entering certain programs or courses. **Home schooled:** Transcript of courses and grades, state high school equivalency certificate required. Conditional enrollment; must provide placement scores. **Learning Disabled:** Coordinated by Vice Chancellor for Student Services.

2011-2012 Annual costs. Tuition/fees: $2,700; $4,290 out-of-state. Per-credit charge: $83 in-state; $136 out-of-state.

Financial aid. Need-based: Work-study available nights, weekends and for part-time students.

Application procedures. Admission: No deadline. No application fee. Admission notification on a rolling basis. **Financial aid:** Priority date 5/1; no closing date.

Academics. Special study options: Cooperative education, distance learning, dual enrollment of high school students, independent study, internships, liberal arts/career combination, study abroad, teacher certification program. License preparation in nursing. **Credit/placement by examination:** AP, CLEP, institutional tests. 30 credit hours maximum toward associate degree. **Support services:** GED preparation and test center, learning center, remedial instruction, study skills assistance, tutoring.

Majors. Business: General, management information systems. **Education:** Middle. **Health services:** EMT paramedic. **Liberal arts:** Arts/sciences.

Computing on campus. Commuter students can connect to campus network. Online course registration, online library, helpline, repair service, wireless network available.

Student life. Freshman orientation: Mandatory. Preregistration for classes offered. **Activities:** Drama, student government.

Student services. Career counseling, services for economically disadvantaged, financial aid counseling, personal counseling, veterans' counselor. **Physically disabled:** Services for visually, speech, hearing impaired. **Transfer:** Re-entry adviser, pre-admission transcript evaluation for new students. Transfer adviser, college fairs on campus for students transferring to 4-year colleges.

Contact. E-mail: rsummers@asun.edu
Phone: (870) 512-7800 Toll-free number: (800) 976-1676
Fax: (870) 512-7825
Robert Summers, Registrar/Director of Admissions, Arkansas State University: Newport, 7648 Victory Boulevard, Newport, AR 72112

Black River Technical College
Pocahontas, Arkansas
www.blackrivertech.edu   CB code: 3879

▶ Public 2-year technical college
▶ Commuter campus in small town

General. Regionally accredited. **Enrollment:** 2,148 degree-seeking undergraduates. **Degrees:** 218 associate awarded. **Location:** 35 miles from Jonesboro. **Calendar:** Semester, extensive summer session. **Full-time faculty:** 68 total. **Part-time faculty:** 65 total.

Transfer out. Colleges most students transferred to 2011: Williams Baptist College, Arkansas State University.

Basis for selection. Open admission, but selective for some programs. High school transcript and standardized test scores most important. **Home schooled:** Transcript of courses and grades required.

2011-2012 Annual costs. Tuition/fees: $2,460; $5,820 out-of-state. Per-credit charge: $70 in-state; $182 out-of-state.

Financial aid. Need-based: Need-based aid available for part-time students. Work-study available nights, weekends and for part-time students. **Non-need-based:** Scholarships awarded for academics, leadership, state residency.

Application procedures. Admission: No deadline. No application fee. **Financial aid:** Priority date 4/1, closing date 6/30. FAFSA required.

Academics. Special study options: Accelerated study, distance learning, dual enrollment of high school students, independent study, internships, weekend college. License preparation in aviation, nursing, paramedic. **Credit/placement by examination:** AP, CLEP, institutional tests. **Support services:** GED preparation and test center, learning center, remedial instruction, study skills assistance, tutoring.

Majors. Business: Accounting, business admin, management information systems. **Education:** Early childhood, elementary. **Protective services:** Police science. **Social sciences:** Economics. **Visual/performing arts:** Art.

Computing on campus. Commuter students can connect to campus network. Online course registration, online library, helpline, wireless network available.

Student life. Freshman orientation: Mandatory. Preregistration for classes offered. **Activities:** Choral groups, music ensembles, student government, student newspaper.

Student services. Career counseling, financial aid counseling, health services, placement for graduates, veterans' counselor. **Physically disabled:** Services for visually, speech, hearing impaired. **Transfer:** Pre-admission transcript evaluation for new students. College fairs on campus for students transferring to 4-year colleges.

Contact. E-mail: shana.akers@blackrivertech.edu
Phone: (870) 248-4000 Fax: (870) 248-4100
Mary Anderson, Academic Advisor, Black River Technical College, Highway 304 East, Pocahontas, AR 72455

Bryan College: Rogers
Rogers, Arkansas
www.bryancolleges.edu

- For-profit 2-year career college
- Small city

General. Regionally accredited; also accredited by ACICS. **Enrollment:** 292 degree-seeking undergraduates. **Degrees:** 44 associate awarded. **Calendar:** Quarter. **Full-time faculty:** 4 total. **Part-time faculty:** 12 total.

Basis for selection. Open admission.

Financial aid. Need-based: Work-study available nights, weekends and for part-time students.

Application procedures. Admission: No deadline. $50 fee. Admission notification on a rolling basis.

Academics. Credit/placement by examination: AP, CLEP.

Majors. Business: Business admin. **Computer sciences:** Networking. **Health services:** Medical assistant.

Contact. Phone: (479) 899-6644
L. Hutchison, Director of Admissions, Bryan College: Rogers, 3704 West Walnut Street, Rogers, AR 72756

College of the Ouachitas
Malvern, Arkansas
www.coto.edu   CB code: 3619

- Public 2-year community and technical college
- Commuter campus in small town

General. Regionally accredited. **Enrollment:** 800 degree-seeking undergraduates; 607 non-degree-seeking students. **Degrees:** 108 associate awarded. **ROTC:** Army. **Location:** 45 miles from Little Rock. **Calendar:** Semester, limited summer session. **Full-time faculty:** 32 total; 9% have terminal degrees, 3% minority, 56% women. **Part-time faculty:** 66 total; 9% have terminal degrees, 9% minority, 62% women.

Student profile. Among degree-seeking undergraduates, 1% already have a bachelor's degree or higher, 153 enrolled as first-time, first-year students, 69 transferred in from other institutions.

Part-time:	29%	Hispanic American:	2%
Out-of-state:	1%	Native American:	1%
Women:	70%	25 or older:	54%
African American:	14%		

Transfer out. Colleges most students transferred to 2011: Henderson State University, University of Central Arkansas.

Basis for selection. Open admission, but selective for some programs. Admission to practical nursing, registered nursing, and cosmetology programs based on test scores.

2011-2012 Annual costs. Tuition/fees: $2,386; $4,246 out-of-state. Per-credit charge: $62 in-state; $124 out-of-state. Books/supplies: $904. Personal expenses: $1,202.

Financial aid. Need-based: Need-based aid available for part-time students. Work-study available nights, weekends and for part-time students.

Application procedures. Admission: No deadline. No application fee. **Financial aid:** No deadline. FAFSA required. Applicants notified on a rolling basis starting 7/1; must reply within 6 week(s) of notification.

Academics. Associate of Arts in General Education and Associate of Applied Science in Criminal Justice offered online. **Special study options:** Distance learning, dual enrollment of high school students, independent study, internships, liberal arts/career combination. License preparation in nursing. **Credit/placement by examination:** AP, CLEP, institutional tests. **Support services:** GED preparation and test center, learning center, remedial instruction, study skills assistance, tutoring.

Majors. Business: General, business admin. **Computer sciences:** General. **Education:** Early childhood. **Health services:** Nursing (RN). **Liberal arts:** Arts/sciences. **Protective services:** Criminal justice, forensics. **Work/family studies:** Child care management.

Most popular majors. Business/marketing 10%, health sciences 40%, interdisciplinary studies 7%, liberal arts 35%.

Computing on campus. 150 workstations in library, computer center. Online library, helpline, wireless network available.

Student life. Freshman orientation: Mandatory. Preregistration for classes offered. Mandatory orientation can be completed online. Optional orientation offered on-campus. **Activities:** Student government.

Student services. Adult student services, alcohol/substance abuse counseling, chaplain/spiritual director, career counseling, services for economically disadvantaged, student employment services, financial aid counseling, personal counseling, placement for graduates, veterans' counselor. **Physically disabled:** Services for visually, speech, hearing impaired. **Transfer:** Pre-admission transcript evaluation for new students. College fairs on campus for students transferring to 4-year colleges.

Contact. E-mail: info@coto.edu
Phone: (501) 337-5000 ext. 1118 Fax: (501) 337-9382
Linda Johnson, Registrar, College of the Ouachitas, One College Circle, Malvern, AR 72104

Cossatot Community College of the University of Arkansas
De Queen, Arkansas
www.cccua.edu   CB code: 3613

- Public 2-year community college
- Commuter campus in small town

General. Regionally accredited. Off-campus sites located in Nashville and Ashdown. **Enrollment:** 1,025 degree-seeking undergraduates. **Degrees:** 104 associate awarded. **Location:** 60 miles from Texarkana. **Calendar:** Semester, limited summer session. **Full-time faculty:** 35 total. **Part-time faculty:** 72 total. **Class size:** 69% < 20, 31% 20-39.

Student profile.

Out-of-state:	2%	25 or older:	38%

Transfer out. Colleges most students transferred to 2011: Henderson State University, Texas A&M - Texarkana, Arkansas Tech University, University of Central Arkansas, Southern Arkansas University.

Basis for selection. Open admission, but selective for some programs. Admission to nursing programs based upon test scores and previous course grades.

High school preparation. 22 units required. Required units include English 4, mathematics 4, social studies 2, history 1, science 3 (laboratory 2), foreign language 1 and academic electives 5.

2011-2012 Annual costs. Tuition/fees: $1,990; $2,320 out-of-district; $4,900 out-of-state. Per-credit charge: $53 in-district; $64 out-of-district; $150 out-of-state. Residents of bordering out-of-state counties may qualify for in-state tuition. Books/supplies: $1,492. Personal expenses: $2,699.

Financial aid. Need-based: Need-based aid available for part-time students. Work-study available nights, weekends and for part-time students. **Additional information:** Active or honorably discharged military and their dependents receive tuition discounts.

Application procedures. Admission: No deadline. No application fee. Admission notification on a rolling basis. **Financial aid:** Priority date 5/1; no closing date. FAFSA, institutional form required. Applicants notified on a rolling basis starting 3/1.

Academics. Special study options: Accelerated study, cooperative education, distance learning, double major, dual enrollment of high school students, ESL, exchange student, independent study, internships, liberal arts/career combination, student-designed major. Bachelor's degree programs available on campus. License preparation in nursing. **Credit/placement by examination:** AP, CLEP, institutional tests. 15 credit hours maximum toward associate degree. **Support services:** GED preparation and test center, learning center, remedial instruction, study skills assistance, tutoring.

Majors. Business: General, management information systems. **Education:** Elementary, middle. **General:** Agribusiness operations, business. **Health services:** Medical assistant, nursing (RN). **Liberal arts:** Arts/sciences. **Protective services:** Forensics, law enforcement admin. **Work/family studies:** Child care management.

Most popular majors. Business/marketing 23%, liberal arts 68%.

Computing on campus. 95 workstations in library, computer center. Commuter students can connect to campus network. Online course registration, online library, helpline, wireless network available.

Student life. Freshman orientation: Available. Preregistration for classes offered. Course offered each semester. **Activities:** Student government, student newspaper, Baptist Collegiate Ministry, Phi Theta Kappa, journalism club, Arkansas Licensed Practical Nursing Association, Amnesty International, SkillsUSA.

Athletics. NAIA. **Intercollegiate:** Rodeo. **Team name:** Colts.

Student services. Adult student services, alcohol/substance abuse counseling, career counseling, services for economically disadvantaged, student employment services, financial aid counseling, minority student services, on-campus daycare, personal counseling, placement for graduates, veterans' counselor. **Physically disabled:** Services for visually, speech, hearing impaired. **Transfer:** Pre-admission transcript evaluation for new students. Transfer adviser, college fairs on campus for students transferring to 4-year colleges.

Contact. E-mail: ncowling@cccua.edu
Phone: (870) 584-4471 Toll-free number: (800) 844-4471
Fax: (870) 642-8766
Shaun Clark, Director of Admissions, Cossatot Community College of the University of Arkansas, 183 Highway 399, De Queen, AR 71832

Crowley's Ridge College
Paragould, Arkansas
www.crc.edu   CB code: 6131

- Private 2-year junior college affiliated with Church of Christ
- Commuter campus in large town

General. Regionally accredited. **Enrollment:** 177 degree-seeking undergraduates. **Degrees:** 1 bachelor's, 17 associate awarded. **Location:** 23 miles from Jonesboro. **Calendar:** Semester, limited summer session. **Full-time faculty:** 13 total. **Part-time faculty:** 12 total.

Transfer out. Colleges most students transferred to 2011: Arkansas State University, Williams Baptist College, Harding University, Freed-Hardeman University.

Basis for selection. Open admission. Placement in freshman composition and algebra determined by ACT and ASSET scores. Development courses required for students with ACT score under 19. Interview required for applicants with less than 2.0 GPA and 15 ACT.

2011-2012 Annual costs. Tuition/fees: $9,860. Per-credit charge: $295. Room/board: $5,980. Books/supplies: $550.

Financial aid. Need-based: Work-study available nights, weekends and for part-time students. **Non-need-based:** Scholarships awarded for academics, leadership, music/drama.

Application procedures. Admission: Closing date 8/10. No application fee. Admission notification on a rolling basis. **Financial aid:** No deadline. FAFSA required.

Academics. Special study options: Dual enrollment of high school students, independent study. **Credit/placement by examination:** AP, CLEP. 34 credit hours maximum toward associate degree. **Support services:** Remedial instruction, study skills assistance, tutoring.

Majors. Education: General. **Liberal arts:** Arts/sciences. **Philosophy/religion:** Religion.

Computing on campus. 15 workstations in dormitories, library, computer center. Dormitories linked to campus network.

Student life. Freshman orientation: Available. Preregistration for classes offered. Takes place second week of August. **Policies:** Chapel attendance required. **Housing:** Guaranteed on-campus for all undergraduates. Single-sex dorms available. $100 deposit. **Activities:** Choral groups, music ensembles, student government.

Athletics. Intercollegiate: Baseball M, basketball, volleyball W. **Intramural:** Baseball M, basketball M, softball W, volleyball W. **Team name:** Pioneers.

Student services. Chaplain/spiritual director, financial aid counseling. **Transfer:** Pre-admission transcript evaluation for new students. College fairs on campus for students transferring to 4-year colleges.

Contact. E-mail: njoneshill@crc.edu
Phone: (870) 236-6901 ext. 14 Toll-free number: (800) 264-1096
Fax: (870) 236-7748
Nancy Joneshill, Admissions Director, Crowley's Ridge College, 100 College Drive, Paragould, AR 72450

East Arkansas Community College
Forrest City, Arkansas
www.eacc.edu   CB code: 0847

- Public 2-year community college
- Commuter campus in large town

General. Founded in 1973. Regionally accredited. **Enrollment:** 1,197 degree-seeking undergraduates. **Degrees:** 114 associate awarded. **Location:** 40 miles from Memphis, Tennessee. **Calendar:** Semester, limited summer session. **Full-time faculty:** 35 total. **Part-time faculty:** 51 total. **Special facilities:** Fine arts center.

Student profile. Among degree-seeking undergraduates, 40% enrolled in a vocational program, 272 enrolled as first-time, first-year students, 3 transferred in from other institutions. Of all enrolled students, 5% already have a bachelor's degree or higher.

Part-time:	45%	Women:	72%
Out-of-state:	1%	25 or older:	47%

Transfer out. 51% of students enrolled in the transfer program go on to 4-year colleges. **Colleges most students transferred to 2011:** Arkansas State University.

Basis for selection. Open admission, but selective for some programs. COMPASS and ACT used in admissions process. Interview required for allied health. **Home schooled:** Transcript of courses and grades, state high school equivalency certificate required.

2011-2012 Annual costs. Tuition/fees: $2,340; $2,610 out-of-district; $3,060 out-of-state. Per-credit charge: $69 in-district; $78 out-of-district; $93 out-of-state. Books/supplies: $1,200. Personal expenses: $1,000.

Financial aid. All financial aid based on need. Need-based aid available for part-time students. Work-study available nights, weekends and for part-time students.

Application procedures. Admission: No deadline. No application fee. Admission notification on a rolling basis. **Financial aid:** Priority date 3/1, closing date 7/1. FAFSA required. Applicants notified on a rolling basis starting 5/15; must reply within 2 week(s) of notification.

Academics. Special study options: Cooperative education, distance learning, dual enrollment of high school students, honors, internships, liberal arts/career combination. Bachelor's degree programs available on campus. License preparation in nursing, paramedic, radiology. **Credit/placement by examination:** AP, CLEP, institutional tests. 12 credit hours maximum toward associate degree. **Support services:** Learning center, remedial instruction, tutoring.

Majors. Business: Administrative services, business admin, finance, management information systems. **Computer sciences:** Web page design. **Education:** Middle, multi-level teacher. **Health services:** EMT paramedic, medical assistant, medical radiologic technology/radiation therapy, nursing (RN), occupational therapy assistant. **Protective services:** Police science. **Work/family studies:** Child care management.

Most popular majors. Business/marketing 18%, education 6%, health sciences 27%, liberal arts 38%, security/protective services 7%.

Computing on campus. 35 workstations in library, computer center. Commuter students can connect to campus network.

Student life. Freshman orientation: Available. Preregistration for classes offered. **Activities:** Choral groups, student government, student newspaper.

Athletics. Intramural: Basketball, softball, tennis, volleyball.

Student services. Career counseling, student employment services, health services, personal counseling, placement for graduates, veterans' counselor. **Physically disabled:** Services for visually, hearing impaired. **Transfer:** Transfer adviser, college fairs on campus for students transferring to 4-year colleges.

Contact. E-mail: scollier@eacc.edu
Phone: (870) 633-4480 ext. 300 Toll-free number: (877) 797-3222
Fax: (870) 633-3840
Sharon Collier, Director of Enrollment Management/IR/Admissions, East Arkansas Community College, 1700 Newcastle Road, Forrest City, AR 72335-2204

Mid-South Community College
West Memphis, Arkansas
www.midsouthcc.edu　　　　　　　　**CB code: 3880**

▸ Public 2-year community and junior college
▸ Commuter campus in large town

General. Regionally accredited. **Enrollment:** 935 full-time, degree-seeking students. **Degrees:** 115 associate awarded. **Location:** 8 miles from Memphis, Tennessee. **Calendar:** Semester, limited summer session. **Full-time faculty:** 32 total. **Part-time faculty:** 97 total. **Class size:** 77% < 20, 23% 20-39.

Student profile.

Out-of-state:	10%	**25 or older:** 53%

Transfer out. Colleges most students transferred to 2011: Arkansas State University, University of Memphis.

Basis for selection. Open admission. **Home schooled:** Transcript of courses and grades required.

2011-2012 Annual costs. Tuition/fees: $2,610; $3,120 out-of-district; $5,220 out-of-state. Per-credit charge: $75 in-district; $92 out-of-district; $162 out-of-state. Books/supplies: $1,000. Personal expenses: $5,500.

Financial aid. Need-based: Need-based aid available for part-time students. Work-study available nights, weekends and for part-time students. **Non-need-based:** Scholarships awarded for academics, state residency.

Application procedures. Admission: No deadline. No application fee. Application must be submitted on paper. Admission notification on a rolling basis. **Financial aid:** Priority date 4/30; no closing date. FAFSA, institutional

---

form required. Applicants notified on a rolling basis starting 6/1; must reply within 2 week(s) of notification.

Academics. Special study options: Cooperative education, distance learning, dual enrollment of high school students, liberal arts/career combination. Bachelor's degree programs available on campus. **Credit/placement by examination:** AP, CLEP, institutional tests. 18 credit hours maximum toward associate degree. **Support services:** GED preparation and test center, learning center, reduced course load, remedial instruction, study skills assistance, tutoring, writing center.

Majors. Business: Office technology. **Computer sciences:** General. **Education:** Middle. **Liberal arts:** Arts/sciences. **Protective services:** Forensics, law enforcement admin.

Computing on campus. 250 workstations in library, computer center, student center. Commuter students can connect to campus network. Online course registration, online library available.

Student life. Freshman orientation: Available. Preregistration for classes offered. **Activities:** Jazz band, choral groups, student newspaper, TV station.

Student services. Adult student services, career counseling, services for economically disadvantaged, student employment services, financial aid counseling, minority student services, veterans' counselor. **Physically disabled:** Services for visually, speech, hearing impaired. **Transfer:** Transfer adviser, college fairs on campus for students transferring to 4-year colleges.

Contact. E-mail: admission@midsouthcc.edu
Phone: (870) 733-6728 Toll-free number: (866) 733-6722
Fax: (870) 733-6719
Jeremy Reece, Director of Admissions and Recruiting, Mid-South Community College, 2000 West Broadway, West Memphis, AR 72301

National Park Community College
Hot Springs, Arkansas
www.npcc.edu　　　　　　　　**CB code: 6243**

▸ Public 2-year liberal arts and technical college
▸ Commuter campus in large town

General. Founded in 1973. Regionally accredited. Located in the Hot Springs National Park. **Enrollment:** 4,168 degree-seeking undergraduates. **Degrees:** 408 associate awarded. **Location:** 53 miles from Little Rock. **Calendar:** Semester, extensive summer session. **Full-time faculty:** 65 total. **Part-time faculty:** 177 total. **Class size:** 63% < 20, 37% 20-39, less than 1% 40-49, less than 1% 50-99.

Student profile.

Out-of-state:	1%	**25 or older:** 56%

Transfer out. Colleges most students transferred to 2011: Henderson State University, Arkadelphia-University of Arkansas, University of Arkansas-Little Rock, University of Arkansas-Fayetteville.

Basis for selection. Open admission, but selective for some programs. Limited admission to allied health programs and nursing. Interview required for some health-related majors. **Home schooled:** State Mandated Notification to High School to be Home-Schooled.

High school preparation. College-preparatory program recommended. 18 units recommended. Recommended units include English 4, mathematics 4, social studies 3, history 2, science 3 (laboratory 3) and foreign language 2.

2011-2012 Annual costs. Tuition/fees: $2,540; $2,840 out-of-district; $4,520 out-of-state. Per-credit charge: $73 in-district; $83 out-of-district; $139 out-of-state. Books/supplies: $700. Personal expenses: $1,420.

Financial aid. Need-based: Need-based aid available for part-time students. Work-study available nights, weekends and for part-time students. **Non-need-based:** Scholarships awarded for academics, minority status, music/drama, state residency.

Application procedures. Admission: No deadline. No application fee. Application must be submitted online. Admission notification on a rolling basis beginning on or about 3/1. **Financial aid:** Priority date 7/1; no closing date. FAFSA, institutional form required. Applicants notified on a rolling basis.

Academics. Special study options: Cooperative education, cross-registration, distance learning, double major, dual enrollment of high school students, honors, independent study, internships, liberal arts/career combination, student-designed major. Bachelor's degree programs available on campus. License preparation in aviation, nursing, paramedic, radiology, real

estate. **Credit/placement by examination:** AP, CLEP, institutional tests. 18 credit hours maximum toward associate degree. **Support services:** Learning center, reduced course load, remedial instruction, study skills assistance, tutoring, writing center.

Majors. Business: Accounting, hospitality admin, hospitality/recreation, office management, office technology. **Computer sciences:** General, applications programming, computer graphics. **Health services:** Clinical lab technology, EMT paramedic, medical assistant, medical radiologic technology/radiation therapy, medical records technology, medical secretary, nursing (RN). **Liberal arts:** Arts/sciences. **Parks/recreation:** General. **Visual/performing arts:** Commercial/advertising art.

Computing on campus. 470 workstations in library, computer center, student center. Online library available.

Student life. Freshman orientation: Mandatory. Preregistration for classes offered. 2 day orientation, held one week prior to beginning of classes. **Activities:** Choral groups, dance, literary magazine, music ensembles, student government, student newspaper, Baptist student union, Black Awareness, Association for Barrier Awareness.

Athletics. Intramural: Baseball, basketball, bowling, skin diving, softball, table tennis, tennis, volleyball.

Student services. Adult student services, career counseling, services for economically disadvantaged, student employment services, financial aid counseling, health services, personal counseling, placement for graduates, veterans' counselor. **Physically disabled:** Services for visually, speech, hearing impaired. **Transfer:** Pre-admission transcript evaluation for new students. Transfer adviser, college fairs on campus for students transferring to 4-year colleges.

Contact. E-mail: admissions@npcc.edu
Phone: (501) 760-4222 ext. 4231 Toll-free number: (800) 761-1825
Fax: (501) 760-4100
Holly Garrett, Director of Admissions, National Park Community College, 101 College Drive, Hot Springs, AR 71913

North Arkansas College
Harrison, Arkansas
www.northark.edu
CB code: 1423

▸ Public 2-year community and technical college
▸ Commuter campus in large town

General. Founded in 1974. Regionally accredited. **Enrollment:** 1,430 full-time, degree-seeking students. **Degrees:** 217 associate awarded. **Location:** 75 miles from Fayetteville. **Calendar:** Semester, limited summer session. **Full-time faculty:** 65 total. **Part-time faculty:** 98 total. **Class size:** 59% < 20, 39% 20-39, 1% 40-49, 1% 50-99. **Special facilities:** Community health resource center, lyric theater.

Student profile.

Out-of-state:	2%	**25 or older:** 44%

Transfer out. Colleges most students transferred to 2011: Arkansas Tech University, University of Arkansas, University of Central Arkansas, Franklin University, Ozark Technical Community College.

Basis for selection. Open admission, but selective for some programs. Allied health programs require separate application. To receive college credit for CLEP exams, student must score at 50th percentile or higher, based on national norms, and may not have earned college credit nor have ever been enrolled in course for which he/she is writing the test.

High school preparation. College-preparatory program required.

2011-2012 Annual costs. Tuition/fees: $1,980; $2,700 out-of-district; $4,830 out-of-state. Per-credit charge: $66 in-district; $90 out-of-district; $161 out-of-state. Books/supplies: $1,050. Personal expenses: $2,294.

Financial aid. Need-based: Need-based aid available for part-time students. Work-study available nights, weekends and for part-time students. **Non-need-based:** Scholarships awarded for academics, athletics, state residency.

Application procedures. Admission: No deadline. No application fee. Application must be submitted on paper. Admission notification on a rolling basis. **Financial aid:** Priority date 5/1; no closing date. FAFSA, institutional form required. Applicants notified on a rolling basis starting 5/1.

Academics. Special study options: Distance learning, dual enrollment of high school students, ESL, honors, independent study, internships, student-designed major. Bachelor's degree programs available on campus. License preparation in nursing, paramedic, radiology, real estate. **Credit/placement by examination:** AP, CLEP, institutional tests. 20 credit hours maximum toward associate degree. Only one-third of the credit hours for a degree can be from Advanced Placement, CLEP, the College Now Program, Challenge Test, various other examinations, or independent studies. Credit for Advanced Placement, CLEP, or Professional Certification Examinations will not be posted to an academic record until the student has successfully completed at least 12 semester credit hours of work. **Support services:** GED preparation and test center, learning center, pre-admission summer program, remedial instruction, study skills assistance, tutoring, writing center.

Majors. Business: General. **Computer sciences:** General. **Education:** Multi-level teacher. **Health services:** Clinical lab technology, EMT paramedic, medical radiologic technology/radiation therapy, nursing (RN), surgical technology. **Liberal arts:** Arts/sciences. **Protective services:** Forensics, law enforcement admin.

Most popular majors. Business/marketing 13%, computer/information sciences 10%, health sciences 30%, liberal arts 41%.

Computing on campus. 250 workstations in library, computer center. Online course registration, online library, wireless network available.

Student life. Freshman orientation: Available. Preregistration for classes offered. **Activities:** Drama, literary magazine, student government, Baptist student union, Future Farmers of America, Health Occupations Students of America, Phi Beta Lambda, Phi Theta Kappa, Pioneer Hands club, Rad Tech club, Skills USA, student nurses association.

Athletics. NJCAA. **Intercollegiate:** Baseball M, basketball, cheerleading M, rodeo, softball W. **Intramural:** Archery, badminton, basketball, football (non-tackle) M, golf, racquetball, softball, table tennis, tennis, volleyball, weight lifting. **Team name:** Pioneers.

Student services. Adult student services, alcohol/substance abuse counseling, career counseling, services for economically disadvantaged, student employment services, financial aid counseling, placement for graduates, veterans' counselor. **Physically disabled:** Services for visually, speech, hearing impaired. **Transfer:** Pre-admission transcript evaluation for new students. Transfer adviser, college fairs on campus for students transferring to 4-year colleges.

Contact. E-mail: admissions@northark.edu
Phone: (870) 391-3505 Toll-free number: (800) 679-6622
Fax: (870) 391-3339
Charla Jennings, Director of Enrollment Services, North Arkansas College, 1515 Pioneer Drive, Harrison, AR 72601

Northwest Arkansas Community College
Bentonville, Arkansas
www.nwacc.edu
CB code: 7101

▸ Public 2-year community college
▸ Commuter campus in small city

General. Regionally accredited. **Enrollment:** 8,528 undergraduates. **Degrees:** 727 associate awarded. **ROTC:** Army, Air Force. **Location:** 30 miles from Fayetteville. **Calendar:** Semester, extensive summer session. **Full-time faculty:** 121 total; 31% have terminal degrees, 8% minority, 60% women. **Part-time faculty:** 328 total; 8% have terminal degrees, 11% minority, 52% women.

Student profile.

Out-of-state:	3%	**25 or older:** 42%

Transfer out. Colleges most students transferred to 2011: University of Arkansas, John Brown University.

Basis for selection. Open admission, but selective for some programs. Additional requirements for nursing, physical therapy, respiratory therapy, emergency medical technician/paramedic programs.

High school preparation. College-preparatory program recommended. 22 units recommended. Recommended units include English 4, mathematics 4, social studies 3, science 3 (laboratory 2), foreign language 2 and academic electives 4.

2012-2013 Annual costs. Tuition/fees (projected): $2,748; $4,098 out-of-district; $5,598 out-of-state. Per-credit charge: $73 in-district; $118 out-of-district; $168 out-of-state. Books/supplies: $1,250. Personal expenses: $3,600.

Financial aid. Need-based: Need-based aid available for part-time students. Work-study available nights, weekends and for part-time students. **Non-need-based:** Scholarships awarded for academics, leadership, music/drama, state residency.

Application procedures. Admission: No deadline. $10 fee. Admission notification on a rolling basis. **Financial aid:** Priority date 4/1; no closing date. FAFSA, institutional form required. Applicants notified on a rolling basis starting 4/1; must reply within 2 week(s) of notification.

Academics. Special study options: Distance learning, double major, dual enrollment of high school students, ESL, honors, independent study, internships, liberal arts/career combination, teacher certification program, weekend college. License preparation in nursing, paramedic, physical therapy. **Credit/placement by examination:** AP, CLEP. 15 credit hours maximum toward associate degree. **Support services:** GED preparation and test center, learning center, remedial instruction, study skills assistance, tutoring, writing center.

Majors. Business: Accounting, administrative services, banking/financial services, business admin. **Computer sciences:** General, LAN/WAN management, programming, webmaster. **Education:** Early childhood, middle. **Engineering:** Environmental. **Health services:** EMT paramedic, nursing (RN), physical therapy assistant, respiratory therapy technology. **Liberal arts:** Arts/sciences. **Protective services:** Criminal justice, firefighting, forensics, homeland security, law enforcement admin. **Visual/performing arts:** Commercial/advertising art. **Work/family studies:** Child care management.

Most popular majors. Business/marketing 9%, health sciences 15%, liberal arts 58%.

Computing on campus. 300 workstations in library, computer center, student center. Commuter students can connect to campus network. Online course registration, online library, helpline, wireless network available.

Student life. Freshman orientation: Mandatory. Preregistration for classes offered. **Activities:** Jazz band, campus ministries, choral groups, drama, international student organizations, literary magazine, music ensembles, musical theater, student government, student newspaper, symphony orchestra.

Athletics. Intramural: Archery, basketball, bowling, golf, soccer, softball, table tennis, volleyball.

Student services. Adult student services, alcohol/substance abuse counseling, career counseling, financial aid counseling, personal counseling, placement for graduates, veterans' counselor. **Transfer:** Transfer center, transfer adviser, college fairs on campus for students transferring to 4-year colleges.

Contact. E-mail: askregistration@nwacc.edu
Phone: (479) 619-4398 Toll-free number: (800) 995-6922
Fax: (479) 619-2229
Michelle Wallace, Director of Admissions, Northwest Arkansas Community College, One College Drive, Bentonville, AR 72712

Ozarka College
Melbourne, Arkansas
www.ozarka.edu   **CB code: 3621**

- Public 2-year community and technical college
- Commuter campus in rural community

General. Regionally accredited. **Enrollment:** 1,600 degree-seeking undergraduates. **Degrees:** 125 associate awarded. **Location:** 125 miles from Little Rock; 160 miles from Memphis, TN. **Calendar:** Semester, limited summer session. **Full-time faculty:** 38 total. **Part-time faculty:** 60 total.

Transfer out. Colleges most students transferred to 2011: Arkansas State University, Lyon College, University of Arkansas, University of Central Arkansas, Williams Baptist College.

Basis for selection. Open admission, but selective for some programs. Admission to licensed practical nursing, Registered Nursing, automotive technology and culinary arts programs based on test scores, and/or essay, interview. **Adult students:** ACT/ASSET/COMPASS/SAT accepted for placement in math and English. **Home schooled:** Transcript of courses and grades required.

2011-2012 Annual costs. Tuition/fees: $2,720; $5,510 out-of-state. Per-credit charge: $75 in-state; $168 out-of-state. Books/supplies: $800. Personal expenses: $1,800.

Financial aid. Need-based: Need-based aid available for part-time students. Work-study available nights, weekends and for part-time students.

Application procedures. Admission: No deadline. No application fee. Admission notification on a rolling basis. **Financial aid:** No deadline. FAFSA required. Applicants notified on a rolling basis; must reply within 2 week(s) of notification.

Academics. Special study options: Cooperative education, distance learning, dual enrollment of high school students, liberal arts/career combination. Bachelor's degree programs available on campus. License preparation in nursing. **Credit/placement by examination:** AP, CLEP, institutional tests. 36 credit hours maximum toward associate degree. **Support services:** GED preparation and test center, learning center, remedial instruction, study skills assistance, tutoring.

Majors. Business: Business admin, information resources management. **Education:** General, elementary, middle. **Health services:** Licensed practical nurse, medical transcription. **Liberal arts:** Arts/sciences. **Protective services:** Law enforcement admin.

Computing on campus. 175 workstations in library, computer center. Commuter students can connect to campus network. Online course registration, helpline, wireless network available.

Student life. Freshman orientation: Mandatory. Preregistration for classes offered. **Activities:** Student government.

Athletics. Team name: Eagles.

Student services. Chaplain/spiritual director, career counseling, services for economically disadvantaged, financial aid counseling, on-campus daycare, veterans' counselor, women's services. **Transfer:** Pre-admission transcript evaluation for new students. College fairs on campus for students transferring to 4-year colleges.

Contact. Phone: (870) 368-2028
Toll-free number: (800) 821-4335 ext. 2028 Fax: (870) 368-2091
Amanda Dobbs, Director of Admissions, Ozarka College, 218 College Drive, Melbourne, AR 72556-0010

Phillips Community College of the University of Arkansas
Helena, Arkansas
www.pccua.edu   **CB code: 6583**

- Public 2-year community college
- Commuter campus in large town

General. Founded in 1965. Regionally accredited. Campuses in Helena, Phillips County, Stuttgart, DeWitt. **Enrollment:** 1,110 degree-seeking undergraduates. **Degrees:** 223 associate awarded. **Location:** 117 miles from Little Rock. **Calendar:** Semester, limited summer session. **Full-time faculty:** 78 total; 4% have terminal degrees, 17% minority, 73% women. **Part-time faculty:** 54 total; 28% minority, 70% women. **Class size:** 90% < 20, 9% 20-39, less than 1% 40-49, less than 1% 50-99. **Special facilities:** Performing arts center.

Student profile. Among degree-seeking undergraduates, 35% enrolled in a transfer program, 52% enrolled in a vocational program, 228 enrolled as first-time, first-year students, 28 transferred in from other institutions.

Part-time:	35%	African American:	49%
Out-of-state:	3%	Hispanic American:	1%
Women:	72%	25 or older:	49%

Basis for selection. Open admission, but selective for some programs. Additional requirements for nursing program. Interview required of applicants with no high school transcript or test scores. **Adult students:** ASSET or COMPASS test required for students taking English or math. **Home schooled:** Transcript of courses and grades, state high school equivalency certificate required.

2011-2012 Annual costs. Tuition/fees: $2,300; $2,630 out-of-district; $3,920 out-of-state. Per-credit charge: $60 in-district; $71 out-of-district; $114 out-of-state. Books/supplies: $1,000. Personal expenses: $4,893.

2010-2011 Financial aid. All financial aid based on need. Need-based aid available for part-time students. Work-study available nights, weekends and for part-time students. **Additional information:** Tuition waivers given to firefighters and law enforcement officers.

Application procedures. Admission: No deadline. No application fee. Admission notification on a rolling basis. **Financial aid:** Priority date 4/12, closing date 6/12. FAFSA required. Applicants notified on a rolling basis starting 4/12; must reply within 2 week(s) of notification.

Academics. **Special study options:** Distance learning, dual enrollment of high school students, honors, independent study, internships, weekend college. Bachelor's degree programs available on campus. License preparation in nursing. **Credit/placement by examination:** AP, CLEP, institutional tests. 30 credit hours maximum toward associate degree. **Support services:** GED preparation and test center, learning center, remedial instruction, study skills assistance, tutoring.

Majors. **Biology:** General. **Business:** General, business admin, office technology. **Communications technology:** Graphic/printing. **Computer sciences:** Computer science, information technology, LAN/WAN management. **Education:** General, early childhood, elementary. **Engineering:** General. **English:** English lit, rhetoric/composition. **Health services:** Nursing (RN), phlebotomy. **Liberal arts:** Arts/sciences. **Math:** General. **Physical sciences:** Chemistry, physics. **Psychology:** General. **Social sciences:** General. **Visual/performing arts:** Printmaking.

Most popular majors. Business/marketing 12%, computer/information sciences 9%, education 20%, health sciences 13%, liberal arts 36%.

Computing on campus. 275 workstations in library, computer center, student center. Commuter students can connect to campus network. Online course registration, wireless network available.

Student life. **Freshman orientation:** Available. Preregistration for classes offered. **Activities:** Choral groups, dance, drama, musical theater, Baptist Collegiate Ministries, Phi Theta Kappa, Arkansas Licensed Practical Nurses Association, National Student Nurses Association, Young Democrats, book club.

Athletics. **Intramural:** Archery, badminton, basketball, football (non-tackle) M, golf, soccer, softball, table tennis, tennis, volleyball.

Student services. Adult student services, career counseling, services for economically disadvantaged, student employment services, financial aid counseling, personal counseling, placement for graduates, veterans' counselor. **Physically disabled:** Services for visually, hearing impaired. **Transfer:** Transfer adviser, college fairs on campus for students transferring to 4-year colleges.

Contact. E-mail: lboone@pccua.edu
Phone: (870) 338-6474 ext. 1336 Fax: (870) 338-7542
Lynn Boone, Vice Chancellor for Student Services/Registrar, Phillips Community College of the University of Arkansas, 1000 Campus Drive, Helena, AR 72342

Pulaski Technical College
North Little Rock, Arkansas
www.pulaskitech.edu   CB code: 3622

▶ Public 2-year community and technical college
▶ Commuter campus in small city

General. Regionally accredited. **Enrollment:** 10,909 degree-seeking undergraduates. **Degrees:** 1,554 associate awarded. **Location:** 4 miles from Little Rock. **Calendar:** Semester, extensive summer session. **Full-time faculty:** 169 total. **Part-time faculty:** 348 total. **Class size:** 55% < 20, 45% 20-39.

Student profile.

Out-of-state:	1%	25 or older:	59%

Transfer out. **Colleges most students transferred to 2011:** University of Arkansas at Little Rock, University of Central Arkansas.

Basis for selection. Open admission, but selective for some programs. Additional requirements for dental assisting, practical nursing, respiratory therapy, occupational therapy assistant and military technology programs. **Adult students:** COMPASS or ACT scores may be used for placement.

2011-2012 Annual costs. Tuition/fees: $2,980; $4,600 out-of-state. Per-credit charge: $84 in-state; $138 out-of-state. Books/supplies: $1,200. Personal expenses: $2,732.

Financial aid. **Need-based:** Need-based aid available for part-time students. Work-study available nights, weekends and for part-time students.

Application procedures. **Admission:** No deadline. No application fee. Admission notification on a rolling basis. **Financial aid:** Closing date 5/15. FAFSA, institutional form required. Applicants notified on a rolling basis starting 5/1; must reply within 2 week(s) of notification.

Academics. **Special study options:** Cooperative education, distance learning, double major, dual enrollment of high school students, external degree,

internships, liberal arts/career combination, weekend college. License preparation in aviation, dental hygiene, nursing, occupational therapy. **Credit/placement by examination:** AP, CLEP, institutional tests. **Support services:** Learning center, pre-admission summer program, remedial instruction, study skills assistance, tutoring.

Majors. **Business:** General, hospitality admin, management information systems. **Education:** Early childhood. **Health services:** Occupational therapy assistant, respiratory therapy technology. **Liberal arts:** Arts/sciences. **Protective services:** Forensics, law enforcement admin. **Work/family studies:** Child care management.

Most popular majors. Business/marketing 13%, liberal arts 69%.

Computing on campus. 281 workstations in library, computer center, student center. Commuter students can connect to campus network. Online course registration, online library, helpline, wireless network available.

Student life. **Freshman orientation:** Available. Preregistration for classes offered. Online orientation is ongoing. **Activities:** Campus ministries, choral groups, literary magazine, student government, Metro student ministries, Culture Shock, philosophy club, student ambassadors, Phi Theta Kappa, College Democrats, Fusion, Phi Beta Lambda.

Student services. Adult student services, career counseling, services for economically disadvantaged, student employment services, financial aid counseling, minority student services, personal counseling, veterans' counselor. **Physically disabled:** Services for visually, hearing impaired. **Transfer:** Transfer adviser, college fairs on campus for students transferring to 4-year colleges.

Contact. E-mail: admissions@pulaskitech.edu
Phone: (501) 812-2231 Fax: (501) 812-2316
Clark Atkins, Director of Admissions, Pulaski Technical College, 3000 West Scenic Drive, North Little Rock, AR 72118-3347

Remington College: Little Rock
Little Rock, Arkansas
www.remingtoncollege.edu/littlerock

▶ For-profit 2-year technical college
▶ Commuter campus in very large city

General. Accredited by ACCSC. **Enrollment:** 362 degree-seeking undergraduates. **Degrees:** 20 associate awarded. **Calendar:** Quarter. **Full-time faculty:** 12 total. **Part-time faculty:** 4 total.

Basis for selection. Open admission, but selective for some programs. Wonderlic Exam required for admission.

Financial aid. **Need-based:** Work-study available nights, weekends and for part-time students.

Application procedures. **Admission:** No deadline. $50 fee. Admission notification on a rolling basis. **Financial aid:** No deadline. FAFSA required.

Academics. **Credit/placement by examination:** AP, CLEP.

Majors. **Computer sciences:** Networking. **Protective services:** Law enforcement admin.

Student life. **Activities:** American Association of Medical Assistants, National Technical Honor Society, Professional Business Leaders of America.

Student services. Career counseling, financial aid counseling.

Contact. E-mail: admissions@remingtoncollege.edu
Phone: (501) 312-0007 Toll-free number: (800) 560-6192
Fax: (501) 225-3819
Jonathan Porter, Director of Admissions, Remington College: Little Rock, 19 Remington Drive, Little Rock, AR 72204

Rich Mountain Community College
Mena, Arkansas
www.rmcc.edu   CB code: 0226

▶ Public 2-year community college
▶ Commuter campus in small town

General. Founded in 1983. Regionally accredited. **Enrollment:** 671 degree-seeking undergraduates; 437 non-degree-seeking students. **Degrees:** 95 associate awarded. **Location:** 85 miles from Fort Smith, 80 miles from Hot Springs. **Calendar:** Semester, limited summer session. **Full-time faculty:** 19 total; 10% have terminal degrees, 58% women. **Part-time faculty:** 60 total; 3% have terminal degrees, 58% women.

Student profile. Among degree-seeking undergraduates, 8% enrolled in a vocational program, 171 enrolled as first-time, first-year students.

Part-time:	32%	Hispanic American:	4%
Out-of-state:	2%	Native American:	4%
Women:	68%	25 or older:	47%
Asian American:	1%		

Transfer out. Colleges most students transferred to 2011: Henderson State University, Arkansas Tech University, University Arkansas Fort Smith, Southern Arkansas University Magnolia.

Basis for selection. Open admission, but selective for some programs. Limited admission to licensed practical nurse program.

2011-2012 Annual costs. Tuition/fees: $2,190; $2,580 out-of-district; $5,640 out-of-state. Per-credit charge: $60 in-district; $73 out-of-district; $175 out-of-state. Books/supplies: $1,400. Personal expenses: $3,045.

Financial aid. Need-based: Need-based aid available for part-time students. Work-study available nights, weekends and for part-time students. **Non-need-based:** Scholarships awarded for academics.

Application procedures. Admission: No deadline. No application fee. Application must be submitted on paper. Admission notification on a rolling basis. **Financial aid:** Priority date 7/1; no closing date. FAFSA, institutional form required. Applicants notified on a rolling basis starting 6/1; must reply within 2 week(s) of notification.

Academics. Special study options: Cooperative education, distance learning, dual enrollment of high school students, external degree, internships, student-designed major. License preparation in nursing. **Credit/placement by examination:** AP, CLEP, institutional tests. 30 credit hours maximum toward associate degree. **Support services:** GED preparation and test center, remedial instruction, study skills assistance, tutoring.

Majors. Business: General, administrative services, management information systems, sales/distribution. **Computer sciences:** Information systems, LAN/WAN management, systems analysis. **Education:** General. **Liberal arts:** Arts/sciences.

Most popular majors. Business/marketing 10%, interdisciplinary studies 21%, liberal arts 58%.

Computing on campus. 73 workstations in library, computer center. Commuter students can connect to campus network. Wireless network available.

Student life. Freshman orientation: Available. Preregistration for classes offered. **Activities:** Radio station, student government, TV station, Baptist student union.

Student services. Adult student services, career counseling, services for economically disadvantaged, financial aid counseling, personal counseling, veterans' counselor. **Physically disabled:** Services for visually, hearing impaired. **Transfer:** Pre-admission transcript evaluation for new students. Transfer adviser, college fairs on campus for students transferring to 4-year colleges.

Contact. Phone: (479) 394-7622 ext. 1440 Fax: (479) 394-2760 Brandon Burk, Director of Admissions, Rich Mountain Community College, 1100 College Drive, Mena, AR 71953

South Arkansas Community College
El Dorado, Arkansas
www.southark.edu   **CB code: 1550**

- Public 2-year community and junior college
- Commuter campus in large town

General. Founded in 1975. Regionally accredited. **Enrollment:** 1,570 degree-seeking undergraduates; 203 non-degree-seeking students. **Degrees:** 134 associate awarded. **Location:** 115 miles from Little Rock. **Calendar:** Semester, limited summer session. **Full-time faculty:** 61 total. **Part-time faculty:** 53 total.

Student profile. Among degree-seeking undergraduates, 234 enrolled as first-time, first-year students.

Part-time:	46%	African American:	42%
Out-of-state:	3%	Hispanic American:	2%
Women:	75%		

Transfer out. Colleges most students transferred to 2011: Southern Arkansas University, Louisiana Tech, University of Arkansas at Monticello.

Basis for selection. Open admission, but selective for some programs. **Home schooled:** Transcript of courses and grades, state high school equivalency certificate required.

High school preparation. College-preparatory program recommended.

2011-2012 Annual costs. Tuition/fees: $2,492; $2,792 out-of-district; $4,832 out-of-state. Per-credit charge: $74 in-district; $84 out-of-district; $152 out-of-state. Books/supplies: $1,200. Personal expenses: $550.

Financial aid. Need-based: Need-based aid available for part-time students. Work-study available nights, weekends and for part-time students.

Application procedures. Admission: Priority date 7/31; no deadline. No application fee. Admission notification on a rolling basis. **Financial aid:** Closing date 7/1. FAFSA, institutional form required. Applicants notified on a rolling basis starting 7/1; must reply within 2 week(s) of notification.

Academics. Special study options: Distance learning, dual enrollment of high school students, liberal arts/career combination. License preparation in nursing, occupational therapy, paramedic, physical therapy, radiology. **Credit/placement by examination:** AP, CLEP, IB, institutional tests. 30 credit hours maximum toward associate degree. **Support services:** GED preparation and test center, learning center, reduced course load, remedial instruction, study skills assistance, tutoring.

Majors. Business: General, administrative services, business admin. **Education:** General, secondary. **Health services:** Clinical lab technology, EMT paramedic, medical radiologic technology/radiation therapy, nursing (RN), occupational therapy assistant, physical therapy assistant, radiologic technology/medical imaging, radiologist assistant, respiratory therapy assistant, surgical technology. **Liberal arts:** Arts/sciences. **Protective services:** Police science.

Most popular majors. Education 7%, health sciences 48%, liberal arts 26%.

Computing on campus. Online course registration, student web hosting, wireless network available.

Student life. Freshman orientation: Available. Preregistration for classes offered. **Activities:** Choral groups, literary magazine, Phi Beta Lambda, Phi Theta Kappa, student leadership group.

Student services. Adult student services, career counseling, services for economically disadvantaged, student employment services, financial aid counseling, personal counseling, veterans' counselor. **Physically disabled:** Services for visually, speech, hearing impaired. **Transfer:** Transfer adviser, college fairs on campus for students transferring to 4-year colleges.

Contact. E-mail: registrar@southark.edu
Phone: (870) 862-8131 Toll-free number: (800) 955-2289
Fax: (870) 864-7137
Dean Inman, Dean of Enrollment Services, South Arkansas Community College, Box 7010, El Dorado, AR 71731-7010

Southeast Arkansas College
Pine Bluff, Arkansas
www.seark.edu   **CB code: 3624**

- Public 2-year community and technical college
- Commuter campus in small city

General. Regionally accredited. **Enrollment:** 1,771 degree-seeking undergraduates; 409 non-degree-seeking students. **Degrees:** 137 associate awarded. **Location:** 42 miles from Little Rock. **Calendar:** Semester, limited summer session. **Full-time faculty:** 42 total; 10% have terminal degrees, 31% minority, 64% women. **Part-time faculty:** 99 total; 3% have terminal degrees, 39% minority, 60% women. **Class size:** 55% < 20, 45% 20-39, less than 1% 40-49, less than 1% 50-99.

Student profile. Among degree-seeking undergraduates, 93% enrolled in a vocational program, 367 enrolled as first-time, first-year students, 150 transferred in from other institutions.

Part-time:	41%	Hispanic American:	1%
Women:	70%	Native American:	1%
African American:	61%		

Transfer out. Colleges most students transferred to 2011: University of Arkansas at Pine Bluff, University of Arkansas at Monticello, University of Arkansas at Little Rock.

Basis for selection. Open admission, but selective for some programs. Additional requirements for some health programs. ACT, ASSET or COMPASS required for placement. **Learning Disabled:** Learning disability must be officially documented.

High school preparation. Recommended units include English 4, mathematics 2, social studies 2, history 2, science 2 and foreign language 1.

2012-2013 Annual costs. Tuition/fees (projected): $2,830; $5,230 out-of-state. Books/supplies: $1,300. Personal expenses: $4,200.

2010-2011 Financial aid. Need-based: 77% of total undergraduate aid awarded as scholarships/grants, 23% as loans/jobs. Need-based aid available for part-time students. Work-study available nights, weekends and for part-time students. **Non-need-based:** Scholarships awarded for academics, leadership, state residency.

Application procedures. Admission: No deadline. No application fee. Application must be submitted on paper. **Financial aid:** Priority date 6/1; no closing date. FAFSA required. Applicants notified on a rolling basis starting 5/1; must reply within 2 week(s) of notification.

Academics. Special study options: Distance learning, dual enrollment of high school students, independent study, internships. License preparation in nursing, paramedic, radiology, real estate. **Credit/placement by examination:** AP, CLEP. 15 credit hours maximum toward associate degree. Credit awarded through challenge exams. **Support services:** Learning center, remedial instruction, study skills assistance, tutoring.

Majors. Business: General, accounting technology, administrative services, business admin. **Computer sciences:** General, networking. **Health services:** EMT paramedic, medical radiologic technology/radiation therapy, nursing (RN), respiratory therapy technology, surgical technology. **Liberal arts:** Arts/sciences. **Protective services:** Criminal justice, forensics, law enforcement admin. **Work/family studies:** Child care service.

Most popular majors. Business/marketing 17%, computer/information sciences 7%, health sciences 26%, liberal arts 30%, security/protective services 17%.

Computing on campus. 100 workstations in library, computer center. Commuter students can connect to campus network. Wireless network available.

Student life. Freshman orientation: Available. Preregistration for classes offered. One-hour program held one weekday morning and one weekday evening before start of classes. **Activities:** Campus ministries, student government.

Student services. Adult student services, alcohol/substance abuse counseling, career counseling, services for economically disadvantaged, student employment services, financial aid counseling, personal counseling, placement for graduates, veterans' counselor. **Physically disabled:** Services for visually, speech, hearing impaired. **Transfer:** Pre-admission transcript evaluation for new students. College fairs on campus for students transferring to 4-year colleges.

Contact. E-mail: bdunn@seark.edu
Phone: (870) 850-8605 Fax: (870) 850-8605
Barbara Dunn, Admissions and Enrollment Management Coordinator, Southeast Arkansas College, 1900 Hazel Street, Pine Bluff, AR 71603

Southern Arkansas University Tech
Camden, Arkansas
www.sautech.edu
CB code: 6704

- Public 2-year community and technical college
- Commuter campus in large town

General. Founded in 1967. Regionally accredited. **Enrollment:** 986 degree-seeking undergraduates; 1,150 non-degree-seeking students. **Degrees:** 140 associate awarded. **Location:** 90 miles from Little Rock. **Calendar:** Semester, limited summer session. **Full-time faculty:** 29 total; 3% have terminal degrees, 7% minority, 48% women. **Part-time faculty:** 75 total; 4% have terminal degrees, 8% minority, 43% women. **Class size:** 61% < 20, 34% 20-39, 5% 40-49, less than 1% 50-99. **Special facilities:** Fire training academy, environmental science academy, law enforcement academy, career technical academy, business and industry center, welding academy. **Partnerships:** Formal partnerships with area businesses/industries and high schools.

Student profile. Among degree-seeking undergraduates, 202 enrolled as first-time, first-year students.

Part-time:	30%	25 or older:	28%
Out-of-state:	2%	Live on campus:	2%
Women:	54%		

Transfer out. Colleges most students transferred to 2011: Southern Arkansas University, Henderson State University, University of Arkansas at Monticello, University of Central Arkansas, South Arkansas Community College.

Basis for selection. Open admission, but selective for some programs. Additional application and testing for Practical Nursing program; additional testing for Welding Academy. **Home schooled:** State high school equivalency certificate required. Applicants must take the GED test.

High school preparation. College-preparatory program recommended. 23 units recommended. Recommended units include English 4, mathematics 4, social studies 2, history 2, science 3, foreign language 2 and academic electives 6.

2011-2012 Annual costs. Tuition/fees: $3,514; $4,834 out-of-state. Per-credit charge: $93 in-state; $137 out-of-state. Books/supplies: $1,400. Personal expenses: $4,500.

Financial aid. Need-based: Need-based aid available for part-time students. Work-study available nights, weekends and for part-time students. **Non-need-based:** Scholarships awarded for academics, state residency.

Application procedures. Admission: Priority date 4/15; deadline 6/1 (postmark date). No application fee. Admission notification on a rolling basis. **Financial aid:** Priority date 6/1; no closing date. FAFSA required. Applicants notified on a rolling basis starting 5/1.

Academics. Special study options: Distance learning, double major, dual enrollment of high school students, honors, independent study, internships. Articulation agreements for Nursing Assistant and Practical Nursing programs. Bachelor's degree programs available on campus. License preparation in aviation, nursing. **Credit/placement by examination:** AP, CLEP, institutional tests. 15 credit hours maximum toward associate degree. **Support services:** GED preparation and test center, learning center, pre-admission summer program, remedial instruction, study skills assistance, tutoring, writing center.

Majors. Business: Business admin, office management. **Computer sciences:** Computer science, networking, programming, web page design. **Education:** Multi-level teacher. **Protective services:** Fire services admin, firefighting. **Work/family studies:** Child care service.

Most popular majors. Business/marketing 18%, computer/information sciences 18%, education 13%, engineering/engineering technologies 29%, liberal arts 10%.

Computing on campus. 250 workstations in library, computer center. Dormitories wired for high-speed internet access and linked to campus network. Commuter students can connect to campus network. Online course registration, online library, helpline, repair service, wireless network available.

Student life. Freshman orientation: Mandatory. Preregistration for classes offered. Eight half-day programs in July or early August. **Housing:** Apartments available. $100 partly refundable deposit, deadline 7/15. Off-campus housing is available. **Activities:** Campus ministries, radio station, student government, TV station, Phi Beta Lambda, Phi Theta Kappa, aviation club, multimedia graphics club, multimedia film/video club, computer club, electronics club, multi-cultural club, student ambassadors, student leadership team, allied health student club.

Athletics. Intramural: Basketball, football (non-tackle), soccer, softball, tennis, volleyball, weight lifting. **Team name:** Varmits.

Student services. Adult student services, chaplain/spiritual director, career counseling, services for economically disadvantaged, student employment services, financial aid counseling, on-campus daycare, personal counseling, placement for graduates, veterans' counselor. **Physically disabled:** Services for visually, speech, hearing impaired. **Transfer:** Re-entry adviser, pre-admission transcript evaluation for new students. Transfer center, transfer adviser, college fairs on campus for students transferring to 4-year colleges.

Contact. E-mail: bellis@sautech.edu
Phone: (870) 574-4558 Fax: (870) 574-4478
Patricia Sindle, Director, Enrollment Services, Southern Arkansas
University Tech, PO Box 3499, Camden, AR 71711-1599

University of Arkansas: Community College at Batesville
Batesville, Arkansas
www.uaccb.edu   CB code: 3628

- Public 2-year community college
- Commuter campus in small town

General. Regionally accredited. **Enrollment:** 1,368 degree-seeking undergraduates. **Degrees:** 243 associate awarded. **Location:** 90 miles from Little Rock. **Calendar:** Semester, limited summer session. **Full-time faculty:** 41 total. **Part-time faculty:** 63 total.

Transfer out. Colleges most students transferred to 2011: Lyon College, Arkansas State University, University of Arkansas, University of Central Arkansas, Arkansas Tech University.

Basis for selection. Open admission, but selective for some programs. Admission to nursing program based on GPA in prerequisite courses and nursing entrance exam. **Home schooled:** Transcript of courses and grades required.

High school preparation. College-preparatory program recommended.

2011-2012 Annual costs. Tuition/fees: $2,440; $2,800 out-of-district; $4,840 out-of-state. Per-credit charge: $60 in-district; $72 out-of-district; $140 out-of-state. Books/supplies: $1,000. Personal expenses: $2,100.

Financial aid. All financial aid based on need. Work-study available nights, weekends and for part-time students.

Application procedures. Admission: No deadline. No application fee. Admission notification on a rolling basis. **Financial aid:** No deadline. FAFSA required. Applicants notified on a rolling basis starting 3/1; must reply within 2 week(s) of notification.

Academics. Special study options: Cooperative education, distance learning, double major, dual enrollment of high school students, ESL, independent study, internships, liberal arts/career combination, weekend college. Bachelor's degree programs available on campus. License preparation in paramedic. **Credit/placement by examination:** AP, CLEP, institutional tests. 30 credit hours maximum toward associate degree. **Support services:** GED preparation and test center, remedial instruction, study skills assistance, tutoring.

Majors. Business: General, accounting, administrative services, business admin. **Computer sciences:** General. **Education:** Early childhood. **Health services:** EMT paramedic, nursing (RN). **Liberal arts:** Arts/sciences. **Protective services:** Criminal justice.

Most popular majors. Business/marketing 14%, health sciences 37%, liberal arts 38%.

Computing on campus. 25 workstations in library, computer center. Online course registration available.

Student life. Freshman orientation: Available. Preregistration for classes offered. **Activities:** Student government, Baptist Collegiate Ministry, Young Democrats, College Republicans.

Student services. Adult student services, career counseling, services for economically disadvantaged, student employment services, financial aid counseling, personal counseling, veterans' counselor. **Physically disabled:** Services for visually, speech, hearing impaired. **Transfer:** College fairs on campus for students transferring to 4-year colleges.

Contact. E-mail: casey.bromley@uaccb.edu
Phone: (870) 612-2000 Toll-free number: (800) 508-7878
Fax: (870) 793-4988
Scott Post, Director of Enrollment Services, University of Arkansas: Community College at Batesville, Box 3350, Batesville, AR 72503

University of Arkansas: Community College at Hope
Hope, Arkansas
www.uacch.edu   CB code: 3629

- Public 2-year community and technical college
- Commuter campus in small town

General. Regionally accredited. **Enrollment:** 1,560 degree-seeking undergraduates. **Degrees:** 134 associate awarded. **Location:** 30 miles from Texarkana. **Calendar:** Semester, limited summer session. **Full-time faculty:** 38 total; 5% have terminal degrees, 8% minority, 45% women. **Part-time faculty:** 23 total; 48% women.

Basis for selection. Open admission, but selective for some programs. Additional requirements for nursing, funeral services, respiratory therapy programs.

2011-2012 Annual costs. Tuition/fees: $2,104; $2,254 out-of-district; $4,114 out-of-state. Per-credit charge: $59 in-district; $64 out-of-district; $126 out-of-state. Books/supplies: $1,492. Personal expenses: $2,519.

Financial aid. Need-based: Need-based aid available for part-time students. Work-study available nights, weekends and for part-time students. **Non-need-based:** Scholarships awarded for academics.

Application procedures. Admission: No deadline. No application fee. Admission notification on a rolling basis. **Financial aid:** Closing date 7/6. FAFSA, institutional form required. Applicants notified on a rolling basis starting 1/1; must reply within 4 week(s) of notification.

Academics. Special study options: Distance learning, double major, dual enrollment of high school students, ESL, independent study, liberal arts/career combination. Bachelor's degree programs available on campus. License preparation in nursing, paramedic. **Credit/placement by examination:** AP, CLEP, institutional tests. **Support services:** GED test center, remedial instruction, study skills assistance, tutoring.

Majors. Business: General. **Education:** Middle. **Health services:** Respiratory therapy technology. **Liberal arts:** Arts/sciences. **Protective services:** Forensics, law enforcement admin, police science. **Work/family studies:** Child care management.

Most popular majors. Business/marketing 7%, health sciences 9%, legal studies 6%, liberal arts 62%, personal/culinary services 7%.

Computing on campus. 20 workstations in library. Commuter students can connect to campus network. Online course registration, online library, helpline, wireless network available.

Student life. Freshman orientation: Available. Preregistration for classes offered. **Activities:** Jazz band, choral groups, drama, music ensembles, student government, student newspaper.

Student services. Adult student services, alcohol/substance abuse counseling, chaplain/spiritual director, career counseling, services for economically disadvantaged, student employment services, financial aid counseling, personal counseling, placement for graduates, veterans' counselor. **Physically disabled:** Services for visually, speech, hearing impaired. **Transfer:** Pre-admission transcript evaluation for new students. College fairs on campus for students transferring to 4-year colleges.

Contact. E-mail: diana.syata@uacch.edu
Phone: (870) 777-5722 Fax: (870) 722-6630
Judy Anderson, Director for Enrollment Services, University of Arkansas: Community College at Hope, 2500 South Main, Hope, AR 71802-0140

University of Arkansas: Community College at Morrilton
Morrilton, Arkansas
www.uaccm.edu   CB code: 3881

- Public 2-year community college
- Commuter campus in small town

General. Regionally accredited. **Enrollment:** 2,204 degree-seeking undergraduates; 92 non-degree-seeking students. **Degrees:** 351 associate awarded. **Location:** 26 miles from Russellville. **Calendar:** Semester, limited summer session. **Full-time faculty:** 68 total; 4% have terminal degrees, 3% minority, 56% women. **Part-time faculty:** 50 total; 8% have terminal degrees, 2% minority, 58% women. **Class size:** 48% < 20, 52% 20-39.

Student profile. Among degree-seeking undergraduates, 49% enrolled in a transfer program, 51% enrolled in a vocational program, 2% already have a bachelor's degree or higher, 584 enrolled as first-time, first-year students, 193 transferred in from other institutions.

Part-time:	34%	Hispanic American:	4%
Women:	60%	International:	1%
African American:	9%	25 or older:	38%
Asian American:	1%		

Transfer out. 11% of students enrolled in the transfer program go on to 4-year colleges. **Colleges most students transferred to 2011:** University of Central Arkansas, Arkansas Tech University, University of Arkansas at Fayetteville, University of Arkansas at Little Rock.

Basis for selection. Open admission. ACT or COMPASS test scores required for placement. **Home schooled:** Transcript of courses and grades required. **Learning Disabled:** Students with documented disability must submit a written request for academic accommodations though the College Counseling Services Office at the beginning of each semester or term.

2011-2012 Annual costs. Tuition/fees: $3,075; $3,285 out-of-district; $4,395 out-of-state. Per-credit charge: $76 in-district; $83 out-of-district; $120 out-of-state. Books/supplies: $1,000. Personal expenses: $2,500.

2011-2012 Financial aid. Need-based: 411 full-time freshmen applied for aid; 356 were judged to have need; 345 of these received aid. Average need met was 61%. Average scholarship/grant was $2,377; average loan $1,528. 85% of total undergraduate aid awarded as scholarships/grants, 15% as loans/jobs. Need-based aid available for part-time students. Work-study available nights, weekends and for part-time students. **Non-need-based:** Awarded to 227 full-time undergraduates, including 134 freshmen. Scholarships awarded for academics, leadership, state residency.

Application procedures. Admission: No deadline. No application fee. Admission notification on a rolling basis. **Financial aid:** Priority date 7/1; no closing date. FAFSA, institutional form required.

Academics. Special study options: Cooperative education, distance learning, dual enrollment of high school students, internships, liberal arts/career combination. License preparation in nursing. **Credit/placement by examination:** AP, CLEP, SAT, ACT, institutional tests. 30 credit hours maximum toward associate degree. **Support services:** GED preparation and test center, learning center, reduced course load, remedial instruction, study skills assistance, tutoring, writing center.

Majors. Business: General. **Education:** Montessori teacher. **Health services:** Nursing (RN). **Liberal arts:** Arts/sciences. **Protective services:** Forensics, law enforcement admin. **Visual/performing arts:** Commercial/advertising art. **Work/family studies:** Child development.

Most popular majors. Business/marketing 8%, engineering/engineering technologies 25%, health sciences 6%, liberal arts 50%, trade and industry 8%.

Computing on campus. Commuter students can connect to campus network. Online library, wireless network available.

Student life. Freshman orientation: Mandatory. Preregistration for classes offered. One-day program, held 2 days before classes start for fall and spring semesters. **Policies:** Alcohol-, tobacco-, and drug-free campus. All students, employees, and visitors are expected to comply with policies and procedures. **Activities:** Campus ministries, choral groups, drama, music ensembles, student government, student newspaper, Baptist Collegiate Ministry, Catholic Campus Ministry, Church of Christ student organization, Young Democrats Club, intramural council, music society, Phi Beta Lambda, Phi Theta Kappa, theatre ensemble.

Athletics. Intramural: Basketball, football (non-tackle), table tennis, volleyball. **Team name:** Timberwolves.

Student services. Alcohol/substance abuse counseling, career counseling, student employment services, financial aid counseling, on-campus daycare, placement for graduates, veterans' counselor. **Physically disabled:** Services for visually, speech, hearing impaired. **Transfer:** College fairs on campus for students transferring to 4-year colleges.

Contact. E-mail: adm@uaccm.edu
Phone: (501) 977-2053 Toll-free number: (800) 264-1094
Fax: (501) 977-2123
Susan Dewey, Director of Admissions, University of Arkansas: Community College at Morrilton, 1537 University Boulevard, Morrilton, AR 72110

California

Allan Hancock College
Santa Maria, California
www.hancockcollege.edu

CB code: 4002

▶ Public 2-year community college
▶ Commuter campus in small city

General. Founded in 1920. Regionally accredited. **Enrollment:** 4,434 degree-seeking undergraduates. **Degrees:** 1,018 associate awarded. **Location:** 70 miles from Santa Barbara, 175 miles from Los Angeles. **Calendar:** Semester, extensive summer session. **Full-time faculty:** 155 total. **Part-time faculty:** 448 total.

Transfer out. Colleges most students transferred to 2011: California Polytechnic State University, San Luis Obispo; UC Santa Barbara, CSU, San Diego; CSU, Northridge; CSU, Fresno.

Basis for selection. Open admission, but selective for some programs. Special requirements for allied health and drama programs. Students required to make separate application for admission to nursing, drama, police academy programs. Interviews required for allied health applicants. Auditions required for drama applicants. **Adult students:** SAT/ACT scores not required.

2011-2012 Annual costs. Tuition/fees: $1,124; $6,824 out-of-state. Per-credit charge: $36 in-state; $226 out-of-state. Books/supplies: $1,656. Personal expenses: $3,114.

Financial aid. All financial aid based on need. Need-based aid available for part-time students. Work-study available nights, weekends and for part-time students.

Application procedures. Admission: No deadline. No application fee. Admission notification on a rolling basis. **Financial aid:** Priority date 5/1; no closing date. FAFSA required. Applicants notified on a rolling basis starting 6/1.

Academics. Special study options: Accelerated study, cooperative education, distance learning, double major, dual enrollment of high school students, ESL, honors, independent study, internships, liberal arts/career combination, study abroad, weekend college. Bachelor's degree programs available on campus. License preparation in dental hygiene, nursing, paramedic, real estate. **Credit/placement by examination:** AP, CLEP, institutional tests. 30 credit hours maximum toward associate degree. **Support services:** GED preparation and test center, learning center, reduced course load, remedial instruction, study skills assistance, tutoring, writing center.

Majors. Architecture: Technology. **Biology:** General. **Business:** General, accounting, administrative services, business admin, international marketing, management information systems, management science, office technology, office/clerical. **Communications technology:** Animation/special effects, graphic/printing, graphics, photo/film/video. **Computer sciences:** General, computer science, information technology. **Conservation:** Environmental studies. **Education:** Early childhood, elementary, physical. **Engineering:** General. **English:** English lit. **Foreign languages:** Spanish. **General:** Agribusiness operations. **Health services:** Dental assistant, licensed practical nurse, medical assistant, medical records admin, medical records technology, nursing (RN), physical therapy assistant. **Liberal arts:** Arts/sciences. **Math:** General, computational. **Parks/recreation:** General. **Physical sciences:** Chemistry, physics. **Protective services:** Fire safety technology. **Psychology:** General. **Social sciences:** General, international relations. **Visual/performing arts:** Art, commercial photography, commercial/advertising art, dance, design, fashion design, film/cinema/video, interior design, music, photography. **Work/family studies:** General, fashion consultant, housing.

Most popular majors. Health sciences 11%, liberal arts 68%, security/protective services 12%.

Computing on campus. 180 workstations in library, computer center. Online library, wireless network available.

Student life. Freshman orientation: Available. Preregistration for classes offered. **Activities:** Bands, choral groups, dance, drama, film society, literary magazine, music ensembles, musical theater, student government, student newspaper.

Athletics. Intercollegiate: Baseball M, basketball, cross-country, football (tackle) M, golf, soccer, softball W, tennis, track and field, volleyball W. **Team name:** Bulldogs.

Student services. Adult student services, career counseling, services for economically disadvantaged, student employment services, health services, on-campus daycare, personal counseling, placement for graduates, veterans' counselor. **Physically disabled:** Services for visually, hearing impaired. **Transfer:** Pre-admission transcript evaluation for new students. Transfer center, transfer adviser, college fairs on campus for students transferring to 4-year colleges.

Contact. Phone: (805) 922-6966 ext. 3248 Fax: (805) 922-3477 Adela Esquivel-Swinson, Director, Admissions and Records, Allan Hancock College, 800 South College Drive, Santa Maria, CA 93454-6399

American Academy of Dramatic Arts: West
Los Angeles, California
www.aada.org

CB code: 7024

▶ Private 2-year performing arts college
▶ Commuter campus in very large city
▶ Application essay, interview required

General. Founded in 1974. Regionally accredited. **Enrollment:** 170 degree-seeking undergraduates. **Degrees:** 14 associate awarded. **Calendar:** Semester, limited summer session. **Full-time faculty:** 9 total. **Part-time faculty:** 32 total. **Class size:** 93% < 20, 7% 20-39. **Special facilities:** Performance theater.

Student profile.

Out-of-state:	25%	25 or older:	20%

Basis for selection. Each candidate evaluated individually; consideration based on dramatic ability and potential, academic qualifications and readiness, in terms of maturity and motivation. Auditions required.

2011-2012 Annual costs. Tuition/fees: $30,500. Books/supplies: $545.

Financial aid. Need-based: Work-study available nights, weekends and for part-time students. **Non-need-based:** Scholarships awarded for academics, music/drama. **Additional information:** The Academy participates in various federal and state financial aid programs and offers a choice of payment plans. The Academy offers a variety of scholarships and assistance opportunities and a choice of payment plans for International Students. The Academy also participates with foreign government aid programs, if available.

Application procedures. Admission: Priority date 3/1; deadline 7/25. $50 fee. Admission notification on a rolling basis. SAT or ACT recommended for applicants attending directly from high school. **Financial aid:** Priority date 7/1; no closing date. Institutional form required. Applicants notified on a rolling basis starting 6/1; must reply within 3 week(s) of notification.

Academics. Select group of students invited to return for additional year of study and performance after graduation in repertory situation. **Special study options:** Cross-registration, exchange student. Students may study 1 year in each of 2 campuses (NY and CA). **Credit/placement by examination:** AP, CLEP. **Support services:** Pre-admission summer program, tutoring, writing center.

Majors. Visual/performing arts: Acting.

Computing on campus. 10 workstations in computer center.

Student life. Freshman orientation: Mandatory. Preregistration for classes offered. Held the Thursday prior to a class start. **Activities:** Student government.

Student services. Alcohol/substance abuse counseling, career counseling, financial aid counseling, personal counseling, veterans' counselor.

Contact. E-mail: khigginbotham@ca.aada.org
Phone: (323) 464-2777 ext. 103 Toll-free number: (800) 222-2867
Fax: (323) 464-1250
Karen Higginbotham, Director of Admissions, American Academy of Dramatic Arts: West, 1336 N. La Brea Avenue, Los Angeles, CA 90028

American River College
Sacramento, California
www.arc.losrios.edu

CB code: 4004

▶ Public 2-year community college
▶ Commuter campus in large city

General. Founded in 1955. Regionally accredited. **Enrollment:** 20,400 degree-seeking undergraduates. **Degrees:** 2,083 associate awarded. **Location:** 10 miles from downtown. **Calendar:** Semester, limited summer session. **Full-time faculty:** 350 total. **Part-time faculty:** 463 total.

Basis for selection. Open admission, but selective for some programs. Limited admission to nursing program. **Home schooled:** Transcript of courses and grades, interview, letter of recommendation (nonparent) required.

2011-2012 Annual costs. Tuition/fees: $1,112; $7,352 out-of-state. Per-credit charge: $36 in-state; $244 out-of-state. Books/supplies: $1,638. Personal expenses: $2,826.

Financial aid. All financial aid based on need. Need-based aid available for part-time students. Work-study available nights, weekends and for part-time students.

Application procedures. **Admission:** No deadline. No application fee in-state; $181 out-of-state. Application must be submitted online. Admission notification on a rolling basis beginning on or about 7/1. **Financial aid:** Priority date 3/2, closing date 6/30. FAFSA required. Applicants notified on a rolling basis starting 7/1; must reply within 2 week(s) of notification.

Academics. **Special study options:** Accelerated study, cooperative education, cross-registration, distance learning, ESL, honors, independent study, internships, liberal arts/career combination, study abroad, weekend college. **Credit/placement by examination:** AP, CLEP, IB. 15 credit hours maximum toward associate degree. **Support services:** Learning center, pre-admission summer program, reduced course load, remedial instruction, study skills assistance, tutoring, writing center.

Majors. **Architecture:** Landscape. **Business:** Accounting, administrative services, fashion, hospitality/recreation, management information systems, office/clerical, real estate. **Communications:** Journalism. **Communications technology:** Graphic/printing. **Computer sciences:** General, database management, networking, programming. **Conservation:** General. **Education:** Teacher assistance. **Health services:** Nursing (RN), respiratory therapy technology. **Liberal arts:** Arts/sciences. **Parks/recreation:** General. **Protective services:** Fire safety technology, police science. **Social sciences:** GIS/cartography. **Visual/performing arts:** Dramatic, interior design. **Work/family studies:** General, child care management, institutional food production.

Computing on campus. Online course registration, helpline available.

Student life. **Freshman orientation:** Available. Preregistration for classes offered. **Activities:** Bands, choral groups, dance, drama, international student organizations, literary magazine, music ensembles, Model UN, musical theater, student government, student newspaper, symphony orchestra.

Athletics. **Intercollegiate:** Baseball M, basketball, cross-country, football (tackle) M, golf, soccer, softball W, swimming, tennis, track and field, volleyball W, water polo M. **Team name:** Beavers.

Student services. Adult student services, career counseling, services for economically disadvantaged, student employment services, financial aid counseling, health services, minority student services, on-campus daycare, personal counseling, placement for graduates, veterans' counselor. **Physically disabled:** Services for visually, speech, hearing impaired. **Transfer:** Transfer center, transfer adviser for students transferring to 4-year colleges.

Contact. E-mail: recadmis@arc.losrios.edu
Phone: (916) 484-8261 Fax: (916) 484-8864
Robin Neal, Dean of Enrollment Services, American River College, 4700 College Oak Drive, Sacramento, CA 95841

Antelope Valley College
Lancaster, California
www.avc.edu   CB code: 4005

▸ Public 2-year liberal arts and technical college
▸ Commuter campus in large city

General. Founded in 1929. Regionally accredited. CSU Bakersfield extension office on campus. **Enrollment:** 10,531 degree-seeking undergraduates. **Degrees:** 890 associate awarded. **Location:** 50 miles from Los Angeles. **Calendar:** Semester, extensive summer session. **Full-time faculty:** 181 total. **Part-time faculty:** 430 total. **Class size:** 22% < 20, 67% 20-39, 7% 40-49, 3% 50-99, less than 1% >100.

Transfer out. Colleges most students transferred to 2011: California State University: Northridge, California State University: Bakersfield, University of California: Los Angeles.

Basis for selection. Open admission, but selective for some programs. Limited enrollment for nursing programs. Selective enrollment for R.N., radiologic technology, and respiratory therapy programs.

2011-2012 Annual costs. Tuition/fees: $1,082; $6,662 out-of-state. Per-credit charge: $36 in-state; $222 out-of-state. Books/supplies: $1,620. Personal expenses: $2,862.

Financial aid. **Need-based:** Need-based aid available for part-time students. Work-study available nights, weekends and for part-time students.

Application procedures. **Admission:** No deadline. No application fee in-state; $186 out-of-state. Admission notification on a rolling basis. **Financial aid:** Closing date 3/2. FAFSA, institutional form required. Applicants notified on a rolling basis starting 7/15; must reply within 2 week(s) of notification.

Academics. **Special study options:** Accelerated study, cooperative education, distance learning, dual enrollment of high school students, ESL, honors, independent study, internships, study abroad, teacher certification program, weekend college. Bachelor's degree programs available on campus. License preparation in aviation, nursing, radiology, real estate. **Credit/placement by examination:** AP, CLEP, institutional tests. Maximum of 4 courses allowed. **Support services:** Learning center, reduced course load, remedial instruction, study skills assistance, tutoring, writing center.

Majors. **Biology:** General. **Business:** General, administrative services, business admin, real estate. **Communications technology:** Graphic/printing. **Computer sciences:** General, computer graphics, computer science, data processing, information systems, programming. **Education:** Teacher assistance. **Engineering:** General. **Foreign languages:** American Sign Language. **General:** Landscaping, ornamental horticulture. **Health services:** Medical assistant, medical secretary, nursing (RN), office assistant. **Liberal arts:** Arts/sciences. **Math:** General. **Parks/recreation:** Health/fitness. **Protective services:** Fire safety technology. **Visual/performing arts:** General, cinematography, interior design, multimedia, music, photography. **Work/family studies:** General, child care management, child care service, child development, clothing/textiles, communication, family resources, food/nutrition, home furnishings.

Computing on campus. 300 workstations in library, computer center, student center. Online course registration, online library available.

Student life. **Freshman orientation:** Available. Preregistration for classes offered. Online orientation available. **Activities:** Bands, choral groups, dance, drama, music ensembles, Model UN, musical theater, student government, student newspaper, symphony orchestra.

Athletics. NAIA. **Intercollegiate:** Baseball M, basketball, cheerleading, cross-country, football (tackle) M, golf, soccer W, softball W, track and field, volleyball W. **Team name:** Marauders.

Student services. Adult student services, career counseling, services for economically disadvantaged, student employment services, financial aid counseling, health services, minority student services, on-campus daycare, personal counseling, veterans' counselor. **Physically disabled:** Services for visually, speech, hearing impaired. **Transfer:** Re-entry adviser for new students. Transfer center, transfer adviser, college fairs on campus for students transferring to 4-year colleges.

Contact. E-mail: registration@avc.edu
Phone: (661) 722-6300 ext. 6504 Fax: (661) 722-6531
LaDonna Trimble, Dean of Enrollment Services, Antelope Valley College, 3041 West Avenue K, Lancaster, CA 93536-5426

Art Institute of California: Los Angeles
Santa Monica, California
www.artinstitutes.edu/losangeles   CB code: 2490

▸ For-profit 2-year visual arts and career college
▸ Commuter campus in large city
▸ Application essay, interview required

General. Accredited by ACICS. **Enrollment:** 2,175 degree-seeking undergraduates. **Degrees:** 206 bachelor's, 111 associate awarded. **Calendar:** Quarter, extensive summer session. **Full-time faculty:** 68 total. **Part-time faculty:** 68 total. **Class size:** 57% < 20, 43% 20-39.

Basis for selection. High school record and general appropriateness of educational background to specific program applied for most important. Portfolio, interview, standardized test scores also important. SAT or ACT recommended.

2011-2012 Annual costs. Tuition/fees: $23,310. Per-credit charge: $518. Apartment-style housing: $2,994/quarter for 2-bedroom. On-campus books and supplies: $1822. Room/board: $8,982. Books/supplies: $1,656.

Financial aid. Need-based: Need-based aid available for part-time students. Work-study available nights, weekends and for part-time students. **Non-need-based:** Scholarships awarded for academics.

Application procedures. Admission: No deadline. No application fee. Admission notification on a rolling basis. **Financial aid:** No deadline. FAFSA required. Applicants notified on a rolling basis.

Academics. Special study options: Independent study, internships, study abroad. Bachelor's degree programs available on campus. **Credit/placement by examination:** AP, CLEP, SAT, ACT, institutional tests. **Support services:** Reduced course load, tutoring, writing center.

Majors. Computer sciences: Computer graphics, web page design. **Visual/performing arts:** Cinematography, commercial/advertising art, design, graphic design.

Computing on campus. 250 workstations in library, computer center. Student web hosting available.

Student life. Freshman orientation: Mandatory. Preregistration for classes offered. One day program before start of quarter. **Housing:** Guaranteed on-campus for all undergraduates. Apartments available. $250 deposit. **Activities:** Literary magazine, gay, lesbian, straight alliance.

Student services. Alcohol/substance abuse counseling, career counseling, student employment services, financial aid counseling, personal counseling, placement for graduates.

Contact. E-mail: ailaadm@aii.edu
Phone: (310) 752-4700 Toll-free number: (888) 646-4610
Fax: (310) 752-4708
Jesus Moreno, Director of Admissions, Art Institute of California: Los Angeles, 2900 31st Street, Santa Monica, CA 90405-3035

Art Institute of California: Sunnyvale
Sunnyvale, California
www.artinstitutes.edu/sunnyvale

- For-profit 2-year culinary school and technical college
- Residential campus in small city

General. Regionally accredited; also accredited by ACICS. Facility formerly campus of Brooks College. **Enrollment:** 726 degree-seeking undergraduates. **Degrees:** 15 associate awarded. **Location:** 45 miles from San Francisco, 10 miles from San Jose. **Calendar:** Quarter, extensive summer session. **Full-time faculty:** 13 total.

Basis for selection. Admission requirements vary by programs. We have the Accuplacer placement system for English and Math. Students can use acceptable ACT or SAT scores to waive this test. **Home schooled:** Transcript of courses and grades, state high school equivalency certificate required.

2011-2012 Annual costs. Tuition/fees: $23,410. Per-credit charge: $518. Room only: $7,200. Books/supplies: $552. Personal expenses: $859.

Financial aid. Need-based: Work-study available nights, weekends and for part-time students.

Application procedures. Admission: Closing date 10/11 (receipt date). $50 fee. Application must be submitted on paper. **Financial aid:** No deadline.

Academics. Special study options: Bachelor's degree programs available on campus. **Credit/placement by examination:** AP, CLEP, SAT, ACT. **Support services:** Tutoring.

Majors. Computer sciences: Web page design. **Visual/performing arts:** Graphic design.

Computing on campus. 30 workstations in library, computer center.

Student life. Freshman orientation: Mandatory. Preregistration for classes offered.

Student services. Financial aid counseling, personal counseling, placement for graduates.

Contact. Phone: (408) 962-6400
Geoff Mahalak, Director of Admissions, Art Institute of California: Sunnyvale, 1120 Kifer Road, Sunnyvale, CA 94086

Bakersfield College
Bakersfield, California
www.bakersfieldcollege.edu   CB code: 4015

- Public 2-year community college
- Commuter campus in large city

General. Founded in 1913. Regionally accredited. **Enrollment:** 9,241 degree-seeking undergraduates. **Degrees:** 920 associate awarded. **Location:** 114 miles from Los Angeles. **Calendar:** Semester, limited summer session. **Full-time faculty:** 252 total. **Part-time faculty:** 287 total. **Special facilities:** Planetarium.

Basis for selection. Open admission, but selective for some programs. Nursing and other allied health programs have additional admission requirements including required coursework.

2011-2012 Annual costs. Tuition/fees: $1,118; $7,208 out-of-state. Per-credit charge: $36 in-state; $239 out-of-state. Books/supplies: $1,638. Personal expenses: $2,150.

Financial aid. Need-based: Work-study available nights, weekends and for part-time students.

Application procedures. Admission: No deadline. No application fee. **Financial aid:** Priority date 3/2, closing date 6/30. FAFSA required. Applicants notified on a rolling basis starting 6/1; must reply within 2 week(s) of notification.

Academics. Special study options: Double major, dual enrollment of high school students. **Credit/placement by examination:** AP, CLEP, institutional tests. 12 credit hours maximum toward associate degree. **Support services:** Learning center, pre-admission summer program, reduced course load, remedial instruction, tutoring, writing center.

Majors. Biology: General, bacteriology. **Business:** Accounting, administrative services, business admin, management information systems, office technology, office/clerical, real estate. **Communications:** Broadcast journalism, journalism. **Communications technology:** General, graphic/printing. **Computer sciences:** Applications programming, data processing. **Conservation:** Forestry. **English:** English lit. **Foreign languages:** German, Spanish. **General:** Agribusiness operations, animal sciences, horticulture, ornamental horticulture. **Health services:** Dental assistant, EMT paramedic, licensed practical nurse, medical radiologic technology/radiation therapy, nursing (RN), predental, premedicine, prepharmacy, preveterinary. **History:** General. **Liberal arts:** Arts/sciences. **Math:** General. **Parks/recreation:** General. **Philosophy/religion:** Philosophy. **Physical sciences:** Chemistry, geology, physics. **Protective services:** Fire safety technology, police science. **Psychology:** General. **Social sciences:** Anthropology, criminology, economics, geography, political science, sociology. **Visual/performing arts:** Interior design, music, photography. **Work/family studies:** General, food/nutrition, institutional food production.

Student life. Activities: Bands, choral groups, dance, drama, literary magazine, music ensembles, radio station, student government, student newspaper.

Athletics. Intercollegiate: Baseball M, basketball, cross-country, diving, football (tackle) M, golf M, softball W, swimming, tennis, track and field, volleyball W, wrestling M. **Team name:** Renegades.

Student services. Career counseling, student employment services, health services, on-campus daycare. **Physically disabled:** Services for visually, speech, hearing impaired.

Contact. Phone: (661) 395-4301
Sue Vaughn, Director of Enrollment Services, Bakersfield College, 1801 Panorama Drive, Bakersfield, CA 93305

Barstow Community College
Barstow, California
www.barstow.edu   CB code: 4020

- Public 2-year community college
- Commuter campus in large town

General. Founded in 1959. Regionally accredited. **Enrollment:** 1,218 degree-seeking undergraduates. **Degrees:** 324 associate awarded. **Location:** 70 miles from San Bernardino. **Calendar:** Semester, limited summer session. **Full-time faculty:** 35 total. **Part-time faculty:** 70 total.

Student profile.

Out-of-state:	10%	25 or older:	43%

Basis for selection. Open admission.

2011-2012 Annual costs. Tuition/fees: $1,080; $6,360 out-of-state. Per-credit charge: $36 in-state; $212 out-of-state. Books/supplies: $1,656. Personal expenses: $2,595.

2010-2011 Financial aid. All financial aid based on need. 99% of total undergraduate aid awarded as scholarships/grants, 1% as loans/jobs. Need-based aid available for part-time students. Work-study available nights, weekends and for part-time students.

Application procedures. Admission: No deadline. No application fee. Admission notification on a rolling basis. **Financial aid:** Closing date 6/17. FAFSA required. Applicants notified on a rolling basis starting 7/1.

Academics. Special study options: Accelerated study, cooperative education, distance learning, double major, dual enrollment of high school students, ESL, independent study, liberal arts/career combination. **Credit/placement by examination:** AP, CLEP, institutional tests. 30 credit hours maximum toward associate degree. **Support services:** Learning center, reduced course load, remedial instruction, study skills assistance, tutoring.

Majors. Biology: General. **Business:** General, accounting, office management, office/clerical. **Computer sciences:** General, applications programming, programming. **Education:** General, elementary, teacher assistance. **Health services:** Medical assistant. **Liberal arts:** Arts/sciences. **Math:** General. **Protective services:** Fire safety technology, police science. **Social sciences:** General. **Work/family studies:** Child care management.

Computing on campus. 40 workstations in library, computer center. Online course registration, online library, wireless network available.

Student life. Freshman orientation: Available. Preregistration for classes offered. **Activities:** Bands, choral groups, dance, drama, music ensembles, musical theater, student government, Christian Club, Alpha Gamma Sigma, Phi Theta Kappa.

Athletics. NJCAA. **Intercollegiate:** Baseball M, basketball M, cross-country, softball W. **Intramural:** Badminton, baseball M, basketball, bowling, soccer, softball, swimming, tennis, volleyball. **Team name:** Vikings.

Student services. Adult student services, career counseling, services for economically disadvantaged, student employment services, financial aid counseling, personal counseling, placement for graduates, veterans' counselor. **Physically disabled:** Services for visually, speech, hearing impaired. **Transfer:** Pre-admission transcript evaluation for new students. Transfer center, transfer adviser, college fairs on campus for students transferring to 4-year colleges.

Contact. E-mail: admit@barstow.edu
Phone: (760) 252-2411 ext. 7236 Fax: (760) 252-6754
Heather Caldon, Director of Enrollment Services, Barstow Community College, 2700 Barstow Road, Barstow, CA 92311-9984

Berkeley City College
Berkeley, California
www.berkeleycitycollege.edu   CB code: 7711

- Public 2-year community college
- Commuter campus in small city

General. Founded in 1974. Regionally accredited. **Enrollment:** 3,243 degree-seeking undergraduates. **Degrees:** 129 associate awarded. **Location:** 15 miles from San Francisco. **Calendar:** Semester, limited summer session. **Full-time faculty:** 49 total. **Part-time faculty:** 137 total.

Basis for selection. Open admission.

2011-2012 Annual costs. Tuition/fees: $1,114; $6,424 out-of-state. Books/supplies: $1,450. Personal expenses: $2,600.

Financial aid. All financial aid based on need. Need-based aid available for part-time students. Work-study available nights, weekends and for part-time students.

Application procedures. Admission: No deadline. No application fee. Admission notification on a rolling basis. **Financial aid:** No deadline. Applicants notified on a rolling basis.

Academics. Special study options: Accelerated study, cooperative education, cross-registration, distance learning, dual enrollment of high school students, ESL, honors, independent study, internships, liberal arts/career combination, study abroad, weekend college. **Credit/placement by examination:** AP, CLEP, institutional tests. 6 credit hours maximum toward associate

degree. **Support services:** Learning center, reduced course load, remedial instruction, study skills assistance, tutoring, writing center.

Majors. Biology: Biotechnology. **Business:** Business admin, office/clerical, small business admin. **Communications technology:** General. **Computer sciences:** General. **English:** English lit. **Foreign languages:** Sign language interpretation, Spanish. **Health services:** Community health services. **Human services:** Social work. **Liberal arts:** Arts/sciences, humanities. **Psychology:** General. **Social sciences:** General, sociology. **Visual/performing arts:** Art.

Computing on campus. Commuter students can connect to campus network. Online course registration, online library, wireless network available.

Student life. Freshman orientation: Mandatory. Preregistration for classes offered. **Housing:** Students can apply for UC Berkeley off-campus co-ops if they intend to transfer. **Activities:** Choral groups, dance, film society, international student organizations, literary magazine, music ensembles, student government, Phi Theta Kappa, Spanish club, X club, Bahai club, black students union, global studies club, associated students club, digital arts club, Milvia Street literary magazine, film club.

Student services. Adult student services, career counseling, services for economically disadvantaged, student employment services, financial aid counseling, health services, minority student services, personal counseling, veterans' counselor. **Physically disabled:** Services for visually, speech, hearing impaired. **Transfer:** Transfer center, transfer adviser, college fairs on campus for students transferring to 4-year colleges.

Contact. E-mail: lnewsom@peralta.edu
Phone: (510) 981-2806 Fax: (510) 841-7333
Loretta Newsom, Admissions and Records Specialist, Berkeley City College, 2050 Center Street, Berkeley, CA 94704

Bryan College: Sacramento
Gold River, California
www.bryancollege.edu

- For-profit 2-year technical college
- Very large city
- Interview required

General. Accredited by ACCSC. **Enrollment:** 505 degree-seeking undergraduates. **Degrees:** 179 associate awarded. **Location:** 10 miles from downtown Sacramento. **Calendar:** Differs by program, limited summer session. **Full-time faculty:** 39 total. **Part-time faculty:** 12 total.

Basis for selection. Open admission. Admission process includes on campus interview, application/meet with director of admissions for recommendation, assessment.

2011-2012 Annual costs. Tuition/fees: $12,183.

Financial aid. Need-based: Work-study available nights, weekends and for part-time students.

Application procedures. Admission: No deadline. No application fee. **Financial aid:** No deadline.

Academics. Special study options: Massage therapy students get hands-on experience in public massage clinic. Personal training students work with fitness professionals to gain field experience. **Credit/placement by examination:** AP, CLEP.

Majors. Biology: Exercise physiology. **Health services:** Massage therapy.

Contact. E-mail: admissions@bryancollege.com
Phone: (916) 649-2400 Toll-free number: (866) 649-2400
Fax: (916) 641-8649
Orquedia Chavez, Director of Admissions, Bryan College: Sacramento, 2317 Gold Meadow Way, Gold River, CA 95670

Bryan University: Los Angeles
Los Angeles, California
www.bryanuniversity.edu

- For-profit 2-year virtual career college
- Commuter campus in very large city

General. Regionally accredited; also accredited by ACICS. **Enrollment:** 988 degree-seeking undergraduates. **Degrees:** 28 associate awarded. **Location:** Downtown. **Calendar:** Quarter, extensive summer session. **Full-time faculty:** 28 total; 89% women. **Part-time faculty:** 10 total; 50% women.

Basis for selection. Open admission, but selective for some programs. **Home schooled:** State high school equivalency certificate required.

2011-2012 Annual costs. Tuition/fees: $12,450. Tuition quoted is one-year cost of the most popular program Advanced Health and Fitness Training (AOS degree, two academic years): $24,900. Health Information Management and Coding (AOS degree, two academic years): $24,900. Court Reporting (AOS degree, 5 academic years): $51,777.

Financial aid. Need-based: Work-study available nights, weekends and for part-time students.

Application procedures. Admission: No deadline. $50 fee. Admission notification on a rolling basis. **Financial aid:** No deadline.

Academics. Special study options: Distance learning. **Credit/placement by examination:** AP, CLEP. **Support services:** Learning center, remedial instruction, study skills assistance, tutoring.

Computing on campus. PC or laptop required. Commuter students can connect to campus network. Online course registration, online library, helpline, repair service, wireless network available.

Student life. Freshman orientation: Mandatory. Preregistration for classes offered. **Activities:** Student newspaper.

Student services. Adult student services, alcohol/substance abuse counseling, career counseling, student employment services, financial aid counseling, health services, legal services, personal counseling, placement for graduates.

Contact. E-mail: info@bryancollege.edu
Phone: (877) 484-8850 Fax: (213) 483-3936
Nadeem Zaidi, Director of Admissions, Bryan University: Los Angeles, 3580 Wilshire Boulevard, Suite 400, Los Angeles, CA 90010

Butte College
Oroville, California
www.butte.edu
CB code: 4226

- Public 2-year community college
- Commuter campus in small city

General. Founded in 1966. Regionally accredited. **Enrollment:** 8,354 degree-seeking undergraduates. **Degrees:** 1,150 associate awarded. **Location:** 100 miles from Sacramento. **Calendar:** Semester, extensive summer session. **Full-time faculty:** 175 total. **Part-time faculty:** 551 total. **Special facilities:** 900-acre wild game refuge, nature trails.

Basis for selection. Open admission, but selective for some programs. Nursing, allied health programs have special requirements. Interviews required for allied health applicants.

2011-2012 Annual costs. Tuition/fees: $1,300; $7,300 out-of-state. Per-credit charge: $36 in-state; $236 out-of-state. Books/supplies: $700. Personal expenses: $1,954.

Financial aid. Need-based: Work-study available nights, weekends and for part-time students.

Application procedures. Admission: No deadline. No application fee. Admission notification on a rolling basis. **Financial aid:** Priority date 5/1; no closing date. FAFSA required. Applicants notified on a rolling basis starting 8/1.

Academics. Special study options: Cooperative education, cross-registration, distance learning, double major, dual enrollment of high school students, ESL, honors, independent study, study abroad. License preparation in nursing, paramedic, real estate. **Credit/placement by examination:** AP, CLEP, institutional tests. 9 credit hours maximum toward associate degree. **Support services:** Learning center, remedial instruction, study skills assistance, tutoring.

Majors. Business: General, accounting, administrative services, business admin, fashion, management information systems, marketing, office technology, real estate, tourism promotion. **Communications:** Broadcast journalism, journalism. **Communications technology:** General, graphic/printing. **Computer sciences:** General, applications programming, networking. **Education:** General, bilingual, early childhood, physical. **English:** English lit. **General:**

Agronomy, animal sciences, business, horticulture, ornamental horticulture. **Health services:** Cardiovascular technology, EMT paramedic, licensed practical nurse, medical assistant, medical secretary, nursing (RN), respiratory therapy technology, substance abuse counseling. **Liberal arts:** Arts/sciences. **Math:** General. **Parks/recreation:** Facilities management. **Protective services:** Fire safety technology, police science. **Social sciences:** General. **Visual/performing arts:** Ceramics, commercial photography, commercial/advertising art, fashion design, photography, studio arts. **Work/family studies:** General, child care management.

Computing on campus. 200 workstations in library, computer center. Wireless network available.

Student life. Activities: Bands, drama, film society, music ensembles, radio station, student government, student newspaper, symphony orchestra, TV station.

Athletics. NJCAA. **Intercollegiate:** Baseball M, basketball, cross-country, field hockey W, football (tackle) M, golf, soccer, softball W, tennis, track and field, volleyball W. **Team name:** Roadrunners.

Student services. Adult student services, career counseling, student employment services, health services, on-campus daycare, personal counseling, placement for graduates, veterans' counselor. **Physically disabled:** Services for visually, speech, hearing impaired. **Transfer:** Re-entry adviser for new students. Transfer center, transfer adviser for students transferring to 4-year colleges.

Contact. E-mail: admissions@butte.edu
Phone: (530) 895-2361 Fax: (530) 895-2411
Clinton Slaughter, Director of Admissions and Records, Butte College, 3536 Butte Campus Drive, Oroville, CA 95965

Cabrillo College
Aptos, California
www.cabrillo.edu
CB code: 4084

- Public 2-year community college
- Commuter campus in large town

General. Founded in 1959. Regionally accredited. Located in the Monterey Bay Area. **Enrollment:** 7,507 degree-seeking undergraduates. **Degrees:** 899 associate awarded. **Location:** 25 miles from San Jose. **Calendar:** Semester, extensive summer session. **Full-time faculty:** 208 total; 20% have terminal degrees. **Part-time faculty:** 383 total. **Special facilities:** Observatory, planetarium, horticulture organic gardens, green technology center.

Student profile.

Out-of-state:	2%	**25 or older:**	52%

Transfer out. Colleges most students transferred to 2011: University of California-Santa Cruz, San Jose State University, California State University-Monterey Bay.

Basis for selection. Open admission, but selective for some programs. Special prerequisite requirements for nursing, dental hygiene, and radiologic technology. International applicants have special admission requirements.

2011-2012 Annual costs. Tuition/fees: $1,143; $6,453 out-of-state. Per-credit charge: $36 in-state; $213 out-of-state. Books/supplies: $1,620. Personal expenses: $3,078.

Financial aid. Need-based: Need-based aid available for part-time students. Work-study available nights, weekends and for part-time students.

Application procedures. Admission: No deadline. No application fee. Admission notification on a rolling basis beginning on or about 6/1. **Financial aid:** No deadline. FAFSA, institutional form required. Applicants notified on a rolling basis starting 7/31; must reply within 3 week(s) of notification.

Academics. Special study options: Cooperative education, distance learning, dual enrollment of high school students, honors, independent study, internships, liberal arts/career combination, study abroad. License preparation in dental hygiene, nursing, radiology. **Credit/placement by examination:** AP, CLEP, institutional tests. **Support services:** Learning center, pre-admission summer program, reduced course load, remedial instruction, study skills assistance, tutoring, writing center.

Majors. Area/ethnic studies: Asian. **Biology:** General. **Business:** General, accounting, banking/financial services, business admin, construction management, entrepreneurial studies, office technology, real estate. **Communications:** Journalism. **Computer sciences:** General, data processing. **English:** English lit, rhetoric/composition. **Foreign languages:** General, French, German, Italian, Japanese, Spanish. **General:** Ornamental horticulture. **Health**

services: Dental hygiene, licensed practical nurse, medical assistant, medical radiologic technology/radiation therapy, nursing (RN). **History:** General. **Liberal arts:** Arts/sciences, library assistant. **Math:** General. **Physical sciences:** Chemistry, physics. **Protective services:** Firefighting, police science. **Psychology:** General. **Social sciences:** General, anthropology, economics, geography, political science, sociology. **Visual/performing arts:** General, art, dance, music, studio arts. **Work/family studies:** General, child care management.

Computing on campus. 350 workstations in library, computer center, student center. Online course registration, wireless network available.

Student life. Freshman orientation: Available. Preregistration for classes offered. **Activities:** Bands, choral groups, dance, drama, music ensembles, musical theater, student government, student newspaper, Various clubs, literacy, recreational, cultural and/or ethnic organizations.

Athletics. Intercollegiate: Baseball M, basketball, cross-country, diving, football (tackle) M, golf M, soccer M, softball W, swimming, tennis, track and field, volleyball W, water polo. **Team name:** Seahawks.

Student services. Adult student services, career counseling, services for economically disadvantaged, student employment services, financial aid counseling, health services, personal counseling, placement for graduates, veterans' counselor. **Physically disabled:** Services for visually, speech, hearing impaired. **Transfer:** Transfer center, transfer adviser, college fairs on campus for students transferring to 4-year colleges.

Contact. Phone: (831) 479-6201 Fax: (831) 479-5782
Tama Bolton, Director of Admissions and Records, Cabrillo College, 6500 Soquel Drive, Aptos, CA 95003

California Culinary Academy
San Francisco, California
www.chefs.edu/San-Francisco   CB code: 2209

- For-profit 2-year culinary school and career college
- Commuter campus in very large city
- Interview required

General. Founded in 1977. Accredited by ACCSC. All programs offered sanctioned by Le Cordon Bleu. **Enrollment:** 900 degree-seeking undergraduates. **Degrees:** 161 associate awarded. **Location:** Downtown. **Calendar:** Differs by program. **Full-time faculty:** 28 total. **Part-time faculty:** 23 total. **Special facilities:** Student-staffed public restaurant, mixology lab, gaming room, professional production kitchens, demonstration kitchens, pastry kitchens, confisseries, butchery lab, culinary library.

Basis for selection. The school has an open enrollment policy but the student needs to complete an interview with an admissions representative, pass a short entrance exam, have a High School diploma or equivalent before starting school. Wonderlic testing required for all programs.

2011-2012 Annual costs. Certificate in Le Cordon Bleu Culinary Arts: Tuition $17,200, Fees $300, STRF $42.50, Application Fee $50, Total Cost $17,592.50. Certificate in Le Cordon Bleu Pâtisserie and Baking: Tuition $17,200, Fees $300, STRF $42.50, Application Fee $50, Total Cost $17,592.50.

Financial aid. Need-based: Work-study available nights, weekends and for part-time students.

Application procedures. Admission: No deadline. $50 fee. Admission notification on a rolling basis. **Financial aid:** No deadline. FAFSA required. Applicants notified on a rolling basis; must reply within 1 week(s) of notification.

Academics. Special study options: Internships. **Credit/placement by examination:** AP, CLEP. **Support services:** Study skills assistance, tutoring.

Computing on campus. Student web hosting, wireless network available.

Student life. Freshman orientation: Mandatory. Preregistration for classes offered. **Housing:** Coed dorms available. $600 fully refundable deposit. **Activities:** Brewing arts association, Cuisine Des Femmes, Asian food club, baking and pastry arts club, dinner club, wine club.

Student services. Career counseling, student employment services, financial aid counseling, placement for graduates. **Transfer:** Re-entry adviser, pre-admission transcript evaluation for new students.

Contact. E-mail: admissions@caculinary.edu
Phone: (415) 771-3500 Toll-free number: (800) 229-2433
Fax: (415) 621-5625
Donna Ingenito, Director of Admissions, California Culinary Academy, 350 Rhode Island Street, San Francisco, CA 94103

Canada College
Redwood City, California
www.canadacollege.edu   CB code: 4109

- Public 2-year community college
- Commuter campus in small city

General. Founded in 1968. Regionally accredited. **Enrollment:** 6,992 undergraduates. **Degrees:** 220 associate awarded. **ROTC:** Army, Air Force. **Location:** 20 miles from San Francisco. **Calendar:** Semester, limited summer session. **Full-time faculty:** 65 total. **Part-time faculty:** 182 total.

Transfer out. Colleges most students transferred to 2011: San Francisco State, San Jose State, College of Notre de Namur, California State University-East Bay.

Basis for selection. Open admission, but selective for some programs. Special admission requirements for radiologic technology programs. middle college and college for working adults.

2011-2012 Annual costs. Tuition/fees: $1,124; $7,214 out-of-state. Per-credit charge: $36 in-state; $239 out-of-state. Books/supplies: $1,638. Personal expenses: $2,772.

Financial aid. Need-based: Work-study available nights, weekends and for part-time students.

Application procedures. Admission: No deadline. No application fee. Admission notification on a rolling basis. **Financial aid:** Priority date 5/1; no closing date. FAFSA required. Applicants notified on a rolling basis starting 7/15; must reply within 2 week(s) of notification.

Academics. Special study options: Cooperative education, cross-registration, distance learning, double major, dual enrollment of high school students, ESL, honors, independent study, internships, study abroad, weekend college. Bachelor's degree programs available on campus. **Credit/placement by examination:** AP, CLEP, IB, institutional tests. 12 credit hours maximum toward associate degree. **Support services:** Learning center, reduced course load, remedial instruction, study skills assistance, tutoring, writing center.

Majors. Biology: General. **Business:** General, accounting, business admin, fashion, management information systems, management science, office technology. **Communications:** Communications/speech/rhetoric, journalism. **Computer sciences:** General. **Education:** Early childhood. **Foreign languages:** Spanish. **Health services:** Medical radiologic technology/radiation therapy, medical transcription. **History:** General. **Liberal arts:** Arts/sciences. **Math:** General. **Philosophy/religion:** Philosophy. **Physical sciences:** Chemistry, physics. **Psychology:** General. **Social sciences:** General, anthropology, archaeology, economics, geography, sociology. **Visual/performing arts:** Art, dramatic, interior design, music.

Computing on campus. 300 workstations in library, computer center. Online course registration, wireless network available.

Student life. Freshman orientation: Available. Preregistration for classes offered. **Activities:** Concert band, choral groups, dance, drama, international student organizations, music ensembles, student government, symphony orchestra, Christian club, People of the Pacific, women in science and engineering, Latino empowerment, veteran's club, political awareness, robotics, interior design, EOPS.

Athletics. Intercollegiate: Baseball M, basketball M, golf W, soccer, volleyball W. **Team name:** Colts.

Student services. Adult student services, career counseling, health services, personal counseling, veterans' counselor. **Physically disabled:** Services for visually, hearing impaired. **Transfer:** Transfer center, transfer adviser, college fairs on campus for students transferring to 4-year colleges.

Contact. E-mail: canadaadmissions@smccd.edu
Phone: (650) 306-3226 Fax: (650) 306-3113
Ruth Miller, Registrar, Canada College, 4200 Farm Hill Boulevard, Redwood City, CA 94061

Carrington College: Antioch
Antioch, California
www.westerncollege.edu   CB code: 3033

- For-profit 2-year technical college
- Commuter campus in small city

General. Regionally accredited. **Enrollment:** 391 degree-seeking undergraduates. **Degrees:** 54 associate awarded. **Calendar:** Differs by program. **Full-time faculty:** 13 total. **Part-time faculty:** 7 total.

Basis for selection. Open admission, but selective for some programs. CPAT results important.

2011-2012 Annual costs. Program cost for the largest program Vocational Nursing: $44,877 (64 weeks). Other programs may vary.

Financial aid. Need-based: Work-study available nights, weekends and for part-time students.

Application procedures. Admission: No deadline. No application fee. Admission notification on a rolling basis. **Financial aid:** No deadline.

Academics. Special study options: Accelerated study, distance learning. License preparation in nursing. **Credit/placement by examination:** AP, CLEP.

Majors. Health services: Licensed practical nurse, massage therapy, medical assistant, medical records technology, pharmacy assistant. **Protective services:** Law enforcement admin.

Contact. Phone: (925) 522-7777
Jeremy McReady, Director of Admissions, Carrington College: Antioch, 2157 Country Hills Drive, Antioch, CA 94531

Carrington College: Citrus Heights
Citrus Heights, California
www.westerncollege.edu

- For-profit 2-year health science and technical college
- Very large city

General. Regionally accredited. **Enrollment:** 520 degree-seeking undergraduates. **Degrees:** 156 associate awarded. **Calendar:** Differs by program. **Full-time faculty:** 13 total. **Part-time faculty:** 11 total.

Basis for selection. Admission requirements vary by programs.

2011-2012 Annual costs. Tuition/fees: $14,280.

Financial aid. Need-based: Work-study available nights, weekends and for part-time students.

Academics. Credit/placement by examination: AP, CLEP.

Majors. Health services: Dental assistant, health care admin, massage therapy, office assistant, pharmacy assistant, sonography, surgical technology, veterinary technology/assistant. **Protective services:** Law enforcement admin.

Contact. Carrington College: Citrus Heights, 7301 Greenback Lane, Suite A, Citrus Heights, CA 95621

Carrington College: Pleasant Hill
Pleasant Hill, California
www.westerncollege.com   CB code: 2922

- For-profit 2-year health science and technical college
- Commuter campus in small city

General. Regionally accredited. **Enrollment:** 399 degree-seeking undergraduates. **Degrees:** 112 associate awarded. **Calendar:** Differs by program. **Full-time faculty:** 9 total. **Part-time faculty:** 9 total.

Basis for selection. CPAT examination important.

2011-2012 Annual costs. Tuition/fees: $14,280.

Financial aid. Need-based: Work-study available nights, weekends and for part-time students.

Application procedures. Admission: No deadline. No application fee. Admission notification on a rolling basis. **Financial aid:** No deadline. Applicants notified on a rolling basis.

Academics. Credit/placement by examination: AP, CLEP.

Majors. Health services: Dental assistant, medical assistant.

Contact. Phone: (925) 609-6650 Toll-free number: (800) 584-4520 Fax: (925) 609-6666
Lashon Wells, Admissions Director/Executive Director, Carrington College: Pleasant Hill, 380 Civic Drive, Suite 300, Pleasant Hill, CA 94523

Carrington College: Sacramento
Sacramento, California
www.westerncollege.edu   CB code: 2917

- For-profit 2-year health science and technical college
- Commuter campus in large city

General. Regionally accredited. **Enrollment:** 1,283 degree-seeking undergraduates. **Degrees:** 284 associate awarded. **Calendar:** Differs by program. **Full-time faculty:** 34 total. **Part-time faculty:** 65 total.

Basis for selection. Admission requirements vary by programs.

2011-2012 Annual costs. Tuition/fees: $14,280. Books/supplies: $448. Personal expenses: $1,686.

Financial aid. Need-based: Work-study available nights, weekends and for part-time students.

Academics. Credit/placement by examination: AP, CLEP.

Majors. Health services: Dental assistant, health care admin, licensed practical nurse, massage therapy, medical assistant, medical records technology, nursing (RN), pharmacy assistant, veterinary technology/assistant.

Contact. E-mail: info@westerncollege.edu
Phone: (800) 321-2386 Toll-free number: (800) 321-2386
Mary Langley, Director of Admissions, Carrington College: Sacramento, 7801 Folsom Blvd #210, Sacramento, CA 95826

Carrington College: San Jose
San Jose, California
www.svcollege.com

- For-profit 2-year technical college
- Commuter campus in very large city

General. Regionally accredited. **Enrollment:** 711 degree-seeking undergraduates. **Degrees:** 170 associate awarded. **Calendar:** Differs by program. **Full-time faculty:** 22 total. **Part-time faculty:** 38 total.

Basis for selection. Limited admission to dental programs.

2011-2012 Annual costs. Tuition/fees: $14,280.

Financial aid. Need-based: Work-study available nights, weekends and for part-time students.

Application procedures. Admission: No deadline. No application fee. Admission notification on a rolling basis.

Academics. Credit/placement by examination: AP, CLEP.

Majors. Computer sciences: Computer graphics. **Health services:** Dental assistant, dental hygiene, massage therapy, medical assistant, medical records technology, pharmacy assistant, surgical technology, veterinary technology/assistant.

Contact. Phone: (408) 360-0840 Fax: (408) 360-0848
Indy Decroos, Admissions Director, Carrington College: San Jose, 6201 San Ignacio Avenue, San Jose, CA 95119

Carrington College: San Leandro
San Leandro, California
www.westerncollege.edu   CB code: 2918

- For-profit 2-year health science and technical college
- Commuter campus in small city
- Interview required

General. Regionally accredited. **Enrollment:** 611 degree-seeking undergraduates. **Degrees:** 106 associate awarded. **Location:** 10 miles from Oakland. **Calendar:** Differs by program. **Full-time faculty:** 20 total. **Part-time faculty:** 15 total. **Special facilities:** Labs.

Basis for selection. CPAT score, interest important. CPAT required.

2011-2012 Annual costs. Tuition/fees: $14,280.

Financial aid. Need-based: Work-study available nights, weekends and for part-time students.

Application procedures. Admission: No deadline. No application fee. Admission notification on a rolling basis. **Financial aid:** No deadline. Applicants notified on a rolling basis.

Academics. Special study options: Distance learning. **Credit/placement by examination:** AP, CLEP. **Support services:** Study skills assistance, tutoring.

Majors. Health services: Licensed practical nurse, medical secretary, pharmacy assistant, veterinary technology/assistant.

Computing on campus. 55 workstations in library, computer center. Online library available.

Student life. Activities: Student newspaper.

Contact. Phone: (510) 276-3888 Toll-free number: (800) 584-4553 Fax: (510) 276-3653
Tiffany Rhodes, Director of Admissions, Carrington College: San Leandro, 1555 East 14th Street Suite 500, San Leandro, CA 94578

Carrington College: Stockton
Stockton, California
www.carrington.edu   CB code: 4886

- For-profit 2-year technical and career college
- Small city
- Application essay, interview required

General. Regionally accredited. **Enrollment:** 416 degree-seeking undergraduates. **Degrees:** 176 associate awarded. **Location:** 40 miles from Sacramento. **Calendar:** Differs by program. **Full-time faculty:** 7 total. **Part-time faculty:** 11 total.

Basis for selection. Admissions decisions are based upon high school diploma (GED or ATB) formal interview with applicant, a completed application and a passing score on an entrance exam.

2011-2012 Annual costs. Tuition/fees: $12,578.

Financial aid. Need-based: Work-study available nights, weekends and for part-time students.

Application procedures. Admission: No deadline. $100 fee.

Academics. Special study options: Accelerated study. **Credit/placement by examination:** AP, CLEP. **Support services:** Learning center, tutoring.

Majors. Health services: Dental assistant, health care admin, massage therapy, medical assistant, pharmacy assistant, veterinary technology/assistant. **Protective services:** Police science.

Computing on campus. 25 workstations in library, computer center. Online library available.

Student life. Freshman orientation: Mandatory. Preregistration for classes offered. **Activities:** Student newspaper.

Contact. Anna Meli, Assistant Director of Admissions, Carrington College: Stockton, 1313 West Robinhood Drive, Suite B, Stockton, CA 95207

Cerritos College
Norwalk, California   CB member
www.cerritos.edu   CB code: 4083

- Public 2-year community college
- Commuter campus in large city

General. Founded in 1955. Regionally accredited. **Enrollment:** 17,309 degree-seeking undergraduates. **Degrees:** 1,157 associate awarded. **Location:** 15 miles from Los Angeles. **Calendar:** Semester, limited summer session. **Full-time faculty:** 284 total. **Part-time faculty:** 456 total. **Special facilities:** Health occupations lab.

Basis for selection. Open admission, but selective for some programs. Limited admissions to nursing program.

2011-2012 Annual costs. Tuition/fees: $1,132; $7,582 out-of-state. Per-credit charge: $36 in-state; $251 out-of-state. Books/supplies: $1,620. Personal expenses: $2,862.

Financial aid. Need-based: Work-study available nights, weekends and for part-time students.

Application procedures. Admission: No deadline. No application fee. Admission notification on a rolling basis. **Financial aid:** Priority date 5/8; no closing date. FAFSA required. Applicants notified on a rolling basis; must reply within 2 week(s) of notification.

Academics. Special study options: Cooperative education, distance learning, dual enrollment of high school students, honors. Bachelor's degree programs available on campus. License preparation in dental hygiene, nursing, physical therapy. **Credit/placement by examination:** AP, CLEP, institutional tests. 12 credit hours maximum toward associate degree. **Support services:** Learning center, remedial instruction, tutoring.

Majors. Area/ethnic studies: Chicano/Hispanic-American/Latino. **Biology:** General, bacteriology, biomedical sciences, botany, zoology. **Business:** General, accounting, administrative services, banking/financial services, business admin, human resources, logistics, office management, office/clerical, real estate. **Communications:** Journalism. **Computer sciences:** General, applications programming, data processing, programming, systems analysis. **Conservation:** Wildlife/wilderness. **Education:** Bilingual, early childhood, special ed, teacher assistance. **English:** English lit, rhetoric/composition. **Foreign languages:** French, German, Spanish. **General:** Ornamental horticulture. **Health services:** Dental assistant, dental hygiene, licensed practical nurse, medical assistant, medical records technology, nursing (RN), physical therapy assistant. **History:** General. **Math:** General. **Parks/recreation:** General. **Philosophy/religion:** Philosophy. **Physical sciences:** Chemistry, geology, physics, planetary. **Protective services:** Police science. **Psychology:** General. **Social sciences:** Anthropology, economics, geography, political science, sociology. **Visual/performing arts:** Art, dramatic, interior design, music, photography. **Work/family studies:** General, clothing/textiles, institutional food production.

Computing on campus. 100 workstations in computer center.

Student life. Activities: Bands, choral groups, dance, drama, film society, literary magazine, music ensembles, musical theater, radio station, student government, student newspaper, symphony orchestra, Ahora, Indian club, Vietnamese club, Black Student Union.

Athletics. NJCAA. **Intercollegiate:** Baseball M, basketball, cross-country, diving, football (tackle) M, golf M, soccer M, softball W, swimming, tennis, track and field, volleyball W, water polo M, wrestling M. **Team name:** Falcons.

Student services. Adult student services, career counseling, financial aid counseling, health services, on-campus daycare, personal counseling, veterans' counselor, women's services. **Physically disabled:** Services for visually, speech, hearing impaired. **Transfer:** Transfer adviser, college fairs on campus for students transferring to 4-year colleges.

Contact. Phone: (562) 860-2451 ext. 2211 Fax: (562) 860-9680
Stephanie Murguia, Dean, Admissions and Records, Cerritos College, 11110 Alondra Boulevard, Norwalk, CA 90650

Cerro Coso Community College
Ridgecrest, California
www.cerrocoso.edu   CB code: 4027

- Public 2-year community college
- Commuter campus in large town

General. Founded in 1973. Regionally accredited. Multiple sites such as in the Kern River Valley, Mammoth, Bishop CA. **Enrollment:** 6,342 undergraduates. **Degrees:** 268 associate awarded. **Location:** 120 miles from Bakersfield. **Calendar:** Semester, limited summer session. **Full-time faculty:** 57 total; 26% have terminal degrees. **Part-time faculty:** 124 total. **Class size:** 44% < 20, 52% 20-39, 3% 40-49, 1% 50-99. **Special facilities:** Nature preserve, sculpture garden.

Student profile.

Out-of-state: 2% 25 or older: 63%

Basis for selection. Open admission. Interview required of nursing majors.

2011-2012 Annual costs. Tuition/fees: $1,080; $6,270 out-of-state. Per-credit charge: $36 in-state; $209 out-of-state. The Mammoth Lakes Foundation operates about 24 apartments on site of the Mammoth Lakes campus. Approximate fee is $700/month. Books/supplies: $1,638. Personal expenses: $2,150.

Financial aid. Need-based: Need-based aid available for part-time students. Work-study available nights, weekends and for part-time students.

Application procedures. Admission: No deadline. No application fee. Admission notification on a rolling basis. **Financial aid:** Priority date 5/15; no closing date. FAFSA required. Applicants notified on a rolling basis starting 6/1; must reply within 2 week(s) of notification.

Academics. Special study options: Cooperative education, distance learning, double major, dual enrollment of high school students, ESL, honors, independent study, internships, study abroad. License preparation in nursing. **Credit/placement by examination:** AP, CLEP. 30 credit hours maximum toward associate degree. **Support services:** GED preparation and test center, learning center, remedial instruction, study skills assistance, tutoring.

Majors. Business: General, administrative services, business admin, office management, office technology, office/clerical. **Computer sciences:** General. **Education:** Early childhood. **Health services:** Licensed practical nurse. **Liberal arts:** Arts/sciences. **Parks/recreation:** Facilities management. **Physical sciences:** General. **Protective services:** Fire safety technology, police science. **Social sciences:** General. **Visual/performing arts:** Art. **Work/family studies:** Child care management.

Most popular majors. Business/marketing 18%, computer/information sciences 6%, health sciences 6%, liberal arts 52%, social sciences 13%.

Computing on campus. Online course registration, online library available.

Student life. Freshman orientation: Available. Preregistration for classes offered. One week before class starts. **Activities:** Bands, choral groups, drama, literary magazine, student government, student newspaper, symphony orchestra.

Athletics. Intercollegiate: Baseball M, basketball W. **Team name:** Coyotes.

Student services. Career counseling, student employment services, financial aid counseling, on-campus daycare, personal counseling, placement for graduates, veterans' counselor. **Physically disabled:** Services for visually, speech, hearing impaired. **Transfer:** Transfer adviser, college fairs on campus for students transferring to 4-year colleges.

Contact. E-mail: jboard@cerrocoso.edu
Phone: (760) 384-6357 Fax: (760) 384-6377
Dave Cornell, Director of Admission and Records, Cerro Coso Community College, 3000 College Heights Boulevard, Ridgecrest, CA 93555-7777

Chabot College
Hayward, California
www.chabotcollege.edu   CB code: 4725

- Public 2-year community college
- Commuter campus in large city

General. Founded in 1961. Regionally accredited. **Enrollment:** 15,004 undergraduates. **Degrees:** 649 associate awarded. **ROTC:** Army, Air Force. **Location:** 30 miles from San Francisco, 15 miles from Berkeley. **Calendar:** Semester, extensive summer session. **Full-time faculty:** 207 total; 27% minority. **Part-time faculty:** 309 total; 26% minority. **Special facilities:** Planetarium.

Student profile.

Out-of-state: 1% 25 or older: 45%

Transfer out. Colleges most students transferred to 2011: CSU: East Bay, San Jose State University, UC: Berkeley, San Francisco State University, UC: Davis.

Basis for selection. Open admission, but selective for some programs. Special requirements for nursing, dental hygiene, and paramedic programs.

2011-2012 Annual costs. Tuition/fees: $1,108; $7,198 out-of-state. Per-credit charge: $36 in-state; $239 out-of-state. Books/supplies: $1,628. Personal expenses: $2,862.

Financial aid. Need-based: Work-study available nights, weekends and for part-time students. **Additional information:** Tuition and/or fee waivers for low-income students.

Application procedures. Admission: No deadline. No application fee. Admission notification on a rolling basis. Early action available for local high school students only. **Financial aid:** Priority date 8/1; no closing date. FAFSA, institutional form required. Applicants notified on a rolling basis.

Academics. Special study options: Cooperative education, cross-registration, distance learning, double major, dual enrollment of high school students, ESL, independent study, internships, liberal arts/career combination, student-designed major, study abroad, weekend college. License preparation in dental hygiene, nursing, real estate. **Credit/placement by examination:** AP, CLEP, institutional tests. 15 credit hours maximum toward associate degree. English and math tests required for placement. **Support services:** Learning center, pre-admission summer program, reduced course load, remedial instruction, study skills assistance, tutoring, writing center.

Majors. Biology: General. **Business:** General, accounting, administrative services, banking/financial services, logistics, management information systems, management science, office management, office technology, office/clerical, real estate, sales/distribution, tourism/travel. **Communications:** Broadcast journalism, journalism. **Communications technology:** General, radio/TV. **Computer sciences:** General, applications programming, computer science, data processing, information systems, programming. **Education:** Early childhood, teacher assistance. **Engineering:** General. **English:** English lit, rhetoric/composition. **Foreign languages:** French, German, Italian, Portuguese, Spanish. **Health services:** Clinical lab technology, dental hygiene, medical assistant, medical records admin, medical records technology, nursing (RN), predental, premedicine, prepharmacy, preveterinary. **History:** General. **Liberal arts:** Arts/sciences, library assistant. **Math:** General. **Parks/recreation:** General. **Philosophy/religion:** Philosophy. **Physical sciences:** Physics. **Protective services:** Firefighting, police science. **Psychology:** General. **Social sciences:** General, criminology, geography, political science, sociology. **Visual/performing arts:** Art, ceramics, commercial/advertising art, dance, dramatic, drawing, music, music performance, painting, photography, sculpture, studio arts. **Work/family studies:** Child care management, clothing/textiles.

Most popular majors. Business/marketing 10%, health sciences 15%, liberal arts 50%.

Computing on campus. Online course registration, wireless network available.

Student life. Freshman orientation: Available. Preregistration for classes offered. Introduction to college experience, programs, services, and registration process. **Activities:** Bands, choral groups, drama, film society, literary magazine, musical theater, radio station, student government, student newspaper, TV station, various religious, political, ethnic, and social service organizations.

Athletics. NJCAA. Intercollegiate: Baseball M, basketball, cross-country, football (tackle) M, golf M, soccer, softball W, swimming, tennis, track and field, volleyball W, water polo W, wrestling M. **Intramural:** Archery, badminton, basketball, bowling, handball, racquetball, soccer, softball, table tennis, tennis, volleyball. **Team name:** Gladiators.

Student services. Adult student services, career counseling, student employment services, on-campus daycare, personal counseling, placement for graduates. **Physically disabled:** Services for visually, speech, hearing impaired. **Transfer:** Re-entry adviser for new students. Transfer center, college fairs on campus for students transferring to 4-year colleges.

Contact. E-mail: ccarcom@chabotcollege.edu
Phone: (510) 723-6700 Fax: (510) 723-7510
Paulette Lino, Director of Admissions & Records, Chabot College, 25555 Hesperian Boulevard, Hayward, CA 94545

Chaffey College
Rancho Cucamonga, California
www.chaffey.edu

CB code: 4046

- Public 2-year community college
- Commuter campus in small city

General. Founded in 1883. Regionally accredited. **Enrollment:** 13,559 degree-seeking undergraduates. **Degrees:** 1,240 associate awarded. **Location:** 50 miles from Los Angeles. **Calendar:** Semester, limited summer session. **Full-time faculty:** 202 total. **Part-time faculty:** 625 total. **Special facilities:** Nature preserve, natural history collection, planetarium, 2 swimming pools, children's center.

Transfer out. Colleges most students transferred to 2011: CSU San Bernardino, California State Polytechnic University: Pomona, CSU Fullerton, University of LaVerne, Loma Linda University.

Basis for selection. Open admission. Assessment testing is recommended.

2011-2012 Annual costs. Tuition/fees: $1,114; $6,604 out-of-state. Per-credit charge: $36 in-state; $219 out-of-state. Books/supplies: $1,638. Personal expenses: $3,096.

Financial aid. Need-based: Need-based aid available for part-time students. Work-study available nights, weekends and for part-time students. **Non-need-based:** Scholarships awarded for academics. **Additional information:** State of California Board of Governors fee waivers to qualified state residents. Criteria for eligibility: households which receive public assistance, meet state's low income guidelines, and demonstrate need as defined by Title IV programs.

Application procedures. Admission: No deadline. No application fee. Admission notification on a rolling basis. **Financial aid:** No deadline. FAFSA required. Applicants notified on a rolling basis starting 7/15; must reply within 2 week(s) of notification.

Academics. Special study options: Accelerated study, cooperative education, dual enrollment of high school students, ESL, honors, independent study, internships, liberal arts/career combination, study abroad, weekend college. License preparation in aviation, nursing. **Credit/placement by examination:** AP, CLEP, institutional tests. **Support services:** GED preparation, learning center, remedial instruction, tutoring, writing center.

Majors. Biology: General. **Business:** Accounting, administrative services, business admin, fashion, office management, sales/distribution. **Communications:** Broadcast journalism, communications/speech/rhetoric. **Computer sciences:** General, applications programming. **Conservation:** Environmental studies. **Education:** General, early childhood, physical. **Engineering:** General. **English:** English lit. **Foreign languages:** French, German, Spanish. **Health services:** Dental assistant, medical radiologic technology/radiation therapy, nursing (RN). **History:** General. **Liberal arts:** Arts/sciences. **Math:** General. **Philosophy/religion:** Philosophy, religion. **Physical sciences:** Chemistry, geology, physics, planetary. **Psychology:** General. **Social sciences:** General, anthropology, economics, geography, political science, sociology. **Visual/performing arts:** Art, commercial/advertising art, dance, design, dramatic, fashion design, graphic design, interior design, multimedia, music, photography, studio arts. **Work/family studies:** General, child care management.

Computing on campus. 950 workstations in library, computer center. Repair service available.

Student life. Freshman orientation: Mandatory. Preregistration for classes offered. 3-hour session covers registration procedures, fees, financial aid, programs and services, counseling, course descriptions. **Activities:** Bands, choral groups, dance, drama, film society, music ensembles, Model UN, musical theater, student government, student newspaper, multicultural organizations, Vietnamese club, MECHA, Alpha Gamma Sigma, Black Student Union, ski club, religious organizations, French club, German club, Spanish club, Lambda.

Athletics. Intercollegiate: Baseball M, basketball, diving, football (tackle) M, softball W, swimming, volleyball W, water polo M. **Team name:** Panthers.

Student services. Alcohol/substance abuse counseling, career counseling, services for economically disadvantaged, student employment services, financial aid counseling, health services, on-campus daycare, personal counseling, veterans' counselor. **Physically disabled:** Services for visually, speech, hearing impaired. **Transfer:** Pre-admission transcript evaluation for new students. Transfer center, transfer adviser, college fairs on campus for students transferring to 4-year colleges.

Contact. Phone: (909) 652-6600 Fax: (909) 652-6006
Cecilia Carrera, Director of Admissions, Chaffey College, 5885 Haven Avenue, Rancho Cucamonga, CA 91701-3002

Citrus College
Glendora, California
www.citruscollege.edu

CB code: 4051

- Public 2-year community college
- Commuter campus in large town

General. Founded in 1915. Regionally accredited. **Enrollment:** 8,407 degree-seeking undergraduates. **Degrees:** 1,126 associate awarded. **Location:** 25 miles from Los Angeles. **Calendar:** Semester, limited summer session. **Full-time faculty:** 158 total; 18% have terminal degrees. **Part-time faculty:** 188 total. **Special facilities:** Performing arts center, golf driving range.

Student profile.

Out-of-state:	3%	25 or older:	29%

Basis for selection. Open admission.

2011-2012 Annual costs. Tuition/fees: $1,148; $7,748 out-of-state. Per-credit charge: $36 in-state; $256 out-of-state. Books/supplies: $1,656. Personal expenses: $3,114.

2010-2011 Financial aid. Need-based: 19% of total undergraduate aid awarded as scholarships/grants, 81% as loans/jobs. Need-based aid available for part-time students. Work-study available nights, weekends and for part-time students.

Application procedures. Admission: No deadline. No application fee. Application must be submitted online. Admission notification on a rolling basis. **Financial aid:** Closing date 3/1. FAFSA required. Applicants notified on a rolling basis; must reply within 2 week(s) of notification.

Academics. Special study options: Cooperative education, distance learning, double major, dual enrollment of high school students, ESL, honors, independent study, study abroad. License preparation in nursing. **Credit/placement by examination:** AP, CLEP, IB. 30 credit hours maximum toward associate degree. **Support services:** Learning center, remedial instruction, tutoring.

Majors. Biology: Botany, zoology. **Business:** General, management information systems, office management, office/clerical. **Computer sciences:** General, data processing. **Conservation:** Forestry. **Engineering:** General. **English:** English lit. **Foreign languages:** French, German, Japanese, Spanish. **Health services:** Dental assistant, licensed practical nurse, medical assistant. **Liberal arts:** Arts/sciences, library assistant. **Math:** General. **Parks/recreation:** Health/fitness. **Physical sciences:** Chemistry, physics. **Protective services:** Criminal justice, law enforcement admin. **Psychology:** General. **Social sciences:** General. **Visual/performing arts:** Art, music, photography, studio arts.

Most popular majors. Business/marketing 17%, English 6%, interdisciplinary studies 15%, liberal arts 13%, social sciences 33%, visual/performing arts 9%.

Computing on campus. 1,100 workstations in library, computer center. Online course registration, online library, wireless network available.

Student life. Freshman orientation: Mandatory. Preregistration for classes offered. **Activities:** Jazz band, dance, drama, international student organizations, literary magazine, music ensembles, musical theater, student government, student newspaper, African American Student Alliance, European heritage club, Get Real Christian Fellowship, Latinos Unidos student association, Latter Day Saints students association, Natives of the Americas student association, Students United for Societal Change.

Athletics. Intercollegiate: Baseball M, basketball, cross-country, football (tackle) M, golf, soccer, softball W, swimming, tennis, track and field, volleyball W, water polo. **Team name:** Owls.

Student services. Career counseling, services for economically disadvantaged, student employment services, financial aid counseling, health services, legal services, minority student services, on-campus daycare, personal counseling, placement for graduates, veterans' counselor. **Physically disabled:** Services for visually, speech, hearing impaired.

Contact. E-mail: admissions@citruscollege.edu
Phone: (626) 914-8511 Fax: (626) 914-8613
Lois Papner, Dean of Admissions, Citrus College, 1000 West Foothill Boulevard, Glendora, CA 91741-1899

City College of San Francisco
San Francisco, California
www.ccsf.edu   CB code: 4052

- Public 2-year community college
- Commuter campus in very large city

General. Founded in 1935. Regionally accredited. **Enrollment:** 19,478 degree-seeking undergraduates. **Degrees:** 1,227 associate awarded. **ROTC:** Army. **Location:** Downtown. **Calendar:** Semester, extensive summer session. **Full-time faculty:** 808 total; 36% minority. **Part-time faculty:** 1,012 total; 40% minority. **Special facilities:** Observatory, Diego Rivera Pan-American Mural.

Student profile.

Out-of-state: 5%   25 or older: 65%

Transfer out. Colleges most students transferred to 2011: San Francisco State University, California State University: East Bay, San Jose State University, University of California: Berkeley, University of California: Davis.

Basis for selection. Open admission, but selective for some programs. If applicant lacks high school diploma or equivalent, must be 18 or older and demonstrate ability to benefit. Program for registered nursing and a few other programs have a competitive/ special admissions process. All students entering the credit program are tested for placement into English or ESL and mathematics courses. **Adult students:** SAT/ACT scores not required. Credit programs require placement tests in English or ESL and mathematics. Free noncredit classes require placement tests depending on intended course of study.

2011-2012 Annual costs. Tuition/fees: $1,114; $6,724 out-of-state. Per-credit charge: $36 in-state; $223 out-of-state. Books/supplies: $1,656. Personal expenses: $3,114.

Financial aid. Need-based: Work-study available nights, weekends and for part-time students. **Additional information:** Board of Governor fee waiver for low income students.

Application procedures. Admission: No deadline. No application fee. Admission notification on a rolling basis. **Financial aid:** Priority date 3/1; no closing date. FAFSA required. Applicants notified on a rolling basis starting 7/1.

Academics. Free, noncredit classes offered in some subjects. Working Adults Degree Program. Bookloan program for low-income students. Intercollegiate Speech and Debate. Learning assistance, diversity, and student success programs. **Special study options:** Accelerated study, distance learning, dual enrollment of high school students, ESL, honors, independent study, internships, liberal arts/career combination, study abroad, weekend college. Credit is available for service-learning. License preparation in dental hygiene, nursing, paramedic, radiology. **Credit/placement by examination:** AP, CLEP, institutional tests. 45 credit hours maximum toward associate degree. Various limitations and stipulations on credit by examination. **Support services:** GED preparation and test center, learning center, pre-admission summer program, remedial instruction, study skills assistance, tutoring, writing center.

Majors. Architecture: Environmental design, interior. **Biology:** General. **Business:** Accounting, administrative services, business admin, fashion, hospitality/recreation, human resources, management information systems, marketing, office technology, office/clerical, operations, real estate, tourism promotion, tourism/travel. **Communications:** Journalism. **Communications technology:** General, graphic/printing. **Computer sciences:** General, computer science. **Education:** Teacher assistance. **Engineering:** General, mechanical. **General:** Floriculture, landscaping, nursery operations, ornamental horticulture. **Health services:** Clinical lab science, dental assistant, EMT paramedic, medical assistant, medical radiologic technology/radiation therapy, medical records admin, medical records technology, medical secretary, nursing (RN), office admin, office assistant, physician assistant, ward clerk. **Liberal arts:** Library assistant. **Physical sciences:** Chemistry. **Protective services:** Fire safety technology, police science. **Visual/performing arts:** Cinematography, graphic design, interior design, photography, printmaking. **Work/family studies:** Child development, human nutrition.

Computing on campus. 750 workstations in library, computer center, student center. Commuter students can connect to campus network. Online course registration, online library, helpline, wireless network available.

Student life. Freshman orientation: Mandatory. Preregistration for classes offered. **Activities:** Jazz band, choral groups, dance, drama, film society, literary magazine, music ensembles, musical theater, opera, radio station, student government, student newspaper, symphony orchestra, TV station, City College Press Club, Cartoon Illustration and Art, La Raza Unida, Chinese Culture Club, Christian Fellowship Club, Le Cercle Francais, African American Changing Times, LBGTstr8 Alliance, Students Linking Education and Activism, Women of Color Organization.

Athletics. NJCAA. **Intercollegiate:** Badminton W, baseball M, basketball, cheerleading, cross-country, football (tackle) M, judo W, soccer, softball W, tennis, track and field, volleyball W. **Intramural:** Archery, badminton, baseball, basketball, cheerleading, fencing, football (non-tackle), golf, gymnastics, judo, racquetball, soccer, swimming, tennis, volleyball, weight lifting. **Team name:** Rams.

Student services. Adult student services, alcohol/substance abuse counseling, career counseling, services for economically disadvantaged, student employment services, financial aid counseling, health services, minority student services, on-campus daycare, personal counseling, placement for graduates, veterans' counselor, women's services. **Physically disabled:** Services for visually, speech, hearing impaired. **Transfer:** Transfer center, transfer adviser, college fairs on campus for students transferring to 4-year colleges.

Contact. E-mail: admits@ccsf.edu
Phone: (415) 239-3285 Fax: (415) 239-3936
MaryLou Leyba-Frank, Dean of Admissions and Records, City College of San Francisco, Office of Admissions and Records E-107, San Francisco, CA 94112

Coastline Community College
Fountain Valley, California   CB member
www.coastline.edu   CB code: 0933

- Public 2-year community college
- Commuter campus in small city

General. Founded in 1976. Regionally accredited. Classes held at community-based sites during the daytime, evenings, weekends, and through extensive distance learning education. **Enrollment:** 11,067 undergraduates. **Degrees:** 1,429 associate awarded. **Location:** 30 miles from Los Angeles. **Calendar:** Semester, limited summer session. **Full-time faculty:** 45 total. **Part-time faculty:** 265 total. **Class size:** 45% < 20, 40% 20-39, 6% 40-49, 6% 50-99, 2% >100. **Special facilities:** Workplace preparation center.

Student profile.

Out-of-state: 1%   25 or older: 73%

Transfer out. Colleges most students transferred to 2011: CSU Fullerton, CSU Long Beach, UC Irvine.

Basis for selection. Open admission. If submitted, SAT/ACT used for placement and counseling, in lieu of college administered English and math tests.

2011-2012 Annual costs. Tuition/fees: $1,112; $6,992 out-of-state. Per-credit charge: $36 in-state; $232 out-of-state. Books/supplies: $1,656. Personal expenses: $3,114.

Financial aid. All financial aid based on need. Need-based aid available for part-time students. Work-study available nights, weekends and for part-time students. **Additional information:** Board of Governor's Grant: statewide fee waiver program for students or dependents receiving HFOL/TANF, SSI, General Relief, or whose income meets set standards or who are considered eligible through Federal needs analysis.

Application procedures. Admission: No deadline. No application fee. Admission notification on a rolling basis. **Financial aid:** Priority date 3/2; no closing date. FAFSA, institutional form required. Applicants notified on a rolling basis starting 8/1; must reply within 2 week(s) of notification.

Academics. Special study options: Accelerated study, cooperative education, distance learning, dual enrollment of high school students, ESL, independent study, liberal arts/career combination, study abroad, weekend college. Midnight college via telecourse delivery. License preparation in physical therapy, real estate. **Credit/placement by examination:** AP, CLEP. 30 credit hours maximum toward associate degree. **Support services:** GED preparation, reduced course load, remedial instruction, tutoring.

Majors. Business: General, accounting, business admin, entrepreneurial studies, management science, office technology, real estate. **Computer sciences:** General. **Liberal arts:** Arts/sciences.

Computing on campus. 100 workstations in computer center.

Student life. Freshman orientation: Available. Preregistration for classes offered. **Activities:** Choral groups, dance, student government.

Student services. Career counseling, services for economically disadvantaged, student employment services, financial aid counseling, health services,

personal counseling, veterans' counselor. **Physically disabled:** Services for hearing impaired. **Transfer:** Transfer center, transfer adviser, college fairs on campus for students transferring to 4-year colleges.

Contact. E-mail: jmcdonald@cccd.edu
Phone: (714) 241-6176 Fax: (714) 241-6288
Jennifer McDonald, Director of Admissions and Records, Coastline Community College, 11460 Warner Avenue, Fountain Valley, CA 92708

Coleman College: San Marcos
San Marcos, California
www.coleman.edu

- For-profit 2-year technical college
- Commuter campus in small city
- Interview required

General. Accredited by ACICS. Branch campus of Coleman College, La Mesa. **Enrollment:** 119 degree-seeking undergraduates. **Degrees:** 17 associate awarded. **Calendar:** Differs by program. **Full-time faculty:** 8 total; 25% minority. **Part-time faculty:** 21 total; 67% minority, 24% women. **Class size:** 100% < 20.

Student profile. Among degree-seeking undergraduates, 16 enrolled as first-time, first-year students, 2 transferred in from other institutions.

Part-time:	13%	Women:	10%
Out-of-state:	1%	25 or older:	59%

Basis for selection. Open admission, but selective for some programs. In addition to HS diploma or GED, applicants required to pass an aptitude test of math and logic. Skills test given during interview.

2011-2012 Annual costs. Tuition/fees: $15,143. Per-credit charge: $325. Tuition quoted is one year cost for undergraduate study. Associate: $35,000. Bachelor's: $58,500. Masters: $23,100. Application Fee: $100.

2011-2012 Financial aid. All financial aid based on need. 13 full-time freshmen applied for aid; 13 were judged to have need; 13 of these received aid. Average need met was 84%. Average scholarship/grant was $3,464; average loan $3,119. 56% of total undergraduate aid awarded as scholarships/grants, 44% as loans/jobs. Need-based aid available for part-time students. Work-study available nights, weekends and for part-time students.

Application procedures. Admission: No deadline. $100 fee. Application must be submitted on paper. **Financial aid:** No deadline. FAFSA, institutional form required. Applicants notified on a rolling basis starting 1/2; must reply within 1 week(s) of notification.

Academics. University uses inverted curriculum with major taken before general curriculum. **Special study options:** Accelerated study, cooperative education, distance learning, double major. **Credit/placement by examination:** AP, CLEP, institutional tests. 36 credit hours maximum toward associate degree. **Support services:** Reduced course load, tutoring, writing center.

Majors. Computer sciences: Web page design.

Computing on campus. Helpline available.

Student life. Freshman orientation: Available. Preregistration for classes offered. Held before start of classes. **Activities:** Student activities committee.

Student services. Career counseling, financial aid counseling, personal counseling, placement for graduates. **Transfer:** Pre-admission transcript evaluation for new students. Transfer adviser for students transferring to 4-year colleges.

Contact. E-mail: admis@coleman.edu
Phone: (760) 747-3990 Toll-free number: (800) 430-2030
Fax: (760) 752-9808
Bobbie Strohm, Director of Admissions, Coleman College: San Marcos, 1284 West San Marcos Boulevard, San Marcos, CA 92069

College of Alameda
Alameda, California
www.alameda.peralta.edu
CB code: 4118

- Public 2-year community college
- Commuter campus in small city

General. Founded in 1970. Regionally accredited. **Enrollment:** 2,879 degree-seeking undergraduates. **Degrees:** 200 associate awarded. **Calendar:**

Semester, limited summer session. **Full-time faculty:** 72 total; 17% have terminal degrees, 42% minority. **Part-time faculty:** 117 total.

Student profile.

Out-of-state:	2%	25 or older:	44%

Basis for selection. Open admission.

High school preparation. College-preparatory program recommended.

2011-2012 Annual costs. Tuition/fees: $1,180; $6,490 out-of-state. Per-credit charge: $36 in-state; $213 out-of-state. Books/supplies: $1,566. Personal expenses: $3,024.

Financial aid. Need-based: Work-study available nights, weekends and for part-time students.

Application procedures. Admission: No deadline. No application fee. Admission notification on a rolling basis. **Financial aid:** Priority date 3/2; no closing date. FAFSA required. Applicants notified on a rolling basis starting 7/1; must reply within 2 week(s) of notification.

Academics. Special study options: Cooperative education, cross-registration, dual enrollment of high school students, honors, independent study, liberal arts/career combination. License preparation in aviation. **Credit/placement by examination:** AP, CLEP, institutional tests. **Support services:** Learning center, remedial instruction, tutoring.

Majors. Area/ethnic studies: African-American. **Biology:** General. **Business:** General, accounting, administrative services, business admin, entrepreneurial studies, fashion, marketing, office/clerical. **Education:** Teacher assistance. **English:** English lit. **Foreign languages:** Spanish. **Health services:** Dental assistant, health aide. **History:** General. **Liberal arts:** Arts/sciences. **Math:** General. **Philosophy/religion:** Philosophy. **Psychology:** General. **Social sciences:** General, anthropology, economics, geography, political science, sociology. **Visual/performing arts:** General, music, studio arts.

Computing on campus. Online course registration available.

Student life. Freshman orientation: Available. Preregistration for classes offered. **Activities:** Jazz band, choral groups, dance, drama, student government, student newspaper.

Athletics. Intercollegiate: Basketball, bowling, cross-country M, fencing, golf, soccer M, tennis, track and field, volleyball. **Intramural:** Golf, sailing, softball W. **Team name:** COUGARS.

Student services. Adult student services, career counseling, services for economically disadvantaged, student employment services, health services, on-campus daycare, personal counseling, placement for graduates, veterans' counselor. **Physically disabled:** Services for visually, speech, hearing impaired. **Transfer:** Transfer adviser, college fairs on campus for students transferring to 4-year colleges.

Contact. E-mail: admissions@peralta.edu
Phone: (510) 748-2228 Fax: (510) 748-5227
Kelly Compton, Vice President of Student Services, College of Alameda, 555 Ralph Appezzato Memorial Parkway, Alameda, CA 94501

College of Marin
Kentfield, California
www.marin.edu
CB code: 4061

- Public 2-year community college
- Commuter campus in small town

General. Founded in 1926. Regionally accredited. Additional campus at Indian Valley - Novato, CA. **Enrollment:** 7,346 undergraduates. **Degrees:** 206 associate awarded. **Location:** 15 miles from San Francisco. **Calendar:** Semester, limited summer session. **Full-time faculty:** 90 total. **Part-time faculty:** 249 total.

Transfer out. Colleges most students transferred to 2011: University of California: Berkeley, San Francisco State, University of California: Davis.

Basis for selection. Open admission, but selective for some programs. Limited admissions to registered nursing program. **Adult students:** SAT/ACT scores not required.

2011-2012 Annual costs. Tuition/fees: $1,116; $7,056 out-of-state. Per-credit charge: $36 in-state; $234 out-of-state. Books/supplies: $1,620. Personal expenses: $3,078.

Financial aid. All financial aid based on need. Need-based aid available for part-time students. Work-study available nights, weekends and for part-time students.

Application procedures. Admission: No deadline. No application fee. Admission notification on a rolling basis. **Financial aid:** Priority date 3/2; no closing date. FAFSA required. Applicants notified on a rolling basis starting 5/15.

Academics. Special study options: Distance learning, ESL. **Credit/placement by examination:** AP, CLEP, institutional tests. **Support services:** GED preparation, remedial instruction, study skills assistance, tutoring, writing center.

Majors. Architecture: Environmental design. **Area/ethnic studies:** General. **Biology:** General, environmental. **Business:** General, accounting, business admin, real estate. **Communications:** Media studies. **Computer sciences:** General, computer science, web page design. **English:** English lit, rhetoric/composition. **Foreign languages:** General, French, Spanish. **General:** Landscaping, nursery operations. **Health services:** Dental assistant, medical assistant, nursing (RN). **History:** General. **Liberal arts:** Arts/sciences. **Math:** General. **Physical sciences:** General, chemistry, physics. **Psychology:** General. **Social sciences:** General, geography. **Visual/performing arts:** Dance, dramatic, music, studio arts. **Work/family studies:** Child care service.

Computing on campus. Online course registration available.

Student life. Activities: Concert band, choral groups, dance, drama, student government, student newspaper.

Athletics. Intercollegiate: Baseball M, basketball, cross-country, diving, soccer, softball, squash, tennis, track and field.

Student services. Career counseling, services for economically disadvantaged, on-campus daycare, personal counseling. **Transfer:** Transfer center, transfer adviser, college fairs on campus for students transferring to 4-year colleges.

Contact. Phone: (415) 485-9412
Robert Balestreri, Dean of Enrollment Services, College of Marin, 835 College Avenue, Kentfield, CA 94904

College of San Mateo
San Mateo, California
www.collegeofsanmateo.edu   CB code: 4070

▶ Public 2-year community college
▶ Commuter campus in small city

General. Founded in 1922. Regionally accredited. **Enrollment:** 11,499 undergraduates. **Degrees:** 320 associate awarded. **ROTC:** Army, Air Force. **Location:** 15 miles from San Francisco. **Calendar:** Semester, limited summer session. **Full-time faculty:** 141 total. **Part-time faculty:** 208 total. **Special facilities:** Planetarium.

Student profile.

Out-of-state:	2%	25 or older:	51%

Basis for selection. Open admission, but selective for some programs. Nursing program has separate requirements.

2011-2012 Annual costs. Tuition/fees: $1,116; $7,206 out-of-state. Per-credit charge: $36 in-state; $239 out-of-state. Books/supplies: $1,638. Personal expenses: $2,772.

Financial aid. Need-based: Work-study available nights, weekends and for part-time students.

Application procedures. Admission: No deadline. No application fee. Admission notification on a rolling basis. Completion of CSM Placement tests for English, reading and mathematics recommended prior to counseling session. **Financial aid:** Closing date 3/2. FAFSA, institutional form required. Applicants notified on a rolling basis starting 6/15.

Academics. Special study options: Cooperative education, cross-registration, distance learning, double major, dual enrollment of high school students, ESL, honors, independent study, liberal arts/career combination, study abroad, weekend college. License preparation in dental hygiene, nursing, real estate. **Credit/placement by examination:** AP, CLEP, IB, institutional tests. 12 credit hours maximum toward associate degree. **Support services:** Learning center, reduced course load, remedial instruction, study skills assistance, tutoring, writing center.

Majors. Biology: General, biomedical sciences. **Business:** General, accounting, entrepreneurial studies, fashion, logistics, management information systems, office/clerical, real estate. **Communications:** Advertising, broadcast journalism. **Communications technology:** General. **Computer sciences:** General, web page design. **Engineering:** General. **English:** English lit, rhetoric/composition. **Foreign languages:** French, German, Spanish. **General:** Horticulture, ornamental horticulture. **Health services:** Dental assistant, medical assistant, nursing (RN), substance abuse counseling. **Liberal arts:** Arts/sciences. **Math:** General. **Physical sciences:** Chemistry, geology, physics. **Protective services:** Fire safety technology. **Social sciences:** General. **Visual/performing arts:** Cinematography, commercial/advertising art, music, painting, photography, studio arts.

Computing on campus. 150 workstations in library, computer center, student center. Online course registration, wireless network available.

Student life. Freshman orientation: Available. Preregistration for classes offered. **Activities:** Bands, choral groups, dance, literary magazine, radio station, student government, student newspaper, symphony orchestra, TV station, Asian student union, Christian Fellowship, ethnic studies society, international students union, Latin American student organization, Arts in Recovery, Ballet Folklorico de CSM, Earth Preservation Committee, Peace Action, Unity Among Brothers.

Athletics. NCAA. **Intercollegiate:** Baseball M, basketball W, cross-country, football (tackle) M, softball W, swimming, tennis W, track and field, water polo. **Team name:** Bulldogs.

Student services. Adult student services, alcohol/substance abuse counseling, career counseling, services for economically disadvantaged, student employment services, financial aid counseling, health services, minority student services, on-campus daycare, personal counseling, veterans' counselor. **Physically disabled:** Services for visually, speech, hearing impaired. **Transfer:** Pre-admission transcript evaluation for new students. Transfer center, transfer adviser, college fairs on campus for students transferring to 4-year colleges.

Contact. E-mail: villarealh@smccd.net
Phone: (650) 574-6165 Fax: (650) 574-6506
Henry Villareal, Dean of Admissions and Records, College of San Mateo, 1700 West Hillsdale Boulevard, San Mateo, CA 94402-3784

College of the Canyons
Santa Clarita, California
www.canyons.edu   CB code: 4117

▶ Public 2-year community college
▶ Commuter campus in large city

General. Founded in 1967. Regionally accredited. **Enrollment:** 8,494 degree-seeking undergraduates. **Degrees:** 1,030 associate awarded. **Location:** 36 miles from Los Angeles. **Calendar:** Semester, extensive summer session. **Full-time faculty:** 188 total. **Part-time faculty:** 463 total. **Class size:** 9% < 20, 83% 20-39, 7% 40-49, less than 1% 50-99. **Special facilities:** Performing arts center, proscenium performing arts stage, experimental "black box" theater, university center for access to upper-division and graduate programs.

Student profile. Among degree-seeking undergraduates, 86% enrolled in a transfer program, 49% enrolled in a vocational program, 3% already have a bachelor's degree or higher, 413 enrolled as first-time, first-year students, 5,124 transferred in from other institutions.

Out-of-state:	3%	Hispanic American:	34%
African American:	5%	International:	1%
Asian American:	9%	25 or older:	42%

Transfer out. Colleges most students transferred to 2011: California State University: Northridge, University of California: Los Angeles, UC San Diego, UC Irvine, University of California: Santa Barbara.

Basis for selection. Open admission, but selective for some programs. Limited admission to nursing program. Nursing applicant selections are made using both multi-criteria screening and random screening. **Home schooled:** Transcript of courses and grades required. Per state guidelines, students must be associated with program approved through Los Angeles County, or must be taught by person holding California teaching credential, or must hold a current private school affidavit filed with the State Superintendent of Public Instruction.

2011-2012 Annual costs. Tuition/fees: $1,108; $6,058 out-of-state. Per-credit charge: $36 in-state; $201 out-of-state.

2011-2012 Financial aid. Need-based: 65% of total undergraduate aid awarded as scholarships/grants, 35% as loans/jobs. Need-based aid available

for part-time students. Work-study available nights, weekends and for part-time students. **Non-need-based:** Scholarships awarded for academics, alumni affiliation, art, athletics, job skills, leadership, minority status, music/drama, religious affiliation, ROTC, state residency.

Application procedures. Admission: No deadline. No application fee. Admission notification on a rolling basis. **Financial aid:** Closing date 3/2. FAFSA, institutional form required. Applicants notified on a rolling basis starting 6/1; must reply within 4 week(s) of notification.

Academics. Special study options: Accelerated study, cooperative education, distance learning, double major, dual enrollment of high school students, ESL, honors, independent study, internships, study abroad, weekend college. Bachelor's degree programs available on campus. License preparation in nursing, real estate. **Credit/placement by examination:** AP, CLEP, institutional tests. 18 credit hours maximum toward associate degree. Applicants must take institutional English, ESL, chemistry, and mathematics placement tests. **Support services:** GED preparation, learning center, remedial instruction, study skills assistance, tutoring, writing center.

Majors. Business: Accounting technology, administrative services, business admin, hospitality admin, hotel/motel admin, real estate, sales/distribution, small business admin. **Communications:** Digital media, journalism, radio/TV. **Communications technology:** Animation/special effects, photo/film/video. **Computer sciences:** Computer science, networking. **Engineering:** Pre-engineering. **English:** English lit. **Foreign languages:** French, sign language interpretation, Spanish. **General:** Landscaping. **Health services:** Nursing (RN). **History:** General. **Liberal arts:** Arts/sciences, humanities, library assistant. **Math:** General. **Parks/recreation:** General, health/fitness. **Protective services:** Fire safety technology, police science. **Psychology:** General. **Social sciences:** General, sociology. **Visual/performing arts:** Art, cinematography, dramatic, graphic design, interior design, multimedia, music, photography.

Most popular majors. Business/marketing 15%, health sciences 11%, interdisciplinary studies 13%, liberal arts 13%, social sciences 12%.

Computing on campus. 1,838 workstations in library, computer center, student center. Online course registration, online library, helpline, wireless network available.

Student life. Freshman orientation: Mandatory. Preregistration for classes offered. **Activities:** Jazz band, choral groups, dance, drama, literary magazine, music ensembles, Model UN, musical theater, student government, symphony orchestra, Future Educators club, political science club, Bible Talk, Grace on Campus, Latter-day Saints Student Association, Progressive Student Alliance, law club, Hands on Earth, Gamma Beta Phi.

Athletics. Intercollegiate: Baseball M, basketball, cross-country, football (tackle) M, golf, soccer, softball W, swimming, track and field, volleyball W. **Team name:** Cougars.

Student services. Adult student services, career counseling, services for economically disadvantaged, student employment services, financial aid counseling, health services, on-campus daycare, personal counseling, placement for graduates, veterans' counselor, women's services. **Physically disabled:** Services for visually, speech, hearing impaired. **Transfer:** Re-entry adviser, pre-admission transcript evaluation for new students. Transfer center, transfer adviser, college fairs on campus for students transferring to 4-year colleges.

Contact. E-mail: jasmine.ruys@canyons.edu
Phone: (661) 362-3280 Fax: (661) 259-8302
Jasmine Ruys, Director, Admissions, Records and Online Services, College of the Canyons, 26455 Rockwell Canyon Road, Santa Clarita, CA 91355

College of the Desert
Palm Desert, California   CB member
www.collegeofthedesert.edu   CB code: 4085

- Public 2-year community college
- Commuter campus in small city

General. Founded in 1958. Regionally accredited. **Enrollment:** 6,808 degree-seeking undergraduates. **Degrees:** 534 associate awarded. **Location:** 20 miles from Palm Springs, 120 miles from Los Angeles. **Calendar:** Semester, limited summer session. **Full-time faculty:** 106 total; 23% have terminal degrees, 17% minority, 47% women. **Part-time faculty:** 307 total; 16% have terminal degrees, 22% minority, 47% women. **Special facilities:** Performing arts center, golf institute, public safety academy.

Student profile.

Out-of-state:	3%	25 or older:	13%

Basis for selection. Open admission, but selective for some programs. Separate application requirements for nursing and golf management and public safety academy. Interviews required for nursing/allied health majors. **Adult students:** SAT/ACT scores not required. **Learning Disabled:** Participation is voluntary. Interested students must meet with the appropriate Disabled Students Programs and Services counselor to apply for these programs.

2011-2012 Annual costs. Tuition/fees: $1,110; $6,600 out-of-state. Per-credit charge: $36 in-state; $219 out-of-state. Books/supplies: $1,656. Personal expenses: $3,114.

Financial aid. Need-based: Need-based aid available for part-time students. Work-study available nights, weekends and for part-time students. **Non-need-based:** Scholarships awarded for academics, art, minority status, music/drama.

Application procedures. Admission: Priority date 5/6; deadline 9/8 (receipt date). No application fee. Application must be submitted online. Admission notification on a rolling basis. **Financial aid:** Priority date 3/2; no closing date. FAFSA required. Applicants notified on a rolling basis starting 7/1.

Academics. Special study options: Cooperative education, distance learning, double major, dual enrollment of high school students, ESL, honors, independent study, liberal arts/career combination. License preparation in nursing. **Credit/placement by examination:** AP, CLEP, institutional tests. **Support services:** GED preparation and test center, learning center, remedial instruction, study skills assistance, tutoring, writing center.

Majors. Architecture: Technology. **Biology:** General. **Business:** Business admin, construction management, hotel/motel admin, managerial economics, office management, restaurant/food services. **Communications:** Communications/speech/rhetoric, journalism, media studies, organizational. **Computer sciences:** General, computer science. **Conservation:** General, environmental science, environmental studies. **English:** American lit, English lit, rhetoric/composition, writing. **Foreign languages:** French, German, Italian, Spanish. **General:** Business, ornamental horticulture, plant sciences, turf management. **Health services:** Dietetic technician, licensed practical nurse, nursing (RN). **History:** General. **Liberal arts:** Arts/sciences. **Math:** General. **Parks/recreation:** General, facilities management, golf management. **Philosophy/religion:** Philosophy. **Physical sciences:** Chemistry, geology, physics. **Protective services:** Fire safety technology, law enforcement admin. **Psychology:** General. **Social sciences:** General, anthropology, economics, geography, political science, sociology. **Visual/performing arts:** Acting, art, art history/conservation, dance, dramatic, drawing, graphic design, music, painting, photography, printmaking, studio arts, theater history. **Work/family studies:** Child care management, food/nutrition, human nutrition.

Most popular majors. Business/marketing 15%, health sciences 32%, psychology 7%, social sciences 12%.

Computing on campus. 125 workstations in library, computer center, student center. Online course registration, online library, wireless network available.

Student life. Freshman orientation: Mandatory. Preregistration for classes offered. **Activities:** Choral groups, dance, drama, international student organizations, music ensembles, musical theater, opera, radio station, student government, student newspaper.

Athletics. Intercollegiate: Baseball M, basketball, cheerleading, cross-country, fencing, football (tackle) M, golf, soccer, softball W, tennis, volleyball W. **Team name:** Roadrunners.

Student services. Adult student services, career counseling, services for economically disadvantaged, financial aid counseling, health services, minority student services, on-campus daycare, personal counseling, placement for graduates, veterans' counselor. **Physically disabled:** Services for visually, speech, hearing impaired. **Transfer:** Re-entry adviser, pre-admission transcript evaluation for new students. Transfer center, transfer adviser, college fairs on campus for students transferring to 4-year colleges.

Contact. Phone: (760) 773-2516 Fax: (760) 862-1379
Sally Tiaga, Admissions & Records Director, College of the Desert, 43500 Monterey Avenue, Palm Desert, CA 92260

College of the Redwoods
Eureka, California
www.redwoods.edu   CB code: 4100

- Public 2-year community college
- Commuter campus in large town

General. Founded in 1964. Regionally accredited. Centers at Fort Bragg and Crescent City; instructional sites in Hoopa, Klamath, downtown Eureka, and Arcata. **Enrollment:** 4,093 degree-seeking undergraduates. **Degrees:** 503 associate awarded. **Location:** 275 miles from San Francisco. **Calendar:** Semester, limited summer session. **Full-time faculty:** 98 total; 19% minority. **Part-time faculty:** 255 total; 37% minority. **Class size:** 53% < 20, 44% 20-39, 1% 40-49, 2% 50-99, less than 1% >100. **Special facilities:** Observatory, fish hatchery, organic farm, fine woodworking shop.

Student profile.

Out-of-state:	4%	Live on campus:	1%
25 or older:	43%		

Transfer out. Colleges most students transferred to 2011: Humboldt State University, California State University: Chico.

Basis for selection. Open admission, but selective for some programs. Admission for nursing applicants based on school record and test scores. **Home schooled:** Must submit a copy of affidavit filed with County Office of Education.

2011-2012 Annual costs. Tuition/fees: $1,104; $7,974 out-of-state. Per-credit charge: $36 in-state; $265 out-of-state. Room/board: $7,117. Books/supplies: $1,638. Personal expenses: $1,638.

Financial aid. Need-based: Need-based aid available for part-time students. Work-study available nights, weekends and for part-time students.

Application procedures. Admission: Priority date 8/13; no deadline. No application fee. Admission notification on a rolling basis. **Financial aid:** Priority date 4/15; no closing date. FAFSA, institutional form required. Applicants notified on a rolling basis starting 5/1; must reply within 6 week(s) of notification.

Academics. Special study options: Cooperative education, cross-registration, distance learning, double major, dual enrollment of high school students, ESL, honors, independent study, teacher certification program. License preparation in nursing. **Credit/placement by examination:** AP, CLEP, institutional tests. **Support services:** GED preparation and test center, learning center, pre-admission summer program, remedial instruction, tutoring, writing center.

Majors. Business: General, administrative services, hospitality admin, managerial economics, office technology, real estate. **Communications:** Journalism. **Computer sciences:** General. **Conservation:** Fisheries, forestry. **Education:** Early childhood. **Engineering:** Electrical. **General:** Agribusiness operations, animal sciences, plant sciences. **Liberal arts:** Arts/sciences. **Physical sciences:** Planetary. **Protective services:** Law enforcement admin. **Visual/performing arts:** Commercial/advertising art.

Most popular majors. Health sciences 21%, liberal arts 62%.

Computing on campus. 578 workstations in dormitories, library, computer center, student center. Dormitories wired for high-speed internet access. Online course registration, online library available.

Student life. Freshman orientation: Available. Preregistration for classes offered. **Housing:** Coed dorms available. Limited housing also available for police academy students. **Activities:** Jazz band, choral groups, dance, student government, student newspaper, Native American club, international students club, apologetics club, Bible study, Latter-day Saints club, veterans club, EOPS club.

Athletics. Intercollegiate: Baseball M, basketball, cross-country, football (tackle) M, golf M, soccer W, track and field, volleyball W. **Intramural:** Badminton, bowling, diving, golf, gymnastics, soccer, volleyball, water polo. **Team name:** Corsairs.

Student services. Career counseling, services for economically disadvantaged, student employment services, financial aid counseling, health services, on-campus daycare, personal counseling, placement for graduates, veterans' counselor. **Physically disabled:** Services for visually, speech, hearing impaired. **Transfer:** Transfer center, transfer adviser, college fairs on campus for students transferring to 4-year colleges.

Contact. E-mail: admissions@redwoods.edu
Phone: (707) 476-4200 Toll-free number: (800) 641-0400
Fax: (707) 476-4406
Kathy Goodlive, Manager, Admissions and Records, College of the Redwoods, 7351 Tompkins Hill Road, Eureka, CA 95501-9300

College of the Sequoias
Visalia, California
www.cos.edu

CB code: 4071

◖ Public 2-year community college
◖ Commuter campus in small city

General. Founded in 1925. Regionally accredited. Broad range of two year transfer, vocational, and basic skill programs offered. **Enrollment:** 8,659 degree-seeking undergraduates. **Degrees:** 998 associate awarded. **ROTC:** Air Force. **Location:** 45 miles from Fresno. **Calendar:** Semester, limited summer session. **Full-time faculty:** 174 total. **Part-time faculty:** 315 total. **Class size:** 33% < 20, 54% 20-39, 5% 40-49, 3% 50-99, 5% >100. **Special facilities:** Self-sufficient farm.

Student profile.

Out-of-state:	3%	25 or older:	39%

Transfer out. Colleges most students transferred to 2011: California State University: Fresno, California State University: Bakersfield, California Polytechnic State University: San Luis Obispo, California State University: Long Beach, California State University: Davis.

Basis for selection. Open admission, but selective for some programs. Limited admission to nursing program. Interviews required for work program, nursing majors. Auditions required for music majors.

High school preparation. College-preparatory program recommended.

2011-2012 Annual costs. Tuition/fees: $1,124; $6,554 out-of-state. Per-credit charge: $36 in-state; $217 out-of-state. Books/supplies: $1,566. Personal expenses: $3,024.

Financial aid. Need-based: Work-study available nights, weekends and for part-time students.

Application procedures. Admission: No deadline. No application fee. Admission notification on a rolling basis. **Financial aid:** Priority date 3/2; no closing date. FAFSA, institutional form required. Applicants notified on a rolling basis starting 6/1; must reply within 2 week(s) of notification.

Academics. Special study options: Distance learning, dual enrollment of high school students, ESL, honors, independent study, internships, student-designed major, study abroad, weekend college. License preparation in nursing, paramedic, physical therapy. **Credit/placement by examination:** AP, CLEP, institutional tests. 12 credit hours maximum toward associate degree. **Support services:** Learning center, pre-admission summer program, reduced course load, remedial instruction, study skills assistance, tutoring, writing center.

Majors. Business: General, accounting, administrative services, management information systems, office/clerical, real estate, sales/distribution. **Communications:** Communications/speech/rhetoric, journalism. **Computer sciences:** Computer science. **Education:** Physical. **Engineering:** General. **English:** English lit, rhetoric/composition. **Foreign languages:** General, French. **General:** Agribusiness operations, landscaping, ornamental horticulture. **Health services:** Nursing (RN). **Liberal arts:** Arts/sciences. **Math:** General. **Parks/recreation:** Facilities management. **Protective services:** Fire safety technology, law enforcement admin. **Social sciences:** General. **Visual/performing arts:** Art, commercial/advertising art, dramatic, multimedia, music, studio arts, theater design. **Work/family studies:** General, child care management.

Most popular majors. Business/marketing 6%, health sciences 22%, liberal arts 49%.

Computing on campus. 325 workstations in library, computer center. Online course registration, helpline, wireless network available.

Student life. Freshman orientation: Available. Preregistration for classes offered. Both online and in person. In person classes are held just before the beginning of each semester. **Activities:** Bands, choral groups, dance, drama, music ensembles, musical theater, student government, student newspaper, symphony orchestra.

Athletics. Intercollegiate: Baseball M, basketball, cross-country, diving, football (tackle) M, golf, soccer W, softball W, swimming, tennis, track and field, volleyball W. **Team name:** Giants.

Student services. Adult student services, alcohol/substance abuse counseling, career counseling, services for economically disadvantaged, student employment services, financial aid counseling, health services, minority student services, personal counseling, placement for graduates, veterans' counselor. **Physically disabled:** Services for visually, speech, hearing impaired.

Transfer: Transfer adviser, college fairs on campus for students transferring to 4-year colleges.

Contact. Phone: (559) 730-3727 Fax: (559) 730-3894
Lisa Hott, Director of Admissions and Records, College of the Sequoias, 915 South Mooney Boulevard, Visalia, CA 93277

College of the Siskiyous
Weed, California
www.siskiyous.edu   **CB code: 4087**

- Public 2-year community and junior college
- Commuter campus in small town

General. Founded in 1957. Regionally accredited. **Enrollment:** 1,419 degree-seeking undergraduates. **Degrees:** 149 associate awarded. **Location:** 285 miles from San Francisco, 80 miles from Medford, Oregon. **Calendar:** Semester, limited summer session. **Full-time faculty:** 48 total; 17% have terminal degrees, 10% minority. **Part-time faculty:** 142 total; 8% have terminal degrees, 11% minority. **Class size:** 57% < 20, 35% 20-39, 3% 40-49, 4% 50-99, less than 1% >100. **Special facilities:** Fire science burn tower and flashover unit, welding lab, emergency services training center, distance learning center.

Student profile.

Out-of-state:	27%	Live on campus:	14%
25 or older:	39%		

Transfer out. Colleges most students transferred to 2011: California State University: Chico, Southern Oregon University, University of California: Davis, Simpson University, Humboldt State University.

Basis for selection. Open admission, but selective for some programs. **Adult students:** SAT/ACT scores not required. SAT/ACT scores not required if out of high school 1 year(s) or more.

2011-2012 Annual costs. Tuition/fees: $1,112; $7,772 out-of-state. Per-credit charge: $36 in-state; $258 out-of-state. Room/board: $8,485. Books/supplies: $1,638. Personal expenses: $2,500.

Financial aid. All financial aid based on need. Need-based aid available for part-time students. Work-study available nights, weekends and for part-time students.

Application procedures. Admission: No deadline. No application fee. **Financial aid:** Priority date 4/30; no closing date. FAFSA required. Applicants notified on a rolling basis starting 6/1; must reply within 2 week(s) of notification.

Academics. Special study options: Cooperative education, distance learning, dual enrollment of high school students, ESL, exchange student, independent study, internships, liberal arts/career combination, student-designed major, study abroad. Bachelor's degree programs available on campus. License preparation in nursing, paramedic. **Credit/placement by examination:** AP, CLEP, institutional tests. 48 credit hours maximum toward associate degree. **Support services:** GED preparation, learning center, pre-admission summer program, reduced course load, remedial instruction, study skills assistance, tutoring, writing center.

Majors. Biology: General. **Business:** General, accounting, accounting technology, administrative services, business admin, management information systems, office management, office/clerical. **Communications:** Broadcast journalism, communications/speech/rhetoric, digital media, media studies, radio/TV. **Communications technology:** General, graphics, radio/TV. **Computer sciences:** General, applications programming, computer science, programming. **Education:** General, early childhood, early childhood special. **Engineering:** General. **English:** English lit, writing. **Foreign languages:** Spanish. **Health services:** EMT paramedic, licensed practical nurse, nursing (RN), predental, premedicine, prenursing, prepharmacy, preveterinary, substance abuse counseling. **History:** General. **Liberal arts:** Arts/sciences, humanities. **Math:** General. **Parks/recreation:** Health/fitness. **Philosophy/religion:** Philosophy. **Physical sciences:** General, chemistry, geology, physics. **Protective services:** Criminal justice, fire safety technology, fire services admin, firefighting, law enforcement admin, police science. **Psychology:** General. **Social sciences:** General, anthropology. **Visual/performing arts:** General, acting, art, digital arts, directing/producing, dramatic, graphic design, music, music performance, studio arts, theater arts management, voice/opera. **Work/family studies:** Child care management, child care service, child development, family studies, family/community services.

Most popular majors. Liberal arts 89%, security/protective services 9%.

Computing on campus. 260 workstations in dormitories, library, computer center. Dormitories wired for high-speed internet access and linked to campus network. Commuter students can connect to campus network. Online course registration, online library, helpline, repair service, wireless network available.

Student life. Freshman orientation: Available. Preregistration for classes offered. Held three months prior to the start of the semester. **Housing:** Guaranteed on-campus for freshmen. Coed dorms, wellness housing available. $100 fully refundable deposit. **Activities:** Bands, choral groups, dance, drama, international student organizations, music ensembles, musical theater, student government, student newspaper, symphony orchestra, TV station, Latino Student Union, Black Student Union, Phi Theta Kappa honor society, intercultural club, American Indian Alliance, intervarsity club, speech club, chess club, disabled student aliance, speech and forensics club.

Athletics. Intercollegiate: Baseball M, basketball, cross-country, football (tackle) M, skiing, softball W, track and field, volleyball W. **Intramural:** Badminton, basketball, bowling, boxing, golf, skiing, softball, tennis, volleyball. **Team name:** Eagles.

Student services. Adult student services, alcohol/substance abuse counseling, career counseling, services for economically disadvantaged, student employment services, financial aid counseling, health services, legal services, on-campus daycare, personal counseling, veterans' counselor. **Physically disabled:** Services for visually, speech, hearing impaired. **Transfer:** Re-entry adviser, pre-admission transcript evaluation for new students. Transfer center, transfer adviser, college fairs on campus for students transferring to 4-year colleges.

Contact. E-mail: registration@siskiyous.edu
Phone: (530) 938-5555 Toll-free number: (888) 397-4339
Fax: (530) 938-5367
Teresa Winkelman, Director of Admissions & Records, College of the Siskiyous, 800 College Avenue, Weed, CA 96094-2899

Columbia College
Sonora, California
www.gocolumbia.edu   **CB code: 4108**

- Public 2-year community college
- Commuter campus in small town

General. Founded in 1968. Regionally accredited. **Enrollment:** 1,773 degree-seeking undergraduates; 1,457 non-degree-seeking students. **Degrees:** 180 associate awarded. **Location:** 100 miles from Sacramento. **Calendar:** Semester, limited summer session. **Full-time faculty:** 49 total; 8% minority. **Part-time faculty:** 118 total. **Class size:** 100% < 20. **Special facilities:** Jogging/fitness trail, arboretum, astronomy dome, seismograph, on-campus fire house.

Student profile. Among degree-seeking undergraduates, 1,022 enrolled as first-time, first-year students.

Part-time:	48%	Hispanic American:	5%
Women:	56%	Native American:	1%
African American:	1%	International:	1%
Asian American:	1%		

Basis for selection. Open admission. Institution uses own assessment test for placement only.

2011-2012 Annual costs. Tuition/fees: $1,108; $7,228 out-of-state. Per-credit charge: $36 in-state; $240 out-of-state. Books/supplies: $1,656. Personal expenses: $3,114.

2010-2011 Financial aid. Need-based: 98% of total undergraduate aid awarded as scholarships/grants, 2% as loans/jobs. Need-based aid available for part-time students. Work-study available nights, weekends and for part-time students. **Non-need-based:** Scholarships awarded for academics.

Application procedures. Admission: No deadline. No application fee. Admission notification on a rolling basis. Matriculation procedures required before new or returning students may register. Early application assures accommodation to new student priority registration periods. **Financial aid:** Priority date 3/2; no closing date. FAFSA, institutional form required. Applicants notified on a rolling basis starting 6/15; must reply within 2 week(s) of notification.

Academics. Special study options: Cooperative education, distance learning, double major, ESL, independent study, internships, liberal arts/career combination. License preparation in paramedic. **Credit/placement by examination:** AP, CLEP, institutional tests. 12 credit hours maximum toward associate degree. **Support services:** GED preparation and test center, learning center, remedial instruction, study skills assistance, tutoring, writing center.

Majors. Biology: General. **Business:** General, accounting technology, administrative services, business admin, hospitality admin. **Communications:** General. **Computer sciences:** General, information technology, programming. **Conservation:** General, environmental science, forest technology, forestry, management/policy. **English:** English lit, rhetoric/composition. **Liberal arts:** Arts/sciences. **Math:** General. **Parks/recreation:** Health/fitness. **Physical sciences:** Chemistry, physics, planetary. **Protective services:** Fire safety technology. **Social sciences:** General. **Visual/performing arts:** Art, music, photography. **Work/family studies:** Child development.

Most popular majors. English 6%, health sciences 6%, liberal arts 51%.

Computing on campus. 60 workstations in library, computer center, student center. Online course registration, online library, wireless network available.

Student life. Freshman orientation: Mandatory. Preregistration for classes offered. 1-hour session prior to registration. **Housing:** Coed dorms, special housing for disabled, apartments available. **Activities:** Bands, choral groups, dance, drama, music ensembles, student government, symphony orchestra.

Athletics. Intercollegiate: Basketball M, volleyball W. **Team name:** Claim Jumpers.

Student services. Adult student services, alcohol/substance abuse counseling, career counseling, services for economically disadvantaged, student employment services, financial aid counseling, health services, on-campus daycare, personal counseling, placement for graduates, veterans' counselor. **Physically disabled:** Services for visually, speech, hearing impaired. **Transfer:** Re-entry adviser for new students. Transfer center, transfer adviser, college fairs on campus for students transferring to 4-year colleges.

Contact. Phone: (209) 588-5231 Fax: (209) 588-5337
Melissa Raby, Dean of Student Services, Columbia College, 11600 Columbia College Drive, Sonora, CA 95370

Concorde Career College: Garden Grove
Garden Grove, California
www.concorde.edu   CB code: 2238

- For-profit 2-year health science and technical college
- Small city

General. Regionally accredited. **Calendar:** Differs by program.

Annual costs/financial aid. Tuition/fees (2011-2012): $21,766. Tuition quoted is nine-month cost for the most popular program Vocational Nursing: $33,857.95 (14 months). Medical Assistant: $14,772.70 (8 months). Dental Assistant: $14,218.01 (36 weeks). Insurance Billing and Coding: $14,050.20 (8 months). Respiratory Therapy: $42,910.29 (20-month Associate degree program).

Contact. Phone: (714) 703-1900
Director of Admissions, 12951 Euclid Street, #101, Garden Grove, CA 92840

Concorde Career College: North Hollywood
North Hollywood, California
www.concorde.edu

- For-profit 2-year health science college
- Large city

General. Accredited by ACCSC. **Enrollment:** 209 degree-seeking undergraduates. **Degrees:** 118 associate awarded. **Calendar:** Differs by program. **Full-time faculty:** 24 total. **Part-time faculty:** 20 total.

Basis for selection. Entrance assessment for all programs. High school graduate or GED for all programs. Institutional exam scores important. CPAT, Wonderlic used.

Financial aid. Need-based: Work-study available nights, weekends and for part-time students.

Application procedures. Admission: No deadline. No application fee. Admission notification on a rolling basis. **Financial aid:** No deadline.

Academics. Credit/placement by examination: AP, CLEP.

Majors. Health services: Respiratory therapy technology.

Contact. Phone: (818) 766-8151 Toll-free number: (800) 464-1212
Fax: (818) 766-1587
Allan Gueco, Director of Admissions, Concorde Career College: North Hollywood, 12412 Victory Boulevard, North Hollywood, CA 91606

Concorde Career College: San Bernardino
San Bernardino, California
www.concorde.edu

- For-profit 2-year technical college
- Small city

General. Regionally accredited. **Calendar:** Differs by program.

Contact. 201 East Airport Dr., San Bernardino, CA 92408

Concorde Career College: San Diego
San Diego, California
www.concorde.edu

- For-profit 2-year health science and nursing college
- Very large city

General. Regionally accredited. **Calendar:** Continuous.

Contact. Director of Admissions, 4393 Imperial Avenue, San Diego, CA 92113

Contra Costa College
San Pablo, California
www.contracosta.edu   CB code: 4943

- Public 2-year community college
- Commuter campus in large town

General. Founded in 1948. Regionally accredited. Middle College High School on-campus. 100% pass rate on NCLEX for nursing program graduates. **Enrollment:** 7,975 undergraduates. **Degrees:** 492 associate awarded. **ROTC:** Naval. **Location:** 20 miles from San Francisco. **Calendar:** Semester, limited summer session. **Full-time faculty:** 105 total. **Part-time faculty:** 194 total. **Special facilities:** Center for scientific excellence.

Transfer out. Colleges most students transferred to 2011: California State University: East Bay, California State University: San Francisco, University of California: Davis, San Jose State University, University of California: Berkeley.

Basis for selection. Open admission.

High school preparation. College-preparatory program recommended.

2011-2012 Annual costs. Tuition/fees: $1,082; $6,782 out-of-state. Per-credit charge: $36 in-state; $226 out-of-state.

Financial aid. Need-based: Work-study available nights, weekends and for part-time students.

Application procedures. Admission: No deadline. No application fee. Admission notification on a rolling basis. **Financial aid:** Priority date 3/2; no closing date. FAFSA required. Applicants notified on a rolling basis; must reply within 2 week(s) of notification.

Academics. Special study options: Cross-registration, dual enrollment of high school students, honors, independent study. License preparation in nursing, paramedic, radiology, real estate. **Credit/placement by examination:** AP, CLEP, institutional tests. 12 credit hours maximum toward associate degree. **Support services:** Learning center, remedial instruction, tutoring.

Majors. Area/ethnic studies: African-American, Chicano/Hispanic-American/Latino. **Biology:** General. **Business:** Administrative services, office/clerical, real estate. **Computer sciences:** General, applications programming. **Education:** Bilingual, teacher assistance. **Engineering:** General. **English:** English lit. **Health services:** Dental assistant, medical assistant, nursing (RN). **History:** General. **Liberal arts:** Arts/sciences. **Math:** General. **Physical sciences:** Chemistry, physics. **Protective services:** Police science. **Psychology:** General. **Social sciences:** Geography, sociology. **Visual/performing arts:** Dramatic, interior design, music. **Work/family studies:** Institutional food production.

Most popular majors. Business/marketing 11%, health sciences 20%, liberal arts 48%.

Student life. Activities: Jazz band, choral groups, dance, drama, international student organizations, literary magazine, music ensembles, musical theater, student government, student newspaper, TV station.

Athletics. NAIA, NCAA, NJCAA. **Intercollegiate:** Baseball M, basketball, football (tackle) M, tennis, track and field. **Team name:** Comets.

Student services. Adult student services, alcohol/substance abuse counseling, career counseling, student employment services, financial aid counseling, health services, minority student services, on-campus daycare, personal counseling, veterans' counselor, women's services. **Transfer:** Re-entry adviser for new students. Transfer center, transfer adviser, college fairs on campus for students transferring to 4-year colleges.

Contact. Phone: (510) 235-7800 ext. 4210 Fax: (510) 236-6768
Mikeal Aldaco, Director of Admissions and Records, Contra Costa College, 2600 Mission Bell Drive, San Pablo, CA 94806

Copper Mountain College
Joshua Tree, California
www.cmccd.edu   CB code: 3889

- Public 2-year community college
- Commuter campus in small town

General. Regionally accredited. **Enrollment:** 2,097 undergraduates. **Degrees:** 138 associate awarded. **Location:** 120 miles from Los Angeles, 45 miles from Palm Springs. **Calendar:** Semester, limited summer session. **Full-time faculty:** 42 total. **Part-time faculty:** 95 total.

Transfer out. Colleges most students transferred to 2011: California State University: San Bernardino.

Basis for selection. Open admission, but selective for some programs. Limited admission to some allied health programs. **Adult students:** Accuplacer assessment tests required.

2011-2012 Annual costs. Tuition/fees: $1,082; $6,362 out-of-state. Per-credit charge: $36 in-state; $212 out-of-state. Books/supplies: $1,656. Personal expenses: $3,114.

Financial aid. Need-based: Need-based aid available for part-time students. Work-study available nights, weekends and for part-time students.

Application procedures. Admission: No deadline. No application fee. Application must be submitted online. Admission notification on a rolling basis. **Financial aid:** Priority date 3/2; no closing date. FAFSA required.

Academics. Special study options: Distance learning, dual enrollment of high school students, ESL, independent study, study abroad. License preparation in nursing, paramedic. **Credit/placement by examination:** AP, CLEP, institutional tests. **Support services:** GED preparation and test center, remedial instruction, study skills assistance, tutoring.

Majors. Business: Business admin. **Communications:** Communications/speech/rhetoric. **Computer sciences:** General, computer science. **English:** English lit. **Foreign languages:** Spanish. **Health services:** Licensed practical nurse. **History:** General. **Liberal arts:** Arts/sciences. **Math:** General. **Philosophy/religion:** Philosophy. **Protective services:** Fire safety technology, law enforcement admin. **Psychology:** General. **Social sciences:** General, anthropology, economics, political science. **Visual/performing arts:** Art.

Computing on campus. 40 workstations in library, computer center.

Student life. Freshman orientation: Mandatory. Preregistration for classes offered. 1.5 hour group orientation offered about 16 times prior to each semester. **Activities:** Literary magazine, student government, student newspaper.

Student services. Adult student services, career counseling, services for economically disadvantaged, student employment services, financial aid counseling, veterans' counselor. **Physically disabled:** Services for visually, speech, hearing impaired. **Transfer:** Pre-admission transcript evaluation for new students. Transfer center, transfer adviser, college fairs on campus for students transferring to 4-year colleges.

Contact. E-mail: lburns@cmccd.edu
Phone: (760) 366-3791 ext. 4232
Toll-free number: (866) 366-3791 ext. 4232 Fax: (760) 366-5257
Gregory Brown, Vice President of Student Services, Copper Mountain College, 6162 Rotary Way, Joshua Tree, CA 92252

Cosumnes River College
Sacramento, California
www.crc.losrios.edu   CB code: 4121

- Public 2-year junior college
- Commuter campus in large city

General. Founded in 1970. Regionally accredited. Classes offered at Folsom Lake Center, El Dorado Center and Folsom Prison. **Enrollment:** 10,291 degree-seeking undergraduates. **Degrees:** 595 associate awarded. **Location:** 12 miles from downtown. **Calendar:** Semester, limited summer session. **Full-time faculty:** 182 total. **Part-time faculty:** 236 total.

Basis for selection. Open admission.

2011-2012 Annual costs. Tuition/fees: $1,112; $7,352 out-of-state. Per-credit charge: $36 in-state; $244 out-of-state. Books/supplies: $1,656. Personal expenses: $3,114.

Financial aid. Need-based: Work-study available nights, weekends and for part-time students.

Application procedures. Admission: No deadline. No application fee. Admission notification on a rolling basis beginning on or about 3/1. First-time students encouraged to participate in orientation and matriculation sessions. English and mathematics tests for placement recommended. **Financial aid:** Priority date 5/1; no closing date. FAFSA required. Applicants notified on a rolling basis starting 7/20; must reply within 4 week(s) of notification.

Academics. Special study options: Cooperative education, distance learning, double major, dual enrollment of high school students, ESL, honors, independent study, internships, study abroad. **Credit/placement by examination:** AP, CLEP. 15 credit hours maximum toward associate degree. **Support services:** Learning center, reduced course load, remedial instruction, tutoring.

Majors. Architecture: Environmental design, interior, landscape. **Area/ethnic studies:** American, women's. **Business:** General, accounting, business admin, entrepreneurial studies, finance, real estate. **Communications:** Advertising, broadcast journalism, journalism, public relations. **Communications technology:** General. **Computer sciences:** Information systems, programming. **Education:** Early childhood. **General:** Animal sciences, business, equestrian studies, horticultural science, plant sciences. **Health services:** Medical assistant, medical records technology. **Liberal arts:** Arts/sciences. **Protective services:** Fire safety technology, law enforcement admin. **Social sciences:** Sociology. **Visual/performing arts:** Art, art history/conservation, cinematography, commercial photography, dramatic, interior design, music, photography, studio arts.

Most popular majors. Business/marketing 8%, health sciences 6%, liberal arts 52%, trade and industry 6%.

Student life. Activities: Bands, choral groups, drama, radio station, student government, student newspaper, TV station, African-American Students Association, Hispanic/Latino Scholars, Asian American Club, Christian Club, earth club.

Athletics. Intercollegiate: Baseball M, basketball, soccer, softball W, tennis, track and field, volleyball W. **Intramural:** Badminton, bowling, fencing, golf, racquetball, skiing, swimming, tennis, track and field, volleyball.

Student services. Adult student services, career counseling, student employment services, health services, on-campus daycare, personal counseling, placement for graduates, veterans' counselor. **Physically disabled:** Services for hearing impaired. **Transfer:** Transfer adviser for students transferring to 4-year colleges.

Contact. Phone: (916) 691-7410 Fax: (916) 691-7467
Celia Esposito-Noy, Vice President, Student Services and Enrollment Management, Cosumnes River College, 8401 Center Parkway, Sacramento, CA 95823

Crafton Hills College
Yucaipa, California
www.craftonhills.edu   CB code: 4126

- Public 2-year community college
- Commuter campus in large town

General. Founded in 1972. Regionally accredited. Located in southern California; offers majors in the liberal arts and sciences, career and technical studies. **Enrollment:** 6,108 undergraduates. **Degrees:** 356 associate awarded. **Location:** 17 miles from San Bernardino, 69 miles from Los Angeles. **Calendar:** Semester, limited summer session. **Full-time faculty:** 70 total; 20%

minority. **Part-time faculty:** 155 total; 29% minority. **Special facilities:** Walking trails, child care services for preschool-aged children.

Basis for selection. Open admission.

High school preparation. College-preparatory program recommended.

2011-2012 Annual costs. Tuition/fees: $1,108; $6,388 out-of-state. Per-credit charge: $36 in-state; $212 out-of-state. Books/supplies: $1,620. Personal expenses: $2,862.

Financial aid. All financial aid based on need. Need-based aid available for part-time students. Work-study available nights, weekends and for part-time students.

Application procedures. Admission: No deadline. No application fee. Application must be submitted online. Admission notification on a rolling basis. Students under 18 admitted with special permission. **Financial aid:** Priority date 4/15, closing date 6/2. FAFSA, institutional form required. Applicants notified on a rolling basis starting 7/31; must reply within 2 week(s) of notification.

Academics. Special study options: Cooperative education, cross-registration, distance learning, double major, dual enrollment of high school students, honors, study abroad. License preparation in paramedic, radiology. **Credit/placement by examination:** AP, CLEP, institutional tests. 36 credit hours maximum toward associate degree. Currently enrolled students who feel that their knowledge is equivalent to the course content of a currently approved course may apply for credit by examination. **Support services:** Learning center, remedial instruction, study skills assistance, tutoring, writing center.

Majors. Biology: General, bacteriology. **Business:** Administrative services, business admin, marketing, office/clerical. **Computer sciences:** General, programming. **Education:** Early childhood, health occupations. **English:** English lit. **Foreign languages:** General, French, Spanish. **Health services:** EMT paramedic, medical radiologic technology/radiation therapy, respiratory therapy technology. **History:** General. **Liberal arts:** Arts/sciences. **Math:** General. **Physical sciences:** Chemistry, geology, physics. **Protective services:** Firefighting, law enforcement admin. **Psychology:** General. **Social sciences:** General, anthropology, economics, geography, political science, sociology. **Visual/performing arts:** Art, dramatic, music.

Most popular majors. Health sciences 16%, interdisciplinary studies 48%, public administration/social services 7%, social sciences 6%.

Computing on campus. 172 workstations in library, computer center. Online course registration, helpline, wireless network available.

Student life. Freshman orientation: Available. Preregistration for classes offered. **Activities:** Jazz band, drama, music ensembles, musical theater, student government, student newspaper.

Student services. Career counseling, student employment services, health services, on-campus daycare, personal counseling, placement for graduates, veterans' counselor. **Physically disabled:** Services for visually, speech, hearing impaired. **Transfer:** Pre-admission transcript evaluation for new students. Transfer center, transfer adviser, college fairs on campus for students transferring to 4-year colleges.

Contact. E-mail: admissions@craftonhills.edu
Phone: (909) 389-3372 Fax: (909) 389-9141
Joe Cabrales, Dean, Student Services, Crafton Hills College, 11711 Sand Canyon Road, Yucaipa, CA 92399-1799

Cuesta College
San Luis Obispo, California
www.cuesta.org   CB code: 4101

- Public 2-year community college
- Commuter campus in large town

General. Founded in 1964. Regionally accredited. Additional North County Campus in Paso Robles and South County Center(s) in Arroyo Grande and Nipomo. **Enrollment:** 7,352 degree-seeking undergraduates. **Degrees:** 666 associate awarded. **Location:** 200 miles from Los Angeles, 6 miles from San Luis Obispo. **Calendar:** Semester, extensive summer session. **Full-time faculty:** 185 total. **Part-time faculty:** 368 total. **Special facilities:** Adobe museum (Chumash Indian).

Student profile.

Out-of-state:	3%	25 or older:	33%

Transfer out. Colleges most students transferred to 2011: California Polytechnic State University: San Luis Obispo, CSU: Chico, San Francisco State University, California State Polytechnic University: Pomona.

Basis for selection. Open admission, but selective for some programs. Nursing program requires critical thinking and math assessments. Prerequisite courses evaluated. **Learning Disabled:** No special admission but must be assessed and qualified to receive services.

2011-2012 Annual costs. Tuition/fees: $1,126; $6,646 out-of-state. Per-credit charge: $36 in-state; $220 out-of-state. Books/supplies: $1,638. Personal expenses: $2,664.

Financial aid. Need-based: Work-study available nights, weekends and for part-time students.

Application procedures. Admission: No deadline. No application fee. Admission notification on a rolling basis. **Financial aid:** Priority date 3/2; no closing date. FAFSA required. Applicants notified on a rolling basis starting 4/15.

Academics. Special study options: Cooperative education, distance learning, double major, ESL, honors, independent study, student-designed major, study abroad, weekend college. Bachelor's degree programs available on campus. **Credit/placement by examination:** AP, CLEP, institutional tests. 12 credit hours maximum toward associate degree. **Support services:** Learning center, remedial instruction, study skills assistance, tutoring, writing center.

Majors. Biology: General. **Business:** General, real estate. **Communications:** Broadcast journalism, communications/speech/rhetoric, journalism. **Computer sciences:** Computer science. **Education:** Art, early childhood, mathematics, physical, special ed. **Engineering:** Electrical. **Health services:** Nursing (RN). **Liberal arts:** Arts/sciences, library assistant. **Math:** General. **Physical sciences:** Chemistry, physics. **Protective services:** Law enforcement admin. **Visual/performing arts:** Interior design.

Computing on campus. 300 workstations in library, computer center, student center. Online course registration, online library available.

Student life. Freshman orientation: Available. Preregistration for classes offered. **Activities:** Jazz band, choral groups, dance, drama, music ensembles, musical theater, radio station, student government, student newspaper, TV station, Alpha Gamma Sigma (honor society).

Athletics. Intercollegiate: Baseball M, basketball, cross-country, diving, soccer W, softball W, swimming, tennis W, track and field, volleyball W, water polo, wrestling M.

Student services. Adult student services, career counseling, student employment services, financial aid counseling, health services, legal services, on-campus daycare, personal counseling, veterans' counselor. **Physically disabled:** Services for visually, speech, hearing impaired. **Transfer:** Re-entry adviser for new students. Transfer center, transfer adviser, college fairs on campus for students transferring to 4-year colleges.

Contact. E-mail: admit@bass.cuesta.cc.ca.us
Phone: (805) 546-3140 Fax: (805) 546-3975
Joy Chambers, Director of Admissions and Records, Cuesta College, Box 8106, San Luis Obispo, CA 93403

Cuyamaca College
El Cajon, California
www.cuyamaca.edu   CB code: 4252

- Public 2-year community college
- Commuter campus in small city

General. Founded in 1978. Regionally accredited. **Enrollment:** 6,378 degree-seeking undergraduates. **Degrees:** 436 associate awarded. **ROTC:** Air Force. **Location:** 18 miles from San Diego. **Calendar:** Semester, limited summer session. **Full-time faculty:** 80 total; 12% have terminal degrees, 20% minority. **Part-time faculty:** 250 total; 10% have terminal degrees, 27% minority. **Special facilities:** Automotive technology facility, water gardens, child care facility, museum.

Transfer out. Colleges most students transferred to 2011: San Diego State University, National University.

Basis for selection. Open admission.

2011-2012 Annual costs. Tuition/fees: $1,120; $6,820 out-of-state. Per-credit charge: $36 in-state; $226 out-of-state. Books/supplies: $1,500. Personal expenses: $2,000.

Two-Year Colleges

Financial aid. **Need-based:** Work-study available nights, weekends and for part-time students.

Application procedures. **Admission:** No deadline. No application fee in-state; $163 out-of-state. Admission notification on a rolling basis. **Financial aid:** Priority date 3/2; no closing date. FAFSA required. Applicants notified on a rolling basis; must reply within 2 week(s) of notification.

Academics. **Special study options:** Cooperative education, cross-registration, distance learning, double major, dual enrollment of high school students, ESL, honors, independent study, internships, study abroad. License preparation in real estate. **Credit/placement by examination:** AP, CLEP, institutional tests. **Support services:** Remedial instruction, tutoring.

Majors. **Business:** Accounting, business admin, real estate. **Communications technology:** General. **Engineering:** General, computer, electrical, surveying. **Foreign languages:** Spanish. **General:** Ornamental horticulture. **Liberal arts:** Arts/sciences. **Physical sciences:** General. **Work/family studies:** Child care management.

Most popular majors. Business/marketing 19%, legal studies 9%, liberal arts 30%, mathematics 6%.

Computing on campus. Online course registration available.

Student life. **Freshman orientation:** Available. Preregistration for classes offered. **Activities:** Concert band, dance, drama, international student organizations, music ensembles, student government, Christian club, Latter-Day Saint student association, MECHA, Multi Culture Union, Sudanese cultural club.

Athletics. **Intercollegiate:** Basketball, cross-country, golf M, soccer, tennis W, track and field, volleyball W. **Team name:** Coyotes.

Student services. Adult student services, career counseling, financial aid counseling, health services, on-campus daycare, personal counseling, veterans' counselor. **Physically disabled:** Services for visually, speech, hearing impaired. **Transfer:** Pre-admission transcript evaluation for new students. Transfer center, transfer adviser, college fairs on campus for students transferring to 4-year colleges.

Contact. Phone: (619) 660-4275 Fax: (619) 660-4575
Susan Topham, Dean, Counseling and Enrollment Services, Cuyamaca College, 900 Rancho San Diego Parkway, El Cajon, CA 92019-4304

Cypress College
Cypress, California
www.cypresscollege.edu

CB code: 4104

- Public 2-year community college
- Commuter campus in small city

General. Founded in 1966. Regionally accredited. **Enrollment:** 11,582 degree-seeking undergraduates. **Degrees:** 869 associate awarded. **Location:** 30 miles from Los Angeles. **Calendar:** Semester, limited summer session. **Full-time faculty:** 199 total; 35% minority, 59% women. **Part-time faculty:** 419 total; 32% minority, 51% women. **Class size:** 20% < 20, 55% 20-39, 19% 40-49, 6% 50-99, less than 1% >100.

Student profile. Among degree-seeking undergraduates, 8% enrolled in a vocational program, 3% already have a bachelor's degree or higher, 1,657 enrolled as first-time, first-year students.

Out-of-state:	5%	Hispanic American:	39%
African American:	6%	Native American:	1%
Asian American:	23%	25 or older:	44%

Transfer out. **Colleges most students transferred to 2011:** CSU Fullerton, CSU Long Beach.

Basis for selection. Open admission. College administered English and math placement exams.

High school preparation. College-preparatory program required.

2011-2012 Annual costs. Tuition/fees: $1,112; $6,602 out-of-state. Per-credit charge: $36 in-state; $219 out-of-state. Books/supplies: $1,386. Personal expenses: $1,898.

2010-2011 Financial aid. **Need-based:** 79% of total undergraduate aid awarded as scholarships/grants, 21% as loans/jobs. Need-based aid available for part-time students. Work-study available nights, weekends and for part-time students.

Application procedures. **Admission:** No deadline. No application fee. Admission notification on a rolling basis. **Financial aid:** FAFSA required.

Academics. **Special study options:** Distance learning, dual enrollment of high school students, ESL, honors, independent study, internships, liberal arts/career combination, study abroad. License preparation in aviation, dental hygiene, nursing, radiology, real estate. **Credit/placement by examination:** AP, CLEP, IB, institutional tests. 12 credit hours maximum toward associate degree. **Support services:** Learning center, reduced course load, remedial instruction, study skills assistance, tutoring, writing center.

Majors. **Area/ethnic studies:** Asian, Latin American. **Business:** General, accounting, administrative services, business admin, hospitality/recreation, management information systems, management science, office technology, office/clerical, tourism promotion. **Communications:** Journalism. **Computer sciences:** General, data processing, information systems. **Education:** General, elementary, physical, secondary, technology/industrial arts. **Engineering:** General. **English:** English lit, rhetoric/composition. **Foreign languages:** French, German, Spanish. **Health services:** Dental assistant, dental hygiene, dental lab technology, medical assistant, medical radiologic technology/radiation therapy, medical records admin, medical records technology, nursing (RN), predental, premedicine, prepharmacy, preveterinary. **History:** General. **Liberal arts:** Arts/sciences. **Math:** General. **Philosophy/religion:** Philosophy. **Physical sciences:** Chemistry, geology, physics. **Psychology:** General. **Social sciences:** Anthropology, economics, geography, political science, sociology. **Visual/performing arts:** General, art, commercial/advertising art, dance, dramatic, music, music performance, theater design. **Work/family studies:** Institutional food production.

Most popular majors. Business/marketing 8%, health sciences 22%, liberal arts 50%, personal/culinary services 8%.

Computing on campus. 200 workstations in library, computer center, student center. Online course registration, helpline, wireless network available.

Student life. **Freshman orientation:** Available. Preregistration for classes offered. **Activities:** Bands, choral groups, dance, drama, international student organizations, literary magazine, music ensembles, musical theater, student government, student newspaper.

Athletics. NJCAA. **Intercollegiate:** Baseball M, basketball, diving, golf, soccer, softball W, swimming, tennis, volleyball W, water polo, wrestling M. **Intramural:** Badminton, baseball M, basketball, softball, volleyball. **Team name:** Chargers.

Student services. Adult student services, career counseling, services for economically disadvantaged, student employment services, financial aid counseling, health services, on-campus daycare, personal counseling, veterans' counselor. **Physically disabled:** Services for visually, speech, hearing impaired. **Transfer:** Re-entry adviser, pre-admission transcript evaluation for new students. Transfer center, transfer adviser, college fairs on campus for students transferring to 4-year colleges.

Contact. Phone: (714) 484-7346 Fax: (714) 484-7446
Dave Wassenaar, Dean of Admissions and Records, Cypress College, 9200 Valley View Street, Cypress, CA 90630

De Anza College
Cupertino, California
www.deanza.edu

CB code: 4286

- Public 2-year community college
- Commuter campus in large town

General. Founded in 1967. Regionally accredited. **Enrollment:** 17,299 degree-seeking undergraduates. **Degrees:** 1,254 associate awarded. **ROTC:** Army, Air Force. **Location:** 5 miles from San Jose, 40 miles from San Francisco. **Calendar:** Quarter, extensive summer session. **Full-time faculty:** 300 total. **Part-time faculty:** 494 total. **Special facilities:** Planetarium, California history center, environmental studies area, advanced technology center, art museum, performing arts facility.

Student profile.

Out-of-state:	2%	25 or older:	37%

Transfer out. **Colleges most students transferred to 2011:** University of California: Davis, San Jose State, San Francisco State, University of California: Berkeley, University of California: Santa Cruz.

Basis for selection. Open admission, but selective for some programs. Limited admission for nursing and physical therapist assistant applicants.

2011-2012 Annual costs. Tuition/fees: $1,180; $7,255 out-of-state. Per-credit charge: $24 in-state; $159 out-of-state. Books/supplies: $1,728. Personal expenses: $2,826.

2010-2011 Financial aid. All financial aid based on need. 69% of total undergraduate aid awarded as scholarships/grants, 31% as loans/jobs. Need-based aid available for part-time students. Work-study available nights, weekends and for part-time students.

Application procedures. Admission: No deadline. No application fee. Admission notification on a rolling basis. **Financial aid:** No deadline. FAFSA required. Applicants notified on a rolling basis starting 5/15; must reply within 2 week(s) of notification.

Academics. Special study options: Cooperative education, cross-registration, distance learning, dual enrollment of high school students, ESL, honors, independent study, internships, study abroad, weekend college. License preparation in nursing, physical therapy, real estate. **Credit/placement by examination:** AP, CLEP, institutional tests. 45 credit hours maximum toward associate degree. **Support services:** Learning center, pre-admission summer program, remedial instruction, study skills assistance, tutoring, writing center.

Majors. Area/ethnic studies: African-American, Asian-American, Chicano/Hispanic-American/Latino, Latin American, Native American. **Biology:** General. **Business:** Accounting, administrative services, business admin, marketing, purchasing, real estate, taxation. **Communications:** Communications/speech/rhetoric. **Computer sciences:** General, applications programming, computer science, programming, systems analysis. **Education:** Early childhood. **Engineering:** General, computer, electrical, mechanical. **English:** English lit, technical writing. **Foreign languages:** French, German, Spanish. **Health services:** Medical assistant, nursing (RN). **History:** General. **Liberal arts:** Arts/sciences. **Math:** General. **Philosophy/religion:** Philosophy. **Physical sciences:** Astronomy, chemistry, geology, physics. **Protective services:** Law enforcement admin, security services. **Psychology:** General. **Social sciences:** Anthropology, economics, geography, political science, sociology. **Visual/performing arts:** Art, art history/conservation, ceramics, cinematography, commercial/advertising art, music, painting, photography, printmaking, sculpture.

Computing on campus. 300 workstations in library, computer center, student center. Online course registration, online library, repair service, wireless network available.

Student life. Freshman orientation: Available. Preregistration for classes offered. Two day counseling course for new, incoming students. **Activities:** Bands, choral groups, dance, drama, international student organizations, literary magazine, music ensembles, student government, student newspaper, symphony orchestra, TV station.

Athletics. Intercollegiate: Baseball M, basketball, cross-country, diving, football (tackle) M, golf, soccer, softball W, swimming, tennis, track and field, volleyball, water polo M. **Intramural:** Badminton, baseball M, basketball, bowling, fencing, gymnastics, racquetball, soccer W, swimming, tennis, volleyball. **Team name:** Dons.

Student services. Adult student services, alcohol/substance abuse counseling, career counseling, services for economically disadvantaged, student employment services, financial aid counseling, health services, legal services, minority student services, on-campus daycare, personal counseling, placement for graduates, veterans' counselor, women's services. **Physically disabled:** Services for visually, speech, hearing impaired. **Transfer:** Re-entry adviser for new students. Transfer center, transfer adviser, college fairs on campus for students transferring to 4-year colleges.

Contact. E-mail: webreg@fhda.edu
Phone: (408) 864-5300 Fax: (408) 864-8329
Kathleen Moberg, Dean of Admissions and Records, De Anza College, 21250 Stevens Creek Boulevard, Cupertino, CA 95014

Deep Springs College
Dyer, Nevada
www.deepsprings.edu   CB code: 4281

- Private 2-year liberal arts college for men
- Residential campus in rural community
- SAT or ACT (ACT writing optional), application essay, interview required

General. Founded in 1917. Regionally accredited. All-male liberal arts college located in California's High Desert; requires students to work ranch and farm, cook, clean, and do routine maintenance, hire faculty, admit students and govern themselves. **Enrollment:** 28 degree-seeking undergraduates. **Degrees:** 9 associate awarded. **Location:** 45 miles from Bishop. **Calendar:**

Differs by program, limited summer session. **Full-time faculty:** 3 total; 100% have terminal degrees, 67% women. **Part-time faculty:** 2 total; 100% have terminal degrees, 100% minority, 50% women. **Class size:** 100% < 20. **Special facilities:** Student-operated 2,600-acre cattle and alfalfa ranch, dairy.

Student profile. Among degree-seeking undergraduates, 95% enrolled in a transfer program, 12 enrolled as first-time, first-year students.

Out-of-state:	74%	International:	11%
Asian American:	7%	Live on campus:	100%

Transfer out. Colleges most students transferred to 2011: Brown University, Yale University.

Basis for selection. Essays most important. School achievement record, interview, extracurricular activities, and recommendations strongly considered. Admissions process created and run by student committee. SAT Subject Tests recommended. International students who cannot take SAT or who have taken equivalent standardized test evaluated on case-by-case basis. 2-round application process: in first round, 3 essays are required. If accepted into second round, additional 4 essays and 3- to 4-day campus visit and interview required.

2012-2013 Annual costs. Deep Springs does not charge tuition, room or board. There are no student fees. A damage deposit of $500 is required of each student. All students receive full scholarship covering tuition, room, and board valued at $56,000. Books/supplies: $1,500.

2011-2012 Financial aid. Need-based: Work-study available nights, weekends and for part-time students. **Non-need-based:** Scholarships awarded for academics.

Application procedures. Admission: Closing date 11/15 (postmark date). No application fee. Application must be submitted on paper. Admission notification by 4/15. Must reply by 5/1. Approximately 40 applicants invited to complete part II of application process between January and March. Includes a 3-day campus visit, interview, and writing 3 additional essays. Foreign students and those with economic hardship may be exempt from visit upon request. Financial aid available for students with economic hardship to visit college for second round interviews. **Financial aid:** No deadline.

Academics. Students required to take 3 classes: composition, public speaking, and summer seminar (interdisciplinary course broadly oriented around questions of political theory). Regular curriculum includes courses in humanities, social sciences and natural sciences. **Special study options:** Independent study. **Credit/placement by examination:** AP, CLEP.

Majors. Liberal arts: Arts/sciences.

Computing on campus. 7 workstations in library, computer center. Online library, helpline, repair service available.

Student life. Freshman orientation: Mandatory. Preregistration for classes offered. **Policies:** All students work on jobs running college or ranch. Student committees organize all community events as well as handle admissions, faculty hiring, public relations, and review/reinvitation process. Students self-govern, managing community issues and each other's conduct. Drugs prohibited. Students do not leave valley during term; familiy and friends may visit outside of term. **Housing:** Guaranteed on-campus for all undergraduates. Special housing for disabled available. Pets allowed in dorm rooms. **Activities:** Jazz band, campus ministries, choral groups, dance, drama, literary magazine, music ensembles, musical theater, student government, student newspaper.

Athletics. Intramural: Basketball M, boxing M, cross-country M, equestrian M, football (non-tackle) M, rifle M, rodeo M, skiing M, soccer M, swimming M, table tennis M, track and field M, volleyball M, weight lifting M, wrestling M.

Student services. Career counseling, health services, personal counseling, placement for graduates. **Transfer:** Transfer center, transfer adviser for students transferring to 4-year colleges.

Contact. E-mail: apcom@deepsprings.edu
Phone: (760) 872-2000 Fax: (760) 874-7077
Cory Myers, Chair, Applications Committee, Deep Springs College, Applications Committee, Dyer, NV 89010-9803

Diablo Valley College
Pleasant Hill, California
www.dvc.edu   CB code: 4295

- Public 2-year community college
- Commuter campus in large town

General. Founded in 1948. Regionally accredited. College for Kids available on-campus which provides enrichment activities for fourth through ninth graders. **Enrollment:** 20,703 undergraduates. **Degrees:** 437 associate awarded. **ROTC:** Army, Naval. **Location:** 25 miles from San Francisco. **Calendar:** Semester, extensive summer session. **Full-time faculty:** 260 total; 36% minority. **Part-time faculty:** 502 total; 41% minority. **Class size:** 21% < 20, 60% 20-39, 15% 40-49, 3% 50-99, less than 1% >100. **Special facilities:** Student-run restaurant and bakery, observatory, planetarium, three art collections, duck pond. **Partnerships:** Formal partnerships with Wells Fargo, Chevron, Pacific Bell, City of San Ramon, Contra Costa/Tri-Valley Telecommunication Incubator.

Transfer out. Colleges most students transferred to 2011: University of California: Berkeley, San Francisco State, University of California: East Bay, California State University: Sacramento, University of California: Davis.

Basis for selection. Open admission. **Adult students:** SAT/ACT scores not required. **Home schooled:** Applicants must supply a copy of their private school affidavit.

2011-2012 Annual costs. Tuition/fees: $1,080; $6,780 out-of-state. Per-credit charge: $36 in-state; $226 out-of-state. Books/supplies: $1,332. Personal expenses: $2,430.

Financial aid. Need-based: Need-based aid available for part-time students. Work-study available nights, weekends and for part-time students.

Application procedures. Admission: Priority date 4/1; no deadline. No application fee. Admission notification on a rolling basis beginning on or about 4/1. **Financial aid:** Priority date 3/2, closing date 5/1. FAFSA, institutional form required. Applicants notified on a rolling basis starting 6/1; must reply within 2 week(s) of notification.

Academics. The college offers a comprehensive educational program that includes courses in general education, transfer, vocational, basic skills, and life-long learning. These courses are offered in flexible formats that include different hours, days, term length, and a variety of instructional delivery methods (classroom and on-line). **Special study options:** Accelerated study, cooperative education, cross-registration, distance learning, dual enrollment of high school students, ESL, honors, independent study, internships, liberal arts/career combination, study abroad, weekend college. Study abroad programs in Florence, Italy; Salamanca, Spain; Capetown, South Africa; Ghana; and London, England. License preparation in dental hygiene. **Credit/placement by examination:** AP, CLEP, institutional tests. **Support services:** Learning center, pre-admission summer program, reduced course load, remedial instruction, study skills assistance, tutoring, writing center.

Majors. Architecture: Technology. **Business:** Business admin. **Communications:** Digital media. **Communications technology:** General. **Computer sciences:** General, computer science, networking. **Education:** Early childhood, physical, special ed. **Health services:** Athletic training. **Math:** General. **Psychology:** General. **Social sciences:** Geography, political science. **Visual/performing arts:** Digital arts, theater design.

Most popular majors. Interdisciplinary studies 84%.

Computing on campus. 1,000 workstations in library, computer center, student center. Commuter students can connect to campus network. Online course registration, online library, helpline, repair service, student web hosting, wireless network available.

Student life. Freshman orientation: Mandatory. Preregistration for classes offered. **Policies:** No smoking except in the quad. **Activities:** Bands, choral groups, dance, drama, film society, international student organizations, literary magazine, music ensembles, musical theater, student government, student newspaper, symphony orchestra, TV station, Alpha Gamma Sigma, Asian student union, DVC Republicans, DVC Democrats, Black student union, Latino students' alliance, Muslim student association, Christians on Campus, Greater China Cultural Association, Taiwan Discovery Club.

Athletics. NJCAA. **Intercollegiate:** Baseball M, basketball, cross-country, football (tackle) M, soccer W, softball W, swimming, tennis, track and field, volleyball W, water polo. **Team name:** Vikings.

Student services. Adult student services, career counseling, services for economically disadvantaged, student employment services, financial aid counseling, on-campus daycare, personal counseling, placement for graduates, veterans' counselor, women's services. **Physically disabled:** Services for visually, speech, hearing impaired. **Transfer:** Re-entry adviser for new students. Transfer center, transfer adviser, college fairs on campus for students transferring to 4-year colleges.

Contact. E-mail: informationcenter@dvc.edu
Phone: (925) 685-1310 Fax: (925) 609-8085
Beth Hauscarriague, Dean of Outreach, Enrollment & Matriculation, Diablo Valley College, 321 Golf Club Road, Pleasant Hill, CA 94523-1529

East Los Angeles College
Monterey Park, California
www.elac.edu

CB member
CB code: 4296

- Public 2-year community college
- Commuter campus in very large city

General. Founded in 1945. Regionally accredited. **Enrollment:** 35,100 undergraduates. **Degrees:** 1,191 associate awarded. **Location:** 7 miles from Los Angeles. **Calendar:** Semester, limited summer session. **Full-time faculty:** 284 total; 18% have terminal degrees, 42% minority. **Part-time faculty:** 549 total; 14% have terminal degrees, 51% minority. **Class size:** 21% < 20, 51% 20-39, 18% 40-49, 10% 50-99. **Special facilities:** Vincent Price art museum.

Transfer out. Colleges most students transferred to 2011: California State University: Los Angeles, California State University: Dominguez Hills, University of California: Los Angeles, California State Polytechnic University: Pomona, University of California: San Diego.

Basis for selection. Open admission, but selective for some programs. Limited admission to nursing and allied health associate programs. Institution uses Assessment Placement Test for English and mathematics placement. Interview required for some nursing, respiratory technology majors. **Adult students:** SAT/ACT scores not required.

2011-2012 Annual costs. Tuition/fees: $1,102; $6,802 out-of-state. Per-credit charge: $36 in-state; $226 out-of-state. Books/supplies: $1,620. Personal expenses: $2,862.

Financial aid. All financial aid based on need. Need-based aid available for part-time students. Work-study available nights, weekends and for part-time students. **Additional information:** Need-based enrollment fee waivers available through a state aid program.

Application procedures. Admission: No deadline. No application fee. **Financial aid:** Priority date 4/30; no closing date. FAFSA, institutional form required. Applicants notified on a rolling basis; must reply within 4.3 week(s) of notification.

Academics. Special study options: Accelerated study, cooperative education, cross-registration, distance learning, double major, dual enrollment of high school students, ESL, honors, independent study, internships, study abroad, weekend college. ITV (Instructional Television) and Saturday classes. License preparation in nursing, paramedic, real estate. **Credit/placement by examination:** AP, CLEP. 15 credit hours maximum toward associate degree. **Support services:** GED preparation, learning center, reduced course load, remedial instruction, study skills assistance, tutoring, writing center.

Majors. Architecture: Technology. **Business:** Accounting technology, administrative services, business admin, insurance, real estate, sales/distribution. **Communications:** Journalism. **Communications technology:** Animation/special effects, desktop publishing, photo/film/video. **Computer sciences:** Information technology. **Health services:** Community health, medical assistant, medical records technology, medical secretary, nursing (RN), respiratory therapy technology. **Liberal arts:** Arts/sciences, humanities. **Math:** General. **Parks/recreation:** Health/fitness. **Protective services:** Firefighting, police science. **Social sciences:** General, anthropology. **Visual/performing arts:** Dramatic, graphic design, music, photography. **Work/family studies:** Child development.

Most popular majors. Health sciences 7%, interdisciplinary studies 6%, liberal arts 51%, security/protective services 11%, social sciences 15%.

Computing on campus. 1,895 workstations in library, computer center, student center. Online course registration, online library, helpline, wireless network available.

Student life. Freshman orientation: Available. Preregistration for classes offered. **Policies:** All Student Life activities conform to Title V, LACCD regulations, LACCD Board Rules, Roberts rules of order, and CA Brown Act. **Activities:** Bands, campus ministries, choral groups, dance, drama, film society, international student organizations, radio station, student government, student newspaper, Associated Students Union, Christians on Campus, Asia club, International Students Club, MEChA, Circle K International, Vietnamese Student Association, Students for Equal Rights, Students for Political Awareness, Students Against Substance Abuse.

Athletics. NJCAA. **Intercollegiate:** Badminton W, baseball M, basketball, cross-country, football (tackle) M, soccer, softball W, track and field, volleyball W, wrestling M. **Intramural:** Cheerleading W. **Team name:** Huskies.

Student services. Adult student services, alcohol/substance abuse counseling, career counseling, services for economically disadvantaged, student

employment services, financial aid counseling, health services, minority student services, on-campus daycare, personal counseling, placement for graduates, veterans' counselor, women's services. **Physically disabled:** Services for visually, speech, hearing impaired. **Transfer:** Pre-admission transcript evaluation for new students. Transfer center, transfer adviser, college fairs on campus for students transferring to 4-year colleges.

Contact. E-mail: admissions2@elac.edu
Phone: (323) 265-8712 Fax: (323) 265-8688
Jeremy Allred, Dean of Admissions, East Los Angeles College, 1301 Avenida Cesar Chavez, Monterey Park, CA 91754-6099

El Camino College
Torrance, California
www.elcamino.edu   **CB code: 4302**

♦ Public 2-year community and junior college
♦ Commuter campus in very large city

General. Founded in 1947. Regionally accredited. **Enrollment:** 12,116 degree-seeking undergraduates. **Degrees:** 1,374 associate awarded. **Location:** 15 miles from Los Angeles. **Calendar:** Semester, limited summer session. **Full-time faculty:** 336 total; 53% women. **Part-time faculty:** 673 total; 51% women. **Special facilities:** Anthropology museum, planetarium, conference center, computer/media center, child development center.

Student profile. Among degree-seeking undergraduates, 75% enrolled in a transfer program, 25% enrolled in a vocational program.

Out-of-state:	5%	25 or older:	35%

Transfer out. Colleges most students transferred to 2011: California State University: Long Beach, California State University: Dominguez Hills, California State University: Fullerton, University of California: Los Angeles.

Basis for selection. Open admission, but selective for some programs. Allied health programs require completion of preparatory courses (anatomy, microbiology, college-level English and mathematics). Interview required for nursing, honors program, x-ray technician, respiratory care majors. **Adult students:** SAT/ACT scores not required. **Home schooled:** Statement describing home school structure and mission, transcript of courses and grades, state high school equivalency certificate, letter of recommendation (nonparent) required. Home school must be registered with state of California. **Learning Disabled:** Contact Special Resources Center and provide evidence of learning disability.

2011-2012 Annual costs. Tuition/fees: $1,115; $6,395 out-of-state. Per-credit charge: $36 in-state; $212 out-of-state. Books/supplies: $1,638. Personal expenses: $2,664.

2010-2011 Financial aid. Need-based: 92% of total undergraduate aid awarded as scholarships/grants, 8% as loans/jobs. Need-based aid available for part-time students. Work-study available nights, weekends and for part-time students. **Non-need-based:** Scholarships awarded for academics, art, athletics, leadership, music/drama. **Additional information:** Students may apply for Pell grants until June 30.

Application procedures. Admission: No deadline. No application fee. Application must be submitted online. Admission notification on a rolling basis beginning on or about 8/20. **Financial aid:** Priority date 3/2, closing date 6/30. FAFSA, institutional form required. Applicants notified on a rolling basis starting 7/15.

Academics. Special study options: Cooperative education, cross-registration, distance learning, double major, dual enrollment of high school students, ESL, honors, independent study, liberal arts/career combination, study abroad, weekend college. License preparation in nursing, paramedic, radiology. **Credit/placement by examination:** AP, CLEP, IB, institutional tests. 15 credit hours maximum toward associate degree. **Support services:** Learning center, remedial instruction, study skills assistance, tutoring, writing center.

Majors. Area/ethnic studies: African-American, American, Asian-American, Chicano/Hispanic-American/Latino, Native American. **Biology:** General, botany, zoology. **Business:** General, administrative services, business admin, office management, real estate, sales/distribution. **Communications:** Journalism. **Communications technology:** General. **Computer sciences:** General, computer science. **Education:** Early childhood. **Engineering:** General. **English:** English lit, rhetoric/composition. **Foreign languages:** French, German, Japanese, Spanish. **General:** Ornamental horticulture. **Health services:** Licensed practical nurse, medical radiologic technology/radiation therapy, nursing (RN), predental, premedicine, prepharmacy, respiratory therapy technology. **History:** General. **Math:** General. **Parks/recreation:** Health/fitness. **Philosophy/religion:** Philosophy. **Physical sciences:** Astronomy, chemistry, geology, physics. **Protective services:**

Fire safety technology, law enforcement admin, police science. **Psychology:** General. **Social sciences:** Anthropology, economics, geography, political science, sociology. **Visual/performing arts:** Art, dance, dramatic, music, photography, studio arts. **Work/family studies:** General.

Most popular majors. Business/marketing 13%, health sciences 11%, liberal arts 37%, social sciences 6%.

Computing on campus. 500 workstations in library, computer center, student center. Online course registration, wireless network available.

Student life. Freshman orientation: Available. Preregistration for classes offered. **Activities:** Bands, choral groups, dance, drama, literary magazine, music ensembles, musical theater, student government, student newspaper, symphony orchestra, Alpha Gamma Sigma, anthropology club, environmental club, Gay-Straight Alliance, Iota Kappa Chi (Nursing), Puente Club, Veterans Club, Muslim Students Association, Native American Club, Tailor Made (Fashion Design).

Athletics. NJCAA. **Intercollegiate:** Badminton W, baseball M, basketball, cross-country, football (tackle) M, golf M, soccer, softball W, swimming, tennis, track and field, volleyball, water polo. **Team name:** Warriors.

Student services. Adult student services, career counseling, services for economically disadvantaged, student employment services, financial aid counseling, health services, on-campus daycare, personal counseling, placement for graduates, veterans' counselor. **Physically disabled:** Services for visually, speech, hearing impaired. **Transfer:** Re-entry adviser, pre-admission transcript evaluation for new students. Transfer center, transfer adviser, college fairs on campus for students transferring to 4-year colleges.

Contact. E-mail: admissionshelp@elcamino.edu
Phone: (310) 660-3414 Fax: (310) 660-3818
Bill Mulrooney, Director of Admissions and Records, El Camino College, 16007 Crenshaw Boulevard, Torrance, CA 90506

Empire College
Santa Rosa, California
www.empcol.edu   **CB code: 4275**

♦ For-profit 2-year business college
♦ Commuter campus in small city
♦ Interview required

General. Accredited by ACICS. **Enrollment:** 260 degree-seeking undergraduates. **Degrees:** 128 associate awarded. **Location:** 55 miles from San Francisco. **Calendar:** Differs by program. **Full-time faculty:** 23 total. **Part-time faculty:** 14 total. **Special facilities:** Law library.

Transfer out. Colleges most students transferred to 2011: Santa Rosa Junior College.

Basis for selection. Open admission, but selective for some programs. Scholastic Level Exam (SLE) administered during admission process. Some programs also have typing speed requirement for entrance.

High school preparation. College-preparatory program required.

2011-2012 Annual costs. Tuition/fees: $10,125. Average lab fee: $1,535. Books/supplies: $2,600. Personal expenses: $211.

Financial aid. All financial aid based on need. Work-study available nights, weekends and for part-time students.

Application procedures. Admission: No deadline. $100 fee. Admission notification on a rolling basis. No fall term, ongoing 5-week application/entry. **Financial aid:** No deadline. FAFSA required. Applicants notified on a rolling basis.

Academics. Special study options: Accelerated study, double major, internships. **Credit/placement by examination:** AP, CLEP. **Support services:** Tutoring.

Majors. Business: Accounting, administrative services. **Computer sciences:** Information systems. **Health services:** Medical secretary.

Computing on campus. 600 workstations in library, computer center. Online library, student web hosting, wireless network available.

Student life. Freshman orientation: Mandatory. Preregistration for classes offered. **Activities:** Student newspaper.

Student services. Career counseling, student employment services, financial aid counseling, placement for graduates. **Transfer:** Re-entry adviser, pre-admission transcript evaluation for new students.

Contact. E-mail: dstraub@empirecollege.com
Phone: (707) 546-4000 ext. 238 Fax: (707) 546-4058
Dahnja Straub, Director of Admissions, Empire College, 3035 Cleveland Avenue, Santa Rosa, CA 95403-2100

Epic Bible College
Sacramento, California
www.tlbc.edu

- Private 2-year Bible college
- Very large city

General. Regionally accredited; also accredited by TRACS. **Enrollment:** 279 degree-seeking undergraduates. **Degrees:** 19 bachelor's, 29 associate awarded. **Calendar:** Quarter. **Full-time faculty:** 5 total. **Part-time faculty:** 15 total.

Basis for selection. Must have expressed personal experience of Christian conversion.

2011-2012 Annual costs. Tuition/fees: $10,605. Per-credit charge: $229. Books/supplies: $1,638.

Financial aid. Need-based: Work-study available nights, weekends and for part-time students.

Application procedures. Admission: Closing date 8/15.

Academics. Special study options: Bachelor's degree programs available on campus. **Credit/placement by examination:** AP, CLEP.

Majors. Philosophy/religion: Christian. **Theology:** Preministerial.

Contact. Phone: (916) 348-4689
Kathy Clarke, Director of Records, Epic Bible College, 5225 Hillsdale Boulevard, Sacramento, CA 95842

Evergreen Valley College
San Jose, California
www.evc.edu   CB code: 4273

- Public 2-year community and junior college
- Commuter campus in very large city

General. Founded in 1975. Regionally accredited. **Enrollment:** 10,551 undergraduates. **Degrees:** 482 associate awarded. **Location:** 7 miles from downtown. **Calendar:** Semester, extensive summer session. **Full-time faculty:** 122 total; 33% have terminal degrees. **Part-time faculty:** 204 total. **Special facilities:** Hiking trails, parks, observatory, natural habitat, cross-country course.

Transfer out. Colleges most students transferred to 2011: San Jose State.

Basis for selection. Open admission, but selective for some programs. Limited admission for nursing and criminal justice programs. **Home schooled:** Interview required. Must complete form R-42 and state affidavit.

2011-2012 Annual costs. Tuition/fees: $1,126; $7,096 out-of-state. Per-credit charge: $36 in-state; $235 out-of-state. Books/supplies: $1,638. Personal expenses: $3,096.

Financial aid. Need-based: Work-study available nights, weekends and for part-time students.

Application procedures. Admission: No deadline. No application fee. Admission notification on a rolling basis. **Financial aid:** Priority date 5/31; no closing date. FAFSA required. Applicants notified on a rolling basis.

Academics. Special study options: Accelerated study, cooperative education, cross-registration, distance learning, double major, dual enrollment of high school students, ESL, honors, independent study, internships, liberal arts/career combination, weekend college. License preparation in nursing, paramedic. **Credit/placement by examination:** AP, CLEP, institutional tests. 12 credit hours maximum toward associate degree. Assessment testing as prescribed by California law required for placement in English and mathematics. **Support services:** Learning center, reduced course load, remedial instruction, study skills assistance, tutoring, writing center.

Majors. Business: Administrative services, fashion, management information systems, office technology, office/clerical. **Computer sciences:** General, applications programming. **Health services:** Nursing (RN). **Liberal arts:** Arts/sciences. **Protective services:** Police science. **Visual/performing arts:** Commercial/advertising art.

Computing on campus. 800 workstations in library, computer center, student center.

Student life. Freshman orientation: Mandatory. Preregistration for classes offered. **Activities:** Choral groups, dance, drama, literary magazine, music ensembles, musical theater, student government, student newspaper, Black Students Union, ASPIRE, Enlace, AFFIRM.

Athletics. NJCAA. **Intercollegiate:** Soccer, track and field, volleyball W, wrestling M. **Intramural:** Basketball, football (non-tackle) M. **Team name:** Hawks.

Student services. Alcohol/substance abuse counseling, career counseling, services for economically disadvantaged, student employment services, financial aid counseling, health services, minority student services, on-campus daycare, personal counseling, veterans' counselor. **Physically disabled:** Services for visually, speech, hearing impaired. **Transfer:** Transfer center, transfer adviser, college fairs on campus for students transferring to 4-year colleges.

Contact. E-mail: lynn.gulkin@evc.edu
Phone: (408) 270-6441 Fax: (408) 223-9351
Octavio Cruz, Dean of Enrollment Services, Evergreen Valley College, 3095 Yerba Buena Road, San Jose, CA 95135

Fashion Careers College
San Diego, California
www.fashioncareerscollege.com   CB code: 3494

- For-profit 2-year visual arts and business college
- Commuter campus in very large city
- Application essay, interview required

General. Accredited by ACICS. **Enrollment:** 67 degree-seeking undergraduates. **Degrees:** 25 associate awarded. **Calendar:** Quarter. **Part-time faculty:** 16 total; 88% women.

Basis for selection. Exam score, essay, interview important. Wonderlic test used for admission.

2012-2013 Annual costs. Tuition/fees: $23,400. Includes books and supplies. Personal expenses: $3,114.

Financial aid. Need-based: Work-study available nights, weekends and for part-time students.

Application procedures. Admission: No deadline. $25 fee. Admission notification on a rolling basis. **Financial aid:** No deadline. FAFSA required.

Academics. Credit/placement by examination: AP, CLEP.

Majors. Business: Fashion. **Visual/performing arts:** Fashion design.

Most popular majors. Business/marketing 50%, visual/performing arts 50%.

Computing on campus. 20 workstations in computer center. Repair service, wireless network available.

Student life. Freshman orientation: Mandatory. Preregistration for classes offered. Held 1 week before classes start.

Student services. Career counseling, financial aid counseling, placement for graduates.

Contact. E-mail: info@fashioncareerscollege.com
Phone: (619) 275-4700 Toll-free number: (888) 322-2999
Fax: (619) 275-0635
Ben Cobos, Director of Admission, Fashion Careers College, 1923 Morena Boulevard, San Diego, CA 92110

Fashion Institute of Design and Merchandising: Los Angeles

Los Angeles, California
www.fidm.edu

CB member
CB code: 4457

♦ For-profit 2-year visual arts and business college
♦ Commuter campus in very large city
♦ Application essay, interview required

General. Founded in 1969. Regionally accredited. Branch campuses in Orange County, San Francisco and San Diego. **Enrollment:** 4,419 degree-seeking undergraduates. **Degrees:** 62 bachelor's, 748 associate awarded. **Calendar:** Quarter, extensive summer session. **Full-time faculty:** 68 total; 31% minority, 32% women. **Part-time faculty:** 258 total; 18% minority, 59% women. **Class size:** 77% < 20, 23% 20-39. **Special facilities:** Hollywood costume collection, costume study collection and museum, textile museum, fragrance bottle collection, fashion library.

Student profile.

Part-time:	11%	Hispanic American:	23%
Out-of-state:	41%	Native American:	1%
Women:	88%	International:	10%
African American:	6%	25 or older:	15%
Asian American:	11%		

Basis for selection. High school transcripts, standardized test scores, references, portfolio or admissions project, essays, and evidence of interest in major area through work experience, high school preparation, or extracurricular activities considered. In addition to transcript evaluation, SAT and/or ACT scores considered to determine if additional testing is required. SAT or ACT recommended. Portfolio or admissions project required. Out-of-state applicants interviewed by telephone. Projects are required of all students. International students not required to interview. **Home schooled:** Statement describing home school structure and mission, interview required. Admissions or standardized testing required. **Learning Disabled:** Interview with Education Specialist to discuss reasonable accommodation.

High school preparation. College-preparatory program recommended.

2012-2013 Annual costs. Tuition/fees (projected): $22,650. Books/supplies: $2,160. Personal expenses: $2,142.

Financial aid. Need-based: Work-study available nights, weekends and for part-time students. **Non-need-based:** Scholarships awarded for academics. **Additional information:** Tuition/fee expenses may be reduced by applying for admission by December 31 of year before student plans to attend.

Application procedures. Admission: No deadline. $225 fee ($375 out-of-state). Admission notification on a rolling basis. **Financial aid:** Priority date 3/1; no closing date. FAFSA, institutional form required. Applicants notified on a rolling basis starting 3/15; must reply within 3 week(s) of notification.

Academics. Faculty and staff come from related industries. Project-oriented courses give students hands-on experience. **Special study options:** Distance learning, ESL, exchange student, independent study, internships, study abroad, weekend college. **Credit/placement by examination:** AP, CLEP, IB, institutional tests. 45 credit hours maximum toward associate degree, 45 toward bachelor's. **Support services:** Learning center, reduced course load, remedial instruction, study skills assistance, tutoring, writing center.

Majors. Business: Fashion, marketing, merchandising, operations, retailing, sales/distribution. **Visual/performing arts:** Design, digital arts, fashion design, fiber arts, graphic design, interior design, metal/jewelry, multimedia, theater design. **Work/family studies:** Apparel marketing, clothing/textiles, fashion consultant, merchandising, textile manufacture, textile science.

Most popular majors. Visual/performing arts 12%.

Computing on campus. 400 workstations in library, computer center, student center. Commuter students can connect to campus network. Online course registration, online library, helpline, wireless network available.

Student life. Freshman orientation: Mandatory. Preregistration for classes offered. **Housing:** Apartments available. **Activities:** International student organizations, student government, student newspaper, honor society, design council, ASID, Phi Theta Kappa.

Student services. Adult student services, alcohol/substance abuse counseling, career counseling, student employment services, financial aid counseling, personal counseling, placement for graduates, women's services. **Physically disabled:** Services for visually, hearing impaired. **Transfer:** Pre-admission transcript evaluation for new students. Transfer center, transfer adviser for students transferring to 4-year colleges.

Contact. E-mail: admissionsdirector@fidm.edu
Phone: (213) 624-1200 Toll-free number: (800) 624-1200
Fax: (213) 624-4799
Susan Aronson, Executive Director of Admissions, Fashion Institute of Design and Merchandising: Los Angeles, 919 South Grand Avenue, Los Angeles, CA 90015-1421

Fashion Institute of Design and Merchandising: San Diego

San Diego, California
www.fidm.edu

CB code: 2949

♦ For-profit 2-year visual arts and business college
♦ Commuter campus in very large city
♦ Application essay, interview required

General. Regionally accredited. Other campuses in Los Angeles, Orange County, and San Francisco. **Enrollment:** 245 degree-seeking undergraduates. **Degrees:** 63 associate awarded. **Calendar:** Quarter, extensive summer session. **Full-time faculty:** 3 total; 67% women. **Part-time faculty:** 24 total; 29% minority, 88% women. **Class size:** 77% < 20, 23% 20-39. **Special facilities:** Hollywood costume study collection and museum, textile museum, historical Annette Green fragrance bottle collection, fashion library.

Student profile. Among degree-seeking undergraduates, 245 enrolled as first-time, first-year students.

Part-time:	7%	Hispanic American:	34%
Out-of-state:	22%	Native American:	1%
Women:	92%	International:	2%
African American:	8%	25 or older:	10%
Asian American:	10%		

Basis for selection. High school transcripts, standardized test scores, references, portfolio or admissions project, essays and evidence of interest in major through work experience, high school preparation, or extracurricular activities considered. In addition to transcript evaluation, SAT and/or ACT scores are considered to determine if additional testing is required. SAT or ACT recommended. Portfolio or admissions project required of all applicants. Out-of-state applicants are interviewed by telephone. International students are not required to interview. **Home schooled:** Statement describing home school structure and mission, interview required. Admissions or standardized testing required. **Learning Disabled:** Interview with Education Specialist to discuss reasonable accommodation.

High school preparation. College-preparatory program recommended.

2012-2013 Annual costs. Tuition/fees (projected): $22,650.

Financial aid. Need-based: Work-study available nights, weekends and for part-time students. **Non-need-based:** Scholarships awarded for academics.

Application procedures. Admission: No deadline. $225 fee ($375 out-of-state). Admission notification on a rolling basis. **Financial aid:** No deadline. FAFSA, institutional form required. Applicants notified on a rolling basis; must reply within 3 week(s) of notification.

Academics. Faculty and staff are recruited from industry. Project-oriented courses provide hands-on learning experiences. **Special study options:** Distance learning, exchange student, independent study, internships, study abroad, weekend college. **Credit/placement by examination:** AP, CLEP, IB, institutional tests. 15 credit hours maximum toward associate degree. **Support services:** Learning center, reduced course load, remedial instruction, study skills assistance, tutoring, writing center.

Majors. Business: Fashion, marketing. **Visual/performing arts:** Design, fashion design, fiber arts, graphic design. **Work/family studies:** Apparel marketing, clothing/textiles, fashion consultant, merchandising, textile manufacture, textile science.

Computing on campus. 35 workstations in library, computer center, student center. Commuter students can connect to campus network. Online course registration, online library, helpline, wireless network available.

Student life. Freshman orientation: Mandatory. Preregistration for classes offered. **Housing:** Apartments available. **Activities:** Honor students society, alumni association, ASID student chapter, Design Council, Phi Theta Kappa, student activities committee.

Student services. Adult student services, alcohol/substance abuse counseling, career counseling, student employment services, financial aid counseling, personal counseling, placement for graduates, women's services. **Physically disabled:** Services for visually, hearing impaired. **Transfer:** Pre-admission transcript evaluation for new students. Transfer center, transfer adviser for students transferring to 4-year colleges.

Contact. E-mail: admissionsdirector@fidm.edu
Phone: (619) 235-2049 Toll-free number: (800) 243-3436
Fax: (619) 232-4322
Susan Aronson, Executive Director of Admissions, Fashion Institute of Design and Merchandising: San Diego, 350 Tenth Avenue, Third Floor, San Diego, CA 92101

Fashion Institute of Design and Merchandising: San Francisco
San Francisco, California
www.fidm.edu   **CB code: 4988**

▶ For-profit 2-year visual arts and business college
▶ Commuter campus in very large city
▶ Application essay, interview required

General. Founded in 1969. Regionally accredited. Other campuses in Los Angeles, Orange County, and San Diego. **Enrollment:** 875 degree-seeking undergraduates. **Degrees:** 346 associate awarded. **Calendar:** Quarter, extensive summer session. **Full-time faculty:** 9 total; 11% minority, 56% women. **Part-time faculty:** 65 total; 15% minority, 62% women. **Class size:** 77% < 20, 23% 20-39. **Special facilities:** Acces to Hollywood costume collection, costume study collection and museum, textiles museum, Annette Green fragrance bottle collection, fashion library.

Student profile. Among degree-seeking undergraduates, 875 enrolled as first-time, first-year students.

Part-time:	13%	Hispanic American:	20%
Out-of-state:	5%	Native American:	1%
Women:	91%	International:	3%
African American:	6%	25 or older:	16%
Asian American:	17%		

Basis for selection. Recommendations and application essay very important. Rigor of secondary school record and academic GPA important. In addition to transcript, SAT and/or ACT scores are considered to determine if additional testing is required. SAT or ACT recommended. Portfolio or admissions project is required of all candidates. Out-of-state applicants are interviewed by telephone. International students are not required to interview. **Home schooled:** Statement describing home school structure and mission, interview required.

High school preparation. College-preparatory program recommended. High school transcripts, standardized test scores, references, portfolio or admissions project, essays, and evidence of interest in major through work experience, high school preparation, or extracurricular activities accepted.

2012-2013 Annual costs. Tuition/fees (projected): $23,175.

Financial aid. **Need-based:** Work-study available nights, weekends and for part-time students. **Non-need-based:** Scholarships awarded for academics.

Application procedures. **Admission:** No deadline. $225 fee ($375 out-of-state). Admission notification on a rolling basis. **Financial aid:** No deadline. FAFSA, institutional form required. Applicants notified on a rolling basis starting 3/15; must reply within 3 week(s) of notification.

Academics. Faculty and staff are recruited from industry. Project oriented courses provide hands-on learning experiences. **Special study options:** Distance learning, ESL, exchange student, independent study, internships, study abroad, weekend college. **Credit/placement by examination:** AP, CLEP, IB, institutional tests. 45 credit hours maximum toward associate degree, 45 toward bachelor's. **Support services:** Learning center, reduced course load, remedial instruction, study skills assistance, tutoring, writing center.

Majors. **Business:** Fashion. **Computer sciences:** Computer graphics, webmaster. **Visual/performing arts:** Design, digital arts, fashion design, fiber arts, graphic design, interior design, metal/jewelry, multimedia, theater design. **Work/family studies:** Apparel marketing, clothing/textiles, fashion consultant, merchandising, textile manufacture, textile science.

Most popular majors. Business/marketing 36%, visual/performing arts 64%.

Computing on campus. 130 workstations in library, computer center, student center. Commuter students can connect to campus network. Online course registration, online library, helpline, wireless network available.

Student life. **Freshman orientation:** Mandatory. Preregistration for classes offered. **Activities:** International student organizations, student government, student newspaper, honor society, design council, ASID student chapter, Phi Theta Kappa.

Student services. Adult student services, alcohol/substance abuse counseling, career counseling, student employment services, financial aid counseling, personal counseling, placement for graduates, women's services. **Physically disabled:** Services for visually, hearing impaired. **Transfer:** Pre-admission transcript evaluation for new students. Transfer center, transfer adviser for students transferring to 4-year colleges.

Contact. E-mail: admissionsdirector@fidm.edu
Phone: (415) 675-5200 Toll-free number: (800) 422-3436
Fax: (415) 394-9700
Sheryl Badalamente, Director of Admissions, Fashion Institute of Design and Merchandising: San Francisco, 55 Stockton Street, San Francisco, CA 94108-5805

Feather River College
Quincy, California
www.frc.edu   **CB code: 4318**

▶ Public 2-year community and liberal arts college
▶ Commuter campus in small town

General. Founded in 1968. Regionally accredited. **Enrollment:** 878 degree-seeking undergraduates. **Degrees:** 173 associate awarded. **Location:** 150 miles from Sacramento, 80 miles from Reno, Nevada. **Calendar:** Semester, limited summer session. **Full-time faculty:** 26 total; 42% women. **Part-time faculty:** 80 total; 6% minority, 49% women. **Class size:** 56% < 20, 38% 20-39, 4% 40-49, 2% 50-99. **Special facilities:** Fish hatchery, horse boarding and training facility, state wildlife preserve.

Transfer out. **Colleges most students transferred to 2011:** CSU: Chico, Humboldt State University, University of Nevada: Reno, California Polytechnic State University: San Luis Obispo.

Basis for selection. Open admission.

2011-2012 Annual costs. Tuition/fees: $1,159; $7,129 out-of-state. Per-credit charge: $36 in-state; $235 out-of-state. Room/board: $7,500. Books/supplies: $1,656. Personal expenses: $2,250.

Financial aid. All financial aid based on need. Need-based aid available for part-time students. Work-study available nights, weekends and for part-time students.

Application procedures. **Admission:** No deadline. No application fee. **Financial aid:** Priority date 3/2; no closing date. FAFSA required. Applicants notified on a rolling basis starting 4/1; must reply within 3 week(s) of notification.

Academics. General education/core courses are offered that satisfy all lower division requirements of California State University, University of California, and University of Nevada system. **Special study options:** Cooperative education, cross-registration, distance learning, double major, dual enrollment of high school students, ESL, honors, independent study, internships, liberal arts/career combination. License preparation in nursing, paramedic. **Credit/placement by examination:** AP, CLEP, institutional tests. 12 credit hours maximum toward associate degree. **Support services:** GED preparation and test center, learning center, reduced course load, remedial instruction, study skills assistance, tutoring.

Majors. **Biology:** General. **Business:** General, administrative services. **Conservation:** General, environmental studies, forestry, wildlife/wilderness. **English:** English lit. **General:** Equine science. **Health services:** Licensed practical nurse. **History:** General. **Liberal arts:** Arts/sciences, humanities. **Math:** General. **Parks/recreation:** General, health/fitness. **Physical sciences:** General. **Protective services:** Police science. **Social sciences:** General. **Visual/performing arts:** General. **Work/family studies:** Child care service, food/nutrition.

Most popular majors. Agriculture 11%, liberal arts 61%, parks/recreation 10%.

Computing on campus. 120 workstations in dormitories, library, computer center, student center. Dormitories wired for high-speed internet access. Online course registration, online library, wireless network available.

Student life. **Freshman orientation:** Mandatory. Preregistration for classes offered. Online orientation available. **Housing:** Apartments available. **Activities:** Student government, Phi Theta Kappa.

Athletics. NJCAA. **Intercollegiate:** Baseball M, basketball, cross-country, football (tackle) M, rodeo, soccer, softball W, track and field W, volleyball W. **Intramural:** Cheerleading W, volleyball W. **Team name:** Golden Eagles.

Student services. Adult student services, career counseling, services for economically disadvantaged, student employment services, financial aid counseling, health services, on-campus daycare, personal counseling, placement for graduates, veterans' counselor. **Physically disabled:** Services for visually, speech, hearing impaired. **Transfer:** Re-entry adviser, pre-admission transcript evaluation for new students. Transfer center, transfer adviser, college fairs on campus for students transferring to 4-year colleges.

Contact. Phone: (530) 283-0202 ext. 600
Toll-free number: (800) 442-9799 ext. 600 Fax: (530) 283-9961
Leslie Mikesell, Registrar, Feather River College, 570 Golden Eagle Avenue, Quincy, CA 95971

Folsom Lake College
Folsom, California
www.flc.losrios.edu
CB code: 4462

- Public 2-year community college
- Commuter campus in small city

General. Regionally accredited. **Enrollment:** 5,843 degree-seeking undergraduates. **Degrees:** 648 associate awarded. **Location:** 25 miles from Sacramento. **Calendar:** Semester, limited summer session. **Full-time faculty:** 104 total. **Part-time faculty:** 176 total. **Special facilities:** Regional visual and performing arts center, observatory.

Transfer out. Colleges most students transferred to 2011: California State University: Sacramento, University of California: Davis.

Basis for selection. Open admission. **Adult students:** SAT/ACT scores not required.

2011-2012 Annual costs. Tuition/fees: $1,112; $7,352 out-of-state. Per-credit charge: $36 in-state; $244 out-of-state. Books/supplies: $1,656. Personal expenses: $3,114.

Financial aid. Need-based: Work-study available nights, weekends and for part-time students.

Application procedures. Admission: No deadline. No application fee. **Financial aid:** Closing date 6/30. FAFSA required.

Academics. Special study options: Cross-registration, distance learning, ESL, internships, study abroad. **Credit/placement by examination:** AP, CLEP, institutional tests. **Support services:** Learning center, remedial instruction, study skills assistance, tutoring, writing center.

Majors. Area/ethnic studies: American, women's. **Biology:** General. **Business:** General, accounting, administrative services, management science, marketing, real estate, small business admin. **Communications:** Organizational. **Computer sciences:** General. **Education:** Early childhood. **English:** English lit. **Liberal arts:** Arts/sciences. **Math:** General. **Physical sciences:** Geology. **Protective services:** Firefighting, law enforcement admin. **Psychology:** General. **Visual/performing arts:** Art, art history/conservation. **Work/family studies:** Aging, family studies.

Computing on campus. 1,300 workstations in library, computer center. Online course registration, online library, wireless network available.

Student life. Freshman orientation: Available. Preregistration for classes offered. **Activities:** Bands, choral groups, dance, drama, international student organizations, music ensembles, student government.

Athletics. Intercollegiate: Golf, tennis. **Team name:** Falcons.

Student services. Services for economically disadvantaged, financial aid counseling, health services, veterans' counselor. **Physically disabled:** Services for visually, speech, hearing impaired. **Transfer:** Transfer center, transfer adviser, college fairs on campus for students transferring to 4-year colleges.

Contact. Phone: (916) 608-6500 Fax: (916) 608-6569
Christine Wurzer, Admissions and Records Supervisor, Folsom Lake College, 10 College Parkway, Folsom, CA 95630

Foothill College
Los Altos Hills, California
www.foothill.edu
CB code: 4315

- Public 2-year community college
- Commuter campus in large town

General. Founded in 1958. Regionally accredited. **Enrollment:** 8,702 degree-seeking undergraduates. **Degrees:** 574 associate awarded. **ROTC:** Army, Naval, Air Force. **Location:** 40 miles from San Francisco. **Calendar:** Quarter, limited summer session. **Full-time faculty:** 193 total; 35% minority, 61% women. **Special facilities:** Center for innovation, Japanese cultural center, observatory, bamboo garden, dental health clinic, travel careers computer lab, math center.

Transfer out. Colleges most students transferred to 2011: San Jose State, University of California: Berkeley, University of California: Santa Cruz, University of California: Los Angeles, University of California: Davis.

Basis for selection. Open admission, but selective for some programs. Allied health programs have special prerequisites: point system used to rank required college-level and general education classes, top 20-40 students selected for admission. Must be 2-year transfer.

2011-2012 Annual costs. Tuition/fees: $1,122; $6,522 out-of-state. Per-credit charge: $24 in-state; $144 out-of-state. Books/supplies: $1,665. Personal expenses: $2,832.

2010-2011 Financial aid. Need-based: 54% of total undergraduate aid awarded as scholarships/grants, 46% as loans/jobs. Need-based aid available for part-time students. Work-study available nights, weekends and for part-time students.

Application procedures. Admission: No deadline. No application fee. Admission notification on a rolling basis. **Financial aid:** Priority date 3/30; no closing date. FAFSA, institutional form required. Applicants notified on a rolling basis starting 5/1; must reply within 3 week(s) of notification.

Academics. NASA Ames Research Center internships available. **Special study options:** Cooperative education, cross-registration, distance learning, ESL, exchange student, honors, independent study, internships, liberal arts/career combination, study abroad, weekend college. Bachelor's degree programs available on campus. License preparation in dental hygiene, paramedic, radiology. **Credit/placement by examination:** AP, CLEP, institutional tests. 20 credit hours maximum toward associate degree. **Support services:** Learning center, remedial instruction, study skills assistance, tutoring, writing center.

Honors college/program. Must have minimum 3.5 cumulative high school GPA or SAT total of at least 2100 or Enhanced ACT Composite of 26 or minimum 3.3 cumulative GPA in 10 or more units completed at another accredited college or university. Minimum AP English score of 3 or 2, minimum score on assessment test of ENGL Reading 93 and ENGL Writing 111 or completion of English 1A with a grade of B or better. Letter of recommendation and personal statement required.

Majors. Area/ethnic studies: American, women's. **Biology:** General, bioinformatics, biotechnology. **Business:** Accounting, business admin, international, office technology, real estate, tourism promotion. **Communications:** Broadcast journalism, communications/speech/rhetoric, media studies, radio/TV. **Computer sciences:** General, computer graphics, computer science, database management, information technology, LAN/WAN management, programming. **Education:** Early childhood. **Engineering:** General, software. **English:** Creative writing, English lit, rhetoric/composition. **Foreign languages:** Chinese, French, Japanese, linguistics, Spanish. **General:** Landscaping, nursery operations, ornamental horticulture. **Health services:** Athletic training, dental assistant, dental hygiene, medical radiologic technology/radiation therapy, pharmacy assistant, physician assistant, predental, premedicine, prepharmacy, preveterinary, radiologic technology/medical imaging, respiratory therapy assistant, respiratory therapy technology, sonography, veterinary technology/assistant. **History:** General. **Liberal arts:** Arts/sciences, library assistant. **Math:** General. **Philosophy/religion:** Philosophy. **Physical sciences:** Chemistry, geology, physics. **Psychology:** General. **Social sciences:** General, anthropology, economics, geography, political science, sociology. **Visual/performing arts:** Art, art history/conservation, commercial/advertising art, dramatic, music, photography, studio arts, theater design. **Work/family studies:** Child development.

Computing on campus. 200 workstations in library, computer center, student center. Commuter students can connect to campus network. Online course registration, online library, wireless network available.

Student life. Freshman orientation: Available. Preregistration for classes offered. **Activities:** Bands, choral groups, dance, drama, film society, music ensembles, musical theater, radio station, student government, student newspaper, symphony orchestra, TV station, 32 different multicultural/ethnic campus clubs.

Athletics. Intercollegiate: Basketball, diving, football (tackle) M, golf, soccer, softball W, swimming, tennis, volleyball W, water polo W. **Intramural:** Basketball, cheerleading, football (non-tackle), soccer, softball, volleyball. **Team name:** Owls.

Student services. Adult student services, alcohol/substance abuse counseling, career counseling, services for economically disadvantaged, student employment services, financial aid counseling, health services, legal services, minority student services, personal counseling, placement for graduates, veterans' counselor. **Physically disabled:** Services for visually, speech, hearing impaired. **Transfer:** Transfer adviser, college fairs on campus for students transferring to 4-year colleges.

Contact. E-mail: balduccilaureen@foothill.edu
Phone: (650) 949-7325 Fax: (650) 949-7048
Laureen Balducci, Dean, Counseling and Matriculation, Foothill College, 12345 El Monte Road, Los Altos Hills, CA 94022

Fremont College: Cerritos
Los Angeles, California
www.fremont.edu
CB code: 3007

- For-profit 2-year branch campus and career college
- Commuter campus in very large city
- Application essay, interview required

General. Regionally accredited; also accredited by ACCSC. Year-round program with starts every 10 weeks. Locations in Los Angeles and Cerritos. **Enrollment:** 348 degree-seeking undergraduates. **Degrees:** 158 associate awarded. **Location:** Downtown. **Calendar:** Quarter, limited summer session. **Full-time faculty:** 2 total. **Part-time faculty:** 10 total. **Class size:** 58% < 20, 42% 20-39.

Student profile. Among degree-seeking undergraduates, 138 enrolled as first-time, first-year students, 171 transferred in from other institutions.

Women:	59%	Hispanic American:	43%
African American:	17%	25 or older:	73%
Asian American:	12%		

Basis for selection. Open admission, but selective for some programs and for out-of-state students. High school diploma or GED and successful completion of CPAt required. **Home schooled:** State high school equivalency certificate required.

2011-2012 Annual costs. Design BA/AA program: $15,750. Business BA/AA/Paralegal AA: $14,760. Sports Rehab Therapy AA/Massage Therapy Diploma: $13,995. $75 registration fee. One time STRF fee of $157.50 for design BA, $80 for Design AA, $75 for Business BA/AA and Paralegal AA, $70 for SRT, $47.50 for Massage. Tuition includes cost of books and supplies. Personal expenses: $2,190.

Financial aid. All financial aid based on need. Work-study available nights, weekends and for part-time students.

Application procedures. Admission: No deadline. $85 fee. **Financial aid:** FAFSA, institutional form required.

Academics. Special study options: Accelerated study, distance learning. **Credit/placement by examination:** AP, CLEP, IB. **Support services:** Learning center, tutoring.

Majors. Business: General. **Parks/recreation:** Exercise sciences.

Computing on campus. PC or laptop required. 30 workstations in library, computer center. Online library, wireless network available.

Student life. Freshman orientation: Mandatory. Preregistration for classes offered.

Student services. Financial aid counseling, placement for graduates. **Transfer:** Pre-admission transcript evaluation for new students.

Contact. E-mail: inquiry@fremont.edu
Phone: (213) 355-8000 Toll-free number: (800) 373-6668
Fax: (213) 355-8088
Mark Dubois, Director of Admissions, Fremont College: Cerritos, 3440 Wilshire Boulevard, 10th floor, Los Angeles, CA 90010

Fresno City College
Fresno, California
www.fresnocitycollege.edu
CB member
CB code: 4311

- Public 2-year community and liberal arts college
- Commuter campus in very large city

General. Founded in 1910. Regionally accredited. **Enrollment:** 9,179 degree-seeking undergraduates. **Degrees:** 1,259 associate awarded. **ROTC:** Army, Air Force. **Location:** 185 miles from San Francisco. **Calendar:** Semester, extensive summer session. **Full-time faculty:** 332 total; 27% minority. **Part-time faculty:** 632 total; 26% minority. **Class size:** 28% < 20, 59% 20-39, 7% 40-49, 4% 50-99, 3% >100. **Special facilities:** Anthropology museum, greenhouse and koi pond, high-tech laboratory for disabled students.

Student profile.

Out-of-state:	2%	25 or older:	39%

Transfer out. Colleges most students transferred to 2011: California State University: Fresno, University of Phoenix, National University, Fresno Pacific University.

Basis for selection. Open admission, but selective for some programs. Limited admission to allied health programs, police academy, and apprenticeship programs.

2011-2012 Annual costs. Tuition/fees: $1,116; $6,396 out-of-state. Per-credit charge: $36 in-state; $212 out-of-state. Books/supplies: $1,640. Personal expenses: $2,818.

Financial aid. All financial aid based on need. Need-based aid available for part-time students. Work-study available nights, weekends and for part-time students. **Additional information:** Board of Governors Grant Program to offset enrollment fees based on untaxed income, low income, or calculated need. Students qualifying for program also automatically exempt from health fees. March 2 application deadline for California grants.

Application procedures. Admission: No deadline. No application fee. Application must be submitted online. Admission notification on a rolling basis. **Financial aid:** Priority date 4/15, closing date 6/30. FAFSA required. Applicants notified on a rolling basis starting 4/1.

Academics. Special study options: Accelerated study, cross-registration, distance learning, double major, dual enrollment of high school students, ESL, honors, independent study, internships, study abroad, weekend college. License preparation in dental hygiene, nursing, radiology, real estate. **Credit/placement by examination:** AP, CLEP, institutional tests. 48 credit hours maximum toward associate degree. **Support services:** Learning center, pre-admission summer program, reduced course load, remedial instruction, study skills assistance, tutoring, writing center.

Majors. Area/ethnic studies: African-American, Chicano/Hispanic-American/Latino, Native American, women's. **Business:** General, accounting, administrative services, banking/financial services, business admin, fashion, insurance, office/clerical, purchasing, real estate. **Communications:** Communications/speech/rhetoric, journalism. **Communications technology:** Graphic/printing. **Computer sciences:** General, computer science, data processing, information systems, programming. **Conservation:** General. **Education:** Bilingual, early childhood, multi-level teacher. **Engineering:** General. **English:** English lit, rhetoric/composition. **Foreign languages:** General, Spanish. **General:** Food science. **Health services:** Clinical lab technology, dental hygiene, medical assistant, medical radiologic technology/radiation therapy, medical records technology, medical secretary, medical transcription, nursing (RN), radiologic technology/medical imaging, respiratory therapy technology, substance abuse counseling. **History:** General. **Human services:** General, social work. **Liberal arts:** Arts/sciences, library assistant. **Math:** General. **Parks/recreation:** General, facilities management. **Physical sciences:** Chemistry. **Protective services:** Corrections, firefighting, law enforcement admin, police science. **Psychology:** General. **Social sciences:** General, anthropology, criminology, geography, sociology. **Visual/performing arts:** General, art, crafts, dance, dramatic, music, music management, photography, piano/keyboard, printmaking, theater design, voice/opera. **Work/family studies:** General, child care management, clothing/textiles, food/nutrition, institutional food production.

Most popular majors. Health sciences 30%, liberal arts 55%.

Computing on campus. 400 workstations in library, computer center. Commuter students can connect to campus network. Online course registration, online library, wireless network available.

Student life. Freshman orientation: Available. Preregistration for classes offered. **Activities:** Bands, choral groups, dance, drama, film society, international student organizations, literary magazine, music ensembles, musical theater, student government, student newspaper, symphony orchestra, TV station, Christian Athletes in Acting, MECHA, Pan American Association, Alpha Gamma Sigma, Phi Theta Kappa.

Athletics. NJCAA. **Intercollegiate:** Badminton, baseball M, basketball, cheerleading, cross-country, football (tackle) M, golf, soccer, softball W, tennis, track and field, volleyball W, wrestling M. **Intramural:** Basketball, football (non-tackle), soccer, softball, table tennis, volleyball, weight lifting. **Team name:** Rams.

Two-Year Colleges

Student services. Adult student services, career counseling, services for economically disadvantaged, student employment services, financial aid counseling, health services, minority student services, on-campus daycare, personal counseling, placement for graduates, veterans' counselor. **Physically disabled:** Services for visually, speech, hearing impaired. **Transfer:** Transfer center, transfer adviser, college fairs on campus for students transferring to 4-year colleges.

Contact. E-mail: info@scccd.com
Phone: (559) 442-4600 Toll-free number: (866) 245-3276
Fax: (559) 237-4232
John Cummings, District Dean of Admissions, Records and Institutional Research, Fresno City College, 1101 East University Avenue, Fresno, CA 93741

Fullerton College
Fullerton, California
www.fullcoll.edu
CB code: 4314

- Public 2-year community and technical college
- Commuter campus in small city
- SAT or ACT required

General. Founded in 1913. Regionally accredited. **Enrollment:** 14,614 degree-seeking undergraduates. **Degrees:** 1,270 associate awarded. **ROTC:** Naval. **Location:** 35 miles from Los Angeles. **Calendar:** Semester, extensive summer session. **Full-time faculty:** 306 total. **Part-time faculty:** 464 total.

Basis for selection. Open admission. College-administered English, reading, and math exams used for placement.

2011-2012 Annual costs. Tuition/fees: $1,112; $6,602 out-of-state. Per-credit charge: $36 in-state; $219 out-of-state. Books/supplies: $1,638. Personal expenses: $3,096.

Financial aid. Need-based: Work-study available nights, weekends and for part-time students.

Application procedures. Admission: No deadline. No application fee. Admission notification on a rolling basis. **Financial aid:** No deadline. FAFSA required. Applicants notified on a rolling basis.

Academics. Special study options: Distance learning, double major, dual enrollment of high school students, ESL, honors, independent study, internships, study abroad. License preparation in real estate. **Credit/placement by examination:** AP, CLEP, institutional tests. 15 credit hours maximum toward associate degree. **Support services:** Learning center, remedial instruction, study skills assistance, tutoring, writing center.

Majors. Architecture: Landscape. **Area/ethnic studies:** Latin American. **Biology:** General, bacteriology, zoology. **Business:** Accounting, administrative services, business admin, fashion, international, management information systems, purchasing, real estate, tourism promotion. **Communications:** Broadcast journalism, communications/speech/rhetoric, journalism. **Communications technology:** Graphic/printing. **Computer sciences:** General, applications programming, data processing. **Conservation:** General, fisheries, forestry. **Education:** Business, trade/industrial. **Engineering:** General. **English:** English lit, rhetoric/composition. **Foreign languages:** General. **General:** Horticulture, nursery operations. **Health services:** Clinical lab science, prenursing. **History:** General. **Liberal arts:** Arts/sciences, library assistant. **Math:** General. **Parks/recreation:** General. **Philosophy/religion:** Philosophy. **Physical sciences:** Astronomy, chemistry, geology, physics. **Protective services:** Police science. **Psychology:** General. **Social sciences:** Anthropology, economics, geography, political science, sociology. **Visual/performing arts:** General, art, commercial/advertising art, dance, design, dramatic, fashion design, music. **Work/family studies:** General, child care management, family studies.

Computing on campus. 400 workstations in library, computer center. Online course registration, helpline, wireless network available.

Student life. Activities: Bands, choral groups, dance, drama, film society, literary magazine, music ensembles, musical theater, radio station, student government, student newspaper, symphony orchestra, TV station, volunteer bureau, Movimiento Estudiantil Chicano de Aztlan.

Athletics. Intercollegiate: Badminton, baseball M, basketball, cross-country, diving, football (tackle) M, golf M, gymnastics, soccer, softball W, swimming, tennis, track and field, volleyball, water polo M. **Team name:** Hornets.

Student services. Adult student services, career counseling, student employment services, health services, on-campus daycare, personal counseling, placement for graduates, veterans' counselor. **Physically disabled:** Services for visually, speech, hearing impaired. **Transfer:** Transfer adviser for students transferring to 4-year colleges.

Contact. E-mail: admissions@fullcoll.edu
Phone: (714) 992-7568
Albert Abutin, Dean, Admissions and Records, Fullerton College, 321 East Chapman Avenue, Fullerton, CA 92832-2095

Gavilan College
Gilroy, California
www.gavilan.edu
CB code: 4678

- Public 2-year community college
- Large town

General. Founded in 1919. Regionally accredited. **Enrollment:** 3,855 degree-seeking undergraduates. **Degrees:** 360 associate awarded. **Location:** 35 miles from San Jose. **Calendar:** Semester, limited summer session. **Full-time faculty:** 78 total; 10% have terminal degrees. **Part-time faculty:** 215 total; 2% have terminal degrees. **Special facilities:** Golf course, hiking trails.

Transfer out. Colleges most students transferred to 2011: San Jose State, California State University: Monterey Bay, University of California: Santa Cruz.

Basis for selection. Open admission.

2011-2012 Annual costs. Tuition/fees: $1,122; $6,522 out-of-state. Per-credit charge: $36 in-state; $216 out-of-state. Books/supplies: $1,638. Personal expenses: $2,772.

Financial aid. Need-based: Work-study available nights, weekends and for part-time students.

Application procedures. Admission: No deadline. No application fee. Application must be submitted on paper. Admission notification on a rolling basis. **Financial aid:** Priority date 6/30; no closing date. FAFSA required. Applicants notified on a rolling basis starting 7/15; must reply within 2 week(s) of notification.

Academics. Special study options: Distance learning, dual enrollment of high school students, ESL, honors, independent study, internships, liberal arts/career combination, study abroad. License preparation in aviation, nursing. **Credit/placement by examination:** AP, CLEP, institutional tests. **Support services:** Learning center, reduced course load, remedial instruction, study skills assistance, tutoring, writing center.

Majors. Biology: General, ecology. **Business:** General. **Communications:** Communications/speech/rhetoric, journalism. **Computer sciences:** General, computer graphics. **English:** English lit. **Foreign languages:** Spanish. **Health services:** Nursing (RN). **History:** General. **Liberal arts:** Arts/sciences. **Math:** General. **Philosophy/religion:** Philosophy. **Physical sciences:** Astronomy, chemistry, geology. **Protective services:** Corrections. **Psychology:** General. **Social sciences:** General, anthropology, economics, geography, political science, sociology. **Visual/performing arts:** Art, art history/conservation, dramatic, music, music performance, studio arts, theater design.

Most popular majors. Education 6%, health sciences 18%, liberal arts 61%, security/protective services 6%.

Computing on campus. 600 workstations in library, computer center. Wireless network available.

Student life. Freshman orientation: Mandatory. Preregistration for classes offered. **Activities:** Choral groups, drama, literary magazine, music ensembles, musical theater, student government, student newspaper, symphony orchestra, TV station.

Athletics. Intercollegiate: Baseball M, basketball, football (tackle) M, golf, soccer W, softball W, tennis, volleyball W. **Team name:** Rams.

Student services. Adult student services, career counseling, services for economically disadvantaged, financial aid counseling, health services, on-campus daycare, personal counseling, veterans' counselor. **Physically disabled:** Services for visually, speech, hearing impaired. **Transfer:** Transfer center, transfer adviser, college fairs on campus for students transferring to 4-year colleges.

Contact. Phone: (408) 848-4735 Fax: (408) 848-4940
Candice Whitney, Director of Admissions and Records, Gavilan College, 5055 Santa Teresa Boulevard, Gilroy, CA 95020

Glendale Community College
Glendale, California
www.glendale.edu
CB code: 4327

◗ Public 2-year community college
◗ Commuter campus in small city

General. Founded in 1927. Regionally accredited. **Enrollment:** 19,523 undergraduates. **Degrees:** 511 associate awarded. **Location:** 10 miles from Los Angeles. **Calendar:** Semester, extensive summer session. **Full-time faculty:** 247 total; 27% minority. **Part-time faculty:** 516 total; 22% minority. **Class size:** 24% < 20, 57% 20-39, 13% 40-49, 5% 50-99, less than 1% >100. **Special facilities:** Science center with planetarium, Baja California (Mexico) field station.

Transfer out. Colleges most students transferred to 2011: California State University: Northridge, University of California: Los Angeles, California State University: Los Angeles, University of Southern California.

Basis for selection. Open admission, but selective for some programs. Nursing program has special requirements.

2011-2012 Annual costs. Tuition/fees: $1,135; $6,565 out-of-state. Per-credit charge: $36 in-state; $217 out-of-state. Books/supplies: $1,638. Personal expenses: $2,550.

Financial aid. All financial aid based on need. Need-based aid available for part-time students. Work-study available nights, weekends and for part-time students.

Application procedures. Admission: Priority date 4/15; no deadline. No application fee. Admission notification on a rolling basis. **Financial aid:** Priority date 4/15; no closing date. FAFSA, institutional form required. Applicants notified on a rolling basis starting 6/15; must reply within 2 week(s) of notification.

Academics. Special study options: Cooperative education, distance learning, dual enrollment of high school students, ESL, honors, independent study, internships, study abroad. License preparation in aviation, nursing, real estate. **Credit/placement by examination:** AP, CLEP, institutional tests. 12 credit hours maximum toward associate degree. **Support services:** GED preparation and test center, learning center, remedial instruction, study skills assistance, tutoring, writing center.

Honors college/program. Scholars program admits academically accomplished students and offers priority transfer opportunites at UCLA, USC, Pepperdine, and others.

Majors. Biology: General. **Business:** General, accounting, administrative services, hospitality/recreation, office management, real estate. **Communications:** Broadcast journalism, journalism. **Computer sciences:** General. **Education:** Early childhood, multi-level teacher. **English:** English lit, writing. **Foreign languages:** General, French, Spanish. **Health services:** Licensed practical nurse, medical assistant, medical secretary, nursing (RN). **History:** General. **Liberal arts:** Arts/sciences, humanities. **Math:** General. **Parks/recreation:** General. **Philosophy/religion:** Philosophy. **Physical sciences:** Chemistry, physics. **Protective services:** Fire safety technology, law enforcement admin, police science. **Psychology:** General. **Social sciences:** General, anthropology, economics, sociology. **Visual/performing arts:** General, commercial/advertising art, dance, theater design. **Work/family studies:** General, child care management, clothing/textiles, food/nutrition.

Most popular majors. Business/marketing 11%, health sciences 20%, liberal arts 49%.

Computing on campus. 1,000 workstations in library, computer center. Online course registration, helpline, repair service, wireless network available.

Student life. Freshman orientation: Available. Preregistration for classes offered. **Activities:** Bands, choral groups, dance, drama, international student organizations, literary magazine, music ensembles, Model UN, musical theater, radio station, student government, student newspaper, TV station, International Student Association, Armenian Student Association, Korean Christian Club, Organization of Latin for Higher Education, Association of Latin American Students.

Athletics. Intercollegiate: Baseball M, basketball, cross-country, football (tackle) M, soccer M, tennis, track and field, volleyball W. **Team name:** Vaqueros.

Student services. Adult student services, career counseling, services for economically disadvantaged, student employment services, financial aid counseling, health services, on-campus daycare, personal counseling, placement for graduates, veterans' counselor. **Physically disabled:** Services for visually, speech, hearing impaired. **Transfer:** Re-entry adviser for new students. Transfer center, transfer adviser, college fairs on campus for students transferring to 4-year colleges.

Contact. E-mail: info@glendale.edu
Phone: (818) 240-1000 ext. 5901 Fax: (818) 549-9436
Sharon Combs, Dean of Admissions and Records, Glendale Community College, 1500 North Verdugo Road, Glendale, CA 91208-2809

Golden West College
Huntington Beach, California
www.goldenwestcollege.edu
CB code: 4339

◗ Public 2-year community college
◗ Commuter campus in small city

General. Founded in 1966. Regionally accredited. **Enrollment:** 13,956 undergraduates. **Degrees:** 629 associate awarded. **Location:** 40 miles from Los Angeles. **Calendar:** Semester, limited summer session. **Full-time faculty:** 134 total. **Part-time faculty:** 315 total. **Class size:** 16% < 20, 58% 20-39, 9% 40-49, 13% 50-99, 3% >100. **Special facilities:** Outdoor amphitheatre, California native garden.

Transfer out. Colleges most students transferred to 2011: California State University: Long Beach, California State University: Dominguez Hills, California State University: Fullerton, University of California: Irvine, University of California: Los Angeles.

Basis for selection. Open admission, but selective for some programs. Any student at least 18 years of age eligible for admission. Limited admission to police academy and nursing program. Nursing applicants accepted on basis of prerequisite courses completed and GPA. SAT or ACT scores can be used for counseling and placement in lieu of institutional placement exams.

2011-2012 Annual costs. Tuition/fees: $1,142; $5,912 out-of-state. Per-credit charge: $36 in-state; $195 out-of-state. Parking fee is $30 per semester. Books/supplies: $700. Personal expenses: $1,800.

Financial aid. Need-based: Work-study available nights, weekends and for part-time students. **Non-need-based:** Scholarships awarded for academics.

Application procedures. Admission: Priority date 4/1; no deadline. No application fee. Admission notification on a rolling basis. **Financial aid:** Priority date 6/1; no closing date. FAFSA, institutional form required. Applicants notified on a rolling basis starting 7/1; must reply within 3 week(s) of notification.

Academics. Special study options: Accelerated study, cooperative education, cross-registration, distance learning, double major, dual enrollment of high school students, ESL, honors, independent study, study abroad, weekend college. License preparation in nursing, real estate. **Credit/placement by examination:** AP, CLEP, institutional tests. 6 credit hours maximum toward associate degree. **Support services:** Learning center, pre-admission summer program, reduced course load, remedial instruction, study skills assistance, tutoring, writing center.

Majors. Biology: General. **Business:** General, accounting, administrative services, business admin, office management, office technology, office/clerical, real estate, sales/distribution. **Communications:** Broadcast journalism, journalism, public relations. **Computer sciences:** General. **Education:** Physical. **English:** English lit, rhetoric/composition. **Foreign languages:** General, French, German, sign language interpretation, Spanish. **General:** Horticultural science. **Health services:** Nursing (RN), predental, premedicine, prepharmacy, preveterinary. **History:** General. **Liberal arts:** Arts/sciences. **Math:** General. **Philosophy/religion:** Philosophy. **Physical sciences:** Astronomy, chemistry, geology. **Protective services:** Criminal justice, law enforcement admin. **Psychology:** General. **Social sciences:** General, anthropology, economics, political science, sociology. **Visual/performing arts:** Art, commercial/advertising art, dance, dramatic, music, music performance, music theory/composition, photography, studio arts.

Computing on campus. Online course registration, online library, wireless network available.

Student life. Freshman orientation: Mandatory. Preregistration for classes offered. Program held prior to enrollment. **Activities:** Bands, choral groups, dance, drama, film society, international student organizations, literary magazine, music ensembles, musical theater, student government, student newspaper, honor society, student nurses organization, cosmetology club, French club, Circle K, Women of Action.

Athletics. NJCAA. Intercollegiate: Baseball M, cross-country, football (tackle) M, soccer, softball W, swimming, track and field, volleyball, water polo. **Team name:** Rustlers.

Student services. Adult student services, career counseling, services for economically disadvantaged, student employment services, health services, on-campus daycare, personal counseling, placement for graduates, veterans' counselor. **Physically disabled:** Services for visually, speech, hearing impaired. **Transfer:** Transfer center, transfer adviser, college fairs on campus for students transferring to 4-year colleges.

Contact. Phone: (714) 895-8306 Fax: (714) 895-8960
Shirley Donnelly, Director Enrollment Services, Golden West College, 15744 Golden West Street, Box 2748, Huntington Beach, CA 92647-2748

Golf Academy of America: San Diego
Carlsbad, California
www.golfacademy.edu   CB code: 3495

- For-profit 2-year college of golf course management
- Small city

General. Accredited by ACICS. **Enrollment:** 251 degree-seeking undergraduates. **Degrees:** 203 associate awarded. **Location:** San Diego, CA - 34 Miles. **Calendar:** Semester, limited summer session. **Full-time faculty:** 6 total. **Part-time faculty:** 13 total. **Special facilities:** Golf Ranges, Updated Golf Technology, Golf Club Repair Lab.

Basis for selection. Open admission. High school diploma or GED required. Application required, reviewed by the Director of Admissions. Serious medical conditions which may prevent a person from swinging a golf club may disqualify a prospective student.

2011-2012 Annual costs. Tuition/fees: $16,664.

Financial aid. Need-based: Work-study available nights, weekends and for part-time students.

Application procedures. Admission: No deadline. $50 fee. **Financial aid:** No deadline.

Academics. Credit/placement by examination: AP, CLEP.

Majors. Parks/recreation: Facilities management.

Student life. Freshman orientation: Available. Preregistration for classes offered.

Contact. E-mail: henry.salgado@golfacademy.edu
Phone: (760) 734-1208 Toll-free number: (800) 342-7342
Henry Salgado, Director of Admissions, Golf Academy of America: San Diego, 1950 Camino Vida Roble, Suite 125, Carlsbad, CA 92008

Grossmont College
El Cajon, California
www.grossmont.edu   CB code: 4334

- Public 2-year community college
- Commuter campus in small city

General. Founded in 1961. Regionally accredited. **Enrollment:** 13,958 degree-seeking undergraduates. **Degrees:** 1,142 associate awarded. **Location:** 25 miles from San Diego. **Calendar:** Semester, extensive summer session. **Full-time faculty:** 224 total; 28% minority, 54% women. **Part-time faculty:** 547 total; 24% minority. **Class size:** 19% < 20, 60% 20-39, 16% 40-49, 4% 50-99, less than 1% >100. **Special facilities:** Observatory.

Student profile.

Out-of-state:	2%	25 or older:	30%

Transfer out. Colleges most students transferred to 2011: San Diego State University, University of California San Diego, National University.

Basis for selection. Open admission, but selective for some programs. Limited admission to health professions programs.

2011-2012 Annual costs. Tuition/fees: $1,110; $6,810 out-of-state. Per-credit charge: $36 in-state; $226 out-of-state. Books/supplies: $1,500. Personal expenses: $2,000.

Financial aid. All financial aid based on need. Need-based aid available for part-time students. Work-study available nights, weekends and for part-time students.

Application procedures. Admission: No deadline. No application fee in-state; $163 out-of-state. Admission notification on a rolling basis. **Financial aid:** Priority date 3/2, closing date 6/30. FAFSA required. Applicants notified on a rolling basis starting 7/15; must reply within 2 week(s) of notification.

Academics. Special study options: Accelerated study, cross-registration, distance learning, double major, dual enrollment of high school students, ESL, honors, independent study, internships, student-designed major, study abroad. License preparation in nursing, occupational therapy. **Credit/placement by examination:** AP, CLEP, institutional tests. Students may earn a maximum of 18 units on the CLEP general examinations. **Support services:** Learning center, reduced course load, remedial instruction, tutoring, writing center.

Majors. Area/ethnic studies: Native American. **Biology:** General. **Business:** General, administrative services, business admin, executive assistant, hospitality admin, international, management science, marketing, sales/distribution, tourism promotion, tourism/travel. **Communications:** Broadcast journalism, communications/speech/rhetoric, digital media, journalism. **Computer sciences:** General, applications programming, computer science, LAN/WAN management, programming, webmaster. **English:** Creative writing, English lit, rhetoric/composition. **Foreign languages:** American Sign Language, Arabic, French, German, Japanese, Russian, Spanish. **Health services:** Athletic training, cardiovascular technology, nursing (RN), occupational therapy assistant, respiratory therapy technology, speech-language pathology assistant. **History:** General. **Liberal arts:** Arts/sciences. **Math:** General. **Parks/recreation:** Exercise sciences. **Philosophy/religion:** Philosophy. **Physical sciences:** Chemistry, geology, physics. **Protective services:** Corrections, forensics, police science, security services. **Social sciences:** Economics, geography, political science. **Visual/performing arts:** Acting, art history/conservation, ceramics, cinematography, dance, digital arts, drawing, jazz, music, musical theater, painting, photography, sculpture, theater design. **Work/family studies:** Child care management, child development.

Most popular majors. Business/marketing 11%, health sciences 14%, liberal arts 45%.

Computing on campus. 500 workstations in library, computer center. Online course registration, wireless network available.

Student life. Freshman orientation: Available. Preregistration for classes offered. **Activities:** Bands, choral groups, dance, drama, music ensembles, musical theater, radio station, student government, student newspaper, symphony orchestra.

Athletics. Intercollegiate: Baseball M, basketball, football (tackle) M, soccer W, softball W, swimming, tennis, volleyball, water polo. **Team name:** Griffins.

Student services. Adult student services, alcohol/substance abuse counseling, career counseling, services for economically disadvantaged, student employment services, financial aid counseling, health services, on-campus daycare, personal counseling, placement for graduates. **Physically disabled:** Services for visually, speech, hearing impaired. **Transfer:** Pre-admission transcript evaluation for new students. Transfer center, transfer adviser, college fairs on campus for students transferring to 4-year colleges.

Contact. Phone: (619) 644-7186 Fax: (619) 644-7933
Wendy Stewart, Dean Counseling and Enrollment Services, Grossmont College, 8800 Grossmont College Drive, El Cajon, CA 92020

Hartnell College
Salinas, California
www.hartnell.edu   CB code: 4340

- Public 2-year community college
- Commuter campus in small city

General. Founded in 1920. Regionally accredited. **Enrollment:** 4,260 degree-seeking undergraduates. **Degrees:** 459 associate awarded. **Location:** 110 miles from San Francisco, 65 miles from San Jose. **Calendar:** Semester, limited summer session. **Full-time faculty:** 88 total. **Part-time faculty:** 219 total.

Basis for selection. Open admission, but selective for some programs. Limited admission to nursing programs. Interview required for nursing, physician's assistant, animal health technician majors.

2011-2012 Annual costs. Tuition/fees: $1,088; $6,368 out-of-state. Per-credit charge: $36 in-state; $212 out-of-state. Books/supplies: $1,656. Personal expenses: $2,853.

Financial aid. Need-based: Work-study available nights, weekends and for part-time students.

Application procedures. Admission: No deadline. No application fee. Admission notification on a rolling basis. **Financial aid:** Priority date 8/1; no closing date. FAFSA required. Applicants notified on a rolling basis.

Academics. Special study options: Cooperative education. **Credit/placement by examination:** AP, CLEP. **Support services:** Learning center, remedial instruction, tutoring.

Majors. Biology: General. **Business:** Administrative services, banking/financial services, business admin, real estate. **Communications:** Digital media. **Computer sciences:** Information technology, programming, system admin, web page design. **Education:** Teacher assistance. **Engineering:** General. **English:** English lit. **General:** Agribusiness operations. **Health services:** Clinical lab technology, dental hygiene, nursing (RN), physician assistant, substance abuse counseling, veterinary technology/assistant. **History:** General. **Liberal arts:** Arts/sciences. **Math:** General. **Physical sciences:** Chemistry, geology, physics. **Protective services:** Corrections, firefighting, law enforcement admin. **Psychology:** General. **Social sciences:** General. **Visual/performing arts:** Art, dramatic, music, photography. **Work/family studies:** Child development.

Student life. Activities: Bands, choral groups, drama, music ensembles, musical theater, student government, student newspaper.

Athletics. Intercollegiate: Baseball M, basketball, cross-country M, football (tackle) M, soccer M. **Team name:** Panthers.

Student services. Career counseling, student employment services, personal counseling, placement for graduates.

Contact. Phone: (831) 755-6711 Fax: (831) 759-6014
Mary Dominguez, Director of Enrollment Services, Hartnell College, 411 Central Avenue, Salinas, CA 93901

Imperial Valley College
Imperial, California
www.imperial.edu

CB member
CB code: 4358

▶ Public 2-year community college
▶ Commuter campus in large town

General. Founded in 1922. Regionally accredited. **Enrollment:** 7,926 degree-seeking undergraduates. **Degrees:** 555 associate awarded. **Location:** 6 miles from El Centro. **Calendar:** Semester, limited summer session. **Full-time faculty:** 105 total; 22% have terminal degrees, 24% minority, 42% women. **Part-time faculty:** 188 total; 4% have terminal degrees, 58% minority, 37% women. **Class size:** 15% < 20, 69% 20-39, 14% 40-49, 2% 50-99. **Partnerships:** Formal partnership with Cisco.

Student profile. Among degree-seeking undergraduates, 1,568 enrolled as first-time, first-year students.

Part-time:	52%	Women:	56%
Out-of-state:	2%	25 or older:	32%

Transfer out. Colleges most students transferred to 2011: San Diego State University, California State Polytechnic University: Pomona, California State University: San Marcos, California State University: San Bernadino, California State University: Long Beach.

Basis for selection. Open admission, but selective for some programs. Limited admission for registered nursing program. **Adult students:** SAT/ACT scores not required.

High school preparation. College-preparatory program recommended.

2011-2012 Annual costs. Tuition/fees: $1,140; $7,710 out-of-state. Per-credit charge: $36 in-state; $255 out-of-state. Books/supplies: $1,656. Personal expenses: $3,105.

2010-2011 Financial aid. All financial aid based on need. 98% of total undergraduate aid awarded as scholarships/grants, 2% as loans/jobs. Need-based aid available for part-time students. Work-study available nights, weekends and for part-time students.

Application procedures. Admission: No deadline. No application fee. Application must be submitted online. Admission notification on a rolling basis. **Financial aid:** Priority date 3/2, closing date 6/30. FAFSA required. Applicants notified on a rolling basis starting 5/1.

Academics. Special study options: Accelerated study, distance learning, double major, dual enrollment of high school students, ESL, liberal arts/

career combination. License preparation in nursing, paramedic. **Credit/placement by examination:** AP, CLEP, institutional tests. 15 credit hours maximum toward associate degree. **Support services:** GED test center, learning center, reduced course load, remedial instruction, study skills assistance, tutoring, writing center.

Majors. Biology: General. **Business:** Accounting technology, administrative services, banking/financial services, business admin, marketing, office technology, office/clerical. **Communications:** Communications/speech/rhetoric, journalism. **Computer sciences:** General, computer science, web page design. **Education:** Early childhood, elementary. **Engineering:** General. **English:** English lit. **Foreign languages:** General, American Sign Language, Arabic, French, Spanish. **General:** Business. **Health services:** EMT paramedic, licensed practical nurse, nursing (RN), substance abuse counseling. **History:** General. **Liberal arts:** Arts/sciences, humanities. **Math:** General. **Parks/recreation:** Health/fitness. **Physical sciences:** General. **Protective services:** Corrections, firefighting, law enforcement admin. **Psychology:** General. **Social sciences:** General, anthropology. **Visual/performing arts:** Art, music. **Work/family studies:** Child development.

Most popular majors. Computer/information sciences 15%, education 18%, family/consumer sciences 7%, health sciences 11%, mathematics 7%, psychology 9%, public administration/social services 13%, security/protective services 6%.

Computing on campus. 90 workstations in library, computer center. Commuter students can connect to campus network. Online course registration, online library, helpline, wireless network available.

Student life. Freshman orientation: Available. Preregistration for classes offered. One day program. **Policies:** Smoke free campus. **Activities:** Jazz band, choral groups, music ensembles, student government, student newspaper, Christian club, Movimiento Estudiantil Chicano de Aztlan, Upward Bound club, French club, Spirit club, Adventure club, Agriculture club, Business club, Educational Talent Search club, Lamplighter's club.

Athletics. NJCAA. Intercollegiate: Baseball M, basketball, cheerleading, cross-country W, soccer, softball W, tennis, volleyball W. **Team name:** Arabs.

Student services. Adult student services, alcohol/substance abuse counseling, career counseling, services for economically disadvantaged, student employment services, financial aid counseling, health services, on-campus daycare, personal counseling, veterans' counselor. **Physically disabled:** Services for visually, speech, hearing impaired. **Transfer:** Pre-admission transcript evaluation for new students. Transfer center, transfer adviser, college fairs on campus for students transferring to 4-year colleges.

Contact. Phone: (760) 352-8320 Fax: (760) 355-2663
Gloria Carmona, Director of Admissions & Records, Imperial Valley College, Box 158, Imperial, CA 92251-0158

Institute of Technology: Clovis
Clovis, California
www.it-colleges.edu

▶ For-profit 2-year culinary school and career college
▶ Small city

General. Regionally accredited; also accredited by ACCSC. **Enrollment:** 1,214 degree-seeking undergraduates. **Degrees:** 330 associate awarded. **Calendar:** Differs by program. **Full-time faculty:** 131 total. **Part-time faculty:** 63 total.

Basis for selection. Admission requirements vary by programs.

2011-2012 Annual costs. Baking and Pastry Specialist: $18,837.50; 40 weeks. Culinary Arts Professional (AOS): $30,892.50; 60 weeks. Culinary Arts Specialist: $18,837.50; 30 weeks. Heating, Ventilation and Air Conditioning: $18,315; 40 weeks. Network Support Technician: $16,986.50; 40 weeks. Web and Graphic Design: $16,986.50; 40 weeks. Medical Billing/Coding Specialist: $16,986.50; 40 weeks. Medical Office Administration: $16,986.50; 40 weeks. Pharmacy Technician: $16,982.50; 40 weeks. Professional Medical Assistant: $16,986.50; 40 weeks. Accounting (AAS): $27,367.50; 75 weeks. Administrative Office Professional: $16,986.50; 40 weeks. Computerized Accounting (Diploma): $16,986.50; 40 weeks. Human Resource Administrator (AAS): $27,367.50; 60 weeks. Criminology/Emergency Response (AAS): $24,135.00; 65 weeks.

Financial aid. Need-based: Work-study available nights, weekends and for part-time students.

Application procedures. Admission: $75 fee.

Academics. **Credit/placement by examination:** AP, CLEP.

Majors. **Business:** Accounting, human resources. **Social sciences:** Criminology.

Contact. E-mail: rgardner@it-email.com
Phone: (559) 297-4500
Ron Gardner, Director of Admissions, Institute of Technology: Clovis,
564 West Herndon Avenue, Clovis, CA 93612

Irvine Valley College
Irvine, California
www.ivc.edu
CB code: 3356

⬧ Public 2-year community college
⬧ Commuter campus in small city

General. Regionally accredited. **Enrollment:** 14,037 undergraduates. **Degrees:** 630 associate awarded. **ROTC:** Air Force. **Location:** 50 miles from Los Angeles. **Calendar:** Semester, extensive summer session. **Full-time faculty:** 125 total. **Part-time faculty:** 356 total. **Special facilities:** Dance studio, Microsoft Office user specialist testing site, telescope, performing arts center.

Transfer out. **Colleges most students transferred to 2011:** University of California: Irvine, California State University: Fullerton.

Basis for selection. Open admission.

2011-2012 Annual costs. Tuition/fees: $1,114; $6,484 out-of-state. Per-credit charge: $36 in-state; $215 out-of-state. Books/supplies: $1,638. Personal expenses: $2,826.

Financial aid. All financial aid based on need. Need-based aid available for part-time students. Work-study available nights, weekends and for part-time students.

Application procedures. **Admission:** No deadline. No application fee. Admission notification on a rolling basis. **Financial aid:** No deadline. FAFSA, institutional form required. Applicants notified on a rolling basis starting 4/30.

Academics. **Special study options:** Accelerated study, cooperative education, cross-registration, distance learning, double major, dual enrollment of high school students, ESL, honors, independent study, internships, study abroad, weekend college. **Credit/placement by examination:** AP, CLEP, institutional tests. 12 credit hours maximum toward associate degree. Minimum 2.0 GPA in at least 12 units completed at IVC required to enroll in credit by examination. **Support services:** Learning center, remedial instruction, study skills assistance, tutoring, writing center.

Majors. **Area/ethnic studies:** Women's. **Biology:** General, ecology. **Business:** General, accounting, business admin, office management, office technology, real estate. **Communications:** Advertising. **Computer sciences:** General, applications programming, networking, programming, systems analysis. **Conservation:** General. **Education:** Early childhood, physical. **English:** British lit, rhetoric/composition, writing. **Foreign languages:** French, Spanish. **History:** General. **Liberal arts:** Arts/sciences. **Math:** General. **Parks/recreation:** Health/fitness. **Philosophy/religion:** Philosophy. **Physical sciences:** Chemistry, geology. **Protective services:** Law enforcement admin, police science. **Psychology:** General. **Social sciences:** Anthropology, economics, geography, political science, sociology. **Visual/performing arts:** General, art, dance, dramatic, music, photography, studio arts, theater design.

Most popular majors. Business/marketing 9%, liberal arts 77%.

Computing on campus. 250 workstations in library, computer center. Commuter students can connect to campus network. Online course registration, online library, helpline available.

Student life. **Freshman orientation:** Mandatory. Preregistration for classes offered. **Housing:** Homestay referral for international students available. **Activities:** Bands, choral groups, dance, drama, literary magazine, music ensembles, musical theater, student government, student newspaper, symphony orchestra, administration of justice club, Phi Theta Kappa honor society, Muslim Student Association, biology society, dance club, geology club, health sciences society, journalism club, Phi Theta Kappa, Psi Beta.

Athletics. **Intercollegiate:** Badminton W, baseball M, basketball, cross-country, golf, soccer, softball W, tennis, volleyball. **Intramural:** Basketball, soccer, tennis, volleyball. **Team name:** Lasers.

Student services. Adult student services, career counseling, services for economically disadvantaged, student employment services, financial aid counseling, health services, on-campus daycare, personal counseling, placement for graduates, veterans' counselor, women's services. **Physically disabled:** Services for visually, speech, hearing impaired. **Transfer:** Re-entry adviser for new students. Transfer center, transfer adviser, college fairs on campus for students transferring to 4-year colleges.

Contact. E-mail: admissions@ivc.edu
Phone: (949) 451-5461 Fax: (949) 451-5443
Arleen Elseroad, Director of Admissions, Records & Enrollment Services, Irvine Valley College, 5500 Irvine Center Drive, Irvine, CA 92618-4399

Kaplan College: Palm Springs
Palm Springs, California
www.kc-palmsprings.com

⬧ For-profit 2-year health science and technical college
⬧ Commuter campus in large town

General. Accredited by ACCSC. **Enrollment:** 652 degree-seeking undergraduates. **Degrees:** 62 associate awarded. **Calendar:** Differs by program. **Full-time faculty:** 11 total. **Part-time faculty:** 21 total.

Basis for selection. Open admission, but selective for some programs. Prospective student must meet with an Admissions Representative, provide a high school diploma or GED, pass an entrance assessment and pay the applicable enrollment fee. Students must also complete the Financial Aid process or make payment arrangements with the college. **Home schooled:** State high school equivalency certificate required.

2011-2012 Annual costs. Tuition varies by program from $13,135 (fees $945) to $28,056 (fees $1,895).

Financial aid. **Need-based:** Work-study available nights, weekends and for part-time students.

Application procedures. **Admission:** $10 fee.

Academics. **Special study options:** Accelerated study, internships. **Credit/placement by examination:** AP, CLEP. **Support services:** Study skills assistance, tutoring.

Student life. **Freshman orientation:** Mandatory. Preregistration for classes offered.

Student services. Financial aid counseling.

Contact. Phone: (760) 327-4562
Leslie Rowden, Director of Admissions, Kaplan College: Palm Springs, 2475 East Tahquitz Canyon Way, Palm Springs, CA 92262

Kaplan College: Panorama City
Panorama City, California
www.panorama-city.kaplancollege.com/
CB code: 3541

⬧ For-profit 2-year junior and technical college
⬧ Commuter campus in very large city
⬧ Interview required

General. Accredited by ACICS. **Degrees:** 26 associate awarded. **Location:** 15 miles from Los Angeles. **Calendar:** Differs by program. **Full-time faculty:** 6 total. **Part-time faculty:** 8 total. **Class size:** 86% < 20, 14% 20-39.

Basis for selection. Open admission. **Home schooled:** Interview required.

2011-2012 Annual costs. Tuition varies by program from $14,240 (fees $408) to $30,126 (fees $1,545).

Financial aid. All financial aid based on need. Work-study available nights, weekends and for part-time students.

Application procedures. **Admission:** No deadline. No application fee. Application must be submitted on paper. **Financial aid:** No deadline. FAFSA, institutional form required.

Academics. **Special study options:** Internships, liberal arts/career combination. **Credit/placement by examination:** AP, CLEP. **Support services:** Learning center, study skills assistance, tutoring.

Majors. **Business:** Accounting, accounting technology, accounting/business management, business admin, office management. **Computer sciences:** Information technology, LAN/WAN management, system admin.

Most popular majors. Business/marketing 17%, computer/information sciences 35%, legal studies 46%.

Computing on campus. 20 workstations in library, computer center. Online library available.

Student life. Freshman orientation: Mandatory. Preregistration for classes offered. **Activities:** Student newspaper.

Student services. Career counseling, student employment services, financial aid counseling, placement for graduates.

Contact. E-mail: enalvarez@kaplan.edu
Phone: (818) 672-3000 Toll-free number: (800) 206-0095
Fax: (818) 672-8919
Enrique Alvarez, Director of Admissions, Kaplan College: Panorama City, 14355 Roscoe Boulevard, Panorama City, CA 91402

Kaplan College: Sacramento
Sacramento, California
www.mariccollege.edu

- For-profit 2-year business and technical college
- Commuter campus in large city

General. Accredited by ACICS. **Degrees:** 51 associate awarded. **Calendar:** Differs by program. **Full-time faculty:** 9 total. **Part-time faculty:** 31 total.

Basis for selection. Open admission, but selective for some programs.

2011-2012 Annual costs. Tuition varies by program from $13,103 (fees $1,602) to $29,965 (fees $1,670).

Financial aid. Need-based: Work-study available nights, weekends and for part-time students.

Application procedures. Admission: No deadline. $10 fee.

Academics. Credit/placement by examination: AP, CLEP.

Student life. Freshman orientation: Available. Preregistration for classes offered.

Contact. E-mail: admissions@mariccollege.edu
Phone: (916) 649-8168
Keever Jankovich, Director of Admissions, Kaplan College: Sacramento, 4330 Watt Avenue, Suite 400, Sacramento, CA 95821

Kaplan College: Salida
Salida, California
www.mariccollege.edu

- For-profit 2-year health science and technical college
- Commuter campus in small city
- Interview required

General. Accredited by ACCSC. **Degrees:** 150 associate awarded. **Calendar:** Differs by program. **Full-time faculty:** 25 total. **Part-time faculty:** 21 total.

Basis for selection. Open admission. **Home schooled:** Transcript of courses and grades required.

2011-2012 Annual costs. Tuition varies by program from $13,185 (fees $943) to $44,260 (fees $3,352).

Financial aid. Need-based: Work-study available nights, weekends and for part-time students.

Application procedures. Admission: No deadline. $45 fee. Application must be submitted on paper.

Academics. Credit/placement by examination: AP, CLEP.

Majors. Health services: Respiratory therapy assistant, surgical technology. **Protective services:** Criminal justice.

Most popular majors. Health sciences 63%.

Computing on campus. 90 workstations in computer center.

Student life. Freshman orientation: Mandatory, $20 fee. Preregistration for classes offered.

Student services. Adult student services, career counseling, financial aid counseling, placement for graduates, veterans' counselor.

Contact. Phone: (209) 543-7000
Doug Stucker, Director of Admissions, Kaplan College: Salida, 5172 Kiernan Court, Salida, CA 95368

Kaplan College: San Diego
San Diego, California
www.kaplancollege.com   **CB code: 3064**

- For-profit 2-year business and health science college
- Commuter campus in very large city

General. Accredited by ACCSC. **Degrees:** 200 associate awarded. **Calendar:** Differs by program. **Full-time faculty:** 48 total. **Part-time faculty:** 46 total.

Basis for selection. Open admission, but selective for some programs.

2011-2012 Annual costs. Diploma programs range from $4,868 to $33,011. Associate programs: Criminal Justice $29,986; Health Information Technology $29,273; Nursing $54,438. Fees, books and supplies included. Personal expenses: $2,925.

Financial aid. Need-based: Work-study available nights, weekends and for part-time students.

Application procedures. Admission: $10 fee.

Academics. Credit/placement by examination: AP, CLEP.

Majors. Business: Business admin.

Student life. Freshman orientation: Available. Preregistration for classes offered.

Contact. Phone: (858) 279-4500 Toll-free number: (800) 400-8232
Fax: (858) 279-4885
Serica Martinez, Director of Admissions, Kaplan College: San Diego, 9055 Balboa Avenue, San Diego, CA 92123

Kaplan College: Vista
Vista, California
www.mariccollege.edu

- For-profit 2-year technical college
- Commuter campus in small city

General. Accredited by ACCSC. **Degrees:** 34 associate awarded. **Calendar:** Differs by program. **Full-time faculty:** 12 total. **Part-time faculty:** 39 total.

Basis for selection. Open admission, but selective for some programs. Institutional entrance exam important. High school diploma/GED required for some programs. Timed institutional examination administered onsite.

2011-2012 Annual costs. Associate degree program: Criminal Justice $28,742. Diploma program: Vocational Nursing $32,093, other diploma program costs range from $4,867-$26,643.

Financial aid. Need-based: Work-study available nights, weekends and for part-time students.

Application procedures. Admission: No deadline. $10 fee.

Academics. Credit/placement by examination: AP, CLEP.

Majors. Computer sciences: LAN/WAN management. **Protective services:** Criminal justice.

Student life. Freshman orientation: Available. Preregistration for classes offered.

Contact. Phone: (760) 630-1555 Fax: (760) 630-1656
Renee Codner, Director of Admissions, Kaplan College: Vista, 2022 University Drive, Vista, CA 92083

Lake Tahoe Community College
South Lake Tahoe, California
www.ltcc.edu   CB code: 4420

- Public 2-year community college
- Commuter campus in large town

General. Founded in 1975. Regionally accredited. The wooded 164-acre campus is located in the Sierra Nevada mountains near the south shore of Lake Tahoe. **Enrollment:** 3,000 undergraduates. **Degrees:** 152 associate awarded. **Location:** 55 miles from Reno, Nevada, 110 miles from Sacramento. **Calendar:** Quarter, limited summer session. **Full-time faculty:** 41 total; 51% women. **Part-time faculty:** 175 total. **Special facilities:** Demonstration garden.

Transfer out. Colleges most students transferred to 2011: California State University, University of California, and University of Nevada: Reno.

Basis for selection. Open admission. Open admission policy for students who are at least 18 or have graduated from high school. Special admission criteria apply to international students. **Learning Disabled:** Assistance is available through the Disability Resource Center.

2011-2012 Annual costs. Tuition/fees: $1,092; $7,347 out-of-state. Per-credit charge: $24 in-state; $163 out-of-state. Out-of-state tuition reduction plan available to Nevada residents. Books/supplies: $1,656. Personal expenses: $3,114.

Financial aid. Need-based: Need-based aid available for part-time students. Work-study available nights, weekends and for part-time students.

Application procedures. Admission: No deadline. No application fee. Application must be submitted online. Admission notification on a rolling basis. **Financial aid:** Priority date 5/1; no closing date. FAFSA required. Applicants notified on a rolling basis starting 7/1; must reply within 2 week(s) of notification.

Academics. Special study options: Cooperative education, distance learning, double major, ESL, internships. License preparation in dental hygiene, real estate. **Credit/placement by examination:** AP, CLEP, institutional tests. **Support services:** GED preparation, learning center, reduced course load, remedial instruction, study skills assistance, tutoring, writing center.

Majors. Business: General, accounting, administrative services, entrepreneurial studies, finance, marketing, office/clerical. **Education:** Early childhood. **English:** English lit. **Foreign languages:** Spanish. **Health services:** Medical assistant, medical records admin, substance abuse counseling. **Liberal arts:** Arts/sciences, humanities. **Math:** General. **Parks/recreation:** Health/fitness. **Protective services:** Firefighting, law enforcement admin. **Psychology:** General. **Social sciences:** General, anthropology, sociology. **Visual/performing arts:** Art, dance, dramatic, music, studio arts.

Computing on campus. 200 workstations in library, computer center, student center. Online course registration, online library, wireless network available.

Student life. Freshman orientation: Available. Preregistration for classes offered. Held during the registration period for each quarter. Orientation, assessment, and advising assist new students to determine the appropriate level of coursework and provide comprehensive information to foster success during the first term of enrollment. **Activities:** Choral groups, dance, drama, music ensembles, musical theater, student government, Alpha Gamma Sigma, art club, international club, math club, Performing Arts League, Rotoract.

Student services. Adult student services, career counseling, services for economically disadvantaged, student employment services, financial aid counseling, minority student services, on-campus daycare, personal counseling, placement for graduates, veterans' counselor. **Physically disabled:** Services for visually, speech, hearing impaired. **Transfer:** Transfer center, transfer adviser, college fairs on campus for students transferring to 4-year colleges.

Contact. E-mail: admissions@ltcc.edu
Phone: (530) 541-4660 ext. 211 Fax: (530) 542-1781
Cheri Jones, Director of Admissions & Records, Lake Tahoe Community College, One College Drive, South Lake Tahoe, CA 96150-4524

Laney College
Oakland, California
www.laney.peralta.edu   CB code: 4406

- Public 2-year community college
- Commuter campus in large city

General. Founded in 1953. Regionally accredited. Vocational programs include programs with PGE and a solar program with UC Lawrence Laboratories. **Enrollment:** 5,670 degree-seeking undergraduates. **Degrees:** 537 associate awarded. **Location:** 10 miles from San Francisco. **Calendar:** Semester, extensive summer session. **Full-time faculty:** 124 total. **Part-time faculty:** 300 total. **Special facilities:** CAD laboratory.

Student profile.

Out-of-state: 2%   **25 or older:**   61%

Transfer out. Colleges most students transferred to 2011: California State University: East Bay, San Francisco State, University of California: Berkeley.

Basis for selection. Open admission.

2011-2012 Annual costs. Tuition/fees: $1,118; $6,428 out-of-state. Per-credit charge: $36 in-state; $213 out-of-state. Books/supplies: $1,656. Personal expenses: $3,096.

Financial aid. Need-based: Work-study available nights, weekends and for part-time students.

Application procedures. Admission: No deadline. No application fee. Admission notification on a rolling basis. **Financial aid:** Priority date 4/1, closing date 6/30. FAFSA, institutional form required. Applicants notified on a rolling basis; must reply within 2 week(s) of notification.

Academics. Special study options: Cooperative education, distance learning, dual enrollment of high school students, ESL, honors, independent study, liberal arts/career combination, weekend college. **Credit/placement by examination:** AP, CLEP, institutional tests. **Support services:** Learning center, remedial instruction, study skills assistance, tutoring.

Majors. Area/ethnic studies: African-American, Asian, Latin American. **Business:** General, accounting, administrative services, banking/financial services, management information systems, office technology, office/clerical, operations, sales/distribution. **Communications:** Broadcast journalism, journalism. **Communications technology:** General, graphic/printing. **Computer sciences:** General, information systems. **Education:** General. **English:** English lit. **Liberal arts:** Arts/sciences. **Math:** General. **Social sciences:** General. **Visual/performing arts:** Art, ceramics, commercial/advertising art, dance, design, dramatic, music.

Computing on campus. 400 workstations in library, computer center, student center. Online course registration, online library available.

Student life. Freshman orientation: Mandatory. Preregistration for classes offered. **Activities:** Pep band, dance, drama, literary magazine, musical theater, student government, student newspaper, TV station.

Athletics. Intercollegiate: Badminton W, baseball M, basketball M, football (tackle) M, softball W, swimming, track and field W, volleyball W, water polo W. **Team name:** Eagles.

Student services. Adult student services, career counseling, services for economically disadvantaged, student employment services, financial aid counseling, health services, minority student services, on-campus daycare, personal counseling, placement for graduates. **Physically disabled:** Services for visually, speech, hearing impaired. **Transfer:** Re-entry adviser for new students. Transfer center, transfer adviser, college fairs on campus for students transferring to 4-year colleges.

Contact. E-mail: admissions@peralta.edu
Phone: (510) 464-3121 Fax: (510) 464-3240
Ron Gerhard, Director of Admissions and Records, Laney College, 900 Fallon Street, Oakland, CA 94607

Las Positas College
Livermore, California
www.laspositascollege.edu   CB code: 6507

- Public 2-year community college
- Commuter campus in small city

General. Founded in 1991. Regionally accredited. **Enrollment:** 9,153 undergraduates. **Degrees:** 529 associate awarded. **Location:** 43 miles from San Francsico, 39 miles from San Jose. **Calendar:** Semester, limited summer session. **Full-time faculty:** 107 total. **Part-time faculty:** 260 total.

Transfer out. Colleges most students transferred to 2011: California State University: East Bay.

Basis for selection. Open admission. High school diploma or GED required for student under 18 years.

2011-2012 Annual costs. Tuition/fees: $1,108; $7,198 out-of-state. Per-credit charge: $36 in-state; $239 out-of-state. Books/supplies: $1,656. Personal expenses: $3,114.

Financial aid. Need-based: Work-study available nights, weekends and for part-time students.

Application procedures. Admission: No deadline. No application fee. Admission notification on a rolling basis. **Financial aid:** Priority date 5/1; no closing date. Institutional form required. Applicants notified on a rolling basis starting 7/1; must reply within 2 week(s) of notification.

Academics. Special study options: Accelerated study, distance learning, dual enrollment of high school students, ESL, honors, independent study, internships, student-designed major. **Credit/placement by examination:** AP, CLEP. **Support services:** Learning center, remedial instruction, tutoring.

Computing on campus. 285 workstations in library, computer center.

Student life. Freshman orientation: Available. Preregistration for classes offered. **Activities:** Jazz band, choral groups, dance, drama, international student organizations, literary magazine, music ensembles, musical theater, student government, student newspaper.

Athletics. Intercollegiate: Basketball, cross-country, soccer. **Intramural:** Basketball, bowling, fencing, handball M, racquetball, skin diving, soccer, swimming, volleyball. **Team name:** Hawks.

Student services. Adult student services, career counseling, student employment services, financial aid counseling, health services, personal counseling, veterans' counselor. **Physically disabled:** Services for visually, speech, hearing impaired. **Transfer:** Transfer center, transfer adviser, college fairs on campus for students transferring to 4-year colleges.

Contact. Phone: (925) 424-1000 Fax: (925) 443-0742
Sylvia Rodriguez, Registrar, Las Positas College, 3033 Collier Canyon Road, Livermore, CA 94551

Lassen Community College
Susanville, California
www.lassencollege.edu   CB code: 4383

- Public 2-year community college
- Small town

General. Founded in 1925. Regionally accredited. **Enrollment:** 1,087 degree-seeking undergraduates. **Degrees:** 130 associate awarded. **Location:** 100 miles from Chico, 84 miles from Reno, Nevada. **Calendar:** Semester, limited summer session. **Full-time faculty:** 40 total. **Part-time faculty:** 97 total.

Student profile.

Out-of-state: 7%   Live on campus: 3%

Basis for selection. Open admission, but selective for some programs. Limited admission to nursing program.

2011-2012 Annual costs. Tuition/fees: $1,103; $7,073 out-of-state. Per-credit charge: $36 in-state; $235 out-of-state. Room/board: $5,564. Books/supplies: $1,620. Personal expenses: $2,250.

Financial aid. Need-based: Work-study available nights, weekends and for part-time students. **Additional information:** Board of Governors Grant: low-income California residents can have registration fees waived.

Application procedures. Admission: No deadline. No application fee. Admission notification on a rolling basis. Institutional placement tests recommended. **Financial aid:** Priority date 7/1; no closing date. FAFSA required. Applicants notified on a rolling basis starting 7/1; must reply within 2 week(s) of notification.

Academics. Gunsmithing and summer NRA programs offered. **Special study options:** Cooperative education, distance learning, dual enrollment of high school students, honors, independent study, internships. **Credit/placement by examination:** AP, CLEP, institutional tests. 15 credit hours maximum toward associate degree. **Support services:** Learning center, pre-admission summer program, reduced course load, remedial instruction, tutoring.

Majors. Business: General, accounting, administrative services, business admin, management information systems, office technology, office/clerical,

real estate. **Communications:** Journalism. **Computer sciences:** General, applications programming. **Education:** General, early childhood, physical. **Health services:** Nursing (RN), nursing assistant. **Liberal arts:** Arts/sciences. **Math:** General. **Protective services:** Corrections, law enforcement admin, police science. **Social sciences:** General. **Visual/performing arts:** Art.

Computing on campus. 40 workstations in computer center.

Student life. Housing: Coed dorms available. **Activities:** Choral groups, drama, film society, student government, student newspaper, over 20 student organizations and clubs.

Athletics. NJCAA. **Intercollegiate:** Baseball M, basketball, cross-country, golf, rifle, softball W, track and field, volleyball W, wrestling M. **Intramural:** Skiing.

Student services. Career counseling, health services, on-campus daycare, personal counseling, veterans' counselor. **Physically disabled:** Services for visually, speech, hearing impaired. **Transfer:** Transfer adviser, college fairs on campus for students transferring to 4-year colleges.

Contact. Phone: (530) 251-8808 Fax: (530) 257-8964
Registrar and Admissions Director, Lassen Community College, Box 3000, Susanville, CA 96130

Le Cordon Bleu College of Culinary Arts: Los Angeles
Pasadena, California
www.chefs.edu/los-angeles

- For-profit 2-year culinary school
- Commuter campus in very large city
- Interview required

General. Regionally accredited; also accredited by ACICS. Le Cordon Bleu college. **Enrollment:** 2,258 degree-seeking undergraduates. **Degrees:** 911 associate awarded. **Location:** 15 miles from downtown Los Angeles. **Calendar:** Differs by program, extensive summer session. **Full-time faculty:** 79 total; 1% have terminal degrees, 30% minority. **Part-time faculty:** 5 total; 80% minority. **Special facilities:** Fine-dining restaurant and casual cafe where students gain practical work experience.

Basis for selection. Open admission. High school diploma/GED, entrance examination required. Students whose first language is not English are required to submit evidence of English Proficiency. This may be done by submitting a TOEFL test score of 500 or higher (for the CPT version, a score of 150 or higher). Entrance Test is required by state agency for diploma programs. Wonderlic SLE Exam used to comply with these regulations. **Learning Disabled:** Students requesting special needs and services required to submit Application for Auxiliary Aid request. Application must include supporting documentation as evidence of disability.

2011-2012 Annual costs. Diploma programs: Culinary Arts $21,576, books and supplies $1,574. Baking and Pastry Arts $26,075, books and supplies $2,077. Associate programs: Culinary Arts $44,717, books and supplies $2,430. Baking and Pastry Arts $34,977, books and supplies $2,501. Restaurant, Culinary, and Catering Management/Manager $31,980, books and supplies $3,028.

Financial aid. Need-based: Need-based aid available for part-time students. Work-study available nights, weekends and for part-time students.

Application procedures. Admission: No deadline. $50 fee. Admission notification on a rolling basis. **Financial aid:** No deadline. FAFSA required. Applicants notified on a rolling basis.

Academics. Credit/placement by examination: AP, CLEP. **Support services:** Learning center, study skills assistance, tutoring.

Computing on campus. 40 workstations in library, computer center, student center. Commuter students can connect to campus network. Online library available.

Student life. Freshman orientation: Mandatory. Preregistration for classes offered. **Activities:** International student organizations, student newspaper.

Student services. Adult student services, career counseling, financial aid counseling, placement for graduates. **Transfer:** Re-entry adviser, pre-admission transcript evaluation for new students.

Two-Year Colleges

Contact. E-mail: admissionsinfo@la.chefs.edu
Phone: (626) 229-1300 Toll-free number: (888) 900-2433
Fax: (626) 585-0486
Ildiko Marschik, Vice President of Admissions, Le Cordon Bleu College of Culinary Arts: Los Angeles, 530 East Colorado Boulevard, Pasadena, CA 91101

Long Beach City College
Long Beach, California
www.lbcc.edu   **CB code: 4388**

◗ Public 2-year community college
◗ Commuter campus in large city

General. Founded in 1927. Regionally accredited. **Enrollment:** 15,186 degree-seeking undergraduates. **Degrees:** 746 associate awarded. **Location:** 20 miles from downtown Los Angeles. **Calendar:** Semester, limited summer session. **Full-time faculty:** 317 total. **Part-time faculty:** 612 total. **Class size:** 35% < 20, 47% 20-39, 10% 40-49, 7% 50-99, 1% >100.

Student profile.

Out-of-state:	1%	25 or older:	51%

Transfer out. Colleges most students transferred to 2011: California State University: Long Beach, California State University: Dominguez Hills, California State University: Los Angeles, California State University: Fullerton, University of California: Los Angeles.

Basis for selection. Open admission.

2011-2012 Annual costs. Tuition/fees: $1,154; $6,644 out-of-state. Per-credit charge: $36 in-state; $219 out-of-state. Books/supplies: $1,620. Personal expenses: $2,862.

Financial aid. All financial aid based on need. Need-based aid available for part-time students. Work-study available nights, weekends and for part-time students.

Application procedures. Admission: No deadline. No application fee. Admission notification on a rolling basis. **Financial aid:** Priority date 5/6; no closing date. FAFSA, institutional form required. Applicants notified on a rolling basis starting 7/6; must reply within 2 week(s) of notification.

Academics. Special study options: Accelerated study, cooperative education, cross-registration, distance learning, dual enrollment of high school students, ESL, honors, independent study, internships, liberal arts/career combination, study abroad, weekend college. License preparation in aviation, nursing, radiology, real estate. **Credit/placement by examination:** AP, CLEP, IB, institutional tests. 40 credit hours maximum toward associate degree. Students must first complete 12 units in residence. **Support services:** GED preparation, learning center, pre-admission summer program, remedial instruction, study skills assistance, tutoring, writing center.

Majors. Biology: General. **Business:** General, accounting, administrative services, business admin, fashion, hotel/motel admin, office technology, office/clerical, real estate, restaurant/food services, sales/distribution, tourism promotion, tourism/travel. **Communications:** Advertising, broadcast journalism, journalism, public relations, publishing. **Communications technology:** General, desktop publishing, graphic/printing. **Computer sciences:** Applications programming, data processing, word processing. **Education:** Teacher assistance. **Engineering:** General. **English:** English lit, rhetoric/composition. **Foreign languages:** General, Spanish. **General:** Ornamental horticulture. **Health services:** Dietetic technician, licensed practical nurse, medical assistant, medical radiologic technology/radiation therapy, nursing (RN). **Human services:** General. **Liberal arts:** Arts/sciences. **Math:** General. **Parks/recreation:** Health/fitness. **Physical sciences:** General. **Protective services:** Fire safety technology, law enforcement admin. **Social sciences:** General. **Visual/performing arts:** Art, commercial photography, commercial/advertising art, dance, design, dramatic, drawing, fashion design, film/cinema/video, interior design, multimedia, music, printmaking, sculpture, theater design. **Work/family studies:** General, child care management, child development, consumer economics, family resources, institutional food production.

Most popular majors. Business/marketing 7%, health sciences 19%, liberal arts 44%, security/protective services 7%.

Computing on campus. 500 workstations in library, computer center, student center. Online course registration, online library, helpline, wireless network available.

Student life. Freshman orientation: Available. Preregistration for classes offered. **Activities:** Bands, campus ministries, choral groups, dance, drama, international student organizations, literary magazine, music ensembles, musical theater, radio station, student government, student newspaper, symphony orchestra, TV station, College Republicans, Students for a Democratic Society.

Athletics. NJCAA. Intercollegiate: Baseball M, basketball, cross-country, football (tackle) M, golf, soccer, softball W, swimming, tennis, track and field, volleyball, water polo. **Intramural:** Archery, badminton, basketball, bowling, golf, racquetball, soccer, softball, swimming, table tennis, tennis, track and field, volleyball, wrestling M. **Team name:** Vikings.

Student services. Career counseling, student employment services, health services, on-campus daycare, personal counseling, veterans' counselor. **Physically disabled:** Services for visually, speech, hearing impaired. **Transfer:** Re-entry adviser for new students. Transfer center, transfer adviser, college fairs on campus for students transferring to 4-year colleges.

Contact. E-mail: rmiyashiro@lbcc.edu
Phone: (562) 938-4485 Fax: (562) 938-4858
Ross Miyashiro, Dean of Admissions and Records, Long Beach City College, 4901 East Carson Street, Long Beach, CA 90808

Los Angeles City College
Los Angeles, California
www.lacitycollege.edu   **CB code: 4391**

◗ Public 2-year community college
◗ Commuter campus in very large city

General. Founded in 1929. Regionally accredited. **Enrollment:** 20,430 undergraduates. **Degrees:** 532 associate awarded. **ROTC:** Army, Naval, Air Force. **Location:** 5 miles from downtown. **Calendar:** Semester, limited summer session. **Full-time faculty:** 223 total; 33% minority. **Part-time faculty:** 406 total; 29% minority.

Basis for selection. Open admission. Auditions required of theater academy, music majors.

2011-2012 Annual costs. Tuition/fees: $1,102; $6,802 out-of-state. Per-credit charge: $36 in-state; $226 out-of-state. Books/supplies: $1,638. Personal expenses: $3,096.

Financial aid. All financial aid based on need. Need-based aid available for part-time students. Work-study available nights, weekends and for part-time students. **Additional information:** Fee waivers available for public assistance and Social Security insurance recipients; fee credits available for low income families.

Application procedures. Admission: Closing date 9/1. No application fee. Admission notification on a rolling basis beginning on or about 4/30. **Financial aid:** Priority date 3/2; no closing date. FAFSA required. Applicants notified by 7/6; Applicants notified on a rolling basis starting 7/6; must reply within 2 week(s) of notification.

Academics. Special study options: Accelerated study, cooperative education, cross-registration, distance learning, dual enrollment of high school students, ESL, honors, independent study. License preparation in dental hygiene, nursing, radiology. **Credit/placement by examination:** AP, CLEP, institutional tests. 15 credit hours maximum toward associate degree. **Support services:** Learning center, remedial instruction, tutoring.

Majors. Area/ethnic studies: African-American, Asian-American. **Biology:** General. **Business:** Accounting, administrative services, banking/financial services, business admin, entrepreneurial studies, management information systems, office technology, office/clerical, real estate, tourism promotion, tourism/travel. **Communications:** Advertising, broadcast journalism, journalism, public relations. **Communications technology:** General. **Computer sciences:** General, applications programming. **Engineering:** General, software. **English:** English lit. **Foreign languages:** Chinese, French, German, Italian, Japanese, Spanish. **Health services:** Dental lab technology, medical radiologic technology/radiation therapy, medical records technology, medical secretary. **Liberal arts:** Arts/sciences. **Math:** General. **Physical sciences:** Chemistry, physics. **Protective services:** Police science. **Psychology:** General. **Visual/performing arts:** Art, cinematography, commercial/advertising art, dramatic, film/cinema/video, music, photography. **Work/family studies:** General, child care management.

Computing on campus. 200 workstations in library, computer center. Wireless network available.

Student life. Activities: Bands, choral groups, dance, drama, film society, literary magazine, music ensembles, musical theater, radio station, student government, student newspaper, TV station, religious, political, ethnic, and foreign student clubs.

Athletics. NJCAA. **Intercollegiate:** Baseball M, basketball M, cross-country, track and field. **Team name:** CUBS.

Student services. Career counseling, student employment services, health services, on-campus daycare, personal counseling, veterans' counselor. **Physically disabled:** Services for visually, speech, hearing impaired. **Transfer:** Transfer adviser, college fairs on campus for students transferring to 4-year colleges.

Contact. Phone: (323) 953-4381 Fax: (323) 953-4013
William Marmolejo, Dean of Admissions, Los Angeles City College, 855 North Vermont Avenue, Los Angeles, CA 90029-3589

Los Angeles County College of Nursing and Allied Health
Los Angeles, California
www.ladhs.org/wps/portal/CollegeOfNursing/   CB code: 4405

▶ Public 2-year nursing and community college
▶ Commuter campus in very large city

General. Clinical component of studies undertaken in cooperation with Los Angeles County Department of Health Services medical centers. Applicants must be residents of the County of Los Angeles. **Enrollment:** 272 degree-seeking undergraduates. **Degrees:** 101 associate awarded. **Location:** 2 miles from Los Angeles. **Calendar:** Semester, limited summer session. **Full-time faculty:** 43 total.

Basis for selection. Admissions criteria include high school diploma or equivalency, prior college experience, minimum cumulative 2.0 GPA in college work, satisfactory score on Test of Essential Academic Skills. Residency in Los Angeles County required. Point system applied when there are more qualified applicants than openings. **Learning Disabled:** Must submit documentation to obtain accommodations.

High school preparation. College-preparatory program recommended. Recommended units include English 3, mathematics 3, social studies 2, history 1, science 3 (laboratory 2), foreign language 2, computer science 1 and academic electives 2.

2011-2012 Annual costs. Tuition/fees: $4,925. Per-credit charge: $240. $125 one-time fee for new students. Estimated books and supplies cost of $1,500 includes uniform, shoes, malpractice insurance fee, second-hand watch along with textbooks and other supplies for 2 years. Books/supplies: $1,419.

Financial aid. **Need-based:** Work-study available nights, weekends and for part-time students.

Application procedures. **Admission:** Closing date 3/1 (receipt date). $5 fee. Application must be submitted on paper. Admission notification by 6/1. Must reply by May 1 or within 2 week(s) if notified thereafter.

Academics. **Special study options:** License preparation in nursing. **Credit/placement by examination:** AP, CLEP, institutional tests. **Support services:** Reduced course load, tutoring.

Majors. **Health services:** Nursing (RN).

Computing on campus. 25 workstations in library, computer center. Wireless network available.

Student life. Freshman orientation: Mandatory. Preregistration for classes offered. **Activities:** Student government.

Student services. Financial aid counseling. **Transfer:** Pre-admission transcript evaluation for new students.

Contact. Phone: (323) 226-4911 Fax: (323) 226-6343
Maria Caballero, Dean, Administrative and Student Services, Los Angeles County College of Nursing and Allied Health, 1237 North Mission Road, Los Angeles, CA 90033-1084

Los Angeles Harbor College
Wilmington, California
www.lahc.edu   CB code: 4395

▶ Public 2-year community college
▶ Commuter campus in small city

General. Founded in 1949. Regionally accredited. **Enrollment:** 10,962 undergraduates. **Degrees:** 571 associate awarded. **Location:** 15 miles from

downtown. **Calendar:** Semester, limited summer session. **Full-time faculty:** 113 total; 19% have terminal degrees, 50% minority, 58% women. **Part-time faculty:** 309 total; 46% minority, 46% women. **Special facilities:** Observatory, nature museum.

Transfer out. Colleges most students transferred to 2011: California State University: Long Beach, California State University: Dominguez Hills.

Basis for selection. Open admission.

High school preparation. 10 units recommended. Recommended units include English 4, mathematics 3, science 2 (laboratory 1). Nursing program requires high school diploma with chemistry and algebra, or college equivalent.

2011-2012 Annual costs. Tuition/fees: $1,104; $6,804 out-of-state. Per-credit charge: $36 in-state; $226 out-of-state. Books/supplies: $1,656. Personal expenses: $4,158.

Financial aid. All financial aid based on need. Need-based aid available for part-time students. Work-study available nights, weekends and for part-time students.

Application procedures. Admission: Closing date 9/10. No application fee. Admission notification on a rolling basis. High school students accepted on part-time basis. **Financial aid:** Priority date 3/2; no closing date. FAFSA, institutional form required. Applicants notified on a rolling basis; must reply within 2 week(s) of notification.

Academics. Special study options: Accelerated study, cooperative education, cross-registration, distance learning, double major, dual enrollment of high school students, ESL, honors, independent study, liberal arts/career combination, study abroad, weekend college. License preparation in nursing, paramedic, physical therapy, real estate. **Credit/placement by examination:** AP, CLEP, IB, institutional tests. **Support services:** GED preparation, learning center, remedial instruction, study skills assistance, tutoring, writing center.

Majors. Architecture: Technology. **Business:** General, accounting, administrative services, business admin, management information systems, office management, office technology, office/clerical, real estate. **Computer sciences:** General, applications programming, data entry, information systems. **Engineering:** Electrical. **Health services:** Medical secretary, nursing (RN). **Liberal arts:** Arts/sciences, library science. **Protective services:** Firefighting, police science. **Psychology:** General. **Visual/performing arts:** Art, interior design. **Work/family studies:** Child care management.

Most popular majors. Health sciences 17%, interdisciplinary studies 12%, liberal arts 57%.

Computing on campus. 660 workstations in library, computer center, student center. Commuter students can connect to campus network. Online course registration, online library, wireless network available.

Student life. Freshman orientation: Available. Preregistration for classes offered. **Activities:** Bands, choral groups, dance, drama, literary magazine, music ensembles, musical theater, student government, student newspaper, TV station, Equal Opportunity Program Student Association.

Athletics. NJCAA. **Intercollegiate:** Baseball M, basketball, football (tackle) M, soccer, volleyball W. **Team name:** Seahawks.

Student services. Adult student services, career counseling, student employment services, health services, legal services, on-campus daycare, personal counseling, placement for graduates, veterans' counselor. **Physically disabled:** Services for visually, speech, hearing impaired. **Transfer:** Transfer center, transfer adviser, college fairs on campus for students transferring to 4-year colleges.

Contact. E-mail: arhelp@lahc.edu
Phone: (310) 233-4090 Fax: (310) 233-4662
David Ching, Dean of Admissions and Records, Los Angeles Harbor College, 1111 Figueroa Place, Wilmington, CA 90744-2397

Los Angeles Mission College
Sylmar, California
www.lamission.edu   CB code: 4404

▶ Public 2-year community college
▶ Large town

General. Founded in 1974. Regionally accredited. College serves nontraditional student body. **Enrollment:** 11,357 undergraduates. **Degrees:** 394 associate awarded. **ROTC:** Army, Air Force. **Location:** 20 miles from Los

Angeles. **Calendar:** Semester, limited summer session. **Full-time faculty:** 81 total. **Part-time faculty:** 310 total.

Basis for selection. Open admission.

2011-2012 Annual costs. Tuition/fees: $1,102; $6,802 out-of-state. Per-credit charge: $36 in-state; $226 out-of-state. Books/supplies: $1,656. Personal expenses: $3,114.

Financial aid. Need-based: Work-study available nights, weekends and for part-time students. **Additional information:** Board of Governors Grant available to those in receipt of AFDC, Social Security Insurance, or General Relief. If not in receipt of program, may qualify based on income.

Application procedures. Admission: Priority date 4/20; no deadline. No application fee. Admission notification on a rolling basis. **Financial aid:** Priority date 8/1; no closing date. FAFSA required. Applicants notified on a rolling basis starting 8/15.

Academics. Bilingual instruction available. **Special study options:** Accelerated study, cooperative education, distance learning, dual enrollment of high school students, ESL, independent study. **Credit/placement by examination:** AP, CLEP, institutional tests. 15 credit hours maximum toward associate degree. **Support services:** Learning center, remedial instruction, tutoring, writing center.

Majors. Business: Accounting, administrative services, business admin, management science, market research, office management, office/clerical, real estate. **Computer sciences:** General. **Education:** Teacher assistance. **English:** English lit. **Foreign languages:** Spanish. **Liberal arts:** Arts/sciences. **Math:** General. **Philosophy/religion:** Philosophy. **Protective services:** Criminal justice. **Psychology:** General. **Visual/performing arts:** Art, interior design. **Work/family studies:** Clothing/textiles, food/nutrition, institutional food production.

Computing on campus. 150 workstations in library, computer center, student center. Online library, repair service, wireless network available.

Student life. Freshman orientation: Mandatory. Preregistration for classes offered. **Activities:** Choral groups, drama, student government.

Athletics. Intercollegiate: Baseball M, softball.

Student services. Career counseling, health services, on-campus daycare, personal counseling, placement for graduates, veterans' counselor. **Physically disabled:** Services for visually, speech, hearing impaired.

Contact. Phone: (818) 364-7661
Joe Ramirez, Vice President, Los Angeles Mission College, 13356 Eldridge Avenue, Sylmar, CA 91342-3245

Los Angeles Pierce College
Woodland Hills, California
www.piercecollege.edu

CB member
CB code: 4398

- Public 2-year community college
- Commuter campus in very large city

General. Founded in 1947. Regionally accredited. **Enrollment:** 14,965 degree-seeking undergraduates. **Degrees:** 932 associate awarded. **Location:** 27 miles from downtown. **Calendar:** Semester, extensive summer session. **Full-time faculty:** 220 total. **Part-time faculty:** 511 total. **Special facilities:** Braille nature trail, life science museum, nature center, weather station, working farm, botanical garden.

Transfer out. Colleges most students transferred to 2011: California State University: Northridge, University of California: Los Angeles.

Basis for selection. Open admission, but selective for some programs. Limited admission to nursing and animal health technology programs. All students required to take English and math placement tests prior to course registration.

2011-2012 Annual costs. Tuition/fees: $1,104; $6,804 out-of-state. Per-credit charge: $36 in-state; $226 out-of-state. International Students are charged additional fees: $35 Application Fee + $25 SEVIS Processing Fee. Books/supplies: $1,620. Personal expenses: $3,114.

Financial aid. All financial aid based on need. Need-based aid available for part-time students. Work-study available nights, weekends and for part-time students.

Application procedures. Admission: Closing date 9/10 (receipt date). No application fee. Admission notification on a rolling basis. **Financial**

aid: Priority date 3/2; no closing date. FAFSA, institutional form required. Applicants notified on a rolling basis starting 8/1.

Academics. Special study options: Accelerated study, cooperative education, distance learning, dual enrollment of high school students, ESL, honors, student-designed major, study abroad. **Credit/placement by examination:** AP, CLEP, institutional tests. 15 credit hours maximum toward associate degree. **Support services:** GED preparation, learning center, pre-admission summer program, remedial instruction, study skills assistance, tutoring, writing center.

Majors. Architecture: Technology. **Area/ethnic studies:** Latin American. **Business:** General, accounting, business admin, management science, marketing. **Communications:** Journalism, photojournalism. **Computer sciences:** General, applications programming, computer science, data processing, programming. **Conservation:** Management/policy. **Education:** Early childhood, kindergarten/preschool. **Engineering:** General. **Foreign languages:** French, Italian, sign language interpretation, Spanish. **General:** Animal health, animal sciences, business, equestrian studies, equine science, greenhouse operations, horticultural science, horticulture, landscaping, ornamental horticulture. **Health services:** Nursing (RN), preveterinary, substance abuse counseling, veterinary technology/assistant. **Liberal arts:** Arts/sciences. **Social sciences:** Criminology. **Visual/performing arts:** Commercial/advertising art, dramatic, industrial design, music, studio arts, theater design.

Computing on campus. Commuter students can connect to campus network. Online course registration, online library, repair service available.

Student life. Freshman orientation: Available. Preregistration for classes offered. **Activities:** Bands, choral groups, dance, drama, international student organizations, literary magazine, music ensembles, musical theater, student government, student newspaper, symphony orchestra, Bible Fellowship, Alpha Gamma Sigma honor society, Phi Theta Kappa honor society, Phi Beta Lambda business association, Hillel, Union of African American Students, Muslim students association.

Athletics. Intercollegiate: Baseball M, basketball, cheerleading, diving, football (tackle) M, soccer W, softball W, swimming, tennis M, volleyball. **Team name:** Brahmas.

Student services. Adult student services, career counseling, services for economically disadvantaged, student employment services, financial aid counseling, health services, on-campus daycare, personal counseling, placement for graduates, veterans' counselor. **Physically disabled:** Services for visually, speech, hearing impaired. **Transfer:** Transfer center, transfer adviser, college fairs on campus for students transferring to 4-year colleges.

Contact. E-mail: pierceinfo@piercecollege.edu
Phone: (818) 719-6404 Fax: (818) 716-1087
Marco De La Garza, Dean of Admissions and Records, Los Angeles Pierce College, 6201 Winnetka Avenue, Woodland Hills, CA 91371

Los Angeles Southwest College
Los Angeles, California
www.lasc.edu

CB code: 4409

- Public 2-year community college
- Commuter campus in very large city

General. Founded in 1967. Regionally accredited. **Enrollment:** 7,591 undergraduates. **Degrees:** 201 associate awarded. **Calendar:** Semester, limited summer session. **Full-time faculty:** 78 total. **Part-time faculty:** 203 total. **Special facilities:** Career services center.

Transfer out. Colleges most students transferred to 2011: Cal State University: Dominguez Hills, Los Angeles, Long Beach, Northridge, UCLA.

Basis for selection. Open admission, but selective for some programs. Limited admission to nursing and allied health programs.

2011-2012 Annual costs. Tuition/fees: $1,094; $6,794 out-of-state. Per-credit charge: $36 in-state; $226 out-of-state. Books/supplies: $1,638. Personal expenses: $3,096.

Financial aid. Need-based: Need-based aid available for part-time students. Work-study available nights, weekends and for part-time students. **Additional information:** Board of Governors Enrollment Fee Waiver available to students receiving AFDC, SSI/SSP, or General Assistance. May also qualify on basis of income.

Application procedures. Admission: No deadline. No application fee. Late registration allowed through third week of classes, if permitted by instructor. **Financial aid:** No deadline. FAFSA required. Applicants notified on a rolling basis; must reply within 2 week(s) of notification.

Two-Year Colleges

Academics. **Special study options:** Accelerated study, cooperative education, cross-registration, double major, dual enrollment of high school students, ESL, honors, independent study, liberal arts/career combination, study abroad, weekend college. **Credit/placement by examination:** AP, CLEP, institutional tests. 15 credit hours maximum toward associate degree. **Support services:** Learning center, reduced course load, remedial instruction, tutoring.

Majors. **Area/ethnic studies:** African-American. **Biology:** General, molecular. **Business:** General, accounting, administrative services, banking/financial services, business admin, insurance, management information systems, office technology, office/clerical, real estate. **Communications:** Advertising, journalism. **Communications technology:** General. **Computer sciences:** General, applications programming, computer graphics, computer science, programming. **Education:** General, early childhood, foreign languages, mathematics, music, teacher assistance. **Engineering:** General, electrical. **English:** English lit. **Foreign languages:** General, French, Spanish. **Health services:** Clinical lab technology, nursing (RN), respiratory therapy technology. **History:** General. **Liberal arts:** Arts/sciences. **Math:** General. **Parks/recreation:** General. **Philosophy/religion:** Philosophy. **Physical sciences:** Chemistry, geology, physics. **Psychology:** General. **Social sciences:** Geography, political science, sociology. **Visual/performing arts:** Art, art history/conservation, commercial/advertising art, dramatic, fashion design, music, photography. **Work/family studies:** Child care management.

Computing on campus. Helpline, repair service available.

Student life. **Freshman orientation:** Available. Preregistration for classes offered. **Activities:** Bands, choral groups, dance, drama, literary magazine, musical theater, student government, student newspaper.

Athletics. NJCAA. **Intercollegiate:** Basketball M, cross-country, football (tackle) M, tennis W, track and field. **Intramural:** Baseball M, basketball, bowling, golf, softball, tennis, track and field, volleyball. **Team name:** Cougars.

Student services. Career counseling, student employment services, on-campus daycare, personal counseling, placement for graduates. **Transfer:** Transfer adviser for students transferring to 4-year colleges.

Contact. Phone: (323) 241-5321
Kim Carpenter, Admissions and Records Supervisor, Los Angeles Southwest College, 1600 West Imperial Highway, Los Angeles, CA 90047-4899

Los Angeles Trade and Technical College
Los Angeles, California
www.lattc.edu   **CB code: 4400**

◆ Public 2-year community and technical college
◆ Commuter campus in very large city

General. Founded in 1925. Regionally accredited. Specialized culinary arts program; fashion, cosmetology, nursing programs. **Enrollment:** 15,734 undergraduates. **Degrees:** 348 associate awarded. **Calendar:** Semester, limited summer session. **Full-time faculty:** 191 total. **Part-time faculty:** 293 total. **Class size:** 46% < 20, 38% 20-39, 9% 40-49, 4% 50-99, 4% >100.

Student profile.

Out-of-state: 8%   25 or older: 60%

Transfer out. **Colleges most students transferred to 2011:** University of California: Los Angeles, California State University: Los Angeles, California State University: Dominguez Hills, University of Southern California.

Basis for selection. Open admission, but selective for some programs. Limited admission to nursing program. Portfolio recommended of commercial art majors.

2011-2012 Annual costs. Tuition/fees: $1,102; $6,802 out-of-state. Per-credit charge: $36 in-state; $226 out-of-state. Books/supplies: $1,638. Personal expenses: $3,096.

Financial aid. All financial aid based on need. Need-based aid available for part-time students. Work-study available nights, weekends and for part-time students.

Application procedures. **Admission:** Closing date 8/31 (receipt date). No application fee. **Financial aid:** Priority date 5/1; no closing date. FAFSA required. Applicants notified on a rolling basis.

Academics. **Special study options:** Accelerated study, cooperative education, cross-registration, distance learning, double major, dual enrollment of high school students, ESL, honors, independent study, liberal arts/career combination, study abroad, weekend college. License preparation in nursing.

Credit/placement by examination: AP, CLEP, institutional tests. 15 credit hours maximum toward associate degree. **Support services:** GED preparation, learning center, pre-admission summer program, reduced course load, remedial instruction, study skills assistance, tutoring, writing center.

Majors. **Business:** General, accounting, administrative services, business admin, entrepreneurial studies, fashion, hospitality/recreation, labor relations, office/clerical, real estate. **Communications:** Journalism. **Communications technology:** General, graphic/printing. **Computer sciences:** General, computer science. **Engineering:** General. **Health services:** Licensed practical nurse. **Human services:** Community org/advocacy. **Liberal arts:** Arts/sciences. **Visual/performing arts:** Commercial/advertising art, fashion design, photography. **Work/family studies:** Clothing/textiles, institutional food production.

Most popular majors. Computer/information sciences 11%, health sciences 11%, liberal arts 34%, trade and industry 30%, visual/performing arts 8%.

Computing on campus. 550 workstations in library, computer center. Commuter students can connect to campus network. Online course registration, wireless network available.

Student life. **Freshman orientation:** Available. Preregistration for classes offered. **Activities:** Dance, student government, student newspaper, political organizations.

Athletics. NJCAA. **Intercollegiate:** Basketball, cross-country, tennis, track and field. **Intramural:** Golf, swimming. **Team name:** Beaver.

Student services. Adult student services, career counseling, services for economically disadvantaged, student employment services, financial aid counseling, health services, minority student services, on-campus daycare, personal counseling, placement for graduates, veterans' counselor. **Physically disabled:** Services for visually, speech, hearing impaired. **Transfer:** Pre-admission transcript evaluation for new students. Transfer center, transfer adviser, college fairs on campus for students transferring to 4-year colleges.

Contact. Phone: (213) 763-7000 Fax: (213) 286-5386
Carolyn Clark, Registrar, Los Angeles Trade and Technical College, 400 West Washington Boulevard, Los Angeles, CA 90015-4181

Los Angeles Valley College
Valley Glen, California
www.lavc.edu   **CB code: 5546**

◆ Public 2-year community college
◆ Commuter campus in very large city

General. Founded in 1949. Regionally accredited. **Enrollment:** 20,676 undergraduates. **Degrees:** 725 associate awarded. **Location:** 15 miles from downtown. **Calendar:** Semester, limited summer session. **Full-time faculty:** 214 total. **Part-time faculty:** 402 total. **Special facilities:** Planetarium.

Student profile.

Out-of-state: 2%   25 or older: 69%

Basis for selection. Open admission, but selective for some programs. Registered nursing program has competitive admission based on points accumulated for prerequisite courses, grades, and placement test scores. Institutional placement tests required of all students.

2011-2012 Annual costs. Tuition/fees: $1,104; $6,804 out-of-state. Per-credit charge: $36 in-state; $226 out-of-state. Books/supplies: $1,638. Personal expenses: $3,096.

Financial aid. All financial aid based on need. Need-based aid available for part-time students. Work-study available nights, weekends and for part-time students.

Application procedures. **Admission:** No deadline. No application fee. Admission notification on a rolling basis. **Financial aid:** Priority date 3/2, closing date 5/1. FAFSA required. Applicants notified on a rolling basis.

Academics. **Special study options:** Cooperative education, dual enrollment of high school students, honors, independent study. License preparation in nursing, paramedic. **Credit/placement by examination:** AP, CLEP, IB, institutional tests. 15 credit hours maximum toward associate degree. **Support services:** Learning center, remedial instruction, study skills assistance, tutoring, writing center.

Majors. **Area/ethnic studies:** American. **Biology:** General. **Business:** General, administrative services, fashion, hospitality/recreation, management information systems, office technology, office/clerical. **Communications:**

Broadcast journalism, journalism. **Computer sciences:** Applications programming, data processing. **English:** English lit. **Foreign languages:** French, German, Italian, Spanish. **Health services:** Nursing (RN), respiratory therapy technology. **History:** General. **Liberal arts:** Arts/sciences. **Math:** General. **Parks/recreation:** General. **Philosophy/religion:** Philosophy. **Physical sciences:** Chemistry, geology, physics, planetary. **Protective services:** Police science. **Psychology:** General. **Social sciences:** Economics, geography, political science, sociology. **Visual/performing arts:** Art, art history/conservation, commercial/advertising art, music. **Work/family studies:** General.

Computing on campus. 300 workstations in library, computer center, student center. Online course registration, wireless network available.

Student life. Freshman orientation: Available. Preregistration for classes offered. **Activities:** Bands, choral groups, dance, drama, film society, literary magazine, music ensembles, musical theater, radio station, student government, student newspaper, symphony orchestra.

Athletics. NJCAA. **Intercollegiate:** Baseball M, basketball, cross-country, diving, football (tackle) M, soccer W, softball W, swimming, track and field, water polo M. **Team name:** Monarchs.

Student services. Career counseling, student employment services, health services, on-campus daycare, personal counseling, placement for graduates, veterans' counselor. **Physically disabled:** Services for visually, speech, hearing impaired. **Transfer:** Transfer adviser, college fairs on campus for students transferring to 4-year colleges.

Contact. E-mail: trudgej@lavc.edu
Phone: (818) 947-2553 Fax: (818) 947-2501
Florentino Manzano, Dean of Enrollment Management, Los Angeles Valley College, 5800 Fulton Avenue, Valley Glen, CA 91401-4096

Los Medanos College
Pittsburg, California
www.losmedanos.edu   **CB code: 4396**

▶ Public 2-year community college
▶ Commuter campus in small city

General. Founded in 1973. Regionally accredited. **Enrollment:** 9,738 undergraduates. **Degrees:** 569 associate awarded. **Location:** 45 miles from San Francisco. **Calendar:** Semester. **Full-time faculty:** 132 total. **Part-time faculty:** 229 total.

Student profile.

Out-of-state:	1%	25 or older:	53%

Basis for selection. Open admission.

2011-2012 Annual costs. Tuition/fees: $1,090; $6,790 out-of-state. Per-credit charge: $36 in-state; $226 out-of-state. Books/supplies: $1,566. Personal expenses: $2,664.

Financial aid. All financial aid based on need. Need-based aid available for part-time students. Work-study available nights, weekends and for part-time students.

Application procedures. Admission: No deadline. Admission notification on a rolling basis. **Financial aid:** Priority date 3/2; no closing date. FAFSA required. Applicants notified on a rolling basis starting 6/1; must reply within 2 week(s) of notification.

Academics. Special study options: Cooperative education, cross-registration, independent study, study abroad. **Credit/placement by examination:** AP, CLEP, institutional tests. 20 credit hours maximum toward associate degree. **Support services:** Learning center, remedial instruction, tutoring.

Majors. Biology: General. **Business:** Accounting, entrepreneurial studies, labor relations, office management, real estate, tourism promotion. **Communications:** Journalism. **Health services:** EMT paramedic, nursing (RN). **Liberal arts:** Arts/sciences. **Math:** General. **Physical sciences:** Chemistry. **Protective services:** Firefighting. **Psychology:** General. **Social sciences:** Anthropology, sociology. **Visual/performing arts:** Commercial/advertising art, music, music performance, studio arts. **Work/family studies:** Child care management.

Most popular majors. Business/marketing 7%, health sciences 18%, liberal arts 60%.

Computing on campus. 150 workstations in computer center.

Student life. Activities: Bands, choral groups, drama, music ensembles, student government, student newspaper.

Athletics. Intercollegiate: Baseball M, basketball, football (tackle) M, soccer M, softball W, volleyball W. **Intramural:** Basketball, softball, tennis.

Student services. Career counseling, student employment services, on-campus daycare, personal counseling, placement for graduates. **Physically disabled:** Services for visually, speech, hearing impaired. **Transfer:** Transfer adviser, college fairs on campus for students transferring to 4-year colleges.

Contact. Phone: (925) 439-2181 ext. 7500 Fax: (925) 427-6351
Robin Armour, Director of Admissions and Records, Los Medanos College, 2700 East Leland Road, Pittsburg, CA 94565

Marymount College Palos Verdes California
Rancho Palos Verdes, California   **CB member**
www.marymountpv.edu   **CB code: 4515**

▶ Private 2-year junior and liberal arts college affiliated with Roman Catholic Church
▶ Residential campus in large town

General. Founded in 1933. Regionally accredited. **Enrollment:** 935 degree-seeking undergraduates; 5 non-degree-seeking students. **Degrees:** 59 associate awarded. **Location:** 30 miles from Los Angeles. **Calendar:** Semester, limited summer session. **Full-time faculty:** 33 total; 48% have terminal degrees, 9% minority, 52% women. **Part-time faculty:** 88 total; 20% have terminal degrees, 18% minority, 51% women. **Class size:** 59% < 20, 41% 20-39.

Student profile. Among degree-seeking undergraduates, 426 enrolled as first-time, first-year students, 67 transferred in from other institutions.

Part-time:	3%	Hispanic American:	19%
Out-of-state:	12%	Native American:	1%
Women:	52%	International:	6%
African American:	9%	25 or older:	2%
Asian American:	5%	Live on campus:	34%

Transfer out. Colleges most students transferred to 2011: University of Southern California, Loyola Marymount University, University of California, California State University, Chapman University.

Basis for selection. High school record, quality of academic preparation, recommendations, student's personal statement, standardized test scores all considered. SAT or ACT recommended. ACCUPLACER used for placement. Interview and essay recommended. **Home schooled:** Transcript of courses and grades, letter of recommendation (nonparent) required. General syllabus of all coursework completed or private tutoring received, statement explaining why family chose home schooling and its advantages and disadvantages, required. SAT or ACT scores and state HS equivalency certificate recommended.

High school preparation. 16 units recommended. Recommended units include English 4, mathematics 3, social studies 2, history 2, science 2, foreign language 2 and academic electives 1.

2011-2012 Annual costs. Tuition/fees: $27,846. Per-credit charge: $1,050. Room/board: $12,074. Books/supplies: $1,656. Personal expenses: $2,278.

2011-2012 Financial aid. Need-based: 276 full-time freshmen applied for aid; 276 were judged to have need; 276 of these received aid. Average need met was 64%. Average scholarship/grant was $23,891. 86% of total undergraduate aid awarded as scholarships/grants, 14% as loans/jobs. Work-study available nights, weekends and for part-time students. **Non-need-based:** Awarded to 172 full-time undergraduates, including 75 freshmen. Scholarships awarded for art, athletics, music/drama.

Application procedures. Admission: Priority date 3/1; no deadline. $40 fee, may be waived for applicants with need. Admission notification on a rolling basis beginning on or about 12/1. Must reply by May 1 or within 2 week(s) if notified thereafter. **Financial aid:** Priority date 3/2; no closing date. FAFSA required. Applicants notified on a rolling basis starting 3/1; must reply by 5/1.

Academics. Special study options: Distance learning, double major, dual enrollment of high school students, ESL, honors, internships, study abroad, urban semester. Bachelor's degree programs available on campus. **Credit/placement by examination:** AP, CLEP, IB, SAT, ACT, institutional tests. 15 credit hours maximum toward associate degree. **Support services:** Learning center, pre-admission summer program, reduced course load, remedial instruction, study skills assistance, tutoring.

Honors college/program. Admitted students are reviewed by the Honors faculty for Honors consideration. Average GPA is 3.3; SAT or ACT scores highly recommended. Approximately 30 students admitted each year. Students may earn their way into the Honors program based on academic success in their first year of college. Honors courses are designated each year. Successful Honors students may join Phi Theta Kappa Honor Society; graduates may secure PTK scholarships upon transfer.

Majors. Liberal arts: Arts/sciences.

Most popular majors. Liberal arts 46%, psychology 19%.

Computing on campus. 77 workstations in library, computer center. Dormitories wired for high-speed internet access and linked to campus network. Commuter students can connect to campus network. Online library, helpline, repair service, wireless network available.

Student life. Freshman orientation: Mandatory, $150 fee. Preregistration for classes offered. **Housing:** Coed dorms, special housing for disabled available. $600 partly refundable deposit. Housing available through volunteers in the community. **Activities:** Jazz band, campus ministries, choral groups, drama, film society, international student organizations, literary magazine, music ensembles, radio station, student government, volunteer club, philosophy discussion club, pre-med club, student integrity council, Phi Theta Kappa, Latinos Unidos, Black Student Union, International Peers, Jewish club, campus ministry leadership team.

Athletics. NJCAA. Intercollegiate: Soccer. **Intramural:** Basketball, football (non-tackle), golf, softball. **Team name:** Mariners.

Student services. Adult student services, alcohol/substance abuse counseling, chaplain/spiritual director, career counseling, student employment services, financial aid counseling, health services, personal counseling. **Physically disabled:** Services for visually, hearing impaired. **Transfer:** Pre-admission transcript evaluation for new students. Transfer center, transfer adviser, college fairs on campus for students transferring to 4-year colleges.

Contact. E-mail: admissions@marymountpv.edu
Phone: (310) 377-5501 Fax: (310) 265-0962
Barbara Layne, Dean of Enrollment Management, Marymount College Palos Verdes California, 30800 Palos Verdes Drive East, Rancho Palos Verdes, CA 90275-6299

Mendocino College
Ukiah, California
www.mendocino.edu   CB code: 4517

- Public 2-year community college
- Commuter campus in large town

General. Founded in 1973. Regionally accredited. **Enrollment:** 2,096 degree-seeking undergraduates; 1,538 non-degree-seeking students. **Degrees:** 287 associate awarded. **Location:** 60 miles from Santa Rosa, 110 miles from San Francisco. **Calendar:** Semester, limited summer session. **Full-time faculty:** 50 total; 18% have terminal degrees, 4% minority, 46% women. **Part-time faculty:** 255 total; 7% minority, 55% women. **Class size:** 45% < 20, 54% 20-39, less than 1% 40-49. **Special facilities:** Gallery and theater complex, point arena field station.

Student profile. Among degree-seeking undergraduates, 55% enrolled in a transfer program, 13% enrolled in a vocational program, 1% already have a bachelor's degree or higher, 359 enrolled as first-time, first-year students, 158 transferred in from other institutions.

Part-time:	60%	Women:	58%
Out-of-state:	4%	25 or older:	50%

Transfer out. 50% of students enrolled in the transfer program go on to 4-year colleges. **Colleges most students transferred to 2011:** Sonoma State University, Humboldt State University, University of California.

Basis for selection. Open admission.

2011-2012 Annual costs. Tuition/fees: $1,100; $6,950 out-of-state. Per-credit charge: $36 in-state; $231 out-of-state. Books/supplies: $1,620. Personal expenses: $3,078.

2011-2012 Financial aid. Need-based: 178 full-time freshmen applied for aid; 160 were judged to have need; 160 of these received aid. Average need met was 100%. Average scholarship/grant was $1,561. 99% of total undergraduate aid awarded as scholarships/grants, 1% as loans/jobs. Need-based aid available for part-time students. Work-study available nights, weekends and for part-time students. **Non-need-based:** Awarded to 141 full-time undergraduates, including 17 freshmen. Scholarships awarded for academics, leadership, music/drama, state residency.

Application procedures. Admission: Priority date 5/1; no deadline. No application fee. Admission notification on a rolling basis beginning on or about 7/1. **Financial aid:** Priority date 5/31; no closing date. FAFSA required. Applicants notified on a rolling basis starting 7/1; must reply within 2 week(s) of notification.

Academics. Special study options: Distance learning, double major, dual enrollment of high school students, ESL, independent study, internships, student-designed major. License preparation in nursing, paramedic, real estate. **Credit/placement by examination:** AP, CLEP, institutional tests. 12 credit hours maximum toward associate degree. **Support services:** GED test center, learning center, pre-admission summer program, remedial instruction, study skills assistance, tutoring.

Majors. Biology: General. **Business:** General, accounting, administrative services, business admin, entrepreneurial studies. **Communications:** Communications/speech/rhetoric. **Computer sciences:** General. **Conservation:** General. **English:** English lit, rhetoric/composition. **Foreign languages:** French, Spanish. **General:** Plant sciences. **Health services:** Substance abuse counseling. **Liberal arts:** Arts/sciences. **Math:** General. **Parks/recreation:** Sports admin. **Protective services:** Law enforcement admin. **Psychology:** General. **Social sciences:** General. **Visual/performing arts:** Art, dramatic, music.

Most popular majors. Business/marketing 17%, family/consumer sciences 6%, health sciences 10%, interdisciplinary studies 8%, liberal arts 23%, psychology 8%, social sciences 10%.

Computing on campus. 144 workstations in library, computer center, student center. Commuter students can connect to campus network. Online course registration, online library, wireless network available.

Student life. Freshman orientation: Available. Preregistration for classes offered. Orientation held before and during first week of class. **Policies:** Smoking restricted to two remote areas. **Activities:** Bands, choral groups, dance, drama, film society, music ensembles, musical theater, radio station, student government.

Athletics. NJCAA. Intercollegiate: Baseball M, basketball, cheerleading M, football (tackle) M, soccer W, softball W, volleyball W. **Team name:** Eagles.

Student services. Adult student services, career counseling, services for economically disadvantaged, student employment services, financial aid counseling, on-campus daycare, personal counseling, placement for graduates, veterans' counselor, women's services. **Physically disabled:** Services for visually, speech, hearing impaired. **Transfer:** Transfer center, transfer adviser, college fairs on campus for students transferring to 4-year colleges.

Contact. E-mail: webaccess@mendocino.edu
Phone: (707) 468-3101 Fax: (707) 468-3120
Kristie Anderson, Director of Admissions and Records, Mendocino College, 1000 Hensley Creek/Box 3000, Ukiah, CA 95482

Merced College
Merced, California
www.mccd.edu   CB code: 4500

- Public 2-year community college
- Commuter campus in small city

General. Founded in 1962. Regionally accredited. Off-campus centers at Los Banos. **Enrollment:** 7,241 degree-seeking undergraduates. **Degrees:** 614 associate awarded. **Location:** 50 miles from Fresno. **Calendar:** Semester, limited summer session. **Full-time faculty:** 172 total. **Part-time faculty:** 351 total.

Transfer out. Colleges most students transferred to 2011: CSU Stanislaus, CSU Fresno, UC Davis.

Basis for selection. Open admission. Institutional placement tests used.

2011-2012 Annual costs. Tuition/fees: $1,114; $7,354 out-of-state. Per-credit charge: $36 in-state; $244 out-of-state. Books/supplies: $1,638. Personal expenses: $3,096.

Financial aid. Need-based: Work-study available nights, weekends and for part-time students. **Non-need-based:** Scholarships awarded for academics.

Application procedures. Admission: No deadline. No application fee. Application must be submitted on paper. Admission notification on a rolling basis. Must reply by May 1 or within 4 week(s) if notified thereafter. **Financial aid:** Priority date 6/1; no closing date. FAFSA required. Applicants notified on a rolling basis starting 1/2; must reply within 3 week(s) of notification.

Academics. **Special study options:** Cooperative education, distance learning, dual enrollment of high school students, honors, internships, study abroad. License preparation in nursing, paramedic, radiology, real estate. **Credit/ placement by examination:** AP, CLEP, institutional tests. 12 credit hours maximum toward associate degree. **Support services:** Learning center, pre-admission summer program, remedial instruction, tutoring.

Majors. **Biology:** General. **Business:** General, accounting, administrative services, business admin, merchandising, real estate. **Communications:** Communications/speech/rhetoric, journalism. **Computer sciences:** General, information systems. **Education:** Early childhood. **Engineering:** General. **English:** English lit. **Foreign languages:** French, German, Spanish. **General:** Agronomy, animal sciences, business, horticulture, ornamental horticulture, soil science. **Health services:** Licensed practical nurse, medical radiologic technology/radiation therapy, medical secretary, nursing (RN), office admin, substance abuse counseling. **History:** General. **Human services:** Social work. **Liberal arts:** Arts/sciences. **Math:** General. **Parks/recreation:** Health/fitness. **Philosophy/religion:** Philosophy. **Physical sciences:** General, chemistry, geology, physics. **Protective services:** Firefighting, police science. **Psychology:** General. **Social sciences:** General, anthropology, archaeology, physical anthropology. **Visual/performing arts:** General, art history/conservation, dramatic, music, photography. **Work/family studies:** General, child development, family studies.

Computing on campus. 400 workstations in library, computer center. Commuter students can connect to campus network. Online library, helpline available.

Student life. **Freshman orientation:** Available. Preregistration for classes offered. **Activities:** Bands, choral groups, dance, drama, international student organizations, music ensembles, musical theater, student government, student newspaper, symphony orchestra, Black student union, Movimiento Estudiantil Chicano de Aztlan, intervarsity Christian group, Rotaract.

Athletics. NJCAA. **Intercollegiate:** Baseball M, basketball, cheerleading M, cross-country, diving, football (tackle) M, golf, softball W, swimming, track and field, volleyball W, water polo. **Team name:** Blue Devils.

Student services. Alcohol/substance abuse counseling, career counseling, services for economically disadvantaged, student employment services, financial aid counseling, health services, on-campus daycare, personal counseling, placement for graduates, veterans' counselor. **Physically disabled:** Services for visually, speech, hearing impaired. **Transfer:** Transfer center, transfer adviser, college fairs on campus for students transferring to 4-year colleges.

Contact. Phone: (209) 384-6187 Fax: (209) 384-6339
Everett Lovelace, Dean of Student Services, Merced College, Lesher Student Services Building, floor 2, Merced, CA 95348

Merritt College
Oakland, California
www.merritt.edu   CB code: 4502

▶ Public 2-year community college
▶ Large city

General. Founded in 1953. Regionally accredited. **Enrollment:** 2,710 degree-seeking undergraduates. **Degrees:** 422 associate awarded. **Location:** 15 miles from San Francisco. **Calendar:** Semester, extensive summer session. **Full-time faculty:** 77 total. **Part-time faculty:** 147 total. **Special facilities:** Anthropology museum, landscape/horticulture complex.

Student profile.

Out-of-state: 5%   25 or older: 60%

Basis for selection. Open admission.

2011-2012 Annual costs. Tuition/fees: $1,084; $6,394 out-of-state. Per-credit charge: $36 in-state; $213 out-of-state. Books/supplies: $1,450. Personal expenses: $2,600.

Financial aid. **Need-based:** Need-based aid available for part-time students. Work-study available nights, weekends and for part-time students.

Application procedures. **Admission:** No deadline. No application fee. Admission notification on a rolling basis. **Financial aid:** Priority date 4/1, closing date 6/30. FAFSA, institutional form required. Applicants notified on a rolling basis starting 6/1.

Academics. **Special study options:** Cooperative education, cross-registration, distance learning, dual enrollment of high school students, honors, independent study. **Credit/placement by examination:** AP, CLEP, institutional tests. 15 credit hours maximum toward associate degree. **Support**

services: Learning center, pre-admission summer program, reduced course load, remedial instruction, tutoring.

Majors. **Area/ethnic studies:** African-American. **Business:** General, real estate. **Computer sciences:** General. **Education:** General, business, early childhood. **Engineering:** Electrical. **English:** English lit. **Foreign languages:** French, Spanish. **General:** Horticultural science, landscaping. **Health services:** Licensed practical nurse, medical radiologic technology/radiation therapy, nursing (RN). **Human services:** Community org/advocacy. **Liberal arts:** Arts/sciences. **Math:** General. **Parks/recreation:** General. **Social sciences:** General. **Work/family studies:** Child care management, family/community services.

Computing on campus. 200 workstations in library, computer center, student center.

Student life. **Activities:** Choral groups, dance, student government, student newspaper, Merritt Christian Fellowship, LaRaza Student Union, Native American Association, Black Student Union, Asian Student Union, Ecology Action Club, Disabled Students Coalition.

Athletics. **Intercollegiate:** Basketball, cross-country, track and field. **Intramural:** Badminton, golf, tennis, volleyball.

Student services. Adult student services, career counseling, student employment services, health services, on-campus daycare, personal counseling, placement for graduates, veterans' counselor. **Physically disabled:** Services for visually, speech, hearing impaired. **Transfer:** Transfer adviser, college fairs on campus for students transferring to 4-year colleges.

Contact. E-mail: admissions@peralta.edu
Phone: (510) 436-2487
Howard Perdue, Dean of Admissions and Records, Merritt College, 12500 Campus Drive, Oakland, CA 94619

MiraCosta College
Oceanside, California
www.miracosta.edu   CB code: 4582

▶ Public 2-year community college
▶ Commuter campus in large city

General. Founded in 1934. Regionally accredited. **Enrollment:** 10,775 degree-seeking undergraduates. **Degrees:** 681 associate awarded. **ROTC:** Army, Naval, Air Force. **Location:** 35 miles from San Diego. **Calendar:** Semester, limited summer session. **Full-time faculty:** 155 total; 28% minority, 51% women. **Part-time faculty:** 154 total; 18% minority, 61% women. **Class size:** 13% < 20, 73% 20-39, 13% 40-49, less than 1% 50-99. **Special facilities:** Bioprocessing training facility, music recording studios, radiation protection technology. **Partnerships:** Formal partnerships with Cisco Academy.

Student profile. Among degree-seeking undergraduates, 77% enrolled in a transfer program, 7% enrolled in a vocational program, 4% already have a bachelor's degree or higher, 2,230 enrolled as first-time, first-year students.

Out-of-state:	2%	Hispanic American:	17%
African American:	4%	Native American:	1%
Asian American:	6%	International:	5%

Transfer out. 38% of students enrolled in the transfer program go on to 4-year colleges. **Colleges most students transferred to 2011:** San Diego State University, Cal State: San Marcos, University of California: San Diego,.

Basis for selection. Open admission, but selective for some programs. Must be either 18 years of age or high school graduate. Concurrently enrolled high school students require principal and parental permission with grade level limitations. Nursing programs require special application with course and GPA requirements. Locally administered tests may be used for placement and counseling. **Home schooled:** Must complete both Math and English placement exams and meet with the Dean of Counseling.

2011-2012 Annual costs. Tuition/fees: $1,124; $6,674 out-of-state. Per-credit charge: $36 in-state; $221 out-of-state.

2010-2011 Financial aid. **Need-based:** 89% of total undergraduate aid awarded as scholarships/grants, 11% as loans/jobs. Need-based aid available for part-time students. Work-study available nights, weekends and for part-time students. **Additional information:** Waiver of in-state fees for eligible low-income students.

Application procedures. **Admission:** No deadline. No application fee. Admission notification on a rolling basis. **Financial aid:** Priority date 4/11; no closing date. FAFSA, institutional form required. Applicants notified on a rolling basis; must reply within 4 week(s) of notification.

Academics. Special study options: Accelerated study, cooperative education, distance learning, double major, dual enrollment of high school students, ESL, honors, independent study, internships, liberal arts/career combination, study abroad, teacher certification program. Study abroad programs in Japan, Mexico, Costa Rica and several countries in Europe. License preparation in nursing, real estate. **Credit/placement by examination:** AP, CLEP, IB, institutional tests. 15 credit hours maximum toward associate degree. **Support services:** GED preparation and test center, learning center, pre-admission summer program, reduced course load, remedial instruction, study skills assistance, tutoring, writing center.

Honors college/program. Students wanting to study at the honors level contract for an honors option in designated courses.

Majors. Architecture: Landscape. **Biology:** General. **Business:** Accounting, administrative services, business admin, hospitality admin, office management, office/clerical, real estate, tourism/travel. **Communications:** Communications/speech/rhetoric. **Computer sciences:** General, computer graphics, computer science, LAN/WAN management, programming. **Education:** Early childhood. **English:** English lit. **Foreign languages:** General, French, German, Japanese, Spanish. **General:** Business, floriculture, landscaping, nursery operations, turf management. **Health services:** Licensed practical nurse, premedicine. **History:** General. **Liberal arts:** Arts/sciences. **Math:** General. **Philosophy/religion:** Philosophy. **Physical sciences:** Chemistry, geology, physics. **Protective services:** Police science. **Psychology:** General. **Social sciences:** General, economics, geography, political science, sociology. **Visual/performing arts:** Art, art history/conservation, commercial/advertising art, dance, dramatic, music, theater design. **Work/family studies:** Child care management.

Most popular majors. Business/marketing 19%, family/consumer sciences 7%, health sciences 20%, liberal arts 26%, personal/culinary services 7%, trade and industry 6%.

Computing on campus. 1,000 workstations in library, computer center, student center. Online course registration, online library, helpline, student web hosting, wireless network available.

Student life. Freshman orientation: Available. Preregistration for classes offered. One-hour session offered 14 times prior to classes each semester. Online orientations and online advising offered 24/7. **Activities:** Bands, choral groups, dance, drama, international student organizations, literary magazine, music ensembles, musical theater, student government, student newspaper, symphony orchestra, Veterans club, MECHA/Latina organization, black student union, Chinese club, Phi Theta Kappa, Single Parents on Campus, Japanese club, Allied Health club, Amnesty International, Gay Straight Alliance.

Athletics. Intercollegiate: Basketball, soccer. **Intramural:** Basketball, soccer, softball, table tennis, tennis, volleyball. **Team name:** Spartans.

Student services. Alcohol/substance abuse counseling, career counseling, services for economically disadvantaged, student employment services, financial aid counseling, health services, on-campus daycare, personal counseling, veterans' counselor. **Physically disabled:** Services for visually, speech, hearing impaired. **Transfer:** Transfer center, transfer adviser, college fairs on campus for students transferring to 4-year colleges.

Contact. E-mail: admissions@miracosta.edu
Phone: (760) 795-6620 Toll-free number: (888) 201-8480
Fax: (760) 795-6626
Alicia Terry, Director of Admissions and Records, MiraCosta College, One Barnard Drive, Oceanside, CA 92056-3899

Mission College
Santa Clara, California
www.missioncollege.org   CB code: 7587

- Public 2-year community college
- Small city

General. Founded in 1975. Regionally accredited. **Enrollment:** 4,689 degree-seeking undergraduates. **Degrees:** 574 associate awarded. **ROTC:** Naval, Air Force. **Location:** 8 miles from San Jose. **Calendar:** Semester, limited summer session. **Full-time faculty:** 146 total. **Part-time faculty:** 189 total.

Transfer out. Colleges most students transferred to 2011: San Jose State.

Basis for selection. Open admission, but selective for some programs. Limited admission to vocational nursing and allied health programs. Interviews required of nursing, psychiatric technician majors.

2011-2012 Annual costs. Tuition/fees: $1,130; $7,250 out-of-state. Per-credit charge: $36 in-state; $240 out-of-state. Books/supplies: $2,388. Personal expenses: $3,096.

Financial aid. Need-based: Work-study available nights, weekends and for part-time students.

Application procedures. Admission: No deadline. No application fee. Admission notification on a rolling basis. **Financial aid:** Priority date 5/1; no closing date. Applicants notified on a rolling basis starting 8/1; must reply within 2 week(s) of notification.

Academics. Special study options: Cooperative education, dual enrollment of high school students, honors, independent study, weekend college. Bachelor's degree programs available on campus. **Credit/placement by examination:** AP, CLEP, institutional tests. 12 credit hours maximum toward associate degree. **Support services:** Learning center, remedial instruction, tutoring.

Majors. Biology: General. **Business:** General, accounting, administrative services, banking/financial services, business admin, management information systems, management science, office management, office/clerical, real estate. **Communications technology:** Graphic/printing. **Computer sciences:** Applications programming, computer science, information systems. **Engineering:** General. **General:** Food science. **Health services:** Licensed practical nurse, nursing (RN). **Liberal arts:** Arts/sciences. **Math:** General. **Physical sciences:** Chemistry, physics. **Protective services:** Fire safety technology. **Social sciences:** General. **Visual/performing arts:** Art, commercial/advertising art.

Student life. Freshman orientation: Available. Preregistration for classes offered. **Activities:** Jazz band, dance, music ensembles, musical theater, student government, TV station.

Athletics. NCAA. **Intercollegiate:** Baseball M, basketball W, soccer M, softball W, tennis. **Team name:** Saints.

Student services. Adult student services, career counseling, student employment services, health services, on-campus daycare, personal counseling, placement for graduates, veterans' counselor. **Transfer:** Transfer center, transfer adviser, college fairs on campus for students transferring to 4-year colleges.

Contact. E-mail: askmc@wvm.edu
Phone: (408) 988-2200 Fax: (408) 980-8980
Rita Grogan, Director of Student Enrollment and Financial Services, Mission College, 3000 Mission College Boulevard, Santa Clara, CA 95054-1897

Modesto Junior College
Modesto, California
www.mjc.edu   CB code: 4486

- Public 2-year community college
- Commuter campus in small city

General. Founded in 1921. Regionally accredited. **Enrollment:** 18,492 undergraduates. **Degrees:** 1,270 associate awarded. **Location:** 90 miles from San Francisco. **Calendar:** Semester, limited summer session. **Full-time faculty:** 243 total. **Part-time faculty:** 354 total. **Special facilities:** Natural history museum.

Transfer out. Colleges most students transferred to 2011: California State University: Stanislaus, California State University: Fresno, California State University: Sacramento, University of California: Davis, University of California: San Diego.

Basis for selection. Open admission, but selective for some programs. Limited admission offered to nursing (RN), dental assisting, medical assisting, and related majors. Selective admission to fire academy.

High school preparation. Certain programs require specific courses.

2011-2012 Annual costs. Tuition/fees: $1,126; $7,366 out-of-state. Per-credit charge: $36 in-state; $244 out-of-state. Books/supplies: $1,620. Personal expenses: $2,514.

Financial aid. All financial aid based on need. Need-based aid available for part-time students. Work-study available nights, weekends and for part-time students. **Additional information:** Modesto Junior College scholarship priority deadline 12/15.

Application procedures. Admission: No deadline. No application fee. Admission notification on a rolling basis. **Financial aid:** Priority date 3/2;

no closing date. FAFSA, institutional form required. Applicants notified on a rolling basis starting 5/1; must reply within 2 week(s) of notification.

Academics. **Special study options:** Cooperative education, distance learning, double major, dual enrollment of high school students, ESL, honors, independent study, internships, liberal arts/career combination, study abroad, weekend college. License preparation in nursing, real estate. **Credit/placement by examination:** AP, CLEP, institutional tests. 30 credit hours maximum toward associate degree. **Support services:** GED preparation, learning center, pre-admission summer program, remedial instruction, study skills assistance, tutoring, writing center.

Majors. **Architecture:** Landscape, urban/community planning. **Business:** General, accounting, administrative services, business admin, fashion, finance, management information systems, marketing, real estate. **Communications:** Broadcast journalism, communications/speech/rhetoric, journalism. **Communications technology:** Graphic/printing. **Computer sciences:** General, computer graphics, computer science, programming. **Conservation:** General, forestry, wildlife/wilderness. **Engineering:** General, electrical. **English:** English lit, rhetoric/composition. **Foreign languages:** General, Spanish. **General:** Agronomy, animal breeding, animal sciences, business, dairy, food science, landscaping, ornamental horticulture, plant sciences, poultry, soil science. **Health services:** Dental assistant, medical assistant, nursing (RN), respiratory therapy technology. **Parks/recreation:** General, health/fitness. **Protective services:** Firefighting, law enforcement admin. **Social sciences:** General. **Visual/performing arts:** General, art, cinematography, commercial photography, commercial/advertising art, dramatic, fashion design, interior design, music, photography, studio arts. **Work/family studies:** General, child care management, clothing/textiles, family/community services, food/nutrition.

Computing on campus. 137 workstations in library, computer center, student center. Commuter students can connect to campus network. Online course registration available.

Student life. **Freshman orientation:** Available. Preregistration for classes offered. One hour, held during registration. **Activities:** Bands, choral groups, dance, drama, film society, international student organizations, music ensembles, musical theater, opera, radio station, student government, student newspaper, symphony orchestra, TV station, Christian Collegiate Fellowship, Able-Disabled Association, foreign, ethnic, minority student and women reentry clubs, Young Farmers.

Athletics. **Intercollegiate:** Baseball M, basketball, cross-country, diving, football (tackle) M, golf, soccer, softball W, swimming, tennis, track and field, volleyball W, water polo, wrestling M. **Team name:** Pirates.

Student services. Adult student services, career counseling, services for economically disadvantaged, student employment services, financial aid counseling, health services, minority student services, on-campus daycare, personal counseling, placement for graduates, veterans' counselor. **Physically disabled:** Services for visually, speech, hearing impaired. **Transfer:** Reentry adviser for new students. Transfer center, transfer adviser, college fairs on campus for students transferring to 4-year colleges.

Contact. Phone: (209) 575-6013 Fax: (209) 575-6859
Martha Robles, Dean of Matriculation, Admissions, and Records, Modesto Junior College, 435 College Avenue, Modesto, CA 95350-5800

Monterey Peninsula College
Monterey, California
www.mpc.edu CB code: 4490

- Public 2-year community college
- Commuter campus in large town

General. Founded in 1947. Regionally accredited. **Enrollment:** 9,674 undergraduates. **Degrees:** 411 associate awarded. **Location:** 120 miles from San Francisco. **Calendar:** Semester, limited summer session. **Full-time faculty:** 114 total. **Part-time faculty:** 274 total.

Basis for selection. Open admission, but selective for some programs. Additional requirements, including interview, for dental assistant, nursing, administrative justice and police academy programs.

2011-2012 Annual costs. Tuition/fees: $1,146; $6,426 out-of-state. Per-credit charge: $36 in-state; $212 out-of-state. Books/supplies: $1,656. Personal expenses: $2,854.

Financial aid. **Need-based:** Need-based aid available for part-time students. Work-study available nights, weekends and for part-time students.

Application procedures. **Admission:** No deadline. No application fee. Admission notification on a rolling basis. **Financial aid:** Closing date 6/30.

FAFSA, institutional form required. Applicants notified on a rolling basis starting 6/1.

Academics. **Special study options:** Cooperative education, cross-registration, distance learning, double major, dual enrollment of high school students, ESL, independent study, weekend college. **Credit/placement by examination:** AP, CLEP, institutional tests. 30 credit hours maximum toward associate degree. **Support services:** Learning center, remedial instruction, tutoring.

Majors. **Area/ethnic studies:** Women's. **Biology:** General. **Business:** General, accounting, business admin, hospitality admin, hospitality/recreation, international, office/clerical, real estate. **Communications:** Communications/speech/rhetoric. **Computer sciences:** General, data processing, LAN/WAN management, programming, web page design, word processing. **English:** English lit. **Foreign languages:** General. **General:** Ornamental horticulture. **Health services:** Dental assistant, medical assistant, nursing (RN), predental, premedicine, prepharmacy, preveterinary. **History:** General. **Liberal arts:** Arts/sciences. **Math:** General. **Philosophy/religion:** Philosophy. **Physical sciences:** Chemistry, physics. **Protective services:** Fire safety technology, law enforcement admin. **Psychology:** General. **Social sciences:** Anthropology, economics, political science, sociology. **Visual/performing arts:** Acting, art, art history/conservation, ceramics, dance, directing/producing, dramatic, drawing, graphic design, interior design, metal/jewelry, music, painting, photography, printmaking, sculpture, studio arts. **Work/family studies:** General, child care service, child development, clothing/textiles, family/community services, fashion consultant, institutional food production.

Student life. **Activities:** Bands, choral groups, dance, drama, music ensembles, musical theater, opera, student government.

Athletics. NJCAA. **Intercollegiate:** Baseball M, basketball, cross-country, football (tackle) M, golf, softball W, swimming, tennis W, track and field, volleyball W. **Team name:** Lobos.

Student services. Career counseling, student employment services, health services, on-campus daycare, personal counseling. **Physically disabled:** Services for visually, speech, hearing impaired. **Transfer:** Transfer center, transfer adviser, college fairs on campus for students transferring to 4-year colleges.

Contact. Phone: (831) 646-4002 Fax: (831) 646-4015
Vera Coleman, Director of Admissions and Records, Monterey Peninsula College, 980 Fremont Street, Monterey, CA 93940-4799

Moorpark College
Moorpark, California
www.moorparkcollege.edu CB code: 4512

- Public 2-year community college
- Commuter campus in small city

General. Founded in 1963. Regionally accredited. **Enrollment:** 10,192 degree-seeking undergraduates. **Degrees:** 1,150 associate awarded. **Location:** 50 miles from Los Angeles. **Calendar:** Semester, limited summer session. **Full-time faculty:** 162 total. **Part-time faculty:** 348 total. **Class size:** 25% 20-39, 50% 40-49, 25% 50-99. **Special facilities:** Exotic animal compound and teaching zoo, observatory.

Student profile.

Out-of-state:	1%	25 or older:	74%

Transfer out. Colleges most students transferred to 2011: California State University, University of Southern California, University of California: Los Angeles, UC Santa Barbara.

Basis for selection. Open admission, but selective for some programs. Limited admission to nursing program, exotic animal training management program, radiologic technology.

2011-2012 Annual costs. Tuition/fees: $1,126; $6,406 out-of-state. Per-credit charge: $36 in-state; $212 out-of-state. Books/supplies: $1,638. Personal expenses: $3,096.

Financial aid. **Need-based:** Work-study available nights, weekends and for part-time students.

Application procedures. **Admission:** Priority date 7/30; no deadline. No application fee. Admission notification on a rolling basis. **Financial aid:** Priority date 5/14; no closing date. FAFSA required. Applicants notified on a rolling basis starting 6/15; must reply within 2 week(s) of notification.

Academics. **Special study options:** Accelerated study, cooperative education, distance learning, honors, independent study, internships, study abroad. License preparation in nursing, paramedic, radiology. **Credit/placement by**

examination: AP, CLEP. 12 credit hours maximum toward associate degree. **Support services:** Learning center, remedial instruction, study skills assistance, tutoring, writing center.

Majors. Biology: General. **Business:** Accounting, administrative services, business admin, management information systems, office management, real estate. **Communications:** Broadcast journalism, communications/speech/rhetoric. **Communications technology:** General, graphic/printing. **Computer sciences:** General, applications programming, information systems. **General:** Animal sciences. **Health services:** Medical radiologic technology/radiation therapy, nursing (RN). **Liberal arts:** Arts/sciences. **Math:** General. **Physical sciences:** Chemistry, geology, physics. **Protective services:** Police science. **Social sciences:** General. **Visual/performing arts:** General, cinematography, commercial/advertising art, dramatic, interior design, music, photography, studio arts. **Work/family studies:** General, child care management, family studies.

Most popular majors. Agriculture 8%, health sciences 9%, liberal arts 66%.

Computing on campus. 400 workstations in library, computer center. Online course registration, online library, helpline, wireless network available.

Student life. Freshman orientation: Available. Preregistration for classes offered. Online orientation. **Activities:** Bands, choral groups, dance, drama, international student organizations, literary magazine, music ensembles, Model UN, musical theater, opera, student government, student newspaper, symphony orchestra, TV station, Alpha Gamma Sigma, Muslim Student Association.

Athletics. Intercollegiate: Baseball M, basketball, cheerleading M, cross-country, football (tackle) M, softball W, track and field, volleyball. **Team name:** Raiders.

Student services. Career counseling, services for economically disadvantaged, student employment services, financial aid counseling, health services, on-campus daycare, personal counseling, veterans' counselor. **Physically disabled:** Services for visually, speech, hearing impaired. **Transfer:** Transfer center, transfer adviser, college fairs on campus for students transferring to 4-year colleges.

Contact. E-mail: mcadmissions@vcccd.net
Phone: (805) 378-1429 Fax: (805) 378-1499
Katherine Colborn, Registrar, Moorpark College, 7075 Campus Road, Moorpark, CA 93021

Moreno Valley College
Moreno Valley, California
www.rcc.edu/morenovalley   CB code: 6512

- Public 2-year community college
- Commuter campus in small city

General. Regionally accredited. **Enrollment:** 5,899 degree-seeking undergraduates. **Degrees:** 292 associate awarded. **Calendar:** Semester, limited summer session. **Full-time faculty:** 75 total; 31% have terminal degrees, 47% minority, 57% women. **Part-time faculty:** 362 total; 31% minority, 38% women.

Basis for selection. Open admission.

2011-2012 Annual costs. Tuition/fees: $1,114; $6,394 out-of-state. Per-credit charge: $36 in-state; $212 out-of-state. Books/supplies: $1,666. Personal expenses: $4,520.

2011-2012 Financial aid. Need-based: 98% of total undergraduate aid awarded as scholarships/grants, 2% as loans/jobs. Work-study available nights, weekends and for part-time students.

Application procedures. Admission: No deadline. No application fee. **Financial aid:** Closing date 3/1.

Academics. Special study options: Distance learning, ESL, honors, weekend college. License preparation in dental hygiene. **Credit/placement by examination:** AP, CLEP. **Support services:** Remedial instruction, tutoring, writing center.

Majors. Business: General, accounting, real estate. **Computer sciences:** Programming. **Education:** Early childhood. **Health services:** Dental hygiene, medical assistant, physician assistant. **Parks/recreation:** Health/fitness. **Protective services:** Firefighting.

Student life. Activities: Student newspaper.

Athletics. Team name: Lions.

Student services. Transfer: Transfer center, transfer adviser, college fairs on campus for students transferring to 4-year colleges.

Contact. Phone: (951) 571-6101
Jamie Clifton, Director, Enrollment Services, Moreno Valley College, 16130 Lasselle Street, Moreno Valley, CA 92551

Mount San Antonio College
Walnut, California
www.mtsac.edu   CB code: 4494

- Public 2-year community college
- Commuter campus in small city

General. Founded in 1946. Regionally accredited. **Enrollment:** 37,172 undergraduates. **Degrees:** 1,938 associate awarded. **ROTC:** Air Force. **Location:** 30 miles from Los Angeles. **Calendar:** Semester, extensive summer session. **Full-time faculty:** 419 total. **Part-time faculty:** 860 total. **Special facilities:** Planetarium, wildlife sanctuary.

Student profile. 5,062 enrolled as first-time, first-year students.

African American:	5%	**Hispanic American:**	49%
Asian American:	21%	**International:**	1%

Transfer out. Colleges most students transferred to 2011: California State Polytechnic University: Pomona, California State University: Los Angeles, California State University: Fullerton.

Basis for selection. Open admission.

2011-2012 Annual costs. Tuition/fees: $1,136; $6,626 out-of-state. Per-credit charge: $36 in-state; $219 out-of-state. Books/supplies: $1,620. Personal expenses: $2,862.

Financial aid. All financial aid based on need. Need-based aid available for part-time students. Work-study available nights, weekends and for part-time students.

Application procedures. Admission: No deadline. No application fee. Admission notification on a rolling basis. **Financial aid:** Priority date 4/15; no closing date. FAFSA required. Applicants notified on a rolling basis starting 7/1.

Academics. Special study options: Cooperative education, cross-registration, distance learning, dual enrollment of high school students, ESL, honors, internships, study abroad, teacher certification program, weekend college. License preparation in aviation, nursing, paramedic, radiology, real estate. **Credit/placement by examination:** AP, CLEP. 12 credit hours maximum toward associate degree. **Support services:** GED preparation, learning center, pre-admission summer program, remedial instruction, study skills assistance, tutoring, writing center.

Majors. Biology: General, marine. **Business:** General, accounting, administrative services, banking/financial services, business admin, entrepreneurial studies, fashion, office/clerical, real estate. **Communications:** Advertising, broadcast journalism, journalism. **Communications technology:** General. **Computer sciences:** Data processing. **Conservation:** General, forestry. **Engineering:** General. **Foreign languages:** Sign language interpretation. **General:** Animal sciences, business, horticulture. **Health services:** EMT paramedic, medical radiologic technology/radiation therapy, medical secretary, nursing (RN), respiratory therapy technology. **Liberal arts:** Arts/sciences. **Parks/recreation:** General, facilities management. **Protective services:** Firefighting, police science. **Visual/performing arts:** Design, interior design, photography. **Work/family studies:** General, clothing/textiles.

Most popular majors. English 14%, health sciences 14%, interdisciplinary studies 19%, liberal arts 12%, social sciences 18%.

Computing on campus. 600 workstations in library, computer center, student center. Commuter students can connect to campus network. Online course registration, online library, helpline, wireless network available.

Student life. Freshman orientation: Mandatory. Preregistration for classes offered. **Activities:** Bands, choral groups, dance, drama, film society, literary magazine, music ensembles, musical theater, radio station, student government, student newspaper, symphony orchestra, TV station, Asian student association, Chinese club, Black student alliance, Indo-Pak club, Democratic club, Republican club, sign language club, MECHA, Muslim student association.

Athletics. Intercollegiate: Baseball M, basketball, cheerleading, cross-country, football (tackle) M, golf W, soccer, softball W, swimming, tennis,

track and field, volleyball, water polo, wrestling M. **Team name:** Mounties.

Student services. Adult student services, alcohol/substance abuse counseling, career counseling, services for economically disadvantaged, student employment services, financial aid counseling, health services, minority student services, on-campus daycare, personal counseling, placement for graduates, veterans' counselor. **Physically disabled:** Services for visually, speech, hearing impaired. **Transfer:** Re-entry adviser, pre-admission transcript evaluation for new students. Transfer center, transfer adviser, college fairs on campus for students transferring to 4-year colleges.

Contact. Phone: (909) 594-5611 ext. 4415 Fax: (909) 468-4068
George Bradshaw, Director of Admissions and Records, Mount San Antonio College, 1100 North Grand Avenue, Walnut, CA 91789

Mount San Jacinto College
San Jacinto, California
www.msjc.edu   CB code: 4501

- Public 2-year community college
- Commuter campus in small city

General. Founded in 1962. Regionally accredited. **Enrollment:** 8,263 degree-seeking undergraduates. **Degrees:** 1,479 associate awarded. **Location:** 35 miles from Riverside, 45 miles from Palm Springs. **Calendar:** Semester, limited summer session. **Full-time faculty:** 127 total. **Part-time faculty:** 570 total. **Class size:** 38% < 20, 54% 20-39, 7% 40-49, less than 1% 50-99.

Transfer out. Colleges most students transferred to 2011: California State University: San Bernardino, University of California: Riverside, California State University: San Marcos, San Diego State University, Azusa Pacific University.

Basis for selection. Open admission, but selective for some programs. Special requirements for nursing and diagnostic medical sonography programs and for concurrently enrolled high school students.

2011-2012 Annual costs. Tuition/fees: $1,080; $6,360 out-of-state. Per-credit charge: $36 in-state; $212 out-of-state. Books/supplies: $1,566. Personal expenses: $3,024.

Financial aid. Need-based: Need-based aid available for part-time students. Work-study available nights, weekends and for part-time students. **Non-need-based:** Scholarships awarded for academics, music/drama. **Additional information:** Board of Governors Grant Program for state residents to defray cost of enrollment fees.

Application procedures. Admission: Closing date 12/18 (receipt date). No application fee. Admission notification on a rolling basis beginning on or about 4/24. **Financial aid:** Priority date 3/2; no closing date. FAFSA, institutional form required. Applicants notified on a rolling basis starting 5/1; must reply within 3 week(s) of notification.

Academics. Special study options: Cross-registration, distance learning, double major, dual enrollment of high school students, ESL, honors, independent study, internships, study abroad, weekend college. License preparation in nursing, paramedic, real estate. **Credit/placement by examination:** AP, CLEP, institutional tests. 12 credit hours maximum toward associate degree. **Support services:** Learning center, reduced course load, remedial instruction, study skills assistance, tutoring, writing center.

Majors. Business: Business admin, real estate. **Computer sciences:** General. **Education:** Early childhood, physical. **General:** Turf management. **Health services:** Nursing (RN), substance abuse counseling. **Liberal arts:** Arts/sciences. **Math:** General. **Protective services:** Police science. **Social sciences:** General. **Visual/performing arts:** Art, dance, dramatic, music, photography.

Computing on campus. 120 workstations in library, computer center. Commuter students can connect to campus network. Online course registration, online library, helpline, wireless network available.

Student life. Freshman orientation: Mandatory. Preregistration for classes offered. 2-hour orientation; online or group session. **Activities:** Bands, dance, drama, international student organizations, musical theater, radio station, student government.

Athletics. NAIA, NCAA. **Intercollegiate:** Baseball M, basketball, football (tackle) M, golf, soccer W, softball W, tennis, volleyball W. **Intramural:** Cheerleading, weight lifting. **Team name:** Eagles.

Student services. Adult student services, career counseling, services for economically disadvantaged, student employment services, financial aid counseling, minority student services, on-campus daycare, veterans' counselor. **Physically disabled:** Services for visually, speech, hearing impaired. **Transfer:** Pre-admission transcript evaluation for new students. Transfer center, transfer adviser, college fairs on campus for students transferring to 4-year colleges.

Contact. E-mail: enrollsvcs@msjc.edu
Phone: (951) 487-3215 Fax: (951) 654-6738
Susan Loomis, Director, Enrollment Services, Mount San Jacinto College, 1499 North State Street, San Jacinto, CA 92583

MTI College
Sacramento, California
www.mticollege.edu   CB code: 3543

- For-profit 2-year business and technical college
- Commuter campus in large city
- Interview required

General. Regionally accredited. **Enrollment:** 791 degree-seeking undergraduates. **Degrees:** 128 associate awarded. **Calendar:** Differs by program, extensive summer session. **Full-time faculty:** 12 total. **Part-time faculty:** 56 total.

Transfer out. Colleges most students transferred to 2011: University of Phoenix, Golden Gate University.

Basis for selection. Interview, talent, ability, character and personal qualities important.

2012-2013 Annual costs. Tuition/fees: $13,577. Books/supplies: $4,875. Personal expenses: $444.

Financial aid. Need-based: Work-study available nights, weekends and for part-time students.

Application procedures. Admission: No deadline. $50 fee. Admission notification on a rolling basis.

Academics. Special study options: Cooperative education, distance learning, internships, liberal arts/career combination. **Credit/placement by examination:** AP, CLEP, institutional tests. **Support services:** Learning center, reduced course load, remedial instruction, study skills assistance, tutoring.

Majors. Business: Office management. **Computer sciences:** Networking.

Most popular majors. Business/marketing 9%, computer/information sciences 27%, legal studies 64%.

Computing on campus. 300 workstations in library, computer center.

Student life. Freshman orientation: Mandatory. Preregistration for classes offered.

Student services. Adult student services, career counseling, financial aid counseling, placement for graduates, veterans' counselor. **Transfer:** Pre-admission transcript evaluation for new students. College fairs on campus for students transferring to 4-year colleges.

Contact. Phone: (916) 339-1500 Fax: (916) 339-0305
Eric Patterson, Director of Admissions, MTI College, 5221 Madison Avenue, Sacramento, CA 95841

Napa Valley College
Napa, California
www.napavalley.edu   CB code: 4530

- Public 2-year community college
- Commuter campus in small city

General. Founded in 1940. Regionally accredited. **Enrollment:** 3,004 degree-seeking undergraduates. **Degrees:** 642 associate awarded. **Location:** 50 miles from San Francisco. **Calendar:** Semester, limited summer session. **Full-time faculty:** 98 total. **Part-time faculty:** 275 total. **Special facilities:** Nature preserve, working vineyard, telecommunications laboratory.

Basis for selection. Open admission, but selective for some programs. Special admission requirements for health occupations programs and athletic program applicants.

2011-2012 Annual costs. Tuition/fees: $1,118; $6,908 out-of-state. Per-credit charge: $36 in-state; $229 out-of-state. Books/supplies: $1,620. Personal expenses: $3,078.

Financial aid. Need-based: Work-study available nights, weekends and for part-time students.

Application procedures. Admission: No deadline. No application fee. Admission notification on a rolling basis. College-administered placement tests recommended for students enrolling in English or mathematics. **Financial aid:** Closing date 5/29. FAFSA required. Applicants notified on a rolling basis starting 6/1; must reply within 3 week(s) of notification.

Academics. Culinary arts program available. **Special study options:** Cooperative education, distance learning, double major, dual enrollment of high school students, ESL, honors, independent study, internships, study abroad, weekend college. Exchange program with Tafe College, Tasmania. **Credit/placement by examination:** AP, CLEP, institutional tests. 12 credit hours maximum toward associate degree. **Support services:** Learning center, remedial instruction, tutoring, writing center.

Majors. Business: General, accounting, administrative services, real estate. **Communications technology:** General. **Computer sciences:** General. **Conservation:** Wildlife/wilderness. **Education:** General, early childhood. **English:** English lit. **Health services:** Licensed practical nurse, nursing (RN), respiratory therapy technology. **Liberal arts:** Arts/sciences. **Protective services:** Police science. **Social sciences:** General.

Computing on campus. 30 workstations in library, computer center.

Student life. Activities: Bands, choral groups, dance, drama, music ensembles, musical theater, student government, student newspaper, symphony orchestra, various religious, ethnic, social service, and special interest organizations including International Student Club, Amnesty International, Hispano-Americano Club.

Athletics. NJCAA. **Intercollegiate:** Baseball M, basketball, diving, golf, soccer, softball W, swimming, tennis, volleyball W. **Intramural:** Volleyball. **Team name:** Storm.

Student services. Adult student services, career counseling, student employment services, on-campus daycare, personal counseling, veterans' counselor. **Physically disabled:** Services for visually, speech, hearing impaired. **Transfer:** Re-entry adviser for new students. Transfer center, transfer adviser, college fairs on campus for students transferring to 4-year colleges.

Contact. Phone: (707) 253-3000 Fax: (707) 253-3064
Director of Admissions, Napa Valley College, 2277 Napa-Vallejo Highway, Napa, CA 94558

Norco College
Norco, California
www.rcc.edu/norco　　　　　　**CB code: 6503**

- Public 2-year community college
- Large town

General. Regionally accredited. **Enrollment:** 6,908 degree-seeking undergraduates. **Degrees:** 399 associate awarded. **Location:** 51 miles from Los Angeles. **Calendar:** Semester, limited summer session. **Full-time faculty:** 68 total; 34% have terminal degrees, 29% minority, 54% women. **Part-time faculty:** 203 total; 39% minority, 48% women.

Basis for selection. Open admission.

2011-2012 Annual costs. Tuition/fees: $1,114; $6,394 out-of-state. Per-credit charge: $36 in-state; $212 out-of-state. Books/supplies: $1,666. Personal expenses: $4,520.

2011-2012 Financial aid. Need-based: 99% of total undergraduate aid awarded as scholarships/grants, 1% as loans/jobs. Work-study available nights, weekends and for part-time students.

Application procedures. Admission: No deadline. No application fee. Admission notification on a rolling basis. **Financial aid:** Closing date 3/1.

Academics. Special study options: Distance learning, dual enrollment of high school students, ESL, honors, study abroad, weekend college. **Credit/placement by examination:** AP, CLEP. **Support services:** Remedial instruction, writing center.

Majors. Business: General, accounting, marketing, real estate. **Computer sciences:** Programming. **Education:** Early childhood.

Student life. Activities: Student newspaper.

Athletics. Team name: mustang.

Student services. Transfer: Transfer center, transfer adviser, college fairs on campus for students transferring to 4-year colleges.

Contact. Phone: (951) 372-7003
Mark DeAsis, Director, Enrollment Services, Norco College, 2001 Third Street, Norco, CA 92860

Ohlone College
Fremont, California
www.ohlone.edu　　　　　　**CB code: 4579**

- Public 2-year community college
- Commuter campus in large city

General. Founded in 1966. Regionally accredited. **Enrollment:** 4,438 degree-seeking undergraduates. **Degrees:** 421 associate awarded. **ROTC:** Air Force. **Location:** 15 miles from San Jose, 40 miles from San Francisco. **Calendar:** Semester, extensive summer session. **Full-time faculty:** 127 total. **Part-time faculty:** 321 total. **Class size:** 54% < 20, 40% 20-39, 2% 40-49, 2% 50-99, less than 1% >100. **Special facilities:** Fine and performing arts center, business and technology center, Newark center for health sciences and technology. **Partnerships:** Formal partnerships with Sun Microsystems, Metatec Inc., Washington Hospital, Fremont Unified School District, Newark Unified School District.

Student profile.

Out-of-state:	1%	25 or older:	45%

Transfer out. Colleges most students transferred to 2011: California State University: East Bay, San Jose State University, University of California: Berkeley, University of California: Davis, San Francisco State University.

Basis for selection. Open admission, but selective for some programs. Nursing, respiratory therapy and physical therapy assisting programs require basic competence in reading comprehension and English skills, basic knowledge of related sciences. All candidates who achieve minimum standards selected by lottery. High school diploma or equivalent not required if applicant is 18 years of age or older.

High school preparation. Nursing and physical therapy assisting programs require anatomy and physiology. Respiratory therapy program requires algebra and physics.

2011-2012 Annual costs. Tuition/fees: $1,134; $7,524 out-of-state. Per-credit charge: $36 in-state; $249 out-of-state. Books/supplies: $1,972. Personal expenses: $3,024.

Financial aid. Need-based: Need-based aid available for part-time students. Work-study available nights, weekends and for part-time students. **Non-need-based:** Scholarships awarded for academics.

Application procedures. Admission: No deadline. No application fee. **Financial aid:** Priority date 7/1; no closing date. FAFSA, institutional form required. Applicants notified on a rolling basis starting 7/30; must reply within 2 week(s) of notification.

Academics. Special study options: Cooperative education, cross-registration, distance learning, double major, dual enrollment of high school students, ESL, independent study, internships, liberal arts/career combination, study abroad, weekend college. License preparation in nursing, physical therapy. **Credit/placement by examination:** AP, CLEP, IB, institutional tests. 10 credit hours maximum toward associate degree. **Support services:** Learning center, pre-admission summer program, reduced course load, remedial instruction, study skills assistance, tutoring, writing center.

Majors. Biology: General. **Business:** General, accounting, administrative services, business admin, marketing, office management, office technology, office/clerical, real estate, receptionist, small business admin. **Communications:** Broadcast journalism, digital media, journalism. **Communications technology:** Desktop publishing. **Computer sciences:** Computer graphics, information systems, LAN/WAN management, programming, system admin. **Education:** Early childhood. **Foreign languages:** American Sign Language. **Health services:** Medical assistant, nursing (RN), physical therapy assistant, respiratory therapy technology. **Liberal arts:** Arts/sciences. **Protective services:** Law enforcement admin. **Social sciences:** General. **Visual/performing arts:** Commercial/advertising art, graphic design, interior design, multimedia, studio arts, theater design. **Work/family studies:** Child care management, food/nutrition, institutional food production.

Most popular majors. Biological/life sciences 21%, business/marketing 10%, health sciences 18%, liberal arts 38%.

Computing on campus. 450 workstations in library, computer center. Commuter students can connect to campus network. Online course registration, online library, helpline, wireless network available.

Student life. Freshman orientation: Mandatory. Preregistration for classes offered. **Activities:** Bands, choral groups, dance, drama, literary magazine, music ensembles, musical theater, radio station, student government, student newspaper, symphony orchestra, TV station, Abundant Life Christian Fellowship, Afghan Students Association, Asian Pacific Islanders Club, Chinese Culture Club, Muslim Student Association, Alpha Gamma Sigma Honor Society, Ohlone Women Engineers and Physical Scientists, Theater and Dance Alliance.

Athletics. Intercollegiate: Baseball M, basketball, soccer, softball W, swimming, tennis, volleyball, water polo. **Team name:** Renegades.

Student services. Adult student services, career counseling, services for economically disadvantaged, student employment services, financial aid counseling, health services, on-campus daycare, personal counseling, placement for graduates, veterans' counselor. **Physically disabled:** Services for visually, hearing impaired. **Transfer:** Pre-admission transcript evaluation for new students. Transfer center, transfer adviser, college fairs on campus for students transferring to 4-year colleges.

Contact. E-mail: admissions@ohlone.edu
Phone: (510) 659-6100 Fax: (510) 659-7231
Christopher Williamson, Director of Admissions and Records, Ohlone College, 43600 Mission Boulevard, Fremont, CA 94539-0390

Orange Coast College
Costa Mesa, California
www.orangecoastcollege.edu   **CB code: 4584**

- Public 2-year community college
- Commuter campus in small city

General. Founded in 1947. Regionally accredited. **Enrollment:** 22,971 degree-seeking undergraduates; 2,441 non-degree-seeking students. **Degrees:** 1,604 associate awarded. **Location:** 40 miles from Los Angeles. **Calendar:** Semester, limited summer session. **Full-time faculty:** 215 total; 24% minority, 48% women. **Part-time faculty:** 543 total; 60% minority, 52% women. **Class size:** 14% < 20, 52% 20-39, 18% 40-49, 10% 50-99, 6% >100. **Special facilities:** Plastination lab, sailing academy, international center.

Student profile. Among degree-seeking undergraduates, 4,205 enrolled as first-time, first-year students.

Part-time:	56%	Asian American:	23%
Out-of-state:	2%	Hispanic American:	24%
Women:	49%	International:	3%
African American:	2%	25 or older:	32%

Transfer out. Colleges most students transferred to 2011: University of California: Irvine, California State University: Fullerton, California State University: Long Beach.

Basis for selection. Open admission. **Home schooled:** Transcript of courses and grades required.

2011-2012 Annual costs. Tuition/fees: $1,111; $6,991 out-of-state. Per-credit charge: $36 in-state; $232 out-of-state. Computer - $900. Books/supplies: $1,656. Personal expenses: $3,115.

2010-2011 Financial aid. Need-based: 1,192 full-time freshmen applied for aid; 1,182 were judged to have need; 1,181 of these received aid. Average need met was 29%. Average scholarship/grant was $4,775; average loan $2,300. 69% of total undergraduate aid awarded as scholarships/grants, 31% as loans/jobs. Need-based aid available for part-time students. Work-study available nights, weekends and for part-time students.

Application procedures. Admission: No deadline. No application fee. Admission notification on a rolling basis. Admission opens January for summer and fall semester, September for spring semester; dates establish registration priority. **Financial aid:** Priority date 3/2, closing date 5/25. FAFSA required. Applicants notified by 2/15; Applicants notified on a rolling basis; must reply within 2 week(s) of notification.

Academics. Student Success Center (individual tutoring, drop-in tutoring, online tutoring, and study skills assistance) available. **Special study options:** Cooperative education, cross-registration, distance learning, ESL, honors, independent study, internships, liberal arts/career combination, student-designed major, study abroad. License preparation in aviation, dental hygiene,

paramedic, radiology, real estate. **Credit/placement by examination:** AP, CLEP, institutional tests. 12 credit hours maximum toward associate degree. **Support services:** Learning center, pre-admission summer program, reduced course load, remedial instruction, study skills assistance, tutoring, writing center.

Honors college/program. Students complete a minimum of 18 units in honors courses for program certification.

Majors. Architecture: Technology. **Biology:** General, ecology. **Business:** General, accounting, administrative services, fashion, hospitality/recreation, international, management information systems, office technology, office/clerical, real estate, sales/distribution, selling, travel services. **Communications:** Advertising, journalism, media studies. **Computer sciences:** General, computer graphics, data entry, information systems, programming. **Education:** Drama/dance, early childhood, kindergarten/preschool, music. **Engineering:** General. **English:** English lit, rhetoric/composition, technical writing. **Foreign languages:** French, German, Italian, Japanese, Spanish. **General:** Ornamental horticulture. **Health services:** Athletic training, cardiovascular technology, dental assistant, dietetic technician, electroencephalograph technology, medical assistant, medical radiologic technology/radiation therapy, medical records technology, radiologic technology/medical imaging, respiratory therapy technology, sonography, speech-language pathology assistant. **History:** General. **Liberal arts:** Arts/sciences, humanities. **Math:** General. **Parks/recreation:** Health/fitness, sports admin. **Philosophy/religion:** Philosophy, religion. **Physical sciences:** Astronomy, chemistry, geology, physics. **Psychology:** General. **Social sciences:** General, anthropology, economics, geography, political science, sociology. **Visual/performing arts:** Art, cinematography, commercial photography, commercial/advertising art, dance, dramatic, fashion design, film/cinema/video, interior design, music, music management, photography, studio arts. **Work/family studies:** General, child care management, clothing/textiles, food/nutrition, institutional food production.

Most popular majors. Health sciences 11%, liberal arts 56%.

Computing on campus. 1,473 workstations in library, computer center, student center. Online course registration, online library, helpline, wireless network available.

Student life. Freshman orientation: Mandatory. Preregistration for classes offered. 3-hour sessions given year round. **Activities:** Bands, choral groups, dance, drama, film society, international student organizations, literary magazine, music ensembles, musical theater, student government, student newspaper, symphony orchestra, Associate Students of Orange Coast College, Doctors of Tomorrow, Circle K International, Spirit of Ability Club, Puente Club, EOPS Honors Club, honors student council, engineering club, Phi Theta Kappa International Honors Society.

Athletics. Intercollegiate: Baseball M, basketball, cheerleading, cross-country, diving, football (tackle) M, golf M, rowing (crew), soccer, softball W, swimming, tennis, track and field, volleyball, water polo. **Team name:** Pirates.

Student services. Adult student services, alcohol/substance abuse counseling, career counseling, services for economically disadvantaged, student employment services, financial aid counseling, health services, minority student services, on-campus daycare, personal counseling, placement for graduates, veterans' counselor. **Physically disabled:** Services for visually, speech, hearing impaired. **Transfer:** Re-entry adviser for new students. Transfer center, transfer adviser, college fairs on campus for students transferring to 4-year colleges.

Contact. E-mail: campustours@occ.cccd.edu
Phone: (714) 432-5072
Efren Galvan, Director of Admissions, Records & Enrollment Technology, Orange Coast College, 2701 Fairview Road, Costa Mesa, CA 92628-5005

Oxnard College
Oxnard, California
www.oxnardcollege.edu   **CB code: 4591**

- Public 2-year community college
- Commuter campus in small city

General. Founded in 1975. Regionally accredited. **Enrollment:** 3,674 degree-seeking undergraduates. **Degrees:** 511 associate awarded. **Location:** 60 miles from Los Angeles. **Calendar:** Semester, limited summer session. **Full-time faculty:** 96 total. **Part-time faculty:** 186 total. **Special facilities:** Marine education center.

Basis for selection. Open admission.

2011-2012 Annual costs. Tuition/fees: $1,126; $6,526 out-of-state. Per-credit charge: $36 in-state; $216 out-of-state. Books/supplies: $1,656. Personal expenses: $3,114.

2010-2011 Financial aid. Need-based: 98% of total undergraduate aid awarded as scholarships/grants, 2% as loans/jobs. Work-study available nights, weekends and for part-time students.

Application procedures. Admission: No deadline. No application fee. Admission notification on a rolling basis. **Financial aid:** Closing date 6/30. FAFSA required. Applicants notified on a rolling basis; must reply within 2 week(s) of notification.

Academics. Special study options: Accelerated study, cross-registration, distance learning, dual enrollment of high school students, independent study. First 2 years of bilingual (English-Spanish) teacher preparatory program. **Credit/placement by examination:** AP, CLEP, institutional tests. 12 credit hours maximum toward associate degree. **Support services:** Learning center, remedial instruction, study skills assistance, tutoring, writing center.

Majors. Biology: General, marine. **Business:** Accounting, administrative services, business admin, hotel/motel admin. **Communications:** Digital media, journalism, public relations, radio/TV. **Computer sciences:** General, information technology, networking, web page design. **Conservation:** Environmental studies. **English:** English lit. **Foreign languages:** Sign language interpretation, Spanish. **Health services:** Dental hygiene, medical records technology, substance abuse counseling. **History:** General. **Liberal arts:** Arts/sciences, humanities. **Math:** General. **Philosophy/religion:** Philosophy. **Protective services:** Firefighting. **Psychology:** General. **Social sciences:** Anthropology, economics, political science, sociology. **Visual/performing arts:** Art, drawing, sculpture. **Work/family studies:** Child development.

Most popular majors. Business/marketing 10%, family/consumer sciences 6%, liberal arts 63%, security/protective services 9%.

Computing on campus. 57 workstations in library, student center. Online course registration available.

Student life. Freshman orientation: Available. Preregistration for classes offered. **Activities:** Jazz band, choral groups, dance, drama, student government, student newspaper, TV station, EconoBus club, film makers club, math club, MECha, chemistry club, culinary club, auto club, chess club, poetry club, theater arts club.

Athletics. Intercollegiate: Baseball M, basketball, cross-country, soccer, softball W, track and field, volleyball W. **Team name:** Condors.

Student services. Services for economically disadvantaged, student employment services, financial aid counseling, health services, on-campus daycare, personal counseling, veterans' counselor. **Physically disabled:** Services for visually, speech, hearing impaired. **Transfer:** Transfer center, transfer adviser, college fairs on campus for students transferring to 4-year colleges.

Contact. E-mail: ocadmissions@vcccd.edu
Phone: (805) 986-5810 Fax: (805) 986-5943
Joel Diaz, Director of Admissions, Oxnard College, 4000 South Rose Avenue, Oxnard, CA 93033

Pacific College of Oriental Medicine: San Diego
San Diego, California
www.pacificcollege.edu

- For-profit 2-year health science and career college
- Very large city

General. Regionally accredited; also accredited by ACCSC. **Enrollment:** 97 degree-seeking undergraduates. **Degrees:** 1 bachelor's, 4 associate awarded; master's, professional offered. **Calendar:** Trimester. **Full-time faculty:** 6 total. **Part-time faculty:** 65 total.

Basis for selection. Admission requirements vary by programs.

2011-2012 Annual costs. Tuition/fees: $27,742. Tuition quoted is based on average cost of tuition and fees for 2 terms.

Financial aid. Need-based: Work-study available nights, weekends and for part-time students.

Application procedures. Admission: $50 fee. **Financial aid:** Priority date 6/29; no closing date.

Academics. Credit/placement by examination: AP, CLEP.

Majors. Health services: Holistic, massage therapy.

Contact. E-mail: admissions-sd@pacificcollege.edu
Phone: (619) 574-6909 Toll-free number: (800) 729-0941
Gina Baxley, Director of Admissions, Pacific College of Oriental Medicine: San Diego, 7445 Mission Valley Road, Suite 105, San Diego, CA 92108

Palo Verde College
Blythe, California
www.paloverde.edu   CB code: 4603

- Public 2-year community college
- Commuter campus in large town

General. Founded in 1947. Regionally accredited. **Enrollment:** 1,060 degree-seeking undergraduates. **Degrees:** 114 associate awarded. **Location:** 120 miles from Palm Springs. **Calendar:** Semester, limited summer session. **Full-time faculty:** 41 total; 15% have terminal degrees. **Part-time faculty:** 95 total; 3% have terminal degrees.

Transfer out. Colleges most students transferred to 2011: CSU: San Bernardino, San Diego State University, University of California: Riverside, Brandman University, University of Phoenix.

Basis for selection. Open admission, but selective for some programs. Limited admission to nursing program. **Adult students:** SAT/ACT scores not required.

2011-2012 Annual costs. Tuition/fees: $1,080; $6,360 out-of-state. Per-credit charge: $36 in-state; $212 out-of-state. Books/supplies: $1,632. Personal expenses: $2,016.

Financial aid. All financial aid based on need. Need-based aid available for part-time students. Work-study available nights, weekends and for part-time students.

Application procedures. Admission: Closing date 8/26. No application fee. Application must be submitted online. Admission notification on a rolling basis. SAT or ACT recommended for placement. **Financial aid:** No deadline. FAFSA, institutional form required. Applicants notified on a rolling basis starting 7/1; must reply within 4 week(s) of notification.

Academics. Special study options: Cooperative education, distance learning, dual enrollment of high school students, ESL, independent study. License preparation in nursing, paramedic, real estate. **Credit/placement by examination:** AP, CLEP, institutional tests. 12 credit hours maximum toward associate degree. **Support services:** GED test center, learning center, remedial instruction, study skills assistance, tutoring, writing center.

Majors. Business: Accounting, business admin, office/clerical. **Computer sciences:** General. **English:** English lit. **History:** General. **Liberal arts:** Arts/sciences. **Protective services:** Firefighting, law enforcement admin. **Visual/performing arts:** Music. **Work/family studies:** Child development.

Most popular majors. Business/marketing 49%, liberal arts 38%, social sciences 6%.

Computing on campus. 125 workstations in library, computer center. Commuter students can connect to campus network. Online course registration, wireless network available.

Student life. Freshman orientation: Mandatory. Preregistration for classes offered. **Activities:** Literary magazine, student government.

Athletics. Intramural: Soccer. **Team name:** Pirates.

Student services. Career counseling, services for economically disadvantaged, student employment services, financial aid counseling, personal counseling, placement for graduates. **Physically disabled:** Services for visually, speech, hearing impaired. **Transfer:** Transfer center, transfer adviser, college fairs on campus for students transferring to 4-year colleges.

Contact. E-mail: mwalnoha@paloverde.edu
Phone: (760) 921-5500
Melinda Walnoha, Registrar, Palo Verde College, One College Drive, Blythe, CA 92225

Palomar College
San Marcos, California   CB member
www.palomar.edu   CB code: 4602

- Public 2-year community college
- Commuter campus in large town

General. Founded in 1946. Regionally accredited. Off-campus sites located throughout North San Diego County area. **Enrollment:** 13,259 degree-seeking undergraduates. **Degrees:** 1,761 associate awarded. **Location:** 40 miles from San Diego. **Calendar:** Semester, extensive summer session. **Full-time faculty:** 280 total. **Part-time faculty:** 930 total. **Special facilities:** Arboretum, observatory.

Transfer out. Colleges most students transferred to 2011: CSU: San Marcos, UC: San Diego, San Diego State University, University of Phoenix.

Basis for selection. Open admission, but selective for some programs. ASSET mathematics and English tests required for nursing applicants. **Adult students:** SAT/ACT scores not required.

2011-2012 Annual costs. Tuition/fees: $1,124; $6,404 out-of-state. Per-credit charge: $36 in-state; $212 out-of-state. Books/supplies: $648. Personal expenses: $1,620.

Financial aid. All financial aid based on need. Need-based aid available for part-time students. Work-study available nights, weekends and for part-time students.

Application procedures. Admission: Priority date 6/11; no deadline. No application fee. Application deadlines for nursing program April 1 for fall semester, November 1 for spring semester. **Financial aid:** Priority date 4/1; no closing date. FAFSA, institutional form required. Applicants notified on a rolling basis starting 6/1.

Academics. Special study options: Cooperative education, distance learning, dual enrollment of high school students, ESL, internships, liberal arts/career combination, study abroad, weekend college. License preparation in nursing, paramedic, real estate. **Credit/placement by examination:** AP, CLEP, IB, institutional tests. 15 credit hours maximum toward associate degree. **Support services:** Learning center, pre-admission summer program, reduced course load, remedial instruction, tutoring, writing center.

Majors. Architecture: Technology. **Area/ethnic studies:** Women's. **Biology:** General. **Business:** General, accounting technology, administrative services, business admin, e-commerce, insurance, international, real estate. **Communications:** Advertising, communications/speech/rhetoric, journalism, radio/TV. **Communications technology:** Animation/special effects, desktop publishing, graphic/printing, photo/film/video. **Computer sciences:** Computer graphics, information technology, networking, programming, web page design. **Education:** General, early childhood special. **Engineering:** Pre-engineering. **English:** English lit. **Foreign languages:** General, French, sign language interpretation. **Health services:** Dental assistant, EMT paramedic, medical secretary, nursing (RN), substance abuse counseling. **Human services:** General. **Liberal arts:** Arts/sciences, humanities, library assistant. **Math:** General. **Parks/recreation:** General, health/fitness. **Physical sciences:** Astronomy, chemistry, geology. **Protective services:** Fire safety technology, forensics, homeland security, police science. **Psychology:** General. **Social sciences:** General, archaeology, economics, GIS/cartography, sociology. **Visual/performing arts:** Art, ceramics, commercial/advertising art, dance, design, dramatic, drawing, fashion design, film/cinema/video, graphic design, interior design, metal/jewelry, music, painting, photography, sculpture. **Work/family studies:** General, apparel marketing, child care management, child care service, family/community services.

Most popular majors. Business/marketing 6%, liberal arts 11%, social sciences 28%, visual/performing arts 22%.

Computing on campus. 922 workstations in library, computer center, student center. Online course registration, online library, wireless network available.

Student life. Freshman orientation: Available. Preregistration for classes offered. **Activities:** Bands, choral groups, dance, drama, literary magazine, music ensembles, musical theater, radio station, student government, student newspaper, symphony orchestra, TV station.

Athletics. NJCAA. **Intercollegiate:** Baseball M, basketball, diving, football (tackle) M, golf M, soccer, softball W, swimming, tennis, track and field M, volleyball, water polo, wrestling M. **Intramural:** Volleyball W. **Team name:** Comets.

Student services. Career counseling, services for economically disadvantaged, student employment services, financial aid counseling, health services, minority student services, on-campus daycare, personal counseling, placement for graduates, veterans' counselor. **Physically disabled:** Services for visually, speech, hearing impaired. **Transfer:** Transfer center, transfer adviser, college fairs on campus for students transferring to 4-year colleges.

Contact. E-mail: admissions@palomar.edu
Phone: (760) 744-1150 ext. 2164 Fax: (760) 761-3536
Herman Lee, Director of Enrollment Services, Palomar College, 1140 West Mission Road, San Marcos, CA 92069-1487

Pasadena City College
Pasadena, California
www.pasadena.edu

CB code: 4604

- Public 2-year community college
- Commuter campus in small city

General. Founded in 1924. Regionally accredited. **Enrollment:** 19,895 degree-seeking undergraduates. **Degrees:** 1,607 associate awarded. **Location:** 10 miles from downtown Los Angeles. **Calendar:** Semester, limited summer session. **Full-time faculty:** 398 total; 24% have terminal degrees. **Part-time faculty:** 658 total; 16% have terminal degrees. **Class size:** 6% < 20, 66% 20-39, 25% 40-49, 2% 50-99, 1% >100. **Special facilities:** Observatory.

Student profile.

Out-of-state:	3%	25 or older:	36%

Transfer out. Colleges most students transferred to 2011: California State University: Los Angeles, Long Beach, Northridge; California State Polytechnic Institute: Pomona.

Basis for selection. Open admission, but selective for some programs. Admission to RN, LVN, dental hygiene programs based on test scores, interview, high school record; minimum 2.0 high school GPA required. School and College Ability Tests, SAT, ACT, or California Achievement Test scores used for admission to some programs. Interview required of dental hygiene majors. Audition required of music majors.

2011-2012 Annual costs. Tuition/fees: $1,104; $6,564 out-of-state. Per-credit charge: $36 in-state; $218 out-of-state. Books/supplies: $1,638. Personal expenses: $3,780.

Financial aid. All financial aid based on need. Work-study available nights, weekends and for part-time students.

Application procedures. Admission: Closing date 8/11. No application fee. Admission notification on a rolling basis beginning on or about 4/1. **Financial aid:** Priority date 5/13; no closing date. FAFSA required. Applicants notified on a rolling basis starting 6/1; must reply within 2 week(s) of notification.

Academics. Special study options: Accelerated study, distance learning, dual enrollment of high school students, ESL, independent study, liberal arts/career combination, study abroad. **Credit/placement by examination:** AP, CLEP, institutional tests. 12 credit hours maximum toward associate degree. **Support services:** Learning center, pre-admission summer program, reduced course load, remedial instruction, study skills assistance, tutoring, writing center.

Majors. Biology: General. **Business:** General, accounting, administrative services, banking/financial services, entrepreneurial studies, fashion, hospitality/recreation, management information systems, office/clerical, real estate, sales/distribution, tourism promotion. **Communications:** Broadcast journalism, communications/speech/rhetoric, journalism. **Communications technology:** General. **Computer sciences:** Applications programming, data processing, programming. **Education:** Early childhood. **English:** Rhetoric/composition. **Health services:** Clinical lab technology, dental assistant, dental hygiene, dental lab technology, licensed practical nurse, medical assistant, medical radiologic technology/radiation therapy, medical secretary, nursing (RN), speech-language pathology assistant. **Liberal arts:** Arts/sciences, library assistant. **Parks/recreation:** General. **Protective services:** Firefighting, police science. **Psychology:** General. **Social sciences:** General. **Visual/performing arts:** Ceramics, commercial photography, commercial/advertising art, crafts, drawing, music, painting, printmaking, sculpture, studio arts.

Computing on campus. 300 workstations in library, computer center, student center.

Student life. Freshman orientation: Available. Preregistration for classes offered. **Activities:** Bands, choral groups, dance, drama, film society, international student organizations, literary magazine, music ensembles, musical theater, radio station, student government, student newspaper, symphony orchestra, TV station, wide variety of religious, political, ethnic, and social service organizations.

Athletics. Intercollegiate: Badminton W, baseball M, basketball, cross-country, football (tackle) M, soccer, softball W, swimming, tennis W, track and field, volleyball W, water polo W. **Team name:** Lancers.

Student services. Career counseling, services for economically disadvantaged, student employment services, financial aid counseling, health services, on-campus daycare, personal counseling, placement for graduates, veterans' counselor. **Physically disabled:** Services for visually, speech, hearing impaired. **Transfer:** Transfer center, transfer adviser, college fairs on campus for students transferring to 4-year colleges.

Contact. Phone: (626) 578-7396 Fax: (626) 585-7912
Associate Dean of Admissions and Records, Pasadena City College, 1570
East Colorado Boulevard, Pasadena, CA 91106

Platt College: Los Angeles
Alhambra, California
www.plattcollege.edu   CB code: 3014

- For-profit 2-year visual arts and technical college
- Commuter campus in very large city
- Application essay, interview required

General. Accredited by ACCSC. **Enrollment:** 258 degree-seeking undergraduates. **Degrees:** 18 bachelor's, 121 associate awarded. **Location:** 10
miles from dowtown Los Angeles. **Calendar:** Differs by program, extensive
summer session. **Full-time faculty:** 6 total. **Part-time faculty:** 21 total.
Class size: 85% < 20, 15% 20-39.

Transfer out. Colleges most students transferred to 2011: University of
LaVerne, University of Phoenix.

Basis for selection. Must score at least 126 on CPAT for admissions.
Multimedia program requires degree. MCSE program requires computer
background. **Learning Disabled:** Students with learning disabilities allowed
30 extra minutes on CPAT examination.

2011-2012 Annual costs. Cost varies by program. Associate degree cost
ranges from $26,967 to $37,995. Bachelor's degree cost ranges from
$73,082.50 to $79,097.50.

Financial aid. Need-based: Need-based aid available for part-time students. Work-study available nights, weekends and for part-time students.

Application procedures. Admission: No deadline. $75 fee. Admission
notification on a rolling basis. **Financial aid:** Priority date 3/2; no closing
date. FAFSA, institutional form required. Applicants notified on a rolling
basis starting 1/1.

Academics. Special study options: Accelerated study, cooperative education, internships. Bachelor's degree programs available on campus. **Credit/
placement by examination:** AP, CLEP, institutional tests. 48 credit hours
maximum toward associate degree. **Support services:** Tutoring.

Majors. Computer sciences: General, computer graphics. **Visual/per-
forming arts:** General, commercial/advertising art.

Computing on campus. 60 workstations in library.

Student life. Freshman orientation: Mandatory. Preregistration for
classes offered. 2-hour program on or around first day of classes.

Student services. Adult student services, career counseling, student
employment services, financial aid counseling, placement for graduates.
Transfer: Re-entry adviser, pre-admission transcript evaluation for new students. Transfer adviser for students transferring to 4-year colleges.

Contact. E-mail: DHarper@PlattCollege.edu
Phone: (626) 300-5444 Toll-free number: (866) 752-8852
Fax: (626) 457-8295
Daryle Harper, Director of Admissions, Platt College: Los Angeles, 1000
South Fremont Avenue A9W, Alhambra, CA 91803

Porterville College
Porterville, California
www.portervillecollege.edu   CB code: 4608

- Public 2-year community college
- Commuter campus in large town

General. Founded in 1927. Regionally accredited. **Enrollment:** 4,320
undergraduates. **Degrees:** 179 associate awarded. **Location:** 75 miles from
Fresno, 50 miles from Bakersfield. **Calendar:** Semester, limited summer
session. **Full-time faculty:** 69 total. **Part-time faculty:** 79 total. **Special
facilities:** Anthropology library.

Basis for selection. Open admission.

2011-2012 Annual costs. Tuition/fees: $1,114; $6,304 out-of-state. Per-
credit charge: $36 in-state; $209 out-of-state. Books/supplies: $1,638. Per-
sonal expenses: $2,150.

Financial aid. Need-based: Work-study available nights, weekends and
for part-time students.

Application procedures. Admission: No deadline. No application fee.
Admission notification on a rolling basis. **Financial aid:** Priority date 3/1;
no closing date. FAFSA required. Applicants notified on a rolling basis; must
reply within 2 week(s) of notification.

Academics. Special study options: Double major, dual enrollment of high
school students. **Credit/placement by examination:** AP, CLEP, institutional
tests. 30 credit hours maximum toward associate degree. **Support services:**
Learning center, reduced course load, remedial instruction, tutoring.

Majors. Biology: General. **Business:** General, administrative services,
banking/financial services, business admin, office/clerical, real estate. **Computer sciences:** General. **Education:** General. **English:** English lit. **Health
services:** Licensed practical nurse. **Liberal arts:** Arts/sciences. **Math:** General. **Physical sciences:** Chemistry. **Protective services:** Police science.
Social sciences: General, criminology. **Visual/performing arts:** General,
commercial/advertising art, music, studio arts. **Work/family studies:** Child
care management.

Computing on campus. 25 workstations in library, computer center.

Student life. Activities: Choral groups, drama, music ensembles, musical
theater, student government, Mexican-American Student Association.

Athletics. NJCAA. **Intercollegiate:** Baseball M, basketball, tennis, volleyball W. **Team name:** Pirates.

Student services. Career counseling, student employment services, health
services, on-campus daycare, personal counseling, placement for graduates,
veterans' counselor. **Physically disabled:** Services for visually, speech, hearing impaired. **Transfer:** Transfer adviser for students transferring to 4-
year colleges.

Contact. Phone: (209) 791-2220 Fax: (209) 784-4779
Virginia Gurrola, Vice President Student Services and Enrollment,
Porterville College, 100 East College Avenue, Porterville, CA 93257

Professional Golfers Career College
Temecula, California
www.golfcollege.edu   CB code: 3548

- For-profit 2-year golf academy
- Commuter campus in small city

General. Accredited by ACICS. **Enrollment:** 146 degree-seeking undergraduates. **Degrees:** 372 associate awarded. **Location:** 60 miles from San
Diego. **Calendar:** Semester. **Full-time faculty:** 6 total; 33% have terminal
degrees. **Part-time faculty:** 18 total; 11% women. **Special facilities:** Pro
shop, video studio.

Student profile. Among degree-seeking undergraduates, 100% enrolled in
a vocational program, 146 enrolled as first-time, first-year students.

Basis for selection. Handicap of 20 or below, 3 letters of personal character reference, 1 letter of recommendation attesting to golf ability required.
Home schooled: Transcript of courses and grades, letter of recommendation
(nonparent) required.

2011-2012 Annual costs. Tuition/fees: $13,000. Books/supplies: $1,000.

Financial aid. Need-based: Work-study available nights, weekends and
for part-time students.

Application procedures. Admission: No deadline. $75 fee. Application
must be submitted on paper. Admission notification on a rolling basis. **Financial aid:** No deadline.

Academics. Special study options: Honors. **Credit/placement by examination:** AP, CLEP.

Majors. Parks/recreation: Facilities management.

Computing on campus. 12 workstations in computer center. Online
library, wireless network available.

Student life. Freshman orientation: Mandatory. Preregistration for
classes offered. **Policies:** PGCC performs a mandatory drug test on all students
in their first semester. The Student Handbook details college regulations
concerning drugs and alcohol.

Student services. Alcohol/substance abuse counseling, career counseling, financial aid counseling, personal counseling, placement for graduates, veterans' counselor.

Contact. E-mail: admin@progolfed.com
Phone: (951) 719-2994 Toll-free number: (800) 877-4380
Fax: (951) 719-1643
Gary Gilleon, Admissions Director, Professional Golfers Career College, 26109 Ynez Road, Temecula, CA 92591

Reedley College
Reedley, California
www.reedleycollege.edu   CB code: 4655

♦ Public 2-year community college
♦ Commuter campus in large town

General. Founded in 1926. Regionally accredited. Courses also offered at community campus sites in Madera, Clovis, Sanger, Easton, Selma, Kerman, Oakhurst, Parlier, Fowler, Orange Cove, Dinuba, Kingsburg, and Sunnyside. **Enrollment:** 6,514 degree-seeking undergraduates. **Degrees:** 591 associate awarded. **Location:** 25 miles from Fresno. **Calendar:** Semester, extensive summer session. **Full-time faculty:** 196 total. **Part-time faculty:** 405 total.

Student profile.

25 or older:	35%	Live on campus:	4%

Transfer out. Colleges most students transferred to 2011: California State University: Fresno, California State University: Long Beach.

Basis for selection. Open admission. **Home schooled:** If under 18, a letter from parent required.

2011-2012 Annual costs. Tuition/fees: $1,114; $7,564 out-of-state. Per-credit charge: $36 in-state; $251 out-of-state. Room/board: $4,490. Books/supplies: $1,566. Personal expenses: $2,600.

Financial aid. All financial aid based on need. Need-based aid available for part-time students. Work-study available nights, weekends and for part-time students. **Additional information:** Board of Governors fee waiver available for low-income students. Book voucher available for EOPS students.

Application procedures. Admission: No deadline. No application fee. Admission notification on a rolling basis. **Financial aid:** Priority date 3/2; no closing date. FAFSA required. Applicants notified on a rolling basis starting 3/2; must reply within 3 week(s) of notification.

Academics. Special study options: Cooperative education, cross-registration, distance learning, double major, dual enrollment of high school students, ESL, honors, independent study, study abroad, weekend college. License preparation in aviation, dental hygiene. **Credit/placement by examination:** AP, CLEP. 48 credit hours maximum toward associate degree. **Support services:** Learning center, pre-admission summer program, reduced course load, remedial instruction, study skills assistance, tutoring, writing center.

Majors. Biology: General. **Business:** Accounting. **Computer sciences:** General, computer science, information systems. **Conservation:** Forestry. **Education:** Early childhood, physical. **English:** English lit. **Foreign languages:** General. **General. Business:** Business, plant sciences. **Health services:** Dental assistant. **Liberal arts:** Arts/sciences. **Math:** General. **Social sciences:** General. **Visual/performing arts:** Art, dramatic, music.

Most popular majors. Interdisciplinary studies 80%.

Computing on campus. 140 workstations in dormitories, library, computer center. Dormitories wired for high-speed internet access and linked to campus network. Commuter students can connect to campus network. Online course registration, online library available.

Student life. Freshman orientation: Available. Preregistration for classes offered. **Housing:** Single-sex dorms available. $140 deposit. **Activities:** Bands, choral groups, drama, music ensembles, musical theater, student government, student newspaper, symphony orchestra.

Athletics. NJCAA. **Intercollegiate:** Baseball M, basketball, equestrian, football (tackle) M, golf, softball W, tennis, track and field, volleyball W. **Team name:** Tigers.

Student services. Adult student services, alcohol/substance abuse counseling, career counseling, services for economically disadvantaged, student employment services, financial aid counseling, health services, minority student services, on-campus daycare, personal counseling, placement for graduates, veterans' counselor, women's services. **Physically disabled:** Services

for visually, speech, hearing impaired. **Transfer:** Transfer adviser, college fairs on campus for students transferring to 4-year colleges.

Contact. Phone: (559) 638-0323 Fax: (559) 638-5040
Leticia Alvarez, Admissions and Records Manager, Reedley College, 995 North Reed Avenue, Reedley, CA 93654

Rio Hondo College
Whittier, California
www.riohondo.edu   CB code: 4663

♦ Public 2-year community college
♦ Commuter campus in small city

General. Founded in 1960. Regionally accredited. **Enrollment:** 8,634 degree-seeking undergraduates. **Degrees:** 784 associate awarded. **Location:** 15 miles from Los Angeles. **Calendar:** Semester, extensive summer session. **Full-time faculty:** 194 total; 44% minority, 50% women. **Part-time faculty:** 315 total; 15% minority, 55% women. **Special facilities:** Observatory, nature preserve.

Student profile. Among degree-seeking undergraduates, 3,732 enrolled as first-time, first-year students.

Out-of-state:	4%	Asian American:	2%
African American:	1%	Hispanic American:	68%

Transfer out. Colleges most students transferred to 2011: Cal State Los Angeles, Cal State Long Beach, Cal State Fullerton, Cal State Polytech, University of California-Los Angeles.

Basis for selection. Open admission, but selective for some programs. Nursing program has special requirements. **Learning Disabled:** Disabled Services Program available to students with disabilities.

2011-2012 Annual costs. Tuition/fees: $1,122; $6,612 out-of-state. Per-credit charge: $36 in-state; $219 out-of-state. Books/supplies: $1,656. Personal expenses: $4,185.

Financial aid. Need-based: Need-based aid available for part-time students. Work-study available nights, weekends and for part-time students.

Application procedures. Admission: No deadline. No application fee. Admission notification on a rolling basis. **Financial aid:** Priority date 7/15; no closing date. FAFSA required. Applicants notified on a rolling basis.

Academics. Special study options: Distance learning, dual enrollment of high school students, ESL, honors, independent study, study abroad, weekend college. License preparation in nursing. **Credit/placement by examination:** AP, CLEP, institutional tests. 12 credit hours maximum toward associate degree. **Support services:** Learning center, pre-admission summer program, remedial instruction, tutoring, writing center.

Majors. Architecture: Environmental design. **Area/ethnic studies:** Chicano/Hispanic-American/Latino. **Business:** Accounting. **Communications:** Journalism, media studies. **Communications technology:** General, graphic/printing. **Computer sciences:** General. **Health services:** Licensed practical nurse, nursing (RN). **Liberal arts:** Arts/sciences, library assistant. **Protective services:** Fire safety technology, police science. **Social sciences:** Geography. **Visual/performing arts:** General, commercial/advertising art, dance, dramatic, music, photography.

Most popular majors. Business/marketing 12%, education 7%, health sciences 14%, interdisciplinary studies 42%, public administration/social services 19%.

Computing on campus. Commuter students can connect to campus network. Online course registration, online library, wireless network available.

Student life. Freshman orientation: Available. Preregistration for classes offered. **Activities:** Jazz band, choral groups, dance, drama, film society, literary magazine, music ensembles, musical theater, radio station, student government, student newspaper, TV station.

Athletics. NJCAA. **Intercollegiate:** Baseball M, basketball, cross-country, golf, soccer, softball W, swimming, tennis, track and field, volleyball W, water polo, wrestling M. **Team name:** Roadrunners.

Student services. Career counseling, student employment services, financial aid counseling, health services, on-campus daycare, personal counseling, veterans' counselor. **Physically disabled:** Services for visually, speech, hearing impaired. **Transfer:** Transfer center, transfer adviser, college fairs on campus for students transferring to 4-year colleges.

Contact. Phone: (562) 692-0921 ext. 3415 Fax: (562) 692-8318
Judy Pearson, Director of Admissions and Records, Rio Hondo College,
3600 Workman Mill Road, Whittier, CA 90601-1699

Riverside Community College
Riverside, California
CB member
www.rcc.edu
CB code: 4658

- Public 2-year community college
- Commuter campus in large city

General. Founded in 1916. Regionally accredited. **Enrollment:** 12,626 degree-seeking undergraduates. **Degrees:** 1,881 associate awarded. **ROTC:** Army, Naval, Air Force. **Location:** 60 miles from Los Angeles. **Calendar:** Semester, limited summer session. **Full-time faculty:** 222 total; 31% have terminal degrees, 30% minority, 50% women. **Part-time faculty:** 443 total; 31% minority, 57% women. **Special facilities:** Planetarium, aquatics complex.

Transfer out. Colleges most students transferred to 2011: University of California: Riverside, California State University: San Bernardino.

Basis for selection. Open admission, but selective for some programs. Limited admission to nursing program.

2011-2012 Annual costs. Tuition/fees: $1,114; $6,394 out-of-state. Per-credit charge: $36 in-state; $212 out-of-state. Books/supplies: $1,666. Personal expenses: $4,520.

2011-2012 Financial aid. Need-based: 98% of total undergraduate aid awarded as scholarships/grants, 2% as loans/jobs. Need-based aid available for part-time students. Work-study available nights, weekends and for part-time students. **Non-need-based:** Scholarships awarded for academics, alumni affiliation, art, leadership, minority status, music/drama, state residency.

Application procedures. Admission: No deadline. No application fee. Admission notification on a rolling basis. **Financial aid:** Priority date 3/1; no closing date. FAFSA, institutional form required. Applicants notified on a rolling basis starting 7/1.

Academics. Special study options: Distance learning, dual enrollment of high school students, ESL, honors, study abroad, weekend college. License preparation in nursing. **Credit/placement by examination:** AP, CLEP, institutional tests. 30 credit hours maximum toward associate degree. **Support services:** Remedial instruction, tutoring, writing center.

Majors. Business: General, accounting, marketing, real estate. **Computer sciences:** General, programming. **Education:** Early childhood. **Foreign languages:** Sign language interpretation. **Health services:** Licensed practical nurse, nursing (RN). **Protective services:** Fire safety technology. **Visual/performing arts:** Photography. **Work/family studies:** General, food/nutrition.

Most popular majors. Health sciences 12%, interdisciplinary studies 76%.

Computing on campus. Online library, wireless network available.

Student life. Activities: Bands, choral groups, dance, drama, music ensembles, Model UN, musical theater, student government, student newspaper, College Democrats, MECHA, Latter-day Saints student association, multicultural advisory council, African American student union.

Athletics. Intercollegiate: Baseball M, basketball, cross-country, diving, football (tackle) M, golf, soccer, softball W, swimming, tennis, track and field, volleyball W, water polo. **Intramural:** Badminton, baseball M, basketball, bowling, golf, racquetball, soccer, tennis, volleyball. **Team name:** Tigers.

Student services. Services for economically disadvantaged, student employment services, financial aid counseling, health services, on-campus daycare, placement for graduates, veterans' counselor. **Physically disabled:** Services for visually, speech, hearing impaired. **Transfer:** Transfer center, transfer adviser, college fairs on campus for students transferring to 4-year colleges.

Contact. E-mail: webmstr@rcc.edu
Phone: (951) 222-8600
Joy Chambers, Dean of Enrollment Services, Riverside Community College, 4800 Magnolia Avenue, Riverside, CA 92506

Sacramento City College
Sacramento, California
www.scc.losrios.edu
CB code: 4670

- Public 2-year community college
- Commuter campus in large city

General. Founded in 1916. Regionally accredited. **Enrollment:** 15,927 degree-seeking undergraduates. **Degrees:** 1,124 associate awarded. **ROTC:** Army, Naval, Air Force. **Location:** 75 miles from San Francisco. **Calendar:** Semester, extensive summer session. **Full-time faculty:** 327 total. **Part-time faculty:** 494 total. **Special facilities:** Observatory.

Student profile.

Out-of-state:	5%	**25 or older:**	68%

Basis for selection. Open admission.

2011-2012 Annual costs. Tuition/fees: $1,112; $6,812 out-of-state. Per-credit charge: $36 in-state; $226 out-of-state. Books/supplies: $1,638. Personal expenses: $2,826.

Financial aid. Need-based: Need-based aid available for part-time students. Work-study available nights, weekends and for part-time students.

Application procedures. Admission: Priority date 7/28; no deadline. No application fee. Admission notification on a rolling basis. **Financial aid:** Priority date 3/2; no closing date. FAFSA required. Applicants notified on a rolling basis starting 7/1; must reply within 2 week(s) of notification.

Academics. Special study options: Accelerated study, cooperative education, cross-registration, distance learning, double major, dual enrollment of high school students, ESL, honors, independent study, internships, study abroad, weekend college. License preparation in aviation, dental hygiene, nursing, physical therapy, real estate. **Credit/placement by examination:** AP, CLEP, institutional tests. 15 credit hours maximum toward associate degree. **Support services:** Learning center, remedial instruction, study skills assistance, tutoring, writing center.

Majors. Area/ethnic studies: Women's. **Business:** General, accounting, administrative services, international marketing, management information systems, office/clerical, real estate. **Communications:** Journalism. **Communications technology:** Graphic/printing. **Computer sciences:** General. **Education:** Bilingual, special ed. **Health services:** Dental assistant, dental hygiene, licensed practical nurse, medical secretary, nursing (RN), occupational therapy assistant, physical therapy assistant. **Liberal arts:** Arts/sciences, library assistant. **Math:** General. **Protective services:** Corrections, police science. **Social sciences:** General. **Visual/performing arts:** General, commercial photography, dramatic, music, music management, studio arts. **Work/family studies:** General, child care management, clothing/textiles, family/community services.

Computing on campus. 350 workstations in library, computer center. Online course registration available.

Student life. Freshman orientation: Available. Preregistration for classes offered. **Activities:** Bands, choral groups, dance, drama, literary magazine, music ensembles, musical theater, student government, student newspaper, minority groups, professional associations, Bible club, gay and lesbian student alliance, special interest groups.

Athletics. Intercollegiate: Baseball M, basketball, cross-country, football (tackle) M, golf W, soccer W, softball W, swimming, tennis, track and field, volleyball W, water polo W, wrestling M. **Intramural:** Badminton, baseball M, basketball, bowling, boxing M, fencing, football (tackle) M, golf, handball, racquetball, softball, swimming, table tennis, tennis, volleyball. **Team name:** Panthers.

Student services. Adult student services, career counseling, services for economically disadvantaged, student employment services, financial aid counseling, health services, on-campus daycare, personal counseling, placement for graduates, veterans' counselor. **Physically disabled:** Services for visually, speech, hearing impaired. **Transfer:** Transfer center, transfer adviser, college fairs on campus for students transferring to 4-year colleges.

Contact. E-mail: sccaeinfo@scc.losrios.edu
Phone: (916) 558-2351 Fax: (916) 558-2190
Catherine Fites, Dean of Enrollment and Student Services, Sacramento City College, 3835 Freeport Boulevard, Sacramento, CA 95822

Saddleback College
Mission Viejo, California
www.saddleback.edu
CB code: 4747

♦ Public 2-year community college
♦ Commuter campus in small city

General. Founded in 1967. Regionally accredited. **Enrollment:** 25,874 undergraduates. **Degrees:** 1,210 associate awarded. **Location:** 55 miles from Los Angeles and San Diego. **Calendar:** Semester, limited summer session. **Full-time faculty:** 233 total. **Part-time faculty:** 556 total. **Special facilities:** Solar observatory, outdoor environmental laboratory, golf driving range, computer/technology centers, greenhouse.

Basis for selection. Open admission, but selective for some programs. Nursing candidates must complete core curriculum with 2.5 GPA or better before screening process. SAT/ACT recommended for placement and counseling.

High school preparation. 10 units recommended. Recommended units include English 3, mathematics 2, social studies 3 and science 2.

2011-2012 Annual costs. Tuition/fees: $1,114; $6,484 out-of-state. Per-credit charge: $36 in-state; $215 out-of-state. Books/supplies: $1,638. Personal expenses: $2,862.

Financial aid. All financial aid based on need. Need-based aid available for part-time students. Work-study available nights, weekends and for part-time students.

Application procedures. Admission: No deadline. No application fee. Admission notification on a rolling basis. **Financial aid:** Closing date 6/30. FAFSA required. Applicants notified on a rolling basis starting 4/1.

Academics. Special study options: Cooperative education, cross-registration, distance learning, double major, dual enrollment of high school students, ESL, honors, independent study, internships, student-designed major, study abroad, weekend college. License preparation in nursing, paramedic, real estate. **Credit/placement by examination:** AP, CLEP, institutional tests. 30 credit hours maximum toward associate degree. **Support services:** Learning center, pre-admission summer program, reduced course load, remedial instruction, study skills assistance, tutoring, writing center.

Honors college/program. Overall GPA of 3.25 in all academic work required.

Majors. Area/ethnic studies: Women's. **Biology:** General. **Business:** General, accounting, administrative services, business admin, fashion, marketing, office management, real estate, tourism/travel. **Communications:** Broadcast journalism, journalism. **Computer sciences:** General, computer science, programming. **Conservation:** General, environmental studies. **Education:** Early childhood, family/consumer sciences, mathematics, music, physical, social science. **Engineering:** General. **English:** British lit, English lit, rhetoric/composition. **Foreign languages:** General, sign language interpretation. **General:** Ornamental horticulture. **Health services:** Medical assistant, nursing (RN), surgical technology. **History:** General. **Liberal arts:** Arts/sciences. **Math:** General. **Parks/recreation:** Health/fitness. **Philosophy/religion:** Philosophy. **Physical sciences:** Astronomy, chemistry, geology, physics. **Psychology:** General. **Social sciences:** General, anthropology, economics, geography, international relations, political science, sociology. **Visual/performing arts:** Art, commercial photography, commercial/advertising art, dance, design, dramatic, fashion design, interior design, music, photography, studio arts. **Work/family studies:** General, food/nutrition.

Most popular majors. Business/marketing 13%, health sciences 11%, liberal arts 42%.

Computing on campus. 1,030 workstations in library, computer center, student center. Commuter students can connect to campus network. Online course registration, online library, wireless network available.

Student life. Activities: Bands, choral groups, dance, drama, literary magazine, music ensembles, musical theater, radio station, student government, student newspaper, symphony orchestra, TV station, Democratic Club, Republican Club, Christian Club, Black United Students, Hillel, Gay and Lesbian Club, Amnesty International, Muslim Student Union, environmental awareness, sign language club.

Athletics. NJCAA. **Intercollegiate:** Baseball M, basketball, cheerleading M, cross-country, diving, football (tackle) M, golf, soccer W, softball W, swimming, tennis, track and field, volleyball W, water polo. **Team name:** Gauchos.

Student services. Adult student services, alcohol/substance abuse counseling, career counseling, services for economically disadvantaged, student employment services, health services, on-campus daycare, personal counseling, placement for graduates, veterans' counselor, women's services. **Physically disabled:** Services for visually, speech, hearing impaired. **Transfer:** Re-entry adviser for new students. Transfer center, transfer adviser, college fairs on campus for students transferring to 4-year colleges.

Contact. E-mail: scadmissions@saddleback.edu
Phone: (949) 582-4555 Fax: (949) 347-8315
Jane Rosenkrans, Director, Admissions, Records and Enrollment Services, Saddleback College, 28000 Marguerite Parkway, Mission Viejo, CA 92692

Sage College
Moreno Valley, California
www.sagecollege.edu

♦ For-profit 2-year technical and career college
♦ Commuter campus in large city

General. Accredited by ACICS. Sage College offers exclusively Court Reporting or Paralegal Studies educational programs. **Enrollment:** 263 full-time, degree-seeking students. **Degrees:** 2 associate awarded. **Location:** 9 miles from Riverside. **Calendar:** Quarter, extensive summer session. **Full-time faculty:** 9 total. **Part-time faculty:** 17 total.

Basis for selection. Open admission. Satisfactory performance on institutional examination required. **Home schooled:** State high school equivalency certificate required.

2011-2012 Annual costs. Tuition/fees: $9,205. Charted figures above represent the three quarters of full time Court Reporting Program. Tuition for the Paralegal Studies Diploma program are based on units; typical three quarters' units are priced at $10,238 (includes textbooks). Required fees: $50. Books/supplies: $875.

Financial aid. Need-based: Work-study available nights, weekends and for part-time students.

Application procedures. Admission: No deadline. $100 fee. Admission notification on a rolling basis.

Academics. Special study options: Distance learning. **Credit/placement by examination:** AP, CLEP.

Computing on campus. 87 workstations in library, computer center.

Student life. Freshman orientation: Mandatory. Preregistration for classes offered.

Student services. Career counseling, financial aid counseling, personal counseling, placement for graduates. **Transfer:** Pre-admission transcript evaluation for new students.

Contact. E-mail: admissions@sagecollege.edu
Phone: (951) 781-2727 Toll-free number: (888) 755-sage
Fax: (951) 781-0570
Lauren Somma, Executive Director, Sage College, 12125 Day Street, Building L, Moreno Valley, CA 92557-6720

Salvation Army College for Officer Training at Crestmont
Rancho Palos Verdes, California
www.crestmont.edu
CB code: 3890

♦ Private 2-year seminary college
♦ Residential campus in small city

General. Regionally accredited. Christian education for Salvation Army officer candidates and others. Officers ordained ministers who manage human service programs and ministries in western US and overseas. Require applicants to have at least 1 year membership in local corps (church). Admissions inquiries should be directed to local Salvation Army community centers. **Enrollment:** 106 degree-seeking undergraduates. **Degrees:** 43 associate awarded. **Calendar:** Quarter. **Full-time faculty:** 16 total. **Part-time faculty:** 11 total. **Special facilities:** Salvation Army museum.

Basis for selection. Open admission, but selective for some programs. High school diploma, Salvation Army officer candidate status required.

2011-2012 Annual costs. Tuition/fees: $4,525. Tuition includes on-campus room and board, extra room and board charge for dependent children. Annual health insurance fee is $275. Books/supplies: $750.

Financial aid. Need-based: Work-study available nights, weekends and for part-time students.

Application procedures. Admission: No deadline. No application fee. **Financial aid:** No deadline.

Academics. Credit/placement by examination: AP, CLEP.

Majors. Theology: Missionary.

Student life. Housing: Housing for both students and families available.

Contact. Phone: (310) 377-0481
Maj. John Brackenbury, Director of Admissions, Salvation Army College for Officer Training at Crestmont, 30840 Hawthorne Boulevard, Rancho Palos Verdes, CA 90275

San Bernardino Valley College
San Bernardino, California
www.valleycollege.edu   CB code: 4679

- Public 2-year community college
- Small city

General. Founded in 1926. Regionally accredited. **Enrollment:** 13,822 undergraduates. **Degrees:** 598 associate awarded. **Location:** 60 miles from Los Angeles. **Calendar:** Semester, limited summer session. **Full-time faculty:** 154 total. **Part-time faculty:** 397 total. **Special facilities:** Planetarium.

Basis for selection. Open admission, but selective for some programs. Special requirements for nursing program. **Home schooled:** Transcript of courses and grades required.

2011-2012 Annual costs. Tuition/fees: $1,126; $6,406 out-of-state. Per-credit charge: $36 in-state; $212 out-of-state. Books/supplies: $1,638. Personal expenses: $2,000.

Financial aid. Need-based: Work-study available nights, weekends and for part-time students.

Application procedures. Admission: No deadline. No application fee. **Financial aid:** Priority date 5/25; no closing date. Applicants notified on a rolling basis starting 5/1; must reply within 2 week(s) of notification.

Academics. Special study options: Cooperative education, cross-registration, distance learning, double major, dual enrollment of high school students, ESL, honors, independent study, internships, liberal arts/career combination, weekend college. Service Members Opportunity College. **Credit/placement by examination:** AP, CLEP, institutional tests. **Support services:** GED preparation, learning center, pre-admission summer program, reduced course load, remedial instruction, study skills assistance, tutoring, writing center.

Majors. Biology: General. **Business:** Accounting, business admin, real estate. **Communications:** Communications/speech/rhetoric. **Computer sciences:** Computer science, systems analysis. **Human services:** Social work. **Liberal arts:** Arts/sciences, library assistant. **Math:** General. **Physical sciences:** Astronomy, chemistry, geology, physics. **Protective services:** Law enforcement admin. **Psychology:** General. **Social sciences:** Geography. **Visual/performing arts:** Commercial/advertising art.

Computing on campus. 180 workstations in library, computer center, student center.

Student life. Freshman orientation: Available. Preregistration for classes offered. **Activities:** Choral groups, drama, literary magazine, music ensembles, musical theater, radio station, student government, student newspaper, TV station, Campus Crusade for Christ, Newman Club, Baptist Student Union, Movimiento Estudiantil Chicano de Aztlan, Black Student Union, Young Democrats, Young Republicans.

Athletics. NCAA. **Intercollegiate:** Baseball M, basketball, cross-country, football (tackle) M, soccer, softball W, track and field, volleyball W. **Team name:** Wolverines.

Student services. Adult student services, career counseling, services for economically disadvantaged, student employment services, financial aid counseling, health services, on-campus daycare, personal counseling, placement for graduates, veterans' counselor. **Physically disabled:** Services for

visually, speech, hearing impaired. **Transfer:** Pre-admission transcript evaluation for new students.

Contact. E-mail: admissions@valleycollege.edu
Phone: (909) 384-4401
Dan Angelo, Associate Dean of Enrollment, San Bernardino Valley College, 701 South Mount Vernon Avenue, San Bernardino, CA 92410

San Diego City College
San Diego, California
www.sdccd.edu

- Public 2-year community and junior college
- Commuter campus in very large city

General. Founded in 1914. Regionally accredited. **Enrollment:** 9,545 degree-seeking undergraduates. **Degrees:** 701 associate awarded. **ROTC:** Army, Air Force. **Location:** Downtown. **Calendar:** Semester, extensive summer session. **Full-time faculty:** 167 total. **Part-time faculty:** 636 total; 35% minority. **Special facilities:** Computerized independent study and learning laboratories, vocational training centers, academic success center.

Student profile.

Out-of-state:	5%	25 or older:	49%

Transfer out. Colleges most students transferred to 2011: San Diego State University, University California San Diego (UCSD), CSU San Marcos, National University.

Basis for selection. Open admission. High school students seeking college admission must submit an approved application certified by parents, principal, registrar, and/or school district official.

2011-2012 Annual costs. Tuition/fees: $1,114; $6,604 out-of-state. Per-credit charge: $36 in-state; $219 out-of-state. Books/supplies: $1,620. Personal expenses: $3,078.

Financial aid. All financial aid based on need. Need-based aid available for part-time students. Work-study available nights, weekends and for part-time students.

Application procedures. Admission: No deadline. No application fee. **Financial aid:** Priority date 4/15; no closing date. FAFSA required. Applicants notified on a rolling basis starting 7/1; must reply within 4 week(s) of notification.

Academics. Special study options: Accelerated study, cooperative education, cross-registration, double major, dual enrollment of high school students, honors, independent study, internships, liberal arts/career combination, student-designed major, study abroad, teacher certification program, weekend college. **Credit/placement by examination:** AP, CLEP, institutional tests. 15 credit hours maximum toward associate degree. **Support services:** Learning center, pre-admission summer program, reduced course load, remedial instruction, study skills assistance, tutoring, writing center.

Majors. Area/ethnic studies: African, African-American, Latin American. **Biology:** General. **Business:** General, accounting, administrative services, business admin, labor relations, management information systems, management science, office technology, office/clerical, operations, purchasing, real estate, tourism promotion. **Communications:** Broadcast journalism. **Communications technology:** General. **Computer sciences:** General, applications programming, data entry, data processing, information systems, systems analysis. **Education:** Bilingual. **Engineering:** General. **English:** English lit, rhetoric/composition. **Foreign languages:** General, French, Italian, Spanish. **Health services:** Nursing (RN), substance abuse counseling. **History:** General. **Liberal arts:** Arts/sciences. **Math:** General, applied. **Parks/recreation:** Health/fitness. **Philosophy/religion:** Philosophy. **Physical sciences:** Chemistry, geology, physics. **Psychology:** General. **Social sciences:** General, anthropology, geography, political science. **Visual/performing arts:** General, art history/conservation, commercial/advertising art, dramatic, music, photography, studio arts. **Work/family studies:** Child care management.

Most popular majors. Family/consumer sciences 6%, foreign language 16%, health sciences 12%, interdisciplinary studies 25%, science technologies 8%, visual/performing arts 6%.

Computing on campus. 150 workstations in library, computer center, student center. Online course registration, online library, helpline, repair service available.

Student life. Freshman orientation: Available. Preregistration for classes offered. **Activities:** Jazz band, choral groups, dance, drama, film society, musical theater, radio station, student government, student newspaper, symphony orchestra, TV station, Arabic club, Italian club, MECHA, National

Society of Black Engineers, Society of Hispanic Professional Engineers, California Coalition Against Poverty, students for labor and solidarity, lesbian, gay, bisexual and transsexual student union.

Athletics. Intercollegiate: Baseball, basketball M, cross-country, football (tackle) M, golf, soccer, softball W, tennis, track and field, volleyball. **Intramural:** Archery, badminton, baseball M, basketball, bowling, racquetball, soccer, tennis, track and field, volleyball, weight lifting. **Team name:** Knights.

Student services. Adult student services, career counseling, student employment services, health services, on-campus daycare, personal counseling, placement for graduates, veterans' counselor. **Physically disabled:** Services for visually, speech, hearing impaired. **Transfer:** Pre-admission transcript evaluation for new students. Transfer center, transfer adviser, college fairs on campus for students transferring to 4-year colleges.

Contact. Phone: (619) 388-3475 Fax: (619) 388-3505
Lou Humphries, Student Services Supervisor II, San Diego City College, 1313 Park Boulevard, San Diego, CA 92101-4787

San Diego Mesa College
San Diego, California
www.sdmesa.edu

CB member
CB code: 4735

- Public 2-year community college
- Commuter campus in very large city

General. Founded in 1964. Regionally accredited. **Enrollment:** 13,526 degree-seeking undergraduates. **Degrees:** 907 associate awarded. **Calendar:** Semester, limited summer session. **Full-time faculty:** 281 total. **Part-time faculty:** 639 total. **Special facilities:** Anthropology museum.

Student profile.

Out-of-state:	1%	25 or older:	43%

Transfer out. Colleges most students transferred to 2011: San Diego State University, University of California San Diego.

Basis for selection. Open admission. Students without high school diploma or equivalent admitted provisionally. **Learning Disabled:** Disabled Student Service Program (DSPS) available.

2011-2012 Annual costs. Tuition/fees: $1,114; $6,604 out-of-state. Per-credit charge: $36 in-state; $219 out-of-state. Books/supplies: $1,620. Personal expenses: $3,078.

Financial aid. Need-based: Work-study available nights, weekends and for part-time students.

Application procedures. Admission: No deadline. No application fee. Admission notification on a rolling basis. Applications not accepted by mail. **Financial aid:** Priority date 3/2; no closing date. FAFSA required. Applicants notified on a rolling basis starting 6/15; must reply within 3 week(s) of notification.

Academics. Special study options: Accelerated study, distance learning, double major, dual enrollment of high school students, honors, independent study, internships, liberal arts/career combination, student-designed major, study abroad, teacher certification program. License preparation in physical therapy, radiology, real estate. **Credit/placement by examination:** AP, CLEP, institutional tests. 15 credit hours maximum toward associate degree. Institutional test required for placement and counseling. **Support services:** Learning center, reduced course load, remedial instruction, study skills assistance, tutoring.

Majors. Architecture: Landscape. **Area/ethnic studies:** African, African-American, Chicano/Hispanic-American/Latino. **Biology:** General. **Business:** General, accounting, business admin, fashion, hotel/motel admin, real estate, tourism/travel. **Computer sciences:** Programming, web page design. **Education:** Physical, sales/marketing, speech. **Engineering:** General. **Foreign languages:** American Sign Language, French, Spanish. **General:** Animal health. **Health services:** Dental assistant, dental lab technology, medical assistant, medical radiologic technology/radiation therapy, physical therapy assistant. **Liberal arts:** Arts/sciences. **Math:** General. **Philosophy/religion:** Philosophy. **Physical sciences:** Chemistry, physics. **Psychology:** General. **Social sciences:** General, anthropology, sociology. **Visual/performing arts:** Art, dramatic, interior design, music, studio arts. **Work/family studies:** Child development.

Most popular majors. Business/marketing 10%, liberal arts 20%.

Computing on campus. Commuter students can connect to campus network. Online library, wireless network available.

Student life. Freshman orientation: Available. Preregistration for classes offered. **Activities:** Bands, choral groups, dance, drama, international student organizations, music ensembles, student government, student newspaper.

Athletics. Intercollegiate: Badminton W, baseball M, basketball, cross-country, diving, football (tackle) M, soccer, softball W, swimming, tennis, track and field, volleyball, water polo. **Team name:** Olympians.

Student services. Adult student services, career counseling, services for economically disadvantaged, financial aid counseling, health services, on-campus daycare, personal counseling, placement for graduates, veterans' counselor. **Physically disabled:** Services for visually, speech, hearing impaired. **Transfer:** Transfer center, transfer adviser, college fairs on campus for students transferring to 4-year colleges.

Contact. E-mail: csawyer@sdccd.edu
Phone: (619) 388-2682 Fax: (619) 388-2960
Ivonne Alvarez, Director of Admissions and Records, San Diego Mesa College, 7250 Mesa College Drive, San Diego, CA 92111

San Diego Miramar College
San Diego, California
www.sdmiramar.edu

CB member
CB code: 4728

- Public 2-year community college
- Commuter campus in very large city

General. Founded in 1969. Regionally accredited. **Enrollment:** 12,360 undergraduates. **Degrees:** 571 associate awarded. **Location:** 9 miles from downtown. **Calendar:** Semester, limited summer session. **Full-time faculty:** 114 total. **Part-time faculty:** 435 total.

Student profile.

Out-of-state:	1%	25 or older:	45%

Basis for selection. Open admission.

2011-2012 Annual costs. Tuition/fees: $1,129; $6,619 out-of-state. Per-credit charge: $36 in-state; $219 out-of-state. Books/supplies: $1,620. Personal expenses: $3,078.

2010-2011 Financial aid. Need-based: 85% of total undergraduate aid awarded as scholarships/grants, 15% as loans/jobs. Need-based aid available for part-time students. Work-study available nights, weekends and for part-time students. **Additional information:** Private scholarships available.

Application procedures. Admission: No deadline. No application fee. Admission notification on a rolling basis. **Financial aid:** Priority date 3/2; no closing date. FAFSA required. Applicants notified on a rolling basis; must reply within 3 week(s) of notification.

Academics. Special study options: Accelerated study, cross-registration, distance learning, dual enrollment of high school students, honors, independent study, weekend college. **Credit/placement by examination:** AP, CLEP. 15 credit hours maximum toward associate degree. Institutional placement tests required. **Support services:** Learning center, remedial instruction, study skills assistance, tutoring.

Majors. Biology: General. **Business:** Administrative services, business admin, marketing, office/clerical. **Communications:** Communications/speech/rhetoric. **Computer sciences:** General. **Education:** Early childhood. **English:** English lit, rhetoric/composition. **Liberal arts:** Humanities. **Math:** General. **Parks/recreation:** Health/fitness. **Physical sciences:** Chemistry, physics. **Protective services:** Corrections, firefighting, law enforcement admin. **Psychology:** General. **Social sciences:** General. **Visual/performing arts:** Studio arts. **Work/family studies:** Family studies.

Most popular majors. Business/marketing 21%, legal studies 9%, liberal arts 43%, psychology 6%, security/protective services 30%, trade and industry 6%.

Computing on campus. 10 workstations in library, computer center.

Student life. Freshman orientation: Mandatory. Preregistration for classes offered. **Activities:** Student government, student newspaper, Amnesty International, Child Development Professionals, Filipino American Association, Latin American club, Miramar Associated Gaming Imagination Club (MAGIC), parent student advisory board, Phi Theta Kappa.

Athletics. Team name: Jets.

Student services. Career counseling, services for economically disadvantaged, health services, on-campus daycare, personal counseling, veterans' counselor. **Physically disabled:** Services for visually, hearing impaired.

Transfer: Transfer adviser, college fairs on campus for students transferring to 4-year colleges.

Contact. E-mail: dstack@sdccd.edu
Phone: (619) 388-7844 Fax: (619) 388-7915
Dana Stack, Student Services Supervisor II, San Diego Miramar College, 10440 Black Mountain Road, San Diego, CA 92126-2999

San Joaquin Delta College
Stockton, California
www.deltacollege.edu   **CB code: 4706**

▶ Public 2-year community college
▶ Commuter campus in large city

General. Founded in 1935. Regionally accredited. 14 off-campus sites located in service district. **Enrollment:** 7,927 degree-seeking undergraduates. **Degrees:** 2,935 associate awarded. **Location:** 45 miles from Sacramento. **Calendar:** Semester, extensive summer session. **Full-time faculty:** 236 total. **Part-time faculty:** 335 total. **Class size:** 48% < 20, 40% 20-39, 7% 40-49, 5% 50-99, less than 1% >100. **Special facilities:** Planetarium, electron microscopy laboratory, farm laboratory, natural resources laboratory, 3 theaters. **Partnerships:** Formal partnerships with Nissan, General Motors, Caterpillar, Cisco.

Transfer out. Colleges most students transferred to 2011: California State University: Stanislaus, California State University: Sacramento, University of the Pacific, California State Polytechnic University, University of California: Davis.

Basis for selection. Open admission, but selective for some programs. Limited admission to registered nursing, psychiatric technician, licensed vocational nursing, radiological technician, and police academy programs.

2011-2012 Annual costs. Tuition/fees: $1,082; $6,362 out-of-state. Per-credit charge: $36 in-state; $212 out-of-state. Books/supplies: $1,566. Personal expenses: $3,024.

2010-2011 Financial aid. Need-based: 2,624 full-time freshmen applied for aid; 2,312 were judged to have need; 2,059 of these received aid. Average need met was 40%. Average scholarship/grant was $5,182; average loan $2,543. 92% of total undergraduate aid awarded as scholarships/grants, 8% as loans/jobs. Need-based aid available for part-time students. Work-study available nights, weekends and for part-time students. **Non-need-based:** Scholarships awarded for academics, athletics. **Additional information:** Enrollment fee waivers available for low-income California residents.

Application procedures. Admission: No deadline. No application fee. Application must be submitted online. Admission notification on a rolling basis beginning on or about 6/5. **Financial aid:** Closing date 6/30. FAFSA, institutional form required. Applicants notified on a rolling basis starting 5/1; must reply within 3 week(s) of notification.

Academics. Special study options: Cooperative education, distance learning, dual enrollment of high school students, ESL, independent study, internships, liberal arts/career combination, study abroad, weekend college. License preparation in nursing, radiology, real estate. **Credit/placement by examination:** AP, CLEP, IB, institutional tests. 15 credit hours maximum toward associate degree. All students taking more than one course must take ASSET or COMPASS for placement. AP and CLEP credit granted after 12 semester hours in residence completed. **Support services:** Learning center, reduced course load, remedial instruction, study skills assistance, tutoring, writing center.

Majors. Architecture: Landscape. **Biology:** General, botany, zoology. **Business:** General, accounting, administrative services, business admin, fashion, management information systems, managerial economics, office technology, office/clerical, real estate. **Communications:** Broadcast journalism, journalism. **Communications technology:** Graphic/printing. **Computer sciences:** General, computer science, data processing, database management, programming. **Conservation:** General, wildlife/wilderness. **Engineering:** General, architectural. **English:** American lit, English lit, rhetoric/composition. **Foreign languages:** French, German, Spanish. **General:** Agribusiness operations, agronomy, animal sciences, business, economics, food science, horticulture, ornamental horticulture, plant protection, plant sciences, soil science. **Health services:** EMT paramedic, medical radiologic technology/radiation therapy, mental health services, nursing (RN). **Human services:** General. **Liberal arts:** Arts/sciences. **Math:** General. **Physical sciences:** Astronomy, chemistry, geology, physics. **Protective services:** Fire safety technology, police science. **Psychology:** General. **Social sciences:** General, anthropology. **Visual/performing arts:** General, crafts, fashion design, interior design, music, photography, studio arts. **Work/family studies:** General, child care management, food/nutrition, institutional food production.

Most popular majors. Business/marketing 9%, health sciences 8%, interdisciplinary studies 7%, liberal arts 62%.

Computing on campus. 220 workstations in library, computer center. Commuter students can connect to campus network. Online course registration, online library, helpline, wireless network available.

Student life. Freshman orientation: Available. Preregistration for classes offered. **Activities:** Bands, choral groups, dance, drama, international student organizations, literary magazine, music ensembles, musical theater, radio station, student government, student newspaper, symphony orchestra, African-American Student Union, Movimiento Estudiantil Chicano de Aztlan, Vietnamese and Asian student clubs.

Athletics. NJCAA. **Intercollegiate:** Baseball M, basketball, cross-country, diving, football (tackle) M, golf M, soccer, softball W, swimming, tennis, track and field, volleyball W, water polo, wrestling M. **Intramural:** Baseball M, basketball, bowling, diving, fencing, golf, softball, swimming, tennis, track and field, volleyball. **Team name:** Mustangs.

Student services. Adult student services, alcohol/substance abuse counseling, career counseling, services for economically disadvantaged, student employment services, financial aid counseling, health services, legal services, minority student services, on-campus daycare, personal counseling, placement for graduates, veterans' counselor. **Physically disabled:** Services for visually, speech, hearing impaired. **Transfer:** Re-entry adviser for new students. Transfer center, transfer adviser, college fairs on campus for students transferring to 4-year colleges.

Contact. Phone: (209) 954-56192 Fax: (209) 954-3769
Catherine Mooney, Registrar, San Joaquin Delta College, 5151 Pacific Avenue, Stockton, CA 95207-6370

San Joaquin Valley College
Visalia, California
www.sjvc.edu   **CB code: 2052**

▶ For-profit 2-year junior college
▶ Commuter campus in small city
▶ Application essay, interview required

General. Regionally accredited. Additional campuses in Bakersfield, Fresno, Modesto, Rancho Cordova, and Rancho Cucamonga. Aviation campus located in Fresno. **Enrollment:** 1,224 undergraduates. **Degrees:** 703 associate awarded. **Calendar:** Semester, extensive summer session. **Full-time faculty:** 96 total. **Part-time faculty:** 73 total.

Basis for selection. Open admission, but selective for some programs. Selective admission to allied health programs. Various programs use either Accuplacer or Wonderlick for placement. ACCUPLACER for placement in Math and English.

2011-2012 Annual costs. Tuition/fees: $14,125. Costs may vary by program, annual tuition includes textbooks and supplies.

Financial aid. Need-based: Work-study available nights, weekends and for part-time students.

Application procedures. Admission: No deadline. No application fee. Admission notification on a rolling basis. **Financial aid:** No deadline. FAFSA, institutional form required.

Academics. Special study options: Independent study, internships, liberal arts/career combination. License preparation in aviation, dental hygiene, nursing. **Credit/placement by examination:** AP, CLEP. **Support services:** Learning center, remedial instruction, study skills assistance, tutoring.

Majors. Business: Business admin, construction management, human resources. **Computer sciences:** Support specialist. **Health services:** Dental assistant, dental hygiene, EMT paramedic, health care admin, insurance coding, licensed practical nurse, massage therapy, medical assistant, medical records admin, medical secretary, nursing (RN), office assistant, pharmacy assistant, physician assistant, respiratory therapy technology, surgical technology, veterinary technology/assistant. **Protective services:** Corrections.

Computing on campus. 100 workstations in library, computer center.

Student life. Freshman orientation: Mandatory. Preregistration for classes offered. Full day on Friday prior to start of classes, continues through first week. **Activities:** Student government, student newspaper.

Student services. Adult student services, career counseling, services for economically disadvantaged, student employment services, financial aid

counseling, personal counseling, placement for graduates. **Transfer:** Pre-admission transcript evaluation for new students.

Contact. Phone: (559) 651-2500 Fax: (559) 651-0574
Susie Topjian, Enrollment Services Director, San Joaquin Valley College, 8400 West Mineral King Avenue, Visalia, CA 93291-9283

San Jose City College
San Jose, California
www.sjcc.edu   CB code: 4686

♦ Public 2-year community college
♦ Commuter campus in very large city

General. Founded in 1921. Regionally accredited. **Enrollment:** 2,751 full-time, degree-seeking students. **Degrees:** 222 associate awarded. **Location:** 55 miles from San Francisco. **Calendar:** Semester, limited summer session. **Full-time faculty:** 124 total. **Part-time faculty:** 288 total. **Partnerships:** Formal partnerships with Intel (Manufacturing Technology program), Laser Electro-Optics Manufacturing Association (Laser Technology program), IntelSemiconductor (Mask Design Technology program).

Transfer out. Colleges most students transferred to 2011: San Jose State University, California State University: East Bay.

Basis for selection. Open admission.

High school preparation. College-preparatory program recommended.

2011-2012 Annual costs. Tuition/fees: $1,114; $7,084 out-of-state. Per-credit charge: $36 in-state; $235 out-of-state. Books/supplies: $1,638. Personal expenses: $3,114.

2010-2011 Financial aid. All financial aid based on need. 89% of total undergraduate aid awarded as scholarships/grants, 11% as loans/jobs. Need-based aid available for part-time students. Work-study available nights, weekends and for part-time students. **Additional information:** Board of Governors Grant (fee waivers) available to all qualified applicants.

Application procedures. Admission: No deadline. No application fee. **Financial aid:** No deadline. FAFSA required. Applicants notified on a rolling basis; must reply within 4 week(s) of notification.

Academics. Special study options: Cooperative education, cross-registration, distance learning, dual enrollment of high school students, ESL, honors, independent study, weekend college. License preparation in real estate. **Credit/placement by examination:** AP, CLEP, IB, institutional tests. 30 credit hours maximum toward associate degree. **Support services:** Learning center, pre-admission summer program, reduced course load, remedial instruction, study skills assistance, tutoring, writing center.

Majors. Business: Accounting, administrative services, banking/financial services, entrepreneurial studies, labor studies, marketing, office technology, office/clerical, real estate. **Communications technology:** General. **Computer sciences:** General, applications programming, data entry, networking, programming. **Education:** Early childhood. **Health services:** Dental assistant, substance abuse counseling. **Liberal arts:** Arts/sciences. **Protective services:** Law enforcement admin. **Psychology:** General. **Social sciences:** General. **Visual/performing arts:** Music, studio arts.

Computing on campus. 250 workstations in library, computer center, student center. Online course registration, helpline, wireless network available.

Student life. Freshman orientation: Available. Preregistration for classes offered. **Activities:** Dance, drama, music ensembles, musical theater, radio station, student government, student newspaper.

Athletics. Intercollegiate: Basketball, cross-country, football (tackle) M, golf M, softball W, track and field, volleyball W. **Team name:** Jaguars.

Student services. Career counseling, services for economically disadvantaged, student employment services, financial aid counseling, health services, minority student services, personal counseling, veterans' counselor. **Physically disabled:** Services for visually, speech, hearing impaired. **Transfer:** Transfer center, transfer adviser, college fairs on campus for students transferring to 4-year colleges.

Contact. E-mail: takeo.kubo@sjcc.edu
Phone: (408) 288-3700 Fax: (408) 298-1935
Takeo Kubo, Dean of Enrollment Services, San Jose City College, 2100 Moorpark Avenue, San Jose, CA 95128-2798

Santa Ana College
Santa Ana, California
www.sac.edu   CB code: 4689

♦ Public 2-year community college
♦ Commuter campus in large city

General. Founded in 1915. Regionally accredited. **Enrollment:** 15,985 undergraduates. **Degrees:** 1,449 associate awarded. **Location:** 40 miles from Los Angeles. **Calendar:** Semester, extensive summer session. **Full-time faculty:** 221 total; 18% have terminal degrees, 37% minority. **Part-time faculty:** 707 total; 27% minority. **Class size:** 33% < 20, 38% 20-39, 16% 40-49, 10% 50-99, 2% >100. **Special facilities:** Planetarium, 2 art galleries, digital media center/digital incubator.

Transfer out. Colleges most students transferred to 2011: California State University: Fullerton, California State University: Long Beach, California State University: Irvine, University of Phoenix.

Basis for selection. Open admission. All students 18 years and older who can benefit from instruction are admitted. **Adult students:** SAT/ACT scores not required.

2011-2012 Annual costs. Tuition/fees: $1,098; $6,378 out-of-state. Per-credit charge: $36 in-state; $212 out-of-state. Books/supplies: $1,500. Personal expenses: $2,928.

Financial aid. Need-based: Work-study available nights, weekends and for part-time students.

Application procedures. Admission: Priority date 4/1; no deadline. No application fee. Admission notification on a rolling basis. **Financial aid:** Priority date 6/30; no closing date. FAFSA required. Applicants notified on a rolling basis starting 6/1; must reply within 2 week(s) of notification.

Academics. Special study options: Cooperative education, distance learning, double major, dual enrollment of high school students, ESL, honors, independent study, internships, liberal arts/career combination, study abroad, weekend college. **Credit/placement by examination:** AP, CLEP, institutional tests. 30 credit hours maximum toward associate degree. **Support services:** GED preparation, learning center, pre-admission summer program, reduced course load, remedial instruction, study skills assistance, tutoring.

Majors. Area/ethnic studies: General, African-American, Chicano/Hispanic-American/Latino, women's. **Biology:** General. **Business:** Accounting, business admin, entrepreneurial studies, fashion, insurance, international, management science, marketing. **Communications:** Advertising, broadcast journalism, communications/speech/rhetoric, journalism. **Computer sciences:** General, computer science, data processing. **Education:** Early childhood. **Engineering:** General. **English:** English lit. **Foreign languages:** General. **Health services:** Medical assistant, nursing (RN), occupational therapy assistant, pharmacy assistant. **History:** General. **Liberal arts:** Arts/sciences, library assistant. **Math:** General. **Parks/recreation:** Exercise sciences. **Philosophy/religion:** Philosophy. **Physical sciences:** Chemistry, geology, physics. **Protective services:** Fire safety technology, fire services admin, firefighting, police science. **Psychology:** General. **Social sciences:** General, anthropology, economics, geography, political science, sociology. **Visual/performing arts:** General, commercial/advertising art, dance, dramatic, fashion design, music, photography. **Work/family studies:** Family/community services, food/nutrition.

Most popular majors. Health sciences 11%, liberal arts 50%, security/protective services 9%.

Computing on campus. 66 workstations in library, computer center. Online course registration, wireless network available.

Student life. Freshman orientation: Available. Preregistration for classes offered. **Activities:** Bands, choral groups, dance, drama, international student organizations, literary magazine, music ensembles, musical theater, radio station, student government, student newspaper, TV station.

Athletics. NJCAA. **Intercollegiate:** Baseball M, basketball, cross-country, football (tackle) M, soccer, softball W, track and field, volleyball, water polo, wrestling M. **Team name:** Dons.

Student services. Adult student services, alcohol/substance abuse counseling, career counseling, services for economically disadvantaged, student employment services, financial aid counseling, health services, minority student services, on-campus daycare, personal counseling, veterans' counselor, women's services. **Physically disabled:** Services for visually, speech, hearing impaired. **Transfer:** Re-entry adviser, pre-admission transcript evaluation for new students. Transfer center, transfer adviser, college fairs on campus for students transferring to 4-year colleges.

Contact. E-mail: adm_records@sac.edu
Phone: (714) 564-6042 Fax: (714) 564-6455
Mark Liang, Director, Admissions and Records, Santa Ana College, 1530 West 17th Street, Santa Ana, CA 92706

Santa Barbara Business College
Santa Barbara, California
www.sbbcollege.edu

- For-profit 2-year junior and career college
- Small city

General. Accredited by ACICS. **Location:** 90 miles from Los Angeles. **Calendar:** Terms begin every 10 weeks.

Annual costs/financial aid. Costs for full programs as follows: Business Administration, Bachelor, $65,227.50. Health Information Technology, Associate, $34,447. Medical Assisting, Associate, $34,627.

Contact. Phone: (805) 967-9677
Director of Admissions, 506 Chapala Street, Santa Barbara, CA 93101

Santa Barbara Business College: Bakersfield
Bakersfield, California
www.sbbcollege.edu

- For-profit 2-year junior and career college
- Commuter campus in large city

General. Accredited by ACICS. **Calendar:** Terms begin every 10 weeks.

Annual costs/financial aid. Costs for full programs as follows: Business Administration, Bachelor, $65,227.50. Health Information Technology, Associate, $34,447. Medical Assisting, Associate, $34,627. Criminal Justice, Bachelor, $64,275. Medical Office Administration, Diploma, $22,147. Office Administration, Diploma, $22,500. Vocational Nursing, Diploma, $35,757. Desktop and Network Support, Diploma, $22,802.50. Early Childhood Education, Associate, $33,670. Network Systems Administration, Associate, $35,182.50. Paralegal Studies, Associate, $34,400.

Contact. Phone: (866) 749-7222
Director of Admissions, 5300 California Avenue, Bakersfield, CA 93304

Santa Barbara Business College: Rancho Mirage
Rancho Mirage, California
www.sbbcollege.edu

- For-profit 2-year junior and career college
- Small city

General. Regionally accredited. **Calendar:** Differs by program.

Annual costs/financial aid. Costs for full programs as follows: Business Administration, Bachelor, $65,227.50. Health Information Technology, Associate, $34,447. Medical Assisting, Associate, $34,627. Criminal Justice, Bachelor, $64,275. Medical Office Administration, Diploma, $22,147. Office Administration, Diploma, $22,500. Vocational Nursing, Diploma, $35,757. Paralegal Studies, Associate, $34,400.

Contact. Phone: (866) 749-7222
Director of Admissions, 75-030 Gerald Ford Drive, Building 2, Palm Desert, CA 92211

Santa Barbara Business College: Santa Maria
Santa Maria, California
www.sbbcollege.edu

- For-profit 2-year junior and career college
- Small city

General. Accredited by ACICS. **Calendar:** Quarter. Terms begin every 10 weeks.

Annual costs/financial aid. Costs for full programs as follows: Business Administration, Bachelor, $65,227.50. Health Information Technology, Associate, $34,447. Medical Assisting, Associate, $34,627. Criminal Justice, Bachelor, $64,275. Medical Office Administration, Diploma, $22,147. Office Administration, Diploma, $22,500. Pharmacy Technology, Associate, $34,307. Vocational Nursing, Diploma, $35,757.

Contact. Phone: (866) 749-7222
Director of Admissions, 303 East Plaza Drive, Santa Maria, CA 93454

Santa Barbara Business College: Ventura
Ventura, California
www.sbbcollege.edu

- For-profit 2-year junior and career college
- Commuter campus in small city

General. Accredited by ACICS. **Location:** 40 miles from Los Angeles. **Calendar:** Quarter. Terms begin every 10 weeks.

Annual costs/financial aid. Costs for full programs as follows: Business Administration, Bachelor, $65,227.50. Health Information Technology, Associate, $34,447. Medical Assisting, Associate, $34,627. Criminal Justice, Bachelor, $64,275. Medical Office Administration, Diploma, $22,147. Office Administration, Diploma, $22,500. Paralegal Studies, Associate, $34,400.

Contact. Phone: (866) 749-7222
Director of Admissions, 4839 Market Street, Ventura, CA 93003

Santa Barbara City College
Santa Barbara, California
www.sbcc.edu   CB code: 4690

- Public 2-year community college
- Commuter campus in small city

General. Founded in 1908. Regionally accredited. **Enrollment:** 12,990 degree-seeking undergraduates. **Degrees:** 1,625 associate awarded. **Location:** 90 miles from Los Angeles. **Calendar:** Semester, limited summer session. **Full-time faculty:** 254 total; 22% minority. **Part-time faculty:** 1,009 total; 10% minority. **Class size:** 19% < 20, 62% 20-39, 12% 40-49, 5% 50-99, 3% >100.

Student profile.

Out-of-state:	6%	25 or older:	29%

Transfer out. Colleges most students transferred to 2011: University of California: Santa Barbara, California State University: Northridge, San Francisco State University, San Diego State University, University of California: Los Angeles.

Basis for selection. Open admission, but selective for some programs. Special requirements for hotel/restaurant/culinary, nursing, radiography, early childhood education, cosmetology, marine diving technology programs. Criteria vary by program. Interview required of nursing, hotel and restaurant management, marine technology majors. Audition required of some music and theater majors. **Adult students:** English assessment test required for placement.

2011-2012 Annual costs. Tuition/fees: $1,114; $7,414 out-of-state. Per-credit charge: $36 in-state; $246 out-of-state. Books/supplies: $1,656. Personal expenses: $3,114.

Financial aid. Need-based: Need-based aid available for part-time students. Work-study available nights, weekends and for part-time students. **Additional information:** California residents may qualify for Board of Governor's Financial Assistance Program, which will allow institutions to waive enrollment fee.

Application procedures. Admission: Priority date 2/1; deadline 8/19 (receipt date). No application fee. Admission notification on a rolling basis beginning on or about 3/1. **Financial aid:** No deadline. FAFSA required. Applicants notified on a rolling basis starting 5/1; must reply within 2 week(s) of notification.

Academics. Special study options: Cooperative education, cross-registration, distance learning, double major, dual enrollment of high school students, ESL, honors, independent study, internships, study abroad. License preparation in nursing, paramedic, radiology, real estate. **Credit/placement by examination:** AP, CLEP, IB, institutional tests. 12 credit hours maximum toward associate degree. **Support services:** Learning center, pre-admission

summer program, reduced course load, remedial instruction, study skills assistance, tutoring, writing center.

Majors. Area/ethnic studies: African-American, Chicano/Hispanic-American/Latino, Native American. **Biology:** General. **Business:** General, accounting, accounting technology, administrative services, banking/financial services, business admin, finance, hospitality/recreation, international, marketing, office management, real estate, sales/distribution, selling, small business admin. **Communications:** Communications/speech/rhetoric, digital media. **Communications technology:** General, computer typography. **Computer sciences:** General, computer science, data processing. **Conservation:** Environmental studies. **Education:** Early childhood, kindergarten/preschool, physical. **Engineering:** General, computer, marine. **English:** English lit, rhetoric/composition. **Foreign languages:** French, Spanish. **General:** Horticulture, landscaping, ornamental horticulture. **Health services:** Athletic training, licensed practical nurse, medical radiologic technology/radiation therapy, nursing (RN), recreational therapy, sonography, substance abuse counseling. **History:** General. **Human services:** General. **Liberal arts:** Arts/sciences. **Math:** General. **Parks/recreation:** General, exercise sciences, health/fitness. **Philosophy/religion:** Philosophy. **Physical sciences:** Chemistry, geology, physics. **Protective services:** Law enforcement admin. **Psychology:** General. **Social sciences:** Anthropology, economics, geography, political science, sociology. **Visual/performing arts:** Art, art history/conservation, commercial/advertising art, dramatic, film/cinema/video, interior design, multimedia, music, studio arts, theater design. **Work/family studies:** Child care management, institutional food production.

Most popular majors. English 7%, health sciences 12%, interdisciplinary studies 10%, liberal arts 40%, social sciences 8%.

Computing on campus. 1,340 workstations in library, computer center, student center. Commuter students can connect to campus network. Online library, helpline, wireless network available.

Student life. Freshman orientation: Mandatory. Preregistration for classes offered. 2-hour on-campus or on-line orientation. **Activities:** Bands, choral groups, dance, drama, literary magazine, music ensembles, musical theater, student government, student newspaper, symphony orchestra, Black Student Union, College Republicans, EOPS, Hillel Club, Latter Day Saint Student Association, Phi Theta Kappa, Shodo Japanese Calligraphy Club, Special Abilities Club, Students Left Alliance Party, Student Sustainability Club, Vaquero Christian Fellowship.

Athletics. Intercollegiate: Baseball M, basketball, cross-country, football (tackle) M, golf, soccer, softball W, tennis, track and field, volleyball. **Team name:** Vaqueros.

Student services. Adult student services, alcohol/substance abuse counseling, career counseling, services for economically disadvantaged, student employment services, financial aid counseling, health services, minority student services, on-campus daycare, personal counseling, placement for graduates, veterans' counselor, women's services. **Physically disabled:** Services for visually, speech, hearing impaired. **Transfer:** Transfer center, transfer adviser, college fairs on campus for students transferring to 4-year colleges.

Contact. E-mail: admissions@sbcc.edu
Phone: (805) 965-0581 ext. 2200 Fax: (805) 963-7222
Allison Curtis, Director of Admissions and Records, Santa Barbara City College, 721 Cliff Drive, Santa Barbara, CA 93109-2394

Santa Monica College
Santa Monica, California
www.smc.edu

CB member
CB code: 4691

- Public 2-year community college
- Commuter campus in small city

General. Founded in 1929. Regionally accredited. Off-campus program at Santa Monica College of Design. **Enrollment:** 23,716 degree-seeking undergraduates. **Degrees:** 1,870 associate awarded. **Location:** 18 miles from Los Angeles. **Calendar:** Semester, extensive summer session. **Full-time faculty:** 318 total; 32% minority, 58% women. **Part-time faculty:** 1,114 total; 22% minority, 54% women. **Special facilities:** Planetarium, photo gallery, humanities center, entertainment technology academy. **Partnerships:** Formal partnerships with DreamWorks, Disney Channel, Sony, 20th Century Fox, and other entertainment industry leaders (for Academy of Entertainment Technology students).

Student profile. Among degree-seeking undergraduates, 4,380 enrolled as first-time, first-year students.

African American:	11%	International:	13%
Asian American:	9%	25 or older:	39%
Hispanic American:	39%		

Transfer out. Colleges most students transferred to 2011: University of California at Los Angeles, California State University-Northridge, University of Southern California.

Basis for selection. Open admission, but selective for some programs. Music, theater arts, entertainment technology programs are competitive with various requirements. Nursing program has course requirements for admission. Audition and portfolio required for music, theater arts.

2011-2012 Annual costs. Tuition/fees: $1,112; $8,282 out-of-state. Per-credit charge: $36 in-state; $275 out-of-state. Books/supplies: $1,566. Personal expenses: $2,862.

Financial aid. Need-based: Need-based aid available for part-time students. Work-study available nights, weekends and for part-time students.

Application procedures. Admission: No deadline. No application fee. Admission notification on a rolling basis. **Financial aid:** No deadline. FAFSA, institutional form required. Applicants notified on a rolling basis starting 7/1; must reply within 2 week(s) of notification.

Academics. Special study options: Accelerated study, cooperative education, distance learning, dual enrollment of high school students, ESL, honors, independent study, internships, study abroad, weekend college. License preparation in nursing. **Credit/placement by examination:** AP, CLEP, institutional tests. 30 credit hours maximum toward associate degree. Math and English placement tests required for some students. **Support services:** Learning center, pre-admission summer program, remedial instruction, study skills assistance, tutoring, writing center.

Majors. Area/ethnic studies: General, women's. **Business:** Accounting, administrative services, business admin, insurance, logistics, selling. **Communications:** Digital media, journalism, radio/TV. **Communications technology:** General, animation/special effects. **Computer sciences:** Computer science, data entry, database management, programming. **Conservation:** Environmental science, environmental studies. **Education:** Early childhood special. **Health services:** Medical assistant, medical secretary, respiratory therapy technology. **Liberal arts:** Arts/sciences, humanities. **Math:** General. **Parks/recreation:** Health/fitness. **Visual/performing arts:** Art, commercial photography, dance, dramatic, fashion design, film/cinema/video, graphic design, interior design, music, photography. **Work/family studies:** Apparel marketing, child development.

Computing on campus. 600 workstations in library, computer center, student center. Commuter students can connect to campus network. Helpline available.

Student life. Freshman orientation: Mandatory. Preregistration for classes offered. **Activities:** Concert band, choral groups, dance, drama, literary magazine, music ensembles, musical theater, opera, radio station, student government, student newspaper.

Athletics. NJCAA. Intercollegiate: Basketball, cross-country M, diving, football (tackle) M, swimming, tennis, track and field, volleyball, water polo M. **Intramural:** Badminton. **Team name:** Corsairs.

Student services. Adult student services, career counseling, services for economically disadvantaged, student employment services, financial aid counseling, health services, minority student services, on-campus daycare, personal counseling, placement for graduates, veterans' counselor. **Physically disabled:** Services for visually, speech, hearing impaired. **Transfer:** Transfer center, transfer adviser, college fairs on campus for students transferring to 4-year colleges.

Contact. Phone: (310) 434-4380 Fax: (310) 434-3645
Kiersten Elliott, Associate Dean of Enrollment Services, Santa Monica College, 1900 Pico Boulevard, Santa Monica, CA 90405-1628

Santa Rosa Junior College
Santa Rosa, California
www.santarosa.edu

CB code: 4692

- Public 2-year community college
- Commuter campus in small city

General. Founded in 1918. Regionally accredited. **Enrollment:** 13,191 degree-seeking undergraduates. **Degrees:** 1,381 associate awarded. **Location:** 55 miles from San Francisco. **Calendar:** Semester, extensive summer session. **Full-time faculty:** 283 total; 17% have terminal degrees, 17% minority, 58% women. **Part-time faculty:** 1,019 total; 12% have terminal degrees, 12% minority, 60% women. **Class size:** 19% < 20, 66% 20-39, 11% 40-49, 4% 50-99, less than 1% >100. **Special facilities:** Native American art museum, college farm, summer repertory theater, planetarium, culinary cafe.

Transfer out. Colleges most students transferred to 2011: Sonoma State University, San Francisco State University, University of California: Davis, California State University: Sacramento, University of California: Berkeley.

Basis for selection. Open admission, but selective for some programs. Audition recommended of music and theater performance courses, some physical education, some communications majors.

2011-2012 Annual costs. Tuition/fees: $1,116; $7,236 out-of-state. Per-credit charge: $36 in-state; $240 out-of-state. Books/supplies: $1,656. Personal expenses: $3,114.

2010-2011 Financial aid. Need-based: 84% of total undergraduate aid awarded as scholarships/grants, 16% as loans/jobs. Need-based aid available for part-time students. Work-study available nights, weekends and for part-time students. **Non-need-based:** Scholarships awarded for academics, art, leadership, music/drama, state residency. **Additional information:** California's Board of Governors Program provides fee waivers for applicants with need.

Application procedures. Admission: No deadline. No application fee. **Financial aid:** Priority date 3/1; no closing date. FAFSA required. Applicants notified on a rolling basis starting 4/15.

Academics. Special study options: Cooperative education, cross-registration, distance learning, double major, dual enrollment of high school students, ESL, independent study, internships, liberal arts/career combination, study abroad, weekend college. License preparation in dental hygiene, nursing, paramedic, radiology, real estate. **Credit/placement by examination:** AP, CLEP, IB, institutional tests. 15 credit hours maximum toward associate degree. Credit will be granted to any student who satisfactorily passes an exam approved or conducted by proper authorities of the college. Such credit may be granted only to a student who is registered at the college and in good standing and only for a course listed in the College Catalog. **Support services:** GED preparation and test center, learning center, pre-admission summer program, reduced course load, remedial instruction, study skills assistance, tutoring.

Majors. Area/ethnic studies: Latin American. **Biology:** General, physiology. **Business:** Business admin. **Computer sciences:** Computer science. **Conservation:** General, environmental studies. **Education:** General, early childhood. **Engineering:** General. **English:** English lit. **Foreign languages:** American Sign Language, Spanish. **General:** Agribusiness operations, equestrian studies, equine science. **Health services:** Dental assistant, dental hygiene, EMT paramedic, licensed practical nurse, medical radiologic technology/radiation therapy, mental health services, nursing (RN), nursing assistant, pharmacy assistant. **History:** General. **Liberal arts:** Arts/sciences. **Math:** General. **Parks/recreation:** General. **Philosophy/religion:** Philosophy. **Physical sciences:** Chemistry, physics. **Protective services:** Firefighting, police science. **Psychology:** General. **Social sciences:** Anthropology, economics, geography, political science, sociology. **Visual/performing arts:** Art, commercial/advertising art, dramatic, fashion design.

Most popular majors. Health sciences 16%, interdisciplinary studies 29%, social sciences 29%.

Computing on campus. 1,900 workstations in library, computer center. Commuter students can connect to campus network. Online course registration, wireless network available.

Student life. Freshman orientation: Available. Preregistration for classes offered. Year round drop-in orientation. Online orientation. **Activities:** Jazz band, choral groups, dance, drama, film society, international student organizations, music ensembles, musical theater, student government, student newspaper, symphony orchestra.

Athletics. Intercollegiate: Badminton W, baseball M, basketball, cross-country, diving, football (tackle) M, golf M, soccer, softball W, swimming, tennis, track and field, volleyball W, water polo, wrestling M. **Team name:** Bear Cubs.

Student services. Adult student services, career counseling, services for economically disadvantaged, student employment services, financial aid counseling, health services, on-campus daycare, personal counseling, placement for graduates, veterans' counselor. **Physically disabled:** Services for visually, speech, hearing impaired. **Transfer:** Re-entry adviser, pre-admission transcript evaluation for new students. Transfer center, transfer adviser, college fairs on campus for students transferring to 4-year colleges.

Contact. E-mail: admininfo@santarosa.edu
Phone: (707) 527-4685 Toll-free number: (800) 564-7752
Fax: (707) 527-4798
Diane Traversi, Director of Enrollment Services, Santa Rosa Junior College, 1501 Mendocino Avenue, Santa Rosa, CA 95401-4395

Santiago Canyon College
Orange, California
www.sccollege.edu   CB code: 2830

- Public 2-year community college
- Commuter campus in small city

General. Regionally accredited. **Enrollment:** 13,123 undergraduates. **Degrees:** 688 associate awarded. **Location:** 30 miles from Los Angeles. **Calendar:** Semester, extensive summer session. **Full-time faculty:** 108 total; 33% minority. **Part-time faculty:** 288 total; 33% minority. **Class size:** 13% < 20, 58% 20-39, 19% 40-49, 8% 50-99, 1% >100.

Transfer out. Colleges most students transferred to 2011: California State University: Fullerton, University of California: Irvine, Chapman University, California State University: Long Beach, University of Phoenix.

Basis for selection. Open admission. **Adult students:** SAT/ACT scores not required. Placement tests for English, math, reading, and chemistry. **Home schooled:** Statement describing home school structure and mission required. Must show private school affidavit confirmation from the California Department of Education.

2011-2012 Annual costs. Tuition/fees: $1,114; $7,114 out-of-state. Per-credit charge: $36 in-state; $236 out-of-state. Books/supplies: $1,500. Personal expenses: $2,300.

Financial aid. All financial aid based on need. Need-based aid available for part-time students. Work-study available nights, weekends and for part-time students.

Application procedures. Admission: No application fee. **Financial aid:** Priority date 7/1; no closing date. FAFSA, institutional form required. Applicants notified on a rolling basis starting 6/1.

Academics. Special study options: Accelerated study, cooperative education, distance learning, double major, dual enrollment of high school students, ESL, honors, weekend college. License preparation in real estate. **Credit/placement by examination:** AP, CLEP, institutional tests. **Support services:** GED preparation and test center, learning center, remedial instruction, study skills assistance, tutoring, writing center.

Majors. Biology: General. **Business:** Accounting, business admin, managerial economics, marketing, selling, tourism/travel. **Communications:** Communications/speech/rhetoric. **Communications technology:** Graphics, photo/film/video. **Computer sciences:** Computer science, information systems, web page design. **Engineering:** General. **English:** English lit, rhetoric/composition. **Foreign languages:** General, American Sign Language, French, Italian, Spanish. **Health services:** Medical assistant. **History:** General. **Liberal arts:** Arts/sciences, library assistant. **Math:** General. **Philosophy/religion:** Philosophy. **Physical sciences:** Chemistry, geology, hydrology, physics. **Protective services:** Fire safety technology. **Psychology:** General. **Social sciences:** General, anthropology, economics, geography, political science, sociology. **Visual/performing arts:** Art, commercial/advertising art, crafts, dance, fashion design, metal/jewelry, music. **Work/family studies:** General.

Most popular majors. Business/marketing 7%, liberal arts 74%.

Computing on campus. Online course registration, wireless network available.

Student life. Freshman orientation: Available. Preregistration for classes offered. **Activities:** Bands, choral groups, dance, drama, music ensembles, student government, student newspaper, TV station.

Athletics. Intercollegiate: Cross-country, golf, soccer, track and field. **Intramural:** Softball, track and field. **Team name:** Hawks.

Student services. Adult student services, alcohol/substance abuse counseling, career counseling, services for economically disadvantaged, student employment services, financial aid counseling, health services, minority student services, on-campus daycare, personal counseling, veterans' counselor, women's services. **Physically disabled:** Services for visually, speech, hearing impaired. **Transfer:** Re-entry adviser, pre-admission transcript evaluation for new students. Transfer center, transfer adviser, college fairs on campus for students transferring to 4-year colleges.

Contact. E-mail: admissions@sccollege.edu
Phone: (714) 628-4901 Fax: (714) 628-4723
Linda Miskovic, Associate Dean of Admissions, Santiago Canyon College, 8045 East Chapman Avenue, Orange, CA 92869

Shasta College
Redding, California
www.shastacollege.edu   **CB code: 4696**

- Public 2-year community and junior college
- Commuter campus in small city

General. Founded in 1948. Regionally accredited. **Enrollment:** 4,964 degree-seeking undergraduates. **Degrees:** 631 associate awarded. **Location:** 160 miles from Sacramento. **Calendar:** Semester, extensive summer session. **Full-time faculty:** 141 total; 10% minority. **Part-time faculty:** 275 total; 8% minority. **Class size:** 41% < 20, 53% 20-39, 3% 40-49, 2% 50-99, less than 1% >100. **Special facilities:** Early childhood education center lab school, college farm.

Student profile.

Out-of-state: 1%   **Live on campus:**   1%
25 or older: 49%

Transfer out. Colleges most students transferred to 2011: California State University: Chico, California State University: Sacramento, Humboldt State University, Simpson University, National University.

Basis for selection. Open admission, but selective for some programs. Applicants to the nursing and dental hygiene programs must have a high school diploma and complete a series of courses as outlined in college catalog. In addition, nursing program applicants must take the National League for Nursing examination.

2011-2012 Annual costs. Tuition/fees: $1,155; $7,125 out-of-state. Per-credit charge: $36 in-state; $235 out-of-state. Room only: $3,920. Books/supplies: $1,620. Personal expenses: $2,000.

Financial aid. All financial aid based on need. Need-based aid available for part-time students. Work-study available nights, weekends and for part-time students.

Application procedures. Admission: No deadline. No application fee. Admission notification on a rolling basis. **Financial aid:** Priority date 3/2; no closing date. FAFSA, institutional form required. Applicants notified on a rolling basis starting 7/1.

Academics. On-campus programs leading to bachelor's degree from California State University: Chico offered. **Special study options:** Cooperative education, distance learning, double major, dual enrollment of high school students, ESL, honors, independent study, internships, liberal arts/career combination, study abroad, weekend college. Bachelor's degree programs available on campus. License preparation in dental hygiene, nursing, paramedic, real estate. **Credit/placement by examination:** AP, CLEP, institutional tests. 12 credit hours maximum toward associate degree. **Support services:** GED preparation, learning center, reduced course load, remedial instruction, study skills assistance, tutoring, writing center.

Majors. Biology: General. **Business:** General, accounting, administrative services, business admin, entrepreneurial studies, executive assistant, hotel/motel admin, management information systems, office management, office technology, office/clerical, restaurant/food services, sales/distribution. **Communications:** Communications/speech/rhetoric, journalism. **Computer sciences:** General, data processing, networking. **Education:** Early childhood, elementary, science. **Engineering:** General. **Foreign languages:** General. **General:** Agribusiness operations, business, equestrian studies, ornamental horticulture. **Health services:** Dental hygiene, EMT paramedic, nursing (RN). **Liberal arts:** Humanities. **Math:** General. **Parks/recreation:** Health/fitness. **Physical sciences:** General, atmospheric science, climatology, geology, oceanography. **Protective services:** Criminal justice, fire safety technology, fire services admin, firefighting, law enforcement admin, police science. **Social sciences:** General. **Visual/performing arts:** Art, commercial/advertising art, dramatic, music, studio arts. **Work/family studies:** General, child care management, child development, family studies, institutional food production.

Most popular majors. Business/marketing 8%, health sciences 11%, liberal arts 56%.

Computing on campus. 191 workstations in library, computer center. Dormitories wired for high-speed internet access and linked to campus network. Commuter students can connect to campus network. Online course registration, online library, helpline, wireless network available.

Student life. Freshman orientation: Mandatory. Preregistration for classes offered. **Housing:** Single-sex dorms available. **Activities:** Bands, choral groups, dance, drama, international student organizations, music ensembles, musical theater, student government, student newspaper, symphony orchestra, Agriculture/Natural Resources Leaders Club, Amigos Unidos Club, Early Childhood Educators Network, Intercultural Club, Intervarsity Christian Fellowship, NATIVE (Native American Tradition in Valued Education) Club, Rotaract, science club, sustainability club, Veterans Organization.

Athletics. NJCAA. **Intercollegiate:** Baseball M, basketball, cross-country, football (tackle) M, golf M, soccer, softball W, swimming, tennis, track and field, volleyball W, wrestling M. **Team name:** Knights.

Student services. Career counseling, services for economically disadvantaged, student employment services, financial aid counseling, health services, on-campus daycare, personal counseling, veterans' counselor. **Physically disabled:** Services for visually, speech, hearing impaired. **Transfer:** Transfer center, transfer adviser, college fairs on campus for students transferring to 4-year colleges.

Contact. E-mail: Admissions@shastacollege.edu
Phone: (530) 242-7650 Fax: (530) 225-4995
Kevin O'Rorke, Dean, Enrollment Services, Shasta College, Box 496006, Redding, CA 96049-6006

Sierra College
Rocklin, California
www.sierracollege.edu   **CB code: 4697**

- Public 2-year community college
- Commuter campus in small city

General. Founded in 1914. Regionally accredited. **Enrollment:** 19,606 undergraduates. **Degrees:** 1,964 associate awarded. **Location:** 25 miles from Sacramento. **Calendar:** Semester, extensive summer session. **Full-time faculty:** 224 total. **Part-time faculty:** 665 total. **Special facilities:** Nature trail, planetarium, science museum displays, learning resource center, cross-country trail.

Student profile.

Out-of-state: 1%   **Live on campus:**   1%

Transfer out. Colleges most students transferred to 2011: California State University: Sacramento, University of California: Davis, California State University: Chico, University of California: Berkeley, San Francisco State University.

Basis for selection. Open admission, but selective for some programs. **Adult students:** SAT/ACT scores not required.

2011-2012 Annual costs. Tuition/fees: $1,124; $6,824 out-of-state. Per-credit charge: $36 in-state; $226 out-of-state. Room/board: $6,700. Books/supplies: $2,222. Personal expenses: $1,800.

Financial aid. Need-based: Need-based aid available for part-time students. Work-study available nights, weekends and for part-time students.

Application procedures. Admission: Closing date 8/1 (receipt date). No application fee. Application must be submitted online. Applicants notified within 4 working days. **Financial aid:** Priority date 3/2; no closing date. FAFSA required. Applicants notified on a rolling basis starting 5/15.

Academics. Special study options: Cross-registration, distance learning, double major, dual enrollment of high school students, ESL, honors, independent study, internships, study abroad, weekend college. License preparation in nursing, real estate. **Credit/placement by examination:** AP, CLEP, institutional tests. 15 credit hours maximum toward associate degree. **Support services:** Learning center, pre-admission summer program, remedial instruction, study skills assistance, tutoring, writing center.

Majors. Area/ethnic studies: Deaf, women's. **Biology:** General. **Business:** General, accounting, administrative services, apparel, business admin, real estate, sales/distribution, small business admin. **Communications:** Digital media. **Computer sciences:** Data entry, information technology, networking, programming, system admin, web page design, webmaster. **Conservation:** Environmental studies. **Education:** Early childhood. **Engineering:** General. **English:** English lit, rhetoric/composition. **Foreign languages:** American Sign Language. **Health services:** Nursing (RN). **History:** General. **Liberal arts:** Arts/sciences, library assistant. **Math:** General. **Parks/recreation:** General, health/fitness. **Philosophy/religion:** Philosophy. **Physical sciences:** Chemistry, geology, physics. **Protective services:** Criminal justice, fire safety technology, firefighting, police science, security services. **Psychology:** General. **Social sciences:** General. **Visual/performing arts:** Art, dramatic, music performance, photography, studio arts. **Work/family studies:** General, child care management.

Most popular majors. Business/marketing 11%, liberal arts 44%, security/protective services 6%, social sciences 8%.

Computing on campus. 300 workstations in dormitories, library, computer center. Dormitories wired for high-speed internet access and linked to campus network. Commuter students can connect to campus network. Online course registration, online library, helpline, wireless network available.

Student life. Freshman orientation: Mandatory. Preregistration for classes offered. **Housing:** Coed dorms available. $250 fully refundable deposit. **Activities:** Concert band, choral groups, drama, international student organizations, music ensembles, student government, student newspaper, symphony orchestra, Persian Cultural Club, Rainbow Alliance, Contemporary Arts Club, Veteran Students Alliance, Environmentally Concerned Students, Freethinkers, Intervarsity Christian Fellowship, Law Club, Circle K International.

Athletics. Intercollegiate: Baseball M, basketball, cross-country W, diving, football (tackle) M, golf, soccer W, softball W, swimming, tennis, volleyball W, water polo W, wrestling M. **Intramural:** Archery, badminton, basketball, cheerleading W, football (non-tackle), golf, softball, tennis, volleyball. **Team name:** Wolverines.

Student services. Adult student services, alcohol/substance abuse counseling, career counseling, services for economically disadvantaged, student employment services, financial aid counseling, health services, on-campus daycare, personal counseling, veterans' counselor. **Physically disabled:** Services for visually, speech, hearing impaired. **Transfer:** Pre-admission transcript evaluation for new students. Transfer center, transfer adviser, college fairs on campus for students transferring to 4-year colleges.

Contact. Phone: (916) 660-7340 Toll-free number: (800) 242-4004 Fax: (916) 630-4500
Gail Modder, Admissions and Records Program Manager, Sierra College, 5000 Rocklin Road, Rocklin, CA 95677-3397

Skyline College
San Bruno, California
www.skylinecollege.edu
CB code: 4746

▶ Public 2-year community college
▶ Commuter campus in small city

General. Founded in 1969. Regionally accredited. **Enrollment:** 5,185 degree-seeking undergraduates. **Degrees:** 522 associate awarded. **Location:** 15 miles from San Francisco. **Calendar:** Semester, limited summer session. **Full-time faculty:** 98 total. **Part-time faculty:** 243 total.

Student profile.

Out-of-state:	1%	**25 or older:**	49%

Transfer out. Colleges most students transferred to 2011: San Francisco State University, San Jose State University, California State University: East Bay, UC Berkeley.

Basis for selection. Open admission, but selective for some programs. Supplemental application must be submitted to automotive technology, cosmetology, and respiratory therapy programs. Selection is made by the department. Concurrent enrollment students must submit a high school permission form. SAT/ACT may be substituted for institutional placement tests. Interview required of respiratory therapy majors. Essay required of full-time international student applicants. **Adult students:** Assessment test required to determine placement for math and English courses. **Home schooled:** State high school equivalency certificate required. **Learning Disabled:** Students may request a skills assessment for best placement in courses.

High school preparation. College-preparatory program recommended.

2011-2012 Annual costs. Tuition/fees: $1,142; $7,232 out-of-state. Per-credit charge: $36 in-state; $239 out-of-state. Books/supplies: $1,638. Personal expenses: $2,772.

Financial aid. Need-based: Need-based aid available for part-time students. Work-study available nights, weekends and for part-time students.

Application procedures. Admission: No deadline. No application fee. Application must be submitted online. Admission notification on a rolling basis. **Financial aid:** Priority date 5/2; no closing date. FAFSA, institutional form required. Applicants notified on a rolling basis starting 5/1; must reply within 2 week(s) of notification.

Academics. Special study options: Cooperative education, cross-registration, distance learning, double major, dual enrollment of high school students, ESL, honors, independent study, liberal arts/career combination, study abroad, weekend college. License preparation in paramedic, real estate. **Credit/placement by examination:** AP, CLEP, institutional tests. 12 credit

---

hours maximum toward associate degree. **Support services:** Learning center, remedial instruction, study skills assistance, tutoring, writing center.

Majors. Business: Accounting, administrative services, business admin, hospitality admin, management information systems, office/clerical. **Communications technology:** General. **Computer sciences:** General, computer science, data processing, information systems, webmaster. **Education:** Early childhood. **English:** English lit, rhetoric/composition. **Foreign languages:** Spanish. **Health services:** Medical secretary, medical transcription, respiratory therapy technology, surgical technology. **Liberal arts:** Arts/sciences. **Math:** General. **Protective services:** Law enforcement admin. **Psychology:** General. **Visual/performing arts:** General, art, dance, music. **Work/family studies:** General, business.

Most popular majors. Business/marketing 13%, health sciences 11%, liberal arts 53%.

Computing on campus. 220 workstations in library, computer center, student center. Online course registration, helpline, repair service, wireless network available.

Student life. Freshman orientation: Available. Preregistration for classes offered. **Activities:** Bands, choral groups, dance, literary magazine, student government, student newspaper.

Athletics. NJCAA. **Intercollegiate:** Baseball M, basketball M, cross-country, soccer M, softball W, track and field, volleyball W, wrestling M. **Team name:** Trojans.

Student services. Adult student services, career counseling, services for economically disadvantaged, student employment services, financial aid counseling, health services, minority student services, on-campus daycare, personal counseling, veterans' counselor, women's services. **Physically disabled:** Services for visually, speech, hearing impaired. **Transfer:** Transfer center, transfer adviser, college fairs on campus for students transferring to 4-year colleges.

Contact. E-mail: Escobar@smccd.edu
Phone: (650) 738-4252 Fax: (650) 738-4200
John Mosby, Dean, Planning Research & Institutional Effectiveness, Skyline College, 3300 College Drive, San Bruno, CA 94066-1662

Solano Community College
Fairfield, California
www.solano.edu
CB code: 4930

▶ Public 2-year community college
▶ Commuter campus in small city

General. Founded in 1945. Regionally accredited. Additional campus centers in Vacaville, Vallejo, and Travis Air Force Base. **Enrollment:** 6,296 degree-seeking undergraduates. **Degrees:** 976 associate awarded. **ROTC:** Air Force. **Location:** 11 miles from Vallejo. **Calendar:** Semester, extensive summer session. **Full-time faculty:** 161 total. **Part-time faculty:** 305 total. **Partnerships:** Formal partnership with Workforce Investment Board of Solano County.

Basis for selection. Open admission, but selective for some programs. Special requirements for nursing program.

2011-2012 Annual costs. Tuition/fees: $1,126; $7,036 out-of-state. Per-credit charge: $36 in-state; $233 out-of-state. Books/supplies: $1,656. Personal expenses: $3,114.

2011-2012 Financial aid. Need-based: Work-study available nights, weekends and for part-time students.

Application procedures. Admission: No deadline. No application fee. Admission notification on a rolling basis. **Financial aid:** Priority date 3/1; no closing date. FAFSA required. Applicants notified on a rolling basis starting 7/1.

Academics. Special study options: Cooperative education, cross-registration, distance learning, double major, dual enrollment of high school students, ESL, honors, independent study, internships, liberal arts/career combination, weekend college. License preparation in nursing, real estate. **Credit/placement by examination:** AP, CLEP, institutional tests. 15 credit hours maximum toward associate degree. Credit-by-examination available for some non-remedial courses, as identified by the appropriate academic division. Credit granted may not exceed the amount listed for the specific course in the college catalog. **Support services:** Learning center, pre-admission summer program, reduced course load, remedial instruction, study skills assistance, tutoring, writing center.

Majors. Area/ethnic studies: African-American, Asian-American, Chicano/Hispanic-American/Latino, Native American. **Biology:** General. **Business:** Accounting, administrative services, banking/financial services, business admin, office management, real estate. **Communications:** Communications/speech/rhetoric, journalism. **Computer sciences:** General, programming. **Education:** Early childhood. **English:** English lit. **Foreign languages:** General, French, German, Spanish. **General:** Landscaping, ornamental horticulture. **Health services:** Medical secretary, nursing (RN). **History:** General. **Liberal arts:** Arts/sciences. **Math:** General. **Parks/recreation:** Health/fitness, sports admin. **Physical sciences:** Chemistry, physics. **Protective services:** Firefighting, police science. **Psychology:** General. **Social sciences:** General, international relations, political science. **Visual/performing arts:** Commercial photography, commercial/advertising art, dramatic, drawing, interior design, music, painting, sculpture, studio arts. **Work/family studies:** General.

Computing on campus. 240 workstations in library, computer center, student center. Commuter students can connect to campus network. Online course registration, helpline, wireless network available.

Student life. Freshman orientation: Available. Preregistration for classes offered. **Policies:** Mandatory attendance at first meeting of class each semester for enrollment verification; failure to appear may result in withdrawal from class. Regular attendance and participation is required of all students. **Activities:** Bands, choral groups, dance, drama, international student organizations, literary magazine, music ensembles, musical theater, radio station, student government, student newspaper, symphony orchestra, Black Student Union, women's change, veterans organization, Sierra club, student nurses, Filipino club, Democratic club, Mathematics, Engineering & Science Achievement club, Asian-Pacific Islander club.

Athletics. Intercollegiate: Baseball M, basketball, cross-country, diving, football (tackle) M, soccer W, softball W, swimming, track and field, volleyball W, water polo M. **Intramural:** Table tennis, tennis. **Team name:** Falcons.

Student services. Career counseling, student employment services, financial aid counseling, health services, on-campus daycare, personal counseling, placement for graduates, veterans' counselor. **Physically disabled:** Services for visually, speech, hearing impaired. **Transfer:** Transfer center for students transferring to 4-year colleges.

Contact. E-mail: admissions@solano.edu
Phone: (707) 864-7171 Fax: (707) 646-2053
Barbara Fountain, Dean, Admissions and Records, Solano Community College, 4000 Suisun Valley Road, Fairfield, CA 94534-3197

South Coast College
Orange, California
www.southcoastcollege.com

▶ For-profit 2-year business and career college
▶ Small city

General. Accredited by ACICS. **Enrollment:** 385 degree-seeking undergraduates. **Degrees:** 17 associate awarded. **Location:** 20 miles from Los Angeles. **Calendar:** Quarter, extensive summer session. **Full-time faculty:** 4 total. **Part-time faculty:** 24 total. **Special facilities:** Computer training center.

Basis for selection. Open admission, but selective for some programs.

2011-2012 Annual costs. Tuition/fees: $9,450. Registration fee: $99. Program cost: $1,050/month (Day), $787.5/month (Night). Books/supplies: $700.

Financial aid. Need-based: Work-study available nights, weekends and for part-time students.

Application procedures. Admission: Closing date 3/31. $99 fee.

Academics. Special study options: Bachelor's degree programs available on campus. **Credit/placement by examination:** AP, CLEP.

Majors. Health services: Medical transcription.

Contact. E-mail: requestinfo@southcoastcollege.com
Phone: (714) 867-5009 Toll-free number: (800) 337-8366
Kevin Magner, Dean of Admissions and Marketing, South Coast College, 2011 West Chapman Avenue, Orange, CA 92868

Southwestern College
Chula Vista, California
www.swccd.edu

CB member
CB code: 4726

▶ Public 2-year community college
▶ Commuter campus in small city

General. Founded in 1961. Regionally accredited. Medical occupation programs accredited by the National League for Nursing Accrediting Commission Inc. (NLNAC). **Enrollment:** 12,456 degree-seeking undergraduates. **Degrees:** 995 associate awarded. **Location:** 10 miles from San Diego. **Calendar:** Semester, extensive summer session. **Full-time faculty:** 249 total. **Part-time faculty:** 689 total. **Class size:** 36% < 20, 49% 20-39, 13% 40-49, 3% 50-99.

Transfer out. Colleges most students transferred to 2011: San Diego State University, University of California: San Diego.

Basis for selection. Open admission, but selective for some programs. Limited admission to nursing and dental hygiene programs.

2011-2012 Annual costs. Tuition/fees: $1,124; $6,824 out-of-state. Per-credit charge: $36 in-state; $226 out-of-state. Books/supplies: $1,656. Personal expenses: $3,114.

Financial aid. Need-based: Need-based aid available for part-time students. Work-study available nights, weekends and for part-time students.

Application procedures. Admission: No deadline. No application fee. Admission notification on a rolling basis. **Financial aid:** Priority date 3/2; no closing date. FAFSA required. Applicants notified on a rolling basis starting 7/1.

Academics. Broad offerings of online and traditional courses. Online credit and non-credit courses available. **Special study options:** Cooperative education, cross-registration, distance learning, double major, dual enrollment of high school students, ESL, honors, independent study, internships, study abroad, weekend college. License preparation in dental hygiene, nursing, paramedic, real estate. **Credit/placement by examination:** AP, CLEP, IB, institutional tests. 15 credit hours maximum toward associate degree. In-house placement test required for some. **Support services:** Learning center, pre-admission summer program, remedial instruction, study skills assistance, tutoring, writing center.

Majors. Architecture: Landscape, technology. **Area/ethnic studies:** African-American, American, Asian-American, Chicano/Hispanic-American/Latino, women's. **Biology:** General, biotechnology. **Business:** Accounting, business admin, construction management, entrepreneurial studies, finance, financial planning, international, market research, office management, office/clerical, real estate, tourism promotion, tourism/travel. **Communications:** Broadcast journalism, communications/speech/rhetoric, journalism. **Communications technology:** General, radio/TV, recording arts. **Computer sciences:** General, applications programming, computer science, information systems, information technology, networking, programming, web page design, webmaster. **Conservation:** Environmental studies. **Education:** General, early childhood, elementary, kindergarten/preschool, physical. **Engineering:** General. **English:** English lit. **Foreign languages:** French, Spanish. **General:** Floriculture, greenhouse operations, landscaping, nursery operations, ornamental horticulture, turf management. **Health services:** Clinical lab technology, dental hygiene, EMT paramedic, insurance coding, licensed practical nurse, medical records admin, medical records technology, medical transcription, nursing (RN), prenursing, surgical technology. **History:** General. **Human services:** Social work. **Liberal arts:** Arts/sciences, humanities. **Math:** General. **Parks/recreation:** General, health/fitness. **Philosophy/religion:** Philosophy. **Physical sciences:** Astronomy, chemistry, geology, physics. **Protective services:** Criminal justice, firefighting, forensics, law enforcement admin. **Psychology:** General. **Social sciences:** Anthropology, economics, geography, political science, sociology. **Visual/performing arts:** Art, cinematography, dance, dramatic, graphic design, music, photography. **Work/family studies:** Child care management, child care service, child development.

Computing on campus. 1,360 workstations in library, computer center. Online course registration, online library, helpline, student web hosting, wireless network available.

Student life. Freshman orientation: Available. Preregistration for classes offered. **Activities:** Jazz band, choral groups, dance, drama, literary magazine, music ensembles, musical theater, student government, student newspaper, over 40 student clubs and organizations available.

Athletics. Intercollegiate: Baseball M, basketball, cross-country, football (tackle) M, soccer, softball W, tennis, track and field, volleyball W, water polo. **Team name:** Jaguars.

Student services. Career counseling, services for economically disadvantaged, student employment services, financial aid counseling, health services, legal services, on-campus daycare, personal counseling, veterans' counselor, women's services. **Physically disabled:** Services for visually, speech, hearing impaired. **Transfer:** Pre-admission transcript evaluation for new students. Transfer center, transfer adviser, college fairs on campus for students transferring to 4-year colleges.

Contact. E-mail: admissions@swccd.edu
Phone: (619) 421-6700 ext. 5215 Fax: (619) 482-6489
Mia McClellan, Dean, Student Services, Southwestern College, 900 Otay Lakes Road, Chula Vista, CA 91910-7297

Taft College
Taft, California
www.taftcollege.edu   CB code: 4820

- Public 2-year community college
- Commuter campus in small town

General. Founded in 1922. Regionally accredited. **Enrollment:** 7,920 undergraduates. **Degrees:** 264 associate awarded. **Location:** 35 miles from Bakersfield. **Calendar:** Semester, limited summer session. **Full-time faculty:** 55 total. **Part-time faculty:** 60 total.

Transfer out. Colleges most students transferred to 2011: California State University: Bakersfield, California State University: Fresno, California Polytechnic State University: San Luis Obispo, University of La Verne.

Basis for selection. Open admission. **Adult students:** SAT/ACT scores not required.

2011-2012 Annual costs. Tuition/fees: $1,080; $6,360 out-of-state. Per-credit charge: $36 in-state; $212 out-of-state. Room/board: $4,172.

Financial aid. Need-based: Need-based aid available for part-time students. Work-study available nights, weekends and for part-time students. **Non-need-based:** Scholarships awarded for academics.

Application procedures. Admission: No deadline. No application fee. Admission notification on a rolling basis. **Financial aid:** No deadline. FAFSA, institutional form required. Applicants notified on a rolling basis; must reply within 4 week(s) of notification.

Academics. Special study options: Distance learning, double major, ESL, independent study. License preparation in dental hygiene, paramedic. **Credit/placement by examination:** AP, CLEP, institutional tests. 12 credit hours maximum toward associate degree. **Support services:** GED preparation and test center, learning center, pre-admission summer program, reduced course load, remedial instruction, study skills assistance, tutoring.

Majors. Business: General, accounting, administrative services, business admin, management information systems, office/clerical. **Communications:** Journalism. **Computer sciences:** General, computer science, information systems. **Education:** General, early childhood, physical, social science. **English:** English lit. **Health services:** Dental hygiene. **Liberal arts:** Arts/sciences. **Math:** General. **Physical sciences:** General. **Protective services:** Corrections, criminal justice. **Social sciences:** General. **Visual/performing arts:** Art, music.

Computing on campus. 121 workstations in dormitories, library, computer center, student center. Dormitories wired for high-speed internet access. Online course registration, online library, helpline, wireless network available.

Student life. Freshman orientation: Available. Preregistration for classes offered. Offered online or by video. **Housing:** Single-sex dorms, special housing for disabled available. $125 fully refundable deposit. **Activities:** Drama, student government, student newspaper, International club, Rotary club, MECHA club, Best Buddies.

Athletics. NJCAA. **Intercollegiate:** Baseball M, basketball W, soccer, softball W, volleyball W. **Team name:** Cougars.

Student services. Adult student services, career counseling, services for economically disadvantaged, student employment services, financial aid counseling, minority student services, on-campus daycare, personal counseling, veterans' counselor. **Physically disabled:** Services for visually, speech, hearing impaired. **Transfer:** Re-entry adviser for new students. Transfer center, transfer adviser, college fairs on campus for students transferring to 4-year colleges.

Contact. E-mail: admissions@taftcollege.edu
Phone: (661) 763-7741 Toll-free number: (800) 379-6784
Fax: (661) 763-7758
Michelle Hines, Director of Academic Records/Assistant Enrollment Services Director, Taft College, 29 Emmons Park Drive, Taft, CA 93268

Ventura College
Ventura, California
www.venturacollege.edu   CB code: 4931

- Public 2-year community college
- Commuter campus in small city

General. Founded in 1925. Regionally accredited. **Enrollment:** 6,656 degree-seeking undergraduates. **Degrees:** 979 associate awarded. **Location:** 60 miles from downtown Los Angeles. **Calendar:** Semester, limited summer session. **Full-time faculty:** 137 total. **Part-time faculty:** 323 total.

Basis for selection. Open admission, but selective for some programs. Limited admission to nursing program.

2011-2012 Annual costs. Tuition/fees: $1,122; $6,402 out-of-state. Per-credit charge: $36 in-state; $212 out-of-state. Books/supplies: $1,638. Personal expenses: $3,096.

Financial aid. Need-based: Need-based aid available for part-time students. Work-study available nights, weekends and for part-time students.

Application procedures. Admission: No deadline. No application fee. Admission notification on a rolling basis. **Financial aid:** Priority date 3/2; no closing date. FAFSA required. Applicants notified on a rolling basis.

Academics. Special study options: Cross-registration, distance learning, dual enrollment of high school students, ESL, independent study, study abroad. **Credit/placement by examination:** AP, CLEP, institutional tests. 12 credit hours maximum toward associate degree. **Support services:** Learning center, reduced course load, remedial instruction, tutoring.

Majors. Biology: General. **Business:** General, accounting, administrative services, business admin, fashion, office management, office/clerical. **Computer sciences:** General. **Conservation:** General. **Education:** Early childhood. **Engineering:** General. **General:** Plant sciences. **Health services:** EMT paramedic, medical secretary, nursing (RN). **Protective services:** Criminal justice. **Social sciences:** International relations. **Visual/performing arts:** Ceramics, commercial/advertising art, dramatic, fashion design, music, photography, studio arts. **Work/family studies:** General, child development.

Computing on campus. Online course registration available.

Student life. Freshman orientation: Available. Preregistration for classes offered. **Housing:** Student housing available off-campus at nearby apartments. **Activities:** Jazz band, choral groups, dance, drama, international student organizations, music ensembles, student government, student newspaper, religious, ethnic, political, special interest organizations, international student club.

Athletics. Intercollegiate: Baseball M, basketball, cheerleading, cross-country, diving, football (tackle) M, golf M, softball W, swimming, tennis, track and field, volleyball M, water polo M. **Team name:** Pirates.

Student services. Adult student services, career counseling, services for economically disadvantaged, student employment services, health services, on-campus daycare, personal counseling, placement for graduates, veterans' counselor. **Physically disabled:** Services for visually, hearing impaired. **Transfer:** Transfer center, transfer adviser, college fairs on campus for students transferring to 4-year colleges.

Contact. Phone: (805) 654-6457 Fax: (805) 654-6357
Susan Bricker, Registrar, Ventura College, 4667 Telegraph Road, Ventura, CA 93003

Victor Valley College
Victorville, California
www.vvc.edu   CB code: 4932

- Public 2-year community college
- Small city

General. Founded in 1960. Regionally accredited. **Enrollment:** 4,345 full-time, degree-seeking students. **Degrees:** 993 associate awarded. **Location:** 38 miles from San Bernardino. **Calendar:** Semester, limited summer session.

Full-time faculty: 116 total. **Part-time faculty:** 442 total. **Class size:** 18% < 20, 67% 20-39, 10% 40-49, 4% 50-99, less than 1% >100. **Special facilities:** Planetarium, mock archaeological dig site.

Student profile.

Out-of-state:	2%	**25 or older:**	35%

Transfer out. Colleges most students transferred to 2011: California State University: San Bernardino.

Basis for selection. Open admission. **Adult students:** SAT/ACT scores not required. **Home schooled:** Must complete concurrent enrollment form with parent signature.

2011-2012 Annual costs. Tuition/fees: $1,090; $6,670 out-of-state. Per-credit charge: $36 in-state; $222 out-of-state. $30 per unit tuition is charged to Nevada residents + an enrollment fee of $36/unit. Books/supplies: $1,656. Personal expenses: $3,114.

Financial aid. Need-based: Need-based aid available for part-time students. Work-study available nights, weekends and for part-time students. **Additional information:** Board of Governors grant pays enrollment fee in full for low-income students.

Application procedures. Admission: No deadline. No application fee. Admission notification on a rolling basis. **Financial aid:** Priority date 3/2; no closing date. FAFSA, institutional form required. Applicants notified on a rolling basis starting 8/1; must reply within 4 week(s) of notification.

Academics. Special study options: Accelerated study, cooperative education, cross-registration, distance learning, double major, dual enrollment of high school students, ESL, honors, independent study, internships, semester at sea, study abroad, weekend college. License preparation in nursing, paramedic. **Credit/placement by examination:** AP, CLEP, institutional tests. 32 credit hours maximum toward associate degree. **Support services:** Learning center, pre-admission summer program, reduced course load, remedial instruction, study skills assistance, tutoring, writing center.

Majors. Business: General, administrative services, business admin, real estate. **General:** Ornamental horticulture. **Health services:** EMT paramedic, medical assistant, nursing (RN), respiratory therapy technology. **Liberal arts:** Arts/sciences. **Math:** General. **Protective services:** Fire safety technology, law enforcement admin. **Visual/performing arts:** Art.

Most popular majors. Business/marketing 12%, health sciences 9%, interdisciplinary studies 18%, liberal arts 48%.

Computing on campus. 350 workstations in computer center, student center. Online course registration, online library, helpline available.

Student life. Freshman orientation: Available. Preregistration for classes offered. **Activities:** Concert band, campus ministries, choral groups, dance, drama, music ensembles, Model UN, musical theater, student government, student newspaper.

Athletics. NJCAA. **Intercollegiate:** Baseball M, basketball, cross-country, football (tackle) M, golf M, soccer, softball W, tennis, track and field, volleyball W, wrestling M. **Team name:** Rams.

Student services. Career counseling, services for economically disadvantaged, student employment services, financial aid counseling, health services, on-campus daycare, personal counseling, placement for graduates, veterans' counselor. **Physically disabled:** Services for visually, speech, hearing impaired. **Transfer:** Re-entry adviser, pre-admission transcript evaluation for new students. College fairs on campus for students transferring to 4-year colleges.

Contact. E-mail: moong@vvc.edu
Phone: (760) 245-4271 ext. 2373 Fax: (760) 843-7707
Greta Moon, Director, Admissions and Records, Victor Valley College, 18422 Bear Valley Road, Victorville, CA 92392-5850

West Hills College: Coalinga
Coalinga, California
www.westhillscollege.com

CB code: 4056

- Public 2-year community college
- Commuter campus in small town

General. Founded in 1932. Regionally accredited. **Enrollment:** 1,800 degree-seeking undergraduates. **Degrees:** 504 associate awarded. **Location:** 60 miles from Fresno. **Calendar:** Semester, limited summer session. **Full-time faculty:** 47 total; 11% minority, 49% women. **Part-time faculty:** 85 total; 20% minority, 42% women. **Class size:** 10% < 20, 90% 20-39.

Student profile.

Out-of-state:	10%	**Live on campus:**	5%
25 or older:	48%		

Transfer out. Colleges most students transferred to 2011: California State University Fresno, California Polytechnic University SLO, University of Phoenix, Fresno Pacific University.

Basis for selection. Open admission. 7-12 students admitted with parental permission and principal of the educational institution recommendation as special students. **Adult students:** SAT/ACT scores not required.

2011-2012 Annual costs. Tuition/fees: $1,080; $6,360 out-of-state. Per-credit charge: $36 in-state; $212 out-of-state. Room/board: $7,977. Books/supplies: $1,400.

2010-2011 Financial aid. Need-based: Need-based aid available for part-time students. Work-study available nights, weekends and for part-time students.

Application procedures. Admission: No deadline. No application fee. Application must be submitted online. Admission notification on a rolling basis. **Financial aid:** Priority date 3/2; no closing date. FAFSA required. Applicants notified on a rolling basis starting 6/1.

Academics. Special study options: Distance learning, double major, dual enrollment of high school students, ESL, honors, independent study, study abroad. License preparation in nursing. **Credit/placement by examination:** AP, CLEP, institutional tests. 15 credit hours maximum toward associate degree. **Support services:** GED preparation, learning center, reduced course load, remedial instruction, tutoring.

Majors. Business: General, accounting, administrative services, business admin, management information systems, office technology, office/clerical. **Communications:** General. **Computer sciences:** General, applications programming. **Education:** Early childhood. **General:** Business. **Liberal arts:** Arts/sciences. **Protective services:** Police science. **Psychology:** General. **Social sciences:** General, criminology, geography. **Visual/performing arts:** Art, commercial/advertising art, studio arts.

Most popular majors. Business/marketing 9%, health sciences 7%, liberal arts 65%.

Computing on campus. 40 workstations in dormitories, library, computer center. Dormitories wired for high-speed internet access. Online course registration, helpline, wireless network available.

Student life. Freshman orientation: Available. Preregistration for classes offered. **Housing:** Single-sex dorms available. $125 fully refundable deposit. **Activities:** Drama, international student organizations, musical theater, student government.

Athletics. NJCAA. **Intercollegiate:** Baseball M, basketball M, football (tackle) M, rodeo, softball W, volleyball W. **Team name:** Falcons.

Student services. Adult student services, career counseling, services for economically disadvantaged, student employment services, financial aid counseling, on-campus daycare, personal counseling, veterans' counselor. **Physically disabled:** Services for visually, speech, hearing impaired. **Transfer:** Transfer center, transfer adviser, college fairs on campus for students transferring to 4-year colleges.

Contact. E-mail: admissions@whccd.edu
Phone: (559) 934-2300 Toll-free number: (800) 266-1114
Fax: (559) 934-2852
Keith Stearns, Associate Vice Chancellor/Registrar, West Hills College: Coalinga, 300 Cherry Lane, Coalinga, CA 93210

West Hills College: Lemoore
Lemoore, California
www.westhillscollege.com

CB code: 5500

- Public 2-year community college
- Large town

General. Candidate for regional accreditation. **Enrollment:** 2,450 degree-seeking undergraduates. **Degrees:** 306 associate awarded. **Location:** 20 miles from Fresno. **Calendar:** Semester, limited summer session. **Full-time faculty:** 47 total; 23% minority, 45% women. **Part-time faculty:** 104 total; 24% minority, 44% women. **Class size:** 4% < 20, 96% 20-39.

Transfer out. Colleges most students transferred to 2011: California State University Fresno, California State University Bakersfield, California State University Chico.

Basis for selection. Open admission. 7-12 students admitted with parental permission and principal of the educational institution recommendation as special students. **Adult students:** SAT/ACT scores not required.

2011-2012 Annual costs. Tuition/fees: $1,080; $6,360 out-of-state. Per-credit charge: $36 in-state; $212 out-of-state. Books/supplies: $1,500. Personal expenses: $1,788.

2010-2011 Financial aid. Need-based: Work-study available nights, weekends and for part-time students.

Application procedures. Admission: No deadline. No application fee. Application must be submitted online. Admission notification on a rolling basis. **Financial aid:** No deadline.

Academics. Special study options: Distance learning, dual enrollment of high school students, ESL, honors, independent study. **Credit/placement by examination:** AP, CLEP, institutional tests. 15 credit hours maximum toward associate degree. **Support services:** GED preparation, learning center, reduced course load, remedial instruction, tutoring.

Majors. Biology: General. **Business:** General, business admin. **Computer sciences:** General. **Engineering:** General. **Health services:** Nursing (RN). **Liberal arts:** Arts/sciences, humanities. **Math:** General. **Protective services:** Law enforcement admin. **Psychology:** General. **Social sciences:** General.

Most popular majors. Business/marketing 12%, health sciences 9%, liberal arts 55%, psychology 6%, security/protective services 13%.

Computing on campus. 60 workstations in library, computer center. Online course registration, wireless network available.

Student life. Freshman orientation: Available. Preregistration for classes offered. **Activities:** Student government, student newspaper.

Athletics. NJCAA. **Intercollegiate:** Cross-country, golf, soccer, wrestling M. **Team name:** Golden Eagles.

Student services. Adult student services, career counseling, services for economically disadvantaged, student employment services, financial aid counseling, on-campus daycare, personal counseling, veterans' counselor. **Physically disabled:** Services for visually, speech, hearing impaired. **Transfer:** Pre-admission transcript evaluation for new students. Transfer center, transfer adviser, college fairs on campus for students transferring to 4-year colleges.

Contact. E-mail: admissions@westhillscollege.com
Phone: (559) 925-3317 Toll-free number: (800) 266-1114
Fax: (559) 925-3837
Keith Stearns, Associate Vice Chancellor/Registrar, West Hills College: Lemoore, 555 College Avenue, Lemoore, CA 93245

West Los Angeles College
Culver City, California
www.wlac.edu   **CB code: 4964**

- Public 2-year community college
- Commuter campus in large town

General. Founded in 1968. Regionally accredited. **Enrollment:** 11,915 undergraduates. **Degrees:** 306 associate awarded. **Location:** 10 miles from Civic Center. **Calendar:** Semester, limited summer session. **Full-time faculty:** 102 total. **Part-time faculty:** 304 total.

Student profile.

Out-of-state:	1%	25 or older:	74%

Basis for selection. Open admission.

2011-2012 Annual costs. Tuition/fees: $1,104; $6,804 out-of-state. Per-credit charge: $36 in-state; $226 out-of-state. Books/supplies: $1,638. Personal expenses: $2,862.

Financial aid. All financial aid based on need. Need-based aid available for part-time students. Work-study available nights, weekends and for part-time students. **Additional information:** California residents may qualify for Board of Governors Grant Program.

Application procedures. Admission: No deadline. No application fee. Admission notification on a rolling basis. **Financial aid:** No deadline. FAFSA required. Applicants notified on a rolling basis; must reply within 4 week(s) of notification.

Academics. Special study options: Accelerated study, cooperative education, distance learning, dual enrollment of high school students, ESL, honors, independent study, internships, student-designed major, study abroad, weekend college. License preparation in aviation, dental hygiene, nursing, paramedic, real estate. **Credit/placement by examination:** AP, CLEP, institutional tests. 15 credit hours maximum toward associate degree. **Support services:** GED preparation, learning center, reduced course load, remedial instruction, study skills assistance, tutoring, writing center.

Majors. Biology: General. **Business:** General, accounting, administrative services, business admin, real estate. **Engineering:** General. **English:** English lit, rhetoric/composition. **Foreign languages:** French, Spanish. **Health services:** Dental hygiene. **History:** General. **Liberal arts:** Arts/sciences. **Parks/recreation:** Health/fitness. **Philosophy/religion:** Philosophy. **Physical sciences:** Chemistry, geology, physics. **Psychology:** General. **Social sciences:** Anthropology, economics, geography, political science, sociology. **Visual/performing arts:** Art, ceramics, music.

Computing on campus. Commuter students can connect to campus network. Online course registration, online library, wireless network available.

Student life. Freshman orientation: Available. Preregistration for classes offered. 2 hour session prior to start of each semester. **Activities:** Bands, choral groups, dance, drama, film society, student government, student newspaper, TV station.

Athletics. Intercollegiate: Baseball M, basketball, cross-country, football (tackle) M, track and field. **Team name:** Oilers.

Student services. Adult student services, career counseling, services for economically disadvantaged, student employment services, financial aid counseling, health services, on-campus daycare, personal counseling, placement for graduates, veterans' counselor. **Physically disabled:** Services for visually, speech, hearing impaired.

Contact. Phone: (310) 287-4501
John Goltermann, Dean, West Los Angeles College, 9000 Overland Avenue, Culver City, CA 90230

West Valley College
Saratoga, California
www.westvalley.edu   **CB code: 4958**

- Public 2-year community college
- Large town

General. Founded in 1963. Regionally accredited. **Enrollment:** 5,261 degree-seeking undergraduates. **Degrees:** 540 associate awarded. **ROTC:** Army, Air Force. **Location:** 13 miles from downtown San Jose. **Calendar:** Semester, limited summer session. **Full-time faculty:** 176 total. **Part-time faculty:** 474 total. **Special facilities:** Planetarium, wireless campus center.

Transfer out. Colleges most students transferred to 2011: University of California: Davis, San Jose State University.

Basis for selection. Open admission.

2011-2012 Annual costs. Tuition/fees: $1,152; $7,272 out-of-state. Per-credit charge: $36 in-state; $240 out-of-state. Books/supplies: $2,406. Personal expenses: $3,114.

Financial aid. All financial aid based on need. Need-based aid available for part-time students. Work-study available nights, weekends and for part-time students.

Application procedures. Admission: Priority date 4/21; no deadline. No application fee. Admission notification on a rolling basis. **Financial aid:** Priority date 5/31; no closing date. FAFSA required. Applicants notified on a rolling basis starting 7/1.

Academics. Special study options: Distance learning, double major, dual enrollment of high school students, ESL, honors, independent study, teacher certification program. License preparation in real estate. **Credit/placement by examination:** AP, CLEP, institutional tests. 12 credit hours maximum toward associate degree. **Support services:** Learning center, pre-admission summer program, remedial instruction, study skills assistance, tutoring, writing center.

Majors. Architecture: Landscape. **Area/ethnic studies:** Women's. **Biology:** General. **Business:** General, accounting, administrative services, business admin, fashion, office management, office technology, office/clerical, real estate. **Computer sciences:** General, programming. **Education:** Early childhood. **Engineering:** General. **English:** English lit, rhetoric/composition. **Foreign languages:** General. **Health services:** Medical assistant. **History:**

General. **Liberal arts:** Arts/sciences. **Math:** General. **Parks/recreation:** Facilities management. **Physical sciences:** Chemistry, geology, physics. **Protective services:** Criminal justice. **Psychology:** General. **Social sciences:** General, sociology. **Visual/performing arts:** Art, dramatic, fashion design, interior design, music. **Work/family studies:** Child care management.

Computing on campus. 150 workstations in library, computer center. Commuter students can connect to campus network. Online course registration, online library, wireless network available.

Student life. Freshman orientation: Available. Preregistration for classes offered. **Activities:** Bands, choral groups, drama, music ensembles, student government, student newspaper, symphony orchestra, TV station, Vietnamese student association, Unlimited Horizons (handicapped), Descendants of Africa, Latin American student association, Alpha Gamma Sigma, Latter-Day Saints, fashion design, Puente, JC Ministries (Christian).

Athletics. Intercollegiate: Baseball M, basketball, cross-country, field hockey W, football (tackle) M, gymnastics W, soccer M, softball W, swimming, tennis, track and field, volleyball, water polo M, wrestling M. **Intramural:** Badminton, basketball, bowling, swimming, tennis, volleyball. **Team name:** Vikings.

Student services. Adult student services, career counseling, student employment services, health services, on-campus daycare, personal counseling, veterans' counselor. **Physically disabled:** Services for visually, speech, hearing impaired. **Transfer:** Re-entry adviser for new students. Transfer center, transfer adviser, college fairs on campus for students transferring to 4-year colleges.

Contact. Phone: (408) 741-2001 Fax: (408) 867-5033
Herlisa Hamp, Director of Admissions, West Valley College, 14000 Fruitvale Avenue, Saratoga, CA 95070-5698

Westwood College: Los Angeles
Los Angeles, California
www.westwood.edu/locations/california/los-angeles-campus

- For-profit 2-year technical college
- Very large city

General. Regionally accredited. **Calendar:** 10-week terms throughout year.

Annual costs/financial aid. Tuition/fees (2011-2012): $15,020. Books/supplies: $1,106.

Contact. Phone: (213) 739-9999
Director of Admissions, 3250 Wilshire Boulevard, Suite 400, Los Angeles, CA 90010

Yuba Community College District
Marysville, California
www.yccd.edu

- Public 2-year community college
- Commuter campus in small city

General. Founded in 1927. Regionally accredited. **Enrollment:** 8,341 undergraduates. **Degrees:** 541 associate awarded. **Location:** 56 miles from Sacramento. **Calendar:** Semester, limited summer session. **Full-time faculty:** 135 total. **Part-time faculty:** 375 total. **Special facilities:** Veterinary technical training clinic, manufacturing technology facilities (factory), college theater. **Partnerships:** Formal partnerships with numerous local businesses.

Transfer out. Colleges most students transferred to 2011: California State University: Sacramento, California State University: Chico, University of California: Davis, American River College.

Basis for selection. Open admission, but selective for some programs. Limited admission to allied health programs. CPT tests recommended for counseling.

2011-2012 Annual costs. Tuition/fees: $1,092; $6,792 out-of-state. Per-credit charge: $36 in-state; $226 out-of-state. Books/supplies: $1,566. Personal expenses: $3,024.

Financial aid. Need-based: Need-based aid available for part-time students. Work-study available nights, weekends and for part-time students. **Non-need-based:** Scholarships awarded for academics, athletics, job skills, minority status, music/drama. **Additional information:** Tuition fee waiver based on Board of Governors Grant.

Application procedures. Admission: No deadline. No application fee. Application must be submitted online. Admission notification on a rolling basis beginning on or about 6/1. **Financial aid:** Closing date 3/1. FAFSA required. Applicants notified on a rolling basis starting 4/1.

Academics. Special study options: Cooperative education, distance learning, ESL. License preparation in nursing, radiology. **Credit/placement by examination:** AP, CLEP, institutional tests. **Support services:** Learning center, remedial instruction, tutoring, writing center.

Majors. Biology: General. **Business:** Accounting, administrative services, business admin, entrepreneurial studies, human resources, taxation. **Communications:** Journalism, media studies. **Computer sciences:** General, computer science. **Education:** Early childhood, physical. **English:** English lit. **General:** Business, landscaping, mechanization, ornamental horticulture. **Health services:** Medical radiologic technology/radiation therapy, medical transcription, nursing (RN), substance abuse counseling, veterinary technology/assistant. **History:** General. **Liberal arts:** Arts/sciences. **Math:** General. **Protective services:** Criminal justice, fire safety technology, police science. **Psychology:** General. **Social sciences:** General. **Visual/performing arts:** Art, dramatic, music, photography, studio arts. **Work/family studies:** Family/community services.

Computing on campus. 300 workstations in library. Online course registration, online library, helpline, wireless network available.

Student life. Freshman orientation: Available. Preregistration for classes offered. **Activities:** Bands, choral groups, drama, music ensembles, musical theater, student government, student newspaper, symphony orchestra, AD Nursing Students Association, Care Club, EOP&S Club, DECA/Marketing Club, Christian students association, Green Society, Future Teachers of America, speech team, photography guild, veterinary technicians association.

Athletics. Intercollegiate: Baseball M, basketball, football (tackle) M, soccer, softball W, track and field, volleyball W. **Team name:** 49'ers.

Student services. Adult student services, career counseling, services for economically disadvantaged, student employment services, financial aid counseling, health services, minority student services, on-campus daycare, personal counseling, veterans' counselor, women's services. **Physically disabled:** Services for visually, speech, hearing impaired. **Transfer:** Transfer adviser, college fairs on campus for students transferring to 4-year colleges.

Contact. E-mail: admissions@yccd.edu
Phone: (530) 741-6720 Fax: (530) 741-6872
Kendyl Magnuson, Director, Admissions and Enrollment Services, Yuba Community College District, 2088 North Beale Road, Marysville, CA 95901

Colorado

Aims Community College
Greeley, Colorado
www.aims.edu

CB member
CB code: 4204

▸ Public 2-year community college
▸ Commuter campus in small city

General. Founded in 1967. Regionally accredited. **Enrollment:** 4,227 degree-seeking undergraduates; 1,010 non-degree-seeking students. **Degrees:** 438 associate awarded. **Location:** 55 miles from Denver. **Calendar:** Semester, extensive summer session. **Full-time faculty:** 90 total; 7% minority, 53% women. **Part-time faculty:** 371 total; 20% minority, 46% women. **Class size:** 70% < 20, 30% 20-39, less than 1% 40-49.

Student profile. Among degree-seeking undergraduates, 47% enrolled in a transfer program, 53% enrolled in a vocational program, 673 enrolled as first-time, first-year students, 191 transferred in from other institutions.

Part-time:	51%	Asian American:	1%
Out-of-state:	3%	Hispanic American:	27%
Women:	56%	Native American:	1%
African American:	2%	25 or older:	45%

Transfer out. Colleges most students transferred to 2011: University of Northern Colorado, Colorado State University, Metropolitan State College.

Basis for selection. Open admission, but selective for some programs. Special admissions requirements for Surgical Technology, Radiologic Technology, Peace Officer Academy, Paramedic, Fire Academy and Nursing. All students must meet assessment requirement by taking computerized placement test, submitting ACT/SAT scores or showing proof of previous college experience.

High school preparation. College-preparatory program recommended. 17 units recommended. Recommended units include English 4, mathematics 4, social studies 3, science 3 (laboratory 2), foreign language 1 and academic electives 2.

2011-2012 Annual costs. Tuition/fees: $2,621; $3,772 out-of-district; $13,358 out-of-state. Per-credit charge: $67 in-district; $106 out-of-district; $425 out-of-state. Books/supplies: $1,475. Personal expenses: $3,375.

2010-2011 Financial aid. Need-based: Work-study available nights, weekends and for part-time students.

Application procedures. Admission: No deadline. No application fee. Admission notification on a rolling basis. **Financial aid:** Priority date 4/15; no closing date. FAFSA required. Applicants notified on a rolling basis starting 6/1.

Academics. Special study options: Cooperative education, distance learning, double major, dual enrollment of high school students, ESL, external degree, honors, independent study, internships, student-designed major. **Credit/placement by examination:** AP, CLEP, IB, institutional tests. 45 credit hours maximum toward associate degree. **Support services:** GED preparation and test center, learning center, remedial instruction, study skills assistance, tutoring, writing center.

Majors. Business: Accounting, accounting technology, administrative services, management information systems, marketing, office technology. **Communications:** Broadcast journalism, digital media, radio/TV. **Communications technology:** General, animation/special effects, graphics, photo/film/video, radio/TV, recording arts. **Education:** Early childhood, educational technology, teacher assistance. **General:** Business, production. **Health services:** EMT paramedic, management/clinical assistant, medical secretary, nursing (RN), radiologic technology/medical imaging, surgical technology. **Liberal arts:** Arts/sciences. **Protective services:** Fire services admin, firefighting, forest/wildland firefighting, law enforcement admin. **Work/family studies:** Child care service, child development.

Most popular majors. Business/marketing 8%, health sciences 15%, liberal arts 53%, trade and industry 8%.

Computing on campus. 500 workstations in library, computer center, student center. Commuter students can connect to campus network. Online course registration, online library, helpline, student web hosting, wireless network available.

Student life. Freshman orientation: Available. Preregistration for classes offered. **Policies:** Student code of conduct, civility statement enforced; parking permits required. **Activities:** Jazz band, dance, drama, international student organizations, music ensembles, radio station, student government, student newspaper, Student United Way, Campus Crusade for Christ, Rotaract club, freethinkers club, LULAC, gay-straight alliance, Helping Hands, veterans club, international club, Women in Transition Together.

Student services. Career counseling, services for economically disadvantaged, financial aid counseling, personal counseling, veterans' counselor. **Physically disabled:** Services for visually, speech, hearing impaired. **Transfer:** Transfer adviser, college fairs on campus for students transferring to 4-year colleges.

Contact. E-mail: admissions.records@aims.edu
Phone: (970) 339-6440 Fax: (970) 506-6958
Stuart Thomas, Director of Admissions, Aims Community College, 5401 West 20th Street, Greeley, CO 80632

Anthem College: Aurora
Aurora, Colorado
www.anthem.edu

CB code: 3201

▸ For-profit 2-year technical college
▸ Commuter campus in small city
▸ Interview required

General. Regionally accredited; also accredited by ACICS. **Enrollment:** 308 degree-seeking undergraduates. **Degrees:** 8 associate awarded. **Calendar:** Differs by program, extensive summer session. **Full-time faculty:** 10 total. **Part-time faculty:** 12 total.

Basis for selection. Open admission.

Financial aid. All financial aid based on need. Work-study available nights, weekends and for part-time students.

Application procedures. Admission: No deadline. $20 fee ($150 out-of-state). Admission notification on a rolling basis. **Financial aid:** No deadline. FAFSA, institutional form required. Applicants notified on a rolling basis.

Academics. Special study options: License preparation in radiology. **Credit/placement by examination:** AP, CLEP. **Support services:** GED preparation.

Majors. Computer sciences: General. **Health services:** Massage therapy, medical assistant, radiologic technology/medical imaging, surgical technology.

Student life. Freshman orientation: Mandatory. Preregistration for classes offered.

Student services. Adult student services, career counseling, student employment services, financial aid counseling, placement for graduates.

Contact. Phone: (720) 859-7900 Toll-free number: (800) 322-4132
Fax: (303) 338-9701
Amy Marshall, Director of Admissions, Anthem College: Aurora, 350 Blackhawk Street, Aurora, CO 80011

Arapahoe Community College
Littleton, Colorado
www.arapahoe.edu

CB code: 4014

▸ Public 2-year community college
▸ Commuter campus in large town

General. Founded in 1965. Regionally accredited. **Enrollment:** 8,107 degree-seeking undergraduates; 2,417 non-degree-seeking students. **Degrees:** 595 associate awarded. **ROTC:** Army, Air Force. **Location:** 10 miles from Denver. **Calendar:** Semester, extensive summer session. **Full-time faculty:** 100 total; 3% minority, 67% women. **Part-time faculty:** 351 total; 7% minority, 55% women. **Class size:** 65% < 20, 33% 20-39, less than 1% 40-49, less than 1% 50-99. **Partnerships:** Formal partnerships with National Cable Telecommunications Institute, Swedish Medical Center, Porter Adventist Hospital, Skyridge Medical Center.

Student profile. Among degree-seeking undergraduates, 1,094 enrolled as first-time, first-year students, 956 transferred in from other institutions.

Part-time:	72%	Hispanic American:		11%
Out-of-state:	11%	Native American:		2%
Women:	55%	International:		1%
African American:	5%	25 or older:		52%
Asian American:	3%			

Transfer out. Colleges most students transferred to 2011: Metropolitan State College, University of Colorado at Denver, Colorado State University, Colorado School of Mines, Adams State College.

Basis for selection. Open admission, but selective for some programs. Allied health, nursing, automotive, legal assistant, and law enforcement programs require interviews and/or test scores.

2011-2012 Annual costs. Tuition/fees: $3,341; $13,194 out-of-state. Per-credit charge: $106 in-state; $434 out-of-state. In-state tuition based upon assumption of Colorado Opportunity Fund waiver of $62 per-credit-hour. Books/supplies: $1,749.

Financial aid. Need-based: Need-based aid available for part-time students. Work-study available nights, weekends and for part-time students. **Non-need-based:** Scholarships awarded for academics, leadership, state residency.

Application procedures. Admission: No deadline. No application fee. Admission notification on a rolling basis. Closing date for nursing applicants February 4. **Financial aid:** Priority date 5/1; no closing date. FAFSA, institutional form required. Applicants notified on a rolling basis starting 5/1; must reply within 3 week(s) of notification.

Academics. Special study options: Accelerated study, cooperative education, distance learning, double major, dual enrollment of high school students, ESL, honors, independent study, internships. License preparation in nursing, occupational therapy, paramedic, physical therapy, real estate. **Credit/placement by examination:** AP, CLEP, IB, institutional tests. No more than half of required credit can be fulfilled through credit for prior learning. **Support services:** GED preparation and test center, learning center, pre-admission summer program, reduced course load, remedial instruction, study skills assistance, tutoring, writing center.

Majors. Business: Accounting technology, administrative services, banking/financial services, hospitality admin, international, management information systems, marketing, office management, selling. **Communications technology:** General. **Computer sciences:** Data entry, LAN/WAN management, networking, web page design. **Health services:** Clinical lab technology, medical records technology, nursing (RN), occupational therapy assistant, office admin, physical therapy assistant. **Liberal arts:** Arts/sciences. **Parks/recreation:** Health/fitness. **Protective services:** Law enforcement admin. **Visual/performing arts:** Graphic design, interior design. **Work/family studies:** Child development.

Most popular majors. Health sciences 23%, liberal arts 43%, trade and industry 6%, visual/performing arts 7%.

Computing on campus. 110 workstations in library, computer center, student center. Online course registration, online library, helpline, wireless network available.

Student life. Freshman orientation: Mandatory. Preregistration for classes offered. **Activities:** Bands, choral groups, international student organizations, literary magazine, music ensembles, student government, symphony orchestra, Phi Theta Kappa, diversity council, Ron Paul society.

Athletics. Team name: Coyotes.

Student services. Adult student services, career counseling, services for economically disadvantaged, student employment services, financial aid counseling, minority student services, on-campus daycare, placement for graduates, veterans' counselor. **Physically disabled:** Services for visually, speech, hearing impaired. **Transfer:** Pre-admission transcript evaluation for new students. Transfer adviser, college fairs on campus for students transferring to 4-year colleges.

Contact. E-mail: admissions@arapahoe.edu
Phone: (303) 797-5621 Fax: (303) 797-5970
Darcy Briggs, Registrar-Director of Enrollment Services, Arapahoe Community College, PO Box 9002, Littleton, CO 80160-9002

Bel-Rea Institute of Animal Technology
Denver, Colorado
www.bel-rea.com   **CB code: 0928**

- For-profit 2-year technical college
- Commuter campus in very large city

General. Accredited by ACCSC. **Enrollment:** 857 degree-seeking undergraduates. **Degrees:** 275 associate awarded. **Calendar:** Differs by program. **Full-time faculty:** 16 total. **Part-time faculty:** 3 total.

Transfer out. Colleges most students transferred to 2011: University of Denver.

Basis for selection. Interview most important, followed by school achievement record. Recommendations considered. 2.5 GPA or GED required. Applicants with below 2.5 GPA or without GED must take entrance exam.

High school preparation. As much science and math as possible recommended. Algebra and chemistry recommended.

2011-2012 Annual costs. Tuition/fees: $10,088. Tuition for full associate program is $26,900. Books/supplies: $1,500. Personal expenses: $1,100.

Financial aid. All financial aid based on need. Work-study available nights, weekends and for part-time students.

Application procedures. Admission: No deadline. No application fee. Admission notification on a rolling basis. **Financial aid:** Priority date 8/31; no closing date. FAFSA required. Applicants notified on a rolling basis starting 8/15.

Academics. Students intern at college-affiliated emergency veterinary hospital. **Special study options:** Internships. **Credit/placement by examination:** AP, CLEP. **Support services:** Reduced course load, study skills assistance, tutoring.

Majors. Health services: Veterinary technology/assistant.

Computing on campus. PC or laptop required. 20 workstations in student center.

Student life. Freshman orientation: Available. Preregistration for classes offered. **Activities:** Student government.

Student services. Career counseling, student employment services, personal counseling, placement for graduates, veterans' counselor.

Contact. E-mail: kaufman@bel-rea.com
Phone: (303) 751-8700 Toll-free number: (800) 950-8001
Fax: (303) 751-9969
Paulette Kaufman, Director, Bel-Rea Institute of Animal Technology, 1681 South Dayton Street, Denver, CO 80247

Boulder College of Massage Therapy
Boulder, Colorado
www.bcmt.org

- Private 2-year health science college
- Residential campus in small city
- Application essay, interview required

General. Accredited by ACCSC. **Enrollment:** 152 degree-seeking undergraduates. **Degrees:** 32 associate awarded. **Location:** 30 miles from Denver. **Calendar:** Quarter, extensive summer session. **Full-time faculty:** 3 total. **Part-time faculty:** 19 total. **Class size:** 97% < 20, 3% 20-39. **Special facilities:** Student massage therapy clinic, wellness bookstore, spa classroom.

Basis for selection. Open admission, but selective for some programs. Health history form required.

Financial aid. All financial aid based on need. Need-based aid available for part-time students. Work-study available nights, weekends and for part-time students.

Application procedures. Admission: No deadline. $75 fee, may be waived for applicants with need. Application must be submitted on paper. Admission notification on a rolling basis. **Financial aid:** No deadline. FAFSA required.

Academics. Special study options: Honors, internships. **Credit/placement by examination:** AP, CLEP. **Support services:** Learning center, reduced course load, study skills assistance, tutoring.

Majors. Health services: Massage therapy.

Computing on campus. 10 workstations in library, computer center. Online library, wireless network available.

Student life. Freshman orientation: Mandatory. Preregistration for classes offered. Held Monday prior to start of quarter. **Activities:** Student government.

Student services. Adult student services, alcohol/substance abuse counseling, career counseling, services for economically disadvantaged, student employment services, financial aid counseling, personal counseling, placement for graduates, veterans' counselor. **Physically disabled:** Services for visually, speech, hearing impaired.

Contact. E-mail: admissions@bcmt.org
Phone: (303) 530-2100 Toll-free number: (800) 442-5131
Fax: (303) 530-2204
Director of Marketing and Admissions, Boulder College of Massage Therapy, 6255 Longbow Drive, Boulder, CO 80301

CollegeAmerica: Denver
Denver, Colorado
www.collegeamerica.com

- For-profit 2-year technical college
- Commuter campus in very large city
- Application essay, interview required

General. Accredited by ACCSC. **Enrollment:** 590 degree-seeking undergraduates. **Degrees:** 37 bachelor's, 97 associate awarded. **Calendar:** Differs by program, extensive summer session. **Full-time faculty:** 14 total. **Part-time faculty:** 40 total. **Class size:** 91% < 20, 9% 20-39.

Basis for selection. Open admission. **Home schooled:** Transcript of courses and grades, state high school equivalency certificate required.

2011-2012 Annual costs. Tuition ranges from $324 to $408 per quarter credit depending on program. Books/supplies: $101. Personal expenses: $1,000.

Financial aid. All financial aid based on need. Work-study available nights, weekends and for part-time students.

Application procedures. Admission: No deadline. No application fee. Application must be submitted on paper. Admission notification on a rolling basis. **Financial aid:** No deadline. FAFSA, institutional form required. Applicants notified on a rolling basis; must reply within 4 week(s) of notification.

Academics. Special study options: Accelerated study, distance learning. Bachelor's degree programs available on campus. License preparation in radiology. **Credit/placement by examination:** AP, CLEP. **Support services:** Tutoring.

Majors. Business: Accounting/business management, business admin. **Computer sciences:** Computer graphics, networking, programming.

Most popular majors. Business/marketing 10%, computer/information sciences 10%, health sciences 80%.

Computing on campus. 50 workstations in library, computer center. Commuter students can connect to campus network. Online course registration, online library, repair service, wireless network available.

Student life. Freshman orientation: Mandatory. Preregistration for classes offered.

Student services. Career counseling, services for economically disadvantaged, student employment services, financial aid counseling, placement for graduates.

Contact. Phone: (303) 691-9756 Toll-free number: (800) 977-5455
Jaclyn Haack, Director of Admissions, CollegeAmerica: Denver, 1385 South Colorado Boulevard, 5th Floor, Denver, CO 80222-1912

Colorado Mountain College
Glenwood Springs, Colorado
www.coloradomtn.edu   CB code: 4112

- Public 2-year community and liberal arts college
- Residential campus in small town

General. Founded in 1965. Regionally accredited. Total of 12 campuses. Three residential campuses are Alpine Campus in Steamboat Springs, Spring Valley Campus in Glenwood Springs, and Timberline Campus in Leadville. Commuter campuses in Aspen, Summit, Vail-Eagle Valley in Edwards, Rifle, Breckinridge, Buena Vista. **Enrollment:** 5,823 degree-seeking undergraduates. **Degrees:** 400 associate awarded. **Location:** 160 miles from Denver. **Calendar:** Semester, limited summer session. **Full-time faculty:** 105 total. **Part-time faculty:** 823 total. **Special facilities:** Outdoor education center, farm for veterinarian technician program, hot springs, climbing wall, ice wall, community theater.

Student profile.

Out-of-state:	10%	**25 or older:**	68%

Transfer out. Colleges most students transferred to 2011: University of Colorado-Boulder, Colorado State University, Mesa State University, Western State College, Fort Lewis College.

Basis for selection. Open admission, but selective for some programs. Special requirements for nursing applicants. Testing requirements for veterinary technology, photography, outdoor recreation leadership, culinary arts, paramedic, and ski area operations.

2011-2012 Annual costs. Tuition/fees: $1,790; $2,870 out-of-district; $8,570 out-of-state. Per-credit charge: $53 in-district; $89 out-of-district; $279 out-of-state. Room/board: $7,928. Books/supplies: $650. Personal expenses: $2,050.

Financial aid. All financial aid based on need. Need-based aid available for part-time students. Work-study available nights, weekends and for part-time students.

Application procedures. Admission: No deadline. No application fee. Application must be submitted on paper. Admission notification on a rolling basis. **Financial aid:** Closing date 3/31. FAFSA required. Applicants notified on a rolling basis starting 5/15; must reply within 4 week(s) of notification.

Academics. Special study options: Distance learning, dual enrollment of high school students, independent study, internships, liberal arts/career combination, study abroad. License preparation in nursing. **Credit/placement by examination:** AP, CLEP, IB, institutional tests. 30 credit hours maximum toward associate degree. Also recognize and accept exam results for DANTES, Excelsior, Institutional Challenge Exams, and credit for life experiences. **Support services:** GED preparation and test center, learning center, reduced course load, remedial instruction, study skills assistance, tutoring.

Majors. Biology: General. **Business:** General, accounting, business admin, hospitality admin, hotel/motel admin, management information systems, real estate, resort management. **Communications:** Photojournalism. **Communications technology:** Animation/special effects, graphic/printing, graphics, photo/film/video. **Computer sciences:** General, applications programming, computer graphics, information technology, networking, programming. **Conservation:** General, forestry, management/policy. **Education:** General, bilingual. **English:** English lit, rhetoric/composition. **General:** Animal health, food processing, food science, soil science. **Health services:** Nursing (RN), prenursing, veterinary technology/assistant. **Liberal arts:** Arts/sciences. **Math:** General. **Parks/recreation:** General, facilities management. **Physical sciences:** Chemistry, geology. **Protective services:** Criminal justice, firefighting. **Social sciences:** General. **Visual/performing arts:** General, art, commercial photography, commercial/advertising art, design, dramatic, graphic design, photography.

Computing on campus. 30 workstations in dormitories, library, computer center, student center. Dormitories wired for high-speed internet access and linked to campus network. Online library, helpline, wireless network available.

Student life. Freshman orientation: Available. Preregistration for classes offered. **Policies:** All students living on-campus must follow housing policies. **Housing:** Guaranteed on-campus for freshmen. Coed dorms, special housing for disabled, wellness housing available. $300 partly refundable deposit, deadline 7/1. **Activities:** Dance, drama, musical theater, student government, student newspaper.

Athletics. NJCAA. **Intercollegiate:** Skiing, soccer. **Intramural:** Basketball, cross-country, skiing, soccer, softball, volleyball. **Team name:** Eagles.

Student services. Adult student services, career counseling, student employment services, financial aid counseling, health services, personal counseling, placement for graduates, veterans' counselor. **Physically disabled:** Services for visually, speech, hearing impaired. **Transfer:** Transfer center, transfer adviser, college fairs on campus for students transferring to 4-year colleges.

Contact. E-mail: joinus@coloradomtn.edu
Phone: (970) 947-8327 Toll-free number: (800) 621-8559 ext. 8327
Fax: (970) 947-8324
Bill Sommers, Assistant Vice President, Enrollment Services, Colorado Mountain College, 831 Grand Avenue, Glenwood Springs, CO 81601

Colorado Northwestern Community College
Rangely, Colorado
www.cncc.edu

CB code: 4665

- Public 2-year community college
- Residential campus in rural community

General. Founded in 1962. Regionally accredited. Additional campus in Craig and 3 off-campus sites in Meeker, Hayden, Oak Creek. **Enrollment:** 990 degree-seeking undergraduates; 378 non-degree-seeking students. **Degrees:** 162 associate awarded. **Location:** 300 miles from Denver, 90 miles from Grand Junction. **Calendar:** Semester, limited summer session. **Full-time faculty:** 33 total; 54% women. **Part-time faculty:** 57 total; 12% minority, 58% women. **Class size:** 86% < 20, 14% 20-39. **Special facilities:** Flight simulator, firearms training simulator, cadaver lab.

Student profile. Among degree-seeking undergraduates, 38% enrolled in a transfer program, 35% enrolled in a vocational program, 1% already have a bachelor's degree or higher, 324 enrolled as first-time, first-year students, 25 transferred in from other institutions.

Part-time:	52%	25 or older:	20%
Out-of-state:	17%	Live on campus:	64%
Women:	64%		

Transfer out. Colleges most students transferred to 2011: University of Northern Colorado, Colorado State University, Mesa State College.

Basis for selection. Open admission, but selective for some programs. Selective admissions to dental hygiene and nursing. Both programs have application deadline and pre-requisite requirements. Interview required of dental hygiene majors. Competitive entry scoring required of nursing majors.

High school preparation. Biological science and/or chemistry required for dental hygiene. Math/science desirable for aviation technology and aviation maintenance.

2011-2012 Annual costs. Tuition/fees: $3,425; $6,543 out-of-state. Per-credit charge: $106 in-state; $210 out-of-state. In-state tuition based upon assumption of Colorado Opportunity Fund waiver of $62 per-credit-hour. Room/board: $5,988. Books/supplies: $1,000. Personal expenses: $1,650.

Financial aid. Need-based: Need-based aid available for part-time students. Work-study available nights, weekends and for part-time students. **Non-need-based:** Scholarships awarded for academics, athletics, leadership, state residency.

Application procedures. Admission: No deadline. No application fee. Admission notification on a rolling basis. Application closing date for dental hygiene program 2/15. **Financial aid:** Priority date 5/1; no closing date. FAFSA, institutional form required. Applicants notified on a rolling basis starting 5/15; must reply within 4 week(s) of notification.

Academics. Special study options: Distance learning, dual enrollment of high school students, independent study, internships, student-designed major. Bachelor's degree programs available on campus. License preparation in aviation, dental hygiene, nursing. **Credit/placement by examination:** AP, CLEP, institutional tests. 30 credit hours maximum toward associate degree. **Support services:** GED preparation and test center, learning center, remedial instruction, study skills assistance, tutoring, writing center.

Majors. Biology: Marine. **Business:** Accounting technology, banking/financial services, entrepreneurial studies, management information systems, office management. **Conservation:** General, management/policy. **Education:** Early childhood. **General:** Equestrian studies. **Health services:** Dental hygiene, EMT paramedic, nursing (RN). **Liberal arts:** Arts/sciences. **Parks/recreation:** Outdoor education. **Protective services:** Law enforcement admin. **Work/family studies:** Child care management.

Computing on campus. 54 workstations in dormitories, library, computer center. Dormitories wired for high-speed internet access and linked to campus network. Online course registration, online library, wireless network available.

Student life. Freshman orientation: Mandatory, $45 fee. Preregistration for classes offered. Two sessions in July, one in August. **Housing:** Guaranteed on-campus for freshmen. Coed dorms, special housing for disabled available. $100 fully refundable deposit. **Activities:** Student government, student newspaper.

Athletics. NJCAA. **Intercollegiate:** Baseball M, basketball, softball W, volleyball W. **Intramural:** Basketball, football (non-tackle), golf, racquetball, rodeo, soccer, softball, table tennis, volleyball. **Team name:** Spartans.

Student services. Adult student services, alcohol/substance abuse counseling, career counseling, student employment services, financial aid counseling, personal counseling, placement for graduates, veterans' counselor. **Physically disabled:** Services for visually, hearing impaired. **Transfer:** Pre-admission transcript evaluation for new students. Transfer adviser, college fairs on campus for students transferring to 4-year colleges.

Contact. E-mail: kelsey.zickefoose@cncc.edu
Phone: (970) 675-3218 Toll-free number: (800) 562-1105
Fax: (970) 975-3343
Tresa England, Director of Student Services/Registrar, Colorado Northwestern Community College, 500 Kennedy Drive, Rangely, CO 81648

Colorado School of Healing Arts
Lakewood, Colorado
www.csha.net

- For-profit 2-year career college
- Commuter campus in small city
- Application essay, interview required

General. Accredited by ACCSC. **Enrollment:** 189 degree-seeking undergraduates; 4 non-degree-seeking students. **Degrees:** 40 associate awarded. **Location:** 7 miles from Denver. **Calendar:** Quarter, extensive summer session. **Part-time faculty:** 35 total. **Class size:** 92% < 20, 8% 20-39.

Student profile. Among degree-seeking undergraduates, 41 enrolled as first-time, first-year students.

Part-time:	21%	Asian American:	1%
Women:	82%	Hispanic American:	7%
African American:	2%	Native American:	3%

Basis for selection. Open admission. **Home schooled:** Interview required.

2011-2012 Annual costs. Tuition/fees: $14,621. Per-credit charge: $197. Books, massage table package, materials fees, State registration fees and 1st year insurance are included in required fees. Books/supplies: $674.

Financial aid. All financial aid based on need. Need-based aid available for part-time students. Work-study available nights, weekends and for part-time students.

Application procedures. Admission: No deadline. $50 fee. Application must be submitted on paper. Admission notification on a rolling basis. **Financial aid:** No deadline. FAFSA required.

Academics. Special study options: Accelerated study. **Credit/placement by examination:** AP, CLEP. **Support services:** Learning center, tutoring.

Majors. Health services: Massage therapy.

Computing on campus. 2 workstations in library. Wireless network available.

Student life. Freshman orientation: Mandatory. Preregistration for classes offered. 4-hour program held prior to start of quarter.

Student services. Career counseling, financial aid counseling.

Contact. E-mail: tiffany@csha.net
Phone: (303) 986-2320 Toll-free number: (800) 233-7114
Fax: (303) 980-6594
Tiffany Layne, Admissions Representative, Colorado School of Healing Arts, 7655 West Mississippi Avenue, Suite 100, Lakewood, CO 80226

Colorado School of Trades
Lakewood, Colorado
www.schooloftrades.edu

CB code: 3211

- For-profit 2-year technical college
- Small city

General. Accredited by ACCSC. **Enrollment:** 165 degree-seeking undergraduates. **Degrees:** 100 associate awarded. **Calendar:** Differs by program. **Full-time faculty:** 12 total. **Part-time faculty:** 1 total.

Basis for selection. Open admission.

2011-2012 Annual costs. For gunsmithing program: tuition, $18,900; tools $3,500; miscellaneous $161.

Financial aid. Need-based: Work-study available nights, weekends and for part-time students.

Application procedures. Admission: No deadline. $25 fee. Admission notification on a rolling basis. **Financial aid:** FAFSA, institutional form required.

Academics. Credit/placement by examination: AP, CLEP.

Majors. Education: Trade/industrial.

Computing on campus. 4 workstations in computer center.

Contact. E-mail: info@schooloftrades.edu
Phone: (800) 234-4594 ext. 45 Toll-free number: (800) 234-4594 ext. 45
Fax: (303) 233-4723
Sunny Duvont-Holt, Director of Admissions, Colorado School of Trades, 1575 Hoyt Street, Lakewood, CO 80215-2945

Community College of Aurora
Aurora, Colorado
www.ccaurora.edu   CB code: 0969

- Public 2-year community college
- Commuter campus in large city

General. Founded in 1983. Regionally accredited. **Enrollment:** 5,596 degree-seeking undergraduates; 2,048 non-degree-seeking students. **Degrees:** 356 associate awarded. **Calendar:** Semester, extensive summer session. **Full-time faculty:** 43 total; 19% have terminal degrees, 14% minority, 54% women. **Part-time faculty:** 391 total; 10% have terminal degrees, 30% minority, 45% women. **Class size:** 41% < 20, 55% 20-39, 2% 40-49, 2% 50-99.

Student profile. Among degree-seeking undergraduates, 1,396 enrolled as first-time, first-year students, 493 transferred in from other institutions.

Part-time:	67%	Hispanic American:	14%
Out-of-state:	3%	Native American:	1%
Women:	59%	International:	1%
African American:	27%	25 or older:	49%
Asian American:	5%		

Transfer out. Colleges most students transferred to 2011: Metropolitan State University, University of Colorado Denver, Colorado State University, University of Northern Colorado.

Basis for selection. Open admission.

2011-2012 Annual costs. Tuition/fees: $3,355; $13,208 out-of-state. Per-credit charge: $106 in-state; $434 out-of-state. In-state tuition based upon assumption of Colorado Opportunity Fund waiver of $62 per-credit-hour. Books/supplies: $1,749. Personal expenses: $3,375.

2010-2011 Financial aid. Need-based: 60% of total undergraduate aid awarded as scholarships/grants, 40% as loans/jobs. Need-based aid available for part-time students. Work-study available nights, weekends and for part-time students. **Non-need-based:** Scholarships awarded for academics, minority status, music/drama, state residency.

Application procedures. Admission: No deadline. No application fee. Admission notification on a rolling basis. **Financial aid:** Priority date 6/1; no closing date. FAFSA required. Applicants notified on a rolling basis starting 7/15.

Academics. Special study options: Accelerated study, distance learning, dual enrollment of high school students, ESL, honors, independent study, internships, weekend college. License preparation in paramedic. **Credit/placement by examination:** AP, CLEP, IB. 30 credit hours maximum toward associate degree. **Support services:** GED preparation, learning center, remedial instruction, tutoring, writing center.

Majors. Business: Accounting technology, marketing, office management. **Computer sciences:** General, computer science, networking, web page design. **Education:** Early childhood. **Health services:** EMT paramedic, respiratory therapy technology. **Liberal arts:** Arts/sciences. **Protective services:** Disaster management, fire services admin, firefighting, law enforcement admin. **Visual/performing arts:** Cinematography, illustration.

Computing on campus. Commuter students can connect to campus network. Online course registration, online library, helpline, wireless network available.

Student life. Freshman orientation: Available. Preregistration for classes offered. **Housing:** $150 deposit. **Activities:** Jazz band, dance, drama, international student organizations, literary magazine, musical theater, student government.

Student services. Physically disabled: Services for visually, speech, hearing impaired. **Transfer:** Transfer adviser, college fairs on campus for students transferring to 4-year colleges.

Contact. Phone: (303) 360-4700 Fax: (303) 361-7432
Kristen Cusack, Registrar, Community College of Aurora, 16000 East CentreTech Parkway, Aurora, CO 80011-9036

Community College of Denver
Denver, Colorado
www.ccd.edu   CB code: 4137

- Public 2-year community college
- Commuter campus in very large city

General. Founded in 1970. Regionally accredited. Library, student center and physical education facilities shared with Metropolitan State College at Denver and University of Colorado/Health Sciences Center at Denver. **Enrollment:** 3,182 full-time, degree-seeking students. **Degrees:** 407 associate awarded. **ROTC:** Army. **Calendar:** Semester, limited summer session. **Full-time faculty:** 114 total; 7% have terminal degrees, 19% minority. **Part-time faculty:** 404 total; 22% minority. **Class size:** 34% < 20, 66% 20-39, less than 1% 40-49.

Student profile. Among full-time, degree-seeking students, 862 transferred in from other institutions.

Out-of-state:	8%	Native American:	1%
African American:	18%	International:	4%
Asian American:	5%	25 or older:	50%
Hispanic American:	25%		

Transfer out. Colleges most students transferred to 2011: Metropolitan State College of Denver, University of Colorado at Denver.

Basis for selection. Open admission, but selective for some programs. Special requirements for health occupations and computer information systems programs.

2011-2012 Annual costs. Tuition/fees: $3,942; $13,795 out-of-state. Per-credit charge: $106 in-state; $434 out-of-state. In-state tuition based upon assumption of Colorado Opportunity Fund waiver of $62 per-credit-hour. Books/supplies: $1,749. Personal expenses: $3,402.

2010-2011 Financial aid. Need-based: 57% of total undergraduate aid awarded as scholarships/grants, 43% as loans/jobs. Need-based aid available for part-time students. Work-study available nights, weekends and for part-time students. **Non-need-based:** Scholarships awarded for academics, leadership, state residency.

Application procedures. Admission: Priority date 8/1; no deadline. No application fee. Admission notification on a rolling basis. **Financial aid:** Priority date 4/15; no closing date. FAFSA, institutional form required. Applicants notified on a rolling basis.

Academics. Special study options: Accelerated study, cooperative education, cross-registration, distance learning, double major, dual enrollment of high school students, ESL, external degree, honors, independent study, internships. **Credit/placement by examination:** AP, CLEP, institutional tests. 45 credit hours maximum toward associate degree. **Support services:** GED preparation and test center, learning center, pre-admission summer program, reduced course load, remedial instruction, study skills assistance, tutoring, writing center.

Majors. Biology: Biomedical sciences. **Business:** Accounting technology, administrative services, business admin, management information systems. **Computer sciences:** General, applications programming. **Education:** Teacher assistance. **Health services:** Dental hygiene, electroencephalograph technology, health aide, nursing (RN), radiologic technology/medical imaging, veterinary technology/assistant. **Liberal arts:** Arts/sciences. **Parks/recreation:** General, health/fitness. **Protective services:** Security services. **Visual/performing arts:** Graphic design. **Work/family studies:** Child development.

Most popular majors. Health sciences 31%, liberal arts 55%.

Computing on campus. 1,032 workstations in library, computer center, student center. Commuter students can connect to campus network. Online course registration available.

Student life. Freshman orientation: Mandatory. Preregistration for classes offered. **Housing:** Dormitory housing available at Lowry campus through cooperative agreement. **Activities:** Choral groups, international student organizations, student government, student newspaper, Mexican-American student organization, African-American student organization, Amnesty International, nursing club.

Student services. Adult student services, career counseling, services for economically disadvantaged, student employment services, financial aid counseling, health services, legal services, minority student services, on-campus daycare, personal counseling, placement for graduates, veterans' counselor, women's services. **Physically disabled:** Services for visually, hearing impaired. **Transfer:** Re-entry adviser, pre-admission transcript evaluation for new students. Transfer center, transfer adviser, college fairs on campus for students transferring to 4-year colleges.

Contact. E-mail: enrollment_services@ccd.edu
Phone: (303) 556-2420 Fax: (303) 556-2431
Michael Rusk, Dean of Students, Community College of Denver, Campus Box 201, PO Box 173363, Denver, CO 80217-3363

Concorde Career College: Aurora
Aurora, Colorado
www.concorde.edu/denver

- For-profit 2-year health science college
- Large city

General. Accredited by ACCSC. **Enrollment:** 651 degree-seeking undergraduates. **Degrees:** 110 associate awarded. **Calendar:** Differs by program. **Full-time faculty:** 33 total. **Part-time faculty:** 8 total.

Basis for selection. Wonderlic and CPAT exams used.

Financial aid. Need-based: Work-study available nights, weekends and for part-time students.

Application procedures. Admission: No deadline. No application fee. Admission notification on a rolling basis.

Academics. Credit/placement by examination: AP, CLEP.

Majors. Health services: Medical radiologic technology/radiation therapy, nursing (RN), respiratory therapy technology.

Contact. Phone: (303) 861-1151
Michael Como, Director of Admissions, Concorde Career College: Aurora, 111 North Havana Street, Aurora, CO 80010

Front Range Community College
Westminster, Colorado
www.frontrange.edu   CB code: 4119

- Public 2-year community college
- Commuter campus in large city

General. Founded in 1968. Regionally accredited. Additional campuses in Brighton, Boulder County, Larimer County. **Enrollment:** 17,650 degree-seeking undergraduates. **Degrees:** 1,120 associate awarded. **ROTC:** Army, Air Force. **Location:** 12 miles from Denver. **Calendar:** Semester, limited summer session. **Full-time faculty:** 212 total; 57% women. **Part-time faculty:** 906 total. **Class size:** 35% < 20, 65% 20-39, less than 1% 40-49. **Special facilities:** Observatories, city/college libraries. **Partnerships:** Formal partnerships with local workforce centers for career training or retraining.

Student profile. Among degree-seeking undergraduates, 41% enrolled in a transfer program, 48% enrolled in a vocational program, 2% already have a bachelor's degree or higher, 3,634 enrolled as first-time, first-year students, 1,726 transferred in from other institutions.

Part-time:	61%	Hispanic American:	13%
Out-of-state:	2%	Native American:	1%
Women:	57%	International:	1%
African American:	2%	25 or older:	43%
Asian American:	3%		

Transfer out. Colleges most students transferred to 2011: Colorado State University, University of Colorado at Boulder, Metropolitan State College, University of Northern Colorado, University of Colorado at Denver Health Sciences.

Basis for selection. Open admission.

2011-2012 Annual costs. Tuition/fees: $3,439; $13,292 out-of-state. Per-credit charge: $106 in-state; $434 out-of-state. In-state tuition based upon assumption of Colorado Opportunity Fund waiver of $62 per-credit-hour. Books/supplies: $1,749.

2010-2011 Financial aid. Need-based: 54% of total undergraduate aid awarded as scholarships/grants, 46% as loans/jobs. Need-based aid available for part-time students. Work-study available nights, weekends and for part-time students. **Non-need-based:** Scholarships awarded for academics, job skills, leadership, ROTC, state residency.

Application procedures. Admission: No deadline. No application fee. Admission notification on a rolling basis. **Financial aid:** Priority date 5/1; no closing date. FAFSA, institutional form required. Applicants notified on a rolling basis starting 4/15; must reply within 3 week(s) of notification.

Academics. Special study options: Accelerated study, cooperative education, cross-registration, distance learning, double major, dual enrollment of high school students, ESL, honors, independent study, internships, liberal arts/career combination, study abroad, teacher certification program, weekend college. License preparation in dental hygiene, nursing, paramedic. **Credit/placement by examination:** AP, CLEP, institutional tests. 30 credit hours maximum toward associate degree. **Support services:** GED preparation and test center, learning center, remedial instruction, study skills assistance, tutoring, writing center.

Majors. Business: Accounting technology, business admin, hospitality admin, management information systems. **Communications technology:** Animation/special effects. **Computer sciences:** General. **Conservation:** Wildlife/wilderness. **Education:** Early childhood. **Foreign languages:** Sign language interpretation. **General:** Animal health, horticulture. **Health services:** EMT paramedic, medical records technology, nursing (RN), office assistant, veterinary technology/assistant. **Liberal arts:** Arts/sciences. **Visual/performing arts:** Interior design.

Most popular majors. Communication technologies 11%, health sciences 18%, liberal arts 60%.

Computing on campus. 233 workstations in library, computer center. Commuter students can connect to campus network. Online course registration, helpline, wireless network available.

Student life. Freshman orientation: Available. Preregistration for classes offered. **Activities:** Campus ministries, dance, drama, international student organizations, music ensembles, student government, student newspaper, interpreters for the deaf, gay/straight alliance, pharmacy tech club, dance club, ski/snowboard club, Phi Theta Kappa, horticulture club, student vet tech association, Latino club, science club.

Student services. Adult student services, career counseling, services for economically disadvantaged, student employment services, financial aid counseling, minority student services, on-campus daycare, personal counseling, veterans' counselor, women's services. **Physically disabled:** Services for visually, speech, hearing impaired. **Transfer:** Transfer center, college fairs on campus for students transferring to 4-year colleges.

Contact. Phone: (303) 404-5414 Fax: (303) 404-5150
Yolanda Espinoza, Registrar, Front Range Community College, 3645 West 112th Avenue, Westminster, CO 80031

Institute of Business & Medical Careers
Fort Collins, Colorado
www.ibmc.edu   CB code: 3566

- For-profit 2-year technical college
- Residential campus in small city
- Application essay, interview required

General. Accredited by ACICS. Additional branch campuses in Greeley, Longmont and Cheyenne, WY. **Enrollment:** 1,115 degree-seeking undergraduates. **Degrees:** 744 associate awarded. **Location:** 60 miles from Denver; 45 miles from Cheyenne, WY. **Calendar:** Differs by program. **Full-time faculty:** 20 total; 15% minority, 85% women. **Part-time faculty:** 55 total; 6% minority, 73% women.

Transfer out. Colleges most students transferred to 2011: Colorado Christian University, Front Range Community College, Aims Community College.

Basis for selection. Open admission, but selective for some programs. Applicants must be able to prove graduation from high school or completion of GED. Students must present certain scores on entrance evaluation exam based on program of study. Institutional entrance exam required for placement. **Home schooled:** State high school equivalency certificate required.

2011-2012 Annual costs. Credit requirements for programs range from 52 to 99 credits, or $15,600 to $29,700 at $300 per credit hour. Books/supplies: $1,400.

Financial aid. Need-based: Work-study available nights, weekends and for part-time students.

Application procedures. Admission: No deadline. $75 fee. Admission notification on a rolling basis.

Academics. Special study options: Internships. **Credit/placement by examination:** AP, CLEP, institutional tests. Up to 50% of total progam credits may be obtained through transfer or test out. **Support services:** GED preparation, learning center, reduced course load, remedial instruction, study skills assistance, tutoring.

Majors. Business: Accounting technology, administrative services, business admin. **Health services:** Massage therapy, medical assistant, medical secretary, pharmacy assistant.

Most popular majors. Business/marketing 8%, health sciences 88%.

Computing on campus. 24 workstations in library, student center. Commuter students can connect to campus network. Wireless network available.

Student life. Freshman orientation: Available. Preregistration for classes offered.

Student services. Career counseling, student employment services, financial aid counseling, placement for graduates. **Transfer:** Pre-admission transcript evaluation for new students.

Contact. E-mail: info@ibmc.edu
Phone: (970) 223-2669 Toll-free number: (800) 495-2669
Kevin McNeil, Director of Admissions, Institute of Business & Medical Careers, 3842 South Mason Street, Fort Collins, CO 80525

IntelliTec College
Colorado Springs, Colorado
www.intelliteccollege.com   **CB code: 2500**

- For-profit 2-year technical college
- Commuter campus in large city

General. Founded in 1965. Accredited by ACCSC. **Enrollment:** 569 degree-seeking undergraduates. **Degrees:** 449 associate awarded. **Location:** 68 miles from Denver. **Calendar:** 6-week cycle. Extensive summer session. **Full-time faculty:** 23 total. **Part-time faculty:** 11 total.

Transfer out. Colleges most students transferred to 2011: Pikes Peak Community College, Denver Technical College.

Basis for selection. Open admission.

2011-2012 Annual costs. HVAC - Refrigeration Technician, $26,400; Computer and Network Systems, $26,880; Automotive Technician, $26,880; Architectural Drafting, $25,200; Mechanical Drafting, $24,480. Books/supplies: $1,200.

Financial aid. All financial aid based on need. Need-based aid available for part-time students. Work-study available nights, weekends and for part-time students.

Application procedures. Admission: No deadline. No application fee. Admission notification on a rolling basis. **Financial aid:** No deadline. FAFSA, institutional form required. Applicants notified on a rolling basis.

Academics. Special study options: Accelerated study, liberal arts/career combination. **Credit/placement by examination:** AP, CLEP. Maximum 50% of required credits may be awarded for prior work and/or life experience. Pre-admission interview required for placement into program. **Support services:** Learning center, tutoring.

Majors. Computer sciences: General, computer science, systems analysis.

Most popular majors. Computer/information sciences 13%, engineering/engineering technologies 21%, trade and industry 66%.

Computing on campus. 125 workstations in library, computer center. Online library, repair service available.

Student life. Freshman orientation: Available. Preregistration for classes offered. **Activities:** Student newspaper.

Student services. Adult student services, career counseling, student employment services, financial aid counseling, personal counseling, placement for graduates, veterans' counselor. **Transfer:** Pre-admission transcript evaluation for new students.

Contact. E-mail: admcs@intellitleccollege.com
Phone: (719) 632-7626 Toll-free number: (800) 748-2282
Fax: (719) 632-7451
Mel Glyman, Director of Admissions, IntelliTec College, 2315 East Pikes Peak Avenue, Colorado Springs, CO 80909

IntelliTec College: Grand Junction
Grand Junction, Colorado
www.intelliteccollege.edu   **CB code: 2489**

- For-profit 2-year technical college
- Commuter campus in small city
- Interview required

General. Accredited by ACCSC. **Enrollment:** 834 degree-seeking undergraduates. **Degrees:** 263 associate awarded. **Location:** 250 miles from Denver, 300 miles from Salt Lake City. **Calendar:** Differs by program, extensive summer session. **Full-time faculty:** 36 total. **Part-time faculty:** 14 total.

Student profile.

Out-of-state:	2%	**25 or older:**	51%

Basis for selection. Open admission. **Home schooled:** Interview required.

2011-2012 Annual costs. Tuition is $240 per credit for all programs. Number of credits required for completion varies by program. Total costs include: Medical Assistant, $23,899; Automotive Technician, $24,873; Administrative Professional, $25,381; Mechanical Drafting, $27,592; Architectural/Structural Drafting $27,500. Total cost of certificate programs: Massage Therapist, $19,777; Dental Assistant, $17,813. Books/supplies: $1,500.

Financial aid. All financial aid based on need. Work-study available nights, weekends and for part-time students.

Application procedures. Admission: No deadline. No application fee. Admission notification on a rolling basis. **Financial aid:** No deadline. FAFSA required. Applicants notified on a rolling basis.

Academics. Special study options: Cooperative education. **Credit/placement by examination:** AP, CLEP. **Support services:** Learning center, tutoring.

Majors. Business: Accounting/business management. **Engineering:** Electrical. **Health services:** Medical assistant.

Computing on campus. 100 workstations in library, computer center.

Student services. Career counseling, student employment services, placement for graduates.

Contact. E-mail: frontdeskGJ@intellitec.edu
Phone: (970) 245-8101 Fax: (970) 243-8074
Carol Earnshaw, Director of Admissions, IntelliTec College: Grand Junction, 772 Horizon Drive, Grand Junction, CO 81506

Kaplan College: Denver
Thornton, Colorado
www.kaplancollege.com

- For-profit 2-year technical and career college
- Very large city

General. Accredited by ACCSC. **Enrollment:** 260 degree-seeking undergraduates. **Degrees:** 25 associate awarded. **Calendar:** Quarter, extensive summer session. **Full-time faculty:** 4 total. **Part-time faculty:** 25 total.

Basis for selection. Open admission, but selective for some programs.

Financial aid. Need-based: Work-study available nights, weekends and for part-time students.

Application procedures. Admission: No deadline. $25 fee. **Financial aid:** FAFSA required.

Two-Year Colleges

Academics. Paralegal program is ABA certified. **Special study options:** Accelerated study, independent study. **Credit/placement by examination:** AP, CLEP. **Support services:** GED preparation, learning center, study skills assistance, tutoring.

Majors. **Protective services:** Law enforcement admin.

Computing on campus. 50 workstations in library, computer center.

Student life. **Freshman orientation:** Mandatory, $20 fee. Preregistration for classes offered.

Student services. Alcohol/substance abuse counseling, personal counseling, women's services.

Contact. Phone: (303) 295-0550 Toll-free number: (800) 848-0550 Fax: (303) 295-0102
Renee Keddington, Director of Admissions, Kaplan College: Denver, 500 East 84th Avenue, Suite W-200, Thornton, CO 80229

Lamar Community College
Lamar, Colorado
www.lamarcc.edu
CB code: 4382

- Public 2-year community college
- Commuter campus in small town

General. Founded in 1937. Regionally accredited. **Enrollment:** 966 degree-seeking undergraduates. **Degrees:** 136 associate awarded. **Location:** 117 miles from Pueblo. **Calendar:** Semester, limited summer session. **Full-time faculty:** 29 total; 3% minority, 38% women. **Part-time faculty:** 32 total; 3% have terminal degrees, 16% minority, 47% women. **Class size:** 81% < 20, 17% 20-39, 2% 50-99.

Student profile. Among degree-seeking undergraduates, 54% enrolled in a transfer program, 46% enrolled in a vocational program, 1% already have a bachelor's degree or higher, 646 enrolled as first-time, first-year students, 57 transferred in from other institutions.

Part-time:	51%	25 or older:	75%
Out-of-state:	10%	Live on campus:	50%
Women:	58%		

Basis for selection. Open admission, but selective for some programs. Admission criteria for horse training management based on riding skills; admission to nursing based on specific prerequisite course grades. Interview required of horse training and management, practical nursing majors.

2011-2012 Annual costs. Tuition/fees: $3,573; $6,691 out-of-state. Per-credit charge: $106 in-state; $210 out-of-state. In-state tuition based upon assumption of Colorado Opportunity Fund waiver of $62 per-credit-hour. Room/board: $5,419. Books/supplies: $1,163. Personal expenses: $420.

2011-2012 Financial aid. **Need-based:** 60% of total undergraduate aid awarded as scholarships/grants, 40% as loans/jobs. Need-based aid available for part-time students. Work-study available nights, weekends and for part-time students.

Application procedures. **Admission:** No application fee. Admission notification on a rolling basis. Applicants to horse training and management and LPN nursing program encouraged to apply early. **Financial aid:** Priority date 4/1; no closing date. FAFSA, institutional form required. Applicants notified on a rolling basis starting 7/1.

Academics. **Special study options:** Cooperative education, distance learning, dual enrollment of high school students, ESL, independent study, internships, student-designed major. **Credit/placement by examination:** AP, CLEP, institutional tests. 16 credit hours maximum toward associate degree. **Support services:** GED preparation and test center, learning center, pre-admission summer program, remedial instruction, tutoring.

Majors. **Biology:** General. **Business:** General, accounting, administrative services, banking/financial services, business admin, office management. **Communications:** Communications/speech/rhetoric. **Computer sciences:** Computer science, information systems. **Education:** General. **English:** English lit. **General:** Agronomy, animal sciences, business, equestrian studies, range science. **Health services:** Medical secretary, predental, prepharmacy, preveterinary. **History:** General. **Human services:** Social work. **Liberal arts:** Arts/sciences. **Math:** General. **Psychology:** General. **Social sciences:** General. **Visual/performing arts:** Art. **Work/family studies:** Child care management.

Computing on campus. 65 workstations in dormitories, library, computer center. Dormitories wired for high-speed internet access. Online course registration, online library, wireless network available.

Student life. **Freshman orientation:** Available. Preregistration for classes offered. **Policies:** All single freshmen under age 21 not living with parent, guardian, or relatives must live in dormitory. **Housing:** Guaranteed on-campus for freshmen. Coed dorms, single-sex dorms available. **Activities:** International student organizations, student government, Christian athletes, horse and rodeo club, Kosmetiques, LPN association, Phi Beta Lambda, nontraditional students club.

Athletics. NJCAA. **Intercollegiate:** Baseball M, basketball, golf M, softball W, volleyball W. **Team name:** Lopes.

Student services. Career counseling, student employment services, health services, personal counseling. **Transfer:** Transfer adviser, college fairs on campus for students transferring to 4-year colleges.

Contact. E-mail: admissions@lamarcc.edu
Phone: (719) 336-1590
Amber Thompson, Admissions Counselor, Lamar Community College, 2401 South Main Street, Lamar, CO 81052-3999

Lincoln College of Technology: Denver
Denver, Colorado
www.dadc.com
CB code: 3133

- For-profit 2-year technical college
- Very large city

General. Accredited by ACCSC. **Degrees:** 238 associate awarded. **Calendar:** Differs by program, extensive summer session. **Full-time faculty:** 40 total. **Part-time faculty:** 1 total. **Special facilities:** Full automotive and diesel lab shops.

Basis for selection. Open admission.

2011-2012 Annual costs. Total program costs range from $13,656 up to $39,904 depending on program. Cost of books and materials included in tuition. Books/supplies: $360. Personal expenses: $1,967.

Financial aid. **Need-based:** Work-study available nights, weekends and for part-time students.

Application procedures. **Admission:** No deadline. $150 fee. Admission notification on a rolling basis.

Academics. **Credit/placement by examination:** AP, CLEP.

Contact. Phone: (303) 722-5724 Toll-free number: (877) 453-5015
Jenn Hash, Director of Admissions, Lincoln College of Technology: Denver, 11194 East 45th Street, Denver, CO 80239

Morgan Community College
Fort Morgan, Colorado
www.morgancc.edu
CB code: 0444

- Public 2-year community college
- Commuter campus in large town

General. Founded in 1967. Regionally accredited. **Enrollment:** 1,050 degree-seeking undergraduates. **Degrees:** 175 associate awarded. **Location:** 81 miles from Denver. **Calendar:** Semester, limited summer session. **Full-time faculty:** 33 total. **Part-time faculty:** 134 total. **Class size:** 69% < 20, 31% 20-39.

Student profile.

Out-of-state:	3%	25 or older:	46%

Basis for selection. Open admission, but selective for some programs. Special requirements for physical therapist assistant, occupational therapy assistant, and nursing programs. Interview required of allied health majors.

2011-2012 Annual costs. Tuition/fees: $3,348; $13,201 out-of-state. Per-credit charge: $106 in-state; $434 out-of-state. In-state tuition based upon assumption of Colorado Opportunity Fund waiver of $62 per-credit-hour. Books/supplies: $675.

Financial aid. **Need-based:** Need-based aid available for part-time students. Work-study available nights, weekends and for part-time students.

Application procedures. **Admission:** No deadline. No application fee. Admission notification on a rolling basis. **Financial aid:** Closing date 4/2. FAFSA required. Applicants notified on a rolling basis.

Academics. Special study options: Distance learning, double major, dual enrollment of high school students, ESL, independent study, internships, liberal arts/career combination, student-designed major, teacher certification program, weekend college. License preparation in nursing, real estate. **Credit/placement by examination:** AP, CLEP, institutional tests. 31 credit hours maximum toward associate degree. **Support services:** GED preparation and test center, learning center, reduced course load, remedial instruction, study skills assistance, tutoring.

Majors. Business: General, accounting. **Computer sciences:** Webmaster. **Education:** General. **Health services:** Nursing (RN), occupational therapy assistant, physical therapy assistant. **Liberal arts:** Arts/sciences. **Visual/performing arts:** Art.

Computing on campus. 50 workstations in library, computer center, student center. Commuter students can connect to campus network. Online course registration available.

Student life. Activities: Student newspaper, TV station, occupational therapy association, vocational industrial collusion association, Phi Theta Kappa, science club, history club, student nursing association, Phi Beta Lambda, health occupation student organization, physical therapy association.

Student services. Career counseling. **Transfer:** Pre-admission transcript evaluation for new students.

Contact. Phone: (970) 542-3156 Fax: (970) 542-3114
Kim Maxwell, Director of Admissions, Morgan Community College, 920 Barlow Road, Fort Morgan, CO 80701

Northeastern Junior College
Sterling, Colorado
www.njc.edu   CB code: 4537

- Public 2-year community and junior college
- Residential campus in large town

General. Founded in 1941. Regionally accredited. **Enrollment:** 1,391 degree-seeking undergraduates; 309 non-degree-seeking students. **Degrees:** 230 associate awarded. **Location:** 125 miles from Denver. **Calendar:** Semester, limited summer session. **Full-time faculty:** 49 total; 4% have terminal degrees, 4% minority, 53% women. **Part-time faculty:** 51 total; 2% have terminal degrees, 12% minority, 76% women. **Class size:** 72% < 20, 27% 20-39, less than 1% 40-49, less than 1% 50-99. **Special facilities:** Equine center, wind technology laboratory, automotive/diesel repair lab, nursing laboratories.

Student profile. Among degree-seeking undergraduates, 64% enrolled in a transfer program, 36% enrolled in a vocational program, 564 enrolled as first-time, first-year students, 79 transferred in from other institutions.

Part-time:	19%	Native American:	1%
Out-of-state:	6%	International:	1%
Women:	57%	25 or older:	23%
African American:	7%	Live on campus:	41%
Hispanic American:	10%		

Transfer out. Colleges most students transferred to 2011: Colorado State University, University of Northern Colorado, University of Colorado, University of Wyoming, Oklahoma State University.

Basis for selection. Open admission, but selective for some programs. Qualifications for programs with limited space, such as licensed practical nursing program, set individually by department. SAT or ACT required for some technical vocational programs. Assessment required by ACCUPLACER, minimum ACT or SAT scores in subject areas, or proof of previous successful college experience. Cooperative admission program with Colorado State University. **Adult students:** ACCUPLACER required. **Home schooled:** Transcript of courses and grades, state high school equivalency certificate required. **Learning Disabled:** IEP required.

2011-2012 Annual costs. Tuition/fees: $3,772; $11,017 out-of-state. Per-credit charge: $106 in-state; $347 out-of-state. In-state tuition based upon assumption of Colorado Opportunity Fund waiver of $62 per-credit-hour. Room/board: $6,010. Books/supplies: $1,749. Personal expenses: $3,402.

2010-2011 Financial aid. Need-based: 56% of total undergraduate aid awarded as scholarships/grants, 44% as loans/jobs. Need-based aid available for part-time students. Work-study available nights, weekends and for part-time students. **Non-need-based:** Scholarships awarded for academics, alumni affiliation, art, athletics, job skills, leadership, music/drama, state residency. **Additional information:** Need-based financial aid available to part-time students taking 6 credits or more per semester.

Application procedures. Admission: No deadline. No application fee. Admission notification on a rolling basis. **Financial aid:** Priority date 3/1; no closing date. FAFSA, institutional form required. Applicants notified on a rolling basis starting 4/15; must reply within 3 week(s) of notification.

Academics. Special study options: Accelerated study, cooperative education, distance learning, double major, dual enrollment of high school students, ESL, honors, independent study, internships, liberal arts/career combination, study abroad, teacher certification program, weekend college. License preparation in nursing, paramedic. **Credit/placement by examination:** AP, CLEP, IB, institutional tests. 45 credit hours maximum toward associate degree. **Support services:** GED preparation and test center, learning center, remedial instruction, study skills assistance, tutoring, writing center.

Majors. Business: Accounting technology, management information systems. **Education:** Early childhood. **General:** Agribusiness operations, farm/ranch, horticulture, mechanization, ornamental horticulture, production. **Health services:** EMT paramedic, nursing (RN). **Liberal arts:** Arts/sciences. **Protective services:** Law enforcement admin. **Work/family studies:** Child development.

Most popular majors. Agriculture 13%, health sciences 8%, liberal arts 72%.

Computing on campus. 302 workstations in library, computer center, student center. Dormitories wired for high-speed internet access and linked to campus network. Online course registration, helpline, student web hosting available.

Student life. Freshman orientation: Mandatory. Preregistration for classes offered. **Policies:** No drugs, alcohol, or smoking on campus. **Housing:** Guaranteed on-campus for freshmen. Coed dorms, single-sex dorms, apartments available. $125 fully refundable deposit, deadline 8/19. Honors house available. **Activities:** Campus ministries, choral groups, dance, drama, literary magazine, music ensembles, student government, student newspaper, Christian fellowship, black student alliance.

Athletics. NJCAA. **Intercollegiate:** Baseball M, basketball, golf, rodeo, soccer, softball W, volleyball W. **Intramural:** Badminton, baseball, basketball, bowling, cheerleading, football (non-tackle) M, racquetball, soccer, softball, tennis, volleyball, weight lifting. **Team name:** Plainswomen, Plainsmen.

Student services. Adult student services, alcohol/substance abuse counseling, career counseling, student employment services, financial aid counseling, health services, personal counseling. **Physically disabled:** Services for visually, speech, hearing impaired. **Transfer:** Pre-admission transcript evaluation for new students. Transfer adviser, college fairs on campus for students transferring to 4-year colleges.

Contact. E-mail: admissions@njc.edu
Phone: (970) 521-7000 Toll-free number: (800) 626-4367
Fax: (970) 521-6715
Andy Long, Director of Admissions, Northeastern Junior College, 100 College Avenue, Sterling, CO 80751-2399

Otero Junior College
La Junta, Colorado
www.ojc.edu   CB code: 4588

- Public 2-year community and junior college
- Commuter campus in small town

General. Founded in 1941. Regionally accredited. **Enrollment:** 1,546 degree-seeking undergraduates. **Degrees:** 186 associate awarded. **Location:** 60 miles from Pueblo, 100 miles from Colorado Springs. **Calendar:** Semester, limited summer session. **Full-time faculty:** 39 total. **Part-time faculty:** 44 total. **Class size:** 74% < 20, 21% 20-39, 2% 40-49, 3% 50-99. **Special facilities:** Koshare Indian kiva museum.

Student profile.

Out-of-state:	7%	Live on campus:	10%
25 or older:	33%		

Basis for selection. Open admission, but selective for some programs. Special admission requirements for nursing program.

2011-2012 Annual costs. Tuition/fees: $3,442; $6,560 out-of-state. Per-credit charge: $106 in-state; $210 out-of-state. In-state tuition based upon assumption of Colorado Opportunity Fund waiver of $62 per-credit-hour. Room/board: $5,462. Books/supplies: $1,100. Personal expenses: $2,500.

Financial aid. Need-based: Need-based aid available for part-time students. Work-study available nights, weekends and for part-time students.

Non-need-based: Scholarships awarded for academics, athletics, state residency.

Application procedures. Admission: No deadline. No application fee. Admission notification on a rolling basis. **Financial aid:** Priority date 4/15; no closing date. FAFSA required. Applicants notified on a rolling basis starting 4/15; must reply within 2 week(s) of notification.

Academics. Special study options: Dual enrollment of high school students. Bachelor's degree programs available on campus. **Credit/placement by examination:** AP, CLEP, institutional tests. 30 credit hours maximum toward associate degree. **Support services:** GED preparation and test center, learning center, reduced course load, remedial instruction, study skills assistance, tutoring.

Majors. Biology: General. **Business:** Administrative services, business admin. **Computer sciences:** General. **Education:** General, early childhood, elementary, secondary, teacher assistance. **Health services:** Medical secretary, nursing (RN), pharmacy assistant, predental, premedicine, prepharmacy, preveterinary, veterinary technology/assistant. **History:** General. **Liberal arts:** Arts/sciences. **Math:** General. **Physical sciences:** Chemistry. **Psychology:** General. **Social sciences:** Political science. **Visual/performing arts:** Dramatic.

Computing on campus. 100 workstations in library, computer center, student center. Dormitories wired for high-speed internet access. Wireless network available.

Student life. Freshman orientation: Available. Preregistration for classes offered. **Housing:** Single-sex dorms available. **Activities:** Dance, drama, student government.

Athletics. NJCAA. **Intercollegiate:** Baseball M, basketball, golf, soccer M, softball W, volleyball W. **Intramural:** Basketball, volleyball. **Team name:** Rattlers.

Student services. Career counseling, student employment services, on-campus daycare, personal counseling, placement for graduates, veterans' counselor. **Physically disabled:** Services for visually, hearing impaired. **Transfer:** Pre-admission transcript evaluation for new students. Transfer adviser, college fairs on campus for students transferring to 4-year colleges.

Contact. E-mail: rana.brown@ojc.edu
Phone: (719) 384-6831 Fax: (719) 384-6933
Rana Brown, Admissions Coordinator, Otero Junior College, 1802 Colorado Avenue, La Junta, CO 81050

Pikes Peak Community College
Colorado Springs, Colorado
www.ppcc.edu
CB code: 4291

- Public 2-year community college
- Commuter campus in large city

General. Founded in 1967. Regionally accredited. **Enrollment:** 14,651 degree-seeking undergraduates. **Degrees:** 1,045 associate awarded. **Location:** 70 miles from Denver. **Calendar:** Semester, extensive summer session. **Full-time faculty:** 171 total. **Part-time faculty:** 307 total. **Class size:** 59% < 20, 41% 20-39, less than 1% 40-49, less than 1% 50-99, less than 1% >100. **Partnerships:** Formal partnership with Cheyenne Mountain Zoo.

Student profile.

Out-of-state:	18%	25 or older:	47%

Transfer out. Colleges most students transferred to 2011: University of Colorado at Colorado Springs, Colorado State University-Pueblo.

Basis for selection. Open admission.

High school preparation. College-preparatory program recommended.

2011-2012 Annual costs. Tuition/fees: $3,450; $13,303 out-of-state. Per-credit charge: $106 in-state; $434 out-of-state. In-state tuition based upon assumption of Colorado Opportunity Fund waiver of $62 per-credit-hour. Books/supplies: $1,163. Personal expenses: $2,547.

Financial aid. Need-based: Need-based aid available for part-time students. Work-study available nights, weekends and for part-time students.

Application procedures. Admission: No deadline. No application fee. Admission notification on a rolling basis. **Financial aid:** Closing date 7/1. FAFSA required. Applicants notified on a rolling basis; must reply within 2 week(s) of notification.

Academics. Special study options: Cooperative education, distance learning, double major, dual enrollment of high school students, ESL, external degree, independent study, internships, study abroad, weekend college. License preparation in nursing, paramedic, radiology, real estate. **Credit/placement by examination:** AP, CLEP, IB, institutional tests. Students may receive up to 75% of total credits for all types of prior learning (testing, work and/or life experience). **Support services:** GED test center, learning center, remedial instruction, study skills assistance, tutoring, writing center.

Majors. Biology: General. **Business:** General, accounting, accounting technology, business admin, customer service support, executive assistant, financial planning, international, management information systems, marketing. **Communications technology:** Graphics, radio/TV. **Computer sciences:** General, computer science, LAN/WAN management, networking. **Conservation:** Management/policy. **English:** American lit, English lit, technical writing. **Foreign languages:** General, sign language interpretation. **Health services:** Dental assistant, EMT paramedic, mental health services, nursing (RN), office admin, premedicine. **History:** General. **Liberal arts:** Arts/sciences, humanities. **Math:** General. **Philosophy/religion:** Philosophy. **Physical sciences:** Chemistry, geology, physics. **Protective services:** Fire safety technology, firefighting, homeland security, law enforcement admin. **Social sciences:** Anthropology, geography, political science, sociology. **Visual/performing arts:** Dance, dramatic, interior design, music, studio arts. **Work/family studies:** Child development.

Most popular majors. Health sciences 12%, liberal arts 58%, security/protective services 13%.

Computing on campus. 180 workstations in library, computer center. Commuter students can connect to campus network. Online course registration, helpline, wireless network available.

Student life. Freshman orientation: Available. Preregistration for classes offered. **Policies:** Dormitory housing available through agreement with University of Colorado at Colorado Springs. **Activities:** Choral groups, dance, drama, music ensembles, radio station, student government, student newspaper, Phi Theta Kappa.

Athletics. Intramural: Soccer, volleyball. **Team name:** Aardvarks.

Student services. Adult student services, alcohol/substance abuse counseling, career counseling, services for economically disadvantaged, student employment services, financial aid counseling, minority student services, on-campus daycare, personal counseling, placement for graduates, veterans' counselor, women's services. **Physically disabled:** Services for visually, speech, hearing impaired. **Transfer:** Re-entry adviser, pre-admission transcript evaluation for new students. Transfer adviser, college fairs on campus for students transferring to 4-year colleges.

Contact. E-mail: admissions@ppcc.edu
Phone: (719) 502-3000 Toll-free number: (800) 456-6847
Jeff Horner, Admissions, Pikes Peak Community College, 5675 South Academy Boulevard, Colorado Springs, CO 80906-5498

Prince Institute
Denver, Colorado
www.princeinstitute.edu
CB code: 3561

- For-profit 2-year college of court reporting
- Commuter campus in small city
- Interview required

General. Accredited by ACICS. **Enrollment:** 149 degree-seeking undergraduates. **Degrees:** 8 associate awarded. **Location:** 8 miles from Denver. **Calendar:** Quarter. **Full-time faculty:** 10 total. **Part-time faculty:** 10 total.

Student profile. Among degree-seeking undergraduates, 100% enrolled in a vocational program, 18 enrolled as first-time, first-year students.

Women:	97%	25 or older:	50%

Basis for selection. Open admission. Must meet with an admissions representative, tour the facility, and inspect the equipment used in the training program.

2011-2012 Annual costs. Tuition $2,750 per quarter, $75 annual enrollment fee. $200 per quarter technology fee. Books/supplies: $450.

Financial aid. Need-based: Work-study available nights, weekends and for part-time students.

Application procedures. Admission: No deadline. $125 fee.

Academics. Special study options: Internships. **Credit/placement by examination:** AP, CLEP.

Computing on campus. PC or laptop required. Online library, wireless network available.

Student life. Freshman orientation: Mandatory. Preregistration for classes offered. **Activities:** Student newspaper.

Student services. Transfer: Pre-admission transcript evaluation for new students.

Contact. E-mail: infoRM@princeinstitute.edu
Phone: (303) 427-5292 Toll-free number: (866) 712-2425
Fax: (303) 427-5383
Susan Williford, Director of Admissions, Prince Institute, 9051 Harlan Street, Unit #20, Westminster, CO 80031

Pueblo Community College
Pueblo, Colorado
www.pueblocc.edu   **CB code: 4634**

▶ Public 2-year community college
▶ Commuter campus in small city

General. Founded in 1933. Regionally accredited. **Enrollment:** 5,595 degree-seeking undergraduates; 898 non-degree-seeking students. **Degrees:** 562 associate awarded. **Location:** 50 miles from Colorado Springs, 100 miles from Denver. **Calendar:** Semester, extensive summer session. **Full-time faculty:** 111 total; 19% minority, 61% women. **Part-time faculty:** 322 total; 14% minority, 57% women. **Class size:** 76% < 20, 22% 20-39, 1% 40-49, less than 1% 50-99. **Special facilities:** Advanced technology center.

Student profile. Among degree-seeking undergraduates, 59% enrolled in a transfer program, 41% enrolled in a vocational program, 2% already have a bachelor's degree or higher, 1,042 enrolled as first-time, first-year students, 387 transferred in from other institutions.

Part-time:	52%	Asian American:	1%
Out-of-state:	1%	Hispanic American:	30%
Women:	61%	Native American:	3%
African American:	2%	25 or older:	58%

Transfer out. Colleges most students transferred to 2011: Colorado State University-Pueblo.

Basis for selection. Open admission, but selective for some programs. Admission to health programs based on GPA, high school courses, test scores. ACT required of dental hygiene applicants; score report by May 1. Assessment testing required for all entering degree- and certificate-seeking students, unless ACT/SAT scores or transcripts showing successful completion of college-level English and math courses provided. Interview required of allied health majors.

2011-2012 Annual costs. Tuition/fees: $3,687; $13,540 out-of-state. Per-credit charge: $106 in-state; $434 out-of-state. In-state tuition based upon assumption of Colorado Opportunity Fund waiver of $62 per-credit-hour. Books/supplies: $1,749. Personal expenses: $3,375.

2010-2011 Financial aid. Need-based: 418 full-time freshmen applied for aid; 314 were judged to have need; 300 of these received aid. Average need met was 50%. Average scholarship/grant was $3,500; average loan $2,000. 65% of total undergraduate aid awarded as scholarships/grants, 35% as loans/jobs. Need-based aid available for part-time students. Work-study available nights, weekends and for part-time students. **Non-need-based:** Awarded to 50 full-time undergraduates, including 20 freshmen. Scholarships awarded for academics, art, job skills, leadership, music/drama.

Application procedures. Admission: Closing date 4/4. No application fee. Admission notification on a rolling basis. Foreign applicants must show evidence of resources sufficient to cover tuition/fees for full academic year before acceptance. Application closing date for allied health programs: 4/1. **Financial aid:** Priority date 3/15; no closing date. FAFSA required. Applicants notified on a rolling basis starting 4/1.

Academics. Special study options: Cooperative education, cross-registration, distance learning, double major, dual enrollment of high school students, honors, independent study, internships. License preparation in dental hygiene, nursing, occupational therapy, paramedic, physical therapy, radiology, real estate. **Credit/placement by examination:** AP, CLEP, institutional tests. All but 15 hour residence requirement for certificate or associate degree may be from credit for prior learning. **Support services:** GED preparation and test center, learning center, reduced course load, remedial instruction, study skills assistance, tutoring, writing center.

Majors. Business: Accounting technology, business admin, entrepreneurial studies, hospitality/recreation, office technology. **Communications technology:** General, animation/special effects. **Computer sciences:** General, web

page design. **Education:** Early childhood. **Health services:** Dental assistant, dental hygiene, EMT paramedic, nursing (RN), occupational therapy assistant, physical therapy assistant, radiologic technology/medical imaging, respiratory therapy technology, sonography. **Liberal arts:** Arts/sciences, library assistant. **Protective services:** Firefighting, law enforcement admin. **Visual/performing arts:** Interior design.

Most popular majors. Business/marketing 7%, health sciences 31%, liberal arts 44%, trade and industry 6%.

Computing on campus. Commuter students can connect to campus network. Online course registration, online library, helpline, wireless network available.

Student life. Freshman orientation: Available. Preregistration for classes offered. **Activities:** Choral groups, dance, drama, student government, student newspaper, TV station.

Athletics. Team name: Panthers.

Student services. Adult student services, career counseling, student employment services, financial aid counseling, health services, personal counseling, placement for graduates. **Physically disabled:** Services for visually, speech, hearing impaired. **Transfer:** Transfer center, transfer adviser, college fairs on campus for students transferring to 4-year colleges.

Contact. E-mail: admissions@pueblocc.edu
Phone: (719) 549-3010 Toll-free number: (888) 642-6017
Fax: (719) 549-3012
Maija Kurtz, Director of Admissions and Records, Pueblo Community College, 900 West Orman Avenue, Pueblo, CO 81004-1499

Red Rocks Community College
Lakewood, Colorado
www.rrcc.edu   **CB code: 4130**

▶ Public 2-year community and career college
▶ Commuter campus in small city

General. Founded in 1969. Regionally accredited. **Enrollment:** 8,240 degree-seeking undergraduates; 1,301 non-degree-seeking students. **Degrees:** 522 associate awarded. **ROTC:** Army, Air Force. **Location:** 10 miles from Denver. **Calendar:** Semester, extensive summer session. **Full-time faculty:** 88 total; 7% minority, 62% women. **Part-time faculty:** 444 total; 8% minority, 50% women. **Class size:** 59% < 20, 41% 20-39, less than 1% 50-99.

Student profile. Among degree-seeking undergraduates, 1,586 enrolled as first-time, first-year students, 864 transferred in from other institutions.

Part-time:	64%	Women:	50%
Out-of-state:	5%	25 or older:	53%

Basis for selection. Open admission.

2011-2012 Annual costs. Tuition/fees: $3,473; $13,326 out-of-state. Per-credit charge: $106 in-state; $434 out-of-state. In-state tuition based upon assumption of Colorado Opportunity Fund waiver of $62 per-credit-hour.

2010-2011 Financial aid. Need-based: 59% of total undergraduate aid awarded as scholarships/grants, 41% as loans/jobs. Need-based aid available for part-time students. Work-study available nights, weekends and for part-time students. **Non-need-based:** Scholarships awarded for academics, leadership, minority status, state residency.

Application procedures. Admission: No deadline. No application fee. Admission notification on a rolling basis. **Financial aid:** Priority date 4/1; no closing date. FAFSA required. Applicants notified on a rolling basis starting 5/1.

Academics. Students in advanced ESL classes may begin some college-level courses early. Scholarships offered for outstanding ESL performance when funds are available. **Special study options:** Accelerated study, cross-registration, distance learning, dual enrollment of high school students, ESL, honors, independent study, internships, liberal arts/career combination, teacher certification program, weekend college. License preparation in paramedic, radiology, real estate. **Credit/placement by examination:** AP, CLEP, IB, institutional tests. **Support services:** GED preparation and test center, learning center, reduced course load, remedial instruction, study skills assistance, tutoring, writing center.

Majors. Business: Accounting technology, business admin, management information systems, real estate. **Communications:** Digital media. **Communications technology:** Animation/special effects. **Computer sciences:** Database management, networking, programming, web page design, webmaster. **Education:** Early childhood, educational technology. **Health services:** EMT

paramedic, holistic, office admin, radiologic technology/medical imaging, sonography. **Liberal arts:** Arts/sciences. **Protective services:** Firefighting, police science. **Visual/performing arts:** Cinematography, game design, interior design, photography, theater design.

Most popular majors. Engineering/engineering technologies 7%, health sciences 11%, liberal arts 56%, security/protective services 8%, trade and industry 8%.

Computing on campus. 128 workstations in library, computer center, student center. Online course registration, online library, helpline, wireless network available.

Student life. Freshman orientation: Available. Preregistration for classes offered. **Activities:** Campus ministries, dance, drama, film society, international student organizations, literary magazine, music ensembles, musical theater, student government.

Student services. Adult student services, career counseling, student employment services, health services, on-campus daycare, personal counseling, placement for graduates, veterans' counselor. **Physically disabled:** Services for visually, speech, hearing impaired. **Transfer:** Transfer adviser, college fairs on campus for students transferring to 4-year colleges.

Contact. E-mail: admissions@rrcc.edu
Phone: (303) 914-6348 Fax: (303) 989-6919
Dean Rathe, Director of Enrollment Services, Red Rocks Community College, 13300 West Sixth Avenue, Lakewood, CO 80228-1255

Redstone College
Broomfield, Colorado
www.redstonecollege.com

- For-profit 2-year technical college
- Commuter campus in small city

General. Accredited by ACCSC. **Enrollment:** 738 degree-seeking undergraduates. **Degrees:** 322 associate awarded. **Location:** 15 miles from Denver and Boulder. **Calendar:** Differs by program. **Full-time faculty:** 36 total. **Part-time faculty:** 29 total.

Basis for selection. Open admission.

2011-2012 Annual costs. Tuition and fees for entire Associates degree program $31,781 to $40,125 depending on program.

Financial aid. All financial aid based on need. Work-study available nights, weekends and for part-time students.

Application procedures. Admission: No deadline. $100 fee. Admission notification on a rolling basis. **Financial aid:** No deadline. FAFSA required. Applicants notified on a rolling basis; must reply within 2 week(s) of notification.

Academics. Special study options: License preparation in aviation. **Credit/placement by examination:** AP, CLEP. **Support services:** Learning center, tutoring.

Computing on campus. 8 workstations in computer center.

Student life. Housing: Apartments available.

Student services. Career counseling, student employment services, placement for graduates, veterans' counselor.

Contact. Phone: (303) 466-1714 Toll-free number: (800) 460-0592
Fax: (303) 469-3797
Cate Clark, Director of Admissions, Redstone College, 10851 West 120th Avenue, Broomfield, CO 80021-3401

Remington College: Colorado Springs
Colorado Springs, Colorado
www.remingtoncollege.edu/coloradosprings CB code: 3565

- For-profit 2-year technical college
- Commuter campus in very large city
- Interview required

General. Accredited by ACICS. **Enrollment:** 149 degree-seeking undergraduates. **Degrees:** 22 associate awarded. **Location:** 60 miles from Denver.

Calendar: Quarter, extensive summer session. **Full-time faculty:** 2 total. **Part-time faculty:** 20 total. **Class size:** 100% < 20.

Basis for selection. Open admission, but selective for some programs.

Financial aid. All financial aid based on need. Need-based aid available for part-time students. Work-study available nights, weekends and for part-time students.

Application procedures. Admission: No deadline. $50 fee. Admission notification on a rolling basis. Non-GED or high school program applicants required to pass Wonderlic assessment. **Financial aid:** No deadline. FAFSA required. Applicants notified on a rolling basis; must reply within 3 week(s) of notification.

Academics. Special study options: Accelerated study, distance learning. Bachelor's degree programs available on campus. **Credit/placement by examination:** AP, CLEP. **Support services:** GED preparation, tutoring.

Majors. Health services: Medical assistant, pharmacy assistant. **Protective services:** Criminal justice.

Computing on campus. 34 workstations in library, computer center. Online library, helpline, repair service available.

Student life. Freshman orientation: Mandatory. Preregistration for classes offered.

Student services. Alcohol/substance abuse counseling, career counseling, student employment services, financial aid counseling, personal counseling, placement for graduates, veterans' counselor. **Transfer:** Pre-admission transcript evaluation for new students.

Contact. E-mail: admissions@remingtoncollege.edu
Phone: (719) 532-1234 ext. 221 Toll-free number: (866) 717-0013
Fax: (719) 264-1234
Shirly McCray, Campus President, Remington College: Colorado Springs, 6050 Erin Park Drive, Colorado Springs, CO 80918

Trinidad State Junior College
Trinidad, Colorado
www.trinidadstate.edu CB code: 4821

- Public 2-year community and junior college
- Commuter campus in small town

General. Founded in 1925. Regionally accredited. **Enrollment:** 1,489 degree-seeking undergraduates; 427 non-degree-seeking students. **Degrees:** 203 associate awarded. **Location:** 90 miles from Pueblo. **Calendar:** Semester, limited summer session. **Full-time faculty:** 38 total. **Part-time faculty:** 89 total. **Special facilities:** Anthropology and geology museum, gunsmithing laboratory, gun range, gun shop, aquaculture farm, line tech field, labs for welding and automotive, heavy equipment operating job site. **Partnerships:** Formal partnership with Brownells for gunsmithing program.

Student profile. Among degree-seeking undergraduates, 74% enrolled in a transfer program, 26% enrolled in a vocational program, 400 enrolled as first-time, first-year students.

Part-time:	35%	Women:	55%
Out-of-state:	10%	Live on campus:	10%

Transfer out. Colleges most students transferred to 2011: Colorado State University-Pueblo, Adams State College, Colorado State University, University of Northern Colorado.

Basis for selection. Open admission, but selective for some programs. Specific grade and class requirements for nursing program. Line tech and gunsmithing programs require deposit. **Adult students:** ACT/SAT or ACCUPLACER required for placement. **Home schooled:** Transcript of courses and grades, state high school equivalency certificate required.

High school preparation. College-preparatory program recommended. 17 units required. Required units include English 4, mathematics 4, social studies 3, science 3, foreign language 1 and academic electives 2.

2011-2012 Annual costs. Tuition/fees: $3,763; $6,881 out-of-state. Per-credit charge: $106 in-state; $210 out-of-state. In-state tuition based upon assumption of Colorado Opportunity Fund waiver of $62 per-credit-hour. Room/board: $5,118.

Financial aid. Need-based: Need-based aid available for part-time students. Work-study available nights, weekends and for part-time students. **Non-need-based:** Scholarships awarded for academics, athletics, state residency.

Application procedures. Admission: No deadline. No application fee. Admission notification on a rolling basis. **Financial aid:** Priority date 5/1; no closing date. FAFSA, institutional form required. Applicants notified on a rolling basis starting 6/15.

Academics. Special study options: Accelerated study, cooperative education, distance learning, double major, dual enrollment of high school students, ESL, independent study, internships, liberal arts/career combination. Bachelor's degree programs available on campus. License preparation in nursing, paramedic. **Credit/placement by examination:** AP, CLEP, institutional tests. 45 credit hours maximum toward associate degree. **Support services:** GED preparation and test center, learning center, reduced course load, remedial instruction, study skills assistance, tutoring, writing center.

Majors. Biology: General. **Business:** General, accounting, business admin. **Communications:** Advertising, journalism. **Computer sciences:** General, computer science, programming, word processing. **Conservation:** General, fisheries. **Education:** General, physical, social studies. **Engineering:** General. **Foreign languages:** Spanish. **Health services:** Massage therapy. **Liberal arts:** Arts/sciences. **Math:** General. **Parks/recreation:** Health/fitness. **Philosophy/religion:** Philosophy. **Physical sciences:** Chemistry. **Protective services:** Criminal justice, law enforcement admin, police science. **Psychology:** General. **Social sciences:** Criminology. **Visual/performing arts:** Commercial/advertising art. **Work/family studies:** Child care management.

Computing on campus. 260 workstations in dormitories, library, student center. Dormitories wired for high-speed internet access and linked to campus network. Commuter students can connect to campus network. Online course registration, helpline, repair service, wireless network available.

Student life. Freshman orientation: Available. Preregistration for classes offered. **Housing:** Guaranteed on-campus for all undergraduates. Single-sex dorms available. $150 partly refundable deposit. Special housing for welding, line tech, and gunsmithing students. **Activities:** Campus ministries, choral groups, drama, music ensembles, musical theater, student government, student newspaper, TV station, MECHA, black student alliance, Christian Challenge.

Athletics. NJCAA. **Intercollegiate:** Baseball M, basketball, golf M, soccer, softball W, volleyball W. **Intramural:** Baseball M, basketball, rifle, soccer, softball, table tennis, tennis, volleyball. **Team name:** Trojans.

Student services. Adult student services, alcohol/substance abuse counseling, career counseling, services for economically disadvantaged, student employment services, financial aid counseling, personal counseling, placement for graduates, veterans' counselor. **Physically disabled:** Services for visually, speech, hearing impaired. **Transfer:** Transfer adviser, college fairs on campus for students transferring to 4-year colleges.

Contact. E-mail: alex.borja@trinidadstate.edu
Phone: (719) 846-5621 Toll-free number: (800) 621-8752
Fax: (719) 846-5620
Kerry Gabrielson, Vice President of Student and Academic Affairs, Trinidad State Junior College, 600 Prospect Street, Trinidad, CO 81082

Connecticut

Asnuntuck Community College
Enfield, Connecticut
www.acc.commnet.edu

CB member
CB code: 3656

▶ Public 2-year community and technical college
▶ Commuter campus in large town

General. Founded in 1972. Regionally accredited. **Enrollment:** 1,311 degree-seeking undergraduates; 376 non-degree-seeking students. **Degrees:** 169 associate awarded. **Location:** 15 miles from Hartford; 10 miles from Springfield, Massachusetts. **Calendar:** Semester, extensive summer session. **Full-time faculty:** 25 total; 32% have terminal degrees, 8% minority, 60% women. **Part-time faculty:** 108 total. **Class size:** 38% < 20, 61% 20-39, less than 1% 40-49.

Student profile. Among degree-seeking undergraduates, 313 enrolled as first-time, first-year students, 149 transferred in from other institutions.

Part-time:	51%	Asian American:	3%
Women:	53%	Hispanic American:	6%
African American:	8%	25 or older:	23%

Transfer out. Colleges most students transferred to 2011: Eastern Connecticut State University, Central Connecticut State University, University of Connecticut, Western New England College.

Basis for selection. Open admission. Special waivers may be granted to applicants without high school diploma/GED who demonstrate the ability to perform academically at college level. **Home schooled:** Transcript of courses and grades required.

High school preparation. College-preparatory program recommended.

2011-2012 Annual costs. Tuition/fees: $3,490; $10,430 out-of-state. Per-credit charge: $129 in-state; $387 out-of-state. Books/supplies: $1,500.

Financial aid. Need-based: Need-based aid available for part-time students. Work-study available nights, weekends and for part-time students.

Application procedures. Admission: No deadline. $20 fee, may be waived for applicants with need. Admission notification on a rolling basis. **Financial aid:** Closing date 6/1. FAFSA, institutional form required. Applicants notified on a rolling basis starting 7/1; must reply within 2 week(s) of notification.

Academics. On-line tutoring available. **Special study options:** Cooperative education, cross-registration, distance learning, double major, dual enrollment of high school students, independent study, internships, liberal arts/career combination, weekend college. License preparation in paramedic, real estate. **Credit/placement by examination:** AP, CLEP, institutional tests. 48 credit hours maximum toward associate degree. **Support services:** Learning center, remedial instruction, study skills assistance, tutoring.

Majors. Business: Accounting, business admin, office technology. **Communications technology:** General, radio/TV. **Computer sciences:** General. **Education:** Early childhood. **Engineering:** Engineering science. **Health services:** Mental health services. **Liberal arts:** Arts/sciences. **Protective services:** Police science. **Work/family studies:** Child care management.

Most popular majors. Business/marketing 31%, family/consumer sciences 7%, liberal arts 47%, security/protective services 7%.

Computing on campus. 111 workstations in library, computer center. Online course registration, online library, wireless network available.

Student life. Freshman orientation: Available. Preregistration for classes offered. **Activities:** Drama, literary magazine, radio station, student government, TV station, human services club, Phi Theta Kappa.

Student services. Career counseling, student employment services, financial aid counseling, minority student services, on-campus daycare, personal counseling, placement for graduates, veterans' counselor. **Physically disabled:** Services for visually, speech, hearing impaired. **Transfer:** Pre-admission transcript evaluation for new students. Transfer adviser, college fairs on campus for students transferring to 4-year colleges.

Contact. E-mail: tstjames@acc.commnet.edu
Phone: (860) 253-3000 ext. 3010 Toll-free number: (800) 501-3967
Fax: (860) 253-3014
Timothy St. James, Director of Admissions and Marketing, Asnuntuck Community College, 170 Elm Street, Enfield, CT 06082

Capital Community College
Hartford, Connecticut
www.ccc.commnet.edu

CB code: 3421

▶ Public 2-year community and technical college
▶ Commuter campus in small city

General. Founded in 1946. Regionally accredited. **Enrollment:** 3,950 degree-seeking undergraduates; 562 non-degree-seeking students. **Degrees:** 430 associate awarded. **ROTC:** Army, Naval, Air Force. **Calendar:** Semester, limited summer session. **Full-time faculty:** 69 total. **Part-time faculty:** 178 total. **Special facilities:** Math development center, computerized English as a Second Language lab, interactive videodisc instruction for nursing students, learning/writing center. **Partnerships:** Formal partnerships with high schools for Tech Prep program.

Student profile. Among degree-seeking undergraduates, 737 enrolled as first-time, first-year students.

Part-time:	71%	Asian American:	3%
Women:	71%	Hispanic American:	30%
African American:	34%	25 or older:	57%

Transfer out. Colleges most students transferred to 2011: University of Connecticut, Central Connecticut State University, University of Hartford, Eastern Connecticut State University.

Basis for selection. Open admission, but selective for some programs. SAT scores used to satisfy admission criteria for nursing, physical therapist assistant, and radiologic technology programs.

High school preparation. Algebra, biology, and chemistry required for nursing program. Physical therapy assistant, radiologic technology, and pre-nursing programs also have specific course requirements. Paramedic program has specific educational and training requirements.

2011-2012 Annual costs. Tuition/fees: $3,490; $10,430 out-of-state. Per-credit charge: $129 in-state; $387 out-of-state. Books/supplies: $850. Personal expenses: $1,965.

Financial aid. All financial aid based on need. Need-based aid available for part-time students. Work-study available nights, weekends and for part-time students.

Application procedures. Admission: No deadline. $20 fee, may be waived for applicants with need. Admission notification on a rolling basis. **Financial aid:** Closing date 7/15. FAFSA required. Applicants notified on a rolling basis starting 7/15; must reply within 2 week(s) of notification.

Academics. Special study options: Accelerated study, cross-registration, distance learning, double major, dual enrollment of high school students, ESL, independent study, internships, liberal arts/career combination, weekend college. Interdisciplinary summer program with Smith College. License preparation in nursing, paramedic, radiology. **Credit/placement by examination:** AP, CLEP, institutional tests. **Support services:** GED preparation, learning center, pre-admission summer program, remedial instruction, study skills assistance, tutoring, writing center.

Majors. Business: Accounting, administrative services, business admin. **Computer sciences:** General. **Education:** Early childhood. **Engineering:** Electrical. **Health services:** EMT paramedic, medical assistant, medical radiologic technology/radiation therapy, mental health services, nursing (RN), physical therapy assistant. **Liberal arts:** Arts/sciences, library assistant. **Protective services:** Fire safety technology.

Most popular majors. Business/marketing 18%, health sciences 40%, liberal arts 26%, public administration/social services 6%.

Computing on campus. 500 workstations in library, computer center, student center. Commuter students can connect to campus network. Online course registration, online library, wireless network available.

Student life. Freshman orientation: Available. Preregistration for classes offered. 3 day program held prior to start of semester. **Policies:** Policies against drugs and alcohol, violence, weapons, and sexual harassment on campus. **Activities:** Choral groups, dance, drama, literary magazine, radio station, student government, TV station, Latin American students association, senior renewal club, early childhood club, pre-professional club, Phi Theta Kappa, nursing club, black student union.

Student services. Adult student services, chaplain/spiritual director, career counseling, services for economically disadvantaged, student employ-ment services, financial aid counseling, minority student services, on-campus daycare, personal counseling, placement for graduates, veterans' counselor, women's services. **Physically disabled:** Services for visually, speech, hearing impaired. **Transfer:** College fairs on campus for students transferring to 4-year colleges.

Contact. E-mail: mball-davis@ccc.commnet.edu
Phone: (860) 906-5126 Toll-free number: (800) 894-6126
Marsha Ball-Davis, Director of Admissions, Capital Community College, 950 Main Street, Hartford, CT 06103-1207

Gateway Community College
New Haven, Connecticut   **CB member**
www.gcc.commnet.edu   **CB code: 3425**

◆ Public 2-year community college
◆ Commuter campus in small city
◆ Application essay, interview required

General. Founded in 1992. Regionally accredited. **Enrollment:** 6,310 degree-seeking undergraduates; 951 non-degree-seeking students. **Degrees:** 539 associate awarded. **Location:** 75 miles from New York City, 130 miles from Boston. **Calendar:** Semester, limited summer session. **Full-time fac-ulty:** 63 total; 24% have terminal degrees, 21% minority, 44% women. **Part-time faculty:** 380 total; 18% minority, 56% women. **Class size:** 24% < 20, 71% 20-39, 4% 40-49, less than 1% 50-99. **Special facilities:** Early childhood learning center, day care center, student operated cafe, student art museum.

Student profile. Among degree-seeking undergraduates, 2% enrolled in a transfer program, 67% enrolled in a vocational program, 1% already have a bachelor's degree or higher, 1,377 enrolled as first-time, first-year students, 53 transferred in from other institutions.

Part-time:	61%	Asian American:	3%
Out-of-state:	1%	Hispanic American:	18%
Women:	59%	International:	1%
African American:	23%	25 or older:	32%

Transfer out. **Colleges most students transferred to 2011:** Southern Con-necticut State University, University of New Haven, Quinnipiac College.

Basis for selection. Open admission, but selective for some programs. Special requirements for radiology, nursing, nuclear medicine technology, diagnostic medical sonography, drug and alcohol rehabilitation counselor. Interview required of radiology, drug and alcohol counseling, nuclear medi-cine technology, diagnostic medical sonography, nursing majors. **Home schooled:** Transcript of courses and grades required.

2011-2012 Annual costs. Tuition/fees: $3,490; $10,430 out-of-state. Per-credit charge: $129 in-state; $387 out-of-state. Books/supplies: $1,200. Per-sonal expenses: $1,100.

Financial aid. All financial aid based on need. Need-based aid available for part-time students. Work-study available nights, weekends and for part-time students.

Application procedures. **Admission:** Priority date 6/1; deadline 9/1. $20 fee, may be waived for applicants with need. Admission notification on a rolling basis beginning on or about 2/1. **Financial aid:** No deadline. FAFSA, institutional form required. Applicants notified on a rolling basis; must reply within 2 week(s) of notification.

Academics. **Special study options:** Accelerated study, cross-registration, distance learning, dual enrollment of high school students, ESL, independent study, internships, liberal arts/career combination, weekend college. License preparation in nursing, radiology. **Credit/placement by examination:** AP, CLEP, institutional tests. 30 credit hours maximum toward associate degree. **Support services:** GED preparation, learning center, pre-admission summer program, reduced course load, remedial instruction, study skills assistance, tutoring, writing center.

Majors. **Business:** Accounting, administrative services, business admin, fashion, hotel/motel admin, office/clerical, restaurant/food services, sales/distribution. **Computer sciences:** Computer science, data processing, infor-mation systems, networking, programming, word processing. **Conservation:** General, environmental science. **Education:** Early childhood, special ed. **Engineering:** Engineering science. **Health services:** Dental hygiene, dietetic technician, environmental health, medical radiologic technology/radiation therapy, medical secretary, nuclear medical technology, nursing (RN), radio-logic technology/medical imaging, sonography, substance abuse counseling. **Liberal arts:** Arts/sciences. **Math:** General. **Parks/recreation:** Sports admin. **Protective services:** Fire services admin. **Visual/performing arts:**

Graphic design, studio arts. **Work/family studies:** Aging, food/nutrition, institutional food production.

Most popular majors. Business/marketing 8%, engineering/engineering technologies 7%, health sciences 27%, liberal arts 49%.

Computing on campus. 650 workstations in library, computer center, student center. Online library, helpline, wireless network available.

Student life. **Freshman orientation:** Available. Preregistration for classes offered. **Activities:** Choral groups, drama, international student organizations, literary magazine, music ensembles, student government, student newspaper, Spanish-American club, math/science club, Phi Theta Kappa, art club, athletic club, veteran's club, biology club, Theater Goers, black student union.

Athletics. NJCAA. **Intercollegiate:** Baseball M, basketball. **Team name:** Ravens.

Student services. Adult student services, career counseling, student employment services, financial aid counseling, health services, on-campus daycare, personal counseling, placement for graduates, veterans' counselor, women's services. **Physically disabled:** Services for visually, speech, hearing impaired. **Transfer:** Transfer adviser for students transferring to 4-year col-leges.

Contact. E-mail: kshea@gwcc.commnet.edu
Phone: (203) 285-2010 Toll-free number: (800) 390-7723
Fax: (203) 285-2018
Shea Kim, Director of Admissions, Gateway Community College, 60 Sargent Drive, New Haven, CT 06511-5970

Goodwin College
East Hartford, Connecticut   **CB member**
www.goodwin.edu   **CB code: 5879**

◆ Private 2-year health science and career college
◆ Commuter campus in small city

General. **Enrollment:** 3,074 degree-seeking undergraduates; 42 non-degree-seeking students. **Degrees:** 332 associate awarded. **Location:** 5 miles from Hartford. **Calendar:** Semester, extensive summer session. **Full-time faculty:** 57 total; 25% have terminal degrees, 16% minority, 67% women. **Part-time faculty:** 204 total; 18% have terminal degrees, 19% minority, 67% women. **Class size:** 88% < 20, 11% 20-39, less than 1% 40-49.

Student profile. Among degree-seeking undergraduates, 11% already have a bachelor's degree or higher, 381 enrolled as first-time, first-year students, 729 transferred in from other institutions.

Part-time:	84%	Asian American:	2%
Out-of-state:	2%	Hispanic American:	19%
Women:	83%	25 or older:	65%
African American:	24%		

Transfer out. **Colleges most students transferred to 2011:** Manchester Community College, Capital Community College, University of Connecticut, Central Connecticut State University, Tunxis Community College.

Basis for selection. Open admission, but selective for some programs. Applicants to nursing, respiratory therapist, and histology technician programs must have successfully completed prerequisite courses prior to application and submit completed application to program desired. Interviews may be required for some programs. **Home schooled:** State high school equivalency certificate required.

2012-2013 Annual costs. Tuition/fees: $19,400. Per-credit charge: $590. Books/supplies: $1,000. Personal expenses: $4,498.

2010-2011 Financial aid. All financial aid based on need. 292 full-time freshmen applied for aid; 285 were judged to have need; 285 of these received aid. Average need met was 25%. Average scholarship/grant was $5,021; average loan $3,235. 44% of total undergraduate aid awarded as scholarships/grants, 56% as loans/jobs. Need-based aid available for part-time students. Work-study available nights, weekends and for part-time students.

Application procedures. **Admission:** No deadline. $50 fee, may be waived for applicants with need. Admission notification on a rolling basis. **Financial aid:** No deadline. FAFSA required. Applicants notified on a rolling basis starting 7/1.

Academics. **Special study options:** Cross-registration, distance learning, double major, ESL, internships. Bachelor's degree programs available on campus. License preparation in nursing, paramedic. **Credit/placement by examination:** AP, CLEP, institutional tests. 30 credit hours maximum toward associate degree, 30 toward bachelor's. **Support services:** Learning center,

pre-admission summer program, reduced course load, remedial instruction, study skills assistance, tutoring, writing center.

Majors. Business: General, administrative services, business admin, entrepreneurial studies, human resources, international, nonprofit/public, office management, selling. **Conservation:** Environmental studies. **Health services:** Insurance coding, medical assistant, nursing (RN), occupational therapy assistant, office admin, office assistant, respiratory therapy technology. **Protective services:** Homeland security, law enforcement admin. **Work/family studies:** Child care management, child development.

Most popular majors. Health sciences 86%.

Computing on campus. 100 workstations in library, computer center, student center. Commuter students can connect to campus network. Online course registration, online library, helpline, repair service, wireless network available.

Student life. Freshman orientation: Available. Preregistration for classes offered. **Activities:** Choral groups, literary magazine, student government, student newspaper.

Athletics. Intramural: Basketball M, football (non-tackle), soccer. **Team name:** Navigators.

Student services. Adult student services, alcohol/substance abuse counseling, career counseling, student employment services, financial aid counseling, personal counseling, placement for graduates, veterans' counselor. **Physically disabled:** Services for visually impaired. **Transfer:** Re-entry adviser, pre-admission transcript evaluation for new students. Transfer adviser for students transferring to 4-year colleges.

Contact. E-mail: nlentino@goodwin.edu
Phone: (860) 727-6765 Toll-free number: (800) 889-3282
Fax: (860) 291-9550
Nicholas Lentino, Director of Admissions, Goodwin College, One Riverside Drive, East Hartford, CT 06118-9980

Housatonic Community College
Bridgeport, Connecticut
www.hcc.commnet.edu

CB member
CB code: 3446

▶ Public 2-year community college
▶ Commuter campus in small city

General. Founded in 1966. Regionally accredited. **Enrollment:** 5,525 degree-seeking undergraduates. **Degrees:** 491 associate awarded. **Location:** 60 miles from Hartford, 60 miles from New York City. **Calendar:** Semester, extensive summer session. **Full-time faculty:** 69 total. **Part-time faculty:** 282 total. **Class size:** 45% < 20, 53% 20-39, 2% 40-49, less than 1% 50-99. **Special facilities:** Art museum.

Basis for selection. Open admission, but selective for some programs. Special requirements for clinical lab science, physical therapist assistant, occupational therapy assistant, nursing programs. Interview required of allied health, computer program majors.

2011-2012 Annual costs. Tuition/fees: $3,490; $10,430 out-of-state. Per-credit charge: $129 in-state; $387 out-of-state. Books/supplies: $700.

Financial aid. All financial aid based on need. Need-based aid available for part-time students. Work-study available nights, weekends and for part-time students.

Application procedures. Admission: No deadline. $20 fee, may be waived for applicants with need. Admission notification on a rolling basis. Application period ends one week after start of classes. **Financial aid:** Priority date 11/1, closing date 5/1. FAFSA required. Applicants notified on a rolling basis starting 6/1.

Academics. Special study options: Cooperative education, distance learning, double major, dual enrollment of high school students, ESL, honors, independent study, internships, weekend college. **Credit/placement by examination:** AP, CLEP, institutional tests. 30 credit hours maximum toward associate degree. New Jersey Basic Skills Placement Test and/or ACCUPLACER used for advising and placement. **Support services:** GED preparation, learning center, reduced course load, remedial instruction, study skills assistance, tutoring, writing center.

Majors. Business: General, accounting, administrative services, business admin. **Computer sciences:** General. **Education:** Early childhood. **Health services:** Mental health services, nursing (RN), physical therapy assistant, substance abuse counseling. **Liberal arts:** Arts/sciences. **Protective services:**

Police science. **Visual/performing arts:** Commercial/advertising art, studio arts. **Work/family studies:** Child care management.

Computing on campus. 140 workstations in library, computer center.

Student life. Freshman orientation: Available. Preregistration for classes offered. **Activities:** Drama, literary magazine, student government, student newspaper.

Student services. Adult student services, career counseling, services for economically disadvantaged, student employment services, financial aid counseling, health services, minority student services, on-campus daycare, personal counseling, placement for graduates, veterans' counselor, women's services. **Transfer:** Transfer adviser, college fairs on campus for students transferring to 4-year colleges.

Contact. E-mail: HO-WAdmissions@hcc.commnet.edu
Phone: (203) 332-5100 Fax: (203) 332-5123
Deloris Curtis, Director of Admissions, Housatonic Community College, 900 Lafayette Boulevard, Bridgeport, CT 06604-4704

Lincoln College of New England: Briarwood
Southington, Connecticut
www.lincolncollegene.edu

CB code: 3121

▶ For-profit 2-year junior college
▶ Commuter campus in large town
▶ Application essay required

General. Founded in 1966. Regionally accredited. **Degrees:** 7 bachelor's, 108 associate awarded. **Location:** 19 miles from Hartford. **Calendar:** Semester, limited summer session. **Full-time faculty:** 35 total. **Part-time faculty:** 132 total.

Student profile.

Out-of-state:	6%	Live on campus:	19%
25 or older:	41%		

Transfer out. Colleges most students transferred to 2011: Central Connecticut State University, Saint Joseph College, Quinnipiac College, Teikyo Post University, University of New Haven, University of Connecticut.

Basis for selection. Open admission, but selective for some programs. Selective admissions to dental hygiene, funeral service management, nuclear medicine technology, and occupational therapy assistant programs.

High school preparation. For occupational therapy assistant program, 2 math, 2 science (including 1 biological science) required.

2011-2012 Annual costs. Tuition/fees: $19,420. Per-credit charge: $700. Room/board: $8,600. Books/supplies: $1,000. Personal expenses: $2,400.

Financial aid. Need-based: Need-based aid available for part-time students. Work-study available nights, weekends and for part-time students. **Non-need-based:** Scholarships awarded for academics, alumni affiliation, leadership.

Application procedures. Admission: No deadline. $125 fee, may be waived for applicants with need. Admission notification on a rolling basis beginning on or about 9/15. **Financial aid:** Priority date 4/30; no closing date. FAFSA required. Applicants notified on a rolling basis starting 3/15; must reply within 2 week(s) of notification.

Academics. Special study options: Double major, ESL, independent study, internships, liberal arts/career combination, weekend college. Bachelor's degree programs available on campus. **Credit/placement by examination:** AP, CLEP, institutional tests. 29 credit hours maximum toward associate degree. **Support services:** Learning center, pre-admission summer program, reduced course load, remedial instruction, study skills assistance, tutoring, writing center.

Majors. Business: General, accounting, administrative services, business admin, fashion, office technology, tourism/travel. **Communications:** Broadcast journalism, communications/speech/rhetoric. **Health services:** Dental assistant, dietetics, medical assistant, medical records technology, medical secretary, occupational therapy assistant. **Liberal arts:** Arts/sciences. **Protective services:** Criminal justice. **Work/family studies:** Child care management.

Computing on campus. 66 workstations in library, computer center. Dormitories wired for high-speed internet access.

Student life. Freshman orientation: Mandatory. Preregistration for classes offered. **Housing:** Coed dorms, apartments, wellness housing available. $100 deposit. Townhouse apartments with kitchens available. **Activities:** Choral groups, radio station, student government, psychology honor society, allied health club.

Athletics. NJCAA. **Intramural:** Basketball M.

Student services. Career counseling, student employment services, financial aid counseling, health services, personal counseling, placement for graduates, veterans' counselor. **Physically disabled:** Services for visually, hearing impaired. **Transfer:** Pre-admission transcript evaluation for new students. Transfer adviser, college fairs on campus for students transferring to 4-year colleges.

Contact. E-mail: admis@briarwood.edu
Phone: (860) 628-4751 ext. 108
Toll-free number: (800) 952-2444 ext. 108 Fax: (860) 628-6444
Rick Einstein, Director of Admissions, Lincoln College of New England: Briarwood, 2279 Mount Vernon Road, Southington, CT 06489-1057

Lincoln College of New England: Suffield
Suffield, Connecticut
www.lincolncollegene.edu   **CB code: 0481**

- For-profit 2-year culinary school and business college
- Residential campus in small town
- Application essay, interview required

General. Regionally accredited. Students can complete degree program in 18-month accelerated format. Cost of attendance includes 6-month paid internship. **Degrees:** 13 associate awarded. **Location:** 50 miles from Hartford. **Calendar:** Differs by program, limited summer session. **Full-time faculty:** 7 total. **Part-time faculty:** 8 total. **Class size:** 95% < 20, 5% 20-39.

Student profile.

Out-of-state:	90%	Live on campus:	90%
25 or older:	40%		

Transfer out. Colleges most students transferred to 2011: University Center Cesar Ritz (Switzerland), Institut Hotelier Cesar Ritz (Switzerland).

Basis for selection. Open admission.

2011-2012 Annual costs. Tuition/fees: $19,420. Hospitality students pay an extra $215 per year. Room/board: $8,600.

Financial aid. Need-based: Need-based aid available for part-time students. Work-study available nights, weekends and for part-time students. **Non-need-based:** Scholarships awarded for academics.

Application procedures. Admission: No deadline. $125 fee, may be waived for applicants with need. Admission notification on a rolling basis. **Financial aid:** No deadline. Applicants notified on a rolling basis starting 1/1.

Academics. Special study options: Accelerated study, cooperative education, internships, liberal arts/career combination, study abroad. **Credit/placement by examination:** AP, CLEP, institutional tests. 18 credit hours maximum toward associate degree. **Support services:** Learning center, remedial instruction, study skills assistance, tutoring, writing center.

Majors. Business: Hospitality admin.

Most popular majors. Business/marketing 68%, personal/culinary services 32%.

Computing on campus. 38 workstations in dormitories, library, computer center, student center. Dormitories wired for high-speed internet access and linked to campus network. Online library, helpline, wireless network available.

Student life. Freshman orientation: Mandatory. Preregistration for classes offered. Half of the first week devoted to orientation. **Housing:** Guaranteed on-campus for freshmen. Coed dorms, wellness housing available. $500 deposit. **Activities:** Film society, student government, Ritz Guild.

Athletics. Intramural: Basketball, soccer, table tennis, tennis, volleyball, weight lifting.

Student services. Adult student services, alcohol/substance abuse counseling, career counseling, student employment services, financial aid counseling, health services, placement for graduates. **Transfer:** Pre-admission transcript evaluation for new students.

Contact. E-mail: admissions@lincolncollegene.edu
Phone: (860) 668-3515 ext. 228 Toll-free number: (800) 955-0809
Fax: (860) 668-7369
Rick Einstein, Director of Admissions, Lincoln College of New England: Suffield, 1760 Mapleton Avenue, Suffield, CT 06078

Manchester Community College
Manchester, Connecticut   **CB member**
www.mcc.commnet.edu   **CB code: 3544**

- Public 2-year community college
- Commuter campus in small city

General. Founded in 1963. Regionally accredited. **Enrollment:** 6,648 degree-seeking undergraduates; 851 non-degree-seeking students. **Degrees:** 812 associate awarded. **Location:** 8 miles from Hartford. **Calendar:** Semester, extensive summer session. **Full-time faculty:** 103 total; 24% have terminal degrees, 58% women. **Part-time faculty:** 400 total; 49% women. **Class size:** 23% < 20, 71% 20-39, 6% 40-49.

Student profile. Among degree-seeking undergraduates, 1,507 enrolled as first-time, first-year students, 881 transferred in from other institutions.

Part-time:	59%	25 or older:	31%
Women:	52%		

Transfer out. Colleges most students transferred to 2011: Central Connecticut State University, University of Connecticut, Eastern Connecticut State University.

Basis for selection. Open admission, but selective for some programs. Interview required of allied health, drug and alcohol rehabilitation counselor majors.

High school preparation. 2 units math and 1 unit laboratory science required of allied health applicants.

2011-2012 Annual costs. Tuition/fees: $3,490; $10,430 out-of-state. Per-credit charge: $129 in-state; $387 out-of-state. Books/supplies: $1,000. Personal expenses: $1,596.

Financial aid. Need-based: Need-based aid available for part-time students. Work-study available nights, weekends and for part-time students.

Application procedures. Admission: No deadline. $20 fee, may be waived for applicants with need. Admission notification on a rolling basis beginning on or about 5/1. **Financial aid:** Priority date 5/15; no closing date. FAFSA required. Applicants notified on a rolling basis starting 5/1; must reply within 2 week(s) of notification.

Academics. Special study options: Cooperative education, cross-registration, distance learning, double major, dual enrollment of high school students, ESL, independent study, internships, semester at sea, student-designed major, weekend college. License preparation in occupational therapy, paramedic. **Credit/placement by examination:** AP, CLEP, SAT, ACT, institutional tests. 45 credit hours maximum toward associate degree. **Support services:** Learning center, reduced course load, remedial instruction, study skills assistance, tutoring, writing center.

Majors. Area/ethnic studies: Women's. **Business:** Accounting, administrative services, business admin, hospitality/recreation, management information systems. **Communications:** Digital media, journalism. **Computer sciences:** Data entry, information systems, networking. **Education:** Early childhood, teacher assistance. **Engineering:** Engineering science. **Health services:** Clinical lab technology, occupational therapy assistant, pharmacy assistant, physical therapy assistant, respiratory therapy technology, substance abuse counseling, surgical technology. **Human services:** Community org/advocacy. **Liberal arts:** Arts/sciences. **Parks/recreation:** Exercise sciences. **Visual/performing arts:** Commercial/advertising art, music. **Work/family studies:** Institutional food production.

Most popular majors. Business/marketing 14%, health sciences 11%, liberal arts 44%, security/protective services 35%.

Computing on campus. 310 workstations in library, computer center. Online course registration, online library, wireless network available.

Student life. Freshman orientation: Available. Preregistration for classes offered. **Activities:** Choral groups, dance, drama, student government, student newspaper, student organization of Latinos, African American Males Achieving Excellence, Muslim student association, Spanish club, political union, PRIDE, Phi Theta Kappa, Veterans Empowering Themselves to Succeed.

Athletics. NJCAA. **Intercollegiate:** Baseball M, basketball W, soccer, softball W. **Team name:** Cougars.

Student services. Adult student services, career counseling, student employment services, health services, on-campus daycare, personal counseling, placement for graduates, veterans' counselor. **Physically disabled:** Services for visually, speech, hearing impaired. **Transfer:** Transfer adviser, college fairs on campus for students transferring to 4-year colleges.

Contact. Phone: (860) 512-3210 Fax: (860) 512-3221
Peter Harris, Director of Admissions, Manchester Community College, Great Path PO Box 1046, MS 12, Manchester, CT 06040-1046

Middlesex Community College
Middletown, Connecticut
www.mxcc.commnet.edu

CB member
CB code: 3551

- Public 2-year community college
- Commuter campus in large town

General. Founded in 1966. **Enrollment:** 1,099 full-time, degree-seeking students. **Degrees:** 288 associate awarded. **Location:** 20 miles from Hartford and New Haven. **Calendar:** Semester, limited summer session. **Full-time faculty:** 44 total. **Part-time faculty:** 144 total. **Class size:** 24% < 20, 76% 20-39. **Special facilities:** Nature trails, art gallery.

Student profile.

Out-of-state:	1%	25 or older:	38%

Transfer out. Colleges most students transferred to 2011: Eastern Connecticut State University, Southern Connecticut State University, University of Connecticut, University of Hartford.

Basis for selection. Open admission, but selective for some programs. Special requirements for radiology technician, broadcast communications, human services, and drug and alcohol rehabilitation counselor programs. Interview recommended of mental health, radiology, drug and alcohol counseling program majors.

High school preparation. College-preparatory program recommended.

2011-2012 Annual costs. Tuition/fees: $3,490; $10,430 out-of-state. Per-credit charge: $129 in-state; $387 out-of-state. Books/supplies: $1,000. Personal expenses: $1,925.

Financial aid. All financial aid based on need. Need-based aid available for part-time students. Work-study available nights, weekends and for part-time students. **Additional information:** Tuition and/or fee waiver for veterans.

Application procedures. Admission: Priority date 7/1; deadline 8/1 (postmark date). $20 fee, may be waived for applicants with need. Admission notification on a rolling basis beginning on or about 1/1. **Financial aid:** Priority date 6/1; no closing date. FAFSA, institutional form required. Applicants notified on a rolling basis starting 7/1; must reply within 2 week(s) of notification.

Academics. Special study options: Cross-registration, dual enrollment of high school students, ESL, independent study, internships, student-designed major. License preparation in radiology. **Credit/placement by examination:** AP, CLEP, institutional tests. 48 credit hours maximum toward associate degree. **Support services:** Pre-admission summer program, reduced course load, remedial instruction, tutoring.

Majors. Biology: Biotechnology. **Business:** Accounting, administrative services, business admin, marketing. **Communications:** Broadcast journalism, communications/speech/rhetoric. **Communications technology:** Radio/TV. **Computer sciences:** Information systems. **Conservation:** General. **Education:** Early childhood. **Engineering:** Engineering science. **Health services:** Medical radiologic technology/radiation therapy, medical secretary, mental health services, ophthalmic lab technology, optician, substance abuse counseling. **Liberal arts:** Arts/sciences. **Protective services:** Police science. **Visual/performing arts:** Art, metal/jewelry, studio arts. **Work/family studies:** Child care management.

Most popular majors. Business/marketing 20%, health sciences 20%, liberal arts 41%.

Computing on campus. Online library, helpline available.

Student life. Freshman orientation: Available. Preregistration for classes offered. **Activities:** Drama, international student organizations, literary magazine, student government, student newspaper, Student Senate, poetry club, national scholastic honor society, student guild, computer club, Minority Opportunities in Education club, art club, human services organization.

Student services. Career counseling, student employment services, financial aid counseling, minority student services, on-campus daycare, personal counseling, placement for graduates, veterans' counselor. **Physically disabled:** Services for visually, hearing impaired. **Transfer:** Transfer adviser, college fairs on campus for students transferring to 4-year colleges.

Contact. E-mail: mshabazz@mxcc.commnet.edu
Phone: (860) 343-5719 Toll-free number: (800) 818-5501
Fax: (860) 344-7488
Mensimah Shabazz, Director of Admissions, Middlesex Community College, 100 Training Hill Road, Middletown, CT 06457-4889

Naugatuck Valley Community College
Waterbury, Connecticut
www.nvcc.commnet.edu

CB member
CB code: 3550

- Public 2-year community and technical college
- Commuter campus in small city

General. Founded in 1992. Regionally accredited. **Enrollment:** 6,710 degree-seeking undergraduates. **Degrees:** 642 associate awarded. **Location:** 32 miles from Hartford. **Calendar:** Semester, limited summer session. **Full-time faculty:** 110 total. **Part-time faculty:** 399 total. **Class size:** 82% < 20, 16% 20-39, 1% 40-49. **Special facilities:** Fine arts center, 2 theaters, music and dance studios, video studios, rehearsal rooms, fire sprinkler laboratory, automotive center, greenhouse laboratory, observatory, arboretum, nature trail.

Transfer out. Colleges most students transferred to 2011: Western Connecticut State University, Southern Connecticut State University, Central Connecticut State University, University of Connecticut, Post University.

Basis for selection. Open admission, but selective for some programs. Admission to nursing, physical therapy assistant, radiology, respiratory care programs based on school achievement, recommendations, test scores, maturity of student, motivation. Interview required of physical therapy majors. Audition recommended of music majors. Portfolio recommended of art majors. **Home schooled:** Statement describing home school structure and mission, interview required. Placement test and interview required.

High school preparation. Recommended units include English 4, mathematics 3, social studies 2, history 2 and science 1. Most allied health programs require high school algebra, biology, chemistry. Engineering technologies require 2 years algebra, 1 year laboratory science (preferably physics or chemistry), and computer literacy.

2011-2012 Annual costs. Tuition/fees: $3,490; $10,430 out-of-state. Per-credit charge: $129 in-state; $387 out-of-state. Books/supplies: $1,400. Personal expenses: $1,507.

Financial aid. All financial aid based on need. Need-based aid available for part-time students. Work-study available nights, weekends and for part-time students.

Application procedures. Admission: Priority date 6/1; no deadline. $20 fee, may be waived for applicants with need. Admission notification on a rolling basis beginning on or about 9/1. **Financial aid:** Priority date 4/1; no closing date. FAFSA required. Applicants notified on a rolling basis starting 6/1.

Academics. Composition, technical writing, literature, computer information systems, math, business law, psychology, astronomy, biology and criminal justice courses available through distance learning. **Special study options:** Cooperative education, cross-registration, distance learning, double major, dual enrollment of high school students, ESL, independent study, internships, study abroad. License preparation in aviation, nursing, physical therapy, radiology, real estate. **Credit/placement by examination:** AP, CLEP, institutional tests. 45 credit hours maximum toward associate degree. **Support services:** Learning center, reduced course load, remedial instruction, study skills assistance, tutoring, writing center.

Majors. Business: Accounting technology, administrative services, banking/financial services, business admin, merchandising. **Computer sciences:** General, networking, web page design. **General:** Horticulture. **Health services:** Medical radiologic technology/radiation therapy, mental health services, nursing (RN), physical therapy assistant, respiratory therapy technology, substance abuse counseling. **Human services:** Social work. **Liberal arts:** Arts/sciences. **Protective services:** Fire safety technology, police science. **Psychology:** General. **Visual/performing arts:** Art, dance, dramatic, multimedia, music. **Work/family studies:** Child development, facilities/event planning, institutional food production.

Most popular majors. Business/marketing 15%, health sciences 25%, liberal arts 25%, security/protective services 6%.

Two-Year Colleges

Computing on campus. 1,100 workstations in library, computer center. Commuter students can connect to campus network. Online course registration, online library, helpline, repair service, wireless network available.

Student life. Freshman orientation: Available. Preregistration for classes offered. **Activities:** Bands, choral groups, dance, drama, literary magazine, music ensembles, musical theater, opera, student government, student newspaper, symphony orchestra, black student union, Hispanic student union, human services club, Phi Theta Kappa, Alpha Beta Gamma, agro-bio club, student nurses clubs, book club.

Student services. Adult student services, career counseling, student employment services, financial aid counseling, health services, personal counseling, placement for graduates, veterans' counselor. **Physically disabled:** Services for visually, speech, hearing impaired. **Transfer:** Pre-admission transcript evaluation for new students. Transfer adviser, college fairs on campus for students transferring to 4-year colleges.

Contact. E-mail: nvcc@nvcc.commnet.edu
Phone: (203) 575-8054 Fax: (203) 596-8766
Linda Stango, Director of Admissions, Naugatuck Valley Community College, 750 Chase Parkway, Waterbury, CT 06708-3089

Northwestern Connecticut Community College
Winsted, Connecticut   **CB member**
www.nwcc.commnet.edu   **CB code: 3652**

▶ Public 2-year community and technical college
▶ Commuter campus in large town

General. Founded in 1965. Regionally accredited. **Enrollment:** 1,307 degree-seeking undergraduates; 394 non-degree-seeking students. **Degrees:** 133 associate awarded. **Location:** 25 miles from Hartford, 25 miles from Waterbury. **Calendar:** Semester, limited summer session. **Full-time faculty:** 24 total. **Part-time faculty:** 104 total.

Student profile. Among degree-seeking undergraduates, 242 enrolled as first-time, first-year students.

| Part-time: | 61% | Women: | 66% |

Basis for selection. Open admission, but selective for some programs. Special requirements for nursing.

2011-2012 Annual costs. Tuition/fees: $3,490; $10,430 out-of-state. Per-credit charge: $129 in-state; $387 out-of-state. Books/supplies: $600. Personal expenses: $1,000.

Financial aid. Need-based: Work-study available nights, weekends and for part-time students.

Application procedures. Admission: No deadline. $20 fee, may be waived for applicants with need. Admission notification on a rolling basis. **Financial aid:** Priority date 6/1; no closing date. FAFSA required. Applicants notified on a rolling basis starting 6/1.

Academics. Career education for the deaf program offers full range of services and participation in all majors by deaf and hearing impaired students. Interpreting major prepares hearing students for National Registry test for interpreters for the deaf. **Special study options:** Cooperative education, cross-registration, distance learning, double major, dual enrollment of high school students, ESL, independent study, internships. **Credit/placement by examination:** AP, CLEP, institutional tests. **Support services:** Learning center, reduced course load, remedial instruction, tutoring.

Majors. Business: Accounting, banking/financial services, business admin, hospitality admin, marketing. **Communications technology:** Animation/special effects, graphics. **Computer sciences:** Systems analysis. **Education:** Early childhood. **Foreign languages:** Sign language interpretation. **Health services:** Medical assistant, nursing (RN), physical therapy assistant, recreational therapy, veterinary technology/assistant. **Liberal arts:** Arts/sciences. **Protective services:** Law enforcement admin.

Student life. Freshman orientation: Available. Preregistration for classes offered. **Activities:** Literary magazine, student government, student newspaper.

Student services. Career counseling, student employment services, personal counseling, veterans' counselor. **Physically disabled:** Services for hearing impaired. **Transfer:** Transfer adviser, college fairs on campus for students transferring to 4-year colleges.

Contact. E-mail: dmartineau@nwcc.commnet.edu
Phone: (860) 738-6330 Fax: (860) 379-4465
Joanne Nardi, Director of Admissions, Northwestern Connecticut Community College, Park Place East, Winsted, CT 06098

Norwalk Community College
Norwalk, Connecticut
www.ncc.commnet.edu   **CB code: 3677**

▶ Public 2-year community and technical college
▶ Commuter campus in small city

General. Founded in 1961. Regionally accredited. Non-credit courses offered through continuing education department. Lifetime Learners Institute for senior citizens. **Enrollment:** 5,083 degree-seeking undergraduates; 1,724 non-degree-seeking students. **Degrees:** 486 associate awarded. **Location:** 45 miles from New York City. **Calendar:** Semester, extensive summer session. **Full-time faculty:** 106 total; 16% minority, 61% women. **Part-time faculty:** 301 total; 15% minority, 52% women. **Class size:** 28% < 20, 72% 20-39, less than 1% 40-49. **Special facilities:** Theater, rotating art and cultural exhibits, culinary arts facility, early childhood education lab/preschool.

Student profile. Among degree-seeking undergraduates, 983 enrolled as first-time, first-year students.

Part-time:	59%	Asian American:	4%
Out-of-state:	1%	Hispanic American:	30%
Women:	60%	International:	2%
African American:	18%	25 or older:	52%

Basis for selection. Open admission, but selective for some programs. Special requirements for nursing, legal assistant, respiratory care programs.

High school preparation. Recommended units include English 4, mathematics 3 and science 2. Chemistry, biology and algebra required for nursing and respiratory therapy applicants. Nursing applicants must have taken chemistry within past 5 years.

2011-2012 Annual costs. Tuition/fees: $3,490; $10,430 out-of-state. Per-credit charge: $129 in-state; $387 out-of-state. Books/supplies: $1,600. Personal expenses: $1,751.

Financial aid. Need-based: Need-based aid available for part-time students. Work-study available nights, weekends and for part-time students. **Non-need-based:** Scholarships awarded for academics, alumni affiliation.

Application procedures. Admission: No deadline. $20 fee, may be waived for applicants with need. Admission notification on a rolling basis. Applicants to nursing program should apply by February 1. **Financial aid:** Priority date 7/1; no closing date. FAFSA, institutional form required. Applicants notified on a rolling basis starting 7/1; must reply within 2 week(s) of notification.

Academics. Special 10-week sessions with longer class hours per day let students finish courses more quickly during fall and spring. **Special study options:** Cooperative education, cross-registration, double major, dual enrollment of high school students, ESL, honors, internships, liberal arts/career combination, weekend college. Early childhood education credential training program. License preparation in nursing, paramedic, real estate. **Credit/placement by examination:** AP, CLEP, IB, institutional tests. 45 credit hours maximum toward associate degree. **Support services:** Learning center, pre-admission summer program, reduced course load, remedial instruction, study skills assistance, tutoring, writing center.

Majors. Business: Accounting, business admin, finance, hospitality admin, management information systems, marketing, office management, office technology. **Communications:** Journalism. **Communications technology:** General. **Computer sciences:** General, applications programming, data processing, information systems, programming, systems analysis. **Education:** Early childhood. **Engineering:** General, architectural, engineering science. **Health services:** Nursing (RN), recreational therapy, respiratory therapy technology. **Liberal arts:** Arts/sciences. **Math:** General. **Parks/recreation:** General. **Protective services:** Fire safety technology, fire services admin, law enforcement admin. **Visual/performing arts:** Art, commercial/advertising art, studio arts.

Most popular majors. Business/marketing 22%, family/consumer sciences 6%, health sciences 18%, liberal arts 33%, visual/performing arts 6%.

Computing on campus. 90 workstations in library, computer center, student center. Commuter students can connect to campus network. Online library, helpline, wireless network available.

Student life. Freshman orientation: Available. Preregistration for classes offered. One-day held before start of semester. **Activities:** Choral groups,

drama, international student organizations, literary magazine, student government, student newspaper, TV station, African culture club, Hay Motivo, Phi Theta Kappa, legal assistants club, early childhood education club, French club, Haitian student association, criminal justice club.

Student services. Adult student services, career counseling, services for economically disadvantaged, student employment services, financial aid counseling, on-campus daycare, placement for graduates, veterans' counselor, women's services. **Physically disabled:** Services for visually, speech, hearing impaired. **Transfer:** Re-entry adviser, pre-admission transcript evaluation for new students. Transfer adviser, college fairs on campus for students transferring to 4-year colleges.

Contact. E-mail: admissions@ncc.commnet.edu
Phone: (203) 857-7060 Fax: (203) 857-3335
Chagnon William, Director of Enrollment Management, Norwalk Community College, 188 Richards Avenue, Norwalk, CT 06854-1655

Quinebaug Valley Community College
Danielson, Connecticut   **CB member**
www.qvcc.commnet.edu   **CB code: 3716**

- Public 2-year community and technical college
- Commuter campus in large town

General. Founded in 1971. Regionally accredited. Instructional Center in downtown Willimantic. **Enrollment:** 1,819 degree-seeking undergraduates; 282 non-degree-seeking students. **Degrees:** 173 associate awarded. **Location:** 50 miles from Hartford; 25 miles from Providence, Rhode Island. **Calendar:** Semester, limited summer session. **Full-time faculty:** 30 total. **Part-time faculty:** 144 total. **Class size:** 30% < 20, 70% 20-39. **Special facilities:** Art museum, plastics laboratory.

Student profile. Among degree-seeking undergraduates, 5% enrolled in a transfer program, 404 enrolled as first-time, first-year students.

Part-time:	65%	Women:	66%
Out-of-state:	1%	25 or older:	40%

Transfer out. Colleges most students transferred to 2011: Eastern Connecticut State University, University of Connecticut, Worcester State College.

Basis for selection. Open admission. Interview recommended. **Learning Disabled:** Meeting with Coordinator of Learning Disability Services recommended.

2011-2012 Annual costs. Tuition/fees: $3,490; $10,430 out-of-state. Per-credit charge: $129 in-state; $387 out-of-state. Books/supplies: $1,300. Personal expenses: $1,200.

Financial aid. All financial aid based on need. Need-based aid available for part-time students. Work-study available nights, weekends and for part-time students.

Application procedures. Admission: No deadline. $20 fee, may be waived for applicants with need. Admission notification on a rolling basis. **Financial aid:** Closing date 10/1. FAFSA required. Applicants notified on a rolling basis starting 5/1.

Academics. Special study options: Distance learning, double major, dual enrollment of high school students, ESL, independent study, internships. License preparation in real estate. **Credit/placement by examination:** AP, CLEP, institutional tests. 30 credit hours maximum toward associate degree. **Support services:** Learning center, pre-admission summer program, reduced course load, remedial instruction, study skills assistance, tutoring, writing center.

Majors. Business: Accounting, administrative services, business admin, office technology. **Computer sciences:** General. **Education:** Early childhood. **Engineering:** Polymer. **Health services:** Community health services, medical assistant. **Liberal arts:** Arts/sciences. **Visual/performing arts:** Graphic design, photography, studio arts.

Most popular majors. Business/marketing 9%, liberal arts 40%, public administration/social services 33%.

Computing on campus. 115 workstations in library, computer center. Commuter students can connect to campus network. Online course registration, online library, helpline, wireless network available.

Student life. Freshman orientation: Available. Preregistration for classes offered. **Activities:** Student government, medical assisting association, Phi Theta Kappa, Alpha Beta Gamma.

Student services. Adult student services, career counseling, student employment services, financial aid counseling, minority student services, on-campus daycare, placement for graduates, veterans' counselor. **Physically disabled:** Services for visually, speech, hearing impaired. **Transfer:** Re-entry adviser, pre-admission transcript evaluation for new students. Transfer adviser, college fairs on campus for students transferring to 4-year colleges.

Contact. E-mail: admissions@qvcc.commnet.edu
Phone: (860) 412-7380 Fax: (860) 774-7768
Alfred Williams, Director of Enrollment Management, Quinebaug Valley Community College, 742 Upper Maple Street, Danielson, CT 06239-1440

St. Vincent's College
Bridgeport, Connecticut
www.stvincentscollege.edu   **CB code: 3789**

- Private 2-year health science and junior college
- Commuter campus in small city
- SAT or ACT with writing, application essay required

General. Regionally accredited. Majority of students are adult learners. Nursing and radiography programs highly competitive; pre-programs available. **Enrollment:** 69 full-time, degree-seeking students. **Degrees:** 106 associate awarded. **Location:** 55 miles from New York City. **Calendar:** Semester, limited summer session. **Full-time faculty:** 13 total. **Part-time faculty:** 43 total.

Transfer out. Colleges most students transferred to 2011: Southern Connecticut State University.

Basis for selection. High school record and GPA most important, followed by character, talents, work and volunteer experience. **Adult students:** SAT/ACT scores not required if out of high school 1 year(s) or more. **Home schooled:** Transcript of courses and grades, letter of recommendation (nonparent) required.

High school preparation. College-preparatory program required. 16 units required. Required units include English 4, mathematics 2, social studies 2, science 2 and academic electives 6.

2011-2012 Annual costs. Tuition/fees: $13,980. Per-credit charge: $440. Books/supplies: $1,400.

Financial aid. Need-based: Work-study available nights, weekends and for part-time students.

Application procedures. Admission: Priority date 5/1; deadline 7/16 (receipt date). $50 fee, may be waived for applicants with need. Admission notification on a rolling basis beginning on or about 10/1. **Financial aid:** Priority date 3/15; no closing date.

Academics. Special study options: Distance learning, internships. Bachelor's degree programs available on campus. License preparation in nursing, radiology. **Credit/placement by examination:** AP, CLEP, institutional tests. 18 credit hours maximum toward associate degree. **Support services:** Learning center, pre-admission summer program, reduced course load, remedial instruction, study skills assistance, tutoring, writing center.

Majors. Health services: Cardiovascular technology, medical assistant, nursing (RN), radiologic technology/medical imaging.

Computing on campus. 40 workstations in computer center, student center. Commuter students can connect to campus network. Online library, wireless network available.

Student life. Freshman orientation: Mandatory. Preregistration for classes offered. Held each spring and fall. **Activities:** Student government, student newspaper.

Student services. Alcohol/substance abuse counseling, chaplain/spiritual director, career counseling, student employment services, financial aid counseling, health services, personal counseling.

Contact. E-mail: admissions@stvincentscollege.edu
Phone: (203) 576-5513 Fax: (203) 576-5318
Joseph Marrone, Admissions Director, St. Vincent's College, 2800 Main Street, Bridgeport, CT 06606

Three Rivers Community College
Norwich, Connecticut
www.trcc.commnet.edu

CB member
CB code: 3558

◆ Public 2-year community and technical college
◆ Commuter campus in large town

General. Founded in 1969. Regionally accredited. **Enrollment:** 4,779 degree-seeking undergraduates; 375 non-degree-seeking students. **Degrees:** 415 associate awarded. **Location:** 45 miles from Hartford. **Calendar:** Semester, limited summer session. **Full-time faculty:** 74 total; 12% have terminal degrees, 12% minority, 53% women. **Part-time faculty:** 231 total; 57% women. **Class size:** 33% < 20, 64% 20-39, 2% 40-49, less than 1% 50-99. **Special facilities:** Nuclear reactor simulator.

Student profile. Among degree-seeking undergraduates, 1,025 enrolled as first-time, first-year students, 362 transferred in from other institutions.

Part-time:	66%	Asian American:	3%
Out-of-state:	1%	Hispanic American:	13%
Women:	58%	Native American:	1%
African American:	8%	25 or older:	45%

Transfer out. Colleges most students transferred to 2011: Eastern Connecticut State University, University of Connecticut, Central Connecticut State University, Southern Illinois University, Sacred Heart University.

Basis for selection. Open admission, but selective for some programs. Admission for nursing program based on successful performance on ATI-TEAS Exam, completion of prerequisite courses, and 2.7 GPA. **Adult students:** SAT or basic skills tests in math and English required for placement unless student has completed college level math and English course. **Home schooled:** Student may take Ability to Benefit Test if standard documentation requirements are not met.

High school preparation. One unit chemistry, biology, and algebra required for nursing program.

2011-2012 Annual costs. Tuition/fees: $3,490; $10,430 out-of-state. Per-credit charge: $129 in-state; $387 out-of-state. Books/supplies: $1,200. Personal expenses: $1,000.

2010-2011 Financial aid. All financial aid based on need. 504 full-time freshmen applied for aid; 404 were judged to have need; 395 of these received aid. Average need met was 50%. Average scholarship/grant was $2,426; average loan $2,619. 84% of total undergraduate aid awarded as scholarships/grants, 16% as loans/jobs. Need-based aid available for part-time students. Work-study available nights, weekends and for part-time students.

Application procedures. Admission: No deadline. $20 fee, may be waived for applicants with need. Admission notification on a rolling basis beginning on or about 3/30. **Financial aid:** Priority date 5/1; no closing date. FAFSA required. Applicants notified on a rolling basis; must reply within 2 week(s) of notification.

Academics. Special study options: Distance learning, double major, dual enrollment of high school students, ESL, honors, independent study, internships, liberal arts/career combination. License preparation in nursing. **Credit/placement by examination:** AP, CLEP, institutional tests. 45 credit hours maximum toward associate degree. **Support services:** Learning center, pre-admission summer program, remedial instruction, study skills assistance, tutoring, writing center.

Majors. Architecture: Technology. **Business:** Accounting, banking/financial services, business admin, construction management, hospitality admin, office technology, restaurant/food services, tourism/travel. **Communications:** Public relations. **Computer sciences:** General, applications programming, information systems. **Conservation:** Environmental science. **Education:** Early childhood, special ed. **Health services:** Nursing (RN). **Liberal arts:** Arts/sciences, library assistant. **Physical sciences:** General. **Protective services:** Criminal justice, fire safety technology, law enforcement admin, police science. **Work/family studies:** Family studies.

Most popular majors. Business/marketing 13%, engineering/engineering technologies 14%, family/consumer sciences 7%, health sciences 20%, liberal arts 38%.

Computing on campus. 300 workstations in library, computer center, student center. Online course registration, online library, helpline, wireless network available.

Student life. Freshman orientation: Available. Preregistration for classes offered. **Policies:** Student government controls student activity fees. **Activities:** Drama, student government, student newspaper, Spanish-American association, Afro-American association, student chapters of professional organizations, gay-straight alliance, volunteer club, golf club, student nurses association, environmentalists club, senior student ambassadors, veterans organization.

Student services. Career counseling, student employment services, financial aid counseling, on-campus daycare, personal counseling. **Physically disabled:** Services for visually, hearing impaired. **Transfer:** Re-entry adviser for new students. Transfer adviser, college fairs on campus for students transferring to 4-year colleges.

Contact. E-mail: admissions@trcc.commnet.edu
Phone: (860) 383-5260
Dan Zaneski, Director of Admissions, Three Rivers Community College, 574 New London Turnpike, Norwich, CT 06360-6598

Tunxis Community College
Farmington, Connecticut
www.tunxis.commnet.edu

CB member
CB code: 3897

◆ Public 2-year community college
◆ Commuter campus in large town

General. Founded in 1970. Regionally accredited. **Enrollment:** 3,916 degree-seeking undergraduates; 824 non-degree-seeking students. **Degrees:** 341 associate awarded. **ROTC:** Army, Naval, Air Force. **Location:** 15 miles from Hartford. **Calendar:** Semester, limited summer session. **Full-time faculty:** 64 total. **Part-time faculty:** 236 total. **Class size:** 29% < 20, 70% 20-39, less than 1% 40-49. **Special facilities:** Early childhood center, art gallery.

Student profile. Among degree-seeking undergraduates, 805 enrolled as first-time, first-year students.

Part-time:	55%	Women:	56%
Out-of-state:	1%	25 or older:	38%

Transfer out. Colleges most students transferred to 2011: Central Connecticut State University, Charter Oak College, St. Joseph College, University of Connecticut.

Basis for selection. Open admission, but selective for some programs. Special requirements for dental hygiene, drug and alcohol rehabilitation counselor, physical therapist assistant, technological studies: television operations option, dental assisting, criminal justice command institute: supervisory leadership programs, and correction pre-service certification. Interview required of dental hygiene, drug and alcohol rehabilitation counselor majors. **Home schooled:** Interview required. Placement test (ACCUPLACER) required. **Learning Disabled:** Contact Academic Support Center prior to placement testing if accommodations are necessary.

High school preparation. College-preparatory program recommended.

2011-2012 Annual costs. Tuition/fees: $3,490; $10,430 out-of-state. Per-credit charge: $129 in-state; $387 out-of-state. Books/supplies: $1,000. Personal expenses: $4,856.

2010-2011 Financial aid. Need-based: 81% of total undergraduate aid awarded as scholarships/grants, 19% as loans/jobs. Need-based aid available for part-time students. Work-study available nights, weekends and for part-time students. **Non-need-based:** Scholarships awarded for academics, leadership. **Additional information:** Financial aid available to all students showing need. Part-time students encouraged to apply.

Application procedures. Admission: No deadline. $20 fee, may be waived for applicants with need. Admission notification on a rolling basis. Dental hygiene program closing date 1/1, notification by 3/1. **Financial aid:** Priority date 6/1; no closing date. FAFSA required. Applicants notified on a rolling basis starting 3/1.

Academics. Special study options: Cross-registration, distance learning, double major, dual enrollment of high school students, ESL, honors, independent study, internships, liberal arts/career combination. License preparation in dental hygiene, physical therapy. **Credit/placement by examination:** AP, CLEP, institutional tests. 30 credit hours maximum toward associate degree. **Support services:** Learning center, pre-admission summer program, reduced course load, remedial instruction, tutoring.

Majors. Business: Accounting, administrative services, business admin, fashion, finance, office/clerical. **Computer sciences:** Applications programming, computer graphics. **Education:** Early childhood. **Engineering:** Engineering science. **Health services:** Dental hygiene, medical secretary, substance abuse counseling. **Liberal arts:** Arts/sciences. **Visual/performing arts:** General, commercial/advertising art.

Most popular majors. Business/marketing 30%, health sciences 17%, liberal arts 32%.

Computing on campus. 200 workstations in library, computer center. Commuter students can connect to campus network. Wireless network available.

Student life. **Freshman orientation:** Available. Preregistration for classes offered. Held once a week during the month before start of classes. **Activities:** Jazz band, literary magazine, student government, student newspaper, minority student alliance, human services club, criminal justice club, dental hygiene group.

Student services. Career counseling, student employment services, financial aid counseling, health services, minority student services, on-campus daycare, personal counseling, placement for graduates. **Physically disabled:** Services for visually impaired. **Transfer:** Transfer adviser, college fairs on campus for students transferring to 4-year colleges.

Contact. E-mail: tx-admissions@txcc.commnet.edu
Phone: (860) 255-3555 Fax: (860) 255-3559
Peter McCluskey, Director of Admissions, Tunxis Community College,
271 Scott Swamp Road, Farmington, CT 06032-3187

Delaware

Delaware College of Art and Design
Wilmington, Delaware
www.dcad.edu   CB code: 5161

▶ Private 2-year visual arts college
▶ Residential campus in large city
▶ Application essay required

General. Regionally accredited. **Enrollment:** 242 degree-seeking undergraduates. **Degrees:** 76 associate awarded. **Location:** 25 miles from Philadelphia. **Calendar:** Semester, limited summer session. **Full-time faculty:** 7 total; 86% have terminal degrees, 29% women. **Part-time faculty:** 24 total; 75% have terminal degrees, 12% minority, 58% women. **Class size:** 82% < 20, 18% 20-39.

Student profile. Among degree-seeking undergraduates, 120 enrolled as first-time, first-year students.

Part-time:	6%	Hispanic American:	5%
Out-of-state:	61%	Native American:	1%
Women:	63%	International:	2%
African American:	21%	25 or older:	2%
Asian American:	2%	Live on campus:	78%

Transfer out. 85% of students enrolled in the transfer program go on to 4-year colleges. **Colleges most students transferred to 2011:** Pratt Institute, Corcoran College of Art and Design, University of the Arts, School of the Visual Arts, Moore College of Art and Design.

Basis for selection. Academic GPA and talent/ability most important. Standardized test scores are recommended but required. Visual art portfolio required. **Adult students:** SAT/ACT scores not required. **Home schooled:** Transcript of courses and grades, state high school equivalency certificate required.

High school preparation. College-preparatory program recommended. Recommended units include English 4, mathematics 3, social studies 4, history 2, science 3, foreign language 2, computer science 2 and visual/performing arts 4.

2012-2013 Annual costs. Tuition/fees: $21,430. Per-credit charge: $875. Room only: $7,650. Books/supplies: $1,090.

Financial aid. Need-based: Work-study available nights, weekends and for part-time students. **Non-need-based:** Scholarships awarded for academics, art.

Application procedures. Admission: Priority date 3/15; no deadline. $40 fee, may be waived for applicants with need. Admission notification on a rolling basis beginning on or about 12/15. Must reply by May 1 or within 2 week(s) if notified thereafter.

Academics. Credit/placement by examination: AP, CLEP, institutional tests. **Support services:** Pre-admission summer program, reduced course load, study skills assistance, tutoring.

Majors. Communications technology: Animation/special effects. **Visual/performing arts:** Graphic design, illustration, interior design, photography, studio arts.

Computing on campus. Dormitories wired for high-speed internet access. Wireless network available.

Student life. Freshman orientation: Mandatory. Preregistration for classes offered. **Housing:** Guaranteed on-campus for all undergraduates. Coed dorms, apartments available. $350 nonrefundable deposit, deadline 5/1. Apartment-style housing with full kitchen/living room, semi-furnished. **Activities:** Dance, drama, film society, literary magazine.

Student services. Financial aid counseling. **Transfer:** Pre-admission transcript evaluation for new students. Transfer adviser, college fairs on campus for students transferring to 4-year colleges.

Contact. E-mail: admissions@dcad.edu
Phone: (302) 622-8867 ext. 118 Fax: (302) 622-8870
Elizabeth Gatti, Director of Admissions, Delaware College of Art and Design, 600 North Market Street, Wilmington, DE 19801

Delaware Technical and Community College: Dover
Dover, Delaware   CB member
www.dtcc.edu   CB code: 5201

▶ Public 2-year community and technical college
▶ Commuter campus in large town

General. Founded in 1972. Regionally accredited. **Enrollment:** 3,194 degree-seeking undergraduates; 129 non-degree-seeking students. **Degrees:** 311 associate awarded. **Location:** 90 miles from Baltimore, 75 miles from Philadelphia. **Calendar:** Semester, limited summer session. **Full-time faculty:** 80 total. **Part-time faculty:** 160 total. **Class size:** 76% < 20, 24% 20-39.

Student profile. Among degree-seeking undergraduates, 767 enrolled as first-time, first-year students, 134 transferred in from other institutions.

Part-time:	56%	Hispanic American:	5%
Women:	65%	Native American:	1%
African American:	28%	International:	1%
Asian American:	2%	25 or older:	45%

Basis for selection. Open admission, but selective for some programs. Special requirements for health/nursing programs.

2011-2012 Annual costs. Tuition/fees: $3,086; $7,200 out-of-state. Per-credit charge: $114 in-state; $286 out-of-state. Books/supplies: $1,500. Personal expenses: $200.

Financial aid. All financial aid based on need. Need-based aid available for part-time students. Work-study available nights, weekends and for part-time students.

Application procedures. Admission: No deadline. $10 fee, may be waived for applicants with need. Admission notification on a rolling basis. **Financial aid:** Priority date 6/15; no closing date. FAFSA required. Applicants notified on a rolling basis starting 7/1; must reply within 2 week(s) of notification.

Academics. Special study options: Distance learning, dual enrollment of high school students, ESL, independent study, internships, study abroad. License preparation in nursing, paramedic. **Credit/placement by examination:** AP, CLEP, institutional tests. **Support services:** GED preparation and test center, learning center, pre-admission summer program, remedial instruction, study skills assistance, tutoring, writing center.

Majors. Business: Accounting, business admin, e-commerce, entrepreneurial studies, hotel/motel admin, human resources, management information systems, marketing, office management. **Communications:** Digital media. **Computer sciences:** General, networking. **Education:** Bilingual, early childhood, elementary, kindergarten/preschool, mathematics, middle, multi-level teacher. **General:** Business. **Health services:** EMT paramedic, medical assistant, nursing (RN), substance abuse counseling. **Protective services:** Law enforcement admin, police science. **Visual/performing arts:** Commercial/advertising art, interior design, photography.

Most popular majors. Business/marketing 12%, education 6%, engineering/engineering technologies 12%, health sciences 32%, personal/culinary services 6%, public administration/social services 9%, security/protective services 6%, visual/performing arts 7%.

Computing on campus. 423 workstations in library, computer center. Commuter students can connect to campus network. Online course registration, online library, helpline available.

Student life. Freshman orientation: Available. Preregistration for classes offered. **Activities:** Campus ministries, international student organizations, student government.

Athletics. NJCAA. **Intercollegiate:** Lacrosse M, soccer, softball W. **Team name:** Hawks.

Student services. Adult student services, career counseling, student employment services, financial aid counseling, personal counseling, placement for graduates, veterans' counselor. **Physically disabled:** Services for visually, hearing impaired. **Transfer:** Transfer adviser for students transferring to 4-year colleges.

Contact. E-mail: t-admissions@dtcc.edu
Phone: (302) 857-1020 Fax: (302) 739-6169
Maria Harris, Admissions Coordinator, Delaware Technical and
Community College: Dover, 100 Campus Drive, Dover, DE 19901

Contact. E-mail: g-admissions@dtcc.edu
Phone: (302) 856-5400 Fax: (302) 855-5961
Claire MacDonald, Admissions Coordinator, Delaware Technical and
Community College: Owens, PO Box 610, Georgetown, DE 19947

Delaware Technical and Community College: Owens
Georgetown, Delaware
www.dtcc.edu **CB code: 5169**

- Public 2-year community and technical college
- Commuter campus in small town

General. Founded in 1967. Regionally accredited. **Enrollment:** 4,291 degree-seeking undergraduates; 450 non-degree-seeking students. **Degrees:** 460 associate awarded. **Location:** 80 miles from Wilmington. **Calendar:** Semester, limited summer session. **Full-time faculty:** 115 total. **Part-time faculty:** 200 total. **Class size:** 72% < 20, 28% 20-39, less than 1% 50-99. **Special facilities:** Maritime exhibit.

Student profile. Among degree-seeking undergraduates, 1,009 enrolled as first-time, first-year students, 162 transferred in from other institutions.

Part-time:	51%	Hispanic American:	6%
Women:	64%	International:	3%
African American:	19%	25 or older:	40%
Asian American:	2%		

Basis for selection. Open admission, but selective for some programs.

2011-2012 Annual costs. Tuition/fees: $3,086; $7,200 out-of-state. Per-credit charge: $114 in-state; $286 out-of-state. Books/supplies: $1,500. Personal expenses: $200.

Financial aid. All financial aid based on need. Need-based aid available for part-time students. Work-study available nights, weekends and for part-time students.

Application procedures. Admission: No deadline. $10 fee, may be waived for applicants with need. Admission notification on a rolling basis. **Financial aid:** Priority date 6/15; no closing date. FAFSA required. Applicants notified on a rolling basis; must reply within 2 week(s) of notification.

Academics. Special study options: Distance learning, dual enrollment of high school students, ESL, independent study, internships, study abroad. License preparation in nursing, occupational therapy, physical therapy, radiology, real estate. **Credit/placement by examination:** AP, CLEP, institutional tests. **Support services:** GED preparation and test center, learning center, pre-admission summer program, remedial instruction, study skills assistance, tutoring, writing center.

Majors. Biology: General. **Business:** General, accounting, construction management, customer service support, e-commerce, entrepreneurial studies, management information systems, marketing, office management, office technology. **Computer sciences:** General. **Education:** Early childhood, elementary, kindergarten/preschool, mathematics, middle, multi-level teacher. **General:** Business, horticulture, poultry, turf management. **Health services:** Clinical lab assistant, EMT paramedic, medical assistant, nursing (RN), occupational therapy assistant, physical therapy assistant, radiologic technology/medical imaging, respiratory therapy assistant, sonography, veterinary technology/assistant. **Protective services:** Law enforcement admin, police science.

Most popular majors. Business/marketing 19%, education 10%, engineering/engineering technologies 9%, health sciences 35%, public administration/social services 7%.

Computing on campus. 728 workstations in library, computer center, student center. Commuter students can connect to campus network. Online course registration, online library, helpline, wireless network available.

Student life. Freshman orientation: Available. Preregistration for classes offered. **Activities:** Bands, campus ministries, choral groups, drama, international student organizations, music ensembles, musical theater, student government, student newspaper.

Athletics. NJCAA. **Intercollegiate:** Baseball M, golf M. **Team name:** Road Runners.

Student services. Adult student services, career counseling, student employment services, financial aid counseling, personal counseling, placement for graduates, veterans' counselor. **Physically disabled:** Services for visually, hearing impaired. **Transfer:** Transfer adviser for students transferring to 4-year colleges.

Delaware Technical and Community College: Stanton/Wilmington
Newark, Delaware
www.dtcc.edu **CB code: 5204**

- Public 2-year community and technical college
- Commuter campus in small city

General. Founded in 1967. Regionally accredited. Multi-location institution. **Enrollment:** 6,556 degree-seeking undergraduates; 422 non-degree-seeking students. **Degrees:** 579 associate awarded. **ROTC:** Air Force. **Location:** 30 miles from Philadelphia. **Calendar:** Semester, limited summer session. **Full-time faculty:** 175 total. **Part-time faculty:** 360 total. **Class size:** 76% < 20, 23% 20-39, less than 1% 40-49, less than 1% 50-99.

Student profile. Among degree-seeking undergraduates, 1,601 enrolled as first-time, first-year students.

Part-time:	59%	Hispanic American:	8%
Women:	59%	International:	2%
African American:	26%	25 or older:	37%
Asian American:	4%		

Basis for selection. Open admission, but selective for some programs. Admission to health technologies program restricted to state residents. Selective admission to allied health, nursing, and culinary arts programs.

2011-2012 Annual costs. Tuition/fees: $3,086; $7,200 out-of-state. Per-credit charge: $114 in-state; $286 out-of-state. Books/supplies: $1,500. Personal expenses: $200.

Financial aid. All financial aid based on need. Need-based aid available for part-time students. Work-study available nights, weekends and for part-time students.

Application procedures. Admission: No deadline. $10 fee, may be waived for applicants with need. Admission notification on a rolling basis. **Financial aid:** Priority date 6/15; no closing date. FAFSA required. Applicants notified on a rolling basis; must reply within 2 week(s) of notification.

Academics. Special study options: Distance learning, double major, dual enrollment of high school students, ESL, independent study, internships, study abroad. License preparation in dental hygiene, nursing, occupational therapy, paramedic, physical therapy, radiology. **Credit/placement by examination:** AP, CLEP, institutional tests. **Support services:** GED preparation and test center, learning center, pre-admission summer program, remedial instruction, study skills assistance, tutoring, writing center.

Majors. Biology: General. **Business:** General, accounting, business admin, construction management, customer service, customer service support, hotel/motel admin, management information systems, management science, marketing, office management, office technology. **Computer sciences:** General, networking. **Education:** Early childhood, elementary, kindergarten/preschool, mathematics, middle, multi-level teacher. **Engineering:** Operations research. **General:** Business. **Health services:** Cardiovascular technology, dental hygiene, electrocardiograph technology, EMT ambulance attendant, EMT paramedic, histologic technology, medical assistant, nuclear medical technology, nursing (RN), occupational therapy assistant, physical therapy assistant, radiologic technology/medical imaging, respiratory therapy assistant, sonography, substance abuse counseling. **Parks/recreation:** Exercise sciences. **Protective services:** Fire safety technology, fire services admin, firefighting, law enforcement admin, police science.

Most popular majors. Business/marketing 17%, education 6%, engineering/engineering technologies 11%, health sciences 43%, security/protective services 7%.

Computing on campus. 1,139 workstations in library, computer center. Commuter students can connect to campus network. Online course registration, online library, helpline, wireless network available.

Student life. Freshman orientation: Available. Preregistration for classes offered. **Activities:** Dance, student government.

Athletics. NJCAA. **Intercollegiate:** Basketball, soccer M, softball W. **Intramural:** Basketball, football (tackle), softball W, volleyball. **Team name:** Spirit.

Student services. Adult student services, career counseling, student employment services, financial aid counseling, health services, personal counseling, placement for graduates, veterans' counselor, women's services. **Physically disabled:** Services for visually, speech, hearing impaired. **Transfer:** Transfer adviser for students transferring to 4-year colleges.

Contact. E-mail: s-admissions@dtcc.edu
Phone: (302) 454-3954 Fax: (302) 453-3084
Rebecca Bailey-Bell, Admissions Representative, Delaware Technical and Community College: Stanton/Wilmington, 400 Stanton-Christiana Road, Newark, DE 19713

Florida

Anthem College: Orlando
Orlando, Florida
www.anthem.edu

- For-profit 2-year health science and technical college
- Commuter campus in large city

General. Regionally accredited; also accredited by ACICS. **Enrollment:** 323 degree-seeking undergraduates. **Degrees:** 2 associate awarded. **Calendar:** Differs by program. **Full-time faculty:** 19 total. **Part-time faculty:** 9 total.

Basis for selection. Open admission.

Financial aid. Need-based: Work-study available nights, weekends and for part-time students.

Academics. Credit/placement by examination: AP, CLEP.

Majors. Computer sciences: General. **Health services:** Surgical technology.

Contact. Phone: (407) 893-7400 Toll-free number: (888) 326-1985 Fax: (407) 895-1804
Nelson Pagan, Admissions Director, Anthem College: Orlando, 3710 Maguire Boulevard, Orlando, FL 32803

ATI Career Training Center: Ft. Lauderdale
Ft. Lauderdale, Florida
www.aticareertraining.edu   CB code: 2945

- For-profit 2-year technical college
- Small city

General. Accredited by ACCSCT. **Calendar:** Differs by program.

Contact. Phone: (954) 973-4760
2890 NW 62nd Street, Fort Lauderdale, FL 33309-9731

ATI Career Training Center: Oakland Park
Oakland Park, Florida
www.aticareertraining.edu   CB code: 3182

- For-profit 2-year technical college
- Very large city

General. Accredited by ACCSCT. **Calendar:** Differs by program.

Contact. Phone: (954) 563-5899
Executive Director, 3501 NW 9th Avenue, Oakland Park, FL 33309

ATI College of Health
Miami, Florida
www.aticareertraining.edu   CB code: 3183

- For-profit 2-year health science and technical college
- Commuter campus in very large city

General. Accredited by ACCSCT. **Calendar:** Semester.

Annual costs/financial aid. Personal expenses: $2,064. Need-based financial aid available to full-time and part-time students.

Contact. Phone: (305) 628-1000
Director of Admissions, 1395 NW 167th Street, Miami, FL 33169-5745

Brevard Community College
Cocoa, Florida
www.brevardcc.edu
CB member
CB code: 5073

- Public 2-year community college
- Commuter campus in large town

General. Founded in 1960. Regionally accredited. Physical campuses in Cocoa, Melbourne, Palm Bay, Titusville. **Enrollment:** 13,973 degree-seeking undergraduates; 3,944 non-degree-seeking students. **Degrees:** 2,962 associate awarded. **ROTC:** Army, Air Force. **Location:** 50 miles from Orlando. **Calendar:** Semester, extensive summer session. **Full-time faculty:** 215 total; 20% have terminal degrees, 11% minority, 60% women. **Part-time faculty:** 822 total; 9% minority, 51% women. **Class size:** 44% < 20, 56% 20-39, less than 1% 40-49, less than 1% 50-99. **Special facilities:** Planetarium, observatory, performing arts center, multicultural center.

Student profile. Among degree-seeking undergraduates, 71% enrolled in a transfer program, 29% enrolled in a vocational program, 15% already have a bachelor's degree or higher, 3,244 enrolled as first-time, first-year students, 441 transferred in from other institutions.

Part-time:	55%	Women:	57%
Out-of-state:	2%	25 or older:	34%

Transfer out. 62% of students enrolled in the transfer program go on to 4-year colleges. **Colleges most students transferred to 2011:** University of Central Florida.

Basis for selection. Open admission, but selective for some programs. Additional application and requirements for limited access programs such as health sciences, law enforcement and corrections programs. CPT required for admission but scores not used. SAT or ACT may be submitted instead of CPT. California Achievement Tests, Stanford Test of Academic Skills, Test of Adult Basic Education required for health program applicants. **Home schooled:** Transcript of courses and grades required. Affidavit of home school completion required. **Learning Disabled:** Students may self-disclose with Office for Students with Disabilities.

High school preparation. Standard high school or equivalent required for degree seeking students. College prep courses required for students testing below college proficiency.

2011-2012 Annual costs. Tuition/fees: $3,060; $11,220 out-of-state. Books/supplies: $800. Personal expenses: $1,224.

2010-2011 Financial aid. Need-based: 65% of total undergraduate aid awarded as scholarships/grants, 35% as loans/jobs. Need-based aid available for part-time students. Work-study available nights, weekends and for part-time students. **Non-need-based:** Scholarships awarded for academics, athletics.

Application procedures. Admission: No deadline. $30 fee. Admission notification on a rolling basis. **Financial aid:** Priority date 4/15, closing date 6/30. FAFSA required. Applicants notified on a rolling basis starting 6/1; must reply within 2 week(s) of notification.

Academics. Special study options: Accelerated study, cooperative education, cross-registration, distance learning, double major, dual enrollment of high school students, ESL, honors, independent study, internships, study abroad, teacher certification program. Bachelor's degree programs available on campus. License preparation in dental hygiene, nursing, paramedic, radiology, real estate. **Credit/placement by examination:** AP, CLEP, IB, institutional tests. 45 credit hours maximum toward associate degree. **Support services:** Learning center, reduced course load, remedial instruction, study skills assistance, tutoring, writing center.

Majors. Business: Administrative services, business admin, management information systems, office management. **Computer sciences:** Programming, systems analysis. **Education:** Early childhood. **Engineering:** General, computer. **Health services:** Clinical lab technology, dental hygiene, EMT paramedic, medical radiologic technology/radiation therapy, nursing (RN). **Protective services:** Firefighting, police science. **Visual/performing arts:** Commercial/advertising art.

Computing on campus. 1,800 workstations in library, computer center, student center. Commuter students can connect to campus network. Online course registration, online library, helpline, student web hosting, wireless network available.

Student life. Freshman orientation: Mandatory. Preregistration for classes offered. **Activities:** Concert band, choral groups, dance, drama, international student organizations, literary magazine, music ensembles, musical theater, student government, TV station, Student Nurses Association of Florida, Phi Theta Kappa, African American Student Association, Phi Mu Alpha.

Athletics. NJCAA. **Intercollegiate:** Baseball M, basketball, golf M, soccer W, softball W, volleyball W. **Team name:** Titans.

Student services. Adult student services, alcohol/substance abuse counseling, career counseling, services for economically disadvantaged, student employment services, financial aid counseling, minority student services, on-campus daycare, personal counseling, veterans' counselor. **Physically disabled:** Services for visually, speech, hearing impaired. **Transfer:** College fairs on campus for students transferring to 4-year colleges.

Contact. E-mail: Registrar@brevardcc.edu
Phone: (321) 632-1111 Toll-free number: (888) 747-2802
Fax: (321) 433-7357
Michelle Loufek, Associate Director, Collegewide Admissions, Brevard Community College, 1519 Clearlake Road, Cocoa, FL 32922-9987

Broward College
Fort Lauderdale, Florida
www.broward.edu

CB member
CB code: 5074

- Public 2-year community college
- Commuter campus in small city

General. Founded in 1959. Regionally accredited. Multilocation institution (3 main campuses and 6 centers as well as 4 overseas centers). **Enrollment:** 37,774 degree-seeking undergraduates; 4,424 non-degree-seeking students. **Degrees:** 67 bachelor's, 5,404 associate awarded. **ROTC:** Army, Air Force. **Location:** 20 miles from Miami. **Calendar:** Semester, extensive summer session. **Full-time faculty:** 396 total; 31% have terminal degrees, 38% minority, 52% women. **Part-time faculty:** 1,331 total; 21% have terminal degrees, 29% minority, 46% women. **Class size:** 46% < 20, 52% 20-39, less than 1% 40-49, less than 1% 50-99, less than 1% >100. **Special facilities:** Concert hall, planetarium, golf course.

Student profile. Among degree-seeking undergraduates, 94% enrolled in a transfer program, 6% enrolled in a vocational program, 6,186 enrolled as first-time, first-year students, 998 transferred in from other institutions.

Part-time:	65%	Asian American:	3%
Out-of-state:	1%	Hispanic American:	33%
Women:	59%	International:	2%
African American:	34%	25 or older:	39%

Transfer out. Colleges most students transferred to 2011: Florida Atlantic University, Florida International University.

Basis for selection. Open admission, but selective for some programs. Limited access and baccalaureate programs require secondary application process. **Home schooled:** Statement describing home school structure and mission required.

High school preparation. Required units include English 4, mathematics 3, science 2 and foreign language 2.

2011-2012 Annual costs. Tuition/fees: $2,937; $10,590 out-of-state. Books/supplies: $617. Personal expenses: $1,973.

2010-2011 Financial aid. Need-based: 72% of total undergraduate aid awarded as scholarships/grants, 28% as loans/jobs. Need-based aid available for part-time students. Work-study available nights, weekends and for part-time students. **Non-need-based:** Scholarships awarded for academics, athletics, leadership, state residency.

Application procedures. Admission: No deadline. $35 fee, may be waived for applicants with need. Admission notification on a rolling basis beginning on or about 2/15. **Financial aid:** Priority date 4/15; no closing date. FAFSA, institutional form required. Applicants notified on a rolling basis starting 6/1.

Academics. Special study options: Accelerated study, cooperative education, distance learning, dual enrollment of high school students, ESL, exchange student, honors, independent study, internships, study abroad, teacher certification program, weekend college. Bachelor's degree programs available on campus. License preparation in aviation, dental hygiene, nursing, paramedic, physical therapy, radiology, real estate. **Credit/placement by examination:** AP, CLEP, IB, institutional tests. 30 credit hours maximum toward associate degree. **Support services:** Learning center, pre-admission summer program, reduced course load, remedial instruction, study skills assistance, tutoring, writing center.

Majors. Architecture: Landscape. **Biology:** General. **Business:** General, accounting, business admin, finance, hospitality admin, international, international marketing, management science, office/clerical, tourism/travel. **Communications:** Broadcast journalism, journalism. **Computer sciences:** General, computer graphics, computer science, data processing, information systems, programming, systems analysis. **Conservation:** Environmental science.

Education: General, early childhood, elementary, mathematics, music, science, special ed. **Engineering:** General, civil, computer, electrical, software. **English:** English lit. **Foreign languages:** General. **Health services:** Athletic training, cardiovascular technology, clinical lab assistant, clinical lab technology, dental hygiene, EMT paramedic, health care admin, medical radiologic technology/radiation therapy, medical records admin, nuclear medical technology, nursing (RN), ophthalmic lab technology, physical therapy assistant, predental, premedicine, prenursing, prepharmacy, preveterinary, recreational therapy, respiratory therapy technology, sonography. **History:** General. **Human services:** Social work. **Liberal arts:** Arts/sciences. **Math:** General. **Parks/recreation:** General. **Philosophy/religion:** Religion. **Physical sciences:** Chemistry, physics. **Protective services:** Criminal justice, firefighting, security services. **Psychology:** General. **Social sciences:** Anthropology, economics, geography, political science, sociology. **Visual/performing arts:** Art, dramatic, interior design, music, music history. **Work/family studies:** Child care management, food/nutrition.

Computing on campus. 6,532 workstations in library, computer center, student center. Commuter students can connect to campus network. Online course registration, online library, helpline, wireless network available.

Student life. Freshman orientation: Available. Preregistration for classes offered. **Activities:** Bands, choral groups, dance, drama, international student organizations, literary magazine, music ensembles, musical theater, opera, student government, student newspaper, symphony orchestra, Phi Theta Kappa, Phi Beta Lambda, African American student union, American Institute of Architecture Students, Catholic club, chess club, HIV peer educators, film club, French club.

Athletics. NJCAA. **Intercollegiate:** Baseball M, basketball, soccer, softball W, tennis W, volleyball W. **Team name:** Seahawks.

Student services. Adult student services, alcohol/substance abuse counseling, career counseling, student employment services, financial aid counseling, health services, on-campus daycare, personal counseling, placement for graduates, veterans' counselor, women's services. **Physically disabled:** Services for visually, speech, hearing impaired. **Transfer:** College fairs on campus for students transferring to 4-year colleges.

Contact. Phone: (954) 201-7541 Fax: (954) 201-7466
Willie Alexander, Associate Vice President for Student Affairs and Registrar, Broward College, 225 East Las Olas Boulevard, Fort Lauderdale, FL 33301

Brown Mackie College: Miami
Miami, Florida
www.brownmackie.edu

- For-profit 2-year business and career college
- Commuter campus in very large city

General. Accredited by ACICS. **Enrollment:** 953 degree-seeking undergraduates. **Degrees:** 15 bachelor's, 175 associate awarded. **Location:** Downtown. **Calendar:** Quarter, extensive summer session. **Full-time faculty:** 18 total. **Part-time faculty:** 30 total.

Basis for selection. Open admission. **Home schooled:** Transcript of courses and grades, state high school equivalency certificate, interview required.

Financial aid. Need-based: Work-study available nights, weekends and for part-time students.

Application procedures. Admission: No deadline. No application fee.

Academics. Special study options: Double major, independent study, internships, liberal arts/career combination. Bachelor's degree programs available on campus. **Credit/placement by examination:** AP, CLEP, institutional tests. **Support services:** Learning center, remedial instruction, study skills assistance, tutoring.

Majors. Business: Accounting, business admin. **Health services:** Medical secretary. **Protective services:** Law enforcement admin.

Computing on campus. 300 workstations in library, computer center, student center. Commuter students can connect to campus network. Online library, wireless network available.

Student life. Freshman orientation: Mandatory. Preregistration for classes offered. **Activities:** Student newspaper.

Athletics. Team name: Lions.

Student services. Adult student services, alcohol/substance abuse counseling, career counseling, student employment services, financial aid counseling, personal counseling, placement for graduates, veterans' counselor. **Transfer:** Re-entry adviser, pre-admission transcript evaluation for new students. Transfer adviser, college fairs on campus for students transferring to 4-year colleges.

Contact. E-mail: bmmiadm@brownmackie.edu
Phone: (305) 341-6600 Toll-free number: (866) 505-0335
Fax: (305) 341-6649
Greg King, Director of Admissions, Brown Mackie College: Miami, One Herald Plaza, Miami, FL 33132

Chipola College
Marianna, Florida
www.chipola.edu   CB code: 5106

- Public 2-year community college
- Commuter campus in small town

General. Founded in 1947. Regionally accredited. **Enrollment:** 1,587 degree-seeking undergraduates; 752 non-degree-seeking students. **Degrees:** 70 bachelor's, 340 associate awarded. **Location:** 70 miles from Tallahassee. **Calendar:** Semester, limited summer session. **Full-time faculty:** 43 total; 33% have terminal degrees, 7% minority, 60% women. **Part-time faculty:** 111 total; 4% have terminal degrees, 21% minority, 45% women.

Student profile. Among degree-seeking undergraduates, 250 enrolled as first-time, first-year students.

Part-time:	46%	Women:	63%
Out-of-state:	10%	Live on campus:	5%

Transfer out. **Colleges most students transferred to 2011:** Florida State University, University of West Florida, University of Florida, Troy State University-Dothan.

Basis for selection. Open admission, but selective for some programs.

High school preparation. Recommended units include English 4, mathematics 3, social studies 3 and science 3.

2011-2012 Annual costs. Tuition/fees: $3,000; $8,557 out-of-state. Tuition and fees for baccalaureate degree programs are slightly higher. Books/supplies: $800. Personal expenses: $1,500.

Financial aid. **Need-based:** Need-based aid available for part-time students. Work-study available nights, weekends and for part-time students. **Non-need-based:** Scholarships awarded for academics, alumni affiliation, art, athletics, job skills, leadership, minority status, music/drama.

Application procedures. **Admission:** Priority date 8/1; no deadline. No application fee. Admission notification on a rolling basis. **Financial aid:** Priority date 5/1; no closing date. FAFSA, institutional form required. Applicants notified on a rolling basis starting 1/2; must reply within 2 week(s) of notification.

Academics. **Special study options:** Accelerated study, cooperative education, distance learning, dual enrollment of high school students, honors, independent study, internships, liberal arts/career combination, teacher certification program. License preparation in nursing, paramedic. **Credit/placement by examination:** AP, CLEP, IB. 45 credit hours maximum toward associate degree, 45 toward bachelor's. **Support services:** Remedial instruction, study skills assistance, tutoring, writing center.

Majors. **Biology:** General. **Business:** Business admin. **Communications:** Communications/speech/rhetoric, journalism. **Computer sciences:** General, computer science, information systems. **Conservation:** Forest sciences. **Education:** General. **Engineering:** General, computer. **Health services:** Nursing (RN). **History:** General. **Math:** General. **Parks/recreation:** General. **Protective services:** Firefighting, law enforcement admin.

Computing on campus. 150 workstations in library, computer center, student center. Dormitories linked to campus network. Online library available.

Student life. **Freshman orientation:** Mandatory. Preregistration for classes offered. **Housing:** Only men's and women's athletic dorms available. **Activities:** Jazz band, campus ministries, choral groups, dance, drama, musical theater, student government, student newspaper, TV station, black student union, Baptist campus ministry, Fellowship of Christian Athletes.

Athletics. NJCAA. **Intercollegiate:** Baseball M, basketball, softball W. **Team name:** Indians.

Student services. Career counseling. **Physically disabled:** Services for visually, hearing impaired. **Transfer:** Pre-admission transcript evaluation for new students.

Contact. Phone: (850) 526-2761 ext. 2233 Fax: (850) 718-2287
Kathy Rehberg, Registrar, Chipola College, 3094 Indian Circle, Marianna, FL 32446

City College: Casselberry
Casselberry, Florida
www.citycollege.edu

- Private 2-year career college
- Large town
- Interview required

General. Accredited by ACICS. **Enrollment:** 294 degree-seeking undergraduates. **Degrees:** 97 associate awarded. **Calendar:** Quarter, extensive summer session. **Full-time faculty:** 4 total. **Part-time faculty:** 30 total.

Basis for selection. Open admission.

2011-2012 Annual costs. Tuition/fees: $12,375. Per-credit charge: $275.

Financial aid. **Need-based:** Work-study available nights, weekends and for part-time students.

Application procedures. **Admission:** No deadline. $25 fee. **Financial aid:** No deadline.

Academics. **Credit/placement by examination:** AP, CLEP.

Majors. **Business:** Business admin, marketing. **Computer sciences:** General. **Protective services:** Security management.

Contact. Phone: (407) 831-8466 Fax: (407) 831-1147
Abby Freeman, Director of Admissions, City College: Casselberry, 853 Semoran Boulevard 436, Casselberry, FL 32707-5353

City College: Gainesville
Gainesville, Florida
www.citycollege.edu   CB code: 3579

- Private 2-year business and health science college
- Commuter campus in small city

General. Accredited by ACICS. **Enrollment:** 484 degree-seeking undergraduates; 14 non-degree-seeking students. **Degrees:** 19 bachelor's, 114 associate awarded. **Location:** 55 miles from Orlando. **Calendar:** Differs by program. **Full-time faculty:** 3 total. **Part-time faculty:** 41 total.

Student profile. Among degree-seeking undergraduates, 412 enrolled as first-time, first-year students.

Part-time:	27%	25 or older:	93%
Women:	79%		

Basis for selection. Open admission.

2011-2012 Annual costs. Tuition/fees: $12,375. Per-credit charge: $275. Books/supplies: $1,377. Personal expenses: $5,688.

2010-2011 Financial aid. **Need-based:** 54% of total undergraduate aid awarded as scholarships/grants, 46% as loans/jobs. Work-study available nights, weekends and for part-time students.

Application procedures. **Admission:** No deadline. $40 fee.

Academics. **Special study options:** Bachelor's degree programs available on campus. **Credit/placement by examination:** AP, CLEP. **Support services:** Tutoring.

Majors. **Business:** Business admin. **Computer sciences:** General. **Health services:** EMT ambulance attendant. **Protective services:** Criminal justice, law enforcement admin.

Computing on campus. Repair service, wireless network available.

Student life. **Freshman orientation:** Mandatory. Preregistration for classes offered.

Student services. Career counseling, student employment services, financial aid counseling, placement for graduates. **Physically disabled:** Services for hearing impaired.

Contact. E-mail: kbowden@citycollege.edu
Phone: (352) 335-4000 ext. 410 Fax: (352) 335-4303
Kim Bowden, Director of Admissions, City College: Gainesville, 7001 NW 4th Boulevard, Gainesville, FL 32607

City College: Miami
Miami, Florida
www.citycollege.edu   CB code: 3580

- Private 2-year business and health science college
- Large city

General. Accredited by ACICS. **Calendar:** Differs by program.

Annual costs/financial aid. Tuition/fees (2011-2012): $12,375. Need-based financial aid available to full-time and part-time students.

Contact. Phone: (305) 666-9242
Director of Admissions, 9300 South Dadeland Boulevard, Miami, FL 33156

College of Business and Technology: Cutler Bay
Cutler Bay, Florida
www.cbt.edu

- For-profit 2-year technical and career college
- Large city

General. Regionally accredited; also accredited by ACICS. **Enrollment:** 185 degree-seeking undergraduates. **Degrees:** 6 associate awarded. **Calendar:** Semester. **Full-time faculty:** 5 total. **Part-time faculty:** 10 total.

Basis for selection. Open admission.

Financial aid. Need-based: Work-study available nights, weekends and for part-time students.

Application procedures. Admission: $25 fee.

Academics. Credit/placement by examination: AP, CLEP.

Majors. Business: Business admin. **Health services:** Medical records admin, medical secretary.

Contact. E-mail: admissions@cbt.edu
Phone: (305) 273-4499
Ivet Rios, Director of Admissions, College of Business and Technology: Cutler Bay, 19151 South Dixie Highway, #203, Cutler Bay, FL 33157

College of Business and Technology: Flagler
Miami, Florida
www.cbt.edu

- For-profit 2-year junior and technical college
- Commuter campus in very large city
- Interview required

General. Accredited by ACICS. **Enrollment:** 240 degree-seeking undergraduates. **Degrees:** 28 associate awarded. **Calendar:** Semester. **Full-time faculty:** 7 total. **Part-time faculty:** 8 total.

Student profile. Among degree-seeking undergraduates, 60% enrolled in a vocational program.

Transfer out. 70% of students enrolled in the transfer program go on to 4-year colleges.

Basis for selection. Open admission. **Home schooled:** Transcript of courses and grades required.

2011-2012 Annual costs. Tuition per semester credit $414.00; additional required fees vary by program.

2011-2012 Financial aid. All financial aid based on need. 46% of total undergraduate aid awarded as scholarships/grants, 54% as loans/jobs. Need-based aid available for part-time students. Work-study available nights, weekends and for part-time students.

Application procedures. Admission: No deadline. $25 fee. **Financial aid:** No deadline. FAFSA required.

Academics. Special study options: ESL. **Credit/placement by examination:** AP, CLEP. **Support services:** Tutoring.

Majors. Business: Accounting, business admin. **Computer sciences:** LAN/WAN management, networking.

Computing on campus. Online library, repair service, wireless network available.

Student life. Freshman orientation: Mandatory. Preregistration for classes offered.

Student services. Career counseling, student employment services, financial aid counseling, placement for graduates.

Contact. E-mail: admissions@cbt.edu
Phone: (305) 273-4499 ext. 2-204 Fax: (305) 485-4411
Ivet Rios, Director of Admission, College of Business and Technology: Flagler, 8230 West Flagler Street, Miami, FL 33144

College of Business and Technology: Hialeah
Hialeah, Florida
www.cbt.edu

- For-profit 2-year business and technical college
- Large city

General. Accredited by ACICS. **Enrollment:** 263 degree-seeking undergraduates. **Degrees:** 17 associate awarded. **Calendar:** Semester. **Full-time faculty:** 5 total; 40% women. **Part-time faculty:** 20 total; 15% women.

Basis for selection. Open admission.

2011-2012 Annual costs. Tuition per semester credit $414.00; additional required fees vary by program.

2011-2012 Financial aid. Need-based: 50% of total undergraduate aid awarded as scholarships/grants, 50% as loans/jobs. Work-study available nights, weekends and for part-time students.

Application procedures. Admission: $25 fee.

Academics. Credit/placement by examination: AP, CLEP.

Majors. Business: Business admin. **Health services:** Medical records technology.

Contact. E-mail: admissions@cbt.edu
Phone: (786) 693-8842 Toll-free number: (866) 457-0073
Fax: (305) 827-9955
Ivet Rios, Admissions Director, College of Business and Technology: Hialeah, 935 West 49th Street Suite 203, Hialeah, FL 33012-3436

College of Business and Technology: Kendall
Miami, Florida
www.cbt.edu

- For-profit 2-year junior and technical college
- Very large city

General. Accredited by ACICS. **Enrollment:** 121 degree-seeking undergraduates. **Degrees:** 26 associate awarded. **Calendar:** Semester. **Full-time faculty:** 4 total; 50% women. **Part-time faculty:** 9 total; 44% women.

Basis for selection. Open admission.

2011-2012 Annual costs. Tuition per semester credit $414.00; additional required fees vary by program.

2011-2012 Financial aid. Need-based: 48% of total undergraduate aid awarded as scholarships/grants, 52% as loans/jobs. Work-study available nights, weekends and for part-time students.

Academics. Credit/placement by examination: AP, CLEP.

Majors. Business: Accounting, business admin. **Computer sciences:** LAN/WAN management. **Health services:** Medical assistant, office admin. **Visual/performing arts:** Graphic design.

Contact. E-mail: admissions@cbt.edu
Phone: (305) 273-4499
Ivet Rios, Admissions Director, College of Business and Technology: Kendall, 8991 SW 107 Avenue, Miami, FL 33176

College of Central Florida
Ocala, Florida
www.cf.edu
CB code: 5127

◆ Public 2-year community college
◆ Commuter campus in small city

General. Founded in 1957. Regionally accredited. **Enrollment:** 7,777 degree-seeking undergraduates; 1,010 non-degree-seeking students. **Degrees:** 1,088 associate awarded. **Location:** 72 miles from Orlando. **Calendar:** Semester, extensive summer session. **Full-time faculty:** 129 total; 22% have terminal degrees, 14% minority, 55% women. **Part-time faculty:** 463 total; 7% have terminal degrees, 16% minority, 43% women. **Partnerships:** Formal partnership with Emergency One Corporation.

Student profile. Among degree-seeking undergraduates, 27% enrolled in a vocational program, 1,015 enrolled as first-time, first-year students.

Part-time:	57%	Asian American:	1%
Out-of-state:	1%	Hispanic American:	10%
Women:	63%	International:	1%
African American:	11%	25 or older:	34%

Transfer out. Colleges most students transferred to 2011: University of Florida, University of Central Florida, Florida State University.

Basis for selection. Open admission, but selective for some programs. Special requirements for registered nursing, dental assisting, physical therapy assistant, child care, criminal justice, practical nursing, surgical technology programs.

High school preparation. College-preparatory program recommended. Recommended units include English 4, mathematics 3, social studies 3 and science 3.

2011-2012 Annual costs. Tuition/fees: $2,956; $11,143 out-of-state. Reported tuition and fees for baccalaureate degree programs are slightly higher. Books/supplies: $1,300. Personal expenses: $3,386.

2010-2011 Financial aid. Need-based: 56% of total undergraduate aid awarded as scholarships/grants, 44% as loans/jobs. Need-based aid available for part-time students. Work-study available nights, weekends and for part-time students. **Non-need-based:** Scholarships awarded for academics, athletics, minority status, music/drama, state residency.

Application procedures. Admission: Closing date 8/9. $30 fee, may be waived for applicants with need. Admission notification on a rolling basis. **Financial aid:** No deadline. FAFSA required.

Academics. Special study options: Accelerated study, cooperative education, distance learning, dual enrollment of high school students, ESL, honors, independent study, internships, liberal arts/career combination, teacher certification program. Bachelor's degrees available through on-campus University Center. Corporate training available through CFCC Institute. Bachelor's degree programs available on campus. License preparation in dental hygiene, nursing, occupational therapy, paramedic, physical therapy, radiology, real estate. **Credit/placement by examination:** AP, CLEP, IB, institutional tests. 21 credit hours maximum toward associate degree. **Support services:** GED preparation and test center, learning center, pre-admission summer program, reduced course load, remedial instruction, study skills assistance, tutoring, writing center.

Majors. Business: Accounting, accounting technology, business admin, executive assistant, restaurant/food services. **Computer sciences:** System admin. **Education:** Early childhood, elementary. **General:** Business, equestrian studies, horticulture, landscaping. **Health services:** EMT paramedic, licensed practical nurse, medical radiologic technology/radiation therapy, medical records technology, mental health services, nuclear medical technology, nursing (RN), physical therapy assistant. **Liberal arts:** Arts/sciences. **Protective services:** Fire safety technology, law enforcement admin. **Work/family studies:** Child care service.

Most popular majors. Health sciences 13%, liberal arts 76%.

Computing on campus. 2,200 workstations in library, computer center, student center. Online library, helpline, wireless network available.

Student life. Freshman orientation: Mandatory. Preregistration for classes offered. Program held prior to beginning of term; also available online. **Housing:** Apartments available. College Square Student Residence Center owned and operated by Central Florida Community College Foundation near campus. **Activities:** Bands, campus ministries, choral groups, dance, drama, international student organizations, literary magazine, music ensembles, musical theater, student government, student newspaper, symphony orchestra, Afro-student union, Hispanic club, Phi Theta Kappa, Community of Scholars, Brain Bowl, Phi Beta Lambda, gay/straight alliance, peer educators.

Athletics. NJCAA. **Intercollegiate:** Baseball M, basketball, softball W, volleyball W. **Team name:** Patriots.

Student services. Adult student services, career counseling, services for economically disadvantaged, student employment services, financial aid counseling, on-campus daycare, personal counseling, placement for graduates, veterans' counselor. **Physically disabled:** Services for visually, speech, hearing impaired. **Transfer:** Transfer adviser, college fairs on campus for students transferring to 4-year colleges.

Contact. E-mail: admissions@cf.edu
Phone: (352) 873-5801 Fax: (352) 873-5875
Teri Little-Berry, Director of Admissions, College of Central Florida, 3001 SW College Road, Ocala, FL 34474-4415

Daytona State College
Daytona Beach, Florida
www.daytonastate.edu
CB code: 5159

◆ Public 2-year community and technical college
◆ Commuter campus in large city

General. Founded in 1958. Regionally accredited. **Enrollment:** 13,736 degree-seeking undergraduates; 1,065 non-degree-seeking students. **Degrees:** 274 bachelor's, 1,849 associate awarded. **ROTC:** Army, Air Force. **Location:** 90 miles from Jacksonville, 65 miles from Orlando. **Calendar:** Semester, extensive summer session. **Full-time faculty:** 334 total; 31% have terminal degrees, 17% minority, 49% women. **Part-time faculty:** 729 total; 9% have terminal degrees, 20% minority, 51% women. **Special facilities:** Museum of photography.

Student profile. Among degree-seeking undergraduates, 28% enrolled in a transfer program, 35% enrolled in a vocational program, 2% already have a bachelor's degree or higher, 2,020 enrolled as first-time, first-year students, 1,112 transferred in from other institutions.

Part-time:	56%	Women:	61%
Out-of-state:	3%	25 or older:	48%

Transfer out. 74% of students enrolled in the transfer program go on to 4-year colleges. **Colleges most students transferred to 2011:** University of Central Florida, University of Northern Florida, University of Florida, University of Southern Florida, Florida State University.

Basis for selection. Open admission, but selective for some programs. Special requirements for limited access programs including Bachelor's degree program.

2011-2012 Annual costs. Tuition/fees: $3,074; $11,595 out-of-state. Baccalaureate degree program tuition is $3,409 (in-state) and $11,595 (out-of-state) per academic year. Books/supplies: $950. Personal expenses: $1,624.

2010-2011 Financial aid. Need-based: Average scholarship/grant was $1,354; average loan $3,776. 60% of total undergraduate aid awarded as scholarships/grants, 40% as loans/jobs. Need-based aid available for part-time students. Work-study available nights, weekends and for part-time students. **Non-need-based:** Scholarships awarded for academics, athletics, leadership, music/drama, state residency.

Application procedures. Admission: No deadline. No application fee. Admission notification on a rolling basis. **Financial aid:** Priority date 5/15; no closing date. FAFSA required. Applicants notified on a rolling basis starting 3/15.

Academics. Special study options: Cooperative education, distance learning, dual enrollment of high school students, ESL, honors, independent study, internships, liberal arts/career combination, study abroad, teacher certification program, weekend college. Bachelor's degree programs available on campus. License preparation in dental hygiene, nursing, occupational therapy, paramedic, physical therapy, radiology. **Credit/placement by examination:** AP, CLEP, IB, institutional tests. 45 credit hours maximum toward associate degree, 45 toward bachelor's. **Support services:** GED preparation and test

center, learning center, pre-admission summer program, remedial instruction, study skills assistance, tutoring, writing center.

Majors. Architecture: Architecture. **Biology:** General, botany, marine, microbiology, zoology. **Business:** Accounting, accounting technology, banking/financial services, business admin, executive assistant, hospitality admin, management information systems, marketing, operations. **Communications technology:** Photo/film/video. **Computer sciences:** General, applications programming, systems analysis. **Education:** General, Deaf/hearing impaired. **Engineering:** General, computer. **Health services:** Dental hygiene, EMT paramedic, medical radiologic technology/radiation therapy, medical records technology, mental health services, nursing (RN), occupational therapy assistant, physical therapy assistant, respiratory therapy technology, veterinary technology/assistant. **Human services:** Social work. **Liberal arts:** Arts/sciences. **Math:** General, statistics. **Philosophy/religion:** Philosophy. **Physical sciences:** General, astronomy, chemistry, meteorology. **Protective services:** Fire safety technology, law enforcement admin. **Psychology:** General. **Social sciences:** Economics, geography, political science, sociology. **Visual/performing arts:** General, acting, art, dance, graphic design, interior design, music, photography, studio arts. **Work/family studies:** Child care service.

Most popular majors. Liberal arts 77%.

Computing on campus. 3,208 workstations in library, computer center, student center. Online course registration, online library, helpline, wireless network available.

Student life. Freshman orientation: Mandatory. Preregistration for classes offered. **Housing:** Off-campus housing available to international students and athletes. **Activities:** Bands, campus ministries, choral groups, dance, drama, international student organizations, music ensembles, musical theater, opera, student government, student newspaper, symphony orchestra, TV station, Baptist campus ministries, Campus Crusade for Christ, Black Student Nurses Association, Global Friends, human services paraprofessional organization, African American student union.

Athletics. NJCAA. Intercollegiate: Baseball M, basketball, golf W, softball W, swimming. **Intramural:** Basketball, football (tackle), soccer, swimming, table tennis, tennis, volleyball, weight lifting. **Team name:** Falcons.

Student services. Adult student services, alcohol/substance abuse counseling, career counseling, student employment services, financial aid counseling, minority student services, on-campus daycare, personal counseling, placement for graduates, veterans' counselor, women's services. **Physically disabled:** Services for visually, speech, hearing impaired. **Transfer:** Transfer adviser, college fairs on campus for students transferring to 4-year colleges.

Contact. E-mail: admissions@daytonastate.edu
Phone: (386) 506-3059 ext. 3059 Fax: (386) 506-4489
Karen Sanders, Director of Admissions, Daytona State College, Daytona State College Admissions Office, Daytona Beach, FL 32114-2811

Edison State College
Fort Myers, Florida
www.edison.edu

CB member
CB code: 5191

♦ Public 2-year liberal arts college
♦ Commuter campus in very large city

General. Founded in 1961. Regionally accredited. Additional campus sites: Charlotte, Hendry Glades, Collier. **Enrollment:** 12,997 degree-seeking undergraduates. **Degrees:** 249 bachelor's, 2,073 associate awarded. **Location:** 35 miles from Naples, 120 miles from Tampa. **Calendar:** Semester, limited summer session. **Full-time faculty:** 140 total. **Part-time faculty:** 637 total. **Class size:** 31% < 20, 35% 20-39, 3% 40-49, 1% 50-99. **Special facilities:** Performing arts hall, observatory, 3-hole instructional golf course.

Student profile.

Out-of-state:	3%	25 or older:	33%

Transfer out. Colleges most students transferred to 2011: University of South Florida, Florida Gulf Coast University, University of Central Florida, Florida State University, University of Florida.

Basis for selection. Open admission, but selective for some programs. Special requirements for allied health programs. **Home schooled:** Applicants must submit affidavit of completion.

High school preparation. 21 units required. Required units include English 4, mathematics 3, social studies 3 and science 3.

2011-2012 Annual costs. Tuition/fees: $3,074; $11,595 out-of-state. Baccalaureate degree program tuition is $3,409 (in-state) and $11,595 (out-of-state) per academic year. Books/supplies: $626. Personal expenses: $1,060.

Financial aid. Need-based: Need-based aid available for part-time students. Work-study available nights, weekends and for part-time students. **Non-need-based:** Scholarships awarded for art, music/drama.

Application procedures. Admission: Closing date 8/15 (receipt date). $25 fee, may be waived for applicants with need. Application must be submitted on paper. Admission notification on a rolling basis. **Financial aid:** Priority date 5/1; no closing date. FAFSA required. Applicants notified on a rolling basis starting 6/1; must reply within 2 week(s) of notification.

Academics. Special study options: Accelerated study, cooperative education, cross-registration, distance learning, double major, dual enrollment of high school students, ESL, honors, independent study, internships, liberal arts/career combination. License preparation in real estate. **Credit/placement by examination:** AP, CLEP, IB, institutional tests. 45 credit hours maximum toward associate degree. Credit by exam not available. **Support services:** Learning center, reduced course load, remedial instruction, tutoring.

Majors. Business: Accounting, business admin, finance, hospitality admin, international, marketing, tourism/travel. **Computer sciences:** General, programming. **Engineering:** General, civil. **Health services:** Cardiovascular technology, dental hygiene, EMT paramedic, medical radiologic technology/radiation therapy, nursing (RN), respiratory therapy technology. **Liberal arts:** Arts/sciences. **Parks/recreation:** Facilities management. **Protective services:** Criminal justice, firefighting, forensics, law enforcement admin.

Most popular majors. Health sciences 10%, liberal arts 75%.

Computing on campus. 80 workstations in library, computer center. Online course registration, online library, helpline available.

Student life. Freshman orientation: Mandatory. Preregistration for classes offered. **Activities:** Bands, choral groups, drama, music ensembles, student government, Black student union, Intervarsity Christian Fellowship, Young Republicans, environmental club, foreign student club, Young Democrats, Rotaract, Latin American student association, student nurses association.

Student services. Career counseling, services for economically disadvantaged, student employment services, financial aid counseling, minority student services, on-campus daycare, placement for graduates, veterans' counselor. **Physically disabled:** Services for visually, speech, hearing impaired. **Transfer:** Transfer adviser, college fairs on campus for students transferring to 4-year colleges.

Contact. E-mail: registrar@edison.edu
Phone: (239) 489-9121 Toll-free number: (800) 749-2322
Fax: (239) 489-9094
Billee Silva, District Registrar, Edison State College, Box 60210, Fort Myers, FL 33906-6210

Florida Career College: Hialeah
Hialeah, Florida
www.careercollege.edu

♦ For-profit 2-year junior and technical college
♦ Commuter campus in very large city
♦ Interview required

General. Accredited by ACICS. **Enrollment:** 1,110 degree-seeking undergraduates. **Degrees:** 5 bachelor's, 70 associate awarded. **Calendar:** Quarter, limited summer session. **Full-time faculty:** 16 total. **Part-time faculty:** 18 total. **Class size:** 69% < 20, 31% 20-39.

Basis for selection. Open admission.

2011-2012 Annual costs. Tuition ranges from $315 - $485 per credit hour, leading to a diploma, associate or bachelor's degree. Books/supplies: $1,000.

Financial aid. Need-based: Work-study available nights, weekends and for part-time students.

Application procedures. Admission: No deadline. $100 fee. Application must be submitted on paper. Admission notification on a rolling basis.

Academics. Special study options: Accelerated study, internships. **Credit/placement by examination:** AP, CLEP. Up to 50% of program credits can be earned through a combination of transfer and/or credit by examination. **Support services:** Learning center, tutoring.

Majors. Computer sciences: Programming, webmaster. **Engineering:** Computer. **Health services:** Office admin.

Computing on campus. 250 workstations in library, computer center. Commuter students can connect to campus network. Online course registration, online library available.

Student life. Freshman orientation: Available. Preregistration for classes offered.

Student services. Financial aid counseling, placement for graduates.

Contact. Phone: (305) 825-3231 Fax: (305) 825-3436
Luis Rodriguez, Director of Admissions, Florida Career College: Hialeah, 3750 West 18th Avenue, Hialeah, FL 33012

Florida Career College: Miami
Miami, Florida
www.careercollege.edu
CB code: 3581

- For-profit 2-year business and technical college
- Large city

General. Accredited by ACICS. **Enrollment:** 1,162 degree-seeking undergraduates. **Degrees:** 16 bachelor's, 75 associate awarded. **Calendar:** Differs by program. **Full-time faculty:** 13 total. **Part-time faculty:** 16 total.

Basis for selection. Open admission.

2011-2012 Annual costs. Tuition ranges from $315 - $485 per credit hour, leading to a diploma, associate or bachelor's degree.

Financial aid. Need-based: Work-study available nights, weekends and for part-time students.

Application procedures. Admission: No deadline. $100 fee.

Academics. Credit/placement by examination: AP, CLEP.

Majors. Computer sciences: General, webmaster. **Engineering:** Computer. **Health services:** Office admin.

Contact. Phone: (305) 553-6065
Heidi Cruz, Director of Admissions, Florida Career College: Miami, 1321 SW 107 Avenue, Suite 201B, Miami, FL 3317-521

Florida Career College: Pembroke Pines
Pembroke Pines, Florida
www.careercollege.edu

- For-profit 2-year business and technical college
- Small city

General. Accredited by ACICS. **Enrollment:** 1,271 degree-seeking undergraduates. **Degrees:** 23 bachelor's, 69 associate awarded. **Calendar:** Differs by program. **Full-time faculty:** 17 total. **Part-time faculty:** 20 total.

Basis for selection. Open admission.

2011-2012 Annual costs. Tuition ranges from $315 - $485 per credit hour, leading to a diploma, associate or bachelor's degree.

Financial aid. Need-based: Work-study available nights, weekends and for part-time students.

Application procedures. Admission: No deadline. $100 fee.

Academics. Credit/placement by examination: AP, CLEP.

Majors. Computer sciences: Programming, webmaster. **Engineering:** Computer. **Health services:** Office admin.

Contact. E-mail: info@careercollege.edu
Phone: (954) 965-7272 Fax: (954) 983-2707
Jarad Held, Director of Admissions, Florida Career College: Pembroke Pines, 7891 Pines Boulevard, Pembroke Pines, FL 33024

Florida Career College: West Palm Beach
West Palm Beach, Florida
www.careercollege.edu

- For-profit 2-year technical college
- Commuter campus in small city

General. Accredited by ACICS. **Enrollment:** 1,474 degree-seeking undergraduates. **Degrees:** 12 bachelor's, 45 associate awarded. **Calendar:** Differs by program. **Full-time faculty:** 16 total. **Part-time faculty:** 17 total.

Basis for selection. Open admission.

2011-2012 Annual costs. Tuition ranges from $315 - $485 per credit hour, leading to a diploma, associate or bachelor's degree.

Financial aid. Need-based: Work-study available nights, weekends and for part-time students.

Application procedures. Admission: No deadline. $100 fee.

Academics. Credit/placement by examination: AP, CLEP.

Majors. Computer sciences: General. **Engineering:** Computer. **Health services:** Office admin.

Contact. Phone: (561) 689-0550 Toll-free number: (888) 852-7272
Fax: (561) 689-0739
Sandeep Kaup, Director of Admissions, Florida Career College: West Palm Beach, 6058 Okeechobee Boulevard, West Palm Beach, FL 33417

Florida College of Natural Health: Bradenton
Bradenton, Florida
www.fcnh.com
CB code: 5024

- For-profit 2-year health science and career college
- Commuter campus in small city

General. Accredited by ACCSC. **Enrollment:** 55 degree-seeking undergraduates. **Degrees:** 30 associate awarded. **Location:** 40 miles from Tampa. **Calendar:** Differs by program, extensive summer session. **Full-time faculty:** 1 total. **Part-time faculty:** 13 total.

Basis for selection. Open admission, but selective for some programs.

2011-2012 Annual costs. Tuition for diploma programs range from $5,166 to $17,480 and programs leading to an associate degree range from $21,600-$22,986. $50 registration fee, books and supplies are not included. Books/supplies: $2,430. Personal expenses: $4,620.

Financial aid. All financial aid based on need. Work-study available nights, weekends and for part-time students.

Application procedures. Admission: No deadline. $50 fee. Admission notification on a rolling basis. **Financial aid:** No deadline. FAFSA required. Applicants notified on a rolling basis.

Academics. Credit/placement by examination: AP, CLEP. **Support services:** Tutoring.

Majors. Health services: Massage therapy.

Computing on campus. 2 workstations in library.

Student life. Freshman orientation: Mandatory. Preregistration for classes offered.

Student services. Career counseling, financial aid counseling, placement for graduates.

Contact. E-mail: sarasota@fcnh.com
Phone: (941) 744-1244 Toll-free number: (800) 966-7117
Fax: (941) 744-1242
Veronica Fulton, Admissions, Florida College of Natural Health: Bradenton, 616 67th Street Circle East, Bradenton, FL 34208

Florida College of Natural Health: Maitland
Maitland, Florida
www.fcnh.com
CB code: 5239

- For-profit 2-year health science and junior college
- Large town
- SAT or ACT required

General. Accredited by ACCSC. **Enrollment:** 375 degree-seeking undergraduates. **Degrees:** 77 associate awarded. **Calendar:** Differs by program. **Full-time faculty:** 4 total. **Part-time faculty:** 17 total.

Basis for selection. Passing score on OLSAT entrance exam or 800 SAT (exclusive of Writing) or 17 ACT required of degree-seeking applicants.

2011-2012 Annual costs. Tuition for diploma programs range from $5,166 to $17,480 and programs leading to an associate degree range from $21,600-$22,986. $50 registration fee, books and supplies are not included. Books/supplies: $2,379. Personal expenses: $2,464.

Financial aid. All financial aid based on need. Work-study available nights, weekends and for part-time students.

Application procedures. Admission: No deadline. No application fee. Admission notification on a rolling basis. **Financial aid:** No deadline. FAFSA required. Applicants notified on a rolling basis.

Academics. Credit/placement by examination: AP, CLEP.

Majors. Health services: Massage therapy.

Contact. E-mail: orlando@fcnh.com
Phone: (407) 261-0319 Toll-free number: (800) 393-7337
Fax: (407) 261-0342
Leonore Barfield, Director of Marketing, Florida College of Natural Health: Maitland, 2600 Lake Lucien Drive; Suite 240, Maitland, FL 32751

Florida College of Natural Health: Miami
Miami, Florida
www.fcnh.com   CB code: 5231

♦ For-profit 2-year branch campus and community college
♦ Very large city

General. Accredited by ACCSCT. **Calendar:** Differs by program.

Annual costs/financial aid. Tuition for diploma programs range from $5,166 to $17,480 and programs leading to an associate degree range from $21,600-$22,986. $50 registration fee, books and supplies are not included. Books/supplies: $2,379. Personal expenses: $2,464. Need-based financial aid available for full-time students.

Contact. Phone: (305) 597-9599
7925 Northwest 12th Street, Suite 201, Miami, FL 33126

Florida College of Natural Health: Pompano Beach
Pompano Beach, Florida
www.fcnh.com   CB code: 5238

♦ For-profit 2-year junior college
♦ Very large city

General. Accredited by ACCSCT. **Calendar:** Differs by program.

Annual costs/financial aid. Tuition for diploma programs range from $5,166 to $17,480 and programs leading to an associate degree range from $21,600-$22,986. $50 registration fee, books and supplies are not included. Books/supplies: $2,379. Need-based financial aid available for full-time students.

Contact. Phone: (954) 975-6400
Chief Operating Officer, 2001 West Sample Road, Suite 100, Pompano Beach, FL 33064

Florida Gateway College
Lake City, Florida   CB member
www.fgc.edu   CB code: 5377

♦ Public 2-year community college
♦ Commuter campus in large town

General. Founded in 1947. Regionally accredited. **Enrollment:** 2,371 degree-seeking undergraduates; 826 non-degree-seeking students. **Degrees:** 378 associate awarded. **Location:** 60 miles from Jacksonville. **Calendar:** Semester, limited summer session. **Full-time faculty:** 60 total; 25% have terminal degrees, 13% minority, 53% women. **Part-time faculty:** 243 total; 13% minority, 44% women. **Class size:** 60% < 20, 40% 20-39, less than 1% 50-99. **Special facilities:** Performing arts center, arboretum. **Partnerships:**

Formal partnership with The Employ Florida Banner Center for Logistics and Distribution.

Student profile. Among degree-seeking undergraduates, 57% enrolled in a transfer program, 43% enrolled in a vocational program, 1% already have a bachelor's degree or higher, 381 enrolled as first-time, first-year students.

Part-time:	57%	Asian American:	1%
Out-of-state:	1%	Hispanic American:	3%
Women:	67%	25 or older:	38%
African American:	13%		

Transfer out. Colleges most students transferred to 2011: University of Florida, Florida State University, University of North Florida.

Basis for selection. Open admission, but selective for some programs. Limited admission to allied health and golf course management programs. Interview recommended for most allied health programs and all golf course operations programs. **Home schooled:** Must supply home school affidavits and/or a GED transcript, and graduation date.

High school preparation. 13 units recommended. Recommended units include English 4, mathematics 3, social studies 3 and science 3.

2011-2012 Annual costs. Tuition/fees: $2,923; $11,169 out-of-state. Books/supplies: $1,000.

Financial aid. Need-based: Need-based aid available for part-time students. Work-study available nights, weekends and for part-time students. **Non-need-based:** Scholarships awarded for academics, leadership, minority status, music/drama, state residency.

Application procedures. Admission: Priority date 8/1; deadline 8/12 (receipt date). No application fee. Application must be submitted on paper. Admission notification on a rolling basis. Some technical programs reach maximum enrollment and close prior to 8/1. **Financial aid:** Priority date 6/1; no closing date. FAFSA, institutional form required. Applicants notified on a rolling basis starting 6/1; must reply within 2 week(s) of notification.

Academics. Special study options: Accelerated study, distance learning, dual enrollment of high school students, independent study, teacher certification program. Bachelor's degree programs available on campus. License preparation in nursing, paramedic, physical therapy. **Credit/placement by examination:** AP, CLEP, IB, institutional tests. 45 credit hours maximum toward associate degree. Restrictions on credits awarded on exams administered prior to July 1, 2001. **Support services:** GED test center, learning center, reduced course load, remedial instruction, study skills assistance, tutoring.

Majors. Business: Business admin, office management, office/clerical. **Computer sciences:** General, computer graphics, programming. **Education:** Early childhood. **General:** Landscaping. **Health services:** EMT paramedic, nursing (RN), physical therapy assistant, veterinary technology/assistant. **Liberal arts:** Arts/sciences. **Parks/recreation:** Golf management. **Protective services:** Law enforcement admin. **Visual/performing arts:** Graphic design.

Most popular majors. Health sciences 26%, liberal arts 66%.

Computing on campus. 320 workstations in library, computer center, student center. Online course registration, online library, wireless network available.

Student life. Freshman orientation: Mandatory. Preregistration for classes offered. **Activities:** Bands, choral groups, drama, literary magazine, music ensembles, student government, TV station, Florida Turf Grass Association, Florida Student Nurses Association, Phi Theta Kappa.

Athletics. Intramural: Basketball, football (non-tackle), soccer. **Team name:** Timberwolves.

Student services. Alcohol/substance abuse counseling, career counseling, student employment services, financial aid counseling, personal counseling, veterans' counselor. **Physically disabled:** Services for visually, speech, hearing impaired. **Transfer:** Transfer adviser, college fairs on campus for students transferring to 4-year colleges.

Contact. E-mail: admissions@fgc.edu
Phone: (386) 754-4287 Fax: (386) 754-4787
Sandra Johnston, Director Enrollment Management, Florida Gateway College, 149 SE College Place, Lake City, FL 32025-2007

Florida Keys Community College
Key West, Florida
www.fkcc.edu   CB code: 5236

♦ Public 2-year nursing and community college
♦ Commuter campus in large town

General. Founded in 1965. Regionally accredited. Branch campuses in Tavernier and Marathon. **Enrollment:** 1,284 degree-seeking undergraduates. **Degrees:** 163 associate awarded. **Location:** 150 miles from Miami. **Calendar:** Semester, limited summer session. **Full-time faculty:** 28 total. **Part-time faculty:** 95 total. **Special facilities:** Fine arts center and theater, ceramics studio, marine propulsion technology center, welding lab, aquatic center, diving program underwater education complex, hyperbaric chamber.

Student profile.

Out-of-state: 1%   25 or older: 47%

Transfer out. Colleges most students transferred to 2011: University of Central Florida, Florida International University, University of Florida, Florida State University, St. Leo's College.

Basis for selection. Open admission, but selective for some programs. Special application, placement examination, physical examination, and interview required for nursing technology applicants. Admission based on objective points system.

High school preparation. Recommended units include English 4, mathematics 3, social studies 3 and science 3.

2011-2012 Annual costs. Tuition/fees: $3,074; $11,595 out-of-state. Books/supplies: $2,300. Personal expenses: $1,000.

Financial aid. Need-based: Need-based aid available for part-time students. Work-study available nights, weekends and for part-time students. **Non-need-based:** Scholarships awarded for academics, art, leadership, minority status.

Application procedures. Admission: No deadline. $30 fee. Admission notification on a rolling basis. **Financial aid:** Priority date 5/1; no closing date. FAFSA, institutional form required. Applicants notified on a rolling basis starting 6/15; must reply within 2 week(s) of notification.

Academics. Special study options: Distance learning, double major, dual enrollment of high school students, ESL, independent study. Bachelor's degree programs available on campus. License preparation in nursing, paramedic. **Credit/placement by examination:** AP, CLEP, IB, institutional tests. 45 credit hours maximum toward associate degree. **Support services:** Learning center, reduced course load, remedial instruction, tutoring, writing center.

Majors. Biology: Marine. **Business:** Business admin. **Computer sciences:** General, programming. **Health services:** Nursing (RN).

Computing on campus. 130 workstations in library, computer center, student center. Online course registration, online library, helpline, wireless network available.

Student life. Freshman orientation: Available. Preregistration for classes offered. **Activities:** Choral groups, student government, student newspaper, nurses pinning club, Florida nurses student association, Mud-Pi ceramics club, Phi Theta Kappa, cyber league, photo guild club, wreckers club, propmasters club.

Athletics. Team name: Wreckers.

Student services. Adult student services, career counseling, student employment services, financial aid counseling, placement for graduates, veterans' counselor. **Physically disabled:** Services for visually, speech, hearing impaired. **Transfer:** Pre-admission transcript evaluation for new students. Transfer adviser, college fairs on campus for students transferring to 4-year colleges.

Contact. E-mail: cheryl.malsheimer@fkcc.edu
Phone: (305) 809-3188 Fax: (305) 292-5155
Cheryl Malsheimer, Director of Enrollment Services, Florida Keys Community College, 5901 College Road, Key West, FL 33040

Florida National College
Hialeah, Florida
www.fnc.edu   **CB code: 2057**

▸ For-profit 2-year junior college
▸ Commuter campus in very large city
▸ Interview required

General. Regionally accredited. **Enrollment:** 2,616 degree-seeking undergraduates; 128 non-degree-seeking students. **Degrees:** 31 bachelor's, 401 associate awarded. **Location:** 12 miles from Miami. **Calendar:** Semester. **Full-time faculty:** 84 total; 12% have terminal degrees, 43% women. **Part-time faculty:** 63 total; 14% have terminal degrees, 44% women. **Class size:** 100% 20-39.

Student profile. Among degree-seeking undergraduates, 30% enrolled in a vocational program, 565 enrolled as first-time, first-year students.

Part-time:	26%	Hispanic American:	88%
Women:	70%	International:	4%
African American:	6%	25 or older:	65%

Transfer out. Colleges most students transferred to 2011: Nova Southeastern University, Florida International University, American Intercontinental University, Miami Institute of Psychology, Carlos Albizu University.

Basis for selection. Open admission, but selective for some programs. Test of Essential Academic Skills (TEAS) for Nursing Program, Radiology Technology, and Diagnostic Medical Sonographer Teachnology.

2011-2012 Annual costs. Tuition/fees: $17,100. Per-credit charge: $525. Books/supplies: $860.

2010-2011 Financial aid. All financial aid based on need. 452 full-time freshmen applied for aid; 447 were judged to have need; 447 of these received aid. Average scholarship/grant was $4,500; average loan $3,500. 33% of total undergraduate aid awarded as scholarships/grants, 67% as loans/jobs. Need-based aid available for part-time students. Work-study available nights, weekends and for part-time students.

Application procedures. Admission: No deadline. No application fee. Admission notification on a rolling basis. **Financial aid:** No deadline. FAFSA, institutional form required. Applicants notified on a rolling basis.

Academics. Special study options: Accelerated study, cooperative education, distance learning, dual enrollment of high school students, ESL, independent study, internships. Bachelor's degree programs available on campus. License preparation in nursing, radiology. **Credit/placement by examination:** AP, CLEP, institutional tests. 9 credit hours maximum toward associate degree, 9 toward bachelor's. **Support services:** GED preparation, reduced course load, remedial instruction, study skills assistance, tutoring, writing center.

Majors. Business: Accounting, business admin, hospitality admin, tourism promotion, tourism/travel. **Computer sciences:** General, programming, system admin, web page design. **Education:** General. **Health services:** Dental hygiene, dental lab technology, health services admin, medical assistant, radiologic technology/medical imaging, respiratory therapy technology, sonography. **Human services:** General. **Protective services:** Criminal justice.

Most popular majors. Business/marketing 23%, health sciences 54%, legal studies 15%, security/protective services 15%.

Computing on campus. Online library available.

Student life. Freshman orientation: Mandatory. Preregistration for classes offered. **Activities:** Student government.

Student services. Career counseling, student employment services, financial aid counseling, placement for graduates. **Transfer:** Re-entry adviser, pre-admission transcript evaluation for new students.

Contact. E-mail: admissions@fnc.edu
Phone: (305) 821-3333 Fax: (305) 362-0595
Guillermo Araya, Admissions Coordinator, Florida National College, 4425 West Jose Regueiro 20th Avenue, Hialeah, FL 33012

Florida State College at Jacksonville
Jacksonville, Florida
www.fscj.edu   **CB code: 5232**

▸ Public 2-year community and junior college
▸ Commuter campus in very large city

General. Founded in 1963. Regionally accredited. 4 campus locations, 6 center sites, online campus. **Enrollment:** 27,950 degree-seeking undergraduates; 2,913 non-degree-seeking students. **Degrees:** 205 bachelor's, 5,418 associate awarded. **ROTC:** Army, Naval. **Calendar:** Semester, extensive summer session. **Full-time faculty:** 407 total; 29% have terminal degrees, 26% minority, 58% women. **Part-time faculty:** 798 total; 29% minority, 52% women. **Class size:** 51% < 20, 49% 20-39, less than 1% 40-49, less than 1% 50-99. **Special facilities:** Performing arts theater, criminal justice center, advanced technology center. **Partnerships:** Formal partnerships with Florida Construction Institute, Florida Home Builders Association, Navy Contracts, GM/ASEP contracts for non-credit (Education-To-Go), NE Florida Credit Union Association, Aviation Professional/Pilot Contract, Cisco Agreement with 2 schools in midwest.

Student profile. Among degree-seeking undergraduates, 70% enrolled in a transfer program, 30% enrolled in a vocational program, 1% already have a bachelor's degree or higher, 4,864 enrolled as first-time, first-year students, 1,071 transferred in from other institutions.

Part-time:	63%	Asian American:	3%
Out-of-state:	6%	Hispanic American:	6%
Women:	60%	International:	1%
African American:	28%	25 or older:	46%

Transfer out. Colleges most students transferred to 2011: University of North Florida, Jacksonville University, University of Florida, Florida State University, Central Florida University.

Basis for selection. Open admission, but selective for some programs. Special requirements for some associate of science programs. Additional program application may be required. SAT/ACT, or the Postsecondary Education Readiness Test (PERT) required for placement. **Home schooled:** Transcript of courses and grades required. Home school letter form required. **Learning Disabled:** Medical documentation required.

High school preparation. 24 units recommended. Recommended units include English 4, mathematics 3, social studies 3, science 3 (laboratory 2), foreign language 2 and academic electives 9. One algebra strongly recommended. Social studies should be .5 U.S. government, .5 economics, 1 U.S. history, 1 world history.

2011-2012 Annual costs. Tuition/fees: $2,940; $11,420 out-of-state. Baccalaureate degree program tuition is $3,224 (in-state) and $11,420 (out-of-state) per academic year. Books/supplies: $900. Personal expenses: $812.

2011-2012 Financial aid. Need-based: 72% of total undergraduate aid awarded as scholarships/grants, 28% as loans/jobs. Need-based aid available for part-time students. Work-study available nights, weekends and for part-time students. **Non-need-based:** Scholarships awarded for academics, alumni affiliation, art, athletics, job skills, leadership, minority status, music/drama.

Application procedures. Admission: Priority date 7/27; no deadline. $25 fee. Admission notification on a rolling basis. **Financial aid:** Priority date 8/1; no closing date. FAFSA, institutional form required.

Academics. Special study options: Accelerated study, cooperative education, cross-registration, distance learning, double major, dual enrollment of high school students, ESL, exchange student, external degree, honors, independent study, internships, liberal arts/career combination, study abroad, teacher certification program, weekend college. Bachelor's degree programs available on campus. License preparation in aviation, dental hygiene, nursing, paramedic, physical therapy, radiology, real estate. **Credit/placement by examination:** AP, CLEP, institutional tests. 45 credit hours maximum toward associate degree. **Support services:** GED preparation and test center, learning center, reduced course load, remedial instruction, study skills assistance, tutoring.

Majors. Architecture: Environmental design, interior. **Biology:** Biomedical sciences. **Business:** Accounting, administrative services, banking/financial services, business admin, fashion, financial planning, hospitality admin, insurance, management information systems, office management, office technology, sales/distribution, tourism/travel. **Communications technology:** Graphic/printing. **Computer sciences:** General, applications programming, computer graphics, data processing, information systems, networking, programming, systems analysis. **Education:** Elementary. **Engineering:** General, civil, computer. **Foreign languages:** Sign language interpretation. **Health services:** Clinical lab technology, dental hygiene, EMT paramedic, medical radiologic technology/radiation therapy, medical records technology, medical secretary, nursing (RN), physical therapy assistant, respiratory therapy technology, sonography, substance abuse counseling. **Protective services:** Criminal justice, fire safety technology, fire services admin, firefighting, law enforcement admin. **Visual/performing arts:** General, cinematography, commercial/advertising art, design, dramatic, interior design, theater design. **Work/family studies:** Clothing/textiles.

Most popular majors. Health sciences 12%, liberal arts 76%.

Computing on campus. 2,500 workstations in library, computer center, student center. Commuter students can connect to campus network. Online course registration, online library, helpline, repair service, student web hosting, wireless network available.

Student life. Freshman orientation: Mandatory. Preregistration for classes offered. **Housing:** Housing assistance available to qualified Talent Grant students. **Activities:** Bands, choral groups, dance, drama, international student organizations, literary magazine, music ensembles, musical theater, radio station, student government, student newspaper, TV station, Phi Theta Kappa, gospel and concert choir, Spanish club, diversity club, German student association.

Athletics. NJCAA. **Intercollegiate:** Baseball M, basketball, softball W, tennis W, volleyball W. **Intramural:** Badminton, basketball, bowling, football (non-tackle), golf, soccer, softball, table tennis, tennis, volleyball. **Team name:** Stars.

Student services. Adult student services, alcohol/substance abuse counseling, career counseling, services for economically disadvantaged, student employment services, financial aid counseling, legal services, minority student services, on-campus daycare, personal counseling, placement for graduates, veterans' counselor, women's services. **Physically disabled:** Services for visually, speech, hearing impaired. **Transfer:** Transfer adviser, college fairs on campus for students transferring to 4-year colleges.

Contact. E-mail: justask@fscj.edu
Phone: (904) 359-5433 Fax: (904) 632-5105
Rosalind Dexter-Harris, Director of Admissions, Florida State College at Jacksonville, 501 West State Street, Jacksonville, FL 32202

Florida Technical College: Deland
Deland, Florida
www.flatech.edu   **CB code: 3589**

- For-profit 2-year junior and technical college
- Small city

General. Accredited by ACICS. **Location:** 30 miles from Orlando, 20 miles from Daytona Beach. **Calendar:** Quarter.

Annual costs/financial aid. Need-based financial aid available to full-time and part-time students.

Contact. Phone: (386) 734-3303
Director of Admissions, 1199 South Woodland Boulevard, Deland, FL 32720

Florida Technical College: Lakeland
Lakeland, Florida
www.flatech.edu   **CB code: 3432**

- For-profit 2-year business and junior college
- Large town

General. Accredited by ACICS. **Calendar:** Differs by program.

Annual costs/financial aid. Need-based financial aid available to full-time and part-time students.

Contact. Phone: (863) 967-8822
School Director, 4715 South Florida Avenue, Lakeland, FL 33813

Florida Technical College: Orlando
Orlando, Florida
www.flatech.edu   **CB code: 3588**

- For-profit 2-year junior and technical college
- Commuter campus in large city

General. Accredited by ACICS. **Location:** 13 miles from downtown. **Calendar:** Differs by program.

Annual costs/financial aid. Need-based financial aid available to full-time and part-time students.

Contact. Phone: (407) 447-7300
Director, 12689 Challenger Parkway, #130, Orlando, FL 32826-2707

Fortis College: Orange Park
Orange Park, Florida
www.fortis.edu

- For-profit 2-year business and health science college
- Large city

General. Regionally accredited. **Calendar:** Continuous.

Contact. Phone: (904) 269-7086
560 Wells Road, Orange Park, FL 32073

Fortis College: Tampa
Tampa, Florida
www.fortis.edu
CB code: 3448

▶ For-profit 2-year technical and career college
▶ Commuter campus in large city

General. Regionally accredited. **Location:** 13 miles from Tampa. **Calendar:** Quarter.

Annual costs/financial aid. Books/supplies: $1,200. Personal expenses: $1,863.

Contact. Phone: (813) 620-1446
Director of Admissions, Director of Admissions, Tampa, FL 33619-1290

Fortis College: Winter Park
Winter Park, Florida
www.fortis.edu

▶ For-profit 2-year technical college
▶ Very large city

General. Regionally accredited. **Calendar:** Differs by program.

Annual costs/financial aid. Need-based financial aid available for full-time students.

Contact. Phone: (407) 843-3984
Director, 1573 West Fairbanks Avenue, Winter Park, FL 32789

Golf Academy of America: Orlando
Altamonte Springs, Florida
www.golfacademy.edu

▶ For-profit 2-year community college
▶ Large town

General. Accredited by ACICS. **Enrollment:** 202 degree-seeking undergraduates. **Degrees:** 184 associate awarded. **Calendar:** Semester. **Full-time faculty:** 3 total. **Part-time faculty:** 12 total.

Basis for selection. Open admission, but selective for some programs.

2011-2012 Annual costs. Tuition/fees: $16,443. Cost for three semesters, $24,650, covers tuition, fees, and textbooks. Typically, students enroll for the calendar year and attend classes for three semesters consecutively. Books/supplies: $700.

Financial aid. Need-based: Work-study available nights, weekends and for part-time students.

Academics. Credit/placement by examination: AP, CLEP.

Majors. Business: Business admin. **Parks/recreation:** Golf management.

Contact. E-mail: sdga@sdgagolf.com
Phone: (480) 905-9288 Toll-free number: (800) 342-7342
Fax: (480) 905-8705
Angel Nguyen, Director of Admissions, Golf Academy of America: Orlando, 7373 North Scottsdale Road, Suite B-100, Scottsdale, AZ 85253

Gulf Coast State College
Panama City, Florida
www.gulfcoast.edu
CB code: 5271

▶ Public 2-year community college
▶ Commuter campus in small city

General. Founded in 1957. Regionally accredited. **Enrollment:** 5,627 degree-seeking undergraduates; 809 non-degree-seeking students. **Degrees:** 800 associate awarded. **Location:** 100 miles from Tallahassee, 100 miles from Pensacola. **Calendar:** Semester, limited summer session. **Full-time faculty:** 114 total; 12% minority, 60% women. **Part-time faculty:** 190 total; 9% minority, 62% women. **Class size:** 45% < 20, 53% 20-39, less than 1% 40-49, less than 1% 50-99, less than 1% >100. **Partnerships:** Formal partnerships with local businesses.

Student profile. Among degree-seeking undergraduates, 653 enrolled as first-time, first-year students.

Part-time:	58%	Asian American:	2%
Out-of-state:	6%	Hispanic American:	8%
Women:	63%	International:	1%
African American:	11%	25 or older:	56%

Transfer out. Colleges most students transferred to 2011: Florida State University, University of Florida, University of Central Florida, University of West Florida.

Basis for selection. Open admission, but selective for some programs. Admission to health science programs determined through high school transcripts, placement test performance and other admissions criteria. Interview required of allied health applicants. Audition recommended for music majors. **Home schooled:** Home School Affidavit must be submitted with parent's signature and notarized.

High school preparation. 13 units recommended. Recommended units include English 4, mathematics 3, social studies 3 and science 3.

2011-2012 Annual costs. Tuition/fees: $2,844; $10,691 out-of-state. Books/supplies: $1,035. Personal expenses: $1,200.

2010-2011 Financial aid. Need-based: 79% of total undergraduate aid awarded as scholarships/grants, 21% as loans/jobs. Need-based aid available for part-time students. Work-study available nights, weekends and for part-time students. **Non-need-based:** Scholarships awarded for academics, athletics, job skills, leadership, minority status, music/drama, state residency.

Application procedures. Admission: No deadline. $20 fee. Admission notification on a rolling basis. Application deadline for nursing program 2/28; dental hygiene 3/15; EMT and paramedic 6/1; radiography 5/15; physical therapist assistant 5/5; surgical technology 10/21. **Financial aid:** Priority date 5/15, closing date 7/1. FAFSA required. Applicants notified on a rolling basis starting 7/1.

Academics. Special study options: Accelerated study, cooperative education, distance learning, dual enrollment of high school students, ESL, honors, independent study, internships, teacher certification program, weekend college. Bachelor's degree programs available on campus. License preparation in dental hygiene, nursing, paramedic, physical therapy, radiology, real estate. **Credit/placement by examination:** AP, CLEP, IB, institutional tests. 45 credit hours maximum toward associate degree. **Support services:** GED preparation, learning center, reduced course load, remedial instruction, study skills assistance, tutoring.

Majors. Area/ethnic studies: Women's. **Biology:** General, entomology, marine. **Business:** Accounting, business admin, e-commerce, hospitality admin, office/clerical. **Communications:** Advertising, broadcast journalism, communications/speech/rhetoric, journalism. **Computer sciences:** General, applications programming, artificial intelligence, computer science, information technology, networking, programming, systems analysis, web page design. **Conservation:** Forestry. **Education:** Biology, business, chemistry, early childhood, elementary, health, mathematics, middle, physical, physics, science, special ed. **Engineering:** General, electrical. **English:** English lit. **Foreign languages:** General. **General:** Landscaping, ornamental horticulture. **Health services:** Chiropractic assistant, clinical lab science, clinical nutrition, dental hygiene, EMT paramedic, medical radiologic technology/radiation therapy, medical records admin, nursing (RN), occupational therapy assistant, optician, physical therapy assistant, predental, premedicine, prepharmacy, preveterinary, radiologic technology/medical imaging, respiratory therapy assistant, sonography. **History:** General. **Human services:** Social work. **Liberal arts:** Arts/sciences. **Math:** General. **Parks/recreation:** General, health/fitness, sports admin. **Philosophy/religion:** Philosophy, religion. **Physical sciences:** Atmospheric science, chemistry, geology, oceanography, physics. **Protective services:** Criminal justice, firefighting, forensics, law enforcement admin. **Psychology:** General. **Social sciences:** Anthropology, archaeology, economics, political science, sociology. **Visual/performing arts:** Art, dramatic, music.

Most popular majors. Health sciences 17%, liberal arts 74%.

Computing on campus. 560 workstations in library, computer center. Commuter students can connect to campus network. Online course registration, online library, helpline, wireless network available.

Student life. Freshman orientation: Available. Preregistration for classes offered. Orientation programs also available on the Internet. **Activities:** Bands, campus ministries, choral groups, dance, drama, international student organizations, literary magazine, music ensembles, musical theater, radio

station, student government, student newspaper, African American student association, Baptist Collegiate Ministries, Gay Straight Alliance, Muslim student association, Rotaract, Spanish club, Visionaries Ink, veterans association, World Philosophy and Religion Association.

Athletics. NJCAA. **Intercollegiate:** Baseball M, basketball, softball W, volleyball W. **Intramural:** Basketball. **Team name:** Commodores.

Student services. Adult student services, career counseling, services for economically disadvantaged, student employment services, financial aid counseling, minority student services, personal counseling, veterans' counselor, women's services. **Physically disabled:** Services for visually, speech, hearing impaired. **Transfer:** Pre-admission transcript evaluation for new students. Transfer adviser, college fairs on campus for students transferring to 4-year colleges.

Contact. Phone: (850) 872-3892 Toll-free number: (800) 311-3685
Fax: (850) 913-3308
Sharon Todd, Director of Enrollment Services, Gulf Coast State College, 5230 West US Highway 98, Panama City, FL 32401-1041

Herzing University: Winter Park
Winter Park, Florida
www.herzing.edu   CB code: 3438

- For-profit 2-year business and health science college
- Commuter campus in very large city
- Interview required

General. Regionally accredited. **Enrollment:** 399 degree-seeking undergraduates. **Degrees:** 6 bachelor's, 110 associate awarded. **Calendar:** Semester, extensive summer session. **Full-time faculty:** 22 total. **Part-time faculty:** 12 total.

Basis for selection. Open admission, but selective for some programs. Entrance test and evaluation for all applicants.

2011-2012 Annual costs. Tuition/fees: $13,440. Per-credit charge: $560. Reported annual tuition is representative. Actual costs vary by program with nursing programs somewhat more expensive.

Financial aid. **Need-based:** Work-study available nights, weekends and for part-time students.

Application procedures. **Admission:** No deadline. No application fee. Admission notification on a rolling basis.

Academics. **Special study options:** Distance learning. Bachelor's degree programs available on campus. **Credit/placement by examination:** AP, CLEP, IB, institutional tests. 52 credit hours maximum toward associate degree, 97 toward bachelor's. **Support services:** Reduced course load, remedial instruction, study skills assistance, tutoring.

Majors. **Business:** General, accounting, business admin. **Computer sciences:** Computer science, information technology, LAN/WAN management, networking, programming. **Health services:** Insurance coding, insurance specialist, massage therapy, medical assistant, nursing (RN), radiologic technology/medical imaging, surgical technology.

Computing on campus. 120 workstations in library, computer center. Online library, wireless network available.

Student life. **Freshman orientation:** Mandatory. Preregistration for classes offered.

Student services. Adult student services, student employment services, financial aid counseling. **Transfer:** Pre-admission transcript evaluation for new students.

Contact. E-mail: info@orl.herzing.edu
Phone: (407) 478-0500 Toll-free number: (800) 574-4446
Fax: (401) 418-0501
Todd Lasota, Director of Admissions, Herzing University: Winter Park, 1595 South Semoran Boulevard, Winter Park, FL 32792

Hillsborough Community College
Tampa, Florida   CB member
www.hccfl.edu   CB code: 5304

- Public 2-year community college
- Commuter campus in large city

General. Founded in 1968. Regionally accredited. **Enrollment:** 26,319 degree-seeking undergraduates; 2,010 non-degree-seeking students. **Degrees:** 2,957 associate awarded. **ROTC:** Army. **Calendar:** Semester, limited summer session. **Full-time faculty:** 278 total; 25% have terminal degrees, 21% minority, 54% women. **Part-time faculty:** 1,167 total; 11% have terminal degrees, 28% minority, 56% women. **Class size:** 20% < 20, 80% 20-39, less than 1% 40-49, less than 1% 50-99.

Student profile. Among degree-seeking undergraduates, 59% enrolled in a transfer program, 41% enrolled in a vocational program, 5,229 enrolled as first-time, first-year students.

Part-time:	56%	Asian American:	3%
Out-of-state:	3%	Hispanic American:	24%
Women:	57%	International:	2%
African American:	20%	25 or older:	45%

Transfer out. Colleges most students transferred to 2011: University of South Florida, University of Central Florida, University of Florida, Florida State University, Florida International University.

Basis for selection. Open admission, but selective for some programs. Limited access to certain health programs. Degree-seeking students must provide assessment/placement scores from PERT, CPT, FCELPT, ACT, or SAT prior to registering for classes. Test scores may be no more than two years old. **Home schooled:** Signed affidavit affirming completion required. **Learning Disabled:** Students should contact Coordinator of Services for students with disabilities to discuss documentation guidelines at least 1 month prior to semester.

High school preparation. 24 units recommended. Recommended units include English 4, mathematics 3, science 3, foreign language 2 and academic electives 8.

2011-2012 Annual costs. Tuition/fees: $3,011; $11,046 out-of-state. Books/supplies: $1,300. Personal expenses: $2,007.

2010-2011 Financial aid. **Need-based:** 63% of total undergraduate aid awarded as scholarships/grants, 37% as loans/jobs. Need-based aid available for part-time students. Work-study available nights, weekends and for part-time students. **Non-need-based:** Scholarships awarded for academics, art, athletics, minority status, music/drama.

Application procedures. **Admission:** Closing date 8/8. No application fee. Application must be submitted online. Admission notification on a rolling basis. **Financial aid:** Priority date 6/1, closing date 7/6. FAFSA, institutional form required. Applicants notified on a rolling basis.

Academics. **Special study options:** Accelerated study, cross-registration, distance learning, double major, dual enrollment of high school students, ESL, honors, independent study, internships, liberal arts/career combination, study abroad, teacher certification program, weekend college. Bachelor's degree programs available on campus. License preparation in dental hygiene, nursing, paramedic. **Credit/placement by examination:** AP, CLEP, IB, institutional tests. Approval required. **Support services:** GED preparation, learning center, remedial instruction, study skills assistance, tutoring, writing center.

Majors. **Business:** Accounting technology, business admin, executive assistant, hospitality admin, management information systems, operations, restaurant/food services. **Computer sciences:** Applications programming, systems analysis. **Education:** Deaf/hearing impaired. **General:** Aquaculture. **Health services:** Dental hygiene, dietician assistant, EMT paramedic, medical radiologic technology/radiation therapy, mental health services, nuclear medical technology, nursing (RN), optician, optometric assistant, respiratory therapy technology, sonography, veterinary technology/assistant. **Liberal arts:** Arts/sciences. **Protective services:** Fire safety technology, law enforcement admin. **Visual/performing arts:** Cinematography. **Work/family studies:** Child care management.

Most popular majors. Health sciences 14%, liberal arts 77%.

Computing on campus. 2,014 workstations in library, computer center, student center. Dormitories wired for high-speed internet access. Commuter students can connect to campus network. Online course registration, online library, helpline, wireless network available.

Student life. **Freshman orientation:** Mandatory. Preregistration for classes offered. **Housing:** Apartments available. **Activities:** Bands, choral groups, dance, drama, international student organizations, literary magazine, music ensembles, radio station, student government, student newspaper, Active Minds, African-American student union, dance club, music club, Phi Theta Kappa, photography club, veterans club.

Athletics. NJCAA. **Intercollegiate:** Baseball M, basketball, softball W, tennis W, volleyball W. **Team name:** Hawks.

Student services. Career counseling, services for economically disadvantaged, student employment services, financial aid counseling, on-campus daycare, personal counseling. **Physically disabled:** Services for visually, speech, hearing impaired. **Transfer:** Transfer center, transfer adviser, college fairs on campus for students transferring to 4-year colleges.

Contact. E-mail: eolmo2@hccfl.edu
Phone: (813) 253-7032 Toll-free number: (877) 736-2575
Fax: (813) 253-7196
Katherine Durkee, Registrar, Hillsborough Community College, Box 31127, Tampa, FL 33631-3127

Indian River State College
Fort Pierce, Florida
www.irsc.edu

CB member
CB code: 5322

- Public 2-year community college
- Commuter campus in small city

General. Founded in 1960. Regionally accredited. Branch campuses in Vero Beach, Stuart, Okeechobee, Port St. Lucie; Criminal Justice Academy, Marine Center in Fort Pierce. **Enrollment:** 14,093 degree-seeking undergraduates; 3,435 non-degree-seeking students. **Degrees:** 242 bachelor's, 2,120 associate awarded. **Location:** 65 miles from West Palm Beach. **Calendar:** Semester, limited summer session. **Full-time faculty:** 211 total. **Part-time faculty:** 756 total. **Special facilities:** Olympic-size pool complex, fine arts center, planetarium.

Student profile. Among degree-seeking undergraduates, 2,123 enrolled as first-time, first-year students.

Part-time:	60%	Asian American:	1%
Out-of-state:	2%	Hispanic American:	15%
Women:	60%	International:	1%
African American:	19%	25 or older:	44%

Transfer out. Colleges most students transferred to 2011: University of Central Florida, University of South Florida, University of Florida, Florida State University, Florida Atlantic University.

Basis for selection. Open admission, but selective for some programs. Testing and academic records determine admission to health science programs.

High school preparation. 24 units recommended. Recommended units include English 4, mathematics 3, social studies 3, history 2, science 3, foreign language 2 and academic electives 7.

2011-2012 Annual costs. Tuition/fees: $2,976; $11,342 out-of-state. Baccalaureate programs tuition and fees are $3,301 for in-state and $15,286 for out-of-state based on academic year of 30 credit hours.

2010-2011 Financial aid. Need-based: Need-based aid available for part-time students. Work-study available nights, weekends and for part-time students. **Non-need-based:** Scholarships awarded for academics, athletics, minority status, music/drama, state residency.

Application procedures. Admission: No deadline. No application fee. Admission notification on a rolling basis. **Financial aid:** Priority date 7/18; no closing date. FAFSA, institutional form required. Applicants notified on a rolling basis starting 5/15.

Academics. Special study options: Accelerated study, distance learning, dual enrollment of high school students, ESL, honors, teacher certification program, weekend college. Bachelor's degree programs available on campus. License preparation in dental hygiene, nursing, paramedic, physical therapy, radiology, real estate. **Credit/placement by examination:** AP, CLEP, IB, institutional tests. 45 credit hours maximum toward associate degree. Degree-seeking students must achieve state-designated cutoff scores on placement test to enter college-level programs, or complete sequence of developmental courses. **Support services:** GED preparation and test center, learning center, pre-admission summer program, reduced course load, remedial instruction, study skills assistance, tutoring.

Majors. Biology: General. **Business:** Accounting, administrative services, business admin, hospitality admin, management information systems, office management, sales/distribution. **Communications:** Public relations. **Communications technology:** Graphic/printing. **Computer sciences:** General, applications programming, computer graphics, information technology, programming, systems analysis, web page design. **Conservation:** Environmental studies. **Education:** General, early childhood, elementary, secondary. **Engineering:** General. **English:** English lit. **Foreign languages:** General. **General:** Business technology, turf management. **Health services:** Clinical lab technology, dental hygiene, dental lab technology, EMT paramedic, medical radiologic technology/radiation therapy, medical records admin, medical records technology, medical transcription, nursing (RN), physical therapy assistant, predental, premedicine, prepharmacy, preveterinary, respiratory therapy technology. **History:** General. **Liberal arts:** Arts/sciences, library assistant. **Math:** General. **Philosophy/religion:** Philosophy. **Physical sciences:** Chemistry, physics. **Protective services:** Criminal justice, fire safety technology. **Psychology:** General. **Social sciences:** Anthropology, economics, political science, sociology. **Visual/performing arts:** Art, commercial/advertising art, dance, dramatic, interior design, music.

Computing on campus. Online course registration, online library available.

Student life. Freshman orientation: Available. Preregistration for classes offered. **Housing:** Apartments available. **Activities:** Bands, choral groups, dance, drama, international student organizations, literary magazine, music ensembles, musical theater, radio station, student government, symphony orchestra, Distributive Education Clubs of America, Vocational International Clubs of America, cultural exchange club, human services club, ambassador club, Bacchus club, Phi Beta Lambda.

Athletics. NJCAA. **Intercollegiate:** Baseball M, basketball, cheerleading W, diving, softball W, swimming, volleyball W. **Team name:** Pioneers.

Student services. Alcohol/substance abuse counseling, career counseling, services for economically disadvantaged, student employment services, financial aid counseling, health services, minority student services, on-campus daycare, placement for graduates, veterans' counselor, women's services. **Physically disabled:** Services for visually, speech, hearing impaired. **Transfer:** Transfer adviser, college fairs on campus for students transferring to 4-year colleges.

Contact. Phone: (772) 462-4740 Toll-free number: (866) 866-4722
Fax: (772) 462-4699
Karen Chapdelaine, Director of Admissions, Indian River State College, 3209 Virginia Avenue, Fort Pierce, FL 34981-5596

Keiser Career College: Greenacres
Greenacres, Florida
www.keisercareer.edu

- For-profit 2-year business and health science college
- Commuter campus in small city

General. Accredited by ACCSCT. **Calendar:** Differs by program.

Contact. Phone: (561) 433-2330
6812 Forest Hill Boulevard, Greenacres, FL 33413

Keiser Career College: Miami Lakes
Miami Lakes, Florida
www.keisercareer.edu

- For-profit 2-year business and health science college
- Commuter campus in large town

General. Accredited by ACCSCT. **Calendar:** Differs by program.

Contact. Phone: (305) 820-5003
17395 NW 59th Avenue, Miami Lakes, FL 33015

Keiser University
Fort Lauderdale, Florida
www.keiseruniversity.edu

CB code: 7004

- Private 2-year health science and career college
- Commuter campus in large city
- SAT or ACT, interview required

General. Founded in 1977. Regionally accredited. **Enrollment:** 16,460 undergraduates. **Degrees:** 546 bachelor's, 3,635 associate awarded; master's, doctoral offered. **Location:** 35 miles from Miami. **Calendar:** Semester, extensive summer session. **Full-time faculty:** 646 total. **Part-time faculty:** 665 total.

Basis for selection. 1430 SAT, 17 ACT, or 35-55 on Otis-Lennon evaluation test required.

Financial aid. Need-based: Need-based aid available for part-time students. Work-study available nights, weekends and for part-time students.

Application procedures. Admission: No deadline. $50 fee. Admission notification on a rolling basis. **Financial aid:** No deadline. FAFSA required.

Academics. Special study options: Accelerated study. **Credit/placement by examination:** AP, CLEP.

Majors. Business: Accounting. **Computer sciences:** General, computer graphics, data processing, information technology, programming. **Engineering:** Computer. **Health services:** Clinical lab technology, health services admin, medical assistant, medical radiologic technology/radiation therapy, medical records admin, nuclear medical technology, nursing (RN), occupational therapy assistant, physical therapy assistant, respiratory therapy assistant, sonography. **Parks/recreation:** Exercise sciences. **Protective services:** Forensics, homeland security, law enforcement admin. **Visual/performing arts:** Game design.

Student life. Activities: Student government.

Student services. Career counseling, student employment services, placement for graduates.

Contact. E-mail: admissions-ftl@keisercollege.edu
Phone: (954) 776-4456 Toll-free number: (800) 749-4456
Fax: (954) 771-4894
Central Admissions, Keiser University, 1500 Northwest 49th Street, Fort Lauderdale, FL 33309

Key College
Dania Beach, Florida
www.keycollege.edu   CB code: 3577

▶ For-profit 2-year business and technical college
▶ Commuter campus in very large city
▶ Interview required

General. Regionally accredited; also accredited by ACICS. **Enrollment:** 113 degree-seeking undergraduates. **Degrees:** 21 associate awarded. **Calendar:** Quarter, extensive summer session. **Full-time faculty:** 6 total. **Part-time faculty:** 6 total.

Student profile.

Out-of-state:	6%	25 or older:	72%

Basis for selection. Admissions based on entrance exam and school record. SAT or ACT recommended. CPAT may be submitted in lieu of SAT/ACT. **Home schooled:** State high school equivalency certificate required.

2011-2012 Annual costs. Tuition/fees: $10,620. Books/supplies: $900. Personal expenses: $3,621.

Financial aid. All financial aid based on need. Need-based aid available for part-time students. Work-study available nights, weekends and for part-time students. **Additional information:** Federal Supplemental Educational Opportunities Grant (FSEOG), PELL grant, ACG, FFEL (federal loan program) available; direct loans offered.

Application procedures. Admission: No deadline. $35 fee. Application must be submitted on paper. Admission notification on a rolling basis. **Financial aid:** No deadline. FAFSA, institutional form required.

Academics. Credit/placement by examination: AP, CLEP, institutional tests. **Support services:** Remedial instruction, study skills assistance.

Majors. Health services: Medical secretary.

Most popular majors. Engineering/engineering technologies 27%, health sciences 9%, legal studies 64%.

Computing on campus. 65 workstations in library, computer center.

Student life. Freshman orientation: Mandatory. Preregistration for classes offered. Held one week prior to beginning of classes for approximately 3 hours. **Activities:** Student newspaper.

Student services. Career counseling, financial aid counseling, personal counseling, veterans' counselor.

Contact. E-mail: admissions@keycollege.edu
Phone: (954) 923-4440 Toll-free number: (800) 581-8292
Fax: (954) 923-9226
Steve Levine, Admissions Specialist, Key College, 225 East Dania Beach Boulevard, Dania Beach, FL 33004-3046

Lake-Sumter Community College
Leesburg, Florida
www.lscc.edu   CB code: 5376

▶ Public 2-year community college
▶ Commuter campus in small city

General. Founded in 1962. Regionally accredited. **Enrollment:** 3,883 degree-seeking undergraduates. **Degrees:** 590 associate awarded. **Location:** 35 miles from Orlando. **Calendar:** Semester, limited summer session. **Full-time faculty:** 84 total; 18% have terminal degrees, 5% minority, 66% women. **Part-time faculty:** 344 total; 14% have terminal degrees, 11% minority, 60% women. **Class size:** 41% < 20, 58% 20-39, less than 1% 40-49, less than 1% 50-99. **Special facilities:** Wellness facilities.

Student profile.

Out-of-state:	1%	25 or older:	29%

Transfer out. Colleges most students transferred to 2011: University of Central Florida, University of Florida, Florida State University, University of South Florida.

Basis for selection. Open admission, but selective for some programs. Special requirements for nursing program. **Home schooled:** Home-schooled affidavit accepted in lieu of high school diploma or GED.

2011-2012 Annual costs. Tuition/fees: $2,997; $11,739 out-of-state. Books/supplies: $1,000. Personal expenses: $2,582.

Financial aid. Need-based: Need-based aid available for part-time students. Work-study available nights, weekends and for part-time students. **Non-need-based:** Scholarships awarded for academics, athletics, minority status, state residency.

Application procedures. Admission: No deadline. $25 fee. Admission notification on a rolling basis. **Financial aid:** Priority date 5/29; no closing date. FAFSA, institutional form required. Applicants notified on a rolling basis.

Academics. Special study options: Cooperative education, distance learning, dual enrollment of high school students, independent study, liberal arts/career combination, teacher certification program. Bachelor's degree programs available on campus. License preparation in nursing, real estate. **Credit/placement by examination:** AP, CLEP, institutional tests. 45 credit hours maximum toward associate degree. **Support services:** Learning center, reduced course load, remedial instruction, study skills assistance, tutoring, writing center.

Majors. Business: Business admin, executive assistant. **Computer sciences:** Applications programming, systems analysis. **Education:** Early childhood. **Health services:** EMT paramedic, medical records technology, nursing (RN). **Liberal arts:** Arts/sciences. **Parks/recreation:** Sports admin. **Protective services:** Fire safety technology, firefighting, law enforcement admin. **Visual/performing arts:** Commercial/advertising art. **Work/family studies:** Child care service.

Most popular majors. Health sciences 14%, liberal arts 80%.

Computing on campus. 825 workstations in library, computer center, student center. Commuter students can connect to campus network. Online course registration, online library, wireless network available.

Student life. Freshman orientation: Mandatory. Preregistration for classes offered. Day, evening, and online sessions available. **Activities:** Bands, campus ministries, choral groups, drama, literary magazine, music ensembles, student government, student newspaper, symphony orchestra, College Democrats, Baptist Collegiate Ministries, community charity club, multicultural student association.

Athletics. NJCAA. **Intercollegiate:** Baseball M, softball W, volleyball W. **Intramural:** Basketball, football (non-tackle), table tennis, volleyball. **Team name:** Lakers.

Student services. Adult student services, career counseling, services for economically disadvantaged, student employment services, financial aid counseling, minority student services, personal counseling, placement for

graduates, veterans' counselor, women's services. **Physically disabled:** Services for visually, speech, hearing impaired. **Transfer:** Pre-admission transcript evaluation for new students. Transfer adviser, college fairs on campus for students transferring to 4-year colleges.

Contact. E-mail: AdmissionsOffice@lscc.edu
Phone: (352) 323-3665 Fax: (352) 365-3553
Lakesher Murphy, Registrar, Lake-Sumter Community College, 9501 U.S. Highway 441, Leesburg, FL 34788-8751

Le Cordon Bleu College of Culinary Arts: Miami
Hollywood, Florida
www.miamiculinary.com

- For-profit 2-year culinary school
- Small city

General. Regionally accredited; also accredited by ACCSC. **Enrollment:** 1,045 degree-seeking undergraduates. **Degrees:** 268 associate awarded. **Calendar:** Differs by program.

Basis for selection. Admission requirements will vary by program.

2011-2012 Annual costs. Tuition/fees: $17,500.

Financial aid. Need-based: Work-study available nights, weekends and for part-time students.

Academics. Credit/placement by examination: AP, CLEP.

Contact. Phone: (954) 438-8882 Toll-free number: (888) 569-3222
Le Cordon Bleu College of Culinary Arts: Miami, 3221 Enterprise Way, Miramar, FL 33025

Le Cordon Bleu College of Culinary Arts: Orlando
Orlando, Florida
www.orlandoculinary.com

- For-profit 2-year culinary school
- Very large city

General. Regionally accredited. **Location:** Downtown. **Calendar:** Differs by program.

Annual costs/financial aid. Tuition/fees (2011-2012): $17,500.

Contact. Phone: (407) 888-4000
8511 Commodity Circle, Suite 100, Orlando, FL 32819

Lincoln College of Technology: West Palm Beach
West Palm Beach, Florida
www.lincolnedu.com   CB code: 0529

- For-profit 2-year technical college
- Commuter campus in small city

General. Founded in 1982. Accredited by ACICS. **Location:** 75 miles from Miami. **Calendar:** Quarter.

Annual costs/financial aid. Total program costs range from $10,050 up to $26,550 depending on program. Cost of books and materials included in tuition. Need-based financial aid available for full-time students.

Contact. Phone: (561) 842-8324
Admissions Director, 2410 Metrocentre Boulevard, West Palm Beach, FL 33407

Miami Dade College
Miami, Florida   CB member
www.mdc.edu/main   CB code: 5457

- Public 2-year community college
- Commuter campus in very large city

General. Founded in 1959. Regionally accredited. **Enrollment:** 59,570 degree-seeking undergraduates; 4,166 non-degree-seeking students. **Degrees:** 440 bachelor's, 9,729 associate awarded. **ROTC:** Army, Air Force. **Calendar:** Semester, limited summer session. **Full-time faculty:** 718 total; 28% have terminal degrees, 62% minority, 53% women. **Part-time faculty:** 1,744 total; 15% have terminal degrees, 70% minority, 49% women. **Class size:** 17% < 20, 70% 20-39, 12% 40-49, less than 1% 50-99, less than 1% >100. **Special facilities:** Environmental demonstration center, bilingual center for dual degree program, greenhouse, fire science tower, fire science burn building, emerging technologies center of the Americas, center for the environment, horticulture center, firearms demonstration lab, earth science museum, studio theater, human patient simulator lab, flight simulator lab, child care labs, culinary institute. **Partnerships:** Formal partnerships with Florida Power and Light's Electrical Power Technology Program, Disney, Center for Financial Training, Homeland Security-TSA.

Student profile. Among degree-seeking undergraduates, 72% enrolled in a transfer program, 28% enrolled in a vocational program, 1% already have a bachelor's degree or higher, 13,498 enrolled as first-time, first-year students, 1,769 transferred in from other institutions.

Part-time:	56%	Asian American:	1%
Out-of-state:	3%	Hispanic American:	71%
Women:	58%	International:	2%
African American:	16%	25 or older:	38%

Transfer out. 84% of students enrolled in the transfer program go on to 4-year colleges. **Colleges most students transferred to 2011:** Florida International University.

Basis for selection. Open admission, but selective for some programs. Special requirements for visual and performing arts, honors, allied health, and bachelor programs. Audition required of performing arts majors. Portfolio required of visual arts majors. **Learning Disabled:** ACCESS office provides, arranges and coordinates accommodations for students with documented disabilities.

High school preparation. 24 units recommended. Recommended units include English 4, mathematics 4, social studies 1, history 2, science 3 (laboratory 2), visual/performing arts 1 and academic electives 8. 1 physical education to include the integration of health. Social Studies: 1 world history, 1 United States history, .5 United States government, .5 economics.

2011-2012 Annual costs. Tuition/fees: $3,074; $11,221 out-of-state. Baccalaureate programs tuition and fees are $3,409 for in-state and $15,526 for out-of-state based on academic year of 30 credit hours. Books/supplies: $1,800. Personal expenses: $2,400.

Financial aid. Need-based: Need-based aid available for part-time students. Work-study available nights, weekends and for part-time students. **Non-need-based:** Scholarships awarded for academics, art, athletics, music/drama, state residency.

Application procedures. Admission: No deadline. $30 fee. Admission notification on a rolling basis. **Financial aid:** Priority date 3/15, closing date 6/30. FAFSA required. Applicants notified on a rolling basis starting 5/15.

Academics. Special study options: Accelerated study, cooperative education, cross-registration, distance learning, dual enrollment of high school students, ESL, honors, independent study, internships, study abroad, teacher certification program, weekend college. Bachelor's degree programs available on campus. License preparation in aviation, dental hygiene, nursing, paramedic, physical therapy, radiology, real estate. **Credit/placement by examination:** AP, CLEP, IB, institutional tests. 45 credit hours maximum toward associate degree, 45 toward bachelor's. **Support services:** GED preparation, learning center, reduced course load, remedial instruction, study skills assistance, tutoring, writing center.

Honors college/program. Combination of grades, test scores, recommendations, essay on assigned topic and personal interview most important. Priority deadline 2/1.

Majors. Architecture: Technology. **Area/ethnic studies:** American, Asian, Latin American. **Biology:** General, biotechnology. **Business:** Accounting, administrative services, banking/financial services, business admin, management science, office management, office/clerical, real estate, tourism promotion, tourism/travel. **Communications:** Broadcast journalism, journalism. **Communications technology:** General, animation/special effects, graphic/printing, graphics, radio/TV. **Computer sciences:** General, applications programming, information systems, information technology, web page design. **Conservation:** Environmental science, forestry. **Education:** Early childhood, elementary, mathematics, physical, science, secondary, special ed, technology/industrial arts. **Engineering:** Architectural, civil, electrical. **English:** American lit, English lit, rhetoric/composition. **Foreign languages:** General, sign language interpretation, translation. **General:** Agribusiness operations, landscaping. **Health services:** Clinical lab technology, dental hygiene, EMT

paramedic, histologic technology, medical assistant, medical radiologic technology/radiation therapy, medical records admin, medical secretary, midwifery, nursing (RN), optician, physician assistant, predental, premedicine, prepharmacy, preveterinary, respiratory therapy technology, veterinary technology/assistant. **History:** General. **Human services:** General, social work. **Liberal arts:** Arts/sciences. **Math:** General. **Parks/recreation:** Exercise sciences. **Philosophy/religion:** Philosophy, religion. **Physical sciences:** Atmospheric science, chemistry, geology, physics. **Protective services:** Criminal justice, fire services admin, forensics. **Psychology:** General. **Social sciences:** Anthropology, economics, international relations, political science, sociology. **Visual/performing arts:** Cinematography, commercial/advertising art, dance, dramatic, music, studio arts. **Work/family studies:** Child development, food/nutrition.

Most popular majors. Health sciences 10%, liberal arts 85%.

Computing on campus. 8,000 workstations in library, computer center. Commuter students can connect to campus network. Online course registration, online library, helpline, wireless network available.

Student life. Freshman orientation: Available. Preregistration for classes offered. Traditionally orientations held before start of term; program-specific sessions held at beginning of term. **Activities:** Bands, campus ministries, choral groups, dance, drama, film society, international student organizations, literary magazine, music ensembles, Model UN, musical theater, radio station, student government, student newspaper, TV station, Newman Club, Chabad Jewish student union, African student union, Phi Beta Lambda, Phi Theta Kappa, Spirit of Faith, Haitian Boukan club, Catholic ministries, Students for Peace.

Athletics. NJCAA. **Intercollegiate:** Baseball M, basketball, softball W, volleyball W. **Intramural:** Basketball, soccer, softball, table tennis, tennis. **Team name:** Sharks.

Student services. Adult student services, career counseling, services for economically disadvantaged, student employment services, financial aid counseling, on-campus daycare, personal counseling, placement for graduates, veterans' counselor. **Physically disabled:** Services for visually, speech, hearing impaired. **Transfer:** Transfer center, transfer adviser, college fairs on campus for students transferring to 4-year colleges.

Contact. E-mail: mdcinfo@mdc.edu
Phone: (305) 237-2206 Fax: (305) 237-2532
Dulce Beltran, College Director, Admissions and Registration Services, Miami Dade College, 11011 SW 104th Street, Miami, FL 33176-3393

North Florida Community College
Madison, Florida
www.nfcc.edu   CB code: 5503

- Public 2-year community college
- Commuter campus in rural community

General. Founded in 1958. Regionally accredited. **Enrollment:** 1,000 degree-seeking undergraduates. **Degrees:** 178 associate awarded. **Location:** 56 miles from Tallahassee. **Calendar:** Semester, limited summer session. **Full-time faculty:** 29 total. **Part-time faculty:** 44 total. **Special facilities:** Nature center.

Transfer out. Colleges most students transferred to 2011: Florida State University, Florida A&M University, Valdosta State University, University of Florida.

Basis for selection. Open admission, but selective for some programs. Limited enrollment for nursing, criminal justice, EMT. Background checks completed by Florida Department of Law Enforcement. Florida College Entry-Level Placement Tests required for all students. Students with satisfactory ACT or SAT scores are exempt from taking FCELPT. **Home schooled:** Statement describing home school structure and mission required. Submit affidavit stating that home education complies with Florida law. **Learning Disabled:** Disabilities must have documentation.

High school preparation. 24 units recommended. Recommended units include English 4, mathematics 4, social studies 3, science 2 (laboratory 1) and foreign language 2. Algebra 1 recommended.

2011-2012 Annual costs. Tuition/fees: $2,745; $10,392 out-of-state. Books/supplies: $500. Personal expenses: $475.

Financial aid. All financial aid based on need. Need-based aid available for part-time students. Work-study available nights, weekends and for part-time students.

Application procedures. Admission: Priority date 7/1; no deadline. $20 fee, may be waived for applicants with need. Application must be submitted on paper. Admission notification on a rolling basis. **Financial aid:** Priority date 5/15; no closing date. FAFSA required. Applicants notified on a rolling basis starting 6/20; must reply within 2 week(s) of notification.

Academics. Special study options: Accelerated study, distance learning, dual enrollment of high school students, independent study, teacher certification program. Bachelor's degree programs available on campus. License preparation in nursing, paramedic, real estate. **Credit/placement by examination:** AP, CLEP, IB, institutional tests. 45 credit hours maximum toward associate degree. **Support services:** GED preparation and test center, reduced course load, remedial instruction, study skills assistance, tutoring, writing center.

Majors. Health services: Nursing assistant. **Liberal arts:** Arts/sciences.

Computing on campus. 65 workstations in library, computer center, student center. Online course registration, online library, wireless network available.

Student life. Freshman orientation: Available. Preregistration for classes offered. **Activities:** Jazz band, choral groups, drama, music ensembles, musical theater, student government, student newspaper, environmental awareness group, African-American Association, veterans club, ASL.

Athletics. NJCAA. **Intercollegiate:** Baseball M, basketball W, softball W. **Team name:** Sentinels.

Student services. Adult student services, career counseling, student employment services, health services, personal counseling, placement for graduates, veterans' counselor. **Physically disabled:** Services for hearing impaired. **Transfer:** Pre-admission transcript evaluation for new students. Transfer adviser, college fairs on campus for students transferring to 4-year colleges.

Contact. Phone: (850) 973-1622 Toll-free number: (866) 937-6322
Fax: (850) 973-1697
Mary Wheeler, Dean of Enrollment Services, North Florida Community College, 325 NW Turner Davis Drive, Madison, FL 32340

Northwest Florida State College
Niceville, Florida
www.nwfsc.edu   CB code: 5526

- Public 2-year business and community college
- Commuter campus in large town

General. Founded in 1963. Regionally accredited. Additional teaching centers at Ft. Walton Beach, Eglin Air Force Base, Hurlburt Field, DeFuniak Springs, Crestview and South Walton County. **Enrollment:** 8,425 undergraduates. **Degrees:** 105 bachelor's, 1,370 associate awarded. **ROTC:** Army. **Location:** 55 miles from Pensacola. **Calendar:** Semester, extensive summer session. **Full-time faculty:** 95 total. **Part-time faculty:** 215 total. **Class size:** 3% < 20, 97% 20-39. **Special facilities:** Fine and performing arts center with 2 theaters and 2 art galleries.

Basis for selection. Open admission. Applicants without high school diploma may be admitted to credit-bearing certificate programs.

High school preparation. Recommended units include English 4, mathematics 3, social studies 3 and science 3.

2011-2012 Annual costs. Tuition/fees: $2,821; $10,944 out-of-state. Reported tuition and fees for baccalaureate degree programs are slightly higher. Books/supplies: $974.

Financial aid. Need-based: Need-based aid available for part-time students. Work-study available nights, weekends and for part-time students.

Application procedures. Admission: Priority date 7/25; no deadline. No application fee. Admission notification on a rolling basis. **Financial aid:** Priority date 4/1; no closing date. FAFSA, institutional form required. Applicants notified on a rolling basis starting 2/1; must reply within 2 week(s) of notification.

Academics. Special study options: Cooperative education, cross-registration, distance learning, dual enrollment of high school students, ESL, independent study, internships, student-designed major, teacher certification program. Bachelor's degree programs available on campus. License preparation in nursing, paramedic, radiology. **Credit/placement by examination:** AP, CLEP, institutional tests. 32 credit hours maximum toward associate degree. **Support services:** GED preparation and test center, learning center, remedial instruction, study skills assistance, tutoring, writing center.

Majors. Biology: General, marine. **Business:** General, accounting, banking/financial services, business admin, fashion, insurance, management information systems, marketing, office management, real estate. **Computer sciences:** General, computer graphics, programming. **Education:** General, early childhood, elementary, secondary. **Engineering:** General, electrical. **Foreign languages:** French, Spanish. **Health services:** Clinical lab science, predental, premedicine, prepharmacy, preveterinary. **Math:** General. **Parks/recreation:** General. **Physical sciences:** Chemistry, geology, physics. **Protective services:** Criminal justice, law enforcement admin. **Theology:** Theology. **Visual/performing arts:** Art, commercial/advertising art, dance, dramatic, interior design, music. **Work/family studies:** General, child care management, housing.

Computing on campus. 900 workstations in library, computer center. Commuter students can connect to campus network. Online course registration, online library, helpline, wireless network available.

Student life. Freshman orientation: Mandatory. Preregistration for classes offered. Orientation can be completed online. **Activities:** Bands, campus ministries, choral groups, dance, drama, literary magazine, music ensembles, musical theater, student government, symphony orchestra, Student Christian Fellowship, African American student association, Circle K, College Republicans, environmental club.

Athletics. NJCAA. **Intercollegiate:** Baseball M, basketball, softball W. **Intramural:** Softball, volleyball. **Team name:** Raiders.

Student services. Adult student services, career counseling, student employment services, on-campus daycare, personal counseling, placement for graduates, veterans' counselor. **Physically disabled:** Services for visually, speech, hearing impaired. **Transfer:** College fairs on campus for students transferring to 4-year colleges.

Contact. E-mail: registrar@nwfsc.edu
Phone: (850) 729-5373 Fax: (850) 729-5215
Christine Bishop, Registrar, Northwest Florida State College, 100 College Boulevard, Niceville, FL 32578-1295

Palm Beach State College
Lake Worth, Florida CB member
www.palmbeachstate.edu CB code: 5531

- Public 2-year community college
- Commuter campus in large town

General. Founded in 1933. Regionally accredited. Multilocation institution with 4 campuses, numerous other locations throughout service area. **Enrollment:** 25,672 degree-seeking undergraduates; 3,682 non-degree-seeking students. **Degrees:** 87 bachelor's, 3,138 associate awarded. **Location:** 30 miles north of Fort Lauderdale. **Calendar:** Semester, limited summer session. **Full-time faculty:** 250 total; 24% have terminal degrees, 28% minority, 57% women. **Part-time faculty:** 1,451 total; 27% minority, 49% women. **Special facilities:** Performing arts centers at 3 campuses.

Student profile. Among degree-seeking undergraduates, 80% enrolled in a transfer program, 20% enrolled in a vocational program, 3,985 enrolled as first-time, first-year students, 1,046 transferred in from other institutions.

Part-time:	59%	Women:	57%
Out-of-state:	6%	25 or older:	40%

Transfer out. Colleges most students transferred to 2011: Florida Atlantic University, University of Florida, Florida State University, University of South Florida.

Basis for selection. Open admission, but selective for some programs. Special requirements for dental, nursing, dietetic, occupational therapy assistant programs. Admission to paramedic, radiography, respiratory care programs based on test scores and GPA. SAT/ACT required for nursing and dental programs. CPT or SAT/ACT used for placement for all. Interview required for nursing, dental, radiography, respiratory care, paramedic majors. Audition required of music majors. **Home schooled:** Home education program affidavit required.

2011-2012 Annual costs. Tuition/fees: $2,880; $10,470 out-of-state. Reported tuition and fees for baccalaureate degree programs are slightly higher. Books/supplies: $1,000. Personal expenses: $400.

2011-2012 Financial aid. Need-based: 98% of total undergraduate aid awarded as scholarships/grants, 2% as loans/jobs. Work-study available nights, weekends and for part-time students. **Non-need-based:** Scholarships awarded for academics, alumni affiliation, athletics, leadership, state residency.

Application procedures. Admission: Closing date 8/23. $20 fee. Admission notification on a rolling basis beginning on or about 3/1. **Financial aid:** Priority date 7/1; no closing date. FAFSA, institutional form required. Applicants notified on a rolling basis; must reply within 2 week(s) of notification.

Academics. Center for Personalized Instruction offers full assistance in all academic areas for students. **Special study options:** Cooperative education, distance learning, double major, dual enrollment of high school students, ESL, honors, independent study, internships, study abroad, weekend college. Bachelor's degree programs available on campus. License preparation in aviation, dental hygiene, nursing, paramedic, radiology, real estate. **Credit/placement by examination:** AP, CLEP, IB, institutional tests. 45 credit hours maximum toward associate degree. **Support services:** Learning center, pre-admission summer program, reduced course load, remedial instruction, study skills assistance, tutoring, writing center.

Majors. Architecture: Interior. **Biology:** General, zoology. **Business:** General, accounting, business admin, finance, hospitality admin, management information systems, marketing, sales/distribution. **Communications:** Broadcast journalism, journalism. **Communications technology:** Graphic/printing. **Computer sciences:** General, applications programming, information systems, programming, systems analysis. **Education:** Art, early childhood, elementary, health, health occupations, music, physical, sales/marketing, science, secondary, social science, voc/tech. **Engineering:** General, electrical. **English:** English lit. **General:** Ornamental horticulture. **Health services:** Clinical lab technology, dental hygiene, dietetics, EMT paramedic, massage therapy, medical radiologic technology/radiation therapy, nursing (RN), occupational therapy assistant, premedicine, respiratory therapy technology. **History:** General. **Human services:** Social work. **Liberal arts:** Arts/sciences. **Math:** General. **Parks/recreation:** General, health/fitness. **Philosophy/religion:** Philosophy. **Physical sciences:** Chemistry, physics. **Protective services:** Fire services admin, firefighting. **Psychology:** General. **Social sciences:** General, anthropology, geography, international relations, political science, sociology. **Visual/performing arts:** General, art history/conservation, cinematography, commercial/advertising art, dance, dramatic, interior design, jazz, music, photography, studio arts. **Work/family studies:** General, child care management.

Most popular majors. Biological/life sciences 10%, health sciences 10%, liberal arts 75%.

Computing on campus. 1,500 workstations in library, computer center. Online course registration, online library, helpline, wireless network available.

Student life. Freshman orientation: Mandatory. Preregistration for classes offered. **Activities:** Bands, choral groups, dance, drama, literary magazine, music ensembles, musical theater, student government, student newspaper, black student union, Students for International Understanding, ASPIRA, Christian Fellowship, Community Earth, Kiskeya Club.

Athletics. NJCAA. **Intercollegiate:** Baseball M, basketball, softball W, volleyball W. **Intramural:** Basketball, softball, volleyball. **Team name:** Panthers.

Student services. Adult student services, alcohol/substance abuse counseling, career counseling, student employment services, financial aid counseling, minority student services, personal counseling, placement for graduates, veterans' counselor. **Physically disabled:** Services for visually, speech, hearing impaired. **Transfer:** Transfer adviser, college fairs on campus for students transferring to 4-year colleges.

Contact. E-mail: admissions@palmbeachstate.edu
Phone: (561) 868-3300 Fax: (561) 868-3584
Edward Mueller, District Registrar, Palm Beach State College, 4200 Congress Avenue, Lake Worth, FL 33461

Pasco-Hernando Community College
New Port Richey, Florida
www.phcc.edu CB code: 5578

- Public 2-year community college
- Commuter campus in large town

General. Founded in 1972. Regionally accredited. District covers counties of Pasco and Hernando; 4 college locations. Distance learning courses offered for variety of courses. **Enrollment:** 12,167 degree-seeking undergraduates. **Degrees:** 1,396 associate awarded. **ROTC:** Army, Naval. **Location:** 35 miles from Tampa. **Calendar:** Semester, limited summer session. **Full-time faculty:** 109 total. **Part-time faculty:** 287 total.

Transfer out. Colleges most students transferred to 2011: University of South Florida, St. Leo University, University of Florida, University of Central Florida, St. Petersburg College.

Basis for selection. Open admission, but selective for some programs. Special requirements for law enforcement, registered nursing, practical nursing, radiography, paramedic, dental hygiene, dental assisting. **Learning Disabled:** Appropriate documentation to Office of Disabilities Services required.

2011-2012 Annual costs. Tuition/fees: $2,844; $11,471 out-of-state. Books/supplies: $1,200. Personal expenses: $1,571.

Financial aid. Need-based: Need-based aid available for part-time students. Work-study available nights, weekends and for part-time students. **Non-need-based:** Scholarships awarded for academics, athletics, minority status. **Additional information:** Childcare assistance grants available to eligible students.

Application procedures. Admission: No deadline. $25 fee. Application must be submitted online. Admission notification on a rolling basis. **Financial aid:** No deadline. FAFSA required. Applicants notified on a rolling basis.

Academics. Special study options: Accelerated study, cross-registration, distance learning, double major, dual enrollment of high school students, external degree, honors, independent study, internships, liberal arts/career combination, study abroad, teacher certification program, weekend college. Bachelor's degree programs available on campus. License preparation in dental hygiene, nursing, paramedic, radiology. **Credit/placement by examination:** AP, CLEP, IB, institutional tests. 45 credit hours maximum toward associate degree. **Support services:** GED preparation and test center, learning center, reduced course load, remedial instruction, study skills assistance, tutoring, writing center.

Majors. Business: Administrative services, business admin, e-commerce, marketing. **Computer sciences:** Information technology, networking, programming, security, systems analysis. **Health services:** Dental hygiene, nursing (RN), radiologic technology/medical imaging. **Liberal arts:** Arts/sciences. **Protective services:** Law enforcement admin.

Computing on campus. Commuter students can connect to campus network. Online course registration, online library, helpline, wireless network available.

Student life. Freshman orientation: Mandatory. Preregistration for classes offered. 3-4 hour program held on variety of days and nights. **Activities:** Pep band, choral groups, drama, literary magazine, music ensembles, student government, 3D-developing, drafters & designers club, Campus Crusade for Christ, Earth awareness organization, Legal Eagles club, Men of Excellence, nursing club, veterans club, science club, human services club.

Athletics. NJCAA. **Intercollegiate:** Baseball M, basketball M, cheerleading M, cross-country W, softball W, volleyball W. **Intramural:** Football (non-tackle), table tennis. **Team name:** Conquistadors.

Student services. Career counseling, services for economically disadvantaged, financial aid counseling, minority student services, on-campus daycare, personal counseling, placement for graduates, veterans' counselor. **Physically disabled:** Services for visually, speech, hearing impaired. **Transfer:** College fairs on campus for students transferring to 4-year colleges.

Contact. E-mail: bullard@phcc.edu
Phone: (727) 816-3261 Toll-free number: (877) 879-7422
Fax: (727) 816-3389
Debra Bullard, Director of Admissions and Student Records, Pasco-Hernando Community College, 10230 Ridge Road, New Port Richey, FL 34654-5199

Pensacola State College
Pensacola, Florida

CB member
www.pensacolastate.edu   **CB code: 5535**

▶ Public 2-year community college
▶ Commuter campus in small city

General. Founded in 1948. Regionally accredited. Additional campuses: Milton, Warrington, Downtown Center, South Santa Rosa Campus, Century Center. **Enrollment:** 9,661 degree-seeking undergraduates; 1,870 non-degree-seeking students. **Degrees:** 1,779 associate awarded. **ROTC:** Army. **Location:** 60 miles from Mobile, AL. **Calendar:** Semester, extensive summer session. **Full-time faculty:** 203 total; 18% have terminal degrees, 16% minority, 58% women. **Part-time faculty:** 431 total; 10% minority, 61% women. **Special facilities:** Science and space theater.

Student profile. Among degree-seeking undergraduates, 1,359 enrolled as first-time, first-year students.

Part-time:	55%	Women:	62%
Out-of-state:	2%	25 or older:	50%

Transfer out. Colleges most students transferred to 2011: University of West Florida, Florida State University, University of Florida, University of South Alabama.

Basis for selection. Open admission, but selective for some programs. Special requirements for health programs. Post-secondary Educational Readiness test (PERT) must be taken for admission; student may submit SAT or ACT in its place. Scores used for placement only. **Home schooled:** State high school equivalency certificate required. Notorized affidavit with verification from school district office.

2011-2012 Annual costs. Tuition/fees: $2,942; $11,088 out-of-state. Baccalaureate programs tuition and fees are $3,409 for in-state and $12,850 for out-of-state based on academic year of 30 credit hours. Books/supplies: $1,100. Personal expenses: $1,170.

Financial aid. Need-based: Need-based aid available for part-time students. Work-study available nights, weekends and for part-time students. **Non-need-based:** Scholarships awarded for academics, athletics, state residency.

Application procedures. Admission: No deadline. $30 fee. Admission notification on a rolling basis. **Financial aid:** Priority date 4/1; no closing date. FAFSA, institutional form required. Applicants notified on a rolling basis starting 7/1; must reply within 2 week(s) of notification.

Academics. Special study options: Accelerated study, cooperative education, cross-registration, distance learning, double major, dual enrollment of high school students, honors, independent study, internships, study abroad, teacher certification program, weekend college. Bachelor's degree programs available on campus. License preparation in dental hygiene, nursing, paramedic, radiology. **Credit/placement by examination:** AP, CLEP, IB, institutional tests. 39 credit hours maximum toward associate degree. No limit but student must earn 25% of program requirement with institutional courses. **Support services:** GED preparation and test center, learning center, reduced course load, remedial instruction, study skills assistance, tutoring, writing center.

Majors. Biology: General, biochemistry, botany, zoology. **Business:** General, accounting, administrative services, banking/financial services, business admin, hospitality/recreation, management information systems, management science, office management. **Communications:** Communications/speech/rhetoric, journalism. **Communications technology:** General. **Computer sciences:** General, computer science, information systems, programming. **Conservation:** Forest resources, forestry, management/policy. **Education:** General, art, early childhood, elementary, music, physical, special ed. **Engineering:** General, civil, computer, electrical. **English:** English lit. **General:** Ornamental horticulture. **Health services:** Dental hygiene, EMT paramedic, health care admin, medical radiologic technology/radiation therapy, medical records admin, nursing (RN), physical therapy assistant, predental, premedicine, prenursing, prepharmacy, preveterinary, sonography. **History:** General. **Liberal arts:** Arts/sciences. **Math:** General. **Philosophy/religion:** Philosophy, religion. **Physical sciences:** Chemistry, geology, physics. **Protective services:** Firefighting, law enforcement admin. **Psychology:** General. **Social sciences:** Sociology. **Visual/performing arts:** Art, commercial/advertising art, dramatic, music. **Work/family studies:** Advocacy, child care management, food/nutrition, institutional food production.

Most popular majors. Health sciences 14%, liberal arts 78%.

Computing on campus. 1,500 workstations in library, computer center. Online course registration, wireless network available.

Student life. Freshman orientation: Mandatory. Preregistration for classes offered. **Activities:** Bands, campus ministries, choral groups, dance, drama, international student organizations, literary magazine, music ensembles, musical theater, student government, student newspaper, symphony orchestra, TV station, African-American student association, Wesley Foundation, Phi Theta Kappa, campus activities board, students for multi-cultural society.

Athletics. NJCAA. **Intercollegiate:** Baseball M, basketball, cheerleading, softball W, volleyball W. **Intramural:** Archery, badminton, basketball, bowling, racquetball, skin diving, soccer, softball W, table tennis, tennis, volleyball, water polo, weight lifting. **Team name:** Pirates.

Student services. Adult student services, alcohol/substance abuse counseling, chaplain/spiritual director, career counseling, services for economically disadvantaged, student employment services, financial aid counseling, health services, minority student services, on-campus daycare, personal counseling, placement for graduates, veterans' counselor, women's services. **Physically disabled:** Services for visually, speech, hearing impaired. **Transfer:** Pre-admission transcript evaluation for new students. Transfer adviser, college fairs on campus for students transferring to 4-year colleges.

Contact. Phone: (850) 484-1601 Toll-free number: (888) 897-3605 Fax: (850) 484-1829
Martha Caughey, Director Admissions and Registrar, Pensacola State College, 1000 College Boulevard, Pensacola, FL 32504-8998

Polk State College
Winter Haven, Florida
www.polk.edu

CB member
CB code: 5548

- Public 2-year community college
- Commuter campus in large town

General. Founded in 1963. Regionally accredited. Branch campus in Lakeland shared with University of South Florida. Additional locations in Lake Wales and Lakeland Airside. **Enrollment:** 9,648 degree-seeking undergraduates; 1,881 non-degree-seeking students. **Degrees:** 22 bachelor's, 1,287 associate awarded. **ROTC:** Army. **Location:** 60 miles from Tampa, 60 miles from Orlando. **Calendar:** Semester, extensive summer session. **Full-time faculty:** 183 total; 23% have terminal degrees, 17% minority, 57% women. **Part-time faculty:** 524 total; 9% have terminal degrees, 20% minority, 50% women. **Class size:** 38% < 20, 61% 20-39, less than 1% 40-49, less than 1% 50-99.

Student profile. Among degree-seeking undergraduates, 51% enrolled in a transfer program, 42% enrolled in a vocational program, 1,548 enrolled as first-time, first-year students, 166 transferred in from other institutions.

Part-time:	62%	Asian American:	2%
Out-of-state:	1%	Hispanic American:	15%
Women:	63%	International:	1%
African American:	20%	25 or older:	36%

Transfer out. Colleges most students transferred to 2011: University of South Florida, University of Central Florida, University of Florida, Florida State University.

Basis for selection. Open admission, but selective for some programs. Limited access to nursing, radiology, physical therapy assistant, occupational therapy assistant, respiratory therapy, paramedic programs, cardiovascular tech, medical sonography. Audition recommended for theater, music majors. Portfolio recommended for graphic arts majors. **Home schooled:** Adheres to FLDOE policy and Florida state statute: affidavit signed by guardian attesting to home school applicant completion required in place of high school diploma. **Learning Disabled:** Students needing classroom accommodations must provide documentation as required.

High school preparation. Recommended units include English 4, mathematics 4, social studies 3, science 3 and foreign language 2.

2011-2012 Annual costs. Tuition/fees: $3,102; $11,413 out-of-state. Reported tuition and fees for baccalaureate degree programs are slightly higher. Books/supplies: $2,000. Personal expenses: $3,696.

Financial aid. Need-based: Need-based aid available for part-time students. Work-study available nights, weekends and for part-time students. **Non-need-based:** Scholarships awarded for academics, athletics, leadership, state residency.

Application procedures. Admission: No deadline. No application fee. Admission notification on a rolling basis. **Financial aid:** Priority date 5/15; no closing date. FAFSA required. Applicants notified on a rolling basis.

Academics. Special study options: Accelerated study, cross-registration, distance learning, double major, dual enrollment of high school students, ESL, honors, independent study, internships. Bachelor's degree programs available on campus. License preparation in nursing, occupational therapy, paramedic, physical therapy, radiology. **Credit/placement by examination:** AP, CLEP, IB. 45 credit hours maximum toward associate degree. **Support services:** Learning center, reduced course load, remedial instruction, study skills assistance, tutoring.

Honors college/program. High school graduates with 3.5 GPA may apply for honors program and designated courses.

Majors. Business: Accounting, administrative services, banking/financial services, business admin, marketing, office management, office/clerical. **Computer sciences:** General, computer graphics, information systems, programming. **Education:** General. **Health services:** Cardiovascular technology, EMT paramedic, medical records technology, nursing (RN), occupational therapy assistant, physical therapy assistant, radiologic technology/medical imaging, respiratory therapy technology, sonography. **Liberal arts:** Arts/sciences. **Protective services:** Corrections, fire safety technology, law enforcement admin, police science. **Visual/performing arts:** Cinematography.

Most popular majors. Health sciences 18%, liberal arts 73%.

Computing on campus. 775 workstations in library, computer center, student center. Online course registration available.

Student life. Freshman orientation: Available. Preregistration for classes offered. **Activities:** Bands, choral groups, drama, music ensembles, musical theater, student government.

Athletics. NJCAA. **Intercollegiate:** Baseball M, basketball M, soccer W, softball W, volleyball W. **Intramural:** Basketball, bowling, football (non-tackle), table tennis, volleyball. **Team name:** Eagles.

Student services. Adult student services, career counseling, services for economically disadvantaged, student employment services, financial aid counseling, personal counseling. **Physically disabled:** Services for visually, speech, hearing impaired. **Transfer:** Re-entry adviser for new students. Transfer adviser, college fairs on campus for students transferring to 4-year colleges.

Contact. E-mail: studentservices@polk.edu
Phone: (863) 297-1010 ext. 5225 Fax: (863) 297-1060
Kathy Bucklew, Registrar, Polk State College, 999 Avenue H NE, Winter Haven, FL 33881-4299

Professional Golfers Career College: Orlando
Winter Garden, Florida
www.golfcollege.edu

- For-profit 2-year branch campus college
- Commuter campus in very large city

General. Accredited by ACICS. **Location:** 16 miles from Orlando. **Calendar:** Semester.

Contact. Phone: (866) 407-7422
Admissions Director, PO Box 892319, Temecula, CA 92589-2319

Saint Johns River State College
Palatka, Florida
www.sjrstate.edu

CB code: 5641

- Public 2-year community college
- Commuter campus in large town

General. Founded in 1957. Regionally accredited. The Florida School of the Arts, is part of St. Johns River State College and offers two year degrees in visual and performing arts. **Enrollment:** 5,951 degree-seeking undergraduates; 311 non-degree-seeking students. **Degrees:** 766 associate awarded. **Location:** 55 miles from Jacksonville and Daytona Beach. **Calendar:** Semester, limited summer session. **Full-time faculty:** 116 total. **Part-time faculty:** 286 total.

Student profile. Among degree-seeking undergraduates, 877 enrolled as first-time, first-year students.

Part-time:	60%	African American:	11%
Out-of-state:	2%	Asian American:	2%
Women:	62%	Hispanic American:	6%

Basis for selection. Open admission, but selective for some programs. Interview, audition, and portfolio required of applicants to Florida School of Arts program. **Home schooled:** Provide proof of a home education program meeting requirements of Florida Statutes 1002.41.

High school preparation. 24 units recommended. Recommended units include English 4, mathematics 3, social studies 3 and science 3.

2011-2012 Annual costs. Tuition/fees: $3,060; $11,548 out-of-state. Baccalaureate programs tuition and fees are $3,405 for in-state and $16,875 for out-of-state based on academic year of 30 credit hours. Books/supplies: $1,210. Personal expenses: $1,677.

Financial aid. Need-based: Need-based aid available for part-time students. Work-study available nights, weekends and for part-time students.

Application procedures. Admission: Priority date 7/15; no deadline. $30 fee. Application must be submitted online. Admission notification on a rolling basis. **Financial aid:** Priority date 7/1; no closing date. FAFSA required. Applicants notified on a rolling basis.

Two-Year Colleges

Academics. **Special study options:** Distance learning, dual enrollment of high school students, honors. Bachelor's degree programs available on campus. **Credit/placement by examination:** AP, CLEP, IB. 45 credit hours maximum toward associate degree. **Support services:** GED preparation, learning center, remedial instruction, tutoring.

Majors. **Business:** Accounting technology, business admin, executive assistant, finance, marketing, operations. **Computer sciences:** Applications programming, systems analysis. **Health services:** EMT paramedic, health care admin, medical radiologic technology/radiation therapy, medical records technology, nursing (RN), respiratory therapy technology. **Liberal arts:** Arts/sciences. **Protective services:** Fire safety technology, law enforcement admin. **Visual/performing arts:** Commercial/advertising art.

Most popular majors. Health sciences 15%, liberal arts 74%.

Computing on campus. Online course registration, online library, helpline, wireless network available.

Student life. **Freshman orientation:** Mandatory. Preregistration for classes offered. **Activities:** Student government, black student union, Phi Theta Kappa, Mathematical Association of America, sailing club, riding club, nature club.

Athletics. NJCAA. **Intercollegiate:** Baseball M, basketball M, softball W, volleyball W. **Team name:** Vikings.

Student services. Career counseling, financial aid counseling, veterans' counselor. **Physically disabled:** Services for visually, hearing impaired. **Transfer:** College fairs on campus for students transferring to 4-year colleges.

Contact. Phone: (386) 312-4030 Fax: (386) 312-4048
Susanne Lineberger, Director of Admission and Records, Saint Johns River State College, 5001 St. Johns Avenue, Palatka, FL 32177-3897

Sanford-Brown Institute: Jacksonville
Jacksonville, Florida
www.sbjacksonville.com

- For-profit 2-year health science and career college
- Commuter campus in very large city
- Interview required

General. Accredited by ACICS. **Enrollment:** 1,566 degree-seeking undergraduates. **Degrees:** 87 associate awarded. **Calendar:** Differs by program. **Full-time faculty:** 12 total. **Part-time faculty:** 33 total.

Basis for selection. Open admission, but selective for some programs. **Home schooled:** Transcript of courses and grades, state high school equivalency certificate, interview required.

Financial aid. **Need-based:** Work-study available nights, weekends and for part-time students.

Application procedures. **Admission:** No deadline. $50 fee, may be waived for applicants with need. Admission notification on a rolling basis.

Academics. **Special study options:** Distance learning, independent study, weekend college. License preparation in nursing. **Credit/placement by examination:** AP, CLEP. **Support services:** Learning center, reduced course load, remedial instruction, study skills assistance, tutoring.

Majors. **Health services:** Cardiovascular technology.

Computing on campus. 60 workstations in library, computer center, student center. Commuter students can connect to campus network. Online library, helpline available.

Student life. **Freshman orientation:** Mandatory. Preregistration for classes offered.

Student services. Adult student services, alcohol/substance abuse counseling, career counseling, student employment services, financial aid counseling, health services, personal counseling, placement for graduates. **Physically disabled:** Services for speech, hearing impaired. **Transfer:** Pre-admission transcript evaluation for new students.

Contact. Phone: (904) 363-6221 Toll-free number: (888) 577-5333 Fax: (904) 363-6824
Jaqueline Pratt, Director of Admissions, Sanford-Brown Institute: Jacksonville, 10255 Fortune Parkway, Suite 501, Jacksonville, FL 32256

Sanford-Brown Institute: Tampa
Tampa, Florida
www.sbtampa.com

- For-profit 2-year health science and community college
- Large city

General. Accredited by ACICS. **Calendar:** Differs by program.

Contact. Phone: (813) 621-0072
Director of Admissions, 5701 East Hillsboro Avenue, Tampa, FL 33610

Santa Fe College
Gainesville, Florida
www.sfcollege.edu
CB member
CB code: 5653

- Public 2-year community college
- Commuter campus in small city

General. Founded in 1965. Regionally accredited. Branch campuses located in Gainesville, Starke, Archer, Keystone Heights, and Alachua. **Enrollment:** 14,225 degree-seeking undergraduates; 1,268 non-degree-seeking students. **Degrees:** 18 bachelor's, 2,569 associate awarded. **ROTC:** Army, Air Force. **Location:** 80 miles from Jacksonville, 110 miles from Orlando. **Calendar:** Semester, extensive summer session. **Full-time faculty:** 230 total; 27% have terminal degrees, 15% minority, 56% women. **Part-time faculty:** 441 total; 17% minority, 54% women. **Class size:** 46% < 20, 54% 20-39, less than 1% 40-49, less than 1% 50-99, less than 1% >100. **Special facilities:** Teaching zoo, planetarium, rock cycle garden, laboratory pre-school.

Student profile. Among degree-seeking undergraduates, 76% enrolled in a transfer program, 6% enrolled in a vocational program, 2,453 enrolled as first-time, first-year students.

Part-time:	58%	Asian American:	2%
Out-of-state:	2%	Hispanic American:	8%
Women:	55%	International:	1%
African American:	12%	25 or older:	30%

Basis for selection. Open admission, but selective for some programs. Computerized placement tests, SAT or ACT required for placement.

2011-2012 Annual costs. Tuition/fees: $3,070; $11,322 out-of-state. Reported tuition and fees for baccalaureate degree programs are slightly higher. Books/supplies: $700. Personal expenses: $3,032.

Financial aid. **Need-based:** Need-based aid available for part-time students. Work-study available nights, weekends and for part-time students. **Non-need-based:** Scholarships awarded for academics, art, athletics, leadership, minority status, music/drama, state residency.

Application procedures. **Admission:** No deadline. No application fee. Application must be submitted online. Admission notification on a rolling basis. High school diploma not required of applicants to most vocational programs. **Financial aid:** Priority date 3/15, closing date 6/30. FAFSA required. Applicants notified by 8/1.

Academics. **Special study options:** Cooperative education, cross-registration, distance learning, dual enrollment of high school students, ESL, honors, independent study, internships, study abroad, teacher certification program, weekend college. Bachelor's degree programs available on campus. License preparation in aviation, dental hygiene, nursing, paramedic, radiology, real estate. **Credit/placement by examination:** AP, CLEP, IB, institutional tests. 30 credit hours maximum toward associate degree. **Support services:** GED preparation, learning center, remedial instruction, tutoring, writing center.

Majors. **Business:** Business admin, executive assistant. **Health services:** Cardiovascular technology, dental hygiene, EMT paramedic, medical radiologic technology/radiation therapy, medical records technology, nuclear medical technology, nursing (RN), respiratory therapy technology, sonography. **Liberal arts:** Arts/sciences. **Protective services:** Fire safety technology, law enforcement admin. **Visual/performing arts:** Cinematography. **Work/family studies:** Child care service.

Most popular majors. Health sciences 11%, liberal arts 82%.

Computing on campus. Commuter students can connect to campus network. Online course registration, online library, helpline, repair service, wireless network available.

Student life. Freshman orientation: Available. Preregistration for classes offered. **Policies:** Students expected to abide by student conduct code. **Activities:** Jazz band, campus ministries, choral groups, film society, international student organizations, literary magazine, music ensembles, Model UN, musical theater, student government, student newspaper, Campus Advent, Christians on Campus, black student union, Hispanic organization of Latino activities, international student cultural association, Democratic Saints, Republican club, Students for Environmental Harmony, Phi Theta Kappa, Circle K International.

Athletics. NJCAA. **Intercollegiate:** Baseball M, basketball, softball W. **Intramural:** Basketball, football (non-tackle), golf, racquetball, soccer, volleyball, weight lifting. **Team name:** Saints.

Student services. Adult student services, alcohol/substance abuse counseling, career counseling, services for economically disadvantaged, student employment services, financial aid counseling, health services, legal services, minority student services, on-campus daycare, personal counseling, placement for graduates, veterans' counselor, women's services. **Physically disabled:** Services for visually, speech, hearing impaired. **Transfer:** Transfer adviser, college fairs on campus for students transferring to 4-year colleges.

Contact. E-mail: admission@sfcollege.edu
Phone: (352) 395-7322 Fax: (352) 395-7300
Michael Hutley, Associate Registrar, Santa Fe College, 3000 NW 83rd Street, R-112, Gainesville, FL 32606-6210

Seminole State College of Florida
Sanford, Florida
www.seminolestate.edu   **CB code: 5662**

▸ Public 2-year community college
▸ Commuter campus in large town

General. Founded in 1965. Regionally accredited. **Enrollment:** 17,709 degree-seeking undergraduates; 1,075 non-degree-seeking students. **Degrees:** 2,146 associate awarded. **Location:** 21 miles from Orlando. **Calendar:** Semester, limited summer session. **Full-time faculty:** 196 total; 17% have terminal degrees, 18% minority, 61% women. **Part-time faculty:** 588 total; 22% minority, 52% women. **Class size:** 16% < 20, 82% 20-39, 2% 40-49, less than 1% 50-99, less than 1% >100. **Special facilities:** Planetarium. **Partnerships:** Formal partnerships with Siemens/Stromberg, local businesses.

Student profile. Among degree-seeking undergraduates, 3,388 enrolled as first-time, first-year students, 1,858 transferred in from other institutions.

Part-time:	53%	Asian American:	2%
Out-of-state:	3%	Hispanic American:	21%
Women:	61%	International:	2%
African American:	18%	25 or older:	48%

Basis for selection. Open admission, but selective for some programs. Limited access to associate of science degrees including nursing, physical therapy, and respiratory care. Interview recommended for respiratory therapy, nursing, and physical therapy majors. **Home schooled:** Affidavit of home school completion required.

High school preparation. College-preparatory program recommended. 24 units required. Required units include English 4, mathematics 4, social studies 3, science 3, visual/performing arts 1 and academic electives 8. PE-1.

2011-2012 Annual costs. Tuition/fees: $3,074; $11,399 out-of-state. Reported tuition and fees for baccalaureate degree programs are slightly higher. Books/supplies: $1,200. Personal expenses: $900.

Financial aid. Need-based: Need-based aid available for part-time students. Work-study available nights, weekends and for part-time students. **Non-need-based:** Scholarships awarded for academics, art, athletics, leadership, minority status, music/drama, state residency.

Application procedures. Admission: Closing date 8/12 (postmark date). No application fee. Admission notification on a rolling basis. **Financial aid:** Priority date 7/1; no closing date. FAFSA required. Applicants notified on a rolling basis starting 4/1.

Academics. Special study options: Accelerated study, cooperative education, cross-registration, distance learning, dual enrollment of high school students, ESL, honors, independent study, study abroad, teacher certification program, weekend college. Bachelor's degree programs available on campus. **Credit/placement by examination:** AP, CLEP, IB, institutional tests. 45 credit hours maximum toward associate degree. **Support services:** GED preparation and test center, learning center, reduced course load, remedial instruction, study skills assistance, tutoring.

Majors. Architecture: Interior. **Business:** Accounting technology, administrative services, banking/financial services, business admin, marketing, office management. **Communications:** Communications/speech/rhetoric. **Communications technology:** General. **Computer sciences:** General, applications programming, computer graphics, computer science, data processing, information systems, networking, programming, systems analysis. **Education:** Kindergarten/preschool. **Engineering:** Electrical, software. **Health services:** EMT paramedic, medical records technology, medical secretary, nursing (RN), physical therapy assistant, respiratory therapy technology. **Liberal arts:** Arts/sciences. **Protective services:** Fire safety technology, firefighting, law enforcement admin. **Visual/performing arts:** Commercial/advertising art, interior design. **Work/family studies:** Child care management.

Most popular majors. Health sciences 11%, liberal arts 74%, trade and industry 7%.

Computing on campus. 100 workstations in library, computer center. Commuter students can connect to campus network. Online course registration, online library, helpline, student web hosting, wireless network available.

Student life. Freshman orientation: Mandatory. Preregistration for classes offered. **Activities:** Bands, choral groups, drama, film society, international student organizations, literary magazine, music ensembles, musical theater, student government, student newspaper, symphony orchestra, African American cultural forum, disabled student association, Hispanic student associations, Muslim student association, Unity Gay Straight Alliance, Fellowship of Christian Athletes, Campus Crusade for Christ, Intervarsity Christian Fellowship, Sigma Phi Gamma.

Athletics. NJCAA. **Intercollegiate:** Baseball M, golf W, softball W. **Team name:** Raider.

Student services. Adult student services, alcohol/substance abuse counseling, career counseling, services for economically disadvantaged, student employment services, financial aid counseling, minority student services, personal counseling, placement for graduates, veterans' counselor. **Physically disabled:** Services for visually, speech, hearing impaired. **Transfer:** Transfer adviser for students transferring to 4-year colleges.

Contact. E-mail: admissions@seminolestate.edu
Phone: (407) 708-2580 Fax: (407) 708-2395
Pamela Mennechey, Associate Vice President of Recruitment and Admissions, Seminole State College of Florida, 100 Weldon Boulevard, Sanford, FL 32773-6199

South Florida Community College
Avon Park, Florida   **CB member**
www.southflorida.edu   **CB code: 5666**

▸ Public 2-year community and technical college
▸ Commuter campus in small town

General. Founded in 1965. Regionally accredited. **Enrollment:** 2,066 degree-seeking undergraduates; 693 non-degree-seeking students. **Degrees:** 531 associate awarded. **Location:** 90 miles from Orlando. **Calendar:** Semester, limited summer session. **Full-time faculty:** 62 total; 24% have terminal degrees, 5% minority, 55% women. **Part-time faculty:** 159 total; 6% have terminal degrees, 20% minority, 50% women. **Class size:** 61% < 20, 37% 20-39, 2% 40-49. **Special facilities:** Museum of Florida Art and Culture, nature walk.

Student profile. Among degree-seeking undergraduates, 57% enrolled in a transfer program, 43% enrolled in a vocational program, 419 enrolled as first-time, first-year students, 98 transferred in from other institutions.

Part-time:	52%	Hispanic American:	27%
Out-of-state:	2%	International:	1%
Women:	62%	25 or older:	23%
African American:	11%	Live on campus:	2%
Asian American:	2%		

Basis for selection. Open admission, but selective for some programs. Some programs have test and prerequisite requirements. Interview recommended for selected programs. **Home schooled:** Students must meet with registrar prior to admission. **Learning Disabled:** Recommend students seek assistance from campus disabilities specialist.

High school preparation. College-preparatory program recommended. 24 units recommended. Recommended units include English 4, mathematics 4, social studies 1, history 2, science 3 (laboratory 2), visual/performing arts 1 and academic electives 9.

2011-2012 Annual costs. Tuition/fees: $2,987; $11,267 out-of-state. Books/supplies: $994. Personal expenses: $1,093.

Two-Year Colleges

2010-2011 Financial aid. Need-based: 71% of total undergraduate aid awarded as scholarships/grants, 29% as loans/jobs. Need-based aid available for part-time students. Work-study available nights, weekends and for part-time students. **Non-need-based:** Scholarships awarded for academics, athletics, leadership, minority status, music/drama, state residency.

Application procedures. Admission: No deadline. No application fee. Admission notification on a rolling basis. **Financial aid:** Priority date 4/15; no closing date. FAFSA required. Applicants notified on a rolling basis starting 4/1.

Academics. Special study options: Accelerated study, cooperative education, distance learning, double major, dual enrollment of high school students, ESL, external degree, honors, independent study, internships, teacher certification program. Bachelor's degree programs available on campus. License preparation in dental hygiene, nursing, paramedic, radiology. **Credit/placement by examination:** AP, CLEP, IB, institutional tests. 30 credit hours maximum toward associate degree. **Support services:** GED preparation and test center, learning center, reduced course load, remedial instruction, study skills assistance, tutoring, writing center.

Majors. Business: Accounting, administrative services, business admin, hospitality admin. **Computer sciences:** LAN/WAN management, programming. **Education:** Teacher assistance. **English:** English lit. **General:** Ornamental horticulture. **Health services:** Dental hygiene, EMT paramedic, medical secretary, nursing (RN), radiologic technology/medical imaging. **Liberal arts:** Arts/sciences. **Protective services:** Firefighting, law enforcement admin. **Work/family studies:** Child care management.

Most popular majors. Health sciences 17%, liberal arts 74%, trade and industry 6%.

Computing on campus. 100 workstations in library, computer center, student center. Online course registration, online library, wireless network available.

Student life. Freshman orientation: Mandatory. Preregistration for classes offered. Online video with review quiz. **Housing:** Single-sex dorms, wellness housing available. **Activities:** Campus ministries, dance, drama, international student organizations, music ensembles, student government, student newspaper, African American association, anime/gaming club, art club, Brain Bowl, HC Panther Ambassadors, Jac Pac, Phi Beta Lambda, Phi Theta Kappa, radiography club, student nurses association.

Athletics. NJCAA. **Intercollegiate:** Softball W, volleyball W. **Intramural:** Baseball M, bowling, football (tackle), soccer, volleyball. **Team name:** Panthers.

Student services. Adult student services, career counseling, services for economically disadvantaged, student employment services, financial aid counseling, minority student services, personal counseling, placement for graduates, veterans' counselor, women's services. **Physically disabled:** Services for visually, speech, hearing impaired. **Transfer:** Transfer adviser, college fairs on campus for students transferring to 4-year colleges.

Contact. E-mail: deborah.fuschetti@southflorida.edu
Phone: (863) 453-6661 ext. 7405 Fax: (863) 453-2365
Deborah Fuschetti, Registrar, South Florida Community College, 600 West College Drive, Avon Park, FL 33825

Southern Career College
Jacksonville, Florida
www.southerncareercollege.edu   CB code: 3590

- For-profit 2-year technical college
- Very large city

General. Regionally accredited. **Calendar:** Differs by program.

Contact. Phone: (904) 724-2229
Campus Director, 9550 Regency Square Boulevard, Jacksonville, FL 32225

Southwest Florida College
Fort Myers, Florida
www.swfc.edu   CB code: 3445

- Private 2-year career college
- Commuter campus in large city

General. Regionally accredited; also accredited by ACICS. Learning site in Estero. **Enrollment:** 1,649 degree-seeking undergraduates. **Degrees:** 68 bachelor's, 650 associate awarded. **Location:** 130 miles from Tampa. **Calendar:** Quarter, extensive summer session. **Full-time faculty:** 44 total; 9% have terminal degrees, 11% minority, 59% women. **Part-time faculty:** 133 total; 8% have terminal degrees, 21% minority, 57% women. **Class size:** 64% < 20, 36% 20-39.

Basis for selection. Open admission, but selective for some programs. Surgical Technology requires interview with program manager prior to acceptance.

2011-2012 Annual costs. Tuition/fees: $16,875. Per-credit charge: $350. Books/supplies: $1,110. Personal expenses: $1,968.

Financial aid. Need-based: Need-based aid available for part-time students. Work-study available nights, weekends and for part-time students.

Application procedures. Admission: No deadline. $25 fee. Application must be submitted on paper. Admission notification on a rolling basis. **Financial aid:** No deadline. FAFSA required. Applicants notified on a rolling basis.

Academics. Online academic assistance availabe to students enrolled in online courses. **Special study options:** Accelerated study, cooperative education, distance learning, double major, internships, liberal arts/career combination, teacher certification program. Bachelor's degree programs available on campus. **Credit/placement by examination:** AP, CLEP, institutional tests. 24 credit hours maximum toward associate degree, 48 toward bachelor's. **Support services:** Learning center, reduced course load, remedial instruction, study skills assistance, tutoring, writing center.

Majors. Business: Accounting, marketing. **Communications technology:** Animation/special effects. **Computer sciences:** Information technology, networking, programming, web page design. **Education:** Early childhood. **Engineering:** Computer. **Health services:** Massage therapy, medical assistant, medical records technology, surgical technology. **Protective services:** Law enforcement admin. **Visual/performing arts:** Interior design.

Most popular majors. Business/marketing 16%, communication technologies 13%, computer/information sciences 9%, education 8%, health sciences 30%, security/protective services 12%, visual/performing arts 6%.

Computing on campus. 195 workstations in library, computer center, student center. Commuter students can connect to campus network. Online library, repair service, wireless network available.

Student life. Freshman orientation: Mandatory. Preregistration for classes offered. Held the Saturday before classes begin and lasts approximately 1-2 hours. **Activities:** Student newspaper.

Student services. Adult student services, career counseling, services for economically disadvantaged, student employment services, financial aid counseling, placement for graduates. **Physically disabled:** Services for visually, speech, hearing impaired. **Transfer:** Re-entry adviser, pre-admission transcript evaluation for new students.

Contact. E-mail: jgonzales@swfc.edu
Phone: (239) 939-4766 Toll-free number: (877) 493-5147
Fax: (239) 936-4040
Jeff Gonzales, Director of Admissions, Southwest Florida College, 1685 Medical Lane, Ft. Myers, FL 33907-1108

Southwest Florida College: Tampa
Tampa, Florida
www.swfc.edu

- Private 2-year branch campus and junior college
- Commuter campus in very large city

General. Accredited by ACICS. **Location:** 15 miles from downtown. **Calendar:** Quarter.

Annual costs/financial aid. Tuition/fees (2011-2012): $16,875. Tuition and fees includes books. Books/supplies: $1,110.

Contact. Phone: (813) 630-4401
Vice President of Admissions, 3910 Riga Boulevard, Tampa, FL 33619

St. Petersburg College

St. Petersburg, Florida

CB member
CB code: 5606
www.spcollege.edu

- Public 2-year community college
- Commuter campus in large city

General. Founded in 1927. Regionally accredited. Campuses include Clearwater, Seminole, St. Petersburg, Tarpon Springs. Health education center in Pinellas Park. Criminal justice/computer complex in St. Petersburg. Corporate training and Cisco at the Epicenter. Downtown and Midtown centers. **Enrollment:** 28,077 degree-seeking undergraduates; 5,051 non-degree-seeking students. **Degrees:** 1,049 bachelor's, 3,624 associate awarded. **Location:** 20 miles from Tampa. **Calendar:** Semester, extensive summer session. **Full-time faculty:** 332 total; 37% have terminal degrees, 20% minority, 56% women. **Part-time faculty:** 1,486 total; 18% minority, 48% women. **Special facilities:** Observatory, planetarium, firing range, college-operated museums, theater, nature preserves.

Student profile. Among degree-seeking undergraduates, 43% enrolled in a transfer program, 32% enrolled in a vocational program, 3,658 enrolled as first-time, first-year students.

Part-time:	65%	Women:	61%
Out-of-state:	3%	25 or older:	50%

Basis for selection. Open admission, but selective for some programs. Limited enrollment to health-related programs. Florida CPT required for all degree-seeking students. Interview recommended for allied health applicants. **Home schooled:** Transcript of courses and grades, state high school equivalency certificate required.

2011-2012 Annual costs. Tuition/fees: $2,907; $11,414 out-of-state. Tuition and fees for baccalaureate degree programs are slightly higher. Books/supplies: $1,600. Personal expenses: $4,337.

Financial aid. Need-based: Need-based aid available for part-time students. Work-study available nights, weekends and for part-time students. **Non-need-based:** Scholarships awarded for academics, art, athletics, minority status, music/drama.

Application procedures. Admission: No deadline. $40 fee. Admission notification on a rolling basis. **Financial aid:** Priority date 4/15; no closing date. FAFSA required. Applicants notified on a rolling basis starting 5/15; must reply within 2 week(s) of notification.

Academics. Special study options: Accelerated study, cooperative education, cross-registration, distance learning, dual enrollment of high school students, ESL, exchange student, honors, independent study, internships, liberal arts/career combination, study abroad, teacher certification program, weekend college. 2-year associate degree program in business and computer science for deaf students. Bachelor's degree programs available on campus. License preparation in dental hygiene, nursing, paramedic, physical therapy, radiology. **Credit/placement by examination:** AP, CLEP, IB, institutional tests. 45 credit hours maximum toward associate degree, 45 toward bachelor's. Florida CPT required for placement. **Support services:** GED preparation, learning center, reduced course load, remedial instruction, study skills assistance, tutoring.

Majors. Business: Banking/financial services, business admin, hospitality admin. **Computer sciences:** Programming, web page design, webmaster. **Education:** Early childhood. **Health services:** Clinical lab technology, dental hygiene, EMT paramedic, medical records admin, nursing (RN), physical therapy assistant, radiologic technology/medical imaging, respiratory therapy technology, substance abuse counseling, veterinary technology/assistant. **Liberal arts:** Arts/sciences. **Parks/recreation:** General. **Protective services:** Firefighting, forensics, law enforcement admin. **Visual/performing arts:** Music, photography.

Most popular majors. Health sciences 18%, liberal arts 74%.

Computing on campus. 4,110 workstations in library, computer center, student center. Commuter students can connect to campus network. Online course registration, online library, helpline, student web hosting, wireless network available.

Student life. Freshman orientation: Mandatory. Preregistration for classes offered. **Activities:** Jazz band, choral groups, dance, drama, film society, international student organizations, literary magazine, music ensembles, student government, student newspaper, Phi Theta Kappa, Harambee black culture club, ethics club, math and science club, American Sign Language club, Rotary club, College Deomocrats, College Republicans, digital artists in motion, hospitality club.

Athletics. NJCAA. **Intercollegiate:** Baseball M, basketball, softball W, tennis W, volleyball W. **Team name:** Titans.

Student services. Career counseling, services for economically disadvantaged, student employment services, financial aid counseling, health services, minority student services, personal counseling, placement for graduates, veterans' counselor, women's services. **Physically disabled:** Services for visually, speech, hearing impaired. **Transfer:** College fairs on campus for students transferring to 4-year colleges.

Contact. E-mail: information@spcollege.edu
Phone: (727) 341-4772
Susan Fell, Director of Admissions and Records, St. Petersburg College, Box 13489, St. Petersburg, FL 33733-3489

State College of Florida, Manatee-Sarasota

Bradenton, Florida

CB member
CB code: 5427
www.scf.edu

- Public 2-year nursing and community college
- Commuter campus in small city

General. Founded in 1957. Regionally accredited. **Enrollment:** 10,154 degree-seeking undergraduates; 1,149 non-degree-seeking students. **Degrees:** 57 bachelor's, 2,271 associate awarded. **Location:** 40 miles from Tampa, 20 miles from St. Petersburg. **Calendar:** Semester, extensive summer session. **Full-time faculty:** 174 total; 24% have terminal degrees, 10% minority, 64% women. **Part-time faculty:** 362 total; 4% have terminal degrees, 10% minority, 59% women.

Student profile. Among degree-seeking undergraduates, 59% enrolled in a transfer program, 41% enrolled in a vocational program, 1,541 enrolled as first-time, first-year students.

Part-time:	55%	Women:	60%
Out-of-state:	2%	25 or older:	40%

Basis for selection. Open admission, but selective for some programs. Limited enrollment in health programs. Interview recommended for nursing, radiologic technology, respiratory therapy, occupational therapy assistant, physical therapist assistant, dental hygiene majors.

High school preparation. Recommended units include English 4, mathematics 3, social studies 2, history 1, science 3 and foreign language 2.

2011-2012 Annual costs. Tuition/fees: $3,074; $11,595 out-of-state. Reported tuition and fees for baccalaureate degree programs are slightly higher. Books/supplies: $1,202. Personal expenses: $1,910.

Financial aid. Need-based: Need-based aid available for part-time students. Work-study available nights, weekends and for part-time students. **Non-need-based:** Scholarships awarded for academics, art, athletics, music/drama, state residency.

Application procedures. Admission: No deadline. No application fee. Admission notification on a rolling basis. **Financial aid:** Priority date 6/1, closing date 7/28. FAFSA required. Applicants notified on a rolling basis starting 3/15.

Academics. Special study options: Accelerated study, cooperative education, distance learning, dual enrollment of high school students, honors, independent study, teacher certification program. License preparation in dental hygiene, nursing, occupational therapy, physical therapy, radiology. **Credit/placement by examination:** AP, CLEP. 30 credit hours maximum toward associate degree. SAT, ACT or CPT (Florida Placement Test) used for placement only. **Support services:** GED preparation, learning center, remedial instruction, study skills assistance, tutoring.

Majors. Biology: Biotechnology. **Business:** Accounting, business admin, hospitality admin. **Computer sciences:** Networking, programming, systems analysis. **Education:** Early childhood. **Engineering:** Civil, computer, engineering science. **Health services:** Dental hygiene, EMT ambulance attendant, medical radiologic technology/radiation therapy, nursing (RN), occupational therapy assistant, physical therapy assistant. **Liberal arts:** Arts/sciences. **Protective services:** Criminal justice, firefighting. **Visual/performing arts:** Graphic design.

Computing on campus. 2,275 workstations in library, computer center. Commuter students can connect to campus network. Online course registration, online library, helpline, repair service, wireless network available.

Student life. Freshman orientation: Mandatory. Preregistration for classes offered. **Activities:** Bands, campus ministries, choral groups, dance, drama, film society, international student organizations, literary magazine, music ensembles, musical theater, opera, student government, student newspaper, symphony orchestra, African-American Student Union, multicultural

student club, art club, student Bible club, Manasota Geographic and Anthropological Society, American Chemical Society, student film club, Hispanic-American club.

Athletics. NJCAA. **Intercollegiate:** Baseball M, basketball M, softball W, volleyball W. **Intramural:** Basketball, golf, soccer, softball, volleyball, weight lifting. **Team name:** Manatees.

Student services. Chaplain/spiritual director, career counseling, student employment services, financial aid counseling, health services, personal counseling, placement for graduates, veterans' counselor. **Physically disabled:** Services for visually, speech, hearing impaired. **Transfer:** Transfer adviser for students transferring to 4-year colleges.

Contact. E-mail: admissions@scf.edu
Phone: (941) 752-5031 Fax: (941) 727-6380
Marilynn Lewy, Registrar, State College of Florida, Manatee-Sarasota, Box 1849, Bradenton, FL 34206-1849

Stenotype Institute: Jacksonville
Jacksonville, Florida
www.stenotype.edu

◗ For-profit 2-year business and community college
◗ Very large city

General. Accredited by ACICS. **Enrollment:** 247 degree-seeking undergraduates. **Degrees:** 7 associate awarded. **Calendar:** Differs by program. **Full-time faculty:** 15 total.

Basis for selection. Admission based on ability, ambition, and character. Prior experience with typing and word processing also important.

Financial aid. Need-based: Work-study available nights, weekends and for part-time students.

Application procedures. Admission: Closing date 5/2. $100 fee.

Academics. Credit/placement by examination: AP, CLEP.

Contact. E-mail: info@thestenotypeinstitute.com
Phone: (904) 398-4141 Toll-free number: (800) 273-5090
Fax: (904) 398-7878
LaNell Derby, Director of Admissions, Stenotype Institute: Jacksonville, 3563 Phillips Highway, Building E, #501, Jacksonville, FL 32207

Stenotype Institute: Orlando
Orlando, Florida
www.stenotype.edu

◗ For-profit 2-year technical college
◗ Very large city

General. Accredited by ACICS. **Enrollment:** 209 degree-seeking undergraduates. **Degrees:** 6 associate awarded. **Calendar:** Semester. **Full-time faculty:** 8 total. **Part-time faculty:** 2 total.

Basis for selection. Open admission.

Financial aid. Need-based: Work-study available nights, weekends and for part-time students.

Academics. Credit/placement by examination: AP, CLEP.

Contact. Phone: (407) 816-5573 Toll-free number: (800) 273-5090
David Miller, Director of Admissions, Stenotype Institute: Orlando, 1636 West Oakridge Road, Orlando, FL 32809

Tallahassee Community College
Tallahassee, Florida
www.tcc.fl.edu   **CB code: 5794**

◗ Public 2-year community college
◗ Commuter campus in small city

General. Founded in 1965. Regionally accredited. **Enrollment:** 13,477 degree-seeking undergraduates. **Degrees:** 2,790 associate awarded. **ROTC:** Army, Naval, Air Force. **Location:** 164 miles from Jacksonville. **Calendar:**

Semester, extensive summer session. **Full-time faculty:** 187 total; 27% have terminal degrees, 27% minority, 57% women. **Part-time faculty:** 681 total; 18% have terminal degrees, 27% minority, 42% women. **Class size:** 14% < 20, 66% 20-39, 15% 40-49, 5% 50-99. **Special facilities:** Center for Health Care Education.

Student profile. Among degree-seeking undergraduates, 24% enrolled in a transfer program, .28% enrolled in a vocational program, 2,642 enrolled as first-time, first-year students, 1,472 transferred in from other institutions.

Part-time:	46%	25 or older:	34%
Women:	53%		

Transfer out. Colleges most students transferred to 2011: Florida State University.

Basis for selection. Open admission, but selective for some programs. Special requirements for nursing, dental hygiene, emergency medical technology, radiologic technology and respiratory therapy programs. Each program requires specific course prerequisites or test scores or required GPA in addition to letters of recommendation. **Home schooled:** Present affidavit verifying completion of high school requirements. **Learning Disabled:** If service or accommodations are needed, documentation required.

2011-2012 Annual costs. Tuition/fees: $2,905; $11,220 out-of-state. Books/supplies: $800. Personal expenses: $1,800.

2010-2011 Financial aid. Need-based: 51% of total undergraduate aid awarded as scholarships/grants, 49% as loans/jobs. Need-based aid available for part-time students. Work-study available nights, weekends and for part-time students. **Non-need-based:** Scholarships awarded for academics, art, athletics, leadership, music/drama, state residency.

Application procedures. Admission: Closing date 8/9 (receipt date). No application fee. Admission notification on a rolling basis. Separate application procedure for health programs. **Financial aid:** Priority date 5/1; no closing date. FAFSA, institutional form required. Applicants notified on a rolling basis starting 5/15.

Academics. Special study options: Cooperative education, cross-registration, distance learning, double major, dual enrollment of high school students, ESL, honors, independent study, liberal arts/career combination, study abroad. Bachelor's degree programs available on campus. License preparation in dental hygiene, nursing, paramedic, radiology, real estate. **Credit/placement by examination:** AP, CLEP, IB, institutional tests. 45 credit hours maximum toward associate degree. **Support services:** GED preparation, learning center, pre-admission summer program, reduced course load, remedial instruction, study skills assistance, tutoring, writing center.

Majors. Business: General, accounting, administrative services, banking/financial services, business admin, management information systems, sales/distribution. **Computer sciences:** Computer graphics, networking, programming. **Education:** Early childhood, health. **Engineering:** General, civil, software. **Health services:** Dental hygiene, EMT paramedic, medical radiologic technology/radiation therapy, nursing (RN), respiratory therapy technology. **Human services:** General. **Liberal arts:** Arts/sciences. **Parks/recreation:** Facilities management. **Protective services:** Criminal justice, law enforcement admin. **Social sciences:** General. **Visual/performing arts:** General, commercial/advertising art, film/cinema/video. **Work/family studies:** Child care service.

Most popular majors. Liberal arts 92%.

Computing on campus. 1,733 workstations in library, computer center, student center. Commuter students can connect to campus network. Online course registration, online library, helpline, wireless network available.

Student life. Freshman orientation: Mandatory. Preregistration for classes offered. All-day event held few days prior to start of term; includes small group meetings and advising. Online orientation also available. **Activities:** Bands, campus ministries, choral groups, dance, drama, international student organizations, literary magazine, music ensembles, musical theater, student government, student newspaper, TV station, Phi Theta Kappa, black student union, Returning Adults Valuing Education, Future Educators of America, students interested in legal careers, College Democrats, BACCHUS, student environmental action coalition.

Athletics. NJCAA. **Intercollegiate:** Baseball M, basketball, softball W. **Intramural:** Basketball, golf, soccer, softball, table tennis, tennis. **Team name:** Eagles.

Student services. Adult student services, career counseling, services for economically disadvantaged, financial aid counseling, minority student services, on-campus daycare, personal counseling, placement for graduates, veterans' counselor. **Physically disabled:** Services for visually, speech, hearing impaired. **Transfer:** Transfer adviser, college fairs on campus for students transferring to 4-year colleges.

Contact. E-mail: enrollment@tcc.fl.edu
Phone: (850) 201-8555 Fax: (850) 201-8474
Sheri Rowland, Dean, Enrollment Services, Tallahassee Community
College, 444 Appleyard Drive, Tallahassee, FL 32304

Valencia College
Orlando, Florida
CB member
www.valenciacollege.edu
CB code: 5869

- Public 2-year community college
- Commuter campus in very large city

General. Founded in 1967. Regionally accredited. **Enrollment:** 36,049
degree-seeking undergraduates; 6,582 non-degree-seeking students. **Degrees:**
6,303 associate awarded. **ROTC:** Army, Air Force. **Location:** 90 miles from
Tampa, 145 miles from Jacksonville. **Calendar:** Semester, extensive summer
session. **Full-time faculty:** 408 total; 21% have terminal degrees, 24% minority, 59% women. **Part-time faculty:** 1,197 total; 35% minority, 53% women.
Class size: 10% < 20, 90% 20-39, less than 1% 40-49, less than 1% 50-99,
less than 1% >100. **Special facilities:** Performing arts center (East Campus).

Student profile. Among degree-seeking undergraduates, 24% enrolled in
a transfer program, 76% enrolled in a vocational program, 8,210 enrolled as
first-time, first-year students, 2,533 transferred in from other institutions.

Part-time:	54%	Asian American:	4%
Out-of-state:	3%	Hispanic American:	32%
Women:	56%	International:	1%
African American:	19%	25 or older:	40%

Transfer out. 60% of students enrolled in the transfer program go on to
4-year colleges. **Colleges most students transferred to 2011:** University of
Central Florida, University of Florida.

Basis for selection. Open admission, but selective for some programs.
Selective admission for high school dual enrollment, criminal justice, dance
performance, film production, health programs and bachelor's degrees. **Home
schooled:** Home school diplomas accepted with official home school verification affidavit.

High school preparation. College-preparatory program recommended.
Recommended units include English 4, mathematics 3, social studies 3 and
science 3.

2011-2012 Annual costs. Tuition/fees: $2,972; $11,257 out-of-state.
Books/supplies: $1,178. Personal expenses: $8,477.

Financial aid. Need-based: Need-based aid available for part-time students. Work-study available nights, weekends and for part-time students.

Application procedures. Admission: Closing date 8/12 (postmark date).
$50 fee. Admission notification on a rolling basis beginning on or about
3/31. **Financial aid:** Closing date 3/15. FAFSA required. Applicants notified
on a rolling basis starting 4/2; must reply within 2 week(s) of notification.

Academics. Special study options: Cooperative education, distance learning, double major, dual enrollment of high school students, ESL, honors,
independent study, internships, student-designed major, study abroad, weekend college. License preparation in dental hygiene, nursing, paramedic, radiology. **Credit/placement by examination:** AP, CLEP, IB, institutional tests.
45 credit hours maximum toward associate degree. Less than 75 percent of
a program's hours may be met with credit by examination and/or other
acceleration mechanisms. **Support services:** Learning center, remedial
instruction, study skills assistance, tutoring, writing center.

Majors. Architecture: Technology. **Business:** Accounting, accounting
technology, business admin, entrepreneurial studies, hospitality admin, human
resources, management information systems, marketing, real estate, restau-
rant/food services, small business admin. **Computer sciences:** General, computer science, information technology, programming, systems analysis, webmaster. **Engineering:** General. **General:** Horticultural science, landscaping.
Health services: Cardiovascular technology, dental hygiene, EMT paramedic, insurance coding, medical records admin, medical records technology,
medical secretary, nursing (RN), radiologic technology/medical imaging,
sonography. **Liberal arts:** Arts/sciences. **Protective services:** Fire safety
technology, law enforcement admin, police science. **Visual/performing arts:**
Dance, graphic design, theater design. **Work/family studies:** Institutional
food production.

Most popular majors. Business/marketing 10%, health sciences 6%, liberal arts 78%.

Computing on campus. 2,500 workstations in library, computer center,
student center. Commuter students can connect to campus network. Online
course registration, online library, helpline, wireless network available.

Student life. Freshman orientation: Mandatory. Preregistration for
classes offered. Two-hour program. **Activities:** Bands, choral groups, dance,
drama, international student organizations, literary magazine, music ensembles, musical theater, student government, student newspaper, symphony
orchestra, African American cultural society, Brain Bowl, Latin American
student organization, student nurses association, volunteer club, Phi Beta
Lambda, Earth club, Muslim student organization, black high achievers club.

Student services. Career counseling, student employment services, financial aid counseling, health services, personal counseling, placement for graduates, veterans' counselor. **Physically disabled:** Services for visually, hearing
impaired. **Transfer:** College fairs on campus for students transferring to 4-
year colleges.

Contact. Phone: (407) 582-1507 Fax: (407) 582-1403
Renee Simpson, Director of Admissions and Records, Valencia College,
PO Box 3028, Orlando, FL 32802-3028

Virginia College at Jacksonville
Jacksonville, Florida
www.jacksonville.vc.edu

- For-profit 2-year technical and career college
- Very large city

General. Regionally accredited; also accredited by ACICS. **Enrollment:**
800 degree-seeking undergraduates. **Degrees:** 26 associate awarded. **Calendar:** Quarter. **Full-time faculty:** 26 total. **Part-time faculty:** 16 total.

Basis for selection. Open admission.

Financial aid. Need-based: Work-study available nights, weekends and
for part-time students.

Application procedures. Admission: $100 fee.

Academics. Credit/placement by examination: AP, CLEP.

Majors. Business: Business admin. **Health services:** Medical records
admin, surgical technology.

Contact. E-mail: jacksonville.info@vc.edu
Phone: (904) 520-7400
Virginia College at Jacksonville, 5940 Beach Boulevard, Jacksonville, FL
32207

Virginia College at Pensacola
Pensacola, Florida
www.vc.edu/pensacola

- For-profit 2-year business and health science college
- Commuter campus in small city

General. Accredited by ACICS. **Enrollment:** 451 degree-seeking undergraduates. **Degrees:** 112 associate awarded. **Calendar:** Quarter, extensive
summer session. **Full-time faculty:** 12 total. **Part-time faculty:** 37 total.

Basis for selection. Open admission.

2011-2012 Annual costs. Tuition/fees: $21,900. Tuition is typical for
full-time attendance for four quarters and depends on program, hours
attempted, and other factors. Tuition includes textbooks and fees.

Financial aid. Need-based: Work-study available nights, weekends and
for part-time students.

Application procedures. Admission: $100 fee.

Academics. Credit/placement by examination: AP, CLEP. **Support services:** Learning center, remedial instruction, tutoring.

Majors. Business: Administrative services, business admin, office management. **Health services:** Medical assistant, medical claims examiner, medical
records technology, office assistant, pharmacy assistant, surgical technology.

Computing on campus. 80 workstations in library, computer center.
Online library available.

Contact. E-mail: hrobbins@vc.edu
Phone: (850) 436-8444 Toll-free number: (888) 208-6932
Fax: (850) 436-4838
Melanie Parlier, Director of Admissions, Virginia College at Pensacola,
19 West Garden Street, Pensacola, FL 32502

Georgia

Abraham Baldwin Agricultural College
Tifton, Georgia
www.abac.edu

CB member
CB code: 5001

- Public 2-year agricultural and community college
- Commuter campus in large town
- SAT or ACT (ACT writing optional) required

General. Founded in 1924. Regionally accredited. **Enrollment:** 3,248 degree-seeking undergraduates. **Degrees:** 24 bachelor's, 447 associate awarded. **Location:** 100 miles from Macon, 50 miles from Albany. **Calendar:** Semester. **Full-time faculty:** 96 total; 5% minority, 55% women. **Part-time faculty:** 74 total. **Class size:** 25% < 20, 65% 20-39, 9% 40-49, less than 1% 50-99. **Special facilities:** 200-acre farm.

Student profile. Among degree-seeking undergraduates, 1,359 enrolled as first-time, first-year students, 100 transferred in from other institutions.

Part-time:	31%	Hispanic American:	6%
Out-of-state:	4%	Native American:	1%
Women:	56%	25 or older:	18%
African American:	18%	Live on campus:	32%
Asian American:	1%		

Basis for selection. 1.8 GPA, 330 SAT verbal and 310 SAT math or 12 ACT English and 14 ACT math necessary to obtain required Freshman Index of 1830. College-preparatory program not required for students pursuing AAS degree. Interview recommended for nursing majors. **Home schooled:** Statement describing home school structure and mission, transcript of courses and grades required. Specific application and portfolio procedures required of home-schooled applicants.

High school preparation. College-preparatory program recommended. 16 units required. Required units include English 4, mathematics 4, social studies 3, science 3 and foreign language 2.

2011-2012 Annual costs. Tuition/fees: $3,778; $11,260 out-of-state. Per-credit charge: $93 in-state; $342 out-of-state. Room/board: $6,810. Books/supplies: $775. Personal expenses: $2,180.

2010-2011 Financial aid. Need-based: 38% of total undergraduate aid awarded as scholarships/grants, 62% as loans/jobs. Work-study available nights, weekends and for part-time students. **Non-need-based:** Scholarships awarded for academics, athletics.

Application procedures. Admission: Closing date 8/1. $20 fee, may be waived for applicants with need. Admission notification on a rolling basis. **Financial aid:** Closing date 11/15. FAFSA, institutional form required. Applicants notified on a rolling basis starting 5/15; must reply within 2 week(s) of notification.

Academics. Special study options: Accelerated study, distance learning, dual enrollment of high school students, honors, internships, study abroad. **Credit/placement by examination:** AP, CLEP, SAT, ACT, institutional tests. **Support services:** Learning center, remedial instruction, tutoring, writing center.

Majors. Biology: General. **Business:** Accounting, business admin, fashion, hospitality admin, office technology, office/clerical. **Communications:** Communications/speech/rhetoric, journalism, media studies. **Computer sciences:** General, applications programming, computer science, data processing, information technology, web page design. **Conservation:** Forest management, forest technology, forestry, wildlife/wilderness. **Education:** General, early childhood. **Engineering:** General, agricultural. **English:** English lit. **Foreign languages:** General. **General:** Animal sciences, business, ornamental horticulture, plant sciences, poultry, turf management. **Health services:** Athletic training, dental hygiene, medical records technology, predental, premedicine, prepharmacy. **History:** General. **Liberal arts:** Arts/sciences. **Math:** General. **Parks/recreation:** Facilities management, health/fitness. **Physical sciences:** Chemistry, physics. **Protective services:** Police science. **Psychology:** General. **Social sciences:** General, sociology. **Visual/performing arts:** General, music, studio arts. **Work/family studies:** General, child care management.

Most popular majors. Agriculture 8%, health sciences 18%, liberal arts 63%, natural resources/environmental science 7%.

Computing on campus. 100 workstations in library. Dormitories wired for high-speed internet access. Commuter students can connect to campus network. Online course registration, wireless network available.

Student life. Freshman orientation: Mandatory, $40 fee. Preregistration for classes offered. **Housing:** Coed dorms, apartments available. $235 nonrefundable deposit. **Activities:** Bands, campus ministries, literary magazine, radio station, student government, student newspaper.

Athletics. NJCAA. **Intercollegiate:** Baseball M, golf M, rodeo, soccer W, softball W, tennis, volleyball W. **Intramural:** Badminton W, basketball, bowling, football (non-tackle) M, softball, tennis, volleyball.

Student services. Adult student services, career counseling, student employment services, health services, personal counseling, placement for graduates, veterans' counselor.

Contact. E-mail: admissions@abac.edu
Phone: (229) 391-5004 Toll-free number: (800) 733-3653
Fax: (229) 391-5002
Debra McCrary, Director of Admissions and Registrar, Abraham Baldwin Agricultural College, ABAC 4, 2802 Moore Highway, Tifton, GA 31793-2601

Albany Technical College
Albany, Georgia
www.albanytech.edu

CB code: 3921

- Public 2-year virtual technical college
- Commuter campus in small city

General. Regionally accredited. Traditional and distance education classes available. **Enrollment:** 4,666 degree-seeking undergraduates; 63 non-degree-seeking students. **Degrees:** 145 associate awarded. **Location:** 3 miles from downtown Albany, 225 miles from Atlanta. **Calendar:** Semester, extensive summer session. **Full-time faculty:** 91 total. **Special facilities:** Logistics education center, culinary arts institute, firefighter training tower, health care and occupational labs.

Student profile. Among degree-seeking undergraduates, 796 enrolled as first-time, first-year students.

Part-time:	39%	Hispanic American:	1%
Women:	63%	25 or older:	65%
African American:	81%		

Transfer out. Colleges most students transferred to 2011: Albany State University.

Basis for selection. Open admission, but selective for some programs. Limited admission to health technology programs. Under certain conditions, ACT or SAT scores may be accepted in lieu of taking the COMPASS or ASSET test.

High school preparation. College-preparatory program recommended. 22 units recommended. Recommended units include English 4, mathematics 3, social studies 3, science 3, foreign language 1 and academic electives 3. 4 tech prep, 1 health science recommended.

2011-2012 Annual costs. Tuition/fees: $2,544; $4,794 out-of-state. Per-credit charge: $75 in-state; $150 out-of-state. Books/supplies: $1,260.

Financial aid. Need-based: Need-based aid available for part-time students. Work-study available nights, weekends and for part-time students. **Non-need-based:** Scholarships awarded for academics, state residency.

Application procedures. Admission: No deadline. $15 fee, may be waived for applicants with need. Admission notification on a rolling basis beginning on or about 8/1. **Financial aid:** No deadline. FAFSA required. Applicants notified on a rolling basis starting 5/1.

Academics. Special study options: Distance learning, dual enrollment of high school students, weekend college. Associates + Bachelors, 2 + 2 agreements with Albany State University in accounting, business administrative technology, business management, computer information systems, early childhood care education, law enforcement, marketing. License preparation in nursing, paramedic, radiology. **Credit/placement by examination:** AP, CLEP, institutional tests. **Support services:** GED preparation and test center, remedial instruction, tutoring.

Majors. Business: Sales/distribution. **Computer sciences:** Data processing, networking. **Conservation:** Forestry. **Education:** Early childhood. **Health services:** Pharmacy assistant. **Protective services:** Criminal justice.

Most popular majors. Business/marketing 38%, computer/information sciences 8%, education 16%, health sciences 12%, security/protective services 25%, trade and industry 8%.

Computing on campus. Online library available.

Student life. Freshman orientation: Available. Preregistration for classes offered. Students contact advisor to register for classes. Advisor registers students via Internet. **Activities:** Choral groups, student government.

Athletics. Intercollegiate: Basketball M. **Team name:** Titans.

Student services. Adult student services, career counseling, services for economically disadvantaged, student employment services, financial aid counseling, on-campus daycare, personal counseling, placement for graduates, veterans' counselor. **Physically disabled:** Services for visually, speech, hearing impaired. **Transfer:** Pre-admission transcript evaluation for new students.

Contact. Phone: (229) 430-3520 Fax: (229) 430-0652
Lisa DeJesus, Director of Admissions, Albany Technical College, 1704 South Slappy Boulevard, Albany, GA 31701-3514

Altamaha Technical College
Jesup, Georgia
www.altamahatech.edu
CB code: 0147

- Public 2-year technical college
- Commuter campus in small town

General. Regionally accredited. **Enrollment:** 1,301 degree-seeking undergraduates; 109 non-degree-seeking students. **Degrees:** 8 associate awarded. **Calendar:** Semester, extensive summer session. **Full-time faculty:** 51 total. **Part-time faculty:** 89 total.

Student profile. Among degree-seeking undergraduates, 262 enrolled as first-time, first-year students.

Part-time:	70%	Hispanic American:	2%
Women:	52%	25 or older:	58%
African American:	30%		

Basis for selection. Open admission. Under certain conditions ACT or SAT may be accepted in lieu of COMPASS or ASSET test for placement. **Home schooled:** Transcript of courses and grades required. Letter from local school superintendent's office verifying the parent/legal guardian complied with state law concerning home schooling.

High school preparation. 22 units recommended. Recommended units include English 4, mathematics 3, social studies 3, science 3, foreign language 1 and academic electives 3. 4 tech prep, 1 health science recommended.

2011-2012 Annual costs. Tuition/fees: $2,520; $4,770 out-of-district; $9,270 out-of-state. Per-credit charge: $75 in-district; $150 out-of-district; $300 out-of-state.

Financial aid. Need-based: Work-study available nights, weekends and for part-time students.

Application procedures. Admission: No deadline. $15 fee.

Academics. Special study options: Distance learning, dual enrollment of high school students, weekend college. License preparation in nursing, paramedic. **Credit/placement by examination:** AP, CLEP. **Support services:** GED preparation and test center, learning center, remedial instruction, study skills assistance, tutoring.

Majors. Business: Accounting, business admin, marketing. **Computer sciences:** Networking, support specialist. **Education:** Early childhood. **Protective services:** Police science.

Most popular majors. Business/marketing 25%, computer/information sciences 50%, education 13%, trade and industry 13%.

Computing on campus. 16 workstations in library. Online library, wireless network available.

Student life. Activities: Student government.

Student services. Career counseling, services for economically disadvantaged, financial aid counseling, personal counseling, placement for graduates.

Contact. E-mail: atcadmissions@altamahatech.edu
Phone: (912) 427-1958 Toll-free number: (800) 645-8284
Fax: (912) 427-1901
Chris Jeancake, Director of Admissions, Altamaha Technical College, 1777 West Cherry Street, Jesup, GA 31545

Andrew College
Cuthbert, Georgia
www.andrewcollege.edu
CB code: 5009

- Private 2-year junior and liberal arts college affiliated with United Methodist Church
- Residential campus in small town
- SAT or ACT (ACT writing recommended) required

General. Founded in 1854. Regionally accredited. **Enrollment:** 320 degree-seeking undergraduates; 1 non-degree-seeking students. **Degrees:** 36 associate awarded. **Location:** 60 miles from Columbus, 40 miles from Albany. **Calendar:** Semester, limited summer session. **Full-time faculty:** 21 total. **Part-time faculty:** 5 total. **Class size:** 75% < 20, 25% 20-39.

Student profile. Among degree-seeking undergraduates, 100% enrolled in a transfer program, 187 enrolled as first-time, first-year students.

Part-time:	1%	Hispanic American:	8%
Women:	49%	Native American:	1%
African American:	44%	International:	2%
Asian American:	1%		

Transfer out. Colleges most students transferred to 2011: Georgia Southwestern State University, Valdosta State University, Georgia Southern University, Columbus State University, Troy State University.

Basis for selection. High school academic record, test scores, school and community activities important. Essay recommended. Interview required of the academically weak. Audition required of music majors. Portfolio recommended for art majors. **Home schooled:** Transcript of courses and grades required.

High school preparation. College-preparatory program recommended. 18 units recommended.

2011-2012 Annual costs. Tuition/fees: $12,111. Room/board: $7,606. Books/supplies: $600. Personal expenses: $1,200.

Financial aid. Need-based: Need-based aid available for part-time students. Work-study available nights, weekends and for part-time students. **Non-need-based:** Scholarships awarded for academics, art, athletics, leadership, music/drama, religious affiliation, state residency.

Application procedures. Admission: Priority date 6/1; deadline 8/1 (receipt date). $20 fee, may be waived for applicants with need. Admission notification on a rolling basis. **Financial aid:** Priority date 4/1, closing date 8/1. FAFSA, institutional form required. Applicants notified on a rolling basis starting 4/15.

Academics. Special study options: Double major, dual enrollment of high school students, ESL, honors. **Credit/placement by examination:** AP, CLEP, SAT, ACT, institutional tests. 24 credit hours maximum toward associate degree. **Support services:** Learning center, pre-admission summer program, remedial instruction, study skills assistance, tutoring, writing center.

Majors. Business: General. **Communications:** Communications/speech/rhetoric. **Computer sciences:** Computer science. **Conservation:** Forestry. **Education:** General. **Engineering:** General. **Health services:** Athletic training, predental, premedicine, prenursing, prepharmacy, preveterinary. **History:** General. **Liberal arts:** Arts/sciences. **Math:** General. **Parks/recreation:** Health/fitness. **Physical sciences:** General. **Psychology:** General. **Social sciences:** General, sociology. **Visual/performing arts:** General, dramatic.

Computing on campus. 100 workstations in dormitories, library, computer center, student center. Dormitories wired for high-speed internet access and linked to campus network. Commuter students can connect to campus network. Online library, repair service, wireless network available.

Student life. Freshman orientation: Mandatory. Preregistration for classes offered. Held selected weekends during summer and beginning of fall term for 3-4 days. **Policies:** No alcohol/illegal drugs allowed on campus. **Housing:** Guaranteed on-campus for all undergraduates. Coed dorms, single-sex dorms available. **Activities:** Campus ministries, choral groups, drama, international student organizations, literary magazine, music ensembles, musical theater, student government, student newspaper, Baptist Student

Union, Wesley Fellowship, Unity, community service group, interdenominational Christian group.

Athletics. NJCAA. **Intercollegiate:** Baseball M, basketball W, cross-country, golf, soccer, softball W, volleyball. **Intramural:** Archery, badminton, basketball, cheerleading, cross-country, football (non-tackle) M, golf, racquetball, soccer, softball, swimming, table tennis, tennis, volleyball, weight lifting. **Team name:** Tigers.

Student services. Alcohol/substance abuse counseling, chaplain/spiritual director, career counseling, services for economically disadvantaged, financial aid counseling, health services, veterans' counselor. **Physically disabled:** Services for speech impaired. **Transfer:** Transfer adviser, college fairs on campus for students transferring to 4-year colleges.

Contact. E-mail: admissions@andrewcollege.edu
Phone: (800) 664-9250 Toll-free number: (800) 664-9250
Fax: (229) 732-2176
Blake Coty, Director of Admissions and Financial Aid, Andrew College, 501 College Street, Cuthbert, GA 39840-1395

Anthem College: Atlanta
Atlanta, Georgia
www.anthem.edu

- For-profit 2-year health science and career college
- Large city

General. Accredited by ACICS. **Calendar:** Differs by program. **Full-time faculty:** 2 total.

Basis for selection. Admission requirements vary by program.

Financial aid. Need-based: Work-study available nights, weekends and for part-time students.

Application procedures. Admission: $20 fee.

Academics. Credit/placement by examination: AP, CLEP.

Majors. Health services: Dental assistant, health care admin, medical assistant, surgical technology.

Contact. Anthem College: Atlanta, 2450 Piedmont Road NE, Atlanta, GA 30324

Ashworth College
Norcross, Georgia
www.ashworthcollege.edu   **CB code: 3912**

- For-profit 2-year community and career college
- Commuter campus in very large city

General. Accredited by DETC. **Enrollment:** 4,630 degree-seeking undergraduates. **Degrees:** 85 bachelor's, 1,500 associate awarded; master's offered. **Location:** 18 miles from Atlanta. **Calendar:** Differs by program, extensive summer session. **Full-time faculty:** 20 total. **Part-time faculty:** 70 total.

Transfer out. Colleges most students transferred to 2011: Ashford University, Phoenix University.

Basis for selection. Open admission. **Home schooled:** Statement describing home school structure and mission, transcript of courses and grades required.

2011-2012 Annual costs. Tuition/fees: $2,400. Cost shown is for 2 semesters of undergraduate program. Associate degree programs require 4 semesters; bachelor's, 8; inclusive of all books and fees.

Financial aid. Need-based: Work-study available nights, weekends and for part-time students.

Application procedures. Admission: No deadline. No application fee. Admission notification on a rolling basis.

Academics. Special study options: Accelerated study, distance learning, weekend college. Bachelor's degree programs available on campus. **Credit/placement by examination:** AP, CLEP. 15 credit hours maximum toward associate degree, 30 toward bachelor's. **Support services:** Reduced course load, study skills assistance, tutoring.

Majors. Business: Accounting, business admin, finance, human resources, marketing. **Education:** Early childhood. **Health services:** Health care admin. **Protective services:** Criminal justice, security management. **Psychology:** General.

Computing on campus. Online library available.

Student life. Freshman orientation: Available. Preregistration for classes offered.

Student services. Transfer: Pre-admission transcript evaluation for new students. Transfer adviser for students transferring to 4-year colleges.

Contact. E-mail: info@ashworthcollege.edu
Phone: (770) 729-8400 Toll-free number: (800) 223-4542
Fax: (770) 729-9389
Eric Ryall, Registrar, Ashworth College, 6625 The Corners Parkway, Norcross, GA 30092-3406

Athens Technical College
Athens, Georgia
www.athenstech.edu   **CB code: 0462**

- Public 2-year technical college
- Commuter campus in small city

General. Founded in 1959. Regionally accredited. **Enrollment:** 4,640 degree-seeking undergraduates; 471 non-degree-seeking students. **Degrees:** 384 associate awarded. **Location:** 65 miles from Atlanta. **Calendar:** Semester, extensive summer session. **Full-time faculty:** 97 total. **Part-time faculty:** 323 total. **Class size:** 61% < 20, 36% 20-39, 1% 40-49, 2% 50-99.

Student profile. Among degree-seeking undergraduates, 634 enrolled as first-time, first-year students.

Part-time:	67%	Asian American:	4%
Women:	66%	Hispanic American:	3%
African American:	23%	25 or older:	57%

Transfer out. Colleges most students transferred to 2011: University of Georgia.

Basis for selection. Open admission, but selective for some programs. Special requirements for radiology, respiratory therapy, nursing, physical therapy assistant, dental hygiene, surgical technology, veterinary technology dental assisting, medical assisting, practical nursing and diagnostic medical sonography. School record, recommendations, standardized test scores, essay, and interview required or recommended depending on program. Under certain conditions, ACT or SAT may be accepted in lieu of COMPASS or ASSET for placement. Interview required of radiology, respiratory therapy, nursing, physical therapy assistant, dental assisting, and dental hygiene majors. **Home schooled:** Must provide documentation of designated home study program activities.

High school preparation. College-preparatory program recommended. 22 units recommended. Recommended units include English 4, mathematics 3, social studies 3, science 3, foreign language 1 and academic electives 3. 4 tech prep and 1 health science recommended.

2011-2012 Annual costs. Tuition/fees: $2,510; $4,760 out-of-state. Per-credit charge: $75 in-state; $150 out-of-state. Books/supplies: $800. Personal expenses: $1,000.

Financial aid. Need-based: Need-based aid available for part-time students. Work-study available nights, weekends and for part-time students. **Non-need-based:** Scholarships awarded for academics, leadership.

Application procedures. Admission: Priority date 8/1; no deadline. $20 fee. Admission notification on a rolling basis. 2/1 deadline for nursing and dental hygiene; 3/1 deadline for dental assistance; 4/1 deadline for radiography, surgical technology, diagnostic medical sonography, nursing accelerated, and veterinary technology; 5/1 deadline for physical therapist assistant, practical nursing; 7/1 deadline for respiratory therapy; 8/1 deadline for medical assistance. **Financial aid:** No deadline. FAFSA required. Applicants notified on a rolling basis starting 6/15; must reply within 2 week(s) of notification.

Academics. Special study options: Distance learning, dual enrollment of high school students, weekend college. License preparation in real estate. **Credit/placement by examination:** AP, CLEP, institutional tests. **Support services:** GED preparation and test center, learning center, reduced course load, remedial instruction, study skills assistance, tutoring.

Majors. Biology: Biotechnology. **Business:** Accounting technology, administrative services, sales/distribution, travel services. **Computer sciences:**

Applications programming, data processing, networking, programming. **Education:** Early childhood. **Health services:** Dental assistant, dental hygiene, nursing (RN), physical therapy assistant, radiologic technology/medical imaging, respiratory therapy technology, sonography, veterinary technology/assistant. **Human services:** Social work. **Protective services:** Law enforcement admin. **Visual/performing arts:** Interior design.

Most popular majors. Business/marketing 19%, computer/information sciences 9%, education 13%, health sciences 28%.

Computing on campus. 346 workstations in computer center. Commuter students can connect to campus network. Online course registration, online library, wireless network available.

Student life. Freshman orientation: Mandatory. Preregistration for classes offered. **Activities:** Student government.

Student services. Adult student services, career counseling, student employment services, financial aid counseling, personal counseling, placement for graduates, veterans' counselor. **Physically disabled:** Services for visually, speech, hearing impaired. **Transfer:** Transfer adviser for students transferring to 4-year colleges.

Contact. E-mail: admissions@athenstech.edu
Phone: (706) 355-5008 Fax: (706) 369-5756
Lenzy Reid, Director of Admissions, Athens Technical College, 800 US Highway 29 North, Athens, GA 30601-1500

Atlanta Metropolitan College
Atlanta, Georgia
www.atlm.edu

CB member
CB code: 5725

▶ Public 2-year junior college
▶ Commuter campus in very large city

General. Founded in 1974. Regionally accredited. **Enrollment:** 2,664 degree-seeking undergraduates. **Degrees:** 276 associate awarded. **Location:** 4 miles from downtown. **Calendar:** Semester, extensive summer session. **Full-time faculty:** 57 total. **Part-time faculty:** 113 total.

Student profile.

Out-of-state:	6%	25 or older:	26%

Basis for selection. Applicants who have followed college preparatory curriculum must have 2.0 GPA. Applicants who have followed technology/career curriculum must have 2.2 GPA. All applicants must meet immunization requirements. Applicants with 430 SAT verbal or 17 ACT English and completion of college preparatory curriculum in English exempt from taking COMPASS Placement Test in English and Reading. Applicants with 400 SAT math or 17 ACT math and completion of college preparatory curriculum in math exempt from taking COMPASS Placement Test in math. **Home schooled:** Transcript of courses and grades required.

High school preparation. 16 units required. Required units include English 4, mathematics 4, social studies 1, history 2, science 3 (laboratory 2) and foreign language 2.

2011-2012 Annual costs. Tuition/fees: $3,400; $10,278 out-of-state. Per-credit charge: $82 in-state; $312 out-of-state. Books/supplies: $1,300.

Financial aid. All financial aid based on need. Need-based aid available for part-time students. Work-study available nights, weekends and for part-time students.

Application procedures. Admission: Priority date 7/15; no deadline. $20 fee. Admission notification on a rolling basis. **Financial aid:** Closing date 6/1. FAFSA required. Applicants notified on a rolling basis; must reply by 6/30.

Academics. Academic and technological workshops provided. Tutorial services available in math, physics, chemistry, English, reading, accounting, and general science. **Special study options:** Distance learning, dual enrollment of high school students, ESL, external degree, honors, independent study, study abroad, weekend college. **Credit/placement by examination:** AP, CLEP. **Support services:** Learning center, remedial instruction, study skills assistance, tutoring, writing center.

Majors. Area/ethnic studies: African-American. **Biology:** General. **Business:** Business admin, office management. **Communications:** Communications/speech/rhetoric. **Computer sciences:** General, computer science. **Education:** Multi-level teacher. **English:** English lit, rhetoric/composition. **Foreign languages:** General. **Health services:** Medical records admin. **History:** General. **Human services:** Social work. **Math:** General. **Parks/recreation:** Health/fitness. **Physical sciences:** Chemistry, physics. **Protective services:**

Law enforcement admin. **Psychology:** General. **Social sciences:** Political science. **Visual/performing arts:** Art, music.

Most popular majors. Liberal arts 94%.

Computing on campus. 580 workstations in library, computer center, student center. Commuter students can connect to campus network. Online course registration, online library, helpline, repair service, wireless network available.

Student life. Freshman orientation: Mandatory. Preregistration for classes offered. Daytime and evening sessions held each semester. **Housing:** Off-campus housing available for college athletes only. **Activities:** Choral groups, dance, drama, international student organizations, student government, student newspaper.

Athletics. NJCAA. **Intercollegiate:** Basketball. **Team name:** Red-Eyed Panthers.

Student services. Adult student services, career counseling, services for economically disadvantaged, financial aid counseling, minority student services, personal counseling, veterans' counselor. **Physically disabled:** Services for visually, speech, hearing impaired. **Transfer:** Pre-admission transcript evaluation for new students. College fairs on campus for students transferring to 4-year colleges.

Contact. E-mail: areid@atlm.edu
Phone: (404) 756-4004 Fax: (404) 756-4407
Audrey Reid, Director of Admissions, Atlanta Metropolitan College, 1630 Metropolitan Parkway, SW, Atlanta, GA 30310-4498

Atlanta Technical College
Atlanta, Georgia
www.atlantatech.edu

CB code: 5030

▶ Public 2-year community and technical college
▶ Commuter campus in very large city

General. Regionally accredited. **Enrollment:** 4,163 degree-seeking undergraduates; 328 non-degree-seeking students. **Degrees:** 176 associate awarded. **Location:** 2 miles from downtown. **Calendar:** Semester, extensive summer session.

Student profile. Among degree-seeking undergraduates, 2.5% already have a bachelor's degree or higher, 748 enrolled as first-time, first-year students.

Part-time:	66%	Asian American:	1%
Women:	59%	Hispanic American:	1%
African American:	94%	25 or older:	66%

Basis for selection. Open admission, but selective for some programs. Requirements vary by program for selective admission majors. Under certain conditions, ACT or SAT may be accepted in lieu of COMPASS or ASSET for placement. **Home schooled:** Letter from superintendent's office confirming compliance with Georgia/TCSG policies and attendance and final exit exam scores from accredited national testing program required.

High school preparation. College-preparatory program recommended. 22 units recommended. Recommended units include English 4, mathematics 3, social studies 3, science 3, foreign language 1 and academic electives 3. 4 tech prep, 1 health science recommended.

2011-2012 Annual costs. Tuition/fees: $2,502; $4,752 out-of-state. Per-credit charge: $75 in-state; $150 out-of-state. Books/supplies: $1,200. Personal expenses: $900.

2011-2012 Financial aid. Need-based: Need-based aid available for part-time students. Work-study available nights, weekends and for part-time students.

Application procedures. Admission: Priority date 9/8; deadline 7/21 (receipt date). $20 fee. Admission notification on a rolling basis. **Financial aid:** Priority date 3/1; no closing date. Applicants notified on a rolling basis starting 4/15.

Academics. Special study options: Distance learning, dual enrollment of high school students, study abroad, weekend college. License preparation in aviation, dental hygiene, nursing, paramedic, radiology, real estate. **Credit/placement by examination:** AP, CLEP, IB, institutional tests. **Support services:** GED test center, learning center, tutoring.

Majors. Business: Accounting, customer service support. **Computer sciences:** General. **Health services:** Pharmacy assistant. **Work/family studies:** Child care service.

Most popular majors. Business/marketing 32%, computer/information sciences 10%, education 26%, health sciences 18%, legal studies 9%.

Computing on campus. 55 workstations in library, computer center. Online library, wireless network available.

Student life. Freshman orientation: Mandatory. Preregistration for classes offered.

Student services. On-campus daycare.

Contact. E-mail: admissions@atlantatech.edu
Phone: (404) 225-4461
Vory Billups, Director of Admissions, Atlanta Technical College, 1560 Metropolitan Parkway, SW, Atlanta, GA 30310-4446

Augusta Technical College
Augusta, Georgia
www.augustatech.edu   **CB code: 2620**

▶ Public 2-year technical college
▶ Commuter campus in large city

General. Founded in 1961. Regionally accredited. Additional campuses in Thomson and Waynesboro. **Enrollment:** 4,319 degree-seeking undergraduates; 73 non-degree-seeking students. **Degrees:** 297 associate awarded. **Location:** 145 miles from Atlanta; 75 miles from Columbia, South Carolina. **Calendar:** Semester, extensive summer session. **Full-time faculty:** 136 total. **Part-time faculty:** 240 total.

Student profile. Among degree-seeking undergraduates, 760 enrolled as first-time, first-year students.

Part-time:	63%	Asian American:	2%
Women:	60%	Hispanic American:	2%
African American:	52%	25 or older:	57%

Basis for selection. Open admission, but selective for some programs. Competitive admission to cardiovascular technology, respiratory therapy care, occupational therapy assistant, radiologic technology, and practical nursing. Requirements vary by program and may include required college courses, placement exam scores, interviews, essays, and GPA. Under certain conditions, ACT or SAT may be accepted in lieu of COMPASS or ASSET for placement.

High school preparation. College-preparatory program recommended. 22 units recommended. Recommended units include English 4, mathematics 3, social studies 3, science 3, foreign language 1 and academic electives 3. Highly recommended that math units include algebra and trigonometry. 4 tech prep and 1 health science recommended.

2011-2012 Annual costs. Tuition/fees: $2,512; $4,762 out-of-state. Per-credit charge: $75 in-state; $150 out-of-state. Books/supplies: $450.

Financial aid. Need-based: Work-study available nights, weekends and for part-time students. **Non-need-based:** Scholarships awarded for state residency.

Application procedures. Admission: No deadline. $20 fee, may be waived for applicants with need. Application deadlines exist for competitive healthcare programs and vary by major. **Financial aid:** No deadline. FAFSA, institutional form required. Must reply within 2 week(s) of notification.

Academics. Special study options: Distance learning, dual enrollment of high school students, weekend college. **Credit/placement by examination:** AP, CLEP, institutional tests. **Support services:** GED preparation and test center, learning center, reduced course load, remedial instruction, tutoring.

Majors. Business: Accounting, administrative services, sales/distribution. **Computer sciences:** Applications programming. **Health services:** Cardiovascular technology, clinical lab technology, EMT paramedic, pharmacy assistant, respiratory therapy technology.

Most popular majors. Business/marketing 32%, computer/information sciences 9%, health sciences 26%, security/protective services 8%, trade and industry 6%.

Computing on campus. Commuter students can connect to campus network. Online course registration, online library available.

Student life. Freshman orientation: Available. Preregistration for classes offered. **Activities:** Student government.

Student services. Career counseling, student employment services, financial aid counseling, on-campus daycare, placement for graduates, veterans'

counselor. **Physically disabled:** Services for visually, speech, hearing impaired. **Transfer:** Pre-admission transcript evaluation for new students.

Contact. E-mail: bcrobert@augustatech.edu
Phone: (706) 771-4150 Fax: (706) 771-4034
Brian Roberts, Director of Admissions, Augusta Technical College, 3200 Augusta Tech Drive, Augusta, GA 30906

Bainbridge College
Bainbridge, Georgia
www.bainbridge.edu   **CB code: 5062**

▶ Public 2-year health science and community college
▶ Commuter campus in large town

General. Founded in 1973. Regionally accredited. **Enrollment:** 3,643 degree-seeking undergraduates. **Degrees:** 206 associate awarded. **Location:** 43 miles from Tallahassee, Florida. **Calendar:** Semester, limited summer session. **Full-time faculty:** 73 total; 26% have terminal degrees, 14% minority, 62% women. **Part-time faculty:** 139 total; 14% have terminal degrees, 15% minority, 76% women. **Class size:** 38% < 20, 62% 20-39, less than 1% 40-49, less than 1% 50-99. **Special facilities:** Nature trail, wellness center.

Student profile. Among degree-seeking undergraduates, 29% enrolled in a transfer program, 71% enrolled in a vocational program, 2% already have a bachelor's degree or higher, 636 enrolled as first-time, first-year students, 976 transferred in from other institutions.

Part-time:	43%	Women:	70%
Out-of-state:	4%	25 or older:	48%

Transfer out. 91% of students enrolled in the transfer program go on to 4-year colleges. **Colleges most students transferred to 2011:** Valdosta State University, Albany State University, Georgia Southwestern University.

Basis for selection. 330 SAT verbal/13 ACT English, 310 SAT math/14 ACT math, or 1.8 GPA required. College preparatory curriculum required for associate of arts degree-seeking students. Limited number admitted who do not meet admission standards. **Adult students:** Compass test required. **Home schooled:** Transcript of courses and grades required. Acceptable scores on COMPASS required.

High school preparation. College-preparatory program recommended. 16 units required. Required units include English 4, mathematics 4, social studies 3, science 3 and foreign language 2. Tech Prep students exempt from foreign language requirement and only requre 3 units of math.

2011-2012 Annual costs. Tuition/fees: $3,358; $10,236 out-of-state. Per-credit charge: $82 in-state; $312 out-of-state. Books/supplies: $600. Personal expenses: $450.

2010-2011 Financial aid. All financial aid based on need. 65% of total undergraduate aid awarded as scholarships/grants, 35% as loans/jobs. Need-based aid available for part-time students. Work-study available nights, weekends and for part-time students.

Application procedures. Admission: Closing date 8/10 (receipt date). No application fee. Admission notification on a rolling basis. **Financial aid:** Priority date 6/1, closing date 8/1. FAFSA, institutional form required. Applicants notified on a rolling basis starting 6/1; must reply within 2 week(s) of notification.

Academics. Academic support services available in the evenings and weekends by request. **Special study options:** Distance learning, double major, dual enrollment of high school students, honors, independent study, internships, study abroad, weekend college. 2-year registered nursing program. Bachelor's degree programs available on campus. License preparation in nursing, paramedic, real estate. **Credit/placement by examination:** AP, CLEP, IB, institutional tests. 18 credit hours maximum toward associate degree. **Support services:** GED preparation, learning center, reduced course load, remedial instruction, study skills assistance, tutoring.

Majors. Business: General, accounting, administrative services, management information systems, marketing. **Communications:** Communications/speech/rhetoric. **Computer sciences:** General. **Education:** General, early childhood, health, middle, physical, secondary. **English:** English lit. **Foreign languages:** General. **Health services:** Medical records technology, nursing (RN). **History:** General. **Math:** General. **Protective services:** Law enforcement admin, police science. **Psychology:** General. **Social sciences:** Political science.

Most popular majors. Biological/life sciences 6%, business/marketing 27%, education 15%, health sciences 16%, security/protective services 7%.

Computing on campus. 300 workstations in library, computer center, student center. Online course registration, online library, wireless network available.

Student life. Freshman orientation: Mandatory. Preregistration for classes offered. Online and on-campus orientations held prior to start of semester. **Activities:** Concert band, choral groups, drama, music ensembles, student government, Delta club, service organizations, Phi Theta Kappa, Sigma Kappa Delta, ALSO club.

Athletics. Intramural: Basketball M, football (non-tackle), softball, table tennis, volleyball.

Student services. Adult student services, alcohol/substance abuse counseling, career counseling, services for economically disadvantaged, student employment services, financial aid counseling, health services, minority student services, personal counseling, placement for graduates, veterans' counselor. **Physically disabled:** Services for visually, speech, hearing impaired. **Transfer:** Transfer adviser, college fairs on campus for students transferring to 4-year colleges.

Contact. E-mail: csnyder@bainbridge.edu
Phone: (229) 248-2504 Fax: (229) 248-2623
Connie Snyder, Dean of Student Services, Bainbridge College, 2500 East Shotwell Street, Bainbridge, GA 39818-0990

Brown Mackie College: Atlanta
Atlanta, Georgia
www.brownmackie.edu

- For-profit 2-year business and health science college
- Very large city

General. Accredited by ACICS. **Calendar:** Quarter.

Annual costs/financial aid. Tuition/fees (2011-2012): $12,996. Books/supplies: $1,275.

Contact. Phone: (404) 799-4500
Senior Director of Admissions, 4370 Peachtree Road NE, Atlanta, GA 30319

Central Georgia Technical College
Macon, Georgia
www.centralgatech.edu   CB code: 1709

- Public 2-year community and technical college
- Commuter campus in small city

General. Regionally accredited. **Enrollment:** 5,798 degree-seeking undergraduates; 240 non-degree-seeking students. **Degrees:** 294 associate awarded. **Location:** 80 miles from Atlanta. **Calendar:** Semester, extensive summer session. **Full-time faculty:** 109 total. **Part-time faculty:** 375 total. **Class size:** 87% < 20, 13% 20-39, less than 1% 40-49. **Partnerships:** Formal partnerships with Cisco and local industries.

Student profile. Among degree-seeking undergraduates, 737 enrolled as first-time, first-year students.

Part-time:	54%	Asian American:	1%
Women:	65%	Hispanic American:	1%
African American:	64%	25 or older:	61%

Basis for selection. Open admission, but selective for some programs. Requirements vary according to program of study. Under certain conditions, ACT or SAT may be accepted in lieu of COMPASS or ASSET for placement.

High school preparation. College-preparatory program recommended. 22 units recommended. Recommended units include English 4, mathematics 3, social studies 3, science 3, foreign language 1 and academic electives 3. 4 tech prep and 1 health science recommended.

2011-2012 Annual costs. Tuition/fees: $2,530; $4,780 out-of-state. Per-credit charge: $75 in-state; $150 out-of-state. Books/supplies: $750.

Financial aid. Need-based: Need-based aid available for part-time students. Work-study available nights, weekends and for part-time students.

Application procedures. Admission: $20 fee, may be waived for applicants with need. Admission notification on a rolling basis. Application closing date is one month prior to first day of attendance. **Financial aid:** Closing date 7/14. FAFSA, institutional form required.

Academics. Special study options: Distance learning, dual enrollment of high school students, weekend college. License preparation in dental hygiene, nursing, paramedic, radiology, real estate. **Credit/placement by examination:** AP, CLEP, institutional tests. Dependent on approval by department/program. **Support services:** GED preparation and test center, reduced course load, remedial instruction, study skills assistance, tutoring, writing center.

Majors. Business: Accounting technology, administrative services, logistics, operations. **Computer sciences:** Data processing, networking, web page design. **Education:** Early childhood. **Health services:** Clinical lab technology, dental hygiene, medical assistant. **Protective services:** Criminal justice.

Most popular majors. Business/marketing 32%, computer/information sciences 10%, education 7%, health sciences 25%, security/protective services 8%, trade and industry 7%.

Computing on campus. 400 workstations in library, computer center. Commuter students can connect to campus network. Online course registration, online library, helpline, repair service, wireless network available.

Student life. Freshman orientation: Mandatory. Preregistration for classes offered. Held prior to each quarterly registration period. **Activities:** Student government.

Student services. Adult student services, career counseling, services for economically disadvantaged, financial aid counseling, on-campus daycare, placement for graduates, veterans' counselor. **Physically disabled:** Services for visually, speech, hearing impaired. **Transfer:** College fairs on campus for students transferring to 4-year colleges.

Contact. E-mail: tcarter@centralgatech.edu
Phone: (478) 757-3408 Fax: (478) 757-3454
Tammy Carter, Director of Admissions, Central Georgia Technical College, 3300 Macon Tech Drive, Macon, GA 31206

Chattahoochee Technical College
Marietta, Georgia
www.chattahoocheetech.edu   CB code: 5441

- Public 2-year community and technical college
- Commuter campus in large city

General. Founded in 1961. Regionally accredited. **Enrollment:** 11,233 degree-seeking undergraduates; 331 non-degree-seeking students. **Degrees:** 526 associate awarded. **Location:** 20 miles from Atlanta. **Calendar:** Semester, extensive summer session. **Full-time faculty:** 178 total. **Part-time faculty:** 392 total.

Student profile. Among degree-seeking undergraduates, 20% enrolled in a transfer program, 80% enrolled in a vocational program, 2,056 enrolled as first-time, first-year students.

Part-time:	67%	Asian American:	2%
Women:	60%	Hispanic American:	6%
African American:	33%		

Transfer out. Colleges most students transferred to 2011: Kennesaw State University, Southern Polytechnica State University.

Basis for selection. Open admission, but selective for some programs. Special requirements for health science programs. Under certain conditions, ACT or SAT may be accepted in lieu of COMPASS or ASSET for placement. **Home schooled:** Transcript of courses and grades required. Documentation of home school registration with state required; SAT/ACT may be required.

High school preparation. College-preparatory program recommended.

2011-2012 Annual costs. Tuition/fees: $2,520; $4,770 out-of-state. Per-credit charge: $75 in-state; $150 out-of-state.

Financial aid. Need-based: Need-based aid available for part-time students. Work-study available nights, weekends and for part-time students.

Application procedures. Admission: Closing date 7/27 (postmark date). $15 fee. Admission notification on a rolling basis. **Financial aid:** No deadline. FAFSA required. Applicants notified on a rolling basis.

Academics. Special study options: Distance learning, dual enrollment of high school students, weekend college. License preparation in nursing. **Credit/placement by examination:** AP, CLEP, IB, institutional tests. **Support services:** GED preparation and test center, learning center, reduced course load, remedial instruction, study skills assistance, tutoring.

Majors. Business: General, accounting, administrative services, marketing, office management. **Computer sciences:** General, applications programming.

Protective services: Criminal justice. **Work/family studies:** Child care management.

Most popular majors. Business/marketing 34%, communication technologies 7%, computer/information sciences 13%, education 6%, engineering/engineering technologies 9%, health sciences 12%, security/protective services 7%, trade and industry 6%.

Computing on campus. 857 workstations in library, computer center, student center. Online course registration, wireless network available.

Student life. Freshman orientation: Available. Preregistration for classes offered. **Activities:** International student organizations, student government.

Athletics. NJCAA. **Intercollegiate:** Basketball, cross-country. **Team name:** Golden Eagles.

Student services. Career counseling, student employment services, financial aid counseling, personal counseling, placement for graduates, veterans' counselor. **Physically disabled:** Services for visually, hearing impaired. **Transfer:** College fairs on campus for students transferring to 4-year colleges.

Contact. E-mail: enroll@chattahoocheetech.edu
Phone: (770) 528-4465
Missy Cusack, Director of Admissions, Chattahoochee Technical College, 980 South Cobb Drive, SE, Marietta, GA 30060-3300

College of Coastal Georgia
Brunswick, Georgia
www.ccga.edu

CB member
CB code: 5078

⟩ Public 2-year liberal arts college
⟩ Commuter campus in large town

General. Founded in 1961. Regionally accredited. Students may take select courses at the Camden Center in Kingsland. **Enrollment:** 3,355 degree-seeking undergraduates; 119 non-degree-seeking students. **Degrees:** 60 bachelor's, 288 associate awarded. **Location:** 70 miles from Savannah; 60 miles from Jacksonville, Florida. **Calendar:** Semester, limited summer session. **Full-time faculty:** 87 total; 52% have terminal degrees, 58% women. **Part-time faculty:** 89 total; 29% have terminal degrees, 60% women. **Class size:** 22% < 20, 64% 20-39, 9% 40-49, 5% 50-99.

Student profile. Among degree-seeking undergraduates, 770 enrolled as first-time, first-year students.

Part-time:	41%	Hispanic American:	4%
Out-of-state:	7%	International:	1%
Women:	69%	25 or older:	38%
African American:	16%	Live on campus:	8%
Asian American:	1%		

Transfer out. Colleges most students transferred to 2011: Armstrong Atlantic State University, Georgia Southern University.

Basis for selection. Open admission, but selective for some programs. Additional requirements for career associate health science programs and all baccalauareate degree programs. SAT/ACT may be used to exempt students from placement testing. **Home schooled:** Statement describing home school structure and mission, transcript of courses and grades, letter of recommendation (nonparent) required. Must take SAT or ACT and score at the average of last year's freshman class. **Learning Disabled:** Students must go through accreditation process with system agency on learning disabilities to receive accommodations.

High school preparation. College-preparatory program recommended. 17 units recommended. Recommended units include English 4, mathematics 4, social studies 3, science 4 (laboratory 2) and foreign language 2.

2011-2012 Annual costs. Tuition/fees: $4,036; $11,518 out-of-state. Per-credit charge: $93 in-state; $342 out-of-state. Room/board: $7,475. Books/supplies: $1,800. Personal expenses: $1,500.

2010-2011 Financial aid. Need-based: 604 full-time freshmen applied for aid; 448 were judged to have need; 448 of these received aid. Average need met was 43%. Average scholarship/grant was $4,434; average loan $2,861. 66% of total undergraduate aid awarded as scholarships/grants, 34% as loans/jobs. Need-based aid available for part-time students. Work-study available nights, weekends and for part-time students. **Non-need-based:** Awarded to 878 full-time undergraduates, including 292 freshmen. Scholarships awarded for academics, athletics, leadership, state residency.

Application procedures. Admission: Closing date 7/15 (postmark date). $25 fee, may be waived for applicants with need. Admission notification on a rolling basis. **Financial aid:** Priority date 5/1; no closing date. FAFSA required. Applicants notified on a rolling basis starting 5/1.

Academics. Special study options: Accelerated study, cooperative education, distance learning, dual enrollment of high school students, independent study, internships, liberal arts/career combination, study abroad, teacher certification program. Bachelor's degree programs available on campus. **Credit/placement by examination:** AP, CLEP, IB, institutional tests. 24 credit hours maximum toward associate degree, 24 toward bachelor's. **Support services:** Learning center, reduced course load, remedial instruction, study skills assistance, tutoring, writing center.

Majors. Biology: General. **Business:** Business admin. **Communications:** Communications/speech/rhetoric. **Computer sciences:** Computer science. **Education:** General, elementary, middle, secondary, special ed. **Engineering:** General. **English:** English lit. **Foreign languages:** General. **General:** Agribusiness operations. **Health services:** Clinical lab technology, medical radiologic technology/radiation therapy, nursing (RN). **History:** General. **Liberal arts:** Arts/sciences. **Math:** General. **Parks/recreation:** General. **Physical sciences:** Chemistry, physics. **Protective services:** Law enforcement admin. **Psychology:** General. **Social sciences:** Sociology. **Visual/performing arts:** Art.

Most popular majors. Health sciences 32%, liberal arts 64%.

Computing on campus. 350 workstations in library, computer center, student center. Dormitories linked to campus network. Commuter students can connect to campus network. Online course registration, online library, helpline, repair service, wireless network available.

Student life. Freshman orientation: Mandatory. Preregistration for classes offered. **Policies:** Exception to no-pets rule made for non-carnivorous fish in reasonable numbers kept in 10 gallon maximum aquarium. **Housing:** Guaranteed on-campus for freshmen. Coed dorms available. **Activities:** Campus ministries, choral groups, drama, international student organizations, literary magazine, student government, student newspaper, minority club.

Athletics. NAIA. **Intercollegiate:** Basketball, cross-country, golf, softball W, tennis, volleyball W. **Intramural:** Basketball, bowling, cheerleading W, football (non-tackle), golf, tennis, volleyball. **Team name:** Mariners.

Student services. Adult student services, career counseling, services for economically disadvantaged, student employment services, financial aid counseling, minority student services, personal counseling, placement for graduates, veterans' counselor. **Physically disabled:** Services for visually, speech, hearing impaired. **Transfer:** College fairs on campus for students transferring to 4-year colleges.

Contact. E-mail: admiss@ccga.edu
Phone: (912) 279-5730 Toll-free number: (800) 675-7235
Fax: (912) 262-3072
Clayton Daniels, Assistant Vice President for Enrollment Management, College of Coastal Georgia, One College Drive, Brunswick, GA 31520

Columbus Technical College
Columbus, Georgia
www.columbustech.edu

CB code: 5704

⟩ Public 2-year technical college
⟩ Commuter campus in small city
⟩ Interview required

General. Founded in 1961. Regionally accredited. **Enrollment:** 3,788 degree-seeking undergraduates; 118 non-degree-seeking students. **Degrees:** 335 associate awarded. **Location:** 110 miles from Atlanta, 86 miles from Albany. **Calendar:** Semester, extensive summer session. **Full-time faculty:** 77 total. **Part-time faculty:** 153 total.

Student profile. Among degree-seeking undergraduates, 620 enrolled as first-time, first-year students.

Part-time:	69%	Asian American:	2%
Women:	69%	Hispanic American:	7%
African American:	45%	25 or older:	53%

Basis for selection. Open admission, but selective for some programs. Special requirements for health programs. Under certain conditions, ACT or SAT may be accepted in lieu of COMPASS or ASSET for placement.

High school preparation. College-preparatory program recommended. 22 units recommended. Recommended units include English 4, mathematics 3, social studies 3, science 3, foreign language 1 and academic electives 3. 4 tech prep and 1 health science recommended.

2011-2012 Annual costs. Tuition/fees: $2,498; $4,748 out-of-state. Per-credit charge: $75 in-state; $150 out-of-state. Books/supplies: $1,600. Personal expenses: $1,100.

Financial aid. Need-based: Need-based aid available for part-time students. Work-study available nights, weekends and for part-time students.

Application procedures. Admission: No deadline. $15 fee. Notification before registration date. **Financial aid:** No deadline. FAFSA required. Applicants notified on a rolling basis.

Academics. Special study options: Distance learning, dual enrollment of high school students, weekend college. License preparation in dental hygiene, nursing, paramedic, radiology, real estate. **Credit/placement by examination:** AP, CLEP. **Support services:** Learning center, remedial instruction, study skills assistance, tutoring.

Majors. Business: Accounting, administrative services, business admin. **Education:** Early childhood. **General:** Horticultural science. **Health services:** Cardiovascular technology, dental hygiene, nursing (RN), surgical technology.

Most popular majors. Business/marketing 18%, computer/information sciences 16%, education 8%, health sciences 40%, trade and industry 6%.

Computing on campus. 40 workstations in library, computer center. Online library available.

Student life. Freshman orientation: Mandatory. Preregistration for classes offered. Three-hour orientation held day before start of classes. **Activities:** Student government.

Student services. Career counseling, student employment services, financial aid counseling, personal counseling, placement for graduates, veterans' counselor. **Physically disabled:** Services for speech, hearing impaired.

Contact. E-mail: admissions@columbustech.edu
Phone: (706) 649-1901 Fax: (404) 649-1885
Nicole Kennedy, Director of Admissions, Columbus Technical College, 928 Manchester Expressway, Columbus, GA 31904-6572

Darton College
Albany, Georgia
www.darton.edu

CB member
CB code: 5026

- Public 2-year community college
- Commuter campus in small city

General. Founded in 1963. Regionally accredited. **Enrollment:** 5,889 degree-seeking undergraduates; 208 non-degree-seeking students. **Degrees:** 625 associate awarded. **Location:** 175 miles from Atlanta. **Calendar:** Semester, extensive summer session. **Full-time faculty:** 121 total; 12% minority. **Part-time faculty:** 161 total; 19% minority. **Class size:** 56% < 20, 41% 20-39, 2% 40-49, less than 1% 50-99, less than 1% >100. **Special facilities:** 50-foot Carolina tower and climbing wall, nature trail, indoor heated pool, bowling alley, racquetball courts.

Student profile. Among degree-seeking undergraduates, 47% enrolled in a transfer program, 53% enrolled in a vocational program, 1% already have a bachelor's degree or higher, 1,303 enrolled as first-time, first-year students, 668 transferred in from other institutions.

Part-time:	49%	Hispanic American:	1%
Out-of-state:	4%	International:	2%
Women:	69%	25 or older:	30%
African American:	42%	Live on campus:	5%
Asian American:	1%		

Transfer out. 60% of students enrolled in the transfer program go on to 4-year colleges. **Colleges most students transferred to 2011:** Georgia Southwestern State University, Albany State University, Florida State University, Valdosta State University.

Basis for selection. Open admission, but selective for some programs. Special requirements for nursing, diagnostic medical sonography, physical therapy, and respiratory care programs. Criminal background check required for all students. Interview, portfolios and essays considered when students do not meet minimum admission requirements but show promise. **Adult students:** Must take COMPASS test if out of high school or college for more than 5 years and do not have 30 transferrable credit hours. **Home schooled:** Transcript of courses and grades required.

High school preparation. College-preparatory program required. 16 units required. Required units include English 4, mathematics 4, social studies 3, science 3 and foreign language 2.

2011-2012 Annual costs. Tuition/fees: $3,534; $10,412 out-of-state. Per-credit charge: $82 in-state; $312 out-of-state. Room/board: $8,450. Books/supplies: $1,100.

Financial aid. Need-based: Need-based aid available for part-time students. Work-study available nights, weekends and for part-time students. **Non-need-based:** Scholarships awarded for academics, alumni affiliation, art, athletics, music/drama, state residency. **Additional information:** Auditions, portfolios, essays, extracurricular activities impact scholarship decisions.

Application procedures. Admission: Priority date 8/1; no deadline. $20 fee. Admission notification on a rolling basis. Applications must be received 10 days prior to registration. **Financial aid:** No deadline. FAFSA, institutional form required. Applicants notified on a rolling basis; must reply within 3 week(s) of notification.

Academics. Career and transfer programs available. Support services available online. **Special study options:** Accelerated study, cooperative education, cross-registration, distance learning, double major, dual enrollment of high school students, ESL, honors, independent study, liberal arts/career combination, weekend college. License preparation in dental hygiene, nursing, occupational therapy, paramedic, physical therapy. **Credit/placement by examination:** AP, CLEP, IB, institutional tests. 18 hours in residence required. **Support services:** Learning center, pre-admission summer program, reduced course load, remedial instruction, study skills assistance, tutoring, writing center.

Majors. Biology: General, biomedical sciences. **Business:** Accounting, administrative services, business admin, entrepreneurial studies, office management. **Communications:** Journalism. **Computer sciences:** General, computer science, information systems, networking. **Conservation:** Environmental studies, forestry. **Education:** Art, business, drama/dance, early childhood, English, foreign languages, mathematics, middle, multi-level teacher, music, science, social science, speech. **Engineering:** Pre-engineering. **English:** English lit, rhetoric/composition. **Foreign languages:** General. **Health services:** Cardiovascular technology, clinical lab science, community health services, dental hygiene, EMT paramedic, histologic assistant, histologic technology, licensed practical nurse, medical radiologic technology/radiation therapy, medical records admin, medical records technology, mental health services, nuclear medical technology, nursing (RN), occupational therapy assistant, physical therapy assistant, polysomnography, predental, premedicine, prepharmacy, prephysical therapy, preveterinary, respiratory therapy assistant, respiratory therapy technology, sonography. **History:** General. **Human services:** Social work. **Math:** General. **Parks/recreation:** General, exercise sciences, health/fitness, sports admin. **Philosophy/religion:** Philosophy. **Physical sciences:** Chemistry, physics. **Protective services:** Criminal justice, forensics. **Psychology:** General. **Social sciences:** Anthropology, economics, geography, political science, sociology. **Visual/performing arts:** Art, dance, dramatic, music.

Most popular majors. Education 12%, health sciences 56%.

Computing on campus. 420 workstations in library, computer center, student center. Dormitories wired for high-speed internet access and linked to campus network. Commuter students can connect to campus network. Online course registration, online library, helpline, wireless network available.

Student life. Freshman orientation: Available. Preregistration for classes offered. Held every semester; required of all students enrolled in learning support classes. **Policies:** All tobacco products banned on campus. **Housing:** Coed dorms available. $200 fully refundable deposit. **Activities:** Bands, choral groups, dance, drama, international student organizations, literary magazine, music ensembles, musical theater, student government, student newspaper, symphony orchestra, cultural exchange club, Democratic/Independent/Republican Team, honors club, Phi Theta Kappa.

Athletics. NJCAA. **Intercollegiate:** Baseball M, basketball W, cross-country, golf M, soccer, softball W, swimming, wrestling M. **Intramural:** Basketball, bowling, football (non-tackle), golf, racquetball, softball, table tennis, tennis, volleyball. **Team name:** Cavaliers.

Student services. Alcohol/substance abuse counseling, career counseling, student employment services, financial aid counseling, health services, minority student services, personal counseling, veterans' counselor. **Physically disabled:** Services for visually, speech, hearing impaired. **Transfer:** Pre-admission transcript evaluation for new students. Transfer adviser, college fairs on campus for students transferring to 4-year colleges.

Contact. E-mail: info@darton.edu
Phone: (229) 317-6740 Toll-free number: (866) 775-1214
Fax: (229) 317-6607
Susan Bowen, Director of Admission, Darton College, 2400 Gillionville Road, Albany, GA 31707-3098

East Georgia College
Swainsboro, Georgia
www.ega.edu

CB member
CB code: 5200

◆ Public 2-year community and junior college
◆ Residential campus in small town

General. Founded in 1973. Regionally accredited. **Enrollment:** 3,436 degree-seeking undergraduates. **Degrees:** 168 associate awarded. **ROTC:** Army. **Location:** 85 miles from Savannah and Augusta. **Calendar:** Semester, limited summer session. **Full-time faculty:** 66 total; 36% have terminal degrees, 11% minority, 47% women. **Part-time faculty:** 49 total; 24% have terminal degrees, 10% minority, 41% women. **Class size:** 9% < 20, 87% 20-39, 4% 40-49. **Special facilities:** Outdoor exercise trail, fitness center, community learning center.

Student profile.

Out-of-state:	6%	Live on campus:	6%
25 or older:	20%		

Transfer out. Colleges most students transferred to 2011: Georgia Southern University.

Basis for selection. Graduation from accredited or approved high school or GED, 17 college prep curriculum units, COMPASS test scores, and 2.0 GPA required. SAT or ACT recommended. **Home schooled:** SAT/ACT, home school portfolio, and letter of completion from primary teacher or program administrator with date of graduation required. GED scores and portfolio required of applicants with GED; SAT/ACT not required. COMPASS placement test may be required.

High school preparation. College-preparatory program recommended. 17 units required. Required and recommended units include English 4, mathematics 4, social studies 3, science 4 and foreign language 2.

2011-2012 Annual costs. Tuition/fees: $3,306; $10,184 out-of-state. Per-credit charge: $82 in-state; $312 out-of-state. Books/supplies: $1,400. Personal expenses: $1,400.

2010-2011 Financial aid. Need-based: 59% of total undergraduate aid awarded as scholarships/grants, 41% as loans/jobs. Need-based aid available for part-time students. Work-study available nights, weekends and for part-time students. **Non-need-based:** Scholarships awarded for academics, leadership, state residency.

Application procedures. Admission: No deadline. $20 fee, may be waived for applicants with need. Admission notification on a rolling basis. **Financial aid:** Priority date 6/1; no closing date. FAFSA, institutional form required. Applicants notified on a rolling basis starting 6/1; must reply within 2 week(s) of notification.

Academics. Special study options: Distance learning, double major, dual enrollment of high school students, honors, independent study, study abroad. Bachelor's degree programs available on campus. License preparation in nursing. **Credit/placement by examination:** AP, CLEP, IB, SAT, ACT, institutional tests. 30 credit hours maximum toward associate degree. **Support services:** Learning center, reduced course load, remedial instruction, study skills assistance, tutoring, writing center.

Majors. Biology: General. **Business:** Business admin. **Computer sciences:** Computer science. **Education:** General, business, multi-level teacher. **English:** English lit. **Foreign languages:** Translation. **Health services:** Prenursing. **History:** General. **Liberal arts:** Arts/sciences. **Math:** General. **Parks/recreation:** General, exercise sciences, health/fitness. **Physical sciences:** Chemistry, geology. **Protective services:** Criminal justice. **Psychology:** General. **Social sciences:** Anthropology, criminology, political science, sociology. **Visual/performing arts:** Art. **Work/family studies:** General.

Computing on campus. 284 workstations in dormitories, library, computer center, student center. Dormitories wired for high-speed internet access and linked to campus network. Commuter students can connect to campus network. Online course registration, online library, helpline, wireless network available.

Student life. Freshman orientation: Mandatory. Preregistration for classes offered. Combined 1-day orientation and registration event. **Policies:** Substance-free campus. **Housing:** Coed dorms available. **Activities:** Pep band, campus ministries, drama, international student organizations, literary magazine, musical theater, student government, student newspaper, Republican Club, Democratic Club, Afro-American union, Earth club, Students in Free Enterprise, Student Professional Association of Georgia Educators, art club, Circle K, non-traditonal club, ECHO club.

Athletics. NJCAA. **Intercollegiate:** Baseball M, basketball, softball W. **Intramural:** Football (non-tackle), table tennis, tennis, volleyball. **Team name:** Bobcats.

Student services. Adult student services, alcohol/substance abuse counseling, career counseling, financial aid counseling, health services, minority student services, personal counseling, veterans' counselor. **Physically disabled:** Services for visually, hearing impaired. **Transfer:** Pre-admission transcript evaluation for new students. Transfer adviser, college fairs on campus for students transferring to 4-year colleges.

Contact. E-mail: kjones@ega.edu
Phone: (478) 289-2017 Fax: (478) 289-2140
Georgia Edmonds, Assistant Director of Admissions, East Georgia College, 131 College Circle, Swainsboro, GA 30401-2699

Gainesville State College
Gainesville, Georgia
www.gsc.edu

CB code: 5273

◆ Public 2-year junior college
◆ Commuter campus in large town

General. Founded in 1964. Regionally accredited. **Enrollment:** 8,241 degree-seeking undergraduates. **Degrees:** 87 bachelor's, 778 associate awarded. **Location:** 45 miles from Atlanta, 40 miles from Athens. **Calendar:** Semester, extensive summer session. **Full-time faculty:** 207 total. **Part-time faculty:** 224 total. **Class size:** 21% < 20, 79% 20-39, less than 1% 40-49, less than 1% 50-99.

Transfer out. Colleges most students transferred to 2011: North Georgia College and State University, University of Georgia, Brenau University, Georgia State University, Georgia Institute of Technology.

Basis for selection. 2.0 GPA required for applicants with college prep curriculum diploma; 2.2 GPA required for applicants with technical prep curriculum diploma. SAT or ACT scores may be used for placement test screening.

High school preparation. College-preparatory program recommended. 16 units required. Required units include English 4, mathematics 4, social studies 3, science 3 (laboratory 3) and foreign language 2.

2011-2012 Annual costs. Tuition/fees: $3,530; $11,012 out-of-state. Per-credit charge: $93 in-state; $342 out-of-state. Books/supplies: $630. Personal expenses: $1,000.

Financial aid. Need-based: Need-based aid available for part-time students. Work-study available nights, weekends and for part-time students. **Non-need-based:** Scholarships awarded for academics, art, leadership, music/drama.

Application procedures. Admission: Closing date 7/1 (postmark date). $35 fee, may be waived for applicants with need. Admission notification on a rolling basis. **Financial aid:** Closing date 6/1. FAFSA required. Applicants notified on a rolling basis starting 5/1; must reply within 2 week(s) of notification.

Academics. Special study options: Distance learning, dual enrollment of high school students, ESL, honors, study abroad, teacher certification program. Bachelor's degree programs available on campus. License preparation in dental hygiene, paramedic. **Credit/placement by examination:** AP, CLEP, SAT, ACT, institutional tests. 30 credit hours maximum toward associate degree. **Support services:** Learning center, remedial instruction, study skills assistance, tutoring, writing center.

Majors. Business: General, accounting, administrative services, business admin. **Communications:** Journalism. **Computer sciences:** General. **Conservation:** Forestry. **Education:** General, art, early childhood, elementary, mathematics, music, physical, science, secondary, social science. **Engineering:** General. **English:** English lit. **General:** Business. **Health services:** Dental hygiene, EMT paramedic. **History:** General. **Human services:** Social work. **Liberal arts:** Arts/sciences. **Math:** General. **Physical sciences:** Chemistry, geology, physics. **Protective services:** Criminal justice. **Psychology:** General. **Social sciences:** Anthropology, political science, sociology. **Visual/performing arts:** Dramatic, music performance, studio arts. **Work/family studies:** Child care management.

Computing on campus. 1,000 workstations in library, computer center, student center. Commuter students can connect to campus network. Online course registration, online library, helpline, student web hosting, wireless network available.

Student life. Freshman orientation: Mandatory. Preregistration for classes offered. **Activities:** Bands, choral groups, drama, film society, international student organizations, literary magazine, music ensembles, musical theater, student government, student newspaper.

Athletics. Intramural: Basketball, bowling, football (non-tackle), golf, softball, tennis, volleyball.

Student services. Adult student services, alcohol/substance abuse counseling, career counseling, student employment services, financial aid counseling, minority student services, personal counseling, placement for graduates, veterans' counselor. **Physically disabled:** Services for visually, speech, hearing impaired. **Transfer:** Transfer adviser, college fairs on campus for students transferring to 4-year colleges.

Contact. E-mail: admissions@gsc.edu
Phone: (678) 717-3641 Fax: (678) 717-3643
Mack Palmour, Director of Admissions, Gainesville State College, PO Box 1358, Gainesville, GA 30503

Georgia Highlands College
Rome, Georgia   **CB member**
www.highlands.edu   **CB code: 5237**

⬧ Public 2-year community and liberal arts college
⬧ Commuter campus in very large city

General. Founded in 1968. Regionally accredited. Classes offered at Cartersville, Marietta, Paulding, Douglasville, and Rome. **Enrollment:** 5,528 degree-seeking undergraduates. **Degrees:** 504 associate awarded. **Location:** 75 miles from Atlanta. **Calendar:** Semester, limited summer session. **Full-time faculty:** 133 total; 26% have terminal degrees, 10% minority, 59% women. **Part-time faculty:** 120 total; 59% women. **Special facilities:** Observatory, wetlands preserve.

Student profile. Among degree-seeking undergraduates, 75% enrolled in a transfer program, 1% already have a bachelor's degree or higher, 1,129 enrolled as first-time, first-year students, 425 transferred in from other institutions.

Part-time:	46%	Asian American:	2%
Out-of-state:	1%	Hispanic American:	5%
Women:	63%	Native American:	1%
African American:	17%	25 or older:	22%

Transfer out. Colleges most students transferred to 2011: Kennesaw State University, State University of West Georgia, Berry College, Shorter College, University of Georgia.

Basis for selection. 2.0 college prep GPA required. SAT/ACT required for nursing and dental hygiene programs. SAT/ACT can be used to exempt COMPASS placement exams. **Home schooled:** Statement describing home school structure and mission, transcript of courses and grades, state high school equivalency certificate required. Must submit SAT scores that are equal to or greater than last year's freshman class average and provide completed home school college prep curriculum evaluation form; portfolio required. **Learning Disabled:** Foreign language college preparatory curriculum may be waived through Georgia Board of Regents Center of Learning Disabilities.

High school preparation. College-preparatory program recommended. 17 units recommended. Recommended units include English 4, mathematics 4, social studies 3, science 4 (laboratory 2) and foreign language 2. College preparatory program required for students planning to transfer to 4-year school.

2011-2012 Annual costs. Tuition/fees: $3,404; $10,282 out-of-state. Per-credit charge: $82 in-state; $312 out-of-state. Books/supplies: $750. Personal expenses: $550.

Financial aid. Need-based: Need-based aid available for part-time students. Work-study available nights, weekends and for part-time students. **Non-need-based:** Scholarships awarded for academics, art.

Application procedures. Admission: Priority date 7/1; no deadline. $20 fee, may be waived for applicants with need. Admission notification on a rolling basis beginning on or about 1/2. **Financial aid:** Closing date 4/1. FAFSA required. Applicants notified on a rolling basis starting 4/1; must reply within 2 week(s) of notification.

Academics. Special study options: Cooperative education, distance learning, double major, dual enrollment of high school students, honors, independent study, liberal arts/career combination, study abroad. License preparation in dental hygiene, nursing. **Credit/placement by examination:** AP, CLEP, IB, SAT, ACT, institutional tests. No limit on credits awarded. **Support**

services: Learning center, pre-admission summer program, remedial instruction, study skills assistance, tutoring, writing center.

Honors college/program. 3.5 GPA, 1100 SAT required.

Majors. Biology: General. **Business:** Accounting technology, business admin, managerial economics, office management, office technology. **Communications:** Communications/speech/rhetoric, journalism. **Computer sciences:** General. **Education:** General, multi-level teacher. **English:** English lit. **Foreign languages:** General. **Health services:** Dental hygiene, nursing (RN), physician assistant, premedicine, prenursing, prepharmacy, preveterinary, radiologic technology/medical imaging, respiratory therapy technology. **History:** General. **Math:** General. **Philosophy/religion:** Philosophy. **Physical sciences:** Chemistry, geology, physics. **Protective services:** Police science. **Psychology:** General. **Social sciences:** Political science, sociology. **Visual/performing arts:** Art.

Most popular majors. Business/marketing 19%, education 15%, health sciences 35%, liberal arts 17%, psychology 6%.

Computing on campus. 100 workstations in library, computer center, student center. Commuter students can connect to campus network. Online course registration, online library, helpline, repair service, wireless network available.

Student life. Freshman orientation: Mandatory. Preregistration for classes offered. **Policies:** Access program tracks all student involvement in school and community activities. Transcripts available for resume use or when transferring to another institution. **Housing:** Marietta Campus housing available through Southern Poly Tech University. **Activities:** Literary magazine, student government, student newspaper, TV station, Baptist student union, College Bowl Team, volunteer opportunity center, black student awareness, Insiders, Phi Theta Kappa.

Athletics. Intramural: Archery, badminton, basketball, bowling, field hockey W, football (tackle) M, golf, sailing, skiing, soccer, softball, table tennis, tennis, volleyball, wrestling M. **Team name:** Chargers.

Student services. Adult student services, alcohol/substance abuse counseling, career counseling, student employment services, financial aid counseling, minority student services, personal counseling, placement for graduates, veterans' counselor. **Physically disabled:** Services for visually, speech, hearing impaired. **Transfer:** Re-entry adviser, pre-admission transcript evaluation for new students. College fairs on campus for students transferring to 4-year colleges.

Contact. E-mail: admitme@highlands.edu
Phone: (706) 295-6339 Toll-free number: (800) 332-2406 ext. 6339
Fax: (706) 295-6341
Sandie Davis, Director of Admissions, Georgia Highlands College, 3175 Cedartown Highway, Rome, GA 30161

Georgia Military College
Milledgeville, Georgia
www.gmc.cc.ga.us   **CB code: 5249**

⬧ Public 2-year community and military college
⬧ Commuter campus in large town

General. Founded in 1879. Regionally accredited. Multiple location institution: Atlanta-Fairburn, Augusta, Columbus, Madison, Milledgeville, Sandersville, Valdosta, Warner Robins, and on-line campus. **Enrollment:** 7,456 undergraduates. **Degrees:** 1,262 associate awarded. **ROTC:** Army. **Location:** 90 miles from Atlanta, 30 miles from Macon. **Calendar:** Quarter, limited summer session. **Full-time faculty:** 118 total; 18% have terminal degrees, 12% minority, 49% women. **Part-time faculty:** 221 total; 10% have terminal degrees, 29% minority, 54% women. **Class size:** 64% < 20, 36% 20-39, less than 1% 40-49.

Student profile.

Out-of-state:	12%	Live on campus:	4%
25 or older:	12%		

Transfer out. Colleges most students transferred to 2011: Georgia College & State University, Macon State University, Georgia State University, Augusta State University.

Basis for selection. Open admission, but selective for some programs. ROTC applicants for early commissioning must have 920 SAT (exclusive of Writing) or 19 ACT and 2.0 GPA. Interview recommended for ROTC cadets. **Home schooled:** Transcript of courses and grades required. List of courses completed and bibliography of textbooks and/or assigned readings required. Must submit writing sample or show successful GED completion.

Learning Disabled: Students with disabilities encouraged to present documentation to disabilities officer prior to enrollment.

2011-2012 Annual costs. Tuition/fees: $5,535; $5,535 out-of-state. Per-credit charge: $114. Books/supplies: $675. Personal expenses: $1,800.

Financial aid. Need-based: Need-based aid available for part-time students. Work-study available nights, weekends and for part-time students. **Non-need-based:** Scholarships awarded for athletics, leadership, ROTC, state residency. **Additional information:** Institutional aid offered to those enrolled in Cadet Corps who reside on campus.

Application procedures. Admission: Priority date 8/1; deadline 9/1 (receipt date). $35 fee, may be waived for applicants with need. Admission notification on a rolling basis. August 1 closing date for cadet applications. Students interested in attending ROTC Basic Camp must apply by May 1. **Financial aid:** No deadline. FAFSA required. Applicants notified on a rolling basis starting 3/1.

Academics. Study of ethics is component of all classes and important part of college mission. **Special study options:** Cross-registration, distance learning, double major, dual enrollment of high school students, external degree, independent study. **Credit/placement by examination:** AP, CLEP, institutional tests. 45 credit hours maximum toward associate degree. **Support services:** Learning center, reduced course load, remedial instruction, study skills assistance, tutoring, writing center.

Majors. Business: Business admin, logistics. **Computer sciences:** General. **Education:** General, early childhood, kindergarten/preschool, secondary. **Health services:** Prenursing, public health ed. **History:** General. **Protective services:** Homeland security, law enforcement admin. **Psychology:** General. **Social sciences:** General, international relations. **Work/family studies:** Family studies.

Most popular majors. Business/marketing 18%, education 13%, health sciences 13%, liberal arts 44%.

Computing on campus. 403 workstations in dormitories, library, computer center, student center. Dormitories wired for high-speed internet access and linked to campus network. Commuter students can connect to campus network. Online course registration, online library, wireless network available.

Student life. Freshman orientation: Available. Preregistration for classes offered. Two summer sessions, college athlete session, Early Commissioning session, State Service Scholarship sessions available. **Policies:** Resident programs only available to members of Corps of Cadets. **Housing:** Single-sex dorms, wellness housing available. $75 fully refundable deposit, deadline 9/1. **Activities:** Marching band, choral groups, drama, literary magazine, music ensembles, student government, student newspaper, Circle-K, Phi Theta Kappa, Alpha Phi Omega, Ranger Challenge, drill team, drama club, officer Christians' fellowship, business club, math club, debate/speech organization.

Athletics. NJCAA. Intercollegiate: Cross-country, football (tackle) M, golf, rifle, soccer, track and field. **Intramural:** Badminton, basketball, bowling, golf, softball, volleyball. **Team name:** Bulldogs.

Student services. Financial aid counseling, health services, veterans' counselor. **Physically disabled:** Services for visually, speech, hearing impaired.

Contact. E-mail: admissionsinfo@gmc.cc.ga.us
Phone: (478) 387-4953 Toll-free number: (800) 342-0413
Fax: (478) 445-6520
Donna Findley, Vice President Admissions and Enrollments, Georgia Military College, 201 East Greene Street, Milledgeville, GA 31061

Georgia Northwestern Technical College
Rome, Georgia
www.gntc.edu

▶ Public 2-year technical college
▶ Large town

General. Regionally accredited. **Enrollment:** 5,838 degree-seeking undergraduates; 347 non-degree-seeking students. **Degrees:** 365 associate awarded. **Calendar:** Semester. **Full-time faculty:** 123 total. **Part-time faculty:** 296 total.

Student profile. Among degree-seeking undergraduates, 997 enrolled as first-time, first-year students.

Part-time:	59%	**Hispanic American:**	4%
Women:	65%	**25 or older:**	57%
African American:	11%		

Basis for selection. Open admission, but selective for some programs. COMPASS placement test or official transcripts showing satisfactory completion of appropriate English and math courses with 2.0 GPA required of applicants without SAT/ACT or ASSET. Under certain conditions, prior scores on the ACT or SAT may be accepted in lieu of COMPASS or ASSET test for placement.

High school preparation. College-preparatory program recommended. 22 units recommended. Recommended units include English 4, mathematics 3, social studies 3, science 3, foreign language 1 and academic electives 3. 4 tech prep, 1 health science recommended.

2011-2012 Annual costs. Tuition/fees: $2,498; $4,748 out-of-state. Per-credit charge: $75 in-state; $150 out-of-state.

Financial aid. Need-based: Work-study available nights, weekends and for part-time students.

Application procedures. Admission: No deadline. $20 fee. **Financial aid:** Closing date 9/1.

Academics. Special study options: Distance learning, dual enrollment of high school students, weekend college. **Credit/placement by examination:** AP, CLEP.

Majors. Business: Marketing. **Health services:** Management/clinical assistant. **Protective services:** Law enforcement admin.

Most popular majors. Business/marketing 22%, computer/information sciences 13%, education 10%, health sciences 36%, security/protective services 8%.

Athletics. Team name: Bobcats.

Contact. E-mail: dmcburnett@gntc.edu
Phone: (706) 295-6933 Toll-free number: (866) 983-4682
David McBurnett, Director of Admissions and Student Placement, Georgia Northwestern Technical College, One Maurice Culberson Drive, Rome, GA 30161

Georgia Perimeter College
Clarkston, Georgia
www.gpc.edu
CB member
CB code: 5711

▶ Public 2-year junior and liberal arts college
▶ Commuter campus in very large city

General. Founded in 1964. Regionally accredited. Additional campuses in Alpharetta, Clarkston, Dunwoody, Decatur, and Newton. Online course/program offerings also available. **Enrollment:** 25,094 degree-seeking undergraduates; 1,902 non-degree-seeking students. **Degrees:** 1,829 associate awarded. **Calendar:** Semester, extensive summer session. **Full-time faculty:** 571 total; 33% have terminal degrees, 29% minority, 57% women. **Part-time faculty:** 646 total; 20% have terminal degrees, 36% minority, 57% women. **Class size:** 33% < 20, 65% 20-39, 2% 40-49, less than 1% 50-99, less than 1% >100. **Special facilities:** Botanical gardens, observatory.

Student profile. Among degree-seeking undergraduates, 98% enrolled in a transfer program, 2% enrolled in a vocational program, 5,274 enrolled as first-time, first-year students, 1,796 transferred in from other institutions.

Part-time:	54%	**Women:**	62%
Out-of-state:	10%	**25 or older:**	31%

Transfer out. Colleges most students transferred to 2011: Georgia State University, University of Georgia.

Basis for selection. Any college preparatory curriculum deficiencies must be satisfied by placement testing or substituting college coursework. Admission to nursing program is competitive; GPA in general education and biology, TEAS scores most important. SAT or ACT recommended. SAT/ACT required for joint enrollment. Interview required for top 50 dental hygiene applicants. **Home schooled:** Transcript of courses and grades required. Detailed portfolio and SAT/ACT required.

High school preparation. College-preparatory program recommended. 16 units required. Required units include English 4, mathematics 4, social studies 3, science 4 (laboratory 4) and foreign language 2.

2011-2012 Annual costs. Tuition/fees: $3,420; $10,298 out-of-state. Per-credit charge: $82 in-state; $312 out-of-state. Books/supplies: $1,400. Personal expenses: $1,200.

2011-2012 Financial aid. Need-based: Need-based aid available for part-time students. Work-study available nights, weekends and for part-time students.

Application procedures. Admission: Closing date 7/1 (postmark date). $20 fee, may be waived for applicants with need. Admission notification on a rolling basis. **Financial aid:** Closing date 6/1. FAFSA required. Applicants notified on a rolling basis; must reply within 3 week(s) of notification.

Academics. Special study options: Accelerated study, distance learning, double major, dual enrollment of high school students, ESL, honors, liberal arts/career combination, study abroad, weekend college. License preparation in dental hygiene, nursing. **Credit/placement by examination:** AP, CLEP, IB, SAT, ACT, institutional tests. 21 credit hours maximum toward associate degree. **Support services:** Learning center, remedial instruction, study skills assistance, tutoring, writing center.

Majors. Biology: General. **Business:** Business admin. **Communications:** Communications/speech/rhetoric, journalism. **Computer sciences:** Computer science. **Education:** General, health, physical. **Engineering:** General. **English:** English lit. **Foreign languages:** General, sign language interpretation. **Health services:** Dental hygiene, nursing (RN), predental, premedicine, prepharmacy. **History:** General. **Liberal arts:** Library assistant. **Math:** General. **Philosophy/religion:** Philosophy. **Physical sciences:** Chemistry, geology, physics. **Protective services:** Fire services admin, law enforcement admin. **Psychology:** General. **Social sciences:** Anthropology, political science, sociology. **Visual/performing arts:** Art, dramatic, film/cinema/video, music.

Most popular majors. Business/marketing 32%, education 12%, health sciences 17%, liberal arts 7%, psychology 8%, social sciences 8%.

Computing on campus. Commuter students can connect to campus network. Online course registration, online library, helpline, wireless network available.

Student life. Freshman orientation: Mandatory, $15 fee. Preregistration for classes offered. 2.5 hour orientations begin one month prior to beginning of term. **Activities:** Bands, choral groups, drama, international student organizations, literary magazine, music ensembles, Model UN, musical theater, student government, student newspaper, symphony orchestra.

Athletics. NJCAA. **Intercollegiate:** Baseball M, basketball, soccer, softball W, tennis. **Team name:** Jaguars.

Student services. Adult student services, career counseling, services for economically disadvantaged, financial aid counseling, minority student services, personal counseling, veterans' counselor. **Physically disabled:** Services for visually, hearing impaired. **Transfer:** Transfer adviser, college fairs on campus for students transferring to 4-year colleges.

Contact. E-mail: gpcrec@gpc.edu
Phone: (404) 631-6585 Toll-free number: (888) 696-2780
Fax: (678) 891-3211
Richard Beaubien, Director of Recruitment & Admissions, Georgia Perimeter College, 555 North Indian Creek Drive, Clarkston, GA 30021-2361

Georgia Piedmont Technical College
Clarkston, Georgia
www.dekalbtech.edu   CB code: 3226

- Public 2-year technical college
- Commuter campus in large city

General. Founded in 1961. Regionally accredited. Second campus located in Covington. **Enrollment:** 4,170 degree-seeking undergraduates; 138 non-degree-seeking students. **Degrees:** 263 associate awarded. **Location:** 17 miles from Atlanta. **Calendar:** Semester, extensive summer session. **Full-time faculty:** 82 total. **Part-time faculty:** 375 total. **Class size:** 88% < 20, 12% 20-39. **Special facilities:** Conference center. **Partnerships:** Formal partnerships with MARTA; Fulton County Government; DeKalb, Rockdale, Newton, Morgan County, Decatur City Schools.

Student profile. Among degree-seeking undergraduates, 601 enrolled as first-time, first-year students.

Part-time:	73%	Asian American:	2%
Women:	60%	Hispanic American:	2%
African American:	77%	25 or older:	67%

Transfer out. Colleges most students transferred to 2011: Georgia State University, Southern Polytechnic State University, DeVry University, Clayton College and State University, Georgia Perimeter College.

Basis for selection. Open admission, but selective for some programs. Limited admission to health technologies programs. Under certain conditions, ACT or SAT may be accepted in lieu of COMPASS or ASSET for placement. Interview recommended.

High school preparation. College-preparatory program recommended. 22 units recommended. Recommended units include English 4, mathematics 3, social studies 3, science 3, foreign language 1 and academic electives 3. 4 tech prep and 1 health science recommended.

2011-2012 Annual costs. Tuition/fees: $2,546; $4,796 out-of-state. Per-credit charge: $75 in-state; $150 out-of-state. Books/supplies: $1,200. Personal expenses: $900.

Financial aid. Need-based: Need-based aid available for part-time students. Work-study available nights, weekends and for part-time students.

Application procedures. Admission: Closing date 8/22 (receipt date). $20 fee. Application must be submitted on paper. Admission notification on a rolling basis. **Financial aid:** Closing date 8/20. FAFSA required. Applicants notified on a rolling basis.

Academics. Special study options: Distance learning, dual enrollment of high school students, weekend college. License preparation in nursing, paramedic, real estate. **Credit/placement by examination:** AP, CLEP, institutional tests. 35 credit hours maximum toward associate degree. **Support services:** GED preparation and test center, learning center, reduced course load, remedial instruction, study skills assistance, tutoring.

Majors. Business: Accounting technology, administrative services, banking/financial services, business admin, human resources, marketing. **Computer sciences:** General, networking, programming, support specialist, system admin. **Education:** Early childhood. **Engineering:** Computer, electrical. **Health services:** Clinical lab technology, ophthalmic lab technology. **Protective services:** Criminal justice.

Most popular majors. Business/marketing 40%, computer/information sciences 14%, education 11%, health sciences 7%, security/protective services 12%, trade and industry 8%.

Computing on campus. 500 workstations in computer center. Online course registration, online library available.

Student life. Freshman orientation: Available. Preregistration for classes offered. **Activities:** Student government, student newspaper, Delta Epsilon Chi, Collegiate Secretaries International, Noon Net-Working of New Connections, Phi Beta Lambda, Student Optical Society, Licensed Practical Nurses Association, Vocational Industrial Clubs of America, Epsilon Delta Phi Honorary Society, Phi Theta Kappa Honor Society.

Student services. Adult student services, career counseling, services for economically disadvantaged, student employment services, financial aid counseling, minority student services, placement for graduates, veterans' counselor, women's services. **Physically disabled:** Services for visually, speech, hearing impaired. **Transfer:** Pre-admission transcript evaluation for new students.

Contact. E-mail: richardt@gptc.edu
Phone: (404) 297-9522 ext. 1229
Toll-free number: (877) 780-3032 ext. 1229 Fax: (404) 294-3424
Terry Richardson, Coordinator of Admissions and Special Services, Georgia Piedmont Technical College, 495 North Indian Creek Drive, Clarkston, GA 30021-2397

Gordon College
Barnesville, Georgia
www.gdn.edu   CB code: 5256

- Public 2-year junior and teachers college
- Commuter campus in small town

General. Founded in 1852. Regionally accredited. **Enrollment:** 4,578 degree-seeking undergraduates. **Degrees:** 73 bachelor's, 440 associate awarded. **Location:** 60 miles from Atlanta. **Calendar:** Semester, limited summer session. **Full-time faculty:** 115 total. **Part-time faculty:** 114 total. **Class size:** 14% < 20, 84% 20-39, 1% 40-49, less than 1% 50-99. **Special facilities:** Georgia book collection, performance theater, indoor pool, ropes course, walking trail, amphitheatre.

Student profile.

Out-of-state:	1%	Live on campus:	26%
25 or older:	19%		

Transfer out. Colleges most students transferred to 2011: Clayton State University, Georgia State University, Griffin Technical College, University of Georgia, University of West Georgia.

Basis for selection. Test scores and GPA considered. Additional requirements for associate degree in nursing and bachelor's of science in education. SAT or ACT, SAT Subject Tests recommended. Interview required for nursing program. Applicants may be asked to interview for admission to B.S. in Education program. **Adult students:** COMPASS placement test used if applicant presents SAT/ACT scores lower than minimum required or if applicant lacks scores. **Home schooled:** Statement describing home school structure and mission required. Portfolio demonstrating completion of college prep curriculum required. Include the following for each course: course descriptions, list of assignments, work samples and grades, and list of educational resources (textbooks and other materials).

High school preparation. College-preparatory program recommended. 16 units recommended. Recommended units include English 4, mathematics 4, social studies 3, science 3 (laboratory 2) and foreign language 2. Foreign language units must be in same language.

2011-2012 Annual costs. Tuition/fees: $3,572; $11,054 out-of-state. Per-credit charge: $93 in-state; $342 out-of-state. Room/board: $5,500. Books/supplies: $950. Personal expenses: $903.

Financial aid. Need-based: Need-based aid available for part-time students. Work-study available nights, weekends and for part-time students. **Non-need-based:** Scholarships awarded for academics, athletics, music/drama, state residency.

Application procedures. Admission: No deadline. $20 fee. Admission notification on a rolling basis. **Financial aid:** Priority date 5/1; no closing date. FAFSA, institutional form required. Applicants notified on a rolling basis starting 5/1.

Academics. Special study options: Distance learning, dual enrollment of high school students, ESL, honors, liberal arts/career combination, study abroad. Bachelor's degree programs available on campus. **Credit/placement by examination:** AP, CLEP, IB, SAT, ACT, institutional tests. 42 credit hours maximum toward associate degree. **Support services:** Tutoring, writing center.

Majors. Biology: General. **Business:** Business admin. **Communications:** Communications/speech/rhetoric. **Computer sciences:** Computer science, information systems. **Conservation:** Environmental science, forestry. **Education:** Multi-level teacher. **English:** English lit. **Foreign languages:** General. **Health services:** Dental hygiene, medical records admin, nuclear medical technology, nursing (RN), physician assistant, prepharmacy, prephysical therapy, radiologic technology/medical imaging, respiratory therapy assistant, sonography. **History:** General. **Human services:** Social work. **Math:** General. **Parks/recreation:** Health/fitness. **Physical sciences:** Astronomy, chemistry, physics. **Protective services:** Criminal justice. **Psychology:** General. **Social sciences:** Political science, sociology. **Visual/performing arts:** Art, dramatic, music.

Most popular majors. Business/marketing 19%, education 18%, health sciences 31%, psychology 9%, social sciences 7%.

Computing on campus. 242 workstations in dormitories, library, computer center, student center. Dormitories wired for high-speed internet access and linked to campus network. Commuter students can connect to campus network. Online course registration, online library, student web hosting, wireless network available.

Student life. Freshman orientation: Mandatory. Preregistration for classes offered. Approximately 5-6 hours in length; held twice prior to start of semester, for students and parents. **Housing:** Coed dorms, single-sex dorms, apartments, wellness housing available. $250 partly refundable deposit, deadline 7/1. **Activities:** Bands, campus ministries, choral groups, dance, drama, international student organizations, literary magazine, music ensembles, musical theater, student government, student newspaper, Baptist Collegiate Ministries, Gordon Christian Fellowship, Association of Nursing Students, art club, education association, Driftwood literary club, Phi Theta Kappa (honor society), science club, history club.

Athletics. NJCAA. **Intercollegiate:** Baseball M, basketball M, cheerleading M, cross-country, soccer, softball W, tennis W. **Intramural:** Basketball M, football (non-tackle), soccer, softball, table tennis. **Team name:** Highlanders.

Student services. Alcohol/substance abuse counseling, career counseling, student employment services, financial aid counseling, health services, minority student services, personal counseling, veterans' counselor. **Physically disabled:** Services for visually, speech, hearing impaired. **Transfer:** College fairs on campus for students transferring to 4-year colleges.

Contact. E-mail: admissions@gdn.edu
Phone: (678) 359-5021 Toll-free number: (800) 282-6504
Fax: (770) 358-5080
Ben Ferguson, Director of Admissions, Gordon College, 419 College Drive, Barnesville, GA 30204

Gupton Jones College of Funeral Service
Decatur, Georgia
www.gupton-jones.edu   CB code: 6200

▶ Private 2-year technical college
▶ Commuter campus in very large city

General. Founded in 1920. Accredited by American Board of Funeral Service Education. **Enrollment:** 225 degree-seeking undergraduates. **Degrees:** 125 associate awarded. **Location:** 18 miles from Atlanta. **Calendar:** Quarter. **Full-time faculty:** 7 total; 29% women. **Part-time faculty:** 1 total; 100% have terminal degrees, 100% women.

Student profile.

Out-of-state:	65%	25 or older:	50%

Basis for selection. Open admission.

2012-2013 Annual costs. Tuition/fees (projected): $9,000. Per-credit charge: $200. Personal expenses: $500.

Financial aid. All financial aid based on need. Need-based aid available for part-time students. Work-study available nights, weekends and for part-time students.

Application procedures. Admission: No deadline. $50 fee. Admission notification on a rolling basis. **Financial aid:** No deadline. FAFSA required. Applicants notified on a rolling basis.

Academics. Special study options: Distance learning. Distance learning for General Studies courses only. **Credit/placement by examination:** AP, CLEP.

Computing on campus. 23 workstations in library, computer center.

Student life. Freshman orientation: Mandatory. Preregistration for classes offered.

Student services. Career counseling, personal counseling, placement for graduates.

Contact. E-mail: gjcfs@mindspring.com
Phone: (770) 593-2257 Fax: (770) 593-1891
Patty Hutcheson, President, Gupton Jones College of Funeral Service, 5141 Snapfinger Woods Drive, Decatur, GA 30035

Gwinnett College
Lilburn, Georgia
www.gwinnettcollege.edu

▶ For-profit 2-year junior and career college
▶ Commuter campus in large city

General. Accredited by ACICS. Additional locations in Sandy Springs and Raleigh, NC. **Enrollment:** 400 full-time, degree-seeking students. **Degrees:** 102 associate awarded. **Location:** 20 miles from Atlanta. **Calendar:** Quarter, extensive summer session. **Full-time faculty:** 8 total. **Part-time faculty:** 40 total.

Transfer out. Colleges most students transferred to 2011: DeVry University, Argosy University, University of Phoenix, Colorado Tech Online, Strayer University.

Basis for selection. Open admission, but selective for some programs. Aptitude testing required for some programs. **Home schooled:** Transcript of courses and grades required.

High school preparation. College-preparatory program recommended.

2012-2013 Annual costs. Tuition/fees (projected): $9,850. Books/supplies: $900. Personal expenses: $220.

Financial aid. Need-based: Need-based aid available for part-time students. Work-study available nights, weekends and for part-time students.

Application procedures. Admission: No deadline. No application fee. Application must be submitted on paper. **Financial aid:** No deadline. FAFSA required. Applicants notified on a rolling basis.

Academics. Special study options: Double major, internships. **Credit/ placement by examination:** AP, CLEP. **Support services:** Reduced course load.

Majors. Business: Business admin. **Computer sciences:** Information technology. **Health services:** Medical assistant, medical secretary.

Computing on campus. PC or laptop required. 100 workstations in library, computer center. Wireless network available.

Student services. Adult student services, financial aid counseling, placement for graduates. **Transfer:** Re-entry adviser, pre-admission transcript evaluation for new students.

Contact. E-mail: admissions@gwinnettcollege.edu
Phone: (770) 381-7200 Fax: (770) 381-0454
Lee Cates, Director of Admissions, Gwinnett College, 4230 Highway 29, Lilburn, GA 30047

Gwinnett Technical College
Lawrenceville, Georgia
www.gwinnetttech.edu

CB member
CB code: 5168

- Public 2-year technical college
- Commuter campus in large town

General. Founded in 1984. Regionally accredited. **Enrollment:** 6,331 degree-seeking undergraduates; 317 non-degree-seeking students. **Degrees:** 668 associate awarded. **Location:** 25 miles from Atlanta. **Calendar:** Semester, extensive summer session. **Full-time faculty:** 91 total; 10% have terminal degrees. **Part-time faculty:** 287 total; 8% have terminal degrees. **Special facilities:** Media center, studio, seminar room with microcomputers and multimedia compilers, life science building. **Partnerships:** Internships and clinicals available with several business industries.

Student profile. Among degree-seeking undergraduates, 100% enrolled in a vocational program, 7% already have a bachelor's degree or higher, 643 enrolled as first-time, first-year students.

Part-time:	61%	Asian American:	6%
Women:	61%	Hispanic American:	10%
African American:	34%	25 or older:	55%

Basis for selection. Open admission, but selective for some programs. Selection criteria vary by program. Competitive screening process for some health science programs. Under certain circumstances, ACT or SAT may be accepted in lieu of COMPASS or ASSET for placement.

High school preparation. College-preparatory program recommended. 22 units recommended. Recommended units include English 4, mathematics 3, social studies 3, science 3, foreign language 1 and academic electives 3. 4 tech prep, 1 health science recommended.

2011-2012 Annual costs. Tuition/fees: $2,564; $4,814 out-of-state. Per-credit charge: $75 in-state; $150 out-of-state. Books/supplies: $1,600. Personal expenses: $2,800.

Financial aid. Need-based: Need-based aid available for part-time students. Work-study available nights, weekends and for part-time students.

Application procedures. Admission: No deadline. $20 fee. Admission notification on a rolling basis. **Financial aid:** Closing date 4/2. FAFSA required.

Academics. Special study options: Distance learning, dual enrollment of high school students, weekend college. License preparation in dental hygiene, nursing, paramedic, radiology. **Credit/placement by examination:** AP, CLEP, institutional tests. **Support services:** GED preparation and test center, learning center, remedial instruction, study skills assistance, tutoring, writing center.

Majors. Biology: Biotechnology. **Business:** Accounting, business admin, construction management, marketing, restaurant/food services, tourism/travel. **Computer sciences:** Networking, programming, security, web page design. **Health services:** Nursing (RN), radiologic technology/medical imaging, respiratory therapy technology, sonography, veterinary technology/assistant. **Protective services:** Police science. **Visual/performing arts:** Game design, interior design, photography.

Most popular majors. Business/marketing 33%, computer/information sciences 19%, education 7%, health sciences 16%.

Computing on campus. 120 workstations in library, computer center, student center. Commuter students can connect to campus network. Online course registration, helpline, repair service, wireless network available.

Student life. Freshman orientation: Mandatory. Preregistration for classes offered. One-hour mandatory session, four 30-minute breakout sessions on advisement, financial aid, registration, and online classes. **Activities:** Student government, student newspaper.

Student services. Adult student services, career counseling, student employment services, financial aid counseling, placement for graduates, veterans' counselor. **Physically disabled:** Services for visually, speech, hearing impaired.

Contact. E-mail: fhalloran@gwinnetttech.edu
Phone: (678) 762-7580 ext. 6600 Fax: (770) 685-1267
Florance Halloran, Director of Admissions, Gwinnett Technical College, 5150 Sugarloaf Parkway, Lawrenceville, GA 30243

ITT Technical Institute: Kennesaw
Kennesaw, Georgia
www.itt-tech.edu

- For-profit 2-year business and technical college
- Large town

General. Accredited by ACICS. **Enrollment:** 570 degree-seeking undergraduates. **Degrees:** 12 bachelor's, 92 associate awarded. **Calendar:** Quarter. **Full-time faculty:** 6 total. **Part-time faculty:** 40 total.

Basis for selection. Admission requirements will vary by program.

2011-2012 Annual costs. Estimated costs as of June 2011: per-credit-hour charge, $493, depending upon level and course of study; academic fee, $300. Certain programs of study require purchase of tools, which could cost an additional $100 to $500. All costs are subject to change.

Financial aid. Need-based: Work-study available nights, weekends and for part-time students.

Academics. Credit/placement by examination: AP, CLEP.

Majors. Computer sciences: Information technology, networking, web page design. **Protective services:** Law enforcement admin. **Visual/performing arts:** Design, game design.

Contact. Toll-free number: (877) 231-6415
ITT Technical Institute: Kennesaw, 2065 ITT Tech Way NW, Kennesaw, GA 30144

Le Cordon Bleu College of Culinary Arts: Atlanta
Tucker, Georgia
www.atlantaculinary.com

- For-profit 2-year branch campus and technical college
- Commuter campus in very large city

General. Regionally accredited. **Location:** 10 miles from Atlanta. **Calendar:** Differs by program.

Contact. Phone: (770) 938-4711
Vice President of Admissions, 1927 Lakeside Parkway, Tucker, GA 30084

Middle Georgia College
Cochran, Georgia
www.mgc.edu

CB code: 5411

- Public 2-year community college
- Commuter campus in small town

General. Founded in 1884. Regionally accredited. **Enrollment:** 3,424 degree-seeking undergraduates. **Degrees:** 29 bachelor's, 34 associate awarded. **Location:** 40 miles from Macon. **Calendar:** Semester, limited summer session. **Full-time faculty:** 115 total. **Part-time faculty:** 55 total. **Class size:** 38% < 20, 59% 20-39, less than 1% 40-49, 2% 50-99.

Student profile.

Out-of-state:	6%	Live on campus:	30%
25 or older:	25%		

Transfer out. Colleges most students transferred to 2011: Georgia College and State University, Macon College, Valdosta State University, Georgia Military College.

Basis for selection. Students graduating with college prep diploma must have 2.0 academic core GPA. Students graduating with tech prep/vocational/general diploma must have 2.2 academic core GPA. Students with college preparatory deficiencies may submit SAT Subject Tests scores in the area of deficiencies. Interview and essay required for applicants to Georgia Academy of Mathematics, Engineering, and Science Program. **Home schooled:** Transcript of courses and grades required. Students must submit home-schooled application and obtain 920 SAT (exclusive of writing) or 19 ACT.

High school preparation. 13 units required; 16 recommended. Required and recommended units include English 4, mathematics 3-4, social studies 1, history 2, science 3 (laboratory 2) and foreign language 2.

2011-2012 Annual costs. Tuition/fees: $3,642; $11,124 out-of-state. Per-credit charge: $93 in-state; $342 out-of-state. Room/board: $7,180. Books/supplies: $800. Personal expenses: $600.

Financial aid. Need-based: Need-based aid available for part-time students. Work-study available nights, weekends and for part-time students. **Non-need-based:** Scholarships awarded for academics, alumni affiliation, art, athletics, job skills, leadership, minority status, music/drama, state residency.

Application procedures. Admission: Closing date 7/19 (receipt date). $20 fee, may be waived for applicants with need. Admission notification on a rolling basis. **Financial aid:** Closing date 4/1. FAFSA required. Applicants notified on a rolling basis starting 5/1.

Academics. Special study options: Accelerated study, cooperative education, distance learning, double major, exchange student, honors, independent study, study abroad, weekend college. Weekend college at Dublin campus only; Georgia Academy of Mathematics, Engineering and Science is 2-year residential joint enrollment program for gifted high school juniors and seniors to pursue associate degree utilizing dual credits. Bachelor's degree programs available on campus. **Credit/placement by examination:** AP, CLEP, institutional tests. 30 credit hours maximum toward associate degree. **Support services:** Learning center, remedial instruction, study skills assistance, tutoring, writing center.

Majors. Architecture: Environmental design. **Biology:** General. **Business:** Accounting, business admin, human resources, merchandising, office technology, sales/distribution. **Communications:** Journalism. **Computer sciences:** General, applications programming, computer science, data entry, information technology, programming. **Conservation:** Forestry. **Education:** Early childhood, elementary, health, middle, secondary, special ed. **Engineering:** General, civil, computer, electrical. **English:** English lit. **Foreign languages:** General. **Health services:** Dental assistant, dental hygiene, licensed practical nurse, medical assistant, medical radiologic technology/radiation therapy, medical records admin, medical records technology, nursing (RN), occupational therapy assistant, pharmacy assistant, physical therapy assistant, predental, premedicine, prenursing, prepharmacy, preveterinary, respiratory therapy technology, surgical technology. **History:** General. **Human services:** General, social work. **Liberal arts:** Arts/sciences. **Math:** General. **Parks/recreation:** General, health/fitness. **Physical sciences:** Chemistry, geology, physics. **Protective services:** Criminal justice, police science. **Psychology:** General. **Social sciences:** Economics, political science, sociology. **Visual/performing arts:** Art, dramatic, music. **Work/family studies:** Family studies.

Most popular majors. Health sciences 24%, liberal arts 67%.

Computing on campus. 464 workstations in dormitories, library. Dormitories wired for high-speed internet access and linked to campus network. Commuter students can connect to campus network. Online course registration, online library, helpline available.

Student life. Freshman orientation: Available, $15 fee. Preregistration for classes offered. One-day sessions held in spring and summer. **Policies:** Alcohol not allowed on campus. Students must live with their immediate families or live in college housing unless given permission to live off-campus. **Housing:** Guaranteed on-campus for all undergraduates. Single-sex dorms, wellness housing available. $100 deposit, deadline 7/1. **Activities:** Campus ministries, choral groups, dance, drama, literary magazine, music ensembles, musical theater, student government, student newspaper, Baptist student union, Wesley Foundation, minority alliance club, Rotaract, cultural relations club, Young Republicans, Young Democrats, Fellowship of Christian Athletes.

Athletics. NJCAA. **Intercollegiate:** Baseball M, basketball, cross-country, soccer, softball W. **Intramural:** Badminton, basketball, football (tackle), golf, handball M, rifle M, softball, tennis, volleyball, weight lifting. **Team name:** Warriors.

Student services. Adult student services, alcohol/substance abuse counseling, career counseling, services for economically disadvantaged, student employment services, financial aid counseling, health services, minority student services, personal counseling, veterans' counselor, women's services. **Physically disabled:** Services for visually, hearing impaired. **Transfer:** College fairs on campus for students transferring to 4-year colleges.

Contact. E-mail: admissions@mgc.edu
Phone: (478) 934-3103 Fax: (478) 934-3403
Jennifer Brannon, Director of Admissions, Middle Georgia College, 1100 Second Street SE, Cochran, GA 31014

Middle Georgia Technical College
Warner Robins, Georgia
www.middlegatech.edu
CB code: 5035

- Public 2-year technical college
- Commuter campus in small city

General. Regionally accredited. **Enrollment:** 3,403 degree-seeking undergraduates; 300 non-degree-seeking students. **Degrees:** 127 associate awarded. **Location:** 105 miles from Atlanta. **Calendar:** Semester, extensive summer session. **Full-time faculty:** 100 total. **Part-time faculty:** 130 total.

Student profile. Among degree-seeking undergraduates, 974 enrolled as first-time, first-year students.

Part-time:	62%	Asian American:	1%
Women:	56%	Hispanic American:	3%
African American:	42%	25 or older:	56%

Basis for selection. Open admission, but selective for some programs. Special requirements for allied health programs. Under certain conditions, ACT or SAT may be accepted in lieu of COMPASS or ASSET for placement.

High school preparation. College-preparatory program recommended. 22 units recommended. Recommended units include English 4, mathematics 3, social studies 3, science 3, foreign language 1 and academic electives 3. 4 tech prep and 1 health science recommended.

2011-2012 Annual costs. Tuition/fees: $2,530; $4,780 out-of-state. Per-credit charge: $75 in-state; $150 out-of-state.

Financial aid. Need-based: Work-study available nights, weekends and for part-time students.

Application procedures. Admission: No deadline. $20 fee. **Financial aid:** FAFSA required.

Academics. Associate of Applied Technology degrees are terminal degrees. Courses cannot be transferred to a higher degree level. **Special study options:** Distance learning, dual enrollment of high school students, weekend college. License preparation in aviation, dental hygiene, radiology. **Credit/placement by examination:** AP, CLEP. **Support services:** GED preparation and test center, learning center, remedial instruction, tutoring.

Majors. Business: Accounting technology, marketing, office technology, office/clerical. **Computer sciences:** LAN/WAN management, support specialist. **Health services:** Dental hygiene, radiologic technology/medical imaging. **Protective services:** Law enforcement admin.

Most popular majors. Business/marketing 55%, health sciences 9%, trade and industry 22%.

Student life. Freshman orientation: Mandatory. Preregistration for classes offered.

Athletics. Team name: Titans.

Student services. Career counseling, financial aid counseling.

Contact. E-mail: info@middlegatech.edu
Phone: (478) 988-6800 ext. 4023 Toll-free number: (800) 474-1031
Fax: (478) 988-6947
Dann Webb, Director of Admissions, Middle Georgia Technical College, 80 Cohen Walker Drive, Warner Robins, GA 31088

North Georgia Technical College
Clarkesville, Georgia
www.northgatech.edu
CB code: 5507

Two-Year Colleges

♦ Public 2-year community and technical college
♦ Commuter campus in small town

General. Regionally accredited. **Enrollment:** 2,493 degree-seeking undergraduates; 38 non-degree-seeking students. **Degrees:** 165 associate awarded. **Location:** 75 miles from of Atlanta. **Calendar:** Semester, extensive summer session. **Full-time faculty:** 71 total. **Part-time faculty:** 96 total.

Student profile. Among degree-seeking undergraduates, 606 enrolled as first-time, first-year students.

Part-time:	55%	Asian American:	1%
Out-of-state:	2%	Hispanic American:	2%
Women:	57%	25 or older:	50%
African American:	7%	Live on campus:	9%

Basis for selection. Open admission, but selective for some programs. Additional requirement for some allied health programs. Under certain conditions, ACT or SAT may be accepted in lieu of COMPASS or ASSET for placement. **Home schooled:** Statement describing home school structure and mission, transcript of courses and grades required. **Learning Disabled:** Documentation of IEP required.

High school preparation. College-preparatory program recommended. 22 units recommended. Recommended units include English 4, mathematics 3, social studies 3, history 2, science 3, foreign language 1 and academic electives 3.

2011-2012 Annual costs. Tuition/fees: $2,526; $4,776 out-of-state. Per-credit charge: $75 in-state; $150 out-of-state. Higher per-credit-hour charges for some programs. Books/supplies: $935.

2010-2011 Financial aid. Need-based: 98% of total undergraduate aid awarded as scholarships/grants, 2% as loans/jobs. Need-based aid available for part-time students. Work-study available nights, weekends and for part-time students.

Application procedures. Admission: Priority date 12/1; deadline 12/1 (receipt date). $15 fee. Admission notification on a rolling basis.

Academics. Special study options: Distance learning, dual enrollment of high school students. License preparation in nursing, paramedic, real estate. **Credit/placement by examination:** AP, CLEP, institutional tests. 50 credit hours maximum toward associate degree. **Support services:** GED preparation and test center, learning center, remedial instruction, tutoring.

Majors. Business: Accounting, business admin, office technology. **Computer sciences:** Networking. **Conservation:** Environmental science. **General:** Turf management. **Health services:** Clinical lab technology. **Protective services:** Law enforcement admin.

Most popular majors. Agriculture 7%, business/marketing 35%, computer/information sciences 7%, engineering/engineering technologies 8%, health sciences 8%, personal/culinary services 7%, security/protective services 7%, trade and industry 10%, visual/performing arts 7%.

Computing on campus. Dormitories wired for high-speed internet access and linked to campus network. Commuter students can connect to campus network. Online course registration, online library, wireless network available.

Student life. Freshman orientation: Mandatory. Preregistration for classes offered. **Housing:** Coed dorms available.

Athletics. NJCAA. **Intercollegiate:** Cross-country. **Intramural:** Basketball, football (tackle), softball. **Team name:** Eagles.

Student services. Career counseling, services for economically disadvantaged, financial aid counseling, placement for graduates. **Physically disabled:** Services for visually, speech, hearing impaired.

Contact. E-mail: amitchell@northgatech.edu
Phone: (706) 754-7724 Fax: (706) 754-7777
Amanda Mitchell, Director of Admissions, North Georgia Technical College, 1500 Highway 197 North, Clarkesville, GA 30523

Oxford College of Emory University
Oxford, Georgia
CB member
www.oxford.emory.edu
CB code: 5186

♦ Private 2-year branch campus and liberal arts college affiliated with United Methodist Church
♦ Residential campus in large town
♦ SAT or ACT with writing, application essay required

General. Founded in 1836. Regionally accredited. One of nine schools within Emory University. Students continue to Emory College after freshman and sophomore years to complete the degree. Selective continuation to Emory School of Business and Emory School of Nursing. **Enrollment:** 937 degree-seeking undergraduates. **Degrees:** 377 associate awarded. **Location:** 38 miles from Atlanta. **Calendar:** Semester, extensive summer session. **Full-time faculty:** 56 total; 86% have terminal degrees, 12% minority, 54% women. **Part-time faculty:** 29 total; 52% have terminal degrees, 10% minority, 55% women. **Class size:** 36% < 20, 63% 20-39, 1% 40-49. **Special facilities:** Center for international studies, two hospitals, regional primate center, Center for Disease Control, museum, park, ethics center, Carter Center.

Student profile. Among degree-seeking undergraduates, 443 enrolled as first-time, first-year students, 5 transferred in from other institutions.

Out-of-state:	50%	Asian American:	29%
Women:	53%	Hispanic American:	6%
African American:	14%	International:	15%

Transfer out. 98% of students enrolled in the transfer program go on to 4-year colleges.

Basis for selection. GED not accepted. GPA, high school curriculum and transcript most important, standardized test scores, letters of recommendation, extracurricular activities, and essays also important. Demonstrated interest also considered. **Adult students:** SAT/ACT scores not required if out of high school 1 year(s) or more. **Home schooled:** Transcript of courses and grades, state high school equivalency certificate required. 3 SAT Subject Tests, including math, required.

High school preparation. College-preparatory program recommended. 16 units recommended. Recommended units include English 4, mathematics 4, social studies 3, science 3 (laboratory 3) and foreign language 2. Math units should include geometry and algebra II.

2011-2012 Annual costs. Tuition/fees: $34,862. Room/board: $10,030. Books/supplies: $1,100.

2010-2011 Financial aid. Need-based: 363 full-time freshmen applied for aid; 363 were judged to have need; 363 of these received aid. Average need met was 100%. Average scholarship/grant was $19,692; average loan $3,500. 88% of total undergraduate aid awarded as scholarships/grants, 12% as loans/jobs. Need-based aid available for part-time students. Work-study available nights, weekends and for part-time students. **Non-need-based:** Scholarships awarded for academics, leadership, religious affiliation, state residency. **Additional information:** Loan reduction program for families with annual assessed incomes of $100,000 or less who demonstrate need. Program reduces amount of money borrowed.

Application procedures. Admission: Priority date 1/15; deadline 1/15 (postmark date). $50 fee, may be waived for applicants with need. Must reply by May 1 or within 3 week(s) if notified thereafter. 11/15 deadline for academic scholarship program. **Financial aid:** Priority date 2/15, closing date 3/1. FAFSA, CSS PROFILE required. Applicants notified on a rolling basis starting 4/1; must reply by 5/1.

Academics. Supplemental instruction program in science and other difficult courses led by students who have excelled in a certain course. All academic services that are conducted outside of the classroom are provided by students who want to help their peers. **Special study options:** Cooperative education, cross-registration, double major, dual enrollment of high school students, independent study, internships, liberal arts/career combination, study abroad. **Credit/placement by examination:** AP, CLEP, IB, institutional tests. 16 credit hours maximum toward associate degree. **Support services:** Reduced course load, study skills assistance, tutoring, writing center.

Majors. Liberal arts: Arts/sciences.

Computing on campus. 80 workstations in dormitories, library, computer center, student center. Dormitories wired for high-speed internet access and linked to campus network. Commuter students can connect to campus network. Online course registration, online library, helpline, repair service, student web hosting, wireless network available.

Student life. Freshman orientation: Mandatory, $125 fee. Preregistration for classes offered. Six-day program held directly prior to start of school

year; includes course registration. **Policies:** Dry campus since all students are under 21. Students required to live on campus both years. All residence halls co-ed by floor or wing. **Housing:** Guaranteed on-campus for all undergraduates. Coed dorms, single-sex dorms, special housing for disabled available. $75 nonrefundable deposit, deadline 5/1. **Activities:** Campus ministries, choral groups, dance, drama, film society, international student organizations, literary magazine, music ensembles, Model UN, musical theater, student government, student newspaper, volunteer club, Christian Fellowship, College Republicans, Circle K, Jewish student union, Catholic student union, Muslim student association, Young Democrats, Hindu student council.

Athletics. NJCAA. **Intercollegiate:** Basketball M, soccer W, tennis. **Intramural:** Badminton, basketball, football (non-tackle), golf, table tennis, volleyball. **Team name:** Eagles.

Student services. Alcohol/substance abuse counseling, chaplain/spiritual director, career counseling, financial aid counseling, health services, minority student services, personal counseling, placement for graduates. **Physically disabled:** Services for visually, speech, hearing impaired.

Contact. E-mail: oxadmission@emory.edu
Phone: (770) 784-8328 Toll-free number: (800) 723-8328
Fax: (770) 784-8359
Jennifer Taylor, Dean of Enrollment Services, Oxford College of Emory University, 100 Hamill Street, Oxford, GA 30054-1418

Savannah Technical College
Savannah, Georgia
www.savannahtech.edu
CB code: 3741

◆ Public 2-year technical college
◆ Commuter campus in large city

General. Regionally accredited. Classes offered at satellite campuses in Liberty and Effingham Counties. **Enrollment:** 4,487 degree-seeking undergraduates; 182 non-degree-seeking students. **Degrees:** 230 associate awarded. **Location:** 250 miles from Atlanta. **Calendar:** Semester, extensive summer session. **Full-time faculty:** 96 total. **Part-time faculty:** 259 total. **Class size:** 100% < 20, 50% 20-39.

Student profile. Among degree-seeking undergraduates, 872 enrolled as first-time, first-year students.

Part-time:	64%	Hispanic American:	6%
Women:	65%	International:	1%
African American:	46%	25 or older:	53%
Asian American:	2%		

Transfer out. Colleges most students transferred to 2011: Savannah State University, Armstrong Atlantic State University.

Basis for selection. Open admission, but selective for some programs. Competitive admissions for allied health programs. Under certain conditions, ACT or SAT may be accepted in lieu of COMPASS or ASSET for placement. **Learning Disabled:** Must meet with disability coordinator.

High school preparation. 22 units recommended. Recommended units include English 4, mathematics 3, social studies 3, science 3, foreign language 1 and academic electives 3. 4 tech prep and 1 science recommended.

2011-2012 Annual costs. Tuition/fees: $2,502; $4,752 out-of-state. Per-credit charge: $75 in-state; $150 out-of-state. Books/supplies: $1,500.

Financial aid. Need-based: Need-based aid available for part-time students. Work-study available nights, weekends and for part-time students. **Non-need-based:** Scholarships awarded for academics, leadership, minority status, state residency.

Application procedures. Admission: No deadline. $15 fee. Application must be submitted on paper. Admission notification on a rolling basis. **Financial aid:** No deadline. FAFSA required. Applicants notified on a rolling basis.

Academics. Special study options: Distance learning, dual enrollment of high school students, weekend college. License preparation in dental hygiene, nursing, paramedic. **Credit/placement by examination:** AP, CLEP, institutional tests. **Support services:** GED preparation and test center, learning center, reduced course load, remedial instruction, study skills assistance, tutoring.

Majors. Business: Accounting technology, administrative services, construction management, office technology, operations, sales/distribution. **Computer sciences:** Data processing, networking. **Education:** Early childhood. **Health services:** Dental hygiene, EMT paramedic, surgical technology. **Protective services:** Criminal justice, firefighting. **Work/family studies:** Child care service.

Most popular majors. Business/marketing 43%, computer/information sciences 16%, education 7%, health sciences 9%, legal studies 7%, security/protective services 8%.

Computing on campus. 100 workstations in library, computer center. Online course registration, online library, helpline, wireless network available.

Student life. Freshman orientation: Available. Preregistration for classes offered. **Activities:** Student government.

Student services. Career counseling, services for economically disadvantaged, student employment services, financial aid counseling, personal counseling, placement for graduates. **Physically disabled:** Services for visually, hearing impaired. **Transfer:** Re-entry adviser, pre-admission transcript evaluation for new students.

Contact. E-mail: gmoore@savannahtech.edu
Phone: (912) 443-5711 Toll-free number: (800) 769-6362
Fax: (912) 443-5705
Gwen Moore, Director of Admissions, Savannah Technical College, 5717 White Bluff Road, Savannah, GA 31401-5521

South Georgia College
Douglas, Georgia
www.sgc.edu
CB code: 5619

◆ Public 2-year community and junior college
◆ Commuter campus in large town

General. Founded in 1906. Regionally accredited. **Enrollment:** 2,218 undergraduates. **Degrees:** 244 associate awarded. **Location:** 212 miles from Atlanta; 140 miles from Jacksonville, FL. **Calendar:** Semester, extensive summer session. **Full-time faculty:** 44 total. **Part-time faculty:** 67 total. **Class size:** 99% < 20, 1% 20-39. **Special facilities:** Mobile nursing clinic, endangered pine/wiregrass plot.

Student profile.

Out-of-state:	3%	Live on campus:	16%
25 or older:	22%		

Transfer out. Colleges most students transferred to 2011: Valdosta State University, Georgia Southern University, University of Georgia.

Basis for selection. Open admission, but selective for some programs. SAT/ACT required of nursing students. COMPASS placement test required of applicants without SAT/ACT. Applicants who score below 400 SAT math (17 ACT math) or 430 SAT verbal (17 ACT English) also required to take placement tests. **Home schooled:** Statement describing home school structure and mission, transcript of courses and grades required. **Learning Disabled:** Documentation required so appropriate services can be provided.

High school preparation. College-preparatory program recommended. 16 units recommended. Recommended units include English 4, mathematics 4, social studies 3, science 3 (laboratory 3) and foreign language 2.

2011-2012 Annual costs. Tuition/fees: $3,500; $10,378 out-of-state. Per-credit charge: $82 in-state; $312 out-of-state. Room/board: $7,715. Books/supplies: $660. Personal expenses: $825.

Financial aid. Need-based: Need-based aid available for part-time students. Work-study available nights, weekends and for part-time students. **Non-need-based:** Scholarships awarded for academics.

Application procedures. Admission: No deadline. $20 fee, may be waived for applicants with need. Admission notification on a rolling basis. **Financial aid:** Priority date 6/1; no closing date. FAFSA, institutional form required. Applicants notified on a rolling basis starting 7/6; must reply within 2 week(s) of notification.

Academics. Special study options: Cooperative education, distance learning, dual enrollment of high school students, independent study, study abroad, teacher certification program. Bachelor's degree programs available on campus. License preparation in nursing. **Credit/placement by examination:** AP, CLEP, IB, SAT, ACT, institutional tests. 30 credit hours maximum toward associate degree. **Support services:** Learning center, reduced course load, remedial instruction, tutoring.

Majors. Biology: General. **Business:** Business admin. **Communications:** Communications/speech/rhetoric, journalism. **Computer sciences:** Computer science, information technology. **Education:** General, early childhood, early childhood special, health, middle, physical, secondary, speech impaired. **English:** English lit. **Foreign languages:** General. **Health services:** Nursing (RN). **History:** General. **Math:** General. **Parks/recreation:** General, health/fitness. **Philosophy/religion:** Philosophy. **Physical sciences:** Chemistry,

physics. **Protective services:** Police science. **Psychology:** General. **Social sciences:** Political science, sociology. **Visual/performing arts:** Dramatic.

Most popular majors. Business/marketing 11%, education 23%, health sciences 35%, liberal arts 8%.

Computing on campus. 80 workstations in library. Dormitories wired for high-speed internet access. Online course registration, online library, wireless network available.

Student life. Freshman orientation: Mandatory. Preregistration for classes offered. **Housing:** Guaranteed on-campus for all undergraduates. Coed dorms, special housing for disabled available. $200 fully refundable deposit. **Activities:** Campus ministries, choral groups, dance, drama, international student organizations, literary magazine, student government, student newspaper, cultural exchange club, debate society, Association of Nursing Students, College Democrats, College Republicans, students for social awareness, student organization for multicultural unity, Phi Beta Lambda.

Athletics. NJCAA. **Intercollegiate:** Baseball M, cross-country, soccer, softball W, tennis W. **Intramural:** Basketball, golf, softball, swimming, synchronized swimming, table tennis, tennis, volleyball. **Team name:** Tigers.

Student services. Financial aid counseling, veterans' counselor. **Physically disabled:** Services for speech impaired. **Transfer:** Pre-admission transcript evaluation for new students. College fairs on campus for students transferring to 4-year colleges.

Contact. E-mail: admissions@sgc.edu
Phone: (912) 260-4206 Toll-free number: (800) 342-6364
Fax: (912) 260-4441
Wes Brown, Director of Enrollment Services, South Georgia College, 100 West College Park Drive, Douglas, GA 31533-5098

Southeastern Technical College
Vidalia, Georgia
www.southeasterntech.edu   CB code: 5652

- Public 2-year technical college
- Commuter campus in large town

General. Regionally accredited. **Enrollment:** 1,609 degree-seeking undergraduates; 217 non-degree-seeking students. **Degrees:** 46 associate awarded. **Location:** 73 miles from Savannah. **Calendar:** Semester. **Full-time faculty:** 70 total. **Part-time faculty:** 80 total. **Class size:** 78% < 20, 22% 20-39.

Student profile. Among degree-seeking undergraduates, 223 enrolled as first-time, first-year students.

Part-time:	65%	Hispanic American:	3%
Women:	72%	25 or older:	50%
African American:	34%		

Basis for selection. Open admission, but selective for some programs. Special requirements for practical nursing and radiologic technology programs. Under certain conditions, ACT or SAT may be accepted in lieu of COMPASS or ASSET for placement. **Home schooled:** Statement describing home school structure and mission required.

High school preparation. College-preparatory program recommended. 22 units recommended. Recommended units include English 4, mathematics 3, social studies 3, science 3, foreign language 1 and academic electives 3. 4 tech prep, 1 health science recommended.

2011-2012 Annual costs. Tuition/fees: $2,498; $4,748 out-of-state. Per-credit charge: $75 in-state; $150 out-of-state.

Financial aid. Need-based: Need-based aid available for part-time students. Work-study available nights, weekends and for part-time students. **Non-need-based:** Scholarships awarded for state residency.

Application procedures. Admission: No deadline. $25 fee. **Financial aid:** No deadline. FAFSA required. Applicants notified on a rolling basis starting 4/6.

Academics. Special study options: Distance learning, dual enrollment of high school students, weekend college. License preparation in dental hygiene, nursing, paramedic, radiology. **Credit/placement by examination:** AP, CLEP, institutional tests. **Support services:** GED preparation and test center, remedial instruction, study skills assistance, tutoring.

Majors. Business: Accounting, business admin, marketing. **Computer sciences:** LAN/WAN management, networking, support specialist. **Conservation:** Forestry. **Education:** Early childhood. **Health services:** Clinical lab

assistant, clinical lab technology, dental hygiene, radiologic technology/medical imaging. **Protective services:** Law enforcement admin.

Most popular majors. Business/marketing 26%, computer/information sciences 17%, education 9%, health sciences 24%, security/protective services 13%, trade and industry 11%.

Computing on campus. 1,400 workstations in library. Commuter students can connect to campus network. Online library, wireless network available.

Student life. Freshman orientation: Mandatory. Preregistration for classes offered. **Activities:** Student government.

Athletics. Intramural: Bowling M, volleyball M.

Student services. Career counseling, student employment services, financial aid counseling, placement for graduates, veterans' counselor. **Physically disabled:** Services for visually, speech, hearing impaired. **Transfer:** Pre-admission transcript evaluation for new students.

Contact. E-mail: brhart@southeasterntech.edu
Phone: (912) 538-3142 Fax: (912) 538-3156
Brad Hart, Director of Enrollment Services, Southeastern Technical College, 3001 East First Street, Vidalia, GA 30474

Southern Crescent Technical College
Griffin, Georgia
www.sctech.edu   CB code: 5670

- Public 2-year technical college
- Small city

General. Regionally accredited. **Enrollment:** 4,995 degree-seeking undergraduates; 160 non-degree-seeking students. **Degrees:** 387 associate awarded. **Calendar:** Semester. **Full-time faculty:** 110 total. **Part-time faculty:** 303 total.

Student profile. Among degree-seeking undergraduates, 756 enrolled as first-time, first-year students.

Part-time:	59%	Asian American:	1%
Women:	67%	Hispanic American:	3%
African American:	42%	25 or older:	57%

Basis for selection. Open admission, but selective for some programs. Admission criteria vary by program. Under certain circumstances, ACT or SAT may be accepted in lieu of COMPASS or ASSET for placement.

High school preparation. College-preparatory program recommended. 22 units recommended. Recommended units include English 4, mathematics 3, social studies 3, science 3, foreign language 1 and academic electives 3. 4 tech prep, 1 health science recommended.

2011-2012 Annual costs. Tuition/fees: $2,498; $4,748 out-of-state. Per-credit charge: $75 in-state; $150 out-of-state. Books/supplies: $150. Personal expenses: $587.

Financial aid. Need-based: Work-study available nights, weekends and for part-time students.

Application procedures. Admission: No deadline. $20 fee. **Financial aid:** FAFSA, institutional form required. Applicants notified on a rolling basis.

Academics. Special study options: Distance learning, dual enrollment of high school students, weekend college. **Credit/placement by examination:** AP, CLEP. **Support services:** GED preparation and test center.

Majors. Business: Accounting, administrative services, business admin, management science. **Computer sciences:** General, information systems. **Health services:** Radiologic technology/medical imaging. **Protective services:** Law enforcement admin.

Most popular majors. Business/marketing 22%, computer/information sciences 14%, education 8%, health sciences 27%, security/protective services 17%, trade and industry 8%.

Student services. Career counseling, services for economically disadvantaged, financial aid counseling, placement for graduates, veterans' counselor.

Contact. E-mail: tkinard@sctech.edu
Phone: (706) 646-6160 Fax: (770) 229-3227
Teri Kinard, Director of Student Affairs, Southern Crescent Technical College, 501 Varsity Road, Griffin, GA 30223

Southwest Georgia Technical College
Thomasville, Georgia
www.southwestgatech.edu   CB code: 3627

▶ Public 2-year technical college
▶ Commuter campus in large town

General. Regionally accredited. **Enrollment:** 1,489 degree-seeking undergraduates; 275 non-degree-seeking students. **Degrees:** 154 associate awarded. **Location:** 35 miles from Tallahassee, Florida. **Calendar:** Semester, extensive summer session. **Full-time faculty:** 48 total. **Part-time faculty:** 81 total. **Partnerships:** Formal partnership with John Deere.

Student profile. Among degree-seeking undergraduates, 251 enrolled as first-time, first-year students.

Part-time:	73%	Hispanic American:	2%
Women:	69%	Native American:	1%
African American:	35%	25 or older:	52%
Asian American:	1%		

Basis for selection. Open admission, but selective for some programs. Most health programs selective due to limited enrollment. Selection process may include required certifications, additional standardized testing, prerequisite courses and physical exam. Under certain conditions, prior official scores on the ACT or SAT may be accepted in lieu of COMPASS or ASSET test for placement. **Learning Disabled:** Students seeking accommodations should provide documentation of learning disability.

High school preparation. College-preparatory program recommended. 22 units recommended. Recommended units include English 4, mathematics 3, social studies 3, science 3, foreign language 1 and academic electives 3. 4 tech prep and 1 health science recommended.

2011-2012 Annual costs. Tuition/fees: $2,498; $4,748 out-of-state. Per-credit charge: $75 in-state; $150 out-of-state. Books/supplies: $990. Personal expenses: $4,400.

Financial aid. Need-based: Need-based aid available for part-time students. Work-study available nights, weekends and for part-time students. **Non-need-based:** Scholarships awarded for state residency.

Application procedures. Admission: No deadline. $15 fee. Admission notification on a rolling basis. **Financial aid:** No deadline. FAFSA, institutional form required. Applicants notified on a rolling basis starting 7/1.

Academics. Special study options: Distance learning, dual enrollment of high school students, weekend college. License preparation in nursing, paramedic, physical therapy, radiology, real estate. **Credit/placement by examination:** AP, CLEP, institutional tests. **Support services:** GED preparation and test center, remedial instruction, tutoring.

Majors. Business: Accounting technology, administrative services, business admin, office/clerical, operations. **Computer sciences:** Data entry, data processing, networking. **Education:** Early childhood. **General:** Equipment technology, power machinery. **Health services:** Clinical lab technology, medical assistant, medical radiologic technology/radiation therapy, nursing (RN), pharmacy assistant, radiologic technology/medical imaging, respiratory therapy technology, surgical technology. **Protective services:** Criminal justice, police science. **Work/family studies:** Child care service.

Most popular majors. Business/marketing 9%, computer/information sciences 7%, health sciences 65%, security/protective services 6%.

Computing on campus. 42 workstations in library. Online course registration, online library available.

Student life. Freshman orientation: Mandatory. Preregistration for classes offered. Held quarterly. **Activities:** Student government, National Vocational honor society, Phi Beta Lambda, SkillsUSA.

Student services. Adult student services, career counseling, services for economically disadvantaged, student employment services, financial aid counseling, personal counseling, placement for graduates. **Physically disabled:** Services for visually, hearing impaired. **Transfer:** Pre-admission transcript evaluation for new students.

Contact. E-mail: info@southwestgatech.edu
Phone: (229) 225-5089 Fax: (229) 227-2666
Wanda Hancock, Director of Admissions, Southwest Georgia Technical College, 15689 US Highway 19N, Thomasville, GA 31792

Virginia College at Augusta
Augusta, Georgia
www.augusta.vc.edu

▶ For-profit 2-year health science and career college
▶ Large city

General. Regionally accredited; also accredited by ACICS. **Enrollment:** 800 degree-seeking undergraduates. **Degrees:** 38 associate awarded. **Calendar:** Quarter. **Full-time faculty:** 10 total. **Part-time faculty:** 58 total.

Basis for selection. Open admission.

Financial aid. Need-based: Work-study available nights, weekends and for part-time students.

Application procedures. Admission: $100 fee.

Academics. Credit/placement by examination: AP, CLEP.

Majors. Business: Business admin. **Health services:** Medical records admin, surgical technology.

Contact. E-mail: augusta.info@vc.edu
Virginia College at Augusta, 2807 Wylds Road, Augusta, GA 30909

Virginia College at Columbus
Columbus, Georgia
www.columbus.vc.edu

▶ For-profit 2-year health science and career college
▶ Small city

General. Regionally accredited; also accredited by ACICS. **Enrollment:** 370 degree-seeking undergraduates. **Calendar:** Quarter.

Basis for selection. Open admission.

Financial aid. Need-based: Work-study available nights, weekends and for part-time students.

Application procedures. Admission: $100 fee.

Academics. Credit/placement by examination: AP, CLEP.

Majors. Business: Business admin. **Health services:** Medical records admin, surgical technology.

Contact. E-mail: columbus.info@vc.edu
Phone: (762) 207-1600
Virginia College at Columbus, 5601 Veterans Parkway, Columbus, GA 31904

Virginia College at Macon
Macon, Georgia
www.macon.vc.edu

▶ For-profit 2-year health science and career college
▶ Small city

General. Accredited by ACICS. **Enrollment:** 400 degree-seeking undergraduates. **Calendar:** Quarter.

Basis for selection. Open admission.

Financial aid. Need-based: Work-study available nights, weekends and for part-time students.

Application procedures. Admission: $100 fee.

Academics. Credit/placement by examination: AP, CLEP.

Majors. Business: Business admin. **Health services:** Medical records admin, surgical technology.

Contact. E-mail: macon.info@vc.edu
Phone: (478) 803-4600
Virginia College at Macon, 1901 Paul Walsh Drive, Macon, GA 31206

Virginia College at Savannah
Savannah, Georgia
www.savannah.vc.edu

- For-profit 2-year culinary school and career college
- Large city

General. Regionally accredited; also accredited by ACICS. **Enrollment:** 400 degree-seeking undergraduates. **Calendar:** Quarter.

Basis for selection. Open admission.

Financial aid. Need-based: Work-study available nights, weekends and for part-time students.

Application procedures. Admission: $100 fee.

Academics. Credit/placement by examination: AP, CLEP.

Majors. Business: Business admin. **Health services:** Medical records admin, surgical technology.

Contact. E-mail: savannah.info@vc.edu
Phone: (912) 721-5600
Virginia College at Savannah, 14045 Abercorn Street, Suite 1503, Savannah, GA 31419

Waycross College
Waycross, Georgia
www.waycross.edu
CB code: 5889

- Public 2-year community and liberal arts college
- Commuter campus in large town

General. Founded in 1976. Regionally accredited. **Enrollment:** 1,109 degree-seeking undergraduates. **Degrees:** 96 associate awarded. **Location:** 70 miles from Jacksonville, FL. **Calendar:** Semester, limited summer session. **Full-time faculty:** 20 total. **Part-time faculty:** 27 total. **Special facilities:** Repository of materials about the Okefenokee Swamp.

Student profile. Among degree-seeking undergraduates, 100% enrolled in a transfer program, 5% already have a bachelor's degree or higher, 220 enrolled as first-time, first-year students.

Part-time:	51%	Women:	69%
Out-of-state:	10%	25 or older:	28%

Transfer out. Colleges most students transferred to 2011: Valdosta State University, Armstrong Atlantic University, Georgia Southern University, University of Georgia.

Basis for selection. Open admission. **Home schooled:** Transcript of courses and grades required.

High school preparation. College-preparatory program recommended. 16 units recommended. Recommended units include English 4, mathematics 4, social studies 3, science 4 and foreign language 2.

2011-2012 Annual costs. Tuition/fees: $3,174; $10,052 out-of-state. Per-credit charge: $82 in-state; $312 out-of-state. Books/supplies: $500. Personal expenses: $900.

Financial aid. Need-based: Need-based aid available for part-time students. Work-study available nights, weekends and for part-time students. **Non-need-based:** Scholarships awarded for academics, alumni affiliation, leadership.

Application procedures. Admission: No deadline. $20 fee, may be waived for applicants with need. Admission notification on a rolling basis. **Financial aid:** Priority date 6/1; no closing date. FAFSA, institutional form required. Applicants notified on a rolling basis; must reply within 2 week(s) of notification.

Academics. Special study options: Dual enrollment of high school students, independent study, liberal arts/career combination, study abroad. Cooperative nursing programs (RN) with South Georgia College, Valdosta State University, Albany State University. Bachelor's degree programs available on campus. **Credit/placement by examination:** AP, CLEP, SAT, ACT, institutional tests. 20 credit hours maximum toward associate degree. SAT Subject Tests used to replace courses students did not take in high school. **Support services:** Learning center, reduced course load, remedial instruction, study skills assistance, tutoring, writing center.

Majors. Biology: General. **Business:** Accounting, business admin. **Computer sciences:** General, programming. **Conservation:** Environmental science. **Education:** General, physical. **English:** English lit. **Health services:** Clinical lab technology, dental hygiene, EMT paramedic, medical radiologic technology/radiation therapy, surgical technology. **History:** General. **Math:** General. **Parks/recreation:** Health/fitness. **Physical sciences:** Chemistry. **Psychology:** General. **Social sciences:** Political science, sociology. **Work/family studies:** Child care management.

Computing on campus. 120 workstations in library, computer center, student center. Online course registration, wireless network available.

Student life. Freshman orientation: Mandatory. Preregistration for classes offered. **Activities:** Drama, literary magazine, student government, student newspaper, Baptist student union, multicultural student alliance, Circle-K.

Athletics. NJCAA. **Intercollegiate:** Basketball M, softball W. **Intramural:** Baseball M, basketball, football (non-tackle), softball. **Team name:** Swamp Fox.

Student services. Adult student services, alcohol/substance abuse counseling, career counseling, student employment services, financial aid counseling, minority student services, personal counseling, placement for graduates, veterans' counselor. **Physically disabled:** Services for visually, speech, hearing impaired. **Transfer:** Pre-admission transcript evaluation for new students. Transfer adviser, college fairs on campus for students transferring to 4-year colleges.

Contact. E-mail: admiss@waycross.edu
Phone: (912) 449-7600 Fax: (912) 449-7610
Robert Wingfield, Director of Admissions and Records, Waycross College, 2001 South Georgia Parkway, Waycross, GA 31503

West Georgia Technical College
Waco, Georgia
www.westgatech.edu
CB code: 3632

- Public 2-year technical college
- Commuter campus in small city

General. Regionally accredited. **Enrollment:** 6,856 degree-seeking undergraduates; 475 non-degree-seeking students. **Degrees:** 32,052 associate awarded. **Location:** 60 miles from Atlanta. **Calendar:** Semester, limited summer session. **Full-time faculty:** 146 total. **Part-time faculty:** 360 total. **Class size:** 80% < 20, 20% 20-39.

Student profile. Among degree-seeking undergraduates, 1,255 enrolled as first-time, first-year students.

Part-time:	72%	Asian American:	1%
Women:	70%	Hispanic American:	3%
African American:	29%	25 or older:	51%

Basis for selection. Open admission, but selective for some programs. Admission to radiology and nursing programs based on examination, interview and space availability. Under certain circumstances, ACT/SAT may be accepted in lieu of COMPASS or ASSET for placement. **Home schooled:** Transcript of courses and grades required. Must provide satisfactory documentation indicating the homeschool is approved. **Learning Disabled:** Disabilities must be documented with the on-site coordinator to receive consideration for accommodation.

High school preparation. College-preparatory program recommended. 22 units recommended. Recommended units include English 4, mathematics 3, social studies 3, science 3, foreign language 1 and academic electives 3. 4 tech prep and 1 health science recommended.

2011-2012 Annual costs. Tuition/fees: $2,522; $4,772 out-of-state. Per-credit charge: $75 in-state; $150 out-of-state. Books/supplies: $1,283. Personal expenses: $1,300.

Financial aid. Need-based: Need-based aid available for part-time students. Work-study available nights, weekends and for part-time students. **Non-need-based:** Scholarships awarded for state residency.

Application procedures. Admission: No deadline. $25 fee. Admission notification on a rolling basis. **Financial aid:** No deadline. FAFSA, institutional form required. Applicants notified on a rolling basis; must reply within 1 week(s) of notification.

Academics. Tutorial program available. **Special study options:** Distance learning, dual enrollment of high school students. License preparation in paramedic, radiology, real estate. **Credit/placement by examination:** AP, CLEP. 15 credit hours maximum toward associate degree. **Support services:**

GED preparation and test center, learning center, study skills assistance, tutoring.

Majors. Business: Accounting, administrative services, business admin, executive assistant, management science. **Computer sciences:** General, data entry, networking, web page design. **Education:** Early childhood. **Health services:** Medical records technology, pharmacy assistant. **Protective services:** Criminal justice, firefighting.

Most popular majors. Business/marketing 26%, computer/information sciences 12%, education 7%, health sciences 31%, security/protective services 12%.

Computing on campus. 100 workstations in library, computer center. Online library available.

Student life. Freshman orientation: Mandatory. Preregistration for classes offered. **Activities:** Student government, TV station, Phi Beta Lambda.

Student services. Adult student services, career counseling, student employment services, financial aid counseling, on-campus daycare, placement for graduates, veterans' counselor, women's services. **Physically disabled:** Services for visually, hearing impaired.

Contact. E-mail: lbasham@westgatech.edu
Phone: (770) 537-5719
Lori Basham, Director of Admission, West Georgia Technical College, 176 Murphy Campus Boulevard, Waco, GA 30182

Wiregrass Georgia Technical College
Valdosta, Georgia
www.wiregrass.edu
CB code: 4557

- Public 2-year technical college
- Commuter campus in small city

General. Regionally accredited. **Enrollment:** 4,332 degree-seeking undergraduates; 198 non-degree-seeking students. **Degrees:** 120 associate awarded. **Calendar:** Semester, extensive summer session. **Full-time faculty:** 120 total. **Part-time faculty:** 171 total. **Class size:** 100% 20-39.

Student profile. Among degree-seeking undergraduates, 100% enrolled in a vocational program, 642 enrolled as first-time, first-year students.

Part-time:	57%	Asian American:	1%
Out-of-state:	1%	Hispanic American:	2%
Women:	68%	25 or older:	54%
African American:	37%		

Basis for selection. Open admission, but selective for some programs. Background checks required for health programs and early childhood education; drug screens required for commercial truck driving; TEAS testing required for nursing. Under certain conditions, prior official scores on the ACT or SAT may be accepted in lieu of COMPASS or ASSET test for placement.

High school preparation. College-preparatory program recommended. 22 units recommended. Recommended units include English 4, mathematics 3, social studies 3, science 3, foreign language 1 and academic electives 3. 4 tech prep and 1 health science recommended.

2011-2012 Annual costs. Tuition/fees: $2,532; $4,782 out-of-state. Per-credit charge: $75 in-state; $150 out-of-state.

2010-2011 Financial aid. Need-based: 99% of total undergraduate aid awarded as scholarships/grants, 1% as loans/jobs. Need-based aid available for part-time students. Work-study available nights, weekends and for part-time students. **Non-need-based:** Scholarships awarded for academics, job skills, state residency.

Application procedures. Admission: No deadline. $15 fee. Admission notification on a rolling basis. **Financial aid:** No deadline. FAFSA, institutional form required. Applicants notified on a rolling basis starting 6/1.

Academics. Special study options: Distance learning, dual enrollment of high school students. License preparation in dental hygiene, nursing, paramedic, radiology, real estate. **Credit/placement by examination:** AP, CLEP, institutional tests. 25 credit hours maximum toward associate degree. **Support services:** GED preparation and test center, learning center, reduced course load, remedial instruction, study skills assistance, tutoring, writing center.

Majors. Communications technology: Graphic/printing. **Computer sciences:** General. **Education:** Early childhood. **Health services:** Clinical lab technology, radiologic technology/medical imaging. **Protective services:** Firefighting.

Most popular majors. Business/marketing 43%, computer/information sciences 13%, education 8%, health sciences 21%, security/protective services 11%.

Computing on campus. 250 workstations in library, computer center, student center. Online course registration, online library, helpline, repair service, wireless network available.

Student life. Freshman orientation: Mandatory. Preregistration for classes offered. **Activities:** Literary magazine, student government.

Student services. Adult student services, alcohol/substance abuse counseling, career counseling, services for economically disadvantaged, student employment services, financial aid counseling, on-campus daycare, personal counseling, placement for graduates, veterans' counselor. **Physically disabled:** Services for visually, speech, hearing impaired.

Contact. E-mail: admissions@wiregrass.edu
Phone: (229) 333-2105 Toll-free number: (800) 575-0567
Fax: (229) 333-2153
Teresa Spires, Executive Director of Admissions, Wiregrass Georgia Technical College, 4089 Val Tech Road, Valdosta, GA 31602

Young Harris College
Young Harris, Georgia
www.yhc.edu
CB code: 5990

- Private 2-year liberal arts college affiliated with United Methodist Church
- Residential campus in rural community
- SAT or ACT (ACT writing recommended) required

General. Founded in 1886. Regionally accredited. Affiliated with the United Methodist Church and welcomes students from all backgrounds. **Enrollment:** 876 degree-seeking undergraduates; 10 non-degree-seeking students. **Degrees:** 38 bachelor's, 86 associate awarded. **Location:** 90 miles from Atlanta. **Calendar:** Semester, limited summer session. **Full-time faculty:** 68 total. **Part-time faculty:** 37 total. **Special facilities:** Planetarium, black box theater, observatory, climbing wall, cross country trail, 18-hole disc golf course, LEED Silver Certified residence hall, predatory beetle lab, bee keeping institute, national forest.

Student profile. Among degree-seeking undergraduates, 311 enrolled as first-time, first-year students, 43 transferred in from other institutions.

Out-of-state:	16%	25 or older:	1%
Women:	55%	Live on campus:	90%

Transfer out. Colleges most students transferred to 2011: University of Georgia, Georgia College & State University, North Georgia College & State University, Kennesaw State University.

Basis for selection. Heavy emphasis on academic GPA and SAT/ACT scores. High school record, interview considered. **Adult students:** SAT/ACT scores not required if out of high school 5 year(s) or more. **Home schooled:** Transcript of courses and grades required. Possible GED requirement dependent upon SAT/ACT scores. **Learning Disabled:** Psycho-educational analysis required.

High school preparation. College-preparatory program recommended. Recommended units include English 4, mathematics 4, social studies 3, science 3 and foreign language 2.

2011-2012 Annual costs. Tuition/fees: $22,000. Per-credit charge: $675. Room/board: $7,480. Books/supplies: $1,000. Personal expenses: $1,100.

2010-2011 Financial aid. Need-based: 313 full-time freshmen applied for aid; 287 were judged to have need; 287 of these received aid. Average need met was 82%. Average scholarship/grant was $15,207; average loan $2,917. 79% of total undergraduate aid awarded as scholarships/grants, 21% as loans/jobs. Need-based aid available for part-time students. Work-study available nights, weekends and for part-time students. **Non-need-based:** Awarded to 337 full-time undergraduates, including 167 freshmen. Scholarships awarded for academics, art, athletics, job skills, leadership, music/drama, state residency.

Application procedures. Admission: Priority date 1/1; no deadline. No application fee. Admission notification on a rolling basis beginning on or about 9/15. **Financial aid:** Priority date 5/1; no closing date. FAFSA, institutional form required. Applicants notified on a rolling basis starting 2/15; must reply within 2 week(s) of notification.

Academics. Special study options: Dual enrollment of high school students, honors, internships, study abroad, teacher certification program. Bachelor's degree programs available on campus. **Credit/placement by examination:** AP, CLEP, IB, institutional tests. Student may exempt computer science

101 but will not receive credit. **Support services:** Pre-admission summer program, reduced course load, remedial instruction, study skills assistance, tutoring, writing center.

Majors. Education: General. **Health services:** Predental, premedicine, prenursing, prepharmacy, preveterinary. **Liberal arts:** Arts/sciences. **Philosophy/religion:** Religion. **Visual/performing arts:** Art.

Computing on campus. 99 workstations in dormitories, library, computer center. Dormitories wired for high-speed internet access and linked to campus network. Commuter students can connect to campus network. Online course registration, online library, helpline, wireless network available.

Student life. Freshman orientation: Mandatory. Preregistration for classes offered. **Housing:** Guaranteed on-campus for all undergraduates. Coed dorms, single-sex dorms, apartments available. $300 fully refundable deposit. **Activities:** Bands, campus ministries, choral groups, dance, drama, literary magazine, music ensembles, musical theater, student government, student newspaper, Wesley Fellowship, Baptist campus ministries, Catholic student association, College Republicans, Bonner Leaders, honor societies.

Athletics. NCAA. **Intercollegiate:** Baseball M, basketball, cheerleading, cross-country, golf, lacrosse, soccer, softball W, tennis. **Intramural:** Basketball, football (non-tackle), soccer, softball, volleyball. **Team name:** Mountain Lions.

Student services. Alcohol/substance abuse counseling, chaplain/spiritual director, career counseling, student employment services, financial aid counseling, health services, personal counseling, women's services. **Physically disabled:** Services for visually, speech, hearing impaired. **Transfer:** Pre-admission transcript evaluation for new students. Transfer adviser for students transferring to 4-year colleges.

Contact. E-mail: admissions@yhc.edu
Phone: (706) 379-3111 Toll-free number: (800) 241-3754
Fax: (706) 379-3108
Clinton Hobbs, Vice President for Enrollment Management, Young Harris College, PO Box 116, Young Harris, GA 30582-0116

Hawaii

Hawaii Tokai International College
Honolulu, Hawaii
www.hawaiitokai.edu
CB code: 2588

- Private 2-year junior and liberal arts college
- Residential campus in large city
- Application essay required

General. Regionally accredited. Students can study abroad in China, Japan or Korea and have the opportunity to complete the Peace Studies Program. **Enrollment:** 71 degree-seeking undergraduates. **Degrees:** 43 associate awarded. **Location:** Downtown Honolulu. **Calendar:** Quarter, limited summer session. **Full-time faculty:** 9 total; 22% have terminal degrees, 33% minority, 44% women. **Part-time faculty:** 17 total; 12% have terminal degrees, 41% minority, 47% women. **Class size:** 100% < 20.

Student profile. Among degree-seeking undergraduates, 93% enrolled in a transfer program, 13 enrolled as first-time, first-year students.

Out-of-state:	3%	25 or older:	1%
Women:	51%	Live on campus:	90%
International:	80%		

Transfer out. 90% of students enrolled in the transfer program go on to 4-year colleges. **Colleges most students transferred to 2011:** University of Hawaii at Manoa, Tokai University, Japan.

Basis for selection. Domestic Students: Personal statement, academic GPA, letters of recommendation, commitment to studies. International Students: Personal statement, academic GPA, letters of recommendation, commitment to studies and interview. SAT/ACT recommended but not required of students. **Home schooled:** Transcript of courses and grades, state high school equivalency certificate required.

2011-2012 Annual costs. Tuition/fees: $10,920. Room/board: $7,020. Books/supplies: $800. Personal expenses: $1,200.

2011-2012 Financial aid. Need-based: Work-study available nights, weekends and for part-time students. **Non-need-based:** Scholarships awarded for academics, leadership.

Application procedures. Admission: Closing date 8/1 (postmark date). $50 fee, may be waived for applicants with need. Application must be submitted on paper. Admission notification on a rolling basis. **Financial aid:** Institutional form required. Applicants notified on a rolling basis.

Academics. Special study options: ESL, study abroad. **Credit/placement by examination:** AP, CLEP, IB, institutional tests. **Support services:** Learning center, study skills assistance, tutoring, writing center.

Majors. Liberal arts: Arts/sciences.

Computing on campus. 60 workstations in library, computer center. Dormitories wired for high-speed internet access and linked to campus network. Commuter students can connect to campus network. Online library, wireless network available.

Student life. Freshman orientation: Mandatory. Preregistration for classes offered. **Policies:** Students must maintain a 2.75 GPA in order to participate in any clubs and organizations. **Housing:** Guaranteed on-campus for all undergraduates. Coed dorms, wellness housing available. $20 nonrefundable deposit. **Activities:** Music ensembles, student government, student newspaper.

Athletics. Team name: T-Wave.

Student services. Alcohol/substance abuse counseling, career counseling, financial aid counseling, health services, personal counseling. **Physically disabled:** Services for visually impaired. **Transfer:** Re-entry adviser, pre-admission transcript evaluation for new students. Transfer center, transfer adviser, college fairs on campus for students transferring to 4-year colleges.

Contact. E-mail: admissions@tokai.edu
Phone: (808) 983-4121 Fax: (808) 983-4173
Laura Sprowls, Director of Student Services, Hawaii Tokai International College, 2241 Kapiolani Boulevard, Honolulu, HI 96826

Remington College: Honolulu
Honolulu, Hawaii
www.remingtoncollege.edu
CB code: 3507

- For-profit 2-year career college
- Commuter campus in very large city
- Interview required

General. Regionally accredited; also accredited by ACCSC. **Enrollment:** 646 degree-seeking undergraduates. **Degrees:** 15 bachelor's, 186 associate awarded. **Calendar:** Quarter. **Full-time faculty:** 16 total. **Part-time faculty:** 39 total.

Basis for selection. Interview most important; CPAT assessment test score also important. CPAT entrance examination required. **Home schooled:** Statement describing home school structure and mission, transcript of courses and grades required.

Financial aid. Need-based: Work-study available nights, weekends and for part-time students.

Application procedures. Admission: No deadline. $50 fee. Admission notification on a rolling basis.

Academics. Special study options: Bachelor's degree programs available on campus. **Credit/placement by examination:** AP, CLEP.

Majors. Business: International. **Computer sciences:** General, networking. **Health services:** Medical assistant. **Protective services:** Criminal justice.

Computing on campus. Online library available.

Student life. Activities: International club.

Student services. Transfer: Pre-admission transcript evaluation for new students.

Contact. E-mail: ken.heinemann@remingtoncollege.edu
Phone: (808) 942-1000 Fax: (808) 533-3064
Louis LaMair, Director of Admissions, Remington College: Honolulu, 1111 Bishop Street, Suite 400, Honolulu, HI 96813-2811

University of Hawaii: Hawaii Community College
Hilo, Hawaii
www.hawcc.hawaii.edu
CB code: 1801

- Public 2-year community college
- Small city

General. Founded in 1969. Regionally accredited. **Enrollment:** 3,933 undergraduates. **Degrees:** 343 associate awarded. **ROTC:** Naval. **Location:** 200 miles from Honolulu. **Calendar:** Semester, limited summer session. **Full-time faculty:** 89 total. **Part-time faculty:** 114 total.

Student profile.

25 or older:	32%	Live on campus:	35%

Basis for selection. Open admission.

2011-2012 Annual costs. Tuition/fees: $2,940; $8,730 out-of-state. Per-credit charge: $97 in-state; $290 out-of-state. Books/supplies: $672. Personal expenses: $953.

Financial aid. All financial aid based on need. Need-based aid available for part-time students. Work-study available nights, weekends and for part-time students. **Additional information:** Hawaii student incentive grants and tuition waivers (merit and need-based) available to Hawaii residents.

Application procedures. Admission: Closing date 7/30. No application fee in-state; $25 out-of-state. Admission notification on a rolling basis. **Financial aid:** Priority date 4/1; no closing date. FAFSA required. Applicants notified on a rolling basis starting 2/1; must reply within 2 week(s) of notification.

Academics. Special study options: Cooperative education, cross-registration, distance learning, double major, dual enrollment of high school students, ESL, honors, independent study. **Credit/placement by examination:** AP, CLEP. 15 credit hours maximum toward associate degree. **Support services:** Learning center, pre-admission summer program, reduced course load, remedial instruction, tutoring.

Majors. Business: Accounting, administrative services, market research, marketing, operations. **Education:** Early childhood. **Health services:** Nursing (RN). **Liberal arts:** Arts/sciences. **Protective services:** Criminal justice, law enforcement admin. **Work/family studies:** Food/nutrition.

Student life. Freshman orientation: Available. Preregistration for classes offered. **Housing:** Coed dorms, special housing for disabled, apartments, wellness housing available. **Activities:** Dance, drama, literary magazine, music ensembles, student government, student newspaper, TV station, Phi Theta Kappa honors society.

Athletics. Team name: Hawaii Hawks (i'eo).

Student services. Adult student services, career counseling, student employment services, financial aid counseling, health services, on-campus daycare, personal counseling, veterans' counselor. **Physically disabled:** Services for hearing impaired. **Transfer:** Transfer adviser, college fairs on campus for students transferring to 4-year colleges.

Contact. E-mail: hawccinf@hawaii.edu
Phone: (808) 974-7661 Fax: (808) 974-7692
David Loeding, Registrar, University of Hawaii: Hawaii Community College, 200 West Kawili Street, Hilo, HI 96720-4091

University of Hawaii: Honolulu Community College
Honolulu, Hawaii
www2.honolulu.hawaii.edu   CB code: 4350

- Public 2-year community and technical college
- Commuter campus in very large city

General. Founded in 1920. Regionally accredited. **Enrollment:** 3,508 degree-seeking undergraduates. **Degrees:** 518 associate awarded. **ROTC:** Army, Air Force. **Calendar:** Semester, limited summer session. **Full-time faculty:** 129 total. **Part-time faculty:** 76 total. **Class size:** 50% < 20, 49% 20-39, less than 1% 50-99.

Student profile.

Out-of-state:	4%	Hispanic American:	7%
African American:	2%	International:	1%
Asian American:	45%	25 or older:	39%

Transfer out. Colleges most students transferred to 2011: University of Hawaii at Manoa, University of Hawaii at Hilo, University of Hawaii West Oahu, Chaminade University, Hawaii Pacific University.

Basis for selection. Open admission, but selective for out-of-state students. Out-of-state and foreign applicants subject to non-resident quota. High school diploma required for cosmetology program.

2011-2012 Annual costs. Tuition/fees: $2,940; $8,730 out-of-state. Per-credit charge: $97 in-state; $290 out-of-state. Books/supplies: $773. Personal expenses: $1,166.

Financial aid. Need-based: Need-based aid available for part-time students. Work-study available nights, weekends and for part-time students. **Non-need-based:** Scholarships awarded for academics, state residency. **Additional information:** Hawaii student incentive grants and tuition waivers (merit and need-based) available to Hawaii residents at participating institutions.

Application procedures. Admission: Priority date 7/1; no deadline. No application fee in-state; $25 out-of-state. Admission notification on a rolling basis beginning on or about 3/1. **Financial aid:** Priority date 4/1; no closing date. FAFSA required. Applicants notified on a rolling basis starting 7/1; must reply within 3 week(s) of notification.

Academics. Special study options: Cooperative education, cross-registration, distance learning, dual enrollment of high school students, ESL, independent study, internships, student-designed major. License preparation in aviation. **Credit/placement by examination:** AP, CLEP, institutional tests. 30 credit hours maximum toward associate degree. **Support services:** Learning center, remedial instruction, study skills assistance, tutoring, writing center.

Majors. Business: Fashion. **Communications technology:** Graphic/printing. **Computer sciences:** General, computer graphics, information systems. **Education:** Early childhood, technology/industrial arts, voc/tech. **Engineering:** Computer, polymer. **Health services:** Occupational health. **Human services:** Community org/advocacy, social work. **Liberal arts:** Arts/sciences. **Protective services:** Criminal justice, fire safety technology, fire services admin, firefighting, law enforcement admin, police science. **Visual/performing arts:** Commercial/advertising art, fashion design. **Work/family studies:** Child care management, institutional food production.

Most popular majors. Engineering/engineering technologies 37%, liberal arts 20%, public administration/social services 8%, security/protective services 11%, trade and industry 16%.

Computing on campus. 135 workstations in library, computer center, student center. Commuter students can connect to campus network. Online course registration, wireless network available.

Student life. Freshman orientation: Mandatory. Preregistration for classes offered. **Housing:** Dorms and apartments available at University of Hawaii at Manoa campus. **Activities:** Literary magazine, student government, student newspaper, Pacific Islander association, Filipino club.

Student services. Alcohol/substance abuse counseling, career counseling, student employment services, financial aid counseling, health services, on-campus daycare, personal counseling, placement for graduates, veterans' counselor. **Physically disabled:** Services for visually, speech, hearing impaired. **Transfer:** Pre-admission transcript evaluation for new students. Transfer center, transfer adviser, college fairs on campus for students transferring to 4-year colleges.

Contact. E-mail: admissions@hcc.hawaii.edu
Phone: (808) 845-9129 Fax: (808) 847-9829
Admissions Counselor, University of Hawaii: Honolulu Community College, 874 Dillingham Boulevard, Honolulu, HI 96817

University of Hawaii: Kapiolani Community College
Honolulu, Hawaii
www.kcc.hawaii.edu   CB code: 4377

- Public 2-year community college
- Commuter campus in very large city

General. Founded in 1957. Regionally accredited. **Enrollment:** 6,242 degree-seeking undergraduates. **Degrees:** 760 associate awarded. **Calendar:** Semester, limited summer session. **Full-time faculty:** 197 total. **Part-time faculty:** 184 total. **Class size:** 55% < 20, 45% 20-39, less than 1% 40-49, less than 1% 50-99.

Student profile.

Out-of-state:	7%	25 or older:	41%

Transfer out. Colleges most students transferred to 2011: University of Hawaii at Manoa.

Basis for selection. Open admission, but selective for some programs. Special requirements for health science and nursing programs. High school diploma required for allied health and nursing programs and for students under age 18. Essay recommended. Interview required of allied health, legal assistant, and nursing programs.

2011-2012 Annual costs. Tuition/fees: $2,970; $8,760 out-of-state. Per-credit charge: $97 in-state; $290 out-of-state. Books/supplies: $725. Personal expenses: $1,143.

Financial aid. All financial aid based on need. Need-based aid available for part-time students. Work-study available nights, weekends and for part-time students. **Additional information:** Hawaii student incentive grants and tuition waivers (merit and need-based) available to Hawaii residents.

Application procedures. Admission: Closing date 7/17 (postmark date). $25 fee. Application must be submitted on paper. Admission notification on a rolling basis. Application deadline April 1 for allied health and legal assistant programs; February 1 for registered nursing program. **Financial aid:** Priority date 4/1; no closing date. FAFSA required. Applicants notified on a rolling basis; must reply within 2 week(s) of notification.

Academics. Special study options: Cross-registration, distance learning, double major, dual enrollment of high school students, ESL, exchange student, external degree, honors, independent study, internships, study abroad, teacher certification program, weekend college. Service learning. License preparation in nursing, paramedic. **Credit/placement by examination:** AP, CLEP, institutional tests. **Support services:** Learning center, remedial instruction, tutoring.

Majors. Business: General, accounting, hospitality/recreation, office technology, sales/distribution. **Computer sciences:** Data processing. **Health services:** Clinical lab technology, dental assistant, dental hygiene, EMT paramedic, licensed practical nurse, medical assistant, medical radiologic technology/radiation therapy, nursing (RN), nursing assistant, occupational therapy assistant, physical therapy assistant, physician assistant, respiratory therapy technology, sonography. **Liberal arts:** Arts/sciences. **Work/family studies:** Institutional food production.

Most popular majors. Business/marketing 30%, computer/information sciences 6%, health sciences 21%, liberal arts 38%.

Computing on campus. 150 workstations in library, computer center, student center. Commuter students can connect to campus network. Online course registration, online library, student web hosting, wireless network available.

Student life. Freshman orientation: Mandatory. Preregistration for classes offered. 15 two-hour sessions, any one of which may be attended by a new student. **Housing:** Coed dorms available. Housing available through University of Hawaii system. **Activities:** Choral groups, dance, drama, literary magazine, music ensembles, student government, student newspaper, international students club, marketing association, music club, Phi Theta Kappa, nursing association, Japanese, Chinese and Korean club, Catholic Ministry Association, pre-engineering club.

Student services. Career counseling, services for economically disadvantaged, student employment services, financial aid counseling, minority student services, on-campus daycare, personal counseling, placement for graduates, veterans' counselor. **Physically disabled:** Services for visually, speech, hearing impaired.

Contact. E-mail: kapinfo@hawaii.edu
Phone: (808) 734-9555 Fax: (808) 734-9896
Sharon Fowler, Coordinator of Enrollment Services, University of Hawaii: Kapiolani Community College, 4303 Diamond Head Road, Honolulu, HI 96816-4421

University of Hawaii: Kauai Community College
Lihue, Hawaii
www.kauai.hawaii.edu　　　　　　　　　**CB code: 4378**

- Public 2-year community college
- Commuter campus in small city

General. Founded in 1928. Regionally accredited. **Enrollment:** 1,261 degree-seeking undergraduates; 169 non-degree-seeking students. **Degrees:** 125 associate awarded. **Location:** 100 miles from Honolulu. **Calendar:** Semester, limited summer session. **Full-time faculty:** 56 total. **Part-time faculty:** 45 total. **Special facilities:** Botanical facilities.

Student profile. Among degree-seeking undergraduates, 60% enrolled in a transfer program, 40% enrolled in a vocational program, 1% already have a bachelor's degree or higher, 332 enrolled as first-time, first-year students.

Part-time:	56%	Asian American:	28%
Out-of-state:	2%	Hispanic American:	12%
Women:	61%	International:	1%
African American:	1%		

Basis for selection. Open admission, but selective for out-of-state students. Special requirements for out-of-state residents in nursing, electrical installation and maintenance technology, facilities engineering technology, nurse's aide, electronics technology programs, and culinary arts.

2011-2012 Annual costs. Tuition/fees: $2,970; $8,760 out-of-state. Per-credit charge: $97 in-state; $290 out-of-state. Books/supplies: $900.

Financial aid. Need-based: Work-study available nights, weekends and for part-time students. **Additional information:** Hawaii student incentive grants and tuition waivers (merit and need-based) available to Hawaii residents.

Application procedures. Admission: Priority date 8/1; no deadline. Admission notification on a rolling basis beginning on or about 3/1. Institutional placement test. **Financial aid:** Priority date 3/1, closing date 5/1. FAFSA, institutional form required. Applicants notified on a rolling basis starting 5/1.

Academics. Special study options: Cooperative education, cross-registration, distance learning, ESL, internships. **Credit/placement by examination:** AP, CLEP, institutional tests. **Support services:** Learning center, tutoring, writing center.

Majors. Business: Accounting, hospitality admin, office/clerical. **Education:** Early childhood. **Health services:** Nursing (RN). **Liberal arts:** Arts/sciences.

Computing on campus. 150 workstations in computer center.

Student life. Freshman orientation: Available. Preregistration for classes offered. **Activities:** Concert band, choral groups, international student organizations, music ensembles, student government, Hawaiian club, Pamantasan club, Hawaiian performing arts club, Japanese club, environmental club.

Athletics. Intramural: Basketball.

Student services. Adult student services, career counseling, student employment services, financial aid counseling, health services, on-campus daycare, personal counseling, placement for graduates, veterans' counselor. **Physically disabled:** Services for visually, speech, hearing impaired. **Transfer:** Transfer adviser, college fairs on campus for students transferring to 4-year colleges.

Contact. E-mail: arkauai@hawaii.edu
Phone: (808) 245-8225 Fax: (808) 245-8297
Leighton Oride, Admissions Officer and Registrar, University of Hawaii: Kauai Community College, 3-1901 Kaumualii Highway, Lihue, HI 96766-9500

University of Hawaii: Leeward Community College
Pearl City, Hawaii
www.lcc.hawaii.edu　　　　　　　　　**CB code: 4410**

- Public 2-year community college
- Commuter campus in large town

General. Founded in 1968. Regionally accredited. **Enrollment:** 5,759 degree-seeking undergraduates. **Degrees:** 597 associate awarded. **ROTC:** Army, Air Force. **Location:** 10 miles from Honolulu. **Calendar:** Semester, limited summer session. **Full-time faculty:** 200 total. **Part-time faculty:** 106 total. **Special facilities:** Observatory.

Student profile.

Out-of-state:	10%	25 or older:	34%

Basis for selection. Open admission.

2011-2012 Annual costs. Tuition/fees: $2,955; $8,745 out-of-state. Per-credit charge: $97 in-state; $290 out-of-state. Books/supplies: $672. Personal expenses: $953.

Financial aid. Need-based: Need-based aid available for part-time students. Work-study available nights, weekends and for part-time students. **Additional information:** Leveraging Educational Assistance Partnership (LEAP) funds or tuition waivers available to students with financial need.

Application procedures. Admission: Closing date 7/15 (postmark date). No application fee in-state; $25 out-of-state. Admission notification on a rolling basis beginning on or about 12/1. **Financial aid:** Priority date 4/15; no closing date. FAFSA required. Applicants notified on a rolling basis starting 6/1; must reply within 2 week(s) of notification.

Academics. Special study options: Cross-registration, distance learning, dual enrollment of high school students, honors, independent study, internships, liberal arts/career combination, weekend college. **Credit/placement by examination:** AP, CLEP, IB, institutional tests. 21 credit hours maximum toward associate degree. **Support services:** Learning center, pre-admission summer program, remedial instruction, study skills assistance, tutoring.

Majors. Business: Accounting, office/clerical. **Communications:** Broadcast journalism. **Computer sciences:** General. **Liberal arts:** Arts/sciences.

Computing on campus. 200 workstations in library, computer center. Commuter students can connect to campus network. Helpline available.

Student life. Activities: Bands, choral groups, dance, drama, film society, literary magazine, music ensembles, musical theater, student government, student newspaper, TV station, Filipino ethnic organization, club for physically handicapped, Campus Crusade for Christ, human services club.

Athletics. Intramural: Bowling, golf, soccer, tennis, volleyball.

Student services. Adult student services, career counseling, student employment services, health services, on-campus daycare, personal counseling, placement for graduates, veterans' counselor. **Physically disabled:** Services for visually, speech, hearing impaired. **Transfer:** Transfer adviser, college fairs on campus for students transferring to 4-year colleges.

Contact. E-mail: lccar@hawaii.edu
Phone: (808) 455-0217 Fax: (808) 454-8804
Warren Mau, Coordinator of Admissions and Records, University of Hawaii: Leeward Community College, 96-045 Ala Ike, Pearl City, HI 96782

University of Hawaii: Maui College
Kahului, Hawaii
www.maui.hawaii.edu   CB code: 4510

- Public 2-year community college
- Commuter campus in small city

General. Founded in 1931. Regionally accredited. Branch campuses on Molokai, Lanai, Lahaina and Hana. **Enrollment:** 4,135 degree-seeking undergraduates; 384 non-degree-seeking students. **Degrees:** 3 bachelor's, 308 associate awarded. **Location:** 150 miles from Honolulu. **Calendar:** Semester, limited summer session. **Full-time faculty:** 124 total. **Part-time faculty:** 1 total.

Student profile. Among degree-seeking undergraduates, 900 enrolled as first-time, first-year students.

Part-time:	61%	Women:	65%
Out-of-state:	1%	Live on campus:	1%

Basis for selection. Open admission, but selective for some programs. Special requirements for nursing program. Interview required of nursing majors.

2011-2012 Annual costs. Tuition/fees: $3,036; $12,126 out-of-state. Per-credit charge: $97 in-state; $400 out-of-state. Books/supplies: $879. Personal expenses: $3,289.

Financial aid. Need-based: Need-based aid available for part-time students. Work-study available nights, weekends and for part-time students.

Application procedures. Admission: Priority date 7/31; no deadline. No application fee in-state; $25 out-of-state. Admission notification on a rolling basis. **Financial aid:** Priority date 4/1; no closing date. FAFSA, institutional form required. Applicants notified on a rolling basis starting 6/1; must reply within 4 week(s) of notification.

Academics. Special study options: Cooperative education, distance learning, double major, dual enrollment of high school students, ESL, independent study, liberal arts/career combination, weekend college. **Credit/placement by examination:** AP, CLEP, institutional tests. 30 credit hours maximum toward associate degree. **Support services:** Learning center, pre-admission summer program, reduced course load, remedial instruction, tutoring.

Majors. Business: General, accounting, tourism/travel. **Education:** Early childhood. **Liberal arts:** Arts/sciences. **Work/family studies:** Apparel marketing, food/nutrition.

Computing on campus. Commuter students can connect to campus network. Online course registration, helpline available.

Student life. Freshman orientation: Available. Preregistration for classes offered. **Housing:** Coed dorms available. **Activities:** Student government, student newspaper, TV station.

Student services. Career counseling, student employment services, health services, on-campus daycare, personal counseling, veterans' counselor. **Physically disabled:** Services for visually, speech, hearing impaired. **Transfer:** Transfer adviser for students transferring to 4-year colleges.

Contact. Phone: (808) 984-3500 Toll-free number: (800) 479-6692
Fax: (808) 242-9618
Stephen Kameda, Admissions Officer/Registrar, University of Hawaii: Maui College, 310 West Kaahumanu Avenue, Kahului, HI 96732-1617

University of Hawaii: Windward Community College
Kaneohe, Hawaii
www.wcc.hawaii.edu   CB code: 4976

- Public 2-year community college
- Commuter campus in small city

General. Founded in 1972. Regionally accredited. **Enrollment:** 2,059 degree-seeking undergraduates. **Degrees:** 153 associate awarded. **ROTC:** Army. **Location:** 10 miles from Honolulu. **Calendar:** Semester, limited summer session. **Full-time faculty:** 42 total; 33% have terminal degrees, 71% minority, 50% women. **Part-time faculty:** 62 total. **Special facilities:** Planetarium, greenhouse, observatory, NASA lab, biomedicinal garden, theater.

Student profile. Among degree-seeking undergraduates, 70% enrolled in a transfer program, 8% enrolled in a vocational program, 6% already have a bachelor's degree or higher.

Out-of-state:	9%	25 or older:	38%

Basis for selection. Open admission. **Adult students:** SAT/ACT scores not required.

2011-2012 Annual costs. Tuition/fees: $2,950; $8,740 out-of-state. Per-credit charge: $97 in-state; $290 out-of-state. Books/supplies: $987. Personal expenses: $1,730.

Financial aid. Need-based: Need-based aid available for part-time students. Work-study available nights, weekends and for part-time students. **Non-need-based:** Scholarships awarded for academics. **Additional information:** Hawaii student incentive grants and tuition waivers (merit and need-based) available to Hawaii residents.

Application procedures. Admission: Priority date 8/1; no deadline. No application fee in-state; $25 out-of-state. Admission notification on a rolling basis. Out-of-state military dependents not required to pay application fee. **Financial aid:** Priority date 4/1; no closing date. FAFSA required. Applicants notified on a rolling basis starting 3/15; must reply within 2 week(s) of notification.

Academics. Special study options: Cooperative education, distance learning, double major, dual enrollment of high school students, independent study, internships, student-designed major, study abroad. **Credit/placement by examination:** AP, CLEP, institutional tests. **Support services:** Learning center, reduced course load, remedial instruction, study skills assistance, tutoring.

Majors. Liberal arts: Arts/sciences.

Computing on campus. 100 workstations in library, computer center, student center. Commuter students can connect to campus network. Online course registration, helpline, wireless network available.

Student life. Freshman orientation: Mandatory. Preregistration for classes offered. **Activities:** Choral groups, drama, literary magazine, student government, student newspaper.

Student services. Adult student services, career counseling, services for economically disadvantaged, student employment services, financial aid counseling, minority student services, personal counseling, placement for graduates, veterans' counselor. **Physically disabled:** Services for visually, speech, hearing impaired. **Transfer:** Pre-admission transcript evaluation for new students. Transfer adviser, college fairs on campus for students transferring to 4-year colleges.

Contact. E-mail: wccinfo@hawaii.edu
Phone: (808) 235-7432 Fax: (808) 235-9148
Geri Imai, Registrar, University of Hawaii: Windward Community College, 45-720 Kea'ahala Road, Kaneohe, HI 96744

Idaho

Broadview University: Boise
Meridian, Idaho
www.broadviewuniversity.edu

- For-profit 2-year university and career college
- Large town

General. Regionally accredited; also accredited by ACICS. **Enrollment:** 124 degree-seeking undergraduates. **Calendar:** Quarter. **Full-time faculty:** 7 total. **Part-time faculty:** 2 total.

Basis for selection. Open admission.

Financial aid. Need-based: Work-study available nights, weekends and for part-time students.

Application procedures. Admission: $50 fee.

Academics. Credit/placement by examination: AP, CLEP.

Majors. Business: Business admin. **Health services:** Massage therapy, medical secretary, veterinary technology/assistant. **Protective services:** Police science.

Contact. Jill Chiddy, Director of Admissions, Broadview University: Boise, 2750 East Gala Court, Meridian, ID 83642

Carrington College: Boise
Boise, Idaho
www.carrington.edu

- For-profit 2-year career college
- Very large city

General. Regionally accredited; also accredited by ACICS. **Degrees:** 195 associate awarded. **Calendar:** Differs by program. **Full-time faculty:** 26 total. **Part-time faculty:** 25 total.

Basis for selection. Admission requirements will vary by program.

Financial aid. Need-based: Work-study available nights, weekends and for part-time students.

Academics. Credit/placement by examination: AP, CLEP.

Majors. Health services: Dental hygiene, physical therapy assistant.

Contact. Phone: (888) 720-5014
Donna Caporaso, Director of Admissions, Carrington College: Boise, 1122 North Liberty Street, Boise, ID 83704-8742

College of Southern Idaho
Twin Falls, Idaho
www.csi.edu
CB code: 4114

- Public 2-year community and junior college
- Commuter campus in large town

General. Founded in 1964. Regionally accredited. **Enrollment:** 6,097 degree-seeking undergraduates. **Degrees:** 634 associate awarded. **Location:** 130 miles from Boise. **Calendar:** Semester, limited summer session. **Full-time faculty:** 170 total. **Part-time faculty:** 213 total. **Special facilities:** Museum and planetarium including anthropology, archeology, fine arts collections.

Student profile.

Out-of-state:	5%	Live on campus:	5%
25 or older:	52%		

Transfer out. Colleges most students transferred to 2011: Boise State University, University of Idaho, Idaho State University, Utah State University, Albertsons College.

Basis for selection. Open admission, but selective for some programs. ACT recommended; letters of reference, letter of intent, and special tests required for applicants to registered nursing program. Interview required of registered nursing, technical majors.

2011-2012 Annual costs. Tuition/fees: $2,640; $6,720 out-of-state. Per-credit charge: $110 in-state; $280 out-of-state. Room/board: $5,070. Books/supplies: $990. Personal expenses: $1,900.

Financial aid. Need-based: Need-based aid available for part-time students. Work-study available nights, weekends and for part-time students. **Additional information:** Out-of-state tuition waivers based on GPA and activities.

Application procedures. Admission: No deadline. No application fee. Admission notification on a rolling basis. **Financial aid:** Priority date 3/1; no closing date. FAFSA required. Applicants notified on a rolling basis starting 4/30; must reply within 3 week(s) of notification.

Academics. Special study options: Distance learning, dual enrollment of high school students, ESL, honors. License preparation in real estate. **Credit/placement by examination:** AP, CLEP. 21 credit hours maximum toward associate degree. **Support services:** GED preparation and test center, learning center, reduced course load, remedial instruction, study skills assistance, tutoring, writing center.

Majors. Biology: General. **Business:** General, accounting, hospitality/recreation, real estate, tourism promotion. **Communications:** Communications/speech/rhetoric. **Computer sciences:** Computer graphics, computer science, LAN/WAN management. **Conservation:** General, forestry, water/wetlands/marine, wildlife/wilderness. **Education:** Bilingual, early childhood, elementary, physical, secondary. **Engineering:** Civil, computer, electrical. **English:** English lit. **Foreign languages:** General, sign language interpretation. **General:** Aquaculture, business, equestrian studies, horticultural science, range science. **Health services:** Dental hygiene, EMT paramedic, nursing (RN), pharmacy assistant, predental, premedicine, prepharmacy, preveterinary, respiratory therapy technology, veterinary technology/assistant. **History:** General. **Liberal arts:** Arts/sciences, library science. **Math:** General. **Parks/recreation:** Health/fitness. **Physical sciences:** Chemistry, geology, physics. **Protective services:** Fire safety technology, law enforcement admin. **Psychology:** General. **Social sciences:** Anthropology, economics, geography, political science, sociology. **Visual/performing arts:** Art, commercial/advertising art, dramatic, music, photography.

Computing on campus. 350 workstations in dormitories, library, computer center, student center. Dormitories wired for high-speed internet access and linked to campus network. Commuter students can connect to campus network. Online course registration, online library, helpline, student web hosting, wireless network available.

Student life. Housing: Coed dorms, apartments, wellness housing available. $100 fully refundable deposit. **Activities:** Pep band, campus ministries, choral groups, drama, international student organizations, student government, student newspaper, Christian Fellowship, Latter-day Saints student association, Ambassadors, Latinos Unidos, Golden Eagle Native Americans, Chi Alpha, accent club.

Athletics. NJCAA. **Intercollegiate:** Baseball M, basketball, equestrian, rodeo, softball, volleyball W. **Intramural:** Basketball, bowling, football (non-tackle), golf, racquetball, soccer, softball, tennis, volleyball. **Team name:** Eagles.

Student services. Adult student services, alcohol/substance abuse counseling, career counseling, student employment services, financial aid counseling, health services, minority student services, on-campus daycare, personal counseling, veterans' counselor. **Physically disabled:** Services for visually, hearing impaired. **Transfer:** Re-entry adviser, pre-admission transcript evaluation for new students. College fairs on campus for students transferring to 4-year colleges.

Contact. Phone: (208) 732-6792 Fax: (208) 736-3014
Gail Schull, Director of Admissions, College of Southern Idaho, Box 1238, Twin Falls, ID 83303-1238

College of Western Idaho
Nampa, Idaho
www.cwidaho.cc
CB member
CB code: 7924

- Public 2-year community and technical college
- Large city

General. Candidate for regional accreditation. **Enrollment:** 7,615 degree-seeking undergraduates; 462 non-degree-seeking students. **Degrees:** 397 associate awarded. **Calendar:** Semester, limited summer session. **Full-time faculty:** 105 total; 3% minority, 51% women. **Part-time faculty:** 349 total; 6% minority, 52% women. **Class size:** 23% < 20, 72% 20-39, less than 1% 40-49, 4% 50-99.

Student profile. Among degree-seeking undergraduates, 2,042 enrolled as first-time, first-year students.

Part-time:	47%	Asian American:	1%
Out-of-state:	1%	Hispanic American:	13%
Women:	55%	Native American:	2%
African American:	2%	25 or older:	51%

Transfer out. 25% of students enrolled in the transfer program go on to 4-year colleges. **Colleges most students transferred to 2011:** Boise State University, Idaho State University, University of Idaho, Louis-Clark State College, Northwest Nazarene University.

Basis for selection. Open admission, but selective for some programs. Limited-enrollment programs may include special admission criteria or space limitations. **Home schooled:** 25 pre-algebra and 62 reading and 32 writing required on Compass.

2012-2013 Annual costs. Tuition/fees (projected): $3,264; $4,264 out-of-district; $7,200 out-of-state. Per-credit charge: $136 in-state; $300 out-of-state. Books/supplies: $990. Personal expenses: $1,050.

2010-2011 Financial aid. **Need-based:** 1,916 full-time freshmen applied for aid; 1,733 were judged to have need; 1,699 of these received aid. Average need met was 56%. Average scholarship/grant was $3,503; average loan $2,417. 49% of total undergraduate aid awarded as scholarships/grants, 51% as loans/jobs. Need-based aid available for part-time students. Work-study available nights, weekends and for part-time students. **Non-need-based:** Awarded to 135 full-time undergraduates, including 70 freshmen. Scholarships awarded for academics, leadership, minority status.

Application procedures. **Admission:** No deadline. $25 fee. Admission notification on a rolling basis. **Financial aid:** Priority date 7/15; no closing date. FAFSA required. Applicants notified on a rolling basis starting 3/1; must reply within 4 week(s) of notification.

Academics. **Special study options:** Distance learning, double major, dual enrollment of high school students, ESL, independent study, internships. **Credit/placement by examination:** AP, CLEP, institutional tests. 21 credit hours maximum toward associate degree. **Support services:** GED preparation and test center, learning center, reduced course load, remedial instruction, study skills assistance, tutoring, writing center.

Majors. **Biology:** General. **Business:** General, accounting, accounting technology, administrative services, marketing. **Communications:** General. **Computer sciences:** LAN/WAN management, networking, security, support specialist, system admin, web page design. **Education:** Early childhood, elementary, physical. **English:** English lit. **General:** Horticulture. **Health services:** Dental assistant, nursing (RN), prepharmacy, surgical technology. **History:** General. **Liberal arts:** Arts/sciences. **Parks/recreation:** Exercise sciences, sports admin. **Physical sciences:** Geology. **Protective services:** Criminal justice, firefighting, forest/wildland firefighting. **Psychology:** General. **Social sciences:** Anthropology, geography, political science, sociology. **Work/family studies:** Child care management.

Computing on campus. 94 workstations in library, computer center. Online course registration, online library, helpline, wireless network available.

Student life. **Freshman orientation:** Available. Preregistration for classes offered. **Activities:** Student government.

Student services. Adult student services, career counseling, services for economically disadvantaged, student employment services, financial aid counseling, health services, personal counseling, placement for graduates, veterans' counselor. **Physically disabled:** Services for visually, speech, hearing impaired. **Transfer:** College fairs on campus for students transferring to 4-year colleges.

Contact. E-mail: onestop@cwidaho.cc
Phone: (208) 562-3000 Fax: (888) 562-3216
Terry Blom, Dean, Enrollment and Student Services, College of Western Idaho, Mail Stop 1000, PO Box 3010, Nampa, ID 83653

Eastern Idaho Technical College
Idaho Falls, Idaho
www.eitc.edu   CB code: 0975

♦ Public 2-year technical college
♦ Commuter campus in small city

General. Founded in 1969. Regionally accredited. **Enrollment:** 663 degree-seeking undergraduates. **Degrees:** 93 associate awarded. **Location:** 280 miles from Boise, 230 miles from Salt Lake City. **Calendar:** Semester, limited summer session. **Full-time faculty:** 39 total; 62% women. **Part-time faculty:** 28 total; 75% women. **Class size:** 81% < 20, 19% 20-39.

Student profile.

African American:	1%	Hispanic American:	12%
Asian American:	1%		

Basis for selection. Open admission, but selective for some programs. COMPASS required of all applicants. Students who score below acceptable level must complete developmental classes before enrolling in degree program. Entrance exam, essay required for nursing.

High school preparation. Recommended units include English 8, mathematics 6 and science 6.

2011-2012 Annual costs. Tuition/fees: $1,932; $7,078 out-of-state. Per-credit charge: $90 in-state; $180 out-of-state.

2010-2011 Financial aid. **Need-based:** 56% of total undergraduate aid awarded as scholarships/grants, 44% as loans/jobs. Need-based aid available for part-time students. Work-study available nights, weekends and for part-time students. **Non-need-based:** Scholarships awarded for academics, job skills, state residency.

Application procedures. **Admission:** No deadline. $10 fee, may be waived for applicants with need. Application must be submitted on paper. Admission notification on a rolling basis. **Financial aid:** Priority date 6/1; no closing date. FAFSA, institutional form required. Applicants notified on a rolling basis starting 6/6.

Academics. **Special study options:** Distance learning, ESL. License preparation in nursing. **Credit/placement by examination:** AP, CLEP, institutional tests. **Support services:** GED preparation and test center, learning center, pre-admission summer program, reduced course load, remedial instruction, study skills assistance, tutoring, writing center.

Majors. **Business:** Accounting, administrative services, marketing. **Computer sciences:** Networking, web page design. **Health services:** Medical assistant, nursing (RN), surgical technology. **Protective services:** Firefighting.

Most popular majors. Business/marketing 24%, computer/information sciences 16%, health sciences 40%, legal studies 10%.

Computing on campus. 209 workstations in library, computer center. Online course registration, online library, helpline, wireless network available.

Student life. **Freshman orientation:** Mandatory. Preregistration for classes offered. **Activities:** Student government.

Student services. Adult student services, alcohol/substance abuse counseling, career counseling, services for economically disadvantaged, student employment services, financial aid counseling, personal counseling, placement for graduates, veterans' counselor, women's services. **Physically disabled:** Services for visually, speech, hearing impaired.

Contact. E-mail: annalea.avery@my.eitc.edu
Phone: (208) 524-3000 ext. 3337 Toll-free number: (800) 662-0261
Fax: (208) 525-7026
Annalea Avery, Director of Admissions and Career Placement, Eastern Idaho Technical College, 1600 South 25th East, Idaho Falls, ID 83404-5788

North Idaho College
Coeur d'Alene, Idaho   CB member
www.nic.edu   CB code: 4539

♦ Public 2-year community college
♦ Commuter campus in large town

General. Founded in 1933. Regionally accredited. **Enrollment:** 5,795 degree-seeking undergraduates; 310 non-degree-seeking students. **Degrees:** 536 associate awarded. **ROTC:** Army. **Location:** 30 miles from Spokane, Washington. **Calendar:** Semester, limited summer session. **Full-time faculty:** 160 total; 11% have terminal degrees, 2% minority, 51% women. **Part-time faculty:** 287 total; 6% have terminal degrees, 6% minority, 53% women. **Partnerships:** Formal partnerships with local businesses.

Student profile. Among degree-seeking undergraduates, 1,500 enrolled as first-time, first-year students, 474 transferred in from other institutions.

Part-time:	42%	Asian American:	1%
Women:	60%	Hispanic American:	4%
African American:	1%	Native American:	3%

Transfer out. Colleges most students transferred to 2011: University of Idaho, Lewis-Clark State College, Boise State University, Eastern Washington University, Spokane Community College.

Basis for selection. RN, LPN and other allied health program applicants must submit 3 references and supplemental statement. Professional technical applicants should be interviewed by counselor. Interview recommended for professional technical majors. **Home schooled:** GED highly recommended. **Learning Disabled:** Contact Disability Support Services at time of application.

High school preparation. Algebra, biology, 2 years chemistry with laboratory, or 1 year chemistry and 1 year physics, with cumulative 2.50 GPA required for registered nursing applicants. Physics, advanced algebra recommended for nursing applicants.

2012-2013 Annual costs. Tuition/fees (projected): $2,764; $3,972 out-of-district; $7,316 out-of-state. Per-credit charge: $70 in-district; $112 out-of-district; $257 out-of-state. Room/board: $6,000. Books/supplies: $1,250. Personal expenses: $1,500.

2011-2012 Financial aid. Need-based: 51% of total undergraduate aid awarded as scholarships/grants, 49% as loans/jobs. Need-based aid available for part-time students. Work-study available nights, weekends and for part-time students. **Non-need-based:** Scholarships awarded for academics, art, athletics, leadership, minority status, music/drama, state residency.

Application procedures. Admission: No deadline. $25 fee, may be waived for applicants with need. Admission notification on a rolling basis. **Financial aid:** Priority date 3/15; no closing date. FAFSA required. Applicants notified on a rolling basis starting 4/1; must reply within 2 week(s) of notification.

Academics. Special study options: Distance learning, dual enrollment of high school students, independent study, internships. Lewis Clark State College and University of Idaho upper division and graduate classes on campus. Bachelor's degree programs available on campus. License preparation in nursing. **Credit/placement by examination:** AP, CLEP, SAT, ACT, institutional tests. 24 credit hours maximum toward associate degree. **Support services:** GED preparation and test center, learning center, reduced course load, remedial instruction, study skills assistance, tutoring, writing center.

Majors. Area/ethnic studies: Native American. **Biology:** General, botany, zoology. **Business:** Administrative services, business admin. **Communications:** Communications/speech/rhetoric, journalism, public relations. **Computer sciences:** General, applications programming, programming. **Conservation:** Fisheries, forestry, wildlife/wilderness. **Education:** General, business, early childhood, elementary, secondary. **Engineering:** General, chemical, civil, electrical. **English:** English lit. **Foreign languages:** General. **Health services:** Clinical lab assistant, medical assistant, medical secretary, medical transcription, mental health services, nursing (RN), pharmacy assistant, physical therapy assistant, predental, premedicine, prepharmacy, preveterinary. **History:** General. **Liberal arts:** Arts/sciences. **Math:** General. **Parks/recreation:** Health/fitness. **Philosophy/religion:** Philosophy. **Physical sciences:** Astronomy, chemistry, geology, physics. **Protective services:** Criminal justice, police science. **Psychology:** General. **Social sciences:** General, anthropology, political science, sociology. **Visual/performing arts:** Commercial/advertising art, music, music performance, music theory/composition, studio arts.

Computing on campus. 150 workstations in dormitories, library, computer center, student center. Dormitories wired for high-speed internet access and linked to campus network. Commuter students can connect to campus network. Online course registration, helpline, repair service, wireless network available.

Student life. Freshman orientation: Available. Preregistration for classes offered. **Housing:** Coed dorms available. $200 deposit. Apartment complex adjacent to campus available. **Activities:** Bands, choral groups, dance, drama, film society, international student organizations, literary magazine, music ensembles, musical theater, student government, student newspaper, Students for Human Equality, creative writers club, nursing student association, veterans club.

Athletics. NJCAA. **Intercollegiate:** Basketball, cheerleading, soccer, softball W, volleyball W, wrestling M. **Intramural:** Basketball, bowling, football (non-tackle), golf, softball, table tennis, tennis, volleyball. **Team name:** Cardinals.

Student services. Adult student services, alcohol/substance abuse counseling, career counseling, services for economically disadvantaged, student employment services, financial aid counseling, health services, legal services, minority student services, on-campus daycare, personal counseling, placement for graduates, veterans' counselor, women's services. **Physically disabled:** Services for visually, speech, hearing impaired. **Transfer:** Transfer adviser, college fairs on campus for students transferring to 4-year colleges.

Contact. E-mail: admit@nic.edu
Phone: (208) 769-3311 Toll-free number: (877) 404-4536
Fax: (208) 769-3399
Director of Admissions, North Idaho College, 1000 West Garden Avenue, Coeur d'Alene, ID 83814-2199

Stevens-Henager College: Boise
Boise, Idaho
www.stevenshenager.edu

▸ For-profit 2-year technical and career college
▸ Commuter campus in small city
▸ Application essay, interview required

General. Enrollment: 834 degree-seeking undergraduates. **Degrees:** 54 bachelor's, 358 associate awarded; master's offered. **Calendar:** Differs by program, extensive summer session. **Full-time faculty:** 15 total. **Part-time faculty:** 45 total.

Student profile. Among degree-seeking undergraduates, 17 transferred in from other institutions.

Out-of-state:	1%	25 or older:	70%

Basis for selection. Open admission, but selective for some programs. All applicants must complete a personal interview and submit a personal statement. **Adult students:** SAT/ACT scores not required. **Home schooled:** Transcript of courses and grades, interview required.

High school preparation. 11 units required; 15 recommended. Required and recommended units include English 4, mathematics 2-3, social studies 1, history 2, science 2-3, foreign language 1 and computer science 1.

2012-2013 Annual costs. Tuition/fees (projected): $16,356. Cost of education is all-inclusive; books, course fees, lab fees, supplies, a laptop, tutoring, career services assistance, parking, and graduation fees are included in the cost of education.

Financial aid. All financial aid based on need. Work-study available nights, weekends and for part-time students.

Application procedures. Admission: No deadline. $75 fee. Application must be submitted on paper. Admission notification on a rolling basis. **Financial aid:** No deadline. FAFSA required.

Academics. Special study options: Accelerated study, distance learning, external degree, liberal arts/career combination. Bachelor's degree programs available on campus. **Credit/placement by examination:** AP, CLEP. **Support services:** GED preparation, learning center, remedial instruction, study skills assistance, tutoring, writing center.

Majors. Business: Accounting, business admin. **Computer sciences:** General. **Health services:** Office assistant. **Visual/performing arts:** Graphic design.

Computing on campus. 35 workstations in library, computer center, student center. Commuter students can connect to campus network. Online library, helpline, repair service, wireless network available.

Student life. Freshman orientation: Mandatory. Preregistration for classes offered. **Activities:** Student newspaper.

Student services. Adult student services, career counseling, student employment services, financial aid counseling, placement for graduates, veterans' counselor. **Transfer:** Pre-admission transcript evaluation for new students. Transfer adviser for students transferring to 4-year colleges.

Contact. E-mail: jaime.davis@stevenshenager.edu
Phone: (208) 383-4540 Toll-free number: (888) 842-7990
Fax: (208) 345-6999
David Breck, Director of Admissions, Stevens-Henager College: Boise, 1444 S Entertainment Avenue, Boise, ID 83709

Illinois

Benedictine University at Springfield
Springfield, Illinois
www.sci.edu
CB code: 1734

- Private 2-year branch campus college affiliated with Roman Catholic Church
- Commuter campus in small town
- SAT or ACT (ACT writing optional) required

General. Founded in 1929. Regionally accredited. **Enrollment:** 800 degree-seeking undergraduates. **Degrees:** 141 bachelor's awarded; master's, professional offered. **Location:** 200 miles from Chicago, 100 miles from St. Louis. **Calendar:** Semester. **Full-time faculty:** 20 total. **Part-time faculty:** 51 total. **Class size:** 87% < 20, 13% 20-39.

Student profile.

Out-of-state:	2%	Live on campus:	11%
25 or older:	47%		

Transfer out. **Colleges most students transferred to 2011:** Southern Illinois University-Edwardsville, University of Illinois-Springfield, Illinois State University, Eastern Illinois University, Southern Illinois University-Carbondale.

Basis for selection. High school course work, test scores, GPA, class rank required criteria. Interview may be recommended for academically weak applicants. Portfolio recommended for art majors. **Adult students:** SAT/ACT scores not required if applicant over 24. **Home schooled:** Transcript of courses and grades, state high school equivalency certificate required. GED required to qualify for federal and state financial aid. **Learning Disabled:** Admission requirements for students with learning disabilities handled on case by case basis.

High school preparation. Recommended units include English 4, mathematics 3, social studies 2, science 2 and academic electives 2. Mathematics and physical science recommended for all applicants, foreign language for some.

2011-2012 Annual costs. Tuition/fees: $10,140. Per-credit charge: $410. 15 meals per week provided plus $50 to use at campus café. Room/board: $6,920. Books/supplies: $1,340. Personal expenses: $2,290.

Financial aid. **Need-based:** Need-based aid available for part-time students. Work-study available nights, weekends and for part-time students. **Non-need-based:** Scholarships awarded for academics, art, athletics, leadership, religious affiliation.

Application procedures. **Admission:** No deadline. $20 fee, may be waived for applicants with need. Admission notification on a rolling basis. **Financial aid:** Priority date 4/15; no closing date. FAFSA required. Applicants notified on a rolling basis starting 4/15; must reply within 2 week(s) of notification.

Academics. **Special study options:** Cross-registration, double major, dual enrollment of high school students, honors, independent study, internships, study abroad. **Credit/placement by examination:** AP, CLEP, ACT, institutional tests. 30 credit hours maximum toward associate degree. **Support services:** Learning center, reduced course load, remedial instruction, study skills assistance, tutoring, writing center.

Majors. **Business:** General, business admin. **Education:** Elementary, secondary. **Health services:** Clinical lab science, predental, premedicine, prenursing, prepharmacy, preveterinary. **Human services:** Social work. **Liberal arts:** Arts/sciences. **Math:** General. **Philosophy/religion:** Religion. **Visual/performing arts:** Art.

Computing on campus. 45 workstations in library, computer center. Dormitories wired for high-speed internet access and linked to campus network. Commuter students can connect to campus network. Online library, helpline, wireless network available.

Student life. **Freshman orientation:** Mandatory. Preregistration for classes offered. Held Friday before classes begin. **Policies:** Alcohol and other drugs prohibited. **Housing:** Single-sex dorms, wellness housing available. $300 nonrefundable deposit. **Activities:** Campus ministries, international student organizations, literary magazine, student government, student newspaper, Student Ambassadors, Phi Theta Kappa, arts and cultural events club, Alpha Sigma Lambda.

Athletics. NAIA. **Intercollegiate:** Baseball M, golf M, soccer, softball W, volleyball W. **Team name:** Bulldogs.

Student services. Alcohol/substance abuse counseling, chaplain/spiritual director, career counseling, financial aid counseling, personal counseling, veterans' counselor. **Transfer:** Pre-admission transcript evaluation for new students. Transfer adviser for students transferring to 4-year colleges.

Contact. E-mail: springadm@ben.edu
Phone: (217) 525-1420 ext. 287 Toll-free number: (800) 635-7289
Fax: (217) 525-1497
Susan Boehler, Director of Enrollment Services, Benedictine University at Springfield, 1500 North Fifth Street, Springfield, IL 62702-2694

Black Hawk College
Moline, Illinois
www.bhc.edu
CB code: 1483

- Public 2-year community college
- Commuter campus in large town

General. Founded in 1946. Regionally accredited. **Enrollment:** 4,505 degree-seeking undergraduates; 1,898 non-degree-seeking students. **Degrees:** 471 associate awarded. **Location:** 160 miles from Chicago, 60 miles from Iowa City. **Calendar:** Semester, limited summer session. **Full-time faculty:** 131 total; 18% have terminal degrees, 9% minority, 55% women. **Part-time faculty:** 179 total; 11% have terminal degrees, 8% minority, 54% women. **Class size:** 53% < 20, 46% 20-39, less than 1% 40-49, less than 1% 50-99. **Special facilities:** Sustainable technologies building.

Student profile. Among degree-seeking undergraduates, 52% enrolled in a transfer program, 48% enrolled in a vocational program, 4% already have a bachelor's degree or higher, 518 enrolled as first-time, first-year students, 225 transferred in from other institutions.

Part-time:	45%	Asian American:	1%
Out-of-state:	8%	Hispanic American:	8%
Women:	61%	International:	1%
African American:	11%	25 or older:	39%

Transfer out. 56% of students enrolled in the transfer program go on to 4-year colleges. **Colleges most students transferred to 2011:** Western Illinois University, St. Ambrose University, Augustana College, University of Illinois, University of Iowa.

Basis for selection. Open admission, but selective for some programs. Special requirements for health care related programs, such as nursing and physical therapy assistant.

High school preparation. 15 units recommended. Recommended units include English 4, mathematics 3, social studies 3 and science 3. 2 years of foreign language, music, or art.

2011-2012 Annual costs. Tuition/fees: $2,955; $6,225 out-of-district; $6,225 out-of-state. Per-credit charge: $89 in-district; $198 out-of-district; $198 out-of-state. Agreement with 5 contiguous Iowa counties for special tuition rate of $123 per credit plus required fees. Online courses (tuition only) are $103 per credit hour in-state; $123, out-of-state. Books/supplies: $1,020. Personal expenses: $2,093.

2010-2011 Financial aid. **Need-based:** 626 full-time freshmen applied for aid; 442 were judged to have need; 404 of these received aid. Average need met was 65%. Average scholarship/grant was $2,342; average loan $1,411. 89% of total undergraduate aid awarded as scholarships/grants, 11% as loans/jobs. Need-based aid available for part-time students. Work-study available nights, weekends and for part-time students. **Non-need-based:** Awarded to 436 full-time undergraduates, including 131 freshmen. Scholarships awarded for academics, art, athletics, leadership, music/drama, state residency. **Additional information:** 5/15 deadline for scholarships.

Application procedures. **Admission:** No deadline. No application fee. Admission notification on a rolling basis beginning on or about 3/1. **Financial aid:** Priority date 5/15; no closing date. FAFSA required. Applicants notified on a rolling basis starting 5/1.

Academics. **Special study options:** Accelerated study, cooperative education, cross-registration, distance learning, dual enrollment of high school students, ESL, honors, independent study, internships, study abroad, weekend college. License preparation in nursing, physical therapy. **Credit/placement by examination:** AP, CLEP, institutional tests. 30 credit hours maximum toward associate degree. Most CLEP credit awarded to students pursuing

associate degree in liberal studies. **Support services:** GED preparation, learning center, reduced course load, remedial instruction, study skills assistance, tutoring.

Majors. Business: Accounting, administrative services, banking/financial services, office technology, retailing, small business admin. **Communications technology:** Radio/TV. **Computer sciences:** Programming. **Education:** Early childhood, mathematics, special ed. **English:** Technical writing. **Foreign languages:** Sign language interpretation. **General:** Business, crop production, equestrian studies, equine science, equipment technology, horticulture, production. **Health services:** Electroencephalograph technology, EMT paramedic, medical records technology, nursing (RN), physical therapy assistant, radiologic technology/medical imaging. **Liberal arts:** Arts/sciences. **Protective services:** Fire services admin, police science. **Visual/performing arts:** Design, interior design. **Work/family studies:** Child care service.

Most popular majors. Agriculture 10%, health sciences 19%, interdisciplinary studies 16%, liberal arts 43%.

Computing on campus. 850 workstations in library, computer center. Commuter students can connect to campus network. Online course registration, online library, wireless network available.

Student life. Freshman orientation: Available. Preregistration for classes offered. **Activities:** Jazz band, choral groups, drama, international student organizations, music ensembles, student government, student newspaper, African Student Association, Association of Latin-American Students, Clean Sphere, College Republicans, Student Wellness Club, Christians on Campus.

Athletics. NJCAA. Intercollegiate: Baseball M, basketball, golf M, softball W, volleyball W. **Team name:** Braves.

Student services. Career counseling, services for economically disadvantaged, student employment services, financial aid counseling, minority student services, personal counseling, placement for graduates, women's services. **Physically disabled:** Services for visually, speech, hearing impaired. **Transfer:** Pre-admission transcript evaluation for new students. Transfer center, transfer adviser, college fairs on campus for students transferring to 4-year colleges.

Contact. Phone: (309) 796-5300 Toll-free number: (800) 334-1311 Fax: (309) 796-5209
Richard Vallandingham, Vice-President of Student Services and Dean of Students, Black Hawk College, 6600-34th Avenue, Moline, IL 61265-5899

Black Hawk College: East Campus
Galva, Illinois
www.bhc.edu   **CB code: 0690**

▶ Public 2-year community college
▶ Commuter campus in small town

General. Founded in 1967. Regionally accredited. **Enrollment:** 980 degree-seeking undergraduates. **Degrees:** 148 associate awarded. **Location:** 45 miles from Peoria, 50 miles from Moline. **Calendar:** Semester, extensive summer session. **Full-time faculty:** 32 total. **Part-time faculty:** 28 total. **Special facilities:** Agricultural facilities for horse boarding.

Transfer out. Colleges most students transferred to 2011: Western Illinois University, Illinois State University, University of Illinois.

Basis for selection. Open admission, but selective for some programs. Special requirements for physical therapy assistant and nursing programs, limited enrollment in practical nursing and truck driving certificates. SAT or ACT may be used in lieu of placement exam. Interview required of nursing and physical therapy assistant majors.

2011-2012 Annual costs. Tuition/fees: $2,955; $6,225 out-of-district; $6,225 out-of-state. Per-credit charge: $89 in-district; $198 out-of-district; $198 out-of-state. Agreement with 5 contiguous Iowa counties for special tuition rate of $123 per credit plus required fees. Online courses (tuition only) are $103 per credit hour in-state; $123, out-of-state. Books/supplies: $1,000.

Financial aid. Need-based: Work-study available nights, weekends and for part-time students.

Application procedures. Admission: No deadline. No application fee. Admission notification on a rolling basis. **Financial aid:** Closing date 5/15. FAFSA required. Applicants notified on a rolling basis; must reply within 2 week(s) of notification.

Academics. Special study options: Cooperative education, cross-registration, distance learning, double major, dual enrollment of high school students, independent study, internships, study abroad. **Credit/placement by examination:** AP, CLEP, institutional tests. 40 credit hours maximum toward associate degree. **Support services:** GED preparation and test center, learning center, pre-admission summer program, reduced course load, remedial instruction, tutoring.

Majors. Biology: General. **Business:** General, accounting, administrative services, office technology. **Communications:** Journalism, public relations. **Computer sciences:** General, data processing, programming. **Education:** Elementary, secondary. **English:** English lit. **General:** Business, equestrian studies, horticulture. **Health services:** Predental, premedicine, prepharmacy. **History:** General. **Liberal arts:** Arts/sciences. **Math:** General. **Physical sciences:** Chemistry, planetary. **Psychology:** General. **Social sciences:** Anthropology, economics, political science, sociology. **Visual/performing arts:** Art, music.

Computing on campus. 101 workstations in computer center.

Student life. Activities: Student government.

Athletics. NJCAA. Intercollegiate: Basketball. **Team name:** Warriors/Lady Warriors.

Student services. Career counseling, student employment services, personal counseling, placement for graduates, veterans' counselor. **Physically disabled:** Services for visually, speech, hearing impaired. **Transfer:** Transfer adviser, college fairs on campus for students transferring to 4-year colleges.

Contact. E-mail: riced@bhc.edu
Phone: (309) 854-1703 Fax: (309) 856-6005
Dede Rice, Assistant Registrar, Black Hawk College: East Campus, 26230 Black Hawk Road, Galva, IL 61434-9476

Carl Sandburg College
Galesburg, Illinois
www.sandburg.edu   **CB code: 1982**

▶ Public 2-year community college
▶ Commuter campus in large town

General. Founded in 1966. Regionally accredited. Branch center in Carthage, extension center in Bushnell. **Enrollment:** 1,939 degree-seeking undergraduates. **Degrees:** 289 associate awarded. **ROTC:** Army. **Location:** 198 miles from Chicago, 47 miles from Peoria. **Calendar:** Semester, limited summer session. **Full-time faculty:** 57 total. **Part-time faculty:** 132 total. **Class size:** 94% < 20, 6% 20-39, less than 1% 40-49, less than 1% 50-99. **Special facilities:** Greenhouse, 22-acre agriculture experience plot.

Student profile.

Out-of-state:	3%	**25 or older:**	39%

Transfer out. Colleges most students transferred to 2011: Western Illinois University, Illinois State University.

Basis for selection. Open admission, but selective for some programs. Special requirements for allied health programs. Interview recommended for radiologic technology, mortuary science, and physical therapy assistant majors.

High school preparation. 15 units recommended. Recommended units include English 4, mathematics 3, social studies 2, science 2 (laboratory 2) and academic electives 2.

2011-2012 Annual costs. Tuition/fees: $4,140; $5,730 out-of-district; $6,930 out-of-state. Per-credit charge: $138 in-district; $191 out-of-district; $231 out-of-state. Books/supplies: $710. Personal expenses: $880.

Financial aid. Need-based: Work-study available nights, weekends and for part-time students. **Non-need-based:** Scholarships awarded for academics, art, athletics, music/drama.

Application procedures. Admission: No deadline. No application fee. Admission notification on a rolling basis. **Financial aid:** Priority date 5/1; no closing date. FAFSA, institutional form required. Applicants notified on a rolling basis starting 5/1; must reply by 8/25 or within 2 week(s) of notification.

Academics. Special study options: Cross-registration, dual enrollment of high school students, ESL, honors, independent study, internships, student-designed major, study abroad, teacher certification program. License preparation in dental hygiene, nursing, paramedic, radiology. **Credit/placement by examination:** AP, CLEP, institutional tests. 20 credit hours maximum toward

associate degree. **Support services:** GED preparation and test center, learning center, remedial instruction, tutoring.

Majors. Business: Accounting, administrative services, banking/financial services, business admin, operations. **Computer sciences:** General. **General:** Business. **Health services:** Nursing (RN). **Protective services:** Firefighting, law enforcement admin. **Work/family studies:** Child care management.

Most popular majors. Business/marketing 8%, health sciences 31%, interdisciplinary studies 17%, liberal arts 32%.

Computing on campus. 69 workstations in library, computer center. Commuter students can connect to campus network. Online library, helpline, wireless network available.

Student life. Activities: Bands, choral groups, drama, literary magazine, music ensembles, student government.

Athletics. NJCAA. **Intercollegiate:** Baseball M, basketball, softball W, volleyball W. **Team name:** Chargers.

Student services. Career counseling, services for economically disadvantaged, student employment services, on-campus daycare, personal counseling, placement for graduates, veterans' counselor. **Physically disabled:** Services for visually, hearing impaired. **Transfer:** Transfer adviser, college fairs on campus for students transferring to 4-year colleges.

Contact. Phone: (309) 344-2518 Fax: (309) 344-3526
Carol Kreider, Dean of Student Support Services, Carl Sandburg College, 2400 Tom L. Wilson Boulevard, Galesburg, IL 61401

City Colleges of Chicago: Harold Washington College
Chicago, Illinois
www.ccc.edu   CB code: 1089

- Public 2-year community college
- Commuter campus in very large city

General. Founded in 1962. Regionally accredited. **Enrollment:** 8,318 degree-seeking undergraduates. **Degrees:** 425 associate awarded. **Calendar:** Semester, limited summer session. **Full-time faculty:** 106 total. **Part-time faculty:** 228 total.

Transfer out. Colleges most students transferred to 2011: University of Illinois-Chicago, DePaul University, Northeastern Illinois University, Columbia College, Roosevelt University.

Basis for selection. Open admission, but selective for some programs. Special requirements for physicians assistant and police programs. All incoming freshmen required to take placement tests.

2011-2012 Annual costs. Tuition/fees: $3,070; $5,607 out-of-district; $7,311 out-of-state. Per-credit charge: $89 in-district; $174 out-of-district; $230 out-of-state. Some courses have specific fees.

2010-2011 Financial aid. All financial aid based on need. 95% of total undergraduate aid awarded as scholarships/grants, 5% as loans/jobs. Need-based aid available for part-time students. Work-study available nights, weekends and for part-time students.

Application procedures. Admission: No deadline. No application fee. **Financial aid:** FAFSA required. Applicants notified on a rolling basis.

Academics. Credit/placement by examination: AP, CLEP, institutional tests. **Support services:** GED preparation, learning center, reduced course load, remedial instruction, study skills assistance, tutoring.

Majors. Business: Accounting, hotel/motel admin. **Communications technology:** Animation/special effects. **Computer sciences:** Information technology. **Education:** Art, early childhood, ESL, music, teacher assistance. **Engineering:** General. **General:** Horticulture. **Health services:** Substance abuse counseling. **Human services:** Social work. **Liberal arts:** Arts/sciences. **Math:** General. **Protective services:** Criminal justice, firefighting. **Visual/performing arts:** Art, music. **Work/family studies:** Child care service.

Most popular majors. Business/marketing 12%, computer/information sciences 7%, family/consumer sciences 17%, interdisciplinary studies 29%.

Student life. Freshman orientation: Mandatory. Preregistration for classes offered. One hour overview. **Activities:** Music ensembles, black student union, Organization of Latin American Students, Berean Bible club, Circle K.

Student services. Adult student services, career counseling, services for economically disadvantaged, student employment services, financial aid counseling, minority student services, personal counseling, placement for graduates, veterans' counselor. **Physically disabled:** Services for visually, speech, hearing impaired.

Contact. Phone: (312) 553-6071 Fax: (312) 553-6077
Robert Brown, Registrar, City Colleges of Chicago: Harold Washington College, 30 East Lake Street, Chicago, IL 60601

City Colleges of Chicago: Harry S. Truman College
Chicago, Illinois
www.ccc.edu   CB code: 1111

- Public 2-year community college
- Commuter campus in very large city

General. Founded in 1956. Regionally accredited. **Enrollment:** 6,691 degree-seeking undergraduates. **Degrees:** 345 associate awarded. **Calendar:** Semester, limited summer session. **Full-time faculty:** 92 total. **Part-time faculty:** 149 total. **Special facilities:** Art gallery for Chicago artists, performing arts theater. **Partnerships:** Formal partnerships with Chamber of Commerce and aldermanic representative for our ward.

Transfer out. Colleges most students transferred to 2011: University of Illinois Chicago, Northeastern Illinois University, DePaul University, Loyola University, Columbia College.

Basis for selection. Open admission, but selective for some programs. Test scores, essay considered for nursing and certain allied health programs. ACT required of nursing applicants. Applicants without high school diploma must obtain GED prior to graduation.

2011-2012 Annual costs. Tuition/fees: $3,070; $5,607 out-of-district; $7,311 out-of-state. Per-credit charge: $89 in-district; $174 out-of-district; $230 out-of-state. Some courses have specific fees.

2010-2011 Financial aid. All financial aid based on need. 94% of total undergraduate aid awarded as scholarships/grants, 6% as loans/jobs. Need-based aid available for part-time students. Work-study available nights, weekends and for part-time students.

Application procedures. Admission: No deadline. No application fee. Admission notification on a rolling basis. **Financial aid:** No deadline. FAFSA required. Applicants notified on a rolling basis.

Academics. Credit/placement by examination: AP, CLEP, institutional tests. 30 credit hours maximum toward associate degree. **Support services:** GED preparation and test center.

Majors. Business: Accounting, business admin. **Computer sciences:** Information technology, networking. **Education:** Mathematics. **Engineering:** General. **Health services:** Nursing (RN). **Liberal arts:** Arts/sciences. **Protective services:** Criminal justice. **Visual/performing arts:** Art. **Work/family studies:** Child care service.

Most popular majors. Health sciences 41%, interdisciplinary studies 8%, liberal arts 38%.

Student life. Freshman orientation: Available. Preregistration for classes offered. **Activities:** Latin American center, refugee center, Native American center.

Contact. Phone: (773) 907-6814 Fax: (773) 907-4757
Mylinh Tran, Registrar, City Colleges of Chicago: Harry S. Truman College, 1145 West Wilson Avenue, Chicago, IL 60640

City Colleges of Chicago: Kennedy-King College
Chicago, Illinois
www.ccc.edu   CB code: 1910

- Public 2-year community college
- Commuter campus in very large city

General. Founded in 1935. Regionally accredited. **Enrollment:** 4,448 degree-seeking undergraduates. **Degrees:** 251 associate awarded. **Calendar:** Semester, limited summer session. **Full-time faculty:** 71 total. **Part-time faculty:** 120 total.

Basis for selection. Open admission. Applicants admitted without high school diploma must pass GED by end of first school year.

2011-2012 Annual costs. Tuition/fees: $3,070; $5,607 out-of-district; $7,311 out-of-state. Per-credit charge: $89 in-district; $174 out-of-district; $230 out-of-state. Some courses have specific fees.

2010-2011 Financial aid. All financial aid based on need. 85% of total undergraduate aid awarded as scholarships/grants, 15% as loans/jobs. Need-based aid available for part-time students. Work-study available nights, weekends and for part-time students.

Application procedures. Admission: No deadline. No application fee. **Financial aid:** No deadline. FAFSA required. Applicants notified on a rolling basis; must reply within 2 week(s) of notification.

Academics. Credit/placement by examination: AP, CLEP, institutional tests. **Support services:** GED preparation.

Majors. Business: Accounting, administrative services, business admin, construction management. **Communications:** Radio/TV. **Communications technology:** Platemaker/imager. **Computer sciences:** Information technology. **Education:** Early childhood, early childhood special. **Health services:** Dental hygiene, nursing (RN), substance abuse counseling. **Human services:** Social work. **Liberal arts:** Arts/sciences. **Protective services:** Criminal justice. **Visual/performing arts:** Dramatic. **Work/family studies:** Child care service.

Most popular majors. Family/consumer sciences 6%, health sciences 20%, liberal arts 52%, personal/culinary services 7%.

Student life. Freshman orientation: Available. Preregistration for classes offered.

Athletics. Team name: Statesman, Lady Statesman.

Contact. Phone: (773) 602-5273 Fax: (773) 602-5247
Marlene Sparrow-Oloko, Registrar, City Colleges of Chicago: Kennedy-King College, 6301 South Halsted Street, Chicago, IL 60621

City Colleges of Chicago: Malcolm X College
Chicago, Illinois
www.ccc.edu
CB code: 1144

- Public 2-year community college
- Commuter campus in very large city

General. Founded in 1911. Regionally accredited. **Enrollment:** 4,960 degree-seeking undergraduates. **Degrees:** 336 associate awarded. **Location:** 3 miles from downtown. **Calendar:** Semester, limited summer session. **Full-time faculty:** 63 total. **Part-time faculty:** 121 total.

Basis for selection. Open admission, but selective for some programs.

2011-2012 Annual costs. Tuition/fees: $3,070; $5,607 out-of-district; $7,311 out-of-state. Per-credit charge: $89 in-district; $174 out-of-district; $230 out-of-state. Some courses have specific fees.

2010-2011 Financial aid. All financial aid based on need. 94% of total undergraduate aid awarded as scholarships/grants, 6% as loans/jobs. Need-based aid available for part-time students. Work-study available nights, weekends and for part-time students.

Application procedures. Admission: No deadline. No application fee. Admission notification on a rolling basis. **Financial aid:** No deadline. FAFSA, institutional form required. Applicants notified on a rolling basis; must reply within 2 week(s) of notification.

Academics. Credit/placement by examination: AP, CLEP, institutional tests. 30 credit hours maximum toward associate degree. **Support services:** GED preparation.

Majors. Computer sciences: Information technology. **Health services:** Dialysis technology, EMT paramedic, nursing (RN), physician assistant, radiologic technology/medical imaging, respiratory therapy technology, surgical technology. **Liberal arts:** Arts/sciences. **Work/family studies:** Child care service.

Most popular majors. Health sciences 47%, liberal arts 43%.

Student life. Freshman orientation: Available. Preregistration for classes offered.

Contact. Phone: (312) 850-7126 Fax: (312) 850-7092
City Colleges of Chicago: Malcolm X College, 1900 West Van Buren Street, Chicago, IL 60612

City Colleges of Chicago: Olive-Harvey College
Chicago, Illinois
www.ccc.edu
CB code: 1584

- Public 2-year community college
- Commuter campus in very large city

General. Founded in 1970. Regionally accredited. **Enrollment:** 3,263 degree-seeking undergraduates. **Degrees:** 210 associate awarded. **Location:** 16 miles from downtown. **Calendar:** Semester, limited summer session. **Full-time faculty:** 54 total. **Part-time faculty:** 55 total.

Basis for selection. Open admission, but selective for some programs.

2011-2012 Annual costs. Tuition/fees: $3,070; $5,607 out-of-district; $7,311 out-of-state. Per-credit charge: $89 in-district; $174 out-of-district; $230 out-of-state. Some courses have specific fees.

2010-2011 Financial aid. Need-based: 92% of total undergraduate aid awarded as scholarships/grants, 8% as loans/jobs. Need-based aid available for part-time students. Work-study available nights, weekends and for part-time students.

Application procedures. Admission: No deadline. No application fee. Admission notification on a rolling basis. **Financial aid:** No deadline. FAFSA required. Applicants notified on a rolling basis.

Academics. Credit/placement by examination: AP, CLEP, institutional tests.

Majors. Business: Accounting, business admin. **Computer sciences:** Information technology. **Health services:** Ophthalmic technology, respiratory therapy technology. **Liberal arts:** Arts/sciences. **Protective services:** Criminal justice. **Work/family studies:** Child care service, family studies.

Most popular majors. Family/consumer sciences 17%, health sciences 7%, interdisciplinary studies 12%, liberal arts 60%.

Student life. Freshman orientation: Available. Preregistration for classes offered.

Contact. Phone: (773) 291-6384 Fax: (773) 291-6185
City Colleges of Chicago: Olive-Harvey College, 10001 South Woodlawn Avenue, Chicago, IL 60628

City Colleges of Chicago: Richard J. Daley College
Chicago, Illinois
www.ccc.edu
CB code: 1093

- Public 2-year community college
- Commuter campus in very large city

General. Founded in 1960. Regionally accredited. **Enrollment:** 4,515 degree-seeking undergraduates. **Degrees:** 294 associate awarded. **Calendar:** Semester, limited summer session. **Full-time faculty:** 59 total. **Part-time faculty:** 98 total.

Basis for selection. Open admission, but selective for some programs.

2011-2012 Annual costs. Tuition/fees: $3,070; $5,607 out-of-district; $7,311 out-of-state. Per-credit charge: $89 in-district; $174 out-of-district; $230 out-of-state. Some courses have specific fees.

2010-2011 Financial aid. Need-based: 95% of total undergraduate aid awarded as scholarships/grants, 5% as loans/jobs. Work-study available nights, weekends and for part-time students.

Application procedures. Admission: No deadline. No application fee. Admission notification on a rolling basis. **Financial aid:** No deadline. FAFSA required. Applicants notified on a rolling basis.

Academics. Credit/placement by examination: AP, CLEP, institutional tests. 30 credit hours maximum toward associate degree.

Majors. Business: Accounting, business admin, sales/distribution. **Computer sciences:** Information technology, networking. **Engineering:** General.

Health services: Nursing (RN). **Liberal arts:** Arts/sciences. **Protective services:** Criminal justice. **Work/family studies:** Child care service.

Most popular majors. Family/consumer sciences 9%, health sciences 30%, liberal arts 33%, security/protective services 14%, trade and industry 7%.

Computing on campus. 250 workstations in library, computer center.

Student life. Freshman orientation: Available. Preregistration for classes offered.

Contact. Phone: (773) 838-7606 Fax: (773) 838-7605
City Colleges of Chicago: Richard J. Daley College, 7500 South Pulaski Road, Chicago, IL 60652

City Colleges of Chicago: Wilbur Wright College
Chicago, Illinois
www.ccc.edu   CB code: 1925

- Public 2-year community college
- Commuter campus in very large city

General. Founded in 1934. Regionally accredited. **Enrollment:** 9,176 degree-seeking undergraduates. **Degrees:** 598 associate awarded. **Location:** 15 miles from downtown. **Calendar:** Semester, limited summer session. **Full-time faculty:** 104 total. **Part-time faculty:** 231 total.

Basis for selection. Open admission.

2011-2012 Annual costs. Tuition/fees: $3,070; $5,607 out-of-district; $7,311 out-of-state. Per-credit charge: $89 in-district; $174 out-of-district; $230 out-of-state. Some courses have specific fees.

2010-2011 Financial aid. Need-based: 98% of total undergraduate aid awarded as scholarships/grants, 2% as loans/jobs. Need-based aid available for part-time students. Work-study available nights, weekends and for part-time students.

Application procedures. Admission: No deadline. No application fee. Admission notification on a rolling basis. **Financial aid:** No deadline. FAFSA, institutional form required. Applicants notified on a rolling basis.

Academics. Credit/placement by examination: AP, CLEP, IB, institutional tests. **Support services:** GED preparation and test center.

Majors. Business: Accounting, business admin, sales/distribution. **Computer sciences:** Information technology. **Engineering:** General. **Health services:** Nursing (RN), occupational therapy assistant, radiologic technology/medical imaging. **Human services:** Social work. **Liberal arts:** Arts/sciences, library assistant. **Visual/performing arts:** Music.

Most popular majors. Interdisciplinary studies 11%, liberal arts 75%.

Student life. Freshman orientation: Available. Preregistration for classes offered.

Athletics. Intercollegiate: Wrestling M.

Contact. Phone: (773) 481-8259 Fax: (773) 481-8053
City Colleges of Chicago: Wilbur Wright College, 4300 North Narragansett Avenue, Chicago, IL 60634-4276

College of DuPage
Glen Ellyn, Illinois
www.cod.edu   CB code: 1083

- Public 2-year community college
- Commuter campus in large town

General. Founded in 1966. Regionally accredited. Continuing education courses at over 50 off-campus locations. Selected internet courses available. Adult fast-track program for students over 21. **Enrollment:** 18,163 degree-seeking undergraduates; 8,046 non-degree-seeking students. **Degrees:** 1,789 associate awarded. **Location:** 25 miles from Chicago. **Calendar:** Semester, extensive summer session. **Full-time faculty:** 273 total. **Part-time faculty:** 1,164 total. **Special facilities:** Older adult institute, prairie-marsh nature preserve, arts center, community recreation center, homeland security center, on-site restaurant and hotel for hospitality and culinary arts students.

Student profile. Among degree-seeking undergraduates, 43% enrolled in a transfer program, 11% enrolled in a vocational program, 10% already have a bachelor's degree or higher, 3,411 enrolled as first-time, first-year students.

Part-time: 56%   **Women:**   52%

Transfer out. 62% of students enrolled in the transfer program go on to 4-year colleges. **Colleges most students transferred to 2011:** Northern Illinois University, Illinois State University, University of Illinois-Chicago, Elmhurst College, Benedictine University.

Basis for selection. Open admission, but selective for some programs. Special requirements for allied health programs.

2011-2012 Annual costs. Tuition/fees: $3,960; $9,570 out-of-district; $11,670 out-of-state. Per-credit charge: $132 in-district; $319 out-of-district; $389 out-of-state. Books/supplies: $1,370. Personal expenses: $1,435.

2010-2011 Financial aid. Need-based: 55% of total undergraduate aid awarded as scholarships/grants, 45% as loans/jobs. Need-based aid available for part-time students. Work-study available nights, weekends and for part-time students. **Non-need-based:** Scholarships awarded for academics, art, leadership, minority status, music/drama, state residency.

Application procedures. Admission: No deadline. $20 fee, may be waived for applicants with need. Admission notification on a rolling basis. **Financial aid:** Priority date 4/30; no closing date. FAFSA required. Applicants notified on a rolling basis starting 6/1; must reply within 2 week(s) of notification.

Academics. Special study options: Accelerated study, cooperative education, cross-registration, distance learning, double major, dual enrollment of high school students, ESL, honors, independent study, internships, student-designed major, study abroad, weekend college. Bachelor's degree programs available on campus. License preparation in dental hygiene, nursing, paramedic, real estate. **Credit/placement by examination:** AP, CLEP, institutional tests. 65 credit hours maximum toward associate degree. **Support services:** GED preparation and test center, learning center, pre-admission summer program, reduced course load, remedial instruction, study skills assistance, tutoring, writing center.

Majors. Business: Accounting, accounting technology, administrative services, business admin, fashion, office management, real estate, sales/distribution, tourism promotion. **Communications technology:** General, graphic/printing. **Computer sciences:** Applications programming. **Engineering:** General. **General:** Horticulture. **Health services:** Dental hygiene, EMT paramedic, medical radiologic technology/radiation therapy, medical records technology, nursing (RN), occupational therapy assistant, physical therapy assistant, respiratory therapy technology, speech-language pathology assistant, substance abuse counseling, surgical technology. **Human services:** Social work. **Liberal arts:** Arts/sciences, library assistant. **Protective services:** Fire safety technology, police science. **Visual/performing arts:** Art, commercial photography, design, music. **Work/family studies:** Child care management.

Most popular majors. Health sciences 15%, interdisciplinary studies 6%, liberal arts 54%.

Computing on campus. 2,403 workstations in library, computer center, student center. Commuter students can connect to campus network. Online course registration, online library, helpline, repair service, wireless network available.

Student life. Freshman orientation: Available. Preregistration for classes offered. Held close to start of term. **Housing:** Housing available in cooperation with nearby private college. **Activities:** Bands, choral groups, dance, drama, international student organizations, literary magazine, music ensembles, Model UN, opera, radio station, student government, student newspaper, symphony orchestra, InterVarsity Christian Fellowship, Endowment for Future Generations, Brothers and Sisters in Christ, black student union, Latino ethnic awareness association, Japanese culture club, La Rencontre Francaise, Muslim student association, Safe Zone for LGBT students.

Athletics. NJCAA. **Intercollegiate:** Baseball M, basketball, cross-country, football (tackle) M, golf M, soccer, softball W, tennis, track and field, volleyball W. **Intramural:** Basketball, softball. **Team name:** Chaparrels.

Student services. Adult student services, career counseling, student employment services, financial aid counseling, health services, on-campus daycare, personal counseling, placement for graduates, veterans' counselor. **Physically disabled:** Services for visually, speech, hearing impaired. **Transfer:** Transfer center, transfer adviser, college fairs on campus for students transferring to 4-year colleges.

Contact. E-mail: admissions@cod.edu
Phone: (630) 942-2482 Fax: (630) 790-2686
Amy Hauenstein, Coordinator of Admission Services, College of DuPage, 425 Fawell Boulevard, Glen Ellyn, IL 60137-6599

College of Lake County
Grayslake, Illinois
www.clcillinois.edu

CB member
CB code: 1983

♦ Public 2-year community college
♦ Commuter campus in large town

General. Founded in 1967. Regionally accredited. **Enrollment:** 13,041 degree-seeking undergraduates; 4,347 non-degree-seeking students. **Degrees:** 1,072 associate awarded. **Location:** 40 miles from Chicago, 45 miles from Milwaukee. **Calendar:** Semester, extensive summer session. **Full-time faculty:** 203 total; 28% have terminal degrees, 22% minority, 55% women. **Part-time faculty:** 824 total; 12% have terminal degrees, 15% minority, 54% women. **Special facilities:** CAD/CAM center, automated industrial center, performing arts center, child care center.

Student profile. Among degree-seeking undergraduates, 1,791 enrolled as first-time, first-year students.

Part-time:	65%	Women:	56%
Out-of-state:	1%	25 or older:	29%

Transfer out. Colleges most students transferred to 2011: Northern Illinois University, University of Wisconsin at Parkside, Northeastern Illinois University, Southern Illinois University, DePaul University.

Basis for selection. Open admission, but selective for some programs. Open admission for certificate and associate of applied science. College-preparatory high school program required for associate of arts and science. Selective admission for health career programs: academic record, class rank, test scores important; recommendations, interview considered. **Learning Disabled:** Accommodations provided when taking proficiency exams.

High school preparation. 15 units recommended. Recommended units include English 4, mathematics 3, social studies 3, (laboratory 3) and academic electives 2. 2 biology and 1 chemistry required for nursing program, mathematics for medical laboratory technician program, chemistry for radiology program. Recommended electives include foreign language, music, vocational education or art.

2012-2013 Annual costs. Tuition/fees (projected): $3,270; $7,470 out-of-district; $9,900 out-of-state. Per-credit charge: $93 in-district; $233 out-of-district; $314 out-of-state. Books/supplies: $1,484. Personal expenses: $1,400.

Financial aid. Need-based: Need-based aid available for part-time students. Work-study available nights, weekends and for part-time students. **Non-need-based:** Scholarships awarded for academics, alumni affiliation, art, athletics, leadership, minority status, music/drama.

Application procedures. Admission: No deadline. No application fee. Admission notification on a rolling basis. Application deadlines vary for health career programs. **Financial aid:** Priority date 6/5; no closing date. FAFSA required. Applicants notified on a rolling basis starting 6/15; must reply within 2 week(s) of notification.

Academics. High school distribution requirement for associate degree applicants may be fulfilled at college. **Special study options:** Accelerated study, cooperative education, cross-registration, distance learning, dual enrollment of high school students, ESL, honors, independent study, internships, student-designed major, study abroad. License preparation in dental hygiene, nursing, paramedic, radiology, real estate. **Credit/placement by examination:** AP, CLEP, institutional tests. 30 credit hours maximum toward associate degree. **Support services:** GED preparation and test center, learning center, reduced course load, remedial instruction, study skills assistance, tutoring, writing center.

Majors. Business: Accounting technology, administrative services, business admin, office technology. **Conservation:** Management/policy. **Education:** Music. **Engineering:** General. **English:** Technical writing. **General:** Landscaping, ornamental horticulture, turf management. **Health services:** Dental hygiene, medical radiologic technology/radiation therapy, nursing (RN), office admin, substance abuse counseling. **Human services:** Social work. **Liberal arts:** Arts/sciences, library assistant. **Protective services:** Fire safety technology, police science. **Visual/performing arts:** Art, music.

Most popular majors. Health sciences 15%, interdisciplinary studies 9%, liberal arts 55%.

Computing on campus. 800 workstations in library, computer center. Online course registration, online library, helpline, wireless network available.

Student life. Freshman orientation: Available. Preregistration for classes offered. **Policies:** Alcohol-free campus, smoking allowed only outside the building. **Activities:** Bands, campus ministries, choral groups, dance, drama, international student organizations, literary magazine, music ensembles, musical theater, radio station, student government, student newspaper, 11 academic organizations, 6 ethnic organizations, 4 religious organizations, 6 health and fitness organizations available.

Athletics. NJCAA. **Intercollegiate:** Baseball M, basketball, cross-country, golf, soccer, softball W, tennis, volleyball W. **Intramural:** Basketball, golf, soccer, table tennis, tennis, volleyball. **Team name:** Lancers.

Student services. Alcohol/substance abuse counseling, career counseling, services for economically disadvantaged, student employment services, financial aid counseling, health services, minority student services, on-campus daycare, personal counseling, placement for graduates, veterans' counselor, women's services. **Physically disabled:** Services for visually, speech, hearing impaired. **Transfer:** Re-entry adviser for new students. Transfer center, transfer adviser, college fairs on campus for students transferring to 4-year colleges.

Contact. E-mail: info@clcillinois.edu
Phone: (847) 543-2061 Fax: (847) 543-3061
Karen Hlavin, Assistant Vice President, College of Lake County, 19351 West Washington Street, Grayslake, IL 60030-1198

College of Office Technology
Chicago, Illinois
www.cot.edu

CB code: 3527

♦ For-profit 2-year career college
♦ Commuter campus in very large city

General. Accredited by ACICS. **Enrollment:** 206 degree-seeking undergraduates. **Degrees:** 3 associate awarded. **Calendar:** Differs by program, limited summer session. **Full-time faculty:** 12 total. **Part-time faculty:** 11 total. **Class size:** 100% < 20.

Basis for selection. Open admission.

2011-2012 Annual costs. Tuition/fees: $11,873. Costs vary by program. Personal expenses: $4,600.

Financial aid. All financial aid based on need. Need-based aid available for part-time students. Work-study available nights, weekends and for part-time students.

Application procedures. Admission: No deadline. $50 fee. Application must be submitted on paper. Admission notification on a rolling basis. **Financial aid:** No deadline. FAFSA required. Applicants notified on a rolling basis.

Academics. Credit/placement by examination: AP, CLEP. **Support services:** Tutoring.

Majors. Computer sciences: Data entry.

Computing on campus. 20 workstations in library.

Student life. Freshman orientation: Mandatory. Preregistration for classes offered.

Student services. Career counseling, personal counseling, placement for graduates.

Contact. E-mail: info@cotedu.com
Phone: (773) 278-0042 Toll-free number: (800) 953-6161
Fax: (773) 278-0143
William Bolton, Director of Admissions, College of Office Technology, 1520 West Division Street, Chicago, IL 60642-3312

Coyne College
Chicago, Illinois
www.coynecollege.edu

♦ For-profit 2-year technical and career college
♦ Commuter campus in very large city

General. Regionally accredited; also accredited by ACCSC. **Enrollment:** 706 full-time, degree-seeking students. **Degrees:** 196 associate awarded. **Location:** 1 mile from downtown. **Calendar:** Differs by program. **Full-time faculty:** 25 total. **Part-time faculty:** 13 total.

Basis for selection. Open admission.

2011-2012 Annual costs. Tuition/fees: $10,125. Per-credit charge: $225. Costs may vary by program.

Financial aid. Need-based: Work-study available nights, weekends and for part-time students.

Academics. Externships are required for courses in the Allied Health programs. Construction trades programs do practical training at school labs in addition to the theory part of the curriculum. **Credit/placement by examination:** AP, CLEP, institutional tests.

Majors. Health services: Medical assistant.

Computing on campus. Wireless network available.

Student life. Freshman orientation: Available. Preregistration for classes offered. **Activities:** Student newspaper.

Contact. E-mail: ppauletti@coynecollege.edu
Phone: (773) 577-8102 Toll-free number: (800) 999-5220
Fax: (312) 226-3818
Peter Pauletti, Director of Admissions, Coyne College, 330 North Green Street, Chicago, IL 60607

Danville Area Community College
Danville, Illinois
www.dacc.edu   CB code: 1160

◆ Public 2-year community college
◆ Commuter campus in large town

General. Founded in 1946. Regionally accredited. **Enrollment:** 2,729 degree-seeking undergraduates. **Degrees:** 278 associate awarded. **Location:** 150 miles from Chicago, 90 miles from Indianapolis. **Calendar:** Semester, limited summer session. **Full-time faculty:** 59 total; 14% have terminal degrees, 15% minority, 46% women. **Part-time faculty:** 90 total; 2% have terminal degrees, 9% minority, 61% women.

Student profile. Among degree-seeking undergraduates, 30% enrolled in a transfer program, 40% enrolled in a vocational program, 94 transferred in from other institutions.

Transfer out. Colleges most students transferred to 2011: Eastern Illinois University, Illinois State University, Southern Illinois University at Carbondale, University of Illinois at Urbana/Champaign.

Basis for selection. Open admission.

High school preparation. College-preparatory program recommended. 15 units recommended. Recommended units include English 4, mathematics 3, social studies 2, science 2 and academic electives 4.

2011-2012 Annual costs. Tuition/fees: $3,435; $6,135 out-of-district; $6,135 out-of-state. Per-credit charge: $95 in-district; $185 out-of-district; $185 out-of-state. Books/supplies: $700. Personal expenses: $1,575.

2010-2011 Financial aid. Need-based: 84% of total undergraduate aid awarded as scholarships/grants, 16% as loans/jobs. Need-based aid available for part-time students. Work-study available nights, weekends and for part-time students. **Non-need-based:** Scholarships awarded for academics, art, athletics, leadership, minority status, music/drama, state residency.

Application procedures. Admission: No deadline. No application fee. Application must be submitted on paper. Admission notification on a rolling basis. **Financial aid:** Priority date 7/1; no closing date. FAFSA, institutional form required. Applicants notified on a rolling basis starting 4/1.

Academics. Special study options: Distance learning, double major, dual enrollment of high school students, ESL, independent study, internships, liberal arts/career combination. License preparation in nursing, radiology. **Credit/placement by examination:** AP, CLEP, IB, institutional tests. 45 credit hours maximum toward associate degree. **Support services:** GED preparation and test center, learning center, remedial instruction, study skills assistance, tutoring, writing center.

Majors. Business: Accounting technology, executive assistant, office technology, selling. **Computer sciences:** Applications programming, data processing, networking. **Education:** Teacher assistance. **Engineering:** General. **General:** Business, floriculture, turf management. **Health services:** Medical records technology, medical secretary, nursing (RN), radiologic technology/medical imaging. **Liberal arts:** Arts/sciences. **Protective services:** Corrections, firefighting, juvenile corrections, police science. **Work/family studies:** Child care service.

Most popular majors. Business/marketing 6%, health sciences 31%, liberal arts 45%.

Computing on campus. 600 workstations in library, computer center, student center. Online course registration, helpline, wireless network available.

Student life. Freshman orientation: Available. Preregistration for classes offered. **Activities:** Choral groups, drama, literary magazine, student government, Fellowship of Christian Athletes, Hispanic Student Association, Minority Teacher Education Association, Power House Campus Ministries, A-Male.

Athletics. NJCAA. **Intercollegiate:** Baseball M, basketball, cheerleading M, cross-country, golf M, soccer M, softball W, volleyball W. **Team name:** Jaguars.

Student services. Adult student services, career counseling, student employment services, financial aid counseling, on-campus daycare, personal counseling, placement for graduates, veterans' counselor. **Physically disabled:** Services for visually, speech, hearing impaired. **Transfer:** Pre-admission transcript evaluation for new students. Transfer adviser, college fairs on campus for students transferring to 4-year colleges.

Contact. E-mail: stacy@dacc.edu
Phone: (217) 443-8800 Fax: (217) 443-8337
Stacy Ehmen, Director, Enrollment Services & Registrar, Danville Area Community College, 2000 East Main Street, Danville, IL 61832

Elgin Community College
Elgin, Illinois   CB member
www.elgin.edu   CB code: 1203

◆ Public 2-year community college
◆ Commuter campus in small city

General. Founded in 1949. Regionally accredited. **Enrollment:** 8,137 degree-seeking undergraduates. **Degrees:** 1,006 associate awarded. **Location:** 35 miles from Chicago. **Calendar:** Semester, extensive summer session. **Full-time faculty:** 125 total. **Part-time faculty:** 370 total. **Class size:** 52% < 20, 48% 20-39. **Special facilities:** Greenhouse, business conference center, visual and performing arts center, student-run gourmet restaurant.

Student profile. Among degree-seeking undergraduates, 68% enrolled in a transfer program, 32% enrolled in a vocational program, 5% already have a bachelor's degree or higher, 558 transferred in from other institutions.

Transfer out. Colleges most students transferred to 2011: Northern Illinois University, Illinois State University, Southern Illinois University-Carbondale, University of Illinois, University of Illinois at Chicago.

Basis for selection. Open admission, but selective for some programs. Additional requirements for nursing and some health professions programs.

High school preparation. College-preparatory program recommended.

2011-2012 Annual costs. Tuition/fees: $2,980; $10,091 out-of-district; $13,368 out-of-state. Per-credit charge: $99 in-district; $336 out-of-district; $445 out-of-state. Books/supplies: $1,700. Personal expenses: $4,130.

Financial aid. Need-based: Need-based aid available for part-time students. Work-study available nights, weekends and for part-time students. **Non-need-based:** Scholarships awarded for academics, alumni affiliation, art, athletics, job skills, leadership, minority status, music/drama, religious affiliation, ROTC, state residency.

Application procedures. Admission: No deadline. No application fee. Admission notification on a rolling basis. **Financial aid:** Priority date 6/1; no closing date. FAFSA, institutional form required. Applicants notified on a rolling basis starting 4/6; must reply within 3 week(s) of notification.

Academics. Special study options: Accelerated study, cooperative education, distance learning, double major, dual enrollment of high school students, ESL, honors, independent study, internships, study abroad, weekend college. Dual admission with selected 4-year schools. Bachelor's degree programs available on campus. License preparation in aviation, dental hygiene, nursing, paramedic, physical therapy, radiology, real estate. **Credit/placement by examination:** AP, CLEP, institutional tests. 30 credit hours maximum toward associate degree. **Support services:** GED preparation and test center, learning center, reduced course load, remedial instruction, study skills assistance, tutoring, writing center.

Honors college/program. Top 20% of class, 3.5 GPA, or 25 ACT/1140 SAT required. Offers smaller class sizes and innovative learning experiences, including multidisciplinary approaches.

Majors. Business: Accounting, business admin, entrepreneurial studies, executive assistant, hotel/motel admin, marketing, retailing. **Computer sciences:** Data entry, security. **Engineering:** General. **Health services:** Clinical lab technology, nursing (RN), physical therapy assistant. **Human services:** Social work. **Liberal arts:** Arts/sciences. **Parks/recreation:** Health/fitness. **Protective services:** Fire services admin, police science. **Visual/performing arts:** Art, design, graphic design.

Most popular majors. Health sciences 14%, interdisciplinary studies 14%, liberal arts 50%, security/protective services 6%.

Computing on campus. 800 workstations in library, computer center, student center. Wireless network available.

Student life. Freshman orientation: Mandatory. Preregistration for classes offered. **Activities:** Bands, choral groups, drama, literary magazine, music ensembles, musical theater, student government, student newspaper, symphony orchestra, Phi Theta Kappa, Alpha Beta Gamma, Latin American organization, United Students of All Cultures, black student association, single parents student group, Advocacy for Disabled and Abled Persons Together, Amnesty International, gay/lesbian/bi-sexual, Earth First.

Athletics. NJCAA. **Intercollegiate:** Baseball M, basketball, cross-country, golf M, soccer, softball W, tennis, volleyball W. **Team name:** Spartans.

Student services. Adult student services, career counseling, services for economically disadvantaged, student employment services, financial aid counseling, minority student services, on-campus daycare, personal counseling, placement for graduates, veterans' counselor. **Physically disabled:** Services for visually, speech, hearing impaired. **Transfer:** Transfer center, transfer adviser, college fairs on campus for students transferring to 4-year colleges.

Contact. E-mail: admissions@elgin.edu
Phone: (847) 214-7385 Fax: (847) 608-5458
Mary Perkins, Associate Dean of Enrollment Management, Elgin Community College, 1700 Spartan Drive, Elgin, IL 60123-7193

Fox College
Bedford Park, Illinois
www.foxcollege.edu   CB code: 2670

- For-profit 2-year junior and technical college
- Commuter campus in very large city

General. Additional degree site in Tinley Park. **Enrollment:** 417 degree-seeking undergraduates. **Degrees:** 190 associate awarded. **Calendar:** Semester. **Full-time faculty:** 19 total. **Part-time faculty:** 14 total.

Basis for selection. Open admission, but selective for some programs. GED not accepted. GED/High school academic record, writing sample, and interview considered for selective programs.

2011-2012 Annual costs. Tuition/fees: $14,880.

Financial aid. Need-based: Work-study available nights, weekends and for part-time students.

Application procedures. Admission: No deadline. $50 fee. **Financial aid:** No deadline.

Academics. Credit/placement by examination: AP, CLEP.

Majors. Business: Accounting, administrative services, hospitality admin, retailing. **Health services:** Medical assistant, physical therapy assistant, veterinary technology/assistant.

Student services. Career counseling, financial aid counseling, placement for graduates.

Contact. E-mail: admissions@foxcollege.edu
Phone: (708) 444-4500
Fox College, 6640 South Cicero Avenue, Bedford Park, IL 60638

Harper College
Palatine, Illinois   CB member
www.harpercollege.edu   CB code: 1932

- Public 2-year community college
- Commuter campus in small city

General. Founded in 1965. Regionally accredited. Program for hearing-impaired offered. **Enrollment:** 7,645 degree-seeking undergraduates; 8,344 non-degree-seeking students. **Degrees:** 1,456 associate awarded. **Location:** 30 miles from Chicago. **Calendar:** Semester, extensive summer session. **Full-time faculty:** 205 total; 11% minority, 58% women. **Part-time faculty:** 687 total; 5% minority, 49% women. **Class size:** 47% < 20, 48% 20-39, 2% 40-49, 2% 50-99, less than 1% >100. **Special facilities:** Observatory. **Partnerships:** Achieving the Dream - Student Success Initiative.

Student profile. Among degree-seeking undergraduates, 1,874 enrolled as first-time, first-year students, 1,264 transferred in from other institutions.

Part-time:	46%	Asian American:	11%
Out-of-state:	1%	Hispanic American:	13%
Women:	52%	25 or older:	39%
African American:	6%		

Transfer out. Colleges most students transferred to 2011: Northern Illinois University, Roosevelt University, Northeastern University, DePaul University, University of Illinois at Chicago.

Basis for selection. Open admission, but selective for some programs. Selective admission to cardiac technology, dental hygiene, emergency medical technician, certified nursing assistant, electrocardiograph technology, emergency medical service paramedic, and diagnostic medical sonography. Pre-nursing examinations for nursing applicants. Critical thinking test for legal technology applicants.

High school preparation. 17 units recommended. Recommended units include English 4, mathematics 4, social studies 2 and science 2.

2011-2012 Annual costs. Tuition/fees: $3,612; $11,322 out-of-district; $13,587 out-of-state. Per-credit charge: $103 in-district; $360 out-of-district; $435 out-of-state. Books/supplies: $1,000. Personal expenses: $1,800.

2010-2011 Financial aid. Need-based: Average need met was 44%. Average scholarship/grant was $5,037; average loan $2,943. 62% of total undergraduate aid awarded as scholarships/grants, 38% as loans/jobs. Need-based aid available for part-time students. Work-study available nights, weekends and for part-time students. **Non-need-based:** Scholarships awarded for academics, art, leadership, minority status, music/drama, state residency.

Application procedures. Admission: No deadline. $25 fee, may be waived for applicants with need. Admission notification on a rolling basis. Priority given to applications to nursing program received by December 1. Priority given to applications received by February 1 for all other limited-enrollment programs. **Financial aid:** Closing date 3/1. FAFSA required. Applicants notified on a rolling basis starting 3/1; must reply within 2 week(s) of notification.

Academics. Cooperative career program with in-district high schools. Students begin specialized training in high school and continue in colleges. Team-taught interdisciplinary courses and courseloads offered each semester. **Special study options:** Accelerated study, cooperative education, distance learning, dual enrollment of high school students, ESL, honors, independent study, internships, study abroad, weekend college. Dual enrollment programs with Northeastern University, Northern Illinois University, Roosevelt University, Western Illinois University. Bachelor's degree programs available on campus. License preparation in dental hygiene, nursing, paramedic, radiology, real estate. **Credit/placement by examination:** AP, CLEP, institutional tests. 30 credit hours maximum toward associate degree. Maximum of 50% total hours in any degree program may be earned through credit by examination. **Support services:** GED preparation and test center, learning center, pre-admission summer program, reduced course load, remedial instruction, study skills assistance, tutoring, writing center.

Majors. Business: Accounting, banking/financial services, business admin, fashion, fashion modeling, hospitality admin, international, sales/distribution, selling, small business admin. **Computer sciences:** General, applications programming, computer science, programming, web page design. **Engineering:** General. **English:** English lit. **Health services:** Cardiovascular technology, dental hygiene, dietetic technician, EMT paramedic, medical secretary, nursing (RN), radiologic technology/medical imaging, sonography. **Liberal arts:** Arts/sciences. **Math:** General. **Philosophy/religion:** Philosophy. **Physical sciences:** General. **Protective services:** Computer forensics, firefighting, homeland security, police science. **Visual/performing arts:** Music, studio arts. **Work/family studies:** Child care service, fashion consultant, institutional food production.

Most popular majors. Biological/life sciences 7%, health sciences 13%, liberal arts 62%, security/protective services 7%.

Computing on campus. 1,698 workstations in library, computer center, student center. Online course registration, online library, helpline, wireless network available.

Student life. Freshman orientation: Mandatory. Preregistration for classes offered. Two-day program includes tour, assessment tests, academic

advising. Optional for part-time students. **Activities:** Bands, campus ministries, choral groups, dance, drama, international student organizations, literary magazine, music ensembles, musical theater, radio station, student government, student newspaper, black student union, Latinos Unidos, Harper Pride (GLBT), Muslim student association, Indian-Pakistani student association, Access & Disabilities Success Club, deaf club, Campus Crusade for Christ, Bible Talk: Life Talk.

Athletics. NJCAA. **Intercollegiate:** Baseball M, basketball, cross-country, football (tackle) M, soccer, softball W, track and field, volleyball W, wrestling M. **Intramural:** Baseball M, basketball M, football (non-tackle) M, racquetball, softball, table tennis, tennis, volleyball. **Team name:** Hawks.

Student services. Adult student services, career counseling, services for economically disadvantaged, student employment services, financial aid counseling, health services, legal services, minority student services, on-campus daycare, personal counseling, veterans' counselor, women's services. **Physically disabled:** Services for visually, speech, hearing impaired. **Transfer:** Transfer adviser, college fairs on campus for students transferring to 4-year colleges.

Contact. E-mail: admissions@harpercollege.edu
Phone: (847) 925-6707 Fax: (847) 925-6044
Robert Parzy, Director of Admissions Outreach, Harper College, 1200 West Algonquin Road, Palatine, IL 60067-7398

Heartland Community College
Normal, Illinois
www.heartland.edu
CB code: 1361

- Public 2-year community college
- Commuter campus in small city

General. Regionally accredited. Green construction and technology employed in construction projects. **Enrollment:** 5,383 degree-seeking undergraduates. **Degrees:** 674 associate awarded. **Calendar:** Semester, extensive summer session. **Full-time faculty:** 95 total. **Part-time faculty:** 230 total. **Class size:** 54% < 20, 46% 20-39, less than 1% 40-49, less than 1% 50-99.

Transfer out. Colleges most students transferred to 2011: Illinois State University.

Basis for selection. Open admission, but selective for some programs. Nursing and radiography programs selective. Placement testing required to determine readiness in reading, English, and math. Developmental courses may be required before proceeding to college-level courses.

High school preparation. Recommended units include English 4, mathematics 3, social studies 2, science 2 and foreign language 2. Social studies units should include history and government.

2011-2012 Annual costs. Tuition/fees: $3,930; $7,620 out-of-district; $11,310 out-of-state. Per-credit charge: $123 in-district; $246 out-of-district; $369 out-of-state. Books/supplies: $1,100. Personal expenses: $950.

Financial aid. Need-based: Need-based aid available for part-time students. Work-study available nights, weekends and for part-time students. **Non-need-based:** Scholarships awarded for academics, alumni affiliation, athletics, job skills, leadership, minority status, state residency.

Application procedures. Admission: Priority date 6/1; no deadline. No application fee. Admission notification on a rolling basis. May defer admission up to one year. Early admission of high school students with recommendation of high school officials. **Financial aid:** Priority date 4/1; no closing date. FAFSA, institutional form required. Applicants notified on a rolling basis starting 5/15; must reply within 2 week(s) of notification.

Academics. Special study options: Distance learning, double major, dual enrollment of high school students, ESL, honors, independent study, internships, liberal arts/career combination, study abroad. License preparation in nursing, paramedic, radiology, real estate. **Credit/placement by examination:** AP, CLEP, institutional tests. 15 credit hours maximum toward associate degree. **Support services:** GED preparation and test center, learning center, remedial instruction, study skills assistance, tutoring, writing center.

Majors. Business: Insurance. **Computer sciences:** Data entry, information technology, networking. **Education:** Mathematics, teacher assistance. **Engineering:** General. **Health services:** Nursing (RN), radiologic technology/medical imaging. **Liberal arts:** Arts/sciences. **Protective services:** Criminal justice. **Visual/performing arts:** Design. **Work/family studies:** Child care service.

Most popular majors. Interdisciplinary studies 12%, liberal arts 76%.

Computing on campus. 70 workstations in library, computer center. Commuter students can connect to campus network. Online course registration, online library, helpline, wireless network available.

Student life. Freshman orientation: Mandatory. Preregistration for classes offered. Multiple half-day sessions for full-time students; reservations required. Online session required for part-time students. Program includes basic skills assessment, academic advising, and registration assistance. **Activities:** Campus ministries, international student organizations, student government, student newspaper, Phi Theta Kappa, Sigma Kappa Delta, Alpha Beta Gamma, Chi Gamma Iota, Rotoract, Toastmasters, culture club, environmental club, outdoor adventure club, Campus Crusade for Christ.

Athletics. NJCAA. **Intercollegiate:** Baseball M, soccer, softball W. **Intramural:** Basketball, softball, volleyball. **Team name:** Hawks.

Student services. Adult student services, alcohol/substance abuse counseling, career counseling, services for economically disadvantaged, student employment services, financial aid counseling, minority student services, on-campus daycare, personal counseling, placement for graduates, veterans' counselor. **Physically disabled:** Services for visually, speech, hearing impaired. **Transfer:** Pre-admission transcript evaluation for new students. Transfer adviser, college fairs on campus for students transferring to 4-year colleges.

Contact. E-mail: soar@heartland.edu
Phone: (309) 268-8000 Fax: (309) 268-7992
Candace Brownlee, Dean of Student Services, Heartland Community College, 1500 West Raab Road, Normal, IL 61761

Highland Community College
Freeport, Illinois
www.highland.edu
CB code: 1233

- Public 2-year community college
- Commuter campus in large town

General. Founded in 1961. Regionally accredited. **Enrollment:** 2,026 degree-seeking undergraduates; 196 non-degree-seeking students. **Degrees:** 334 associate awarded. **Location:** 100 miles from Chicago, 38 miles from Rockford. **Calendar:** Semester, limited summer session. **Full-time faculty:** 45 total; 13% have terminal degrees, 7% minority, 31% women. **Part-time faculty:** 97 total; 3% have terminal degrees, 4% minority, 67% women. **Class size:** 75% < 20, 22% 20-39, 2% 40-49, less than 1% 50-99. **Special facilities:** Regional arboretum, YMCA on campus, wind turbine training facility.

Student profile. Among degree-seeking undergraduates, 55% enrolled in a transfer program, 45% enrolled in a vocational program, 4% already have a bachelor's degree or higher, 450 enrolled as first-time, first-year students, 64 transferred in from other institutions.

Part-time:	42%	Asian American:	1%
Out-of-state:	2%	Hispanic American:	1%
Women:	62%	Native American:	2%
African American:	11%	25 or older:	39%

Transfer out. Colleges most students transferred to 2011: Illinois State University, University of Wisconsin-Platteville, Northern Illinois University, Western Illinois University, Columbia College.

Basis for selection. Open admission, but selective for some programs. Special criteria for acceptance into nursing program: based on points accumulated by taking prerequisite courses, class rank, and test scores considered. Special criteria for wind turbine program: based on pre-requisites, GPA, and letters of recommendation. **Home schooled:** Transcript of courses and grades required.

High school preparation. College-preparatory program recommended. 15 units recommended. Recommended units include English 4, mathematics 3, social studies 2, science 2 (laboratory 2) and academic electives 4.

2011-2012 Annual costs. Tuition/fees: $3,240; $4,740 out-of-district; $5,220 out-of-state. Per-credit charge: $99 in-district; $149 out-of-district; $165 out-of-state.

2010-2011 Financial aid. Need-based: 331 full-time freshmen applied for aid; 274 were judged to have need; 259 of these received aid. Average need met was 32%. Average scholarship/grant was $4,516; average loan $2,596. Need-based aid available for part-time students. Work-study available nights, weekends and for part-time students. **Non-need-based:** Awarded to 658 full-time undergraduates, including 191 freshmen. Scholarships awarded for academics, athletics.

Application procedures. Admission: No deadline. No application fee. Admission notification on a rolling basis. **Financial aid:** No deadline. FAFSA, institutional form required. Applicants notified on a rolling basis starting 8/1; must reply within 2 week(s) of notification.

Academics. Special study options: Distance learning, dual enrollment of high school students, ESL, honors, independent study, internships, liberal arts/career combination, student-designed major. Bachelor's degree programs available on campus. License preparation in nursing, real estate. **Credit/placement by examination:** AP, CLEP, institutional tests. 21 credit hours maximum toward associate degree. **Support services:** GED preparation, learning center, remedial instruction, study skills assistance, tutoring, writing center.

Majors. Business: Accounting, administrative services. **Computer sciences:** Information technology. **Education:** Early childhood, learning disabled, mathematics. **Engineering:** General. **General:** Business. **Health services:** EMT paramedic, medical assistant, medical records technology, nursing (RN). **Liberal arts:** Arts/sciences. **Visual/performing arts:** Graphic design. **Work/family studies:** Child care service.

Most popular majors. Health sciences 20%, interdisciplinary studies 21%, liberal arts 36%, trade and industry 9%.

Computing on campus. 366 workstations in library, computer center, student center. Commuter students can connect to campus network. Online course registration, online library, helpline, repair service, wireless network available.

Student life. Freshman orientation: Available. Preregistration for classes offered. **Activities:** Bands, campus ministries, choral groups, dance, drama, international student organizations, literary magazine, music ensembles, musical theater, radio station, student government, student newspaper, current issues club, environmental awareness, religious fellowship, People of Color, pride club, student senate.

Athletics. NJCAA. **Intercollegiate:** Baseball M, basketball, golf M, softball W, volleyball W. **Intramural:** Basketball, volleyball. **Team name:** Cougars.

Student services. Adult student services, alcohol/substance abuse counseling, career counseling, services for economically disadvantaged, student employment services, financial aid counseling, on-campus daycare, personal counseling, veterans' counselor. **Physically disabled:** Services for visually, speech, hearing impaired. **Transfer:** Pre-admission transcript evaluation for new students. Transfer center, transfer adviser, college fairs on campus for students transferring to 4-year colleges.

Contact. E-mail: registration@highland.edu
Phone: (815) 235-6121 ext. 3414 Fax: (815) 235-6130
Jeremy Bradt, Director of Enrollment and Records, Highland Community College, 2998 West Pearl City Road, Freeport, IL 61032-9341

Illinois Central College
East Peoria, Illinois
www.icc.edu   CB code: 1312

- Public 2-year community college
- Commuter campus in large town

General. Founded in 1966. Regionally accredited. **Enrollment:** 9,705 degree-seeking undergraduates; 2,536 non-degree-seeking students. **Degrees:** 1,687 associate awarded. **Location:** 150 miles from Chicago, 5 miles from Peoria. **Calendar:** Semester, extensive summer session. **Full-time faculty:** 192 total; 17% have terminal degrees, 12% minority, 51% women. **Part-time faculty:** 658 total; 6% have terminal degrees, 7% minority, 57% women. **Class size:** 57% < 20, 38% 20-39, 5% 40-49, less than 1% 50-99, less than 1% >100. **Partnerships:** Formal partnerships with Caterpillar Tractor Company and General Motors.

Student profile.

Part-time:	54%	Women:	58%
Out-of-state:	1%	25 or older:	35%

Transfer out. Colleges most students transferred to 2011: Illinois State University, Bradley University, Western Illinois University, Southern Illinois University: Carbondale, University of Illinois: Urbana-Champaign.

Basis for selection. Open admission, but selective for some programs. Special requirements for health occupation programs and diesel mechanics. Some programs require ACT for admission and placement. Audition required of music majors. **Home schooled:** Transcript of courses and grades required.

High school preparation. 15 units recommended. Recommended units include English 4, mathematics 3, social studies 2, science 2, foreign language 1, visual/performing arts 1 and academic electives 2.

2012-2013 Annual costs. Tuition/fees (projected): $3,060; $6,750 out-of-district; $6,750 out-of-state. Per-credit charge: $102 in-district; $225 out-of-district; $225 out-of-state. Books/supplies: $1,200. Personal expenses: $1,200.

Financial aid. Need-based: Need-based aid available for part-time students. Work-study available nights, weekends and for part-time students. **Non-need-based:** Scholarships awarded for academics, athletics, minority status, music/drama, state residency.

Application procedures. Admission: No deadline. No application fee. **Financial aid:** Priority date 6/1; no closing date. FAFSA required. Applicants notified on a rolling basis starting 5/1; must reply within 2 week(s) of notification.

Academics. Team-taught, multidisciplinary program available for transfers. **Special study options:** Distance learning, ESL, honors, independent study, internships, study abroad, weekend college. Bachelor's degree programs available on campus. License preparation in dental hygiene, nursing, occupational therapy, paramedic, physical therapy, radiology, real estate. **Credit/placement by examination:** AP, CLEP, institutional tests. 30 credit hours maximum toward associate degree. **Support services:** GED preparation, learning center, reduced course load, remedial instruction, study skills assistance, tutoring, writing center.

Majors. Architecture: Interior. **Business:** General, accounting, administrative services, banking/financial services, business admin, international, real estate. **Communications:** Broadcast journalism, journalism. **Computer sciences:** General, applications programming, programming. **Conservation:** General. **Education:** Elementary, physical, secondary, special ed. **Engineering:** General, electrical. **English:** English lit, rhetoric/composition. **Foreign languages:** General. **General:** Business, horticulture. **Health services:** Clinical lab technology, dental hygiene, health care admin, medical radiologic technology/radiation therapy, medical records technology, occupational therapy assistant, physical therapy assistant, predental, premedicine, prepharmacy, preveterinary, respiratory therapy technology, surgical technology. **Liberal arts:** Arts/sciences, library assistant. **Math:** General. **Physical sciences:** Chemistry, geology, physics, planetary. **Protective services:** Criminal justice, fire safety technology. **Visual/performing arts:** Dance, dramatic, music, studio arts. **Work/family studies:** General, child care management, food/nutrition.

Most popular majors. Education 11%, health sciences 43%, liberal arts 22%, security/protective services 9%.

Computing on campus. 500 workstations in library, computer center. Wireless network available.

Student life. Freshman orientation: Available. Preregistration for classes offered. **Housing:** Apartments available. **Activities:** Bands, campus ministries, choral groups, dance, drama, international student organizations, literary magazine, music ensembles, student government, student newspaper, TV station, College Democrats, Campus Crusade for Christ, Chi Alpha Fellowship, Areopagus.

Athletics. NJCAA. **Intercollegiate:** Baseball M, basketball, cross-country, golf M, soccer, softball W, volleyball W. **Intramural:** Basketball, bowling, football (non-tackle). **Team name:** Cougars.

Student services. Adult student services, career counseling, services for economically disadvantaged, student employment services, financial aid counseling, health services, on-campus daycare, personal counseling, placement for graduates, veterans' counselor. **Physically disabled:** Services for visually, speech, hearing impaired. **Transfer:** Transfer center, transfer adviser, college fairs on campus for students transferring to 4-year colleges.

Contact. E-mail: enroll@icc.edu
Phone: (309) 694-5354 Fax: (309) 694-8461
Guy Goodman, Dean, Student Services, Illinois Central College, One College Drive, East Peoria, IL 61635-0001

Illinois Eastern Community Colleges: Frontier Community College
Fairfield, Illinois
www.iecc.edu/fcc   CB code: 1894

- Public 2-year community college
- Commuter campus in small town

General. Founded in 1976. Regionally accredited. **Enrollment:** 500 degree-seeking undergraduates; 1,694 non-degree-seeking students. **Degrees:** 79 associate awarded. **Location:** 110 miles from St. Louis. **Calendar:** Semester, extensive summer session. **Full-time faculty:** 5 total. **Part-time faculty:** 230 total.

Student profile. Among degree-seeking undergraduates, 53% enrolled in a transfer program, 47% enrolled in a vocational program, 108 enrolled as first-time, first-year students.

Part-time:	48%	25 or older:	49%
Women:	61%		

Basis for selection. Open admission, but selective for some programs. Special requirements for nursing and radiography programs. Preference given to regional residents. Interview recommended for nursing and radiography technology.

High school preparation. Recommended units include English 3, mathematics 2 and science 1.

2011-2012 Annual costs. Tuition/fees: $2,590; $7,258 out-of-district; $9,423 out-of-state. Per-credit charge: $71 in-district; $227 out-of-district; $299 out-of-state. Books/supplies: $1,000. Personal expenses: $1,120.

Financial aid. Need-based: Need-based aid available for part-time students. Work-study available nights, weekends and for part-time students. **Non-need-based:** Scholarships awarded for academics, state residency.

Application procedures. Admission: No deadline. No application fee. Admission notification on a rolling basis beginning on or about 8/1. **Financial aid:** No deadline. FAFSA, institutional form required. Applicants notified on a rolling basis starting 8/1; must reply within 2 week(s) of notification.

Academics. Students, with counselors' aid, design own academic programs through nontraditional alternatives to classroom study. **Special study options:** Distance learning, double major, dual enrollment of high school students, ESL, honors, independent study, student-designed major, study abroad, teacher certification program, weekend college. License preparation in nursing. **Credit/placement by examination:** AP, CLEP, institutional tests. 32 credit hours maximum toward associate degree. **Support services:** GED preparation, learning center, remedial instruction, study skills assistance, tutoring.

Majors. Business: Administrative services, office technology. **Computer sciences:** General, information systems. **Engineering:** General. **Health services:** EMT ambulance attendant, medical records technology, mental health services. **Liberal arts:** Arts/sciences. **Protective services:** Firefighting.

Most popular majors. Liberal arts 75%, trade and industry 7%.

Computing on campus. 40 workstations in library, computer center. Commuter students can connect to campus network. Helpline available.

Student life. Freshman orientation: Available. Preregistration for classes offered. Freshman orientation strongly recommended. **Activities:** Bands, choral groups, drama, music ensembles, musical theater, student government, student newspaper.

Student services. Adult student services, career counseling, services for economically disadvantaged, student employment services, financial aid counseling, minority student services, personal counseling, placement for graduates, veterans' counselor. **Physically disabled:** Services for visually, speech, hearing impaired. **Transfer:** Pre-admission transcript evaluation for new students. Transfer adviser, college fairs on campus for students transferring to 4-year colleges.

Contact. Phone: (618) 842-3711 Toll-free number: (877) 464-3687 Fax: (618) 842-6340
Mary Atkins, Director of Registration and Records, Illinois Eastern Community Colleges: Frontier Community College, Two Frontier Drive, Fairfield, IL 62837-9801

Illinois Eastern Community Colleges: Lincoln Trail College
Robinson, Illinois
www.iecc.edu/ltc
CB code: 0758

▪ Public 2-year community college
▪ Commuter campus in small town

General. Founded in 1969. Regionally accredited. **Enrollment:** 614 degree-seeking undergraduates; 452 non-degree-seeking students. **Degrees:** 113 associate awarded. **Location:** 200 miles from Indianapolis, 110 miles from

---

St. Louis. **Calendar:** Semester, extensive summer session. **Full-time faculty:** 18 total. **Part-time faculty:** 68 total.

Student profile. Among degree-seeking undergraduates, 53% enrolled in a transfer program, 47% enrolled in a vocational program, 176 enrolled as first-time, first-year students.

Part-time:	28%	Women:	58%
Out-of-state:	1%	25 or older:	40%

Basis for selection. Open admission, but selective for some programs.

High school preparation. Recommended units include English 3, mathematics 2 and science 1.

2011-2012 Annual costs. Tuition/fees: $2,590; $7,258 out-of-district; $9,423 out-of-state. Per-credit charge: $71 in-district; $227 out-of-district; $299 out-of-state. Books/supplies: $1,000. Personal expenses: $1,120.

Financial aid. Need-based: Need-based aid available for part-time students. Work-study available nights, weekends and for part-time students. **Non-need-based:** Scholarships awarded for academics, athletics, state residency.

Application procedures. Admission: No deadline. No application fee. Admission notification on a rolling basis beginning on or about 8/1. **Financial aid:** No deadline. FAFSA, institutional form required. Applicants notified on a rolling basis starting 8/1; must reply within 2 week(s) of notification.

Academics. Students (with counselors' aid) design academic programs through nontraditional alternatives to classroom study. **Special study options:** Distance learning, double major, dual enrollment of high school students, ESL, honors, independent study, internships, student-designed major, study abroad, weekend college. License preparation in nursing. **Credit/placement by examination:** AP, CLEP, institutional tests. 32 credit hours maximum toward associate degree. **Support services:** GED preparation, learning center, remedial instruction, study skills assistance, tutoring.

Majors. Business: Administrative services, office technology. **Computer sciences:** General, networking. **Education:** Teacher assistance. **Engineering:** General. **General:** Horticulture. **Health services:** Clinical lab technology. **Liberal arts:** Arts/sciences.

Most popular majors. Engineering/engineering technologies 16%, liberal arts 70%.

Computing on campus. 91 workstations in library, computer center. Commuter students can connect to campus network. Helpline available.

Student life. Freshman orientation: Available. Preregistration for classes offered. **Activities:** Bands, choral groups, drama, music ensembles, musical theater, student government, student newspaper.

Athletics. NJCAA. **Intercollegiate:** Baseball M, basketball, softball W. **Intramural:** Basketball, softball. **Team name:** Statesmen.

Student services. Career counseling, services for economically disadvantaged, student employment services, financial aid counseling, minority student services, personal counseling, placement for graduates, veterans' counselor. **Physically disabled:** Services for visually, speech, hearing impaired. **Transfer:** Pre-admission transcript evaluation for new students. Transfer adviser, college fairs on campus for students transferring to 4-year colleges.

Contact. Phone: (618) 544-8657 Toll-free number: (866) 582-4322 Fax: (618) 544-3957
Becky Mikeworth, Director of Admissions, Illinois Eastern Community Colleges: Lincoln Trail College, 11220 State Highway 1, Robinson, IL 62454-5707

Illinois Eastern Community Colleges: Olney Central College
Olney, Illinois
www.iecc.edu/occ
CB code: 0827

▪ Public 2-year community college
▪ Commuter campus in small town

General. Founded in 1962. Regionally accredited. **Enrollment:** 987 degree-seeking undergraduates; 537 non-degree-seeking students. **Degrees:** 324 associate awarded. **Location:** 200 miles from St. Louis. **Calendar:** Semester, extensive summer session. **Full-time faculty:** 42 total. **Part-time faculty:** 75 total.

Student profile. Among degree-seeking undergraduates, 59% enrolled in a transfer program, 41% enrolled in a vocational program, 270 enrolled as first-time, first-year students.

Part-time:	27%	Women:	63%
Out-of-state:	1%	25 or older:	41%

Basis for selection. Open admission, but selective for some programs. Special requirements for nursing, radiology programs. Preference given to Illinois Eastern Community College region residents. Interview recommended for nursing, radiology technology majors.

High school preparation. Recommended units include English 3, mathematics 2 and science 1.

2011-2012 Annual costs. Tuition/fees: $2,590; $7,258 out-of-district; $9,423 out-of-state. Per-credit charge: $71 in-district; $227 out-of-district; $299 out-of-state. Books/supplies: $1,000. Personal expenses: $1,120.

Financial aid. Need-based: Need-based aid available for part-time students. Work-study available nights, weekends and for part-time students. **Non-need-based:** Scholarships awarded for academics, athletics, state residency.

Application procedures. Admission: No deadline. No application fee. Admission notification on a rolling basis beginning on or about 8/1. **Financial aid:** No deadline. FAFSA, institutional form required. Applicants notified on a rolling basis starting 8/1; must reply within 2 week(s) of notification.

Academics. Students design academic programs with aid of counselors through nontraditional alternatives to classroom study. **Special study options:** Distance learning, double major, dual enrollment of high school students, ESL, honors, independent study, internships, student-designed major, study abroad, weekend college. License preparation in nursing, radiology. **Credit/placement by examination:** AP, CLEP, institutional tests. 32 credit hours maximum toward associate degree. **Support services:** GED preparation, learning center, remedial instruction, study skills assistance, tutoring.

Majors. Business: Accounting, administrative services, office technology. **Engineering:** General. **Health services:** Clinical lab technology, medical radiologic technology/radiation therapy, medical secretary, nursing (RN). **Liberal arts:** Arts/sciences. **Protective services:** Police science.

Most popular majors. Health sciences 40%, liberal arts 42%, trade and industry 7%.

Computing on campus. 125 workstations in library, computer center. Commuter students can connect to campus network. Helpline available.

Student life. Freshman orientation: Available. Preregistration for classes offered. **Activities:** Bands, choral groups, drama, music ensembles, musical theater, student government, student newspaper.

Athletics. NJCAA. **Intercollegiate:** Baseball M, basketball, softball W. **Intramural:** Basketball, softball. **Team name:** Blue Knights.

Student services. Career counseling, services for economically disadvantaged, student employment services, financial aid counseling, minority student services, on-campus daycare, personal counseling, placement for graduates, veterans' counselor. **Physically disabled:** Services for visually, speech, hearing impaired. **Transfer:** Pre-admission transcript evaluation for new students. Transfer adviser, college fairs on campus for students transferring to 4-year colleges.

Contact. Phone: (618) 395-7777 Toll-free number: (866) 622-4322 Fax: (618) 392-5212
Chris Webber, Assistant Dean of Student Services, Illinois Eastern Community Colleges: Olney Central College, 305 North West Street, Olney, IL 62450

Illinois Eastern Community Colleges: Wabash Valley College
Mount Carmel, Illinois
www.iecc.edu/wvc   **CB code: 1936**

▶ Public 2-year community college
▶ Commuter campus in small town

General. Founded in 1960. Regionally accredited. **Enrollment:** 828 degree-seeking undergraduates; 4,628 non-degree-seeking students. **Degrees:** 196 associate awarded. **Location:** 40 miles from Evansville, Indiana. **Calendar:** Semester, extensive summer session. **Full-time faculty:** 35 total. **Part-time faculty:** 91 total.

Student profile. Among degree-seeking undergraduates, 55% enrolled in a transfer program, 45% enrolled in a vocational program, 251 enrolled as first-time, first-year students.

Part-time:	28%	Women:	48%
Out-of-state:	4%	25 or older:	58%

Basis for selection. Open admission, but selective for some programs. Special requirements for nursing, radiology programs. Preference given to Illinois Eastern Community College region residents. Interview recommended for nursing, radiology technology majors.

High school preparation. Recommended units include English 3, mathematics 2 and science 1.

2012-2013 Annual costs. Tuition/fees: $2,590; $7,258 out-of-district; $9,423 out-of-state. Per-credit charge: $71 in-district; $227 out-of-district; $299 out-of-state. Books/supplies: $1,000. Personal expenses: $1,120.

Financial aid. Need-based: Need-based aid available for part-time students. Work-study available nights, weekends and for part-time students. **Non-need-based:** Scholarships awarded for academics, athletics, state residency.

Application procedures. Admission: No deadline. No application fee. Admission notification on a rolling basis beginning on or about 8/1. **Financial aid:** No deadline. FAFSA, institutional form required. Applicants notified on a rolling basis starting 8/1; must reply within 2 week(s) of notification.

Academics. Students, with counselor's aid, design own academic programs through nontraditional alternatives to classroom study. **Special study options:** Distance learning, double major, dual enrollment of high school students, ESL, honors, independent study, internships, student-designed major, study abroad, weekend college. License preparation in nursing, real estate. **Credit/placement by examination:** AP, CLEP, institutional tests. 32 credit hours maximum toward associate degree. **Support services:** GED preparation, learning center, remedial instruction, study skills assistance, tutoring.

Majors. Business: Accounting technology, administrative services, office technology. **Communications:** Broadcast journalism. **Engineering:** General. **General:** Business technology, horticulture, production. **Human services:** Social work. **Liberal arts:** Arts/sciences. **Visual/performing arts:** Music. **Work/family studies:** Child care management.

Most popular majors. Agriculture 8%, business/marketing 7%, engineering/engineering technologies 6%, interdisciplinary studies 19%, liberal arts 37%, trade and industry 13%.

Computing on campus. 100 workstations in library, computer center. Commuter students can connect to campus network. Helpline available.

Student life. Freshman orientation: Available. Preregistration for classes offered. **Activities:** Bands, choral groups, drama, music ensembles, musical theater, radio station, student government, student newspaper, TV station.

Athletics. NJCAA. **Intercollegiate:** Baseball M, basketball, softball W. **Intramural:** Basketball, softball. **Team name:** Warriors.

Student services. Career counseling, services for economically disadvantaged, student employment services, financial aid counseling, minority student services, on-campus daycare, personal counseling, placement for graduates, veterans' counselor. **Physically disabled:** Services for visually, speech, hearing impaired. **Transfer:** Pre-admission transcript evaluation for new students. Transfer adviser, college fairs on campus for students transferring to 4-year colleges.

Contact. Phone: (618) 262-8641 Toll-free number: (866) 982-4322 Fax: (618) 262-5347
Diana Spear, Assistant Dean for Student Services, Illinois Eastern Community Colleges: Wabash Valley College, 2200 College Drive, Mount Carmel, IL 62863-2657

Illinois Valley Community College
Oglesby, Illinois   **CB member**
www.ivcc.edu   **CB code: 1397**

▶ Public 2-year community college
▶ Commuter campus in small town

General. Founded in 1966. Regionally accredited. **Enrollment:** 2,753 degree-seeking undergraduates; 1,602 non-degree-seeking students. **Degrees:** 559 associate awarded. **Location:** 60 miles from Peoria, 95 miles from Chicago. **Calendar:** Semester, extensive summer session. **Full-time faculty:** 91 total; 11% have terminal degrees, 6% minority, 53% women. **Part-time faculty:** 179 total; 5% have terminal degrees, 3% minority, 52% women.

Student profile. Among degree-seeking undergraduates, 41% enrolled in a transfer program, 59% enrolled in a vocational program, 2% already have a bachelor's degree or higher, 368 enrolled as first-time, first-year students.

Part-time:	43%	Asian American:	1%
Women:	60%	Hispanic American:	8%
African American:	3%	25 or older:	32%

Transfer out. 70% of students enrolled in the transfer program go on to 4-year colleges. **Colleges most students transferred to 2011:** Illinois State University, Northern Illinois University, Western Illinois University, University of Illinois/Urbana-Champaign, Eastern Illinois University.

Basis for selection. Open admission, but selective for some programs. Applicants to nursing programs must have 2.0 GPA for LPN, 2.5 GPA for RN and background in laboratory science; 2.0 GPA required for dental assisting. **Home schooled:** Transcript of courses and grades required.

2011-2012 Annual costs. Tuition/fees: $2,506; $7,203 out-of-district; $8,057 out-of-state. Per-credit charge: $76 in-district; $233 out-of-district; $261 out-of-state. Books/supplies: $1,400. Personal expenses: $1,350.

2010-2011 Financial aid. Need-based: 73% of total undergraduate aid awarded as scholarships/grants, 27% as loans/jobs. Need-based aid available for part-time students. Work-study available nights, weekends and for part-time students. **Non-need-based:** Scholarships awarded for academics, art, athletics, leadership, music/drama.

Application procedures. Admission: No deadline. No application fee. Admission notification on a rolling basis. **Financial aid:** Priority date 3/1; no closing date. FAFSA required. Applicants notified on a rolling basis starting 3/1.

Academics. Special study options: Cross-registration, distance learning, dual enrollment of high school students, honors, independent study, internships, study abroad. License preparation in nursing, real estate. **Credit/placement by examination:** AP, CLEP, institutional tests. 16 credit hours maximum toward associate degree. **Support services:** GED preparation and test center, learning center, pre-admission summer program, reduced course load, remedial instruction, study skills assistance, tutoring, writing center.

Majors. Biology: General. **Business:** Management science. **Communications:** Communications/speech/rhetoric, journalism. **Computer sciences:** General, applications programming, information systems. **Education:** General. **Engineering:** General. **English:** American lit, English lit, rhetoric/composition, writing. **Foreign languages:** General. **Health services:** Athletic training, nursing (RN). **History:** General. **Human services:** Social work. **Math:** General. **Parks/recreation:** Health/fitness, sports admin. **Physical sciences:** Chemistry, geology, oceanography, physics, planetary. **Protective services:** Law enforcement admin, police science. **Psychology:** General. **Social sciences:** General, political science, sociology. **Visual/performing arts:** General, art, art history/conservation, dramatic, music, music history, music performance, studio arts. **Work/family studies:** Child care management.

Most popular majors. Health sciences 9%, interdisciplinary studies 40%, liberal arts 26%, trade and industry 9%.

Computing on campus. 242 workstations in library, computer center. Commuter students can connect to campus network. Online course registration, online library, helpline, wireless network available.

Student life. Freshman orientation: Available. Preregistration for classes offered. Sessions held in spring and fall. **Activities:** Bands, choral groups, drama, literary magazine, music ensembles, musical theater, student government, student newspaper, Amnesty International, gay/straight alliance, People of the World End Racism (POWER), student nurses association, Young Republicans.

Athletics. NJCAA. **Intercollegiate:** Baseball M, basketball, golf M, softball W, tennis, volleyball W. **Intramural:** Basketball, softball, volleyball. **Team name:** Eagles.

Student services. Career counseling, student employment services, financial aid counseling, on-campus daycare, personal counseling, placement for graduates, veterans' counselor. **Physically disabled:** Services for visually, hearing impaired. **Transfer:** Transfer adviser for students transferring to 4-year colleges.

Contact. E-mail: mark_grzybowski@ivcc.edu
Phone: (815) 224-0439 Fax: (815) 224-6091
Mark Gryzbowski, Director of Admissions and Records, Illinois Valley Community College, 815 North Orlando Smith Avenue, Oglesby, IL 61348-9693

John A. Logan College
Carterville, Illinois
www.jalc.edu — **CB code: 1357**

- Public 2-year community college
- Commuter campus in small town

General. Founded in 1967. Regionally accredited. **Enrollment:** 1,996 full-time, degree-seeking students. **Degrees:** 579 associate awarded. **ROTC:** Army, Air Force. **Location:** 10 miles from Carbondale. **Calendar:** Semester, limited summer session. **Full-time faculty:** 107 total. **Part-time faculty:** 218 total. **Class size:** 53% < 20, 44% 20-39, less than 1% 40-49, less than 1% 50-99, less than 1% >100.

Student profile.

Out-of-state:	1%	25 or older:	47%

Transfer out. Colleges most students transferred to 2011: Southern Illinois University at Carbondale.

Basis for selection. Open admission, but selective for some programs. Admission to allied health programs competitive, unique criteria depending on program. ASSET and/or COMPASS accepted in place of SAT or ACT.

High school preparation. College preparatory program required of 2-year transfer degree applicants. Must have 15 high school course units: 4 English, 3 math, 3 laboratory science, 3 social science, 2 electives.

2011-2012 Annual costs. Tuition/fees: $2,760; $6,492 out-of-district; $8,337 out-of-state. Per-credit charge: $92 in-district; $216 out-of-district; $278 out-of-state. Books/supplies: $1,234. Personal expenses: $617.

Financial aid. All financial aid based on need. Need-based aid available for part-time students. Work-study available nights, weekends and for part-time students.

Application procedures. Admission: No deadline. No application fee. Admission notification on a rolling basis. **Financial aid:** Priority date 5/1; no closing date. FAFSA, institutional form required. Applicants notified on a rolling basis starting 5/1.

Academics. Special study options: Distance learning, double major, dual enrollment of high school students, liberal arts/career combination, study abroad. Bachelor's degree programs available on campus. License preparation in dental hygiene, nursing, occupational therapy, paramedic, real estate. **Credit/placement by examination:** AP, CLEP, institutional tests. 30 credit hours maximum toward associate degree. **Support services:** GED preparation and test center, remedial instruction, study skills assistance, tutoring, writing center.

Majors. Biology: General. **Business:** Accounting technology, business admin, executive assistant, office management. **Communications:** Journalism. **Computer sciences:** General, data entry, information technology. **Education:** Art, early childhood, elementary, history, mathematics, physical, secondary, social studies, special ed, teacher assistance. **Engineering:** General. **English:** English lit. **Health services:** Clinical lab technology, dental hygiene, medical records technology, nursing (RN), occupational therapy assistant, prepharmacy, sonography. **Human services:** Social work. **Liberal arts:** Arts/sciences. **Math:** General. **Physical sciences:** Chemistry, physics. **Protective services:** Corrections, criminal justice. **Psychology:** General. **Social sciences:** Economics, international relations, political science, sociology. **Visual/performing arts:** Art, dramatic, music.

Most popular majors. Business/marketing 15%, health sciences 13%, interdisciplinary studies 9%, liberal arts 23%, security/protective services 6%, trade and industry 14%.

Computing on campus. Commuter students can connect to campus network. Online course registration, wireless network available.

Student life. Freshman orientation: Available. Preregistration for classes offered. **Housing:** Housing at Southern Illinois University - Carbondale. **Activities:** Concert band, choral groups, drama, music ensembles, musical theater, student government, student newspaper.

Athletics. NJCAA. **Intercollegiate:** Baseball M, basketball, golf, softball W, volleyball W. **Team name:** Volunteers.

Student services. Adult student services, career counseling, student employment services, financial aid counseling, minority student services, on-campus daycare, placement for graduates, veterans' counselor. **Physically disabled:** Services for visually, hearing impaired. **Transfer:** Transfer center, college fairs on campus for students transferring to 4-year colleges.

Contact. E-mail: terrycrain@jalc.edu
Phone: (618) 985-3741 ext. 8298 Fax: (618) 985-4433
Terry Crain, Dean for Student Services, John A. Logan College, 700
Logan College Road, Carterville, IL 62918

John Wood Community College
Quincy, Illinois
www.jwcc.edu   **CB code: 1374**

- Public 2-year community college
- Commuter campus in large town

General. Founded in 1974. Regionally accredited. Additional extension
sites in Pittsfield and Mt. Sterling. **Enrollment:** 2,022 degree-seeking undergraduates; 368 non-degree-seeking students. **Degrees:** 371 associate awarded.
Location: 140 miles from St. Louis, 100 miles from Springfield. **Calendar:**
Semester, extensive summer session. **Full-time faculty:** 56 total; 7% have
terminal degrees, 2% minority, 52% women. **Part-time faculty:** 202 total;
4% have terminal degrees, 2% minority, 54% women. **Class size:** 59% < 20,
41% 20-39. **Special facilities:** Workforce development center, truck driver
training facility, greenhouse, agricultural center, G.E.D. center.

Student profile. Among degree-seeking undergraduates, 66% enrolled in
a transfer program, 34% enrolled in a vocational program, 3% already have
a bachelor's degree or higher, 530 enrolled as first-time, first-year students,
368 transferred in from other institutions.

Part-time:	42%	Asian American:	1%
Out-of-state:	7%	Hispanic American:	1%
Women:	59%	25 or older:	38%
African American:	4%		

Transfer out. 66% of students enrolled in the transfer program go on to 4-
year colleges. **Colleges most students transferred to 2011:** Western Illinois
University, Eastern Illinois University, University of Illinois-Springfield,
Quincy University.

Basis for selection. Open admission, but selective for some programs.
Limited enrollment in certificate programs in dietary management, practical
nursing, nurse assistant and in associate degree programs in nursing and
truck driver training.

High school preparation. Recommended units include English 4, mathematics 3, social studies 3 and science 4.

2011-2012 Annual costs. Tuition/fees: $3,900; $7,200 out-of-state. Per-
credit charge: $120 in-state; $230 out-of-state. Books/supplies: $2,040. Per-
sonal expenses: $879.

2010-2011 Financial aid. Need-based: 67% of total undergraduate aid
awarded as scholarships/grants, 33% as loans/jobs. Need-based aid available
for part-time students. Work-study available nights, weekends and for part-
time students.

Application procedures. Admission: No deadline. No application fee.
Admission notification on a rolling basis. **Financial aid:** No deadline. FAFSA
required. Applicants notified on a rolling basis starting 3/1.

Academics. Special study options: Distance learning, dual enrollment of
high school students, ESL, independent study, internships, liberal arts/career
combination, student-designed major, study abroad. License preparation in
nursing, paramedic, radiology, real estate. **Credit/placement by examination:** AP, CLEP, institutional tests. 30 credit hours maximum toward associate
degree. **Support services:** GED preparation and test center, learning center,
reduced course load, remedial instruction, study skills assistance, tutoring,
writing center.

Majors. Biology: General. **Business:** General, accounting, accounting technology, administrative services, business admin, executive assistant, sales/
distribution. **Communications:** Communications/speech/rhetoric. **Engineering:** General. **Foreign languages:** Spanish. **General:** Animal sciences,
business, horticulture. **Health services:** Clinical lab technology, EMT paramedic, medical radiologic technology/radiation therapy, medical secretary,
nursing (RN). **History:** General. **Liberal arts:** Arts/sciences. **Math:** General.
Parks/recreation: Health/fitness. **Physical sciences:** General, physics. **Protective services:** Fire safety technology, homeland security, police science.
Psychology: General. **Social sciences:** Economics, sociology. **Visual/per-
forming arts:** Art, graphic design, music. **Work/family studies:** Child
care management.

Most popular majors. Health sciences 13%, liberal arts 38%.

Computing on campus. 400 workstations in library, computer center.
Commuter students can connect to campus network. Online course registration, online library, helpline, wireless network available.

Student life. Freshman orientation: Mandatory. Preregistration for
classes offered. **Activities:** Bands, choral groups, drama, music ensembles,
musical theater, student government, service organizations, honor society,
Phi Theta Kappa, Campus Crusade for Christ.

Athletics. NJCAA. **Intercollegiate:** Baseball M, basketball, cheerleading,
softball W. **Intramural:** Basketball, bowling, football (non-tackle), volleyball. **Team name:** Trail Blazers.

Student services. Adult student services, career counseling, services for
economically disadvantaged, student employment services, financial aid
counseling, minority student services, veterans' counselor. **Physically disabled:** Services for visually, speech, hearing impaired. **Transfer:** Transfer
adviser, college fairs on campus for students transferring to 4-year colleges.

Contact. E-mail: admissions@jwcc.edu
Phone: (217) 641-4338 Fax: (217) 224-4208
Lee Wibbell, Director of Admissions, John Wood Community College,
1301 South 48th Street, Quincy, IL 62305-8736

Joliet Junior College
Joliet, Illinois
www.jjc.edu   **CB code: 1346**

- Public 2-year community and junior college
- Commuter campus in small city

General. Founded in 1901. Regionally accredited. **Enrollment:** 6,407 full-
time, degree-seeking students. **Degrees:** 1,431 associate awarded. **Location:**
45 miles from Chicago. **Calendar:** Semester, extensive summer session.
Full-time faculty: 211 total. **Part-time faculty:** 653 total. **Class size:** 48%
< 20, 51% 20-39, less than 1% 40-49, less than 1% 50-99, less than 1%
>100. **Special facilities:** Planetarium, nature trail, arboretum, working farm,
fitness center.

Student profile.

Out-of-state:	1%	25 or older:	42%

Transfer out. Colleges most students transferred to 2011: Northern Illinois University, Illinois State University, University of St. Francis, Lewis
University, Governors State University.

Basis for selection. Open admission, but selective for some programs
and for out-of-state students. Preference given to cooperative programs and
in-district applicants. Nursing applicants must have 20 ACT if in top third
of high school class or 21 ACT if in top half of class. Interview recommended
for some.

High school preparation. 15 units recommended. Recommended units
include English 4, mathematics 3, social studies 3, science 3 and academic
electives 2.

2011-2012 Annual costs. Tuition/fees: $3,090; $8,285 out-of-district;
$9,035 out-of-state. Per-credit charge: $76 in-district; $249 out-of-district;
$274 out-of-state. Additional course fees may apply. Personal expenses:
$1,500.

Financial aid. Need-based: Need-based aid available for part-time students. Work-study available nights, weekends and for part-time students.
Non-need-based: Scholarships awarded for academics.

Application procedures. Admission: No deadline. No application fee.
Admission notification on a rolling basis. **Financial aid:** Closing date 5/1.
FAFSA, institutional form required. Applicants notified on a rolling basis
starting 5/15.

Academics. Special study options: Cooperative education, distance learning, dual enrollment of high school students, ESL, honors, independent study,
internships, study abroad. License preparation in nursing, paramedic, radiology, real estate. **Credit/placement by examination:** AP, CLEP, institutional
tests. 45 credit hours maximum toward associate degree. **Support services:**
GED preparation, learning center, pre-admission summer program, reduced
course load, remedial instruction, study skills assistance, tutoring, writing
center.

Majors. Biology: General. **Business:** Accounting, administrative services,
business admin, office management, office technology, office/clerical. **Computer sciences:** General, information systems, programming. **Education:**
Early childhood, elementary, secondary, special ed, teacher assistance. **Engineering:** Electrical. **English:** English lit. **General:** Greenhouse operations,
horticulture, landscaping, nursery operations, ornamental horticulture, supplies, turf management. **Health services:** Medical secretary, nursing (RN),
veterinary technology/assistant. **History:** General. **Liberal arts:** Arts/sci-
ences. **Math:** General. **Physical sciences:** Chemistry. **Protective services:**

Law enforcement admin. **Psychology:** General. **Social sciences:** Political science, sociology. **Visual/performing arts:** Art, interior design, music. **Work/family studies:** Clothing/textiles.

Most popular majors. Business/marketing 7%, health sciences 15%, liberal arts 49%.

Computing on campus. Helpline, repair service available.

Student life. Freshman orientation: Available. Preregistration for classes offered. **Activities:** Bands, choral groups, drama, literary magazine, music ensembles, musical theater, student government, student newspaper, campus ministry, black student organization, Intervarsity Christian Fellowship, Latinos Unidos, Latter Day Saints association, unity club.

Athletics. NJCAA. **Intercollegiate:** Baseball M, basketball, cross-country, football (tackle) M, soccer, softball W, tennis, volleyball W. **Team name:** Wolves.

Student services. Career counseling, services for economically disadvantaged, student employment services, financial aid counseling, minority student services, on-campus daycare, personal counseling, placement for graduates, veterans' counselor, women's services. **Physically disabled:** Services for visually, speech, hearing impaired. **Transfer:** Transfer center, transfer adviser for students transferring to 4-year colleges.

Contact. E-mail: jkloberd@jjc.edu
Phone: (815) 729-9020 Fax: (815) 744-5507
Jennifer Kloberdanz, Director of Admissions and Recruitment, Joliet Junior College, 1215 Houbolt Road, Joliet, IL 60431-8938

Kankakee Community College
Kankakee, Illinois
www.kcc.edu   CB code: 1380

▶ Public 2-year community college
▶ Commuter campus in large town

General. Founded in 1966. Regionally accredited. **Enrollment:** 3,655 degree-seeking undergraduates. **Degrees:** 319 associate awarded. **ROTC:** Army. **Location:** 60 miles from Chicago. **Calendar:** Semester, extensive summer session. **Full-time faculty:** 73 total. **Part-time faculty:** 123 total. **Special facilities:** Greenhouse.

Student profile.

Out-of-state:	2%	25 or older:	44%

Transfer out. Colleges most students transferred to 2011: Illinois State University, Governors State University, Olivet Nazarene University, University of Illinois, Eastern Illinois University.

Basis for selection. Open admission, but selective for some programs. Criteria for health career programs may include prerequisite coursework, high school record and test scores; separate application and COMPASS required. COMPASS or ACT test required of all students for placement. **Adult students:** COMPASS test required.

High school preparation. 15 units recommended. Recommended units include English 4, mathematics 3, social studies 2, science 2 (laboratory 1) and academic electives 4.

2011-2012 Annual costs. Tuition/fees: $3,210; $4,848 out-of-district; $13,173 out-of-state. Per-credit charge: $97 in-district; $152 out-of-district; $429 out-of-state. Books/supplies: $1,090. Personal expenses: $1,400.

Financial aid. Need-based: Need-based aid available for part-time students. Work-study available nights, weekends and for part-time students. **Non-need-based:** Scholarships awarded for athletics.

Application procedures. Admission: No deadline. No application fee. Admission notification on a rolling basis. **Financial aid:** Closing date 7/13. FAFSA required. Applicants notified on a rolling basis; must reply within 4 week(s) of notification.

Academics. Special study options: Cross-registration, distance learning, dual enrollment of high school students, ESL, honors, independent study, internships, study abroad, teacher certification program. License preparation in nursing, paramedic, physical therapy, radiology. **Credit/placement by examination:** AP, CLEP, institutional tests. 16 credit hours maximum toward associate degree. **Support services:** GED preparation and test center, learning center, pre-admission summer program, reduced course load, remedial instruction, study skills assistance, tutoring, writing center.

Majors. Biology: General. **Business:** Administrative services, business admin, construction management. **Communications technology:** Desktop publishing. **Education:** General, early childhood, elementary, mathematics, secondary, special ed, teacher assistance. **Engineering:** General. **General:** Horticultural science. **Health services:** Clinical lab technology, EMT paramedic, medical assistant, nursing (RN), physical therapy assistant, radiologic technology/medical imaging, respiratory therapy technology. **Math:** General. **Protective services:** Police science. **Psychology:** General. **Social sciences:** Political science. **Visual/performing arts:** General, art, studio arts.

Most popular majors. Business/marketing 6%, education 7%, health sciences 34%, liberal arts 31%, security/protective services 6%, trade and industry 7%.

Computing on campus. 1,100 workstations in library, computer center, student center. Commuter students can connect to campus network. Online course registration, online library, helpline, wireless network available.

Student life. Freshman orientation: Available. Preregistration for classes offered. Two-hour orientation class held multiple dates and times at beginning of term. **Activities:** Radio station, student government.

Athletics. NJCAA. **Intercollegiate:** Baseball M, basketball, soccer M, softball W, volleyball W. **Intramural:** Basketball, golf. **Team name:** Cavaliers.

Student services. Adult student services, career counseling, services for economically disadvantaged, student employment services, financial aid counseling, minority student services, on-campus daycare, placement for graduates, veterans' counselor. **Physically disabled:** Services for visually, speech, hearing impaired. **Transfer:** Pre-admission transcript evaluation for new students. Transfer center, transfer adviser, college fairs on campus for students transferring to 4-year colleges.

Contact. E-mail: admissions@kcc.edu
Phone: (815) 802-8520 Fax: (815) 802-8521
Michelle Driscoll, Assistant Dean of Student Services, Kankakee Community College, 100 College Drive, Kankakee, IL 60901-6505

Kaskaskia College
Centralia, Illinois
www.kaskaskia.edu   CB code: 1108

▶ Public 2-year community college
▶ Commuter campus in large town

General. Founded in 1966. Regionally accredited. **Enrollment:** 3,375 degree-seeking undergraduates; 1,911 non-degree-seeking students. **Degrees:** 522 associate awarded. **Location:** 60 miles from St. Louis, MO. **Calendar:** Semester, limited summer session. **Full-time faculty:** 76 total; 7% have terminal degrees, 4% minority, 47% women. **Part-time faculty:** 153 total; 7% have terminal degrees, 6% minority, 54% women. **Class size:** 82% < 20, 17% 20-39, less than 1% 40-49, less than 1% 50-99, less than 1% >100. **Special facilities:** Fitness trail. **Partnerships:** Formal partnerships with local businesses, hospitals, factories/industries, correctional institutions.

Student profile. Among degree-seeking undergraduates, 51% enrolled in a transfer program, 49% enrolled in a vocational program, 4% already have a bachelor's degree or higher, 1,305 enrolled as first-time, first-year students, 1,706 transferred in from other institutions.

Part-time:	41%	Asian American:	1%
Out-of-state:	1%	Hispanic American:	1%
Women:	64%	25 or older:	33%
African American:	6%		

Transfer out. Colleges most students transferred to 2011: Southern Illinois University at Carbondale, Southern Illinois University at Edwardsville, Milliken University, McKendree University, University of Illinois.

Basis for selection. Open admission, but selective for some programs. Special requirements for health-related programs. COMPASS or ACT test recommended for practical nursing, cosmetology, dental, radiologic technology, physical therapy assistant program applicants. ACT, COMPASS or ASSET required for nursing assistant; English and math requirements and/or COMPASS required for diagnostic medical sonography; English and math requirements for respiratory therapy applicants. Interview required of allied health majors.

High school preparation. 15 units recommended. Recommended units include English 4, mathematics 3, social studies 3, science 3, foreign language 2 and academic electives 2. Specific requirements for allied health.

2011-2012 Annual costs. Tuition/fees: $2,910; $5,340 out-of-district; $12,090 out-of-state. Per-credit charge: $84 in-district; $165 out-of-district; $390 out-of-state.

2011-2012 Financial aid. Need-based: 702 full-time freshmen applied for aid; 702 were judged to have need; 668 of these received aid. Average need met was 65%. Average scholarship/grant was $1,450; average loan $1,880. 22% of total undergraduate aid awarded as scholarships/grants, 78% as loans/jobs. Need-based aid available for part-time students. Work-study available nights, weekends and for part-time students. **Non-need-based:** Scholarships awarded for academics, athletics, state residency.

Application procedures. Admission: No deadline. No application fee. Application must be submitted on paper. Admission notification on a rolling basis. Allied health programs have specific closing dates. **Financial aid:** Priority date 5/15; no closing date. FAFSA required. Applicants notified on a rolling basis starting 4/1; must reply within 2 week(s) of notification.

Academics. Learning communities available. **Special study options:** Accelerated study, cooperative education, distance learning, double major, dual enrollment of high school students, ESL, honors, independent study, internships, liberal arts/career combination, student-designed major, weekend college. License preparation in nursing, paramedic, physical therapy, radiology. **Credit/placement by examination:** AP, CLEP, institutional tests. 30 credit hours maximum toward associate degree. **Support services:** GED preparation and test center, learning center, reduced course load, remedial instruction, study skills assistance, tutoring.

Majors. Business: General, accounting, executive assistant, office technology. **Computer sciences:** Information systems, system admin, webmaster. **Education:** Mathematics, teacher assistance. **Engineering:** General. **Health services:** Clinical lab technology, EMT paramedic, medical records technology, nursing (RN), occupational therapy assistant, physical therapy assistant, radiologic technology/medical imaging, respiratory therapy technology, veterinary technology/assistant. **Liberal arts:** Arts/sciences. **Protective services:** Juvenile corrections, law enforcement admin. **Work/family studies:** Child care service.

Most popular majors. Business/marketing 7%, health sciences 28%, liberal arts 44%.

Computing on campus. 186 workstations in library, computer center, student center. Commuter students can connect to campus network. Online library, helpline, repair service, wireless network available.

Student life. Freshman orientation: Available, $96 fee. Preregistration for classes offered. Three 15 week formats offered both on-line and face-to-face; assists students acclimation to college. **Activities:** Bands, choral groups, drama, international student organizations, music ensembles, student government, student newspaper, Brothers and Sisters in Christ, Black Student Association.

Athletics. NJCAA. **Intercollegiate:** Baseball M, basketball, cheerleading, cross-country, golf, soccer, softball W, tennis M, volleyball W. **Team name:** Blue Devils.

Student services. Adult student services, career counseling, services for economically disadvantaged, student employment services, financial aid counseling, minority student services, on-campus daycare, personal counseling, placement for graduates, veterans' counselor. **Physically disabled:** Services for visually, speech, hearing impaired. **Transfer:** Pre-admission transcript evaluation for new students. Transfer center, transfer adviser, college fairs on campus for students transferring to 4-year colleges.

Contact. E-mail: kcadmissions@kaskaskia.edu
Phone: (618) 545-3040 Fax: (618) 532-1135
Cheryl Boehne, Director of Admissions and Registration, Kaskaskia College, 27210 College Road, Centralia, IL 62801

Kishwaukee College
Malta, Illinois
www.kishwaukeecollege.edu   CB code: 0511

- Public 2-year community college
- Commuter campus in rural community

General. Founded in 1967. Regionally accredited. **Enrollment:** 5,100 undergraduates. **Degrees:** 501 associate awarded. **ROTC:** Army. **Location:** 7 miles from DeKalb. **Calendar:** Semester, limited summer session. **Full-time faculty:** 73 total. **Part-time faculty:** 164 total.

Student profile.

Out-of-state:	1%	25 or older:	32%

Transfer out. Colleges most students transferred to 2011: Northern Illinois University.

Basis for selection. Open admission, but selective for some programs. Special requirements, including interview, for nursing, radiologic technology and therapeutic massage programs. Portfolio recommended for art majors. **Learning Disabled:** Students with learning disabilities should contact disabilities service office at least 30 days before enrollment to assist student with reasonable accommodations.

High school preparation. 15 units recommended. Recommended units include English 4, mathematics 3, social studies 3, science 3 and foreign language 2. High school diploma or equivalency required for nursing, radiologic technology, and therapeutic massage applicants.

2011-2012 Annual costs. Tuition/fees: $2,940; $9,480 out-of-district; $12,840 out-of-state. Per-credit charge: $80 in-district; $307 out-of-district; $419 out-of-state. Books/supplies: $1,000. Personal expenses: $1,000.

Financial aid. Need-based: Need-based aid available for part-time students. Work-study available nights, weekends and for part-time students. **Non-need-based:** Scholarships awarded for academics, athletics, leadership, music/drama, state residency.

Application procedures. Admission: No deadline. No application fee. Admission notification on a rolling basis. **Financial aid:** Priority date 5/1; no closing date. FAFSA, institutional form required. Applicants notified on a rolling basis starting 5/1; must reply within 2 week(s) of notification.

Academics. Cross-registration with Northern Illinois University and nearby community colleges. Distance Learning Consortium, member Illinois Virtual College (IVC). **Special study options:** Cross-registration, distance learning, double major, dual enrollment of high school students, ESL, independent study, internships, study abroad. License preparation in aviation, nursing, radiology, real estate. **Credit/placement by examination:** AP, CLEP, institutional tests. 48 credit hours maximum toward associate degree. Must complete 15 hours residency prior to posting proficiency credit. **Support services:** GED preparation and test center, learning center, pre-admission summer program, reduced course load, remedial instruction, study skills assistance, tutoring.

Majors. Architecture: Landscape. **Business:** General, accounting, human resources, management information systems, office management, office/clerical, operations. **Communications:** Communications/speech/rhetoric, journalism. **Computer sciences:** Applications programming. **Education:** General, early childhood, elementary, physical, secondary, special ed. **Engineering:** General. **English:** English lit. **Foreign languages:** General, French, Spanish. **General:** Agribusiness operations, animal breeding, business, greenhouse operations, horticultural science, horticulture, landscaping, nursery operations, ornamental horticulture, supplies. **Health services:** Medical radiologic technology/radiation therapy, nursing (RN), predental, premedicine, prenursing, prepharmacy, preveterinary. **History:** General. **Human services:** Social work. **Liberal arts:** Arts/sciences. **Math:** General. **Parks/recreation:** Health/fitness. **Physical sciences:** Astronomy, chemistry, physics. **Protective services:** Fire safety technology, firefighting, police science. **Psychology:** General. **Social sciences:** General, criminology, economics, political science, sociology. **Visual/performing arts:** General, art, dramatic, music. **Work/family studies:** General, child care management.

Most popular majors. Agriculture 7%, health sciences 10%, interdisciplinary studies 51%, liberal arts 29%.

Computing on campus. 376 workstations in library, computer center. Online library, helpline available.

Student life. Freshman orientation: Available. Preregistration for classes offered. Five sessions held during summer. **Activities:** Choral groups, drama, literary magazine, music ensembles, musical theater, student government, student newspaper, international student club, Nurses Christian Fellowship, Phi Theta Kappa, black student union, Vocational Industrial Clubs of America, Christian Fellowship, agriculture club, horticulture club, student nurses organization, student radiographers association.

Athletics. NJCAA. **Intercollegiate:** Baseball M, basketball, golf, soccer M, softball W, volleyball W. **Intramural:** Badminton, basketball, softball, volleyball. **Team name:** Kougars.

Student services. Adult student services, career counseling, services for economically disadvantaged, student employment services, financial aid counseling, health services, minority student services, on-campus daycare, personal counseling, placement for graduates, veterans' counselor, women's services. **Physically disabled:** Services for visually, speech, hearing impaired. **Transfer:** Re-entry adviser, pre-admission transcript evaluation for new students. Transfer center, transfer adviser, college fairs on campus for students transferring to 4-year colleges.

Contact. Phone: (815) 825-2086 ext. 218 Fax: (815) 825-2306
Jill Bier, Director of Admissions, Registration and Records, Kishwaukee College, 21193 Malta Road, Malta, IL 60150-9699

Lake Land College
Mattoon, Illinois
www.lakelandcollege.edu   CB code: 1424

▶ Public 2-year community college
▶ Commuter campus in large town

General. Founded in 1966. Regionally accredited. **Enrollment:** 6,874 degree-seeking undergraduates. **Degrees:** 827 associate awarded. **Location:** 45 miles from Decatur, 45 miles from Champaign. **Calendar:** Semester, extensive summer session. **Full-time faculty:** 125 total. **Part-time faculty:** 404 total. **Class size:** 55% < 20, 45% 20-39.

Student profile. Among degree-seeking undergraduates, 38% enrolled in a transfer program, 40% enrolled in a vocational program.

Out-of-state: 3%   25 or older: 46%

Transfer out. Colleges most students transferred to 2011: Eastern Illinois University, Southern Illinois University, University of Illinois.

Basis for selection. Open admission, but selective for some programs. Special requirements for dental hygiene, nursing, physical therapist assistant, John Deere agricultural technology, massage therapy, and cosmetology programs. ACT required of dental hygiene applicants for placement only. **Adult students:** Assessment battery test required.

High school preparation. Recommended units include English 4, mathematics 3, social studies 3, history 3, science 3 (laboratory 3), foreign language 2 and academic electives 2. Math and biology required for dental hygiene and nursing applicants.

2011-2012 Annual costs. Tuition/fees: $2,904; $6,197 out-of-district; $11,257 out-of-state. Per-credit charge: $78 in-district; $187 out-of-district; $356 out-of-state. Books/supplies: $318.

Financial aid. Need-based: Need-based aid available for part-time students. Work-study available nights, weekends and for part-time students. **Non-need-based:** Scholarships awarded for academics, athletics.

Application procedures. Admission: No deadline. No application fee. Admission notification on a rolling basis. **Financial aid:** Priority date 5/1; no closing date. FAFSA required. Applicants notified on a rolling basis starting 6/1.

Academics. Special study options: Accelerated study, cooperative education, distance learning, dual enrollment of high school students, ESL, honors, independent study, internships, study abroad, weekend college. License preparation in dental hygiene, nursing, physical therapy. **Credit/placement by examination:** AP, CLEP, institutional tests. 32 credit hours maximum toward associate degree. **Support services:** GED preparation, learning center, reduced course load, remedial instruction, study skills assistance, tutoring.

Majors. Business: General, administrative services, human resources. **Communications:** Broadcast journalism, journalism. **Computer sciences:** LAN/WAN management, networking. **Conservation:** Wildlife/wilderness. **Education:** General, mathematics, social science. **Engineering:** General, civil. **English:** Rhetoric/composition. **Health services:** Dental hygiene, nursing (RN), physical therapy assistant, premedicine, prepharmacy, preveterinary. **Liberal arts:** Arts/sciences. **Math:** General. **Protective services:** Police science. **Psychology:** General. **Social sciences:** General, economics. **Visual/performing arts:** Studio arts. **Work/family studies:** General, child care management.

Computing on campus. 500 workstations in library, computer center. Online course registration available.

Student life. Freshman orientation: Available. Preregistration for classes offered. Mandatory for degree-seeking students; approximately 4 hours in length. **Activities:** Choral groups, radio station, student government, student newspaper, Phi Theta Kappa.

Athletics. NJCAA. **Intercollegiate:** Baseball M, basketball, softball W, volleyball W. **Team name:** Lakers.

Student services. Career counseling, student employment services, health services, on-campus daycare, personal counseling, placement for graduates, veterans' counselor. **Physically disabled:** Services for visually, speech, hearing impaired. **Transfer:** Transfer adviser, college fairs on campus for students transferring to 4-year colleges.

Contact. E-mail: admissions@lakeland.cc.il.us
Phone: (217) 234-5434 Fax: (217) 234-5390
Jon VanDyke, Dean of Admission Services, Lake Land College, 5001 Lake Land Boulevard, Mattoon, IL 61938-9366

Le Cordon Bleu College of Culinary Arts: Chicago
Chicago, Illinois
www.chefs.edu   CB code: 2564

▶ For-profit 2-year culinary school
▶ Commuter campus in very large city
▶ Interview required

General. Regionally accredited. Affiliated with Le Cordon Bleu. **Enrollment:** 1,153 degree-seeking undergraduates. **Degrees:** 363 associate awarded. **Location:** Downtown. **Calendar:** Differs by program, extensive summer session. **Full-time faculty:** 27 total. **Part-time faculty:** 25 total. **Special facilities:** Student-run restaurant.

Student profile.

Out-of-state: 29%   25 or older: 46%

Basis for selection. Open admission. **Home schooled:** Portfolio required. **Learning Disabled:** Documentation of learning disability and special accommodations needed must be provided.

2011-2012 Annual costs. Books/supplies: $2,800. Personal expenses: $2,116.

Financial aid. Need-based: Need-based aid available for part-time students. Work-study available nights, weekends and for part-time students.

Application procedures. Admission: No deadline. $50 fee. Admission notification on a rolling basis. **Financial aid:** No deadline. FAFSA, institutional form required. Applicants notified on a rolling basis.

Academics. All levels of developmental learning provided. **Special study options:** All programs contain an externship course. **Credit/placement by examination:** AP, CLEP. 12 credit hours maximum toward associate degree. **Support services:** Learning center, remedial instruction, tutoring.

Computing on campus. 70 workstations in library, computer center, student center. Commuter students can connect to campus network. Online library, wireless network available.

Student life. Freshman orientation: Mandatory. Preregistration for classes offered. **Activities:** Student newspaper.

Student services. Career counseling, student employment services, financial aid counseling, placement for graduates, veterans' counselor.

Contact. Phone: (312) 944-0882 Toll-free number: (877) 828-7772 Fax: (312) 944-8557
Christopher Heath, Senior Director of Admissions, Le Cordon Bleu College of Culinary Arts: Chicago, 361 West Chestnut, Chicago, IL 60610-3050

Lewis and Clark Community College
Godfrey, Illinois   CB member
www.lc.edu   CB code: 0623

▶ Public 2-year community college
▶ Commuter campus in large town

General. Founded in 1970. Regionally accredited. **Enrollment:** 7,612 degree-seeking undergraduates. **Degrees:** 769 associate awarded. **ROTC:** Army. **Location:** 30 miles from St. Louis. **Calendar:** Semester, limited summer session. **Full-time faculty:** 96 total. **Part-time faculty:** 223 total.

Student profile. Among degree-seeking undergraduates, 486 enrolled as first-time, first-year students.

Part-time: 78%   25 or older: 44%
Women: 54%

Transfer out. Colleges most students transferred to 2011: Southern Illinois University: Edwardsville.

Basis for selection. Open admission, but selective for some programs. Special requirements for nursing and other allied health programs. Interview required for radio broadcasting, music majors. Audition required for music majors.

High school preparation. Recommended units include English 4, mathematics 3 and science 2.

2011-2012 Annual costs. Tuition/fees: $3,300; $8,880 out-of-district; $11,670 out-of-state. Per-credit charge: $93 in-district; $279 out-of-district; $372 out-of-state. Books/supplies: $435. Personal expenses: $1,100.

Financial aid. Need-based: Need-based aid available for part-time students. Work-study available nights, weekends and for part-time students.

Application procedures. Admission: No deadline. No application fee. Admission notification on a rolling basis. **Financial aid:** Priority date 6/1; no closing date. FAFSA required. Applicants notified on a rolling basis starting 8/1; must reply within 3 week(s) of notification.

Academics. Special study options: Cooperative education, cross-registration, distance learning, double major, dual enrollment of high school students, internships, liberal arts/career combination, student-designed major. Bachelor's degree programs available on campus. License preparation in dental hygiene, nursing, occupational therapy, paramedic, real estate. **Credit/placement by examination:** AP, CLEP, institutional tests. 32 credit hours maximum toward associate degree. **Support services:** GED preparation, learning center, remedial instruction, study skills assistance, tutoring, writing center.

Majors. Business: General, accounting, banking/financial services, business admin, office/clerical. **Communications:** Radio/TV. **Computer sciences:** General, computer graphics, computer science, data processing, information technology, LAN/WAN management, web page design, webmaster. **Education:** General, early childhood, teacher assistance. **Health services:** Dental hygiene, nursing (RN), occupational therapy assistant, predental, premedicine, prenursing, prepharmacy. **Liberal arts:** Arts/sciences. **Protective services:** Criminal justice, firefighting. **Visual/performing arts:** Music, studio arts. **Work/family studies:** Child care management.

Computing on campus. 300 workstations in library, computer center. Online course registration, online library, wireless network available.

Student life. Freshman orientation: Available. Preregistration for classes offered. **Activities:** Bands, choral groups, dance, drama, music ensembles, radio station, student government, student newspaper, TV station, veterans organization, Christian Campus Fellowship, disabled students organization, black student association, political action club.

Athletics. NJCAA. **Intercollegiate:** Baseball M, basketball, golf M, soccer, softball W, tennis, volleyball W. **Team name:** Trailblazers.

Student services. Adult student services, career counseling, student employment services, health services, on-campus daycare, personal counseling, placement for graduates, veterans' counselor. **Physically disabled:** Services for visually, hearing impaired. **Transfer:** Pre-admission transcript evaluation for new students. Transfer center, transfer adviser, college fairs on campus for students transferring to 4-year colleges.

Contact. E-mail: enroll@lc.edu
Phone: (618) 468-2222 Toll-free number: (800) 500-5222
Fax: (618) 468-2310
Kim Widman, Assistant Director of Admissions and Registration, Lewis and Clark Community College, 5800 Godfrey Road, Godfrey, IL 62035-2466

Lincoln College
Lincoln, Illinois
www.lincolncollege.edu   CB code: 1406

- Private 2-year junior and liberal arts college
- Residential campus in large town
- SAT or ACT (ACT writing optional) required

General. Founded in 1865. Regionally accredited. Associates in Liberal Arts and Science degree programs offered at Lincoln campus. Bachelor Degree and vocational programs available at Normal campus. **Enrollment:** 1,179 degree-seeking undergraduates. **Degrees:** 51 bachelor's, 180 associate awarded. **Location:** 185 miles from Chicago, 125 miles from St. Louis. **Calendar:** Semester, limited summer session. **Full-time faculty:** 46 total. **Part-time faculty:** 77 total. **Class size:** 67% < 20, 32% 20-39, 1% 40-49. **Special facilities:** Lincoln Heritage Museum, museum of the presidents.

Transfer out. Colleges most students transferred to 2011: Illinois State University, Southern Illinois University, Eastern Illinois University, Northern Illinois University, Western Illinois University.

Basis for selection. Test scores and high school transcripts are given the most weight. Letters of recommendation and/or personal statement or interview may be required. Normal campus requires 18 ACT score for resident students. Interview and personal statement recommended for applicants whom do not meet the minimum admissions requirement of a 16 ACT, 2.0 GPA.

Adult students: SAT/ACT scores not required if applicant over 23. **Home schooled:** Transcript of courses and grades, state high school equivalency certificate required. **Learning Disabled:** Upon acceptance students may submit documentation to the Office of Disability Services for consideration for the ACCESS program or to receive services through the Office of Disability Services.

High school preparation. College-preparatory program recommended. Recommended units include English 4, mathematics 3, social studies 2, history 2, science 3 (laboratory 1), foreign language 2 and computer science 2.

2011-2012 Annual costs. Tuition/fees: $23,000. Per-credit charge: $260. Room/board: $6,900. Personal expenses: $1,886.

Financial aid. Need-based: Need-based aid available for part-time students. Work-study available nights, weekends and for part-time students. **Non-need-based:** Scholarships awarded for academics, alumni affiliation, art, athletics, leadership, music/drama. **Additional information:** Auditions recommended for music, speech, theater, broadcasting, and dance scholarship candidates, portfolios recommended for art and technical theater scholarship candidates.

Application procedures. Admission: Priority date 7/1; no deadline. $25 fee, may be waived for applicants with need. Admission notification on a rolling basis. Upon receipt of official high school transcripts and ACT scores, application can be reviewed. Additional information may be requested by the Director of Admissions. **Financial aid:** Priority date 4/1, closing date 6/1. FAFSA required. Applicants notified on a rolling basis starting 6/1; must reply within 3 week(s) of notification.

Academics. Special study options: Dual enrollment of high school students, honors, independent study, study abroad. Bachelor's degree programs available on campus. **Credit/placement by examination:** AP, CLEP, SAT, ACT, institutional tests. 15 credit hours maximum toward associate degree. **Support services:** Learning center, pre-admission summer program, reduced course load, remedial instruction, study skills assistance, tutoring.

Majors. Biology: General. **Business:** General, accounting, business admin, tourism promotion, tourism/travel. **Communications:** Communications/speech/rhetoric, journalism. **Computer sciences:** Computer science. **Conservation:** General, environmental studies. **Education:** General, art, elementary, multi-level teacher. **English:** American lit, English lit, rhetoric/composition, writing. **History:** General. **Liberal arts:** Arts/sciences. **Math:** General. **Parks/recreation:** Health/fitness. **Philosophy/religion:** Philosophy, religion. **Physical sciences:** Chemistry, physics. **Protective services:** Law enforcement admin, police science. **Psychology:** General. **Social sciences:** General, economics, geography, sociology. **Visual/performing arts:** General, art, art history/conservation, ceramics, dance, dramatic, drawing, jazz, music, music history, music performance, music theory/composition, painting, photography, piano/keyboard, sculpture, studio arts, theater design, voice/opera.

Computing on campus. 130 workstations in library, computer center, student center. Dormitories wired for high-speed internet access and linked to campus network. Commuter students can connect to campus network. Helpline available.

Student life. Freshman orientation: Mandatory. Preregistration for classes offered. 1-day event for freshman and transfers held in May, June, and July. **Housing:** Guaranteed on-campus for all undergraduates. Single-sex dorms available. $125 fully refundable deposit, deadline 8/1. **Activities:** Bands, choral groups, dance, drama, literary magazine, music ensembles, musical theater, radio station, student government, student newspaper, Black Student Union, Rotaract, Mosaic (Christian group), Phi Theta Kappa.

Athletics. NJCAA. **Intercollegiate:** Baseball M, basketball, cross-country, diving, golf, soccer, softball W, swimming, track and field, volleyball W, wrestling M. **Intramural:** Baseball M, basketball, football (non-tackle), soccer, softball, table tennis, volleyball. **Team name:** Lynx.

Student services. Adult student services, alcohol/substance abuse counseling, career counseling, financial aid counseling, health services, personal counseling, placement for graduates. **Transfer:** Pre-admission transcript evaluation for new students. Transfer center, transfer adviser, college fairs on campus for students transferring to 4-year colleges.

Contact. E-mail: admissions@lincolncollege.edu
Phone: (800) 569-0556 Fax: (217) 732-7715
Gretchen Bree, Director of Admissions, Lincoln College, 300 Keokuk Street, Lincoln, IL 62656

Lincoln Land Community College
Springfield, Illinois
www.llcc.edu   CB code: 1428

- Public 2-year community and junior college
- Commuter campus in small city

General. Founded in 1967. Regionally accredited. **Enrollment:** 6,455 degree-seeking undergraduates. **Degrees:** 740 associate awarded. **ROTC:** Army, Naval, Air Force. **Location:** 180 miles from Chicago, 96 miles from St. Louis. **Calendar:** Semester, extensive summer session. **Full-time faculty:** 130 total; 92% have terminal degrees, 6% minority, 47% women. **Part-time faculty:** 228 total; 52% women. **Class size:** 74% < 20, 25% 20-39, less than 1% 40-49, less than 1% 50-99. **Special facilities:** Museum.

Transfer out. Colleges most students transferred to 2011: University of Illinois: Springfield, Southern Illinois University: Carbondale, Eastern Illinois University, Western Illinois University, Illinois State University.

Basis for selection. Open admission, but selective for some programs. Nursing and allied health program applicants must rank in top half of high school class and have 20 ACT. Admissions assessment not required of students with 22 ACT or above.

High school preparation. Recommended units include English 4, mathematics 3, social studies 2, science 2 (laboratory 2) and academic electives 2.

2011-2012 Annual costs. Tuition/fees: $3,015; $5,700 out-of-district; $8,370 out-of-state. Per-credit charge: $90 in-district; $179 out-of-district; $268 out-of-state. Books/supplies: $840.

Financial aid. Need-based: Need-based aid available for part-time students. Work-study available nights, weekends and for part-time students. **Non-need-based:** Scholarships awarded for academics, athletics, minority status, state residency.

Application procedures. Admission: No deadline. No application fee. Application must be submitted on paper. Admission notification on a rolling basis. **Financial aid:** Priority date 5/1; no closing date. FAFSA, institutional form required. Applicants notified on a rolling basis starting 4/15; must reply within 2 week(s) of notification.

Academics. Special study options: Accelerated study, cooperative education, distance learning, double major, dual enrollment of high school students, ESL, honors, independent study, internships, liberal arts/career combination, study abroad, United Nations semester. License preparation in nursing, occupational therapy, paramedic, physical therapy, radiology, real estate. **Credit/placement by examination:** AP, CLEP, institutional tests. 30 credit hours maximum toward associate degree. **Support services:** GED preparation, learning center, reduced course load, remedial instruction, study skills assistance, tutoring, writing center.

Majors. Business: General, accounting, administrative services, hospitality admin, office technology. **Computer sciences:** Applications programming, networking, programming. **Education:** Teacher assistance. **Engineering:** General. **General:** Landscaping, production. **Health services:** Nursing (RN), occupational therapy assistant, office assistant, radiologic technology/medical imaging. **Liberal arts:** Arts/sciences. **Protective services:** Firefighting, police science. **Visual/performing arts:** Graphic design, music, studio arts. **Work/family studies:** Child care service.

Most popular majors. Health sciences 18%, interdisciplinary studies 24%, liberal arts 45%.

Computing on campus. 325 workstations in library, computer center, student center. Commuter students can connect to campus network. Online course registration, online library, helpline, wireless network available.

Student life. Freshman orientation: Available. Preregistration for classes offered. Half-day program offered at beginning of semester. **Activities:** Bands, choral groups, dance, drama, international student organizations, literary magazine, music ensembles, musical theater, student government, student newspaper.

Athletics. NJCAA. **Intercollegiate:** Baseball M, basketball, cheerleading M, soccer M, softball W, volleyball W. **Team name:** Loggers.

Student services. Adult student services, career counseling, services for economically disadvantaged, student employment services, financial aid counseling, minority student services, on-campus daycare, personal counseling, placement for graduates, veterans' counselor. **Physically disabled:** Services for visually, speech, hearing impaired. **Transfer:** Pre-admission transcript evaluation for new students. Transfer adviser, college fairs on campus for students transferring to 4-year colleges.

Contact. E-mail: ron.gregoire@llcc.cc.il.us
Phone: (217) 786-2290 Toll-free number: (800) 727-4161
Fax: (217) 786-2492
Ron Gregoire, Director of Admissions and Records, Lincoln Land Community College, 5250 Shepherd Road, Springfield, IL 62794-9256

MacCormac College
Chicago, Illinois
www.maccormac.edu   CB code: 1520

- Private 2-year junior college
- Commuter campus in very large city
- Interview required

General. Founded in 1904. Regionally accredited. **Enrollment:** 176 degree-seeking undergraduates. **Degrees:** 35 associate awarded. **Calendar:** Semester, extensive summer session. **Full-time faculty:** 5 total. **Part-time faculty:** 21 total.

Student profile.

Out-of-state:	1%	25 or older:	30%

Transfer out. Colleges most students transferred to 2011: Loyola University, DePaul University, Roosevelt University.

Basis for selection. Minimum typing speed required for court reporting. ACT recommended.

High school preparation. 13 units required; 15 recommended. Required and recommended units include English 4, mathematics 2-3, social studies 3-4, history 1, science 2 (laboratory 1).

2011-2012 Annual costs. Tuition/fees: $12,100. Per-credit charge: $500. Books/supplies: $1,000.

Financial aid. Need-based: Work-study available nights, weekends and for part-time students. **Non-need-based:** Scholarships awarded for academics, leadership.

Application procedures. Admission: No deadline. $20 fee, may be waived for applicants with need. Admission notification on a rolling basis. **Financial aid:** Closing date 8/15. FAFSA required. Must reply within 2 week(s) of notification.

Academics. Special study options: ESL, internships. **Credit/placement by examination:** AP, CLEP, IB, institutional tests. 36 credit hours maximum toward associate degree. **Support services:** Learning center, study skills assistance, tutoring.

Majors. Business: General, accounting, administrative services, business admin, hospitality admin, international, international marketing, management information systems, marketing, office management, office technology, office/clerical, tourism promotion, tourism/travel. **Computer sciences:** General, computer science, information systems. **Health services:** Medical transcription.

Most popular majors. Business/marketing 80%, legal studies 15%.

Computing on campus. 118 workstations in library, computer center.

Student life. Freshman orientation: Mandatory. Preregistration for classes offered. **Activities:** Student government, student activities committee, Phi Theta Kappa.

Student services. Career counseling, student employment services, financial aid counseling, personal counseling, placement for graduates. **Transfer:** Transfer adviser for students transferring to 4-year colleges.

Contact. E-mail: admissions@maccormac.edu
Phone: (312) 922-1884 Fax: (312) 922-3196
Marcus Troutman, Director of Admissions, MacCormac College, 29 East Madison Street, Chicago, IL 60602

McHenry County College
Crystal Lake, Illinois
www.mchenry.edu   CB code: 1525

- Public 2-year community college
- Commuter campus in large town

General. Founded in 1967. Regionally accredited. **Enrollment:** 5,651 degree-seeking undergraduates; 898 non-degree-seeking students. **Degrees:** 746 associate awarded. **Location:** 50 miles from Chicago. **Calendar:** Semester, limited summer session. **Full-time faculty:** 94 total; 6% minority, 49% women. **Part-time faculty:** 268 total; 8% minority, 57% women. **Special facilities:** Planetarium, weather cam, art galleries.

Student profile. Among degree-seeking undergraduates, 69% enrolled in a transfer program, 6% enrolled in a vocational program, 1,312 enrolled as first-time, first-year students.

Part-time:	53%	Hispanic American:	10%
Women:	56%	International:	1%
African American:	1%	25 or older:	28%
Asian American:	2%		

Transfer out. Colleges most students transferred to 2011: Northern Illinois University, Illinois State University, University of Illinois at Chicago, Southern Illinois University, Columbia College.

Basis for selection. Open admission, but selective for some programs. Selective admission to RN program. **Adult students:** SAT/ACT scores not required. **Learning Disabled:** Students requesting accommodations from the Special Needs Department must present appropriate documentation during an intake appointment.

High school preparation. College-preparatory program recommended. 18 units recommended. Recommended units include English 4, mathematics 3, social studies 3, science 3 (laboratory 3) and academic electives 2. 2 units in foreign language, music, vocational education, or art recommended.

2012-2013 Annual costs. Tuition/fees (projected): $2,984; $8,050 out-of-district; $9,775 out-of-state. Per-credit charge: $90 in-district; $259 out-of-district; $316 out-of-state. Books/supplies: $800. Personal expenses: $1,362.

Financial aid. Need-based: Need-based aid available for part-time students. Work-study available nights, weekends and for part-time students. **Non-need-based:** Scholarships awarded for academics, athletics, leadership, music/drama, state residency. **Additional information:** Students can apply throughout the award year for federal and state aid. Students with physical handicaps or learning disabilities may apply for special needs scholarship.

Application procedures. Admission: No deadline. $15 fee. Admission notification on a rolling basis. **Financial aid:** Priority date 6/1; no closing date. FAFSA, institutional form required. Applicants notified on a rolling basis starting 5/1.

Academics. Special study options: Accelerated study, cooperative education, distance learning, dual enrollment of high school students, ESL, honors, independent study, internships, liberal arts/career combination, study abroad. Cooperative programs (tech prep) with Education for Employment. License preparation in nursing, paramedic. **Credit/placement by examination:** AP, CLEP, institutional tests. 30 credit hours maximum toward associate degree. Local proficiency exams available for occupational course credit, DANTES exams accepted. **Support services:** GED preparation and test center, learning center, pre-admission summer program, reduced course load, remedial instruction, study skills assistance, tutoring, writing center.

Majors. Business: Accounting technology, administrative services, business admin, operations, real estate, selling. **Computer sciences:** Applications programming. **Engineering:** General. **General:** Horticulture. **Health services:** EMT paramedic, nursing (RN). **Liberal arts:** Arts/sciences. **Protective services:** Firefighting, police science. **Visual/performing arts:** Art, music. **Work/family studies:** Child care service.

Computing on campus. 153 workstations in library, computer center, student center. Commuter students can connect to campus network. Online course registration, online library, wireless network available.

Student life. Freshman orientation: Available. Preregistration for classes offered. Admitted students from local high schools invited to participate in orientation and preregistration during April and May. **Activities:** Bands, campus ministries, choral groups, drama, literary magazine, music ensembles, student government, student newspaper, Latinos Unidos, Phi Theta Kappa, campus activities board, campus Christian fellowship, Club Concordia, Pride Alliance, black student alliance, Latter-day Saint student association, Special Needs Action Program.

Athletics. NJCAA. **Intercollegiate:** Baseball M, basketball, soccer M, softball W, tennis, volleyball W. **Intramural:** Basketball. **Team name:** Fighting Scots.

Student services. Adult student services, career counseling, student employment services, financial aid counseling, minority student services, on-campus daycare, personal counseling, placement for graduates, veterans' counselor. **Physically disabled:** Services for visually, speech, hearing impaired. **Transfer:** Pre-admission transcript evaluation for new students. Transfer center, transfer adviser, college fairs on campus for students transferring to 4-year colleges.

Contact. E-mail: admissions@mchenry.edu
Phone: (815) 455-8530 Fax: (815) 455-3766
Jared Wacker, Coordinator of Admissions, McHenry County College, 8900 US Highway 14, Crystal Lake, IL 60012-2738

Moraine Valley Community College
Palos Hills, Illinois
www.morainevalley.edu   **CB code: 1524**

- Public 2-year community and junior college
- Commuter campus in large town

General. Founded in 1967. Regionally accredited. **Enrollment:** 10,790 degree-seeking undergraduates; 7,379 non-degree-seeking students. **Degrees:** 1,532 associate awarded. **Location:** 25 miles from Chicago. **Calendar:** Semester, extensive summer session. **Full-time faculty:** 178 total; 10% have terminal degrees, 10% minority, 60% women. **Part-time faculty:** 575 total; 6% have terminal degrees, 9% minority, 48% women. **Class size:** 43% < 20, 57% 20-39, less than 1% 40-49, less than 1% 50-99. **Special facilities:** Nature study area, center for contemporary technology, fine and performing arts center, business and conference center.

Student profile. Among degree-seeking undergraduates, 62% enrolled in a transfer program, 34% enrolled in a vocational program, 3% already have a bachelor's degree or higher, 1,194 enrolled as first-time, first-year students, 239 transferred in from other institutions.

Part-time:	52%	Hispanic American:	16%
Women:	53%	International:	2%
African American:	10%	25 or older:	32%
Asian American:	2%		

Transfer out. 88% of students enrolled in the transfer program go on to 4-year colleges. **Colleges most students transferred to 2011:** Governors State University, St. Xavier University, University of Illinois Chicago, Illinois State University, Lewis University.

Basis for selection. Open admission, but selective for some programs. Some health science programs have special admission requirements and limited enrollment. Placement tests may be waived for students with specified ACT scores. COMPASS tests required of all full-time students. **Learning Disabled:** Students should register with Center for Disability Services before May 1.

High school preparation. College-preparatory program recommended. 15 units required. Required units include English 4, mathematics 2, social studies 2, science 2 (laboratory 2) and academic electives 5.

2012-2013 Annual costs. Tuition/fees: $3,396; $8,016 out-of-district; $9,336 out-of-state. Per-credit charge: $113 in-district; $267 out-of-district; $311 out-of-state. Books/supplies: $1,608. Personal expenses: $1,724.

2010-2011 Financial aid. Need-based: 89% of total undergraduate aid awarded as scholarships/grants, 11% as loans/jobs. Need-based aid available for part-time students. Work-study available nights, weekends and for part-time students. **Non-need-based:** Scholarships awarded for academics, athletics, leadership.

Application procedures. Admission: No deadline. No application fee. Admission notification on a rolling basis. **Financial aid:** Priority date 5/1; no closing date. FAFSA, institutional form required. Applicants notified on a rolling basis starting 3/1; must reply within 4 week(s) of notification.

Academics. Special study options: Accelerated study, cooperative education, distance learning, double major, dual enrollment of high school students, ESL, honors, independent study, internships, liberal arts/career combination, study abroad, weekend college. License preparation in paramedic. **Credit/placement by examination:** AP, CLEP, institutional tests. **Support services:** GED preparation and test center, learning center, reduced course load, remedial instruction, study skills assistance, tutoring, writing center.

Majors. Business: General, administrative services, business admin, hospitality admin, human resources, management information systems, retailing, small business admin, tourism/travel. **Computer sciences:** LAN/WAN management, security, webmaster. **Education:** Mathematics, science, special ed, teacher assistance. **Health services:** EMT paramedic, medical records technology, nursing (RN), radiologic technology/medical imaging, recreational therapy, respiratory therapy technology, substance abuse counseling. **Liberal arts:** Arts/sciences. **Parks/recreation:** Facilities management. **Protective services:** Fire safety technology, firefighting, police science. **Visual/performing arts:** General, graphic design. **Work/family studies:** Child care service.

Most popular majors. Health sciences 11%, interdisciplinary studies 44%, liberal arts 28%.

Computing on campus. 2,000 workstations in library, computer center, student center. Commuter students can connect to campus network. Online course registration, online library, helpline, wireless network available.

Student life. Freshman orientation: Available. Preregistration for classes offered. Students registering for 12 or more credit hours required to participate in orientation program prior to first registration. **Activities:** Bands, choral groups, dance, drama, international student organizations, literary magazine, music ensembles, musical theater, student government, student newspaper, Action Social and Political Empowerment club, green club, Inter-club Council, International Women's club, Peers Educating Peers, Muslim student association, Alliance for African-American students, Latin and Arab student groups.

Athletics. NJCAA. **Intercollegiate:** Baseball M, basketball, cross-country, golf M, soccer, softball W, tennis, volleyball W. **Intramural:** Badminton W, basketball, football (non-tackle) M, volleyball. **Team name:** Cyclones.

Student services. Adult student services, career counseling, services for economically disadvantaged, student employment services, financial aid counseling, minority student services, on-campus daycare, personal counseling, placement for graduates, women's services. **Physically disabled:** Services for visually, speech, hearing impaired. **Transfer:** Transfer center, transfer adviser, college fairs on campus for students transferring to 4-year colleges.

Contact. E-mail: admissions@morainevalley.edu
Phone: (708) 974-5355 Fax: (708) 974-0974
Mary Lou Griffin, Director of Registration, Moraine Valley Community College, 9000 West College Parkway, Palos Hills, IL 60465-2478

Morrison Institute of Technology
Morrison, Illinois
www.morrisontech.edu   CB code: 1269

- Private 2-year technical college
- Residential campus in small town

General. Founded in 1973. Accredited by Technology Accreditation Commission of Accreditation Board of Engineering and Technology. **Enrollment:** 91 degree-seeking undergraduates. **Degrees:** 34 associate awarded. **Location:** 100 miles from Chicago, 50 miles from Davenport, Iowa. **Calendar:** Semester, limited summer session. **Full-time faculty:** 1 total. **Part-time faculty:** 8 total. **Class size:** 46% < 20, 54% 20-39. **Special facilities:** 4 computer-aided design (CAD) laboratories.

Student profile.

Out-of-state:	6%	Live on campus:	70%
25 or older:	10%		

Transfer out. Colleges most students transferred to 2011: Bradley University, University of Wisconsin at Platteville.

Basis for selection. Open admission. Interview recommended.

High school preparation. Recommended units include mathematics 2 and science 1. Algebra, geometry and drafting recommended.

2011-2012 Annual costs. Tuition/fees: $15,100. Per-credit charge: $579. Room only: $2,900. Books/supplies: $850. Personal expenses: $900.

Financial aid. Need-based: Need-based aid available for part-time students. Work-study available nights, weekends and for part-time students. **Non-need-based:** Scholarships awarded for academics.

Application procedures. Admission: Priority date 8/1; no deadline. $30 fee. Admission notification on a rolling basis. **Financial aid:** No deadline. FAFSA, institutional form required. Applicants notified on a rolling basis; must reply within 2 week(s) of notification.

Academics. Special study options: Double major. **Credit/placement by examination:** AP, CLEP, IB, institutional tests. 25 credit hours maximum toward associate degree. SOC approved guidelines. **Support services:** Reduced course load, tutoring.

Majors. Architecture: Technology. **Computer sciences:** LAN/WAN management.

Computing on campus. 80 workstations in library, computer center. Dormitories wired for high-speed internet access and linked to campus network. Wireless network available.

Student life. Freshman orientation: Mandatory. Preregistration for classes offered. Five 1-hour presentations during first 5 weeks of semester. **Housing:** Guaranteed on-campus for all undergraduates. Coed dorms, special housing for disabled, wellness housing available. $100 deposit. **Activities:** Student government, student newspaper, professional societies, student chapters.

Athletics. Intramural: Basketball M, bowling, volleyball.

Student services. Career counseling, student employment services, personal counseling, placement for graduates. **Transfer:** Transfer adviser, college fairs on campus for students transferring to 4-year colleges.

Contact. E-mail: admissions@morrison.tec.il.us
Phone: (815) 772-7218 ext. 206 Fax: (815) 772-7548
Jodie Eaker, Director of Admissions, Morrison Institute of Technology, 701 Portland Avenue, Morrison, IL 61270-2959

Morton College
Cicero, Illinois   CB member
www.morton.edu   CB code: 1489

- Public 2-year community college
- Commuter campus in small city

General. Founded in 1924. Regionally accredited. **Enrollment:** 5,321 undergraduates. **Degrees:** 338 associate awarded. **Location:** 6 miles from Chicago Loop. **Calendar:** Semester, limited summer session. **Full-time faculty:** 52 total. **Part-time faculty:** 218 total. **Class size:** 44% < 20, 55% 20-39, less than 1% 40-49, less than 1% 50-99, less than 1% >100. **Special facilities:** Planetarium, natural history museum, aquarium, Western Electric museum, internet cafe. **Partnerships:** Partnership with UPS.

Transfer out. Colleges most students transferred to 2011: University of Illinois at Chicago, Northeastern Illinois University, Triton Community College, DePaul University, Moraine Valley Community College.

Basis for selection. Open admission, but selective for some programs and for out-of-state students. Nursing and physical therapist assistant programs have limited space. Preference given to in-district applicants using class rank, mathematics and science course prerequisites, and placement tests as guides.

High school preparation. 15 units required. Required units include English 4, mathematics 3, social studies 3, science 3 and academic electives 2.

2011-2012 Annual costs. Tuition/fees: $3,188; $7,284 out-of-district; $9,332 out-of-state. Per-credit charge: $79 in-district; $207 out-of-district; $271 out-of-state. Books/supplies: $1,225.

Financial aid. Need-based: Need-based aid available for part-time students. Work-study available nights, weekends and for part-time students.

Application procedures. Admission: No deadline. $10 fee. Admission notification on a rolling basis. **Financial aid:** Priority date 6/1; no closing date. FAFSA, institutional form required. Applicants notified on a rolling basis starting 8/3.

Academics. Special study options: Distance learning, double major, dual enrollment of high school students, ESL, internships, weekend college. License preparation in nursing, physical therapy. **Credit/placement by examination:** AP, CLEP, IB, institutional tests. 30 credit hours maximum toward associate degree. **Support services:** GED preparation, learning center, pre-admission summer program, remedial instruction, tutoring, writing center.

Majors. Business: Accounting, administrative services, business admin. **Computer sciences:** Information technology. **Education:** Early childhood. **English:** English lit. **Health services:** Nursing (RN), physical therapy assistant. **Liberal arts:** Arts/sciences. **Protective services:** Police science. **Visual/performing arts:** Studio arts. **Work/family studies:** Child care service.

Most popular majors. Health sciences 22%, interdisciplinary studies 13%, liberal arts 46%, security/protective services 6%.

Computing on campus. 314 workstations in library, computer center, student center. Wireless network available.

Student life. Freshman orientation: Available. Preregistration for classes offered. **Activities:** Jazz band, choral groups, dance, drama, music ensembles, musical theater, student government, student newspaper, nursing students association, Phi Theta Kappa, College Bowl, film club, Anime Gamers Union, belly dance club, Broadway club, Kosho Ryu Kempo, language and culture club, Morton Ambassador Program.

Athletics. NJCAA. **Intercollegiate:** Baseball M, basketball, cross-country, soccer M, softball W, volleyball W. **Team name:** Panthers.

Student services. Career counseling, services for economically disadvantaged, student employment services, financial aid counseling, on-campus daycare, personal counseling, placement for graduates. **Physically disabled:** Services for visually, speech, hearing impaired. **Transfer:** Pre-admission

transcript evaluation for new students. Transfer center, transfer adviser, college fairs on campus for students transferring to 4-year colleges.

Contact. E-mail: enroll@morton.edu
Phone: (708) 656-8000 ext. 346 Fax: (708) 656-9592
Victor Sanchez, Director of Student Development, Morton College, 3801 South Central Avenue, Cicero, IL 60804-4398

Northwestern College
Chicago, Illinois
www.northwesterncollege.edu   CB code: 2433

- For-profit 2-year technical and career college
- Commuter campus in very large city
- Interview required

General. Founded in 1902. Regionally accredited. Additional campuses in Bridgeview and Naperville; on-line programs available. **Enrollment:** 1,548 degree-seeking undergraduates; 221 non-degree-seeking students. **Degrees:** 194 associate awarded. **Calendar:** Quarter, extensive summer session. **Full-time faculty:** 45 total; 9% have terminal degrees, 33% minority, 67% women. **Part-time faculty:** 97 total; 13% have terminal degrees, 47% minority, 74% women. **Special facilities:** Health sciences laboratories.

Student profile. Among degree-seeking undergraduates, 401 enrolled as first-time, first-year students.

Part-time:	56%	Asian American:	2%
Women:	83%	Hispanic American:	33%
African American:	38%	Native American:	1%

Basis for selection. Open admission, but selective for some programs. Students must have a 15 ACT, 740 SAT or achieve an established score on placement exam. COMPASS or ASSET used for placement.

2011-2012 Annual costs. Tuition/fees: $20,365. Tuition may be higher for some classes.

2011-2012 Financial aid. Need-based: 62% of total undergraduate aid awarded as scholarships/grants, 38% as loans/jobs. Need-based aid available for part-time students. Work-study available nights, weekends and for part-time students. **Non-need-based:** Scholarships awarded for academics. **Additional information:** State grant programs for Illinois residents and alternative loans offered.

Application procedures. Admission: No deadline. $25 fee. Admission notification on a rolling basis. **Financial aid:** Priority date 6/30; no closing date. FAFSA, institutional form required. Applicants notified on a rolling basis starting 8/15; must reply within 4 week(s) of notification.

Academics. Students wishing to graduate early may attend summer quarter. **Special study options:** Distance learning, double major, honors, internships. **Credit/placement by examination:** AP, CLEP, institutional tests. 50 credit hours maximum toward associate degree. No more than 50 percent of the credits in the major may be earned through proficiency examinations. **Support services:** Learning center, reduced course load, remedial instruction, study skills assistance, tutoring, writing center.

Majors. Business: Accounting, business admin, human resources. **Health services:** Massage therapy, medical assistant, medical records technology, nursing education, radiologic technology/medical imaging. **Protective services:** Police science.

Most popular majors. Business/marketing 41%, health sciences 19%, legal studies 19%, security/protective services 20%.

Computing on campus. 411 workstations in library, computer center, student center. Commuter students can connect to campus network. Online course registration, wireless network available.

Student life. Freshman orientation: Mandatory. Preregistration for classes offered. Three-hour program offered day and evening. **Activities:** Honor society, clubs related to majors available.

Student services. Alcohol/substance abuse counseling, career counseling, student employment services, financial aid counseling, personal counseling, placement for graduates. **Physically disabled:** Services for visually, speech, hearing impaired. **Transfer:** Pre-admission transcript evaluation for new students. Transfer center, transfer adviser, college fairs on campus for students transferring to 4-year colleges.

Contact. Phone: (773) 481-3730 Toll-free number: (888) 205-2283 Fax: (773) 777-2861
Shahed Kasem, Director of Admissions, Northwestern College, 4829 North Lipps Ave, Chicago, IL 60630

Oakton Community College
Des Plaines, Illinois
www.oakton.edu   CB code: 1573

- Public 2-year community college
- Commuter campus in small city

General. Founded in 1969. Regionally accredited. **Enrollment:** 3,253 full-time, degree-seeking students. **Degrees:** 564 associate awarded. **Location:** 15 miles from Chicago. **Calendar:** Semester, limited summer session. **Full-time faculty:** 159 total. **Part-time faculty:** 517 total. **Special facilities:** Wildlife preserve, visual arts center, performing arts center.

Student profile.

Out-of-state:	7%	25 or older:	45%

Transfer out. Colleges most students transferred to 2011: University of Illinois-Chicago, Northeastern Illinois University, DePaul University, Loyola University-Chicago.

Basis for selection. Open admission, but selective for some programs. Special requirements for health career programs and international students. Interview required of non-nursing health career majors. **Adult students:** SAT/ACT scores not required. **Learning Disabled:** After applying for admission, students provide documentation of disability and arrange meetings for testing and registration.

2011-2012 Annual costs. Tuition/fees: $2,814; $8,720 out-of-district; $10,528 out-of-state. Per-credit charge: $91 in-district; $288 out-of-district; $348 out-of-state. Books/supplies: $800. Personal expenses: $1,000.

2010-2011 Financial aid. Need-based: 95% of total undergraduate aid awarded as scholarships/grants, 5% as loans/jobs. Need-based aid available for part-time students. Work-study available nights, weekends and for part-time students. **Non-need-based:** Scholarships awarded for academics, art, athletics, leadership, minority status, music/drama, state residency.

Application procedures. Admission: No deadline. $25 fee. Admission notification on a rolling basis. **Financial aid:** Priority date 3/1; no closing date. FAFSA, institutional form required. Applicants notified on a rolling basis starting 3/1; must reply within 2 week(s) of notification.

Academics. Special study options: Accelerated study, distance learning, dual enrollment of high school students, exchange student, honors, independent study, internships, study abroad, teacher certification program, weekend college. License preparation in nursing. **Credit/placement by examination:** AP, CLEP, institutional tests. 30 credit hours maximum toward associate degree. **Support services:** GED preparation, learning center, remedial instruction, study skills assistance, tutoring, writing center.

Majors. Business: Accounting, business admin, international, office management. **Computer sciences:** General, data processing. **Education:** Early childhood. **Engineering:** General. **Health services:** Clinical lab assistant, medical records technology, nursing (RN), physical therapy assistant. **Liberal arts:** Arts/sciences. **Protective services:** Firefighting, police science. **Visual/performing arts:** Commercial/advertising art, music.

Computing on campus. 1,100 workstations in library, computer center, student center. Commuter students can connect to campus network. Online course registration, online library, helpline, wireless network available.

Student life. Freshman orientation: Available. Preregistration for classes offered. **Activities:** Jazz band, choral groups, drama, literary magazine, music ensembles, student government, student newspaper, Christian student association, Indian student association, political science forum, black student union, Hillel, Japanese club, desktop publishing club.

Athletics. NJCAA. **Intercollegiate:** Baseball M, basketball, cross-country, golf M, soccer, softball W, tennis, track and field, volleyball W. **Intramural:** Basketball, volleyball. **Team name:** Raiders.

Student services. Adult student services, alcohol/substance abuse counseling, career counseling, student employment services, financial aid counseling, health services, minority student services, on-campus daycare, personal counseling, placement for graduates, veterans' counselor. **Transfer:** Transfer center, transfer adviser, college fairs on campus for students transferring to 4-year colleges.

Contact. E-mail: admiss@oakton.edu
Phone: (847) 635-1700 Fax: (847) 635-1706
Michele Brown, Director of Student Recruitment & Outreach, Oakton Community College, Enrollment Center, Des Plaines, IL 60016

Parkland College
Champaign, Illinois
www.parkland.edu
CB code: 1619

- Public 2-year community college
- Commuter campus in small city
- Interview required

General. Founded in 1966. Regionally accredited. Students have access to resources at University of Illinois and within certain guidelines may enroll in University of Illinois classes. **Enrollment:** 9,368 undergraduates. **Degrees:** 828 associate awarded. **ROTC:** Army, Naval, Air Force. **Location:** 136 miles from Chicago, 122 miles from Indianapolis. **Calendar:** Semester, extensive summer session. **Full-time faculty:** 169 total. **Part-time faculty:** 442 total. **Class size:** 64% < 20, 34% 20-39, less than 1% 40-49, less than 1% 50-99, less than 1% >100. **Special facilities:** Planetarium, nature preserve, agricultural technology applications center, land laboratory, theater. **Partnerships:** Formal partnerships with local businesses including CISCO Systems, Case Corporation, Microsoft, Ford ASSET, LINUX Professional Institute.

Student profile.

Out-of-state:	65%	**25 or older:**	33%

Transfer out. Colleges most students transferred to 2011: University of Illinois at Urbana-Champaign, Eastern Illinois University, Illinois State University, Southern Illinois University-Carbondale, Southern Illinois University-Edwardsville.

Basis for selection. Open admission, but selective for some programs. Acceptance does not ensure admission into particular major or enrollment in specific course. There is limited admissions to health professions and trade union programs. ACT required for health programs. **Home schooled:** Recommended that students meet with admissions adviser. **Learning Disabled:** Encouraged to contact learning disabilities specialist prior to enrolling.

High school preparation. 15 units required. Required units include English 4, mathematics 3, social studies 2, science 2, foreign language 2 and academic electives 2.

2011-2012 Annual costs. Tuition/fees: $2,970; $7,530 out-of-district; $12,450 out-of-state. Per-credit charge: $99 in-district; $251 out-of-district; $415 out-of-state. Books/supplies: $1,200. Personal expenses: $1,500.

Financial aid. Need-based: Work-study available nights, weekends and for part-time students. **Non-need-based:** Scholarships awarded for academics, art, athletics, leadership, minority status, music/drama, state residency.

Application procedures. Admission: No deadline. No application fee. Admission notification on a rolling basis. **Financial aid:** Closing date 3/1. FAFSA, institutional form required. Applicants notified on a rolling basis starting 6/1; must reply within 2 week(s) of notification.

Academics. Special study options: Accelerated study, cross-registration, distance learning, double major, dual enrollment of high school students, ESL, honors, independent study, internships, student-designed major, study abroad. Bachelor's degree programs available on campus. License preparation in dental hygiene, nursing, paramedic. **Credit/placement by examination:** AP, CLEP, SAT, ACT, institutional tests. 25 credit hours maximum toward associate degree. Institutionally-prepared proficiency exams are available. **Support services:** GED preparation and test center, learning center, reduced course load, remedial instruction, study skills assistance, tutoring, writing center.

Majors. Business: General, accounting technology, business admin, executive assistant, hotel/motel admin, marketing, selling. **Communications:** Radio/TV. **Communications technology:** Radio/TV. **Computer sciences:** Applications programming, networking. **Education:** Art, music. **Engineering: General. General:** Animal husbandry, business, landscaping, mechanization. **Health services:** Dental hygiene, nursing (RN), occupational therapy assistant, radiologic technology/medical imaging, respiratory therapy technology, surgical technology, veterinary technology/assistant. **Human services:** Social work. **Liberal arts:** Arts/sciences. **Protective services:** Fire safety technology, police science. **Visual/performing arts:** Art, commercial/advertising art, music. **Work/family studies:** Child care service.

Most popular majors. Business/marketing 14%, education 7%, health sciences 18%, interdisciplinary studies 20%, liberal arts 14%.

Computing on campus. 1,425 workstations in library, computer center. Online course registration available.

Student life. Freshman orientation: Mandatory. Preregistration for classes offered. Held at beginning of semester. **Policies:** Students may take part in activities at University of Illinois. **Housing:** Housing available at University of Illinois facilities. **Activities:** Bands, choral groups, dance, drama, international student organizations, literary magazine, music ensembles, musical theater, radio station, student government, student newspaper, TV station, black student association, Phi Theta Kappa, student nurses association, veterinary technology association, Christian Fellowship, Colours, dental assisting association, dental hygienists association.

Athletics. NJCAA. **Intercollegiate:** Baseball M, basketball, golf M, soccer, softball W, volleyball W. **Intramural:** Basketball, bowling, softball, tennis, volleyball. **Team name:** Cobras.

Student services. Adult student services, career counseling, services for economically disadvantaged, student employment services, financial aid counseling, minority student services, on-campus daycare, personal counseling, placement for graduates, veterans' counselor, women's services. **Physically disabled:** Services for visually, speech, hearing impaired. **Transfer:** Re-entry adviser, pre-admission transcript evaluation for new students. Transfer center, transfer adviser, college fairs on campus for students transferring to 4-year colleges.

Contact. E-mail: rwilhour@parkland.edu
Phone: (217) 351-2208 Toll-free number: (800) 346-8089
Fax: (217) 353-2640
Reo Wilhour, Director of Admissions and Records, Parkland College, 2400 West Bradley Avenue, Champaign, IL 61821-1899

Prairie State College
Chicago Heights, Illinois
www.prairiestate.edu
CB code: 1077

- Public 2-year community college
- Commuter campus in large town

General. Founded in 1957. Regionally accredited. **Enrollment:** 5,063 degree-seeking undergraduates. **Degrees:** 361 associate awarded. **Location:** 30 miles from Chicago. **Calendar:** Semester, limited summer session. **Full-time faculty:** 85 total. **Part-time faculty:** 200 total.

Student profile. Among degree-seeking undergraduates, 59% enrolled in a transfer program, 41% enrolled in a vocational program, 2% already have a bachelor's degree or higher.

Transfer out. Colleges most students transferred to 2011: Governors State University, University of Illinois - Urbana, Eastern Illinois University, University of Illinois - Chicago, Chicago State University.

Basis for selection. Open admission, but selective for some programs. Admission to nursing and dental hygiene programs based on GPA in required courses and test scores.

High school preparation. One unit each of chemistry and algebra required for nursing and dental programs, plus 1 unit biology for nursing.

2011-2012 Annual costs. Tuition/fees: $3,170; $8,180 out-of-district; $10,370 out-of-state. Per-credit charge: $104 in-district; $271 out-of-district; $344 out-of-state. Books/supplies: $1,680. Personal expenses: $1,700.

Financial aid. Need-based: Need-based aid available for part-time students. Work-study available nights, weekends and for part-time students.

Application procedures. Admission: No deadline. $10 fee, may be waived for applicants with need. Admission notification on a rolling basis. **Financial aid:** Closing date 7/1. FAFSA, institutional form required. Applicants notified on a rolling basis; must reply within 2 week(s) of notification.

Academics. Students completing an Associate in Arts or Science degree are guaranteed their classes will transfer to other Illinois colleges. **Special study options:** Cross-registration, distance learning, dual enrollment of high school students, ESL, honors, independent study, internships, study abroad, weekend college. License preparation in dental hygiene, nursing. **Credit/placement by examination:** AP, CLEP, institutional tests. 45 credit hours maximum toward associate degree. **Support services:** GED preparation and test center, learning center, pre-admission summer program, reduced course load, remedial instruction, study skills assistance, tutoring.

Majors. Business: Business admin. **Communications technology:** Graphics. **Computer sciences:** Information technology. **Education:** Mathematics, teacher assistance. **Health services:** Dental hygiene, EMT ambulance attendant, nursing (RN). **Liberal arts:** Arts/sciences. **Parks/recreation:** Exercise sciences. **Protective services:** Firefighting, police science. **Visual/performing arts:** Commercial photography, studio arts. **Work/family studies:** Child care service.

Most popular majors. Business/marketing 12%, education 7%, health sciences 29%, liberal arts 19%, public administration/social services 7%.

Computing on campus. 248 workstations in library, computer center, student center. Helpline available.

Student life. Freshman orientation: Available. Preregistration for classes offered. **Activities:** Jazz band, choral groups, dance, drama, musical theater, student government, student newspaper, symphony orchestra, All Latin Alliance, Black Student Union.

Athletics. Intercollegiate: Baseball M, basketball, cheerleading M, cross-country, golf M, soccer M, softball W, tennis M, volleyball W. **Team name:** Pioneers.

Student services. Career counseling, services for economically disadvantaged, student employment services, financial aid counseling, minority student services, on-campus daycare, personal counseling, placement for graduates, veterans' counselor. **Physically disabled:** Services for visually, speech, hearing impaired. **Transfer:** Transfer center, transfer adviser, college fairs on campus for students transferring to 4-year colleges.

Contact. Phone: (708) 709-3516
Jaime Miller, Director of Admissions, Prairie State College, 202 South Halsted Street, Chicago Heights, IL 60411

Rasmussen College: Aurora
Aurora, Illinois
www.rasmussen.edu

- For-profit 2-year technical college
- Small city

General. Regionally accredited. **Degrees:** 25 associate awarded. **Calendar:** Quarter. **Full-time faculty:** 3 total. **Part-time faculty:** 29 total.

Basis for selection. Open admission, but selective for some programs.

2011-2012 Annual costs. Tuition/fees: $15,750. Per-credit charge: $350. Full-time tuition varies according to program of study. Examples of per-credit-hour charges include Early Childhood Education ($310), Medical Lab Technician, Surgical Technician, Practical Nursing ($395), Professional Nursing, Information Systems Management, Multimedia Technician ($395).

Financial aid. Need-based: Work-study available nights, weekends and for part-time students.

Application procedures. Admission: No deadline. $40 fee.

Academics. Credit/placement by examination: AP, CLEP.

Majors. Business: Accounting, business admin. **Computer sciences:** Information technology, web page design. **Health services:** Massage therapy, medical transcription, pharmacy assistant. **Protective services:** Law enforcement admin.

Contact. Phone: (630) 888-3500
Susan Hammerstrom, Director of Admissions, Rasmussen College: Aurora, 2363 Sequoia Drive, Suite 131, Aurora, IL 60506

Rasmussen College: Rockford
Rockford, Illinois
www.rasmussen.edu   CB code: 5753

- For-profit 2-year technical college
- Small city

General. Regionally accredited. **Enrollment:** 879 degree-seeking undergraduates. **Degrees:** 140 associate awarded. **Calendar:** Quarter. **Full-time faculty:** 7 total. **Part-time faculty:** 34 total.

Basis for selection. Open admission, but selective for some programs.

2011-2012 Annual costs. Tuition/fees: $15,750. Per-credit charge: $350. Full-time tuition varies according to program of study. Examples of per-credit-hour charges include Early Childhood Education ($310), Medical Lab Technician, Surgical Technician, Practical Nursing ($395), Professional Nursing, Information Systems Management, Multimedia Technician ($395).

Financial aid. Need-based: Work-study available nights, weekends and for part-time students.

Application procedures. Admission: No deadline. $40 fee.

Academics. Credit/placement by examination: AP, CLEP.

Majors. Business: Accounting, business admin. **Computer sciences:** Information technology, webmaster. **Health services:** Massage therapy, medical records technology, medical transcription, pharmacy assistant. **Protective services:** Law enforcement admin.

Contact. Phone: (815) 316-4800
Susan Hammerstrom, Director of Admissions, Rasmussen College: Rockford, 6000 East State Street, Fourth Floor, Rockford, IL 61108-2513

Rasmussen College: Romeoville/Joliet
Romeoville, Illinois
www.rasmussen.edu

- For-profit 2-year career college
- Large town

General. Regionally accredited. **Enrollment:** 437 degree-seeking undergraduates. **Degrees:** 3 associate awarded. **Calendar:** Quarter. **Full-time faculty:** 1 total. **Part-time faculty:** 9 total.

Basis for selection. Open admission, but selective for some programs.

2011-2012 Annual costs. Tuition/fees: $15,750. Per-credit charge: $350. Full-time tuition varies according to program of study. Examples of per-credit-hour charges include Early Childhood Education ($310), Medical Lab Technician, Surgical Technician, Practical Nursing ($395), Professional Nursing, Information Systems Management, Multimedia Technician ($395).

Financial aid. Need-based: Work-study available nights, weekends and for part-time students.

Application procedures. Admission: No deadline. $40 fee.

Academics. Credit/placement by examination: AP, CLEP.

Contact. Susan Hammerstrom, Director of Admissions, Rasmussen College: Romeoville/Joliet, 400 West Normantown Road, Romeoville, IL 60446

Rend Lake College
Ina, Illinois
www.rlc.edu   CB code: 1673

- Public 2-year community college
- Commuter campus in rural community

General. Founded in 1955. Regionally accredited. Satellite campuses located in Mt. Vernon and Pinckneyville. **Enrollment:** 4,512 undergraduates. **Degrees:** 702 associate awarded. **Location:** 45 miles from Carbondale, 85 miles from St. Louis. **Calendar:** Semester, limited summer session. **Full-time faculty:** 66 total. **Part-time faculty:** 139 total. **Class size:** 68% < 20, 29% 20-39, 2% 40-49, less than 1% 50-99. **Special facilities:** Fitness center, aquatics center, walking/bicycle paths. **Partnerships:** Formal partnerships to provide technical training for employees of General Tire (Mt. Vernon) and Walgreens Distribution Center; mandated federal training provided to Department of Natural Resources-Mines and Minerals.

Student profile.

Out-of-state:	1%	Live on campus:	1%
25 or older:	70%		

Transfer out. Colleges most students transferred to 2011: Southern Illinois University-Carbondale, Southern Illinois University-Edwardsville, Eastern Illinois University, Southeast Missouri State University, Murray State University.

Basis for selection. Open admission, but selective for some programs. Special requirements for allied health programs. SAT, ACT, ASSET, or COMPASS scores required for degree-seeking students for placement. **Home schooled:** Provide certified documentation stating the student has never had or has officially severed his or her connection with the school system.

High school preparation. 15 units required. Required units include English 4, mathematics 3, social studies 3, science 3 (laboratory 3) and academic electives 2. Social studies units should include history and government. Electives may include foreign language, vocational education, music, or art. Lowest level math accepted is algebra 1.

2011-2012 Annual costs. Tuition/fees: $2,880; $4,360 out-of-district; $4,590 out-of-state. Per-credit charge: $93 in-district; $143 out-of-district; $150 out-of-state. Books/supplies: $900. Personal expenses: $1,636.

Financial aid. Need-based: Need-based aid available for part-time students. Work-study available nights, weekends and for part-time students. **Non-need-based:** Scholarships awarded for academics, art, athletics, leadership, music/drama, state residency.

Application procedures. Admission: No deadline. No application fee. Admission notification on a rolling basis. **Financial aid:** No deadline. FAFSA required. Applicants notified on a rolling basis starting 3/15; must reply within 4 week(s) of notification.

Academics. Special study options: Cooperative education, distance learning, dual enrollment of high school students, ESL, honors, independent study, internships, study abroad, teacher certification program. Bachelor's degree programs available on campus. License preparation in nursing, occupational therapy, paramedic, radiology, real estate. **Credit/placement by examination:** AP, CLEP, institutional tests. 16 credit hours maximum toward associate degree. Credits awarded for CLEP, proficiency exams and AP scores. **Support services:** GED preparation, learning center, remedial instruction, study skills assistance, tutoring.

Majors. Architecture: Technology. **Business:** Administrative services, business admin. **Computer sciences:** Applications programming, LAN/WAN management. **Engineering:** General. **General:** Business, horticulture, mechanization, production. **Health services:** Clinical lab technology, EMT paramedic, medical records technology, nursing (RN), occupational therapy assistant. **Liberal arts:** Arts/sciences. **Protective services:** Corrections, fire services admin, police science. **Visual/performing arts:** Art, commercial/advertising art. **Work/family studies:** Child development.

Computing on campus. 496 workstations in library, computer center. Commuter students can connect to campus network. Online library, wireless network available.

Student life. Freshman orientation: Mandatory. Preregistration for classes offered. **Activities:** Bands, choral groups, dance, drama, music ensembles, musical theater, student government, student newspaper, symphony orchestra, culinary arts club, Active College Christians, practical nursing club, automotive club, horticulture club, art league, criminal justice club.

Athletics. NJCAA. **Intercollegiate:** Baseball M, basketball, cheerleading M, cross-country, golf, softball W, tennis W, track and field, volleyball W, wrestling M. **Team name:** Warriors.

Student services. Adult student services, career counseling, services for economically disadvantaged, student employment services, financial aid counseling, on-campus daycare, personal counseling, placement for graduates, veterans' counselor. **Physically disabled:** Services for visually, speech, hearing impaired. **Transfer:** Pre-admission transcript evaluation for new students. Transfer adviser, college fairs on campus for students transferring to 4-year colleges.

Contact. E-mail: admiss@rlc.edu
Phone: (618) 437-5321 ext. 1230 Fax: (618) 437-5677
Vickie Schulte, Director of Student Records, Rend Lake College, 468 North Ken Gray Parkway, Ina, IL 62846

Richland Community College
Decatur, Illinois   **CB member**
www.richland.edu   **CB code: 0738**

- Public 2-year community college
- Commuter campus in small city

General. Founded in 1971. Regionally accredited. **Enrollment:** 3,632 undergraduates. **Degrees:** 378 associate awarded. **Location:** 180 miles from Chicago, 120 miles from St. Louis. **Calendar:** Semester, limited summer session. **Full-time faculty:** 99 total; 7% have terminal degrees, 8% minority, 48% women. **Part-time faculty:** 143 total; 6% have terminal degrees, 6% minority, 54% women. **Class size:** 76% < 20, 24% 20-39, less than 1% 40-49. **Special facilities:** Human patient simulators for allied health students.

Transfer out. Colleges most students transferred to 2011: Illinois State University, Millikin University, Southern Illinois University-Carbondale, Eastern Illinois University, University of Illinois-Springfield.

Basis for selection. Open admission, but selective for some programs. Separate admission process for allied health programs.

High school preparation. Required units include English 4, mathematics 3, social studies 3, science 3 and foreign language 2.

2011-2012 Annual costs. Tuition/fees: $2,880; $14,306 out-of-district; $18,072 out-of-state. Per-credit charge: $91 in-district; $472 out-of-district; $597 out-of-state. Books/supplies: $1,000.

Financial aid. Need-based: Need-based aid available for part-time students. Work-study available nights, weekends and for part-time students. **Non-need-based:** Scholarships awarded for academics, art, leadership, music/drama.

Application procedures. Admission: No deadline. No application fee. Admission notification on a rolling basis. **Financial aid:** Closing date 6/30. FAFSA required. Applicants notified on a rolling basis starting 3/20.

Academics. Special study options: Accelerated study, cooperative education, distance learning, double major, dual enrollment of high school students, ESL, honors, independent study, internships, liberal arts/career combination, study abroad, teacher certification program. Bachelor's degree programs available on campus. License preparation in nursing, paramedic, radiology. **Credit/placement by examination:** AP, CLEP, institutional tests. **Support services:** GED preparation, learning center, reduced course load, remedial instruction, study skills assistance, tutoring, writing center.

Majors. Biology: General. **Business:** General, accounting, hospitality admin, management information systems. **Communications:** Journalism. **Computer sciences:** General, computer graphics, computer science, data entry, programming. **Education:** General. **Engineering:** General. **English:** American lit, English lit, rhetoric/composition, writing. **Foreign languages:** French, German, Spanish. **General:** Business, horticultural science, horticulture. **Health services:** EMT paramedic, nursing (RN), radiologic technology/medical imaging, surgical technology. **History:** General. **Liberal arts:** Arts/sciences. **Math:** General. **Philosophy/religion:** Philosophy. **Physical sciences:** Planetary. **Protective services:** Criminal justice, firefighting, police science. **Psychology:** General. **Social sciences:** General, anthropology, archaeology, economics, geography, political science, sociology. **Visual/performing arts:** General, art, art history/conservation, ceramics, drawing, music, painting, sculpture.

Most popular majors. Health sciences 26%, interdisciplinary studies 24%, liberal arts 27%.

Computing on campus. 245 workstations in library, computer center. Commuter students can connect to campus network. Online course registration, online library, helpline, wireless network available.

Student life. Freshman orientation: Mandatory. Preregistration for classes offered. 2 hours, includes registering for courses, variety of times available. **Activities:** Jazz band, dance, drama, literary magazine, radio station, student government, student newspaper.

Athletics. Team name: Knights.

Student services. Adult student services, career counseling, services for economically disadvantaged, student employment services, financial aid counseling, minority student services, on-campus daycare, personal counseling, placement for graduates, veterans' counselor, women's services. **Physically disabled:** Services for visually, speech, hearing impaired. **Transfer:** Pre-admission transcript evaluation for new students. Transfer center, transfer adviser, college fairs on campus for students transferring to 4-year colleges.

Contact. E-mail: admissions@richland.edu
Phone: (217) 875-7200 ext. 257 Fax: (217) 875-7783
Cathy Sebok, Director of Admissions, Richland Community College, One College Park, Decatur, IL 62521

Rock Valley College
Rockford, Illinois   **CB member**
www.rockvalleycollege.edu   **CB code: 1674**

- Public 2-year community college
- Commuter campus in small city

General. Founded in 1964. Regionally accredited. **Enrollment:** 7,774 degree-seeking undergraduates; 1,075 non-degree-seeking students. **Degrees:** 965 associate awarded. **Location:** 85 miles from Chicago. **Calendar:** Semester, limited summer session. **Full-time faculty:** 157 total; 18% have terminal degrees, 11% minority, 52% women. **Part-time faculty:** 267 total; 4% have terminal degrees, 9% minority, 46% women. **Special facilities:** Outdoor theater with retractable roof. **Partnerships:** Formal partnership with CISCO.

Student profile. Among degree-seeking undergraduates, 3% already have a bachelor's degree or higher, 1,429 enrolled as first-time, first-year students, 278 transferred in from other institutions.

Part-time:	50%	Asian American:	1%
Out-of-state:	2%	Hispanic American:	9%
Women:	57%	25 or older:	40%
African American:	11%		

Transfer out. Colleges most students transferred to 2011: Northern Illinois University, Illinois State University, Western Illinois University, Rockford College, University of Illinois.

Basis for selection. Open admission, but selective for some programs. Special requirements for nursing, respiratory therapy, dental hygiene, and surgical technology programs. **Adult students:** Must submit ACT or SAT scores, proof of successful performance in college, or complete ACCUPLACER placement test. **Learning Disabled:** Students are encouraged to access services through the coordinator of disability services.

High school preparation. College-preparatory program recommended. 15 units required. Required units include English 4, mathematics 3, social studies 3, science 3 (laboratory 3) and academic electives 2.

2011-2012 Annual costs. Tuition/fees: $2,804; $8,234 out-of-district; $13,994 out-of-state. Books/supplies: $1,400. Personal expenses: $900.

2010-2011 Financial aid. Need-based: 74% of total undergraduate aid awarded as scholarships/grants, 26% as loans/jobs. Need-based aid available for part-time students. Work-study available nights, weekends and for part-time students. **Non-need-based:** Scholarships awarded for academics, ROTC.

Application procedures. Admission: No deadline. No application fee. Admission notification on a rolling basis. **Financial aid:** Closing date 5/1. FAFSA required. Applicants notified on a rolling basis starting 4/1; must reply within 4 week(s) of notification.

Academics. Special study options: Cooperative education, distance learning, dual enrollment of high school students, ESL, external degree, honors, independent study, internships, liberal arts/career combination, student-designed major, study abroad. License preparation in aviation, dental hygiene, nursing. **Credit/placement by examination:** AP, CLEP, institutional tests. 39 credit hours maximum toward associate degree. **Support services:** GED preparation, learning center, reduced course load, remedial instruction, study skills assistance, tutoring, writing center.

Majors. Business: General, accounting, administrative services, business admin, logistics, marketing. **Computer sciences:** General. **Health services:** Medical records technology, nursing (RN), respiratory therapy technology. **Liberal arts:** Arts/sciences. **Protective services:** Firefighting, law enforcement admin. **Work/family studies:** Child care management.

Most popular majors. Health sciences 10%, interdisciplinary studies 14%, liberal arts 58%.

Computing on campus. 225 workstations in library, computer center, student center. Commuter students can connect to campus network. Online course registration, online library, helpline, wireless network available.

Student life. Freshman orientation: Available. Preregistration for classes offered. 2-part process with educational planning session followed by a multi-week College Success course. **Activities:** Bands, choral groups, dance, drama, international student organizations, literary magazine, music ensembles, musical theater, opera, student government, student newspaper, 26 student clubs.

Athletics. NJCAA. **Intercollegiate:** Baseball M, basketball, golf M, softball W, tennis, volleyball W. **Team name:** Eagles.

Student services. Adult student services, career counseling, student employment services, financial aid counseling, personal counseling, placement for graduates, veterans' counselor. **Physically disabled:** Services for visually, speech, hearing impaired. **Transfer:** Pre-admission transcript evaluation for new students. Transfer adviser, college fairs on campus for students transferring to 4-year colleges.

Contact. E-mail: RVC-Admissions@rockvalleycollege.edu
Phone: (815) 921-4250 Fax: (815) 921-4269
Jennifer Thompson, Admissions Director, Rock Valley College, 3301 North Mulford Road, Rockford, IL 61114-5699

Rockford Career College
Rockford, Illinois
www.rockfordcareercollege.edu

CB code: 2459

- For-profit 2-year career college
- Commuter campus in small city
- Interview required

General. Founded in 1862. Accredited by ACICS. **Enrollment:** 670 degree-seeking undergraduates; 21 non-degree-seeking students. **Degrees:** 144 associate awarded. **Location:** 90 miles from Chicago, 75 miles from Madison, Wisconsin. **Calendar:** Quarter, extensive summer session. **Full-time faculty:** 17 total; 6% have terminal degrees, 18% minority, 59% women. **Part-time faculty:** 39 total; 3% have terminal degrees, 5% minority, 62% women. **Class size:** 88% < 20, 11% 20-39, 1% 40-49.

Student profile. Among degree-seeking undergraduates, 100% enrolled in a vocational program, 1% already have a bachelor's degree or higher, 100 enrolled as first-time, first-year students.

Part-time:	61%	Asian American:	1%
Women:	82%	Hispanic American:	8%
African American:	32%	25 or older:	34%

Transfer out. Colleges most students transferred to 2011: Upper Iowa University, Judson University.

Basis for selection. Open admission.

2011-2012 Annual costs. Tuition/fees: $9,000. Per-credit charge: $250. Books/supplies: $800. Personal expenses: $2,880.

2010-2011 Financial aid. All financial aid based on need. 671 full-time freshmen applied for aid; 621 were judged to have need; 621 of these received aid. Average need met was 29%. Average scholarship/grant was $5,550; average loan $9,500. 31% of total undergraduate aid awarded as scholarships/grants, 69% as loans/jobs. Need-based aid available for part-time students. Work-study available nights, weekends and for part-time students.

Application procedures. Admission: No deadline. $150 fee. Application must be submitted on paper. Admission notification on a rolling basis. **Financial aid:** No deadline. FAFSA required. Applicants notified on a rolling basis.

Academics. Special study options: Distance learning, independent study, internships. **Credit/placement by examination:** AP, CLEP, IB, institutional tests. 50 credit hours maximum toward associate degree. **Support services:** Study skills assistance, tutoring.

Majors. Business: Accounting, business admin, marketing. **Computer sciences:** General, data processing, information systems. **Health services:** Massage therapy, medical assistant, medical secretary, pharmacy assistant, veterinary technology/assistant.

Most popular majors. Business/marketing 14%, computer/information sciences 8%, health sciences 46%.

Computing on campus. 75 workstations in library, computer center. Online library, repair service, wireless network available.

Student life. Freshman orientation: Mandatory. Preregistration for classes offered. **Activities:** Student newspaper.

Student services. Career counseling, student employment services, financial aid counseling, placement for graduates. **Transfer:** Pre-admission transcript evaluation for new students.

Contact. E-mail: info@rockfordcareercollege.edu
Phone: (815) 965-8616 Toll-free number: (866) 722-4632
Fax: (815) 965-0360
David Julius, Director of Admissions, Rockford Career College, 1130 South Alpine Road, Rockford, IL 61108

Sauk Valley Community College
Dixon, Illinois
www.svcc.edu

CB code: 1780

- Public 2-year community college
- Commuter campus in large town

General. Founded in 1965. Regionally accredited. **Enrollment:** 2,063 degree-seeking undergraduates; 441 non-degree-seeking students. **Degrees:** 267 associate awarded. **Location:** 110 miles from Chicago. **Calendar:** Semester, limited summer session. **Full-time faculty:** 40 total; 12% have

terminal degrees, 2% minority, 45% women. **Part-time faculty:** 106 total; 8% have terminal degrees, 6% minority, 60% women. **Class size:** 60% < 20, 36% 20-39, 3% 40-49, less than 1% 50-99. **Special facilities:** Observatory, prairie plots.

Student profile. Among degree-seeking undergraduates, 51% enrolled in a transfer program, 49% enrolled in a vocational program, 1% already have a bachelor's degree or higher, 337 enrolled as first-time, first-year students, 1 transferred in from other institutions.

Part-time:	47%	Hispanic American:	7%
Women:	60%	25 or older:	58%
African American:	4%	Live on campus:	1%
Asian American:	1%		

Transfer out. 54% of students enrolled in the transfer program go on to 4-year colleges. **Colleges most students transferred to 2011:** Northern Illinois University, Illinois State University, Western Illinois University, University of Illinois, Southern Illinois University.

Basis for selection. Open admission, but selective for some programs. Special requirements for health programs: academic record, state residency important; class rank, test scores considered. Placement exam required of all students who plan to enroll in English or math courses. **Home schooled:** Transcript of courses and grades required.

High school preparation. 15 units recommended. Recommended units include English 4, mathematics 3, social studies 2, science 2 (laboratory 2) and academic electives 4. Special course requirements for health programs.

2011-2012 Annual costs. Tuition/fees: $2,970; $7,650 out-of-district; $8,970 out-of-state. Per-credit charge: $99 in-district; $255 out-of-district; $289 out-of-state. Books/supplies: $1,237. Personal expenses: $1,575.

2010-2011 Financial aid. Need-based: 182 full-time freshmen applied for aid; 164 were judged to have need; 141 of these received aid. Average need met was 41%. Average scholarship/grant was $4,655; average loan $2,033. 82% of total undergraduate aid awarded as scholarships/grants, 18% as loans/jobs. Work-study available nights, weekends and for part-time students. **Non-need-based:** Awarded to 557 full-time undergraduates, including 96 freshmen. Scholarships awarded for academics, athletics, minority status, state residency.

Application procedures. Admission: No deadline. No application fee. Admission notification on a rolling basis. **Financial aid:** Priority date 3/1; no closing date. FAFSA, institutional form required. Applicants notified on a rolling basis starting 5/1; must reply within 4 week(s) of notification.

Academics. Special study options: Cooperative education, distance learning, dual enrollment of high school students, ESL, honors, independent study, internships. License preparation in nursing, paramedic, radiology. **Credit/placement by examination:** AP, CLEP, institutional tests. 30 credit hours maximum toward associate degree. Both CLEP and DANTES exams are used. **Support services:** GED preparation and test center, learning center, remedial instruction, study skills assistance, tutoring, writing center.

Majors. Business: Accounting, administrative services, business admin, selling. **Communications:** General, media studies. **Communications technology:** Desktop publishing. **Computer sciences:** Data entry, LAN/WAN management, programming. **Education:** Mathematics, special ed, teacher assistance. **Engineering:** General. **General:** Business. **Health services:** EMT paramedic, medical secretary, nursing (RN), radiologic technology/medical imaging. **Human services:** Social work. **Liberal arts:** Arts/sciences. **Protective services:** Corrections, police science. **Visual/performing arts:** Music, studio arts. **Work/family studies:** Child care service.

Most popular majors. Business/marketing 9%, health sciences 21%, interdisciplinary studies 38%, liberal arts 20%.

Computing on campus. 120 workstations in library, computer center, student center. Dormitories wired for high-speed internet access. Online library, helpline, wireless network available.

Student life. Freshman orientation: Mandatory, $99 fee. Preregistration for classes offered. 15 hours held throughout first semester or prior to start of semester. **Housing:** Apartments available. **Activities:** Bands, choral groups, drama, music ensembles, student government, symphony orchestra, Association of Latin American Students, Campus Crusade for Christ, Phi Theta Kappa.

Athletics. NJCAA. **Intercollegiate:** Baseball M, basketball, cheerleading M, cross-country, golf M, softball W, tennis, volleyball W. **Team name:** Skyhawks.

Student services. Adult student services, career counseling, services for economically disadvantaged, student employment services, financial aid counseling, minority student services, veterans' counselor. **Physically disabled:** Services for visually, speech, hearing impaired. **Transfer:** Preadmission transcript evaluation for new students. Transfer center, transfer adviser, college fairs on campus for students transferring to 4-year colleges.

Contact. E-mail: admissionsvc@svcc.edu
Phone: (815) 288-5511 ext. 343 Fax: (815) 288-3190
Pamela Medema, Registrar, Sauk Valley Community College, 173 Illinois Route 2, Dixon, IL 61021-9112

Shawnee Community College
Ullin, Illinois
www.shawneecc.edu　　　　　　　　　　　　**CB code: 0882**

▶ Public 2-year community college
▶ Commuter campus in rural community

General. Founded in 1967. Regionally accredited. Extension centers in Anna, Cairo, and Metropolis. **Enrollment:** 1,937 degree-seeking undergraduates. **Degrees:** 276 associate awarded. **ROTC:** Army, Naval, Air Force. **Location:** 40 miles from Paducah, Kentucky. **Calendar:** Semester, extensive summer session. **Full-time faculty:** 39 total; 3% have terminal degrees, 3% minority, 72% women. **Part-time faculty:** 139 total; 5% have terminal degrees, 12% minority, 55% women. **Class size:** 86% < 20, 11% 20-39, 2% 40-49, less than 1% 50-99, less than 1% >100.

Student profile. Among degree-seeking undergraduates, 73% enrolled in a transfer program, 8% enrolled in a vocational program, 10% already have a bachelor's degree or higher.

African American:	17%	Hispanic American:	3%

Basis for selection. Open admission, but selective for some programs. Applicants for allied health programs selected on basis of entrance examination score. ACT recommended for placement and counseling. Interview recommended for art, music, speech majors. Audition recommended for speech and music majors. Portfolio recommended for art majors.

High school preparation. 15 units recommended. Recommended units include English 4, mathematics 3, social studies 3, science 3 and foreign language 2. 2 units recommended in foreign language, music, or art. Transfer program applicants must have state mandated high school course requirements or demonstrate proficiency through placement tests.

2011-2012 Annual costs. Tuition/fees: $2,760; $4,140 out-of-district; $4,620 out-of-state. Per-credit charge: $92 in-district; $138 out-of-district; $154 out-of-state. Books/supplies: $972. Personal expenses: $623.

2011-2012 Financial aid. All financial aid based on need. 81 full-time freshmen applied for aid; 80 were judged to have need; 80 of these received aid. Average scholarship/grant was $1,265. 99% of total undergraduate aid awarded as scholarships/grants, 1% as loans/jobs. Need-based aid available for part-time students. Work-study available nights, weekends and for part-time students.

Application procedures. Admission: No deadline. No application fee. Admission notification on a rolling basis beginning on or about 1/15. **Financial aid:** Priority date 9/1; no closing date. FAFSA required. Applicants notified on a rolling basis; must reply within 2 week(s) of notification.

Academics. Special study options: Cooperative education, distance learning, dual enrollment of high school students, honors, independent study, internships, liberal arts/career combination. License preparation in nursing, occupational therapy, paramedic, real estate. **Credit/placement by examination:** AP, CLEP, institutional tests. 15 credit hours maximum toward associate degree. **Support services:** GED preparation and test center, learning center, pre-admission summer program, remedial instruction, study skills assistance, tutoring, writing center.

Majors. Business: General, accounting, management science. **Conservation:** Forestry, wildlife/wilderness. **General:** Business, horticulture. **Health services:** Medical records technology, medical secretary. **Liberal arts:** Arts/sciences. **Work/family studies:** Family/community services, food/nutrition.

Computing on campus. 120 workstations in library, computer center, student center. Online course registration, online library, helpline, wireless network available.

Student life. Freshman orientation: Mandatory. Preregistration for classes offered. **Activities:** Concert band, choral groups, dance, drama, music ensembles, musical theater, student government, student newspaper.

Athletics. NJCAA. **Intercollegiate:** Baseball M, basketball, softball W, volleyball W. **Intramural:** Baseball M, basketball, volleyball. **Team name:** Saints.

Student services. Career counseling, services for economically disadvantaged, student employment services, financial aid counseling, on-campus daycare, personal counseling, placement for graduates, veterans' counselor. **Physically disabled:** Services for visually, speech, hearing impaired. **Transfer:** Pre-admission transcript evaluation for new students. Transfer center, transfer adviser, college fairs on campus for students transferring to 4-year colleges.

Contact. E-mail: admissions@shawneecc.edu
Phone: (618) 634-3247 Fax: (618) 634-3346
Dee Blakely, Dean of Student Services, Shawnee Community College, 8364 Shawnee College Road, Ullin, IL 62992

South Suburban College of Cook County
South Holland, Illinois
www.ssc.edu
CB code: 1806

- Public 2-year community college
- Commuter campus in large town

General. Founded in 1927. Regionally accredited. **Enrollment:** 2,769 full-time, degree-seeking students. **Degrees:** 390 associate awarded. **Location:** 20 miles from downtown. **Calendar:** Semester, limited summer session. **Full-time faculty:** 282 total. **Part-time faculty:** 418 total.

Student profile.

Out-of-state:	5%	25 or older:	54%

Transfer out. Colleges most students transferred to 2011: Governors State University, University of Illinois-Chicago, Purdue University-Calumet, Chicago State University.

Basis for selection. Open admission, but selective for some programs. Separate requirements for health career programs. Audition recommended for music majors. **Home schooled:** Transcript of courses and grades required. Notorized. **Learning Disabled:** Students need to self-declare with counseling center. Accommodations provided as needed.

High school preparation. 15 units required; 18 recommended. Required and recommended units include English 4, mathematics 2-3, social studies 2, science 2 (laboratory 1) and academic electives 4.

2011-2012 Annual costs. Tuition/fees: $3,773; $9,113 out-of-district; $10,763 out-of-state. Per-credit charge: $110 in-district; $288 out-of-district; $343 out-of-state. Chicago residents or those residing or employed in Lake County, Indiana, may qualify for tuition rate of $115 per credit hour for some programs. Books/supplies: $1,200. Personal expenses: $1,200.

2011-2012 Financial aid. Need-based: 162 full-time freshmen applied for aid; 160 were judged to have need; 160 of these received aid. Average need met was 70%. Average scholarship/grant was $4,893. 99% of total undergraduate aid awarded as scholarships/grants, 1% as loans/jobs. Need-based aid available for part-time students. Work-study available nights, weekends and for part-time students. **Non-need-based:** Scholarships awarded for academics, art, athletics, music/drama, state residency.

Application procedures. Admission: No deadline. No application fee. Application must be submitted on paper. Admission notification on a rolling basis. **Financial aid:** Priority date 7/11; no closing date. FAFSA required. Applicants notified on a rolling basis starting 5/1.

Academics. Special study options: Distance learning, double major, dual enrollment of high school students, ESL, honors, internships, liberal arts/career combination, study abroad. License preparation in nursing, occupational therapy, paramedic, radiology, real estate. **Credit/placement by examination:** AP, CLEP, institutional tests. 15 credit hours maximum toward associate degree. ECEP (institutional evaluation/award process), DANTES accepted. **Support services:** GED preparation and test center, learning center, reduced course load, remedial instruction, study skills assistance, tutoring, writing center.

Majors. Biology: General, biomedical sciences. **Business:** General, accounting, administrative services, fashion, finance, marketing, office management. **Computer sciences:** General. **Education:** General, early childhood, special ed, teacher assistance. **Engineering:** General, engineering science. **English:** English lit. **Foreign languages:** Spanish. **Health services:** Medical radiologic technology/radiation therapy, nursing (RN), occupational therapy assistant, pharmacy assistant. **History:** General. **Liberal arts:** Arts/sciences. **Math:** General. **Parks/recreation:** Health/fitness, sports admin. **Philosophy/religion:** Philosophy. **Physical sciences:** Astronomy, chemistry, geology, physics. **Protective services:** Criminal justice. **Psychology:** General. **Social sciences:** Anthropology, economics, geography, political science, sociology. **Visual/performing arts:** Dramatic, music, studio arts.

Computing on campus. 1,500 workstations in library, computer center, student center. Online course registration, online library, helpline, repair service, wireless network available.

Student life. Freshman orientation: Mandatory. Preregistration for classes offered. Continuous orientation program; specialized high school student success program in summer. **Activities:** Bands, choral groups, drama, literary magazine, music ensembles, student government, TV station, business professionals, veterans organization, paralegal association, occupational therapy organization, human service club, Creative Dimensions, nursing club.

Athletics. NJCAA. **Intercollegiate:** Baseball M, basketball, soccer M, softball W, volleyball W. **Intramural:** Baseball M, basketball, softball, volleyball. **Team name:** Bulldogs.

Student services. Career counseling, student employment services, financial aid counseling, on-campus daycare, personal counseling, veterans' counselor. **Physically disabled:** Services for visually, speech, hearing impaired. **Transfer:** Transfer center, transfer adviser, college fairs on campus for students transferring to 4-year colleges.

Contact. E-mail: admissions@ssc.edu
Phone: (708) 596-2000 ext. 2329 Fax: (708) 225-5806
Robin Rihacek, Director of Enrollment Services, South Suburban College of Cook County, 15800 South State Street, South Holland, IL 60473

Southeastern Illinois College
Harrisburg, Illinois
www.sic.edu
CB code: 1777

- Public 2-year community college
- Commuter campus in small town

General. Founded in 1960. Regionally accredited. **Enrollment:** 1,067 degree-seeking undergraduates. **Degrees:** 196 associate awarded. **Location:** 45 miles from Carbondale, 65 miles from Evansville, Indiana. **Calendar:** Semester, extensive summer session. **Full-time faculty:** 48 total; 12% have terminal degrees, 4% minority, 44% women. **Part-time faculty:** 72 total; 4% have terminal degrees, 4% minority, 60% women. **Class size:** 77% < 20, 21% 20-39, 1% 40-49, less than 1% 50-99, less than 1% >100. **Special facilities:** Game preserve management facility, archery range, fire science center, burn tunnel. **Partnerships:** Formal partnership with Cummins Corporation for diesel technology.

Student profile.

African American:	4%	Hispanic American:	1%
Asian American:	1%	25 or older:	60%

Transfer out. Colleges most students transferred to 2011: Southern Illinois University at Carbondale.

Basis for selection. Open admission, but selective for some programs. Special requirements for nursing, medical records, health information technology, surgical nurse, occupational therapy assistant, and conservation game management programs. Psychological Services Bureau-Health Occupations Examination required for medical laboratory technician, ASSET for health information systems. TEAS test required for associate degree and practical nursing programs. **Home schooled:** Transcript of courses and grades required.

High school preparation. 15 units recommended. Recommended units include English 4, mathematics 3, social studies 3, science 3 and academic electives 2.

2011-2012 Annual costs. Tuition/fees: $2,760; $4,290 out-of-district; $4,530 out-of-state. Per-credit charge: $88 in-district; $139 out-of-district; $147 out-of-state. Books/supplies: $450. Personal expenses: $1,357.

2010-2011 Financial aid. Need-based: 89 full-time freshmen applied for aid; 66 were judged to have need; 65 of these received aid. Average need met was 48%. Average scholarship/grant was $3,389. Need-based aid available for part-time students. Work-study available nights, weekends and for part-time students. **Non-need-based:** Awarded to 298 full-time undergraduates, including 84 freshmen. Scholarships awarded for academics, alumni affiliation, art, athletics, music/drama.

Application procedures. Admission: No deadline. No application fee. Admission notification on a rolling basis beginning on or about 5/1. **Financial aid:** No deadline. FAFSA required. Applicants notified on a rolling basis starting 4/15; must reply within 2 week(s) of notification.

Academics. Special study options: Cross-registration, distance learning, double major, dual enrollment of high school students, independent study, internships, student-designed major. Bachelor's degree programs available

on campus. License preparation in nursing. **Credit/placement by examination:** AP, CLEP, institutional tests. 29 credit hours maximum toward associate degree. **Support services:** GED preparation and test center, learning center, pre-admission summer program, reduced course load, remedial instruction, tutoring.

Majors. Business: Administrative services, business admin, office technology. **Computer sciences:** Information systems, LAN/WAN management. **Conservation:** Wildlife/wilderness. **Education:** General. **Health services:** Clinical lab technology, medical records technology, nursing (RN), occupational therapy assistant, office assistant. **Liberal arts:** Arts/sciences. **Math:** General. **Protective services:** Police science. **Work/family studies:** Child care management.

Most popular majors. Health sciences 14%, trade and industry 13%.

Computing on campus. 75 workstations in library, computer center. Online course registration, repair service, wireless network available.

Student life. Freshman orientation: Available. Preregistration for classes offered. Individual orientation/advisement/registration appointments held for degree-seeking students. **Activities:** Concert band, choral groups, drama, music ensembles, musical theater, student government, student newspaper, art club, math and science club, BASIC, Students in Free Enterprise, Phi Theta Kappa, Phi Beta Lambda, Theta Sigma Phi, Student Association of Family and Consumer Sciences, forensics club.

Athletics. NJCAA. **Intercollegiate:** Baseball M, basketball, softball W. **Intramural:** Basketball. **Team name:** Falcons.

Student services. Career counseling, student employment services, financial aid counseling, on-campus daycare, personal counseling, placement for graduates, veterans' counselor. **Physically disabled:** Services for visually, hearing impaired. **Transfer:** Transfer adviser, college fairs on campus for students transferring to 4-year colleges.

Contact. E-mail: admissions@sic.edu
Phone: (618) 252-5400 ext. 2441 Toll-free number: (866) 338-2742
Fax: (618) 252-3062
Tabitha Neal, Admission Specialist, Southeastern Illinois College, 3575 College Road, Harrisburg, IL 62946

Southwestern Illinois College
Belleville, Illinois
www.swic.edu   CB code: 1057

▶ Public 2-year community college
▶ Commuter campus in small city

General. Founded in 1946. Regionally accredited. Campuses at Belleville, Granite City and Red Bud. Extension centers in 24 locations throughout the district. **Enrollment:** 12,779 undergraduates. **Degrees:** 1,304 associate awarded. **ROTC:** Army, Air Force. **Location:** 20 miles from St. Louis. **Calendar:** Semester, limited summer session. **Full-time faculty:** 1 total. **Part-time faculty:** 8 total. **Class size:** 69% < 20, 30% 20-39, less than 1% 40-49, less than 1% 50-99, less than 1% >100. **Special facilities:** Greenhouse solar collector, native tree arboretum, interactive video classrooms, art center.

Student profile.

Out-of-state: 1%   **25 or older:**   45%

Basis for selection. Open admission, but selective for some programs. Special requirements for health career programs and associate degrees in arts, fine arts, teaching, science, or engineering science. All applicants required to take COMPASS and ASSET tests. Applicants to allied health programs to contact college advisor. **Home schooled:** Must take a placement test or submit ACT or SAT scores.

High school preparation. 15 units recommended. Recommended units include English 4, mathematics 2, social studies 3, science 3 and foreign language 1. 1 of music, art, or vocational education recommended.

2011-2012 Annual costs. Tuition/fees: $2,970; $7,050 out-of-district; $11,250 out-of-state. Per-credit charge: $95 in-district; $231 out-of-district; $371 out-of-state. Books/supplies: $500. Personal expenses: $1,320.

Financial aid. Need-based: Need-based aid available for part-time students. Work-study available nights, weekends and for part-time students. **Non-need-based:** Scholarships awarded for academics, athletics.

Application procedures. Admission: No deadline. No application fee. Application must be submitted on paper. Admission notification on a rolling basis beginning on or about 4/16. **Financial aid:** Closing date 5/31. FAFSA,

institutional form required. Applicants notified on a rolling basis starting 7/1; must reply within 2 week(s) of notification.

Academics. Special study options: Accelerated study, distance learning, double major, dual enrollment of high school students, ESL, independent study, internships, study abroad, weekend college. **Credit/placement by examination:** AP, CLEP, institutional tests. 16 credit hours maximum toward associate degree. 30 hours of credit may be awarded for successful completion of CLEP tests. **Support services:** Learning center, reduced course load, remedial instruction, study skills assistance, tutoring, writing center.

Majors. Biology: General. **Business:** General, accounting, business admin, hospitality admin, management information systems, management science, office/clerical, sales/distribution. **Communications:** Communications/speech/rhetoric. **Communications technology:** General. **Computer sciences:** General, applications programming, computer science, data processing, information systems, programming. **Education:** Early childhood, elementary, middle, secondary. **Engineering:** General. **English:** English lit, rhetoric/composition. **Foreign languages:** General. **General:** Greenhouse operations, horticulture, landscaping, nursery operations, turf management. **Health services:** Clinical lab assistant, clinical lab technology, EMT paramedic, medical assistant, medical radiologic technology/radiation therapy, medical records technology, nursing (RN), physical therapy assistant, premedicine, prepharmacy, preveterinary, respiratory therapy technology. **History:** General. **Human services:** Social work. **Liberal arts:** Arts/sciences. **Math:** General. **Parks/recreation:** Health/fitness. **Philosophy/religion:** Philosophy. **Physical sciences:** Astronomy, chemistry, physics. **Protective services:** Firefighting, police science, security services. **Psychology:** General. **Social sciences:** Anthropology, archaeology, economics, geography, political science, sociology. **Visual/performing arts:** Art, dramatic, music, photography, studio arts. **Work/family studies:** Child care management.

Computing on campus. 250 workstations in library, computer center. Wireless network available.

Student life. Freshman orientation: Mandatory. Preregistration for classes offered. **Activities:** Bands, choral groups, drama, literary magazine, music ensembles, student government, student newspaper, minority transfer center, Black Affairs Council, physically challenged organization, Campus Christian Fellowship, international student organization.

Athletics. NJCAA. **Intercollegiate:** Baseball M, basketball, golf, soccer, softball W, volleyball W. **Intramural:** Basketball, bowling, football (non-tackle), softball, tennis, volleyball. **Team name:** Blue Storm.

Student services. Adult student services, career counseling, student employment services, minority student services, on-campus daycare, personal counseling, placement for graduates, veterans' counselor. **Physically disabled:** Services for visually, speech, hearing impaired. **Transfer:** Transfer adviser, college fairs on campus for students transferring to 4-year colleges.

Contact. E-mail: admissions@swic.edu
Phone: (618) 235-2700 ext. 5526 Fax: (618) 222-9768
Michelle Birk, Director of Admissions, Southwestern Illinois College, 2500 Carlyle Avenue, Belleville, IL 62221-5899

Spoon River College
Canton, Illinois
www.src.edu   CB code: 1154

▶ Public 2-year community college
▶ Commuter campus in large town

General. Founded in 1959. Regionally accredited. **Enrollment:** 1,966 undergraduates. **Degrees:** 235 associate awarded. **ROTC:** Army. **Location:** 35 miles from Peoria. **Calendar:** Semester, limited summer session. **Full-time faculty:** 34 total. **Part-time faculty:** 123 total. **Special facilities:** Natural arboretum, walking trail, agricultural test plots.

Transfer out. Colleges most students transferred to 2011: Western Illinois University.

Basis for selection. Open admission, but selective for some programs. Special requirements for nursing program. All students must take COMPASS exam for placement; if score indicates, student must be remediated before taking college-level courses. College-preparatory program recommended for transfer degree programs. Vocational students not required to have specific high school courses.

High school preparation. College-preparatory program recommended. 15 units recommended. Recommended units include English 4, mathematics 3, social studies 3, science 3 (laboratory 3) and academic electives 2.

2011-2012 Annual costs. Tuition/fees: $3,090; $6,960 out-of-district; $8,040 out-of-state. Per-credit charge: $91 in-district; $220 out-of-district; $256 out-of-state. Books/supplies: $600.

Financial aid. Need-based: Need-based aid available for part-time students. Work-study available nights, weekends and for part-time students. **Non-need-based:** Scholarships awarded for academics, art, athletics, music/drama, state residency. **Additional information:** Students who have submitted all required forms by the processing deadline are guaranteed to have aid eligibility established by the tuition deadline. All forms submitted after the processing deadline are processed in the order received on a continuing basis.

Application procedures. Admission: No deadline. No application fee. Admission notification on a rolling basis. **Financial aid:** Closing date 7/1. FAFSA required. Applicants notified on a rolling basis starting 5/15.

Academics. Special study options: Distance learning, dual enrollment of high school students, ESL, honors, internships. License preparation in nursing. **Credit/placement by examination:** AP, CLEP, IB, institutional tests. 32 credit hours maximum toward associate degree. Maximum 50% of credit hours toward degree may be awarded through CLEP. **Support services:** GED preparation, learning center, reduced course load, remedial instruction, study skills assistance, tutoring, writing center.

Majors. Business: General, administrative services, managerial economics. **Computer sciences:** Information technology, web page design. **Conservation:** Management/policy. **Education:** Early childhood, ESL. **English:** English lit. **General:** Business, equipment technology. **Health services:** Health care admin. **History:** General. **Protective services:** Law enforcement admin. **Visual/performing arts:** Art.

Computing on campus. 100 workstations in library, computer center, student center. Online course registration, online library, helpline, wireless network available.

Student life. Freshman orientation: Available. Preregistration for classes offered. Offered prior to fall semester and online. **Activities:** Drama, literary magazine, student government, agriculture fraternity, honors fraternity, peer ambassador program, diesel fraternity, intramurals.

Athletics. NJCAA. **Intercollegiate:** Baseball M, golf M, softball W. **Intramural:** Basketball.

Student services. Adult student services, career counseling, student employment services, financial aid counseling, on-campus daycare, personal counseling, placement for graduates, veterans' counselor. **Physically disabled:** Services for visually, speech, hearing impaired. **Transfer:** Pre-admission transcript evaluation for new students. Transfer adviser, college fairs on campus for students transferring to 4-year colleges.

Contact. E-mail: admissions@src.edu
Phone: (309) 649-7020 Toll-free number: (800) 334-7337
Fax: (309) 649-6393
Melissa Wilkinson, Director of Admissions and Records, Spoon River College, 23235 North County Road 22, Canton, IL 61520

Taylor Business Institute
Chicago, Illinois
www.tbiil.edu
CB code: 2488

▸ For-profit 2-year business college
▸ Very large city

General. Accredited by ACICS. **Enrollment:** 322 undergraduates. **Degrees:** 63 associate awarded. **Calendar:** Differs by program. **Full-time faculty:** 8 total. **Part-time faculty:** 15 total.

Basis for selection. Admissions assessment based on individual strengths; CPAT used. CPAT required for placement and assessment after admission.

2011-2012 Annual costs. Tuition/fees: $13,500. Books/supplies: $450.

Financial aid. Need-based: Work-study available nights, weekends and for part-time students.

Application procedures. Admission: No deadline. $25 fee, may be waived for applicants with need. **Financial aid:** FAFSA, institutional form required.

Academics. Credit/placement by examination: AP, CLEP.

Majors. Business: Accounting. **Health services:** Insurance coding. **Protective services:** Law enforcement admin.

Student life. Freshman orientation: Available. Preregistration for classes offered.

Student services. Alcohol/substance abuse counseling, career counseling, services for economically disadvantaged, student employment services, financial aid counseling, minority student services, personal counseling, placement for graduates, veterans' counselor, women's services.

Contact. Phone: (312) 658-5100
Franklin Parker, Vice President, Taylor Business Institute, 318 West Adams Street, 5th Floor, Chicago, IL 60606

Triton College
River Grove, Illinois
www.triton.edu
CB member
CB code: 1821

▸ Public 2-year community and junior college
▸ Commuter campus in large town

General. Founded in 1964. Regionally accredited. **Enrollment:** 10,590 degree-seeking undergraduates; 5,042 non-degree-seeking students. **Degrees:** 1,009 associate awarded. **Location:** 5 miles from Chicago. **Calendar:** Semester, extensive summer session. **Full-time faculty:** 111 total; 22% have terminal degrees, 18% minority, 55% women. **Part-time faculty:** 623 total; 11% have terminal degrees, 18% minority, 48% women. **Class size:** 64% < 20, 35% 20-39, less than 1% 40-49, less than 1% 50-99, less than 1% >100. **Special facilities:** Earth and space center with planetarium, theater, performing arts center, botanical gardens, educational technology resource center, culinary arts operated dining facility. **Partnerships:** Formal partnerships with Toyota, General Motors, Disney Corporation, over 24 hospitals and health care providers in Chicago area.

Student profile. Among degree-seeking undergraduates, 2,614 enrolled as first-time, first-year students.

Part-time:	61%	**African American:**	23%
Out-of-state:	1%	**Asian American:**	3%
Women:	58%	**Hispanic American:**	25%

Transfer out. Colleges most students transferred to 2011: Northern Illinois University, Northeastern Illinois University, University of Illinois at Chicago, DePaul University, Eastern Illinois University.

Basis for selection. Open admission, but selective for some programs. Special requirements for most health programs and two manufacturer-related automotive programs. Applicants to allied health program must attend information session. **Learning Disabled:** Students must self-identify.

High school preparation. 15 units required. Required units include English 4, mathematics 3, social studies 3, science 3 and academic electives 2. Biology, chemistry, or algebra required for most allied health programs. 15 specified units required for university transfer programs.

2011-2012 Annual costs. Tuition/fees: $3,132; $7,656 out-of-district; $9,515 out-of-state. Per-credit charge: $93 in-district; $244 out-of-district; $306 out-of-state. Books/supplies: $1,154. Personal expenses: $1,632.

Financial aid. Need-based: Need-based aid available for part-time students. Work-study available nights, weekends and for part-time students. **Non-need-based:** Scholarships awarded for academics, athletics.

Application procedures. Admission: Closing date 9/15. No application fee. Admission notification on a rolling basis. **Financial aid:** Priority date 4/15; no closing date. FAFSA, institutional form required. Applicants notified on a rolling basis starting 4/1; must reply within 2 week(s) of notification.

Academics. Special study options: Accelerated study, cooperative education, cross-registration, distance learning, dual enrollment of high school students, ESL, exchange student, external degree, honors, independent study, internships, liberal arts/career combination, study abroad, teacher certification program, weekend college. Bachelor's degree programs available on campus. License preparation in nursing, paramedic, radiology, real estate. **Credit/placement by examination:** AP, CLEP, SAT, ACT, institutional tests. 30 credit hours maximum toward associate degree. **Support services:** GED preparation, learning center, reduced course load, remedial instruction, study skills assistance, tutoring, writing center.

Honors college/program. 25 ACT and/or 3.35 GPA required; about 25 admitted each year.

Majors. Business: Accounting, business admin, construction management, financial planning, hospitality admin, hotel/motel admin, human resources,

restaurant/food services. **Computer sciences:** Information systems, networking. **Education:** General, early childhood, mathematics, teacher assistance. **Foreign languages:** General, French, Italian, Spanish. **General:** Ornamental horticulture. **Health services:** Clinical lab technology, EMT paramedic, medical assistant, nuclear medical technology, nursing (RN), ophthalmic technology, radiologic technology/medical imaging, respiratory therapy technology, sonography, substance abuse counseling. **Liberal arts:** Arts/sciences. **Parks/recreation:** Facilities management. **Protective services:** Firefighting, law enforcement admin, police science. **Visual/performing arts:** Commercial photography, design, interior design, music, studio arts. **Work/family studies:** Child care service.

Most popular majors. Business/marketing 8%, health sciences 19%, interdisciplinary studies 16%, liberal arts 36%, security/protective services 6%, trade and industry 9%.

Computing on campus. 946 workstations in library, computer center. Commuter students can connect to campus network. Online course registration, online library, helpline, wireless network available.

Student life. Freshman orientation: Available. Preregistration for classes offered. Sessions held throughout summer months. **Activities:** Jazz band, campus ministries, choral groups, dance, drama, international student organizations, music ensembles, Model UN, musical theater, radio station, student government, student newspaper, over 30 clubs and organizations available.

Athletics. NJCAA. **Intercollegiate:** Baseball M, basketball, soccer, softball W, volleyball W, wrestling M. **Team name:** Trojans.

Student services. Career counseling, services for economically disadvantaged, student employment services, financial aid counseling, health services, minority student services, on-campus daycare, personal counseling, placement for graduates, veterans' counselor. **Physically disabled:** Services for visually, speech, hearing impaired. **Transfer:** Pre-admission transcript evaluation for new students. Transfer center, transfer adviser, college fairs on campus for students transferring to 4-year colleges.

Contact. E-mail: triton@triton.edu
Phone: (708) 456-0300 ext. 3130 Fax: (708) 583-3162
Mary-Rita Moore, Dean, Enrollment Services, Triton College, 2000 North Fifth Avenue, River Grove, IL 60171

Vatterott College: Quincy
Quincy, Illinois
www.vatterott-college.edu   **CB code: 3640**

▸ For-profit 2-year technical college
▸ Commuter campus in small city

General. Accredited by ACCSCT. **Calendar:** Differs by program.

Annual costs/financial aid. Estimated program costs as of June 2011: diploma (60 weeks) $21,840 - $25,600; associate degree (70 weeks) $27,100 - $33,350, (90 weeks) $37,250 - $38,150. All costs, which include tuition, fees, books and supplies, and taxes, are subject to change.

Contact. Phone: (217) 224-0600
Director of Admissions, 3609 North Marx Drive, Quincy, IL 62305

Waubonsee Community College
Sugar Grove, Illinois
www.waubonsee.edu   **CB code: 1938**

▸ Public 2-year community and junior college
▸ Commuter campus in small town

General. Founded in 1966. Regionally accredited. Comprehensive community college. **Enrollment:** 8,423 degree-seeking undergraduates; 2,294 non-degree-seeking students. **Degrees:** 774 associate awarded. **ROTC:** Army. **Location:** 9 miles from Aurora. **Calendar:** 4-4-1 semester system. Extensive summer session. **Full-time faculty:** 114 total; 12% have terminal degrees, 11% minority, 59% women. **Part-time faculty:** 646 total; 7% have terminal degrees, 13% minority, 58% women. **Special facilities:** Observatory, nature trail. **Partnerships:** Formal partnership with Valley Education for Employment System.

Student profile. Among degree-seeking undergraduates, 55% enrolled in a transfer program, 45% enrolled in a vocational program, 7% already have a bachelor's degree or higher, 1,673 enrolled as first-time, first-year students, 280 transferred in from other institutions.

Part-time:	57%	Asian American:	2%
Women:	56%	Hispanic American:	25%
African American:	8%	25 or older:	35%

Transfer out. Colleges most students transferred to 2011: Northern Illinois University, Illinois State University, Aurora University-Illinois, University of Illinois at Urbana-Champaign, University of Illinois at Chicago.

Basis for selection. Open admission, but selective for some programs. Limited enrollment to certain programs based on specific assessment testing and/or successful completion of prerequisite coursework.

High school preparation. College-preparatory program recommended. 15 units recommended. Recommended units include English 4, mathematics 3, social studies 3, science 3 and academic electives 2.

2011-2012 Annual costs. Tuition/fees: $3,000; $8,083 out-of-district; $8,848 out-of-state. Per-credit charge: $95 in-district; $264 out-of-district; $290 out-of-state. Books/supplies: $1,300. Personal expenses: $1,330.

2010-2011 Financial aid. Need-based: 71% of total undergraduate aid awarded as scholarships/grants, 29% as loans/jobs. Need-based aid available for part-time students. Work-study available nights, weekends and for part-time students. **Non-need-based:** Scholarships awarded for academics, art, athletics, leadership, minority status, music/drama, state residency.

Application procedures. Admission: No deadline. No application fee. Admission notification on a rolling basis. **Financial aid:** Priority date 3/1; no closing date. FAFSA required. Applicants notified on a rolling basis starting 4/1.

Academics. Review classes offered for various levels of math, English, and reading. **Special study options:** Accelerated study, distance learning, dual enrollment of high school students, ESL, honors, independent study, internships, liberal arts/career combination, study abroad, weekend college. License preparation in nursing. **Credit/placement by examination:** AP, CLEP, institutional tests. 30 credit hours maximum toward associate degree. Student must be enrolled before scores can be recorded on transcript. Recording fee may apply. **Support services:** GED preparation and test center, learning center, reduced course load, remedial instruction, study skills assistance, tutoring, writing center.

Majors. Business: Accounting, business admin, construction management, executive assistant, human resources, logistics, office technology, retailing, small business admin. **Communications technology:** Radio/TV. **Computer sciences:** Programming, web page design. **Education:** Mathematics, multi-level teacher, music, special ed, teacher assistance. **Engineering:** General. **Foreign languages:** Sign language interpretation. **Health services:** Community health services, EMT ambulance attendant, massage therapy, medical records technology, nursing (RN). **Human services:** Social work. **Liberal arts:** Arts/sciences, library assistant. **Parks/recreation:** Health/fitness. **Protective services:** Firefighting, police science. **Visual/performing arts:** Graphic design, music, studio arts. **Work/family studies:** Child care service.

Most popular majors. Health sciences 12%, interdisciplinary studies 45%, liberal arts 27%.

Computing on campus. 140 workstations in library, computer center, student center. Commuter students can connect to campus network. Online course registration, helpline, wireless network available.

Student life. Freshman orientation: Available. Preregistration for classes offered. Three hour orientation for new students and mandatory 45 minute online tutorial for registration and planning. **Activities:** Bands, choral groups, dance, drama, literary magazine, music ensembles, musical theater, opera, student government, student newspaper, Latino Unidos, Christian fellowship, Amnesty International, African cultural alliance, model Illinois government, Students for a Diverse Society.

Athletics. NJCAA. **Intercollegiate:** Baseball M, basketball, cheerleading, cross-country, golf M, soccer, softball W, tennis, volleyball W, wrestling M. **Intramural:** Basketball, table tennis, volleyball. **Team name:** Chiefs.

Student services. Career counseling, services for economically disadvantaged, student employment services, financial aid counseling, minority student services, on-campus daycare, personal counseling, veterans' counselor. **Physically disabled:** Services for visually, speech, hearing impaired. **Transfer:** Transfer adviser, college fairs on campus for students transferring to 4-year colleges.

Contact. E-mail: admissions@waubonsee.edu
Phone: (630) 466-7900 ext. 5756 Fax: (630) 466-6663
Joy Sanders, Admissions Manager, Waubonsee Community College, Route 47 at Waubonsee Drive, Sugar Grove, IL 60554-9454

Indiana

Ancilla College
Donaldson, Indiana
www.ancilla.edu
CB code: 1015

- Private 2-year junior and liberal arts college affiliated with Roman Catholic Church
- Commuter campus in rural community

General. Founded in 1937. Regionally accredited. **Enrollment:** 518 degree-seeking undergraduates. **Degrees:** 103 associate awarded. **Location:** 30 miles from South Bend, 7 miles from Plymouth. **Calendar:** Semester, limited summer session. **Full-time faculty:** 20 total; 35% have terminal degrees, 60% women. **Part-time faculty:** 30 total; 27% have terminal degrees, 3% minority. **Class size:** 69% < 20, 31% 20-39.

Student profile. Among degree-seeking undergraduates, 136 enrolled as first-time, first-year students.

Part-time:	30%	Women:	67%
Out-of-state:	10%	25 or older:	39%

Transfer out. Colleges most students transferred to 2011: Indiana University South Bend, Indiana-Purdue University Indianapolis, Ball State University, Indiana University Kokomo, Bethel College.

Basis for selection. Open admission, but selective for some programs. Special requirements for nursing program. **Home schooled:** Transcript of courses and grades required.

High school preparation. College-preparatory program recommended.

2011-2012 Annual costs. Tuition/fees: $13,880. Per-credit charge: $455. Books/supplies: $1,070. Personal expenses: $2,488.

2011-2012 Financial aid. Need-based: 48% of total undergraduate aid awarded as scholarships/grants, 52% as loans/jobs. Need-based aid available for part-time students. Work-study available nights, weekends and for part-time students. **Non-need-based:** Scholarships awarded for academics, athletics, job skills, leadership.

Application procedures. Admission: No deadline. No application fee. Admission notification on a rolling basis. **Financial aid:** Closing date 3/1. FAFSA, institutional form required. Applicants notified on a rolling basis starting 3/1; must reply within 2 week(s) of notification.

Academics. Special study options: Double major, dual enrollment of high school students, independent study, liberal arts/career combination. License preparation in real estate. **Credit/placement by examination:** AP, CLEP, institutional tests. 12 credit hours maximum toward associate degree. **Support services:** Learning center, reduced course load, remedial instruction, study skills assistance, tutoring, writing center.

Majors. Biology: General. **Business:** Business admin. **Communications:** Media studies. **Education:** General, early childhood, elementary, secondary. **Health services:** Nursing (RN), prenursing. **History:** General. **Liberal arts:** Arts/sciences. **Protective services:** Law enforcement admin.

Most popular majors. Business/marketing 15%, education 8%, health sciences 45%, liberal arts 10%, psychology 9%.

Computing on campus. 53 workstations in library, computer center. Online library, wireless network available.

Student life. Freshman orientation: Mandatory. Preregistration for classes offered. **Activities:** Campus ministries, literary magazine, student government, student newspaper, student ambassadors, Phi Theta Kappa.

Athletics. NJCAA. **Intercollegiate:** Baseball M, basketball, cheerleading, golf, soccer M, softball W, volleyball W. **Team name:** Chargers.

Student services. Chaplain/spiritual director, career counseling, financial aid counseling, personal counseling. **Transfer:** Transfer adviser for students transferring to 4-year colleges.

Contact. E-mail: admissions@ancilla.edu
Phone: (574) 936-8898 ext. 330
Toll-free number: (866) 262-4552 ext. 330 Fax: (574) 935-1773
Sarah Lawrence, Assistant Director of Admissions, Ancilla College, 9001 Union Road, Donaldson, IN 46513

Brown Mackie College: Fort Wayne
Fort Wayne, Indiana
www.brownmackie.com
CB code: 3379

- For-profit 2-year branch campus and business college
- Large city

General. Accredited by ACICS. **Calendar:** Quarter.

Annual costs/financial aid. Books/supplies: $1,275.

Contact. Phone: (260) 484-4400
Director of Admissions, 3000 Coliseum Boulevard, Suite 100, Fort Wayne, IN 46805

Brown Mackie College: Merrillville
Merrillville, Indiana
www.brownmackie.edu
CB code: 7115

- For-profit 2-year business college
- Small city

General. Accredited by ACICS. **Calendar:** Differs by program.

Annual costs/financial aid. Books/supplies: $1,275. Personal expenses: $845.

Contact. Phone: (219) 769-3321
Director of Admissions, 1000 East 80th Place, Suite 101N, Merrillville, IN 46410

Brown Mackie College: Michigan City
Michigan City, Indiana
www.cbcaec.com
CB code: 3345

- For-profit 2-year branch campus college
- Large town

General. Accredited by ACICS. **Calendar:** Differs by program.

Annual costs/financial aid. Books/supplies: $1,275. Personal expenses: $2,664.

Contact. Phone: (219) 877-3100
Director of Admissions, 325 East US Highway 20, Michigan City, IN 46360-7362

Brown Mackie College: South Bend
South Bend, Indiana
www.brownmackie.edu
CB code: 3140

- For-profit 2-year community and technical college
- Commuter campus in small city

General. Founded in 1882. Accredited by ACICS. **Location:** 90 miles from Chicago, 150 miles from Indianapolis. **Calendar:** Quarter.

Annual costs/financial aid. Books/supplies: $1,275. Need-based financial aid available to full-time and part-time students.

Contact. Phone: (574) 237-0774
Director of Admissions, 3454 Douglas Road, South Bend, IN 46635

College of Court Reporting
Hobart, Indiana
www.ccr.edu
CB code: 3532

- For-profit 2-year business and technical college
- Commuter campus in small city

General. Accredited by ACICS. **Enrollment:** 274 degree-seeking under-graduates. **Degrees:** 13 associate awarded. **Calendar:** Semester, extensive summer session. **Full-time faculty:** 5 total. **Part-time faculty:** 30 total.

Student profile. Among degree-seeking undergraduates, 100% enrolled in a vocational program.

Basis for selection. Open admission. **Home schooled:** Transcript of courses and grades, state high school equivalency certificate required.

High school preparation. College-preparatory program recommended.

2011-2012 Annual costs. Tuition/fees: $8,550. Per-credit charge: $350. Required annual fee of $150 quoted above is for on-site students. Online students pay required fees of $600 annually. Books/supplies: $1,500.

Financial aid. Need-based: Work-study available nights, weekends and for part-time students.

Application procedures. Admission: Closing date 9/30 (receipt date). $50 fee. Application must be submitted on paper. Admission notification on a rolling basis.

Academics. Special study options: Distance learning, internships. **Credit/placement by examination:** AP, CLEP.

Majors. Business: Office technology. **Health services:** Medical transcription.

Computing on campus. PC or laptop required. Online library, helpline, wireless network available.

Student life. Freshman orientation: Mandatory. Preregistration for classes offered. **Activities:** Student newspaper.

Student services. Adult student services, student employment services, financial aid counseling, placement for graduates. **Transfer:** Pre-admission transcript evaluation for new students.

Contact. E-mail: information@ccr.edu
Phone: (219) 942-1459 Toll-free number: (866) 294-3974
Fax: (219) 942-1631
Nicky Rodriguez, Director of Admissions, College of Court Reporting, 111 West 10th Street, Suite 111, Hobart, IN 46342

Fortis College: Indianapolis
Indianapolis, Indiana
www.fortis.edu

- For-profit 2-year career college
- Very large city

General. Regionally accredited; also accredited by ACCSC. **Enrollment:** 105 degree-seeking undergraduates. **Calendar:** Quarter. **Full-time faculty:** 8 total. **Part-time faculty:** 14 total.

Basis for selection. Open admission.

2011-2012 Annual costs. Tuition/fees: $10,740. Per-credit charge: $290. Books/supplies: $1,185. Personal expenses: $3,046.

Financial aid. Need-based: Work-study available nights, weekends and for part-time students.

Application procedures. Admission: No deadline. $25 fee. **Financial aid:** No deadline.

Academics. Credit/placement by examination: AP, CLEP.

Majors. Health services: Dental assistant, medical assistant, nursing (RN).

Contact. Phone: (317) 808-4800 Toll-free number: (855) 436-7847
Alan Schultz, Director of Admissions, Fortis College: Indianapolis, 9001 North Wesleyan Road, Suite 101, Indianapolis, IN 46268

Harrison College: Anderson
Anderson, Indiana
www.harrison.edu   CB code: 3364

- For-profit 2-year business and health science college
- Commuter campus in small city
- Interview required

General. Accredited by ACICS. **Enrollment:** 300 degree-seeking under-graduates. **Degrees:** 58 associate awarded. **Location:** 45 miles from Indianapolis. **Calendar:** Quarter, extensive summer session. **Full-time faculty:** 6 total. **Part-time faculty:** 14 total.

Basis for selection. Open admission, but selective for some programs.

2011-2012 Annual costs. Tuition/fees: $12,865. Tuition varies by program. Examples of per-credit hour charges include: business management $355; culinary arts $335; information technology $360; medical assistant $365; nursing $400. Examples of quarterly tuition charges include: medical laboratory technology $4,880; occupational medical Spanish $4,070. Books/supplies: $1,650.

Financial aid. Need-based: Need-based aid available for part-time students. Work-study available nights, weekends and for part-time students. **Additional information:** Work-study programs available.

Application procedures. Admission: No deadline. $50 fee. Admission notification on a rolling basis. **Financial aid:** No deadline. FAFSA required. Applicants notified on a rolling basis.

Academics. Special study options: Distance learning, dual enrollment of high school students, internships. Bachelor's degree programs available on campus. **Credit/placement by examination:** AP, CLEP, institutional tests. Free test-out program is available to high school seniors. Test-outs are available to all other students for a $30 fee. **Support services:** Tutoring.

Majors. Business: Accounting, accounting/finance, administrative services, banking/financial services, business admin, human resources, marketing. **Health services:** Insurance coding, insurance specialist, medical assistant, medical records technology. **Protective services:** Law enforcement admin.

Most popular majors. Business/marketing 27%, health sciences 46%, security/protective services 10%.

Student life. Housing: Apartments available. **Activities:** Student government.

Student services. Career counseling, student employment services, financial aid counseling, placement for graduates.

Contact. Phone: (765) 644-7514 Toll-free number: (800) 422-4723
Fax: (765) 644-5724
Charlene Stacy, Executive Director, Harrison College: Anderson, 140 East 53rd Street, Anderson, IN 46013

Harrison College: Columbus
Columbus, Indiana
www.harrison.edu   CB code: 3349

- For-profit 2-year business and health science college
- Commuter campus in large town

General. Accredited by ACICS. **Location:** 50 miles from Indianapolis. **Calendar:** Quarter.

Annual costs/financial aid. Tuition/fees (2011-2012): $12,865. Tuition varies by program. Examples of per-credit hour charges include: business management $355; culinary arts $335; information technology $360; medical assistant $365; nursing $400. Examples of quarterly tuition charges include: medical laboratory yechnology $4,880; occupational medical spanish $4,070. Books/supplies: $1,650. Need-based financial aid available to full-time and part-time students.

Contact. Phone: (812) 379-9000
Director of Admissions, 2222 Poshard Drive, Columbus, IN 47203

Harrison College: Elkhart
Elkhart, Indiana
www.harrison.edu

- For-profit 2-year business and health science college
- Commuter campus in small city

General. Regionally accredited. **Location:** 15 miles from South Bend, 100 miles from Fort Wayne. **Calendar:** Quarter.

Annual costs/financial aid. Tuition/fees (2011-2012): $12,865. Tuition varies by program. Examples of per-credit hour charges include: business management $355; culinary arts $335; information technology $360; medical

assistant $365; nursing $400. Examples of quarterly tuition charges include: medical laboratory technology $4,880; occupational medical Spanish $4,070. Books/supplies: $1,650.

Contact. Phone: (574) 522-0397
56075 Parkway Ave., Elkhart, IN 46516

Harrison College: Evansville
Evansville, Indiana
www.harrison.edu   CB code: 3346

⬦ For-profit 2-year business and health science college
⬦ Commuter campus in small city

General. Accredited by ACICS. **Calendar:** Quarter.

Annual costs/financial aid. Tuition/fees (2011-2012): $12,865. Tuition varies by program. Examples of per-credit hour charges include: business management $355; culinary arts $335; information technology $360; medical assistant $365; nursing $400. Examples of quarterly tuition charges include: medical laboratory technology $4,880; occupational medical Spanish $4,070. Books/supplies: $1,650. Need-based financial aid available to full-time and part-time students.

Contact. Phone: (812) 476-6000
Director of Admissions, 4601 Theater Drive, Evansville, IN 47715

Harrison College: Fort Wayne
Fort Wayne, Indiana
www.harrison.edu   CB code: 3867

⬦ For-profit 2-year business and health science college
⬦ Commuter campus in large city

General. Accredited by ACICS. **Calendar:** Quarter.

Annual costs/financial aid. Tuition/fees (2011-2012): $12,865. Tuition varies by program. Examples of per-credit hour charges include: business management $355; culinary arts $335; information technology $360; medical assistant $365; nursing $400. Examples of quarterly tuition charges include: medical laboratory technology $4,880; occupational medical Spanish $4,070. Books/supplies: $1,575. Need-based financial aid available to full-time and part-time students.

Contact. Phone: (260) 471-7667
Executive Director, 6413 North Clinton Street, Fort Wayne, IN 46825

Harrison College: Indianapolis
Indianapolis, Indiana
www.harrison.edu   CB code: 2317

⬦ For-profit 2-year business and health science college
⬦ Commuter campus in very large city

General. Founded in 1902. Accredited by ACICS. **Calendar:** Quarter.

Annual costs/financial aid. Tuition/fees (2011-2012): $12,865. Tuition varies by program. Examples of per-credit hour charges include: business management $355; culinary arts $335; information technology $360; medical assistant $365; nursing $400. Examples of quarterly tuition charges include: medical laboratory technology $4,880; occupational medical Spanish $4,070. Need-based financial aid available to full-time and part-time students.

Contact. Phone: (317) 264-5656
Director of Admissions, 550 East Washington Street, Indianapolis, IN 46204

Harrison College: Indianapolis East
Indianapolis, Indiana
www.harrison.edu   CB code: 3370

⬦ For-profit 2-year health science college
⬦ Commuter campus in very large city

General. Accredited by ACICS. **Calendar:** Quarter.

Annual costs/financial aid. Tuition/fees (2011-2012): $12,865. Tuition varies by program. Examples of per-credit hour charges include: business management $355; culinary arts $335; information technology $360; medical assistant $365; nursing $400. Examples of quarterly tuition charges include: medical laboratory technology $4,880; occupational medical Spanish $4,070. Books/supplies: $1,850. Need-based financial aid available to full-time and part-time students.

Contact. Phone: (317) 375-8000
8150 Brookville Road, Indianapolis, IN 46239

Harrison College: Indianapolis Northwest
Indianapolis, Indiana
www.harrison.edu

⬦ For-profit 2-year health science college
⬦ Very large city

General. Accredited by ACICS. **Calendar:** Quarter.

Annual costs/financial aid. Tuition/fees (2011-2012): $12,865. Tuition varies by program. Examples of per-credit hour charges include: business management $355; culinary arts $335; information technology $360; medical assistant $365; nursing $400. Examples of quarterly tuition charges include: medical laboratory technology $4,880; occupational medical Spanish $4,070. Books/supplies: $1,500. Need-based financial aid available for full-time students.

Contact. Phone: (317) 873-6500
Director of Admissions, 6300 Technology Center Drive, Indianapolis, IN 46278

Harrison College: Lafayette
Lafayette, Indiana
www.harrison.edu   CB code: 3353

⬦ For-profit 2-year business and health science college
⬦ Commuter campus in small city

General. Accredited by ACICS. **Location:** 60 miles from Indianapolis. **Calendar:** Quarter.

Annual costs/financial aid. Tuition/fees (2011-2012): $12,865. Tuition varies by program. Examples of per-credit hour charges include: business management $355; culinary arts $335; information technology $360; medical assistant $365; nursing $400. Examples of quarterly tuition charges include: medical laboratory technology $4,880; occupational medical Spanish $4,070. Books/supplies: $1,650. Need-based financial aid available to full-time and part-time students.

Contact. Phone: (765) 447-9550
Director of Admissions, 4705 Meijer Court, Lafayette, IN 47905

Harrison College: Muncie
Muncie, Indiana
www.harrison.edu   CB code: 3347

⬦ For-profit 2-year business and health science college
⬦ Commuter campus in small city

General. Accredited by ACICS. **Calendar:** Quarter.

Annual costs/financial aid. Tuition/fees (2011-2012): $12,865. Tuition varies by program. Examples of per-credit hour charges include: business management $355; culinary arts $335; information technology $360; medical assistant $365; nursing $400. Examples of quarterly tuition charges include: medical laboratory technology $4,880; occupational medical Spanish $4,070. Books/supplies: $1,650. Need-based financial aid available to full-time and part-time students.

Contact. Phone: (765) 288-8681
Associate Director of Admissions, 411 West Riggin Road, Muncie, IN 47303

Two-Year Colleges

Two-Year Colleges

Harrison College: Terre Haute
Terre Haute, Indiana
www.harrison.edu   **CB code: 3348**

- For-profit 2-year business and health science college
- Commuter campus in small city

General. Accredited by ACICS. **Calendar:** Quarter.

Annual costs/financial aid. Tuition/fees (2011-2012): $12,865. Tuition varies by program. Examples of per-credit hour charges include: business management $355; culinary arts $335; information technology $360; medical assistant $365; nursing $400. Examples of quarterly tuition charges include: medical laboratory technology $4,880; occupational medical Spanish $4,070. Books/supplies: $1,600. Need-based financial aid available to full-time and part-time students.

Contact. Phone: (812) 877-2100
Regional Director, 1378 South State Road 46, Terre Haute, IN 47803

International Business College: Indianapolis
Indianapolis, Indiana
www.intlbusinesscollege.com   **CB code: 3374**

- For-profit 2-year business college
- Commuter campus in very large city

General. Accredited by ACICS. Branch campus of International Business College. **Enrollment:** 355 degree-seeking undergraduates. **Degrees:** 151 associate awarded. **Calendar:** Differs by program. **Full-time faculty:** 10 total. **Part-time faculty:** 3 total.

Basis for selection. Interview and Wonderlic evaluation are main admission criteria.

2011-2012 Annual costs. Tuition/fees: $13,620. Room only: $6,480. Books/supplies: $2,000.

Financial aid. Need-based: Work-study available nights, weekends and for part-time students.

Application procedures. Admission: No deadline. $50 fee.

Academics. Credit/placement by examination: AP, CLEP.

Majors. Business: Business admin. **Computer sciences:** General.

Contact. Phone: (317) 841-6400
International Business College: Indianapolis, 7205 Shadeland Station, Indianapolis, IN 46256

ITT Technical Institute: Newburgh
Newburgh, Indiana
www.itt-tech.edu   **CB code: 7311**

- For-profit 2-year business and technical college
- Small town

General. Accredited by ACICS. **Enrollment:** 565 undergraduates. **Degrees:** 17 bachelor's, 97 associate awarded. **Calendar:** Quarter. **Full-time faculty:** 13 total. **Part-time faculty:** 33 total.

Basis for selection. Selective admissions to certain programs.

2011-2012 Annual costs. Estimated costs as of June 2011: per-credit-hour charge, $493, depending upon level and course of study; academic fee, $200. Certain programs of study require purchase of tools, which could cost an additional $100 to $655. All costs are subject to change.

Financial aid. Need-based: Work-study available nights, weekends and for part-time students.

Academics. Credit/placement by examination: AP, CLEP.

Majors. Computer sciences: Networking, programming, web page design. **Health services:** Nursing (RN). **Protective services:** Law enforcement admin. **Visual/performing arts:** Design.

Contact. Toll-free number: (800) 832-4488
ITT Technical Institute: Newburgh, 10999 Stahl Road, Newburgh, IN 47630

Ivy Tech Community College: Bloomington
Bloomington, Indiana
www.ivytech.edu   **CB code: 1455**

- Public 2-year community college
- Commuter campus in small city

General. **Enrollment:** 5,458 degree-seeking undergraduates; 760 non-degree-seeking students. **Degrees:** 477 associate awarded. **Calendar:** Semester, extensive summer session. **Full-time faculty:** 73 total. **Part-time faculty:** 270 total.

Student profile. Among degree-seeking undergraduates, 1,048 enrolled as first-time, first-year students.

Part-time:	50%	Hispanic American:	3%
Women:	57%	Native American:	1%
African American:	5%	25 or older:	45%
Asian American:	1%		

Transfer out. Colleges most students transferred to 2011: Indiana University-Bloomington.

Basis for selection. Open admission, but selective for some programs. Special requirements for human services and health technology programs based on test scores and prior academic work.

2012-2013 Annual costs. Tuition/fees (projected): $3,455; $7,302 out-of-state. Per-credit charge: $111 in-state; $239 out-of-state.

Financial aid. Need-based: Need-based aid available for part-time students. Work-study available nights, weekends and for part-time students.

Application procedures. Admission: No deadline. No application fee. Admission notification on a rolling basis. Application closing date for international students at least 60 days prior to start of semester. **Financial aid:** Priority date 3/1; no closing date. FAFSA required. Applicants notified on a rolling basis starting 7/1.

Academics. Special study options: Distance learning, dual enrollment of high school students, internships, liberal arts/career combination, teacher certification program, weekend college. License preparation in nursing. **Credit/placement by examination:** AP, CLEP, institutional tests. 45 credit hours maximum toward associate degree. 15 credits must be earned in residence. **Support services:** Learning center, reduced course load, remedial instruction, tutoring.

Majors. Biology: Biotechnology. **Business:** Accounting technology, business admin, executive assistant, hospitality admin. **Computer sciences:** General, information technology. **Education:** General, early childhood. **Health services:** EMT paramedic, medical radiologic technology/radiation therapy, medical records technology, mental health services, nursing (RN), respiratory therapy technology. **Liberal arts:** Arts/sciences, library assistant. **Parks/recreation:** Exercise sciences. **Protective services:** Criminal justice.

Most popular majors. Business/marketing 29%, computer/information sciences 8%, engineering/engineering technologies 8%, health sciences 23%, liberal arts 17%.

Computing on campus. 884 workstations in library, computer center. Online course registration, online library, helpline, repair service, student web hosting available.

Student life. Freshman orientation: Available. Preregistration for classes offered. **Activities:** Student government, Phi Theta Kappa, College Democrats, student leadership academy, Christian Challenge, computer club, cultural awareness.

Student services. Adult student services, career counseling, student employment services, financial aid counseling, minority student services, placement for graduates, veterans' counselor. **Physically disabled:** Services for visually, speech, hearing impaired. **Transfer:** Transfer center, transfer adviser, college fairs on campus for students transferring to 4-year colleges.

Contact. E-mail: bpless@ivytech.edu
Phone: (812) 330-6023 Toll-free number: (800) 447-0700 ext. 6350
Fax: (812) 330-106
Beth Pless, Director of Enrollment Services, Ivy Tech Community College: Bloomington, 200 Daniels Way, Bloomington, IN 47404-1511

Ivy Tech Community College: Central Indiana
Indianapolis, Indiana
www.ivytech.edu
CB code: 1311

- Public 2-year community college
- Commuter campus in very large city

General. Founded in 1966. Regionally accredited. Branch location at Lawrence. **Enrollment:** 20,835 degree-seeking undergraduates; 1,519 non-degree-seeking students. **Degrees:** 1,184 associate awarded. **Location:** 2 miles from downtown. **Calendar:** Semester, extensive summer session. **Full-time faculty:** 178 total. **Part-time faculty:** 648 total.

Student profile. Among degree-seeking undergraduates, 3,002 enrolled as first-time, first-year students.

Part-time:	65%	Asian American:	2%
Out-of-state:	1%	Hispanic American:	5%
Women:	59%	25 or older:	53%
African American:	29%		

Transfer out. Colleges most students transferred to 2011: Indiana University-Purdue University Indianapolis, Vincennes University, Indiana University-Bloomington, Purdue University-West Lafayette, Ball State University.

Basis for selection. Open admission, but selective for some programs. Special requirements for human services and health technology programs based on test scores and prior academic work.

2012-2013 Annual costs. Tuition/fees (projected): $3,455; $7,302 out-of-state. Per-credit charge: $111 in-state; $239 out-of-state.

Financial aid. Need-based: Need-based aid available for part-time students. Work-study available nights, weekends and for part-time students.

Application procedures. Admission: No deadline. No application fee. Admission notification on a rolling basis. Application closing date for undergraduate international students at least 60 days prior to start of semester. **Financial aid:** Priority date 3/1; no closing date. FAFSA required. Applicants notified on a rolling basis starting 7/1.

Academics. Special study options: Cooperative education, distance learning, dual enrollment of high school students, ESL, internships, liberal arts/career combination, teacher certification program, weekend college. License preparation in nursing, radiology. **Credit/placement by examination:** AP, CLEP, institutional tests. 45 credit hours maximum toward associate degree. 15 credits must be earned in residence. **Support services:** GED preparation and test center, learning center, reduced course load, remedial instruction, tutoring.

Majors. Biology: Biotechnology. **Business:** Accounting technology, business admin, executive assistant, hospitality admin, logistics. **Computer sciences:** General, information technology. **Education:** General, early childhood. **Health services:** EMT paramedic, medical assistant, medical radiologic technology/radiation therapy, medical records technology, mental health services, nursing (RN), respiratory therapy technology, surgical technology. **Liberal arts:** Arts/sciences, library assistant. **Protective services:** Criminal justice, homeland security. **Visual/performing arts:** Design.

Most popular majors. Business/marketing 20%, engineering/engineering technologies 6%, health sciences 26%, liberal arts 9%, trade and industry 20%.

Computing on campus. 1,599 workstations in library, computer center. Online course registration, online library, helpline, repair service, student web hosting, wireless network available.

Student life. Freshman orientation: Available. Preregistration for classes offered. **Activities:** Student government, Phi Theta Kappa, accounting association, human service club, radiology technology club, student leadership academy, black student union, Veterans Association.

Student services. Adult student services, career counseling, student employment services, financial aid counseling, minority student services, placement for graduates, veterans' counselor. **Physically disabled:** Services for visually, speech, hearing impaired. **Transfer:** Transfer center, transfer adviser, college fairs on campus for students transferring to 4-year colleges.

Contact. E-mail: tfunk@ivytech.edu
Phone: (317) 921-4882 Toll-free number: (800) 732-1470
Fax: (317) 921-4753
Tracy Funk, Director of Admissions, Ivy Tech Community College: Central Indiana, 50 West Fall Creek Parkway North Drive, Indianapolis, IN 46208-5752

Ivy Tech Community College: Columbus
Columbus, Indiana
www.ivytech.edu
CB code: 1286

- Public 2-year community college
- Commuter campus in large town

General. Founded in 1963. Regionally accredited. **Enrollment:** 4,121 degree-seeking undergraduates; 1,432 non-degree-seeking students. **Degrees:** 363 associate awarded. **Location:** 40 miles from Indianapolis. **Calendar:** Semester, extensive summer session. **Full-time faculty:** 56 total. **Part-time faculty:** 235 total. **Special facilities:** Visual communications gallery.

Student profile. Among degree-seeking undergraduates, 788 enrolled as first-time, first-year students.

Part-time:	57%	Asian American:	1%
Out-of-state:	1%	Hispanic American:	2%
Women:	69%	25 or older:	53%
African American:	2%		

Transfer out. Colleges most students transferred to 2011: Indiana University-Purdue University Indianapolis, Indiana University-Bloomington, Purdue University, Vincennes University, Indiana State University.

Basis for selection. Open admission, but selective for some programs. Special requirements for human services and health technology programs based on test scores and prior academic work.

2012-2013 Annual costs. Tuition/fees (projected): $3,455; $7,302 out-of-state. Per-credit charge: $111 in-state; $239 out-of-state.

Financial aid. Need-based: Need-based aid available for part-time students. Work-study available nights, weekends and for part-time students.

Application procedures. Admission: No deadline. No application fee. Admission notification on a rolling basis. Application closing date for international students at least 60 days prior to start of semester. **Financial aid:** Priority date 3/1; no closing date. FAFSA required. Applicants notified on a rolling basis starting 7/1.

Academics. Special study options: Distance learning, dual enrollment of high school students, internships, liberal arts/career combination, teacher certification program, weekend college. License preparation in dental hygiene, nursing, paramedic, radiology. **Credit/placement by examination:** AP, CLEP, institutional tests. 45 credit hours maximum toward associate degree. 15 credits must be earned in residence. **Support services:** Learning center, reduced course load, remedial instruction, tutoring.

Majors. Business: Accounting technology, business admin, executive assistant. **Computer sciences:** General, information technology. **Education:** General, early childhood. **Health services:** EMT paramedic, medical assistant, medical radiologic technology/radiation therapy, mental health services, nursing (RN), ophthalmic technology, surgical technology. **Liberal arts:** Arts/sciences, library assistant. **Protective services:** Criminal justice. **Visual/performing arts:** Design, interior design.

Most popular majors. Business/marketing 18%, computer/information sciences 7%, engineering/engineering technologies 6%, health sciences 50%.

Computing on campus. 524 workstations in library, computer center. Online course registration, online library, helpline, repair service, student web hosting available.

Student life. Freshman orientation: Available. Preregistration for classes offered. **Activities:** Student government, student newspaper, Phi Theta Kappa, student leadership academy.

Student services. Adult student services, career counseling, student employment services, financial aid counseling, minority student services, placement for graduates, veterans' counselor. **Physically disabled:** Services for visually, speech, hearing impaired. **Transfer:** Transfer adviser, college fairs on campus for students transferring to 4-year colleges.

Contact. E-mail: nbagadio@ivytech.edu
Phone: (812) 374-5129 Toll-free number: (800) 922-4838
Fax: (812) 372-0311
Neil Bagadiong, Director of Admissions/Assistant Director of Student Affairs, Ivy Tech Community College: Columbus, 4475 Central Avenue, Columbus, IN 47203-1868

Ivy Tech Community College: East Central
Muncie, Indiana
www.ivytech.edu/eastcentral/   CB code: 1279

♦ Public 2-year community college
♦ Commuter campus in small city

General. Founded in 1968. Regionally accredited. Campuses also at Anderson and Marion. **Enrollment:** 8,307 degree-seeking undergraduates; 595 non-degree-seeking students. **Degrees:** 551 associate awarded. **Location:** 50 miles from Indianapolis. **Calendar:** Semester, extensive summer session. **Full-time faculty:** 112 total. **Part-time faculty:** 436 total.

Student profile. Among degree-seeking undergraduates, 1,690 enrolled as first-time, first-year students.

Part-time:	48%	Asian American:	1%
Out-of-state:	1%	Hispanic American:	2%
Women:	63%	25 or older:	52%
African American:	9%		

Transfer out. Colleges most students transferred to 2011: Ball State University, Purdue University-West Lafayette, Indiana University-Kokomo.

Basis for selection. Open admission, but selective for some programs. Special requirements for human services and health technology programs based on test scores and prior academic work. **Adult students:** SAT/ACT scores not required.

2012-2013 Annual costs. Tuition/fees (projected): $3,455; $7,302 out-of-state. Per-credit charge: $111 in-state; $239 out-of-state.

Financial aid. Need-based: Need-based aid available for part-time students. Work-study available nights, weekends and for part-time students. **Additional information:** Higher Education Aid (HEA), Child of Disabled/Deceased Veterans (CDV), Ivy Tech Scholarships (IVTC) and grants, vocational rehabilitation and veteran's assistance available. None require repayment.

Application procedures. Admission: No deadline. No application fee. Admission notification on a rolling basis. Application closing date for international students at least 60 days prior to start of semester. **Financial aid:** Priority date 3/1; no closing date. FAFSA required. Applicants notified on a rolling basis starting 7/1.

Academics. Special study options: Distance learning, dual enrollment of high school students, internships, liberal arts/career combination, teacher certification program, weekend college. License preparation in dental hygiene, nursing, physical therapy, radiology. **Credit/placement by examination:** AP, CLEP, institutional tests. 45 credit hours maximum toward associate degree. 15 credits must be earned in residence. **Support services:** GED preparation and test center, learning center, reduced course load, remedial instruction, tutoring.

Majors. Business: Accounting technology, business admin, executive assistant, hospitality admin. **Computer sciences:** General, information technology. **Education:** General, early childhood. **Health services:** Medical assistant, medical radiologic technology/radiation therapy, mental health services, nursing (RN), physical therapy assistant, respiratory therapy technology, surgical technology. **Liberal arts:** Arts/sciences, library assistant. **Protective services:** Criminal justice.

Most popular majors. Business/marketing 18%, engineering/engineering technologies 11%, health sciences 47%, liberal arts 8%, security/protective services 6%.

Computing on campus. 1,481 workstations in library, computer center. Online course registration, online library, helpline, repair service, student web hosting available.

Student life. Freshman orientation: Available. Preregistration for classes offered. **Activities:** Student government, Phi Theta Kappa, Skills USA-VICA, early childhood education club, human services club, student leadership academy.

Student services. Adult student services, career counseling, student employment services, financial aid counseling, minority student services, placement for graduates, veterans' counselor. **Physically disabled:** Services for visually, speech, hearing impaired. **Transfer:** Transfer center, transfer adviser, college fairs on campus for students transferring to 4-year colleges.

Contact. E-mail: csharp@ivytech.edu
Phone: (765) 289-2291 ext. 1479 Toll-free number: (800) 589-8324
Fax: (765) 289-2292 ext. 502
Corey Sharp, Director of Enrollment Management, Ivy Tech Community College: East Central, 4301 South Cowan Road, Muncie, IN 47302-9448

Ivy Tech Community College: Kokomo
Kokomo, Indiana
www.ivytech.edu   CB code: 1329

♦ Public 2-year community college
♦ Commuter campus in large town

General. Founded in 1968. Regionally accredited. Campus also at Logansport. Branch location at Wabash. **Enrollment:** 5,047 degree-seeking undergraduates; 356 non-degree-seeking students. **Degrees:** 554 associate awarded. **Location:** 50 miles from Indianapolis. **Calendar:** Semester, extensive summer session. **Full-time faculty:** 75 total. **Part-time faculty:** 263 total.

Student profile. Among degree-seeking undergraduates, 816 enrolled as first-time, first-year students.

Part-time:	57%	Hispanic American:	2%
Women:	65%	Native American:	1%
African American:	7%	25 or older:	63%
Asian American:	1%		

Transfer out. Colleges most students transferred to 2011: Indiana University-Kokomo, Purdue University-West Lafayette, Ball State University.

Basis for selection. Open admission, but selective for some programs. Special requirements for human services and health technology programs based on test scores and prior academic work.

2012-2013 Annual costs. Tuition/fees (projected): $3,455; $7,302 out-of-state. Per-credit charge: $111 in-state; $239 out-of-state.

Financial aid. Need-based: Need-based aid available for part-time students. Work-study available nights, weekends and for part-time students.

Application procedures. Admission: No deadline. No application fee. Admission notification on a rolling basis. Application closing date for international students at least 60 days prior to start of semester. **Financial aid:** Priority date 3/1; no closing date. FAFSA required. Applicants notified on a rolling basis starting 7/1.

Academics. Special study options: Distance learning, dual enrollment of high school students, independent study, internships, liberal arts/career combination, teacher certification program, weekend college. License preparation in nursing, paramedic, physical therapy. **Credit/placement by examination:** AP, CLEP, institutional tests. 45 credit hours maximum toward associate degree. 15 credits must be earned in residence. **Support services:** Learning center, reduced course load, remedial instruction, tutoring.

Majors. Business: Accounting technology, business admin, executive assistant. **Communications:** Communications/speech/rhetoric. **Computer sciences:** General, information technology. **Education:** General, early childhood. **Health services:** EMT paramedic, medical assistant, mental health services, nursing (RN), surgical technology. **Liberal arts:** Arts/sciences, library assistant. **Protective services:** Criminal justice. **Visual/performing arts:** Design.

Most popular majors. Business/marketing 18%, computer/information sciences 6%, engineering/engineering technologies 9%, health sciences 37%, trade and industry 8%.

Computing on campus. 699 workstations in library, computer center. Online course registration, online library, helpline, repair service, student web hosting available.

Student life. Freshman orientation: Available. Preregistration for classes offered. **Activities:** Student government, Phi Theta Kappa, student leadership academy, business administration student organization, professional and trade organization.

Student services. Adult student services, career counseling, student employment services, financial aid counseling, minority student services, placement for graduates, veterans' counselor. **Physically disabled:** Services for visually, speech, hearing impaired. **Transfer:** Transfer adviser, college fairs on campus for students transferring to 4-year colleges.

Contact. E-mail: sdillman@ivytech.edu
Phone: (765) 459-0561 ext. 318 Toll-free number: (800) 459-0561
Fax: (765) 454-5111
Mike Federspill, Director of Admissions, Ivy Tech Community College: Kokomo, 1815 East Morgan Street, Kokomo, IN 46903-1373

Ivy Tech Community College: Lafayette
Lafayette, Indiana
www.ivytech.edu
CB code: 1282

- Public 2-year community college
- Commuter campus in large town

General. Founded in 1968. Regionally accredited. **Enrollment:** 6,436 degree-seeking undergraduates; 903 non-degree-seeking students. **Degrees:** 614 associate awarded. **Location:** 60 miles from Indianapolis. **Calendar:** Semester, extensive summer session. **Full-time faculty:** 101 total. **Part-time faculty:** 330 total. **Special facilities:** Multimedia laboratory.

Student profile. Among degree-seeking undergraduates, 1,231 enrolled as first-time, first-year students.

Part-time:	46%	Asian American:	1%
Out-of-state:	1%	Hispanic American:	6%
Women:	57%	Native American:	1%
African American:	5%	25 or older:	45%

Transfer out. Colleges most students transferred to 2011: Purdue University-West Lafayette, Indiana University-Purdue University Indianapolis.

Basis for selection. Open admission, but selective for some programs. Special requirements for human services and health technology programs based on test scores and prior academic work.

2012-2013 Annual costs. Tuition/fees (projected): $3,455; $7,302 out-of-state. Per-credit charge: $111 in-state; $239 out-of-state.

Financial aid. Need-based: Need-based aid available for part-time students. Work-study available nights, weekends and for part-time students.

Application procedures. Admission: No deadline. No application fee. Admission notification on a rolling basis. Application closing date for international students at least 60 days prior to start of semester. **Financial aid:** Priority date 3/1; no closing date. FAFSA required. Applicants notified on a rolling basis starting 7/1.

Academics. Special study options: Distance learning, dual enrollment of high school students, internships, liberal arts/career combination, teacher certification program, weekend college. License preparation in dental hygiene, nursing. **Credit/placement by examination:** AP, CLEP, institutional tests. 45 credit hours maximum toward associate degree. 15 credits must be earned in residence. **Support services:** Learning center, reduced course load, remedial instruction, tutoring.

Majors. Biology: Biotechnology. **Business:** Accounting technology, business admin, executive assistant. **Computer sciences:** General, information technology. **Education:** General, early childhood. **Health services:** Medical assistant, medical records technology, mental health services, nursing (RN), respiratory therapy technology, surgical technology. **Liberal arts:** Arts/sciences, library assistant. **Protective services:** Criminal justice.

Most popular majors. Business/marketing 21%, computer/information sciences 9%, engineering/engineering technologies 10%, health sciences 27%, liberal arts 8%, security/protective services 8%, trade and industry 10%.

Computing on campus. 1,313 workstations in library, computer center. Online course registration, online library, helpline, repair service, student web hosting available.

Student life. Freshman orientation: Available. Preregistration for classes offered. **Activities:** Student government, Phi Theta Kappa, American Chemical Society, Dental Assistant Society, Respiratory Care Society, student leadership academy, culture club.

Student services. Adult student services, career counseling, student employment services, financial aid counseling, minority student services, placement for graduates, veterans' counselor. **Physically disabled:** Services for visually, speech, hearing impaired. **Transfer:** Transfer center, transfer adviser for students transferring to 4-year colleges.

Contact. E-mail: jdoppelf@ivytech.edu
Phone: (765) 269-5200 Toll-free number: (800) 669-4882 ext. 5200
Fax: (765) 772-9293
Ivan Hernadez, Director of Admissions, Ivy Tech Community College: Lafayette, 3101 South Creasy Lane, Lafayette, IN 47905-6299

Ivy Tech Community College: North Central
South Bend, Indiana
www.ivytech.edu
CB code: 1280

- Public 2-year community college
- Commuter campus in small city

General. Founded in 1968. Regionally accredited. Campuses also at Warsaw and Elkhart. **Enrollment:** 8,132 degree-seeking undergraduates; 530 non-degree-seeking students. **Degrees:** 579 associate awarded. **Location:** 100 miles from Chicago. **Calendar:** Semester, extensive summer session. **Full-time faculty:** 104 total. **Part-time faculty:** 329 total.

Student profile. Among degree-seeking undergraduates, 1,375 enrolled as first-time, first-year students.

Part-time:	66%	Asian American:	1%
Out-of-state:	2%	Hispanic American:	8%
Women:	63%	Native American:	1%
African American:	20%	25 or older:	62%

Transfer out. Colleges most students transferred to 2011: Indiana University-South Bend, Indiana University-Purdue University Fort Wayne, Purdue University-West Lafayette, Purdue University-North Central.

Basis for selection. Open admission, but selective for some programs. Special requirements for human services and health technology programs based on test scores and prior academic work. Comparative Guidance and Placement Program required for admission of allied health applicants. Interview required of allied health majors. Portfolio recommended for photographic technology and graphic arts technology majors.

High school preparation. Medical laboratory assistant program requires 1 chemistry and 1 algebra.

2012-2013 Annual costs. Tuition/fees (projected): $3,455; $7,302 out-of-state. Per-credit charge: $111 in-state; $239 out-of-state.

Financial aid. Need-based: Need-based aid available for part-time students. Work-study available nights, weekends and for part-time students.

Application procedures. Admission: No deadline. No application fee. Admission notification on a rolling basis. **Financial aid:** Priority date 3/1; no closing date. FAFSA required. Applicants notified on a rolling basis starting 7/1.

Academics. Industrial training division offers customized courses and seminars to companies and corporations in surrounding community. **Special study options:** Distance learning, dual enrollment of high school students, ESL, internships, liberal arts/career combination, teacher certification program, weekend college. License preparation in nursing. **Credit/placement by examination:** AP, CLEP, institutional tests. 45 credit hours maximum toward associate degree. 15 credits must be earned in residence. **Support services:** Learning center, reduced course load, remedial instruction, tutoring.

Majors. Biology: Biotechnology. **Business:** Accounting technology, business admin, executive assistant, hospitality admin. **Computer sciences:** General, information technology. **Education:** General, early childhood. **Health services:** Clinical lab technology, EMT paramedic, medical assistant, medical radiologic technology/radiation therapy, mental health services, nursing (RN), respiratory therapy technology. **Liberal arts:** Arts/sciences, library assistant. **Protective services:** Criminal justice. **Visual/performing arts:** Design, interior design.

Most popular majors. Business/marketing 25%, computer/information sciences 8%, engineering/engineering technologies 9%, health sciences 28%, trade and industry 16%.

Computing on campus. 1,178 workstations in library, computer center. Online course registration, online library, helpline, repair service, student web hosting available.

Student life. Freshman orientation: Available. Preregistration for classes offered. **Activities:** Student government, Phi Theta Kappa, student leadership academy, student ad club.

Student services. Adult student services, career counseling, student employment services, financial aid counseling, minority student services, placement for graduates, veterans' counselor. **Physically disabled:** Services for visually, speech, hearing impaired. **Transfer:** Transfer adviser, college fairs on campus for students transferring to 4-year colleges.

Contact. E-mail: jaustin@ivytech.edu
Phone: (574) 289-7001 Toll-free number: (888) 489-5463
Fax: (574) 236-7177
Janice Austin, Director of Admissions, Ivy Tech Community College: North Central, 220 Dean Johnson Boulevard, South Bend, IN 46601-3415

Ivy Tech Community College: Northeast
Fort Wayne, Indiana
www.ivytech.edu   CB code: 1278

- Public 2-year community college
- Commuter campus in small city

General. Founded in 1963. Regionally accredited. **Enrollment:** 10,660 degree-seeking undergraduates; 878 non-degree-seeking students. **Degrees:** 780 associate awarded. **Location:** 120 miles from Indianapolis. **Calendar:** Semester, extensive summer session. **Full-time faculty:** 130 total. **Part-time faculty:** 417 total.

Student profile. Among degree-seeking undergraduates, 2,040 enrolled as first-time, first-year students.

Part-time:	57%	Asian American:	2%
Out-of-state:	3%	Hispanic American:	5%
Women:	60%	Native American:	1%
African American:	19%	25 or older:	55%

Transfer out. Colleges most students transferred to 2011: Indiana University, Purdue University-Ft. Wayne, Ball State University.

Basis for selection. Open admission, but selective for some programs. Special requirements for human services and health technology programs based on test scores and prior academic work.

2012-2013 Annual costs. Tuition/fees (projected): $3,455; $7,302 out-of-state. Per-credit charge: $111 in-state; $239 out-of-state.

Financial aid. Need-based: Need-based aid available for part-time students. Work-study available nights, weekends and for part-time students.

Application procedures. Admission: No deadline. No application fee. Admission notification on a rolling basis. Application closing dates for international students at least 60 days prior to start of semester. **Financial aid:** Priority date 3/1; no closing date. FAFSA required. Applicants notified on a rolling basis starting 7/1.

Academics. Special study options: Distance learning, dual enrollment of high school students, ESL, internships, liberal arts/career combination, teacher certification program, weekend college. License preparation in nursing. **Credit/placement by examination:** AP, CLEP, institutional tests. 45 credit hours maximum toward associate degree. 15 credits must be completed in residence. **Support services:** GED preparation and test center, learning center, reduced course load, remedial instruction, tutoring.

Majors. Business: Accounting technology, business admin, executive assistant, hospitality admin. **Computer sciences:** General, information technology. **Education:** General, early childhood. **Health services:** EMT paramedic, massage therapy, medical assistant, mental health services, nursing (RN), respiratory therapy technology. **Liberal arts:** Arts/sciences, library assistant. **Protective services:** Criminal justice.

Most popular majors. Business/marketing 24%, engineering/engineering technologies 7%, health sciences 41%, trade and industry 8%.

Computing on campus. 1,511 workstations in library, computer center. Online course registration, online library, helpline, repair service, student web hosting available.

Student life. Freshman orientation: Available. Preregistration for classes offered. **Activities:** Student government, student newspaper, Phi Theta Kappa, multi-cultural organization, Society of Manufacturing Engineers, student leadership academy, Association of Construction Technology Students.

Student services. Adult student services, career counseling, student employment services, financial aid counseling, minority student services, placement for graduates, veterans' counselor. **Physically disabled:** Services for visually, speech, hearing impaired. **Transfer:** Transfer center, transfer adviser, college fairs on campus for students transferring to 4-year colleges.

Contact. E-mail: sscheer@ivytech.edu
Phone: (260) 480-4221 Toll-free number: (800) 859-4882 ext. 4268
Fax: (260) 480-2053
Steve Scheer, Director of Admissions, Ivy Tech Community College: Northeast, 3800 North Anthony Boulevard, Fort Wayne, IN 46805-1489

Ivy Tech Community College: Northwest
Gary, Indiana
www.ivytech.edu   CB code: 1281

- Public 2-year community college
- Commuter campus in small city

General. Founded in 1968. Regionally accredited. Campuses also at East Chicago, Valparaiso, and Michigan City. **Enrollment:** 9,323 degree-seeking undergraduates; 557 non-degree-seeking students. **Degrees:** 601 associate awarded. **Location:** 30 miles from Chicago. **Calendar:** Semester, extensive summer session. **Full-time faculty:** 126 total. **Part-time faculty:** 321 total.

Student profile. Among degree-seeking undergraduates, 54% enrolled in a transfer program, 46% enrolled in a vocational program, 2,096 enrolled as first-time, first-year students, 532 transferred in from other institutions.

Part-time:	61%	Asian American:	1%
Out-of-state:	1%	Hispanic American:	11%
Women:	64%	25 or older:	56%
African American:	27%		

Transfer out. Colleges most students transferred to 2011: Purdue University- Calumet, Indiana University-Northwest, Purdue University-North Central.

Basis for selection. Open admission, but selective for some programs. Special requirements for human services and health technology programs based on test scores and prior academic work.

2012-2013 Annual costs. Tuition/fees (projected): $3,455; $7,302 out-of-state. Per-credit charge: $111 in-state; $239 out-of-state.

Financial aid. Need-based: Need-based aid available for part-time students. Work-study available nights, weekends and for part-time students.

Application procedures. Admission: No deadline. No application fee. Admission notification on a rolling basis. Application closing date for international students at least 60 days prior to start of semester. **Financial aid:** Priority date 3/1; no closing date. FAFSA required. Applicants notified on a rolling basis starting 7/1.

Academics. Special study options: Distance learning, dual enrollment of high school students, internships, liberal arts/career combination, teacher certification program, weekend college. License preparation in nursing, physical therapy, real estate. **Credit/placement by examination:** AP, CLEP, institutional tests. 45 credit hours maximum toward associate degree. 15 credits must be earned in residence. **Support services:** Learning center, reduced course load, remedial instruction, tutoring.

Majors. Business: Accounting technology, administrative services, business admin, executive assistant, hospitality admin. **Computer sciences:** General, information technology. **Education:** General, early childhood. **Engineering:** General. **Health services:** EMT paramedic, medical assistant, medical radiologic technology/radiation therapy, mental health services, nursing (RN), physical therapy assistant, respiratory therapy technology, surgical technology. **Liberal arts:** Arts/sciences, library assistant. **Protective services:** Criminal justice.

Most popular majors. Business/marketing 19%, engineering/engineering technologies 9%, health sciences 32%, trade and industry 23%.

Computing on campus. 419 workstations in library, computer center. Online course registration, online library, helpline, repair service, student web hosting available.

Student life. Freshman orientation: Available. Preregistration for classes offered. **Activities:** Student government, Phi Theta Kappa, computer club, business club, culinary arts club, medical assistants, mortuary science club, student leadership academy, early childhood development club, nursing club.

Student services. Adult student services, career counseling, student employment services, financial aid counseling, minority student services, placement for graduates, veterans' counselor. **Physically disabled:** Services for visually, speech, hearing impaired. **Transfer:** Transfer adviser, college fairs on campus for students transferring to 4-year colleges.

Contact. E-mail: tlewis@ivytech.edu
Phone: (219) 981-1111 ext. 2216 Toll-free number: (888) 489-5463
Fax: (219) 981-4415
John Johnson, Director of Admissions, Ivy Tech Community College: Northwest, 1440 East 35th Avenue, Gary, IN 46409-1499

Ivy Tech Community College: Richmond
Richmond, Indiana
www.ivytech.edu   CB code: 1283

- Public 2-year community college
- Commuter campus in large town

General. Founded in 1968. Regionally accredited. Branch location at Connersville. **Enrollment:** 3,573 degree-seeking undergraduates; 310 non-degree-seeking students. **Degrees:** 314 associate awarded. **Location:** 70 miles from Indianapolis; 45 miles from Dayton, Ohio. **Calendar:** Semester, extensive summer session. **Full-time faculty:** 42 total. **Part-time faculty:** 163 total. **Special facilities:** Student-operated restaurant.

Student profile. Among degree-seeking undergraduates, 674 enrolled as first-time, first-year students.

Part-time:	62%	Hispanic American:	1%
Out-of-state:	6%	Native American:	1%
Women:	66%	25 or older:	64%
African American:	4%		

Transfer out. Colleges most students transferred to 2011: Indiana University East, Purdue University-West Lafayette.

Basis for selection. Open admission, but selective for some programs. Special requirements for human services and health technology programs based on test scores and prior academic work.

2012-2013 Annual costs. Tuition/fees (projected): $3,455; $7,302 out-of-state. Per-credit charge: $111 in-state; $239 out-of-state.

Financial aid. **Need-based:** Need-based aid available for part-time students. Work-study available nights, weekends and for part-time students.

Application procedures. **Admission:** No deadline. No application fee. Admission notification on a rolling basis. Application closing date for international students at least 60 days prior to start of semester. **Financial aid:** Priority date 3/1; no closing date. FAFSA required. Applicants notified on a rolling basis starting 7/1.

Academics. **Special study options:** Distance learning, dual enrollment of high school students, independent study, internships, liberal arts/career combination, teacher certification program, weekend college. License preparation in nursing. **Credit/placement by examination:** AP, CLEP, institutional tests. 45 credit hours maximum toward associate degree. 15 credits must be earned in residence. **Support services:** Learning center, reduced course load, remedial instruction, tutoring.

Majors. **Business:** Accounting technology, business admin, executive assistant. **Computer sciences:** General, information technology. **Education:** General, early childhood. **Health services:** EMT paramedic, medical assistant, medical radiologic technology/radiation therapy, mental health services, nursing (RN), respiratory therapy technology. **Liberal arts:** Arts/sciences, library assistant. **Protective services:** Criminal justice.

Most popular majors. Business/marketing 29%, computer/information sciences 6%, engineering/engineering technologies 8%, health sciences 37%, liberal arts 7%.

Computing on campus. 857 workstations in library, computer center. Online course registration, online library, helpline, repair service, student web hosting available.

Student life. **Freshman orientation:** Available. Preregistration for classes offered. **Activities:** Student government, Phi Theta Kappa, Business Professionals of America, student computer association, Student Chapter of the Institute of Management Accounts, Refrigeration Service Engineers Society, student leadership academy, multicultural student organization.

Student services. Adult student services, career counseling, student employment services, financial aid counseling, minority student services, placement for graduates, veterans' counselor. **Physically disabled:** Services for visually, speech, hearing impaired. **Transfer:** Transfer adviser for students transferring to 4-year colleges.

Contact. E-mail: jplaster@ivytech.edu
Phone: (765) 966-2656 ext. 1212 Toll-free number: (800) 659-4562
Fax: (765) 962-8741
Christine Seger, Director of Admissions, Ivy Tech Community College: Richmond, 2357 Chester Boulevard, Richmond, IN 47374-1298

Ivy Tech Community College: South Central
Sellersburg, Indiana
www.ivytech.edu   CB code: 1273

▸ Public 2-year community college
▸ Commuter campus in small town

General. Founded in 1968. Regionally accredited. **Enrollment:** 4,952 degree-seeking undergraduates; 461 non-degree-seeking students. **Degrees:**

---

563 associate awarded. **Location:** 10 miles from Louisville, Kentucky. **Calendar:** Semester, extensive summer session. **Full-time faculty:** 60 total. **Part-time faculty:** 183 total.

Student profile. Among degree-seeking undergraduates, 1,043 enrolled as first-time, first-year students.

Part-time:	62%	Asian American:	1%
Out-of-state:	13%	Hispanic American:	2%
Women:	58%	Native American:	1%
African American:	8%	25 or older:	57%

Transfer out. Colleges most students transferred to 2011: Indiana University Southeast.

Basis for selection. Open admission, but selective for some programs. Special requirements for human services and health technology programs based on test scores and prior academic work.

2012-2013 Annual costs. Tuition/fees (projected): $3,455; $7,302 out-of-state. Per-credit charge: $111 in-state; $239 out-of-state.

Financial aid. **Need-based:** Need-based aid available for part-time students. Work-study available nights, weekends and for part-time students.

Application procedures. **Admission:** No deadline. No application fee. Admission notification on a rolling basis. Application closing date for international students at least 60 days prior to start of semester. **Financial aid:** Priority date 3/1; no closing date. FAFSA required. Applicants notified on a rolling basis starting 7/1.

Academics. **Special study options:** Cooperative education, distance learning, dual enrollment of high school students, internships, liberal arts/career combination, teacher certification program, weekend college. License preparation in nursing, real estate. **Credit/placement by examination:** AP, CLEP, institutional tests. 45 credit hours maximum toward associate degree. 15 credits must be earned in residence. **Support services:** GED preparation and test center, learning center, reduced course load, remedial instruction, tutoring.

Majors. **Business:** Accounting technology, business admin, executive assistant. **Computer sciences:** General, information technology. **Education:** General, early childhood. **Health services:** Clinical lab technology, medical assistant, medical radiologic technology/radiation therapy, mental health services, nursing (RN), respiratory therapy technology. **Liberal arts:** Arts/sciences, library assistant. **Protective services:** Criminal justice. **Visual/performing arts:** Design.

Most popular majors. Business/marketing 12%, engineering/engineering technologies 6%, health sciences 46%, liberal arts 12%, trade and industry 11%.

Computing on campus. 505 workstations in library, computer center. Online course registration, online library, helpline, repair service, student web hosting available.

Student life. **Freshman orientation:** Mandatory. Preregistration for classes offered. **Activities:** Student government, student newspaper, Phi Theta Kappa, art club, Christian Student Fellowship, C.A.R.E. club, ASN club, Business Professionals of America, human services club, computer information club, student leadership academy.

Student services. Career counseling, student employment services, financial aid counseling, minority student services, placement for graduates, veterans' counselor. **Transfer:** Transfer center, transfer adviser, college fairs on campus for students transferring to 4-year colleges.

Contact. E-mail: pfawcett@ivytech.edu
Phone: (812) 246-3301 ext. 4136 Toll-free number: (800) 321-9021
Fax: (812) 246-9905
Pat Fawcett, Director of Enrollment Services, Ivy Tech Community College: South Central, 8204 Highway 311, Sellersburg, IN 47172-1897

Ivy Tech Community College: Southeast
Madison, Indiana
www.ivytech.edu   CB code: 1334

▸ Public 2-year community college
▸ Commuter campus in large town

General. Founded in 1968. Regionally accredited. Branch in Lawrenceburg. **Enrollment:** 2,592 degree-seeking undergraduates; 224 non-degree-seeking students. **Degrees:** 268 associate awarded. **Location:** 46 miles from Columbus, Ohio; 88 miles from Indianapolis. **Calendar:** Semester, extensive summer session. **Full-time faculty:** 47 total. **Part-time faculty:** 151 total. **Special facilities:** Gaming training center in Aurora, Indiana.

Student profile. Among degree-seeking undergraduates, 502 enrolled as first-time, first-year students.

Part-time:	53%	African American:	1%
Out-of-state:	5%	Hispanic American:	1%
Women:	70%	25 or older:	51%

Transfer out. Colleges most students transferred to 2011: Indiana University-Southeast.

Basis for selection. Open admission, but selective for some programs. Special requirements for human services and health technology programs based on test scores and prior academic work.

2012-2013 Annual costs. Tuition/fees (projected): $3,455; $7,302 out-of-state. Per-credit charge: $111 in-state; $239 out-of-state.

Financial aid. Need-based: Need-based aid available for part-time students. Work-study available nights, weekends and for part-time students.

Application procedures. Admission: No deadline. No application fee. Admission notification on a rolling basis. Application closing date for international students at least 60 days prior to start of semester. **Financial aid:** Priority date 3/1; no closing date. FAFSA required. Applicants notified on a rolling basis starting 7/1.

Academics. Special study options: Distance learning, dual enrollment of high school students, internships, liberal arts/career combination, teacher certification program, weekend college. License preparation in nursing. **Credit/placement by examination:** AP, CLEP, institutional tests. 45 credit hours maximum toward associate degree. 15 credit hours must be earned in residence. **Support services:** Learning center, reduced course load, remedial instruction, tutoring.

Majors. Business: Accounting technology, business admin, executive assistant. **Computer sciences:** General, information technology. **Education:** General, early childhood. **Health services:** Medical assistant, mental health services, nursing (RN). **Liberal arts:** Arts/sciences, library assistant. **Protective services:** Criminal justice.

Most popular majors. Business/marketing 28%, computer/information sciences 7%, education 6%, engineering/engineering technologies 7%, health sciences 41%, liberal arts 6%.

Computing on campus. 710 workstations in library, computer center. Online course registration, online library, helpline, repair service, student web hosting available.

Student life. Freshman orientation: Available. Preregistration for classes offered. **Activities:** Student government, Phi Theta Kappa, student leadership academy, computer club, fitness club.

Student services. Career counseling, student employment services, financial aid counseling, minority student services, placement for graduates, veterans' counselor. **Physically disabled:** Services for visually, speech, hearing impaired. **Transfer:** Transfer adviser, college fairs on campus for students transferring to 4-year colleges.

Contact. E-mail: chutcher@ivytech.edu
Phone: (812) 265-2580 ext. 4142 Toll-free number: (800) 403-2190
Fax: (812) 265-4028
Cindy Hutcherson, Assistant Director of Admission/Career Services, Ivy Tech Community College: Southeast, 590 Ivy Tech Drive, Madison, IN 47250-1881

Ivy Tech Community College: Southwest
Evansville, Indiana
www.ivytech.edu
CB code: 1277

▸ Public 2-year community college
▸ Commuter campus in small city

General. Founded in 1968. Regionally accredited. Branch location at Tell City. **Enrollment:** 5,855 degree-seeking undergraduates; 432 non-degree-seeking students. **Degrees:** 540 associate awarded. **Location:** 180 miles from Indianapolis; 112 miles from Louisville, Kentucky. **Calendar:** Semester, extensive summer session. **Full-time faculty:** 85 total. **Part-time faculty:** 256 total. **Special facilities:** Plastics lab, computer integrated manufacturing lab.

Student profile. Among degree-seeking undergraduates, 966 enrolled as first-time, first-year students.

Part-time:	58%	Asian American:	1%
Out-of-state:	3%	Hispanic American:	2%
Women:	56%	25 or older:	56%
African American:	10%		

Transfer out. Colleges most students transferred to 2011: University of Southern Indiana, Vincennes University, Indiana State University.

Basis for selection. Open admission, but selective for some programs. Special requirements for human services and health technology programs based on test scores and prior academic work.

2012-2013 Annual costs. Tuition/fees (projected): $3,455; $7,302 out-of-state. Per-credit charge: $111 in-state; $239 out-of-state.

Financial aid. Need-based: Need-based aid available for part-time students. Work-study available nights, weekends and for part-time students.

Application procedures. Admission: No deadline. No application fee. Admission notification on a rolling basis. Application closing date for international students at least 60 days prior to start of semester. **Financial aid:** Priority date 3/1; no closing date. FAFSA required. Applicants notified on a rolling basis starting 7/1.

Academics. Special study options: Cooperative education, distance learning, dual enrollment of high school students, independent study, internships, liberal arts/career combination, teacher certification program, weekend college. License preparation in nursing, paramedic. **Credit/placement by examination:** AP, CLEP, institutional tests. 45 credit hours maximum toward associate degree. 15 credit hours must be earned in residence. **Support services:** Learning center, reduced course load, remedial instruction, tutoring.

Majors. Biology: Biotechnology. **Business:** Accounting technology, business admin, executive assistant, hospitality admin. **Computer sciences:** General, information technology. **Education:** General, early childhood. **Engineering:** General. **Health services:** EMT paramedic, medical assistant, mental health services, nursing (RN), surgical technology. **Liberal arts:** Arts/sciences, library assistant. **Protective services:** Criminal justice. **Visual/performing arts:** Design, interior design.

Most popular majors. Business/marketing 17%, engineering/engineering technologies 8%, health sciences 21%, trade and industry 27%, visual/performing arts 7%.

Computing on campus. 1,021 workstations in library, computer center. Online course registration, online library, helpline, repair service, student web hosting available.

Student life. Freshman orientation: Available. Preregistration for classes offered. **Housing:** Housing available at University of Southern Indiana. **Activities:** Student government, Phi Theta Kappa, American Institute of Architectural Students, National Association of Industrial Technicians, International Association of Administrative Professionals, human services club, student leadership academy, art and design club.

Student services. Adult student services, career counseling, student employment services, financial aid counseling, minority student services, placement for graduates, veterans' counselor. **Physically disabled:** Services for visually, speech, hearing impaired. **Transfer:** Transfer adviser, college fairs on campus for students transferring to 4-year colleges.

Contact. E-mail: ajohnson@ivytech.edu
Phone: (812) 429-1430 Toll-free number: (888) 489-5463
Fax: (812) 429-9878
Denise Johnson-Kincaid, Director of Admissions, Ivy Tech Community College: Southwest, 3501 First Avenue, Evansville, IN 47710-3398

Ivy Tech Community College: Wabash Valley
Terre Haute, Indiana
www.ivytech.edu
CB code: 1284

▸ Public 2-year community college
▸ Commuter campus in small city

General. Founded in 1966. Regionally accredited. Branch location at Greencastle. **Enrollment:** 5,371 degree-seeking undergraduates; 763 non-degree-seeking students. **Degrees:** 581 associate awarded. **Location:** 80 miles from Indianapolis. **Calendar:** Semester, extensive summer session. **Full-time faculty:** 95 total. **Part-time faculty:** 185 total. **Special facilities:** Plastics productivity center.

Student profile. Among degree-seeking undergraduates, 842 enrolled as first-time, first-year students.

Part-time:	50%	Asian American:	1%
Out-of-state:	5%	Hispanic American:	1%
Women:	61%	25 or older:	53%
African American:	4%		

Transfer out. Colleges most students transferred to 2011: Indiana State University, Vincennes University, Purdue University-West Lafayette.

Basis for selection. Open admission, but selective for some programs. Special requirements for human services and health technology programs based on test scores and prior academic work.

2012-2013 Annual costs. Tuition/fees (projected): $3,455; $7,302 out-of-state. Per-credit charge: $111 in-state; $239 out-of-state.

Financial aid. Need-based: Need-based aid available for part-time students. Work-study available nights, weekends and for part-time students.

Application procedures. Admission: No deadline. No application fee. Admission notification on a rolling basis. Application closing date for international students is at least 60 days prior to start of semester. **Financial aid:** Priority date 3/1; no closing date. FAFSA required. Applicants notified on a rolling basis starting 7/1.

Academics. Special study options: Distance learning, dual enrollment of high school students, internships, liberal arts/career combination, teacher certification program, weekend college. License preparation in aviation, nursing, paramedic, radiology. **Credit/placement by examination:** AP, CLEP, institutional tests. 45 credit hours maximum toward associate degree. 15 credits must be earned in residence. **Support services:** Learning center, reduced course load, remedial instruction, tutoring.

Majors. Biology: Biotechnology. **Business:** Accounting technology, business admin, executive assistant. **Computer sciences:** General, information technology. **Education:** General, early childhood. **Health services:** Clinical lab technology, EMT paramedic, medical assistant, medical radiologic technology/radiation therapy, mental health services, nursing (RN), respiratory therapy technology, surgical technology. **Liberal arts:** Arts/sciences, library assistant. **Protective services:** Criminal justice. **Visual/performing arts:** Design.

Most popular majors. Business/marketing 14%, education 6%, health sciences 39%, trade and industry 18%.

Computing on campus. 1,589 workstations in library, computer center. Online course registration, online library, helpline, repair service, student web hosting, wireless network available.

Student life. Freshman orientation: Available. Preregistration for classes offered. **Activities:** Student government, Phi Theta Kappa, student leadership academy, practical nurses class organization.

Student services. Adult student services, career counseling, student employment services, financial aid counseling, minority student services, on-campus daycare, placement for graduates, veterans' counselor. **Physically disabled:** Services for visually, speech, hearing impaired. **Transfer:** Transfer center, transfer adviser, college fairs on campus for students transferring to 4-year colleges.

Contact. E-mail: mfisher@ivytech.edu
Phone: (812) 298-2300 Toll-free number: (800) 377-4882
Fax: (812) 299-5723
Michael Fisher, Director of Admissions, Ivy Tech Community College: Wabash Valley, 8000 South Education Drive, Terre Haute, IN 47802-4898

Kaplan College: Hammond
Hammond, Indiana
www.kaplan.com   CB code: 2461

- For-profit 2-year business and technical college
- Commuter campus in small city
- Interview required

General. Founded in 1969. Accredited by ACICS. Branch campus in Merrillville. **Degrees:** 101 associate awarded. **Location:** 30 miles from Chicago, 15 miles from Merrillville. **Calendar:** Quarter, extensive summer session. **Full-time faculty:** 7 total. **Part-time faculty:** 30 total.

Basis for selection. Personal interview with admissions representative and passing score on entrance examination required.

Financial aid. Need-based: Work-study available nights, weekends and for part-time students.

Application procedures. Admission: No deadline. $10 fee. Admission notification on a rolling basis. **Financial aid:** FAFSA required. Applicants notified on a rolling basis.

Academics. Special study options: Internships. **Credit/placement by examination:** AP, CLEP, institutional tests. 24 credit hours maximum toward associate degree. Institutional placement test score must be at least 81%. **Support services:** Remedial instruction, study skills assistance, tutoring.

Majors. Business: Accounting, administrative services. **Computer sciences:** General. **Health services:** Massage therapy, medical assistant, medical secretary.

Most popular majors. Business/marketing 48%, computer/information sciences 52%.

Computing on campus. 70 workstations in computer center.

Student life. Activities: Student newspaper.

Student services. Career counseling, student employment services, personal counseling, placement for graduates. **Transfer:** Pre-admission transcript evaluation for new students.

Contact. Phone: (219) 844-0100 Fax: (219) 844-0105
Rodger Schilling, Admissions Director, Kaplan College: Hammond, 7833 Indianapolis Boulevard, Hammond, IN 46324

Kaplan College: Indianapolis
Indianapolis, Indiana
www.kaplancollege.com   CB code: 7700

- For-profit 2-year health science and nursing college
- Commuter campus in very large city
- Application essay, interview required

General. Accredited by ACCSC. **Location:** Northwest Indianapolis, Indiana. **Calendar:** Differs by program. **Full-time faculty:** 15 total. **Part-time faculty:** 7 total.

Basis for selection. Open admission, but selective for some programs. Interview most important. Class rank, school record, recommendations, standardized test scores, and essay also important.

Financial aid. All financial aid based on need. Work-study available nights, weekends and for part-time students.

Application procedures. Admission: No deadline. $10 fee. Admission notification on a rolling basis.

Academics. Special study options: Accelerated study, internships. **Credit/placement by examination:** AP, CLEP.

Majors. Business: Administrative services, business admin. **Computer sciences:** General, applications programming, data entry, information technology. **Health services:** Dental assistant, massage therapy, medical assistant, medical secretary, office admin.

Computing on campus. 30 workstations in library, computer center.

Student services. Financial aid counseling, placement for graduates.

Contact. E-mail: rmagaruh@kaplan.edu
Phone: (317) 299-6001 Fax: (317) 298-6342
Jerry Rasberry, Director of Admissions, Kaplan College: Indianapolis, 7302 Woodland Drive, Indianapolis, IN 46278-1736

Kaplan College: Merrillville
Merrillville, Indiana
www.sawyercollege.edu   CB code: 3381

- For-profit 2-year technical college
- Commuter campus in large town
- Interview required

General. Accredited by ACICS. **Enrollment:** 295 undergraduates. **Degrees:** 47 associate awarded. **Location:** 35 miles from Chicago. **Calendar:** Quarter. **Full-time faculty:** 5 total. **Part-time faculty:** 14 total.

Basis for selection. Open admission. **Home schooled:** State high school equivalency certificate required.

2011-2012 Annual costs. Books/supplies: $1,324.

Financial aid. Need-based: Need-based aid available for part-time students. Work-study available nights, weekends and for part-time students.

Application procedures. Admission: No deadline. $20 fee. Admission notification on a rolling basis. **Financial aid:** No deadline. FAFSA required. Applicants notified on a rolling basis.

Academics. Special study options: Liberal arts/career combination. **Credit/placement by examination:** AP, CLEP. 50 credit hours maximum toward associate degree. **Support services:** Reduced course load, study skills assistance, tutoring.

Majors. Health services: Massage therapy, medical assistant, office admin.

Computing on campus. 72 workstations in library, computer center. Online library available.

Student life. Freshman orientation: Mandatory. Preregistration for classes offered.

Student services. Adult student services, career counseling, student employment services, financial aid counseling, placement for graduates. **Transfer:** Pre-admission transcript evaluation for new students.

Contact. Phone: (219) 736-0436 Toll-free number: (800) 964-0218
Fax: (219) 942-3762
Sonya Vance-Brown, Director of Admissions, Kaplan College: Merrillville, 3803 East Lincoln Highway, Merrillville, IN 46410

Lincoln College of Technology: Indianapolis
Indianapolis, Indiana
www.lincolntech.com   CB code: 3058

◗ For-profit 2-year technical college
◗ Very large city

General. Accredited by ACCSC. **Degrees:** 329 associate awarded. **Calendar:** Differs by program. **Full-time faculty:** 45 total. **Part-time faculty:** 9 total.

Basis for selection. Open admission.

2011-2012 Annual costs. Total program costs range from $12,200 up to $32,945 depending on program. Cost of books and materials included in tuition. Books/supplies: $1,815.

Financial aid. Need-based: Work-study available nights, weekends and for part-time students.

Application procedures. Admission: No deadline. $100 fee.

Academics. Credit/placement by examination: AP, CLEP.

Contact. Phone: (317) 632-5553 Toll-free number: (800) 554-4465
Fax: (317) 634-1089
David Cahill, Vice President of Admissions, Lincoln College of Technology: Indianapolis, 7225 Winton Drive, Building 128, Indianapolis, IN 46268

Mid-America College of Funeral Service
Jeffersonville, Indiana
www.mid-america.edu   CB code: 0644

◗ Private 2-year school of mortuary science
◗ Commuter campus in large town

General. Founded in 1905. **Enrollment:** 90 degree-seeking undergraduates. **Degrees:** 16 bachelor's, 47 associate awarded. **Location:** 5 miles from Louisville, Kentucky. **Calendar:** Quarter. **Full-time faculty:** 3 total. **Part-time faculty:** 2 total.

Basis for selection. Open admission. **Home schooled:** Transcript of courses and grades required.

2011-2012 Annual costs. Tuition/fees: $9,000. Cost of entire program leading to associate degree: $18,000; cost of bachelor's degree completion for those with sufficient transfer credit also $18,000. Personal expenses: $2,520.

Financial aid. Need-based: Work-study available nights, weekends and for part-time students.

Application procedures. Admission: No deadline. $50 fee. Admission notification on a rolling basis. **Financial aid:** No deadline. FAFSA required. Applicants notified on a rolling basis.

Academics. Credit/placement by examination: AP, CLEP.

Computing on campus. 15 workstations in library, computer center.

Student life. Activities: Student government.

Student services. Student employment services, personal counseling, placement for graduates. **Transfer:** Pre-admission transcript evaluation for new students.

Contact. E-mail: macfs@mindspring.com
Phone: (812) 288-8878 Toll-free number: (800) 221-6158
Fax: (812) 288-5942
Amanda Christiansen, Director of Admissions, Mid-America College of Funeral Service, 3111 Hamburg Pike, Jeffersonville, IN 47130

National College: Indianapolis
Indianapolis, Indiana
www.national-college.edu

◗ For-profit 2-year branch campus college
◗ Very large city

General. Regionally accredited; also accredited by ACICS. **Enrollment:** 127 degree-seeking undergraduates. **Degrees:** 2 bachelor's, 54 associate awarded. **Calendar:** Quarter. **Full-time faculty:** 4 total. **Part-time faculty:** 26 total.

Basis for selection. Open admission, but selective for some programs.

2011-2012 Annual costs. Tuition/fees: $13,770. Per-credit charge: $305.

Financial aid. Need-based: Work-study available nights, weekends and for part-time students.

Application procedures. Admission: No deadline. $50 fee.

Academics. Credit/placement by examination: AP, CLEP.

Majors. Business: Accounting/business management, administrative services, business admin. **Health services:** Medical assistant, medical records technology, pharmacy assistant, surgical technology.

Contact. Phone: (317) 578-7353
Patricia Young, Regional Director of Admissions, National College: Indianapolis, 6060 Castleway Drive West, Indianapolis, IN 46250

Vincennes University
Vincennes, Indiana   CB member
www.vinu.edu   CB code: 1877

◗ Public 2-year junior college
◗ Residential campus in large town

General. Founded in 1801. Regionally accredited. Additional campuses/sites: Jasper (VUJC), Aviation Technology Center at Indianapolis International Airport; American Sign Language program at Indiana School for the Deaf (Indianapolis), Indiana Center for Applied Technology, Gibson County Center for Advanced Manufacturing and Logistics, Plainfield Logistics Training and Education Center. Extensive military education program and 27 online degree programs. **Enrollment:** 16,825 undergraduates. **Degrees:** 91 bachelor's, 1,256 associate awarded. **ROTC:** Army, Air Force. **Location:** 55 miles from Evansville, 120 miles from Indianapolis. **Calendar:** Semester, extensive summer session. **Full-time faculty:** 269 total; 3% minority, 48% women. **Part-time faculty:** 891 total; 6% minority, 55% women. **Special facilities:** Airport, performing arts center, Indiana Center for Applied Technology, physical education complex, robotics lab, diesel technology/agricultural facility, welding facility. **Partnerships:** Formal partnerships with Haas Haas Automation, Incorporated, ABB Robotics, John Deere, Associated Builders and Contractors, WorkOne.

Student profile. 57% enrolled in a vocational program.

Out-of-state:	16%	International:	1%
African American:	11%	25 or older:	38%
Asian American:	1%	Live on campus:	21%
Hispanic American:	3%		

Transfer out. **Colleges most students transferred to 2011:** Indiana University, Indiana State University, Purdue University, University of Southern Indiana, Ball State University.

Basis for selection. Open admission, but selective for some programs. Admission to health occupation programs is based primarily on high school transcripts, test scores, school and community activities, and special talents/ skills. Audition required of music majors. Portfolio recommended for fine arts, commercial art, design majors, and graduates of non-traditional high schools. **Adult students:** SAT/ACT scores not required. **Home schooled:** Statement describing home school structure and mission, transcript of courses and grades required. Documentation should include course/curriculum descriptions and an academic portfolio. **Learning Disabled:** Students needing special accommodations are required to submit psychometric testing indicating diagnosis of specific disability, along with a list of any special services required.

High school preparation. College-preparatory program recommended. Recommended units include English 4, mathematics 3, social studies 2, history 2, science 3 (laboratory 2) and foreign language 2.

2012-2013 Annual costs. Tuition/fees (projected): $4,616; $11,213 out-of-state. Per-credit charge: $154 in-state; $374 out-of-state. Projected tuition for students from Crawford, Richland, Lawrence and Wabash counties in Illinois is $240 per-credit hour (including capital improvement and technology fees, not including student activity fee). Room/board: $8,151. Books/supplies: $1,098. Personal expenses: $1,020.

Financial aid. **Need-based:** Need-based aid available for part-time students. Work-study available nights, weekends and for part-time students. **Non-need-based:** Scholarships awarded for academics, art, athletics, leadership, music/drama, state residency.

Application procedures. **Admission:** No deadline. $20 fee, may be waived for applicants with need. Admission notification on a rolling basis. **Financial aid:** Priority date 3/1; no closing date. FAFSA required. Applicants notified on a rolling basis starting 5/1; must reply by 8/24.

Academics. **Special study options:** Accelerated study, distance learning, double major, dual enrollment of high school students, ESL, external degree, honors, independent study, internships, student-designed major. Bachelor's degree programs available on campus. License preparation in aviation, nursing, paramedic, real estate. **Credit/placement by examination:** AP, CLEP, IB, institutional tests. **Support services:** GED test center, learning center, pre-admission summer program, reduced course load, remedial instruction, study skills assistance, tutoring, writing center.

Honors college/program. 1100 SAT (exclusive of Writing), 25 ACT, leadership qualities, writing sample, 3 references. 20 students admitted for fall.

Majors. **Biology:** General, biochemistry, biotechnology. **Business:** General, accounting technology, administrative services, business admin, fashion, hospitality admin, hotel/motel admin, logistics. **Communications:** Journalism, photojournalism, public relations. **Communications technology:** Graphic/ printing, radio/TV, recording arts. **Computer sciences:** General, computer science, networking, programming, webmaster. **Conservation:** General. **Education:** Art, business, chemistry, early childhood, elementary, English, family/consumer sciences, health, mathematics, music, physical, secondary, special ed, speech, teacher assistance, technology/industrial arts. **Engineering:** Agricultural, biomedical, chemical, civil, electrical, mechanical, surveying. **English:** English lit. **Foreign languages:** General, American Sign Language. **General:** Business, food processing, food science, horticulture. **Health services:** Art therapy, dietetics, EMT paramedic, environmental health, health care admin, massage therapy, medical radiologic technology/ radiation therapy, medical records technology, nuclear medical technology, nursing (RN), pharmacy assistant, physical therapy assistant, predental, premedicine, prepharmacy, preveterinary, surgical technology. **History:** General. **Human services:** General, social work. **Liberal arts:** Arts/sciences. **Math:** General. **Parks/recreation:** Health/fitness, sports admin. **Philosophy/ religion:** Philosophy. **Physical sciences:** Chemistry, geology, physics. **Protective services:** Firefighting, police science, security management, security services. **Psychology:** General. **Social sciences:** General, anthropology, economics, geography, political science, sociology. **Visual/performing arts:** Art, commercial/advertising art, dramatic, music performance, theater design. **Work/family studies:** General, child care management.

Most popular majors. Business/marketing 10%, engineering/engineering technologies 8%, health sciences 16%, liberal arts 24%, security/protective services 8%, trade and industry 10%.

Computing on campus. 1,500 workstations in dormitories, library, computer center, student center. Dormitories wired for high-speed internet access and linked to campus network. Commuter students can connect to campus network. Online library, wireless network available.

Student life. **Freshman orientation:** Mandatory. Preregistration for classes offered. Held the weekend prior to first day of classes; includes study skills, social activities, both student and parent sessions, tours, move-in, and entertainment. **Policies:** Tobacco use is only permitted in designated areas. Facilities and grounds are tobacco-free zones. **Housing:** Coed dorms, single-sex dorms, special housing for disabled, cooperative housing, fraternity/ sorority housing, wellness housing available. $150 partly refundable deposit. **Activities:** Bands, campus ministries, choral groups, dance, drama, international student organizations, literary magazine, music ensembles, musical theater, radio station, student government, student newspaper, TV station, Black Male Initiative, College Republicans, Christian Campus Fellowship, Democrat Club, Today's Black Women, Women of Essence and Gospel Choir, Embracing Latino Heritage, VU Pride (GLBT).

Athletics. NJCAA. **Intercollegiate:** Baseball M, basketball, bowling, cheerleading, cross-country, golf M, tennis M, track and field, volleyball W. **Intramural:** Baseball M, basketball, bowling, cross-country, football (non-tackle) M, golf, gymnastics, handball, racquetball, skiing, softball, swimming, table tennis, tennis, track and field, volleyball, wrestling M. **Team name:** Trailblazers.

Student services. Adult student services, alcohol/substance abuse counseling, chaplain/spiritual director, career counseling, services for economically disadvantaged, student employment services, financial aid counseling, health services, minority student services, personal counseling, placement for graduates, veterans' counselor. **Physically disabled:** Services for visually, speech, hearing impaired. **Transfer:** Pre-admission transcript evaluation for new students. Transfer adviser for students transferring to 4-year colleges.

Contact. E-mail: vuadmit@vinu.edu
Phone: (812) 888-4313 Toll-free number: (800) 742-9198
Fax: (812) 888-5707
Christian Blome, Director of Admissions, Vincennes University, 1002 North First Street, Vincennes, IN 47591

Iowa

AIB College of Business
Des Moines, Iowa
www.aib.edu   CB code: 7302

▶ Private 2-year business college
▶ Commuter campus in large city

General. Founded in 1921. Regionally accredited. **Enrollment:** 828 degree-seeking undergraduates; 12 non-degree-seeking students. **Degrees:** 197 bachelor's, 180 associate awarded. **Location:** 1 mile from downtown. **Calendar:** Quarter, extensive summer session. **Full-time faculty:** 21 total; 5% have terminal degrees, 67% women. **Part-time faculty:** 44 total; 7% have terminal degrees, 4% minority, 59% women. **Class size:** 71% < 20, 29% 20-39. **Special facilities:** Steno and voice captioning labs.

Student profile. Among degree-seeking undergraduates, 1% already have a bachelor's degree or higher, 119 enrolled as first-time, first-year students, 99 transferred in from other institutions.

Part-time:	31%	Hispanic American:	4%
Out-of-state:	8%	Native American:	1%
Women:	67%	25 or older:	38%
African American:	3%	Live on campus:	32%
Asian American:	3%		

Transfer out. Colleges most students transferred to 2011: University of Northern Iowa, Iowa State University, Grand View University, Upper Iowa University, Des Moines Area Community College.

Basis for selection. High school record important, test scores considered. ACT recommended. Institution's own test administered for students without ACT or with less than 18 ACT. **Adult students:** Must be transfer student or take institutional admission exam. **Home schooled:** Transcript of courses and grades required. **Learning Disabled:** Accommodations require documentation of disability from health care professional.

High school preparation. Business classes recommended.

2012-2013 Annual costs. Tuition/fees: $14,040. Per-credit charge: $256. Room only: $3,525. Books/supplies: $1,440. Personal expenses: $1,281.

2010-2011 Financial aid. Need-based: 106 full-time freshmen applied for aid; 99 were judged to have need; 99 of these received aid. Average need met was 80%. Average scholarship/grant was $10,382; average loan $2,440. 57% of total undergraduate aid awarded as scholarships/grants, 43% as loans/jobs. Need-based aid available for part-time students. Work-study available nights, weekends and for part-time students. **Non-need-based:** Awarded to 472 full-time undergraduates, including 73 freshmen. Scholarships awarded for academics, alumni affiliation, athletics, leadership, minority status.

Application procedures. Admission: Closing date 8/15 (receipt date). No application fee. Admission notification on a rolling basis beginning on or about 9/15. **Financial aid:** Priority date 4/1; no closing date. FAFSA, institutional form required. Applicants notified on a rolling basis starting 3/1; must reply within 2 week(s) of notification.

Academics. Students can complete bachelor's degree in 3 years. Steno court reporting program approved by the National Court Reporters Association. Online bachelor's programs available in Accounting and Business Administration. **Special study options:** Distance learning, double major, dual enrollment of high school students, independent study, internships. Evening program. Bachelor's degree programs available on campus. **Credit/placement by examination:** AP, CLEP, ACT, institutional tests. 72 credit hours maximum toward associate degree, 27 toward bachelor's. 18 quarter hours can be earned through assessment of prior learning towards associate's degree and bachelor's degree. **Support services:** Reduced course load, remedial instruction, study skills assistance, tutoring.

Majors. Business: Accounting, accounting/business management, accounting/finance, administrative services, business admin, finance, hospitality admin, international, marketing, organizational leadership, sales/distribution, selling, tourism/travel. **Communications technology:** General. **Computer sciences:** General, programming. **Health services:** Medical records admin. **Parks/recreation:** Sports admin.

Most popular majors. Business/marketing 77%, legal studies 9%.

Computing on campus. 372 workstations in dormitories, library, computer center, student center. Dormitories wired for high-speed internet access and linked to campus network. Commuter students can connect to campus network. Online library, helpline, repair service, wireless network available.

Student life. Freshman orientation: Mandatory. Preregistration for classes offered. One-day sessions held in summer for students and families. **Housing:** Guaranteed on-campus for all undergraduates. Coed dorms, special housing for disabled, apartments available. $200 fully refundable deposit. **Activities:** International student organizations, student government, international student organization, non-traditional student organization, Students in Free Enterprise, pride alliance.

Athletics. NAIA. **Intercollegiate:** Basketball, cheerleading, golf, soccer, volleyball W. **Intramural:** Badminton, basketball, bowling, football (non-tackle), softball, table tennis, volleyball. **Team name:** Eagles.

Student services. Adult student services, alcohol/substance abuse counseling, career counseling, student employment services, financial aid counseling, personal counseling, placement for graduates. **Physically disabled:** Services for visually, speech, hearing impaired. **Transfer:** Re-entry adviser, pre-admission transcript evaluation for new students.

Contact. E-mail: admissions@aib.edu
Phone: (515) 246-5358 Toll-free number: (800) 444-1921
Fax: (515) 244-6773
Steve Olsen, Director of Admissions, AIB College of Business, 2500 Fleur Drive, Des Moines, IA 50321-1799

Clinton Community College
Clinton, Iowa
www.eicc.edu   CB code: 6100

▶ Public 2-year community college
▶ Commuter campus in large town

General. Founded in 1946. Regionally accredited. **Enrollment:** 783 full-time, degree-seeking students. **Degrees:** 125 associate awarded. **Location:** 40 miles from Davenport. **Calendar:** Semester, limited summer session. **Full-time faculty:** 32 total. **Part-time faculty:** 97 total. **Class size:** 90% < 20, 9% 20-39, less than 1% 40-49.

Student profile.

Out-of-state:	12%	25 or older:	35%

Transfer out. Colleges most students transferred to 2011: Ashford University, University of Iowa, Iowa State University, University of Northern Iowa, St. Ambrose University.

Basis for selection. Open admission, but selective for some programs. Special requirements for nursing program. Interview recommended.

2011-2012 Annual costs. Tuition/fees: $3,840; $5,760 out-of-state. Per-credit charge: $128 in-state; $192 out-of-state. Online course tuition: $150 per credit-hour. Books/supplies: $1,140. Personal expenses: $1,090.

Financial aid. Need-based: Work-study available nights, weekends and for part-time students.

Application procedures. Admission: No deadline. No application fee. Admission notification on a rolling basis beginning on or about 9/1. **Financial aid:** Priority date 4/20; no closing date. FAFSA, institutional form required. Applicants notified on a rolling basis starting 5/15; must reply within 2 week(s) of notification.

Academics. Special study options: Accelerated study, cooperative education, cross-registration, distance learning, double major, dual enrollment of high school students, ESL, honors, independent study, study abroad, weekend college. License preparation in nursing, paramedic, real estate. **Credit/placement by examination:** AP, CLEP, institutional tests. 30 credit hours maximum toward associate degree. **Support services:** GED preparation and test center, learning center, reduced course load, remedial instruction, study skills assistance, tutoring.

Majors. Business: Administrative services, business admin. **Communications technology:** Graphic/printing, graphics. **Computer sciences:** Applications programming. **General:** Equine science. **Health services:** Dental hygiene, electroencephalograph technology, EMT paramedic, nuclear medical technology, nursing (RN), physical therapy assistant, radiologic technology/medical imaging, sonography. **Liberal arts:** Arts/sciences. **Protective services:** Firefighting, police science.

Most popular majors. Health sciences 11%, liberal arts 77%.

Computing on campus. 55 workstations in library, computer center. Commuter students can connect to campus network. Online course registration, helpline, wireless network available.

Student life. Freshman orientation: Available. Preregistration for classes offered. **Activities:** Drama, literary magazine, student government, student newspaper, Phi Beta Lambda, Phi Theta Kappa, student senate, peer ambassadors, drama/fine arts club, S.N.A.P., drafting club, nursing club, graphic arts/printer club, Leadership Connection.

Athletics. NJCAA. **Intercollegiate:** Basketball M, volleyball W. **Intramural:** Basketball, bowling, softball, table tennis, tennis, volleyball. **Team name:** Cougars.

Student services. Career counseling, student employment services, financial aid counseling, personal counseling, placement for graduates, veterans' counselor. **Physically disabled:** Services for visually, speech, hearing impaired. **Transfer:** Transfer adviser, college fairs on campus for students transferring to 4-year colleges.

Contact. E-mail: esnyder@eicc.edu
Phone: (888) 336-3907 Toll-free number: (888) 336-3907
Fax: (563) 244-7107
Erin Snyder, Communication Center Manager, Clinton Community College, 1000 Lincoln Boulevard, Clinton, IA 52732

Des Moines Area Community College
Ankeny, Iowa
www.dmacc.edu   CB code: 6177

- Public 2-year community college
- Commuter campus in large town

General. Founded in 1966. Regionally accredited. Multilocation institution with campuses at Boone, Des Moines, West Des Moines, Carroll, and Newton. Ankeny campus is primary location and administrative center. **Enrollment:** 17,457 degree-seeking undergraduates; 7,968 non-degree-seeking students. **Degrees:** 2,036 associate awarded. **Location:** 15 miles from downtown Des Moines, 25 miles from Ames. **Calendar:** Semester, extensive summer session. **Full-time faculty:** 340 total; 11% have terminal degrees, 6% minority, 48% women. **Part-time faculty:** 1,073 total; 13% have terminal degrees, 7% minority, 55% women. **Special facilities:** Wireless computer technology campus, career academies.

Student profile. Among degree-seeking undergraduates, 1% already have a bachelor's degree or higher, 3,017 enrolled as first-time, first-year students.

Part-time:	47%	Native American:	1%
Women:	56%	International:	1%
African American:	11%	25 or older:	24%
Asian American:	3%	Live on campus:	1%
Hispanic American:	5%		

Transfer out. Colleges most students transferred to 2011: Iowa State University, Grand View College, University of Northern Iowa.

Basis for selection. Open admission, but selective for some programs. Special requirements for dental hygiene, commercial art, nursing, CAP programs. Interview required of dental hygiene, commercial art majors. Portfolio required of commercial art majors.

High school preparation. Recommended units include English 4, mathematics 3 and science 3.

2011-2012 Annual costs. Tuition/fees: $3,936; $7,860 out-of-state. Per-credit charge: $131 in-state; $262 out-of-state. Books/supplies: $1,160. Personal expenses: $1,922.

2010-2011 Financial aid. Need-based: 39% of total undergraduate aid awarded as scholarships/grants, 61% as loans/jobs. Need-based aid available for part-time students. Work-study available nights, weekends and for part-time students. **Non-need-based:** Scholarships awarded for academics, athletics, state residency.

Application procedures. Admission: No deadline. No application fee. Admission notification on a rolling basis. **Financial aid:** Priority date 4/1; no closing date. FAFSA required. Applicants notified on a rolling basis starting 4/1; must reply within 2 week(s) of notification.

Academics. Special study options: Cooperative education, cross-registration, distance learning, dual enrollment of high school students, ESL, honors, independent study, internships, liberal arts/career combination, study abroad, weekend college. Bachelor's degree programs available on campus. License preparation in dental hygiene, nursing, paramedic, real estate. **Credit/placement by examination:** AP, CLEP, institutional tests. 28 credit hours

maximum toward associate degree. **Support services:** GED preparation and test center, learning center, pre-admission summer program, reduced course load, remedial instruction, study skills assistance, tutoring, writing center.

Majors. Biology: Biotechnology. **Business:** Accounting, accounting technology, apparel, business admin, hospitality admin, marketing, office management, sales/distribution. **Communications technology:** Desktop publishing. **Computer sciences:** Information technology. **Engineering:** Surveying. **Foreign languages:** Translation. **General:** Supplies. **Health services:** Clinical lab technology, dental hygiene, health care admin, medical records technology, medical secretary, nursing (RN), respiratory therapy technology, veterinary technology/assistant. **Human services:** Community org/advocacy. **Liberal arts:** Arts/sciences. **Parks/recreation:** Sports admin. **Protective services:** Fire safety technology, police science. **Visual/performing arts:** Commercial/advertising art. **Work/family studies:** Child care service.

Most popular majors. Business/marketing 9%, health sciences 10%, liberal arts 56%, trade and industry 6%.

Computing on campus. 200 workstations in library, computer center. Dormitories wired for high-speed internet access and linked to campus network. Commuter students can connect to campus network. Online course registration, online library, helpline, wireless network available.

Student life. Freshman orientation: Available. Preregistration for classes offered. Half-day program offered. **Policies:** Student Action Board responsible for many on-campus professional and social activities. **Housing:** Coed dorms available. **Activities:** Choral groups, drama, literary magazine, student government, student newspaper.

Athletics. NJCAA. **Intercollegiate:** Baseball M, basketball, volleyball W. **Intramural:** Badminton, basketball, bowling, football (non-tackle), golf, softball, table tennis, tennis, volleyball. **Team name:** Bears (Boone campus only).

Student services. Adult student services, career counseling, student employment services, financial aid counseling, health services, on-campus daycare, personal counseling, placement for graduates, veterans' counselor. **Physically disabled:** Services for visually, speech, hearing impaired. **Transfer:** Transfer adviser, college fairs on campus for students transferring to 4-year colleges.

Contact. E-mail: admissions@dmacc.edu
Phone: (515) 964-6241 Toll-free number: (800) 362-2127 ext. 6241
Fax: (515) 964-6391
Michael Lentsch, Director of Enrollment Management, Des Moines Area Community College, 2006 South Ankeny Boulevard, Ankeny, IA 50023-3993

Ellsworth Community College
Iowa Falls, Iowa
www.iavalley.cc.ia.us/ecc   CB code: 5528

- Public 2-year community college
- Residential campus in small town

General. Founded in 1890. Regionally accredited. **Enrollment:** 1,046 degree-seeking undergraduates. **Degrees:** 160 associate awarded. **Location:** 70 miles from Des Moines. **Calendar:** Semester, limited summer session. **Full-time faculty:** 40 total. **Part-time faculty:** 51 total. **Special facilities:** 80-acre wildlife area.

Transfer out. Colleges most students transferred to 2011: University of Northern Iowa, Buena Vista University, Iowa State University, Wartburg College, University of Iowa.

Basis for selection. Open admission, but selective for some programs. Special requirements for some nursing programs.

2011-2012 Annual costs. Tuition/fees: $4,950; $5,910 out-of-state. Per-credit charge: $139 in-state; $171 out-of-state. Room/board: $4,978. Books/supplies: $700. Personal expenses: $1,400.

Financial aid. Need-based: Need-based aid available for part-time students. Work-study available nights, weekends and for part-time students. **Non-need-based:** Scholarships awarded for academics, art, athletics, leadership, minority status, music/drama.

Application procedures. Admission: No deadline. No application fee. Admission notification on a rolling basis. COMPASS required of applicants without SAT or ACT. **Financial aid:** Closing date 4/1. FAFSA, institutional form required. Applicants notified on a rolling basis starting 2/15; must reply within 4 week(s) of notification.

Academics. Special study options: Cooperative education, cross-registration, distance learning, double major, dual enrollment of high school students, ESL, honors, independent study, internships, liberal arts/career combination. Bachelor's degree programs available on campus. License preparation in nursing. **Credit/placement by examination:** AP, CLEP, institutional tests. 24 credit hours maximum toward associate degree. **Support services:** GED preparation and test center, learning center, remedial instruction, study skills assistance, tutoring, writing center.

Majors. Biology: General, biotechnology. **Business:** General, accounting, administrative services, fashion, insurance, office technology, office/clerical. **Communications:** Communications/speech/rhetoric. **Computer sciences:** General, computer graphics, computer science, data processing, information systems, LAN/WAN management, programming. **Conservation:** General, wildlife/wilderness. **Education:** General, agricultural, biology, business, chemistry, elementary, family/consumer sciences, history, mathematics, middle, multi-level teacher, physical, physics, science, secondary, social science, social studies, teacher assistance. **Engineering:** General. **English:** English lit. **General:** Business, equestrian studies, farm/ranch. **Health services:** Athletic training, medical secretary, nursing (RN), predental, premedicine, prepharmacy, preveterinary. **History:** General. **Human services:** Social work. **Liberal arts:** Arts/sciences. **Math:** General. **Parks/recreation:** Health/fitness. **Physical sciences:** Chemistry, physics. **Protective services:** Criminal justice, law enforcement admin. **Psychology:** General. **Social sciences:** General, criminology, sociology. **Visual/performing arts:** Art, commercial/advertising art, dramatic, studio arts. **Work/family studies:** General, clothing/textiles, family/community services.

Most popular majors. Business/marketing 10%, health sciences 10%, liberal arts 59%.

Computing on campus. 100 workstations in dormitories, library, computer center, student center. Dormitories wired for high-speed internet access and linked to campus network. Commuter students can connect to campus network. Online library, repair service, wireless network available.

Student life. Freshman orientation: Mandatory. Preregistration for classes offered. Various dates to chose from for orientation, advising, and preregistration. **Housing:** Guaranteed on-campus for freshmen. Single-sex dorms available. $200 deposit. **Activities:** Bands, choral groups, dance, drama, international student organizations, literary magazine, music ensembles, musical theater, student government, student newspaper, Young Democrats, Young Republicans, minority student organization, human services club, agricultural science club, criminal justice club.

Athletics. NJCAA. **Intercollegiate:** Baseball M, basketball, cross-country, football (tackle) M, golf, softball W, volleyball W, wrestling M. **Intramural:** Badminton, basketball, bowling, football (non-tackle), handball, racquetball, swimming, tennis, volleyball. **Team name:** Panthers.

Student services. Adult student services, alcohol/substance abuse counseling, career counseling, services for economically disadvantaged, student employment services, financial aid counseling, health services, personal counseling, placement for graduates, veterans' counselor. **Transfer:** Pre-admission transcript evaluation for new students. Transfer adviser, college fairs on campus for students transferring to 4-year colleges.

Contact. Phone: (641) 648-4611 ext. 431
Toll-free number: (800) 322-9253 Fax: (641) 648-3128
Annie Kalous, Director of Admissions, Ellsworth Community College, 1100 College Avenue, Iowa Falls, IA 50126

Hawkeye Community College
Waterloo, Iowa
www.hawkeyecollege.edu   **CB code: 6288**

▶ Public 2-year community and technical college
▶ Commuter campus in small city

General. Founded in 1966. Regionally accredited. **Enrollment:** 4,330 degree-seeking undergraduates; 1,801 non-degree-seeking students. **Degrees:** 910 associate awarded. **ROTC:** Army, Naval, Air Force. **Location:** 120 miles from Des Moines, 70 miles from Cedar Rapids. **Calendar:** Semester, limited summer session. **Full-time faculty:** 119 total; 11% have terminal degrees, 3% minority, 49% women. **Part-time faculty:** 225 total; 4% have terminal degrees, 6% minority, 64% women.

Student profile. Among degree-seeking undergraduates, 56% enrolled in a transfer program, 44% enrolled in a vocational program, 1,118 enrolled as first-time, first-year students.

Part-time:	30%	Asian American:	1%
Out-of-state:	1%	Hispanic American:	3%
Women:	54%	25 or older:	23%
African American:	9%		

Transfer out. Colleges most students transferred to 2011: University of Northern Iowa, University of Iowa, Iowa State University.

Basis for selection. Open admission, but selective for some programs. Selective admission to health, engineering and information systems programs. ACT required for admission to medical laboratory technician and dental hygiene programs. Specific placement scores may be required in reading, writing and math for selective programs. **Home schooled:** Transcript of courses and grades required.

High school preparation. 1 year biology for nursing and medical laboratory technicians. 1 year chemistry for nursing, 1 semester physics for physical therapist assistant.

2011-2012 Annual costs. Tuition/fees: $4,170; $4,920 out-of-state. Per-credit charge: $133 in-state; $158 out-of-state. Books/supplies: $1,000. Personal expenses: $1,700.

Financial aid. Need-based: Work-study available nights, weekends and for part-time students. **Non-need-based:** Scholarships awarded for academics, state residency.

Application procedures. Admission: No deadline. No application fee. Application must be submitted online. Admission notification on a rolling basis. Accepted students asked to pay first-semester tuition in August to confirm fall enrollment or enter into a tuition payment plan. **Financial aid:** Priority date 7/1; no closing date. FAFSA required. Applicants notified on a rolling basis starting 5/1; must reply within 2 week(s) of notification.

Academics. Special study options: Cooperative education, distance learning, dual enrollment of high school students, external degree, independent study, internships, liberal arts/career combination, study abroad. License preparation in dental hygiene, nursing, occupational therapy, physical therapy. **Credit/placement by examination:** AP, CLEP, institutional tests. 30 credit hours maximum toward associate degree. **Support services:** GED preparation and test center, learning center, reduced course load, remedial instruction, study skills assistance, tutoring.

Majors. Business: Accounting, executive assistant, human resources, sales/distribution. **Communications technology:** Graphics. **Computer sciences:** General, networking, web page design. **Conservation:** Management/policy. **General:** Animal husbandry, horticulture, power machinery, supplies. **Health services:** Clinical lab technology, dental hygiene, medical secretary, nursing (RN), occupational therapy assistant, physical therapy assistant, respiratory therapy technology. **Liberal arts:** Arts/sciences. **Protective services:** Police science. **Visual/performing arts:** Commercial photography, interior design. **Work/family studies:** Child care service.

Most popular majors. Health sciences 16%, liberal arts 45%, trade and industry 7%.

Computing on campus. 2,100 workstations in library, computer center, student center. Commuter students can connect to campus network. Online course registration, wireless network available.

Student life. Freshman orientation: Mandatory. Preregistration for classes offered. Held week before classes begin. **Activities:** Choral groups, dance, international student organizations, student government.

Athletics. Intramural: Badminton, basketball, bowling, football (non-tackle), golf, softball, table tennis, volleyball.

Student services. Alcohol/substance abuse counseling, career counseling, services for economically disadvantaged, student employment services, financial aid counseling, health services, on-campus daycare, personal counseling, placement for graduates, veterans' counselor. **Physically disabled:** Services for visually, speech, hearing impaired. **Transfer:** Pre-admission transcript evaluation for new students. Transfer center, transfer adviser, college fairs on campus for students transferring to 4-year colleges.

Contact. E-mail: admission@hawkeyecollege.edu
Phone: (319) 296-4000 Toll-free number: (800) 670-4769 ext. 4000
Fax: (319) 296-4490
David Ball, Director of Admissions & Recruiting, Hawkeye Community College, Box 8015, Waterloo, IA 50704-8015

Iowa Central Community College
Fort Dodge, Iowa
www.iowacentral.edu   **CB code: 6217**

▶ Public 2-year community college
▶ Commuter campus in large town

General. Founded in 1966. Regionally accredited. Courses available at 2 branch campuses: Webster City and Storm Lake. **Enrollment:** 6,298 degree-seeking undergraduates. **Degrees:** 790 associate awarded. **Location:** 90 miles from Des Moines. **Calendar:** Semester, limited summer session. **Full-time faculty:** 86 total. **Part-time faculty:** 342 total. **Special facilities:** Broadcasting suite, criminal justice simulator, Willow Ridge Golf Course (for Turf Grass, Culinary Arts and Restaurant & Hospitality Management).

Student profile.

Out-of-state:	5%	Live on campus:	25%

Transfer out. Colleges most students transferred to 2011: Buena Vista University, Iowa State University, University of Northern Iowa.

Basis for selection. Open admission.

2011-2012 Annual costs. Tuition/fees: $4,200; $6,090 out-of-state. Per-credit charge: $126 in-state; $189 out-of-state. Room/board: $5,350. Books/supplies: $850. Personal expenses: $1,550.

Financial aid. Need-based: Need-based aid available for part-time students. Work-study available nights, weekends and for part-time students. **Non-need-based:** Scholarships awarded for academics, art, athletics, leadership, music/drama.

Application procedures. Admission: No deadline. No application fee. Admission notification on a rolling basis. **Financial aid:** Priority date 3/8; no closing date. FAFSA required. Applicants notified on a rolling basis starting 4/15; must reply within 2 week(s) of notification.

Academics. Special study options: Accelerated study, cooperative education, cross-registration, distance learning, dual enrollment of high school students, external degree, independent study, internships, study abroad. 2 Plus 2 Agreements with Iowa State University and the University of Iowa, University of Iowa College of Nursing RN-BSN program. Bachelor's degree programs available on campus. License preparation in aviation, dental hygiene, nursing, paramedic, radiology. **Credit/placement by examination:** AP, CLEP. 30 credit hours maximum toward associate degree. ACT may be submitted for placement in lieu of COMPASS or ASSET. **Support services:** GED preparation and test center, learning center, pre-admission summer program, reduced course load, remedial instruction, study skills assistance, tutoring.

Majors. Business: Accounting, administrative services, business admin, logistics, operations. **Communications technology:** General, desktop publishing, radio/TV. **Computer sciences:** Web page design, webmaster. **General:** Agribusiness operations, turf management. **Health services:** Clinical lab technology, EMT paramedic, medical assistant, medical radiologic technology/radiation therapy, nursing (RN), occupational therapy assistant, physical therapy assistant, premedicine, prepharmacy, preveterinary, radiologic technology/medical imaging. **Human services:** Social work. **Liberal arts:** Arts/sciences. **Protective services:** Firefighting, police science.

Computing on campus. 500 workstations in library, computer center, student center. Dormitories wired for high-speed internet access and linked to campus network. Commuter students can connect to campus network. Online course registration, helpline available.

Student life. Freshman orientation: Mandatory. Preregistration for classes offered. **Housing:** Coed dorms, single-sex dorms, special housing for disabled, apartments available. $100 nonrefundable deposit. **Activities:** Bands, choral groups, dance, drama, music ensembles, musical theater, radio station, student government, student newspaper, symphony orchestra.

Athletics. NJCAA. **Intercollegiate:** Baseball M, basketball, cross-country, football (tackle) M, golf, rodeo, soccer, softball W, swimming, track and field, volleyball W, wrestling M. **Intramural:** Basketball, bowling, golf, volleyball. **Team name:** Tritons.

Student services. Career counseling, services for economically disadvantaged, student employment services, financial aid counseling, health services, minority student services, personal counseling, placement for graduates, veterans' counselor. **Physically disabled:** Services for visually, speech, hearing impaired. **Transfer:** Pre-admission transcript evaluation for new students. Transfer adviser, college fairs on campus for students transferring to 4-year colleges.

Contact. Phone: (515) 576-7201 ext. 1008
Toll-free number: (800) 362-2793 ext. 1008 Fax: (515) 576-7724
Sara Condon, Director of Admissions, Iowa Central Community College, One Triton Circle, Fort Dodge, IA 50501

Iowa Lakes Community College
Estherville, Iowa
www.iowalakes.edu

CB code: 6196

- Public 2-year community college
- Commuter campus in small town

General. Founded in 1967. Regionally accredited. 3 campuses with dormitories and food service operating in Emmetsburg, Estherville and Spencer. Classes also offered at campuses located in Algona and Spirit Lake. **Enrollment:** 2,205 degree-seeking undergraduates; 897 non-degree-seeking students. **Degrees:** 439 associate awarded. **Location:** 100 miles from Mason City; 100 miles from Sioux Falls, SD. **Calendar:** Semester, limited summer session. **Full-time faculty:** 228 total; 59% women. **Part-time faculty:** 197 total; 76% women. **Special facilities:** 360-acre farm, print collection, wind turbine.

Student profile. Among degree-seeking undergraduates, 46% enrolled in a transfer program, 54% enrolled in a vocational program, 20% already have a bachelor's degree or higher, 490 enrolled as first-time, first-year students, 414 transferred in from other institutions.

Part-time:	26%	25 or older:	30%
Out-of-state:	23%	Live on campus:	15%
Women:	52%		

Transfer out. 11% of students enrolled in the transfer program go on to 4-year colleges. **Colleges most students transferred to 2011:** University of Northern Iowa, Iowa State University, University of Iowa, South Dakota State University, Buena Vista University.

Basis for selection. Open admission, but selective for some programs. Special requirements for nursing, aviation/airport management, wind turbine technology programs. ACT required for nursing students. Interview required of career programs. Audition recommended for music majors. Portfolio recommended for advertising design majors. **Home schooled:** Transcript of courses and grades, state high school equivalency certificate required.

High school preparation. College-preparatory program recommended.

2012-2013 Annual costs. Tuition/fees (projected): $5,004; $5,068 out-of-state. Per-credit charge: $139 in-state; $141 out-of-state. Room/board: $5,000. Books/supplies: $1,300. Personal expenses: $3,400.

2011-2012 Financial aid. All financial aid based on need. Need-based aid available for part-time students. Work-study available nights, weekends and for part-time students.

Application procedures. Admission: No deadline. No application fee. Admission notification on a rolling basis. **Financial aid:** Priority date 4/22; no closing date. FAFSA, institutional form required. Applicants notified on a rolling basis starting 4/15.

Academics. Special study options: Cooperative education, cross-registration, distance learning, dual enrollment of high school students, ESL, honors, internships, liberal arts/career combination, weekend college. Evening college. License preparation in aviation, nursing, paramedic, real estate. **Credit/placement by examination:** AP, CLEP, institutional tests. 30 credit hours maximum toward associate degree. **Support services:** GED preparation and test center, learning center, reduced course load, remedial instruction, study skills assistance, tutoring.

Majors. Business: Accounting, business admin, hotel/motel admin, office management, restaurant/food services, sales/distribution. **Communications:** Broadcast journalism, journalism. **Computer sciences:** Applications programming, networking. **Conservation:** Environmental studies. **Engineering:** Agricultural. **General:** Landscaping, power machinery, production, supplies. **Health services:** EMT paramedic, health care admin, nursing (RN). **Liberal arts:** Arts/sciences. **Parks/recreation:** Facilities management. **Protective services:** Police science. **Social sciences:** GIS/cartography. **Visual/performing arts:** Commercial/advertising art, photography. **Work/family studies:** Child care service.

Most popular majors. Agriculture 6%, business/marketing 15%, engineering/engineering technologies 6%, health sciences 15%, history 10%, liberal arts 31%, trade and industry 7%.

Computing on campus. 800 workstations in library, computer center, student center. Dormitories wired for high-speed internet access. Online course registration, online library, helpline, repair service, wireless network available.

Student life. Freshman orientation: Mandatory. Preregistration for classes offered. **Housing:** Coed dorms, special housing for disabled, apartments available. **Activities:** Bands, choral groups, drama, international student organizations, literary magazine, music ensembles, musical theater, radio station, student government, student newspaper, TV station.

Athletics. NJCAA. **Intercollegiate:** Baseball M, basketball, cross-country, golf, soccer, softball W, swimming, volleyball W, wrestling M. **Intramural:** Basketball, bowling, racquetball, skiing, softball, table tennis, volleyball. **Team name:** Lakers.

Student services. Adult student services, alcohol/substance abuse counseling, career counseling, services for economically disadvantaged, financial aid counseling, personal counseling, placement for graduates, veterans' counselor, women's services. **Transfer:** Pre-admission transcript evaluation for new students. Transfer adviser, college fairs on campus for students transferring to 4-year colleges.

Contact. E-mail: info@iowalakes.edu
Phone: (712) 362-7945 Toll-free number: (800) 521-5054
Julie Williams, Dean of Students, Iowa Lakes Community College, 300 South 18th Street, Estherville, IA 51334-2725

Iowa Western Community College
Council Bluffs, Iowa
www.iwcc.edu   **CB code: 6302**

- Public 2-year community and technical college
- Commuter campus in small city

General. Founded in 1966. Regionally accredited. Branch campus at Clarinda offers liberal arts and vocational programs in nursing. Centers in Harlan and Atlantic offer evening programs in liberal arts and business administration. Practical nursing offered at Harlan. Design Technology program offered at Atlantic. **Enrollment:** 6,023 degree-seeking undergraduates. **Degrees:** 687 associate awarded. **ROTC:** Army, Air Force. **Location:** 10 miles from Omaha, Nebraska. **Calendar:** Semester, extensive summer session. **Full-time faculty:** 129 total. **Part-time faculty:** 233 total. **Special facilities:** Center for advanced nursing and allied health programs, cyber library and cafe, arts center, athletic complex.

Student profile.

Out-of-state:	10%	**Live on campus:**	21%

Transfer out. Colleges most students transferred to 2011: Bellevue University, University of Nebraska at Lincoln, University of Iowa, Iowa State University, Northwest Missouri State University.

Basis for selection. Open admission, but selective for some programs. Limited admission to some vocational-technical programs, including nursing, dental hygiene, automotive technology, veterinary technology, medical assisting, surgical technology, design technology, and dental assisting. COMPASS or ACT/SAT required for placement. Academic enrichment courses available. **Home schooled:** Transcript of courses and grades required.

High school preparation. College-preparatory program recommended. Specific subject requirements for some career programs.

2011-2012 Annual costs. Tuition/fees: $4,180; $4,320 out-of-state. Per-credit charge: $126 in-state; $131 out-of-state. Room/board: $7,480. Books/supplies: $1,040. Personal expenses: $1,728.

2010-2011 Financial aid. Need-based: 43% of total undergraduate aid awarded as scholarships/grants, 57% as loans/jobs. Need-based aid available for part-time students. Work-study available nights, weekends and for part-time students. **Non-need-based:** Scholarships awarded for athletics, music/drama.

Application procedures. Admission: No deadline. No application fee. Admission notification on a rolling basis. Applicants for limited-enrollment programs considered on first applied, first accepted basis. **Financial aid:** No deadline. FAFSA required. Applicants notified on a rolling basis starting 3/1; must reply within 3 week(s) of notification.

Academics. Special study options: Cooperative education, distance learning, dual enrollment of high school students, ESL, independent study, internships, student-designed major. License preparation in aviation, dental hygiene, nursing, paramedic. **Credit/placement by examination:** AP, CLEP, institutional tests. 40 credit hours maximum toward associate degree. **Support services:** GED preparation and test center, learning center, reduced course load, remedial instruction, study skills assistance, tutoring, writing center.

Majors. Area/ethnic studies: Spanish/Iberian. **Biology:** General, botany, microbiology, molecular. **Business:** Business admin, fashion, hotel/motel/restaurant management, human resources, marketing, office management, sales/distribution. **Communications:** General, broadcast journalism, media studies, radio/TV, sports. **Communications technology:** Graphic/printing. **Computer sciences:** Computer science, programming, security, system admin, web page design. **Education:** General. **English:** General lit. **Foreign languages:** Sign language interpretation. **General:** Agribusiness operations,

business. **Health services:** Athletic training, dental hygiene, nursing (RN), premedicine, preoccupational therapy, prepharmacy, prephysical therapy, substance abuse counseling, surgical technology, veterinary technology/assistant. **Human services:** Social work. **Liberal arts:** Arts/sciences. **Math:** General. **Physical sciences:** Chemistry. **Protective services:** Firefighting, forensics. **Psychology:** General. **Social sciences:** General, political science, sociology. **Visual/performing arts:** Art, music, theater arts management. **Work/family studies:** Child care management, institutional food production.

Computing on campus. 250 workstations in dormitories, library, computer center, student center. Dormitories wired for high-speed internet access and linked to campus network. Commuter students can connect to campus network. Online course registration, online library, helpline, wireless network available.

Student life. Freshman orientation: Available. Preregistration for classes offered. **Housing:** Coed dorms, single-sex dorms, apartments available. $200 fully refundable deposit. **Activities:** Bands, choral groups, dance, drama, international student organizations, literary magazine, music ensembles, musical theater, radio station, student government, student newspaper, TV station, Christian Fellowship, special interest clubs, Phi Theta Kappa, Multicultural Student Alliance.

Athletics. NJCAA. **Intercollegiate:** Baseball M, basketball, cheerleading, cross-country, football (tackle) M, golf, soccer, softball W, track and field, volleyball W, wrestling M. **Intramural:** Basketball, bowling, football (non-tackle), softball, table tennis, tennis, volleyball. **Team name:** Reivers.

Student services. Career counseling, services for economically disadvantaged, student employment services, financial aid counseling, health services, on-campus daycare, personal counseling, placement for graduates, veterans' counselor. **Physically disabled:** Services for visually, speech, hearing impaired. **Transfer:** Pre-admission transcript evaluation for new students. Transfer center, transfer adviser, college fairs on campus for students transferring to 4-year colleges.

Contact. E-mail: admissions@iwcc.edu
Phone: (712) 325-3277 Toll-free number: (800) 432-5852
Fax: (712) 325-3720
Chris LaFerla, Director of Admissions, Iowa Western Community College, 2700 College Road, Council Bluffs, IA 51502-3004

Kaplan University: Cedar Rapids
Cedar Rapids, Iowa
www.kucampus.edu   **CB code: 3384**

- For-profit 2-year liberal arts college
- Commuter campus in small city
- Application essay, interview required

General. Regionally accredited. **Enrollment:** 553 degree-seeking undergraduates. **Degrees:** 90 bachelor's, 246 associate awarded. **Calendar:** Continuous, extensive summer session. **Full-time faculty:** 9 total. **Part-time faculty:** 26 total. **Class size:** 49% < 20, 51% 20-39.

Basis for selection. Open admission, but selective for some programs. **Home schooled:** State high school equivalency certificate required.

2011-2012 Annual costs. Estimated tuition and fees ranges for entire programs as of July 2011: certificate and diploma programs beginning with 5-week terms, $24,798-$25,085; certificate and diploma programs beginning with 10-week terms, $19,770-$23,676; associate degree programs beginning with 5-week terms, $32,586-$33,645; associate degree programs beginning with 10-week terms, $30,654-$35,763; bachelor's degree programs beginning with 5-week terms, $65,358; bachelor's degree programs beginning with 10-week terms, $66,417; does not include books and supplies, which vary by program. All costs subject to change at any time.

Financial aid. Need-based: Need-based aid available for part-time students. Work-study available nights, weekends and for part-time students. **Non-need-based:** Scholarships awarded for academics.

Application procedures. Admission: No deadline. $20 fee. Application must be submitted on paper. Admission notification on a rolling basis. **Financial aid:** Priority date 6/30; no closing date. FAFSA, institutional form required. Applicants notified on a rolling basis.

Academics. Special study options: Accelerated study, distance learning, honors, independent study, internships. Bachelor's degree programs available on campus. License preparation in nursing. **Credit/placement by examination:** AP, CLEP, institutional tests. Combined credit by examination and for life/work experiences shall not exceed 25% of program requirements. **Support services:** Learning center, remedial instruction, tutoring.

Majors. Business: Accounting, business admin. **Computer sciences:** Information technology. **Health services:** Medical assistant. **Protective services:** Criminal justice.

Most popular majors. Business/marketing 19%, computer/information sciences 14%, health sciences 34%, security/protective services 19%.

Computing on campus. 207 workstations in library. Commuter students can connect to campus network. Online library available.

Student life. Freshman orientation: Mandatory, $20 fee. Preregistration for classes offered.

Student services. Adult student services, career counseling, student employment services, financial aid counseling, placement for graduates. **Physically disabled:** Services for visually, hearing impaired. **Transfer:** Re-entry adviser for new students.

Contact. Phone: (319) 363-0481 Toll-free number: (800) 728-0481
Fax: (319) 363-3812
Dave Ruddy, Director of Admissions, Kaplan University: Cedar Rapids, 3165 Edgewood Parkway, SW, Cedar Rapids, IA 52404

Kirkwood Community College
Cedar Rapids, Iowa
www.kirkwood.edu   **CB code: 6027**

- Public 2-year community college
- Commuter campus in small city

General. Founded in 1966. Regionally accredited. Off-campus sites in Iowa City, Vinton, Tipton, Williamsburg, Monticello, Washington, Belle Plaine, Marion, Cedar Rapids. **Enrollment:** 17,610 undergraduates. **Degrees:** 2,114 associate awarded. **Location:** 128 miles from Des Moines. **Calendar:** Semester, extensive summer session. **Full-time faculty:** 284 total. **Part-time faculty:** 615 total. **Special facilities:** Recreational center, raptor center, equestrian center, hotel. **Partnerships:** Formal partnerships with CISCO LAN Management.

Student profile.

| Out-of-state: | 2% | 25 or older: | 29% |

Transfer out. Colleges most students transferred to 2011: University of Iowa, University of Northern Iowa, Iowa State University, Mount Mercy College, Coe College.

Basis for selection. Open admission, but selective for some programs. Some health science programs require minimum scores on COMPASS exam for admission to program. Interview required of vocational-technical, career option applicants.

2011-2012 Annual costs. Tuition/fees: $3,840; $4,590 out-of-state. Per-credit charge: $128 in-state; $153 out-of-state. Books/supplies: $1,410.

Financial aid. Need-based: Need-based aid available for part-time students. Work-study available nights, weekends and for part-time students. **Non-need-based:** Scholarships awarded for art, athletics, leadership, music/drama.

Application procedures. Admission: Priority date 3/15; no deadline. No application fee. Admission notification on a rolling basis. **Financial aid:** Closing date 6/30. FAFSA required. Applicants notified on a rolling basis starting 4/1.

Academics. Special study options: Accelerated study, cooperative education, cross-registration, distance learning, dual enrollment of high school students, ESL, exchange student, external degree, honors, independent study, internships, liberal arts/career combination, student-designed major, study abroad, weekend college. License preparation in dental hygiene, nursing, paramedic, physical therapy, real estate. **Credit/placement by examination:** AP, CLEP, IB, institutional tests. 21 credit hours maximum toward associate degree. **Support services:** GED preparation and test center, learning center, pre-admission summer program, reduced course load, remedial instruction, study skills assistance, tutoring, writing center.

Majors. Biology: Biotechnology. **Business:** Accounting, administrative services, business admin, fashion, finance, office technology, sales/distribution. **Communications technology:** General, graphic/printing. **Computer sciences:** Applications programming. **Conservation:** General. **Engineering:** General. **Foreign languages:** Sign language interpretation. **General:** Equestrian studies, nursery operations, supplies, turf management. **Health services:** Dental assistant, dental hygiene, dental lab technology, electroencephalograph technology, EMT ambulance attendant, EMT paramedic, medical assistant, medical records technology, medical secretary, nursing (RN), occupational

therapy assistant, physical therapy assistant, respiratory therapy technology, surgical technology, veterinary technology/assistant. **Human services:** Community org/advocacy. **Liberal arts:** Arts/sciences. **Protective services:** Fire services admin, firefighting, police science. **Work/family studies:** Child care management, institutional food production.

Computing on campus. 1,000 workstations in library, computer center, student center. Commuter students can connect to campus network. Online course registration, online library, helpline, wireless network available.

Student life. Freshman orientation: Available. Preregistration for classes offered. Various group sessions held throughout the year. Additional 2-day session held week before fall classes start. **Activities:** Bands, campus ministries, choral groups, drama, film society, literary magazine, music ensembles, musical theater, radio station, student government, student newspaper, symphony orchestra, TV station, over 50 organizations.

Athletics. NJCAA. **Intercollegiate:** Baseball M, basketball, golf M, softball W, volleyball W. **Intramural:** Basketball, cheerleading, handball, racquetball, soccer, volleyball. **Team name:** Eagles.

Student services. Adult student services, alcohol/substance abuse counseling, career counseling, services for economically disadvantaged, student employment services, financial aid counseling, health services, minority student services, on-campus daycare, personal counseling, placement for graduates, veterans' counselor. **Physically disabled:** Services for visually, speech, hearing impaired. **Transfer:** Pre-admission transcript evaluation for new students. Transfer center, transfer adviser, college fairs on campus for students transferring to 4-year colleges.

Contact. E-mail: info@kirkwood.edu
Phone: (319) 398-5517 Toll-free number: (800) 332-2055 ext. 5517
Fax: (319) 398-1244
Doug Bannon, Director of Admissions Services, Kirkwood Community College, 6301 Kirkwood Boulevard SW, Cedar Rapids, IA 52406

Marshalltown Community College
Marshalltown, Iowa
www.iavalley.edu/mcc/   **CB code: 6394**

- Public 2-year community college
- Residential campus in large town

General. Founded in 1927. Regionally accredited. **Enrollment:** 2,026 degree-seeking undergraduates. **Degrees:** 284 associate awarded. **Location:** 50 miles from Des Moines. **Calendar:** Semester, limited summer session. **Full-time faculty:** 45 total. **Part-time faculty:** 81 total. **Special facilities:** Prairie, challenge course.

Transfer out. Colleges most students transferred to 2011: Iowa State University, University of Northern Iowa, University of Iowa.

Basis for selection. Open admission, but selective for some programs. Special requirements for health career programs. Interview recommended for health careers majors.

2011-2012 Annual costs. Tuition/fees: $4,950; $5,250 out-of-state. Per-credit charge: $139 in-state; $149 out-of-state. Room/board: $5,680. Books/supplies: $425.

Financial aid. Need-based: Work-study available nights, weekends and for part-time students.

Application procedures. Admission: No deadline. No application fee. Admission notification on a rolling basis. **Financial aid:** Closing date 3/1. Institutional form required. Applicants notified on a rolling basis starting 6/1; must reply within 2 week(s) of notification.

Academics. Special study options: Accelerated study, cooperative education, cross-registration, distance learning, dual enrollment of high school students, ESL, honors, independent study, internships, liberal arts/career combination, study abroad. Bachelor's degree programs available on campus. License preparation in nursing, real estate. **Credit/placement by examination:** AP, CLEP, institutional tests. 30 credit hours maximum toward associate degree. **Support services:** GED preparation and test center, learning center, reduced course load, remedial instruction, study skills assistance, tutoring, writing center.

Majors. Biology: General, botany. **Business:** General, accounting, administrative services, business admin. **Communications:** Journalism. **Communications technology:** General. **Computer sciences:** General, networking, systems analysis. **Conservation:** Forestry. **Education:** General, elementary, physical, secondary. **Engineering:** General. **English:** English lit. **Foreign languages:** Spanish. **General:** Business. **Health services:** Nursing (RN),

predental, premedicine, prenursing, prepharmacy, preveterinary, surgical technology. **Human services:** Community org/advocacy. **Liberal arts:** Arts/ sciences. **Math:** General. **Protective services:** Law enforcement admin, police science. **Psychology:** General. **Social sciences:** General. **Visual/per-forming arts:** General, music, studio arts. **Work/family studies:** General, child care management.

Most popular majors. Computer/information sciences 7%, education 8%, health sciences 10%, liberal arts 65%.

Computing on campus. 250 workstations in dormitories, library, computer center. Commuter students can connect to campus network. Online library, helpline available.

Student life. Freshman orientation: Available. Preregistration for classes offered. **Housing:** Special housing for disabled, apartments available. $300 deposit. **Activities:** Concert band, choral groups, drama, international student organizations, radio station, student government, student newspaper, TV station.

Athletics. NJCAA. **Intercollegiate:** Baseball M, basketball, golf, soccer M, softball W. **Intramural:** Basketball, racquetball. **Team name:** Tigers.

Student services. Adult student services, career counseling, services for economically disadvantaged, student employment services, financial aid counseling, health services, on-campus daycare, personal counseling, placement for graduates, veterans' counselor. **Physically disabled:** Services for visually, speech, hearing impaired. **Transfer:** College fairs on campus for students transferring to 4-year colleges.

Contact. Phone: (641) 752-7106 ext. 216 Fax: (641) 752-8149 Angela Redmond, Director of Admissions, Marshalltown Community College, 3700 South Center Street, Marshalltown, IA 50158

Muscatine Community College
Muscatine, Iowa
www.eicc.edu   **CB code: 6422**

- Public 2-year community college
- Commuter campus in large town

General. Founded in 1929. Regionally accredited. **Enrollment:** 767 full-time, degree-seeking students. **Degrees:** 145 associate awarded. **Location:** 30 miles from Davenport. **Calendar:** Semester, extensive summer session. **Full-time faculty:** 34 total. **Part-time faculty:** 100 total. **Class size:** 28% < 20, 4% 20-39, 68% 40-49.

Student profile.

Out-of-state:	5%	Live on campus:	5%
25 or older:	26%		

Basis for selection. Open admission, but selective for some programs. Special requirements for nursing program.

2011-2012 Annual costs. Tuition/fees: $3,840; $5,760 out-of-state. Online course tuition: $150 per credit-hour. Room only: $4,370. Books/supplies: $900.

Financial aid. Need-based: Work-study available nights, weekends and for part-time students.

Application procedures. Admission: No deadline. No application fee. Admission notification on a rolling basis beginning on or about 9/1. **Financial aid:** Priority date 4/20; no closing date. FAFSA required. Applicants notified on a rolling basis starting 5/15; must reply within 2 week(s) of notification.

Academics. Special study options: Accelerated study, cooperative education, cross-registration, distance learning, double major, dual enrollment of high school students, ESL, honors, independent study, internships, study abroad. Bachelor's degree programs available on campus. License preparation in nursing, real estate. **Credit/placement by examination:** AP, CLEP, institutional tests. 30 credit hours maximum toward associate degree. **Support services:** Learning center, reduced course load, remedial instruction, tutoring.

Majors. Business: Accounting, administrative services, business admin, logistics. **Computer sciences:** Applications programming. **Conservation:** General. **General:** Horticulture, production, supplies. **Health services:** Dental hygiene, electroencephalograph technology, EMT paramedic, nuclear medical technology, physical therapy assistant, radiologic technology/medical imaging, respiratory therapy technology, sonography, veterinary technology/ assistant. **Liberal arts:** Arts/sciences. **Protective services:** Firefighting, police science. **Work/family studies:** Child care service.

Most popular majors. Agriculture 11%, liberal arts 82%.

Computing on campus. 60 workstations in library, computer center. Dormitories wired for high-speed internet access and linked to campus network. Commuter students can connect to campus network. Online course registration, online library, helpline available.

Student life. Freshman orientation: Available. Preregistration for classes offered. **Housing:** Apartments, cooperative housing available. **Activities:** Choral groups, drama, film society, music ensembles, student government, student newspaper, TV station, agriculture technology club, All Kinds of People, College Democrats, College Republicans, Delta Epsilon Chi, Business Professionals of America, horticulture club, Phi Theta Kappa.

Athletics. NJCAA. **Intercollegiate:** Baseball M, softball W. **Intramural:** Bowling, football (non-tackle), golf, skiing, soccer, table tennis. **Team name:** Cardinals.

Student services. Adult student services, career counseling, student employment services, financial aid counseling, on-campus daycare, placement for graduates. **Physically disabled:** Services for visually, speech, hearing impaired. **Transfer:** Transfer adviser, college fairs on campus for students transferring to 4-year colleges.

Contact. Phone: (563) 288-6000 Toll-free number: (888) 336-3907 Fax: (563) 264-8341 Katie Watson, Executive Director of External Affairs, Muscatine Community College, 152 Colorado Street, Muscatine, IA 52761-5396

North Iowa Area Community College
Mason City, Iowa
www.niacc.edu   **CB code: 6400**

- Public 2-year community college
- Commuter campus in large town

General. Founded in 1918. Regionally accredited. **Enrollment:** 3,455 degree-seeking undergraduates; 102 non-degree-seeking students. **Degrees:** 1,056 associate awarded. **Location:** 120 miles from Des Moines, 120 miles from Minneapolis-St. Paul. **Calendar:** Semester, limited summer session. **Full-time faculty:** 84 total; 10% have terminal degrees, 1% minority, 36% women. **Part-time faculty:** 172 total; 5% have terminal degrees, 2% minority, 49% women. **Class size:** 63% < 20, 34% 20-39, 2% 40-49, less than 1% 50-99, less than 1% >100. **Special facilities:** Manufacturing technology center, entrepreneurial center, community auditorium, business incubator, recreation center.

Student profile. Among degree-seeking undergraduates, 771 enrolled as first-time, first-year students, 118 transferred in from other institutions.

Part-time:	45%	Hispanic American:	4%
Out-of-state:	6%	International:	1%
Women:	56%	25 or older:	22%
African American:	3%	Live on campus:	10%
Asian American:	1%		

Transfer out. Colleges most students transferred to 2011: University of Northern Iowa, Iowa State University, University of Iowa.

Basis for selection. Open admission, but selective for some programs. Nursing and physical therapy assistant programs have additional requirements. Applicants missing requirements accepted as pre-major students until all requirements are met.

2011-2012 Annual costs. Tuition/fees: $5,143; $6,977 out-of-state. Per-credit charge: $122 in-state; $183 out-of-state. Room/board: $5,197. Books/supplies: $859. Personal expenses: $1,738.

2011-2012 Financial aid. Need-based: 641 full-time freshmen applied for aid; 501 were judged to have need; 485 of these received aid. Average need met was 21%. Average scholarship/grant was $3,380; average loan $2,089. 49% of total undergraduate aid awarded as scholarships/grants, 51% as loans/jobs. Need-based aid available for part-time students. Work-study available nights, weekends and for part-time students. **Non-need-based:** Scholarships awarded for academics, art, athletics, leadership, music/drama.

Application procedures. Admission: No deadline. No application fee. Admission notification on a rolling basis. **Financial aid:** Priority date 3/1; no closing date. FAFSA, institutional form required. Applicants notified on a rolling basis starting 4/1; must reply within 2 week(s) of notification.

Academics. Special study options: Cooperative education, distance learning, dual enrollment of high school students, honors, internships, liberal arts/ career combination, student-designed major, study abroad. Bachelor's degree programs available on campus. **Credit/placement by examination:** AP, CLEP, institutional tests. 30 credit hours maximum toward associate degree.

Support services: GED preparation and test center, learning center, remedial instruction, study skills assistance, tutoring, writing center.

Majors. Business: Accounting, administrative services, business admin, entrepreneurial studies, hospitality admin. **Computer sciences:** System admin. **Education:** General, early childhood, physical, secondary. **General:** Agribusiness operations, business, farm/ranch, production, supplies. **Health services:** Clinical lab technology, EMT paramedic, nursing (RN), physical therapy assistant. **Liberal arts:** Arts/sciences. **Parks/recreation:** Sports admin. **Protective services:** Fire services admin, police science. **Social sciences:** General, criminology, geography, political science, sociology. **Work/family studies:** General.

Computing on campus. 400 workstations in dormitories, library, computer center. Dormitories wired for high-speed internet access and linked to campus network. Commuter students can connect to campus network. Online course registration, online library, helpline, wireless network available.

Student life. Freshman orientation: Mandatory. Preregistration for classes offered. **Housing:** Coed dorms, apartments, wellness housing available. $50 partly refundable deposit. **Activities:** Bands, campus ministries, choral groups, dance, drama, music ensembles, student government, student newspaper, symphony orchestra.

Athletics. NJCAA. **Intercollegiate:** Baseball M, basketball, cross-country, golf, soccer M, softball W, track and field, volleyball W, wrestling M. **Team name:** Trojans.

Student services. Adult student services, alcohol/substance abuse counseling, career counseling, student employment services, financial aid counseling, health services, personal counseling, placement for graduates, veterans' counselor. **Physically disabled:** Services for visually, speech, hearing impaired. **Transfer:** Transfer adviser, college fairs on campus for students transferring to 4-year colleges.

Contact. E-mail: admisoff@niacc.edu
Phone: (641) 422-4245 Toll-free number: (888) 466-4222
Fax: (641) 422-4385
Rachel McGuire, Director of Admissions, North Iowa Area Community College, 500 College Drive, Mason City, IA 50401

Northeast Iowa Community College
Calmar, Iowa   **CB member**
www.nicc.edu   **CB code: 6754**

▶ Public 2-year community college
▶ Commuter campus in rural community

General. Founded in 1966. Regionally accredited. Branch campus in Peosta. **Enrollment:** 3,300 degree-seeking undergraduates; 1,751 non-degree-seeking students. **Degrees:** 570 associate awarded. **Location:** 75 miles from Waterloo, 13 miles from Dubuque. **Calendar:** Semester, extensive summer session. **Full-time faculty:** 114 total; 6% have terminal degrees, 3% minority, 59% women. **Part-time faculty:** 210 total; 6% have terminal degrees, less than 1% minority, 61% women. **Class size:** 69% < 20, 31% 20-39. **Special facilities:** Nature preserve, prairie, wetland. **Partnerships:** Formal partnership with John Deere.

Student profile. Among degree-seeking undergraduates, 39% enrolled in a transfer program, 61% enrolled in a vocational program, 778 enrolled as first-time, first-year students, 357 transferred in from other institutions.

Part-time:	35%	African American:	3%
Out-of-state:	9%	Hispanic American:	2%
Women:	63%	25 or older:	26%

Transfer out. 21% of students enrolled in the transfer program go on to 4-year colleges. **Colleges most students transferred to 2011:** University of Northern Iowa-Cedar Falls, Upper Iowa University, University of Dubuque, University of Iowa, Clarke College.

Basis for selection. Open admission, but selective for some programs. Health students required to meet program specific admission criteria. Students admitted to the electrical program must have high school diploma or GED. All degree-seeking students required to submit placement test scores.

2011-2012 Annual costs. Tuition/fees: $5,130; $5,130 out-of-state. Per-credit charge: $145. Books/supplies: $1,600. Personal expenses: $1,652.

2010-2011 Financial aid. **Need-based:** 41% of total undergraduate aid awarded as scholarships/grants, 59% as loans/jobs. Need-based aid available for part-time students. Work-study available nights, weekends and for part-time students. **Non-need-based:** Scholarships awarded for academics, leadership, state residency.

Application procedures. Admission: No deadline. No application fee. Admission notification on a rolling basis. **Financial aid:** Priority date 7/1; no closing date. FAFSA required. Applicants notified on a rolling basis starting 5/1.

Academics. Dental assisting certification exam given on-campus. **Special study options:** Distance learning, double major, dual enrollment of high school students, external degree, honors, internships, liberal arts/career combination. License preparation in nursing, paramedic, radiology. **Credit/placement by examination:** AP, CLEP, SAT, ACT. **Support services:** GED preparation and test center, learning center, reduced course load, remedial instruction, study skills assistance, tutoring, writing center.

Majors. Business: Accounting, administrative services, business admin, office technology, sales/distribution. **Communications technology:** Desktop publishing. **Computer sciences:** Applications programming. **General:** Agribusiness operations, crop production, dairy husbandry, power machinery, production, products processing. **Health services:** Clinical lab technology, EMT paramedic, medical records technology, nursing (RN), radiologic technology/medical imaging, respiratory therapy technology. **Human services:** Social work. **Liberal arts:** Arts/sciences. **Protective services:** Firefighting.

Most popular majors. Agriculture 12%, business/marketing 13%, health sciences 26%, liberal arts 37%, trade and industry 6%.

Computing on campus. Commuter students can connect to campus network. Online course registration, helpline, repair service, wireless network available.

Student life. Freshman orientation: Mandatory. Preregistration for classes offered. One-day program with different interest sessions available. **Policies:** Smoke-free campuses. **Activities:** Choral groups, student government, student newspaper.

Athletics. Intramural: Basketball, bowling, football (non-tackle) M, golf, skiing, softball, volleyball. **Team name:** Cougars.

Student services. Adult student services, career counseling, services for economically disadvantaged, student employment services, financial aid counseling, on-campus daycare, personal counseling, placement for graduates. **Physically disabled:** Services for visually, speech, hearing impaired. **Transfer:** Pre-admission transcript evaluation for new students. Transfer adviser, college fairs on campus for students transferring to 4-year colleges.

Contact. Phone: (563) 562-3263 ext. 307
Toll-free number: (800) 728-2256 ext. 307 Fax: (563) 562-4369
Kristi Strief, Admissions Manager, Northeast Iowa Community College, Box 400, Calmar, IA 52132

Northwest Iowa Community College
Sheldon, Iowa
www.nwicc.edu   **CB code: 1359**

▶ Public 2-year community college
▶ Commuter campus in small town

General. Founded in 1966. Regionally accredited. **Enrollment:** 912 degree-seeking undergraduates; 632 non-degree-seeking students. **Degrees:** 190 associate awarded. **Location:** 60 miles from Sioux City; 65 miles from Sioux Falls, South Dakota. **Calendar:** Semester, extensive summer session. **Full-time faculty:** 40 total; 32% women. **Part-time faculty:** 100 total; 1% minority, 58% women.

Student profile. Among degree-seeking undergraduates, 280 enrolled as first-time, first-year students.

Part-time:	22%	Women:	51%

Basis for selection. Open admission, but selective for some programs. 2.0 GPA and 2 science required for LPN and Radiologic Technology programs. Minimum COMPASS scores for ADN, Radiologic Technology, and Powerline programs. **Home schooled:** Transcript of courses and grades required.

2011-2012 Annual costs. Tuition/fees: $4,800; $5,460 out-of-state. Per-credit charge: $132 in-state; $154 out-of-state. Room/board: $4,340. Books/supplies: $716. Personal expenses: $854.

Financial aid. Need-based: Need-based aid available for part-time students. Work-study available nights, weekends and for part-time students.

Application procedures. Admission: No deadline. No application fee. Admission notification on a rolling basis. **Financial aid:** Priority date 4/1; no closing date. FAFSA, institutional form required. Applicants notified on a rolling basis starting 5/1.

Academics. Special study options: Cooperative education, distance learning, dual enrollment of high school students, ESL, independent study, liberal arts/career combination. Bachelor's degree programs available on campus. License preparation in nursing, radiology. **Credit/placement by examination:** AP, CLEP, institutional tests. 30 credit hours maximum toward associate degree. **Support services:** GED preparation and test center, learning center, pre-admission summer program, reduced course load, remedial instruction, study skills assistance, tutoring.

Majors. Business: Accounting, business admin. **Computer sciences:** Networking, system admin. **Conservation:** General. **Health services:** Medical records technology, nursing (RN), radiologic technology/medical imaging. **Liberal arts:** Arts/sciences.

Computing on campus. 433 workstations in dormitories, library, computer center, student center. Dormitories wired for high-speed internet access. Online course registration, online library, wireless network available.

Student life. Freshman orientation: Available. Preregistration for classes offered. **Policies:** Student housing is non-smoking; no alcohol allowed. **Housing:** Apartments available. $190 deposit. **Activities:** Student government, student newspaper, Campus Crusade for Christ.

Athletics. Intramural: Basketball, bowling, football (non-tackle), volleyball. **Team name:** Thunder.

Student services. Career counseling, student employment services, financial aid counseling, minority student services, personal counseling, placement for graduates, veterans' counselor. **Physically disabled:** Services for visually, speech, hearing impaired. **Transfer:** Pre-admission transcript evaluation for new students. Transfer adviser, college fairs on campus for students transferring to 4-year colleges.

Contact. E-mail: studentservices@nwicc.edu
Phone: (712) 324-5061 ext. 132
Toll-free number: (800) 352-4907 ext. 132 Fax: (712) 324-4136
Lisa Story, Director of Enrollment, Northwest Iowa Community College, 603 West Park Street, Sheldon, IA 51201

Scott Community College
Bettendorf, Iowa
www.eicc.edu   CB code: 0282

- Public 2-year community college
- Commuter campus in small city

General. Founded in 1966. Regionally accredited. **Enrollment:** 2,575 full-time, degree-seeking students. **Degrees:** 465 associate awarded. **Location:** 3 miles from Davenport. **Calendar:** Semester, extensive summer session. **Full-time faculty:** 73 total. **Part-time faculty:** 255 total. **Class size:** 80% < 20, 20% 20-39, less than 1% 40-49, less than 1% 50-99.

Student profile.

Out-of-state:	11%	25 or older:	40%

Transfer out. Colleges most students transferred to 2011: University of Iowa, Iowa State University, University of Northern Iowa, St. Ambrose University, Western Illinois University.

Basis for selection. Open admission, but selective for some programs. Admission to some programs, particularly health occupations, based on academic achievement and previous courses. Interview required for radiologic technology and medical laboratory technician; recommended for nursing, electroneuro diagnostic technology and pharmacy technician.

2011-2012 Annual costs. Tuition/fees: $3,840; $5,760 out-of-state. Per-credit charge: $128 in-state; $192 out-of-state. Online course tuition: $150 per credit-hour. Books/supplies: $1,140. Personal expenses: $1,090.

Financial aid. Need-based: Work-study available nights, weekends and for part-time students.

Application procedures. Admission: No deadline. No application fee. Admission notification on a rolling basis beginning on or about 9/1. **Financial aid:** Priority date 4/20; no closing date. FAFSA required. Applicants notified on a rolling basis starting 5/15; must reply within 2 week(s) of notification.

Academics. Special study options: Accelerated study, cooperative education, cross-registration, distance learning, double major, dual enrollment of high school students, ESL, honors, independent study, internships, liberal arts/career combination, study abroad, weekend college. License preparation in nursing, real estate. **Credit/placement by examination:** AP, CLEP, institutional tests. 30 credit hours maximum toward associate degree. **Support**

services: GED preparation and test center, learning center, reduced course load, remedial instruction, tutoring.

Majors. Business: Accounting, administrative services, hospitality admin, logistics. **Communications technology:** General. **Computer sciences:** Applications programming. **Foreign languages:** Sign language interpretation. **General:** Equine science. **Health services:** Dental hygiene, electroencephalograph technology, EMT paramedic, medical records technology, nuclear medical technology, nursing (RN), physical therapy assistant, radiologic technology/medical imaging, respiratory therapy technology, sonography. **Liberal arts:** Arts/sciences. **Protective services:** Police science. **Visual/performing arts:** Interior design. **Work/family studies:** Child care service.

Most popular majors. Business/marketing 8%, health sciences 18%, liberal arts 58%, trade and industry 6%.

Computing on campus. 125 workstations in library, computer center, student center. Commuter students can connect to campus network. Online course registration, helpline, wireless network available.

Student life. Freshman orientation: Available. Preregistration for classes offered. **Activities:** Campus ministries, international student organizations, literary magazine, student government, student newspaper, auto collision repair club, volunteer club, Phi Theta Kappa, nursing club, RadTech club, environmental club, dental assisting club.

Athletics. Intercollegiate: Golf, soccer. **Team name:** Eagles.

Student services. Career counseling, student employment services, financial aid counseling, on-campus daycare, personal counseling, placement for graduates, veterans' counselor. **Physically disabled:** Services for visually, speech, hearing impaired. **Transfer:** Transfer adviser, college fairs on campus for students transferring to 4-year colleges.

Contact. Phone: (563) 441-4004 Toll-free number: (888) 336-3907
Fax: (563) 441-4101
Ladrina Wilson, Admissions Officer, Scott Community College, 500 Belmont Road, Bettendorf, IA 52722-6804

Southeastern Community College: North Campus
West Burlington, Iowa
www.scciowa.edu   CB code: 6048

- Public 2-year community and junior college
- Commuter campus in large town

General. Founded in 1966. Regionally accredited. Campuses in West Burlington, Keokuk, Mt. Pleasant, and Ft. Madison. **Enrollment:** 3,193 degree-seeking undergraduates; 148 non-degree-seeking students. **Degrees:** 566 associate awarded. **Location:** 200 miles from Des Moines, 300 miles from Chicago. **Calendar:** Semester, limited summer session. **Full-time faculty:** 70 total; 7% have terminal degrees, 7% minority. **Part-time faculty:** 88 total; 4% have terminal degrees, 2% minority. **Class size:** 61% < 20, 34% 20-39, 4% 40-49, 1% 50-99. **Special facilities:** Greenhouse, college operated farm.

Student profile. Among degree-seeking undergraduates, 399 enrolled as first-time, first-year students, 94 transferred in from other institutions.

Part-time:	45%	Hispanic American:	4%
Out-of-state:	13%	Native American:	1%
Women:	61%	International:	1%
African American:	5%	25 or older:	32%
Asian American:	1%	Live on campus:	2%

Transfer out. Colleges most students transferred to 2011: University of Iowa, Western Illinois University, Iowa State University, University of Northern Iowa, Iowa Wesleyan College.

Basis for selection. Open admission, but selective for some programs. Special requirements for nursing, electronic technology, medical assistant, medical coding and billing, medical transcription, chemical dependency counselor, EMT-paramedic, and respiratory care.

2011-2012 Annual costs. Tuition/fees: $4,050; $4,200 out-of-state. Per-credit charge: $135 in-state; $140 out-of-state. Room/board: $4,800. Books/supplies: $1,040. Personal expenses: $1,728.

2011-2012 Financial aid. Need-based: 306 full-time freshmen applied for aid; 260 were judged to have need; 260 of these received aid. Average scholarship/grant was $4,600; average loan $2,789. 67% of total undergraduate aid awarded as scholarships/grants, 33% as loans/jobs. Need-based aid available for part-time students. Work-study available nights, weekends and

for part-time students. **Non-need-based:** Awarded to 323 full-time undergraduates, including 99 freshmen. Scholarships awarded for academics, art, athletics, minority status.

Application procedures. Admission: No deadline. No application fee, Admission notification on a rolling basis. **Financial aid:** Priority date 7/1; no closing date. FAFSA required. Applicants notified on a rolling basis starting 3/1; must reply within 4 week(s) of notification.

Academics. Special study options: Cooperative education, cross-registration, distance learning, dual enrollment of high school students, ESL, independent study, internships, student-designed major. Bachelor's degree programs available on campus. License preparation in dental hygiene, nursing, occupational therapy, paramedic, physical therapy, radiology, real estate. **Credit/placement by examination:** AP, CLEP, ACT, institutional tests. 30 credit hours maximum toward associate degree. **Support services:** GED preparation and test center, learning center, pre-admission summer program, reduced course load, remedial instruction, study skills assistance, tutoring.

Majors. Business: General, accounting, administrative services, business admin, construction management, executive assistant, office management, office technology, office/clerical, receptionist. **Communications:** Digital media, journalism. **Communications technology:** Desktop publishing, graphics. **Computer sciences:** Computer graphics, data processing, networking, programming, web page design. **Engineering:** Electrical, engineering mechanics. **General:** Business, supplies. **Health services:** EMT paramedic, medical assistant, medical radiologic technology/radiation therapy, nursing (RN), substance abuse counseling. **Liberal arts:** Arts/sciences. **Protective services:** Law enforcement admin. **Work/family studies:** Child care management.

Most popular majors. Business/marketing 7%, health sciences 21%, liberal arts 58%.

Computing on campus. 100 workstations in library, computer center. Dormitories wired for high-speed internet access. Helpline, wireless network available.

Student life. Freshman orientation: Mandatory. Preregistration for classes offered. Two-hour session offered both day and evening before term begins. **Housing:** Coed dorms, single-sex dorms, special housing for disabled, apartments available. $300 partly refundable deposit. **Activities:** Choral groups, drama, international student organizations, music ensembles, musical theater, student government, student newspaper, Campus Crusade for Christ, multicultural club.

Athletics. NJCAA. **Intercollegiate:** Baseball M, basketball, golf, softball W, volleyball W. **Intramural:** Basketball, bowling, cheerleading, football (non-tackle), softball, volleyball. **Team name:** Black Hawks.

Student services. Career counseling, services for economically disadvantaged, student employment services, financial aid counseling, minority student services, on-campus daycare, personal counseling, placement for graduates, veterans' counselor. **Physically disabled:** Services for visually, speech, hearing impaired. **Transfer:** Pre-admission transcript evaluation for new students. Transfer adviser, college fairs on campus for students transferring to 4-year colleges.

Contact. E-mail: admoff@scciowa.edu
Phone: (319) 208-5010 Toll-free number: (866) 722-4692 ext. 5012
Fax: (319) 758-6725
Dana Chrisman, Senior Enrollment Officer, Southeastern Community College: North Campus, 1500 West Agency Road, West Burlington, IA 52655-0605

Southwestern Community College
Creston, Iowa
www.swcciowa.edu
CB code: 6122

⦁ Public 2-year community college
⦁ Commuter campus in small town

General. Founded in 1966. Regionally accredited. **Enrollment:** 1,133 degree-seeking undergraduates. **Degrees:** 237 associate awarded. **Location:** 75 miles from Des Moines; 110 miles from Omaha, Nebraska. **Calendar:** Semester, limited summer session. **Full-time faculty:** 43 total. **Part-time faculty:** 80 total. **Class size:** 79% < 20, 18% 20-39, 2% 40-49, 1% 50-99. **Special facilities:** Recording studio.

Student profile.

Out-of-state:	4%	Live on campus:	5%
25 or older:	38%		

Transfer out. Colleges most students transferred to 2011: Northwest Missouri State University, Buena Vista University, Iowa State University, Graceland College, University of Northern Iowa.

Basis for selection. Open admission, but selective for some programs. Special requirements for nursing. LPN criteria includes date nursing application is received and date COMPASS test scores are achieved. ADN requirements contingent upon application, COMPASS test scores, and ranking selection process. **Adult students:** Students must take COMPASS test for placement.

High school preparation. One chemistry required for health programs.

2011-2012 Annual costs. Tuition/fees: $4,230; $4,635 out-of-state. Per-credit charge: $129 in-state; $143 out-of-state. Room/board: $5,400. Books/supplies: $1,230. Personal expenses: $1,766.

Financial aid. Need-based: Need-based aid available for part-time students. Work-study available nights, weekends and for part-time students. **Non-need-based:** Scholarships awarded for academics, athletics, leadership, music/drama, state residency.

Application procedures. Admission: Priority date 8/1; no deadline. No application fee. Admission notification on a rolling basis. **Financial aid:** Closing date 7/1. FAFSA required. Applicants notified on a rolling basis starting 6/1; must reply within 2 week(s) of notification.

Academics. Special study options: Cooperative education, distance learning, double major, dual enrollment of high school students, independent study, internships, liberal arts/career combination. License preparation in nursing. **Credit/placement by examination:** AP, CLEP. 30 credit hours maximum toward associate degree. Arts and science students without 19 ACT required to take ASSET exam. **Support services:** GED preparation and test center, learning center, reduced course load, remedial instruction, study skills assistance, tutoring.

Majors. Business: General, accounting, administrative services, marketing. **Computer sciences:** Applications programming, information systems, webmaster. **Education:** General. **General:** Business, production. **Health services:** Medical transcription, nursing (RN). **Liberal arts:** Arts/sciences. **Visual/performing arts:** Music performance.

Most popular majors. Business/marketing 10%, computer/information sciences 6%, health sciences 20%, liberal arts 43%, trade and industry 12%.

Computing on campus. 140 workstations in dormitories, library, computer center, student center. Dormitories wired for high-speed internet access and linked to campus network. Helpline, repair service, wireless network available.

Student life. Freshman orientation: Mandatory. Preregistration for classes offered. **Housing:** Coed dorms, single-sex dorms, wellness housing available. $100 deposit. **Activities:** Bands, choral groups, music ensembles, student government, student newspaper.

Athletics. NJCAA. **Intercollegiate:** Baseball M, basketball, cross-country, golf M, softball W, volleyball W. **Intramural:** Basketball, table tennis, tennis, volleyball. **Team name:** Spartans.

Student services. Adult student services, career counseling, services for economically disadvantaged, student employment services, health services, legal services, personal counseling, placement for graduates, veterans' counselor. **Physically disabled:** Services for visually, speech, hearing impaired. **Transfer:** Pre-admission transcript evaluation for new students. Transfer adviser, college fairs on campus for students transferring to 4-year colleges.

Contact. Phone: (641) 782-7081 ext. 421
Toll-free number: (800) 247-4023 Fax: (641) 782-3312
Lisa Carstens, Director of Admissions, Southwestern Community College, 1501 West Townline Street, Creston, IA 50801

St. Luke's College
Sioux City, Iowa
www.stlukescollege.edu
CB code: 3625

⦁ Private 2-year health science college
⦁ Commuter campus in small city
⦁ SAT or ACT (ACT writing optional), application essay, interview required

General. Regionally accredited. Offers hospital-based health care provider programs. **Enrollment:** 190 degree-seeking undergraduates; 12 non-degree-seeking students. **Degrees:** 62 associate awarded. **Location:** 90 miles from Omaha. **Calendar:** Semester, limited summer session. **Full-time faculty:**

19 total; 10% have terminal degrees, 90% women. **Part-time faculty:** 22 total; 14% have terminal degrees, 82% women. **Class size:** 69% < 20, 31% 20-39.

Student profile. Among degree-seeking undergraduates, 32% enrolled in a transfer program, 68% enrolled in a vocational program, 8% already have a bachelor's degree or higher, 4 enrolled as first-time, first-year students, 18 transferred in from other institutions.

Part-time:	22%	Asian American:	4%
Out-of-state:	35%	Hispanic American:	5%
Women:	88%	Native American:	1%
African American:	1%	25 or older:	28%

Transfer out. 62% of students enrolled in the transfer program go on to 4-year colleges. **Colleges most students transferred to 2011:** Morningside College, Briar Cliff College, Western Iowa Tech Community College, Dordt College.

Basis for selection. Degree programs require 2.5 GPA or GED and 19 ACT. **Learning Disabled:** Job shadowing recommended.

High school preparation. College-preparatory program recommended. 8 units recommended. Recommended units include English 4, mathematics 2 and science 2. Electives recommended include psychology, computer operations, typing or keyboarding.

2012-2013 Annual costs. Tuition/fees (projected): $16,990. Per-credit charge: $445. Books/supplies: $1,250. Personal expenses: $1,245.

Financial aid. Need-based: Need-based aid available for part-time students. Work-study available nights, weekends and for part-time students. **Non-need-based:** Scholarships awarded for academics, job skills, leadership.

Application procedures. Admission: Closing date 8/1 (receipt date). $100 fee, may be waived for applicants with need. Admission notification on a rolling basis. Must reply within 2 weeks of acceptance. **Financial aid:** Priority date 3/1; no closing date. FAFSA required. Applicants notified on a rolling basis starting 4/1; must reply within 2 week(s) of notification.

Academics. Students can attend any bachelor's nursing program in Iowa after graduating with associate degree in nursing. Local college offers students access to learning and writing center. **Special study options:** Internships. License preparation in nursing. **Credit/placement by examination:** AP, CLEP. 22 credit hours maximum toward associate degree. **Support services:** Reduced course load, study skills assistance, tutoring.

Majors. Health services: Medical radiologic technology/radiation therapy, nursing (RN), respiratory therapy technology.

Computing on campus. 12 workstations in library, computer center, student center. Commuter students can connect to campus network. Online library, helpline, wireless network available.

Student life. Freshman orientation: Mandatory, $20 fee. Preregistration for classes offered. Held prior to classes. **Policies:** Alcohol- and drug-free campus. **Activities:** Community service participation.

Student services. Alcohol/substance abuse counseling, chaplain/spiritual director, student employment services, financial aid counseling, health services, on-campus daycare, personal counseling. **Transfer:** Pre-admission transcript evaluation for new students.

Contact. E-mail: mccartsj@stlukescollege.edu
Phone: (712) 279-3158 Toll-free number: (800) 352-4660 ext. 3158
Fax: (712) 233-8017
Sherry McCarthy, Enrollment Coordinator, St. Luke's College, 2720 Stone Park Boulevard, Sioux City, IA 51104

Vatterott College: Des Moines
Des Moines, Iowa
www.vatterott-college.edu   CB code: 2909

▶ For-profit 2-year health science and technical college
▶ Commuter campus in large city

General. Accredited by ACCSCT. **Calendar:** Differs by program.

Annual costs/financial aid. Estimated program costs as of June 2011: diploma (40 weeks) $14,800 - $17,600, (60 weeks) $21,840 - $25,403; associate degree (70 weeks) $28,568 - $37,166, (90 weeks) $37,359. All costs, which include tuition, fees, books and supplies, and taxes, are subject to change. Need-based financial aid available for full-time students.

Contact. Phone: (515) 309-9000
Director of Admissions, 7000 Fleur Drive, Des Moines, IA 50321

Western Iowa Tech Community College
Sioux City, Iowa   CB member
www.witcc.com   CB code: 6950

▶ Public 2-year community college
▶ Commuter campus in small city

General. Founded in 1966. Regionally accredited. **Enrollment:** 3,936 degree-seeking undergraduates; 2,851 non-degree-seeking students. **Degrees:** 511 associate awarded. **Location:** 200 miles from Des Moines; 90 miles from Omaha, Nebraska. **Calendar:** Semester, extensive summer session. **Full-time faculty:** 76 total; 12% have terminal degrees, 4% minority, 53% women. **Part-time faculty:** 287 total; 7% have terminal degrees, 3% minority, 56% women. **Class size:** 60% < 20, 38% 20-39, 2% 40-49, less than 1% 50-99, less than 1% >100.

Student profile. Among degree-seeking undergraduates, 37% enrolled in a transfer program, 63% enrolled in a vocational program, 801 enrolled as first-time, first-year students.

Part-time:	34%	Women:	62%
Out-of-state:	10%		

Transfer out. Colleges most students transferred to 2011: Iowa State University, Briar Cliff College, Morningside College, University of Northern Iowa, Bellevue University.

Basis for selection. Open admission, but selective for some programs. Special requirements for nursing, surgical technician, dental assistant, physical therapy assistant, childcare supervision and management, emergency medical technician, police science, forensics, corrections, emergency disaster management, emergency medical services, and business. CPT or ACT required of all diploma and degree-seeking students and those taking English composition and math courses.

High school preparation. Recommended units include English 4, mathematics 3, social studies 3, history 2, science 3 and foreign language 1.

2011-2012 Annual costs. Tuition/fees: $4,185; $4,455 out-of-state. Per-credit charge: $124 in-state; $133 out-of-state. Room/board: $4,540. Books/supplies: $1,050. Personal expenses: $1,170.

2010-2011 Financial aid. Need-based: Need-based aid available for part-time students. Work-study available nights, weekends and for part-time students. **Non-need-based:** Scholarships awarded for academics, leadership, music/drama.

Application procedures. Admission: No deadline. No application fee. Admission notification on a rolling basis. **Financial aid:** No deadline. FAFSA required. Applicants notified on a rolling basis starting 4/1.

Academics. Special study options: Accelerated study, distance learning, double major, dual enrollment of high school students, ESL, honors, independent study, internships. License preparation in nursing, paramedic. **Credit/placement by examination:** AP, CLEP, institutional tests. **Support services:** GED preparation and test center, learning center, pre-admission summer program, reduced course load, remedial instruction, study skills assistance, tutoring.

Majors. Biology: Biotechnology. **Business:** Accounting, administrative services, business admin, finance, human resources, office technology, sales/distribution. **Communications technology:** Animation/special effects, desktop publishing. **Computer sciences:** Applications programming, web page design. **General:** Supplies, turf management. **Health services:** Dental hygiene, EMT paramedic, medical secretary, office admin, physical therapy assistant, surgical technology. **Liberal arts:** Arts/sciences. **Protective services:** Firefighting, juvenile corrections, police science. **Visual/performing arts:** Interior design. **Work/family studies:** Child care service.

Most popular majors. Business/marketing 12%, health sciences 27%, interdisciplinary studies 8%, liberal arts 26%, security/protective services 9%.

Computing on campus. 1,700 workstations in dormitories, library, computer center, student center. Dormitories wired for high-speed internet access and linked to campus network. Commuter students can connect to campus network. Online course registration, online library, helpline, wireless network available.

Student life. Freshman orientation: Available. Preregistration for classes offered. **Housing:** Coed dorms, apartments available. $125 nonrefundable

deposit. **Activities:** Choral groups, dance, drama, international student organizations, music ensembles, radio station, student government, celebrations, multicultural group, sociology club.

Athletics. Intramural: Basketball, bowling, football (non-tackle), golf, soccer, softball, volleyball, wrestling. **Team name:** Comets.

Student services. Adult student services, career counseling, services for economically disadvantaged, student employment services, financial aid counseling, minority student services, personal counseling, placement for graduates, veterans' counselor. **Physically disabled:** Services for visually, speech, hearing impaired. **Transfer:** Transfer center, transfer adviser, college fairs on campus for students transferring to 4-year colleges.

Contact. E-mail: Admissions@witcc.edu
Phone: (712) 274-6403 Toll-free number: (800) 352-4649 ext. 6403
Fax: (712) 274-6441
Lora VanderZwaag, Director of Admissions, Western Iowa Tech
Community College, Box 5199, Sioux City, IA 51102-5199

Kansas

Allen County Community College
Iola, Kansas
www.allencc.edu
CB code: 6305

- Public 2-year community college
- Commuter campus in small town

General. Founded in 1923. Regionally accredited. **Enrollment:** 2,914 degree-seeking undergraduates. **Degrees:** 314 associate awarded. **Location:** 100 miles from Kansas City. **Calendar:** Semester, limited summer session. **Full-time faculty:** 36 total. **Part-time faculty:** 145 total. **Special facilities:** Allen owns a 240 acre farm located 6 miles north of Iola. This is a working farm where 8 students have an opportunity to live in the Zahn Scholarship House.

Student profile.

Out-of-state:	3%	Live on campus:	20%
25 or older:	31%		

Transfer out. Colleges most students transferred to 2011: Pittsburg State University, Kansas State University, Emporia State University, University of Kansas, Washburn University.

Basis for selection. Open admission. TOEFL score of 520 or higher required for admission of non-English-speaking students. **Home schooled:** Transcript of courses and grades required. Placement test required (ACT, COMPASS or ASSET). **Learning Disabled:** Copies of a high school IEP are helpful, but not required.

2011-2012 Annual costs. Tuition/fees: $1,950; $1,950 out-of-district; $1,950 out-of-state. Per-credit charge: $47 in-district; $47 out-of-district; $47 out-of-state. Room/board: $4,350. Books/supplies: $300. Personal expenses: $1,620.

Financial aid. Need-based: Need-based aid available for part-time students. Work-study available nights, weekends and for part-time students. **Non-need-based:** Scholarships awarded for academics, art, athletics, music/drama, state residency. **Additional information:** Scholarships for livestock judging, cheerleading, choir, dance, drama, art, academic challenge, and student ambassadors.

Application procedures. Admission: No deadline. No application fee. Admission notification on a rolling basis. **Financial aid:** Closing date 6/1. FAFSA required. Applicants notified on a rolling basis starting 6/1; must reply within 2 week(s) of notification.

Academics. Special study options: Cooperative education, distance learning, double major, dual enrollment of high school students, independent study, internships, liberal arts/career combination, student-designed major, weekend college. Bachelor's degree programs available on campus. **Credit/placement by examination:** AP, CLEP, institutional tests. 12 credit hours maximum toward associate degree. **Support services:** GED preparation and test center, learning center, reduced course load, remedial instruction, study skills assistance, tutoring, writing center.

Majors. Biology: General. **Business:** Accounting, administrative services, business admin, office management, sales/distribution. **Computer sciences:** General, computer science. **Education:** Mathematics, music, secondary. **Engineering:** Electrical. **General:** Farm/ranch. **Health services:** EMT paramedic, nursing assistant. **History:** General. **Liberal arts:** Library science. **Math:** General. **Physical sciences:** Chemistry, physics. **Protective services:** Police science. **Social sciences:** Economics, geography, sociology. **Visual/performing arts:** Art, ceramics, crafts, drawing, music, painting, studio arts, voice/opera.

Most popular majors. Business/marketing 28%, communications/journalism 16%, education 12%, health sciences 12%, liberal arts 13%.

Computing on campus. 100 workstations in dormitories, library, computer center, student center. Dormitories wired for high-speed internet access. Online library, repair service, wireless network available.

Student life. Freshman orientation: Mandatory. Preregistration for classes offered. **Housing:** Coed dorms, apartments available. $125 fully refundable deposit, deadline 7/7. **Activities:** Bands, choral groups, dance, drama, music ensembles, musical theater, student government, student newspaper, Aggie club, biology club, Phi Theta Kappa, Academic Challenge, student senate, Allen Flame.

Athletics. NJCAA. **Intercollegiate:** Baseball M, basketball, cheerleading, cross-country, golf M, soccer, softball W, track and field, volleyball W. **Intramural:** Basketball, football (non-tackle), softball, table tennis, tennis, volleyball. **Team name:** Red Devils.

Student services. Adult student services, alcohol/substance abuse counseling, career counseling, services for economically disadvantaged, student employment services, financial aid counseling, minority student services, personal counseling, placement for graduates, veterans' counselor, women's services. **Physically disabled:** Services for visually, hearing impaired. **Transfer:** Pre-admission transcript evaluation for new students. Transfer adviser, college fairs on campus for students transferring to 4-year colleges.

Contact. E-mail: bilderback@allencc.edu
Phone: (620) 365-5116 ext. 268 Fax: (620) 365-3284
Rebecca Bilderback, Director of Admissions and Marketing, Allen County Community College, 1801 North Cottonwood, Iola, KS 66749

Barton County Community College
Great Bend, Kansas
www.bartonccc.edu
CB code: 0784

- Public 2-year community college
- Commuter campus in large town

General. Founded in 1965. Regionally accredited. **Enrollment:** 5,516 undergraduates. **Degrees:** 493 associate awarded. **Location:** 125 miles from Wichita. **Calendar:** Semester, limited summer session. **Full-time faculty:** 70 total; 9% have terminal degrees, 7% minority, 41% women. **Part-time faculty:** 139 total; 3% have terminal degrees, 4% minority, 57% women. **Class size:** 82% < 20, 16% 20-39, less than 1% 40-49, 1% 50-99, less than 1% >100. **Special facilities:** Natatorium, planetarium.

Student profile.

Out-of-state:	5%	Live on campus:	8%
25 or older:	46%		

Transfer out. Colleges most students transferred to 2011: Fort Hays State University, Kansas State University, University of Kansas, Wichita State University, Emporia State University.

Basis for selection. Open admission, but selective for some programs. Special requirements for medical laboratory technician, nursing, and mobile intensive care technician programs. ACT, SAT, ASSET or ACCUPLACER required for placement in math or English courses. Interview required of nursing majors.

2011-2012 Annual costs. Tuition/fees: $2,620; $3,540 out-of-state. Per-credit charge: $57 in-state; $88 out-of-state. Room/board: $4,784. Books/supplies: $1,133. Personal expenses: $2,041.

Financial aid. Need-based: Need-based aid available for part-time students. Work-study available nights, weekends and for part-time students. **Non-need-based:** Scholarships awarded for academics, athletics.

Application procedures. Admission: No deadline. No application fee. Application must be submitted on paper. Admission notification on a rolling basis. **Financial aid:** Priority date 3/1; no closing date. FAFSA required. Applicants notified on a rolling basis starting 6/1; must reply within 4 week(s) of notification.

Academics. Special study options: Accelerated study, cooperative education, distance learning, dual enrollment of high school students, ESL, honors, independent study, internships. License preparation in nursing, paramedic, real estate. **Credit/placement by examination:** AP, CLEP, IB, institutional tests. ACT, SAT, ASSET, or ACCUPLACER is required for enrollment in Math or English coursework. **Support services:** GED preparation and test center, learning center, remedial instruction, tutoring.

Majors. Biology: General, wildlife. **Business:** General, accounting, accounting technology, administrative services, business admin, human resources, operations. **Communications:** Communications/speech/rhetoric, journalism. **Computer sciences:** Computer science, information systems, networking. **Conservation:** Forestry. **Education:** General. **Engineering:** General. **English:** English lit. **Foreign languages:** General. **General:** Agribusiness operations, plant protection. **Health services:** Athletic training, clinical lab technology, dietetics, EMT paramedic, medical assistant, medical records admin, nursing (RN), office assistant, predental, premedicine, prenursing, prepharmacy, preveterinary. **History:** General. **Human services:** General, social work. **Liberal arts:** Arts/sciences. **Math:** General. **Parks/**

recreation: Exercise sciences, health/fitness, sports admin. **Philosophy/religion:** Philosophy. **Physical sciences:** General, chemistry, physics. **Protective services:** Corrections, firefighting, police science, security management. **Psychology:** General. **Social sciences:** Anthropology, economics, political science, sociology. **Visual/performing arts:** Art, dance, dramatic, graphic design, music. **Work/family studies:** Child care management.

Computing on campus. 350 workstations in dormitories, library, computer center, student center. Dormitories wired for high-speed internet access and linked to campus network. Commuter students can connect to campus network. Online course registration, online library, helpline, wireless network available.

Student life. Freshman orientation: Mandatory. Preregistration for classes offered. **Housing:** Guaranteed on-campus for freshmen. Coed dorms, wellness housing available. $120 fully refundable deposit. **Activities:** Bands, choral groups, dance, drama, literary magazine, music ensembles, musical theater, student government, student newspaper, Newman Club, Fellowship of Christian Athletes, Campus Christian Fellowship, Student Ambassadors.

Athletics. NJCAA. **Intercollegiate:** Baseball M, basketball, cheerleading, cross-country, golf, soccer, softball W, tennis, track and field, volleyball W. **Intramural:** Baseball M, basketball, football (non-tackle), softball, table tennis, tennis, volleyball. **Team name:** Cougars.

Student services. Adult student services, alcohol/substance abuse counseling, career counseling, services for economically disadvantaged, student employment services, financial aid counseling, health services, on-campus daycare, personal counseling, placement for graduates, veterans' counselor. **Physically disabled:** Services for hearing impaired. **Transfer:** Pre-admission transcript evaluation for new students. Transfer adviser, college fairs on campus for students transferring to 4-year colleges.

Contact. E-mail: admissions@bartonccc.edu
Phone: (620) 792-2701 ext. 286 Toll-free number: (800) 722-6842
Fax: (620) 786-1160
Tana Cooper, Director of Marketing, Barton County Community College, 245 North East 30th Road, Great Bend, KS 67530-9283

Brown Mackie College: Salina
Salina, Kansas
www.brownmackie.edu/Salina/   CB code: 3366

▸ For-profit 2-year junior college
▸ Commuter campus in large town

General. Regionally accredited. **Location:** 90 miles from Wichita, 108 miles from Topeka. **Calendar:** Quarter.

Annual costs/financial aid. Books/supplies: $1,440. Personal expenses: $1,520.

Contact. Phone: (785) 825-5422
Director of Admissions, 2106 South Ninth Street, Salina, KS 67401

Bryan College: Topeka
Topeka, Kansas
www.bryancolleges.com

▸ For-profit 2-year technical and career college
▸ Small city

General. Regionally accredited. **Calendar:** Quarter.

Contact. Phone: (785) 272-0889
Director of Admission, 1527 SW Fairlawn Road, Topeka, KS 66604

Butler Community College
El Dorado, Kansas
www.butlercc.edu   CB code: 6191

▸ Public 2-year community college
▸ Commuter campus in large town

General. Founded in 1927. Regionally accredited. Off-campus sites at Andover, McConnell, Augusta, Flint Hills, Rose Hill and 20 other smaller locations. **Enrollment:** 7,228 degree-seeking undergraduates. **Degrees:** 886 associate awarded. **Location:** 25 miles from Wichita. **Calendar:** Semester, extensive summer session. **Full-time faculty:** 152 total. **Class size:** 70% < 20, 30% 20-39, less than 1% 40-49, less than 1% 50-99.

Student profile.

| Out-of-state: | 1% | Live on campus: | 2% |
| 25 or older: | 38% | | |

Transfer out. Colleges most students transferred to 2011: Wichita State University, Kansas State University, Emporia State University, University of Kansas, Kansas Newman College.

Basis for selection. Open admission, but selective for some programs. Nursing applicants admitted based on GPA in prerequisite courses.

2011-2012 Annual costs. Tuition/fees: $2,565; $2,565 out-of-district; $4,185 out-of-state. Per-credit charge: $70 in-district; $70 out-of-district; $124 out-of-state. Room/board: $5,250. Books/supplies: $1,000. Personal expenses: $1,350.

Financial aid. Need-based: Need-based aid available for part-time students. Work-study available nights, weekends and for part-time students. **Non-need-based:** Scholarships awarded for academics, art, athletics, music/drama.

Application procedures. Admission: No deadline. No application fee. Admission notification on a rolling basis. **Financial aid:** Priority date 4/1; no closing date. FAFSA, institutional form required. Applicants notified on a rolling basis starting 5/1; must reply within 2 week(s) of notification.

Academics. Special study options: Accelerated study, cooperative education, distance learning, dual enrollment of high school students, ESL, honors, independent study, internships, liberal arts/career combination, weekend college. License preparation in nursing, paramedic. **Credit/placement by examination:** AP, CLEP, institutional tests. 30 credit hours maximum toward associate degree. **Support services:** GED preparation, learning center, reduced course load, remedial instruction, study skills assistance, tutoring, writing center.

Majors. Business: Accounting, business admin, hospitality admin, hospitality/recreation, office/clerical. **Communications:** Journalism. **Computer sciences:** General, computer science. **Education:** Business, early childhood, elementary, physical, secondary, teacher assistance. **Engineering:** General. **English:** Rhetoric/composition, writing. **Foreign languages:** General, Spanish. **General:** Animal sciences, farm/ranch. **Health services:** Licensed practical nurse, nursing (RN), premedicine. **History:** General. **Human services:** Social work. **Liberal arts:** Arts/sciences. **Math:** General. **Physical sciences:** Chemistry, physics. **Protective services:** Criminal justice, firefighting, police science. **Psychology:** General. **Social sciences:** Economics, political science. **Visual/performing arts:** Art, dramatic, music. **Work/family studies:** Child care management.

Most popular majors. Health sciences 15%, liberal arts 75%.

Computing on campus. 130 workstations in dormitories, library, computer center, student center. Dormitories wired for high-speed internet access and linked to campus network. Commuter students can connect to campus network. Online course registration, online library, helpline, repair service available.

Student life. Freshman orientation: Mandatory. Preregistration for classes offered. **Housing:** Coed dorms, single-sex dorms, special housing for disabled, wellness housing available. $75 fully refundable deposit. **Activities:** Bands, choral groups, dance, drama, literary magazine, music ensembles, musical theater, radio station, student government, student newspaper, TV station, international student association, Campus Crusade for Christ.

Athletics. NJCAA. **Intercollegiate:** Baseball M, basketball, cross-country, football (tackle) M, soccer W, softball W, track and field, volleyball W. **Intramural:** Basketball, bowling, soccer, softball, table tennis, volleyball. **Team name:** Grizzlies.

Student services. Adult student services, career counseling, student employment services, financial aid counseling, health services, on-campus daycare, personal counseling, placement for graduates, veterans' counselor. **Physically disabled:** Services for visually, speech, hearing impaired. **Transfer:** Pre-admission transcript evaluation for new students. Transfer adviser, college fairs on campus for students transferring to 4-year colleges.

Contact. E-mail: admissions@butlercc.edu
Phone: (316) 322-3255 Fax: (316) 322-3316
Kirsten Allen, Director of Enrollment Management, Butler Community College, 901 South Haverhill Road, El Dorado, KS 67042-3280

Cloud County Community College
Concordia, Kansas
www.cloud.edu   CB code: 6137

♦ Public 2-year community college
♦ Commuter campus in small town

General. Founded in 1965. Regionally accredited. **Enrollment:** 1,233 degree-seeking undergraduates; 1,465 non-degree-seeking students. **Degrees:** 221 associate awarded. **Location:** 200 miles from Kansas City, 140 miles from Topeka. **Calendar:** Semester, limited summer session. **Full-time faculty:** 45 total. **Part-time faculty:** 217 total. **Class size:** 80% < 20, 19% 20-39, less than 1% 40-49, less than 1% 50-99. **Special facilities:** Theater, observatory, children's center, human cadaver lab.

Student profile. Among degree-seeking undergraduates, 78% enrolled in a transfer program, 22% enrolled in a vocational program, 385 enrolled as first-time, first-year students.

Part-time:	26%	Hispanic American:	8%
Out-of-state:	6%	Native American:	1%
Women:	60%	International:	2%
African American:	11%	25 or older:	35%
Asian American:	1%	Live on campus:	4%

Transfer out. Colleges most students transferred to 2011: Kansas State University, Fort Hays State University, Wichita State University, Kansas Wesleyan University, Kansas University.

Basis for selection. Open admission.

High school preparation. 18 units recommended. Recommended units include English 4, mathematics 3, social studies 2 and science 4.

2011-2012 Annual costs. Tuition/fees: $2,640; $2,640 out-of-state. Per-credit charge: $69 in-state; $133 out-of-state. Room/board: $5,380. Books/supplies: $1,000. Personal expenses: $1,650.

Financial aid. Need-based: Need-based aid available for part-time students. Work-study available nights, weekends and for part-time students.

Application procedures. Admission: No deadline. No application fee. Admission notification on a rolling basis. **Financial aid:** Priority date 4/1; no closing date. FAFSA required. Applicants notified on a rolling basis starting 5/1; must reply within 4 week(s) of notification.

Academics. Special study options: Cooperative education, distance learning, dual enrollment of high school students, ESL, independent study, internships. License preparation in nursing. **Credit/placement by examination:** AP, CLEP, institutional tests. 30 credit hours maximum toward associate degree. **Support services:** GED preparation and test center, learning center, remedial instruction, study skills assistance, tutoring, writing center.

Majors. Business: Administrative services, business admin. **Communications:** Journalism. **Communications technology:** Radio/TV. **Computer sciences:** LAN/WAN management, web page design. **Education:** Teacher assistance. **General:** Equine science, production, supplies. **Health services:** Nursing (RN). **Liberal arts:** Arts/sciences. **Protective services:** Police science. **Visual/performing arts:** Graphic design. **Work/family studies:** Child care management.

Most popular majors. Health sciences 13%, liberal arts 67%, trade and industry 9%.

Computing on campus. 294 workstations in library, computer center. Dormitories wired for high-speed internet access and linked to campus network. Commuter students can connect to campus network. Online course registration, online library, wireless network available.

Student life. Freshman orientation: Mandatory. Preregistration for classes offered. One-day prior to classes each fall semester, from 9am to 3pm. **Housing:** Single-sex dorms, apartments available. $100 fully refundable deposit. **Activities:** Bands, choral groups, dance, drama, music ensembles, radio station, student government, student newspaper, Fellowship of Christian Athletes.

Athletics. NJCAA. **Intercollegiate:** Baseball M, basketball, cheerleading, cross-country, rodeo, soccer, softball W, track and field, volleyball W. **Intramural:** Basketball, football (non-tackle), volleyball. **Team name:** Thunderbirds.

Student services. Career counseling, services for economically disadvantaged, student employment services, financial aid counseling, health services, on-campus daycare, personal counseling, veterans' counselor. **Physically disabled:** Services for visually, hearing impaired. **Transfer:** Pre-admission transcript evaluation for new students. College fairs on campus for students transferring to 4-year colleges.

Contact. E-mail: admit@cloud.edu
Phone: (785) 243-1435 ext. 212
Toll-free number: (800) 729-5101 ext. 212 Fax: (785) 243-9380
Kim Reynolds, Director of Admissions, Cloud County Community College, 2221 Campus Drive, Concordia, KS 66901-1002

Coffeyville Community College
Coffeyville, Kansas
www.coffeyville.edu   CB code: 6102

♦ Public 2-year community and technical college
♦ Commuter campus in large town

General. Founded in 1923. Regionally accredited. **Enrollment:** 1,323 degree-seeking undergraduates. **Degrees:** 250 associate awarded. **Location:** 75 miles from Tulsa, Oklahoma, 137 miles from Wichita. **Calendar:** Semester, limited summer session. **Full-time faculty:** 160 total. **Part-time faculty:** 37 total. **Class size:** 64% < 20, 33% 20-39, less than 1% 40-49, 3% 50-99. **Special facilities:** Greenhouse, commercial television station. **Partnerships:** Formal partnership with Wal-Mart.

Student profile.

Out-of-state:	15%	Live on campus:	31%

Transfer out. Colleges most students transferred to 2011: Pittsburg State University, Kansas State University, University of Kansas.

Basis for selection. Open admission. **Home schooled:** ACT or placement test required for placement. **Learning Disabled:** Require IEP.

High school preparation. 20 units recommended. Recommended units include English 4, mathematics 4, social studies 3, history 2, science 3 (laboratory 2), foreign language 1, computer science 1 and visual/performing arts 1.

2011-2012 Annual costs. Tuition/fees: $1,800; $3,045 out-of-state. Per-credit charge: $27 in-state; $69 out-of-state. Room/board: $4,926. Books/supplies: $700. Personal expenses: $1,200.

Financial aid. Need-based: Need-based aid available for part-time students. Work-study available nights, weekends and for part-time students. **Non-need-based:** Scholarships awarded for academics, alumni affiliation, art, athletics, leadership, music/drama, state residency.

Application procedures. Admission: No deadline. No application fee. Admission notification on a rolling basis. **Financial aid:** Priority date 8/1; no closing date. FAFSA required. Applicants notified on a rolling basis starting 6/20.

Academics. Special study options: Distance learning, double major, dual enrollment of high school students, ESL, honors, independent study, internships, liberal arts/career combination, student-designed major. License preparation in nursing, paramedic. **Credit/placement by examination:** AP, CLEP, institutional tests. **Support services:** GED preparation, learning center, reduced course load, remedial instruction, study skills assistance, tutoring.

Honors college/program. Application for Presidential Scholarship, minimum ACT score of 24, minimum 3.5 high school GPA, essay required. Top 12-15 applicants accepted each fall.

Majors. Biology: General. **Business:** General, accounting, administrative services, business admin, entrepreneurial studies, management information systems, office management, office/clerical, retailing. **Communications:** Broadcast journalism, communications/speech/rhetoric, journalism. **Communications technology:** General. **Computer sciences:** General, networking. **Education:** General, early childhood, elementary, multi-level teacher, physical, secondary, speech. **Engineering:** General. **English:** English lit, rhetoric/composition. **Foreign languages:** General, Spanish. **General:** Business, horticulture, supplies. **Health services:** Athletic training, EMT paramedic, nursing assistant, predental, premedicine, prenursing, prepharmacy, preveterinary. **History:** General. **Human services:** Social work. **Liberal arts:** Arts/sciences. **Math:** General. **Parks/recreation:** Health/fitness. **Physical sciences:** Chemistry, physics. **Psychology:** General. **Social sciences:** General, economics, political science, sociology. **Visual/performing arts:** General, art, dramatic, music, studio arts. **Work/family studies:** General, institutional food production.

Computing on campus. 100 workstations in dormitories, library, computer center, student center. Dormitories wired for high-speed internet access. Online course registration, wireless network available.

Student life. Freshman orientation: Mandatory. Preregistration for classes offered. **Housing:** Single-sex dorms, apartments available. $100 partly refundable deposit. **Activities:** Bands, choral groups, dance, drama, film society, international student organizations, music ensembles, musical theater, student government, TV station, Phi Theta Kappa, agriculture club.

Athletics. NJCAA. **Intercollegiate:** Baseball M, basketball, cheerleading, cross-country, football (tackle) M, golf, rodeo, soccer, softball W, track and field, volleyball W. **Intramural:** Basketball, bowling, golf, table tennis, volleyball. **Team name:** Red Ravens.

Student services. Adult student services, career counseling, student employment services, financial aid counseling, health services, personal counseling, veterans' counselor. **Physically disabled:** Services for visually, speech, hearing impaired. **Transfer:** Transfer adviser, college fairs on campus for students transferring to 4-year colleges.

Contact. E-mail: admissions@coffeyville.edu
Phone: (620) 252-7047 Toll-free number: (877) 517-2836
Fax: (620) 252-7399
Kelli Bauer, Admissions Coordinator, Coffeyville Community College, 400 West 11th Street, Coffeyville, KS 67337-5064

Colby Community College
Colby, Kansas
www.colbycc.edu   CB code: 6129

- Public 2-year community college
- Commuter campus in small town

General. Founded in 1964. Regionally accredited. **Enrollment:** 714 degree-seeking undergraduates. **Degrees:** 252 associate awarded. **Location:** 100 miles from Hays, 200 miles from Denver. **Calendar:** Semester, limited summer session. **Full-time faculty:** 56 total. **Part-time faculty:** 81 total. **Class size:** 72% < 20, 26% 20-39, less than 1% 40-49, less than 1% 50-99. **Special facilities:** Cultural arts center, fitness laboratory, college swimming pool.

Student profile. Among degree-seeking undergraduates, 60% enrolled in a transfer program, 40% enrolled in a vocational program, 5% already have a bachelor's degree or higher, 80 transferred in from other institutions.

Part-time:	24%	25 or older:	12%
Out-of-state:	30%	Live on campus:	30%
Women:	60%		

Transfer out. Colleges most students transferred to 2011: Fort Hays State University, Kansas State University, University of Kansas.

Basis for selection. Open admission, but selective for some programs. Interview required for physical therapist assistant, veterinary technology, dental hygiene, and nursing programs. Audition recommended for music majors. Portfolios recommended for art majors. **Adult students:** COMPASS required if 2 or more years since ACT/SAT was taken. **Home schooled:** Transcript of courses and grades, state high school equivalency certificate required.

2011-2012 Annual costs. Tuition/fees: $2,830; $4,390 out-of-state. Per-credit charge: $57 in-state; $109 out-of-state. Nebraska, Colorado, Oklahoma, Texas and Missouri pay a reduced border rate of $76 per credit hour for tuition. Room/board: $4,910. Books/supplies: $888. Personal expenses: $850.

2010-2011 Financial aid. Need-based: 257 full-time freshmen applied for aid; 209 were judged to have need; 207 of these received aid. Average need met was 80%. Average scholarship/grant was $5,438; average loan $1,405. 60% of total undergraduate aid awarded as scholarships/grants, 40% as loans/jobs. Need-based aid available for part-time students. Work-study available nights, weekends and for part-time students. **Non-need-based:** Awarded to 202 full-time undergraduates, including 151 freshmen. Scholarships awarded for academics, athletics, leadership, music/drama.

Application procedures. Admission: No deadline. No application fee. Admission notification on a rolling basis. **Financial aid:** Priority date 6/1; no closing date. FAFSA required. Applicants notified on a rolling basis starting 5/1.

Academics. Special study options: Cooperative education, distance learning, dual enrollment of high school students, independent study, internships, liberal arts/career combination. License preparation in dental hygiene, nursing. **Credit/placement by examination:** AP, CLEP, institutional tests. 15 credit hours maximum toward associate degree. **Support services:** GED preparation and test center, learning center, pre-admission summer program, reduced course load, remedial instruction, study skills assistance, tutoring, writing center.

Majors. Biology: General, wildlife. **Business:** Administrative services, business admin. **Communications:** General, journalism, media studies, persuasive communications, radio/TV. **Computer sciences:** General. **Conservation:** Forestry, wildlife/wilderness. **Education:** General, agricultural, art, business, elementary, health, mathematics, middle, multi-level teacher, music, physical, sales/marketing, secondary. **English:** English lit. **General:** Agribusiness operations, equine science, farm/ranch. **Health services:** Dental hygiene, nursing (RN), physical therapy assistant, substance abuse counseling, veterinary technology/assistant. **History:** General. **Human services:** Social work. **Liberal arts:** Arts/sciences. **Math:** General. **Parks/recreation:** Exercise sciences, health/fitness. **Philosophy/religion:** Philosophy. **Physical sciences:** General, chemistry, geology, physics. **Protective services:** Police science. **Psychology:** General, developmental. **Social sciences:** General, sociology. **Visual/performing arts:** General, graphic design. **Work/family studies:** Child care management.

Most popular majors. Health sciences 20%, liberal arts 67%.

Computing on campus. 100 workstations in dormitories, library, computer center, student center. Dormitories wired for high-speed internet access. Online course registration, online library, helpline, repair service, wireless network available.

Student life. Freshman orientation: Mandatory, $15 fee. Preregistration for classes offered. **Housing:** Coed dorms, special housing for disabled, wellness housing available. $100 fully refundable deposit. **Activities:** Bands, choral groups, dance, international student organizations, literary magazine, music ensembles, musical theater, radio station, student government, student newspaper, OPTIC (Ordinary People Together in Christ), Catholic Youth.

Athletics. NJCAA. **Intercollegiate:** Baseball M, basketball, cheerleading, cross-country, equestrian, golf, rodeo, softball W, track and field, volleyball W, wrestling M. **Intramural:** Basketball, softball, volleyball. **Team name:** Trojans.

Student services. Adult student services, alcohol/substance abuse counseling, career counseling, services for economically disadvantaged, student employment services, financial aid counseling, health services, personal counseling, placement for graduates, veterans' counselor. **Physically disabled:** Services for visually, speech, hearing impaired. **Transfer:** Pre-admission transcript evaluation for new students. Transfer adviser, college fairs on campus for students transferring to 4-year colleges.

Contact. E-mail: admissions@colbycc.edu
Phone: (785) 460-4690 Toll-free number: (888) 634-9350
Fax: (785) 460-4691
Nikol Nolan, Director of Admissions, Colby Community College, 1255 South Range Avenue, Colby, KS 67701

Cowley County Community College
Arkansas City, Kansas
www.cowley.edu   CB code: 6008

- Public 2-year community and technical college
- Commuter campus in large town

General. Founded in 1922. Regionally accredited. **Enrollment:** 3,883 degree-seeking undergraduates; 445 non-degree-seeking students. **Degrees:** 548 associate awarded. **Location:** 50 miles from Wichita. **Calendar:** Semester, limited summer session. **Full-time faculty:** 48 total; 2% minority, 50% women. **Part-time faculty:** 204 total; 8% minority, 60% women. **Class size:** 64% < 20, 35% 20-39, less than 1% 40-49, less than 1% 50-99, less than 1% >100.

Student profile. Among degree-seeking undergraduates, 79% enrolled in a transfer program, 21% enrolled in a vocational program, 1% already have a bachelor's degree or higher, 1,010 enrolled as first-time, first-year students.

Part-time:	41%	Hispanic American:	8%
Out-of-state:	7%	Native American:	1%
Women:	62%	International:	1%
African American:	9%	25 or older:	42%
Asian American:	2%	Live on campus:	11%

Transfer out. Colleges most students transferred to 2011: Wichita State University, Southwestern College, University of Kansas, Kansas State University, Oklahoma State University.

Basis for selection. Open admission, but selective for some programs. Special requirements for mobile intensive care training program. **Home schooled:** Transcript of courses and grades required.

2011-2012 Annual costs. Tuition/fees: $2,220; $2,520 out-of-district; $3,930 out-of-state. Per-credit charge: $48 in-district; $58 out-of-district;

$105 out-of-state. Oklahoma border county resident tuition: $63 per-credit-hour. Room/board: $4,450. Books/supplies: $1,000. Personal expenses: $900.

2011-2012 Financial aid. Need-based: 562 full-time freshmen applied for aid; 422 were judged to have need; 422 of these received aid. Average scholarship/grant was $4,388; average loan $2,138. 61% of total undergraduate aid awarded as scholarships/grants, 39% as loans/jobs. Need-based aid available for part-time students. Work-study available nights, weekends and for part-time students. **Non-need-based:** Awarded to 639 full-time undergraduates, including 299 freshmen. Scholarships awarded for academics, alumni affiliation, art, athletics, leadership, music/drama, state residency.

Application procedures. Admission: No deadline. No application fee. Admission notification on a rolling basis. **Financial aid:** Priority date 4/15; no closing date. FAFSA required. Applicants notified on a rolling basis starting 1/15; must reply within 2 week(s) of notification.

Academics. Special study options: Cooperative education, distance learning, double major, dual enrollment of high school students, independent study, internships, teacher certification program. Area vocational-technical school programs available. **Credit/placement by examination:** AP, CLEP. 15 credit hours maximum toward associate degree. Students must complete 12 credit hours with a GPA of 2.0 or higher before CLEP credit is listed on the transcript. **Support services:** GED preparation and test center, learning center, reduced course load, remedial instruction, study skills assistance, tutoring.

Majors. Biology: General. **Business:** General, administrative services, business admin, customer service support, entrepreneurial studies, office/clerical, organizational behavior. **Communications:** Communications/speech/rhetoric, journalism. **Computer sciences:** Networking. **Education:** General. **Engineering:** General, robotics. **English:** English lit. **Foreign languages:** General, sign language interpretation. **General:** Farm/ranch. **Health services:** EMT paramedic, medical records technology, medical transcription, nursing assistant. **History:** General. **Human services:** Social work. **Liberal arts:** Arts/sciences. **Math:** General. **Philosophy/religion:** Philosophy, religion. **Physical sciences:** General, chemistry. **Protective services:** Corrections, law enforcement admin, police science. **Psychology:** General. **Social sciences:** General. **Visual/performing arts:** General, art, design, music. **Work/family studies:** Child care management.

Most popular majors. Liberal arts 83%.

Computing on campus. 100 workstations in dormitories, library, computer center, student center. Dormitories wired for high-speed internet access and linked to campus network. Commuter students can connect to campus network. Online course registration, online library, wireless network available.

Student life. Freshman orientation: Available. Preregistration for classes offered. **Housing:** Single-sex dorms, wellness housing available. $75 nonrefundable deposit. **Activities:** Bands, choral groups, drama, music ensembles, student government, student newspaper, Academic Civic Engagement through Service, Campus Christian Fellowship, Black Student Union, Young Democrats, College Republicans.

Athletics. NJCAA. **Intercollegiate:** Baseball M, basketball, cheerleading, cross-country, soccer, softball W, tennis, track and field, volleyball W. **Intramural:** Basketball, football (non-tackle), softball, volleyball. **Team name:** Tigers.

Student services. Career counseling, student employment services, health services, personal counseling, placement for graduates, veterans' counselor.

Contact. E-mail: admissions@cowley.edu
Phone: (620) 442-0430 Toll-free number: (800) 593-2222
Fax: (620) 441-5350
Lory West, Director of Admissions, Cowley County Community College, PO Box 1147, Arkansas City, KS 67005-1147

Dodge City Community College
Dodge City, Kansas
www.dc3.edu   CB code: 6166

▶ Public 2-year community and technical college
▶ Commuter campus in large town

General. Founded in 1935. Regionally accredited. **Enrollment:** 1,924 degree-seeking undergraduates. **Degrees:** 163 associate awarded. **Location:** 150 miles from Wichita. **Calendar:** Semester, limited summer session. **Full-time faculty:** 56 total. **Part-time faculty:** 69 total. **Class size:** 25% < 20, 75% 20-39. **Special facilities:** Federal depository of books and documents, horse barn, rodeo practice arena.

Student profile.

Out-of-state:	5%	Live on campus:	33%
25 or older:	45%		

Transfer out. Colleges most students transferred to 2011: Kansas State University, Fort Hays State University, University of Kansas, Pittsburg State University, Wichita State University.

Basis for selection. Open admission, but selective for some programs. Special requirements for nursing program. Students without GED or high school diploma must take test to demonstrate ability to benefit. CELSEA assessment test given to ESL students. Interview recommended for nursing majors. Audition recommended for music majors. Portfolio recommended for art majors.

High school preparation. Recommended units include English 4, mathematics 3, social studies 3 and science 3.

2011-2012 Annual costs. Tuition/fees: $2,280; $2,580 out-of-state. Per-credit charge: $35 in-district; $35 out-of-district; $45 out-of-state. Room/board: $4,622. Books/supplies: $800. Personal expenses: $1,000.

Financial aid. Need-based: Need-based aid available for part-time students. Work-study available nights, weekends and for part-time students. **Non-need-based:** Scholarships awarded for academics, athletics, music/drama, state residency.

Application procedures. Admission: No deadline. No application fee. Admission notification on a rolling basis. **Financial aid:** Priority date 3/15; no closing date. FAFSA, institutional form required. Applicants notified on a rolling basis; must reply within 2 week(s) of notification.

Academics. Special study options: Distance learning, double major, dual enrollment of high school students, ESL, independent study. Bachelor's degree programs available on campus. License preparation in nursing. **Credit/placement by examination:** AP, CLEP. 30 credit hours maximum toward associate degree. **Support services:** GED preparation and test center, learning center, reduced course load, remedial instruction, tutoring, writing center.

Majors. Biology: General. **Business:** General, accounting, banking/financial services, management information systems, office management. **Communications:** Broadcast journalism, journalism. **Computer sciences:** General, computer science, data processing. **Education:** General, elementary, secondary. **Engineering:** General. **General:** Agribusiness operations, business, equestrian studies, farm/ranch, horticulture. **Health services:** Athletic training, licensed practical nurse, medical records technology, nursing (RN), nursing assistant, premedicine, prepharmacy, preveterinary, substance abuse counseling. **Math:** General. **Parks/recreation:** Health/fitness. **Physical sciences:** Chemistry. **Protective services:** Firefighting. **Social sciences:** General, economics, sociology. **Visual/performing arts:** Art, music. **Work/family studies:** Child care management.

Computing on campus. 125 workstations in dormitories, library, computer center, student center. Dormitories wired for high-speed internet access.

Student life. Freshman orientation: Mandatory. Preregistration for classes offered. Held 2 days before classes begins. **Housing:** Guaranteed on-campus for freshmen. Single-sex dorms, wellness housing available. **Activities:** Bands, choral groups, dance, drama, music ensembles, radio station, student government, student newspaper, TV station, Black student union, Fellowship of Christian Athletes, Hispanic American leadership organization.

Athletics. NJCAA. **Intercollegiate:** Baseball M, basketball, cross-country, football (tackle) M, golf, soccer, softball W, track and field, volleyball W. **Intramural:** Basketball, racquetball, softball W. **Team name:** Conquistadors.

Student services. Adult student services, career counseling, student employment services, financial aid counseling, veterans' counselor. **Physically disabled:** Services for visually, speech, hearing impaired. **Transfer:** Transfer adviser, college fairs on campus for students transferring to 4-year colleges.

Contact. E-mail: admit@dc3.edu
Phone: (620) 227-9208 Toll-free number: (800) 367-3222
Fax: (620) 227-9277
Tammy Tabor, Director of Admissions, Dodge City Community College, 2501 North 14th Avenue, Dodge City, KS 67801-2399

Donnelly College
Kansas City, Kansas
www.donnelly.edu

CB code: 6167

- Private 2-year junior and liberal arts college affiliated with Roman Catholic Church
- Commuter campus in large city

General. Founded in 1949. Regionally accredited. **Enrollment:** 588 degree-seeking undergraduates. **Degrees:** 21 bachelor's, 25 associate awarded. **Location:** 5 miles from downtown. **Calendar:** Semester, limited summer session. **Full-time faculty:** 18 total. **Part-time faculty:** 36 total. **Class size:** 91% < 20, 9% 20-39.

Student profile.

Out-of-state:	17%	Live on campus:	3%
25 or older:	72%		

Transfer out. Colleges most students transferred to 2011: University of Kansas, University of Missouri-Kansas City, Kansas City Kansas Community College, Kansas State, Johnson County Community College.

Basis for selection. Open admission. **Home schooled:** Must take the Ability to Benefit test or have a GED.

2011-2012 Annual costs. Tuition/fees: $5,992. Per-credit charge: $214. Room/board: $5,774. Books/supplies: $830.

Financial aid. Need-based: Need-based aid available for part-time students. Work-study available nights, weekends and for part-time students. **Non-need-based:** Scholarships awarded for academics, religious affiliation.

Application procedures. Admission: No deadline. No application fee. Admission notification on a rolling basis. **Financial aid:** Priority date 4/1; no closing date. FAFSA, institutional form required. Applicants notified on a rolling basis starting 7/1.

Academics. Special study options: Distance learning, double major, dual enrollment of high school students, ESL, liberal arts/career combination, weekend college. Bachelor's degree programs available on campus. **Credit/placement by examination:** AP, CLEP, institutional tests. 20 credit hours maximum toward associate degree. **Support services:** GED preparation, learning center, reduced course load, remedial instruction, study skills assistance, tutoring, writing center.

Majors. Biology: General. **Business:** General, accounting, office/clerical. **Computer sciences:** Data processing, programming. **Education:** Elementary. **Engineering:** General. **English:** English lit, rhetoric/composition. **Health services:** Prenursing. **Math:** General. **Physical sciences:** General. **Psychology:** General. **Social sciences:** General.

Most popular majors. Biological/life sciences 11%, business/marketing 19%, education 8%, English 6%, liberal arts 47%, social sciences 6%.

Computing on campus. 75 workstations in library, computer center. Dormitories wired for high-speed internet access and linked to campus network. Commuter students can connect to campus network. Online library, wireless network available.

Student life. Freshman orientation: Mandatory. Preregistration for classes offered. **Housing:** Single-sex dorms available. $100 nonrefundable deposit, deadline 8/1. **Activities:** Campus ministries, organization of student leadership.

Student services. Chaplain/spiritual director, career counseling, services for economically disadvantaged, student employment services, financial aid counseling, personal counseling, placement for graduates, veterans' counselor. **Physically disabled:** Services for visually, speech, hearing impaired. **Transfer:** Pre-admission transcript evaluation for new students. Transfer adviser, college fairs on campus for students transferring to 4-year colleges.

Contact. E-mail: admissions@donnelly.edu
Phone: (913) 621-8700 Fax: (913) 621-8719
Edward Marquez, Director of Admissions, Donnelly College, 608 North 18th Street, Kansas City, KS 66102-4210

Fort Scott Community College
Fort Scott, Kansas
www.fortscott.edu

CB code: 6219

- Public 2-year community college
- Commuter campus in small town

General. Founded in 1919. Regionally accredited. **Enrollment:** 1,977 degree-seeking undergraduates. **Degrees:** 270 associate awarded. **Location:** 25 miles from Pittsburg. **Calendar:** Semester, limited summer session. **Full-time faculty:** 60 total. **Part-time faculty:** 75 total. **Special facilities:** Indoor and outdoor rodeo training facilities.

Student profile.

Out-of-state:	14%	Live on campus:	14%

Basis for selection. Open admission.

2011-2012 Annual costs. Tuition/fees: $2,430; $4,110 out-of-state. Per-credit charge: $44 in-state; $100 out-of-state. Room/board: $5,300. Books/supplies: $550. Personal expenses: $1,020.

Financial aid. Need-based: Work-study available nights, weekends and for part-time students.

Application procedures. Admission: No deadline. No application fee. Application must be submitted online. Admission notification on a rolling basis. **Financial aid:** No deadline. Applicants notified on a rolling basis starting 10/1.

Academics. Special study options: Cooperative education, distance learning, dual enrollment of high school students, ESL, independent study, internships, weekend college. **Credit/placement by examination:** AP, CLEP. 18 credit hours maximum toward associate degree. **Support services:** GED test center, learning center, pre-admission summer program, remedial instruction, tutoring.

Majors. Business: General, administrative services, business admin, management information systems. **Communications:** Communications/speech/rhetoric, public relations. **Communications technology:** Graphic/printing. **Computer sciences:** General. **Conservation:** General. **Education:** General. **General:** Business, mechanization. **Health services:** Licensed practical nurse. **History:** General. **Liberal arts:** Arts/sciences. **Protective services:** Law enforcement admin.

Computing on campus. Dormitories wired for high-speed internet access. Wireless network available.

Student life. Freshman orientation: Available. Preregistration for classes offered. **Housing:** Coed dorms available. **Activities:** Bands, choral groups, dance, drama, music ensembles, musical theater, symphony orchestra, Christians on Campus.

Athletics. NJCAA. **Intercollegiate:** Baseball M, basketball, cheerleading M, football (tackle) M, rodeo, softball W, volleyball W. **Intramural:** Basketball, bowling, racquetball. **Team name:** Greyhounds.

Student services. Adult student services, services for economically disadvantaged, student employment services, financial aid counseling. **Transfer:** Transfer adviser, college fairs on campus for students transferring to 4-year colleges.

Contact. Phone: (620) 223-2700 ext. 3530 Fax: (620) 223-6530
Mert Barrows, Director of Admissions, Fort Scott Community College, 2108 South Horton Street, Fort Scott, KS 66701

Garden City Community College
Garden City, Kansas
www.gcccks.edu

CB code: 6246

- Public 2-year community college
- Commuter campus in large town

General. Founded in 1919. Regionally accredited. **Enrollment:** 1,330 degree-seeking undergraduates; 557 non-degree-seeking students. **Degrees:** 231 associate awarded. **Location:** 200 miles from Wichita. **Calendar:** Semester, limited summer session. **Full-time faculty:** 67 total; 49% women. **Part-time faculty:** 80 total; 59% women. **Class size:** 82% < 20, 18% 20-39, less than 1% 50-99, less than 1% >100. **Special facilities:** Cadaver lab, fire arms training system, fire training tower. **Partnerships:** Formal partnerships with John Deere Company and dealers (John Deere Agricultural technical program,) Centers of excellence in automotive, cosmetology and broadcasting offered in cooperation with area high schools, and Ford Motor Company.

Student profile. Among degree-seeking undergraduates, 418 enrolled as first-time, first-year students, 35 transferred in from other institutions.

Part-time:	31%	Hispanic American:	35%
Out-of-state:	9%	Native American:	1%
Women:	54%	International:	1%
African American:	7%	25 or older:	25%
Asian American:	2%	Live on campus:	14%

Transfer out. Colleges most students transferred to 2011: Fort Hays State University, Kansas State University, Kansas University, Wichita State University, Newman University.

Basis for selection. Open admission, but selective for some programs. Additional requirements and/or an additional application is required for Nursing, Automotive Technology, Industrial Maintenance Technology, Emergency Medical Services Technology, Information Technology, and John Deere Agricultural Technology programs. Michigan English Placement Test required. Audition recommended for music majors. Portfolio recommended for art and photography majors.

High school preparation. College-preparatory program recommended. Recommended units include English 4, mathematics 2, social studies 2 and science 2.

2011-2012 Annual costs. Tuition/fees: $2,130; $2,730 out-of-state. Per-credit charge: $45 in-state; $65 out-of-state. Room/board: $4,500. Books/supplies: $840. Personal expenses: $1,645.

2011-2012 Financial aid. Need-based: 77% of total undergraduate aid awarded as scholarships/grants, 23% as loans/jobs. Need-based aid available for part-time students. Work-study available nights, weekends and for part-time students. **Non-need-based:** Scholarships awarded for academics, art, athletics, job skills, leadership, minority status, music/drama, state residency.

Application procedures. Admission: No deadline. No application fee. Application must be submitted on paper. Admission notification on a rolling basis. **Financial aid:** Priority date 3/1; no closing date. FAFSA, institutional form required. Applicants notified on a rolling basis starting 4/15; must reply within 2 week(s) of notification.

Academics. Special study options: Cooperative education, cross-registration, distance learning, dual enrollment of high school students, ESL, internships, liberal arts/career combination, student-designed major. License preparation in nursing, paramedic, radiology. **Credit/placement by examination:** AP, CLEP. 30 credit hours maximum toward associate degree. **Support services:** GED preparation and test center, learning center, remedial instruction, study skills assistance, tutoring, writing center.

Majors. Biology: General. **Business:** General. **Communications:** Communications/speech/rhetoric, journalism. **Computer sciences:** General, computer science, networking. **Conservation:** Forestry, management/policy, wildlife/wilderness. **Education:** General, art, business, chemistry, early childhood, elementary, health, history, mathematics, middle, music, physical, physics, reading, science, secondary, social science, social studies. **Engineering:** General, engineering science. **English:** English lit. **General:** Agronomy, animal sciences, business, farm/ranch. **Health services:** Athletic training, nursing (RN). **Liberal arts:** Arts/sciences. **Math:** General. **Parks/recreation:** Health/fitness. **Physical sciences:** General, chemistry. **Protective services:** Firefighting, law enforcement admin, police science. **Psychology:** General. **Social sciences:** General. **Visual/performing arts:** General, art, dramatic, music. **Work/family studies:** General, child care management.

Most popular majors. Agriculture 14%, business/marketing 8%, education 8%, health sciences 23%, liberal arts 23%.

Computing on campus. 325 workstations in dormitories, library, student center. Dormitories wired for high-speed internet access. Commuter students can connect to campus network. Online course registration available.

Student life. Freshman orientation: Available. Preregistration for classes offered. Held prior to start of classes. **Policies:** Smoke free buildings. **Housing:** Coed dorms, apartments, wellness housing available. $300 deposit, deadline 8/1. **Activities:** Bands, choral groups, drama, literary magazine, music ensembles, musical theater, radio station, student government, student newspaper, Newman Club, Hispanic American Leadership Organization, Black Student Union.

Athletics. NJCAA. **Intercollegiate:** Baseball M, basketball, cheerleading, cross-country, football (tackle) M, golf M, rodeo, soccer W, softball W, track and field, volleyball W. **Intramural:** Basketball, bowling, handball, racquetball, rifle, soccer, softball, table tennis, tennis, volleyball. **Team name:** Broncbusters.

Student services. Career counseling, services for economically disadvantaged, student employment services, financial aid counseling, health services, on-campus daycare, personal counseling, veterans' counselor. **Physically disabled:** Services for visually, speech, hearing impaired. **Transfer:** Transfer adviser, college fairs on campus for students transferring to 4-year colleges.

Contact. E-mail: nikki.geier@gcccks.edu
Phone: (620) 276-9608 Toll-free number: (800) 658-1696
Fax: (620) 276-9650
Nikki Geier, Director of Admissions, Garden City Community College, 801 Campus Drive, Garden City, KS 67846-6333

Hesston College
Hesston, Kansas
www.hesston.edu

CB code: 6274

◗ Private 2-year junior and liberal arts college affiliated with Mennonite Church
◗ Residential campus in small town

General. Founded in 1909. Regionally accredited. **Enrollment:** 468 degree-seeking undergraduates. **Degrees:** 125 associate awarded. **Location:** 35 miles from Wichita. **Calendar:** Semester, limited summer session. **Full-time faculty:** 37 total. **Part-time faculty:** 12 total. **Class size:** 63% < 20, 31% 20-39, 6% 40-49. **Special facilities:** Arboretum, retreat center. **Partnerships:** Formal partnerships with schools in the Mennonite Secondary Education Council.

Student profile.

Out-of-state:	49%	Live on campus:	75%
25 or older:	14%		

Transfer out. Colleges most students transferred to 2011: Eastern Mennonite College, Goshen College, Wichita State University, Bethel College.

Basis for selection. Open admission, but selective for some programs. Special requirements for nursing and pastoral ministries programs. A supplementary application is required for admission to the nursing and pastoral ministries programs. **Home schooled:** Must provide ACT, SAT, ASSET, or COMPASS scores.

High school preparation. Recommended units include English 4, mathematics 3, social studies 3 and science 3.

2011-2012 Annual costs. Tuition/fees: $21,652. Room/board: $7,166. Books/supplies: $1,500. Personal expenses: $1,500.

Financial aid. Need-based: Need-based aid available for part-time students. Work-study available nights, weekends and for part-time students. **Non-need-based:** Scholarships awarded for academics, alumni affiliation, art, athletics, job skills, music/drama.

Application procedures. Admission: Priority date 6/1; no deadline. $15 fee. Admission notification on a rolling basis. **Financial aid:** Closing date 4/1. FAFSA required. Applicants notified on a rolling basis starting 2/1; must reply within 4 week(s) of notification.

Academics. Special study options: Cooperative education, ESL, independent study, internships, liberal arts/career combination. License preparation in aviation, nursing. **Credit/placement by examination:** AP, CLEP, IB, institutional tests. 12 credit hours maximum toward associate degree. **Support services:** Learning center, reduced course load, remedial instruction, study skills assistance, tutoring, writing center.

Majors. Business: General. **Computer sciences:** General. **Education:** Early childhood. **Health services:** Nursing (RN). **Liberal arts:** Arts/sciences. **Theology:** Theology.

Computing on campus. 78 workstations in library, computer center, student center. Dormitories wired for high-speed internet access and linked to campus network. Online library, wireless network available.

Student life. Freshman orientation: Mandatory. Preregistration for classes offered. One day prior to the beginning of classes. All new first-time students are required to enroll during the first semester in either College Orientation/Success or College Learning Strategies. **Policies:** Use of alcohol, drugs, smoking and possession of firearms/fireworks prohibited. Decency in dress and appearance is expected. Chapel attendance is required. Religious observance required. **Housing:** Guaranteed on-campus for all undergraduates. Single-sex dorms, wellness housing available. $50 deposit. **Activities:** Bands, choral groups, drama, music ensembles, musical theater, student newspaper, peace and service club, International Christian Fellowship, Students for Responsible Citizenship.

Athletics. NJCAA. **Intercollegiate:** Baseball M, basketball, cross-country, soccer, softball W, tennis, volleyball W. **Intramural:** Basketball, cross-country, soccer, volleyball. **Team name:** Larks.

Student services. Alcohol/substance abuse counseling, chaplain/spiritual director, career counseling, financial aid counseling, minority student services, personal counseling, veterans' counselor. **Physically disabled:** Services for hearing impaired. **Transfer:** Pre-admission transcript evaluation for new students. Transfer adviser, college fairs on campus for students transferring to 4-year colleges.

Contact. E-mail: admissions@hesston.edu
Phone: (620) 327-8222 Toll-free number: (800) 995-2757
Fax: (620) 327-8300
Rachel Swartzendruber, Vice President of Admissions, Hesston College,
Box 3000, Hesston, KS 67062-2093

Highland Community College
Highland, Kansas
www.highlandcc.edu
CB code: 6276

- Public 2-year community college
- Residential campus in rural community

General. Founded in 1857. Regionally accredited. **Enrollment:** 2,313
degree-seeking undergraduates; 975 non-degree-seeking students. **Degrees:**
250 associate awarded. **Location:** 26 miles from St. Joseph, Missouri. **Calendar:** Semester, limited summer session. **Full-time faculty:** 38 total; 8% have
terminal degrees, 3% minority, 50% women. **Part-time faculty:** 192 total;
5% have terminal degrees, 4% minority, 55% women. **Class size:** 90%
< 20, 9% 20-39, less than 1% 40-49, less than 1% 50-99. **Special facilities:**
Photography studio, sports medicine/athletic trainer facilities, learning skills
center, communication technology complex.

Student profile. Among degree-seeking undergraduates, 80% enrolled in
a transfer program, 12% enrolled in a vocational program, 800 enrolled as
first-time, first-year students, 451 transferred in from other institutions.

Part-time:	48%	25 or older:	29%
Out-of-state:	7%	Live on campus:	19%
Women:	61%		

Transfer out. 61% of students enrolled in the transfer program go on to
4-year colleges. **Colleges most students transferred to 2011:** Kansas State
University, Emporia State University, University of Kansas, Washburn University, Missouri Western State College.

Basis for selection. Open admission, but selective for out-of-state students. Out-of-state applicants must be in top two-thirds of graduating class
or have 14 ACT or 660 SAT (exclusive of Writing). Placement tests determine
program eligibility. **Adult students:** Full Compass Placement. **Home
schooled:** Transcript of courses and grades required. **Learning Disabled:**
Students are asked to self-identify if they have an IEP or other verified
disability. There are no special requirements or procedures.

High school preparation. College-preparatory program recommended.
11 units recommended. Recommended units include English 3, mathematics
2, social studies 2 and science 4.

2011-2012 Annual costs. Tuition/fees: $2,430; $2,820 out-of-district;
$4,350 out-of-state. Per-credit charge: $47 in-district; $60 out-of-district;
$111 out-of-state. Out-of-state within 150 miles: $73 per-credit-hour. Room/
board: $5,070. Books/supplies: $580. Personal expenses: $1,800.

2010-2011 Financial aid. Need-based: Average scholarship/grant was
$2,051; average loan $1,483. 58% of total undergraduate aid awarded as
scholarships/grants, 42% as loans/jobs. Need-based aid available for part-time students. Work-study available nights, weekends and for part-time students. **Non-need-based:** Scholarships awarded for academics, alumni affiliation, art, athletics, job skills, leadership, music/drama. **Additional information:** Auditions and portfolios important for certain scholarship candidates.

Application procedures. Admission: Priority date 7/1; no deadline. No
application fee. Admission notification on a rolling basis beginning on or
about 4/1. Application deadline for out-of-state applicants August 1, must
reply within 2 weeks. SAT or ACT recommended, ACT preferred. Score
report by August 1. **Financial aid:** Priority date 4/1; no closing date. FAFSA,
institutional form required. Applicants notified on a rolling basis starting
4/15; must reply within 4 week(s) of notification.

Academics. Special study options: Cooperative education, distance learning, double major, dual enrollment of high school students, independent
study, internships, liberal arts/career combination, student-designed major.
License preparation in nursing, paramedic. **Credit/placement by examination:** AP, CLEP, institutional tests. 15 credit hours maximum toward associate
degree. **Support services:** GED preparation and test center, learning center,
pre-admission summer program, reduced course load, remedial instruction,
study skills assistance, tutoring.

Majors. Business: Accounting, business admin, marketing. **Computer sciences:** Data entry. **Education:** Early childhood. **General:** Agribusiness operations, economics, farm/ranch. **Health services:** Licensed practical nurse,
nursing assistant. **Math:** General. **Protective services:** Law enforcement
admin. **Visual/performing arts:** Commercial photography, graphic design.

Most popular majors. Business/marketing 13%, education 12%, health
sciences 19%, liberal arts 34%.

Computing on campus. 96 workstations in library, computer center.
Dormitories linked to campus network. Commuter students can connect to
campus network. Online course registration, repair service available.

Student life. Freshman orientation: Mandatory. Preregistration for
classes offered. **Housing:** Coed dorms, single-sex dorms, apartments, wellness housing available. $150 fully refundable deposit. **Activities:** Bands,
campus ministries, choral groups, dance, drama, music ensembles, musical
theater, student government, campus Christian fellowship, Gay/Straight Alliance.

Athletics. NJCAA. **Intercollegiate:** Baseball M, basketball, cheerleading,
cross-country, football (tackle) M, softball W, track and field, volleyball
W. **Intramural:** Badminton, basketball, football (non-tackle), softball, table
tennis, tennis, volleyball. **Team name:** Scotties.

Student services. Adult student services, career counseling, services for
economically disadvantaged, student employment services, financial aid
counseling, personal counseling, placement for graduates, veterans' counselor.
Physically disabled: Services for visually, speech, hearing impaired. **Transfer:** Transfer adviser, college fairs on campus for students transferring to 4-year colleges.

Contact. E-mail: mscott@highlandcc.edu
Phone: (785) 442-6020 Fax: (785) 442-6106
Cheryl Rasmussen, Vice President for Student Services, Highland
Community College, 606 West Main Street, Highland, KS 66035

Hutchinson Community College
Hutchinson, Kansas
www.hutchcc.edu
CB code: 6281

- Public 2-year community college
- Commuter campus in large town

General. Founded in 1928. Regionally accredited. Additional centers in
Newton, McPherson. **Enrollment:** 4,409 degree-seeking undergraduates;
1,151 non-degree-seeking students. **Degrees:** 680 associate awarded. **Location:** 45 miles from Wichita, 200 miles from Kansas City. **Calendar:** Semester, limited summer session. **Full-time faculty:** 116 total; 12% have terminal
degrees, 4% minority, 49% women. **Part-time faculty:** 280 total; 2% have
terminal degrees, 4% minority, 52% women. **Class size:** 77% < 20, 22% 20-
39, 1% 40-49. **Special facilities:** Cosmosphere space center, Kansas state
fair, underground salt mine museum.

Student profile. Among degree-seeking undergraduates, 52% enrolled in
a transfer program, 48% enrolled in a vocational program, 4% already have
a bachelor's degree or higher, 1,208 enrolled as first-time, first-year students,
552 transferred in from other institutions.

Part-time:	40%	Hispanic American:	7%
Out-of-state:	7%	Native American:	1%
Women:	58%	25 or older:	37%
African American:	7%	Live on campus:	11%
Asian American:	1%		

Transfer out. 73% of students enrolled in the transfer program go on to
4-year colleges. **Colleges most students transferred to 2011:** Kansas State
University, University of Kansas, Wichita State University, Emporia State
University, Fort Hays State University.

Basis for selection. Open admission, but selective for some programs.
Special requirements for nursing, radiology, emergency medical sciences
paramedic, health information technology, licensed practical nursing, physical
therapy assistant, and surgical technology. C-NET exam required for nursing
program applicants. Interview required for nursing, radiology, paramedic,
health information technology, physical therapy assistant, and surgical technology programs. **Home schooled:** Provide home school/high school diploma
or GED.

2011-2012 Annual costs. Tuition/fees: $2,460; $3,390 out-of-state. Per-credit charge: $65 in-state; $96 out-of-state. Room/board: $5,020. Books/
supplies: $1,200. Personal expenses: $1,200.

Financial aid. Need-based: Need-based aid available for part-time students. Work-study available nights, weekends and for part-time students.
Non-need-based: Scholarships awarded for academics, athletics, minority
status, state residency.

Application procedures. Admission: No deadline. No application fee.
Admission notification on a rolling basis. Priority application dates: 2/15 or
10/15 practical nursing, 2/20 or 8/20 nursing, 5/21 physical therapy assistant,

5/24 radiology, 6/1 health information. **Financial aid:** Priority date 2/1; no closing date. FAFSA, institutional form required. Applicants notified on a rolling basis starting 4/1; must reply within 2 week(s) of notification.

Academics. **Special study options:** Cooperative education, distance learning, double major, dual enrollment of high school students, ESL, honors, independent study, internships, weekend college. Bachelor's degree programs available on campus. **Credit/placement by examination:** AP, CLEP, institutional tests. 16 credit hours maximum toward associate degree. **Support services:** GED preparation and test center, learning center, remedial instruction, study skills assistance, tutoring, writing center.

Majors. **Biology:** General, biotechnology. **Business:** General, accounting technology, administrative services, personal/financial services, small business admin. **Communications:** Communications/speech/rhetoric. **Communications technology:** General, graphics, radio/TV. **Computer sciences:** General, networking, systems analysis, web page design. **Education:** General. **Engineering:** General. **English:** English lit. **Foreign languages:** General. **General:** Farm/ranch, power machinery. **Health services:** EMT paramedic, medical radiologic technology/radiation therapy, medical records technology, nursing (RN), physical therapy assistant. **Liberal arts:** Arts/sciences. **Math:** General. **Parks/recreation:** General. **Physical sciences:** General. **Protective services:** Fire safety technology, homeland security, police science. **Psychology:** General. **Social sciences:** General. **Visual/performing arts:** General, music. **Work/family studies:** General, child care management.

Most popular majors. Biological/life sciences 8%, business/marketing 12%, health sciences 23%, liberal arts 21%, security/protective services 8%.

Computing on campus. 600 workstations in dormitories, library, computer center, student center. Dormitories wired for high-speed internet access. Helpline, wireless network available.

Student life. **Freshman orientation:** Available. Preregistration for classes offered. **Housing:** Single-sex dorms available. $100 deposit, deadline 7/15. **Activities:** Bands, choral groups, dance, drama, literary magazine, music ensembles, student government, student newspaper, symphony orchestra, Black Cultural Society, Hispanic American leadership organization, Hutchinson Christian Fellowship, Campus Crusade for Christ, Right to Life.

Athletics. NJCAA. **Intercollegiate:** Baseball M, basketball, cross-country, football (tackle) M, golf M, soccer W, softball W, track and field, volleyball W. **Intramural:** Badminton, basketball, bowling, racquetball, soccer, softball, table tennis, tennis, track and field, volleyball. **Team name:** Blue Dragons.

Student services. Adult student services, career counseling, student employment services, financial aid counseling, health services, on-campus daycare, personal counseling, placement for graduates, veterans' counselor. **Physically disabled:** Services for visually, speech, hearing impaired. **Transfer:** Pre-admission transcript evaluation for new students. Transfer adviser, college fairs on campus for students transferring to 4-year colleges.

Contact. E-mail: info@hutchcc.edu
Phone: (620) 665-3536 Toll-free number: (800) 289-3501
Fax: (620) 665-3301
Corbin Strobel, Director of Admissions, Hutchinson Community College, 1300 North Plum, Hutchinson, KS 67501

Independence Community College
Independence, Kansas
www.indycc.edu   **CB code: 6304**

▸ Public 2-year community and junior college
▸ Commuter campus in large town

General. Founded in 1925. Regionally accredited. **Enrollment:** 736 degree-seeking undergraduates. **Degrees:** 101 associate awarded. **Location:** 110 miles from Tulsa, Oklahoma. **Calendar:** Semester, extensive summer session. **Full-time faculty:** 26 total. **Part-time faculty:** 69 total. **Special facilities:** Collection of original manuscripts, press clippings, personal books and recordings of playwright William Inge.

Student profile.

Out-of-state:	9%	Live on campus:	10%
25 or older:	53%		

Transfer out. **Colleges most students transferred to 2011:** Pittsburg State University, Emporia State University, Wichita State University, Kansas State University, University of Kansas.

Basis for selection. Open admission.

High school preparation. 17 units recommended. Recommended units include English 4, mathematics 4, social studies 2, history 2, science 2 (laboratory 1) and foreign language 2.

2011-2012 Annual costs. Tuition/fees: $2,040; $2,130 out-of-district; $3,330 out-of-state. Per-credit charge: $30 in-district; $33 out-of-district; $73 out-of-state. Room/board: $4,700. Books/supplies: $700.

Financial aid. **Need-based:** Need-based aid available for part-time students. Work-study available nights, weekends and for part-time students. **Non-need-based:** Scholarships awarded for academics, athletics.

Application procedures. **Admission:** No deadline. No application fee. Admission notification on a rolling basis beginning on or about 5/1. **Financial aid:** Priority date 4/1; no closing date. FAFSA required. Applicants notified on a rolling basis.

Academics. **Special study options:** Distance learning, double major, dual enrollment of high school students, ESL, independent study, internships. Bachelor's degree programs available on campus. **Credit/placement by examination:** AP, CLEP, institutional tests. **Support services:** GED preparation and test center, learning center, reduced course load, remedial instruction, study skills assistance, tutoring, writing center.

Majors. **Biology:** General, botany, zoology. **Business:** General, accounting, administrative services, business admin, office technology, office/clerical. **Communications:** Advertising, broadcast journalism, communications/speech/rhetoric, journalism. **Computer sciences:** General, data processing, information systems, programming, systems analysis. **Education:** General, art, biology, chemistry, computer, early childhood, elementary, English, health, history, mathematics, middle, music, physical, sales/marketing, school counseling, science, social science, social studies, technology/industrial arts, voc/tech. **Engineering:** General, architectural, chemical, civil. **English:** American lit, English lit, technical writing, writing. **Foreign languages:** General, French, Spanish. **General:** Business. **Health services:** EMT paramedic, medical secretary, nursing assistant. **History:** General. **Human services:** Social work. **Liberal arts:** Arts/sciences. **Math:** General, applied, statistics. **Physical sciences:** Chemistry. **Psychology:** General. **Social sciences:** General, economics, political science, sociology. **Visual/performing arts:** Art, dramatic, music, studio arts. **Work/family studies:** Child care management.

Most popular majors. Business/marketing 30%, education 10%, liberal arts 52%.

Computing on campus. 130 workstations in library, computer center, student center. Online course registration available.

Student life. **Freshman orientation:** Mandatory, $15 fee. Preregistration for classes offered. **Housing:** Coed dorms available. $50 deposit. **Activities:** Bands, choral groups, drama, music ensembles, musical theater, radio station, student government, student newspaper.

Athletics. NJCAA. **Intercollegiate:** Baseball M, basketball, football (tackle) M, softball W, tennis, track and field, volleyball W. **Intramural:** Basketball. **Team name:** Pirates.

Student services. Adult student services, career counseling, student employment services, financial aid counseling, personal counseling, placement for graduates, veterans' counselor. **Transfer:** Pre-admission transcript evaluation for new students. Transfer adviser, college fairs on campus for students transferring to 4-year colleges.

Contact. E-mail: admissions@indycc.edu
Phone: (620) 331-4100 Toll-free number: (800) 842-6063 ext. 5400
Fax: (620) 331-0946
Sheila Smither, Director of Admissions, Independence Community College, 1057 West College Avenue, Independence, KS 67301

Johnson County Community College
Overland Park, Kansas
www.jccc.edu   **CB code: 6325**

▸ Public 2-year community college
▸ Commuter campus in very large city

General. Founded in 1967. Regionally accredited. **Enrollment:** 7,021 full-time, degree-seeking students. **Degrees:** 1,412 associate awarded. **Location:** 20 miles from Kansas City. **Calendar:** Semester, extensive summer session. **Full-time faculty:** 330 total. **Part-time faculty:** 556 total. **Special facilities:** National academy of railroad sciences.

Student profile.

Out-of-state:	6%	25 or older:	37%

Two-Year Colleges

Transfer out. **Colleges most students transferred to 2011:** Kansas University, Kansas State University.

Basis for selection. Open admission, but selective for some programs. Special requirements for some allied health programs. ACT required for admission for nursing and dental hygiene applicants. Interview required for nursing, dental hygiene, emergency medical intensive care technician, respiratory therapy, and paralegal programs. Portfolio required of art majors. **Adult students:** SAT/ACT scores not required. **Home schooled:** Transcript of courses and grades required. **Learning Disabled:** Access services office assists students with documented disabilities.

2011-2012 Annual costs. Tuition/fees: $2,430; $2,880 out-of-district; $5,670 out-of-state. Per-credit charge: $81 in-district; $96 out-of-district; $189 out-of-state. Books/supplies: $1,000. Personal expenses: $1,500.

2011-2012 Financial aid. **Need-based:** Need-based aid available for part-time students. Work-study available nights, weekends and for part-time students. **Non-need-based:** Scholarships awarded for academics.

Application procedures. **Admission:** No deadline. No application fee. Admission notification on a rolling basis. **Financial aid:** Priority date 4/1; no closing date. FAFSA required. Applicants notified on a rolling basis starting 4/15; must reply within 2 week(s) of notification.

Academics. Wide variety of telecourses and courses offered by special arrangement. **Special study options:** Cooperative education, cross-registration, distance learning, double major, dual enrollment of high school students, ESL, exchange student, honors, independent study, internships, study abroad, weekend college. License preparation in dental hygiene, nursing, paramedic, radiology, real estate. **Credit/placement by examination:** AP, CLEP, institutional tests. 30 credit hours maximum toward associate degree. **Support services:** GED preparation and test center, learning center, reduced course load, remedial instruction, tutoring, writing center.

Majors. **Business:** Accounting, administrative services, business admin, entrepreneurial studies, logistics, sales/distribution. **Communications technology:** Animation/special effects. **Computer sciences:** Applications programming, modeling/simulation, networking. **Education:** Early childhood. **Foreign languages:** Sign language interpretation. **General:** Horticulture. **Health services:** Dental assistant, dental hygiene, EMT paramedic, medical radiologic technology/radiation therapy, medical records technology, nursing (RN), occupational therapy assistant, physical therapy assistant, respiratory therapy technology, surgical technology, veterinary technology/assistant. **Liberal arts:** Arts/sciences. **Protective services:** Firefighting, police science. **Visual/performing arts:** Commercial/advertising art, fashion design, game design, graphic design, interior design. **Work/family studies:** Child care management, institutional food production.

Most popular majors. Business/marketing 7%, family/consumer sciences 8%, health sciences 12%, liberal arts 60%.

Computing on campus. 800 workstations in library, computer center, student center. Online course registration, online library, helpline, wireless network available.

Student life. **Freshman orientation:** Available. Preregistration for classes offered. **Activities:** Bands, choral groups, dance, drama, international student organizations, literary magazine, Model UN, radio station, student government, student newspaper.

Athletics. NJCAA. **Intercollegiate:** Baseball M, basketball, cross-country, golf M, soccer M, softball W, tennis, track and field, volleyball W. **Intramural:** Basketball M, bowling, handball, racquetball, softball M, table tennis M, tennis M, volleyball M. **Team name:** Cavaliers.

Student services. Adult student services, career counseling, student employment services, on-campus daycare, personal counseling, placement for graduates, veterans' counselor. **Physically disabled:** Services for visually, hearing impaired. **Transfer:** Transfer adviser, college fairs on campus for students transferring to 4-year colleges.

Contact. E-mail: jcccadmissions@jccc.edu
Phone: (913) 469-3803 Toll-free number: (866) 896-5893
Fax: (913) 469-2524
Pete Belk, Director of Admission, Johnson County Community College, 12345 College Boulevard, Overland Park, KS 66210-1299

Kansas City Kansas Community College
Kansas City, Kansas
www.kckcc.edu
CB member
CB code: 6333

- Public 2-year community and career college
- Commuter campus in very large city

General. Founded in 1923. Regionally accredited. **Enrollment:** 6,220 degree-seeking undergraduates; 1,341 non-degree-seeking students. **Degrees:** 593 associate awarded. **Calendar:** Semester, extensive summer session. **Full-time faculty:** 156 total; 25% minority, 55% women. **Part-time faculty:** 309 total; 25% minority, 48% women. **Class size:** 88% < 20, 11% 20-39, less than 1% 40-49, less than 1% 50-99. **Partnerships:** Formal partnership with American Hotel and Lodging Educational Institute.

Student profile. Among degree-seeking undergraduates, 970 enrolled as first-time, first-year students, 282 transferred in from other institutions.

Part-time:	56%	Hispanic American:	10%
Out-of-state:	5%	Native American:	1%
Women:	64%	International:	2%
African American:	29%	25 or older:	52%
Asian American:	2%		

Basis for selection. Open admission, but selective for some programs. Special requirements for nursing program. **Home schooled:** Interview required. Admission based on ACT, SAT, or GED scores and interview.

High school preparation. 21 units recommended. Recommended units include English 4, mathematics 4, social studies 4, history 4, science 3 and foreign language 2.

2011-2012 Annual costs. Tuition/fees: $2,130; $5,250 out-of-state. Per-credit charge: $58 in-state; $162 out-of-state. Books/supplies: $920. Personal expenses: $2,250.

2010-2011 Financial aid. **Need-based:** Need-based aid available for part-time students. Work-study available nights, weekends and for part-time students. **Non-need-based:** Scholarships awarded for academics, art, athletics, music/drama.

Application procedures. **Admission:** No deadline. No application fee. Admission notification on a rolling basis. **Financial aid:** Priority date 4/15; no closing date. FAFSA required. Applicants notified on a rolling basis starting 5/1; must reply within 4 week(s) of notification.

Academics. Extensive online classes. **Special study options:** Cooperative education, distance learning, dual enrollment of high school students, ESL, external degree, honors, internships, liberal arts/career combination, weekend college. **Credit/placement by examination:** AP, CLEP, IB, institutional tests. 15 credit hours maximum toward associate degree. **Support services:** GED preparation and test center, learning center, reduced course load, remedial instruction, study skills assistance, tutoring, writing center.

Majors. **Business:** Accounting/business management, administrative services, business admin, marketing. **Communications technology:** Desktop publishing, recording arts. **Computer sciences:** Networking. **Health services:** EMT paramedic, nursing (RN), physical therapy assistant, respiratory therapy assistant, respiratory therapy technology, substance abuse counseling. **Liberal arts:** Arts/sciences. **Protective services:** Corrections, fire safety technology, firefighting, police science. **Work/family studies:** Child care management.

Most popular majors. Business/marketing 6%, health sciences 27%, liberal arts 43%.

Computing on campus. 900 workstations in library, computer center. Commuter students can connect to campus network. Online course registration, online library, helpline, wireless network available.

Student life. **Freshman orientation:** Mandatory, $59 fee. Preregistration for classes offered. One credit hour course taken in first semester. **Activities:** Bands, choral groups, drama, international student organizations, music ensembles, musical theater, student government, student newspaper, TV station, African American Student Union, International Student Organization, Campus Forum, Christian Student Union, Phi Theta Kappa, Student Senate, Out Questioning & Straight Diversity Club, Student Organization of Latinos, Economics Club, Students in Free Enterprise.

Athletics. NJCAA. **Intercollegiate:** Baseball M, basketball, cross-country, golf M, soccer M, softball W, track and field, volleyball W. **Team name:** Blue Devils.

Student services. Adult student services, alcohol/substance abuse counseling, career counseling, services for economically disadvantaged, student employment services, financial aid services, health services, on-campus daycare, personal counseling, veterans' counselor, women's services. **Physically disabled:** Services for visually, speech, hearing impaired. **Transfer:** Transfer adviser, college fairs on campus for students transferring to 4-year colleges.

Contact. E-mail: admiss@kckcc.edu
Phone: (913) 288-7600 Fax: (913) 288-7648
Denise McDowell, Dean of Enrollment Management and Registrar, Kansas City Kansas Community College, 7250 State Avenue, Kansas City, KS 66112

Labette Community College
Parsons, Kansas
www.labette.edu   CB code: 6576

- Public 2-year community college
- Commuter campus in large town

General. Founded in 1923. Regionally accredited. **Enrollment:** 1,266 degree-seeking undergraduates. **Degrees:** 166 associate awarded. **Location:** 130 miles from Kansas City, 50 miles from Tulsa, Oklahoma. **Calendar:** Semester, extensive summer session. **Full-time faculty:** 34 total. **Part-time faculty:** 117 total. **Class size:** 78% < 20, 22% 20-39, less than 1% 40-49. **Special facilities:** Recording technology program equipment and health science equipment. **Partnerships:** Formal partnerships with local businesses.

Student profile.

Out-of-state: 5%   Live on campus: 3%
25 or older: 41%

Transfer out. Colleges most students transferred to 2011: Pittsburg State, Emporia State, Wichita State, Kansas University, Kansas State University.

Basis for selection. Open admission, but selective for some programs. Special requirements for health and commercial music programs. ACT, school and College Ability Tests required of nursing applicants. COMPASS also used to measure language proficiency. Interview required for nursing, radiology, respiratory therapy programs, and commercial music programs. **Home schooled:** Transcript of courses and grades required. GED and ACT scores may be considered. Placement testing available. **Learning Disabled:** Student must notify campus ADA coordinator at least 30 days prior to first day of classes (earlier in special circumstances).

2011-2012 Annual costs. Tuition/fees: $2,340; $3,090 out-of-state. Books/supplies: $1,050. Personal expenses: $2,500.

Financial aid. Need-based: Need-based aid available for part-time students. Work-study available nights, weekends and for part-time students. **Non-need-based:** Scholarships awarded for academics, leadership.

Application procedures. Admission: No deadline. No application fee. Admission notification on a rolling basis. **Financial aid:** No deadline. FAFSA required. Applicants notified on a rolling basis starting 4/4; must reply within 2 week(s) of notification.

Academics. Extensive PLATO learning system available. Four-year bachelor's program with Emporia State University, Washburn University. **Special study options:** Distance learning, dual enrollment of high school students, liberal arts/career combination. License preparation in nursing, radiology. **Credit/placement by examination:** AP, CLEP, institutional tests. 12 credit hours maximum toward associate degree. **Support services:** GED preparation and test center, learning center, remedial instruction, study skills assistance, tutoring, writing center.

Majors. Biology: General. **Business:** Accounting, business admin, office/clerical. **Communications:** Journalism. **Computer sciences:** General, data processing, LAN/WAN management, networking, programming. **Education:** General, business, early childhood, elementary, music, secondary. **English:** English lit. **Health services:** Medical secretary, nursing (RN), radiologic technology/medical imaging, respiratory therapy technology. **History:** General. **Liberal arts:** Arts/sciences. **Protective services:** Corrections, firefighting, law enforcement admin. **Psychology:** General. **Social sciences:** General, political science. **Visual/performing arts:** Commercial/advertising art, music, music management, studio arts.

Most popular majors. Business/marketing 11%, education 15%, health sciences 53%.

Computing on campus. 150 workstations in library, computer center, student center. Commuter students can connect to campus network. Online library, helpline, student web hosting, wireless network available.

Student life. Freshman orientation: Mandatory. Preregistration for classes offered. **Activities:** Bands, choral groups, dance, drama, music ensembles, student government, Christian Club, Phi Beta Lambda, Phi Theta Kappa.

Athletics. NJCAA. **Intercollegiate:** Baseball M, basketball, cheerleading, softball W, tennis W, volleyball W, wrestling M. **Team name:** Cardinals.

Student services. Adult student services, career counseling, services for economically disadvantaged, student employment services, financial aid counseling, personal counseling, placement for graduates, veterans' counselor. **Physically disabled:** Services for visually, speech, hearing impaired. **Transfer:** Transfer adviser, college fairs on campus for students transferring to 4-year colleges.

Contact. Phone: (620) 421-6700 Toll-free number: (888) 522-3883 Fax: (620) 421-0180
Angela Holmes, Director of Admissions, Labette Community College, 200 South 14th Street, Parsons, KS 67357

Manhattan Area Technical College
Manhattan, Kansas
www.matc.net

- Public 2-year technical college
- Commuter campus in large town

General. Enrollment: 731 degree-seeking undergraduates. **Degrees:** 97 associate awarded. **Location:** 125 miles from Kansas City. **Calendar:** Semester, limited summer session. **Full-time faculty:** 24 total. **Part-time faculty:** 12 total.

Basis for selection. Open admission, but selective for some programs. Practical Nursing applicants must meet testing requirements and be KS licensed Certified Nurse Aide; Associate Degree/Registered Nurse applicants must be KS licensed Practical Nurses; Electric Power & Distribution applicants must be 18 years of age prior to June 1 of their year of enrollment and have or be eligible to receive a Commercial Drivers License by the same date.

2011-2012 Annual costs. Tuition/fees: $4,212; $4,212 out-of-state. Per-credit charge: $82 in-state; $82 out-of-state. Books/supplies: $1,900. Personal expenses: $2,500.

Financial aid. Need-based: Need-based aid available for part-time students. Work-study available nights, weekends and for part-time students. **Non-need-based:** Scholarships awarded for academics, leadership.

Application procedures. Admission: No deadline. $40 fee. Application must be submitted on paper. Admission notification on a rolling basis. **Financial aid:** No deadline. FAFSA, institutional form required. Applicants notified on a rolling basis.

Academics. Special study options: Cooperative education. License preparation in nursing. **Credit/placement by examination:** AP, CLEP, institutional tests. 9 credit hours maximum toward associate degree. **Support services:** Learning center, reduced course load, study skills assistance, tutoring.

Majors. Business: Administrative services, executive assistant. **Computer sciences:** General. **Health services:** Nursing (RN).

Most popular majors. Business/marketing 10%, communication technologies 15%, computer/information sciences 20%, engineering/engineering technologies 20%, health sciences 9%, trade and industry 14%.

Computing on campus. 16 workstations in library, student center. Commuter students can connect to campus network. Online library, wireless network available.

Student life. Freshman orientation: Mandatory. Preregistration for classes offered. Approximately 6-8 weeks prior to beginning of semester. Half day sessions include pre-enrollment, and pre-testing.

Student services. Career counseling, financial aid counseling, personal counseling, placement for graduates. **Transfer:** Pre-admission transcript evaluation for new students.

Contact. E-mail: nicolefischer@matc.net
Phone: (785) 587-2800 ext. 104
Toll-free number: (800) 352-7575 ext. 104 Fax: (785) 587-2804
Nicole Fischer, Director of Admissions, Manhattan Area Technical College, 3136 Dickens Avenue, Manhattan, KS 66503-2499

Neosho County Community College
Chanute, Kansas
www.neosho.edu   CB code: 6093

- Public 2-year community college
- Commuter campus in small town

General. Founded in 1936. Regionally accredited. **Enrollment:** 2,550 degree-seeking undergraduates. **Degrees:** 210 associate awarded. **Location:** Approximately 100 miles from both Kansas City, Missouri and Wichita, Kansas. **Calendar:** Semester, limited summer session. **Full-time faculty:** 53 total. **Part-time faculty:** 140 total.

Student profile.

Out-of-state:	14%	**Live on campus:**	28%

Transfer out. Colleges most students transferred to 2011: Pittsburg State University, Emporia State University, Kansas State University, University of Kansas, Wichita State University.

Basis for selection. Open admission, but selective for some programs. Special requirements for nursing program, nursing entrance test (NET) required. **Home schooled:** Must take GED or have ACT score of 20 or SAT score of 850.

2011-2012 Annual costs. Tuition/fees: $2,220; $2,580 out-of-district; $3,240 out-of-state. Room/board: $4,900. Books/supplies: $430. Personal expenses: $800.

2010-2011 Financial aid. Need-based: 60% of total undergraduate aid awarded as scholarships/grants, 40% as loans/jobs. Need-based aid available for part-time students. Work-study available nights, weekends and for part-time students. **Non-need-based:** Scholarships awarded for academics, art, athletics, job skills, leadership, music/drama, state residency.

Application procedures. Admission: Priority date 8/15; no deadline. No application fee. Admission notification on a rolling basis. **Financial aid:** Priority date 4/1; no closing date. FAFSA required. Applicants notified on a rolling basis; must reply within 6 week(s) of notification.

Academics. Special study options: Cooperative education, distance learning, dual enrollment of high school students, ESL, honors, independent study, liberal arts/career combination, weekend college. License preparation in nursing, real estate. **Credit/placement by examination:** AP, CLEP, institutional tests. 15 credit hours maximum toward associate degree. **Support services:** GED preparation and test center, learning center, reduced course load, remedial instruction, study skills assistance, tutoring, writing center.

Majors. Biology: General. **Business:** Accounting, administrative services, banking/financial services, business admin, office management. **Communications:** Communications/speech/rhetoric. **Computer sciences:** General. **Education:** General, secondary. **English:** English lit. **Foreign languages:** General. **Health services:** Athletic training, health care admin, licensed practical nurse, nursing (RN). **Human services:** Social work. **Liberal arts:** Arts/sciences. **Math:** General. **Parks/recreation:** Exercise sciences. **Physical sciences:** Chemistry. **Psychology:** General. **Social sciences:** General. **Visual/performing arts:** Art, dramatic, music, studio arts. **Work/family studies:** General.

Computing on campus. 120 workstations in dormitories, library, computer center, student center. Dormitories wired for high-speed internet access. Online library, helpline, wireless network available.

Student life. Freshman orientation: Mandatory. Preregistration for classes offered. **Housing:** Guaranteed on-campus for freshmen. Coed dorms available. $125 nonrefundable deposit. Home stays with host families for international students. **Activities:** Choral groups, dance, drama, music ensembles, musical theater, student government.

Athletics. NJCAA. **Intercollegiate:** Baseball M, basketball, cheerleading, cross-country, soccer, softball W, track and field, volleyball W, wrestling M. **Team name:** Panthers.

Student services. Adult student services, career counseling, student employment services, financial aid counseling, personal counseling, placement for graduates, veterans' counselor. **Physically disabled:** Services for visually, speech, hearing impaired. **Transfer:** Pre-admission transcript evaluation for new students. Transfer center, transfer adviser, college fairs on campus for students transferring to 4-year colleges.

Contact. E-mail: admissions@neosho.edu
Phone: (620) 431-2820 ext. 233 Toll-free number: (800) 729-6222
Fax: (620)
Sarah Cadwallader, Director of Admission, Neosho County Community College, 800 West 14th Street, Chanute, KS 66720

North Central Kansas Technical College
Beloit, Kansas
www.ncktc.edu CB code: 2616

⬧ Public 2-year technical college
⬧ Small town

General. Regionally accredited. Multicampus institution. **Enrollment:** 658 degree-seeking undergraduates. **Degrees:** 121 associate awarded. **Location:** 107 miles from Hays, 175 miles from Topeka. **Calendar:** Semester, limited summer session. **Full-time faculty:** 45 total. **Part-time faculty:** 12 total.

Basis for selection. Open admission. **Home schooled:** Transcript of courses and grades required. **Learning Disabled:** Students must present written documentation from certified professional identifying disability with recommendations for accommodations.

2011-2012 Annual costs. Tuition/fees: $4,886; $4,886 out-of-state. Room/board: $4,450. Books/supplies: $800.

Financial aid. All financial aid based on need. Need-based aid available for part-time students. Work-study available nights, weekends and for part-time students.

Application procedures. Admission: No deadline. $50 fee. Admission notification on a rolling basis. **Financial aid:** No deadline. FAFSA required.

Academics. Credit/placement by examination: AP, CLEP. **Support services:** Learning center, remedial instruction, tutoring.

Majors. General: Equipment technology. **Health services:** Nursing (RN).

Computing on campus. 50 workstations in library, computer center. Dormitories wired for high-speed internet access. Repair service available.

Student life. Freshman orientation: Available. Preregistration for classes offered. **Housing:** Coed dorms available. **Activities:** Student government.

Athletics. Intramural: Basketball M, football (non-tackle) M, volleyball, wrestling M.

Student services. Career counseling, financial aid counseling, placement for graduates.

Contact. E-mail: dhughes@ncktc.edu
Phone: (800) 658-4655 Toll-free number: (800) 658-4655
Fax: (785) 738-2903
David Hughes, Admissions Director, North Central Kansas Technical College, PO Box 507, Beloit, KS 67420

Northwest Kansas Technical College
Goodland, Kansas
www.nwktc.edu

⬧ Public 2-year technical college
⬧ Residential campus in small town

General. Regionally accredited. **Enrollment:** 332 degree-seeking undergraduates; 141 non-degree-seeking students. **Degrees:** 75 associate awarded. **Location:** 144 miles from Hays. **Calendar:** Semester, limited summer session. **Full-time faculty:** 30 total. **Part-time faculty:** 2 total. **Special facilities:** Rodeo practice arena.

Student profile. Among degree-seeking undergraduates, 16% enrolled in a transfer program, 70% enrolled in a vocational program, .6% already have a bachelor's degree or higher, 204 enrolled as first-time, first-year students.

Women:	28%	**25 or older:**	34%

Transfer out. Colleges most students transferred to 2011: Pittsburg State University, Fort Hays State University, Kansas State University.

Basis for selection. Open admission, but selective for some programs. ACT or COMPASS very important. **Home schooled:** Transcript of courses and grades required.

2011-2012 Annual costs. Tuition/fees: $2,970; $5,940 out-of-state. Per-credit charge: $99 in-state; $198 out-of-state.

Financial aid. Need-based: Work-study available nights, weekends and for part-time students.

Application procedures. Admission: Closing date 8/13 (postmark date). $25 fee. **Financial aid:** Closing date 8/1.

Academics. Special study options: Distance learning, dual enrollment of high school students, ESL, honors, internships, teacher certification program. **Credit/placement by examination:** AP, CLEP, institutional tests. **Support services:** GED preparation, learning center, remedial instruction, study skills assistance, tutoring.

Majors. Communications technology: General. **Computer sciences:** Computer graphics.

Computing on campus. PC or laptop required. Dormitories wired for high-speed internet access and linked to campus network. Online course registration, helpline, repair service, wireless network available.

Student life. Freshman orientation: Mandatory. Preregistration for classes offered. **Housing:** Guaranteed on-campus for freshmen. Single-sex dorms, special housing for disabled, apartments, wellness housing available. **Activities:** Campus ministries, choral groups, dance, student government, student newspaper.

Athletics. NJCAA. Intercollegiate: Basketball, cheerleading, golf, rodeo, soccer, wrestling. **Intramural:** Badminton, baseball, football (non-tackle), racquetball, softball, volleyball, weight lifting. **Team name:** Mavericks.

Student services. Adult student services, alcohol/substance abuse counseling, career counseling, services for economically disadvantaged, student employment services, financial aid counseling, on-campus daycare, personal counseling, placement for graduates. **Physically disabled:** Services for hearing impaired. **Transfer:** Pre-admission transcript evaluation for new students. Transfer adviser for students transferring to 4-year colleges.

Contact. E-mail: admissions@nwktc.edu
Phone: (785) 890-3641 Toll-free number: (800) 316-4127
Fax: (785) 899-5711
Reina Branum, Assistant Vice President for Student Affairs, Northwest Kansas Technical College, 1209 Harrison, Goodland, KS 67735

Pratt Community College
Pratt, Kansas
www.prattcc.edu   CB code: 6581

▸ Public 2-year community and technical college
▸ Commuter campus in small town

General. Founded in 1938. Regionally accredited. **Enrollment:** 744 full-time, degree-seeking students. **Degrees:** 265 associate awarded. **Location:** 70 miles from Wichita. **Calendar:** Semester, limited summer session. **Full-time faculty:** 48 total. **Part-time faculty:** 5 total. **Class size:** 64% < 20, 33% 20-39, 2% 40-49, less than 1% 50-99. **Special facilities:** Indoor and outdoor rodeo facilities, electrical powerlineman training facility.

Student profile.

Out-of-state:	11%	Live on campus:	40%
25 or older:	20%		

Transfer out. Colleges most students transferred to 2011: Fort Hays State University, Emporia State University, Kansas State University.

Basis for selection. Open admission, but selective for some programs. Special requirements for nursing, agriculture power technology, and electrical power distribution programs. Interview required of nursing majors. Audition required of music and drama majors. Portfolio recommended for art majors. **Home schooled:** Transcript of courses and grades required. **Learning Disabled:** IEP's must be submitted to admissions before initial enrollment and request of services.

2011-2012 Annual costs. Tuition/fees: $2,550; $2,730 out-of-state. Per-credit charge: $51 in-state; $57 out-of-state. Room/board: $5,058. Books/supplies: $800. Personal expenses: $1,000.

Financial aid. Need-based: Need-based aid available for part-time students. Work-study available nights, weekends and for part-time students. **Non-need-based:** Scholarships awarded for academics, art, athletics, leadership, minority status, music/drama, state residency.

Application procedures. Admission: No deadline. No application fee. Admission notification on a rolling basis beginning on or about 1/1. **Financial aid:** Priority date 5/1, closing date 8/1. FAFSA, institutional form required. Applicants notified on a rolling basis starting 2/1; must reply within 2 week(s) of notification.

Academics. Special study options: Distance learning, dual enrollment of high school students, honors, independent study, internships, liberal arts/career combination, weekend college. Bachelor's degree programs available on campus. License preparation in nursing. **Credit/placement by examination:** AP, CLEP, IB, institutional tests. 15 credit hours maximum toward associate degree. **Support services:** GED preparation, learning center, remedial instruction, tutoring.

Majors. Biology: General, botany. **Business:** Accounting, business admin, entrepreneurial studies, office management, office technology, office/clerical. **Communications:** Communications/speech/rhetoric, journalism. **Computer sciences:** General. **Conservation:** Wildlife/wilderness. **Education:** General, early childhood, elementary, secondary. **Engineering:** General. **English:** English lit, rhetoric/composition. **General:** Animal sciences, business, farm/ranch, range science. **Health services:** Licensed practical nurse, medical secretary, nursing (RN), predental, premedicine, prepharmacy, preveterinary. **History:** General. **Liberal arts:** Arts/sciences. **Math:** General. **Physical**

sciences: Chemistry. **Psychology:** General. **Social sciences:** General, political science, sociology. **Visual/performing arts:** General, ceramics, commercial/advertising art, dramatic, drawing, music, painting, studio arts.

Most popular majors. Agriculture 9%, business/marketing 6%, education 7%, health sciences 39%, trade and industry 18%.

Computing on campus. 125 workstations in dormitories, library, computer center. Dormitories wired for high-speed internet access and linked to campus network. Commuter students can connect to campus network. Online course registration, online library, helpline, wireless network available.

Student life. Freshman orientation: Available. Preregistration for classes offered. One to 2 days before classes begin in each fall and spring semester. **Policies:** 2 MMR (Measle, Mumps, Rubella) inoculations and Meningitis inoculations required for dorm students. **Housing:** Coed dorms, single-sex dorms, wellness housing available. $200 deposit. **Activities:** Bands, choral groups, dance, drama, international student organizations, literary magazine, music ensembles, musical theater, student government, student newspaper, Christian Challenge, Student Senate, Student Ambassadors, Rotaract.

Athletics. NJCAA. Intercollegiate: Baseball M, basketball, cheerleading, cross-country, rodeo, soccer, softball W, track and field, volleyball W, wrestling M. **Intramural:** Basketball, football (non-tackle), rodeo, softball, table tennis, volleyball. **Team name:** Beavers.

Student services. Adult student services, career counseling, student employment services, financial aid counseling, health services, personal counseling, placement for graduates, veterans' counselor. **Physically disabled:** Services for visually, speech, hearing impaired. **Transfer:** College fairs on campus for students transferring to 4-year colleges.

Contact. E-mail: lynnp@prattcc.edu
Phone: (620) 672-5641 ext. 217
Toll-free number: (800) 794-3091 ext. 217 Fax: (620) 672-5288
Ann Ruder, Director of Admissions, Pratt Community College, 348 Northeast State Road 61, Pratt, KS 67124-8317

Seward County Community College
Liberal, Kansas
www.sccc.edu   CB code: 0286

▸ Public 2-year community college
▸ Commuter campus in large town

General. Founded in 1967. Regionally accredited. Off-campus classes offered in 7 locations, adult learning center with ESL classes, interactive television classrooms to off-site locations, adult basic education classes, GED testing available. **Enrollment:** 1,268 degree-seeking undergraduates. **Degrees:** 228 associate awarded. **Location:** 210 miles from Wichita, 150 miles from Amarillo, Texas. **Calendar:** Semester, limited summer session. **Full-time faculty:** 62 total. **Part-time faculty:** 85 total. **Class size:** 83% < 20, 16% 20-39, less than 1% 40-49, less than 1% 50-99. **Special facilities:** Wellness center.

Student profile.

Out-of-state:	19%	Live on campus:	15%

Transfer out. Colleges most students transferred to 2011: Kansas State University, Texas Christian University, University of Texas-Arlington, University of Central Oklahoma, Fort Hays State University.

Basis for selection. Open admission.

High school preparation. 20 units recommended. Recommended units include English 4, mathematics 3, social studies 2, science 2 and foreign language 1.

2011-2012 Annual costs. Tuition/fees: $1,950; $2,850 out-of-state. Per-credit charge: $40 in-state; $70 out-of-state. Residents of neighboring counties in OK, TX and CO pay per-credit-hour rate of $55. Room/board: $4,200. Books/supplies: $700. Personal expenses: $1,000.

Financial aid. Need-based: Need-based aid available for part-time students. Work-study available nights, weekends and for part-time students. **Non-need-based:** Scholarships awarded for academics, athletics.

Application procedures. Admission: Priority date 4/1; no deadline. No application fee. Admission notification on a rolling basis. **Financial aid:** Priority date 4/1; no closing date. FAFSA, institutional form required. Applicants notified on a rolling basis starting 6/15; must reply within 4 week(s) of notification.

Academics. **Special study options:** Cooperative education, cross-registration, distance learning, double major, dual enrollment of high school students, ESL, external degree, honors, independent study, internships, liberal arts/career combination. Bachelor's degree programs available on campus. License preparation in nursing, paramedic. **Credit/placement by examination:** AP, CLEP, institutional tests. 24 credit hours maximum toward associate degree. **Support services:** GED preparation and test center, learning center, remedial instruction, study skills assistance, tutoring, writing center.

Majors. **Biology:** General. **Business:** General, accounting, administrative services, business admin, fashion, finance, hospitality admin, office management, office technology, office/clerical, sales/distribution. **Communications:** Communications/speech/rhetoric, journalism. **Computer sciences:** General, applications programming, computer graphics, computer science, data entry, data processing, information technology, programming. **Conservation:** Forestry, wildlife/wilderness. **Education:** General, teacher assistance. **Engineering:** General. **English:** English lit. **General:** Animal sciences, business, farm/ranch. **Health services:** Athletic training, clinical lab assistant, clinical lab technology, dental hygiene, medical secretary, nursing (RN), predental, premedicine, prenursing, prepharmacy, preveterinary, respiratory therapy technology. **History:** General. **Human services:** Social work. **Liberal arts:** Arts/sciences, library assistant. **Math:** General. **Parks/recreation:** General, exercise sciences, health/fitness. **Philosophy/religion:** Religion. **Physical sciences:** Chemistry, physics. **Protective services:** Law enforcement admin, police science. **Psychology:** General. **Social sciences:** General, economics, sociology. **Visual/performing arts:** General, art, ceramics, dramatic, music, music performance, painting, studio arts, voice/opera.

Computing on campus. 450 workstations in dormitories, library, computer center, student center. Dormitories wired for high-speed internet access. Commuter students can connect to campus network. Online course registration, online library, wireless network available.

Student life. **Freshman orientation:** Mandatory. Preregistration for classes offered. **Housing:** Coed dorms available. $100 deposit, deadline 6/30. **Activities:** Bands, choral groups, drama, film society, literary magazine, music ensembles, musical theater, student government, student newspaper, symphony orchestra, TV station.

Athletics. NJCAA. **Intercollegiate:** Baseball M, basketball, softball W, tennis, volleyball W. **Intramural:** Basketball, bowling, football (non-tackle), golf, soccer, swimming, table tennis, volleyball. **Team name:** Saints.

Student services. Adult student services, career counseling, student employment services, financial aid counseling, personal counseling, veterans' counselor. **Transfer:** Transfer adviser, college fairs on campus for students transferring to 4-year colleges.

Contact. E-mail: jr.doney@sccc.edu
Phone: (620) 417-1102 Toll-free number: (800) 373-9951 ext. 1102
Fax: (620) 417-1079
JR Doney, Director of Marketing and Admissions, Seward County Community College, 1801 North Kansas Avenue, Liberal, KS 67905-1137

Wichita Area Technical College
Wichita, Kansas
www.watc.edu

- Public 2-year technical college
- Large city

General. Regionally accredited. **Enrollment:** 978 full-time, degree-seeking students. **Degrees:** 57 associate awarded. **Calendar:** Semester. **Full-time faculty:** 51 total. **Part-time faculty:** 101 total.

Basis for selection. Open admission, but selective for some programs.

2011-2012 Annual costs. Tuition for general education courses is $60 per credit hour and fees are $27 per credit hour. Tuition costs vary by program.

Financial aid. **Need-based:** Work-study available nights, weekends and for part-time students.

Academics. **Credit/placement by examination:** AP, CLEP.

Majors. **Business:** Accounting technology, business admin, entrepreneurial studies, office/clerical. **Health services:** Dental assistant, licensed practical nurse, medical assistant, surgical technology. **Visual/performing arts:** Interior design.

Contact. E-mail: info@watc.edu
Andy McFayden, Director of Admissions, Wichita Area Technical College, 4004 North Webb Road, Suite 100, Wichita, KS 67226

Kentucky

Ashland Community and Technical College
Ashland, Kentucky
www.ashland.kctcs.edu   CB code: 0703

▶ Public 2-year community college
▶ Commuter campus in large town

General. Founded in 1957. Regionally accredited. Off-campus classes in surrounding counties. **Enrollment:** 2,800 degree-seeking undergraduates. **Degrees:** 410 associate awarded. **Location:** 120 miles from Lexington; 15 miles from Huntington, WV. **Calendar:** Semester, limited summer session. **Full-time faculty:** 95 total. **Part-time faculty:** 113 total. **Special facilities:** 3 open computer labs, learning assistance center, early intervention program for students at risk.

Student profile.

Out-of-state: 26%   **25 or older:**   43%

Transfer out. Colleges most students transferred to 2011: Morehead State University, Marshall University, Shawnee State University.

Basis for selection. Open admission, but selective for some programs. Admission to nursing program based on test scores and academic record. Interview recommended.

High school preparation. 11 units recommended. Recommended units include English 4, mathematics 3, social studies 2, science 2 (laboratory 2).

2011-2012 Annual costs. Tuition/fees: $4,050; $13,950 out-of-state. Per-credit charge: $135 in-state; $465 out-of-state. Books/supplies: $750. Personal expenses: $800.

Financial aid. Need-based: Work-study available nights, weekends and for part-time students. **Non-need-based:** Scholarships awarded for academics, job skills, leadership, minority status, music/drama. **Additional information:** In-state 100% disabled or deceased veterans' children receive tuition waiver from state.

Application procedures. Admission: No deadline. No application fee. Admission notification on a rolling basis. Nursing applications due by 3/1. **Financial aid:** Priority date 3/15; no closing date. FAFSA, institutional form required. Applicants notified on a rolling basis starting 5/1; must reply within 3 week(s) of notification.

Academics. Special study options: Cooperative education, cross-registration, distance learning, dual enrollment of high school students, honors, internships, liberal arts/career combination, weekend college. **Credit/placement by examination:** AP, CLEP, institutional tests. 40 credit hours maximum toward associate degree. **Support services:** GED test center, learning center, pre-admission summer program, reduced course load, remedial instruction, study skills assistance, tutoring.

Honors college/program. Participants have option of taking selected honors courses.

Majors. Business: Accounting, banking/financial services, business admin, management information systems, office/clerical, real estate. **Computer sciences:** Information systems, vendor certification. **Health services:** Medical secretary, nursing (RN), physical therapy assistant, respiratory therapy technology. **Liberal arts:** Arts/sciences. **Protective services:** Police science.

Most popular majors. Biological/life sciences 14%, business/marketing 16%, health sciences 49%, liberal arts 16%.

Computing on campus. 138 workstations in library, computer center. Commuter students can connect to campus network. Online course registration, helpline available.

Student life. Freshman orientation: Mandatory. Preregistration for classes offered. **Activities:** Choral groups, drama, literary magazine, music ensembles, musical theater, student government, student newspaper, Baptist student union/students for Christ, Circle K, drama club, multicultural student affairs, Phi Theta Kappa, students in free enterprise.

Athletics. Intramural: Basketball, bowling, fencing, softball, table tennis, tennis, volleyball.

Student services. Adult student services, career counseling, student employment services, financial aid counseling, health services, minority student services, on-campus daycare, personal counseling, placement for graduates, veterans' counselor. **Physically disabled:** Services for visually, speech, hearing impaired. **Transfer:** Re-entry adviser for new students. Transfer center, transfer adviser for students transferring to 4-year colleges.

Contact. E-mail: willie.mccullough@kctcs.net
Phone: (606) 326-2000 Toll-free number: (800) 370-7191
Fax: (606) 325-8124
Willie McCullough, Dean for Student Affairs, Ashland Community and Technical College, 1400 College Drive, Ashland, KY 41101-3683

Big Sandy Community and Technical College
Prestonsburg, Kentucky
www.bigsandy.kctcs.edu   CB code: 0869

▶ Public 2-year community and technical college
▶ Commuter campus in small town

General. Founded in 1964. Regionally accredited. Four campuses located at Hager Hill, Paintsville, Pikeville, and Prestonsburg. **Enrollment:** 3,418 degree-seeking undergraduates. **Degrees:** 349 associate awarded. **Location:** 120 miles from Lexington. **Calendar:** Semester, limited summer session. **Full-time faculty:** 128 total. **Part-time faculty:** 86 total. **Special facilities:** East Kentucky Science Center, planetarium, nature trail.

Student profile.

Out-of-state: 1%   **25 or older:**   36%

Basis for selection. Open admission, but selective for some programs. 20 ACT required for nursing and dental hygiene programs. All others required to submit COMPASS, ASSET, ACT or SAT for placement.

2011-2012 Annual costs. Tuition/fees: $4,050; $13,950 out-of-state. Per-credit charge: $135 in-state; $465 out-of-state. Books/supplies: $450. Personal expenses: $3,000.

Financial aid. Need-based: Need-based aid available for part-time students. Work-study available nights, weekends and for part-time students. **Non-need-based:** Scholarships awarded for academics.

Application procedures. Admission: No deadline. No application fee. Admission notification on a rolling basis. Must have completed junior year of high school prior to enrolling full-time; may audit courses as sophomores or juniors. **Financial aid:** Priority date 4/1; no closing date. FAFSA required. Applicants notified on a rolling basis; must reply within 2 week(s) of notification.

Academics. Special study options: Cooperative education, distance learning, dual enrollment of high school students, independent study, internships, liberal arts/career combination, weekend college. Bachelor's degree programs available on campus. **Credit/placement by examination:** AP, CLEP, institutional tests. 36 credit hours maximum toward associate degree. **Support services:** GED preparation and test center, learning center, remedial instruction, study skills assistance, tutoring, writing center.

Majors. Business: Accounting, administrative services, management information systems, management science, real estate. **Computer sciences:** Information technology, networking, programming, webmaster. **Health services:** Dental hygiene, nursing (RN). **Liberal arts:** Arts/sciences. **Protective services:** Police science.

Computing on campus. 575 workstations in library, computer center, student center. Online course registration, online library, wireless network available.

Student life. Freshman orientation: Available. Preregistration for classes offered. **Activities:** Choral groups, drama, literary magazine, student government, Baptist Student Union, Phi Theta Kappa, Phi Beta Lambda, Kentucky Association of Nursing Students, CARE, law enforcement club.

Student services. Career counseling, services for economically disadvantaged, financial aid counseling, personal counseling, veterans' counselor. **Physically disabled:** Services for visually, speech, hearing impaired. **Transfer:** Pre-admission transcript evaluation for new students. Transfer center, transfer adviser, college fairs on campus for students transferring to 4-year colleges.

Contact. E-mail: jimmy.wright@kctcs.edu
Phone: (606) 886-3863 ext. 67366
Toll-free number: (888) 641-4132 ext. 67366 Fax: (606) 886-6943
Jimmy Wright, Associate Dean of Admissions, Big Sandy Community and Technical College, One Bert T. Combs Drive, Prestonsburg, KY 41653

Bluegrass Community and Technical College
Lexington, Kentucky
www.bluegrass.kctcs.edu

CB code: 0645

- Public 2-year community and technical college
- Commuter campus in large city

General. Founded in 1965. Regionally accredited. Locations include Danville, Georgetown, Lawrenceburg, Lexington, Nicholasville, and Winchester. **Enrollment:** 12,377 degree-seeking undergraduates. **Degrees:** 1,106 associate awarded. **Location:** 90 miles from Cincinnati, 75 miles from Louisville. **Calendar:** Semester, extensive summer session. **Full-time faculty:** 269 total. **Part-time faculty:** 405 total. **Special facilities:** North American Racing Academy located at Kentucky Horse Park. **Partnerships:** Industrial maintenance internship with Toyota; pre-hire assessments conducted for local companies; short-term training offered for local businesses (computer skills, HVAC skills, etc.).

Student profile. Among degree-seeking undergraduates, 2,591 enrolled as first-time, first-year students.

Part-time:	48%	Women:	59%
Out-of-state:	1%	25 or older:	47%

Transfer out. Colleges most students transferred to 2011: University of Kentucky, Eastern Kentucky University, Midway College, Morehead University, University of Phoenix.

Basis for selection. Open admission, but selective for some programs. Special requirements for computer information systems, health technologies, nursing, nuclear medicine, radiography, respiratory care, dental hygiene, dental laboratory technology. ACT required for admission to some health programs. NLN preadmission test may be used for nursing rather than ACT. **Home schooled:** ACT/SAT scores (or COMPASS) and transcript including grading scale required.

High school preparation. Students strongly encouraged to follow state pre-college curriculum.

2011-2012 Annual costs. Tuition/fees: $4,050; $13,950 out-of-state. Per-credit charge: $135 in-state; $465 out-of-state. Room/board: $6,976. Books/supplies: $750. Personal expenses: $800.

Financial aid. Need-based: Need-based aid available for part-time students. Work-study available nights, weekends and for part-time students. **Non-need-based:** Scholarships awarded for academics, minority status, state residency.

Application procedures. Admission: Closing date 8/1 (receipt date). No application fee. Admission notification on a rolling basis. **Financial aid:** Priority date 4/15; no closing date. FAFSA, institutional form required. Applicants notified on a rolling basis starting 6/5; must reply within 3 week(s) of notification.

Academics. Six nationally accredited programs offered in allied health and nursing. **Special study options:** Cooperative education, distance learning, double major, dual enrollment of high school students, ESL, exchange student, internships, study abroad, weekend college. License preparation in dental hygiene, nursing, radiology, real estate. **Credit/placement by examination:** AP, CLEP, institutional tests. **Support services:** GED preparation and test center, learning center, remedial instruction, study skills assistance, tutoring, writing center.

Majors. Architecture: Landscape. **Area/ethnic studies:** Latin American, Russian/Slavic. **Biology:** General, biochemistry. **Business:** Administrative services, business admin, executive assistant. **Communications:** Communications/speech/rhetoric, journalism, radio/TV. **Computer sciences:** General, data processing, information technology. **Conservation:** General, forest sciences, wildlife/wilderness. **Education:** Teacher assistance. **English:** English lit, rhetoric/composition. **Foreign languages:** French, German, Italian, linguistics, Russian, Spanish. **General:** Economics, equestrian studies. **Health services:** Dental hygiene, dental lab technology, medical assistant, medical radiologic technology/radiation therapy, medical secretary, nuclear medical technology, nursing (RN), respiratory therapy technology, surgical technology. **Human services:** Social work. **Liberal arts:** Arts/sciences. **Math:** General. **Philosophy/religion:** Philosophy, religion. **Physical sciences:** General, chemistry, geology, physics. **Protective services:** Fire safety technology, firefighting. **Psychology:** General. **Visual/performing arts:** General, art history/conservation, commercial/advertising art, dramatic, interior design, music, music history, music performance, music theory/composition, studio arts, studio arts management. **Work/family studies:** Child care service.

Most popular majors. Business/marketing 9%, health sciences 23%, interdisciplinary studies 6%, liberal arts 43%, trade and industry 6%.

Computing on campus. 370 workstations in library, computer center. Commuter students can connect to campus network. Online course registration, online library, helpline, repair service, wireless network available.

Student life. Freshman orientation: Mandatory. Preregistration for classes offered. Four-hour session held periodically throughout summer. **Housing:** Coed dorms, single-sex dorms, apartments available. Students apply for and are assigned housing at University of Kentucky. Applications submitted to Office of Student Housing, University of Kentucky. **Activities:** Choral groups, drama, international student organizations, student government, student newspaper, Christian Fellowship, College Republicans, Students for Peace and Earth Justice.

Athletics. Intramural: Basketball, soccer.

Student services. Adult student services, alcohol/substance abuse counseling, career counseling, services for economically disadvantaged, student employment services, financial aid counseling, health services, minority student services, on-campus daycare, personal counseling, placement for graduates, veterans' counselor. **Physically disabled:** Services for visually, speech, hearing impaired. **Transfer:** Pre-admission transcript evaluation for new students. Transfer center, transfer adviser, college fairs on campus for students transferring to 4-year colleges.

Contact. E-mail: shelbie.hugle@kctcs.edu
Phone: (859) 246-6210 Toll-free number: (866) 774-4872 ext. 56210
Fax: (859) 246-4666
Shelbie Hugle, Director of Admissions, Bluegrass Community and Technical College, 200 Oswald Building, Cooper Drive, Lexington, KY 40506-0235

Brown Mackie College: Hopkinsville
Hopkinsville, Kentucky
www.brownmackie.edu

CB code: 5375

- For-profit 2-year business and junior college
- Large town

General. Accredited by ACICS. **Calendar:** Quarter.

Annual costs/financial aid. Tuition/fees (2011-2012): $13,905. Costs vary by program. Quoted tuition and per-credit-hour charge are for most programs. Need-based financial aid available for full-time students.

Contact. Phone: (270) 886-1302
4001 Fort Campbell Boulevard, Hopkinsville, KY 42240

Brown Mackie College: Louisville
Louisville, Kentucky
www.brownmackie.edu

CB code: 0305

- For-profit 2-year technical college
- Commuter campus in large city

General. Founded in 1972. Accredited by ACICS. **Calendar:** Quarter.

Annual costs/financial aid. Tuition/fees (2011-2012): $13,905. Room/board: $8,760. Books/supplies: $1,275.

Contact. Phone: (502) 968-7191
Admissions Director, 3605 Fern Valley Road, Louisville, KY 40219

Brown Mackie College: North Kentucky
Fort Mitchell, Kentucky
www.brownmackie.edu

CB code: 3419

- For-profit 2-year business and health science college
- Small town

General. Accredited by ACICS. **Location:** 8 miles from Cincinnati. **Calendar:** Differs by program.

Annual costs/financial aid. Tuition/fees (2011-2012): $13,905. Tuition for regular programs $294 per hour; Nursing and OTA $361 per hour; Surgical Tech $340 per hour. Required fees for regular programs $15 per hour; Nursing $25 per hour. Room/board: $5,613. Books/supplies: $1,380.

Contact. Phone: (859) 341-5627
309 Buttermilk Pike, Fort Mitchell, KY 41017

Daymar College: Bowling Green
Bowling Green, Kentucky
www.daymarcollege.edu　　　　**CB code: 3399**

- For-profit 2-year branch campus and career college
- Commuter campus in small city

General. Regionally accredited; also accredited by ACICS. **Enrollment:** 600 degree-seeking undergraduates. **Degrees:** 233 associate awarded. **Location:** 90 miles from Louisville; 60 miles from Nashville, TN. **Calendar:** Quarter, extensive summer session. **Full-time faculty:** 15 total. **Part-time faculty:** 13 total. **Class size:** 92% < 20, 8% 20-39.

Student profile.

Out-of-state:　　　　1%　　**25 or older:**　　　　80%

Transfer out. Colleges most students transferred to 2011: Western Kentucky University, Lindsey Wilson College, Kentucky Advanced Technology Institute.

Basis for selection. Open admission. SAT/ACT scores used for placement and counseling in remedial work.

2011-2012 Annual costs. Tuition/fees: $15,345. Per-credit charge: $325. Books/supplies: $2,100.

Financial aid. All financial aid based on need. Need-based aid available for part-time students. Work-study available nights, weekends and for part-time students.

Application procedures. Admission: No deadline. No application fee. Admission notification on a rolling basis. **Financial aid:** No deadline. FAFSA required.

Academics. Special study options: Distance learning, double major, internships. Bachelor's degree programs available on campus. **Credit/placement by examination:** AP, CLEP, institutional tests. 16 credit hours maximum toward associate degree. **Support services:** Learning center, reduced course load, remedial instruction, tutoring.

Majors. Business: Accounting technology, business admin. **Computer sciences:** General, system admin, webmaster. **Health services:** Cardiovascular technology, insurance coding, medical assistant, medical secretary, pharmacy assistant. **Protective services:** Law enforcement admin.

Most popular majors. Business/marketing 20%, computer/information sciences 10%, health sciences 64%, legal studies 6%, security/protective services 9%.

Computing on campus. 75 workstations in library, computer center. Online library, wireless network available.

Student life. Freshman orientation: Mandatory. Preregistration for classes offered. One-day session held 1 week prior to beginning of quarter. **Activities:** Student newspaper.

Student services. Adult student services, career counseling, financial aid counseling, personal counseling, placement for graduates. **Transfer:** Re-entry adviser, pre-admission transcript evaluation for new students. Transfer adviser for students transferring to 4-year colleges.

Contact. E-mail: thenderson@daymarcollege.edu
Phone: (270) 843-6750 Toll-free number: (800) 541-0296
Fax: (270) 843-6976
Traci Henderson, Admissions, Daymar College: Bowling Green, 2421 Fitzgerald Industrial Drive, Bowling Green, KY 42101

Daymar College: Louisville
Louisville, Kentucky
www.daymarcollege.edu　　　　**CB code: 3407**

- For-profit 2-year business college
- Large city

General. Accredited by ACICS. **Calendar:** Quarter.

Annual costs/financial aid. Tuition/fees (2011-2012): $15,850. Per-credit-hour charge (tuition only): $325 per quarter credit hour for most courses. $390 per quarter credit hour for 300-400 level courses. $365 per quarter credit hour for LAW specific courses. $410 per quarter credit hour for Information Technology and Personal Fitness Training specific courses. $475 per quarter credit hour for Associate Degree in Nursing specific courses. Books/supplies: $3,000.

Contact. Phone: (502) 495-1040
Director of Admissions, 4112 Fern Valley Road, Louisville, KY 40219-1973

Daymar College: Owensboro
Owensboro, Kentucky
www.daymarcollege.edu　　　　**CB code: 0772**

- For-profit 2-year business and junior college
- Commuter campus in small city
- Interview required

General. Founded in 1963. Accredited by ACICS. Provides hands-on training with practical theory. Medical assisting-clinical track students have 3 classes at Owensboro Medical Health System. **Enrollment:** 470 undergraduates. **Degrees:** 92 associate awarded. **Location:** 120 miles from Louisville; 35 miles from Evansville, IN. **Calendar:** Quarter, extensive summer session. **Full-time faculty:** 12 total. **Part-time faculty:** 23 total.

Basis for selection. Open admission. Must have diploma or GED. SAT, ACT, or Wonderlic Scholastic Level Exam required for placement. **Learning Disabled:** Copy of IEP required.

High school preparation. Recommended units include English 3, mathematics 1, social studies 1 and science 1. One human relations also recommended.

2011-2012 Annual costs. Tuition/fees: $15,850. Per-credit charge: $325. Per-credit-hour charge (tuition only): $325 per quarter credit hour for most courses. $390 per quarter credit hour for 300-400 level courses. $365 per quarter credit hour for LAW specific courses. $410 per quarter credit hour for Information Technology and Personal Fitness Training specific courses. $475 per quarter credit hour for Associate Degree in Nursing specific courses. Books/supplies: $3,000.

Financial aid. All financial aid based on need. Need-based aid available for part-time students. Work-study available nights, weekends and for part-time students.

Application procedures. Admission: No deadline. No application fee. Admission notification on a rolling basis. **Financial aid:** No deadline. FAFSA required. Applicants notified on a rolling basis.

Academics. Special study options: Cooperative education, distance learning, double major, dual enrollment of high school students, honors, independent study, internships. **Credit/placement by examination:** AP, CLEP, institutional tests. 12 credit hours maximum toward associate degree. **Support services:** GED preparation, remedial instruction, tutoring.

Majors. Business: Administrative services, business admin, office management, office technology, office/clerical, operations. **Computer sciences:** General, data processing, information systems, networking, systems analysis. **Health services:** Medical assistant, medical secretary, pharmacy assistant.

Most popular majors. Business/marketing 14%, computer/information sciences 36%, health sciences 32%, legal studies 19%.

Computing on campus. 115 workstations in library, computer center.

Student life. Freshman orientation: Mandatory. Preregistration for classes offered. **Activities:** Student newspaper.

Student services. Alcohol/substance abuse counseling, career counseling, student employment services, financial aid counseling, personal counseling, placement for graduates. **Physically disabled:** Services for visually, hearing impaired. **Transfer:** Re-entry adviser, pre-admission transcript evaluation for new students. Transfer adviser for students transferring to 4-year colleges.

Contact. Phone: (270) 926-4040 Toll-free number: (800) 960-4090
Fax: (270) 685-4090
Latasha Shemwell, Director of Admissions, Daymar College: Owensboro, 3361 Buckland Square, Owensboro, KY 42301

Daymar College: Paducah
Paducah, Kentucky
www.daymarcollege.edu   CB code: 0669

◆ For-profit 2-year technical college
◆ Commuter campus in small city
◆ Interview required

General. Founded in 1964. Accredited by ACICS. Associate program completes 3 academic years in 2 calendar years. **Enrollment:** 430 degree-seeking undergraduates. **Degrees:** 92 associate awarded. **Location:** 150 miles from St. Louis and Nashville, TN. **Calendar:** Quarter, extensive summer session. **Full-time faculty:** 12 total. **Part-time faculty:** 23 total.

Basis for selection. Open admission.

2011-2012 Annual costs. Tuition/fees: $15,850. Per-credit charge: $325. Per-credit-hour charge (tuition only): $325 per quarter credit hour for most courses. $390 per quarter credit hour for 300-400 level courses. $365 per quarter credit hour for LAW specific courses. $410 per quarter credit hour for Information Technology and Personal Fitness Training specific courses. $475 per quarter credit hour for Associate Degree in Nursing specific courses. Books/supplies: $3,000.

Financial aid. Need-based: Work-study available nights, weekends and for part-time students.

Application procedures. Admission: No deadline. No application fee. Admission notification on a rolling basis. **Financial aid:** No deadline. FAFSA, CSS PROFILE required. Applicants notified on a rolling basis; must reply within 3 week(s) of notification.

Academics. Special study options: Distance learning, internships. **Credit/placement by examination:** AP, CLEP. **Support services:** Learning center, tutoring.

Majors. Engineering: Electrical. **Health services:** Insurance coding, insurance specialist, pharmacy assistant.

Computing on campus. 50 workstations in library, computer center. Commuter students can connect to campus network. Online library, helpline, wireless network available.

Student life. Freshman orientation: Mandatory. Preregistration for classes offered.

Student services. Alcohol/substance abuse counseling, career counseling, student employment services, financial aid counseling, personal counseling, placement for graduates, veterans' counselor. **Transfer:** Pre-admission transcript evaluation for new students.

Contact. Phone: (270) 444-9676 Toll-free number: (800) 995-4438
Fax: (270) 441-7202
Connie Holley, Director of Admission, Daymar College: Paducah, 509 South 30th Street, Paducah, KY 42001

Elizabethtown Community and Technical College
Elizabethtown, Kentucky
www.elizabethtown.kctcs.edu   CB code: 1211

◆ Public 2-year community and technical college
◆ Commuter campus in large town

General. Founded in 1964. Regionally accredited. Off-campus locations at Fort Knox, Bardstown, Leitchfield, Hardinsburg, and Brandenburg. **Enrollment:** 5,187 degree-seeking undergraduates. **Degrees:** 696 associate awarded. **ROTC:** Army. **Location:** 40 miles from Louisville. **Calendar:** Semester, limited summer session. **Full-time faculty:** 158 total. **Part-time faculty:** 226 total. **Special facilities:** Regional Home for the Arts center.

Student profile.

Out-of-state:	1%	25 or older:	52%

Transfer out. Colleges most students transferred to 2011: Western Kentucky University, University of Louisville, University of Kentucky.

Basis for selection. Open admission, but selective for some programs. All nursing, radiography and dental hygiene programs have selective criteria. Enrolled freshmen must take ACT, ACT/Career Planning Profile or ASSET

by start of second semester. **Learning Disabled:** ADA counselor assists those with special needs or disabilities.

High school preparation. College-preparatory program recommended.

2011-2012 Annual costs. Tuition/fees: $4,050; $13,950 out-of-state. Per-credit charge: $135 in-state; $465 out-of-state. Books/supplies: $1,358.

2010-2011 Financial aid. All financial aid based on need. Need-based aid available for part-time students. Work-study available nights, weekends and for part-time students.

Application procedures. Admission: No deadline. No application fee. Admission notification on a rolling basis. Early admission available for specially qualified high school students on part-time basis. **Financial aid:** Priority date 8/1; no closing date. FAFSA required. Applicants notified on a rolling basis starting 6/1; must reply within 2 week(s) of notification.

Academics. Special study options: Cooperative education, distance learning, dual enrollment of high school students, honors, internships, liberal arts/career combination, teacher certification program, weekend college. Bachelor's degree programs available on campus. License preparation in dental hygiene, nursing, radiology, real estate. **Credit/placement by examination:** AP, CLEP, institutional tests. 6 credit hours maximum toward associate degree. **Support services:** GED test center, learning center, remedial instruction, study skills assistance, tutoring, writing center.

Majors. Business: Business admin, executive assistant, real estate. **Computer sciences:** General. **Education:** Early childhood, teacher assistance. **Health services:** Dental hygiene, medical radiologic technology/radiation therapy, medical secretary, nursing (RN). **Human services:** Social work. **Liberal arts:** Arts/sciences. **Protective services:** Firefighting, law enforcement admin. **Work/family studies:** Child care service.

Computing on campus. 87 workstations in library, computer center, student center. Online library, helpline, wireless network available.

Student life. Freshman orientation: Available. Preregistration for classes offered. Online orientation or on-campus orientation available. **Activities:** Choral groups, drama, literary magazine, student government, student newspaper, Baptist campus ministry, Association of Nursing Students, Phi Theta Kappa, Phi Beta Lambda, gay straight alliance, Students in Free Enterprise, Skills USA, Phoenix club.

Student services. Adult student services, career counseling, services for economically disadvantaged, financial aid counseling, personal counseling, placement for graduates, veterans' counselor, women's services. **Physically disabled:** Services for visually, speech, hearing impaired. **Transfer:** Transfer adviser, college fairs on campus for students transferring to 4-year colleges.

Contact. E-mail: Elizabethtown-Admissions@kctcs.edu
Phone: (270) 769-1632 Toll-free number: (877) 246-2322
Fax: (270) 769-1618
Bryan Smith, Counselor, Elizabethtown Community and Technical College, 600 College Street Road, Elizabethtown, KY 42701

Gateway Community and Technical College
Florence, Kentucky
www.gateway.kctcs.edu   CB code: 0596

◆ Public 2-year community and technical college
◆ Commuter campus in large city

General. Candidate for regional accreditation. **Enrollment:** 3,216 degree-seeking undergraduates. **Degrees:** 291 associate awarded. **Calendar:** Semester, limited summer session. **Full-time faculty:** 91 total. **Part-time faculty:** 198 total. **Class size:** 69% < 20, 30% 20-39, less than 1% 40-49.

Student profile. Among degree-seeking undergraduates, 19% enrolled in a transfer program, 81% enrolled in a vocational program.

Part-time:	58%	Asian American:	1%
Out-of-state:	6%	Hispanic American:	1%
Women:	63%	25 or older:	57%
African American:	12%		

Basis for selection. Open admission, but selective for some programs. ACT COMPASS used for placement.

2011-2012 Annual costs. Tuition/fees: $4,090; $13,990 out-of-state. Per-credit charge: $135 in-state; $465 out-of-state. Returning enrollees from the fall 2010 and/or spring 2011 semesters will pay $130 per credit hour. Books/supplies: $1,000.

Financial aid. Need-based: Work-study available nights, weekends and for part-time students.

Application procedures. Admission: No deadline. No application fee.

Academics. Special study options: Cooperative education, distance learning, internships. **Credit/placement by examination:** AP, CLEP. **Support services:** GED preparation and test center, remedial instruction, tutoring.

Majors. Business: Business admin. **Computer sciences:** Information technology. **Education:** Early childhood. **Health services:** Medical assistant, nursing (RN). **Protective services:** Criminal justice. **Visual/performing arts:** Design.

Most popular majors. Business/marketing 11%, computer/information sciences 9%, engineering/engineering technologies 7%, health sciences 19%, liberal arts 20%, security/protective services 10%, trade and industry 15%.

Computing on campus. Online library, helpline, wireless network available.

Student life. Freshman orientation: Available. Preregistration for classes offered. **Activities:** Student government.

Student services. Career counseling, financial aid counseling, personal counseling, placement for graduates, veterans' counselor. **Transfer:** Transfer center, college fairs on campus for students transferring to 4-year colleges.

Contact. Phone: (859) 442-1134 Fax: (859) 442-1107
Andre Washington, Director of Admissions and Enrollment Management, Gateway Community and Technical College, 790 Thomas More Parkway, Edgewood, KY 41017

Hazard Community and Technical College
Hazard, Kentucky
www.hazard.kctcs.edu   CB code: 0815

- Public 2-year community and technical college
- Commuter campus in small town

General. Founded in 1968. Regionally accredited. **Enrollment:** 2,702 degree-seeking undergraduates. **Degrees:** 411 associate awarded. **Location:** 100 miles from Lexington. **Calendar:** Semester, limited summer session. **Full-time faculty:** 96 total. **Part-time faculty:** 173 total.

Transfer out. Colleges most students transferred to 2011: Morehead State University, Eastern Kentucky University, University of Kentucky, Lindsey Wilson College.

Basis for selection. Open admission, but selective for some programs and for out-of-state students. GPA, ACT/COMPASS, and pre-admissions conference required for applicants to allied health programs. Out-of-state applicants must rank in top 50% of high school class or have 3.0 GPA.

High school preparation. 11 units recommended. Recommended units include English 4, mathematics 3, social studies 1, history 1 and science 2.

2011-2012 Annual costs. Tuition/fees: $4,050; $13,950 out-of-state. Per-credit charge: $135 in-state; $465 out-of-state. Books/supplies: $1,000. Personal expenses: $800.

Financial aid. All financial aid based on need. Need-based aid available for part-time students. Work-study available nights, weekends and for part-time students.

Application procedures. Admission: Priority date 8/1; no deadline. No application fee. Admission notification on a rolling basis beginning on or about 6/15. **Financial aid:** Priority date 4/1; no closing date. FAFSA required. Applicants notified on a rolling basis starting 6/15; must reply within 2 week(s) of notification.

Academics. Special study options: Cooperative education, distance learning, dual enrollment of high school students, honors, independent study, internships, liberal arts/career combination. 2+2 bachelor's degree programs in business administration, elementary education and University Studies with Morehead State University; 2+2 bachelor's degree program in criminal justice, Individualized studies, nursing and social work with Eastern Kentucky University; 2+2 bachelor's degree in Arts/Human Services and Counseling with Lindsey Wilson and a Master of Education in Mental Health Counseling with Lindsey Wilson. Bachelor's degree programs available on campus. **Credit/placement by examination:** AP, CLEP, institutional tests. **Support services:** GED test center, learning center, remedial instruction, study skills assistance, tutoring, writing center.

Majors. Business: Marketing. **Computer sciences:** General. **Education:** Early childhood. **Health services:** Medical radiologic technology/radiation therapy, nursing (RN), physical therapy assistant. **Liberal arts:** Arts/sciences.

Computing on campus. 494 workstations in library, computer center, student center.

Student life. Freshman orientation: Available. Preregistration for classes offered. **Activities:** Student government.

Student services. Physically disabled: Services for visually, speech, hearing impaired. **Transfer:** Pre-admission transcript evaluation for new students. College fairs on campus for students transferring to 4-year colleges.

Contact. Phone: (606) 436-5721 ext. 73525
Toll-free number: (800) 246-7521 ext. 73525 Fax: (606) 666-4312
Scott Gross, Director of Admissions, Hazard Community and Technical College, One Community College Drive, Hazard, KY 41701

Henderson Community College
Henderson, Kentucky
www.hencc.kctcs.edu   CB code: 1307

- Public 2-year community college
- Commuter campus in large town

General. Founded in 1960. Regionally accredited. **Enrollment:** 2,142 degree-seeking undergraduates. **Degrees:** 294 associate awarded. **Location:** 10 miles from Evansville, IN. **Calendar:** Semester, limited summer session. **Full-time faculty:** 47 total. **Part-time faculty:** 86 total. **Special facilities:** Fine arts center hosting variety of social and cultural activities in visual and performing arts.

Transfer out. Colleges most students transferred to 2011: Western Kentucky University, Murray State University, University of Kentucky, University of Southern Indiana, Wesley University.

Basis for selection. Open admission, but selective for some programs. Dental hygiene, nursing and clinical lab technician programs selective; test scores and high school GPA important admissions criteria. Interview required for nursing program.

2011-2012 Annual costs. Tuition/fees: $4,050; $13,950 out-of-state. Per-credit charge: $135 in-state; $465 out-of-state. Books/supplies: $1,250.

Financial aid. Need-based: Work-study available nights, weekends and for part-time students.

Application procedures. Admission: Closing date 8/1. No application fee. Admission notification on a rolling basis beginning on or about 3/1. **Financial aid:** Closing date 7/15. FAFSA required. Applicants notified on a rolling basis starting 5/1.

Academics. Special study options: Cooperative education, cross-registration, distance learning, double major, dual enrollment of high school students, honors, independent study, liberal arts/career combination, weekend college. Bachelor's degree programs available on campus. License preparation in dental hygiene, nursing. **Credit/placement by examination:** AP, CLEP. **Support services:** GED preparation and test center, learning center, pre-admission summer program, reduced course load, remedial instruction, study skills assistance, tutoring, writing center.

Majors. Business: Administrative services, business admin, management information systems. **Communications:** Communications/speech/rhetoric. **Computer sciences:** Data processing. **Education:** Early childhood. **General:** Business technology. **Health services:** Clinical lab technology. **Human services:** Community org/advocacy, social work. **Liberal arts:** Arts/sciences.

Computing on campus. 99 workstations in library, computer center, student center. Commuter students can connect to campus network. Online course registration, online library, repair service available.

Student life. Freshman orientation: Available. Preregistration for classes offered. **Activities:** Choral groups, literary magazine, student government, student newspaper, Baptist student union.

Student services. Career counseling, financial aid counseling, minority student services, personal counseling, placement for graduates, veterans' counselor. **Transfer:** Re-entry adviser, pre-admission transcript evaluation for new students. Transfer center, transfer adviser, college fairs on campus for students transferring to 4-year colleges.

Contact. Phone: (270) 830-5256
Cary Conley, Admissions Counselor, Henderson Community College, 2660 South Green Street, Henderson, KY 42420

Hopkinsville Community College
Hopkinsville, Kentucky
www.hopkinsville.kctcs.edu   **CB code: 1274**

- Public 2-year community college
- Commuter campus in small city

General. Founded in 1965. Regionally accredited. **Enrollment:** 3,933 degree-seeking undergraduates; 449 non-degree-seeking students. **Degrees:** 430 associate awarded. **Location:** 70 miles from Nashville, TN, 25 miles from Clarksville, TN. **Calendar:** Semester, limited summer session. **Full-time faculty:** 65 total; 12% have terminal degrees, 9% minority, 46% women. **Part-time faculty:** 56 total. **Class size:** 42% < 20, 58% 20-39.

Student profile. Among degree-seeking undergraduates, 49% enrolled in a transfer program, 51% enrolled in a vocational program, 770 enrolled as first-time, first-year students, 315 transferred in from other institutions.

Part-time:	50%	African American:	10%
Out-of-state:	34%	Hispanic American:	5%
Women:	70%	25 or older:	57%

Transfer out. 19% of students enrolled in the transfer program go on to 4-year colleges. **Colleges most students transferred to 2011:** Murray State University, Austin Peay State University, Western Kentucky University, Kentucky State University, University of Kentucky.

Basis for selection. Open admission, but selective for some programs. Selective admissions to practical and registered nursing programs. **Learning Disabled:** Must be documented to receive services.

2011-2012 Annual costs. Tuition/fees: $4,050; $13,950 out-of-state. Per-credit charge: $135 in-state; $465 out-of-state. Books/supplies: $1,000. Personal expenses: $2,820.

2010-2011 Financial aid. **Need-based:** Need-based aid available for part-time students. Work-study available nights, weekends and for part-time students. **Non-need-based:** Scholarships awarded for academics, leadership, minority status, state residency. **Additional information:** ACT required for academic scholarships.

Application procedures. **Admission:** No deadline. No application fee. Admission notification on a rolling basis. **Financial aid:** No deadline. FAFSA required. Applicants notified on a rolling basis starting 7/1.

Academics. **Special study options:** Cooperative education, distance learning, dual enrollment of high school students, independent study, internships. License preparation in nursing. **Credit/placement by examination:** AP, CLEP. **Support services:** GED preparation and test center, learning center, remedial instruction, study skills assistance, tutoring, writing center.

Majors. **Architecture:** Architecture. **Biology:** General. **Business:** General, accounting, business admin, executive assistant, management science, office management. **Communications:** Communications/speech/rhetoric, journalism. **Computer sciences:** General. **Conservation:** Forest sciences. **Education:** Art, elementary, health, middle, physical, special ed, speech impaired, teacher assistance. **Engineering:** General, civil. **English:** English lit. **Foreign languages:** Linguistics. **General:** Production. **Health services:** Dental hygiene, nuclear medical technology, nursing (RN), pharmacy assistant, physical therapy. **History:** American. **Human services:** Social work. **Liberal arts/sciences:** Math: General. **Parks/recreation:** Exercise sciences. **Philosophy/religion:** Philosophy, religion. **Physical sciences:** General, chemistry, geology, physics. **Protective services:** Law enforcement admin. **Psychology:** General. **Social sciences:** General, economics, political science, sociology. **Visual/performing arts:** Music, studio arts. **Work/family studies:** Child care service, food/nutrition.

Most popular majors. Business/marketing 10%, health sciences 9%, liberal arts 55%.

Computing on campus. Online course registration, online library, help-line, wireless network available.

Student life. **Freshman orientation:** Available. Preregistration for classes offered. On-campus orientations held prior to start of semester. **Activities:** Campus ministries, literary magazine, student government, student newspaper, TV station, Ag Tech, amateur radio, ballroom dance, Baptist campus ministries, Black Men United, College Democrats, College Republicans, criminal justice organization, Pi Gamma Epsilon, Donovan Scholars, HKANS.

Student services. Career counseling, student employment services, financial aid counseling, minority student services, placement for graduates, veterans' counselor. **Physically disabled:** Services for visually, speech, hearing impaired. **Transfer:** Transfer adviser for students transferring to 4-year colleges.

Contact. E-mail: melissa.stevenson@kctcs.edu
Phone: (270) 707-3810 Fax: (270) 886-0237
Melissa Stevenson, Registrar, Hopkinsville Community College, PO Box 2100, Hopkinsville, KY 42241-2100

Jefferson Community and Technical College
Louisville, Kentucky
www.jefferson.kctcs.edu   **CB code: 1328**

- Public 2-year community and technical college
- Commuter campus in large city

General. Founded in 1968. Regionally accredited. **Location:** Downtown. **Calendar:** Semester.

Annual costs/financial aid. Tuition/fees (2011-2012): $4,050; $13,950 out-of-state. Books/supplies: $1,000. Personal expenses: $800. Need-based financial aid available to full-time and part-time students.

Contact. Phone: (502) 213-5333
Dean of Student Affairs, 109 East Broadway, Louisville, KY 40202

Lincoln College of Technology: Florence
Florence, Kentucky
www.swcollege.net   **CB code: 2482**

- For-profit 2-year health science and career college
- Residential campus in small city
- Interview required

General. Accredited by ACICS. **Degrees:** 44 associate awarded. **Location:** 5 miles from Cincinnati. **Calendar:** Quarter, extensive summer session. **Full-time faculty:** 10 total; 50% have terminal degrees, 20% minority, 60% women. **Part-time faculty:** 14 total.

Transfer out. Colleges most students transferred to 2011: Brown Mackie, Beckfield, Northern Kentucky University, Gateway Technical Community College.

Basis for selection. Open admission. **Home schooled:** State high school equivalency certificate required.

High school preparation. College-preparatory program required.

2011-2012 Annual costs. Tuition/fees: $14,375. Tuition includes cost of books and supplies. Per-credit-hour charge (tuition only): $318 Practical Nursing, $300 Dental Assisting.

Financial aid. All financial aid based on need. Need-based aid available for part-time students. Work-study available nights, weekends and for part-time students.

Application procedures. **Admission:** No deadline. $125 fee. Application must be submitted on paper. Admission notification on a rolling basis. **Financial aid:** No deadline. FAFSA required. Applicants notified on a rolling basis.

Academics. **Special study options:** Independent study, liberal arts/career combination. **Credit/placement by examination:** AP, CLEP. **Support services:** GED preparation, study skills assistance, tutoring.

Majors. **Business:** Business admin. **Computer sciences:** General. **Health services:** Medical assistant. **Protective services:** Law enforcement admin.

Computing on campus. 50 workstations in library, computer center. Online library available.

Student life. **Freshman orientation:** Mandatory. Preregistration for classes offered. Held on campus before each quarter in mornings and evenings. **Activities:** Student government, student newspaper.

Student services. Career counseling, services for economically disadvantaged, student employment services, financial aid counseling, placement for graduates. **Transfer:** Pre-admission transcript evaluation for new students.

Contact. E-mail: mdurkin@swcollege.net
Phone: (859) 282-9999 Fax: (859) 282-7940
Melissa Durkin, Director of Admissions, Lincoln College of Technology:
Florence, 8095 Connector Drive, Florence, KY 41042

Madisonville Community College
Madisonville, Kentucky
www.madisonville.kctcs.edu   **CB code: 1606**

- Public 2-year community college
- Commuter campus in large town

General. Founded in 1968. Regionally accredited. Campuses include: North Campus, Health Campus, and Muhlenberg County Campus. **Enrollment:** 3,025 degree-seeking undergraduates. **Degrees:** 432 associate awarded. **Location:** 50 miles from Evansville, Indiana. **Calendar:** Semester, extensive summer session. **Full-time faculty:** 112 total. **Part-time faculty:** 146 total. **Special facilities:** Center for the arts.

Student profile.

Out-of-state: 1%   25 or older: 50%

Transfer out. Colleges most students transferred to 2011: Murray State University, Western Kentucky University, University of Kentucky.

Basis for selection. Open admission, but selective for some programs. ACT or Compass required for placement/counseling. Special requirements for nursing, physical therapy assistant, radiography, respiratory, occupational therapy assistant, clinical lab technology. Interview recommended for nursing and physical therapy assistant applicants. **Adult students:** ACT or COMPASS placement scores must be less than 5 years old. **Home schooled:** Encouraged to apply for early admissions status prior to completion of high school credential. **Learning Disabled:** Disability resources provided for qualified students.

High school preparation. 14 units recommended. Recommended units include English 4, mathematics 3, social studies 2, history 2, science 2 (laboratory 1).

2011-2012 Annual costs. Tuition/fees: $4,050; $13,950 out-of-state. Per-credit charge: $135 in-state; $465 out-of-state. Personal expenses: $1,000.

Financial aid. Need-based: Need-based aid available for part-time students. Work-study available nights, weekends and for part-time students. **Non-need-based:** Scholarships awarded for minority status.

Application procedures. Admission: Closing date 8/1 (receipt date). No application fee. Admission notification on a rolling basis. **Financial aid:** Priority date 3/15; no closing date. FAFSA, institutional form required. Applicants notified on a rolling basis; must reply within 3 week(s) of notification.

Academics. Adult and continuing education programs available both on- and off-campus. Tech prep and school-to-work programs available. Classes also offered at area high schools and other off-campus locations, including KET telecourses and online. **Special study options:** Cooperative education, distance learning, double major, dual enrollment of high school students, honors, independent study, internships, liberal arts/career combination, weekend college. Bachelor's degree programs available on campus. License preparation in nursing, occupational therapy, paramedic, physical therapy, radiology, real estate. **Credit/placement by examination:** AP, CLEP, institutional tests. **Support services:** GED preparation and test center, learning center, remedial instruction, study skills assistance, tutoring, writing center.

Majors. Business: Accounting, administrative services, business admin, finance, management information systems, real estate, sales/distribution. **Computer sciences:** General. **Education:** General, early childhood. **General:** Production. **Health services:** Clinical lab science, clinical lab technology, medical radiologic technology/radiation therapy, medical secretary, nursing (RN), occupational therapy assistant, physical therapy assistant, respiratory therapy technology. **Liberal arts:** Arts/sciences. **Protective services:** Law enforcement admin. **Work/family studies:** Child care service.

Most popular majors. Business/marketing 14%, health sciences 39%, liberal arts 36%.

Computing on campus. 200 workstations in library, computer center, student center. Commuter students can connect to campus network. Online course registration, online library, helpline, wireless network available.

Student life. Freshman orientation: Mandatory. Preregistration for classes offered. First Semester Experience held throughout June and July for new students. **Activities:** Campus ministries, choral groups, drama, literary magazine, musical theater, student government, student newspaper, multicultural student organization, Lions Club, student ambassadors, Socratic Society, Phi Theta Kappa, Baptist student union.

Student services. Adult student services, career counseling, services for economically disadvantaged, student employment services, financial aid counseling, health services, minority student services, personal counseling, placement for graduates, veterans' counselor. **Physically disabled:** Services for visually, speech, hearing impaired. **Transfer:** Pre-admission transcript evaluation for new students. Transfer center, transfer adviser, college fairs on campus for students transferring to 4-year colleges.

Contact. Phone: (270) 821-2250 Toll-free number: (866) 227-4812
Fax: (270) 825-8553
Aimee Wilkerson, Director of Enrollment Management, Madisonville Community College, 2000 College Drive, Madisonville, KY 42431

Maysville Community and Technical College
Maysville, Kentucky
www.maysville.kctcs.edu   **CB code: 0693**

- Public 2-year community and technical college
- Commuter campus in small town

General. Founded in 1968. Regionally accredited. Access to Kentucky Virtual Library. **Enrollment:** 4,525 undergraduates. **Degrees:** 266 associate awarded. **Location:** 60 miles from Lexington, 60 miles from Cincinnati. **Calendar:** Semester, limited summer session. **Full-time faculty:** 95 total. **Part-time faculty:** 90 total.

Basis for selection. Open admission, but selective for some programs. ACT considered for nursing program. Some occupational/technical programs have additional requirements. ACT or COMPASS may be required for placement in degree-seeking programs. Interview required of nursing majors. **Home schooled:** Transcript of courses and grades required.

High school preparation. College-preparatory program recommended. Recommended units include English 4, mathematics 3, social studies 2, history 1, science 2 (laboratory 1), foreign language 2 and academic electives 5.

2011-2012 Annual costs. Tuition/fees: $4,050; $13,950 out-of-state. Per-credit charge: $135 in-state; $465 out-of-state. Books/supplies: $4,000.

Financial aid. Need-based: Need-based aid available for part-time students. Work-study available nights, weekends and for part-time students. **Non-need-based:** Scholarships awarded for academics.

Application procedures. Admission: No deadline. No application fee. Admission notification on a rolling basis. 3/1 priority date for nursing applicants. **Financial aid:** Priority date 4/1; no closing date. FAFSA, institutional form required. Applicants notified on a rolling basis starting 3/1; must reply within 3 week(s) of notification.

Academics. Special study options: Cooperative education, distance learning, double major, dual enrollment of high school students, honors, independent study, internships. Bachelor's degree programs available on campus. License preparation in nursing, real estate. **Credit/placement by examination:** AP, CLEP, institutional tests. **Support services:** GED preparation and test center, learning center, reduced course load, remedial instruction, study skills assistance, tutoring, writing center.

Majors. Business: General, accounting, business admin, e-commerce, executive assistant, office management. **Computer sciences:** General. **Education:** Early childhood. **Engineering:** Industrial, manufacturing. **Health services:** Medical secretary, nursing (RN). **Liberal arts:** Arts/sciences.

Computing on campus. 375 workstations in library, computer center. Commuter students can connect to campus network. Online library, wireless network available.

Student life. Freshman orientation: Mandatory. Preregistration for classes offered. **Activities:** Student government, Phi Theta Kappa, Phi Beta Lambda, Christian student fellowship.

Student services. Adult student services, career counseling, services for economically disadvantaged, financial aid counseling. **Physically disabled:** Services for hearing impaired. **Transfer:** Transfer adviser, college fairs on campus for students transferring to 4-year colleges.

Contact. E-mail: patee.massie@kctcs.edu
Phone: (606) 759-7141 ext. 66186 Fax: (606) 759-5818
Patricia Massie, Associate Dean of Student Development/Registrar/ Admissions Officer, Maysville Community and Technical College, 1755 US HIghway 68, Maysville, KY 41056

National College: Danville
Danville, Kentucky
www.ncbt.edu   CB code: 3413

◆ For-profit 2-year business college
◆ Commuter campus in large town

General. Accredited by ACICS. **Enrollment:** 236 degree-seeking under-graduates. **Degrees:** 84 associate awarded. **Calendar:** Quarter, extensive summer session. **Full-time faculty:** 1 total. **Part-time faculty:** 18 total.

Basis for selection. Open admission. Interviews highly recommended.

2011-2012 Annual costs. Tuition/fees: $13,770. Per-credit charge: $305. Books/supplies: $1,500.

Financial aid. All financial aid based on need. Need-based aid available for part-time students. Work-study available nights, weekends and for part-time students.

Application procedures. Admission: No deadline. $50 fee, may be waived for applicants with need. Admission notification on a rolling basis. **Financial aid:** No deadline. FAFSA required. Applicants notified on a rolling basis.

Academics. Special study options: Double major, internships, liberal arts/career combination. **Credit/placement by examination:** AP, CLEP, institutional tests. **Support services:** Learning center, remedial instruction, tutoring.

Majors. Business: Accounting, administrative services, business admin. **Computer sciences:** Computer science. **Health services:** Medical assistant, medical secretary, physician assistant.

Computing on campus. 35 workstations in library, computer center.

Student life. Freshman orientation: Mandatory. Preregistration for classes offered. **Activities:** Student government.

Student services. Career counseling, student employment services, financial aid counseling, personal counseling, placement for graduates, veterans' counselor.

Contact. E-mail: market@educorp.edu
Phone: (859) 236-6991 Toll-free number: (800) 664-1886
Fax: (859) 236-1063
Jeannie Martin, Director of Admissions, National College: Danville, PO Box 6400, Roanoke, VA 24017

National College: Florence
Florence, Kentucky
www.ncbt.edu   CB code: 3408

◆ For-profit 2-year business college
◆ Commuter campus in large town

General. Accredited by ACICS. **Enrollment:** 133 degree-seeking under-graduates. **Degrees:** 31 associate awarded. **Calendar:** Quarter, limited summer session. **Full-time faculty:** 4 total. **Part-time faculty:** 24 total.

Basis for selection. Open admission. Interview highly recommended.

2011-2012 Annual costs. Tuition/fees: $13,770. Per-credit charge: $305. Books/supplies: $1,500.

Financial aid. All financial aid based on need. Need-based aid available for part-time students. Work-study available nights, weekends and for part-time students.

Application procedures. Admission: No deadline. $50 fee. Admission notification on a rolling basis. **Financial aid:** No deadline. FAFSA required. Applicants notified on a rolling basis.

Academics. Special study options: Double major, internships. **Credit/placement by examination:** AP, CLEP, institutional tests. **Support services:** Learning center, remedial instruction, tutoring.

Majors. Business: Accounting, administrative services, business admin. **Computer sciences:** Computer science. **Health services:** Medical assistant, medical secretary.

Computing on campus. 35 workstations in library, computer center.

Student life. Freshman orientation: Mandatory. Preregistration for classes offered. **Activities:** Student government.

Student services. Career counseling, student employment services, financial aid counseling, personal counseling, placement for graduates, veterans' counselor.

Contact. E-mail: market@educorp.edu
Phone: (606) 525-6510 Fax: (606) 525-8961
Regina Becker, Director of Admissions, National College: Florence, PO Box 6400, Roanoke, VA 24017

National College: Lexington
Lexington, Kentucky
www.ncbt.edu   CB code: 0987

◆ For-profit 2-year business and junior college
◆ Commuter campus in small city

General. Founded in 1941. Accredited by ACICS. **Enrollment:** 391 degree-seeking undergraduates. **Degrees:** 25 bachelor's, 121 associate awarded. **Location:** 100 miles from Cincinnati. **Calendar:** Quarter, limited summer session. **Full-time faculty:** 5 total. **Part-time faculty:** 44 total.

Basis for selection. Open admission, but selective for some programs. Interview recommended.

2011-2012 Annual costs. Tuition/fees: $13,770. Per-credit charge: $305. Books/supplies: $1,500.

Financial aid. All financial aid based on need. Need-based aid available for part-time students. Work-study available nights, weekends and for part-time students.

Application procedures. Admission: No deadline. $50 fee, may be waived for applicants with need. Admission notification on a rolling basis. **Financial aid:** No deadline. FAFSA required. Applicants notified on a rolling basis.

Academics. Special study options: Double major, internships. **Credit/placement by examination:** AP, CLEP, institutional tests. **Support services:** Learning center, remedial instruction, tutoring.

Majors. Business: Accounting, administrative services, business admin, office management, office/clerical. **Computer sciences:** Computer science. **Health services:** Medical assistant, medical secretary, physician assistant.

Computing on campus. 35 workstations in library, computer center.

Student life. Freshman orientation: Mandatory. Preregistration for classes offered. **Activities:** Student government.

Student services. Career counseling, student employment services, personal counseling, placement for graduates, veterans' counselor.

Contact. E-mail: market@educorp.edu
Phone: (859) 253-0621 Toll-free number: (800) 664-1886
Fax: (859) 233-3054
Jim McGee, Director of Admissions, National College: Lexington, PO Box 6400, Roanoke, VA 24017

National College: Louisville
Louisville, Kentucky
www.ncbt.edu   CB code: 3415

◆ For-profit 2-year business college
◆ Commuter campus in large city

General. Accredited by ACICS. **Enrollment:** 471 degree-seeking under-graduates. **Degrees:** 13 bachelor's, 118 associate awarded. **Calendar:** Quarter, limited summer session. **Full-time faculty:** 3 total. **Part-time faculty:** 41 total.

Basis for selection. Open admission, but selective for some programs. Interviews highly recommended.

2011-2012 Annual costs. Tuition/fees: $13,770. Per-credit charge: $305. Books/supplies: $1,500.

Financial aid. All financial aid based on need. Need-based aid available for part-time students. Work-study available nights, weekends and for part-time students.

Application procedures. Admission: No deadline. $50 fee, may be waived for applicants with need. Admission notification on a rolling basis. **Financial aid:** No deadline. FAFSA required. Applicants notified on a rolling basis.

Academics. Special study options: Internships. **Credit/placement by examination:** AP, CLEP, institutional tests. **Support services:** Learning center, remedial instruction, tutoring.

Majors. Business: Accounting, administrative services, business admin. **Computer sciences:** Computer science. **Health services:** Medical assistant, medical secretary.

Computing on campus. 35 workstations in library, computer center.

Student life. Freshman orientation: Mandatory. Preregistration for classes offered. **Activities:** Student government.

Student services. Career counseling, student employment services, personal counseling, placement for graduates, veterans' counselor.

Contact. E-mail: market@educorp.edu
Phone: (502) 447-7634 Toll-free number: (800) 664-1886
Fax: (502) 447-7665
Trent Ramey, Regional Director of Admissions, National College: Louisville, PO Box 6400, Roanoke, VA 24017

National College: Pikeville
Pikeville, Kentucky
www.ncbt.edu   CB code: 3412

- For-profit 2-year business college
- Commuter campus in large town

General. Accredited by ACICS. **Enrollment:** 231 degree-seeking undergraduates. **Degrees:** 38 associate awarded. **Calendar:** Quarter, extensive summer session. **Full-time faculty:** 5 total. **Part-time faculty:** 25 total.

Basis for selection. Open admission, but selective for some programs. Interviews highly recommended.

2011-2012 Annual costs. Tuition/fees: $13,770. Per-credit charge: $305. Books/supplies: $1,500.

Financial aid. All financial aid based on need. Need-based aid available for part-time students. Work-study available nights, weekends and for part-time students.

Application procedures. Admission: No deadline. $50 fee, may be waived for applicants with need. Admission notification on a rolling basis. **Financial aid:** No deadline. FAFSA required.

Academics. Special study options: Double major, internships. **Credit/placement by examination:** AP, CLEP, institutional tests. **Support services:** Learning center, remedial instruction, tutoring.

Majors. Business: Accounting, administrative services, business admin. **Health services:** Medical assistant, medical secretary.

Computing on campus. 35 workstations in library, computer center.

Student life. Freshman orientation: Mandatory. Preregistration for classes offered. **Activities:** Student government.

Student services. Career counseling, student employment services, financial aid counseling, personal counseling, placement for graduates, veterans' counselor.

Contact. E-mail: market@educorp.edu
Phone: (606) 432-5477 Toll-free number: (800) 664-1886
Fax: (606) 437-4952
Leigh Ann Harris, Director of Admissions, National College: Pikeville, PO Box 6400, Roanoke, VA 24017

National College: Richmond
Richmond, Kentucky
www.ncbt.edu   CB code: 3414

- For-profit 2-year business college
- Commuter campus in large town

General. Accredited by ACICS. **Enrollment:** 236 degree-seeking undergraduates. **Degrees:** 68 associate awarded. **Calendar:** Quarter, limited summer session. **Full-time faculty:** 1 total. **Part-time faculty:** 28 total.

Basis for selection. Open admission. Interviews highly recommended.

2011-2012 Annual costs. Tuition/fees: $13,770. Per-credit charge: $305. Books/supplies: $1,500.

Financial aid. All financial aid based on need. Need-based aid available for part-time students. Work-study available nights, weekends and for part-time students.

Application procedures. Admission: No deadline. $50 fee, may be waived for applicants with need. Admission notification on a rolling basis. **Financial aid:** No deadline. FAFSA required. Applicants notified on a rolling basis.

Academics. Special study options: Double major, internships. **Credit/placement by examination:** AP, CLEP, institutional tests. **Support services:** Learning center, remedial instruction, tutoring.

Majors. Business: Accounting, administrative services, business admin. **Computer sciences:** Computer science. **Health services:** Medical assistant, medical secretary.

Computing on campus. 35 workstations in library, computer center.

Student life. Freshman orientation: Mandatory. Preregistration for classes offered. **Activities:** Student government.

Student services. Career counseling, student employment services, financial aid counseling, personal counseling, placement for graduates, veterans' counselor.

Contact. E-mail: market@educorp.edu
Phone: (859) 623-8956 Toll-free number: (800) 664-1886
Fax: (859) 624-5544
Virgie Douglas, Director of Admissions, National College: Richmond, PO Box 6400, Roanoke, VA 24017

Owensboro Community and Technical College
Owensboro, Kentucky
www.owensboro.kctcs.edu   CB code: 0613

- Public 2-year community and technical college
- Commuter campus in small city

General. Founded in 1986. Regionally accredited. **Enrollment:** 3,367 degree-seeking undergraduates. **Degrees:** 569 associate awarded. **Location:** 120 miles from Louisville; 40 miles from Evansville, IN. **Calendar:** Semester, extensive summer session. **Full-time faculty:** 98 total. **Part-time faculty:** 114 total. **Special facilities:** Outdoor classroom/nature area, early Headstart program.

Transfer out. Colleges most students transferred to 2011: Western Kentucky University, Kentucky Wesleyan College, Brescia University, University of Southern Indiana, University of Kentucky.

Basis for selection. Open admission, but selective for some programs. ACT scores required for nursing, radiography, diagnostic medical sonography, surgical technology, and early childhood education programs. **Home schooled:** Documentation of courses required.

High school preparation. 11 units recommended. Recommended units include English 4, mathematics 3, social studies 2, science 2 (laboratory 2).

2011-2012 Annual costs. Tuition/fees: $4,050; $13,950 out-of-state. Per-credit charge: $135 in-state; $465 out-of-state. Contiguous counties pay $270 per credit hour. Books/supplies: $1,100. Personal expenses: $1,040.

Financial aid. Need-based: Need-based aid available for part-time students. Work-study available nights, weekends and for part-time students. **Non-need-based:** Scholarships awarded for academics, state residency.

Application procedures. Admission: Priority date 4/1; deadline 8/15 (receipt date). No application fee. Admission notification on a rolling basis beginning on or about 3/1. **Financial aid:** Priority date 3/16; no closing date. FAFSA required. Must reply within 2 week(s) of notification.

Academics. Special study options: Cooperative education, distance learning, double major, dual enrollment of high school students, independent study, internships, study abroad. License preparation in nursing, paramedic, radiology, real estate. **Credit/placement by examination:** AP, CLEP, institutional tests. **Support services:** GED preparation and test center, learning center, remedial instruction, study skills assistance, tutoring.

Majors. Biology: Biotechnology. **Business:** General, accounting, administrative services, business admin, management information systems, office/clerical. **Computer sciences:** Information systems. **Education:** General, early childhood. **General:** Business. **Health services:** Medical radiologic technology/radiation therapy, medical secretary, medical transcription, nursing (RN), office assistant, sonography. **Human services:** Social work. **Liberal arts:** Arts/sciences. **Protective services:** Police science.

Most popular majors. Health sciences 20%, liberal arts 53%.

Computing on campus. 350 workstations in library, computer center, student center. Commuter students can connect to campus network. Online course registration, online library, helpline, wireless network available.

Student life. Freshman orientation: Mandatory. Preregistration for classes offered. Half-day session conducted a month before classes begin. **Activities:** Choral groups, drama, literary magazine, radio station, student government, student newspaper, TV station.

Athletics. Intramural: Basketball, softball.

Student services. Career counseling, services for economically disadvantaged, student employment services, financial aid counseling, minority student services, on-campus daycare, personal counseling, placement for graduates, veterans' counselor. **Physically disabled:** Services for visually, speech, hearing impaired. **Transfer:** Pre-admission transcript evaluation for new students. Transfer adviser, college fairs on campus for students transferring to 4-year colleges.

Contact. E-mail: octc.info@kctcs.edu
Phone: (270) 686-4527 Toll-free number: (866) 755-6282
Fax: (270) 686-4648
Kevin Beardmore, Vice President of Student Affairs, Owensboro Community and Technical College, 4800 New Hartford Road, Owensboro, KY 42303-1899

Somerset Community College
Somerset, Kentucky
www.somerset.kctcs.edu　　　　　　　**CB code: 1779**

◗ Public 2-year community and technical college
◗ Commuter campus in large town

General. Founded in 1965. Regionally accredited. One of 16 community colleges and 12 technical colleges consolidated under one administration. **Enrollment:** 7,153 degree-seeking undergraduates. **Degrees:** 614 associate awarded. **Location:** 70 miles from Lexington. **Calendar:** Semester, limited summer session. **Full-time faculty:** 185 total; 11% have terminal degrees, 5% minority, 55% women. **Part-time faculty:** 160 total. **Class size:** 54% < 20, 39% 20-39, 2% 40-49, 4% 50-99, less than 1% >100.

Student profile.

Out-of-state:	1%	25 or older:	43%

Transfer out. Colleges most students transferred to 2011: Morehead State University, University of Kentucky, Western Kentucky University, Eastern Kentucky University.

Basis for selection. Open admission, but selective for some programs. Test scores, letters of recommendation, and interview required for limited enrollment programs in allied health. ACT required in admissions process but not ordinarily used as selective criterion.

High school preparation. 20 units recommended. Recommended units include English 4, mathematics 3, social studies 2, science 2 and academic electives 9.

2011-2012 Annual costs. Tuition/fees: $4,050; $13,950 out-of-state. Per-credit charge: $135 in-state; $465 out-of-state. Books and supplies for residents (on-campus) is $750. Books/supplies: $1,000. Personal expenses: $800.

2011-2012 Financial aid. All financial aid based on need. 53% of total undergraduate aid awarded as scholarships/grants, 47% as loans/jobs. Need-based aid available for part-time students. Work-study available nights, weekends and for part-time students.

Application procedures. Admission: No deadline. No application fee. Admission notification on a rolling basis. Admitted students in nursing, clinical laboratory techniques, and physical therapy assisting must reply within 10 days. **Financial aid:** Priority date 3/1; no closing date. FAFSA required. Applicants notified on a rolling basis starting 5/1; must reply within 2 week(s) of notification.

Academics. Special study options: Cooperative education, distance learning, dual enrollment of high school students, ESL, external degree, independent study, internships, liberal arts/career combination. Bachelor's degree programs available on campus. License preparation in aviation, dental hygiene, nursing, physical therapy, radiology, real estate. **Credit/placement by examination:** AP, CLEP. 12 credit hours maximum toward associate degree. **Support services:** GED preparation and test center, learning center, reduced course load, remedial instruction, study skills assistance, tutoring, writing center.

Majors. Business: Business admin, executive assistant. **Communications technology:** Graphics, printing management. **Computer sciences:** General. **Education:** General, teacher assistance. **Health services:** Clinical lab assistant, clinical lab technology, licensed practical nurse, medical assistant, medical secretary, nursing (RN), physical therapy assistant. **Liberal arts:** Arts/sciences. **Protective services:** Law enforcement admin, police science. **Work/family studies:** Child care management, child care service.

Computing on campus. 947 workstations in library, computer center, student center. Commuter students can connect to campus network. Online course registration, online library, repair service, wireless network available.

Student life. Freshman orientation: Mandatory. Preregistration for classes offered. **Activities:** Choral groups, drama, film society, music ensembles, student government, student newspaper, Baptist Student Union, Student Government Association, Students for Free Enterprise, Phi Beta Lambda, Phi Theta Kappa, criminal justice student organization.

Athletics. Intramural: Basketball, football (non-tackle), racquetball, softball, volleyball. **Team name:** Cougars.

Student services. Adult student services, career counseling, services for economically disadvantaged, student employment services, financial aid counseling, minority student services, personal counseling, placement for graduates, veterans' counselor. **Physically disabled:** Services for visually, speech, hearing impaired. **Transfer:** Pre-admission transcript evaluation for new students. Transfer center, transfer adviser, college fairs on campus for students transferring to 4-year colleges.

Contact. E-mail: somerset-admissions@kctcs.edu
Phone: (606) 451-6630 Toll-free number: (877) 629-9722
Fax: (606) 679-4369
Tracy Casada, Dean of Student Affairs, Somerset Community College, 808 Monticello Street, Somerset, KY 42501

Southeast Kentucky Community and Technical College
Cumberland, Kentucky
www.southeast.kctcs.edu　　　　　　　**CB code: 1770**

◗ Public 2-year community and technical college
◗ Commuter campus in small town

General. Founded in 1960. Regionally accredited. Branch campuses at Harlan, Middlesboro, Pineville and Whitesburg. **Enrollment:** 2,730 degree-seeking undergraduates; 2,486 non-degree-seeking students. **Degrees:** 395 associate awarded. **Location:** 150 miles from Lexington. **Calendar:** Semester, limited summer session. **Full-time faculty:** 110 total; 13% have terminal degrees, 12% minority, 46% women. **Part-time faculty:** 90 total; 3% have terminal degrees, 4% minority, 40% women. **Class size:** 31% < 20, 55% 20-39, 10% 40-49, 4% 50-99. **Special facilities:** Appalachian archives.

Student profile. Among degree-seeking undergraduates, 33% enrolled in a transfer program, 67% enrolled in a vocational program, 725 enrolled as first-time, first-year students.

Part-time:	46%	African American:	2%
Out-of-state:	4%	Native American:	1%
Women:	52%	25 or older:	40%

Transfer out. 24% of students enrolled in the transfer program go on to 4-year colleges. **Colleges most students transferred to 2011:** Lincoln

Memorial University, University of Louisville, Eastern Kentucky University.

Basis for selection. Open admission, but selective for some programs. ACT required for nursing, radiography, respiratory care and physical therapy programs. **Home schooled:** Transcript of courses and grades required.

High school preparation. 12 units recommended. Recommended units include English 4, mathematics 3, history 2, science 2 (laboratory 1).

2011-2012 Annual costs. Tuition/fees: $4,050; $13,950 out-of-state. Per-credit charge: $135 in-state; $465 out-of-state. Books/supplies: $600. Personal expenses: $1,100.

Financial aid. All financial aid based on need. Need-based aid available for part-time students. Work-study available nights, weekends and for part-time students. **Additional information:** March 15 deadline for state financial aid.

Application procedures. Admission: No deadline. No application fee. Admission notification on a rolling basis. **Financial aid:** Priority date 3/15; no closing date. FAFSA required. Must reply within 2 week(s) of notification.

Academics. Special study options: Cross-registration, distance learning, dual enrollment of high school students, internships, liberal arts/career combination. License preparation in nursing. **Credit/placement by examination:** AP, CLEP, institutional tests. 30 credit hours maximum toward associate degree. **Support services:** GED preparation and test center, learning center, pre-admission summer program, reduced course load, remedial instruction, study skills assistance, tutoring, writing center.

Majors. Business: Administrative services, banking/financial services, business admin, finance, management information systems. **Computer sciences:** General, data processing. **Health services:** Clinical lab assistant, medical radiologic technology/radiation therapy, nursing (RN), physical therapy assistant, respiratory therapy technology. **Liberal arts:** Arts/sciences. **Protective services:** Police science.

Most popular majors. Business/marketing 10%, health sciences 30%, liberal arts 50%.

Computing on campus. 60 workstations in library, computer center. Commuter students can connect to campus network. Online course registration, wireless network available.

Student life. Freshman orientation: Mandatory. Preregistration for classes offered. **Activities:** Choral groups, dance, drama, student government, student newspaper, Christian student union, black student union, Professional Business Leaders, wilderness club, nursing club.

Student services. Adult student services, career counseling, financial aid counseling, personal counseling, placement for graduates, veterans' counselor. **Physically disabled:** Services for visually impaired. **Transfer:** Transfer adviser, college fairs on campus for students transferring to 4-year colleges.

Contact. Phone: (606) 589-2145 Toll-free number: (888) 274-7332 Fax: (606) 589-5423
Veria Baldwin, Director of Admissions, Southeast Kentucky Community and Technical College, 700 College Road, Cumberland, KY 40823

Spencerian College
Louisville, Kentucky
www.spencerian.edu   **CB code: 3422**

- For-profit 2-year career college
- Commuter campus in large city

General. Accredited by ACICS. **Enrollment:** 1,008 degree-seeking undergraduates; 4 non-degree-seeking students. **Degrees:** 147 associate awarded. **Location:** 10 miles from downtown. **Calendar:** Quarter, extensive summer session. **Full-time faculty:** 47 total; 6% have terminal degrees, 8% minority, 81% women. **Part-time faculty:** 54 total; 2% have terminal degrees, 7% minority, 78% women. **Special facilities:** Radiology digital lab, X-ray lab, surgical technology lab, massage therapy lab, medical laboratory technology and cardiovascular technology lab.

Student profile. Among degree-seeking undergraduates, 100% enrolled in a vocational program, 266 enrolled as first-time, first-year students.

Part-time:	33%	Women:	86%

Basis for selection. Open admission, but selective for some programs. Requirements vary for medical programs. Minimum entrance test scores required for some programs. Interview may be required for selective programs such as nursing, medical laboratory technology, invasive cardiovascular technology, respiratory care, and surgical technology programs. **Home schooled:**

Transcript of courses and grades required. Students may be asked to provide copies of letters notifying school district for each year they were home schooled.

2011-2012 Annual costs. Tuition/fees: $16,410. Per-credit charge: $265. Room/board: $7,740. Books/supplies: $2,100. Personal expenses: $2,500.

Financial aid. Need-based: Need-based aid available for part-time students. Work-study available nights, weekends and for part-time students. **Non-need-based:** Scholarships awarded for academics.

Application procedures. Admission: No deadline. $100 fee, may be waived for applicants with need. Admission notification on a rolling basis. **Financial aid:** No deadline. FAFSA, institutional form required.

Academics. Special study options: Distance learning, internships. **Credit/placement by examination:** AP, CLEP, institutional tests. **Support services:** Learning center, tutoring.

Majors. Business: Accounting, business admin. **Health services:** Cardiovascular technology, clinical lab technology, insurance specialist, massage therapy, medical radiologic technology/radiation therapy, office admin, respiratory therapy technology, surgical technology.

Most popular majors. Health sciences 95%.

Computing on campus. 86 workstations in library. Commuter students can connect to campus network.

Student life. Freshman orientation: Mandatory. Preregistration for classes offered. One day and one evening session held week before classes begin. Make-up orientation held second week of quarter. **Housing:** $95 deposit.

Student services. Career counseling, financial aid counseling, placement for graduates. **Transfer:** Re-entry adviser, pre-admission transcript evaluation for new students.

Contact. Phone: (502) 447-1000 Toll-free number: (800) 264-1799 Fax: (502) 447-4574
Kathleen Belanger, Director of Admissions, Spencerian College, 4627 Dixie Highway, Louisville, KY 40216

Spencerian College: Lexington
Lexington, Kentucky
www.spencerian.edu   **CB code: 3424**

- For-profit 2-year branch campus and technical college
- Commuter campus in small city
- Interview required

General. Accredited by ACICS. **Enrollment:** 621 degree-seeking undergraduates. **Degrees:** 117 associate awarded. **Location:** 72 miles from Louisville. **Calendar:** Quarter, limited summer session. **Full-time faculty:** 30 total; 3% have terminal degrees, 13% minority, 57% women. **Part-time faculty:** 31 total; 16% minority, 52% women. **Class size:** 91% < 20, 9% 20-39.

Student profile. Among degree-seeking undergraduates, 294 enrolled as first-time, first-year students.

Part-time:	7%	Women:	57%

Transfer out. Colleges most students transferred to 2011: Lexington Community College, University of Kentucky, Eastern Kentucky University.

Basis for selection. Open admission, but selective for some programs. 16 ACT or passing score on CPAt required for selective programs. HOBET required for certain programs. **Home schooled:** Transcript of courses and grades, state high school equivalency certificate required. **Learning Disabled:** Potential students need to submit IEP or 504.

2012-2013 Annual costs. Tuition/fees (projected): $14,839. Per-credit charge: $360. Room/board: $7,205. Books/supplies: $1,300.

Financial aid. All financial aid based on need. Need-based aid available for part-time students. Work-study available nights, weekends and for part-time students.

Application procedures. Admission: No deadline. $100 fee, may be waived for applicants with need. Admission notification on a rolling basis. **Financial aid:** No deadline. FAFSA, institutional form required. Applicants notified on a rolling basis starting 1/1.

Academics. Special study options: Cooperative education, double major, independent study, internships, weekend college. License preparation in radiology. **Credit/placement by examination:** AP, CLEP, IB. 23 credit hours maximum toward associate degree. **Support services:** Reduced course load, study skills assistance, tutoring.

Majors. Biology: Biomedical sciences. **Computer sciences:** Computer graphics. **Engineering:** Electrical. **Visual/performing arts:** Commercial/advertising art.

Most popular majors. Architecture 11%, computer/information sciences 30%, engineering/engineering technologies 17%, health sciences 19%.

Computing on campus. PC or laptop required. 170 workstations in library, computer center. Commuter students can connect to campus network. Online library, helpline, wireless network available.

Student life. Freshman orientation: Available. Preregistration for classes offered. Four-hour session held at beginning of quarter. **Policies:** Students must be under the age of 21 to live in dorm. **Housing:** Guaranteed on-campus for freshmen. Coed dorms, special housing for disabled, apartments available. $95 nonrefundable deposit. **Activities:** Student newspaper, Healing Hands student organization, Skeleton Crew (radiography), CADD student organization, allied health student organization.

Student services. Adult student services, career counseling, student employment services, financial aid counseling, placement for graduates, veterans' counselor. **Physically disabled:** Services for visually, speech, hearing impaired. **Transfer:** Pre-admission transcript evaluation for new students.

Contact. Phone: (859) 223-9608 ext. 5460
Toll-free number: (800) 456-3253 ext. 5460 Fax: (859) 224-7744
Christine Wildes, Director of Admissions, Spencerian College: Lexington, 1575 Winchester Road, Lexington, KY 40505

Sullivan College of Technology and Design
Louisville, Kentucky
www.sctd.edu　　　　　　　　　　　　　　**CB code: 1501**

- For-profit 2-year technical and career college
- Commuter campus in very large city
- Interview required

General. Founded in 1961. Regionally accredited; also accredited by ACICS. **Enrollment:** 581 degree-seeking undergraduates; 1 non-degree-seeking students. **Degrees:** 19 bachelor's, 166 associate awarded. **Location:** 7 miles from downtown. **Calendar:** Quarter, extensive summer session. **Full-time faculty:** 34 total; 6% minority, 35% women. **Part-time faculty:** 44 total; 18% minority, 43% women. **Class size:** 97% < 20, 3% 20-39. **Special facilities:** Laboratories for computer-aided graphics, computer-aided drafting, electronics, computer networking, computer security and forensics, robotics and heating-ventilation-air conditioning-refrigeration.

Student profile. Among degree-seeking undergraduates, 100% enrolled in a vocational program, 4% already have a bachelor's degree or higher, 121 enrolled as first-time, first-year students, 57 transferred in from other institutions.

Part-time:	38%	**25 or older:**	48%
Out-of-state:	11%	**Live on campus:**	3%
Women:	34%		

Transfer out. 45% of students enrolled in the transfer program go on to 4-year colleges. **Colleges most students transferred to 2011:** Sullivan University.

Basis for selection. Entrance test (CPAt), previous school record and interview most important. Equivalent ACT/SAT scores may be accepted in place of CPAt. **Home schooled:** State high school equivalency certificate required. In-state applicants must have certificate of completion or high school diploma provided by local public school district. Applicants from other states must have certificate of completion or high school diploma provided by local school district or state's Department of Education. Applicants who cannot meet these requirements must obtain GED. **Learning Disabled:** Students seeking special accommodations must provide documentation from professional analysis indicating level of disability and types of recommended accommodations.

High school preparation. Recommended units include English 4, mathematics 4, social studies 2, science 3, computer science 1 and visual/performing arts 1.

2012-2013 Annual costs. The full-program tuition rate ranges from $16,890 to $19,705 depending upon program of study. The per-credit-hour

tuition rate ranges from $395 to $460 depending upon program of study. The approximated cost of books and supplies ranges from $1,500 to $2,500 depending upon program of study. Required fees: $540 plus fee of $200 for online courses. Room/board: $8,595. Books/supplies: $1,500. Personal expenses: $2,400.

2010-2011 Financial aid. Need-based: 151 full-time freshmen applied for aid; 151 were judged to have need; 151 of these received aid. Average scholarship/grant was $3,512. 38% of total undergraduate aid awarded as scholarships/grants, 62% as loans/jobs. Need-based aid available for part-time students. Work-study available nights, weekends and for part-time students. **Non-need-based:** Scholarships awarded for academics, art, job skills.

Application procedures. Admission: No deadline. $100 fee, may be waived for applicants with need. Application must be submitted on paper. Admission notification on a rolling basis. **Financial aid:** No deadline. FAFSA required. Applicants notified on a rolling basis; must reply within 2 week(s) of notification.

Academics. Special study options: Accelerated study, cooperative education, double major, dual enrollment of high school students, internships. Bachelor's degree programs available on campus. **Credit/placement by examination:** AP, CLEP, SAT, ACT, institutional tests. 75 credit hours maximum toward associate degree, 145 toward bachelor's. **Support services:** Learning center, reduced course load, remedial instruction, study skills assistance, tutoring.

Majors. Architecture: Interior. **Communications technology:** Animation/special effects, desktop publishing, graphics. **Computer sciences:** Computer graphics, information systems, information technology, LAN/WAN management, security, system admin, vendor certification, web page design. **Engineering:** Architectural. **Visual/performing arts:** Graphic design, interior design.

Most popular majors. Computer/information sciences 39%, engineering/engineering technologies 41%, visual/performing arts 20%.

Computing on campus. 250 workstations in dormitories, library, computer center. Dormitories wired for high-speed internet access. Commuter students can connect to campus network. Online library, helpline, repair service, wireless network available.

Student life. Freshman orientation: Mandatory. Preregistration for classes offered. Three-hour program held at start of quarter. **Housing:** Coed dorms, apartments, wellness housing available. $95 nonrefundable deposit. **Activities:** SkillsUSA student chapter, American Design Drafting Association, American Society of Interior Designers, International Interior Design Association, ad federation, greener living club.

Student services. Adult student services, career counseling, services for economically disadvantaged, student employment services, financial aid counseling, placement for graduates, veterans' counselor. **Physically disabled:** Services for speech, hearing impaired. **Transfer:** Re-entry adviser, pre-admission transcript evaluation for new students.

Contact. E-mail: achauhdri@sctd.edu
Phone: (502) 456-6509 Toll-free number: (800) 844-6528
Fax: (502) 456-2341
Aamer Chauhdri, Director of Admissions, Sullivan College of Technology and Design, 3901 Atkinson Square Drive, Louisville, KY 40218-4524

West Kentucky Community and Technical College
Paducah, Kentucky
www.westkentucky.kctcs.edu　　　　　　　　**CB code: 1620**

- Public 2-year community and technical college
- Commuter campus in large town

General. Founded in 1932. Regionally accredited. **Enrollment:** 4,488 degree-seeking undergraduates; 791 non-degree-seeking students. **Degrees:** 557 associate awarded. **Location:** 140 miles from Nashville, TN. **Calendar:** Semester, limited summer session. **Full-time faculty:** 124 total. **Part-time faculty:** 121 total.

Student profile. Among degree-seeking undergraduates, 871 enrolled as first-time, first-year students, 125 transferred in from other institutions.

Part-time:	44%	**African American:**	5%
Out-of-state:	4%	**Hispanic American:**	1%
Women:	65%	**25 or older:**	39%

Basis for selection. Open admission, but selective for some programs. 19 ACT required for nursing and physical therapist assistant applicants. CPP

placement test required for non-traditional students. ACT, when required, must be received by 8/25. Interview required of nursing applicants.

High school preparation. 20 units recommended. Recommended units include English 4, mathematics 3, social studies 2 and science 2.

2011-2012 Annual costs. Tuition/fees: $4,050; $13,950 out-of-state. Per-credit charge: $135 in-state; $465 out-of-state. Books/supplies: $500. Personal expenses: $425.

Financial aid. Need-based: Need-based aid available for part-time students. Work-study available nights, weekends and for part-time students.

Application procedures. Admission: No deadline. No application fee. Admission notification on a rolling basis beginning on or about 4/1. **Financial aid:** Priority date 4/1, closing date 7/15. FAFSA required. Applicants notified on a rolling basis starting 7/15; must reply within 4 week(s) of notification.

Academics. Special study options: Accelerated study, cooperative education, distance learning, dual enrollment of high school students, ESL, honors, weekend college. License preparation in real estate. **Credit/placement by examination:** AP, CLEP. **Support services:** GED preparation and test center, learning center, reduced course load, remedial instruction, tutoring.

Majors. Business: Accounting, administrative services, banking/financial services, business admin, management information systems, office technology, real estate. **Communications:** Communications/speech/rhetoric. **Computer sciences:** General, applications programming. **Health services:** Clinical lab technology, medical radiologic technology/radiation therapy, nursing (RN), physical therapy assistant, physics/radiologic health, respiratory therapy technology, sonography. **Liberal arts:** Arts/sciences.

Computing on campus. 70 workstations in library, computer center.

Student life. Freshman orientation: Mandatory. Preregistration for classes offered. **Activities:** Choral groups, drama, musical theater, radio station, student government, student newspaper, TV station.

Athletics. Intramural: Basketball M, golf, volleyball.

Student services. Adult student services, career counseling, student employment services, personal counseling, placement for graduates, veterans' counselor. **Physically disabled:** Services for visually, speech, hearing impaired. **Transfer:** Transfer adviser for students transferring to 4-year colleges.

Contact. Phone: (270) 534-3264 Fax: (270) 534-6304
Maria Rosa, Director of Admissions, West Kentucky Community and Technical College, 4810 Alben Barkley Drive, Paducah, KY 42002-7380

Louisiana

Baton Rouge Community College
Baton Rouge, Louisiana
www.mybrcc.edu
CB code: 6023

◆ Public 2-year community college
◆ Commuter campus in large city

General. Regionally accredited. **Enrollment:** 8,089 degree-seeking undergraduates. **Degrees:** 388 associate awarded. **Location:** 60 miles from New Orleans. **Calendar:** Semester, extensive summer session. **Full-time faculty:** 148 total. **Part-time faculty:** 171 total. **Class size:** 18% < 20, 75% 20-39, 7% 40-49, less than 1% 50-99. **Special facilities:** Sonography lab, process technology glass lab, health and wellness facility with full-sized basketball court, rock climbing wall, weight room, dance and fitness rooms, academic learning center, black box theater, gaming and animation center, green house, student success center.

Student profile. Among degree-seeking undergraduates, 2,030 enrolled as first-time, first-year students.

Part-time:	47%	Asian American:	2%
Out-of-state:	1%	Hispanic American:	1%
Women:	57%	International:	2%
African American:	38%	25 or older:	31%

Transfer out. Colleges most students transferred to 2011: Louisiana State University, Southern University, Southeastern University.

Basis for selection. Open admission. **Home schooled:** GED or documentation from state verifying completion of SBESE-approved home study program required. **Learning Disabled:** Students self-identify with disability services.

2011-2012 Annual costs. Tuition/fees: $2,472; $5,760 out-of-state. Books/supplies: $1,200. Personal expenses: $1,819.

Financial aid. **Need-based:** Need-based aid available for part-time students. Work-study available nights, weekends and for part-time students. **Non-need-based:** Scholarships awarded for academics, athletics, leadership, minority status, state residency.

Application procedures. **Admission:** Closing date 8/18 (receipt date). $7 fee. Admission notification on a rolling basis. **Financial aid:** Priority date 4/15, closing date 6/30. FAFSA, institutional form required. Applicants notified on a rolling basis.

Academics. **Special study options:** Cross-registration, distance learning, double major, dual enrollment of high school students, honors, internships, study abroad, teacher certification program, weekend college. License preparation in aviation, nursing. **Credit/placement by examination:** AP, CLEP, institutional tests. **Support services:** Learning center, remedial instruction, study skills assistance, tutoring, writing center.

Majors. **Business:** General, accounting technology, construction management, office technology. **Computer sciences:** General. **Education:** General. **Health services:** Nursing (RN). **Liberal arts:** Arts/sciences. **Protective services:** Police science. **Visual/performing arts:** Cinematography.

Most popular majors. Business/marketing 35%, engineering/engineering technologies 13%, health sciences 9%, liberal arts 39%.

Computing on campus. 175 workstations in library, computer center, student center. Online course registration, online library, helpline, wireless network available.

Student life. **Freshman orientation:** Mandatory. Preregistration for classes offered. **Policies:** All student club members must maintain 2.0 GPA to be active in campus clubs. All student government association officers must maintain 2.5 GPA to remain in office. **Activities:** Jazz band, dance, drama, international student organizations, literary magazine, music ensembles, student government, student newspaper, Christian student association, future educators club, center for peace, peer advisors and leaders, poetry club, self-esteem club, twenty-five plus society, student government association, production assistance club, Christian student association.

Athletics. NJCAA. **Intercollegiate:** Baseball M, basketball. **Intramural:** Football (non-tackle) M, soccer, volleyball. **Team name:** Bears.

Student services. Career counseling, student employment services, financial aid counseling, personal counseling, placement for graduates, veterans' counselor. **Physically disabled:** Services for visually, speech, hearing impaired. **Transfer:** College fairs on campus for students transferring to 4-year colleges.

Contact. E-mail: clayn@mybrcc.edu
Phone: (225) 216-8700
Nancy Clay, Executive Director of Enrollment Services, Baton Rouge Community College, 201 Community College Drive, Baton Rouge, LA 70806

Baton Rouge School of Computers
Baton Rouge, Louisiana
www.brsc.net
CB code: 3197

◆ For-profit 2-year technical college
◆ Small city

General. Accredited by ACCSC. **Enrollment:** 39 full-time, degree-seeking students. **Degrees:** 22 associate awarded. **Calendar:** Differs by program. **Full-time faculty:** 17 total. **Part-time faculty:** 2 total.

Basis for selection. Open admission.

2011-2012 Annual costs. $16,504 tuition for diploma program, $33,008 for associate degree. Additional charge for textbooks. Books/supplies: $300.

Financial aid. **Need-based:** Work-study available nights, weekends and for part-time students.

Application procedures. **Admission:** No deadline. $25 fee, may be waived for applicants with need.

Academics. **Credit/placement by examination:** AP, CLEP.

Majors. **Business:** General. **Computer sciences:** General.

Student life. **Freshman orientation:** Mandatory. Preregistration for classes offered.

Contact. Phone: (225) 923-2525 Fax: (225) 923-2979
Brenda Boss, Director of Admissions, Baton Rouge School of Computers, 10425 Plaza Americana, Baton Rouge, LA 70816

Blue Cliff College: Metairie
Metairie, Louisiana
www.bluecliffcollege.com

◆ For-profit 2-year technical college
◆ Commuter campus in large town

General. Accredited by ACCSC. **Enrollment:** 387 full-time, degree-seeking students. **Degrees:** 3 associate awarded. **Calendar:** Quarter. **Full-time faculty:** 10 total. **Part-time faculty:** 33 total.

Basis for selection. Open admission. Wonderlic test given as skills assessment before enrollment.

2011-2012 Annual costs. Medical Assisting tuition $14,336; program fees $1,200. Massage Therapy tuition $13,144; program fees $1,200. Dental Assisting tuition $13,216; program fees $1,000. Dialysis tuition $15,232; program fees $1,200.

Financial aid. **Need-based:** Work-study available nights, weekends and for part-time students.

Application procedures. **Admission:** No deadline. No application fee.

Academics. **Credit/placement by examination:** AP, CLEP.

Majors. **Health services:** Massage therapy. **Protective services:** Criminal justice.

Student services. **Transfer:** Pre-admission transcript evaluation for new students.

Contact. E-mail: pattyr@bluecliffcollege.com
Phone: (504) 456-3141 Toll-free number: (800) 517-8176
Fax: (504) 456-7849
Lisa Francis, Admissions Officer, Blue Cliff College: Metairie, 3200 Cleary Avenue, Metairie, LA 70002

Blue Cliff College: Shreveport
Shreveport, Louisiana
www.bluecliffcollege.com

▶ For-profit 2-year technical college
▶ Commuter campus in small city

General. Accredited by ACCSC. **Enrollment:** 135 full-time, degree-seeking students. **Calendar:** Quarter. **Full-time faculty:** 14 total. **Part-time faculty:** 9 total.

Basis for selection. Open admission.

2011-2012 Annual costs. Medical Assisting tuition $14,336, program fees $1,200. Massage Therapy tuition $13,144, program fees $1,200.

Financial aid. Need-based: Work-study available nights, weekends and for part-time students.

Application procedures. Admission: No deadline. $25 fee. Admission notification on a rolling basis.

Academics. Credit/placement by examination: AP, CLEP.

Majors. Health services: Massage therapy, medical assistant.

Contact. Phone: (318) 425-7941
Admissions Representative, Blue Cliff College: Shreveport, 8731 Park Plaza Drive, Shreveport, LA 71105-5682

Bossier Parish Community College
Bossier City, Louisiana
www.bpcc.edu   CB code: 0787

▶ Public 2-year community college
▶ Commuter campus in small city

General. Founded in 1966. Regionally accredited. **Enrollment:** 6,476 degree-seeking undergraduates; 601 non-degree-seeking students. **Degrees:** 336 associate awarded. **Location:** 6 miles from downtown Shreveport. **Calendar:** Semester, extensive summer session. **Full-time faculty:** 132 total; 13% have terminal degrees, 11% minority, 61% women. **Part-time faculty:** 267 total; 4% have terminal degrees, 23% minority. **Class size:** 47% < 20, 51% 20-39, 1% 40-49, less than 1% 50-99. **Partnerships:** Formal partnerships with General Motors, Libby Glass.

Student profile. Among degree-seeking undergraduates, 1,799 enrolled as first-time, first-year students, 487 transferred in from other institutions.

Part-time:	34%	Asian American:	1%
Out-of-state:	3%	Hispanic American:	3%
Women:	65%	Native American:	1%
African American:	39%	25 or older:	39%

Transfer out. Colleges most students transferred to 2011: Louisiana State University in Shreveport, Northwestern State University of Louisiana, Louisiana Tech University, Southern Arkansas University, Grambling State University.

Basis for selection. Open admission, but selective for out-of-state students. **Adult students:** SAT/ACT scores not required. **Home schooled:** Students generally expected to complete requirements for GED.

2011-2012 Annual costs. Tuition/fees: $2,392; $5,460 out-of-state.

Financial aid. Need-based: Need-based aid available for part-time students. Work-study available nights, weekends and for part-time students. **Non-need-based:** Scholarships awarded for academics, alumni affiliation, athletics, minority status, music/drama.

Application procedures. Admission: Closing date 8/10 (postmark date). No application fee. Admission notification on a rolling basis. **Financial aid:** Priority date 6/1, closing date 7/1. FAFSA, institutional form required. Applicants notified on a rolling basis starting 3/1.

Academics. Special study options: Accelerated study, distance learning, double major, dual enrollment of high school students, internships, teacher certification program. License preparation in nursing, paramedic. **Credit/placement by examination:** AP, CLEP, institutional tests. 30 credit hours maximum toward associate degree. **Support services:** GED preparation, learning center, remedial instruction, study skills assistance, tutoring, writing center.

Majors. Business: General, construction management. **Communications technology:** Recording arts. **Computer sciences:** Information systems, LAN/WAN management, security, system admin, web page design, webmaster. **Education:** General. **Health services:** EMT paramedic, facilities admin, medical assistant, nursing (RN), occupational therapy assistant, pharmacy assistant, physical therapy assistant, respiratory therapy technology. **Protective services:** Criminal justice. **Work/family studies:** Child care service.

Most popular majors. Business/marketing 14%, communication technologies 9%, computer/information sciences 9%, health sciences 12%, interdisciplinary studies 11%, liberal arts 32%, security/protective services 9%.

Computing on campus. 120 workstations in library. Online course registration, online library, wireless network available.

Student life. Freshman orientation: Available. Preregistration for classes offered. **Activities:** Bands, campus ministries, choral groups, dance, drama, international student organizations, literary magazine, music ensembles, musical theater, radio station, student government, student newspaper, TV station, College Republicans, gospel choir, ADAPTS, Maroon Jackets, NAACP, FCA, SGA.

Athletics. NJCAA. **Intercollegiate:** Baseball M, basketball M, cheerleading, softball W. **Team name:** Cavaliers.

Student services. Career counseling, services for economically disadvantaged, student employment services, financial aid counseling, personal counseling, veterans' counselor. **Physically disabled:** Services for visually, speech, hearing impaired. **Transfer:** Re-entry adviser, pre-admission transcript evaluation for new students. College fairs on campus for students transferring to 4-year colleges.

Contact. E-mail: admissions@bpcc.edu
Phone: (318) 678-6004 Fax: (318) 678-6390
Patty Stewart, Admissions Officer, Bossier Parish Community College, 6220 East Texas Street, Bossier City, LA 71111-6922

Delgado Community College
New Orleans, Louisiana
www.dcc.edu   CB code: 6176

▶ Public 2-year community college
▶ Commuter campus in very large city

General. Founded in 1921. Regionally accredited. **Enrollment:** 19,009 degree-seeking undergraduates; 1,443 non-degree-seeking students. **Degrees:** 1,116 associate awarded. **Calendar:** Semester, extensive summer session. **Full-time faculty:** 488 total; 6% have terminal degrees, 27% minority, 62% women. **Part-time faculty:** 452 total; 33% minority, 51% women. **Class size:** 48% < 20, 49% 20-39, 2% 40-49, 1% 50-99. **Special facilities:** Ship simulator, fine arts gallery.

Student profile. Among degree-seeking undergraduates, 3,762 enrolled as first-time, first-year students.

Part-time:	50%	Asian American:	2%
Out-of-state:	3%	Hispanic American:	6%
Women:	67%	International:	1%
African American:	42%	25 or older:	47%

Transfer out. Colleges most students transferred to 2011: Southeastern Louisiana University, University of New Orleans, Southern University at New Orleans, Nicholls State University.

Basis for selection. Open admission, but selective for some programs. Special requirements for health-related programs. **Adult students:** SAT/ACT scores not required if applicant over 25. Adult students without high school diploma or GED required to pass Ability to Benefit Exam. **Home schooled:** Applicants who have not completed state or regionally approved program required to have GED or successfully pass Ability to Benefit Exam.

2011-2012 Annual costs. Tuition/fees: $3,330; $6,858 out-of-state. Books/supplies: $1,200. Personal expenses: $3,224.

Financial aid. Need-based: Need-based aid available for part-time students. Work-study available nights, weekends and for part-time students. **Non-need-based:** Scholarships awarded for academics, athletics, leadership, music/drama, state residency.

Application procedures. Admission: No deadline. $25 fee. Admission notification on a rolling basis. **Financial aid:** Priority date 5/1, closing date 7/15. FAFSA, institutional form required. Applicants notified on a rolling basis starting 4/1; must reply within 2 week(s) of notification.

Academics. Special study options: Cooperative education, cross-registration, distance learning, double major, dual enrollment of high school students, ESL, honors, independent study, internships, liberal arts/career combination, student-designed major, weekend college. License preparation in nursing, paramedic, physical therapy, real estate. **Credit/placement by examination:** AP, CLEP, institutional tests. 24 credit hours maximum toward associate degree. **Support services:** GED preparation, learning center, pre-admission summer program, remedial instruction, tutoring, writing center.

Majors. Business: General, accounting technology, administrative services, business admin, construction management, hospitality admin. **Computer sciences:** Data processing, networking. **Education:** General. **Foreign languages:** Sign language interpretation. **General:** Horticulture. **Health services:** Clinical lab technology, dietetic technician, EMT paramedic, medical radiologic technology/radiation therapy, medical records technology, nursing (RN), occupational therapy assistant, physical therapy assistant, radiologic technology/medical imaging, respiratory therapy technology, veterinary technology/assistant. **Protective services:** Firefighting, police science. **Visual/performing arts:** Graphic design, interior design, music, studio arts. **Work/family studies:** Child care service.

Most popular majors. Business/marketing 17%, health sciences 44%, liberal arts 10%, security/protective services 6%.

Computing on campus. 555 workstations in library, computer center, student center. Online library, wireless network available.

Student life. Freshman orientation: Available. Preregistration for classes offered. **Activities:** Concert band, choral groups, dance, drama, film society, music ensembles, musical theater, radio station, student government, student newspaper, religious organizations available.

Athletics. NJCAA. **Intercollegiate:** Baseball M, basketball M, cheerleading. **Intramural:** Archery, badminton, baseball M, basketball, golf, soccer, softball, swimming, table tennis, tennis, volleyball. **Team name:** Dolphins.

Student services. Adult student services, career counseling, services for economically disadvantaged, student employment services, financial aid counseling, health services, on-campus daycare, personal counseling, placement for graduates, veterans' counselor. **Physically disabled:** Services for visually, speech, hearing impaired. **Transfer:** Re-entry adviser for new students. Transfer center, transfer adviser, college fairs on campus for students transferring to 4-year colleges.

Contact. E-mail: enroll@dcc.edu
Phone: (504) 671-5099 Fax: (504) 483-1895
Gwen Boutte, Director of Admissions & Enrollment Services, Delgado Community College, 615 City Park Avenue, New Orleans, LA 70119

Delta College of Arts & Technology
Baton Rouge, Louisiana
www.deltacollege.com
CB code: 3131

- For-profit 2-year visual arts and technical college
- Large city

General. Accredited by ACCSC. **Enrollment:** 635 degree-seeking undergraduates. **Degrees:** 13 associate awarded. **Calendar:** Differs by program. **Full-time faculty:** 21 total. **Part-time faculty:** 22 total.

Basis for selection. Open admission.

2011-2012 Annual costs. Tuition for full programs ranges from $9,750 to $22,500 and includes books and supplies. Registration fee $100. Books/supplies: $775. Personal expenses: $250.

Financial aid. Need-based: Work-study available nights, weekends and for part-time students.

Application procedures. Admission: No deadline. $100 fee. Admission notification on a rolling basis. **Financial aid:** No deadline.

Academics. Credit/placement by examination: AP, CLEP.

Majors. Health services: Licensed practical nurse. **Visual/performing arts:** General.

Student life. Freshman orientation: Available, $100 fee. Preregistration for classes offered.

Contact. E-mail: admissions@deltacollege.com
Phone: (225) 928-7770 Fax: (225) 927-9096
David Clark, General Manager, Delta College of Arts & Technology, 7380 Exchange Place, Baton Rouge, LA 70806

Delta School of Business & Technology
Lake Charles, Louisiana
www.deltatech.edu
CB code: 2252

- For-profit 2-year business and technical college
- Small city

General. Founded in 1970. Accredited by ACICS. **Location:** 128 miles from Baton Rouge. **Calendar:** Differs by program.

Annual costs/financial aid. Cost of associate degree program $9,590 per year, plus books and fees of approximately $2,540; IT program $9,590 per year, plus books and fees of approximately $2,790. One-year diploma programs also available at similar cost.

Contact. Phone: (337) 439-5765
Director of Admissions, 517 Broad Street, Lake Charles, LA 70601

Gretna Career College
Gretna, Louisiana
www.gccla.edu

- For-profit 2-year technical college
- Commuter campus in large town

General. Accredited by ACCSC. **Enrollment:** 150 degree-seeking undergraduates. **Degrees:** 4 associate awarded. **Calendar:** Quarter. **Full-time faculty:** 8 total. **Part-time faculty:** 4 total.

Basis for selection. Open admission, but selective for some programs.

2011-2012 Annual costs. Tuition/fees: $13,050. Tuition and fees vary by program and range from $8,700-$14,400 for certificate and diploma programs; $26,150-$26,970 for associate degree programs. Costs include books, supplies, uniforms, and lab fees. Tuition charged for all programs - by quarter - not by quarter credits. The difference in costs of programs comes from other fees: books/lab/uniforms/tools (auto). Books/supplies: $1,562. Personal expenses: $1,770.

Financial aid. Need-based: Work-study available nights, weekends and for part-time students.

Application procedures. Admission: $50 fee. Admission notification on a rolling basis. **Financial aid:** No deadline.

Academics. Credit/placement by examination: AP, CLEP.

Majors. Business: Business admin. **Health services:** Medical secretary, office assistant.

Contact. E-mail: admissions@gretnacareercollege.edu
Phone: (504) 366-5409 ext. 23
Admissions Team, Gretna Career College, 1415 Whitney Avenue, Gretna, LA 70037

ITI Technical College
Baton Rouge, Louisiana
www.iticollege.edu

- For-profit 2-year technical college
- Commuter campus in large city
- Interview required

General. Accredited by ACCSC. **Enrollment:** 400 degree-seeking undergraduates. **Degrees:** 72 associate awarded. **Calendar:** Continuous. **Full-time faculty:** 20 total; 25% minority, 20% women. **Part-time faculty:** 30 total; 13% minority, 10% women.

Student profile.

Out-of-state:	1%	**25 or older:**	49%

Basis for selection. Open admission, but selective for some programs. Applicant completes application, must interview and tour campus, complete entrance evaluation, settle funding, sign enrollment agreement. **Home schooled:** Students must have acceptable certificate or diploma at time of enrollment. **Learning Disabled:** Students must meet with school director regarding special needs and referral for assistance.

2011-2012 Annual costs. Full-time tuition varies by program from $13,350 to $26,650.

2010-2011 Financial aid. All financial aid based on need. 39% of total undergraduate aid awarded as scholarships/grants, 61% as loans/jobs. Work-study available nights, weekends and for part-time students.

Application procedures. Admission: No deadline. No application fee. Admission notification on a rolling basis. **Financial aid:** No deadline. FAFSA required.

Academics. Special study options: Internships. **Credit/placement by examination:** AP, CLEP. **Support services:** Study skills assistance, tutoring.

Majors. Business: Administrative services, business admin, executive assistant, office management, office technology. **Communications technology:** General. **Computer sciences:** Data processing, information systems. **Health services:** Insurance coding, insurance specialist, medical records admin, medical records technology, medical secretary, medical transcription, office admin, office assistant, office computer specialist, receptionist.

Computing on campus. 5 workstations in library. Repair service available.

Student life. Freshman orientation: Mandatory. Preregistration for classes offered.

Student services. Career counseling, financial aid counseling, placement for graduates.

Contact. E-mail: admissions@iticollege.edu
Phone: (225) 752-4233 Toll-free number: (800) 467-4484
Fax: (225) 756-0903
Marcia Stevens, Director of Admissions, ITI Technical College, 13944 Airline Highway, Baton Rouge, LA 70817

Louisiana State University at Eunice
Eunice, Louisiana
www.lsue.edu   CB code: 6386

- Public 2-year branch campus and community college
- Commuter campus in large town

General. Founded in 1964. Regionally accredited. **Enrollment:** 2,982 degree-seeking undergraduates. **Degrees:** 270 associate awarded. **Location:** 40 miles from Lafayette, 90 miles from Baton Rouge. **Calendar:** Semester, limited summer session. **Full-time faculty:** 65 total. **Part-time faculty:** 76 total.

Student profile.

Out-of-state:	1%	25 or older:	37%

Transfer out. Colleges most students transferred to 2011: Louisiana State University-Baton Rouge, University of Louisiana at Lafayette, McNeese State University, Southern University.

Basis for selection. Open admission, but selective for some programs. Test scores, school achievement record, interview considered for admission to nursing and respiratory care programs. **Home schooled:** Transcript of courses and grades required. Applicants must be from nationally recognized program from accredited agency and have GED or ACT score equal to or greater than current state average.

2011-2012 Annual costs. Tuition/fees: $2,756; $7,220 out-of-state. Room/board: $8,236. Books/supplies: $1,300.

Financial aid. Need-based: Need-based aid available for part-time students. Work-study available nights, weekends and for part-time students.

Application procedures. Admission: Closing date 8/25. $25 fee. Admission notification on a rolling basis. **Financial aid:** Priority date 6/1; no closing date. FAFSA, institutional form required. Applicants notified on a rolling basis starting 4/1; must reply within 2 week(s) of notification.

Academics. Special study options: Distance learning, dual enrollment of high school students, honors, independent study, liberal arts/career combination. Bachelor's degree programs available on campus. License preparation in nursing, physical therapy. **Credit/placement by examination:** AP, CLEP, institutional tests. 30 credit hours maximum toward associate degree. **Support services:** Learning center, remedial instruction, study skills assistance, tutoring.

Majors. Business: General, administrative services. **Computer sciences:** General. **Education:** Early childhood. **Health services:** Licensed practical nurse, medical radiologic technology/radiation therapy, respiratory therapy technology. **Liberal arts:** Arts/sciences. **Protective services:** Criminal justice, fire safety technology.

Computing on campus. 150 workstations in library, computer center. Commuter students can connect to campus network. Online course registration, helpline available.

Student life. Freshman orientation: Available, $15 fee. Preregistration for classes offered. **Activities:** Drama, student government, student newspaper, Circle-K, Baptist collegiate ministry, Newman Club, Rotoract, African American student alliance, Students in Free Enterprise, Catholic student center.

Athletics. NJCAA. **Intercollegiate:** Baseball M, basketball W. **Intramural:** Baseball M, basketball, football (non-tackle) M, softball W, tennis W, volleyball. **Team name:** Bengals.

Student services. Adult student services, chaplain/spiritual director, career counseling, financial aid counseling, health services, personal counseling, placement for graduates, veterans' counselor. **Physically disabled:** Services for visually, hearing impaired. **Transfer:** Transfer adviser, college fairs on campus for students transferring to 4-year colleges.

Contact. E-mail: rryder@lsue.edu
Phone: (337) 550-1305 Toll-free number: (888) 367-5783
Fax: (337) 550-1306
Admissions Director, Louisiana State University at Eunice, Box 1129, Eunice, LA 70535

Nunez Community College
Chalmette, Louisiana   CB member
www.nunez.edu   CB code: 0295

- Public 2-year community and technical college
- Commuter campus in large town

General. Founded in 1992. Regionally accredited. **Enrollment:** 1,561 degree-seeking undergraduates; 855 non-degree-seeking students. **Degrees:** 120 associate awarded. **Location:** 11 miles from New Orleans. **Calendar:** Semester, limited summer session. **Full-time faculty:** 38 total; 13% minority, 58% women. **Part-time faculty:** 43 total; 33% minority, 40% women. **Class size:** 52% < 20, 46% 20-39, 1% 40-49, 1% 50-99. **Special facilities:** Methanol plant for industrial/process technology students.

Student profile. Among degree-seeking undergraduates, 287 enrolled as first-time, first-year students.

Part-time:	40%	Hispanic American:	3%
Women:	68%	Native American:	1%
African American:	46%	25 or older:	29%
Asian American:	1%		

Transfer out. Colleges most students transferred to 2011: University of New Orleans, Southern University of New Orleans, Louisiana State University-Baton Rouge, Our Lady of Holy Cross College, Loyola University of New Orleans.

Basis for selection. Open admission, but selective for some programs. Additional requirements for Practical Nursing, Emergency Medical Technician and Associate of Science in Teaching (Grades 1-5).

2011-2012 Annual costs. Tuition/fees: $2,280; $5,122 out-of-state. Books/supplies: $1,800. Personal expenses: $1,819.

2011-2012 Financial aid. Need-based: 135 full-time freshmen applied for aid; 103 were judged to have need; 97 of these received aid. Average need met was 24%. Average scholarship/grant was $2,319; average loan $1,205. 87% of total undergraduate aid awarded as scholarships/grants, 13% as loans/jobs. Need-based aid available for part-time students. Work-study available nights, weekends and for part-time students. **Additional information:** Pell Grants, Stafford Loans, campus work-study, and tuition waiver scholarships available. Louisiana National Guard tuition exemption, teacher tuition exemption, dependents of injured fire-police tuition waivers available.

Application procedures. Admission: Priority date 8/1; no deadline. $10 fee. Application must be submitted on paper. Admission notification on a rolling basis. **Financial aid:** Priority date 6/1, closing date 8/1. FAFSA required.

Academics. Special study options: Cooperative education, cross-registration, distance learning, double major, dual enrollment of high school students, honors, independent study, internships, student-designed major. License preparation in nursing, paramedic. **Credit/placement by examination:** AP, CLEP, institutional tests. 24 credit hours maximum toward associate

degree. **Support services:** Learning center, reduced course load, remedial instruction, study skills assistance, tutoring.

Majors. Business: General. **Computer sciences:** Computer science, information systems. **Education:** General. **Health services:** Office admin. **Work/family studies:** Child care service.

Most popular majors. Business/marketing 10%, education 12%, health sciences 8%, liberal arts 28%, trade and industry 29%.

Computing on campus. 75 workstations in library, computer center, student center. Online library, helpline, wireless network available.

Student life. Freshman orientation: Mandatory. Preregistration for classes offered. Two-hour orientation offered during registration period. **Activities:** Concert band, drama, student government, student newspaper.

Athletics. Team name: Pelicans.

Student services. Career counseling, financial aid counseling, personal counseling, placement for graduates, veterans' counselor. **Physically disabled:** Services for visually, hearing impaired. **Transfer:** Transfer adviser, college fairs on campus for students transferring to 4-year colleges.

Contact. E-mail: bmaillet@nunez.edu
Phone: (504) 278-6467 Fax: (504) 278-6487
Becky Maillet, Director of Admissions and Registration, Nunez Community College, 3710 Paris Road, Chalmette, LA 70043

Remington College: Baton Rouge
Baton Rouge, Louisiana
www.remingtoncollege.edu/batonrouge/   CB code: 3428

- For-profit 2-year technical college
- Commuter campus in large city
- Interview required

General. Regionally accredited; also accredited by ACCSC. **Enrollment:** 409 degree-seeking undergraduates. **Degrees:** 54 associate awarded. **Calendar:** Quarter. **Full-time faculty:** 20 total. **Part-time faculty:** 7 total.

Basis for selection. Open admission, but selective for some programs.

Financial aid. All financial aid based on need. Work-study available nights, weekends and for part-time students.

Application procedures. Admission: No deadline. $50 fee. Admission notification on a rolling basis. **Financial aid:** No deadline. FAFSA required. Applicants notified on a rolling basis; must reply within 1 week(s) of notification.

Academics. Special study options: Liberal arts/career combination. **Credit/placement by examination:** AP, CLEP. **Support services:** Tutoring.

Majors. Computer sciences: General, information systems, LAN/WAN management.

Computing on campus. PC or laptop required.

Student life. Freshman orientation: Mandatory. Preregistration for classes offered. **Activities:** Student government.

Student services. Financial aid counseling, placement for graduates.

Contact. Phone: (225) 922-3990 Fax: (225) 922-6569
Monica Butler-Johnson, Director of Admissions, Remington College: Baton Rouge, 10551 Coursey Boulevard, Baton Rouge, LA 70816

Remington College: Lafayette
Lafayette, Louisiana
www.remingtoncollege.edu/lafayette/   CB code: 7117

- For-profit 2-year junior college
- Commuter campus in small city
- Interview required

General. Founded in 1940. Regionally accredited; also accredited by ACCSC. **Enrollment:** 420 degree-seeking undergraduates. **Degrees:** 51 associate awarded. **Location:** 50 miles from Baton Rouge. **Calendar:** Quarter, extensive summer session. **Full-time faculty:** 19 total. **Part-time faculty:** 10 total.

Basis for selection. Open admission, but selective for some programs. **Home schooled:** State high school equivalency certificate required.

Financial aid. All financial aid based on need. Work-study available nights, weekends and for part-time students.

Application procedures. Admission: No deadline. $50 fee. Application must be submitted on paper. Admission notification on a rolling basis. **Financial aid:** No deadline. FAFSA, institutional form required.

Academics. Laptop computer provided to each student. **Special study options:** Accelerated study, independent study, liberal arts/career combination. **Credit/placement by examination:** AP, CLEP. **Support services:** GED preparation, tutoring.

Majors. Business: Business admin. **Computer sciences:** General. **Protective services:** Law enforcement admin.

Computing on campus. 110 workstations in library, computer center. Online library, helpline, repair service available.

Student life. Freshman orientation: Mandatory. Preregistration for classes offered. **Activities:** National Vocational Technical Society (associate degree honors society), Nightingale Medical Honor Society (diploma honors society).

Student services. Student employment services, financial aid counseling, placement for graduates. **Transfer:** Pre-admission transcript evaluation for new students.

Contact. E-mail: admissions@remingtoncollege.edu
Phone: (337) 981-4010 Fax: (337) 983-7130
Joseph Howanski, Director of Admissions, Remington College: Lafayette, 303 Rue Louis XIV, Lafayette, LA 70508

Remington College: Shreveport
Shreveport, Louisiana
www.remingtoncollege.edu/shreveport/

- For-profit 2-year technical college
- Small city

General. Regionally accredited; also accredited by ACCSC. **Enrollment:** 445 degree-seeking undergraduates. **Degrees:** 51 associate awarded. **Calendar:** Differs by program. **Full-time faculty:** 28 total. **Part-time faculty:** 5 total.

Basis for selection. Open admission, but selective for some programs.

Financial aid. Need-based: Work-study available nights, weekends and for part-time students.

Application procedures. Admission: No deadline. $50 fee. **Financial aid:** No deadline.

Academics. Credit/placement by examination: AP, CLEP.

Majors. Business: Business admin. **Protective services:** Law enforcement admin.

Contact. E-mail: admissions@remingtoncollege.edu
Jason Stanley, Director of Admissions, Remington College: Shreveport, 2106 Bert Kouns Industrial Loop, Shreveport, LA 71118

River Parishes Community College
Sorrento, Louisiana
www.rpcc.edu

- Public 2-year community college
- Commuter campus in rural community

General. Regionally accredited. **Enrollment:** 1,827 degree-seeking undergraduates. **Degrees:** 108 associate awarded. **Location:** 20 miles from Baton Rouge, 40 miles from New Orleans. **Calendar:** Semester, extensive summer session. **Full-time faculty:** 48 total. **Part-time faculty:** 51 total.

Student profile.

Out-of-state:	1%	**25 or older:**	27%

Basis for selection. Open admission, but selective for some programs. **Home schooled:** Transcript of courses and grades required.

2011-2012 Annual costs. Tuition/fees: $2,472; $5,400 out-of-state. Books/supplies: $1,200. Personal expenses: $1,726.

Financial aid. Need-based: Work-study available nights, weekends and for part-time students.

Application procedures. Admission: $10 fee. Admission notification on a rolling basis. **Financial aid:** Priority date 4/15; no closing date. FAFSA required. Applicants notified on a rolling basis starting 3/1.

Academics. Credit/placement by examination: AP, CLEP, SAT, ACT.

Majors. Liberal arts: Arts/sciences.

Most popular majors. Liberal arts 96%.

Computing on campus. Online library, wireless network available.

Student life. Freshman orientation: Mandatory. Preregistration for classes offered. Orientation held prior to each semester.

Student services. Personal counseling, veterans' counselor. **Physically disabled:** Services for visually, speech, hearing impaired.

Contact. Phone: (225) 675-8270 Fax: (225) 675-5478
Dianna Gilbert, Admissions Director, River Parishes Community College, PO Box 310, Sorrento, LA 70778

South Louisiana Community College
Lafayette, Louisiana
www.southlouisiana.edu   **CB code: 4521**

◆ Public 2-year community college
◆ Commuter campus in small city

General. Regionally accredited. Additional campus in New Iberia. **Enrollment:** 3,359 degree-seeking undergraduates. **Degrees:** 211 associate awarded. **Calendar:** Semester, extensive summer session. **Full-time faculty:** 58 total. **Part-time faculty:** 110 total. **Class size:** 47% < 20, 51% 20-39, 2% 40-49, less than 1% 50-99.

Student profile.

Out-of-state:	5%	25 or older:	21%

Basis for selection. Open admission, but selective for some programs. Specific admissions criteria for EMT-Paramedic, Midwifery, and Associate of Science in Teaching programs.

High school preparation. College-preparatory program recommended.

2011-2012 Annual costs. Tuition/fees: $2,602; $5,038 out-of-state. Books/supplies: $1,200. Personal expenses: $1,819.

Financial aid. Need-based: Need-based aid available for part-time students. Work-study available nights, weekends and for part-time students. **Non-need-based:** Scholarships awarded for academics, leadership, state residency.

Application procedures. Admission: Priority date 7/1; no deadline. No application fee. Application must be submitted on paper. Admission notification on a rolling basis. **Financial aid:** Priority date 5/15; no closing date. FAFSA, institutional form required.

Academics. Special study options: Cross-registration, distance learning, double major, dual enrollment of high school students, independent study, internships. **Credit/placement by examination:** AP, CLEP, IB, ACT, institutional tests. **Support services:** Learning center, remedial instruction, study skills assistance, tutoring, writing center.

Majors. Business: General. **Education:** Kindergarten/preschool. **Health services:** EMT paramedic. **Liberal arts:** Arts/sciences. **Protective services:** Criminal justice. **Work/family studies:** Child care service.

Most popular majors. Business/marketing 9%, education 39%, engineering/engineering technologies 9%, health sciences 6%, liberal arts 31%.

Computing on campus. 50 workstations in library, student center. Online library, helpline, wireless network available.

Student life. Freshman orientation: Mandatory. Preregistration for classes offered. **Activities:** Literary magazine, student government.

Student services. Career counseling, student employment services, financial aid counseling, personal counseling. **Physically disabled:** Services for

visually, speech, hearing impaired. **Transfer:** Pre-admission transcript evaluation for new students. College fairs on campus for students transferring to 4-year colleges.

Contact. E-mail: admissions@southlouisiana.edu
Phone: (337) 521-8923 Fax: (337) 262-2101
Susan Butler, Director of Admissions, South Louisiana Community College, 320 Devalcourt, Lafayette, LA 70506-4124

Southern University at Shreveport
Shreveport, Louisiana   **CB member**
www.susla.edu   **CB code: 0322**

◆ Public 2-year community college
◆ Commuter campus in small city

General. Founded in 1964. Regionally accredited. **Enrollment:** 2,599 degree-seeking undergraduates. **Degrees:** 274 associate awarded. **Calendar:** Semester, limited summer session. **Full-time faculty:** 92 total. **Part-time faculty:** 86 total.

Basis for selection. Open admission, but selective for some programs. Students may only apply to selective programs once enrolled and after general education credits are complete.

2011-2012 Annual costs. Tuition/fees: $2,996; $4,126 out-of-state. Per-credit charge: $514. Room/board: $5,114. Books/supplies: $600.

Financial aid. Need-based: Work-study available nights, weekends and for part-time students.

Application procedures. Admission: No deadline. $20 fee ($15 out-of-state). Admission notification on a rolling basis. **Financial aid:** Priority date 4/1; no closing date. FAFSA required. Applicants notified on a rolling basis.

Academics. Special study options: Cross-registration, internships. License preparation in dental hygiene, nursing, radiology. **Credit/placement by examination:** AP, CLEP, institutional tests. 3 credit hours maximum toward associate degree. **Support services:** GED preparation, remedial instruction, study skills assistance, tutoring, writing center.

Majors. Biology: General. **Business:** Accounting, banking/financial services, business admin. **Computer sciences:** General, applications programming, computer science. **Education:** Early childhood. **Health services:** Clinical lab technology, dental hygiene, medical radiologic technology/radiation therapy, medical records technology, respiratory therapy technology, surgical technology. **Liberal arts:** Arts/sciences. **Physical sciences:** Chemistry. **Protective services:** Law enforcement admin. **Social sciences:** General, sociology.

Most popular majors. Business/marketing 20%, education 9%, health sciences 41%, liberal arts 15%.

Computing on campus. 50 workstations in library, computer center. Commuter students can connect to campus network. Online course registration, online library available.

Student life. Freshman orientation: Mandatory. Preregistration for classes offered. **Activities:** Choral groups, dance, student government, student newspaper, Baptist student union, Afro-American society.

Athletics. NJCAA. **Intercollegiate:** Basketball. **Team name:** Jaguars.

Student services. Health services, personal counseling, placement for graduates, veterans' counselor.

Contact. Phone: (318) 674-3342 Fax: (318) 674-3489
Rhalanda Jackson, Associate Vice Chancellor Enrollment Management, Southern University at Shreveport, 3050 Martin Luther King, Jr. Drive, Shreveport, LA 71107

Virginia College at Baton Rouge
Baton Rouge, Louisiana
www.batonrouge.vc.edu

◆ For-profit 2-year health science and career college
◆ Very large city

General. Regionally accredited; also accredited by ACICS. **Enrollment:** 900 degree-seeking undergraduates. **Calendar:** Quarter.

Basis for selection. Open admission.

Financial aid. Need-based: Work-study available nights, weekends and for part-time students.

Application procedures. Admission: $100 fee.

Academics. Credit/placement by examination: AP, CLEP.

Majors. Business: Office management. **Health services:** Massage therapy, medical records admin, office admin, surgical technology.

Contact. E-mail: batonrouge.info@vc.edu
Phone: (225) 236-3900
Virginia College at Baton Rouge, 9501 Cortana Place, Baton Rouge, LA 70815

Maine

Beal College
Bangor, Maine
www.bealcollege.edu   CB code: 3114

▶ For-profit 2-year junior and career college
▶ Commuter campus in large town

General. Founded in 1891. Accredited by ACICS. **Enrollment:** 364 degree-seeking undergraduates. **Degrees:** 105 associate awarded. **Location:** 250 miles from Boston. **Calendar:** Six 8-week modules per year. Extensive summer session. **Full-time faculty:** 7 total. **Part-time faculty:** 20 total. **Class size:** 59% < 20, 41% 20-39.

Basis for selection. Open admission. Interview recommended. **Home schooled:** Students who earned high school diploma through home school education must provide passing GED scores.

High school preparation. Recommended units include English 4, mathematics 4 and science 1.

2011-2012 Annual costs. Tuition/fees: $7,040. Per-credit charge: $187. Books/supplies: $1,200. Personal expenses: $700.

Financial aid. Need-based: Work-study available nights, weekends and for part-time students.

Application procedures. Admission: No deadline. $30 fee, may be waived for applicants with need. Admission notification on a rolling basis. **Financial aid:** No deadline. FAFSA, institutional form required. Applicants notified on a rolling basis starting 6/15; must reply within 2 week(s) of notification.

Academics. Students in medical assisting program must complete 160-hour practicum. **Special study options:** Accelerated study, double major, independent study. Externships. **Credit/placement by examination:** AP, CLEP, institutional tests. 30 credit hours maximum toward associate degree. **Support services:** Tutoring.

Majors. Business: Accounting, administrative services, business admin, office management, sales/distribution, tourism promotion. **Education:** Early childhood. **Health services:** Medical assistant, medical secretary. **Protective services:** Police science. **Work/family studies:** Child care service, family/community services.

Computing on campus. 45 workstations in library, computer center. Wireless network available.

Student life. Freshman orientation: Available. Preregistration for classes offered.

Student services. Adult student services, career counseling, student employment services, placement for graduates, veterans' counselor. **Transfer:** Pre-admission transcript evaluation for new students.

Contact. E-mail: admissions@bealcollege.edu
Phone: (207) 947-4591 Fax: (207) 947-0208
Erin Leighton, Director of Admissions, Beal College, 99 Farm Road, Bangor, ME 04401

Central Maine Community College
Auburn, Maine   CB member
www.cmcc.edu   CB code: 3309

▶ Public 2-year community and technical college
▶ Commuter campus in small city

General. Founded in 1964. Regionally accredited. **Enrollment:** 2,456 degree-seeking undergraduates. **Degrees:** 441 associate awarded. **Location:** One mile from downtown. **Calendar:** Semester, limited summer session. **Full-time faculty:** 54 total. **Part-time faculty:** 174 total. **Partnerships:** Formal partnership with Verizon Telecommunications Technology program.

Student profile.

Out-of-state: 2%   Live on campus: 13%
25 or older: 32%

Transfer out. Colleges most students transferred to 2011: University of Maine System.

Basis for selection. Open admission, but selective for some programs. Special requirements for nursing and radiologic technology. Many other academic programs have specific academic prerequisites but are not selective in terms of admission to the program. **Home schooled:** Transcript of courses and grades required. A copy of the state department of education correspondence granting approval of homeschooling program and the most recent teacher certification recognizing student's grade level and/or appropriate test results required. **Learning Disabled:** Applicants with documented disabilities should contact the college's disability coordinator.

High school preparation. Recommended units include English 4, mathematics 2, social studies 1, history 1 and science 2.

2011-2012 Annual costs. Tuition/fees: $3,324; $5,904 out-of-state. Per-credit charge: $86 in-state; $172 out-of-state. Additional lab and technology fees may apply to specific programs and courses. Room/board: $7,976. Books/supplies: $1,200. Personal expenses: $1,400.

Financial aid. All financial aid based on need. Need-based aid available for part-time students. Work-study available nights, weekends and for part-time students. **Additional information:** Tuition and/or fee waivers may be available to orphans, Native Americans, fire fighters, police, disabled veterans, dependents or survivors of veterans killed in line of duty.

Application procedures. Admission: No deadline. $20 fee, may be waived for applicants with need. Admission notification on a rolling basis beginning on or about 10/1. **Financial aid:** Priority date 5/8; no closing date. FAFSA, institutional form required. Applicants notified on a rolling basis starting 3/15; must reply within 2 week(s) of notification.

Academics. Special study options: Distance learning, ESL, independent study, internships, liberal arts/career combination. License preparation in nursing, radiology, real estate. **Credit/placement by examination:** AP, CLEP, IB, institutional tests. Up to 75% of credits may meet curriculum requirements; 25% of credits must be completed in residence. **Support services:** Learning center, reduced course load, remedial instruction, study skills assistance, tutoring, writing center.

Majors. Business: Accounting, business admin, hospitality admin, office technology. **Communications technology:** Graphic/printing. **Computer sciences:** Data entry, LAN/WAN management. **Education:** Early childhood, teacher assistance. **Health services:** Medical assistant, medical radiologic technology/radiation therapy, nursing (RN). **Liberal arts:** Arts/sciences. **Protective services:** Law enforcement admin.

Most popular majors. Business/marketing 24%, engineering/engineering technologies 9%, family/consumer sciences 6%, health sciences 23%, liberal arts 11%, trade and industry 22%.

Computing on campus. 400 workstations in library, computer center. Dormitories wired for high-speed internet access and linked to campus network. Commuter students can connect to campus network. Online library, helpline, wireless network available.

Student life. Freshman orientation: Available. Preregistration for classes offered. **Policies:** Student code of conduct observed. **Housing:** Single-sex dorms, apartments available. $50 nonrefundable deposit. **Activities:** Drama, literary magazine, student government.

Athletics. USCAA. **Intercollegiate:** Baseball M, basketball. **Intramural:** Basketball, skiing. **Team name:** Mustangs.

Student services. Career counseling, services for economically disadvantaged, student employment services, financial aid counseling, personal counseling, placement for graduates, women's services. **Physically disabled:** Services for visually, speech, hearing impaired. **Transfer:** Transfer adviser, college fairs on campus for students transferring to 4-year colleges.

Contact. E-mail: enroll@cmcc.edu
Phone: (207) 755-5273 Toll-free number: (800) 891-2002 ext. 273
Fax: (207) 755-5493
Betsy Libby, Director of Admissions, Central Maine Community College, 1250 Turner Street, Auburn, ME 04210

Central Maine Medical Center College of Nursing and Health Professions

Lewiston, Maine   **CB member**
www.cmmccollege.edu   **CB code: 3302**

- Private 2-year health science and nursing college
- Commuter campus in large town
- SAT or ACT (ACT writing optional), application essay required

General. Founded in 1891. Regionally accredited. **Enrollment:** 180 degree-seeking undergraduates. **Degrees:** 53 associate awarded. **Location:** 35 miles from Portland. **Calendar:** Semester, limited summer session. **Full-time faculty:** 19 total; 5% have terminal degrees, 90% women. **Part-time faculty:** 4 total; 25% have terminal degrees, 100% women.

Basis for selection. Test scores required. Essay, academic ability very important. SAT or ACT may be waived if applicant has completed 12 academic college credits with minimum grade of 2.0. Interview required for Medical Imaging programs. **Home schooled:** High school diploma or GED required.

High school preparation. College-preparatory program recommended. Required units include mathematics 2 and science 2.

2011-2012 Annual costs. Tuition/fees: $8,530. Per-credit charge: $230. Room only: $1,960.

Financial aid. All financial aid based on need. Need-based aid available for part-time students. Work-study available nights, weekends and for part-time students.

Application procedures. Admission: Closing date 1/15 (receipt date). $40 fee, may be waived for applicants with need. Application must be submitted on paper. Admission notification by 3/15. Must reply by 5/1. **Financial aid:** Closing date 7/1. FAFSA, institutional form required. Applicants notified on a rolling basis starting 4/1; must reply within 2 week(s) of notification.

Academics. Special study options: Distance learning, internships. License preparation in nursing, radiology. **Credit/placement by examination:** AP, CLEP. 15 credit hours maximum toward associate degree. **Support services:** Learning center, remedial instruction, study skills assistance, tutoring.

Majors. Health services: Nursing (RN), radiologic technology/medical imaging.

Computing on campus. PC or laptop required. 20 workstations in computer center. Wireless network available.

Student life. Freshman orientation: Mandatory. Preregistration for classes offered. One-day program held in June. **Policies:** Entire campus is smoke-free; zero tolerance for alcohol, drugs, weapons. **Housing:** Coed dorms, apartments, wellness housing available. $60 fully refundable deposit, deadline 8/15. Single rooms available at extra cost. **Activities:** Student government.

Student services. Financial aid counseling, health services, personal counseling, veterans' counselor. **Transfer:** Pre-admission transcript evaluation for new students.

Contact. E-mail: jenisod@cmhc.org
Phone: (207) 795-2843 Fax: (207) 795-2849
Jacqueline Collins, Admissions Committee Chairperson, Central Maine Medical Center College of Nursing and Health Professions, 70 Middle Street, Lewiston, ME 04240

Eastern Maine Community College

Bangor, Maine   **CB member**
www.emcc.edu   **CB code: 3372**

- Public 2-year community and technical college
- Commuter campus in large town
- Application essay required

General. Founded in 1966. Regionally accredited. **Enrollment:** 1,904 degree-seeking undergraduates. **Degrees:** 345 associate awarded. **ROTC:** Army. **Location:** 250 miles from Boston, 130 miles from Portland. **Calendar:** Semester, limited summer session. **Full-time faculty:** 54 total. **Part-time faculty:** 115 total.

Student profile. Among degree-seeking undergraduates, 43% enrolled in a transfer program, 57% enrolled in a vocational program, 1% already have a bachelor's degree or higher.

Transfer out. 14% of students enrolled in the transfer program go on to 4-year colleges. **Colleges most students transferred to 2011:** University of Maine-Orono, Husson College.

Basis for selection. Open admission, but selective for some programs. School record, recommendations, and essays most important. Entrance requirements vary by program. SAT required for engineering technologies, registered nursing, and medical radiography applicants; score report preferred by April 30. Interview recommended for some majors.

High school preparation. Recommended units include English 4, mathematics 3 and science 2. Academic requirements vary by program.

2011-2012 Annual costs. Tuition/fees: $3,519; $6,099 out-of-state. Per-credit charge: $86 in-state; $172 out-of-state. Additional lab and technology fees may apply to specific programs and courses. Room/board: $6,490. Books/supplies: $800. Personal expenses: $1,500.

Financial aid. All financial aid based on need. Need-based aid available for part-time students. Work-study available nights, weekends and for part-time students.

Application procedures. Admission: No deadline. $20 fee, may be waived for applicants with need. Admission notification on a rolling basis. Must reply by May 1 or within 4 week(s) if notified thereafter. Deposit refundable up to 60 days before program begins. **Financial aid:** Priority date 5/1; no closing date. FAFSA, institutional form required. Applicants notified on a rolling basis starting 5/1; must reply within 3 week(s) of notification.

Academics. Special study options: Distance learning, dual enrollment of high school students, ESL, external degree, internships, student-designed major, study abroad. **Credit/placement by examination:** AP, CLEP, institutional tests. Maximum of 40% of required credit total in student's field of study may be obtained through credit by examination. **Support services:** Learning center, reduced course load, remedial instruction, study skills assistance, tutoring.

Majors. Business: General, administrative services, banking/financial services, business admin, office management. **Education:** Early childhood. **General:** Food science. **Health services:** Medical radiologic technology/radiation therapy, nursing (RN), preop/surgical nursing. **Liberal arts:** Arts/sciences. **Protective services:** Firefighting.

Most popular majors. Business/marketing 36%, computer/information sciences 17%, health sciences 22%, interdisciplinary studies 11%, personal/culinary services 14%.

Computing on campus. 150 workstations in dormitories, library, computer center. Dormitories wired for high-speed internet access. Commuter students can connect to campus network. Online course registration, online library, helpline, wireless network available.

Student life. Freshman orientation: Available. Preregistration for classes offered. **Housing:** Coed dorms available. $50 nonrefundable deposit, deadline 7/1. **Activities:** Student government, student newspaper, Student Veterans Association, International Club, Phi Theta Kappa.

Athletics. Intercollegiate: Basketball, golf, soccer. **Intramural:** Badminton, basketball, bowling, cheerleading, ice hockey M, skiing, softball, table tennis, volleyball. **Team name:** Golden Eagles.

Student services. Adult student services, alcohol/substance abuse counseling, career counseling, student employment services, financial aid counseling, health services, on-campus daycare, personal counseling, placement for graduates, veterans' counselor.

Contact. E-mail: admissions@emcc.edu
Phone: (207) 974-4680 Toll-free number: (800) 286-9357
Fax: (207) 974-4683
Elizabeth Russell, Director of Admissions, Eastern Maine Community College, 354 Hogan Road, Bangor, ME 04401

Kaplan University: South Portland

South Portland, Maine
www.kaplanuniversity.edu   **CB code: 0688**

- For-profit 2-year business and junior college
- Commuter campus in small city
- Interview required

General. Founded in 1966. Regionally accredited. **Enrollment:** 389 degree-seeking undergraduates. **Degrees:** 290 associate awarded. **Location:** 115 miles from Boston. **Calendar:** Quarter, extensive summer session. **Full-time faculty:** 7 total. **Part-time faculty:** 41 total. **Class size:** 98% < 20, 2% 20-39.

Student profile.

Out-of-state:	4%	25 or older:	90%

Transfer out. Colleges most students transferred to 2011: University of Southern Maine.

Basis for selection. Open admission, but selective for some programs. Students must take entrance assessment and receive a minimum score to gain entrance. **Home schooled:** Transcript of courses and grades, state high school equivalency certificate, interview required. **Learning Disabled:** Must submit documentation to the Director of the Academic Center.

2011-2012 Annual costs. Estimated tuition and fees ranges for entire programs as of July 2011: associate degree programs, $20,700; bachelor's degree programs, $41,400; does not include books and supplies, which vary by program. All costs subject to change at any time. Books/supplies: $1,250.

Financial aid. All financial aid based on need. Work-study available nights, weekends and for part-time students. **Additional information:** Work-study positions available.

Application procedures. Admission: No deadline. $20 fee. **Financial aid:** No deadline. FAFSA required. Applicants notified on a rolling basis.

Academics. Special study options: Accelerated study, cooperative education, distance learning, double major, independent study, internships, liberal arts/career combination. **Credit/placement by examination:** AP, CLEP, institutional tests. 12 credit hours maximum toward associate degree. **Support services:** Learning center, reduced course load, remedial instruction, study skills assistance, tutoring, writing center.

Majors. Business: Accounting, administrative services, business admin, hospitality admin, hospitality/recreation, office management, office technology, office/clerical, tourism promotion, tourism/travel. **Computer sciences:** General, computer science, data processing, programming. **Education:** Early childhood. **Health services:** Medical assistant, medical records admin, medical records technology, medical secretary, medical transcription. **Protective services:** Criminal justice, law enforcement admin, police science. **Work/family studies:** Child care management.

Computing on campus. 90 workstations in library, computer center, student center. Helpline, wireless network available.

Student life. Freshman orientation: Mandatory, $20 fee. Preregistration for classes offered. **Activities:** Student newspaper, Phi Beta Lambda, C.O.P.S. (criminal justice), APPEAL paralegal professionals, college student advisors.

Student services. Adult student services, career counseling, student employment services, financial aid counseling, personal counseling, placement for graduates. **Physically disabled:** Services for hearing impaired. **Transfer:** Pre-admission transcript evaluation for new students.

Contact. E-mail: enroll@andovercollege.edu
Phone: (207) 774-6126 Toll-free number: (800) 639-3110
Fax: (207) 774-1715
Craig MacMunn, Assistant Director of Admissions, Kaplan University: South Portland, 265 Western Avenue, South Portland, ME 04106

Kennebec Valley Community College
Fairfield, Maine
www.kvcc.me.edu   **CB code: 3475**

‣ Public 2-year community and technical college
‣ Commuter campus in small town

General. Founded in 1969. Regionally accredited. **Enrollment:** 1,746 degree-seeking undergraduates; 783 non-degree-seeking students. **Degrees:** 319 associate awarded. **Location:** 24 miles from Augusta, 75 miles from Portland. **Calendar:** Semester, limited summer session. **Full-time faculty:** 40 total; 5% have terminal degrees, 5% minority, 65% women. **Part-time faculty:** 117 total; 5% have terminal degrees, 2% minority, 51% women. **Class size:** 71% < 20, 29% 20-39, less than 1% 40-49.

Student profile. Among degree-seeking undergraduates, 34% enrolled in a transfer program, 66% enrolled in a vocational program, 318 enrolled as first-time, first-year students.

Part-time:	55%	Asian American:	1%
Women:	67%	Hispanic American:	1%
African American:	1%	Native American:	1%

Basis for selection. Open admission, but selective for some programs. Special requirements for nursing and allied health programs. **Adult students:** SAT/ACT scores not required. **Home schooled:** Transcript of courses and grades required.

2011-2012 Annual costs. Tuition/fees: $3,174; $5,754 out-of-state. Per-credit charge: $86 in-state; $172 out-of-state. Additional lab and technology fees apply to specific programs and courses. Books/supplies: $1,098.

2010-2011 Financial aid. All financial aid based on need. 338 full-time freshmen applied for aid; 307 were judged to have need; 294 of these received aid. Average need met was 53%. Average scholarship/grant was $5,108; average loan $2,792. 68% of total undergraduate aid awarded as scholarships/grants, 32% as loans/jobs. Need-based aid available for part-time students. Work-study available nights, weekends and for part-time students.

Application procedures. Admission: No deadline. $20 fee, may be waived for applicants with need. Admission notification on a rolling basis. Only allied health programs have application deadline. **Financial aid:** Priority date 4/1; no closing date. FAFSA, institutional form required. Applicants notified on a rolling basis starting 5/1.

Academics. Special study options: Cooperative education, cross-registration, distance learning, dual enrollment of high school students, internships, liberal arts/career combination. License preparation in nursing, occupational therapy, paramedic, physical therapy, radiology. **Credit/placement by examination:** AP, CLEP. **Support services:** Learning center, reduced course load, remedial instruction, study skills assistance, tutoring, writing center.

Majors. Biology: General. **Business:** Accounting technology, management information systems, marketing. **Conservation:** Forest technology. **Education:** Teacher assistance. **Health services:** EMT paramedic, medical assistant, medical records technology, nursing (RN), occupational therapy assistant, physical therapy assistant, radiologic technology/medical imaging, respiratory therapy technology. **Liberal arts:** Arts/sciences. **Work/family studies:** Child development.

Most popular majors. Business/marketing 16%, health sciences 53%, liberal arts 11%, trade and industry 7%.

Computing on campus. 400 workstations in library, computer center, student center. Commuter students can connect to campus network. Online course registration, online library, helpline, wireless network available.

Student life. Freshman orientation: Mandatory, $30 fee. Preregistration for classes offered. **Activities:** Choral groups, student government.

Athletics. Intramural: Basketball, bowling, cross-country, football (non-tackle), golf, softball, volleyball. **Team name:** Lynx.

Student services. Career counseling, services for economically disadvantaged, student employment services, financial aid counseling, on-campus daycare, personal counseling, placement for graduates. **Transfer:** Transfer center, transfer adviser, college fairs on campus for students transferring to 4-year colleges.

Contact. E-mail: jbourgoin@kvcc.me.edu
Phone: (207) 453-5131 Toll-free number: (800) 528-5882
Fax: (207) 453-5010
Jim Bourgoin, Director of Admissions, Kennebec Valley Community College, 92 Western Avenue, Fairfield, ME 04937-1367

Landing School of Boatbuilding and Design
Kennebunkport, Maine
www.landingschool.edu

‣ Private 2-year career college
‣ Commuter campus in small town

General. Regionally accredited; also accredited by ACCSC. **Enrollment:** 68 degree-seeking undergraduates. **Degrees:** 4 associate awarded. **Location:** 20 miles from Portland, 30 miles from Portsmouth, NH. **Calendar:** Semester. **Full-time faculty:** 10 total.

Student profile. Among degree-seeking undergraduates, 100% enrolled in a vocational program, 12 enrolled as first-time, first-year students.

Basis for selection. Open admission, but selective for some programs.

2011-2012 Annual costs. Tuition/fees: $18,000. Fees vary by program $500-$1,835. Books/supplies: $1,700. Personal expenses: $2,050.

2011-2012 Financial aid. All financial aid based on need. 60% of total undergraduate aid awarded as scholarships/grants, 40% as loans/jobs. Work-study available nights, weekends and for part-time students.

Application procedures. Admission: No deadline. No application fee. Admission notification on a rolling basis. **Financial aid:** Priority date 4/1; no closing date. FAFSA required. Applicants notified on a rolling basis starting 3/1; must reply within 3 week(s) of notification.

Academics. Credit/placement by examination: AP, CLEP.

Computing on campus. 8 workstations in library. Wireless network available.

Contact. E-mail: info@landingschool.edu
Phone: (207) 985-7976
Kristin Potter, Admissions Representative, Landing School of Boatbuilding and Design, 286 River Road, Arundel, ME 04046

Northern Maine Community College
Presque Isle, Maine
www.nmcc.edu
CB code: 3631

- Public 2-year community and technical college
- Commuter campus in small town
- Application essay, interview required

General. Founded in 1961. Regionally accredited. **Enrollment:** 988 degree-seeking undergraduates. **Degrees:** 197 associate awarded. **Location:** 165 miles from Bangor. **Calendar:** Semester, limited summer session. **Full-time faculty:** 44 total. **Part-time faculty:** 54 total.

Basis for selection. School achievement record and test scores important.

High school preparation. Required units include English 4 and mathematics 2.

2011-2012 Annual costs. Tuition/fees: $3,268; $5,848 out-of-state. Per-credit charge: $86 in-state; $172 out-of-state. Additional lab and technology fees may apply to specific programs and courses. Room/board: $6,260. Books/supplies: $1,400. Personal expenses: $1,200.

Financial aid. Need-based: Need-based aid available for part-time students. Work-study available nights, weekends and for part-time students.

Application procedures. Admission: No deadline. $20 fee, may be waived for applicants with need. Admission notification on a rolling basis. **Financial aid:** No deadline. FAFSA, institutional form required. Applicants notified on a rolling basis starting 4/15; must reply within 2 week(s) of notification.

Academics. Special study options: Cross-registration, double major, internships, liberal arts/career combination. **Credit/placement by examination:** AP, CLEP. 15 credit hours maximum toward associate degree. **Support services:** Learning center, pre-admission summer program, reduced course load, remedial instruction, tutoring.

Majors. Business: Accounting, administrative services, business admin, management information systems, office management, office technology, operations. **Computer sciences:** Applications programming, data processing, programming. **Education:** Early childhood. **General:** Business. **Health services:** Medical secretary, nursing (RN).

Computing on campus. Commuter students can connect to campus network.

Student life. Freshman orientation: Mandatory, $35 fee. Preregistration for classes offered. Held both in fall and spring semester. **Housing:** Coed dorms, apartments available. $25 deposit. **Activities:** Student government, student newspaper.

Athletics. Intercollegiate: Basketball M, golf, ice hockey, soccer. **Intramural:** Archery, badminton, baseball M, basketball M, racquetball, softball, table tennis, tennis, volleyball. **Team name:** Falcons.

Student services. Adult student services, alcohol/substance abuse counseling, career counseling, student employment services, financial aid counseling, health services, personal counseling, placement for graduates, veterans' counselor. **Transfer:** Transfer adviser for students transferring to 4-year colleges.

Contact. E-mail: nemcclus@nmcc.edu
Phone: (207) 768-2785 Toll-free number: (800) 535-6682
Fax: (207) 768-2848
Eugene McCluskey, Director of Admissions, Northern Maine Community College, 33 Edgemont Drive, Presque Isle, ME 04769

Southern Maine Community College
South Portland, Maine
CB member
www.smccme.edu
CB code: 3535

- Public 2-year community and technical college
- Commuter campus in large town

General. Founded in 1946. Regionally accredited. **Enrollment:** 6,182 degree-seeking undergraduates; 1,300 non-degree-seeking students. **Degrees:** 687 associate awarded. **Location:** 3 miles from Portland, 120 miles from Boston. **Calendar:** Semester, extensive summer session. **Full-time faculty:** 109 total. **Part-time faculty:** 392 total.

Student profile. Among degree-seeking undergraduates, 1,401 enrolled as first-time, first-year students.

Part-time:	47%	Asian American:	2%
Women:	52%	Hispanic American:	2%
African American:	5%	Native American:	1%

Basis for selection. Open admission, but selective for some programs. Special requirements for allied health science programs. Must have prerequisites completed prior to being accepted into the programs.

High school preparation. College-preparatory program recommended. Recommended units include English 4, mathematics 3, science 1 (laboratory 1). Academic subject requirements vary by program.

2011-2012 Annual costs. Tuition/fees: $3,341; $5,921 out-of-state. Per-credit charge: $86 in-state; $172 out-of-state. Additional lab and technology fees may apply to specific programs and courses. Room/board: $8,226. Books/supplies: $1,200.

Financial aid. All financial aid based on need. Need-based aid available for part-time students. Work-study available nights, weekends and for part-time students.

Application procedures. Admission: Priority date 7/15; no deadline. $20 fee, may be waived for applicants with need. Admission notification on a rolling basis. Must reply by May 1 or within 4 week(s) if notified thereafter. **Financial aid:** Priority date 3/30; no closing date. FAFSA required. Applicants notified on a rolling basis; must reply by 5/1 or within 2 week(s) of notification.

Academics. Special study options: Cross-registration, distance learning, double major, dual enrollment of high school students, honors, independent study, internships, liberal arts/career combination. License preparation in nursing, paramedic, radiology. **Credit/placement by examination:** AP, CLEP, institutional tests. **Support services:** Learning center, reduced course load, remedial instruction, study skills assistance, tutoring.

Majors. Biology: Biotechnology, marine. **Business:** Business admin, hotel/motel admin. **Communications:** Digital media. **Education:** Early childhood. **General:** Horticulture. **Health services:** Cardiovascular technology, dietetic technician, EMT paramedic, medical assistant, medical radiologic technology/radiation therapy, nursing (RN), radiologic technology/medical imaging, respiratory therapy technology, surgical technology. **Protective services:** Firefighting, police science.

Computing on campus. 400 workstations in library, computer center, student center. Dormitories wired for high-speed internet access and linked to campus network. Commuter students can connect to campus network. Online course registration, online library, helpline, wireless network available.

Student life. Freshman orientation: Available. Preregistration for classes offered. **Housing:** Coed dorms available. $250 nonrefundable deposit. **Activities:** Choral groups, international student organizations, literary magazine, student government, student newspaper.

Athletics. USCAA. Intercollegiate: Baseball M, basketball, golf, soccer, softball W. **Intramural:** Basketball, ice hockey M, soccer, volleyball. **Team name:** Seawolves.

Student services. Career counseling, student employment services, financial aid counseling, on-campus daycare, personal counseling, placement for graduates, veterans' counselor. **Physically disabled:** Services for visually, speech, hearing impaired. **Transfer:** Pre-admission transcript evaluation for new students. Transfer center, transfer adviser, college fairs on campus for students transferring to 4-year colleges.

Contact. E-mail: admissions@smccME.edu
Phone: (207) 741-5800 Toll-free number: (877) 282-2182
Fax: (207) 741-5760
Staci Grasky, Associate Dean for Information and Enrollment Services /
Registrar, Southern Maine Community College, 2 Fort Road, South
Portland, ME 04106

Washington County Community College
Calais, Maine
www.wccc.me.edu   CB code: 3961

- Public 2-year community and technical college
- Commuter campus in small town

General. Founded in 1969. Regionally accredited. **Enrollment:** 355 degree-
seeking undergraduates. **Degrees:** 64 associate awarded. **Location:** 98 miles
from Bangor, 75 miles from St. John, Canada. **Calendar:** Semester, limited
summer session. **Full-time faculty:** 21 total; 5% have terminal degrees, 29%
women. **Part-time faculty:** 20 total.

Transfer out. Colleges most students transferred to 2011: University of
Maine at Machias, University of Maine at Augusta, Husson College.

Basis for selection. Open admission, but selective for some programs.
Algebra I required or placement in the equivalent of MAT106 on
ACCUPLACER exam for Residential and Commercial Electricity program.
Home schooled: Applicants required to take GED exam or equivalent.

High school preparation. 20 units recommended. Recommended units
include English 4, mathematics 2, social studies 1, history 2 and science 2.
Program-specific requirements apply in some areas.

2011-2012 Annual costs. Tuition/fees: $3,194; $5,774 out-of-state. Per-
credit charge: $86 in-state; $172 out-of-state. Additional lab and technology
fees may apply to specific programs and courses. Room only: $3,600. Books/
supplies: $1,900. Personal expenses: $1,669.

Financial aid. Need-based: Need-based aid available for part-time students. Work-study available nights, weekends and for part-time students.
Non-need-based: Scholarships awarded for academics.

Application procedures. Admission: Closing date 8/19 (receipt date).
$20 fee, may be waived for applicants with need. Admission notification on
a rolling basis. **Financial aid:** Priority date 4/1; no closing date. FAFSA,
institutional form required. Applicants notified on a rolling basis starting
6/1; must reply within 2 week(s) of notification.

Academics. Special study options: Cooperative education, distance learning, double major, dual enrollment of high school students, independent
study, liberal arts/career combination. Offer license preparation program in
heating and plumbing. **Credit/placement by examination:** AP, CLEP, IB.
Support services: GED preparation and test center, learning center, reduced
course load, remedial instruction, study skills assistance, tutoring, writing
center.

Majors. Business: Business admin, small business admin. **Education:** Early
childhood. **Health services:** Medical assistant. **Liberal arts:** Arts/sciences.

Computing on campus. 117 workstations in dormitories, library, computer center, student center. Dormitories wired for high-speed internet access
and linked to campus network. Helpline, wireless network available.

Student life. Freshman orientation: Mandatory. Preregistration for
classes offered. **Policies:** Drug/alcohol/tobacco free apartments. **Housing:**
Guaranteed on-campus for all undergraduates. Special housing for disabled,
apartments available. $150 fully refundable deposit. **Activities:** Drama, stu-
dent government, student senate, Skills USA, Phi Theta Kappa.

Athletics. Intercollegiate: Wrestling. **Intramural:** Baseball M, basketball,
golf, rifle, skiing, soccer, volleyball, wrestling. **Team name:** Polar Bears.

Student services. Adult student services, alcohol/substance abuse counseling, career counseling, services for economically disadvantaged, student
employment services, financial aid counseling, on-campus daycare, personal
counseling, placement for graduates, veterans' counselor. **Physically disabled:** Services for visually, speech, hearing impaired. **Transfer:** Pre-
admission transcript evaluation for new students. College fairs on campus
for students transferring to 4-year colleges.

Contact. E-mail: admissions@wccc.me.edu
Phone: (207) 454-1000 Toll-free number: (800) 210-6932
Fax: (207) 454-1092
Susan Mingo, Associate Dean for Enrollment Services, Washington
County Community College, One College Drive, Calais, ME 04619

York County Community College
Wells, Maine   **CB member**
www.yccc.edu   **CB code: 3990**

- Public 2-year community and technical college
- Commuter campus in small town

General. Regionally accredited. **Enrollment:** 1,296 degree-seeking undergraduates; 335 non-degree-seeking students. **Degrees:** 117 associate awarded.
Location: 30 miles from Portland, 75 miles from Boston, MA. **Calendar:**
Semester, extensive summer session. **Full-time faculty:** 18 total; 28% have
terminal degrees, 39% women. **Part-time faculty:** 98 total; 7% have terminal
degrees, 55% women. **Partnerships:** Agreements with Portsmouth Naval
Shipyard.

Student profile. Among degree-seeking undergraduates, 490 enrolled as
first-time, first-year students, 133 transferred in from other institutions.

Part-time:	51%	Asian American:	1%
Out-of-state:	3%	Hispanic American:	2%
Women:	65%	Native American:	1%
African American:	1%		

Transfer out. Colleges most students transferred to 2011: University of
Southern Maine, University of New England, Southern New Hampshire
University, Husson University.

Basis for selection. Open admission. **Home schooled:** Transcript of
courses and grades, state high school equivalency certificate required.

2011-2012 Annual costs. Tuition/fees: $3,186; $5,766 out-of-state. Per-
credit charge: $86 in-state; $172 out-of-state. Additional lab and technology
fees may apply to specific programs and courses. Books/supplies: $1,000.
Personal expenses: $1,000.

2010-2011 Financial aid. Need-based: 172 full-time freshmen applied
for aid; 149 were judged to have need; 140 of these received aid. Average
need met was 54%. Average scholarship/grant was $4,812; average loan
$2,824. 64% of total undergraduate aid awarded as scholarships/grants, 36%
as loans/jobs. Need-based aid available for part-time students. Work-study
available nights, weekends and for part-time students. **Non-need-based:**
Awarded to 10 full-time undergraduates, including 4 freshmen. Scholarships
awarded for academics, art, leadership.

Application procedures. Admission: No deadline. No application fee.
Financial aid: Priority date 5/1; no closing date. FAFSA required. Must
reply within 2 week(s) of notification.

Academics. Special study options: Distance learning, dual enrollment of
high school students, internships, liberal arts/career combination. License
preparation in nursing. **Credit/placement by examination:** AP, CLEP, institutional tests. 45 credit hours maximum toward associate degree. **Support
services:** Learning center, remedial instruction, study skills assistance,
tutoring, writing center.

Majors. Business: Accounting, business admin, management information
systems. **Education:** Teacher assistance. **Health services:** Medical assistant.
Protective services: Criminal justice. **Visual/performing arts:** Design.
Work/family studies: Child development.

Most popular majors. Business/marketing 22%, family/consumer sciences 6%, liberal arts 39%, visual/performing arts 11%.

Computing on campus. 160 workstations in library, computer center,
student center. Online course registration, online library, wireless network
available.

Student life. Freshman orientation: Available. Preregistration for classes
offered. **Activities:** Literary magazine, student government, student newspaper.

Athletics. Intramural: Basketball, football (non-tackle), ice hockey, soccer. **Team name:** Coyotes.

Student services. Career counseling, services for economically disadvantaged, student employment services, financial aid counseling, veterans' counselor. **Physically disabled:** Services for speech, hearing impaired. **Transfer:**
Transfer adviser, college fairs on campus for students transferring to 4-
year colleges.

Contact. E-mail: admissions@yccc.edu
Phone: (207) 216-4409 Toll-free number: (800) 580-3820
Fax: (207) 641-0837
Fred Quistgard, Director of Admissions, York County Community
College, 112 College Drive, Wells, ME 04090

Maryland

Allegany College of Maryland
Cumberland, Maryland
www.allegany.edu
CB code: 5028

▸ Public 2-year community college
▸ Commuter campus in large town

General. Founded in 1961. Regionally accredited. **Enrollment:** 3,182 degree-seeking undergraduates. **Degrees:** 603 associate awarded. **ROTC:** Army. **Location:** 150 miles from Baltimore, 150 miles from Washington, DC. **Calendar:** Semester, limited summer session. **Full-time faculty:** 115 total. **Part-time faculty:** 186 total. **Class size:** 74% < 20, 24% 20-39, 1% 40-49, less than 1% 50-99, less than 1% >100. **Special facilities:** Greenhouse, arboretum, wetlands, Appalachian Room, labyrinth and serenity garden.

Student profile.

Out-of-state:	54%	Live on campus:	7%
25 or older:	32%		

Transfer out. Colleges most students transferred to 2011: Frostburg State University, Shippensburg University, University of Pittsburgh at Johnstown.

Basis for selection. Open admission, but selective for some programs. Admission to allied health programs based on high school records, test scores.

2011-2012 Annual costs. Tuition/fees: $3,266; $5,906 out-of-district; $7,046 out-of-state. Per-credit charge: $102 in-district; $190 out-of-district; $228 out-of-state. Books/supplies: $1,200. Personal expenses: $2,041.

2011-2012 Financial aid. Need-based: Need-based aid available for part-time students. Work-study available nights, weekends and for part-time students. **Non-need-based:** Scholarships awarded for academics, athletics, leadership, state residency.

Application procedures. Admission: No deadline. No application fee. Admission notification on a rolling basis. High school and/or college transcript and placement tests in English, reading, and mathematics required. **Financial aid:** Priority date 3/1; no closing date. FAFSA, institutional form required. Applicants notified on a rolling basis starting 4/15; must reply within 2 week(s) of notification.

Academics. Special study options: Accelerated study, distance learning, double major, dual enrollment of high school students, ESL, honors, independent study, internships, liberal arts/career combination. Bachelor's degree programs available on campus. License preparation in dental hygiene, nursing, occupational therapy, physical therapy, radiology, real estate. **Credit/placement by examination:** AP, CLEP, institutional tests. 30 credit hours maximum toward associate degree. **Support services:** Learning center, reduced course load, remedial instruction, study skills assistance, tutoring.

Majors. Biology: General. **Business:** General, accounting, accounting technology, administrative services, business admin, hospitality admin, hospitality/recreation, management information systems, managerial economics, marketing. **Communications:** Communications/speech/rhetoric. **Communications technology:** General. **Computer sciences:** General, computer science, information systems. **Conservation:** Forest management. **Education:** Early childhood, elementary, health, physical, secondary. **Engineering:** General. **English:** English lit. **Foreign languages:** Spanish. **Health services:** Clinical lab technology, dental hygiene, massage therapy, medical assistant, medical radiologic technology/radiation therapy, medical secretary, medical transcription, mental health services, nursing (RN), occupational therapy assistant, physical therapy assistant, prepharmacy, respiratory therapy technology. **History:** General. **Human services:** Social work. **Liberal arts:** Arts/sciences. **Math:** General. **Parks/recreation:** Facilities management. **Physical sciences:** Chemistry, physics. **Protective services:** Police science. **Psychology:** General. **Social sciences:** General, economics, political science, sociology. **Visual/performing arts:** Art.

Most popular majors. Business/marketing 14%, health sciences 45%, liberal arts 23%.

Computing on campus. 450 workstations in library, computer center. Online course registration, online library, student web hosting, wireless network available.

Student life. Freshman orientation: Available, $4 fee. Preregistration for classes offered. **Housing:** Apartments, wellness housing available. $300 partly refundable deposit, deadline 8/26. **Activities:** Choral groups, dance, literary magazine, student government, forestry club, Older and Wiser Club, Phi Theta Kappa-Honors Society, Christian Fellowship, chess club, respiratory therapy club, dental hygiene club, medical laboratory technology club.

Athletics. NJCAA. **Intercollegiate:** Baseball M, basketball, soccer M, softball W, volleyball W. **Team name:** Trojans.

Student services. Career counseling, student employment services, financial aid counseling, on-campus daycare, personal counseling, placement for graduates, veterans' counselor, women's services. **Physically disabled:** Services for visually, speech, hearing impaired. **Transfer:** Pre-admission transcript evaluation for new students. Transfer adviser, college fairs on campus for students transferring to 4-year colleges.

Contact. E-mail: cnolan@allegany.edu
Phone: (301) 784-5199 Fax: (301) 784-5027
Cathy Nolan, Director of Admissions and Registration, Allegany College of Maryland, 12401 Willowbrook Road, SE, Cumberland, MD 21502

Anne Arundel Community College
Arnold, Maryland
www.aacc.edu
CB member
CB code: 5019

▸ Public 2-year community college
▸ Commuter campus in large town

General. Founded in 1964. Regionally accredited. 3 off-campus academic/student services centers: Fort Meade Army Education Center, Glen Burnie Town Center and Arundel Mills. Hospitality, Culinary Arts and Tourism Institute, Entrepreneurial Studies Institute. **Enrollment:** 15,335 degree-seeking undergraduates; 2,622 non-degree-seeking students. **Degrees:** 1,505 associate awarded. **ROTC:** Army, Air Force. **Location:** 20 miles from Baltimore, 8 miles from Annapolis. **Calendar:** Semester, limited summer session. **Full-time faculty:** 264 total; 38% have terminal degrees, 16% minority, 58% women. **Part-time faculty:** 804 total; 18% minority, 58% women. **Special facilities:** Off-campus workforce center at Baltimore-Washington international airport, environmental center, astronomy laboratory, center for performing arts, fine arts academic center, allied health/public services center, technology center, STEM center and cyber center.

Student profile. Among degree-seeking undergraduates, 55% enrolled in a transfer program, 30% enrolled in a vocational program, 6% already have a bachelor's degree or higher, 3,084 enrolled as first-time, first-year students.

Part-time:	65%	Hispanic American:	5%
Women:	61%	Native American:	1%
African American:	19%	International:	1%
Asian American:	3%		

Transfer out. Colleges most students transferred to 2011: University of Maryland-Baltimore County, Towson University, University of Maryland-College Park, Salisbury University, University of Maryland University College.

Basis for selection. Open admission, but selective for some programs. Special requirements for certain allied health programs. International students must provide certification of finances. Interview recommended for applicants to nursing, human services, radiologic technology, physician's assistant programs, EMT, physical therapy assistant.

2011-2012 Annual costs. Tuition/fees: $3,160; $5,650 out-of-district; $9,640 out-of-state. Per-credit charge: $90 in-district; $173 out-of-district; $306 out-of-state. Books/supplies: $1,484. Personal expenses: $1,778.

2010-2011 Financial aid. Need-based: 47% of total undergraduate aid awarded as scholarships/grants, 53% as loans/jobs. Need-based aid available for part-time students. Work-study available nights, weekends and for part-time students.

Application procedures. Admission: No deadline. No application fee. Admission notification on a rolling basis. **Financial aid:** Priority date 5/15; no closing date. FAFSA, institutional form required. Applicants notified on a rolling basis starting 7/1; must reply within 2 week(s) of notification.

Academics. Special study options: Accelerated study, cooperative education, distance learning, double major, dual enrollment of high school students, ESL, honors, independent study, internships, liberal arts/career combination, student-designed major, teacher certification program, weekend college. Bachelor's degree programs available on campus. License preparation in nursing, paramedic, radiology, real estate. **Credit/placement by examination:** AP, CLEP, IB, institutional tests. 15 credit hours maximum toward

associate degree. **Support services:** GED preparation, learning center, pre-admission summer program, reduced course load, remedial instruction, study skills assistance, tutoring, writing center.

Majors. Architecture: Interior. **Area/ethnic studies:** American. **Business:** General, accounting technology, entrepreneurial studies, hotel/motel admin, management information systems. **Communications technology:** General, graphics, photo/film/video. **Computer sciences:** General, security. **Conservation:** Environmental science. **Education:** General, chemistry, elementary, English, mathematics, physics, secondary, Spanish. **Engineering:** General. **Health services:** Clinical lab technology, medical assistant, medical radiologic technology/radiation therapy, medical records technology, medical secretary, mental health services, nursing (RN), physical therapy assistant, substance abuse counseling, surgical technology. **Liberal arts:** Arts/sciences. **Math:** General. **Parks/recreation:** Health/fitness. **Protective services:** Fire safety technology, law enforcement admin, police science. **Visual/performing arts:** Commercial/advertising art, graphic design, interior design. **Work/family studies:** Child care management.

Most popular majors. Business/marketing 18%, health sciences 15%, liberal arts 42%.

Computing on campus. 2,008 workstations in library, computer center, student center. Commuter students can connect to campus network. Online library, helpline, wireless network available.

Student life. Freshman orientation: Mandatory. Preregistration for classes offered. One day program. **Activities:** Bands, campus ministries, choral groups, dance, drama, international student organizations, literary magazine, music ensembles, musical theater, opera, student government, student newspaper, symphony orchestra, Agape Campus Christian Fellowship, Anime, Apostolic Campus Ministries, BACCHUS, Baptist campus ministries, Black Student Union, Campus Crusade for Christ, Caribbean Student Association, Democrats club, Hispanos Unidos de AACC.

Athletics. NJCAA. **Intercollegiate:** Baseball M, basketball, golf M, lacrosse, soccer, softball W, volleyball W. **Intramural:** Weight lifting. **Team name:** Pioneers.

Student services. Adult student services, alcohol/substance abuse counseling, career counseling, student employment services, financial aid counseling, health services, minority student services, on-campus daycare, personal counseling, placement for graduates, veterans' counselor. **Physically disabled:** Services for visually, speech, hearing impaired. **Transfer:** Transfer center, transfer adviser, college fairs on campus for students transferring to 4-year colleges.

Contact. E-mail: admissions@aacc.edu
Phone: (410) 777-2831 Fax: (410) 777-2018
Thomas McGinn, Director of Enrollment Development and Admissions, Anne Arundel Community College, 101 College Parkway, Arnold, MD 21012-1895

Baltimore City Community College
Baltimore, Maryland
www.bccc.edu   **CB code: 5051**

⦁ Public 2-year community college
⦁ Commuter campus in very large city

General. Founded in 1947. Regionally accredited. Numerous sites throughout Baltimore. **Enrollment:** 7,085 degree-seeking undergraduates. **Degrees:** 473 associate awarded. **Location:** 50 miles from Washington, DC, 75 miles from Philadelphia. **Calendar:** Semester, extensive summer session. **Full-time faculty:** 108 total. **Part-time faculty:** 278 total. **Special facilities:** Greenhouse, planetarium.

Student profile.

Out-of-state:	1%	25 or older:	58%

Transfer out. Colleges most students transferred to 2011: Coppin State University, Morgan State University, University of Baltimore, Towson University, University of Maryland Baltimore County.

Basis for selection. Open admission, but selective for some programs. Special requirements for nursing and allied health programs. SAT and ACT scores may be used in place of reading, math, and English proficiency tests required of all first-time students. Interview recommended for applicants to allied health, paralegal, emergency medical services programs. Portfolio recommended for art, fashion design majors.

2011-2012 Annual costs. Tuition/fees: $3,062; $6,722 out-of-state. Books/supplies: $700.

Financial aid. All financial aid based on need. Need-based aid available for part-time students. Work-study available nights, weekends and for part-time students.

Application procedures. Admission: Closing date 8/27. $10 fee, may be waived for applicants with need. Admission notification on a rolling basis. **Financial aid:** Priority date 6/1; no closing date. FAFSA, institutional form required. Applicants notified on a rolling basis starting 7/1; must reply within 2 week(s) of notification.

Academics. Adults without diploma or GED become eligible for degree programs after successfully completing 15 college-level credits. **Special study options:** Cooperative education, distance learning, double major, dual enrollment of high school students, ESL, honors, independent study, internships, liberal arts/career combination, study abroad, teacher certification program, weekend college. License preparation in dental hygiene, nursing, paramedic, physical therapy. **Credit/placement by examination:** AP, CLEP, IB, institutional tests. 15 credit hours maximum toward associate degree. **Support services:** GED preparation, learning center, pre-admission summer program, reduced course load, remedial instruction, study skills assistance, tutoring, writing center.

Majors. Biology: Biotechnology. **Business:** General, accounting, administrative services, business admin, fashion, hospitality admin, management information systems, marketing, office management, office technology. **Computer sciences:** General, computer graphics, computer science, information systems, systems analysis. **Education:** General, early childhood, multi-level teacher. **Engineering:** General. **Health services:** Dental hygiene, EMT paramedic, health care admin, licensed practical nurse, medical records admin, medical records technology, medical secretary, nursing (RN), physical therapy assistant, respiratory therapy technology. **Human services:** Social work. **Liberal arts:** Arts/sciences. **Protective services:** Corrections, law enforcement admin, police science. **Visual/performing arts:** Art, fashion design, music. **Work/family studies:** Clothing/textiles.

Most popular majors. Business/marketing 22%, health sciences 32%, liberal arts 27%.

Computing on campus. 926 workstations in library, computer center, student center. Online library, wireless network available.

Student life. Freshman orientation: Mandatory. Preregistration for classes offered. **Activities:** Choral groups, drama, international student organizations, musical theater, radio station, student government, student newspaper, fashion club, human services club, media club, civic organizations, computer club.

Athletics. NJCAA. **Intercollegiate:** Baseball M, basketball, volleyball W. **Team name:** Panthers.

Student services. Career counseling, student employment services, financial aid counseling, health services, on-campus daycare, personal counseling, placement for graduates, veterans' counselor. **Physically disabled:** Services for visually, speech, hearing impaired. **Transfer:** Pre-admission transcript evaluation for new students. Transfer adviser, college fairs on campus for students transferring to 4-year colleges.

Contact. E-mail: admissions@bccc.edu
Phone: (410) 462-8300 Toll-free number: (888) 203-1261
Fax: (410) 462-8345
Deneen Dangerfield, Director of Admissions, Baltimore City Community College, 2901 Liberty Heights Avenue, Baltimore, MD 21215-7893

Carroll Community College
Westminster, Maryland
www.carrollcc.edu   **CB code: 5797**

⦁ Public 2-year community college
⦁ Commuter campus in large town

General. Founded in 1993. Regionally accredited. **Enrollment:** 3,891 degree-seeking undergraduates; 150 non-degree-seeking students. **Degrees:** 534 associate awarded. **Location:** 30 miles from Baltimore. **Calendar:** Semester, extensive summer session. **Full-time faculty:** 75 total; 12% have terminal degrees, 5% minority, 67% women. **Part-time faculty:** 200 total; 10% minority, 64% women. **Class size:** 49% < 20, 50% 20-39, 1% 40-49. **Special facilities:** Theater, amphitheatre, art gallery.

Student profile. Among degree-seeking undergraduates, 83% enrolled in a transfer program, 17% enrolled in a vocational program, 818 enrolled as first-time, first-year students, 303 transferred in from other institutions.

Part-time:	58%	Asian American:	1%
Out-of-state:	1%	Hispanic American:	2%
Women:	62%	25 or older:	29%
African American:	4%		

Transfer out. Colleges most students transferred to 2011: Towson University, McDaniel College, University of Maryland College Park, University of Maryland Baltimore County, Salisbury University.

Basis for selection. Open admission, but selective for some programs.

2011-2012 Annual costs. Tuition/fees: $3,696; $5,352 out-of-district; $7,512 out-of-state. Per-credit charge: $123 in-district; $178 out-of-district; $250 out-of-state. Books/supplies: $1,200. Personal expenses: $1,000.

2010-2011 Financial aid. Need-based: 98% of total undergraduate aid awarded as scholarships/grants, 2% as loans/jobs. Need-based aid available for part-time students. Work-study available nights, weekends and for part-time students. **Non-need-based:** Scholarships awarded for academics, art, job skills, leadership, state residency.

Application procedures. Admission: No deadline. No application fee. Application must be submitted on paper. Admission notification on a rolling basis. **Financial aid:** Priority date 3/1; no closing date. FAFSA required. Applicants notified by 6/1; must reply within 2 week(s) of notification.

Academics. Special study options: Distance learning, dual enrollment of high school students, ESL, honors, independent study. License preparation in nursing, physical therapy. **Credit/placement by examination:** AP, CLEP, institutional tests. 30 credit hours maximum toward associate degree. **Support services:** GED preparation, learning center, remedial instruction, study skills assistance, tutoring, writing center.

Majors. Business: General, accounting technology, international, management information systems. **Computer sciences:** Computer graphics. **Education:** General, chemistry, early childhood, elementary, English, mathematics, secondary, Spanish. **Engineering:** Computer, electrical. **Health services:** EMT ambulance attendant, medical records technology, nuclear medical technology, nursing (RN), physical therapy assistant, prenursing, radiologic technology/medical imaging, respiratory therapy technology, sonography, surgical technology. **Liberal arts:** Arts/sciences. **Parks/recreation:** Exercise sciences. **Protective services:** Forensics, police science. **Psychology:** General. **Visual/performing arts:** Art, commercial/advertising art, music, theater design. **Work/family studies:** Child care management.

Most popular majors. Business/marketing 14%, education 6%, health sciences 15%, liberal arts 62%.

Computing on campus. 684 workstations in library, computer center, student center. Commuter students can connect to campus network. Online library, helpline, wireless network available.

Student life. Freshman orientation: Available. Preregistration for classes offered. One-day program in late August. **Policies:** Smoke free campus. **Activities:** Jazz band, choral groups, drama, film society, literary magazine, music ensembles, musical theater, student government, symphony orchestra, BACCHUS, Christian club, Leadership Challenge, campus activities board, outdoor club, Green Team, game design, Student Art Society, soccer club, serving learning club.

Student services. Career counseling, student employment services, financial aid counseling, on-campus daycare. **Physically disabled:** Services for visually, speech, hearing impaired. **Transfer:** Re-entry adviser, pre-admission transcript evaluation for new students. Transfer center, transfer adviser, college fairs on campus for students transferring to 4-year colleges.

Contact. E-mail: cedwards@carrollcc.edu
Phone: (410) 386-8430 Toll-free number: (888) 221-9748
Fax: (410) 386-8446
Candace Edwards, Coordinator of Admissions, Carroll Community College, 1601 Washington Road, Westminster, MD 21157

Cecil College
North East, Maryland
www.my.cecil.edu   **CB code: 5091**

- Public 2-year community college
- Commuter campus in large town

General. Founded in 1968. Regionally accredited. **Enrollment:** 2,441 degree-seeking undergraduates; 104 non-degree-seeking students. **Degrees:** 235 associate awarded. **Location:** 50 miles from Baltimore, 50 miles from Philadelphia. **Calendar:** Semester, limited summer session. **Full-time faculty:** 47 total; 28% have terminal degrees, 13% minority, 68% women. **Part-time faculty:** 220 total; 10% minority, 59% women. **Class size:** 83% < 20, 16% 20-39, less than 1% 40-49, less than 1% 50-99.

Student profile. Among degree-seeking undergraduates, 48% enrolled in a transfer program, 52% enrolled in a vocational program, 761 enrolled as first-time, first-year students, 1 transferred in from other institutions.

Part-time:	57%	Asian American:	1%
Out-of-state:	9%	Hispanic American:	4%
Women:	62%	25 or older:	33%
African American:	9%		

Basis for selection. Open admission, but selective for some programs. Admission to nursing programs based on high school record, test scores, required interview. All students must take Cecil College placement tests.

High school preparation. College-preparatory program recommended.

2011-2012 Annual costs. Tuition/fees: $3,080; $5,780 out-of-district; $7,130 out-of-state. Per-credit charge: $90 in-district; $180 out-of-district; $225 out-of-state. Books/supplies: $1,100. Personal expenses: $2,300.

2010-2011 Financial aid. Need-based: 59% of total undergraduate aid awarded as scholarships/grants, 41% as loans/jobs. Work-study available nights, weekends and for part-time students. **Non-need-based:** Scholarships awarded for academics, alumni affiliation, athletics, job skills, state residency.

Application procedures. Admission: No deadline. No application fee. Admission notification on a rolling basis. Application deadline for nursing program March 1. **Financial aid:** Priority date 8/1; no closing date. FAFSA required. Applicants notified on a rolling basis; must reply within 2 week(s) of notification.

Academics. Special study options: Accelerated study, cooperative education, distance learning, double major, dual enrollment of high school students, ESL, honors, independent study, internships, teacher certification program, weekend college. Bachelor's degree programs available on campus. License preparation in aviation, nursing. **Credit/placement by examination:** AP, CLEP, institutional tests. 45 credit hours maximum toward associate degree. **Support services:** Learning center, reduced course load, remedial instruction, tutoring, writing center.

Majors. Biology: Biotechnology. **Business:** General, accounting technology, administrative services, business admin, communications, financial planning, human resources, management information systems, marketing, office management, purchasing, transportation. **Computer sciences:** General, applications programming, programming, web page design. **Education:** General, early childhood, elementary, English, secondary. **General:** Equine science. **Health services:** EMT paramedic, nursing (RN). **Liberal arts:** Arts/sciences. **Math:** General. **Physical sciences:** Chemistry, physics. **Protective services:** Firefighting, police science. **Visual/performing arts:** Commercial photography, design, drawing, photography, studio arts. **Work/family studies:** Child care management.

Most popular majors. Business/marketing 17%, health sciences 26%, liberal arts 38%, visual/performing arts 7%.

Computing on campus. 200 workstations in library, computer center, student center. Commuter students can connect to campus network. Online course registration, online library available.

Student life. Freshman orientation: Available. Preregistration for classes offered. **Activities:** Dance, drama, musical theater, student government, student newspaper.

Athletics. NJCAA. **Intercollegiate:** Baseball M, basketball, cheerleading M, soccer, softball W, tennis, volleyball W. **Team name:** Seahawks.

Student services. Adult student services, alcohol/substance abuse counseling, career counseling, student employment services, financial aid counseling, legal services, minority student services, personal counseling, placement for graduates, veterans' counselor. **Transfer:** Transfer adviser, college fairs on campus for students transferring to 4-year colleges.

Contact. E-mail: cmishoe@cecil.edu
Phone: (410) 287-6060 Fax: (410) 287-1026
Diane Lane, Vice President of Student Services, Cecil College, One Seahawk Drive, North East, MD 21901

Chesapeake College
Wye Mills, Maryland
www.chesapeake.edu   **CB code: 5143**

- Public 2-year community college
- Commuter campus in rural community

General. Founded in 1965. Regionally accredited. Coursework at undergraduate and graduate levels offered by University of Maryland, University

College, University of Maryland Eastern Shore, Salisbury University and Grant's College available at this location. **Enrollment:** 2,635 degree-seeking undergraduates; 347 non-degree-seeking students. **Degrees:** 251 associate awarded. **Location:** 50 miles from Washington, DC, 50 miles from Baltimore. **Calendar:** Semester, limited summer session. **Full-time faculty:** 61 total; 36% have terminal degrees, 8% minority, 64% women. **Part-time faculty:** 86 total; 13% have terminal degrees, 8% minority, 50% women. **Class size:** 45% < 20, 55% 20-39. **Special facilities:** Performing arts center.

Student profile. Among degree-seeking undergraduates, 39% enrolled in a transfer program, 49% enrolled in a vocational program, 672 enrolled as first-time, first-year students.

Part-time:	63%	Asian American:	1%
Women:	66%	Hispanic American:	3%
African American:	18%	25 or older:	47%

Transfer out. Colleges most students transferred to 2011: Salisbury University, Towson University, Frostburg State College, University of Maryland.

Basis for selection. Open admission, but selective for some programs. Admission to radiological technology, surgical technology, physical therapist assistant and nursing programs based on specific high school courses, cumulative grade point averages, and/or test scores.

2011-2012 Annual costs. Tuition/fees: $3,754; $5,824 out-of-district; $8,134 out-of-state. Per-credit charge: $101 in-district; $169 out-of-district; $246 out-of-state. Books/supplies: $1,400. Personal expenses: $1,000.

2010-2011 Financial aid. Need-based: Need-based aid available for part-time students. Work-study available nights, weekends and for part-time students. **Non-need-based:** Scholarships awarded for academics, art, athletics, state residency.

Application procedures. Admission: No deadline. No application fee. Application must be submitted on paper. Early application advised for radiologic technology and nursing programs. **Financial aid:** Priority date 5/5; no closing date. FAFSA, institutional form required. Applicants notified on a rolling basis starting 5/5; must reply within 2 week(s) of notification.

Academics. Special study options: Cooperative education, cross-registration, distance learning, dual enrollment of high school students, ESL, honors, independent study, internships, student-designed major. License preparation in nursing, paramedic, physical therapy, radiology. **Credit/placement by examination:** AP, CLEP, institutional tests. 32 credit hours maximum toward associate degree. **Support services:** GED test center, learning center, reduced course load, remedial instruction, study skills assistance, tutoring, writing center.

Majors. Business: General, accounting technology, business admin, hotel/motel/restaurant management. **Computer sciences:** General, data processing, networking, security, web page design. **Conservation:** Environmental science. **Education:** General, chemistry, elementary, English, mathematics, physics, secondary. **Health services:** Clinical lab technology, medical radiologic technology/radiation therapy, medical records technology, mental health services, nursing (RN), physical therapy assistant. **Liberal arts:** Arts/sciences. **Parks/recreation:** General. **Protective services:** Criminal justice, police science. **Psychology:** General. **Social sciences:** General. **Work/family studies:** Child care management.

Most popular majors. Business/marketing 12%, education 8%, health sciences 24%, liberal arts 47%.

Computing on campus. Commuter students can connect to campus network. Helpline, wireless network available.

Student life. Freshman orientation: Available. Preregistration for classes offered. **Activities:** Campus ministries, choral groups, drama, literary magazine, student government, Happy Hands, Gay/Straight Alliance, African American student union (UHURU), Phi Theta Kappa honor society, Best Buddies, Green Team, Students for the Arts.

Athletics. NJCAA. **Intercollegiate:** Baseball M, basketball, soccer M, softball W, volleyball W. **Team name:** Skipjacks.

Student services. Adult student services, career counseling, student employment services, financial aid counseling, minority student services, on-campus daycare, personal counseling, placement for graduates, veterans' counselor. **Physically disabled:** Services for visually, speech, hearing impaired. **Transfer:** Transfer adviser, college fairs on campus for students transferring to 4-year colleges.

Contact. E-mail: kpetrichenko@chesapeake.edu
Phone: (410) 822-5400 ext. 287 Fax: (410) 827-5875
Kathy Petrichenko, Dean of Recruitment, Chesapeake College, Box 8, Wye Mills, MD 21679-0008

College of Southern Maryland
La Plata, Maryland
www.csmd.edu   **CB code: 5144**

- Public 2-year community college
- Commuter campus in large town

General. Founded in 1958. Regionally accredited. Additional campuses located in Charles County, Calvert County, and St. Mary's County. **Enrollment:** 8,216 degree-seeking undergraduates; 937 non-degree-seeking students. **Degrees:** 821 associate awarded. **Location:** 30 miles from Washington, DC. **Calendar:** Semester, limited summer session. **Full-time faculty:** 124 total; 23% have terminal degrees, 18% minority, 56% women. **Part-time faculty:** 433 total; 8% have terminal degrees, 18% minority, 59% women. **Class size:** 29% < 20, 70% 20-39, less than 1% 40-49, less than 1% 50-99.

Student profile. Among degree-seeking undergraduates, 55% enrolled in a transfer program, 33% enrolled in a vocational program, 1,817 enrolled as first-time, first-year students, 356 transferred in from other institutions.

Part-time:	61%	Hispanic American:	5%
Women:	62%	Native American:	1%
African American:	25%	25 or older:	35%
Asian American:	2%		

Transfer out. Colleges most students transferred to 2011: University of Maryland: University College, University of Maryland: College Park, Towson University, Salisbury University, St. Mary's College of Maryland.

Basis for selection. Open admission, but selective for some programs. Specific requirements for clinical nursing courses include high school diploma or GED, special testing (ACT), minimum 2.0 GPA in high school. Students must take the college skills assessment test unless they have taken the SAT, scored 550 in English and math or the ACT, scored 21 or higher. Interview required of early admission and nursing applicants. **Adult students:** SAT/ACT scores not required.

2011-2012 Annual costs. Tuition/fees: $3,948; $6,827 out-of-district; $8,819 out-of-state. Per-credit charge: $107 in-district; $185 out-of-district; $239 out-of-state. Books/supplies: $1,400. Personal expenses: $1,591.

Financial aid. Need-based: Need-based aid available for part-time students. Work-study available nights, weekends and for part-time students. **Non-need-based:** Scholarships awarded for academics, athletics, state residency.

Application procedures. Admission: No deadline. No application fee. Admission notification on a rolling basis. **Financial aid:** Priority date 3/1; no closing date. FAFSA required. Applicants notified on a rolling basis starting 5/15; must reply within 2 week(s) of notification.

Academics. Special study options: Accelerated study, cooperative education, distance learning, dual enrollment of high school students, honors, independent study, liberal arts/career combination, weekend college. Bachelor's degree programs available on campus. License preparation in nursing, paramedic, physical therapy, radiology. **Credit/placement by examination:** AP, CLEP, institutional tests. 30 credit hours maximum toward associate degree. **Support services:** Learning center, reduced course load, remedial instruction, study skills assistance, tutoring.

Majors. Business: General, accounting technology, business admin, hospitality admin. **Computer sciences:** General, information technology, programming, security. **Education:** General, early childhood, elementary. **Engineering:** General. **Health services:** Clinical lab technology, EMT paramedic, licensed practical nurse, massage therapy, nursing (RN), physical therapy assistant. **Liberal arts:** Arts/sciences. **Parks/recreation:** Health/fitness. **Protective services:** Firefighting, law enforcement admin. **Work/family studies:** Child care management.

Most popular majors. Business/marketing 17%, health sciences 12%, liberal arts 52%.

Computing on campus. 1,200 workstations in library, computer center. Commuter students can connect to campus network. Online course registration, helpline available.

Student life. Freshman orientation: Available. Preregistration for classes offered. **Activities:** Jazz band, choral groups, drama, literary magazine, music ensembles, musical theater, student government, student newspaper, BACCHUS Peer Education Network, Black Student Union, Association of Future Educators Club, Nursing Student Association, Phi Theta Kappa, Fellowship of Christian Athletes, English Honor Society, National Society of Leadership and Success, Service Learning Club, Student Ambassador Club.

Athletics. NJCAA. **Intercollegiate:** Baseball M, basketball, golf, soccer, softball W, tennis, volleyball W. **Team name:** Hawks.

Student services. Adult student services, career counseling, student employment services, financial aid counseling, personal counseling, placement for graduates, veterans' counselor. **Physically disabled:** Services for visually, speech, hearing impaired. **Transfer:** Re-entry adviser for new students. Transfer adviser, college fairs on campus for students transferring to 4-year colleges.

Contact. E-mail: info@csmd.edu
Phone: (301) 934-7765 Toll-free number: (800) 933-9177 ext. 7765
Fax: (301) 934-7698
Joan Middleton, Associate Vice President, Enrollment Management, College of Southern Maryland, College of Southern Maryland-AOD, La Plata, MD 20646-0910

Community College of Baltimore County

Baltimore, Maryland   **CB member**
www.ccbcmd.edu   **CB code: 5137**

⬥ Public 2-year community college
⬥ Commuter campus in very large city

General. Founded in 1956. Regionally accredited. 3 campuses-Catonsville, Dundalk and Essex; 3 extension centers in Owings Mills, Hunt Valley, and Randallstown. **Enrollment:** 24,087 degree-seeking undergraduates; 2,184 non-degree-seeking students. **Degrees:** 1,854 associate awarded. **Location:** 8 miles from Baltimore. **Calendar:** Semester, limited summer session. **Full-time faculty:** 426 total; 23% have terminal degrees, 20% minority, 59% women. **Part-time faculty:** 990 total; 1% have terminal degrees, 22% minority, 56% women. **Special facilities:** Planetarium, occupational training center, performing arts theater, computer integrated manufacturing center. **Partnerships:** Formal partnership with the Baltimore County Public Schools for the Early Assessment and Intervention Project.

Student profile. Among degree-seeking undergraduates, 4,799 enrolled as first-time, first-year students.

Part-time:	64%	Hispanic American:	3%
Women:	62%	International:	3%
African American:	39%	25 or older:	44%
Asian American:	4%		

Transfer out. Colleges most students transferred to 2011: University of Baltimore, University of Maryland Baltimore County, Towson University, Morgan State University.

Basis for selection. Open admission, but selective for some programs. Additional requirements for School of Health Professions. In-house placement tests required of applicants not presenting SAT or ACT scores. Score reports preferred by July 1. Interview recommended for applicants under age 16 and early admission applicants.

High school preparation. 21 units recommended. Recommended units include English 4, mathematics 3, social studies 4, science 3, foreign language 2 and academic electives 6.

2011-2012 Annual costs. Tuition/fees: $3,772; $6,562 out-of-district; $9,502 out-of-state. Per-credit charge: $103 in-district; $196 out-of-district; $294 out-of-state. Books/supplies: $1,400. Personal expenses: $1,400.

Financial aid. Need-based: Need-based aid available for part-time students. Work-study available nights, weekends and for part-time students. **Non-need-based:** Scholarships awarded for academics, athletics, state residency. **Additional information:** On-campus employment typically available.

Application procedures. Admission: No deadline. No application fee. Admission notification on a rolling basis. **Financial aid:** Closing date 3/1. FAFSA required. Applicants notified on a rolling basis starting 5/1; must reply within 2 week(s) of notification.

Academics. Special study options: Cooperative education, cross-registration, distance learning, dual enrollment of high school students, ESL, honors, independent study, internships, liberal arts/career combination, study abroad, teacher certification program. Weekend Courses available. License preparation in aviation, dental hygiene, nursing, occupational therapy. **Credit/placement by examination:** AP, CLEP, institutional tests. 30 credit hours maximum toward associate degree. **Support services:** GED preparation, learning center, reduced course load, remedial instruction, tutoring.

Majors. Business: General, accounting technology, administrative services, business admin, hotel/motel admin, labor relations, management information systems. **Computer sciences:** General, computer graphics, networking, security. **Education:** General, chemistry, early childhood, elementary, mathematics, physics, Spanish. **Engineering:** General. **Foreign languages:** Sign language interpretation. **General:** Horticulture. **Health services:** Clinical lab technology, dental hygiene, EMT paramedic, massage therapy, medical informatics, medical radiologic technology/radiation therapy, medical secretary, mental health services, nursing (RN), occupational therapy, respiratory therapy technology, substance abuse counseling, veterinary technology/assistant. **Human services:** General. **Liberal arts:** Arts/sciences. **Parks/recreation:** General. **Protective services:** Police science. **Social sciences:** Geography. **Visual/performing arts:** General, commercial/advertising art. **Work/family studies:** Child care management.

Computing on campus. Online course registration, online library available.

Student life. Freshman orientation: Mandatory. Preregistration for classes offered. **Activities:** Choral groups, dance, drama, international student organizations, literary magazine, music ensembles, musical theater, radio station, student government, student newspaper, TV station, Black student union, Adventure Society, Christian fellowship.

Athletics. NJCAA. **Intercollegiate:** Baseball M, basketball, lacrosse, soccer, softball W, volleyball W.

Student services. Career counseling, services for economically disadvantaged, student employment services, financial aid counseling, minority student services, on-campus daycare, personal counseling, placement for graduates, veterans' counselor. **Physically disabled:** Services for visually, speech, hearing impaired. **Transfer:** Pre-admission transcript evaluation for new students. Transfer adviser, college fairs on campus for students transferring to 4-year colleges.

Contact. E-mail: catonsvilleadmissions@ccbcmd.edu
Phone: (443) 840-4991 Fax: (443) 840-5046
Diane Drake, Director of Admissions, Community College of Baltimore County, 800 South Rolling Road, Baltimore, MD 21228

Frederick Community College

Frederick, Maryland   **CB member**
www.frederick.edu   **CB code: 5230**

⬥ Public 2-year community college
⬥ Commuter campus in small city

General. Founded in 1957. Regionally accredited. **Enrollment:** 5,206 degree-seeking undergraduates; 1,063 non-degree-seeking students. **Degrees:** 778 associate awarded. **Location:** 40 miles from Washington, DC, 40 miles from Baltimore. **Calendar:** Semester, extensive summer session. **Full-time faculty:** 97 total. **Part-time faculty:** 425 total. **Special facilities:** Culinary arts institute, advanced workforce training center.

Student profile. Among degree-seeking undergraduates, 1,362 enrolled as first-time, first-year students.

Part-time:	58%	Asian American:	4%
Out-of-state:	1%	Hispanic American:	6%
Women:	58%	Native American:	1%
African American:	14%	25 or older:	50%

Transfer out. Colleges most students transferred to 2011: Hood College, Mount St. Mary's University, Towson University, University of Maryland: College Park, Frostburg University.

Basis for selection. Open admission, but selective for some programs. All nursing, respiratory therapy, and surgical technology programs have special requirements. Students must show successful completion of appropriate general education requirements. Score of 550 or higher on either SAT math or verbal will exempt student from appropriate assessment. Interview required of nursing, respiratory therapy applicants. **Home schooled:** Transcript of courses and grades required. **Learning Disabled:** Meet with Office of Services for Students with Disabilities staff prior to testing/registration.

2011-2012 Annual costs. Tuition/fees: $3,806; $7,526 out-of-district; $9,986 out-of-state. Per-credit charge: $106 in-district; $230 out-of-district; $312 out-of-state. Books/supplies: $1,200. Personal expenses: $1,000.

Financial aid. Need-based: Need-based aid available for part-time students. Work-study available nights, weekends and for part-time students. **Non-need-based:** Scholarships awarded for academics, athletics, state residency.

Application procedures. Admission: No deadline. No application fee. Admission notification on a rolling basis beginning on or about 1/1. Application deadline for nursing applicants December 15, surgical technology and emergency medical services applicants February 1. **Financial aid:** Priority date 6/1; no closing date. FAFSA, institutional form required. Applicants notified on a rolling basis starting 5/15; must reply within 2 week(s) of notification.

Academics. **Special study options:** Cooperative education, distance learning, dual enrollment of high school students, ESL, honors, independent study, internships, liberal arts/career combination, study abroad, teacher certification program, weekend college. License preparation in nursing, real estate. **Credit/placement by examination:** AP, CLEP, institutional tests. 30 credit hours maximum toward associate degree. **Support services:** GED preparation, learning center, pre-admission summer program, reduced course load, remedial instruction, study skills assistance, tutoring, writing center.

Majors. **Biology:** General. **Business:** Accounting, banking/financial services, business admin, hospitality admin, international. **Communications:** Communications/speech/rhetoric. **Communications technology:** General. **Computer sciences:** General, applications programming, computer science, information systems, information technology, system admin, systems analysis. **Education:** General, early childhood, multi-level teacher, physical, Spanish. **Engineering:** General. **English:** English lit, rhetoric/composition. **Health services:** Nuclear medical technology, nursing (RN), prenursing, prepharmacy, respiratory therapy technology, surgical technology. **History:** General. **Liberal arts:** Arts/sciences. **Math:** General. **Philosophy/religion:** Philosophy. **Physical sciences:** Chemistry. **Protective services:** Criminal justice, fire services admin, homeland security, police science. **Psychology:** General. **Social sciences:** Economics, political science, sociology. **Visual/performing arts:** Art, dramatic. **Work/family studies:** Child care management.

Most popular majors. Business/marketing 18%, health sciences 17%, liberal arts 47%.

Computing on campus. 230 workstations in library, computer center. Commuter students can connect to campus network. Online course registration, online library, wireless network available.

Student life. **Freshman orientation:** Mandatory. Preregistration for classes offered. Held throughout summer; include advisement and pre-registration. **Activities:** Jazz band, choral groups, dance, drama, film society, literary magazine, music ensembles, student government, student newspaper, multicultural student union, Christian students club, chess club, community service club, environmental awareness club, honors student association, international students club, gay/lesbian/bisexual group, nursing club, young Democrats and Republicans.

Athletics. NJCAA. **Intercollegiate:** Baseball M, basketball, golf, soccer, softball W, volleyball W. **Team name:** Cougars.

Student services. Adult student services, alcohol/substance abuse counseling, career counseling, student employment services, financial aid counseling, minority student services, on-campus daycare, personal counseling, placement for graduates, veterans' counselor, women's services. **Physically disabled:** Services for visually, speech, hearing impaired. **Transfer:** Transfer center, transfer adviser, college fairs on campus for students transferring to 4-year colleges.

Contact. E-mail: sasmith@frederick.edu
Phone: (301) 846-2431 Fax: (301) 624-2799
Sandra Smith, Associate Vice President/Enrollment Management, Frederick Community College, 7932 Opossumtown Pike, Frederick, MD 21702

Garrett College
McHenry, Maryland
www.garrettcollege.edu   CB code: 5279

- Public 2-year community college
- Commuter campus in rural community

General. Founded in 1971. Regionally accredited. **Enrollment:** 669 degree-seeking undergraduates; 233 non-degree-seeking students. **Degrees:** 98 associate awarded. **Location:** 45 miles from Cumberland, 40 miles from Morgantown, West Virginia. **Calendar:** Semester, limited summer session. **Full-time faculty:** 19 total; 32% have terminal degrees, 10% minority, 37% women. **Part-time faculty:** 58 total; 7% have terminal degrees, 60% women. **Class size:** 55% < 20, 43% 20-39, 3% 40-49. **Special facilities:** Community Aquatic and Recreational Complex.

Student profile. Among degree-seeking undergraduates, 70% enrolled in a transfer program, 30% enrolled in a vocational program, 269 enrolled as first-time, first-year students, 61 transferred in from other institutions.

Part-time:	13%	Hispanic American:	2%
Out-of-state:	18%	25 or older:	20%
Women:	47%	Live on campus:	19%
African American:	21%		

Transfer out. Colleges most students transferred to 2011: Frostburg State University, Allegeny College of Maryland, West Virginia University.

Basis for selection. **Adult students:** SAT/ACT scores not required. **Home schooled:** Transcript of courses and grades, state high school equivalency certificate required. **Learning Disabled:** We encourage students to register as a 504 student, with our Associate Dean of Academic Affairs.

2011-2012 Annual costs. Tuition/fees: $3,450; $7,230 out-of-district; $8,400 out-of-state. Per-credit charge: $90 in-district; $216 out-of-district; $255 out-of-state. Room/board: $5,770. Books/supplies: $1,400. Personal expenses: $2,000.

2010-2011 Financial aid. **Need-based:** 242 full-time freshmen applied for aid; 212 were judged to have need; 212 of these received aid. Average need met was 26%. Average scholarship/grant was $4,916; average loan $1,732. 74% of total undergraduate aid awarded as scholarships/grants, 26% as loans/jobs. Need-based aid available for part-time students. Work-study available nights, weekends and for part-time students. **Non-need-based:** Awarded to 213 full-time undergraduates, including 96 freshmen. Scholarships awarded for academics, athletics, leadership. **Additional information:** Many local scholarships both merit and need based.

Application procedures. **Admission:** No deadline. No application fee. Application must be submitted on paper. Admission notification on a rolling basis. **Financial aid:** Priority date 3/1; no closing date. FAFSA required. Applicants notified on a rolling basis starting 6/1; must reply within 2 week(s) of notification.

Academics. **Special study options:** Distance learning, double major, dual enrollment of high school students, honors, independent study, internships, semester at sea. License preparation in paramedic. **Credit/placement by examination:** AP, CLEP, institutional tests. 30 credit hours maximum toward associate degree. **Support services:** GED preparation and test center, learning center, pre-admission summer program, reduced course load, remedial instruction, tutoring, writing center.

Majors. **Business:** General, business admin, management information systems, office technology. **Conservation:** Wildlife/wilderness. **Education:** General, early childhood, elementary. **Engineering:** Electrical. **Liberal arts:** Arts/sciences. **Parks/recreation:** Sports admin. **Protective services:** Corrections.

Most popular majors. Business/marketing 18%, education 16%, liberal arts 44%, natural resources/environmental science 7%, physical sciences 9%, security/protective services 9%.

Computing on campus. 48 workstations in library. Dormitories wired for high-speed internet access. Commuter students can connect to campus network. Online library, wireless network available.

Student life. **Freshman orientation:** Available. Preregistration for classes offered. **Housing:** Coed dorms, special housing for disabled, wellness housing available. $200 fully refundable deposit. **Activities:** International student organizations, student government, student newspaper.

Athletics. NJCAA. **Intercollegiate:** Baseball M, basketball, golf M, softball W, volleyball W. **Team name:** Lakers.

Student services. Alcohol/substance abuse counseling, career counseling, student employment services, financial aid counseling, health services, personal counseling, veterans' counselor. **Physically disabled:** Services for visually, speech, hearing impaired. **Transfer:** Transfer center, transfer adviser, college fairs on campus for students transferring to 4-year colleges.

Contact. E-mail: admissions@garrettcollege.edu
Phone: (301) 387-3044 Toll-free number: (866) 554-2773
Fax: (301) 387-3038
Rachelle Davis, Director of Admission, Garrett College, 687 Mosser Road, McHenry, MD 21541

Hagerstown Community College
Hagerstown, Maryland
www.hagerstowncc.edu   CB code: 5290

- Public 2-year community college
- Commuter campus in small city

General. Founded in 1946. Regionally accredited. **Enrollment:** 4,216 degree-seeking undergraduates; 498 non-degree-seeking students. **Degrees:** 492 associate awarded. **Location:** 70 miles from Baltimore. **Calendar:** Semester, extensive summer session. **Full-time faculty:** 77 total; 20% have terminal degrees, 10% minority, 64% women. **Part-time faculty:** 185 total; 3% minority, 58% women. **Special facilities:** Technology center, distance learning classrooms, amphitheater, biotechnology/wet labs.

Student profile. Among degree-seeking undergraduates, 62% enrolled in a transfer program, 38% enrolled in a vocational program, 979 enrolled as first-time, first-year students, 453 transferred in from other institutions.

Part-time:	66%	Women:	61%
Out-of-state:	21%	25 or older:	42%

Transfer out. Colleges most students transferred to 2011: Frostburg State University, Towson State University, Shepherd University, Shippensburg University, University of Maryland.

Basis for selection. Open admission, but selective for some programs. Selective criteria and admission requirements for LPN, RN, Radiography and Paramedic Emergency Services/EMT programs. **Adult students:** SAT/ACT scores not required.

High school preparation. College-preparatory program recommended. 16 units recommended. Recommended units include English 4, mathematics 3, social studies 1, history 1, science 3 (laboratory 2) and academic electives 2. 1 chemistry, 1 biology, 2 algebra required of nursing applicants; 1 physics, 1 chemistry, 2 algebra required of radiologic technologies applicants.

2011-2012 Annual costs. Tuition/fees: $3,440; $5,180 out-of-district; $6,710 out-of-state. Per-credit charge: $103 in-district; $161 out-of-district; $212 out-of-state. Books/supplies: $1,300. Personal expenses: $1,200.

Financial aid. All financial aid based on need. Need-based aid available for part-time students. Work-study available nights, weekends and for part-time students.

Application procedures. Admission: No deadline. No application fee. Admission notification on a rolling basis. **Financial aid:** Priority date 3/1; no closing date. FAFSA required. Applicants notified on a rolling basis starting 5/1.

Academics. Special study options: Accelerated study, cooperative education, cross-registration, distance learning, double major, dual enrollment of high school students, ESL, honors, independent study, internships, liberal arts/career combination. License preparation in nursing, paramedic, radiology, real estate. **Credit/placement by examination:** AP, CLEP, institutional tests. 30 credit hours maximum toward associate degree. **Support services:** GED preparation and test center, learning center, pre-admission summer program, reduced course load, remedial instruction, study skills assistance, tutoring.

Majors. Business: General, accounting technology, banking/financial services, business admin, management information systems, transportation. **Communications technology:** Animation/special effects. **Computer sciences:** General, web page design. **Education:** General, early childhood, elementary. **Engineering:** General. **Health services:** EMT paramedic, medical radiologic technology/radiation therapy, medical secretary, mental health services, nursing (RN). **Liberal arts:** Arts/sciences. **Protective services:** Police science. **Visual/performing arts:** Commercial/advertising art. **Work/family studies:** Child care management.

Most popular majors. Business/marketing 19%, health sciences 20%, liberal arts 45%.

Computing on campus. 500 workstations in library, computer center, student center. Commuter students can connect to campus network. Online course registration, online library, helpline, repair service, wireless network available.

Student life. Freshman orientation: Available. Preregistration for classes offered. **Activities:** Jazz band, choral groups, drama, international student organizations, literary magazine, musical theater, student government, student newspaper.

Athletics. NJCAA. **Intercollegiate:** Baseball M, basketball, cheerleading, cross-country, golf, soccer, softball W, tennis, track and field, volleyball W. **Team name:** Hawks.

Student services. Adult student services, career counseling, services for economically disadvantaged, student employment services, financial aid counseling, health services, on-campus daycare, personal counseling, placement for graduates, veterans' counselor. **Physically disabled:** Services for visually, speech, hearing impaired. **Transfer:** Pre-admission transcript evaluation for new students. Transfer adviser, college fairs on campus for students transferring to 4-year colleges.

Contact. E-mail: admissions@hagerstowncc.edu
Phone: (240) 500-2238 Toll-free number: (301) 766-4422
Fax: (301) 791-9165
Jennifer Haughie, Director of Admissions, Records and Registration, Hagerstown Community College, 11400 Robinwood Drive, Hagerstown, MD 21742-6514

Harford Community College
Bel Air, Maryland
www.harford.edu
CB code: 5303

♦ Public 2-year community college
♦ Commuter campus in small city

General. Founded in 1957. Regionally accredited. **Enrollment:** 6,094 degree-seeking undergraduates; 1,038 non-degree-seeking students. **Degrees:** 772 associate awarded. **Location:** 25 miles from Baltimore. **Calendar:** Semester, limited summer session. **Full-time faculty:** 101 total; 23% have terminal degrees, 8% minority, 52% women. **Part-time faculty:** 286 total; 8% have terminal degrees, 10% minority, 55% women. **Special facilities:** Observatory, theater. **Partnerships:** Partnerships with local employers who provide co-op opportunities.

Student profile. Among degree-seeking undergraduates, 54% enrolled in a transfer program, 32% enrolled in a vocational program, 5% already have a bachelor's degree or higher, 1,527 enrolled as first-time, first-year students, 381 transferred in from other institutions.

Part-time:	56%	Asian American:	2%
Out-of-state:	3%	Hispanic American:	4%
Women:	61%	25 or older:	33%
African American:	15%		

Transfer out. Colleges most students transferred to 2011: Towson University, University of Maryland at College Park, Salisbury University, University of Maryland Baltimore County, Stevenson University.

Basis for selection. Open admission, but selective for some programs. Some restrictions apply for applicants under 16 years old and international students. Nursing program has specific selection criteria. Students with a SAT score of 550 or higher in the critical reading portion or the math section will be exempt from the corresponding Accuplacer section of the assessment. Students not meeting basic requirements must complete transitional courses. **Adult students:** SAT/ACT scores not required. **Home schooled:** If under 16, Assessment Testing with a qualified college-level score and an interview.

High school preparation. 14 units recommended. Recommended units include English 4, mathematics 4, social studies 3 and science 3.

2011-2012 Annual costs. Tuition/fees: $2,760; $5,220 out-of-district; $7,680 out-of-state. Per-credit charge: $82 in-district; $164 out-of-district; $246 out-of-state. Required fees based on $82 per credit in-county fee. Books/supplies: $1,300. Personal expenses: $1,000.

2010-2011 Financial aid. Need-based: 87% of total undergraduate aid awarded as scholarships/grants, 13% as loans/jobs. Need-based aid available for part-time students. Work-study available nights, weekends and for part-time students.

Application procedures. Admission: No deadline. No application fee. Admission notification on a rolling basis. Application deadline for nursing June 1. Notification within 30 days. **Financial aid:** Priority date 3/15; no closing date. FAFSA, institutional form required. Applicants notified on a rolling basis starting 4/1; must reply within 2 week(s) of notification.

Academics. Special study options: Cooperative education, distance learning, double major, dual enrollment of high school students, ESL, honors, independent study, internships, student-designed major, study abroad. License preparation in nursing. **Credit/placement by examination:** AP, CLEP, IB, institutional tests. 30 credit hours maximum toward associate degree. **Support services:** GED preparation and test center, learning center, pre-admission summer program, remedial instruction, study skills assistance, tutoring, writing center.

Majors. Biology: General. **Business:** General, accounting technology, business admin, management information systems. **Communications:** Media studies. **Computer sciences:** General, computer science, security. **Conservation:** Environmental science, environmental studies. **Education:** General, chemistry, early childhood, elementary, mathematics, physics, secondary. **Engineering:** General. **English:** English lit. **General:** Business, equestrian studies, landscaping, turf management. **Health services:** Electroencephalograph technology, licensed practical nurse, medical assistant, nursing (RN). **History:** General. **Human services:** Social work. **Liberal arts:** Arts/sciences. **Math:** General. **Parks/recreation:** Golf management. **Philosophy/religion:** Philosophy. **Physical sciences:** Chemistry, physics. **Protective services:** Police science. **Psychology:** General. **Social sciences:** Anthropology, international relations, political science, sociology. **Visual/performing arts:** General, commercial photography, design, interior design, music, studio arts, theater design.

Most popular majors. Business/marketing 16%, health sciences 17%, liberal arts 43%, visual/performing arts 7%.

Two-Year Colleges

Computing on campus. 750 workstations in library, computer center, student center. Commuter students can connect to campus network. Online course registration, online library, helpline, student web hosting, wireless network available.

Student life. Freshman orientation: Available. Preregistration for classes offered. **Activities:** Bands, choral groups, dance, drama, music ensembles, musical theater, radio station, student government, student newspaper, TV station, Political awareness association, Phi Theta Kappa, Campus Christian Life club, Multicultural student association, Campus Lions club, Vowlunteers.

Athletics. NJCAA. **Intercollegiate:** Baseball M, basketball, golf M, lacrosse, soccer, softball W, tennis, volleyball W. **Intramural:** Badminton, basketball, football (non-tackle), soccer, softball, tennis, volleyball. **Team name:** Fighting Owls.

Student services. Career counseling, student employment services, financial aid counseling, on-campus daycare, personal counseling, placement for graduates, veterans' counselor. **Physically disabled:** Services for visually, speech, hearing impaired. **Transfer:** Transfer adviser, college fairs on campus for students transferring to 4-year colleges.

Contact. E-mail: sendinfo@harford.edu
Phone: (443) 412-2109 Fax: (443) 412-2169
Brian Hammond, Coordinator of Admissions, Harford Community College, 401 Thomas Run Road, Bel Air, MD 21015

Howard Community College
Columbia, Maryland
www.howardcc.edu

CB code: 5308

- Public 2-year community college
- Commuter campus in small city

General. Founded in 1966. Regionally accredited. **Enrollment:** 9,244 degree-seeking undergraduates; 837 non-degree-seeking students. **Degrees:** 872 associate awarded. **Location:** 20 miles from Baltimore, 30 miles from Washington, DC. **Calendar:** Semester, extensive summer session. **Full-time faculty:** 173 total; 30% have terminal degrees, 24% minority, 66% women. **Part-time faculty:** 679 total; 13% have terminal degrees, 26% minority, 63% women. **Class size:** 55% < 20, 43% 20-39, 2% 40-49, less than 1% 50-99, less than 1% >100. **Special facilities:** Practice rooms, recital hall, black box theater, art and dance studios, child care facility, center for entrepreneurial and business excellence, wellness center, mediation and conflict resolution center, World Languages Institute, transfer center, Howard County African American cultural center research library and archives. **Partnerships:** Formal partnerships with Microsoft Authorized Academic Training Program, Comp Tia Authorized Education Partner, Regional Cisco Networking Academy, Castle Worldwide.

Student profile. Among degree-seeking undergraduates, 71% enrolled in a transfer program, 29% enrolled in a vocational program, 13% already have a bachelor's degree or higher, 1,541 enrolled as first-time, first-year students.

Part-time:	62%	Hispanic American:	7%
Women:	57%	International:	5%
African American:	28%	25 or older:	36%
Asian American:	11%		

Transfer out. 67% of students enrolled in the transfer program go on to 4-year colleges. **Colleges most students transferred to 2011:** University of Maryland-College Park, University of Maryland-Baltimore County, Towson University, Salisbury University.

Basis for selection. Open admission, but selective for some programs. Special requirements for clinical nursing, radiologic technology, emergency medical services, cardiovascular technology applicants. Selective admission to honors programs. SAT or ACT required for admission to Scholars Program. Mandatory assessment policy. Most students must complete placement testing before completing 12 credits. Placement test exemptions allowed based on SAT/ACT scores. Interview and portfolio recommended for some selective admissions programs. **Adult students:** SAT/ACT scores not required.

High school preparation. Recommended units include English 4, mathematics 4, social studies 4, history 3, science 3 (laboratory 2) and foreign language 3. Computer related course involving skills such as word-processing, databases and spreadsheets, as well as the Internet.

2011-2012 Annual costs. Tuition/fees: $4,168; $6,658 out-of-district; $8,008 out-of-state. Books/supplies: $1,800. Personal expenses: $1,600.

2010-2011 Financial aid. Need-based: 75% of total undergraduate aid awarded as scholarships/grants, 25% as loans/jobs. Need-based aid available for part-time students. Work-study available nights, weekends and for part-time students.

Application procedures. Admission: No deadline. $25 fee, may be waived for applicants with need. Admission notification on a rolling basis. Specific deadlines may apply for applications to honors programs, clinical nursing program and most allied health programs. **Financial aid:** Priority date 3/1; no closing date. FAFSA required. Applicants notified on a rolling basis starting 5/1.

Academics. Pre-admission summer program for disabled students only. **Special study options:** Accelerated study, cooperative education, distance learning, dual enrollment of high school students, ESL, external degree, honors, independent study, internships, liberal arts/career combination, study abroad, teacher certification program, weekend college. License preparation in nursing, paramedic, radiology. **Credit/placement by examination:** AP, CLEP, IB, institutional tests. 30 credit hours maximum toward associate degree. **Support services:** GED preparation, learning center, pre-admission summer program, reduced course load, remedial instruction, study skills assistance, tutoring, writing center.

Majors. Area/ethnic studies: American, women's. **Biology:** Bioinformatics, biotechnology. **Business:** Accounting technology, business admin, casino management, entrepreneurial studies, financial planning, hospitality admin, hotel/motel admin, international, office management, office technology, restaurant/food services. **Communications:** Communications/speech/rhetoric, journalism, organizational, persuasive communications. **Computer sciences:** Computer science, data entry, information technology, networking, programming, support specialist, vendor certification, web page design. **Conservation:** Environmental science. **Education:** Chemistry, early childhood, early childhood special, elementary, elementary special ed, English, mathematics, physics, secondary, Spanish. **Engineering:** General, biomedical, computer, electrical. **English:** English lit. **Foreign languages:** Arabic, Spanish. **General:** Food science, horticultural science. **Health services:** Alternative medicine, athletic training, cardiovascular technology, clinical nutrition, community health, dietetic technician, EMT paramedic, health care admin, licensed practical nurse, massage therapy, nursing (RN), physical therapy assistant, predental, premedicine, prenursing, preoptometry, prepharmacy, preveterinary, radiologic technology/medical imaging, respiratory therapy technology, substance abuse counseling, surgical technology. **History:** General. **Liberal arts:** Arts/sciences. **Math:** General, applied. **Parks/recreation:** Exercise sciences, health/fitness, sports admin. **Philosophy/religion:** General. **Physical sciences:** General. **Protective services:** Criminal justice, police science. **Psychology:** General. **Social sciences:** General, anthropology, international economics, sociology. **Visual/performing arts:** Art, art history/conservation, cinematography, dance, digital arts, dramatic, film/cinema/video, game design, graphic design, interior design, multimedia, music, music technology, musical theater, photography, studio arts, studio arts management, theater design.

Most popular majors. Business/marketing 11%, education 6%, health sciences 17%, liberal arts 59%.

Computing on campus. 200 workstations in library, computer center, student center. Commuter students can connect to campus network. Online course registration, online library, helpline, student web hosting, wireless network available.

Student life. Freshman orientation: Available. Preregistration for classes offered. 3-4 hour day or evening program the week before start of fall and spring semesters or optional online orientation. **Policies:** Drug- and alcohol-free campus, code of conduct, academic honesty. **Activities:** Jazz band, campus ministries, choral groups, dance, drama, international student organizations, literary magazine, music ensembles, musical theater, radio station, student government, student newspaper, TV station, Christian fellowship, Muslim student association, Black student union, Hispanic student union, peace/human rights club, environmental club, nursing club, anthropology & archaeology society, gay straight alliance, U.S. Green Building Council club.

Athletics. NJCAA. **Intercollegiate:** Basketball, cross-country, lacrosse, soccer, track and field, volleyball W. **Team name:** Dragons.

Student services. Adult student services, career counseling, services for economically disadvantaged, student employment services, financial aid counseling, on-campus daycare, personal counseling, placement for graduates, veterans' counselor, women's services. **Physically disabled:** Services for visually, speech, hearing impaired. **Transfer:** Pre-admission transcript evaluation for new students. Transfer center, transfer adviser, college fairs on campus for students transferring to 4-year colleges.

Contact. E-mail: adm-adv@howardcc.edu
Phone: (443) 518-1200 Fax: (443) 518-4589
Christy Thomson, Assistant Director of Admissions (Outreach), Howard Community College, 10901 Little Patuxent Parkway, Columbia, MD 21044-3197

Kaplan University: Hagerstown
Hagerstown, Maryland
www.Hagerstown.KaplanUniversity.edu — CB code: 0804

- For-profit 2-year business and junior college
- Commuter campus in large town
- Interview required

General. Founded in 1938. Regionally accredited. **Enrollment:** 284 full-time, degree-seeking students. **Degrees:** 39 bachelor's, 276 associate awarded. **Location:** 70 miles from Baltimore, 70 miles from Washington, DC. **Calendar:** Quarter, limited summer session. **Full-time faculty:** 12 total. **Part-time faculty:** 31 total. **Special facilities:** Firearms training simulator, forensic recovery and evidence detection lab.

Student profile.

Out-of-state:	60%	Live on campus:	3%
25 or older:	55%		

Basis for selection. Open admission, but selective for some programs.

2011-2012 Annual costs. Estimated tuition and fees ranges for entire programs as of July 2011: diploma programs, $16,065 -$22,491; associate degree programs, $32,130; bachelor's degree programs, $64,260; does not include books and supplies, which vary by program. All costs subject to change at any time. Books/supplies: $875. Personal expenses: $960.

Financial aid. Need-based: Need-based aid available for part-time students. Work-study available nights, weekends and for part-time students.

Application procedures. Admission: No deadline. $20 fee. Admission notification on a rolling basis. **Financial aid:** No deadline. FAFSA, institutional form required. Applicants notified on a rolling basis starting 6/1; must reply within 2 week(s) of notification.

Academics. College includes allied health, legal, business, criminal justice, computer forensics and information technology divisions. Several bachelor's programs offered in online courses. **Special study options:** Distance learning, double major, internships. Bachelor's degree programs available on campus. **Credit/placement by examination:** AP, CLEP, institutional tests. 15 credit hours maximum toward associate degree. **Support services:** Reduced course load, remedial instruction, tutoring.

Majors. Business: Accounting, administrative services, business admin, office technology. **Computer sciences:** Computer graphics, data processing, LAN/WAN management, system admin, webmaster. **Health services:** Medical assistant, medical records technology, medical secretary, medical transcription. **Protective services:** Criminal justice, forensics, law enforcement admin.

Most popular majors. Business/marketing 22%, computer/information sciences 28%, health sciences 39%, legal studies 11%.

Computing on campus. 85 workstations in library, computer center.

Student life. Freshman orientation: Mandatory. Preregistration for classes offered. **Housing:** Coed dorms available. $150 deposit. **Activities:** Student government.

Student services. Career counseling, student employment services, financial aid counseling, personal counseling, placement for graduates.

Contact. E-mail: info@ku-hagerstown.edu
Phone: (301) 739-2670 Toll-free number: (800) 422-2670
Fax: (301) 791-7661
Jim Klein, Director of Admissions, Kaplan University: Hagerstown, 18618 Crestwood Drive, Hagerstown, MD 21742

Montgomery College
Rockville, Maryland — CB member
www.montgomerycollege.edu — CB code: 5440

- Public 2-year community college
- Commuter campus in very large city

General. Founded in 1946. Regionally accredited. Campuses in Takoma Park/Silver Spring, Rockville, and Germantown. **Enrollment:** 21,446 degree-seeking undergraduates. **Degrees:** 2,184 associate awarded. **Location:** 5 miles from Washington, DC. **Calendar:** Semester, extensive summer session. **Full-time faculty:** 523 total; 35% have terminal degrees, 29% minority, 57% women. **Part-time faculty:** 786 total; 29% have terminal degrees, 29% minority, 56% women. **Class size:** 36% < 20, 62% 20-39, less than 1% 40-49, 2% 50-99. **Special facilities:** Performing arts center, child care center, planetarium.

Student profile. Among degree-seeking undergraduates, 75% enrolled in a transfer program, 25% enrolled in a vocational program, 2% already have a bachelor's degree or higher, 1,037 transferred in from other institutions.

Out-of-state:	4%	25 or older:	36%

Transfer out. 67% of students enrolled in the transfer program go on to 4-year colleges. **Colleges most students transferred to 2011:** University of Maryland: College Park, University of Maryland: Baltimore County, Towson State University, University of Maryland: University College, Salisbury University.

Basis for selection. Open admission, but selective for some programs. Admission to allied medical health programs considers standardized test scores, secondary school record, geographical residence, and state residence. Montgomery County residents get first priority; GPA rank within residency category is important. Audition required for music majors and School of Art & Design admissions process requires a portfolio review/interview.

High school preparation. College-preparatory program recommended. Recommended units include English 4, mathematics 3 and science 2.

2011-2012 Annual costs. Tuition/fees: $4,380; $8,520 out-of-district; $11,508 out-of-state. Books/supplies: $1,200. Personal expenses: $1,380.

2010-2011 Financial aid. Need-based: 98% of total undergraduate aid awarded as scholarships/grants, 2% as loans/jobs. Need-based aid available for part-time students. Work-study available nights, weekends and for part-time students. **Non-need-based:** Scholarships awarded for academics, alumni affiliation, art, athletics, leadership, minority status, music/drama, state residency.

Application procedures. Admission: No deadline. $25 fee, may be waived for applicants with need. Admission notification on a rolling basis. **Financial aid:** Priority date 5/15; no closing date. FAFSA, institutional form required. Applicants notified on a rolling basis starting 5/30.

Academics. Special study options: Accelerated study, cooperative education, distance learning, double major, dual enrollment of high school students, ESL, honors, independent study, internships, study abroad, teacher certification program. License preparation in nursing, physical therapy, radiology, real estate. **Credit/placement by examination:** AP, CLEP, institutional tests. 45 credit hours maximum toward associate degree. **Support services:** GED preparation, learning center, pre-admission summer program, remedial instruction, study skills assistance, tutoring, writing center.

Majors. Architecture: Technology. **Biology:** Biochemistry. **Business:** General, accounting technology, business admin, construction management, hospitality admin, hotel/motel admin, international, management information systems. **Communications:** Advertising, broadcast journalism. **Communications technology:** Desktop publishing, graphic/printing, graphics. **Computer sciences:** General, computer graphics, computer science, information systems, programming. **Education:** General, early childhood, science. **Engineering:** General, civil. **Foreign languages:** American Sign Language. **Health services:** Medical radiologic technology/radiation therapy, medical records technology, nursing (RN), physical therapy assistant, predental, premedicine, prepharmacy, sonography, surgical technology. **Liberal arts:** Arts/sciences. **Math:** General. **Parks/recreation:** Exercise sciences. **Physical sciences:** Physics. **Protective services:** Firefighting, law enforcement admin. **Visual/performing arts:** General, art history/conservation, commercial photography, commercial/advertising art, dance, game design, interior design, music, photography, studio arts, theater design. **Work/family studies:** Child care management, institutional food production.

Most popular majors. Business/marketing 18%, engineering/engineering technologies 6%, health sciences 11%, liberal arts 52%.

Computing on campus. 400 workstations in library, computer center. Commuter students can connect to campus network. Online course registration, online library, helpline, wireless network available.

Student life. Freshman orientation: Available. Preregistration for classes offered. **Activities:** Concert band, choral groups, dance, drama, international student organizations, music ensembles, musical theater, radio station, student government, student newspaper, TV station, Jewish student association, progressive student alliance, Christian fellowship, lesbian student alliance, Students Against Driving Drunk, African-American student organization, Hispanic student organization, Asian student organization.

Athletics. NJCAA. **Intercollegiate:** Baseball M, basketball, soccer M, softball W, tennis, track and field, volleyball W. **Intramural:** Basketball.

Student services. Adult student services, career counseling, services for economically disadvantaged, student employment services, financial aid

counseling, minority student services, on-campus daycare, personal counseling, placement for graduates, veterans' counselor. **Physically disabled:** Services for visually, speech, hearing impaired. **Transfer:** Re-entry adviser, preadmission transcript evaluation for new students. Transfer center, transfer adviser, college fairs on campus for students transferring to 4-year colleges.

Contact. Phone: (240) 567-5034 Fax: (240) 567-5037
Rochelle Moore, Director of Enrollment Management, Montgomery College, 51 Mannakee Street, Rockville, MD 20850

Prince George's Community College

Largo, Maryland
www.pgcc.edu

CB member
CB code: 5545

- Public 2-year community college
- Commuter campus in very large city

General. Founded in 1958. Regionally accredited. Extension center at Andrews Air Force Base serves both military and civilian personnel. **Enrollment:** 14,647 undergraduates. **Degrees:** 807 associate awarded. **ROTC:** Army, Air Force. **Location:** 10 miles from Washington, DC. **Calendar:** Semester, limited summer session. **Full-time faculty:** 239 total. **Part-time faculty:** 694 total. **Class size:** 64% < 20, 35% 20-39, less than 1% 40-49, less than 1% 50-99. **Special facilities:** Natatorium, art gallery.

Student profile.

Out-of-state:	4%	25 or older:	47%

Transfer out. Colleges most students transferred to 2011: University of Maryland-College Park, Bowie State University, University of Maryland-University College, Morgan State University, Howard University.

Basis for selection. Open admission, but selective for some programs. Special requirements for health technology programs and for international students. Health technology program requires high school diploma or GED. For some scholarship awards or honors program consideration, SAT combined score of 1050 or above (exclusive of writing) required. SAT or ACT scores may be used in place of college's placement tests.

High school preparation. Recommended units include English 4, mathematics 4, social studies 3, history 3, science 3 (laboratory 2) and academic electives 4. One computer literacy recommended.

2011-2012 Annual costs. Tuition/fees: $3,920; $6,050 out-of-district; $8,690 out-of-state. Per-credit charge: $96 in-district; $167 out-of-district; $255 out-of-state. Books/supplies: $723.

Financial aid. All financial aid based on need. Need-based aid available for part-time students. Work-study available nights, weekends and for part-time students.

Application procedures. Admission: No deadline. $25 fee. Admission notification on a rolling basis. **Financial aid:** Priority date 6/1; no closing date. FAFSA, institutional form required. Applicants notified on a rolling basis starting 6/1; must reply within 2 week(s) of notification.

Academics. Special study options: Cooperative education, distance learning, double major, dual enrollment of high school students, ESL, honors, independent study, liberal arts/career combination, teacher certification program, weekend college. License preparation in nursing, paramedic, radiology, real estate. **Credit/placement by examination:** AP, CLEP, institutional tests. 30 credit hours maximum toward associate degree. **Support services:** GED preparation, learning center, reduced course load, remedial instruction, study skills assistance, tutoring, writing center.

Majors. Area/ethnic studies: African-American, American, women's. **Biology:** General. **Business:** Accounting, administrative services, business admin, marketing, office management, office technology. **Computer sciences:** General, computer science, information systems, programming, systems analysis. **Education:** Business, early childhood, elementary, health, mathematics, physical, science, secondary. **Engineering:** General. **Health services:** EMT paramedic, medical radiologic technology/radiation therapy, medical records admin, medical records technology, medical secretary, nuclear medical technology, nursing (RN), premedicine, prepharmacy, respiratory therapy technology. **Liberal arts:** Arts/sciences. **Physical sciences:** Chemistry. **Protective services:** Criminal justice, forensics. **Psychology:** General. **Visual/performing arts:** Commercial/advertising art, music, studio arts. **Work/family studies:** Child care management.

Computing on campus. 950 workstations in library, computer center, student center. Commuter students can connect to campus network. Online course registration, helpline, repair service available.

Student life. Freshman orientation: Available. Preregistration for classes offered. **Activities:** Choral groups, drama, film society, international student organizations, literary magazine, music ensembles, musical theater, opera, student government, student newspaper, TV station, Union of Black Scholars, Active Seniors (for senior citizens), student program board, Spanish club, French club, Caribbean students club, Muslim society, women's Bible study.

Athletics. NJCAA. **Intercollegiate:** Baseball M, basketball, bowling, golf, soccer, softball W, tennis M, volleyball W. **Intramural:** Basketball, bowling, golf, racquetball, soccer, table tennis, volleyball. **Team name:** Owls.

Student services. Adult student services, career counseling, services for economically disadvantaged, student employment services, financial aid counseling, health services, minority student services, on-campus daycare, personal counseling, placement for graduates, veterans' counselor. **Physically disabled:** Services for visually, speech, hearing impaired. **Transfer:** Re-entry adviser for new students. Transfer center, transfer adviser, college fairs on campus for students transferring to 4-year colleges.

Contact. E-mail: enrollmentservices@pgcc.edu
Phone: (301) 322-0801 Fax: (301) 322-0119
Vera Bagley, Director of Admissions and Records, Prince George's Community College, 301 Largo Road, Largo, MD 20774

TESST College of Technology: Baltimore

Baltimore, Maryland
www.tesst.com/tesstPortal

- For-profit 2-year technical college
- Very large city

General. Regionally accredited; also accredited by ACCSC. **Degrees:** 37 associate awarded. **Calendar:** Semester. **Full-time faculty:** 7 total. **Part-time faculty:** 34 total.

Basis for selection. Open admission, but selective for some programs. Institutional evaluation test may be accepted in lieu of SAT/ACT.

Financial aid. Need-based: Work-study available nights, weekends and for part-time students.

Application procedures. Admission: No deadline. $10 fee. Admission notification on a rolling basis. **Financial aid:** No deadline.

Academics. Credit/placement by examination: AP, CLEP.

Majors. Computer sciences: Information systems.

Contact. Phone: (410) 644-6400 Toll-free number: (800) 988-2650
Fax: (410) 644-6481
William Scott, Director of Admissions, TESST College of Technology: Baltimore, 1520 South Caton Avenue, Baltimore, MD 21227-1063

TESST College of Technology: Beltsville

Beltsville, Maryland
www.tesst.com

- For-profit 2-year technical college
- Large town

General. Accredited by ACCSC. **Degrees:** 112 associate awarded. **Calendar:** Semester. **Full-time faculty:** 5 total. **Part-time faculty:** 45 total.

Basis for selection. Open admission.

Financial aid. Need-based: Work-study available nights, weekends and for part-time students.

Application procedures. Admission: $10 fee.

Academics. Credit/placement by examination: AP, CLEP.

Majors. Computer sciences: Data entry, information systems.

Contact. E-mail: dedmonds@tesst.com
Phone: (301) 937-8448 Toll-free number: (800) 488-3778
Cathy McKinney, Director of Admissions, TESST College of Technology: Beltsville, 4600 Powder Mill Road, Beltsville, MD 20705

Two-Year Colleges

TESST College of Technology: Towson
Towson, Maryland
www.tesst.com

- For-profit 2-year technical college
- Small city
- Interview required

General. Accredited by ACCSC. **Degrees:** 36 associate awarded. **Location:** 15 miles from Baltimore. **Calendar:** Semester. **Full-time faculty:** 8 total. **Part-time faculty:** 14 total.

Basis for selection. Open admission, but selective for some programs. **Adult students:** CPAT for all students.

Financial aid. Need-based: Work-study available nights, weekends and for part-time students.

Application procedures. Admission: No deadline. $10 fee. Admission notification on a rolling basis.

Academics. Credit/placement by examination: AP, CLEP. **Support services:** Tutoring.

Majors. Business: Management information systems. **Protective services:** Law enforcement admin.

Student life. Freshman orientation: Mandatory. Preregistration for classes offered.

Student services. Career counseling, student employment services, financial aid counseling, placement for graduates, veterans' counselor.

Contact. Phone: (410) 296-5350 Fax: (410) 296-5356
Nicholaus Buzzard, Director of Admissions, TESST College of Technology: Towson, 803 Glen Eagles Court, Towson, MD 21286

Wor-Wic Community College
Salisbury, Maryland
www.worwic.edu   CB code: 1613

- Public 2-year community college
- Commuter campus in large town

General. Founded in 1975. Regionally accredited. **Enrollment:** 3,657 degree-seeking undergraduates; 406 non-degree-seeking students. **Degrees:** 371 associate awarded. **Location:** 110 miles from Baltimore, 120 miles from Washington, DC. **Calendar:** Semester, limited summer session. **Full-time faculty:** 68 total; 25% have terminal degrees, 9% minority, 63% women. **Part-time faculty:** 134 total; 6% have terminal degrees, 11% minority, 66% women. **Class size:** 35% < 20, 56% 20-39, 6% 40-49, 3% 50-99. **Partnerships:** Formal partnership with local medical center to provide financial and clinical support to the college's health programs.

Student profile. Among degree-seeking undergraduates, 41% enrolled in a transfer program, 59% enrolled in a vocational program, 5% already have a bachelor's degree or higher, 800 enrolled as first-time, first-year students.

Part-time:	65%	Asian American:	2%
Out-of-state:	2%	Hispanic American:	3%
Women:	64%	25 or older:	44%
African American:	25%		

Transfer out. 15% of students enrolled in the transfer program go on to 4-year colleges. **Colleges most students transferred to 2011:** Salisbury University, University of Maryland Eastern Shore.

Basis for selection. Open admission, but selective for some programs. Special requirements for emergency medical services, nursing and radiologic technology programs.

High school preparation. College-preparatory program recommended.

2011-2012 Annual costs. Tuition/fees: $2,951; $6,318 out-of-district; $7,728 out-of-state. Per-credit charge: $91 in-district; $203 out-of-district; $250 out-of-state. Books/supplies: $1,600. Personal expenses: $1,900.

Financial aid. Need-based: Need-based aid available for part-time students. Work-study available nights, weekends and for part-time students. **Non-need-based:** Scholarships awarded for academics, state residency.

Application procedures. Admission: No deadline. No application fee. Admission notification on a rolling basis. **Financial aid:** Priority date 6/1; no closing date. FAFSA, institutional form required. Applicants notified on a rolling basis starting 4/1.

Academics. Special study options: Distance learning, double major, dual enrollment of high school students, ESL, honors, internships. License preparation in nursing, paramedic, radiology. **Credit/placement by examination:** AP, CLEP, institutional tests. 30 credit hours maximum toward associate degree. **Support services:** Learning center, reduced course load, remedial instruction, tutoring, writing center.

Majors. Business: General, accounting technology, administrative services, business admin, hospitality admin. **Computer sciences:** General, systems analysis. **Education:** General, early childhood, elementary. **Health services:** EMT paramedic, medical radiologic technology/radiation therapy, nursing (RN), substance abuse counseling. **Liberal arts:** Arts/sciences. **Protective services:** Police science. **Work/family studies:** Child care management.

Most popular majors. Business/marketing 21%, education 7%, health sciences 28%, liberal arts 29%.

Computing on campus. 657 workstations in library, computer center, student center. Commuter students can connect to campus network. Online library available.

Student life. Freshman orientation: Available. Preregistration for classes offered. **Activities:** Choral groups, drama, literary magazine, student government, student newspaper.

Student services. Career counseling, student employment services, financial aid counseling, on-campus daycare, personal counseling, placement for graduates, veterans' counselor. **Physically disabled:** Services for visually, speech, hearing impaired. **Transfer:** College fairs on campus for students transferring to 4-year colleges.

Contact. E-mail: admissions@worwic.edu
Phone: (410) 334-2895 Fax: (410) 334-2954
Richard Webster, Director of Admissions, Wor-Wic Community College, 32000 Campus Drive, Salisbury, MD 21804

Massachusetts

Bay State College
Boston, Massachusetts
www.baystate.edu

CB code: 3120

- For-profit 2-year career college
- Commuter campus in very large city
- Interview required

General. Founded in 1946. Regionally accredited. **Enrollment:** 1,203 degree-seeking undergraduates. **Degrees:** 57 bachelor's, 144 associate awarded. **Calendar:** Semester, limited summer session. **Full-time faculty:** 36 total. **Part-time faculty:** 96 total.

Student profile. Among degree-seeking undergraduates, 261 enrolled as first-time, first-year students.

Part-time:	35%	Hispanic American:	13%
Women:	73%	International:	3%
African American:	23%	25 or older:	13%
Asian American:	4%	Live on campus:	31%

Basis for selection. Students must meet acceptance criteria and interview with admissions.

High school preparation. Recommended units include English 4, mathematics 4, social studies 4, history 4, science 4 (laboratory 1).

2011-2012 Annual costs. Tuition/fees: $22,355. Per-credit charge: $731. Room/board: $11,800. Books/supplies: $1,500. Personal expenses: $2,388.

2010-2011 Financial aid. Need-based: 43% of total undergraduate aid awarded as scholarships/grants, 57% as loans/jobs. Need-based aid available for part-time students. Work-study available nights, weekends and for part-time students. **Non-need-based:** Scholarships awarded for academics, job skills, leadership.

Application procedures. Admission: No deadline. $40 fee, may be waived for applicants with need. Admission notification on a rolling basis. **Financial aid:** Priority date 3/15, closing date 6/30. FAFSA required. Applicants notified on a rolling basis starting 3/1.

Academics. Special study options: Accelerated study, distance learning, honors, independent study, internships, study abroad. Bachelor's degree programs available on campus. License preparation in nursing, physical therapy. **Credit/placement by examination:** AP, CLEP, IB, institutional tests. 30 credit hours maximum toward associate degree, 30 toward bachelor's. **Support services:** Learning center, reduced course load, study skills assistance, tutoring.

Majors. Business: Business admin, fashion, hospitality/recreation, retailing. **Education:** Early childhood. **Health services:** General, licensed practical nurse, medical assistant, physical therapy assistant. **Protective services:** Law enforcement admin. **Visual/performing arts:** Fashion design, music management.

Most popular majors. Business/marketing 22%, education 6%, health sciences 36%, visual/performing arts 19%.

Computing on campus. 62 workstations in dormitories, library, computer center, student center.

Student life. Freshman orientation: Mandatory. Preregistration for classes offered. **Housing:** Coed dorms, single-sex dorms available. $300 nonrefundable deposit. **Activities:** Literary magazine, clubs associated with majors, student activities club, international club, community service.

Student services. Adult student services, career counseling, student employment services, financial aid counseling, health services, personal counseling, placement for graduates, veterans' counselor. **Transfer:** Pre-admission transcript evaluation for new students. Transfer adviser, college fairs on campus for students transferring to 4-year colleges.

Contact. E-mail: admissions@baystate.edu
Phone: (617) 217-9000 Toll-free number: (800) 815-3276
Fax: (617) 249-0400
Kim Olds, Director of College-Wide Admissions, Bay State College, 122 Commonwealth Avenue, Boston, MA 02116

Benjamin Franklin Institute of Technology
Boston, Massachusetts
www.bfit.edu

CB member
CB code: 3394

- Private 2-year technical college
- Commuter campus in very large city
- Application essay required

General. Founded in 1908. Regionally accredited. Prepares students for careers in automotive, computer, industrial, and engineering technologies. **Enrollment:** 564 degree-seeking undergraduates. **Degrees:** 5 bachelor's, 120 associate awarded. **Calendar:** Semester, limited summer session. **Full-time faculty:** 34 total. **Part-time faculty:** 32 total. **Special facilities:** Extensive learning laboratories for automotive, architecture, computer, electronic, electrical, optician, pharmacy, and mechanical engineering technologies.

Student profile.

Out-of-state:	6%	Live on campus:	10%
25 or older:	14%		

Transfer out. Colleges most students transferred to 2011: University of Massachusetts at Lowell, Wentworth Institute, Boston Architectural College, University of Massachusetts at Dartmouth, University of Massachusetts at Boston.

Basis for selection. High school academic performance and motivation most important. After conditional admission, all students required to take placement testing to determine English and math-level placement. Math requirements vary by academic program. SAT or ACT recommended. Interview recommended. **Home schooled:** State high school equivalency certificate, letter of recommendation (nonparent) required.

High school preparation. College-preparatory program recommended. 17 units required; 20 recommended. Required and recommended units include English 4, mathematics 3-4, social studies 2, history 1, science 3 (laboratory 2), foreign language 2 and computer science 2. Level of math and science required varies by program.

2011-2012 Annual costs. Tuition/fees: $15,950. Per-credit charge: $665. Cost shown is for Associate and Certificate programs. Bachelor degree tuition is $17,190 for the third and fourth year courses. Room/board: $9,300. Books/supplies: $1,000.

Financial aid. Need-based: Need-based aid available for part-time students. Work-study available nights, weekends and for part-time students. **Non-need-based:** Scholarships awarded for academics, leadership.

Application procedures. Admission: Priority date 5/1; no deadline. $25 fee, may be waived for applicants with need, free for online applicants. Admission notification on a rolling basis beginning on or about 11/15. **Financial aid:** Priority date 4/1; no closing date. FAFSA required. Applicants notified on a rolling basis starting 3/1; must reply within 4 week(s) of notification.

Academics. Special study options: Accelerated study, double major, dual enrollment of high school students, ESL, internships, liberal arts/career combination. Bachelor's degree programs available on campus. **Credit/placement by examination:** AP, CLEP, IB, institutional tests. **Support services:** Learning center, pre-admission summer program, reduced course load, remedial instruction, study skills assistance, tutoring.

Majors. Architecture: Technology. **Biology:** Biomedical sciences. **Computer sciences:** General, programming. **Health services:** Ophthalmic technology, optician.

Computing on campus. 120 workstations in library, computer center. Dormitories wired for high-speed internet access and linked to campus network. Commuter students can connect to campus network. Online library, helpline, wireless network available.

Student life. Freshman orientation: Mandatory. Preregistration for classes offered. Two-day program held in late-August or early-September prior to first day of class. **Housing:** Coed dorms available. $200 nonrefundable deposit, deadline 6/1. **Activities:** Student government, student newspaper.

Athletics. NJCAA. **Intercollegiate:** Soccer M. **Intramural:** Basketball, football (non-tackle), skiing, table tennis. **Team name:** Shockers.

Student services. Career counseling, student employment services, financial aid counseling, personal counseling, placement for graduates, veterans' counselor, women's services. **Transfer:** Pre-admission transcript evaluation for new students. Transfer adviser, college fairs on campus for students transferring to 4-year colleges.

Contact. E-mail: admissions@bfit.edu
Phone: (617) 423-4630 ext. 121
Toll-free number: (877) 400-2348 ext. 121 Fax: (617) 482-3706
Michael Bosco, Dean of Admissions, Benjamin Franklin Institute of
Technology, 41 Berkeley Street, Boston, MA 02116

Berkshire Community College
Pittsfield, Massachusetts
CB member
www.berkshirecc.edu
CB code: 3102

◆ Public 2-year community college
◆ Commuter campus in large town

General. Founded in 1960. Regionally accredited. Elderhostel program site,
lead institution for Osher Lifelong Learning Institute. **Enrollment:** 2,157
degree-seeking undergraduates; 409 non-degree-seeking students. **Degrees:**
263 associate awarded. **Location:** 45 miles from Albany, NY. **Calendar:**
Semester, limited summer session. **Full-time faculty:** 51 total; 100% have
terminal degrees, 2% minority, 67% women. **Part-time faculty:** 144 total;
88% have terminal degrees, 5% minority, 55% women. **Class size:** 16%
< 20, 84% 20-39. **Special facilities:** Global positioning laboratory, nature
trails, renewable energy technology resource training center, public recreational facility. **Partnerships:** Formal partnerships with Plastics Network,
Applied Technology Council, Berkshire Works, Tech-Prep programs, service
learning programs.

Student profile. Among degree-seeking undergraduates, 33% enrolled in
a transfer program, 67% enrolled in a vocational program, 527 enrolled as
first-time, first-year students, 140 transferred in from other institutions.

Part-time:	51%	Asian American:	2%
Out-of-state:	3%	Hispanic American:	6%
Women:	62%	International:	1%
African American:	6%	25 or older:	42%

Transfer out. 41% of students enrolled in the transfer program go on to
4-year colleges. **Colleges most students transferred to 2011:** University of
Massachusetts-Amherst, Massachusetts College of Liberal Arts, Westfield
State College, State University of New York, Sage Colleges.

Basis for selection. Open admission, but selective for some programs.
Special requirements for nursing and allied health programs. **Home schooled:**
State high school equivalency certificate required.

High school preparation. 1 chemistry, 1 biology, 1 algebra, demonstrated
college level English skills required for nursing and health program applicants.

2011-2012 Annual costs. Tuition/fees: $5,190; $12,810 out-of-state. Per-
credit charge: $26 in-state; $280 out-of-state. Books/supplies: $825. Personal
expenses: $2,615.

2010-2011 Financial aid. Need-based: Average need met was 58%. Average scholarship/grant was $3,281; average loan $2,415. 72% of total undergraduate aid awarded as scholarships/grants, 28% as loans/jobs. Need-based
aid available for part-time students. Work-study available nights, weekends
and for part-time students. **Non-need-based:** Scholarships awarded for academics, job skills, leadership, state residency. **Additional information:** "Free
College" Financial aid pledge to cover 100% of tuition and fees up to 12
credits/semester for students who file FAFSA by May 1 each year and who
become eligible for Federal Pell grant.

Application procedures. Admission: No deadline. $10 fee ($35 out-of-
state), may be waived for applicants with need. Application must be submitted
on paper. Admission notification on a rolling basis. High school students
may enroll in Dual Enrollment program and may take full time credit load
(12 credits or more). **Financial aid:** Priority date 5/1; no closing date. FAFSA
required. Applicants notified on a rolling basis starting 5/10.

Academics. Special study options: Cross-registration, distance learning,
double major, dual enrollment of high school students, ESL, honors, independent study, internships, liberal arts/career combination, student-designed
major, study abroad. License preparation in nursing, occupational therapy,
physical therapy. **Credit/placement by examination:** AP, CLEP, IB, institutional tests. 30 credit hours maximum toward associate degree. **Support
services:** GED test center, learning center, pre-admission summer program,
reduced course load, remedial instruction, study skills assistance, tutoring,
writing center.

Majors. Business: General, business admin, hospitality admin, office technology. **Computer sciences:** General. **Conservation:** Environmental science.
Engineering: General. **Health services:** Nursing (RN), physical therapy
assistant, respiratory therapy technology. **Human services:** Community org/
advocacy. **Liberal arts:** Arts/sciences. **Protective services:** Criminal justice,
firefighting. **Visual/performing arts:** General.

Most popular majors. Business/marketing 13%, health sciences 29%,
legal studies 8%, liberal arts 25%, security/protective services 8%, social
sciences 6%.

Computing on campus. 387 workstations in library, computer center,
student center. Commuter students can connect to campus network. Online
course registration, online library, helpline, wireless network available.

Student life. Freshman orientation: Mandatory. Preregistration for
classes offered. Variety of options, including 1-day orientation/registration
and 2-week summer transition program. **Policies:** Alcohol-free campus.
Activities: Jazz band, choral groups, dance, drama, international student
organizations, literary magazine, music ensembles, musical theater, student
government, TV station, Phi Theta Kappa honor society.

Student services. Adult student services, alcohol/substance abuse counseling, career counseling, services for economically disadvantaged, student
employment services, financial aid counseling, minority student services, on-
campus daycare, personal counseling, placement for graduates, veterans'
counselor, women's services. **Physically disabled:** Services for visually,
speech, hearing impaired. **Transfer:** Re-entry adviser, pre-admission transcript evaluation for new students. Transfer adviser, college fairs on campus
for students transferring to 4-year colleges.

Contact. E-mail: admissions@berkshirecc.edu
Phone: (413) 236-1630 Toll-free number: (800) 816-1233 ext. 1630
Fax: (413) 496-9511
Michael Bullock, Dean of Student Affairs and Enrollment Services,
Berkshire Community College, 1350 West Street, Pittsfield, MA
01201-5786

Bristol Community College
Fall River, Massachusetts
CB member
www.bristolcc.edu
CB code: 3110

◆ Public 2-year community college
◆ Commuter campus in small city

General. Founded in 1965. Regionally accredited. **Enrollment:** 4,416 full-
time, degree-seeking students. **Degrees:** 911 associate awarded. **Location:**
48 miles from Boston; 17 miles from Providence, Rhode Island. **Calendar:**
Semester, extensive summer session. **Full-time faculty:** 100 total. **Part-
time faculty:** 330 total. **Special facilities:** Planetarium, greenhouse, robotics
laboratory, aquaculture laboratory, cyber cafe. **Partnerships:** Formal partnerships with local businesses and non-profit organizations.

Student profile.

Out-of-state:	15%	25 or older:	49%

Basis for selection. Open admission, but selective for some programs.
Special requirements for health science and culinary arts programs. SAT
scores required for allied health programs. Essay or personal statement
required for applicants to occupational therapy assistant program. **Home
schooled:** Transcript of courses and grades required. Letter of approval from
student's school district that authenticates home school education required.

High school preparation. College-preparatory program required. Health
science programs require certain grades on specified courses.

2011-2012 Annual costs. Tuition/fees: $4,454; $10,634 out-of-state. Per-
credit charge: $24 in-state; $230 out-of-state. Books/supplies: $1,000. Per-
sonal expenses: $4,840.

Financial aid. Need-based: Need-based aid available for part-time students. Work-study available nights, weekends and for part-time students.
Non-need-based: Scholarships awarded for academics, art, leadership,
minority status, music/drama.

Application procedures. Admission: No deadline. $10 fee ($35 out-of-
state), may be waived for applicants with need, free for online applicants.
Admission notification on a rolling basis beginning on or about 12/1. Must
reply by May 1 or within 2 week(s) if notified thereafter. **Financial aid:**
Priority date 5/1; no closing date. FAFSA, institutional form required. Applicants notified on a rolling basis starting 5/1; must reply within 2 week(s)
of notification.

Academics. Students must complete general education requirement core
curriculum prior to graduation. **Special study options:** Cooperative education, cross-registration, distance learning, dual enrollment of high school
students, ESL, honors, independent study, internships, student-designed
major, weekend college. **Credit/placement by examination:** AP, CLEP,
institutional tests. 30 credit hours maximum toward associate degree. **Support
services:** GED preparation and test center, learning center, pre-admission

summer program, reduced course load, remedial instruction, tutoring, writing center.

Majors. Business: Accounting, banking/financial services, business admin. **Communications:** Communications/speech/rhetoric. **Computer sciences:** General, computer science, data processing, information systems, programming. **Education:** Early childhood, elementary, kindergarten/preschool. **Engineering:** General. **Foreign languages:** American Sign Language. **Health services:** Clinical lab technology, dental hygiene, medical records technology, medical secretary, nursing (RN), occupational therapy assistant. **Liberal arts:** Arts/sciences. **Protective services:** Criminal justice, firefighting. **Visual/performing arts:** Art, dramatic. **Work/family studies:** Child care management.

Most popular majors. Business/marketing 23%, education 8%, health sciences 12%, liberal arts 31%, security/protective services 9%.

Computing on campus. Dormitories linked to campus network. Commuter students can connect to campus network. Online course registration, online library, helpline available.

Student life. Freshman orientation: Available. Preregistration for classes offered. **Activities:** Campus ministries, choral groups, dance, drama, international student organizations, radio station, student government, student newspaper, TV station, Catholic student association, Christian Fellowship, water watch, international club, Portuguese club, Latino club, Cambodian association, human services club, coalition for social justice.

Athletics. NJCAA. **Intercollegiate:** Basketball, soccer. **Team name:** Bristol Bee's.

Student services. Adult student services, alcohol/substance abuse counseling, chaplain/spiritual director, career counseling, student employment services, financial aid counseling, health services, minority student services, on-campus daycare, personal counseling, placement for graduates, veterans' counselor. **Physically disabled:** Services for visually, speech, hearing impaired. **Transfer:** Transfer adviser, college fairs on campus for students transferring to 4-year colleges.

Contact. E-mail: admissions@bristolcc.edu
Phone: (508) 678-2811 ext. 2516 Toll-free number: (800) 462-0035
Fax: (508) 730-3265
Ben Baumann, Dean of Admissions, Bristol Community College, 777 Elsbree Street, Fall River, MA 02720-7395

Bunker Hill Community College
Boston, Massachusetts
www.bhcc.mass.edu

CB member
CB code: 3123

▶ Public 2-year community college
▶ Commuter campus in very large city

General. Founded in 1973. Regionally accredited. **Enrollment:** 11,348 degree-seeking undergraduates. **Degrees:** 815 associate awarded. **Location:** 5 miles from downtown. **Calendar:** Semester, extensive summer session. **Full-time faculty:** 142 total. **Part-time faculty:** 549 total. **Class size:** 40% < 20, 60% 20-39, less than 1% 40-49, less than 1% 50-99.

Transfer out. Colleges most students transferred to 2011: University of Massachusetts Boston, Northeastern University, Salem State College, Suffolk University, Cambridge College.

Basis for selection. Open admission, but selective for some programs. Selective admissions to nursing, medical imaging, respiratory therapy, medical laboratory technician, surgical technology, medical assistant, phlebotomy technician, medical interpreting, patient care technician, electrical power utility, and paralegal certificate program. **Home schooled:** Transcript of courses and grades required. Must submit evidence that program was approved by school district's superintendent or school committee. If under the age of 16, a letter from school district's superintendent or school committee required as well.

2011-2012 Annual costs. Tuition/fees: $4,230; $10,410 out-of-state. Per-credit charge: $24 in-state; $230 out-of-state. New England Regional Tuition: $153 per-credit-hour. Books/supplies: $1,800. Personal expenses: $1,800.

Financial aid. Need-based: Need-based aid available for part-time students. Work-study available nights, weekends and for part-time students. **Non-need-based:** Scholarships awarded for academics.

Application procedures. Admission: Priority date 5/1; no deadline. $10 fee ($35 out-of-state), may be waived for applicants with need. Admission notification on a rolling basis. Must reply by May 1 or within 2 week(s) if notified thereafter. **Financial aid:** Priority date 4/15; no closing date. FAFSA

required. Applicants notified on a rolling basis starting 6/1; must reply within 2 week(s) of notification.

Academics. Some courses taught off-campus in the community. **Special study options:** Cross-registration, distance learning, double major, dual enrollment of high school students, ESL, external degree, honors, independent study, internships, liberal arts/career combination, study abroad, weekend college. License preparation in nursing, paramedic, radiology, real estate. **Credit/placement by examination:** AP, CLEP, institutional tests. 45 credit hours maximum toward associate degree. **Support services:** GED preparation, learning center, pre-admission summer program, reduced course load, remedial instruction, study skills assistance, tutoring, writing center.

Majors. Biology: General. **Business:** Accounting, business admin, finance, hospitality admin, international, office/clerical, operations, tourism/travel. **Communications:** Communications/speech/rhetoric. **Computer sciences:** Applications programming, computer science, data entry, networking, system admin, web page design, word processing. **Education:** General. **Engineering:** General, biomedical. **English:** English lit. **Foreign languages:** General. **Health services:** Cardiovascular technology, medical radiologic technology/radiation therapy, medical secretary, nuclear medical technology, nursing (RN), respiratory therapy technology, sonography. **History:** General. **Math:** General. **Physical sciences:** Chemistry, physics. **Protective services:** Corrections, law enforcement admin, security management. **Psychology:** General. **Social sciences:** Sociology. **Visual/performing arts:** Art, design, dramatic, music.

Most popular majors. Business/marketing 28%, health sciences 28%, liberal arts 9%.

Computing on campus. 731 workstations in library, computer center. Commuter students can connect to campus network. Online course registration, online library, helpline, wireless network available.

Student life. Freshman orientation: Available. Preregistration for classes offered. **Activities:** Jazz band, choral groups, dance, drama, film society, international student organizations, literary magazine, music ensembles, radio station, student government, African American cultural society, African students club, Alpha Kappa, Arab students association, Asian students association, Brazilian club, criminal justice society, multicultural club, Veterans of All Nations club, sustainabillity club, Cape Verdean club.

Athletics. NJCAA. **Intercollegiate:** Baseball M, basketball, golf, soccer, softball W. **Intramural:** Basketball, table tennis, tennis. **Team name:** Bulldogs.

Student services. Adult student services, career counseling, services for economically disadvantaged, student employment services, financial aid counseling, health services, on-campus daycare, personal counseling, placement for graduates, veterans' counselor. **Physically disabled:** Services for visually, speech, hearing impaired. **Transfer:** Re-entry adviser, pre-admission transcript evaluation for new students. Transfer center, transfer adviser, college fairs on campus for students transferring to 4-year colleges.

Contact. E-mail: admissions@bhcc.mass.edu
Phone: (617) 228-2422 Fax: (617) 228-2082
William Sakamoto, Director of Admissions, Bunker Hill Community College, 250 New Rutherford Avenue, Boston, MA 02129-2925

Cape Cod Community College
West Barnstable, Massachusetts
www.capecod.edu

CB member
CB code: 3289

▶ Public 2-year community college
▶ Commuter campus in small town

General. Founded in 1961. Regionally accredited. **Enrollment:** 1,710 full-time, degree-seeking students. **Degrees:** 433 associate awarded. **Location:** 79 miles from Boston; 80 miles from Providence, Rhode Island. **Calendar:** Semester, limited summer session. **Full-time faculty:** 68 total; 66% women. **Part-time faculty:** 258 total; 64% women. **Class size:** 36% < 20, 63% 20-39, less than 1% 40-49, less than 1% 50-99. **Special facilities:** Source collection for Cape Cod history, marshland nature preserve, maritime studies collection, art gallery. **Partnerships:** Formal partnerships with Tech Prep, School-to-Career, Cape Cod Technology Council Apprenticeship Program.

Transfer out. Colleges most students transferred to 2011: Bridgewater State College, University of Massachusetts (Amherst, Boston, Dartmouth), Suffolk University.

Basis for selection. Open admission, but selective for some programs. Special requirements for dental hygiene and nursing programs; priority given to Massachusetts residents. Interview recommended for dental hygiene and nursing programs. **Home schooled:** Ability To Benefit assessment required.

High school preparation. Chemistry with lab and algebra required for dental hygiene and nursing programs. Nursing also requires biology with anatomy and physiology unit labs.

2011-2012 Annual costs. Tuition/fees: $4,830; $11,010 out-of-state. Per-credit charge: $24 in-state; $230 out-of-state. Books/supplies: $1,000. Personal expenses: $1,344.

Financial aid. Need-based: Need-based aid available for part-time students. Work-study available nights, weekends and for part-time students. **Non-need-based:** Scholarships awarded for academics, art, job skills, leadership, music/drama, state residency.

Application procedures. Admission: Priority date 8/10; no deadline. No application fee. Application must be submitted on paper. Admission notification on a rolling basis. Must reply by May 1 or within 4 week(s) if notified thereafter. January 5 application priority date for nursing, February 1 for dental hygiene. **Financial aid:** Priority date 5/1; no closing date. FAFSA required. Applicants notified on a rolling basis starting 5/1.

Academics. Special study options: Accelerated study, cooperative education, cross-registration, distance learning, dual enrollment of high school students, ESL, honors, independent study, internships, study abroad. Bachelor's degree programs available on campus. License preparation in dental hygiene, nursing, paramedic, real estate. **Credit/placement by examination:** AP, CLEP, institutional tests. 30 credit hours maximum toward associate degree. **Support services:** GED preparation and test center, learning center, reduced course load, remedial instruction, study skills assistance, tutoring, writing center.

Honors college/program. Students invited based on GPA at end of first semester or CPT results.

Majors. Business: Accounting, accounting/business management, administrative services, business admin, executive assistant, hotel/motel admin, management science, marketing, office management, office/clerical. **Communications:** Communications/speech/rhetoric, journalism, media studies, public relations. **Computer sciences:** General, applications programming, computer science, information systems, information technology, LAN/WAN management, networking, web page design, webmaster. **Conservation:** General, environmental science, environmental studies. **Education:** General, early childhood, kindergarten/preschool. **Engineering:** General. **English:** English lit. **Foreign languages:** General. **Health services:** Dental hygiene, EMT paramedic, medical secretary, nursing (RN), predental, prenursing. **History:** General. **Liberal arts:** Arts/sciences. **Math:** General. **Philosophy/religion:** Philosophy. **Physical sciences:** General. **Protective services:** Criminal justice, fire safety technology, firefighting, law enforcement admin. **Psychology:** General. **Social sciences:** General, sociology. **Visual/performing arts:** General, commercial/advertising art, dance, dramatic, graphic design, music.

Most popular majors. Business/marketing 14%, health sciences 23%, liberal arts 22%.

Computing on campus. 400 workstations in library, computer center, student center. Commuter students can connect to campus network. Helpline, wireless network available.

Student life. Freshman orientation: Mandatory. Preregistration for classes offered. Half-day program includes meeting with assigned adviser. **Policies:** All clubs must perform one item of community service in order to maintain recognition. **Activities:** Choral groups, dance, drama, literary magazine, music ensembles, musical theater, radio station, student government, student newspaper, TV station, Phi Theta Kappa honor society, service learning, unity club, academic support club, recycling club, rotary club, sustainability club, gay-straight alliance.

Athletics. Intramural: Basketball, racquetball, table tennis, tennis, volleyball. **Team name:** Helmsmen.

Student services. Adult student services, alcohol/substance abuse counseling, career counseling, services for economically disadvantaged, student employment services, financial aid counseling, health services, minority student services, on-campus daycare, personal counseling, placement for graduates, veterans' counselor, women's center. **Physically disabled:** Services for visually, speech, hearing impaired. **Transfer:** Re-entry adviser, pre-admission transcript evaluation for new students. Transfer adviser, college fairs on campus for students transferring to 4-year colleges.

Contact. E-mail: admiss@capecod.edu
Phone: (508) 362-2131 ext. 4311
Toll-free number: (877) 846-3672 ext. 4311 Fax: (508) 375-4089
Susan Kline-Symington, Director of Admissions, Cape Cod Community College, 2240 Iyannough Road, West Barnstable, MA 02668-1599

Dean College
Franklin, Massachusetts
www.dean.edu

CB member
CB code: 3352

- Private 2-year liberal arts college
- Residential campus in large town
- SAT or ACT (ACT writing optional), application essay required

General. Founded in 1865. Regionally accredited. ARCH program for students with diagnosed learning disabilities (10% of student population), Pathway program for students needing additional academic support in the college transition (5% of student population), Honors Program available (5% of student population). **Enrollment:** 1,088 degree-seeking undergraduates. **Degrees:** 34 bachelor's, 221 associate awarded. **Location:** 30 miles from Boston; 30 miles from Providence, Rhode Island. **Calendar:** Semester, limited summer session. **Full-time faculty:** 39 total. **Part-time faculty:** 78 total. **Class size:** 63% < 20, 36% 20-39, less than 1% 40-49. **Special facilities:** Telecommunications center, childcare center, radio station. **Partnerships:** Formal partnerships with Putnam Investments (students may earn associate degree while working).

Student profile.

Out-of-state:	49%	**Live on campus:**	90%

Transfer out. Colleges most students transferred to 2011: Suffolk University, Northeastern University, University of Massachusetts Amherst, Emerson College, Bridgewater State University.

Basis for selection. School achievement record, recommendations most important. Interview recommended. **Adult students:** Test scores may be waived for adult students on a case-by-case basis. **Learning Disabled:** Arch program applicants must submit appropriate materials that identify and describe the student's learning abilities and any issues relevant to successful completion of a college program.

High school preparation. College-preparatory program recommended. Required units include English 4, mathematics 3, social studies 3, science 3 (laboratory 1).

2011-2012 Annual costs. Tuition/fees: $30,570. Room/board: $13,050. Books/supplies: $1,500. Personal expenses: $200.

Financial aid. Need-based: Need-based aid available for part-time students. Work-study available nights, weekends and for part-time students. **Non-need-based:** Scholarships awarded for academics, athletics, leadership, music/drama, state residency.

Application procedures. Admission: Priority date 3/1; deadline 8/15. $35 fee, may be waived for applicants with need. Admission notification on a rolling basis beginning on or about 11/1. Must reply by May 1 or within 2 week(s) if notified thereafter. **Financial aid:** Priority date 3/15; no closing date. FAFSA required. Applicants notified on a rolling basis starting 3/6; must reply by 5/1 or within 2 week(s) of notification.

Academics. Special study options: Double major, ESL, honors, independent study, internships, New York semester, student-designed major, study abroad, Washington semester. Bachelor's degree programs available on campus. **Credit/placement by examination:** AP, CLEP, IB, SAT, ACT, institutional tests. **Support services:** Learning center, reduced course load, remedial instruction, study skills assistance, tutoring, writing center.

Majors. Business: General, business admin. **Communications:** Communications/speech/rhetoric. **Computer sciences:** General. **Conservation:** Environmental science. **Education:** Early childhood, physical. **Health services:** Athletic training. **History:** General. **Liberal arts:** Arts/sciences. **Math:** General. **Parks/recreation:** Health/fitness, sports admin. **Physical sciences:** General. **Protective services:** Criminal justice, law enforcement admin. **Psychology:** General. **Visual/performing arts:** Dance, dramatic.

Most popular majors. Business/marketing 24%, liberal arts 24%, visual/performing arts 52%.

Computing on campus. PC or laptop required. Helpline, wireless network available.

Student life. Freshman orientation: Mandatory. Preregistration for classes offered. **Housing:** Guaranteed on-campus for all undergraduates. Coed dorms, single-sex dorms, apartments, wellness housing available. $500 nonrefundable deposit, deadline 5/1. Off-campus condos. **Activities:** Jazz band, choral groups, dance, drama, international student organizations, literary magazine, music ensembles, musical theater, radio station, student government, TV station, Hillel, Christian Fellowship.

Athletics. NJCAA. **Intercollegiate:** Baseball M, basketball, football (tackle) M, golf M, lacrosse, soccer, softball W. **Intramural:** Basketball, soccer, softball W. **Team name:** Bulldogs.

Student services. Adult student services, alcohol/substance abuse counseling, career counseling, financial aid counseling, health services, personal counseling, placement for graduates, veterans' counselor. **Physically disabled:** Services for visually, speech, hearing impaired. **Transfer:** Transfer center, transfer adviser, college fairs on campus for students transferring to 4-year colleges.

Contact. E-mail: admissions@dean.edu
Phone: (508) 541-1508 Toll-free number: (877) 879-3326
Fax: (508) 541-8726
James Fowler, Assistant Vice President of Enrollment, Dean College, 99 Main Street, Franklin, MA 02038-1994

Fisher College
Boston, Massachusetts
www.fisher.edu
CB code: 3391

- Private 2-year business and liberal arts college
- Residential campus in very large city

General. Founded in 1903. Regionally accredited. Branch campuses in Boston, North Attleboro and New Bedford. **Enrollment:** 1,605 degree-seeking undergraduates; 207 non-degree-seeking students. **Degrees:** 85 bachelor's, 175 associate awarded. **ROTC:** Army. **Location:** Downtown Boston. **Calendar:** Semester, limited summer session. **Full-time faculty:** 29 total; 31% have terminal degrees, 52% women. **Part-time faculty:** 136 total; 5% have terminal degrees, 52% women. **Class size:** 72% < 20, 28% 20-39. **Special facilities:** Fashion laboratory. **Partnerships:** Formal agreements with TechPrep programs in Massachusetts.

Student profile. Among degree-seeking undergraduates, 379 enrolled as first-time, first-year students, 71 transferred in from other institutions.

Part-time:	34%	Hispanic American:	8%
Out-of-state:	34%	International:	8%
Women:	72%	25 or older:	5%
African American:	12%	Live on campus:	42%
Asian American:	2%		

Basis for selection. High school GPA, test scores, personal essays and recommendation letters reviewed. Essay recommended. **Home schooled:** Statement describing home school structure and mission required. **Learning Disabled:** Accommodation review available upon request. Students requesting review should submit latest IEP as well as current psychoeducational testing.

High school preparation. Required units include English 4, mathematics 3, social studies 3 and science 2.

2011-2012 Annual costs. Tuition/fees: $25,778. Per-credit charge: $825. Room/board: $13,786. Books/supplies: $2,000. Personal expenses: $1,310.

2011-2012 Financial aid. Need-based: 79% of total undergraduate aid awarded as scholarships/grants, 21% as loans/jobs. Need-based aid available for part-time students. Work-study available nights, weekends and for part-time students. **Non-need-based:** Scholarships awarded for academics.

Application procedures. Admission: No deadline. $50 fee, may be waived for applicants with need, free for online applicants. Admission notification on a rolling basis beginning on or about 11/15. **Financial aid:** Priority date 5/1; no closing date. FAFSA required. Applicants notified on a rolling basis starting 3/1.

Academics. Special study options: Accelerated study, distance learning, dual enrollment of high school students, ESL, honors, independent study, internships, study abroad, weekend college. Bachelor's degree programs available on campus. **Credit/placement by examination:** AP, CLEP, IB, institutional tests. 30 credit hours maximum toward associate degree, 75 toward bachelor's. Institution follows ACE guide for credit by examination. **Support services:** Learning center, reduced course load, remedial instruction, study skills assistance, tutoring, writing center.

Majors. Business: Accounting, business admin, fashion, hospitality admin. **Computer sciences:** General. **Education:** Early childhood. **Liberal arts:** Arts/sciences. **Psychology:** General. **Work/family studies:** Clothing/textiles, fashion consultant.

Most popular majors. Education 9%, health sciences 14%, history 32%, liberal arts 34%.

Computing on campus. 60 workstations in dormitories, library, computer center, student center. Dormitories wired for high-speed internet access and linked to campus network. Online course registration, helpline, repair service available.

Student life. Freshman orientation: Mandatory. Preregistration for classes offered. Several 1-day preregistration days scheduled throughout summer with full 2-day orientation program prior to start of classes. **Housing:** Coed dorms, single-sex dorms available. $500 fully refundable deposit, deadline 5/14. **Activities:** Choral groups, dance, drama, literary magazine, student government.

Athletics. NAIA. **Intercollegiate:** Baseball M, basketball, soccer, softball W. **Team name:** Falcons.

Student services. Adult student services, alcohol/substance abuse counseling, career counseling, student employment services, financial aid counseling, health services, personal counseling, placement for graduates, veterans' counselor. **Transfer:** Re-entry adviser, pre-admission transcript evaluation for new students. Transfer adviser, college fairs on campus for students transferring to 4-year colleges.

Contact. E-mail: admissions@fisher.edu
Phone: (617) 236-8818 Toll-free number: (866) 266-6007
Fax: (617) 236-5473
Robert Melaragni, Dean of Admissions, Fisher College, Office of Admissions, Boston, MA 02116

Greenfield Community College
Greenfield, Massachusetts
www.gcc.mass.edu
CB member
CB code: 3420

- Public 2-year community college
- Commuter campus in large town

General. Founded in 1962. Regionally accredited. Students may enroll in credit courses taught at Smith College, Veterans Hospital (Northampton), Massachusetts College of Art. **Enrollment:** 2,285 degree-seeking undergraduates; 226 non-degree-seeking students. **Degrees:** 297 associate awarded. **Location:** 40 miles from Springfield. **Calendar:** Semester, limited summer session. **Full-time faculty:** 62 total; 64% women. **Part-time faculty:** 136 total. **Class size:** 62% < 20, 37% 20-39, less than 1% 40-49, less than 1% 50-99.

Student profile. Among degree-seeking undergraduates, 506 enrolled as first-time, first-year students, 230 transferred in from other institutions.

Part-time:	56%	Hispanic American:	5%
Women:	59%	Native American:	1%
African American:	3%	25 or older:	43%
Asian American:	4%		

Transfer out. 60% of students enrolled in the transfer program go on to 4-year colleges. **Colleges most students transferred to 2011:** University of Massachusetts: Amherst, Westfield State College, Massachusetts College of Liberal Arts, Smith College, Elms College.

Basis for selection. Open admission, but selective for some programs. Special entrance requirements for occupational technology, nursing, paramedic, massage therapy, outdoor leadership programs. **Home schooled:** State high school equivalency certificate required.

High school preparation. College-preparatory program recommended. Students from public high schools in the Commonwealth must be MCAS graduates, or demonstrate an ability to benefit.

2011-2012 Annual costs. Tuition/fees: $5,717; $13,367 out-of-state. Per-credit charge: $26 in-state; $281 out-of-state. Books/supplies: $850. Personal expenses: $1,560.

Financial aid. All financial aid based on need. Need-based aid available for part-time students. Work-study available nights, weekends and for part-time students.

Application procedures. Admission: No deadline. No application fee. Admission notification on a rolling basis. Limited space available in nursing and outdoor leadership programs. Application priority date 2/1. **Financial aid:** Priority date 4/15; no closing date. FAFSA, institutional form required. Applicants notified on a rolling basis starting 5/1; must reply within 2 week(s) of notification.

Academics. Special study options: Cooperative education, cross-registration, distance learning, double major, dual enrollment of high school students, ESL, independent study, internships, liberal arts/career combination. License preparation in nursing, paramedic, real estate. **Credit/placement by**

examination: AP, CLEP, institutional tests. 15 credit hours maximum toward associate degree. **Support services:** GED test center, learning center, reduced course load, remedial instruction, study skills assistance, tutoring.

Majors. Business: General, accounting, administrative services, business admin. **Computer sciences:** General. **Conservation:** General, environmental science. **Education:** Early childhood. **Engineering:** Engineering science. **Health services:** Nursing (RN), occupational therapy assistant. **Liberal arts:** Arts/sciences. **Protective services:** Police science. **Visual/performing arts:** Commercial/advertising art.

Most popular majors. Business/marketing 10%, health sciences 12%, liberal arts 49%, security/protective services 8%, visual/performing arts 9%.

Computing on campus. 272 workstations in library, computer center, student center. Commuter students can connect to campus network. Online library, helpline, wireless network available.

Student life. Freshman orientation: Available. Preregistration for classes offered. **Activities:** Jazz band, choral groups, dance, drama, international student organizations, music ensembles, student government.

Student services. Adult student services, career counseling, services for economically disadvantaged, student employment services, financial aid counseling, health services, personal counseling, placement for graduates, veterans' counselor, women's services. **Physically disabled:** Services for visually, speech, hearing impaired. **Transfer:** Re-entry adviser, pre-admission transcript evaluation for new students. Transfer adviser, college fairs on campus for students transferring to 4-year colleges.

Contact. E-mail: admissions@gcc.mass.edu
Phone: (413) 775-1809 Fax: (413) 773-5129
Herbert Hentz, Director of Admissions, Greenfield Community College, One College Drive, Greenfield, MA 01301

Holyoke Community College
Holyoke, Massachusetts   **CB member**
www.hcc.edu   **CB code: 3437**

▸ Public 2-year community college
▸ Commuter campus in large town

General. Founded in 1946. Regionally accredited. **Enrollment:** 6,785 degree-seeking undergraduates; 334 non-degree-seeking students. **Degrees:** 940 associate awarded. **ROTC:** Army, Air Force. **Location:** 8 miles from Springfield. **Calendar:** Semester, extensive summer session. **Full-time faculty:** 130 total; 31% have terminal degrees, 12% minority, 59% women. **Part-time faculty:** 388 total; 16% have terminal degrees, 9% minority, 55% women. **Class size:** 52% < 20, 48% 20-39, less than 1% 40-49. **Special facilities:** Art gallery.

Student profile. Among degree-seeking undergraduates, 1,730 enrolled as first-time, first-year students, 541 transferred in from other institutions.

Part-time:	48%	Asian American:	2%
Out-of-state:	1%	Hispanic American:	19%
Women:	62%	Native American:	1%
African American:	7%	25 or older:	34%

Transfer out. Colleges most students transferred to 2011: University of Massachusetts-Amherst, Western New England College, American International College, Westfield State College, Elms College.

Basis for selection. Open admission, but selective for some programs. Special requirements for nursing, radiography, animal sciences, practical nursing, medical assistant, medical coding, graphic art certificate, and culinary programs. Audition required of music majors. Portfolio required of fine arts majors. **Home schooled:** Transcript of courses and grades required. Letter required from Superintendent stating student is approved to be home schooled.

2011-2012 Annual costs. Tuition/fees: $4,290; $10,470 out-of-state. Per-credit charge: $24 in-state; $230 out-of-state. Books/supplies: $1,200. Personal expenses: $3,800.

2010-2011 Financial aid. Need-based: 77% of total undergraduate aid awarded as scholarships/grants, 23% as loans/jobs. Need-based aid available for part-time students. Work-study available nights, weekends and for part-time students. **Non-need-based:** Scholarships awarded for academics, art, leadership, music/drama.

Application procedures. Admission: No deadline. No application fee. Admission notification on a rolling basis. **Financial aid:** Priority date 5/1; no closing date. FAFSA required. Applicants notified on a rolling basis starting 5/1; must reply within 2 week(s) of notification.

Academics. Special study options: Cooperative education, cross-registration, distance learning, double major, dual enrollment of high school students, ESL, honors, independent study, internships, liberal arts/career combination, student-designed major, study abroad, teacher certification program, weekend college. License preparation in nursing. **Credit/placement by examination:** AP, CLEP, institutional tests. 30 credit hours maximum toward associate degree. **Support services:** GED preparation and test center, learning center, reduced course load, remedial instruction, study skills assistance, tutoring, writing center.

Majors. Business: Accounting technology, administrative services, hospitality admin, human resources, restaurant/food services, retailing. **Computer sciences:** Applications programming. **Engineering:** General. **Health services:** Medical radiologic technology/radiation therapy, nursing (RN), optician, veterinary technology/assistant. **Human services:** Social work. **Liberal arts:** Arts/sciences. **Parks/recreation:** Health/fitness, sports admin. **Protective services:** Criminal justice. **Social sciences:** Geography. **Visual/performing arts:** Art, music. **Work/family studies:** Child care management.

Most popular majors. Business/marketing 19%, health sciences 8%, liberal arts 49%, security/protective services 9%.

Computing on campus. 67 workstations in computer center. Commuter students can connect to campus network. Online course registration, online library, helpline, wireless network available.

Student life. Freshman orientation: Mandatory. Preregistration for classes offered. **Activities:** Jazz band, choral groups, drama, literary magazine, music ensembles, musical theater, radio station, student government, student newspaper, symphony orchestra, more than 30 clubs and organizations available.

Athletics. NJCAA. **Intercollegiate:** Baseball M, basketball, cross-country, golf, soccer, softball W, volleyball W. **Intramural:** Basketball, soccer, softball, volleyball. **Team name:** Cougars.

Student services. Adult student services, alcohol/substance abuse counseling, chaplain/spiritual director, career counseling, services for economically disadvantaged, student employment services, financial aid counseling, health services, minority student services, on-campus daycare, personal counseling, placement for graduates, veterans' counselor, women's services. **Physically disabled:** Services for visually, speech, hearing impaired. **Transfer:** Transfer adviser, college fairs on campus for students transferring to 4-year colleges.

Contact. E-mail: admissions@hcc.edu
Phone: (413) 552-2321 Fax: (413) 552-2045
Marcia Rosbury-Henne, Director of Admissions and Transfer Affairs, Holyoke Community College, 303 Homestead Avenue, Holyoke, MA 01040

ITT Technical Institute: Norwood
Norwood, Massachusetts
www.itt-tech.edu   **CB code: 2699**

▸ For-profit 2-year technical college
▸ Commuter campus in small city
▸ Interview required

General. Accredited by ACICS. **Enrollment:** 597 undergraduates. **Degrees:** 8 bachelor's, 153 associate awarded. **Calendar:** Quarter, extensive summer session. **Full-time faculty:** 3 total. **Part-time faculty:** 65 total.

Basis for selection. Satisfactory scores from on-site tests in English and math required.

2011-2012 Annual costs. Estimated costs as of July 2011: per-credit-hour charge, $493, depending upon level and course of study; academic fee, $200. Certain programs of study require purchase of tools, which could cost an additional $100 to $500. All costs are subject to change.

Financial aid. Need-based: Work-study available nights, weekends and for part-time students.

Application procedures. Admission: No deadline. No application fee. Admission notification on a rolling basis. **Financial aid:** FAFSA, institutional form required. Applicants notified on a rolling basis.

Academics. Credit/placement by examination: AP, CLEP. **Support services:** Learning center, tutoring.

Majors. Computer sciences: LAN/WAN management, networking, programming, web page design, webmaster.

Computing on campus. Online library available.

Student life. Freshman orientation: Available. Preregistration for classes offered.

Student services. Career counseling, student employment services, placement for graduates.

Contact. Phone: (781) 278-7200 Toll-free number: (800) 879-8324 Tom Ryan, Director of Recruitment, ITT Technical Institute: Norwood, 333 Providence Highway, Norwood, MA 02062

ITT Technical Institute: Wilmington
Wilmington, Massachusetts
www.itt-tech.edu

CB member
CB code: 7989

▶ For-profit 2-year technical and career college
▶ Large town

General. Regionally accredited; also accredited by ACICS. **Enrollment:** 547 undergraduates. **Degrees:** 17 bachelor's, 143 associate awarded. **Calendar:** Quarter. **Full-time faculty:** 4 total. **Part-time faculty:** 64 total.

Basis for selection. Satisfactory scores from on-site tests in English and math required.

2011-2012 Annual costs. Estimated costs as of June 2011: per-credit-hour charge, $493, depending upon level and course of study; academic fee, $200. Certain programs of study require purchase of tools, which could cost an additional $100 to $500. All costs are subject to change.

Financial aid. Need-based: Work-study available nights, weekends and for part-time students.

Academics. Credit/placement by examination: AP, CLEP.

Majors. Computer sciences: Networking, web page design.

Contact. ITT Technical Institute: Wilmington, 200 Ballardvale Street, Building 1 Suite 200, Wilmington, MA 01887

Laboure College
Dorchester, Massachusetts
www.laboure.edu

CB code: 3287

▶ Private 2-year health science and junior college affiliated with Roman Catholic Church
▶ Commuter campus in very large city

General. Founded in 1971. Regionally accredited. Affiliated with more than 100 health care agencies in Greater Boston area. **Enrollment:** 699 degree-seeking undergraduates; 32 non-degree-seeking students. **Degrees:** 3 bachelor's, 117 associate awarded. **Location:** 5 miles from downtown. **Calendar:** Semester, limited summer session. **Full-time faculty:** 22 total; 9% have terminal degrees, 4% minority, 77% women. **Part-time faculty:** 48 total; 4% have terminal degrees, 8% minority, 83% women. **Class size:** 67% < 20, 31% 20-39, 1% 40-49, 1% 50-99.

Student profile. Among degree-seeking undergraduates, 10 enrolled as first-time, first-year students, 123 transferred in from other institutions.

Part-time:	93%	Asian American:	3%
Out-of-state:	1%	Hispanic American:	7%
Women:	91%	25 or older:	70%
African American:	24%		

Transfer out. 87% of students enrolled in the transfer program go on to 4-year colleges.

Basis for selection. School achievement record, recommendations, interview important; work/life experience considered. **Home schooled:** Transcript of courses and grades, state high school equivalency certificate, letter of recommendation (nonparent) required.

High school preparation. College-preparatory program recommended. 10 units required; 16 recommended. Required and recommended units include English 4, mathematics 3, science 1-2 (laboratory 1).

2011-2012 Annual costs. Per-credit charge: $675. Cost of full-time, 4-term academic year is $25,945, inclusive of fees.

2011-2012 Financial aid. Need-based: 1 full-time freshmen applied for aid; 1 were judged to have need; 1 of these received aid. Average scholarship/grant was $1,475; average loan $3,500. 18% of total undergraduate aid awarded as scholarships/grants, 82% as loans/jobs. Need-based aid available for part-time students. Work-study available nights, weekends and for part-time students. **Non-need-based:** Scholarships awarded for academics, alumni affiliation, leadership, religious affiliation.

Application procedures. Admission: Priority date 7/1; no deadline. $50 fee, may be waived for applicants with need. Application must be submitted on paper. Admission notification on a rolling basis. Within 1 month of acceptance. **Financial aid:** Priority date 4/1; no closing date. FAFSA required. Applicants notified on a rolling basis starting 6/15; must reply within 2 week(s) of notification.

Academics. Special study options: Accelerated study, distance learning, independent study, liberal arts/career combination. Bachelor's degree programs available on campus. License preparation in nursing. **Credit/placement by examination:** AP, CLEP, institutional tests. 23 credit hours maximum toward associate degree. **Support services:** Learning center, pre-admission summer program, reduced course load, remedial instruction, tutoring.

Majors. Health services: Dietetics, medical records technology, nursing (RN).

Computing on campus. 20 workstations in library, computer center. Online library, wireless network available.

Student life. Freshman orientation: Available, $100 fee. Preregistration for classes offered. One-day information session and tour held prior to term. **Policies:** Student Conduct Policy in effect; each student expected to respect the rights and privileges of others, to adhere to acceptable standards of personal conduct, and to follow the moral and ethical standards of health care professions as reflected in the Catholic philosophy of the college, in both academic and non-academic matters. **Housing:** $200 nonrefundable deposit. **Activities:** Campus ministries, student government, student newspaper, National Student Nurses Association.

Student services. Adult student services, chaplain/spiritual director, career counseling, financial aid counseling, personal counseling. **Physically disabled:** Services for visually, speech, hearing impaired. **Transfer:** Pre-admission transcript evaluation for new students.

Contact. E-mail: admissions@laboure.edu
Phone: (617) 296-8300 ext. 4016 Toll-free number: (617) 296-7947
Fax: (617) 296-7947
Gina Morrissette, Director of Admissions, Laboure College, 2120 Dorchester Avenue, Dorchester, MA 02124-5698

Marian Court College
Swampscott, Massachusetts
www.mariancourt.edu

CB member
CB code: 9100

▶ Private 2-year junior college affiliated with Roman Catholic Church
▶ Commuter campus in large town

General. Founded in 1964. Regionally accredited. Evening division on quarter system. **Enrollment:** 187 full-time, degree-seeking students. **Degrees:** 62 associate awarded. **Location:** 15 miles from Boston. **Calendar:** Semester, limited summer session. **Full-time faculty:** 7 total. **Part-time faculty:** 20 total.

Basis for selection. High school grades and interview important. SAT/ACT is optional. Institutional English and math tests used for placement.

High school preparation. College-preparatory program recommended.

2012-2013 Annual costs. Tuition/fees (projected): $16,200. Books/supplies: $900.

Financial aid. Need-based: Need-based aid available for part-time students. Work-study available nights, weekends and for part-time students. **Non-need-based:** Scholarships awarded for academics.

Application procedures. Admission: Priority date 5/1; no deadline. No application fee. Admission notification on a rolling basis. Must reply by May 1 or within 2 week(s) if notified thereafter. **Financial aid:** Priority date 4/1; no closing date. FAFSA, institutional form required. Applicants notified on a rolling basis starting 4/15.

Academics. Freshman seminar required. **Special study options:** Cross-registration, double major, dual enrollment of high school students, honors, independent study, internships, liberal arts/career combination. Member

Northeast Consortium of Colleges and Universities in Massachusetts (NEC-CUM). **Credit/placement by examination:** AP, CLEP, IB, institutional tests. 15 credit hours maximum toward associate degree. **Support services:** Reduced course load, study skills assistance, tutoring, writing center.

Majors. Business: Accounting, business admin, entrepreneurial studies, fashion, hospitality admin, marketing. **Computer sciences:** Data entry. **Health services:** Office admin. **Liberal arts:** Arts/sciences. **Protective services:** Law enforcement admin.

Computing on campus. 53 workstations in library, computer center. Wireless network available.

Student life. Freshman orientation: Mandatory. Preregistration for classes offered. One-day program held prior to start of semester. **Policies:** Obligatory community service component to first year seminar. **Activities:** Campus ministries, literary magazine, student government.

Student services. Adult student services, career counseling, student employment services, financial aid counseling, placement for graduates. **Transfer:** Pre-admission transcript evaluation for new students. Transfer adviser, college fairs on campus for students transferring to 4-year colleges.

Contact. E-mail: info@mariancourt.edu
Phone: (781) 309-5200 Fax: (781) 595-3560
Peter Schilling, Director of Admissions, Marian Court College, 35 Little's Point Road, Swampscott, MA 01907-2896

Massachusetts Bay Community College
Wellesley Hills, Massachusetts
www.massbay.edu

CB member
CB code: 3294

- Public 2-year community college
- Commuter campus in large town

General. Founded in 1961. Regionally accredited. Study abroad opportunities in Asia, Europe, and the Americas. **Enrollment:** 5,320 degree-seeking undergraduates; 76 non-degree-seeking students. **Degrees:** 435 associate awarded. **Location:** 13 miles from Boston. **Calendar:** Semester, extensive summer session. **Full-time faculty:** 80 total; 62% women. **Part-time faculty:** 269 total; 52% women. **Class size:** 42% < 20, 57% 20-39, less than 1% 40-49, less than 1% 50-99. **Special facilities:** Technology and health science laboratories. **Partnerships:** Formal partnerships with Toyota, Chrysler, General Motors, EMC2.

Student profile. Among degree-seeking undergraduates, 1,151 enrolled as first-time, first-year students, 311 transferred in from other institutions.

Part-time:	60%	Women:	57%
Out-of-state:	1%	25 or older:	38%

Transfer out. Colleges most students transferred to 2011: Framingham State College, University of Massachusetts-Boston, Northeastern University, Bentley College.

Basis for selection. Open admission, but selective for some programs. Special requirements for nursing, radiologic technology, paramedic, respiratory therapy programs.

High school preparation. Some programs require special academic preparation.

2011-2012 Annual costs. Tuition/fees: $5,220; $11,400 out-of-state. Books/supplies: $1,200. Personal expenses: $3,638.

2010-2011 Financial aid. Need-based: 555 full-time freshmen applied for aid; 478 were judged to have need; 464 of these received aid. Average need met was 35%. Average scholarship/grant was $4,307; average loan $2,132. 73% of total undergraduate aid awarded as scholarships/grants, 27% as loans/jobs. Need-based aid available for part-time students. Work-study available nights, weekends and for part-time students. **Non-need-based:** Awarded to 21 full-time undergraduates, including 17 freshmen.

Application procedures. Admission: No deadline. $20 fee, may be waived for applicants with need. Admission notification on a rolling basis. **Financial aid:** Priority date 5/1; no closing date. FAFSA required. Applicants notified on a rolling basis starting 7/1.

Academics. Special study options: Cooperative education, distance learning, dual enrollment of high school students, honors, internships, liberal arts/career combination, study abroad. License preparation in nursing, paramedic, physical therapy, radiology. **Credit/placement by examination:** AP, CLEP, IB, institutional tests. 30 credit hours maximum toward associate degree. **Support services:** Learning center, reduced course load, remedial instruction, study skills assistance, tutoring, writing center.

Majors. Biology: Marine. **Business:** General, accounting, business admin, hospitality admin. **Communications:** Communications/speech/rhetoric. **Computer sciences:** General, computer science, information systems. **Health services:** Medical informatics, medical radiologic technology/radiation therapy, nursing (RN), physical therapy assistant, respiratory therapy technology. **Liberal arts:** Arts/sciences. **Protective services:** Forensics, law enforcement admin. **Social sciences:** General. **Work/family studies:** Child care management.

Most popular majors. Business/marketing 14%, engineering/engineering technologies 10%, health sciences 22%, liberal arts 40%, security/protective services 9%.

Computing on campus. 550 workstations in library, computer center, student center. Commuter students can connect to campus network. Wireless network available.

Student life. Freshman orientation: Available. Preregistration for classes offered. **Activities:** Drama, student government, student newspaper, volunteer service corps, Christian Fellowship, Hillel, New World club, Latino club, sexual orientation support group.

Athletics. NJCAA. **Intercollegiate:** Baseball M, basketball, cheerleading M, golf, soccer, softball W. **Intramural:** Ice hockey M. **Team name:** Buccaneers.

Student services. Adult student services, career counseling, student employment services, financial aid counseling, health services, minority student services, personal counseling, placement for graduates, veterans' counselor. **Physically disabled:** Services for visually, speech, hearing impaired. **Transfer:** Pre-admission transcript evaluation for new students. Transfer adviser, college fairs on campus for students transferring to 4-year colleges.

Contact. E-mail: info@massbay.edu
Phone: (781) 239-2500 Fax: (781) 239-1047
Donna Raposa, Director for Admissions, Massachusetts Bay Community College, 50 Oakland Street, Wellesley Hills, MA 02481

Massasoit Community College
Brockton, Massachusetts
www.massasoit.mass.edu

CB member
CB code: 3549

- Public 2-year community college
- Commuter campus in small city

General. Founded in 1966. Regionally accredited. Second campus located in Canton, 10 miles from Boston. **Enrollment:** 6,521 degree-seeking undergraduates. **Degrees:** 785 associate awarded. **Location:** 25 miles from Boston. **Calendar:** Semester, extensive summer session. **Full-time faculty:** 115 total. **Part-time faculty:** 518 total. **Special facilities:** Theater, conference center, arts museum.

Student profile.

Out-of-state:	1%	25 or older:	39%

Transfer out. Colleges most students transferred to 2011: Bridgewater State College, University of Massachusetts Boston, University of Massachusetts Amherst, Stonehill College, Northeastern University.

Basis for selection. Open admission, but selective for some programs. Special requirements for allied health programs. Interview recommended for allied health applicants.

2011-2012 Annual costs. Tuition/fees: $4,650; $10,830 out-of-state. Per-credit charge: $24 in-state; $230 out-of-state. Books/supplies: $800. Personal expenses: $1,800.

Financial aid. All financial aid based on need. Work-study available nights, weekends and for part-time students.

Application procedures. Admission: No deadline. No application fee. Application must be submitted on paper. Admission notification on a rolling basis. Application priority date of 2/1 for nursing and radiology programs. **Financial aid:** Priority date 4/15; no closing date. FAFSA required. Applicants notified on a rolling basis starting 6/1.

Academics. Special study options: Accelerated study, cooperative education, cross-registration, distance learning, dual enrollment of high school students, ESL, honors, independent study, internships, liberal arts/career combination, weekend college. License preparation in dental hygiene, nursing, radiology, real estate. **Credit/placement by examination:** AP, CLEP, institutional tests. 30 credit hours maximum toward associate degree. **Support services:** GED preparation and test center, learning center, pre-admission

summer program, reduced course load, remedial instruction, study skills assistance, tutoring, writing center.

Majors. Business: Accounting, administrative services, business admin, hospitality admin, marketing, office management, tourism/travel. **Communications:** Media studies. **Computer sciences:** General, programming. **Education:** Teacher assistance. **Health services:** Medical radiologic technology/radiation therapy, nursing (RN), respiratory therapy technology. **Liberal arts:** Arts/sciences. **Protective services:** Firefighting, police science. **Visual/performing arts:** Commercial/advertising art, dramatic, studio arts. **Work/family studies:** Child care management.

Most popular majors. Business/marketing 19%, health sciences 20%, liberal arts 26%, security/protective services 10%.

Computing on campus. 280 workstations in library, computer center, student center. Commuter students can connect to campus network. Helpline, repair service, student web hosting, wireless network available.

Student life. Freshman orientation: Available. Preregistration for classes offered. **Activities:** Jazz band, choral groups, dance, drama, literary magazine, music ensembles, musical theater, opera, radio station, student government, student newspaper, TV station, Phi Theta Kappa, art and museum association, Helping Hands, International Touch, senior center, women's resource center, Top of the Rainbow.

Athletics. NJCAA. **Intercollegiate:** Baseball M, basketball, soccer, softball W. **Intramural:** Swimming, weight lifting. **Team name:** Warriors.

Student services. Adult student services, alcohol/substance abuse counseling, career counseling, services for economically disadvantaged, student employment services, financial aid counseling, health services, minority student services, on-campus daycare, personal counseling, placement for graduates, veterans' counselor, women's services. **Physically disabled:** Services for visually, speech, hearing impaired. **Transfer:** Transfer adviser, college fairs on campus for students transferring to 4-year colleges.

Contact. E-mail: admoffice@massasoit.mass.edu
Phone: (508) 588-9100 ext. 1411 Fax: (508) 427-1255
Michelle Hughes, Director of Admissions, Massasoit Community College, One Massasoit Boulevard, Brockton, MA 02302-3996

Middlesex Community College

Bedford, Massachusetts
www.middlesex.mass.edu

CB member
CB code: 3554

- Public 2-year community college
- Commuter campus in small city

General. Founded in 1969. Regionally accredited. Second main campus located in Lowell. **Enrollment:** 9,000 degree-seeking undergraduates; 840 non-degree-seeking students. **Degrees:** 896 associate awarded. **ROTC:** Army, Air Force. **Location:** 16 miles from Boston. **Calendar:** Semester, limited summer session. **Full-time faculty:** 134 total; 14% have terminal degrees, 14% minority, 64% women. **Special facilities:** Dental clinic, law center. **Partnerships:** Formal partnerships with business and industry links.

Student profile. Among degree-seeking undergraduates, 81% enrolled in a transfer program, 19% enrolled in a vocational program, 2,076 enrolled as first-time, first-year students.

Part-time:	57%	Asian American:	11%
Out-of-state:	1%	Hispanic American:	16%
Women:	57%	International:	1%
African American:	7%	25 or older:	49%

Transfer out. Colleges most students transferred to 2011: University of Massachusetts Lowell, Salem State College, Northern Essex Community College, University of Massachusetts Boston, Bunker Hill Community College, University of Massachusetts Amherst.

Basis for selection. Open admission, but selective for some programs. Admission to some health programs based on prerequisite courses in math and science and placement test or program specific test scores. Some health, counseling, and biotechnology programs require essays, letters of reference and interview. **Home schooled:** Must have successfully completed approved home school program in accordance with their state laws or pass federally-approved Ability-to-Benefit Test.

High school preparation. For some health programs, 1 unit each of biology and chemistry required in addition to 2 units of math at Algebra I level and above.

2011-2012 Annual costs. Tuition/fees: $5,100; $11,280 out-of-state. Per-credit charge: $170 in-state; $376 out-of-state. Books/supplies: $900. Personal expenses: $600.

Financial aid. All financial aid based on need. Need-based aid available for part-time students. Work-study available nights, weekends and for part-time students. **Additional information:** Application priority date 5/1 for Massachusetts state funds.

Application procedures. Admission: No deadline. No application fee. Admission notification on a rolling basis. Closing date first Friday in December for dental hygiene, radiologic technology and diagnostic medical sonography. Applications received later considered on space-available basis. Applicants must reply within 2 weeks of acceptance. **Financial aid:** Priority date 5/1; no closing date. FAFSA, institutional form required. Applicants notified on a rolling basis starting 6/1; must reply within 2 week(s) of notification.

Academics. Academic support available online. **Special study options:** Accelerated study, cooperative education, cross-registration, distance learning, dual enrollment of high school students, ESL, exchange student, honors, independent study, internships, liberal arts/career combination, study abroad, weekend college. License preparation in dental hygiene, nursing, paramedic, radiology. **Credit/placement by examination:** AP, CLEP, institutional tests. 45 credit hours maximum toward associate degree. **Support services:** GED preparation, learning center, pre-admission summer program, reduced course load, remedial instruction, study skills assistance, tutoring, writing center.

Majors. Biology: Biotechnology. **Business:** Accounting, business admin, fashion, hospitality admin, office management, office technology. **Communications:** General. **Communications technology:** Desktop publishing, graphic/printing. **Computer sciences:** Computer science, networking. **Education:** Early childhood. **Engineering:** Engineering science. **Health services:** Dental assistant, dental hygiene, dental lab technology, medical assistant, medical radiologic technology/radiation therapy, nursing (RN), sonography. **Liberal arts:** Arts/sciences. **Physical sciences:** General. **Protective services:** Fire safety technology, law enforcement admin. **Psychology:** General. **Visual/performing arts:** General, commercial/advertising art, dramatic, studio arts.

Most popular majors. Business/marketing 19%, education 6%, health sciences 19%, liberal arts 12%, social sciences 11%.

Computing on campus. 350 workstations in library, computer center. Commuter students can connect to campus network. Online course registration, helpline, wireless network available.

Student life. Freshman orientation: Available. Preregistration for classes offered. **Activities:** Choral groups, dance, drama, international student organizations, musical theater, student government, international club, student activities, mental health club, early childhood education club, art club, MassPIRG.

Athletics. Intramural: Basketball, bowling, soccer, volleyball.

Student services. Adult student services, alcohol/substance abuse counseling, career counseling, services for economically disadvantaged, student employment services, financial aid counseling, health services, legal services, minority student services, personal counseling, placement for graduates, veterans' counselor. **Physically disabled:** Services for visually, speech, hearing impaired. **Transfer:** Re-entry adviser, pre-admission transcript evaluation for new students. Transfer adviser, college fairs on campus for students transferring to 4-year colleges.

Contact. E-mail: admissions@middlesex.mass.edu
Phone: (978) 656-3207 Toll-free number: (800) 818-3434
Fax: (978) 656-3322
Marilynn Gallagan, Dean of Admissions, Middlesex Community College, 33 Kearney Square, Lowell, MA 01852-1987

Mount Wachusett Community College

Gardner, Massachusetts
www.mwcc.edu

CB member
CB code: 3545

- Public 2-year community college
- Commuter campus in large town

General. Founded in 1963. Regionally accredited. **Enrollment:** 4,277 degree-seeking undergraduates; 478 non-degree-seeking students. **Degrees:** 470 associate awarded. **Location:** 59 miles from Boston. **Calendar:** Semester, extensive summer session. **Full-time faculty:** 73 total; 4% minority, 66% women. **Part-time faculty:** 164 total; 5% minority, 65% women. **Class size:** 67% < 20, 33% 20-39, less than 1% 40-49. **Special facilities:** On-site child-care facility, theater, fitness and wellness center, pool. **Partnerships:** Formal partnership with Tech Prep (high school articulation programs), Nypro, Adams and Associates.

Student profile. Among degree-seeking undergraduates, 1,010 enrolled as first-time, first-year students, 281 transferred in from other institutions.

Part-time:	55%	Asian American:	2%
Out-of-state:	4%	Hispanic American:	13%
Women:	65%	International:	1%
African American:	7%	25 or older:	46%

Transfer out. Colleges most students transferred to 2011: Fitchburg State College, University of Massachusetts Amherst, Worcester State College, University of Massachusetts Lowell.

Basis for selection. Open admission, but selective for some programs. Special requirements for all health science programs with emphasis on college level academic coursework, life science or other science programs, other academic preparation and work experience. Interview required for early admission of high school students. Portfolio recommended for art programs. **Home schooled:** Statement describing home school structure and mission, transcript of courses and grades, interview required. Applicants must submit copies of curriculum approvals from local secondary school district. **Learning Disabled:** Students advised to meet with coordinator of disabilities services during admissions process.

High school preparation. College-preparatory program recommended. 16 units recommended. Recommended units include English 4, mathematics 3, social studies 1, history 1, science 2 (laboratory 2), foreign language 2 and academic electives 3.

2011-2012 Annual costs. Tuition/fees: $5,840; $11,990 out-of-state. Per-credit charge: $25 in-state; $230 out-of-state. New England resident tuition is $1,125. Books/supplies: $1,000. Personal expenses: $2,000.

2010-2011 Financial aid. All financial aid based on need. 580 full-time freshmen applied for aid; 469 were judged to have need; 461 of these received aid. Average need met was 94%. Average scholarship/grant was $4,938; average loan $1,341. 81% of total undergraduate aid awarded as scholarships/grants, 19% as loans/jobs. Need-based aid available for part-time students. Work-study available nights, weekends and for part-time students.

Application procedures. **Admission:** Priority date 4/1; no deadline. $10 fee, may be waived for applicants with need, free for online applicants. Admission notification on a rolling basis beginning on or about 2/1. Must reply by May 1 or within 2 week(s) if notified thereafter. Nursing, Dental Hygiene must apply by February 1. Clinical Laboratory Science, Physical Therapy Assistant, and Massage Therapy must apply by March 1. **Financial aid:** Priority date 4/15; no closing date. FAFSA, institutional form required. Applicants notified on a rolling basis starting 5/1.

Academics. **Special study options:** Accelerated study, cooperative education, cross-registration, distance learning, double major, dual enrollment of high school students, ESL, honors, independent study, internships, liberal arts/career combination, study abroad, weekend college. License preparation in dental hygiene, nursing, physical therapy. **Credit/placement by examination:** AP, CLEP, IB, institutional tests. 30 credit hours maximum toward associate degree. **Support services:** GED preparation and test center, learning center, pre-admission summer program, reduced course load, remedial instruction, study skills assistance, tutoring, writing center.

Majors. **Biology:** Biotechnology. **Business:** General, business admin. **Communications technology:** Radio/TV. **Computer sciences:** General, computer graphics, web page design. **Conservation:** Environmental studies. **Engineering:** General. **Health services:** Clinical lab technology, dental hygiene, medical assistant, mental health services, nursing (RN), physical therapy assistant, yoga therapy. **Liberal arts:** Arts/sciences. **Protective services:** Corrections, fire safety technology, law enforcement admin. **Visual/performing arts:** Art. **Work/family studies:** Child care management, child development.

Most popular majors. Business/marketing 18%, computer/information sciences 7%, health sciences 33%, liberal arts 17%.

Computing on campus. 415 workstations in library, computer center. Commuter students can connect to campus network. Online course registration, online library, helpline, wireless network available.

Student life. **Freshman orientation:** Available. Preregistration for classes offered. One-day session held week before start of classes. **Housing:** Limited housing available on campus of Fitchburg State College. **Activities:** Drama, international student organizations, literary magazine, musical theater, radio station, student government, student newspaper, art club, nursing clubs, student government association, pride club, dental hygiene club, green society, Campus Crusade for Christ, campus activities team for students, MassPIRG, ALANA club.

Athletics. **Intramural:** Badminton, basketball, football (tackle), soccer, softball, table tennis, volleyball, water polo. **Team name:** Mountain Lions.

Student services. Adult student services, alcohol/substance abuse counseling, chaplain/spiritual director, career counseling, services for economically disadvantaged, student employment services, financial aid counseling, health services, minority student services, on-campus daycare, personal counseling, placement for graduates, veterans' counselor, women's services. **Physically disabled:** Services for visually, speech, hearing impaired. **Transfer:** Pre-admission transcript evaluation for new students. Transfer adviser, college fairs on campus for students transferring to 4-year colleges.

Contact. E-mail: admissions@mwcc.mass.edu
Phone: (978) 630-9554 Fax: (978) 630-9554
Ryan Forsythe, Mount Wachusett Community College, 444 Green Street, Gardner, MA 01440-1000

New England College of Business and Finance
Boston, Massachusetts
www.necb.edu
CB code: 3376

- For-profit 2-year business college
- Large city

General. Founded in 1909. Regionally accredited. Programs designed for adult learners. Undergraduate courses delivered in 8-week format; graduate courses delivered in 5-week format. **Enrollment:** 131 full-time, degree-seeking students. **Degrees:** 35 bachelor's, 54 associate awarded; master's offered. **Calendar:** Differs by program, extensive summer session. **Full-time faculty:** 6 total; 100% have terminal degrees, 17% minority, 17% women. **Part-time faculty:** 40 total; 25% have terminal degrees, 12% minority, 50% women. **Partnerships:** Formal partnerships with several financial services companies.

Basis for selection. Open admission, but selective for some programs. Placement exams or equivalent completion of applicable college credits required.

2011-2012 Annual costs. Books/supplies: $800.

Financial aid. **Need-based:** Work-study available nights, weekends and for part-time students. **Additional information:** No college-administered financial aid. 90% of students receive tuition reimbursement from employer.

Application procedures. **Admission:** No deadline. $50 fee, may be waived for applicants with need. Application must be submitted online. Admission notification on a rolling basis.

Academics. **Special study options:** Accelerated study, distance learning, dual enrollment of high school students, independent study. Bachelor's degree programs available on campus. **Credit/placement by examination:** AP, CLEP, IB, institutional tests. **Support services:** Remedial instruction, tutoring.

Majors. **Business:** General, banking/financial services, business admin.

Computing on campus. PC or laptop required. Online library available.

Student life. **Activities:** Literary magazine.

Student services. Career counseling, financial aid counseling, personal counseling. **Transfer:** Pre-admission transcript evaluation for new students. Transfer adviser for students transferring to 4-year colleges.

Contact. Phone: (617) 951-2350 Fax: (617) 951-2533
Pamela Dellaporta, Director of Admissions and Student Services, New England College of Business and Finance, 10 High Street, Suite 204, Boston, MA 02110

North Shore Community College
Danvers, Massachusetts
CB member
www.northshore.edu
CB code: 3651

- Public 2-year community college
- Commuter campus in small city

General. Founded in 1965. Regionally accredited. Additional campus in Lynn, corporate training center in Beverly. **Enrollment:** 7,340 degree-seeking undergraduates; 634 non-degree-seeking students. **Degrees:** 803 associate awarded. **Location:** 25 miles from Boston. **Calendar:** Semester, limited summer session. **Full-time faculty:** 131 total. **Part-time faculty:** 384 total. **Class size:** 44% < 20, 55% 20-39, less than 1% 40-49, less than 1% 50-99. **Special facilities:** Agricultural facility for horticulture, animal science, culinary arts. **Partnerships:** Formal partnership with Verizon, area high

schools for Tech Prep, consortium providing distance learning opportunities.

Student profile. Among degree-seeking undergraduates, 40% enrolled in a transfer program, 51% enrolled in a vocational program, 1,549 enrolled as first-time, first-year students, 644 transferred in from other institutions.

Part-time:	55%	Asian American:	4%
Out-of-state:	2%	Hispanic American:	19%
Women:	60%	25 or older:	40%
African American:	9%		

Transfer out. Colleges most students transferred to 2011: Salem State College, University of Massachusetts-Boston, University of Massachusetts-Lowell, Suffolk University, Northeastern University, Lesley College.

Basis for selection. Open admission, but selective for some programs. School achievement record considered for health, engineering, computer science programs; some prerequisite course requirements exist. Pre-Nursing Assessment Test required for pre-nursing program; Nurse Entrance Exam required for LPN program. Essay and/or interview may be required in some programs, including health and human services. **Home schooled:** Home program must be affiliated with accredited agency or local school system. **Learning Disabled:** Students must identify disability, individual test administration available.

High school preparation. One algebra, 1 biology, and 1 chemistry required for some health programs and for biotechnology. Trigonometry, physics, chemistry required for engineering. Trigonometry, computer literacy required for computer science.

2011-2012 Annual costs. Tuition/fees: $4,850; $11,810 out-of-state. Per-credit charge: $25 in-state; $257 out-of-state. New England Regional Tuition: $174.50 per credit. Books/supplies: $1,200. Personal expenses: $1,500.

2010-2011 Financial aid. All financial aid based on need. Need-based aid available for part-time students. Work-study available nights, weekends and for part-time students.

Application procedures. Admission: No deadline. No application fee. Admission notification on a rolling basis. We accept high school seniors as conditional students. Once the student provides proof of high school graduation, the conditional status will be removed. **Financial aid:** Priority date 4/15; no closing date. FAFSA required. Applicants notified on a rolling basis starting 4/1; must reply within 2 week(s) of notification.

Academics. Participation in state dual enrollment program which allows high school juniors and seniors to take credit courses contingent upon approval of high school principal. Tuition and fees paid by state. **Special study options:** Accelerated study, cross-registration, distance learning, double major, dual enrollment of high school students, ESL, honors, independent study, internships, student-designed major, study abroad, weekend college. License preparation in aviation, nursing, occupational therapy, physical therapy, radiology, real estate. **Credit/placement by examination:** AP, CLEP, institutional tests. 45 credit hours maximum toward associate degree. DANTES, Excelsior, CLEP tests accepted. CLEP tests in Freshman Composition and Analyzing and Interpreting Literature must be accompanied by essay; lab credit not awarded for Biology and Chemistry tests. **Support services:** GED preparation and test center, learning center, reduced course load, remedial instruction, study skills assistance, tutoring, writing center.

Majors. Business: Accounting technology, business admin, executive assistant, hospitality admin, hotel/motel admin, marketing. **Computer sciences:** General, computer science, programming. **Education:** Early childhood, elementary, kindergarten/preschool, teacher assistance. **Engineering:** General. **Health services:** Dietetic technician, medical secretary, mental health services, nursing (RN), occupational therapy assistant, physical therapy assistant, radiologic technology/medical imaging, respiratory therapy technology, substance abuse counseling, veterinary technology/assistant. **Liberal arts:** Arts/sciences. **Protective services:** Criminal justice, fire safety technology. **Visual/performing arts:** Graphic design. **Work/family studies:** Aging, child care service.

Most popular majors. Business/marketing 10%, family/consumer sciences 6%, health sciences 27%, liberal arts 25%, security/protective services 16%.

Computing on campus. 300 workstations in library, computer center, student center. Commuter students can connect to campus network. Online course registration, online library, helpline, wireless network available.

Student life. Freshman orientation: Available. Preregistration for classes offered. All-day event includes placement testing, adviser assistance. **Activities:** Campus ministries, drama, literary magazine, Model UN, musical theater, student government, student newspaper, students against drug abuse, early childhood club, marketing club, engineering club, women in transition club, multicultural society, poets and writers club, gerontology club, occupational therapy assistant club.

Athletics. Intramural: Basketball, soccer. **Team name:** Seahawks.

Student services. Adult student services, career counseling, services for economically disadvantaged, student employment services, financial aid counseling, health services, on-campus daycare, personal counseling, placement for graduates, veterans' counselor, women's services. **Physically disabled:** Services for visually, speech, hearing impaired. **Transfer:** Pre-admission transcript evaluation for new students. Transfer adviser, college fairs on campus for students transferring to 4-year colleges.

Contact. E-mail: info@northshore.edu
Phone: (978) 762-4188 Fax: (978) 762-4015
Jennifer Kirk, Director of Recruitment, North Shore Community College, One Ferncroft Road, Danvers, MA 01923-0840

Northern Essex Community College
Haverhill, Massachusetts CB member
www.necc.mass.edu CB code: 3674

- Public 2-year community and junior college
- Commuter campus in small city

General. Founded in 1960. Regionally accredited. Additional campus in Lawrence. **Enrollment:** 6,382 degree-seeking undergraduates; 654 non-degree-seeking students. **Degrees:** 640 associate awarded. **Location:** 40 miles from Boston. **Calendar:** Semester, extensive summer session. **Full-time faculty:** 99 total; 11% minority, 62% women. **Part-time faculty:** 388 total; 6% minority, 58% women. **Class size:** 36% < 20, 64% 20-39, less than 1% 40-49.

Student profile. Among degree-seeking undergraduates, 40% enrolled in a transfer program, 60% enrolled in a vocational program, 7% already have a bachelor's degree or higher, 1,185 enrolled as first-time, first-year students, 365 transferred in from other institutions.

Part-time:	61%	Women:	62%
Out-of-state:	18%		

Basis for selection. Open admission, but selective for some programs. Special requirements for technology studies (engineering, computer, computer maintenance, electronics) and health and human services. Interview required of health and human services majors.

High school preparation. Health and technologies programs have specific math and/or science requirements.

2011-2012 Annual costs. Tuition/fees: $4,410; $11,640 out-of-state. Per-credit charge: $25 in-state; $266 out-of-state. New England residents pay $160 per credit hour. Books/supplies: $800. Personal expenses: $850.

Financial aid. Need-based: Need-based aid available for part-time students. Work-study available nights, weekends and for part-time students. **Non-need-based:** Scholarships awarded for academics.

Application procedures. Admission: Priority date 2/1; no deadline. $25 fee, may be waived for applicants with need. Admission notification on a rolling basis. Entrance examination required for schools of practical/vocational nursing. **Financial aid:** Priority date 5/1; no closing date. FAFSA, institutional form required. Must reply within 2 week(s) of notification.

Academics. Special study options: Accelerated study, cooperative education, cross-registration, distance learning, double major, dual enrollment of high school students, ESL, exchange student, honors, internships, liberal arts/career combination, study abroad, weekend college. License preparation in dental hygiene, nursing, paramedic, radiology, real estate. **Credit/placement by examination:** AP, CLEP, institutional tests. 36 credit hours maximum toward associate degree. **Support services:** GED preparation and test center, learning center, pre-admission summer program, reduced course load, remedial instruction, study skills assistance, tutoring, writing center.

Majors. Biology: General. **Business:** General, accounting, administrative services, business admin, finance, international, logistics, marketing, office management, office technology, tourism promotion, tourism/travel. **Communications:** Broadcast journalism, journalism. **Communications technology:** General. **Computer sciences:** General, computer graphics, computer science, information systems, programming. **Education:** Business, early childhood. **Engineering:** Engineering science. **Foreign languages:** Sign language interpretation. **Health services:** EMT paramedic, medical records admin, medical secretary, mental health services, nursing (RN), respiratory therapy technology, substance abuse counseling. **Human services:** Social work. **Liberal arts:** Arts/sciences. **Parks/recreation:** Sports admin. **Protective services:** Criminal justice. **Psychology:** General. **Visual/performing arts:** Commercial/advertising art, design. **Work/family studies:** Child care management.

Computing on campus. 500 workstations in library, computer center, student center. Commuter students can connect to campus network. Online course registration, online library, helpline, wireless network available.

Student life. Freshman orientation: Mandatory. Preregistration for classes offered. **Activities:** Choral groups, dance, drama, literary magazine, student government, student newspaper, American Sign Language club, Hispanic cultural club, women's resource network, social club (students with disabilities), Bible club.

Athletics. NJCAA. **Intercollegiate:** Baseball M, basketball, track and field, volleyball W. **Intramural:** Basketball, football (non-tackle), soccer, table tennis, volleyball. **Team name:** Scarlet Knights.

Student services. Adult student services, career counseling, services for economically disadvantaged, student employment services, financial aid counseling, health services, on-campus daycare, placement for graduates, veterans' counselor, women's services. **Physically disabled:** Services for visually, speech, hearing impaired. **Transfer:** Transfer adviser, college fairs on campus for students transferring to 4-year colleges.

Contact. E-mail: admissions@necc.mass.edu
Phone: (978) 556-3600
Nora Sheridan, Dean of Admissions, Northern Essex Community College, 100 Elliott Street, Haverhill, MA 01830-2399

Quincy College
Quincy, Massachusetts
www.quincycollege.edu

CB member
CB code: 3713

▸ Public 2-year community college
▸ Commuter campus in small city

General. Founded in 1956. Regionally accredited. Branch campus in Plymouth. **Enrollment:** 3,852 degree-seeking undergraduates; 822 non-degree-seeking students. **Degrees:** 479 associate awarded. **Location:** 10 miles from downtown Boston. **Calendar:** Semester, extensive summer session. **Full-time faculty:** 43 total. **Part-time faculty:** 264 total.

Student profile. Among degree-seeking undergraduates, 639 enrolled as first-time, first-year students.

Part-time:	56%	25 or older:	46%
Women:	68%		

Basis for selection. Open admission, but selective for some programs. Admission to health career programs based on test scores, class rank and high school record. College-preparatory program with anatomy and physiology I with lab or biology with lab and introductory or general chemistry with lab required for associate degree in nursing program.

2011-2012 Annual costs. Tuition/fees: $5,100; $5,100 out-of-state. Books/supplies: $1,550. Personal expenses: $500.

Financial aid. Need-based: Work-study available nights, weekends and for part-time students.

Application procedures. Admission: No deadline. $30 fee, may be waived for applicants with need. Admission notification on a rolling basis. **Financial aid:** No deadline. FAFSA required. Applicants notified on a rolling basis starting 5/1; must reply within 2 week(s) of notification.

Academics. Special study options: Accelerated study, distance learning, dual enrollment of high school students, independent study, internships. **Credit/placement by examination:** AP, CLEP, institutional tests. 30 credit hours maximum toward associate degree. **Support services:** Learning center, reduced course load, remedial instruction, tutoring.

Majors. Business: Accounting, business admin. **Computer sciences:** Computer science. **Education:** Early childhood, elementary. **Health services:** Health care admin, nursing (RN). **Liberal arts:** Arts/sciences. **Parks/recreation:** Exercise sciences. **Protective services:** Criminal justice. **Visual/performing arts:** Studio arts.

Most popular majors. Business/marketing 24%, computer/information sciences 6%, health sciences 29%, liberal arts 25%, security/protective services 7%.

Computing on campus. 60 workstations in library, computer center, student center. Commuter students can connect to campus network. Online library, wireless network available.

Student life. Freshman orientation: Available. Preregistration for classes offered. **Activities:** Drama, international student organizations, student government, student newspaper.

Athletics. Intramural: Basketball.

Student services. Adult student services, alcohol/substance abuse counseling, career counseling, student employment services, financial aid counseling, minority student services. **Transfer:** Pre-admission transcript evaluation for new students. Transfer adviser, college fairs on campus for students transferring to 4-year colleges.

Contact. E-mail: admissions@quincycollege.edu
Phone: (617) 984-1710 Toll-free number: (800) 698-1700
Fax: (617) 984-1794
Lisa Stack, Director of Enrollment, Quincy College, 24 Saville Avenue, Quincy, MA 02169

Quinsigamond Community College
Worcester, Massachusetts
www.qcc.edu

CB member
CB code: 3714

▸ Public 2-year community college
▸ Commuter campus in small city

General. Founded in 1963. Regionally accredited. Additional location in Southbridge. **Enrollment:** 7,921 degree-seeking undergraduates; 1,209 non-degree-seeking students. **Degrees:** 856 associate awarded. **ROTC:** Army, Air Force. **Location:** 45 miles from Boston. **Calendar:** Semester, extensive summer session. **Full-time faculty:** 127 total; 9% have terminal degrees, 13% minority, 67% women. **Part-time faculty:** 419 total; 13% have terminal degrees, 10% minority, 51% women. **Class size:** 67% < 20, 33% 20-39, less than 1% 40-49, less than 1% 50-99. **Special facilities:** Dental hygiene clinic, athletic center, child care center. **Partnerships:** Formal partnerships with Intel Corporation, Verizon, National Grid.

Student profile. Among degree-seeking undergraduates, 6% already have a bachelor's degree or higher, 1,923 enrolled as first-time, first-year students, 558 transferred in from other institutions.

Part-time:	52%	Asian American:	4%
Out-of-state:	1%	Hispanic American:	15%
Women:	58%	25 or older:	35%
African American:	11%		

Transfer out. Colleges most students transferred to 2011: Worcester State College, University of Massachusetts-Amherst, Nichols College, Clark University, Framingham State College.

Basis for selection. Open admission, but selective for some programs. Students without high school diploma may be considered for admission under Ability to Benefit. **Home schooled:** Transcript of courses and grades required. Letter from district superintendent appoving home school curriculum required. **Learning Disabled:** Students encouraged to contact Disability Services office prior to enrollment.

High school preparation. College-preparatory program recommended. Recommended units include English 4, mathematics 3, social studies 2, history 1, science 3 (laboratory 2), foreign language 2 and computer science 1. English, college math, and laboratory sciences required for health programs. English and math required for business, technology, and early childhood education.

2011-2012 Annual costs. Tuition/fees: $5,340; $11,520 out-of-state. Per-credit charge: $24 in-state; $230 out-of-state. Books/supplies: $900. Personal expenses: $1,440.

Financial aid. Need-based: Need-based aid available for part-time students. Work-study available nights, weekends and for part-time students. **Non-need-based:** Scholarships awarded for academics, leadership, minority status. **Additional information:** All Pell Grant eligible students applying by May 1 will receive enough grant aid to cover tuition, fees and books.

Application procedures. Admission: No deadline. $20 fee ($50 out-of-state), may be waived for applicants with need. Admission notification on a rolling basis beginning on or about 10/1. Must reply by May 1 or within 2 week(s) if notified thereafter. **Financial aid:** Priority date 4/1; no closing date. FAFSA required. Applicants notified on a rolling basis starting 4/1.

Academics. Specialized academic support to those with disabilities. Online academic tutoring available in most subjects. **Special study options:** Accelerated study, cooperative education, cross-registration, distance learning, double major, dual enrollment of high school students, ESL, honors, independent study, internships, liberal arts/career combination, weekend college. Member 13-school Worcester consortium. License preparation in dental hygiene, nursing, occupational therapy, paramedic, radiology. **Credit/placement by examination:** AP, CLEP, IB, institutional tests. **Support services:** GED preparation and test center, learning center, reduced course load, remedial instruction, study skills assistance, tutoring, writing center.

Majors. **Biology:** Biotechnology. **Business:** General, business admin, executive assistant, hospitality admin, restaurant/food services. **Communications technology:** Graphics. **Computer sciences:** Applications programming, computer graphics, computer science, security, systems analysis, web page design. **Education:** Kindergarten/preschool. **Health services:** Dental hygiene, EMT paramedic, medical secretary, nursing (RN), occupational therapy, radiologic technology/medical imaging, respiratory therapy technology. **Liberal arts:** Arts/sciences. **Protective services:** Fire services admin, police science.

Most popular majors. Business/marketing 20%, engineering/engineering technologies 7%, health sciences 21%, liberal arts 26%, security/protective services 11%.

Computing on campus. 400 workstations in library, computer center. Helpline, wireless network available.

Student life. **Freshman orientation:** Available. Preregistration for classes offered. Half-day program; some academic majors hold specialized orientation programs. **Activities:** Campus ministries, choral groups, drama, literary magazine, student government, student newspaper, multicultural club, several occupational groups, academic clubs.

Athletics. NJCAA. **Intercollegiate:** Baseball M, basketball, softball W. **Intramural:** Basketball, football (non-tackle), soccer, volleyball. **Team name:** Wyverns.

Student services. Chaplain/spiritual director, career counseling, student employment services, financial aid counseling, minority student services, on-campus daycare, personal counseling, placement for graduates, veterans' counselor. **Physically disabled:** Services for visually, speech, hearing impaired. **Transfer:** Transfer adviser, college fairs on campus for students transferring to 4-year colleges.

Contact. E-mail: admissions@qcc.mass.edu
Phone: (508) 854-4262 Fax: (508) 854-7525
Michelle Tufau, Associate Dean of Enrollment Management, Quinsigamond Community College, 670 West Boylston Street, Worcester, MA 01606

Roxbury Community College
Roxbury Crossing, Massachusetts
www.rcc.mass.edu

CB member
CB code: 3740

- Public 2-year community college
- Commuter campus in very large city

General. Founded in 1973. Regionally accredited. **Enrollment:** 2,597 degree-seeking undergraduates; 182 non-degree-seeking students. **Degrees:** 295 associate awarded. **ROTC:** Army. **Calendar:** Semester, extensive summer session. **Full-time faculty:** 49 total. **Part-time faculty:** 106 total. **Class size:** 73% < 20, 27% 20-39. **Special facilities:** Indoor track and field facilities. **Partnerships:** Formal partnerships with local employers.

Student profile. Among degree-seeking undergraduates, 69% enrolled in a transfer program, 31% enrolled in a vocational program, 571 enrolled as first-time, first-year students, 42 transferred in from other institutions.

Part-time:	60%	Hispanic American:	17%
Women:	67%	International:	1%
African American:	48%	25 or older:	61%
Asian American:	2%		

Transfer out. 20% of students enrolled in the transfer program go on to 4-year colleges.

Basis for selection. Open admission, but selective for some programs. Specific admissions criteria for nursing and radiologic technology programs.

2011-2012 Annual costs. Tuition/fees: $4,800; $12,450 out-of-state. Per-credit charge: $26 in-state; $247 out-of-state. Books/supplies: $800. Personal expenses: $1,800.

Financial aid. All financial aid based on need. Need-based aid available for part-time students. Work-study available nights, weekends and for part-time students.

Application procedures. **Admission:** No deadline. $10 fee ($35 out-of-state), may be waived for applicants with need. Admission notification on a rolling basis. **Financial aid:** Closing date 5/1. FAFSA, institutional form required. Applicants notified on a rolling basis starting 6/15; must reply within 2 week(s) of notification.

Academics. **Special study options:** Cross-registration, double major, dual enrollment of high school students, ESL, honors, independent study, internships, liberal arts/career combination. License preparation in nursing. **Credit/**

---

placement by examination: AP, CLEP, institutional tests. **Support services:** GED preparation and test center, learning center, remedial instruction, study skills assistance, tutoring, writing center.

Majors. **Architecture:** Technology. **Biology:** General. **Business:** Accounting, administrative services, business admin, hospitality/recreation, management information systems, office management, office technology. **Communications technology:** Radio/TV. **Computer sciences:** General, applications programming. **Conservation:** General. **Education:** Early childhood. **English:** English lit. **Foreign languages:** French. **Health services:** Medical secretary, nursing (RN), prenursing. **Liberal arts:** Arts/sciences, humanities. **Math:** General. **Physical sciences:** General. **Protective services:** Law enforcement admin. **Social sciences:** General. **Visual/performing arts:** General, music. **Work/family studies:** Child care management.

Most popular majors. Business/marketing 28%, health sciences 28%, liberal arts 30%, security/protective services 11%.

Computing on campus. 52 workstations in library, computer center.

Student life. **Freshman orientation:** Available. Preregistration for classes offered. **Activities:** Choral groups, dance, drama, student government, student newspaper, Union Estudiantil Latina, Christian ministry.

Athletics. NJCAA. **Intercollegiate:** Basketball, soccer M. **Team name:** Tigers.

Student services. Career counseling, student employment services, financial aid counseling, health services, on-campus daycare, personal counseling, placement for graduates. **Transfer:** Transfer adviser, college fairs on campus for students transferring to 4-year colleges.

Contact. Phone: (617) 541-5310 Fax: (617) 541-5316
Charles Diggs, Director of Admissions, Roxbury Community College, 1234 Columbus Avenue, Roxbury Crossing, MA 02120-3400

Springfield Technical Community College
Springfield, Massachusetts
www.stcc.edu

CB code: 3791

- Public 2-year community and technical college
- Commuter campus in small city

General. Founded in 1967. Regionally accredited. STCC has an extensive selection of degree programs, degree options and certificate programs - many of which are not available anywhere else in the region. **Enrollment:** 6,021 degree-seeking undergraduates. **Degrees:** 858 associate awarded. **Location:** 90 miles from Boston; 30 miles from Hartford, Connecticut. **Calendar:** Semester, limited summer session. **Full-time faculty:** 150 total. **Part-time faculty:** 252 total. **Special facilities:** Springfield Armory Museum (national historic site). **Partnerships:** Formal partnerships with Verizon, Microsoft, Novell, A+, Cisco, IBM.

Student profile.

Part-time:	51%	Hispanic American:	22%
Out-of-state:	3%	Native American:	1%
Women:	58%	International:	1%
African American:	14%	25 or older:	48%
Asian American:	2%		

Transfer out. **Colleges most students transferred to 2011:** University of Massachusetts-Amherst, Westfield State University, Elms College, American International College, Springfield College.

Basis for selection. Open admission, but selective for some programs. Special requirements for certain health, engineering and science programs. SAT required for selective health and engineering programs.

High school preparation. Math, chemistry, biology and/or physics required for many competitive programs.

2011-2012 Annual costs. Tuition/fees: $4,776; $11,286 out-of-state. Per-credit charge: $25 in-state; $242 out-of-state. New England reciprocal rate $259 per credit hour, including fees. Books/supplies: $1,200. Personal expenses: $1,836.

2010-2011 Financial aid. **Need-based:** 74% of total undergraduate aid awarded as scholarships/grants, 26% as loans/jobs. Need-based aid available for part-time students. Work-study available nights, weekends and for part-time students.

Application procedures. **Admission:** No deadline. $10 fee ($35 out-of-state), may be waived for applicants with need. Admission notification on a rolling basis beginning on or about 3/1. Applicants must reply within 3

weeks of notification of admission. **Financial aid:** Priority date 5/1; no closing date. FAFSA required. Applicants notified on a rolling basis starting 7/1.

Academics. Special study options: Cooperative education, cross-registration, distance learning, dual enrollment of high school students, ESL, honors, independent study, internships, liberal arts/career combination. License preparation in nursing, radiology. **Credit/placement by examination:** AP, CLEP, institutional tests. 45 credit hours maximum toward associate degree. **Support services:** GED preparation and test center, learning center, reduced course load, remedial instruction, study skills assistance, tutoring, writing center.

Majors. Biology: General, biotechnology. **Business:** General, accounting, administrative services, business admin, executive assistant, finance, marketing, small business admin. **Communications technology:** Animation/special effects, radio/TV, recording arts. **Computer sciences:** Applications programming, computer science, data processing, security, system admin, web page design. **Education:** Early childhood, elementary, secondary. **Engineering:** General, architectural. **General:** Landscaping. **Health services:** Clinical lab technology, dental hygiene, insurance coding, massage therapy, medical assistant, medical secretary, nuclear medical technology, nursing (RN), occupational therapy assistant, physical therapy assistant, premedicine, radiologic technology/medical imaging, respiratory therapy technology, sonography, surgical technology. **Liberal arts:** Arts/sciences. **Math:** General. **Parks/recreation:** Sports admin. **Physical sciences:** Chemistry, physics. **Protective services:** Fire safety technology, police science. **Visual/performing arts:** Commercial photography, commercial/advertising art, studio arts.

Most popular majors. Business/marketing 11%, computer/information sciences 6%, engineering/engineering technologies 14%, health sciences 26%, liberal arts 22%, security/protective services 9%.

Computing on campus. 1,627 workstations in library, student center. Commuter students can connect to campus network. Online course registration, online library, helpline, repair service, wireless network available.

Student life. Freshman orientation: Available. Preregistration for classes offered. Half-day session held 3 weeks before start of classes. **Policies:** No alcohol permitted. **Activities:** Drama, student government, student newspaper, TV station, student government association, student ambassadors, Latino culture club, gay/lesbian/bisexual/transgender alliance, Christian Fellowship, Phi Theta Kappa, Campus Civitan, Gallery Players.

Athletics. NJCAA. **Intercollegiate:** Basketball, golf, soccer, wrestling M. **Team name:** Rams.

Student services. Adult student services, alcohol/substance abuse counseling, career counseling, services for economically disadvantaged, student employment services, financial aid counseling, health services, on-campus daycare, personal counseling, placement for graduates, veterans' counselor, women's services. **Physically disabled:** Services for visually, speech, hearing impaired. **Transfer:** Pre-admission transcript evaluation for new students. Transfer center, transfer adviser, college fairs on campus for students transferring to 4-year colleges.

Contact. E-mail: admissions@stcc.edu
Phone: (413) 755-4202
Louisa Davis-Freeman, Dean of Admissions, Springfield Technical Community College, One Armory Square, Springfield, MA 01102-9000

Urban College of Boston
Boston, Massachusetts
www.urbancollege.edu

CB code: 3630

- Private 2-year community college
- Commuter campus in very large city

General. Regionally accredited. **Enrollment:** 1,200 undergraduates. **Degrees:** 83 associate awarded. **Calendar:** Semester, limited summer session. **Full-time faculty:** 2 total. **Part-time faculty:** 40 total. **Class size:** 57% < 20, 43% 20-39.

Transfer out. Colleges most students transferred to 2011: Lesley College, Springfield College, Cambridge College.

Basis for selection. Open admission.

2011-2012 Annual costs. Tuition/fees: $5,900. Per-credit charge: $196. Books/supplies: $1,100. Personal expenses: $2,860.

Financial aid. All financial aid based on need. Need-based aid available for part-time students. Work-study available nights, weekends and for part-time students.

Application procedures. Admission: No deadline. $10 fee, may be waived for applicants with need. Admission notification on a rolling basis. **Financial aid:** Priority date 12/10; no closing date. FAFSA required. Applicants notified on a rolling basis starting 4/15.

Academics. Special study options: Independent study, internships. **Credit/placement by examination:** AP, CLEP, IB. **Support services:** Learning center, study skills assistance, tutoring.

Majors. Education: Early childhood. **Liberal arts:** Arts/sciences.

Most popular majors. Education 82%, public administration/social services 15%.

Computing on campus. 2 workstations in library, computer center.

Student life. Freshman orientation: Available. Preregistration for classes offered. **Policies:** Drug and alcohol use prohibited.

Student services. Career counseling, services for economically disadvantaged, financial aid counseling, minority student services, personal counseling, placement for graduates. **Transfer:** Transfer adviser for students transferring to 4-year colleges.

Contact. E-mail: information@urbancollege.edu
Phone: (617) 348-6359 Fax: (617) 423-4758
Henry Johnson, Dean of Enrollment Services, Urban College of Boston, 178 Tremont Street, Seventh Floor, Boston, MA 02111

Michigan

Alpena Community College
Alpena, Michigan
www.alpenacc.edu   CB code: 1011

▸ Public 2-year community college
▸ Commuter campus in large town

General. Founded in 1952. Regionally accredited. **Enrollment:** 2,200 degree-seeking undergraduates. **Degrees:** 303 associate awarded. **Location:** 240 miles from Detroit. **Calendar:** Semester, limited summer session. **Full-time faculty:** 59 total. **Part-time faculty:** 105 total. **Special facilities:** Museum, planetarium.

Student profile.

Out-of-state:	1%	Live on campus:	3%
25 or older:	48%		

Transfer out. Colleges most students transferred to 2011: Lake Superior State University, Central Michigan University, Michigan State University, Ferris State University, Saginaw Valley State University.

Basis for selection. Open admission, but selective for some programs. Special requirements for practical nursing, registered nursing, and utility technician programs. ACT may be used for scholarship consideration or as basis for corroboration of institutional placement exam results. Placement test requirement waived for applicants with ACT composite score of 20 or higher.

High school preparation. High school diploma or equivalent required for nursing applicants.

2011-2012 Annual costs. Tuition/fees: $3,510; $5,160 out-of-district; $6,480 out-of-state. Per-credit charge: $99 in-district; $154 out-of-district; $198 out-of-state. Tuition and fees are per contact hour. Books/supplies: $500. Personal expenses: $600.

Financial aid. Need-based: Need-based aid available for part-time students. Work-study available nights, weekends and for part-time students. **Non-need-based:** Scholarships awarded for academics, art, athletics, job skills, leadership, music/drama.

Application procedures. Admission: Priority date 6/15; no deadline. No application fee. Admission notification on a rolling basis beginning on or about 2/15. **Financial aid:** Priority date 8/1; no closing date. FAFSA required. Applicants notified on a rolling basis starting 5/15; must reply within 3 week(s) of notification.

Academics. Special study options: Distance learning, double major, dual enrollment of high school students, internships, liberal arts/career combination. Bachelor's degree programs available on campus. License preparation in nursing. **Credit/placement by examination:** AP, CLEP, institutional tests. 30 credit hours maximum toward associate degree. **Support services:** Learning center, reduced course load, remedial instruction, study skills assistance, tutoring, writing center.

Majors. Business: Accounting, business admin, management information systems. **Communications technology:** Graphic/printing. **Computer sciences:** General, information systems, LAN/WAN management, networking. **Education:** General. **Engineering:** General. **Health services:** Medical assistant, nursing (RN). **Liberal arts:** Arts/sciences. **Protective services:** Corrections, law enforcement admin.

Computing on campus. 75 workstations in library, computer center. Commuter students can connect to campus network. Online library available.

Student life. Freshman orientation: Available. Preregistration for classes offered. One-day program during week prior to start of each semester. **Housing:** Apartments available. $410 deposit, deadline 8/1. **Activities:** Jazz band, dance, drama, musical theater, student government, student newspaper.

Athletics. NJCAA. **Intercollegiate:** Basketball, golf M, softball W, volleyball W. **Intramural:** Basketball, bowling, softball, volleyball. **Team name:** Lumberjacks.

Student services. Adult student services, alcohol/substance abuse counseling, career counseling, student employment services, financial aid counseling, personal counseling, placement for graduates, veterans' counselor, women's services. **Transfer:** Pre-admission transcript evaluation for new students. Transfer adviser, college fairs on campus for students transferring to 4-year colleges.

Contact. E-mail: kollienm@alpenacc.edu
Phone: (989) 358-7339 Toll-free number: (888) 468-6222
Fax: (989) 358-7540
Michael Kollien, Director of Admissions, Alpena Community College, 665 Johnson Street, Alpena, MI 49707

Bay de Noc Community College
Escanaba, Michigan
www.baycollege.edu   CB code: 1049

▸ Public 2-year community college
▸ Commuter campus in large town

General. Founded in 1962. Regionally accredited. **Enrollment:** 2,749 degree-seeking undergraduates. **Degrees:** 367 associate awarded. **Location:** 110 miles from Green Bay, Wisconsin. **Calendar:** Semester, limited summer session. **Full-time faculty:** 48 total. **Part-time faculty:** 119 total. **Class size:** 57% < 20, 42% 20-39, less than 1% 40-49, less than 1% 50-99. **Special facilities:** Reading, writing, math and computer-assisted instructional laboratories, center for performing arts, supplemental instruction math and science lab.

Student profile.

Out-of-state:	5%	Live on campus:	2%
25 or older:	33%		

Transfer out. Colleges most students transferred to 2011: Northern Michigan University, Lake Superior State University, Michigan Technological University.

Basis for selection. Open admission, but selective for some programs. Special requirements for nursing program.

High school preparation. College-preparatory program recommended.

2011-2012 Annual costs. Tuition/fees: $3,240; $5,490 out-of-district; $9,227 out-of-state. Per-credit charge: $97 in-district; $172 out-of-district; $297 out-of-state. Tuition and instructional fees based on contact hours. Room only: $2,800. Books/supplies: $1,072. Personal expenses: $500.

Financial aid. Need-based: Need-based aid available for part-time students. Work-study available nights, weekends and for part-time students. **Non-need-based:** Scholarships awarded for academics.

Application procedures. Admission: Closing date 8/15. No application fee. Admission notification on a rolling basis. **Financial aid:** Priority date 4/1; no closing date. FAFSA required. Applicants notified on a rolling basis starting 2/1; must reply within 2 week(s) of notification.

Academics. Special study options: Cooperative education, distance learning, dual enrollment of high school students, honors, independent study, internships, liberal arts/career combination. Bachelor's degree programs available on campus. License preparation in nursing. **Credit/placement by examination:** AP, CLEP, institutional tests. 40 credit hours maximum toward associate degree. **Support services:** Pre-admission summer program, reduced course load, remedial instruction, study skills assistance, tutoring, writing center.

Majors. Biology: Biotechnology. **Business:** Accounting, accounting technology, administrative services, business admin, hospitality admin, marketing, sales/distribution, small business admin. **Communications:** Advertising, broadcast journalism, communications/speech/rhetoric, journalism. **Computer sciences:** Applications programming, data processing, networking. **Conservation:** General, wildlife/wilderness, wood science. **Education:** Kindergarten/preschool. **Health services:** Clinical lab assistant, medical secretary, nursing (RN), prenursing, radiologic technology/medical imaging, sonography. **Liberal arts:** Arts/sciences. **Physical sciences:** Astronomy. **Protective services:** Corrections, criminal justice, law enforcement admin. **Work/family studies:** Child care management, child development.

Most popular majors. Business/marketing 21%, engineering/engineering technologies 8%, health sciences 26%, liberal arts 26%, security/protective services 9%.

Computing on campus. 535 workstations in library, computer center. Dormitories wired for high-speed internet access and linked to campus network. Commuter students can connect to campus network. Online course registration, online library, helpline, wireless network available.

Student life. Freshman orientation: Available. Preregistration for classes offered. Students meet with counselors, financial aid officers, student services representatives to determine course of study and expenses. **Housing:** Apartments available. $150 partly refundable deposit, deadline 8/15. **Activities:** Campus ministries, choral groups, drama, literary magazine, Model UN, student government, student newspaper, student volunteer association, nurses association, student activities board, history club, water tech club, art club.

Student services. Adult student services, career counseling, student employment services, financial aid counseling, on-campus daycare, personal counseling, veterans' counselor. **Physically disabled:** Services for visually, hearing impaired. **Transfer:** Transfer adviser, college fairs on campus for students transferring to 4-year colleges.

Contact. E-mail: carterc@baycollege.edu
Phone: (906) 217-4134 Toll-free number: (800) 221-2001
Fax: (906) 217-1714
Cynthia Carter, Director of Admissions, Bay de Noc Community College, 2001 North Lincoln Road, Escanaba, MI 49829-2511

Bay Mills Community College
Brimley, Michigan
www.bmcc.edu   **CB code: 2101**

- Public 2-year community college
- Commuter campus in rural community

General. Regionally accredited. **Enrollment:** 575 degree-seeking undergraduates. **Degrees:** 43 associate awarded. **Location:** 20 miles from Sault Ste. Marie. **Calendar:** Semester, limited summer session. **Full-time faculty:** 18 total; 56% women. **Part-time faculty:** 26 total.

Transfer out. Colleges most students transferred to 2011: Lake Superior State University.

Basis for selection. Open admission. All newly admitted degree-seeking students must complete the COMPASS test or provide results of previous testing or have successfully completed college courses in mathematics and English. **Home schooled:** Transcript of courses and grades required. **Learning Disabled:** Students with documented disabilities must contact the Student Services Office to receive assistance and accommodations.

2011-2012 Annual costs. Tuition/fees: $2,910; $2,910 out-of-state. Per-credit charge: $85 in-state; $85 out-of-state. Books/supplies: $200.

Financial aid. Need-based: Work-study available nights, weekends and for part-time students.

Application procedures. Admission: Closing date 8/26 (receipt date). No application fee. Admission notification on a rolling basis. **Financial aid:** Priority date 6/30; no closing date. FAFSA required.

Academics. Special study options: Cooperative education, distance learning, double major, dual enrollment of high school students, independent study, internships. License preparation in paramedic. **Credit/placement by examination:** AP, CLEP, institutional tests. A minimum of 60% of credits required for any BMCC degree or certificate program must be earned through the successful completion of BMCC courses. **Support services:** GED preparation and test center, learning center, remedial instruction, study skills assistance, tutoring.

Majors. Area/ethnic studies: Native American. **Business:** Business admin. **Computer sciences:** Information technology. **Education:** Early childhood. **Parks/recreation:** Health/fitness. **Protective services:** Corrections.

Computing on campus. 30 workstations in library, computer center. Online library, repair service, wireless network available.

Student life. Freshman orientation: Mandatory. Preregistration for classes offered. **Activities:** Student government.

Student services. Career counseling, financial aid counseling. **Transfer:** Pre-admission transcript evaluation for new students. College fairs on campus for students transferring to 4-year colleges.

Contact. E-mail: elehre@bmcc.edu
Phone: (906) 248-3354 ext. 8422 Toll-free number: (800) 844-2622
Fax: (906) 248-3351
Elaine Lehre, Admissions Officer, Bay Mills Community College, 12214 West Lakeshore Drive, Brimley, MI 49715

Delta College
University Center, Michigan
www.delta.edu   **CB code: 1816**

- Public 2-year community college
- Commuter campus in small city

General. Founded in 1957. Regionally accredited. Classes offered at 21 off-campus sites, including 3 major off-campus facilities. **Enrollment:** 9,599 degree-seeking undergraduates; 1,879 non-degree-seeking students. **Degrees:** 1,464 associate awarded. **Location:** 10 miles from Saginaw, 12 miles from Midland. **Calendar:** Semester, limited summer session. **Full-time faculty:** 216 total; 95% have terminal degrees, 11% minority, 57% women. **Part-time faculty:** 367 total; 7% minority, 47% women. **Class size:** 44% < 20, 55% 20-39, less than 1% 40-49, less than 1% 50-99. **Special facilities:** Planetarium, on-site dental clinic. **Partnerships:** Formal partnership with General Motors (ASEP program for automotive students).

Student profile. Among degree-seeking undergraduates, 1,634 enrolled as first-time, first-year students.

Part-time:	58%	Hispanic American:	6%
Out-of-state:	2%	Native American:	1%
Women:	55%	International:	1%
African American:	11%	25 or older:	37%
Asian American:	1%		

Transfer out. Colleges most students transferred to 2011: Central Michigan University, Saginaw Valley State University, Northwood University, University of Michigan, Michigan State University.

Basis for selection. Open admission. ACT, ASSET or COMPASS required of all students for counseling purposes.

2011-2012 Annual costs. Tuition/fees: $3,120; $4,410 out-of-district; $6,150 out-of-state. Books/supplies: $1,500. Personal expenses: $855.

Financial aid. Need-based: Need-based aid available for part-time students. Work-study available nights, weekends and for part-time students. **Non-need-based:** Scholarships awarded for academics, athletics.

Application procedures. Admission: No deadline. $20 fee, may be waived for applicants with need. Admission notification on a rolling basis. **Financial aid:** No deadline. FAFSA required. Applicants notified on a rolling basis; must reply within 2 week(s) of notification.

Academics. Special study options: Cooperative education, distance learning, double major, dual enrollment of high school students, honors, independent study, internships, liberal arts/career combination, student-designed major, study abroad, weekend college. License preparation in dental hygiene, nursing, occupational therapy, physical therapy, radiology, real estate. **Credit/placement by examination:** AP, CLEP, IB, institutional tests. 38 credit hours maximum toward associate degree. **Support services:** GED preparation and test center, learning center, reduced course load, remedial instruction, study skills assistance, tutoring, writing center.

Majors. Architecture: Technology. **Biology:** General, biotechnology. **Business:** General, accounting, administrative services, business admin, construction management, international, marketing, merchandising, office management, office technology, small business admin. **Communications:** Journalism. **Communications technology:** General, graphic/printing. **Computer sciences:** General, computer science, information systems, information technology, networking, programming, web page design, webmaster. **Conservation:** General, environmental science, forestry, water/wetlands/marine. **Education:** Art, business, elementary, kindergarten/preschool, music, physical, secondary, special ed, technology/industrial arts. **Engineering:** General, architectural, mechanical. **English:** English lit. **Foreign languages:** General. **General:** Business. **Health services:** Clinical lab science, dental assistant, dental hygiene, dietetics, licensed practical nurse, medical assistant, medical radiologic technology/radiation therapy, medical secretary, nursing (RN), office assistant, optometric assistant, pharmacy assistant, physical therapy assistant, physics/radiologic health, predental, premedicine, prenursing, prepharmacy, preveterinary, respiratory therapy assistant, respiratory therapy technology, sonography, surgical technology. **Human services:** Social work. **Liberal arts:** Arts/sciences. **Math:** General. **Parks/recreation:** Health/fitness. **Physical sciences:** General, chemistry, geology. **Protective services:** Corrections, fire safety technology, fire services admin, firefighting, law enforcement admin, police science. **Psychology:** General. **Social sciences:** Economics, geography, sociology. **Visual/performing arts:** Art, dramatic, graphic design, interior design, music, photography. **Work/family studies:** Child development.

Computing on campus. 350 workstations in library, computer center, student center. Commuter students can connect to campus network. Online course registration, online library, helpline, wireless network available.

Student life. Freshman orientation: Mandatory. Preregistration for classes offered. General campus overview and individual academic counseling/advising. Assessment required prior to orientation. **Activities:** Choral groups, drama, radio station, student government, student newspaper, TV station, Black student union, Chi Alpha, Delta Collegiate, Delta Epsilon Chi, health care organizations, InterVarsity Christian Fellowship, Phi Theta Kappa International, Society of Hispanic Leaders, student senate, trilogy club.

Athletics. NJCAA. **Intercollegiate:** Basketball, golf M, soccer W, softball W. **Team name:** Pioneers.

Student services. Adult student services, career counseling, services for economically disadvantaged, student employment services, financial aid counseling, minority student services, personal counseling, placement for graduates, veterans' counselor. **Physically disabled:** Services for visually, speech, hearing impaired. **Transfer:** Transfer center, transfer adviser, college fairs on campus for students transferring to 4-year colleges.

Contact. E-mail: admit@delta.edu
Phone: (989) 686-9093 Toll-free number: (800) 285-1704
Fax: (989) 667-2202
Gary Brasseur, Director of Enrollment Services, Delta College, 1961 Delta Road D101, University Center, MI 48710

Glen Oaks Community College
Centreville, Michigan   **CB member**
www.glenoaks.edu   **CB code: 1261**

- Public 2-year community college
- Commuter campus in rural community

General. Founded in 1965. Regionally accredited. **Enrollment:** 1,400 degree-seeking undergraduates. **Degrees:** 157 associate awarded. **Location:** 35 miles from Kalamazoo. **Calendar:** Semester, limited summer session. **Full-time faculty:** 35 total. **Part-time faculty:** 42 total. **Special facilities:** Fitness center, nature trails and habitat.

Student profile.

Out-of-state:	18%	25 or older:	82%

Transfer out. Colleges most students transferred to 2011: Western Michigan University, Grand Valley State University, Kalamazoo Valley Community College, Kellogg Community College, Michigan State University.

Basis for selection. Open admission, but selective for some programs. Admission to nursing program based on pre-admission test, high school grades, and health form. ACCUPLACER test requested for certain programs. ACT or SAT may be considered in lieu of ACCUPLACER.

2011-2012 Annual costs. Tuition/fees: $3,300; $4,590 out-of-district; $5,550 out-of-state. Per-credit charge: $85 in-district; $128 out-of-district; $160 out-of-state. Books/supplies: $500. Personal expenses: $775.

Financial aid. Need-based: Need-based aid available for part-time students. Work-study available nights, weekends and for part-time students. **Non-need-based:** Scholarships awarded for academics, art, athletics, leadership.

Application procedures. Admission: No deadline. No application fee. Admission notification on a rolling basis. **Financial aid:** No deadline. FAFSA, institutional form required. Applicants notified on a rolling basis.

Academics. Special study options: Accelerated study, distance learning, double major, dual enrollment of high school students, independent study, internships, liberal arts/career combination. Bachelor's degree programs available on campus. License preparation in nursing. **Credit/placement by examination:** AP, CLEP, institutional tests. 47 credit hours maximum toward associate degree. **Support services:** Learning center, pre-admission summer program, remedial instruction, study skills assistance, tutoring.

Majors. Business: General. **Education:** Early childhood. **Engineering:** Engineering science. **Health services:** Nursing (RN). **Liberal arts:** Arts/sciences. **Work/family studies:** Child care management.

Most popular majors. Business/marketing 26%, engineering/engineering technologies 6%, health sciences 27%, liberal arts 38%.

Computing on campus. 150 workstations in library, computer center, student center. Commuter students can connect to campus network. Online course registration, online library, wireless network available.

Student life. Freshman orientation: Mandatory. Preregistration for classes offered. **Activities:** Choral groups, student government, academic honorary society, Phi Theta Kappa, veterans club.

Athletics. NJCAA. **Intercollegiate:** Baseball M, basketball, cross-country, golf, softball W. **Intramural:** Table tennis. **Team name:** Vikings.

Student services. Adult student services, career counseling, services for economically disadvantaged, student employment services, financial aid counseling, personal counseling, women's services. **Physically disabled:** Services for visually, speech, hearing impaired. **Transfer:** Transfer adviser, college fairs on campus for students transferring to 4-year colleges.

Contact. E-mail: thowden@glenoaks.edu
Phone: (269) 294-4230 Toll-free number: (888) 994-7818 ext. 320
Fax: (269) 467-9068
Tonya Howden, Director of Admissions, Glen Oaks Community College, 62249 Shimmel Road, Centreville, MI 49032-9719

Gogebic Community College
Ironwood, Michigan
www.gogebic.edu   **CB code: 1250**

- Public 2-year community college
- Commuter campus in small town

General. Founded in 1932. Regionally accredited. **Enrollment:** 1,043 degree-seeking undergraduates; 104 non-degree-seeking students. **Degrees:** 167 associate awarded. **Location:** 100 miles from Duluth, Minnesota, 150 miles from Marquette. **Calendar:** Semester, limited summer session. **Full-time faculty:** 28 total. **Part-time faculty:** 11 total. **Class size:** 72% < 20, 27% 20-39, less than 1% 40-49, less than 1% 50-99. **Special facilities:** Arboretum, ski hill, terrain park, tubing park, cross-country ski trails, snowshoeing trails.

Student profile. Among degree-seeking undergraduates, 43% enrolled in a transfer program, 49% enrolled in a vocational program, 259 enrolled as first-time, first-year students.

Part-time:	31%	Asian American:	1%
Out-of-state:	20%	Hispanic American:	1%
Women:	59%	Native American:	3%
African American:	2%		

Transfer out. Colleges most students transferred to 2011: Northern Michigan University, University of Wisconsin-Superior, Northland College, Michigan Technological University.

Basis for selection. Open admission, but selective for some programs. Students applying to nursing programs required to show competency in biology and chemistry. Admission based on assessment test scores and academic achievement. Interview recommended. **Home schooled:** Interview required.

High school preparation. Nursing applicants must have background in chemistry, math, and biology.

2011-2012 Annual costs. Tuition/fees: $3,430; $4,390 out-of-district; $5,290 out-of-state. Per-credit charge: $96 in-district; $128 out-of-district; $158 out-of-state. Room only: $4,004. Books/supplies: $1,000. Personal expenses: $3,300.

2010-2011 Financial aid. Need-based: 69% of total undergraduate aid awarded as scholarships/grants, 31% as loans/jobs. Need-based aid available for part-time students. Work-study available nights, weekends and for part-time students. **Non-need-based:** Scholarships awarded for academics, art, athletics, job skills, leadership, music/drama, state residency.

Application procedures. Admission: No deadline. $10 fee, may be waived for applicants with need. Admission notification on a rolling basis. **Financial aid:** Priority date 5/1; no closing date. FAFSA required. Applicants notified on a rolling basis starting 3/15; must reply within 2 week(s) of notification.

Academics. Special study options: Cooperative education, distance learning, double major, dual enrollment of high school students, honors, internships, student-designed major. License preparation in nursing, paramedic. **Credit/placement by examination:** AP, CLEP, institutional tests. 12 credit hours maximum toward associate degree. AP exam scores not listed in policy evaluated on individual basis. **Support services:** GED test center, learning center, reduced course load, remedial instruction, study skills assistance, tutoring.

Majors. Biology: General. **Business:** General, accounting, business admin, entrepreneurial studies, office management, office technology. **Communications technology:** Graphics. **Computer sciences:** Computer science, IT project management. **Conservation:** General, forestry. **Education:** General, early childhood, elementary, secondary, special ed, teacher assistance. **Engineering:** General. **Health services:** Clinical lab science, EMT paramedic,

nursing (RN), predental, premedicine, prenursing, prepharmacy, preveterinary. **History:** General. **Human services:** Social work. **Liberal arts:** Arts/sciences. **Math:** General. **Parks/recreation:** Facilities management. **Physical sciences:** General, chemistry, physics. **Protective services:** Law enforcement admin. **Psychology:** General. **Social sciences:** Sociology. **Visual/performing arts:** Art, commercial/advertising art.

Computing on campus. 240 workstations in dormitories, library, computer center, student center. Dormitories wired for high-speed internet access and linked to campus network. Commuter students can connect to campus network. Wireless network available.

Student life. Freshman orientation: Mandatory. Preregistration for classes offered. Early orientation held in April for accepted students who have completed assessment. Other orientation programs in August and June. **Housing:** Coed dorms available. **Activities:** Campus ministries, drama, music ensembles, student government, student newspaper, student senate, student nurses association.

Athletics. NJCAA. **Intercollegiate:** Basketball, cross-country. **Intramural:** Basketball, bowling, cheerleading, football (non-tackle) M, golf, skiing, soccer, softball, tennis, volleyball. **Team name:** Samsons.

Student services. Alcohol/substance abuse counseling, career counseling, services for economically disadvantaged, student employment services, financial aid counseling, personal counseling, placement for graduates, veterans' counselor. **Physically disabled:** Services for visually, hearing impaired. **Transfer:** Re-entry adviser for new students. Transfer adviser, college fairs on campus for students transferring to 4-year colleges.

Contact. E-mail: debbiej@gogebic.edu
Phone: (906) 932-4231 ext. 207
Toll-free number: (800) 682-5910 ext. 207 Fax: (906) 932-2339
Jeanne Graham, Dean of Students, Gogebic Community College, E4946 Jackson Road, Ironwood, MI 49938

Grand Rapids Community College
Grand Rapids, Michigan
www.grcc.edu

CB member
CB code: 1254

- Public 2-year community college
- Commuter campus in small city

General. Founded in 1914. Regionally accredited. Courses offered at several off-campus sites in Western Michigan. **Enrollment:** 16,809 degree-seeking undergraduates; 766 non-degree-seeking students. **Degrees:** 1,837 associate awarded. **Location:** 70 miles from Lansing, 180 miles from Chicago. **Calendar:** Semester, extensive summer session. **Full-time faculty:** 241 total; 13% have terminal degrees, 13% minority, 53% women. **Part-time faculty:** 622 total; 8% have terminal degrees, 9% minority, 50% women. **Class size:** 20% < 20, 79% 20-39, less than 1% 40-49, less than 1% 50-99.

Student profile. Among degree-seeking undergraduates, 35% enrolled in a transfer program, 65% enrolled in a vocational program, 3,919 enrolled as first-time, first-year students.

Part-time:	61%	Women:	53%
Out-of-state:	1%	25 or older:	36%

Transfer out. Colleges most students transferred to 2011: Grand Valley State University, Ferris State University, Western Michigan University, Michigan State University, Aquinas College.

Basis for selection. Open admission, but selective for some programs. Certain health-related programs require 2.5 high school GPA and completion of certain math and science courses before admission. **Home schooled:** Assessment exam required.

High school preparation. Recommended units include English 4, mathematics 4, social studies 3 and science 4.

2011-2012 Annual costs. Tuition/fees: $2,959; $6,379 out-of-district; $9,499 out-of-state. Per-credit charge: $96 in-district; $210 out-of-district; $314 out-of-state. Books/supplies: $1,566.

Financial aid. Need-based: Need-based aid available for part-time students. Work-study available nights, weekends and for part-time students. **Non-need-based:** Scholarships awarded for academics, alumni affiliation, art, athletics, leadership, minority status, music/drama, state residency. **Additional information:** Tuition reimbursement and/or child-care services for single parents and displaced homemakers who meet Perkins guidelines.

Application procedures. Admission: No deadline. No application fee. Admission notification on a rolling basis. **Financial aid:** Priority date 4/1;

no closing date. FAFSA required. Applicants notified on a rolling basis starting 5/1; must reply within 3 week(s) of notification.

Academics. Liberal arts and pre-professional curricula along with extensive work-force training and technical seminars offered. **Special study options:** Cooperative education, distance learning, dual enrollment of high school students, ESL, independent study, internships, study abroad. License preparation in dental hygiene, nursing, occupational therapy, radiology. **Credit/placement by examination:** AP, CLEP, institutional tests. 47 credit hours maximum toward associate degree. **Support services:** GED test center, learning center, reduced course load, remedial instruction, study skills assistance, tutoring, writing center.

Majors. Architecture: Architecture. **Biology:** General. **Business:** General, accounting technology, business admin, executive assistant, fashion, sales/distribution. **Communications:** Journalism. **Computer sciences:** General, applications programming, LAN/WAN management, programming, webmaster. **Conservation:** General, forestry. **Education:** Elementary, multi-level teacher, music, physical, teacher assistance. **Engineering:** General. **English:** English lit, rhetoric/composition. **Foreign languages:** General. **General:** Landscaping. **Health services:** Clinical lab science, dental assistant, dental hygiene, licensed practical nurse, medical radiologic technology/radiation therapy, nursing (RN), occupational therapy, occupational therapy assistant, physical therapy, predental, premedicine, prepharmacy, preveterinary, surgical technology. **Human services:** Social work. **Liberal arts:** Arts/sciences, library science. **Math:** General. **Physical sciences:** Chemistry, geology, oceanography, physics. **Protective services:** Corrections, law enforcement admin, police science. **Psychology:** General. **Social sciences:** Economics, geography, political science, sociology. **Visual/performing arts:** Art, commercial/advertising art, dramatic, interior design, music, music management, music performance, photography, piano/keyboard, studio arts, voice/opera. **Work/family studies:** Child care management.

Most popular majors. Business/marketing 13%, health sciences 12%, liberal arts 35%.

Computing on campus. 1,500 workstations in library, computer center. Commuter students can connect to campus network. Online course registration, online library, helpline, wireless network available.

Student life. Freshman orientation: Available. Preregistration for classes offered. Provides campus tours and general information about the college. **Policies:** No smoking on campus. **Activities:** Bands, choral groups, dance, drama, film society, international student organizations, literary magazine, music ensembles, musical theater, student government, student newspaper, symphony orchestra, TV station, Black student organization, Hispanic student organization, Native American student organization, Vietnamese student organization, Christian Fellowship, content area student organizations, service learning.

Athletics. NJCAA. **Intercollegiate:** Baseball M, basketball, football (tackle) M, golf M, softball W, tennis, volleyball W. **Intramural:** Basketball, racquetball, skiing, soccer M, swimming. **Team name:** Raiders.

Student services. Adult student services, career counseling, student employment services, financial aid counseling, on-campus daycare, personal counseling, placement for graduates. **Physically disabled:** Services for visually, speech, hearing impaired. **Transfer:** Pre-admission transcript evaluation for new students. Transfer adviser, college fairs on campus for students transferring to 4-year colleges.

Contact. E-mail: admissions@grcc.edu
Phone: (616) 234-3300 Fax: (616) 234-4107
Diane Patrick, Director of Admissions, Grand Rapids Community College, 143 Bostwick Avenue NE, Grand Rapids, MI 49503-3295

Henry Ford Community College
Dearborn, Michigan
www.hfcc.edu

CB code: 1293

- Public 2-year community college
- Commuter campus in small city

General. Founded in 1938. Regionally accredited. **Enrollment:** 17,500 degree-seeking undergraduates. **Degrees:** 1,360 associate awarded. **Location:** 8 miles from downtown. **Calendar:** Semester, extensive summer session. **Full-time faculty:** 193 total. **Part-time faculty:** 744 total.

Student profile.

Out-of-state:	2%	25 or older:	47%

Transfer out. Colleges most students transferred to 2011: The University of Michigan-Dearborn, Wayne State University, Eastern Michigan University, Michigan State University.

Basis for selection. Open admission, but selective for some programs. Special requirements for specific allied health programs.

High school preparation. College-preparatory program recommended. Recommended units include English 4, mathematics 4, social studies 3, science 4, foreign language 1 and computer science 1. For allied health programs: 1 year high school biology, chemistry, and algebra.

2011-2012 Annual costs. Tuition/fees: $2,792; $4,592 out-of-district; $4,742 out-of-state. Per-credit charge: $75 in-district; $135 out-of-district; $140 out-of-state.

Financial aid. Need-based: Work-study available nights, weekends and for part-time students.

Application procedures. Admission: No deadline. $30 fee, may be waived for applicants with need. Admission notification on a rolling basis. **Financial aid:** Priority date 4/1; no closing date. FAFSA required. Applicants notified on a rolling basis starting 3/1.

Academics. Special study options: Accelerated study, cooperative education, distance learning, double major, dual enrollment of high school students, ESL, honors, independent study. License preparation in nursing, paramedic, physical therapy, radiology. **Credit/placement by examination:** AP, CLEP. 20 credit hours maximum toward associate degree. **Support services:** Learning center, pre-admission summer program, reduced course load, remedial instruction, study skills assistance, tutoring, writing center.

Majors. Architecture: Technology. **Business:** General, accounting, business admin, executive assistant, hospitality admin, management science, office/clerical, real estate. **Communications:** Broadcast journalism. **Communications technology:** Animation/special effects. **Computer sciences:** General, security. **Conservation:** Environmental studies. **Education:** Early childhood, elementary, secondary, special ed. **Engineering:** General. **Health services:** EMT paramedic, licensed practical nurse, management/clinical assistant, medical records technology, nursing (RN), office admin, physical therapy assistant, prepharmacy, radiologic technology/medical imaging, respiratory therapy technology, surgical technology. **Liberal arts:** Arts/sciences. **Parks/recreation:** Exercise sciences. **Philosophy/religion:** Religion. **Physical sciences:** Chemistry. **Protective services:** Firefighting, law enforcement admin, security management. **Visual/performing arts:** Art, commercial/advertising art, dramatic, interior design, studio arts. **Work/family studies:** Child development.

Computing on campus. Commuter students can connect to campus network. Online course registration, online library, helpline, wireless network available.

Student life. Freshman orientation: Available. Preregistration for classes offered. **Activities:** Bands, choral groups, dance, drama, film society, international student organizations, literary magazine, music ensembles, musical theater, radio station, student government, student newspaper, Muslim student association, African American association, community service club, Campus Crusade for Christ, Students for a Democratic Society, Crazy Antics club, Yemen student association, multicultural club, diversity club.

Athletics. NJCAA. **Intercollegiate:** Baseball M, basketball, golf, softball W, volleyball W. **Intramural:** Basketball, bowling, golf, table tennis, tennis, track and field, volleyball. **Team name:** Hawks.

Student services. Adult student services, career counseling, services for economically disadvantaged, student employment services, financial aid counseling, on-campus daycare, personal counseling, placement for graduates, veterans' counselor. **Physically disabled:** Services for visually, hearing impaired. **Transfer:** Re-entry adviser, pre-admission transcript evaluation for new students. Transfer center, transfer adviser, college fairs on campus for students transferring to 4-year colleges.

Contact. Phone: (313) 845-9613 Toll-free number: (800) 585-4322 Fax: (313) 845-9891
Douglas Freed, Director of Enrollment Management, Henry Ford Community College, 5101 Evergreen Road, Dearborn, MI 48128

ITT Technical Institute: Canton
Canton, Michigan
www.itt-tech.edu

- For-profit 2-year business and technical college
- Commuter campus in small city

General. Accredited by ACICS. **Enrollment:** 809 undergraduates. **Degrees:** 76 bachelor's, 196 associate awarded. **Calendar:** Quarter. **Full-time faculty:** 16 total. **Part-time faculty:** 63 total.

Basis for selection. Selective admissions to some programs.

2011-2012 Annual costs. Estimated costs as of June 2011: per-credit-hour charge, $493, depending upon level and course of study; academic fee, $200. Certain programs of study require purchase of tools, which could cost an additional $100 to $700. All costs are subject to change.

Financial aid. Need-based: Work-study available nights, weekends and for part-time students.

Academics. Credit/placement by examination: AP, CLEP.

Majors. Business: Business admin. **Computer sciences:** General, networking, web page design. **Health services:** Nursing (RN). **Protective services:** Law enforcement admin. **Visual/performing arts:** Design.

Contact. ITT Technical Institute: Canton, 1905 South Haggerty Road, Canton, MI 48188

ITT Technical Institute: Troy
Troy, Michigan
www.itt-tech.edu
CB code: 2784

- For-profit 2-year technical college
- Commuter campus in small city
- Interview required

General. Accredited by ACICS. **Enrollment:** 1,434 undergraduates. **Degrees:** 82 bachelor's, 315 associate awarded. **Calendar:** Quarter, extensive summer session. **Full-time faculty:** 16 total. **Part-time faculty:** 129 total.

Basis for selection. Satisfactory scores from on-site tests in English and mathematics required.

2011-2012 Annual costs. Estimated costs as of June 2011: per-credit-hour charge, $493, depending upon level and course of study; academic fee, $200. Certain programs of study require purchase of tools, which could cost an additional $100 to $500. All costs are subject to change.

Financial aid. Need-based: Work-study available nights, weekends and for part-time students.

Application procedures. Admission: No deadline. No application fee. Admission notification on a rolling basis. **Financial aid:** No deadline. FAFSA, institutional form required. Applicants notified on a rolling basis.

Academics. Credit/placement by examination: AP, CLEP. **Support services:** Learning center, tutoring.

Majors. Business: Business admin. **Computer sciences:** Networking, programming, web page design. **Protective services:** Law enforcement admin. **Visual/performing arts:** Design.

Computing on campus. Online library available.

Student life. Freshman orientation: Available. Preregistration for classes offered.

Student services. Career counseling, student employment services, placement for graduates.

Contact. Phone: (248) 524-1800 Toll-free number: (800) 832-6817 Fax: (248) 524-1965
Patricia Hyman, Director of Recruitment, ITT Technical Institute: Troy, 1522 East Big Beaver Road, Troy, MI 48083-1905

Jackson Community College
Jackson, Michigan
www.jccmi.edu
CB code: 1340

- Public 2-year community college
- Commuter campus in small city

General. Founded in 1928. Regionally accredited. Off-campus locations in Hillsdale County and Lenawee County. **Enrollment:** 6,551 degree-seeking undergraduates; 437 non-degree-seeking students. **Degrees:** 698 associate awarded. **Location:** 6 miles from downtown. **Calendar:** Semester, limited summer session. **Full-time faculty:** 96 total; 5% minority, 53% women. **Part-time faculty:** 356 total; 6% minority, 56% women. **Class size:** 60% < 20, 38% 20-39, 1% 40-49. **Partnerships:** Formal partnership with Foote Health University to provide education and training for employees.

Two-Year Colleges

Student profile. Among degree-seeking undergraduates, 1,415 enrolled as first-time, first-year students.

Part-time:	53%	Asian American:	1%
Out-of-state:	1%	Hispanic American:	4%
Women:	61%	Native American:	1%
African American:	9%	25 or older:	45%

Transfer out. **Colleges most students transferred to 2011:** Michigan State University, Spring Arbor University, Eastern Michigan University, Siena Heights University, Western Michigan University.

Basis for selection. Open admission, but selective for some programs. Special requirements for allied health programs and nursing program. ACT scores used for placement if submitted. Students not submitting ACT scores are required to take college-administered placement tests. Second admit programs require interviews and specific academic prerequisites.

2011-2012 Annual costs. Tuition/fees: $3,945; $5,175 out-of-district; $6,930 out-of-state. Per-credit charge: $101 in-district; $142 out-of-district; $200 out-of-state. Books/supplies: $672. Personal expenses: $720.

Financial aid. **Need-based:** Need-based aid available for part-time students. Work-study available nights, weekends and for part-time students. **Non-need-based:** Scholarships awarded for academics, art, leadership, music/drama, state residency.

Application procedures. **Admission:** No deadline. No application fee. Admission notification on a rolling basis. **Financial aid:** Priority date 6/15; no closing date. FAFSA, institutional form required. Applicants notified on a rolling basis starting 3/1.

Academics. Extensive on-line offerings. Students may also complete bachelor's degrees on-campus from partner universities. **Special study options:** Distance learning, dual enrollment of high school students, ESL, independent study, internships, liberal arts/career combination. Bachelor's degree programs available on campus. License preparation in aviation, nursing, paramedic, radiology. **Credit/placement by examination:** AP, CLEP, IB, institutional tests. 30 credit hours maximum toward associate degree. **Support services:** GED preparation and test center, learning center, pre-admission summer program, remedial instruction, study skills assistance, tutoring, writing center.

Majors. **Business:** General, accounting, business admin, finance. **Computer sciences:** Applications programming, computer graphics, data processing, programming, web page design. **Education:** Early childhood. **Health services:** EMT paramedic, medical assistant, medical transcription, nursing (RN), radiologic technology/medical imaging, sonography. **Liberal arts:** Arts/sciences. **Protective services:** Criminal justice. **Visual/performing arts:** Graphic design.

Most popular majors. Business/marketing 12%, health sciences 28%, liberal arts 39%, trade and industry 9%.

Computing on campus. 356 workstations in library, computer center, student center. Online course registration, helpline available.

Student life. **Freshman orientation:** Available. Preregistration for classes offered. 2- to 3-hour program prior to each semester. **Activities:** Bands, choral groups, dance, drama, music ensembles, musical theater, student government, student newspaper.

Athletics. **Intramural:** Basketball M, football (non-tackle) M, soccer M. **Team name:** Golden Jets.

Student services. Adult student services, career counseling, services for economically disadvantaged, financial aid counseling, minority student services, on-campus daycare. **Physically disabled:** Services for visually, speech, hearing impaired. **Transfer:** Pre-admission transcript evaluation for new students. Transfer center, transfer adviser, college fairs on campus for students transferring to 4-year colleges.

Contact. E-mail: admissions@jccmi.edu
Phone: (517) 796-8425 Toll-free number: (888) 522-7344
Fax: (517) 796-8631
Julie Hand, Enrollment Services Team Leader, Jackson Community College, 2111 Emmons Road, Jackson, MI 49201-8399

Kalamazoo Valley Community College
Kalamazoo, Michigan
www.kvcc.edu   CB code: 1378

▶ Public 2-year community college
▶ Commuter campus in small city

General. Founded in 1966. Regionally accredited. Additional campus downtown. **Enrollment:** 10,645 degree-seeking undergraduates. **Degrees:** 927 associate awarded. **Location:** 130 miles from Detroit, 150 miles from Chicago. **Calendar:** Semester, limited summer session. **Full-time faculty:** 138 total. **Part-time faculty:** 455 total. **Class size:** 30% < 20, 59% 20-39, 10% 40-49, less than 1% 50-99. **Special facilities:** Museum, nature trails.

Student profile.

Out-of-state:	1%	25 or older:	50%

Transfer out. **Colleges most students transferred to 2011:** Western Michigan University.

Basis for selection. Open admission.

2011-2012 Annual costs. Tuition/fees: $2,385; $3,960 out-of-district; $5,400 out-of-state. Per-credit charge: $80 in-district; $132 out-of-district; $180 out-of-state. Books/supplies: $1,350. Personal expenses: $1,282.

Financial aid. **Need-based:** Need-based aid available for part-time students. Work-study available nights, weekends and for part-time students. **Non-need-based:** Scholarships awarded for academics, athletics.

Application procedures. **Admission:** No deadline. No application fee. Admission notification on a rolling basis. **Financial aid:** Priority date 6/1; no closing date. FAFSA, institutional form required. Applicants notified on a rolling basis starting 5/1; must reply within 2 week(s) of notification.

Academics. **Special study options:** Cooperative education, cross-registration, distance learning, dual enrollment of high school students, ESL, honors, independent study, internships, liberal arts/career combination, week-end college. License preparation in dental hygiene, nursing. **Credit/placement by examination:** AP, CLEP, institutional tests. 32 credit hours maximum toward associate degree. Michigan Language Assessment Battery may be used for placement. **Support services:** Learning center, reduced course load, remedial instruction, tutoring, writing center.

Majors. **Business:** Accounting, administrative services, business admin, management information systems. **Communications technology:** General. **Computer sciences:** Computer graphics, data processing, programming. **Education:** General. **Engineering:** General. **Health services:** Dental hygiene, licensed practical nurse, medical assistant, medical secretary, nursing (RN), respiratory therapy technology. **Liberal arts:** Arts/sciences. **Physical sciences:** General. **Protective services:** Firefighting, law enforcement admin, police science. **Visual/performing arts:** Commercial/advertising art. **Work/family studies:** Family studies.

Most popular majors. Business/marketing 11%, education 11%, engineering/engineering technologies 7%, health sciences 12%, liberal arts 43%.

Computing on campus. 1,000 workstations in library, computer center, student center. Online course registration, wireless network available.

Student life. **Freshman orientation:** Available. Preregistration for classes offered. **Activities:** Choral groups, dance, Fellowship of Christian Athletes, Student American Dental Hygiene Association, data processing association, African American association, Latino student association, Native American association, deaf student association.

Athletics. NJCAA. **Intercollegiate:** Baseball M, basketball, golf M, softball W, tennis, volleyball W. **Intramural:** Basketball M, tennis W, volleyball W. **Team name:** Cougars.

Student services. Career counseling, services for economically disadvantaged, student employment services, financial aid counseling, minority student services, on-campus daycare, personal counseling, placement for graduates, women's services. **Physically disabled:** Services for visually, speech, hearing impaired. **Transfer:** Transfer adviser, college fairs on campus for students transferring to 4-year colleges.

Contact. E-mail: admissions@kvcc.edu
Phone: (269) 488-4400 Fax: (269) 488-4161
Michael McCall, Director of Admissions, Registration and Records, Kalamazoo Valley Community College, 6767 West O Avenue, Kalamazoo, MI 49003-4070

Kellogg Community College
Battle Creek, Michigan
www.kellogg.edu   CB code: 1375

▶ Public 2-year community college
▶ Commuter campus in small city

General. Founded in 1956. Regionally accredited. Academic centers in Coldwater, Hastings and Albion. Regional manufacturing technical center with open entry/open exit programs in 7 different technical areas. **Enrollment:** 5,992 degree-seeking undergraduates. **Degrees:** 739 associate awarded. **Location:** 20 miles from Kalamazoo, 80 miles from Grand Rapids. **Calendar:** Semester, limited summer session. **Full-time faculty:** 87 total. **Part-time faculty:** 309 total.

Transfer out. Colleges most students transferred to 2011: Western Michigan University, Michigan State University, Ferris State University, Grand Valley State University, Central Michigan University.

Basis for selection. Open admission, but selective for some programs. Allied health and nursing program applicants must supply high school record, previous college transcripts, ACT/SAT test scores, and meet specific academic criteria.

High school preparation. College-preparatory program recommended. Recommended units include English 4, mathematics 4, social studies 1, history 3, science 4 (laboratory 1), foreign language 1 and academic electives 6.

2012-2013 Annual costs. Tuition/fees (projected): $2,935; $4,350 out-of-district; $6,015 out-of-state. Per-credit charge: $87.5 in-district; $137 out-of-district; $192.5 out-of-state. Books/supplies: $1,300. Personal expenses: $5,782.

Financial aid. Need-based: Need-based aid available for part-time students. Work-study available nights, weekends and for part-time students. **Non-need-based:** Scholarships awarded for academics, athletics, minority status.

Application procedures. Admission: Priority date 8/1; no deadline. No application fee. Admission notification on a rolling basis. **Financial aid:** Priority date 4/1; no closing date. FAFSA, institutional form required. Applicants notified on a rolling basis starting 4/1.

Academics. Special study options: Accelerated study, cooperative education, double major, dual enrollment of high school students, honors, independent study, internships, liberal arts/career combination. Bachelor's degree programs available on campus. License preparation in dental hygiene, nursing, paramedic, physical therapy, radiology. **Credit/placement by examination:** AP, CLEP, IB, institutional tests. Must be 2.0 or above for credit. **Support services:** Learning center, reduced course load, remedial instruction, study skills assistance, tutoring, writing center.

Majors. Business: Accounting, administrative services, business admin. **Communications technology:** General. **Computer sciences:** Programming. **English:** English lit. **Health services:** Clinical lab technology, dental hygiene, EMT paramedic, medical radiologic technology/radiation therapy, medical secretary, nursing (RN), physical therapy assistant. **Human services:** Social work. **Liberal arts:** Arts/sciences. **Protective services:** Corrections, fire safety technology, police science. **Visual/performing arts:** Commercial/advertising art. **Work/family studies:** Child care management.

Most popular majors. Business/marketing 12%, health sciences 27%, liberal arts 47%.

Computing on campus. 1,000 workstations in library, computer center. Commuter students can connect to campus network. Online course registration, online library, helpline, wireless network available.

Student life. Freshman orientation: Mandatory. Preregistration for classes offered. **Activities:** Bands, campus ministries, choral groups, drama, film society, international student organizations, literary magazine, music ensembles, musical theater, student newspaper, military student support group, tech club, Phi Theta Kappa, Kampus Activities board, Spectrum, film club, art league, Encore Theatre Company, human services club, international studies club.

Athletics. NJCAA. **Intercollegiate:** Baseball M, basketball, soccer M, softball W, volleyball W. **Team name:** Bruins.

Student services. Adult student services, alcohol/substance abuse counseling, career counseling, student employment services, financial aid counseling, personal counseling, placement for graduates, veterans' counselor. **Physically disabled:** Services for visually, speech, hearing impaired. **Transfer:** Pre-admission transcript evaluation for new students. Transfer adviser, college fairs on campus for students transferring to 4-year colleges.

Contact. E-mail: admissions@kellogg.edu
Phone: (269) 965-4153 Fax: (269) 966-4089
Meredith Stravers, Director of Enrollment Services, Kellogg Community College, 450 North Avenue, Battle Creek, MI 49017-3397

Kirtland Community College
Roscommon, Michigan
www.kirtland.edu   CB code: 1382

▶ Public 2-year community college
▶ Commuter campus in rural community

General. Founded in 1966. Regionally accredited. Additional sites in Roscommon, West Branch, Grayling and Gaylord. **Enrollment:** 1,747 degree-seeking undergraduates; 68 non-degree-seeking students. **Degrees:** 193 associate awarded. **Location:** 192 miles from Detroit, 150 miles from Grand Rapids. **Calendar:** Semester, extensive summer session. **Full-time faculty:** 39 total; 10% have terminal degrees, 8% minority, 51% women. **Part-time faculty:** 100 total; 4% minority, 52% women. **Class size:** 77% < 20, 22% 20-39, less than 1% 40-49, less than 1% 50-99. **Special facilities:** Fitness and nature trail, firing range, Michigan Technical Education Center.

Student profile. Among degree-seeking undergraduates, 17% enrolled in a transfer program, 81% enrolled in a vocational program, 298 enrolled as first-time, first-year students, 209 transferred in from other institutions.

Part-time:	57%	Hispanic American:	2%
Women:	64%	Native American:	1%
African American:	1%	25 or older:	43%

Transfer out. Colleges most students transferred to 2011: Central Michigan University, Saginaw Valley State University, North Central Michigan College, Delta College, North Central Michigan College.

Basis for selection. Open admission, but selective for some programs. Special requirements for nursing (levels I and II), pre-corrections, criminal justice administration, criminal justice pre-services, cardiovascular sonography, surgical technology and corrections administration programs. **Home schooled:** Transcript or record of courses and grades requested.

High school preparation. 10 units recommended. Recommended units include English 4, mathematics 2, social studies 2 and science 2.

2011-2012 Annual costs. Tuition/fees: $2,850; $4,840 out-of-district; $6,210 out-of-state. Books/supplies: $1,000. Personal expenses: $1,951.

2010-2011 Financial aid. Need-based: 349 full-time freshmen applied for aid; 339 were judged to have need; 329 of these received aid. Average need met was 38%. Average scholarship/grant was $3,918; average loan $1,977. 72% of total undergraduate aid awarded as scholarships/grants, 28% as loans/jobs. Need-based aid available for part-time students. Work-study available nights, weekends and for part-time students. **Non-need-based:** Awarded to 37 full-time undergraduates, including 11 freshmen. Scholarships awarded for academics, athletics, minority status. **Additional information:** Federal and institutional work-study programs available.

Application procedures. Admission: No deadline. No application fee. Admission notification on a rolling basis. **Financial aid:** Priority date 5/1; no closing date. FAFSA required. Applicants notified on a rolling basis.

Academics. Special study options: Accelerated study, cooperative education, distance learning, dual enrollment of high school students, ESL, honors, independent study, internships. License preparation in nursing. **Credit/placement by examination:** AP, CLEP, institutional tests. 45 credit hours maximum toward associate degree. **Support services:** Learning center, reduced course load, remedial instruction, study skills assistance, tutoring, writing center.

Majors. Business: Administrative services, business admin, management information systems. **Computer sciences:** Systems analysis, webmaster, word processing. **Education:** Multi-level teacher, teacher assistance. **Engineering:** Computer. **Health services:** Cardiovascular technology, medical assistant, medical secretary, medical transcription, nursing (RN), predental, premedicine, prepharmacy, preveterinary, sonography, surgical technology. **Liberal arts:** Arts/sciences, humanities. **Protective services:** Correctional facilities, corrections, fire services admin, law enforcement admin, police science. **Visual/performing arts:** Graphic design, industrial design.

Most popular majors. Business/marketing 15%, computer/information sciences 6%, health sciences 49%, liberal arts 20%, security/protective services 13%.

Computing on campus. 210 workstations in library, computer center, student center. Commuter students can connect to campus network. Online course registration, online library, helpline, wireless network available.

Student life. Freshman orientation: Available. Preregistration for classes offered. Held in August for students and parents. **Activities:** Choral groups, drama, literary magazine, student government, student newspaper, student senate, Phi Theta Kappa, Christian Fellowship, student activities committee, student medieval club, criminal justice club.

Two-Year Colleges

Athletics. NJCAA. **Intercollegiate:** Basketball, cross-country, golf. **Team name:** Firebirds.

Student services. Adult student services, career counseling, services for economically disadvantaged, student employment services, financial aid counseling, on-campus daycare, personal counseling, placement for graduates, veterans' counselor. **Physically disabled:** Services for visually, speech, hearing impaired. **Transfer:** Transfer adviser, college fairs on campus for students transferring to 4-year colleges.

Contact. E-mail: admissions@kirtland.edu
Phone: (989) 275-5000 ext. 280 Fax: (989) 275-6727
Michelle Devine, Admissions Recruiter, Kirtland Community College, 10775 North Saint Helen Road, Roscommon, MI 48653

Lake Michigan College
Benton Harbor, Michigan
www.lakemichigancollege.edu

CB code: 1137

◗ Public 2-year community college
◗ Commuter campus in large town

General. Founded in 1946. Regionally accredited. Additional campuses located in South Haven and Bertrand Crossing in Niles, Michigan. Technical Education Center (M-TEC) located in Benton Harbor. **Enrollment:** 3,545 degree-seeking undergraduates; 1,117 non-degree-seeking students. **Degrees:** 380 associate awarded. **Location:** 80 miles from Grand Rapids, 40 miles from South Bend, IN. **Calendar:** Semester, limited summer session. **Full-time faculty:** 57 total; 30% have terminal degrees, 4% minority, 49% women. **Part-time faculty:** 299 total; 5% have terminal degrees, 7% minority, 48% women. **Class size:** 81% < 20, 19% 20-39, less than 1% 40-49, less than 1% 50-99. **Special facilities:** Video production facility, nature area. **Partnerships:** Formal partnerships with Four Winds Casino for Casino Management program, Whirlpool Corporation for Best Ticket Program, and American Electric Power for Energy Program.

Student profile. Among degree-seeking undergraduates, 48% enrolled in a transfer program, 2.7% already have a bachelor's degree or higher, 799 enrolled as first-time, first-year students, 187 transferred in from other institutions.

Part-time:	58%	Asian American:	1%
Out-of-state:	2%	Hispanic American:	6%
Women:	63%	Native American:	1%
African American:	21%	25 or older:	49%

Transfer out. Colleges most students transferred to 2011: Western Michigan University, Grand Valley State University, Michigan State University, Ferris State University, Siena Heights University.

Basis for selection. Open admission, but selective for some programs. Admission to health sciences programs based on GPA ranking in specific courses. Interview required for dental assistant, radiologic technology, nursing majors. **Home schooled:** Transcript of courses and grades required.

2011-2012 Annual costs. Tuition/fees: $3,480; $4,710 out-of-district; $5,820 out-of-state. Per-credit charge: $81 in-district; $122 out-of-district; $159 out-of-state. Books/supplies: $1,600. Personal expenses: $1,400.

2010-2011 Financial aid. Need-based: 446 full-time freshmen applied for aid; 380 were judged to have need; 356 of these received aid. Average need met was 59%. Average scholarship/grant was $6,757; average loan $3,058. 82% of total undergraduate aid awarded as scholarships/grants, 18% as loans/jobs. Need-based aid available for part-time students. Work-study available nights, weekends and for part-time students. **Non-need-based:** Awarded to 111 full-time undergraduates, including 54 freshmen.

Application procedures. Admission: No deadline. No application fee. Admission notification on a rolling basis. **Financial aid:** Priority date 3/1; no closing date. FAFSA required. Applicants notified on a rolling basis starting 4/1; must reply within 2 week(s) of notification.

Academics. Special study options: Cooperative education, cross-registration, distance learning, double major, dual enrollment of high school students, honors, independent study, internships, liberal arts/career combination. License preparation in nursing, paramedic, radiology. **Credit/placement by examination:** AP, CLEP, institutional tests. 30 credit hours maximum toward associate degree. **Support services:** GED test center, learning center, remedial instruction, study skills assistance, tutoring.

Majors. Biology: General. **Business:** Accounting technology, administrative services, business admin, casino management, hospitality admin, marketing. **Communications:** General. **Computer sciences:** Computer science, information technology, programming, system admin, web page design. **Conservation:** Environmental science. **Education:** Early childhood, elementary,

secondary. **Engineering:** Pre-engineering. **English:** English lit. **Foreign languages:** General. **General:** Horticulture, landscaping, turf management, viticulture. **Health services:** Dental assistant, EMT paramedic, MRI technology, nursing (RN), office assistant, prechiropractic, predental, premedicine, preoptometry, prepharmacy, prephysical therapy, preveterinary, radiologic technology/medical imaging, sonography. **History:** General. **Liberal arts:** Arts/sciences, humanities. **Math:** General. **Parks/recreation:** Health/fitness. **Philosophy/religion:** Philosophy. **Physical sciences:** General, chemistry, geology, physics. **Protective services:** Corrections, police science. **Psychology:** General. **Social sciences:** Geography, political science, sociology. **Visual/performing arts:** Art, dramatic, graphic design, music.

Most popular majors. Business/marketing 18%, engineering/engineering technologies 11%, health sciences 24%, interdisciplinary studies 7%, liberal arts 22%.

Computing on campus. 100 workstations in library, student center. Commuter students can connect to campus network. Online course registration, online library, helpline, wireless network available.

Student life. Freshman orientation: Available. Preregistration for classes offered. Offered fall, spring and summer. **Activities:** Bands, choral groups, drama, music ensembles, student government.

Athletics. NJCAA. **Intercollegiate:** Baseball M, basketball, softball W, volleyball W. **Team name:** Indians.

Student services. Adult student services, career counseling, services for economically disadvantaged, student employment services, financial aid counseling, on-campus daycare, placement for graduates, veterans' counselor. **Physically disabled:** Services for visually, hearing impaired. **Transfer:** Transfer center, college fairs on campus for students transferring to 4-year colleges.

Contact. E-mail: admissions@lakemichigancollege.edu
Phone: (269) 927-8626 Toll-free number: (800) 252-1562
Fax: (269) 927-6718
Louis Thomas, Lead Admissions Specialist, Lake Michigan College, 2755 East Napier Avenue, Benton Harbor, MI 49022-1899

Lansing Community College
Lansing, Michigan
www.lcc.edu

CB member
CB code: 1414

◗ Public 2-year community college
◗ Commuter campus in small city

General. Founded in 1957. Regionally accredited. **Enrollment:** 19,993 degree-seeking undergraduates; 647 non-degree-seeking students. **Degrees:** 1,585 associate awarded. **ROTC:** Army, Air Force. **Location:** 90 miles from Detroit. **Calendar:** Semester, extensive summer session. **Full-time faculty:** 212 total; 16% minority, 52% women. **Part-time faculty:** 2,060 total; 13% minority, 54% women. **Class size:** 54% < 20, 45% 20-39, less than 1% 40-49, less than 1% 50-99, less than 1% >100. **Special facilities:** Planetarium, observatory, science concepts laboratory, computer-integrated manufacturing institute, in-depth photography institute, truck driver training range, technical library.

Student profile. Among degree-seeking undergraduates, 18% enrolled in a transfer program, 5,121 enrolled as first-time, first-year students, 174 transferred in from other institutions.

Part-time:	71%	25 or older:	32%
Women:	55%		

Transfer out. Colleges most students transferred to 2011: Michigan State University, Central Michigan University, Ferris University.

Basis for selection. Open admission, but selective for some programs. Special requirements for health, aviation, music, police academy programs, fire academy. MELAB required of foreign students. TOEFL also accepted. Interview required of health program applicants and international applicants. Audition recommended for music, dance, theater majors. Portfolio recommended for art majors.

2011-2012 Annual costs. Tuition/fees: $2,420; $4,790 out-of-district; $7,160 out-of-state. Per-credit charge: $79 in-district; $158 out-of-district; $237 out-of-state. The cost for attending a course is determined by the course's billing hours, instead of credit hours. A billing hour represents an amount of time that a student spends in direct contact with an instructor or with laboratory equipment. Books/supplies: $800. Personal expenses: $2,000.

Financial aid. Need-based: Need-based aid available for part-time students. Work-study available nights, weekends and for part-time students. **Non-need-based:** Scholarships awarded for academics, athletics.

Application procedures. Admission: Closing date 8/10 (receipt date). No application fee. Admission notification on a rolling basis. SAT or ACT recommended for assessment waivers and counseling. **Financial aid:** Closing date 7/18. FAFSA required. Applicants notified on a rolling basis starting 4/3.

Academics. Several 4-year degree course studies available, students complete 3 years at LCC and 4th year at a 4-year degree institution. **Special study options:** Accelerated study, cooperative education, cross-registration, distance learning, double major, dual enrollment of high school students, ESL, exchange student, honors, independent study, internships, study abroad, teacher certification program, weekend college. External bachelor's degree with Northwood Institute, 3+1 degree program, 2+2 degree program, University Center (partnership between Lansing Community College and six four-year universities). Bachelor's degree programs available on campus. License preparation in aviation, dental hygiene, nursing, paramedic, radiology, real estate. **Credit/placement by examination:** AP, CLEP, IB, institutional tests. 40 credit hours maximum toward associate degree. **Support services:** Learning center, pre-admission summer program, reduced course load, remedial instruction, study skills assistance, tutoring, writing center.

Majors. Architecture: Technology. **Area/ethnic studies:** African-American, American. **Biology:** General, biotechnology. **Business:** General, accounting technology, administrative services, banking/financial services, business admin, customer service support, e-commerce, fashion, hotel/motel admin, human resources, international, management information systems, real estate, sales/distribution, selling. **Communications technology:** Animation/special effects. **Computer sciences:** General, applications programming, networking. **Conservation:** General. **Education:** Elementary, secondary, teacher assistance. **Engineering:** General. **English:** English lit. **Foreign languages:** General, sign language interpretation. **General:** Business. **Health services:** Dental hygiene, EMT paramedic, histologic assistant, licensed practical nurse, nursing (RN), premedicine, radiologic technology/medical imaging, sonography, surgical technology, veterinary technology/assistant. **History:** General. **Human services:** Community org/advocacy. **Liberal arts:** Arts/sciences, humanities. **Math:** General. **Parks/recreation:** Health/fitness. **Philosophy/religion:** Philosophy, religion. **Physical sciences:** Chemistry. **Protective services:** Corrections, firefighting, juvenile corrections, police science. **Psychology:** General. **Social sciences:** General, economics, geography, international relations, political science, sociology. **Visual/performing arts:** Art, art history/conservation, cinematography, dramatic, graphic design, music, music performance, photography. **Work/family studies:** Child care service.

Most popular majors. Business/marketing 8%, health sciences 32%, liberal arts 27%, trade and industry 11%.

Computing on campus. 2,500 workstations in library, computer center. Commuter students can connect to campus network. Online course registration, helpline, wireless network available.

Student life. Freshman orientation: Mandatory. Preregistration for classes offered. Four-hour sessions offered select days during registration (June-August). Online orientation also available during these times. **Activities:** Bands, choral groups, dance, drama, film society, international student organizations, music ensembles, musical theater, radio station, student government, student newspaper, symphony orchestra, TV station, Adventist Student Fellowship, veterans association, Native American student alliance, Campus Disciples, Gay-Straight Alliance, international club, Friends of the Listening Ear, People for Positive Social Change, Students for Political Involvement, Black student delegates.

Athletics. NJCAA. **Intercollegiate:** Baseball M, basketball, cross-country, softball W, track and field, volleyball W. **Team name:** Stars.

Student services. Adult student services, career counseling, services for economically disadvantaged, student employment services, financial aid counseling, minority student services, personal counseling, placement for graduates, veterans' counselor, women's services. **Physically disabled:** Services for visually, speech, hearing impaired. **Transfer:** Transfer adviser, college fairs on campus for students transferring to 4-year colleges.

Contact. E-mail: Admissions@lcc.edu
Phone: (517) 483-1200 Toll-free number: (800) 644-4522 ext. 2
Fax: (517) 483-1170
Tammy Grossbauer, Director of Admissions, Lansing Community College, 1121 Enrollment Services, Lansing, MI 48901-7210

Macomb Community College
Warren, Michigan
www.macomb.edu   CB code: 1722

- Public 2-year community college
- Commuter campus in small city

General. Founded in 1954. Regionally accredited. **Enrollment:** 14,394 degree-seeking undergraduates; 9,575 non-degree-seeking students. **Degrees:** 2,799 associate awarded. **Location:** 20 miles from Detroit. **Calendar:** Semester, extensive summer session. **Full-time faculty:** 229 total. **Part-time faculty:** 803 total. **Special facilities:** Nature preserves, center for performing arts.

Student profile. Among degree-seeking undergraduates, 1,360 enrolled as first-time, first-year students.

Part-time:	64%	Hispanic American:	2%
Women:	49%	Native American:	1%
African American:	10%	International:	1%
Asian American:	3%	25 or older:	39%

Transfer out. Colleges most students transferred to 2011: Central Michigan University, Oakland University, Walsh College, Wayne State University, Michigan State University.

Basis for selection. Open admission, but selective for some programs. Special requirements for nursing, physical therapy assistant, occupational therapy assistant, respiratory therapy assistant, veterinarian technician programs; combination of GPA and test scores considered.

2011-2012 Annual costs. Tuition/fees: $2,620; $3,940 out-of-district; $5,110 out-of-state. Per-credit charge: $84 in-district; $128 out-of-district; $167 out-of-state. Books/supplies: $719.

2010-2011 Financial aid. Need-based: Need-based aid available for part-time students. Work-study available nights, weekends and for part-time students. **Non-need-based:** Scholarships awarded for academics, athletics, leadership, music/drama, state residency.

Application procedures. Admission: No deadline. No application fee. Admission notification on a rolling basis. January 31 closing date for nursing and physical therapy assistant programs. **Financial aid:** Priority date 4/15; no closing date. FAFSA, institutional form required. Applicants notified on a rolling basis starting 5/15; must reply within 2 week(s) of notification.

Academics. Courses toward bachelor's degrees offered on campus by University of Detroit, Walsh College of Accountancy and Business Administration, Wayne State University, Central Michigan University, Oakland University, University of Detroit Mercy, Davenport University, Rochester College. On-line degree program with Franklin University. **Special study options:** Cooperative education, cross-registration, distance learning, dual enrollment of high school students, ESL, independent study, internships, liberal arts/career combination, study abroad, weekend college. **Credit/placement by examination:** AP, CLEP, institutional tests. 47 credit hours maximum toward associate degree. **Support services:** Learning center, reduced course load, remedial instruction, tutoring.

Majors. Biology: General. **Business:** General, accounting, administrative services, business admin, marketing, office technology, operations. **Communications:** Broadcast journalism, communications/speech/rhetoric, public relations. **Communications technology:** Graphic/printing. **Computer sciences:** General, data entry, networking, programming, web page design. **Health services:** EMT paramedic, medical assistant, medical secretary, nursing (RN), occupational therapy assistant, physical therapy assistant, respiratory therapy technology, surgical technology, veterinary technology/assistant. **Liberal arts:** Arts/sciences. **Math:** General. **Physical sciences:** Chemistry. **Protective services:** Fire safety technology, firefighting, forensics, police science. **Visual/performing arts:** Commercial/advertising art, music. **Work/family studies:** Child care management.

Most popular majors. Business/marketing 12%, engineering/engineering technologies 6%, health sciences 13%, liberal arts 51%.

Computing on campus. 1,800 workstations in library, computer center. Commuter students can connect to campus network.

Student life. Freshman orientation: Available. Preregistration for classes offered. Held beginning of semester. **Activities:** Bands, choral groups, dance, drama, music ensembles, musical theater, symphony orchestra, student activities board, College Republicans, service learning and volunteerism, Newman Club, Campus Crusade for Christ, Young Democrats, African American alliance, Phi Theta Kappa.

Athletics. NJCAA. **Intercollegiate:** Baseball M, basketball, cross-country, soccer M, softball W, volleyball W.

Student services. Chaplain/spiritual director, career counseling, student employment services, financial aid counseling, health services, personal counseling, placement for graduates. **Physically disabled:** Services for visually, speech, hearing impaired. **Transfer:** Transfer adviser, college fairs on campus for students transferring to 4-year colleges.

Contact. Phone: (586) 445-7999 Toll-free number: (866) 622-6621
Fax: (586) 445-7157
Ronald Hughes, Director of Enrollment Services, Macomb Community
College, 14500 East Twelve Mile Road, Warren, MI 48088-3896

Mid Michigan Community College
Harrison, Michigan
www.midmich.edu

CB code: 1523

- Public 2-year community college
- Commuter campus in rural community

General. Founded in 1965. Regionally accredited. Two additional locations
in Mt. Pleasant. **Enrollment:** 4,145 degree-seeking undergraduates; 740 non-
degree-seeking students. **Degrees:** 499 associate awarded. **Location:** 30 miles
from Mount Pleasant, 100 miles from Lansing. **Calendar:** Semester, limited
summer session. **Full-time faculty:** 44 total. **Part-time faculty:** 211 total.

Student profile. Among degree-seeking undergraduates, 1,336 enrolled as
first-time, first-year students.

Part-time:	49%	**Women:**	59%
Out-of-state:	5%	**25 or older:**	65%

Transfer out. Colleges most students transferred to 2011: Central Michigan University, Ferris State University, Saginaw Valley State University.

Basis for selection. Open admission, but selective for some programs.
Admission for health occupation majors based on prerequisite course completion and grades. High school diploma or GED recommended. Interview
required of health program applicants. **Learning Disabled:** Students referred
to counselor to address special needs.

High school preparation. Recommended units include English 4, mathematics 4, social studies 2, history 1, science 3 (laboratory 2) and foreign
language 1. One unit chemistry, 1 algebra, 1 biology required for health
occupations majors.

2011-2012 Annual costs. Tuition/fees: $2,788; $5,280 out-of-district;
$9,466 out-of-state. Per-credit charge: $88 in-district; $171 out-of-district;
$313 out-of-state. Books/supplies: $1,222. Personal expenses: $1,755.

Financial aid. Need-based: Need-based aid available for part-time students. Work-study available nights, weekends and for part-time students.
Non-need-based: Scholarships awarded for academics, art.

Application procedures. Admission: No deadline. No application fee.
Admission notification on a rolling basis. **Financial aid:** Priority date 5/1;
no closing date. FAFSA, institutional form required. Applicants notified on
a rolling basis starting 4/1; must reply within 2 week(s) of notification.

Academics. Special study options: Distance learning, double major, dual
enrollment of high school students, independent study, internships, liberal
arts/career combination. License preparation in nursing, paramedic, physical
therapy, radiology. **Credit/placement by examination:** AP, CLEP, institutional tests. 15 credit hours maximum toward associate degree. **Support
services:** Learning center, reduced course load, remedial instruction, study
skills assistance, tutoring, writing center.

Majors. Biology: General, biotechnology. **Business:** Accounting, administrative services, banking/financial services, business admin, entrepreneurial
studies, marketing. **Communications:** Communications/speech/rhetoric.
Computer sciences: General, applications programming, computer science.
Conservation: General, fisheries. **Education:** Elementary, secondary,
teacher assistance. **Engineering:** General. **English:** Rhetoric/composition.
Health services: EMT paramedic, medical assistant, medical radiologic tech-
nology/radiation therapy, medical secretary, medical transcription, nursing
(RN), prepharmacy. **Liberal arts:** Arts/sciences. **Math:** General. **Physical
sciences:** Chemistry. **Protective services:** Firefighting, police science. **Psychology:** General. **Social sciences:** Sociology. **Visual/performing arts:** General, commercial/advertising art, dramatic. **Work/family studies:** Child
care management.

Computing on campus. 450 workstations in library, computer center.
Commuter students can connect to campus network. Online library, helpline,
wireless network available.

Student life. Freshman orientation: Available. Preregistration for classes
offered. Scheduled before each semester. **Housing:** Community-wide housing
bulletin available on request. **Activities:** Drama, student government, Phi
Theta Kappa.

Athletics. Team name: Lakers.

Student services. Adult student services, career counseling, services for
economically disadvantaged, student employment services, financial aid
counseling, personal counseling, veterans' counselor. **Physically disabled:**
Services for visually, speech, hearing impaired. **Transfer:** Pre-admission
transcript evaluation for new students. Transfer adviser, college fairs on
campus for students transferring to 4-year colleges.

Contact. E-mail: admissions@midmich.edu
Phone: (989) 386-6661 Fax: (989) 386-6613
Jessica Gordon, Director of Marketing and Admissions, Mid Michigan
Community College, 1375 South Clare Avenue, Harrison, MI 48625

Monroe County Community College
Monroe, Michigan
www.monroeccc.edu

CB code: 1514

- Public 2-year community college
- Commuter campus in large town
- Interview required

General. Founded in 1964. Regionally accredited. Off-campus site at Whitman Center. **Enrollment:** 4,440 degree-seeking undergraduates. **Degrees:**
509 associate awarded. **Location:** 45 miles from Detroit, 20 miles from
Toledo, Ohio. **Calendar:** Semester, limited summer session. **Full-time faculty:** 62 total. **Part-time faculty:** 125 total.

Student profile. Among degree-seeking undergraduates, 50% enrolled in
a transfer program, 50% enrolled in a vocational program.

Out-of-state:	11%	**25 or older:**	42%

Transfer out. Colleges most students transferred to 2011: Eastern Michigan University, University of Toledo, Siena Heights University, Western
Michigan University, University of Michigan.

Basis for selection. Open admission, but selective for some programs.
Selective admission for nursing, respiratory therapy, medical assistance and
culinary skills program. Test scores required by March 31. Interview required
of respiratory therapy and culinary program applicants.

High school preparation. Recommended units include English 4, mathematics 4, social studies 3, history 1 and science 3. Nursing and respiratory
therapy applicants must have 1 unit chemistry and 1 biology. Strong science
background highly recommended.

2011-2012 Annual costs. Tuition/fees: $2,520; $4,170 out-of-district;
$4,590 out-of-state. Per-credit charge: $83 in-district; $138 out-of-district;
$152 out-of-state. Tuition and fees reported are for 30 contact hours. Books/
supplies: $1,000. Personal expenses: $560.

Financial aid. Need-based: Need-based aid available for part-time students. Work-study available nights, weekends and for part-time students.
Non-need-based: Scholarships awarded for academics, alumni affiliation,
art, leadership, music/drama, state residency.

Application procedures. Admission: Priority date 5/1; no deadline. No
application fee. Admission notification on a rolling basis. Closing date for
nursing and respiratory therapy applications: 5/10. **Financial aid:** Priority
date 4/1; no closing date. FAFSA, institutional form required. Applicants
notified on a rolling basis starting 4/1; must reply within 2 week(s) of notification.

Academics. Special study options: Accelerated study, cooperative education, dual enrollment of high school students, independent study. Bachelor's
degree programs available on campus. License preparation in nursing, paramedic, real estate. **Credit/placement by examination:** AP, CLEP, institutional tests. 30 credit hours maximum toward associate degree. **Support
services:** Learning center, reduced course load, remedial instruction, tutoring,
writing center.

Majors. Business: Accounting, administrative services, banking/financial
services, business admin, office technology, office/clerical. **Computer sciences:** General, applications programming, programming. **Education:** Early
childhood. **Engineering:** Electrical. **Health services:** Medical secretary,
nursing (RN), respiratory therapy technology. **Liberal arts:** Arts/sciences.
Visual/performing arts: Studio arts. **Work/family studies:** Child care management.

Computing on campus. 150 workstations in library, computer center,
student center. Helpline, wireless network available.

Student life. Freshman orientation: Available. Preregistration for classes
offered. **Activities:** Concert band, choral groups, drama, international student

organizations, radio station, student government, student newspaper, symphony orchestra, respiratory therapy club, nursing club, Society of Automotive Engineers, campus Bible study.

Athletics. Team name: Huskies.

Student services. Career counseling, student employment services, on-campus daycare, personal counseling, placement for graduates. **Physically disabled:** Services for visually, speech, hearing impaired. **Transfer:** Transfer adviser, college fairs on campus for students transferring to 4-year colleges.

Contact. E-mail: mhall@monroeccc.edu
Phone: (734) 384-4104 Toll-free number: (877) 937-6222
Fax: (734) 242-9711
Mark Hall, Director of Admissions and Guidance Services, Monroe County Community College, 1555 South Raisinville Road, Monroe, MI 48161-9746

Montcalm Community College
Sidney, Michigan
www.montcalm.edu   CB code: 1522

- Public 2-year community and liberal arts college
- Commuter campus in rural community

General. Founded in 1965. Regionally accredited. Off-campus centers in Ionia, Howard City, and Greenville. **Enrollment:** 1,720 degree-seeking undergraduates; 342 non-degree-seeking students. **Degrees:** 233 associate awarded. **Location:** 50 miles from Grand Rapids, 65 miles from Lansing. **Calendar:** Semester, limited summer session. **Full-time faculty:** 30 total; 97% have terminal degrees, 57% women. **Part-time faculty:** 108 total; 59% have terminal degrees, 2% minority, 59% women. **Special facilities:** Marked nature preserves and trails, barn theatre.

Student profile. Among degree-seeking undergraduates, 65% enrolled in a transfer program, 35% enrolled in a vocational program, 235 enrolled as first-time, first-year students.

Part-time:	60%	African American:	1%
Women:	68%		

Transfer out. Colleges most students transferred to 2011: Central Michigan University, Ferris State University, Grand Valley State University, Davenport University.

Basis for selection. Open admission, but selective for some programs. Applicants to nursing program must score at least 44 on COMPASS pre-algebra and 82 on COMPASS reading.

2011-2012 Annual costs. Tuition/fees: $2,760; $4,860 out-of-district; $7,110 out-of-state. Per-credit charge: $83 in-district; $153 out-of-district; $228 out-of-state. Books/supplies: $901. Personal expenses: $1,072.

Financial aid. Need-based: Need-based aid available for part-time students. Work-study available nights, weekends and for part-time students. **Non-need-based:** Scholarships awarded for academics, state residency.

Application procedures. Admission: No deadline. No application fee. Admission notification on a rolling basis. **Financial aid:** Priority date 2/15; no closing date. FAFSA, institutional form required. Applicants notified on a rolling basis starting 6/15; must reply within 2 week(s) of notification.

Academics. Special study options: Cooperative education, distance learning, dual enrollment of high school students, independent study, internships, liberal arts/career combination, study abroad. License preparation in nursing, paramedic. **Credit/placement by examination:** AP, CLEP, institutional tests. **Support services:** GED test center, learning center, reduced course load, remedial instruction, study skills assistance, tutoring.

Majors. Business: Accounting, administrative services, business admin, construction management, entrepreneurial studies, executive assistant, information resources management, management information systems, office technology. **Computer sciences:** General, data processing. **Education:** Teacher assistance. **Health services:** Medical secretary, nursing (RN). **Liberal arts:** Arts/sciences. **Protective services:** Criminal justice. **Visual/performing arts:** Music. **Work/family studies:** Child care management.

Most popular majors. Business/marketing 24%, education 6%, health sciences 21%, liberal arts 36%.

Computing on campus. 450 workstations in library, computer center. Online course registration, helpline, wireless network available.

Student life. Freshman orientation: Available. Preregistration for classes offered. **Activities:** Jazz band, choral groups, drama, music ensembles, musical theater, student newspaper, Phi Theta Kappa, future business professionals club, Native American club, nursing club, judo club.

Athletics. Intramural: Volleyball.

Student services. Career counseling, financial aid counseling. **Physically disabled:** Services for visually, speech, hearing impaired. **Transfer:** Pre-admission transcript evaluation for new students. Transfer adviser, college fairs on campus for students transferring to 4-year colleges.

Contact. E-mail: admissions@montcalm.edu
Phone: (989) 328-1250 Toll-free number: (877) 328-2111
Fax: (989) 328-2950
Debra Alexander, Associate Dean of Student Services, Montcalm Community College, 2800 College Drive, Sidney, MI 48885

Mott Community College
Flint, Michigan   CB member
www.mcc.edu   CB code: 1225

- Public 2-year community college
- Commuter campus in small city

General. Founded in 1923. Regionally accredited. Extension centers located in Fenton, Lapeer and Clio. **Enrollment:** 9,073 degree-seeking undergraduates; 2,687 non-degree-seeking students. **Degrees:** 1,576 associate awarded. **Location:** 66 miles from Detroit. **Calendar:** Semester, extensive summer session. **Full-time faculty:** 140 total; 25% have terminal degrees, 17% minority, 61% women. **Part-time faculty:** 432 total; 6% have terminal degrees, 20% minority, 56% women. **Special facilities:** Geology museum, regional technology center, dental clinic, visual arts and design center, greenhouse, student-operated cosmetology/nail technology salon, hospital wing replica, SimMan control room, esthetician labs, student-operated fine dining restaurant.

Student profile. Among degree-seeking undergraduates, 20% enrolled in a transfer program, 78% enrolled in a vocational program, 705 enrolled as first-time, first-year students.

Part-time:	63%	Hispanic American:	3%
Women:	60%	Native American:	1%
African American:	21%	25 or older:	50%

Transfer out. Colleges most students transferred to 2011: University of Michigan-Flint, Ferris State University, Central Michigan University, Saginaw Valley State University, Eastern Michigan University.

Basis for selection. Open admission, but selective for some programs. Special requirements for nursing and allied health programs. Audition recommended for music majors. **Learning Disabled:** Students must request assistance, provide documentation of disabilities, and register with Disability Services before classes begin.

2011-2012 Annual costs. Tuition/fees: $3,327; $4,799 out-of-district; $6,281 out-of-state. Per-credit charge: $99 in-district; $148 out-of-district; $197 out-of-state. Tuition and fees are based on 30 contact hours.

2010-2011 Financial aid. Need-based: 59% of total undergraduate aid awarded as scholarships/grants, 41% as loans/jobs. Need-based aid available for part-time students. Work-study available nights, weekends and for part-time students. **Non-need-based:** Scholarships awarded for academics, alumni affiliation, art, athletics, leadership, minority status, music/drama, state residency.

Application procedures. Admission: No deadline. No application fee. Admission notification on a rolling basis. **Financial aid:** Priority date 6/1; no closing date. FAFSA required. Applicants notified on a rolling basis starting 5/1.

Academics. Distance learning and open entry/open exit modular courses being expanded in Regional Technology Center. Late-start semester classes. **Special study options:** Cooperative education, distance learning, double major, dual enrollment of high school students, ESL, honors, independent study, internships, liberal arts/career combination. Bachelor's degree programs available on campus. License preparation in dental hygiene, nursing, occupational therapy, physical therapy. **Credit/placement by examination:** AP, CLEP, institutional tests. 16 credit hours maximum toward associate degree. **Support services:** GED preparation, learning center, remedial instruction, study skills assistance, tutoring, writing center.

Majors. Biology: General. **Business:** General, accounting technology, administrative services, business admin, entrepreneurial studies, marketing. **Communications technology:** General. **Computer sciences:** Applications

programming, networking, programming, web page design. **Education:** Early childhood. **Foreign languages:** Sign language interpretation. **Health services:** Community health services, dental assistant, dental hygiene, EMT paramedic, histologic assistant, medical radiologic technology/radiation therapy, medical records technology, nursing (RN), occupational therapy assistant, physical therapy assistant, respiratory therapy technology. **Liberal arts:** Arts/sciences. **Protective services:** Fire safety technology, police science. **Visual/performing arts:** Cinematography, graphic design, photography. **Work/family studies:** Child care service, institutional food production.

Most popular majors. Biological/life sciences 10%, business/marketing 8%, health sciences 14%, liberal arts 42%, security/protective services 6%.

Computing on campus. 1,388 workstations in library, computer center, student center. Commuter students can connect to campus network. Online course registration, online library, helpline, wireless network available.

Student life. Freshman orientation: Mandatory. Preregistration for classes offered. Orientation is conducted in a group format, and lasts approximately three hours. **Activities:** Bands, campus ministries, choral groups, dance, music ensembles, student government, student newspaper, criminal justice club, Phi Theta Kappa, Student Nurses Association, dental hygiene club, gardening association, social work club, Ballroomers/Steppers, travel club, Future Teachers Association, Gay-Straight Alliance.

Athletics. NJCAA. **Intercollegiate:** Baseball M, basketball, cross-country, golf M, softball W, volleyball W. **Team name:** Bears.

Student services. Career counseling, services for economically disadvantaged, student employment services, financial aid counseling, health services, personal counseling, placement for graduates. **Physically disabled:** Services for visually, speech, hearing impaired. **Transfer:** Pre-admission transcript evaluation for new students. Transfer adviser, college fairs on campus for students transferring to 4-year colleges.

Contact. Phone: (810) 762-0315 Toll-free number: (800) 852-8614 Fax: (810) 232-9442
Troy Boquette, Executive Dean, Student Services, Mott Community College, 1401 East Court Street, Flint, MI 48503-2089

Muskegon Community College
Muskegon, Michigan
www.muskegoncc.edu CB code: 1495

- Public 2-year community college
- Commuter campus in small city

General. Founded in 1926. Regionally accredited. Bachelor's and graduate programs offered on-campus with participating 4-year institutions. **Enrollment:** 3,871 degree-seeking undergraduates; 1,708 non-degree-seeking students. **Degrees:** 415 associate awarded. **Location:** 41 miles from Grand Rapids. **Calendar:** Semester, limited summer session. **Full-time faculty:** 100 total. **Part-time faculty:** 218 total. **Special facilities:** Planetarium, nature preserve, herbal garden, observatory.

Student profile. Among degree-seeking undergraduates, 47% enrolled in a transfer program, 53% enrolled in a vocational program, 716 enrolled as first-time, first-year students.

Part-time:	62%	Asian American:	1%
Women:	56%	Hispanic American:	5%
African American:	11%	Native American:	1%

Transfer out. Colleges most students transferred to 2011: Grand Valley State University, Central Michigan University, Ferris State University, Western Michigan University.

Basis for selection. Open admission, but selective for some programs. Reading proficiency required for select programs and courses. High school diploma, GED or completion of 15 credits with at least a C average required for degree-seeking candidates. Additional prerequisites required for nursing applicants. **Adult students:** SAT/ACT scores not required. **Home schooled:** Transcript of courses and grades required.

High school preparation. College-preparatory program recommended.

2011-2012 Annual costs. Tuition/fees: $2,920; $4,765 out-of-district; $6,355 out-of-state. Per-credit charge: $82 in-district; $143 out-of-district; $196 out-of-state. Students also assessed contact hour fees, which vary according to residency status, and course fees, which vary. Books/supplies: $1,100. Personal expenses: $1,200.

Financial aid. Need-based: Need-based aid available for part-time students. Work-study available nights, weekends and for part-time students.

Application procedures. Admission: Priority date 5/12; no deadline. No application fee. Admission notification on a rolling basis. **Financial aid:** Priority date 5/1; no closing date. FAFSA, institutional form required. Applicants notified on a rolling basis starting 6/1; must reply within 2 week(s) of notification.

Academics. Supplemental Instruction (SI) is offered each semester in various academic areas at pre-arranged times. Information about SI can be acquired by contacting MCC's Tutoring Center. **Special study options:** Cooperative education, cross-registration, distance learning, double major, dual enrollment of high school students, honors, independent study, internships. Bachelor's degree programs available on campus. License preparation in nursing, real estate. **Credit/placement by examination:** AP, CLEP, institutional tests. 30 credit hours maximum toward associate degree. **Support services:** Learning center, remedial instruction, study skills assistance, tutoring, writing center.

Majors. Business: Accounting, administrative services, international, marketing. **Communications technology:** Graphic/printing. **Computer sciences:** General, data processing. **Education:** Early childhood. **Health services:** Licensed practical nurse, medical secretary, nursing (RN), respiratory therapy technology. **Protective services:** Law enforcement admin. **Visual/performing arts:** Commercial/advertising art.

Computing on campus. 88 workstations in library, computer center, student center. Online course registration, helpline, wireless network available.

Student life. Freshman orientation: Available. Preregistration for classes offered. Offered year-round. **Activities:** Concert band, choral groups, dance, drama, international student organizations, music ensembles, musical theater, student government, student newspaper, TV station, Christian Fellowship, Black student alliance, Gay Straight Alliance, Hispanic Students, Veteran Students.

Athletics. NJCAA. **Intercollegiate:** Baseball M, basketball, golf, softball W, tennis W, volleyball W, wrestling M. **Intramural:** Baseball M, basketball, bowling, golf, softball W, table tennis. **Team name:** Jayhawks.

Student services. Adult student services, career counseling, student employment services, financial aid counseling, health services, personal counseling, veterans' counselor. **Physically disabled:** Services for visually, speech, hearing impaired. **Transfer:** Pre-admission transcript evaluation for new students. College fairs on campus for students transferring to 4-year colleges.

Contact. E-mail: darlene.peklar@muskegoncc.edu
Phone: (231) 777-0366 Toll-free number: (866) 711-4622 Fax: (231) 777-0443
Cindy Reuss, Dean of Admissions, Muskegon Community College, 221 South Quarterline Road, Muskegon, MI 49442

North Central Michigan College
Petoskey, Michigan
www.ncmich.edu CB code: 1569

- Public 2-year community college
- Commuter campus in small town

General. Founded in 1958. Regionally accredited. **Enrollment:** 2,572 degree-seeking undergraduates. **Degrees:** 294 associate awarded. **Location:** 40 miles from Mackinaw City, 60 miles from Traverse City. **Calendar:** Semester, limited summer session. **Full-time faculty:** 32 total. **Part-time faculty:** 174 total. **Class size:** 100% 20-39. **Special facilities:** Nature preserve.

Student profile.

Out-of-state:	5%	Live on campus:	5%
25 or older:	57%		

Transfer out. Colleges most students transferred to 2011: Lake Superior State University, Grand Valley State University, Central Michigan University, Northern Michigan University, Ferris State University.

Basis for selection. Open admission, but selective for some programs. All degree-seeking students must provide ACT, SAT or COMPASS scores for mandatory placement. Special requirements for most health science/ allied health programs.

High school preparation. Recommended units include English 3, mathematics 3 and science 3. Chemistry recommended for nursing applicants.

2011-2012 Annual costs. Tuition/fees: $2,790; $4,245 out-of-district; $5,318 out-of-state. Per-credit charge: $75 in-district; $123 out-of-district;

$159 out-of-state. Tuition is based on contact hours and may vary by program. Room/board: $6,110. Books/supplies: $1,050. Personal expenses: $650.

Financial aid. Need-based: Need-based aid available for part-time students. Work-study available nights, weekends and for part-time students.

Application procedures. Admission: No deadline. No application fee. Application must be submitted online. Admission notification on a rolling basis. **Financial aid:** Closing date 4/1. FAFSA, institutional form required. Applicants notified on a rolling basis starting 4/30.

Academics. Special study options: Cooperative education, cross-registration, distance learning, dual enrollment of high school students, independent study, internships. Bachelor's degree programs available on campus. **Credit/placement by examination:** AP, CLEP, IB. 15 credit hours maximum toward associate degree. **Support services:** Learning center, remedial instruction, tutoring.

Majors. Business: General, accounting, administrative services, business admin, office/clerical. **Computer sciences:** General. **Education:** Early childhood. **Health services:** EMT paramedic, nursing (RN). **Liberal arts:** Arts/sciences.

Most popular majors. Health sciences 21%, liberal arts 71%.

Computing on campus. 133 workstations in dormitories, library, computer center, student center. Dormitories wired for high-speed internet access and linked to campus network. Commuter students can connect to campus network. Online course registration, wireless network available.

Student life. Freshman orientation: Available. Preregistration for classes offered. Held in summer before classes begin. **Housing:** Coed dorms available. $50 deposit. **Activities:** Student government, student newspaper, nursing student association, Phi Theta Kappa, Campus Crusade.

Athletics. Intramural: Basketball, volleyball.

Student services. Career counseling, services for economically disadvantaged, financial aid counseling, personal counseling, veterans' counselor, women's services. **Physically disabled:** Services for visually, speech, hearing impaired. **Transfer:** Transfer adviser, college fairs on campus for students transferring to 4-year colleges.

Contact. E-mail: advisor@ncmich.edu
Phone: (231) 348-6600 Toll-free number: (888) 298-6605
Fax: (231) 348-6672
Renee DeYoung, Director Enrollment Management, North Central Michigan College, 1515 Howard Street, Petoskey, MI 49770

Northwestern Michigan College
Traverse City, Michigan
www.nmc.edu   CB code: 1564

- Public 2-year community and maritime college
- Commuter campus in large town

General. Founded in 1951. Regionally accredited. **Enrollment:** 4,843 degree-seeking undergraduates. **Degrees:** 600 associate awarded. **Location:** 180 miles from Lansing, 265 miles from Detroit. **Calendar:** Semester, extensive summer session. **Full-time faculty:** 81 total. **Part-time faculty:** 242 total. **Class size:** 100% 20-39. **Special facilities:** Maritime academy, pilot training center, observatory, museum, fresh water studies institute, renewable energy facilities, automotive with hybrid repair and welding.

Student profile. Among degree-seeking undergraduates, 373 transferred in from other institutions.

Out-of-state:	5%	Live on campus:	3%
25 or older:	64%		

Transfer out. Colleges most students transferred to 2011: Michigan State University, Grand Valley State University, Ferris State University, Central Michigan University.

Basis for selection. Open admission, but selective for some programs. Admission for maritime, nursing, dental assistant and aviation programs based on school GPA, recommendation and test scores. ACT or SAT required for maritime program. **Adult students:** SAT/ACT scores not required. **Home schooled:** Transcript of courses and grades required. **Learning Disabled:** COMPASS testing to show ability to benefit.

2011-2012 Annual costs. Tuition/fees: $2,793; $5,112 out-of-district; $6,458 out-of-state. Per-credit charge: $82 in-district; $159 out-of-district; $204 out-of-state. Room/board: $8,652. Books/supplies: $690. Personal expenses: $690.

Financial aid. Need-based: Need-based aid available for part-time students. Work-study available nights, weekends and for part-time students. **Non-need-based:** Scholarships awarded for academics, art, job skills, leadership, minority status, music/drama, ROTC, state residency.

Application procedures. Admission: No deadline. $20 fee, may be waived for applicants with need. Admission notification on a rolling basis. **Financial aid:** Priority date 4/1; no closing date. FAFSA required. Applicants notified on a rolling basis starting 5/1; must reply within 2 week(s) of notification.

Academics. Great Lakes Maritime Academy (4-year deck officer and maritime engineer training program) for service in shipping industry on campus. 9 months spent aboard commercial vessels. Bachelor's degree awarded to maritime academy graduates in conjunction with Ferris State University. **Special study options:** Cooperative education, cross-registration, distance learning, dual enrollment of high school students, ESL, honors, independent study, internships, liberal arts/career combination, study abroad. Study broad includes two summer programs - Germany for the Business Division and Russia for the pre-engineering students. Bachelor's degree programs available on campus. License preparation in aviation, real estate. **Credit/placement by examination:** AP, CLEP, institutional tests. 32 credit hours maximum toward associate degree. **Support services:** Learning center, pre-admission summer program, reduced course load, remedial instruction, study skills assistance, tutoring, writing center.

Majors. Biology: General. **Business:** General, accounting, accounting technology, business admin, management information systems, office technology. **Communications:** Communications/speech/rhetoric. **Computer sciences:** Information systems. **Education:** General. **Engineering:** General. **English:** English lit. **General:** Crop production, landscaping, nursery operations, turf management, viticulture. **Health services:** Dental assistant, nursing (RN), respiratory therapy assistant. **Liberal arts:** Arts/sciences. **Math:** General. **Physical sciences:** General. **Protective services:** Law enforcement admin, police science. **Social sciences:** General. **Visual/performing arts:** Art, commercial/advertising art, dramatic, music, piano/keyboard, studio arts, voice/opera.

Most popular majors. Health sciences 19%, liberal arts 52%.

Computing on campus. 675 workstations in dormitories, library, computer center, student center. Dormitories wired for high-speed internet access and linked to campus network. Commuter students can connect to campus network. Online course registration, online library, helpline, wireless network available.

Student life. Freshman orientation: Mandatory. Preregistration for classes offered. Multiple one-day sessions prior to the start of each semester. **Housing:** Guaranteed on-campus for freshmen. Coed dorms, single-sex dorms, special housing for disabled, apartments available. $250 fully refundable deposit. **Activities:** Bands, campus ministries, choral groups, dance, drama, international student organizations, literary magazine, music ensembles, musical theater, radio station, student government, student newspaper, symphony orchestra, residence hall council, propeller club, Phi Theta Kappa, engineer club, botany club, law enforcement club, diverse student body group, Native American student group.

Student services. Adult student services, career counseling, student employment services, health services, minority student services, personal counseling, placement for graduates, veterans' counselor. **Physically disabled:** Services for visually, speech, hearing impaired. **Transfer:** Re-entry adviser, pre-admission transcript evaluation for new students. Transfer adviser, college fairs on campus for students transferring to 4-year colleges.

Contact. E-mail: jbensley@nmc.edu
Phone: (231) 995-1054 Toll-free number: (800) 748-0566
Fax: (231) 995-1339
James Bensley, Director of Admissions, Northwestern Michigan College, 1701 East Front Street, Traverse City, MI 49686

Oakland Community College
Bloomfield Hills, Michigan
www.oaklandcc.edu   CB code: 1607

- Public 2-year community college
- Commuter campus in very large city

General. Founded in 1964. Regionally accredited. Multicampus institution with locations in Auburn Hills, Farmington Hills, Southfield, Royal Oak, and Waterford. CREST (Combined Regional Emergency Services Training Center) located in Auburn Hills. **Enrollment:** 17,199 degree-seeking undergraduates; 11,959 non-degree-seeking students. **Degrees:** 2,284 associate awarded. **Location:** 30 miles from Detroit. **Calendar:** Semester, limited summer session. **Full-time faculty:** 250 total. **Part-time faculty:** 1,015 total.

Student profile. Among degree-seeking undergraduates, 11% enrolled in a transfer program, 62% enrolled in a vocational program, 1% already have a bachelor's degree or higher, 3,908 enrolled as first-time, first-year students, 1,803 transferred in from other institutions.

Part-time:	67%	Hispanic American:	3%
Out-of-state:	1%	Native American:	1%
Women:	60%	International:	5%
African American:	28%	25 or older:	55%
Asian American:	2%		

Transfer out. 38% of students enrolled in the transfer program go on to 4-year colleges. **Colleges most students transferred to 2011:** Oakland University, Wayne State University, Central Michigan University, Macomb Community College, Michigan State University.

Basis for selection. Open admission. Interview recommended. **Home schooled:** English and math placement testing mandatory.

2011-2012 Annual costs. Tuition/fees: $2,071; $3,457 out-of-district; $4,822 out-of-state. Per-credit charge: $68 in-district; $113 out-of-district; $158 out-of-state. Books/supplies: $1,050. Personal expenses: $725.

2011-2012 Financial aid. Need-based: 1,527 full-time freshmen applied for aid; 1,358 were judged to have need; 1,304 of these received aid. Average need met was 43%. Average scholarship/grant was $4,876; average loan $586. 97% of total undergraduate aid awarded as scholarships/grants, 3% as loans/jobs. Need-based aid available for part-time students. Work-study available nights, weekends and for part-time students. **Non-need-based:** Awarded to 262 full-time undergraduates, including 122 freshmen. Scholarships awarded for academics, athletics, job skills.

Application procedures. Admission: No deadline. No application fee. Admission notification on a rolling basis. **Financial aid:** Priority date 4/15; no closing date. FAFSA required. Applicants notified on a rolling basis starting 4/15.

Academics. Special study options: Cooperative education, distance learning, dual enrollment of high school students, ESL, internships, study abroad. Saturday classes offered. License preparation in dental hygiene, nursing, occupational therapy, paramedic, physical therapy, radiology. **Credit/placement by examination:** AP, CLEP, institutional tests. Last 15 credit hours toward degree program must be satisfied with institution's coursework, not credit by exam. **Support services:** Learning center, reduced course load, remedial instruction, study skills assistance, tutoring, writing center.

Majors. Business: Accounting technology, accounting/business management, business admin, construction management, entrepreneurial studies, hotel/motel admin, international, office technology, restaurant/food services. **Communications technology:** Photo/film/video, radio/TV. **Computer sciences:** Data processing, information technology, programming, security, systems analysis. **Engineering:** General. **Foreign languages:** Sign language interpretation. **General:** Landscaping. **Health services:** Community health services, dental hygiene, EMT paramedic, health care admin, histologic technology, massage therapy, medical assistant, medical radiologic technology/radiation therapy, medical transcription, nuclear medical technology, nursing (RN), occupational therapy assistant, pharmacy assistant, physical therapy assistant, respiratory therapy technology, sonography, surgical technology, veterinary technology/assistant. **Liberal arts:** Arts/sciences, library assistant. **Parks/recreation:** Exercise sciences. **Protective services:** Corrections, criminalistics, firefighting, police science. **Visual/performing arts:** Ceramics, dramatic, graphic design, interior design, music performance, music theory/composition, photography, voice/opera. **Work/family studies:** Child care management.

Most popular majors. Business/marketing 14%, health sciences 20%, liberal arts 44%.

Computing on campus. 2,501 workstations in library, computer center, student center. Commuter students can connect to campus network. Online course registration, online library, helpline, wireless network available.

Student life. Freshman orientation: Available. Preregistration for classes offered. Held in the first two weeks of class. **Activities:** Bands, choral groups, dance, drama, film society, international student organizations, literary magazine, music ensembles, student government, symphony orchestra, PTK, film society, Writers Block, student mentor program, dance team, Rhythm of the Cultures, anime club, Gamers Guild, psychology club.

Athletics. NJCAA. **Intercollegiate:** Basketball, cross-country, golf M, softball W, tennis W, volleyball W. **Intramural:** Cross-country, racquetball. **Team name:** Raiders.

Student services. Career counseling, services for economically disadvantaged, student employment services, financial aid counseling, on-campus daycare, personal counseling, placement for graduates, veterans' counselor, women's services. **Physically disabled:** Services for visually, speech, hearing impaired. **Transfer:** Pre-admission transcript evaluation for new students.

Transfer center, transfer adviser, college fairs on campus for students transferring to 4-year colleges.

Contact. Phone: (248) 341-2200 Fax: (248) 341-2099
Stephen Linden, College Registrar, Oakland Community College, 2480 Opdyke Road, Bloomfield Hills, MI 48304-2266

Saginaw Chippewa Tribal College
Mount Pleasant, Michigan
www.sagchip.edu

- Public 2-year community college
- Commuter campus in large town

General. Enrollment: 155 degree-seeking undergraduates. **Degrees:** 15 associate awarded. **Calendar:** Semester, limited summer session. **Full-time faculty:** 5 total. **Part-time faculty:** 12 total.

Basis for selection. Open admission.

2011-2012 Annual costs. Tuition/fees: $2,550; $2,550 out-of-state. Per-credit charge: $60 in-state; $60 out-of-state.

Financial aid. Need-based: Work-study available nights, weekends and for part-time students.

Application procedures. Admission: No deadline. $25 fee. Application must be submitted on paper. Admission notification on a rolling basis. **Financial aid:** No deadline.

Academics. Special study options: Dual enrollment of high school students. **Credit/placement by examination:** AP, CLEP, institutional tests. **Support services:** Remedial instruction, tutoring.

Majors. Area/ethnic studies: Native American. **Business:** Business admin.

Computing on campus. Commuter students can connect to campus network.

Student life. Freshman orientation: Available. Preregistration for classes offered. **Activities:** Student government.

Student services. Financial aid counseling.

Contact. E-mail: reed.tracy@sagchip.edu
Phone: (989) 775-4123 Fax: (989) 775-4528
Tracy Reed, Admissions Officer/Registrar, Saginaw Chippewa Tribal College, 2274 Enterprise Drive, Mount Pleasant, MI 48858

Schoolcraft College
Livonia, Michigan   **CB member**
www.schoolcraft.edu   **CB code: 1764**

- Public 2-year community college
- Commuter campus in small city

General. Founded in 1961. Regionally accredited. **Enrollment:** 14,000 degree-seeking undergraduates. **Degrees:** 1,426 associate awarded. **Location:** 20 miles from Ann Arbor. **Calendar:** Semester, limited summer session. **Full-time faculty:** 94 total. **Part-time faculty:** 435 total. **Special facilities:** Scanning electron microscope, biotech center.

Transfer out. Colleges most students transferred to 2011: Henry Ford Community College, Oakland Community College, Eastern Michigan University, Michigan State University, Wayne State University.

Basis for selection. Open admission, but selective for some programs. International students advised to start application process 3 months prior to start date of semester. **Home schooled:** Interview required.

2011-2012 Annual costs. Tuition/fees: $2,740; $3,910 out-of-district; $5,650 out-of-state. Per-credit charge: $84 in-district; $123 out-of-district; $181 out-of-state. Books/supplies: $1,217.

Financial aid. Need-based: Need-based aid available for part-time students. Work-study available nights, weekends and for part-time students. **Non-need-based:** Scholarships awarded for academics, athletics, leadership, music/drama, state residency.

Application procedures. Admission: No deadline. No application fee. Admission notification on a rolling basis. **Financial aid:** No deadline. FAFSA required. Applicants notified on a rolling basis starting 6/1.

Academics. Special study options: Accelerated study, cooperative education, distance learning, double major, dual enrollment of high school students, ESL, external degree, honors, liberal arts/career combination, weekend college. **Credit/placement by examination:** AP, CLEP, institutional tests. 30 credit hours maximum toward associate degree. **Support services:** GED preparation and test center, learning center, remedial instruction, tutoring.

Honors college/program. Minimum 3.5 GPA, 25 ACT or 1100 SAT (exclusive of Writing), writing sample, personal interview and 2 letters of recommendation required.

Majors. Business: General, accounting technology, administrative services, business admin, entrepreneurial studies, executive assistant, marketing, office technology, small business admin. **Communications technology:** Radio/TV, recording arts. **Computer sciences:** General, applications programming, computer graphics, programming, web page design. **Education:** General. **Engineering:** General. **Health services:** EMT paramedic, licensed practical nurse, massage therapy, medical records technology, nursing (RN), occupational therapy assistant. **Protective services:** Corrections, firefighting, police science, security services. **Work/family studies:** Child care management, child development.

Most popular majors. Business/marketing 18%, education 10%, health sciences 16%, liberal arts 28%, security/protective services 10%.

Computing on campus. 930 workstations in library, computer center.

Student life. Freshman orientation: Mandatory. Preregistration for classes offered. **Activities:** Concert band, choral groups, drama, literary magazine, music ensembles, musical theater, student newspaper, music club, beekeepers club, international students club, quilting club, student activities board, Phi Theta Kappa, honors society, gourmet club, occupational therapy club.

Athletics. NJCAA. **Intercollegiate:** Basketball, bowling, cross-country W, golf, soccer, volleyball W. **Team name:** Ocelots.

Student services. Adult student services, career counseling, services for economically disadvantaged, student employment services, financial aid counseling, health services, legal services, on-campus daycare, personal counseling, placement for graduates, veterans' counselor, women's services. **Physically disabled:** Services for visually, speech, hearing impaired. **Transfer:** College fairs on campus for students transferring to 4-year colleges.

Contact. E-mail: admissions@schoolcraft.edu
Phone: (734) 462-4426 Fax: (734) 462-4553
Nicole Wilson-Fennell, Director of Enrollment Management, Schoolcraft College, 18600 Haggerty Road, Livonia, MI 48152-2696

Southwestern Michigan College
Dowagiac, Michigan
www.swmich.edu   **CB code: 1783**

▶ Public 2-year community college
▶ Commuter campus in small town

General. Founded in 1964. Regionally accredited. Two traditional semesters (fall and winter) and one optional spring term. Bachelor's degree programs offered in agreement with 4-year colleges and universities including Bethel College and Ferris State University. **Enrollment:** 2,698 degree-seeking undergraduates; 331 non-degree-seeking students. **Degrees:** 264 associate awarded. **Location:** 30 miles from South Bend, Indiana. **Calendar:** Semester, extensive summer session. **Full-time faculty:** 58 total; 28% have terminal degrees, 5% minority, 45% women. **Part-time faculty:** 96 total; 18% have terminal degrees, 10% minority, 67% women. **Special facilities:** Museum, wooded trails.

Student profile. Among degree-seeking undergraduates, 43% enrolled in a transfer program, 57% enrolled in a vocational program, 635 enrolled as first-time, first-year students, 224 transferred in from other institutions.

Part-time:	45%	Hispanic American:	3%
Out-of-state:	12%	Native American:	1%
Women:	62%	International:	1%
African American:	9%	25 or older:	38%
Asian American:	1%	Live on campus:	10%

Transfer out. Colleges most students transferred to 2011: Western Michigan University, Ferris State University, Indiana University of South Bend, Bethel College, Grand Valley State University.

Basis for selection. Open admission, but selective for some programs. Students who test below a specific score on the College's basic assessment tests in reading, writing, and math will be admitted as provisional students only and will be advised to demonstrate competency. Students may be exempted based upon ACT/SAT scores. Special requirements for nursing programs. Interview required for nursing applicants.

2011-2012 Annual costs. Tuition/fees: $4,118; $4,988 out-of-district; $5,333 out-of-state. Per-credit charge: $99 in-district; $128 out-of-district; $140 out-of-state.

Financial aid. Need-based: Need-based aid available for part-time students. Work-study available nights, weekends and for part-time students. **Non-need-based:** Scholarships awarded for academics, art, leadership, music/drama.

Application procedures. Admission: No deadline. No application fee. Admission notification on a rolling basis. **Financial aid:** Priority date 7/1; no closing date. FAFSA, institutional form required. Applicants notified on a rolling basis starting 4/1; must reply within 2 week(s) of notification.

Academics. Special study options: Accelerated study, cooperative education, distance learning, double major, dual enrollment of high school students, ESL, independent study, internships, weekend college. Bachelor's degree programs available on campus. License preparation in nursing, paramedic. **Credit/placement by examination:** AP, CLEP, institutional tests. 13 credit hours maximum toward associate degree. Credit for specific courses may be earned through ACE (Achieved Credit by Examination) testing. **Support services:** Learning center, reduced course load, remedial instruction, study skills assistance, tutoring, writing center.

Majors. Business: Accounting technology, business admin, construction management, event planning, executive assistant, hotel/motel admin. **Communications technology:** Graphic/printing. **Computer sciences:** Networking, programming. **Education:** Early childhood, teacher assistance. **Engineering:** Robotics. **English:** Technical writing. **Health services:** Medical assistant, medical records technology, nursing (RN), prenursing. **Human services:** Social work. **Liberal arts:** Arts/sciences. **Protective services:** Firefighting. **Visual/performing arts:** Theater design.

Most popular majors. Business/marketing 8%, engineering/engineering technologies 8%, health sciences 21%, liberal arts 50%.

Computing on campus. 103 workstations in dormitories, library, computer center, student center. Dormitories wired for high-speed internet access and linked to campus network. Commuter students can connect to campus network. Online course registration, online library, helpline, repair service, wireless network available.

Student life. Freshman orientation: Available. Preregistration for classes offered. Several half-day sessions available. **Housing:** Coed dorms, wellness housing available. $275 nonrefundable deposit, deadline 7/1. **Activities:** Bands, choral groups, dance, drama, music ensembles, musical theater, student newspaper, Phi Theta Kappa, Business Professionals of America, Christian Bible Study, dance club, Green club, Alpha Kappa Omega, library club.

Athletics. Intramural: Basketball, football (non-tackle), golf, soccer, softball, tennis, volleyball.

Student services. Career counseling, student employment services, financial aid counseling. **Physically disabled:** Services for visually, speech, hearing impaired. **Transfer:** Transfer adviser, college fairs on campus for students transferring to 4-year colleges.

Contact. E-mail: enrollment@swmich.edu
Phone: (269) 782-1413 Toll-free number: (800) 456-8675 ext. 1413
Fax: (269) 782-1371
Angela Palsak, Associate Dean of Students, Southwestern Michigan College, 58900 Cherry Grove Road, Dowagiac, MI 49047-9793

St. Clair County Community College
Port Huron, Michigan
www.sc4.edu   **CB code: 1628**

▶ Public 2-year community college
▶ Commuter campus in large town

General. Founded in 1923. Regionally accredited. **Enrollment:** 4,053 degree-seeking undergraduates. **Degrees:** 653 associate awarded. **Location:** 55 miles from Detroit. **Calendar:** Semester, limited summer session. **Full-time faculty:** 71 total. **Part-time faculty:** 231 total. **Special facilities:** Fine arts facility, natural history museum.

Student profile. Among degree-seeking undergraduates, 22% enrolled in a transfer program, 50% enrolled in a vocational program, 877 enrolled as first-time, first-year students.

Out-of-state: .1% **25 or older:** 36%

Transfer out. **Colleges most students transferred to 2011:** Central Michigan University, Saginaw Valley Sate University, Ferris State University, University of Michigan-Flint and Walsh College.

Basis for selection. Open admission, but selective for some programs. Nursing programs are selective admission.

2011-2012 Annual costs. Tuition/fees: $3,083; $5,663 out-of-district; $8,093 out-of-state. Per-credit charge: $91 in-district; $177 out-of-district; $258 out-of-state. Residents of Lambton County, Canada pay in-state, out-of-district rate for tuition. Lambton County residents pay in-district tuition rate if enrolled in program of study not offered at Lambton College. Books/supplies: $1,103. Personal expenses: $546.

2011-2012 Financial aid. **Need-based:** 71% of total undergraduate aid awarded as scholarships/grants, 29% as loans/jobs. Work-study available nights, weekends and for part-time students.

Application procedures. **Admission:** No deadline. No application fee. Admission notification on a rolling basis. **Financial aid:** Priority date 6/1; no closing date. FAFSA required. Applicants notified on a rolling basis starting 5/15; must reply within 2 week(s) of notification.

Academics. **Special study options:** Accelerated study, cooperative education, cross-registration, distance learning, double major, dual enrollment of high school students, honors, internships, weekend college. Bachelor's degree programs available on campus. License preparation in nursing, radiology. **Credit/placement by examination:** AP, CLEP, institutional tests. 47 credit hours maximum toward associate degree. **Support services:** Learning center, reduced course load, remedial instruction, study skills assistance, tutoring, writing center.

Majors. **Business:** General, accounting technology, executive assistant, marketing, office management. **Communications:** Broadcast journalism, journalism. **Communications technology:** Radio/TV. **Computer sciences:** Data processing, networking, programming, webmaster. **Education:** Kindergarten/preschool. **Engineering:** General. **General:** Landscaping. **Health services:** Massage therapy, medical radiologic technology/radiation therapy, medical secretary, nursing (RN). **Liberal arts:** Arts/sciences. **Protective services:** Corrections, firefighting, law enforcement admin. **Visual/performing arts:** Commercial/advertising art, studio arts. **Work/family studies:** Child care management.

Computing on campus. 300 workstations in library, computer center, student center. Online course registration, online library, helpline, wireless network available.

Student life. **Freshman orientation:** Mandatory. Preregistration for classes offered. **Activities:** Concert band, choral groups, drama, music ensembles, radio station, student government, student newspaper, symphony orchestra, TV station, global awareness club.

Athletics. NJCAA. **Intercollegiate:** Baseball M, basketball, golf, softball W, volleyball W. **Team name:** Skippers.

Student services. Adult student services, career counseling, services for economically disadvantaged, student employment services, financial aid counseling, minority student services, on-campus daycare, personal counseling, placement for graduates, veterans' counselor. **Physically disabled:** Services for visually, speech, hearing impaired. **Transfer:** Pre-admission transcript evaluation for new students. Transfer adviser, college fairs on campus for students transferring to 4-year colleges.

Contact. E-mail: enrollment@sc4.edu
Phone: (810) 989-5500 Fax: (810) 984-4730
Carrie Bearss, Registrar, St. Clair County Community College, 323 Erie Street, Port Huron, MI 48061-5015

Location: 40 miles from Detroit. **Calendar:** Semester, extensive summer session. **Full-time faculty:** 171 total. **Part-time faculty:** 724 total.

Transfer out. **Colleges most students transferred to 2011:** Eastern Michigan University, University of Michigan.

Basis for selection. Open admission, but selective for some programs. Special requirements for health service technologies programs and some computer technology programs.

High school preparation. 15 units recommended. Recommended units include English 4, mathematics 4, social studies 2, science 4 and foreign language 1. Biology, chemistry, and algebra required for health programs. Trigonometry and drafting required for technical programs.

2011-2012 Annual costs. Tuition/fees: $2,760; $4,290 out-of-district; $5,580 out-of-state. Per-credit charge: $92 in-district; $143 out-of-district; $186 out-of-state. Books/supplies: $600. Personal expenses: $2,000.

Financial aid. **Need-based:** Work-study available nights, weekends and for part-time students. **Non-need-based:** Scholarships awarded for academics.

Application procedures. **Admission:** Priority date 8/12; no deadline. No application fee. Admission notification on a rolling basis beginning on or about 2/20. **Financial aid:** Priority date 6/1, closing date 7/1. FAFSA, institutional form required. Applicants notified on a rolling basis.

Academics. **Special study options:** Cooperative education, cross-registration, distance learning, dual enrollment of high school students, ESL, honors, independent study, internships, liberal arts/career combination, weekend college. **Credit/placement by examination:** AP, CLEP, institutional tests. 45 credit hours maximum toward associate degree. **Support services:** GED preparation and test center, learning center, remedial instruction, study skills assistance, tutoring, writing center.

Majors. **Architecture:** Technology. **Business:** Accounting, administrative services, business admin. **Communications technology:** Graphic/printing. **Computer sciences:** General, applications programming, computer graphics, computer science, data processing, information systems, LAN/WAN management, networking, programming, security, web page design. **Education:** Early childhood, elementary, secondary. **Engineering:** General, engineering mechanics, engineering science. **English:** Technical writing. **Health services:** Medical radiologic technology/radiation therapy, medical records admin, nursing (RN), premedicine, respiratory therapy technology, substance abuse counseling. **Liberal arts:** Arts/sciences. **Protective services:** Corrections, law enforcement admin, police science. **Social sciences:** General. **Visual/performing arts:** Commercial photography, photography.

Computing on campus. 211 workstations in library, computer center, student center. Commuter students can connect to campus network. Online course registration, online library, helpline, repair service, student web hosting, wireless network available.

Student life. **Freshman orientation:** Mandatory. Preregistration for classes offered. **Activities:** Jazz band, choral groups, dance, drama, literary magazine, musical theater, radio station, student government, student newspaper, African-American student association, Christian Challenge Student Advisory Council, international student association, Phi Theta Kappa, student assembly.

Student services. Adult student services, alcohol/substance abuse counseling, career counseling, services for economically disadvantaged, student employment services, financial aid counseling, minority student services, on-campus daycare, personal counseling, placement for graduates, veterans' counselor, women's services. **Physically disabled:** Services for visually, speech, hearing impaired. **Transfer:** Pre-admission transcript evaluation for new students. Transfer center, transfer adviser, college fairs on campus for students transferring to 4-year colleges.

Contact. E-mail: studrec@wccnet.org
Phone: (734) 973-3543 Fax: (734) 677-5414
Larry Aeilts, Director of Admissions, Washtenaw Community College, 4800 East Huron River Drive, Ann Arbor, MI 48105-4800

Washtenaw Community College
Ann Arbor, Michigan **CB member**
www.wccnet.edu **CB code: 1935**

- Public 2-year community college
- Commuter campus in small city

General. Founded in 1965. Regionally accredited. Classes taught in Brighton, Saline, Chelsea, Ypsilanti and Hartland. **Enrollment:** 11,095 degree-seeking undergraduates. **Degrees:** 1,150 associate awarded. **ROTC:** Army.

Wayne County Community College
Detroit, Michigan
www.wcccd.edu **CB code: 1937**

- Public 2-year community and liberal arts college
- Commuter campus in very large city

General. Founded in 1967. Regionally accredited. Five campuses and extension site. **Enrollment:** 16,370 degree-seeking undergraduates; 4,070 non-degree-seeking students. **Degrees:** 1,401 associate awarded. **Calendar:**

Semester, extensive summer session. **Full-time faculty:** 95 total. **Part-time faculty:** 1,120 total. **Class size:** 36% < 20, 52% 20-39, 10% 40-49, 2% 50-99. **Partnerships:** Formal partnerships with corporations and high schools.

Student profile. Among degree-seeking undergraduates, 3,615 enrolled as first-time, first-year students.

Part-time:	74%	Asian American:	1%
Women:	68%	Hispanic American:	2%
African American:	61%	25 or older:	59%

Transfer out. Colleges most students transferred to 2011: Wayne State University, University of Michigan Dearborn, Oakland University, University Of Detroit Mercy, Eastern Michigan University.

Basis for selection. Open admission, but selective for some programs. Competitive career programs require interviews and prerequisite classes. **Adult students:** COMPASS placement exam required. **Home schooled:** Transcript of courses and grades, state high school equivalency certificate required. **Learning Disabled:** Students with learning disabilities must register with the campus Learning Center Coordinator and provide appropriate documentation.

2011-2012 Annual costs. Tuition/fees: $3,040; $3,670 out-of-district; $4,570 out-of-state. Per-credit charge: $89 in-district; $110 out-of-district; $140 out-of-state. Books/supplies: $2,300. Personal expenses: $260.

Financial aid. Need-based: Need-based aid available for part-time students. Work-study available nights, weekends and for part-time students. **Additional information:** High school diploma, GED, or passing grade on ABT required for financial aid.

Application procedures. Admission: No deadline. No application fee. **Financial aid:** Priority date 5/1; no closing date. FAFSA required. Applicants notified on a rolling basis starting 5/1.

Academics. Special study options: Accelerated study, distance learning, double major, dual enrollment of high school students, honors, independent study, internships, liberal arts/career combination, study abroad, weekend college. License preparation in dental hygiene, nursing, occupational therapy, paramedic, real estate. **Credit/placement by examination:** AP, CLEP, institutional tests. Recommendation of CAO or program chair. **Support services:** GED preparation, learning center, remedial instruction, study skills assistance, tutoring.

Majors. Business: Accounting, business admin, e-commerce, labor relations, office management. **Computer sciences:** General, applications programming, artificial intelligence, database management, networking, support specialist, system admin, web page design, webmaster. **Education:** Elementary. **Engineering:** General. **Health services:** Dental hygiene, dietetic technician, EMT paramedic, insurance specialist, mental health services, nursing (RN), occupational therapy assistant, pharmacy assistant, surgical technology, trauma nursing, veterinary technology/assistant. **Human services:** Social work. **Liberal arts:** Arts/sciences. **Philosophy/religion:** Religion. **Protective services:** Corrections, fire safety technology, law enforcement admin, police science. **Social sciences:** General. **Visual/performing arts:** Directing/producing, dramatic. **Work/family studies:** Child care management, institutional food production.

Most popular majors. Business/marketing 7%, health sciences 21%, liberal arts 17%, social sciences 24%, visual/performing arts 22%.

Computing on campus. Commuter students can connect to campus network. Online course registration, online library, helpline, repair service, wireless network available.

Student life. Freshman orientation: Available. Preregistration for classes offered. Includes assessment testing. **Policies:** Students must follow the student code of conduct. **Activities:** Dance, drama, student government.

Student services. Adult student services, career counseling, services for economically disadvantaged, student employment services, financial aid counseling, on-campus daycare, personal counseling, placement for graduates, veterans' counselor, women's services. **Physically disabled:** Services for visually, speech, hearing impaired. **Transfer:** Re-entry adviser, pre-admission transcript evaluation for new students. Transfer adviser, college fairs on campus for students transferring to 4-year colleges.

Contact. Phone: (313) 496-2600
Brian Singleton, Vice Chancellor Student Services, Wayne County Community College, 801 West Fort Street, Detroit, MI 48226

West Shore Community College
Scottville, Michigan
www.westshore.edu   CB code: 1941

▶ Public 2-year community college
▶ Commuter campus in rural community

General. Founded in 1967. Regionally accredited. **Enrollment:** 1,222 degree-seeking undergraduates. **Degrees:** 185 associate awarded. **Location:** 54 miles from Muskegon. **Calendar:** Semester, limited summer session. **Full-time faculty:** 24 total. **Part-time faculty:** 70 total.

Transfer out. Colleges most students transferred to 2011: Grand Valley State University, Ferris State University, Davenport College, Central Michigan University.

Basis for selection. Open admission, but selective for some programs. Applicants to nursing programs must complete prerequisite course work with minimum 2.0 GPA.

2011-2012 Annual costs. Tuition/fees: $2,592; $4,362 out-of-district; $5,772 out-of-state. Per-credit charge: $79 in-district; $138 out-of-district; $185 out-of-state. Books/supplies: $700. Personal expenses: $650.

Financial aid. Need-based: Need-based aid available for part-time students. Work-study available nights, weekends and for part-time students.

Application procedures. Admission: No deadline. $15 fee. Admission notification on a rolling basis. Applicants for associate degree in nursing must apply by January 1, practical nursing applicants by June 1. **Financial aid:** Priority date 3/15; no closing date. FAFSA required. Applicants notified on a rolling basis starting 5/15; must reply within 2 week(s) of notification.

Academics. Special study options: Distance learning, dual enrollment of high school students, honors, independent study, internships. Bachelor's degree programs available on campus. License preparation in nursing, paramedic. **Credit/placement by examination:** AP, CLEP, institutional tests. 10 credit hours maximum toward associate degree. **Support services:** GED test center, learning center, reduced course load, remedial instruction, study skills assistance, tutoring.

Majors. Business: General, accounting, administrative services, management information systems, marketing, office technology, office/clerical. **Computer sciences:** Data processing. **Education:** General. **Health services:** EMT paramedic, nursing (RN), nursing assistant, prepharmacy. **Liberal arts:** Arts/sciences. **Math:** General. **Protective services:** Law enforcement admin.

Computing on campus. 300 workstations in library, computer center, student center. Commuter students can connect to campus network. Helpline, wireless network available.

Student life. Freshman orientation: Mandatory. Preregistration for classes offered. Each student meets one-on-one with academic counselor during registration period before classes begin. **Activities:** Bands, choral groups, drama, music ensembles, musical theater, student government, student newspaper, Phi Theta Kappa honor society, law enforcement club, art club, science club, additional special interest clubs.

Athletics. Intramural: Basketball, racquetball, softball, volleyball.

Student services. Career counseling, student employment services, personal counseling, placement for graduates, veterans' counselor. **Physically disabled:** Services for visually, speech, hearing impaired. **Transfer:** Pre-admission transcript evaluation for new students. Transfer adviser, college fairs on campus for students transferring to 4-year colleges.

Contact. E-mail: admissions@westshore.edu
Phone: (231) 845-6211 ext. 5503 Fax: (231) 845-3944
West Shore Community College, 3000 North Stiles Road, Scottville, MI 49454-0277

Minnesota

Academy College
Bloomington, Minnesota
www.academycollege.edu   CB code: 3311

▸ For-profit 2-year junior and career college
▸ Commuter campus in large city
▸ Interview required

General. Accredited by ACICS. **Enrollment:** 240 degree-seeking undergraduates. **Degrees:** 11 bachelor's, 14 associate awarded. **Calendar:** Quarter, extensive summer session. **Part-time faculty:** 23 total.

Student profile.

Out-of-state: 27%   25 or older: 65%

Basis for selection. Open admission.

2011-2012 Annual costs. Tuition ranges from $350 to $440 per credit hour depending on program. Required fees for academic year, $400, include one-time student activity fee, $280, required of all entering students, as well as technology fee, $120, required of all students. Books/supplies: $1,100. Personal expenses: $2,200.

Financial aid. Need-based: Need-based aid available for part-time students. Work-study available nights, weekends and for part-time students.

Application procedures. Admission: No deadline. $40 fee. Application must be submitted on paper. Admission notification on a rolling basis. **Financial aid:** No deadline. FAFSA, institutional form required. Applicants notified on a rolling basis.

Academics. Special study options: Distance learning, internships. License preparation in aviation. **Credit/placement by examination:** AP, CLEP. **Support services:** Learning center, reduced course load, study skills assistance, tutoring.

Majors. Business: Accounting, business admin, finance, sales/distribution, training/development. **Communications technology:** General, animation/special effects. **Computer sciences:** General, computer graphics, programming, system admin, web page design. **Visual/performing arts:** General, commercial/advertising art.

Computing on campus. PC or laptop required. 50 workstations in library, computer center. Online library, wireless network available.

Student life. Freshman orientation: Mandatory. Preregistration for classes offered.

Student services. Placement for graduates. **Transfer:** Re-entry adviser, pre-admission transcript evaluation for new students.

Contact. E-mail: admissions@academycollege.edu
Phone: (952) 851-0066 Toll-free number: (800) 292-9149
Fax: (952) 851-0094
Dan Erhardt, Director of Admissions, Academy College, 1101 East 78th Street, Bloomington, MN 55420

Alexandria Technical and Community College
Alexandria, Minnesota
www.alextech.edu   CB code: 0771

▸ Public 2-year community and technical college
▸ Commuter campus in large town
▸ Interview required

General. Founded in 1961. Regionally accredited. **Enrollment:** 1,744 degree-seeking undergraduates. **Degrees:** 411 associate awarded. **Location:** 135 miles from Minneapolis-St. Paul. **Calendar:** Semester, limited summer session. **Full-time faculty:** 66 total; 3% have terminal degrees, 39% women. **Part-time faculty:** 40 total; 5% have terminal degrees, 60% women.

Student profile.

Out-of-state: 4%   25 or older: 24%

Basis for selection. Open admission, but selective for some programs. Application, high school transcript/GED/or Ability to Benefit Test required. Mechanical Reasoning test required for Diesel and Marine and Small Engine students; physical agility test required for Law Enforcement students. Applicants considered in order of applications received. Portfolio required for communications art and design students.

2011-2012 Annual costs. Tuition/fees: $5,169; $5,169 out-of-state. Per-credit charge: $155. Laptop lease required for some programs; approximately $800 annually. Books/supplies: $1,200. Personal expenses: $7,100.

Financial aid. All financial aid based on need. Need-based aid available for part-time students. Work-study available nights, weekends and for part-time students.

Application procedures. Admission: Priority date 8/1; no deadline. $20 fee, may be waived for applicants with need. Admission notification on a rolling basis. **Financial aid:** Priority date 5/1; no closing date. FAFSA, institutional form required. Applicants notified on a rolling basis starting 6/30; must reply within 2 week(s) of notification.

Academics. Special study options: Distance learning, double major, independent study, internships, liberal arts/career combination, student-designed major. Bachelor's degree programs available on campus. License preparation in nursing. **Credit/placement by examination:** AP, CLEP, IB, institutional tests. No separate limits on CLEP and credit by exam. **Support services:** Reduced course load, remedial instruction, study skills assistance, tutoring, writing center.

Majors. Business: Accounting, banking/financial services, business admin, credit management, fashion, hotel/motel/restaurant management, marketing, office management, operations, sales/distribution. **Computer sciences:** Information systems, networking, web page design. **Health services:** Clinical lab technology, medical secretary, nursing (RN). **Liberal arts:** Arts/sciences. **Parks/recreation:** Physical fitness technician. **Protective services:** Police science. **Visual/performing arts:** Commercial/advertising art, interior design. **Work/family studies:** Child development.

Most popular majors. Business/marketing 27%, computer/information sciences 7%, health sciences 11%, liberal arts 6%, security/protective services 27%, visual/performing arts 9%.

Computing on campus. 1,100 workstations in library, computer center. Online course registration, online library, helpline, repair service, wireless network available.

Student life. Freshman orientation: Available. Preregistration for classes offered. **Activities:** Campus ministries, choral groups, student government, Phi Theta Kappa, Business Professionals of America, Delta Epsilon Chi, Skills USA, student senate.

Athletics. Intramural: Basketball, football (tackle), softball, volleyball.

Student services. Alcohol/substance abuse counseling, career counseling, services for economically disadvantaged, student employment services, financial aid counseling, health services, minority student services, personal counseling, placement for graduates, veterans' counselor. **Physically disabled:** Services for visually, speech, hearing impaired. **Transfer:** Pre-admission transcript evaluation for new students. Transfer adviser, college fairs on campus for students transferring to 4-year colleges.

Contact. E-mail: admissionsrep@alextech.edu
Phone: (320) 762-4520 Toll-free number: (888) 234-1222
Fax: (320) 762-4603
Charles (Tex) Claymore, Director of Admissions, Alexandria Technical and Community College, 1601 Jefferson Street, Alexandria, MN 56308-3799

Anoka Technical College
Anoka, Minnesota
www.anokatech.edu   CB code: 6084

▸ Public 2-year technical college
▸ Commuter campus in large town

General. Regionally accredited. **Enrollment:** 1,956 degree-seeking undergraduates. **Degrees:** 293 associate awarded. **Location:** 25 miles from Minneapolis-St. Paul. **Calendar:** Semester, limited summer session. **Full-time faculty:** 61 total. **Part-time faculty:** 53 total.

Basis for selection. Open admission, but selective for some programs. Testing and score requirements for admission to the Surgical Technology, Occupational Therapy Assistant, and Practical Nursing Programs. If seeking an associate's degree in the Practical Nursing Program, additional biology requirement needed. All new students required to take Accuplacer to determine skill level in mathematics, reading and writing or meet exemption criteria as described on the college's website. The student may begin a program regardless of test scores unless the program requires placement testing as a program pre-requisite. **Adult students:** SAT/ACT scores not required.

2011-2012 Annual costs. Tuition/fees: $5,506; $5,506 out-of-state. Per-credit charge: $161.

Financial aid. All financial aid based on need. Need-based aid available for part-time students. Work-study available nights, weekends and for part-time students.

Application procedures. **Admission:** No deadline. $20 fee, may be waived for applicants with need. Admission notification on a rolling basis. **Financial aid:** No deadline. FAFSA required. Applicants notified on a rolling basis starting 7/1.

Academics. **Special study options:** Distance learning, internships, liberal arts/career combination. License preparation in nursing, occupational therapy. **Credit/placement by examination:** AP, CLEP, institutional tests. **Support services:** GED preparation and test center, learning center, reduced course load, remedial instruction, study skills assistance, tutoring, writing center.

Majors. **Business:** Accounting, administrative services, office management. **General:** Landscaping. **Health services:** Licensed practical nurse, medical assistant, medical records technology, medical secretary, occupational therapy assistant, surgical technology. **Parks/recreation:** Golf management. **Work/family studies:** Developmental services.

Most popular majors. Business/marketing 9%, engineering/engineering technologies 22%, health sciences 52%, legal studies 8%, parks/recreation 6%.

Computing on campus. 250 workstations in library, computer center, student center. Online library, wireless network available.

Student life. **Freshman orientation:** Mandatory. Preregistration for classes offered. **Activities:** Student government.

Student services. Career counseling, student employment services, financial aid counseling, health services, personal counseling, placement for graduates, veterans' counselor. **Physically disabled:** Services for visually, speech, hearing impaired.

Contact. E-mail: info@anokatech.edu
Phone: (763) 576-4850 Fax: (763) 576-4756
LeAnn Brown, Director of Admission, Anoka Technical College, 1355 West Highway 10, Anoka, MN 55303

Anoka-Ramsey Community College
Coon Rapids, Minnesota
www.anokaramsey.edu CB code: 6024

- Public 2-year community college
- Commuter campus in small city

General. Founded in 1965. Regionally accredited. Courses offered at 15 locations in east central Minnesota and the north metro. **Enrollment:** 6,980 degree-seeking undergraduates. **Degrees:** 987 associate awarded. **ROTC:** Army, Naval, Air Force. **Location:** 20 miles from Minneapolis-St. Paul. **Calendar:** Semester, extensive summer session. **Full-time faculty:** 117 total. **Part-time faculty:** 179 total. **Special facilities:** Glass-blowing studio, native prairie ground.

Transfer out. Colleges most students transferred to 2011: University of Minnesota-Twin Cities, St. Cloud State University, Metropolitan State University.

Basis for selection. Open admission, but selective for some programs. Special requirements for nursing, biomedical technology, and computer networking and telecommunications programs.

2011-2012 Annual costs. Tuition/fees: $4,738; $4,738 out-of-state. Per-credit charge: $139.

Financial aid. All financial aid based on need. Need-based aid available for part-time students. Work-study available nights, weekends and for part-time students.

Application procedures. **Admission:** No deadline. $20 fee. Admission notification on a rolling basis. **Financial aid:** Priority date 4/1; no closing date. FAFSA, institutional form required. Applicants notified on a rolling basis; must reply within 2 week(s) of notification.

Academics. **Special study options:** Cooperative education, cross-registration, distance learning, double major, dual enrollment of high school students, honors, independent study, internships, study abroad, weekend college. Bachelor's degree programs available on campus. **Credit/placement by examination:** AP, CLEP, institutional tests. 10 credit hours maximum toward associate degree. **Support services:** Learning center, reduced course load, remedial instruction, study skills assistance, tutoring, writing center.

Majors. **Biology:** General. **Business:** General, accounting, accounting technology, business admin, human resources, sales/distribution. **Computer sciences:** Computer science, networking. **Conservation:** Environmental science. **Engineering:** Biomedical, pre-engineering. **Health services:** Community health, holistic, nursing (RN), physical therapy assistant. **Liberal arts:** Arts/sciences. **Visual/performing arts:** Dramatic, music, studio arts.

Most popular majors. Business/marketing 10%, health sciences 24%, liberal arts 58%.

Computing on campus. Commuter students can connect to campus network. Wireless network available.

Student life. **Freshman orientation:** Mandatory. Preregistration for classes offered. **Activities:** Bands, choral groups, drama, international student organizations, literary magazine, music ensembles, musical theater, student government, student newspaper, symphony orchestra, Phi Theta Kappa, Gay Straight Alliance.

Athletics. NJCAA. **Intercollegiate:** Baseball M, basketball, soccer, softball W, volleyball W. **Intramural:** Baseball M, basketball, bowling, football (tackle), golf, ice hockey, soccer, softball, tennis, volleyball. **Team name:** Golden Rams.

Student services. Adult student services, career counseling, student employment services, financial aid counseling, personal counseling, veterans' counselor. **Physically disabled:** Services for visually, speech, hearing impaired. **Transfer:** Transfer adviser, college fairs on campus for students transferring to 4-year colleges.

Contact. E-mail: admissions@anokaramsey.edu
Phone: (763) 433-1300
Ashley Weatherspoon, Director of Enrollment Services, Anoka-Ramsey Community College, 11200 Mississippi Boulevard NW, Coon Rapids, MN 55433

Anthem College: Minneapolis
Saint Louis Park, Minnesota
www.anthem.edu CB code: 3042

- For-profit 2-year technical and career college
- Commuter campus in small city
- Interview required

General. Regionally accredited; also accredited by ACICS. **Enrollment:** 202 full-time, degree-seeking students. **Degrees:** 12 associate awarded. **Location:** 8 miles from downtown. **Calendar:** Quarter, extensive summer session. **Full-time faculty:** 19 total; 16% have terminal degrees, 47% women. **Part-time faculty:** 7 total; 14% have terminal degrees, 14% minority, 43% women.

Student profile. Among full-time, degree-seeking students, 100% enrolled in a vocational program. Of all enrolled students, 1% already have a bachelor's degree or higher.

African American:	21%	Native American:	2%
Asian American:	13%	International:	6%
Hispanic American:	2%		

Basis for selection. Open admission. Applicants must meet with an admissions representative for an initial interview and must achieve a passing score on the entrance assessment. Must also have a high school diploma or equivalent or have an associates or higher degree from an institution recognized by the US Department of Education.

2012-2013 Annual costs. Cost of attendance includes text books, supplies, uniforms and testing fees (where applicable). Program tution ranges from $30,900 to $42,300 for an Associate of Applied Science degree and from $15,900 to $20,923 for a Diploma.

Financial aid. **Need-based:** Work-study available nights, weekends and for part-time students.

Application procedures. Admission: No deadline. $20 fee. Admission notification on a rolling basis.

Academics. Credit/placement by examination: AP, CLEP. **Support services:** Tutoring.

Majors. Health services: Insurance coding, massage therapy, medical assistant, pharmacy assistant, surgical technology.

Computing on campus. Online library available.

Student services. Career counseling, student employment services, financial aid counseling, placement for graduates.

Contact. Phone: (952) 417-2200 Toll-free number: (855) 331-7769 Todd Paulson, Director of Admissions, Anthem College: Minneapolis, 5100 Gamble Drive, St. Louis Park, MN 55416

Central Lakes College
Brainerd, Minnesota
www.clcmn.edu   CB code: 6045

◆ Public 2-year community and technical college
◆ Commuter campus in large town

General. Founded in 1938. Regionally accredited. Access to 1.5 million book titles through participation in online catalog system with 28 other libraries. **Enrollment:** 2,963 degree-seeking undergraduates. **Degrees:** 612 associate awarded. **Location:** 125 miles from Minneapolis-St. Paul. **Calendar:** Semester, limited summer session. **Full-time faculty:** 105 total. **Part-time faculty:** 70 total. **Class size:** 41% < 20, 50% 20-39, 6% 40-49, 2% 50-99. **Special facilities:** Conservatory, American Indian studies center.

Student profile. Among degree-seeking undergraduates, 40% enrolled in a transfer program, 42% enrolled in a vocational program, 290 transferred in from other institutions.

Basis for selection. Open admission, but selective for some programs. Applicants to mobility nursing program must have graduate license in practical nursing (LPN). Practical nurse program grades and college grades considered. Instructor and employer references, practical to registered nursing mobility profile, and mathematics test scores also considered.

2011-2012 Annual costs. Tuition/fees: $5,209; $5,209 out-of-state. Per-credit charge: $153. Books/supplies: $800. Personal expenses: $1,500.

2010-2011 Financial aid. Need-based: 43% of total undergraduate aid awarded as scholarships/grants, 57% as loans/jobs. Need-based aid available for part-time students. Work-study available nights, weekends and for part-time students.

Application procedures. Admission: No deadline. $20 fee. Admission notification on a rolling basis. **Financial aid:** Priority date 6/1; no closing date. FAFSA, institutional form required. Applicants notified on a rolling basis starting 6/10; must reply within 2 week(s) of notification.

Academics. Special study options: Distance learning, dual enrollment of high school students, independent study, internships, liberal arts/career combination. Bachelor's degree programs available on campus. License preparation in nursing. **Credit/placement by examination:** AP, CLEP, IB, institutional tests. **Support services:** Learning center, remedial instruction, study skills assistance, tutoring, writing center.

Majors. Business: Accounting, administrative services, business admin, tourism/travel. **Communications technology:** Photo/film/video. **Computer sciences:** Data processing, networking, programming. **Conservation:** General. **Education:** Teacher assistance. **Engineering:** General. **General:** Horticulture. **Health services:** Medical secretary, nursing (RN). **Liberal arts:** Arts/sciences. **Protective services:** Criminal justice, criminalistics, police science. **Visual/performing arts:** Commercial/advertising art. **Work/family studies:** Child care management.

Most popular majors. Business/marketing 8%, health sciences 12%, liberal arts 57%.

Computing on campus. 150 workstations in library, computer center. Commuter students can connect to campus network. Online course registration, online library, helpline, repair service, wireless network available.

Student life. Freshman orientation: Mandatory. Preregistration for classes offered. Online orientation required. Orientations also held in-person throughout spring and summer. **Activities:** Bands, choral groups, drama, international student organizations, music ensembles, musical theater, student government, student newspaper, Anishinabe Student Association, campus ambassadors, law enforcement club, mentoring, theater club, Phi Theta Kappa, Spanish club, minority student forum.

Athletics. NJCAA. **Intercollegiate:** Baseball M, basketball, football (tackle) M, golf, softball W, volleyball W. **Intramural:** Baseball M, basketball, bowling, golf, softball, volleyball. **Team name:** Raiders.

Student services. Adult student services, career counseling, services for economically disadvantaged, financial aid counseling, health services, minority student services, on-campus daycare, personal counseling, placement for graduates, veterans' counselor, women's services. **Physically disabled:** Services for visually, speech, hearing impaired. **Transfer:** Pre-admission transcript evaluation for new students. Transfer adviser, college fairs on campus for students transferring to 4-year colleges.

Contact. E-mail: rtretter@clcmn.edu
Phone: (218) 855-8037 Toll-free number: (800) 933-0346
Fax: (218) 855-8230
Charlotte Daniels, Director of Admissions, Central Lakes College, 501 West College Drive, Brainerd, MN 56401

Century College
White Bear Lake, Minnesota
www.century.edu   CB code: 6388

◆ Public 2-year community and technical college
◆ Commuter campus in large town

General. Founded in 1967. Regionally accredited. **Enrollment:** 10,073 degree-seeking undergraduates; 634 non-degree-seeking students. **Degrees:** 1,136 associate awarded. **ROTC:** Air Force. **Location:** 16 miles from Minneapolis-St. Paul. **Calendar:** Semester, limited summer session. **Full-time faculty:** 204 total; 7% minority, 57% women. **Part-time faculty:** 187 total; 9% minority, 51% women. **Class size:** 32% < 20, 58% 20-39, 8% 40-49, 2% 50-99. **Special facilities:** 92-acre nature area, walking trail.

Student profile. Among degree-seeking undergraduates, 36% enrolled in a transfer program, 64% enrolled in a vocational program, 2% already have a bachelor's degree or higher, 1,671 enrolled as first-time, first-year students, 1,085 transferred in from other institutions.

Part-time:	56%	**Hispanic American:**	6%
Out-of-state:	6%	**Native American:**	1%
Women:	55%	**International:**	1%
African American:	11%	**25 or older:**	42%
Asian American:	15%		

Transfer out. Colleges most students transferred to 2011: Metropolitan State University, University of Minnesota, University of Wisconsin-River Falls, MN State University-Mankato, Hamline University.

Basis for selection. Open admission, but selective for some programs. Special requirements for nursing, radiology, orthotics, prosthetics, paramedic, dental assist and dental hygiene programs. LOEP used to determine English proficiency. **Learning Disabled:** Documentation of disability must be provided within the first semester of service.

2011-2012 Annual costs. Tuition/fees: $5,201; $5,201 out-of-state. Per-credit charge: $155. Books/supplies: $1,000.

Financial aid. All financial aid based on need. Need-based aid available for part-time students. Work-study available nights, weekends and for part-time students. **Additional information:** Minnesota resident out of high school or not enrolled in college for 7 years without bachelor's or other higher degree offered cost of tuition and books for 1 course in 1 semester up to maximum of 5 credits.

Application procedures. Admission: No deadline. $20 fee, may be waived for applicants with need. Admission notification on a rolling basis. **Financial aid:** Priority date 5/1; no closing date. FAFSA required. Applicants notified on a rolling basis starting 5/15.

Academics. Special study options: Distance learning, dual enrollment of high school students, ESL, honors, internships, liberal arts/career combination. License preparation in dental hygiene, nursing, paramedic, radiology. **Credit/placement by examination:** AP, CLEP, IB. **Support services:** Learning center, remedial instruction, study skills assistance, tutoring, writing center.

Majors. Business: Accounting, administrative services, business admin, e-commerce, marketing. **Communications:** Digital media. **Computer sciences:** Computer science, information systems, networking, security. **Education:** General, teacher assistance. **Engineering:** General. **Foreign languages:** Translation. **General:** Greenhouse operations, horticultural science, landscaping. **Health services:** Dental assistant, dental hygiene, EMT paramedic,

medical secretary, nursing (RN), orthotics/prosthetics, radiologic technology/ medical imaging, substance abuse counseling. **Liberal arts:** Arts/sciences. **Protective services:** Criminal justice, criminalistics, police science. **Visual/ performing arts:** Interior design, music, studio arts.

Most popular majors. Business/marketing 9%, health sciences 21%, liberal arts 47%, security/protective services 8%.

Computing on campus. 1,550 workstations in library, computer center. Commuter students can connect to campus network. Online course registration, wireless network available.

Student life. Freshman orientation: Mandatory. Preregistration for classes offered. Two-part orientation includes advising/registration session, welcome day/workshops, tours and speakers. **Activities:** Bands, choral groups, drama, literary magazine, student government, student newspaper, symphony orchestra, Asian student association, intercultural club, student senate, Phi Theta Kappa, planning activities committee, dental assisting, Alpha Omega, orthotics/prosthetics, nursing club, Black student association.

Athletics. NJCAA. **Intercollegiate:** Baseball M, soccer, softball W. **Intramural:** Badminton, basketball, bowling, soccer, softball, table tennis, volleyball. **Team name:** Wood Ducks.

Student services. Adult student services, career counseling, student employment services, financial aid counseling, health services, minority student services, on-campus daycare, personal counseling. **Physically disabled:** Services for visually, speech, hearing impaired. **Transfer:** Transfer adviser, college fairs on campus for students transferring to 4-year colleges.

Contact. E-mail: admissions@century.edu
Phone: (651) 779-1700 Toll-free number: (800) 228-1978
Fax: (651) 779-1796
Christine Paulos, Director of Admissions, Century College, 3300 Century Avenue North, White Bear Lake, MN 55110

Dakota County Technical College
Rosemount, Minnesota
www.dctc.edu   CB code: 7149

- Public 2-year technical college
- Commuter campus in large town

General. Regionally accredited. **Enrollment:** 2,760 degree-seeking undergraduates; 320 non-degree-seeking students. **Degrees:** 440 associate awarded. **Location:** 20 miles from Minneapolis-St. Paul. **Calendar:** Semester, limited summer session. **Full-time faculty:** 80 total; 12% have terminal degrees, 2% minority, 45% women. **Part-time faculty:** 68 total; 15% have terminal degrees, 4% minority, 47% women. **Class size:** 61% < 20, 39% 20-39, less than 1% 40-49. **Special facilities:** Greenhouse, skid pad. **Partnerships:** Formal partnership with General Motors for Automotive Service Education Program/Body Service Education Program.

Student profile. Among degree-seeking undergraduates, 881 enrolled as first-time, first-year students, 560 transferred in from other institutions.

Part-time:	41%	25 or older:	51%
Women:	48%		

Transfer out. Colleges most students transferred to 2011: St. Mary's University, Metropolitan State University, Concordia University.

Basis for selection. Open admission, but selective for some programs. Students must achieve qualifying scores on the Accuplacer Assessment for entrance into medical assistant and practical nursing programs. TOEFL required for international students. Admissions visit including meeting with the program instructor(s) not required but strongly recommended. **Home schooled:** Transcript of courses and grades required.

2011-2012 Annual costs. Tuition/fees: $5,521; $5,521 out-of-state. Per-credit charge: $163. Books/supplies: $1,625. Personal expenses: $2,250.

Financial aid. Need-based: Need-based aid available for part-time students. Work-study available nights, weekends and for part-time students. **Non-need-based:** Scholarships awarded for academics, leadership.

Application procedures. Admission: No deadline. $20 fee, may be waived for applicants with need. Admission notification on a rolling basis. **Financial aid:** No deadline. FAFSA required. Applicants notified on a rolling basis starting 3/15.

Academics. Special study options: Accelerated study, cross-registration, distance learning, double major, ESL, independent study, internships, liberal arts/career combination, student-designed major. Bachelor's degree programs available on campus. License preparation in nursing. **Credit/placement by**

---

examination: AP, CLEP, IB, institutional tests. **Support services:** Learning center, pre-admission summer program, reduced course load, remedial instruction, study skills assistance, tutoring, writing center.

Majors. Business: Accounting, business admin, executive assistant, management information systems, marketing, real estate, resort management, tourism/travel, travel services. **Communications:** Digital media. **Computer sciences:** Networking, programming. **General:** Landscaping. **Health services:** Dental assistant, licensed practical nurse, medical assistant, medical secretary. **Parks/recreation:** Exercise sciences. **Visual/performing arts:** Commercial/advertising art, graphic design, interior design, photography. **Work/family studies:** Child care service.

Most popular majors. Business/marketing 26%, computer/information sciences 8%, engineering/engineering technologies 11%, health sciences 15%, trade and industry 13%, visual/performing arts 13%.

Computing on campus. 200 workstations in library, computer center, student center. Online course registration, online library, helpline, wireless network available.

Student life. Freshman orientation: Mandatory. Preregistration for classes offered. Sessions available 2-3 months prior to semester. **Activities:** Campus ministries, international student organizations, student government, Multicultural Student Leadership Association, veterans center, student senate, Christians on Campus, Lion's Club, Student Ambassadors, Gay Straight Alliance.

Athletics. NJCAA. **Intercollegiate:** Baseball M, basketball M, soccer, softball W, volleyball W. **Team name:** Blue Knights.

Student services. Alcohol/substance abuse counseling, career counseling, services for economically disadvantaged, student employment services, financial aid counseling, health services, minority student services, personal counseling, placement for graduates, veterans' counselor. **Physically disabled:** Services for visually, speech, hearing impaired. **Transfer:** Re-entry adviser, pre-admission transcript evaluation for new students. College fairs on campus for students transferring to 4-year colleges.

Contact. E-mail: admissions@dctc.edu
Phone: (651) 423-8301 Toll-free number: (877) 937-3282
Fax: (651) 423-8775
Patrick Lair, Admissions Director, Dakota County Technical College, 1300 145th Street East, Rosemount, MN 55068

Duluth Business University
Duluth, Minnesota
www.dbumn.edu   CB code: 3312

- For-profit 2-year business and career college
- Residential campus in small city
- Interview required

General. Accredited by ACICS. **Enrollment:** 329 degree-seeking undergraduates. **Degrees:** 67 associate awarded. **Location:** 150 miles from Minneapolis-St. Paul. **Calendar:** Quarter, extensive summer session. **Full-time faculty:** 17 total. **Part-time faculty:** 29 total.

Student profile. Among degree-seeking undergraduates, 2% already have a bachelor's degree or higher, 32 enrolled as first-time, first-year students.

Part-time:	45%	Women:	80%

Transfer out. 1% of students enrolled in the transfer program go on to 4-year colleges.

Basis for selection. High school diploma or GED and interview required.

2011-2012 Annual costs. Tuition/fees: $15,750. Per-credit charge: $350. Vet tech and Graphics programs $370 per-credit hour. Books/supplies: $1,462.

Financial aid. Need-based: Work-study available nights, weekends and for part-time students.

Application procedures. Admission: No deadline. $35 fee. Application must be submitted on paper. Admission notification on a rolling basis. **Financial aid:** No deadline.

Academics. Special study options: Distance learning, internships, weekend college. **Credit/placement by examination:** AP, CLEP. **Support services:** Remedial instruction, tutoring.

Majors. Business: Business admin. **Health services:** Massage therapy, medical assistant, medical records technology, phlebotomy, veterinary technology/assistant. **Visual/performing arts:** Commercial/advertising art.

Most popular majors. Business/marketing 12%, health sciences 88%.

Computing on campus. Helpline, wireless network available.

Student life. Freshman orientation: Mandatory. Preregistration for classes offered.

Student services. Career counseling. **Transfer:** Re-entry adviser, pre-admission transcript evaluation for new students.

Contact. E-mail: info@dbumn.edu
Phone: (218) 722-4000 Toll-free number: (800) 777-8406
Fax: (218) 628-2127
Bonnie Kupczynski, Campus Director, Duluth Business University, 4727 Mike Colalillo Drive, Duluth, MN 55807

Dunwoody College of Technology
Minneapolis, Minnesota
www.dunwoody.edu
CB code: 2265

- Private 2-year technical college
- Commuter campus in very large city
- Application essay, interview required

General. Founded in 1914. Regionally accredited. **Enrollment:** 1,055 degree-seeking undergraduates. **Degrees:** 37 bachelor's, 363 associate awarded. **Calendar:** Continuous, limited summer session. **Full-time faculty:** 88 total; 8% have terminal degrees, 9% minority, 24% women. **Part-time faculty:** 50 total; 6% have terminal degrees, 10% minority, 12% women. **Class size:** 93% < 20, 7% 20-39.

Student profile. Among degree-seeking undergraduates, 100% enrolled in a vocational program, 152 enrolled as first-time, first-year students.

Part-time:	16%	Asian American:	7%
Out-of-state:	2%	Hispanic American:	2%
Women:	13%	Native American:	1%
African American:	8%	25 or older:	42%

Transfer out. Colleges most students transferred to 2011: Minneapolis Community and Technical College, Normandale Community College, University of Minnesota-Twin Cities, Inver Hills Community College, Century College.

Basis for selection. Institutional entrance test or ACT test results required. Rank in upper-half of high school class preferred. ACT recommended. Essay or personal statement required at time of admissions testing. **Home schooled:** Transcript of courses and grades required. **Learning Disabled:** Students must submit official documentation.

High school preparation. College-preparatory program recommended. 8 units required; 20 recommended. Required and recommended units include English 3-4, mathematics 3-4, social studies 2, history 2, science 1-2 (laboratory 1-2) and academic electives 4.

2011-2012 Annual costs. Tuition/fees: $17,562. Per-credit charge: $352. Books/supplies: $900.

2010-2011 Financial aid. Need-based: Need-based aid available for part-time students. Work-study available nights, weekends and for part-time students. **Non-need-based:** Scholarships awarded for academics.

Application procedures. Admission: Closing date 8/15 (postmark date). $50 fee, may be waived for applicants with need. Admission notification on a rolling basis. **Financial aid:** Priority date 6/1; no closing date. FAFSA required. Applicants notified on a rolling basis starting 2/1; must reply within 4 week(s) of notification.

Academics. Special study options: Distance learning, double major, independent study, internships, study abroad. Bachelor's degree programs available on campus. **Credit/placement by examination:** AP, CLEP, IB, institutional tests. **Support services:** Learning center, pre-admission summer program, reduced course load, remedial instruction, study skills assistance, tutoring, writing center.

Majors. Architecture: Technology. **Communications technology:** Desktop publishing, printing press operator. **Computer sciences:** Networking, web page design. **Health services:** Medical radiologic technology/radiation therapy. **Visual/performing arts:** Graphic design.

Most popular majors. Architecture 7%, computer/information sciences 18%, engineering/engineering technologies 25%, trade and industry 44%.

Computing on campus. PC or laptop required. 1,900 workstations in library, computer center. Commuter students can connect to campus network. Online library, helpline, repair service, wireless network available.

Student life. Freshman orientation: Mandatory. Preregistration for classes offered. One-day program, offered multiple times. **Activities:** Student government.

Student services. Career counseling, student employment services, financial aid counseling, minority student services, personal counseling, placement for graduates, veterans' counselor, women's services. **Transfer:** Re-entry adviser, pre-admission transcript evaluation for new students. Transfer adviser for students transferring to 4-year colleges.

Contact. E-mail: info@dunwoody.edu
Phone: (612) 374-5800 Toll-free number: (800) 292-4625
Fax: (612) 677-3131
Bonney Bielen, Admissions Manager, Dunwoody College of Technology, 818 Dunwoody Boulevard, Minneapolis, MN 55403-1192

Fond du Lac Tribal and Community College
Cloquet, Minnesota
www.fdltcc.edu
CB code: 2047

- Public 2-year community college
- Commuter campus in large town

General. Founded in 1987. Regionally accredited. Combined state community college and tribal college. **Enrollment:** 1,178 degree-seeking undergraduates. **Degrees:** 236 associate awarded. **Location:** 16 miles from Duluth. **Calendar:** Semester, limited summer session. **Full-time faculty:** 34 total. **Part-time faculty:** 28 total. **Special facilities:** 21,000 acre environmental study area.

Student profile.

Out-of-state:	5%	Live on campus:	8%
25 or older:	34%		

Basis for selection. Open admission. ACCUPLACER testing required in Reading, Math, and English.

High school preparation. Recommended units include English 4, mathematics 3 and foreign language 4.

2011-2012 Annual costs. Tuition/fees: $5,036; $5,036 out-of-state. Per-credit charge: $153. Room only: $3,536. Books/supplies: $876.

Financial aid. Need-based: Need-based aid available for part-time students. Work-study available nights, weekends and for part-time students. **Non-need-based:** Scholarships awarded for academics.

Application procedures. Admission: No deadline. $20 fee, may be waived for applicants with need. Admission notification on a rolling basis. **Financial aid:** Priority date 3/15; no closing date. FAFSA, institutional form required. Applicants notified on a rolling basis starting 4/15.

Academics. Special study options: Cooperative education, distance learning, dual enrollment of high school students, liberal arts/career combination, weekend college. Bachelor's degree programs available on campus. License preparation in nursing. **Credit/placement by examination:** AP, CLEP, IB, institutional tests. 24 credit hours maximum toward associate degree. **Support services:** Learning center, remedial instruction, study skills assistance, tutoring.

Majors. Business: Administrative services. **Computer sciences:** Security. **Conservation:** Environmental science. **Health services:** Nursing (RN). **Liberal arts:** Arts/sciences. **Parks/recreation:** Physical fitness technician. **Protective services:** Corrections, police science. **Social sciences:** GIS/cartography. **Visual/performing arts:** Studio arts. **Work/family studies:** Child development, food/nutrition.

Computing on campus. 100 workstations in dormitories, library, computer center, student center. Dormitories linked to campus network.

Student life. Freshman orientation: Mandatory. Preregistration for classes offered. **Housing:** Coed dorms, special housing for disabled, apartments available. $150 deposit, deadline 6/15. **Activities:** Choral groups, drama, student government, student newspaper, Phi Theta Kappa Honor Society, law enforcement club, human services club, science club, volunteer information program, Anishinaabe Congress, math club, veterans club, American Indian Business Leaders.

Athletics. Intramural: Bowling, softball, volleyball.

Student services. Adult student services, career counseling, student employment services, financial aid counseling, health services, minority student services, on-campus daycare, personal counseling, placement for graduates, veterans' counselor. **Physically disabled:** Services for visually, speech, hearing impaired. **Transfer:** Pre-admission transcript evaluation for new students. Transfer adviser, college fairs on campus for students transferring to 4-year colleges.

Contact. E-mail: admissions@fdltcc.edu
Phone: (218) 879-0808 Toll-free number: (800) 657-3712
Fax: (218) 879-0814
Kathy Jubie, Admissions Representative, Fond du Lac Tribal and Community College, 2101 14th Street, Cloquet, MN 55720

Hennepin Technical College
Brooklyn Park, Minnesota
www.hennepintech.edu   CB code: 6290

♦ Public 2-year technical college
♦ Commuter campus in small city

General. Regionally accredited. **Enrollment:** 6,759 degree-seeking undergraduates. **Degrees:** 700 associate awarded. **Location:** 10 miles from Minneapolis-St. Paul. **Calendar:** Semester, limited summer session. **Full-time faculty:** 145 total. **Part-time faculty:** 269 total.

Student profile. Among degree-seeking undergraduates, 100% enrolled in a vocational program.

Basis for selection. Open admission, but selective for some programs. Special requirements for nursing and dental program. Accuplacer for placement only.

2011-2012 Annual costs. Tuition/fees: $4,835; $4,835 out-of-state. Per-credit charge: $151. Books/supplies: $1,000.

Financial aid. All financial aid based on need. Work-study available nights, weekends and for part-time students.

Application procedures. Admission: No deadline. $20 fee, may be waived for applicants with need. Admission notification on a rolling basis. **Financial aid:** No deadline. FAFSA, institutional form required. Applicants notified on a rolling basis starting 3/1.

Academics. Special study options: Accelerated study, cross-registration, distance learning, dual enrollment of high school students, ESL, honors, independent study, internships, student-designed major. License preparation in nursing. **Credit/placement by examination:** AP, CLEP, IB. **Support services:** Learning center, reduced course load, remedial instruction, study skills assistance, tutoring, writing center.

Majors. Business: Accounting, accounting technology, office technology, office/clerical. **Communications:** Advertising, digital media, publishing. **Communications technology:** General, desktop publishing, graphic/printing, graphics, photo/film/video, printing press operator, recording arts. **Computer sciences:** General, applications programming, computer graphics, data processing, information systems, programming, security, systems analysis, web page design. **General:** Floriculture, landscaping, nursery operations. **Health services:** Dental assistant, EMT paramedic, licensed practical nurse, medical secretary, office admin, ward clerk. **Work/family studies:** Child development.

Most popular majors. Business/marketing 7%, computer/information sciences 13%, engineering/engineering technologies 20%, health sciences 28%, trade and industry 16%.

Computing on campus. 150 workstations in library, computer center, student center. Commuter students can connect to campus network. Online course registration, online library, wireless network available.

Student life. Freshman orientation: Mandatory. Preregistration for classes offered. A week before school starts. **Activities:** Student government.

Student services. Career counseling, student employment services, financial aid counseling, personal counseling, placement for graduates, veterans' counselor. **Physically disabled:** Services for visually, speech, hearing impaired. **Transfer:** Pre-admission transcript evaluation for new students. Transfer adviser, college fairs on campus for students transferring to 4-year colleges.

Contact. E-mail: info@hennepintech.edu
Phone: (763) 488-2500 Toll-free number: (800) 345-4655
Fax: (763) 488-2944
Monir Johnson, Director of Admissions, Hennepin Technical College, 9000 Brooklyn Boulevard, Brooklyn Park, MN 55455

Herzing University: Minneapolis
Minneapolis, Minnesota
www.herzing.edu

♦ For-profit 2-year technical college
♦ Large city

General. Regionally accredited. **Enrollment:** 375 degree-seeking undergraduates. **Degrees:** 11 bachelor's, 70 associate awarded. **Calendar:** Semester. **Full-time faculty:** 22 total. **Part-time faculty:** 34 total.

Basis for selection. Open admission, but selective for some programs. Admissions decisions based on applicant's interest, professional attitude, and performance on standardized tests. Applicants who don't submit SAT or ACT scores must complete an entrance examination for admission.

2011-2012 Annual costs. Tuition/fees: $13,800. Per-credit charge: $460. Reported annual tuition is representative. Actual costs vary by program with nursing programs somewhat more expensive.

Financial aid. Need-based: Work-study available nights, weekends and for part-time students.

Application procedures. Admission: No deadline. No application fee. Admission notification on a rolling basis. **Financial aid:** No deadline.

Academics. Credit/placement by examination: AP, CLEP.

Majors. Business: Accounting, business admin. **Computer sciences:** System admin. **Health services:** Dental assistant, dental hygiene, insurance coding, medical assistant, occupational therapy assistant, office admin, surgical technology.

Contact. E-mail: info@mpls.herzing.edu
Phone: (763) 535-3000
Shelly Larson, Director of Admissions, Herzing University: Minneapolis, 5700 West Broadway, Minneapolis, MN 55428

Hibbing Community College
Hibbing, Minnesota
www.hibbing.edu   CB code: 6275

♦ Public 2-year community and technical college
♦ Commuter campus in large town

General. Founded in 1916. Regionally accredited. **Enrollment:** 1,598 degree-seeking undergraduates. **Degrees:** 231 associate awarded. **Location:** 75 miles from Duluth. **Calendar:** Semester, limited summer session. **Full-time faculty:** 113 total. **Part-time faculty:** 60 total.

Student profile.

Out-of-state:	13%	Live on campus:	10%
25 or older:	40%		

Transfer out. Colleges most students transferred to 2011: Bemidji State University, University of Minnesota: Duluth, College of St. Scholastica, University of Wisconsin-Superior.

Basis for selection. Open admission, but selective for some programs. Academic placement test required. Special requirements for nursing, dental assistant and law enforcement programs. **Home schooled:** Transcript of courses and grades required.

2011-2012 Annual costs. Tuition/fees: $5,111; $6,248 out-of-state. Per-credit charge: $152 in-state; $189 out-of-state. Room only: $3,000. Books/supplies: $900.

Financial aid. Need-based: Work-study available nights, weekends and for part-time students.

Application procedures. Admission: Priority date 4/15; no deadline. $20 fee, may be waived for applicants with need. Admission notification on a rolling basis. **Financial aid:** Priority date 7/1; no closing date. FAFSA required. Applicants notified on a rolling basis starting 6/30; must reply within 2 week(s) of notification.

Academics. Special study options: Cooperative education, cross-registration, distance learning, dual enrollment of high school students, honors, independent study, internships, liberal arts/career combination, study abroad. Bachelor's degree programs available on campus. License preparation in aviation, nursing. **Credit/placement by examination:** AP, CLEP, institutional tests. 12 credit hours maximum toward associate degree. **Support services:** Learning center, pre-admission summer program, reduced course load, remedial instruction, study skills assistance, tutoring.

Majors. Business: Administrative services, business admin, office/clerical. **Computer sciences:** General, security. **Education:** General. **Engineering:** General. **English:** English lit. **Health services:** Clinical lab technology, dental assistant, medical secretary, nursing (RN). **Liberal arts:** Arts/sciences. **Protective services:** Police science.

Computing on campus. 100 workstations in dormitories, library, computer center. Dormitories wired for high-speed internet access. Commuter students can connect to campus network. Online course registration, online library, wireless network available.

Student life. Freshman orientation: Available. Preregistration for classes offered. Registration orientation held throughout summer; all-student orientation held before fall & spring classes begin. **Housing:** Apartments available. $250 fully refundable deposit. **Activities:** Choral groups, student government, Phi Theta Kappa.

Athletics. NJCAA. **Intercollegiate:** Baseball M, basketball, golf, softball W, volleyball W. **Intramural:** Basketball, bowling, volleyball. **Team name:** Cardinals.

Student services. Adult student services, career counseling, services for economically disadvantaged, student employment services, financial aid counseling, personal counseling, placement for graduates, veterans' counselor. **Physically disabled:** Services for visually, speech, hearing impaired. **Transfer:** Transfer adviser, college fairs on campus for students transferring to 4-year colleges.

Contact. E-mail: admissions@hibbing.edu
Phone: (218) 262-7207 Toll-free number: (800) 224-4422
Fax: (218) 263-2992
Sarah Merhar, Admissions Representative, Hibbing Community College, 1515 East 25th Street, Hibbing, MN 55746

Institute of Production and Recording
Minneapolis, Minnesota
www.ipr.edu   CB code: 6461

▶ For-profit 2-year career college
▶ Commuter campus in large city
▶ Interview required

General. Regionally accredited; also accredited by ACCSC. **Enrollment:** 432 degree-seeking undergraduates; 24 non-degree-seeking students. **Degrees:** 191 associate awarded. **Calendar:** Quarter. **Full-time faculty:** 17 total. **Part-time faculty:** 28 total; 7% have terminal degrees.

Student profile. Among degree-seeking undergraduates, 127 enrolled as first-time, first-year students.

Part-time:	10%	Asian American:	2%
Out-of-state:	8%	Hispanic American:	5%
Women:	12%	Native American:	1%
African American:	8%		

Basis for selection. Completion of our Dynamic Needs Assessment survey required. ACCUPLACER required of all applicants unless documentation of a minimum ACT composite score of 21 or documentation of a minimum composite score of 1485 on the SAT is presented.

Financial aid. Need-based: Work-study available nights, weekends and for part-time students.

Application procedures. Admission: No deadline. $50 fee. Admission notification on a rolling basis.

Academics. Special study options: Internships. Academic remediation, summer session for credit. **Credit/placement by examination:** AP, CLEP. **Support services:** Remedial instruction, study skills assistance, tutoring, writing center.

Majors. Communications technology: Recording arts. **Visual/performing arts:** Music management.

Most popular majors. Communication technologies 85%, visual/performing arts 15%.

Computing on campus. 119 workstations in library, computer center, student center. Online library, helpline, wireless network available.

Student life. Freshman orientation: Mandatory. Preregistration for classes offered.

Student services. Financial aid counseling, placement for graduates.

Contact. E-mail: sferkingstad@ipr.edu
Phone: (612) 375-1900 Toll-free number: (866) 477-4840
Sue Ferkingstad, Director of Admissions, Institute of Production and Recording, 312 Washington Avenue North, Minneapolis, MN 55401

Inver Hills Community College
Inver Grove Heights, Minnesota   CB member
www.inverhills.edu   CB code: 6300

▶ Public 2-year community college
▶ Commuter campus in large town

General. Founded in 1967. Regionally accredited. **Enrollment:** 4,943 degree-seeking undergraduates; 1,120 non-degree-seeking students. **Degrees:** 699 associate awarded. **ROTC:** Army, Air Force. **Location:** 6 miles from Minneapolis-St. Paul. **Calendar:** Semester, limited summer session. **Full-time faculty:** 111 total. **Part-time faculty:** 122 total. **Class size:** 27% < 20, 69% 20-39, 4% 40-49, less than 1% 50-99.

Student profile. Among degree-seeking undergraduates, 729 enrolled as first-time, first-year students, 539 transferred in from other institutions.

Part-time:	59%	Asian American:	6%
Out-of-state:	2%	Hispanic American:	5%
Women:	59%	Native American:	1%
African American:	12%	25 or older:	43%

Transfer out. Colleges most students transferred to 2011: University of Minnesota, Metro State University, St. Thomas/St. Catherine's University, University of Wisconsin-River Falls, Minnesota State University-Mankato.

Basis for selection. Open admission, but selective for some programs. Special requirements for nursing and emergency medical service programs, computer and networking technology, and international students. **Adult students:** SAT/ACT scores not required. **Home schooled:** Transcript of courses and grades, state high school equivalency certificate required.

2012-2013 Annual costs. Tuition/fees (projected): $5,542; $6,322 out-of-state. Per-credit charge: $168 in-state; $194 out-of-state. Books/supplies: $1,500.

2010-2011 Financial aid. All financial aid based on need. 96% of total undergraduate aid awarded as scholarships/grants, 4% as loans/jobs. Need-based aid available for part-time students. Work-study available nights, weekends and for part-time students.

Application procedures. Admission: Priority date 8/1; no deadline. $20 fee, may be waived for applicants with need. Admission notification on a rolling basis. **Financial aid:** No deadline. FAFSA required. Applicants notified on a rolling basis starting 4/1.

Academics. Special study options: Accelerated study, distance learning, double major, dual enrollment of high school students, ESL, honors, independent study, internships, liberal arts/career combination, student-designed major, study abroad. License preparation in nursing, paramedic. **Credit/placement by examination:** AP, CLEP, IB, institutional tests. 40 credit hours maximum toward associate degree. Accept ACE, DSST, CLEP, TCEP, Excelsior Exams, NYUFLP, NOCTI, AP, and other forms of credits earned through non-formal learning. **Support services:** GED test center, learning center, pre-admission summer program, reduced course load, remedial instruction, study skills assistance, tutoring, writing center.

Majors. Biology: General. **Business:** General, accounting, construction management. **Computer sciences:** Computer science, networking, programming, support specialist. **Education:** General, physical. **Engineering:** Pre-engineering. **Health services:** EMT paramedic, nursing (RN). **Liberal arts:** Arts/sciences. **Parks/recreation:** Exercise sciences. **Physical sciences:** Chemistry. **Protective services:** Criminal justice, police science. **Visual/performing arts:** Studio arts.

Most popular majors. Security/protective services 7%.

Computing on campus. 85 workstations in library, computer center, student center. Commuter students can connect to campus network. Online course registration, online library, helpline, wireless network available.

Student life. Freshman orientation: Mandatory. Preregistration for classes offered. Orientation is held prior to start of the semester. Online orientation also available. **Activities:** Campus ministries, choral groups, dance, drama, international student organizations, music ensembles, musical theater, student government, Asian Diversity club, Black Student Union, Ethiopian student association, international student club, Muslim student association, Native American club, Somali student club, Spanish club, Volunteering Individuals Bring Empowerment (VIBE), Student Organization for Leadership (SOLD).

Athletics. Intramural: Bowling, football (non-tackle), golf, ice hockey, softball, table tennis, volleyball.

Student services. Adult student services, career counseling, services for economically disadvantaged, student employment services, financial aid counseling, health services, minority student services, personal counseling, placement for graduates, veterans' counselor. **Physically disabled:** Services for visually, speech, hearing impaired. **Transfer:** Pre-admission transcript evaluation for new students. Transfer adviser, college fairs on campus for students transferring to 4-year colleges.

Contact. E-mail: iseekinfo@inverhills.edu
Phone: (651) 450-3503 Fax: (651) 450-3677
Matt Traxler, Director of Enrollment Services, Inver Hills Community College, 2500 80th Street East, Inver Grove Heights, MN 55076-3224

Itasca Community College
Grand Rapids, Minnesota
www.itascacc.edu   CB code: 6309

- Public 2-year junior and liberal arts college
- Commuter campus in large town

General. Founded in 1922. Regionally accredited. **Enrollment:** 1,296 undergraduates. **Degrees:** 275 associate awarded. **Location:** 80 miles from Duluth, 180 miles from Minneapolis-St. Paul. **Calendar:** Semester, limited summer session. **Full-time faculty:** 41 total; 5% have terminal degrees, 5% minority, 44% women. **Part-time faculty:** 46 total; 48% women. **Special facilities:** Educational wetland habitat, University of Minnesota agricultural station, U.S. Forest Service shared campus, 500-acre experimental forest. **Partnerships:** Formal partnerships with local businesses for training, partnership council with area high schools.

Student profile.

Out-of-state:	7%	Live on campus:	9%
25 or older:	28%		

Transfer out. Colleges most students transferred to 2011: Bemidji State University, College of St. Scholastica, University of Minnesota: Duluth, St. Cloud State University, University of North Dakota.

Basis for selection. Open admission, but selective for some programs. College-level reading and English testing required for class act teacher education program. **Adult students:** SAT/ACT scores not required.

High school preparation. College-preparatory program recommended. 12 units recommended. Recommended units include English 4, mathematics 2, social studies 2, science 2 and foreign language 2. Computer skills recommended.

2012-2013 Annual costs. Tuition/fees (projected): $5,310; $6,422 out-of-state. Per-credit charge: $158 in-state; $195 out-of-state. Room/board: $6,214. Books/supplies: $700. Personal expenses: $1,962.

2010-2011 Financial aid. Need-based: 62% of total undergraduate aid awarded as scholarships/grants, 38% as loans/jobs. Need-based aid available for part-time students. Work-study available nights, weekends and for part-time students. **Non-need-based:** Scholarships awarded for academics, leadership, music/drama, state residency.

Application procedures. Admission: Priority date 8/1; deadline 8/28 (postmark date). $20 fee, may be waived for applicants with need. Admission notification on a rolling basis. **Financial aid:** Priority date 5/1; no closing date. FAFSA required. Applicants notified on a rolling basis starting 4/20.

Academics. Special study options: Cooperative education, dual enrollment of high school students, independent study, internships, liberal arts/career combination, study abroad. Bachelor's degree programs available on campus. License preparation in nursing, real estate. **Credit/placement by examination:** AP, CLEP, IB, institutional tests. 10 credit hours maximum toward associate degree. **Support services:** GED test center, learning center, pre-admission summer program, reduced course load, remedial instruction, study skills assistance, tutoring.

Majors. Area/ethnic studies: Native American. **Business:** Accounting, business admin. **Communications:** Media studies. **Conservation:** General, forestry. **Education:** General, early childhood. **Engineering:** General. **Health services:** Prenursing. **Human services:** Social work. **Liberal arts:** Arts/sciences. **Psychology:** General. **Social sciences:** Geography.

Computing on campus. 275 workstations in dormitories, library, computer center, student center. Dormitories wired for high-speed internet access and linked to campus network. Commuter students can connect to campus network. Online course registration, online library, wireless network available.

Student life. Freshman orientation: Available. Preregistration for classes offered. Held day before classes begin. **Housing:** Coed dorms available. $200 nonrefundable deposit, deadline 6/30. Apartment complex adjacent to campus housing available for ICC students. It is not owned by the campus. **Activities:** Literary magazine, student government, Circle-K, business club, Student Ambassadors, Global Ed, engineering club, psychology club, leadership club, natural resources club, GSA, minority student club.

Athletics. NJCAA. Intercollegiate: Baseball M, basketball, football (tackle) M, softball W, volleyball W, wrestling M. **Intramural:** Basketball M, bowling, football (non-tackle), soccer, softball, table tennis, volleyball. **Team name:** Vikings.

Student services. Adult student services, career counseling, student employment services, financial aid counseling, minority student services, personal counseling. **Physically disabled:** Services for visually, speech, hearing impaired. **Transfer:** Transfer adviser for students transferring to 4-year colleges.

Contact. E-mail: info@itascacc.edu
Phone: (218) 322-2340 Toll-free number: (800) 996-6422
Fax: (218) 322-2332
Candace Perry, Director of Enrollment Services, Itasca Community College, 1851 Highway 169 East, Grand Rapids, MN 55744

ITT Technical Institute: Eden Prairie
Eden Prairie, Minnesota
www.itt-tech.edu/campus/school.cfm?lloc_num=27

- For-profit 2-year technical college
- Commuter campus in small city

General. Accredited by ACICS. **Enrollment:** 704 undergraduates. **Degrees:** 50 bachelor's, 168 associate awarded. **Calendar:** Quarter. **Full-time faculty:** 10 total. **Part-time faculty:** 66 total.

Basis for selection. To be admitted into a program of study offered by ITT Technical Institute, an individual must satisfy all of the admission requirements applicable to that program of study.

2011-2012 Annual costs. Estimated costs as of July 2011: per-credit-hour charge, $493, depending upon level and course of study; academic fee, $200. Certain programs of study require purchase of tools, which could cost an additional $100 to $500. All costs are subject to change.

Financial aid. Need-based: Work-study available nights, weekends and for part-time students.

Application procedures. Admission: No application fee.

Academics. Credit/placement by examination: AP, CLEP. **Support services:** Remedial instruction.

Majors. Business: General. **Computer sciences:** LAN/WAN management, networking, programming, web page design. **Protective services:** Criminalistics, law enforcement admin. **Visual/performing arts:** Design, graphic design.

Most popular majors. Computer/information sciences 66%, engineering/engineering technologies 34%.

Student services. Career counseling, student employment services, placement for graduates.

Contact. Phone: (952) 914-5300 Toll-free number: (888) 488-9646
ITT Technical Institute: Eden Prairie, 8911 Columbine Road, Eden Prairie, MN 55347

Lake Superior College
Duluth, Minnesota
www.lsc.edu   CB code: 6352

- Public 2-year community and technical college
- Commuter campus in small city

General. Regionally accredited. **Enrollment:** 3,859 degree-seeking undergraduates; 590 non-degree-seeking students. **Degrees:** 714 associate awarded. **Location:** 150 miles from Minneapolis-St. Paul. **Calendar:** Semester, limited summer session. **Full-time faculty:** 94 total; 5% have terminal degrees, 7% minority, 56% women. **Part-time faculty:** 127 total; 10% have terminal degrees, 5% minority, 56% women. **Class size:** 53% < 20, 46% 20-39, 1% 40-49. **Special facilities:** 100 acre wooded site, interpretative hiking and snowshoe trails, trout stream, access to city-run golf course.

Student profile. Among degree-seeking undergraduates, 39% enrolled in a transfer program, 61% enrolled in a vocational program, 690 enrolled as first-time, first-year students, 823 transferred in from other institutions.

Part-time:	43%	Asian American:	1%
Out-of-state:	14%	Hispanic American:	1%
Women:	57%	Native American:	3%
African American:	4%	25 or older:	42%

Basis for selection. Open admission, but selective for some programs. Many health programs have special requirements including coursework and GPA. After admission, the ACCUPLACER computerized placement test is required for all students unless transcript shows completion of college-level math and English composition. **Home schooled:** Ability to Benefit test required for Wisconsin home schooled applicants.

High school preparation. College-preparatory program recommended.

2011-2012 Annual costs. Tuition/fees: $4,872; $9,119 out-of-state. Per-credit charge: $142 in-state; $283 out-of-state. Books/supplies: $1,500. Personal expenses: $4,346.

Financial aid. Need-based: Need-based aid available for part-time students. Work-study available nights, weekends and for part-time students. **Non-need-based:** Scholarships awarded for academics, leadership.

Application procedures. Admission: No deadline. $20 fee, may be waived for applicants with need. Admission notification on a rolling basis. **Financial aid:** Priority date 5/1; no closing date. FAFSA required. Applicants notified on a rolling basis starting 5/1.

Academics. Special study options: Accelerated study, distance learning, double major, dual enrollment of high school students, independent study, internships, liberal arts/career combination, study abroad. License preparation in aviation, dental hygiene, nursing, paramedic, physical therapy, radiology, real estate. **Credit/placement by examination:** AP, CLEP, institutional tests. 30 credit hours maximum toward associate degree. **Support services:** Learning center, reduced course load, remedial instruction, study skills assistance, tutoring, writing center.

Majors. Business: Accounting, business admin, management information systems, office management, office technology. **Computer sciences:** System admin, web page design. **Health services:** Clinical lab technology, dental hygiene, medical secretary, nursing (RN), physical therapy assistant, radiologic technology/medical imaging, respiratory therapy technology, sonography, surgical technology. **Liberal arts:** Arts/sciences. **Protective services:** Fire safety technology. **Visual/performing arts:** Studio arts.

Computing on campus. 514 workstations in library, computer center, student center. Commuter students can connect to campus network. Online course registration, online library, helpline, repair service, student web hosting, wireless network available.

Student life. Freshman orientation: Available. Preregistration for classes offered. Half day each semester prior to start of term. **Policies:** Students have a role in the allocation of student activity fees. Students are involved in the College's decision making processes through shared governance. **Activities:** Choral groups, student government, Intervarsity Christian Fellowship, Phi Theta Kappa, Teachers of Tomorrow, United Multicultural Group, art club, skills, nursing, dental hygiene club, radiology club.

Athletics. Intramural: Baseball, basketball, bowling, ice hockey, skiing, softball, volleyball. **Team name:** Huskies.

Student services. Adult student services, alcohol/substance abuse counseling, career counseling, services for economically disadvantaged, student employment services, financial aid counseling, health services, minority student services, on-campus daycare, personal counseling, placement for graduates, veterans' counselor. **Physically disabled:** Services for visually, speech, hearing impaired. **Transfer:** Pre-admission transcript evaluation for new

students. Transfer center, transfer adviser, college fairs on campus for students transferring to 4-year colleges.

Contact. E-mail: enroll@lsc.edu
Phone: (218) 733-7601 Toll-free number: (800) 432-2884
Fax: (218) 733-5945
Melissa Leno, Director of Admissions, Lake Superior College, 2101 Trinity Road, Duluth, MN 55811

Le Cordon Bleu College of Culinary Arts: Minneapolis-St. Paul
Mendota Heights, Minnesota
www.chefs.edu/Minneapolis-St-Paul

- For-profit 2-year culinary school and career college
- Commuter campus in very large city
- Interview required

General. Accredited by ACCSC. **Enrollment:** 750 degree-seeking undergraduates. **Degrees:** 225 associate awarded. **Location:** 12 miles from Minneapolis-St. Paul. **Calendar:** Quarter, extensive summer session. **Full-time faculty:** 28 total. **Part-time faculty:** 4 total.

Basis for selection. Open admission. **Home schooled:** Statement describing home school structure and mission, transcript of courses and grades, interview required. **Learning Disabled:** Current IEP.

High school preparation. College-preparatory program recommended. Recommended units include English 3, mathematics 2, social studies 1, history 1 and science 1.

2011-2012 Annual costs. Tuition and fees for both culinary and patisserie programs: $10,800.

Financial aid. Need-based: Work-study available nights, weekends and for part-time students. **Non-need-based:** Scholarships awarded for academics, job skills, leadership.

Application procedures. Admission: No deadline. $50 fee, may be waived for applicants with need. Admission notification on a rolling basis. **Financial aid:** No deadline.

Academics. Special study options: Internships. **Credit/placement by examination:** AP, CLEP. **Support services:** Remedial instruction, study skills assistance, tutoring.

Computing on campus. 40 workstations in library, computer center. Online library, wireless network available.

Student life. Freshman orientation: Mandatory. Preregistration for classes offered. Several options for orientation including the Saturday prior to beginning of classes. **Activities:** Student government.

Student services. Adult student services, alcohol/substance abuse counseling, career counseling, student employment services, financial aid counseling, legal services, personal counseling, placement for graduates, veterans' counselor. **Transfer:** Re-entry adviser, pre-admission transcript evaluation for new students.

Contact. E-mail: info@msp.chefs.edu
Phone: (651) 675-4700 Toll-free number: (800) 931-6855
Fax: (651) 452-5282
David Peterson, Director of Admissions, Le Cordon Bleu College of Culinary Arts: Minneapolis-St. Paul, 1315 Mendota Heights Road, Mendota Heights, MN 55120

Leech Lake Tribal College
Cass Lake, Minnesota
www.lltc.edu   CB code: 3931

- Public 2-year Tribal College grounded in Anishinaabe values.
- Commuter campus in small town

General. Regionally accredited. Chartered by the Leech Lake Band of Ojibwe. **Enrollment:** 192 degree-seeking undergraduates; 14 non-degree-seeking students. **Degrees:** 23 associate awarded. **Location:** 15 miles from Bemidji. **Calendar:** Semester, limited summer session. **Full-time faculty:** 12 total; 33% minority, 33% women. **Part-time faculty:** 9 total; 44% minority, 44% women. **Class size:** 100% < 20.

Student profile. Among degree-seeking undergraduates, 44 enrolled as first-time, first-year students, 13 transferred in from other institutions.

Part-time:	7%	Native American:	88%
Women:	58%	25 or older:	62%
Asian American:	1%		

Transfer out. Colleges most students transferred to 2011: Bemidji State Universtiy.

Basis for selection. Open admission. **Home schooled:** Documentation of high school classes required.

2012-2013 Annual costs. Tuition/fees: $4,432; $4,432 out-of-state. Per-credit charge: $140. Books/supplies: $600. Personal expenses: $2,000.

Financial aid. Need-based: Need-based aid available for part-time students. Work-study available nights, weekends and for part-time students.

Application procedures. Admission: Closing date 8/13 (postmark date). $15 fee. Application must be submitted on paper. Admission notification on a rolling basis. **Financial aid:** No deadline. FAFSA, institutional form required. Applicants notified on a rolling basis; must reply within 4 week(s) of notification.

Academics. Special study options: Cooperative education, double major, independent study, internships, liberal arts/career combination, teacher certification program. **Credit/placement by examination:** AP, CLEP, institutional tests. **Support services:** GED test center, learning center, reduced course load, remedial instruction, study skills assistance, tutoring.

Majors. Area/ethnic studies: Native American. **Business:** Business admin. **Education:** Early childhood. **Health services:** Clinical nutrition. **Liberal arts:** Arts/sciences. **Protective services:** Police science.

Most popular majors. Liberal arts 65%, physical sciences 22%.

Computing on campus. 31 workstations in library, computer center, student center.

Student life. Freshman orientation: Available. Preregistration for classes offered. **Activities:** Choral groups, student government.

Student services. Adult student services, financial aid counseling, personal counseling. **Transfer:** Transfer adviser for students transferring to 4-year colleges.

Contact. Phone: (218) 335-4222 Fax: (218) 335-4217
Mandy Schram, Registrar, Leech Lake Tribal College, PO Box 180, Cass Lake, MN 56633

Mesabi Range Community and Technical College
Virginia, Minnesota
www.mesabirange.edu   CB code: 6432

▶ Public 2-year community and technical college
▶ Commuter campus in large town

General. Founded in 1918. Regionally accredited. Career/technical programs offered at Eveleth campus. **Enrollment:** 1,689 undergraduates. **Degrees:** 187 associate awarded. **Location:** 60 miles from Duluth. **Calendar:** Semester, limited summer session. **Full-time faculty:** 47 total; 15% minority. **Part-time faculty:** 42 total. **Special facilities:** Iron Range Engineering.

Student profile.

Out-of-state:	9%	Live on campus:	8%
25 or older:	26%		

Transfer out. Colleges most students transferred to 2011: University of Minnesota-Duluth, Bemidji State University, St. Cloud State University, Mankato State University, University of Minnesota-Minneapolis.

Basis for selection. Open admission.

2011-2012 Annual costs. Tuition/fees: $5,111; $6,248 out-of-state. Per-credit charge: $152 in-state; $189 out-of-state. Books/supplies: $1,000. Personal expenses: $1,000.

Financial aid. Need-based: Need-based aid available for part-time students. Work-study available nights, weekends and for part-time students. **Non-need-based:** Scholarships awarded for state residency.

Application procedures. Admission: No deadline. $20 fee, may be waived for applicants with need. Admission notification on a rolling basis beginning on or about 1/1. **Financial aid:** Priority date 4/22; no closing date. FAFSA, institutional form required. Applicants notified on a rolling basis starting 5/1; must reply within 2 week(s) of notification.

Academics. Special study options: Dual enrollment of high school students, independent study, internships, liberal arts/career combination, study abroad. Bachelor's degree programs available on campus. License preparation in nursing, paramedic. **Credit/placement by examination:** AP, CLEP, institutional tests. **Support services:** Learning center, reduced course load, remedial instruction, study skills assistance, tutoring.

Majors. Biology: General. **Business:** General, administrative services, marketing, office technology. **Communications technology:** Graphic/printing. **Computer sciences:** General, programming, systems analysis. **Education:** General, teacher assistance. **Engineering:** Computer. **Health services:** Substance abuse counseling. **Liberal arts:** Arts/sciences. **Parks/recreation:** Exercise sciences.

Computing on campus. Dormitories linked to campus network. Online course registration, helpline, wireless network available.

Student life. Freshman orientation: Mandatory. Preregistration for classes offered. **Housing:** Apartments available. $300 fully refundable deposit, deadline 9/1. **Activities:** Bands, choral groups, dance, drama, literary magazine, music ensembles, musical theater, student government, student newspaper, symphony orchestra.

Athletics. NJCAA. **Intercollegiate:** Baseball M, basketball, football (tackle) M, softball W, volleyball W. **Intramural:** Badminton, basketball, bowling, field hockey W, ice hockey, racquetball, softball, table tennis, volleyball. **Team name:** Norseman.

Student services. Career counseling, student employment services, minority student services, on-campus daycare, personal counseling, placement for graduates. **Physically disabled:** Services for visually, hearing impaired. **Transfer:** Pre-admission transcript evaluation for new students.

Contact. E-mail: s.twaddle@mr.mnscu.edu
Phone: (218) 749-0315 Fax: (218) 749-0318
Brenda Kochevar, Director of Enrollment Services, Mesabi Range Community and Technical College, 1001 Chestnut Street West, Virginia, MN 55792-3448

Minneapolis Business College
Roseville, Minnesota
www.minneapolisbusinesscollege.edu   CB code: 7126

▶ For-profit 2-year business and technical college
▶ Residential campus in very large city

General. Founded in 1874. Accredited by ACICS. **Enrollment:** 386 degree-seeking undergraduates. **Degrees:** 191 associate awarded. **Location:** 10 miles from Minneapolis-St. Paul. **Calendar:** Semester, limited summer session. **Full-time faculty:** 8 total. **Part-time faculty:** 8 total.

Student profile.

Out-of-state:	20%	Live on campus:	12%

Basis for selection. Open admission. Interview recommended.

2011-2012 Annual costs. Tuition/fees: $14,040. Room only: $6,780. Books/supplies: $1,000.

Financial aid. Need-based: Work-study available nights, weekends and for part-time students. **Additional information:** Individual financial planning available for all students to meet the cost of education.

Application procedures. Admission: No deadline. $50 fee. Admission notification on a rolling basis beginning on or about 7/1. **Financial aid:** No deadline. Applicants notified on a rolling basis.

Academics. Externships related to career available. 14-month associate of applied science degree options. **Credit/placement by examination:** AP, CLEP.

Majors. Business: Accounting, administrative services, hospitality admin, management information systems, office management, tourism/travel. **Computer sciences:** Applications programming. **Health services:** Medical assistant. **Visual/performing arts:** Commercial/advertising art.

Student life. Freshman orientation: Mandatory. Preregistration for classes offered. **Housing:** Single-sex dorms available. $100 partly refundable deposit. **Activities:** Student government, student newspaper.

Student services. Career counseling, placement for graduates.

Contact. Phone: (651) 636-7406 Toll-free number: (800) 279-5200 Fax: (651) 636-8185
Lisa Stuart, Admissions Supervisor, Minneapolis Business College, 1711 West County Road B, Roseville, MN 55113

Minneapolis Community and Technical College
Minneapolis, Minnesota
www.minneapolis.edu   **CB code: 6434**

▶ Public 2-year community and technical college
▶ Commuter campus in large city

General. Founded in 1965. Regionally accredited. **Enrollment:** 9,558 degree-seeking undergraduates; 433 non-degree-seeking students. **Degrees:** 841 associate awarded. **Location:** Downtown. **Calendar:** Semester, limited summer session. **Full-time faculty:** 158 total. **Part-time faculty:** 319 total. **Class size:** 47% < 20, 43% 20-39, 7% 40-49, 4% 50-99.

Student profile. Among degree-seeking undergraduates, 64% enrolled in a vocational program, 1,548 enrolled as first-time, first-year students, 1,236 transferred in from other institutions.

Part-time:	61%	**Hispanic American:**	8%
Women:	53%	**Native American:**	2%
African American:	32%	**International:**	2%
Asian American:	5%		

Basis for selection. Open admission, but selective for some programs. Admission to the college does not guarantee admission to a career program/major. Some programs have additional requirements for admission.

2011-2012 Annual costs. Tuition/fees: $5,192; $5,192 out-of-state. Per-credit charge: $151. Books/supplies: $1,200. Personal expenses: $3,150.

2010-2011 Financial aid. All financial aid based on need. 40% of total undergraduate aid awarded as scholarships/grants, 60% as loans/jobs. Need-based aid available for part-time students. Work-study available nights, weekends and for part-time students.

Application procedures. Admission: No deadline. $20 fee, may be waived for applicants with need. Admission notification on a rolling basis. **Financial aid:** Priority date 5/1; no closing date. FAFSA required. Applicants notified on a rolling basis starting 7/1.

Academics. Special study options: Accelerated study, cross-registration, distance learning, dual enrollment of high school students, ESL, honors, independent study, internships, liberal arts/career combination, teacher certification program, weekend college. License preparation in dental hygiene, nursing. **Credit/placement by examination:** AP, CLEP, IB, institutional tests. **Support services:** Learning center, remedial instruction, study skills assistance, tutoring, writing center.

Majors. Biology: General, biotechnology. **Business:** Accounting technology, business admin, office technology, restaurant/food services. **Communications technology:** Animation/special effects, recording arts. **Computer sciences:** Programming, security, system admin, web page design. **Education:** General. **Health services:** Electroencephalograph technology, nursing (RN), polysomnography, substance abuse counseling. **Human services:** Community org/advocacy. **Liberal arts:** Arts/sciences, library assistant. **Math:** General. **Philosophy/religion:** Philosophy. **Physical sciences:** Chemistry. **Protective services:** Criminal justice, police science. **Visual/performing arts:** Cinematography, commercial photography, design, dramatic, play/screenwriting, studio arts. **Work/family studies:** Child development.

Most popular majors. Business/marketing 10%, health sciences 17%, liberal arts 27%, trade and industry 9%, visual/performing arts 10%.

Computing on campus. 279 workstations in library, computer center, student center. Online course registration, online library, helpline, repair service, wireless network available.

Student life. Freshman orientation: Mandatory. Preregistration for classes offered. **Activities:** Jazz band, choral groups, drama, film society, international student organizations, literary magazine, music ensembles, student government, student newspaper, Phi Theta Kappa Honor Society, Skills USA, Association of Black Collegiates, Student Nurses Association, United Nations of Indian Tribes for Education, Bicycle Collective, Chicanos Latinos Unidos, Three-Legged Frog Environmental Club.

Student services. Adult student services, career counseling, services for economically disadvantaged, student employment services, financial aid counseling, health services, legal services, minority student services, personal counseling, placement for graduates, veterans' counselor. **Physically disabled:** Services for visually, speech, hearing impaired. **Transfer:** Transfer adviser, college fairs on campus for students transferring to 4-year colleges.

Contact. E-mail: admissions.office@minneapolis.edu
Phone: (612) 659-6200 Toll-free number: (800) 247-0911
Fax: (612) 659-6210
Kerri Carlson, Director of Admissions, Minneapolis Community and Technical College, 1501 Hennepin Avenue, Minneapolis, MN 55403-1779

Minnesota School of Business: Brooklyn Center
Brooklyn Center, Minnesota
www.msbcollege.edu   **CB code: 3314**

▶ For-profit 2-year career college
▶ Commuter campus in large town
▶ Interview required

General. Accredited by ACICS. **Enrollment:** 442 degree-seeking undergraduates. **Degrees:** 47 bachelor's, 64 associate awarded. **Calendar:** Differs by program. **Full-time faculty:** 10 total. **Part-time faculty:** 35 total.

Basis for selection. Personal interview and assessment examination most important. SAT or ACT recommended. Applicants must submit ACT scores of 17 or above, SAT equivalent, or take an entrance exam. **Adult students:** SAT/ACT scores not required.

2011-2012 Annual costs. Tuition/fees: $19,575. Per-credit charge: $435. Books/supplies: $1,800.

Financial aid. All financial aid based on need. Need-based aid available for part-time students. Work-study available nights, weekends and for part-time students.

Application procedures. Admission: No deadline. $50 fee. Admission notification on a rolling basis. **Financial aid:** FAFSA required.

Academics. Special study options: Bachelor's degree programs available on campus. **Credit/placement by examination:** AP, CLEP. **Support services:** Tutoring.

Majors. Business: Business admin. **Visual/performing arts:** General.

Contact. Phone: (763) 566-7777 Toll-free number: (877) 655-7676
Kelly O'Brien, Director of Admissions, Minnesota School of Business: Brooklyn Center, 5910 Shingle Creek Parkway, Brooklyn Center, MN 55430

Minnesota State College - Southeast Technical
Winona, Minnesota
www.southeastmn.edu/index.aspx   **CB code: 7123**

▶ Public 2-year technical college
▶ Commuter campus in large town

General. Founded in 1949. Regionally accredited. Unique programs include: musical string instrument repair, band instrument repair, mobile electronics installation. **Enrollment:** 2,177 degree-seeking undergraduates; 60 non-degree-seeking students. **Degrees:** 278 associate awarded. **Location:** 55 miles from Rochester. **Calendar:** Semester, limited summer session. **Full-time faculty:** 67 total; 3% minority, 55% women. **Part-time faculty:** 116 total; 2% minority, 55% women. **Class size:** 65% < 20, 33% 20-39, 2% 40-49, less than 1% 50-99.

Student profile. Among degree-seeking undergraduates, 612 enrolled as first-time, first-year students, 1,091 transferred in from other institutions.

Part-time:	38%	**Asian American:**	2%
Out-of-state:	27%	**Hispanic American:**	1%
Women:	61%	**Native American:**	1%
African American:	4%	**25 or older:**	47%

Transfer out. Colleges most students transferred to 2011: Rochester Community and Technical College, Winona State University, Metropolitan State University.

Basis for selection. Open admission, but selective for some programs. Nursing, radiography, and truck driving have requirements for admission to program. **Home schooled:** Transcript of courses and grades required. **Learning Disabled:** Disability documentation required to receive accommodations.

High school preparation. College-preparatory program recommended. 7 units recommended. Recommended units include English 4, mathematics 2 and science 1.

2011-2012 Annual costs. Tuition/fees: $5,133; $5,133 out-of-state. Per-credit charge: $161. Books/supplies: $900. Personal expenses: $3,654.

Financial aid. Need-based: Need-based aid available for part-time students. Work-study available nights, weekends and for part-time students. **Non-need-based:** Scholarships awarded for academics, leadership.

Application procedures. Admission: No deadline. $20 fee, may be waived for applicants with need. Admission notification on a rolling basis. **Financial aid:** Priority date 5/15, closing date 6/30. FAFSA, institutional form required. Applicants notified on a rolling basis; must reply within 3 week(s) of notification.

Academics. Special study options: Distance learning, double major, dual enrollment of high school students, internships, liberal arts/career combination. **Credit/placement by examination:** AP, CLEP, IB, institutional tests. **Support services:** Learning center, pre-admission summer program, remedial instruction, tutoring.

Majors. Business: Accounting, accounting technology, administrative services, business admin, retailing, sales/distribution, selling. **Computer sciences:** Networking, programming, web page design. **Education:** Early childhood. **Health services:** Massage therapy, medical secretary, nursing (RN), radiologic technology/medical imaging. **Protective services:** Criminal justice.

Most popular majors. Business/marketing 22%, computer/information sciences 10%, education 11%, health sciences 39%.

Computing on campus. 100 workstations in library. Online course registration, online library, wireless network available.

Student life. Freshman orientation: Mandatory. Preregistration for classes offered. **Housing:** Cooperative housing available. For Winona campus students, dormitories are available at Winona State University. For Red Wing campus students, a privately-owned dormitory near college is available. **Activities:** Student government, student newspaper, Student Senate, Business Professionals of America (BPA), Skills USA, Delta Epsilon Chi (DEX), Guild of American Luthiers, Association of Stringed Instrument Artisans, Violin Society of America, Musical Instrument Technicians Association (MITA), National Association of Professional Band Instrument Repair Technicians (NAPBIRT), Data Processing Management Association.

Student services. Adult student services, alcohol/substance abuse counseling, career counseling, services for economically disadvantaged, student employment services, financial aid counseling, health services, minority student services, personal counseling, placement for graduates, veterans' counselor. **Physically disabled:** Services for visually, speech, hearing impaired. **Transfer:** Re-entry adviser, pre-admission transcript evaluation for new students.

Contact. E-mail: enrollmentservices@southeastmn.edu
Phone: (507) 453-2700 Toll-free number: (877) 853-8324
Fax: (507) 453-2715
Gale Lanning, Director of Admissions, Minnesota State College - Southeast Technical, 1250 Homer Road, Winona, MN 55987-0409

Minnesota State Community and Technical College
Fergus Falls, Minnesota
www.minnesota.edu   CB code: 2110

- Public 2-year community and technical college
- Commuter campus in large town

General. Founded in 1960. Regionally accredited. Campuses in Detroit Lakes, Fergus Falls, Moorhead, and Wadena. Online programs available through E campus and we offer credit and non-credit courses through customized tranining/CTS and our Business Entrepreneur Center. **Enrollment:** 5,457 degree-seeking undergraduates; 1,145 non-degree-seeking students. **Degrees:** 1,080 associate awarded. **Location:** 180 miles from Minneapolis-St. Paul, 60 miles from Fargo, ND. **Calendar:** Semester, limited summer session. **Full-time faculty:** 181 total. **Part-time faculty:** 169 total. **Partnerships:** Formal partnerships with local high schools and local and national corporations.

Student profile. Among degree-seeking undergraduates, 1,052 enrolled as first-time, first-year students, 719 transferred in from other institutions.

Part-time:	39%	25 or older:	34%
Out-of-state:	30%	Live on campus:	4%
Women:	59%		

Transfer out. Colleges most students transferred to 2011: Minnesota State University: Moorhead, St. Cloud State University, Bemidji State University, Minnesota State University: Mankato, University of Minnesota: Twin Cities.

Basis for selection. Open admission. **Home schooled:** Transcript of courses and grades required. **Learning Disabled:** Special accommodations available for students during placement assessment tests.

2011-2012 Annual costs. Tuition/fees: $5,162; $5,162 out-of-state. Per-credit charge: $155. Room only: $2,850.

2010-2011 Financial aid. Need-based: 47% of total undergraduate aid awarded as scholarships/grants, 53% as loans/jobs. Need-based aid available for part-time students. Work-study available nights, weekends and for part-time students. **Non-need-based:** Scholarships awarded for academics, art, leadership, minority status, music/drama, state residency.

Application procedures. Admission: $20 fee, may be waived for applicants with need. Admission notification on a rolling basis. **Financial aid:** Priority date 6/1; no closing date. FAFSA required. Applicants notified on a rolling basis starting 7/1.

Academics. Special study options: Accelerated study, distance learning, double major, dual enrollment of high school students, ESL, honors, independent study, internships, liberal arts/career combination, study abroad. Bachelor's degree programs available on campus. License preparation in dental hygiene, nursing, radiology. **Credit/placement by examination:** AP, CLEP, IB, institutional tests. **Support services:** Learning center, pre-admission summer program, reduced course load, remedial instruction, study skills assistance, tutoring, writing center.

Majors. Biology: General. **Business:** General, accounting, administrative services, banking/financial services, business admin, entrepreneurial studies, fashion, human resources, office technology, sales/distribution, selling. **Computer sciences:** Information technology, networking, programming, security, web page design. **Conservation:** Environmental studies. **Education:** Teacher assistance. **General:** Products processing. **Health services:** Clinical lab technology, dental hygiene, licensed practical nurse, medical records technology, medical secretary, nursing (RN), pharmacy assistant, radiologic technology/medical imaging. **Liberal arts:** Arts/sciences. **Protective services:** Criminal justice. **Visual/performing arts:** Graphic design, music, studio arts.

Most popular majors. Business/marketing 25%, computer/information sciences 11%, engineering/engineering technologies 9%, health sciences 16%, trade and industry 14%.

Computing on campus. PC or laptop required. 600 workstations in library, computer center, student center. Dormitories wired for high-speed internet access and linked to campus network. Commuter students can connect to campus network. Online course registration, online library, helpline, repair service, wireless network available.

Student life. Freshman orientation: Mandatory. Preregistration for classes offered. 5-8 hour session held in summer. **Policies:** Alcoholic beverages prohibited in dorms. **Housing:** Coed dorms, apartments available. **Activities:** Bands, choral groups, drama, music ensembles, musical theater, student government, student newspaper, CACTUS (campus diversity organization), United for Africa, Phi Theta Kappa, Business Professionals of America, Ignite (Campus Crusade for Christ), Delta Epsilon Chi, nursing student organizations, Skills USA.

Athletics. NJCAA. **Intercollegiate:** Baseball M, basketball, football (tackle) M, golf, softball W, volleyball W. **Intramural:** Basketball, bowling, football (non-tackle), football (tackle) M, golf, soccer, softball, volleyball. **Team name:** Spartans.

Student services. Adult student services, alcohol/substance abuse counseling, career counseling, student employment services, financial aid counseling, minority student services, personal counseling, placement for graduates, veterans' counselor, women's services. **Physically disabled:** Services for visually, speech, hearing impaired. **Transfer:** Pre-admission transcript evaluation for new students. Transfer adviser, college fairs on campus for students transferring to 4-year colleges.

Contact. E-mail: enroll@minnesota.edu
Phone: (877) 450-3322 Toll-free number: (877) 450-3322
Fax: (218) 347-6236
Anthony Schaffhauser, Dean of Student Services and Enrollment, Minnesota State Community and Technical College, 150 2nd St. SW, Suite B, Perham, MN 56573

Minnesota West Community and Technical College
Pipestone, Minnesota
www.mnwest.edu
CB code: 6945

▶ Public 2-year community and technical college
▶ Commuter campus in large town

General. Founded in 1936. Regionally accredited. Campuses at Canby, Granite Falls, Jackson, Pipestone, and Worthington and learning centers in Fairmont, Luverne and Marshall, and Redwood Falls Minnesota. **Enrollment:** 2,250 degree-seeking undergraduates. **Degrees:** 364 associate awarded. **Location:** 200 miles from Minneapolis-St. Paul, 60 miles from Sioux Falls, South Dakota. **Calendar:** Semester, extensive summer session. **Full-time faculty:** 90 total. **Part-time faculty:** 120 total.

Transfer out. Colleges most students transferred to 2011: Southwest Minnesota State University, Minnesota State University - Mankato, South Dakota State University.

Basis for selection. Open admission, but selective for some programs. PSB-Aptitude for Practical Nursing Examination required of nursing applicants. Test scores not required for continuing education students. Interview recommended. **Home schooled:** Transcript of courses and grades required.

2011-2012 Annual costs. Tuition/fees: $5,422; $10,373 out-of-state. Per-credit charge: $165 in-state; $330 out-of-state. Books/supplies: $1,200. Personal expenses: $1,908.

Financial aid. Need-based: Need-based aid available for part-time students. Work-study available nights, weekends and for part-time students.

Application procedures. Admission: No deadline. $20 fee. Admission notification on a rolling basis. Priority deadline for practical nursing applicants is 2/15. **Financial aid:** Priority date 6/9; no closing date. FAFSA required. Applicants notified on a rolling basis starting 4/9; must reply within 2 week(s) of notification.

Academics. Special study options: Cooperative education, cross-registration, distance learning, double major, dual enrollment of high school students, independent study, internships, liberal arts/career combination, student-designed major. License preparation in nursing, radiology. **Credit/placement by examination:** AP, CLEP, IB, institutional tests. **Support services:** Learning center, pre-admission summer program, reduced course load, remedial instruction, study skills assistance, tutoring.

Majors. Biology: General. **Business:** General, accounting, accounting/business management, accounting/finance, administrative services, business admin, executive assistant, office management. **Communications:** Communications/speech/rhetoric, media studies. **Computer sciences:** General. **Education:** General, business, elementary, physical, secondary, special ed. **Engineering:** General. **English:** English lit. **General:** Agronomy, business, equipment technology, farm/ranch, plant sciences, production. **Health services:** Clinical lab technology, dental assistant, medical assistant, medical secretary, nursing (RN), predental, premedicine, prenursing, prepharmacy, preveterinary, radiologic technology/medical imaging. **History:** General. **Liberal arts:** Arts/sciences. **Math:** General. **Philosophy/religion:** Philosophy. **Physical sciences:** Chemistry, physics. **Protective services:** Corrections, law enforcement admin, police science. **Psychology:** General. **Social sciences:** Economics, geography, political science, sociology. **Visual/performing arts:** General, art, music. **Work/family studies:** Child care management.

Computing on campus. Online course registration, online library, helpline, wireless network available.

Student life. Freshman orientation: Mandatory. Preregistration for classes offered. Orientation is provided at each campus location and generally takes 3 hours to complete. Online orientation available for off-campus students. **Housing:** Subsidized apartments adjacent to campus. **Activities:** Jazz band, choral groups, drama, music ensembles, musical theater, student government, TV station, non-traditional student club, student senate, Phi Beta Kappa.

Athletics. NJCAA. **Intercollegiate:** Basketball, cheerleading, football (tackle) M, golf, softball W, volleyball W, wrestling M. **Team name:** Blue Jays.

Student services. Adult student services, career counseling, services for economically disadvantaged, student employment services, financial aid counseling, minority student services, veterans' counselor. **Physically disabled:** Services for visually, speech, hearing impaired. **Transfer:** Pre-admission transcript evaluation for new students. Transfer adviser, college fairs on campus for students transferring to 4-year colleges.

Contact. Phone: (800) 658-2330 Toll-free number: (800) 658-2330 Fax: (507) 825-4656
Dean of Admissions, Minnesota West Community and Technical College, 1314 North Hiawatha Avenue, Pipestone, MN 56164

Normandale Community College
Bloomington, Minnesota
www.normandale.edu
CB code: 6501

▶ Public 2-year community college
▶ Commuter campus in very large city

General. Founded in 1968. Regionally accredited. **Enrollment:** 9,871 degree-seeking undergraduates. **Degrees:** 1,082 associate awarded. **ROTC:** Army, Naval, Air Force. **Location:** 12 miles from Minneapolis-St. Paul. **Calendar:** Semester, extensive summer session. **Full-time faculty:** 193 total; 11% minority, 51% women. **Part-time faculty:** 165 total; 10% minority, 58% women. **Class size:** 31% < 20, 52% 20-39, 15% 40-49, 2% 50-99. **Special facilities:** Japanese garden, career and academic planning center, classroom technology, language and learning labs, exercise/workout facility.

Student profile. Among degree-seeking undergraduates, 1,359 enrolled as first-time, first-year students.

Part-time:	56%	**Asian American:**	9%
Out-of-state:	1%	**Hispanic American:**	4%
Women:	55%	**Native American:**	1%
African American:	16%	**25 or older:**	35%

Transfer out. Colleges most students transferred to 2011: University of Minnesota, University of St. Thomas, Minnesota State University: Mankato, St. Cloud State University, Metropolitan State University.

Basis for selection. Open admission, but selective for some programs. Admission to health-related programs (dental hygiene, nursing, dietetic technology) based on cumulative GPA of college level courses and completion of specific course requirements. In-house placement tests in English, mathematics, reading may also be required. **Adult students:** SAT/ACT scores not required. **Home schooled:** Must provide immunization information. **Learning Disabled:** No special requirement for admission. For those seeking accommodations, once admitted must make an appointment with the Office for Students with Disabilities for an intake interview and to present documentation of the disability. Accommodations determined on a case by case basis.

2011-2012 Annual costs. Tuition/fees: $5,448; $5,448 out-of-state. Per-credit charge: $157. Books/supplies: $1,160. Personal expenses: $5,348.

2010-2011 Financial aid. Need-based: 65% of total undergraduate aid awarded as scholarships/grants, 35% as loans/jobs. Need-based aid available for part-time students. Work-study available nights, weekends and for part-time students. **Non-need-based:** Scholarships awarded for academics, art, leadership, music/drama, state residency.

Application procedures. Admission: Closing date 8/15 (postmark date). $20 fee, may be waived for applicants with need. Admission notification on a rolling basis. **Financial aid:** Priority date 4/1; no closing date. FAFSA required. Applicants notified on a rolling basis starting 4/15.

Academics. Tutoring provided by faculty, professional staff and peer tutors, English for Academic Purposes, world languages and more. Online tutoring provided by online tutoring service available 24/7 for selected subjects. Supplemental Instruction study sessions (informal student seminars in which students review notes, discuss readings, learn study sills and prepare for exams) also available. **Special study options:** Accelerated study, cooperative education, distance learning, double major, dual enrollment of high school students, ESL, honors, independent study, internships, liberal arts/career combination, study abroad, teacher certification program, weekend college. Bachelor's degree programs available on campus. License preparation in dental hygiene, nursing. **Credit/placement by examination:** AP, CLEP, IB, institutional tests. No limit to the number of credits that can be applied toward a student's degree, provided the student meets the college's credits-in-residence requirement. **Support services:** Learning center, reduced course load, remedial instruction, study skills assistance, tutoring, writing center.

Majors. Business: Business admin, hospitality admin, marketing. **Computer sciences:** General, computer science. **Education:** General, elementary, special ed. **Engineering:** General. **Health services:** Dental hygiene, dietetics, nursing (RN). **Liberal arts:** Arts/sciences. **Protective services:** Criminal justice, police science. **Visual/performing arts:** Dramatic, music, studio arts.

Most popular majors. Health sciences 15%, liberal arts 69%, security/protective services 6%.

Computing on campus. 575 workstations in library, computer center, student center. Commuter students can connect to campus network. Online

course registration, online library, helpline, repair service, wireless network available.

Student life. Freshman orientation: Mandatory, $25 fee. Preregistration for classes offered. Advising and Registration session held prior to the beginning of fall and spring semesters. Approximately 3 hours in length. **Activities:** Bands, choral groups, drama, literary magazine, music ensembles, musical theater, student government, student newspaper, Black Student Alliance, Campus Crusade for Christ, College Democrats, diversity student club, Ethiopian student union, Gay and Straight Alliance, InterVarsity Christian Fellowship, Latter-day Saints association, Muslim student association, Somali student association, Club Latino.

Athletics. Intramural: Archery, badminton, baseball, basketball, bowling, boxing, cross-country, fencing, field hockey, football (non-tackle), golf, handball, ice hockey, judo, racquetball, skiing, soccer, softball, table tennis, tennis, volleyball, weight lifting. **Team name:** Lions.

Student services. Adult student services, career counseling, services for economically disadvantaged, student employment services, financial aid counseling, on-campus daycare, personal counseling, placement for graduates, veterans' counselor. **Physically disabled:** Services for visually, speech, hearing impaired. **Transfer:** Pre-admission transcript evaluation for new students. Transfer adviser, college fairs on campus for students transferring to 4-year colleges.

Contact. E-mail: admissions@normandale.edu
Phone: (952) 358-8201 Toll-free number: (866) 880-8740
Fax: (952) 358-8230
Nancy Pates, Director of Admissions, Normandale Community College, 9700 France Avenue South, Bloomington, MN 55431

North Hennepin Community College
Brooklyn Park, Minnesota
www.nhcc.edu   CB code: 6498

- Public 2-year community college
- Commuter campus in small city

General. Founded in 1966. Regionally accredited. **Enrollment:** 6,789 degree-seeking undergraduates; 577 non-degree-seeking students. **Degrees:** 751 associate awarded. **ROTC:** Army, Naval, Air Force. **Location:** 12 miles from downtown. **Calendar:** Semester, limited summer session. **Full-time faculty:** 110 total; 11% minority, 62% women. **Part-time faculty:** 141 total; 36% minority, 46% women. **Class size:** 29% < 20, 61% 20-39, 6% 40-49, 4% 50-99, less than 1% >100. **Special facilities:** Greenhouse.

Student profile. Among degree-seeking undergraduates, 1% already have a bachelor's degree or higher, 1,170 enrolled as first-time, first-year students, 976 transferred in from other institutions.

Part-time:	66%	Asian American:	11%
Out-of-state:	2%	Hispanic American:	4%
Women:	56%	International:	1%
African American:	18%	25 or older:	48%

Transfer out. 69% of students enrolled in the transfer program go on to 4-year colleges. **Colleges most students transferred to 2011:** University of MN-TC, Metropolitan State University, St. Cloud State University, Concordia, University of St. Thomas.

Basis for selection. Open admission, but selective for some programs. Competitive admission for medical programs: nursing, medical lab technician, histo technician and graphic design. Must show proof of immunization to be enrolled in classes. Assessment test or approved waiver required for registration. **Home schooled:** State high school equivalency certificate required.

High school preparation. 1 unit chemistry and algebra are required for nursing program.

2011-2012 Annual costs. Tuition/fees: $5,220; $5,220 out-of-state. Per-credit charge: $160. Books/supplies: $1,000.

Financial aid. Need-based: Need-based aid available for part-time students. Work-study available nights, weekends and for part-time students. **Non-need-based:** Scholarships awarded for academics, art, leadership. **Additional information:** Computerized financial aid application.

Application procedures. Admission: No deadline. $20 fee. Admission notification on a rolling basis. **Financial aid:** Priority date 4/15; no closing date. FAFSA required. Applicants notified on a rolling basis starting 6/1.

Academics. Special study options: Accelerated study, cross-registration, distance learning, double major, dual enrollment of high school students,

ESL, honors, independent study, internships, student-designed major, study abroad, weekend college. Bachelor's degree programs available on campus. License preparation in nursing. **Credit/placement by examination:** AP, CLEP, IB, institutional tests. 30 credit hours maximum toward associate degree. **Support services:** GED test center, learning center, reduced course load, remedial instruction, study skills assistance, tutoring, writing center.

Majors. Biology: General. **Business:** Accounting, accounting technology, business admin, entrepreneurial studies, finance, management information systems, marketing. **Computer sciences:** Computer science. **Education:** Physical. **Engineering:** General. **Health services:** Clinical lab technology, histologic technology, nursing (RN). **Liberal arts:** Arts/sciences. **Math:** General. **Physical sciences:** Chemistry. **Protective services:** Criminal justice, police science. **Visual/performing arts:** Dramatic, graphic design, studio arts.

Most popular majors. Business/marketing 20%, health sciences 18%, liberal arts 43%, security/protective services 8%.

Computing on campus. 850 workstations in library, computer center, student center. Online course registration, online library, wireless network available.

Student life. Freshman orientation: Mandatory. Preregistration for classes offered. 3 to 4 hour sessions held prior to the start of each term. **Activities:** Choral groups, drama, international student organizations, literary magazine, musical theater, student government.

Athletics. Intramural: Basketball, bowling, football (non-tackle), soccer, softball, table tennis, volleyball, weight lifting.

Student services. Career counseling, student employment services, financial aid counseling, personal counseling, placement for graduates, veterans' counselor. **Physically disabled:** Services for visually, speech, hearing impaired. **Transfer:** Pre-admission transcript evaluation for new students. Transfer adviser, college fairs on campus for students transferring to 4-year colleges.

Contact. E-mail: admissions@nhcc.edu
Phone: (763) 424-0720 Toll-free number: (800) 818-0395
Fax: (763) 493-0563
Lori Kirkeby, Registrar, North Hennepin Community College, 7411 85th Avenue North, Brooklyn Park, MN 55445

Northland Community & Technical College
Thief River Falls, Minnesota
www.northlandcollege.edu   CB code: 6500

- Public 2-year community and technical college
- Commuter campus in small town

General. Founded in 1965. Regionally accredited. Campuses in East Grand Forks and Thief River Falls. First college in the nation to offer training in Unmanned Aircraft Systems Maintenance. **Enrollment:** 3,083 degree-seeking undergraduates. **Degrees:** 567 associate awarded. **Location:** 55 miles from Grand Forks, North Dakota. **Calendar:** Semester, limited summer session. **Full-time faculty:** 128 total. **Part-time faculty:** 106 total. **Class size:** 50% < 20, 48% 20-39, 2% 40-49, less than 1% 50-99, less than 1% >100. **Special facilities:** On-campus radio station.

Student profile.

Out-of-state:	36%	25 or older:	40%

Transfer out. Colleges most students transferred to 2011: University of North Dakota, North Dakota State University, Bemidji State University, University of Minnesota: Crookston, Moorhead State University, St. Cloud State University.

Basis for selection. Open admission, but selective for some programs. Special requirements for cardiovascular technology, firefighter-paramedic, nursing, occupational therapy assistant, intensive care paramedic, pharmacy technology, physical therapist assistant, practical nursing, radiology, respiratory therapy, and surgical technology. Students admitted on first-come, first-served basis determined by program application date. Students required to go through ACCUPLACER assessment program to determine level of mathematics, reading and English skills for course placement purposes. **Home schooled:** Transcript of courses and grades required.

2011-2012 Annual costs. Tuition/fees: $5,253; $5,253 out-of-state. Per-credit charge: $159. Books/supplies: $600. Personal expenses: $1,350.

Financial aid. All financial aid based on need. Need-based aid available for part-time students. Work-study available nights, weekends and for part-time students.

Application procedures. Admission: No deadline. $20 fee. Admission notification on a rolling basis. **Financial aid:** Priority date 5/1; no closing date. FAFSA, institutional form required. Applicants notified on a rolling basis starting 5/15.

Academics. Special study options: Distance learning, double major, dual enrollment of high school students, external degree, internships, liberal arts/career combination. License preparation in aviation, nursing, occupational therapy, paramedic, physical therapy, radiology. **Credit/placement by examination:** AP, CLEP, IB, institutional tests. 40 credit hours maximum toward associate degree. **Support services:** GED test center, learning center, reduced course load, remedial instruction, study skills assistance, tutoring, writing center.

Majors. Architecture: Technology. **Biology:** General. **Business:** Accounting, accounting technology, administrative services, management information systems, marketing, office/clerical, sales/distribution. **Communications:** Broadcast journalism, communications/speech/rhetoric, journalism, media studies, radio/TV. **Computer sciences:** Networking. **Conservation:** Environmental science, management/policy. **Education:** General, early childhood. **Engineering:** General, electrical. **English:** English lit. **Foreign languages:** General. **General:** Business, economics, farm/ranch. **Health services:** Cardiovascular technology, clinical lab science, clinical lab technology, EMT ambulance attendant, EMT paramedic, insurance coding, licensed practical nurse, medical assistant, medical secretary, medical transcription, nursing (RN), occupational therapy assistant, office assistant, pharmacy assistant, physical therapy assistant, radiologic technology/medical imaging, respiratory therapy assistant, respiratory therapy technology, surgical technology. **Liberal arts:** Arts/sciences. **Math:** General. **Parks/recreation:** General. **Protective services:** Corrections, criminal justice, law enforcement admin, police science. **Psychology:** General. **Social sciences:** General. **Visual/performing arts:** General, art, music, studio arts. **Work/family studies:** Child care service.

Most popular majors. Business/marketing 6%, health sciences 57%, liberal arts 23%.

Computing on campus. 356 workstations in library, computer center, student center. Online course registration, online library, helpline, repair service, wireless network available.

Student life. Freshman orientation: Mandatory. Preregistration for classes offered. **Activities:** Bands, choral groups, dance, music ensembles, musical theater, radio station, student government, Phi Theta Kappa honor society, multicultural club, SOS club, diversity committee.

Athletics. NJCAA. **Intercollegiate:** Baseball M, basketball, football (tackle) M, softball W, volleyball W. **Intramural:** Basketball, bowling, golf, ice hockey M, softball, tennis, volleyball. **Team name:** Pioneers.

Student services. Career counseling, financial aid counseling, minority student services, personal counseling, veterans' counselor, women's services. **Physically disabled:** Services for visually, speech, hearing impaired. **Transfer:** Re-entry adviser, pre-admission transcript evaluation for new students. Transfer adviser, college fairs on campus for students transferring to 4-year colleges.

Contact. E-mail: admissions@northlandcollege.edu
Phone: (218) 683-8554 Toll-free number: (800) 959-6282
Fax: (218) 683-8980
Eugene Klinke, Director of Enrollment Management and Multicultural Services, Northland Community & Technical College, 1101 Highway One East, Thief River Falls, MN 56701

Northwest Technical College
Bemidji, Minnesota
www.ntcmn.edu   CB code: 3626

- Public 2-year technical college
- Commuter campus in large town

General. Regionally accredited. Northwest Technical College is affiliated with Bemidji State University. **Enrollment:** 946 degree-seeking undergraduates; 438 non-degree-seeking students. **Degrees:** 166 associate awarded. **Location:** 229 miles from Minneapolis-St. Paul, 152 miles from Duluth. **Calendar:** Semester, limited summer session. **Full-time faculty:** 27 total; 7% minority, 67% women. **Part-time faculty:** 39 total; 3% minority, 56% women. **Class size:** 77% < 20, 22% 20-39, 1% 40-49. **Special facilities:** American Indian resource center.

Student profile. Among degree-seeking undergraduates, 142 enrolled as first-time, first-year students, 205 transferred in from other institutions.

Part-time:	46%	Hispanic American:	3%
Out-of-state:	8%	Native American:	9%
Women:	67%	25 or older:	48%
African American:	2%	Live on campus:	4%

Transfer out. Colleges most students transferred to 2011: Bemidji State University, Northland Community and Technical College, Minnesota State Community and Technical College.

Basis for selection. Open admission, but selective for some programs. Health programs require a background check. **Learning Disabled:** Learners with learning disabilities are encouraged to have an IEP on file with the Learning Services Coordinator and meet with the coordinator prior to the start of the semester to develop a Personal Education Plan.

2011-2012 Annual costs. Tuition/fees: $5,329; $5,329 out-of-state. Per-credit charge: $168. Room/board: $2,480. Books/supplies: $1,200. Personal expenses: $2,500.

2010-2011 Financial aid. All financial aid based on need. 59% of total undergraduate aid awarded as scholarships/grants, 41% as loans/jobs. Need-based aid available for part-time students. Work-study available nights, weekends and for part-time students.

Application procedures. Admission: No deadline. $20 fee. Admission notification on a rolling basis. High school learners can attend the college under the Post-Secondary Enrollment Options program. **Financial aid:** Priority date 6/1; no closing date. FAFSA, institutional form required. Applicants notified on a rolling basis.

Academics. NTC learners can take General Education courses from Bemidji State University and/or online from a regional consortium of colleges in fulfillment of general education requirements of degrees at NTC. **Special study options:** Cross-registration, distance learning, double major, dual enrollment of high school students, ESL, exchange student, independent study, liberal arts/career combination. Study abroad options are available through our partnership with Bemidji State University. License preparation in nursing. **Credit/placement by examination:** AP, CLEP, IB, institutional tests. A maximum of 25% of the required credits for a program major is allowed for credit for experiential learning. **Support services:** Learning center, reduced course load, remedial instruction, study skills assistance, tutoring.

Majors. Business: Accounting, administrative services, business admin, sales/distribution. **General:** Landscaping. **Health services:** Licensed practical nurse, massage therapy, medical secretary, nursing (RN). **Work/family studies:** Child care management, child care service.

Most popular majors. Business/marketing 11%, engineering/engineering technologies 15%, health sciences 65%.

Computing on campus. PC or laptop required. 140 workstations in dormitories, library, computer center, student center. Dormitories wired for high-speed internet access. Commuter students can connect to campus network. Online course registration, online library, helpline, repair service, wireless network available.

Student life. Freshman orientation: Mandatory. Preregistration for classes offered. One day orientation/registration sessions are held periodically during the 6 months prior to the start of fall and spring semesters. **Housing:** Coed dorms, special housing for disabled, wellness housing available. $150 nonrefundable deposit. NTC learners may reside in Bemidji State University residence halls. **Activities:** Student government, Phi Theta Kappa, Skills USA.

Student services. Adult student services, career counseling, services for economically disadvantaged, student employment services, financial aid counseling, health services, minority student services, personal counseling, placement for graduates, veterans' counselor. **Physically disabled:** Services for visually, speech, hearing impaired. **Transfer:** Re-entry adviser, pre-admission transcript evaluation for new students. Transfer adviser, college fairs on campus for students transferring to 4-year colleges.

Contact. E-mail: sue.ludwig@ntcmn.edu
Phone: (218) 333-6647 Toll-free number: (800) 942-8324
Fax: (218) 333-6697
Sue Ludwig, Admissions Specialist, Northwest Technical College, 905 Grant Avenue Southeast, Bemidji, MN 56601-4907

Northwest Technical Institute
Eagan, Minnesota
www.nti.edu   CB code: 1388

- For-profit 2-year technical college
- Commuter campus in small city

General. Founded in 1957. Accredited by ACCSCT. **Location:** 10 miles from Minneapolis-St. Paul. **Calendar:** Semester.

Annual costs/financial aid. Tuition/fees (2011-2012): $18,950. Required fees include the cost of textbooks. Books/supplies: $650. Personal expenses: $3,192. Need-based financial aid available to full-time and part-time students.

Contact. Phone: (952) 944-0080
President, 950 Blue Gentian Road, Eagan, MN 55121

Pine Technical College
Pine City, Minnesota
www.pinetech.edu   CB code: 7118

- Public 2-year technical college
- Commuter campus in small town

General. Regionally accredited. **Enrollment:** 736 degree-seeking undergraduates. **Degrees:** 24 associate awarded. **Location:** 60 miles from Minneapolis-St. Paul. **Calendar:** Semester, limited summer session. **Full-time faculty:** 20 total. **Part-time faculty:** 23 total. **Class size:** 77% < 20, 18% 20-39, 2% 40-49, 2% 50-99.

Student profile.

Out-of-state:	11%	25 or older:	35%

Transfer out. Colleges most students transferred to 2011: St. Cloud Technical College, Anoka-Ramsey Community College, Lake Superior Community College, Mesabi Community College, North Hennepin College.

Basis for selection. Open admission, but selective for some programs. Additional requirements for some majors; criminal history check. **Home schooled:** State high school equivalency certificate required.

2011-2012 Annual costs. Tuition/fees: $4,925; $9,365 out-of-state. Per-credit charge: $148 in-state; $296 out-of-state. Books/supplies: $800. Personal expenses: $600.

Financial aid. Need-based: Need-based aid available for part-time students. Work-study available nights, weekends and for part-time students. **Non-need-based:** Scholarships awarded for academics, state residency.

Application procedures. Admission: No deadline. $20 fee, may be waived for applicants with need. Admission notification on a rolling basis. **Financial aid:** Priority date 5/5; no closing date. FAFSA, institutional form required. Applicants notified on a rolling basis starting 6/5.

Academics. Special study options: Cross-registration, distance learning, double major, dual enrollment of high school students, honors, independent study, internships, liberal arts/career combination. License preparation in nursing. **Credit/placement by examination:** AP, CLEP, institutional tests. 35 credit hours maximum toward associate degree. **Support services:** Learning center, reduced course load, remedial instruction, study skills assistance, tutoring.

Majors. Biology: Biotechnology. **Business:** Accounting, business admin. **Computer sciences:** Data processing, information systems, programming. **Health services:** Insurance coding. **Work/family studies:** Child care management.

Most popular majors. Business/marketing 62%, family/consumer sciences 31%.

Computing on campus. 100 workstations in library, computer center. Commuter students can connect to campus network. Online course registration, online library, helpline, wireless network available.

Student life. Freshman orientation: Mandatory. Preregistration for classes offered. **Activities:** Student government.

Athletics. Intercollegiate: Rifle. **Intramural:** Rifle, tennis. **Team name:** Pines.

Student services. Career counseling, services for economically disadvantaged, student employment services, financial aid counseling, on-campus daycare, personal counseling, placement for graduates. **Physically disabled:** Services for visually, hearing impaired. **Transfer:** Pre-admission transcript evaluation for new students. Transfer adviser, college fairs on campus for students transferring to 4-year colleges.

Contact. E-mail: information@pinetech.edu
Phone: (320) 629-5100 Toll-free number: (800) 521-7463
Fax: (320) 629-5101
Dani Chandonnet, Director of Admissions, Pine Technical College, 900 Fourth Street, SE, Pine City, MN 55063

Rainy River Community College
International Falls, Minnesota
www.rrcc.mnscu.edu   CB code: 1637

- Public 2-year community and technical college
- Commuter campus in small town

General. Founded in 1967. Regionally accredited. **Enrollment:** 344 degree-seeking undergraduates. **Degrees:** 57 associate awarded. **Location:** 300 miles from Minneapolis-St. Paul, 150 miles from Duluth. **Calendar:** Semester, limited summer session. **Full-time faculty:** 10 total; 10% have terminal degrees, 50% women. **Part-time faculty:** 13 total; 8% have terminal degrees, 31% women.

Student profile.

Part-time:	22%	Asian American:	1%
Women:	62%	Hispanic American:	1%
African American:	13%	Native American:	5%

Transfer out. Colleges most students transferred to 2011: St. Cloud State University, Bemidji State University, University of Minnesota-Duluth.

Basis for selection. Open admission.

2011-2012 Annual costs. Tuition/fees: $5,141; $6,278 out-of-state. Per-credit charge: $152 in-state; $189 out-of-state. Room/board: $3,700. Books/supplies: $800. Personal expenses: $1,800.

Financial aid. Need-based: Need-based aid available for part-time students. Work-study available nights, weekends and for part-time students. **Non-need-based:** Scholarships awarded for academics, alumni affiliation, leadership, minority status, state residency. **Additional information:** Many scholarship and employment opportunities for applicants showing little or no need.

Application procedures. Admission: No deadline. $20 fee. Admission notification on a rolling basis. **Financial aid:** Priority date 6/1; no closing date. FAFSA, institutional form required. Applicants notified on a rolling basis starting 5/1; must reply within 3 week(s) of notification.

Academics. Special study options: Distance learning, dual enrollment of high school students, honors, independent study, internships, liberal arts/career combination. License preparation in nursing. **Credit/placement by examination:** AP, CLEP, IB, institutional tests. **Support services:** Learning center, pre-admission summer program, reduced course load, remedial instruction, study skills assistance, tutoring, writing center.

Majors. Area/ethnic studies: Native American. **Education:** Science. **Liberal arts:** Arts/sciences. **Math:** General.

Computing on campus. 100 workstations in dormitories, library, computer center, student center. Dormitories wired for high-speed internet access. Online course registration available.

Student life. Freshman orientation: Mandatory. Preregistration for classes offered. **Housing:** Special housing for disabled, apartments available. $200 deposit. Student housing lobby equipped with computers, wireless available throughout building. **Activities:** Choral groups, drama, literary magazine, music ensembles, musical theater, student government, Black Student Association club, Native Student club, environment club.

Athletics. NJCAA. **Intercollegiate:** Baseball M, basketball, ice hockey W, softball W, volleyball W. **Intramural:** Archery, badminton, bowling, cheerleading, cross-country, golf, racquetball, skiing, softball, table tennis, tennis, volleyball. **Team name:** Voyageurs.

Student services. Adult student services, career counseling, services for economically disadvantaged, student employment services, financial aid counseling, minority student services, personal counseling, placement for graduates, veterans' counselor. **Physically disabled:** Services for visually, speech, hearing impaired. **Transfer:** Re-entry adviser, pre-admission transcript evaluation for new students. Transfer adviser, college fairs on campus for students transferring to 4-year colleges.

Two-Year Colleges

Contact. E-mail: admissions@rrcc.mnscu.edu
Phone: (218) 285-2207 Toll-free number: (800) 456-3996
Fax: (218) 285-2314
Berta Hagen, Registrar, Rainy River Community College, 1501 Highway 71, International Falls, MN 56649

Rasmussen College: Bloomington
Bloomington, Minnesota
www.rasmussen.edu
CB member
CB code: 2448

- For-profit 2-year career college
- Commuter campus in small city

General. Regionally accredited. **Enrollment:** 611 degree-seeking undergraduates. **Degrees:** 17 bachelor's, 138 associate awarded. **Location:** 10 miles from Minneapolis-St. Paul. **Calendar:** Quarter, extensive summer session. **Full-time faculty:** 18 total. **Part-time faculty:** 20 total.

Basis for selection. Open admission, but selective for some programs. Programs in allied health, justice studies, and education require students to complete a background check. **Adult students:** SAT/ACT scores not required.

2011-2012 Annual costs. Tuition/fees: $17,775. Per-credit charge: $395. Full-time tuition varies according to program of study. Examples of per-credit-hour charges include Early Childhood Education ($310), Medical Lab Technician, Surgical Technician, Practical Nursing ($395), Professional Nursing, Information Systems Mgmt, Multimedia Technician ($395). Personal expenses: $2,214.

Financial aid. Need-based: Need-based aid available for part-time students. Work-study available nights, weekends and for part-time students.

Application procedures. Admission: No deadline. $40 fee. Admission notification on a rolling basis. **Financial aid:** No deadline. FAFSA, institutional form required. Applicants notified on a rolling basis.

Academics. Special study options: Distance learning, double major, honors, independent study, internships. **Credit/placement by examination:** AP, CLEP. 45 credit hours maximum toward associate degree, 90 toward bachelor's. Credit limited to specific programs and to courses for which examinations are available. 50% of the student's program credits must be completed through coursework at Rasmussen College. **Support services:** Learning center, remedial instruction, study skills assistance, tutoring, writing center.

Majors. Business: Accounting, administrative services, business admin. **Computer sciences:** Web page design. **Health services:** Massage therapy, medical assistant, medical records technology, medical secretary, medical transcription, pharmacy assistant. **Work/family studies:** Child care management.

Computing on campus. 100 workstations in library, computer center, student center. Online course registration, online library, helpline, wireless network available.

Student life. Freshman orientation: Mandatory. Preregistration for classes offered.

Student services. Adult student services, career counseling, services for economically disadvantaged, student employment services, financial aid counseling, placement for graduates.

Contact. E-mail: jeff.lust@rasmussen.edu
Phone: (952) 545-2000 Toll-free number: (800) 852-0929
Susan Hammerstrom, Director of Admissions, Rasmussen College: Bloomington, 4400 West 78th Street, Eden Prairie, MN 55435

Rasmussen College: Brooklyn Park
Brooklyn Park, Minnesota
www.rasmussen.edu
CB code: 6730

- For-profit 2-year career college
- Commuter campus in small city

General. Regionally accredited. **Enrollment:** 1,016 degree-seeking undergraduates. **Degrees:** 22 bachelor's, 246 associate awarded. **Location:** 10 miles from Minneapolis-St. Paul. **Calendar:** Quarter, extensive summer session. **Full-time faculty:** 18 total. **Part-time faculty:** 27 total.

Basis for selection. Open admission, but selective for some programs. Programs in allied health, justice studies, and education require students to complete a background check. **Adult students:** SAT/ACT scores not required.

2011-2012 Annual costs. Tuition/fees: $17,775. Per-credit charge: $395. Full-time tuition varies according to program of study. Examples of per-credit-hour charges include Early Childhood Education ($310), Medical Lab Technician, Surgical Technician, Practical Nursing ($395), Professional Nursing, Information Systems Mgmt, Multimedia Technician ($395). Personal expenses: $2,214.

Financial aid. Need-based: Need-based aid available for part-time students. Work-study available nights, weekends and for part-time students.

Application procedures. Admission: No deadline. $40 fee. Admission notification on a rolling basis. **Financial aid:** No deadline. FAFSA, institutional form required. Applicants notified on a rolling basis.

Academics. Special study options: Distance learning, double major, honors, independent study, internships. **Credit/placement by examination:** AP, CLEP, institutional tests. 45 credit hours maximum toward associate degree, 90 toward bachelor's. Credit limited to specific programs and to courses for which examinations are available. 50% of a student's program credits must be completed through coursework at Rasmussen College. **Support services:** Learning center, remedial instruction, study skills assistance, tutoring, writing center.

Majors. Business: Accounting, administrative services, business admin. **Computer sciences:** Web page design. **Health services:** Clinical lab assistant, licensed practical nurse, massage therapy, medical assistant, medical records technology, medical secretary, medical transcription, pharmacy assistant, surgical technology. **Work/family studies:** Child care management.

Computing on campus. 100 workstations in library, computer center, student center. Online course registration, online library, helpline, wireless network available.

Student life. Freshman orientation: Mandatory. Preregistration for classes offered.

Student services. Adult student services, career counseling, services for economically disadvantaged, student employment services, financial aid counseling, placement for graduates.

Contact. Phone: (763) 493-4500 Toll-free number: (877) 495-4500
Susan Hammerstrom, Director of Admissions, Rasmussen College: Brooklyn Park, 8301 93rd Avenue North, Brooklyn Park, MN 55445

Rasmussen College: Eagan
Eagan, Minnesota
www.rasmussen.edu
CB code: 2449

- For-profit 2-year career college
- Commuter campus in small city

General. Regionally accredited. **Enrollment:** 924 degree-seeking undergraduates. **Degrees:** 29 bachelor's, 175 associate awarded. **Location:** 12 miles from Minneapolis-St. Paul. **Calendar:** Quarter, extensive summer session. **Full-time faculty:** 14 total. **Part-time faculty:** 53 total.

Basis for selection. Open admission, but selective for some programs. The Practical Nursing AAS program has selective admissions requirements, including entrance examinations, background checks, and health screenings. Some additional programs in allied health, justice studies, and education require students to complete a background check. **Adult students:** SAT/ACT scores not required.

2011-2012 Annual costs. Tuition/fees: $17,775. Per-credit charge: $395. Full-time tuition varies according to program of study. Examples of per-credit-hour charges include Early Childhood Education ($310), Medical Lab Technician, Surgical Technician, Practical Nursing ($395), Professional Nursing, Information Systems Mgmt, Multimedia Technician ($395). Personal expenses: $2,214.

Financial aid. Need-based: Need-based aid available for part-time students. Work-study available nights, weekends and for part-time students.

Application procedures. Admission: No deadline. $40 fee. Admission notification on a rolling basis. **Financial aid:** No deadline. FAFSA, institutional form required. Applicants notified on a rolling basis.

Academics. Special study options: Distance learning, double major, honors, independent study, internships. **Credit/placement by examination:** AP, CLEP, institutional tests. 45 credit hours maximum toward associate degree, 90 toward bachelor's. Credit limited to specific programs and to courses for which examinations are available. 50% of the student's program credits must be completed through coursework at Rasmussen College. **Support services:**

Learning center, remedial instruction, study skills assistance, tutoring, writing center.

Majors. Business: Accounting, administrative services, business admin. **Computer sciences:** Web page design. **Health services:** Licensed practical nurse, massage therapy, medical assistant, medical records technology, medical secretary, medical transcription, pharmacy assistant. **Work/family studies:** Child care management.

Computing on campus. 100 workstations in library, computer center, student center. Online course registration, online library, helpline, wireless network available.

Student life. Freshman orientation: Mandatory. Preregistration for classes offered.

Student services. Adult student services, career counseling, services for economically disadvantaged, student employment services, financial aid counseling, placement for graduates.

Contact. Phone: (651) 687-9000 Toll-free number: (800) 852-6367 Fax: (651) 687-0507
Susan Hammerstrom, Director of Admissions, Rasmussen College: Eagan, 3500 Federal Drive, Eagan, MN 55122

Rasmussen College: Mankato
Mankato, Minnesota
www.rasmussen.edu   CB code: 2453

- For-profit 2-year career college
- Commuter campus in large town

General. Founded in 1983. Regionally accredited. **Enrollment:** 797 degree-seeking undergraduates. **Degrees:** 29 bachelor's, 227 associate awarded. **Location:** 60 miles from Minneapolis-St. Paul. **Calendar:** Quarter, extensive summer session. **Full-time faculty:** 16 total. **Part-time faculty:** 35 total.

Basis for selection. Open admission, but selective for some programs. The Medical Laboratory Technician and Practical Nursing AAS programs have selective admissions requirements, including entrance examinations, background checks, and health screenings. Some additional programs in allied health, justice studies, and education require students to complete a background check. **Adult students:** SAT/ACT scores not required.

2011-2012 Annual costs. Tuition/fees: $17,775. Per-credit charge: $395. Full-time tuition varies according to program of study. Examples of per-credit-hour charges include Early Childhood Education ($310), Medical Lab Technician, Surgical Technician, Practical Nursing ($395), Professional Nursing, Information Systems Mgmt, Multimedia Technician ($395). Personal expenses: $2,214.

Financial aid. Need-based: Need-based aid available for part-time students. Work-study available nights, weekends and for part-time students.

Application procedures. Admission: No deadline. $40 fee. Admission notification on a rolling basis. **Financial aid:** No deadline. FAFSA, institutional form required. Applicants notified on a rolling basis.

Academics. Special study options: Distance learning, double major, honors, independent study, internships. **Credit/placement by examination:** AP, CLEP, IB, institutional tests. 45 credit hours maximum toward associate degree, 90 toward bachelor's. Credit limited to specific programs and to courses for which examinations are available. 50% of the student's program must be completed through coursework at Rasmussen College. **Support services:** Learning center, remedial instruction, study skills assistance, tutoring, writing center.

Majors. Business: Accounting, administrative services, business admin. **Health services:** Clinical lab technology, licensed practical nurse, massage therapy, medical assistant, medical records technology, medical secretary, medical transcription, pharmacy assistant. **Work/family studies:** Child care management.

Computing on campus. 100 workstations in library, computer center, student center. Online course registration, online library, helpline available.

Student life. Freshman orientation: Mandatory. Preregistration for classes offered.

Student services. Adult student services, career counseling, services for economically disadvantaged, student employment services, financial aid counseling, placement for graduates.

Contact. Phone: (507) 625-6556 Toll-free number: (800) 657-6767 Fax: (507) 625-6557
Susan Hammerstrom, Director of Admissions, Rasmussen College: Mankato, 130 Saint Andrews Drive, Mankato, MN 56001

Rasmussen College: St. Cloud
St. Cloud, Minnesota
www.rasmussen.edu   CB code: 3315

- For-profit 2-year community and career college
- Commuter campus in small city

General. Regionally accredited. **Enrollment:** 1,018 degree-seeking undergraduates. **Degrees:** 24 bachelor's, 258 associate awarded. **Location:** 60 miles from Minneapolis-St. Paul. **Calendar:** Quarter, extensive summer session. **Full-time faculty:** 14 total. **Part-time faculty:** 24 total.

Basis for selection. Open admission, but selective for some programs. Medical Laboratory Technician, Surgical Technologist, and Practical Nursing AAS programs have additional requirements, including entrance examinations, background checks, and health screenings. Other programs in allied health, justice studies, and education require students to complete a background check. **Adult students:** SAT/ACT scores not required.

2011-2012 Annual costs. Tuition/fees: $17,775. Per-credit charge: $395. Full-time tuition varies according to program of study. Examples of per-credit-hour charges include Early Childhood Education ($310), Medical Lab Technician, Surgical Technician, Practical Nursing ($395), Professional Nursing, Information Systems Mgmt, Multimedia Technician ($395). Personal expenses: $2,214.

Financial aid. Need-based: Need-based aid available for part-time students. Work-study available nights, weekends and for part-time students.

Application procedures. Admission: No deadline. $40 fee. Admission notification on a rolling basis. **Financial aid:** No deadline. FAFSA, institutional form required. Applicants notified on a rolling basis.

Academics. Special study options: Distance learning, double major, honors, independent study, internships. **Credit/placement by examination:** AP, CLEP, institutional tests. 45 credit hours maximum toward associate degree, 90 toward bachelor's. Credit limited to specific programs and to courses for which examinations are available. 50% of a student's program credits must be completed through coursework at Rasmussen College. **Support services:** Learning center, remedial instruction, study skills assistance, tutoring, writing center.

Majors. Business: Accounting, administrative services, business admin. **Computer sciences:** Web page design. **Health services:** Clinical lab technology, licensed practical nurse, massage therapy, medical assistant, medical records technology, medical secretary, medical transcription, pharmacy assistant, surgical technology. **Work/family studies:** Child care management.

Computing on campus. 100 workstations in library, computer center, student center. Online course registration, online library, helpline, wireless network available.

Student life. Freshman orientation: Mandatory. Preregistration for classes offered.

Student services. Adult student services, career counseling, services for economically disadvantaged, student employment services, financial aid counseling, placement for graduates.

Contact. Phone: (320) 251-5600 Toll-free number: (800) 852-0460 Fax: (320) 251-3702
Susan Hammerstrom, Director of Admissions, Rasmussen College: St. Cloud, 226 Park Avenue South, St. Cloud, MN 56301-3713

Ridgewater College
Willmar, Minnesota
www.ridgewater.edu   CB code: 4924

- Public 2-year community and technical college
- Commuter campus in large town

General. Founded in 1961. Regionally accredited. **Location:** 100 miles from Minneapolis-St. Paul. **Calendar:** Semester.

Annual costs/financial aid. Tuition/fees (2011-2012): $5,173; $5,173 out-of-state. Need-based financial aid available to full-time and part-time students.

Contact. Phone: (320) 222-5976
Director of Admissions, 2101 15th Avenue Northwest, Willmar, MN 56201

Riverland Community College
Austin, Minnesota
www.riverland.edu
CB code: 6017

- Public 2-year community and technical college
- Commuter campus in large town

General. Founded in 1996. Regionally accredited. **Enrollment:** 3,329 undergraduates. **Degrees:** 396 associate awarded. **Location:** 90 miles from Minneapolis-St. Paul. **Calendar:** Semester, limited summer session. **Full-time faculty:** 72 total. **Part-time faculty:** 128 total. **Class size:** 68% < 20, 29% 20-39, 2% 40-49, less than 1% 50-99.

Student profile.

Out-of-state:	2%	Live on campus:	3%
25 or older:	46%		

Transfer out. Colleges most students transferred to 2011: Mankato State University, Winona State University, Southwest Minnesota State University.

Basis for selection. Open admission, but selective for some programs. Special requirements for human services, nursing, corrections, radiography, and construction electrician, wind turbine technician programs. **Home schooled:** Transcript of courses and grades required.

High school preparation. Chemistry required of nursing applicants.

2011-2012 Annual costs. Tuition/fees: $5,332; $5,332 out-of-state. Per-credit charge: $159. $400 laptop charge for each term. Personal expenses: $4,346.

Financial aid. Need-based: Need-based aid available for part-time students. Work-study available nights, weekends and for part-time students. **Non-need-based:** Scholarships awarded for alumni affiliation, art, job skills, leadership, music/drama, state residency. **Additional information:** One class tuition-free for Minnesota residents over 25 who have not attended college for at least 7 years.

Application procedures. Admission: No deadline. $20 fee, may be waived for applicants with need. Admission notification on a rolling basis. **Financial aid:** Priority date 5/15; no closing date. FAFSA required. Applicants notified on a rolling basis; must reply within 5 week(s) of notification.

Academics. Special study options: Cross-registration, distance learning, double major, dual enrollment of high school students, ESL, internships, liberal arts/career combination, study abroad, weekend college. Bachelor's degree programs available on campus. License preparation in nursing, radiology. **Credit/placement by examination:** AP, CLEP, IB, institutional tests. **Support services:** Learning center, reduced course load, remedial instruction, study skills assistance, tutoring, writing center.

Majors. Business: Accounting, administrative services, management science. **Computer sciences:** General, LAN/WAN management. **Engineering:** Software. **Health services:** Medical radiologic technology/radiation therapy, medical secretary, nursing (RN). **Liberal arts:** Arts/sciences. **Protective services:** Police science.

Most popular majors. Business/marketing 6%, health sciences 26%, liberal arts 53%, security/protective services 7%.

Computing on campus. 250 workstations in library, computer center, student center. Online course registration, helpline, wireless network available.

Student life. Freshman orientation: Mandatory. Preregistration for classes offered. **Housing:** Coed dorms, wellness housing available. $350 partly refundable deposit, deadline 9/1. College foundation-owned student housing. **Activities:** Concert band, choral groups, drama, music ensembles, musical theater, student government, student newspaper, diversity club, DEEDS (Human Service) club, Criminal Justice Society, RIOT (Christian Fellowship) club, Amnesty International, Student Ambassadors, Older, Wiser Learners, Phi Theta Kappa.

Athletics. NJCAA. **Intercollegiate:** Baseball M, basketball, soccer M, softball W, volleyball W. **Intramural:** Basketball, football (tackle) M, weight lifting. **Team name:** Blue Devils.

Student services. Alcohol/substance abuse counseling, career counseling, services for economically disadvantaged, student employment services, financial aid counseling, minority student services, on-campus daycare, personal counseling, placement for graduates, veterans' counselor, women's services. **Physically disabled:** Services for visually, speech, hearing impaired. **Transfer:** Transfer adviser, college fairs on campus for students transferring to 4-year colleges.

Contact. E-mail: admissions@riverland.edu
Phone: (507) 433-0517 Toll-free number: (800) 247-5039
Fax: (507) 433-0515
Sue Jech, Director of Enrollment Services/Registrar, Riverland Community College, 1900 Eighth Avenue, NW, Austin, MN 55912-1407

Rochester Community and Technical College
Rochester, Minnesota
www.roch.edu
CB code: 6610

- Public 2-year community and technical college
- Commuter campus in small city

General. Founded in 1915. Regionally accredited. **Enrollment:** 6,081 degree-seeking undergraduates. **Degrees:** 818 associate awarded. **Location:** 80 miles from Minneapolis-St. Paul. **Calendar:** Semester, limited summer session. **Full-time faculty:** 174 total; 47% have terminal degrees, 8% minority, 52% women. **Part-time faculty:** 165 total; 7% minority, 52% women. **Class size:** 57% < 20, 42% 20-39, less than 1% 40-49, less than 1% 50-99, less than 1% >100. **Special facilities:** Observatory, dental clinic, horticulture technology facility, regional sports center.

Student profile. Among degree-seeking undergraduates, 66% enrolled in a transfer program, 34% enrolled in a vocational program, 2,162 enrolled as first-time, first-year students.

Out-of-state:	5%	Hispanic American:	4%
African American:	9%	International:	1%
Asian American:	3%	25 or older:	37%

Transfer out. 32% of students enrolled in the transfer program go on to 4-year colleges. **Colleges most students transferred to 2011:** Winona State University, Minnesota State College: Mankato, University of Minnesota.

Basis for selection. Open admission, but selective for some programs. Admission to allied health and technology programs based on course work, class rank, institutional placement test scores. **Adult students:** SAT/ACT scores not required.

High school preparation. Biology, chemistry, algebra and/or English required for some programs.

2011-2012 Annual costs. Tuition/fees: $5,435; $5,435 out-of-state. Per-credit charge: $159. South Dakota residents pay $183.92 per-credit hour charges. Books/supplies: $1,400. Personal expenses: $3,475.

Financial aid. Need-based: Need-based aid available for part-time students. Work-study available nights, weekends and for part-time students.

Application procedures. Admission: Priority date 6/1; deadline 8/10 (postmark date). $20 fee, may be waived for applicants with need. Admission notification on a rolling basis. **Financial aid:** Priority date 4/15; no closing date. FAFSA required. Applicants notified on a rolling basis.

Academics. Special study options: Distance learning, dual enrollment of high school students, honors, independent study, internships, study abroad. 2+2 and other career pathways spanning certificate to master's degree programs through a partnership with Winona State University and other 4-year institutions. Bachelor's degree programs available on campus. License preparation in dental hygiene, nursing, paramedic. **Credit/placement by examination:** AP, CLEP, institutional tests. 16 credit hours maximum toward associate degree. **Support services:** Learning center, reduced course load, remedial instruction, study skills assistance, tutoring, writing center.

Majors. Biology: Biomedical sciences. **Business:** Accounting, administrative services, business admin, retailing, special products marketing. **Communications:** Digital media, media studies. **Computer sciences:** General, computer science, web page design. **Conservation:** Environmental science. **Education:** Music, teacher assistance. **Engineering:** General. **General:** Equine science, greenhouse operations, horticultural science, turf management. **Health services:** Cardiovascular technology, dental assistant, dental hygiene, electroencephalograph technology, EMT paramedic, medical records technology, medical secretary, mental health services, nursing (RN), radiologic technology/medical imaging, surgical technology, veterinary technology/assistant. **Liberal arts:** Arts/sciences. **Parks/recreation:** Sports admin. **Protective services:** Criminal justice, police science. **Visual/performing arts:**

Graphic design, music management, music theory/composition. **Work/family studies:** Child care management.

Computing on campus. 450 workstations in library, computer center. Commuter students can connect to campus network. Online course registration, online library, helpline available.

Student life. Freshman orientation: Available. Preregistration for classes offered. **Housing:** Non-college-affiliated student-only housing available near campus. **Activities:** Bands, choral groups, dance, drama, international student organizations, music ensembles, musical theater, radio station, student government, student newspaper, student senate, ECHO (student newspaper), Asian student association, African student organization, Muslim student association, environmentalism club, Armed Forces and Veterans club, Circle of Friends-GLBTQA, international student association, law enforcement club.

Athletics. NJCAA. **Intercollegiate:** Baseball M, basketball, football (tackle) M, golf, soccer W, softball W, volleyball W, wrestling M. **Intramural:** Badminton, basketball, football (non-tackle), golf, soccer, softball, volleyball. **Team name:** Yellowjackets.

Student services. Alcohol/substance abuse counseling, career counseling, services for economically disadvantaged, financial aid counseling, health services, minority student services, on-campus daycare, personal counseling, veterans' counselor. **Physically disabled:** Services for visually, speech, hearing impaired. **Transfer:** Pre-admission transcript evaluation for new students. Transfer adviser, college fairs on campus for students transferring to 4-year colleges.

Contact. Phone: (507) 285-7265 Fax: (507) 280-3529
Holly Bigelow, Registrar, Rochester Community and Technical College, 851 30th Avenue SE, Rochester, MN 55904-4999

South Central College
North Mankato, Minnesota
www.southcentral.edu   **CB code: 7124**

▶ Public 2-year community and technical college
▶ Commuter campus in large town

General. Founded in 1946. Regionally accredited. Campuses in North Mankato and Faribault, MN. **Enrollment:** 3,921 undergraduates. **Degrees:** 463 associate awarded. **Location:** 80 miles from Minneapolis-St. Paul. **Calendar:** Semester, limited summer session. **Full-time faculty:** 99 total. **Part-time faculty:** 119 total.

Basis for selection. Open admission. **Home schooled:** State high school equivalency certificate required.

High school preparation. College-preparatory program recommended.

2011-2012 Annual costs. Tuition/fees: $5,169; $5,169 out-of-state. Per-credit charge: $155.

Financial aid. Need-based: Need-based aid available for part-time students. Work-study available nights, weekends and for part-time students.

Application procedures. Admission: Priority date 8/15; no deadline. $20 fee. Admission notification on a rolling basis. **Financial aid:** Priority date 5/1; no closing date. FAFSA required. Applicants notified on a rolling basis starting 6/1.

Academics. Special study options: Distance learning, dual enrollment of high school students, honors, independent study, internships, liberal arts/career combination. License preparation in nursing, paramedic. **Credit/placement by examination:** AP, CLEP, IB, institutional tests. **Support services:** GED preparation and test center, learning center, reduced course load, remedial instruction, study skills assistance, tutoring, writing center.

Majors. Business: Accounting, accounting technology, administrative services, business admin, marketing, restaurant/food services. **Communications technology:** Graphic/printing. **Computer sciences:** Data processing, information technology, LAN/WAN management. **General:** Animal sciences, equipment technology, production. **Health services:** Clinical lab technology, dental assistant, EMT paramedic, licensed practical nurse, nursing (RN). **Liberal arts:** Arts/sciences. **Visual/performing arts:** Commercial/advertising art, graphic design. **Work/family studies:** Child development.

Computing on campus. 100 workstations in library, computer center, student center. Commuter students can connect to campus network. Online course registration, online library, helpline, wireless network available.

Student life. Freshman orientation: Mandatory. Preregistration for classes offered. **Activities:** Music ensembles, student government, student newspaper.

Student services. Alcohol/substance abuse counseling, career counseling, student employment services, financial aid counseling, personal counseling, placement for graduates, veterans' counselor. **Physically disabled:** Services for visually, speech, hearing impaired. **Transfer:** Pre-admission transcript evaluation for new students. Transfer adviser for students transferring to 4-year colleges.

Contact. E-mail: admissions@southcentral.edu
Phone: (507) 389-7451 Toll-free number: (800) 722-9359
Fax: (507) 388-9951
David Miller, Admissions Director, South Central College, 1920 Lee Boulevard, North Mankato, MN 56003

St. Cloud Technical and Community College
St Cloud, Minnesota
www.sctcc.edu   **CB code: 1986**

▶ Public 2-year community and technical college
▶ Commuter campus in small city

General. Founded in 1948. Regionally accredited. **Enrollment:** 4,275 degree-seeking undergraduates; 403 non-degree-seeking students. **Degrees:** 635 associate awarded. **Location:** 65 miles from Minneapolis-St. Paul. **Calendar:** Semester, limited summer session. **Full-time faculty:** 102 total; 4% have terminal degrees, 2% minority, 40% women. **Part-time faculty:** 143 total; 6% have terminal degrees, 3% minority, 51% women. **Class size:** 18% < 20, 76% 20-39, 6% 40-49, less than 1% 50-99.

Student profile. Among degree-seeking undergraduates, 39% enrolled in a transfer program, 61% enrolled in a vocational program, 1% already have a bachelor's degree or higher, 1,587 enrolled as first-time, first-year students.

| Part-time: | 45% | Women: | 54% |
| Out-of-state: | 15% | 25 or older: | 29% |

Transfer out. Colleges most students transferred to 2011: St. Cloud State University, Southwest MN State University, Bemidji State University, University of Minnesota.

Basis for selection. Open admission, but selective for some programs. Paramedicine applicants must complete EMT basic and emergency cardiac care courses prior to acceptance. Echocardiography, sonography, cardiovascular technician, practical nursing, dental assisting, and dental hygiene all require prerequisite courses to be completed prior to admission to the major. Programs such as echocardiography, sonography and cardiovascular technician require that students are interviewed as part of the acceptance process. **Home schooled:** Proof of high school graduation required. **Learning Disabled:** Students with developmental disabilities may take the course placement test with accommodations.

High school preparation. Recommended units include English 2, mathematics 2, science 1 (laboratory 1). Mathematics and science classes recommended for technical programs; algebra required for civil engineering; dental hygiene applicants must have all science and nutrition coursework completed; anatomy and physiology, college algebra, and physics required for echocardiography, sonography, and cardiovascular technology.

2011-2012 Annual costs. Tuition/fees: $5,149; $5,149 out-of-state. Per-credit charge: $154. Books/supplies: $950. Personal expenses: $1,000.

2010-2011 Financial aid. Need-based: 56% of total undergraduate aid awarded as scholarships/grants, 44% as loans/jobs. Need-based aid available for part-time students. Work-study available nights, weekends and for part-time students. **Non-need-based:** Scholarships awarded for academics, leadership, state residency.

Application procedures. Admission: Closing date 8/7 (postmark date). $20 fee. Admission notification on a rolling basis beginning on or about 10/7. **Financial aid:** No deadline. FAFSA required. Applicants notified on a rolling basis starting 6/1.

Academics. Special study options: Cooperative education, cross-registration, distance learning, double major, dual enrollment of high school students, ESL, independent study, internships, liberal arts/career combination. Bachelor's degree programs available on campus. License preparation in dental hygiene, nursing, paramedic. **Credit/placement by examination:** AP, CLEP, institutional tests. **Support services:** Learning center, pre-admission summer program, reduced course load, remedial instruction, study skills assistance, tutoring, writing center.

Majors. Business: Accounting, banking/financial services, business admin, executive assistant, sales/distribution. **Communications:** Advertising. **Computer sciences:** Networking, programming. **Education:** Teacher assistance. **Health services:** Cardiovascular technology, dental assistant, dental hygiene, EMT paramedic, licensed practical nurse, medical records technology, sonography, surgical technology. **Work/family studies:** Child care management.

Most popular majors. Business/marketing 16%, communications/journalism 6%, engineering/engineering technologies 11%, health sciences 33%, liberal arts 16%, trade and industry 6%.

Computing on campus. 486 workstations in library, computer center, student center. Commuter students can connect to campus network. Online course registration, online library, helpline, repair service, wireless network available.

Student life. Freshman orientation: Mandatory. Preregistration for classes offered. **Housing:** Privately-owned dormitory next to campus. Housing also available at St. Cloud State University. **Activities:** Student government, student newspaper, TV station, Student senate, Beta Xi Gamma, Somali student club, student veterans club.

Athletics. NJCAA. **Intercollegiate:** Baseball M, basketball, softball W, volleyball W. **Intramural:** Basketball, football (non-tackle), football (tackle), golf, ice hockey, racquetball, soccer, softball, tennis, track and field, volleyball. **Team name:** Cyclones.

Student services. Adult student services, career counseling, student employment services, financial aid counseling, on-campus daycare, personal counseling, placement for graduates, veterans' counselor. **Physically disabled:** Services for visually, speech, hearing impaired. **Transfer:** Pre-admission transcript evaluation for new students. Transfer adviser for students transferring to 4-year colleges.

Contact. E-mail: enroll@sctcc.edu
Phone: (320) 308-5089 Toll-free number: (800) 222-1009 ext. 5089
Fax: (320) 308-5981
Jodi Elness, Director of Enrollment Management, St. Cloud Technical and Community College, 1540 Northway Drive, St. Cloud, MN 56303

St. Paul College
Saint Paul, Minnesota
www.saintpaul.edu

CB code: 0534

◆ Public 2-year community and technical college
◆ Commuter campus in large city

General. Founded in 1919. Regionally accredited. **Enrollment:** 5,886 degree-seeking undergraduates. **Degrees:** 426 associate awarded. **Calendar:** Semester, limited summer session. **Full-time faculty:** 118 total. **Part-time faculty:** 118 total. **Class size:** 35% < 20, 61% 20-39, 4% 40-49, less than 1% 50-99.

Student profile.

Out-of-state:	1%	25 or older:	54%

Transfer out. Colleges most students transferred to 2011: Metropolitan State University, Century Community and Technical College, Inver Hills Community College.

Basis for selection. Open admission, but selective for some programs. ACT considered for placement if submitted; scores must be received by July 1. Limited enrollment and additional requirements for the Medical Laboratory Technician, Watchmaking and MicroMechanical Technology, Respiratory Care Practitioner, and Practical Nursing programs. Our $20 application fee is non-refundable, however due to challenging economic times this fee is waived until further notice. Interview recommended for selected programs. **Home schooled:** Transcript of courses and grades required.

High school preparation. College-preparatory program recommended. Recommended units include English 3, mathematics 2, social studies 3 and history 3.

2011-2012 Annual costs. Tuition/fees: $4,986; $4,986 out-of-state. Per-credit charge: $156. Books/supplies: $800. Personal expenses: $1,640.

Financial aid. Need-based: Need-based aid available for part-time students. Work-study available nights, weekends and for part-time students. **Non-need-based:** Scholarships awarded for leadership.

Application procedures. Admission: Priority date 7/1; no deadline. $20 fee. Application must be submitted online. Admission notification on a rolling basis. **Financial aid:** No deadline. FAFSA required. Applicants notified on a rolling basis starting 6/1.

Academics. Special study options: Distance learning, dual enrollment of high school students, ESL, honors, internships. License preparation in nursing. **Credit/placement by examination:** AP, CLEP, IB, institutional tests. **Support services:** Learning center, reduced course load, remedial instruction, study skills assistance, tutoring, writing center.

Majors. Business: General, accounting, administrative services, business admin, entrepreneurial studies, hospitality admin, human resources, international marketing, logistics, management information systems, office management. **Communications technology:** Animation/special effects. **Computer sciences:** Applications programming, computer graphics, computer science, networking, programming. **Foreign languages:** American Sign Language, sign language interpretation. **Health services:** Athletic training, clinical lab technology, licensed practical nurse, massage therapy, medical records technology, office assistant, respiratory therapy technology. **Liberal arts:** Arts/sciences. **Work/family studies:** Child care management.

Most popular majors. Business/marketing 16%, engineering/engineering technologies 6%, family/consumer sciences 11%, foreign language 8%, health sciences 23%, liberal arts 21%, personal/culinary services 7%.

Computing on campus. 1,000 workstations in library, computer center. Commuter students can connect to campus network. Online course registration, online library, helpline, repair service, wireless network available.

Student life. Freshman orientation: Available. Preregistration for classes offered. **Activities:** Drama, student government, Student Senate, Asian student association, Phi Theta Kappa, Environmental Action Society.

Student services. Adult student services, alcohol/substance abuse counseling, career counseling, student employment services, financial aid counseling, on-campus daycare, personal counseling, placement for graduates, veterans' counselor. **Physically disabled:** Services for visually, speech, hearing impaired. **Transfer:** Pre-admission transcript evaluation for new students. Transfer center, transfer adviser, college fairs on campus for students transferring to 4-year colleges.

Contact. E-mail: admissions@saintpaul.edu
Phone: (651) 846-1555 Toll-free number: (800) 227-6029
Fax: (651) 846-1468
Sarah Carrico, Director of Office of Enrollment Services, St. Paul College, 235 Marshall Avenue, Saint Paul, MN 55102-1800

Vermilion Community College
Ely, Minnesota
www.vcc.edu

CB code: 6194

◆ Public 2-year community and technical college
◆ Residential campus in small town

General. Founded in 1922. Regionally accredited. **Enrollment:** 600 degree-seeking undergraduates. **Degrees:** 90 associate awarded. **Location:** 100 miles from Duluth. **Calendar:** Semester, limited summer session. **Full-time faculty:** 21 total. **Part-time faculty:** 16 total. **Special facilities:** 40-acre outdoor learning center near Boundary Waters Canoe Area.

Student profile.

Out-of-state:	5%	Live on campus:	40%
25 or older:	18%		

Basis for selection. Open admission. Interview required for law enforcement, natural resources, parks and recreation students.

2011-2012 Annual costs. Tuition/fees: $5,141; $6,278 out-of-state. Per-credit charge: $152 in-state; $189 out-of-state. Room/board: $5,040. Books/supplies: $900. Personal expenses: $1,862.

2011-2012 Financial aid. Need-based: 49% of total undergraduate aid awarded as scholarships/grants, 51% as loans/jobs. Need-based aid available for part-time students. Work-study available nights, weekends and for part-time students.

Application procedures. Admission: No deadline. $20 fee, may be waived for applicants with need. Admission notification on a rolling basis beginning on or about 1/1. **Financial aid:** Priority date 4/15; no closing date. FAFSA, institutional form required. Applicants notified on a rolling basis starting 4/1.

Academics. Special study options: Cooperative education, cross-registration, dual enrollment of high school students, honors, independent study, internships, liberal arts/career combination. **Credit/placement by examination:** AP, CLEP. **Support services:** Learning center, pre-admission summer program, reduced course load, remedial instruction, tutoring.

Majors. Biology: General. **Business:** General, accounting, business admin. **Communications:** Communications/speech/rhetoric, journalism. **Conservation:** General, environmental studies, fisheries, forest resources, forestry, management/policy, wildlife/wilderness. **Education:** General, art, biology, business, chemistry, computer, elementary, geography, health, history, kindergarten/preschool, mathematics, middle, physics, science, secondary, social studies. **Engineering:** Civil. **English:** English lit. **Health services:** Environmental health, predental, premedicine, preveterinary. **History:** General. **Parks/recreation:** General, facilities management. **Physical sciences:** General, astronomy, chemistry, geology, physics. **Protective services:** Criminal justice, law enforcement admin, police science. **Psychology:** General. **Social sciences:** General, criminology, geography, political science. **Visual/performing arts:** Dramatic. **Work/family studies:** General.

Computing on campus. 110 workstations in dormitories, library, computer center, student center. Dormitories wired for high-speed internet access and linked to campus network. Helpline, wireless network available.

Student life. Freshman orientation: Mandatory. Preregistration for classes offered. 6 different programs from April through start of classes. **Housing:** Coed dorms available. $200 partly refundable deposit. On-campus, apartment style student housing available. **Activities:** Choral groups, drama, musical theater, student government, student newspaper, Campus Crusaders, GLBT Allies.

Athletics. NJCAA. **Intercollegiate:** Baseball M, basketball, football (tackle) M, softball W, volleyball W. **Intramural:** Basketball, bowling, softball, tennis, volleyball. **Team name:** Ironmen, Ironwomen.

Student services. Alcohol/substance abuse counseling, career counseling, student employment services, personal counseling, placement for graduates, veterans' counselor. **Physically disabled:** Services for visually, speech, hearing impaired. **Transfer:** Transfer adviser, college fairs on campus for students transferring to 4-year colleges.

Contact. E-mail: admissions@vcc.edu
Phone: (218) 235-2191 Toll-free number: (800) 657-3608
Fax: (218) 235-2173
Jeff Nelson, Director of Enrollment Services, Vermilion Community College, 1900 East Camp Street, Ely, MN 55731-9989

White Earth Tribal and Community College
Mahnomen, Minnesota
www.wetcc.edu

- Private 2-year community college
- Commuter campus in rural community

General. Location: 70 miles from Fargo/Moorhead. **Calendar:** Semester.

Annual costs/financial aid. Tuition/fees (2011-2012): $3,285. Books/supplies: $850. Personal expenses: $1,725.

Contact. Phone: (218) 935-0417 ext. 303
Admission's Coordinator, PO Box 478, Mahnomen, MN 56557

Mississippi

Antonelli College: Hattiesburg
Hattiesburg, Mississippi
www.antonellicollege.edu
CB code: 3195

- For-profit 2-year branch campus and technical college
- Commuter campus in large town

General. Accredited by ACCSCT. **Location:** 90 miles from Jackson. **Calendar:** Quarter.

Annual costs/financial aid. Tuition/fees (2011-2012): $14,850. Books/supplies: $1,200.

Contact. Phone: (601) 583-4100
Director of Admissions, 1500 North 31st Avenue, Hattiesburg, MS 39401

Antonelli College: Jackson
Jackson, Mississippi
www.antonellicollege.edu
CB code: 3193

- For-profit 2-year technical and career college
- Commuter campus in small city
- Interview required

General. Accredited by ACCSC. **Enrollment:** 347 degree-seeking undergraduates. **Degrees:** 149 associate awarded. **Calendar:** Quarter. **Full-time faculty:** 17 total. **Part-time faculty:** 22 total.

Basis for selection. Open admission. **Home schooled:** Transcript of courses and grades required.

2011-2012 Annual costs. Tuition/fees: $14,000. Books/supplies: $1,200.

Financial aid. Need-based: Work-study available nights, weekends and for part-time students.

Application procedures. Admission: No deadline. $50 fee. **Financial aid:** No deadline.

Academics. Special study options: Distance learning, double major, honors, internships. **Credit/placement by examination:** AP, CLEP, institutional tests. 14 credit hours maximum toward associate degree. **Support services:** Study skills assistance, tutoring.

Majors. Business: Accounting, office technology. **Computer sciences:** Computer graphics, data entry, networking, security, web page design, webmaster. **Health services:** Insurance coding, massage therapy, medical assistant, medical transcription. **Visual/performing arts:** Graphic design, interior design.

Computing on campus. PC or laptop required. 100 workstations in library, computer center. Commuter students can connect to campus network. Online course registration, online library, repair service, wireless network available.

Student life. Freshman orientation: Mandatory. Preregistration for classes offered. 2 days prior to start of class. **Activities:** Student newspaper.

Student services. Student employment services, financial aid counseling, placement for graduates.

Contact. Phone: (601) 362-9991
Jason Davis, Admissions Director, Antonelli College: Jackson, 2323 Lakeland Drive, Jackson, MS 39232

Blue Cliff College: Gulfport
Gulfport, Mississippi
www.bluecliffcollege.com

- For-profit 2-year career college
- Commuter campus in small city

General. Accredited by ACCSCT. **Calendar:** Quarter.

Annual costs/financial aid. Medical assisting: $14,336 tuition, $1,200 program fees; massage therapist: $13,144 tuition, $1,200 program fees; dialysis technician: $13,144 tuition, $1,200 program fees; cosmetologist: $12,270 tuition, $1,500 program fees. Covers cost of entire program. Need-based financial aid available to full-time and part-time students.

Contact. Phone: (288) 896-9727
Director of Admissions, 12251 Bernard Parkway, Gulfport, MS 39503

Coahoma Community College
Clarksdale, Mississippi
www.coahomacc.edu
CB code: 1126

- Public 2-year community college
- Commuter campus in large town

General. Founded in 1949. Regionally accredited. **Enrollment:** 3,000 degree-seeking undergraduates. **Degrees:** 291 associate awarded. **Location:** 65 miles from Memphis, Tennessee. **Calendar:** Semester, limited summer session. **Full-time faculty:** 77 total. **Part-time faculty:** 54 total.

Transfer out. Colleges most students transferred to 2011: Alcorn State University, Delta State University, Jackson State University, Mississippi Valley State University, University of Mississippi.

Basis for selection. Open admission, but selective for some programs. High school record most important for admission to degree programs. Open admissions to vocational programs. Limited admission to associate degree nursing, licensed practical nursing, and respiratory therapy. ACT/SAT required for nursing. Interview required for nursing students; audition required for music students. **Home schooled:** Transcript of courses and grades, letter of recommendation (nonparent) required.

High school preparation. College-preparatory program required. Recommended units include English 4, mathematics 3, social studies 2, science 3 (laboratory 3) and foreign language 1.

2011-2012 Annual costs. Tuition/fees: $2,040; $4,940 out-of-state. Per-credit charge: $100. Room/board: $3,714. Books/supplies: $800. Personal expenses: $700.

Financial aid. All financial aid based on need. Need-based aid available for part-time students. Work-study available nights, weekends and for part-time students.

Application procedures. Admission: No deadline. No application fee. Admission notification on a rolling basis. **Financial aid:** Priority date 4/1; no closing date. FAFSA, institutional form required. Applicants notified on a rolling basis starting 7/1.

Academics. Special study options: Distance learning, dual enrollment of high school students. License preparation in nursing. **Credit/placement by examination:** AP, CLEP. **Support services:** GED preparation and test center, reduced course load, remedial instruction, tutoring, writing center.

Majors. Biology: General. **Business:** General, accounting, hotel/motel admin, office technology. **Communications:** Broadcast journalism, journalism. **Computer sciences:** General, computer science. **Education:** General, art, business, early childhood, elementary, health, mathematics, music, physical, science, social science. **Health services:** Clinical lab science, medical records admin, nursing (RN), predental, premedicine, prenursing, prepharmacy, preveterinary, respiratory therapy technology. **Human services:** Social work. **Math:** General. **Parks/recreation:** Sports admin. **Physical sciences:** Chemistry. **Protective services:** Criminal justice. **Social sciences:** General. **Visual/performing arts:** General. **Work/family studies:** Child care management.

Most popular majors. Business/marketing 16%, education 41%, health sciences 15%, public administration/social services 11%.

Computing on campus. Dormitories wired for high-speed internet access and linked to campus network. Online course registration, online library, helpline, wireless network available.

Student life. Freshman orientation: Mandatory. Preregistration for classes offered. Semester-long course offered each semester. **Housing:** Single-sex dorms, special housing for disabled, wellness housing available. $100 deposit, deadline 8/1. **Activities:** Bands, choral groups, music ensembles, student government, student newspaper, Baptist student union, Wesley Foundation, Black literary society.

Athletics. NJCAA. **Intercollegiate:** Baseball M, basketball, football (tackle) M, softball W. **Intramural:** Badminton, basketball, bowling, cheerleading W, football (non-tackle) M, football (tackle) M, softball, table tennis, volleyball. **Team name:** Tigers.

Student services. Career counseling, services for economically disadvantaged, financial aid counseling, health services, personal counseling. **Physically disabled:** Services for visually, speech, hearing impaired. **Transfer:** Pre-admission transcript evaluation for new students. Transfer adviser, college fairs on campus for students transferring to 4-year colleges.

Contact. E-mail: wholmes@coahomacc.edu
Phone: (662) 621-4205 Toll-free number: (800) 844-1222
Fax: (800) 844-1222
Delores Richard, Director of Admissions, Coahoma Community College, 3240 Friars Point Road, Clarksdale, MS 38614-9799

Copiah-Lincoln Community College
Wesson, Mississippi
www.colin.edu   CB code: 1142

▶ Public 2-year community college
▶ Commuter campus in small town

General. Founded in 1928. Regionally accredited. Branch campuses in Natchez and Simpson County. **Enrollment:** 3,506 degree-seeking undergraduates; 212 non-degree-seeking students. **Degrees:** 506 associate awarded. **Location:** 45 miles from Jackson. **Calendar:** Semester, limited summer session. **Full-time faculty:** 122 total. **Part-time faculty:** 77 total. **Special facilities:** Walking trail, golf course. **Partnerships:** Formal partnerships with over 300 local businesses and industries, health occupation affiliates, government agencies, and public service groups.

Student profile. Among degree-seeking undergraduates, 911 enrolled as first-time, first-year students.

Part-time:	14%	25 or older:	29%
Out-of-state:	6%	Live on campus:	18%
Women:	63%		

Transfer out. Colleges most students transferred to 2011: University of Southern Mississippi, Alcorn State University, University of Mississippi, Mississippi State University, Jackson State University.

Basis for selection. Open admission, but selective for some programs. ACT required for certain technology and health occupation programs. **Adult students:** If ACT score not available, placement test required. **Home schooled:** Transcript of courses and grades required. ACT required.

2011-2012 Annual costs. Tuition/fees: $2,100; $3,900 out-of-state. Per-credit charge: $108 in-state; $183 out-of-state. Room/board: $3,300. Books/supplies: $800.

Financial aid. Need-based: Need-based aid available for part-time students. Work-study available nights, weekends and for part-time students. **Non-need-based:** Scholarships awarded for academics, art, athletics, job skills, leadership, music/drama, state residency.

Application procedures. Admission: No deadline. No application fee. Application must be submitted on paper. Admission notification on a rolling basis. **Financial aid:** Priority date 4/1; no closing date. FAFSA required. Applicants notified on a rolling basis starting 4/1; must reply within 2 week(s) of notification.

Academics. Special study options: Accelerated study, distance learning, dual enrollment of high school students, honors. License preparation in nursing, paramedic, radiology. **Credit/placement by examination:** AP, CLEP, institutional tests. 24 credit hours maximum toward associate degree. **Support services:** GED preparation and test center, learning center, remedial instruction, study skills assistance, tutoring.

Majors. Business: Accounting technology, business admin, hotel/motel/restaurant management, marketing, office technology. **Computer sciences:** Data entry, networking. **Health services:** Clinical lab science, clinical lab technology, medical radiologic technology/radiation therapy, nursing (RN), respiratory therapy technology. **Liberal arts:** Arts/sciences. **Work/family studies:** Child care management.

Computing on campus. 519 workstations in library, computer center. Dormitories wired for high-speed internet access and linked to campus network. Commuter students can connect to campus network. Online course registration, online library, helpline, student web hosting, wireless network available.

Student life. Freshman orientation: Mandatory. Preregistration for classes offered. 3 times during the summer and before fall and spring registration. **Housing:** Guaranteed on-campus for all undergraduates. Single-sex dorms, special housing for disabled, apartments, wellness housing available. $50 nonrefundable deposit. **Activities:** Bands, campus ministries, choral groups, literary magazine, music ensembles, radio station, student government, student newspaper, Baptist student union, Wesley Foundation, student Christian association, African-American Studies Club, College Republicans.

Athletics. NJCAA. **Intercollegiate:** Baseball M, basketball, cheerleading, football (tackle) M, golf, soccer, softball W, tennis, track and field M. **Intramural:** Basketball, softball M, volleyball. **Team name:** Wolves.

Student services. Chaplain/spiritual director, career counseling, services for economically disadvantaged, financial aid counseling, health services, on-campus daycare, personal counseling, veterans' counselor. **Physically disabled:** Services for visually, speech, hearing impaired. **Transfer:** Pre-admission transcript evaluation for new students. College fairs on campus for students transferring to 4-year colleges.

Contact. E-mail: gay.langham@colin.edu
Phone: (601) 643-8307 Fax: (601) 643-8225
Christopher Warren, Director of Admissions, Copiah-Lincoln Community College, PO Box 649, Wesson, MS 39191

East Central Community College
Decatur, Mississippi
www.eccc.edu   CB code: 1196

▶ Public 2-year community college
▶ Commuter campus in rural community

General. Founded in 1928. Regionally accredited. **Location:** 30 miles from Meridian, 85 miles from Jackson. **Calendar:** Semester.

Annual costs/financial aid. Tuition/fees (2011-2012): $1,980; $2,290 out-of-state. Room/board: $3,190. Books/supplies: $800. Personal expenses: $900.

Contact. Phone: (601) 635-2111 ext. 392
Director of Admissions, Box 129, Decatur, MS 39327

East Mississippi Community College
Scooba, Mississippi
www.eastms.edu   CB code: 1197

▶ Public 2-year community college
▶ Residential campus in rural community

General. Founded in 1927. Regionally accredited. **Enrollment:** 4,968 degree-seeking undergraduates. **Degrees:** 850 associate awarded. **ROTC:** Naval. **Location:** 37 miles from Meridian. **Calendar:** Semester, extensive summer session. **Full-time faculty:** 105 total. **Part-time faculty:** 137 total.

Basis for selection. Open admission, but selective for some programs. Special requirements for practical nursing, cosmetology, and funeral service technology. **Adult students:** SAT/ACT scores not required if applicant over 21.

2011-2012 Annual costs. Tuition/fees: $2,450; $4,500 out-of-state. Per-credit charge: $135 in-state; $139 out-of-state. Room/board: $3,500. Books/supplies: $900. Personal expenses: $2,200.

Financial aid. Need-based: Need-based aid available for part-time students. Work-study available nights, weekends and for part-time students. **Non-need-based:** Scholarships awarded for academics, art, athletics, leadership, music/drama, state residency.

Application procedures. Admission: No deadline. No application fee. Admission notification on a rolling basis. **Financial aid:** Priority date 4/1; no closing date. FAFSA, institutional form required. Applicants notified on a rolling basis starting 4/1; must reply within 2 week(s) of notification.

Academics. Special study options: Distance learning, dual enrollment of high school students, honors. License preparation in nursing. **Credit/placement by examination:** AP, CLEP, institutional tests. **Support services:** GED preparation and test center, learning center, reduced course load, remedial instruction, tutoring.

Majors. Business: Banking/financial services. **Computer sciences:** General, programming.

Most popular majors. Business/marketing 17%, education 12%, health sciences 24%, liberal arts 21%, personal/culinary services 6%.

Computing on campus. 60 workstations in library, computer center. Dormitories wired for high-speed internet access. Online library, helpline, wireless network available.

Student life. Freshman orientation: Mandatory. Preregistration for classes offered. **Housing:** Single-sex dorms available. $50 deposit. **Activities:** Marching band, choral groups, drama, literary magazine, music ensembles, student government, student newspaper, Gospel Choir, Interdenominational Christian Fellowship Group, Fellowship of Christian Athletes.

Athletics. NJCAA. **Intercollegiate:** Baseball M, basketball, cheerleading, football (tackle) M, golf, rodeo, softball W. **Team name:** Lions.

Student services. Adult student services, career counseling, services for economically disadvantaged, financial aid counseling, health services, personal counseling, placement for graduates. **Transfer:** Pre-admission transcript evaluation for new students. Transfer adviser, college fairs on campus for students transferring to 4-year colleges.

Contact. E-mail: kbriggs@eastms.edu
Phone: (662) 476-5040 Fax: (662) 476-5038
Karen Briggs, Director of Admissions, East Mississippi Community College, Admissions Office, Scooba, MS 39358

Hinds Community College
Raymond, Mississippi
www.hindscc.edu   CB code: 1296

- Public 2-year branch campus and community college
- Commuter campus in small town

General. Founded in 1917. Regionally accredited. 6 campus locations: Raymond, Utica, Rankin (Pearl), Jackson Academic/Technical Center, Nursing/Allied Health Center (Jackson), and Vicksburg-Warren County Center. **Enrollment:** 12,714 degree-seeking undergraduates. **Degrees:** 1,318 associate awarded. **ROTC:** Army. **Location:** 10 miles from Jackson. **Calendar:** Semester, extensive summer session. **Full-time faculty:** 431 total. **Part-time faculty:** 312 total. **Class size:** 45% < 20, 48% 20-39, 5% 40-49, less than 1% 50-99, less than 1% >100.

Student profile.

Out-of-state:	1%	Live on campus:	16%
25 or older:	43%		

Transfer out. Colleges most students transferred to 2011: Mississippi State University, University of Southern Mississippi, Jackson State, University of Mississippi, Mississippi College.

Basis for selection. Open admission, but selective for some programs. Special requirements for allied health and data processing programs. ACT not required for placement in vocational programs. 19 high school units, ACT composite score of 18 may be substituted for diploma. Interview required for allied health and some vocational majors.

High school preparation. 19 units recommended. Recommended units include English 4, mathematics 2, social studies 2 and science 2.

2011-2012 Annual costs. Tuition/fees: $2,060; $4,660 out-of-state. Per-credit charge: $100 in-state; $200 out-of-state. Room/board: $3,510. Books/supplies: $420. Personal expenses: $1,500.

2011-2012 Financial aid. Need-based: Need-based aid available for part-time students. Work-study available nights, weekends and for part-time students. **Non-need-based:** Scholarships awarded for academics, art, athletics, job skills, leadership, minority status, music/drama, state residency.

Application procedures. Admission: No deadline. No application fee. Admission notification on a rolling basis beginning on or about 3/1. **Financial aid:** Priority date 4/1; no closing date. FAFSA required. Applicants notified on a rolling basis starting 5/15; must reply within 2 week(s) of notification.

Academics. Special study options: Accelerated study, cooperative education, distance learning, double major, dual enrollment of high school students, honors, independent study, internships, liberal arts/career combination, study abroad. License preparation in nursing. **Credit/placement by examination:** AP, CLEP, institutional tests. 18 credit hours maximum toward associate degree. **Support services:** GED preparation and test center, learning center, remedial instruction, tutoring.

Majors. Biology: General. **Business:** Administrative services, fashion, finance, management information systems, office management, operations,

sales/distribution, tourism promotion. **Communications:** Journalism. **Communications technology:** General, graphic/printing. **Computer sciences:** General, data processing. **Education:** Business, elementary, physical, secondary, trade/industrial. **Engineering:** General. **English:** English lit, rhetoric/composition. **Foreign languages:** Sign language interpretation. **General:** Agribusiness operations, animal breeding, food science, landscaping. **Health services:** Clinical lab assistant, clinical lab technology, dental assistant, EMT paramedic, licensed practical nurse, medical records technology, nursing assistant, respiratory therapy technology, surgical technology, veterinary technology/assistant. **History:** General. **Liberal arts:** Arts/sciences. **Math:** General. **Physical sciences:** Chemistry, geology, physics. **Protective services:** Criminal justice, fire safety technology. **Psychology:** General. **Social sciences:** Political science, sociology. **Visual/performing arts:** Art, commercial/advertising art, dramatic, music. **Work/family studies:** General, child care management, institutional food production.

Most popular majors. Business/marketing 12%, health sciences 28%, liberal arts 45%.

Computing on campus. 55 workstations in library, computer center. Online course registration, helpline, repair service available.

Student life. Freshman orientation: Available, $65 fee. Preregistration for classes offered. **Housing:** Single-sex dorms available. $50 deposit. **Activities:** Bands, choral groups, dance, drama, music ensembles, musical theater, student government, student newspaper, Baptist Student Union, Afro-American Cultural Society, Catholic Student Organization, College Independents, College Republicans, Fellowship of Christian Athletes, Class/Leadership/Authority and Womanhood, Campus Christian Fellowship.

Athletics. NJCAA. **Intercollegiate:** Baseball M, basketball, football (tackle) M, golf M, soccer M, softball W, tennis, track and field M. **Intramural:** Basketball, football (tackle) M, softball M, volleyball. **Team name:** Eagles.

Student services. Career counseling, student employment services, minority student services, personal counseling, placement for graduates, veterans' counselor. **Physically disabled:** Services for visually, speech, hearing impaired. **Transfer:** Transfer adviser, college fairs on campus for students transferring to 4-year colleges.

Contact. E-mail: records@hindscc.edu
Phone: (601) 857-3212 Toll-free number: (800) 446-3722
Fax: (601) 857-3539
Randall Harris, Director of Admissions and Records, Hinds Community College, 505 East Main Street, Raymond, MS 39154-1100

Holmes Community College
Goodman, Mississippi
www.holmescc.edu   CB code: 1299

- Public 2-year community college
- Residential campus in rural community

General. Founded in 1925. Regionally accredited. Additional campuses in Ridgeland and Grenada. **Enrollment:** 6,495 degree-seeking undergraduates. **Degrees:** 949 associate awarded. **Location:** 40 miles from Jackson. **Calendar:** Semester, extensive summer session. **Full-time faculty:** 149 total. **Part-time faculty:** 186 total. **Special facilities:** Observatory.

Student profile.

Out-of-state:	5%	Live on campus:	25%
25 or older:	33%		

Transfer out. Colleges most students transferred to 2011: Mississippi State University, University of Mississippi, Delta State University, University of Southern Mississippi.

Basis for selection. Open admission, but selective for some programs. Associate degree nursing applicants required to have ACT composite score of 18, and 17 math sub-score and 18 reading sub-score. Practical nurse applicants must have composite ACT score of 16 with math and reading sub-scores of 12. Adjustments made for scores pre-dating October 1989. ACT or SAT is required for placement. **Adult students:** SAT/ACT scores not required if applicant over 21. **Home schooled:** Transcript of courses and grades required.

High school preparation. College-preparatory program required. 21 units required. Required units include English 4, mathematics 4, social studies 1, history 2, science 3, computer science 1, visual/performing arts 1, academic electives 4.5. .5 unit in health.

2011-2012 Annual costs. Tuition/fees: $2,210; $4,790 out-of-state. Room/board: $2,433. Books/supplies: $600. Personal expenses: $3,610.

2010-2011 Financial aid. Need-based: 79% of total undergraduate aid awarded as scholarships/grants, 21% as loans/jobs. Work-study available nights, weekends and for part-time students. **Non-need-based:** Scholarships awarded for academics, athletics.

Application procedures. Admission: No deadline. No application fee. Admission notification on a rolling basis. **Financial aid:** Priority date 6/1; no closing date. FAFSA, institutional form required. Applicants notified on a rolling basis.

Academics. Special study options: Cooperative education, distance learning, dual enrollment of high school students, honors, internships, liberal arts/career combination, weekend college. License preparation in nursing, paramedic. **Credit/placement by examination:** AP, CLEP, institutional tests. **Support services:** GED test center, learning center, reduced course load, remedial instruction, study skills assistance, tutoring, writing center.

Majors. Business: Administrative services, business admin, fashion. **Computer sciences:** General, computer science, programming. **Conservation:** Forestry. **Education:** Elementary, secondary. **Engineering:** General, architectural, electrical. **Health services:** Predental, premedicine, prepharmacy, preveterinary. **Liberal arts:** Arts/sciences. **Math:** General.

Computing on campus. 400 workstations in library, computer center. Dormitories linked to campus network. Commuter students can connect to campus network. Online course registration, online library, helpline, repair service, wireless network available.

Student life. Freshman orientation: Available. Preregistration for classes offered. **Housing:** Single-sex dorms available. $50 partly refundable deposit. **Activities:** Bands, campus ministries, choral groups, dance, drama, literary magazine, music ensembles, musical theater, student government, student newspaper, Baptist Student Union, Wesley Foundation, College Republican Club, Fellowship of Christian Athletes.

Athletics. NJCAA. **Intercollegiate:** Baseball M, basketball, cheerleading, football (tackle) M, golf M, soccer, softball W, tennis, track and field. **Intramural:** Basketball, football (tackle) M, soccer M, softball, track and field M, volleyball. **Team name:** Bulldogs.

Student services. Adult student services, career counseling, services for economically disadvantaged, personal counseling, veterans' counselor. **Physically disabled:** Services for visually, speech, hearing impaired. **Transfer:** Pre-admission transcript evaluation for new students. Transfer adviser, college fairs on campus for students transferring to 4-year colleges.

Contact. E-mail: progers@holmescc.edu
Phone: (662) 472-9073 Toll-free number: (800) 465-6374
Fax: (662) 472-9152
Joshua Guest, Director of Admissions and Records, Holmes Community College, Box 398, Goodman, MS 39079

Itawamba Community College
Fulton, Mississippi
www.iccms.edu   CB code: 1326

- Public 2-year community and technical college
- Commuter campus in small town

General. Founded in 1948. Regionally accredited. Additional campuses in Fulton, Tupelo, as well as online instruction. **Enrollment:** 6,842 degree-seeking undergraduates. **Degrees:** 1,229 associate awarded. **Location:** 115 miles from Memphis, Tennessee, 135 miles from Birmingham, Alabama. **Calendar:** Semester, limited summer session. **Full-time faculty:** 169 total. **Part-time faculty:** 280 total. **Class size:** 51% < 20, 43% 20-39, 5% 40-49, 1% 50-99.

Transfer out. Colleges most students transferred to 2011: Mississippi State University, University of Mississippi.

Basis for selection. Open admission, but selective for some programs. Special requirements for health science programs, including minimum test scores on ACT or other discipline-specific tests and grade of at least 2.0 in program prerequisite courses. **Home schooled:** Must complete GED or appeal to Admissions and Guidance Committee. **Learning Disabled:** Developmental courses recommended. Assistance provided by special needs counselor.

2011-2012 Annual costs. Tuition/fees: $2,020; $3,770 out-of-state. Room/board: $3,230. Books/supplies: $900. Personal expenses: $180.

Financial aid. Need-based: Need-based aid available for part-time students. Work-study available nights, weekends and for part-time students. **Non-need-based:** Scholarships awarded for academics, art, athletics, leadership, music/drama, state residency.

Application procedures. Admission: No deadline. No application fee. Admission notification on a rolling basis. **Financial aid:** Priority date 4/30, closing date 7/31. FAFSA, institutional form required. Applicants notified on a rolling basis starting 4/15.

Academics. Special study options: Accelerated study, cooperative education, distance learning, double major, dual enrollment of high school students, ESL, honors, independent study, internships. License preparation in nursing, paramedic, physical therapy, radiology, real estate. **Credit/placement by examination:** AP, CLEP, institutional tests. 15 credit hours maximum toward associate degree. **Support services:** GED preparation and test center, learning center, reduced course load, remedial instruction, study skills assistance, tutoring, writing center.

Majors. Business: General, accounting, administrative services, management information systems, office/clerical. **Communications:** Broadcast journalism, journalism, public relations. **Computer sciences:** General, computer science, data processing, programming. **Conservation:** Forestry. **Education:** Art, biology, business, chemistry, elementary, French, health, history, mathematics, music, physical, physics, science, secondary, social studies, Spanish, special ed, speech. **Engineering:** General, electrical. **Foreign languages:** French, sign language interpretation, Spanish. **General:** Business. **Health services:** EMT paramedic, medical radiologic technology/radiation therapy, medical records admin, medical records technology, nursing (RN), occupational health, physical therapy assistant, predental, premedicine, prepharmacy, preveterinary, respiratory therapy technology, sonography, surgical technology. **History:** General. **Human services:** Social work. **Liberal arts:** Arts/sciences, library science. **Math:** General. **Philosophy/religion:** Philosophy. **Physical sciences:** Chemistry, geology, physics. **Protective services:** Criminal justice. **Psychology:** General. **Social sciences:** Economics, sociology. **Visual/performing arts:** Art, music. **Work/family studies:** General, child care management.

Most popular majors. Business/marketing 11%, family/consumer sciences 6%, health sciences 36%, liberal arts 42%.

Computing on campus. 600 workstations in dormitories, library, computer center. Dormitories wired for high-speed internet access and linked to campus network. Commuter students can connect to campus network. Online course registration, online library, helpline, wireless network available.

Student life. Freshman orientation: Available. Preregistration for classes offered. **Housing:** Single-sex dorms, wellness housing available. $50 deposit. **Activities:** Bands, choral groups, dance, drama, literary magazine, music ensembles, musical theater, student government, student newspaper.

Athletics. NJCAA. **Intercollegiate:** Baseball M, basketball, cheerleading, football (tackle) M, golf M, soccer M, softball W. **Intramural:** Basketball. **Team name:** Indians.

Student services. Alcohol/substance abuse counseling, chaplain/spiritual director, career counseling, services for economically disadvantaged, student employment services, financial aid counseling, minority student services, on-campus daycare, placement for graduates, veterans' counselor, women's services. **Physically disabled:** Services for visually, hearing impaired. **Transfer:** Transfer adviser, college fairs on campus for students transferring to 4-year colleges.

Contact. E-mail: hgjefcoat@iccms.edu
Phone: (662) 862-8031 Fax: (662) 862-8036
Cay Lollar, Director of Admissions, Itawamba Community College, 602 West Hill Street, Fulton, MS 38843-1099

Jones County Junior College
Ellisville, Mississippi
www.jcjc.edu   CB code: 1347

- Public 2-year community and junior college
- Commuter campus in small town

General. Founded in 1927. Regionally accredited. **Location:** 7 miles from Laurel, 20 miles from Hattiesburg. **Calendar:** Semester.

Annual costs/financial aid. Tuition/fees (2011-2012): $2,380; $4,380 out-of-state. Room/board: $3,474. Books/supplies: $600. Personal expenses: $1,299. Need-based financial aid available to full-time and part-time students.

Contact. Phone: (601) 477-4025
Director of Admissions & Records, 900 South Court Street, Ellisville, MS 39437

Meridian Community College
Meridian, Mississippi
www.meridiancc.edu

CB member
CB code: 1461

◆ Public 2-year community college
◆ Commuter campus in large town

General. Founded in 1937. Regionally accredited. On-line degree programs. **Enrollment:** 2,999 full-time, degree-seeking students. **Degrees:** 545 associate awarded. **Location:** 90 miles from Jackson, 90 miles from Tuscaloosa, Alabama. **Calendar:** Semester, extensive summer session. **Full-time faculty:** 162 total; 14% minority, 72% women. **Part-time faculty:** 57 total; 14% minority, 54% women. **Special facilities:** Fitness center & natatorium, workforce development center, student success center.

Basis for selection. Open admission, but selective for some programs. Specific programs may have admission criteria required for entrance to the program. Test scores, recommendations, background checks, prerequisite coursework all considered for health education applicants. Interview recommended for broadcast technology, data processing, graphic communication technology, and health programs majors. **Adult students:** SAT/ACT scores not required. ACCUPLACER given for placement if no SAT/ACT test scores are available,.

High school preparation. Recommended units include English 4, mathematics 3, social studies 3, science 3 and academic electives 2. .5 unit computer applications recommended.

2011-2012 Annual costs. Tuition/fees: $2,220; $3,600 out-of-state. Per-credit charge: $100 in-state; $157 out-of-state. Room/board: $3,300.

2011-2012 Financial aid. **Need-based:** Need-based aid available for part-time students. Work-study available nights, weekends and for part-time students. **Non-need-based:** Scholarships awarded for academics, art, athletics, leadership, music/drama, state residency.

Application procedures. **Admission:** No deadline. No application fee. Admission notification on a rolling basis. **Financial aid:** Priority date 6/1; no closing date. FAFSA, institutional form required. Applicants notified on a rolling basis starting 5/15; must reply within 2 week(s) of notification.

Academics. **Special study options:** Accelerated study, distance learning, dual enrollment of high school students, ESL, independent study, internships, weekend college. License preparation in dental hygiene, nursing, occupational therapy, physical therapy, radiology, real estate. **Credit/placement by examination:** AP, CLEP. 45 credit hours maximum toward associate degree. **Support services:** GED preparation and test center, learning center, remedial instruction, study skills assistance, tutoring.

Majors. **Business:** Administrative services, hotel/motel/restaurant management, marketing. **Communications technology:** Graphics, radio/TV. **Computer sciences:** General, LAN/WAN management, programming. **Education:** Early childhood. **Health services:** Clinical lab technology, dental hygiene, insurance coding, insurance specialist, medical radiologic technology/radiation therapy, medical records technology, medical secretary, nursing (RN), physical therapy assistant, radiologic technology/medical imaging, respiratory therapy assistant, respiratory therapy technology. **Protective services:** Firefighting.

Computing on campus. 85 workstations in library, computer center. Dormitories wired for high-speed internet access and linked to campus network. Commuter students can connect to campus network. Online course registration, online library, helpline, repair service, wireless network available.

Student life. Freshman orientation: Mandatory. Preregistration for classes offered. Orientation sessions specific to certain programs and for first-time freshmen available. **Housing:** Single-sex dorms, special housing for disabled, apartments, wellness housing available. $100 fully refundable deposit. **Activities:** Bands, campus ministries, choral groups, drama, international student organizations, literary magazine, music ensembles, musical theater, radio station, student government, student newspaper, TV station, Baptist Student Union, T.J. Harris Organization, Wesley Foundation, Fellowship of Christian Athletes, Phi Theta Kappa, multicultural student association, Future Teachers of America, health occupation organizations, HOSA.

Athletics. NJCAA. **Intercollegiate:** Baseball M, basketball, cheerleading, golf, soccer, softball W, tennis. **Intramural:** Basketball, softball W, tennis, volleyball. **Team name:** Eagles.

Student services. Career counseling, student employment services, financial aid counseling, personal counseling, placement for graduates, veterans' counselor. **Physically disabled:** Services for visually, speech, hearing impaired. **Transfer:** Pre-admission transcript evaluation for new students.

Transfer adviser, college fairs on campus for students transferring to 4-year colleges.

Contact. E-mail: apayne@meridiancc.edu
Phone: (601) 484-8895 Toll-free number: (800) 622-8431
Fax: (601) 484-8838
Angela Payne, Director of Admissions, Meridian Community College, 910 Highway 19 North, Meridian, MS 39307-5890

Mississippi Delta Community College
Moorhead, Mississippi
www.msdelta.edu

CB code: 1742

◆ Public 2-year community college
◆ Commuter campus in rural community

General. Founded in 1926. Regionally accredited. **Enrollment:** 3,364 degree-seeking undergraduates. **Degrees:** 392 associate awarded. **Location:** 20 miles from Greenwood. **Calendar:** Semester, limited summer session. **Full-time faculty:** 116 total. **Part-time faculty:** 108 total.

Student profile.

Out-of-state:	3%	Live on campus:	25%

Transfer out. Colleges most students transferred to 2011: Delta State University, Mississippi State University, University of Mississippi, University of Southern Mississippi.

Basis for selection. Open admission, but selective for some programs. Test scores most important. Open admission to vocational programs. Limited admission to health occupations and computer technology curriculum.

High school preparation. 19 units recommended. Recommended units include English 3, mathematics 3, social studies 3, science 3, foreign language 3 and academic electives 4. 12 of the recommended units may be distributed in any combination in mathematics, science, foreign language, social studies, and history.

2011-2012 Annual costs. Tuition/fees: $2,330; $3,938 out-of-state. Room/board: $2,690. Books/supplies: $450. Personal expenses: $400.

Financial aid. **Need-based:** Work-study available nights, weekends and for part-time students. **Non-need-based:** Scholarships awarded for academics, athletics, state residency.

Application procedures. **Admission:** Priority date 7/1; no deadline. No application fee. Admission notification on a rolling basis beginning on or about 5/30. **Financial aid:** Closing date 8/1. FAFSA, institutional form required. Applicants notified on a rolling basis; must reply within 2 week(s) of notification.

Academics. **Special study options:** Distance learning. License preparation in nursing. **Credit/placement by examination:** AP, CLEP. 15 credit hours maximum toward associate degree. **Support services:** GED preparation and test center, reduced course load, remedial instruction.

Majors. **Area/ethnic studies:** American. **Biology:** General. **Business:** Accounting, administrative services. **Communications:** Advertising, communications/speech/rhetoric. **Computer sciences:** Programming. **Conservation:** Forestry. **Education:** General, art, business, elementary, health, physical, secondary, special ed, speech. **Engineering:** General. **English:** English lit. **General:** Business, economics, farm/ranch, horticulture. **Health services:** Clinical lab technology, dental hygiene, EMT paramedic, medical radiologic technology/radiation therapy, medical records admin, predental, prepharmacy, preveterinary. **History:** General. **Human services:** Social work. **Liberal arts:** Arts/sciences. **Protective services:** Law enforcement admin. **Psychology:** General. **Social sciences:** General, sociology. **Visual/performing arts:** Music, studio arts. **Work/family studies:** General.

Student life. Freshman orientation: Available. Preregistration for classes offered. **Housing:** Single-sex dorms available. **Activities:** Bands, choral groups, dance, drama, student government, student newspaper, Baptist Student Union, Wesley Foundation, Vocational Industrial Clubs of America.

Athletics. NJCAA. **Intercollegiate:** Baseball M, basketball, football (tackle) M, golf M, soccer M, softball W, tennis, track and field M. **Intramural:** Basketball, softball, tennis, track and field, volleyball.

Student services. Career counseling, student employment services, personal counseling, placement for graduates, veterans' counselor. **Transfer:** Transfer adviser for students transferring to 4-year colleges.

Two-Year Colleges

Contact. E-mail: admissions@msdelta.edu
Phone: (662) 246-6306 Fax: (662) 246-6321
Joe Ray, Chief Admissions Officer, Mississippi Delta Community
College, Box 668, Moorhead, MS 38761

Mississippi Gulf Coast Community College
Perkinston, Mississippi **CB member**
www.mgccc.edu **CB code: 1353**

- Public 2-year community college
- Commuter campus in large city

General. Founded in 1965. Regionally accredited. 3 campuses and 4 centers. **Enrollment:** 9,980 degree-seeking undergraduates. **Degrees:** 1,904 associate awarded. **Location:** 30 miles from Biloxi, 90 miles from New Orleans. **Calendar:** Semester, limited summer session. **Full-time faculty:** 308 total. **Part-time faculty:** 230 total.

Student profile.

Out-of-state:	3%	Live on campus:	8%
25 or older:	36%		

Transfer out. Colleges most students transferred to 2011: University of Southern MS; Mississippi State University; University of South Alabama.

Basis for selection. Open admission, but selective for some programs. Background check and substance tests, reading and math proficiency required for nursing.

High school preparation. 19 units recommended. Recommended units include English 3, mathematics 3 and science 3.

2011-2012 Annual costs. Tuition/fees: $2,772; $4,618 out-of-state. Per-credit charge: $115 in-state; $192 out-of-state. Room/board: $3,810. Books/supplies: $860. Personal expenses: $1,050.

Financial aid. All financial aid based on need. Work-study available nights, weekends and for part-time students.

Application procedures. Admission: No deadline. No application fee. **Financial aid:** Priority date 6/1; no closing date. Institutional form required. Applicants notified on a rolling basis starting 7/1.

Academics. Special study options: Accelerated study, cooperative education, distance learning, dual enrollment of high school students, honors, weekend college. License preparation in nursing, paramedic, radiology. **Credit/placement by examination:** AP, CLEP. 32 credit hours maximum toward associate degree. **Support services:** GED preparation and test center, learning center, reduced course load, remedial instruction, study skills assistance, tutoring.

Majors. Biology: General, biotechnology. **Business:** General, accounting, administrative services, banking/financial services, business admin, fashion, management information systems, marketing, office technology. **Communications:** Communications/speech/rhetoric. **Computer sciences:** General. **Conservation:** Fisheries, forestry. **Education:** General, art, business, elementary, mathematics, multi-level teacher, science, secondary, trade/industrial. **Engineering:** General. **General:** Food science, landscaping, ornamental horticulture, turf management. **Health services:** Clinical lab science, clinical lab technology, EMT paramedic, medical radiologic technology/radiation therapy, medical records admin, medical secretary, nursing (RN), optician, orthotics/prosthetics, prepharmacy, respiratory therapy technology, veterinary technology/assistant. **Human services:** Social work. **Liberal arts:** Arts/sciences. **Math:** General. **Protective services:** Criminal justice, fire safety technology. **Psychology:** General. **Visual/performing arts:** Art, commercial/advertising art, interior design, music, sculpture.

Most popular majors. Business/marketing 15%, education 15%, engineering/engineering technologies 10%, health sciences 19%, liberal arts 27%.

Computing on campus. 750 workstations in library, computer center, student center. Dormitories wired for high-speed internet access and linked to campus network. Commuter students can connect to campus network. Online course registration, wireless network available.

Student life. Freshman orientation: Mandatory. Preregistration for classes offered. **Housing:** Single-sex dorms, special housing for disabled available. $50 nonrefundable deposit. **Activities:** Bands, campus ministries, choral groups, dance, drama, music ensembles, musical theater, student government, student newspaper, Baptist student union, Wesley Foundation, Newman Club, A.D.U.L.T.

Athletics. NJCAA. **Intercollegiate:** Baseball M, basketball, cheerleading, football (tackle) M, golf M, softball, tennis. **Intramural:** Baseball, basketball, football (tackle), softball, tennis. **Team name:** Bulldogs.

Student services. Adult student services, career counseling, student employment services, financial aid counseling, health services, on-campus daycare, personal counseling, placement for graduates, veterans' counselor. **Physically disabled:** Services for visually, hearing impaired. **Transfer:** Transfer adviser, college fairs on campus for students transferring to 4-year colleges.

Contact. E-mail: nichol.green@mgccc.edu
Phone: (601) 928-6333 Toll-free number: (866) 735-1122
Fax: (601) 928-6345
Nichol Green, Director of Admissions, Mississippi Gulf Coast Community College, PO Box 548, Perkinston, MS 39573

Northeast Mississippi Community College
Booneville, Mississippi
www.nemcc.edu **CB code: 1557**

- Public 2-year community college
- Commuter campus in small town

General. Founded in 1948. Regionally accredited. **Enrollment:** 3,733 degree-seeking undergraduates. **Degrees:** 523 associate awarded. **Location:** 30 miles from Tupelo, 110 miles from Memphis, Tennessee. **Calendar:** Semester, extensive summer session. **Full-time faculty:** 180 total. **Part-time faculty:** 27 total.

Basis for selection. Open admission, but selective for some programs. Admission to nursing, dental hygiene, and medical laboratory, medical assistance, practical nursing, radiologic technology, and respiratory technician programs based on test scores. Interview required for dental hygiene, medical laboratory technology, and nursing students. **Adult students:** SAT/ACT scores not required if applicant over 21.

High school preparation. 18 units recommended. Recommended units include English 4, mathematics 2, social studies 2 and science 2.

2011-2012 Annual costs. Tuition/fees: $2,145; $4,245 out-of-state. Per-credit charge: $117 in-state; $224 out-of-state. Room/board: $3,180. Books/supplies: $1,250. Personal expenses: $1,200.

Financial aid. Need-based: Work-study available nights, weekends and for part-time students.

Application procedures. Admission: No deadline. No application fee. Application must be submitted on paper. Admission notification on a rolling basis. **Financial aid:** Priority date 4/1; no closing date. FAFSA, institutional form required. Applicants notified on a rolling basis.

Academics. Special study options: Distance learning, dual enrollment of high school students, study abroad, weekend college. License preparation in dental hygiene, nursing, occupational therapy, radiology. **Credit/placement by examination:** AP, CLEP, institutional tests. 18 credit hours maximum toward associate degree. **Support services:** GED preparation and test center, learning center, pre-admission summer program, reduced course load, remedial instruction, study skills assistance, tutoring.

Majors. Architecture: Building sciences. **Biology:** General. **Business:** Accounting, business admin, fashion modeling. **Communications:** Communications/speech/rhetoric, journalism. **Computer sciences:** General, programming, web page design. **Conservation:** Forestry. **Education:** Agricultural, art, business, elementary, English, family/consumer sciences, foreign languages, mathematics, music, physical, science, social science, special ed. **Engineering:** General, geological. **English:** Writing. **Foreign languages:** General. **General:** Business. **Health services:** Athletic training, clinical lab technology, licensed practical nurse, nursing (RN), premedicine, prepharmacy, preveterinary, radiologic technology/medical imaging, respiratory therapy technology. **History:** General. **Human services:** Social work. **Liberal arts:** Arts/sciences, library science. **Math:** General. **Physical sciences:** Chemistry, physics. **Protective services:** Criminal justice. **Psychology:** General. **Social sciences:** Political science, sociology. **Theology:** Theology. **Visual/performing arts:** Art, interior design, music, musical theater, photography. **Work/family studies:** General, clothing/textiles.

Computing on campus. Dormitories wired for high-speed internet access and linked to campus network. Commuter students can connect to campus network. Online course registration, online library, helpline, wireless network available.

Student life. Freshman orientation: Available, $25 fee. Preregistration for classes offered. Two one-day orientation/registration sessions for entering

freshman and transfer students; students will attend sessions according to major. **Housing:** Single-sex dorms available. $100 fully refundable deposit. **Activities:** Bands, choral groups, dance, drama, film society, music ensembles, musical theater, radio station, student government, student newspaper.

Athletics. NJCAA. **Intercollegiate:** Baseball M, basketball, football (tackle) M, golf M, softball W, tennis. **Intramural:** Basketball, softball, table tennis, volleyball. **Team name:** Tigers.

Student services. Adult student services, career counseling, student employment services, health services, on-campus daycare, personal counseling, placement for graduates. **Physically disabled:** Services for visually, speech, hearing impaired. **Transfer:** Transfer adviser for students transferring to 4-year colleges.

Contact. E-mail: admitme@nemcc.edu
Phone: (662) 720-7290 Toll-free number: (800) 555-2154
Fax: (662) 728-1165
Robert Gibson, Director of Enrollment Services/Registrar, Northeast Mississippi Community College, 101 Cunningham Boulevard, Booneville, MS 38829

Northwest Mississippi Community College
Senatobia, Mississippi
www.northwestms.edu   CB code: 1562

- Public 2-year community college
- Commuter campus in small town

General. Founded in 1927. Regionally accredited. **Location:** 30 miles from Memphis, Tennessee. **Calendar:** Semester.

Annual costs/financial aid. Tuition/fees (2011-2012): $1,950; $3,950 out-of-state. Room/board: $2,700. Books/supplies: $600. Personal expenses: $375. Need-based financial aid available for full-time students.

Contact. Phone: (601) 562-3200 ext. 3219
Registrar, 4975 Highway 51 North, Senatobia, MS 38668

Pearl River Community College
Poplarville, Mississippi
www.prcc.edu   CB code: 1622

- Public 2-year community college
- Commuter campus in small town

General. Founded in 1921. Regionally accredited. **Enrollment:** 5,500 undergraduates. **Degrees:** 579 associate awarded. **Location:** 35 miles from Hattiesburg, 70 miles from New Orleans. **Calendar:** Semester, limited summer session. **Full-time faculty:** 260 total. **Part-time faculty:** 112 total.

Student profile.

Out-of-state:	9%	Live on campus:	25%
25 or older:	23%		

Basis for selection. Open admission, but selective for some programs. Special requirements for health occupation programs. Interview recommended for nursing majors.

2011-2012 Annual costs. Tuition/fees: $2,186; $4,584 out-of-state. Per-credit charge: $100 in-state; $200 out-of-state. Room/board: $3,700. Books/supplies: $500.

Financial aid. Need-based: Need-based aid available for part-time students. Work-study available nights, weekends and for part-time students. **Non-need-based:** Scholarships awarded for academics, alumni affiliation, athletics, leadership, music/drama, state residency.

Application procedures. Admission: No deadline. No application fee. Admission notification on a rolling basis. **Financial aid:** Priority date 4/17; no closing date. FAFSA, institutional form required. Applicants notified on a rolling basis.

Academics. Special study options: Cooperative education, dual enrollment of high school students. License preparation in dental hygiene, nursing, occupational therapy, physical therapy, radiology. **Credit/placement by examination:** AP, CLEP, ACT. 30 credit hours maximum toward associate degree. **Support services:** GED preparation and test center, learning center, reduced course load, remedial instruction, tutoring.

Majors. Business: Business admin, management information systems, office technology. **Computer sciences:** Applications programming, data processing. **Education:** Multi-level teacher. **Health services:** Licensed practical nurse, medical secretary, respiratory therapy technology. **Liberal arts:** Arts/sciences.

Computing on campus. 150 workstations in library, computer center. Dormitories wired for high-speed internet access and linked to campus network. Commuter students can connect to campus network. Online course registration, helpline, wireless network available.

Student life. Freshman orientation: Available, $25 fee. Preregistration for classes offered. **Housing:** Single-sex dorms, special housing for disabled available. $50 deposit. **Activities:** Bands, choral groups, drama, music ensembles, student government, student newspaper, Black Student Union, Wesley and Newman Clubs, Phi Theta Kappa, Afro-American Club, Baptist Student Union.

Athletics. NJCAA. **Intercollegiate:** Baseball M, basketball, football (tackle) M, golf M, softball W, tennis. **Intramural:** Badminton, basketball, softball, table tennis, tennis, volleyball. **Team name:** Wildcats.

Student services. Career counseling, student employment services, health services, personal counseling, placement for graduates, veterans' counselor.

Contact. E-mail: dford@prcc.edu
Phone: (601) 403-1214 Fax: (601) 403-1339
Dow Ford, Director of Admissions, Pearl River Community College, 101 Highway 11 North, Poplarville, MS 39470

Southwest Mississippi Community College
Summit, Mississippi
www.smcc.edu   CB code: 1729

- Public 2-year community college
- Commuter campus in rural community

General. Founded in 1918. Regionally accredited. **Enrollment:** 1,693 degree-seeking undergraduates; 364 non-degree-seeking students. **Degrees:** 343 associate awarded. **Location:** 76 miles from Jackson, 100 miles from New Orleans. **Calendar:** Semester, limited summer session. **Full-time faculty:** 84 total. **Part-time faculty:** 16 total. **Class size:** 58% < 20, 31% 20-39, 5% 40-49, 5% 50-99. **Special facilities:** Observatory.

Student profile. Among degree-seeking undergraduates, 55% enrolled in a transfer program, 45% enrolled in a vocational program, 567 enrolled as first-time, first-year students.

Part-time:	7%	African American:	45%
Out-of-state:	10%	25 or older:	28%
Women:	60%	Live on campus:	20%

Transfer out. Colleges most students transferred to 2011: The University of Southern Mississippi, Southeastern Louisiana University, Mississippi State University, The University of Mississippi, Jackson State University.

Basis for selection. Open admission, but selective for some programs. Some career-technical programs have additional requirements for admission, such as minimum ACT scores and/or sufficient grades in prerequisite courses. For ability to benefit from career programs, high school graduation or GED preferred. **Home schooled:** Transcript of courses and grades required. ACT scores highly recommended.

High school preparation. College-preparatory program recommended.

2011-2012 Annual costs. Tuition/fees: $2,090; $4,790 out-of-state. Per-credit charge: $100 in-state; $215 out-of-state. Room/board: $2,730. Books/supplies: $600. Personal expenses: $2,840.

Financial aid. Need-based: Need-based aid available for part-time students. Work-study available nights, weekends and for part-time students.

Application procedures. Admission: Priority date 8/1; no deadline. No application fee. Application must be submitted on paper. Admission notification on a rolling basis. **Financial aid:** No deadline. FAFSA required. Applicants notified on a rolling basis.

Academics. Special study options: Distance learning, dual enrollment of high school students. License preparation in nursing. **Credit/placement by examination:** AP, CLEP. 24 credit hours maximum toward associate degree. **Support services:** GED preparation and test center, learning center, reduced course load, remedial instruction, tutoring.

Majors. Business: Marketing, office/clerical. **Computer sciences:** Data processing. **Health services:** Insurance specialist, massage therapy, medical

records admin, medical records technology, nursing (RN). **Liberal arts:** Arts/sciences.

Most popular majors. Business/marketing 8%, engineering/engineering technologies 9%, family/consumer sciences 6%, health sciences 31%, liberal arts 40%.

Computing on campus. 150 workstations in library, computer center. Dormitories wired for high-speed internet access. Online course registration, wireless network available.

Student life. Freshman orientation: Mandatory. Preregistration for classes offered. 4-hour sessions offered during summer and week before class begins. **Housing:** Single-sex dorms available. $60 partly refundable deposit, deadline 8/1. **Activities:** Bands, campus ministries, choral groups, dance, music ensembles, student government, student newspaper, Baptist student union, Wesley Foundation.

Athletics. NJCAA. **Intercollegiate:** Baseball M, basketball, football (tackle) M, soccer, softball W. **Intramural:** Basketball, football (non-tackle), table tennis, tennis M, volleyball. **Team name:** Bears.

Student services. Career counseling, health services, personal counseling, placement for graduates, veterans' counselor. **Physically disabled:** Services for visually, speech, hearing impaired. **Transfer:** Transfer adviser, college fairs on campus for students transferring to 4-year colleges.

Contact. E-mail: mattc@smcc.edu
Phone: (601) 276-2001 Fax: (601) 276-3888
Matthew Calhoun, Vice President of Admissions, Southwest Mississippi Community College, 1156 College Drive, Summit, MS 39666

Virginia College at Jackson
Jackson, Mississippi
www.vc.edu

- For-profit 2-year community college
- Small city

General. Regionally accredited; also accredited by ACICS. **Enrollment:** 439 degree-seeking undergraduates. **Degrees:** 60 associate awarded. **Calendar:** Quarter. **Full-time faculty:** 30 total. **Part-time faculty:** 43 total.

Basis for selection. Passing score on CPAT exam required.

2011-2012 Annual costs. Tuition/fees: $21,900. Tuition is typical for full-time attendance for four quarters and depends on program, hours attempted, and other factors. Tuition includes textbooks and fees.

Financial aid. Need-based: Work-study available nights, weekends and for part-time students.

Application procedures. Admission: No deadline. $100 fee.

Academics. Credit/placement by examination: AP, CLEP.

Majors. Business: Business admin, office management. **Computer sciences:** LAN/WAN management, networking, system admin. **Health services:** Office admin, surgical technology.

Contact. E-mail: mtlittle@vc.edu
Phone: (601) 977-0960 Fax: (601) 977-2719
Lawrence Brown, Director of Admissions, Virginia College at Jackson, 4795 Interstate 55 North, Jackson, MS 39206

Virginia College Gulf Coast
Biloxi, Mississippi
www.vc.edu/gulfcoast/index.cfm

- For-profit 2-year business and health science college
- Small city

General. Accredited by ACICS. **Enrollment:** 524 degree-seeking undergraduates. **Degrees:** 96 associate awarded. **Calendar:** Quarter. **Full-time faculty:** 9 total. **Part-time faculty:** 32 total.

Basis for selection. Admission requirements vary by program.

2011-2012 Annual costs. Tuition/fees: $21,900. Tuition is typical for full-time attendance for four quarters and depends on program, hours attempted, and other factors. Tuition includes textbooks and fees.

Financial aid. Need-based: Work-study available nights, weekends and for part-time students.

Application procedures. Admission: No deadline.

Academics. Credit/placement by examination: AP, CLEP.

Majors. Business: Administrative services, business admin, office management. **Health services:** Office assistant, surgical technology.

Contact. Phone: (228) 392-2994
Betina Yurkus, Director of Admissions, Virginia College Gulf Coast, 920 Cedar Lake Road, BIloxi, MS 39532

Missouri

Anthem College: Kansas City
Kansas City, Missouri
www.anthem.edu

- For-profit 2-year technical college
- Commuter campus in very large city

General. Regionally accredited; also accredited by ACICS. **Enrollment:** 200 degree-seeking undergraduates. **Degrees:** 2 associate awarded. **Calendar:** Differs by program. **Full-time faculty:** 13 total. **Part-time faculty:** 7 total.

Basis for selection. Open admission.

Financial aid. Need-based: Work-study available nights, weekends and for part-time students.

Application procedures. Admission: No deadline. $20 fee.

Academics. Credit/placement by examination: AP, CLEP. **Support services:** GED preparation, study skills assistance, tutoring.

Majors. Health services: Dental assistant, insurance coding, surgical technology.

Computing on campus. Online library, helpline available.

Student life. Freshman orientation: Mandatory. Preregistration for classes offered. **Activities:** Alpha Beta Kappa, student organization.

Contact. Phone: (816) 444-4300
AJ Sare, Director of Admissions, Anthem College: Kansas City, 9001 State Line Road, Kansas City, MO 64114

Bolivar Technical College
Bolivar, Missouri
www.bolivarcollege.org

- Private 2-year branch campus and technical college
- Commuter campus in small town
- Application essay required

General. Accredited by ACICS. Home campus in Houston Missouri. Consortium agreement with Drury University. **Enrollment:** 84 degree-seeking undergraduates. **Degrees:** 5 associate awarded. **Location:** 120 miles from Kansas City. **Calendar:** Semester. **Full-time faculty:** 7 total. **Part-time faculty:** 9 total.

Transfer out. Colleges most students transferred to 2011: Missouri State University, Ozarks Technical Community College.

Basis for selection. Open admission, but selective for some programs. Admission based on composite score of 75% or higher on institutional entrance exams; requires a minimum passing score on each section of the exam. CPAt exam administered to all admitted students; additional testing for nursing students. **Home schooled:** Transcript of courses and grades required. ACT score of 18 or higher required. **Learning Disabled:** High school IEP from the junior or senior year allowed; adult diagnosis of special needs required if out of high school 2 or more years.

2011-2012 Annual costs. Tuition/fees: $12,348. Per-credit charge: $399. Tuition varies by program, $160-$399 per credit hour. Books/supplies: $2,000.

Financial aid. All financial aid based on need. Need-based aid available for part-time students. Work-study available nights, weekends and for part-time students.

Application procedures. Admission: No deadline. $45 fee. **Financial aid:** Priority date 4/1; no closing date. FAFSA, institutional form required.

Academics. Special study options: Internships. License preparation in nursing, paramedic. **Credit/placement by examination:** AP, CLEP, institutional tests. **Support services:** Remedial instruction, study skills assistance, tutoring.

Majors. Business: Accounting. **Health services:** EMT paramedic, medical secretary, nursing (RN).

Computing on campus. 40 workstations in library, computer center. Commuter students can connect to campus network. Online course registration, online library available.

Student life. Freshman orientation: Mandatory. Preregistration for classes offered. **Activities:** Student newspaper.

Student services. Financial aid counseling. **Transfer:** Pre-admission transcript evaluation for new students.

Contact. E-mail: info@bolivarcollege.org
Phone: (417) 777-5062 Toll-free number: (800) 440-6135
Fax: (417) 777-8908
Charlotte Gray, Admissions Director, Bolivar Technical College, PO Box 592, Bolivar, MO 65613

Brown Mackie College: St. Louis
Fenton, Missouri
www.brownmackie.edu

- For-profit 2-year career college
- Very large city

General. Regionally accredited. **Calendar:** Quarter.

Annual costs/financial aid. Tuition/fees (2011-2012): $11,353.

Contact. Director of Admissions, #2 Soccer Park Road, Fenton, MO 63026

Colorado Technical University: North Kansas City
North Kansas City, Missouri
www.ctukansascity.com   CB code: 3322

- For-profit 2-year health science and technical college
- Rural community

General. Calendar: Quarter.

Annual costs/financial aid. Tuition/fees (2011-2012): $10,700. Books/supplies: $1,620.

Contact. Phone: (816) 472-7400
Admissions Director, 520 East 19th Avenue, North Kansas City, MO 64116

Concorde Career College: Kansas City
Kansas City, Missouri
www.concorde.edu/kansas   CB code: 3126

- For-profit 2-year business and health science college
- Large city

General. Accredited by ACCSCT. **Calendar:** Differs by program.

Annual costs/financial aid. Books/supplies: $348.

Contact. Phone: (816) 531-5223
Campus Director, 3239 Broadway, Kansas City, MO 64111

Cottey College
Nevada, Missouri   CB member
www.cottey.edu   CB code: 6120

- Private 2-year junior and liberal arts college for women
- Residential campus in small town
- SAT or ACT (ACT writing optional) required

General. Founded in 1884. Regionally accredited. Sponsored and supported by P.E.O. Sisterhood, nonsectarian philanthropic educational organization. College owned and supported by women for women. **Enrollment:** 319 degree-seeking undergraduates; 5 non-degree-seeking students. **Degrees:** 107 associate awarded. **Location:** 100 miles from Kansas City, 60 miles from Joplin. **Calendar:** Semester. **Full-time faculty:** 36 total; 89% have terminal degrees, 14% minority, 50% women. **Part-time faculty:** 4 total; 25% have terminal degrees, 25% women. **Special facilities:** 33-acre wooded area with lodge for outings and nature laboratory, women's leadership center.

Student profile. Among degree-seeking undergraduates, 177 enrolled as first-time, first-year students.

Out-of-state:	90%	Hispanic American:	10%
Women:	100%	Native American:	1%
African American:	5%	International:	13%
Asian American:	3%	Live on campus:	99%

Transfer out. 95% of students enrolled in the transfer program go on to 4-year colleges. **Colleges most students transferred to 2011:** Smith College, Hood College, Truman State University, Boston University, Mount Holyoke College.

Basis for selection. High school course of study most important; GPA and test scores also important. Recommendations, essay and interviews considered when other criteria not met. Interview recommended for all students. Audition recommended for music students; portfolio recommended for art students. Essay requested sometimes. **Home schooled:** Statement describing home school structure and mission, transcript of courses and grades required. Students should take GED examination.

High school preparation. College-preparatory program required. 18 units required. Required units include English 4, mathematics 3, social studies 2, science 2 (laboratory 2) and foreign language 2. Mathematics should include algebra I, algebra II, geometry.

2012-2013 Annual costs. Tuition/fees: $17,400. Per-credit charge: $200. Room/board: $6,400. Books/supplies: $1,000. Personal expenses: $900.

2010-2011 Financial aid. Need-based: 133 full-time freshmen applied for aid; 117 were judged to have need; 117 of these received aid. Average need met was 86%. Average scholarship/grant was $14,138; average loan $2,700. 76% of total undergraduate aid awarded as scholarships/grants, 24% as loans/jobs. Need-based aid available for part-time students. Work-study available nights, weekends and for part-time students. **Non-need-based:** Awarded to 104 full-time undergraduates, including 55 freshmen. Scholarships awarded for academics, alumni affiliation, art, athletics, leadership, music/drama.

Application procedures. Admission: Priority date 3/1; no deadline. $20 fee, may be waived for applicants with need. Admission notification on a rolling basis. Tuition deposit of $100 required to reserve spot in class and in student housing. **Financial aid:** Priority date 3/1; no closing date. FAFSA required. Applicants notified on a rolling basis starting 4/1; must reply within 2 week(s) of notification.

Academics. Special study options: Cross-registration, dual enrollment of high school students, independent study, internships. Bachelor's degree programs available on campus. **Credit/placement by examination:** AP, CLEP, IB, SAT, ACT, institutional tests. **Support services:** Reduced course load, study skills assistance, tutoring, writing center.

Majors. Liberal arts: Arts/sciences.

Computing on campus. 62 workstations in dormitories, library, computer center, student center. Commuter students can connect to campus network. Wireless network available.

Student life. Freshman orientation: Mandatory. Preregistration for classes offered. Held in late August, 5 days prior to the first day of class. **Housing:** Guaranteed on-campus for all undergraduates. Wellness housing available. $100 fully refundable deposit, deadline 5/1. **Activities:** Jazz band, campus ministries, choral groups, dance, drama, international student organizations, literary magazine, music ensembles, opera, student government, student newspaper, 35 campus service and social organizations available.

Athletics. NJCAA. **Intercollegiate:** Basketball W, softball W, volleyball W. **Intramural:** Badminton W, basketball W, cheerleading W, golf W, soccer W, softball W, swimming W, synchronized swimming W, table tennis W, tennis W, volleyball W. **Team name:** Comets.

Student services. Alcohol/substance abuse counseling, chaplain/spiritual director, career counseling, student employment services, financial aid counseling, health services, personal counseling. **Transfer:** Pre-admission transcript evaluation for new students. Transfer center, transfer adviser, college fairs on campus for students transferring to 4-year colleges.

Contact. E-mail: enrollmgt@cottey.edu
Phone: (417) 667-8181 Toll-free number: (888) 526-8839
Fax: (417) 448-1025
Judi Steege, Director of Admission, Cottey College, 1000 West Austin Boulevard, Nevada, MO 64772

Crowder College
Neosho, Missouri
www.crowder.edu

CB code: 6138

- Public 2-year community and liberal arts college
- Commuter campus in small town

General. Founded in 1963. Regionally accredited. Water resource school with active/passive solar program. **Enrollment:** 4,137 degree-seeking undergraduates; 1,082 non-degree-seeking students. **Degrees:** 488 associate awarded. **Location:** 70 miles from Springfield, 28 miles from Joplin. **Calendar:** Semester, limited summer session. **Full-time faculty:** 99 total; 11% have terminal degrees, 3% minority, 60% women. **Part-time faculty:** 347 total; 4% have terminal degrees, 5% minority, 57% women. **Class size:** 60% < 20, 39% 20-39, less than 1% 40-49, less than 1% 50-99.

Student profile. Among degree-seeking undergraduates, 1,111 enrolled as first-time, first-year students, 232 transferred in from other institutions.

Part-time:	41%	Live on campus:	10%
Women:	64%		

Transfer out. Colleges most students transferred to 2011: Missouri Southern State College, Pittsburg State University, Southwest Missouri State University.

Basis for selection. Open admission, but selective for some programs. Interview, 2.75 GPA, and minimum 19 ACT score required for nursing program. **Home schooled:** Must pass GED.

High school preparation. Recommended units include English 4, mathematics 3 and science 3.

2011-2012 Annual costs. Tuition/fees: $2,550; $3,360 out-of-district; $4,200 out-of-state. Per-credit charge: $73 in-district; $100 out-of-district; $128 out-of-state. Room/board: $4,000. Books/supplies: $800.

Financial aid. All financial aid based on need. Need-based aid available for part-time students. Work-study available nights, weekends and for part-time students.

Application procedures. Admission: No deadline. $25 fee, may be waived for applicants with need. Admission notification on a rolling basis. **Financial aid:** Priority date 7/1; no closing date. FAFSA, institutional form required. Applicants notified on a rolling basis starting 5/15.

Academics. Special study options: Distance learning, dual enrollment of high school students, ESL, honors, independent study, internships, liberal arts/career combination, study abroad, weekend college. License preparation in nursing. **Credit/placement by examination:** AP, CLEP, institutional tests. 15 credit hours maximum toward associate degree. **Support services:** GED preparation and test center, learning center, reduced course load, remedial instruction, study skills assistance, tutoring.

Majors. Biology: General. **Business:** General, administrative services, office/clerical. **Communications:** Journalism, public relations. **Computer sciences:** General, system admin. **Education:** Elementary, physical, secondary. **Engineering:** General. **Foreign languages:** Spanish. **General:** Agribusiness operations, farm/ranch, poultry, production. **Health services:** Environmental health, nursing (RN), office assistant. **History:** General. **Liberal arts:** Arts/sciences. **Math:** General. **Physical sciences:** General, chemistry, physics. **Psychology:** General. **Social sciences:** General. **Visual/performing arts:** Art, music, theater arts management.

Most popular majors. Business/marketing 13%, education 6%, health sciences 19%, liberal arts 49%.

Computing on campus. 1,000 workstations in dormitories, library, computer center. Dormitories wired for high-speed internet access. Online library, helpline, wireless network available.

Student life. Freshman orientation: Mandatory. Preregistration for classes offered. **Housing:** Guaranteed on-campus for all undergraduates. Single-sex dorms, wellness housing available. $150 deposit. **Activities:** Bands, choral groups, dance, drama, literary magazine, music ensembles, musical theater, student government, student newspaper, Aggies (agricultural club), art club, Baptist student union, Students in Free Enterprise, Student-Missouri State Teacher's Association, Phi Theta Kappa, Latino union, Habitat for Humanity.

Athletics. NJCAA. **Intercollegiate:** Baseball M, basketball W, soccer M, softball W. **Team name:** Roughriders.

Student services. Career counseling, student employment services, financial aid counseling, personal counseling, placement for graduates. **Transfer:** Transfer adviser, college fairs on campus for students transferring to 4-year colleges.

Contact. E-mail: admissions@crowder.edu
Phone: (417) 455-5718 Toll-free number: (866) 238-7788
Fax: (417) 455-2439
Jim Riggs, Director of Admission, Crowder College, 601 LaClede Avenue, Neosho, MO 64850

East Central College
Union, Missouri
www.eastcentral.edu

CB member
CB code: 0845

- Public 2-year community college
- Commuter campus in large town

General. Founded in 1968. Regionally accredited. **Enrollment:** 3,167 degree-seeking undergraduates; 960 non-degree-seeking students. **Degrees:** 441 associate awarded. **Location:** 45 miles from St. Louis. **Calendar:** Semester, limited summer session. **Full-time faculty:** 76 total. **Part-time faculty:** 178 total. **Special facilities:** Learning and assessment center, observatory, natural prairie.

Student profile. Among degree-seeking undergraduates, 858 enrolled as first-time, first-year students.

Part-time:	37%	Women:	63%

Basis for selection. Open admission, but selective for some programs. Special requirements for nursing and teaching programs. Accuplacer required for placement for all associate degree and most certificate programs. **Home schooled:** 21 ACT required without GED.

2011-2012 Annual costs. Tuition/fees: $2,280; $3,120 out-of-district; $4,530 out-of-state. Per-credit charge: $66 in-district; $94 out-of-district; $141 out-of-state.

Financial aid. Need-based: Need-based aid available for part-time students. Work-study available nights, weekends and for part-time students. **Non-need-based:** Scholarships awarded for academics, alumni affiliation, art, athletics, music/drama, state residency.

Application procedures. Admission: No deadline. No application fee. Application must be submitted on paper. Admission notification on a rolling basis. **Financial aid:** Priority date 3/1; no closing date. FAFSA required. Applicants notified on a rolling basis starting 3/15.

Academics. Special study options: Distance learning, dual enrollment of high school students, ESL, honors, independent study, internships, liberal arts/career combination. Central Methodist University classes offered on campus and may count toward 4-year degree. Bachelor's degree programs available on campus. License preparation in nursing, paramedic, radiology. **Credit/placement by examination:** AP, CLEP, institutional tests. **Support services:** GED preparation and test center, learning center, reduced course load, remedial instruction, study skills assistance, tutoring, writing center.

Majors. Business: General, accounting technology, administrative services, management information systems. **Computer sciences:** Networking. **Education:** General, voc/tech. **Engineering:** General. **Health services:** EMT paramedic, medical radiologic technology/radiation therapy, medical records technology, nursing (RN), occupational therapy assistant, respiratory therapy technology. **Protective services:** Firefighting. **Visual/performing arts:** Commercial/advertising art, studio arts. **Work/family studies:** Child care management.

Computing on campus. Online course registration, online library, wireless network available.

Student life. Freshman orientation: Mandatory. Preregistration for classes offered. Held prior to start of classes, includes tours, seminars, advisor activities, social activities. **Activities:** Bands, choral groups, drama, music ensembles, musical theater, student government, student newspaper, TV station, Phi Theta Kappa honor society, variety of religious and social clubs.

Athletics. NJCAA. **Intercollegiate:** Soccer M, softball W, volleyball W. **Team name:** Falcons.

Student services. Adult student services, career counseling, student employment services, financial aid counseling, personal counseling, placement for graduates, veterans' counselor. **Physically disabled:** Services for

visually, hearing impaired. **Transfer:** Pre-admission transcript evaluation for new students. Transfer adviser, college fairs on campus for students transferring to 4-year colleges.

Contact. E-mail: admissions@eastcentral.edu
Phone: (636) 584-6563 Fax: (636) 584-7347
Megen Poynter, Admissions Coordinator, East Central College, 1964 Prairie Dell Road, Union, MO 63084-0529

ITT Technical Institute: Kansas City
Kansas City, Missouri
www.itt-tech.edu

- For-profit 2-year business and technical college
- Large city

General. Accredited by ACICS. **Enrollment:** 827 degree-seeking undergraduates. **Degrees:** 54 bachelor's, 240 associate awarded. **Calendar:** Quarter. **Full-time faculty:** 16 total. **Part-time faculty:** 65 total.

Basis for selection. Admission requirements will vary by program.

2011-2012 Annual costs. Estimated costs as of June 2011: per-credit-hour charge, $493, depending upon level and course of study; academic fee, $200. Certain programs of study require purchase of tools, which could cost an additional $100 to $500. All costs are subject to change.

Financial aid. Need-based: Work-study available nights, weekends and for part-time students.

Academics. Credit/placement by examination: AP, CLEP.

Majors. Computer sciences: Networking, programming, system admin. **Protective services:** Forensics, law enforcement admin. **Visual/performing arts:** Design, graphic design.

Contact. Toll-free number: (877) 488-1442
ITT Technical Institute: Kansas City, 9150 East 41st Terrace, Kansas City, MO 64133

Jefferson College
Hillsboro, Missouri
www.jeffco.edu

CB code: 6320

- Public 2-year community and technical college
- Commuter campus in rural community

General. Founded in 1963. Regionally accredited. Serves as county area vocational school. **Enrollment:** 5,786 degree-seeking undergraduates; 293 non-degree-seeking students. **Degrees:** 775 associate awarded. **Location:** 30 miles from St. Louis. **Calendar:** Semester, limited summer session. **Full-time faculty:** 89 total; 17% have terminal degrees, 3% minority, 51% women. **Part-time faculty:** 285 total; 4% have terminal degrees, 4% minority, 52% women. **Class size:** 48% < 20, 51% 20-39, less than 1% 40-49, less than 1% 50-99, less than 1% >100. **Special facilities:** Outdoor theater, facility for computer-related technologies, graphic design lab, veterinary technology clinic, law enforcement academy, emergency medical technician lab/classroom, CNA lab/classroom, college operated television station, olympic size pool, adult basic education center, business and technology training center.

Student profile. Among degree-seeking undergraduates, 55% enrolled in a transfer program, 46% enrolled in a vocational program, 1,440 enrolled as first-time, first-year students.

Part-time:	47%	Hispanic American:	1%
Out-of-state:	1%	Native American:	1%
Women:	60%	25 or older:	40%
African American:	2%	Live on campus:	1%
Asian American:	1%		

Transfer out. Colleges most students transferred to 2011: University of Missouri: St. Louis, Missouri Baptist University, Southeast Missouri State University, Saint Louis University.

Basis for selection. Open admission, but selective for some programs. Special requirements for the nursing program, veterinary technology program, health and occupational programs, law enforcement academy, and emergency medical technician. Interview required for health services technologies students. **Home schooled:** Minimum placement test scores if high school transcript is not from an approved accrediting body. **Learning Disabled:** Suggested that students with disabilities meet with the campus Disability Support Services Coordinator prior to enrollment.

High school preparation. College-preparatory program required. Elementary algebra required for electronics; chemistry required for nursing and veterinary technology.

2011-2012 Annual costs. Tuition/fees: $2,700; $4,050 out-of-district; $5,400 out-of-state. Per-credit charge: $90 in-district; $135 out-of-district; $180 out-of-state. Room/board: $5,794. Books/supplies: $1,200. Personal expenses: $1,000.

2010-2011 Financial aid. Need-based: 1,144 full-time freshmen applied for aid; 832 were judged to have need; 815 of these received aid. Average need met was 57%. Average scholarship/grant was $2,097; average loan $2,703. 61% of total undergraduate aid awarded as scholarships/grants, 39% as loans/jobs. Need-based aid available for part-time students. Work-study available nights, weekends and for part-time students. **Non-need-based:** Awarded to 612 full-time undergraduates, including 262 freshmen. Scholarships awarded for academics, art, athletics, leadership, music/drama, state residency.

Application procedures. Admission: No deadline. $25 fee, may be waived for applicants with need. Admission notification on a rolling basis. **Financial aid:** Priority date 4/1; no closing date. FAFSA required. Applicants notified on a rolling basis starting 4/15.

Academics. Advising and Retention Center available. **Special study options:** Cooperative education, distance learning, dual enrollment of high school students, ESL, honors, independent study, internships, liberal arts/career combination, teacher certification program. Cooperative agreement with 2 neighboring community colleges. Bachelor's degree programs available on campus. License preparation in nursing, occupational therapy, paramedic, physical therapy. **Credit/placement by examination:** AP, CLEP, IB, institutional tests. 30 credit hours maximum toward associate degree. **Support services:** GED preparation and test center, learning center, remedial instruction, study skills assistance, tutoring, writing center.

Majors. Business: General, administrative services, office/clerical. **Computer sciences:** General, security. **Education:** Early childhood, secondary. **Engineering:** General. **Health services:** EMT paramedic, medical secretary, nursing (RN), veterinary technology/assistant. **Liberal arts:** Arts/sciences. **Protective services:** Fire safety technology, law enforcement admin, police science. **Work/family studies:** Child care management.

Most popular majors. Health sciences 8%, liberal arts 23%, security/protective services 9%.

Computing on campus. 250 workstations in dormitories, library, computer center, student center. Dormitories wired for high-speed internet access and linked to campus network. Commuter students can connect to campus network. Online course registration, online library, helpline, wireless network available.

Student life. Freshman orientation: Mandatory. Preregistration for classes offered. **Housing:** Apartments, wellness housing available. $200 partly refundable deposit. **Activities:** Bands, choral groups, drama, literary magazine, music ensembles, musical theater, student government, student newspaper, TV station, Phi Theta Kappa, College Ambassadors, Habitat for Humanity, academic clubs, cultural clubs, Missouri Student National Educational Association.

Athletics. NJCAA. **Intercollegiate:** Baseball M, basketball W, soccer M, softball W, volleyball W. **Team name:** Vikings.

Student services. Adult student services, alcohol/substance abuse counseling, career counseling, services for economically disadvantaged, student employment services, financial aid counseling, on-campus daycare, personal counseling, placement for graduates, veterans' counselor. **Physically disabled:** Services for visually, speech, hearing impaired. **Transfer:** Re-entry adviser, pre-admission transcript evaluation for new students. Transfer adviser, college fairs on campus for students transferring to 4-year colleges.

Contact. E-mail: admissions@jeffco.edu
Phone: (636) 481-3217 Fax: (636) 789-5103
Kimberly Harvey, Director of Admissions and Student Records, Jefferson College, 1000 Viking Drive, Hillsboro, MO 63050-2441

L'Ecole Culinaire
St. Louis, Missouri
www.lecoleculinaire.com

- For-profit 2-year culinary school
- Commuter campus in large city

General. Accredited by ACCSCT. **Calendar:** Quarter.

Annual costs/financial aid. Estimated program costs as of April 2011: diploma (60 weeks) $29,150; associate degree (70 weeks) $33,750, (90 weeks) $42,650. All costs, which include tuition, fees, books and supplies, and taxes, are subject to change.

Contact. 9811 South Outer Forty Drive, St. Louis, MO 63124

Linn State Technical College
Linn, Missouri
www.linnstate.edu

- Public 2-year community and technical college
- Commuter campus in rural community

General. Enrollment: 1,120 degree-seeking undergraduates; 48 non-degree-seeking students. **Degrees:** 348 associate awarded. **Location:** 30 miles from Jefferson City. **Calendar:** Semester, limited summer session. **Full-time faculty:** 83 total; 25% women. **Part-time faculty:** 3 total. **Class size:** 60% < 20, 40% 20-39. **Special facilities:** 3,600 feet hard surface runway, hangers, and fixed base operations. **Partnerships:** Formal partnerships with Caterpillar Inc., Haas Technical Education Center, Cisco Systems.

Student profile. Among degree-seeking undergraduates, 498 enrolled as first-time, first-year students, 103 transferred in from other institutions.

Part-time:	11%	Native American:	1%
Out-of-state:	2%	25 or older:	15%
Women:	11%	Live on campus:	15%
African American:	2%		

Basis for selection. Open admission, but selective for some programs. Some programs have additional requirements and are filled on a competitive basis. Some programs require essays, interviews and other information. **Learning Disabled:** Students with learning disabilities must meet entrance requirements established for each program. Accommodations are available if a student provides proper documentation.

High school preparation. College-preparatory program recommended. 24 units recommended. Recommended units include English 4, mathematics 3, social studies 3, science 3 (laboratory 1), visual/performing arts 1 and academic electives 7. 1 practical arts, 1 physical education, .5 health education, .5 personal finance recommended.

2011-2012 Annual costs. Tuition/fees: $5,040; $9,510 out-of-state. Per-credit charge: $149 in-state; $298 out-of-state. Room/board: $5,070. Books/supplies: $1,170. Personal expenses: $1,600.

2010-2011 Financial aid. Need-based: 427 full-time freshmen applied for aid; 332 were judged to have need; 332 of these received aid. Average need met was 19%. Average scholarship/grant was $4,036; average loan $2,563. 56% of total undergraduate aid awarded as scholarships/grants, 44% as loans/jobs. Need-based aid available for part-time students. Work-study available nights, weekends and for part-time students. **Non-need-based:** Scholarships awarded for academics, alumni affiliation, state residency.

Application procedures. Admission: No deadline. No application fee. Admission notification on a rolling basis. **Financial aid:** Priority date 4/1; no closing date. FAFSA required. Applicants notified on a rolling basis starting 4/1; must reply within 3 week(s) of notification.

Academics. Academic support services and technical skill tutoring provided at no cost. **Special study options:** Distance learning, dual enrollment of high school students, independent study, internships. License preparation in aviation, physical therapy. **Credit/placement by examination:** AP, CLEP, institutional tests. CLEP credit not accepted; internal equivalency examination system in place. No limit to number of credits earned by examination that may be counted towards degree. **Support services:** Learning center, remedial instruction, study skills assistance, tutoring, writing center.

Majors. Business: Management information systems. **Computer sciences:** Networking, programming. **General:** Turf management. **Health services:** Physical therapy assistant.

Most popular majors. Computer/information sciences 11%, engineering/engineering technologies 14%, science technologies 11%, trade and industry 56%.

Computing on campus. 51 workstations in library, student center. Dormitories wired for high-speed internet access. Helpline, wireless network available.

Student life. Freshman orientation: Mandatory. Preregistration for classes offered. Orientation sessions offered simultaneously with registration sessions throughout summer. One day orientation also available day before

classes start. **Policies:** Drug and alcohol free campus. **Housing:** Coed dorms available. $350 fully refundable deposit. **Activities:** Student government.

Athletics. Intramural: Archery, basketball, football (non-tackle), softball, volleyball.

Student services. Transfer: Pre-admission transcript evaluation for new students. College fairs on campus for students transferring to 4-year colleges.

Contact. E-mail: admissions@linnstate.edu
Phone: (573) 897-5196 Toll-free number: (800) 743-8324
Fax: (573) 897-5026
Kathy Scheulen, Assistant Dean of Enrollment Management, Linn State Technical College, One Technology Drive, Linn, MO 65051

Metro Business College
Cape Girardeau, Missouri
www.metrobusinesscollege.edu

CB code: 3316

- For-profit 2-year business and career college
- Commuter campus in large town
- Interview required

General. Accredited by ACICS. Parent campus in Cape Girardeau. **Enrollment:** 170 degree-seeking undergraduates. **Degrees:** 55 associate awarded. **Location:** 125 miles from St. Louis. **Calendar:** Differs by program. **Full-time faculty:** 11 total. **Part-time faculty:** 2 total.

Basis for selection. Open admission. **Home schooled:** State high school equivalency certificate required.

2011-2012 Annual costs. Tuition/fees: $9,850.

Financial aid. Need-based: Work-study available nights, weekends and for part-time students.

Application procedures. Admission: No deadline. $25 fee.

Academics. Credit/placement by examination: AP, CLEP. **Support services:** Study skills assistance, tutoring.

Majors. Business: Business admin.

Computing on campus. Online library available.

Student life. Freshman orientation: Mandatory. Preregistration for classes offered.

Student services. Adult student services, alcohol/substance abuse counseling, career counseling, services for economically disadvantaged, student employment services, financial aid counseling, minority student services, personal counseling, placement for graduates, veterans' counselor. **Physically disabled:** Services for visually impaired.

Contact. E-mail: randy@metrobusinesscollege.edu
Phone: (573) 334-9181 Toll-free number: (800) 467-0785
Fax: (573) 334-0617
Denise Acey, Director of Admissions, Metro Business College, 1732 North Kingshighway, Cape Girardeau, MO 36701

Metro Business College: Jefferson City
Jefferson City, Missouri
www.metrobusinesscollege.edu

CB code: 3318

- For-profit 2-year business and health science college
- Commuter campus in large town
- Interview required

General. Accredited by ACICS. **Enrollment:** 224 degree-seeking undergraduates. **Degrees:** 90 associate awarded. **Location:** 35 miles from Columbia. **Calendar:** Quarter, extensive summer session. **Full-time faculty:** 10 total. **Part-time faculty:** 11 total. **Class size:** 100% 40-49.

Basis for selection. Open admission, but selective for some programs. Students must take entrance exam. Required scores vary by program.

2011-2012 Annual costs. Tuition/fees: $9,850.

Financial aid. Need-based: Need-based aid available for part-time students. Work-study available nights, weekends and for part-time students.

Application procedures. Admission: No deadline. $25 fee. Application must be submitted on paper. Admission notification on a rolling basis. **Financial aid:** No deadline. FAFSA, institutional form required. Applicants notified on a rolling basis.

Academics. Credit/placement by examination: AP, CLEP. **Support services:** Reduced course load, remedial instruction, study skills assistance, tutoring.

Majors. Business: Business admin. **Computer sciences:** Data entry. **Health services:** Office assistant.

Most popular majors. Computer/information sciences 55%, health sciences 45%.

Computing on campus. 16 workstations in library, computer center. Online library, repair service available.

Student life. Freshman orientation: Mandatory. Preregistration for classes offered. **Activities:** Student government.

Student services. Adult student services, alcohol/substance abuse counseling, services for economically disadvantaged, student employment services, financial aid counseling, personal counseling, placement for graduates. **Transfer:** Pre-admission transcript evaluation for new students.

Contact. E-mail: infojeff@metrobusinesscollege.edu
Phone: (573) 635-6600 Toll-free number: (888) 436-3876
Fax: (573) 635-6999
Francie Balk, Admissions Coordinator, Metro Business College: Jefferson City, 210 El Mercado Plaza, Jefferson City, MO 65109

Metro Business College: Rolla
Rolla, Missouri
www.metrobusinesscollege.edu

CB code: 3317

- For-profit 2-year business college
- Large town

General. Accredited by ACICS. **Enrollment:** 180 degree-seeking undergraduates. **Degrees:** 36 associate awarded. **Calendar:** Differs by program. **Full-time faculty:** 7 total. **Part-time faculty:** 2 total.

Basis for selection. Open admission.

2011-2012 Annual costs. Tuition/fees: $9,850.

Financial aid. Need-based: Work-study available nights, weekends and for part-time students.

Application procedures. Admission: No deadline. $25 fee.

Academics. Credit/placement by examination: AP, CLEP.

Majors. Business: Business admin.

Contact. E-mail: dana@metrobusinesscollege.edu
Phone: (573) 364-8464 Toll-free number: (888) 436-3876
Fax: (573) 364-8077
Karla Lindeman, Director, Metro Business College: Rolla, 1202 East Highway 72, Rolla, MO 65401

Metropolitan Community College: Blue River
Independence, Missouri
www.mcckc.edu

CB code: 6060

- Public 2-year community college
- Commuter campus in small city

General. Regionally accredited. **Enrollment:** 2,888 degree-seeking undergraduates; 595 non-degree-seeking students. **Degrees:** 270 associate awarded. **Location:** 25 miles from Kansas City. **Calendar:** Semester, limited summer session. **Full-time faculty:** 42 total; 24% have terminal degrees, 12% minority, 57% women. **Part-time faculty:** 193 total; 2% have terminal degrees, 8% minority, 36% women. **Class size:** 28% < 20, 71% 20-39, less than 1% 50-99.

Student profile. Among degree-seeking undergraduates, 85% enrolled in a transfer program, 15% enrolled in a vocational program, 2% already have a bachelor's degree or higher, 788 enrolled as first-time, first-year students, 124 transferred in from other institutions.

Part-time:	51%	Asian American:	1%
Women:	61%	Hispanic American:	7%
African American:	6%	25 or older:	25%

Basis for selection. Open admission. **Home schooled:** Statement describing home school structure and mission, transcript of courses and grades, interview required. Provide proof of graduation requirements. Applicants under age 16 must meet with Dean of Student Services and bring student portfolio.

High school preparation. 16 units recommended. Recommended units include English 4, mathematics 3, social studies 3, science 3, foreign language 2 and visual/performing arts 1.

2011-2012 Annual costs. Tuition/fees: $2,630; $4,700 out-of-district; $6,320 out-of-state. Per-credit charge: $82 in-district; $151 out-of-district; $205 out-of-state. Books/supplies: $1,000. Personal expenses: $3,279.

Financial aid. Need-based: Need-based aid available for part-time students. Work-study available nights, weekends and for part-time students. **Non-need-based:** Scholarships awarded for academics, athletics, leadership.

Application procedures. Admission: No deadline. No application fee. Admission notification on a rolling basis. **Financial aid:** Priority date 5/30, closing date 6/30. FAFSA, institutional form required. Applicants notified on a rolling basis starting 4/8.

Academics. Special study options: Accelerated study, cooperative education, cross-registration, distance learning, dual enrollment of high school students, honors, independent study, internships, weekend college. **Credit/placement by examination:** AP, CLEP, institutional tests. 30 credit hours maximum toward associate degree. **Support services:** GED test center, learning center, remedial instruction, tutoring.

Majors. Business: General, business admin. **Computer sciences:** General, programming. **Education:** General. **Engineering:** General. **Liberal arts:** Arts/sciences. **Protective services:** Firefighting, law enforcement admin, police science.

Most popular majors. Liberal arts 77%, security/protective services 9%.

Computing on campus. 375 workstations in library, computer center. Commuter students can connect to campus network. Online course registration, online library, helpline available.

Student life. Freshman orientation: Available. Preregistration for classes offered. **Activities:** Choral groups, student government, student newspaper.

Athletics. NJCAA. **Intercollegiate:** Soccer. **Team name:** Trail Blazers.

Student services. Adult student services, career counseling, student employment services, personal counseling, placement for graduates, veterans' counselor. **Physically disabled:** Services for visually, speech, hearing impaired. **Transfer:** Transfer adviser for students transferring to 4-year colleges.

Contact. Phone: (816) 604-6550
Rowdy Pyle, Enrollment Manager, Metropolitan Community College: Blue River, 3200 Broadway Boulevard, Kansas City, MO 64111-2429

Metropolitan Community College: Business & Technology
Kansas City, Missouri
www.mcckc.edu

- Public 2-year community college
- Commuter campus in very large city

General. Regionally accredited. **Enrollment:** 695 degree-seeking undergraduates; 157 non-degree-seeking students. **Degrees:** 56 associate awarded. **Calendar:** Semester. **Full-time faculty:** 18 total; 39% women. **Part-time faculty:** 67 total; 8% minority, 24% women. **Class size:** 85% < 20, 15% 20-39.

Student profile. Among degree-seeking undergraduates, 15% enrolled in a transfer program, 85% enrolled in a vocational program, 8% already have a bachelor's degree or higher, 160 enrolled as first-time, first-year students, 23 transferred in from other institutions.

Part-time:	65%	Asian American:	2%
Out-of-state:	3%	Hispanic American:	6%
Women:	12%	Native American:	1%
African American:	14%	25 or older:	68%

Basis for selection. Open admission. **Home schooled:** Statement describing home school structure and mission, transcript of courses and grades, interview required.

High school preparation. College-preparatory program recommended. 16 units recommended. Recommended units include English 4, mathematics 3, social studies 3, science 3, foreign language 2 and visual/performing arts 1.

2011-2012 Annual costs. Tuition/fees: $2,630; $4,700 out-of-district; $6,320 out-of-state. Per-credit charge: $82 in-district; $151 out-of-district; $205 out-of-state. Books/supplies: $1,000. Personal expenses: $3,279.

Financial aid. Need-based: Work-study available nights, weekends and for part-time students.

Application procedures. Admission: No deadline. No application fee. Admission notification on a rolling basis. **Financial aid:** Closing date 2/1.

Academics. Special study options: Cross-registration, distance learning, dual enrollment of high school students, internships, weekend college. **Credit/placement by examination:** AP, CLEP, institutional tests. 30 credit hours maximum toward associate degree. **Support services:** GED test center, remedial instruction, tutoring.

Majors. Business: General, construction management. **Computer sciences:** Programming.

Most popular majors. Computer/information sciences 21%, engineering/engineering technologies 76%.

Computing on campus. 327 workstations in library, computer center. Online course registration, online library available.

Student life. Freshman orientation: Available. Preregistration for classes offered.

Student services. Adult student services, career counseling, student employment services, veterans' counselor. **Physically disabled:** Services for visually, speech, hearing impaired.

Contact. Phone: (816) 604-5200
Karen Moore, Associate Dean of Student Services, Metropolitan Community College: Business & Technology, 1775 Universal Avenue, Kansas City, MO 64120-2429

Metropolitan Community College: Longview
Lee's Summit, Missouri
www.mcckc.edu   **CB code: 6359**

- Public 2-year community college
- Commuter campus in small city

General. Founded in 1968. Regionally accredited. **Enrollment:** 5,066 degree-seeking undergraduates; 1,143 non-degree-seeking students. **Degrees:** 481 associate awarded. **Location:** 10 miles from Kansas City. **Calendar:** Semester, extensive summer session. **Full-time faculty:** 84 total; 18% have terminal degrees, 12% minority. **Part-time faculty:** 271 total; 31% have terminal degrees, 7% minority. **Class size:** 37% < 20, 61% 20-39, 2% 40-49, less than 1% 50-99.

Student profile. Among degree-seeking undergraduates, 88% enrolled in a transfer program, 12% enrolled in a vocational program, 3% already have a bachelor's degree or higher, 1,392 enrolled as first-time, first-year students, 210 transferred in from other institutions.

Part-time:	51%	Asian American:	1%
Out-of-state:	1%	Hispanic American:	6%
Women:	57%	25 or older:	29%
African American:	18%		

Basis for selection. Open admission. **Home schooled:** Statement describing home school structure and mission, transcript of courses and grades, interview required. Provide proof of graduation requirements. Applicants under the age of 16 must meet with Dean of Student Services and bring student portfolio.

High school preparation. 16 units recommended. Recommended units include English 4, mathematics 3, social studies 3, science 3, foreign language 2 and visual/performing arts 1.

2011-2012 Annual costs. Tuition/fees: $2,630; $4,700 out-of-district; $6,320 out-of-state. Per-credit charge: $82 in-district; $151 out-of-district; $205 out-of-state. Books/supplies: $1,000. Personal expenses: $3,279.

Financial aid. **Need-based:** Work-study available nights, weekends and for part-time students. **Non-need-based:** Scholarships awarded for academics, athletics, leadership.

Application procedures. **Admission:** No deadline. No application fee. Admission notification on a rolling basis. **Financial aid:** Priority date 5/30, closing date 6/30. FAFSA, institutional form required. Applicants notified on a rolling basis starting 4/8.

Academics. **Special study options:** Accelerated study, cooperative education, cross-registration, distance learning, dual enrollment of high school students, honors, independent study, internships, weekend college. **Credit/placement by examination:** AP, CLEP, institutional tests. 30 credit hours maximum toward associate degree. **Support services:** GED test center, learning center, remedial instruction, tutoring.

Majors. **Business:** General, accounting, administrative services, business admin, office management, office technology, sales/distribution. **Computer sciences:** General, applications programming. **Education:** General. **Engineering:** General. **General:** Turf management. **Liberal arts:** Arts/sciences. **Protective services:** Corrections, criminal justice.

Most popular majors. Business/marketing 8%, education 6%, liberal arts 75%, trade and industry 6%.

Computing on campus. 663 workstations in library, computer center. Commuter students can connect to campus network. Online course registration, helpline available.

Student life. **Freshman orientation:** Available. Preregistration for classes offered. **Activities:** Choral groups, drama, literary magazine, student government, student newspaper.

Athletics. NJCAA. **Intercollegiate:** Baseball M, volleyball W. **Intramural:** Basketball, swimming, volleyball. **Team name:** Lakers.

Student services. Adult student services, career counseling, student employment services, on-campus daycare, personal counseling, placement for graduates, veterans' counselor. **Physically disabled:** Services for visually, hearing impaired. **Transfer:** Transfer adviser for students transferring to 4-year colleges.

Contact. Phone: (816) 604-2568 Fax: (816) 672-2025
David Fritz, Admissions Supervisor, Metropolitan Community College: Longview, 500 Longview Road, Lee's Summit, MO 64081-2105

Metropolitan Community College: Maple Woods
Kansas City, Missouri
www.mcckc.edu   CB code: 6436

- Public 2-year community college
- Commuter campus in large city

General. Founded in 1968. Regionally accredited. **Enrollment:** 4,135 degree-seeking undergraduates; 1,197 non-degree-seeking students. **Degrees:** 408 associate awarded. **Location:** 15 miles from downtown. **Calendar:** Semester, limited summer session. **Full-time faculty:** 54 total; 20% have terminal degrees, 13% minority. **Part-time faculty:** 179 total; 5% have terminal degrees, 6% minority. **Class size:** 36% < 20, 63% 20-39, less than 1% 40-49, less than 1% 50-99, less than 1% >100.

Student profile. Among degree-seeking undergraduates, 91% enrolled in a transfer program, 9% enrolled in a vocational program, 4% already have a bachelor's degree or higher, 1,198 enrolled as first-time, first-year students, 189 transferred in from other institutions.

Part-time:	52%	**Asian American:**	3%
Women:	59%	**Hispanic American:**	7%
African American:	7%	**Native American:**	1%

Basis for selection. Open admission, but selective for some programs. Special requirements for animal health technology program. **Home schooled:** Provide proof of high school graduation. If under 16 years old must meet with Dean of Student Services and bring student portfolio.

High school preparation. 16 units recommended. Recommended units include English 4, mathematics 3, social studies 3, science 3 and foreign language 2. 1 unit in visual/performing arts recommended.

2011-2012 Annual costs. Tuition/fees: $2,630; $4,700 out-of-district; $6,320 out-of-state. Per-credit charge: $82 in-district; $151 out-of-district; $205 out-of-state. Books/supplies: $1,000. Personal expenses: $3,279.

Financial aid. **Need-based:** Need-based aid available for part-time students. Work-study available nights, weekends and for part-time students. **Non-need-based:** Scholarships awarded for academics, athletics, leadership.

Application procedures. **Admission:** No deadline. No application fee. Admission notification on a rolling basis. Separate application required for animal health technology; deadline March 1. **Financial aid:** Priority date 5/30, closing date 6/30. FAFSA, institutional form required. Applicants notified on a rolling basis.

Academics. **Special study options:** Cross-registration, distance learning, dual enrollment of high school students, exchange student, honors, internships. **Credit/placement by examination:** AP, CLEP, institutional tests. 30 credit hours maximum toward associate degree. **Support services:** GED test center, learning center, reduced course load, remedial instruction, tutoring.

Majors. **Business:** General, administrative services, business admin, office technology, sales/distribution. **Computer sciences:** General, applications programming. **Education:** General. **Engineering:** General. **Foreign languages:** Sign language interpretation. **Health services:** Veterinary technology/assistant. **Liberal arts:** Arts/sciences. **Physical sciences:** General. **Protective services:** Criminal justice, law enforcement admin.

Most popular majors. Education 8%, liberal arts 83%.

Computing on campus. 300 workstations in computer center. Commuter students can connect to campus network. Online course registration, online library, helpline available.

Student life. **Freshman orientation:** Available. Preregistration for classes offered. **Activities:** Choral groups, drama, student government, student newspaper.

Athletics. NJCAA. **Intercollegiate:** Baseball M, soccer, softball W. **Intramural:** Softball, volleyball W. **Team name:** Centaurs.

Student services. Adult student services, career counseling, student employment services, personal counseling, placement for graduates, veterans' counselor. **Physically disabled:** Services for visually, speech, hearing impaired. **Transfer:** Transfer adviser, college fairs on campus for students transferring to 4-year colleges.

Contact. Phone: (816) 604-3167 Fax: (816) 437-3049
Tyson Schank, Enrollment Manager, Metropolitan Community College: Maple Woods, 2601 NE Barry Road, Kansas City, MO 64156-1299

Metropolitan Community College: Penn Valley
Kansas City, Missouri
www.mcckc.edu   CB code: 6324

- Public 2-year community college
- Commuter campus in large city

General. Regionally accredited. **Enrollment:** 4,637 degree-seeking undergraduates; 772 non-degree-seeking students. **Degrees:** 396 associate awarded. **Location:** 2 miles from downtown. **Calendar:** Semester, extensive summer session. **Full-time faculty:** 93 total; 23% have terminal degrees, 22% minority, 62% women. **Part-time faculty:** 190 total; 33% have terminal degrees, 32% minority, 60% women. **Class size:** 48% < 20, 50% 20-39, less than 1% 40-49, 1% 50-99.

Student profile. Among degree-seeking undergraduates, 75% enrolled in a transfer program, 25% enrolled in a vocational program, 7% already have a bachelor's degree or higher, 1,048 enrolled as first-time, first-year students, 242 transferred in from other institutions.

Part-time:	67%	**Asian American:**	3%
Out-of-state:	3%	**Hispanic American:**	9%
Women:	70%	**International:**	2%
African American:	41%	**25 or older:**	59%

Basis for selection. Open admission, but selective for some programs. Special requirements for allied health programs. ACT or ASSET required for placement and counseling. **Home schooled:** Statement describing home school structure and mission, transcript of courses and grades, interview required. Students under 16 must bring portfolio to Dean of Student Services.

High school preparation. 16 units recommended. Recommended units include English 4, mathematics 3, social studies 3, science 3 and foreign language 2. One unit visual/performing arts recommended.

2011-2012 Annual costs. Tuition/fees: $2,630; $4,700 out-of-district; $6,320 out-of-state. Per-credit charge: $82 in-district; $151 out-of-district; $205 out-of-state. Books/supplies: $1,000. Personal expenses: $3,279.

Financial aid. Need-based: Work-study available nights, weekends and for part-time students. **Non-need-based:** Scholarships awarded for academics, athletics, leadership.

Application procedures. Admission: No deadline. No application fee. Admission notification on a rolling basis. **Financial aid:** Priority date 5/30, closing date 6/30. FAFSA, institutional form required. Applicants notified on a rolling basis starting 4/8.

Academics. Special study options: Cross-registration, distance learning, dual enrollment of high school students, ESL, honors, internships, liberal arts/career combination, weekend college. Cooperative programs in allied health with Johnson County Community College. License preparation in dental hygiene, nursing, occupational therapy, paramedic, physical therapy, radiology. **Credit/placement by examination:** AP, CLEP, institutional tests. 30 credit hours maximum toward associate degree. **Support services:** GED test center, learning center, reduced course load, remedial instruction, tutoring.

Majors. Business: General, accounting, administrative services, business admin, customer service support, fashion, office management, office technology, sales/distribution. **Computer sciences:** General. **Education:** General. **Engineering:** General. **Health services:** Dental assistant, EMT paramedic, medical radiologic technology/radiation therapy, mental health services, nursing (RN), occupational therapy assistant, physical therapy assistant, respiratory therapy technology. **Liberal arts:** Arts/sciences. **Protective services:** Corrections, criminal justice, law enforcement admin. **Visual/performing arts:** Commercial/advertising art, fashion design, graphic design. **Work/family studies:** Child care management.

Most popular majors. Family/consumer sciences 6%, health sciences 60%, liberal arts 23%.

Computing on campus. 1,133 workstations in library, computer center.

Student life. Freshman orientation: Available. Preregistration for classes offered. **Activities:** Jazz band, drama, music ensembles, opera, student government, student newspaper, Black student association, Los Americanos.

Athletics. NJCAA. **Intercollegiate:** Basketball M, golf M. **Team name:** Scouts.

Student services. Career counseling, student employment services, on-campus daycare, personal counseling, placement for graduates, veterans' counselor. **Physically disabled:** Services for visually, speech, hearing impaired.

Contact. Phone: (816) 604-4079 Fax: (816) 759-4161
Carlton Fowler, Registrar, Metropolitan Community College: Penn Valley, 3201 Southwest Trafficway, Kansas City, MO 64111-2429

Mineral Area College
Park Hills, Missouri
www.mineralarea.edu   **CB code: 6323**

▶ Public 2-year community college
▶ Commuter campus in small town

General. Founded in 1922. Regionally accredited. **Enrollment:** 3,011 degree-seeking undergraduates. **Degrees:** 540 associate awarded. **Location:** 60 miles from St. Louis. **Calendar:** Semester, limited summer session. **Full-time faculty:** 97 total. **Part-time faculty:** 201 total. **Class size:** 49% < 20, 51% 20-39.

Student profile.

Out-of-state:	1%	Live on campus:	4%
25 or older:	34%		

Transfer out. Colleges most students transferred to 2011: Central Methodist College at Park Hills, Southeast Missouri State University, Southwest Missouri State University, University of Missouri - St. Louis, University of Missouri - Columbia.

Basis for selection. Open admission, but selective for some programs. Special requirements for nursing program. Interview required for health majors and law enforcement academy. **Home schooled:** Must submit documentation as required by Missouri State Statute 167.031.

2012-2013 Annual costs. Tuition/fees (projected): $2,610; $3,450 out-of-district; $4,290 out-of-state. Per-credit charge: $87 in-district; $115 out-of-district; $143 out-of-state. Room/board: $5,995. Books/supplies: $1,400.

Financial aid. Need-based: Need-based aid available for part-time students. Work-study available nights, weekends and for part-time students. **Non-need-based:** Scholarships awarded for academics, alumni affiliation, art, athletics, leadership, music/drama, state residency.

Application procedures. Admission: Priority date 8/1; no deadline. $15 fee. Admission notification on a rolling basis beginning on or about 2/15. **Financial aid:** Closing date 4/1. FAFSA required. Applicants notified on a rolling basis starting 2/15; must reply within 4 week(s) of notification.

Academics. Special study options: Cross-registration, distance learning, dual enrollment of high school students, honors, independent study, internships, liberal arts/career combination, study abroad. Bachelor's degree programs available on campus. License preparation in nursing, paramedic. **Credit/placement by examination:** AP, CLEP, institutional tests. 30 credit hours maximum toward associate degree. Credit held in escrow for 1 semester. **Support services:** GED test center, learning center, pre-admission summer program, reduced course load, remedial instruction, study skills assistance, tutoring, writing center.

Majors. Business: General, accounting, administrative services, banking/financial services, business admin. **Communications technology:** Graphic/printing. **Computer sciences:** Networking, programming. **Education:** Voc/tech. **English:** English lit. **General:** Horticulture, production. **Health services:** Clinical lab technology, nursing (RN), respiratory therapy technology. **Liberal arts:** Arts/sciences. **Protective services:** Firefighting, police science. **Social sciences:** General. **Work/family studies:** Child development.

Computing on campus. Dormitories wired for high-speed internet access. Online course registration, helpline available.

Student life. Freshman orientation: Mandatory. Preregistration for classes offered. One-day program for students and parents. **Housing:** Coed dorms, wellness housing available. $200 deposit. Privatized housing available. **Activities:** Bands, choral groups, drama, music ensembles, musical theater, student government, Young Democrats, Young Republicans, Baptist Youth.

Athletics. NJCAA. **Intercollegiate:** Baseball M, basketball, volleyball W. **Team name:** Cardinals.

Student services. Adult student services, career counseling, student employment services, financial aid counseling, personal counseling, placement for graduates, veterans' counselor. **Physically disabled:** Services for visually, speech, hearing impaired. **Transfer:** Pre-admission transcript evaluation for new students. Transfer adviser, college fairs on campus for students transferring to 4-year colleges.

Contact. E-mail: admissions@mineralarea.edu
Phone: (573) 518-2206 Fax: (573) 518-2166
Julie Sheets, Admissions Officer, Mineral Area College, PO Box 1000, Park Hills, MO 63601-1000

Missouri College
Brentwood, Missouri
www.missouricollege.com   **CB code: 3074**

▶ For-profit 2-year technical college
▶ Commuter campus in large city

General. Accredited by ACCSCT. **Calendar:** Differs by program.

Annual costs/financial aid. Need-based financial aid available to full-time and part-time students.

Contact. Phone: (314) 821-7700
Director of Admissions, 1405 South Hanley Road, Brentwood, MO 63144

Missouri State University: West Plains
West Plains, Missouri
www.wp.missouristate.edu   **CB code: 6662**

▶ Public 2-year branch campus and liberal arts college
▶ Commuter campus in large town

General. Regionally accredited. The open admissions 2-year campus in Missouri State University system. **Enrollment:** 1,698 degree-seeking undergraduates; 444 non-degree-seeking students. **Degrees:** 345 associate awarded.

Location: 110 miles from Springfield. **Calendar:** Semester, limited summer session. **Full-time faculty:** 33 total; 21% have terminal degrees, 9% minority, 52% women. **Part-time faculty:** 81 total; 11% have terminal degrees, 60% women. **Class size:** 28% < 20, 71% 20-39, less than 1% 40-49. **Partnerships:** Partnership with West Plains High School.

Student profile. Among degree-seeking undergraduates, 50% enrolled in a transfer program, 583 enrolled as first-time, first-year students, 91 transferred in from other institutions.

Part-time:	25%	25 or older:	38%
Out-of-state:	7%	Live on campus:	3%
Women:	61%		

Transfer out. 52% of students enrolled in the transfer program go on to 4-year colleges. **Colleges most students transferred to 2011:** Missouri State University: Springfield.

Basis for selection. Open admission, but selective for some programs. Nursing and respiratory therapy programs require separate application and applicants are considered competitively. **Home schooled:** Transcript of courses and grades required. Must submit ACT score (minimum 18) or official GED transcript.

2011-2012 Annual costs. Tuition/fees: $3,504; $6,714 out-of-state. Per-credit charge: $107 in-state; $214 out-of-state. Room/board: $5,116. Books/supplies: $1,072. Personal expenses: $2,848.

2010-2011 Financial aid. Need-based: 602 full-time freshmen applied for aid; 376 were judged to have need; 363 of these received aid. 70% of total undergraduate aid awarded as scholarships/grants, 30% as loans/jobs. Need-based aid available for part-time students. Work-study available nights, weekends and for part-time students. **Non-need-based:** Scholarships awarded for academics, athletics, state residency.

Application procedures. Admission: Closing date 8/20 (receipt date). $15 fee, may be waived for applicants with need. Admission notification on a rolling basis. **Financial aid:** Priority date 3/31; no closing date. FAFSA, institutional form required. Applicants notified on a rolling basis; must reply by 4/15.

Academics. Special study options: Distance learning, dual enrollment of high school students, honors, independent study, internships, liberal arts/career combination, student-designed major, study abroad. Early degree for High School students to earn high school diploma and A.A. degree concurrently. Bachelor's degree programs available on campus. License preparation in nursing. **Credit/placement by examination:** AP, CLEP, IB, institutional tests. 15 credit hours maximum toward associate degree. **Support services:** GED test center, learning center, remedial instruction, study skills assistance, tutoring, writing center.

Majors. Business: General, entrepreneurial studies. **Communications technology:** Animation/special effects. **Computer sciences:** General. **Education:** General. **General:** Business, food science, horticultural science. **Health services:** Nursing (RN), respiratory therapy technology. **Liberal arts:** Arts/sciences. **Protective services:** Police science. **Work/family studies:** Child care management.

Most popular majors. Health sciences 15%, liberal arts 75%.

Computing on campus. 104 workstations in dormitories, library, computer center, student center. Dormitories wired for high-speed internet access and linked to campus network. Commuter students can connect to campus network. Online course registration, online library, helpline, repair service, wireless network available.

Student life. Freshman orientation: Mandatory. Preregistration for classes offered. Half-day sessions held throughout summer. **Housing:** Coed dorms, special housing for disabled, wellness housing available. $100 fully refundable deposit. **Activities:** Campus ministries, choral groups, drama, international student organizations, student government, Campus Crusade for Christ, Christian Campus House, Wesley Club, College Democrats, College Republicans,.

Athletics. NJCAA. **Intercollegiate:** Basketball M, cheerleading, volleyball W. **Team name:** Grizzlies.

Student services. Career counseling, services for economically disadvantaged, student employment services, financial aid counseling, health services, legal services, minority student services, personal counseling, placement for graduates, veterans' counselor. **Physically disabled:** Services for visually, hearing impaired. **Transfer:** Transfer adviser, college fairs on campus for students transferring to 4-year colleges.

Contact. E-mail: wpadmissions@missouristate.edu
Phone: (417) 255-7955 Toll-free number: (888) 466-7897
Fax: (417) 255-7959
Melissa Jett, Coordinator of Admissions, Missouri State University: West Plains, 128 Garfield Avenue, West Plains, MO 65775-2715

Moberly Area Community College
Moberly, Missouri
www.macc.edu

CB code: 6414

▸ Public 2-year community college
▸ Commuter campus in large town

General. Founded in 1927. Regionally accredited. **Enrollment:** 5,659 degree-seeking undergraduates. **Degrees:** 627 associate awarded. **Location:** 35 miles from Columbia. **Calendar:** Semester, extensive summer session. **Full-time faculty:** 69 total. **Part-time faculty:** 247 total. **Special facilities:** Multimedia/instructional television center, graphic arts/fine arts gallery, alumni museum.

Student profile.

Out-of-state:	2%	Live on campus:	2%
25 or older:	24%		

Transfer out. Colleges most students transferred to 2011: Central Methodist University, Columbia College, University of Missouri.

Basis for selection. Open admission, but selective for some programs. Special requirements for allied health and law enforcement programs. ACT scores required for admission to nursing programs. Degree-seeking students, or those taking 14 or more credits, must have ACT or ASSET score for placement purposes; tests also required for students enrolling in English or math courses. **Home schooled:** Transcript of courses and grades, state high school equivalency certificate required. Applicants must provide transcript outlining educational process or take GED.

2011-2012 Annual costs. Tuition/fees: $2,430; $3,360 out-of-district; $4,860 out-of-state. Per-credit charge: $70 in-district; $101 out-of-district; $151 out-of-state. Board plan covers breakfast and lunch, five-days-a-week. Room/board: $4,200. Books/supplies: $800. Personal expenses: $1,500.

Financial aid. Need-based: Need-based aid available for part-time students. Work-study available nights, weekends and for part-time students. **Non-need-based:** Scholarships awarded for academics, alumni affiliation, art, athletics, leadership, music/drama.

Application procedures. Admission: No deadline. No application fee. Admission notification on a rolling basis. **Financial aid:** Priority date 4/1; no closing date. FAFSA required. Applicants notified on a rolling basis starting 4/1; must reply by 7/15 or within 2 week(s) of notification.

Academics. Special study options: Cooperative education, distance learning, dual enrollment of high school students, honors, internships, study abroad, teacher certification program. License preparation in nursing, paramedic. **Credit/placement by examination:** AP, CLEP, IB, institutional tests. 30 credit hours maximum toward associate degree. **Support services:** GED preparation and test center, learning center, remedial instruction, study skills assistance, tutoring.

Majors. Business: Accounting technology, marketing, office/clerical. **Communications:** Journalism. **Communications technology:** Graphic/printing. **Computer sciences:** Programming. **Education:** Voc/tech. **Engineering:** General. **Health services:** Nursing (RN). **Liberal arts:** Arts/sciences. **Work/family studies:** Child care management.

Most popular majors. Business/marketing 6%, liberal arts 74%.

Computing on campus. 750 workstations in dormitories, library, computer center. Dormitories wired for high-speed internet access. Commuter students can connect to campus network. Online library, helpline, repair service, wireless network available.

Student life. Freshman orientation: Available. Preregistration for classes offered. Half-day program held during late summer. **Housing:** Single-sex dorms, wellness housing available. $150 partly refundable deposit, deadline 8/20. Limited housing available. **Activities:** Choral groups, drama, literary magazine, student government, student newspaper, Phi Theta Kappa, Association for the Education of Young Children, Brothers OX, service organizations, multicultural club.

Athletics. NJCAA. **Intercollegiate:** Basketball, cheerleading. **Intramural:** Basketball, volleyball. **Team name:** Greyhounds.

Student services. Adult student services, career counseling, services for economically disadvantaged, student employment services, financial aid counseling, placement for graduates. **Physically disabled:** Services for visually, speech, hearing impaired. **Transfer:** Pre-admission transcript evaluation for new students. Transfer adviser, college fairs on campus for students transferring to 4-year colleges.

Contact. E-mail: info@macc.edu
Phone: (660) 263-4110 ext. 270
Toll-free number: (800) 622-2070 ext. 270 Fax: (660) 263-2406
James Grant, Dean of Student Services, Moberly Area Community
College, 101 College Avenue, Moberly, MO 65270-1304

North Central Missouri College
Trenton, Missouri
www.ncmissouri.edu   **CB code: 6830**

▶ Public 2-year community college
▶ Commuter campus in small town

General. Founded in 1925. Regionally accredited. Evening classes offered
at outreach sites in many area communities. **Enrollment:** 1,351 degree-
seeking undergraduates; 451 non-degree-seeking students. **Degrees:** 249
associate awarded. **Location:** 90 miles from Kansas City. **Calendar:** Semester, limited summer session. **Full-time faculty:** 29 total. **Part-time faculty:**
75 total.

Student profile. Among degree-seeking undergraduates, 30% enrolled in
a transfer program, 70% enrolled in a vocational program, 447 enrolled as
first-time, first-year students.

Part-time:	27%	25 or older:	28%
Out-of-state:	2%	Live on campus:	8%
Women:	73%		

Transfer out. Colleges most students transferred to 2011: Missouri
Western State College, Northwest Missouri State University, Missouri State
University, University of Central Missouri.

Basis for selection. Open admission, but selective for some programs.
Special requirements for associate and certificate programs in nursing. Interview required for nursing students. **Home schooled:** Statement describing
home school structure and mission required.

2011-2012 Annual costs. Tuition/fees: $2,700; $3,660 out-of-district;
$4,800 out-of-state. Per-credit charge: $70 in-district; $102 out-of-district;
$140 out-of-state. Room/board: $5,323. Books/supplies: $800. Personal
expenses: $1,029.

Financial aid. Need-based: Need-based aid available for part-time students. Work-study available nights, weekends and for part-time students.
Non-need-based: Scholarships awarded for academics, athletics, leadership,
music/drama.

Application procedures. Admission: Priority date 8/5; deadline 8/15
(receipt date). $20 fee. Application must be submitted online. Admission
notification on a rolling basis beginning on or about 2/1. **Financial aid:**
Priority date 7/1; no closing date. FAFSA, institutional form required. Applicants notified on a rolling basis starting 3/15.

Academics. Special study options: Distance learning, dual enrollment of
high school students, internships, liberal arts/career combination. Bachelor's
degree programs available on campus. License preparation in nursing, occupational therapy. **Credit/placement by examination:** AP, CLEP, institutional
tests. 30 credit hours maximum toward associate degree. **Support services:**
Learning center, reduced course load, remedial instruction, study skills assistance, tutoring.

Majors. Business: Accounting, business admin, office technology, office/
clerical. **Education:** General. **General:** Agribusiness operations. **Health services:** EMT paramedic, health care admin, medical radiologic technology/
radiation therapy, medical secretary, nursing (RN), office assistant, pharmacy
assistant, physical therapy assistant, surgical technology. **Liberal arts:** Arts/
sciences. **Protective services:** Criminal justice. **Work/family studies:** Child
care service.

Most popular majors. Business/marketing 9%, health sciences 38%, liberal arts 40%.

Computing on campus. 163 workstations in dormitories, library, computer center, student center. Dormitories wired for high-speed internet access.
Online course registration, helpline, wireless network available.

Student life. Freshman orientation: Available. Preregistration for classes
offered. **Housing:** Single-sex dorms, wellness housing available. $100 partly
refundable deposit. **Activities:** Student government, Baptist student union,
Fellowship of Christian Athletes.

Athletics. NJCAA. **Intercollegiate:** Baseball M, basketball, softball W.
Intramural: Volleyball. **Team name:** Pirates.

Student services. Career counseling, student employment services, financial aid counseling. **Physically disabled:** Services for visually, speech, hearing impaired. **Transfer:** Transfer adviser, college fairs on campus for students
transferring to 4-year colleges.

Contact. E-mail: admissions@mail.ncmissouri.edu
Phone: (660) 359-3948 ext. 1401
Toll-free number: (800) 880-6180 ext. 1401 Fax: (660) 359-2211
Karla McCollum, Admission Director, North Central Missouri College,
1301 Main Street, Trenton, MO 64683

Ozarks Technical Community College
Springfield, Missouri
www.otc.edu   **CB code: 2583**

▶ Public 2-year community and technical college
▶ Commuter campus in small city

General. Regionally accredited. **Enrollment:** 7,447 full-time, degree-
seeking students. **Degrees:** 1,251 associate awarded. **Location:** 160 miles
from Kansas City, 250 miles from St. Louis. **Calendar:** Semester, extensive
summer session. **Full-time faculty:** 188 total. **Part-time faculty:** 479 total.
Class size: 43% < 20, 56% 20-39, less than 1% 40-49, less than 1% 50-99.

Transfer out. Colleges most students transferred to 2011: Drury University, Evangel University, Missouri State University.

Basis for selection. Open admission, but selective for some programs.
Special requirements for some allied health programs.

2011-2012 Annual costs. Tuition/fees: $3,150; $4,155 out-of-district;
$5,280 out-of-state. Per-credit charge: $88 in-district; $122 out-of-district;
$159 out-of-state. Books/supplies: $800. Personal expenses: $1,100.

Financial aid. All financial aid based on need. Need-based aid available
for part-time students. Work-study available nights, weekends and for part-
time students.

Application procedures. Admission: No deadline. No application fee.
Admission notification on a rolling basis. **Financial aid:** Closing date 3/31.
FAFSA, institutional form required. Applicants notified on a rolling basis
starting 5/16.

Academics. Special study options: Cooperative education, distance learning, dual enrollment of high school students, ESL, honors, independent study,
internships, study abroad. License preparation in dental hygiene, nursing,
paramedic. **Credit/placement by examination:** AP, CLEP, IB, institutional
tests. **Support services:** GED preparation and test center, learning center,
reduced course load, remedial instruction, study skills assistance, tutoring,
writing center.

Honors college/program. ACT greater than 27; High School GPA greater
than or equal to 3.75; 2 letters of recommendation.

Majors. Biology: General. **Business:** Accounting technology, administrative services, marketing. **Communications technology:** General, graphic/
printing, graphics. **Computer sciences:** Networking, programming. **Education:** Voc/tech. **Engineering:** General. **General:** Turf management. **Health
services:** Dental assistant, dental hygiene, EMT paramedic, medical records
technology, nursing (RN), occupational therapy assistant, physical therapy
assistant, respiratory therapy technology, surgical technology. **Liberal arts:**
Arts/sciences. **Physical sciences:** Chemistry. **Protective services:** Firefighting. **Work/family studies:** Child care service.

Most popular majors. Education 7%, health sciences 12%, liberal arts
53%.

Computing on campus. 325 workstations in library, computer center.
Commuter students can connect to campus network. Online course registration, online library, helpline, repair service, wireless network available.

Student life. Freshman orientation: Mandatory. Preregistration for
classes offered. **Activities:** Drama, student government, student newspaper,
Phi Theta Kappa, National Honor Society, Women in Construction, nursing
students groups, Phi Beta Lambda, national business organizations, electronics club, Society of Manufacturing Engineers.

Athletics. Team name: Eagles.

Student services. Career counseling, student employment services, financial aid counseling, health services, on-campus daycare, personal counseling,
placement for graduates, veterans' counselor. **Physically disabled:** Services
for visually, speech, hearing impaired. **Transfer:** Re-entry adviser for new

students. Transfer adviser, college fairs on campus for students transferring to 4-year colleges.

Contact. Phone: (417) 447-6900 Fax: (417) 447-6906
Joan Barrett, Associate Provost for Student Affairs, Ozarks Technical Community College, 1001 East Chestnut Expressway, Springfield, MO 65802

Pinnacle Career Institute: Kansas City
Kansas City, Missouri
www.pcitraining.edu   CB code: 2271

- For-profit 2-year technical and career college
- Commuter campus in very large city
- Interview required

General. Accredited by ACCSC. Second campus in Kansas City, in addition to the main location, and campus in Lawrence, KS. Offer distance education programs. **Enrollment:** 1,253 degree-seeking undergraduates. **Degrees:** 328 associate awarded. **Location:** Downtown. **Calendar:** Quarter, limited summer session. **Full-time faculty:** 10 total. **Part-time faculty:** 11 total. **Class size:** 100% >100.

Student profile. Among degree-seeking undergraduates, 100% enrolled in a vocational program, 32% already have a bachelor's degree or higher.

Basis for selection. Open admission. **Home schooled:** Transcript of courses and grades, state high school equivalency certificate, interview required.

2011-2012 Annual costs. Tuition/fees: $13,350. Books/supplies: $1,500.

Financial aid. **Need-based:** Work-study available nights, weekends and for part-time students.

Application procedures. **Admission:** No deadline. No application fee. Admission notification on a rolling basis. **Financial aid:** No deadline.

Academics. **Special study options:** Distance learning, weekend college. **Credit/placement by examination:** AP, CLEP. **Support services:** Study skills assistance, tutoring.

Majors. **Business:** Executive assistant. **Computer sciences:** Information technology. **Health services:** Medical assistant. **Parks/recreation:** Exercise sciences.

Most popular majors. Health sciences 54%, physical sciences 28%.

Computing on campus. 30 workstations in computer center. Online library, helpline, wireless network available.

Student life. **Freshman orientation:** Mandatory. Preregistration for classes offered. **Activities:** Student newspaper.

Student services. Career counseling, services for economically disadvantaged, student employment services, financial aid counseling, placement for graduates, veterans' counselor. **Transfer:** Pre-admission transcript evaluation for new students.

Contact. E-mail: bricks@pcitraining.edu
Phone: (816) 331-5700 Toll-free number: (800) 676-7912
Fax: (816) 331-2026
Keith Elliott, Director of Admissions, Pinnacle Career Institute: Kansas City, 1001 East 101st Terrace, Suite 325, Kansas City, MO 64131-3367

Ranken Technical College
St. Louis, Missouri
www.ranken.edu   CB code: 7028

- Private 2-year technical college
- Commuter campus in very large city

General. Founded in 1907. Regionally accredited. **Enrollment:** 2,119 degree-seeking undergraduates. **Degrees:** 22 bachelor's, 325 associate awarded. **Location:** 3 miles from downtown. **Calendar:** Semester, limited summer session. **Full-time faculty:** 61 total; 5% minority, 7% women. **Part-time faculty:** 74 total; 7% have terminal degrees, 14% minority, 19% women. **Partnerships:** Partnerships with General Motors, JM&A Group, Customer Direct, bioMerieux, Toyota Technical Education Network, National Automotive Technicians Education Foundation , National Institute for Automotive

Service Excellence, Shearwater High School, Hunter Engineering, American Honda Motor Company,.

Student profile. Among degree-seeking undergraduates, 506 enrolled as first-time, first-year students.

Part-time:	38%	Asian American:	1%
Out-of-state:	43%	Hispanic American:	1%
Women:	3%	25 or older:	23%
African American:	24%	Live on campus:	3%

Transfer out. **Colleges most students transferred to 2011:** Webster University, Lindenwood, University of Missouri: St. Louis, Southern Illinois University.

Basis for selection. Open admission. Institutional placement test, counseling session, and tour recommended. Interviews recommended. **Home schooled:** State high school equivalency certificate required. **Learning Disabled:** Special accommodations available with appropriate documentation.

High school preparation. College-preparatory program recommended. Recommended units include English 4 and mathematics 3. Recommend industrial arts elective.

2011-2012 Annual costs. Tuition/fees: $13,833. Per-credit charge: $567. Room/board: $6,836. Books/supplies: $1,700. Personal expenses: $1,774.

2011-2012 Financial aid. **Need-based:** 36% of total undergraduate aid awarded as scholarships/grants, 64% as loans/jobs. Need-based aid available for part-time students. Work-study available nights, weekends and for part-time students.

Application procedures. **Admission:** No deadline. $25 fee, may be waived for applicants with need, free for online applicants. Admission notification on a rolling basis. Interview and tour recommended for new applicants. **Financial aid:** No deadline. FAFSA, institutional form required. Applicants notified on a rolling basis starting 4/1.

Academics. **Special study options:** Accelerated study, cooperative education, distance learning, double major, dual enrollment of high school students, independent study, internships, study abroad. Bachelor's degree programs available on campus. **Credit/placement by examination:** AP, CLEP, IB, institutional tests. Enrolled students are reviewed on an individual case basis. **Support services:** Learning center, pre-admission summer program, reduced course load, remedial instruction, study skills assistance, tutoring, writing center.

Majors. **Architecture:** Environmental design. **Communications technology:** General. **Computer sciences:** General, LAN/WAN management, webmaster.

Computing on campus. 100 workstations in dormitories, library, computer center, student center. Dormitories wired for high-speed internet access and linked to campus network. Commuter students can connect to campus network. Online course registration, online library, helpline, repair service, wireless network available.

Student life. **Freshman orientation:** Mandatory. Preregistration for classes offered. Four hour session held the week before classes begin. **Housing:** Guaranteed on-campus for all undergraduates. Coed dorms, special housing for disabled available. $150 fully refundable deposit. **Activities:** Student government, Women's support program, Phi Theta Kappa.

Athletics. **Intramural:** Baseball, basketball, football (non-tackle).

Student services. Adult student services, alcohol/substance abuse counseling, career counseling, services for economically disadvantaged, student employment services, financial aid counseling, minority student services, personal counseling, placement for graduates, veterans' counselor, women's services. **Physically disabled:** Services for visually, speech, hearing impaired. **Transfer:** Pre-admission transcript evaluation for new students. Transfer adviser, college fairs on campus for students transferring to 4-year colleges.

Contact. E-mail: admissions@ranken.edu
Phone: (314) 286-4809 Toll-free number: (866) 472-6536
Fax: (314) 371-0241
Michael Hawley, Director of Admissions, Ranken Technical College, 4431 Finney Avenue, St. Louis, MO 63113

Sanford-Brown College
Fenton, Missouri
www.sbcfenton.com   CB code: 3320

- For-profit 2-year business and health science college
- Commuter campus in small town

General. Regionally accredited. **Calendar:** Differs by program.

Annual costs/financial aid. Books/supplies: $1,714. Need-based financial aid available to full-time and part-time students.

Contact. Phone: (636) 349-4900
Dean, 1345 Smizer Mill Road, Fenton, MO 63026-1583

Sanford-Brown College: Hazelwood
Hazelwood, Missouri
www.sanford-brown.edu   CB code: 3321

- For-profit 2-year technical and career college
- Large city

General. Accredited by ACICS. **Calendar:** Quarter.

Annual costs/financial aid. Books/supplies: $909.

Contact. Phone: (314) 687-2900
Director of Admissions, 75 Village Square, Hazelwood, MO 63042

Sanford-Brown College: St. Peters
St. Peters, Missouri
www.sbcstpeters.com   CB code: 3323

- For-profit 2-year career college
- Commuter campus in small city

General. Accredited by ACICS. **Location:** 40 miles from St. Louis. **Calendar:** Differs by program.

Contact. Phone: (636) 696-2300
Director of Admissions, 100 Richmond Center Boulevard, St. Peters, MO 63376

Southeast Missouri Hospital College of Nursing and Health Sciences
Cape Girardeau, Missouri
www.southeastmissourihospitalcollege.edu   CB code: 4459

- Private 2-year health science and nursing college
- Commuter campus in large town

General. **Location:** 125 miles from St. Louis. **Calendar:** Semester.

Annual costs/financial aid. Tuition/fees (2011-2012): $10,791. Costs vary by program. Books/supplies: $1,000.

Contact. Phone: (573) 334-6825 ext. 23
Registrar/Enrollment Counselor, 2001 William Street, Second Floor, Cape Girardeau, MO 63703-5815

St. Charles Community College
Cottleville, Missouri
www.stchas.edu   CB code: 0168

- Public 2-year community college
- Commuter campus in small city

General. Founded in 1986. Regionally accredited. **Enrollment:** 7,380 degree-seeking undergraduates; 880 non-degree-seeking students. **Degrees:** 636 associate awarded. **Location:** 35 miles from St. Louis. **Calendar:** Semester, limited summer session. **Full-time faculty:** 98 total; 26% have terminal degrees, 4% minority, 59% women. **Part-time faculty:** 308 total; 16% have terminal degrees, 8% minority, 56% women. **Class size:** 33% < 20, 66% 20-39, less than 1% 40-49.

Student profile. Among degree-seeking undergraduates, 87% enrolled in a transfer program, 13% enrolled in a vocational program, 1,986 enrolled as first-time, first-year students.

Part-time:	46%	Hispanic American:	3%
Women:	57%	International:	1%
African American:	6%	25 or older:	30%
Asian American:	2%		

Transfer out. 52% of students enrolled in the transfer program go on to 4-year colleges. **Colleges most students transferred to 2011:** University of Missouri: St. Louis, Lindenwood University, University of Missouri: Columbia.

Basis for selection. Open admission, but selective for some programs. Must submit ACT scores for allied health and nursing programs. **Home schooled:** Transcript of courses and grades required.

2011-2012 Annual costs. Tuition/fees: $2,550; $3,840 out-of-district; $5,790 out-of-state. Per-credit charge: $85 in-district; $128 out-of-district; $191 out-of-state. Books/supplies: $1,200. Personal expenses: $1,800.

2010-2011 Financial aid. Need-based: 75% of total undergraduate aid awarded as scholarships/grants, 25% as loans/jobs. Need-based aid available for part-time students. Work-study available nights, weekends and for part-time students. **Non-need-based:** Scholarships awarded for academics, art, athletics, leadership, music/drama.

Application procedures. Admission: No deadline. $10 fee. Application must be submitted online. Admission notification on a rolling basis. **Financial aid:** Priority date 6/1; no closing date. FAFSA, institutional form required. Applicants notified on a rolling basis starting 4/1; must reply by 8/1.

Academics. Special study options: Distance learning, double major, dual enrollment of high school students, ESL, independent study, internships, liberal arts/career combination, study abroad, teacher certification program. License preparation in nursing, occupational therapy, real estate. **Credit/placement by examination:** AP, CLEP, institutional tests. 39 credit hours maximum toward associate degree. **Support services:** GED preparation and test center, learning center, pre-admission summer program, remedial instruction, study skills assistance, tutoring, writing center.

Majors. Biology: General. **Business:** Accounting technology, marketing, office management. **Communications:** General. **Computer sciences:** Programming. **Education:** General, teacher assistance. **Engineering:** General, civil, mechanical, pre-engineering. **English:** English lit. **Foreign languages:** General, French, Spanish. **Health services:** EMT paramedic, massage therapy, medical records technology, medical secretary, nursing (RN), occupational therapy assistant. **History:** General. **Human services:** Social work. **Liberal arts:** Arts/sciences. **Math:** General. **Philosophy/religion:** Philosophy. **Physical sciences:** Chemistry. **Protective services:** Firefighting, police science. **Psychology:** General. **Social sciences:** Economics, political science, sociology. **Visual/performing arts:** Commercial/advertising art, dramatic, music history. **Work/family studies:** Child care management.

Most popular majors. Health sciences 12%, liberal arts 72%.

Computing on campus. 131 workstations in library, computer center, student center. Commuter students can connect to campus network. Online course registration, online library, helpline, wireless network available.

Student life. Freshman orientation: Mandatory, $80 fee. Preregistration for classes offered. One credit hour, multiple formats, with online campus tour. **Activities:** Bands, campus ministries, choral groups, drama, international student organizations, literary magazine, music ensembles, musical theater, student government, student newspaper, Campus Crusade for Christ, Fellowship of Christian Athletes, Global Student Network, SCC Young Democrats, Cougars Care, Tau Upsilon Alpha, Student Senate.

Athletics. NJCAA. **Intercollegiate:** Baseball M, soccer, softball W. **Team name:** Cougars.

Student services. Adult student services, alcohol/substance abuse counseling, career counseling, student employment services, financial aid counseling, on-campus daycare, personal counseling, placement for graduates, veterans' counselor. **Physically disabled:** Services for visually, speech, hearing impaired. **Transfer:** Pre-admission transcript evaluation for new students. College fairs on campus for students transferring to 4-year colleges.

Contact. E-mail: adm-reg@stchas.edu
Phone: (636) 922-8237 Fax: (636) 922-8236
Kathy Brockgreitens-Gober, Dean of Enrollment Services, St. Charles Community College, 4601 Mid Rivers Mall Drive, Cottleville, MO 63376

St. Louis Community College
Saint Louis, Missouri   CB member
www.stlcc.edu   CB code: 6226

- Public 2-year community and junior college
- Commuter campus in large city

General. Founded in 1962. Regionally accredited. Four campus locations: Forest Park (St. Louis), Florissant Valley (Ferguson), Meramec (Kirkwood),

Two-Year Colleges

and Wildwood (Wildwood). **Enrollment:** 8,823 undergraduates. **Degrees:** 1,975 associate awarded. **Calendar:** Semester, extensive summer session. **Full-time faculty:** 132 total. **Part-time faculty:** 401 total.

Student profile.

Out-of-state: 4%   25 or older: 52%

Transfer out. Colleges most students transferred to 2011: St. Louis University, Washington University, University of Missouri: St. Louis, University of Missouri: Columbia, Webster University.

Basis for selection. Open admission.

2011-2012 Annual costs. Tuition/fees: $2,640; $4,020 out-of-district; $5,370 out-of-state. Per-credit charge: $88 in-district; $134 out-of-district; $179 out-of-state. Books/supplies: $800. Personal expenses: $2,100.

Financial aid. Need-based: Need-based aid available for part-time students. Work-study available nights, weekends and for part-time students. **Non-need-based:** Scholarships awarded for academics, art, athletics, leadership, music/drama.

Application procedures. Admission: No deadline. No application fee. Admission notification on a rolling basis beginning on or about 4/1. **Financial aid:** Priority date 4/15; no closing date. FAFSA required. Applicants notified on a rolling basis starting 4/1.

Academics. Special study options: Cross-registration, distance learning, double major, dual enrollment of high school students, ESL, honors, independent study, liberal arts/career combination, study abroad, weekend college. License preparation in dental hygiene, nursing, paramedic, radiology, real estate. **Credit/placement by examination:** AP, CLEP, institutional tests. 30 credit hours maximum toward associate degree. **Support services:** GED preparation and test center, learning center, remedial instruction, study skills assistance, tutoring, writing center.

Majors. Biology: General. **Business:** General, accounting, administrative services, banking/financial services, international, organizational behavior, tourism/travel. **Communications:** Communications/speech/rhetoric. **Communications technology:** Graphic/printing. **Computer sciences:** General, data processing, programming, systems analysis. **Education:** Teacher assistance. **Engineering:** General. **Health services:** Clinical lab science, dental assistant, dental hygiene, EMT paramedic, medical radiologic technology/radiation therapy, respiratory therapy technology, sonography, surgical technology. **Liberal arts:** Arts/sciences. **Math:** General. **Physical sciences:** Chemistry, physics. **Protective services:** Fire safety technology. **Psychology:** General. **Social sciences:** General. **Visual/performing arts:** Music, photography, studio arts. **Work/family studies:** Child care management, food/nutrition, institutional food production.

Most popular majors. Business/marketing 7%, computer/information sciences 9%, health sciences 20%, liberal arts 34%, personal/culinary services 12%.

Computing on campus. Commuter students can connect to campus network. Online course registration, online library available.

Student life. Freshman orientation: Available. Preregistration for classes offered. **Activities:** Choral groups, drama, literary magazine, musical theater, student government, student newspaper, TV station.

Athletics. NJCAA. **Intercollegiate:** Baseball M, basketball, soccer M, softball W. **Team name:** Highlanders.

Student services. Career counseling, services for economically disadvantaged, student employment services, financial aid counseling, health services, on-campus daycare, personal counseling, placement for graduates, veterans' counselor. **Physically disabled:** Services for visually, speech, hearing impaired. **Transfer:** Transfer adviser, college fairs on campus for students transferring to 4-year colleges.

Contact. E-mail: gmarshall@stlcc.edu
Phone: (314) 644-9127 Fax: (314) 644-9375
Glenn Marshall, Manager, Admissions/Registration, St. Louis Community College, 300 South Broadway, St. Louis, MO 63102-2800

St. Louis Community College at Florissant Valley
St. Louis, Missouri
www.stlcc.edu   CB code: 6225

- Public 2-year branch campus and community college
- Commuter campus in large city

General. Founded in 1962. Regionally accredited. **Enrollment:** 7,440 degree-seeking undergraduates. **Degrees:** 147 associate awarded. **ROTC:** Army. **Location:** 17 miles from downtown. **Calendar:** Semester, extensive summer session. **Full-time faculty:** 140 total. **Part-time faculty:** 250 total. **Special facilities:** Observatory, child development center.

Student profile.

Out-of-state: 2%   25 or older: 48%

Basis for selection. Open admission, but selective for some programs. Nursing program applicants required to pass institutional test.

2011-2012 Annual costs. Tuition/fees: $2,640; $4,020 out-of-district; $5,370 out-of-state. Per-credit charge: $88 in-district; $134 out-of-district; $179 out-of-state. Books/supplies: $1,000. Personal expenses: $2,100.

Financial aid. Need-based: Work-study available nights, weekends and for part-time students.

Application procedures. Admission: No deadline. No application fee. Admission notification on a rolling basis. **Financial aid:** Closing date 8/1. FAFSA required. Applicants notified on a rolling basis starting 5/1.

Academics. Special study options: Cooperative education, cross-registration, distance learning, dual enrollment of high school students, ESL, exchange student, honors, independent study, internships, study abroad, teacher certification program, weekend college. Bachelor's degree programs available on campus. **Credit/placement by examination:** AP, CLEP, institutional tests. 49 credit hours maximum toward associate degree. **Support services:** Learning center, remedial instruction, tutoring.

Majors. Biology: General. **Business:** Administrative services, banking/financial services, business admin, fashion, management information systems, office technology. **Communications:** Advertising, broadcast journalism, communications/speech/rhetoric, journalism, public relations. **Communications technology:** Graphic/printing. **Computer sciences:** General, applications programming, data processing, programming, systems analysis. **Education:** Early childhood, teacher assistance. **Engineering:** General. **English:** Rhetoric/composition, technical writing. **Foreign languages:** Sign language interpretation. **Health services:** Predental, premedicine, prepharmacy. **Liberal arts:** Arts/sciences. **Math:** General. **Physical sciences:** Chemistry, physics. **Protective services:** Fire safety technology, police science. **Psychology:** General. **Social sciences:** General. **Visual/performing arts:** General, commercial/advertising art, dramatic, music, studio arts. **Work/family studies:** Child care management.

Student life. Activities: Concert band, drama, musical theater, radio station, student government, student newspaper, TV station, Black student association.

Athletics. NJCAA. **Intercollegiate:** Baseball M, basketball, cross-country, soccer, softball W, track and field, volleyball W.

Student services. Career counseling, student employment services, health services, on-campus daycare, personal counseling, placement for graduates. **Physically disabled:** Services for visually, speech, hearing impaired. **Transfer:** Transfer adviser, college fairs on campus for students transferring to 4-year colleges.

Contact. Phone: (314) 513-4244 Fax: (314) 513-4724
Brenda Davenport, Manager of Admissions/Registration, St. Louis Community College at Florissant Valley, 3400 Pershall Road, St. Louis, MO 63135

St. Louis Community College at Meramec
St. Louis, Missouri
www.stlcc.edu   CB code: 6430

- Public 2-year community college
- Commuter campus in large city

General. Founded in 1963. Regionally accredited. Off-campus site at South County Education Center. **Enrollment:** 3,891 full-time, degree-seeking students. **Degrees:** 1,030 associate awarded. **ROTC:** Army, Air Force. **Location:** 15 miles from St. Louis. **Calendar:** Semester, extensive summer session. **Full-time faculty:** 190 total. **Part-time faculty:** 500 total. **Special facilities:** Center for advanced imaging.

Student profile.

Out-of-state: 1%   25 or older: 66%

Basis for selection. Open admission, but selective for some programs. Nursing, occupational therapy assistant, physical therapist assistant, paramedic technology programs have specific admission requirements. SAT or ACT score used to waive Accuplacer Test. Interview required for some health programs. **Home schooled:** Transcript of courses and grades, interview required.

High school preparation. 22 units recommended. Recommended units include English 4, mathematics 2, social studies 3 and science 2.

2011-2012 Annual costs. Tuition/fees: $2,640; $4,020 out-of-district; $5,370 out-of-state. Per-credit charge: $88 in-district; $134 out-of-district; $179 out-of-state. Books/supplies: $800. Personal expenses: $2,100.

Financial aid. Need-based: Need-based aid available for part-time students. Work-study available nights, weekends and for part-time students.

Application procedures. Admission: Priority date 8/1; no deadline. No application fee. Admission notification on a rolling basis beginning on or about 3/1. **Financial aid:** Closing date 6/30. FAFSA, institutional form required. Applicants notified on a rolling basis starting 2/1.

Academics. Special study options: Accelerated study, cross-registration, distance learning, dual enrollment of high school students, ESL, honors, independent study, internships, study abroad. **Credit/placement by examination:** AP, CLEP, institutional tests. 49 credit hours maximum toward associate degree. **Support services:** GED preparation, learning center, pre-admission summer program, reduced course load, remedial instruction, tutoring, writing center.

Majors. Architecture: Interior. **Business:** General, accounting, administrative services, banking/financial services, management information systems, office technology, office/clerical, real estate. **Communications:** Communications/speech/rhetoric. **Computer sciences:** General, applications programming, data processing. **Education:** General, elementary, secondary. **Engineering:** General. **General.** Horticultural science, ornamental horticulture. **Health services:** EMT paramedic, occupational therapy assistant, physical therapy assistant. **Human services:** Social work. **Liberal arts:** Arts/sciences. **Math:** General. **Protective services:** Criminal justice, police science. **Social sciences:** General. **Visual/performing arts:** Commercial/advertising art, music, photography, studio arts.

Computing on campus. 420 workstations in library, computer center.

Student life. Freshman orientation: Mandatory. Preregistration for classes offered. **Activities:** Bands, choral groups, drama, literary magazine, music ensembles, musical theater, student government, student newspaper, symphony orchestra, Phi Theta Kappa, international club, Intervarsity Christian Fellowship, horticulture club, bridge club, engineering club, photo club, scuba club, Student Ambassadors.

Athletics. NJCAA. **Intercollegiate:** Baseball M, basketball, soccer W, softball W, volleyball W. **Intramural:** Volleyball. **Team name:** Magic.

Student services. Career counseling, student employment services, financial aid counseling, health services, on-campus daycare, personal counseling, placement for graduates, veterans' counselor. **Physically disabled:** Services for visually, speech, hearing impaired. **Transfer:** Transfer adviser, college fairs on campus for students transferring to 4-year colleges.

Contact. Phone: (314) 984-7601 Fax: (314) 984-7051
Michael Cundiff, Director of Admission, St. Louis Community College at Meramec, 11333 Big Bend Road, Kirkwood, MO 63122-5799

State Fair Community College
Sedalia, Missouri
www.sfccmo.edu   CB code: 6709

▶ Public 2-year community college
▶ Commuter campus in large town

General. Founded in 1966. Regionally accredited. Academic Quality Improvement Program (AQIP) institution. **Enrollment:** 4,506 degree-seeking undergraduates. **Degrees:** 544 associate awarded. **ROTC:** Army. **Location:** 78 miles from Kansas City. **Calendar:** Semester, limited summer session. **Full-time faculty:** 69 total. **Part-time faculty:** 307 total. **Special facilities:** Contemporary art museum.

Student profile.

Out-of-state:	2%	Live on campus:	3%
25 or older:	41%		

Transfer out. Colleges most students transferred to 2011: University of Central Missouri, Missouri State University.

Basis for selection. Open admission, but selective for some programs. Special requirements for some health programs. Mechanical knowledge test required of all auto mechanics program students. ACT, ASSET, or COMPASS score current within the last five years required of full-time students and all degree-seeking students. Mechanical knowledge test required for auto mechanics program. Interview required for radiologic technology program applicants. **Learning Disabled:** Students encouraged to establish documentation two weeks prior to first day of semester to receive accommodations.

2011-2012 Annual costs. Tuition/fees: $2,700; $3,600 out-of-district; $5,370 out-of-state. Per-credit charge: $72 in-district; $102 out-of-district; $161 out-of-state. Room/board: $6,150. Books/supplies: $1,400. Personal expenses: $3,381.

Financial aid. Need-based: Need-based aid available for part-time students. Work-study available nights, weekends and for part-time students. **Non-need-based:** Scholarships awarded for academics, art, athletics, music/drama, state residency.

Application procedures. Admission: No deadline. $25 fee, may be waived for applicants with need. Admission notification on a rolling basis. **Financial aid:** Priority date 7/1; no closing date. FAFSA required. Applicants notified on a rolling basis starting 7/15; must reply within 3 week(s) of notification.

Academics. Special study options: Cooperative education, cross-registration, distance learning, dual enrollment of high school students, ESL, internships. License preparation in dental hygiene, nursing, occupational therapy, paramedic, physical therapy, radiology, real estate. **Credit/placement by examination:** AP, CLEP, institutional tests. 30 credit hours maximum toward associate degree. Students may earn a maximum of 30 hours in combination from credit by exam or nontraditional credit toward an AA or AAS degree. **Support services:** GED preparation, learning center, reduced course load, remedial instruction, study skills assistance, tutoring, writing center.

Majors. Business: Accounting, business admin, special products marketing. **Computer sciences:** Applications programming, networking, web page design. **Education:** Teacher assistance, voc/tech. **Engineering:** General. **General:** Agribusiness operations. **Health services:** Dental hygiene, medical records technology, nursing (RN), occupational therapy assistant, physical therapy assistant, radiologic technology/medical imaging. **Liberal arts:** Arts/sciences. **Protective services:** Firefighting, police science. **Work/family studies:** Child care management.

Most popular majors. Business/marketing 9%, health sciences 20%, liberal arts 53%.

Computing on campus. 520 workstations in dormitories, library, computer center, student center. Dormitories wired for high-speed internet access and linked to campus network. Commuter students can connect to campus network. Online course registration, online library, helpline, wireless network available.

Student life. Freshman orientation: Available. Preregistration for classes offered. **Housing:** Coed dorms, wellness housing available. $100 nonrefundable deposit, deadline 7/15. **Activities:** Jazz band, choral groups, drama, music ensembles, student government.

Athletics. NJCAA. **Intercollegiate:** Basketball, cheerleading M. **Intramural:** Basketball, football (tackle), softball, table tennis, volleyball. **Team name:** Roadrunners.

Student services. Career counseling, services for economically disadvantaged, student employment services, financial aid counseling, minority student services, on-campus daycare, personal counseling, placement for graduates, veterans' counselor. **Physically disabled:** Services for visually, speech, hearing impaired. **Transfer:** Pre-admission transcript evaluation for new students. Transfer adviser, college fairs on campus for students transferring to 4-year colleges.

Contact. E-mail: mcarter@sfccmo.edu
Phone: (660) 530-5833 Toll-free number: (877) 311-7322
Fax: (660) 596-7472
Mark Carter, Director of Admissions, State Fair Community College, 3201 West 16th Street, Sedalia, MO 65301-2199

Stevens Institute of Business & Arts
St. Louis, Missouri
www.siba.edu   CB code: 3319

▶ For-profit 2-year business and liberal arts college
▶ Commuter campus in very large city
▶ Application essay, interview required

General. Regionally accredited; also accredited by ACICS. **Enrollment:** 267 full-time, degree-seeking students. **Degrees:** 34 bachelor's, 45 associate awarded. **Location:** Downtown. **Calendar:** Quarter, extensive summer session. **Full-time faculty:** 8 total. **Part-time faculty:** 19 total. **Class size:** 97% < 20, 3% 20-39.

Student profile.

Out-of-state: 26%   25 or older: 39%

Transfer out. Colleges most students transferred to 2011: Fontbonne University, Lindenwood University, Maryville University, University of Phoenix, Webster University.

Basis for selection. Open admission, but selective for some programs. Every applicant interviewed by admissions staff. High school and college transcripts are analyzed, as are attendance records and SAT and ACT scores. Achievements in community and workplace considered. SAT or ACT scores only required of students enrolling in bachelor's degree program with less than 90 quarter hours in transfer credits. SAT or ACT scores are not required for students enrolling in AAS program. SAT or ACT scores are only required of students enrolling in a bachelor's degree program with less than 90 quarter hours in transfer credits. SAT or ACT scores are not required for students enrolling in an AAS program. **Home schooled:** Statement describing home school structure and mission, transcript of courses and grades, state high school equivalency certificate, interview required.

2011-2012 Annual costs. Tuition/fees: $10,125. Per-credit charge: $225.

Financial aid. All financial aid based on need. Need-based aid available for part-time students. Work-study available nights, weekends and for part-time students.

Application procedures. Admission: No deadline. $15 fee. Application must be submitted on paper. Admission notification on a rolling basis. **Financial aid:** No deadline. FAFSA required. Applicants notified on a rolling basis.

Academics. Special study options: Accelerated study, independent study, internships, liberal arts/career combination. Bachelor's degree programs available on campus. **Credit/placement by examination:** AP, CLEP. **Support services:** Reduced course load, study skills assistance, tutoring.

Majors. Business: Business admin, fashion, hospitality admin, retailing, tourism/travel, travel services. **Visual/performing arts:** Interior design.

Most popular majors. Business/marketing 57%, legal studies 11%.

Computing on campus. 42 workstations in library, computer center. Commuter students can connect to campus network. Online library, wireless network available.

Student life. Freshman orientation: Mandatory. Preregistration for classes offered. Held each quarter before start of classes. **Policies:** Dress code and attendance policies enforced.

Student services. Adult student services, alcohol/substance abuse counseling, career counseling, student employment services, financial aid counseling, placement for graduates. **Transfer:** Pre-admission transcript evaluation for new students. Transfer adviser, college fairs on campus for students transferring to 4-year colleges.

Contact. E-mail: admissions@siba.edu
Phone: (314) 421-0949 ext. 1119
Toll-free number: (800) 871-0949 ext. 1119 Fax: (314) 421-0304
John Willmon, Director of Admissions, Stevens Institute of Business & Arts, 1521 Washington Avenue, St. Louis, MO 63103

Texas County Technical Institute
Houston, Missouri
www.texascountytech.edu

▶ Private 2-year nursing and technical college
▶ Commuter campus in small town

General. Accredited by ACICS. **Enrollment:** 55 degree-seeking undergraduates. **Degrees:** 8 associate awarded. **Calendar:** Semester. **Full-time faculty:** 11 total. **Part-time faculty:** 18 total.

Basis for selection. Open admission. **Home schooled:** Transcript of courses and grades required.

2011-2012 Annual costs. Tuition/fees: $12,348. Per-credit charge: $345. Books/supplies: $1,000. Personal expenses: $1,083.

Financial aid. All financial aid based on need. Need-based aid available for part-time students. Work-study available nights, weekends and for part-time students.

Application procedures. Admission: No deadline. $45 fee. Application must be submitted on paper. Admission notification on a rolling basis. **Financial aid:** No deadline. FAFSA, institutional form required.

Academics. Special study options: License preparation in nursing, paramedic. **Credit/placement by examination:** AP, CLEP.

Majors. Business: Accounting, administrative services. **Computer sciences:** Data processing. **Health services:** EMT paramedic, medical secretary, nursing (RN).

Most popular majors. Health sciences 27%.

Student life. Freshman orientation: Available. Preregistration for classes offered. **Activities:** Student newspaper.

Student services. Career counseling, financial aid counseling.

Contact. E-mail: info@texascountytech.edu
Phone: (417) 967-5466 Toll-free number: (800) 835-1130
Fax: (417) 967-4604
Clarice Casebeer, Director of Admissions, Texas County Technical Institute, 6915 South Highway 63, Houston, MO 65483

Three Rivers Community College
Poplar Bluff, Missouri
www.trcc.edu   **CB code: 6836**

▶ Public 2-year community college
▶ Commuter campus in large town

General. Founded in 1966. Regionally accredited. Selected courses offered at area high schools, vocational schools and other off-campus facilities. **Enrollment:** 4,234 undergraduates. **Degrees:** 426 associate awarded. **Location:** 160 miles from St. Louis. **Calendar:** Semester, limited summer session. **Full-time faculty:** 63 total; 5% minority, 64% women. **Part-time faculty:** 157 total; 2% minority, 51% women.

Student profile.

Out-of-state:	2%	Live on campus:	6%
25 or older:	35%		

Transfer out. Colleges most students transferred to 2011: Southeast Missouri State University, Arkansas State University, Southwest Missouri State University.

Basis for selection. Open admission, but selective for some programs. Special requirements for allied health programs and nursing. **Home schooled:** Statement describing home school structure and mission required.

2011-2012 Annual costs. Tuition/fees: $3,120; $4,470 out-of-district; $5,280 out-of-state. Per-credit charge: $72 in-district; $117 out-of-district; $144 out-of-state. Book rental: $30 per book. Room only: $3,324. Books/supplies: $450. Personal expenses: $1,249.

Financial aid. Need-based: Need-based aid available for part-time students. Work-study available nights, weekends and for part-time students. **Non-need-based:** Scholarships awarded for academics, athletics, state residency.

Application procedures. Admission: No deadline. No application fee. Application must be submitted on paper. Admission notification on a rolling basis. **Financial aid:** Priority date 5/1; no closing date. FAFSA, institutional form required. Applicants notified on a rolling basis starting 6/1; must reply within 2 week(s) of notification.

Academics. Special study options: Accelerated study, distance learning, dual enrollment of high school students, independent study, internships, liberal arts/career combination. Bachelor's degree programs available on campus. License preparation in nursing, paramedic. **Credit/placement by examination:** AP, CLEP. 30 credit hours maximum toward associate degree. **Support services:** GED test center, learning center, remedial instruction, study skills assistance, tutoring, writing center.

Majors. Biology: General. **Business:** Accounting, administrative services, entrepreneurial studies, management information systems, marketing. **Education:** General. **English:** English lit, rhetoric/composition. **Foreign languages:** General. **General:** Business. **Health services:** Clinical lab technology, nursing (RN), premedicine, prepharmacy, preveterinary. **History:** General. **Liberal arts:** Arts/sciences, library assistant. **Math:** General. **Parks/recreation:**

Health/fitness. **Philosophy/religion:** Philosophy. **Physical sciences:** Chemistry. **Protective services:** Police science. **Psychology:** General. **Social sciences:** Economics, geography, political science, sociology. **Visual/performing arts:** Music, studio arts.

Most popular majors. Business/marketing 9%, health sciences 22%, liberal arts 50%, trade and industry 6%.

Computing on campus. 100 workstations in dormitories, library, computer center, student center. Dormitories wired for high-speed internet access.

Student life. Freshman orientation: Available. Preregistration for classes offered. Mini orientation activities are held for incoming freshmen during registration. Orientation for new students offered at beginning of each semester for students, family and friends. **Housing:** Apartments, wellness housing available. $200 partly refundable deposit. **Activities:** Concert band, choral groups, drama, music ensembles, student government, Student Senate, Phi Theta Kappa, Marketing Management Association,.

Athletics. NJCAA. **Intercollegiate:** Baseball M, basketball, softball W. **Intramural:** Baseball M, basketball, volleyball W. **Team name:** Raiders.

Student services. Career counseling, student employment services, placement for graduates, veterans' counselor. **Transfer:** Transfer adviser, college fairs on campus for students transferring to 4-year colleges.

Contact. E-mail: mfields@trcc.edu
Phone: (573) 840-9605 Toll-free number: (877) 879-8722 ext. 605
Fax: (573) 840-9058
Marcia Fields, Director of Admissions, Three Rivers Community College, 2080 Three Rivers Boulevard, Poplar Bluff, MO 63901-1308

Vatterott College: Berkeley
Berkeley, Missouri
www.vatterott-college.edu   CB code: 2507

- For-profit 2-year technical college
- Large city

General. Accredited by ACCSCT. **Location:** 20 miles from St. Louis, 310 miles from Chicago. **Calendar:** Differs by program.

Annual costs/financial aid. Estimated program costs as of April 2011: diploma (50 weeks) $17,565, (60 weeks) $17,565 - $25,925; associate degree (70 weeks) $33,325, (90 weeks) $35,600 - $39,060; bachelor's degree (170 weeks) $73,550. All costs, which include tuition, fees, books and supplies, and taxes, are subject to change.

Contact. Phone: (314) 264-1040
Director of Admissions, 8580 Evans Avenue, Berkeley, MO 63134

Vatterott College: Joplin
Joplin, Missouri
www.vatterott-college.com   CB code: 3635

- For-profit 2-year technical college
- Large town

General. Accredited by ACCSCT. **Calendar:** Differs by program.

Annual costs/financial aid. Estimated program costs as of June 2011: diploma (50 weeks) $18,400, (60 weeks) $18,400 - $24,100; associate degree (70 weeks) $27,100 - $33,350, (90 weeks) $36,100 - $36,750. All costs, which include tuition, fees, books and supplies, and taxes, are subject to change.

Contact. Phone: (417) 781-5633
Director of Admissions, 809 Illinois Avenue, Joplin, MO 64801

Vatterott College: Kansas City
Kansas City, Missouri
www.vatterott-college.edu   CB code: 2893

- For-profit 2-year technical college
- Large city

General. Accredited by ACCSCT. **Calendar:** Differs by program.

Annual costs/financial aid. Estimated program costs as of June 2011: diploma (60 weeks) $21,840 - $25,600; associate degree (70 weeks) $27,100 - $33,350, (90 weeks) $37,250 - $38,150. All costs, which include tuition, fees, books and supplies, and taxes, are subject to change.

Contact. Phone: (816) 861-1000
Director of Admissions, 8955 East 38th Terrace, Kansas City, MO 64129

Vatterott College: O'Fallon
Saint Charles, Missouri
www.vatterott-college.edu

- For-profit 2-year branch campus and technical college
- Small city

General. Accredited by ACCSC. **Enrollment:** 291 full-time, degree-seeking students. **Degrees:** 82 associate awarded. **Location:** 30 miles from St. Louis. **Calendar:** Differs by program. **Full-time faculty:** 15 total. **Part-time faculty:** 11 total.

Basis for selection. Open admission.

Financial aid. Need-based: Work-study available nights, weekends and for part-time students.

Academics. Credit/placement by examination: AP, CLEP.

Majors. Computer sciences: Networking. **Health services:** Medical assistant.

Contact. E-mail: ofallon@vatterott-college.edu
Phone: (636) 978-7488 Toll-free number: (888) 766-3601
Fax: (636) 978-5121
Gertrude Bogan-Jones, Director of Admissions, Vatterott College: O'Fallon, 3350 West Clay Street, St. Charles, MO 63301

Vatterott College: Springfield
Springfield, Missouri
www.vatterott-college.edu   CB code: 2895

- For-profit 2-year branch campus and technical college
- Commuter campus in small city

General. Accredited by ACCSCT. **Calendar:** Quarter.

Annual costs/financial aid. Estimated program costs as of June 2011: diploma (40 weeks) $16,000, (60 weeks) $24,300 - $25,500; associate degree (70 weeks) $27,100 - $33,800, (90 weeks) $36,700 - $37,950. All costs, which include tuition, fees, books and supplies, and taxes, are subject to change. Books/supplies: $2,388. Personal expenses: $2,289.

Contact. Phone: (417) 831-8116
Director of Admissions, 3850 South Campbell, Springfield, MO 65807

Vatterott College: St. Joseph
Saint Joseph, Missouri
www.vatterott-college.edu   CB code: 2896

- For-profit 2-year branch campus and technical college
- Commuter campus in small city

General. Accredited by ACCSC. **Enrollment:** 341 undergraduates. **Degrees:** 91 associate awarded. **Location:** 50 miles from Kansas City. **Calendar:** Quarter, extensive summer session. **Full-time faculty:** 9 total. **Part-time faculty:** 19 total.

Basis for selection. Open admission.

2011-2012 Annual costs. Estimated program costs as of June 2011: diploma (30 weeks) $13,200, (50 weeks) $20,265, (60 weeks) $20,265 - $21,840; associate degree (70 weeks) $27,100 - $33,600. All costs, which include tuition, fees, books and supplies, and taxes, are subject to change. Personal expenses: $1,288.

Financial aid. Need-based: Need-based aid available for part-time students. Work-study available nights, weekends and for part-time students.

Application procedures. Admission: No deadline. No application fee. **Financial aid:** No deadline. FAFSA required.

Academics. Credit/placement by examination: AP, CLEP, institutional tests. 36 credit hours maximum toward associate degree. **Support services:** Tutoring.

Majors. Computer sciences: General. **Health services:** Medical secretary.

Student life. Freshman orientation: Mandatory. Preregistration for classes offered. Held first day of classes. Students are briefed on policies and procedures and are introduced to the directors, career services, instructors and financial aid paperwork.

Student services. Career counseling, student employment services, financial aid counseling, placement for graduates, veterans' counselor.

Contact. E-mail: jaymi.evans@vatterott-college.edu
Phone: (816) 364-5399 Toll-free number: (800) 282-5327
Fax: (816) 364-1593
Jaymi Evans, Director of Admissions, Vatterott College: St. Joseph, 3131 Frederick Avenue, St. Joseph, MO 64506

Vatterott College: Sunset Hills
Sunset Hills, Missouri
www.vatterott-college.com   **CB code: 2898**

▸ For-profit 2-year branch campus and technical college
▸ Very large city

General. Accredited by ACCSCT. **Calendar:** Differs by program.

Annual costs/financial aid. Estimated program costs as of April 2011: diploma (60 weeks) $21,840 - $26,065; associate degree (70 weeks) $33,300 - $34,750, (90 weeks) $37,750 - $39,290; bachelor's degree (170 weeks) $74,550 - $75,450. All costs, which include tuition, fees, books and supplies, and taxes, are subject to change.

Contact. Phone: (314) 843-4200
Director, 12900 Maurer Industrial Drive, Sunset Hills, MO 63127

Wentworth Military Junior College
Lexington, Missouri   **CB member**
www.wma.edu/college   **CB code: 6934**

▸ Private 2-year junior and military college
▸ Commuter campus in small town
▸ Interview required

General. Founded in 1880. Regionally accredited. Adult evening program open to both men and women. **Enrollment:** 265 degree-seeking undergraduates. **Degrees:** 48 associate awarded. **ROTC:** Army. **Location:** 40 miles from Kansas City. **Calendar:** Semester, extensive summer session. **Full-time faculty:** 13 total; 8% minority, 31% women. **Part-time faculty:** 27 total; 7% have terminal degrees, 22% women. **Class size:** 100% < 20. **Special facilities:** Nature trail, military history library, indoor rifle range, athletic facilities.

Student profile.

Out-of-state:	55%	**Live on campus:**	23%
25 or older:	30%		

Transfer out. Colleges most students transferred to 2011: Central Missouri State University, Texas A&M University, University of Kansas, Kansas State University, University of Missouri.

Basis for selection. Open admission, but selective for some programs. Admittees to senior ROTC programs must meet ROTC admission criteria. ACT/SAT required of applicants to ROTC commissioning program for admission, placement, counseling. Score report by August 1. **Home schooled:** Transcript of courses and grades, letter of recommendation (nonparent) required.

High school preparation. 24 units recommended. Recommended units include English 4, mathematics 3, social studies 3, science 2 (laboratory 2), foreign language 2 and academic electives 8.

2011-2012 Annual costs. Tuition/fees: $19,000. Room/board: $6,800. Books/supplies: $2,000. Personal expenses: $4,830.

Financial aid. All financial aid based on need. Work-study available nights, weekends and for part-time students.

Application procedures. Admission: No deadline. $25 fee. Admission notification on a rolling basis. **Financial aid:** Closing date 4/30. FAFSA required. Applicants notified on a rolling basis.

Academics. Service academy preparatory program. **Special study options:** Accelerated study, distance learning, dual enrollment of high school students, ESL, independent study, liberal arts/career combination. License preparation in nursing. **Credit/placement by examination:** AP, CLEP, institutional tests. 30 credit hours maximum toward associate degree. **Support services:** Tutoring.

Majors. Liberal arts: Arts/sciences.

Computing on campus. 50 workstations in library, computer center. Dormitories wired for high-speed internet access and linked to campus network. Commuter students can connect to campus network. Helpline, wireless network available.

Student life. Freshman orientation: Available. Preregistration for classes offered. **Policies:** Religious observance required. **Housing:** Single-sex dorms available. $1,500 deposit, deadline 6/30. **Activities:** Bands, choral groups, dance, drama, music ensembles, student government, student newspaper.

Athletics. NJCAA. **Intercollegiate:** Cross-country, rifle M, track and field, wrestling M. **Intramural:** Baseball M, basketball M, cheerleading W, football (non-tackle) M, golf, racquetball, rifle, soccer, swimming, tennis, volleyball, weight lifting M. **Team name:** Red Dragons.

Student services. Career counseling, financial aid counseling, health services, personal counseling. **Transfer:** Transfer adviser, college fairs on campus for students transferring to 4-year colleges.

Contact. E-mail: admissions@wma.edu
Phone: (660) 259-2221 Toll-free number: (800) 962-7682
Fax: (660) 259-2677
Robert Harmon, Admissions Director, Wentworth Military Junior College, 1880 Washington Avenue, Lexington, MO 64067-1799

Montana

Aaniiih Nakoda College
Harlem, Montana
www.fbcc.edu

- Public 2-year community college
- Commuter campus in rural community

General. Regionally accredited. **Enrollment:** 162 degree-seeking undergraduates. **Degrees:** 17 associate awarded. **Location:** On Fort Belknap Reservation. **Calendar:** Semester. **Full-time faculty:** 16 total. **Part-time faculty:** 3 total. **Special facilities:** Native American cultural center.

Transfer out. Colleges most students transferred to 2011: University of Missoula.

Basis for selection. Open admission. COMPASS Placement Test required. **Home schooled:** Transcript of courses and grades, state high school equivalency certificate required.

2011-2012 Annual costs. Tuition/fees: $2,410; $2,410 out-of-state. Per-credit charge: $70. Books/supplies: $910. Personal expenses: $960.

Financial aid. Need-based: Work-study available nights, weekends and for part-time students.

Application procedures. Admission: No deadline. $10 fee. Admission notification on a rolling basis. **Financial aid:** No deadline. Applicants notified on a rolling basis.

Academics. Special study options: Dual enrollment of high school students. **Credit/placement by examination:** AP, CLEP. **Support services:** GED preparation, learning center, tutoring.

Majors. Area/ethnic studies: Native American. **Business:** General, office technology. **Computer sciences:** Data processing. **Conservation:** Management/policy. **Education:** Elementary. **Health services:** Substance abuse counseling. **Liberal arts:** Arts/sciences.

Most popular majors. Biological/life sciences 21%, business/marketing 7%, computer/information sciences 29%, education 7%, liberal arts 7%, natural resources/environmental science 21%, psychology 7%.

Student life. Freshman orientation: Mandatory. Preregistration for classes offered. **Activities:** Student government.

Student services. Career counseling, financial aid counseling.

Contact. Phone: (406) 353-2607 Fax: (406) 353-2898
Dixie Brockie, Registrar/Admissions Officer, Aaniiih Nakoda College, Box 159, Harlem, MT 59526-0159

Blackfeet Community College
Browning, Montana
www.bfcc.org   **CB code: 0379**

- Public 2-year community college
- Commuter campus in small town

General. Founded in 1976. Regionally accredited. Tribally controlled college located on Blackfeet Indian reservation. **Enrollment:** 472 degree-seeking undergraduates. **Degrees:** 58 associate awarded. **Location:** 126 miles from Great Falls. **Calendar:** Semester, limited summer session. **Full-time faculty:** 27 total. **Part-time faculty:** 24 total. **Class size:** 77% < 20, 22% 20-39, less than 1% 40-49.

Basis for selection. Open admission. **Home schooled:** State high school equivalency certificate required.

2011-2012 Annual costs. Tuition/fees: $2,190; $2,190 out-of-state. Per-credit charge: $75. Books/supplies: $750.

Financial aid. Need-based: Need-based aid available for part-time students. Work-study available nights, weekends and for part-time students.

Application procedures. Admission: No deadline. $20 fee. Application must be submitted on paper. Admission notification on a rolling basis. **Financial aid:** No deadline. FAFSA, institutional form required.

Academics. Special study options: Distance learning, double major, internships. 2-2 teacher training program with Montana University System. **Credit/placement by examination:** AP, CLEP. 3 credit hours maximum toward associate degree. **Support services:** GED preparation and test center, learning center, pre-admission summer program, remedial instruction, tutoring, writing center.

Majors. Area/ethnic studies: Native American. **Business:** Business admin, entrepreneurial studies, hospitality admin, office management, small business admin. **Computer sciences:** General, networking. **Conservation:** General, environmental science, forestry. **Education:** Early childhood, elementary. **Health services:** Prenursing, substance abuse counseling. **Human services:** Social work. **Liberal arts:** Arts/sciences. **Parks/recreation:** Health/fitness. **Protective services:** Criminal justice, homeland security.

Most popular majors. Business/marketing 30%, computer/information sciences 8%, education 14%, engineering/engineering technologies 12%, health sciences 14%, natural resources/environmental science 8%.

Computing on campus. 5 workstations in library, computer center, student center.

Student life. Freshman orientation: Mandatory. Preregistration for classes offered. **Activities:** Literary magazine, student government, student newspaper.

Athletics. Intercollegiate: Basketball, cross-country, rodeo. **Intramural:** Basketball.

Student services. Adult student services, career counseling, financial aid counseling, personal counseling. **Transfer:** Transfer adviser for students transferring to 4-year colleges.

Contact. Phone: (406) 338-5421 ext. 243
Toll-free number: (800) 549-7457 Fax: (406) 338-3272
Deana McNabb, Registrar/Admissions Officer, Blackfeet Community College, 504 SE Boundary, Browning, MT 59417

Chief Dull Knife College
Lame Deer, Montana
www.cdkc.edu   **CB code: 5938**

- Public 2-year junior college
- Commuter campus in rural community

General. Regionally accredited. **Enrollment:** 242 degree-seeking undergraduates. **Degrees:** 28 associate awarded. **Location:** 110 miles from Billings. **Calendar:** Semester, limited summer session. **Full-time faculty:** 13 total. **Part-time faculty:** 12 total.

Basis for selection. Open admission.

2011-2012 Annual costs. Tuition/fees: $2,240; $2,240 out-of-state. Per-credit charge: $70. Books/supplies: $1,000. Personal expenses: $4,000.

Financial aid. Need-based: Need-based aid available for part-time students. Work-study available nights, weekends and for part-time students. **Non-need-based:** Scholarships awarded for academics.

Application procedures. Admission: No deadline. No application fee. Application must be submitted on paper. Admission notification on a rolling basis. **Financial aid:** Priority date 3/1; no closing date. FAFSA, institutional form required. Applicants notified on a rolling basis; must reply within 2 week(s) of notification.

Academics. Special study options: Cooperative education, double major, internships. Bachelor's degree programs available on campus. **Credit/placement by examination:** AP, CLEP, institutional tests. 9 credit hours maximum toward associate degree. **Support services:** GED preparation and test center, learning center, remedial instruction, tutoring.

Majors. Business: General, office management.

Computing on campus. 25 workstations in library, computer center. Online library available.

Student life. Freshman orientation: Mandatory. Preregistration for classes offered. **Activities:** Student government, student newspaper.

Athletics. Intramural: Basketball.

Student services. Career counseling, financial aid counseling, on-campus daycare, personal counseling, veterans' counselor. **Transfer:** Transfer adviser for students transferring to 4-year colleges.

Contact. E-mail: zspang@cdkc.edu
Phone: (406) 477-6215 Fax: (406) 477-6219
Zane Spang, Dean of Student Affairs, Chief Dull Knife College, Box 98, Lame Deer, MT 59043

Dawson Community College
Glendive, Montana
www.dawson.edu
CB code: 4280

❥ Public 2-year community college
❥ Commuter campus in small town

General. Founded in 1940. Regionally accredited. **Enrollment:** 437 degree-seeking undergraduates. **Degrees:** 118 associate awarded. **Location:** 220 miles from Billings, 200 miles from Bismarck, North Dakota. **Calendar:** Semester, limited summer session. **Full-time faculty:** 23 total. **Part-time faculty:** 3 total.

Student profile.

Out-of-state: 15%   Live on campus: 48%

Transfer out. Colleges most students transferred to 2011: Dickinson State University, Montana State University-Bozeman, Montana State University-Billings, University of Montana.

Basis for selection. Open admission.

2011-2012 Annual costs. Tuition/fees: $3,083; $4,245 out-of-district; $9,135 out-of-state. Per-credit charge: $55 in-district; $94 out-of-district; $257 out-of-state. Room only: $2,300. Books/supplies: $1,000. Personal expenses: $1,048.

Financial aid. Need-based: Work-study available nights, weekends and for part-time students. **Non-need-based:** Scholarships awarded for academics, art, athletics, music/drama.

Application procedures. Admission: No deadline. $30 fee. Admission notification on a rolling basis. **Financial aid:** Priority date 3/1; no closing date. FAFSA required. Applicants notified on a rolling basis starting 5/15; must reply within 2 week(s) of notification.

Academics. Special study options: Distance learning, double major, dual enrollment of high school students, independent study, internships. **Credit/placement by examination:** AP, CLEP, institutional tests. 15 credit hours maximum toward associate degree. **Support services:** GED preparation and test center, learning center, reduced course load, remedial instruction, study skills assistance, tutoring.

Majors. Business: General, administrative services. **Computer sciences:** General, vendor certification. **Education:** Early childhood. **General:** Business, equestrian studies, farm/ranch, power machinery. **Health services:** Medical transcription, substance abuse counseling. **Liberal arts:** Arts/sciences. **Protective services:** Police science. **Visual/performing arts:** Music technology.

Most popular majors. Liberal arts 60%.

Computing on campus. 70 workstations in dormitories, library, computer center. Dormitories wired for high-speed internet access and linked to campus network. Wireless network available.

Student life. Freshman orientation: Mandatory. Preregistration for classes offered. Held during June and July. **Housing:** Coed dorms available. $150 deposit. Student dormitories include kitchen facilities. **Activities:** Bands, choral groups, drama, music ensembles, musical theater, student government, human services club, law enforcement club, Intervarsity Christian Fellowship.

Athletics. NJCAA. **Intercollegiate:** Baseball M, basketball, rodeo, softball W. **Intramural:** Basketball, bowling, golf, racquetball, softball, table tennis, tennis, volleyball. **Team name:** Buccaneers.

Student services. Adult student services, career counseling, student employment services, placement for graduates, veterans' counselor. **Physically disabled:** Services for visually, speech, hearing impaired. **Transfer:** Pre-admission transcript evaluation for new students. College fairs on campus for students transferring to 4-year colleges.

Contact. E-mail: myers@dawson.edu
Phone: (406) 377-3396 ext. 410
Toll-free number: (800) 821-8320 ext. 410 Fax: (406) 377-8132
Jolene Myers, Director of Admissions, Dawson Community College, 300 College Drive, Glendive, MT 59330

Flathead Valley Community College
Kalispell, Montana
www.fvcc.edu
CB code: 4317

❥ Public 2-year community college
❥ Commuter campus in large town

General. Founded in 1967. Regionally accredited. **Enrollment:** 2,043 degree-seeking undergraduates. **Degrees:** 353 associate awarded. **Location:** 238 miles from Spokane, Washington. **Calendar:** Semester, limited summer session. **Full-time faculty:** 48 total. **Part-time faculty:** 172 total. **Class size:** 75% < 20, 25% 20-39. **Partnerships:** Formal partnerships with area high schools for Early College programs.

Student profile.

Out-of-state: 2%   **25 or older:**   51%

Transfer out. Colleges most students transferred to 2011: University of Montana, Montana State University - Bozeman.

Basis for selection. Open admission, but selective for some programs. Culinary Arts Program requires COMPASS scores of 78 in reading, 71 in writing, and 47 in pre-algebra, or completion of appropriate remedial coursework. Heavy Equipment Operator students must pass a physical and drug screen. Paramedicine requires a valid EMT-B License, Basic A&P and college level math, entrance exam, interview with selection committee, and a background check. Practical Nursing requires the completion of specific courses, with grades of C or higher; GPA of at least 2.75 in all prerequisite courses. Pharmacy Technology requires COMPASS scores of 30 in Algebra and 74 in Reading or completion of appropriate remedial coursework. Comprehensive background check required. Application essay and letter of reference required for Culinary Arts Program. Essay, references, and interview required for Radiologic and Surgical Technology students. **Home schooled:** Applicants must have GED or COMPASS test scores.

2011-2012 Annual costs. Tuition/fees: $3,657; $5,029 out-of-district; $10,797 out-of-state. Books/supplies: $1,000. Personal expenses: $2,240.

Financial aid. Need-based: Need-based aid available for part-time students. Work-study available nights, weekends and for part-time students. **Non-need-based:** Scholarships awarded for academics, athletics.

Application procedures. Admission: No deadline. $15 fee. Application must be submitted on paper. Admission notification on a rolling basis. **Financial aid:** Priority date 3/1; no closing date. FAFSA required. Applicants notified on a rolling basis starting 4/15; must reply within 2 week(s) of notification.

Academics. Special study options: Distance learning, dual enrollment of high school students, honors, independent study, internships, liberal arts/career combination, study abroad. Bachelor's degree programs available on campus. License preparation in nursing, paramedic, radiology, real estate. **Credit/placement by examination:** AP, CLEP, IB, institutional tests. 12 AP credits allowed toward associate degree. **Support services:** GED preparation and test center, learning center, reduced course load, remedial instruction, study skills assistance, tutoring, writing center.

Majors. Business: Accounting, administrative services, business admin, executive assistant, small business admin. **Computer sciences:** Information technology, web page design. **Conservation:** Management/policy. **Education:** Early childhood. **Health services:** EMT paramedic, licensed practical nurse, medical assistant, medical radiologic technology/radiation therapy, medical secretary, office assistant, receptionist, substance abuse counseling, surgical technology. **Liberal arts:** Arts/sciences, humanities. **Protective services:** Criminal justice. **Visual/performing arts:** Graphic design, metal/jewelry.

Most popular majors. Health sciences 14%, liberal arts 65%, trade and industry 7%.

Computing on campus. 175 workstations in library, computer center. Commuter students can connect to campus network. Online course registration, online library, helpline, wireless network available.

Student life. Freshman orientation: Available. Preregistration for classes offered. 4 half-day summer advising and registration programs. **Activities:**

Campus ministries, choral groups, drama, student government, student newspaper, Phi Theta Kappa, veterans organization, forestry club, Bitta club (Native American), human service club, international student association.

Athletics. NJCAA. **Intercollegiate:** Cross-country. **Intramural:** Basketball, bowling, skiing, soccer, softball, table tennis, volleyball. **Team name:** Eagles.

Student services. Adult student services, career counseling, services for economically disadvantaged, student employment services, financial aid counseling, health services, minority student services, on-campus daycare, personal counseling, placement for graduates, veterans' counselor. **Physically disabled:** Services for visually, hearing impaired. **Transfer:** Pre-admission transcript evaluation for new students. Transfer adviser for students transferring to 4-year colleges.

Contact. E-mail: mstoltz@fvcc.edu
Phone: (406) 756-3846 Toll-free number: (800) 313-3822
Fax: (406) 756-3965
Marlene Stoltz, Registrar/Admissions and Records Coordinator, Flathead Valley Community College, 777 Grandview Drive, Kalispell, MT 59901

Fort Peck Community College
Poplar, Montana
www.fpcc.edu

♦ Public 2-year community college
♦ Commuter campus in rural community

General. Regionally accredited. Tribally controlled college. Transfer degrees and Vocational Degrees also offered. **Enrollment:** 380 degree-seeking undergraduates. **Degrees:** 35 associate awarded. **Location:** 70 miles from Williston, North Dakota; 300 miles from Billings. **Calendar:** Semester, limited summer session. **Full-time faculty:** 25 total. **Part-time faculty:** 15 total.

Transfer out. Colleges most students transferred to 2011: Rocky Mountain College.

Basis for selection. Open admission. Interview recommended.

2011-2012 Annual costs. Tuition/fees: $2,250; $2,250 out-of-state. Per-credit charge: $70. Books/supplies: $700. Personal expenses: $2,000.

Financial aid. All financial aid based on need. Need-based aid available for part-time students. Work-study available nights, weekends and for part-time students.

Application procedures. Admission: No deadline. $15 fee. Application must be submitted on paper. Admission notification on a rolling basis. **Financial aid:** No deadline. FAFSA required. Applicants notified on a rolling basis; must reply within 2 week(s) of notification.

Academics. Special study options: Distance learning, double major, dual enrollment of high school students, independent study, internships, teacher certification program. **Credit/placement by examination:** AP, CLEP. **Support services:** GED preparation and test center, learning center, remedial instruction, study skills assistance, tutoring.

Majors. Area/ethnic studies: Native American. **Biology:** Biomedical sciences. **Business:** General, administrative services, business admin. **Computer sciences:** Computer graphics, data processing. **Conservation:** General, management/policy. **Education:** General, science. **Health services:** Substance abuse counseling. **Visual/performing arts:** Studio arts.

Most popular majors. Business/marketing 43%, liberal arts 50%.

Computing on campus. 65 workstations in library, computer center.

Student life. Freshman orientation: Available. Preregistration for classes offered. **Activities:** Student government, student newspaper, American Indian Business Leaders.

Athletics. Team name: Buffalo Chasers.

Student services. Adult student services, career counseling, student employment services, on-campus daycare, personal counseling, placement for graduates, veterans' counselor. **Transfer:** Pre-admission transcript evaluation for new students. Transfer adviser, college fairs on campus for students transferring to 4-year colleges.

Contact. Phone: (406) 768-6300 Fax: (406) 738-6301
Linda Hansen, Registrar, Fort Peck Community College, Box 398, 605 Indian, Poplar, MT 59255-0398

Little Big Horn College
Crow Agency, Montana
www.lbhc.edu
CB code: 0536

♦ Private 2-year community college
♦ Commuter campus in rural community

General. Founded in 1980. Regionally accredited. Provides education for Crow Indian community. Crow lifeways, economic environment, history, language, and culture emphasized with standard curriculum. **Enrollment:** 337 degree-seeking undergraduates. **Degrees:** 63 associate awarded. **Location:** 60 miles from Billings. **Calendar:** Quarter. **Full-time faculty:** 17 total. **Part-time faculty:** 12 total.

Basis for selection. Open admission.

2011-2012 Annual costs. Tuition/fees: $3,180. Per-credit charge: $75. Books/supplies: $600. Personal expenses: $600.

Financial aid. Need-based: Need-based aid available for part-time students. Work-study available nights, weekends and for part-time students.

Application procedures. Admission: No deadline. No application fee. Admission notification on a rolling basis. **Financial aid:** No deadline. Applicants notified on a rolling basis.

Academics. Bilingual methodologies approach in some course work. **Special study options:** Distance learning, exchange student, internships. **Credit/placement by examination:** AP, CLEP, institutional tests. **Support services:** Remedial instruction, tutoring.

Majors. Area/ethnic studies: Native American. **Biology:** General. **Business:** General, business admin, management information systems. **Computer sciences:** Data processing, information systems. **Health services:** Substance abuse counseling. **Liberal arts:** Arts/sciences. **Math:** General. **Psychology:** General. **Social sciences:** General. **Work/family studies:** General, child care management.

Most popular majors. Business/marketing 10%, liberal arts 90%.

Student life. Policies: Native religious ceremonies offered. **Activities:** Student government.

Athletics. Intercollegiate: Basketball.

Student services. Career counseling, student employment services, personal counseling. **Transfer:** Transfer adviser, college fairs on campus for students transferring to 4-year colleges.

Contact. E-mail: tina@lbhc.edu
Phone: (406) 638-3116 Fax: (406) 638-3169
Tina Pretty On Top, Admissions Officer, Little Big Horn College, Box 370, Crow Agency, MT 59022

Miles Community College
Miles City, Montana
www.milescc.edu
CB code: 4081

♦ Public 2-year community college
♦ Commuter campus in small town

General. Founded in 1939. Regionally accredited. **Enrollment:** 459 degree-seeking undergraduates; 32 non-degree-seeking students. **Degrees:** 117 associate awarded. **Location:** 150 miles east of Billings. **Calendar:** Semester, limited summer session. **Full-time faculty:** 21 total. **Part-time faculty:** 25 total.

Student profile. Among degree-seeking undergraduates, 127 enrolled as first-time, first-year students, 46 transferred in from other institutions.

Part-time:	30%	25 or older:	31%
Out-of-state:	20%	Live on campus:	25%
Women:	62%		

Transfer out. Colleges most students transferred to 2011: Montana State University-Billings, Montana State University-Bozeman, Dickinson State University, University of Montana, South Dakota State University.

Basis for selection. Open admission, but selective for some programs. Special requirements for nursing program: National League for Nursing Pre-Admission Examination and nurse's aide certification required. COMPASS required for all students. **Home schooled:** Minimum COMPASS scores:

Writing, 32; Reading, 62; Pre-Algebra/Number Skills, 25; may be used in lieu of high school diploma or GED.

2011-2012 Annual costs. Tuition/fees: $3,630; $4,590 out-of-district; $7,380 out-of-state. Per-credit charge: $77 in-district; $109 out-of-district; $202 out-of-state. Room/board: $4,850. Books/supplies: $800. Personal expenses: $630.

Financial aid. Need-based: Need-based aid available for part-time students. Work-study available nights, weekends and for part-time students. **Non-need-based:** Scholarships awarded for academics, athletics, leadership.

Application procedures. Admission: No deadline. $30 fee. Admission notification on a rolling basis. **Financial aid:** Priority date 3/1; no closing date. FAFSA required. Applicants notified on a rolling basis starting 4/15; must reply within 4 week(s) of notification.

Academics. Special study options: Cooperative education, cross-registration, distance learning, dual enrollment of high school students, ESL, independent study, internships. License preparation in nursing. **Credit/placement by examination:** AP, CLEP, IB, institutional tests. 15 credit hours maximum toward associate degree. **Support services:** GED preparation and test center, learning center, pre-admission summer program, reduced course load, remedial instruction, study skills assistance, tutoring, writing center.

Majors. Biology: General. **Business:** Administrative services, business admin, office management, office/clerical. **Communications:** Journalism. **Computer sciences:** General, computer graphics, data processing. **Conservation:** General, forestry, wildlife/wilderness. **Education:** General. **Engineering:** General. **English:** American lit, English lit, rhetoric/composition. **Foreign languages:** General. **General:** Business. **Health services:** Medical secretary, nursing (RN), prenursing. **Human services:** General, social work. **Liberal arts:** Arts/sciences. **Math:** General. **Parks/recreation:** Health/fitness. **Physical sciences:** General. **Psychology:** General. **Social sciences:** General, economics, political science. **Visual/performing arts:** Art, crafts, dramatic, photography. **Work/family studies:** General.

Computing on campus. 90 workstations in library, computer center. Dormitories wired for high-speed internet access. Commuter students can connect to campus network. Online course registration, helpline, wireless network available.

Student life. Freshman orientation: Mandatory. Preregistration for classes offered. **Housing:** Coed dorms available. $200 deposit. **Activities:** Campus ministries, choral groups, dance, drama, international student organizations, student government, Phi Theta Kappa, rodeo club, student senate, student ambassadors.

Athletics. NJCAA. **Intercollegiate:** Baseball M, basketball, cheerleading, golf, rodeo. **Intramural:** Basketball, bowling, fencing, golf, handball, ice hockey, racquetball, soccer, tennis, volleyball, weight lifting. **Team name:** Pioneers.

Student services. Adult student services, career counseling, student employment services, financial aid counseling, health services, placement for graduates, veterans' counselor. **Transfer:** Pre-admission transcript evaluation for new students. College fairs on campus for students transferring to 4-year colleges.

Contact. Phone: (406) 874-6217 Toll-free number: (800) 541-9281 Fax: (406) 874-6283
Darren Pitcher, Vice President of Student Success, Miles Community College, 2715 Dickinson Street, Miles City, MT 59301

Montana State University: Great Falls College of Technology
Great Falls, Montana
www.msugf.edu   CB code: 4482

- Public 2-year community and technical college
- Commuter campus in small city

General. Founded in 1969. Regionally accredited. **Enrollment:** 1,703 degree-seeking undergraduates; 171 non-degree-seeking students. **Degrees:** 246 associate awarded. **Location:** 200 miles from Billings, 150 miles from Missoula. **Calendar:** Semester, limited summer session. **Full-time faculty:** 43 total; 9% have terminal degrees, 7% minority, 65% women. **Part-time faculty:** 116 total; 9% have terminal degrees, 4% minority, 66% women. **Class size:** 55% < 20, 45% 20-39.

Student profile. Among degree-seeking undergraduates, 34% enrolled in a transfer program, 66% enrolled in a vocational program, 5% already have a bachelor's degree or higher, 338 enrolled as first-time, first-year students, 178 transferred in from other institutions.

Part-time:	43%	Asian American:	1%
Out-of-state:	3%	Hispanic American:	4%
Women:	71%	Native American:	6%
African American:	1%	25 or older:	58%

Transfer out. 60% of students enrolled in the transfer program go on to 4-year colleges. **Colleges most students transferred to 2011:** Montana State University, Montana State University - Northern, Montana State University - Billings, University of Great Falls.

Basis for selection. Open admission, but selective for some programs. Special admissions requirements for dental assistant, dental hygiene, radiologic technology, practical nursing, dental assistant, surgical technology, and physical therapist assistant programs. **Adult students:** COMPASS test used to determine placement in courses. All placement tests must have been taken within the past three years. **Home schooled:** Transcript of courses and grades, letter of recommendation (nonparent) required. Notarized copy of the home school curriculum, 2 letters of recommendation from non-family members, parental approval form if under 18 required.

2011-2012 Annual costs. Tuition/fees: $3,069; $9,321 out-of-state. Per-credit charge: $104 in-state; $364 out-of-state. Books/supplies: $1,200. Personal expenses: $3,238.

2010-2011 Financial aid. Need-based: 182 full-time freshmen applied for aid; 161 were judged to have need; 159 of these received aid. Average need met was 59%. Average scholarship/grant was $4,978; average loan $2,749. 54% of total undergraduate aid awarded as scholarships/grants, 46% as loans/jobs. Need-based aid available for part-time students. Work-study available nights, weekends and for part-time students. **Non-need-based:** Awarded to 17 full-time undergraduates, including 2 freshmen. Scholarships awarded for academics, leadership.

Application procedures. Admission: No deadline. $30 fee. Application must be submitted on paper. Admission notification on a rolling basis. **Financial aid:** Priority date 3/1; no closing date. FAFSA, institutional form required. Applicants notified on a rolling basis starting 4/15.

Academics. Special study options: Distance learning, double major, dual enrollment of high school students, independent study, internships. License preparation in dental hygiene, nursing, paramedic, physical therapy, radiology. **Credit/placement by examination:** AP, CLEP, institutional tests. 45 credit hours maximum toward associate degree. **Support services:** Learning center, remedial instruction, study skills assistance, tutoring.

Majors. Business: Accounting, business admin. **Computer sciences:** Information technology, networking, web page design. **Health services:** Dental hygiene, dietetic technician, EMT paramedic, insurance specialist, licensed practical nurse, medical assistant, medical records admin, medical transcription, physical therapy assistant, radiologic technology/medical imaging, respiratory therapy assistant, respiratory therapy technology, surgical technology. **Protective services:** Firefighting. **Visual/performing arts:** Graphic design, interior design.

Most popular majors. Business/marketing 14%, health sciences 42%, liberal arts 28%.

Computing on campus. 465 workstations in library, computer center. Commuter students can connect to campus network. Online course registration, online library, helpline, wireless network available.

Student life. Freshman orientation: Available. Preregistration for classes offered. Held prior to the fall and spring semesters. Students attend mandatory sessions selected by the college and then have optional sections to choose from. Students able to choose the days and times for their sessions; sessions will be offered in the week prior to the beginning of the semester. **Activities:** Student government, Phi Theta Kappa, Health Occupations Students of America, interior design club, LPN club, Student Association of Dental Hygiene, Native American student group, Christian Bible study group, veterans center, Anime club, Lambda COT.

Student services. Career counseling, services for economically disadvantaged, student employment services, financial aid counseling, placement for graduates, veterans' counselor. **Physically disabled:** Services for visually, speech, hearing impaired. **Transfer:** Pre-admission transcript evaluation for new students. Transfer adviser, college fairs on campus for students transferring to 4-year colleges.

Contact. E-mail: admissions@msugf.edu
Phone: (406) 771-4420 Toll-free number: (800) 446-2698
Fax: (406) 771-4329
Dana Freshly, Director of Admissions, Montana State University: Great Falls College of Technology, 2100 16th Avenue South, Great Falls, MT 59405

Stone Child College
Box Elder, Montana
www.stonechild.edu   **CB code: 7044**

- Public 2-year community and junior college
- Commuter campus in rural community

General. Founded in 1984. Regionally accredited. Tribally-controlled college located on the Rocky Boys Indian Reservation. **Enrollment:** 177 degree-seeking undergraduates. **Degrees:** 20 associate awarded. **Location:** 26 miles from Havre, 100 miles from Great Falls. **Calendar:** Semester, limited summer session. **Full-time faculty:** 10 total; 100% have terminal degrees, 10% minority, 40% women. **Part-time faculty:** 25 total. **Class size:** 80% < 20, 20% 20-39.

Student profile.

Out-of-state: 2%   25 or older: 48%

Transfer out. Colleges most students transferred to 2011: Montana State University-Northern, Montana State University-Billings, University of Montana, University of Great Falls.

Basis for selection. Open admission. **Adult students:** COMPASS testing required of all incoming students.

High school preparation. College-preparatory program recommended. 22 units recommended. Recommended units include English 4, mathematics 3, social studies 3, history 4, science 3, foreign language 1 and academic electives 4.

2011-2012 Annual costs. Tuition/fees: $2,450; $2,450 out-of-state. Per-credit charge: $60. Books/supplies: $800. Personal expenses: $1,520.

Financial aid. Need-based: Need-based aid available for part-time students. Work-study available nights, weekends and for part-time students. **Non-need-based:** Scholarships awarded for academics. **Additional information:** Scholarships available to high school and GED graduates who apply for college admission during the first term after graduation.

Application procedures. Admission: No deadline. No application fee. Admission notification on a rolling basis. **Financial aid:** Priority date 3/1; no closing date. FAFSA, institutional form required. Applicants notified on a rolling basis.

Academics. Special study options: Double major, dual enrollment of high school students, independent study, liberal arts/career combination. **Credit/placement by examination:** AP, CLEP, institutional tests. 12 credit hours maximum toward associate degree. **Support services:** Learning center, remedial instruction, tutoring.

Majors. Area/ethnic studies: Native American. **Business:** General, management information systems, office/clerical. **Computer sciences:** Information systems. **Conservation:** General. **Education:** Elementary. **Health services:** Substance abuse counseling. **Liberal arts:** Arts/sciences. **Math:** General.

Most popular majors. Business/marketing 30%, education 30%, health sciences 17%, liberal arts 9%.

Computing on campus. 35 workstations in library, computer center, student center.

Student life. Freshman orientation: Mandatory. Preregistration for classes offered. Half-day program held before regular registration, introduces new students to programs and services. **Activities:** Student government.

Athletics. Intercollegiate: Basketball. **Intramural:** Basketball. **Team name:** Bear Paws.

Student services. Career counseling, financial aid counseling, on-campus daycare, personal counseling. **Transfer:** Transfer adviser, college fairs on campus for students transferring to 4-year colleges.

Contact. Phone: (406) 395-4313 ext. 222 Fax: (406) 395-4836
Gaile Torres, Registrar, Stone Child College, 8294 Upper Box Elder Road, Box Elder, MT 59521

University of Montana: Helena College of Technology
Helena, Montana
www.umhelena.edu   **CB code: 2022**

- Public 2-year community and technical college
- Commuter campus in large town

General. Founded in 1939. Regionally accredited. **Enrollment:** 1,306 degree-seeking undergraduates. **Degrees:** 173 associate awarded. **Location:** 90 miles from Great Falls. **Calendar:** Semester, limited summer session. **Full-time faculty:** 40 total. **Part-time faculty:** 93 total.

Student profile. Among degree-seeking undergraduates, 37% enrolled in a transfer program, 41% enrolled in a vocational program, 1% already have a bachelor's degree or higher, 117 transferred in from other institutions.

Basis for selection. Open admission. Graduates of non-accredited high schools may be required to provide GED scores or meet Ability to Benefit requirements. **Home schooled:** May be required to provide GED scores or meet Ability to Benefit Requirements.

High school preparation. Recommended units include English 3 and mathematics 3.

2011-2012 Annual costs. Tuition/fees: $3,061; $8,357 out-of-state. Per-credit charge: $79 in-state; $255 out-of-state. Books/supplies: $1,200.

2011-2012 Financial aid. Need-based: 36% of total undergraduate aid awarded as scholarships/grants, 64% as loans/jobs. Need-based aid available for part-time students. Work-study available nights, weekends and for part-time students.

Application procedures. Admission: Closing date 8/12 (receipt date). $30 fee. Application must be submitted on paper. Admission notification on a rolling basis. **Financial aid:** Priority date 3/1; no closing date. FAFSA, institutional form required. Applicants notified on a rolling basis starting 5/1.

Academics. Special study options: Dual enrollment of high school students, independent study, internships. Bachelor's degree programs available on campus. License preparation in aviation, nursing. **Credit/placement by examination:** AP, CLEP. **Support services:** Learning center, pre-admission summer program, remedial instruction, study skills assistance, tutoring, writing center.

Majors. Business: Accounting, administrative services, office technology. **Computer sciences:** Programming. **Conservation:** Water/wetlands/marine. **Health services:** Medical secretary, nursing (RN). **Liberal arts:** Arts/sciences. **Protective services:** Firefighting.

Computing on campus. 160 workstations in library, computer center. Commuter students can connect to campus network. Online course registration, online library, helpline, wireless network available.

Student life. Freshman orientation: Available. Preregistration for classes offered. **Activities:** Student government, student newspaper, Circle K, Associated Students of UM-Helena, College Christian Fellowship.

Student services. Adult student services, career counseling, student employment services, financial aid counseling, personal counseling, placement for graduates, veterans' counselor. **Physically disabled:** Services for visually, speech, hearing impaired. **Transfer:** Transfer adviser, college fairs on campus for students transferring to 4-year colleges.

Contact. E-mail: admissions@umhelena.edu
Phone: (406) 444-6800 Toll-free number: (800) 241-4882
Fax: (406) 444-6892
Michael Brown, Assistant Dean of Student Services, University of Montana: Helena College of Technology, 1115 North Roberts Street, Helena, MT 59601-3098

Two-Year Colleges

Nebraska

Central Community College
Grand Island, Nebraska
www.cccneb.edu

- Public 2-year community and technical college
- Commuter campus in large town

General. Founded in 1966. Regionally accredited. Multi-campus institution with campuses in Columbus, Grand Island, and Hastings. Learning Centers located in Holdrege, Kearney, and Lexington. Multiple starting dates for most programs and courses. **Enrollment:** 4,919 degree-seeking undergraduates; 2,699 non-degree-seeking students. **Degrees:** 576 associate awarded. **Location:** 100 miles from Lincoln. **Calendar:** Semester, extensive summer session. **Full-time faculty:** 170 total; 4% have terminal degrees, 2% minority, 53% women. **Part-time faculty:** 126 total; 4% have terminal degrees, 2% minority, 61% women.

Student profile. Among degree-seeking undergraduates, 28% enrolled in a transfer program, 72% enrolled in a vocational program, 1,023 enrolled as first-time, first-year students.

Part-time:	47%	Asian American:	1%
Out-of-state:	1%	Hispanic American:	9%
Women:	64%	25 or older:	35%
African American:	2%	Live on campus:	20%

Transfer out. Colleges most students transferred to 2011: University of Nebraska-Kearney, University of Nebraska-Lincoln, University of Nebraska-Omaha, Bellevue University.

Basis for selection. Open admission, but selective for some programs and for out-of-state students. Special admission requirements for: dental assisting, dental hygiene, health information management services, medical assisting, medical laboratory technician, occupational therapy assistant, practical nursing, associate degree nursing, truck driving. Interview required for some programs.

2011-2012 Annual costs. Tuition/fees: $2,580; $3,750 out-of-state. Per-credit charge: $78 in-state; $117 out-of-state. Room/board: $6,194. Books/supplies: $1,200. Personal expenses: $1,380.

Financial aid. Need-based: Need-based aid available for part-time students. Work-study available nights, weekends and for part-time students. **Non-need-based:** Scholarships awarded for academics, art, athletics, job skills, leadership, music/drama. **Additional information:** All students are eligible to apply for a Pell Grant. Students enrolled for at least six semester hours (half-time) are eligible to apply for grants, loans, work study, and scholarships. To be considered for full-time benefits, students must be enrolled for at least 12 credit hours during the semester.

Application procedures. Admission: No deadline. No application fee. Admission notification on a rolling basis. Application deadlines for the following programs only: February 1 for Dental Hygiene and April 15th for Occupational Therapy Assistant. **Financial aid:** Priority date 3/1; no closing date. FAFSA, institutional form required. Applicants notified on a rolling basis starting 2/1; must reply within 2 week(s) of notification.

Academics. Special study options: Accelerated study, cooperative education, distance learning, double major, dual enrollment of high school students, ESL, honors, independent study, internships, weekend college. License preparation in dental hygiene, nursing, occupational therapy, real estate. **Credit/placement by examination:** AP, CLEP, institutional tests. 48 credit hours maximum toward associate degree. **Support services:** GED preparation and test center, learning center, reduced course load, remedial instruction, study skills assistance, tutoring.

Majors. Business: Administrative services, business admin, vehicle parts marketing. **Communications:** Digital media. **Computer sciences:** General. **General:** Business, horticulture. **Health services:** Clinical lab technology, dental assistant, dental hygiene, licensed practical nurse, medical assistant, medical records technology, nursing (RN). **Liberal arts:** Arts/sciences. **Protective services:** Criminal justice. **Visual/performing arts:** Commercial/advertising art. **Work/family studies:** General, child care management.

Most popular majors. Business/marketing 14%, health sciences 27%, liberal arts 22%, trade and industry 17%.

Computing on campus. Dormitories linked to campus network. Commuter students can connect to campus network. Online course registration, online library, helpline available.

Student life. Freshman orientation: Available. Preregistration for classes offered. **Housing:** Coed dorms, single-sex dorms, apartments, wellness housing available. $150 partly refundable deposit. **Activities:** Jazz band, choral groups, dance, drama, music ensembles, musical theater, radio station, student government, student newspaper, Multicultural Student Association, FOCUS (Friendships of Culturally Unique Students), Campus Crusade for Christ.

Athletics. NJCAA. **Intercollegiate:** Basketball M, golf M, softball W, volleyball W. **Intramural:** Basketball, bowling, table tennis, volleyball, weight lifting. **Team name:** Raiders.

Student services. Adult student services, career counseling, services for economically disadvantaged, student employment services, financial aid counseling, health services, minority student services, on-campus daycare, personal counseling, placement for graduates, veterans' counselor, women's services. **Physically disabled:** Services for visually, speech, hearing impaired. **Transfer:** Pre-admission transcript evaluation for new students. Transfer adviser, college fairs on campus for students transferring to 4-year colleges.

Contact. E-mail: admissions@cccneb.edu
Phone: (308) 398-7406 Toll-free number: (877) 222-0780
Fax: (308) 398-7398
Michelle Lubken, Admissions Director, Central Community College, 3134 West Highway 34, Grand Island, NE 68802-4903

Kaplan University: Lincoln
Lincoln, Nebraska
www.kucampus.edu
CB code: 3385

- For-profit 2-year branch campus college
- Commuter campus in small city

General. Founded in 1884. **Enrollment:** 381 degree-seeking undergraduates. **Degrees:** 31 bachelor's, 169 associate awarded. **Calendar:** Differs by program, extensive summer session. **Full-time faculty:** 10 total. **Part-time faculty:** 49 total. **Class size:** 83% < 20, 17% 20-39.

Student profile.

Out-of-state:	2%	25 or older:	54%

Transfer out. Colleges most students transferred to 2011: Southeast Community College.

Basis for selection. Open admission, but selective for some programs. CPAT required of all applicants. Students must pass entrance exam.

2011-2012 Annual costs. Tuition/fees: $15,352. Per-credit charge: $405. Cost of books and supplies is included in tuition. Personal expenses: $1,968.

Financial aid. All financial aid based on need. Need-based aid available for part-time students. Work-study available nights, weekends and for part-time students.

Application procedures. Admission: No deadline. $20 fee. Admission notification on a rolling basis. **Financial aid:** No deadline. FAFSA, institutional form required. Applicants notified on a rolling basis starting 2/1.

Academics. Special study options: Internships. Bachelor's degree programs available on campus. License preparation in nursing. **Credit/placement by examination:** AP, CLEP. **Support services:** Learning center, study skills assistance, tutoring.

Majors. Business: Accounting, administrative services, business admin. **Computer sciences:** Information technology. **Health services:** Medical assistant. **Protective services:** Criminal justice.

Most popular majors. Business/marketing 20%, computer/information sciences 11%, health sciences 31%, legal studies 9%, security/protective services 23%.

Computing on campus. 70 workstations in library, computer center.

Student life. Freshman orientation: Mandatory, $20 fee. Preregistration for classes offered. Orientation held on first day of classes for all new students. **Housing:** $150 deposit. **Activities:** Tour and travel club, medical club, Association of Information Technology Professionals, business club, legal assisting club.

Student services. Career counseling, student employment services, financial aid counseling, placement for graduates, veterans' counselor. **Physically**

disabled: Services for visually, hearing impaired. **Transfer:** Pre-admission transcript evaluation for new students.

Contact. E-mail: kfrette@kaplan.edu
Phone: (402) 474-5315 Toll-free number: (800) 742-7738
Fax: (402) 474-0896
Michael Klacik, Director of Admissions, Kaplan University: Lincoln, 1821 K Street, Lincoln, NE 68508

Kaplan University: Omaha
Omaha, Nebraska
www.omaha.kaplanuniversity.edu
CB code: 3326

▸ For-profit 2-year career college
▸ Commuter campus in large city
▸ Interview required

General. **Enrollment:** 595 degree-seeking undergraduates. **Degrees:** 48 bachelor's, 241 associate awarded; master's offered. **Calendar:** Quarter, extensive summer session. **Full-time faculty:** 15 total. **Part-time faculty:** 45 total. **Class size:** 54% < 20, 46% 20-39. **Special facilities:** Firearms training simulator, dental assisting lab with 4 operatories, nursing lab.

Basis for selection. Open admission, but selective for some programs. **Home schooled:** Transcript of courses and grades, state high school equivalency certificate required.

High school preparation. College-preparatory program required.

2011-2012 Annual costs. Tuition/fees: $15,352. Per-credit charge: $405.

Financial aid. All financial aid based on need. Need-based aid available for part-time students. Work-study available nights, weekends and for part-time students.

Application procedures. **Admission:** No deadline. $20 fee. Application must be submitted on paper. Admission notification on a rolling basis. **Financial aid:** No deadline. FAFSA, institutional form required. Applicants notified on a rolling basis.

Academics. **Special study options:** Accelerated study, distance learning, internships, liberal arts/career combination. Bachelor's degree programs available on campus. License preparation in nursing. **Credit/placement by examination:** AP, CLEP, institutional tests. 32 credit hours maximum toward associate degree. **Support services:** Learning center, reduced course load, remedial instruction, study skills assistance, tutoring, writing center.

Majors. **Business:** Accounting, business admin. **Computer sciences:** Data processing. **Health services:** Medical assistant. **Protective services:** Criminal justice.

Most popular majors. Security/protective services 14%.

Computing on campus. 120 workstations in library, computer center, student center. Commuter students can connect to campus network. Online course registration, online library, helpline, wireless network available.

Student life. **Freshman orientation:** Mandatory. Preregistration for classes offered. **Activities:** Student government, student newspaper.

Student services. Adult student services, career counseling, services for economically disadvantaged, student employment services, financial aid counseling, placement for graduates, veterans' counselor. **Physically disabled:** Services for visually, speech, hearing impaired. **Transfer:** Pre-admission transcript evaluation for new students.

Contact. E-mail: zlorenzen@kaplan.edu
Phone: (402) 431-6100 Toll-free number: (800) 642-1456
Fax: (402) 573-6482
Zac Lorenzen, Director of Admissions, Kaplan University: Omaha, 5425 North 103rd Street, Omaha, NE 68134

Little Priest Tribal College
Winnebago, Nebraska
www.littlepriest.edu
CB code: 3616

▸ Private 2-year community college
▸ Commuter campus in rural community

General. Regionally accredited. **Enrollment:** 171 undergraduates. **Degrees:** 16 associate awarded. **Location:** 30 miles from Sioux City, Iowa.

Calendar: Semester, limited summer session. **Full-time faculty:** 5 total. **Class size:** 82% < 20, 18% 20-39.

Transfer out. **Colleges most students transferred to 2011:** Wayne State College, Haskell Indian Nations University.

Basis for selection. Open admission.

High school preparation. 11 units recommended. Recommended units include English 3, mathematics 3, social studies 3 and science 2.

2011-2012 Annual costs. Tuition/fees: $3,750. Per-credit charge: $100. Books/supplies: $700.

Financial aid. **Need-based:** Need-based aid available for part-time students. Work-study available nights, weekends and for part-time students.

Application procedures. **Admission:** No deadline. $20 fee. **Financial aid:** No deadline. FAFSA, institutional form required.

Academics. **Special study options:** Dual enrollment of high school students, independent study, liberal arts/career combination. **Credit/placement by examination:** AP, CLEP. **Support services:** GED preparation and test center, learning center, reduced course load, remedial instruction, study skills assistance, tutoring.

Majors. **Area/ethnic studies:** Native American. **Business:** General. **Computer sciences:** General. **Conservation:** General. **Education:** General. **English:** English lit. **Health services:** Substance abuse counseling. **Liberal arts:** Arts/sciences. **Math:** General.

Most popular majors. Area/ethnic studies 20%, business/marketing 20%, health sciences 20%, liberal arts 40%.

Computing on campus. 20 workstations in library, computer center, student center.

Student life. **Freshman orientation:** Available. Preregistration for classes offered. **Activities:** Student government, student newspaper.

Student services. Adult student services, financial aid counseling, personal counseling. **Transfer:** Pre-admission transcript evaluation for new students. College fairs on campus for students transferring to 4-year colleges.

Contact. Phone: (402) 878-2380 ext. 160 Fax: (402) 878-2355
Darla LaPointe, Dean of Admissions, Little Priest Tribal College, PO Box 270, Winnebago, NE 68071

Metropolitan Community College
Omaha, Nebraska
www.mccneb.edu
CB code: 5755

▸ Public 2-year community and technical college
▸ Commuter campus in large city

General. Founded in 1974. Regionally accredited. Additional locations: Fort Omaha, Elkhorn Valley, South Omaha, Applied Technology Center, Fremont Area Center, Sarpy Center in La Vista. **Enrollment:** 15,161 degree-seeking undergraduates. **Degrees:** 1,144 associate awarded. **Location:** 50 miles from Lincoln. **Calendar:** Quarter, extensive summer session. **Full-time faculty:** 248 total. **Part-time faculty:** 869 total. **Class size:** 63% < 20, 37% 20-39, less than 1% 40-49, less than 1% 50-99. **Special facilities:** CAD/CAM and electronic graphics facilities.

Student profile.

Out-of-state:	3%	Live on campus:	1%
25 or older:	46%		

Transfer out. **Colleges most students transferred to 2011:** University of Nebraska-Omaha, Bellevue University.

Basis for selection. Open admission, but selective for some programs. Admission to nursing and allied health programs based on test scores and references. Assessment testing and standardized RN entrance examination required for nursing associate degree programs. Human services programs require a "C" and approval from Human Services Faculty Review Committee. Certain programs may require preparatory work before attending classes. Interview required for nursing and allied health programs.

High school preparation. High school diploma or GED required of nursing and allied health applicants.

2011-2012 Annual costs. Tuition/fees: $2,385; $3,443 out-of-state. Per-credit charge: $48 in-state; $72 out-of-state. Discounted rates available for

persons 62 years of age or older and other discounted rates available (see Catalog). Room/board: $3,555. Books/supplies: $1,800. Personal expenses: $1,404.

Financial aid. Need-based: Need-based aid available for part-time students. Work-study available nights, weekends and for part-time students. **Non-need-based:** Scholarships awarded for academics.

Application procedures. Admission: No deadline. No application fee. Admission notification on a rolling basis. **Financial aid:** Priority date 3/15; no closing date. FAFSA, institutional form required. Applicants notified on a rolling basis starting 4/15.

Academics. Individualized, self-paced instruction. Degree through online available. **Special study options:** Cooperative education, distance learning, double major, dual enrollment of high school students, ESL, honors, independent study, internships, weekend college. License preparation in nursing. **Credit/placement by examination:** AP, CLEP, institutional tests. 81 credit hours maximum toward associate degree. **Support services:** GED preparation and test center, learning center, remedial instruction, tutoring, writing center.

Majors. Architecture: Interior. **Business:** General, accounting, administrative services, business admin, management information systems. **Communications technology:** Graphic/printing. **Computer sciences:** General, networking. **Foreign languages:** Sign language interpretation. **General:** Horticulture, nursery operations. **Health services:** Nursing (RN), respiratory therapy technology. **Human services:** Social work. **Liberal arts:** Arts/sciences. **Protective services:** Fire services admin, police science. **Visual/performing arts:** Commercial photography, commercial/advertising art, studio arts, theater arts management. **Work/family studies:** Child care management, institutional food production.

Most popular majors. Business/marketing 16%, health sciences 15%, liberal arts 29%, security/protective services 6%, trade and industry 9%, visual/performing arts 7%.

Computing on campus. 1,550 workstations in library, computer center. Dormitories wired for high-speed internet access. Commuter students can connect to campus network. Online course registration, online library, helpline available.

Student life. Freshman orientation: Available. Preregistration for classes offered. **Housing:** Coed dorms, single-sex dorms, wellness housing available. $200 fully refundable deposit. **Activities:** Phi Theta Kappa scholastic honor society.

Student services. Adult student services, career counseling, services for economically disadvantaged, student employment services, financial aid counseling, minority student services, personal counseling, placement for graduates, veterans' counselor, women's services. **Physically disabled:** Services for visually, speech, hearing impaired. **Transfer:** Transfer adviser for students transferring to 4-year colleges.

Contact. E-mail: info@mccneb.edu
Phone: (402) 457-2422 Toll-free number: (800) 228-9553
Fax: (402) 457-2616
Maria Vazquez, Associate Vice President for Student Affairs,
Metropolitan Community College, Box 3777, Omaha, NE 68103-0777

Mid-Plains Community College Area
North Platte, Nebraska
www.mpcc.edu   **CB code: 6497**

- Public 2-year community and technical college
- Commuter campus in large town

General. Founded in 1964. Regionally accredited. Two major sites, North Platte and McCook; extended campus sites in Broken Bow, Imperial, Ogallala, and Valentine. **Enrollment:** 1,310 degree-seeking undergraduates; 1,313 non-degree-seeking students. **Degrees:** 296 associate awarded. **Location:** 230 miles from Lincoln, 270 miles from Denver. **Calendar:** Semester, limited summer session. **Full-time faculty:** 68 total; 6% have terminal degrees, 50% women. **Part-time faculty:** 241 total. **Class size:** 39% < 20, 61% 20-39. **Partnerships:** Formal partnership with Union Pacific Railroad for apprenticeships, technical training, continuing education.

Student profile. Among degree-seeking undergraduates, 59% enrolled in a transfer program, 41% enrolled in a vocational program, 5% already have a bachelor's degree or higher, 444 enrolled as first-time, first-year students.

Part-time:	32%	Native American:	1%
Out-of-state:	5%	International:	1%
Women:	60%	25 or older:	65%
African American:	5%	Live on campus:	5%
Hispanic American:	7%		

Transfer out. Colleges most students transferred to 2011: University of Nebraska at Lincoln, University of Nebraska at Kearney, Chadron State College.

Basis for selection. Open admission, but selective for some programs. Psychological Corporation Pre-Nursing Examination required of applicants to nursing program. Minimum ACT score of 17 required for licensed practical nursing and 21 for associate degree nursing. Minimum ASSET score of 40 in all areas required for medical laboratory technology program. **Adult students:** SAT/ACT scores not required. **Home schooled:** State high school equivalency certificate required. **Learning Disabled:** Student should have physician's documentation of learning disability.

High school preparation. College-preparatory program recommended. Recommended units include English 4, mathematics 4, social studies 1, history 1, science 2, foreign language 1, computer science 1 and visual/performing arts 1.

2011-2012 Annual costs. Tuition/fees: $2,670; $3,330 out-of-state. Per-credit charge: $74 in-state; $96 out-of-state. Room/board: $5,300. Books/supplies: $1,000. Personal expenses: $750.

Financial aid. Need-based: Need-based aid available for part-time students. Work-study available nights, weekends and for part-time students. **Non-need-based:** Scholarships awarded for academics, art, athletics, music/drama.

Application procedures. Admission: No deadline. No application fee. Admission notification on a rolling basis. **Financial aid:** Priority date 5/1; no closing date. FAFSA, institutional form required. Applicants notified on a rolling basis starting 5/1; must reply within 3 week(s) of notification.

Academics. Special study options: Cooperative education, distance learning, dual enrollment of high school students, exchange student, honors, independent study, internships, liberal arts/career combination. Bachelor's degree programs available on campus. License preparation in dental hygiene, nursing, paramedic, real estate. **Credit/placement by examination:** AP, CLEP. 20 credit hours maximum toward associate degree. **Support services:** GED preparation and test center, remedial instruction, study skills assistance, tutoring.

Majors. Business: Business admin, office management. **Computer sciences:** Information technology. **Health services:** Clinical lab technology, dental assistant, nursing (RN). **Liberal arts:** Arts/sciences, library assistant. **Protective services:** Firefighting, police science. **Visual/performing arts:** Graphic design. **Work/family studies:** Child care management.

Computing on campus. 100 workstations in dormitories, library, computer center, student center. Dormitories wired for high-speed internet access. Commuter students can connect to campus network. Online library, wireless network available.

Student life. Freshman orientation: Available. Preregistration for classes offered. **Policies:** Drugs, alcohol, tobacco strictly prohibited. **Housing:** Coed dorms, single-sex dorms, special housing for disabled, apartments available. $200 deposit, deadline 8/15. **Activities:** Bands, choral groups, drama, music ensembles, student government, student newspaper.

Athletics. NJCAA. **Intercollegiate:** Baseball M, basketball, golf M, softball W, volleyball W. **Intramural:** Basketball, volleyball. **Team name:** McCook Indians & North Platte Knights.

Student services. Career counseling, services for economically disadvantaged, student employment services, financial aid counseling, on-campus daycare, placement for graduates. **Transfer:** Transfer adviser for students transferring to 4-year colleges.

Contact. E-mail: rippenk@mpcc.edu
Phone: (308) 535-3609 Toll-free number: (800) 658-4308 ext. 3609
Fax: (308) 534-5767
Kelly Rippen, Area Admissions Coordinator, Mid-Plains Community College Area, 1101 Halligan Drive, North Platte, NE 69101

Myotherapy Institute
Lincoln, Nebraska
www.myotherapy.edu

- For-profit 2-year health science and community college
- Small city

General. Accredited by ACCSCT. **Calendar:** Differs by program.

Annual costs/financial aid. Diploma program $10,800. Associate program $12,300.

Contact. Phone: (402) 421-7410
Director, 6020 South 58th Street, Lincoln, NE 68516

Nebraska College of Technical Agriculture
Curtis, Nebraska
www.ncta.unl.edu

CB code: 1305

- Public 2-year agricultural college
- Residential campus in rural community

General. Founded in 1965. Regionally accredited. **Enrollment:** 251 degree-seeking undergraduates; 82 non-degree-seeking students. **Degrees:** 57 associate awarded. **Location:** 40 miles from North Platte, 40 miles from McCook. **Calendar:** Semester, extensive summer session. **Full-time faculty:** 13 total; 31% have terminal degrees, 46% women. **Part-time faculty:** 10 total; 10% have terminal degrees, 40% women. **Special facilities:** Farm, community golf course, land lab, cattle working facilities, indoor arena, horticulture greenhouse, vet tech surgery and lab facilities.

Student profile. Among degree-seeking undergraduates, 7% enrolled in a transfer program, 93% enrolled in a vocational program, 85 enrolled as first-time, first-year students, 18 transferred in from other institutions.

Part-time:	3%	25 or older:	5%
Out-of-state:	22%	Live on campus:	25%
Women:	54%		

Transfer out. 7% of students enrolled in the transfer program go on to 4-year colleges. **Colleges most students transferred to 2011:** University of Nebraska-Lincoln, Oklahoma Panhandle State University.

Basis for selection. Open admission. **Home schooled:** Transcript of courses and grades, state high school equivalency certificate required.

High school preparation. College-preparatory program recommended. 14 units recommended. Recommended units include English 4, mathematics 3, social studies 3, science 3 (laboratory 1).

2011-2012 Annual costs. Tuition/fees: $4,144; $7,474 out-of-state. Per-credit charge: $112 in-state; $223 out-of-state. Room/board: $6,260.

2010-2011 Financial aid. All financial aid based on need. 45% of total undergraduate aid awarded as scholarships/grants, 55% as loans/jobs. Need-based aid available for part-time students. Work-study available nights, weekends and for part-time students.

Application procedures. Admission: Priority date 3/1; no deadline. $25 fee. Application must be submitted on paper. Admission notification on a rolling basis. **Financial aid:** Priority date 4/1; no closing date. FAFSA required. Applicants notified on a rolling basis starting 5/1; must reply within 2 week(s) of notification.

Academics. Special study options: Cooperative education, distance learning, double major, dual enrollment of high school students, ESL, internships. **Credit/placement by examination:** AP, CLEP, institutional tests. **Support services:** Reduced course load, remedial instruction, study skills assistance, tutoring, writing center.

Majors. Conservation: Management/policy. **General:** Agribusiness operations, animal health, business, equestrian studies, greenhouse operations, horticultural science, horticulture, landscaping, nursery operations, ornamental horticulture, turf management. **Health services:** Veterinary technology/assistant.

Computing on campus. 99 workstations in dormitories, library, computer center, student center. Dormitories wired for high-speed internet access and linked to campus network. Online course registration, online library, repair service, wireless network available.

Student life. Freshman orientation: Mandatory. Preregistration for classes offered. 2-day program. **Housing:** Guaranteed on-campus for freshmen. Coed dorms, single-sex dorms, wellness housing available. $250 partly refundable deposit, deadline 7/1. **Activities:** Student government, student newspaper.

Athletics. USCAA. **Intercollegiate:** Basketball, equestrian, golf M, rodeo, volleyball W. **Intramural:** Basketball, volleyball W. **Team name:** Aggies.

Student services. Alcohol/substance abuse counseling, career counseling, student employment services, financial aid counseling, health services, personal counseling, placement for graduates, veterans' counselor. **Transfer:** Pre-admission transcript evaluation for new students. Transfer adviser, college fairs on campus for students transferring to 4-year colleges.

Contact. E-mail: snichols3@unl.edu
Phone: (308) 367-4124 ext. 281 Toll-free number: (800) 328-7847
Fax: (308) 367-5203
Scott Mickelsen, Admissions Counselor, Nebraska College of Technical Agriculture, 404 East 7th Street, Curtis, NE 69025-0069

Nebraska Indian Community College
Macy, Nebraska
www.thenicc.edu

CB code: 1431

- Public 2-year Tribal college
- Commuter campus in rural community

General. Founded in 1979. Regionally accredited. Bachelor's degrees offered on campus through Bellevue University and UNK. **Enrollment:** 149 degree-seeking undergraduates. **Degrees:** 10 associate awarded. **Location:** 70 miles from Omaha, 30 miles from Sioux City, Iowa. **Calendar:** Semester, limited summer session. **Full-time faculty:** 10 total. **Part-time faculty:** 11 total. **Class size:** 100% < 20.

Student profile.

Out-of-state:	23%	25 or older:	69%

Basis for selection. Open admission.

High school preparation. College-preparatory program required. Strong background in English, mathematics, and science recommended.

2011-2012 Annual costs. Per-credit charge: $170. Tuition is a flat rate of $170 per credit hour, which includes books, tuition, and fees. Books/supplies: $900. Personal expenses: $700.

Financial aid. All financial aid based on need. Need-based aid available for part-time students. Work-study available nights, weekends and for part-time students.

Application procedures. Admission: No deadline. $50 fee, may be waived for applicants with need. Admission notification on a rolling basis. **Financial aid:** Closing date 6/30. FAFSA, institutional form required. Applicants notified on a rolling basis starting 8/30; must reply within 2 week(s) of notification.

Academics. Special study options: Accelerated study, double major, dual enrollment of high school students, independent study, internships. Bachelor's degree programs available on campus. **Credit/placement by examination:** AP, CLEP, institutional tests. 15 credit hours maximum toward associate degree. **Support services:** Remedial instruction, study skills assistance, tutoring.

Majors. Area/ethnic studies: Native American. **Business:** Business admin. **Computer sciences:** General, data entry. **Conservation:** General. **Education:** Early childhood. **Human services:** Social work. **Liberal arts:** Arts/sciences. **Protective services:** Police science.

Most popular majors. Business/marketing 20%, history 20%, liberal arts 60%.

Computing on campus. 40 workstations in library, computer center.

Student life. Freshman orientation: Available. Preregistration for classes offered. **Activities:** Student government, student newspaper.

Student services. Adult student services, career counseling, financial aid counseling. **Transfer:** Pre-admission transcript evaluation for new students. Transfer adviser, college fairs on campus for students transferring to 4-year colleges.

Contact. E-mail: sscahayes@thenicc.edu
Phone: (402) 494-2311 ext. 2569 Fax: (402) 837-4183
Annette Loche, Registrar/Financial Aid Director, Nebraska Indian Community College, PO Box 428, Macy, NE 68039

Northeast Community College
Norfolk, Nebraska
www.northeast.edu

CB code: 6473

- Public 2-year community college
- Residential campus in large town

General. Founded in 1973. Regionally accredited. **Enrollment:** 2,806 degree-seeking undergraduates; 2,355 non-degree-seeking students. **Degrees:**

709 associate awarded. **Location:** 110 miles from Omaha. **Calendar:** Semester, limited summer session. **Full-time faculty:** 110 total. **Part-time faculty:** 290 total. **Class size:** 78% < 20, 22% 20-39, less than 1% 40-49, less than 1% >100. **Special facilities:** College farm.

Student profile. Among degree-seeking undergraduates, 40% enrolled in a transfer program, 60% enrolled in a vocational program, 894 enrolled as first-time, first-year students.

Part-time:	24%	25 or older:	40%
Out-of-state:	5%	Live on campus:	20%
Women:	54%		

Transfer out. Colleges most students transferred to 2011: Wayne State College, University of Nebraska-Lincoln, University of Nebraska-Omaha, University of Nebraska-Kearney, University of South Dakota.

Basis for selection. Open admission, but selective for some programs. Special requirements for nursing programs, physical therapy assistant program, and veterinary technician program. ACT or ASSET scores required for placement for students enrolling in 6 or more credit hours.

2011-2012 Annual costs. Tuition/fees: $2,655; $3,203 out-of-state. Per-credit charge: $73 in-state; $91 out-of-state. Room/board: $5,936. Books/supplies: $1,187. Personal expenses: $900.

Financial aid. Need-based: Need-based aid available for part-time students. Work-study available nights, weekends and for part-time students. **Non-need-based:** Scholarships awarded for academics, athletics, music/drama.

Application procedures. Admission: No deadline. No application fee. Admission notification on a rolling basis. **Financial aid:** No deadline. FAFSA, institutional form required. Applicants notified on a rolling basis; must reply within 2 week(s) of notification.

Academics. Off-campus credit classes available. Lifelong Learning Center offers students opportunity to earn advanced degrees on NECC campus. **Special study options:** Accelerated study, cooperative education, cross-registration, distance learning, dual enrollment of high school students, ESL, independent study, internships, liberal arts/career combination. License preparation in nursing, paramedic, physical therapy, real estate. **Credit/placement by examination:** AP, CLEP, institutional tests. **Support services:** GED preparation and test center, learning center, reduced course load, remedial instruction, study skills assistance, tutoring, writing center.

Majors. Biology: General. **Business:** Accounting, administrative services, banking/financial services, business admin, entrepreneurial studies, international, marketing, merchandising, office/clerical, real estate. **Communications:** Journalism. **Communications technology:** Radio/TV, recording arts. **Computer sciences:** General, computer science, programming, support specialist. **Education:** Early childhood, elementary, music, secondary. **Engineering:** General. **English:** English lit, rhetoric/composition. **General:** Agribusiness operations, agronomy, animal sciences, business, equipment technology, farm/ranch, horticultural science, horticulture, livestock, mechanization, production. **Health services:** Dietetics, EMT paramedic, medical radiologic technology/radiation therapy, medical records technology, medical secretary, nursing (RN), physical therapy assistant, predental, premedicine, prenursing, prepharmacy, preveterinary, surgical technology, veterinary technology/assistant. **Liberal arts:** Arts/sciences, library assistant. **Math:** General. **Parks/recreation:** Health/fitness. **Physical sciences:** Chemistry, physics. **Protective services:** Corrections. **Psychology:** General. **Social sciences:** General. **Visual/performing arts:** Art, dramatic, music, music management, music performance.

Most popular majors. Agriculture 10%, business/marketing 12%, education 7%, engineering/engineering technologies 8%, health sciences 19%, liberal arts 8%, trade and industry 21%.

Computing on campus. 300 workstations in dormitories, library, computer center, student center. Dormitories linked to campus network. Online course registration, online library, helpline, wireless network available.

Student life. Freshman orientation: Mandatory. Preregistration for classes offered. **Housing:** Coed dorms, special housing for disabled, apartments, wellness housing available. $25 nonrefundable deposit. **Activities:** Bands, choral groups, dance, drama, music ensembles, musical theater, radio station, student government, student newspaper, symphony orchestra, TV station, Habitat for Humanity, HOPE, multicultural club, Campus Crusade for Christ, Christian Student Fellowship.

Athletics. NJCAA. **Intercollegiate:** Basketball. **Intramural:** Basketball, soccer, softball. **Team name:** Hawks.

Student services. Adult student services, career counseling, student employment services, financial aid counseling, health services, minority student services, on-campus daycare, personal counseling, placement for graduates, veterans' counselor. **Physically disabled:** Services for visually, speech,

hearing impaired. **Transfer:** Pre-admission transcript evaluation for new students. Transfer adviser for students transferring to 4-year colleges.

Contact. E-mail: admission@northeast.edu
Phone: (402) 844-7260 Toll-free number: (800) 348-9033
Fax: (402) 844-7400
Sandy Hilliges, Coordinator of Admissions Services, Northeast Community College, 801 East Benjamin Avenue, Norfolk, NE 68702-0469

Two-Year Colleges

Southeast Community College
Lincoln, Nebraska
www.southeast.edu   **CB code: 1189**

> Public 2-year community college
> Commuter campus in small city

General. Founded in 1973. Regionally accredited. Extensive adult and continuing education programs, both credit and noncredit. Additional campuses in Beatrice and Milford. **Enrollment:** 9,110 degree-seeking undergraduates. **Degrees:** 1,341 associate awarded. **Location:** 50 miles from Omaha. **Calendar:** Quarter, extensive summer session. **Full-time faculty:** 359 total. **Part-time faculty:** 405 total. **Special facilities:** Fire service training facility.

Student profile.

Out-of-state:	2%	25 or older:	26%

Transfer out. Colleges most students transferred to 2011: University of Nebraska, Doane-Lincoln College, College of St. Mary, Nebraska Wesleyan, University of Nebraska-Kearney.

Basis for selection. Open admission. **Home schooled:** Transcript of courses and grades required.

2011-2012 Annual costs. Tuition/fees: $2,351; $2,891 out-of-state. Per-credit charge: $51 in-state; $63 out-of-state. Room/board: $7,800. Books/supplies: $1,000.

Financial aid. Need-based: Need-based aid available for part-time students. Work-study available nights, weekends and for part-time students. **Non-need-based:** Scholarships awarded for academics.

Application procedures. Admission: No deadline. No application fee. Admission notification on a rolling basis. **Financial aid:** No deadline. FAFSA, institutional form required. Applicants notified on a rolling basis; must reply within 2 week(s) of notification.

Academics. Academic transfer courses (liberal arts) offered on Saturdays. **Special study options:** Cooperative education, distance learning, dual enrollment of high school students, independent study, internships, liberal arts/career combination, weekend college. License preparation in nursing, paramedic, physical therapy, radiology. **Credit/placement by examination:** AP, CLEP, institutional tests. 30 credit hours maximum toward associate degree. Most applicants required to take COMPASS or ASSET for placement purposes. ACT may be substituted for ASSET. **Support services:** GED preparation and test center, learning center, reduced course load, remedial instruction, study skills assistance, tutoring, writing center.

Majors. Business: Administrative services, business admin, marketing, office/clerical, vehicle parts marketing. **Communications technology:** Radio/TV. **Computer sciences:** Information systems. **General:** Business. **Health services:** Clinical lab technology, medical radiologic technology/radiation therapy, nursing (RN), respiratory therapy technology, surgical technology. **Liberal arts:** Arts/sciences. **Protective services:** Criminal justice, fire safety technology. **Visual/performing arts:** Commercial/advertising art. **Work/family studies:** Child care management.

Computing on campus. 300 workstations in dormitories, library, computer center, student center. Dormitories wired for high-speed internet access and linked to campus network. Online course registration, online library, helpline, wireless network available.

Student life. Freshman orientation: Mandatory. Preregistration for classes offered. **Housing:** Single-sex dorms available. $100 fully refundable deposit. **Activities:** Choral groups, drama, radio station, student government, student newspaper, multicultural student organization.

Athletics. NJCAA. **Intercollegiate:** Baseball M, basketball, golf M, softball W, volleyball W. **Intramural:** Baseball M, basketball, softball W, table tennis, tennis, volleyball. **Team name:** Storm.

Student services. Career counseling, student employment services, financial aid counseling, on-campus daycare, placement for graduates, veterans' counselor. **Physically disabled:** Services for visually, speech, hearing

impaired. **Transfer:** Transfer adviser, college fairs on campus for students transferring to 4-year colleges.

Contact. Phone: (402) 437-2600 Toll-free number: (800) 642-4075 Fax: (402) 437-2402
Robin Moore, Dean of Student Services, Southeast Community College, 8800 O Street, Lincoln, NE 68520

Vatterott College: Spring Valley
Omaha, Nebraska
www.vatterott-college.com

▶ For-profit 2-year community and technical college
▶ Large city

General. Accredited by ACCSCT. **Calendar:** Quarter.

Contact. Phone: (402) 891-9411
Director of Admissions, 11818 I Street, Omaha, NE 68137

Western Nebraska Community College
Scottsbluff, Nebraska
www.wncc.edu   CB code: 6648

▶ Public 2-year community college
▶ Commuter campus in large town

General. Founded in 1926. Regionally accredited. Additional campuses at Sidney and Alliance. Advanced Technology Center in Scottsbluff. **Enrollment:** 1,755 degree-seeking undergraduates; 486 non-degree-seeking students. **Degrees:** 222 associate awarded. **Location:** 100 miles from Cheyenne, Wyoming. **Calendar:** Semester, extensive summer session. **Full-time faculty:** 77 total; 9% have terminal degrees, 5% minority, 51% women. **Part-time faculty:** 57 total; 7% minority, 51% women. **Class size:** 69% < 20, 31% 20-39, less than 1% 40-49.

Student profile. Among degree-seeking undergraduates, 78% enrolled in a transfer program, 22% enrolled in a vocational program, 466 enrolled as first-time, first-year students, 75 transferred in from other institutions.

Part-time:	38%	Hispanic American:	18%
Out-of-state:	14%	Native American:	1%
Women:	66%	International:	4%
African American:	2%	25 or older:	41%
Asian American:	1%	Live on campus:	13%

Transfer out. 44% of students enrolled in the transfer program go on to 4-year colleges. **Colleges most students transferred to 2011:** Chadron State College, University of Nebraska-Lincoln, University of Wyoming.

Basis for selection. Open admission, but selective for some programs. Special requirements for practical nursing, Associate Degree-Nursing, and radiologic technologies programs. **Adult students:** COMPASS used for proper course placement in writing, mathematics, and classes with a reading prerequisite; ACT, SAT, or ASSET accepted in lieu of COMPASS. **Learning Disabled:** Students should contact the Director of Counseling to discuss the process required to request assistance and arrange for reasonable accommodations.

High school preparation. Recommended units include English 4, mathematics 4, social studies 3, history 3, science 4 (laboratory 2) and foreign language 1.

2011-2012 Annual costs. Tuition/fees: $2,760; $3,180 out-of-state. Per-credit charge: $77 in-state; $91 out-of-state. Border states Colorado, Wyoming & South Dakota pay in-state, out-of district tuition. Room/board: $6,250. Books/supplies: $1,080. Personal expenses: $2,183.

2011-2012 Financial aid. **Need-based:** 299 full-time freshmen applied for aid; 256 were judged to have need; 256 of these received aid. Average need met was 97%. Average scholarship/grant was $4,686; average loan $2,308. 77% of total undergraduate aid awarded as scholarships/grants, 23% as loans/jobs. Need-based aid available for part-time students. Work-study available nights, weekends and for part-time students. **Non-need-based:** Awarded to 475 full-time undergraduates, including 257 freshmen. Scholarships awarded for academics, art, athletics, leadership, music/drama, state residency.

Application procedures. **Admission:** No deadline. No application fee. Application must be submitted online. Admission notification on a rolling basis. **Financial aid:** Priority date 3/1; no closing date. FAFSA required. Applicants notified on a rolling basis starting 4/1.

Academics. **Special study options:** Cooperative education, distance learning, double major, dual enrollment of high school students, ESL, independent study, internships, liberal arts/career combination, student-designed major. Radiological technology program at Regional West Medical Center. License preparation in aviation, nursing, paramedic, radiology, real estate. **Credit/placement by examination:** AP, CLEP, IB, institutional tests. 25 credit hours maximum toward associate degree. **Support services:** GED preparation and test center, learning center, pre-admission summer program, reduced course load, remedial instruction, study skills assistance, tutoring, writing center.

Majors. **Biology:** General. **Business:** General, accounting, administrative services, business admin, office/clerical. **Communications:** Journalism. **Computer sciences:** General, computer science, programming. **Conservation:** Forestry. **Education:** General, art, early childhood, elementary, music, physical, secondary. **Engineering:** General. **English:** English lit. **Foreign languages:** French, Spanish. **Health services:** Athletic training, medical radiologic technology/radiation therapy, medical records technology, nursing (RN), predental, premedicine, prenursing, prepharmacy, preveterinary. **History:** General. **Human services:** Social work. **Liberal arts:** Arts/sciences. **Math:** General. **Physical sciences:** Chemistry, physics. **Protective services:** Police science. **Psychology:** General. **Social sciences:** Anthropology, economics, geography, political science, sociology. **Visual/performing arts:** Art, music performance. **Work/family studies:** Food/nutrition.

Computing on campus. 518 workstations in dormitories, library, computer center. Dormitories wired for high-speed internet access and linked to campus network. Commuter students can connect to campus network. Online course registration, online library, helpline, wireless network available.

Student life. **Freshman orientation:** Available. Preregistration for classes offered. 6 hours held the weekday before classes begin. **Policies:** All buildings are smoke-free. Coed dorms, wellness housing available. $150 fully refundable deposit, deadline 8/15. **Activities:** Jazz band, choral groups, drama, literary magazine, music ensembles, musical theater, student government, student newspaper, Campus Ventures, College Republicans, Student Ambassadors, United Leaders for Cultural Diversity, student senate, student council.

Athletics. NJCAA. **Intercollegiate:** Baseball M, basketball, soccer, softball W, volleyball W. **Intramural:** Basketball, football (non-tackle), volleyball. **Team name:** Cougars.

Student services. Adult student services, alcohol/substance abuse counseling, career counseling, student employment services, financial aid counseling, minority student services, on-campus daycare, personal counseling, placement for graduates, veterans' counselor. **Physically disabled:** Services for visually, speech, hearing impaired. **Transfer:** Pre-admission transcript evaluation for new students. Transfer adviser, college fairs on campus for students transferring to 4-year colleges.

Contact. E-mail: admissions@wncc.edu
Phone: (308) 635-6183 Toll-free number: (800) 348-4435 ext. 6183
Fax: (308) 635-6732
Gretchen Foster, Admissions Director, Western Nebraska Community College, 1601 East 27th Street, Scottsbluff, NE 69361

Nevada

Career College of Northern Nevada
Reno, Nevada
www.ccnn.edu   CB code: 3202

- For-profit 2-year career college
- Commuter campus in large city

General. Accredited by ACCSCT. **Calendar:** Quarter.

Annual costs/financial aid. Tuition/fees (2011-2012): $9,675. Quoted tuition amount doesn't include required fees $434 to $1,649. Tuition for associate of occupational studies programs range from $21,285 to $26,875; diploma programs, $11,825 to $16,340. Total estimated fees range from $819 to $2,346. Books/supplies: $1,500. Personal expenses: $1,832. Need-based financial aid available for full-time students.

Contact. Phone: (775) 856-2266
Director of Admissions, 1421 Pullman Drive, Sparks, NV 89434

Carrington College: Las Vegas
Las Vegas, Nevada
www.carrington.edu

- For-profit 2-year career college
- Very large city

General. Regionally accredited; also accredited by ACICS. **Degrees:** 120 associate awarded. **Calendar:** Differs by program. **Full-time faculty:** 10 total. **Part-time faculty:** 12 total.

Basis for selection. Admission requirements will vary by program.

2011-2012 Annual costs. Tuition/fees: $14,914. Program cost $44,542 (96 weeks). Costs are provided for the largest program. Other programs may vary.

Financial aid. Need-based: Work-study available nights, weekends and for part-time students.

Academics. Credit/placement by examination: AP, CLEP.

Majors. Health services: Physical therapy assistant, respiratory therapy technology.

Contact. Phone: (888) 720-5014
William Hale, Director of Admissions, Carrington College: Las Vegas, 5740 South Eastern Avenue, Las Vegas, NV 89119-1642

Carrington College: Reno
Reno, Nevada
www.carrington.edu/nevada/reno/home

- For-profit 2-year nursing college
- Large city

General. Regionally accredited; also accredited by ACICS. **Degrees:** 42 associate awarded. **Calendar:** Semester. **Full-time faculty:** 17 total. **Part-time faculty:** 16 total.

Basis for selection. Admission requirements will vary by program.

2011-2012 Annual costs. Tuition/fees: $15,500. Program cost $46,500 (90 weeks). Costs are provided for the largest program. Other programs may vary.

Financial aid. Need-based: Work-study available nights, weekends and for part-time students.

Application procedures. Admission: No deadline. No application fee. **Financial aid:** Priority date 8/27; no closing date.

Academics. Credit/placement by examination: AP, CLEP.

Majors. Health services: Medical assistant, nursing (RN).

Contact. E-mail: brossini@carrington.edu
Phone: (775) 335-2900
Becki Rossini, Director of Admissions, Carrington College: Reno, 5580 Kietzke Lane, Reno, NV 89511

College of Southern Nevada
Las Vegas, Nevada
www.csn.edu   CB code: 4136

- Public 2-year community college
- Commuter campus in very large city

General. Founded in 1971. Regionally accredited. Three major campuses serve the entire Las Vegas valley. Three High-Tech Centers located throughout the city. **Enrollment:** 29,134 degree-seeking undergraduates. **Degrees:** 20 bachelor's, 2,030 associate awarded. **ROTC:** Army. **Location:** 6 miles from downtown. **Calendar:** Semester, limited summer session. **Full-time faculty:** 477 total; 21% minority, 45% women. **Part-time faculty:** 996 total; 28% minority, 55% women. **Special facilities:** Planetarium, ornamental horticulture demonstration facilities, culinary facilities, telecommunications/ multimedia center, automotive technology center, occupational therapy labs, dental practice, massage therapy practice.

Student profile.

Out-of-state:	2%	25 or older:	54%

Transfer out. Colleges most students transferred to 2011: University of Nevada Las Vegas.

Basis for selection. Open admission, but selective for some programs. Special requirements for nursing, dental hygiene, and health professions programs. Associate degree and certification required for BS dental hygiene program.

2011-2012 Annual costs. Tuition/fees: $2,513; $9,008 out-of-state. Per-credit charge: $69. Discounted tuition available for residents of western states participating in Western Undergraduate Exchange: Alaska, Arizona, California, Colorado, Hawaii, Idaho, Montana, Nevada, New Mexico, North Dakota, Oregon, South Dakota, Utah, Washington, Wyoming. Books/supplies: $900. Personal expenses: $1,800.

Financial aid. Need-based: Work-study available nights, weekends and for part-time students. **Non-need-based:** Scholarships awarded for state residency.

Application procedures. Admission: No deadline. $5 fee, may be waived for applicants with need. Admission notification on a rolling basis. **Financial aid:** Priority date 5/1, closing date 6/30. FAFSA required. Applicants notified on a rolling basis starting 7/15; must reply within 2 week(s) of notification.

Academics. Special study options: Cooperative education, cross-registration, distance learning, double major, dual enrollment of high school students, ESL, honors, independent study, internships, liberal arts/career combination, student-designed major, weekend college. Bachelor's degree programs available on campus. License preparation in aviation, dental hygiene, nursing, occupational therapy, paramedic, physical therapy, radiology, real estate. **Credit/placement by examination:** AP, CLEP, institutional tests. 15 credit hours maximum toward associate degree. **Support services:** GED preparation and test center, learning center, remedial instruction, study skills assistance, tutoring, writing center.

Majors. Architecture: Technology. **Biology:** General. **Business:** General, accounting, administrative services, banking/financial services, business admin, hospitality admin, hospitality/recreation, management information systems, office management, real estate, sales/distribution. **Communications:** Communications/speech/rhetoric. **Communications technology:** Animation/special effects, computer typography, graphic/printing. **Computer sciences:** Computer graphics, data processing, database management, information systems, LAN/WAN management, networking, programming, systems analysis, webmaster. **Education:** Deaf/hearing impaired, early childhood, kindergarten/preschool. **Engineering:** Electrical, software. **English:** English lit. **General:** Landscaping, ornamental horticulture. **Health services:** Clinical lab assistant, clinical lab technology, dental hygiene, EMT paramedic, medical records technology, nursing (RN), optician, orthotics/prosthetics, physical therapy assistant. **Liberal arts:** Arts/sciences. **Protective services:** Corrections, criminal justice, fire safety technology, firefighting, police science, security services. **Psychology:** General. **Social sciences:** General. **Visual/performing arts:** Art, commercial photography, commercial/advertising art, studio arts.

Computing on campus. 650 workstations in library, computer center. Commuter students can connect to campus network. Online course registration, online library, helpline, wireless network available.

Student life. Freshman orientation: Mandatory. Preregistration for classes offered. Orientation is mandatory for degree-seeking students only. **Activities:** Jazz band, choral groups, dance, drama, literary magazine, music ensembles, musical theater, student government, student newspaper.

Athletics. NJCAA. **Intercollegiate:** Baseball M, softball W. **Team name:** Coyotes.

Student services. Adult student services, career counseling, student employment services, financial aid counseling, on-campus daycare, personal counseling, placement for graduates, veterans' counselor, women's services. **Physically disabled:** Services for visually, speech, hearing impaired. **Transfer:** Re-entry adviser, pre-admission transcript evaluation for new students. Transfer center, transfer adviser, college fairs on campus for students transferring to 4-year colleges.

Contact. E-mail: admrec@csn.edu
Phone: (702) 651-5610 Fax: (702) 651-4811
Patricia Zozaya, Registrar, College of Southern Nevada, 6375 West Charleston Boulevard, Las Vegas, NV 89146-1164

Kaplan College: Las Vegas
Las Vegas, Nevada
www.kaplancollege.com   **CB code: 3167**

- For-profit 2-year career college
- Commuter campus in very large city
- Interview required

General. Accredited by ACCSC. **Degrees:** 39 associate awarded. **Calendar:** Differs by program. **Full-time faculty:** 17 total. **Part-time faculty:** 31 total.

Basis for selection. Open admission, but selective for some programs. Clean legal record required for pharmacy technician, practical nursing and criminal justice programs. Wonderlic SLE exam required for all applicants; cut-off scores vary by program. **Adult students:** All students must take a Wonderlic Scholastic Level Exam.

2011-2012 Annual costs. Tuition/fees: $14,821. Per-credit charge: $315. Personal expenses: $2,925.

Financial aid. Need-based: Need-based aid available for part-time students. Work-study available nights, weekends and for part-time students.

Application procedures. Admission: No deadline. $10 fee. **Financial aid:** No deadline. FAFSA, institutional form required.

Academics. Credit/placement by examination: AP, CLEP. **Support services:** Learning center, study skills assistance, tutoring.

Majors. Health services: Insurance coding, office assistant, pharmacy assistant. **Protective services:** Law enforcement admin.

Computing on campus. 90 workstations in library, computer center. Online library available.

Student life. Freshman orientation: Available. Preregistration for classes offered. Held one week to a few days before start of class; on-campus; attendance strongly encouraged. **Activities:** Student government.

Student services. Adult student services, career counseling, student employment services, financial aid counseling, placement for graduates.

Contact. Phone: (702) 368-2338 Toll-free number: (888) 727-7863
Fax: (702) 368-3853
Derrick Perry, Director of Admissions, Kaplan College: Las Vegas, 3535 West Sahara Avenue, Las Vegas, NV 89102

Truckee Meadows Community College
Reno, Nevada
www.tmcc.edu   **CB code: 1096**

- Public 2-year community and technical college
- Commuter campus in large city

General. Founded in 1971. Regionally accredited. Classes offered at over 30 sites in Reno-Sparks area. **Enrollment:** 9,939 degree-seeking undergraduates. **Degrees:** 1,103 associate awarded. **ROTC:** Army. **Location:** 9 miles from downtown. **Calendar:** Semester, limited summer session. **Full-time faculty:** 172 total; 11% minority. **Part-time faculty:** 409 total; 10% minority. **Class size:** 29% < 20, 69% 20-39, 2% 40-49, less than 1% 50-99.

Transfer out. Colleges most students transferred to 2011: University of Nevada-Reno, University of Nevada-Las Vegas.

Basis for selection. Open admission, but selective for some programs. High school diploma or GED required if student under 18 years of age. Competitive admission to nursing, dental assistant, and radiological technician programs. **Learning Disabled:** Applicants must contact Disabled Students Office. Accommodations provided according to documentation.

2011-2012 Annual costs. Tuition/fees: $2,513; $9,008 out-of-state. Per-credit charge: $69. Discounted tuition available for residents of western states participating in Western Undergraduate Exchange: Alaska, Arizona, California, Colorado, Hawaii, Idaho, Montana, Nevada, New Mexico, North Dakota, Oregon, South Dakota, Utah, Washington, Wyoming. Books/supplies: $800. Personal expenses: $1,298.

Financial aid. Need-based: Work-study available nights, weekends and for part-time students. **Non-need-based:** Scholarships awarded for academics, art, leadership, minority status, music/drama, state residency. **Additional information:** Institutional grants to state residents, short-term emergency loans available. Work-study applications must reply within 10 days of notification.

Application procedures. Admission: No deadline. $10 fee. Admission notification on a rolling basis. Application fee is paid at time of registration for first class. **Financial aid:** Priority date 1/15; no closing date. FAFSA, institutional form required.

Academics. Special study options: Cooperative education, distance learning, dual enrollment of high school students, ESL, honors, internships, liberal arts/career combination, weekend college. License preparation in dental hygiene, nursing, radiology, real estate. **Credit/placement by examination:** AP, CLEP, IB, institutional tests. 15 credit hours maximum toward associate degree. **Support services:** GED preparation and test center, learning center, reduced course load, remedial instruction, study skills assistance, tutoring, writing center.

Majors. Architecture: Landscape. **Business:** General, accounting, administrative services, business admin, office management, office technology, real estate. **Computer sciences:** General, data processing, programming. **Conservation:** Environmental studies. **Education:** Early childhood, elementary, secondary. **Health services:** Dental assistant, dental hygiene, medical radiologic technology/radiation therapy, medical secretary, nursing (RN), radiologic technology/medical imaging, substance abuse counseling. **Parks/recreation:** Facilities management. **Protective services:** Corrections, criminal justice, firefighting, juvenile corrections, law enforcement admin, police science. **Social sciences:** Anthropology. **Visual/performing arts:** Design, dramatic, music. **Work/family studies:** Child care management, institutional food production.

Most popular majors. Health sciences 11%, liberal arts 58%, physical sciences 9%, security/protective services 7%.

Computing on campus. 558 workstations in library, computer center. Helpline, repair service available.

Student life. Freshman orientation: Mandatory. Preregistration for classes offered. **Housing:** Housing available 2 miles away at University of Nevada: Reno, for students enrolled for 12 or more credits. **Activities:** Concert band, choral groups, drama, literary magazine, music ensembles, student government, student newspaper, symphony orchestra, social organization for handicapped students.

Student services. Adult student services, career counseling, student employment services, financial aid counseling, health services, on-campus daycare, personal counseling, placement for graduates, veterans' counselor. **Physically disabled:** Services for visually, speech, hearing impaired. **Transfer:** Re-entry adviser for new students. Transfer adviser, college fairs on campus for students transferring to 4-year colleges.

Contact. E-mail: admissions@tmcc.edu
Phone: (775) 673-7042 Fax: (775) 673-7028
Ty Moore, Director of Admissions/Registrar, Truckee Meadows Community College, 7000 Dandini Boulevard, Reno, NV 89512

Western Nevada College
Carson City, Nevada
www.wnc.edu   CB code: 4972

- Public 2-year community college
- Commuter campus in small city

General. Founded in 1971. Regionally accredited. Three campuses and 6 teaching centers. **Enrollment:** 3,531 degree-seeking undergraduates; 746 non-degree-seeking students. **Degrees:** 6 bachelor's, 445 associate awarded. **Location:** 30 miles from Reno. **Calendar:** Semester, limited summer session. **Full-time faculty:** 116 total; 21% women. **Part-time faculty:** 114 total; 25% women. **Class size:** 50% < 20, 47% 20-39, 2% 40-49, less than 1% 50-99. **Special facilities:** Observatory, fitness center, baseball field. **Partnerships:** Formal partnerships with selected high schools for dual credit.

Student profile. Among degree-seeking undergraduates, 89% enrolled in a transfer program, 598 enrolled as first-time, first-year students, 548 transferred in from other institutions.

Part-time:	61%	Asian American:	2%
Out-of-state:	5%	Hispanic American:	16%
Women:	61%	Native American:	3%
African American:	2%	25 or older:	51%

Transfer out. 20% of students enrolled in the transfer program go on to 4-year colleges. **Colleges most students transferred to 2011:** University of Nevada-Reno.

Basis for selection. Open admission, but selective for some programs. SAT and ACT scores accepted, but not required, for math and English placement. Special requirements for nursing program.

2011-2012 Annual costs. Tuition/fees: $2,513; $9,008 out-of-state. Per-credit charge: $78. Books/supplies: $1,400. Personal expenses: $2,160.

Financial aid. Need-based: Need-based aid available for part-time students. Work-study available nights, weekends and for part-time students. **Non-need-based:** Scholarships awarded for academics, state residency.

Application procedures. Admission: No deadline. $15 fee. No notification sent to applicants except by request. **Financial aid:** Priority date 4/1; no closing date. FAFSA required. Applicants notified on a rolling basis; must reply within 3 week(s) of notification.

Academics. Special study options: Distance learning, double major, dual enrollment of high school students, ESL, honors, independent study, internships. Bachelor's degree programs available on campus. License preparation in nursing, real estate. **Credit/placement by examination:** AP, CLEP, institutional tests. 30 credit hours maximum toward associate degree, 30 toward bachelor's. **Support services:** GED preparation and test center, learning center, remedial instruction, study skills assistance, tutoring.

Majors. Business: Accounting, business admin, management science, office technology, real estate. **Communications technology:** Graphics. **Computer sciences:** General, LAN/WAN management, webmaster. **Conservation:** General. **Education:** Early childhood. **Engineering:** General. **Health services:** Nursing (RN). **Liberal arts:** Arts/sciences. **Math:** General. **Physical sciences:** Chemistry, physics. **Protective services:** Police science. **Visual/performing arts:** Music.

Most popular majors. Business/marketing 10%, health sciences 9%, liberal arts 54%.

Computing on campus. 678 workstations in library, computer center, student center. Commuter students can connect to campus network. Online course registration, online library, student web hosting, wireless network available.

Student life. Freshman orientation: Available. Preregistration for classes offered. **Activities:** Bands, choral groups, dance, drama, musical theater, student government.

Athletics. NJCAA. **Intercollegiate:** Baseball M, softball W. **Team name:** Wildcats.

Student services. Adult student services, alcohol/substance abuse counseling, career counseling, services for economically disadvantaged, student employment services, financial aid counseling, health services, on-campus daycare, personal counseling, placement for graduates, veterans' counselor, women's services. **Physically disabled:** Services for visually, speech, hearing impaired. **Transfer:** Pre-admission transcript evaluation for new students. Transfer center, transfer adviser for students transferring to 4-year colleges.

Contact. E-mail: admissions.records@wnc.edu
Phone: (775) 445-3277 Fax: (775) 887-3147
Dianne Hilliard, Director, Admissions and Records, Western Nevada College, 2201 West College Parkway, Carson City, NV 89703-7399

New Hampshire

Great Bay Community College
Portsmouth, New Hampshire
www.greatbay.edu   CB code: 3661

- Public 2-year community and technical college
- Commuter campus in small town

General. Founded in 1945. Regionally accredited. **Enrollment:** 2,132 undergraduates. **Degrees:** 184 associate awarded. **Location:** 45 miles from Boston. **Calendar:** Semester, limited summer session. **Full-time faculty:** 33 total. **Part-time faculty:** 197 total. **Special facilities:** Biotechnology lab.

Transfer out. Colleges most students transferred to 2011: University of New Hampshire, Southern New Hampshire University, Keene State College, Plymouth State University, Granite State College.

Basis for selection. Open admission, but selective for some programs. Selective admission to allied health and automotive programs. National League for Nursing Pre-Admission Assessment for Registered Nursing required for applicants to RN program. ACT-PEP Nursing Fundamentals Test required for admission to associate degree nursing program as advanced standing students. Career Guidance Placement Test given to technical majors on selected basis. Interview required for allied health and education applicants.

High school preparation. Recommended units include English 4, mathematics 2, social studies 2 and science 2. High school vocational and college-preparatory courses recommended. For mechanical-technical majors, algebra I and II and geometry recommended. For associate nursing applicants and surgical technology, biology, chemistry, algebra I required. For vet tech, algebra, biology and chemistry are required. For business management, typing or keyboarding skills required.

2011-2012 Annual costs. Tuition/fees: $6,570; $14,610 out-of-state. Per-credit charge: $210 in-state; $478 out-of-state. New England Regional tuition: $315 per credit hour. Books/supplies: $600.

Financial aid. All financial aid based on need. Need-based aid available for part-time students. Work-study available nights, weekends and for part-time students.

Application procedures. Admission: No deadline. $20 fee, may be waived for applicants with need, free for online applicants. Admission notification on a rolling basis. **Financial aid:** No deadline. FAFSA, institutional form required. Applicants notified on a rolling basis; must reply within 2 week(s) of notification.

Academics. Special study options: Accelerated study, distance learning, double major, dual enrollment of high school students, ESL, independent study, internships, liberal arts/career combination. License preparation in nursing. **Credit/placement by examination:** AP, CLEP, institutional tests. **Support services:** GED preparation, learning center, pre-admission summer program, reduced course load, remedial instruction, study skills assistance, tutoring, writing center.

Majors. Biology: Biotechnology. **Business:** General, accounting, administrative services, business admin, hospitality admin, management science, marketing. **Computer sciences:** Information systems, programming, web page design. **Education:** Early childhood, social science. **Health services:** Massage therapy, nursing (RN), surgical technology, veterinary technology/assistant. **Liberal arts:** Arts/sciences. **Protective services:** Law enforcement admin. **Work/family studies:** Child care management.

Computing on campus. 140 workstations in library, computer center. Online library, helpline, wireless network available.

Student life. Freshman orientation: Available. Preregistration for classes offered. **Activities:** Literary magazine, student government, student senate, Phi Theta Kappa.

Student services. Career counseling, student employment services, placement for graduates. **Transfer:** Pre-admission transcript evaluation for new students. Transfer adviser, college fairs on campus for students transferring to 4-year colleges.

Contact. E-mail: askgreatbay@ccsnh.edu
Phone: (603) 772-1194 Toll-free number: (800) 522-1194
Fax: (603) 772-1198
Sandy Ho, Admissions Coordinator, Great Bay Community College, 320 Corporate Drive, Portsmouth, NH 03801

Lakes Region Community College
Laconia, New Hampshire
www.lrcc.edu   CB code: 3850

- Public 2-year community and technical college
- Commuter campus in small city

General. Founded in 1967. Regionally accredited. Numerous satellite programs at various locations. **Enrollment:** 1,100 undergraduates. **Degrees:** 190 associate awarded. **Location:** 95 miles from Boston, 25 miles from Concord. **Calendar:** Semester, limited summer session. **Full-time faculty:** 45 total. **Part-time faculty:** 30 total. **Special facilities:** Student operated restaurant.

Student profile.

Out-of-state:	25%	**25 or older:**	50%

Basis for selection. Open admission, but selective for some programs. Competitive admission to nursing program.

High school preparation. College-preparatory program recommended. Required and recommended units include English 4, mathematics 2-3, social studies 2 and science 4.

2011-2012 Annual costs. Tuition/fees: $6,480; $14,520 out-of-state. Per-credit charge: $210 in-state; $478 out-of-state. New England regional tuition: $315 per-credit-hour. Books/supplies: $500.

Financial aid. Need-based: Need-based aid available for part-time students. Work-study available nights, weekends and for part-time students.

Application procedures. Admission: No deadline. $10 fee, may be waived for applicants with need, free for online applicants. Admission notification on a rolling basis beginning on or about 10/1. Must reply by May 1 or within 4 week(s) if notified thereafter. **Financial aid:** Priority date 5/1; no closing date. FAFSA, institutional form required.

Academics. Special study options: Cooperative education, distance learning, double major, honors, independent study, internships, liberal arts/career combination. License preparation in nursing. **Credit/placement by examination:** AP, CLEP, IB, institutional tests. 12 credit hours maximum toward associate degree. **Support services:** Learning center, reduced course load, remedial instruction, study skills assistance, tutoring.

Majors. Business: Accounting, business admin, hospitality/recreation. **Communications technology:** Graphic/printing. **Computer sciences:** General, data processing, programming. **Education:** Early childhood. **Human services:** Social work. **Liberal arts:** Arts/sciences. **Protective services:** Fire safety technology, fire services admin, firefighting. **Visual/performing arts:** Commercial/advertising art, studio arts.

Computing on campus. 100 workstations in library, computer center. Online course registration, wireless network available.

Student life. Freshman orientation: Mandatory, $30 fee. Preregistration for classes offered. **Activities:** Literary magazine, student government.

Athletics. NJCAA. **Intercollegiate:** Basketball M, golf, track and field. **Intramural:** Soccer, table tennis. **Team name:** Centurions.

Student services. Career counseling, student employment services, financial aid counseling, personal counseling, placement for graduates, veterans' counselor. **Physically disabled:** Services for hearing impaired. **Transfer:** Pre-admission transcript evaluation for new students. Transfer adviser, college fairs on campus for students transferring to 4-year colleges.

Contact. E-mail: wfraser@ccsnh.edu
Phone: (603) 524-3207 ext. 767 Toll-free number: (800) 357-2992
Fax: (603) 524-8084
Wayne Fraser, Director of Admissions, Lakes Region Community College, 379 Belmont Road, Laconia, NH 03246-9204

Lebanon College
Lebanon, New Hampshire
www.lebanoncollege.edu

- Private 2-year health science and community college
- Commuter campus in large town
- Application essay, interview required

General. Regionally accredited; also accredited by ACICS. **Enrollment:** 116 degree-seeking undergraduates; 113 non-degree-seeking students. **Degrees:** 27 associate awarded. **Location:** 125 miles from Boston. **Calendar:** Trimester, extensive summer session. **Full-time faculty:** 6 total; 17% have terminal degrees, 83% women. **Part-time faculty:** 44 total; 4% have terminal degrees, 9% minority, 41% women. **Class size:** 99% < 20, 1% 20-39.

Student profile. Among degree-seeking undergraduates, 62 enrolled as first-time, first-year students.

Part-time:	34%	Women:	58%
Out-of-state:	31%	25 or older:	60%

Basis for selection. Open admission, but selective for some programs. Additional requirements and documentation may apply for specialty programs such as radiography and sonography. **Home schooled:** State high school equivalency certificate required.

2012-2013 Annual costs. Tuition/fees (projected): $6,998. Per-credit charge: $180. Trimester school with three fifteen week terms; amount listed is for three terms. Books/supplies: $610. Personal expenses: $5,810.

2011-2012 Financial aid. **Need-based:** 21 full-time freshmen applied for aid; 21 were judged to have need; 21 of these received aid. Average need met was 50%. Average scholarship/grant was $700; average loan $4,500. 50% of total undergraduate aid awarded as scholarships/grants, 50% as loans/jobs. Need-based aid available for part-time students. Work-study available nights, weekends and for part-time students.

Application procedures. **Admission:** No deadline. $40 fee, may be waived for applicants with need. Admission notification on a rolling basis. **Financial aid:** No deadline. FAFSA, institutional form required. Applicants notified on a rolling basis.

Academics. **Special study options:** Double major, dual enrollment of high school students, ESL, independent study. License preparation in radiology. **Credit/placement by examination:** AP, CLEP. **Support services:** Remedial instruction, tutoring.

Majors. **Business:** Accounting, business admin. **Computer sciences:** General. **Education:** Teacher assistance. **English:** Creative writing. **Health services:** Radiologic technology/medical imaging. **Protective services:** Criminal justice. **Visual/performing arts:** Photography, studio arts.

Most popular majors. Business/marketing 7%, computer/information sciences 11%, education 7%, health sciences 56%, liberal arts 11%.

Computing on campus. 6 workstations in library. Wireless network available.

Student life. Freshman orientation: Available. Preregistration for classes offered.

Student services. Services for economically disadvantaged, student employment services, financial aid counseling, minority student services. **Transfer:** Pre-admission transcript evaluation for new students.

Contact. E-mail: admissions@lebanoncollege.edu
Phone: (603) 448-2445 ext. 103 Fax: (603) 448-2491
Phoebe Buskey, Admissions Director, Lebanon College, 15 Hanover Street, Lebanon, NH 03766

Manchester Community College
Manchester, New Hampshire
www.mccnh.edu

CB member
CB code: 3660

- Public 2-year community and technical college
- Commuter campus in small city

General. Founded in 1945. Regionally accredited. **Enrollment:** 2,800 undergraduates. **Degrees:** 223 associate awarded. **Location:** 50 miles from Boston. **Calendar:** Semester, limited summer session. **Full-time faculty:** 54 total. **Part-time faculty:** 260 total. **Partnerships:** Formal partnerships with local businesses.

Basis for selection. Open admission, but selective for some programs. National League for Nursing Pre-Admission Examination-RN required for nursing applicants. **Learning Disabled:** A Disabilities Counselor is available for students with learning and other disabilities.

High school preparation. Recommended units include English 4, mathematics 3 and science 2. Chemistry, algebra, geometry and biology required for some programs.

2011-2012 Annual costs. Tuition/fees: $6,540; $14,580 out-of-state. Per-credit charge: $210 in-state; $478 out-of-state. New England Regional tuition: $315 per credit hour. Books/supplies: $550.

Financial aid. All financial aid based on need. Need-based aid available for part-time students. Work-study available nights, weekends and for part-time students.

Application procedures. **Admission:** No deadline. $20 fee, may be waived for applicants with need. Admission notification on a rolling basis. **Financial aid:** Priority date 5/1; no closing date. FAFSA, institutional form required. Applicants notified on a rolling basis starting 4/15; must reply within 2 week(s) of notification.

Academics. **Special study options:** Cooperative education, cross-registration, distance learning, double major, dual enrollment of high school students, ESL, external degree, independent study, internships, liberal arts/career combination, student-designed major. License preparation in nursing. **Credit/placement by examination:** AP, CLEP, institutional tests. 32 credit hours maximum toward associate degree. **Support services:** Learning center, reduced course load, remedial instruction, study skills assistance, tutoring, writing center.

Majors. **Business:** Accounting, administrative services, business admin, management science, marketing, office management. **Communications technology:** Desktop publishing, graphics. **Computer sciences:** General. **Education:** Early childhood. **Health services:** Medical assistant, medical records technology, nursing (RN), prenursing. **Liberal arts:** Arts/sciences. **Parks/recreation:** Exercise sciences. **Visual/performing arts:** Commercial/advertising art, interior design.

Computing on campus. 75 workstations in library, computer center. Online library, helpline, wireless network available.

Student life. Freshman orientation: Available, $25 fee. Preregistration for classes offered. **Activities:** Literary magazine, student government, student newspaper, honor society, community service club, Alternative Spring Break, international club, student senate, medical assisting club, business honor society.

Athletics. Intramural: Skiing, soccer, volleyball.

Student services. Career counseling, services for economically disadvantaged, financial aid counseling, minority student services, on-campus daycare. **Physically disabled:** Services for visually, hearing impaired. **Transfer:** Pre-admission transcript evaluation for new students. Transfer adviser, college fairs on campus for students transferring to 4-year colleges.

Contact. E-mail: jpoirier@ccsnh.edu
Phone: (603) 206-8100 Toll-free number: (800) 924-3445
Fax: (603) 668-5354
Larissa Baia, AVP Enrollment Management, Manchester Community College, 1066 Front Street, Manchester, NH 03102-8518

Nashua Community College
Nashua, New Hampshire
www.nashuacc.edu

CB member
CB code: 3643

- Public 2-year community and technical college
- Commuter campus in small city
- Interview required

General. Founded in 1967. Regionally accredited. **Enrollment:** 2,208 degree-seeking undergraduates. **Degrees:** 232 associate awarded. **Location:** 20 miles from Lowell, Massachusetts. **Calendar:** Semester, limited summer session. **Full-time faculty:** 43 total. **Part-time faculty:** 140 total.

Transfer out. Colleges most students transferred to 2011: University of Southern New Hampshire, University of New Hampshire, Keene State College, Plymouth State College.

Basis for selection. Open admission, but selective for some programs. Prerequisite courses, references, interview, exam required for nursing program. Clean driving record required for Honda program.

High school preparation. One unit algebra required for business and technical programs, 2 for computer/engineering technology.

2011-2012 Annual costs. Tuition/fees: $6,780; $14,820 out-of-state. Per-credit charge: $210 in-state; $478 out-of-state. New England regional tuition: $315 per credit hour. Books/supplies: $500. Personal expenses: $500.

Financial aid. All financial aid based on need. Need-based aid available for part-time students. Work-study available nights, weekends and for part-time students.

Application procedures. Admission: No deadline. $20 fee, may be waived for applicants with need. Admission notification on a rolling basis. Application priority date of 12/31 for nursing applicants. **Financial aid:** Priority date 5/1; no closing date. FAFSA required. Applicants notified on a rolling basis starting 3/1; must reply within 2 week(s) of notification.

Academics. Special study options: Distance learning, double major, dual enrollment of high school students, ESL, honors, independent study, internships, student-designed major, weekend college. License preparation in aviation, nursing. **Credit/placement by examination:** AP, CLEP, institutional tests. 48 credit hours maximum toward associate degree. **Support services:** Learning center, pre-admission summer program, reduced course load, remedial instruction, study skills assistance, tutoring, writing center.

Majors. Business: Accounting, business admin. **Computer sciences:** General, applications programming, computer science, data entry, data processing, information systems, networking, webmaster. **Education:** Early childhood. **Engineering:** Electrical. **Health services:** Nursing (RN). **Liberal arts:** Arts/sciences.

Computing on campus. 150 workstations in library, computer center. Student web hosting, wireless network available.

Student life. Freshman orientation: Mandatory, $30 fee. Preregistration for classes offered. One-day session held prior to beginning of each semester. **Housing:** Student housing available near campus. **Activities:** Drama, literary magazine, radio station, student government, Phi Theta Kappa, Rotoract.

Athletics. Intercollegiate: Basketball. **Intramural:** Basketball, volleyball. **Team name:** Jaguars.

Student services. Adult student services, career counseling, student employment services, financial aid counseling, personal counseling, placement for graduates, veterans' counselor. **Transfer:** Pre-admission transcript evaluation for new students. Transfer adviser, college fairs on campus for students transferring to 4-year colleges.

Contact. E-mail: nashua@ccsnh.edu
Phone: (603) 578-8908 Fax: (603) 882-8690
Patricia Goodman, Vice President of Student Services, Nashua Community College, 505 Amherst Street, Nashua, NH 03063-1026

NHTI-Concord's Community College
Concord, New Hampshire
www.nhti.edu   **CB code: 3647**

⬧ Public 2-year community and technical college
⬧ Commuter campus in large town

General. Founded in 1965. Regionally accredited. **Enrollment:** 4,324 degree-seeking undergraduates. **Degrees:** 556 associate awarded. **Location:** 75 miles from Boston. **Calendar:** Semester, extensive summer session. **Full-time faculty:** 130 total. **Part-time faculty:** 200 total. **Special facilities:** Planetarium, wellness center. **Partnerships:** Formal partnerships with New Hampshire businesses for internships, practicums, and clinicals.

Student profile.

Out-of-state:	2%	Live on campus:	8%

Transfer out. Colleges most students transferred to 2011: University of New Hampshire, Southern New Hampshire University, Plymouth State College, Keene State College, Granite State College.

Basis for selection. Open admission, but selective for some programs. Requirements vary by program. Nursing and allied health programs require special testing and interviews. National League for Nursing Pre-Nursing Test, special challenge test for practical nursing required. Institutional assessment test required of all students. Interview required for health program applicants, recommended for others. **Home schooled:** Transcript of courses and grades required. Must submit portfolio of work approved by school district.

High school preparation. Recommended units include English 4, mathematics 3 and science 2. High school academic subject requirements vary according to program. Strong background in mathematics and natural sciences recommended.

2011-2012 Annual costs. Tuition/fees: $6,900; $14,940 out-of-state. Per-credit charge: $210 in-state; $478 out-of-state. New England Regional tuition: $315 per credit hour. Room/board: $8,336. Books/supplies: $600. Personal expenses: $1,600.

Financial aid. All financial aid based on need. Need-based aid available for part-time students. Work-study available nights, weekends and for part-time students. **Additional information:** 60% of students who apply receive some form of financial aid. State school; all financial aid need-based, primarily from federal sources. No scholarships awarded.

Application procedures. Admission: No deadline. $20 fee, may be waived for applicants with need. Admission notification on a rolling basis. Must reply by May 1 or within 4 week(s) if notified thereafter. Applicants must make a $100 deposit within 30 days of acceptance. **Financial aid:** Priority date 5/1; no closing date. FAFSA, institutional form required. Applicants notified on a rolling basis starting 6/1; must reply within 2 week(s) of notification.

Academics. Support services available for ESOL students and students with declared disabilities. **Special study options:** Distance learning, double major, dual enrollment of high school students, ESL, honors, internships, teacher certification program. License preparation in dental hygiene, nursing, paramedic, radiology, real estate. **Credit/placement by examination:** AP, CLEP, IB, institutional tests. **Support services:** Learning center, pre-admission summer program, reduced course load, remedial instruction, study skills assistance, tutoring, writing center.

Majors. Business: Accounting, business admin, hospitality admin, hospitality/recreation, marketing, tourism promotion, tourism/travel. **Communications technology:** General. **Computer sciences:** Information technology. **Education:** General, early childhood, special ed. **Health services:** Dental hygiene, EMT paramedic, nursing (RN), radiologic technology/medical imaging, sonography, substance abuse counseling. **Liberal arts:** Arts/sciences. **Parks/recreation:** Sports admin. **Protective services:** Law enforcement admin.

Most popular majors. Business/marketing 15%, computer/information sciences 7%, engineering/engineering technologies 14%, health sciences 39%, liberal arts 8%, security/protective services 7%.

Computing on campus. 225 workstations in dormitories, library, computer center. Dormitories wired for high-speed internet access. Helpline, wireless network available.

Student life. Freshman orientation: Mandatory, $25 fee. Preregistration for classes offered. Session held before start of semester. **Housing:** Coed dorms, wellness housing available. $300 deposit. **Activities:** Drama, literary magazine, musical theater, student government, NHTI alliance, environmental action, Phi Theta Kappa, student nurses association, human service club, alternative spring break, criminal justice club, Christian club, cultural exchange club.

Athletics. Intercollegiate: Baseball M, basketball, soccer, softball W, volleyball. **Intramural:** Basketball, football (non-tackle) M, volleyball. **Team name:** Capitals.

Student services. Career counseling, financial aid counseling, health services, on-campus daycare, personal counseling, placement for graduates, veterans' counselor. **Physically disabled:** Services for visually, speech, hearing impaired. **Transfer:** Pre-admission transcript evaluation for new students. Transfer adviser, college fairs on campus for students transferring to 4-year colleges.

Contact. E-mail: nhtiadm@nhctc.edu
Phone: (603) 271-7134 Toll-free number: (800) 247-0179
Fax: (603) 271-7139
Frank Meyer, Director of Admissions, NHTI-Concord's Community College, 31 College Drive, Concord, NH 03301

River Valley Community College
Claremont, New Hampshire
www.rivervalley.edu   **CB code: 3684**

⬧ Public 2-year community college
⬧ Commuter campus in large town

General. Founded in 1967. Regionally accredited. **Enrollment:** 791 degree-seeking undergraduates. **Degrees:** 138 associate awarded. **Location:** 50 miles from Concord. **Calendar:** Semester, limited summer session. **Full-time faculty:** 26 total. **Part-time faculty:** 76 total.

Basis for selection. Open admission, but selective for some programs. ACCUPLACER test used for placement. Special requirements for nursing program.

High school preparation. Typing required for medical assistant, chemistry required for nursing and medical laboratory programs. Algebra recommended for all applicants.

2011-2012 Annual costs. Tuition/fees: $6,450; $14,490 out-of-state. Per-credit charge: $210 in-state; $478 out-of-state. New England Regional tuition: $315 per credit hour. Books/supplies: $550. Personal expenses: $1,100.

Financial aid. All financial aid based on need. Need-based aid available for part-time students. Work-study available nights, weekends and for part-time students.

Application procedures. Admission: No deadline. $20 fee, may be waived for applicants with need. Admission notification on a rolling basis. **Financial aid:** Closing date 5/1. FAFSA required. Applicants notified on a rolling basis; must reply within 2 week(s) of notification.

Academics. Special study options: Accelerated study, cooperative education, distance learning, double major, independent study, internships, student-designed major. Joint associate degree program in restaurant management with Les Roches, 2-2 program in teacher education with Keene State College. **Credit/placement by examination:** AP, CLEP, institutional tests. 16 credit hours maximum toward associate degree. **Support services:** Learning center, reduced course load, study skills assistance, tutoring.

Majors. Business: General, accounting, office technology. **Health services:** Clinical lab technology, nursing (RN), occupational therapy assistant, physical therapy assistant, respiratory therapy technology. **Liberal arts:** Arts/sciences. **Parks/recreation:** General. **Work/family studies:** General, child care service.

Most popular majors. Health sciences 87%.

Computing on campus. 45 workstations in library, computer center. Wireless network available.

Student life. Freshman orientation: Available, $30 fee. Preregistration for classes offered. **Activities:** Student government.

Student services. Adult student services, student employment services, financial aid counseling, veterans' counselor.

Contact. Phone: (603) 542-7744 Toll-free number: (800) 837-0658 Fax: (603) 543-1844
Chuck Kusselow, Director of Admissions, River Valley Community College, One College Drive, Claremont, NH 03743-9707

White Mountains Community College
Berlin, New Hampshire
www.wmcc.edu   CB code: 3646

- Public 2-year community college
- Commuter campus in large town

General. Founded in 1966. Regionally accredited. **Enrollment:** 790 degree-seeking undergraduates; 132 non-degree-seeking students. **Degrees:** 140 associate awarded. **Location:** 110 miles from Concord; 100 miles from Portland, Maine. **Calendar:** Semester, limited summer session. **Full-time faculty:** 30 total. **Part-time faculty:** 225 total.

Student profile. Among degree-seeking undergraduates, 189 enrolled as first-time, first-year students.

Part-time:	56%	Women:	65%

Basis for selection. Open admission, but selective for some programs. Pre-admission exam required for nursing students; ACCUPLACER required for placement for all others. **Home schooled:** Statement describing home school structure and mission, transcript of courses and grades, state high school equivalency certificate required.

2011-2012 Annual costs. Tuition/fees: $6,840; $14,880 out-of-state. Per-credit charge: $210 in-state; $478 out-of-state. New England Regional tuition: $315 per credit hour. Books/supplies: $1,500.

2010-2011 Financial aid. All financial aid based on need. 43% of total undergraduate aid awarded as scholarships/grants, 57% as loans/jobs. Need-based aid available for part-time students. Work-study available nights, weekends and for part-time students.

Application procedures. Admission: No deadline. $20 fee, may be waived for applicants with need. Admission notification on a rolling basis. **Financial aid:** Priority date 5/1; no closing date. FAFSA, institutional form required. Applicants notified on a rolling basis starting 5/1; must reply within 2 week(s) of notification.

Academics. Special study options: Cooperative education, double major, dual enrollment of high school students, independent study, internships, student-designed major. Bachelor's degree programs available on campus. **Credit/placement by examination:** AP, CLEP, institutional tests. **Support services:** Learning center, reduced course load, remedial instruction, study skills assistance, tutoring.

Majors. Business: Accounting, administrative services, business admin, office management, office technology, office/clerical, restaurant/food services. **Computer sciences:** General. **Conservation:** Environmental science. **Education:** Early childhood, multi-level teacher. **Health services:** Nursing (RN), office admin. **Liberal arts:** Arts/sciences. **Protective services:** Law enforcement admin.

Computing on campus. 45 workstations in library, computer center. Online course registration, online library, wireless network available.

Student life. Freshman orientation: Mandatory, $30 fee. Preregistration for classes offered. **Activities:** Student government.

Student services. Adult student services, career counseling, financial aid counseling, on-campus daycare, personal counseling, veterans' counselor. **Physically disabled:** Services for visually, hearing impaired. **Transfer:** Transfer adviser for students transferring to 4-year colleges.

Contact. E-mail: wmcc@ccsnh.edu
Phone: (603) 752-1113 Toll-free number: (800) 445-4525
Fax: (603) 752-6335
Mark Desmarais, Admissions Director, White Mountains Community College, 2020 Riverside Drive, Berlin, NH 03570

New Jersey

Assumption College for Sisters
Mendham, New Jersey
www.acs350.org   CB code: 2009

▶ Private 2-year junior and liberal arts college for women affiliated with Roman Catholic Church
▶ Residential campus in small town
▶ Application essay required

General. Founded in 1953. Regionally accredited. **Enrollment:** 30 degree-seeking undergraduates; 10 non-degree-seeking students. **Degrees:** 10 associate awarded. **Location:** 35 miles from New York City. **Calendar:** Semester, limited summer session. **Part-time faculty:** 12 total; 17% have terminal degrees, 92% women. **Class size:** 100% < 20.

Student profile. Among degree-seeking undergraduates, 12% already have a bachelor's degree or higher, 9 enrolled as first-time, first-year students.

Part-time:	13%	International:	93%
Women:	100%	25 or older:	97%
Hispanic American:	3%		

Basis for selection. Interview, recommendations, school achievement record, test scores, commitment to obligations of religious vocation as well as acceptance of applicant by a religious community important.

High school preparation. 16 units required. Required and recommended units include English 4, mathematics 2-3, history 2, science 2-3, foreign language 2, visual/performing arts 1 and academic electives 4.

2011-2012 Annual costs. Tuition/fees: $5,000. Per-credit charge: $150. International summer students may request assistance with off-campus housing in homes of parishioners or with Sisters of Christian Charity. Books/supplies: $101.

2010-2011 Financial aid. Need-based: Work-study available nights, weekends and for part-time students.

Application procedures. Admission: No deadline. $50 fee, may be waived for applicants with need. Admission notification on a rolling basis. **Financial aid:** No deadline.

Academics. Special study options: ESL. **Credit/placement by examination:** AP, CLEP, SAT. **Support services:** Reduced course load, remedial instruction, study skills assistance, tutoring.

Majors. Liberal arts: Arts/sciences. **Theology:** Theology.

Computing on campus. 21 workstations in library, computer center, student center. Online library, helpline, repair service, wireless network available.

Student life. Freshman orientation: Mandatory. Preregistration for classes offered. **Policies:** Students reside with their religious congregations or with the Sisters of Christian Charity. Religious observance required.

Student services. Transfer: Pre-admission transcript evaluation for new students. Transfer adviser for students transferring to 4-year colleges.

Contact. E-mail: deanregistrar@acs350.org
Phone: (973) 543-6528 ext. 228 Fax: (973) 543-1738
Sr. Gerardine Tantsits, Academic Dean/Registrar, Assumption College for Sisters, 350 Bernardsville Road, Mendham, NJ 07945-2923

Atlantic Cape Community College
Mays Landing, New Jersey   CB member
www.atlantic.edu   CB code: 2024

▶ Public 2-year culinary school and community college
▶ Commuter campus in small town

General. Founded in 1964. Regionally accredited. Instruction and student/academic support services delivered at all 3 campuses (Mays Landing, Atlantic City, Cape May). **Enrollment:** 7,034 degree-seeking undergraduates; 558 non-degree-seeking students. **Degrees:** 871 associate awarded. **Location:** 15 miles from Atlantic City, 49 miles from Philadelphia. **Calendar:** Semester, limited summer session. **Full-time faculty:** 80 total. **Part-time faculty:** 282 total. **Class size:** 42% < 20, 57% 20-39, less than 1% 40-49, less than 1% 50-99. **Special facilities:** Gourmet student-run restaurant.

Student profile. Among degree-seeking undergraduates, 1,556 enrolled as first-time, first-year students, 236 transferred in from other institutions.

Part-time:	56%	Asian American:	8%
Women:	58%	Hispanic American:	14%
African American:	14%	25 or older:	32%

Transfer out. 67% of students enrolled in the transfer program go on to 4-year colleges. **Colleges most students transferred to 2011:** Richard Stockton State College of New Jersey, Rowan University, Rutgers University.

Basis for selection. Open admission, but selective for some programs. Admission to allied health and nursing programs based upon entrance exam scores and GPA. ACCUPLACER exam used for placement only. All students must take college basic skills exam after completing 12th credit or when they officially matriculate. Students who score 500 on SAT Verbal, and 470 on SAT Math exempt from basic skills testing. **Home schooled:** Students must be in certified homeschooling program. Letter from certifying school district approving courses required. **Learning Disabled:** Student must self-identify.

2011-2012 Annual costs. Tuition/fees: $3,558; $6,474 out-of-district; $12,306 out-of-state. Per-credit charge: $97 in-district; $194 out-of-district; $389 out-of-state. Books/supplies: $1,600.

2010-2011 Financial aid. Need-based: Need-based aid available for part-time students. Work-study available nights, weekends and for part-time students. **Additional information:** Installment plan available for culinary arts majors. Employees of Atlantic City casinos may attend ACCC at in-county rates regardless of residence.

Application procedures. Admission: No deadline. $35 fee, may be waived for applicants with need. Admission notification on a rolling basis. **Financial aid:** Priority date 5/1; no closing date. FAFSA, institutional form required. Applicants notified on a rolling basis starting 5/1.

Academics. 15 associate degrees available through distance education. **Special study options:** Cooperative education, distance learning, double major, dual enrollment of high school students, ESL, independent study, internships, liberal arts/career combination. Bachelor's degree programs available on campus. License preparation in nursing, paramedic, real estate. **Credit/placement by examination:** AP, CLEP, institutional tests. 32 credit hours maximum toward associate degree. **Support services:** GED preparation and test center, learning center, pre-admission summer program, reduced course load, remedial instruction, study skills assistance, tutoring, writing center.

Majors. Business: Accounting, administrative services, business admin, hotel/motel admin, management information systems. **Computer sciences:** Data processing, programming. **Health services:** Nursing (RN), respiratory therapy technology. **Liberal arts:** Arts/sciences. **Protective services:** Police science.

Most popular majors. Business/marketing 13%, education 7%, health sciences 7%, liberal arts 36%, security/protective services 6%.

Computing on campus. 635 workstations in library, computer center, student center. Commuter students can connect to campus network. Online course registration, online library, helpline, wireless network available.

Student life. Freshman orientation: Available. Preregistration for classes offered. Online orentation available. **Activities:** Choral groups, drama, international student organizations, literary magazine, music ensembles, radio station, student government, student newspaper, human services club, African American coalition, Jewish association of students, Phi Theta Kappa, Alpha and Omega Christian clubs, Shades of Brown of Atlantic City.

Athletics. NJCAA. **Intercollegiate:** Archery, baseball M, basketball, soccer M, softball W, volleyball W. **Intramural:** Basketball, bowling, soccer, softball, volleyball. **Team name:** Buccaneers.

Student services. Adult student services, career counseling, student employment services, health services, on-campus daycare, personal counseling, placement for graduates, veterans' counselor. **Physically disabled:** Services for visually, speech, hearing impaired. **Transfer:** Pre-admission transcript evaluation for new students. Transfer adviser, college fairs on campus for students transferring to 4-year colleges.

Contact. E-mail: accadmit@atlantic.edu
Phone: (609) 343-5000 Fax: (609) 343-4921
Regina Skinner, Director, Admission and College Recruitment, Atlantic
Cape Community College, 5100 Black Horse Pike, Mays Landing, NJ
08330-2699

Bergen Community College
Paramus, New Jersey
www.bergen.edu
CB code: 2032

- Public 2-year community college
- Commuter campus in large town

General. Founded in 1965. Regionally accredited. Center for Deaf Education with counselors and specialized equipment. **Enrollment:** 17,271 degree-seeking undergraduates. **Degrees:** 1,953 associate awarded. **Location:** 12 miles from New York City. **Calendar:** Semester, extensive summer session. **Full-time faculty:** 346 total. **Part-time faculty:** 666 total.

Transfer out. Colleges most students transferred to 2011: Montclair State University, William Paterson University, Rutgers University, Ramapo College.

Basis for selection. Open admission, but selective for some programs. Admission to allied health programs based on academic record and specific courses taken. Priority given to county residents. High school diploma not required for students over 18 years old. **Learning Disabled:** Students must provide documentation of disability to Office of Specialized Services.

High school preparation. Math, biology, chemistry required for most allied health programs.

2011-2012 Annual costs. Tuition/fees: $4,914; $9,030 out-of-district; $9,420 out-of-state. Per-credit charge: $125 in-district; $262 out-of-district; $275 out-of-state. Books/supplies: $1,200.

Financial aid. Need-based: Work-study available nights, weekends and for part-time students.

Application procedures. Admission: No deadline. No application fee. Admission notification on a rolling basis. Application closing date for nursing and dental hygiene March 1. **Financial aid:** No deadline. FAFSA required. Applicants notified on a rolling basis starting 6/1.

Academics. Special study options: Cooperative education, distance learning, dual enrollment of high school students, ESL, honors, internships, study abroad. **Credit/placement by examination:** AP, CLEP, institutional tests. **Support services:** Learning center, pre-admission summer program, reduced course load, remedial instruction, tutoring, writing center.

Majors. Area/ethnic studies: Women's. **Biology:** General, biotechnology. **Business:** Accounting technology, administrative services, banking/financial services, hotel/motel admin, marketing, sales/distribution, special products marketing. **Communications:** Communications/speech/rhetoric, journalism. **Communications technology:** Animation/special effects, radio/TV, recording arts. **Computer sciences:** General, applications programming, computer graphics, information technology, system admin. **Conservation:** Environmental science. **Education:** General, early childhood. **Engineering:** General. **English:** English lit. **Foreign languages:** General. **General:** Horticulture. **Health services:** Clinical lab technology, dental hygiene, medical assistant, medical radiologic technology/radiation therapy, nursing (RN), physical therapy assistant, respiratory therapy technology, sonography, veterinary technology/assistant. **History:** General. **Liberal arts:** Arts/sciences. **Math:** General. **Philosophy/religion:** Philosophy, religion. **Physical sciences:** General, chemistry, physics. **Protective services:** Corrections, police science. **Psychology:** General. **Social sciences:** Economics, sociology. **Visual/performing arts:** General, commercial/advertising art, film/cinema/video, music, theater arts management.

Most popular majors. Health sciences 21%, liberal arts 62%.

Student life. Freshman orientation: Available. Preregistration for classes offered. **Activities:** Choral groups, dance, drama, literary magazine, music ensembles, musical theater, student government, student newspaper, TV station.

Athletics. NJCAA. **Intercollegiate:** Baseball M, basketball, cross-country, golf M, soccer M, softball W, tennis M, track and field, volleyball W, wrestling M. **Team name:** Bulldogs.

Student services. Career counseling, student employment services, financial aid counseling, health services, on-campus daycare, personal counseling, placement for graduates, veterans' counselor. **Physically disabled:** Services

for visually, speech, hearing impaired. **Transfer:** Transfer adviser, college fairs on campus for students transferring to 4-year colleges.

Contact. E-mail: admsoffice@bergen.edu
Phone: (201) 447-7195 Fax: (201) 670-7973
Office of Enrollment Services, Bergen Community College, 400 Paramus Road, Paramus, NJ 07652-1595

Brookdale Community College
Lincroft, New Jersey
www.brookdalecc.edu
CB member
CB code: 2181

- Public 2-year community college
- Commuter campus in small city

General. Founded in 1967. Regionally accredited. **Enrollment:** 13,194 degree-seeking undergraduates; 1,758 non-degree-seeking students. **Degrees:** 1,946 associate awarded. **ROTC:** Army, Air Force. **Location:** 5 miles from Red Bank, 25 miles from New Brunswick. **Calendar:** Semester, extensive summer session. **Full-time faculty:** 234 total; 11% minority, 57% women. **Part-time faculty:** 722 total; 11% minority, 58% women.

Student profile. Among degree-seeking undergraduates, 65% enrolled in a transfer program, 35% enrolled in a vocational program, 1% already have a bachelor's degree or higher.

Part-time:	38%	Asian American:	3%
Out-of-state:	1%	Hispanic American:	12%
Women:	53%	International:	1%
African American:	11%	25 or older:	38%

Transfer out. 68% of students enrolled in the transfer program go on to 4-year colleges. **Colleges most students transferred to 2011:** Monmouth University, Rutgers University, Kean University.

Basis for selection. Open admission, but selective for some programs. Special requirements for culinary, dental hygiene, nursing, respiratory therapy, radiologic technology, and automotive technology. Applicants 18 or older may be admitted without high school diploma or GED.

High school preparation. One unit high school or college algebra, 1 chemistry, 1 biology required for allied health programs.

2011-2012 Annual costs. Tuition/fees: $4,408; $7,963 out-of-district; $8,713 out-of-state. Per-credit charge: $119 in-district; $237 out-of-district; $262 out-of-state. Books/supplies: $1,200. Personal expenses: $4,370.

Financial aid. Need-based: Need-based aid available for part-time students. Work-study available nights, weekends and for part-time students. **Non-need-based:** Scholarships awarded for academics, athletics.

Application procedures. Admission: No deadline. $25 fee. Admission notification on a rolling basis. **Financial aid:** Priority date 5/1; no closing date. FAFSA, institutional form required. Applicants notified on a rolling basis starting 5/1; must reply within 2 week(s) of notification.

Academics. Special study options: Cooperative education, distance learning, dual enrollment of high school students, ESL, honors, independent study, internships, study abroad. License preparation in dental hygiene, nursing, radiology. **Credit/placement by examination:** AP, CLEP, institutional tests. **Support services:** GED preparation and test center, reduced course load, remedial instruction, tutoring, writing center.

Majors. Architecture: Architecture. **Business:** General, accounting technology, business admin, fashion, marketing. **Communications technology:** Animation/special effects, radio/TV. **Computer sciences:** General, system admin. **Education:** General, teacher assistance. **Engineering:** General. **Health services:** Clinical lab technology, dental hygiene, medical radiologic technology/radiation therapy, medical records technology, nursing (RN), respiratory therapy technology, sonography. **Human services:** Social work. **Liberal arts:** Arts/sciences. **Protective services:** Police science. **Social sciences:** General. **Visual/performing arts:** Graphic design, interior design, music technology, studio arts.

Computing on campus. 1,100 workstations in library, computer center. Commuter students can connect to campus network. Helpline, wireless network available.

Student life. Freshman orientation: Available. Preregistration for classes offered. **Activities:** Dance, drama, film society, literary magazine, musical theater, radio station, student government, student newspaper, TV station.

Athletics. NJCAA. **Intercollegiate:** Baseball M, basketball, cross-country, soccer, softball W, tennis. **Intramural:** Basketball, golf M, volleyball. **Team name:** Blues.

Student services. Career counseling, student employment services, financial aid counseling, health services, on-campus daycare, personal counseling, placement for graduates, veterans' counselor. **Physically disabled:** Services for visually, speech, hearing impaired. **Transfer:** Transfer adviser for students transferring to 4-year colleges.

Contact. E-mail: recruitment@brookdalecc.edu
Phone: (732) 224-2375 Fax: (732) 224-2271
Kim Toomey, Registrar, Brookdale Community College, 765 Newman Springs Road, Lincroft, NJ 07738

Burlington County College
Pemberton, New Jersey
www.bcc.edu

CB member
CB code: 2180

▶ Public 2-year community college
▶ Commuter campus in small town

General. Founded in 1966. Regionally accredited. Credit courses offered at main campus in Pemberton, Mount Laurel Campus, Willingboro Center, Mount Holly Center, educational centers at Bordentown Regional High School and McGuire AFB, as well as various other county high schools. **Enrollment:** 9,341 degree-seeking undergraduates; 937 non-degree-seeking students. **Degrees:** 1,263 associate awarded. **Location:** 30 miles from Philadelphia, 80 miles from New York City. **Calendar:** Semester, limited summer session. **Full-time faculty:** 55 total; 14% minority, 47% women. **Part-time faculty:** 403 total; 17% minority, 54% women. **Class size:** 20% < 20, 68% 20-39, 4% 40-49, 7% 50-99. **Special facilities:** Culinary arts, hospitality and tourism facility, sculpture garden, outdoor amphitheatre, small business science and high technology incubators, NASA laboratory. **Partnerships:** Formal partnerships with Police Academy, Global Corporate College.

Student profile. Among degree-seeking undergraduates, 2,303 enrolled as first-time, first-year students.

Part-time:	43%	Women:	58%
Out-of-state:	1%	25 or older:	31%

Transfer out. Colleges most students transferred to 2011: Rutgers University, Richard Stockton College of New Jersey, Rowan University, Drexel University, Rider University.

Basis for selection. Open admission, but selective for some programs. Academic high school background required of nursing program applicants. Criminal background check required for all allied health students.

2011-2012 Annual costs. Tuition/fees: $3,615; $4,095 out-of-district; $6,045 out-of-state. Per-credit charge: $92 in-district; $108 out-of-district; $173 out-of-state. Special Rates for Culinary courses. Books/supplies: $1,200. Personal expenses: $1,610.

2011-2012 Financial aid. All financial aid based on need. Need-based aid available for part-time students. Work-study available nights, weekends and for part-time students.

Application procedures. Admission: No deadline. $20 fee, may be waived for applicants with need, free for online applicants. Admission notification on a rolling basis. **Financial aid:** No deadline. FAFSA required. Applicants notified on a rolling basis.

Academics. Special study options: Cooperative education, distance learning, double major, dual enrollment of high school students, ESL, independent study, study abroad, weekend college. Bachelor's degree programs available on campus. License preparation in dental hygiene, nursing, radiology. **Credit/placement by examination:** AP, CLEP, institutional tests. 30 credit hours maximum toward associate degree. **Support services:** GED preparation and test center, learning center, pre-admission summer program, reduced course load, remedial instruction, study skills assistance, tutoring, writing center.

Majors. Biology: Biotechnology. **Business:** General, accounting, accounting technology, business admin, hospitality admin, management information systems, real estate, restaurant/food services, sales/distribution. **Communications technology:** Animation/special effects, photo/film/video. **Computer sciences:** Computer graphics, computer science, data processing, information systems. **Foreign languages:** Sign language interpretation. **General:** Agribusiness operations. **Health services:** Dental hygiene, medical radiologic technology/radiation therapy, medical records technology, nursing (RN), respiratory therapy technology, sonography. **Liberal arts:** Arts/sciences. **Physical sciences:** General. **Protective services:** Firefighting, police science. **Social sciences:** GIS/cartography. **Visual/performing arts:** Art, fashion design, graphic design, music, photography.

Most popular majors. Security/protective services 6%.

Computing on campus. 1,600 workstations in library, computer center, student center. Commuter students can connect to campus network. Online library, helpline, wireless network available.

Student life. Freshman orientation: Available. Preregistration for classes offered. **Activities:** Concert band, choral groups, dance, drama, international student organizations, literary magazine, music ensembles, musical theater, radio station, student government, minority student union, veterans club, Phi Theta Kappa, student nurses association, Collegiate Republicans, Young Democrats, Circle K, students for ecological action, Christian student club.

Athletics. NJCAA. **Intercollegiate:** Baseball M, basketball, golf M, soccer, softball W. **Team name:** Barons.

Student services. Adult student services, career counseling, services for economically disadvantaged, student employment services, financial aid counseling, health services, minority student services, placement for graduates, veterans' counselor. **Physically disabled:** Services for visually, speech, hearing impaired. **Transfer:** Transfer center, transfer adviser, college fairs on campus for students transferring to 4-year colleges.

Contact. Phone: (609) 894-9311 ext. 1200 Fax: (609) 894-8356
Mary Lou Mascarin, Executive Director, Enrollment Management and Marketing, Burlington County College, 601 Pemberton-Browns Mills Road, Pemberton, NJ 08068-1599

Camden County College
Blackwood, New Jersey
www.camdencc.edu

CB member
CB code: 2121

▶ Public 2-year community college
▶ Commuter campus in large town

General. Founded in 1966. Regionally accredited. Additional campus locations in Camden and Cherry Hill. **Enrollment:** 14,259 degree-seeking undergraduates. **Degrees:** 1,727 associate awarded. **Location:** 15 miles from Philadelphia, 13 miles from Camden. **Calendar:** Semester, extensive summer session. **Full-time faculty:** 138 total. **Part-time faculty:** 617 total. **Special facilities:** Integrated manufacturing building, laser technology institute for education and research, computer graphics laboratories.

Student profile.

Out-of-state:	1%	25 or older:	39%

Transfer out. Colleges most students transferred to 2011: Rowan University, Rutgers University-Camden, Temple University, Widener University.

Basis for selection. Open admission, but selective for some programs. Special requirements for allied health, dental, and nursing programs. Interview recommended for various health programs and the General Motors programs.

2011-2012 Annual costs. Tuition/fees: $3,990; $4,110 out-of-district; $6,060 out-of-state. Per-credit charge: $101 in-district; $105 out-of-district; $170 out-of-state.

Financial aid. Need-based: Need-based aid available for part-time students. Work-study available nights, weekends and for part-time students.

Application procedures. Admission: No deadline. No application fee. Admission notification on a rolling basis beginning on or about 2/3. **Financial aid:** Priority date 5/1, closing date 7/1. FAFSA, institutional form required. Applicants notified on a rolling basis starting 7/1.

Academics. Strong program in robotics, laser/electro optics technology, and computer graphics. **Special study options:** Cooperative education, cross-registration, distance learning, double major, dual enrollment of high school students, ESL, honors, independent study, internships, liberal arts/career combination, weekend college. General Motors automotive service education program. License preparation in dental hygiene, nursing, paramedic, real estate. **Credit/placement by examination:** AP, CLEP, institutional tests. 30 credit hours maximum toward associate degree. New Jersey College Basic Skills placement test required. **Support services:** GED preparation and test center, learning center, pre-admission summer program, reduced course load, remedial instruction, study skills assistance, tutoring.

Majors. Business: Accounting, banking/financial services, business admin, management information systems, marketing, sales/distribution. **Computer sciences:** General, computer graphics. **Engineering:** Engineering science. **Foreign languages:** Sign language interpretation. **Health services:** Clinical lab technology, dental assistant, dental hygiene, nursing (RN), optician, respiratory therapy technology, veterinary technology/assistant. **Human services:** Social work. **Liberal arts:** Arts/sciences. **Protective services:** Fire safety technology, police science. **Visual/performing arts:** Photography.

Computing on campus. 800 workstations in library, computer center. Online course registration, online library, wireless network available.

Student life. Freshman orientation: Available. Preregistration for classes offered. **Activities:** Concert band, choral groups, dance, drama, international student organizations, literary magazine, music ensembles, radio station, student government, student newspaper.

Athletics. NJCAA. **Intercollegiate:** Baseball M, basketball, soccer, softball W. **Team name:** Cougars.

Student services. Career counseling, student employment services, financial aid counseling, health services, on-campus daycare, placement for graduates, veterans' counselor. **Physically disabled:** Services for visually, speech, hearing impaired. **Transfer:** Re-entry adviser, pre-admission transcript evaluation for new students. Transfer center, transfer adviser, college fairs on campus for students transferring to 4-year colleges.

Contact. Phone: (856) 227-7200 ext. 4200
Toll-free number: (888) 228-2466 Fax: (856) 374-4917
Sharon Wedington, Admissions Director, Camden County College, Box 200, Blackwood, NJ 08012

County College of Morris
Randolph, New Jersey
www.ccm.edu

CB member
CB code: 2124

- Public 2-year community college
- Commuter campus in small city

General. Founded in 1965. Regionally accredited. Courses available at off-campus sites. **Enrollment:** 7,470 degree-seeking undergraduates; 1,084 non-degree-seeking students. **Degrees:** 1,130 associate awarded. **Location:** 40 miles from New York City. **Calendar:** Semester, extensive summer session. **Full-time faculty:** 166 total. **Part-time faculty:** 373 total. **Special facilities:** Planetarium.

Student profile. Among degree-seeking undergraduates, 66% enrolled in a transfer program, 34% enrolled in a vocational program, 1,865 enrolled as first-time, first-year students, 521 transferred in from other institutions.

Part-time:	40%	Women:	48%
Out-of-state:	1%	25 or older:	25%

Transfer out. Colleges most students transferred to 2011: Montclair State University, William Paterson University of New Jersey, Rutgers University, Kean University, Fairleigh Dickinson University, New Jersey Institute of Technology.

Basis for selection. Open admission, but selective for some programs. Restricted admissions to nursing, medical lab technology, radiography, respiratory therapy, and veterinary technology on space-available basis. Applicants who are not native speakers of English required to take LOEP test (Levels of English Proficiency) for placement. SAT required for honors programs. Students who submit SAT section scores of 500 exempt from basic skills placement test. Audition required for music programs. **Adult students:** Placements test required for all students, however students are exempt if they have 540 SAT Critical Reading or 530 SAT Math. **Learning Disabled:** Students may apply to Horizons program if they want accommodations.

High school preparation. 16 units recommended. Some programs require 2 to 4 units math and 1 to 2 units laboratory science.

2011-2012 Annual costs. Tuition/fees: $4,088; $7,508 out-of-district; $10,388 out-of-state. Per-credit charge: $115 in-district; $230 out-of-district; $326 out-of-state. Books/supplies: $100. Personal expenses: $1,220.

Financial aid. Need-based: Need-based aid available for part-time students. Work-study available nights, weekends and for part-time students. **Non-need-based:** Scholarships awarded for athletics.

Application procedures. Admission: No deadline. $30 fee. Admission notification on a rolling basis. **Financial aid:** Priority date 3/1; no closing date. FAFSA required. Applicants notified on a rolling basis starting 5/1.

Academics. Special study options: Accelerated study, cooperative education, distance learning, double major, dual enrollment of high school students, ESL, exchange student, external degree, honors, independent study, internships, liberal arts/career combination, study abroad, teacher certification program, weekend college. License preparation in aviation, nursing, radiology. **Credit/placement by examination:** AP, CLEP, institutional tests. **Support services:** GED preparation, learning center, pre-admission summer program, reduced course load, remedial instruction, study skills assistance, tutoring, writing center.

Majors. Business: Business admin, management information systems. **Communications:** Journalism. **Communications technology:** General. **Computer sciences:** General. **Education:** Biology, chemistry, drama/dance, early childhood, French, German, history, physics, Spanish. **Engineering:** Engineering science. **General:** Business. **Health services:** Clinical lab technology, nursing (RN), respiratory therapy technology. **Human services:** General. **Liberal arts:** Arts/sciences. **Math:** General. **Parks/recreation:** Health/fitness. **Protective services:** Police science. **Social sciences:** General. **Visual/performing arts:** General.

Computing on campus. 650 workstations in library, computer center. Commuter students can connect to campus network. Online course registration, online library, helpline, wireless network available.

Student life. Freshman orientation: Available. Preregistration for classes offered. Half-day sessions held 1 week prior to start of academic year. **Activities:** Bands, campus ministries, choral groups, dance, drama, international student organizations, literary magazine, music ensembles, musical theater, radio station, student government, student newspaper, symphony orchestra, Phi Theta Kappa, United Latino organization, student ambassadors, black student union, Asian students association, Jewish students association, Christian Fellowship, IEEE, Muslim student club, Alpha Beta Gamma.

Athletics. NJCAA. **Intercollegiate:** Baseball M, basketball, golf, ice hockey M, lacrosse M, soccer, softball W, tennis M, volleyball W. **Intramural:** Badminton, basketball, bowling, football (non-tackle), soccer W, softball, table tennis, volleyball. **Team name:** Titans.

Student services. Adult student services, alcohol/substance abuse counseling, career counseling, services for economically disadvantaged, student employment services, financial aid counseling, health services, minority student services, on-campus daycare, personal counseling, placement for graduates, veterans' counselor, women's services. **Physically disabled:** Services for visually, hearing impaired. **Transfer:** Pre-admission transcript evaluation for new students. Transfer adviser, college fairs on campus for students transferring to 4-year colleges.

Contact. E-mail: admis@ccm.edu
Phone: (973) 328-5100 Fax: (973) 328-5199
Jessica Chambers, Director of Admissions, County College of Morris, 214 Center Grove Road, Randolph, NJ 07869-2086

Cumberland County College
Vineland, New Jersey
www.cccnj.edu

CB member
CB code: 2118

- Public 2-year community college
- Commuter campus in small city

General. Founded in 1963. Regionally accredited. **Enrollment:** 4,188 degree-seeking undergraduates. **Degrees:** 555 associate awarded. **Location:** 35 miles from Philadelphia. **Calendar:** Semester, extensive summer session. **Full-time faculty:** 50 total. **Part-time faculty:** 258 total. **Class size:** 47% < 20, 46% 20-39, 6% 40-49, less than 1% 50-99. **Special facilities:** Fine and performing arts center, conference center.

Transfer out. Colleges most students transferred to 2011: Rowan University, Stockton State College, Rutgers University, University of Delaware.

Basis for selection. Open admission, but selective for some programs. Special requirements for nursing program; National League for Nursing pre-entrance examination required.

High school preparation. College-preparatory program recommended.

2011-2012 Annual costs. Tuition/fees: $4,020; $6,420 out-of-district; $13,470 out-of-state. Per-credit charge: $105 in-district; $185 out-of-district; $420 out-of-state. Students who provide proof of residence may get out of county per credit hour charge-back rate of $115. Books/supplies: $1,300. Personal expenses: $2,006.

Financial aid. Need-based: Need-based aid available for part-time students. Work-study available nights, weekends and for part-time students. **Non-need-based:** Scholarships awarded for academics.

Application procedures. Admission: No deadline. $25 fee, may be waived for applicants with need. Admission notification on a rolling basis. **Financial aid:** No deadline. FAFSA required. Applicants notified on a rolling basis; must reply within 3 week(s) of notification.

Academics. Special study options: Accelerated study, distance learning, double major, dual enrollment of high school students, ESL, honors, independent study. Project Assist for students with learning disabilities. Bachelor's

Two-Year Colleges

degree programs available on campus. License preparation in nursing, radiology. **Credit/placement by examination:** AP, CLEP, institutional tests. 32 credit hours maximum toward associate degree. **Support services:** GED preparation and test center, learning center, pre-admission summer program, reduced course load, remedial instruction, study skills assistance, tutoring, writing center.

Majors. Biology: Biomedical sciences. **Business:** Accounting, administrative services, business admin, hospitality/recreation, management information systems, marketing, office management, operations, tourism/travel. **Communications:** Journalism, radio/TV. **Computer sciences:** General, computer science, information technology, LAN/WAN management, networking, vendor certification. **Education:** Art, early childhood, multi-level teacher. **Engineering:** General. **General:** Ornamental horticulture. **Health services:** Medical radiologic technology/radiation therapy, medical records admin, nursing (RN), respiratory therapy assistant. **Human services:** General, social work. **Liberal arts:** Arts/sciences, humanities. **Math:** General. **Protective services:** Corrections, criminal justice, forensics, homeland security, police science. **Social sciences:** General. **Visual/performing arts:** Acting, art, ceramics, cinematography, commercial/advertising art, dramatic, graphic design, music, studio arts.

Most popular majors. Business/marketing 9%, health sciences 13%, liberal arts 47%, public administration/social services 12%, social sciences 8%.

Computing on campus. 400 workstations in library, computer center, student center. Commuter students can connect to campus network. Online course registration, online library, helpline, wireless network available.

Student life. Freshman orientation: Mandatory. Preregistration for classes offered. **Policies:** Comprehensive support center for learning disabled students. **Activities:** Choral groups, drama, literary magazine, musical theater, student government, student newspaper, symphony orchestra, multicultural club, Latin American club, African American club.

Athletics. NJCAA. **Intercollegiate:** Baseball M, basketball, cross-country, soccer, softball W, track and field. **Intramural:** Cross-country. **Team name:** Dukes, Lady Dukes.

Student services. Career counseling, services for economically disadvantaged, student employment services, financial aid counseling, personal counseling, placement for graduates. **Physically disabled:** Services for visually, speech, hearing impaired. **Transfer:** Pre-admission transcript evaluation for new students. Transfer adviser, college fairs on campus for students transferring to 4-year colleges.

Contact. Phone: (609) 691-8986 Fax: (609) 691-6157
Maud Fried-Goodnight, Executive Director of Enrollment and Student Support Services, Cumberland County College, PO Box 1500, Vineland, NJ 08362-9912

Eastern International College
Jersey City, New Jersey
www.eicollege.edu

▶ For-profit 2-year health science and nursing college
▶ Very large city

General. Regionally accredited. **Enrollment:** 80 degree-seeking undergraduates. **Degrees:** 5 associate awarded. **Calendar:** Semester. **Full-time faculty:** 11 total. **Part-time faculty:** 11 total.

Basis for selection. Open admission.

Financial aid. Need-based: Work-study available nights, weekends and for part-time students.

Academics. Credit/placement by examination: AP, CLEP.

Majors. Health services: Medical assistant, nursing (RN), sonography.

Contact. E-mail: eicollege@verizon.net
Phone: (201) 216-9901 Fax: (201) 216-9225
Vanessa Chance, Director of Admissions, Eastern International College, 3000 JF Kennedy Boulevard, Jersey City, NJ 07306

Essex County College
Newark, New Jersey
www.essex.edu
CB code: 2237

▶ Public 2-year community college
▶ Commuter campus in large city

General. Founded in 1966. Regionally accredited. Classes also given at West Caldwell campus and several locations in Essex County and Newark. **Enrollment:** 11,504 degree-seeking undergraduates; 992 non-degree-seeking students. **Degrees:** 1,172 associate awarded. **Location:** 12 miles from New York City. **Calendar:** Semester, limited summer session. **Full-time faculty:** 126 total; 54% minority, 52% women. **Part-time faculty:** 510 total; 69% minority, 44% women. **Special facilities:** Police academy, Africana Institute.

Student profile. Among degree-seeking undergraduates, 60% enrolled in a transfer program, 29% enrolled in a vocational program, 1% already have a bachelor's degree or higher, 2,547 enrolled as first-time, first-year students, 275 transferred in from other institutions.

Part-time:	34%	Asian American:	3%
Out-of-state:	2%	Hispanic American:	27%
Women:	59%	International:	9%
African American:	46%	25 or older:	42%

Transfer out. 75% of students enrolled in the transfer program go on to 4-year colleges. **Colleges most students transferred to 2011:** Rutgers University at Newark, Montclair University, Kean University, New Jersey Institute of Technology.

Basis for selection. Open admission, but selective for some programs. Special requirements for allied health programs. Priority given to allied health program applications received by April 15. National League for Nursing test required of nursing students. Interview recommended for nursing, ophthalmic science, physical therapy programs. **Adult students:** Companion Placement Test required.

2012-2013 Annual costs. Tuition/fees (projected): $4,051; $7,305 out-of-district; $7,305 out-of-state. Books/supplies: $1,000. Personal expenses: $1,061.

Financial aid. Need-based: Need-based aid available for part-time students. Work-study available nights, weekends and for part-time students.

Application procedures. Admission: No deadline. $25 fee, may be waived for applicants with need. Admission notification on a rolling basis. **Financial aid:** Priority date 6/30; no closing date. FAFSA, institutional form required. Applicants notified on a rolling basis starting 6/15; must reply within 3 week(s) of notification.

Academics. Special study options: Cooperative education, cross-registration, double major, dual enrollment of high school students, ESL, honors, independent study, internships, teacher certification program, weekend college. Cross-registration with other institutions in Council of Higher Education in Newark; civil construction engineering program with New Jersey Institute of Technology; criminal justice program with Rutgers: State University of New Jersey. License preparation in nursing, physical therapy, radiology. **Credit/placement by examination:** AP, CLEP, institutional tests. 30 credit hours maximum toward associate degree. Maximum credits accepted must be 30 credits less than number required for degree at Essex County College; may not include more than half credits required in major field. **Support services:** GED preparation and test center, learning center, reduced course load, remedial instruction, study skills assistance, tutoring, writing center.

Majors. Biology: General. **Business:** Accounting, accounting technology, administrative services, business admin, hospitality admin, office technology, tourism/travel. **Communications:** Journalism, media studies. **Computer sciences:** General, programming. **Education:** General, elementary, kindergarten/preschool, music, physical, secondary. **Engineering:** General, civil, electrical. **Health services:** Dental hygiene, EMT paramedic, health care admin, medical radiologic technology/radiation therapy, medical secretary, nursing (RN), optician, physical therapy assistant, premedicine, respiratory therapy technology. **Human services:** Social work. **Liberal arts:** Arts/sciences. **Math:** General. **Physical sciences:** Chemistry. **Protective services:** Criminal justice, firefighting, law enforcement admin, police science. **Social sciences:** General. **Visual/performing arts:** Art, commercial/advertising art, dramatic, music, studio arts, theater design.

Most popular majors. Business/marketing 18%, education 14%, engineering/engineering technologies 6%, health sciences 21%, liberal arts 12%, social sciences 9%.

Computing on campus. 870 workstations in library, computer center. Commuter students can connect to campus network. Online course registration available.

Student life. Freshman orientation: Available. Preregistration for classes offered. **Activities:** Choral groups, drama, music ensembles, musical theater, student government, student newspaper, French club, Islamic student organization, Latin student union, Distributive Education Club of America, criminal justice organization, black student association, social science club, fashion entertainment board, Phi Theta Kappa.

Athletics. NJCAA. **Intercollegiate:** Basketball, soccer M, track and field. **Intramural:** Basketball, table tennis, volleyball. **Team name:** Wolverines.

Student services. Alcohol/substance abuse counseling, career counseling, student employment services, financial aid counseling, on-campus daycare, personal counseling, placement for graduates, veterans' counselor, women's services. **Physically disabled:** Services for visually, speech, hearing impaired. **Transfer:** Transfer center, transfer adviser, college fairs on campus for students transferring to 4-year colleges.

Contact. Phone: (973) 877-3100 Fax: (973) 623-6449
Marva Mack, Director of Admissions, Essex County College, 303 University Avenue, Newark, NJ 07102

Gloucester County College
Sewell, New Jersey
www.gccnj.edu

CB member
CB code: 2281

- Public 2-year community and liberal arts college
- Commuter campus in large town

General. Founded in 1966. Regionally accredited. **Enrollment:** 6,329 degree-seeking undergraduates. **Degrees:** 880 associate awarded. **Location:** 12 miles from Camden, 16 miles from Philadelphia. **Calendar:** Semester, limited summer session. **Full-time faculty:** 72 total. **Part-time faculty:** 247 total. **Special facilities:** Learning resource center, 60-station computer room for multimedia course delivery and Internet access, interactive television (ITV) distance learning classroom.

Student profile.

Out-of-state:	1%	**25 or older:** 27%

Transfer out. Colleges most students transferred to 2011: Rowan University, Rutgers University, Richard Stockton College of New Jersey, Drexel University.

Basis for selection. Open admission, but selective for some programs. Special requirements for certain programs including allied health and automotive technology programs. Special-need students, deaf or hearing-impaired evaluated for support college can offer. Institutional placement tests may be used. **Home schooled:** Eligible, but admission determined on individual basis.

High school preparation. Biology and chemistry required for nursing applicants. Algebra also required for respiratory therapy, nuclear medicine, and diagnostic medical sonography applicants.

2011-2012 Annual costs. Tuition/fees: $3,390; $3,780 out-of-district; $6,780 out-of-state. Per-credit charge: $87 in-district; $100 out-of-district; $200 out-of-state. Books/supplies: $1,000. Personal expenses: $800.

Financial aid. All financial aid based on need. Need-based aid available for part-time students. Work-study available nights, weekends and for part-time students.

Application procedures. Admission: No deadline. $20 fee, may be waived for applicants with need. Admission notification on a rolling basis beginning on or about 2/28. Application closing dates for selective admission programs vary per program. **Financial aid:** Priority date 5/1; no closing date. FAFSA, institutional form required. Applicants notified on a rolling basis starting 3/20.

Academics. Through New Jersey Virtual Community College Consortium, students can take online courses from any New Jersey community college and receive GCC credit at no extra cost. **Special study options:** Accelerated study, cooperative education, distance learning, dual enrollment of high school students, ESL, independent study, internships, weekend college. Bachelor's degree programs available on campus. License preparation in nursing. **Credit/placement by examination:** AP, CLEP, institutional tests. 16 credit hours maximum toward associate degree. **Support services:** GED preparation and test center, learning center, pre-admission summer program, reduced course load, remedial instruction, study skills assistance, tutoring.

Majors. Biology: General. **Business:** General, accounting, administrative services, business admin, finance, hospitality admin, marketing, office management, office technology, office/clerical, sales/distribution. **Communications:** Communications/speech/rhetoric, journalism. **Computer sciences:** General, computer graphics, computer science, data processing, LAN/WAN management, web page design. **Education:** General, early childhood, multilevel teacher, physical, special ed. **Engineering:** General, engineering science. **English:** English lit. **Health services:** Medical secretary, nuclear medical technology, nursing (RN), respiratory therapy technology, sonography.

History: General. **Liberal arts:** Arts/sciences. **Math:** General. **Parks/recreation:** Exercise sciences, health/fitness. **Physical sciences:** General, chemistry. **Protective services:** Police science. **Psychology:** General. **Social sciences:** Political science, sociology. **Visual/performing arts:** Art, commercial/advertising art, dramatic.

Computing on campus. 750 workstations in library, computer center. Commuter students can connect to campus network. Online course registration, online library, wireless network available.

Student life. Freshman orientation: Available. Preregistration for classes offered. **Activities:** Choral groups, drama, literary magazine, musical theater, radio station, student government, student newspaper, student activities board, student government association, human services club, equal opportunity club, Phi Theta Kappa, paralegal club.

Athletics. NJCAA. **Intercollegiate:** Baseball M, basketball, cross-country, soccer, softball W, tennis, track and field, wrestling M. **Intramural:** Golf, volleyball. **Team name:** Road Runners.

Student services. Career counseling, services for economically disadvantaged, student employment services, financial aid counseling, health services, on-campus daycare, veterans' counselor. **Physically disabled:** Services for visually, speech, hearing impaired. **Transfer:** Pre-admission transcript evaluation for new students. Transfer adviser, college fairs on campus for students transferring to 4-year colleges.

Contact. Phone: (856) 415-2209 Fax: (856) 468-8498
Judith Atkinson, Director of Admissions, Gloucester County College, 1400 Tanyard Road, Sewell, NJ 08080

Hudson County Community College
Jersey City, New Jersey
www.hccc.edu

CB code: 2291

- Public 2-year community college
- Commuter campus in small city

General. Founded in 1974. Regionally accredited. HACU Hispanic-serving institution. **Enrollment:** 9,414 degree-seeking undergraduates. **Degrees:** 739 associate awarded. **Location:** 10 miles from New York City. **Calendar:** Semester, limited summer session. **Full-time faculty:** 96 total. **Part-time faculty:** 350 total. **Special facilities:** Culinary arts classroom, conference center.

Student profile.

Out-of-state:	2%	**25 or older:** 38%

Transfer out. Colleges most students transferred to 2011: New Jersey City University, St. Peter's College.

Basis for selection. Open admission. High school diploma required if applicant is less than 18 years of age.

2011-2012 Annual costs. Tuition/fees: $4,378; $7,573 out-of-district; $10,768 out-of-state. Per-credit charge: $107 in-district; $213 out-of-district; $320 out-of-state. Books/supplies: $1,500. Personal expenses: $1,500.

Financial aid. All financial aid based on need. Need-based aid available for part-time students. Work-study available nights, weekends and for part-time students.

Application procedures. Admission: No deadline. $15 fee, may be waived for applicants with need. Application must be submitted on paper. Admission notification on a rolling basis. **Financial aid:** Priority date 7/15; no closing date. FAFSA required. Applicants notified on a rolling basis starting 6/1; must reply within 1 week(s) of notification.

Academics. Students may earn second degree by completing 24 additional credits, including all requirements for second major. **Special study options:** Cross-registration, distance learning, dual enrollment of high school students, ESL, honors, independent study, internships, liberal arts/career combination, teacher certification program, weekend college. License preparation in nursing, paramedic. **Credit/placement by examination:** AP, CLEP, IB, institutional tests. 12 credit hours maximum toward associate degree. **Support services:** Pre-admission summer program, reduced course load, remedial instruction, study skills assistance, tutoring, writing center.

Majors. Biology: General. **Business:** Accounting, administrative services, business admin, hospitality admin, management information systems. **Computer sciences:** Computer science, data processing. **Education:** Early childhood. **Engineering:** Engineering science. **Health services:** Medical assistant, medical records technology, nursing (RN), respiratory therapy technology. **History:** General. **Liberal arts:** Arts/sciences. **Math:** General. **Physical**

sciences: Chemistry. **Protective services:** Criminal justice. **Psychology:** General. **Social sciences:** Sociology. **Visual/performing arts:** Studio arts. **Work/family studies:** Child care management.

Most popular majors. Business/marketing 10%, health sciences 20%, liberal arts 60%.

Computing on campus. 645 workstations in library, computer center. Commuter students can connect to campus network. Online library, wireless network available.

Student life. Freshman orientation: Mandatory. Preregistration for classes offered. **Activities:** Drama, film society, international student organizations, literary magazine, student government, student newspaper, South Asian society, black history and art society, law club, French club, Hispanos Unidos para el Progreso, women's awareness organization, hospitality club, health information and technology club, medical assisting club.

Student services. Adult student services, career counseling, student employment services, financial aid counseling, personal counseling, placement for graduates, veterans' counselor. **Physically disabled:** Services for visually, speech, hearing impaired. **Transfer:** Pre-admission transcript evaluation for new students. Transfer center, transfer adviser, college fairs on campus for students transferring to 4-year colleges.

Contact. E-mail: admissions@hccc.edu
Phone: (201) 714-7200 Fax: (201) 714-2136
Nelson Vieira, Director of Admissions, Hudson County Community College, 70 Sip Avenue, 1st Floor, Jersey City, NJ 07306

Mercer County Community College
Trenton, New Jersey
www.mccc.edu

CB member
CB code: 2444

- Public 2-year community college
- Commuter campus in small city

General. Founded in 1966. Regionally accredited. Courses also available at downtown Trenton location. External degree program for military service members. **Enrollment:** 8,603 degree-seeking undergraduates; 778 non-degree-seeking students. **Degrees:** 969 associate awarded. **Location:** 35 miles from Philadelphia, 60 miles from New York City. **Calendar:** Semester, extensive summer session. **Full-time faculty:** 127 total; 12% minority, 55% women. **Part-time faculty:** 517 total; 21% minority, 48% women. **Class size:** 48% < 20, 50% 20-39, less than 1% 40-49, less than 1% 50-99. **Special facilities:** CAD laboratory, computer graphics laboratory, greenhouse complex, mortuary science lab.

Student profile. Among degree-seeking undergraduates, 57% enrolled in a transfer program, 35% enrolled in a vocational program, 2,174 enrolled as first-time, first-year students, 38 transferred in from other institutions.

Part-time:	57%	Asian American:	5%
Out-of-state:	2%	Hispanic American:	13%
Women:	53%	International:	4%
African American:	26%	25 or older:	29%

Transfer out. Colleges most students transferred to 2011: The College of New Jersey, Rider University, Rutgers University, Rowan University, Thomas Edison State College.

Basis for selection. Open admission. Applicants without high school diploma or GED must be 18 or older and have completed the New Jersey Basic Skills Placement Examination. Designation of provisional status dependent on skills scores and/or high school units. Interview required for nursing and funeral service programs; recommended for all others.

2012-2013 Annual costs. Tuition/fees: $4,140; $5,475 out-of-district; $8,085 out-of-state. Per-credit charge: $109 in-district; $154 out-of-district; $241 out-of-state. Books/supplies: $1,040. Personal expenses: $1,900.

Financial aid. Need-based: Need-based aid available for part-time students. Work-study available nights, weekends and for part-time students. **Non-need-based:** Scholarships awarded for academics, athletics, state residency.

Application procedures. Admission: No deadline. No application fee. Admission notification on a rolling basis. **Financial aid:** Closing date 5/1. FAFSA required. Applicants notified on a rolling basis.

Academics. Cross-registration with area hospitals for nursing. **Special study options:** Cooperative education, cross-registration, distance learning, double major, dual enrollment of high school students, ESL, external degree, independent study, internships, liberal arts/career combination, weekend college. License preparation in aviation, nursing, occupational therapy, physical

therapy, radiology. **Credit/placement by examination:** AP, CLEP, institutional tests. 45 credit hours maximum toward associate degree. **Support services:** GED preparation and test center, learning center, pre-admission summer program, reduced course load, remedial instruction, study skills assistance, tutoring, writing center.

Majors. Biology: General. **Business:** General, accounting, administrative services, business admin, hotel/motel admin, management information systems, restaurant/food services. **Communications technology:** Radio/TV. **Computer sciences:** Networking, programming. **General:** Ornamental horticulture, plant sciences. **Health services:** Clinical lab technology, medical radiologic technology/radiation therapy, nursing (RN), physical therapy assistant, respiratory therapy technology. **Liberal arts:** Arts/sciences. **Math:** General. **Parks/recreation:** Exercise sciences. **Protective services:** Fire safety technology, police science. **Visual/performing arts:** General, commercial/advertising art.

Most popular majors. Business/marketing 19%, health sciences 20%, liberal arts 35%, security/protective services 7%, visual/performing arts 6%.

Computing on campus. 1,100 workstations in library, computer center. Commuter students can connect to campus network. Online course registration, online library, helpline, wireless network available.

Student life. Freshman orientation: Available. Preregistration for classes offered. **Activities:** Bands, choral groups, dance, drama, international student organizations, literary magazine, music ensembles, musical theater, radio station, student government, student newspaper, TV station, Christian Fellowship, bilingual club, African-American student organization, Fuerza Latina, ecology club, educational opportunity fund club, gay/straight alliance.

Athletics. NJCAA. **Intercollegiate:** Baseball M, basketball, soccer, softball W, tennis, track and field. **Intramural:** Basketball, softball, volleyball. **Team name:** Vikings.

Student services. Adult student services, career counseling, services for economically disadvantaged, student employment services, financial aid counseling, minority student services, personal counseling, placement for graduates, veterans' counselor. **Physically disabled:** Services for visually, speech, hearing impaired. **Transfer:** Transfer center, transfer adviser, college fairs on campus for students transferring to 4-year colleges.

Contact. E-mail: admiss@mccc.edu
Phone: (609) 570-3795 Fax: (609) 570-3861
Joan Guggenheim, Registrar, Enrollment Services, Mercer County Community College, Box B, Trenton, NJ 08690-1099

Middlesex County College
Edison, New Jersey
www.middlesexcc.edu

CB member
CB code: 2441

- Public 2-year community college
- Commuter campus in small city

General. Founded in 1964. Regionally accredited. **Enrollment:** 12,732 degree-seeking undergraduates. **Degrees:** 1,479 associate awarded. **ROTC:** Army. **Location:** 5 miles from New Brunswick, 30 miles from New York City. **Calendar:** Semester, extensive summer session. **Full-time faculty:** 177 total. **Part-time faculty:** 410 total. **Class size:** 23% < 20, 77% 20-39, less than 1% 40-49, less than 1% >100. **Special facilities:** Ecological walking path.

Transfer out. Colleges most students transferred to 2011: Rutgers State University, New Jersey Institute of Technology, Montclair State University, Kean University, Farleigh Dickinson University.

Basis for selection. Open admission, but selective for some programs. Special requirements for dental hygiene, nursing, radiography, respiratory care, psychosocial rehabilitation and treatment, medical laboratory technology, automotive technology programs. Allied Health Aptitude Test required for radiography education, dental hygiene and respiratory care applicants. National League of Nursing Exam (NLN) required for nursing applicants. **Learning Disabled:** Must submit separate application to Project Connections Office to be eligible for learning disabilities program.

High school preparation. Recommended units include English 4, mathematics 3, social studies 2, history 2, science 3 (laboratory 3) and foreign language 2. Math and science units required for some programs.

2011-2012 Annual costs. Tuition/fees: $4,065; $7,095 out-of-state. Per-credit charge: $101 in-state; $202 out-of-state. Out-of-county and out-of-state students pay additional $1,005 in required fees, based on 30 credit hours. Books/supplies: $1,557. Personal expenses: $3,555.

Two-Year Colleges

Financial aid. Need-based: Need-based aid available for part-time students. Work-study available nights, weekends and for part-time students.

Application procedures. Admission: Priority date 8/1; no deadline. $25 fee, may be waived for applicants with need. Admission notification on a rolling basis. **Financial aid:** Priority date 4/1; no closing date. FAFSA, institutional form required. Applicants notified on a rolling basis starting 5/4.

Academics. Special study options: Cooperative education, cross-registration, distance learning, double major, dual enrollment of high school students, ESL, independent study, internships, study abroad. License preparation in dental hygiene, nursing. **Credit/placement by examination:** AP, CLEP, institutional tests. 45 credit hours maximum toward associate degree. **Support services:** Learning center, pre-admission summer program, reduced course load, remedial instruction, tutoring.

Majors. Business: Accounting, business admin, fashion, office management. **Communications:** Communications/speech/rhetoric, journalism. **Computer sciences:** General, computer graphics, programming. **Education:** General, teacher assistance. **Engineering:** Civil, engineering science. **Health services:** Clinical lab technology, dental hygiene, nursing (RN), pharmacy assistant, respiratory therapy technology. **Parks/recreation:** Health/fitness. **Physical sciences:** Chemistry, physics. **Protective services:** Corrections, firefighting, law enforcement admin. **Social sciences:** Political science, sociology. **Visual/performing arts:** Commercial photography, commercial/advertising art, dance, dramatic, music performance, studio arts.

Most popular majors. Business/marketing 21%, education 11%, health sciences 9%, liberal arts 33%, physical sciences 9%, security/protective services 9%.

Computing on campus. 1,255 workstations in library, computer center. Commuter students can connect to campus network. Online library, helpline available.

Student life. Freshman orientation: Available. Preregistration for classes offered. One-day program scheduled 1 week prior to start of classes. **Activities:** Jazz band, choral groups, dance, drama, literary magazine, music ensembles, musical theater, radio station, student government, student newspaper, Third World student association, Hispanic club, foreign student association.

Athletics. NJCAA. Intercollegiate: Baseball M, basketball, cross-country, golf, soccer, softball W, track and field, wrestling M. **Team name:** Blue Colts.

Student services. Alcohol/substance abuse counseling, career counseling, student employment services, financial aid counseling, health services, minority student services, on-campus daycare, personal counseling, placement for graduates, veterans' counselor. **Physically disabled:** Services for visually, speech, hearing impaired. **Transfer:** Transfer adviser, college fairs on campus for students transferring to 4-year colleges.

Contact. E-mail: admissions@middlesexcc.edu
Phone: (732) 906-4243 Toll-free number: (888) 968-4622
Fax: (732) 956-7728
Aretha Watson, Assistant Dean Admissions, Middlesex County College, 2600 Woodbridge Avenue, Edison, NJ 08818-3050

Ocean County College
Toms River, New Jersey
www.ocean.edu

CB member
CB code: 2630

- Public 2-year community college
- Commuter campus in small city

General. Founded in 1964. Regionally accredited. 11 off-campus sites in Ocean County. **Enrollment:** 10,317 degree-seeking undergraduates. **Degrees:** 1,567 associate awarded. **Location:** 60 miles from Philadelphia, 80 miles from New York City. **Calendar:** Semester, extensive summer session. **Full-time faculty:** 106 total; 31% have terminal degrees, 8% minority, 61% women. **Part-time faculty:** 430 total; 26% have terminal degrees, 5% minority, 49% women. **Special facilities:** Planetarium, arts and community center. **Partnerships:** Formal partnerships through Jump Start program that allows high school juniors/seniors to enroll for college credits.

Student profile. Among degree-seeking undergraduates, 364 transferred in from other institutions.

Transfer out. Colleges most students transferred to 2011: Kean University, Richard Stockton College of New Jersey, Rutgers University, Georgian Court University, New Jersey Institute of Technology.

Basis for selection. Open admission, but selective for some programs. Admission to nursing and honors programs based on test scores and academic record. SAT or ACT required of nursing and honors program applicants.

Score report by May 30. **Learning Disabled:** Students invited to share learning disability needs with Disability Resource Center, which then makes appropriate accommodations.

High school preparation. Algebra, chemistry, biology required of nursing applicants.

2011-2012 Annual costs. Tuition/fees: $3,710; $4,670 out-of-district; $7,070 out-of-state. Per-credit charge: $94 in-district; $126 out-of-district; $206 out-of-state. Books/supplies: $1,600. Personal expenses: $1,500.

2010-2011 Financial aid. Need-based: 57% of total undergraduate aid awarded as scholarships/grants, 43% as loans/jobs. Need-based aid available for part-time students. Work-study available nights, weekends and for part-time students. **Non-need-based:** Scholarships awarded for academics, state residency.

Application procedures. Admission: No deadline. No application fee. Admission notification on a rolling basis. **Financial aid:** Priority date 5/31; no closing date. FAFSA required. Applicants notified on a rolling basis starting 7/15; must reply within 1 week(s) of notification.

Academics. Special study options: Distance learning, dual enrollment of high school students, ESL, honors, independent study, internships, liberal arts/career combination, study abroad, weekend college. Bachelor's degree programs available on campus. License preparation in nursing. **Credit/placement by examination:** AP, CLEP, institutional tests. 32 credit hours maximum toward associate degree. **Support services:** GED preparation and test center, learning center, pre-admission summer program, reduced course load, remedial instruction, study skills assistance, tutoring, writing center.

Honors college/program. For liberal arts students only; admission based on GPA, test scores, class rank, interview.

Majors. Business: General, business admin. **Communications:** Broadcast journalism. **Computer sciences:** General. **Conservation:** Environmental science. **Engineering:** General. **Foreign languages:** Sign language interpretation. **Health services:** Nursing (RN). **Liberal arts:** Arts/sciences. **Protective services:** Fire safety technology, homeland security, police science.

Most popular majors. Business/marketing 6%, health sciences 8%, liberal arts 73%, security/protective services 7%.

Computing on campus. 1,800 workstations in library, computer center. Commuter students can connect to campus network. Online course registration, online library, helpline, wireless network available.

Student life. Freshman orientation: Available. Preregistration for classes offered. **Activities:** Concert band, choral groups, dance, drama, literary magazine, musical theater, radio station, student government, student newspaper, symphony orchestra, TV station, EOF Alliance, Circle K, Organization for Black Unity, East Asian Student Alliance, Sign Language Society, Student Alliance for Latino Unity and Achievement, Student Learning About Politics, Veterans Club, Single Parenting, Native American Studies Society.

Athletics. NJCAA. Intercollegiate: Baseball M, basketball, cross-country, golf, soccer, softball W, swimming, tennis. **Intramural:** Basketball, soccer, volleyball. **Team name:** Vikings.

Student services. Adult student services, alcohol/substance abuse counseling, career counseling, services for economically disadvantaged, student employment services, financial aid counseling, health services, minority student services, on-campus daycare, personal counseling, placement for graduates, veterans' counselor, women's services. **Physically disabled:** Services for visually, speech, hearing impaired. **Transfer:** Re-entry adviser, pre-admission transcript evaluation for new students. Transfer adviser, college fairs on campus for students transferring to 4-year colleges.

Contact. Phone: (732) 255-0304 Fax: (732) 255-0444
Jacklyn Rodemann, Director of Admissions and Recruitment, Ocean County College, College Drive, Toms River, NJ 08754-2001

Passaic County Community College
Paterson, New Jersey
www.pccc.edu

CB member
CB code: 2694

- Public 2-year community college
- Commuter campus in small city

General. Founded in 1968. Regionally accredited. **Enrollment:** 9,257 degree-seeking undergraduates; 755 non-degree-seeking students. **Degrees:** 557 associate awarded. **Location:** 15 miles from New York City. **Calendar:** Semester, limited summer session. **Full-time faculty:** 99 total. **Part-time faculty:** 549 total. **Special facilities:** 2 art galleries, playhouse, poetry center.

Student profile. Among degree-seeking undergraduates, 64% enrolled in a transfer program, 36% enrolled in a vocational program, 1,628 enrolled as first-time, first-year students, 354 transferred in from other institutions.

Part-time:	66%	Asian American:	4%
Out-of-state:	.4%	Hispanic American:	47%
Women:	61%	International:	1%
African American:	18%	25 or older:	40%

Transfer out. Colleges most students transferred to 2011: William Paterson University, Rutgers University, Montclair State University, Bergen County College, Kean University.

Basis for selection. Open admission, but selective for some programs. Special requirements for nursing and other allied health programs. Interview recommended.

2011-2012 Annual costs. Tuition/fees: $3,954; $6,969 out-of-state. Per-credit charge: $101 in-state; $201 out-of-state. Books/supplies: $1,150. Personal expenses: $2,358.

Financial aid. Need-based: Need-based aid available for part-time students. Work-study available nights, weekends and for part-time students. **Non-need-based:** Scholarships awarded for academics. **Additional information:** Limited scholarship funds available for low income students eligible for federal or state aid.

Application procedures. Admission: No deadline. No application fee. Admission notification on a rolling basis. Early admissions available to high school students based on decisions made by high school guidance counselor and college's director of admissions. **Financial aid:** Priority date 8/1; no closing date. FAFSA required. Applicants notified on a rolling basis starting 8/1; must reply within 2 week(s) of notification.

Academics. Special study options: Cooperative education, cross-registration, distance learning, double major, dual enrollment of high school students, ESL, honors, independent study, internships, liberal arts/career combination, student-designed major, study abroad, weekend college. License preparation in nursing, radiology. **Credit/placement by examination:** AP, CLEP, institutional tests. 12 credit hours maximum toward associate degree. New Jersey Basic Skills test required for placement. **Support services:** Learning center, reduced course load, remedial instruction, study skills assistance, tutoring, writing center.

Majors. Biology: General. **Business:** General, accounting, accounting technology, administrative services, management information systems, marketing, sales/distribution. **Communications:** Communications/speech/rhetoric. **Computer sciences:** General, applications programming. **Education:** Early childhood. **Engineering:** Engineering science. **English:** English lit. **Health services:** Medical radiologic technology/radiation therapy, nursing (RN), nursing education, prenursing, radiologic technology/medical imaging, respiratory therapy technology. **Human services:** Social work. **Liberal arts:** Arts/sciences, humanities. **Math:** General. **Protective services:** Corrections, fire safety technology, police science. **Psychology:** General. **Social sciences:** Sociology.

Most popular majors. Business/marketing 16%, family/consumer sciences 8%, health sciences 17%, liberal arts 45%, security/protective services 6%.

Computing on campus. 900 workstations in computer center.

Student life. Freshman orientation: Available. Preregistration for classes offered. **Activities:** Dance, international student organizations, student government, student newspaper, Latin American club, Organization of African Ancestry, Phi Theta Kappa, Arabic club, Christian Fellowship Club, LGBT Club, Muslim Student Association.

Athletics. NJCAA. **Intercollegiate:** Basketball, soccer M. **Intramural:** Basketball M, volleyball W. **Team name:** Panthers.

Student services. Adult student services, career counseling, services for economically disadvantaged, student employment services, financial aid counseling, minority student services, on-campus daycare, personal counseling, placement for graduates, veterans' counselor, women's services. **Transfer:** Transfer adviser, college fairs on campus for students transferring to 4-year colleges.

Contact. E-mail: admissions@pccc.edu
Phone: (973) 684-6868 Fax: (973) 684-6778
Stephanie Decker, Director of Admissions, Passaic County Community College, 1 College Boulevard, Paterson, NJ 07505-1179

Raritan Valley Community College
Somerville, New Jersey
www.raritanval.edu　　　　　　　CB code: 2867

▶ Public 2-year community college
▶ Commuter campus in large town

General. Founded in 1966. Regionally accredited. **Enrollment:** 7,172 degree-seeking undergraduates; 1,198 non-degree-seeking students. **Degrees:** 964 associate awarded. **ROTC:** Army, Air Force. **Location:** 36 miles from New York City. **Calendar:** Semester, extensive summer session. **Full-time faculty:** 114 total; 11% minority, 57% women. **Part-time faculty:** 385 total; 17% minority, 46% women. **Special facilities:** Planetarium, professional theater, pool, fitness center. **Partnerships:** Formal partnership with area high schools for articulated credit program.

Student profile. Among degree-seeking undergraduates, 55% enrolled in a transfer program, 45% enrolled in a vocational program, 4% already have a bachelor's degree or higher, 1,588 enrolled as first-time, first-year students, 569 transferred in from other institutions.

Part-time:	47%	Asian American:	6%
Out-of-state:	1%	Hispanic American:	15%
Women:	51%	International:	2%
African American:	10%		

Transfer out. Colleges most students transferred to 2011: Rutgers State University, Kean University, Montclair State University, College of New Jersey, Rider University.

Basis for selection. Open admission, but selective for some programs. Special requirements for nursing program; interview recommended. Matriculated students must take Accuplacer Placement Test. **Adult students:** SAT/ACT scores not required; however, based on scores, students may be exempt from taking college's placement test. **Home schooled:** Must provide home school portfolio.

2011-2012 Annual costs. Tuition/fees: $3,720; $4,020 out-of-state. Per-credit charge: $102 in-state; $112 out-of-state. Books/supplies: $1,200. Personal expenses: $1,000.

Financial aid. Need-based: Need-based aid available for part-time students. Work-study available nights, weekends and for part-time students. **Non-need-based:** Scholarships awarded for academics.

Application procedures. Admission: No deadline. $25 fee, may be waived for applicants with need. Admission notification on a rolling basis. **Financial aid:** No deadline. FAFSA required. Applicants notified on a rolling basis starting 4/1.

Academics. Special study options: Accelerated study, cooperative education, distance learning, double major, dual enrollment of high school students, ESL, external degree, honors, independent study, weekend college. Service learning. Bachelor's degree programs available on campus. License preparation in nursing. **Credit/placement by examination:** AP, CLEP, institutional tests. 45 credit hours maximum toward associate degree. **Support services:** GED test center, learning center, pre-admission summer program, remedial instruction, study skills assistance, tutoring, writing center.

Majors. Biology: Biotechnology. **Business:** General, accounting technology, business admin, management information systems, marketing. **Communications:** Digital media. **Communications technology:** Animation/special effects. **Computer sciences:** Information technology. **Education:** Kindergarten/preschool. **Engineering:** Engineering science. **English:** English lit. **Health services:** Dental hygiene, medical assistant, medical records technology, nursing (RN), optician, respiratory therapy technology. **Liberal arts:** Arts/sciences. **Parks/recreation:** Exercise sciences. **Protective services:** Law enforcement admin, police science. **Visual/performing arts:** Dance, interior design, music, studio arts.

Most popular majors. Business/marketing 14%, education 12%, health sciences 11%, interdisciplinary studies 9%, liberal arts 32%, security/protective services 7%.

Computing on campus. 844 workstations in library, computer center, student center. Commuter students can connect to campus network. Online course registration, online library, helpline, wireless network available.

Student life. Freshman orientation: Available. Preregistration for classes offered. Three-hour sessions available. **Activities:** Choral groups, dance, drama, international student organizations, music ensembles, musical theater, radio station, student government, student newspaper, Black Student Association, Student Nurses Association, students for environmental awareness, BLGT club, Christian Fellowship, Islamic culture association, performing artist club, Orgullo Latino/Latin pride club, social justice club.

Athletics. NJCAA. **Intercollegiate:** Baseball M, basketball, golf, soccer, softball W. **Intramural:** Basketball, softball W, volleyball. **Team name:** Golden Lions.

Student services. Adult student services, alcohol/substance abuse counseling, career counseling, student employment services, financial aid counseling, on-campus daycare, personal counseling, placement for graduates, veterans' counselor. **Physically disabled:** Services for visually, speech, hearing impaired. **Transfer:** Re-entry adviser, pre-admission transcript evaluation for new students. Transfer center, transfer adviser, college fairs on campus for students transferring to 4-year colleges.

Contact. E-mail: registrar@raritanval.edu
Phone: (908) 526-1200 ext. 8935 Fax: (908) 704-3442
Mary O'Malley, Executive Director, Enrollment Services, Raritan Valley Community College, PO Box 3300, Somerville, NJ 08876-1265

Salem Community College
Carneys Point, New Jersey
www.salemcc.edu

CB member
CB code: 2868

▶ Public 2-year community college
▶ Commuter campus in small town

General. Founded in 1972. Regionally accredited. **Enrollment:** 1,321 degree-seeking undergraduates. **Degrees:** 183 associate awarded. **Location:** 12 miles from Wilmington, Delaware. **Calendar:** Semester, limited summer session. **Full-time faculty:** 25 total; 16% have terminal degrees, 8% minority, 52% women. **Part-time faculty:** 64 total. **Special facilities:** Glass education center, science laboratories, computer graphic arts lab, sustainable energy center, PSEG energy and environmental resource center, nursing center.

Student profile. Among degree-seeking undergraduates, 380 enrolled as first-time, first-year students.

Part-time:	39%	Asian American:	1%
Out-of-state:	10%	Hispanic American:	3%
Women:	60%	25 or older:	28%
African American:	22%		

Transfer out. Colleges most students transferred to 2011: Wilmington University, Rowan University, Richard Stockton College of New Jersey, Rutgers University, Cumberland County College.

Basis for selection. Open admission, but selective for some programs. Interview suggested for scientific glassblowing and glass art programs. **Learning Disabled:** Students must file release form and documentation of disability to be granted special accommodations.

2012-2013 Annual costs. Tuition/fees (projected): $3,924; $4,734 out-of-state. Books/supplies: $975. Personal expenses: $1,150.

Financial aid. Need-based: Need-based aid available for part-time students. Work-study available nights, weekends and for part-time students. **Non-need-based:** Scholarships awarded for academics, athletics, state residency.

Application procedures. Admission: No deadline. $27 fee, may be waived for applicants with need. Admission notification on a rolling basis. **Financial aid:** Priority date 6/1; no closing date. FAFSA, institutional form required. Applicants notified on a rolling basis starting 4/1; must reply within 2 week(s) of notification.

Academics. Special study options: Cooperative education, distance learning, double major, dual enrollment of high school students, ESL, honors, independent study, internships, teacher certification program. License preparation in nursing. **Credit/placement by examination:** AP, CLEP, institutional tests. 30 credit hours maximum toward associate degree. **Support services:** GED preparation and test center, learning center, reduced course load, remedial instruction, study skills assistance, tutoring, writing center.

Majors. Biology: Biotechnology. **Business:** Business admin. **Communications:** Journalism. **Computer sciences:** Computer graphics, computer science. **Education:** General, early childhood. **English:** English lit. **General:** Agribusiness operations. **Health services:** Nursing (RN). **History:** General. **Human services:** Community org/advocacy. **Liberal arts:** Arts/sciences, humanities. **Math:** General. **Parks/recreation:** Health/fitness. **Physical sciences:** Chemistry, physics. **Protective services:** Forensics. **Psychology:** General. **Social sciences:** General, criminology, political science, sociology. **Visual/performing arts:** Industrial design.

Most popular majors. Business/marketing 11%, health sciences 23%, liberal arts 60%.

Computing on campus. 300 workstations in library, computer center. Online course registration, online library, helpline, wireless network available.

Student life. Freshman orientation: Available. Preregistration for classes offered. Held at beginning of semester. **Activities:** Choral groups, drama, student government, Chi Alpha Epsilon, Educational Opportunity Fund Students, institutional diversity committee, Phi Theta Kappa, multicultural club.

Athletics. NJCAA. **Intercollegiate:** Baseball M, basketball, golf M, soccer W, softball W. **Team name:** Oaks.

Student services. Adult student services, career counseling, services for economically disadvantaged, student employment services, financial aid counseling, minority student services, personal counseling, veterans' counselor. **Physically disabled:** Services for visually, speech, hearing impaired. **Transfer:** Re-entry adviser, pre-admission transcript evaluation for new students. Transfer center, transfer adviser, college fairs on campus for students transferring to 4-year colleges.

Contact. E-mail: sccinfo@salemcc.edu
Phone: (856) 351-2703 Fax: (856) 299-9193
Lynn Fishlock, Director of Admissions and Records, Salem Community College, 460 Hollywood Avenue, Carneys Point, NJ 08069-2799

Sussex County Community College
Newton, New Jersey
www.sussex.edu

CB member
CB code: 2711

▶ Public 2-year community college
▶ Commuter campus in small town

General. Founded in 1981. Regionally accredited. Extension sites at Sussex County Technical School, several area high schools, and other locations. **Enrollment:** 3,318 degree-seeking undergraduates. **Degrees:** 504 associate awarded. **Location:** 70 miles from New York City. **Calendar:** Semester, limited summer session. **Full-time faculty:** 44 total. **Part-time faculty:** 206 total. **Special facilities:** 10 computer laboratories (including graphic design). **Partnerships:** Formal partnerships with Oracle database administration training program, Unix operating system training program, Cisco network training program.

Student profile.

Out-of-state:	11%	25 or older:	25%

Transfer out. Colleges most students transferred to 2011: Montclair State University, William Paterson University of New Jersey, Rutgers University, Ramapo College of New Jersey, Centenary College.

Basis for selection. Open admission, but selective for some programs. Special requirements for nursing program. Incoming freshmen must pass ACCUPLACER placement test for admission to program of study; those failing any part of test must satisfactorily complete remedial study in appropriate areas before being admitted to program.

2011-2012 Annual costs. Tuition/fees: $4,470; $8,070 out-of-district; $8,070 out-of-state. Per-credit charge: $120 in-district; $240 out-of-district; $240 out-of-state. Residents of Wayne, Monroe and Pike County (PA): $180 per credit hour. Books/supplies: $1,400. Personal expenses: $2,400.

Financial aid. All financial aid based on need. Need-based aid available for part-time students. Work-study available nights, weekends and for part-time students.

Application procedures. Admission: No deadline. $15 fee, may be waived for applicants with need. Admission notification on a rolling basis. **Financial aid:** Closing date 6/1. FAFSA, institutional form required. Applicants notified on a rolling basis; must reply within 2 week(s) of notification.

Academics. Special study options: Distance learning, double major, dual enrollment of high school students, ESL, honors, independent study, internships, teacher certification program. Bachelor's degree programs available on campus. License preparation in nursing, paramedic. **Credit/placement by examination:** AP, CLEP, IB, institutional tests. 30 credit hours maximum toward associate degree. **Support services:** GED preparation and test center, learning center, reduced course load, remedial instruction, study skills assistance, tutoring, writing center.

Majors. Biology: General. **Business:** Accounting, business admin. **Communications:** Journalism. **Computer sciences:** General, applications programming. **Conservation:** Environmental studies. **Education:** Early childhood, elementary, secondary. **Engineering:** General. **English:** English lit. **Health services:** Clinical lab technology, predental, premedicine, prepharmacy, respiratory therapy technology. **Human services:** Social work. **Liberal**

arts: Arts/sciences. **Math:** General. **Physical sciences:** Chemistry. **Protective services:** Criminal justice, firefighting. **Psychology:** General. **Social sciences:** General. **Visual/performing arts:** Art, commercial/advertising art, studio arts.

Computing on campus. 250 workstations in library, computer center, student center. Commuter students can connect to campus network. Online course registration, online library, wireless network available.

Student life. Freshman orientation: Available. Preregistration for classes offered. Half-day program held 2 days before start of classes. **Activities:** Concert band, campus ministries, choral groups, dance, drama, international student organizations, literary magazine, music ensembles, musical theater, opera, student government, student newspaper, symphony orchestra, TV station, student ambassadors, arts club, broadcasting club, criminal justice Ccub, law & justice society, Phi Theta Kappa, Rainbows in the Dark, psychology club, University Mothers Against Drunk Driving, Strengths Without Violence.

Athletics. NJCAA. **Intercollegiate:** Baseball M, basketball M, soccer, softball W. **Intramural:** Archery, badminton, basketball, soccer, softball, table tennis, volleyball. **Team name:** Skylanders.

Student services. Adult student services, career counseling, student employment services, financial aid counseling, personal counseling, placement for graduates, veterans' counselor, women's services. **Physically disabled:** Services for visually, speech, hearing impaired. **Transfer:** Pre-admission transcript evaluation for new students. Transfer adviser, college fairs on campus for students transferring to 4-year colleges.

Contact. E-mail: tpoltersdorf@sussex.edu
Phone: (973) 300-2216 Fax: (973) 579-5226
Todd Poltersdorf, Director of Admissions, Sussex County Community College, One College Hill Road, Newton, NJ 07860

Union County College
Cranford, New Jersey
www.ucc.edu

CB code: 2921

- Public 2-year community college
- Commuter campus in large town

General. Founded in 1933. Regionally accredited. Branch campuses in Elizabeth, Plainfield, and Scotch Plains. **Enrollment:** 10,839 degree-seeking undergraduates; 1,577 non-degree-seeking students. **Degrees:** 1,002 associate awarded. **ROTC:** Air Force. **Location:** 20 miles from New York City. **Calendar:** Semester, extensive summer session. **Full-time faculty:** 176 total; 32% have terminal degrees, 22% minority, 60% women. **Part-time faculty:** 388 total; 24% have terminal degrees, 31% minority, 50% women.

Student profile. Among degree-seeking undergraduates, 78% enrolled in a transfer program, 22% enrolled in a vocational program, 2,114 enrolled as first-time, first-year students, 685 transferred in from other institutions.

Part-time:	50%	Hispanic American:	26%
Out-of-state:	3%	Native American:	1%
Women:	64%	International:	2%
African American:	27%	25 or older:	45%
Asian American:	4%		

Transfer out. 66% of students enrolled in the transfer program go on to 4-year colleges. **Colleges most students transferred to 2011:** Kean University, Rutgers University, Montclair State University, Jersey City State University.

Basis for selection. Open admission, but selective for some programs. Special requirements for allied health and nursing programs. SAT required of dental hygiene program applicants; score report required by April. Essay, interview recommended for nursing, interpreter for the deaf programs.

High school preparation. 19 units recommended. Recommended units include English 4, mathematics 3, history 3, science 2 (laboratory 2), foreign language 2 and academic electives 5. Chemistry and biology required of health program applicants. Trigonometry, geometry, algebra, physics and chemistry required of engineering and physical science applicants. Level 3 proficiency in American Sign Language required of interpreter for the deaf program applicants. Algebra and geometry recommended for business majors.

2011-2012 Annual costs. Tuition/fees: $4,373; $7,643 out-of-state. Per-credit charge: $109 in-state; $218 out-of-state. Books/supplies: $1,200. Personal expenses: $2,000.

2011-2012 Financial aid. All financial aid based on need. Need-based aid available for part-time students. Work-study available nights, weekends and for part-time students.

Application procedures. Admission: No deadline. $35 fee. Admission notification on a rolling basis. **Financial aid:** Priority date 5/1; no closing date. FAFSA, institutional form required. Must reply within 2 week(s) of notification.

Academics. Special study options: Accelerated study, cross-registration, distance learning, dual enrollment of high school students, ESL, honors, internships, liberal arts/career combination, weekend college. Dual admissions agreements with Rutgers University, Montclair State University, New Jersey Institute of Technology, New Jersey City University, Kean University, Fairleigh Dickinson University. License preparation in dental hygiene, nursing, paramedic, physical therapy, radiology. **Credit/placement by examination:** AP, CLEP, institutional tests. 32 credit hours maximum toward associate degree. **Support services:** GED preparation and test center, learning center, reduced course load, remedial instruction, study skills assistance, tutoring, writing center.

Majors. Biology: General. **Business:** General, accounting technology, administrative services, business admin, customer service support, hospitality admin, marketing. **Communications:** Media studies. **Communications technology:** Animation/special effects, recording arts. **Computer sciences:** Computer science, information technology. **Engineering:** General. **Foreign languages:** American Sign Language, sign language interpretation, translation. **Health services:** Dental hygiene, EMT paramedic, medical radiologic technology/radiation therapy, nuclear medical technology, nursing (RN), physical therapy assistant, radiologic technology/medical imaging, respiratory therapy technology, sonography. **Liberal arts:** Arts/sciences. **Math:** General. **Parks/recreation:** Sports admin. **Physical sciences:** Chemistry. **Protective services:** Fire safety technology, law enforcement admin. **Visual/performing arts:** Game design.

Most popular majors. Business/marketing 17%, health sciences 29%, liberal arts 33%, security/protective services 6%.

Computing on campus. 1,024 workstations in library, computer center, student center. Commuter students can connect to campus network. Online library, helpline, wireless network available.

Student life. Freshman orientation: Available. Preregistration for classes offered. **Activities:** Drama, international student organizations, literary magazine, radio station, student government, student newspaper, Catholic student organization, Christian Fellowship, student volunteer organization, Phi Theta Kappa, Phi Beta, Union of African Students, gerontology club, French club, Spanish club.

Athletics. NJCAA. **Intercollegiate:** Baseball M, basketball, golf, soccer M, volleyball W. **Team name:** Owls; Lady Owls.

Student services. Alcohol/substance abuse counseling, career counseling, services for economically disadvantaged, student employment services, financial aid counseling, minority student services, personal counseling, placement for graduates, veterans' counselor. **Physically disabled:** Services for visually, speech, hearing impaired. **Transfer:** Re-entry adviser, pre-admission transcript evaluation for new students. Transfer adviser, college fairs on campus for students transferring to 4-year colleges.

Contact. Phone: (908) 709-7500 Fax: (908) 709-7125
Nina Hernandez, Director Admissions/Records/Registration, Union County College, 1033 Springfield Avenue, Cranford, NJ 07016-1599

Warren County Community College
Washington, New Jersey
www.warren.edu

CB code: 2722

- Public 2-year community college
- Commuter campus in small town

General. Founded in 1981. Regionally accredited. **Enrollment:** 2,159 degree-seeking undergraduates; 17 non-degree-seeking students. **Degrees:** 240 associate awarded. **Location:** 10 miles from Phillipsburg. **Calendar:** Semester, extensive summer session. **Full-time faculty:** 23 total; 17% have terminal degrees, 4% minority, 56% women. **Part-time faculty:** 82 total.

Student profile. Among degree-seeking undergraduates, 748 enrolled as first-time, first-year students.

Part-time:	55%	Women:	59%
Out-of-state:	2%	25 or older:	43%

Transfer out. Colleges most students transferred to 2011: Centenary College, Rutgers-New Brunswick, East Stroudsburg University.

Basis for selection. Open admission, but selective for some programs. Interview recommended.

High school preparation. High school diploma or GED strongly recommended.

2012-2013 Annual costs. Tuition/fees (projected): $3,901; $4,201 out-of-district; $4,801 out-of-state. Per-credit charge: $106 in-district; $116 out-of-district; $136 out-of-state. Books/supplies: $700. Personal expenses: $900.

2011-2012 Financial aid. All financial aid based on need. 84% of total undergraduate aid awarded as scholarships/grants, 16% as loans/jobs. Need-based aid available for part-time students. Work-study available nights, weekends and for part-time students.

Application procedures. Admission: No deadline. $25 fee, may be waived for applicants with need. Application must be submitted on paper. Admission notification on a rolling basis. Early admission students ages 16-18 must provide written permission from parent/guardian and high school official. **Financial aid:** Closing date 7/1. FAFSA, institutional form required. Applicants notified on a rolling basis; must reply within 2 week(s) of notification.

Academics. Special study options: Cooperative education, cross-registration, distance learning, double major, dual enrollment of high school students, ESL, independent study, internships, liberal arts/career combination, weekend college. Bachelor's degree programs available on campus. License preparation in dental hygiene, nursing, real estate. **Credit/placement by examination:** AP, CLEP, IB, institutional tests. Challenge exams. **Support services:** GED preparation, learning center, pre-admission summer program, reduced course load, remedial instruction, tutoring, writing center.

Majors. Biology: General. **Business:** General, accounting, entrepreneurial studies. **Computer sciences:** General. **Conservation:** General, environmental studies. **Education:** General, early childhood. **English:** English lit. **Health services:** Nursing (RN). **Liberal arts:** Arts/sciences. **Physical sciences:** Chemistry. **Protective services:** Criminal justice. **Social sciences:** General. **Visual/performing arts:** Studio arts.

Most popular majors. Health sciences 10%, liberal arts 63%.

Computing on campus. 100 workstations in library, computer center. Online library, wireless network available.

Student life. Freshman orientation: Mandatory. Preregistration for classes offered. **Activities:** Literary magazine, student government, student newspaper, Phi Theta Kappa honor society, criminal justice association.

Athletics. Team name: Golden Eagles.

Student services. Adult student services, career counseling, student employment services, financial aid counseling, personal counseling, placement for graduates, veterans' counselor. **Physically disabled:** Services for visually, speech, hearing impaired. **Transfer:** Transfer adviser, college fairs on campus for students transferring to 4-year colleges.

Contact. Phone: (908) 835-9222 Fax: (908) 689-5824
Shannon Horwath, Associate Director of Admissions, Warren County Community College, Route 57 West, Washington, NJ 07882-4343

New Mexico

Brookline College: Albuquerque
Albuquerque, New Mexico
www.brooklinecollege.edu

▶ For-profit 2-year branch campus and career college
▶ Commuter campus in large city
▶ Interview required

General. Accredited by ACICS. Additional campuses in Phoenix, Tempe, Tucson, and Oklahoma City. **Enrollment:** 407 degree-seeking undergraduates. **Degrees:** 43 associate awarded. **Calendar:** Differs by program, extensive summer session. **Full-time faculty:** 15 total. **Part-time faculty:** 15 total.

Basis for selection. Open admission. **Home schooled:** Letter of attestation is required.

2011-2012 Annual costs. Tuition/fees: $13,750. Tuition shown is an average; actual tuition and fees may vary by program. Personal expenses: $5,880.

Financial aid. All financial aid based on need. Work-study available nights, weekends and for part-time students.

Application procedures. Admission: No deadline. No application fee. Admission notification on a rolling basis. **Financial aid:** No deadline. FAFSA, institutional form required.

Academics. Special study options: Accelerated study. **Credit/placement by examination:** AP, CLEP, institutional tests. **Support services:** GED preparation and test center, learning center, remedial instruction, tutoring.

Majors. Business: Accounting, business admin. **Protective services:** Law enforcement admin.

Most popular majors. Business/marketing 35%, legal studies 30%, security/protective services 35%.

Computing on campus. Commuter students can connect to campus network. Online library available.

Student life. Freshman orientation: Mandatory. Preregistration for classes offered.

Student services. Career counseling, services for economically disadvantaged, financial aid counseling, placement for graduates. **Transfer:** Preadmission transcript evaluation for new students.

Contact. E-mail: awebb@brooklinecollege.edu
Phone: (505) 880-2877 Toll-free number: (888) 660-2428
Fax: (505) 352-0199
Andrew Webb, Campus Director, Brookline College: Albuquerque, 4201 Central Avenue NW, Suite J, Albuquerque, NM 87105-1649

Carrington College: Albuquerque
Albuquerque, New Mexico
www.carrington.edu

▶ For-profit 2-year career college
▶ Very large city

General. Regionally accredited; also accredited by ACICS. **Enrollment:** 778 degree-seeking undergraduates. **Degrees:** 172 associate awarded. **Calendar:** Differs by program. **Full-time faculty:** 19 total. **Part-time faculty:** 53 total.

Basis for selection. Applicants must be at least 18 in New Mexico by the first day of classes, have a high school diploma or its equivalent, interview with an Enrollment Services Representative, complete admission testing, and fulfill additional program-specific requirements.

Financial aid. Need-based: Work-study available nights, weekends and for part-time students.

Academics. Credit/placement by examination: AP, CLEP.

Majors. Health services: Nursing (RN), office admin, physical therapy assistant.

Contact. Phone: (888) 720-5014
Micki Pyszkowski, Director of Admissions, Carrington College: Albuquerque, 1001 Menaul Boulevard, N.E., Albuquerque, NM 87107-1642

Central New Mexico Community College
Albuquerque, New Mexico   **CB member**
www.cnm.edu   **CB code: 3387**

▶ Public 2-year community and technical college
▶ Commuter campus in very large city

General. Founded in 1965. Regionally accredited. **Enrollment:** 27,145 degree-seeking undergraduates; 2,146 non-degree-seeking students. **Degrees:** 2,051 associate awarded. **ROTC:** Army, Naval, Air Force. **Calendar:** Trimester, extensive summer session. **Full-time faculty:** 322 total. **Part-time faculty:** 764 total. **Class size:** 20% < 20, 75% 20-39, 2% 40-49, 3% 50-99.

Student profile. Among degree-seeking undergraduates, 50% enrolled in a transfer program, 50% enrolled in a vocational program, 3,868 enrolled as first-time, first-year students, 1,694 transferred in from other institutions.

Part-time:	65%	Hispanic American:	43%
Women:	56%	Native American:	7%
African American:	4%	International:	2%
Asian American:	2%	25 or older:	51%

Transfer out. Colleges most students transferred to 2011: University of New Mexico.

Basis for selection. Open admission.

2011-2012 Annual costs. Tuition/fees: $1,243; $6,102 out-of-state. Per-credit charge: $48 in-state; $251 out-of-state. $10 per credit hour for career, technical and developmental education courses. Books/supplies: $772.

2010-2011 Financial aid. Need-based: 62% of total undergraduate aid awarded as scholarships/grants, 38% as loans/jobs. Need-based aid available for part-time students. Work-study available nights, weekends and for part-time students. **Non-need-based:** Scholarships awarded for academics, state residency.

Application procedures. Admission: No deadline. No application fee. Admission notification on a rolling basis. **Financial aid:** Priority date 5/1; no closing date. FAFSA required. Applicants notified on a rolling basis starting 5/1.

Academics. Special study options: Cooperative education, distance learning, double major, dual enrollment of high school students, ESL, internships, liberal arts/career combination, teacher certification program. Apprenticeships. License preparation in aviation, dental hygiene, nursing, paramedic, radiology, real estate. **Credit/placement by examination:** AP, CLEP, institutional tests. **Support services:** GED preparation and test center, learning center, remedial instruction, study skills assistance, tutoring, writing center.

Majors. Biology: Biotechnology. **Business:** Accounting, administrative services, banking/financial services, business admin, hospitality admin. **Computer sciences:** Data processing, information systems, systems analysis. **Education:** Elementary, technology/industrial arts. **Engineering:** General, environmental. **Health services:** Clinical lab technology, medical radiologic technology/radiation therapy, medical records admin, nursing (RN), respiratory therapy technology, sonography, veterinary technology/assistant. **Liberal arts:** Arts/sciences. **Parks/recreation:** General. **Protective services:** Criminal justice, fire safety technology. **Work/family studies:** Child care management.

Most popular majors. Business/marketing 14%, health sciences 15%, liberal arts 46%.

Computing on campus. Commuter students can connect to campus network. Online course registration, online library, student web hosting, wireless network available.

Student life. Freshman orientation: Mandatory. Preregistration for classes offered. **Activities:** Drama, literary magazine, student government, student newspaper.

Athletics. Team name: Suncats.

Student services. Adult student services, career counseling, services for economically disadvantaged, student employment services, financial aid counseling, health services, minority student services, placement for graduates. **Physically disabled:** Services for visually, speech, hearing impaired. **Transfer:** Transfer adviser for students transferring to 4-year colleges.

Contact. Phone: (505) 224-3160 Fax: (505) 224-3237
Jane Campbell, Registrar/Director of Enrollment Services, Central New Mexico Community College, 525 Buena Vista Drive, SE, Albuquerque, NM 87106

Clovis Community College
Clovis, New Mexico
www.clovis.edu

CB member
CB code: 4921

♦ Public 2-year community and junior college
♦ Commuter campus in large town

General. Founded in 1990. Regionally accredited. **Enrollment:** 2,169 degree-seeking undergraduates; 1,745 non-degree-seeking students. **Degrees:** 170 associate awarded. **Location:** 200 miles from Albuquerque, 100 miles from Lubbock, Texas. **Calendar:** Semester, limited summer session. **Full-time faculty:** 52 total. **Part-time faculty:** 119 total. **Class size:** 56% < 20, 43% 20-39, 1% 50-99, less than 1% >100. **Special facilities:** Art collection representing multiple cultures of New Mexico, college-operated art gallery.

Student profile. Among degree-seeking undergraduates, 6% enrolled in a transfer program, 2% already have a bachelor's degree or higher, 255 enrolled as first-time, first-year students, 239 transferred in from other institutions.

Part-time:	59%	**Women:**	68%
Out-of-state:	9%	**25 or older:**	56%

Transfer out. Colleges most students transferred to 2011: Eastern New Mexico University, New Mexico State University, University of New Mexico, Texas Tech University, West Texas A&M University.

Basis for selection. Open admission, but selective for some programs. Nursing and radiologic technology are selective; criteria include GPA, performance in related science courses. Test of Adult Basic Education (TABE) or ACCUPLACER required for vocational programs. **Home schooled:** Home-schooled students will be required to present documented grade level status from a nationally accredited home school curriculum provider. **Learning Disabled:** Students with learning disabilities are encouraged but not required to register with the Office of Special Services. Students so registered may obtain special diagnostic services and modifications to include assistance with testing, note taking, and intervention with instructors.

2011-2012 Annual costs. Tuition/fees: $1,048; $1,120 out-of-district; $2,248 out-of-state. Books/supplies: $800. Personal expenses: $1,800.

2010-2011 Financial aid. Need-based: 91% of total undergraduate aid awarded as scholarships/grants, 9% as loans/jobs. Need-based aid available for part-time students. Work-study available nights, weekends and for part-time students. **Non-need-based:** Scholarships awarded for academics, state residency. **Additional information:** Endowment of over $1,000,000 to assist nursing students.

Application procedures. Admission: No deadline. No application fee. Admission notification on a rolling basis. **Financial aid:** Priority date 9/1; no closing date. FAFSA required. Applicants notified on a rolling basis starting 4/15.

Academics. Special study options: Cooperative education, distance learning, double major, dual enrollment of high school students, ESL, independent study, internships, teacher certification program, weekend college. Bachelor's degree programs available on campus. License preparation in nursing, paramedic, radiology. **Credit/placement by examination:** AP, CLEP, institutional tests. 32 credit hours maximum toward associate degree. **Support services:** GED preparation and test center, learning center, remedial instruction, study skills assistance, tutoring, writing center.

Majors. Business: Business admin, office management, office/clerical. **Computer sciences:** General, system admin, web page design. **Education:** General, early childhood, teacher assistance. **Engineering:** Electrical. **Health services:** EMT ambulance attendant, medical records technology, nursing (RN), radiologist assistant. **Liberal arts:** Arts/sciences, library assistant. **Math:** General. **Parks/recreation:** Health/fitness. **Protective services:** Firefighting, police science. **Psychology:** General. **Visual/performing arts:** Commercial/advertising art, studio arts.

Most popular majors. Business/marketing 9%, health sciences 39%, liberal arts 31%, personal/culinary services 14%.

Computing on campus. 280 workstations in library, computer center, student center. Online course registration, helpline, wireless network available.

Student life. Freshman orientation: Available. Preregistration for classes offered. 3 hours prior to semester. **Activities:** Drama, literary magazine, musical theater, student government, Hispanic advisory council, Phi Theta Kappa, social committee, international awareness organization, student ambassadors.

Student services. Adult student services, career counseling, services for economically disadvantaged, student employment services, financial aid counseling, minority student services, on-campus daycare, personal counseling, placement for graduates, veterans' counselor. **Physically disabled:** Services for visually, speech, hearing impaired. **Transfer:** Re-entry adviser for new students. Transfer adviser, college fairs on campus for students transferring to 4-year colleges.

Contact. E-mail: admissions@clovis.edu
Phone: (575) 769-4025 Fax: (575) 769-4190
Rosie Corrie, Director of Admissions/Registrar, Clovis Community College, 417 Schepps Boulevard, Clovis, NM 88101-8381

Dona Ana Community College of New Mexico State University
Las Cruces, New Mexico
www.dacc.nmsu.edu

CB code: 6296

♦ Public 2-year branch campus and community college
♦ Commuter campus in small city

General. Founded in 1973. Regionally accredited. Access to New Mexico State University facilities and activities. **Enrollment:** 8,891 degree-seeking undergraduates. **Degrees:** 923 associate awarded. **ROTC:** Army, Air Force. **Location:** 42 miles from El Paso, Texas. **Calendar:** Semester, limited summer session. **Full-time faculty:** 132 total. **Part-time faculty:** 244 total.

Student profile. Among degree-seeking undergraduates, 2,087 enrolled as first-time, first-year students.

Part-time:	55%	**Women:**	43%

Basis for selection. Open admission, but selective for some programs. Applicants to radiology technology, EMT-paramedic, and respiratory care programs selected on basis of COMPASS scores, Health Occupations Aptitude Test scores, resume, 3 letters of recommendation, clinical observation, and interview. Applicants to nursing program selected on basis of nursing entrance exam scores and completion of requirements. COMPASS required for placement if ACT or SAT not taken.

2011-2012 Annual costs. Tuition/fees: $1,488; $1,776 out-of-district; $4,656 out-of-state. Per-credit charge: $62 in-district; $74 out-of-district; $194 out-of-state. Room/board: $6,620. Books/supplies: $664. Personal expenses: $1,215.

Financial aid. Need-based: Need-based aid available for part-time students. Work-study available nights, weekends and for part-time students.

Application procedures. Admission: No deadline. $15 fee, may be waived for applicants with need. Admission notification on a rolling basis. February 15th application deadline for radiology technology, EMT-paramedic, nursing, and respiratory care programs. **Financial aid:** Priority date 3/1; no closing date. FAFSA required. Applicants notified on a rolling basis starting 5/1.

Academics. Special study options: Cooperative education, cross-registration, distance learning, double major, dual enrollment of high school students, ESL, independent study, internships. License preparation in dental hygiene, nursing, paramedic, radiology. **Credit/placement by examination:** AP, CLEP, institutional tests. 30 credit hours maximum toward associate degree. **Support services:** GED preparation and test center, learning center, pre-admission summer program, remedial instruction, study skills assistance, tutoring.

Majors. Business: Administrative services, business admin, fashion, hospitality admin, marketing, office management. **Computer sciences:** Computer graphics, computer science, data processing. **Education:** General, early childhood. **Engineering:** Electrical. **General:** Landscaping. **Health services:** EMT paramedic, medical radiologic technology/radiation therapy, medical secretary, nursing (RN), respiratory therapy technology. **Liberal arts:** Library assistant. **Protective services:** Firefighting.

Most popular majors. Liberal arts 97%.

Computing on campus. 460 workstations in library, computer center. Commuter students can connect to campus network. Online course registration, online library, helpline, repair service, wireless network available.

Student life. Freshman orientation: Available. Preregistration for classes offered. **Housing:** Coed dorms, single-sex dorms, special housing for disabled, apartments available. Housing available on adjacent New Mexico State University campus. **Activities:** Student government, student newspaper, Vocational Industrial Clubs of America, Distributive Education Clubs of America, Phi Theta Kappa, fraternities and sororities available through New Mexico State University.

Student services. Adult student services, career counseling, student employment services, health services, personal counseling, placement for graduates, veterans' counselor. **Physically disabled:** Services for visually, speech, hearing impaired. **Transfer:** Transfer adviser, college fairs on campus for students transferring to 4-year colleges.

Contact. E-mail: admissions@dacc.nmsu.edu
Phone: (575) 527-7710 Fax: (575) 527-7515
Geraldine Martinez, Director, Admissions, Dona Ana Community College of New Mexico State University, MSC-3DA, Las Cruces, NM 88003-8001

Eastern New Mexico University: Roswell

Roswell, New Mexico — **CB member**
www.roswell.enmu.edu — **CB code: 4662**

- Public 2-year branch campus and community college
- Commuter campus in large town

General. Founded in 1958. Regionally accredited. Online and on-site classes available from main campus, allowing students to continue upper-division classes without travel. **Enrollment:** 2,696 degree-seeking undergraduates; 1,317 non-degree-seeking students. **Degrees:** 306 associate awarded. **Location:** 200 miles from Albuquerque. **Calendar:** Semester, limited summer session. **Full-time faculty:** 52 total; 6% have terminal degrees, 12% minority, 50% women. **Part-time faculty:** 153 total; 3% have terminal degrees, 16% minority, 54% women. **Class size:** 69% < 20, 25% 20-39, 4% 40-49, 2% 50-99, less than 1% >100.

Student profile. Among degree-seeking undergraduates, 1% already have a bachelor's degree or higher, 617 enrolled as first-time, first-year students, 172 transferred in from other institutions.

Part-time:	56%	Native American:	1%
Women:	60%	International:	2%
African American:	3%	25 or older:	49%
Asian American:	1%	Live on campus:	5%
Hispanic American:	54%		

Transfer out. 10% of students enrolled in the transfer program go on to 4-year colleges. **Colleges most students transferred to 2011:** Eastern New Mexico University-Portales, New Mexico State University, University of New Mexico, New Mexico Highlands University.

Basis for selection. Open admission, but selective for some programs. Students must pass university skills placement test to enroll in math or English courses. Remedial reading course required if test not passed. Student may be exempt based on ACT scores. Some health services programs require completion of a pre-admission series of courses, have minimum course grades and GPAs. **Adult students:** Some programs require completion of placement testing as prerequisite. **Home schooled:** ACT score of 15 or more and high school transcript with graduation date required. **Learning Disabled:** Services based on need and disability documentation. Students requiring special services asked to provide information on needs as soon as possible to avoid delays in receiving service.

2012-2013 Annual costs. Tuition/fees (projected): $1,507; $1,566 out-of-district; $5,272 out-of-state. Per-credit charge: $57 in-district; $59 out-of-district; $214 out-of-state. Room/board: $6,832. Books/supplies: $1,200. Personal expenses: $3,000.

2011-2012 Financial aid. Need-based: 87% of total undergraduate aid awarded as scholarships/grants, 13% as loans/jobs. Need-based aid available for part-time students. Work-study available nights, weekends and for part-time students.

Application procedures. Admission: No deadline. No application fee. Admission notification on a rolling basis. **Financial aid:** Priority date 4/1; no closing date. FAFSA required. Applicants notified on a rolling basis starting 7/1; must reply within 3 week(s) of notification.

Academics. Special study options: Distance learning, dual enrollment of high school students, ESL, independent study, internships, liberal arts/career

---

combination. Bachelor's degree programs available on campus. License preparation in aviation, nursing, occupational therapy, paramedic. **Credit/placement by examination:** AP, CLEP, IB, institutional tests. 30 credit hours maximum toward associate degree. Credits earned through CLEP and Advanced Placement must be mutually exclusive. **Support services:** GED preparation and test center, learning center, remedial instruction, study skills assistance, tutoring, writing center.

Majors. Business: General, accounting, administrative services. **Communications technology:** Animation/special effects. **Computer sciences:** General. **Education:** General, teacher assistance. **Health services:** EMT paramedic, medical assistant, medical records technology, occupational therapy assistant, phlebotomy, respiratory therapy assistant. **Human services:** Social work. **Liberal arts:** Arts/sciences. **Protective services:** Criminal justice, fire safety technology, police science. **Work/family studies:** Child care management.

Most popular majors. Business/marketing 8%, health sciences 33%, liberal arts 10%, trade and industry 32%.

Computing on campus. 700 workstations in dormitories, library, computer center. Dormitories wired for high-speed internet access. Commuter students can connect to campus network. Online course registration, online library, helpline, wireless network available.

Student life. Freshman orientation: Available. Preregistration for classes offered. One-day program before classes commence. **Housing:** Coed dorms, apartments available. $150 deposit, deadline 8/1. **Activities:** Concert band, choral groups, drama, student government, art club, ski club, computer club, Spanish club, science club, Student Nurses Association, residence hall council, psychology club, electronics club, occupational therapy assistants, SkillsUSA club.

Athletics. Intramural: Basketball M, football (non-tackle) M, racquetball, softball W, tennis, volleyball, weight lifting M.

Student services. Career counseling, services for economically disadvantaged, student employment services, financial aid counseling, health services, on-campus daycare, personal counseling, placement for graduates, veterans' counselor. **Physically disabled:** Services for visually, speech, hearing impaired. **Transfer:** College fairs on campus for students transferring to 4-year colleges.

Contact. E-mail: admissions@roswell.enmu.edu
Phone: (575) 624-7142 Toll-free number: (800) 243-6687 ext. 142
Fax: (575) 624-7144
Lily Quezada, Director of Admissions and Records, Eastern New Mexico University: Roswell, Box 6000, Roswell, NM 88202-6000

Luna Community College

Las Vegas, New Mexico
www.luna.edu — **CB code: 2591**

- Public 2-year community and liberal arts college
- Commuter campus in large town

General. Regionally accredited. **Enrollment:** 939 degree-seeking undergraduates; 791 non-degree-seeking students. **Degrees:** 87 associate awarded. **Location:** 60 miles North of Santa Fe. **Calendar:** Semester, extensive summer session. **Full-time faculty:** 26 total; 58% minority, 73% women. **Part-time faculty:** 103 total; 58% minority, 57% women. **Class size:** 88% < 20, 11% 20-39, less than 1% 40-49.

Student profile. Among degree-seeking undergraduates, 127 enrolled as first-time, first-year students.

Part-time:	47%	Asian American:	1%
Out-of-state:	4%	Hispanic American:	77%
Women:	58%	Native American:	2%
African American:	1%	25 or older:	36%

Basis for selection. Open admission, but selective for some programs and for out-of-state students. The nursing program requires a 2.7 College GPA and passing scores from an approved nursing entrance exam. **Home schooled:** State high school equivalency certificate required.

2011-2012 Annual costs. Tuition/fees: $886; $1,198 out-of-district; $2,230 out-of-state. Books/supplies: $500. Personal expenses: $572.

Financial aid. Need-based: Work-study available nights, weekends and for part-time students.

Application procedures. Admission: No deadline. No application fee. Admission notification on a rolling basis.

Academics. **Special study options:** Accelerated study, distance learning, double major, dual enrollment of high school students, liberal arts/career combination. License preparation in dental hygiene, nursing. **Credit/placement by examination:** AP, CLEP, institutional tests. **Support services:** GED preparation, learning center, remedial instruction, tutoring.

Majors. **Business:** General, accounting, business admin, office management. **Communications:** Media studies. **Computer sciences:** General. **Education:** Early childhood. **Engineering:** Electrical. **General:** Equestrian studies. **Health services:** Clinical lab technology. **Math:** General.

Most popular majors. Business/marketing 15%, education 16%, health sciences 19%, liberal arts 18%, parks/recreation 8%.

Computing on campus. 100 workstations in library, computer center, student center. Commuter students can connect to campus network. Online course registration, online library, helpline, repair service, wireless network available.

Student life. **Freshman orientation:** Mandatory. Preregistration for classes offered. **Activities:** Student government, student newspaper.

Athletics. NJCAA. **Intercollegiate:** Baseball M, softball W. **Team name:** Rough Riders.

Student services. Career counseling, financial aid counseling, minority student services, on-campus daycare.

Contact. E-mail: mmarquez@luna.edu
Phone: (505) 454-2550
Moses Marquez, Director of Admissions, Luna Community College, 366 Luna Drive, Las Vegas, NM 87701

Mesalands Community College
Tucumcari, New Mexico
www.mesalands.edu   CB code: 3618

- Public 2-year community and technical college
- Commuter campus in small town

General. Regionally accredited. **Enrollment:** 567 degree-seeking undergraduates. **Degrees:** 85 associate awarded. **Location:** 175 miles from Albuquerque, 110 miles from Amarillo, Texas. **Calendar:** Semester, extensive summer session. **Full-time faculty:** 15 total. **Part-time faculty:** 16 total. **Special facilities:** Museum, foundry, production wind turbine, farrier, equine science facility.

Basis for selection. Open admission. Mesalands has an open admissions policy however the COMPASS placement test must be taken by all incoming students. **Home schooled:** Ability to Benefit Test or GED required. **Learning Disabled:** Students must submit an IEP.

2011-2012 Annual costs. Tuition/fees: $1,665; $2,775 out-of-state. Per-credit charge: $44 in-state; $81 out-of-state. Personal expenses: $1,427.

Financial aid. **Need-based:** Need-based aid available for part-time students. Work-study available nights, weekends and for part-time students. **Non-need-based:** Scholarships awarded for academics, athletics, leadership, minority status, state residency.

Application procedures. **Admission:** No deadline. No application fee. Admission notification on a rolling basis. **Financial aid:** Priority date 4/1; no closing date. FAFSA required. Applicants notified on a rolling basis starting 4/1; must reply within 3 week(s) of notification.

Academics. **Special study options:** Distance learning, dual enrollment of high school students, ESL, independent study, internships. Bachelor's degree programs available on campus. **Credit/placement by examination:** AP, CLEP, institutional tests. 18 credit hours maximum toward associate degree. **Support services:** GED preparation and test center, learning center, remedial instruction, study skills assistance, tutoring.

Majors. **Business:** Business admin. **Education:** General. **Engineering:** General. **Liberal arts:** Arts/sciences. **Physical sciences:** Geology, paleontology. **Protective services:** Law enforcement admin.

Computing on campus. 48 workstations in library, computer center. Online course registration, wireless network available.

Student life. **Freshman orientation:** Mandatory. Preregistration for classes offered. **Activities:** Student government.

Athletics. NCAA. **Intercollegiate:** Rodeo. **Team name:** Stampede.

Student services. Adult student services, financial aid counseling. **Physically disabled:** Services for visually, hearing impaired.

Contact. Phone: (575) 461-4413
Robin Alden, Director of Enrollment Management, Mesalands Community College, 911 South Tenth Street, Tucumcari, NM 88401

Navajo Technical College
Crownpoint, New Mexico
www.navajotech.edu

- Public 2-year community and technical college
- Commuter campus in rural community

General. Tribal college. **Enrollment:** 1,174 degree-seeking undergraduates. **Degrees:** 35 associate awarded. **Location:** 28 miles from Thoreau, 71 miles from Farmington. **Calendar:** Semester, limited summer session. **Full-time faculty:** 44 total. **Class size:** 73% < 20, 18% 20-39, 2% 40-49, 4% 50-99, 2% >100. **Partnerships:** Formal partnerships with TeraGrid, SC08, Navajo Head Start, University of New Mexico, New Mexico Computing Applications Center, Navajo Rural Systemic Initiative, Navajo Workforce Development, Office of Dine Youth, Lewis and Clark University (Illinois), Southern University (Louisiana), National Museum of the American Indian, UNM Telemedicine Consortium, New Mexico State University's Extension Program, Sandia National Laboratories.

Basis for selection. Open admission. ACCUPLACER required for all students to identify any remedial education requirements. **Home schooled:** Statement describing home school structure and mission, transcript of courses and grades, interview required. **Learning Disabled:** Special needs assessment conducted if disability is declared.

High school preparation. College-preparatory program recommended.

2011-2012 Annual costs. Tuition/fees: $1,200. Figures quoted are for members of federally recognized tribes. Non-members pay $2,160 in tuition. Room/board: $5,392. Books/supplies: $800.

Financial aid. **Need-based:** Need-based aid available for part-time students. Work-study available nights, weekends and for part-time students. **Non-need-based:** Scholarships awarded for academics.

Application procedures. **Admission:** Closing date 6/25 (postmark date). No application fee. Application must be submitted on paper. Admission notification by 9/9. Admission notification on a rolling basis. Must reply by May 1 or within 1 week(s) if notified thereafter. **Financial aid:** Closing date 6/25. FAFSA, institutional form required. Applicants notified on a rolling basis starting 8/5; must reply by 11/30 or within 4 week(s) of notification.

Academics. **Special study options:** Accelerated study, distance learning, double major, dual enrollment of high school students, honors, independent study, internships, teacher certification program. Bachelor's degree programs available on campus. License preparation in nursing. **Credit/placement by examination:** AP, CLEP. **Support services:** GED preparation and test center, remedial instruction, study skills assistance, tutoring.

Majors. **Business:** Accounting, administrative services. **Computer sciences:** General, information technology. **Education:** Early childhood. **Health services:** Nursing (RN), nursing assistant, veterinary technology/assistant. **Human services:** General. **Social sciences:** GIS/cartography.

Most popular majors. Agriculture 6%, business/marketing 16%, computer/information sciences 22%, education 10%, health sciences 6%, legal studies 28%, personal/culinary services 8%.

Computing on campus. 68 workstations in dormitories, library, computer center, student center. Dormitories wired for high-speed internet access and linked to campus network. Commuter students can connect to campus network. Online course registration, online library, helpline, repair service, wireless network available.

Student life. **Freshman orientation:** Mandatory. Preregistration for classes offered. 3 day event held one week before classes start. First time applicants must attend orientation before registering for classes. **Housing:** Guaranteed on-campus for all undergraduates. Single-sex dorms, special housing for disabled, apartments available. $250 fully refundable deposit, deadline 9/29. **Activities:** International student organizations, student government, student newspaper, Native American Church.

Athletics. USCAA. **Intercollegiate:** Cross-country, rodeo. **Intramural:** Basketball, softball, volleyball. **Team name:** Skyhawks.

Student services. Adult student services, alcohol/substance abuse counseling, career counseling, services for economically disadvantaged, student

employment services, financial aid counseling, on-campus daycare, personal counseling, placement for graduates, veterans' counselor. **Physically disabled:** Services for visually, speech, hearing impaired. **Transfer:** Pre-admission transcript evaluation for new students. Transfer adviser for students transferring to 4-year colleges.

Contact. E-mail: rdamon@navajotech.edu
Phone: (505) 786-4326 Fax: (505) 786-5644
Delores Becenti, Registrar, Navajo Technical College, PO Box 849, Crownpoint, NM 87313

New Mexico Junior College
Hobbs, New Mexico
www.nmjc.edu
CB code: 4553

 Public 2-year community and technical college
 Commuter campus in large town

General. Founded in 1965. Regionally accredited. **Enrollment:** 2,978 degree-seeking undergraduates. **Degrees:** 216 associate awarded. **Location:** 110 miles from Roswell, 100 miles from Lubbock, Texas. **Calendar:** Semester, extensive summer session. **Full-time faculty:** 66 total. **Part-time faculty:** 120 total. **Special facilities:** Western Heritage Museum, Cowboy Hall of Fame.

Student profile. Among degree-seeking undergraduates, 60% enrolled in a transfer program, 40% enrolled in a vocational program, 164 transferred in from other institutions.

Out-of-state:	10%	Live on campus:	8%
25 or older:	51%		

Transfer out. **Colleges most students transferred to 2011:** College of the Southwest, Eastern New Mexico University, Texas Tech University, University of New Mexico, New Mexico State University.

Basis for selection. Open admission, but selective for some programs. Special requirements for nursing, law enforcement, and automotive service education programs. Applicants admitted without high school diploma or GED must pass GED before completion of degree program. Interview required for nursing, medical laboratory technician, automotive service education programs. **Home schooled:** Transcript of courses and grades required.

High school preparation. 18 units recommended. Recommended units include English 4, mathematics 3, social studies 4, science 2 and academic electives 5.

2011-2012 Annual costs. Tuition/fees: $1,272; $1,728 out-of-district; $1,920 out-of-state. Per-credit charge: $33 in-district; $52 out-of-district; $60 out-of-state. Room/board: $4,100. Books/supplies: $1,000. Personal expenses: $1,575.

Financial aid. **Need-based:** Need-based aid available for part-time students. Work-study available nights, weekends and for part-time students. **Non-need-based:** Scholarships awarded for academics, art, athletics, leadership, music/drama.

Application procedures. **Admission:** No deadline. No application fee. Admission notification on a rolling basis. **Financial aid:** Priority date 6/1; no closing date. FAFSA required. Applicants notified on a rolling basis; must reply within 2 week(s) of notification.

Academics. **Special study options:** Cooperative education, cross-registration, distance learning, dual enrollment of high school students, ESL, honors, internships, weekend college. License preparation in nursing, paramedic, real estate. **Credit/placement by examination:** AP, CLEP, institutional tests. 30 credit hours maximum toward associate degree. **Support services:** GED preparation and test center, learning center, pre-admission summer program, reduced course load, remedial instruction, study skills assistance, tutoring, writing center.

Majors. Biology: General. **Business:** General, accounting, administrative services, banking/financial services, business admin, office management, office technology, real estate. **Communications:** Communications/speech/rhetoric. **Computer sciences:** General, applications programming, computer graphics, programming. **Education:** General, early childhood, elementary, middle, physical, secondary. **Engineering:** General. **Foreign languages:** Spanish. **Health services:** Athletic training, clinical lab assistant, clinical lab technology, EMT paramedic, medical radiologic technology/radiation therapy, predental, premedicine, prepharmacy. **Liberal arts:** Arts/sciences. **Math:** General. **Physical sciences:** Chemistry, physics. **Protective services:** Criminal justice, police science. **Psychology:** General. **Social sciences:** General. **Visual/performing arts:** Commercial/advertising art, music, studio arts.

Most popular majors. Agriculture 6%, business/marketing 11%, education 13%, health sciences 24%, liberal arts 10%, mathematics 7%, trade and industry 13%.

Computing on campus. 275 workstations in dormitories, library, computer center, student center. Dormitories wired for high-speed internet access. Commuter students can connect to campus network. Helpline available.

Student life. Freshman orientation: Mandatory. Preregistration for classes offered. **Housing:** Single-sex dorms, special housing for disabled, wellness housing available. **Activities:** Concert band, choral groups, drama, music ensembles, student government, Young Republicans, Young Democrats, student nurses, ambassadors.

Athletics. NJCAA. **Intercollegiate:** Baseball M, basketball, golf M. **Intramural:** Badminton, basketball, bowling, golf, handball, racquetball, skiing, soccer, softball, swimming, table tennis, tennis, volleyball. **Team name:** Thunderbirds.

Student services. Career counseling, student employment services, financial aid counseling, health services, personal counseling, placement for graduates, veterans' counselor. **Physically disabled:** Services for visually, speech, hearing impaired. **Transfer:** Pre-admission transcript evaluation for new students. Transfer adviser, college fairs on campus for students transferring to 4-year colleges.

Contact. Phone: (575) 392-5113 Toll-free number: (800) 657-6260
Fax: (575) 392-0322
Michele Clingman, Dean of Enrollment Management, New Mexico Junior College, 5317 Lovington Highway, Hobbs, NM 88240

New Mexico Military Institute
Roswell, New Mexico
www.nmmi.edu
CB member
CB code: 4534

 Public 2-year junior and military college
 Residential campus in large town
 ACT (writing optional), interview required

General. Founded in 1891. Regionally accredited. Nation's only state-supported, nationally accredited military junior college with embedded service academy preparatory program that serves all five national service academies and offers the US Army ROTC 2-Year Early Commissioning Program (ECP). **Enrollment:** 463 degree-seeking undergraduates. **Degrees:** 88 associate awarded. **ROTC:** Army. **Location:** 200 miles from Albuquerque, 200 miles from El Paso, Texas. **Calendar:** Semester, limited summer session. **Full-time faculty:** 78 total. **Class size:** 64% < 20, 34% 20-39, 3% 40-49. **Special facilities:** Leadership center, museum; high and low ropes courses, leader reaction course, fitness factory, obstacle course, golf course.

Transfer out. **Colleges most students transferred to 2011:** University of New Mexico, New Mexico State University, Texas A&M University, University of Colorado.

Basis for selection. 2.0 GPA, 19 ACT or 920 SAT (exclusive of Writing) for participation in Advanced Army ROTC. 17 ACT or 800 SAT (exclusive of Writing) for Basic Army ROTC program. Preference given to in-state applicants. Maximum age of 22 for enrollment. Students cannot be married or have children.

High school preparation. College-preparatory program recommended. 21 units recommended. Recommended units include English 4, mathematics 3, social studies 1, history 2, science 2 (laboratory 2), foreign language 2 and academic electives 5. Computer science 0.5 unit recommended.

2011-2012 Annual costs. Tuition/fees: $5,985; $10,260 out-of-state. Room/board: $4,670. Books/supplies: $700. Personal expenses: $1,000.

Financial aid. **Need-based:** Work-study available nights, weekends and for part-time students. **Non-need-based:** Scholarships awarded for academics, alumni affiliation, athletics, leadership, minority status, ROTC, state residency.

Application procedures. **Admission:** No deadline. $85 fee, may be waived for applicants with need, free for online applicants. Admission notification on a rolling basis beginning on or about 9/1. Advanced Army ROTC applicants must pass Army physical examination. **Financial aid:** Priority date 4/1; no closing date. FAFSA required. Applicants notified on a rolling basis starting 5/1; must reply within 3 week(s) of notification.

Academics. **Special study options:** Dual enrollment of high school students. **Credit/placement by examination:** AP, CLEP, institutional tests. 30 credit hours maximum toward associate degree. **Support services:** Learning center, remedial instruction, tutoring, writing center.

Majors. **Liberal arts:** Arts/sciences.

Computing on campus. 100 workstations in dormitories, library, computer center, student center. Dormitories linked to campus network. Helpline, repair service available.

Student life. **Freshman orientation:** Mandatory. Preregistration for classes offered. **Policies:** Student life governed by the Cadet Rules and Regulations and the Cadet Honor Code. All students must live in college housing. **Housing:** Guaranteed on-campus for all undergraduates. Single-sex dorms available. $350 nonrefundable deposit. **Activities:** Bands, campus ministries, choral groups, film society, literary magazine, music ensembles, student government, student newspaper, symphony orchestra, Fellowship of Christian Athletes, African-American club, Native American club, Mexican club, Pacific Islander club, Corps of Cadets Community Service.

Athletics. NJCAA. **Intercollegiate:** Baseball M, basketball M, fencing, football (tackle) M, golf, rifle, tennis, track and field, volleyball W. **Intramural:** Fencing, football (tackle) M, handball, racquetball, skiing, soccer, softball, swimming, tennis, track and field, volleyball. **Team name:** Broncos.

Student services. Alcohol/substance abuse counseling, chaplain/spiritual director, career counseling, financial aid counseling, health services, personal counseling. **Transfer:** Pre-admission transcript evaluation for new students.

Contact. E-mail: admissions@nmmi.edu
Phone: (505) 624-8435 Toll-free number: (800) 421-5376
Fax: (505) 624-8058
Lt. Col. Sonya Rodriguez, Director of Admissions & Financial Aid, New Mexico Military Institute, 101 West College Boulevard, Roswell, NM 88201-5173

New Mexico State University at Alamogordo
Alamogordo, New Mexico
www.nmsua.edu/
CB code: 4012

- Public 2-year branch campus college
- Commuter campus in large town

General. Founded in 1958. Regionally accredited. **Enrollment:** 3,474 degree-seeking undergraduates. **Degrees:** 234 associate awarded. **ROTC:** Air Force. **Location:** 65 miles from Las Cruces, 85 miles from El Paso, Texas. **Calendar:** Semester, limited summer session. **Full-time faculty:** 50 total; 16% have terminal degrees, 22% minority, 64% women. **Part-time faculty:** 117 total; 5% have terminal degrees, 13% minority, 56% women. **Class size:** 49% < 20, 51% 20-39. **Special facilities:** Planetarium.

Student profile. Among degree-seeking undergraduates, 75% enrolled in a transfer program, 18% enrolled in a vocational program, 2% already have a bachelor's degree or higher, 454 enrolled as first-time, first-year students, 170 transferred in from other institutions.

Part-time:	43%	Hispanic American:	38%
Out-of-state:	14%	Native American:	3%
Women:	64%	International:	2%
African American:	4%	25 or older:	47%
Asian American:	2%		

Transfer out. Colleges most students transferred to 2011: New Mexico State University.

Basis for selection. Open admission, but selective for some programs. Special requirements for nursing.

2011-2012 Annual costs. Tuition/fees: $1,824; $2,160 out-of-district; $4,872 out-of-state. Per-credit charge: $72 in-district; $86 out-of-district; $199 out-of-state. Books/supplies: $1,038. Personal expenses: $2,253.

Financial aid. **Need-based:** Need-based aid available for part-time students. Work-study available nights, weekends and for part-time students. **Non-need-based:** Scholarships awarded for academics, state residency.

Application procedures. **Admission:** No deadline. $20 fee. Admission notification on a rolling basis. **Financial aid:** Priority date 3/1; no closing date. FAFSA, institutional form required. Applicants notified by 6/1.

Academics. **Special study options:** Cooperative education, cross-registration, distance learning, double major, dual enrollment of high school students, honors, independent study, internships, liberal arts/career combination, weekend college. License preparation in nursing, paramedic. **Credit/placement by examination:** AP, CLEP, institutional tests. 30 credit hours maximum toward associate degree. **Support services:** GED preparation and test center, learning center, reduced course load, remedial instruction, study skills assistance, tutoring, writing center.

Majors. **Business:** General, administrative services, office/clerical. **Communications technology:** Animation/special effects, photo/film/video. **Computer sciences:** Data processing, information technology, programming, webmaster. **Education:** General, early childhood. **Protective services:** Criminal justice. **Visual/performing arts:** Graphic design, studio arts.

Most popular majors. Business/marketing 6%, health sciences 20%, liberal arts 53%.

Computing on campus. 203 workstations in library, computer center, student center. Commuter students can connect to campus network. Online course registration, online library, helpline, repair service, wireless network available.

Student life. **Freshman orientation:** Mandatory. Preregistration for classes offered. **Activities:** Jazz band, choral groups, drama, music ensembles, student government.

Student services. Career counseling, student employment services, financial aid counseling, personal counseling, placement for graduates, veterans' counselor. **Physically disabled:** Services for visually, speech, hearing impaired. **Transfer:** Transfer adviser, college fairs on campus for students transferring to 4-year colleges.

Contact. E-mail: admissions@nmsua.nmsu.edu
Phone: (575) 439-3700
Tina Truong, Admissions Coordinator, New Mexico State University at Alamogordo, 2400 North Scenic Drive, Alamogordo, NM 88310

New Mexico State University at Carlsbad
Carlsbad, New Mexico
www.cavern.nmsu.edu
CB code: 4547

- Public 2-year branch campus and community college
- Commuter campus in large town

General. Founded in 1950. Regionally accredited. **Enrollment:** 1,292 degree-seeking undergraduates; 452 non-degree-seeking students. **Degrees:** 30 associate awarded. **Location:** 165 miles from El Paso, Texas. **Calendar:** Semester, limited summer session. **Full-time faculty:** 37 total. **Part-time faculty:** 52 total.

Student profile. Among degree-seeking undergraduates, 68% enrolled in a transfer program, 15% enrolled in a vocational program, 1% already have a bachelor's degree or higher, 242 enrolled as first-time, first-year students, 68 transferred in from other institutions.

Part-time:	64%	Women:	69%
Out-of-state:	3%	25 or older:	28%

Transfer out. Colleges most students transferred to 2011: New Mexico State University.

Basis for selection. Open admission, but selective for some programs. Special admission process for nursing applicants; ACT and prerequisite courses required. **Adult students:** SAT/ACT scores not required. **Home schooled:** Copy of document verifying registration as homeschooled student and academic transcript outlining 9th-12th grade courses and grades required.

High school preparation. 10 units recommended. Recommended units include English 4, mathematics 3, science 2 and foreign language 1.

2011-2012 Annual costs. Tuition/fees: $1,036; $1,636 out-of-district; $3,388 out-of-state. Per-credit charge: $39 in-district; $64 out-of-district; $134 out-of-state. Books/supplies: $1,038. Personal expenses: $2,253.

Financial aid. **Need-based:** Need-based aid available for part-time students. Work-study available nights, weekends and for part-time students. **Non-need-based:** Scholarships awarded for academics, state residency.

Application procedures. **Admission:** No deadline. No application fee. Admission notification on a rolling basis. **Financial aid:** Priority date 3/1; no closing date. FAFSA required. Applicants notified on a rolling basis starting 5/1; must reply within 4 week(s) of notification.

Academics. **Special study options:** Distance learning, double major, dual enrollment of high school students, ESL, independent study, internships, student-designed major. Bachelor's degree programs available on campus. License preparation in nursing. **Credit/placement by examination:** AP, CLEP, institutional tests. 30 credit hours maximum toward associate degree. **Support services:** GED preparation and test center, learning center, reduced course load, remedial instruction, study skills assistance, tutoring, writing center.

Majors. Business: General, administrative services, office/clerical. **Education:** General, early childhood, teacher assistance. **Engineering:** General. **Health services:** Nursing (RN), prenursing. **Protective services:** Criminal justice.

Most popular majors. Business/marketing 11%, health sciences 22%, liberal arts 50%, security/protective services 7%.

Computing on campus. 365 workstations in library, computer center. Commuter students can connect to campus network. Online course registration, online library, helpline, wireless network available.

Student life. Freshman orientation: Available. Preregistration for classes offered. **Activities:** Choral groups, literary magazine, student government, student newspaper, student nursing association, criminal justice association, Phi Theta Kappa, MEChA.

Athletics. Team name: Aggies.

Student services. Career counseling, services for economically disadvantaged, student employment services, financial aid counseling, health services, minority student services, personal counseling. **Physically disabled:** Services for visually, speech, hearing impaired. **Transfer:** Transfer adviser, college fairs on campus for students transferring to 4-year colleges.

Contact. E-mail: mcleary@nmsu.edu
Phone: (575) 234-9223 Toll-free number: (888) 888-2199
Fax: (575) 885-4951
Michael Cleary, Vice President for Student Services, New Mexico State University at Carlsbad, 1500 University Drive, Carlsbad, NM 88220

New Mexico State University at Grants
Grants, New Mexico
www.grants.nmsu.edu   **CB code: 0461**

▶ Public 2-year branch campus and community college
▶ Commuter campus in small town

General. Founded in 1968. Regionally accredited. **Enrollment:** 1,247 degree-seeking undergraduates. **Degrees:** 75 associate awarded. **Location:** 75 miles from Albuquerque. **Calendar:** Semester, limited summer session. **Full-time faculty:** 18 total. **Part-time faculty:** 51 total. **Special facilities:** Judicial district law library.

Basis for selection. Open admission.

High school preparation. 15 units recommended. Recommended units include English 3, mathematics 3, social studies 1 and science 1.

2011-2012 Annual costs. Tuition/fees: $1,704; $1,872 out-of-district; $3,528 out-of-state. Per-credit charge: $71 in-district; $78 out-of-district; $139 out-of-state. Books/supplies: $400.

Financial aid. Need-based: Need-based aid available for part-time students. Work-study available nights, weekends and for part-time students.

Application procedures. Admission: Closing date 8/28. $20 fee, may be waived for applicants with need. Admission notification on a rolling basis beginning on or about 8/3. **Financial aid:** Priority date 3/5; no closing date. FAFSA, institutional form required. Applicants notified on a rolling basis starting 6/15; must reply by 8/28.

Academics. Special study options: Distance learning, double major, dual enrollment of high school students, student-designed major, weekend college. Bachelor's degree programs available on campus. License preparation in nursing. **Credit/placement by examination:** AP, CLEP, institutional tests. 30 credit hours maximum toward associate degree. **Support services:** GED preparation and test center, learning center, reduced course load, remedial instruction, tutoring.

Majors. Business: General, office management. **Communications:** Digital media. **Computer sciences:** Programming. **Education:** General. **Protective services:** Law enforcement admin. **Visual/performing arts:** Art.

Most popular majors. Business/marketing 12%, interdisciplinary studies 13%, liberal arts 52%, public administration/social services 11%.

Computing on campus. 230 workstations in computer center. Online library available.

Student life. Freshman orientation: Available. Preregistration for classes offered. **Activities:** Student government, student newspaper.

Athletics. Team name: Aggies.

Student services. Adult student services, career counseling, student employment services, personal counseling, veterans' counselor. **Transfer:** Pre-admission transcript evaluation for new students. Transfer adviser, college fairs on campus for students transferring to 4-year colleges.

Contact. E-mail: ilutz@grants.nmsu.edu
Phone: (505) 287-7981 Toll-free number: (888) 450-6678
Fax: (505) 287-2329
Beth Armstead, Vice President for Student Services, New Mexico State University at Grants, 1500 North Third Street, Grants, NM 87020

Northern New Mexico College
Espanola, New Mexico
www.nnmc.edu   **CB code: 0425**

▶ Public 2-year community college
▶ Commuter campus in small town

General. Founded in 1909. Regionally accredited. Off-site facilities in seven locations. **Enrollment:** 1,826 undergraduates. **Degrees:** 10 bachelor's, 107 associate awarded. **Location:** 24 miles from Santa Fe. **Calendar:** Semester, limited summer session. **Full-time faculty:** 59 total. **Part-time faculty:** 179 total.

Student profile.

Out-of-state:	25%	Live on campus:	1%
25 or older:	43%		

Basis for selection. Open admission, but selective for some programs and for out-of-state students. Nursing, radiography, massage therapy, engineering, business, environmental science, education, barbering, and cosmetology programs require separate applications subsequent to admission. 2-year nursing program requires 2.5 GPA and pre-admission test. Pre-requisite for BSN program is an RN. Limited number of out-of-state applicants considered. **Home schooled:** Transcript of courses and grades, state high school equivalency certificate required. Applicant must be at least 16. **Learning Disabled:** Students may provide an IEP and are offered accommodations for a course placement test.

2011-2012 Annual costs. Tuition/fees: $2,871; $10,671 out-of-state. Per-credit charge: $100 in-state; $425 out-of-state. Books/supplies: $2,168. Personal expenses: $1,144.

Financial aid. All financial aid based on need. Work-study available nights, weekends and for part-time students.

Application procedures. Admission: Closing date 8/15 (receipt date). No application fee. Application must be submitted online. Admission notification on a rolling basis. **Financial aid:** Priority date 3/1; no closing date. FAFSA required. Applicants notified on a rolling basis starting 6/1; must reply within 2 week(s) of notification.

Academics. Special study options: Distance learning, double major, dual enrollment of high school students, ESL, internships, teacher certification program. Bachelor's degree programs available on campus. License preparation in nursing, radiology. **Credit/placement by examination:** AP, CLEP, IB, institutional tests. 15 credit hours maximum toward associate degree, 30 toward bachelor's. **Support services:** GED preparation and test center, learning center, remedial instruction, study skills assistance, tutoring, writing center.

Majors. Area/ethnic studies: Regional. **Business:** General, accounting, administrative services, business admin, management information systems. **Computer sciences:** General. **Conservation:** General, forestry, management/policy. **Education:** Early childhood, elementary. **Health services:** Medical radiologic technology/radiation therapy, substance abuse counseling. **Human services:** Social work. **Liberal arts:** Arts/sciences, library assistant. **Physical sciences:** General. **Protective services:** Criminal justice. **Visual/performing arts:** General, art, design, fiber arts, studio arts.

Computing on campus. 24 workstations in library, computer center. Dormitories wired for high-speed internet access and linked to campus network. Commuter students can connect to campus network. Online course registration, online library, wireless network available.

Student life. Freshman orientation: Mandatory. Preregistration for classes offered. Four hour sessions held on Tuesdays prior to term. **Housing:** Single-sex dorms, wellness housing available. **Activities:** Bands, dance, drama, film society, international student organizations, music ensembles, student government, student newspaper, Phi Theta Kappa, American Indian organization.

Athletics. NAIA. **Intercollegiate:** Basketball, cross-country, golf. **Intramural:** Basketball, soccer, softball, volleyball. **Team name:** Eagles.

Student services. Services for economically disadvantaged, student employment services, financial aid counseling, minority student services, veterans' counselor. **Physically disabled:** Services for visually, speech, hearing impaired. **Transfer:** Re-entry adviser, pre-admission transcript evaluation for new students. Transfer adviser, college fairs on campus for students transferring to 4-year colleges.

Contact. E-mail: forona@nnmc.edu
Phone: (505) 747-2112 Fax: (505) 747-5449
Frank Orona, Director of Admissions, Northern New Mexico College, 921 Paseo de Onate, Espanola, NM 87532

San Juan College
Farmington, New Mexico
www.sanjuancollege.edu

CB member
CB code: 4732

- Public 2-year community college
- Commuter campus in large town

General. Founded in 1956. Regionally accredited. **Enrollment:** 6,246 degree-seeking undergraduates; 2,517 non-degree-seeking students. **Degrees:** 506 associate awarded. **Location:** 183 miles from Albuquerque. **Calendar:** Semester, limited summer session. **Full-time faculty:** 155 total; 17% have terminal degrees, 14% minority, 49% women. **Part-time faculty:** 357 total; 14% minority, 54% women. **Special facilities:** Planetarium, Southwestern books and materials collection, geographic information system, art gallery and 800-seat performance hall, fire tower for specialized training, commercial truck driving training range, drilling rig, clean room for instrumentation training, plant operations equipment.

Student profile. Among degree-seeking undergraduates, 44% enrolled in a transfer program, 56% enrolled in a vocational program, 982 enrolled as first-time, first-year students.

Part-time:	56%	Hispanic American:	13%
Women:	63%	Native American:	36%
African American:	1%		

Basis for selection. Open admission. **Home schooled:** Transcript of courses and grades required. Minimum score on ACCUPLACER showing ability to benefit required.

High school preparation. 13 units recommended. Recommended units include English 4, mathematics 3, social studies 3, science 2 and foreign language 1.

2011-2012 Annual costs. Tuition/fees: $1,410; $3,330 out-of-state. Per-credit charge: $41 in-state; $105 out-of-state. Books/supplies: $1,200. Personal expenses: $1,350.

2010-2011 Financial aid. Need-based: 70% of total undergraduate aid awarded as scholarships/grants, 30% as loans/jobs. Need-based aid available for part-time students. Work-study available nights, weekends and for part-time students. **Non-need-based:** Scholarships awarded for academics, state residency.

Application procedures. Admission: No deadline. $10 fee. Admission notification on a rolling basis. High school students may enroll as Early Admit or Dual Credit students. **Financial aid:** No deadline. FAFSA required. Applicants notified on a rolling basis starting 7/1; must reply within 2 week(s) of notification.

Academics. Special study options: Cooperative education, distance learning, dual enrollment of high school students, ESL, external degree, honors, independent study, internships, liberal arts/career combination, teacher certification program. Bachelor's degree programs available on campus. License preparation in dental hygiene, nursing, paramedic, physical therapy. **Credit/placement by examination:** AP, CLEP, institutional tests. 30 credit hours maximum toward associate degree. **Support services:** GED preparation and test center, learning center, reduced course load, remedial instruction, study skills assistance, tutoring, writing center.

Majors. Biology: General. **Business:** Accounting technology, business admin. **Computer sciences:** Data processing. **Education:** Elementary, secondary, special ed. **Engineering:** General. **General:** Landscaping. **Health services:** Clinical lab technology, dental hygiene, medical records technology, nursing (RN), physical therapy assistant, premedicine, respiratory therapy technology, surgical technology, veterinary technology/assistant. **Human services:** Social work. **Liberal arts:** Arts/sciences. **Math:** General. **Parks/recreation:** General, health/fitness. **Physical sciences:** General, chemistry, geology, physics. **Protective services:** Firefighting. **Psychology:** General. **Social sciences:** Geography. **Visual/performing arts:** Commercial/advertising art, theater design. **Work/family studies:** Child care service.

Most popular majors. Business/marketing 7%, engineering/engineering technologies 16%, health sciences 26%, liberal arts 19%, trade and industry 11%.

Computing on campus. 980 workstations in library, computer center, student center. Commuter students can connect to campus network. Online course registration, online library, helpline, wireless network available.

Student life. Freshman orientation: Mandatory. Preregistration for classes offered. One-day session held prior to beginning of semester. **Activities:** Bands, choral groups, dance, drama, film society, music ensembles, musical theater, radio station, student government, student newspaper, Native American club, Student Ambassadors, Phi Theta Kappa honor society, Latino club.

Athletics. Intramural: Archery, badminton, baseball M, basketball, bowling, cross-country, golf, handball, racquetball, skiing, softball, table tennis, tennis, volleyball.

Student services. Career counseling, services for economically disadvantaged, student employment services, financial aid counseling, minority student services, on-campus daycare, personal counseling, placement for graduates, veterans' counselor. **Physically disabled:** Services for visually, speech, hearing impaired. **Transfer:** Transfer adviser, college fairs on campus for students transferring to 4-year colleges.

Contact. E-mail: admissions@sanjuancollege.edu
Phone: (505) 566-3300 Fax: (505) 566-3500
Jon Betz, Senior Director of Enrollment Management, San Juan College, 4601 College Boulevard, Farmington, NM 87402-4699

Santa Fe Community College
Santa Fe, New Mexico
www.sfcc.edu

CB member
CB code: 4816

- Public 2-year community college
- Commuter campus in small city

General. Founded in 1983. Regionally accredited. LEED certified new construction and 90% bio-fueled heating system. **Enrollment:** 3,897 degree-seeking undergraduates; 2,297 non-degree-seeking students. **Degrees:** 287 associate awarded. **Location:** 50 miles from Albuquerque. **Calendar:** Semester, limited summer session. **Full-time faculty:** 68 total; 26% minority, 62% women. **Part-time faculty:** 270 total; 19% minority, 58% women. **Class size:** 50% < 20, 47% 20-39, 3% 40-49, less than 1% 50-99. **Special facilities:** Planetarium, art galleries, fine arts studios, fitness center, swimming pools, child development center, trades and advanced technology center. **Partnerships:** Formal partnerships with businesses and state agencies.

Student profile. Among degree-seeking undergraduates, 25% enrolled in a transfer program, 75% enrolled in a vocational program, 35% already have a bachelor's degree or higher, 570 enrolled as first-time, first-year students, 306 transferred in from other institutions.

Part-time:	58%	Asian American:	2%
Out-of-state:	11%	Hispanic American:	46%
Women:	64%	Native American:	34%
African American:	2%	25 or older:	60%

Transfer out. 20% of students enrolled in the transfer program go on to 4-year colleges. **Colleges most students transferred to 2011:** University of New Mexico, New Mexico State University.

Basis for selection. Open admission, but selective for some programs. Selective admissions to nursing program. Essay and interview required for international students. **Home schooled:** State high school equivalency certificate required.

2011-2012 Annual costs. Tuition/fees: $1,329; $1,689 out-of-district; $3,084 out-of-state. Per-credit charge: $40 in-district; $52 out-of-district; $98 out-of-state. Books/supplies: $600. Personal expenses: $1,500.

Financial aid. Need-based: Need-based aid available for part-time students. Work-study available nights, weekends and for part-time students. **Non-need-based:** Scholarships awarded for academics, state residency.

Application procedures. Admission: No deadline. No application fee. Admission notification on a rolling basis. **Financial aid:** Priority date 5/1; no closing date. FAFSA, institutional form required. Applicants notified on a rolling basis starting 6/1; must reply within 4 week(s) of notification.

Academics. Special study options: Accelerated study, cooperative education, cross-registration, distance learning, double major, dual enrollment of high school students, ESL, honors, independent study, internships, liberal

Two-Year Colleges

arts/career combination, teacher certification program. Bachelor's degree programs available on campus. License preparation in nursing, paramedic. **Credit/placement by examination:** AP, CLEP, institutional tests. 30 credit hours maximum toward associate degree. **Support services:** GED preparation and test center, reduced course load, remedial instruction, study skills assistance, tutoring, writing center.

Majors. Area/ethnic studies: Regional. **Biology:** General. **Business:** Accounting, banking/financial services, business admin. **Computer sciences:** General. **Conservation:** Environmental studies. **Education:** General, kindergarten/preschool. **Engineering:** General. **Foreign languages:** Sign language interpretation, Spanish. **Health services:** Dental assistant, nursing (RN), respiratory therapy technology. **Human services:** Social work. **Liberal arts:** Arts/sciences. **Parks/recreation:** Health/fitness. **Physical sciences:** General. **Protective services:** Criminal justice, police science. **Psychology:** General. **Visual/performing arts:** Art, art history/conservation, design, interior design, studio arts management.

Most popular majors. Business/marketing 21%, education 6%, health sciences 23%, liberal arts 6%, public administration/social services 8%, visual/performing arts 13%.

Computing on campus. 200 workstations in library, computer center, student center. Commuter students can connect to campus network. Online course registration, online library, helpline, wireless network available.

Student life. Freshman orientation: Mandatory. Preregistration for classes offered. **Activities:** Choral groups, drama, film society, international student organizations, literary magazine, music ensembles, radio station, student government, TV station, Phi Theta Kappa, Native American student association, student nursing association, student council, Movimiento Estudiantil Chiemo de Aztlan, fine arts club, Los Tournants, sign language interpreters club, student ambassadors, veterans club.

Student services. Adult student services, career counseling, services for economically disadvantaged, student employment services, financial aid counseling, minority student services, on-campus daycare, personal counseling, placement for graduates, veterans' counselor, women's services. **Physically disabled:** Services for visually, speech, hearing impaired. **Transfer:** Transfer adviser, college fairs on campus for students transferring to 4-year colleges.

Contact. E-mail: enroll@sfcc.edu
Phone: (505) 428-1278 Fax: (505) 428-1468
Cheryl Drangmeister, Asst. VP for Enrollment Management, Santa Fe Community College, 6401 Richards Avenue, Santa Fe, NM 87508-4887

Southwestern Indian Polytechnic Institute
Albuquerque, New Mexico
www.sipi.edu   **CB code: 7047**

▶ Public 2-year community and technical college
▶ Residential campus in large city

General. Founded in 1971. Regionally accredited. National Indian Community College serving American Indians from federally recognized Indian tribes across the United States. Students must show membership by either a certificate of Indian blood or Tribal enrollment card. **Enrollment:** 377 degree-seeking undergraduates; 103 non-degree-seeking students. **Degrees:** 65 associate awarded. **Calendar:** Trimester, extensive summer session. **Full-time faculty:** 13 total; 15% have terminal degrees, 62% minority, 38% women. **Part-time faculty:** 34 total; 24% have terminal degrees, 38% minority, 41% women.

Student profile. Among degree-seeking undergraduates, 35% enrolled in a transfer program, 33% enrolled in a vocational program, 121 enrolled as first-time, first-year students, 27 transferred in from other institutions.

Part-time:	18%	Native American:	100%
Out-of-state:	34%	25 or older:	42%
Women:	54%	Live on campus:	59%

Transfer out. Colleges most students transferred to 2011: University of New Mexico, New Mexico State University, New Mexico Highlands University, Fort Lewis College.

Basis for selection. Open admission. ACT-COMPASS and TABE required for placement of new students. Applicants must have valid membership in U.S. federally recognized Indian tribe. **Home schooled:** Transcript of courses and grades, state high school equivalency certificate required.

High school preparation. College-preparatory program recommended.

2012-2013 Annual costs. Only accepts registered members of Federally-recognized tribes and is tuition free. Students are responsible for required

fees: full-time Lodge student, $560; full-time commuter, $450; part-time, $300. Room only: $110. Books/supplies: $1,200. Personal expenses: $6,000.

Financial aid. Need-based: Need-based aid available for part-time students. Work-study available nights, weekends and for part-time students. **Non-need-based:** Scholarships awarded for academics, leadership, minority status. **Additional information:** Students with valid membership in recognized Indian tribe attend tuition-free.

Application procedures. Admission: Closing date 7/31 (receipt date). No application fee. Admission notification on a rolling basis. **Financial aid:** Closing date 3/1. FAFSA, institutional form required. Applicants notified on a rolling basis starting 9/30.

Academics. Special study options: Cooperative education, distance learning, double major, honors, liberal arts/career combination. **Credit/placement by examination:** AP, CLEP. **Support services:** GED preparation, learning center, remedial instruction, study skills assistance, tutoring.

Majors. Business: General, accounting technology, business admin, hospitality admin, management information systems, office technology. **Computer sciences:** LAN/WAN management. **Education:** Early childhood. **Engineering:** General. **Health services:** Optician. **Liberal arts:** Arts/sciences. **Social sciences:** GIS/cartography.

Most popular majors. Business/marketing 29%, computer/information sciences 9%, education 22%, health sciences 8%, liberal arts 20%, natural resources/environmental science 8%.

Computing on campus. 15 workstations in dormitories, library, computer center, student center. Dormitories linked to campus network. Wireless network available.

Student life. Freshman orientation: Mandatory. Preregistration for classes offered. Held week prior to start of classes. **Policies:** Zero tolerance policy on alcohol and drugs. **Housing:** Single-sex dorms available. $55 fully refundable deposit, deadline 7/30. **Activities:** Dance, student government, natural resources club, Native American political action council, Phi Theta Kappa, dance club, AISES, inter-tribal pow-wow club, music and art club, Four Winds and Golden Eagle Lodge Council.

Athletics. Intramural: Basketball, softball, volleyball, weight lifting. **Team name:** Eagles.

Student services. Alcohol/substance abuse counseling, career counseling, student employment services, financial aid counseling, health services, personal counseling. **Transfer:** Pre-admission transcript evaluation for new students. Transfer adviser, college fairs on campus for students transferring to 4-year colleges.

Contact. E-mail: joseph.carpio@bie.edu
Phone: (505) 346-2338 Toll-free number: (800) 586-7474
Fax: (505) 346-2373
Joseph Carpio, Registrar, Southwestern Indian Polytechnic Institute, PO Box 10146, Albuquerque, NM 87184

New York

Adirondack Community College
Queensbury, New York
www.sunyacc.edu

CB member
CB code: 2017

- Public 2-year community college
- Commuter campus in large town

General. Founded in 1960. Regionally accredited. **Enrollment:** 3,389 degree-seeking undergraduates. **Degrees:** 475 associate awarded. **Location:** 50 miles from Albany, 1 mile from Glens Falls. **Calendar:** Semester, limited summer session. **Full-time faculty:** 89 total. **Part-time faculty:** 187 total. **Special facilities:** Solar botany lab, challenge course, fitness trail, pond preserve, arboretum, weather station, forensic science lab.

Student profile.

Out-of-state:	1%	25 or older:	21%

Basis for selection. Open admission, but selective for some programs. Minimum high school average of 80 or minimum GPA of 2.5 for acceptance into nursing program. If submitted, SAT or ACT and SAT Subject Tests used for placement and counseling. **Home schooled:** State high school equivalency certificate required. Must take and pass GED or successfuly complete ability to benefit test.

High school preparation. College-preparatory program recommended. 22 units recommended. Recommended units include English 4, mathematics 3, social studies 4, history 2, science 3, foreign language 1 and academic electives 5. Allied health programs require Regents biology, chemistry examinations. Engineering requires Regents biology, chemistry and mathematics through pre-calculus. Computer science, mechanical and electrical technology require mathematics through advanced algebra. Forestry requires Regents biology, chemistry, and mathematics through intermediate algebra.

2011-2012 Annual costs. Tuition/fees: $3,828; $7,384 out-of-state. Per-credit charge: $149 in-state; $298 out-of-state. Books/supplies: $1,200. Personal expenses: $807.

Financial aid. Need-based: Need-based aid available for part-time students. Work-study available nights, weekends and for part-time students. **Non-need-based:** Scholarships awarded for academics, state residency.

Application procedures. Admission: No deadline. $50 fee, may be waived for applicants with need. Admission notification on a rolling basis. **Financial aid:** Priority date 4/15; no closing date. FAFSA, institutional form required. Applicants notified on a rolling basis starting 5/1.

Academics. Special study options: Cross-registration, distance learning, double major, dual enrollment of high school students, independent study, internships, liberal arts/career combination. Bachelor's degree programs available on campus. **Credit/placement by examination:** AP, CLEP, IB, institutional tests. 34 credit hours maximum toward associate degree. **Support services:** Learning center, reduced course load, remedial instruction, study skills assistance, tutoring, writing center.

Majors. Business: Accounting, business admin, hospitality/recreation, marketing, tourism promotion. **Communications:** Broadcast journalism, media studies. **Computer sciences:** General, data processing, information systems, information technology, programming. **Engineering:** General. **Health services:** Nursing (RN), radiologic technology/medical imaging. **Liberal arts:** Arts/sciences. **Protective services:** Police science. **Visual/performing arts:** Music.

Most popular majors. Business/marketing 18%, communications/journalism 6%, health sciences 15%, liberal arts 46%, security/protective services 6%.

Computing on campus. 600 workstations in library, computer center, student center. Commuter students can connect to campus network. Online course registration, online library, wireless network available.

Student life. Freshman orientation: Mandatory. Preregistration for classes offered. **Activities:** Bands, choral groups, dance, drama, literary magazine, music ensembles, musical theater, radio station, student government, student newspaper.

Athletics. NJCAA. **Intercollegiate:** Baseball M, basketball, bowling, golf M, soccer, softball W, tennis, volleyball W. **Intramural:** Badminton, basketball, football (non-tackle), softball, volleyball. **Team name:** Timberwolves.

Student services. Adult student services, career counseling, student employment services, financial aid counseling, on-campus daycare, personal counseling, placement for graduates, veterans' counselor. **Physically disabled:** Services for visually, speech, hearing impaired. **Transfer:** Transfer adviser, college fairs on campus for students transferring to 4-year colleges.

Contact. E-mail: info@acc.sunyacc.edu
Phone: (518) 743-2264 Fax: (518) 832-7602
Sara Jane Linehan, Director of Enrollment Management, Adirondack Community College, 640 Bay Road, Queensbury, NY 12804

American Academy McAllister Institute of Funeral Service
New York, New York
www.funeraleducation.org

CB code: 0774

- Private 2-year school of mortuary science
- Commuter campus in very large city
- Application essay required

General. Founded in 1926. **Enrollment:** 395 degree-seeking undergraduates. **Degrees:** 125 associate awarded. **Calendar:** Semester, extensive summer session. **Part-time faculty:** 25 total; 4% have terminal degrees, 12% minority, 48% women. **Class size:** 67% 20-39, 33% 40-49.

Student profile. Among degree-seeking undergraduates, 10% enrolled in a vocational program, 30% already have a bachelor's degree or higher, 395 enrolled as first-time, first-year students, 40 transferred in from other institutions.

Part-time:	62%	Asian American:	1%
Out-of-state:	26%	Hispanic American:	10%
Women:	53%	Native American:	1%
African American:	20%	25 or older:	39%

Basis for selection. Interview recommended. **Home schooled:** Transcript of courses and grades required.

2011-2012 Annual costs. Tuition/fees: $11,370. Books/supplies: $709. Personal expenses: $2,635.

Financial aid. All financial aid based on need. Work-study available nights, weekends and for part-time students.

Application procedures. Admission: No deadline. $50 fee. Admission notification on a rolling basis. **Financial aid:** FAFSA required. Applicants notified on a rolling basis starting 7/1; must reply by 9/1 or within 3 week(s) of notification.

Academics. Special study options: Cross-registration, distance learning. **Credit/placement by examination:** AP, CLEP. **Support services:** Study skills assistance, tutoring.

Computing on campus. 12 workstations in library.

Student life. Freshman orientation: Mandatory. Preregistration for classes offered. **Activities:** Student government.

Student services. Personal counseling, placement for graduates. **Transfer:** Pre-admission transcript evaluation for new students. Transfer adviser for students transferring to 4-year colleges.

Contact. E-mail: info@funeraleducation.org
Phone: (212) 757-1190 Toll-free number: (866) 932-2264
Fax: (212) 765-5923
Andre Rampaul, Director of Admissions and Registrar, American Academy McAllister Institute of Funeral Service, 619 West 54th Street, 2nd Floor, New York, NY 10019-3602

American Academy of Dramatic Arts
New York, New York
www.aada.org

CB code: 2603

- Private 2-year junior and performing arts college
- Commuter campus in very large city
- Application essay, interview required

General. Founded in 1884. Regionally accredited. Offers practical conservatory and training. Additional campus in Hollywood, CA. **Enrollment:** 224 degree-seeking undergraduates. **Degrees:** 88 associate awarded. **Location:** Midtown Manhattan. **Calendar:** Semester, limited summer session. **Full-time faculty:** 8 total; 38% have terminal degrees, 12% minority, 75% women. **Part-time faculty:** 19 total; 21% have terminal degrees, 16% minority, 53% women. **Class size:** 100% < 20. **Special facilities:** 3 theaters, dance studio, costume department, property/production areas, audio/visual center, state-of-the-art television studio.

Student profile. Among degree-seeking undergraduates, 12% enrolled in a transfer program, 4% already have a bachelor's degree or higher, 66 enrolled as first-time, first-year students, 58 transferred in from other institutions.

Out-of-state:	64%	Hispanic American:	5%
Women:	57%	International:	18%
African American:	7%	25 or older:	12%
Asian American:	1%		

Transfer out. 6% of students enrolled in the transfer program go on to 4-year colleges.

Basis for selection. Dramatic ability or potential, academic qualifications, maturity and motivation very important. Audition required; regional audition/interview may be arranged. **Home schooled:** Transcript of courses and grades, interview, letter of recommendation (nonparent) required.

2011-2012 Annual costs. Tuition/fees: $30,500. Books/supplies: $700. Personal expenses: $1,100.

Financial aid. All financial aid based on need. Work-study available nights, weekends and for part-time students. **Additional information:** Need-based incentive grants of $200-$2,000 for first-year students.

Application procedures. Admission: No deadline. $50 fee. Admission notification on a rolling basis. **Financial aid:** No deadline. FAFSA, institutional form required. Applicants notified on a rolling basis.

Academics. 2-year professional actor training program offered with associate of occupational studies degree. Third year, available by faculty invitation, forms showcase Academy Company. **Special study options:** Students may study 1 year at each of 2 campuses. **Credit/placement by examination:** AP, CLEP. **Support services:** Tutoring.

Majors. Visual/performing arts: Acting.

Computing on campus. 6 workstations in library.

Student life. Freshman orientation: Mandatory. Preregistration for classes offered. **Activities:** Drama, student government, student newspaper, various arts-related organizations available.

Student services. Career counseling, student employment services, placement for graduates.

Contact. E-mail: admissions-ny@aada.org
Phone: (212) 686-9244 Toll-free number: (800) 463-8990
Fax: (212) 685-8093
Karen Higginbotham, Director of Admissions, American Academy of Dramatic Arts, 120 Madison Avenue, New York, NY 10016

Art Institute of New York City
New York, New York — CB member
www.ainyc.artinstitutes.edu — CB code: 3106

- For-profit 2-year culinary school and technical college
- Commuter campus in very large city
- Application essay, interview required

General. Accredited by ACICS. **Enrollment:** 1,650 degree-seeking undergraduates. **Degrees:** 207 associate awarded. **Calendar:** Quarter, extensive summer session. **Full-time faculty:** 80 total. **Part-time faculty:** 25 total.

Basis for selection. Open admission. Accuplacer may be used in placement for certain programs of study. **Home schooled:** Transcript of courses and grades, state high school equivalency certificate required.

2011-2012 Annual costs. Tuition/fees: $24,670. Per-credit charge: $546. Students are required to purchase a "starter" kit of items needed for their program of study. Prices range from $755 to $1,995. Books/supplies: $650.

Financial aid. Need-based: Work-study available nights, weekends and for part-time students.

Application procedures. Admission: No deadline. $50 fee. Admission notification on a rolling basis.

Academics. Special study options: Cooperative education, internships. **Credit/placement by examination:** AP, CLEP. **Support services:** Learning center, remedial instruction, study skills assistance.

Majors. Visual/performing arts: Cinematography, fashion design, graphic design, interior design, multimedia.

Computing on campus. 40 workstations in library, computer center. Online library, helpline, repair service available.

Student life. Freshman orientation: Mandatory. Preregistration for classes offered. Scheduled prior to class start or in first week. **Activities:** Film society, student newspaper.

Student services. Adult student services, career counseling, student employment services, financial aid counseling, personal counseling, placement for graduates. **Transfer:** Re-entry adviser, pre-admission transcript evaluation for new students.

Contact. E-mail: mgrillo@aii.edu
Phone: (212) 226-5500 Toll-free number: (800) 654-2433
Fax: (212) 625-6065
Mary Ann Grillo, Senior Director of Admissions, Art Institute of New York City, 11 Beach Street, New York, NY 10013-1917

ASA Institute of Business and Computer Technology
Brooklyn, New York
www.asa.edu

- For-profit 2-year technical and career college
- Commuter campus in very large city
- Interview required

General. Regionally accredited; also accredited by ACICS. Externships are included in every program. **Enrollment:** 5,039 degree-seeking undergraduates; 33 non-degree-seeking students. **Degrees:** 1,279 associate awarded. **Location:** Located in New York City. **Calendar:** Semester, extensive summer session. **Full-time faculty:** 76 total. **Part-time faculty:** 245 total. **Class size:** 64% < 20, 36% 20-39.

Student profile. Among degree-seeking undergraduates, 1,265 enrolled as first-time, first-year students, 54 transferred in from other institutions.

Part-time:	5%	Hispanic American:	41%
Out-of-state:	4%	International:	7%
Women:	67%	25 or older:	49%
African American:	39%	Live on campus:	1%
Asian American:	6%		

Transfer out. Colleges most students transferred to 2011: St. Joseph's College.

Basis for selection. Open admission. Candidates accorded individual consideration through assessment testing results. **Learning Disabled:** Meet with Director, Office of Students with Disability Services.

2012-2013 Annual costs. Tuition/fees (projected): $12,099. Per-credit charge: $495. Books/supplies: $1,500. Personal expenses: $4,985.

2010-2011 Financial aid. Need-based: 68% of total undergraduate aid awarded as scholarships/grants, 32% as loans/jobs. Need-based aid available for part-time students. Work-study available nights, weekends and for part-time students. **Non-need-based:** Scholarships awarded for academics, alumni affiliation, leadership, state residency.

Application procedures. Admission: No deadline. $25 fee. Application must be submitted on paper. **Financial aid:** No deadline. FAFSA required. Applicants notified on a rolling basis starting 7/6; must reply by 10/6.

Academics. Special study options: Accelerated study, distance learning, ESL, internships. **Credit/placement by examination:** AP, CLEP. **Support services:** GED preparation, learning center, reduced course load, remedial instruction, study skills assistance, tutoring, writing center.

Majors. Business: Accounting/business management, business admin. **Computer sciences:** Networking, programming. **Health services:** Health care admin, medical assistant, medical records admin, nursing practice, pharmacy assistant. **Protective services:** Criminal justice.

Most popular majors. Business/marketing 18%, computer/information sciences 7%, health sciences 53%, legal studies 22%.

Computing on campus. 700 workstations in dormitories, library, computer center. Online library, helpline available.

Student life. Freshman orientation: Mandatory. Preregistration for classes offered. **Housing:** Coed dorms available. **Activities:** Drama, literary magazine, student government.

Athletics. NJCAA. **Intercollegiate:** Basketball, soccer M. **Team name:** Avengers.

Student services. Adult student services, career counseling, services for economically disadvantaged, student employment services, financial aid counseling, personal counseling, placement for graduates.

Contact. E-mail: vkostyukov@asa.edu
Phone: (718) 522-9073 Toll-free number: (877) 867-5327
Fax: (718) 532-1432
Victoria Kostyukov, Vice President of Marketing and Admissions, ASA Institute of Business and Computer Technology, 81 Willoughby Street, Brooklyn, NY 11201

Bramson ORT College
Forest Hills, New York
www.bramsonort.edu
CB code: 0944

- Private 2-year junior and technical college affiliated with Jewish faith
- Commuter campus in very large city

General. Founded in 1977. Regionally accredited. Extensions in Brooklyn and Queens. **Enrollment:** 846 full-time, degree-seeking students. **Degrees:** 275 associate awarded. **Calendar:** Semester, extensive summer session. **Full-time faculty:** 65 total. **Part-time faculty:** 58 total. **Special facilities:** Ophthalmic laboratory.

Basis for selection. High school diploma and placement examination required. English and mathematics placement tests required. Interview recommended.

2011-2012 Annual costs. Tuition/fees: $10,970.

Financial aid. Need-based: Work-study available nights, weekends and for part-time students.

Application procedures. Admission: No deadline. $50 fee. Admission notification on a rolling basis. **Financial aid:** No deadline. Institutional form required. Applicants notified on a rolling basis; must reply within 3 week(s) of notification.

Academics. Special study options: Accelerated study, double major, ESL, internships. **Credit/placement by examination:** AP, CLEP, institutional tests. 50% of total hours needed for degree may be maximum of earned by examination. **Support services:** Learning center, pre-admission summer program, reduced course load, remedial instruction, tutoring.

Majors. Business: Accounting, administrative services, business admin, financial planning, management information systems. **Computer sciences:** General, applications programming, data processing, programming. **Engineering:** Electrical.

Computing on campus. 87 workstations in library, computer center.

Student life. Activities: Student government, student newspaper.

Student services. Adult student services, career counseling, student employment services, personal counseling, placement for graduates, veterans' counselor. **Physically disabled:** Services for visually, speech, hearing impaired.

Contact. Phone: (718) 261-5800 Fax: (718) 575-5118
Aleksandra Kagan, Director of Admissions, Bramson ORT College, 6930 Austin Street, Forest Hills, NY 11375

Broome Community College
Binghamton, New York
CB member
www.sunybroome.edu
CB code: 2048

- Public 2-year community college
- Commuter campus in small city

General. Founded in 1946. Regionally accredited. SUNY institution. **Enrollment:** 5,659 degree-seeking undergraduates. **Degrees:** 986 associate awarded. **Location:** 3 miles from downtown. **Calendar:** Semester, extensive summer session. **Full-time faculty:** 166 total. **Part-time faculty:** 287 total. **Class size:** 67% < 20, 31% 20-39, less than 1% 40-49, less than 1% 50-99, less than 1% >100. **Special facilities:** College-operated ice rink.

Student profile.

Out-of-state:	4%	25 or older:	28%

Transfer out. Colleges most students transferred to 2011: Binghamton University, Rochester Institute of Technology, State University of New York Cortland, State University of New York Utica-Rome, Ithaca College.

Basis for selection. Open admission, but selective for some programs. Entry into certain health sciences programs (nursing, physical therapy assistant, medical lab technology, medical assistant, radiologic technology, health information technology, dental hygiene) limited on space-available basis. Interview recommended for computer science and health science programs. **Home schooled:** Provide either 1) letter from superintendent of the school district in which student resides attesting to completion of program meeting requirements of Section 100.10 of the Regulations of the Commissioner of Education or 2) a passing score on GED (and diploma itself when available). Also may be admitted on ability-to-benefit basis.

2011-2012 Annual costs. Tuition/fees: $4,111; $7,805 out-of-state. Per-credit charge: $154 in-state; $308 out-of-state. Books/supplies: $1,400. Personal expenses: $1,004.

Financial aid. Need-based: Need-based aid available for part-time students. Work-study available nights, weekends and for part-time students.

Application procedures. Admission: No deadline. No application fee. Admission notification on a rolling basis. Health Science students should apply and have all transcripts sent by March 15 prior to the fall semester. **Financial aid:** Priority date 3/1; no closing date. FAFSA required. Applicants notified on a rolling basis starting 3/15; must reply within 2 week(s) of notification.

Academics. Special study options: Cooperative education, distance learning, dual enrollment of high school students, ESL, exchange student, honors, independent study, internships, student-designed major, study abroad, weekend college. License preparation in dental hygiene, nursing, paramedic, physical therapy, radiology, real estate. **Credit/placement by examination:** AP, CLEP, institutional tests. Contact division dean for assessment of experiential learning or portfolio assessment. **Support services:** Learning center, reduced course load, remedial instruction, study skills assistance, tutoring, writing center.

Majors. Business: Accounting technology, business admin, executive assistant, financial planning, hotel/motel admin, international finance. **Communications:** Communications/speech/rhetoric. **Computer sciences:** General, data processing, information systems. **Engineering:** Engineering science. **Health services:** Clinical lab technology, dental hygiene, EMT paramedic, medical assistant, medical radiologic technology/radiation therapy, medical records technology, nursing (RN), physical therapy assistant, substance abuse counseling. **Liberal arts:** Arts/sciences. **Protective services:** Corrections, firefighting, police science. **Work/family studies:** Child care management.

Most popular majors. Business/marketing 17%, engineering/engineering technologies 8%, health sciences 19%, liberal arts 40%.

Computing on campus. 500 workstations in library, computer center. Commuter students can connect to campus network. Online course registration, helpline, wireless network available.

Student life. Freshman orientation: Available. Preregistration for classes offered. **Activities:** Bands, campus ministries, choral groups, dance, drama, international student organizations, music ensembles, musical theater, student government, student newspaper, black student union, Phi Theta Kappa, Ski Extreme, writing club, chess club, Alpha Beta Gamma, computer club, music association.

Athletics. NJCAA. **Intercollegiate:** Baseball M, basketball, cheerleading, cross-country, golf M, ice hockey M, lacrosse M, soccer, tennis M, volleyball W. **Intramural:** Badminton, basketball, bowling, golf, soccer, tennis, volleyball. **Team name:** Hornets.

Student services. Adult student services, career counseling, services for economically disadvantaged, student employment services, financial aid counseling, health services, on-campus daycare, personal counseling, placement for graduates, veterans' counselor. **Physically disabled:** Services for visually, speech, hearing impaired. **Transfer:** Transfer adviser, college fairs on campus for students transferring to 4-year colleges.

Contact. E-mail: admissions@sunybroome.edu
Phone: (607) 778-5001 Toll-free number: (800) 836-0689
Fax: (607) 778-5310
Janae Schmidt, Director of Admissions, Broome Community College, Box 1017, Binghamton, NY 13902

Bryant & Stratton College: Albany
Albany, New York
www.bryantstratton.edu   **CB code: 2018**

♦ For-profit 2-year business college
♦ Commuter campus in small city
♦ Application essay, interview required

General. Founded in 1854. Regionally accredited. **Enrollment:** 769 degree-seeking undergraduates. **Degrees:** 222 associate awarded. **Location:** 2 miles from Albany, 28 miles from Saratoga. **Calendar:** Semester, extensive summer session. **Full-time faculty:** 23 total; 44% have terminal degrees, 17% minority, 44% women. **Part-time faculty:** 50 total; 22% have terminal degrees, 12% minority, 52% women.

Student profile. Among degree-seeking undergraduates, 106 enrolled as first-time, first-year students.

Part-time:	37%	25 or older:	46%
Women:	76%		

Basis for selection. High school record, entrance examination score, personal interview and personal essay considered. Portfolio recommended.

High school preparation. Business courses recommended. Mathematics concentration preferred.

2011-2012 Annual costs. Tuition/fees: $15,570.

Financial aid. All financial aid based on need. Need-based aid available for part-time students. Work-study available nights, weekends and for part-time students.

Application procedures. Admission: No deadline. No application fee. Admission notification on a rolling basis. **Financial aid:** No deadline. FAFSA required. Applicants notified on a rolling basis.

Academics. Special study options: Distance learning, double major, independent study, internships. Bachelor's degree programs available on campus. **Credit/placement by examination:** AP, CLEP. 31 credit hours maximum toward associate degree. **Support services:** GED preparation, learning center, reduced course load, remedial instruction, study skills assistance, tutoring, writing center.

Majors. Business: Accounting, administrative services, business admin, human resources. **Computer sciences:** General. **Health services:** Medical assistant. **Protective services:** Law enforcement admin.

Most popular majors. Business/marketing 21%, computer/information sciences 7%, health sciences 35%, legal studies 37%, security/protective services 23%.

Computing on campus. 200 workstations in library, computer center. Wireless network available.

Student life. Freshman orientation: Mandatory. Preregistration for classes offered.

Student services. Alcohol/substance abuse counseling, career counseling, student employment services, financial aid counseling, personal counseling, placement for graduates, veterans' counselor. **Physically disabled:** Services for visually impaired. **Transfer:** Pre-admission transcript evaluation for new students. Transfer adviser, college fairs on campus for students transferring to 4-year colleges.

Contact. E-mail: rpferrell@bryantstratton.edu
Phone: (518) 437-1802 ext. 203 Fax: (518) 437-1049
Robert Ferrell, Director of Admissions, Bryant & Stratton College: Albany, 1259 Central Avenue, Albany, NY 12205

Bryant & Stratton College: Amherst
Getzville, New York
www.bryantstratton.edu   **CB code: 3331**

♦ For-profit 2-year business and career college
♦ Small town

General. Regionally accredited. **Enrollment:** 507 degree-seeking undergraduates. **Degrees:** 20 bachelor's, 124 associate awarded. **Calendar:** Trimester.

Basis for selection. Students conditionally accepted if all admissions requirements are received except for the official transcripts as long as a College official is able to verbally verify the graduation status or receipt of the GED from the granting institution.

2011-2012 Annual costs. Tuition/fees: $15,570. Books/supplies: $1,200.

Financial aid. Need-based: Work-study available nights, weekends and for part-time students.

Academics. Special study options: Distance learning, internships. Bachelor's degree programs available on campus. **Credit/placement by examination:** AP, CLEP. **Support services:** Learning center.

Majors. Business: Business admin. **Computer sciences:** General. **Visual/performing arts:** General.

Computing on campus. Wireless network available.

Student services. Placement for graduates.

Contact. Phone: (716) 625-6300 Fax: (716) 689-6078
Brian Dioguardi, Director of Admissions, Bryant & Stratton College: Amherst, 3650 Millersport Highway, Getzville, NY 14068

Bryant & Stratton College: Buffalo
Buffalo, New York
www.bryantstratton.edu   **CB code: 2058**

♦ For-profit 2-year business and career college
♦ Commuter campus in large city
♦ Interview required

General. Founded in 1854. Regionally accredited. Branch campuses in Amherst (NY) and Orchard Park. **Enrollment:** 874 degree-seeking undergraduates. **Degrees:** 20 bachelor's, 173 associate awarded. **Calendar:** Semester, extensive summer session. **Full-time faculty:** 16 total. **Part-time faculty:** 53 total.

Transfer out. Colleges most students transferred to 2011: Erie Community College.

Basis for selection. Open admission. **Learning Disabled:** Students with special needs are invited to discuss their needs with their student services advisor prior to registration. Students requesting accommodations are required to provide current documentation in order to determine reasonable accommodations where appropriate.

2011-2012 Annual costs. Tuition/fees: $15,570.

Financial aid. Need-based: Work-study available nights, weekends and for part-time students.

Application procedures. Admission: No deadline. $35 fee, may be waived for applicants with need. Admission notification on a rolling basis. **Financial aid:** No deadline. Applicants notified on a rolling basis.

Academics. Special study options: Distance learning, internships, weekend college. Bachelor's degree programs available on campus. **Credit/placement by examination:** AP, CLEP, institutional tests. **Support services:** Learning center, remedial instruction, study skills assistance, tutoring, writing center.

Majors. Business: General, administrative services. **Computer sciences:** General. **Health services:** Medical assistant.

Computing on campus. 150 workstations in library, computer center. Online library, repair service, wireless network available.

Student life. Freshman orientation: Mandatory. Preregistration for classes offered. **Activities:** Student government, student newspaper, numerous special interest clubs.

Athletics. Intramural: Bowling, skiing, softball, swimming.

Student services. Career counseling, student employment services, financial aid counseling, personal counseling, placement for graduates. **Physically disabled:** Services for visually, hearing impaired. **Transfer:** Re-entry adviser, pre-admission transcript evaluation for new students. Transfer adviser, college fairs on campus for students transferring to 4-year colleges.

Contact. E-mail: mbrobinson@bryantstratton.edu
Phone: (716) 884-9120 Fax: (716) 884-0091
Philip Struebel, Director of Admissions, Bryant & Stratton College:
Buffalo, 465 Main Street, Suite 400, Buffalo, NY 14203

Bryant & Stratton College: Henrietta
Rochester, New York
www.bryantstratton.edu

- For-profit 2-year business college
- Commuter campus in small city

General. **Enrollment:** 431 degree-seeking undergraduates. **Degrees:** 130 associate awarded. **Calendar:** Semester. **Full-time faculty:** 22 total. **Part-time faculty:** 39 total.

Basis for selection. Interview, entrance evaluation important.

2011-2012 Annual costs. Tuition/fees: $15,570.

Financial aid. **Need-based:** Work-study available nights, weekends and for part-time students.

Application procedures. **Admission:** No deadline. No application fee.

Academics. Credit/placement by examination: AP, CLEP.

Majors. **Business:** Accounting, administrative services, human resources. **Computer sciences:** Information technology. **Health services:** Medical assistant, medical secretary. **Protective services:** Law enforcement admin. **Visual/performing arts:** Graphic design.

Contact. Phone: (585) 292-5627
Dave Profita, Admissions Director, Bryant & Stratton College: Henrietta, 1225 Jefferson Road, Rochester, NY 14623

Bryant & Stratton College: Rochester
Rochester, New York
www.bryantstratton.edu   CB code: 7327

- For-profit 2-year business and career college
- Commuter campus in large city
- Interview required

General. Founded in 1973. Regionally accredited. Two campuses in Rochester. Degree program runs 4 consecutive semesters. **Enrollment:** 432 degree-seeking undergraduates. **Degrees:** 80 associate awarded. **Calendar:** Differs by program, extensive summer session. **Full-time faculty:** 2 total. **Part-time faculty:** 26 total.

Basis for selection. Character, previous scholastic record, and counselor recommendation important. CPAt required for admission.

2011-2012 Annual costs. Tuition/fees: $15,570. Books/supplies: $1,000.

Financial aid. **Need-based:** Work-study available nights, weekends and for part-time students.

Application procedures. **Admission:** No deadline. No application fee. Admission notification on a rolling basis. **Financial aid:** No deadline. FAFSA required. Applicants notified on a rolling basis.

Academics. **Special study options:** Accelerated study, distance learning, double major, internships. **Credit/placement by examination:** AP, CLEP. **Support services:** Learning center, reduced course load, study skills assistance, tutoring.

Majors. **Business:** Accounting, administrative services, business admin, customer service, office technology. **Computer sciences:** Information technology, webmaster. **Health services:** Office admin. **Visual/performing arts:** Design.

Computing on campus. 10 workstations in computer center. Commuter students can connect to campus network.

Student life. **Freshman orientation:** Available. Preregistration for classes offered. **Activities:** Student government, professional interest clubs.

Athletics. **Team name:** Bobcats.

Student services. Career counseling, financial aid counseling, personal counseling, placement for graduates. **Transfer:** Pre-admission transcript evaluation for new students. Transfer adviser for students transferring to 4-year colleges.

Contact. Phone: (585) 292-5627
Brandon DiNell, Director of Admissions, Bryant & Stratton College: Rochester, 1225 Jefferson Road, Rochester, NY 14623

Bryant & Stratton College: Southtowns
Orchard Park, New York
www.bryantstratton.edu   CB code: 3328

- For-profit 2-year business college
- Commuter campus in large town

General. Regionally accredited. **Enrollment:** 529 degree-seeking undergraduates. **Degrees:** 18 bachelor's, 168 associate awarded. **Location:** 11 miles from downtown Buffalo. **Calendar:** Differs by program, extensive summer session. **Full-time faculty:** 10 total. **Part-time faculty:** 42 total.

Basis for selection. Open admission.

2011-2012 Annual costs. Tuition/fees: $15,570. Books/supplies: $1,200.

Financial aid. **Need-based:** Work-study available nights, weekends and for part-time students.

Application procedures. **Admission:** No deadline. $25 fee.

Academics. **Special study options:** Distance learning, double major. **Credit/placement by examination:** AP, CLEP. **Support services:** Learning center, study skills assistance, tutoring.

Majors. **Business:** Business admin. **Computer sciences:** General.

Computing on campus. Online library available.

Student life. **Freshman orientation:** Mandatory. Preregistration for classes offered. **Activities:** Student government, student newspaper.

Student services. Career counseling, student employment services, financial aid counseling. **Physically disabled:** Services for visually, hearing impaired. **Transfer:** Pre-admission transcript evaluation for new students.

Contact. E-mail: prkehr@bryantstratton.edu
Phone: (716) 677-9500 Fax: (716) 677-9599
Paul Kehr, Director of Admissions, Bryant & Stratton College: Southtowns, 200 Redtail, Orchard Park, NY 14127

Bryant & Stratton College: Syracuse
Syracuse, New York
www.bryantstratton.edu   CB code: 0654

- For-profit 2-year business and junior college
- Commuter campus in small city

General. Founded in 1854. Regionally accredited. **Enrollment:** 772 degree-seeking undergraduates. **Degrees:** 174 associate awarded. **Location:** 75 miles from Rochester. **Calendar:** Trimester, extensive summer session. **Full-time faculty:** 23 total. **Part-time faculty:** 38 total. **Class size:** 54% < 20, 46% 20-39.

Student profile.

Out-of-state:	2%	Live on campus:	10%
25 or older:	45%		

Basis for selection. Open admission.

2011-2012 Annual costs. Tuition/fees: $15,570. Books/supplies: $700.

Financial aid. All financial aid based on need. Work-study available nights, weekends and for part-time students.

Application procedures. **Admission:** No deadline. No application fee. Application must be submitted on paper. Admission notification on a rolling basis. **Financial aid:** No deadline. FAFSA required. Applicants notified on a rolling basis starting 10/1.

Academics. **Special study options:** Cross-registration, distance learning, honors, internships. **Credit/placement by examination:** AP, CLEP. **Support**

services: Learning center, reduced course load, remedial instruction, study skills assistance, tutoring.

Majors. Business: Accounting, administrative services, business admin, hotel/motel admin, marketing, office management, sales/distribution, tourism promotion, tourism/travel. **Computer sciences:** General. **Health services:** Medical assistant, medical secretary. **Protective services:** Police science.

Most popular majors. Business/marketing 61%, health sciences 35%.

Computing on campus. 230 workstations in dormitories, library, computer center. Dormitories wired for high-speed internet access and linked to campus network. Commuter students can connect to campus network. Online library available.

Student life. Freshman orientation: Mandatory. Preregistration for classes offered. **Housing:** Single-sex dorms available. $100 fully refundable deposit. **Activities:** Student newspaper.

Athletics. NJCAA. **Intercollegiate:** Soccer. **Team name:** Bobcats.

Student services. Career counseling, student employment services, financial aid counseling, personal counseling, placement for graduates. **Physically disabled:** Services for visually, speech, hearing impaired. **Transfer:** Re-entry adviser, pre-admission transcript evaluation for new students. Transfer adviser, college fairs on campus for students transferring to 4-year colleges.

Contact. Phone: (315) 472-6603 Fax: (315) 474-4383
Andy Cunningham, Director of Admissions, Bryant & Stratton College: Syracuse, 953 James Street, Syracuse, NY 13203

Bryant & Stratton College: Syracuse North
Liverpool, New York
www.bryantstratton.edu

- For-profit 2-year career college
- Commuter campus in small city
- Interview required

General. Enrollment: 536 degree-seeking undergraduates. **Degrees:** 185 associate awarded. **Location:** 5 miles from Syracuse. **Calendar:** Semester, extensive summer session. **Full-time faculty:** 11 total. **Part-time faculty:** 42 total.

Transfer out. Colleges most students transferred to 2011: Onondaga Community College.

Basis for selection. Acceptance based on the completion of the required admissions paperwork. This process includes the admissions application, interview, and entrance evaluation. **Home schooled:** State high school equivalency certificate, interview required. **Learning Disabled:** Testing accommodations made when students disclose they have a learning disability.

High school preparation. College-preparatory program recommended.

2011-2012 Annual costs. Tuition/fees: $15,570.

Financial aid. All financial aid based on need. Need-based aid available for part-time students. Work-study available nights, weekends and for part-time students.

Application procedures. Admission: No deadline. No application fee. Application must be submitted on paper. Admission notification on a rolling basis beginning on or about 9/20. **Financial aid:** No deadline. FAFSA, institutional form required.

Academics. Special study options: Accelerated study, internships. **Credit/placement by examination:** AP, CLEP. **Support services:** GED preparation, learning center, study skills assistance, tutoring.

Majors. Business: General, accounting, administrative services. **Computer sciences:** System admin. **Visual/performing arts:** Graphic design.

Computing on campus. Online library available.

Student life. Freshman orientation: Mandatory. Preregistration for classes offered.

Athletics. NJCAA. **Intercollegiate:** Cross-country, soccer. **Team name:** Bobcats.

Student services. Career counseling, financial aid counseling, placement for graduates. **Transfer:** Pre-admission transcript evaluation for new students. College fairs on campus for students transferring to 4-year colleges.

Contact. Phone: (315) 652-6500
Heather Macknick, Admissions Director, Bryant & Stratton College: Syracuse North, 8687 Carling Road, Liverpool, NY 13090

Business Informatics Center
Valley Stream, New York
www.thecollegeforbusiness.com

- For-profit 2-year business and community college
- Commuter campus in large town
- Interview required

General. Accredited by ACCSC. **Enrollment:** 135 degree-seeking undergraduates. **Degrees:** 51 associate awarded. **Calendar:** Quarter. **Full-time faculty:** 10 total. **Part-time faculty:** 12 total. **Class size:** 92% < 20, 8% 20-39.

Transfer out. Colleges most students transferred to 2011: Briarcliff College, Katharine Gibbs.

Basis for selection. Open admission.

2011-2012 Annual costs. Tuition/fees: $12,500.

Financial aid. Need-based: Work-study available nights, weekends and for part-time students.

Application procedures. Admission: No deadline. $50 fee, may be waived for applicants with need. Admission notification on a rolling basis. **Financial aid:** No deadline.

Academics. Credit/placement by examination: AP, CLEP, institutional tests. **Support services:** Tutoring.

Majors. Business: Office technology.

Most popular majors. Business/marketing 77%, legal studies 23%.

Computing on campus. 50 workstations in library, computer center.

Student life. Freshman orientation: Mandatory. Preregistration for classes offered. **Activities:** Student government.

Student services. Financial aid counseling, placement for graduates. **Transfer:** Transfer center for students transferring to 4-year colleges.

Contact. Phone: (516) 561-0050
Hank Meaney, Admissions Director, Business Informatics Center, 134 South Central Avenue, Valley Stream, NY 11580-5431

Cayuga Community College
Auburn, New York
www.cayuga-cc.edu   **CB code: 2010**

- Public 2-year community college
- Commuter campus in large town

General. Founded in 1953. Regionally accredited. **Enrollment:** 3,307 degree-seeking undergraduates. **Degrees:** 536 associate awarded. **Location:** 30 miles from Syracuse. **Calendar:** Semester, limited summer session. **Full-time faculty:** 59 total. **Part-time faculty:** 203 total. **Class size:** 63% < 20, 36% 20-39, less than 1% 40-49, less than 1% 50-99. **Special facilities:** Nature trail, multitrack recording studio and video-editing suites, NASA Institute for the Application of Geospatial Technology.

Student profile. Among degree-seeking undergraduates, 65% enrolled in a transfer program, 35% enrolled in a vocational program, 324 transferred in from other institutions.

Out-of-state: 1%   **25 or older:**   34%

Transfer out. Colleges most students transferred to 2011: SUNY Oswego, SUNY Cortland, SUNY Brockport, Rochester Institute of Technology, SUNY Institute of Technology.

Basis for selection. Open admission, but selective for some programs. Special requirements for nursing; interview required. All new students with no prior college credits must take placement tests in English and Math. **Home schooled:** 1) official final high school transcript from student's school district indicating graduation or 2) letter on district letterhead from relevant district superintendent certifying that student has documented satisfactory completion of equivalent of 4-year high school program or 3) taking college's placement

test; and if Ability to Benefit scores set by college met/exceeded, may matriculate and be considered for financial aid and work toward satisfying 24-credit option prescribed by New York State Education Department.

High school preparation. Recommended units include English 4, mathematics 2, social studies 3 and science 1.

2011-2012 Annual costs. Tuition/fees: $4,196; $8,016 out-of-state. Per-credit charge: $150 in-state; $300 out-of-state. Books/supplies: $1,000. Personal expenses: $940.

Financial aid. All financial aid based on need. Need-based aid available for part-time students. Work-study available nights, weekends and for part-time students.

Application procedures. Admission: No deadline. No application fee. Admission notification on a rolling basis. **Financial aid:** Priority date 4/15, closing date 5/1. FAFSA required. Applicants notified on a rolling basis starting 3/15.

Academics. Special study options: Accelerated study, distance learning, double major, dual enrollment of high school students, honors, independent study, internships, liberal arts/career combination, study abroad, weekend college. License preparation in nursing. **Credit/placement by examination:** AP, CLEP, institutional tests. 30 credit hours maximum toward associate degree. **Support services:** Learning center, pre-admission summer program, reduced course load, remedial instruction, study skills assistance, tutoring, writing center.

Majors. Biology: General. **Business:** Accounting technology, business admin. **Communications:** Broadcast journalism, radio/TV. **Communications technology:** General, photo/film/video, recording arts. **Computer sciences:** General, computer science, web page design. **Education:** Early childhood. **Health services:** Nursing (RN). **Liberal arts:** Arts/sciences. **Math:** General. **Physical sciences:** Chemistry, geology. **Protective services:** Corrections, police science. **Social sciences:** GIS/cartography. **Visual/performing arts:** Art, studio arts.

Most popular majors. Business/marketing 10%, legal studies 17%, liberal arts 51%.

Computing on campus. 450 workstations in library, computer center. Online library, wireless network available.

Student life. Freshman orientation: Available. Preregistration for classes offered. Held week before classes begin. **Activities:** Choral groups, drama, musical theater, radio station, student government, student newspaper, TV station, honor fraternity, business society, nursing club, multicultural association, criminal justice club, alumni association, diversity club.

Athletics. NJCAA. **Intercollegiate:** Basketball, golf M, lacrosse, soccer, volleyball W. **Intramural:** Racquetball, skiing, volleyball. **Team name:** Spartans.

Student services. Chaplain/spiritual director, career counseling, student employment services, financial aid counseling, health services, on-campus daycare, personal counseling, placement for graduates, veterans' counselor. **Transfer:** Pre-admission transcript evaluation for new students. Transfer adviser, college fairs on campus for students transferring to 4-year colleges.

Contact. E-mail: admissions@cayuga-cc.edu
Phone: (315) 255-1743 ext. 2241 Fax: (315) 255-2117
Bruce Blodgett, Director of Admissions, Cayuga Community College, 197 Franklin Street, Auburn, NY 13021-3099

City University of New York: Borough of Manhattan Community College

New York, New York **CB member**
www.bmcc.cuny.edu **CB code: 2063**

▶ Public 2-year community college
▶ Commuter campus in very large city

General. Founded in 1963. Regionally accredited. **Enrollment:** 23,888 degree-seeking undergraduates; 575 non-degree-seeking students. **Degrees:** 3,180 associate awarded. **Calendar:** Semester, limited summer session. **Full-time faculty:** 404 total; 59% have terminal degrees, 42% minority, 56% women. **Part-time faculty:** 1,006 total; 17% have terminal degrees, 38% minority, 46% women. **Class size:** 8% < 20, 91% 20-39, less than 1% 40-49, less than 1% 50-99. **Special facilities:** 2 theaters, media center, gymnasium with intercollegiate-size swimming pool.

Student profile. Among degree-seeking undergraduates, 6,270 enrolled as first-time, first-year students, 1,242 transferred in from other institutions.

Part-time:	34%	Asian American:	11%
Women:	58%	Hispanic American:	38%
African American:	32%	International:	7%

Transfer out. Colleges most students transferred to 2011: Baruch College, Brooklyn College, City College, Hunter College, Lehman College.

Basis for selection. Open admission, but selective for some programs. Special requirements for associate degree programs in nursing; admission to clinical sequence of AAS degree programs competitive, based on college GPA. SAT or ACT recommended.

High school preparation. 16 units recommended. Recommended units include English 4, mathematics 3, social studies 4, science 2 (laboratory 2) and foreign language 2. One unit of fine arts recommended.

2011-2012 Annual costs. Tuition/fees: $3,918; $7,518 out-of-state. Per-credit charge: $150 in-state; $240 out-of-state. Books/supplies: $1,125.

2011-2012 Financial aid. All financial aid based on need. 4,552 full-time freshmen applied for aid; 4,367 were judged to have need; 4,162 of these received aid. 84% of total undergraduate aid awarded as scholarships/grants, 16% as loans/jobs. Need-based aid available for part-time students. Work-study available nights, weekends and for part-time students.

Application procedures. Admission: Priority date 2/1; no deadline. $65 fee, may be waived for applicants with need. Admission notification on a rolling basis beginning on or about 2/1. All CUNY schools operate on a rolling admission basis; therefore colleges and programs may close before the deadline date. **Financial aid:** Priority date 5/1; no closing date. FAFSA, institutional form required. Applicants notified on a rolling basis starting 4/15.

Academics. Special study options: Accelerated study, cooperative education, cross-registration, distance learning, dual enrollment of high school students, ESL, exchange student, independent study, internships, liberal arts/career combination, study abroad, weekend college. License preparation in nursing. **Credit/placement by examination:** AP, CLEP, institutional tests. 30 credit hours maximum toward associate degree. **Support services:** GED preparation and test center, learning center, pre-admission summer program, remedial instruction, study skills assistance, tutoring, writing center.

Majors. Business: Accounting technology, administrative services, business admin, small business admin. **Communications technology:** Radio/TV. **Computer sciences:** General, computer science, networking, web page design. **Education:** Teacher assistance. **Engineering:** General. **English:** English lit. **Health services:** EMT paramedic, medical records technology, nursing (RN), respiratory therapy assistant. **Human services:** Community org/advocacy. **Liberal arts:** Arts/sciences. **Math:** General. **Physical sciences:** General. **Protective services:** Forensics, police science. **Visual/performing arts:** General.

Most popular majors. Business/marketing 30%, computer/information sciences 6%, education 6%, health sciences 8%, liberal arts 38%.

Computing on campus. 1,500 workstations in library, computer center, student center. Commuter students can connect to campus network. Online course registration, online library, wireless network available.

Student life. Freshman orientation: Available. Preregistration for classes offered. **Activities:** Concert band, campus ministries, choral groups, dance, drama, literary magazine, Model UN, student government, student newspaper, numerous organizations.

Athletics. NJCAA. **Intercollegiate:** Baseball, basketball, soccer M, volleyball. **Intramural:** Basketball, cricket, football (non-tackle), soccer, table tennis, triathlon, volleyball. **Team name:** Panthers.

Student services. Alcohol/substance abuse counseling, career counseling, services for economically disadvantaged, student employment services, financial aid counseling, health services, legal services, on-campus daycare, personal counseling, placement for graduates, veterans' counselor, women's services. **Physically disabled:** Services for visually, speech, hearing impaired. **Transfer:** Pre-admission transcript evaluation for new students. Transfer center, transfer adviser, college fairs on campus for students transferring to 4-year colleges.

Contact. E-mail: ebarrios@bmcc.cuny.edu
Phone: (212) 220-1265 Fax: (212) 220-2366
Eugenio Barrios, Director of Enrollment Management, City University of New York: Borough of Manhattan Community College, 199 Chambers Street, New York, NY 10007-1097

City University of New York: Bronx Community College
Bronx, New York
www.bcc.cuny.edu/

CB member
CB code: 2051

▸ Public 2-year community college
▸ Commuter campus in very large city

General. Founded in 1957. Regionally accredited. **Enrollment:** 11,450 degree-seeking undergraduates. **Degrees:** 1,128 associate awarded. **Calendar:** Semester, limited summer session. **Full-time faculty:** 325 total. **Part-time faculty:** 450 total. **Special facilities:** Hall of Fame for Great Americans.

Student profile.

Out-of-state:	9%	Asian American:	3%
African American:	33%	Hispanic American:	61%

Transfer out. Colleges most students transferred to 2011: Lehman College, City College, Baruch College, Hunter College, John Jay College of Criminal Justice.

Basis for selection. Open admission. Units recommended for admission must be acquired before graduation from any CUNY community college.

High school preparation. College-preparatory program recommended. 9 units recommended. Recommended units include English 3, mathematics 2 and science 1.

2011-2012 Annual costs. Tuition/fees: $3,954; $7,554 out-of-state. Per-credit charge: $150 in-state; $240 out-of-state. Books/supplies: $759. Personal expenses: $2,100.

Financial aid. All financial aid based on need. Need-based aid available for part-time students. Work-study available nights, weekends and for part-time students.

Application procedures. Admission: $60 fee. Admission notification on a rolling basis beginning on or about 2/1. All CUNY schools operate on a rolling admission basis; therefore colleges and programs may close before the deadline date. **Financial aid:** Closing date 6/30. FAFSA required. Applicants notified on a rolling basis starting 8/1.

Academics. Special study options: Cooperative education, cross-registration, distance learning, double major, dual enrollment of high school students, ESL, external degree, honors, independent study, internships, liberal arts/career combination, student-designed major, study abroad, weekend college. License preparation in nursing. **Credit/placement by examination:** AP, CLEP, IB, institutional tests. 30 credit hours maximum toward associate degree. **Support services:** GED preparation and test center, learning center, pre-admission summer program, reduced course load, remedial instruction, study skills assistance, tutoring, writing center.

Majors. Business: General, accounting, administrative services, management information systems, office technology. **Computer sciences:** Computer science, data processing. **Education:** Teacher assistance. **General:** Horticultural science. **Health services:** Clinical lab technology, medical assistant, medical radiologic technology/radiation therapy, nuclear medical technology, nursing (RN). **Liberal arts:** Arts/sciences. **Visual/performing arts:** Commercial/advertising art.

Most popular majors. Business/marketing 21%, computer/information sciences 6%, health sciences 14%, liberal arts 27%, public administration/social services 15%.

Computing on campus. 490 workstations in library, computer center, student center. Commuter students can connect to campus network. Online course registration, online library, wireless network available.

Student life. Freshman orientation: Available. Preregistration for classes offered. **Activities:** Choral groups, dance, drama, literary magazine, music ensembles, radio station, student government, student newspaper.

Athletics. Intercollegiate: Baseball M, basketball, cheerleading, soccer M, track and field. **Team name:** BCC Broncos.

Student services. Chaplain/spiritual director, career counseling, student employment services, financial aid counseling, health services, on-campus daycare, personal counseling, placement for graduates, veterans' counselor. **Physically disabled:** Services for visually, speech impaired. **Transfer:** Transfer adviser, college fairs on campus for students transferring to 4-year colleges.

Contact. E-mail: admission@bcc.cuny.edu
Phone: (718) 289-5895 Fax: (718) 289-6352
Alba Cancetty, Director of Admissions, City University of New York: Bronx Community College, 2155 University Avenue, Bronx, NY 10453

City University of New York: Hostos Community College
Bronx, New York
www.hostos.cuny.edu

CB member
CB code: 2303

▸ Public 2-year community college
▸ Commuter campus in very large city

General. Founded in 1970. Regionally accredited. Bilingual Spanish/English liberal arts program. **Enrollment:** 6,480 degree-seeking undergraduates; 598 non-degree-seeking students. **Degrees:** 676 associate awarded. **Calendar:** Semester, limited summer session. **Full-time faculty:** 169 total; 54% have terminal degrees, 52% minority, 53% women. **Part-time faculty:** 246 total; 24% have terminal degrees, 65% minority, 47% women. **Class size:** 26% < 20, 69% 20-39, 5% 40-49.

Student profile. Among degree-seeking undergraduates, 28% enrolled in a transfer program, 61% enrolled in a vocational program, 1,230 enrolled as first-time, first-year students, 570 transferred in from other institutions.

Part-time:	36%	Asian American:	3%
Out-of-state:	1%	Hispanic American:	57%
Women:	68%	International:	5%
African American:	26%	25 or older:	37%

Transfer out. 10% of students enrolled in the transfer program go on to 4-year colleges. **Colleges most students transferred to 2011:** CUNY Lehman College, CUNY City College, CUNY John Jay College.

Basis for selection. Open admission, but selective for some programs. Admission to allied health programs based on Freshman Skills Assessment and subsequent performance in courses.

High school preparation. 16 units recommended. Recommended units include English 4, mathematics 3, social studies 4, science 2 and foreign language 2. 2 fine arts required. High school biology, chemistry, math required of allied health applicants.

2011-2012 Annual costs. Tuition/fees: $3,955; $7,555 out-of-state. Per-credit charge: $150 in-state; $240 out-of-state. Books/supplies: $1,179. Personal expenses: $2,838.

Financial aid. Need-based: Need-based aid available for part-time students. Work-study available nights, weekends and for part-time students.

Application procedures. Admission: $70 fee, may be waived for applicants with need. Admission notification on a rolling basis beginning on or about 2/1. All CUNY schools operate on a rolling admission basis; therefore colleges and programs may close before the deadline date. **Financial aid:** Priority date 7/1; no closing date. FAFSA required. Applicants notified on a rolling basis; must reply within 3 week(s) of notification.

Academics. Dual enrollment programs with City College, John Jay College. **Special study options:** Cooperative education, distance learning, dual enrollment of high school students, ESL, honors, independent study, internships, liberal arts/career combination, student-designed major, study abroad, weekend college. Serrano scholars program. License preparation in dental hygiene, nursing, radiology. **Credit/placement by examination:** AP, CLEP, institutional tests. **Support services:** GED preparation and test center, learning center, pre-admission summer program, remedial instruction, study skills assistance, tutoring, writing center.

Majors. Business: General, accounting, administrative services, business admin, office technology. **Education:** Early childhood. **Engineering:** Chemical, electrical. **Health services:** Community health, dental hygiene, medical radiologic technology/radiation therapy, medical secretary, nursing (RN). **Human services:** General. **Liberal arts:** Arts/sciences. **Math:** General. **Protective services:** Criminal justice, forensics. **Visual/performing arts:** Digital arts.

Most popular majors. Business/marketing 9%, education 14%, engineering/engineering technologies 8%, health sciences 21%, liberal arts 33%.

Computing on campus. 1,000 workstations in library, computer center, student center. Commuter students can connect to campus network. Online course registration, online library, helpline, wireless network available.

Student life. Freshman orientation: Available. Preregistration for classes offered. Held once a week each semester. **Activities:** Marching band, dance, drama, student government, student newspaper, TV station, Puerto Rican club, Christian club, black student union, Dominican association, South American student union, Ecuadorean student association, dental hygiene club, nursing club, Mexican club, Cuban club.

Athletics. NJCAA. **Intercollegiate:** Baseball M, basketball, soccer, volleyball W. **Intramural:** Basketball, volleyball W. **Team name:** Caimans.

Student services. Alcohol/substance abuse counseling, chaplain/spiritual director, career counseling, services for economically disadvantaged, student employment services, financial aid counseling, health services, on-campus daycare, personal counseling, placement for graduates, veterans' counselor, women's services. **Physically disabled:** Services for visually, speech, hearing impaired. **Transfer:** Re-entry adviser, pre-admission transcript evaluation for new students. Transfer adviser, college fairs on campus for students transferring to 4-year colleges.

Contact. E-mail: admissions@hostos.cuny.edu
Phone: (718) 518-4405 Fax: (718) 518-6643
Roland Velez, Director of Admissions/Recruitment, City University of New York: Hostos Community College, 500 Grand Concourse, Bronx, NY 10451

City University of New York: Kingsborough Community College
Brooklyn, New York   **CB member**
www.kbcc.cuny.edu   **CB code: 2358**

- Public 2-year community college
- Commuter campus in very large city

General. Founded in 1963. Regionally accredited. **Enrollment:** 14,997 degree-seeking undergraduates; 4,264 non-degree-seeking students. **Degrees:** 2,534 associate awarded. **Location:** 10 miles from midtown. **Calendar:** Semester, extensive summer session. **Full-time faculty:** 343 total; 55% have terminal degrees, 27% minority, 54% women. **Part-time faculty:** 590 total; 13% have terminal degrees, 19% minority, 53% women. **Class size:** 25% < 20, 61% 20-39, 14% 40-49. **Special facilities:** Private beach on campus. **Partnerships:** Formal partnership with College Now program for high school seniors.

Student profile. Among degree-seeking undergraduates, 2,702 enrolled as first-time, first-year students, 1,721 transferred in from other institutions.

Part-time:	26%	Asian American:	12%
Out-of-state:	1%	Hispanic American:	16%
Women:	56%	International:	4%
African American:	35%	25 or older:	23%

Transfer out. **Colleges most students transferred to 2011:** City University of New York: Brooklyn College, Long Island University, Pace University, City University of New York: College of Staten Island, City University of New York: Baruch College.

Basis for selection. Open admission. Units recommended for admission must be acquired before graduation from any CUNY community college.

High school preparation. 16 units recommended. Recommended units include English 4, mathematics 3, social studies 4, science 2 and foreign language 2. One unit fine arts.

2012-2013 Annual costs. Tuition/fees (projected): $4,300; $7,550 out-of-state. Books/supplies: $1,179. Personal expenses: $2,912.

Financial aid. All financial aid based on need. Need-based aid available for part-time students. Work-study available nights, weekends and for part-time students.

Application procedures. **Admission:** $65 fee, may be waived for applicants with need. Admission notification on a rolling basis beginning on or about 2/1. All CUNY schools operate on a rolling admission basis; therefore colleges and programs may close before the deadline date. **Financial aid:** Closing date 4/30. FAFSA required. Applicants notified on a rolling basis; must reply within 2 week(s) of notification.

Academics. **Special study options:** Accelerated study, cross-registration, dual enrollment of high school students, ESL, honors, independent study, internships, student-designed major. My Turn Program for senior citizens, New Start Program for students academically dismissed from 4-year institutions. License preparation in nursing. **Credit/placement by examination:** AP, CLEP, institutional tests. 16 credit hours maximum toward associate degree. **Support services:** GED preparation, learning center, pre-admission summer program, reduced course load, remedial instruction, tutoring, writing center.

Majors. **Biology:** General. **Business:** Accounting, business admin, fashion, office management, tourism promotion, tourism/travel. **Communications:** Broadcast journalism, journalism. **Computer sciences:** Computer science, data processing. **Education:** Early childhood, elementary, teacher assistance. **Engineering:** General. **Health services:** Community health services, mental health services, nursing (RN), physical therapy assistant, prenursing, surgical technology. **Liberal arts:** Arts/sciences. **Math:** General. **Parks/recreation:**

General, exercise sciences. **Physical sciences:** Chemistry, physics. **Protective services:** Law enforcement admin. **Visual/performing arts:** General, commercial/advertising art, studio arts.

Most popular majors. Business/marketing 19%, health sciences 15%, liberal arts 39%.

Computing on campus. 900 workstations in library, computer center. Online course registration available.

Student life. **Freshman orientation:** Available. Preregistration for classes offered. **Activities:** Bands, choral groups, dance, drama, film society, literary magazine, music ensembles, musical theater, opera, radio station, student government, student newspaper, symphony orchestra, over 60 ethnic, academic, religious, and political groups.

Athletics. NJCAA. **Intercollegiate:** Baseball M, basketball, soccer M, softball W, tennis, track and field, volleyball W. **Intramural:** Basketball, bowling, football (non-tackle), racquetball, soccer, softball, swimming, table tennis, tennis, volleyball, weight lifting.

Student services. Adult student services, career counseling, student employment services, health services, on-campus daycare, personal counseling, placement for graduates, veterans' counselor. **Physically disabled:** Services for visually, speech, hearing impaired. **Transfer:** Transfer adviser for students transferring to 4-year colleges.

Contact. E-mail: info@kbcc.cuny.edu
Phone: (718) 368-4600 Fax: (718) 368-5356
Robert Ingenito, Admissions Information Center Director, City University of New York: Kingsborough Community College, 2001 Oriental Boulevard, Brooklyn, NY 11235

City University of New York: LaGuardia Community College
Long Island City, New York
www.lagcc.cuny.edu   **CB code: 2246**

- Public 2-year community college
- Commuter campus in very large city

General. Founded in 1970. Regionally accredited. **Enrollment:** 16,224 degree-seeking undergraduates; 1,339 non-degree-seeking students. **Degrees:** 2,034 associate awarded. **Calendar:** Semester, limited summer session. **Full-time faculty:** 333 total; 54% have terminal degrees, 40% minority, 56% women. **Part-time faculty:** 795 total; 11% have terminal degrees, 40% minority, 52% women. **Class size:** 25% < 20, 75% 20-39, less than 1% 40-49. **Special facilities:** LaGuardia and Wagner archives.

Student profile. Among degree-seeking undergraduates, 63% enrolled in a transfer program, 37% enrolled in a vocational program, 3,190 enrolled as first-time, first-year students, 1,641 transferred in from other institutions.

Part-time:	37%	Hispanic American:	37%
Out-of-state:	2%	Native American:	1%
Women:	59%	International:	6%
African American:	16%	25 or older:	29%
Asian American:	14%		

Transfer out. 62% of students enrolled in the transfer program go on to 4-year colleges. **Colleges most students transferred to 2011:** Queens College, Baruch College, Hunter College, York College, John Jay College.

Basis for selection. Open admission. **Adult students:** SAT/ACT scores not required. **Home schooled:** Transcript of courses and grades required. Submit a letter from their school district superintendent confirming that all high school graduation requirements of the district have been met. **Learning Disabled:** Students are encouraged to contact the office for Students with Disabilities before completing the application to ensure accommodations are addressed throughout the application and matriculation process.

High school preparation. 13 units recommended. Recommended units include English 4, mathematics 2, social studies 2, science 1 and academic electives 4.

2011-2012 Annual costs. Tuition/fees: $3,942; $7,542 out-of-state. Per-credit charge: $150 in-state; $240 out-of-state. Books/supplies: $1,146. Personal expenses: $1,744.

2010-2011 Financial aid. All financial aid based on need. 2,169 full-time freshmen applied for aid; 2,066 were judged to have need; 1,996 of these received aid. Average need met was 41%. Average scholarship/grant was $4,397; average loan $1,080. 88% of total undergraduate aid awarded as scholarships/grants, 12% as loans/jobs. Need-based aid available for part-time

students. Work-study available nights, weekends and for part-time students.

Application procedures. Admission: $65 fee, may be waived for applicants with need. Admission notification on a rolling basis beginning on or about 2/1. All CUNY schools operate on a rolling admission basis; therefore colleges and programs may close before the deadline date. **Financial aid:** Priority date 4/15; no closing date. FAFSA, institutional form required. Applicants notified on a rolling basis starting 3/1; must reply within 4 week(s) of notification.

Academics. Special study options: Accelerated study, cooperative education, cross-registration, distance learning, dual enrollment of high school students, ESL, honors, independent study, internships, liberal arts/career combination, student-designed major. Summer program with Vassar College. License preparation in nursing, paramedic. **Credit/placement by examination:** AP, CLEP, institutional tests. 10 credit hours maximum toward associate degree. **Support services:** GED preparation and test center, learning center, pre-admission summer program, reduced course load, remedial instruction, tutoring, writing center.

Majors. Biology: General. **Business:** Accounting technology, administrative services, business admin, restaurant/food services, tourism/travel. **Communications:** Communications/speech/rhetoric. **Communications technology:** Recording arts. **Computer sciences:** Computer science, data entry, programming. **Conservation:** Environmental science. **Education:** Teacher assistance. **Engineering:** Civil, electrical, mechanical. **English:** English lit. **Foreign languages:** Spanish. **Health services:** Dietetic technician, EMT paramedic, medical radiologic technology/radiation therapy, mental health services, nursing (RN), occupational therapy assistant, physical therapy assistant, veterinary technology/assistant. **Liberal arts:** Arts/sciences. **Philosophy/religion:** Philosophy. **Physical sciences:** General. **Protective services:** Criminal justice. **Visual/performing arts:** Commercial photography, dramatic, industrial design, studio arts. **Work/family studies:** Aging.

Most popular majors. Business/marketing 33%, computer/information sciences 6%, health sciences 15%, liberal arts 24%, personal/culinary services 6%.

Computing on campus. 1,236 workstations in library, computer center. Online course registration, online library, helpline, wireless network available.

Student life. Freshman orientation: Available. Preregistration for classes offered. **Activities:** Dance, drama, film society, international student organizations, literary magazine, music ensembles, Model UN, radio station, student government, student newspaper, Muslim, Christian, Buddhist, Phi Theta Kappa, Jewish, Catholic clubs.

Athletics. Intramural: Basketball, football (non-tackle) M, football (tackle) M, handball, soccer, softball, swimming, table tennis, volleyball.

Student services. Adult student services, career counseling, student employment services, financial aid counseling, health services, on-campus daycare, personal counseling, placement for graduates, veterans' counselor, women's services. **Physically disabled:** Services for visually, speech, hearing impaired. **Transfer:** Transfer center, transfer adviser, college fairs on campus for students transferring to 4-year colleges.

Contact. E-mail: admissions@lagcc.cuny.edu
Phone: (718) 482-7206 Fax: (718) 482-2033
LaVora Desvigne, Director of Admissions, City University of New York: LaGuardia Community College, 31-10 Thomson Avenue, Long Island City, NY 11101

City University of New York: Queensborough Community College
Bayside, New York
www.qcc.cuny.edu
CB code: 2751

- Public 2-year community college
- Commuter campus in very large city

General. Founded in 1958. Regionally accredited. **Enrollment:** 15,147 degree-seeking undergraduates. **Degrees:** 1,701 associate awarded. **Location:** 10 miles from midtown Manhattan. **Calendar:** Semester, limited summer session. **Full-time faculty:** 357 total. **Part-time faculty:** 540 total. **Special facilities:** Resource center for Holocaust studies, observatory, art museum. **Partnerships:** Formal partnership with Verizon for Next Step associate degree program in telecommunication technology for Verizon employees.

Student profile.

Out-of-state:	1%	25 or older:	32%

Transfer out. Colleges most students transferred to 2011: CUNY Queens College, St. John's University.

Basis for selection. Open admission. Units recommended for admission must be acquired before graduation from CUNY.

High school preparation. 15 units recommended. Recommended units include English 4, mathematics 3, social studies 2, science 2 (laboratory 2) and academic electives 4.

2011-2012 Annual costs. Tuition/fees: $3,940; $7,540 out-of-state. Per-credit charge: $150 in-state; $240 out-of-state. Books/supplies: $500. Personal expenses: $2,100.

Financial aid. Need-based: Work-study available nights, weekends and for part-time students.

Application procedures. Admission: $65 fee, may be waived for applicants with need. Admission notification on a rolling basis beginning on or about 2/1. All CUNY schools operate on a rolling admission basis; therefore colleges and programs may close before the deadline date. **Financial aid:** No deadline. FAFSA, institutional form required. Applicants notified on a rolling basis starting 7/15.

Academics. Special study options: Cooperative education, dual enrollment of high school students, ESL, independent study, internships, liberal arts/career combination, student-designed major. External education for homebound students, honors program for high school seniors. License preparation in nursing. **Credit/placement by examination:** AP, CLEP, institutional tests. **Support services:** Learning center, pre-admission summer program, remedial instruction, tutoring.

Majors. Biology: General. **Business:** General, accounting, administrative services, business admin, office management. **Communications technology:** General, recording arts. **Computer sciences:** General, data processing, information systems, programming. **Engineering:** Computer. **Health services:** Clinical lab technology, environmental health, nursing (RN). **History:** General. **Liberal arts:** Arts/sciences. **Physical sciences:** Chemistry. **Psychology:** General. **Social sciences:** Political science, sociology. **Visual/performing arts:** General, art, dance, dramatic, music history, photography.

Computing on campus. 143 workstations in library, computer center. Online course registration, helpline, wireless network available.

Student life. Freshman orientation: Available. Preregistration for classes offered. **Activities:** Bands, choral groups, dance, drama, film society, music ensembles, musical theater, student government, student newspaper, symphony orchestra, architecture club, Asian society, biology club, Chi Alpha Christian, drama society, future teachers society, Hillel club, Muslim student association, Newman club.

Athletics. NJCAA. Intercollegiate: Baseball M, basketball, cross-country, soccer M, softball W, tennis, track and field, volleyball. **Intramural:** Badminton, basketball, soccer, softball, swimming, table tennis, tennis, track and field, volleyball. **Team name:** Tigers.

Student services. Adult student services, career counseling, student employment services, health services, on-campus daycare, personal counseling, placement for graduates, veterans' counselor. **Physically disabled:** Services for visually, speech, hearing impaired. **Transfer:** Transfer adviser, college fairs on campus for students transferring to 4-year colleges.

Contact. Phone: (718) 281-5000 Fax: (718) 281-5189
Winston Yarde, Director of Admissions, City University of New York: Queensborough Community College, Springfield Boulevard & 56th Avenue, Bayside, NY 11364-1497

Clinton Community College
Plattsburgh, New York
www.clinton.edu
CB code: 2135

- Public 2-year community college
- Commuter campus in large town

General. Founded in 1966. Regionally accredited. SUNY (State University of New York) institution. **Enrollment:** 1,621 degree-seeking undergraduates; 713 non-degree-seeking students. **Degrees:** 336 associate awarded. **Location:** 60 miles from Montreal, Canada, 30 miles from Burlington, Vermont. **Calendar:** Semester, limited summer session. **Full-time faculty:** 56 total. **Part-time faculty:** 115 total. **Class size:** 18% < 20, 81% 20-39, less than 1% 50-99. **Special facilities:** Science and technology center. **Partnerships:** Formal partnership with area high schools in collaboration with College Advancement Program (CAP).

Two-Year Colleges

Student profile. Among degree-seeking undergraduates, 47% enrolled in a transfer program, 53% enrolled in a vocational program, 507 enrolled as first-time, first-year students, 58 transferred in from other institutions.

Part-time:	21%	Asian American:	1%
Women:	55%	Hispanic American:	1%
African American:	9%	Native American:	1%

Transfer out. Colleges most students transferred to 2011: SUNY at Plattsburgh.

Basis for selection. Essay and recommendations required for nursing program. Test scores may exempt students from taking placement test. **Home schooled:** State high school equivalency certificate required. Must take Ability-to-Benefit test.

High school preparation. Recommended units include English 4, mathematics 3, social studies 4, history 4, science 2 (laboratory 2) and foreign language 2. Chemistry and biology recommended for nursing.

2011-2012 Annual costs. Tuition/fees: $4,072; $8,952 out-of-state. Per-credit charge: $151 in-state; $350 out-of-state. Books/supplies: $800. Personal expenses: $634.

Financial aid. All financial aid based on need. Need-based aid available for part-time students. Work-study available nights, weekends and for part-time students.

Application procedures. Admission: No deadline. No application fee. Admission notification on a rolling basis. **Financial aid:** Priority date 6/11; no closing date. FAFSA required. Applicants notified on a rolling basis starting 4/11; must reply within 2 week(s) of notification.

Academics. Special study options: Cross-registration, distance learning, dual enrollment of high school students, honors, independent study, liberal arts/career combination, student-designed major. Basic skills program. License preparation in nursing. **Credit/placement by examination:** AP, CLEP, IB, institutional tests. 30 credit hours maximum toward associate degree. **Support services:** Reduced course load, remedial instruction, study skills assistance, tutoring, writing center.

Majors. Business: Accounting, business admin. **Computer sciences:** General, networking. **Health services:** Nursing (RN). **Liberal arts:** Arts/sciences. **Math:** General. **Protective services:** Law enforcement admin.

Computing on campus. 350 workstations in library, computer center. Dormitories wired for high-speed internet access and linked to campus network. Commuter students can connect to campus network. Online library, helpline, wireless network available.

Student life. Freshman orientation: Mandatory. Preregistration for classes offered. Each session lasts about 3 hours and takes place during the 2 weeks before classes begin. **Housing:** Guaranteed on-campus for freshmen. Coed dorms, special housing for disabled available. $200 nonrefundable deposit. **Activities:** Choral groups, drama, international student organizations, musical theater, student government, student newspaper.

Athletics. NJCAA. **Intercollegiate:** Baseball M, basketball, soccer, softball W. **Team name:** Cougars.

Student services. Adult student services, alcohol/substance abuse counseling, career counseling, financial aid counseling, health services, on-campus daycare, personal counseling, placement for graduates, veterans' counselor. **Physically disabled:** Services for visually, speech, hearing impaired. **Transfer:** Transfer adviser, college fairs on campus for students transferring to 4-year colleges.

Contact. E-mail: admissions@clinton.edu
Phone: (518) 562-4170 Toll-free number: (800) 552-1160
Fax: (518) 562-4373
Tobi Hay, Director of Admissions, Clinton Community College, 136 Clinton Point Drive, Plattsburgh, NY 12901-4297

Cochran School of Nursing
Yonkers, New York
www.cochranschoolofnursing.us   **CB code: 2894**

- Private 2-year nursing college
- Commuter campus in small city
- Application essay, interview required

General. Founded in 1894. Access to all clinical facilities at St. John's Riverside Hospital. **Enrollment:** 157 degree-seeking undergraduates. **Degrees:** 97 associate awarded. **Location:** 20 miles from New York City.

Calendar: Semester, limited summer session. **Full-time faculty:** 17 total; 6% have terminal degrees, 18% minority, 100% women. **Part-time faculty:** 26 total; 42% minority, 96% women. **Class size:** 6% < 20, 94% 20-39.

Student profile. Among degree-seeking undergraduates, 24 transferred in from other institutions.

Part-time:	73%	Asian American:	13%
Women:	87%	Hispanic American:	23%
African American:	28%	25 or older:	91%

Transfer out. Colleges most students transferred to 2011: Mercy College, College of New Rochelle, College of Mount St. Vincent, Adelphi University.

Basis for selection. School achievement record, test scores, interview most important. Completion of prerequisite with B grade or better. **Learning Disabled:** Must submit necessary documentation of disabilities at time of admission to disability officer.

High school preparation. 16 units required. Required and recommended units include English 4, mathematics 4, social studies 2, history 2, science 2 and foreign language 2. Math units should include 1 algebra, science units should include 1 biology and 1 chemistry. 2 units of laboratory recommended.

2011-2012 Annual costs. Tuition and required fees for full 2-year AAS program is $27,446. Books/supplies: $1,800.

Financial aid. All financial aid based on need. Need-based aid available for part-time students. Work-study available nights, weekends and for part-time students.

Application procedures. Admission: Closing date 6/1 (postmark date). $35 fee. Application must be submitted on paper. Admission notification on a rolling basis. **Financial aid:** No deadline. FAFSA required. Applicants notified on a rolling basis.

Academics. Special testing program facilitates career goals of LPNs who want to become RNs. **Special study options:** Accelerated study, liberal arts/career combination. License preparation in nursing. **Credit/placement by examination:** AP, CLEP, IB, institutional tests. 27 credit hours maximum toward associate degree. **Support services:** Learning center, tutoring.

Majors. Health services: Nursing (RN).

Computing on campus. 22 workstations in library, computer center, student center. Online course registration, online library available.

Student life. Freshman orientation: Mandatory. Preregistration for classes offered. **Activities:** Student government, student newspaper.

Student services. Adult student services, career counseling, health services, personal counseling. **Transfer:** Pre-admission transcript evaluation for new students. College fairs on campus for students transferring to 4-year colleges.

Contact. E-mail: admissions@cochranschoolofnursing.us
Phone: (914) 964-4296 ext. 4296 Fax: (914) 964-4796
Kathy Vitola, Admissions Counselor, Cochran School of Nursing, 967 North Broadway, Yonkers, NY 10701

College of Westchester
White Plains, New York
www.cw.edu   **CB code: 1023**

- For-profit 2-year business and career college
- Commuter campus in small city

General. Founded in 1915. Regionally accredited. **Location:** 30 miles from New York City. **Calendar:** Semester.

Annual costs/financial aid. Tuition/fees (2011-2012): $22,300. Books/supplies: $1,000. Need-based financial aid available to full-time and part-time students.

Contact. Phone: (914) 831-0200
Director of Admissions, 325 Central Park Avenue, White Plains, NY 10602

Columbia-Greene Community College
Hudson, New York
www.sunycgcc.edu

CB member
CB code: 2138

- Public 2-year community college
- Commuter campus in small town

General. Founded in 1966. Regionally accredited. SUNY institution. **Enrollment:** 1,583 degree-seeking undergraduates; 515 non-degree-seeking students. **Degrees:** 317 associate awarded. **Location:** 40 miles from Albany. **Calendar:** Semester, limited summer session. **Full-time faculty:** 49 total. **Part-time faculty:** 86 total. **Class size:** 54% < 20, 45% 20-39, less than 1% 40-49, less than 1% 50-99. **Special facilities:** 4 art galleries, Hudson River biological field station.

Student profile. Among degree-seeking undergraduates, 386 enrolled as first-time, first-year students.

Part-time:	34%	Asian American:	1%
Women:	64%	Hispanic American:	6%
African American:	7%		

Transfer out. Colleges most students transferred to 2011: SUNY Albany, SUNY New Paltz, College of Saint Rose.

Basis for selection. Admission to some programs based on school achievement record, test scores, and recommendations. Interview recommended. **Adult students:** SAT/ACT scores not required. **Home schooled:** Transcript of courses and grades, interview required.

High school preparation. Recommended units include English 3, mathematics 3, science 3 and foreign language 3.

2011-2012 Annual costs. Tuition/fees: $3,978; $7,626 out-of-state. Per-credit charge: $152 in-state; $304 out-of-state. Books/supplies: $1,200. Personal expenses: $950.

Financial aid. Need-based: Need-based aid available for part-time students. Work-study available nights, weekends and for part-time students. **Non-need-based:** Scholarships awarded for academics, state residency.

Application procedures. Admission: No deadline. No application fee. Admission notification on a rolling basis. **Financial aid:** Priority date 5/1; no closing date. FAFSA, institutional form required. Applicants notified on a rolling basis starting 7/1; must reply within 2 week(s) of notification.

Academics. Special study options: Cooperative education, cross-registration, distance learning, dual enrollment of high school students, honors, independent study, internships, student-designed major. License preparation in nursing. **Credit/placement by examination:** AP, CLEP, institutional tests. 30 credit hours maximum toward associate degree. **Support services:** Learning center, pre-admission summer program, remedial instruction, study skills assistance, tutoring, writing center.

Honors college/program. Program offers the opportunity to work closely with faculty, conduct research, and participate in seminars and conferences with an interdisciplinary focus.

Majors. Business: Accounting, administrative services, business admin. **Computer sciences:** Computer science, information technology. **Conservation:** Environmental science. **Education:** Multi-level teacher, physical. **Health services:** Massage therapy, nursing (RN). **Human services:** Social work. **Liberal arts:** Arts/sciences. **Protective services:** Criminal justice, law enforcement admin. **Visual/performing arts:** Studio arts.

Most popular majors. Security/protective services 6%.

Computing on campus. 150 workstations in library, computer center. Commuter students can connect to campus network. Online library, wireless network available.

Student life. Freshman orientation: Available. Preregistration for classes offered. Held 1 week prior to start of fall classes. **Activities:** Choral groups, dance, drama, music ensembles, musical theater, radio station, student government, International Rotary Club, minority alliance group, College Union Board.

Athletics. NJCAA. **Intercollegiate:** Baseball M, basketball, bowling, soccer W, softball W. **Intramural:** Basketball, bowling, fencing, table tennis, tennis, volleyball. **Team name:** Twins.

Student services. Adult student services, alcohol/substance abuse counseling, career counseling, student employment services, health services, on-campus daycare, personal counseling, placement for graduates, veterans' counselor. **Physically disabled:** Services for visually, hearing impaired.

Transfer: Transfer adviser, college fairs on campus for students transferring to 4-year colleges.

Contact. E-mail: pepitone@sunycgcc.edu
Phone: (518) 828-4181 ext. 5513 Fax: (518) 828-8543
Christine Pepitone, Director of Admissions, Columbia-Greene Community College, 4400 Route 23, Hudson, NY 12534

Corning Community College
Corning, New York
www.corning-cc.edu

CB code: 2106

- Public 2-year community college
- Commuter campus in large town

General. Founded in 1956. Regionally accredited. SUNY institution. **Enrollment:** 3,450 degree-seeking undergraduates; 1,848 non-degree-seeking students. **Degrees:** 685 associate awarded. **Location:** 70 miles from Binghamton. **Calendar:** Semester, limited summer session. **Full-time faculty:** 99 total; 6% minority, 46% women. **Part-time faculty:** 154 total; 6% minority, 50% women. **Class size:** 62% < 20, 35% 20-39, less than 1% 40-49, 2% 50-99, less than 1% >100. **Special facilities:** 200-acre nature center, criminal justice complex, observatory with historic working model of Hale telescope, planetarium.

Student profile. Among degree-seeking undergraduates, 917 enrolled as first-time, first-year students, 211 transferred in from other institutions.

Part-time:	32%	Asian American:	1%
Out-of-state:	5%	Hispanic American:	2%
Women:	58%	25 or older:	35%
African American:	5%		

Transfer out. Colleges most students transferred to 2011: Mansfield University, Keuka College, Rochester Institute of Technology, SUNY Empire State College, Elmira College.

Basis for selection. Open admission, but selective for some programs. Applicants without diploma or GED evaluated on individual basis. **Adult students:** SAT/ACT scores not required. **Home schooled:** Ability to Benefit testing required. **Learning Disabled:** Students should contact disability services to arrange accommodations, including accommodations for placement tests.

High school preparation. Recommended units include English 4, mathematics 1, social studies 4, science 1 (laboratory 1). 4 math and 4 science required of engineering science applicants; 1 algebra and 1 biology required of nursing applicants.

2011-2012 Annual costs. Tuition/fees: $4,220; $8,090 out-of-state. Per-credit charge: $161 in-state; $322 out-of-state. Books/supplies: $1,000. Personal expenses: $700.

Financial aid. All financial aid based on need. Need-based aid available for part-time students. Work-study available nights, weekends and for part-time students.

Application procedures. Admission: No deadline. No application fee. Admission notification on a rolling basis. **Financial aid:** Priority date 4/1; no closing date. FAFSA required. Applicants notified on a rolling basis starting 4/1; must reply within 4 week(s) of notification.

Academics. Special study options: Distance learning, double major, dual enrollment of high school students, honors, independent study, internships, liberal arts/career combination, student-designed major, study abroad, weekend college. License preparation in nursing, paramedic, real estate. **Credit/placement by examination:** AP, CLEP, institutional tests. 30 credit hours maximum toward associate degree. **Support services:** Learning center, reduced course load, remedial instruction, study skills assistance, tutoring, writing center.

Majors. Business: Accounting, administrative services, business admin. **Computer sciences:** General, computer graphics, computer science, programming. **Education:** Early childhood, elementary, health, physical. **Engineering:** Engineering science. **Health services:** EMT paramedic, nursing (RN), substance abuse counseling. **Liberal arts:** Arts/sciences, humanities. **Math:** General. **Parks/recreation:** Health/fitness. **Physical sciences:** General. **Protective services:** Criminal justice, fire safety technology, law enforcement admin. **Social sciences:** General. **Work/family studies:** Child care management.

Most popular majors. Business/marketing 12%, health sciences 10%, liberal arts 46%, public administration/social services 6%, security/protective services 10%.

Computing on campus. 400 workstations in library, computer center, student center. Online course registration, online library, helpline, wireless network available.

Student life. Freshman orientation: Available. Preregistration for classes offered. One-day transition course offered in January, end of August. **Activities:** Campus ministries, choral groups, drama, literary magazine, music ensembles, radio station, student government, student newspaper, human services club, law society, Christian club, College Republicans, Phi Theta Kappa, nursing society, multicultural society, environmental club.

Athletics. NJCAA. **Intercollegiate:** Baseball M, basketball, bowling, golf, soccer, softball W, volleyball W. **Intramural:** Badminton, basketball, soccer, volleyball. **Team name:** Red Barons.

Student services. Adult student services, alcohol/substance abuse counseling, chaplain/spiritual director, career counseling, services for economically disadvantaged, student employment services, financial aid counseling, health services, personal counseling, placement for graduates. **Physically disabled:** Services for visually, speech, hearing impaired. **Transfer:** Transfer center, transfer adviser, college fairs on campus for students transferring to 4-year colleges.

Contact. E-mail: admissions@corning-cc.edu
Phone: (607) 962-9151 Toll-free number: (800) 358-7171 ext. 151
Fax: (607) 962-9582
Karen Brown, Director of Admissions, Corning Community College, One Academic Drive, Corning, NY 14830

Dutchess Community College
Poughkeepsie, New York
www.sunydutchess.edu

CB member
CB code: 2198

- Public 2-year community college
- Commuter campus in large town

General. Founded in 1957. Regionally accredited. Extension programs at 2 sites. **Enrollment:** 7,644 degree-seeking undergraduates; 2,672 non-degree-seeking students. **Degrees:** 1,076 associate awarded. **Location:** 70 miles from New York City. **Calendar:** Semester, limited summer session. **Full-time faculty:** 131 total; 24% have terminal degrees, 13% minority, 55% women. **Part-time faculty:** 360 total; 52% women. **Special facilities:** Biological experimentation site on Hudson River. **Partnerships:** Formal partnership with Verizon.

Student profile. Among degree-seeking undergraduates, 67% enrolled in a transfer program, 33% enrolled in a vocational program, 2,148 enrolled as first-time, first-year students.

Part-time:	35%	Women:	54%
Out-of-state:	1%	25 or older:	22%

Transfer out. Colleges most students transferred to 2011: State University of New York at Paltz, Marist College, Mount St. Mary's College, State University of New York at Albany.

Basis for selection. Open admission, but selective for some programs. Special requirements for nursing and engineering programs. **Home schooled:** Students must pass entrance test unless they have local diploma or diploma from accredited school.

High school preparation. Recommended units include English 4, mathematics 3, social studies 4, science 3 and foreign language 2.

2011-2012 Annual costs. Tuition/fees: $3,320; $6,220 out-of-state. Per-credit charge: $121 in-state; $242 out-of-state. Books/supplies: $1,250. Personal expenses: $1,400.

2010-2011 Financial aid. Need-based: 76% of total undergraduate aid awarded as scholarships/grants, 24% as loans/jobs. Need-based aid available for part-time students. Work-study available nights, weekends and for part-time students. **Non-need-based:** Scholarships awarded for academics.

Application procedures. Admission: No deadline. No application fee. Admission notification on a rolling basis. **Financial aid:** Priority date 5/1; no closing date. FAFSA required. Applicants notified on a rolling basis starting 5/15; must reply within 2 week(s) of notification.

Academics. Special study options: Cooperative education, cross-registration, distance learning, dual enrollment of high school students, ESL, honors, independent study, internships, liberal arts/career combination. Combined degree in education with SUNY at New Paltz. License preparation in aviation, nursing, paramedic. **Credit/placement by examination:** AP, CLEP, institutional tests. 40 credit hours maximum toward associate degree. **Support services:** GED preparation and test center, learning center, pre-admission

---

summer program, reduced course load, remedial instruction, study skills assistance, tutoring, writing center.

Majors. Business: Accounting, administrative services, business admin, office technology, sales/distribution, tourism promotion, tourism/travel, travel services. **Communications:** Communications/speech/rhetoric. **Computer sciences:** General, computer science. **Education:** Biology, chemistry, early childhood, elementary, English, French, German, kindergarten/preschool, mathematics, middle, science, secondary, social studies, Spanish, teacher assistance. **Engineering:** Electrical, engineering science. **Health services:** Clinical lab technology, EMT paramedic, mental health services, nursing (RN), physical therapy assistant. **Liberal arts:** Arts/sciences, humanities. **Math:** General. **Parks/recreation:** General, exercise sciences, facilities management. **Physical sciences:** General. **Protective services:** Criminal justice. **Visual/performing arts:** Commercial/advertising art, dramatic. **Work/family studies:** Child care management.

Most popular majors. Business/marketing 14%, education 10%, health sciences 14%, liberal arts 34%, security/protective services 10%.

Computing on campus. 1,000 workstations in library, computer center. Online course registration, online library, helpline, repair service, wireless network available.

Student life. Freshman orientation: Available. Preregistration for classes offered. **Housing:** Coed dorms available. **Activities:** Jazz band, choral groups, dance, drama, film society, international student organizations, literary magazine, music ensembles, musical theater, radio station, student government, student newspaper, TV station, foreign student organization, special interest clubs.

Athletics. NJCAA. **Intercollegiate:** Baseball M, basketball M, bowling M, golf M, soccer M, softball W, tennis, volleyball W. **Intramural:** Archery, badminton, basketball, bowling, fencing, racquetball, soccer, softball, tennis, volleyball, weight lifting. **Team name:** Falcons.

Student services. Adult student services, career counseling, services for economically disadvantaged, student employment services, financial aid counseling, health services, minority student services, on-campus daycare, personal counseling, placement for graduates, veterans' counselor. **Physically disabled:** Services for visually, speech, hearing impaired. **Transfer:** Pre-admission transcript evaluation for new students. Transfer adviser, college fairs on campus for students transferring to 4-year colleges.

Contact. E-mail: admissions@sunydutchess.edu
Phone: (845) 431-8010 Toll-free number: (800) 378-9707
Fax: (845) 431-8605
Michael Roe, Director of Admissions, Dutchess Community College, 53 Pendell Road, Poughkeepsie, NY 12601-1595

Elmira Business Institute
Elmira, New York
www.ebi-college.com

CB code: 3332

- For-profit 2-year business and technical college
- Commuter campus in large town
- Interview required

General. Accredited by ACICS. **Enrollment:** 189 degree-seeking undergraduates. **Degrees:** 78 associate awarded. **Calendar:** Trimester. **Full-time faculty:** 23 total. **Part-time faculty:** 28 total.

Student profile.

Out-of-state:	37%	25 or older:	72%

Basis for selection. Open admission. High school diploma or GED required along with a career planning session. **Home schooled:** State high school equivalency certificate required.

2011-2012 Annual costs. Tuition/fees: $11,900. Per-credit charge: $390. Tuition varies by program. Medical Assisting Program has a one-time fee of $700.

Financial aid. All financial aid based on need. Need-based aid available for part-time students. Work-study available nights, weekends and for part-time students.

Application procedures. Admission: No deadline. No application fee. Admission notification on a rolling basis. **Financial aid:** Closing date 5/1. FAFSA, institutional form required.

Academics. Special study options: Internships, weekend college. **Credit/placement by examination:** AP, CLEP, institutional tests. **Support services:** Reduced course load, remedial instruction, tutoring.

Majors. Business: Accounting. **Health services:** Clinical lab assistant, insurance coding, medical assistant, medical records admin, medical records technology, medical secretary, medical transcription.

Computing on campus. 70 workstations in library, computer center.

Student life. Freshman orientation: Mandatory. Preregistration for classes offered.

Student services. Career counseling, financial aid counseling, personal counseling, placement for graduates. **Transfer:** Pre-admission transcript evaluation for new students. College fairs on campus for students transferring to 4-year colleges.

Contact. E-mail: lroan@ebi-college.com
Phone: (607) 733-7177 Toll-free number: (800) 843-1812
Fax: (607) 733-7178
Lisa Roan, Director of Admissions, Elmira Business Institute, 303 North Main Street, Elmira, NY 14901

Elmira Business Institute: Vestal
Vestal, New York
www.ebi-college.com

♦ For-profit 2-year business and technical college
♦ Commuter campus in small city
♦ Interview required

General. Accredited by ACICS. **Enrollment:** 225 degree-seeking undergraduates. **Degrees:** 55 associate awarded. **Calendar:** Trimester, extensive summer session. **Full-time faculty:** 23 total. **Part-time faculty:** 28 total.

Transfer out. Colleges most students transferred to 2011: Broome Community College.

Basis for selection. Open admission. **Home schooled:** Statement describing home school structure and mission required. Must have a letter from school superintendent or principal.

2011-2012 Annual costs. Tuition/fees: $11,900. Per-credit charge: $390. Tuition varies by program. Medical Assisting Program has a onetime fee of $700.

Financial aid. All financial aid based on need. Need-based aid available for part-time students. Work-study available nights, weekends and for part-time students.

Application procedures. Admission: No deadline. No application fee. **Financial aid:** No deadline. FAFSA, institutional form required. Applicants notified on a rolling basis.

Academics. Credit/placement by examination: AP, CLEP, institutional tests. **Support services:** Reduced course load, remedial instruction, study skills assistance, tutoring.

Majors. Business: Accounting technology. **Health services:** Clinical lab assistant, insurance coding.

Computing on campus. Online library available.

Student life. Freshman orientation: Mandatory. Preregistration for classes offered.

Student services. Transfer: Pre-admission transcript evaluation for new students.

Contact. Phone: (607) 729-8915
Susan Reinbold, Director of Admissions, Elmira Business Institute: Vestal, 4100 Vestal Road, Vestal, NY 13850

Erie Community College
Buffalo, New York
www.ecc.edu   CB code: 2213

♦ Public 2-year community college
♦ Commuter campus in large city

General. Founded in 1971. Regionally accredited. SUNY institution. Main campus located in Buffalo. Additional campuses in Williamsville and Orchard

Park. **Enrollment:** 11,950 degree-seeking undergraduates; 2,226 non-degree-seeking students. **Degrees:** 1,955 associate awarded. **ROTC:** Army. **Calendar:** Semester, limited summer session. **Full-time faculty:** 327 total; 10% minority, 50% women. **Part-time faculty:** 619 total; 8% minority, 43% women. **Special facilities:** Natatorium (City Campus), vehicle training technology center, corporate training facility, athletic fields (North and South Campus), dental hygiene clinic (North Campus), gourmet restaurant (City and North Campus). **Partnerships:** Formal partnerships with Ford Motor Company, Daimler Chrysler, Verizon.

Student profile. Among degree-seeking undergraduates, 50% enrolled in a transfer program, 50% enrolled in a vocational program, 2,899 enrolled as first-time, first-year students.

Part-time:	23%	**Hispanic American:**	6%
Out-of-state:	1%	**Native American:**	1%
Women:	51%	**International:**	3%
African American:	17%	**25 or older:**	33%
Asian American:	1%		

Transfer out. Colleges most students transferred to 2011: SUNY College at Buffalo, SUNY College at Fredonia, SUNY College at Brockport, SUNY Buffalo.

Basis for selection. Open admission, but selective for some programs. Special requirements for nursing and radiologic technology programs, occupational therapy, dental hygiene and dental lab tech; interview required. Students scoring 500 or higher on SAT Critical Reading waived from English placement test; students scoring 500 or higher on SAT Math waived from Math placement test. International students must be at least 17 years of age. **Home schooled:** Applicants follow same criteria as applicants with GED.

2011-2012 Annual costs. Tuition/fees: $4,070; $7,670 out-of-state. Per-credit charge: $150 in-state; $300 out-of-state. Books/supplies: $1,300. Personal expenses: $900.

2010-2011 Financial aid. All financial aid based on need. 76% of total undergraduate aid awarded as scholarships/grants, 24% as loans/jobs. Need-based aid available for part-time students. Work-study available nights, weekends and for part-time students.

Application procedures. Admission: Priority date 8/1; no deadline. No application fee. Admission notification on a rolling basis. **Financial aid:** Priority date 5/1; no closing date. FAFSA required. Applicants notified on a rolling basis starting 4/1; must reply within 2 week(s) of notification.

Academics. Special study options: Cooperative education, cross-registration, distance learning, double major, dual enrollment of high school students, ESL, exchange student, honors, independent study, internships, liberal arts/career combination, student-designed major, study abroad, teacher certification program, weekend college. Dual admissions with 4-year institutions. License preparation in dental hygiene, nursing, occupational therapy, paramedic, radiology. **Credit/placement by examination:** AP, CLEP, institutional tests. **Support services:** GED preparation and test center, learning center, pre-admission summer program, reduced course load, remedial instruction, study skills assistance, tutoring, writing center.

Majors. Business: Business admin, construction management, office management. **Communications:** Communications/speech/rhetoric. **Communications technology:** Graphic/printing. **Computer sciences:** General, information technology. **Conservation:** Environmental science. **Education:** Middle, physical. **Engineering:** General. **Health services:** Clinical lab technology, community health services, dental hygiene, dental lab technology, dietician assistant, EMT paramedic, medical radiologic technology/radiation therapy, medical records technology, nursing (RN), occupational therapy assistant, office admin, optician, respiratory therapy technology, substance abuse counseling. **Liberal arts:** Arts/sciences, humanities. **Physical sciences:** General. **Protective services:** Fire services admin, police science. **Work/family studies:** Child care management.

Most popular majors. Business/marketing 12%, health sciences 16%, liberal arts 43%, trade and industry 9%.

Computing on campus. 1,260 workstations in library, computer center. Commuter students can connect to campus network. Online course registration, online library, helpline, repair service, student web hosting, wireless network available.

Student life. Freshman orientation: Mandatory, $50 fee. Preregistration for classes offered. **Activities:** Bands, campus ministries, choral groups, dance, drama, literary magazine, music ensembles, musical theater, radio station, student government, student newspaper, Muslim international student association, honors association, Phi Theta Kappa, veterans club.

Athletics. NJCAA. **Intercollegiate:** Baseball M, basketball, bowling, cheerleading M, diving, football (tackle) M, ice hockey M, lacrosse W, soccer, softball W, swimming, volleyball W. **Team name:** Kats.

Student services. Adult student services, career counseling, services for economically disadvantaged, student employment services, financial aid counseling, health services, minority student services, on-campus daycare, personal counseling, placement for graduates, veterans' counselor, women's services. **Physically disabled:** Services for visually, speech, hearing impaired. **Transfer:** Pre-admission transcript evaluation for new students. Transfer adviser, college fairs on campus for students transferring to 4-year colleges.

Contact. E-mail: daquino@ecc.edu
Phone: (716) 851-1155 Fax: (716) 270-2821
Erik D'Aquino, Director of Admissions, Erie Community College, 121 Ellicott Street, Buffalo, NY 14203-2698

Finger Lakes Community College
Canandaigua, New York
www.flcc.edu   **CB code: 2134**

▶ Public 2-year community college
▶ Commuter campus in small town

General. Founded in 1965. Regionally accredited. SUNY institution. **Enrollment:** 4,861 degree-seeking undergraduates; 1,950 non-degree-seeking students. **Degrees:** 911 associate awarded. **Location:** 25 miles from Rochester. **Calendar:** Semester, extensive summer session. **Full-time faculty:** 120 total; 2% minority, 49% women. **Part-time faculty:** 282 total; 57% women. **Class size:** 67% < 20, 33% 20-39, less than 1% 40-49, less than 1% 50-99, less than 1% >100. **Special facilities:** Outdoor classrooms, nature trails, music recording studio, performing arts center. **Partnerships:** Formal partnerships with local hospitals for nursing clinics; more informally for cooperative studies and placement of interns.

Student profile. Among degree-seeking undergraduates, 63% enrolled in a transfer program, 37% enrolled in a vocational program, 1,627 enrolled as first-time, first-year students.

Part-time:	22%	Asian American:	1%
Out-of-state:	1%	Hispanic American:	5%
Women:	54%	25 or older:	28%
African American:	7%	Live on campus:	7%

Transfer out. Colleges most students transferred to 2011: SUNY at Brockport, SUNY at Geneseo, St. John Fisher College, Nazareth College, Rochester Institute of Technology.

Basis for selection. Open admission, but selective for some programs. Admission to nursing program based on high school curriculum and GPA. Competitive admission to therapeutic massage/integrated health care program. Interview recommended for all; portfolio recommended for graphic arts program. **Home schooled:** State high school equivalency certificate required.

High school preparation. 1 each biology, chemistry, and algebra required of nursing applicants. Students without high school diploma or GED must pass federally approved Ability to Benefit test prior to acceptance. 1 biology required for therapeutic massage/integrated health care applicants.

2011-2012 Annual costs. Tuition/fees: $3,894; $7,378 out-of-state. Per-credit charge: $132 in-state; $264 out-of-state. Books/supplies: $900. Personal expenses: $790.

2010-2011 Financial aid. All financial aid based on need. 1,355 full-time freshmen applied for aid; 1,187 were judged to have need; 1,170 of these received aid. 69% of total undergraduate aid awarded as scholarships/grants, 31% as loans/jobs. Need-based aid available for part-time students. Work-study available nights, weekends and for part-time students.

Application procedures. Admission: No deadline. $20 fee, may be waived for applicants with need. Application must be submitted online. Admission notification on a rolling basis beginning on or about 11/1. Must reply by May 1 or within 4 week(s) if notified thereafter. Application closing date for Nursing and Therapeutic Massage programs is February 1. **Financial aid:** Priority date 3/15; no closing date. FAFSA required. Applicants notified on a rolling basis starting 3/1; must reply within 2 week(s) of notification.

Academics. Special study options: Cooperative education, cross-registration, distance learning, double major, dual enrollment of high school students, ESL, honors, independent study, internships. Credit-bearing travel opportunities. License preparation in nursing, paramedic. **Credit/placement by examination:** AP, CLEP, IB, institutional tests. 32 credit hours maximum toward associate degree. **Support services:** GED preparation, learning center, pre-admission summer program, reduced course load, remedial instruction, study skills assistance, tutoring, writing center.

Majors. Biology: Biotechnology. **Business:** General, accounting, administrative services, business admin, e-commerce, hospitality/recreation, hotel/motel admin, marketing, sales/distribution, tourism promotion, tourism/travel.

Communications: Broadcast journalism, communications/speech/rhetoric. **Communications technology:** Recording arts. **Computer sciences:** General, computer science, information systems, programming. **Conservation:** General, environmental studies, fisheries, management/policy. **Education:** Elementary, physical. **Engineering:** General, engineering science. **General:** Ornamental horticulture, viticulture. **Health services:** Athletic training, EMT paramedic, massage therapy, nursing (RN), substance abuse counseling. **Liberal arts:** Arts/sciences. **Math:** General. **Parks/recreation:** Sports admin. **Physical sciences:** Chemistry. **Protective services:** Criminal justice. **Social sciences:** General. **Visual/performing arts:** Commercial/advertising art, dramatic, music, studio arts.

Most popular majors. Business/marketing 16%, health sciences 12%, liberal arts 30%, natural resources/environmental science 11%, security/protective services 6%, visual/performing arts 10%.

Computing on campus. 650 workstations in library, computer center, student center. Commuter students can connect to campus network. Online course registration, online library, helpline, student web hosting, wireless network available.

Student life. Freshman orientation: Available. Preregistration for classes offered. One-day program with faculty and student leaders. **Policies:** Student code of conduct policy, grievance procedures, procedures for services for students with disabilities. **Housing:** Coed dorms available. **Activities:** Bands, choral groups, drama, music ensembles, musical theater, student government, TV station, Phi Theta Kappa international honor society, Sigma Alpha Pi, nursing club, social science/human services club, College Democrats, Finger Lakes Environmental Action, veterans club, massage therapy club, ASL club, viticulture club, horticulture club.

Athletics. NJCAA. **Intercollegiate:** Baseball M, basketball, cross-country, lacrosse M, soccer, softball W, track and field, volleyball W. **Intramural:** Badminton, basketball, football (non-tackle), soccer, softball, tennis, volleyball, weight lifting.

Student services. Adult student services, career counseling, services for economically disadvantaged, student employment services, financial aid counseling, health services, legal services, on-campus daycare, personal counseling, placement for graduates, veterans' counselor. **Physically disabled:** Services for visually, speech, hearing impaired. **Transfer:** Pre-admission transcript evaluation for new students. Transfer center, transfer adviser, college fairs on campus for students transferring to 4-year colleges.

Contact. E-mail: admissions@flcc.edu
Phone: (585) 785-1278 Fax: (585) 394-5005
Bonnie Ritts, Admissions Office, Finger Lakes Community College, 3325 Marvin Sands Drive, Canandaigua, NY 14424-8395

Fulton-Montgomery Community College
Johnstown, New York
www.fmcc.suny.edu   **CB code: 2254**

▶ Public 2-year community college
▶ Commuter campus in large town

General. Founded in 1963. Regionally accredited. **Enrollment:** 2,334 degree-seeking undergraduates; 508 non-degree-seeking students. **Degrees:** 381 associate awarded. **Location:** 40 miles from Albany, 200 miles from New York City. **Calendar:** Semester, extensive summer session. **Full-time faculty:** 55 total. **Part-time faculty:** 113 total. **Class size:** 36% < 20, 57% 20-39, 5% 40-49, 1% 50-99. **Special facilities:** Regional history study center.

Student profile. Among degree-seeking undergraduates, 63% enrolled in a transfer program, 37% enrolled in a vocational program, 795 enrolled as first-time, first-year students.

Part-time:	22%	Hispanic American:	9%
Women:	42%	International:	5%
African American:	8%	25 or older:	29%
Asian American:	1%	Live on campus:	5%

Transfer out. Colleges most students transferred to 2011: State University of New York at Plattsburgh, College of Saint Rose, SUNY College at Oneonta, University at Albany.

Basis for selection. Open admission, but selective for some programs. Admission for the Nursing and Radiologic Technology programs is based on high school GPA, class rank, any college experience and meeting program prerequisites. COMPASS test used for placement in math and English courses, Focal Skills Test used for ESL placement. Interview recommended. **Home schooled:** Applicants applying for financial aid may be required to complete Ability to Benefit Test. Applicants from accredited home school who have received or will receive diploma may not be required to take test.

2011-2012 Annual costs. Tuition/fees: $3,938; $7,332 out-of-state. Per-credit charge: $141 in-state; $282 out-of-state.

Financial aid. Need-based: Need-based aid available for part-time students. Work-study available nights, weekends and for part-time students. **Non-need-based:** Scholarships awarded for academics.

Application procedures. Admission: No deadline. No application fee. Admission notification on a rolling basis. **Financial aid:** Priority date 6/1; no closing date. FAFSA required. Applicants notified on a rolling basis starting 6/15; must reply within 2 week(s) of notification.

Academics. Fulton-Montgomery offers a career-oriented individual studies program (COCAL). In this approach to career learning, students learn career skills in fields in which jobs are available locally. Although similar to cooperative education and internship programs, COCAL requires that students learn basic career skills at job sites without pay. Students learn from practicing professionals who follow competency guidelines prescribed by the College and based on O*NET online specifications, national competency catalogs, and employer input. Students can also complete a bachelor's degree online through Empire State College (SUNY). Advising for this is available on campus. **Special study options:** Accelerated study, cooperative education, cross-registration, distance learning, double major, dual enrollment of high school students, ESL, external degree, honors, independent study, internships, student-designed major, study abroad. Bachelor's degree programs available on campus. License preparation in nursing, radiology. **Credit/placement by examination:** AP, CLEP, institutional tests. 30 credit hours maximum toward associate degree. **Support services:** Learning center, reduced course load, remedial instruction, study skills assistance, tutoring, writing center.

Majors. Business: General, accounting technology, administrative services, business admin. **Communications:** Communications/speech/rhetoric, journalism. **Communications technology:** Graphic/printing. **Computer sciences:** General, information systems. **Education:** Elementary, kindergarten/preschool, secondary. **Engineering:** General. **English:** English lit. **Health services:** Medical radiologic technology/radiation therapy, nursing (RN), office admin. **Human services:** Community org/advocacy. **Liberal arts:** Arts/sciences. **Parks/recreation:** Health/fitness. **Protective services:** Criminal justice. **Visual/performing arts:** Art, commercial/advertising art. **Work/family studies:** Child care management.

Computing on campus. 400 workstations in library, computer center, student center. Commuter students can connect to campus network. Helpline, wireless network available.

Student life. Freshman orientation: Available. Preregistration for classes offered. A one-day orientation is held just before classes begin. **Housing:** $250 nonrefundable deposit. **Activities:** Choral groups, drama, musical theater, student government, student newspaper, Phi Theta Kappa, Alpha Omega, international student union, business club, fencing club.

Athletics. NJCAA. **Intercollegiate:** Baseball M, basketball, soccer, softball W, volleyball W. **Intramural:** Basketball M, volleyball. **Team name:** Raiders.

Student services. Adult student services, career counseling, student employment services, financial aid counseling, on-campus daycare, personal counseling, veterans' counselor. **Physically disabled:** Services for visually, speech, hearing impaired. **Transfer:** Pre-admission transcript evaluation for new students. Transfer center, college fairs on campus for students transferring to 4-year colleges.

Contact. E-mail: geninfo@fmcc.suny.edu
Phone: (518) 736-3622 ext. 8301
Laura LaPorte, Associate Dean of Enrollment Management, Fulton-Montgomery Community College, 2805 State Highway 67, Johnstown, NY 12095

Genesee Community College
Batavia, New York
www.genesee.edu

CB code: 2272

● Public 2-year community college
● Commuter campus in large town

General. Founded in 1966. Regionally accredited. SUNY institution. Mall-type campus, suited to disabled. Seven campus sites in Genesee, Livingston, Orleans, and Wyoming counties. **Enrollment:** 4,515 degree-seeking undergraduates; 2,685 non-degree-seeking students. **Degrees:** 781 associate awarded. **Location:** 35 miles from Buffalo, 35 miles from Rochester. **Calendar:** Semester, limited summer session. **Full-time faculty:** 82 total. **Part-time faculty:** 284 total. **Special facilities:** Nature trail, center for the arts, art gallery.

Student profile. Among degree-seeking undergraduates, 1,291 enrolled as first-time, first-year students.

Part-time:	24%	Hispanic American:	2%
Out-of-state:	1%	Native American:	1%
Women:	65%	International:	3%
African American:	9%	25 or older:	31%
Asian American:	1%		

Transfer out. Colleges most students transferred to 2011: SUNY: Brockport, Buffalo State, Geneseo, University of Buffalo, Empire State College.

Basis for selection. Open admission, but selective for some programs. Admission to nursing, physical therapist assistant, paralegal, and respiratory care programs based on academic achievement, test scores, interview, and school and community activities. ACT and COMPASS used for placement. Although SAT not used as placement test, students scoring above 500 on each part exempted from remedial courses. Portfolio recommended for digital art program.

High school preparation. Recommended units include English 4, mathematics 3, social studies 4, science 3 and foreign language 2. Additional units of math and science recommended for students planning to transfer to 4-year programs. 18 units, including biology and chemistry, required for nursing applicants. 18 units, including biology and physics, required for physical therapist assistant applicants.

2011-2012 Annual costs. Tuition/fees: $3,720; $4,320 out-of-state. Per-credit charge: $140 in-state; $160 out-of-state. Books/supplies: $985. Personal expenses: $1,010.

2010-2011 Financial aid. Need-based: 977 full-time freshmen applied for aid; 805 were judged to have need; 805 of these received aid. Average need met was 88%. Average scholarship/grant was $4,625; average loan $3,225. 59% of total undergraduate aid awarded as scholarships/grants, 41% as loans/jobs. Need-based aid available for part-time students. Work-study available nights, weekends and for part-time students. **Non-need-based:** Awarded to 160 full-time undergraduates, including 107 freshmen. Scholarships awarded for academics, alumni affiliation, athletics, leadership, state residency.

Application procedures. Admission: No deadline. No application fee. Admission notification on a rolling basis beginning on or about 11/15. **Financial aid:** Priority date 3/1, closing date 5/1. FAFSA required. Applicants notified on a rolling basis starting 4/15; must reply within 2 week(s) of notification.

Academics. Special study options: Cooperative education, cross-registration, distance learning, double major, dual enrollment of high school students, ESL, honors, independent study, internships, liberal arts/career combination. License preparation in nursing, physical therapy. **Credit/placement by examination:** AP, CLEP, IB, institutional tests. 31 credit hours maximum toward associate degree. **Support services:** GED preparation, learning center, reduced course load, remedial instruction, study skills assistance, tutoring, writing center.

Majors. Biology: Biotechnology. **Business:** Accounting, accounting technology, administrative services, business admin, customer service, fashion, retailing, tourism/travel. **Communications:** Communications/speech/rhetoric. **Computer sciences:** Information systems, webmaster. **Education:** Teacher assistance. **Engineering:** Engineering science. **Health services:** Medical secretary, nursing (RN), occupational therapy assistant, physical therapy assistant, polysomnography, recreational therapy, respiratory therapy technology, substance abuse counseling, veterinary technology/assistant. **Human services:** Community org/advocacy. **Liberal arts:** Arts/sciences, humanities. **Parks/recreation:** Health/fitness. **Protective services:** Law enforcement admin. **Visual/performing arts:** Art, digital arts, dramatic, theater design.

Most popular majors. Business/marketing 14%, health sciences 25%, liberal arts 35%, public administration/social services 6%, security/protective services 10%.

Computing on campus. 350 workstations in dormitories, library, computer center, student center. Dormitories wired for high-speed internet access and linked to campus network. Commuter students can connect to campus network. Online course registration, online library, helpline, wireless network available.

Student life. Freshman orientation: Mandatory. Preregistration for classes offered. Day-long orientation before classes begin. **Policies:** Residence life regulations covered in housing license signed by students. **Housing:** Single-sex dorms, special housing for disabled, wellness housing available. Global living community, quiet building. **Activities:** Choral groups, drama, film society, international student organizations, literary magazine, musical theater, radio station, student government, student newspaper, African American student union, Native American student organization, Christian Students

United, New Age Circle, Enjoying Children Through Recreation and Education, Phi Theta Kappa, Distribution Education Clubs of America, adult student group, Habitat for Humanity, adult student group.

Athletics. NJCAA. **Intercollegiate:** Baseball M, basketball, diving, golf, lacrosse, soccer, softball W, swimming, volleyball W. **Intramural:** Basketball, cheerleading, football (non-tackle), golf, skiing, soccer, softball, table tennis, tennis, volleyball. **Team name:** Cougars.

Student services. Adult student services, career counseling, student employment services, financial aid counseling, health services, on-campus daycare, personal counseling, placement for graduates, veterans' counselor. **Physically disabled:** Services for visually, speech, hearing impaired. **Transfer:** Re-entry adviser for new students. Transfer center, transfer adviser, college fairs on campus for students transferring to 4-year colleges.

Contact. E-mail: tmlanemartin@genesee.edu
Phone: (585) 345-6800 Toll-free number: (866) 225-5422
Fax: (585) 345-6842
Tanya Lane-Martin, Director of Admissions and Recruitment/Assistant Dean for Enrollment Services, Genesee Community College, One College Road, Batavia, NY 14020-9704

Helene Fuld College of Nursing
New York, New York
www.helenefuld.edu   CB code: 2327

▶ Private 2-year nursing and junior college
▶ Commuter campus in very large city

General. Founded in 1945. Regionally accredited. One-year, full-time associate degree program accredited by National League for Nursing Accrediting Commission and Middle States Association of Colleges and Schools. Career ladder for LPNs. Part-time accredited study also offered. **Enrollment:** 365 degree-seeking undergraduates. **Degrees:** 362 associate awarded. **Location:** Uptown. **Calendar:** Quarter, limited summer session. **Full-time faculty:** 17 total. **Part-time faculty:** 23 total. **Class size:** 6% < 20, 47% 20-39, 29% 40-49, 18% 50-99.

Basis for selection. Must be licensed practical nurse with 1 year work experience. Require satisfactory performance on pre-entrance exams on practical nursing equivalent, mathematics, and English and completion of a prerequisite chemistry and mathematics course. After all entrance requirements fulfilled, including successful completion of testing, 18 credits granted for practical nursing. ATI testing required for entrance to nursing program.

2011-2012 Annual costs. Tuition/fees: $15,704. Books/supplies: $2,047.

Financial aid. All financial aid based on need. Need-based aid available for part-time students. Work-study available nights, weekends and for part-time students.

Application procedures. Admission: No deadline. $110 fee. Admission notification on a rolling basis. **Financial aid:** No deadline. FAFSA required. Applicants notified on a rolling basis.

Academics. Special study options: Accelerated study, liberal arts/career combination. License preparation in nursing. **Credit/placement by examination:** AP, CLEP, institutional tests. **Support services:** Learning center, reduced course load, study skills assistance, tutoring.

Majors. Health services: Nursing (RN).

Computing on campus. 24 workstations in library, computer center. Commuter students can connect to campus network. Wireless network available.

Student life. Freshman orientation: Mandatory. Preregistration for classes offered. 2 weeks before term starts. **Activities:** Student government.

Student services. Adult student services, career counseling, financial aid counseling, personal counseling. **Transfer:** Pre-admission transcript evaluation for new students. College fairs on campus for students transferring to 4-year colleges.

Contact. E-mail: sandra.senior@helenefuld.edu
Phone: (212) 616-7200
Gladys Pineda, Assistant Director of Student Services, Helene Fuld College of Nursing, 24 East 120th Street, New York, NY 10035

Herkimer County Community College
Herkimer, New York
www.herkimer.edu   CB code: 2316

▶ Public 2-year community college
▶ Commuter campus in small town

General. Founded in 1966. Regionally accredited. **Enrollment:** 2,880 degree-seeking undergraduates; 806 non-degree-seeking students. **Degrees:** 570 associate awarded. **ROTC:** Army. **Location:** 10 miles from Utica, 55 miles from Syracuse. **Calendar:** Semester, limited summer session. **Full-time faculty:** 73 total. **Part-time faculty:** 96 total. **Special facilities:** 500-acre nature center, natural history museum, archeology museum.

Student profile. Among degree-seeking undergraduates, 1,008 enrolled as first-time, first-year students.

Part-time:	16%	Women:	59%
Out-of-state:	3%	Live on campus:	18%

Transfer out. Colleges most students transferred to 2011: SUNY Institute of Technology, SUNY Oneonta, SUNY Brockport, SUNY Oswego, SUNY Cortland.

Basis for selection. Open admission, but selective for some programs. SAT and ACT scores may be used to waive required college placement test. Students from Herkimer County must have proof of graduation or a GED certificate. Students from outside Herkimer County must have a 68 GPA or 2400 or higher on the GED. ACCUPLACER used to help determine placement into developmental courses. Interview recommended for emergency medical technician, occupational/physical therapy assistant programs. Audition required for performance and sound engineering majors. **Home schooled:** Transcript of courses and grades, letter of recommendation (nonparent) required. Letter from superintendent of home district stating student meets the requirements.

High school preparation. Physical/occupational therapist assistant applicants should contact admissions office to review high school course requirements.

2011-2012 Annual costs. Tuition/fees: $4,100; $6,360 out-of-state. Per-credit charge: $129 in-state; $233 out-of-state. Books/supplies: $1,200. Personal expenses: $610.

Financial aid. Need-based: Need-based aid available for part-time students. Work-study available nights, weekends and for part-time students.

Application procedures. Admission: Priority date 7/1; deadline 7/31. No application fee. Admission notification on a rolling basis. **Financial aid:** Closing date 4/1. FAFSA required. Applicants notified on a rolling basis starting 4/1; must reply within 2 week(s) of notification.

Academics. Online tutoring and late night writing lab (via Angel) available after 6:00. Regular Academic Support Center open weekdays. **Special study options:** Distance learning, dual enrollment of high school students, ESL, honors, independent study, internships, liberal arts/career combination. License preparation in paramedic. **Credit/placement by examination:** AP, CLEP, institutional tests. 32 credit hours maximum toward associate degree. **Support services:** GED preparation, learning center, reduced course load, remedial instruction, study skills assistance, tutoring.

Honors college/program. Applicants need high school average of 88. Students must maintain GPA of 3.5.

Majors. Area/ethnic studies: Women's. **Business:** Accounting, accounting technology, administrative services, business admin, entrepreneurial studies, fashion, human resources, international, travel services. **Communications:** Broadcast journalism. **Communications technology:** Photo/film/video. **Computer sciences:** Data processing, networking, webmaster. **Education:** Kindergarten/preschool. **Health services:** EMT paramedic, physical therapy assistant. **Human services:** Community org/advocacy. **Liberal arts:** Arts/sciences, humanities. **Math:** General. **Parks/recreation:** Health/fitness. **Protective services:** Computer forensics, forensics, law enforcement admin. **Visual/performing arts:** General, art, music management, studio arts.

Most popular majors. Business/marketing 24%, liberal arts 35%, security/protective services 16%.

Computing on campus. 560 workstations in dormitories, library, computer center, student center. Dormitories wired for high-speed internet access and linked to campus network. Commuter students can connect to campus network. Online library, helpline, wireless network available.

Student life. Freshman orientation: Mandatory. Preregistration for classes offered. **Housing:** Coed dorms available. $350 partly refundable

deposit. **Activities:** Pep band, dance, drama, literary magazine, musical theater, radio station, student government, student newspaper, TV station, Students for a Better World, social issues club, Students Against Drunk Driving, Campus Christian Fellowship, cultural exchange club, Black student union, Phi Theta Kappa.

Athletics. NJCAA. **Intercollegiate:** Baseball M, basketball, cross-country, diving, field hockey W, lacrosse, soccer, softball W, swimming, tennis, track and field, volleyball W. **Intramural:** Badminton, baseball M, basketball, bowling, lacrosse, soccer, softball, swimming, tennis, volleyball. **Team name:** Generals.

Student services. Adult student services, alcohol/substance abuse counseling, career counseling, student employment services, financial aid counseling, health services, on-campus daycare, personal counseling, placement for graduates, veterans' counselor. **Physically disabled:** Services for visually, hearing impaired. **Transfer:** Re-entry adviser, pre-admission transcript evaluation for new students. Transfer adviser, college fairs on campus for students transferring to 4-year colleges.

Contact. E-mail: admissions@herkimer.edu
Phone: (315) 866-0300 ext. 8278
Toll-free number: (888) 464-4222 ext. 8278 Fax: (315) 866-0062
Robert Palmieri, Director of Admissions, Herkimer County Community College, 100 Reservoir Road, Herkimer, NY 13350-1598

Hudson Valley Community College

Troy, New York	**CB member**
www.hvcc.edu	**CB code: 2300**

- Public 2-year community college
- Commuter campus in small city

General. Founded in 1953. Regionally accredited. SUNY institution. **Enrollment:** 10,164 degree-seeking undergraduates. **Degrees:** 1,799 associate awarded. **ROTC:** Army, Air Force. **Location:** 10 miles from Albany. **Calendar:** Semester, limited summer session. **Full-time faculty:** 277 total. **Part-time faculty:** 440 total. **Special facilities:** Language laboratory, computer laboratories.

Basis for selection. Open admission, but selective for some programs. Admission to some programs based on school achievement record and test scores. Interview also considered for some programs.

High school preparation. Requirements vary for selective programs.

2011-2012 Annual costs. Tuition/fees: $4,278; $11,678 out-of-state. Per-credit charge: $154 in-state; $462 out-of-state. Books/supplies: $550. Personal expenses: $800.

Financial aid. Need-based: Work-study available nights, weekends and for part-time students.

Application procedures. Admission: No deadline. $30 fee, may be waived for applicants with need. Admission notification on a rolling basis. **Financial aid:** Priority date 5/30; no closing date. FAFSA required. Applicants notified on a rolling basis starting 5/1; must reply within 2 week(s) of notification.

Academics. Special study options: Accelerated study, cooperative education, cross-registration, distance learning, double major, internships, student-designed major. License preparation in dental hygiene, nursing, paramedic, radiology. **Credit/placement by examination:** AP, CLEP. 30 credit hours maximum toward associate degree. **Support services:** GED preparation, learning center, pre-admission summer program, reduced course load, remedial instruction, tutoring.

Majors. Business: General, accounting, administrative services, business admin, finance, insurance, international, office technology, real estate. **Computer sciences:** Data processing, networking. **Conservation:** Environmental studies. **Education:** Physical. **Engineering:** General, engineering science. **Health services:** Clinical lab science, clinical lab technology, dental hygiene, medical radiologic technology/radiation therapy, medical secretary, nursing (RN), physician assistant, respiratory therapy technology, substance abuse counseling. **Human services:** Community org/advocacy, social work. **Physical sciences:** Chemistry. **Protective services:** Forensics. **Social sciences:** General. **Work/family studies:** Child care management.

Computing on campus. 1,000 workstations in library, computer center.

Student life. Activities: Drama, radio station, student government, student newspaper, TV station.

Athletics. NJCAA. **Intercollegiate:** Baseball M, basketball, bowling, cross-country, football (tackle) M, golf, ice hockey M, lacrosse M, soccer, softball W, tennis, track and field, volleyball W. **Intramural:** Baseball M, basketball, bowling, cross-country, field hockey W, golf, ice hockey, lacrosse, racquetball, skiing, soccer, softball, table tennis, tennis, track and field, volleyball, wrestling M.

Student services. Adult student services, career counseling, student employment services, health services, on-campus daycare, personal counseling, placement for graduates, veterans' counselor. **Physically disabled:** Services for visually, speech, hearing impaired.

Contact. E-mail: admissions@hvcc.edu
Phone: (518) 629-7309 Toll-free number: (877) 325-4822
Fax: (518) 629-4576
Mary Bauer, Director of Admissions, Hudson Valley Community College, 80 Vandenburgh Avenue, Troy, NY 12180

Institute of Design and Construction

Brooklyn, New York	
www.idc.edu	**CB code: 0677**

- Private 2-year junior and technical college
- Commuter campus in very large city

General. Founded in 1947. Regionally accredited. Classes and seminars available for candidates preparing for Architect Registration Exam. **Enrollment:** 104 degree-seeking undergraduates; 20 non-degree-seeking students. **Degrees:** 13 associate awarded. **Calendar:** Semester, limited summer session. **Part-time faculty:** 26 total; 62% have terminal degrees, 15% minority, 12% women. **Class size:** 98% < 20, 2% 20-39.

Student profile. Among degree-seeking undergraduates, 100% enrolled in a vocational program, 2% already have a bachelor's degree or higher, 7 enrolled as first-time, first-year students, 14 transferred in from other institutions.

Part-time:	44%	Asian American:	9%
Out-of-state:	3%	Hispanic American:	18%
Women:	16%	International:	3%
African American:	41%	25 or older:	60%

Transfer out. 25% of students enrolled in the transfer program go on to 4-year colleges. **Colleges most students transferred to 2011:** CUNY New York City College of Technology.

Basis for selection. Open admission. Interview recommended. **Adult students:** SAT/ACT scores not required.

High school preparation. Recommended units include English 4, mathematics 4, science 3 and foreign language 4. One unit of drafting or architecture recommended.

2011-2012 Annual costs. Tuition/fees: $9,130. Per-credit charge: $300. Books/supplies: $900. Personal expenses: $750.

2010-2011 Financial aid. All financial aid based on need. 72% of total undergraduate aid awarded as scholarships/grants, 28% as loans/jobs. Need-based aid available for part-time students. Work-study available nights, weekends and for part-time students.

Application procedures. Admission: No deadline. $30 fee, may be waived for applicants with need. Application must be submitted on paper. Admission notification on a rolling basis. **Financial aid:** No deadline. FAFSA, institutional form required. Applicants notified on a rolling basis starting 3/1; must reply within 4 week(s) of notification.

Academics. Work and study plan available. Students can spend 2 full-time semesters in accelerated study, then complete degree through part-time evening study while working during the day in the architecture/construction industries. Credits transferable to Pratt Institute and New York City College of Technology. **Special study options:** Double major. **Credit/placement by examination:** AP, CLEP, institutional tests. **Support services:** Reduced course load, remedial instruction, tutoring.

Computing on campus. 18 workstations in library, computer center. Online library, wireless network available.

Student life. Freshman orientation: Available. Preregistration for classes offered.

Student services. Career counseling, student employment services, financial aid counseling, personal counseling, placement for graduates, veterans' counselor. **Transfer:** Pre-admission transcript evaluation for new students. Transfer adviser for students transferring to 4-year colleges.

Contact. E-mail: kgiannetti@idc.edu
Phone: (718) 855-3661 ext. 16 Fax: (718) 852-5889
Kevin Giannetti, Director of Admissions, Institute of Design and
Construction, 141 Willoughby Street, Brooklyn, NY 11201-5380

Island Drafting and Technical Institute
Amityville, New York
www.idti.edu   **CB code: 3048**

▶ For-profit 2-year technical and career college
▶ Commuter campus in large town
▶ Interview required

General. Accredited by ACCSC. **Enrollment:** 122 degree-seeking undergraduates. **Degrees:** 74 associate awarded. **Location:** 25 miles from New
York City. **Calendar:** Semester, extensive summer session. **Full-time faculty:** 5 total. **Part-time faculty:** 3 total.

Basis for selection. Open admission. School-administered test for CADD/
Architecture students. **Home schooled:** Interview required.

High school preparation. Recommended units include English 2 and
mathematics 2.

2011-2012 Annual costs. Tuition/fees: $15,200. Per-credit charge: $495.
Books/supplies: $600.

Financial aid. All financial aid based on need. Work-study available nights,
weekends and for part-time students.

Application procedures. Admission: No deadline. $25 fee. Application
must be submitted on paper. Admission notification on a rolling basis. **Financial aid:** No deadline. Applicants notified on a rolling basis.

Academics. Credit/placement by examination: AP, CLEP, institutional
tests. **Support services:** Learning center.

Majors. Computer sciences: Computer graphics. **Engineering:** Electrical.

Computing on campus. 100 workstations in library, computer center.
Wireless network available.

Student life. Freshman orientation: Mandatory. Preregistration for
classes offered.

Student services. Alcohol/substance abuse counseling, career counseling,
student employment services, financial aid counseling, personal counseling,
placement for graduates, veterans' counselor.

Contact. E-mail: info@idti.edu
Phone: (631) 691-8733 Fax: (631) 691-8738
Jaimie Laudicina, Admissions, Island Drafting and Technical Institute,
128 Broadway, Amityville, NY 11701-2704

ITT Technical Institute: Albany
Albany, New York
www.itt-tech.edu   **CB code: 2689**

▶ For-profit 2-year technical college
▶ Commuter campus in large city
▶ Interview required

General. Accredited by ACICS. **Enrollment:** 518 undergraduates.
Degrees: 103 associate awarded. **Calendar:** Quarter, extensive summer session. **Full-time faculty:** 7 total. **Part-time faculty:** 38 total.

Basis for selection. Satisfactory scores from on-site tests in English and
mathematics required.

2011-2012 Annual costs. Estimated costs as of June 2011: per-credit-
hour charge, $493, depending upon level and course of study; academic fee,
$200. Certain programs of study require purchase of tools, which could cost
an additional $100 to $500. All costs are subject to change.

Financial aid. Need-based: Work-study available nights, weekends and
for part-time students.

Application procedures. Admission: No deadline. No application fee.
Admission notification on a rolling basis. **Financial aid:** FAFSA, institutional
form required. Applicants notified on a rolling basis.

Academics. Credit/placement by examination: AP, CLEP. **Support services:** Learning center, tutoring.

Majors. Computer sciences: Networking, web page design. **Visual/per-
forming arts:** Design.

Computing on campus. Online library available.

Student life. Freshman orientation: Available. Preregistration for
classes offered.

Student services. Career counseling, student employment services, placement for graduates.

Contact. Phone: (518) 452-9300 Toll-free number: (800) 489-1191
Fax: (518) 452-9393
John Henebry, Director of Recruitment, ITT Technical Institute: Albany,
13 Airline Drive, Albany, NY 12205

ITT Technical Institute: Getzville
Getzville, New York
www.itt-tech.edu   **CB code: 2704**

▶ For-profit 2-year technical college
▶ Commuter campus in rural community
▶ Interview required

General. Accredited by ACICS. **Enrollment:** 668 undergraduates.
Degrees: 187 associate awarded. **Calendar:** Quarter, extensive summer session. **Full-time faculty:** 9 total. **Part-time faculty:** 40 total.

Basis for selection. Satisfactory scores from on-site tests in English and
mathematics required.

2011-2012 Annual costs. Estimated costs as of June 2011: per-credit-
hour charge, $493, depending upon level and course of study; academic fee,
$200. Certain programs of study require purchase of tools, which could cost
an additional $100 to $500. All costs are subject to change.

Financial aid. Need-based: Work-study available nights, weekends and
for part-time students.

Application procedures. Admission: No deadline. No application fee.
Admission notification on a rolling basis. **Financial aid:** No deadline.
FAFSA, institutional form required. Applicants notified on a rolling basis.

Academics. Credit/placement by examination: AP, CLEP. **Support services:** Learning center, tutoring.

Majors. Computer sciences: Networking, web page design. **Protective
services:** Law enforcement admin. **Visual/performing arts:** Design.

Computing on campus. Online library available.

Student services. Career counseling, student employment services, placement for graduates.

Contact. Phone: (716) 689-2200 Toll-free number: (800) 469-7593
Fax: (716) 689-2828
Scott Jaskier, Director of Recruitment, ITT Technical Institute: Getzville,
2295 Millersport Highway, PO Box 327, Getzville, NY 14068

ITT Technical Institute: Liverpool
Liverpool, New York
www.itt-tech.edu   **CB code: 2725**

▶ For-profit 2-year technical college
▶ Commuter campus in small town
▶ Interview required

General. Accredited by ACICS. **Enrollment:** 386 undergraduates.
Degrees: 126 associate awarded. **Calendar:** Quarter, extensive summer session. **Full-time faculty:** 7 total. **Part-time faculty:** 19 total.

Basis for selection. Satisfactory scores from on-site tests in English and
mathematics required.

2011-2012 Annual costs. Estimated costs as of June 2011: per-credit-
hour charge, $493, depending upon level and course of study; academic fee,
$200. Certain programs of study require purchase of tools, which could

cost an additional $100 to $500. All costs are subject to change. Books/supplies: $3,300.

Financial aid. Need-based: Work-study available nights, weekends and for part-time students.

Application procedures. Admission: No deadline. Admission notification on a rolling basis. **Financial aid:** No deadline. FAFSA, institutional form required. Applicants notified on a rolling basis.

Academics. Credit/placement by examination: AP, CLEP. **Support services:** Learning center, tutoring.

Majors. Computer sciences: Networking, web page design. **Visual/performing arts:** Design.

Computing on campus. Online library available.

Student life. Freshman orientation: Available. Preregistration for classes offered.

Student services. Career counseling, student employment services, placement for graduates.

Contact. Phone: (315) 461-8000 Toll-free number: (877) 488-0011 Fax: (315) 461-80008
Terry Riesel, Director of Recruitment, ITT Technical Institute: Liverpool, 235 Greenfield Parkway, Liverpool, NY 13088-6651

Jamestown Business College
Jamestown, New York
www.jamestownbusinesscollege.edu   CB code: 2346

- For-profit 2-year business and junior college
- Commuter campus in large town

General. Founded in 1886. Regionally accredited. JBC offers programming outside of general curriculum to enhance student and professional experiences. **Enrollment:** 317 degree-seeking undergraduates. **Degrees:** 20 bachelor's, 141 associate awarded. **Location:** 80 miles from Buffalo, 60 miles from Erie, Pennsylvania. **Calendar:** Quarter, limited summer session. **Full-time faculty:** 7 total; 14% have terminal degrees, 57% minority, 86% women. **Part-time faculty:** 10 total; 40% minority, 70% women. **Class size:** 42% < 20, 58% 20-39.

Student profile. Among degree-seeking undergraduates, 70 enrolled as first-time, first-year students, 42 transferred in from other institutions.

Part-time:	4%	Asian American:	1%
Out-of-state:	11%	Hispanic American:	4%
Women:	70%	Native American:	2%
African American:	2%	25 or older:	52%

Basis for selection. Class rank and academic record important. School and community activities considered. College uses Comparative Guidance and Placement program in admission process. Interview recommended.

2011-2012 Annual costs. Tuition/fees: $11,100. Books/supplies: $1,500. Personal expenses: $2,000.

2011-2012 Financial aid. Need-based: 69% of total undergraduate aid awarded as scholarships/grants, 31% as loans/jobs. Need-based aid available for part-time students. Work-study available nights, weekends and for part-time students. **Non-need-based:** Scholarships awarded for academics.

Application procedures. Admission: No deadline. $25 fee. Application must be submitted on paper. Admission notification on a rolling basis. **Financial aid:** No deadline. FAFSA required. Applicants notified on a rolling basis starting 2/15.

Academics. Special study options: Bachelor's degree programs available on campus. **Credit/placement by examination:** AP, CLEP, institutional tests. **Support services:** Reduced course load, study skills assistance, tutoring.

Majors. Business: Accounting, administrative services, business admin, marketing. **Computer sciences:** General, data processing. **Health services:** Medical secretary.

Computing on campus. 100 workstations in library, computer center. Commuter students can connect to campus network. Online library, wireless network available.

Student life. Freshman orientation: Mandatory. Preregistration for classes offered.

Athletics. Intramural: Basketball, swimming, tennis, volleyball.

Student services. Adult student services, career counseling, student employment services, financial aid counseling, personal counseling, placement for graduates. **Transfer:** Pre-admission transcript evaluation for new students. Transfer adviser for students transferring to 4-year colleges.

Contact. E-mail: admissions@jamestownbusinesscollege.edu
Phone: (716) 664-5100 Fax: (716) 664-3144
Brenda Salemme, Director of Admissions, Jamestown Business College, 7 Fairmount Avenue, Jamestown, NY 14701

Jamestown Community College
Jamestown, New York
www.sunyjcc.edu   CB code: 2335

- Public 2-year community college
- Commuter campus in large town

General. Founded in 1950. Regionally accredited. SUNY institution. Branch campus at Olean for Cattaraugus County. Extensions in Dunkirk, NY and Warren, PA. **Enrollment:** 3,658 degree-seeking undergraduates; 268 non-degree-seeking students. **Degrees:** 789 associate awarded. **Location:** 70 miles from Buffalo and Erie, Pennsylvania. **Calendar:** Semester, extensive summer session. **Full-time faculty:** 83 total; 2% minority, 66% women. **Part-time faculty:** 331 total; 4% minority, 57% women. **Class size:** 54% < 20, 45% 20-39, less than 1% 40-49, less than 1% 50-99. **Special facilities:** Roger Tory Peterson Institute of Natural History, manufacturing technology institute. **Partnerships:** Formal partnerships with Jones Memorial Hospital, Bradford Regional Medical Center, Olean General Hospital, WCA Hospital.

Student profile. Among degree-seeking undergraduates, 69% enrolled in a transfer program, 31% enrolled in a vocational program, 1,152 enrolled as first-time, first-year students, 247 transferred in from other institutions.

Part-time:	25%	Hispanic American:	5%
Out-of-state:	9%	Native American:	1%
Women:	58%	25 or older:	30%
African American:	3%	Live on campus:	6%
Asian American:	1%		

Transfer out. 55% of students enrolled in the transfer program go on to 4-year colleges. **Colleges most students transferred to 2011:** SUNY Fredonia, SUNY Empire State, St. Bonaventure University, University at Buffalo, SUNY Buffalo State College.

Basis for selection. Open admission, but selective for some programs. Preference given to area students in highly subscribed programs. Competitive admission to Nursing and Occupational Therapy Assistant programs with school achievement record very important. ACT and ASSET scores used for placement.

2011-2012 Annual costs. Tuition/fees: $4,355; $8,255 out-of-state. Per-credit charge: $163 in-state; $294 out-of-state. Room/board: $9,100. Books/supplies: $1,000. Personal expenses: $680.

2010-2011 Financial aid. Need-based: 1,008 full-time freshmen applied for aid; 880 were judged to have need; 880 of these received aid. 77% of total undergraduate aid awarded as scholarships/grants, 23% as loans/jobs. Need-based aid available for part-time students. Work-study available nights, weekends and for part-time students. **Non-need-based:** Awarded to 167 full-time undergraduates, including 102 freshmen. Scholarships awarded for academics, alumni affiliation, art, athletics, music/drama, state residency.

Application procedures. Admission: No deadline. No application fee. Admission notification on a rolling basis. Must reply by May 1 or within 2 week(s) if notified thereafter. **Financial aid:** Priority date 3/1; no closing date. FAFSA required. Applicants notified on a rolling basis starting 4/15.

Academics. Strong liberal arts tradition, with a balance between transfer and career-oriented programs. **Special study options:** Cross-registration, distance learning, dual enrollment of high school students, honors, independent study, internships, liberal arts/career combination, study abroad, weekend college. English immersion program during the summer. English language Instruction courses offered each fall and spring. License preparation in nursing, occupational therapy. **Credit/placement by examination:** AP, CLEP, institutional tests. 36 credit hours maximum toward associate degree. **Support services:** Learning center, pre-admission summer program, reduced course load, remedial instruction, study skills assistance, tutoring.

Majors. Business: Accounting, administrative services, business admin. **Communications:** Communications/speech/rhetoric. **Computer sciences:** Data processing, programming. **Education:** Early childhood, elementary, kindergarten/preschool, physical. **Engineering:** General. **Health services:** Medical records technology, nursing (RN), occupational therapy assistant.

Human services: Community org/advocacy. **Liberal arts:** Arts/sciences, humanities. **Protective services:** Criminal justice, fire safety technology, law enforcement admin, police science. **Visual/performing arts:** Design, music, studio arts.

Most popular majors. Business/marketing 10%, health sciences 18%, liberal arts 47%, security/protective services 10%.

Computing on campus. 450 workstations in library, computer center, student center. Dormitories wired for high-speed internet access and linked to campus network. Commuter students can connect to campus network. Online course registration, online library, helpline, wireless network available.

Student life. Freshman orientation: Mandatory. Preregistration for classes offered. **Housing:** Coed dorms available. $200 nonrefundable deposit. Suite-style dorms available to students. **Activities:** Bands, choral groups, dance, drama, music ensembles, musical theater, radio station, student government, environmental club, InterVarsity Christian Fellowship, Early Childhood Educators, Political Awareness, Nursing club, Humanities club, criminal justice club, multicultural club, occupational therapy assistant club, human services club, Animal Rights Consortium, College Republican club, Japanese culture club, community service club, teacher education club, Latino Outreach.

Athletics. NJCAA. **Intercollegiate:** Baseball M, basketball, cross-country, diving, golf, soccer, softball W, swimming, volleyball W, wrestling M. **Intramural:** Basketball, bowling, football (non-tackle), softball, table tennis, tennis, volleyball. **Team name:** Jayhawks.

Student services. Adult student services, alcohol/substance abuse counseling, career counseling, services for economically disadvantaged, student employment services, financial aid counseling, health services, personal counseling, placement for graduates, veterans' counselor. **Physically disabled:** Services for visually, speech, hearing impaired. **Transfer:** Transfer adviser, college fairs on campus for students transferring to 4-year colleges.

Contact. E-mail: admissions@mail.sunyjcc.edu
Phone: (716) 338-1001 Toll-free number: (800) 388-8557
Fax: (716) 338-1450
Wendy Present, Director of Admissions, Jamestown Community College, 525 Falconer Street, Jamestown, NY 14701-0020

Jefferson Community College
Watertown, New York
www.sunyjefferson.edu

CB member
CB code: 2345

▸ Public 2-year community college
▸ Commuter campus in large town

General. Founded in 1961. Regionally accredited. **Enrollment:** 3,179 degree-seeking undergraduates; 847 non-degree-seeking students. **Degrees:** 574 associate awarded. **Location:** 70 miles from Syracuse. **Calendar:** Semester, limited summer session. **Full-time faculty:** 83 total. **Part-time faculty:** 145 total.

Student profile. Among degree-seeking undergraduates, 941 enrolled as first-time, first-year students, 311 transferred in from other institutions.

Part-time:	30%	Women:	63%
Out-of-state:	2%	25 or older:	36%

Transfer out. Colleges most students transferred to 2011: SUNY Empire State College, SUNY Oswego, SUNY Potsdam.

Basis for selection. Open admission, but selective for some programs. Admission to some programs based on grades, class rank, test scores, school recommendation, personal interview. Waiting list available for nursing program. Interview recommended for engineering science, nursing programs.

High school preparation. Strong background in math and science required for engineering science, computer science, nursing, and science laboratory technologies programs.

2011-2012 Annual costs. Tuition/fees: $4,119; $6,279 out-of-state. Per-credit charge: $152 in-state; $242 out-of-state.

Financial aid. All financial aid based on need. Need-based aid available for part-time students. Work-study available nights, weekends and for part-time students.

Application procedures. Admission: No deadline. No application fee. Admission notification on a rolling basis. **Financial aid:** Priority date 4/1, closing date 8/15. FAFSA, institutional form required. Applicants notified on a rolling basis starting 4/15; must reply within 2 week(s) of notification.

Academics. Students in engineering science, computer science, and computer information systems programs required to purchase or lease microcomputers. **Special study options:** Cooperative education, distance learning, double major, dual enrollment of high school students, honors, independent study, internships, student-designed major, weekend college. Bachelor's degree programs available on campus. **Credit/placement by examination:** AP, CLEP, IB, institutional tests. 30 credit hours maximum toward associate degree. **Support services:** Learning center, reduced course load, remedial instruction, study skills assistance, tutoring.

Majors. Business: Accounting technology, administrative services, business admin, tourism promotion. **Computer sciences:** General, computer science, information systems. **Engineering:** General. **General:** Animal husbandry. **Health services:** EMT paramedic, medical secretary, nursing (RN). **Human services:** Community org/advocacy. **Liberal arts:** Arts/sciences. **Protective services:** Fire services admin, law enforcement admin.

Most popular majors. Business/marketing 19%, health sciences 6%, liberal arts 53%, security/protective services 9%.

Computing on campus. 354 workstations in library, computer center, student center. Online course registration, online library, helpline, wireless network available.

Student life. Freshman orientation: Available. Preregistration for classes offered. Half-day program held in August and January. **Housing:** Privately owned apartments available. **Activities:** Bands, choral groups, drama, literary magazine, music ensembles, student government, student newspaper, veterans club, multicultural club, human services club, environmental club, European excursion club, business club, office technology association, political clubs, Brothers and Sisters in Christ.

Athletics. NJCAA. **Intercollegiate:** Baseball M, basketball, golf, lacrosse, soccer, softball W, tennis W, volleyball W. **Intramural:** Badminton, basketball, soccer, softball, volleyball. **Team name:** Cannoneers.

Student services. Adult student services, chaplain/spiritual director, career counseling, student employment services, financial aid counseling, health services, on-campus daycare, personal counseling, placement for graduates, veterans' counselor. **Physically disabled:** Services for visually, speech, hearing impaired. **Transfer:** Transfer adviser, college fairs on campus for students transferring to 4-year colleges.

Contact. E-mail: admissions@sunyjefferson.edu
Phone: (315) 786-2277 Fax: (315) 786-2459
Rosanne Weir, Director of Admissions, Jefferson Community College, 1220 Coffeen Street, Watertown, NY 13601

Long Island Business Institute
Flushing, New York
www.libi.edu

▸ For-profit 2-year business and career college
▸ Commuter campus in very large city
▸ Interview required

General. Regionally accredited; also accredited by ACICS. Additional campus in Commack, Long Island, 38 miles from Manhattan. **Enrollment:** 566 degree-seeking undergraduates; 30 non-degree-seeking students. **Degrees:** 223 associate awarded. **Location:** 8 miles from Manhattan for our Main Flushing Campus and 38 miles from Manhattan for our LI Commack additional site. **Calendar:** Semester, extensive summer session. **Full-time faculty:** 19 total; 63% minority, 63% women. **Part-time faculty:** 71 total; 1% have terminal degrees, 39% minority, 48% women. **Class size:** 59% < 20, 41% 20-39. **Special facilities:** ESL Language lab, computer learning center, student business club owned and operated cafe.

Student profile. Among degree-seeking undergraduates, 100% enrolled in a vocational program, 7% already have a bachelor's degree or higher, 150 enrolled as first-time, first-year students, 9 transferred in from other institutions.

Part-time:	36%	25 or older:	65%
Women:	80%		

Basis for selection. Must pass COMPASS or CELSA entrance exams. All students with high school diploma or GED welcome. A limited number of students without a high school diploma may be admitted to select programs if they meet admissions requirements under the Ability to Benefit program. Minimum scores on aptitude test required for ESL-based study or for students needing developmental English. **Home schooled:** State high school equivalency certificate required.

2011-2012 Annual costs. Tuition/fees: $13,899. Books/supplies: $600.

2011-2012 Financial aid. Need-based: Average need met was 87%. Average scholarship/grant was $2,500; average loan $1,300. 84% of total undergraduate aid awarded as scholarships/grants, 16% as loans/jobs. Need-based aid available for part-time students. Work-study available nights, weekends and for part-time students. **Non-need-based:** Scholarships awarded for academics.

Application procedures. Admission: No deadline. $55 fee, may be waived for applicants with need. Admission notification on a rolling basis. **Financial aid:** Closing date 5/1. FAFSA required. Applicants notified by 1/1; must reply by 4/30.

Academics. Special study options: ESL. **Credit/placement by examination:** AP, CLEP, institutional tests. **Support services:** Learning center, reduced course load, remedial instruction, study skills assistance, tutoring.

Majors. Business: General, office technology. **Protective services:** Homeland security.

Most popular majors. Business/marketing 65%, health sciences 24%, legal studies 11%.

Computing on campus. 335 workstations in library, computer center, student center.

Student life. Freshman orientation: Available. Preregistration for classes offered. **Activities:** Student newspaper.

Student services. Career counseling, student employment services, financial aid counseling, placement for graduates, veterans' counselor.

Contact. E-mail: eyang@libi.edu
Phone: (718) 939-5100 Fax: (718) 939-9235
William Chong, Enrollment Manager, Long Island Business Institute, 136-18 39th Avenue, 5th Floor, Flushing, NY 11354

Maria College
Albany, New York
www.mariacollege.edu

CB member
CB code: 2434

- Private 2-year health science and liberal arts college
- Commuter campus in small city
- SAT or ACT (ACT writing optional), application essay, interview required

General. Founded in 1958. Regionally accredited. **Enrollment:** 886 degree-seeking undergraduates; 19 non-degree-seeking students. **Degrees:** 135 associate awarded. **ROTC:** Army, Naval, Air Force. **Location:** 150 miles from New York City and Boston. **Calendar:** Semester, limited summer session. **Full-time faculty:** 30 total. **Part-time faculty:** 59 total. **Class size:** 58% < 20, 35% 20-39, less than 1% 40-49, 6% 50-99.

Student profile. Among degree-seeking undergraduates, 46 enrolled as first-time, first-year students.

Part-time:	73%	African American:	16%
Out-of-state:	3%	Asian American:	3%
Women:	87%	Hispanic American:	3%

Transfer out. Colleges most students transferred to 2011: College of Saint Rose, State University at Albany, Hudson Valley Community College, The Sage Colleges, Schenectady County Community College.

Basis for selection. School achievement record, test scores, interviews, recommendations important. Test required for students with scores on SAT Verbal less than 480, Math less than 490, or ACT Composite less than 19. Dual interview required for Occupational Therapy Assistant. **Adult students:** Applicants who did not take SAT or ACT may be required to take an admissions test, which may be waived based on prior college credit. **Home schooled:** Transcript of courses and grades, state high school equivalency certificate, interview, letter of recommendation (nonparent) required. SAT or ACT scores or applicant must take College admissions test for placement purposes. **Learning Disabled:** Must provide documentation regarding specific diagnosis and services/accommodations being requested. Documentation must be within 3 years of acceptance. Must meet with the Dean of Student Services for coordination of support services.

High school preparation. College-preparatory program recommended. 21 units required. Required and recommended units include English 4, mathematics 2-3, social studies 4, science 2-3 (laboratory 3). Requirements vary with program.

2011-2012 Annual costs. Tuition/fees: $10,300. Per-credit charge: $415. Books/supplies: $1,000. Personal expenses: $500.

2011-2012 Financial aid. All financial aid based on need. Average scholarship/grant was $6,690; average loan $2,721. 54% of total undergraduate aid awarded as scholarships/grants, 46% as loans/jobs. Need-based aid available for part-time students. Work-study available nights, weekends and for part-time students.

Application procedures. Admission: Priority date 8/1; deadline 8/15 (receipt date). $35 fee, may be waived for applicants with need. Admission notification on a rolling basis. Must reply by May 1 or within 4 week(s) if notified thereafter. Tuition deposit deadline 30 days after acceptance. High school seniors have until May 1. **Financial aid:** No deadline. FAFSA required. Applicants notified on a rolling basis starting 2/1; must reply within 2 week(s) of notification.

Academics. Special study options: Accelerated study, cross-registration, distance learning, dual enrollment of high school students, independent study, internships, liberal arts/career combination, weekend college. Advanced placement program in nursing for licensed practical nurse and New York State LPN to ADN Nursing Bridge Course. Bachelor's degree programs available on campus. License preparation in nursing, occupational therapy. **Credit/placement by examination:** AP, CLEP, IB, SAT, ACT, institutional tests. 16 credit hours maximum toward associate degree. **Support services:** Learning center, pre-admission summer program, reduced course load, remedial instruction, study skills assistance, tutoring.

Majors. Business: General, accounting, business admin. **Computer sciences:** General. **Education:** Early childhood, teacher assistance. **Health services:** Nursing (RN), occupational therapy assistant. **Liberal arts:** Arts/sciences.

Most popular majors. Business/marketing 6%, health sciences 81%, liberal arts 8%.

Computing on campus. 72 workstations in library, computer center. Commuter students can connect to campus network. Online course registration, online library, wireless network available.

Student life. Freshman orientation: Mandatory. Preregistration for classes offered. Held one day prior to the beginning of the semester.

Student services. Adult student services, alcohol/substance abuse counseling, chaplain/spiritual director, career counseling, student employment services, financial aid counseling, personal counseling, placement for graduates. **Physically disabled:** Services for visually impaired. **Transfer:** Re-entry adviser, pre-admission transcript evaluation for new students. Transfer adviser, college fairs on campus for students transferring to 4-year colleges.

Contact. E-mail: laurieg@mariacollege.edu
Phone: (518) 438-3111 ext. 217 Fax: (518) 453-1366
Laurie Gilmore, Director of Admissions, Maria College, 700 New Scotland Avenue, Albany, NY 12208

Mildred Elley
Albany, New York
www.mildred-elley.edu

CB code: 3335

- For-profit 2-year junior and career college
- Commuter campus in very large city
- Interview required

General. Accredited by ACICS. **Enrollment:** 506 degree-seeking undergraduates; 332 non-degree-seeking students. **Degrees:** 82 associate awarded. **Location:** 147 miles from New York City. **Calendar:** Semester, limited summer session. **Full-time faculty:** 16 total; 25% have terminal degrees, 25% minority, 94% women. **Part-time faculty:** 52 total; 14% have terminal degrees, 10% minority, 52% women. **Class size:** 71% < 20, 29% 20-39.

Student profile. Among degree-seeking undergraduates, 91 enrolled as first-time, first-year students, 7 transferred in from other institutions.

Part-time:	3%	Asian American:	1%
Out-of-state:	2%	Hispanic American:	9%
Women:	72%	Native American:	1%
African American:	38%	25 or older:	80%

Basis for selection. Open admission, but selective for some programs. Additional requirements for Massage Therapy and Practical Nursing programs. **Home schooled:** Transcript of courses and grades, state high school equivalency certificate required.

2011-2012 Annual costs. Tuition/fees: $11,375. Per-credit charge: $354. Books/supplies: $800.

2010-2011 Financial aid. All financial aid based on need. 106 full-time freshmen applied for aid; 106 were judged to have need; 106 of these received

aid. Average scholarship/grant was $4,700; average loan $1,700. 48% of total undergraduate aid awarded as scholarships/grants, 52% as loans/jobs. Need-based aid available for part-time students. Work-study available nights, weekends and for part-time students.

Application procedures. Admission: No deadline. $25 fee, may be waived for applicants with need. Application must be submitted on paper. Admission notification on a rolling basis. **Financial aid:** No deadline. FAFSA required.

Academics. Special study options: Accelerated study, cooperative education, double major, independent study, internships, weekend college. License preparation in nursing. **Credit/placement by examination:** AP, CLEP, institutional tests. **Support services:** GED preparation, learning center, remedial instruction, study skills assistance, tutoring, writing center.

Majors. Business: Business admin. **Computer sciences:** General, information systems. **Health services:** Massage therapy, medical assistant. **Visual/performing arts:** Design, game design.

Most popular majors. Business/marketing 28%, computer/information sciences 10%, health sciences 46%, legal studies 12%.

Computing on campus. PC or laptop required. 120 workstations in library, computer center, student center. Commuter students can connect to campus network. Online library, helpline, repair service, wireless network available.

Student life. Freshman orientation: Mandatory. Preregistration for classes offered. **Activities:** Student government.

Student services. Adult student services, alcohol/substance abuse counseling, career counseling, financial aid counseling, legal services, personal counseling, placement for graduates, veterans' counselor, women's services. **Transfer:** Re-entry adviser, pre-admission transcript evaluation for new students. College fairs on campus for students transferring to 4-year colleges.

Contact. E-mail: admissions@mildred-elley.edu
Phone: (518) 786-3171 Toll-free number: (800) 622-6327
Fax: (518) 786-0011
George Chakmakas, Admissions Director, Mildred Elley, 855 Central Avenue, Albany, NY 12206-1513

Mohawk Valley Community College
Utica, New York
www.mvcc.edu   **CB code: 2414**

- Public 2-year community college
- Commuter campus in small city

General. Founded in 1946. Regionally accredited. SUNY institution. Branch campus in Rome, New York. **Enrollment:** 6,087 degree-seeking undergraduates; 619 non-degree-seeking students. **Degrees:** 832 associate awarded. **ROTC:** Army, Air Force. **Location:** 55 miles from Syracuse, 95 miles from Albany. **Calendar:** Semester, limited summer session. **Full-time faculty:** 146 total; 20% have terminal degrees, 6% minority, 45% women. **Part-time faculty:** 339 total; 10% have terminal degrees, 6% minority, 47% women. **Class size:** 49% < 20, 47% 20-39, 3% 40-49, less than 1% 50-99. **Special facilities:** Human cadaver lab, welding facilities, airframe and powerplant hangar facilities. **Partnerships:** Formal partnership with Verizon for NEXT STEP, a virtual university program for Verizon employees to earn an associate in telecommunications.

Student profile. Among degree-seeking undergraduates, 37% enrolled in a transfer program, 63% enrolled in a vocational program, 2% already have a bachelor's degree or higher, 1,766 enrolled as first-time, first-year students, 387 transferred in from other institutions.

Part-time:	20%	Native American:	1%
Women:	55%	International:	1%
African American:	9%	25 or older:	32%
Asian American:	3%	Live on campus:	8%
Hispanic American:	6%		

Transfer out. 70% of students enrolled in the transfer program go on to 4-year colleges. **Colleges most students transferred to 2011:** SUNY Institute of Technology, Utica College, SUNY Oswego, SUNY Morrisville, SUNY Oneonta.

Basis for selection. Open admission, but selective for some programs. Applicants' records reviewed for completion of program-specific prerequisites to determine regular or underprepared acceptance to program. Interview recommended for all, required for airframe & powerplant tech applicants. **Home schooled:** State high school equivalency certificate required. Must pass ability-to-benefit test prior to acceptance if the state high school equivalency

certificate letter is not provided. **Learning Disabled:** Learning-disabled applicants should forward copy of IEP to Coordinator of Disabilities Services.

High school preparation. College-preparatory program recommended. 15 units recommended. Recommended units include English 4, mathematics 2, social studies 4, science 2, foreign language 1 and academic electives 2. Requirements vary for admission to nursing and certain other programs.

2011-2012 Annual costs. Tuition/fees: $4,010; $7,490 out-of-state. Per-credit charge: $120 in-state; $240 out-of-state. Room/board: $8,660. Books/supplies: $2,000. Personal expenses: $540.

2011-2012 Financial aid. Need-based: 1,543 full-time freshmen applied for aid; 1,047 were judged to have need; 1,031 of these received aid. Average need met was 91%. Average scholarship/grant was $5,244; average loan $3,544. 72% of total undergraduate aid awarded as scholarships/grants, 28% as loans/jobs. Need-based aid available for part-time students. Work-study available nights, weekends and for part-time students. **Non-need-based:** Awarded to 4 full-time undergraduates, including 1 freshmen. Scholarships awarded for academics, alumni affiliation, art, leadership, state residency. **Additional information:** Students in families that are above the threshold of the federal and state allowances for full grant aid (and thus receive little or no grant funding) may be eligible to receive assistance with books, fees, or other expenses.

Application procedures. Admission: No deadline. No application fee. Admission notification on a rolling basis beginning on or about 12/1. Within 30 days of date of acceptance due to limited housing availability on campus. **Financial aid:** Priority date 4/15; no closing date. FAFSA, institutional form required. Applicants notified on a rolling basis starting 3/1; must reply within 2 week(s) of notification.

Academics. Special study options: Cross-registration, distance learning, double major, dual enrollment of high school students, ESL, honors, independent study, internships, student-designed major. License preparation in aviation, nursing. **Credit/placement by examination:** AP, CLEP, institutional tests. Each center has its own policy for the awarding of credit. **Support services:** Learning center, reduced course load, remedial instruction, study skills assistance, tutoring, writing center.

Majors. Business: Accounting technology, administrative services, banking/financial services, business admin, entrepreneurial studies, hotel/motel admin, management information systems. **Communications:** Advertising. **Computer sciences:** General, programming, webmaster. **Education:** Elementary, secondary. **Engineering:** General. **Foreign languages:** Sign language interpretation. **Health services:** EMT paramedic, medical assistant, medical radiologic technology/radiation therapy, nursing (RN), respiratory therapy technology, substance abuse counseling. **Human services:** General, community org/advocacy. **Liberal arts:** Arts/sciences, humanities. **Parks/recreation:** Facilities management. **Protective services:** Fire services admin, law enforcement admin. **Visual/performing arts:** Art, commercial photography, commercial/advertising art, digital arts, dramatic. **Work/family studies:** Institutional food production.

Most popular majors. Business/marketing 15%, engineering/engineering technologies 6%, health sciences 13%, liberal arts 34%, security/protective services 8%, visual/performing arts 8%.

Computing on campus. 116 workstations in library, computer center. Dormitories wired for high-speed internet access. Commuter students can connect to campus network. Online course registration, online library, helpline, wireless network available.

Student life. Freshman orientation: Available. Preregistration for classes offered. Orientation mandatory for residence hall students, with a $40 charge. A 4-hour commuter student orientation and 2-day dorm student orientation held in January and August. **Housing:** Coed dorms, special housing for disabled, wellness housing available. $100 fully refundable deposit. Pets allowed in dorm rooms. Housing eligibility based on academic standing for initial acceptance and continued eligibility. All halls nonsmoking; 1 residence hall has extended quiet hours. Limited visitation suites available. On-campus housing is on first-come, first-served basis. **Activities:** Concert band, dance, drama, international student organizations, musical theater, student government, student newspaper, Black student union, bowling club, chemical dependency club, chess club, drama club, international club, Kidz-N-Coaches, Phi Beta Kappa, Rome student activities association, Student Congress program board.

Athletics. NJCAA. **Intercollegiate:** Baseball M, basketball, bowling, cross-country, golf, ice hockey M, lacrosse, soccer, softball W, tennis, track and field, volleyball W. **Intramural:** Basketball, football (non-tackle), racquetball, soccer, tennis, volleyball, weight lifting. **Team name:** Hawks.

Student services. Adult student services, alcohol/substance abuse counseling, career counseling, student employment services, financial aid counseling, health services, on-campus daycare, personal counseling, placement for graduates, veterans' counselor. **Physically disabled:** Services for visually,

speech, hearing impaired. **Transfer:** Pre-admission transcript evaluation for new students. Transfer center, transfer adviser, college fairs on campus for students transferring to 4-year colleges.

Contact. E-mail: admissions@mvcc.edu
Phone: (315) 792-5354 Toll-free number: (800) 733-6822
Fax: (315) 792-5527
Daniel Ianno, Director of Admissions, Mohawk Valley Community College, 1101 Sherman Drive, Utica, NY 13501-5394

Monroe Community College
Rochester, New York **CB member**
www.monroecc.edu **CB code: 2429**

- Public 2-year community college
- Commuter campus in large city

General. Founded in 1961. Regionally accredited. SUNY institution. Off-campus extension centers in 4 area high schools, branch campus in downtown Rochester. Applied technology center. **Enrollment:** 15,968 degree-seeking undergraduates; 1,731 non-degree-seeking students. **Degrees:** 2,717 associate awarded. **ROTC:** Army, Naval, Air Force. **Location:** 4 miles from downtown. **Calendar:** Semester, limited summer session. **Full-time faculty:** 329 total; 15% have terminal degrees, 16% minority, 56% women. **Part-time faculty:** 630 total; 7% have terminal degrees, 13% minority, 51% women. **Class size:** 30% < 20, 63% 20-39, 5% 40-49, 2% 50-99. **Special facilities:** Human ecology habitat, human performance laboratory, electronic learning center. **Partnerships:** Formal partnerships with Xerox, Kodak, Frontier, Wegman's.

Student profile. Among degree-seeking undergraduates, 4,206 enrolled as first-time, first-year students.

Part-time:	31%	Hispanic American:	8%
Out-of-state:	5%	International:	1%
Women:	54%	25 or older:	40%
African American:	19%	Live on campus:	2%
Asian American:	3%		

Transfer out. Colleges most students transferred to 2011: SUNY College at Brockport, Rochester Institute of Technology, St. John Fisher College, SUNY College at Geneseo, Nazareth College.

Basis for selection. Open admission, but selective for some programs. Admissions to certain programs based on high school records, with preference given to county residents. Applicants to engineering and computer science must have precalculus, chemistry and physics. **Home schooled:** Transcript of courses and grades required. Must meet Federal Ability to Benefit guidelines on placement exam if not issued a regular high school diploma.

High school preparation. Recommended units include English 4, mathematics 4, social studies 4 and science 4. Individual programs have specific math and science requirements.

2011-2012 Annual costs. Tuition/fees: $3,458; $6,518 out-of-state. Per-credit charge: $128 in-state; $256 out-of-state. Room only: $6,300. Books/supplies: $1,000.

Financial aid. All financial aid based on need. Need-based aid available for part-time students. Work-study available nights, weekends and for part-time students.

Application procedures. Admission: Priority date 3/1; no deadline. $20 fee, may be waived for applicants with need. Admission notification on a rolling basis. Application deadline for healthcare programs: 1/31 for fall term, 10/31 for spring term. Applicants to nursing program are encouraged to apply 1 year prior to registration. **Financial aid:** Priority date 3/30; no closing date. FAFSA required. Applicants notified on a rolling basis starting 3/15; must reply within 2 week(s) of notification.

Academics. Special study options: Accelerated study, cooperative education, cross-registration, distance learning, dual enrollment of high school students, ESL, exchange student, honors, independent study, internships, liberal arts/career combination, weekend college. License preparation in aviation, dental hygiene, nursing, paramedic, radiology. **Credit/placement by examination:** AP, CLEP, institutional tests. 30 credit hours maximum toward associate degree. **Support services:** Learning center, pre-admission summer program, reduced course load, remedial instruction, study skills assistance, tutoring, writing center.

Majors. Architecture: Landscape. **Biology:** General. **Business:** General, accounting, administrative services, international, marketing, sales/distribution, tourism promotion, tourism/travel. **Communications:** Advertising,

communications/speech/rhetoric, public relations. **Communications technology:** General, radio/TV. **Computer sciences:** Computer science, information technology, networking, programming, systems analysis. **Education:** Health, music, physical. **Engineering:** Engineering science. **Health services:** Dental hygiene, medical records technology, nursing (RN), physics/radiologic health. **History:** General. **Liberal arts:** Arts/sciences. **Math:** General. **Parks/recreation:** Health/fitness. **Physical sciences:** Chemistry, optics, physics. **Protective services:** Corrections, criminal justice, fire safety technology, police science. **Social sciences:** General, political science. **Visual/performing arts:** Commercial/advertising art, interior design, music performance, photography, studio arts. **Work/family studies:** Child care service, institutional food production.

Most popular majors. Business/marketing 17%, health sciences 10%, liberal arts 50%.

Computing on campus. 150 workstations in library, computer center, student center. Dormitories wired for high-speed internet access and linked to campus network. Commuter students can connect to campus network. Helpline, wireless network available.

Student life. Freshman orientation: Available. Preregistration for classes offered. Orientation held 1 week prior to beginning of semester. **Housing:** Coed dorms available. **Activities:** Bands, choral groups, drama, literary magazine, musical theater, radio station, student government, student newspaper, symphony orchestra, Christian, Jewish, and Christian Science groups; Latin American, Italian-American, Black, and international student organizations; veterans and handicapped student clubs; honor society.

Athletics. NJCAA. **Intercollegiate:** Baseball M, basketball, diving, golf M, ice hockey M, lacrosse M, soccer, softball W, swimming, tennis, volleyball W. **Intramural:** Archery, basketball, bowling, cheerleading W, cross-country, diving, lacrosse, racquetball, rugby M, skiing, soccer, softball, swimming, tennis, volleyball, water polo M. **Team name:** Tribunes.

Student services. Adult student services, career counseling, student employment services, financial aid counseling, health services, on-campus daycare, personal counseling, placement for graduates, veterans' counselor. **Physically disabled:** Services for visually, hearing impaired. **Transfer:** Transfer center, transfer adviser, college fairs on campus for students transferring to 4-year colleges.

Contact. Phone: (585) 292-2200 Fax: (585) 292-3860
Andrew Freeman, Director of Admissions, Monroe Community College, Office of Admissions-Monroe Community College, Rochester, NY 14692-8908

Nassau Community College
Garden City, New York **CB member**
www.ncc.edu **CB code: 2563**

- Public 2-year community college
- Commuter campus in large town

General. Founded in 1959. Regionally accredited. SUNY institution. Students may attend some courses at off-campus locations. **Enrollment:** 23,226 degree-seeking undergraduates. **Degrees:** 2,635 associate awarded. **Location:** 25 miles from New York City. **Calendar:** Semester, extensive summer session. **Full-time faculty:** 557 total. **Part-time faculty:** 886 total. **Class size:** 100% 20-39. **Special facilities:** Firehouse gallery. **Partnerships:** Formal partnerships with local businesses and industry to provide on-site training to employees.

Transfer out. Colleges most students transferred to 2011: Hofstra University, Adelphi University, SUNY Old Westbury, SUNY Stony Brook, Dowling College.

Basis for selection. Open admission, but selective for some programs. Class rank and fulfillment of mathematics and science requirements important for admission to accounting, business, engineering, nursing, allied health, mortuary science, civil technology, computer information systems, computer science, electrical technology, paralegal, and telecommunications technology programs. Students without high school diploma or equivalent may apply for GED after successful completion of 24 college credits. SAT scores may result in exemption from placement testing. Interview required for allied health programs; audition required for music program; portfolio review required for fashion apparel design program. **Adult students:** Placement test in reading, English, and math required unless applicant has prior associate or bachelor's degree or prior college credit for English composition and college-level math. **Home schooled:** Transcript of courses and grades, state high school equivalency certificate required. **Learning Disabled:** Students must submit a copy of their I.E.P. in order to get services through our Center for Students with Disabilities.

High school preparation. Recommended units include English 4, mathematics 4, social studies 4, science 4 (laboratory 4), foreign language 3 and academic electives 4.

2011-2012 Annual costs. Tuition/fees: $4,330; $8,320 out-of-state. Per-credit charge: $167 in-state; $334 out-of-state. Books/supplies: $1,400. Personal expenses: $2,200.

Financial aid. Need-based: Need-based aid available for part-time students. Work-study available nights, weekends and for part-time students. **Non-need-based:** Scholarships awarded for academics, minority status.

Application procedures. Admission: No deadline. $40 fee. Admission notification on a rolling basis beginning on or about 2/1. **Financial aid:** Priority date 6/7; no closing date. FAFSA required. Applicants notified on a rolling basis; must reply within 1 week(s) of notification.

Academics. Special study options: Cooperative education, cross-registration, distance learning, ESL, honors, internships, study abroad, weekend college. Cooperative programs with SUNY College of Technology at Utica-Rome and SUNY at New Paltz, New York State Chiropractic College, Fashion Institute of Technology, Adelphi University; joint admissions with SUNY at Stony Brook and SUNY College at Old Westbury. License preparation in nursing, physical therapy, radiology, real estate. **Credit/placement by examination:** AP, CLEP, IB, institutional tests. 33 credit hours maximum toward associate degree. **Support services:** GED preparation and test center, learning center, reduced course load, remedial instruction, study skills assistance, tutoring, writing center.

Honors college/program. Honors applicants must rank in the top 20% of their graduating class and have 3 years of Regents math, English, science and high grades in each.

Majors. Area/ethnic studies: African. **Business:** Accounting, administrative services, business admin, fashion, management information systems, sales/distribution. **Communications:** Communications/speech/rhetoric, media studies. **Computer sciences:** General, computer science, programming. **Education:** Early childhood, elementary, middle, secondary. **Engineering:** General, electrical. **Foreign languages:** American Sign Language. **Health services:** Medical radiologic technology/radiation therapy, medical secretary, nursing (RN), physical therapy assistant, respiratory therapy technology, surgical technology. **Liberal arts:** Arts/sciences. **Math:** General. **Protective services:** Law enforcement admin. **Visual/performing arts:** Art, digital arts, graphic design, interior design, music performance, photography. **Work/family studies:** Food/nutrition.

Most popular majors. Business/marketing 11%, family/consumer sciences 6%, health sciences 11%, liberal arts 57%.

Computing on campus. 1,300 workstations in library, computer center. Commuter students can connect to campus network. Online course registration, online library, helpline, wireless network available.

Student life. Freshman orientation: Available. Preregistration for classes offered. Full-day program. **Activities:** Bands, choral groups, dance, drama, literary magazine, music ensembles, musical theater, radio station, student government, student newspaper, symphony orchestra, TV station, Haraya Caribbean students organizations, Asian American society, Irish American club, NYPIRG, women center, Association Catholic Community, Jewish students organization, organization of Latinos, multicultural club, Intervarsity Christian Fellowship.

Athletics. NJCAA. **Intercollegiate:** Baseball M, basketball, bowling, cross-country, football (tackle) M, golf, lacrosse, soccer, softball W, tennis, track and field, volleyball W, wrestling M. **Intramural:** Badminton, baseball M, basketball, football (non-tackle) M, handball, judo, racquetball, soccer, softball, swimming, table tennis, tennis, volleyball. **Team name:** Lions.

Student services. Adult student services, career counseling, student employment services, financial aid counseling, health services, minority student services, on-campus daycare, personal counseling, placement for graduates, veterans' counselor, women's services. **Physically disabled:** Services for visually, speech, hearing impaired. **Transfer:** Pre-admission transcript evaluation for new students. Transfer center, transfer adviser, college fairs on campus for students transferring to 4-year colleges.

Contact. E-mail: admissions@ncc.edu
Phone: (516) 572-7345 Fax: (516) 572-9743
Tika Esler, Dean of Academic Student Services, Nassau Community College, One Education Drive, Garden City, NY 11530

New York Career Institute
New York, New York
www.nyci.edu

CB code: 5324

- For-profit 2-year junior college
- Commuter campus in very large city
- Interview required

General. Accredited by New York State Board of Regents. **Enrollment:** 722 degree-seeking undergraduates. **Degrees:** 23 associate awarded. **Calendar:** Trimester, extensive summer session. **Full-time faculty:** 11 total. **Part-time faculty:** 35 total.

Basis for selection. Open admission. CPAt examination performance important for all students who enter without college credit in English and/or mathematics. All applicants take English and math placement examinations (CPAt). **Adult students:** SAT/ACT scores not required.

2011-2012 Annual costs. Tuition/fees: $12,450. Tuition for paralegal and medical evening programs $390 per credit hour. Books/supplies: $1,000. Personal expenses: $4,000.

Financial aid. All financial aid based on need. Need-based aid available for part-time students. Work-study available nights, weekends and for part-time students.

Application procedures. Admission: No deadline. $50 fee. Admission notification on a rolling basis. **Financial aid:** No deadline. Applicants notified on a rolling basis.

Academics. Special study options: Internships. **Credit/placement by examination:** AP, CLEP, institutional tests. **Support services:** Remedial instruction, study skills assistance.

Majors. Health services: Medical secretary.

Computing on campus. Online library, repair service available.

Student life. Freshman orientation: Mandatory. Preregistration for classes offered.

Student services. Career counseling, student employment services, financial aid counseling, personal counseling, placement for graduates. **Transfer:** Pre-admission transcript evaluation for new students.

Contact. E-mail: lstieglitz@nyci.edu
Phone: (212) 962-0002 ext. 100 Fax: (212) 385-7574
Larry Steiglitz, Director of Admissions, New York Career Institute, 11 Park Place, New York, NY 10007

Niagara County Community College
Sanborn, New York
www.niagaracc.suny.edu

CB member
CB code: 2568

- Public 2-year community college
- Commuter campus in rural community

General. Founded in 1962. Regionally accredited. SUNY institution. **Enrollment:** 5,597 degree-seeking undergraduates; 1,580 non-degree-seeking students. **Degrees:** 970 associate awarded. **ROTC:** Army. **Location:** 10 miles from Niagara Falls. **Calendar:** Semester, limited summer session. **Full-time faculty:** 106 total; 27% have terminal degrees, 8% minority, 55% women. **Part-time faculty:** 280 total; 5% have terminal degrees, 5% minority, 61% women. **Special facilities:** Biofeedback laboratory.

Student profile. Among degree-seeking undergraduates, 1,588 enrolled as first-time, first-year students, 427 transferred in from other institutions.

Part-time:	22%	Hispanic American:	2%
Out-of-state:	1%	Native American:	2%
Women:	58%	25 or older:	27%
African American:	12%	Live on campus:	4%
Asian American:	1%		

Transfer out. Colleges most students transferred to 2011: Buffalo State College, Niagara University, SUNY Buffalo, Brockport, Fredonia.

Basis for selection. Open admission, but selective for some programs. Admission to nursing, physical therapist assistant, radiologic technology, and surgical technology programs based on school achievement record and test scores, on a space-available basis. SAT/ACT reviewed for placement if submitted. Interview recommended.

High school preparation. 1 drafting required for drafting applicants; 1 biology or chemistry required for nursing applicants; 3 mathematics for engineering technology; 1 biology, 1 chemistry and 2 mathematics for physical therapist assistant; 1 chemistry, 1 biology, 2 mathematics for radiologic technology; 1 biology for surgical technician; 3 mathematics for business administration.

2011-2012 Annual costs. Tuition/fees: $3,958; $7,582 out-of-state. Per-credit charge: $151 in-state; $302 out-of-state. Books/supplies: $1,000. Personal expenses: $650.

2010-2011 Financial aid. All financial aid based on need. 61% of total undergraduate aid awarded as scholarships/grants, 39% as loans/jobs. Need-based aid available for part-time students. Work-study available nights, weekends and for part-time students. **Additional information:** Assistance offered with placing students in part-time employment through the Job Locator office. Students can charge books and food coupons.

Application procedures. Admission: Closing date 8/31. No application fee. Admission notification on a rolling basis beginning on or about 8/1. Must reply by May 1 or within 4 week(s) if notified thereafter. **Financial aid:** Priority date 4/1; no closing date. FAFSA required. Applicants notified on a rolling basis starting 5/1; must reply within 2 week(s) of notification.

Academics. Orientation program for Distance Learning students. **Special study options:** Cooperative education, cross-registration, distance learning, double major, dual enrollment of high school students, honors, independent study, internships, study abroad. License preparation in nursing. **Credit/placement by examination:** AP, CLEP, IB, institutional tests. 30 credit hours maximum toward associate degree. **Support services:** Learning center, pre-admission summer program, reduced course load, remedial instruction, study skills assistance, tutoring, writing center.

Majors. Business: Accounting, administrative services, business admin, hospitality admin, retailing, tourism/travel. **Communications:** Communications/speech/rhetoric, digital media. **Computer sciences:** General, computer science. **Conservation:** Environmental studies. **Education:** Elementary. **Health services:** Medical assistant, medical radiologic technology/radiation therapy, nursing (RN), physical therapy assistant, surgical technology. **Liberal arts:** Arts/sciences, humanities. **Parks/recreation:** General, health/fitness, sports admin. **Protective services:** Criminalistics, law enforcement admin. **Visual/performing arts:** Dramatic, music, studio arts.

Most popular majors. Business/marketing 21%, health sciences 30%, liberal arts 22%, security/protective services 9%.

Computing on campus. 500 workstations in library, computer center, student center. Dormitories wired for high-speed internet access and linked to campus network. Commuter students can connect to campus network. Online course registration, online library, helpline, student web hosting, wireless network available.

Student life. Freshman orientation: Available. Preregistration for classes offered. One-day orientation in August. **Housing:** Guaranteed on-campus for all undergraduates. Coed dorms available. $275 partly refundable deposit. **Activities:** Jazz band, choral groups, dance, drama, international student organizations, music ensembles, musical theater, radio station, student government, student newspaper, disabled student association, comeback club, African American student association, Native American club, human services club, international club, outdoor adventure club, student ambassadors, student nurses association, tanzen dance club.

Athletics. NJCAA. **Intercollegiate:** Baseball M, basketball, bowling, golf, lacrosse, soccer, softball W, volleyball W, wrestling M. **Intramural:** Basketball, racquetball, soccer, swimming, tennis. **Team name:** Trailblazers.

Student services. Adult student services, alcohol/substance abuse counseling, career counseling, student employment services, financial aid counseling, health services, on-campus daycare, personal counseling, placement for graduates, veterans' counselor. **Physically disabled:** Services for visually, speech, hearing impaired. **Transfer:** Pre-admission transcript evaluation for new students. Transfer adviser, college fairs on campus for students transferring to 4-year colleges.

Contact. E-mail: admissions@niagaracc.suny.edu
Phone: (716) 614-6200 Fax: (716) 614-6820
Kathy Saunders, Director of Admissions, Niagara County Community College, 3111 Saunders Settlement Road, Sanborn, NY 14132-9460

North Country Community College
Saranac Lake, New York
www.nccc.edu

CB member
CB code: 2571

▶ Public 2-year community college
▶ Commuter campus in small town

General. Founded in 1967. Regionally accredited. SUNY institution. Campuses in Saranac Lake, Malone, and Ticonderoga. **Enrollment:** 1,289 degree-seeking undergraduates. **Degrees:** 273 associate awarded. **Location:** 150 miles from Albany, 50 miles from Plattsburgh. **Calendar:** Semester, limited summer session. **Full-time faculty:** 48 total. **Part-time faculty:** 96 total. **Class size:** 75% < 20, 24% 20-39, 1% 40-49. **Partnerships:** Formal partnerships with local high schools through College Bridge Program.

Student profile.

Out-of-state:	2%	**Live on campus:**	6%
25 or older:	26%		

Transfer out. Colleges most students transferred to 2011: SUNY Colleges at Plattsburgh, Potsdam, Cobleskill, Geneseo; SUNY at Buffalo.

Basis for selection. Open admission, but selective for some programs. Special requirements for nursing, radiologic technology, and massage therapy. SAT or ACT and placement tests recommended for competitive programs. **Home schooled:** Must complete and score in appropriate ranges on College Board Descriptive Tests System in math, English, and reading.

High school preparation. 16 units recommended. Recommended units include English 4, mathematics 3, social studies 4, science 3 (laboratory 1) and foreign language 3. 5 units of math and science recommended (3 math and 2 science or 2 math and 3 science).

2011-2012 Annual costs. Tuition/fees: $4,980; $10,680 out-of-state. Per-credit charge: $163 in-state; $400 out-of-state. Annual room rate based on single-occupancy bedroom within suite; no double-occupancy rooms available. Room/board: $9,100. Books/supplies: $800. Personal expenses: $800.

Financial aid. All financial aid based on need. Need-based aid available for part-time students. Work-study available nights, weekends and for part-time students.

Application procedures. Admission: Priority date 2/1; no deadline. No application fee. Admission notification on a rolling basis. Must reply by May 1 or within 4 week(s) if notified thereafter. **Financial aid:** Priority date 4/1; no closing date. FAFSA required. Applicants notified on a rolling basis starting 4/1; must reply within 3 week(s) of notification.

Academics. 23-42 credit hours required in major, 62-70 required for graduation depending on field of study. **Special study options:** Distance learning, double major, dual enrollment of high school students, internships, liberal arts/career combination, student-designed major. License preparation in nursing, radiology. **Credit/placement by examination:** AP, CLEP, institutional tests. 31 credit hours maximum toward associate degree. **Support services:** Learning center, reduced course load, remedial instruction, study skills assistance, tutoring.

Majors. Business: General, business admin, office/clerical. **Computer sciences:** Computer graphics. **Health services:** Massage therapy, medical radiologic technology/radiation therapy, nursing (RN). **Liberal arts:** Arts/sciences. **Parks/recreation:** Facilities management. **Protective services:** Criminal justice.

Most popular majors. Security/protective services 12%.

Computing on campus. 200 workstations in dormitories, library, computer center, student center. Dormitories linked to campus network. Commuter students can connect to campus network. Online library, helpline, wireless network available.

Student life. Freshman orientation: Mandatory. Preregistration for classes offered. Day-long session held 1 day prior to start of classes. **Housing:** Coed dorms, wellness housing available. $250 nonrefundable deposit. **Activities:** Drama, literary magazine, music ensembles, student government, student newspaper.

Athletics. NJCAA. **Intercollegiate:** Basketball M, ice hockey M, soccer, softball W. **Intramural:** Badminton, basketball, bowling, golf, soccer, softball, swimming, volleyball, weight lifting. **Team name:** Saints.

Student services. Adult student services, alcohol/substance abuse counseling, career counseling, student employment services, financial aid counseling, personal counseling, placement for graduates. **Physically disabled:** Services for visually, speech, hearing impaired. **Transfer:** Pre-admission transcript evaluation for new students. Transfer adviser, college fairs on campus for students transferring to 4-year colleges.

Contact. E-mail: info@nccc.edu
Phone: (518) 891-2915 ext. 233 Toll-free number: (888) 879-6222
Fax: (518) 891-0898
Edwin Trathen, Vice President for Enrollment and Student Services, North Country Community College, 23 Santanoni Avenue, Saranac Lake, NY 12983

Olean Business Institute
Olean, New York
www.obi.edu

CB code: 0630

- For-profit 2-year business college
- Commuter campus in large town

General. Founded in 1961. Accredited by ACICS. **Location:** 90 miles from Buffalo, 90 miles from Erie, Pennsylvania. **Calendar:** Semester.

Annual costs/financial aid. Tuition/fees (2011-2012): $11,325. Books/supplies: $700.

Contact. Phone: (716) 372-7978
Director of Admissions, 301 North Union Street, Olean, NY 14760

Onondaga Community College
Syracuse, New York
www.sunyocc.edu

CB member
CB code: 2627

- Public 2-year community college
- Commuter campus in small city

General. Founded in 1962. Regionally accredited. **Enrollment:** 8,745 degree-seeking undergraduates; 3,986 non-degree-seeking students. **Degrees:** 1,157 associate awarded. **ROTC:** Army, Air Force. **Location:** 4 miles from downtown Syracuse. **Calendar:** Semester, extensive summer session. **Full-time faculty:** 176 total; 8% minority, 52% women. **Part-time faculty:** 508 total; 6% minority, 52% women. **Class size:** 49% < 20, 50% 20-39, 1% 40-49, less than 1% 50-99, less than 1% >100. **Special facilities:** Children's learning center, applied technology center, multicultural center. **Partnerships:** Formal partnerships with Syracuse public schools, Manufacturers Association of Central New York, Disney.

Student profile. Among degree-seeking undergraduates, 69% enrolled in a transfer program, 31% enrolled in a vocational program, 2,497 enrolled as first-time, first-year students, 656 transferred in from other institutions.

Part-time:	24%	Hispanic American:	5%
Out-of-state:	1%	Native American:	1%
Women:	50%	International:	1%
African American:	13%	25 or older:	28%
Asian American:	2%	Live on campus:	7%

Transfer out. 20% of students enrolled in the transfer program go on to 4-year colleges. **Colleges most students transferred to 2011:** SUNY Oswego, SUNY Cortland, SUNY Buffalo, Le Moyne College, Syracuse University.

Basis for selection. Open admission, but selective for some programs. Admission to some programs based on high school GPA, test scores, and specific program prerequisites. Mandatory developmental skills courses required as condition of acceptance for students lacking adequate academic background. School achievement record, test scores, special talents considered for placement only. Information session required for nursing and recommended for physical therapy assistant; audition required for music. **Adult students:** SAT/ACT scores not required. **Home schooled:** Letter of substantial equivalency from local school district.

High school preparation. 15 units recommended. Recommended units include English 4, mathematics 3, science 3 and foreign language 2. Algebra, biology, chemistry required of respiratory care, surgical technology, nursing applicants. 4 math required for engineering, science, computer science and physical therapy assistant applicants. Language required for humanities.

2011-2012 Annual costs. Tuition/fees: $4,484; $8,414 out-of-state. Per-credit charge: $158 in-state; $316 out-of-state. Books/supplies: $1,230. Personal expenses: $700.

2010-2011 Financial aid. All financial aid based on need. 2,076 full-time freshmen applied for aid; 1,834 were judged to have need; 1,738 of these received aid. Average need met was 80%. Average scholarship/grant was $5,098; average loan $2,850. 73% of total undergraduate aid awarded as scholarships/grants, 27% as loans/jobs. Need-based aid available for part-time students. Work-study available nights, weekends and for part-time students.

Application procedures. Admission: Closing date 8/13 (receipt date). No application fee. Admission notification on a rolling basis. **Financial aid:** Priority date 2/15; no closing date. FAFSA required. Applicants notified on a rolling basis starting 4/15; must reply within 4 week(s) of notification.

Academics. Special study options: Accelerated study, cooperative education, cross-registration, distance learning, double major, dual enrollment of high school students, ESL, honors, independent study, internships, liberal arts/career combination, New York semester, study abroad. License preparation in nursing, physical therapy. **Credit/placement by examination:** AP, CLEP, IB, institutional tests. 30 credit hours maximum toward associate degree. **Support services:** GED preparation, learning center, pre-admission summer program, reduced course load, remedial instruction, study skills assistance, tutoring, writing center.

Majors. Architecture: Technology. **Business:** Accounting technology, business admin. **Communications:** Communications/speech/rhetoric, radio/TV. **Computer sciences:** General, computer science. **Education:** Multi-level teacher. **Engineering:** Engineering science. **Health services:** Medical records technology, nursing (RN), physical therapy assistant, respiratory therapy technology. **Liberal arts:** Humanities. **Parks/recreation:** General. **Protective services:** Criminal justice, fire safety technology, forensics, law enforcement admin, police science. **Visual/performing arts:** Interior design, music, photography.

Most popular majors. Business/marketing 13%, health sciences 8%, liberal arts 31%, public administration/social services 9%, security/protective services 11%, visual/performing arts 8%.

Computing on campus. 1,000 workstations in library, computer center, student center. Dormitories wired for high-speed internet access and linked to campus network. Commuter students can connect to campus network. Online course registration, online library, helpline, repair service, student web hosting, wireless network available.

Student life. Freshman orientation: Available. Preregistration for classes offered. Programs held for half day in fall and spring prior to start of classes. **Policies:** Dorms are alcohol free. **Housing:** Coed dorms, wellness housing available. $300 nonrefundable deposit. Suite-style housing available. **Activities:** Bands, choral groups, drama, film society, international student organizations, music ensembles, musical theater, radio station, student government, student newspaper, international students, minority, veterans, interreligious, older/returning student clubs.

Athletics. NJCAA. **Intercollegiate:** Baseball M, basketball, lacrosse, soccer, softball W, tennis, volleyball W. **Intramural:** Badminton, basketball, golf, skiing, swimming, table tennis, tennis, volleyball. **Team name:** Lazers.

Student services. Alcohol/substance abuse counseling, chaplain/spiritual director, career counseling, services for economically disadvantaged, student employment services, financial aid counseling, health services, minority student services, on-campus daycare, personal counseling, placement for graduates, veterans' counselor. **Physically disabled:** Services for visually, speech, hearing impaired. **Transfer:** Pre-admission transcript evaluation for new students. Transfer adviser, college fairs on campus for students transferring to 4-year colleges.

Contact. E-mail: OCCadmissions@sunyocc.edu
Phone: (315) 498-2202 Fax: (315) 498-2107
Katherine Perry, Director of Recruitment & Admissions, Onondaga Community College, 4585 West Seneca Turnpike, Syracuse, NY 13215-4585

Orange County Community College
Middletown, New York
www.sunyorange.edu

CB code: 2625

- Public 2-year community college
- Commuter campus in large town

General. Founded in 1950. Regionally accredited. **Enrollment:** 5,907 degree-seeking undergraduates; 1,399 non-degree-seeking students. **Degrees:** 768 associate awarded. **ROTC:** Army. **Location:** 25 miles from Newburgh, 60 miles from New York City. **Calendar:** Semester, limited summer session. **Full-time faculty:** 156 total. **Part-time faculty:** 278 total. **Class size:** 59% < 20, 41% 20-39.

Student profile. Among degree-seeking undergraduates, 1,984 enrolled as first-time, first-year students, 377 transferred in from other institutions.

Part-time:	39%	Asian American:	2%
Women:	57%	Hispanic American:	21%
African American:	12%	25 or older:	26%

Transfer out. Colleges most students transferred to 2011: SUNY College at New Paltz, Mount Saint Mary College, Marist College, Dominican College of Blauvelt.

Basis for selection. Open admission, but selective for some programs. Admission to allied health and nursing programs based on academic record, assessment scores and, to some extent, residency. **Home schooled:** Must have letter from school district supervisor attesting that the student has completed 4 years of high school study.

High school preparation. Regents biology recommended for physical therapist assistant, occupational therapy assistant, radiologic technologist and dental hygienist. Regents chemistry recommended for dental hygiene.

2011-2012 Annual costs. Tuition/fees: $4,336; $8,236 out-of-state. Per-credit charge: $163 in-state; $326 out-of-state. Books/supplies: $1,500. Personal expenses: $1,766.

2010-2011 Financial aid. Need-based: 58% of total undergraduate aid awarded as scholarships/grants, 42% as loans/jobs. Need-based aid available for part-time students. Work-study available nights, weekends and for part-time students.

Application procedures. Admission: Closing date 8/20 (receipt date). $30 fee, may be waived for applicants with need. Admission notification on a rolling basis. February 1 application closing date for allied health/nursing program. Notification by March 15, must reply within 2 weeks. **Financial aid:** Priority date 4/15, closing date 7/1. FAFSA, institutional form required. Applicants notified on a rolling basis starting 4/1; must reply within 4 week(s) of notification.

Academics. Agreement with Franklin University (Ohio) for bachelor's completion program. **Special study options:** Cooperative education, distance learning, dual enrollment of high school students, ESL, honors, independent study, internships. License preparation in dental hygiene, nursing, real estate. **Credit/placement by examination:** AP, CLEP, institutional tests. 30 credit hours maximum toward associate degree. **Support services:** GED preparation and test center, learning center, reduced course load, remedial instruction, study skills assistance, tutoring, writing center.

Majors. Business: General, accounting, administrative services, business admin, e-commerce, finance, office technology, sales/distribution. **Communications:** Communications/speech/rhetoric. **Computer sciences:** General, data processing. **Education:** General, elementary. **Engineering:** General. **Foreign languages:** General, French, Spanish. **Health services:** Clinical lab science, clinical lab technology, dental hygiene, medical radiologic technology/radiation therapy, occupational therapy assistant, physical therapy assistant. **Liberal arts:** Arts/sciences. **Math:** General. **Parks/recreation:** Exercise sciences, facilities management. **Protective services:** Criminal justice, police science. **Work/family studies:** Child care management.

Computing on campus. 300 workstations in library, computer center, student center. Online course registration, online library, helpline, wireless network available.

Student life. Freshman orientation: Mandatory. Preregistration for classes offered. **Activities:** Bands, choral groups, dance, drama, music ensembles, musical theater, radio station, student government, student newspaper, black and Latino organization, Helping Hands, social service organization, Habitat for Humanity.

Athletics. NJCAA. **Intercollegiate:** Baseball M, basketball, golf, soccer, softball W, swimming, tennis, volleyball W. **Intramural:** Football (non-tackle), racquetball, soccer M, softball, tennis, volleyball. **Team name:** Colts.

Student services. Adult student services, alcohol/substance abuse counseling, career counseling, services for economically disadvantaged, student employment services, financial aid counseling, health services, on-campus daycare, personal counseling, placement for graduates, veterans' counselor. **Physically disabled:** Services for visually, speech, hearing impaired. **Transfer:** Transfer adviser, college fairs on campus for students transferring to 4-year colleges.

Contact. E-mail: apply@sunyorange.edu
Phone: (845) 341-4030 Fax: (845) 342-8662
Orange County Community College, 115 South Street, Middletown, NY 10940-0115

Phillips Beth Israel School of Nursing
New York, New York
www.futurenursebi.org   **CB code: 2031**

- Private 2-year nursing college
- Commuter campus in very large city
- Application essay, interview required

General. Founded in 1904. **Enrollment:** 265 degree-seeking undergraduates. **Degrees:** 83 associate awarded. **Calendar:** Semester, limited summer session. **Full-time faculty:** 9 total; 11% have terminal degrees, 11% minority, 100% women. **Part-time faculty:** 35 total; 11% have terminal degrees, 54% minority, 83% women. **Class size:** 12% < 20, 68% 20-39, 21% 40-49.

Student profile. Among degree-seeking undergraduates, 100% enrolled in a transfer program, 50% already have a bachelor's degree or higher, 16 enrolled as first-time, first-year students, 123 transferred in from other institutions.

Part-time:	92%	Asian American:	11%
Out-of-state:	15%	Hispanic American:	10%
Women:	77%	25 or older:	50%
African American:	19%		

Transfer out. 70% of students enrolled in the transfer program go on to 4-year colleges. **Colleges most students transferred to 2011:** Pace University, New York University, New York City College of Technology, Excelsior College.

Basis for selection. Academic achievement, aptitude test scores, personal interview, recommendations, and prior experience of primary consideration. 55th percentile score on National League for Nursing's Preadmission Examination-RN mandatory (65th percentile score recommended). Standing in top half of high school class recommended. High school minimum average of 75 percent required, college GPA of 2.5 or better, GED minimum score of 250. **Home schooled:** Statement describing home school structure and mission, transcript of courses and grades, state high school equivalency certificate required.

High school preparation. College-preparatory program recommended. 16 units required. Required units include English 4, mathematics 2, social studies 2, science 2 (laboratory 2). Chemistry and biology required.

2011-2012 Annual costs. Tuition/fees: $19,160. Per-credit charge: $400. Books/supplies: $1,600.

2011-2012 Financial aid. Need-based: 42% of total undergraduate aid awarded as scholarships/grants, 58% as loans/jobs. Need-based aid available for part-time students. Work-study available nights, weekends and for part-time students.

Application procedures. Admission: Closing date 3/1 (postmark date). $50 fee, may be waived for applicants with need. Application must be submitted on paper. Admission notification on a rolling basis beginning on or about 2/1. Must reply by May 1 or within 2 week(s) if notified thereafter. **Financial aid:** Closing date 6/1. FAFSA, institutional form required. Applicants notified by 8/1; must reply within 3 week(s) of notification.

Academics. Special study options: Honors, weekend college. License preparation in nursing. **Credit/placement by examination:** AP, CLEP, institutional tests. 24 credit hours maximum toward associate degree. **Support services:** Learning center, pre-admission summer program, reduced course load, remedial instruction, study skills assistance, tutoring.

Majors. Health services: Nursing (RN).

Computing on campus. PC or laptop required. 40 workstations in library, computer center. Commuter students can connect to campus network. Online course registration, wireless network available.

Student life. Freshman orientation: Mandatory. Preregistration for classes offered. 2 full days the week before classes start. **Activities:** Choral groups, student government, student newspaper, National Student Nurses Association Chapter.

Student services. Alcohol/substance abuse counseling, career counseling, financial aid counseling, health services, personal counseling. **Physically disabled:** Services for visually, speech, hearing impaired. **Transfer:** Pre-admission transcript evaluation for new students. Transfer adviser, college fairs on campus for students transferring to 4-year colleges.

Contact. E-mail: mgallo@chpnet.org
Phone: (212) 614-6114 Fax: (212) 614-6109
Bernice Pass-Stern, Assistant Dean, Phillips Beth Israel School of Nursing, 776 Sixth Avenue, Fourth Floor, New York, NY 10001

Plaza College
Jackson Heights, New York
www.plazacollege.edu   **CB code: 0545**

- For-profit 2-year business and junior college
- Commuter campus in very large city
- Application essay, interview required

General. Founded in 1916. Regionally accredited. **Enrollment:** 704 full-time, degree-seeking students. **Degrees:** 47 bachelor's, 168 associate awarded. **Calendar:** Semester, extensive summer session. **Full-time faculty:** 14 total. **Part-time faculty:** 45 total.

Basis for selection. Essay, interview, and test scores most important. Student must pass entrance examination. COMPASS and college-administered writing test required of all students.

2011-2012 Annual costs. Tuition/fees: $11,350. 3 semesters required in academic year; costs quoted for 2 of 3 semesters. Books/supplies: $1,100. Personal expenses: $5,102.

Financial aid. Need-based: Work-study available nights, weekends and for part-time students.

Application procedures. Admission: No deadline. $100 fee, may be waived for applicants with need, free for online applicants. Admission notification on a rolling basis. **Financial aid:** No deadline. FAFSA, institutional form required. Applicants notified on a rolling basis.

Academics. Special study options: Accelerated study, internships. Bachelor's degree programs available on campus. **Credit/placement by examination:** AP, CLEP, institutional tests. 30 credit hours maximum toward associate degree. **Support services:** Learning center, reduced course load, remedial instruction, study skills assistance, tutoring, writing center.

Majors. Business: Accounting, business admin. **Computer sciences:** Information systems. **Health services:** Medical assistant.

Most popular majors. Business/marketing 71%, health sciences 29%.

Computing on campus. 200 workstations in library, computer center, student center. Commuter students can connect to campus network. Online library, wireless network available.

Student life. Freshman orientation: Mandatory. Preregistration for classes offered. **Activities:** Literary magazine.

Student services. Career counseling, financial aid counseling, personal counseling, placement for graduates. **Physically disabled:** Services for visually, speech, hearing impaired. **Transfer:** Transfer adviser for students transferring to 4-year colleges.

Contact. E-mail: plazainfo@plazacollege.edu
Phone: (718) 779-1430 Fax: (718) 779-7423
Vanessa Lopez, Director of Admission, Plaza College, 74-09 37th Avenue, Jackson Heights, NY 11372

Professional Business College
New York, New York
www.pbcny.edu

- Private 2-year business college
- Commuter campus in very large city

General. Regionally accredited; also accredited by ACICS. **Enrollment:** 847 degree-seeking undergraduates. **Degrees:** 185 associate awarded. **Calendar:** Semester, extensive summer session. **Full-time faculty:** 32 total. **Part-time faculty:** 38 total.

Basis for selection. Applicants required to have high school diploma or its equivalent. Limited number of students who are not high school graduates, but who qualify for admission under "ability to benefit" (atb) guidelines. Ability-to-benefit students required to achieve a satisfactory score on the Career Programs Assessment test (CPAt).

2011-2012 Annual costs. Tuition/fees: $9,805. Cost reported is for associate degree program. Books/supplies: $1,782. Personal expenses: $5,471.

Financial aid. Need-based: Work-study available nights, weekends and for part-time students.

Application procedures. Admission: No deadline. No application fee. Application deadline is anytime within the first 5 days of any new semester.

Academics. Credit/placement by examination: AP, CLEP. **Support services:** Learning center, remedial instruction, study skills assistance, tutoring, writing center.

Majors. Business: Accounting, business admin, office technology.

Computing on campus. 175 workstations in library, computer center.

Student life. Freshman orientation: Mandatory. Preregistration for classes offered.

Student services. Adult student services, career counseling, services for economically disadvantaged, student employment services, financial aid counseling, minority student services, personal counseling, placement for graduates.

Contact. E-mail: dwang@pbcny.edu
David Wang, Admissions Director, Professional Business College, 408 Broadway, New York, NY 10013

Rockland Community College
Suffern, New York **CB member**
www.sunyrockland.edu **CB code: 2767**

- Public 2-year community college
- Commuter campus in large town

General. Founded in 1959. Regionally accredited. SUNY institution. Extension sites/centers located throughout Rockland County. **Enrollment:** 6,847 degree-seeking undergraduates; 1,139 non-degree-seeking students. **Degrees:** 1,035 associate awarded. **Location:** 35 miles from New York City. **Calendar:** Semester, extensive summer session. **Full-time faculty:** 115 total; 16% minority, 62% women. **Part-time faculty:** 587 total; 14% minority, 43% women. **Class size:** 50% < 20, 50% 20-39, less than 1% 40-49.

Student profile. Among degree-seeking undergraduates, 1,581 enrolled as first-time, first-year students, 667 transferred in from other institutions.

Part-time:	31%	**Asian American:**	5%
Out-of-state:	2%	**Hispanic American:**	19%
Women:	53%	**International:**	2%
African American:	20%	**25 or older:**	35%

Transfer out. Colleges most students transferred to 2011: SUNY New Paltz, Ramapo College, Dominican College.

Basis for selection. Open admission. Students required to take assessment examination before enrolling full-time. **Adult students:** SAT/ACT scores not required. **Home schooled:** Mathematics and English placement exams. **Learning Disabled:** Students with disabilities encouraged to self-report to our Disabilities Services Office, which arranges for appropriate accommodations with faculty.

High school preparation. College-preparatory program required. 18 units recommended. Recommended units include English 4, mathematics 2, social studies 4, history 4, science 2, foreign language 1 and academic electives 4.

2011-2012 Annual costs. Tuition/fees: $4,108; $7,923 out-of-state. Per-credit charge: $158 in-state; $316 out-of-state. Books/supplies: $1,200. Personal expenses: $600.

2011-2012 Financial aid. Need-based: Average need met was 64%. Average scholarship/grant was $3,081; average loan $3,547. Need-based aid available for part-time students. Work-study available nights, weekends and for part-time students.

Application procedures. Admission: Priority date 8/1; no deadline. $30 fee, may be waived for applicants with need. Admission notification on a rolling basis. **Financial aid:** Priority date 5/31; no closing date. FAFSA, institutional form required. Applicants notified on a rolling basis starting 6/1; must reply within 3 week(s) of notification.

Academics. Special study options: Cooperative education, distance learning, double major, dual enrollment of high school students, ESL, exchange student, external degree, honors, independent study, internships, liberal arts/career combination, study abroad, weekend college. License preparation in nursing. **Credit/placement by examination:** AP, CLEP, IB. 45 credit hours maximum toward associate degree. **Support services:** Learning center, remedial instruction, study skills assistance, tutoring, writing center.

Honors college/program. Mentor/Talented honors program. Business honors degree requires minimum combined SAT score of 1100 (exclusive of Writing) and at least 90 average; interviews, auditions and portfolios recommended.

Majors. Business: General, accounting, accounting technology, administrative services, business admin, hospitality admin, tourism/travel. **Communications:** Communications/speech/rhetoric. **Computer sciences:** Computer graphics, data processing, programming. **Conservation:** Environmental science. **Education:** Elementary, physical. **Health services:** EMT paramedic, medical assistant, medical records technology, nursing (RN), occupational therapy assistant, respiratory therapy technology. **Liberal arts:** Arts/sciences. **Protective services:** Criminal justice, fire safety technology. **Social sciences:** General. **Visual/performing arts:** Commercial photography, commercial/advertising art, dramatic, music, photography, studio arts. **Work/family studies:** Food/nutrition, institutional food production.

Most popular majors. Business/marketing 10%, health sciences 14%, liberal arts 55%.

Computing on campus. 177 workstations in library, computer center. Commuter students can connect to campus network. Online library, wireless network available.

Student life. Freshman orientation: Available. Preregistration for classes offered. **Activities:** Bands, campus ministries, choral groups, dance, drama, international student organizations, literary magazine, music ensembles, radio station, student government, student newspaper, TV station, special interest clubs.

Athletics. NJCAA. **Intercollegiate:** Baseball M, basketball, bowling, golf M, soccer, softball W, table tennis, tennis, volleyball W. **Intramural:** Basketball, bowling, racquetball, soccer, softball, table tennis, track and field, volleyball. **Team name:** Hawks.

Student services. Adult student services, alcohol/substance abuse counseling, chaplain/spiritual director, career counseling, services for economically disadvantaged, student employment services, financial aid counseling, health services, minority student services, on-campus daycare, personal counseling, placement for graduates, veterans' counselor. **Physically disabled:** Services for visually, speech, hearing impaired. **Transfer:** Pre-admission transcript evaluation for new students. Transfer adviser, college fairs on campus for students transferring to 4-year colleges.

Contact. E-mail: info@sunyrockland.edu
Phone: (845) 574-4462 Toll-free number: (800) 722-7666
Fax: (845) 574-4433
Dana Stilley, Dean of Enrollment Management, Rockland Community College, 145 College Road, Suffern, NY 10901-3699

Sanford-Brown Institute: Melville
Melville, New York
www.sbmelville.com
CB code: 1039

- For-profit 2-year junior college
- Small town

General. Founded in 1911. Accredited by ACICS. **Location:** 40 miles from New York City. **Calendar:** Quarter.

Annual costs/financial aid. Books/supplies: $700.

Contact. Phone: (631) 370-3300
Director of Admissions, 320 South Service Road, Melville, NY 11747

Schenectady County Community College
Schenectady, New York
www.sunysccc.edu
CB code: 2879

- Public 2-year community college
- Commuter campus in small city

General. Founded in 1968. Regionally accredited. SUNY institution. **Enrollment:** 3,816 degree-seeking undergraduates. **Degrees:** 482 associate awarded. **ROTC:** Air Force. **Location:** 150 miles from New York City, 20 miles from Albany. **Calendar:** Semester, limited summer session. **Full-time faculty:** 66 total. **Part-time faculty:** 177 total.

Transfer out. Colleges most students transferred to 2011: SUNY Albany, College of Saint Rose, Siena College, Sage College of Albany.

Basis for selection. Open admission, but selective for some programs. Special requirements for music program. Interview recommended for all; audition required for music, music merchandising programs. **Home schooled:** Letter from school district superintendent where they reside attesting to home school equivalency of public system.

High school preparation. Certain programs have specific mathematics and science prerequisites.

2011-2012 Annual costs. Tuition/fees: $3,681; $7,065 out-of-state. Books/supplies: $800. Personal expenses: $900.

Financial aid. All financial aid based on need. Need-based aid available for part-time students. Work-study available nights, weekends and for part-time students.

Application procedures. Admission: No deadline. No application fee. Admission notification on a rolling basis. **Financial aid:** Priority date 5/1; no closing date. FAFSA required. Applicants notified on a rolling basis starting 4/15; must reply by 8/31.

Academics. 25-32 credit hours required in major depending on program. 60-66 credit hours required for graduation depending on program. **Special study options:** Cooperative education, cross-registration, distance learning, dual enrollment of high school students, ESL, honors, independent study, internships, liberal arts/career combination, teacher certification program. License preparation in aviation. **Credit/placement by examination:** AP, CLEP, institutional tests. 30 credit hours maximum toward associate degree. **Support services:** GED preparation and test center, learning center, reduced course load, remedial instruction, tutoring.

Majors. Business: General, tourism promotion, travel services. **Computer sciences:** General, computer science, programming. **Education:** Early childhood, multi-level teacher. **Liberal arts:** Arts/sciences. **Physical sciences:** General. **Protective services:** Criminal justice, security services. **Social sciences:** General. **Visual/performing arts:** Music.

Computing on campus. 400 workstations in library, computer center, student center.

Student life. Freshman orientation: Available. Preregistration for classes offered. **Activities:** Bands, choral groups, drama, literary magazine, music ensembles, student government, Black and Latino student alliance, Christian Fellowship, human services club, disabled student awareness committee, culinary club.

Athletics. NJCAA. **Intercollegiate:** Baseball M, basketball, bowling, softball W. **Team name:** The Royals.

Student services. Adult student services, alcohol/substance abuse counseling, career counseling, services for economically disadvantaged, student employment services, financial aid counseling, minority student services, on-campus daycare, personal counseling, placement for graduates, veterans' counselor. **Physically disabled:** Services for visually, speech, hearing impaired. **Transfer:** Transfer adviser, college fairs on campus for students transferring to 4-year colleges.

Contact. E-mail: sampsondg@gw.sunysccc.edu
Phone: (518) 381-1366 Fax: (518) 346-0379
David Sampson, Director of Admissions, Schenectady County Community College, 78 Washington Avenue, Schenectady, NY 12305

St. Elizabeth College of Nursing
Utica, New York
www.secon.edu
CB code: 2847

- Private 2-year nursing college affiliated with Roman Catholic Church
- Commuter campus in small city
- SAT or ACT (ACT writing optional) required

General. Regionally accredited. **Enrollment:** 218 degree-seeking undergraduates. **Degrees:** 78 associate awarded. **Location:** 40 miles from Albany, 50 miles from Syracuse. **Calendar:** Semester. **Full-time faculty:** 17 total; 94% women. **Part-time faculty:** 2 total; 100% women.

Student profile. Among degree-seeking undergraduates, 17% already have a bachelor's degree or higher, 17 enrolled as first-time, first-year students, 97 transferred in from other institutions.

Part-time:	33%	Hispanic American:	1%
Out-of-state:	20%	Native American:	1%
Women:	88%	International:	2%
African American:	1%	25 or older:	46%
Asian American:	2%		

Basis for selection. Rigor of high school record, test scores most important. SAT Subject Tests recommended. **Adult students:** SAT/ACT scores not required. **Home schooled:** Transcript of courses and grades, state high school equivalency certificate required. Strong math and science background required, including coursework in chemistry, biology and equivalent of Math Level 1 and 2. **Learning Disabled:** Self-reporting highly recommended. We have a learning disabilities coordinator on campus.

High school preparation. Required and recommended units include English 4, mathematics 2-3, social studies 4, history 4, science 2 (laboratory 2) and foreign language 1.

2011-2012 Annual costs. Tuition/fees: $13,750. Per-credit charge: $375. Books/supplies: $1,700. Personal expenses: $1,300.

2011-2012 Financial aid. Need-based: 29% of total undergraduate aid awarded as scholarships/grants, 71% as loans/jobs. Need-based aid available for part-time students. Work-study available nights, weekends and for part-time students.

Application procedures. Admission: Priority date 5/30; no deadline. $65 fee, may be waived for applicants with need. Admission notification on a rolling basis. Must reply by May 1 or within 2 week(s) if notified thereafter. Admission application fee $25 if submitted before 2/1. **Financial aid:** No deadline. FAFSA required. Applicants notified on a rolling basis starting 1/1; must reply within 2 week(s) of notification.

Academics. One 6-week summer session at end of first year. **Special study options:** Distance learning, liberal arts/career combination, weekend college. Articulation agreements with upper division BSN colleges. License preparation in nursing. **Credit/placement by examination:** AP, CLEP. **Support services:** Remedial instruction, study skills assistance, tutoring.

Majors. Health services: Nursing (RN).

Computing on campus. 20 workstations in library, computer center. Commuter students can connect to campus network. Online library, repair service available.

Student life. Freshman orientation: Mandatory. Preregistration for classes offered. Held week prior to classes. **Housing:** Option of staying on campus at affiliated college available. **Activities:** Student government, National League of Nursing.

Student services. Alcohol/substance abuse counseling, chaplain/spiritual director, financial aid counseling, health services, on-campus daycare. **Transfer:** Pre-admission transcript evaluation for new students. Transfer adviser for students transferring to 4-year colleges.

Contact. E-mail: conadmis@stemc.org
Phone: (315) 798-8347 Fax: (315) 235-7431
Donna Ernst, Recruitment Director, St. Elizabeth College of Nursing, 2215 Genesee Street, Utica, NY 13501

St. Joseph's College of Nursing
Syracuse, New York
www.sjhsyr.org/nursing
CB code: 2825

- Private 2-year nursing college affiliated with Roman Catholic Church
- Commuter campus in small city
- SAT or ACT (ACT writing optional), application essay, interview required

General. Founded in 1898. Practice in a variety of settings including medical/surgical, maternity, pediatrics, oncology, psychiatry, ambulatory care clinics, and home care and outpatient experiences. **Enrollment:** 299 degree-seeking undergraduates. **Degrees:** 108 associate awarded. **Calendar:** Semester, limited summer session. **Full-time faculty:** 26 total; 92% women. **Part-time faculty:** 8 total; 12% have terminal degrees, 100% women. **Class size:** 57% 20-39, 29% 40-49, 14% 50-99. **Special facilities:** Cardiovascular lab, electro-physiology lab, home care, outpatient services, 462-bed teaching hospital.

Transfer out. Colleges most students transferred to 2011: SUNY New York Upstate Medical University, SUNY College of Technology at Utica-Rome, Le Moyne College.

Basis for selection. High school record, SAT/ACT test scores or pre-entrance examination, and personal interview very important. **Adult students:** SAT/ACT scores not required. **Home schooled:** Transcript of courses and grades, state high school equivalency certificate, letter of recommendation (nonparent) required.

High school preparation. College-preparatory program recommended. 13 units required. Required and recommended units include English 4, mathematics 2-3, social studies 4 and science 2-3. Science units must be in biology and chemistry; advanced biology and/or physics recommended.

2011-2012 Annual costs. Tuition/fees: $14,000. Per-credit charge: $465. Room only: $4,200. Books/supplies: $1,000. Personal expenses: $4,656.

Financial aid. All financial aid based on need. Need-based aid available for part-time students. Work-study available nights, weekends and for part-time students.

Application procedures. Admission: No deadline. $50 fee. Application must be submitted on paper. Admission notification on a rolling basis. **Financial aid:** Priority date 3/1; no closing date. FAFSA required. Applicants notified on a rolling basis starting 6/15.

Academics. Weekend program meets every other Friday, Saturday and Sunday year-round for 2 years. **Special study options:** Liberal arts/career combination, weekend college. License preparation in nursing. **Credit/placement by examination:** AP, CLEP. **Support services:** Reduced course load, study skills assistance, tutoring.

Majors. Health services: Nursing (RN).

Computing on campus. 31 workstations in dormitories, library, computer center. Dormitories wired for high-speed internet access and linked to campus network. Commuter students can connect to campus network. Online library, helpline, wireless network available.

Student life. Freshman orientation: Mandatory. Preregistration for classes offered. 3 days one week prior to start of classes. **Housing:** Guaranteed on-campus for all undergraduates. Coed dorms, wellness housing available. $200 fully refundable deposit. **Activities:** Student government.

Student services. Adult student services, alcohol/substance abuse counseling, chaplain/spiritual director, career counseling, student employment services, financial aid counseling, health services, personal counseling, placement for graduates, veterans' counselor. **Physically disabled:** Services for visually, speech, hearing impaired. **Transfer:** Pre-admission transcript evaluation for new students. Transfer adviser, college fairs on campus for students transferring to 4-year colleges.

Contact. E-mail: rhonda.reader@sjhsyr.org
Phone: (315) 448-5040 Fax: (315) 448-5745
Rhonda Reader, Assistant Dean of Admissions, St. Joseph's College of Nursing, 206 Prospect Avenue, Syracuse, NY 13203

Suffolk County Community College
Selden, New York
www.sunysuffolk.edu
CB member
CB code: 2827

- Public 2-year community college
- Commuter campus in large town

General. Founded in 1959. Regionally accredited. 3 campuses in Suffolk County: Brentwood, Selden, Riverhead. Downtown center in Sayville dedicated to nursing, downtown center in Riverhead dedicated to culinary arts. **Enrollment:** 23,332 degree-seeking undergraduates. **Degrees:** 3,159 associate awarded. **Location:** 60 miles from New York City. **Calendar:** Semester, extensive summer session. **Full-time faculty:** 326 total. **Part-time faculty:** 1,186 total. **Special facilities:** Planetarium.

Student profile.

Out-of-state:	2%	25 or older:	51%

Transfer out. Colleges most students transferred to 2011: SUNY Stony Brook, Hofstra University, St. Joseph's College, Dowling College, Adelphi University.

Basis for selection. Open admission, but selective for some programs. Admission tests may be used for admission or placement in certain programs in conjunction with high school record. Portfolio required for visual arts program; interview recommended for broadcast telecommunications, fine arts, health career, and paralegal assistant programs. Audition recommended for performing arts programs. **Home schooled:** State high school equivalency certificate required. Appropriate scores on the CPT test to indicate Ability To Benefit.

High school preparation. Special course requirements vary by program.

2011-2012 Annual costs. Tuition/fees: $4,458; $8,448 out-of-state. Per-credit charge: $167 in-state; $334 out-of-state. Books/supplies: $900. Personal expenses: $1,048.

Financial aid. Need-based: Need-based aid available for part-time students. Work-study available nights, weekends and for part-time students. **Non-need-based:** Scholarships awarded for academics, art, leadership, minority status, music/drama, state residency.

Application procedures. Admission: No deadline. $40 fee, may be waived for applicants with need. Admission notification on a rolling basis. **Financial aid:** Priority date 4/15, closing date 6/1. FAFSA required. Applicants notified on a rolling basis starting 4/15; must reply within 2 week(s) of notification.

Academics. Special study options: Cooperative education, distance learning, dual enrollment of high school students, ESL, honors, independent study, internships, study abroad, weekend college. Joint admission with other SUNY schools and private institutions. License preparation in nursing. **Credit/placement by examination:** AP, CLEP, IB, institutional tests. 30 credit hours

maximum toward associate degree. **Support services:** GED preparation and test center, learning center, pre-admission summer program, reduced course load, remedial instruction, study skills assistance, tutoring, writing center.

Majors. Architecture: Environmental design, interior. **Area/ethnic studies:** Women's. **Biology:** General. **Business:** General, accounting, business admin, finance, human resources, management science, marketing, office management, office technology, sales/distribution. **Communications:** Broadcast journalism, communications/speech/rhetoric. **Communications technology:** General. **Computer sciences:** General, computer graphics, computer science, information systems, information technology, webmaster. **Conservation:** Environmental science, environmental studies. **Education:** Early childhood, secondary. **Engineering:** Electrical, engineering science. **Foreign languages:** Sign language interpretation. **Health services:** Athletic training, clinical lab science, dietetic technician, EMT paramedic, medical records technology, nursing (RN), occupational therapy assistant, physical therapy assistant, substance abuse counseling, veterinary technology/assistant. **History:** General. **Liberal arts:** Arts/sciences. **Math:** General. **Physical sciences:** Astronomy, chemistry, geology, meteorology, physics, planetary. **Protective services:** Firefighting. **Psychology:** General. **Social sciences:** General, economics, political science. **Visual/performing arts:** Commercial/advertising art, dramatic, interior design, music, studio arts, theater design. **Work/family studies:** Food/nutrition.

Computing on campus. 1,785 workstations in library, computer center, student center. Commuter students can connect to campus network. Online course registration, online library, helpline, wireless network available.

Student life. Freshman orientation: Available. Preregistration for classes offered. **Activities:** Bands, choral groups, drama, international student organizations, literary magazine, music ensembles, musical theater, radio station, student government, student newspaper, over 60 clubs available.

Athletics. NJCAA. **Intercollegiate:** Baseball M, basketball, bowling M, cross-country, golf M, lacrosse M, soccer M, softball, tennis, track and field, triathlon W. **Intramural:** Basketball, bowling, softball.

Student services. Adult student services, career counseling, services for economically disadvantaged, student employment services, financial aid counseling, health services, minority student services, on-campus daycare, personal counseling, placement for graduates, veterans' counselor. **Physically disabled:** Services for visually, speech, hearing impaired. **Transfer:** Pre-admission transcript evaluation for new students. Transfer adviser, college fairs on campus for students transferring to 4-year colleges.

Contact. E-mail: admissions@sunysuffolk.edu
Phone: (631) 451-4000 Fax: (631) 451-4415
Kate Rowe, College Dean of Enrollment Management, Suffolk County Community College, 533 College Road, Selden, NY 11784

Sullivan County Community College
Loch Sheldrake, New York
www.sullivan.suny.edu | CB code: 2855

- Public 2-year community college
- Commuter campus in small town

General. Founded in 1962. Regionally accredited. **Enrollment:** 1,373 degree-seeking undergraduates; 331 non-degree-seeking students. **Degrees:** 230 associate awarded. **Location:** 100 miles from New York City, 90 miles from Binghamton. **Calendar:** 4-1-4, limited summer session. **Full-time faculty:** 50 total. **Part-time faculty:** 62 total. **Class size:** 100% < 20. **Special facilities:** Complete kitchens, dining room for hospitality programs, mini-travel agency for travel and tourism program, color and black and white darkrooms, computer graphics labs, TV studio for communications and media arts program.

Student profile. Among degree-seeking undergraduates, 49% enrolled in a transfer program, 51% enrolled in a vocational program, 448 enrolled as first-time, first-year students, 84 transferred in from other institutions.

Part-time:	19%	Asian American:	2%
Out-of-state:	2%	Hispanic American:	14%
Women:	59%	Native American:	1%
African American:	23%	25 or older:	30%

Basis for selection. Open admission, but selective for some programs. Special requirements for nursing program and university parallel business administration program. Out-of-county applicants must have 68 or better high school grade point average. SAT or ACT recommended for placement and counseling. Interview recommended.

High school preparation. Liberal arts applicants entering science programs should have 3 each in math and science. Computer science applicants,

---

3 math and 1 chemistry or physics. Nursing applicants, 1 laboratory biology. Engineering science, 3.5 math and 1 chemistry or physics.

2011-2012 Annual costs. Tuition/fees: $4,742; $6,832 out-of-state. Per-credit charge: $163 in-state; $244 out-of-state. Books/supplies: $1,400. Personal expenses: $1,020.

2011-2012 Financial aid. Need-based: 71% of total undergraduate aid awarded as scholarships/grants, 29% as loans/jobs. Need-based aid available for part-time students. Work-study available nights, weekends and for part-time students. **Additional information:** 60% of students hold part-time jobs locally.

Application procedures. Admission: No deadline. No application fee. Admission notification on a rolling basis. Recommended priority application date for nursing department is December 1. **Financial aid:** Priority date 4/15; no closing date. FAFSA required. Applicants notified on a rolling basis starting 5/15; must reply within 2 week(s) of notification.

Academics. Practical experience in class laboratory situations emphasized in technical programs. **Special study options:** Dual enrollment of high school students, exchange student, honors, independent study, internships. **Credit/placement by examination:** AP, CLEP, institutional tests. 31 credit hours maximum toward associate degree. **Support services:** Learning center, reduced course load, remedial instruction, tutoring, writing center.

Majors. Business: General, accounting, business admin, insurance, management information systems, office management, office technology, sales/distribution. **Communications:** Broadcast journalism, communications/speech/rhetoric. **Computer sciences:** General, data processing. **Conservation:** General, forestry. **Education:** Early childhood, elementary. **Engineering:** General, engineering science. **Health services:** Nursing (RN), predental, premedicine, prepharmacy, preveterinary, substance abuse counseling. **History:** General. **Liberal arts:** Arts/sciences. **Math:** General. **Parks/recreation:** Facilities management. **Philosophy/religion:** Philosophy. **Protective services:** Criminal justice, police science. **Psychology:** General. **Social sciences:** General, sociology. **Visual/performing arts:** Commercial photography, commercial/advertising art. **Work/family studies:** Child care management, institutional food production.

Most popular majors. Business/marketing 8%, health sciences 25%, liberal arts 32%.

Computing on campus. 80 workstations in library, computer center. Online course registration, wireless network available.

Student life. Freshman orientation: Mandatory, $30 fee. Preregistration for classes offered. **Policies:** 45 percent of students are county residents. **Housing:** College-approved housing adjacent to campus. **Activities:** Drama, radio station, student government, student newspaper, black student union, Latin student union.

Athletics. NJCAA. **Intercollegiate:** Basketball, golf, softball W, track and field, volleyball W. **Intramural:** Archery, badminton, basketball, bowling, equestrian, golf, handball, racquetball, skiing, soccer, softball, swimming, table tennis, tennis, volleyball. **Team name:** Generals.

Student services. Adult student services, career counseling, student employment services, financial aid counseling, health services, personal counseling, placement for graduates, veterans' counselor. **Transfer:** Transfer adviser, college fairs on campus for students transferring to 4-year colleges.

Contact. E-mail: admissions@sullivan.suny.edu
Phone: (845) 434-5750 ext. 4287 Toll-free number: (800) 577-5243
Fax: (845) 434-0923
Sari Rosenheck, Director of Admissions and Registration Services, Sullivan County Community College, 112 College Road, Loch Sheldrake, NY 12759-5151

SUNY College of Agriculture and Technology at Cobleskill
Cobleskill, New York
www.cobleskill.edu | CB code: 2524

- Public 2-year agricultural and technical college
- Residential campus in small town

General. Founded in 1911. Regionally accredited. **Enrollment:** 2,566 degree-seeking undergraduates. **Degrees:** 208 bachelor's, 296 associate awarded. **Location:** 35 miles from Albany, 29 miles from Oneonta. **Calendar:** Semester, limited summer session. **Full-time faculty:** 100 total. **Part-time faculty:** 75 total. **Class size:** 35% < 20, 51% 20-39, 7% 40-49, 7% 50-99, less than 1% >100. **Special facilities:** Arboretum, 14 greenhouses, livestock pavilion, 350-acre farm, modern chemical and biological technology

laboratories, student-operated restaurant, fish hatchery, ski area, equestrian center, child care and development center. **Partnerships:** Formal partnership with John Deere Company for agricultural engineering.

Student profile.

Out-of-state:	7%	**Live on campus:**	59%
25 or older:	9%		

Transfer out. Colleges most students transferred to 2011: Cornell University, College of St. Rose, SUNY Albany, SUNY Oneonta, SUNY Plattsburgh.

Basis for selection. Strength of high school curriculum most important. GPA, SAT/ACT scores considered. Letters of recommendation, interview recommended. SAT scores required for all applicants to the degree-seeking bachelor's program. SAT or ACT recommended. SAT or ACT optional for associate degree students, depending on degree. SAT required for bachelor degree seeking students. **Home schooled:** Transcript of courses and grades, letter of recommendation (nonparent) required. Letter of certification from local high school required.

High school preparation. College-preparatory program recommended. 10 units required; 16 recommended. Required and recommended units include English 3-4, mathematics 2-3, social studies 1, history 1, science 2-3 (laboratory 2-3) and foreign language 1. Additional recommendations for some programs.

2011-2012 Annual costs. Tuition/fees: $6,751; $11,221 out-of-state. Per-credit charge: $220 in-state; $406 out-of-state. Out-of-state tuition for bachelor's program: $14,320; per-credit-hour $597. Room/board: $10,466. Books/supplies: $1,000. Personal expenses: $1,092.

Financial aid. Need-based: Need-based aid available for part-time students. Work-study available nights, weekends and for part-time students. **Non-need-based:** Scholarships awarded for academics, alumni affiliation, leadership, state residency. **Additional information:** Application deadline for scholarships March 15. Separate application required, available through admissions office.

Application procedures. Admission: No deadline. $40 fee, may be waived for applicants with need. Admission notification on a rolling basis beginning on or about 11/1. Must reply by May 1 or within 2 week(s) if notified thereafter. **Financial aid:** Closing date 2/15. FAFSA, institutional form required. Applicants notified on a rolling basis starting 3/20; must reply within 2 week(s) of notification.

Academics. Special study options: Cross-registration, distance learning, ESL, exchange student, honors, internships, study abroad, weekend college. **Credit/placement by examination:** AP, CLEP, institutional tests. 33 credit hours maximum toward associate degree, 60 toward bachelor's. **Support services:** Learning center, pre-admission summer program, reduced course load, remedial instruction, study skills assistance, tutoring, writing center.

Majors. Business: Accounting technology, business admin, hotel/motel admin, travel services. **Communications:** Communications/speech/rhetoric. **Computer sciences:** General, information systems. **Conservation:** General, fisheries. **General:** Agribusiness operations, agronomy, animal sciences, mechanization, ornamental horticulture, poultry. **Health services:** EMT paramedic. **Human services:** Social work. **Liberal arts:** Arts/sciences, humanities. **Visual/performing arts:** Commercial/advertising art. **Work/family studies:** Child care management, institutional food production.

Most popular majors. Agriculture 29%, business/marketing 15%, family/consumer sciences 9%, health sciences 7%, liberal arts 17%, personal/culinary services 7%.

Computing on campus. 270 workstations in dormitories, library, computer center, student center. Dormitories wired for high-speed internet access and linked to campus network. Commuter students can connect to campus network. Online course registration, online library, helpline, repair service, student web hosting, wireless network available.

Student life. Freshman orientation: Mandatory. Preregistration for classes offered. 2-day academic and social program held first week of classes. **Housing:** Guaranteed on-campus for freshmen. Coed dorms, single-sex dorms, special housing for disabled, wellness housing available. $55 fully refundable deposit. Designated quiet study, sophomore experience, upperclass experience. **Activities:** Jazz band, campus ministries, choral groups, drama, international student organizations, literary magazine, music ensembles, student government, student newspaper, TV station, Phi Theta Kappa, activities team, community club, Student Christian Fellowship, student medical response team, X-Pressions of Kolor, Black and Latino alliance.

Athletics. NCAA. **Intercollegiate:** Basketball, cross-country, diving, golf, lacrosse M, soccer, softball W, swimming, track and field, volleyball W. **Intramural:** Bowling, football (non-tackle), soccer, softball. **Team name:** Tigers.

Student services. Adult student services, alcohol/substance abuse counseling, chaplain/spiritual director, career counseling, student employment services, financial aid counseling, health services, on-campus daycare, personal counseling, placement for graduates, veterans' counselor. **Physically disabled:** Services for visually, speech, hearing impaired. **Transfer:** Pre-admission transcript evaluation for new students. Transfer adviser, college fairs on campus for students transferring to 4-year colleges.

Contact. E-mail: admissions@cobleskill.edu
Phone: (518) 255-5525 Toll-free number: (800) 295-8988
Fax: (518) 255-6769
Christopher Tacea, Director of Admissions and Marketing, SUNY College of Agriculture and Technology at Cobleskill, Knapp Hall, Cobleskill, NY 12043

SUNY College of Agriculture and Technology at Morrisville
Morrisville, New York
www.morrisville.edu   CB code: 2527

- Public 2-year agricultural and technical college
- Residential campus in small town

General. Founded in 1908. Regionally accredited. **Enrollment:** 3,090 degree-seeking undergraduates. **Degrees:** 148 bachelor's, 512 associate awarded. **ROTC:** Army. **Location:** 30 miles from Syracuse and Utica. **Calendar:** Semester, limited summer session. **Full-time faculty:** 139 total. **Part-time faculty:** 85 total. **Class size:** 45% < 20, 48% 20-39, 2% 40-49, 4% 50-99, less than 1% >100. **Special facilities:** Arboretum, archery range, Helyar Pond, 2 ice arenas, Nelson Farms country store (owned by college and operated by SUNY Morrisville students), observatory, walking trail, wildlife museum, dairy facilities, equestrian center, architecture center.

Student profile.

Out-of-state:	7%	**Live on campus:**	62%
25 or older:	21%		

Transfer out. Colleges most students transferred to 2011: Cornell University, Rochester Institute of Technology, Clarkson, State University of New York.

Basis for selection. High school record most important. SAT required for bachelor's degree applicants, SAT or ACT required for students seeking academic scholarship. Essays or interviews not required, but students welcome to submit essay or visit for interview. **Home schooled:** State high school equivalency certificate required. GED required for students without supporting documentation.

High school preparation. Recommended units include English 4, mathematics 3, social studies 4 and science 3. Requirements depend on program. Math and science preparation important for technical majors.

2011-2012 Annual costs. Tuition/fees: $6,472; $10,942 out-of-state. Per-credit charge: $220 in-state; $406 out-of-state. Out-of-state tuition for bachelor's program: $14,320; per credit hour $597. Room/board: $9,980. Books/supplies: $1,000. Personal expenses: $1,150.

Financial aid. Need-based: Need-based aid available for part-time students. Work-study available nights, weekends and for part-time students. **Non-need-based:** Scholarships awarded for academics.

Application procedures. Admission: No deadline. $50 fee, may be waived for applicants with need. Admission notification on a rolling basis beginning on or about 11/1. Housing deposit refundable only through June 1. **Financial aid:** Priority date 2/1; no closing date. FAFSA required. Applicants notified on a rolling basis.

Academics. Think-Pad university in partnership with IBM. Students wishing to enroll in Morrisville programs not offered at the Norwich Campus may take general education or elective courses that can be applied to Morrisville State College (main campus) associate or bachelor's degree programs. **Special study options:** Accelerated study, cooperative education, distance learning, double major, dual enrollment of high school students, ESL, exchange student, honors, internships, liberal arts/career combination, student-designed major, study abroad, weekend college. Joint program with SUNY Forest Technology School at Wanakena, 2-2 transfer program with SUNY College of Environmental Science and Forestry. Bachelor's degree programs available on campus. License preparation in nursing. **Credit/placement by examination:** AP, CLEP, institutional tests. 21 credit hours maximum toward associate degree. **Support services:** Learning center, pre-admission summer program, reduced course load, remedial instruction, study skills assistance, tutoring.

Majors. Architecture: Landscape, technology. **Biology:** General, conservation, marine. **Business:** General, accounting, accounting technology, accounting/business management, accounting/finance, administrative services, business admin, office management, office technology, restaurant/food services, tourism promotion, tourism/travel, travel services. **Communications:** Journalism. **Computer sciences:** General, applications programming, computer science, information technology, programming. **Conservation:** General, environmental science, environmental studies, fisheries, forest management, forest sciences, forest technology, forestry, management/policy, wood science. **Engineering:** General, architectural, computer, computer hardware, construction, electrical, engineering mechanics, engineering science, polymer, software. **English:** English lit, technical writing. **General:** Agribusiness operations, animal husbandry, animal sciences, aquaculture, business, business technology, dairy, dairy husbandry, equestrian studies, equine science, equipment technology, farm/ranch, floriculture, greenhouse operations, horticultural science, horticulture, landscaping, livestock, mechanization, nursery operations, ornamental horticulture, power machinery. **Health services:** Clinical lab technology, massage therapy, nursing (RN), prenursing. **Liberal arts:** Arts/sciences, humanities. **Math:** General. **Parks/recreation:** Exercise sciences, facilities management, health/fitness, sports admin. **Physical sciences:** Chemistry, physics. **Psychology:** General. **Social sciences:** General. **Work/family studies:** Food/nutrition.

Most popular majors. Agriculture 24%, business/marketing 13%, health sciences 14%, interdisciplinary studies 8%, liberal arts 15%, trade and industry 12%.

Computing on campus. 140 workstations in dormitories, library, computer center, student center. Dormitories linked to campus network. Commuter students can connect to campus network. Online library, helpline, repair service, wireless network available.

Student life. Freshman orientation: Mandatory, $85 fee. Preregistration for classes offered. **Housing:** Guaranteed on-campus for all undergraduates. Coed dorms, special housing for disabled, wellness housing available. $50 fully refundable deposit, deadline 5/1. Special interest housing available. **Activities:** Bands, choral groups, dance, drama, literary magazine, music ensembles, musical theater, radio station, student government, student newspaper, Newman Society, Latin American student organization, African student union/black alliance.

Athletics. NCAA. **Intercollegiate:** Basketball, diving, equestrian, field hockey W, football (tackle) M, ice hockey M, lacrosse, soccer, softball W, swimming W, volleyball W. **Intramural:** Archery, badminton, basketball, diving, equestrian, golf, handball, racquetball, rifle, soccer, swimming, table tennis, tennis, volleyball, wrestling M. **Team name:** Mustangs.

Student services. Adult student services, alcohol/substance abuse counseling, chaplain/spiritual director, career counseling, services for economically disadvantaged, student employment services, financial aid counseling, health services, minority student services, on-campus daycare, personal counseling, placement for graduates, veterans' counselor, women's services. **Physically disabled:** Services for visually, speech, hearing impaired. **Transfer:** Pre-admission transcript evaluation for new students. Transfer center, transfer adviser, college fairs on campus for students transferring to 4-year colleges.

Contact. E-mail: admissions@morrisville.edu
Phone: (315) 684-6046 Toll-free number: (800) 258-0111
Fax: (315) 684-6427
Thomas VerDow, Dean of Enrollment Management, SUNY College of Agriculture and Technology at Morrisville, PO Box 901, Morrisville, NY 13408-0901

SUNY College of Technology at Alfred
Alfred, New York
www.alfredstate.edu   CB code: 2522

 ▶ Public 2-year liberal arts and technical college
 ▶ Residential campus in rural community
 ▶ Application essay required

General. Founded in 1908. Regionally accredited. School of Applied Technology located in Wellsville. **Enrollment:** 3,531 degree-seeking undergraduates; 86 non-degree-seeking students. **Degrees:** 206 bachelor's, 747 associate awarded. **ROTC:** Army. **Location:** 75 miles from Rochester, 90 miles from Buffalo. **Calendar:** Semester, limited summer session. **Full-time faculty:** 181 total; 19% have terminal degrees, 6% minority, 30% women. **Part-time faculty:** 38 total; 29% have terminal degrees, 5% minority, 50% women. **Class size:** 44% < 20, 51% 20-39, 2% 40-49, 2% 50-99, less than 1% >100. **Special facilities:** 750-acre working farm, motorsports facility, center for organic and sustainable agriculture.

Student profile. Among degree-seeking undergraduates, 14% enrolled in a transfer program, 23% enrolled in a vocational program, 1% already have a bachelor's degree or higher, 1,083 enrolled as first-time, first-year students, 289 transferred in from other institutions.

Part-time:	7%	Asian American:	2%
Out-of-state:	6%	Hispanic American:	5%
Women:	37%	25 or older:	15%
African American:	9%	Live on campus:	74%

Transfer out. Colleges most students transferred to 2011: Alfred University, Clarkson University, SUNY Brockport, SUNY Fredonia, SUNY Oswego.

Basis for selection. School achievement record most important, test scores, class rank, school and community service considered. SAT or ACT recommended. SAT or ACT required for students applying for baccalaureate degree programs and consideration for some academic scholarships, recommended for associate degree programs. Interview, essay is required on supplemental application, and letters of reference recommended. **Adult students:** SAT/ACT scores not required if applicant has graduated high school and completed at least one semester of college. **Home schooled:** Applicant must provide one of the following: letter from superintendent of home school district; passing score on GED exam; 24 college credit hours in appropriate courses; college degree; or passed 5 Regents exams (NY).

High school preparation. Recommended units include English 4, mathematics 4, social studies 4 and science 4. Course requirements vary depending on program.

2012-2013 Annual costs. Tuition/fees (projected): $6,842; $11,986 out-of-state. Per-credit charge: $232 in-state; $447 out-of-state. Tuition for bachelor degree: full-time, out-of-state $15,180; per-credit-hour $633. Room/board: $10,450. Books/supplies: $1,200. Personal expenses: $800.

2010-2011 Financial aid. Need-based: 1,226 full-time freshmen applied for aid; 1,086 were judged to have need; 1,072 of these received aid. Average need met was 53%. Average scholarship/grant was $5,937; average loan $3,220. 39% of total undergraduate aid awarded as scholarships/grants, 61% as loans/jobs. Need-based aid available for part-time students. Work-study available nights, weekends and for part-time students. **Non-need-based:** Awarded to 794 full-time undergraduates, including 335 freshmen. Scholarships awarded for academics, alumni affiliation, job skills, minority status.

Application procedures. Admission: No deadline. $50 fee, may be waived for applicants with need. Admission notification on a rolling basis beginning on or about 11/1. Must reply by May 1 or within 4 week(s) if notified thereafter. Reply within 30 days of acceptance; full refund of deposit if requested in writing by May 1. Early application recommended for applied technology programs. **Financial aid:** No deadline. FAFSA required. Applicants notified on a rolling basis starting 3/15; must reply by 3/15 or within 4 week(s) of notification.

Academics. Special study options: Cooperative education, cross-registration, distance learning, ESL, honors, independent study, internships, liberal arts/career combination, student-designed major, study abroad. Bachelor's degree programs available on campus. License preparation in nursing. **Credit/placement by examination:** AP, CLEP, IB, SAT, ACT, institutional tests. **Support services:** Learning center, reduced course load, remedial instruction, study skills assistance, tutoring, writing center.

Majors. Architecture: Interior. **Biology:** General. **Business:** Accounting, accounting technology, banking/financial services, business admin, entrepreneurial studies, finance, marketing. **Communications:** Digital media. **Computer sciences:** General, computer science, data processing. **Conservation:** Environmental science, urban forestry. **Engineering:** General. **General:** Agribusiness operations, agronomy, animal sciences, dairy, sustainable agriculture. **Health services:** Medical records technology, nursing (RN), veterinary technology/assistant. **Human services:** Community org/advocacy. **Liberal arts:** Arts/sciences, humanities. **Parks/recreation:** Sports admin. **Visual/performing arts:** Digital arts, interior design.

Most popular majors. Agriculture 7%, business/marketing 8%, engineering/engineering technologies 33%, health sciences 10%, social sciences 6%, trade and industry 17%.

Computing on campus. 100 workstations in dormitories, library, student center. Dormitories wired for high-speed internet access and linked to campus network. Commuter students can connect to campus network. Online course registration, online library, helpline, repair service, student web hosting, wireless network available.

Student life. Freshman orientation: Mandatory, $100 fee. Preregistration for classes offered. Day-long summer program in mid-July, followed by pre-entry orientation/Welcome Week in August. Parallel January program for mid-year entrants. **Housing:** Guaranteed on-campus for all undergraduates. Coed dorms, special housing for disabled, apartments, fraternity/sorority housing, wellness housing available. $50 deposit. Extended stay, quiet study,

over 21 or over 24, single-room options available. **Activities:** Bands, campus ministries, choral groups, dance, drama, film society, international student organizations, literary magazine, music ensembles, musical theater, radio station, student government, student newspaper, symphony orchestra, sustainability club, international club, Black student union, Alfred State response team, cultural life committee, student senate, political alliance club, Bacchus peer education network.

Athletics. NJCAA. **Intercollegiate:** Baseball M, basketball, cross-country, diving, equestrian, football (tackle) M, lacrosse M, soccer, softball W, swimming, track and field, volleyball W, wrestling M. **Intramural:** Basketball, football (non-tackle), football (tackle) M, golf, handball, soccer, softball, tennis, volleyball. **Team name:** Pioneers.

Student services. Adult student services, alcohol/substance abuse counseling, chaplain/spiritual director, career counseling, services for economically disadvantaged, student employment services, financial aid counseling, health services, minority student services, personal counseling, placement for graduates, veterans' counselor, women's services. **Physically disabled:** Services for visually, hearing impaired. **Transfer:** Pre-admission transcript evaluation for new students. Transfer center, transfer adviser, college fairs on campus for students transferring to 4-year colleges.

Contact. E-mail: admissions@alfredstate.edu
Phone: (607) 587-4215 Toll-free number: (800) 425-3733 ext. 1
Fax: (607) 587-4299
Deborah Goodrich, Associate Vice President for Enrollment Management, SUNY College of Technology at Alfred, Huntington Administration Building, Alfred, NY 14802-1196

SUNY College of Technology at Canton
Canton, New York
www.canton.edu   CB code: 2523

▸ Public 2-year technical college
▸ Residential campus in small town

General. Founded in 1906. Regionally accredited. Offers master's degrees in conjunction with SUNY Institute of Technology at Utica/Rome. **Enrollment:** 3,549 degree-seeking undergraduates; 312 non-degree-seeking students. **Degrees:** 252 bachelor's, 491 associate awarded. **ROTC:** Army, Air Force. **Location:** 135 miles from Syracuse, 120 miles from Montreal, Canada. **Calendar:** Semester, limited summer session. **Full-time faculty:** 117 total; 44% have terminal degrees, 14% minority, 39% women. **Part-time faculty:** 83 total; 10% have terminal degrees, 2% minority, 58% women. **Class size:** 37% < 20, 49% 20-39, 10% 40-49, 4% 50-99. **Special facilities:** Cross-country trails. **Partnerships:** Formal partnership with Polaris.

Student profile. Among degree-seeking undergraduates, 4% already have a bachelor's degree or higher, 953 enrolled as first-time, first-year students, 442 transferred in from other institutions.

Part-time:	17%	25 or older:	23%
Out-of-state:	2%	Live on campus:	32%
Women:	51%		

Transfer out. **Colleges most students transferred to 2011:** SUNY College at Potsdam, Clarkson University, SUNY Institute of Technology at Utica/Rome, Rochester Institute of Technology, SUNY College at Plattsburgh.

Basis for selection. High school record most important. Admission requirements vary according to program of study. Some enrolled freshmen must complete ACCUPLACER placement test on campus before classes begin. Students notified of testing dates and whether they need ACCUPLACER. SAT or ACT required of bachelor's degree program applicants. SAT, ACT, SAT Subject Test scores received on rolling basis. Interview recommended. **Home schooled:** Transcript of courses and grades required. Applicants must do 1 of following: present letter from superintendent from school district they reside in indicating completion of program equivalent to high school diploma; take GED exam; take 5 Regents Exams indicated in SUNY policy; complete 24 credit-hour program to earn GED. **Learning Disabled:** Students with documented needs should request accommodations through coordinator of Accommodative Services.

High school preparation. College-preparatory program recommended. 16 units required; 17 recommended. Required and recommended units include English 4, mathematics 3, social studies 3, history 1, science 3 (laboratory 1-2) and foreign language 1. Required high school courses vary with major. Engineering science technologies, health, and life sciences stress math and science; business technologies stress algebra.

2011-2012 Annual costs. Tuition/fees: $6,597; $11,067 out-of-state. Per-credit charge: $220 in-state; $406 out-of-state. Laundry fee of $90 annually added to the bill for room and board. Out-of-state tuition for bachelor's

degree program: $14,320; $597 per credit hour. Room/board: $10,340. Books/supplies: $1,200. Personal expenses: $1,200.

2011-2012 Financial aid. **Need-based:** 886 full-time freshmen applied for aid; 796 were judged to have need; 791 of these received aid. Average scholarship/grant was $6,610; average loan $3,244. 50% of total undergraduate aid awarded as scholarships/grants, 50% as loans/jobs. Need-based aid available for part-time students. Work-study available nights, weekends and for part-time students. **Non-need-based:** Scholarships awarded for academics, alumni affiliation, leadership, minority status, state residency.

Application procedures. **Admission:** Priority date 3/1; no deadline. $40 fee, may be waived for applicants with need. Admission notification on a rolling basis beginning on or about 11/1. Must reply by May 1 or within 4 week(s) if notified thereafter. **Financial aid:** Priority date 3/15; no closing date. FAFSA required. Applicants notified on a rolling basis starting 2/15; must reply within 4 week(s) of notification.

Academics. **Special study options:** Cross-registration, distance learning, dual enrollment of high school students, independent study, internships, liberal arts/career combination, student-designed major. Criminal justice students can complete Police Academy during spring semester of senior year. Bachelor's degree programs available on campus. License preparation in dental hygiene, nursing, physical therapy. **Credit/placement by examination:** AP, CLEP, IB, SAT, ACT, institutional tests. Student must take at least 15 credit hours at SUNY Canton to earn an associate degree and 30 hours to earn a bachelor's degree. Maximum number of credits awarded for prior work and/or life experience of 30 hours is for a bachelor's degree. Maximum hours for an associate degree is 15 credits. **Support services:** Learning center, reduced course load, remedial instruction, study skills assistance, tutoring, writing center.

Majors. **Business:** Accounting technology, business admin. **Computer sciences:** Information systems. **Education:** Early childhood. **Engineering:** General. **Health services:** Dental hygiene, nursing (RN), physical therapy assistant, veterinary technology/assistant. **Liberal arts:** Arts/sciences. **Protective services:** Police science.

Most popular majors. Business/marketing 16%, engineering/engineering technologies 8%, health sciences 37%, liberal arts 26%, security/protective services 14%.

Computing on campus. 300 workstations in library. Dormitories wired for high-speed internet access. Online library, helpline, wireless network available.

Student life. **Freshman orientation:** Mandatory, $60 fee. Preregistration for classes offered. For students entering in the fall, 2-day orientation for traditional students, 1-day orientation for non-traditional students. 1-day orientation for students entering in the spring. **Policies:** All full-time students must live in college housing unless requirement waived by Residence Life office. **Housing:** Guaranteed on-campus for freshmen. Coed dorms, special housing for disabled, fraternity/sorority housing, wellness housing available. $105 nonrefundable deposit, deadline 5/1. Pets allowed in dorm rooms. Some all-male or all-female floors and wings available. **Activities:** Campus ministries, choral groups, dance, drama, international student organizations, student government, student newspaper, Newman Club, Chinese culture club, Brother 2 Brother, Afro Latin Society, Caribbean United, African student union, Habitat for Humanity, Peer Educators.

Athletics. NAIA. **Intercollegiate:** Baseball M, basketball, cross-country, golf M, ice hockey M, lacrosse, soccer, softball W, volleyball W. **Intramural:** Basketball, football (non-tackle), soccer, volleyball. **Team name:** Kangaroos.

Student services. Adult student services, alcohol/substance abuse counseling, chaplain/spiritual director, career counseling, services for economically disadvantaged, student employment services, financial aid counseling, health services, minority student services, personal counseling, placement for graduates, veterans' counselor. **Physically disabled:** Services for visually, speech, hearing impaired. **Transfer:** Pre-admission transcript evaluation for new students. Transfer adviser, college fairs on campus for students transferring to 4-year colleges.

Contact. E-mail: admissions@canton.edu
Phone: (315) 386-7123 Toll-free number: (800) 388-7123
Fax: (315) 386-7929
Nicole Campbell, Director of Admissions, SUNY College of Technology at Canton, 34 Cornell Drive, Canton, NY 13617-1098

SUNY College of Technology at Delhi
Delhi, New York
www.delhi.edu
                                                 CB code: 2525

▸ Public 2-year liberal arts and technical college
▸ Residential campus in rural community

General. Founded in 1913. Regionally accredited. Students can earn bachelor degrees in selected programs on main campus as well as at remote sites and online. **Enrollment:** 3,204 degree-seeking undergraduates; 226 non-degree-seeking students. **Degrees:** 198 bachelor's, 557 associate awarded. **Location:** 70 miles from Albany and Binghamton. **Calendar:** Semester, limited summer session. **Full-time faculty:** 123 total; 27% have terminal degrees, 9% minority, 40% women. **Part-time faculty:** 100 total; 7% have terminal degrees, 1% minority, 63% women. **Class size:** 55% < 20, 40% 20-39, 2% 40-49, 2% 50-99, less than 1% >100. **Special facilities:** Demonstration forest and arboretum, student-operated restaurant, veterinary science laboratories, golf course, CAD laboratory, architecture laboratories, golf swing lab.

Student profile. Among degree-seeking undergraduates, 85% enrolled in a transfer program, 15% enrolled in a vocational program, 910 enrolled as first-time, first-year students, 395 transferred in from other institutions.

Part-time:	13%	Hispanic American:	11%
Out-of-state:	3%	Native American:	1%
Women:	51%	International:	1%
African American:	14%	25 or older:	17%
Asian American:	3%	Live on campus:	60%

Basis for selection. Special requirements for 4-year programs. Enrollment limits in some programs. Once a program is full, academically admissable students can defer admission to the next available semester. SAT or ACT recommended. Interview recommended. **Home schooled:** Transcript of courses and grades, state high school equivalency certificate required.

High school preparation. College-preparatory program recommended. 18 units recommended. Recommended units include English 4, mathematics 4, social studies 2, history 2, science 3 (laboratory 2) and foreign language 1. Requirements vary by program.

2011-2012 Annual costs. Tuition/fees: $6,800; $11,270 out-of-state. Per-credit charge: $220 in-state; $406 out-of-state. Out-of-state tuition for bachelor's program: $14,320; per-credit-hour $597. Room/board: $10,120. Books/supplies: $1,300. Personal expenses: $1,410.

2011-2012 Financial aid. Need-based: 57% of total undergraduate aid awarded as scholarships/grants, 43% as loans/jobs. Need-based aid available for part-time students. Work-study available nights, weekends and for part-time students.

Application procedures. Admission: Priority date 8/1; no deadline. $50 fee, may be waived for applicants with need. Admission notification on a rolling basis beginning on or about 11/1. Deposit is required within four weeks of acceptance and is fully refundable until May 1st. **Financial aid:** Priority date 2/15; no closing date. FAFSA required. Applicants notified on a rolling basis starting 3/1; must reply within 2 week(s) of notification.

Academics. Special study options: Cross-registration, distance learning, double major, dual enrollment of high school students, ESL, honors, independent study, internships, liberal arts/career combination, study abroad. Bachelor's degree programs available on campus. License preparation in nursing. **Credit/placement by examination:** AP, CLEP, IB, institutional tests. 50 credit hours maximum toward associate degree, 50 toward bachelor's. Maximum of 50 percent of credits required for degree may be earned by combination of transfer, life experience and credit by examination. **Support services:** Learning center, reduced course load, remedial instruction, study skills assistance, tutoring, writing center.

Majors. Architecture: Landscape, technology. **Business:** Accounting, administrative services, business admin, management information systems, marketing, tourism promotion, tourism/travel. **Computer sciences:** Data processing. **Education:** Early childhood, elementary, physical, secondary. **General:** Horticultural science, horticulture, landscaping, ornamental horticulture, turf management. **Health services:** Nursing (RN), veterinary technology/assistant. **Liberal arts:** Arts/sciences. **Math:** General. **Parks/recreation:** Facilities management. **Work/family studies:** Institutional food production.

Most popular majors. Business/marketing 11%, engineering/engineering technologies 10%, health sciences 19%, liberal arts 15%, trade and industry 25%.

Computing on campus. 230 workstations in library, computer center. Dormitories wired for high-speed internet access and linked to campus network. Commuter students can connect to campus network. Online course registration, online library, helpline, repair service, student web hosting, wireless network available.

Student life. Freshman orientation: Available, $75 fee. Preregistration for classes offered. Several pre-orientation dates throughout the spring and summer. In addition, students take part in a 3-day orientation immediately prior to the beginning of the fall semester. **Housing:** Guaranteed on-campus for freshmen. Coed dorms, apartments, wellness housing available. $100 nonrefundable deposit, deadline 6/1. **Activities:** Bands, campus ministries, choral groups, dance, drama, international student organizations, literary

magazine, musical theater, radio station, student government, student newspaper, TV station, Delhi Interfaith Council, Black student union, Latin student association, West Indian coalition.

Athletics. NAIA, NJCAA. **Intercollegiate:** Basketball, cross-country, golf, lacrosse M, soccer, softball W, swimming, tennis, track and field, volleyball W. **Intramural:** Badminton, basketball, bowling, boxing, football (nontackle) M, golf, handball, racquetball, soccer, softball, swimming, table tennis, tennis, volleyball. **Team name:** Broncos.

Student services. Adult student services, alcohol/substance abuse counseling, chaplain/spiritual director, career counseling, services for economically disadvantaged, student employment services, financial aid counseling, health services, minority student services, on-campus daycare, personal counseling, placement for graduates, veterans' counselor, women's services. **Physically disabled:** Services for visually, hearing impaired. **Transfer:** Preadmission transcript evaluation for new students. Transfer adviser, college fairs on campus for students transferring to 4-year colleges.

Contact. E-mail: enroll@delhi.edu
Phone: (607) 746-4550 Toll-free number: (800) 963-3544
Fax: (607) 746-4104
Robert Mazzei, Director of Admissions, SUNY College of Technology at Delhi, 2 Main Street, Delhi, NY 13753-1190

Swedish Institute
New York, New York
www.swedishinstitute.edu

- For-profit 2-year health science college
- Very large city
- Interview required

General. Accredited by ACCSC. **Enrollment:** 475 degree-seeking undergraduates. **Calendar:** Semester, extensive summer session. **Full-time faculty:** 17 total. **Part-time faculty:** 35 total.

Basis for selection. GPA, recommendations considered.

2011-2012 Annual costs. Tuition/fees: $11,450. Students generally attend 3 semesters/year.

Financial aid. All financial aid based on need. Need-based aid available for part-time students. Work-study available nights, weekends and for part-time students.

Application procedures. Admission: No deadline. $100 fee. **Financial aid:** No deadline. FAFSA, institutional form required.

Academics. Credit/placement by examination: AP, CLEP, institutional tests. **Support services:** Reduced course load, study skills assistance, tutoring.

Majors. Health services: Asian bodywork therapy, massage therapy.

Computing on campus. 7 workstations in library, computer center.

Contact. E-mail: admissions@swedishinstitute.edu
Phone: (212) 924-5900 Fax: (212) 924-7600
Jennifer Apicella, Director of Admissions, Swedish Institute, 226 West 26th Street, 5th Floor, New York, NY 10001-6700

Technical Career Institutes
New York, New York
www.tcicollege.edu   CB code: 2755

- For-profit 2-year technical and career college
- Commuter campus in very large city

General. Founded in 1909. Regionally accredited. **Enrollment:** 4,196 degree-seeking undergraduates. **Degrees:** 1,168 associate awarded. **Calendar:** Trimester, extensive summer session. **Full-time faculty:** 91 total; 20% have terminal degrees. **Part-time faculty:** 172 total; 17% have terminal degrees.

Student profile.

Part-time:	10%	Women:	39%

Basis for selection. Open admission, but selective for some programs. Students without a high school diploma, GED, or other high school equivalency credential must pass ACCUPLACER to be admitted. **Home schooled:**

Transcript of courses and grades, state high school equivalency certificate, interview required.

2011-2012 Annual costs. Tuition/fees: $12,285. Per-credit charge: $496. Required fees $265/year for second-year students.

Financial aid. Need-based: Work-study available nights, weekends and for part-time students. **Non-need-based:** Scholarships awarded for academics, alumni affiliation.

Application procedures. Admission: No deadline. No application fee. Admission notification on a rolling basis. **Financial aid:** No deadline. FAFSA, institutional form required. Applicants notified on a rolling basis.

Academics. Special study options: Double major. **Credit/placement by examination:** AP, CLEP, institutional tests. **Support services:** Learning center, reduced course load, remedial instruction, tutoring.

Majors. Business: Accounting technology, administrative services, banking/financial services, business admin, marketing. **Communications:** Digital media. **Health services:** Medical records technology, office computer specialist, optometric assistant. **Protective services:** Security management.

Most popular majors. Business/marketing 15%, engineering/engineering technologies 28%, health sciences 19%, legal studies 8%, public administration/social services 10%, trade and industry 14%.

Computing on campus. PC or laptop required. Commuter students can connect to campus network. Online library, student web hosting, wireless network available.

Student life. Freshman orientation: Available. Preregistration for classes offered. **Activities:** Student government, Student chapter of Institute of Electrical and Electronics Engineering, Electronics Technicians Association, Tau Alpha Pi Honor Fraternity for Engineering Technology, Future Business Leaders, Society of Women Engineers, Dare to Dream Volunteer Project, and American Society of Heating, Refrigeration & Air Conditioning Engineers.

Student services. Adult student services, chaplain/spiritual director, career counseling, services for economically disadvantaged, student employment services, financial aid counseling, health services, minority student services, personal counseling, placement for graduates, veterans' counselor. **Transfer:** Transfer adviser for students transferring to 4-year colleges.

Contact. E-mail: admissions@tcicollege.edu
Phone: (212) 594-4000 Toll-free number: (800) 878-8246
Fax: (212) 629-3937
Bernard Price, Vice President of Admissions, Technical Career Institutes, 320 West 31st Street, New York, NY 10001

Tompkins Cortland Community College
Dryden, New York
www.TC3.edu

CB member
CB code: 2904

- Public 2-year community college
- Commuter campus in small town

General. Founded in 1968. Regionally accredited. SUNY institution. **Enrollment:** 3,478 degree-seeking undergraduates; 364 non-degree-seeking students. **Degrees:** 698 associate awarded. **Location:** 45 miles from Syracuse, 12 miles from Ithaca. **Calendar:** Semester, extensive summer session. **Full-time faculty:** 68 total. **Part-time faculty:** 268 total. **Class size:** 60% < 20, 40% 20-39, less than 1% 40-49, less than 1% 50-99.

Student profile. Among degree-seeking undergraduates, 1,091 enrolled as first-time, first-year students, 348 transferred in from other institutions.

Part-time:	19%	Hispanic American:	8%
Out-of-state:	1%	International:	4%
Women:	54%	25 or older:	29%
African American:	10%	Live on campus:	26%
Asian American:	1%		

Transfer out. Colleges most students transferred to 2011: SUNY Cortland, Ithaca College, Cornell University, SUNY Binghamton, SUNY Oswego.

Basis for selection. Open admission, but selective for some programs. Special requirements for nursing students. Nursing requires high school average of B or better, plus math and science prerequisites, and ACT. Interview recommended for nursing. **Home schooled:** Letter of recommendation (nonparent) required. Completion of an IHIP pursuant to section 100.10 of the Regulations of the Commissions of Education required.

High school preparation. College-preparatory program recommended.

2011-2012 Annual costs. Tuition/fees: $4,605; $8,855 out-of-state. Per-credit charge: $143 in-state; $296 out-of-state.

Financial aid. Need-based: Need-based aid available for part-time students. Work-study available nights, weekends and for part-time students. **Non-need-based:** Scholarships awarded for academics.

Application procedures. Admission: No deadline. $15 fee, may be waived for applicants with need, free for online applicants. Admission notification on a rolling basis. **Financial aid:** Priority date 4/15; no closing date. FAFSA, institutional form required. Applicants notified on a rolling basis starting 3/15; must reply within 4 week(s) of notification.

Academics. Special study options: Cooperative education, cross-registration, distance learning, dual enrollment of high school students, ESL, honors, independent study, internships, liberal arts/career combination, study abroad. Bachelor's degree programs available on campus. License preparation in nursing, real estate. **Credit/placement by examination:** AP, CLEP, IB, institutional tests. 47 credit hours maximum toward associate degree. **Support services:** GED preparation, learning center, reduced course load, remedial instruction, study skills assistance, tutoring, writing center.

Honors college/program. All applicants to the honors college will be individually evaluated based on their academic achievement and potential for further achievement.

Majors. Biology: Biotechnology. **Business:** Accounting technology, business admin, hotel/motel admin, international, labor relations, retailing. **Communications:** Advertising, broadcast journalism, communications/speech/rhetoric. **Communications technology:** Radio/TV. **Computer sciences:** General, information systems, support specialist, webmaster. **Conservation:** General. **Education:** Early childhood, kindergarten/preschool, secondary. **Engineering:** General. **English:** English lit. **Health services:** Nursing (RN), substance abuse counseling. **Human services:** Community org/advocacy. **Liberal arts:** Arts/sciences, humanities. **Parks/recreation:** Facilities management, sports admin. **Protective services:** Forensics, police science. **Visual/performing arts:** Commercial/advertising art, photography. **Work/family studies:** Child care management.

Most popular majors. Business/marketing 18%, health sciences 8%, liberal arts 39%, security/protective services 9%.

Computing on campus. 400 workstations in library, computer center, student center. Dormitories wired for high-speed internet access and linked to campus network. Commuter students can connect to campus network. Online course registration, online library, helpline, wireless network available.

Student life. Freshman orientation: Available. Preregistration for classes offered. Held prior to each semester. Multiple sessions offered: new students, international students, and adult students. **Policies:** All campus organizations must apply for recognition, must have staff advisor, and are funded by the activity fee through faculty-student association and student government. **Housing:** Coed dorms, special housing for disabled, apartments, wellness housing available. $250 fully refundable deposit, deadline 5/15. **Activities:** Choral groups, dance, drama, film society, literary magazine, radio station, student government, student advisory board, Students Acting for a Greener Earth, drama club, outdoor adventure club, nursing club, accounting and business association, Alpha Omega Christian fellowship, gay straight alliance, Habitat for Humanity, Otaku cafe.

Athletics. NJCAA. **Intercollegiate:** Baseball M, basketball, golf, lacrosse M, soccer, softball W, volleyball W. **Intramural:** Archery, badminton, basketball, bowling, football (non-tackle), golf, handball, lacrosse, racquetball, skiing, soccer, softball, squash, swimming, table tennis, tennis, volleyball, water polo, weight lifting, wrestling. **Team name:** Panthers.

Student services. Adult student services, alcohol/substance abuse counseling, career counseling, services for economically disadvantaged, student employment services, financial aid counseling, health services, minority student services, on-campus daycare, personal counseling, placement for graduates, veterans' counselor. **Physically disabled:** Services for visually, speech, hearing impaired. **Transfer:** Re-entry adviser, pre-admission transcript evaluation for new students. Transfer center, transfer adviser, college fairs on campus for students transferring to 4-year colleges.

Contact. E-mail: admissions@tc3.edu
Phone: (607) 844-6580 Toll-free number: (888) 567-8211
Fax: (607) 844-6541
Sandy Drumluk, Director of Admissions, Tompkins Cortland Community College, 170 North Street, Dryden, NY 13053-0139

Trocaire College
Buffalo, New York
www.trocaire.edu

CB code: 2856

- Private 2-year junior college affiliated with Roman Catholic Church
- Commuter campus in large city

General. Founded in 1958. Regionally accredited. Affiliated with Sisters of Mercy, Buffalo Diocese. Although offering primarily 2-year degrees, Trocaire does offer several 4-year Bachelor's degree programs. **Enrollment:** 1,420 degree-seeking undergraduates. **Degrees:** 217 associate awarded. **Location:** Located within the City of Buffalo. **Calendar:** Semester, limited summer session. **Full-time faculty:** 52 total. **Part-time faculty:** 96 total. **Class size:** 79% < 20, 21% 20-39.

Basis for selection. Open admission, but selective for some programs. Special requirements for health-related fields.

High school preparation. 16 units required. Laboratory science and mathematics required for some programs.

2011-2012 Annual costs. Tuition/fees: $13,900. Per-credit charge: $550. Books/supplies: $1,200. Personal expenses: $700.

Financial aid. Need-based: Need-based aid available for part-time students. Work-study available nights, weekends and for part-time students. **Non-need-based:** Scholarships awarded for academics, alumni affiliation.

Application procedures. Admission: No deadline. $25 fee, may be waived for applicants with need, free for online applicants. Admission notification on a rolling basis. Must reply by May 1 or within 4 week(s) if notified thereafter. **Financial aid:** No deadline. FAFSA required. Applicants notified on a rolling basis starting 3/1; must reply within 2 week(s) of notification.

Academics. Special study options: Cross-registration, dual enrollment of high school students, independent study, internships. Bachelor's degree programs available on campus. License preparation in nursing, radiology. **Credit/placement by examination:** AP, CLEP, institutional tests. 30 credit hours maximum toward associate degree. **Support services:** Learning center, reduced course load, remedial instruction, study skills assistance, tutoring.

Majors. Business: Administrative services, business admin, office management, sales/distribution. **Education:** Early childhood. **Health services:** Massage therapy, medical assistant, medical radiologic technology/radiation therapy, medical records technology, nursing (RN), surgical technology. **Liberal arts:** Arts/sciences.

Most popular majors. Business/marketing 16%, education 7%, health sciences 71%.

Computing on campus. 114 workstations in library, computer center, student center. Helpline available.

Student life. Freshman orientation: Mandatory. Preregistration for classes offered. **Activities:** Student government.

Student services. Adult student services, career counseling, student employment services, health services, personal counseling, placement for graduates, veterans' counselor. **Physically disabled:** Services for visually, hearing impaired. **Transfer:** Pre-admission transcript evaluation for new students. Transfer center, transfer adviser, college fairs on campus for students transferring to 4-year colleges.

Contact. E-mail: info@trocaire.edu
Phone: (716) 827-2545 Fax: (716) 828-6107
Maria Povlock, Director of Admissions, Trocaire College, 360 Choate Avenue, Buffalo, NY 14220

Ulster County Community College
Stone Ridge, New York
www.sunyulster.edu

CB code: 2938

- Public 2-year community college
- Commuter campus in small town

General. Founded in 1963. Regionally accredited. SUNY institution. **Enrollment:** 2,298 degree-seeking undergraduates; 1,321 non-degree-seeking students. **Degrees:** 484 associate awarded. **Location:** 8 miles from Kingston. **Calendar:** Semester, extensive summer session. **Full-time faculty:** 64 total. **Part-time faculty:** 149 total. **Class size:** 65% < 20, 34% 20-39, less than 1% 40-49, less than 1% 50-99. **Special facilities:** Computer art graphics laboratory, small-business incubator, Mid-Hudson Health and Safety

Institute. **Partnerships:** Formal partnership with Cisco Networking Academy, the Microsoft IT Academy program.

Student profile. Among degree-seeking undergraduates, 79% enrolled in a transfer program, 21% enrolled in a vocational program, 683 enrolled as first-time, first-year students, 148 transferred in from other institutions.

Part-time:	31%	Hispanic American:	11%
Women:	59%	Native American:	1%
African American:	6%	International:	1%
Asian American:	1%	25 or older:	30%

Transfer out. Colleges most students transferred to 2011: SUNY New Paltz, SUNY Albany, Marist College, Mount St. Mary's College, College of Saint Rose.

Basis for selection. Open admission, but selective for some programs. Special requirements for nursing and honors programs, with school achievement record very important. SAT or ACT recommended for all applicants. Entry into nursing program is competitive and based on the results of the ATI - TEAS exam. Interview required for nursing, honors program, early admissions applicants; recommended for others. Portfolio recommended for graphic arts.

High school preparation. 18 units recommended. Recommended units include English 4 and social studies 4. 3 math and 3 science, including chemistry and physics, required of engineering applicants. 4 English, 3 math, 3 language required of honors program applicants.

2011-2012 Annual costs. Tuition/fees: $4,628; $8,618 out-of-state. Per-credit charge: $142 in-state; $284 out-of-state. Books/supplies: $1,000. Personal expenses: $800.

Financial aid. Need-based: Need-based aid available for part-time students. Work-study available nights, weekends and for part-time students.

Application procedures. Admission: No deadline. No application fee. Admission notification on a rolling basis. **Financial aid:** Priority date 6/1; no closing date. FAFSA required. Applicants notified on a rolling basis starting 6/1; must reply within 2 week(s) of notification.

Academics. Special study options: Cooperative education, cross-registration, distance learning, double major, dual enrollment of high school students, ESL, honors, independent study, internships, student-designed major. License preparation in nursing. **Credit/placement by examination:** AP, CLEP, institutional tests. 30 credit hours maximum toward associate degree. **Support services:** Learning center, pre-admission summer program, reduced course load, remedial instruction, study skills assistance, tutoring, writing center.

Majors. Business: General, accounting technology, business admin, entrepreneurial studies, managerial economics, office/clerical. **Communications:** Communications/speech/rhetoric. **Computer sciences:** Computer science, system admin. **Conservation:** Environmental studies. **Education:** Biology, chemistry, elementary, English, kindergarten/preschool, mathematics, middle, science, social studies, Spanish. **Engineering:** General. **Health services:** EMT paramedic, nursing (RN), substance abuse counseling, veterinary technology/assistant. **Human services:** Community org/advocacy. **Liberal arts:** Arts/sciences, humanities. **Math:** General. **Parks/recreation:** General. **Protective services:** Homeland security, law enforcement admin. **Social sciences:** General. **Visual/performing arts:** General, commercial/advertising art, dramatic, music.

Most popular majors. Business/marketing 12%, education 7%, health sciences 13%, liberal arts 41%, visual/performing arts 8%.

Computing on campus. 600 workstations in library, computer center, student center. Wireless network available.

Student life. Freshman orientation: Available. Preregistration for classes offered. **Activities:** Bands, choral groups, drama, music ensembles, musical theater, student government, child care club, environmental awareness club, business club, improv club, Phi Theta Kappa, LGBTA, vet tech club, tomorrow's teachers, psychology club, nursing club.

Athletics. NJCAA. **Intercollegiate:** Baseball M, basketball M, golf, soccer, softball W, tennis, volleyball W. **Intramural:** Basketball M. **Team name:** Senators.

Student services. Adult student services, career counseling, services for economically disadvantaged, student employment services, financial aid counseling, health services, on-campus daycare, personal counseling, placement for graduates, veterans' counselor. **Physically disabled:** Services for visually, speech, hearing impaired. **Transfer:** Transfer adviser, college fairs on campus for students transferring to 4-year colleges.

Two-Year Colleges

Contact. E-mail: admissions@sunyulster.edu
Phone: (845) 687-5022 Toll-free number: (800) 724-5022
Fax: (845) 687-5090
Matthew Green, Director of Admissions, Ulster County Community
College, Cottekill Road, Stone Ridge, NY 12484

University of Rochester School of Nursing
Rochester, New York
www.son.rochester.edu

- Private 1-year university and nursing college
- Large city

General. Students with only high school diploma and transfer students
are not accepted for admission. Applicants must have either a non-nursing
bachelor's degree or a registered nurse (RN) license. Accelerated (12-month)
bachelor's degree in nursing program available to those with a prior non-
nursing bachelor's degree. RN to BS program (4 continuous semesters) available to those with a 2-year (community college) nursing degree. **Enrollment:**
242 degree-seeking undergraduates. **Degrees:** 196 bachelor's awarded; master's, professional, doctoral offered. **Calendar:** Semester. **Full-time faculty:**
50 total. **Part-time faculty:** 50 total.

Basis for selection. Each applicant's unique capabilities and objectives
are considered in addition to traditional academic criteria.

Financial aid. Need-based: Need-based aid available for part-time students. Work-study available nights, weekends and for part-time students.

Academics. Credit/placement by examination: AP, CLEP.

Contact. E-mail: son_admissions@urmc.rochester.edu
Phone: (585) 275-2375
Elaine Andolina, Director of Admissions, University of Rochester School
of Nursing, Box SON, Rochester, NY 14642

Utica School of Commerce
Utica, New York
www.uscny.edu   CB code: 0343

- For-profit 2-year business college
- Commuter campus in small city
- Interview required

General. Founded in 1896. Regionally accredited. Branch campuses in
Oneonta and Canastota. **Enrollment:** 405 degree-seeking undergraduates.
Degrees: 107 associate awarded. **Location:** 50 miles from Syracuse. **Calendar:** Semester, extensive summer session. **Full-time faculty:** 16 total. **Part-
time faculty:** 51 total. **Special facilities:** Museum of business education.

Student profile.

Out-of-state:	1%	25 or older:	30%

Transfer out. Colleges most students transferred to 2011: SUNY College
of Technology, St. Rose College, SUNY at Oneonta.

Basis for selection. Open admission. Admissions interview required.
High School diploma or GED required.

2011-2012 Annual costs. Tuition/fees: $12,470. Per-credit charge: $499.
Books/supplies: $1,185.

Financial aid. All financial aid based on need. Work-study available nights,
weekends and for part-time students.

Application procedures. Admission: No deadline. No application fee.
Admission notification on a rolling basis. Must reply by May 1 or within 3
week(s) if notified thereafter. **Financial aid:** No deadline. FAFSA, institutional form required. Applicants notified on a rolling basis.

Academics. Special study options: Accelerated study, dual enrollment of
high school students, liberal arts/career combination. Joint admissions with
SUNY Institute of Technology. **Credit/placement by examination:** AP,
CLEP, institutional tests. 30 credit hours maximum toward associate degree.
Support services: Learning center, reduced course load, remedial instruc-
tion, tutoring.

Majors. Business: General, accounting, administrative services, business
admin, executive assistant, management information systems, nonprofit/pub-
lic, retailing, sales/distribution. **Computer sciences:** General, data processing, programming, word processing. **Health services:** Health care admin,
medical records technology, medical secretary.

Most popular majors. Business/marketing 81%, computer/information
sciences 19%.

Computing on campus. 168 workstations in library, computer center.

Student life. Freshman orientation: Mandatory. Preregistration for
classes offered. **Activities:** Student government, student newspaper, future
secretaries association, accounting association.

Student services. Career counseling, student employment services, personal counseling, placement for graduates, veterans' counselor. **Physically
disabled:** Services for visually, hearing impaired. **Transfer:** Transfer adviser,
college fairs on campus for students transferring to 4-year colleges.

Contact. E-mail: admissions@uscny.edu
Phone: (315) 733-2307 Toll-free number: (800) 321-4872
Fax: (315) 733-9281
Leslie Crosley, Director of Admissions, Utica School of Commerce, 201
Bleecker Street, Utica, NY 13501

Villa Maria College of Buffalo
Buffalo, New York
www.villa.edu   CB code: 2962

- Private 2-year visual arts and music college affiliated with Roman Catho-
lic Church
- Commuter campus in large city
- Interview required

General. Founded in 1960. Regionally accredited. **Enrollment:** 451 degree-
seeking undergraduates; 6 non-degree-seeking students. **Degrees:** 14 bachelor's, 71 associate awarded. **Location:** 2 miles from downtown Buffalo.
Calendar: Semester, limited summer session. **Full-time faculty:** 30 total;
37% have terminal degrees, 53% women. **Part-time faculty:** 51 total; 39%
have terminal degrees, 4% minority, 43% women. **Class size:** 88% < 20,
12% 20-39. **Special facilities:** Interior design resource center, education
resource center, recording studio, recital hall, digital photography lab, art
shop, photography studio, apparel construction lab, computer animation lab,
stop action lab.

Student profile. Among degree-seeking undergraduates, 3% already have
a bachelor's degree or higher, 91 enrolled as first-time, first-year students,
59 transferred in from other institutions.

Part-time:	18%	Hispanic American:	4%
Out-of-state:	2%	Native American:	1%
Women:	65%	25 or older:	24%
African American:	16%	Live on campus:	12%
Asian American:	1%		

Transfer out. 50% of students enrolled in the transfer program go on to
4-year colleges. **Colleges most students transferred to 2011:** SUNY at
Buffalo, Buffalo State College, Medaille College, Hilbert College, Canisius College.

Basis for selection. Admission based on academic records, learning experience, and assessment and advisement program results where applicable.
Interview, recommendations also considered. Physical therapist assistant program requires 3.5 GPA. Animation requires interview with program personnel. Interview and audition required for associate and bachelor's level music
programs. Essay, portfolio and interview with faculty required for all BFA
programs and associate level interior design program. **Adult students:** SAT/
ACT scores not required. **Home schooled:** Statement describing home school
structure and mission, transcript of courses and grades, interview required.
Letter required verifying completion of all requirements from the school
district in which home schooled individual resides, or a passing GED score.
Learning Disabled: Must submit all documentation to Coordinator for Students with Disabilities. Coordinator follows through with placement and
accommodations.

High school preparation. Recommended units include English 4, mathematics 3, social studies 4, history 4 and science 3. General physics with lab
required for physical therapist assistant applicants.

2012-2013 Annual costs. Tuition/fees (projected): $17,150. Per-credit
charge: $560. Books/supplies: $1,200. Personal expenses: $700.

2010-2011 Financial aid. Need-based: 104 full-time freshmen applied for aid; 103 were judged to have need; 88 of these received aid. Average need met was 42%. Average scholarship/grant was $4,513. 41% of total undergraduate aid awarded as scholarships/grants, 59% as loans/jobs. Need-based aid available for part-time students. Work-study available nights, weekends and for part-time students. **Non-need-based:** Awarded to 113 full-time undergraduates, including 34 freshmen. Scholarships awarded for academics, alumni affiliation, art, leadership, minority status, music/drama.

Application procedures. Admission: No deadline. No application fee. Admission notification on a rolling basis. **Financial aid:** No deadline. FAFSA required. Applicants notified on a rolling basis starting 2/15; must reply within 2 week(s) of notification.

Academics. Implemented Adviser/Advisee Action Plan provides early identification of students encountering difficulty with scheduling, finances, academic skills, personal problems, and employment. **Special study options:** Cooperative education, cross-registration, double major, dual enrollment of high school students, internships, liberal arts/career combination, study abroad. Bachelor's degree programs available on campus. License preparation in physical therapy. **Credit/placement by examination:** AP, CLEP, institutional tests. 30 credit hours maximum toward associate degree, 30 toward bachelor's. **Support services:** Learning center, pre-admission summer program, reduced course load, study skills assistance, tutoring.

Majors. Business: Business admin. **Education:** General, early childhood. **Health services:** Physical therapy assistant. **Liberal arts:** Arts/sciences, humanities. **Physical sciences:** General. **Visual/performing arts:** Commercial/advertising art, interior design, jazz, music management, music performance, photography, studio arts.

Most popular majors. Business/marketing 14%, communication technologies 6%, education 10%, health sciences 25%, visual/performing arts 41%.

Computing on campus. 150 workstations in library, computer center. Commuter students can connect to campus network. Online library, wireless network available.

Student life. Freshman orientation: Mandatory, $50 fee. Preregistration for classes offered. One-day program for first-time students and their parents; half day for transfer students. **Housing:** Apartments available. $300 fully refundable deposit. Housing is offered at Collegiate Village (college affiliated), located a mile off-campus; van service to campus available. No on-campus housing. **Activities:** Jazz band, campus ministries, choral groups, literary magazine, music ensembles, student government, Helping Adults' New Dreams Succeed, Students Actively Striving for Success, Students Against Destructive Decision Making, Multicultural Club.

Student services. Adult student services, alcohol/substance abuse counseling, chaplain/spiritual director, career counseling, services for economically disadvantaged, student employment services, financial aid counseling, health services, personal counseling, placement for graduates, veterans' counselor. **Transfer:** Pre-admission transcript evaluation for new students. Transfer adviser, college fairs on campus for students transferring to 4-year colleges.

Contact. E-mail: admissions@villa.edu
Phone: (716) 896-0700 ext. 1805 Fax: (716) 896-0705
Kevin Donovan, Director of Admissions, Villa Maria College of Buffalo, 240 Pine Ridge Road, Buffalo, NY 14225-3999

Westchester Community College
Valhalla, New York
www.sunywcc.edu

CB member
CB code: 2972

- Public 2-year community college
- Commuter campus in large town

General. Founded in 1946. Regionally accredited. SUNY institution. **Enrollment:** 12,108 degree-seeking undergraduates; 1,861 non-degree-seeking students. **Degrees:** 1,159 associate awarded. **Location:** 30 miles from New York City, 6 miles from White Plains. **Calendar:** Semester, extensive summer session. **Full-time faculty:** 161 total. **Part-time faculty:** 960 total. **Special facilities:** On-campus child care center.

Student profile. Among degree-seeking undergraduates, 2,726 enrolled as first-time, first-year students, 967 transferred in from other institutions.

| Part-time: | 41% | Women: | 52% |
| Out-of-state: | 1% | 25 or older: | 32% |

Transfer out. Colleges most students transferred to 2011: Mercy College, CUNY Lehman, SUNY Purchase, Pace University, Iona College.

Basis for selection. Open admission, but selective for some programs. Competitive programs in allied health curricula. High school diploma or GED required of applicants 18 years of age or older. Interview recommended. **Home schooled:** Statement describing home school structure and mission required. Students must submit letter from superintendent of district in which they reside certifying that home instruction program is equivalent of high school program.

2011-2012 Annual costs. Tuition/fees: $4,513; $12,813 out-of-state. Per-credit charge: $173 in-state; $519 out-of-state. Books/supplies: $1,600. Personal expenses: $600.

2010-2011 Financial aid. Need-based: 88% of total undergraduate aid awarded as scholarships/grants, 12% as loans/jobs. Need-based aid available for part-time students. Work-study available nights, weekends and for part-time students. **Non-need-based:** Scholarships awarded for academics.

Application procedures. Admission: No deadline. $35 fee, may be waived for applicants with need. Application must be submitted on paper. Admission notification on a rolling basis beginning on or about 2/1. **Financial aid:** No deadline. FAFSA, institutional form required. Applicants notified on a rolling basis; must reply within 4 week(s) of notification.

Academics. Extensive ESL program and online tutoring. **Special study options:** Accelerated study, cooperative education, cross-registration, distance learning, double major, ESL, honors, independent study, internships, liberal arts/career combination, student-designed major, study abroad. Cambridge University summer program; Italian language study program in Italy. License preparation in nursing, paramedic, radiology, real estate. **Credit/placement by examination:** AP, CLEP, IB, institutional tests. 32 credit hours maximum toward associate degree. **Support services:** Learning center, reduced course load, remedial instruction, study skills assistance, tutoring, writing center.

Majors. Business: Accounting, administrative services, business admin, international, marketing, merchandising, office/clerical, sales/distribution. **Communications:** Communications/speech/rhetoric. **Computer sciences:** General, computer science, information systems, LAN/WAN management, security. **Education:** Early childhood. **Engineering:** General, engineering science. **Health services:** EMT paramedic, medical radiologic technology/radiation therapy, nursing (RN), nursing assistant, respiratory therapy technology, substance abuse counseling. **Human services:** Social work. **Liberal arts:** Arts/sciences. **Physical sciences:** General. **Protective services:** Corrections, police science. **Social sciences:** General. **Visual/performing arts:** General, dramatic, music performance. **Work/family studies:** Child care management, food/nutrition, institutional food production.

Computing on campus. 3,034 workstations in library, computer center, student center. Online library, helpline, wireless network available.

Student life. Freshman orientation: Available. Preregistration for classes offered. Held last week in August for fall semester, usually 2-day event. **Activities:** Choral groups, dance, drama, literary magazine, musical theater, radio station, student government, student newspaper, TV station, international friendship club, Black student union, Brazilian club, Haitian club, El Club Hispano Americano, Irish society, Jamaican club, Il Club Italiano, French club, Amnesty International.

Athletics. NJCAA. **Intercollegiate:** Baseball M, basketball, bowling, golf M, soccer M, softball W, volleyball W. **Intramural:** Basketball M, soccer M, softball, volleyball. **Team name:** Westcos.

Student services. Adult student services, alcohol/substance abuse counseling, career counseling, student employment services, financial aid counseling, health services, minority student services, on-campus daycare, personal counseling, placement for graduates, veterans' counselor, women's services. **Physically disabled:** Services for visually, speech, hearing impaired. **Transfer:** Pre-admission transcript evaluation for new students. Transfer center, transfer adviser, college fairs on campus for students transferring to 4-year colleges.

Contact. E-mail: admissions@sunywcc.edu
Phone: (914) 606-6735 Fax: (914) 606-6540
Gloria Leon, Director of Admissions, Westchester Community College, 75 Grasslands Road, Valhalla, NY 10595

Wood Tobe-Coburn School
New York, New York
www.woodtobecoburn.edu

CB code: 2913

- For-profit 2-year career college
- Commuter campus in very large city
- Interview required

General. Founded in 1879. Regionally accredited. **Enrollment:** 483 degree-seeking undergraduates. **Degrees:** 217 associate awarded. **Calendar:** Semester. **Full-time faculty:** 6 total. **Part-time faculty:** 19 total.

Student profile.

Out-of-state: 5%   25 or older: 5%

Basis for selection. Evaluation of high school or college transcript and/or GED. Portfolio recommended.

2011-2012 Annual costs. Tuition/fees: $16,730. Books/supplies: $1,165. Personal expenses: $2,110.

Financial aid. Need-based: Work-study available nights, weekends and for part-time students.

Application procedures. Admission: No deadline. $50 fee, may be waived for applicants with need. Application must be submitted on paper. Admission notification on a rolling basis. **Financial aid:** No deadline. Applicants notified on a rolling basis.

Academics. 16-month accelerated program available for fashion students, and 8 weeks of supervised on-the-job training each year. **Special study options:** Accelerated study, internships. Externships. **Credit/placement by examination:** AP, CLEP.

Majors. Business: Accounting, administrative services, fashion. **Computer sciences:** Networking, programming. **Engineering:** Software. **Health services:** Medical assistant. **Visual/performing arts:** Fashion design.

Most popular majors. Business/marketing 59%, visual/performing arts 41%.

Computing on campus. 154 workstations in library, computer center.

Student life. Freshman orientation: Mandatory. Preregistration for classes offered.

Student services. Career counseling, student employment services, placement for graduates.

Contact. Phone: (212) 686-9040 Toll-free number: (800) 394-9663 Fax: (212) 686-9171
Sandra Andujar-Wendland, Director of Admissions, Wood Tobe-Coburn School, 8 East 40th Street, New York, NY 10016-0190

North Carolina

Alamance Community College
Graham, North Carolina
www.alamancecc.edu   CB code: 5790

‣ Public 2-year community college
‣ Commuter campus in large town

General. Founded in 1958. Regionally accredited. **Enrollment:** 4,399 degree-seeking undergraduates; 865 non-degree-seeking students. **Degrees:** 445 associate awarded. **Location:** 4 miles from Burlington, 30 miles from Greensboro. **Calendar:** Semester, extensive summer session. **Full-time faculty:** 115 total; 6% have terminal degrees, 10% minority, 64% women. **Part-time faculty:** 320 total; 1% have terminal degrees, 13% minority, 53% women. **Class size:** 81% < 20, 19% 20-39.

Student profile. Among degree-seeking undergraduates, 22% enrolled in a transfer program, 78% enrolled in a vocational program, 636 enrolled as first-time, first-year students.

Part-time:	46%	Asian American:	1%
Out-of-state:	1%	Hispanic American:	2%
Women:	63%	Native American:	1%
African American:	24%	25 or older:	54%

Transfer out. Colleges most students transferred to 2011: University of North Carolina System.

Basis for selection. Open admission, but selective for some programs. Special requirements for Dental and Nursing. SAT or ACT score may waive required testing for placement. Portfolio recommended for advertising design, commercial art majors. **Learning Disabled:** Disabilities must be documented with special needs counselor. Contact Student Development Office.

High school preparation. 21 units recommended. Recommended units include English 4, mathematics 3, social studies 2, history 1, science 3 (laboratory 1), foreign language 2 and academic electives 6. Biology, chemistry required for nursing.

2011-2012 Annual costs. Tuition/fees: $2,055; $7,815 out-of-state. Per-credit charge: $67 in-state; $259 out-of-state. Books/supplies: $800. Personal expenses: $800.

2011-2012 Financial aid. Need-based: 330 full-time freshmen applied for aid; 320 were judged to have need; 310 of these received aid. Average need met was 30%. Average scholarship/grant was $4,500; average loan $3,000. 98% of total undergraduate aid awarded as scholarships/grants, 2% as loans/jobs. Need-based aid available for part-time students. Work-study available nights, weekends and for part-time students. **Non-need-based:** Awarded to 70 full-time undergraduates, including 30 freshmen. Scholarships awarded for academics, state residency.

Application procedures. Admission: No deadline. No application fee. Application must be submitted online. Admission notification on a rolling basis. **Financial aid:** Priority date 5/15; no closing date. FAFSA required. Applicants notified on a rolling basis starting 3/15; must reply within 2 week(s) of notification.

Academics. Special study options: Cooperative education, distance learning, double major, dual enrollment of high school students, ESL, independent study, internships, weekend college. License preparation in nursing. **Credit/placement by examination:** AP, CLEP, IB, institutional tests. 18 credit hours maximum toward associate degree. Maximum 25% of hours for degree by examination. **Support services:** GED preparation and test center, learning center, reduced course load, remedial instruction, study skills assistance, tutoring.

Majors. Biology: Biotechnology. **Business:** General, accounting, administrative services, banking/financial services, business admin, management science, office management, sales/distribution. **Computer sciences:** Information systems. **Education:** Early childhood. **Engineering:** Electrical. **General:** Horticultural science, horticulture. **Health services:** Clinical lab assistant, clinical lab technology, medical records admin, medical secretary, nursing (RN). **Liberal arts:** Arts/sciences. **Protective services:** Criminal justice, firefighting, law enforcement admin. **Visual/performing arts:** Music.

Most popular majors. Business/marketing 21%, health sciences 21%, liberal arts 20%.

Computing on campus. 152 workstations in library, computer center, student center. Wireless network available.

Student life. Freshman orientation: Available. Preregistration for classes offered. General orientation available; some programs have additional orientations. **Activities:** Student government, student newspaper, ethnic student association, marketing club, Phi Beta Lambda (service organization), criminal justice club, early childhood education club, Phi Theta Kappa, nursing club, medical assisting club, Sigma Psi, animal care club, biotechnology, college transfer student club.

Student services. Career counseling, student employment services, financial aid counseling, health services, on-campus daycare, personal counseling, placement for graduates, veterans' counselor. **Physically disabled:** Services for visually, speech, hearing impaired. **Transfer:** Pre-admission transcript evaluation for new students. Transfer adviser, college fairs on campus for students transferring to 4-year colleges.

Contact. E-mail: accadmissions@alamancecc.edu
Phone: (336) 506-4270 Fax: (336) 506-4264
Elizabeth Brehler, Director of Enrollment Management, Alamance Community College, Box 8000, Graham, NC 27253

Asheville-Buncombe Technical Community College
Asheville, North Carolina   CB member
www.abtech.edu   CB code: 5033

‣ Public 2-year community and technical college
‣ Commuter campus in small city

General. Founded in 1959. Regionally accredited. Certain credit courses offered at the Enka and Madison Sites. **Enrollment:** 6,001 degree-seeking undergraduates; 2,055 non-degree-seeking students. **Degrees:** 728 associate awarded. **Location:** 115 miles from Charlotte. **Calendar:** Semester, limited summer session. **Full-time faculty:** 175 total; 6% have terminal degrees, 1% minority. **Part-time faculty:** 514 total; 4% have terminal degrees, 8% minority.

Student profile. Among degree-seeking undergraduates, 638 enrolled as first-time, first-year students.

Part-time:	58%	Women:	58%
Out-of-state:	2%	25 or older:	47%

Basis for selection. Open admission, but selective for some programs. Computerized Placement Test (CPT) administered by college. SAT and/or ACT scores may be used in lieu of CPT for English and math placement. For allied health programs, tests used to earn admission through point system. Provisional or unconditional admission to individual programs will be determined by scores on the test requirements. Placement interview required of all entering students; interview required for all medical programs.

High school preparation. 8 units recommended. Recommended units include English 4, mathematics 2 and science 2. Algebra I and algebra II or geometry for engineering; algebra I, chemistry and biology for nursing, medical laboratory and dental programs; algebra I for radiologic technology; biology and 1 mathematics for practical nursing.

2011-2012 Annual costs. Tuition/fees: $2,068; $7,828 out-of-state. Per-credit charge: $67 in-state; $259 out-of-state. Books/supplies: $1,000. Personal expenses: $7,367.

Financial aid. Need-based: Work-study available nights, weekends and for part-time students. **Non-need-based:** Scholarships awarded for academics, leadership.

Application procedures. Admission: No deadline. No application fee. **Financial aid:** Priority date 3/15, closing date 3/31. FAFSA required. Applicants notified on a rolling basis starting 5/1; must reply within 2 week(s) of notification.

Academics. Special study options: Cooperative education, cross-registration, distance learning, double major, dual enrollment of high school students, independent study, internships, liberal arts/career combination. License preparation in dental hygiene, nursing. **Credit/placement by examination:** AP, CLEP, institutional tests. **Support services:** GED preparation and test center, learning center, pre-admission summer program, reduced course load, remedial instruction, tutoring.

Majors. Business: Accounting, administrative services, business admin, management information systems, office technology, office/clerical, operations, sales/distribution. **Computer sciences:** Applications programming. **Health services:** Clinical lab technology, dental hygiene, EMT paramedic,

medical radiologic technology/radiation therapy, nursing (RN). **Human services:** Social work. **Liberal arts:** Arts/sciences. **Protective services:** Police science. **Work/family studies:** Child care management, institutional food production.

Most popular majors. Business/marketing 13%, computer/information sciences 9%, engineering/engineering technologies 14%, health sciences 29%, liberal arts 9%, trade and industry 13%.

Computing on campus. 300 workstations in library, computer center.

Student life. Activities: Drama, literary magazine, student government, student newspaper.

Student services. Career counseling, student employment services, on-campus daycare, personal counseling, placement for graduates, veterans' counselor. **Physically disabled:** Services for visually, speech, hearing impaired. **Transfer:** Transfer adviser, college fairs on campus for students transferring to 4-year colleges.

Contact. E-mail: admissions@abtech.edu
Phone: (828) 254-1921 ext. 7523 Fax: (828) 251-6718
Scott Douglas, Director, Enrollment Management, Asheville-Buncombe Technical Community College, 340 Victoria Road, Asheville, NC 28801-4897

Beaufort County Community College
Washington, North Carolina
www.beaufortccc.edu
CB code: 7307

- Public 2-year community college
- Commuter campus in small town

General. Founded in 1967. Regionally accredited. **Enrollment:** 1,074 full-time, degree-seeking students. **Degrees:** 163 associate awarded. **Location:** 23 miles from Greenville. **Calendar:** Semester, limited summer session. **Full-time faculty:** 61 total. **Part-time faculty:** 147 total. **Special facilities:** ECU/Wachovia Partnership East hub site.

Transfer out. Colleges most students transferred to 2011: East Carolina University.

Basis for selection. Open admission, but selective for some programs. Special admission requirements for allied health programs and basic law enforcement training. **Adult students:** SAT/ACT scores may be substituted for College Placement Testing (Accuplacer). **Home schooled:** Must provide proof that the home school is registered with the appropriate state agencies.

High school preparation. One unit chemistry required for nursing and medical technology applicants.

2011-2012 Annual costs. Tuition/fees: $2,059; $7,819 out-of-state. Per-credit charge: $67 in-state; $259 out-of-state. Books/supplies: $944. Personal expenses: $2,247.

Financial aid. Need-based: Need-based aid available for part-time students. Work-study available nights, weekends and for part-time students. **Non-need-based:** Scholarships awarded for academics.

Application procedures. Admission: No deadline. No application fee. **Financial aid:** Closing date 7/1. FAFSA, institutional form required. Applicants notified on a rolling basis starting 5/1; must reply within 2 week(s) of notification.

Academics. Special study options: Cooperative education, distance learning, dual enrollment of high school students, ESL, internships, liberal arts/career combination. Bachelor's degree programs available on campus. License preparation in nursing. **Credit/placement by examination:** AP, CLEP, institutional tests. **Support services:** GED preparation and test center, learning center, remedial instruction, study skills assistance, tutoring, writing center.

Majors. Business: Accounting, administrative services, business admin. **Computer sciences:** Applications programming, information systems, networking, programming, vendor certification. **Education:** General, early childhood. **General:** Mechanization. **Health services:** Clinical lab technology, medical secretary, nursing (RN), office admin. **Liberal arts:** Arts/sciences. **Protective services:** Criminal justice. **Work/family studies:** Child care management, child development.

Computing on campus. Commuter students can connect to campus network. Online library, wireless network available.

Student life. Freshman orientation: Available. Preregistration for classes offered. **Activities:** Literary magazine, student government.

Student services. Career counseling, services for economically disadvantaged, student employment services, financial aid counseling, personal counseling, placement for graduates, veterans' counselor. **Transfer:** Pre-admission transcript evaluation for new students. Transfer adviser, college fairs on campus for students transferring to 4-year colleges.

Contact. E-mail: garyb@beaufortccc.edu
Phone: (252) 940-6237 Fax: (252) 940-6393
Gary Burbage, Director of Admissions and Recruitment, Beaufort County Community College, Box 1069, Washington, NC 27889

Bladen Community College
Dublin, North Carolina
www.bladencc.edu
CB code: 3082

- Public 2-year community college
- Commuter campus in rural community

General. Founded in 1967. Regionally accredited. **Enrollment:** 1,801 degree-seeking undergraduates. **Degrees:** 136 associate awarded. **Location:** 35 miles from Fayetteville. **Calendar:** Semester, limited summer session. **Full-time faculty:** 116 total; 3% have terminal degrees, 10% minority. **Part-time faculty:** 42 total; 10% have terminal degrees, 38% minority. **Class size:** 82% < 20, 18% 20-39.

Transfer out. Colleges most students transferred to 2011: University of North Carolina-Wilmington, University of North Carolina-Pembroke, Fayetteville State University, East Carolina University, North Carolina State University.

Basis for selection. Open admission, but selective for some programs. Practical nursing program requires submission of appropriate test results and completion of high school biology and algebra courses with grade of C or better. ADN program requires biology and algebra, plus general chemistry. Biology and chemistry must be within last 5 years for ADN.

High school preparation. 26 units recommended. Recommended units include English 4, mathematics 3, social studies 1, history 2, science 3 (laboratory 1), foreign language 2, computer science 1 and academic electives 10.

2011-2012 Annual costs. Tuition/fees: $2,015; $7,775 out-of-state. Per-credit charge: $67 in-state; $259 out-of-state. Books/supplies: $800. Personal expenses: $725.

Financial aid. Need-based: Need-based aid available for part-time students. Work-study available nights, weekends and for part-time students.

Application procedures. Admission: Priority date 8/15; no deadline. No application fee. Admission notification on a rolling basis beginning on or about 6/15. **Financial aid:** Priority date 6/1; no closing date. FAFSA required. Applicants notified on a rolling basis starting 8/1; must reply within 2 week(s) of notification.

Academics. Special study options: Cooperative education, distance learning, double major, dual enrollment of high school students, ESL, independent study, internships, liberal arts/career combination, weekend college. Bachelor's degree programs available on campus. **Credit/placement by examination:** AP, CLEP, institutional tests. 10 credit hours maximum toward associate degree. **Support services:** GED preparation and test center, learning center, reduced course load, remedial instruction, study skills assistance, tutoring, writing center.

Majors. Biology: Biotechnology. **Business:** Business admin, office technology, office/clerical. **Computer sciences:** General, applications programming, programming. **Education:** General. **General:** Agribusiness operations, business. **Health services:** Nursing (RN). **Liberal arts:** Arts/sciences. **Protective services:** Law enforcement admin. **Work/family studies:** Child care service.

Computing on campus. 100 workstations in library, computer center, student center. Online course registration, helpline, wireless network available.

Student life. Freshman orientation: Mandatory. Preregistration for classes offered. **Activities:** Drama, literary magazine, student government, student newspaper.

Athletics. Team name: Eagles.

Student services. Adult student services, alcohol/substance abuse counseling, career counseling, services for economically disadvantaged, student employment services, financial aid counseling, minority student services, personal counseling, placement for graduates, veterans' counselor. **Physically**

disabled: Services for visually, speech, hearing impaired. **Transfer:** Pre-admission transcript evaluation for new students. Transfer center, transfer adviser, college fairs on campus for students transferring to 4-year colleges.

Contact. E-mail: ywilloughby@bladencc.edu
Phone: (910) 879-5593 Fax: (910) 879-5564
Barry Priest, Dean of Enrollment Management, Bladen Community College, Post Office Box 266, Dublin, NC 28332-0266

Blue Ridge Community College
Flat Rock, North Carolina
www.blueridge.edu　　　　　　　**CB code: 5644**

- Public 2-year community and technical college
- Commuter campus in large town

General. Founded in 1969. Regionally accredited. **Enrollment:** 2,097 degree-seeking undergraduates. **Degrees:** 201 associate awarded. **Location:** 25 miles from Asheville. **Calendar:** Semester, limited summer session. **Full-time faculty:** 72 total. **Part-time faculty:** 246 total. **Class size:** 81% < 20, 19% 20-39, less than 1% 40-49. **Special facilities:** CAVE - virtual reality training center.

Student profile.

Out-of-state:	2%	25 or older:	29%

Basis for selection. Open admission, but selective for some programs. Mathematics and science requirements for allied health programs in surgical technology, pharmacy technology, nursing.

High school preparation. 3 units of science, one of which must be lab, required for allied health programs only.

2011-2012 Annual costs. Tuition/fees: $2,077; $7,837 out-of-state. Per-credit charge: $67 in-state; $259 out-of-state. Books/supplies: $1,200.

Financial aid. Need-based: Need-based aid available for part-time students. Work-study available nights, weekends and for part-time students. **Non-need-based:** Scholarships awarded for academics, athletics, leadership, minority status, state residency.

Application procedures. Admission: No deadline. No application fee. Admission notification on a rolling basis. **Financial aid:** Priority date 6/30; no closing date. FAFSA, institutional form required. Applicants notified on a rolling basis starting 2/1; must reply within 4 week(s) of notification.

Academics. Special study options: Cooperative education, distance learning, double major, dual enrollment of high school students, ESL, study abroad, teacher certification program. Bachelor's degree programs available on campus. License preparation in nursing, paramedic, physical therapy, real estate. **Credit/placement by examination:** AP, CLEP, institutional tests. Maximum of 50% of credit hours by examination may be counted toward degree. **Support services:** GED preparation and test center, learning center, reduced course load, remedial instruction, study skills assistance, tutoring.

Majors. Business: General, administrative services, sales/distribution, tourism promotion. **Computer sciences:** Information systems, programming. **Conservation:** General. **Engineering:** Electrical. **Foreign languages:** Sign language interpretation. **General:** Horticulture. **Health services:** Nursing (RN), surgical technology. **Liberal arts:** Arts/sciences. **Protective services:** Fire safety technology. **Visual/performing arts:** Game design. **Work/family studies:** Child care management.

Most popular majors. Business/marketing 17%, computer/information sciences 27%, health sciences 12%, liberal arts 23%.

Computing on campus. 200 workstations in library, computer center. Commuter students can connect to campus network. Online course registration, helpline, wireless network available.

Student life. Freshman orientation: Mandatory. Preregistration for classes offered. **Activities:** Drama, literary magazine, student government, Circle-K, Rotaract, Phi Theta Kappa, National Vocational-Technical Honor Society.

Athletics. NJCAA. **Intercollegiate:** Bowling M, volleyball W. **Team name:** Bears.

Student services. Adult student services, career counseling, student employment services, financial aid counseling, on-campus daycare, personal counseling, placement for graduates, veterans' counselor. **Physically disabled:** Services for visually, speech, hearing impaired. **Transfer:** Pre-admission transcript evaluation for new students. Transfer adviser, college fairs on campus for students transferring to 4-year colleges.

Contact. E-mail: kirstenb@blueridge.edu
Phone: (828) 694-1800 Fax: (828) 694-1693
Marcia Stoneman, Dean for Student Services, Blue Ridge Community College, 180 West Campus Drive, Flat Rock, NC 28731-9624

Brunswick Community College
Supply, North Carolina
www.brunswickcc.edu　　　　　　　**CB code: 7314**

- Public 2-year community college
- Commuter campus in small town

General. Founded in 1979. Regionally accredited. **Enrollment:** 1,238 degree-seeking undergraduates; 312 non-degree-seeking students. **Degrees:** 68 associate awarded. **Location:** 25 miles from Wilmington, 30 miles from Myrtle Beach, South Carolina. **Calendar:** Semester, limited summer session. **Full-time faculty:** 42 total; 24% have terminal degrees, 7% minority, 64% women. **Part-time faculty:** 113 total; 8% have terminal degrees, 8% minority, 62% women. **Class size:** 74% < 20, 26% 20-39. **Special facilities:** Nature walk, fitness and aquatics center.

Student profile. Among degree-seeking undergraduates, 73% enrolled in a transfer program, 27% enrolled in a vocational program, 279 enrolled as first-time, first-year students, 610 transferred in from other institutions.

Part-time:	43%	Hispanic American:	2%
Out-of-state:	3%	Native American:	1%
Women:	62%	25 or older:	45%
African American:	14%		

Transfer out. Colleges most students transferred to 2011: University of North Carolina at Wilmington.

Basis for selection. Open admission, but selective for some programs. Phlebotomy, Basic Law Enforcement Technology, Practical Nursing, Associate Degree Nursing, and Health Information Technology program applicants must have completed specific course work before they are considered. Limited slots. May also enter based on test scores. No interview necessary. **Adult students:** SAT/ACT scores not required. **Home schooled:** Transcript of courses and grades required. **Learning Disabled:** Requests for any accommodations should be made at least 2 weeks prior to beginning of applicant's first semester.

2011-2012 Annual costs. Tuition/fees: $2,080; $7,840 out-of-state. Per-credit charge: $67 in-state; $259 out-of-state. Books/supplies: $1,500. Personal expenses: $3,307.

2011-2012 Financial aid. Need-based: 96% of total undergraduate aid awarded as scholarships/grants, 4% as loans/jobs. Need-based aid available for part-time students. Work-study available nights, weekends and for part-time students. **Non-need-based:** Scholarships awarded for academics, state residency. **Additional information:** Attendance required at financial aid orientation session for those receiving federal student aid.

Application procedures. Admission: No deadline. No application fee. Admission notification on a rolling basis. **Financial aid:** Priority date 6/1, closing date 6/15. FAFSA, institutional form required. Applicants notified on a rolling basis starting 3/1; must reply by 6/30 or within 2 week(s) of notification.

Academics. Special study options: Cooperative education, distance learning, double major, dual enrollment of high school students, ESL, internships. License preparation in nursing, paramedic, real estate. **Credit/placement by examination:** AP, CLEP, SAT, institutional tests. No limits on credit by examination hours that may be applied toward an associate degree. **Support services:** GED preparation and test center, learning center, reduced course load, remedial instruction, study skills assistance, tutoring.

Majors. Business: Administrative services, business admin, small business admin. **Computer sciences:** Information systems, programming. **Education:** Early childhood. **General:** Aquaculture, horticultural science, turf management. **Health services:** Medical records technology, nursing (RN). **Liberal arts:** Arts/sciences.

Most popular majors. Health sciences 21%, liberal arts 61%.

Computing on campus. 146 workstations in library, computer center. Helpline, wireless network available.

Student life. Freshman orientation: Available. Preregistration for classes offered. **Policies:** All facilities are nonsmoking. Smoking allowed in designated outdoor areas only. **Activities:** Jazz band, choral groups, dance, drama, radio station, student government, student newspaper, National Technical Honor Society, Phi Theta Kappa, science club, journalism club, drama club, art club.

Athletics. NJCAA. **Intercollegiate:** Baseball M, basketball, golf, volleyball W. **Team name:** Dolphins.

Student services. Alcohol/substance abuse counseling, career counseling, student employment services, financial aid counseling, minority student services, on-campus daycare, personal counseling, placement for graduates, veterans' counselor. **Physically disabled:** Services for visually, speech, hearing impaired. **Transfer:** Pre-admission transcript evaluation for new students. Transfer adviser, college fairs on campus for students transferring to 4-year colleges.

Contact. E-mail: Coxc@brunswickcc.edu
Phone: (910) 755-7324 Toll-free number: (800) 754-1050 ext. 324
Fax: (910) 754-9609
Christen Cox, Admissions Counselor, Brunswick Community College, PO Box 30, Supply, NC 28462

Caldwell Community College and Technical Institute
Hudson, North Carolina
www.cccti.edu   CB code: 5146

- Public 2-year community and technical college
- Commuter campus in small town

General. Founded in 1964. Regionally accredited. **Enrollment:** 3,973 degree-seeking undergraduates; 960 non-degree-seeking students. **Degrees:** 588 associate awarded. **Location:** 90 miles from Charlotte. **Calendar:** Semester, limited summer session. **Full-time faculty:** 130 total. **Part-time faculty:** 290 total. **Class size:** 68% < 20, 31% 20-39, 1% 40-49, less than 1% 50-99, less than 1% >100. **Special facilities:** Civic center.

Student profile. Among degree-seeking undergraduates, 27% enrolled in a transfer program, 83% enrolled in a vocational program, 2% already have a bachelor's degree or higher, 799 enrolled as first-time, first-year students, 454 transferred in from other institutions.

Part-time:	55%	Women:	58%
Out-of-state:	2%	25 or older:	43%

Basis for selection. Open admission, but selective for some programs. Limited number of applicants are admitted to health science programs. These students are accepted based on competitive admissions.

2011-2012 Annual costs. Tuition/fees: $2,071; $7,831 out-of-state. Per-credit charge: $67 in-state; $259 out-of-state. Books/supplies: $1,100. Personal expenses: $1,350.

Financial aid. All financial aid based on need. Need-based aid available for part-time students. Work-study available nights, weekends and for part-time students.

Application procedures. Admission: No deadline. No application fee. Admission notification on a rolling basis. **Financial aid:** Closing date 5/1. FAFSA required. Applicants notified on a rolling basis starting 6/30.

Academics. Special study options: Cooperative education, distance learning, dual enrollment of high school students, independent study. Bachelor's degree programs available on campus. License preparation in aviation, nursing, paramedic, physical therapy, radiology. **Credit/placement by examination:** AP, CLEP, institutional tests. 16 credit hours maximum toward associate degree. **Support services:** GED preparation and test center, learning center, reduced course load, remedial instruction, study skills assistance, tutoring, writing center.

Majors. Business: Accounting, administrative services, business admin. **Computer sciences:** Applications programming, data processing, programming. **Education:** Early childhood. **Health services:** Cardiovascular technology, medical radiologic technology/radiation therapy, medical secretary, nuclear medical technology, nursing (RN), physical therapy assistant, sonography, speech-language pathology assistant. **Liberal arts:** Arts/sciences. **Math:** General. **Visual/performing arts:** Art, music.

Most popular majors. Business/marketing 23%, computer/information sciences 12%, health sciences 38%, liberal arts 16%.

Computing on campus. 750 workstations in library, computer center. Commuter students can connect to campus network. Online course registration, helpline, wireless network available.

Student life. Freshman orientation: Mandatory. Preregistration for classes offered. Day/evening sessions held during the early registration time over a one week period each semester. **Activities:** Choral groups, drama, literary magazine, student government, student newspaper, TV station, Ebony

Kinship, Phi Theta Kappa, Alpha Omega (non-denominational religious organization), special interest clubs.

Athletics. NJCAA. **Intercollegiate:** Basketball. **Team name:** Cobras.

Student services. Adult student services, career counseling, services for economically disadvantaged, student employment services, financial aid counseling, minority student services, personal counseling, placement for graduates, veterans' counselor. **Physically disabled:** Services for visually, speech, hearing impaired. **Transfer:** Pre-admission transcript evaluation for new students. Transfer center, transfer adviser, college fairs on campus for students transferring to 4-year colleges.

Contact. E-mail: CCCTIAdmissions@cccti.edu
Phone: (828) 726-2200 Fax: (828) 726-2709
Dena Holman, Director, Enrollment Management Services, Caldwell Community College and Technical Institute, 2855 Hickory Boulevard, Hudson, NC 28638-2672

Cape Fear Community College
Wilmington, North Carolina
www.cfcc.edu   CB code: 5094

- Public 2-year community college
- Commuter campus in small city

General. Founded in 1959. Regionally accredited. Campuses at Burgaw and North Campus. **Enrollment:** 8,560 degree-seeking undergraduates; 756 non-degree-seeking students. **Degrees:** 1,002 associate awarded. **Location:** 125 miles from Raleigh. **Calendar:** Semester, limited summer session. **Full-time faculty:** 284 total. **Part-time faculty:** 417 total.

Student profile. Among degree-seeking undergraduates, 40% enrolled in a transfer program, 60% enrolled in a vocational program, 1,414 enrolled as first-time, first-year students, 1,603 transferred in from other institutions.

Part-time:	51%	Asian American:	1%
Out-of-state:	5%	Hispanic American:	4%
Women:	55%	Native American:	1%
African American:	14%	25 or older:	31%

Transfer out. Colleges most students transferred to 2011: University of North Carolina at Wilmington.

Basis for selection. Open admission, but selective for some programs. Special requirements for health science programs: Psychological Services Bureau Examination and interview required. **Home schooled:** A copy of approval from North Carolina Department of Non-Public Instruction required or similar documents from states other than North Carolina. **Learning Disabled:** Students must register with Disability Services.

2011-2012 Annual costs. Tuition/fees: $2,092; $7,852 out-of-state. Per-credit charge: $67 in-state; $259 out-of-state. Books/supplies: $1,300. Personal expenses: $4,300.

2011-2012 Financial aid. Need-based: 54% of total undergraduate aid awarded as scholarships/grants, 46% as loans/jobs. Need-based aid available for part-time students. Work-study available nights, weekends and for part-time students. **Non-need-based:** Scholarships awarded for academics, athletics, job skills, leadership, music/drama, religious affiliation.

Application procedures. Admission: No deadline. No application fee. Admission notification on a rolling basis. **Financial aid:** Priority date 6/1; no closing date. FAFSA required. Applicants notified on a rolling basis starting 4/1; must reply within 2 week(s) of notification.

Academics. Special study options: Cooperative education, distance learning, dual enrollment of high school students, ESL, independent study, internships. Bachelor's degree programs available on campus. License preparation in dental hygiene, nursing, occupational therapy, paramedic, radiology, real estate. **Credit/placement by examination:** AP, CLEP, IB, institutional tests. **Support services:** GED preparation and test center, learning center, remedial instruction, study skills assistance, tutoring.

Majors. Architecture: Interior, landscape, urban/community planning. **Business:** Accounting technology, administrative services, business admin, executive assistant, hospitality admin, hotel/motel admin, restaurant/food services. **Computer sciences:** Information technology. **Conservation:** General. **Education:** General. **General:** Landscaping. **Health services:** Dental hygiene, medical radiologic technology/radiation therapy, nursing (RN), occupational therapy assistant, pharmacy assistant, sonography. **Liberal arts:** Arts/sciences. **Physical sciences:** Oceanography. **Protective services:** Police science. **Visual/performing arts:** Cinematography, interior design. **Work/family studies:** Child care management, institutional food production.

Most popular majors. Health sciences 12%, liberal arts 67%.

Computing on campus. 90 workstations in library, computer center. Online course registration, helpline, wireless network available.

Student life. Freshman orientation: Available. Preregistration for classes offered. Half-day program held in July and December. **Policies:** CFCC is a smoke-free campus. **Activities:** Student government, student newspaper, Phi Theta Kappa Honor Society.

Athletics. NJCAA. **Intercollegiate:** Basketball M, golf, volleyball W. **Intramural:** Cheerleading, soccer. **Team name:** Sea Devils.

Student services. Alcohol/substance abuse counseling, career counseling, student employment services, financial aid counseling, on-campus daycare, personal counseling, placement for graduates, veterans' counselor. **Physically disabled:** Services for visually, speech, hearing impaired. **Transfer:** Pre-admission transcript evaluation for new students. Transfer adviser, college fairs on campus for students transferring to 4-year colleges.

Contact. E-mail: admissions@cfcc.edu
Phone: (910) 362-7557 Fax: (910) 362-7080
Linda Kasyan, Director of Enrollment Management, Cape Fear Community College, 411 North Front Street, Wilmington, NC 28401-3910

Carolinas College of Health Sciences
Charlotte, North Carolina
www.carolinascollege.edu   **CB code: 6211**

♦ Public 2-year health science and junior college
♦ Commuter campus in very large city

General. Regionally accredited. The institution is supported by Carolinas Medical Center and specializes in health careers such as nursing, radiologic technology, radiation therapy, surgical technology and medical laboratory sciences. **Enrollment:** 402 degree-seeking undergraduates; 22 non-degree-seeking students. **Degrees:** 126 associate awarded. **Calendar:** Semester, limited summer session. **Full-time faculty:** 23 total; 4% minority, 87% women. **Part-time faculty:** 20 total; 25% minority, 75% women. **Class size:** 40% < 20, 57% 20-39, 3% 40-49. **Special facilities:** Simuation center.

Student profile. Among degree-seeking undergraduates, 100% enrolled in a vocational program, 34% already have a bachelor's degree or higher, 8 enrolled as first-time, first-year students, 284 transferred in from other institutions.

Part-time:	85%	Asian American:	3%
Women:	86%	Hispanic American:	4%
African American:	12%		

Transfer out. Colleges most students transferred to 2011: Queens University of Charlotte, University of North Carolina at Charlotte, Winston-Salem State University, Central Piedmont Community College, Mercy School of Nursing.

Basis for selection. Open admission, but selective for some programs. Selection based on SAT/ACT test scores, high school GPA, college GPA. A number ranking system is used. Only students with permanent resident status will be considered for enrollment.

High school preparation. College-preparatory program recommended. 15 units required. Required units include English 4, mathematics 1, social studies 2, history 2, science 2 (laboratory 2) and foreign language 2. Algebra, biology, chemistry required.

2011-2012 Annual costs. Tuition/fees: $8,615; $8,615 out-of-state. Per-credit charge: $275. Books/supplies: $1,072.

2010-2011 Financial aid. Need-based: 10% of total undergraduate aid awarded as scholarships/grants, 90% as loans/jobs. Need-based aid available for part-time students. Work-study available nights, weekends and for part-time students. **Non-need-based:** Scholarships awarded for academics.

Application procedures. Admission: Closing date 12/12 (receipt date). $50 fee. Admission notification on a rolling basis beginning on or about 3/15. Must reply by May 1 or within 4 week(s) if notified thereafter. Application deadlines vary by program. **Financial aid:** Priority date 5/1; no closing date. FAFSA, institutional form required. Applicants notified on a rolling basis starting 5/1.

Academics. Post-bachelor's certificate in Medical Technology available. **Special study options:** Distance learning, independent study, liberal arts/career combination. License preparation in nursing, radiology. **Credit/placement by examination:** AP, CLEP, IB, institutional tests. 25 credit hours

maximum toward associate degree. **Support services:** Learning center, study skills assistance, tutoring.

Majors. Health services: Medical radiologic technology/radiation therapy, nursing (RN).

Computing on campus. 30 workstations in computer center. Online course registration, online library, wireless network available.

Student life. Freshman orientation: Mandatory. Preregistration for classes offered. **Housing:** Apartments available. **Activities:** Student government.

Student services. Alcohol/substance abuse counseling, chaplain/spiritual director, career counseling, student employment services, financial aid counseling, health services, personal counseling, placement for graduates, veterans' counselor. **Transfer:** Pre-admission transcript evaluation for new students. College fairs on campus for students transferring to 4-year colleges.

Contact. E-mail: cchsinformation@carolinas.org
Phone: (704) 355-5583 Fax: (704) 355-9336
Rhoda Rillorta, Admissions Coordinator, Carolinas College of Health Sciences, PO Box 32861, Charlotte, NC 28232

Carteret Community College
Morehead City, North Carolina
www.carteret.edu   **CB code: 5092**

♦ Public 2-year community and technical college
♦ Commuter campus in small town

General. Founded in 1963. Regionally accredited. Aquaculture technology and marine technical trades programs. **Enrollment:** 1,617 degree-seeking undergraduates. **Degrees:** 198 associate awarded. **Location:** 150 miles from Raleigh, 87 miles from Wilmington. **Calendar:** Semester, limited summer session. **Full-time faculty:** 95 total; 43% have terminal degrees, 5% minority, 48% women. **Part-time faculty:** 84 total; 36% have terminal degrees, 12% minority, 67% women. **Special facilities:** Carteret County historical research center, center for marine science and technology, North Carolina marine technical education center. **Partnerships:** Formal partnerships with the North Carolina State Department of Public Instruction and the North Carolina Community College System.

Student profile.

Out-of-state:	2%	25 or older:	48%

Transfer out. Colleges most students transferred to 2011: University of North Carolina at Wilmington, East Carolina University, North Carolina State University, Pitt Community College, Cape Fear Community College.

Basis for selection. Open admission, but selective for some programs. General college acceptance to all applicants with complete admissions files. Specific admissions programs have additional requirements. **Home schooled:** Transcript of courses and grades required. **Learning Disabled:** Students must present proper documentation and follow the procedures to request reasonable accommodations.

High school preparation. College-preparatory program recommended. Extensive science and mathematics recommended for allied health programs, particularly respiratory therapy, radiography, and nursing.

2011-2012 Annual costs. Tuition/fees: $2,043; $7,803 out-of-state. Per-credit charge: $67 in-state; $259 out-of-state. Books/supplies: $950. Personal expenses: $1,081.

Financial aid. Need-based: Need-based aid available for part-time students. Work-study available nights, weekends and for part-time students. **Non-need-based:** Scholarships awarded for academics, leadership, minority status, state residency. **Additional information:** Institutional student loan program administered by college. Student may charge up to $600 for books, supplies and tuition per quarter. Repayment due by 11th week of semester.

Application procedures. Admission: No deadline. No application fee. Admission notification on a rolling basis. **Financial aid:** No deadline. FAFSA, institutional form required. Applicants notified on a rolling basis starting 7/1; must reply within 2 week(s) of notification.

Academics. Special study options: Cooperative education, cross-registration, distance learning, double major, dual enrollment of high school students, ESL, independent study, internships, liberal arts/career combination, teacher certification program. License preparation in nursing, paramedic, radiology, real estate. **Credit/placement by examination:** AP, CLEP, institutional tests. **Support services:** GED preparation and test center, learning

center, pre-admission summer program, reduced course load, remedial instruction, study skills assistance, tutoring, writing center.

Majors. Biology: Biotechnology. **Business:** General, administrative services, hotel/motel admin, office/clerical. **Communications:** Photojournalism. **Communications technology:** Photo/film/video. **Computer sciences:** General, information technology, LAN/WAN management, web page design, webmaster, word processing. **Education:** General, teacher assistance. **General:** Greenhouse operations, horticultural science, horticulture. **Health services:** EMT ambulance attendant, massage therapy, medical radiologic technology/radiation therapy, office admin, predental, premedicine, prenursing, prepharmacy, preveterinary, radiologic technology/medical imaging, recreational therapy, respiratory therapy technology. **Liberal arts:** Arts/sciences. **Math:** General. **Protective services:** Criminal justice, police science. **Psychology:** General. **Visual/performing arts:** General, interior design, photography. **Work/family studies:** Child care management, child care service, child development.

Computing on campus. 225 workstations in library, computer center, student center. Commuter students can connect to campus network. Online course registration, online library, helpline, student web hosting, wireless network available.

Student life. Freshman orientation: Available. Preregistration for classes offered. **Activities:** Drama, literary magazine, student government, student newspaper, Psi Beta (honorary society for psychology majors), Phi Beta Lambda (business organization), Sigma Kappa Delta (honorary society for English majors), Phi Theta Kappa - Beta Delta Pi (honors fraternity).

Student services. Adult student services, alcohol/substance abuse counseling, career counseling, services for economically disadvantaged, student employment services, financial aid counseling, minority student services, personal counseling, placement for graduates, veterans' counselor. **Physically disabled:** Services for visually, speech, hearing impaired. **Transfer:** Pre-admission transcript evaluation for new students. Transfer center, transfer adviser, college fairs on campus for students transferring to 4-year colleges.

Contact. E-mail: admissions@carteret.edu
Phone: (252) 222-6154 Fax: (252) 222-6265
Joseph Croom, Admissions Officer, Carteret Community College, 3505 Arendell Street, Morehead City, NC 28557-2989

Catawba Valley Community College
Hickory, North Carolina
www.cvcc.edu   CB code: 5098

◗ Public 2-year community college
◗ Commuter campus in large town

General. Founded in 1960. Regionally accredited. **Enrollment:** 4,297 degree-seeking undergraduates; 817 non-degree-seeking students. **Degrees:** 592 associate awarded. **ROTC:** Air Force. **Location:** 50 miles from Charlotte. **Calendar:** Semester, limited summer session. **Full-time faculty:** 154 total; 4% minority, 51% women. **Part-time faculty:** 394 total; 6% minority, 54% women. **Class size:** 84% < 20, 16% 20-39, less than 1% 40-49. **Special facilities:** Regional simulated hospital.

Student profile. Among degree-seeking undergraduates, 35% enrolled in a transfer program, 65% enrolled in a vocational program, 2% already have a bachelor's degree or higher, 856 enrolled as first-time, first-year students, 558 transferred in from other institutions.

Part-time:	57%	**Hispanic American:**	5%
Women:	59%	**Native American:**	1%
African American:	9%	**25 or older:**	40%
Asian American:	8%		

Basis for selection. Open admission, but selective for some programs. Special requirements for nursing, emergency medical science, surgical technology, respiratory care, health information technology, dental hygiene, speech-language pathology assistant, advertising and graphic design, electroneurodiagnostic technology, polysomnography, radiography. Interview required for health program applicants, advertising and graphic design applicants, and photography applicants; recommended for all others. **Home schooled:** Transcript of courses and grades, state high school equivalency certificate required.

2011-2012 Annual costs. Tuition/fees: $2,082; $7,842 out-of-state. Per-credit charge: $67 in-state; $259 out-of-state. Books/supplies: $1,150. Personal expenses: $3,280.

2010-2011 Financial aid. Need-based: 460 full-time freshmen applied for aid; 424 were judged to have need; 361 of these received aid. 77% of total undergraduate aid awarded as scholarships/grants, 23% as loans/jobs. Need-based aid available for part-time students. Work-study available nights, weekends and for part-time students. **Non-need-based:** Awarded to 139 full-time undergraduates, including 99 freshmen. Scholarships awarded for academics, athletics, leadership, music/drama.

Application procedures. Admission: No deadline. No application fee. Admission notification on a rolling basis. **Financial aid:** Closing date 3/15. FAFSA required. Applicants notified on a rolling basis starting 5/15.

Academics. Special study options: Cooperative education, distance learning, double major, dual enrollment of high school students, ESL, honors, independent study, student-designed major, teacher certification program, weekend college. License preparation in dental hygiene, nursing, paramedic, real estate. **Credit/placement by examination:** AP, CLEP, IB, institutional tests. Maximum of 65 percent of total credit hours required for degree may be obtained by examination. **Support services:** GED preparation and test center, learning center, reduced course load, remedial instruction, study skills assistance, tutoring, writing center.

Majors. Business: Accounting technology, banking/financial services, business admin, customer service, e-commerce, management information systems, office management, operations, real estate. **Communications technology:** Photo/film/video. **Computer sciences:** Information systems, information technology, LAN/WAN management, programming. **Education:** Early childhood. **Engineering:** Industrial. **General:** Horticultural science, turf management. **Health services:** Dental hygiene, electroencephalograph technology, EMT paramedic, medical radiologic technology/radiation therapy, medical records technology, nursing (RN), office admin, respiratory therapy technology. **Liberal arts:** Arts/sciences. **Protective services:** Criminal justice, fire safety technology, forensics. **Visual/performing arts:** Commercial/advertising art.

Most popular majors. Business/marketing 10%, education 6%, engineering/engineering technologies 6%, health sciences 22%, liberal arts 39%.

Computing on campus. 1,360 workstations in library, computer center. Commuter students can connect to campus network. Online course registration, online library, helpline, repair service, wireless network available.

Student life. Freshman orientation: Available. Preregistration for classes offered. Held a few days prior to the first day of semester. Lasts 1-2 hours. **Activities:** Choral groups, drama, international student organizations, music ensembles, student government, Phi Theta Kappa, association of nursing students, Certifiable club, Rotaract club, Student American Dental Hygiene Association, Students in Free Enterprise, theater arts club, student photographic society club, Seeds of Service, Hmong student association.

Athletics. NJCAA. **Intercollegiate:** Baseball M, basketball, volleyball W. **Team name:** Buccaneers.

Student services. Career counseling, services for economically disadvantaged, student employment services, financial aid counseling, minority student services, personal counseling, placement for graduates, veterans' counselor, women's services. **Physically disabled:** Services for visually, hearing impaired. **Transfer:** Pre-admission transcript evaluation for new students. Transfer adviser, college fairs on campus for students transferring to 4-year colleges.

Contact. E-mail: admissions@cvcc.edu
Phone: (828) 327-7000 Fax: (828) 327-7276
Laurie Wegner, Director of Admissions, Catawba Valley Community College, 2550 Highway 70 SE, Hickory, NC 28602

Central Carolina Community College
Sanford, North Carolina
www.cccc.edu   CB code: 5147

◗ Public 2-year community college
◗ Commuter campus in large town

General. Founded in 1958. Regionally accredited. **Enrollment:** 4,350 degree-seeking undergraduates. **Degrees:** 440 associate awarded. **Location:** 45 miles from Raleigh. **Calendar:** Semester, limited summer session. **Full-time faculty:** 165 total. **Part-time faculty:** 462 total. **Class size:** 78% < 20, 21% 20-39, less than 1% 40-49, less than 1% 50-99.

Transfer out. Colleges most students transferred to 2011: East Carolina University, NC State, University of NC-Greenville, University of NC-Wilmington, Appalachian State University.

Basis for selection. Open admission, but selective for some programs. Special requirements for veterinary technician, dental, nursing education, radio-television broadcasting, laser electro-optic, electronics and instrumentation technology, cosmetology, medical assisting programs. ACT/SAT scores

Two-Year Colleges

may exempt student from placement tests. **Home schooled:** Must be registered with local county Board of Education and NC Non-public Education office; must submit documentation of successful completion of NC Competency Exam, copies of transcript and high school diploma. **Learning Disabled:** Students must sign up with special populations office and request accommodations and services.

High school preparation. Strong background in mathematics, biology, and chemistry required for veterinary technician and nursing education option programs.

2011-2012 Annual costs. Tuition/fees: $2,083; $7,843 out-of-state. Per-credit charge: $67 in-state; $259 out-of-state. Books/supplies: $750.

2010-2011 Financial aid. Need-based: Need-based aid available for part-time students. Work-study available nights, weekends and for part-time students. **Non-need-based:** Scholarships awarded for academics.

Application procedures. Admission: No deadline. No application fee. Admission notification on a rolling basis. **Financial aid:** Priority date 7/7; no closing date. FAFSA, institutional form required. Applicants notified on a rolling basis starting 7/1; must reply within 2 week(s) of notification.

Academics. Special study options: Distance learning, dual enrollment of high school students, honors, independent study, internships, liberal arts/career combination. License preparation in dental hygiene, nursing. **Credit/placement by examination:** AP, CLEP, institutional tests. Placement interview required. **Support services:** GED preparation, learning center, reduced course load, remedial instruction, study skills assistance, tutoring, writing center.

Majors. Business: Accounting, administrative services, business admin, office/clerical. **Computer sciences:** Applications programming, information systems, networking, programming. **Education:** General, early childhood. **Engineering:** Civil, computer. **General:** Sustainable agriculture. **Health services:** Licensed practical nurse, medical assistant, medical secretary, nursing (RN), veterinary technology/assistant. **Liberal arts:** Arts/sciences. **Protective services:** Criminal justice. **Work/family studies:** Child care management.

Computing on campus. Online library, helpline, wireless network available.

Student life. Freshman orientation: Mandatory. Preregistration for classes offered. **Activities:** Radio station, student government, TV station, Student Nurses Association, Student Ambassador Program, Veterinary Medical Technician Student Organization.

Athletics. NJCAA. **Intercollegiate:** Basketball, golf, softball, volleyball. **Intramural:** Basketball M, bowling, golf, softball, tennis M, volleyball. **Team name:** Cougars.

Student services. Career counseling, student employment services, financial aid counseling, personal counseling, placement for graduates, veterans' counselor. **Physically disabled:** Services for visually, speech, hearing impaired. **Transfer:** Transfer adviser for students transferring to 4-year colleges.

Contact. E-mail: khoyle@cccc.edu
Phone: (919) 775-5401 Toll-free number: (800) 682-8353
Fax: (919) 718-7379
Jamee Stiffler, Director of Admissions, Central Carolina Community College, 1105 Kelly Drive, Sanford, NC 27330

Central Piedmont Community College

Charlotte, North Carolina   **CB member**
www.cpcc.edu   **CB code: 5102**

▶ Public 2-year community college
▶ Commuter campus in very large city

General. Founded in 1963. Regionally accredited. **Enrollment:** 17,413 degree-seeking undergraduates; 2,464 non-degree-seeking students. **Degrees:** 1,511 associate awarded. **Location:** 247 miles from Atlanta. **Calendar:** Semester, extensive summer session. **Full-time faculty:** 403 total. **Part-time faculty:** 1,420 total.

Student profile. Among degree-seeking undergraduates, 2,379 enrolled as first-time, first-year students.

Part-time:	60%	**Women:**	57%
Out-of-state:	2%	**25 or older:**	45%

Basis for selection. Open admission, but selective for some programs. Placement test scores used for admission to some programs with specific requirements.

High school preparation. Recommended units include English 4, mathematics 3, social studies 3 and science 3.

2011-2012 Annual costs. Tuition/fees: $2,090; $7,850 out-of-state. Per-credit charge: $67 in-state; $259 out-of-state. Books/supplies: $1,195. Personal expenses: $3,066.

Financial aid. Need-based: Need-based aid available for part-time students. Work-study available nights, weekends and for part-time students. **Non-need-based:** Scholarships awarded for academics, minority status.

Application procedures. Admission: No deadline. No application fee. Admission notification on a rolling basis. **Financial aid:** Priority date 4/1, closing date 6/1. FAFSA required. Applicants notified on a rolling basis.

Academics. Special study options: Cooperative education, cross-registration, distance learning, double major, dual enrollment of high school students, ESL, honors, independent study, internships, study abroad, weekend college. **Credit/placement by examination:** AP, CLEP, institutional tests. **Support services:** GED preparation and test center, learning center, reduced course load, remedial instruction, study skills assistance, tutoring, writing center.

Majors. Business: Accounting technology, administrative services, business admin, hospitality admin, international, management information systems, real estate, retailing, tourism/travel. **Communications technology:** Graphic/printing. **Computer sciences:** Database management, information technology, LAN/WAN management, programming, webmaster. **Education:** Early childhood. **Foreign languages:** Sign language interpretation. **General:** Horticulture, turf management. **Health services:** Cardiovascular technology, clinical lab assistant, cytotechnology, dental hygiene, medical assistant, medical records technology, mental health services, nursing (RN), physical therapy assistant, respiratory therapy technology, substance abuse counseling. **Liberal arts:** Arts/sciences. **Parks/recreation:** Facilities management. **Protective services:** Corrections, fire safety technology. **Visual/performing arts:** Commercial/advertising art, interior design. **Work/family studies:** Child care management.

Most popular majors. Business/marketing 8%, health sciences 18%, liberal arts 49%.

Computing on campus. 2,591 workstations in library, computer center, student center. Commuter students can connect to campus network. Online course registration, helpline, wireless network available.

Student life. Freshman orientation: Available. Preregistration for classes offered. **Activities:** Bands, campus ministries, choral groups, dance, drama, film society, international student organizations, literary magazine, music ensembles, musical theater, opera, radio station, student government, student newspaper, symphony orchestra, TV station, Afro-American Cultural Club, Baptist Student Union, Chess Club, Phi Theta Kappa.

Athletics. NJCAA. **Intramural:** Soccer.

Student services. Adult student services, chaplain/spiritual director, career counseling, student employment services, financial aid counseling, personal counseling, placement for graduates, veterans' counselor, women's services. **Physically disabled:** Services for visually, speech, hearing impaired. **Transfer:** Re-entry adviser, pre-admission transcript evaluation for new students. Transfer center, transfer adviser, college fairs on campus for students transferring to 4-year colleges.

Contact. Phone: (704) 330-2722 Fax: (704) 330-6007
Greg Stanley, Associate Dean of Admissions & Registration, Central Piedmont Community College, Box 35009, Charlotte, NC 28235-5009

Cleveland Community College

Shelby, North Carolina   **CB member**
www.clevelandcommunitycollege.edu   **CB code: 5140**

▶ Public 2-year community college
▶ Commuter campus in large town

General. Founded in 1965. Regionally accredited. **Enrollment:** 2,733 degree-seeking undergraduates; 686 non-degree-seeking students. **Degrees:** 218 associate awarded. **Location:** 45 miles from Charlotte. **Calendar:** Semester, limited summer session. **Full-time faculty:** 83 total. **Part-time faculty:** 269 total.

Two-Year Colleges

Student profile. Among degree-seeking undergraduates, 678 enrolled as first-time, first-year students.

Part-time:	34%	Women:	64%
Out-of-state:	1%	25 or older:	44%

Transfer out. **Colleges most students transferred to 2011:** Gardner-Webb University, University of North Carolina-Charlotte, Appalachian State University, Western Carolina University, North Carolina State University.

Basis for selection. Open admission, but selective for some programs. Special requirements for allied health programs. Interview required for nursing, radiography, surgical technology, and phlebotomy programs.

2011-2012 Annual costs. Tuition/fees: $2,087; $7,847 out-of-state. Per-credit charge: $67 in-state; $259 out-of-state. Books/supplies: $1,400. Personal expenses: $400.

2011-2012 Financial aid. **Need-based:** 99% of total undergraduate aid awarded as scholarships/grants, 1% as loans/jobs. Need-based aid available for part-time students. Work-study available nights, weekends and for part-time students.

Application procedures. **Admission:** No deadline. No application fee. Applicants notified immediately except for allied health applicants. **Financial aid:** Priority date 6/28; no closing date. FAFSA required. Applicants notified on a rolling basis starting 5/1.

Academics. **Special study options:** Accelerated study, cooperative education, cross-registration, distance learning, double major, dual enrollment of high school students, ESL, honors, independent study, internships, liberal arts/career combination. Bachelor's degree programs available on campus. License preparation in nursing, paramedic, real estate. **Credit/placement by examination:** AP, CLEP, IB, institutional tests. Credit determined on individual basis. Students may not receive Credit By Exam for more than 20 percent of the total number of credits required for program. **Support services:** GED preparation and test center, learning center, reduced course load, remedial instruction, study skills assistance, tutoring.

Majors. **Business:** Accounting, banking/financial services, business admin, entrepreneurial studies, marketing, office management, operations. **Communications technology:** Radio/TV. **Computer sciences:** Information systems, information technology, networking, security. **Education:** Early childhood, elementary. **Engineering:** Pre-engineering. **Foreign languages:** Translation. **Health services:** Nursing (RN), office admin, prenursing, radiologic technology/medical imaging. **Liberal arts:** Arts/sciences. **Protective services:** Criminal justice, fire safety technology.

Computing on campus. Online library, wireless network available.

Student life. **Freshman orientation:** Available. Preregistration for classes offered. **Activities:** Drama, student government, student newspaper, TV station, black awareness club, communications club, criminal justice club, radiologic technology club, nursing club, Students in Free Enterprise, Mu Epsilon Delta, Campus Crusade for Christ.

Student services. Adult student services, career counseling, student employment services, financial aid counseling, placement for graduates, veterans' counselor. **Physically disabled:** Services for visually, speech, hearing impaired. **Transfer:** Transfer adviser, college fairs on campus for students transferring to 4-year colleges.

Contact. E-mail: blantonb@clevelandcommunitycollege.edu
Phone: (704) 484-4103 Fax: (704) 484-5305
Emily Arey, Admissions Coordinator, Cleveland Community College, 137 South Post Road, Shelby, NC 28152-6224

Coastal Carolina Community College
Jacksonville, North Carolina
www.coastalcarolina.edu   CB code: 5134

- Public 2-year community college
- Commuter campus in large town

General. Founded in 1964. Regionally accredited. Off-campus classes available at Camp Lejeune Marine Corps Base and New River Marine Corps Air Station. **Enrollment:** 4,121 degree-seeking undergraduates; 607 non-degree-seeking students. **Degrees:** 586 associate awarded. **Location:** 100 miles from Raleigh. **Calendar:** Semester, limited summer session. **Full-time faculty:** 127 total; 13% have terminal degrees, 9% minority, 56% women. **Part-time faculty:** 158 total; 11% have terminal degrees, 10% minority, 63% women. **Class size:** 67% < 20, 33% 20-39.

Student profile. Among degree-seeking undergraduates, 797 enrolled as first-time, first-year students.

Part-time:	50%	Women:	66%
Out-of-state:	31%	25 or older:	44%

Transfer out. **Colleges most students transferred to 2011:** University of North Carolina - Wilmington, East Carolina University, North Carolina State University.

Basis for selection. Open admission, but selective for some programs. Admission to limited enrollment programs based on examination. **Adult students:** SAT/ACT scores not required. **Home schooled:** Transcript of courses and grades required.

High school preparation. 20 units recommended. Recommended units include English 4, mathematics 3, social studies 2, history 1, science 3 (laboratory 1) and academic electives 6. Recommended units may vary by college.

2011-2012 Annual costs. Tuition/fees: $2,025; $7,785 out-of-state. Per-credit charge: $67 in-state; $259 out-of-state. Books/supplies: $1,476. Personal expenses: $1,934.

2010-2011 Financial aid. **Need-based:** 99% of total undergraduate aid awarded as scholarships/grants, 1% as loans/jobs. Need-based aid available for part-time students. Work-study available nights, weekends and for part-time students. **Non-need-based:** Scholarships awarded for academics, state residency.

Application procedures. **Admission:** No deadline. No application fee. Admission notification on a rolling basis beginning on or about 2/15. **Financial aid:** Priority date 5/15; no closing date. FAFSA, institutional form required. Applicants notified on a rolling basis starting 5/15; must reply within 2 week(s) of notification.

Academics. **Special study options:** Cooperative education, distance learning, dual enrollment of high school students, independent study, internships, liberal arts/career combination. License preparation in dental hygiene, nursing, paramedic. **Credit/placement by examination:** AP, CLEP, IB, institutional tests. 30 credit hours maximum toward associate degree. **Support services:** GED preparation and test center, learning center, reduced course load, remedial instruction, tutoring.

Majors. **Business:** Accounting technology, administrative services, business admin, information resources management. **Computer sciences:** Information systems. **Education:** Early childhood. **Health services:** Clinical lab technology, dental hygiene, EMT paramedic, nursing (RN). **Liberal arts:** Arts/sciences. **Protective services:** Fire safety technology, police science.

Most popular majors. Business/marketing 6%, health sciences 18%, liberal arts 60%.

Computing on campus. 720 workstations in library, computer center, student center. Commuter students can connect to campus network. Online library, helpline available.

Student life. **Freshman orientation:** Available. Preregistration for classes offered. Orientation sessions available throughout the month prior to start of each term. **Activities:** Concert band, choral groups, drama, music ensembles, student government, Phi Theta Kappa, Star of Life, Association of Nursing Students, social science club, Practical Nursing Students, fine arts society, Extreme Science, SGA, Fellowship of Christian Athletes.

Student services. Adult student services, alcohol/substance abuse counseling, career counseling, services for economically disadvantaged, student employment services, financial aid counseling, minority student services, personal counseling, placement for graduates, veterans' counselor. **Physically disabled:** Services for visually, speech, hearing impaired. **Transfer:** Transfer adviser, college fairs on campus for students transferring to 4-year colleges.

Contact. E-mail: admissions@coastalcarolina.edu
Phone: (910) 938-6332 Fax: (910) 455-2767
Don Herring, Division Chair for Admissions, Coastal Carolina Community College, 444 Western Boulevard, Jacksonville, NC 28546-6877

College of the Albemarle
Elizabeth City, North Carolina
www.albemarle.edu   CB code: 5133

- Public 2-year branch campus and community college
- Commuter campus in large town

General. Founded in 1960. Regionally accredited. The college has campuses in Elizabeth City, Manteo/Roanoke Island (Dare County), and Edenton (Chowan County) with a new facility opening school in Currituck County for Aviation Technologies. **Enrollment:** 2,586 degree-seeking undergraduates; 401 non-degree-seeking students. **Degrees:** 222 associate awarded. **Location:** 45 miles from Norfolk, Virginia. **Calendar:** Semester, limited summer session. **Full-time faculty:** 72 total; 56% women. **Part-time faculty:** 285 total; 54% women. **Special facilities:** Community center auditorium.

Student profile. Among degree-seeking undergraduates, 46% enrolled in a transfer program, 29% enrolled in a vocational program, 737 enrolled as first-time, first-year students, 1,514 transferred in from other institutions.

Part-time:	53%	Asian American:	1%
Out-of-state:	3%	Hispanic American:	3%
Women:	67%	International:	3%
African American:	22%	25 or older:	40%

Transfer out. Colleges most students transferred to 2011: Elizabeth City State University, East Carolina University, North Carolina State University, UNC-Chapel Hill, UNC-Wilmington.

Basis for selection. Open admission, but selective for some programs. All degree-seeking students required to take placement test. Students may waive placement test if scores for SAT or ACT are acceptable. Limited enrollment programs have additional admissions criteria. Admission limited to fall semester for associate degree in nursing, practical nursing, associate degree nursing, electrical/electronics technology, AC/HR, machining technology, surgical technology, medical assisting, and phlebotomy. New students admitted to cosmetology program as spaces become available. Interview required for allied health programs.

High school preparation. Recommended units include English 4, mathematics 3, social studies 3, history 3, science 3 and academic electives 6.

2011-2012 Annual costs. Tuition/fees: $2,061; $7,821 out-of-state. Per-credit charge: $67 in-state; $259 out-of-state. Books/supplies: $1,000.

Financial aid. Need-based: Need-based aid available for part-time students. Work-study available nights, weekends and for part-time students. **Non-need-based:** Scholarships awarded for academics, art, leadership, minority status, music/drama, state residency. **Additional information:** Separate application must be submitted for COA Private Scholarships.

Application procedures. Admission: No deadline. No application fee. Admission notification on a rolling basis. Application deadline for allied health January 15 prior to fall semester. **Financial aid:** Priority date 3/15, closing date 6/1. FAFSA required. Applicants notified on a rolling basis starting 5/1; must reply within 2 week(s) of notification.

Academics. Special study options: Cooperative education, distance learning, double major, dual enrollment of high school students, ESL, honors, independent study, internships, liberal arts/career combination. Agreement with Elizabeth City State University to offer the first 2 years of Elementary Education. License preparation in nursing, real estate. **Credit/placement by examination:** AP, CLEP, institutional tests. 30 credit hours maximum toward associate degree. Credit by examination not granted until examinee has enrolled at COA and passed 12 credit hours with 2.0 or better grade point average. **Support services:** GED preparation and test center, learning center, reduced course load, remedial instruction, study skills assistance, tutoring, writing center.

Majors. Architecture: Technology. **Business:** Administrative services, business admin, office/clerical. **Computer sciences:** General, applications programming, information systems, networking, programming. **Conservation:** Fisheries. **Education:** General, early childhood. **Engineering:** Computer. **Health services:** Clinical lab science, medical assistant, medical secretary, nursing (RN), office admin. **Liberal arts:** Arts/sciences. **Protective services:** Law enforcement admin. **Visual/performing arts:** Art, dramatic, music.

Computing on campus. 553 workstations in library, computer center, student center. Commuter students can connect to campus network. Online course registration, online library, helpline, wireless network available.

Student life. Freshman orientation: Available. Preregistration for classes offered. Monthly information sessions held for all COA programs. **Activities:** Bands, drama, literary magazine, musical theater, student government, Phi Theta Kappa, environmental club, literacy round table, nursing club, SADD, Spanish club.

Athletics. NJCAA. **Intercollegiate:** Baseball M, softball W. **Intramural:** Archery, badminton, baseball, basketball, bowling, football (non-tackle), golf, racquetball, sailing, soccer, softball, swimming, tennis, volleyball, weight lifting M. **Team name:** Dolphins.

Student services. Adult student services, career counseling, services for economically disadvantaged, student employment services, financial aid counseling, personal counseling, placement for graduates, veterans' counselor. **Physically disabled:** Services for visually, speech, hearing impaired. **Transfer:** Pre-admission transcript evaluation for new students. College fairs on campus for students transferring to 4-year colleges.

Contact. Phone: (252) 335-0821 ext. 2290 Fax: (252) 335-2011 Kenneth Krentz, Assistant Dean for Admissions and Testing, College of the Albemarle, 1208 North Road Street, Elizabeth City, NC 27906-2327

Craven Community College
New Bern, North Carolina
www.cravencc.edu   CB code: 5148

- Public 2-year community college
- Commuter campus in large town

General. Founded in 1965. Campuses in New Bern and Havelock. **Enrollment:** 2,986 degree-seeking undergraduates. **Degrees:** 353 associate awarded. **Location:** 100 miles from Raleigh, 45 miles from Greenville. **Calendar:** Semester, limited summer session. **Full-time faculty:** 92 total. **Part-time faculty:** 245 total. **Special facilities:** Nursing simulation laboratory, Institute of Aeronautical Technology.

Transfer out. Colleges most students transferred to 2011: East Carolina University, University of North Carolina: Wilmington, North Carolina State University.

Basis for selection. Open admission, but selective for some programs. Open admission policy except for Nursing, Practical Nursing, Health Information Technology, Pharmacy Technology, and Physical Therapist Assistant programs.

2011-2012 Annual costs. Tuition/fees: $2,091; $7,851 out-of-state. Per-credit charge: $67 in-state; $259 out-of-state. Books/supplies: $1,270. Personal expenses: $3,582.

Financial aid. Need-based: Work-study available nights, weekends and for part-time students.

Application procedures. Admission: No deadline. No application fee. Admission notification on a rolling basis. **Financial aid:** Closing date 6/1.

Academics. Special study options: Cooperative education, distance learning, dual enrollment of high school students, ESL, independent study, teacher certification program. Bachelor's degree programs available on campus. License preparation in aviation, nursing, physical therapy, real estate. **Credit/placement by examination:** AP, CLEP, institutional tests. **Support services:** GED preparation and test center; learning center, reduced course load, remedial instruction, study skills assistance, tutoring, writing center.

Majors. Business: Accounting, banking/financial services, business admin, office management, operations. **Computer sciences:** Information systems, information technology, LAN/WAN management, networking, programming. **Education:** Early childhood, elementary, special ed. **Engineering:** Pre-engineering. **Health services:** Medical assistant, medical records technology, nursing (RN), office admin, physical therapy assistant. **Liberal arts:** Arts/sciences. **Protective services:** Criminal justice.

Computing on campus. Online library, helpline, wireless network available.

Student life. Freshman orientation: Mandatory. Preregistration for classes offered. **Activities:** Choral groups, radio station, student government.

Athletics. NJCAA. **Team name:** Panthers.

Student services. Financial aid counseling, personal counseling. **Transfer:** Pre-admission transcript evaluation for new students. College fairs on campus for students transferring to 4-year colleges.

Contact. Phone: (252) 638-7200 Fax: (252) 638-4649 John Smith, Director of Enrollment Services, Craven Community College, 800 College Court, New Bern, NC 28562

Davidson County Community College
Lexington, North Carolina
www.davidsonccc.edu   CB code: 5170

- Public 2-year community college
- Commuter campus in large town

General. Founded in 1958. Regionally accredited. Davie Campus in Mocksville has 3 buildings and an emergency services training facility on 45 acres. **Enrollment:** 3,728 degree-seeking undergraduates. **Degrees:** 478 associate awarded. **Location:** 30 miles from Greensboro. **Calendar:** Semester, limited summer session. **Full-time faculty:** 90 total. **Part-time faculty:** 131 total. **Class size:** 59% < 20, 39% 20-39, less than 1% 40-49, less than 1% 50-99.

Student profile.

Out-of-state:	1%	25 or older:	46%

Transfer out. **Colleges most students transferred to 2011:** University of North Carolina-Greensboro, University of North Carolina-Charlotte, High Point University, Winston-Salem State University, Catawba College.

Basis for selection. Open admission, but selective for some programs. ASSET required unless acceptable test scores submitted. Admissions to nursing program under points system; based on test scores and grades.

High school preparation. Recommended units include English 4, mathematics 3, social studies 2, history 2, science 3 and foreign language 2.

2011-2012 Annual costs. Tuition/fees: $2,092; $7,852 out-of-state. Per-credit charge: $67 in-state; $259 out-of-state. Books/supplies: $1,000. Personal expenses: $600.

Financial aid. **Need-based:** Need-based aid available for part-time students. Work-study available nights, weekends and for part-time students. **Non-need-based:** Scholarships awarded for academics, leadership.

Application procedures. **Admission:** No deadline. No application fee. Admission notification on a rolling basis. Nursing program deadline 1/31, Allied Health program deadlines 3/15 to 5/15. **Financial aid:** Priority date 6/30; no closing date. FAFSA, institutional form required. Applicants notified on a rolling basis starting 7/31; must reply within 2 week(s) of notification.

Academics. **Special study options:** Distance learning, dual enrollment of high school students, ESL, independent study. License preparation in nursing, paramedic, real estate. **Credit/placement by examination:** AP, CLEP, institutional tests. Students must complete 25% of hours required for graduation in residence. **Support services:** GED preparation and test center, learning center, pre-admission summer program, reduced course load, remedial instruction, study skills assistance, tutoring, writing center.

Majors. **Biology:** Zoology. **Business:** Accounting, business admin, human resources. **Computer sciences:** Information technology, networking, programming. **Education:** Early childhood. **Health services:** Clinical lab technology, EMT paramedic, medical assistant, medical records technology, nursing (RN). **Liberal arts:** Arts/sciences. **Protective services:** Criminal justice, fire safety technology.

Computing on campus. 450 workstations in library, computer center. Commuter students can connect to campus network. Helpline available.

Student life. **Freshman orientation:** Available. Preregistration for classes offered. **Activities:** Literary magazine, student government, criminal justice club, association of nursing students, Phi Theta Kappa, Rotaract, spanish club, cosmetology club, Christian organization, computer system technology association, future educators club.

Athletics. **Intramural:** Basketball, golf.

Student services. Career counseling, student employment services, financial aid counseling, on-campus daycare, personal counseling, placement for graduates, veterans' counselor. **Physically disabled:** Services for visually, speech, hearing impaired. **Transfer:** Pre-admission transcript evaluation for new students. Transfer adviser, college fairs on campus for students transferring to 4-year colleges.

Contact. E-mail: admissions@davidsonccc.edu
Phone: (336) 249-8186 ext. 6731 Fax: (336) 224-0240
Lori Blevins, Director of Admissions, Davidson County Community College, PO Box 1287, Lexington, NC 27293-1287

Durham Technical Community College
Durham, North Carolina
www.durhamtech.edu   **CB code: 5172**

♦ Public 2-year community and technical college
♦ Commuter campus in small city

General. Founded in 1958. Regionally accredited. Most programs are structured to begin in fall and continue for 5 or 6 consecutive semesters. Satellite sites in northern Durham and Orange Counties. **Enrollment:** 4,511 degree-seeking undergraduates. **Degrees:** 346 associate awarded. **Location:** 25 miles

from Raleigh, 50 miles from Greensboro. **Calendar:** Semester, limited summer session. **Full-time faculty:** 163 total. **Part-time faculty:** 416 total.

Transfer out. **Colleges most students transferred to 2011:** University of North Carolina - Chapel Hill, North Carolina Central University, North Carolina State University.

Basis for selection. Open admission, but selective for some programs. Placement testing required. ASSET and COMPASS used. Admission to some allied health programs based on placement test and completion of prerequisite courses. **Home schooled:** Documentation of state recognition of home school required.

High school preparation. Algebra, chemistry, and biology required for allied health programs. Algebra and science courses recommended for most associate degree programs.

2011-2012 Annual costs. Tuition/fees: $2,045; $7,805 out-of-state. Per-credit charge: $67 in-state; $259 out-of-state. Books/supplies: $1,300. Personal expenses: $562.

Financial aid. **Need-based:** Need-based aid available for part-time students. Work-study available nights, weekends and for part-time students. **Non-need-based:** Scholarships awarded for academics, minority status, state residency. **Additional information:** Special funds available to single parents for tuition, fees, books, supplies and child care expenses.

Application procedures. **Admission:** Closing date 8/8 (receipt date). No application fee. Admission notification on a rolling basis. **Financial aid:** FAFSA required. Applicants notified on a rolling basis starting 1/31; must reply within 3 week(s) of notification.

Academics. **Special study options:** Distance learning, dual enrollment of high school students, ESL, weekend college. License preparation in nursing, occupational therapy, paramedic, real estate. **Credit/placement by examination:** AP, CLEP, institutional tests. Maximum of 10% of total curriculum hours of credit by examination may be counted toward degree. **Support services:** GED preparation and test center, learning center, remedial instruction, study skills assistance, tutoring.

Majors. **Architecture:** Technology. **Biology:** Biotechnology. **Business:** Accounting, administrative services, business admin, operations. **Computer sciences:** Applications programming, data processing, information technology, networking, programming, security, systems analysis. **Education:** Early childhood, teacher assistance. **Engineering:** Electrical. **Health services:** Dental lab technology, environmental health, medical records admin, medical secretary, nursing (RN), occupational health, occupational therapy assistant, office admin, optician, respiratory therapy assistant, respiratory therapy technology. **Liberal arts:** Arts/sciences.

Student life. **Freshman orientation:** Available. Preregistration for classes offered. **Activities:** Drama, literary magazine, student government.

Student services. Career counseling, services for economically disadvantaged, financial aid counseling, minority student services, personal counseling, veterans' counselor. **Physically disabled:** Services for visually, speech, hearing impaired. **Transfer:** College fairs on campus for students transferring to 4-year colleges.

Contact. E-mail: admissions@durhamtech.edu
Phone: (919) 536-7202 Fax: (919) 686-3669
Penny Augustine, Director of Admissions & Student Records, Durham Technical Community College, 1637 Lawson Street, Durham, NC 27703

Edgecombe Community College
Tarboro, North Carolina   **CB member**
www.edgecombe.edu   **CB code: 5199**

♦ Public 2-year community college
♦ Commuter campus in large town

General. Founded in 1967. Regionally accredited. Branch campus in Rocky Mount. **Enrollment:** 3,307 degree-seeking undergraduates. **Degrees:** 235 associate awarded. **Location:** 75 miles from Raleigh. **Calendar:** Semester, limited summer session. **Full-time faculty:** 82 total; 11% have terminal degrees, 46% minority. **Part-time faculty:** 124 total; 6% have terminal degrees, 32% minority. **Class size:** 77% < 20, 20% 20-39, 2% 40-49, less than 1% 50-99. **Special facilities:** Wildlife preserve.

Student profile.

Out-of-state:	1%	25 or older:	46%

Transfer out. Colleges most students transferred to 2011: East Carolina University, Pitt Community College, NC Wesleyan College, North Carolina Agricultural and Technical State University.

Basis for selection. Open admission, but selective for some programs. Special requirements for allied health programs and networking technology. TEAS Nursing Test required for nursing applicants.

2011-2012 Annual costs. Tuition/fees: $2,059; $7,819 out-of-state. Per-credit charge: $67 in-state; $259 out-of-state. Books/supplies: $1,500. Personal expenses: $2,000.

Financial aid. All financial aid based on need. Need-based aid available for part-time students. Work-study available nights, weekends and for part-time students.

Application procedures. Admission: No deadline. No application fee. Admission notification on a rolling basis. **Financial aid:** No deadline. FAFSA, institutional form required. Applicants notified on a rolling basis starting 8/15; must reply within 3 week(s) of notification.

Academics. Special study options: Cooperative education, distance learning, double major, dual enrollment of high school students, ESL, independent study. License preparation in nursing, radiology. **Credit/placement by examination:** AP, CLEP, institutional tests. 24 credit hours maximum toward associate degree. **Support services:** GED preparation and test center, learning center, reduced course load, remedial instruction, study skills assistance, tutoring.

Majors. Business: Accounting, administrative services, business admin. **Computer sciences:** General, information systems, networking. **Education:** Early childhood, teacher assistance. **Engineering:** Manufacturing. **Health services:** Medical assistant, medical radiologic technology/radiation therapy, medical records technology, nursing (RN), respiratory therapy technology. **Liberal arts:** Arts/sciences. **Protective services:** Criminal justice. **Work/family studies:** Child care management.

Most popular majors. Business/marketing 13%, education 14%, health sciences 48%, liberal arts 13%.

Computing on campus. 120 workstations in library, computer center. Online library, helpline available.

Student life. Activities: Drama, student government.

Athletics. Team name: Eagles.

Student services. Alcohol/substance abuse counseling, career counseling, student employment services, financial aid counseling, minority student services, personal counseling, placement for graduates, veterans' counselor. **Physically disabled:** Services for visually, hearing impaired. **Transfer:** Pre-admission transcript evaluation for new students. Transfer adviser, college fairs on campus for students transferring to 4-year colleges.

Contact. Phone: (252) 823-5166 ext. 254 Fax: (252) 823-6817 Ginny McLendon, Dean of Enrollment Management, Edgecombe Community College, 2009 West Wilson Street, Tarboro, NC 27886

Fayetteville Technical Community College

Fayetteville, North Carolina   **CB member**
www.faytechcc.edu   **CB code: 5208**

▶ Public 2-year community and technical college
▶ Commuter campus in large city

General. Founded in 1961. Regionally accredited. Offers the only funeral services curriculum in the North Carolina Community College System. Offers Imaging 3-D program support to educational programs. **Enrollment:** 9,750 degree-seeking undergraduates; 1,987 non-degree-seeking students. **Degrees:** 850 associate awarded. **Location:** 60 miles from Raleigh, 20 miles from Lumberton. **Calendar:** Semester, limited summer session. **Full-time faculty:** 313 total; 9% have terminal degrees, 27% minority, 62% women. **Part-time faculty:** 496 total; 2% have terminal degrees, 40% minority, 62% women. **Class size:** 59% < 20, 41% 20-39, less than 1% 40-49, less than 1% 50-99. **Special facilities:** Center for applied technology, virtual college center, horticulture educational center, Spring Lake campus. **Partnerships:** Formal partnership with ITCAP to provide college credit for prior learning. The FTCC Special Warfare Center provides accelerated degree completion for active duty military.

Student profile. Among degree-seeking undergraduates, 20% enrolled in a transfer program, 68% enrolled in a vocational program, 1% already have a bachelor's degree or higher, 1,812 enrolled as first-time, first-year students, 2,379 transferred in from other institutions.

| Part-time: | 52% | Women: | 68% |
| Out-of-state: | 11% | 25 or older: | 50% |

Transfer out. Colleges most students transferred to 2011: Fayetteville State University, UNC: Pembroke, UNC: Chapel Hill, East Carolina University, Methodist University.

Basis for selection. Open admission, but selective for some programs. Admission of health applicants based on transcripts, academic average, interview, and institutional assessment of reading, writing, and math. Group interview required for allied health programs. **Home schooled:** Transcript of courses and grades required. Must submit a copy of the home school's approved registration from the state in which they are registered and an official transcript including the graduation date and documentation of completion of competency. **Learning Disabled:** Documentation of disability required if applicant desires any academic accommodations.

High school preparation. Engineering and College Transfer programs require 2 algebra courses. Health programs require up to 2 algebra, 1 biology, and 1 chemistry course.

2011-2012 Annual costs. Tuition/fees: $2,055; $7,815 out-of-state. Per-credit charge: $67 in-state; $259 out-of-state. Books/supplies: $1,750.

2010-2011 Financial aid. Need-based: 846 full-time freshmen applied for aid; 792 were judged to have need; 746 of these received aid. Average need met was 47%. Average scholarship/grant was $1,000; average loan $3,500. 58% of total undergraduate aid awarded as scholarships/grants, 42% as loans/jobs. Need-based aid available for part-time students. Work-study available nights, weekends and for part-time students.

Application procedures. Admission: No deadline. No application fee. Application must be submitted online. Admission notification on a rolling basis. Deadline for health program applicants is January 30. Applicants admitted to these programs must reply immediately upon notification. High school students enroll only on a part-time basis while simultaneously attending high school. **Financial aid:** Priority date 6/1, closing date 7/15. FAFSA required. Applicants notified on a rolling basis starting 4/1; must reply by 6/1.

Academics. Web-based online tutoring (supplemental instruction) available to students 24 hours a day, seven days a week. **Special study options:** Cooperative education, distance learning, double major, dual enrollment of high school students, ESL, independent study, liberal arts/career combination, student-designed major, weekend college. License preparation in dental hygiene, nursing, paramedic, physical therapy, radiology. **Credit/placement by examination:** AP, CLEP, IB, institutional tests. 75 credit hours maximum toward associate degree. Up to 75 credit hours allowed, however students must complete at least 25% of program requirements at Fayetteville Technical Community College. **Support services:** GED preparation and test center, learning center, pre-admission summer program, reduced course load, remedial instruction, study skills assistance, tutoring.

Majors. Business: Accounting, banking/financial services, business admin, e-commerce, hotel/motel/restaurant management, human resources, marketing, office management, operations. **Computer sciences:** Information systems, information technology, networking, programming, security. **Education:** Early childhood, elementary. **General:** Horticulture. **Health services:** Dental hygiene, EMT paramedic, medical records technology, nuclear medical technology, nursing (RN), office admin, physical therapy assistant, radiologic technology/medical imaging, respiratory therapy technology, speech-language pathology assistant, surgical technology. **Human services:** General. **Liberal arts:** Arts/sciences. **Protective services:** Criminal justice, disaster management, fire safety technology, forensics. **Visual/performing arts:** Commercial/advertising art, game design.

Most popular majors. Business/marketing 14%, education 8%, health sciences 27%, liberal arts 27%.

Computing on campus. 1,450 workstations in library, computer center, student center. Commuter students can connect to campus network. Online course registration, online library, helpline, wireless network available.

Student life. Freshman orientation: Available. Preregistration for classes offered. Two hours, held the first day of new student registration. Three orientation sessions are held (June, July and August) for new students entering during the Fall term. **Activities:** Choral groups, drama, international student organizations, student government, student newspaper, TV station, African-American Heritage club, Democratic club, Nos-Ostros (Latino Cultural Organization), Parents for Higher Education, Students Against Destructive Decisions, intercultural club, veterans club.

Athletics. Intramural: Basketball, bowling, football (non-tackle), golf, softball, tennis, volleyball.

Student services. Adult student services, alcohol/substance abuse counseling, career counseling, student employment services, financial aid counseling, minority student services, on-campus daycare, personal counseling, placement for graduates, veterans' counselor. **Physically disabled:** Services for visually, speech, hearing impaired. **Transfer:** Pre-admission transcript evaluation for new students. Transfer adviser, college fairs on campus for students transferring to 4-year colleges.

Contact. E-mail: admissions@faytechcc.edu
Phone: (910) 678-8473 Fax: (910) 678-8407
Melissa Jones, Registrar, Fayetteville Technical Community College, PO Box 35236, Fayetteville, NC 28303-0236

Forsyth Technical Community College
Winston-Salem, North Carolina   **CB member**
www.forsythtech.edu   **CB code: 5234**

▸ Public 2-year community and technical college
▸ Commuter campus in small city

General. Founded in 1964. Regionally accredited. **Enrollment:** 9,689 degree-seeking undergraduates. **Degrees:** 835 associate awarded. **Location:** 32 miles from Greensboro, 85 miles from Charlotte. **Calendar:** Semester, extensive summer session. **Full-time faculty:** 214 total. **Part-time faculty:** 805 total.

Transfer out. Colleges most students transferred to 2011: Winston-Salem State University, Gardner-Webb University, High Point University, Appalachian State University, North Carolina A&T State University.

Basis for selection. Open admission, but selective for some programs. Admission to health program based on school record and test scores. Health information session attendance required. SAT or ACT used for admission to health and developmental programs and for placement in other programs. **Home schooled:** NCDPI registration information or similar information from the respective state's department of education authorizing the home school to provide instruction.

High school preparation. Algebra I required for allied health and engineering programs. Biology and chemistry required for allied health programs.

2011-2012 Annual costs. Tuition/fees: $2,057; $7,817 out-of-state. Per-credit charge: $67 in-state; $259 out-of-state. Books/supplies: $938. Personal expenses: $1,194.

Financial aid. Need-based: Need-based aid available for part-time students. Work-study available nights, weekends and for part-time students. **Non-need-based:** Scholarships awarded for academics, state residency. **Additional information:** Apply for aid as close to January 1 as possible for best consideration.

Application procedures. Admission: No deadline. No application fee. Admission notification on a rolling basis. **Financial aid:** Closing date 6/1. FAFSA, institutional form required. Applicants notified on a rolling basis starting 7/1; must reply within 2 week(s) of notification.

Academics. Special study options: Cooperative education, cross-registration, distance learning, double major, dual enrollment of high school students, ESL, exchange student, external degree, honors, independent study, internships, liberal arts/career combination, student-designed major. License preparation in dental hygiene, nursing, radiology, real estate. **Credit/placement by examination:** AP, CLEP, institutional tests. **Support services:** GED preparation and test center, learning center, pre-admission summer program, reduced course load, remedial instruction, study skills assistance, tutoring, writing center.

Majors. Biology: Biophysics. **Business:** Accounting, banking/financial services, business admin, executive assistant, international, logistics, office/clerical. **Computer sciences:** General, applications programming, information technology, networking. **Education:** Early childhood, science, special ed. **General:** Horticulture. **Health services:** Cardiovascular technology, dental hygiene, EMT paramedic, licensed practical nurse, massage therapy, medical assistant, medical radiologic technology/radiation therapy, nuclear medical technology, nursing (RN), office admin, radiologic technology/medical imaging, respiratory therapy technology, sonography. **Liberal arts:** Arts/sciences. **Protective services:** Criminal justice, fire safety technology, forensics. **Visual/performing arts:** Graphic design, interior design.

Computing on campus. 400 workstations in library, computer center. Online library, wireless network available.

Student life. Freshman orientation: Available. Preregistration for classes offered. **Activities:** Student government, student newspaper, Circle-K, Afro-American Society, minority male mentoring program, women's center.

Athletics. Intercollegiate: Basketball M, softball. **Intramural:** Basketball, bowling, golf, softball, volleyball. **Team name:** Tech Tigers.

Student services. Adult student services, alcohol/substance abuse counseling, career counseling, services for economically disadvantaged, student employment services, financial aid counseling, health services, minority student services, personal counseling, placement for graduates, veterans' counselor, women's services. **Physically disabled:** Services for visually, speech, hearing impaired. **Transfer:** Transfer adviser, college fairs on campus for students transferring to 4-year colleges.

Contact. E-mail: admissions@forsythtech.edu
Phone: (336) 734-7253 Fax: (336) 734-7291
Jean Groome, Dean of Enrollment Management, Forsyth Technical Community College, 2100 Silas Creek Parkway, Winston-Salem, NC 27103

Gaston College
Dallas, North Carolina
www.gaston.edu   **CB code: 5262**

▸ Public 2-year community college
▸ Commuter campus in small town

General. Founded in 1963. Regionally accredited. Branch campus at Lincolnton. **Enrollment:** 5,702 degree-seeking undergraduates. **Degrees:** 655 associate awarded. **Location:** 25 miles from Charlotte. **Calendar:** Semester, limited summer session. **Full-time faculty:** 161 total. **Part-time faculty:** 410 total.

Student profile.

Out-of-state:	1%	**25 or older:**	54%

Basis for selection. Open admission, but selective for some programs. Admission to health services programs, including nursing, based on ACT scores and interview. Basic literacy must be demonstrated, after admission, in order to take certain courses. Interview recommended for emergency medical technician, medical assistant, nursing programs; audition recommended for music programs; portfolio recommended for art programs.

2011-2012 Annual costs. Tuition/fees: $2,049; $7,809 out-of-state. Per-credit charge: $67 in-state; $259 out-of-state. Books/supplies: $1,000. Personal expenses: $1,000.

Financial aid. Need-based: Work-study available nights, weekends and for part-time students. **Non-need-based:** Scholarships awarded for academics, state residency. **Additional information:** Grants/scholarships available for women pursuing nontraditional roles.

Application procedures. Admission: No deadline. No application fee. Admission notification on a rolling basis. **Financial aid:** Priority date 3/15, closing date 6/30. FAFSA, institutional form required. Applicants notified on a rolling basis.

Academics. Special study options: Cooperative education, cross-registration, distance learning, double major, dual enrollment of high school students, ESL, independent study, internships, weekend college. **Credit/placement by examination:** AP, CLEP, institutional tests. 18 credit hours maximum toward associate degree. **Support services:** GED preparation and test center, learning center, reduced course load, remedial instruction, study skills assistance, tutoring, writing center.

Majors. Architecture: Technology. **Business:** Accounting, administrative services, business admin. **Communications:** Broadcast journalism. **Computer sciences:** Applications programming, information technology, programming. **Education:** Early childhood. **Health services:** Dietetic technician, EMT paramedic, massage therapy, medical assistant, medical secretary, nursing (RN), office admin, veterinary technology/assistant. **Human services:** Social work. **Liberal arts:** Arts/sciences. **Protective services:** Fire safety technology.

Computing on campus. 233 workstations in library, computer center.

Student life. Freshman orientation: Available. Preregistration for classes offered. **Activities:** Literary magazine, music ensembles, radio station, student government.

Student services. Adult student services, career counseling, student employment services, financial aid counseling, on-campus daycare, placement for graduates, veterans' counselor. **Physically disabled:** Services for visually, speech, hearing impaired. **Transfer:** Transfer adviser, college fairs on campus for students transferring to 4-year colleges.

Contact. E-mail: wray.michelle@gaston.edu
Phone: (704) 922-6214 Fax: (704) 922-2344
Terry Bracier, Director of Admissions/Enrollment Management, Gaston College, 201 Highway 321 South, Dallas, NC 28034-1499

Guilford Technical Community College
Jamestown, North Carolina
www.gtcc.edu | **CB code: 5275**

- Public 2-year community and technical college
- Commuter campus in large city
- Interview required

General. Founded in 1958. Regionally accredited. Campuses in Greensboro and High Point. **Enrollment:** 14,136 degree-seeking undergraduates; 609 non-degree-seeking students. **Degrees:** 1,025 associate awarded. **Location:** 2 miles from Greensboro, 5 miles from High Point. **Calendar:** Semester, limited summer session. **Full-time faculty:** 367 total. **Part-time faculty:** 785 total. **Class size:** 13% < 20, 79% 20-39, 2% 40-49, 6% 50-99. **Special facilities:** Observatory.

Student profile. Among degree-seeking undergraduates, 52% enrolled in a transfer program, 48% enrolled in a vocational program, 1,849 enrolled as first-time, first-year students.

Part-time:	39%	25 or older:	45%
Women:	57%		

Transfer out. Colleges most students transferred to 2011: University of North Carolina-Greensboro, University of North Carolina-Charlotte, North Carolina A&T, University of North Carolina-Wilmington, and Winston-Salem State University.

Basis for selection. Open admission, but selective for some programs. Admission to allied health programs is highly competitive. Each program has specific requirements that must be met to be considered for admission. **Home schooled:** Proof of NC home-school registry from the NC Department of Non-Public Instruction. **Learning Disabled:** Contact Disability Access Services office.

High school preparation. Allied health programs have specific course requirements that vary according to program.

2011-2012 Annual costs. Tuition/fees: $2,062; $7,822 out-of-state. Per-credit charge: $67 in-state; $259 out-of-state. Books/supplies: $1,024. Personal expenses: $5,040.

2010-2011 Financial aid. Need-based: 54% of total undergraduate aid awarded as scholarships/grants, 46% as loans/jobs. Need-based aid available for part-time students. Work-study available nights, weekends and for part-time students.

Application procedures. Admission: No deadline. No application fee. Admission notification on a rolling basis. Applicants for limited enrollment programs (nursing, aviation maintenance/mechanic, dental hygiene, dental assistant, medical assistant, surgical technology cosmetology, emergency medical science) advised to apply before December 31. **Financial aid:** Priority date 3/15, closing date 8/1. FAFSA required. Applicants notified on a rolling basis starting 7/1; must reply within 2 week(s) of notification.

Academics. Special study options: Cooperative education, cross-registration, distance learning, double major, dual enrollment of high school students, ESL, internships, liberal arts/career combination, teacher certification program. License preparation in aviation, dental hygiene, nursing, paramedic, physical therapy, radiology, real estate. **Credit/placement by examination:** AP, CLEP, IB, institutional tests. 60 credit hours maximum toward associate degree. **Support services:** GED preparation and test center, learning center, reduced course load, remedial instruction, study skills assistance, tutoring, writing center.

Majors. Business: Accounting technology, business admin, executive assistant, human resources, management information systems. **Communications technology:** Recording arts. **Computer sciences:** Information systems. **Education:** General, early childhood. **General:** Power machinery, turf management. **Health services:** Dental hygiene, EMT paramedic, medical assistant, mental health services, nursing (RN), physical therapy assistant, substance abuse counseling, surgical technology. **Liberal arts:** Arts/sciences. **Protective services:** Criminal justice, fire safety technology. **Visual/performing arts:** Commercial/advertising art, music management.

Computing on campus. 130 workstations in library, computer center. Commuter students can connect to campus network. Online course registration, online library, helpline, wireless network available.

Student life. Freshman orientation: Mandatory. Preregistration for classes offered. **Activities:** Campus ministries, choral groups, drama, international student organizations, music ensembles, student government, Ambassadors for Christ, American Muslim Student Association, Nurses Christian Fellowship, Fellowship of Christian Athletes, International Students Association, Political Science Club, Rotaract, Phi Theta Kappa, Veteran's and Civilians Organized Network.

Athletics. NJCAA. **Intercollegiate:** Baseball M, basketball, volleyball W. **Team name:** Titans.

Student services. Alcohol/substance abuse counseling, career counseling, services for economically disadvantaged, student employment services, financial aid counseling, minority student services, on-campus daycare, personal counseling, placement for graduates, veterans' counselor, women's services. **Physically disabled:** Services for visually, speech, hearing impaired. **Transfer:** Pre-admission transcript evaluation for new students. Transfer adviser, college fairs on campus for students transferring to 4-year colleges.

Contact. E-mail: jlcross@gtcc.edu
Phone: (336) 334-4822 ext. 31125 Fax: (336) 819-2022
Jesse Cross, Director of Admissions, Guilford Technical Community College, PO Box 309, Jamestown, NC 27282

Halifax Community College
Weldon, North Carolina
www.halifaxcc.edu | **CB code: 0621**

- Public 2-year community college
- Small town

General. Founded in 1967. Regionally accredited. **Enrollment:** 1,560 degree-seeking undergraduates. **Degrees:** 137 associate awarded. **Location:** 83 miles from Raleigh. **Calendar:** Semester, limited summer session. **Full-time faculty:** 57 total; 5% have terminal degrees, 53% minority. **Part-time faculty:** 52 total. **Special facilities:** Performing arts auditorium. **Partnerships:** Formal partnerships with Small Business Center, Continue Education, Huskins Program, and high schools.

Basis for selection. Open admission, but selective for some programs. Special requirements for nursing and allied health programs.

High school preparation. High school chemistry or equivalent and developmental mathematics required for nursing applicants.

2011-2012 Annual costs. Tuition/fees: $2,085; $7,845 out-of-state. Per-credit charge: $67 in-state; $259 out-of-state. Books/supplies: $1,200. Personal expenses: $1,294.

Financial aid. Need-based: Work-study available nights, weekends and for part-time students.

Application procedures. Admission: No deadline. No application fee. Admission notification on a rolling basis. **Financial aid:** Priority date 6/1; no closing date. Applicants notified on a rolling basis starting 8/1; must reply within 2 week(s) of notification.

Academics. Special study options: Distance learning, dual enrollment of high school students, ESL, independent study, internships. Huskins Program. License preparation in dental hygiene, nursing, paramedic, real estate. **Credit/placement by examination:** AP, CLEP, institutional tests. **Support services:** GED preparation and test center, learning center, reduced course load, remedial instruction, tutoring.

Majors. Business: Accounting, business admin, office management, office technology, office/clerical. **Communications:** Advertising. **Computer sciences:** General. **Conservation:** Wood science. **Education:** Early childhood, multi-level teacher, teacher assistance. **Health services:** Clinical lab technology, medical secretary, nursing (RN), phlebotomy. **Human services:** Social work. **Liberal arts:** Arts/sciences. **Visual/performing arts:** Commercial/advertising art, interior design.

Most popular majors. Business/marketing 7%, education 9%, engineering/engineering technologies 8%, health sciences 41%, liberal arts 18%, social sciences 6%.

Computing on campus. 100 workstations in computer center.

Student life. Freshman orientation: Available. Preregistration for classes offered. **Activities:** Student government, student newspaper.

Student services. Career counseling, student employment services, personal counseling, placement for graduates, veterans' counselor. **Transfer:**

Transfer adviser, college fairs on campus for students transferring to 4-year colleges.

Contact. E-mail: washingtonj@halifaxcc.edu
Phone: (252) 536-7220 Fax: (252) 538-4311
James Washington, Director of Admissions and Recruitment, Halifax Community College, 100 College Drive, Drawer 809, Weldon, NC 27890

Haywood Community College
Clyde, North Carolina
www.haywood.edu
CB code: 5289

- Public 2-year community and technical college
- Commuter campus in rural community

General. Founded in 1965. Regionally accredited. **Enrollment:** 1,860 degree-seeking undergraduates. **Degrees:** 254 associate awarded. **Location:** 25 miles from Asheville. **Calendar:** Semester, extensive summer session. **Full-time faculty:** 79 total. **Part-time faculty:** 183 total. **Class size:** 85% < 20, 14% 20-39, less than 1% 40-49.

Student profile.

Out-of-state: 14%   25 or older: 39%

Transfer out. Colleges most students transferred to 2011: Western Carolina University, Appalachian State University, University of North Carolina - Asheville.

Basis for selection. Open admission, but selective for some programs. Completion of Accuplacer, SAT score of 500 or higher on each section, ACT composite score of 21 or higher, or official transcript with "C" or better in college-level English and algebra required. Admission to nursing program based on admission test scores, high school record, GPA, prerequisite courses, and health occupations aptitude examination. Informational interview required for electrical engineering technology, manufacturing engineering technology, cosmetology, and professional crafts programs. **Learning Disabled:** Accommodations made upon request.

High school preparation. Algebra, biology and chemistry required for nursing. Algebra recommended for electrical and manufacturing engineering, microcomputer systems and college transfer.

2011-2012 Annual costs. Tuition/fees: $2,092; $7,852 out-of-state. Per-credit charge: $67 in-state; $259 out-of-state. Books/supplies: $1,000. Personal expenses: $1,656.

Financial aid. Need-based: Need-based aid available for part-time students. Work-study available nights, weekends and for part-time students. **Non-need-based:** Scholarships awarded for academics. **Additional information:** Complete FAFSA by priority filing date for consideration for institutional scholarships.

Application procedures. Admission: No deadline. No application fee. Admission notification on a rolling basis. **Financial aid:** Priority date 4/1; no closing date. FAFSA, institutional form required. Applicants notified on a rolling basis starting 4/15; must reply within 2 week(s) of notification.

Academics. Special study options: Cooperative education, distance learning, dual enrollment of high school students, independent study, internships. **Credit/placement by examination:** AP, CLEP, institutional tests. 18 credit hours maximum toward associate degree. **Support services:** GED preparation and test center, learning center, reduced course load, remedial instruction, tutoring.

Majors. Business: Accounting, administrative services, business admin. **Computer sciences:** Applications programming, networking. **Conservation:** Fisheries, forest resources, forestry, wildlife/wilderness, wood science. **Engineering:** Computer. **General:** Horticulture. **Health services:** Medical assistant, nursing (RN). **Liberal arts:** Arts/sciences. **Protective services:** Criminal justice. **Visual/performing arts:** Ceramics, fiber arts, metal/jewelry. **Work/family studies:** Child care management.

Most popular majors. Agriculture 6%, business/marketing 10%, engineering/engineering technologies 7%, family/consumer sciences 6%, health sciences 10%, liberal arts 15%, natural resources/environmental science 19%, trade and industry 8%, visual/performing arts 8%.

Computing on campus. 10 workstations in library.

Student life. Freshman orientation: Available. Preregistration for classes offered. **Activities:** Student government, Phi Theta Kappa, Phi Beta Lambda.

Student services. Career counseling, student employment services, financial aid counseling, on-campus daycare, personal counseling, placement for

graduates, veterans' counselor. **Physically disabled:** Services for visually, speech, hearing impaired. **Transfer:** Transfer adviser for students transferring to 4-year colleges.

Contact. E-mail: enrollment@haywood.edu
Phone: (828) 627-4505 Toll-free number: (866) 468-6422
Fax: (828) 627-4513
Jennifer Herrera, Director of Enrollment Management, Haywood Community College, 185 Freelander Drive, Clyde, NC 28721-9454

Isothermal Community College
Spindale, North Carolina
www.isothermal.edu
CB code: 5319

- Public 2-year community college
- Commuter campus in small town

General. Founded in 1964. Regionally accredited. **Enrollment:** 1,923 degree-seeking undergraduates. **Degrees:** 319 associate awarded. **Location:** 65 miles from Charlotte, 48 miles from Asheville. **Calendar:** Semester, extensive summer session. **Full-time faculty:** 68 total. **Part-time faculty:** 102 total. **Class size:** 69% < 20, 31% 20-39. **Partnerships:** Formal partnership with Rutherford County Schools.

Basis for selection. Open admission, but selective for some programs. Open general admission. Selective admission requirements for BLET, LPN, RN, and Surgical Technology programs. **Home schooled:** Transcript of courses and grades required. Copy of license to operate as provided by the state required.

2011-2012 Annual costs. Tuition/fees: $2,033; $7,793 out-of-state. Per-credit charge: $67 in-state; $259 out-of-state. Books/supplies: $864. Personal expenses: $765.

Financial aid. Need-based: Need-based aid available for part-time students. Work-study available nights, weekends and for part-time students. **Non-need-based:** Scholarships awarded for academics, job skills, leadership, minority status, music/drama, state residency.

Application procedures. Admission: No deadline. No application fee. Admission notification on a rolling basis. **Financial aid:** Priority date 5/31, closing date 7/1. FAFSA, institutional form required. Applicants notified on a rolling basis starting 4/30; must reply within 4 week(s) of notification.

Academics. Special study options: Cooperative education, distance learning, dual enrollment of high school students, ESL, independent study. Bachelor's degree programs available on campus. License preparation in nursing, real estate. **Credit/placement by examination:** AP, CLEP, institutional tests. 12 credit hours maximum toward associate degree. **Support services:** GED preparation and test center, learning center, reduced course load, remedial instruction, tutoring, writing center.

Majors. Business: Banking/financial services, business admin, customer service support, e-commerce, entrepreneurial studies, marketing, office management, operations. **Communications technology:** Radio/TV. **Computer sciences:** Information systems, information technology, LAN/WAN management, networking, programming, security. **Education:** Early childhood, elementary, trade/industrial. **Health services:** Nursing (RN), office admin. **Liberal arts:** Arts/sciences. **Protective services:** Criminal justice. **Visual/performing arts:** Commercial/advertising art.

Most popular majors. Business/marketing 13%, education 6%, engineering/engineering technologies 10%, health sciences 17%, liberal arts 43%.

Computing on campus. 44 workstations in library, computer center. Commuter students can connect to campus network. Online library, helpline, wireless network available.

Student life. Freshman orientation: Available. Preregistration for classes offered. **Activities:** Literary magazine, radio station, student government, TV station, art and computer design club, Afro-American club, chess club, Student Nurses' Association, International Association of Administrative Professionals, Isothermal Education Society, math club, Phi Theta Kappa, Phi Beta Lambda, Twin Phoenix Karate Club.

Athletics. Intramural: Basketball, football (non-tackle), table tennis, volleyball.

Student services. Career counseling, financial aid counseling, personal counseling, placement for graduates, veterans' counselor. **Physically disabled:** Services for visually, speech, hearing impaired. **Transfer:** Transfer adviser, college fairs on campus for students transferring to 4-year colleges.

Contact. E-mail: admissions@isothermal.edu
Phone: (828) 286-3636 ext. 251 Fax: (828) 286-8109
Alice McCluney, Director, Enrollment Management, Isothermal
Community College, PO Box 804, Spindale, NC 28160-0804

James Sprunt Community College
Kenansville, North Carolina
www.jamessprunt.edu   **CB code: 6256**

▶ Public 2-year community college
▶ Commuter campus in rural community

General. Founded in 1964. Regionally accredited. **Enrollment:** 1,175
degree-seeking undergraduates; 412 non-degree-seeking students. **Degrees:**
155 associate awarded. **Location:** 75 miles from Raleigh, 45 miles from
Wilmington. **Calendar:** Semester, limited summer session. **Full-time faculty:** 58 total; 5% have terminal degrees, 24% minority, 57% women. **Part-time faculty:** 77 total; 3% have terminal degrees, 31% minority, 54% women.
Class size: 55% < 20, 45% 20-39, less than 1% 40-49, less than 1% 50-99.

Student profile. Among degree-seeking undergraduates, 27% enrolled in
a transfer program, 46% enrolled in a vocational program, 212 enrolled as
first-time, first-year students, 292 transferred in from other institutions.

Part-time:	36%	Hispanic American:	4%
Out-of-state:	1%	Native American:	1%
Women:	76%	25 or older:	41%
African American:	50%		

Transfer out. 70% of students enrolled in the transfer program go on to
4-year colleges. **Colleges most students transferred to 2011:** University of
North Carolina at Wilmington, East Carolina University, Mount Olive College, North Carolina State University, Fayetteville State University.

Basis for selection. Open admission, but selective for some programs.
Test of Essential Academic Skills (TEAS), current Nursing Assistant I certification and 2.0 GPA in biology, chemistry, and algebra required for nursing
applicants. SAT or ACT accepted in lieu of academic placement tests. Credit
may be awarded for graphic arts classes based on portfolio. **Home schooled:**
Letter from State Board of Education giving approval for home school.
Learning Disabled: Submit letter from professional stating disabilities.

2011-2012 Annual costs. Tuition/fees: $2,033; $7,793 out-of-state. Per-credit charge: $67 in-state; $259 out-of-state. Books/supplies: $1,500. Personal expenses: $1,500.

2010-2011 Financial aid. All financial aid based on need. 274 full-time
freshmen applied for aid; 261 were judged to have need; 261 of these received
aid. Average need met was 100%. Average scholarship/grant was $5,775;
average loan $3,500. 74% of total undergraduate aid awarded as scholarships/
grants, 26% as loans/jobs. Need-based aid available for part-time students.
Work-study available nights, weekends and for part-time students.

Application procedures. Admission: No deadline. No application fee.
Admission notification on a rolling basis. **Financial aid:** Priority date 7/1;
no closing date. FAFSA, institutional form required. Applicants notified on
a rolling basis starting 6/15; must reply within 2 week(s) of notification.

Academics. Special study options: Cooperative education, distance learning, double major, dual enrollment of high school students, ESL, independent
study, internships, liberal arts/career combination. License preparation in
nursing. **Credit/placement by examination:** AP, CLEP, institutional tests.
16 credit hours maximum toward associate degree. **Support services:** GED
preparation and test center, learning center, pre-admission summer program,
reduced course load, remedial instruction, study skills assistance, tutoring.

Majors. Business: Accounting, administrative services, business admin,
office management. **Computer sciences:** Information technology. **Education:** Early childhood, elementary. **General:** Agribusiness operations, animal
husbandry, viticulture. **Health services:** Medical assistant, nursing (RN).
Liberal arts: Arts/sciences. **Protective services:** Criminal justice, police
science. **Visual/performing arts:** Commercial/advertising art. **Work/family
studies:** Child development.

Most popular majors. Business/marketing 17%, education 11%, health
sciences 16%, liberal arts 39%.

Computing on campus. 260 workstations in library, computer center.

Student life. Freshman orientation: Mandatory. Preregistration for
classes offered. Held prior to regular registration day; students must pre-register with counselors. **Activities:** Student government, student newspaper,
Phi Theta Kappa, Student Nurses Association, National Vocational-Technical
Honor Society, Ambassador Program, Criminal Justice Club.

Athletics. Intercollegiate: Softball, volleyball.

Student services. Career counseling, services for economically disadvantaged, student employment services, financial aid counseling, personal counseling, placement for graduates, veterans' counselor. **Physically disabled:**
Services for visually, hearing impaired. **Transfer:** Pre-admission transcript
evaluation for new students. Transfer adviser, college fairs on campus for
students transferring to 4-year colleges.

Contact. E-mail: lmatthews@jamessprunt.edu
Phone: (910) 296-2500 Fax: (910) 296-1222
Lea Matthews, Admissions Specialist, James Sprunt Community College,
PO Box 398, Kenansville, NC 28349-0398

Johnston Community College
Smithfield, North Carolina   **CB member**
www.johnstoncc.edu   **CB code: 0727**

▶ Public 2-year community and technical college
▶ Commuter campus in large town

General. Founded in 1969. Regionally accredited. **Enrollment:** 3,764
degree-seeking undergraduates; 534 non-degree-seeking students. **Degrees:**
413 associate awarded. **Location:** 30 miles from Raleigh. **Calendar:** Semester, limited summer session. **Full-time faculty:** 142 total. **Part-time faculty:**
245 total. **Class size:** 70% < 20, 30% 20-39, less than 1% 40-49, less than
1% 50-99. **Special facilities:** Howell woods.

Student profile. Among degree-seeking undergraduates, 53% enrolled in
a transfer program, 47% enrolled in a vocational program, 660 enrolled as
first-time, first-year students.

Part-time:	41%	Women:	66%
Out-of-state:	1%		

Transfer out. Colleges most students transferred to 2011: East Carolina
University, University of North Carolina at Wilmington, North Carolina
State University.

Basis for selection. Open admission, but selective for some programs.
Admission to health programs based on test scores, high school record and
related completed courses. PSB required for admission to nursing and radiologic technology programs. Placement interview required for all applicants;
interview required for health programs.

2011-2012 Annual costs. Tuition/fees: $2,090; $7,850 out-of-state. Per-credit charge: $67 in-state; $259 out-of-state. Books/supplies: $1,152. Personal expenses: $1,619.

2010-2011 Financial aid. All financial aid based on need. 72% of total
undergraduate aid awarded as scholarships/grants, 28% as loans/jobs. Need-based aid available for part-time students. Work-study available nights, weekends and for part-time students.

Application procedures. Admission: Priority date 8/1; no deadline. No
application fee. Admission notification on a rolling basis. **Financial aid:**
Priority date 5/31; no closing date. FAFSA, institutional form required.
Applicants notified on a rolling basis starting 6/1; must reply within 2 week(s)
of notification.

Academics. Special study options: Cross-registration, distance learning,
double major, dual enrollment of high school students, internships. **Credit/
placement by examination:** AP, CLEP, IB, institutional tests. **Support
services:** GED preparation and test center, learning center, pre-admission
summer program, reduced course load, remedial instruction, tutoring.

Majors. Business: Accounting, business admin, office management. **Computer sciences:** Networking, programming. **Education:** Early childhood,
teacher assistance. **Foreign languages:** Translation. **Health services:** Cardiopulmonary technology, cardiovascular technology, medical assistant, nuclear
medical technology, nursing (RN), office admin, pharmacy assistant, radiologic technology/medical imaging. **Liberal arts:** Arts/sciences. **Protective
services:** Criminal justice. **Visual/performing arts:** Commercial/advertising art.

Most popular majors. Business/marketing 11%, health sciences 20%,
legal studies 12%, liberal arts 31%, security/protective services 8%, trade
and industry 7%.

Computing on campus. 115 workstations in library, computer center.
Commuter students can connect to campus network. Online course registration available.

Student life. Freshman orientation: Mandatory. Preregistration for
classes offered. **Activities:** Jazz band, choral groups, student government.

Athletics. NJCAA. **Intercollegiate:** Basketball M, golf M, volleyball W. **Team name:** Jaguars.

Student services. Chaplain/spiritual director, career counseling, student employment services, financial aid counseling, minority student services, on-campus daycare, personal counseling, placement for graduates, veterans' counselor. **Physically disabled:** Services for visually, speech, hearing impaired. **Transfer:** Pre-admission transcript evaluation for new students. College fairs on campus for students transferring to 4-year colleges.

Contact. Phone: (919) 209-2128 Fax: (919) 989-7862
Joan McLendon, Director of Admissions and Counseling, Johnston Community College, PO Box 2350, Smithfield, NC 27577

King's College
Charlotte, North Carolina
www.kingscollegecharlotte.edu   CB code: 5361

- For-profit 2-year career college
- Large city
- Interview required

General. Accredited by ACICS. **Enrollment:** 529 degree-seeking undergraduates. **Degrees:** 190 associate awarded. **Calendar:** Semester. **Full-time faculty:** 10 total. **Part-time faculty:** 15 total.

Basis for selection. Interview required, class rank and standardized test scores important.

2011-2012 Annual costs. Tuition/fees: $13,540. Room/board: $6,380. Books/supplies: $2,300.

Financial aid. Need-based: Work-study available nights, weekends and for part-time students.

Application procedures. Admission: No deadline. $50 fee. Admission notification on a rolling basis.

Academics. Credit/placement by examination: AP, CLEP.

Majors. Business: Accounting, administrative services, tourism/travel. **Computer sciences:** Applications programming. **Health services:** Medical secretary. **Visual/performing arts:** Commercial/advertising art.

Student life. Freshman orientation: Mandatory. Preregistration for classes offered. Held on the day prior to the start of classes. **Policies:** Dress code observed; no alcoholic beverages or drugs on campus. **Housing:** Single-sex dorms available. **Activities:** Student government, Sigma Chi Kappa, Lambda Epsilon Chi.

Student services. Career counseling, financial aid counseling, placement for graduates.

Contact. Phone: (704) 372-0266 Toll-free number: (800) 768-2255 Fax: (704) 348-2029
Diane Ryon, Director of Admissions, King's College , 322 Lamar Avenue, Charlotte, NC 28204

Lenoir Community College
Kinston, North Carolina
www.lenoircc.edu   CB code: 5378

- Public 2-year community college
- Commuter campus in large town

General. Founded in 1958. Regionally accredited. Extension campuses in Jones and Greene Counties. **Enrollment:** 2,344 degree-seeking undergraduates; 1,163 non-degree-seeking students. **Degrees:** 329 associate awarded. **Location:** 75 miles from Raleigh, 25 miles from Greenville. **Calendar:** Semester, extensive summer session. **Full-time faculty:** 90 total; 60% women. **Part-time faculty:** 263 total. **Class size:** 73% < 20, 26% 20-39, 1% 40-49, less than 1% 50-99. **Special facilities:** Facility for local history, genealogy collection.

Student profile. Among degree-seeking undergraduates, 491 enrolled as first-time, first-year students.

Part-time:	39%	Women:	62%
Out-of-state:	2%		

Transfer out. Colleges most students transferred to 2011: East Carolina University.

Basis for selection. Open admission, but selective for some programs. Special requirements for allied health programs. Interview required for surgical technology program.

High school preparation. Recommended units include English 4, mathematics 2, social studies 2, history 1, science 2 (laboratory 1). One biology, 1 chemistry required for registered nursing program.

2011-2012 Annual costs. Tuition/fees: $2,091; $7,851 out-of-state. Per-credit charge: $67 in-state; $259 out-of-state. Books/supplies: $1,700. Personal expenses: $1,450.

Financial aid. Need-based: Need-based aid available for part-time students. Work-study available nights, weekends and for part-time students. **Non-need-based:** Scholarships awarded for academics, athletics, leadership, state residency.

Application procedures. Admission: No deadline. No application fee. Admission notification on a rolling basis. Separate application required for allied health programs. January 31 deadline for nursing and April 30 for surgical technology. **Financial aid:** Priority date 7/1, closing date 8/15. Institutional form required. Applicants notified on a rolling basis starting 8/1; must reply within 2 week(s) of notification.

Academics. Special study options: Cooperative education, distance learning, dual enrollment of high school students, honors, liberal arts/career combination, study abroad, weekend college. License preparation in aviation, nursing, paramedic, real estate. **Credit/placement by examination:** AP, CLEP, IB, institutional tests. **Support services:** GED preparation and test center, learning center, pre-admission summer program, reduced course load, remedial instruction, tutoring.

Majors. Business: Accounting, administrative services, business admin, e-commerce, executive assistant, management information systems. **Computer sciences:** Data processing, programming. **Conservation:** Water/wetlands/marine. **Education:** General, art, biology, chemistry, early childhood, elementary, health, history, physical, social science, teacher assistance. **Engineering:** General. **General:** Horticulture. **Health services:** Massage therapy, medical assistant, medical secretary, nursing (RN), radiologic technology/medical imaging. **Human services:** Social work. **Liberal arts:** Arts/sciences. **Math:** General. **Psychology:** General. **Visual/performing arts:** Commercial/advertising art, studio arts. **Work/family studies:** Child care management.

Computing on campus. 100 workstations in library, computer center, student center. Commuter students can connect to campus network. Online course registration available.

Student life. Freshman orientation: Available. Preregistration for classes offered. **Activities:** Choral groups, student government, student newspaper, Phi Theta Kappa, various clubs related to major fields of study.

Athletics. NJCAA. **Intercollegiate:** Baseball M, basketball, volleyball W. **Team name:** Lancers.

Student services. Adult student services, career counseling, student employment services, financial aid counseling, health services, minority student services, personal counseling, placement for graduates, veterans' counselor. **Transfer:** Pre-admission transcript evaluation for new students. Transfer adviser, college fairs on campus for students transferring to 4-year colleges.

Contact. E-mail: pmazingo@lenoircc.edu
Phone: (252) 527-6223 ext. 309 Fax: (252) 233-6879 ext. 323
Pam Mazingo, Director of Enrollment Management, Lenoir Community College, PO Box 188, Kinston, NC 28502-0188

Louisburg College
Louisburg, North Carolina   CB member
www.louisburg.edu   CB code: 5369

- Private 2-year junior college affiliated with United Methodist Church
- Residential campus in small town
- SAT or ACT (ACT writing optional) required

General. Founded in 1787. Regionally accredited. Small classes with individual approach. **Enrollment:** 689 degree-seeking undergraduates. **Degrees:** 76 associate awarded. **ROTC:** Army. **Location:** 25 miles from Raleigh. **Calendar:** Semester, limited summer session. **Full-time faculty:** 31 total; 19% have terminal degrees, 58% women. **Part-time faculty:** 24 total; 8% have terminal degrees, 25% minority, 71% women.

Student profile. Among degree-seeking undergraduates, 100% enrolled in a transfer program, 367 enrolled as first-time, first-year students.

Part-time:	1%	25 or older:	2%
Out-of-state:	20%	Live on campus:	84%
Women:	34%		

Transfer out. 95% of students enrolled in the transfer program go on to 4-year colleges. **Colleges most students transferred to 2011:** North Carolina State University, East Carolina University, Appalachian State University, University of North Carolina at Wilmington, University of North Carolina at Greensboro.

Basis for selection. School achievement most important, followed by test scores and recommendations. Interview recommended for some applicants. SAT or ACT scores may not be required of International students if they submit the TOEFL. **Adult students:** SAT/ACT scores not required if out of high school 1 year(s) or more. **Home schooled:** Transcript of courses and grades required. Submission of SAT verbal and mathematics scores required. **Learning Disabled:** Comprehensive tutorial program available for learning-disabled students. Interested students must contact the Learning Partners program for testing and consideration.

High school preparation. College-preparatory program required. 20 units recommended. Recommended units include English 4, mathematics 3, social studies 3, science 2 and foreign language 2.

2011-2012 Annual costs. Tuition/fees: $14,722. Room/board: $8,962. Books/supplies: $100.

Financial aid. **Need-based:** Work-study available nights, weekends and for part-time students. **Non-need-based:** Scholarships awarded for academics, art, athletics, leadership, minority status, music/drama, religious affiliation, ROTC, state residency. **Additional information:** Job location and development program helps students obtain work in the community.

Application procedures. **Admission:** Priority date 7/1; deadline 8/15 (postmark date). $25 fee, may be waived for applicants with need. Admission notification on a rolling basis. Must reply by May 1 or within 2 week(s) if notified thereafter. **Financial aid:** Priority date 3/1; no closing date. FAFSA required.

Academics. **Special study options:** Cooperative education, dual enrollment of high school students, independent study. Louisburg Learning Partners for Students with Learning Differences. **Credit/placement by examination:** AP, CLEP, institutional tests. 30 credit hours maximum toward associate degree. Computer Literacy and Internet Literacy. **Support services:** Learning center, pre-admission summer program, reduced course load, remedial instruction, study skills assistance, tutoring, writing center.

Majors. **Biology:** General. **Business:** General. **Liberal arts:** Arts/sciences.

Most popular majors. Biological/life sciences 6%, business/marketing 8%, liberal arts 86%.

Computing on campus. 75 workstations in library, computer center, student center. Dormitories wired for high-speed internet access and linked to campus network. Online library, helpline, wireless network available.

Student life. **Freshman orientation:** Mandatory. Preregistration for classes offered. **Policies:** Non-resident undergraduates under 21 must live on campus or at home. **Housing:** Guaranteed on-campus for all undergraduates. Single-sex dorms available. $200 partly refundable deposit, deadline 7/1. **Activities:** Campus ministries, choral groups, dance, drama, literary magazine, music ensembles, musical theater, radio station, student government, student newspaper, Christian Life Council, Spanish Club, Workers Actively Volunteering Energetic Services, Phi Theta Kappa, Ecological Concerns Club.

Athletics. NJCAA. **Intercollegiate:** Baseball M, basketball, cheerleading, cross-country, golf M, soccer, softball W, volleyball W. **Intramural:** Basketball, football (tackle), soccer, softball, table tennis, volleyball. **Team name:** Hurricanes.

Student services. Adult student services, alcohol/substance abuse counseling, chaplain/spiritual director, career counseling, student employment services, financial aid counseling, health services, personal counseling, veterans' counselor. **Transfer:** Transfer adviser, college fairs on campus for students transferring to 4-year colleges.

Contact. E-mail: admissions@louisburg.edu
Phone: (919) 497-3222 Toll-free number: (800) 775-0208
Fax: (919) 496-1788
Stephanie Tolbert, Vice President of Enrollment Management, Louisburg College, 501 North Main Street, Louisburg, NC 27549

Martin Community College
Williamston, North Carolina
www.martincc.edu

CB member
CB code: 5445

- Public 2-year community and technical college
- Commuter campus in small town

General. Founded in 1967. Regionally accredited. **Enrollment:** 667 degree-seeking undergraduates; 143 non-degree-seeking students. **Degrees:** 67 associate awarded. **Location:** 30 miles from Greenville, 100 miles from Raleigh. **Calendar:** Semester, limited summer session. **Full-time faculty:** 23 total; 9% have terminal degrees, 61% women. **Part-time faculty:** 44 total; 7% have terminal degrees, 54% women. **Special facilities:** Equine arena, bull riding, rodeos.

Student profile. Among degree-seeking undergraduates, 163 enrolled as first-time, first-year students, 185 transferred in from other institutions.

Part-time:	29%	Hispanic American:	1%
Women:	72%	25 or older:	43%
African American:	46%		

Transfer out. **Colleges most students transferred to 2011:** East Carolina University.

Basis for selection. Open admission, but selective for some programs. Limited enrollment in physical therapy assistant program. Selection based on high school record, placement test results, completion of required courses and interview. Selection of Dental Assisting applications includes high school record, completion of required courses, and an interview. COMPASS required of some students. Interview required for physical therapist assistant applicants and dental assisting applicants. **Home schooled:** Statement describing home school structure and mission, transcript of courses and grades required.

High school preparation. 22 units recommended. Recommended units include English 4, mathematics 3, social studies 2, history 1, science 3 (laboratory 1) and academic electives 9.

2011-2012 Annual costs. Tuition/fees: $2,015; $7,775 out-of-state. Per-credit charge: $67 in-state; $259 out-of-state. Books/supplies: $1,000. Personal expenses: $400.

2010-2011 Financial aid. **Need-based:** 99% of total undergraduate aid awarded as scholarships/grants, 1% as loans/jobs. Need-based aid available for part-time students. Work-study available nights, weekends and for part-time students. **Non-need-based:** Scholarships awarded for academics.

Application procedures. **Admission:** No deadline. No application fee. Admission notification on a rolling basis. **Financial aid:** No deadline. FAFSA required. Applicants notified on a rolling basis starting 5/1.

Academics. **Special study options:** Cooperative education, distance learning, double major, dual enrollment of high school students, ESL, independent study, internships, liberal arts/career combination, teacher certification program. License preparation in paramedic, physical therapy, real estate. **Credit/placement by examination:** AP, CLEP, institutional tests. No more than half of credits required in program of study may be earned through credit by exam (including CLEP). **Support services:** GED preparation and test center, learning center, reduced course load, remedial instruction, study skills assistance, tutoring.

Majors. **Business:** Accounting technology, business admin, executive assistant, management information systems. **Computer sciences:** Information systems. **Education:** General, early childhood, elementary, secondary. **General:** Equestrian studies. **Health services:** Medical assistant, medical secretary, physical therapy assistant. **Liberal arts:** Arts/sciences.

Most popular majors. Agriculture 6%, business/marketing 7%, education 13%, health sciences 31%, liberal arts 15%, trade and industry 23%.

Computing on campus. 31 workstations in library, computer center. Commuter students can connect to campus network. Wireless network available.

Student life. **Freshman orientation:** Available. Preregistration for classes offered. Offered on registration day. **Activities:** Student government, physical therapist assistant club, Phi Theta Kappa, equine club, medical assisting club, Alpha Beta Gamma.

Athletics. **Team name:** Screaming Eagles.

Student services. Career counseling, services for economically disadvantaged, student employment services, financial aid counseling, on-campus daycare, personal counseling, placement for graduates, veterans' counselor. **Transfer:** Pre-admission transcript evaluation for new students. Transfer adviser, college fairs on campus for students transferring to 4-year colleges.

Two-Year Colleges

Contact. E-mail: admissions@martincc.edu
Phone: (252) 792-1521 ext. 268 Fax: (252) 792-0826
Brian Busch, Director of Student Services, Martin Community College, 1161 Kehukee Park Road, Williamston, NC 27892-9988

Mayland Community College

Spruce Pine, North Carolina   **CB member**
www.mayland.edu   **CB code: 0795**

- Public 2-year community college
- Commuter campus in rural community

General. Founded in 1971. Regionally accredited. Mayland Community College serves three counties with a main campus (Spruce Pine), an Avery Campus (Newland) and a Yancey Campus (Burnsville). MCC also has an early college, Mayland Early College High School, which serves selective high school students from all three counties. **Enrollment:** 1,563 degree-seeking undergraduates. **Degrees:** 85 associate awarded. **Location:** 50 miles from Asheville. **Calendar:** Semester, limited summer session. **Full-time faculty:** 40 total. **Part-time faculty:** 50 total. **Class size:** 71% < 20, 29% 20-39.

Student profile. Among degree-seeking undergraduates, 32% enrolled in a transfer program, 68% enrolled in a vocational program.

Transfer out. 11% of students enrolled in the transfer program go on to 4-year colleges. **Colleges most students transferred to 2011:** Appalachian State University, University of North Carolina-Asheville, Western Carolina University, East Tennessee State University, Gardner Webb University.

Basis for selection. Open admission, but selective for some programs. Placement assessment required of all degree-seeking students. Admission to associate degree nursing program and practical nursing program based on competitive ranking system. Medical assisting admissions based on completion of requirements and timely application. **Home schooled:** Transcript of courses and grades required.

2011-2012 Annual costs. Tuition/fees: $2,091; $7,851 out-of-state. Per-credit charge: $67 in-state; $259 out-of-state. Books/supplies: $1,778. Personal expenses: $1,087.

Financial aid. **Need-based:** Need-based aid available for part-time students. Work-study available nights, weekends and for part-time students.

Application procedures. Admission: No deadline. No application fee. Admission notification on a rolling basis beginning on or about 3/1. Medical Assisting Applications due July 15th. Allied Health Transition students due December 9. ADN Adminission students due December 16-March 20. **Financial aid:** Priority date 3/15, closing date 6/30. FAFSA, institutional form required. Applicants notified on a rolling basis starting 6/15.

Academics. Special study options: Cooperative education, cross-registration, distance learning, double major, dual enrollment of high school students, independent study, internships, liberal arts/career combination. Bachelor's degree programs available on campus. License preparation in nursing, real estate. **Credit/placement by examination:** AP, CLEP, institutional tests. Maximum 25% of program hours can be earned via credit by examination. **Support services:** GED preparation and test center, learning center, pre-admission summer program, reduced course load, remedial instruction, study skills assistance, tutoring, writing center.

Majors. Business: Accounting, administrative services, business admin. **Computer sciences:** Systems analysis. **Education:** Early childhood. **Engineering:** Electrical. **General:** Horticulture. **Health services:** Medical secretary, nursing (RN). **Liberal arts:** Arts/sciences.

Most popular majors. Business/marketing 9%, engineering/engineering technologies 7%, family/consumer sciences 6%, health sciences 33%, liberal arts 33%.

Computing on campus. 150 workstations in library, computer center, student center. Commuter students can connect to campus network. Online course registration, online library, helpline, student web hosting available.

Student life. Freshman orientation: Mandatory. Preregistration for classes offered. Most majors at MCC require a mandatory orientation class during the first term of enrollment. **Activities:** Literary magazine, student government, Association of student medical assistants, criminal justice association, early childhood association, human services organization, Phi Theta Kappa, student ambassadors association, student nurses' association, Circle K, Kiwanis Satellite.

Student services. Career counseling, services for economically disadvantaged, student employment services, financial aid counseling, personal counseling, placement for graduates, veterans' counselor. **Physically disabled:** Services for visually, speech, hearing impaired. **Transfer:** Pre-admission transcript evaluation for new students. Transfer center, transfer adviser, college fairs on campus for students transferring to 4-year colleges.

Contact. E-mail: jvance@mayland.edu
Phone: (828) 765-7351 ext. 222
Toll-free number: (800) 462-9526 ext. 222 Fax: (828) 765-0728
Monica Boyd, Director of Enrollment Management, Mayland Community College, Box 547, Spruce Pine, NC 28777

McDowell Technical Community College

Marion, North Carolina
www.mcdowelltech.edu   **CB code: 0789**

- Public 2-year community and technical college
- Commuter campus in small town

General. Founded in 1964. Regionally accredited. **Enrollment:** 1,264 degree-seeking undergraduates. **Degrees:** 160 associate awarded. **Location:** 35 miles from Asheville. **Calendar:** Semester, limited summer session. **Full-time faculty:** 49 total. **Part-time faculty:** 95 total; 2% minority. **Special facilities:** Color and black/white photography laboratories.

Student profile.

Out-of-state:	2%	**25 or older:**	58%

Basis for selection. Open admission, but selective for some programs. Special requirements for allied health programs. Interview required for some allied health programs. **Adult students:** Must take required placement tests. **Home schooled:** Transcript of courses and grades required.

2011-2012 Annual costs. Tuition/fees: $2,047; $7,807 out-of-state. Per-credit charge: $67 in-state; $259 out-of-state. Books/supplies: $1,000. Personal expenses: $4,212.

Financial aid. All financial aid based on need. Need-based aid available for part-time students. Work-study available nights, weekends and for part-time students.

Application procedures. Admission: No deadline. No application fee. Application must be submitted on paper. Admission notification on a rolling basis. **Financial aid:** Priority date 3/15; no closing date. FAFSA, institutional form required. Applicants notified on a rolling basis starting 7/1.

Academics. Special study options: Cooperative education, distance learning, double major, dual enrollment of high school students, independent study, internships, liberal arts/career combination. Bachelor's degree programs available on campus. License preparation in nursing. **Credit/placement by examination:** AP, CLEP, institutional tests. 20 credit hours maximum toward associate degree. **Support services:** GED preparation and test center, learning center, reduced course load, remedial instruction, tutoring.

Majors. Business: General, accounting, office/clerical. **Communications technology:** Graphic/printing. **Computer sciences:** Applications programming, programming. **Education:** General. **Health services:** Nursing (RN). **Liberal arts:** Arts/sciences. **Visual/performing arts:** Commercial photography, commercial/advertising art.

Most popular majors. Business/marketing 13%, computer/information sciences 6%, education 16%, health sciences 25%, liberal arts 14%, trade and industry 20%.

Computing on campus. 80 workstations in library, computer center.

Student life. Freshman orientation: Available. Preregistration for classes offered. Two-hour orientation held one day prior to registration day. **Activities:** Student government.

Student services. Adult student services, career counseling, student employment services, on-campus daycare, personal counseling, placement for graduates, veterans' counselor. **Physically disabled:** Services for visually, speech, hearing impaired. **Transfer:** Transfer adviser for students transferring to 4-year colleges.

Contact. E-mail: rickw@mcdowelltech.edu
Phone: (828) 652-0632 Fax: (828) 652-1014
Rick Wilson, Director of Admissions, McDowell Technical Community College, 54 College Drive, Marion, NC 28752

Miller-Motte College: Cary
Cary, North Carolina
www.mmccary.net

- For-profit 2-year technical and career college
- Commuter campus in small city

General. Regionally accredited; also accredited by ACICS. **Enrollment:** 541 degree-seeking undergraduates. **Degrees:** 79 associate awarded. **Location:** 10 miles from downtown Raleigh. **Calendar:** Quarter. **Full-time faculty:** 10 total. **Part-time faculty:** 23 total.

Basis for selection. Open admission, but selective for some programs. High school diploma is required and GED is accepted. **Home schooled:** Interview required.

2011-2012 Annual costs. Tuition/fees: $12,672. Per-credit charge: $264.

Financial aid. Need-based: Work-study available nights, weekends and for part-time students.

Application procedures. Admission: No deadline. $40 fee. **Financial aid:** No deadline.

Academics. Credit/placement by examination: AP, CLEP. **Support services:** Tutoring.

Majors. Health services: Insurance coding, massage therapy, medical assistant, surgical technology.

Computing on campus. 25 workstations in library.

Student life. Freshman orientation: Preregistration for classes offered.

Student services. Physically disabled: Services for visually impaired.

Contact. Tim Horn, Admissions Director, Miller-Motte College: Cary, 2205 Walnut Street, Cary, NC 27518

Miller-Motte College: Fayetteville
Fayetteville, North Carolina
www.miller-motte.edu

- For-profit 2-year branch campus and technical college
- Large city

General. Regionally accredited; also accredited by ACICS. **Enrollment:** 515 full-time, degree-seeking students. **Calendar:** Quarter. **Full-time faculty:** 5 total. **Part-time faculty:** 38 total.

Basis for selection. Admission requirements vary by programs.

Financial aid. Need-based: Work-study available nights, weekends and for part-time students.

Application procedures. Admission: $40 fee.

Academics. Credit/placement by examination: AP, CLEP.

Majors. Health services: Medical assistant. **Protective services:** Law enforcement admin.

Contact. Michael McCollum, Director of Admissions, Miller-Motte College: Fayetteville, 3725 Ramsey Street, Suite 103A, Fayetteville, NC 28311

Mitchell Community College
Statesville, North Carolina
www.mitchellcc.edu

CB member
CB code: 5412

- Public 2-year community college
- Commuter campus in large town

General. Founded in 1852. Regionally accredited. **Enrollment:** 2,959 degree-seeking undergraduates. **Degrees:** 280 associate awarded. **Location:** 40 miles from Charlotte, 40 miles from Winston-Salem. **Calendar:** Semester, limited summer session. **Full-time faculty:** 92 total. **Part-time faculty:** 250 total.

Student profile.

Out-of-state:	8%	25 or older:	40%

Transfer out. Colleges most students transferred to 2011: University of North Carolina-Charlotte, Appalachian State University, Gardner-Webb University, Lenoir-Rhyne University.

Basis for selection. Open admission, but selective for some programs. All applicants must take college placement tests to determine readiness for college-level studies. Nursing program applicants must meet minimum admissions requirements; interview and essay required.

2011-2012 Annual costs. Tuition/fees: $2,065; $7,825 out-of-state. Per-credit charge: $67 in-state; $259 out-of-state. Books/supplies: $900. Personal expenses: $1,448.

Financial aid. Need-based: Need-based aid available for part-time students. Work-study available nights, weekends and for part-time students.

Application procedures. Admission: No deadline. No application fee. Admission notification on a rolling basis. **Financial aid:** No deadline. FAFSA, institutional form required. Applicants notified on a rolling basis starting 3/1; must reply within 2 week(s) of notification.

Academics. Special study options: Cooperative education, distance learning, dual enrollment of high school students, independent study, weekend college. License preparation in nursing, paramedic, real estate. **Credit/placement by examination:** AP, CLEP, institutional tests. 20 credit hours maximum toward associate degree. **Support services:** GED preparation and test center, learning center, reduced course load, remedial instruction, tutoring.

Majors. Business: Accounting, administrative services, business admin, operations. **Computer sciences:** Information systems, programming. **Education:** Early childhood, teacher assistance. **Engineering:** Electrical. **Health services:** Nursing (RN), predental, premedicine, prepharmacy, preveterinary. **Liberal arts:** Arts/sciences. **Protective services:** Police science. **Visual/performing arts:** Studio arts.

Most popular majors. Business/marketing 15%, computer/information sciences 13%, engineering/engineering technologies 6%, health sciences 26%, liberal arts 18%, personal/culinary services 8%.

Computing on campus. 45 workstations in library, computer center.

Student life. Freshman orientation: Available. Preregistration for classes offered. Usually held immediately prior to fall semester for approximately 2.5 hours. **Activities:** Concert band, choral groups, literary magazine, student government, Circle-K, Christian Student Fellowship, Ebony Kinship.

Student services. Chaplain/spiritual director, career counseling, student employment services, financial aid counseling, personal counseling, placement for graduates, veterans' counselor. **Physically disabled:** Services for visually, hearing impaired. **Transfer:** College fairs on campus for students transferring to 4-year colleges.

Contact. E-mail: kmoore@mitchellcc.edu
Phone: (704) 878-3243 Fax: (704) 878-0872
Kirby Moore, Director of Admissions and Records, Mitchell Community College, 500 West Broad Street, Statesville, NC 28677

Montgomery Community College
Troy, North Carolina
www.montgomery.edu

CB code: 0785

- Public 2-year community college
- Commuter campus in small town

General. Founded in 1967. Regionally accredited. **Enrollment:** 657 degree-seeking undergraduates; 99 non-degree-seeking students. **Degrees:** 77 associate awarded. **Location:** 50 miles from Greensboro, 62 miles from Charlotte. **Calendar:** Semester, limited summer session. **Full-time faculty:** 38 total. **Part-time faculty:** 34 total. **Special facilities:** Rifle/pistol firing range.

Student profile. Among degree-seeking undergraduates, 16% enrolled in a transfer program, 71% enrolled in a vocational program, 90 enrolled as first-time, first-year students.

Part-time:	43%	Asian American:	2%
Out-of-state:	1%	Hispanic American:	2%
Women:	63%	Native American:	1%
African American:	25%	25 or older:	53%

Transfer out. Colleges most students transferred to 2011: Pfeiffer University, Gardner-Webb University, University of North Carolina at Greensboro.

Basis for selection. Open admission, but selective for some programs. Special requirements for nursing program. Secondary school record and test scores considered. **Home schooled:** Home school must provide copy of "Notification of intent to operate" card from NC Department of Non-Public Education.

High school preparation. 28 units recommended. Recommended units include English 4, mathematics 4, social studies 3, science 3 (laboratory 1) and academic electives 13.

2011-2012 Annual costs. Tuition/fees: $2,053; $7,813 out-of-state. Per-credit charge: $67 in-state; $259 out-of-state. Books/supplies: $1,467. Personal expenses: $1,600.

2010-2011 Financial aid. Need-based: 99% of total undergraduate aid awarded as scholarships/grants, 1% as loans/jobs. Need-based aid available for part-time students. Work-study available nights, weekends and for part-time students. **Non-need-based:** Scholarships awarded for academics, minority status, state residency.

Application procedures. Admission: No deadline. No application fee. Admission notification on a rolling basis. Practical Nursing program applicants must apply by October 15 for following fall program. **Financial aid:** Priority date 7/1, closing date 7/1. FAFSA, institutional form required. Applicants notified on a rolling basis starting 6/1.

Academics. Special study options: Distance learning, dual enrollment of high school students. Bachelor's degree programs available on campus. License preparation in nursing. **Credit/placement by examination:** AP, CLEP, institutional tests. 16 credit hours maximum toward associate degree. **Support services:** GED preparation and test center, learning center, reduced course load, remedial instruction, tutoring.

Majors. Business: Accounting, business admin, office management. **Computer sciences:** Information technology. **Conservation:** Forest technology. **Education:** Early childhood. **Health services:** Medical assistant. **Liberal arts:** Arts/sciences. **Protective services:** Criminal justice. **Visual/performing arts:** Crafts.

Most popular majors. Business/marketing 12%, education 12%, health sciences 9%, liberal arts 33%, natural resources/environmental science 17%, security/protective services 6%, trade and industry 8%.

Computing on campus. 125 workstations in library, computer center. Commuter students can connect to campus network. Wireless network available.

Student life. Freshman orientation: Available. Preregistration for classes offered. **Activities:** Student government, gunsmithing society, forestry club, phi beta lambda, practical nursing club, medical assisting club.

Athletics. Team name: Trailblazers.

Student services. Career counseling, student employment services, financial aid counseling, personal counseling, veterans' counselor. **Physically disabled:** Services for visually, speech, hearing impaired. **Transfer:** Transfer adviser, college fairs on campus for students transferring to 4-year colleges.

Contact. E-mail: fryek@montgomery.edu
Phone: (910) 576-6222 ext. 240 Toll-free number: (800) 839-6222
Fax: (910) 576-2176
Karen Frye, Admissions Officer, Montgomery Community College, 1011 Page Street, Troy, NC 27371-0787

Nash Community College
Rocky Mount, North Carolina
www.nashcc.edu
CB member
CB code: 5881

▶ Public 2-year community college
▶ Commuter campus in small city

General. Founded in 1967. Regionally accredited. **Enrollment:** 2,900 degree-seeking undergraduates. **Degrees:** 250 associate awarded. **Location:** 55 miles from Raleigh. **Calendar:** Semester, limited summer session. **Full-time faculty:** 75 total. **Part-time faculty:** 150 total. **Class size:** 54% < 20, 46% 20-39. **Partnerships:** Formal partnership with high schools to provide students opportunity to earn college credit.

Student profile. Among degree-seeking undergraduates, 28% enrolled in a transfer program, 86% enrolled in a vocational program.

Out-of-state: 1% **25 or older:** 52%

Transfer out. Colleges most students transferred to 2011: University of North Carolina system universities.

Basis for selection. Open admission, but selective for some programs. Special requirements for nursing, physical therapy assistant, phlebotomy, cosmetology programs. **Adult students:** College recommends ASSET or COMPASS placement test if student does not have SAT scores.

High school preparation. Appropriate biology courses required for nursing and physical therapist assistant programs.

2011-2012 Annual costs. Tuition/fees: $2,091; $7,851 out-of-state. Per-credit charge: $67 in-state; $259 out-of-state. Books/supplies: $1,000. Personal expenses: $2,000.

Financial aid. Need-based: Need-based aid available for part-time students. Work-study available nights, weekends and for part-time students. **Non-need-based:** Scholarships awarded for academics.

Application procedures. Admission: No deadline. No application fee. Admission notification on a rolling basis. **Financial aid:** Priority date 6/30; no closing date. FAFSA, institutional form required. Applicants notified on a rolling basis starting 7/15.

Academics. Special study options: Accelerated study, distance learning, dual enrollment of high school students, ESL, liberal arts/career combination. License preparation in nursing, paramedic, physical therapy, real estate. **Credit/placement by examination:** AP, CLEP, IB, institutional tests. **Support services:** GED preparation and test center, learning center, reduced course load, remedial instruction, study skills assistance, tutoring.

Majors. Architecture: Technology. **Business:** Accounting, administrative services, business admin, hotel/motel admin, management information systems. **Computer sciences:** Information systems. **Education:** General, early childhood, teacher assistance. **Engineering:** Electrical. **Health services:** Licensed practical nurse, medical secretary, nursing (RN). **Liberal arts:** Arts/sciences. **Protective services:** Police science. **Work/family studies:** Child care management.

Most popular majors. Business/marketing 18%, computer/information sciences 8%, engineering/engineering technologies 16%, health sciences 21%, liberal arts 21%, social sciences 7%.

Computing on campus. 110 workstations in library, computer center, student center. Online library, helpline, wireless network available.

Student life. Freshman orientation: Mandatory. Preregistration for classes offered. **Activities:** Drama, radio station, student government.

Student services. Career counseling, services for economically disadvantaged, student employment services, financial aid counseling, on-campus daycare, placement for graduates, veterans' counselor. **Physically disabled:** Services for visually, speech, hearing impaired. **Transfer:** Pre-admission transcript evaluation for new students. Transfer adviser, college fairs on campus for students transferring to 4-year colleges.

Contact. E-mail: dgardner@nashcc.edu
Phone: (252) 443-4011 ext. 300 Fax: (252) 451-8401
Dot Gardner, Admissions Officer, Nash Community College, Box 7488, Rocky Mount, NC 27804-0488

Pamlico Community College
Grantsboro, North Carolina
www.pamlicocc.edu
CB code: 0864

▶ Public 2-year community college
▶ Commuter campus in rural community
▶ Interview required

General. Founded in 1962. Regionally accredited. **Enrollment:** 491 degree-seeking undergraduates. **Degrees:** 58 associate awarded. **Location:** 20 miles from New Bern. **Calendar:** Semester, limited summer session. **Full-time faculty:** 29 total. **Part-time faculty:** 41 total.

Transfer out. Colleges most students transferred to 2011: Craven Community College.

Basis for selection. Open admission. Students talk to admission counselor and adviser. **Home schooled:** Transcript of courses and grades required.

High school preparation. College-preparatory program recommended. 24 units required.

2011-2012 Annual costs. Tuition/fees: $2,030; $7,790 out-of-state. Per-credit charge: $67 in-state; $259 out-of-state. Books/supplies: $1,000. Personal expenses: $1,630.

Financial aid. Need-based: Work-study available nights, weekends and for part-time students. **Additional information:** Jobs Training Partner Act and Displaced Homemaker Programs cover tuition, books, fees.

Application procedures. Admission: No deadline. No application fee. Application must be submitted on paper. Admission notification on a rolling basis. **Financial aid:** Priority date 3/15; no closing date. FAFSA required. Applicants notified on a rolling basis.

Academics. Special study options: Cooperative education, distance learning, dual enrollment of high school students, ESL, independent study, internships. **Credit/placement by examination:** AP, CLEP, institutional tests. **Support services:** GED preparation and test center, learning center, reduced course load, remedial instruction, tutoring.

Majors. Business: Accounting, business admin, office/clerical. **Conservation:** General. **Education:** General, early childhood. **Engineering:** Electrical.

Computing on campus. 40 workstations in library. Online library, wireless network available.

Student life. Freshman orientation: Available. Preregistration for classes offered. **Activities:** Student government, student newspaper.

Student services. Career counseling, student employment services, financial aid counseling, personal counseling, placement for graduates, veterans' counselor. **Transfer:** Pre-admission transcript evaluation for new students. College fairs on campus for students transferring to 4-year colleges.

Contact. E-mail: jgibbs@pamlicocc.edu
Phone: (252) 249-1851 Fax: (252) 249-2377
Jamie Gibbs, Vice President of Student Services, Pamlico Community College, PO Box 185, Grantsboro, NC 28529

Piedmont Community College
Roxboro, North Carolina
www.piedmontcc.edu   **CB code: 5518**

- Public 2-year community college
- Small town

General. Founded in 1970. Regionally accredited. Branch campus in Caswell County. Correctional education in Foodservice Technology offered in Hillsborough. **Enrollment:** 1,781 degree-seeking undergraduates. **Degrees:** 191 associate awarded. **Location:** 30 miles from Durham, 45 miles from Chapel Hill. **Calendar:** Semester, limited summer session. **Full-time faculty:** 86 total. **Part-time faculty:** 106 total. **Special facilities:** 4-mile nature trail.

Student profile. Among degree-seeking undergraduates, 310 enrolled as first-time, first-year students.

Out-of-state:	1%	25 or older:	46%

Basis for selection. Open admission, but selective for some programs. Admission for nursing based on test scores, interview and recommendations. Nursing applicants must provide health data.

2011-2012 Annual costs. Tuition/fees: $2,035; $7,795 out-of-state. Per-credit charge: $67 in-state; $259 out-of-state. Books/supplies: $1,200. Personal expenses: $750.

Financial aid. Need-based: Work-study available nights, weekends and for part-time students.

Application procedures. Admission: No deadline. No application fee. Admission notification on a rolling basis. Certain certificate programs do not require high school diploma. **Financial aid:** Priority date 4/15; no closing date. FAFSA required. Applicants notified on a rolling basis; must reply within 2 week(s) of notification.

Academics. Special study options: Cooperative education, cross-registration, distance learning, double major, dual enrollment of high school students, independent study, internships, weekend college. License preparation in nursing. **Credit/placement by examination:** AP, CLEP, institutional tests. Maximum of 50% of coursework may be completed through credit by examination. **Support services:** GED preparation and test center, learning center, reduced course load, remedial instruction, study skills assistance, tutoring.

Majors. Biology: Biotechnology. **Business:** General, accounting, administrative services, business admin, international, office technology. **Computer sciences:** Applications programming, programming. **Health services:** Medical secretary, nursing (RN). **Human services:** Social work. **Liberal arts:** Arts/sciences. **Protective services:** Criminal justice. **Visual/performing arts:** Cinematography, studio arts.

Computing on campus. 140 workstations in library, computer center.

Student life. Freshman orientation: Available. Preregistration for classes offered. **Activities:** Dance, drama, student government, student newspaper, Phi Theta Kappa, Student Nursing Assoc., C.A.R.E. (Human Services), film/video production technology club, ACM Student Siggraph Chapter, criminal justice club, Phi Beta Lambda, PCC Engage (Warriors for Christ), Minority Male Mentoring Initiative (3MI), athletic club.

Athletics. Team name: Pacers.

Student services. Career counseling, services for economically disadvantaged, student employment services, financial aid counseling, on-campus daycare, personal counseling, placement for graduates, veterans' counselor. **Physically disabled:** Services for visually, hearing impaired. **Transfer:** Transfer center, transfer adviser, college fairs on campus for students transferring to 4-year colleges.

Contact. Phone: (336) 599-1181 Fax: (336) 598-9283
Shelia Williamson, Coordinator of Admissions, Piedmont Community College, 1715 College Drive, Roxboro, NC 27573-1197

Pitt Community College
Greenville, North Carolina   **CB member**
www.pittcc.edu   **CB code: 5556**

- Public 2-year community and technical college
- Commuter campus in small city

General. Founded in 1961. Regionally accredited. **Enrollment:** 8,544 degree-seeking undergraduates. **Degrees:** 796 associate awarded. **ROTC:** Army. **Location:** 85 miles from Raleigh. **Calendar:** Semester, limited summer session. **Full-time faculty:** 226 total. **Part-time faculty:** 429 total. **Class size:** 66% < 20, 34% 20-39, less than 1% 40-49, less than 1% 50-99.

Student profile.

Out-of-state:	2%	25 or older:	39%

Transfer out. Colleges most students transferred to 2011: East Carolina University, University of North Carolina at Wilmington, Barton College.

Basis for selection. Open admission, but selective for some programs. Special admission requirements for some allied health programs. SAT and/or ACT may be used in lieu of the college's placement test for placement into English and Math courses.

2011-2012 Annual costs. Tuition/fees: $2,069; $7,829 out-of-state. Per-credit charge: $67 in-state; $259 out-of-state. Books/supplies: $1,600.

Financial aid. Need-based: Need-based aid available for part-time students. Work-study available nights, weekends and for part-time students. **Non-need-based:** Scholarships awarded for academics, athletics, ROTC.

Application procedures. Admission: No deadline. No application fee. Admission notification on a rolling basis. **Financial aid:** Priority date 3/15; no closing date. FAFSA required. Applicants notified on a rolling basis starting 2/1.

Academics. Special study options: Cooperative education, distance learning, double major, dual enrollment of high school students, ESL, independent study, internships, weekend college. License preparation in nursing, occupational therapy, paramedic, radiology, real estate. **Credit/placement by examination:** AP, CLEP, institutional tests. 40 credit hours maximum toward associate degree. Credit by examination can not be included in the 25% residency requirement. **Support services:** GED preparation and test center, learning center, remedial instruction, tutoring.

Majors. Business: Accounting, business admin, e-commerce, human resources, marketing, office management, operations, sales/distribution, training/development. **Computer sciences:** Applications programming, information systems, vendor certification. **Education:** Early childhood. **Health services:** Medical assistant, medical radiologic technology/radiation therapy, medical records technology, medical secretary, mental health services, nuclear medical technology, nursing (RN), occupational therapy assistant, office admin, respiratory therapy assistant, respiratory therapy technology, sonography. **Liberal arts:** Arts/sciences. **Protective services:** Criminal justice, police science. **Visual/performing arts:** Commercial/advertising art.

Most popular majors. Business/marketing 10%, computer/information sciences 10%, engineering/engineering technologies 10%, health sciences 33%, liberal arts 20%, trade and industry 15%.

Computing on campus. 50 workstations in library, computer center. Helpline available.

Student life. Freshman orientation: Available. Preregistration for classes offered. **Activities:** Student government, Gamma Beta Phi, student government association, Southern Organization of Human Services Organization, Society of Advancement of Management, Delta Epsilon Chi, multicultural/international Club, Students Monitoring Students.

Athletics. NJCAA. **Intercollegiate:** Baseball M, basketball M, golf M, softball W, volleyball W. **Intramural:** Basketball M. **Team name:** Bulldogs.

Student services. Adult student services, alcohol/substance abuse counseling, career counseling, services for economically disadvantaged, student employment services, financial aid counseling, minority student services, on-campus daycare, personal counseling, veterans' counselor. **Physically disabled:** Services for visually, speech, hearing impaired. **Transfer:** Transfer adviser, college fairs on campus for students transferring to 4-year colleges.

Contact. E-mail: pittadm@email.pittcc.edu
Phone: (252) 493-7232 Fax: (252) 321-4209
Joanne Ceres, Director of Admissions and Records, Pitt Community College, PO Drawer 7007, Greenville, NC 27835-7007

Randolph Community College
Asheboro, North Carolina
www.randolph.edu   **CB code: 5585**

- Public 2-year community and technical college
- Commuter campus in large town

General. Founded in 1962. Regionally accredited. **Enrollment:** 3,409 degree-seeking undergraduates. **Degrees:** 391 associate awarded. **Location:** 65 miles from Charlotte, 26 miles from Greensboro. **Calendar:** Semester, limited summer session. **Full-time faculty:** 88 total. **Part-time faculty:** 287 total.

Transfer out. Colleges most students transferred to 2011: University of North Carolina-Greensboro, High Point University, Guilford College, University of North Carolina-Charlotte.

Basis for selection. Open admission, but selective for some programs. Admission to nursing and radiography program based primarily on competitive admission. Admission into the cosmetology program requires students to complete RED 090 or have an acceptable reading placement score. Medical Assisting requires keyboard proficiency and biology competency with a grade of C or higher. Basic Law Enforcement Training requires 20 or older, clean criminal history, and background check, valid license, medical exam, and reading placement assessment. **Home schooled:** Transcript of courses and grades required. Copy of certificate of home school operation or a Notice of Intent (to operate a home school) is required to have been sent to the North Carolina Non-Public Education Office.

High school preparation. College-preparatory program recommended.

2011-2012 Annual costs. Tuition/fees: $2,078; $7,838 out-of-state. Per-credit charge: $67 in-state; $259 out-of-state. Books/supplies: $1,043. Personal expenses: $2,700.

Financial aid. Need-based: Need-based aid available for part-time students. Work-study available nights, weekends and for part-time students. **Non-need-based:** Scholarships awarded for academics, leadership, minority status, state residency.

Application procedures. Admission: No deadline. No application fee. Admission notification on a rolling basis. Students are required to complete placement testing or send official placement test scores taken within the last 3 years prior to enrolling. **Financial aid:** No deadline. FAFSA required. Applicants notified on a rolling basis starting 3/1.

Academics. Special study options: Cooperative education, distance learning, double major, dual enrollment of high school students, ESL, independent study, internships, liberal arts/career combination, weekend college. **Credit/placement by examination:** AP, CLEP, IB, institutional tests. 16 credit hours maximum toward associate degree. **Support services:** GED preparation and test center, learning center, remedial instruction, study skills assistance, tutoring, writing center.

Majors. Business: Accounting, administrative services, business admin, management information systems. **Communications technology:** Photo/

film/video. **Computer sciences:** Networking. **Foreign languages:** Sign language interpretation. **Health services:** EMT paramedic, nursing (RN). **Liberal arts:** Arts/sciences. **Protective services:** Police science. **Visual/performing arts:** Commercial photography, commercial/advertising art, interior design, photography, studio arts. **Work/family studies:** Child care management.

Most popular majors. Business/marketing 8%, computer/information sciences 8%, education 8%, health sciences 13%, liberal arts 21%, security/protective services 6%, trade and industry 7%, visual/performing arts 21%.

Computing on campus. Online course registration, online library, wireless network available.

Student life. Freshman orientation: Mandatory. Preregistration for classes offered. 30 minute overview of policies and procedures scheduled online or on campus. Students are notified by mail about scheduled dates and times. **Activities:** Student government, student newspaper.

Athletics. Team name: Armadillos.

Student services. Adult student services, career counseling, student employment services, financial aid counseling, personal counseling, placement for graduates, veterans' counselor. **Physically disabled:** Services for visually, speech, hearing impaired. **Transfer:** Pre-admission transcript evaluation for new students. Transfer adviser, college fairs on campus for students transferring to 4-year colleges.

Contact. E-mail: masmith@randolph.edu
Phone: (336) 633-0200 ext. 239 Fax: (336) 629-9547
Brandi Hagerman, Director of Enrollment Management / Registrar, Randolph Community College, PO Box 1009, Asheboro, NC 27204

Richmond Community College
Hamlet, North Carolina   **CB member**
www.richmondcc.edu   **CB code: 5588**

- Public 2-year community college
- Commuter campus in small town

General. Founded in 1964. Regionally accredited. **Enrollment:** 2,170 degree-seeking undergraduates. **Degrees:** 199 associate awarded. **Location:** 75 miles from Charlotte. **Calendar:** Semester, limited summer session. **Full-time faculty:** 68 total. **Part-time faculty:** 5 total. **Special facilities:** Health science building with exam rooms and simulation areas.

Student profile. Among degree-seeking undergraduates, 2,162 enrolled as first-time, first-year students.

Transfer out. Colleges most students transferred to 2011: UNC-Pembroke, Gardner-Webb University, UNC-Charlotte, Fayetteville State.

Basis for selection. Open admission, but selective for some programs. Admission to nursing program based on academic record and completion of admission requirements, interview required. **Home schooled:** Transcript of courses and grades required.

2011-2012 Annual costs. Tuition/fees: $2,051; $7,811 out-of-state. Per-credit charge: $67 in-state; $259 out-of-state. Books/supplies: $600. Personal expenses: $900.

Financial aid. Need-based: Need-based aid available for part-time students. Work-study available nights, weekends and for part-time students. **Non-need-based:** Scholarships awarded for academics, leadership.

Application procedures. Admission: No deadline. No application fee. Admission notification on a rolling basis. **Financial aid:** Closing date 7/25. FAFSA, institutional form required. Applicants notified on a rolling basis starting 7/8; must reply within 2 week(s) of notification.

Academics. Special study options: Cooperative education, cross-registration, distance learning, double major, dual enrollment of high school students, ESL, independent study, internships, student-designed major, teacher certification program. Bachelor's degree programs available on campus. License preparation in nursing. **Credit/placement by examination:** AP, CLEP, institutional tests. 15 credit hours maximum toward associate degree. Interview required for placement and counseling. **Support services:** GED preparation and test center, learning center, reduced course load, remedial instruction, study skills assistance, tutoring, writing center.

Majors. Business: Accounting, administrative services, business admin, management information systems. **Computer sciences:** Information systems, networking. **Engineering:** Electrical. **Health services:** Medical assistant,

mental health services, nursing (RN). **Human services:** Social work. **Liberal arts:** Arts/sciences. **Work/family studies:** Child care management.

Computing on campus. 250 workstations in library, computer center.

Student life. Freshman orientation: Mandatory. Preregistration for classes offered. **Activities:** Drama, student government, student newspaper.

Athletics. Team name: Panthers.

Student services. Career counseling, student employment services, financial aid counseling, health services, minority student services, personal counseling, placement for graduates, veterans' counselor. **Physically disabled:** Services for visually, hearing impaired. **Transfer:** Transfer adviser, college fairs on campus for students transferring to 4-year colleges.

Contact. Phone: (910) 410-1736 Fax: (910) 582-7102
Daphne Stancil, Director of Admissions, Richmond Community College, Box 1189, Hamlet, NC 28345

Roanoke-Chowan Community College
Ahoskie, North Carolina
www.roanokechowan.edu   CB code: 5564

- Public 2-year community college
- Commuter campus in small town

General. Founded in 1967. Regionally accredited. **Enrollment:** 918 degree-seeking undergraduates; 45 non-degree-seeking students. **Degrees:** 52 associate awarded. **Location:** 60 miles from Greenville, 65 miles from Norfolk, Virginia. **Calendar:** Semester, limited summer session. **Full-time faculty:** 36 total. **Part-time faculty:** 44 total. **Class size:** 70% < 20, 29% 20-39, 2% 40-49. **Special facilities:** Arboretum/environmental science outdoor laboratory.

Student profile. Among degree-seeking undergraduates, 15% enrolled in a transfer program, 85% enrolled in a vocational program, 96 enrolled as first-time, first-year students, 90 transferred in from other institutions.

Part-time:	46%	25 or older:	45%
Women:	69%		

Transfer out. Colleges most students transferred to 2011: Elizabeth City State University, Pitt Community College, East Carolina University.

Basis for selection. Open admission, but selective for some programs. Special requirements for nursing applicants. **Adult students:** SAT/ACT scores not required. **Home schooled:** Statement describing home school structure and mission, transcript of courses and grades required.

2011-2012 Annual costs. Tuition/fees: $2,092; $7,852 out-of-state. Per-credit charge: $67 in-state; $259 out-of-state. Books/supplies: $800. Personal expenses: $1,555.

Financial aid. Need-based: Need-based aid available for part-time students. Work-study available nights, weekends and for part-time students. **Non-need-based:** Scholarships awarded for academics.

Application procedures. Admission: No deadline. No application fee. Admission notification on a rolling basis. **Financial aid:** Priority date 3/15; no closing date. FAFSA required. Applicants notified on a rolling basis starting 7/1.

Academics. Special study options: Cooperative education, distance learning, dual enrollment of high school students, independent study, internships. License preparation in nursing. **Credit/placement by examination:** AP, CLEP, institutional tests. **Support services:** GED preparation and test center, learning center, reduced course load, remedial instruction, study skills assistance, tutoring.

Majors. Architecture: Technology. **Business:** Administrative services, business admin, management information systems. **Computer sciences:** Information systems. **Conservation:** Environmental science. **Education:** Early childhood, teacher assistance. **Health services:** Mental health services, nursing (RN), substance abuse counseling. **Liberal arts:** Arts/sciences. **Protective services:** Criminal justice. **Work/family studies:** Child care management.

Most popular majors. Business/marketing 10%, education 15%, health sciences 52%, liberal arts 8%, security/protective services 6%.

Computing on campus. 200 workstations in library, computer center. Online library available.

Student life. Freshman orientation: Available. Preregistration for classes offered. **Activities:** Student government.

Student services. Career counseling, services for economically disadvantaged, student employment services, financial aid counseling, minority student services, personal counseling, veterans' counselor, women's services. **Transfer:** Pre-admission transcript evaluation for new students.

Contact. Phone: (252) 862-1200 Fax: (252) 862-1355
Amy Wiggins, Director of Admissions/Counseling, Roanoke-Chowan Community College, 109 Community College Road, Ahoskie, NC 27910-9522

Robeson Community College
Lumberton, North Carolina
www.robeson.edu   CB code: 5594

- Public 2-year community college
- Commuter campus in large town

General. Founded in 1965. Regionally accredited. **Enrollment:** 2,747 degree-seeking undergraduates. **Degrees:** 205 associate awarded. **Location:** 30 miles from Fayetteville. **Calendar:** Semester, limited summer session. **Full-time faculty:** 91 total; 2% have terminal degrees. **Part-time faculty:** 251 total; 2% have terminal degrees.

Basis for selection. Open admission, but selective for some programs. Special requirements for allied health programs. Interview recommended. **Adult students:** SAT/ACT scores not required.

2011-2012 Annual costs. Tuition/fees: $2,063; $7,823 out-of-state. Per-credit charge: $67 in-state; $259 out-of-state. Books/supplies: $1,300. Personal expenses: $75.

Financial aid. Need-based: Need-based aid available for part-time students. Work-study available nights, weekends and for part-time students.

Application procedures. Admission: Closing date 7/12. No application fee. Admission notification on a rolling basis. **Financial aid:** Priority date 5/15, closing date 7/19. FAFSA required. Applicants notified on a rolling basis starting 7/31.

Academics. Special study options: Distance learning, double major, dual enrollment of high school students. License preparation in nursing, radiology. **Credit/placement by examination:** AP, CLEP, IB, institutional tests. 40 credit hours maximum toward associate degree. **Support services:** GED preparation and test center, learning center, reduced course load, remedial instruction, study skills assistance, tutoring, writing center.

Majors. Business: Business admin. **Computer sciences:** Information technology. **Health services:** EMT paramedic, nursing (RN), radiologic technology/medical imaging, respiratory therapy technology, surgical technology. **Protective services:** Criminal justice.

Computing on campus. 50 workstations in library. Commuter students can connect to campus network. Online library, helpline, wireless network available.

Student life. Freshman orientation: Available. Preregistration for classes offered. **Activities:** Choral groups, student government, student newspaper.

Student services. Adult student services, career counseling, services for economically disadvantaged, student employment services, financial aid counseling, health services, personal counseling, placement for graduates, veterans' counselor. **Physically disabled:** Services for visually, hearing impaired. **Transfer:** Pre-admission transcript evaluation for new students. Transfer adviser, college fairs on campus for students transferring to 4-year colleges.

Contact. E-mail: jrevels@robeson.cc.nc.us
Phone: (910) 272-3700 ext. 3347 Fax: (910) 618-5686
Judith Revels, Director of Admissions, Robeson Community College, PO Box 1420, Lumberton, NC 28359

Rockingham Community College
Wentworth, North Carolina
www.rockinghamcc.edu   CB code: 5582

- Public 2-year community college
- Commuter campus in rural community

General. Founded in 1963. Regionally accredited. **Enrollment:** 2,087 degree-seeking undergraduates; 346 non-degree-seeking students. **Degrees:** 173 associate awarded. **Location:** 26 miles from Greensboro. **Calendar:**

Semester, extensive summer session. **Full-time faculty:** 66 total. **Part-time faculty:** 54 total.

Student profile. Among degree-seeking undergraduates, 478 enrolled as first-time, first-year students.

Part-time:	49%	Women:	63%

Transfer out. Colleges most students transferred to 2011: University of North Carolina at Greensboro, North Carolina A&T University.

Basis for selection. Open admission, but selective for some programs. All allied health programs and some other programs require all or some of the following: qualifying high school and college GPA, placement testing, specific high school courses, professional certification, other exams. Interview required for nursing and occupational therapy assistant programs. **Home schooled:** Need complete record of all courses taken in grades 9-12.

High school preparation. Recommended units include English 4, mathematics 3, social studies 2, history 1, science 3 (laboratory 1) and foreign language 2.

2011-2012 Annual costs. Tuition/fees: $2,091; $7,851 out-of-state. Per-credit charge: $67 in-state; $259 out-of-state. Books/supplies: $1,500. Personal expenses: $4,100.

Financial aid. Need-based: Need-based aid available for part-time students. Work-study available nights, weekends and for part-time students. **Non-need-based:** Scholarships awarded for academics.

Application procedures. Admission: No deadline. No application fee. Admission notification on a rolling basis. **Financial aid:** Priority date 3/15; no closing date. FAFSA, institutional form required. Must reply within 2 week(s) of notification.

Academics. Special study options: Cooperative education, distance learning, dual enrollment of high school students, independent study. Preengineering program leading to transfer to North Carolina State University, North Carolina Agricultural and Technical State University, or University of North Carolina at Charlotte. License preparation in nursing. **Credit/placement by examination:** AP, CLEP, institutional tests. **Support services:** GED preparation and test center, learning center, reduced course load, remedial instruction, study skills assistance, tutoring.

Majors. Biology: Biotechnology. **Business:** Accounting, business admin, financial planning, office technology, office/clerical. **Computer sciences:** Information systems. **Education:** Early childhood. **Engineering:** Electrical. **Health services:** Medical secretary, nursing (RN), respiratory therapy technology. **Liberal arts:** Arts/sciences. **Protective services:** Law enforcement admin. **Visual/performing arts:** Studio arts.

Most popular majors. Security/protective services 7%.

Computing on campus. 1,022 workstations in library, computer center. Wireless network available.

Student life. Freshman orientation: Available. Preregistration for classes offered. **Activities:** Student government, student newspaper, Phi Theta Kappa, art club, criminal justice club, early childhood educators club, musicians guild, NC Assoc of Nursing Students, practical nursing club, science club, Sigma Kappa Delta, Students in Free Enterprise.

Athletics. NJCAA. **Intercollegiate:** Baseball M, basketball M, cheerleading M, golf, volleyball W. **Intramural:** Basketball, table tennis, tennis, volleyball. **Team name:** Eagles.

Student services. Career counseling, services for economically disadvantaged, student employment services, financial aid counseling, personal counseling, placement for graduates, veterans' counselor. **Physically disabled:** Services for visually, hearing impaired. **Transfer:** Transfer adviser, college fairs on campus for students transferring to 4-year colleges.

Contact. E-mail: bouldinc@rockinghamcc.edu
Phone: (336) 342-4261 ext. 2333 Fax: (336) 342-1809
Derrick Satterfield, Director of Enrollment Services, Rockingham Community College, Box 38, Wentworth, NC 27375-0038

Rowan-Cabarrus Community College
Salisbury, North Carolina
www.rowancabarrus.edu   **CB code: 5589**

- Public 2-year community and technical college
- Commuter campus in large town

General. Founded in 1961. Regionally accredited. **Enrollment:** 7,383 degree-seeking undergraduates. **Degrees:** 616 associate awarded. **Location:** 40 miles from Charlotte. **Calendar:** Semester, extensive summer session. **Full-time faculty:** 157 total. **Part-time faculty:** 437 total. **Class size:** 58% < 20, 39% 20-39, 2% 40-49, less than 1% 50-99.

Transfer out. Colleges most students transferred to 2011: University of North Carolina-Charlotte, Pfeiffer University, Catawba College.

Basis for selection. Open admission, but selective for some programs. Interview required for allied health programs.

2011-2012 Annual costs. Tuition/fees: $2,051; $7,811 out-of-state. Per-credit charge: $67 in-state; $259 out-of-state. Books/supplies: $750.

Financial aid. Need-based: Need-based aid available for part-time students. Work-study available nights, weekends and for part-time students. **Non-need-based:** Scholarships awarded for academics, job skills, state residency.

Application procedures. Admission: No deadline. No application fee. Admission notification on a rolling basis. **Financial aid:** Priority date 3/15; no closing date. FAFSA required. Applicants notified on a rolling basis starting 5/1; must reply within 3 week(s) of notification.

Academics. Special study options: Cooperative education, distance learning, dual enrollment of high school students, ESL, liberal arts/career combination, teacher certification program. License preparation in nursing, radiology, real estate. **Credit/placement by examination:** AP, CLEP, institutional tests. 75 credit hours maximum toward associate degree. Student must complete 25% of credits required for graduation in resident classes. **Support services:** GED preparation and test center, learning center, reduced course load, remedial instruction, tutoring, writing center.

Majors. Business: Accounting, business admin, office technology. **Computer sciences:** Information systems, programming. **Education:** Early childhood. **Health services:** Nursing (RN), radiologic technology/medical imaging. **Protective services:** Criminal justice, fire safety technology.

Student life. Freshman orientation: Available. Preregistration for classes offered. Fall and spring orientation. **Activities:** Student government.

Student services. Career counseling, student employment services, on-campus daycare, personal counseling, placement for graduates, veterans' counselor. **Physically disabled:** Services for visually, speech, hearing impaired. **Transfer:** Pre-admission transcript evaluation for new students. College fairs on campus for students transferring to 4-year colleges.

Contact. Phone: (704) 216-3602 Fax: (704) 633-6804
Rob Dunnam, Director, Admissions and Recruitment, Rowan-Cabarrus Community College, Box 1595, Salisbury, NC 28145

Sampson Community College
Clinton, North Carolina
www.sampsoncc.edu   **CB code: 0505**

- Public 2-year community college
- Commuter campus in small town
- Interview required

General. Founded in 1965. Regionally accredited. **Enrollment:** 1,623 degree-seeking undergraduates. **Degrees:** 137 associate awarded. **Location:** 30 miles from Fayetteville. **Calendar:** Semester, limited summer session. **Full-time faculty:** 72 total. **Part-time faculty:** 47 total.

Student profile. Among degree-seeking undergraduates, 253 enrolled as first-time, first-year students.

Part-time:	54%	Women:	72%
Out-of-state:	1%	25 or older:	47%

Transfer out. Colleges most students transferred to 2011: Fayetteville State University, UNC-Wilmington, Campbell University, Mt. Olive College, East Carolina University.

Basis for selection. Open admission, but selective for some programs. Special requirements for nursing and practical nursing; secondary school record and test scores important. Interview required for nursing programs.

High school preparation. 15 units recommended. Recommended units include English 4, mathematics 3, social studies 3, science 4 and foreign language 2. Algebra, chemistry and biology required for nursing programs.

2011-2012 Annual costs. Tuition/fees: $2,059; $7,819 out-of-state. Per-credit charge: $67 in-state; $259 out-of-state. Books/supplies: $600. Personal expenses: $900.

Financial aid. Need-based: Need-based aid available for part-time students. Work-study available nights, weekends and for part-time students. **Non-need-based:** Scholarships awarded for academics, state residency.

Application procedures. Admission: No deadline. No application fee. Admission notification on a rolling basis. **Financial aid:** Priority date 7/1; no closing date. FAFSA required. Applicants notified on a rolling basis starting 7/15; must reply within 2 week(s) of notification.

Academics. Special study options: Cooperative education, distance learning, dual enrollment of high school students, independent study, internships, liberal arts/career combination, weekend college. License preparation in nursing. **Credit/placement by examination:** AP, CLEP, institutional tests. 15 credit hours maximum toward associate degree. **Support services:** GED preparation and test center, learning center, pre-admission summer program, reduced course load, remedial instruction, study skills assistance, tutoring.

Majors. Business: Accounting, administrative services, business admin, office/clerical. **Computer sciences:** General, applications programming, information systems. **Education:** General, early childhood. **General:** Horticulture, ornamental horticulture. **Health services:** Licensed practical nurse, nursing (RN).

Computing on campus. 110 workstations in library, computer center.

Student life. Freshman orientation: Mandatory. Preregistration for classes offered. **Activities:** Student government, student newspaper.

Student services. Adult student services, career counseling, student employment services, financial aid counseling, personal counseling, placement for graduates, veterans' counselor. **Physically disabled:** Services for visually, speech, hearing impaired. **Transfer:** Pre-admission transcript evaluation for new students. Transfer adviser, college fairs on campus for students transferring to 4-year colleges.

Contact. Phone: (910) 592-8084 Fax: (910) 592-8048
Oscar Rodriguez, Director of Admissions, Sampson Community College, PO Box 318, Clinton, NC 28329

Sandhills Community College
Pinehurst, North Carolina
www.sandhills.edu   CB code: 5649

▶ Public 2-year community college
▶ Commuter campus in large town

General. Founded in 1963. Regionally accredited. **Enrollment:** 3,685 degree-seeking undergraduates. **Degrees:** 450 associate awarded. **Location:** 41 miles from Fayetteville, 71 miles from Raleigh. **Calendar:** Semester, limited summer session. **Full-time faculty:** 122 total. **Part-time faculty:** 185 total. **Class size:** 51% < 20, 46% 20-39, 1% 40-49, 2% 50-99. **Special facilities:** Student maintained 30-acre garden, culinary arts lab.

Student profile.

Out-of-state:	1%	25 or older:	41%

Transfer out. Colleges most students transferred to 2011: University of North Carolina-Chapel Hill, University of North Carolina-Charlotte, University of North Carolina-Pembroke, North Carolina State University, Appalachian State University.

Basis for selection. Open admission, but selective for some programs. Placement testing required for all students who wish to enroll in curriculum programs and all non-degree seeking students who enroll in English, mathematics, or other restricted courses. Students with a minimum SAT score of 500 Writing, 500 Critical Reading, 500 Math or ACT score of 21 Writing, 21 Reading, 21 Math may be placed into college level English and math classes without taking a placement test. **Adult students:** SAT/ACT scores not required. **Home schooled:** Transcript of courses and grades required. Copy of state registration required. **Learning Disabled:** Students with learning disabilities recommended to take classes in Continuing Education Program first.

2011-2012 Annual costs. Tuition/fees: $2,092; $7,852 out-of-state. Per-credit charge: $67 in-state; $259 out-of-state. Books/supplies: $1,024. Personal expenses: $924.

Financial aid. Need-based: Need-based aid available for part-time students. Work-study available nights, weekends and for part-time students. **Non-need-based:** Scholarships awarded for academics.

Application procedures. Admission: No deadline. No application fee. Admission notification on a rolling basis. **Financial aid:** Closing date 6/1. FAFSA required. Applicants notified on a rolling basis starting 5/1; must reply by 8/1 or within 4 week(s) of notification.

Academics. Weekend support services held at satellite campus. **Special study options:** Cooperative education, distance learning, double major, dual enrollment of high school students, ESL, honors, independent study, internships, liberal arts/career combination, teacher certification program. Third and fourth year courses offered on campus evenings by St. Andrews Presbyterian College and UNC Pembroke. Bachelor's degree programs available on campus. License preparation in nursing, paramedic, radiology. **Credit/placement by examination:** AP, CLEP, institutional tests. **Support services:** GED preparation and test center, learning center, reduced course load, remedial instruction, study skills assistance, tutoring.

Majors. Architecture: Technology. **Biology:** General. **Business:** Accounting, administrative services, business admin, e-commerce, hotel/motel admin, restaurant/food services. **Computer sciences:** General, applications programming, computer science, information systems, programming, webmaster. **Education:** Biology, chemistry, early childhood, elementary, history, science, secondary, social science, social studies, teacher assistance. **General:** Landscaping, turf management. **Health services:** Clinical lab technology, EMT ambulance attendant, EMT paramedic, massage therapy, medical radiologic technology/radiation therapy, medical records admin, nursing (RN), predental, premedicine, prenursing, prepharmacy, preveterinary, respiratory therapy technology, substance abuse counseling, surgical technology. **Human services:** Social work. **Liberal arts:** Arts/sciences. **Math:** General. **Parks/recreation:** Health/fitness. **Protective services:** Criminal justice. **Psychology:** General. **Social sciences:** General. **Visual/performing arts:** Art, music. **Work/family studies:** Child care management.

Most popular majors. Business/marketing 8%, computer/information sciences 6%, health sciences 42%, liberal arts 11%, trade and industry 11%.

Computing on campus. 400 workstations in library, computer center, student center. Commuter students can connect to campus network. Wireless network available.

Student life. Freshman orientation: Available. Preregistration for classes offered. 2-hour information session, course planning, and registration. **Activities:** Bands, choral groups, music ensembles, student government, student newspaper, symphony orchestra, Minority Students for Academic and Cultural Enrichment, Circle-K, Young Democrats, Young Republicans, Phi Theta Kappa, Nursing Club, Rotaract.

Athletics. NJCAA. **Intercollegiate:** Basketball M, golf, volleyball W. **Team name:** Flyers.

Student services. Adult student services, alcohol/substance abuse counseling, career counseling, services for economically disadvantaged, student employment services, financial aid counseling, minority student services, personal counseling, placement for graduates, veterans' counselor. **Physically disabled:** Services for visually, hearing impaired. **Transfer:** Pre-admission transcript evaluation for new students. Transfer adviser, college fairs on campus for students transferring to 4-year colleges.

Contact. E-mail: greenec@sandhills.edu
Phone: (910) 692-6185 Toll-free number: (800) 338-3944
Fax: (910) 695-3981
Cary Greene, Director of Admissions, Sandhills Community College, 3395 Airport Road, Pinehurst, NC 28374

Shepherds Theological Seminary
Cary, North Carolina
www.shepherdsseminary.org

▶ Private 2-year seminary college affiliated with Christian Church
▶ Commuter campus in small city
▶ Interview required

General. Regionally accredited; also accredited by TRACS. Associate and Bachelor of Theology students enroll in classes with MA and MDiv students. **Enrollment:** 6 degree-seeking undergraduates. **Location:** 10 miles from Raleigh. **Calendar:** Semester, limited summer session. **Full-time faculty:** 3 total; 100% have terminal degrees. **Part-time faculty:** 6 total; 67% have terminal degrees. **Class size:** 100% < 20. **Special facilities:** Church of 4,000 attendees, ministry opportunities.

Basis for selection. Open admission. **Home schooled:** State high school equivalency certificate, interview required.

2011-2012 Annual costs. Tuition/fees: $4,350. Per-credit charge: $235. Books/supplies: $400.

Financial aid. Need-based: Work-study available nights, weekends and for part-time students.

Application procedures. Admission: Closing date 8/15. $30 fee, may be waived for applicants with need. **Financial aid:** No deadline.

Academics. Special study options: Distance learning. **Credit/placement by examination:** AP, CLEP.

Computing on campus. 4 workstations in library. Wireless network available.

Student life. Freshman orientation: Mandatory. Preregistration for classes offered. **Policies:** Students required to be members of a church and engage in mentored internship programs. Religious observance required. **Activities:** Campus ministries, student government.

Student services. Chaplain/spiritual director, career counseling, financial aid counseling, personal counseling.

Contact. E-mail: info@shepherds.edu
Phone: (919) 573-1555 Toll-free number: (800) 672-3060
Fax: (919) 573-1438
Randall McKinion, Registrar, Shepherds Theological Seminary, 6051 Tryon Road, Cary, NC 27518

South College
Asheville, North Carolina
www.southcollegenc.edu   CB code: 0508

▶ For-profit 2-year health science and technical college
▶ Commuter campus in small city
▶ Interview required

General. Founded in 1905. Candidate for regional accreditation; also accredited by ACICS. **Enrollment:** 203 degree-seeking undergraduates. **Degrees:** 2 bachelor's, 62 associate awarded. **Location:** 4 miles from downtown. **Calendar:** Quarter, extensive summer session. **Full-time faculty:** 15 total. **Part-time faculty:** 29 total. **Class size:** 91% < 20, 9% 20-39.

Student profile. Of all enrolled students, 12% already have a bachelor's degree or higher.

Transfer out. Colleges most students transferred to 2011: Asheville-Buncombe Technical Community College, Blue Ridge Community College, Mars Hill College, Montreat College.

Basis for selection. Open admission, but selective for some programs. College-administered exam required of all applicants. Scores used for admission and program placement. **Home schooled:** Copy of homeschool diploma required.

2011-2012 Annual costs. Bachelor programs: Legal Studies $71,600, Radiological Sciences $71,600. Associate programs: Accounting $40,000, Business Administration $40,000, Criminal Justice $40,000, Medical Assisting $40,000, Nursing $42,000, Paralegal Studies $40,000, Physical Therapist Assistant $42,400, Radiologic Technology $42,400. Certificate program: Surgical Technology $25,700. Tuition amounts include fees. Books and supplies costs vary by program. Books/supplies: $2,000. Personal expenses: $3,069.

Financial aid. Need-based: Need-based aid available for part-time students. Work-study available nights, weekends and for part-time students.

Application procedures. Admission: No deadline. $50 fee, may be waived for applicants with need. Application must be submitted on paper. Admission notification on a rolling basis. **Financial aid:** No deadline. FAFSA required. Applicants notified on a rolling basis.

Academics. Special study options: Accelerated study, cooperative education, double major, internships, liberal arts/career combination. Bachelor's degree programs available on campus. License preparation in nursing, physical therapy, radiology. **Credit/placement by examination:** AP, CLEP, institutional tests. Varies with program, but no more than 60% of any program. **Support services:** Reduced course load, study skills assistance, tutoring, writing center.

Majors. Business: Accounting, business admin. **Computer sciences:** General. **Health services:** Medical assistant. **Protective services:** Law enforcement admin.

Computing on campus. 28 workstations in library, computer center. Wireless network available.

Student life. Freshman orientation: Mandatory. Preregistration for classes offered. Orientation is held prior to each quarter.

Student services. Career counseling, student employment services, financial aid counseling, placement for graduates, veterans' counselor. **Transfer:** Pre-admission transcript evaluation for new students.

Contact. Phone: (828) 398-2500 Fax: (828) 277-6151
Debra Kasey, Director of Admissions, South College, 140 Sweeten Creek Road, Asheville, NC 28803

South Piedmont Community College
Polkton, North Carolina
www.spcc.edu   CB code: 3623

▶ Public 2-year community college
▶ Commuter campus in small city

General. Founded in 1962. Regionally accredited. Multiple campus locations near Charlotte. **Enrollment:** 2,054 degree-seeking undergraduates. **Degrees:** 201 associate awarded. **Location:** 60 miles from Charlotte. **Calendar:** Semester, limited summer session. **Full-time faculty:** 75 total. **Part-time faculty:** 200 total.

Student profile.

Out-of-state:	1%	Hispanic American:	7%
African American:	24%	25 or older:	57%
Asian American:	1%		

Basis for selection. Open admission, but selective for some programs. Special requirements for health technology programs. **Home schooled:** Students should have state certification number, successful completion of competency exam, registered with local board of education, copy of transcript and diploma.

2011-2012 Annual costs. Tuition/fees: $2,091; $7,851 out-of-state. Per-credit charge: $67 in-state; $259 out-of-state. Books/supplies: $800. Personal expenses: $900.

2011-2012 Financial aid. Need-based: 98% of total undergraduate aid awarded as scholarships/grants, 2% as loans/jobs. Need-based aid available for part-time students. Work-study available nights, weekends and for part-time students. **Additional information:** Small amount of non-federal scholarship aid available. FAFSA applications received before June 1 will receive first priority.

Application procedures. Admission: No deadline. No application fee. Admission notification on a rolling basis. **Financial aid:** Priority date 6/1; no closing date. FAFSA required. Applicants notified on a rolling basis.

Academics. Special study options: Cooperative education, distance learning, dual enrollment of high school students, independent study. **Credit/placement by examination:** AP, CLEP, institutional tests. **Support services:** GED preparation and test center, learning center, reduced course load, remedial instruction, study skills assistance, tutoring.

Majors. Business: Accounting, business admin. **Computer sciences:** General. **Education:** Early childhood, elementary. **Health services:** Massage therapy, medical assistant, nursing (RN), office assistant, sonography. **Liberal arts:** Arts/sciences. **Protective services:** Criminal justice. **Visual/performing arts:** Commercial/advertising art. **Work/family studies:** Child care service.

Computing on campus. 200 workstations in library, computer center. Wireless network available.

Student life. Freshman orientation: Available. Preregistration for classes offered. **Activities:** Student government, student newspaper, Phi Beta Lambda business organization, criminal justice student association, social services club, Phi Theta Kappa.

Athletics. Team name: Patriots.

Student services. Alcohol/substance abuse counseling, career counseling, student employment services, financial aid counseling, personal counseling, placement for graduates, veterans' counselor. **Physically disabled:** Services for visually, hearing impaired. **Transfer:** Transfer adviser for students transferring to 4-year colleges.

Contact. E-mail: admissions@spcc.edu
Phone: (704) 272-5324 Toll-free number: (800) 766-0319
Fax: (704) 272-5303
Tracie Boone, Director of Enrollment Services, South Piedmont Community College, PO Box 126, Polkton, NC 28135

Southeastern Community College
Whiteville, North Carolina
www.sccnc.edu   CB code: 5651

- Public 2-year community college
- Commuter campus in small town

General. Founded in 1964. Regionally accredited. **Enrollment:** 1,611 degree-seeking undergraduates. **Degrees:** 82 associate awarded. **Location:** 50 miles from Wilmington. **Calendar:** Semester, extensive summer session. **Full-time faculty:** 56 total. **Part-time faculty:** 74 total. **Special facilities:** Hardwood and pine forest with signed nature trail, greenhouses. **Partnerships:** Formal partnership with Columbus County School System - Early College High School.

Student profile.

Out-of-state: 1%   25 or older: 42%

Transfer out. Colleges most students transferred to 2011: University of North Carolina at Wilmington, University of North Carolina at Pembroke, Fayetteville State University, East Carolina University.

Basis for selection. Open admission, but selective for some programs. Basic law Enforcement Training: Age 21 and Reading test requirements. Allied Health: Reading, Math, CNA 1 certification, points requirements. SAT may be substituted for placement test. **Home schooled:** Transcript of courses and grades required. Documentation from state showing authorization. **Learning Disabled:** Applicant must provide proof of disability from specialist, and list of required accommodations from specialist, and list of requested accommodations from student.

High school preparation. Recommended units include English 6, mathematics 6, social studies 6 and science 6.

2011-2012 Annual costs. Tuition/fees: $2,079; $7,839 out-of-state. Per-credit charge: $67 in-state; $259 out-of-state. Books/supplies: $910. Personal expenses: $972.

Financial aid. Need-based: Need-based aid available for part-time students. Work-study available nights, weekends and for part-time students. **Non-need-based:** Scholarships awarded for academics, athletics, leadership, music/drama, state residency.

Application procedures. Admission: No deadline. No application fee. Admission notification on a rolling basis. **Financial aid:** Priority date 4/1; no closing date. FAFSA required. Applicants notified on a rolling basis starting 6/1; must reply within 2 week(s) of notification.

Academics. Special study options: Cooperative education, distance learning, dual enrollment of high school students, independent study. License preparation in nursing. **Credit/placement by examination:** AP, CLEP, institutional tests. Credit by exam, in combination with credits transferred from other post-secondary institutions, should not exceed 25% of degree awarded. **Support services:** GED preparation and test center, learning center, reduced course load, remedial instruction, study skills assistance, tutoring.

Majors. Biology: General. **Business:** Business admin, office management. **Communications:** Communications/speech/rhetoric. **Communications technology:** Radio/TV. **Computer sciences:** General, information technology, networking, web page design. **Conservation:** Environmental science, forest technology. **Education:** Early childhood, elementary, secondary. **English:** English lit. **Health services:** Clinical lab technology, massage therapy, nursing assistant, prenursing. **History:** General. **Liberal arts:** Arts/sciences. **Math:** General. **Physical sciences:** Chemistry. **Protective services:** Law enforcement admin. **Psychology:** General. **Social sciences:** General. **Visual/performing arts:** Music performance, studio arts. **Work/family studies:** Child care management.

Computing on campus. 395 workstations in library, computer center. Online library, helpline, wireless network available.

Student life. Freshman orientation: Available. Preregistration for classes offered. **Activities:** Concert band, choral groups, literary magazine, student government, student newspaper, Student Ambassadors, Environmental Action Club, Phi Beta Lambda, early childhood organization, medical lab, technology club, Spanish club, Student Nurses Association, cosmetology club, art club.

Athletics. NJCAA. **Intercollegiate:** Baseball M, volleyball W. **Team name:** Rams.

Student services. Career counseling, services for economically disadvantaged, student employment services, financial aid counseling, on-campus daycare, veterans' counselor. **Physically disabled:** Services for visually, speech, hearing impaired. **Transfer:** Pre-admission transcript evaluation for new students. Transfer center, college fairs on campus for students transferring to 4-year colleges.

Contact. E-mail: jgiles@sccnc.edu
Phone: (910) 642-7141 ext. 265 Fax: (910) 642-1267
Kelly Kingry, Dean of Students, Southeastern Community College, 4564 Chadbourn Highway, Whiteville, NC 28472-0151

Southwestern Community College
Sylva, North Carolina
www.southwesterncc.edu   CB code: 5667

- Public 2-year community college
- Commuter campus in rural community

General. Founded in 1964. Regionally accredited. Five off-campus sites serve two adjoining counties. **Enrollment:** 2,641 degree-seeking undergraduates. **Degrees:** 340 associate awarded. **Location:** 48 miles from Asheville. **Calendar:** Semester, limited summer session. **Full-time faculty:** 83 total. **Part-time faculty:** 184 total. **Class size:** 80% < 20, 20% 20-39.

Student profile.

Out-of-state: 1%   25 or older: 46%

Transfer out. Colleges most students transferred to 2011: Western Carolina University.

Basis for selection. Open admission, but selective for some programs. Admission to allied health programs based on test scores, academic record, interview, and recommendations. Interview required for allied health applicants; recommended for all others.

High school preparation. Algebra, biology, and chemistry required for allied health program applicants.

2011-2012 Annual costs. Tuition/fees: $2,029; $7,789 out-of-state. Per-credit charge: $67 in-state; $259 out-of-state. Books/supplies: $750. Personal expenses: $1,238.

Financial aid. Need-based: Need-based aid available for part-time students. Work-study available nights, weekends and for part-time students.

Application procedures. Admission: No deadline. No application fee. Admission notification on a rolling basis. **Financial aid:** Closing date 6/30. FAFSA required. Applicants notified on a rolling basis starting 5/1; must reply within 2 week(s) of notification.

Academics. Special study options: Cooperative education, double major, dual enrollment of high school students, ESL, independent study, internships, liberal arts/career combination. License preparation in nursing, paramedic, physical therapy, radiology, real estate. **Credit/placement by examination:** AP, CLEP, institutional tests. **Support services:** GED preparation and test center, learning center, reduced course load, remedial instruction, tutoring.

Majors. Business: Accounting, administrative services, business admin, marketing. **Computer sciences:** General, networking, programming. **Education:** General, early childhood, trade/industrial. **Engineering:** Computer, electrical, surveying. **Health services:** Clinical lab science, clinical lab technology, EMT paramedic, medical radiologic technology/radiation therapy, medical records technology, mental health services, nursing (RN), physical therapy assistant, respiratory therapy assistant, respiratory therapy technology, sonography, substance abuse counseling. **Liberal arts:** Arts/sciences. **Parks/recreation:** General. **Protective services:** Criminal justice. **Visual/performing arts:** Commercial/advertising art. **Work/family studies:** Child care management.

Most popular majors. Business/marketing 7%, health sciences 35%, liberal arts 22%, security/protective services 10%.

Computing on campus. 200 workstations in computer center. Commuter students can connect to campus network.

Student life. Freshman orientation: Mandatory. Preregistration for classes offered. One-day live orientation held on Jackson Campus at beginning of Fall Semester for all students enrolling for first time. New students enrolling in Spring or Summer semesters take on-line orientation program. **Activities:** Literary magazine, student government, Phi Theta Kappa, Native American Society, Spanish Club.

Student services. Career counseling, services for economically disadvantaged, student employment services, financial aid counseling, on-campus daycare, personal counseling, placement for graduates, veterans' counselor.

Physically disabled: Services for visually, speech, hearing impaired. **Transfer:** Pre-admission transcript evaluation for new students. Transfer adviser for students transferring to 4-year colleges.

Contact. Phone: (828) 586-4091 ext. 352
Toll-free number: (800) 447-4091 Fax: (828) 586-3129
Phil Weast, Dean of Student Services, Southwestern Community College, 447 College Drive, Sylva, NC 28779

Stanly Community College
Albemarle, North Carolina
www.stanly.edu　　　　　　　　　　　**CB code: 0496**

▶ Public 2-year community college
▶ Commuter campus in large town

General. Founded in 1971. Regionally accredited. **Enrollment:** 3,116 degree-seeking undergraduates. **Degrees:** 388 associate awarded. **Location:** 30 miles from Charlotte. **Calendar:** Semester, limited summer session. **Full-time faculty:** 100 total. **Part-time faculty:** 230 total.

Transfer out. Colleges most students transferred to 2011: University of North Carolina at Charlotte, Pfeiffer University.

Basis for selection. Open admission, but selective for some programs. Special requirements for nursing, radiography, respiratory therapy, and medical lab assistant majors. **Learning Disabled:** Written verification of disability, no more than five years old, required at least 60 days prior to enrollment.

2011-2012 Annual costs. Tuition/fees: $2,060; $7,820 out-of-state. Per-credit charge: $67 in-state; $259 out-of-state. Books/supplies: $900. Personal expenses: $1,050.

Financial aid. All financial aid based on need. Need-based aid available for part-time students. Work-study available nights, weekends and for part-time students.

Application procedures. Admission: No deadline. No application fee. Admission notification on a rolling basis. **Financial aid:** No deadline. FAFSA, institutional form required. Applicants notified on a rolling basis starting 6/1; must reply within 2 week(s) of notification.

Academics. Special study options: Distance learning, dual enrollment of high school students, ESL, weekend college. **Credit/placement by examination:** AP, CLEP, institutional tests. **Support services:** GED preparation and test center, remedial instruction, study skills assistance, tutoring.

Majors. Business: Accounting, business admin, human resources. **Computer sciences:** Computer graphics, information systems, information technology, LAN/WAN management, networking, security. **Education:** Early childhood, elementary, special ed. **Health services:** Clinical lab assistant, EMT paramedic, medical assistant, nursing (RN), radiologic technology/medical imaging, respiratory therapy technology. **Liberal arts:** Arts/sciences. **Protective services:** Computer forensics, criminal justice. **Visual/performing arts:** Game design, graphic design. **Work/family studies:** General.

Most popular majors. Business/marketing 11%, computer/information sciences 6%, education 13%, health sciences 32%, liberal arts 18%, security/protective services 13%.

Computing on campus. 100 workstations in library, computer center, student center. Commuter students can connect to campus network. Online library, helpline, wireless network available.

Student life. Freshman orientation: Available. Preregistration for classes offered. **Activities:** Student government.

Athletics. NJCAA. **Intercollegiate:** Baseball M, soccer, softball W. **Team name:** Eagles.

Student services. Adult student services, alcohol/substance abuse counseling, career counseling, services for economically disadvantaged, student employment services, financial aid counseling, minority student services, personal counseling, placement for graduates, veterans' counselor, women's services. **Transfer:** Pre-admission transcript evaluation for new students. Transfer adviser, college fairs on campus for students transferring to 4-year colleges.

Contact. E-mail: sccadmissions@stanly.edu
Phone: (704) 991-0226 Fax: (704) 991-0255
Denise Ross, Associate Dean of Admissions and Counseling, Stanly Community College, 141 College Drive, Albemarle, NC 28001

Surry Community College
Dobson, North Carolina
www.surry.edu　　　　　　　　　　　**CB code: 5656**

▶ Public 2-year community college
▶ Commuter campus in rural community

General. Founded in 1964. Regionally accredited. **Enrollment:** 2,640 degree-seeking undergraduates. **Degrees:** 362 associate awarded. **Location:** 40 miles from Winston-Salem. **Calendar:** Semester, extensive summer session. **Full-time faculty:** 100 total. **Part-time faculty:** 268 total. **Special facilities:** Working vineyard and wine-making facilities, NC center for viticulture and enology.

Transfer out. Colleges most students transferred to 2011: Appalachian State University, Gardner-Webb University, Lees-McRae University, University of North Carolina-Greensboro, Winston-Salem State University.

Basis for selection. Open admission, but selective for some programs. Competitive admission to associate degree nursing program (RN) and practical nursing program (LPN) based primarily on academic standing; test scores considered. Special admissions also required for Physical Therapy Assistant includes prerequisites, Teas testing and interviews. Competitive admissions for Medical Assisting. Portfolio required for admission to advertising and graphic design programs. **Home schooled:** Proof of homeschool registration from the state of NC required.

2011-2012 Annual costs. Tuition/fees: $2,064; $7,824 out-of-state. Per-credit charge: $67 in-state; $259 out-of-state. Books/supplies: $1,200. Personal expenses: $1,000.

Financial aid. Need-based: Need-based aid available for part-time students. Work-study available nights, weekends and for part-time students. **Non-need-based:** Scholarships awarded for academics.

Application procedures. Admission: No deadline. No application fee. Admission notification on a rolling basis. **Financial aid:** Closing date 5/1. FAFSA, institutional form required. Applicants notified on a rolling basis starting 6/1; must reply within 2 week(s) of notification.

Academics. Special study options: Accelerated study, cooperative education, distance learning, double major, dual enrollment of high school students, ESL, independent study, internships, weekend college. Bachelor's degree programs available on campus. License preparation in nursing, paramedic, physical therapy, real estate. **Credit/placement by examination:** AP, CLEP, institutional tests. **Support services:** GED preparation and test center, learning center, reduced course load, remedial instruction, study skills assistance, tutoring.

Majors. Business: Accounting, business admin, office/clerical, real estate. **Computer sciences:** Information systems. **Education:** Early childhood, early childhood special. **Engineering:** Computer, electrical. **Foreign languages:** Translation. **General:** Horticulture. **Health services:** Medical assistant, nursing (RN), office admin, physical therapy assistant. **Liberal arts:** Arts/sciences. **Protective services:** Law enforcement admin. **Visual/performing arts:** Commercial/advertising art, game design.

Computing on campus. 500 workstations in library, computer center. Online library, helpline, wireless network available.

Student life. Freshman orientation: Mandatory. Preregistration for classes offered. **Activities:** Choral groups, literary magazine, student government.

Athletics. NJCAA. **Intercollegiate:** Baseball M, golf, softball W, volleyball W. **Intramural:** Basketball M. **Team name:** Knights.

Student services. Adult student services, career counseling, services for economically disadvantaged, student employment services, financial aid counseling, personal counseling, placement for graduates, veterans' counselor. **Physically disabled:** Services for visually, hearing impaired. **Transfer:** Transfer adviser, college fairs on campus for students transferring to 4-year colleges.

Contact. E-mail: hazelwoodr@surry.edu
Phone: (336) 386-3392 Fax: (336) 386-8951
Renita Hazelwood, Director of Admissions, Surry Community College, ATTN: Admissions Offfice 630 South Main Street, Dobson, NC 27017

Tri-County Community College
Murphy, North Carolina
www.tricountycc.edu　　　　　　　　　**CB code: 5785**

▶ Public 2-year community college
▶ Commuter campus in rural community

General. Founded in 1964. Regionally accredited. **Enrollment:** 1,069 degree-seeking undergraduates. **Degrees:** 146 associate awarded. **Location:** 110 miles from Asheville, 96 miles from Chattanooga, Tennessee. **Calendar:** Semester, extensive summer session. **Full-time faculty:** 34 total. **Part-time faculty:** 137 total. **Class size:** 22% < 20, 57% 20-39, 20% 40-49, 1% 50-99.

Student profile.

Out-of-state:	9%	25 or older:	54%

Transfer out. Colleges most students transferred to 2011: Western Carolina University, Southwestern Community College.

Basis for selection. Open admission. **Learning Disabled:** Tutoring is available.

2011-2012 Annual costs. Tuition/fees: $2,043; $7,803 out-of-state. Per-credit charge: $67 in-state; $259 out-of-state. Books/supplies: $350. Personal expenses: $450.

Financial aid. All financial aid based on need. Need-based aid available for part-time students. Work-study available nights, weekends and for part-time students.

Application procedures. Admission: No deadline. No application fee. Admission notification on a rolling basis. **Financial aid:** Priority date 6/30; no closing date. FAFSA required. Applicants notified on a rolling basis starting 6/1; must reply within 4 week(s) of notification.

Academics. Special study options: Double major, dual enrollment of high school students, independent study, internships. License preparation in nursing, paramedic, real estate. **Credit/placement by examination:** AP, CLEP, institutional tests. 6 credit hours maximum toward associate degree. **Support services:** GED preparation and test center, learning center, reduced course load, remedial instruction, study skills assistance, tutoring.

Majors. Business: Accounting, administrative services, business admin. **Computer sciences:** Information systems. **Health services:** EMT paramedic, medical assistant, nursing (RN). **Liberal arts:** Arts/sciences.

Most popular majors. Business/marketing 24%, liberal arts 43%, trade and industry 35%.

Computing on campus. 42 workstations in library, computer center, student center. Online library available.

Student life. Freshman orientation: Mandatory. Preregistration for classes offered. **Activities:** Student government, student newspaper, honor society.

Student services. Adult student services, career counseling, services for economically disadvantaged, student employment services, financial aid counseling, on-campus daycare, personal counseling, placement for graduates, veterans' counselor. **Physically disabled:** Services for visually, hearing impaired. **Transfer:** Pre-admission transcript evaluation for new students. College fairs on campus for students transferring to 4-year colleges.

Contact. E-mail: dstafford@tricountycc.edu
Phone: (828) 837-6810 Toll-free number: (828) 835-4208
Fax: (828) 837-3266
Dotie Stafford-Ortega, Director of Student Affairs, Tri-County Community College, 21 Campus Circle, Murphy, NC 28906

Vance-Granville Community College
Henderson, North Carolina
www.vgcc.edu

CB member
CB code: 0617

- Public 2-year community college
- Commuter campus in large town

General. Founded in 1969. Regionally accredited. 4 rural counties served with satellite campuses in Warrenton, Butner and Louisburg. **Enrollment:** 3,321 degree-seeking undergraduates. **Degrees:** 315 associate awarded. **Location:** 42 miles from Raleigh. **Calendar:** Semester, limited summer session. **Full-time faculty:** 132 total. **Part-time faculty:** 231 total.

Basis for selection. Open admission, but selective for some programs. Admission to nursing, radiologic technology, and medical assisting is based on academic record, health education aptitude test, and other criteria. Interview recommended for nursing, radiologic technology programs.

2011-2012 Annual costs. Tuition/fees: $2,057; $7,817 out-of-state. Per-credit charge: $67 in-state; $259 out-of-state. Books/supplies: $800. Personal expenses: $400.

Financial aid. Need-based: Need-based aid available for part-time students. Work-study available nights, weekends and for part-time students. **Non-need-based:** Scholarships awarded for academics.

Application procedures. Admission: No deadline. No application fee. Admission notification on a rolling basis. Application deadlines apply and may vary for Allied Health programs. College placement examinations required of all students, unless acceptable scores on SAT/ACT or special students. **Financial aid:** Closing date 3/15. FAFSA required. Applicants notified on a rolling basis starting 5/1; must reply within 2 week(s) of notification.

Academics. Special study options: Cooperative education, distance learning, double major, dual enrollment of high school students, ESL, independent study, internships. License preparation in nursing, radiology, real estate. **Credit/placement by examination:** AP, CLEP, institutional tests. **Support services:** GED preparation and test center, learning center, pre-admission summer program, reduced course load, remedial instruction, study skills assistance, tutoring.

Majors. Business: Accounting, administrative services, business admin, office technology. **Computer sciences:** Information technology, networking, security, web page design. **Education:** General, early childhood, teacher assistance. **Engineering:** Electrical. **Health services:** Medical assistant, medical radiologic technology/radiation therapy, nursing (RN), recreational therapy. **Liberal arts:** Arts/sciences. **Parks/recreation:** General. **Protective services:** Law enforcement admin. **Work/family studies:** Child care management.

Most popular majors. Business/marketing 17%, computer/information sciences 9%, education 14%, health sciences 21%, liberal arts 8%, security/protective services 7%.

Computing on campus. 48 workstations in library, computer center.

Student life. Activities: Drama, student government, departmental clubs.

Student services. Adult student services, career counseling, student employment services, financial aid counseling, on-campus daycare, personal counseling, placement for graduates, veterans' counselor. **Physically disabled:** Services for visually, hearing impaired. **Transfer:** Transfer adviser for students transferring to 4-year colleges.

Contact. E-mail: waddlet@vgcc.edu
Phone: (252) 492-2061 Fax: (252) 430-0460
Tonya Waddle, Director of Admissions and Records, Vance-Granville Community College, Box 917, Henderson, NC 27536

Wake Technical Community College
Raleigh, North Carolina
www.waketech.edu

CB code: 5928

- Public 2-year community and technical college
- Commuter campus in large city

General. Founded in 1958. Regionally accredited. **Enrollment:** 18,615 degree-seeking undergraduates; 693 non-degree-seeking students. **Degrees:** 1,260 associate awarded. **ROTC:** Army. **Location:** 10 miles from Raleigh. **Calendar:** Semester, extensive summer session. **Full-time faculty:** 520 total. **Part-time faculty:** 836 total.

Student profile. Among degree-seeking undergraduates, 33% enrolled in a transfer program, 67% enrolled in a vocational program, 9% already have a bachelor's degree or higher, 6,471 transferred in from other institutions.

Part-time:	55%	25 or older:	51%
Women:	53%		

Transfer out. Colleges most students transferred to 2011: North Carolina State University, University of North Carolina at Chapel Hill, East Carolina University, University of North Carolina at Greensboro, Appalachian State University.

Basis for selection. Open admission, but selective for some programs. Admission to health programs based on standardized test scores, post-secondary coursework. Placement tests required of all degree and diploma students with SAT scores below 520 verbal or 600 math, or below ACT math 21, reading 21, and writing 21. Interview recommended. **Home schooled:** Must include transcript and test scores.

High school preparation. Recommended units include English 4 and mathematics 4. 1 chemistry required for health sciences associate degree programs.

2011-2012 Annual costs. Tuition/fees: $2,067; $7,827 out-of-state. Per-credit charge: $67 in-state; $259 out-of-state. Books/supplies: $1,000. Personal expenses: $1,350.

Financial aid. Need-based: Need-based aid available for part-time students. Work-study available nights, weekends and for part-time students. **Non-need-based:** Scholarships awarded for academics, job skills, leadership, ROTC, state residency.

Application procedures. Admission: No deadline. No application fee. Admission notification on a rolling basis. Application fee for international students requesting issuance of I-20. **Financial aid:** Priority date 3/15; no closing date. FAFSA, institutional form required. Applicants notified on a rolling basis starting 4/1; must reply within 2 week(s) of notification.

Academics. Special study options: Cooperative education, distance learning, double major, dual enrollment of high school students, ESL, honors, liberal arts/career combination. License preparation in dental hygiene, nursing, paramedic, radiology. **Credit/placement by examination:** AP, CLEP, IB, institutional tests. 25% of degree requirement must be taken in residence. **Support services:** GED preparation and test center, learning center, pre-admission summer program, reduced course load, remedial instruction, study skills assistance, tutoring, writing center.

Majors. Architecture: Landscape. **Business:** General, accounting, administrative services, hospitality/recreation. **Computer sciences:** General, applications programming, computer graphics, programming. **Conservation:** General. **Education:** Early childhood. **Health services:** Clinical lab technology, dental hygiene, EMT paramedic, medical assistant, medical radiologic technology/radiation therapy, medical records technology, medical secretary, nursing (RN). **Liberal arts:** Arts/sciences. **Protective services:** Police science.

Most popular majors. Business/marketing 22%, computer/information sciences 15%, engineering/engineering technologies 17%, health sciences 15%, liberal arts 25%.

Computing on campus. 62 workstations in library, computer center, student center. Online course registration, helpline, wireless network available.

Student life. Freshman orientation: Available. Preregistration for classes offered. Held on first day of class. **Activities:** Choral groups, drama, international student organizations, student government, student newspaper.

Athletics. NJCAA. **Intercollegiate:** Baseball M, basketball, cheerleading, cross-country, golf, soccer M, volleyball W. **Team name:** Eagles.

Student services. Career counseling, student employment services, financial aid counseling, minority student services, personal counseling, placement for graduates, veterans' counselor. **Physically disabled:** Services for visually, speech, hearing impaired. **Transfer:** Transfer adviser, college fairs on campus for students transferring to 4-year colleges.

Contact. E-mail: admissions@waketech.edu
Phone: (919) 866-5500 Fax: (919) 661-0117
Susan Bloomfield, Director of Admissions, Wake Technical Community College, 9101 Fayetteville Road, Raleigh, NC 27603

Wayne Community College
Goldsboro, North Carolina
www.waynecc.edu   CB code: 5926

- Public 2-year community college
- Commuter campus in large town

General. Founded in 1957. Regionally accredited. **Enrollment:** 3,335 degree-seeking undergraduates; 379 non-degree-seeking students. **Degrees:** 367 associate awarded. **Location:** 55 miles from Raleigh. **Calendar:** Semester, limited summer session. **Full-time faculty:** 133 total; 4% have terminal degrees, 20% minority, 63% women. **Part-time faculty:** 202 total; less than 1% have terminal degrees, 30% minority, 52% women. **Class size:** 45% < 20, 53% 20-39, 2% 40-49, less than 1% 50-99.

Student profile. Among degree-seeking undergraduates, 686 enrolled as first-time, first-year students, 414 transferred in from other institutions.

Part-time:	53%	Women:	62%
Out-of-state:	11%	25 or older:	40%

Transfer out. Colleges most students transferred to 2011: East Carolina University, Mount Olive College, Campbell University, North Carolina State.

Basis for selection. Open admission, but selective for some programs. Admission to allied health programs based on placement test and academic record.

High school preparation. 14 units recommended. Recommended units include English 4, mathematics 3, social studies 1, history 1, science 3 (laboratory 1) and foreign language 2.

2011-2012 Annual costs. Tuition/fees: $2,067; $7,827 out-of-state. Per-credit charge: $67 in-state; $259 out-of-state. Books/supplies: $800. Personal expenses: $400.

2010-2011 Financial aid. Need-based: 99% of total undergraduate aid awarded as scholarships/grants, 1% as loans/jobs. Need-based aid available for part-time students. Work-study available nights, weekends and for part-time students. **Non-need-based:** Scholarships awarded for academics, job skills.

Application procedures. Admission: No deadline. No application fee. Admission notification on a rolling basis. **Financial aid:** Priority date 3/15, closing date 5/1. FAFSA, institutional form required. Applicants notified on a rolling basis starting 6/1; must reply within 2 week(s) of notification.

Academics. Special study options: Accelerated study, cooperative education, distance learning, double major, dual enrollment of high school students, ESL, honors, internships, teacher certification program, weekend college. License preparation in aviation, dental hygiene, nursing, occupational therapy, paramedic, real estate. **Credit/placement by examination:** AP, CLEP, IB, institutional tests. **Support services:** GED preparation and test center, learning center, reduced course load, remedial instruction, study skills assistance, tutoring, writing center.

Majors. Business: Accounting, business admin, marketing, office management, operations. **Computer sciences:** Information technology, networking. **Conservation:** Forest technology. **Education:** Early childhood, elementary. **General:** Agribusiness operations, animal husbandry, poultry, sustainable agriculture, turf management. **Health services:** Dental hygiene, medical assistant, mental health services, nursing (RN), office admin, substance abuse counseling. **Liberal arts:** Arts/sciences. **Protective services:** Criminal justice, disaster management, forensics. **Visual/performing arts:** Game design.

Most popular majors. Business/marketing 11%, health sciences 32%, liberal arts 35%.

Computing on campus. 400 workstations in library, computer center. Online course registration available.

Student life. Freshman orientation: Mandatory. Preregistration for classes offered. **Policies:** Student government organizes sports program. **Activities:** Concert band, choral groups, student government, student newspaper.

Athletics. Intramural: Basketball, bowling, golf, softball, table tennis, tennis, volleyball. **Team name:** Bisons.

Student services. Adult student services, career counseling, student employment services, financial aid counseling, health services, minority student services, on-campus daycare, personal counseling, placement for graduates, veterans' counselor, women's services. **Physically disabled:** Services for visually, speech, hearing impaired. **Transfer:** Transfer center, transfer adviser, college fairs on campus for students transferring to 4-year colleges.

Contact. E-mail: msm@waynecc.edu
Phone: (919) 735-5151 ext. 6720 Fax: (919) 736-9425
Susan Sasser, Director of Admissions and Records, Wayne Community College, PO Box 8002, Goldsboro, NC 27533-8002

Western Piedmont Community College
Morganton, North Carolina
www.wpcc.edu   CB code: 5922

- Public 2-year community college
- Commuter campus in large town

General. Founded in 1964. Regionally accredited. **Enrollment:** 2,616 degree-seeking undergraduates. **Degrees:** 130 associate awarded. **Location:** 60 miles from Charlotte. **Calendar:** Semester, extensive summer session. **Full-time faculty:** 79 total; 6% have terminal degrees, 5% minority. **Part-time faculty:** 354 total; less than 1% have terminal degrees, 5% minority. **Special facilities:** Greenhouses, fitness and nature trails, alpine climbing tower, Senator Sam J. Ervin Jr. library and museum.

Student profile.

Out-of-state:	20%	25 or older:	51%

Transfer out. Colleges most students transferred to 2011: Appalachian State University, Gardner-Webb University, Western Carolina University, Lenoir-Rhyne College, Lees McRae.

Basis for selection. Open admission, but selective for some programs. Special requirements for health programs.

2011-2012 Annual costs. Tuition/fees: $2,022; $7,782 out-of-state. Per-credit charge: $67 in-state; $259 out-of-state. Books/supplies: $1,104. Personal expenses: $2,482.

Financial aid. Need-based: Need-based aid available for part-time students. Work-study available nights, weekends and for part-time students. **Non-need-based:** Scholarships awarded for academics.

Application procedures. Admission: No deadline. No application fee. Admission notification on a rolling basis. Application closing date for nursing, medical laboratory applicants is January 1 for fall admission. **Financial aid:** No deadline. FAFSA required. Applicants notified on a rolling basis starting 6/15; must reply within 2 week(s) of notification.

Academics. Special study options: Cooperative education, distance learning, dual enrollment of high school students. License preparation in nursing. **Credit/placement by examination:** AP, CLEP, IB, institutional tests. 15 credit hours maximum toward associate degree. **Support services:** GED preparation and test center, learning center, reduced course load, remedial instruction, tutoring.

Majors. Business: Accounting, administrative services, business admin, office technology, office/clerical, operations, sales/distribution. **Computer sciences:** Computer science, data processing, information systems, systems analysis. **Conservation:** General. **Education:** Early childhood. **Engineering:** General. **General:** Horticulture. **Health services:** Clinical lab assistant, medical assistant, nursing (RN), office admin, recreational therapy. **Liberal arts:** Arts/sciences. **Protective services:** Criminal justice. **Visual/performing arts:** Interior design, studio arts. **Work/family studies:** Child care management.

Most popular majors. Business/marketing 24%, education 6%, health sciences 28%, liberal arts 30%, security/protective services 9%.

Computing on campus. 280 workstations in library, computer center. Commuter students can connect to campus network. Online library, wireless network available.

Student life. Freshman orientation: Available. Preregistration for classes offered. **Activities:** Drama, student government, Phi Beta Lambda, Phi Theta Kappa, African American Students Association, Students for Christ.

Athletics. Team name: Pioneers.

Student services. Adult student services, career counseling, services for economically disadvantaged, student employment services, financial aid counseling, personal counseling, placement for graduates, veterans' counselor. **Physically disabled:** Services for visually, speech, hearing impaired. **Transfer:** Transfer adviser, college fairs on campus for students transferring to 4-year colleges.

Contact. E-mail: arushin@wpcc.edu
Phone: (828) 448-6051 Fax: (828) 448-6170
Jennifer Propst, Director of Enrollment Management, Western Piedmont Community College, 1001 Burkemont Avenue, Morganton, NC 28655-4504

Wilkes Community College
Wilkesboro, North Carolina
www.wilkescc.edu   CB code: 5921

▶ Public 2-year community college
▶ Commuter campus in small town

General. Founded in 1965. Regionally accredited. **Enrollment:** 2,429 degree-seeking undergraduates. **Degrees:** 352 associate awarded. **Location:** 50 miles from Winston-Salem. **Calendar:** Semester, limited summer session. **Full-time faculty:** 84 total. **Part-time faculty:** 261 total. **Class size:** 80% < 20, 19% 20-39, 1% 40-49, less than 1% 50-99. **Special facilities:** Community center.

Student profile.

Out-of-state:	1%	25 or older:	39%

Transfer out. Colleges most students transferred to 2011: Appalachian State University, Gardner-Webb University, Winston-Salem State University.

Basis for selection. Open admission, but selective for some programs. High school diploma or its equivalency required. Special requirements for nursing program.

High school preparation. 20 units recommended. Recommended units include English 4, mathematics 4, social studies 3, history 2, science 3 (laboratory 1), foreign language 2 and academic electives 2.

2011-2012 Annual costs. Tuition/fees: $2,092; $7,852 out-of-state. Per-credit charge: $67 in-state; $259 out-of-state. Books/supplies: $1,200. Personal expenses: $500.

Financial aid. Need-based: Need-based aid available for part-time students. Work-study available nights, weekends and for part-time students. **Non-need-based:** Scholarships awarded for academics, art, job skills, leadership, minority status, music/drama, state residency.

Application procedures. Admission: No deadline. No application fee. Admission notification on a rolling basis. **Financial aid:** Closing date 5/15. FAFSA required. Applicants notified on a rolling basis starting 4/1; must reply by 8/1.

Academics. Special study options: Cooperative education, distance learning, double major, dual enrollment of high school students, ESL, independent study, internships. Bachelor's degree programs available on campus. License preparation in nursing, paramedic, real estate. **Credit/placement by examination:** AP, CLEP, IB, institutional tests. 16 credit hours maximum toward associate degree. **Support services:** GED preparation and test center, learning center, pre-admission summer program, reduced course load, remedial instruction, study skills assistance, tutoring, writing center.

Majors. Business: Accounting, business admin, marketing, office management. **Communications technology:** Radio/TV. **Computer sciences:** Computer graphics, information systems, information technology, LAN/WAN management, programming. **Education:** Early childhood, elementary. **General:** Horticulture. **Health services:** Medical assistant, nursing (RN). **Liberal arts:** Arts/sciences. **Protective services:** Criminal justice.

Most popular majors. Business/marketing 18%, education 7%, engineering/engineering technologies 11%, health sciences 16%, liberal arts 26%, trade and industry 9%.

Computing on campus. 150 workstations in library, computer center, student center.

Student life. Freshman orientation: Mandatory. Preregistration for classes offered. **Activities:** Choral groups, drama, literary magazine, music ensembles, musical theater, radio station, student government, student newspaper, Baptist student union, Ye Hosts food service club, camera club, Phi Theta Kappa, Association of Information Technology Professionals, Rotaract, human services club, medical assisting club, student government association, Student Ambassadors.

Athletics. NJCAA. **Intercollegiate:** Baseball M, basketball, volleyball W. **Intramural:** Basketball, table tennis, tennis, volleyball. **Team name:** Cougars.

Student services. Adult student services, career counseling, services for economically disadvantaged, student employment services, financial aid counseling, minority student services, personal counseling, placement for graduates, veterans' counselor. **Physically disabled:** Services for visually, speech, hearing impaired. **Transfer:** Pre-admission transcript evaluation for new students. Transfer adviser, college fairs on campus for students transferring to 4-year colleges.

Contact. E-mail: mac.warren@wilkescc.edu
Phone: (336) 838-6135 Fax: (336) 838-6547
Scott Johnson, Director of Admissions, Wilkes Community College, 1328 South Collegiate Drive, Wilkesboro, NC 28697-0120

Wilson Community College
Wilson, North Carolina
www.wilsoncc.edu   CB code: 5930

▶ Public 2-year community college
▶ Commuter campus in large town

General. Founded in 1958. Regionally accredited. **Enrollment:** 1,538 degree-seeking undergraduates; 361 non-degree-seeking students. **Degrees:** 191 associate awarded. **Location:** 50 miles from Raleigh. **Calendar:** Semester, limited summer session. **Full-time faculty:** 50 total; 6% have terminal degrees, 18% minority, 74% women. **Part-time faculty:** 177 total; 28% minority, 58% women. **Special facilities:** Student services green building

featuring sustainable energy technologies such as a vertical axis wind turbine and photovoltaic solar panels.

Student profile. Among degree-seeking undergraduates, 21% enrolled in a transfer program, 4% already have a bachelor's degree or higher, 262 enrolled as first-time, first-year students, 330 transferred in from other institutions.

Part-time:	41%	Asian American:	1%
Out-of-state:	1%	Hispanic American:	5%
Women:	70%	Native American:	1%
African American:	45%	25 or older:	51%

Basis for selection. Open admission, but selective for some programs. Admission for nursing based on test scores, high school record, skills, and experience. Health requirement for emergency medical technology. Interview recommended. **Adult students:** SAT/ACT scores not required.

High school preparation. High school diploma not required for certificate programs.

2011-2012 Annual costs. Tuition/fees: $2,098; $7,858 out-of-state. Per-credit charge: $67 in-state; $259 out-of-state. Books/supplies: $1,000. Personal expenses: $7,800.

Financial aid. Need-based: Need-based aid available for part-time students. Work-study available nights, weekends and for part-time students. **Non-need-based:** Scholarships awarded for academics.

Application procedures. Admission: No deadline. No application fee. Admission notification on a rolling basis beginning on or about 1/1. Applicants accepted to nursing program must reply by May 1. **Financial aid:** Priority date 3/15; no closing date. FAFSA, institutional form required. Applicants notified on a rolling basis.

Academics. Special program assistance for hearing-impaired students. **Special study options:** Cooperative education, distance learning, double major, dual enrollment of high school students, ESL, liberal arts/career combination. License preparation in nursing. **Credit/placement by examination:** AP, CLEP, institutional tests. **Support services:** GED preparation and test center, learning center, reduced course load, remedial instruction, tutoring.

Majors. Business: Accounting, business admin, office management. **Computer sciences:** Information technology, networking, security. **Education:** Early childhood, elementary. **Foreign languages:** Sign language interpretation. **Health services:** Nursing (RN), office admin, surgical technology. **Liberal arts:** Arts/sciences. **Protective services:** Criminal justice, fire safety technology. **Visual/performing arts:** Game design.

Most popular majors. Business/marketing 12%, computer/information sciences 8%, education 10%, foreign language 6%, health sciences 19%, liberal arts 19%, security/protective services 16%.

Computing on campus. 33 workstations in library, computer center. Online course registration, helpline, wireless network available.

Student life. Freshman orientation: Available. Preregistration for classes offered. **Activities:** Choral groups, student government.

Student services. Career counseling, services for economically disadvantaged, student employment services, placement for graduates, veterans' counselor. **Physically disabled:** Services for hearing impaired. **Transfer:** Transfer adviser, college fairs on campus for students transferring to 4-year colleges.

Contact. E-mail: lmansfield@wilsoncc.edu
Phone: (252) 246-1285 Fax: (252) 246-1384
Leonard Mansfield, Director of Admissions and Registration, Wilson Community College, Box 4305, Wilson, NC 27893-0305

North Dakota

Bismarck State College
Bismarck, North Dakota
www.bismarckstate.edu

CB code: 6041

- Public 2-year community college
- Commuter campus in small city

General. Founded in 1939. Regionally accredited. **Enrollment:** 4,392 degree-seeking undergraduates. **Degrees:** 32 bachelor's, 989 associate awarded. **Location:** 200 miles from Fargo. **Calendar:** Semester, limited summer session. **Full-time faculty:** 124 total. **Part-time faculty:** 246 total. **Special facilities:** Aquatic and wellness center.

Student profile. Among degree-seeking undergraduates, 912 enrolled as first-time, first-year students.

Part-time:	40%	25 or older:	30%
Out-of-state:	11%	Live on campus:	11%
Women:	46%		

Basis for selection. Open admission, but selective for some programs. Test scores required for selective admission programs in air conditioning, heating and refrigeration, automotive technology, automotive collision technology, carpentry, electronics technology, line worker (electrical), power plant technology, process plant technology, welding, commercial art. Interview recommended for some programs; portfolio recommended for graphic arts program. **Adult students:** Students aged 25 or older must submit COMPASS assessment scores in the areas of English, math, and reading.

High school preparation. Recommended units include English 4, mathematics 3, social studies 3, science 3 and foreign language 2.

2011-2012 Annual costs. Tuition/fees: $4,007; $9,625 out-of-state. Per-credit charge: $112 in-state; $299 out-of-state. Room/board: $5,146. Books/supplies: $750. Personal expenses: $1,900.

Financial aid. All financial aid based on need. Need-based aid available for part-time students. Work-study available nights, weekends and for part-time students.

Application procedures. Admission: No deadline. $35 fee. Admission notification on a rolling basis beginning on or about 1/1. **Financial aid:** Priority date 3/15; no closing date. FAFSA required. Applicants notified on a rolling basis starting 6/1; must reply within 3 week(s) of notification.

Academics. Academic advising focus over the summer with 20+ sessions offered to students who are enrolling for the following fall session. Online academic support services available. **Special study options:** Cooperative education, distance learning, dual enrollment of high school students, internships, liberal arts/career combination. Bachelor's degree programs available on campus. License preparation in nursing, paramedic. **Credit/placement by examination:** AP, CLEP, institutional tests. 30 credit hours maximum toward associate degree. **Support services:** Learning center, remedial instruction, study skills assistance, tutoring, writing center.

Majors. Business: General, administrative services, office technology, transportation. **Communications:** Public relations. **Computer sciences:** Networking, web page design. **Education:** Teacher assistance. **General:** Business, farm/ranch. **Health services:** Clinical lab technology, EMT paramedic, licensed practical nurse, medical secretary, nursing (RN), surgical technology. **Liberal arts:** Arts/sciences. **Protective services:** Criminal justice. **Social sciences:** GIS/cartography. **Visual/performing arts:** Commercial/advertising art.

Computing on campus. 450 workstations in library, computer center, student center. Dormitories wired for high-speed internet access. Commuter students can connect to campus network. Online course registration, online library, helpline, wireless network available.

Student life. Freshman orientation: Available. Preregistration for classes offered. **Housing:** Coed dorms, single-sex dorms, wellness housing available. $100 partly refundable deposit. **Activities:** Bands, choral groups, dance, drama, literary magazine, music ensembles, musical theater, student government, student newspaper.

Athletics. NJCAA. **Intercollegiate:** Baseball M, basketball, golf, soccer, softball W, tennis, volleyball W. **Intramural:** Basketball, bowling, golf, soccer, softball, table tennis, volleyball. **Team name:** Mystics.

Student services. Adult student services, alcohol/substance abuse counseling, career counseling, student employment services, financial aid counseling, minority student services, personal counseling, placement for graduates, veterans' counselor. **Physically disabled:** Services for visually, speech, hearing impaired. **Transfer:** Pre-admission transcript evaluation for new students. Transfer adviser, college fairs on campus for students transferring to 4-year colleges.

Contact. E-mail: BSC.Admissions@bismarckstate.edu
Phone: (701) 224-5429 Toll-free number: (800) 445-5073
Fax: (701) 224-5643
Karen Erickson, Director of Admissions and Enrollment Services, Bismarck State College, PO Box 5587, Bismarck, ND 58506-5587

Cankdeska Cikana Community College
Fort Totten, North Dakota
www.littlehoop.edu

CB code: 1306

- Public 2-year community college
- Residential campus in rural community

General. Founded in 1974. Regionally accredited. **Enrollment:** 219 degree-seeking undergraduates. **Degrees:** 47 associate awarded. **Location:** 13 miles from Devils Lake. **Calendar:** Semester, limited summer session. **Full-time faculty:** 19 total. **Part-time faculty:** 10 total.

Basis for selection. Open admission.

2011-2012 Annual costs. Tuition/fees: $2,770; $2,770 out-of-state. Per-credit charge: $105. Books/supplies: $700. Personal expenses: $3,000.

Financial aid. All financial aid based on need. Need-based aid available for part-time students. Work-study available nights, weekends and for part-time students.

Application procedures. Admission: No deadline. No application fee. **Financial aid:** Closing date 8/20. FAFSA, institutional form required. Applicants notified on a rolling basis.

Academics. Special study options: Cooperative education, independent study, internships. **Credit/placement by examination:** AP, CLEP. **Support services:** GED preparation and test center, learning center, remedial instruction, study skills assistance, tutoring.

Majors. Area/ethnic studies: Native American. **Business:** General, administrative services, auditing, business admin, office technology. **Computer sciences:** General, applications programming. **Education:** Early childhood. **Engineering:** Pre-engineering. **Health services:** Medical assistant, prenursing. **Liberal arts:** Arts/sciences. **Visual/performing arts:** Digital arts, studio arts.

Computing on campus. 30 workstations in library, computer center. Repair service, wireless network available.

Student life. Freshman orientation: Available. Preregistration for classes offered. **Activities:** Student government, Indian organization.

Athletics. Intramural: Volleyball.

Student services. Career counseling, financial aid counseling, on-campus daycare, personal counseling. **Transfer:** Transfer adviser, college fairs on campus for students transferring to 4-year colleges.

Contact. E-mail: Ermen_Brown@littlehoop.edu
Phone: (701) 766-1342 Fax: (701) 766-1344
Ermen Brown, Registrar, Cankdeska Cikana Community College, Box 269, Fort Totten, ND 58335

Dakota College at Bottineau
Bottineau, North Dakota
www.dakotacollege.edu

CB code: 1540

- Public 2-year nursing and junior college
- Residential campus in small town

General. Founded in 1907. Regionally accredited. **Enrollment:** 812 degree-seeking undergraduates. **Degrees:** 106 associate awarded. **Location:** 80 miles

Two-Year Colleges

from Minot. **Calendar:** Semester, limited summer session. **Full-time faculty:** 27 total; 7% have terminal degrees, 44% women. **Part-time faculty:** 50 total; 6% have terminal degrees, 6% minority, 70% women. **Special facilities:** Headquarters for North Dakota Forest Service, outdoor laboratories on state and federally owned refuges, forests, parklands.

Basis for selection. Open admission. **Adult students:** Must take math and English placement tests.

2011-2012 Annual costs. Tuition/fees: $3,857; $5,417 out-of-state. Per-credit charge: $130 in-state; $195 out-of-state. Room/board: $4,930. Books/supplies: $1,000. Personal expenses: $3,300.

2011-2012 Financial aid. **Need-based:** Need-based aid available for part-time students. Work-study available nights, weekends and for part-time students. **Non-need-based:** Scholarships awarded for academics, alumni affiliation, athletics, minority status, music/drama, state residency.

Application procedures. **Admission:** No deadline. $35 fee. Admission notification on a rolling basis. **Financial aid:** Priority date 4/15; no closing date. FAFSA required. Applicants notified on a rolling basis starting 6/1; must reply within 2 week(s) of notification.

Academics. **Special study options:** Cooperative education, distance learning, double major, dual enrollment of high school students, independent study, internships, liberal arts/career combination. License preparation in nursing, paramedic. **Credit/placement by examination:** AP, CLEP, institutional tests. **Support services:** Learning center, reduced course load, remedial instruction, study skills assistance, tutoring.

Majors. **Biology:** General, botany, wildlife, zoology. **Business:** Accounting technology, accounting/business management, administrative services, business admin, office/clerical, receptionist. **Communications:** Advertising. **Computer sciences:** Information technology, webmaster. **Conservation:** General, environmental studies, management/policy, wildlife/wilderness. **Education:** General, teacher assistance. **Engineering:** Surveying. **English:** English lit. **General:** Floriculture, greenhouse operations, landscaping, turf management. **Health services:** EMT paramedic, medical assistant, medical secretary, nursing (RN), premedicine, prenursing, prepharmacy, preveterinary. **History:** General. **Liberal arts:** Arts/sciences. **Math:** General. **Parks/recreation:** General, facilities management, health/fitness. **Physical sciences:** General. **Psychology:** General. **Social sciences:** General. **Work/family studies:** Child care service.

Most popular majors. Agriculture 18%, health sciences 23%, liberal arts 56%.

Computing on campus. 60 workstations in library, computer center, student center. Dormitories wired for high-speed internet access. Online course registration, online library, repair service, wireless network available.

Student life. **Freshman orientation:** Mandatory. Preregistration for classes offered. **Housing:** Guaranteed on-campus for all undergraduates. Single-sex dorms, wellness housing available. $100 nonrefundable deposit. **Activities:** Campus ministries, drama, student government, student newspaper.

Athletics. NJCAA. **Intercollegiate:** Baseball M, basketball, football (tackle) M, ice hockey M, softball W, volleyball W. **Intramural:** Badminton, basketball, bowling, football (non-tackle), racquetball, skiing, soccer, softball, volleyball. **Team name:** Lumberjacks and Ladyjacks.

Student services. Adult student services, alcohol/substance abuse counseling, career counseling, student employment services, financial aid counseling, health services, personal counseling, veterans' counselor. **Transfer:** Transfer adviser, college fairs on campus for students transferring to 4-year colleges.

Contact. E-mail: admissions@dakotacollege.edu
Phone: (701) 228-5488 Toll-free number: (800) 542-6866
Fax: (701) 228-5499
Paula Berg, Associate Dean, Dakota College at Bottineau, 105 Simrall Boulevard, Bottineau, ND 58318-1198

Fort Berthold Community College
New Town, North Dakota
www.fortbertholdcc.edu
CB code: 7304

- Public 2-year community college
- Small town

General. Founded in 1973. Regionally accredited. Affiliated with American Indian Higher Education Consortium. **Enrollment:** 200 undergraduates. **Degrees:** 24 associate awarded. **Location:** 80 miles from Minot, 150 miles from Bismarck. **Calendar:** Semester, limited summer session. **Full-time faculty:** 14 total. **Part-time faculty:** 11 total.

Basis for selection. Open admission.

2011-2012 Annual costs. Tuition/fees: $4,010; $4,010 out-of-state. Per-credit charge: $150. Books/supplies: $400. Personal expenses: $800.

Financial aid. **Need-based:** Work-study available nights, weekends and for part-time students.

Application procedures. **Admission:** No deadline. $25 fee.

Academics. **Special study options:** Double major, independent study. **Credit/placement by examination:** AP, CLEP. **Support services:** GED preparation and test center, remedial instruction, tutoring.

Majors. **Area/ethnic studies:** Native American. **Business:** Business admin, office technology. **Education:** Elementary. **Health services:** Medical secretary, nursing assistant. **Human services:** General.

Student life. **Activities:** Drama, student government.

Athletics. **Intercollegiate:** Basketball, cross-country.

Student services. Adult student services, personal counseling, veterans' counselor. **Transfer:** Transfer adviser for students transferring to 4-year colleges.

Contact. E-mail: taulau@fbcc.bia.edu
Phone: (701) 627-4738 ext. 286 Fax: (701) 627-4790
Kathy Kraft, Registrar and Data Manager, Fort Berthold Community College, Box 490, New Town, ND 58763

Lake Region State College
Devils Lake, North Dakota
www.lrsc.edu
CB code: 6163

- Public 2-year community and technical college
- Commuter campus in small town

General. Founded in 1941. Regionally accredited. Satellite campus at Grand Forks Air Force Base. **Enrollment:** 736 degree-seeking undergraduates; 1,320 non-degree-seeking students. **Degrees:** 172 associate awarded. **Location:** 90 miles from Grand Forks, 400 miles from Minneapolis-St. Paul. **Calendar:** Semester, limited summer session. **Full-time faculty:** 34 total; 12% have terminal degrees, 3% minority, 47% women. **Part-time faculty:** 139 total; 9% have terminal degrees, 4% minority, 64% women. **Class size:** 89% < 20, 11% 20-39. **Partnerships:** Formal partnership with CISCO.

Student profile. Among degree-seeking undergraduates, 70% enrolled in a transfer program, 30% enrolled in a vocational program, 1% already have a bachelor's degree or higher, 211 enrolled as first-time, first-year students, 182 transferred in from other institutions.

Part-time:	32%	25 or older:	24%
Out-of-state:	17%	Live on campus:	20%
Women:	55%		

Transfer out. 40% of students enrolled in the transfer program go on to 4-year colleges. **Colleges most students transferred to 2011:** Mayville State University, Minot State University, University of North Dakota, North Dakota State University, Valley City State University.

Basis for selection. Open admission, but selective for some programs. Selective to some programs. **Adult students:** SAT/ACT scores not required if applicant over 24. COMPASS test required of new adult students. **Home schooled:** Transcript of courses and grades required.

High school preparation. College-preparatory program recommended. Recommended units include English 4, mathematics 3, social studies 3, science 3 (laboratory 2) and foreign language 2.

2011-2012 Annual costs. Tuition/fees: $3,908; $3,908 out-of-state. Per-credit charge: $128 in-state; $128 out-of-state. Room/board: $5,160. Books/supplies: $1,000. Personal expenses: $3,342.

2011-2012 Financial aid. **Need-based:** Average need met was 57%. Average scholarship/grant was $4,404; average loan $2,945. 51% of total undergraduate aid awarded as scholarships/grants, 49% as loans/jobs. Need-based aid available for part-time students. Work-study available nights, weekends and for part-time students. **Non-need-based:** Scholarships awarded for academics, athletics, leadership, minority status, music/drama.

Application procedures. Admission: No deadline. $35 fee. Admission notification on a rolling basis. **Financial aid:** Priority date 3/15; no closing date. FAFSA required. Applicants notified on a rolling basis starting 5/15; must reply within 2 week(s) of notification.

Academics. Special study options: Cooperative education, distance learning, dual enrollment of high school students, ESL, honors, internships, liberal arts/career combination. Bachelor's degree programs available on campus. License preparation in nursing. **Credit/placement by examination:** AP, CLEP, institutional tests. 15 credit hours maximum toward associate degree. May not take a CLEP subject exam after enrolling in that course. **Support services:** GED preparation and test center, learning center, reduced course load, remedial instruction, study skills assistance, tutoring, writing center.

Majors. Business: Accounting, accounting technology, administrative services, business admin, executive assistant, fashion, management information systems, market research, office management, office/clerical, sales/distribution, small business admin. **Computer sciences:** General, computer science, data processing, networking, vendor certification. **Engineering:** Electrical. **Health services:** Licensed practical nurse, medical secretary. **Liberal arts:** Arts/sciences. **Parks/recreation:** Physical fitness technician. **Protective services:** Police science. **Work/family studies:** Child care management, child care service.

Most popular majors. Business/marketing 10%, health sciences 14%, liberal arts 59%.

Computing on campus. 250 workstations in dormitories, library, computer center, student center. Dormitories wired for high-speed internet access and linked to campus network. Commuter students can connect to campus network. Online course registration, online library, helpline, wireless network available.

Student life. Freshman orientation: Mandatory, $10 fee. Preregistration for classes offered. Summer orientation available. Mandatory session the day before classes start. **Policies:** Smoke-free campus; alcohol not allowed on campus. **Housing:** Single-sex dorms, special housing for disabled, apartments, wellness housing available. $50 nonrefundable deposit, deadline 9/1. **Activities:** Campus ministries, choral groups, drama, international student organizations, literary magazine, musical theater, student government, symphony orchestra, Delta Epsilon Chi, Skills USA, Students Other than Average, business club, Int'l students club, student nurse organization, simulator maintenance technician club, Campus Crusade for Christ, Phi Theta Kappa.

Athletics. NJCAA. **Intercollegiate:** Basketball. **Intramural:** Archery, basketball, bowling, football (non-tackle), golf, ice hockey, soccer, softball, swimming, table tennis, volleyball. **Team name:** Royals.

Student services. Adult student services, career counseling, services for economically disadvantaged, student employment services, financial aid counseling, on-campus daycare, personal counseling, placement for graduates, veterans' counselor. **Physically disabled:** Services for speech, hearing impaired. **Transfer:** Transfer adviser, college fairs on campus for students transferring to 4-year colleges.

Contact. E-mail: lrsc.admissions@lrsc.edu
Phone: (701) 662-1514 Toll-free number: (800) 443-1313 ext. 1514
Fax: (701) 662-1581
Stephanie Shock, Director of Admissions and Enrollment Management, Lake Region State College, 1801 College Drive North, Devils Lake, ND 58301-1598

North Dakota State College of Science
Wahpeton, North Dakota
www.ndscs.edu   CB code: 6476

- Public 2-year junior and technical college
- Residential campus in small town

General. Founded in 1903. Regionally accredited. NDSCS has the look and feel of a four-year institution, but offers associate degrees. **Enrollment:** 3,127 degree-seeking undergraduates. **Degrees:** 518 associate awarded. **Location:** 50 miles from Fargo, 200 miles from Sioux Falls, South Dakota. **Calendar:** Semester, limited summer session. **Full-time faculty:** 117 total; 3% have terminal degrees, 3% minority, 38% women. **Part-time faculty:** 165 total; 6% have terminal degrees, 2% minority, 60% women. **Class size:** 63% < 20, 31% 20-39, 4% 40-49, 2% 50-99, less than 1% >100. **Partnerships:** Formal partnerships with Caterpillar Corporation, John Deere and Snap-On.

Student profile. Among degree-seeking undergraduates, 17% enrolled in a transfer program, 53% enrolled in a vocational program, 758 enrolled as first-time, first-year students.

Part-time:	43%	25 or older:	79%
Out-of-state:	41%	Live on campus:	52%
Women:	43%		

Transfer out. Colleges most students transferred to 2011: Minnesota State University Moorhead, North Dakota State University, University of North Dakota, Valley City State University.

Basis for selection. Open admission, but selective for some programs. Special requirements for allied health programs. **Adult students:** SAT/ACT scores not required if applicant over 25.

High school preparation. Chemistry, English, and anatomy & physiology required for dental hygiene.

2011-2012 Annual costs. Tuition/fees: $3,921; $9,544 out-of-state. Per-credit charge: $112 in-state; $300 out-of-state. Room/board: $5,196. Books/supplies: $1,000. Personal expenses: $2,230.

2010-2011 Financial aid. Need-based: 462 full-time freshmen applied for aid; 372 were judged to have need; 367 of these received aid. Average need met was 67%. Average scholarship/grant was $4,160; average loan $3,644. 41% of total undergraduate aid awarded as scholarships/grants, 59% as loans/jobs. Need-based aid available for part-time students. Work-study available nights, weekends and for part-time students. **Non-need-based:** Awarded to 580 full-time undergraduates, including 221 freshmen. Scholarships awarded for academics, alumni affiliation, athletics, leadership, minority status, music/drama, state residency.

Application procedures. Admission: No deadline. $35 fee. Admission notification on a rolling basis. **Financial aid:** Priority date 3/15; no closing date. FAFSA, institutional form required. Applicants notified on a rolling basis starting 6/1; must reply within 2 week(s) of notification.

Academics. Special study options: Cooperative education, distance learning, dual enrollment of high school students, ESL, independent study, internships, liberal arts/career combination. License preparation in dental hygiene, nursing, occupational therapy, paramedic. **Credit/placement by examination:** AP, CLEP, institutional tests. 32 credit hours maximum toward associate degree. **Support services:** Learning center, pre-admission summer program, reduced course load, remedial instruction, study skills assistance, tutoring, writing center.

Majors. Business: Administrative services, business admin, e-commerce. **Computer sciences:** General, data entry, networking, programming. **General:** Business, equipment technology. **Health services:** Dental hygiene, EMT paramedic, insurance coding, licensed practical nurse, mental health services, nursing (RN), occupational therapy assistant, pharmacy assistant. **Liberal arts:** Arts/sciences.

Most popular majors. Agriculture 7%, engineering/engineering technologies 17%, health sciences 25%, liberal arts 20%, trade and industry 21%.

Computing on campus. 550 workstations in dormitories, library, computer center, student center. Dormitories wired for high-speed internet access and linked to campus network. Commuter students can connect to campus network. Online course registration, online library, helpline, wireless network available.

Student life. Freshman orientation: Mandatory, $25 fee. Preregistration for classes offered. Orientation held the day before classes start. **Housing:** Guaranteed on-campus for freshmen. Coed dorms, single-sex dorms, special housing for disabled, apartments available. $25 fully refundable deposit. Honors floor available. **Activities:** Bands, campus ministries, choral groups, drama, music ensembles, student government, Intervarsity Christian Fellowship.

Athletics. NJCAA. **Intercollegiate:** Basketball, football (tackle) M, volleyball W. **Intramural:** Basketball, racquetball, softball, volleyball. **Team name:** Wildcats.

Student services. Alcohol/substance abuse counseling, career counseling, student employment services, financial aid counseling, health services, on-campus daycare, personal counseling, placement for graduates, veterans' counselor. **Physically disabled:** Services for visually, hearing impaired. **Transfer:** Pre-admission transcript evaluation for new students. Transfer adviser, college fairs on campus for students transferring to 4-year colleges.

Contact. E-mail: ndscs.admissions@ndscs.edu
Phone: (701) 671-2203 Toll-free number: (800) 342-4325 ext. 32203
Fax: (701) 671-2332
Karen Reilly, Director of Enrollment Services and Records, North Dakota State College of Science, 800 North 6th Street, Wahpeton, ND 58076-0001

Two-Year Colleges

Rasmussen College: Bismarck
Bismarck, North Dakota
www.rasmussen.edu

- For-profit 2-year career college
- Commuter campus in small city

General. **Enrollment:** 289 degree-seeking undergraduates. **Degrees:** 14 bachelor's, 73 associate awarded. **Calendar:** Quarter, extensive summer session. **Full-time faculty:** 7 total. **Part-time faculty:** 40 total.

Basis for selection. Open admission, but selective for some programs. Placement exams required for some programs.

2011-2012 Annual costs. Full-time tuition varies according to program of study. Examples of per-credit-hour charges include Early Childhood Education ($310), Medical Lab Technician, Surgical Technician, Practical Nursing ($395), Professional Nursing, Information Systems Mgmt, Multemedia Technician ($395). Personal expenses: $2,214.

Financial aid. **Need-based:** Need-based aid available for part-time students. Work-study available nights, weekends and for part-time students.

Application procedures. **Admission:** No deadline. $40 fee. Admission notification on a rolling basis. **Financial aid:** No deadline. FAFSA, institutional form required. Applicants notified on a rolling basis.

Academics. **Special study options:** Distance learning, double major, honors, independent study, internships. **Credit/placement by examination:** AP, CLEP, institutional tests. 45 credit hours maximum toward associate degree, 90 toward bachelor's. Credit limited to specific programs, and to courses for which examinations are available. 50% of the student's program must be completed through coursework at institution. **Support services:** Learning center, remedial instruction, study skills assistance, tutoring, writing center.

Majors. **Business:** Accounting, administrative services, business admin. **Health services:** Clinical lab technology, massage therapy, medical records technology, medical secretary, medical transcription.

Computing on campus. 100 workstations in library, computer center, student center. Online course registration, online library, helpline, wireless network available.

Student life. **Freshman orientation:** Mandatory. Preregistration for classes offered.

Student services. Adult student services, career counseling, services for economically disadvantaged, student employment services, financial aid counseling, placement for graduates.

Contact. Phone: (701) 530-9600 Toll-free number: (877) 530-9600 Fax: (701) 530-9604
Susan Hammerstrom, Director of Admissions, Rasmussen College: Bismarck, 1701 East Century Avenue, Bismarck, ND 58503

Sitting Bull College
Fort Yates, North Dakota
www.sittingbull.edu   CB code: 0310

- Public 2-year community college
- Commuter campus in small town

General. Founded in 1971. Regionally accredited. **Enrollment:** 317 degree-seeking undergraduates. **Degrees:** 15 bachelor's, 32 associate awarded. **Location:** 75 miles from Bismarck, 60 miles from Mobridge, South Dakota. **Calendar:** Semester, limited summer session. **Full-time faculty:** 23 total; 17% have terminal degrees, 35% minority, 35% women. **Part-time faculty:** 20 total; 10% have terminal degrees, 40% minority, 55% women. **Class size:** 99% < 20, 1% 20-39.

Transfer out. **Colleges most students transferred to 2011:** Northern State College, Black Hills State College, Bismarck State College, United Tribes Technical College.

Basis for selection. Open admission. COMPASS test required of students without 2-year college degree. High school students may enroll with approval of Vice President of Academic Affairs and parents; letters of recommendation from high school counselor or principal required. **Adult students:** COMPASS required for placement in math and English.

2011-2012 Annual costs. Tuition/fees: $3,910; $3,910 out-of-state. Per-credit charge: $125. Books/supplies: $1,200. Personal expenses: $1,170.

Financial aid. **Need-based:** Need-based aid available for part-time students. Work-study available nights, weekends and for part-time students.

Application procedures. **Admission:** No deadline. $25 fee. Application must be submitted on paper. Admission notification on a rolling basis. **Financial aid:** Priority date 5/1; no closing date. FAFSA, institutional form required. Applicants notified on a rolling basis starting 7/15; must reply within 6 week(s) of notification.

Academics. **Special study options:** Dual enrollment of high school students, independent study. Bachelor's degree programs available on campus. **Credit/placement by examination:** AP, CLEP. **Support services:** GED preparation and test center, learning center, remedial instruction, study skills assistance, tutoring, writing center.

Majors. **Area/ethnic studies:** Native American. **Business:** Business admin, entrepreneurial studies, office technology. **Computer sciences:** Applications programming. **Conservation:** Environmental science, wildlife/wilderness. **Education:** Early childhood, elementary, multi-level teacher. **General:** Agribusiness operations. **Health services:** Licensed practical nurse. **Protective services:** Law enforcement admin.

Most popular majors. Business/marketing 30%, computer/information sciences 8%, education 15%, liberal arts 15%, natural resources/environmental science 12%, public administration/social services 8%.

Computing on campus. 75 workstations in library, computer center, student center. Online course registration, wireless network available.

Student life. **Housing:** Very limited housing available for single parents or married students. **Activities:** Model UN, student government, culture club, rodeo club.

Athletics. **Team name:** Suns.

Student services. Career counseling, student employment services, on-campus daycare, personal counseling, placement for graduates, veterans' counselor. **Transfer:** Transfer adviser for students transferring to 4-year colleges.

Contact. E-mail: melodya@sbci.edu
Phone: (701) 854-8020 Fax: (701) 854-3403
Melody Azure, Director of Admissions/Registrar, Sitting Bull College, 9299 Hwy 24, Fort Yates, ND 58538

Turtle Mountain Community College
Belcourt, North Dakota
www.tm.edu   CB code: 0352

- Private 2-year community college
- Commuter campus in rural community

General. Regionally accredited. **Calendar:** Semester.

Annual costs/financial aid. Tuition/fees (2011-2012): $2,000. Room/board: $3,664. Books/supplies: $400.

Contact. Phone: (701) 477-7862
Admissions/Records Officer, PO Box 340, Belcourt, ND 58316

United Tribes Technical College
Bismarck, North Dakota
www.uttc.edu   CB code: 4915

- Private 2-year technical college
- Residential campus in small city

General. Regionally accredited. Native American college. **Enrollment:** 583 degree-seeking undergraduates. **Degrees:** 7 bachelor's, 143 associate awarded. **Location:** One mile south of Bismarck on University Drive. **Calendar:** Semester, limited summer session. **Full-time faculty:** 57 total. **Part-time faculty:** 6 total. **Special facilities:** Elementary school on campus.

Basis for selection. Open admission, but selective for some programs. Some programs have limited enrollment and/or more stringent academic, medical, and legal requirements. Admittance priority given to those who are members of recognized tribe. **Home schooled:** Statement describing home school structure and mission, transcript of courses and grades, state high school equivalency certificate required.

2011-2012 Annual costs. Books/supplies: $1,200. Personal expenses: $1,880.

Financial aid. Need-based: Need-based aid available for part-time students. Work-study available nights, weekends and for part-time students.

Application procedures. Admission: No deadline. No application fee. Application must be submitted on paper. Admission notification on a rolling basis. **Financial aid:** Priority date 5/29, closing date 6/30. FAFSA required. Applicants notified on a rolling basis starting 5/29; must reply within 2 week(s) of notification.

Academics. Special study options: Accelerated study, distance learning. Bachelor's degree programs available on campus. **Credit/placement by examination:** AP, CLEP. **Support services:** Learning center, remedial instruction, study skills assistance, tutoring.

Majors. Business: Administrative services, business admin. **Education:** General. **Health services:** Licensed practical nurse. **Protective services:** Law enforcement admin.

Computing on campus. 40 workstations in computer center. Commuter students can connect to campus network. Online course registration, repair service available.

Student life. Freshman orientation: Mandatory. Preregistration for classes offered. **Housing:** Coed dorms, single-sex dorms, wellness housing available. **Activities:** Student newspaper.

Athletics. NJCAA. **Intercollegiate:** Basketball, cross-country. **Team name:** Thunderbirds.

Student services. Adult student services, alcohol/substance abuse counseling, chaplain/spiritual director, career counseling, financial aid counseling, health services, on-campus daycare, personal counseling, placement for graduates, women's services. **Transfer:** Pre-admission transcript evaluation for new students.

Contact. E-mail: dlambert@uttc.edu
Phone: (701) 255-3285 ext. 1334 Toll-free number: (800) 643-8882
Fax: (701) 530-0640
Donovan Lambert, Director of Admissions, United Tribes Technical College, 3315 University Drive, Bismarck, ND 58504

Williston State College
Williston, North Dakota
www.willistonstate.edu   CB code: 6905

▶ Public 2-year community and junior college
▶ Commuter campus in large town

General. Founded in 1957. Regionally accredited. Baccalaureate, post-baccalaureate programs from other campuses available on-campus, all via interactive video network. **Enrollment:** 355 full-time, degree-seeking students. **Degrees:** 158 associate awarded. **Location:** 250 miles from Bismarck, 130 miles from Minot. **Calendar:** Semester, limited summer session. **Full-time faculty:** 31 total; 48% women. **Part-time faculty:** 49 total; 69% women. **Class size:** 78% < 20, 22% 20-39, less than 1% 40-49.

Student profile.

Out-of-state:	20%	Live on campus:	20%
25 or older:	27%		

Transfer out. Colleges most students transferred to 2011: University of North Dakota, Minot State University, Dickinson State University, North Dakota State University, Montana State University-Bozeman.

Basis for selection. Open admission, but selective for some programs. Special requirements for practical nursing, speech language pathology assistant, mental health addictions technician, and massage therapy programs. **Adult students:** SAT/ACT scores not required if applicant over 25. **Home schooled:** Transcript of courses and grades required.

High school preparation. 15 units recommended. Recommended units include English 4, mathematics 3, social studies 3, science 3 (laboratory 1) and foreign language 1.

2011-2012 Annual costs. Tuition/fees: $3,811; $3,811 out-of-state. Per-credit charge: $101 in-state; $101 out-of-state. Room/board: $6,376. Books/supplies: $900. Personal expenses: $500.

Financial aid. Need-based: Need-based aid available for part-time students. Work-study available nights, weekends and for part-time students.

Non-need-based: Scholarships awarded for academics, athletics, music/drama.

Application procedures. Admission: No deadline. $35 fee. Admission notification on a rolling basis. **Financial aid:** Priority date 3/15; no closing date. FAFSA required. Applicants notified on a rolling basis starting 5/15.

Academics. Special study options: Cooperative education, cross-registration, distance learning, double major, dual enrollment of high school students, internships, liberal arts/career combination, student-designed major. Bachelor's degree programs available on campus. License preparation in nursing. **Credit/placement by examination:** AP, CLEP, institutional tests. 15 credit hours maximum toward associate degree. **Support services:** GED preparation and test center, learning center, reduced course load, remedial instruction, study skills assistance, tutoring, writing center.

Majors. Business: Accounting technology, administrative services, entrepreneurial studies, marketing. **Computer sciences:** Data processing, system admin, systems analysis, vendor certification, web page design. **General:** Agribusiness operations, farm/ranch. **Health services:** Massage therapy, medical records technology, medical transcription, nursing (RN), physical therapy assistant, speech-language pathology assistant. **Liberal arts:** Arts/sciences.

Computing on campus. 70 workstations in dormitories, library, computer center. Dormitories wired for high-speed internet access and linked to campus network. Online course registration, online library, wireless network available.

Student life. Freshman orientation: Mandatory. Preregistration for classes offered. Activities take place on the day prior to first day of fall semester. **Housing:** Coed dorms, single-sex dorms, apartments available. $35 nonrefundable deposit. **Activities:** Bands, campus ministries, choral groups, dance, drama, literary magazine, music ensembles, student government, student newspaper, Campus Crusade.

Athletics. NJCAA. **Intercollegiate:** Baseball M, basketball, volleyball W. **Intramural:** Basketball, field hockey, football (non-tackle), ice hockey, racquetball, rifle, rugby, soccer, softball, table tennis, volleyball. **Team name:** Tetons.

Student services. Alcohol/substance abuse counseling, career counseling, services for economically disadvantaged, student employment services, financial aid counseling, minority student services, personal counseling, veterans' counselor. **Physically disabled:** Services for visually, speech, hearing impaired. **Transfer:** Pre-admission transcript evaluation for new students. Transfer adviser, college fairs on campus for students transferring to 4-year colleges.

Contact. E-mail: Dorisann.lindvig@willistonstate.edu
Phone: (701) 774-210 Toll-free number: (888) 863-9455
Fax: (701) 774-4211
Kaylyn Bondy, Director for Admission & Records, Williston State College, 1410 University Avenue, Williston, ND 58801

Ohio

Akron Institute of Herzing University
Akron, Ohio
www.akroninstitute.com

CB code: 7277

- For-profit 2-year career college
- Commuter campus in small city

General. Regionally accredited. **Enrollment:** 613 degree-seeking undergraduates. **Degrees:** 162 associate awarded. **Calendar:** Semester, extensive summer session. **Full-time faculty:** 28 total. **Part-time faculty:** 23 total.

Basis for selection. Secondary school record very important, test scores recommended.

2011-2012 Annual costs. Tuition/fees: $10,560. Per-credit charge: $440. Reported annual tuition is representative. Actual costs vary by program with nursing programs somewhat more expensive.

Financial aid. Need-based: Work-study available nights, weekends and for part-time students.

Application procedures. Admission: No deadline.

Academics. Special study options: Accelerated study, internships. License preparation in aviation, nursing. **Credit/placement by examination:** AP, CLEP, institutional tests. **Support services:** Reduced course load, remedial instruction, study skills assistance, tutoring, writing center.

Majors. Business: Business admin. **Computer sciences:** Security. **Health services:** Dental assistant, insurance coding, insurance specialist, medical assistant, medical records admin, office admin. **Protective services:** Police science.

Computing on campus. 5 workstations in library. Online library, helpline, repair service, wireless network available.

Student life. Freshman orientation: Mandatory. Preregistration for classes offered. **Activities:** Student government.

Student services. Adult student services, career counseling, student employment services, financial aid counseling, placement for graduates.

Contact. E-mail: info@akr.herzing.edu
Phone: (330) 724-1600 Toll-free number: (800) 311-0512
Fax: (330) 724-9688
Maribeth Graham, Director of Admissions, Akron Institute of Herzing University, 1600 South Arlington Street, Suite 100, Akron, OH 44306

Antonelli College: Cincinnati
Cincinnati, Ohio
www.antonellicollege.edu

- For-profit 2-year visual arts and technical college
- Commuter campus in large city

General. Founded in 1947. Regionally accredited. **Location:** 55 miles from Dayton; 90 miles from Lexington, Kentucky. **Calendar:** Quarter.

Contact. Phone: (513) 241-4338
Registrar, 124 East Seventh Street, Cincinnati, OH 45202

Art Institute of Cincinnati
Cincinnati, Ohio
www.aic-arts.edu

CB code: 3181

- For-profit 2-year visual arts college
- Commuter campus in large city
- Application essay, interview required

General. Accredited by ACCSC. **Enrollment:** 30 degree-seeking undergraduates. **Degrees:** 24 associate awarded. **Location:** 12 miles from downtown. **Calendar:** Quarter. **Full-time faculty:** 8 total; 12% women. **Part-time faculty:** 5 total; 80% women.

Student profile. Among degree-seeking undergraduates, 7% already have a bachelor's degree or higher, 13 enrolled as first-time, first-year students.

Out-of-state:	23%	25 or older:	13%
Women:	57%		

Transfer out. 5% of students enrolled in the transfer program go on to 4-year colleges.

Basis for selection. Admission determined by applicant's artistic ability. Portfolio, letter of recommendation from art teacher required. **Adult students:** SAT/ACT scores not required if applicant over 25. **Home schooled:** Portfolio presentation of at least 10 pieces of art with variety of media and subject matter.

High school preparation. Required and recommended units include English 2-3, mathematics 1, social studies 1, history 1, science 1 and foreign language 1.

2012-2013 Annual costs. Tuition/fees (projected): $22,346. Books/supplies: $700.

2010-2011 Financial aid. Need-based: 8 full-time freshmen applied for aid; 8 were judged to have need; 8 of these received aid. Average scholarship/grant was $5,270; average loan $3,500. 38% of total undergraduate aid awarded as scholarships/grants, 62% as loans/jobs. Work-study available nights, weekends and for part-time students. **Non-need-based:** Awarded to 1 full-time undergraduates, including 1 freshmen. Scholarships awarded for academics, art.

Application procedures. Admission: No deadline. $100 fee. Application must be submitted on paper. Admission notification on a rolling basis. **Financial aid:** No deadline. FAFSA required. Applicants notified on a rolling basis starting 9/1; must reply within 1 week(s) of notification.

Academics. Special study options: Accelerated study. **Credit/placement by examination:** AP, CLEP, SAT, ACT, institutional tests. **Support services:** Pre-admission summer program, remedial instruction, study skills assistance, writing center.

Majors. Computer sciences: Computer graphics. **Visual/performing arts:** Design.

Computing on campus. Online library, student web hosting, wireless network available.

Student life. Freshman orientation: Mandatory. Preregistration for classes offered. **Activities:** Student government.

Student services. Career counseling, financial aid counseling, personal counseling, placement for graduates. **Transfer:** Pre-admission transcript evaluation for new students.

Contact. E-mail: admissions@aic-arts.edu
Phone: (513) 751-1206 Fax: (513) 751-1209
Cyndi Mendell, Vice President, Admissions, Art Institute of Cincinnati, 1171 East Kemper Road, Cincinnati, OH 45246

Art Institute of Ohio: Cincinnati
Cincinnati, Ohio
www.artinstitutes.edu/cincinnati

CB code: 4895

- For-profit 2-year culinary school and visual arts college
- Commuter campus in very large city
- Application essay, interview required

General. Regionally accredited; also accredited by ACICS, ACCSC. **Enrollment:** 725 degree-seeking undergraduates. **Degrees:** 10 bachelor's, 138 associate awarded. **Calendar:** Quarter, extensive summer session. **Full-time faculty:** 25 total. **Part-time faculty:** 22 total.

Basis for selection. 2.0 GPA required. **Home schooled:** Transcript of courses and grades required.

Financial aid. Need-based: Work-study available nights, weekends and for part-time students.

Application procedures. Admission: No deadline. $50 fee. Application must be submitted on paper. Admission notification on a rolling basis.

Academics. Special study options: Accelerated study, distance learning, independent study, internships. Bachelor's degree programs available on campus. **Credit/placement by examination:** AP, CLEP, SAT, ACT, institutional tests. **Support services:** Learning center, reduced course load, remedial instruction, study skills assistance, tutoring.

Majors. Business: Fashion. **Visual/performing arts:** Cinematography, graphic design, interior design, multimedia.

Student life. Freshman orientation: Available. Preregistration for classes offered. **Housing:** Apartments available.

Student services. Career counseling, student employment services, financial aid counseling, personal counseling, placement for graduates. **Physically disabled:** Services for visually, speech, hearing impaired. **Transfer:** Re-entry adviser, pre-admission transcript evaluation for new students.

Contact. E-mail: trucker@aii.edu
Phone: (513) 833-2400 Toll-free number: (866) 613-5184
Fax: (513) 833-2411
Tasha Rucker, Senior Director of Admissions, Art Institute of Ohio: Cincinnati, 8845 Governors Hill Drive, Cincinnati, OH 45249-3317

ATS Institute of Technology
Highland Heights, Ohio
www.atsinstitute.com

- For-profit 2-year nursing and technical college
- Commuter campus in very large city

General. Accredited by ACICS. **Calendar:** Semester.

Annual costs/financial aid. Books/supplies: $900.

Contact. Phone: (440) 449-1700
Academic Director, 325 Alpha Park, Highland Heights, OH 44143

Aultman College of Nursing and Health Sciences
Canton, Ohio
www.aultmancollege.edu   CB code: 3203

- Private 2-year health science and nursing college
- Commuter campus in small city
- SAT or ACT (ACT writing optional) required

General. Candidate for regional accreditation. Affiliated with Aultman Hospital. **Enrollment:** 307 degree-seeking undergraduates; 7 non-degree-seeking students. **Degrees:** 80 associate awarded. **Location:** 50 miles from Cleveland. **Calendar:** Semester, limited summer session. **Full-time faculty:** 15 total; 7% have terminal degrees, 7% minority, 100% women. **Part-time faculty:** 14 total; 29% have terminal degrees, 14% minority, 43% women. **Class size:** 41% < 20, 59% 20-39.

Student profile. Among degree-seeking undergraduates, 5 enrolled as first-time, first-year students, 113 transferred in from other institutions.

Part-time:	84%	Hispanic American:	1%
Women:	83%	25 or older:	63%
African American:	6%	Live on campus:	1%
Asian American:	1%		

Transfer out. Colleges most students transferred to 2011: Stark State College of Technology, University of Akron, Kent State University.

Basis for selection. Cumulative GPA of 3.0 or greater and an ACT composite score of 20 or greater (or SAT combined score of 950 or greater) OR a college cumulative GPA of 2.5 or greater on their most recent college transcript. COMPASS placement testing required.

2011-2012 Annual costs. Tuition/fees: $14,175. Per-credit charge: $465. Books/supplies: $1,800.

2010-2011 Financial aid. All financial aid based on need. 32% of total undergraduate aid awarded as scholarships/grants, 68% as loans/jobs. Need-based aid available for part-time students. Work-study available nights, weekends and for part-time students.

Application procedures. Admission: Closing date 1/15 (receipt date). $30 fee, may be waived for applicants with need. Must reply by May 1 or within 2 week(s) if notified thereafter. **Financial aid:** Priority date 3/1,

closing date 10/1. FAFSA, institutional form required. Applicants notified on a rolling basis starting 6/15; must reply within 2 week(s) of notification.

Academics. Special study options: License preparation in nursing. **Credit/placement by examination:** AP, CLEP, institutional tests. **Support services:** Learning center, reduced course load, remedial instruction, study skills assistance, tutoring, writing center.

Majors. Health services: Nursing (RN), radiologic technology/medical imaging.

Computing on campus. 47 workstations in library, computer center. Online library, wireless network available.

Student life. Freshman orientation: Mandatory. Preregistration for classes offered. One-day program held in Fall, Spring, and Summer. **Activities:** Student government, student newspaper.

Athletics. Intramural: Basketball.

Student services. Chaplain/spiritual director, financial aid counseling, health services.

Contact. E-mail: lcelik@aultman.com
Phone: (330) 363-5075 Fax: (330) 580-6654
Nicole Boatright, Enrollment Manager, Aultman College of Nursing and Health Sciences, 2600 Sixth Street SW, Canton, OH 44710-1799

Belmont Technical College
St. Clairsville, Ohio
www.btc.edu   CB code: 1072

- Public 2-year community and technical college
- Commuter campus in small town
- Interview required

General. Founded in 1969. Regionally accredited. **Enrollment:** 2,063 degree-seeking undergraduates. **Degrees:** 292 associate awarded. **Location:** 15 miles from Wheeling, West Virginia. **Calendar:** Quarter, limited summer session. **Full-time faculty:** 40 total. **Part-time faculty:** 131 total. **Class size:** 79% < 20, 20% 20-39, less than 1% 40-49, less than 1% 50-99.

Student profile.

Out-of-state:	15%	25 or older:	45%

Transfer out. Colleges most students transferred to 2011: Wheeling Jesuit University, Ohio University Eastern Campus, West Liberty State College.

Basis for selection. Open admission, but selective for some programs. Admission to registered nursing and LPN programs predicated on completion of remediation with grade of C or better and completion of selected general courses with C or better, based on ACCUPLACER placement test scores. Interview required for nursing and paramedic applicants after admission to program, recommended for all others. **Home schooled:** State high school equivalency certificate required.

2011-2012 Annual costs. Tuition/fees: $3,908; $6,799 out-of-state. Per-credit charge: $64 in-state; $128 out-of-state. Books/supplies: $1,500. Personal expenses: $1,800.

Financial aid. Need-based: Need-based aid available for part-time students. Work-study available nights, weekends and for part-time students. **Non-need-based:** Scholarships awarded for state residency.

Application procedures. Admission: No deadline. No application fee. Admission notification on a rolling basis. **Financial aid:** No deadline. FAFSA required. Applicants notified on a rolling basis starting 6/1; must reply within 2 week(s) of notification.

Academics. Special study options: Cross-registration, distance learning, double major, dual enrollment of high school students, internships, student-designed major, weekend college. **Credit/placement by examination:** AP, CLEP, institutional tests. **Support services:** GED test center, learning center, reduced course load, remedial instruction, study skills assistance, tutoring, writing center.

Majors. Business: General, accounting, office/clerical. **Computer sciences:** General, computer graphics, programming. **Education:** Early childhood. **Engineering:** Civil, electrical. **Health services:** EMT paramedic, medical assistant, nursing (RN).

Most popular majors. Business/marketing 15%, computer/information sciences 11%, engineering/engineering technologies 18%, health sciences 10%, security/protective services 6%, social sciences 7%.

Computing on campus. Online library, wireless network available.

Student life. Freshman orientation: Available. Preregistration for classes offered. **Activities:** Phi Theta Kappa.

Athletics. Intercollegiate: Football (non-tackle).

Student services. Adult student services, career counseling, student employment services, financial aid counseling, on-campus daycare, personal counseling, placement for graduates, veterans' counselor. **Physically disabled:** Services for visually, hearing impaired. **Transfer:** Pre-admission transcript evaluation for new students. Transfer adviser, college fairs on campus for students transferring to 4-year colleges.

Contact. E-mail: info@btc.edu
Phone: (740) 695-9500 ext. 1563 Fax: (740) 699-3049
Michael Sterling, Director of Admissions, Belmont Technical College, 120 Fox Shannon Place, St. Clairsville, OH 43950

Bowling Green State University: Firelands College
Huron, Ohio
www.firelands.bgsu.edu
CB code: 0749

- Public 2-year branch campus college
- Commuter campus in small town

General. Founded in 1967. Regionally accredited. **Enrollment:** 1,924 degree-seeking undergraduates; 487 non-degree-seeking students. **Degrees:** 211 associate awarded. **Location:** 50 miles from Cleveland, 60 miles from Toledo. **Calendar:** Semester, limited summer session. **Full-time faculty:** 53 total; 11% minority, 55% women. **Part-time faculty:** 118 total. **Class size:** 54% < 20, 45% 20-39, less than 1% 40-49.

Student profile. Among degree-seeking undergraduates, 30% enrolled in a transfer program, 70% enrolled in a vocational program, 3% already have a bachelor's degree or higher, 388 enrolled as first-time, first-year students, 132 transferred in from other institutions.

Part-time:	36%	Hispanic American:	5%
Women:	68%	Native American:	1%
African American:	9%	25 or older:	33%
Asian American:	1%		

Basis for selection. Open admission. **Home schooled:** Statement describing home school structure and mission, transcript of courses and grades required. Home school program must be accredited.

High school preparation. College-preparatory program recommended. 16 units recommended. Recommended units include English 4, mathematics 3, social studies 3, science 3 (laboratory 2) and foreign language 2. One visual or performing arts recommended.

2011-2012 Annual costs. Tuition/fees: $4,686; $11,994 out-of-state. Per-credit charge: $186 in-state; $491 out-of-state. Books/supplies: $1,000. Personal expenses: $2,616.

2010-2011 Financial aid. All financial aid based on need. 307 full-time freshmen applied for aid; 288 were judged to have need; 288 of these received aid. Average need met was 59%. Average scholarship/grant was $4,267; average loan $5,956. 37% of total undergraduate aid awarded as scholarships/grants, 63% as loans/jobs. Need-based aid available for part-time students. Work-study available nights, weekends and for part-time students. **Additional information:** Scholarship application deadline May 1. Technology computer loan program available. Based on need, students may receive computer on semester by semester loan basis.

Application procedures. Admission: Closing date 8/12 (receipt date). $45 fee, may be waived for applicants with need. Admission notification on a rolling basis. **Financial aid:** Priority date 3/1; no closing date. FAFSA required. Applicants notified on a rolling basis starting 4/15; must reply within 2 week(s) of notification.

Academics. Nursing programs (RN, LPN, and RN-to-BSN) are available through affiliate agreements with Firelands Regional Medical Center, Lorain County Community College, and University of Toledo. Bachelor degree programs available in eight additional areas: Applied Health Science, Applied Health Science - Respiratory Care, Business Administration, Criminal Justice, Early Childhood Education, Liberal Studies, Social Work, and Visual Communication Technology. Fully online Associate of Arts degree. **Special study**

options: Cross-registration, distance learning, dual enrollment of high school students, independent study, internships, liberal arts/career combination, student-designed major, teacher certification program. Satellite associate degree registered nurse program from Lorain County Community College and Firelands Regional Medical Center. Bachelor's degree programs available on campus. License preparation in nursing, radiology. **Credit/placement by examination:** AP, CLEP, institutional tests. 15 credit hours maximum toward associate degree. **Support services:** Learning center, reduced course load, remedial instruction, study skills assistance, tutoring, writing center.

Majors. Business: General, accounting, administrative services, business admin, operations. **Communications technology:** General. **Computer sciences:** Programming. **Engineering:** Electrical. **Health services:** Medical radiologic technology/radiation therapy, medical records technology, nursing (RN), respiratory therapy technology, sonography. **Liberal arts:** Arts/sciences. **Protective services:** Criminal justice. **Social sciences:** General.

Most popular majors. Business/marketing 10%, health sciences 22%, liberal arts 48%.

Computing on campus. 300 workstations in library, computer center. Commuter students can connect to campus network. Online course registration, online library, helpline, wireless network available.

Student life. Freshman orientation: Available. Preregistration for classes offered. **Activities:** Drama, musical theater, student government, student newspaper, allied health club, Campus Fellowship, theater group, writing center, peace and justice club, virtual communication technology organization, women's resource group.

Athletics. Intramural: Basketball, football (non-tackle) M, table tennis, volleyball.

Student services. Adult student services, career counseling, student employment services, financial aid counseling, personal counseling, placement for graduates. **Physically disabled:** Services for visually, speech, hearing impaired. **Transfer:** Transfer adviser, college fairs on campus for students transferring to 4-year colleges.

Contact. E-mail: fireadm@bgsu.edu
Phone: (419) 433-5560 ext. 20607 Toll-free number: (800) 322-4787
Fax: (419) 372-0604
Debralee Divers, Director of Enrollment Mgmt & Student Retention Services, Bowling Green State University: Firelands College, One University Drive, Huron, OH 44839-9719

Bradford School
Columbus, Ohio
www.bradfordschoolcolumbus.edu
CB code: 3952

- For-profit 2-year business and technical college
- Commuter campus in very large city

General. Founded in 1911. Accredited by ACICS. **Enrollment:** 705 degree-seeking undergraduates. **Degrees:** 304 associate awarded. **Calendar:** Semester, extensive summer session. **Full-time faculty:** 15 total. **Part-time faculty:** 10 total.

Basis for selection. Open admission. Interview required to ensure interest in business, health care or culinary education.

Financial aid. Need-based: Work-study available nights, weekends and for part-time students.

Application procedures. Admission: No deadline. $50 fee. Admission notification on a rolling basis.

Academics. Credit/placement by examination: AP, CLEP.

Majors. Business: Accounting, office management. **Computer sciences:** LAN/WAN management, programming. **Health services:** Veterinary technology/assistant.

Student life. Housing: Single-sex dorms available.

Student services. Career counseling, financial aid counseling, placement for graduates.

Contact. E-mail: bradfordcols@bradfordschoolcolumbus.edu
Phone: (614) 416-6200 Toll-free number: (800) 678-7981
Fax: (614) 416-6210
Raeann Lee, Director of Admissions, Bradford School, 2469 Stelzer Road, Columbus, OH 43219

Brown Mackie College: Akron
Akron, Ohio
www.brownmackie.edu   CB code: 3266

- For-profit 2-year business college
- Commuter campus in small city

General. Accredited by ACICS. **Calendar:** Quarter.

Annual costs/financial aid. Books/supplies: $1,000. Personal expenses: $2,664.

Contact. Phone: (330) 733-8766
Director of Admissions, 755 White Pond Drive, Suite 101, Akron, OH 44320

Brown Mackie College: Cincinnati
Cincinnati, Ohio
www.brownmackie.edu   CB code: 3576

- For-profit 2-year business and nursing college
- Commuter campus in large city

General. Founded in 1927. Accredited by ACICS. **Location:** 10 miles from downtown. **Calendar:** Quarter.

Annual costs/financial aid. Tuition/fees (2011-2012): $13,230. Tuition, which varies according to area of study, is $294 per credit hour for most programs. Books/supplies: $1,275. Personal expenses: $2,700. Need-based financial aid available to full-time and part-time students.

Contact. Phone: (513) 771-2424
Director of Admissions, 1011 Glendale-Milford Road, Cincinnati, OH 45215

Brown Mackie College: Findlay
Findlay, Ohio
www.brownmackie.edu

- For-profit 2-year business and junior college
- Commuter campus in small city

General. Accredited by ACICS. **Location:** 20 miles Bowling Green, 48 miles from Toledo. **Calendar:** Quarter.

Annual costs/financial aid. Books/supplies: $1,850. Personal expenses: $2,700. Need-based financial aid available to full-time and part-time students.

Contact. Phone: (419) 423-2211
Senior Admissions Director, 1700 Fostoria Avenue, Suite 100, Findlay, OH 45840

Brown Mackie College: North Canton
Canton, Ohio
www.brownmackie.edu   CB code: 3148

- For-profit 2-year career college
- Commuter campus in small city

General. Accredited by ACICS. **Calendar:** Differs by program.

Annual costs/financial aid. Tuition/fees (2011-2012): $13,590. Tuition, which varies according to area of study, is $294 per credit hour for most programs. Books/supplies: $1,275.

Contact. Phone: (330) 494-1214
Director of Admissions, 4300 Munson Street Northwest, Canton, OH 44718-3674

Bryant & Stratton College: Cleveland
Cleveland, Ohio
www.bryantstratton.edu   CB code: 0814

- For-profit 2-year technical and career college
- Commuter campus in very large city
- Interview required

General. Founded in 1929. Regionally accredited. **Enrollment:** 1,080 degree-seeking undergraduates. **Degrees:** 25 bachelor's, 109 associate awarded. **Location:** Downtown. **Calendar:** Trimester, extensive summer session. **Full-time faculty:** 21 total. **Part-time faculty:** 39 total. **Class size:** 79% < 20, 21% 20-39.

Transfer out. **Colleges most students transferred to 2011:** ITT Technical Institute, Cuyahoga Community College, Myer University, Cleveland State University.

Basis for selection. Open admission, but selective for some programs. Institutional test scores and interview most important. Passing scores on entrance exams required. **Home schooled:** Transcript of courses and grades, interview required.

2011-2012 Annual costs. Tuition/fees: $15,570. Books/supplies: $1,800. Personal expenses: $1,530.

Financial aid. **Need-based:** Need-based aid available for part-time students. Work-study available nights, weekends and for part-time students. **Non-need-based:** Scholarships awarded for academics.

Application procedures. **Admission:** No deadline. No application fee. Admission notification on a rolling basis. **Financial aid:** No deadline. FAFSA, institutional form required. Applicants notified on a rolling basis starting 5/1; must reply within 2 week(s) of notification.

Academics. **Special study options:** Distance learning, double major, internships, liberal arts/career combination. Bachelor's degree programs available on campus. **Credit/placement by examination:** AP, CLEP, institutional tests. 26 credit hours maximum toward associate degree. **Support services:** GED preparation and test center, learning center, reduced course load, remedial instruction, study skills assistance, tutoring, writing center.

Majors. **Business:** General, administrative services. **Computer sciences:** Information technology.

Most popular majors. Computer/information sciences 60%, engineering/engineering technologies 40%.

Computing on campus. 106 workstations in dormitories, library, computer center. Online library, helpline, wireless network available.

Student life. **Freshman orientation:** Available. Preregistration for classes offered. Three-hour session 1 week prior to start of semester. **Housing:** Apartments available. **Activities:** Student government.

Athletics. **Intramural:** Softball. **Team name:** Bobcats.

Student services. Adult student services, alcohol/substance abuse counseling, career counseling, student employment services, financial aid counseling, personal counseling, placement for graduates. **Transfer:** Pre-admission transcript evaluation for new students. Transfer adviser, college fairs on campus for students transferring to 4-year colleges.

Contact. E-mail: bacassidy@bryantstratton.edu
Phone: (216) 771-1700 Fax: (216) 771-7787
William Cassidy, Director of Admissions, Bryant & Stratton College: Cleveland, 3121 Euclid Avenue, Cleveland, OH 44115

Central Ohio Technical College
Newark, Ohio
www.cotc.edu   CB code: 7321

- Public 2-year technical college
- Commuter campus in large town

General. Founded in 1971. Regionally accredited. Additional campuses at Coshocton, Knox, Pataskala, and Newark. **Enrollment:** 3,990 degree-seeking undergraduates; 261 non-degree-seeking students. **Degrees:** 503 associate awarded. **Location:** 45 miles from Columbus. **Calendar:** Quarter, limited summer session. **Full-time faculty:** 61 total; 16% have terminal degrees, 7% minority, 62% women. **Part-time faculty:** 284 total; 8% have terminal degrees, 6% minority, 57% women. **Class size:** 85% < 20, 15% 20-39, less than 1% 50-99.

Student profile. Among degree-seeking undergraduates, 698 enrolled as first-time, first-year students.

Part-time:	53%	Asian American:	1%
Out-of-state:	1%	Hispanic American:	1%
Women:	72%	25 or older:	52%
African American:	9%	Live on campus:	1%

Transfer out. Colleges most students transferred to 2011: Franklin University, Mount Vernon Nazarene, Ohio State University.

Basis for selection. Open admission, but selective for some programs.

High school preparation. Each selective admission program has separate high school course requirements.

2011-2012 Annual costs. Tuition/fees: $3,978; $6,678 out-of-state. Per-credit charge: $110 in-state; $185 out-of-state. Books/supplies: $1,650. Personal expenses: $3,303.

Financial aid. Need-based: Need-based aid available for part-time students. Work-study available nights, weekends and for part-time students. **Non-need-based:** Scholarships awarded for academics, state residency.

Application procedures. Admission: Priority date 6/15; no deadline. $20 fee, may be waived for applicants with need. Admission notification on a rolling basis. **Financial aid:** Priority date 2/15; no closing date. FAFSA required. Applicants notified on a rolling basis starting 5/1; must reply within 3 week(s) of notification.

Academics. Special study options: Cooperative education, distance learning, double major, dual enrollment of high school students, ESL, internships, weekend college. License preparation in nursing, paramedic, radiology. **Credit/placement by examination:** AP, CLEP, IB, institutional tests. 45 credit hours maximum toward associate degree. **Support services:** Learning center, reduced course load, remedial instruction, study skills assistance, tutoring.

Majors. Business: Accounting, business admin. **Communications technology:** Desktop publishing. **Computer sciences:** Applications programming, data entry, web page design. **Education:** Early childhood. **Health services:** Medical radiologic technology/radiation therapy, nursing (RN), sonography, surgical technology. **Human services:** Social work. **Liberal arts:** Arts/sciences. **Protective services:** Criminal justice, firefighting, forensics, law enforcement admin.

Most popular majors. Business/marketing 12%, health sciences 61%, public administration/social services 16%, security/protective services 6%.

Computing on campus. 40 workstations in library, computer center. Commuter students can connect to campus network. Online course registration, helpline, wireless network available.

Student life. Freshman orientation: Mandatory. Preregistration for classes offered. Three-hour program. **Housing:** Apartments available. **Activities:** Choral groups, drama, music ensembles, student government, student newspaper, Phi Theta Kappa, theatre arts association, student nurses organization, criminal justice club, rad tech club, Habitat for Humanity College Chapter, ski club, Students in Free Enterprise.

Athletics. NJCAA. **Intercollegiate:** Baseball M, basketball, cross-country, golf, soccer M, softball W, volleyball. **Intramural:** Badminton, basketball, bowling, football (non-tackle), softball, table tennis, tennis, volleyball.

Student services. Career counseling, student employment services, financial aid counseling, minority student services, personal counseling, placement for graduates, veterans' counselor. **Physically disabled:** Services for visually, speech, hearing impaired. **Transfer:** Transfer adviser, college fairs on campus for students transferring to 4-year colleges.

Contact. E-mail: cotcadmissions@cotc.edu
Phone: (740) 366-9222 Fax: (740) 366-5047
Tara Houdeshell, Director of Gateway Operations, Central Ohio Technical College, 1179 University Drive, Newark, OH 43055

Chatfield College
St. Martin, Ohio
www.chatfield.edu   CB code: 1143

- Private 2-year liberal arts college affiliated with Roman Catholic Church
- Commuter campus in rural community

General. Founded in 1970. Regionally accredited. **Enrollment:** 433 degree-seeking undergraduates. **Degrees:** 42 associate awarded. **Location:** 40 miles from Cincinnati. **Calendar:** Semester, limited summer session. **Full-time faculty:** 3 total. **Part-time faculty:** 82 total.

Transfer out. Colleges most students transferred to 2011: Wilmington College, Xavier University, Mount St. Joseph, Northern Kentucky University.

Basis for selection. Open admission. Interview recommended. **Home schooled:** Official documentation of home school program required.

High school preparation. 16 units recommended. Recommended units include English 4, mathematics 3, social studies 3, science 3 and foreign language 2. Computer science recommended.

2011-2012 Annual costs. Tuition/fees: $10,246. Per-credit charge: $328. Books/supplies: $750. Personal expenses: $1,922.

Financial aid. Need-based: Need-based aid available for part-time students. Work-study available nights, weekends and for part-time students. **Non-need-based:** Scholarships awarded for academics, leadership. **Additional information:** Institutional grants/scholarships given primarily to first-year students to reduce debt load during initial year.

Application procedures. Admission: No deadline. $10 fee. Admission notification on a rolling basis. **Financial aid:** Priority date 5/1, closing date 8/3. FAFSA, institutional form required. Applicants notified on a rolling basis starting 4/1; must reply within 2 week(s) of notification.

Academics. Special study options: Cooperative education, cross-registration, dual enrollment of high school students, independent study, internships, liberal arts/career combination. Cooperative programs leading to bachelor's in business and liberal studies with 2 local institutions. Third-year option: student can complete junior year at school through arrangements with several regional 4-year colleges. **Credit/placement by examination:** AP, CLEP, institutional tests. **Support services:** Learning center, remedial instruction, study skills assistance, tutoring, writing center.

Majors. Business: Business admin. **Education:** Early childhood. **Liberal arts:** Arts/sciences.

Computing on campus. 58 workstations in library, computer center, student center.

Student life. Freshman orientation: Available. Preregistration for classes offered. **Activities:** Campus ministries, choral groups, student newspaper.

Student services. Adult student services, career counseling, financial aid counseling, personal counseling. **Transfer:** Transfer adviser, college fairs on campus for students transferring to 4-year colleges.

Contact. E-mail: admissions@chatfield.edu
Phone: (513) 875-3344 Fax: (513) 875-3912
John Penrose, Director of Admissions, Chatfield College, 20918 State Route 251, St. Martin, OH 45118

Cincinnati College of Mortuary Science
Cincinnati, Ohio
www.ccms.edu   CB code: 0945

- Private 2-year school of mortuary science
- Commuter campus in large city

General. Founded in 1882. Regionally accredited. **Enrollment:** 118 degree-seeking undergraduates. **Degrees:** 37 bachelor's, 73 associate awarded. **Location:** 5 miles from downtown. **Calendar:** Quarter, extensive summer session. **Full-time faculty:** 4 total. **Part-time faculty:** 1 total. **Class size:** 100% 50-99.

Student profile. Among degree-seeking undergraduates, 24% enrolled in a transfer program, 26% already have a bachelor's degree or higher, 5 enrolled as first-time, first-year students, 12 transferred in from other institutions.

Out-of-state:	20%	African American:	8%
Women:	60%		

Basis for selection. 2.0 GPA and test scores important. SAT or ACT recommended. **Home schooled:** Transcript of courses and grades, state high school equivalency certificate required. **Learning Disabled:** Documentation of the disability.

High school preparation. College-preparatory program recommended. 16 units recommended. Recommended units include English 3, mathematics 1, social studies 2 and science 2.

2011-2012 Annual costs. Per-credit charge: $225. Tuition for 4-qtr. A.A.S. $16,875; 5-qtr. B.M.S. $20,250. $100.00 lab fee per quarter. Books/supplies: $1,500.

Financial aid. All financial aid based on need. Work-study available nights, weekends and for part-time students.

Application procedures. Admission: Closing date 8/31 (postmark date). $40 fee. Application must be submitted on paper. Admission notification by 9/15. Admission notification on a rolling basis. **Financial aid:** No deadline. FAFSA required.

Academics. Program of study contingent on licensing requirements of state in which student will practice. **Special study options:** Cooperative education. **Credit/placement by examination:** AP, CLEP.

Computing on campus. 12 workstations in library.

Student life. Freshman orientation: Mandatory. Preregistration for classes offered. **Housing:** Some housing available in local funeral homes.

Student services. Transfer: Pre-admission transcript evaluation for new students.

Contact. E-mail: psullivan@ccms.edu
Phone: (513) 761-2020 Toll-free number: (888) 377-8433
Fax: (513) 761-3333
Pat Sullivan, Executive Director, Enrollment Management, Cincinnati College of Mortuary Science, 645 West North Bend Road, Cincinnati, OH 45224-1428

Cincinnati State Technical and Community College
Cincinnati, Ohio
www.cincinnatistate.edu   **CB code: 1984**

▶ Public 2-year community and technical college
▶ Commuter campus in large city

General. Founded in 1966. Regionally accredited. **Enrollment:** 9,843 degree-seeking undergraduates; 738 non-degree-seeking students. **Degrees:** 1,155 associate awarded. **ROTC:** Army. **Location:** 5 miles from downtown. **Calendar:** Five 10-week terms. Extensive summer session. **Full-time faculty:** 188 total; 10% have terminal degrees, 15% minority, 57% women. **Part-time faculty:** 576 total. **Class size:** 67% < 20, 32% 20-39, less than 1% 40-49. **Special facilities:** Aviation maintenance facility, culinary facility, television studio.

Student profile. Among degree-seeking undergraduates, 13% enrolled in a transfer program, 87% enrolled in a vocational program, 5% already have a bachelor's degree or higher, 1,424 enrolled as first-time, first-year students.

Part-time:	63%	Hispanic American:	2%
Out-of-state:	10%	Native American:	1%
Women:	54%	International:	1%
African American:	30%	25 or older:	55%
Asian American:	1%		

Transfer out. Colleges most students transferred to 2011: University of Cincinnati, Northern Kentucky University, Wilmington College, College of Mount St. Joseph, Xavier University.

Basis for selection. Open admission, but selective for some programs. Health technology programs require biology and chemistry courses to have been taken in last 7 years. COMPASS test required for placement. **Home schooled:** Statement describing home school structure and mission, transcript of courses and grades required.

High school preparation. Specific course prerequisites for some programs.

2011-2012 Annual costs. Tuition/fees: $4,258; $8,259 out-of-state. Per-credit charge: $89 in-state; $178 out-of-state. Books/supplies: $3,000. Personal expenses: $3,108.

Financial aid. Need-based: Need-based aid available for part-time students. Work-study available nights, weekends and for part-time students. **Non-need-based:** Scholarships awarded for academics, athletics, state residency.

Application procedures. Admission: No deadline. No application fee. Admission notification on a rolling basis. **Financial aid:** Priority date 2/15; no closing date. FAFSA required. Applicants notified on a rolling basis starting 3/15; must reply within 4 week(s) of notification.

Academics. Special study options: Cooperative education, cross-registration, distance learning, double major, dual enrollment of high school students, ESL, honors, independent study, internships, student-designed major. Bachelor's degree programs available on campus. License preparation in aviation, nursing, occupational therapy, paramedic, real estate. **Credit/placement by examination:** AP, CLEP, IB, institutional tests. 55 credit hours maximum toward associate degree. **Support services:** GED preparation and test center, reduced course load, remedial instruction, study skills assistance, tutoring, writing center.

Majors. Business: Accounting, accounting technology, business admin, executive assistant, finance, hotel/motel admin, international, marketing, office management, office/clerical, purchasing, real estate, restaurant/food services. **Communications technology:** Desktop publishing. **Computer sciences:** General, applications programming, networking. **Education:** Deaf/hearing impaired, early childhood. **English:** Technical writing. **Foreign languages:** Sign language interpretation. **General:** Landscaping, turf management. **Health services:** Clinical lab assistant, clinical lab technology, dietetic technician, EMT paramedic, massage therapy, medical records technology, nursing (RN), occupational therapy assistant, respiratory therapy technology, sonography, surgical technology, ward clerk. **Liberal arts:** Arts/sciences. **Protective services:** Firefighting. **Visual/performing arts:** Cinematography, commercial/advertising art, music. **Work/family studies:** Child care management, institutional food production.

Most popular majors. Business/marketing 17%, engineering/engineering technologies 22%, health sciences 21%, liberal arts 16%, personal/culinary services 7%.

Computing on campus. 175 workstations in library, computer center, student center. Commuter students can connect to campus network. Online course registration, online library, helpline, wireless network available.

Student life. Freshman orientation: Available. Preregistration for classes offered. Day and evening sessions held for 2-3 hours before start of classes. **Activities:** Drama, student government, TV station, United African American Association, international students, Phi Theta Kappa, adult learners on campus, environmental club, students in free enterprise.

Athletics. NJCAA. **Intercollegiate:** Basketball, golf, soccer. **Team name:** Surge.

Student services. Adult student services, alcohol/substance abuse counseling, career counseling, services for economically disadvantaged, student employment services, financial aid counseling, on-campus daycare, personal counseling, veterans' counselor. **Physically disabled:** Services for visually, speech, hearing impaired. **Transfer:** College fairs on campus for students transferring to 4-year colleges.

Contact. E-mail: adm@cincinnatistate.edu
Phone: (513) 861-7700 Fax: (513) 569-1562
Gabriele Boeckermann, Director of Admission, Cincinnati State Technical and Community College, 3520 Central Parkway, Cincinnati, OH 45223-2690

Clark State Community College
Springfield, Ohio
www.clarkstate.edu   **CB code: 0777**

▶ Public 2-year community college
▶ Commuter campus in small city

General. Founded in 1966. Regionally accredited. **Enrollment:** 3,917 degree-seeking undergraduates; 799 non-degree-seeking students. **Degrees:** 432 associate awarded. **Location:** 30 miles from Dayton, 45 miles from Columbus. **Calendar:** Quarter, limited summer session. **Full-time faculty:** 71 total; 16% have terminal degrees, 14% minority, 68% women. **Part-time faculty:** 457 total; 4% have terminal degrees, 8% minority, 55% women. **Class size:** 58% < 20, 40% 20-39, 1% 40-49, less than 1% 50-99. **Special facilities:** Performing arts center.

Student profile. Among degree-seeking undergraduates, 17% enrolled in a transfer program, 83% enrolled in a vocational program, 1,642 enrolled as first-time, first-year students.

Part-time:	54%	Women:	68%
Out-of-state:	1%	25 or older:	52%

Transfer out. Colleges most students transferred to 2011: Wright State University.

Basis for selection. Open admission, but selective for some programs. Nursing and allied health applicants must have high school chemistry; allied health must also have algebra or equivalent with grade of 2.0 or better. Mathematics placement test with score of 12 or better required for nursing.

High school preparation. Chemistry required for nursing and medical technology. Algebra required for medical technology. 2 math units required for engineering programs.

2011-2012 Annual costs. Tuition/fees: $3,845; $7,152 out-of-state. Per-credit charge: $74 in-state; $147 out-of-state. Books/supplies: $1,200. Personal expenses: $550.

Two-Year Colleges

Financial aid. Need-based: Work-study available nights, weekends and for part-time students.

Application procedures. Admission: No deadline. $15 fee. Admission notification on a rolling basis. Early admission open to high school sophomores, juniors and seniors. Placement test, high school approval, and 3.0 GPA required. **Financial aid:** Priority date 6/15; no closing date. FAFSA required. Applicants notified on a rolling basis.

Academics. Special study options: Accelerated study, cooperative education, cross-registration, distance learning, double major, dual enrollment of high school students, honors, independent study, internships, liberal arts/career combination, study abroad. Bachelor's degree programs available on campus. License preparation in aviation, nursing, paramedic, physical therapy, real estate. **Credit/placement by examination:** AP, CLEP, institutional tests. 24 credit hours maximum toward associate degree. **Support services:** GED test center, learning center, reduced course load, remedial instruction, study skills assistance, tutoring.

Majors. Business: Accounting technology, business admin, human resources, logistics, marketing. **Computer sciences:** Applications programming, database management, information systems, networking. **Education:** General, early childhood, kindergarten/preschool. **Engineering:** Agricultural. **English:** English lit. **General:** Business, horticulture. **Health services:** Clinical lab technology, EMT paramedic, medical assistant, medical secretary, nursing (RN), physical therapy assistant. **Human services:** Social work. **Liberal arts:** Arts/sciences, library assistant. **Protective services:** Corrections, law enforcement admin. **Visual/performing arts:** Commercial/advertising art.

Most popular majors. Business/marketing 11%, computer/information sciences 7%, health sciences 43%, liberal arts 18%.

Computing on campus. Commuter students can connect to campus network. Online course registration, online library, helpline, wireless network available.

Student life. Freshman orientation: Available. Preregistration for classes offered. Held prior to the beginning of each quarter. **Activities:** Campus ministries, choral groups, dance, drama, international student organizations, student government, student newspaper, professional and technological fraternities and sororities, minority student forum, Phi Theta Kappa, social work club.

Athletics. NJCAA. **Intercollegiate:** Baseball M, basketball, softball W, volleyball W. **Intramural:** Basketball, volleyball. **Team name:** Eagles.

Student services. Adult student services, chaplain/spiritual director, career counseling, services for economically disadvantaged, student employment services, financial aid counseling, health services, minority student services, on-campus daycare, personal counseling, placement for graduates, veterans' counselor. **Physically disabled:** Services for visually, speech, hearing impaired. **Transfer:** Pre-admission transcript evaluation for new students. Transfer adviser, college fairs on campus for students transferring to 4-year colleges.

Contact. E-mail: admissions@clarkstate.edu
Phone: (937) 328-6028 Fax: (937) 328-6133
Corey Holliday, Director of Admissions, Clark State Community College, Box 570, Springfield, OH 45501-0570

Cleveland Institute of Electronics
Cleveland, Ohio
www.cie-wc.edu   CB code: 0802

▸ For-profit 2-year technical college
▸ Very large city

General. Founded in 1934. Accredited by DETC. Curriculum completed entirely through distance learning. **Enrollment:** 1,769 full-time, degree-seeking students. **Degrees:** 54 associate awarded. **Calendar:** Differs by program. **Full-time faculty:** 4 total. **Part-time faculty:** 75 total.

Basis for selection. Open admission.

2011-2012 Annual costs. Tuition/fees: $3,770. Associate degree tuition $1,885 per 6 month term.

Financial aid. Need-based: Work-study available nights, weekends and for part-time students.

Application procedures. Admission: No deadline. No application fee. Admission notification on a rolling basis. High school students permitted to enroll with signed approval of parents and guidance counselors (if students are minors).

Academics. Special study options: Accelerated study, distance learning, independent study. **Credit/placement by examination:** AP, CLEP.

Majors. Computer sciences: Programming.

Computing on campus. Online course registration available.

Student life. Activities: Student newspaper.

Student services. Student employment services, veterans' counselor.

Contact. E-mail: instruct@cie-wc.edu
Phone: (216) 781-9400 Toll-free number: (800) 243-6446
Fax: (216) 781-0331
Keith Conn, Admissions Director, Cleveland Institute of Electronics, 1776 East 17th Street, Cleveland, OH 44114-3679

Columbus State Community College
Columbus, Ohio
www.cscc.edu   CB code: 1148

▸ Public 2-year community and technical college
▸ Commuter campus in very large city

General. Founded in 1967. Regionally accredited. Courses offered at 10 off-campus centers. **Enrollment:** 17,100 degree-seeking undergraduates. **Degrees:** 1,991 associate awarded. **ROTC:** Army, Air Force. **Location:** 2 miles from downtown. **Calendar:** Quarter, extensive summer session. **Full-time faculty:** 345 total. **Part-time faculty:** 1,398 total. **Class size:** 48% < 20, 51% 20-39, less than 1% 40-49, less than 1% 50-99, less than 1% >100. **Special facilities:** College-owned building for aviation maintenance program at Bolton Field Airport.

Student profile. Among degree-seeking undergraduates, 29% enrolled in a transfer program, 65% enrolled in a vocational program, 3% already have a bachelor's degree or higher.

Transfer out. Colleges most students transferred to 2011: Ohio State University.

Basis for selection. Open admission, but selective for some programs. Select applicant populations such as underage, international, felon, and dismissed transfer students may be required to submit documentation to determine admission status. Some technology programs have special admission requirements. COMPASS required for placement. English as a Second Language applicants required to complete ESL placement test. Placement testing required for all students who plan to take courses that have an English, math, and/or reading prerequisite. Interview required for chef apprenticeship and some health and human service technology programs. **Home schooled:** Some academic programs may require completion of GED. Recommend completing COMPASS Ability to Benefit Placement Test if applying for financial aid. **Learning Disabled:** Students must provide documentation and register with Disability Services to receive services.

High school preparation. Algebra required for transfer programs and engineering, health, and business technology programs. Chemistry and biology required for health programs.

2011-2012 Annual costs. Tuition/fees: $3,605; $7,925 out-of-state. Per-credit charge: $79 in-state; $175 out-of-state. Books/supplies: $1,050. Personal expenses: $180.

Financial aid. Need-based: Need-based aid available for part-time students. Work-study available nights, weekends and for part-time students. **Non-need-based:** Scholarships awarded for athletics, state residency.

Application procedures. Admission: No deadline. No application fee. Application must be submitted online. Admission notification on a rolling basis. Many health programs admit qualified students on space-available basis; students advised to apply early. **Financial aid:** Priority date 7/15; no closing date. FAFSA required. Applicants notified on a rolling basis starting 4/1.

Academics. Special study options: Cooperative education, cross-registration, distance learning, double major, dual enrollment of high school students, ESL, honors, independent study, internships, liberal arts/career combination, student-designed major, study abroad, teacher certification program, weekend college. Bachelor's degree programs available on campus. License preparation in dental hygiene, nursing, paramedic, real estate. **Credit/placement by examination:** AP, CLEP, IB, institutional tests. **Support services:**

GED preparation and test center, learning center, reduced course load, remedial instruction, study skills assistance, tutoring, writing center.

Majors. Architecture: Landscape. **Business:** Accounting, accounting technology, administrative services, business admin, entrepreneurial studies, hospitality admin, hospitality/recreation, human resources, logistics, marketing, office management, office/clerical, purchasing, real estate, sales/distribution, tourism promotion, tourism/travel. **Communications technology:** General, graphic/printing. **Computer sciences:** General, applications programming, computer graphics, information systems, programming. **Conservation:** Environmental studies. **Education:** Early childhood. **Foreign languages:** Sign language interpretation. **Health services:** Clinical lab assistant, dental hygiene, dental lab technology, EMT paramedic, medical radiologic technology/radiation therapy, medical records admin, medical records technology, medical secretary, mental health services, nuclear medical technology, nursing (RN), respiratory therapy technology, substance abuse counseling, surgical technology, veterinary technology/assistant. **Human services:** General. **Liberal arts:** Arts/sciences. **Parks/recreation:** Exercise sciences, sports admin. **Protective services:** Corrections, fire safety technology, firefighting, law enforcement admin, police science. **Visual/performing arts:** Commercial photography. **Work/family studies:** Aging, child development.

Most popular majors. Business/marketing 8%, health sciences 12%, liberal arts 16%.

Computing on campus. Commuter students can connect to campus network. Online course registration, online library, helpline, wireless network available.

Student life. Freshman orientation: Available. Preregistration for classes offered. **Housing:** Students may live in residence halls of other local colleges if space is available. **Activities:** Concert band, choral groups, dance, drama, international student organizations, literary magazine, music ensembles, musical theater, student government, student newspaper.

Athletics. NJCAA. **Intercollegiate:** Basketball, golf M, volleyball W. **Intramural:** Basketball, soccer, volleyball. **Team name:** Cougars.

Student services. Adult student services, alcohol/substance abuse counseling, career counseling, services for economically disadvantaged, student employment services, financial aid counseling, minority student services, on-campus daycare, personal counseling, placement for graduates, veterans' counselor. **Physically disabled:** Services for visually, speech, hearing impaired. **Transfer:** Transfer adviser, college fairs on campus for students transferring to 4-year colleges.

Contact. E-mail: information@cscc.edu
Phone: (614) 287-2669 Toll-free number: (800) 621-6407 ext. 2669
Fax: (614) 287-6019
Tari Blaney, Director of Admissions, Columbus State Community College, 550 East Spring Street, Columbus, OH 43216-1609

Cuyahoga Community College: Eastern
Highland Hills, Ohio
www.tri-c.edu   CB code: 1978

- Public 2-year branch campus and community college
- Commuter campus in large city

General. Founded in 1971. Regionally accredited. **Location:** 3 miles from Cleveland. **Calendar:** Semester.

Annual costs/financial aid. Tuition/fees (2011-2012): $2,737; $3,554 out-of-district; $7,068 out-of-state. Books/supplies: $900. Personal expenses: $1,504. Need-based financial aid available to full-time and part-time students.

Contact. Phone: (216) 987-2024
Director of Admissions, 4250 Richmond Road, Highland Hills, OH 44122

Cuyahoga Community College: Metropolitan
Cleveland, Ohio   CB member
www.tri-c.edu   CB code: 1159

- Public 2-year community college
- Commuter campus in very large city

General. Founded in 1963. Regionally accredited. Additional campuses in Highland Hills, Westlake, Brunswick, and Parma. **Enrollment:** 15,107 degree-seeking undergraduates; 16,154 non-degree-seeking students. **Degrees:** 2,278 associate awarded. **ROTC:** Naval, Air Force. **Location:** Downtown. **Calendar:** Semester, limited summer session. **Full-time faculty:**

361 total; 19% have terminal degrees, 22% minority, 59% women. **Part-time faculty:** 1,457 total; 10% have terminal degrees, 20% minority, 53% women. **Class size:** 55% < 20, 42% 20-39, 2% 40-49, less than 1% 50-99. **Special facilities:** Technology center.

Student profile. Among degree-seeking undergraduates, 26% enrolled in a transfer program, 74% enrolled in a vocational program, 2,970 enrolled as first-time, first-year students, 1,242 transferred in from other institutions.

Part-time:	58%	Hispanic American:	4%
Women:	60%	Native American:	1%
African American:	33%	International:	1%
Asian American:	2%	25 or older:	50%

Transfer out. 68% of students enrolled in the transfer program go on to 4-year colleges. **Colleges most students transferred to 2011:** Cleveland State University, Baldwin-Wallace College, Kent State University, University of Akron.

Basis for selection. Open admission, but selective for some programs. Special requirements for some health technology programs (SAT or ACT required). English placement test required.

2011-2012 Annual costs. Tuition/fees: $2,737; $3,554 out-of-district; $7,068 out-of-state. Per-credit charge: $79 in-district; $106 out-of-district; $224 out-of-state. Books/supplies: $1,700. Personal expenses: $1,105.

2010-2011 Financial aid. Need-based: Average need met was 100%. Average scholarship/grant was $4,764; average loan $3,063. 73% of total undergraduate aid awarded as scholarships/grants, 27% as loans/jobs. Need-based aid available for part-time students. Work-study available nights, weekends and for part-time students. **Non-need-based:** Awarded to 67 full-time undergraduates, including 29 freshmen. Scholarships awarded for academics, art, athletics, leadership, minority status, music/drama.

Application procedures. Admission: No deadline. No application fee. Admission notification on a rolling basis. **Financial aid:** No deadline. FAFSA, institutional form required. Applicants notified on a rolling basis starting 5/12.

Academics. Special study options: Cooperative education, cross-registration, distance learning, dual enrollment of high school students, ESL, honors, independent study. **Credit/placement by examination:** AP, CLEP, institutional tests. 30 credit hours maximum toward associate degree. **Support services:** GED preparation and test center, learning center, reduced course load, remedial instruction, study skills assistance, tutoring, writing center.

Majors. Business: General, accounting, administrative services, business admin, entrepreneurial studies, hospitality admin, management information systems, real estate. **Communications technology:** General. **Computer sciences:** General. **Education:** Early childhood. **Foreign languages:** Sign language interpretation. **General:** Horticulture. **Health services:** Clinical lab technology, dental assistant, dental hygiene, dental lab technology, EMT paramedic, medical assistant, medical records admin, medical records technology, nursing (RN), occupational therapy assistant, optician, pharmacy assistant, physical therapy assistant, surgical technology. **Liberal arts:** Arts/sciences. **Math:** General. **Protective services:** Corrections, fire safety technology, police science. **Visual/performing arts:** Commercial/advertising art, music, photography. **Work/family studies:** Child care management.

Most popular majors. Business/marketing 9%, health sciences 30%, liberal arts 45%.

Computing on campus. 1,500 workstations in library, computer center, student center. Online course registration, online library, helpline available.

Student life. Freshman orientation: Mandatory. Preregistration for classes offered. **Activities:** Bands, choral groups, dance, drama, musical theater, student government, student newspaper, Hillel, Afro-American society, veterans service fraternity, Young Socialist Alliance, Student Coalition Against Racism, National Education Association, Hispanic club, Phi Theta Kappa.

Athletics. NJCAA. **Intercollegiate:** Baseball M, basketball, cross-country, soccer, softball W, track and field, volleyball W, wrestling M. **Intramural:** Baseball M, basketball, bowling, gymnastics, handball, racquetball, softball, tennis, volleyball, weight lifting. **Team name:** Challengers.

Student services. Adult student services, alcohol/substance abuse counseling, career counseling, student employment services, financial aid counseling, health services, minority student services, on-campus daycare, personal counseling, placement for graduates, veterans' counselor, women's services. **Physically disabled:** Services for visually, speech, hearing impaired. **Transfer:** Transfer adviser, college fairs on campus for students transferring to 4-year colleges.

Contact. E-mail: customerservice@tri-c.edu
Phone: (216) 987-4200 Toll-free number: (800) 954-8742
Fax: (216) 696-2567
Rena Mason, Director of Admissions, Cuyahoga Community College:
Metropolitan, 2900 Community College Avenue, Cleveland, OH
44115-2878

Cuyahoga Community College: Western
Parma, Ohio
www.tri-c.edu   **CB code: 1985**

◆ Public 2-year community college
◆ Commuter campus in small city

General. Founded in 1966. Regionally accredited. **Location:** 15 miles from
Cleveland. **Calendar:** Semester.

Annual costs/financial aid. Tuition/fees (2011-2012): $2,737; $3,554
out-of-district; $7,068 out-of-state. Books/supplies: $900. Personal expenses:
$1,504. Need-based financial aid available to full-time and part-time students.

Contact. Phone: (216) 987-5150
Director of Admissions and Records, 11000 Pleasant Valley Road, Parma,
OH 44130

Davis College
Toledo, Ohio
www.daviscollege.edu   **CB code: 2155**

◆ For-profit 2-year junior college
◆ Commuter campus in large city
◆ Interview required

General. Founded in 1858. Regionally accredited. **Enrollment:** 383 degree-
seeking undergraduates; 2 non-degree-seeking students. **Degrees:** 122 associate awarded. **Location:** 6 miles from downtown, 45 miles from Detroit.
Calendar: Quarter, limited summer session. **Full-time faculty:** 16 total;
12% minority, 75% women. **Part-time faculty:** 21 total; 52% women. **Class
size:** 90% < 20, 10% 20-39.

Student profile. Among degree-seeking undergraduates, 45 enrolled as
first-time, first-year students, 92 transferred in from other institutions.

Part-time:	63%	African American:	43%
Out-of-state:	1%	Hispanic American:	3%
Women:	81%	25 or older:	63%

Transfer out. 30% of students enrolled in the transfer program go on to 4-
year colleges. **Colleges most students transferred to 2011:** Lourdes College,
Spring Arbor University, University of Toledo, Owens Community College,
Monroe Community College.

Basis for selection. Character and personal qualities very important; CPAt
score, interview, talent and ability important. School and College Ability
Tests (CPAt) required. Portfolio required for some graphic design degree
programs. **Home schooled:** State high school equivalency certificate required.

2011-2012 Annual costs. Tuition/fees: $19,410. Per-credit charge: $408.
Books/supplies: $1,350. Personal expenses: $1,980.

Financial aid. All financial aid based on need. Need-based aid available
for part-time students. Work-study available nights, weekends and for part-
time students.

Application procedures. **Admission:** Closing date 9/1 (receipt date). $30
fee. Admission notification on a rolling basis. **Financial aid:** No deadline.
FAFSA required. Applicants notified on a rolling basis.

Academics. **Special study options:** Distance learning, internships, liberal
arts/career combination. **Credit/placement by examination:** AP, CLEP,
institutional tests. 16 credit hours maximum toward associate degree. **Support
services:** Reduced course load, remedial instruction, tutoring.

Majors. **Business:** Accounting technology, administrative services, business
admin, fashion, human resources, insurance, marketing. **Computer sciences:**
Networking, webmaster. **Education:** Early childhood. **Health services:**
Insurance coding, medical assistant, medical secretary. **Visual/performing
arts:** Graphic design, interior design.

Most popular majors. Business/marketing 30%, health sciences 48%,
visual/performing arts 11%.

Computing on campus. 111 workstations in library, computer center.
Wireless network available.

Student life. **Freshman orientation:** Mandatory. Preregistration for
classes offered.

Student services. Career counseling, student employment services, financial aid counseling, personal counseling, placement for graduates, veterans'
counselor. **Transfer:** Pre-admission transcript evaluation for new students.

Contact. E-mail: dstern@daviscollege.edu
Phone: (419) 473-2700 Toll-free number: (800) 477-7021
Fax: (419) 473-2472
Dana Stern, Senior Career Coordinator, Davis College, 4747 Monroe
Street, Toledo, OH 43623

Daymar College: Chillicothe
Chillicothe, Ohio
www.samuelstephencollege.edu   **CB code: 2468**

◆ For-profit 2-year business college
◆ Commuter campus in large town

General. Founded in 1962. Regionally accredited. **Location:** 45 miles from
Columbus, 90 miles from Cincinnati. **Calendar:** Quarter.

Annual costs/financial aid. Tuition/fees (2011-2012): $15,850. Per-
credit-hour charge (tuition only): $325 per quarter credit hour for most
courses. $390 per quarter credit hour for 300-400 level courses. $365 per
quarter credit hour for LAW specific courses. $410 per quarter credit hour
for Information Technology and Personal Fitness Training specific courses.
$475 per quarter credit hour for Associate Degree in Nursing specific courses.
Need-based financial aid available to full-time and part-time students.

Contact. Phone: (740) 774-6300
Admissions Representative, 1410 Industrial Drive, Chillicothe, OH 45601

Eastern Gateway Community College
Steubenville, Ohio
www.egcc.edu   **CB code: 2264**

◆ Public 2-year community college
◆ Commuter campus in large town

General. Founded in 1966. Regionally accredited. **Enrollment:** 1,868
degree-seeking undergraduates. **Degrees:** 195 associate awarded. **Location:**
40 miles from Pittsburgh, PA. **Calendar:** Semester, limited summer session.
Full-time faculty: 35 total. **Part-time faculty:** 197 total.

Transfer out. **Colleges most students transferred to 2011:** Franciscan
University of Steubenville, Franklin University, West Liberty State College,
Kent State University.

Basis for selection. Open admission, but selective for some programs.
Special requirements for all allied health technologies programs. ACT
required for admission to radiology, respiratory, practical nursing, medical
laboratory, medical assisting, dental assisting technologies. **Home schooled:**
Final transcript showing successful home school completion signed and dated
by home school principal required.

2011-2012 Annual costs. Tuition/fees: $2,970; $3,150 out-of-district;
$3,960 out-of-state. Per-credit charge: $99 in-district; $105 out-of-district;
$133 out-of-state. Residents of 5 neighboring West Virginia counties eligible
for in-state, out-of-district tuition rates. Books/supplies: $1,000. Personal
expenses: $400.

Financial aid. All financial aid based on need. Need-based aid available
for part-time students. Work-study available nights, weekends and for part-
time students.

Application procedures. **Admission:** No deadline. $20 fee. Admission
notification on a rolling basis. **Financial aid:** Priority date 4/1; no closing
date. FAFSA, institutional form required. Applicants notified on a rolling
basis starting 6/15.

Academics. **Special study options:** Accelerated study, distance learning,
double major, dual enrollment of high school students, external degree,
honors, independent study, internships. Bachelor's degree programs available
on campus. License preparation in paramedic, radiology, real estate. **Credit/
placement by examination:** AP, CLEP, institutional tests. 42 credit hours
maximum toward associate degree. **Support services:** GED preparation and

test center, learning center, pre-admission summer program, remedial instruction, study skills assistance, tutoring, writing center.

Majors. Biology: General. **Business:** Accounting, administrative services, business admin, office management. **Computer sciences:** General, applications programming, computer science, data processing, information systems, systems analysis. **Education:** Early childhood. **Engineering:** General, engineering science, systems. **Health services:** Clinical lab technology, dental assistant, EMT paramedic, licensed practical nurse, medical assistant, medical radiologic technology/radiation therapy, respiratory therapy technology. **Liberal arts:** Arts/sciences. **Protective services:** Police science.

Computing on campus. 50 workstations in library, computer center. Online library, wireless network available.

Student life. Freshman orientation: Mandatory. Preregistration for classes offered. **Activities:** Student government, student newspaper.

Athletics. Intramural: Basketball M, football (non-tackle) M, softball. **Team name:** Gators.

Student services. Adult student services, career counseling, services for economically disadvantaged, student employment services, financial aid counseling, health services, on-campus daycare, veterans' counselor. **Physically disabled:** Services for visually, hearing impaired. **Transfer:** Re-entry adviser, pre-admission transcript evaluation for new students. Transfer center, transfer adviser, college fairs on campus for students transferring to 4-year colleges.

Contact. E-mail: admissions@egcc.edu
Phone: (740) 264-5591 ext. 212
Toll-free number: (800) 682-6553 ext. 212 Fax: (740) 266-2944
Marlana Haynes, Director of Admissions, Eastern Gateway Community College, Eastern Gateway Community College- Jefferson County Campus, Steubenville, OH 43952

Edison State Community College
Piqua, Ohio
www.edisonohio.edu   CB code: 1191

▶ Public 2-year community college
▶ Commuter campus in large town

General. Founded in 1973. Regionally accredited. **Enrollment:** 2,789 degree-seeking undergraduates; 669 non-degree-seeking students. **Degrees:** 402 associate awarded. **Location:** 30 miles from Dayton. **Calendar:** Semester, extensive summer session. **Full-time faculty:** 55 total; 14% have terminal degrees, 6% minority, 58% women. **Part-time faculty:** 188 total; 10% have terminal degrees, 4% minority, 58% women. **Class size:** 77% < 20, 23% 20-39, less than 1% 40-49, less than 1% 50-99. **Partnerships:** Formal partnership with Tech Prep.

Student profile. Among degree-seeking undergraduates, 35% enrolled in a transfer program, 65% enrolled in a vocational program, 2% already have a bachelor's degree or higher, 639 enrolled as first-time, first-year students, 76 transferred in from other institutions.

Part-time:	59%	Asian American:	1%
Out-of-state:	1%	Hispanic American:	1%
Women:	66%	25 or older:	45%
African American:	2%		

Transfer out. 55% of students enrolled in the transfer program go on to 4-year colleges. **Colleges most students transferred to 2011:** Wright State University, Ohio State University, Sinclair Community College, Franklin University, Bluffton University.

Basis for selection. Open admission, but selective for some programs. Special admissions requirements for nursing and other health care programs, early childhood education, and social services program. **Adult students:** Math and English placement with Compass. **Home schooled:** State high school equivalency certificate required.

High school preparation. College-preparatory program recommended. Recommended units include English 4, mathematics 3, social studies 3, science 3 and foreign language 2. 1 fine arts recommended.

2011-2012 Annual costs. Tuition/fees: $3,819; $7,029 out-of-state. Per-credit charge: $127 in-state; $234 out-of-state. Books/supplies: $1,520. Personal expenses: $756.

Financial aid. Need-based: Need-based aid available for part-time students. Work-study available nights, weekends and for part-time students. **Non-need-based:** Scholarships awarded for academics, athletics, job skills, minority status, state residency.

Application procedures. Admission: No deadline. $20 fee, may be waived for applicants with need. Admission notification on a rolling basis. **Financial aid:** Priority date 5/2; no closing date. FAFSA, institutional form required. Applicants notified on a rolling basis starting 5/15.

Academics. Special study options: Accelerated study, cooperative education, cross-registration, distance learning, double major, dual enrollment of high school students, ESL, independent study, internships, student-designed major. Bachelor's degree programs available on campus. License preparation in nursing, real estate. **Credit/placement by examination:** AP, CLEP, institutional tests. 30 credit hours maximum toward associate degree. DANTE, DSST and professional exams recommended by American Council on Education accepted. **Support services:** Learning center, pre-admission summer program, reduced course load, remedial instruction, study skills assistance, tutoring, writing center.

Majors. Business: Accounting, business admin, executive assistant, human resources, logistics, marketing, real estate, sales/distribution. **Communications:** Communications/speech/rhetoric. **Computer sciences:** General, networking, programming, security, web page design. **Education:** General. **Health services:** Clinical lab technology, medical assistant, medical secretary, nursing (RN), physical therapy assistant, prenursing. **Human services:** Social work. **Liberal arts:** Arts/sciences. **Protective services:** Police science. **Visual/performing arts:** Art, commercial/advertising art, dramatic. **Work/family studies:** Child development.

Most popular majors. Business/marketing 13%, computer/information sciences 7%, engineering/engineering technologies 7%, health sciences 31%, liberal arts 26%.

Computing on campus. 67 workstations in library, student center. Commuter students can connect to campus network. Online course registration, online library, helpline, wireless network available.

Student life. Freshman orientation: Mandatory. Preregistration for classes offered. **Activities:** Drama, student government, Phi Theta Kappa, photo society, writers club, student ambassadors, StageLight Players, international club, digital media club, Arts League, Society of Human Resource Management, Campus Crusade for Christ.

Athletics. NJCAA. **Intercollegiate:** Basketball, volleyball W. **Team name:** Chargers.

Student services. Adult student services, career counseling, student employment services, financial aid counseling, health services, on-campus daycare, personal counseling, placement for graduates, veterans' counselor. **Physically disabled:** Services for visually, speech, hearing impaired. **Transfer:** Pre-admission transcript evaluation for new students. Transfer adviser, college fairs on campus for students transferring to 4-year colleges.

Contact. E-mail: info@edisonohio.edu
Phone: (937) 778-7868 Toll-free number: (800) 922-3722 ext. 7868
Fax: (937) 778-1920
Teresa Roth, Director of Admissions, Edison State Community College, 1973 Edison Drive, Piqua, OH 45356-9253

ETI Technical College of Niles
Niles, Ohio
www.eticollege.edu   CB code: 3149

▶ For-profit 2-year technical college
▶ Commuter campus in large city
▶ Interview required

General. Accredited by ACCSC. **Enrollment:** 138 degree-seeking undergraduates; 74 non-degree-seeking students. **Degrees:** 67 associate awarded. **Location:** 50 miles from Cleveland and Pittsburgh. **Calendar:** Semester. **Full-time faculty:** 9 total; 56% women. **Part-time faculty:** 20 total; 5% minority, 65% women.

Student profile. Among degree-seeking undergraduates, 100% enrolled in a vocational program, 34 enrolled as first-time, first-year students.

Women:	70%	Asian American:	1%
African American:	9%	Hispanic American:	4%

Basis for selection. Open admission, but selective for some programs.

2012-2013 Annual costs. Tuition/fees (projected): $8,880. Per-credit charge: $330. Books/supplies: $1,800. Personal expenses: $2,140.

2011-2012 Financial aid. Need-based: 34 full-time freshmen applied for aid; 34 were judged to have need; 34 of these received aid. Average need met was 100%. Average scholarship/grant was $3,550; average loan $3,500.

62% of total undergraduate aid awarded as scholarships/grants, 38% as loans/jobs. Need-based aid available for part-time students. Work-study available nights, weekends and for part-time students. **Non-need-based:** Scholarships awarded for academics.

Application procedures. Admission: No deadline. $50 fee. Admission notification on a rolling basis. **Financial aid:** No deadline. FAFSA required. Applicants notified on a rolling basis; must reply within 4 week(s) of notification.

Academics. Special study options: Internships. License preparation in real estate. **Credit/placement by examination:** AP, CLEP. **Support services:** GED preparation, tutoring.

Majors. Business: Accounting, administrative services. **Computer sciences:** Information technology, web page design. **Health services:** Insurance coding, medical assistant, medical secretary, medical transcription.

Most popular majors. Business/marketing 12%, engineering/engineering technologies 15%, health sciences 55%, legal studies 18%.

Student life. Freshman orientation: Mandatory. Preregistration for classes offered. **Activities:** Student government.

Student services. Career counseling, financial aid counseling, placement for graduates.

Contact. E-mail: etiadmissionsdir@hotmail.com
Phone: (330) 652-9919 Fax: (330) 652-4399
Diane Marsteller, Director of Admissions, ETI Technical College of Niles, 2076 Youngstown Warren Road, Niles, OH 44446-4398

Fortis College: Centerville
Centerville, Ohio
www.fortis.edu   **CB code: 1610**

- For-profit 2-year junior and technical college
- Commuter campus in large town

General. Founded in 1953. Regionally accredited; also accredited by ACCSC. **Enrollment:** 833 degree-seeking undergraduates. **Degrees:** 883 associate awarded. **Location:** 15 miles from Dayton. **Calendar:** Continuous, extensive summer session. **Full-time faculty:** 37 total. **Part-time faculty:** 63 total.

Basis for selection. Open admission. High school diploma or GED required for associate degree programs. Students without diploma or GED must pass Ability to Benefit test in order to enter diploma program. Students must have interview before submitting application for admission.

2011-2012 Annual costs. Books/supplies: $950. Personal expenses: $945.

Financial aid. All financial aid based on need. Need-based aid available for part-time students. Work-study available nights, weekends and for part-time students.

Application procedures. Admission: No deadline. $100 fee, may be waived for applicants with need. Admission notification on a rolling basis. **Financial aid:** No deadline. FAFSA, institutional form required. Applicants notified on a rolling basis.

Academics. Special study options: Internships. **Credit/placement by examination:** AP, CLEP, institutional tests. 16 credit hours maximum toward associate degree. **Support services:** GED preparation, remedial instruction, tutoring.

Majors. Computer sciences: General, computer science. **Engineering:** Electrical. **Health services:** Medical assistant, nursing (RN).

Computing on campus. 176 workstations in library, computer center.

Student life. Freshman orientation: Mandatory. Preregistration for classes offered. Held first day of classes. **Activities:** Student government, student newspaper.

Student services. Adult student services, alcohol/substance abuse counseling, career counseling, student employment services, financial aid counseling, personal counseling, placement for graduates, veterans' counselor. **Transfer:** Pre-admission transcript evaluation for new students.

Contact. E-mail: twallace@fortiscolleg.edu
Phone: (937) 433-3410 Toll-free number: (800) 837-7387
Sean Kuhn, Director, Fortis College: Centerville, 555 East Alex Bell Road, Centerville, OH 45459-9627

Fortis College: Cuyahoga
Cuyahoga Falls, Ohio
www.fortis.edu

- For-profit 2-year nursing and technical college
- Commuter campus in small city

General. Regionally accredited. **Calendar:** Differs by program.

Contact. Phone: (330) 923-9959 ext. 4660
Director of Admissions, 2545 Bailey Road, Cuyahoga Falls, OH 44221

Fortis College: Ravenna
Ravenna, Ohio
www.fortis.edu   **CB code: 2195**

- For-profit 2-year business college
- Large town

General. Regionally accredited. **Calendar:** Five 10-week sessions per calendar year.

Annual costs/financial aid. Need-based financial aid available to full-time and part-time students.

Contact. Phone: (330) 297-7319
Director of Admissions, 326 East Main Street, Ravenna, OH 44266

Gallipolis Career College
Gallipolis, Ohio
www.gallipoliscareercollege.com   **CB code: 2469**

- For-profit 2-year business and technical college
- Commuter campus in small town

General. Accredited by ACICS. **Location:** 45 miles from Huntington, West Virginia. **Calendar:** Quarter.

Annual costs/financial aid. Tuition/fees (2011-2012): $11,090. Books/supplies: $1,400. Personal expenses: $4,000. Need-based financial aid available to full-time and part-time students.

Contact. Phone: (740) 446-4367 ext. 12
Director of Admissions, 1176 Jackson Pike, Suite 312, Gallipolis, OH 45631

Good Samaritan College of Nursing and Health Science
Cincinnati, Ohio
www.gscollege.edu   **CB code: 1259**

- Private 2-year nursing college affiliated with Roman Catholic Church
- Commuter campus in very large city
- SAT or ACT (ACT writing optional) required

General. Hospital-based program. **Enrollment:** 313 degree-seeking undergraduates. **Degrees:** 92 associate awarded. **Calendar:** Semester, limited summer session. **Full-time faculty:** 26 total. **Part-time faculty:** 9 total.

Basis for selection. Test scores very important. COMPASS and ATI critical thinking used for advising only. **Adult students:** SAT/ACT scores not required if out of high school 5 year(s) or more.

High school preparation. College-preparatory program recommended. 14 units required. Required and recommended units include English 4, mathematics 4, social studies 3, history 2, science 3, foreign language 2 and computer science 1.

2011-2012 Annual costs. Tuition/fees: $20,400. Books/supplies: $1,350.

Financial aid. Need-based: Work-study available nights, weekends and for part-time students.

Application procedures. Admission: No deadline. $40 fee. Admission notification on a rolling basis.

Academics. Credit/placement by examination: AP, CLEP. **Support services:** Learning center, study skills assistance, tutoring.

Majors. Health services: Nursing (RN).

Computing on campus. Online course registration, wireless network available.

Student life. Freshman orientation: Mandatory. Preregistration for classes offered.

Student services. Student employment services, financial aid counseling, health services, personal counseling.

Contact. E-mail: linda_hayes@trihealth.com
Phone: (513) 862-2743
Linda Hayes, Dean of Enrollment Management, Good Samaritan College of Nursing and Health Science, 375 Dixmyth Avenue, Cincinnati, OH 45220

Hocking College
Nelsonville, Ohio
www.hocking.edu
CB code: 1822

- Public 2-year technical college
- Commuter campus in small town

General. Founded in 1968. Regionally accredited. **Enrollment:** 5,631 degree-seeking undergraduates. **Degrees:** 793 associate awarded. **ROTC:** Army, Air Force. **Location:** 15 miles from Athens, 55 miles from Columbus. **Calendar:** Quarter, extensive summer session. **Full-time faculty:** 179 total. **Part-time faculty:** 141 total. **Class size:** 61% < 20, 34% 20-39, 2% 40-49, 3% 50-99, less than 1% >100. **Special facilities:** Nature center, living history village, land lab, firing range, burn building, early learning center, fish hatchery.

Student profile.

Out-of-state:	3%	Live on campus:	13%
25 or older:	38%		

Transfer out. Colleges most students transferred to 2011: Ohio University, Rio Grande University, Franklin University.

Basis for selection. Open admission, but selective for some programs. Special admissions requirements to nursing program (based on test scores), physical therapist assistant program (based on grades), and radiologic and surgical/operating room technology (based on test scores and grades). Some programs have additional admission requirements. Interview recommended. **Home schooled:** Applicants to health and public safety technology must have GED before classes begin. **Learning Disabled:** Documentation required for services in the Access Center - Office of Disability Services.

High school preparation. Recommended units include English 4, mathematics 3 and science 3. 1 algebra, 1 biology highly recommended for recreation/wildlife and forestry applicants.

2011-2012 Annual costs. Tuition/fees: $3,993; $7,986 out-of-state. Per-credit charge: $76 in-state; $187 out-of-state. Books/supplies: $1,200. Personal expenses: $550.

Financial aid. Need-based: Need-based aid available for part-time students. Work-study available nights, weekends and for part-time students. **Non-need-based:** Scholarships awarded for academics, minority status, state residency.

Application procedures. Admission: No deadline. $15 fee. Admission notification on a rolling basis. **Financial aid:** Priority date 2/28; no closing date. FAFSA, institutional form required. Applicants notified on a rolling basis starting 4/15.

Academics. Self paced online courses available. Enrollment possible any day college is in session. **Special study options:** Accelerated study, cooperative education, cross-registration, distance learning, double major, dual enrollment of high school students, ESL, exchange student, honors, independent study, internships, student-designed major, study abroad. Bachelor's degree programs available on campus. License preparation in nursing, paramedic, physical therapy, radiology, real estate. **Credit/placement by examination:** AP, CLEP, institutional tests. 60 credit hours maximum toward associate

degree. **Support services:** GED preparation and test center, learning center, pre-admission summer program, reduced course load, remedial instruction, study skills assistance, tutoring, writing center.

Majors. Architecture: Landscape. **Biology:** Biomedical sciences. **Business:** General, accounting technology, administrative services, hotel/motel admin. **Communications technology:** Radio/TV. **Computer sciences:** Networking, programming. **Conservation:** General, fisheries, forest management, management/policy, wildlife/wilderness. **Education:** Teacher assistance. **General:** Equestrian studies. **Health services:** EMT paramedic, massage therapy, medical assistant, medical records technology, nursing (RN), optician, physical therapy assistant. **Parks/recreation:** Sports admin. **Physical sciences:** Materials science. **Protective services:** Corrections, firefighting, police science. **Visual/performing arts:** Art, music.

Most popular majors. Agriculture 7%, business/marketing 15%, health sciences 31%, natural resources/environmental science 23%, personal/culinary services 6%, security/protective services 16%.

Computing on campus. 177 workstations in dormitories, library, computer center, student center. Dormitories wired for high-speed internet access and linked to campus network. Commuter students can connect to campus network. Online course registration, online library, helpline, repair service, wireless network available.

Student life. Freshman orientation: Mandatory, $20 fee. Preregistration for classes offered. **Policies:** All students have full use of student center. Clubs must be sanctioned by college. **Housing:** Coed dorms, wellness housing available. $100 partly refundable deposit. **Activities:** Campus ministries, choral groups, dance, drama, international student organizations, literary magazine, music ensembles, radio station, student government, student newspaper, Phi Theta Kappa, Kappa Beta Delta, SIFE, Unity Board, technology based clubs, Hocking Heights hall council.

Athletics. Intramural: Basketball, football (non-tackle), golf, soccer, softball, swimming, table tennis, tennis, volleyball, weight lifting, wrestling.

Student services. Adult student services, alcohol/substance abuse counseling, chaplain/spiritual director, career counseling, student employment services, financial aid counseling, health services, legal services, on-campus daycare, personal counseling, placement for graduates, veterans' counselor, women's services. **Physically disabled:** Services for visually, speech, hearing impaired. **Transfer:** Pre-admission transcript evaluation for new students. Transfer center, transfer adviser, college fairs on campus for students transferring to 4-year colleges.

Contact. E-mail: admissions@hocking.edu
Phone: (740) 753-7049 Toll-free number: (877) 462-5464
Fax: (740) 753-7065
Sally Lozada, Dean of Enrollment Services, Hocking College, 3301 Hocking Parkway, Nelsonville, OH 45764-9704

Hondros College
Westerville, Ohio
www.hondros.edu
CB code: 3255

- For-profit 2-year nursing and career college
- Commuter campus in very large city
- Application essay, interview required

General. Accredited by ACICS. **Enrollment:** 1,139 degree-seeking undergraduates. **Degrees:** 164 associate awarded. **Location:** 10 miles from Columbus. **Calendar:** Quarter, extensive summer session. **Full-time faculty:** 70 total. **Part-time faculty:** 88 total. **Class size:** 15% < 20, 53% 20-39, less than 1% 40-49, 31% 50-99.

Student profile. Among degree-seeking undergraduates, 1% already have a bachelor's degree or higher, 70 enrolled as first-time, first-year students.

Part-time:	14%	Hispanic American:	1%
Women:	88%	Native American:	1%
African American:	25%	25 or older:	69%
Asian American:	1%		

Transfer out. Colleges most students transferred to 2011: University of Phoenix, Devry University.

Basis for selection. Nursing program 2.0 GPA required. Special requirements for allied health related programs. **Adult students:** SAT/ACT scores not required. **Home schooled:** State high school equivalency certificate required.

2011-2012 Annual costs. Books/supplies: $1,565.

2010-2011 Financial aid. Need-based: 50 full-time freshmen applied for aid; 48 were judged to have need; 48 of these received aid. Average scholarship/grant was $1,250. 26% of total undergraduate aid awarded as scholarships/grants, 74% as loans/jobs. Need-based aid available for part-time students. Work-study available nights, weekends and for part-time students.

Application procedures. Admission: No deadline. $25 fee. Admission notification on a rolling basis. **Financial aid:** No deadline. FAFSA required.

Academics. Special study options: Distance learning, liberal arts/career combination. Bachelor's degree programs available on campus. License preparation in nursing, real estate. **Credit/placement by examination:** AP, CLEP. **Support services:** Remedial instruction, study skills assistance, tutoring.

Majors. Business: Real estate. **Health services:** Nursing (RN).

Most popular majors. Business/marketing 25%, health sciences 75%.

Computing on campus. PC or laptop required. 15 workstations in library, computer center, student center. Online course registration, online library, helpline, wireless network available.

Student life. Freshman orientation: Mandatory. Preregistration for classes offered. Held approximately one week prior to the quarter start. **Activities:** Student newspaper.

Student services. Career counseling, financial aid counseling, placement for graduates. **Transfer:** Re-entry adviser, pre-admission transcript evaluation for new students.

Contact. E-mail: admissions@hondros.edu
Phone: (888) 466-3767 Toll-free number: (888) 466-3767
Fax: (614) 508-7280
Joshua Moore, Director of Admissions, Hondros College, 4140 Executive Parkway, Westerville, OH 43081-3855

International College of Broadcasting
Dayton, Ohio
www.icbcollege.com   CB code: 3047

▸ For-profit 2-year technical college
▸ Commuter campus in small city

General. Accredited by ACCSC. **Enrollment:** 83 degree-seeking undergraduates. **Degrees:** 51 associate awarded. **Location:** 50 miles from Cincinnati, 70 miles from Columbus. **Calendar:** Semester, limited summer session. **Full-time faculty:** 11 total. **Part-time faculty:** 4 total. **Class size:** 100% < 20.

Student profile. Among degree-seeking undergraduates, 100% enrolled in a vocational program. Of all enrolled students, 1% already have a bachelor's degree or higher.

Out-of-state: 19%   **25 or older:**   20%

Basis for selection. Open admission. Tour of the campus and interview required before admission.

2011-2012 Annual costs. Tuition/fees: $14,660. Tuition and fees include books. Personal expenses: $2,862.

Financial aid. Need-based: Need-based aid available for part-time students. Work-study available nights, weekends and for part-time students.

Application procedures. Admission: No deadline. $100 fee. **Financial aid:** No deadline. FAFSA required. Applicants notified on a rolling basis starting 11/1.

Academics. Credit/placement by examination: AP, CLEP. **Support services:** Reduced course load.

Majors. Communications: Communications/speech/rhetoric, radio/TV. **Visual/performing arts:** General.

Computing on campus. Wireless network available.

Contact. E-mail: admissions@icbcollege.com
Phone: (937) 258-8251 ext. 202 Fax: (937) 258-8714
James Stringfield, Director of Admissions, International College of Broadcasting, 6 South Smithville Road, Dayton, OH 45431

ITT Technical Institute: Dayton
Dayton, Ohio
www.itt-tech.edu   CB code: 7312

▸ For-profit 2-year technical college
▸ Commuter campus in small city
▸ Interview required

General. Founded in 1935. Accredited by ACICS. **Enrollment:** 534 undergraduates. **Degrees:** 164 associate awarded. **Location:** 5 miles from downtown. **Calendar:** Quarter, extensive summer session. **Full-time faculty:** 12 total. **Part-time faculty:** 33 total.

Basis for selection. Satisfactory scores from on-site tests in English and mathematics required.

2011-2012 Annual costs. Estimated costs as of June 2011: per-credit-hour charge, $493, depending upon level and course of study; academic fee, $200. Certain programs of study require purchase of tools, which could cost an additional $100 to $500. All costs are subject to change.

Financial aid. Need-based: Work-study available nights, weekends and for part-time students.

Application procedures. Admission: No deadline. No application fee. Admission notification on a rolling basis. **Financial aid:** No deadline. FAFSA, institutional form required. Applicants notified on a rolling basis.

Academics. Credit/placement by examination: AP, CLEP. **Support services:** Learning center, tutoring.

Majors. Business: Business admin. **Computer sciences:** Computer graphics, LAN/WAN management, networking, programming, web page design, webmaster. **Protective services:** Criminal justice. **Visual/performing arts:** Design.

Computing on campus. Online library available.

Student life. Freshman orientation: Available. Preregistration for classes offered.

Student services. Career counseling, student employment services, placement for graduates.

Contact. Phone: (937) 454-2267 Toll-free number: (800) 568-3241
Fax: (937) 454-2278
Joe Graham, Director of Recruitment, ITT Technical Institute: Dayton, 3325 Stop Eight Road, Dayton, OH 45414

ITT Technical Institute: Hilliard
Hilliard, Ohio
www.itt-tech.edu

▸ For-profit 2-year business and technical college
▸ Large town

General. Accredited by ACICS. **Enrollment:** 543 undergraduates. **Degrees:** 152 associate awarded. **Calendar:** Quarter. **Full-time faculty:** 10 total. **Part-time faculty:** 62 total.

Basis for selection. Secondary school record very important.

2011-2012 Annual costs. Estimated costs as of June 2011: per-credit-hour charge, $493, depending upon level and course of study; academic fee, $200. Certain programs of study require purchase of tools, which could cost an additional $100 to $655. All costs are subject to change.

Financial aid. Need-based: Work-study available nights, weekends and for part-time students.

Academics. Credit/placement by examination: AP, CLEP.

Majors. Business: Business admin. **Computer sciences:** Networking, programming, web page design. **Protective services:** Criminal justice. **Visual/performing arts:** Design.

Contact. ITT Technical Institute: Hilliard, 3781 Park Mill Run Drive, Suite 1, Hilliard, OH 43026

ITT Technical Institute: Norwood
Norwood, Ohio
www.itt-tech.edu   CB code: 2739

- For-profit 2-year technical college
- Commuter campus in large town
- Interview required

General. Accredited by ACICS. **Enrollment:** 699 undergraduates. **Degrees:** 189 associate awarded. **Calendar:** Quarter, extensive summer session. **Full-time faculty:** 14 total. **Part-time faculty:** 45 total.

Basis for selection. Satisfactory scores from on-site tests in English and mathematics required.

2011-2012 Annual costs. Estimated costs as of June 2011: per-credit-hour charge, $493, depending upon level and course of study; academic fee, $200. Certain programs of study require purchase of tools, which could cost an additional $100 to $500. All costs are subject to change.

Financial aid. Need-based: Work-study available nights, weekends and for part-time students.

Application procedures. Admission: No deadline. No application fee. Admission notification on a rolling basis. **Financial aid:** No deadline. FAFSA, institutional form required. Applicants notified on a rolling basis.

Academics. Credit/placement by examination: AP, CLEP. **Support services:** Learning center, tutoring.

Majors. Business: Accounting technology, business admin. **Computer sciences:** Computer graphics, networking, programming, web page design, webmaster. **Protective services:** Criminal justice. **Visual/performing arts:** Design.

Computing on campus. Online library available.

Student life. Freshman orientation: Available. Preregistration for classes offered.

Student services. Career counseling, student employment services, placement for graduates.

Contact. Phone: (513) 531-8300 Toll-free number: (800) 314-8324
Greg Hitt, Director of Recruitment, ITT Technical Institute: Norwood, 4750 Wesley Avenue, Norwood, OH 45212

ITT Technical Institute: Strongsville
Strongsville, Ohio
www.itt-tech.edu   CB code: 2773

- For-profit 2-year technical college
- Commuter campus in large town
- Interview required

General. Accredited by ACICS. **Enrollment:** 513 undergraduates. **Degrees:** 173 associate awarded. **Calendar:** Quarter, extensive summer session. **Full-time faculty:** 10 total. **Part-time faculty:** 46 total.

Basis for selection. Satisfactory scores from on-site tests in English and mathematics required.

2011-2012 Annual costs. Estimated costs as of June 2011: per-credit-hour charge, $493, depending upon level and course of study; academic fee, $200. Certain programs of study require purchase of tools, which could cost an additional $100 to $655. All costs are subject to change.

Financial aid. Need-based: Work-study available nights, weekends and for part-time students.

Application procedures. Admission: No deadline. No application fee. Admission notification on a rolling basis. **Financial aid:** No deadline. FAFSA, institutional form required. Applicants notified on a rolling basis.

Academics. Credit/placement by examination: AP, CLEP. **Support services:** Learning center, tutoring.

Majors. Business: Accounting technology, business admin. **Computer sciences:** Computer graphics, LAN/WAN management, networking, programming, web page design, webmaster. **Protective services:** Criminal justice. **Visual/performing arts:** Design.

Computing on campus. Online library available.

Student life. Freshman orientation: Available. Preregistration for classes offered.

Student services. Career counseling, student employment services, placement for graduates.

Contact. Phone: (440) 234-9091 Toll-free number: (800) 331-1488
Fax: (440) 234-7568
Joanne Dyer, Director of Recruitment, ITT Technical Institute: Strongsville, 14955 Sprague Road, Strongsville, OH 44136

ITT Technical Institute: Youngstown
Youngstown, Ohio
www.itt-tech.edu

- For-profit 2-year technical college
- Commuter campus in small city
- Interview required

General. Founded in 1967. Accredited by ACICS. **Enrollment:** 784 undergraduates. **Degrees:** 2 bachelor's, 227 associate awarded. **Location:** 60 miles from Cleveland, 60 miles from Pittsburgh. **Calendar:** Quarter, extensive summer session. **Full-time faculty:** 12 total. **Part-time faculty:** 74 total.

Basis for selection. Satisfactory scores from on-site tests in English and mathematics required.

2011-2012 Annual costs. Estimated costs as of June 2011: per-credit-hour charge, $493, depending upon level and course of study; academic fee, $200. Certain programs of study require purchase of tools, which could cost an additional $100 to $655. All costs are subject to change.

Financial aid. Need-based: Work-study available nights, weekends and for part-time students.

Application procedures. Admission: No deadline. No application fee. Admission notification on a rolling basis. **Financial aid:** No deadline. FAFSA, institutional form required. Applicants notified on a rolling basis.

Academics. Credit/placement by examination: AP, CLEP. **Support services:** Learning center, tutoring.

Majors. Business: Business admin. **Computer sciences:** LAN/WAN management, networking, programming, web page design, webmaster. **Protective services:** Law enforcement admin. **Visual/performing arts:** Design.

Computing on campus. Online library available.

Student life. Freshman orientation: Available. Preregistration for classes offered.

Student services. Career counseling, student employment services, placement for graduates.

Contact. Phone: (330) 270-1600 Toll-free number: (800) 832-5001
Fax: (330) 270-8333
Tom Flynn, Director of Recruitment, ITT Technical Institute: Youngstown, 1030 North Meridian Road, Youngstown, OH 44509

James A. Rhodes State College
Lima, Ohio
www.rhodesstate.edu   CB code: 0754

- Public 2-year community and technical college
- Commuter campus in large town

General. Founded in 1971. Regionally accredited. **Enrollment:** 3,679 degree-seeking undergraduates; 371 non-degree-seeking students. **Degrees:** 525 associate awarded. **Location:** 75 miles from Dayton, 75 miles from Toledo. **Calendar:** Quarter, limited summer session. **Full-time faculty:** 70 total; 4% have terminal degrees, 4% minority, 67% women. **Part-time faculty:** 165 total; 4% minority, 68% women. **Class size:** 66% < 20, 28% 20-39, 5% 40-49, 2% 50-99. **Special facilities:** Ambulance simulator. **Partnerships:** Formal partnerships with Central Ohio Regional Healthcare Alliance, Tech Prep/PSEOP, Ford Training Center, Lima City High School, Allen County Health Partners, Agile Manufacturing, West Ohio Manufacturing Consortium.

Student profile. Among degree-seeking undergraduates, 3% enrolled in a transfer program, 97% enrolled in a vocational program, 3% already have a bachelor's degree or higher, 669 enrolled as first-time, first-year students, 228 transferred in from other institutions.

Part-time:	42%	Asian American:	1%
Out-of-state:	1%	Hispanic American:	2%
Women:	70%	25 or older:	44%
African American:	8%	Live on campus:	1%

Transfer out. Colleges most students transferred to 2011: Ohio State University, Bowling Green State University, Wright State University, Owens Community College, Northwest State Community College.

Basis for selection. Open admission, but selective for some programs. Special requirements for nursing and health programs (ACT required); interview recommended. **Home schooled:** State high school equivalency certificate required. **Learning Disabled:** Students must self-disclose; accommodations are available.

High school preparation. Recommended units include English 4, mathematics 3, social studies 3 and science 3.

2011-2012 Annual costs. Tuition/fees: $4,413; $8,826 out-of-state. Per-credit charge: $98 in-state; $196 out-of-state. Books/supplies: $1,800. Personal expenses: $3,082.

Financial aid. **Need-based:** Need-based aid available for part-time students. Work-study available nights, weekends and for part-time students. **Non-need-based:** Scholarships awarded for academics.

Application procedures. **Admission:** No deadline. $25 fee ($25 out-of-state). Admission notification on a rolling basis. **Financial aid:** Priority date 2/15; no closing date. FAFSA required. Applicants notified on a rolling basis starting 5/1; must reply within 2 week(s) of notification.

Academics. **Special study options:** Cooperative education, cross-registration, distance learning, double major, dual enrollment of high school students, independent study, internships, liberal arts/career combination, student-designed major. License preparation in dental hygiene, nursing, occupational therapy, paramedic, physical therapy, radiology, real estate. **Credit/placement by examination:** AP, CLEP, institutional tests. 15 credit hours maximum toward associate degree. **Support services:** Learning center, pre-admission summer program, reduced course load, remedial instruction, study skills assistance, tutoring.

Majors. **Business:** General, accounting, administrative services, business admin, finance, management information systems, marketing, office management. **Computer sciences:** General, LAN/WAN management, networking, programming, security, web page design. **Education:** Early childhood. **Engineering:** General. **Health services:** Dental assistant, EMT paramedic, medical assistant, medical radiologic technology/radiation therapy, medical secretary, nursing (RN), occupational therapy assistant, office assistant, phlebotomy, physical therapy assistant, radiologic technology/medical imaging, respiratory therapy assistant. **Liberal arts:** Arts/sciences. **Protective services:** Corrections, law enforcement admin, police science. **Social sciences:** GIS/cartography. **Work/family studies:** Child development, family/community services.

Most popular majors. Business/marketing 18%, computer/information sciences 7%, engineering/engineering technologies 11%, health sciences 50%.

Computing on campus. 332 workstations in library, computer center. Commuter students can connect to campus network. Online course registration, online library, helpline, repair service, wireless network available.

Student life. **Freshman orientation:** Mandatory. Preregistration for classes offered. Orientation programs held before each quarter begins; specific dates and times mailed after application is made. **Activities:** Campus ministries, choral groups, drama, music ensembles, student government, academic area organizations, political party clubs, special interest clubs, fellowship and bible study.

Athletics. **Intramural:** Baseball M, basketball, bowling, football (non-tackle), softball, volleyball. **Team name:** Barons.

Student services. Career counseling, student employment services, financial aid counseling, on-campus daycare, placement for graduates, veterans' counselor. **Physically disabled:** Services for visually, speech, hearing impaired. **Transfer:** Pre-admission transcript evaluation for new students. College fairs on campus for students transferring to 4-year colleges.

Contact. E-mail: admissions@rhodesstate.edu
Phone: (419) 995-8320 Fax: (419) 995-8098
Traci Cox, Director of Admissions, James A. Rhodes State College, 4240 Campus Drive, PS 148, Lima, OH 45804-3597

Kaplan College: Columbus
Columbus, Ohio
www.kc-columbus.com
CB code: 3035

- For-profit 2-year technical and career college
- Commuter campus in very large city
- Application essay, interview required

General. Accredited by ACCSC. **Degrees:** 68 associate awarded. **Calendar:** Quarter, extensive summer session. **Full-time faculty:** 2 total. **Part-time faculty:** 37 total.

Basis for selection. Open admission.

Financial aid. All financial aid based on need. Need-based aid available for part-time students. Work-study available nights, weekends and for part-time students.

Application procedures. **Admission:** No deadline. $10 fee. Admission notification on a rolling basis. **Financial aid:** No deadline. FAFSA, institutional form required. Applicants notified on a rolling basis.

Academics. **Credit/placement by examination:** AP, CLEP. **Support services:** GED preparation, learning center, study skills assistance, tutoring.

Majors. **Health services:** Medical assistant. **Protective services:** Police science.

Computing on campus. 100 workstations in library, computer center, student center. Online library, helpline available.

Student life. **Freshman orientation:** Mandatory. Preregistration for classes offered.

Student services. Career counseling, student employment services, financial aid counseling, personal counseling, placement for graduates.

Contact. Phone: (614) 456-4600 Toll-free number: (800) 838-3233
Fax: (614) 456-4640
Angela Turner, Director of Admissions, Kaplan College: Columbus, 2745 Winchester Pike, Columbus, OH 43232

Kaplan College: Dayton
Dayton, Ohio
www.dayton.kaplancollege.com
CB code: 3380

- For-profit 2-year technical college
- Commuter campus in very large city
- Interview required

General. Founded in 1971. Accredited by ACCSC. **Enrollment:** 406 undergraduates. **Degrees:** 126 associate awarded. **Location:** 55 miles from Cincinnati, 80 miles from Columbus. **Calendar:** Quarter, extensive summer session. **Full-time faculty:** 36 total; 17% minority, 58% women. **Part-time faculty:** 32 total; 12% minority, 38% women. **Special facilities:** Photographic laboratories and computer laboratory for digital imaging, pharmacy technician laboratory, dental assisting laboratory and stick house for Electrical Technician program.

Student profile.

Out-of-state:	19%	25 or older:	33%

Basis for selection. Open admission, but selective for some programs. Entrance exam and interview required. Criminal Justice or Pharmacy Technician programs must also pass a background check. Essay and portfolio recommended.

2011-2012 Annual costs. Books/supplies: $1,350. Personal expenses: $1,701.

Financial aid. **Need-based:** Need-based aid available for part-time students. Work-study available nights, weekends and for part-time students.

Application procedures. **Admission:** No deadline. $10 fee. Admission notification on a rolling basis. **Financial aid:** No deadline. FAFSA, institutional form required. Applicants notified on a rolling basis starting 3/1.

Academics. Training directed toward technical and professional aspects of photography. **Special study options:** Double major, internships. **Credit/placement by examination:** AP, CLEP. **Support services:** GED preparation, tutoring.

Majors. Computer sciences: Networking. **Protective services:** Law enforcement admin. **Visual/performing arts:** Commercial photography, photography.

Computing on campus. 36 workstations in library. Online library available.

Student life. Freshman orientation: Available. Preregistration for classes offered. Held for 3 hours, prior to first day of classes.

Student services. Adult student services, career counseling, student employment services, financial aid counseling, placement for graduates. **Transfer:** Pre-admission transcript evaluation for new students. Transfer adviser for students transferring to 4-year colleges.

Contact. Phone: (937) 294-6155 Toll-free number: (800) 932-9698 Fax: (937) 294-2259
Curtis Kirby, Director of Admissions, Kaplan College: Dayton, 2800 East River Road, Dayton, OH 45439

Kent State University: Ashtabula
Ashtabula, Ohio
www.ashtabula.kent.edu　　　　　　**CB code: 1485**

▶ Public 2-year branch campus college
▶ Commuter campus in large town

General. Founded in 1958. Regionally accredited. Off-site courses available. **Enrollment:** 2,375 degree-seeking undergraduates; 76 non-degree-seeking students. **Degrees:** 188 associate awarded. **Location:** 50 miles from Cleveland. **Calendar:** Semester, limited summer session. **Full-time faculty:** 52 total; 4% minority, 56% women. **Part-time faculty:** 74 total; 4% minority, 65% women. **Class size:** 51% < 20, 41% 20-39, 5% 40-49, 3% 50-99, less than 1% >100. **Special facilities:** Interactive television link with all county high schools.

Student profile. Among degree-seeking undergraduates, 419 enrolled as first-time, first-year students, 204 transferred in from other institutions.

Part-time:	49%	Asian American:	1%
Out-of-state:	2%	Hispanic American:	3%
Women:	65%	25 or older:	57%
African American:	7%		

Transfer out. Colleges most students transferred to 2011: Lakeland Community College, Mount Union College, University of Akron.

Basis for selection. Open admission, but selective for some programs. Special requirements for nursing, human services, physical therapy assisting programs. **Home schooled:** Transcript of courses and grades required.

High school preparation. College-preparatory program recommended. 16 units recommended. Recommended units include English 4, mathematics 3, social studies 3, science 3 (laboratory 2), foreign language 2 and visual/performing arts 1. One art unit recommended.

2011-2012 Annual costs. Tuition/fees: $5,288; $13,248 out-of-state. Per-credit charge: $241 in-state; $603 out-of-state. Books/supplies: $1,320. Personal expenses: $2,400.

2011-2012 Financial aid. Need-based: 250 full-time freshmen applied for aid; 240 were judged to have need; 238 of these received aid. Average need met was 45%. Average scholarship/grant was $4,813; average loan $3,031. 50% of total undergraduate aid awarded as scholarships/grants, 50% as loans/jobs. Need-based aid available for part-time students. Work-study available nights, weekends and for part-time students. **Non-need-based:** Awarded to 31 full-time undergraduates, including 9 freshmen. Scholarships awarded for academics, alumni affiliation, art, athletics, job skills, leadership, minority status, music/drama, ROTC, state residency.

Application procedures. Admission: No deadline. $30 fee, may be waived for applicants with need. Admission notification on a rolling basis beginning on or about 10/1. **Financial aid:** Priority date 3/1; no closing date. FAFSA required. Applicants notified on a rolling basis starting 3/15; must reply within 2 week(s) of notification.

Academics. Special study options: Accelerated study, distance learning, double major, dual enrollment of high school students, independent study, internships, liberal arts/career combination, New York semester, student-designed major, Washington semester. Bachelor's degree programs available on campus. License preparation in nursing, occupational therapy, physical therapy, radiology. **Credit/placement by examination:** AP, CLEP, institutional tests. 12 credit hours maximum toward associate degree. **Support services:** Learning center, remedial instruction, tutoring.

Majors. Business: General, accounting technology, administrative services. **Computer sciences:** Applications programming. **Education:** Early childhood. **Health services:** Health care admin, nursing (RN), physical therapy assistant, preop/surgical nursing. **Liberal arts:** Arts/sciences. **Protective services:** Criminal justice.

Most popular majors. Business/marketing 11%, health sciences 64%, liberal arts 15%.

Computing on campus. 82 workstations in library, computer center. Online course registration, online library, helpline, student web hosting available.

Student life. Freshman orientation: Available. Preregistration for classes offered. **Activities:** Literary magazine, student government, TV station, world affairs club, social issues club.

Athletics. Intramural: Basketball, football (non-tackle), softball W, volleyball, weight lifting. **Team name:** Golden Flashes.

Student services. Adult student services, career counseling, student employment services, on-campus daycare, personal counseling, placement for graduates, veterans' counselor. **Physically disabled:** Services for visually impaired. **Transfer:** Transfer adviser for students transferring to 4-year colleges.

Contact. E-mail: tdhanna@kent.edu
Phone: (440) 964-4217 Toll-free number: (800) 988-5368
Fax: (440) 964-4269
Kelly Anthony, Director, Enrollment Management, Kent State University: Ashtabula, 3300 Lake Road West, Ashtabula, OH 44004

Kent State University: East Liverpool
East Liverpool, Ohio
www.eliv.kent.edu　　　　　　**CB code: 0328**

▶ Public 2-year branch campus college
▶ Commuter campus in large town

General. Founded in 1965. Regionally accredited. **Enrollment:** 1,357 degree-seeking undergraduates; 134 non-degree-seeking students. **Degrees:** 124 associate awarded. **Location:** 45 miles from Youngstown, 40 miles from Pittsburgh. **Calendar:** Semester, extensive summer session. **Full-time faculty:** 26 total; 4% minority, 54% women. **Part-time faculty:** 51 total; 63% women. **Class size:** 66% < 20, 31% 20-39, 2% 40-49, 2% 50-99.

Student profile. Among degree-seeking undergraduates, 146 enrolled as first-time, first-year students, 90 transferred in from other institutions.

Part-time:	36%	African American:	4%
Out-of-state:	5%	Hispanic American:	1%
Women:	70%	25 or older:	50%

Transfer out. Colleges most students transferred to 2011: Youngstown State University, Jefferson Community College, West Virginia Northern Community College, Hannah Mullins School of Nursing.

Basis for selection. Open admission, but selective for some programs. Special requirements for nursing, occupational therapy, and physical therapy applicants. Interview recommended. **Home schooled:** Transcript of courses and grades required.

High school preparation. College-preparatory program recommended. 16 units recommended. Recommended units include English 4, mathematics 3, social studies 3, science 3 (laboratory 2), foreign language 2 and visual/performing arts 1. One unit algebra, 1 unit chemistry, 1 unit biology required for nursing applicants. One unit algebra, 1 unit biology required for physical therapy and occupational therapy. One art unit recommended for all.

2011-2012 Annual costs. Tuition/fees: $5,288; $13,248 out-of-state. Per-credit charge: $241 in-state; $603 out-of-state. Books/supplies: $550. Personal expenses: $2,400.

2011-2012 Financial aid. Need-based: 123 full-time freshmen applied for aid; 117 were judged to have need; 115 of these received aid. Average need met was 49%. Average scholarship/grant was $4,742; average loan $3,140. 52% of total undergraduate aid awarded as scholarships/grants, 48% as loans/jobs. Need-based aid available for part-time students. Work-study available nights, weekends and for part-time students. **Non-need-based:** Awarded to 22 full-time undergraduates, including 2 freshmen. Scholarships awarded for academics, alumni affiliation, art, athletics, leadership, minority status, music/drama, ROTC, state residency.

Application procedures. Admission: Priority date 8/1; no deadline. $30 fee, may be waived for applicants with need. Admission notification on a

rolling basis beginning on or about 9/15. All new applicants must complete basic skills assessment tests. **Financial aid:** Priority date 3/1; no closing date. FAFSA required. Applicants notified on a rolling basis starting 3/15; must reply within 2 week(s) of notification.

Academics. Special study options: Accelerated study, distance learning, double major, dual enrollment of high school students, honors, independent study, internships, New York semester, student-designed major, Washington semester. Bachelor's degree programs available on campus. License preparation in nursing, occupational therapy, physical therapy. **Credit/placement by examination:** AP, CLEP, institutional tests. 14 credit hours maximum toward associate degree. **Support services:** Learning center, pre-admission summer program, reduced course load, remedial instruction, study skills assistance, tutoring, writing center.

Honors college/program. 3.5 GPA, 24 ACT, recommendation, interview, placement exam required. Various course offerings plus Freshman Year Colloquium to replace university composition requirement.

Majors. Business: General, accounting technology. **Computer sciences:** Applications programming. **Health services:** Nursing (RN), occupational therapy assistant, physical therapy assistant. **Liberal arts:** Arts/sciences. **Protective services:** Criminal justice.

Most popular majors. Computer/information sciences 6%, health sciences 73%, history 6%, liberal arts 7%.

Computing on campus. 114 workstations in library, computer center. Online course registration, online library, helpline, student web hosting available.

Student life. Freshman orientation: Available. Preregistration for classes offered. **Activities:** Student government, student newspaper.

Athletics. Team name: Golden Flashes.

Student services. Career counseling, student employment services, placement for graduates, veterans' counselor. **Transfer:** Transfer adviser, college fairs on campus for students transferring to 4-year colleges.

Contact. E-mail: admissions@eliv.kent.edu
Phone: (330) 382-7400 Toll-free number: (800) 988-5368
Fax: (330) 382-7562
Michelle Lingenfelter, Director, Enrollment Management, Kent State University: East Liverpool, 400 East Fourth Street, East Liverpool, OH 43920

Kent State University: Geauga
Burton, Ohio
www.geauga.kent.edu   CB code: 6979

▸ Public 2-year branch campus college
▸ Commuter campus in rural community

General. Regionally accredited. **Enrollment:** 2,422 degree-seeking undergraduates; 155 non-degree-seeking students. **Degrees:** 83 associate awarded. **Calendar:** Semester. **Full-time faculty:** 28 total; 7% have terminal degrees, 7% minority, 71% women. **Part-time faculty:** 98 total; 12% minority, 53% women. **Class size:** 68% < 20, 32% 20-39.

Student profile. Among degree-seeking undergraduates, 264 enrolled as first-time, first-year students, 154 transferred in from other institutions.

Part-time:	41%	Hispanic American:	2%
Out-of-state:	1%	Native American:	1%
Women:	67%	International:	1%
African American:	10%	25 or older:	46%
Asian American:	1%	Live on campus:	1%

Basis for selection. Open admission, but selective for some programs. Special requirements for nursing progams. **Home schooled:** Transcript of courses and grades required.

High school preparation. College-preparatory program recommended. 16 units recommended. Recommended units include English 4, mathematics 3, social studies 3, science 3 (laboratory 2), foreign language 2 and visual/performing arts 1.

2011-2012 Annual costs. Tuition/fees: $5,288; $13,248 out-of-state. Per-credit charge: $241 in-state; $603 out-of-state. Books/supplies: $1,280. Personal expenses: $2,400.

2011-2012 Financial aid. Need-based: 165 full-time freshmen applied for aid; 144 were judged to have need; 144 of these received aid. Average need met was 45%. Average scholarship/grant was $4,150; average loan

$3,112. 43% of total undergraduate aid awarded as scholarships/grants, 57% as loans/jobs. Need-based aid available for part-time students. Work-study available nights, weekends and for part-time students. **Non-need-based:** Awarded to 23 full-time undergraduates, including 3 freshmen. Scholarships awarded for academics, alumni affiliation, art, athletics, leadership, minority status, music/drama, ROTC, state residency.

Application procedures. Admission: No deadline. $30 fee, may be waived for applicants with need. Admission notification on a rolling basis beginning on or about 9/15. **Financial aid:** Priority date 3/1; no closing date. FAFSA required. Must reply within 2 week(s) of notification.

Academics. Special study options: Accelerated study, distance learning, double major, dual enrollment of high school students, internships, New York semester, student-designed major, teacher certification program, Washington semester, weekend college. License preparation in nursing. **Credit/placement by examination:** AP, CLEP, institutional tests. 30 credit hours maximum toward bachelor's degree. **Support services:** Learning center, pre-admission summer program, reduced course load, remedial instruction, study skills assistance, tutoring, writing center.

Honors college/program. 3.5 GPA, 24 ACT, recommendation, interview, placement exam required. Various course offerings, freshman year colloquium to replace university composition requirement.

Majors. General: Horticultural science. **Health services:** EMT paramedic. **Liberal arts:** Arts/sciences.

Most popular majors. Computer/information sciences 18%, health sciences 67%, liberal arts 13%.

Computing on campus. Online course registration, online library, helpline, student web hosting available.

Student life. Freshman orientation: Available. Preregistration for classes offered. **Activities:** Campus ministries, student government.

Athletics. Team name: Golden Flashes.

Student services. Physically disabled: Services for visually, speech, hearing impaired. **Transfer:** Transfer adviser, college fairs on campus for students transferring to 4-year colleges.

Contact. E-mail: info@geauga.kent.edu
Phone: (440) 834-3716 Toll-free number: (800) 988-5368
Thomas Hoiles, Director, Enrollment Management, Kent State University: Geauga, Office of Admissions, Burton, OH 44021

Kent State University: Salem
Salem, Ohio
www.salem.kent.edu   CB code: 0683

▸ Public 2-year branch campus college
▸ Commuter campus in large town

General. Founded in 1962. Regionally accredited. **Enrollment:** 1,851 degree-seeking undergraduates; 167 non-degree-seeking students. **Degrees:** 38 bachelor's, 115 associate awarded. **Location:** 25 miles from Youngstown, 40 miles from Canton. **Calendar:** Semester, limited summer session. **Full-time faculty:** 45 total; 2% minority, 56% women. **Part-time faculty:** 88 total; 68% women. **Class size:** 70% < 20, 28% 20-39, 2% 40-49. **Special facilities:** Writers' workshop, science and math lab, academic center.

Student profile. Among degree-seeking undergraduates, 267 enrolled as first-time, first-year students, 148 transferred in from other institutions.

Part-time:	28%	Asian American:	1%
Out-of-state:	1%	Hispanic American:	2%
Women:	72%	Native American:	1%
African American:	4%	25 or older:	46%

Transfer out. Colleges most students transferred to 2011: Youngstown State University, Stark State College of Technology, University of Akron, Ohio State University, ITT Technical Institute.

Basis for selection. Open admission, but selective for some programs. Radiologic technology program requires 2.5 GPA, completion of certain courses, SAT/ACT. Nursing program requires 2.5 GPA, SAT/ACT. **Home schooled:** Transcript of courses and grades required.

High school preparation. College-preparatory program recommended. 16 units recommended. Recommended units include English 4, mathematics 3, social studies 3, science 3 (laboratory 2), foreign language 2 and visual/performing arts 1. One visual or performing arts may be substituted for 1 foreign language.

2011-2012 Annual costs. Tuition/fees: $5,288; $13,248 out-of-state. Per-credit charge: $241 in-state; $603 out-of-state. Books/supplies: $700. Personal expenses: $2,400.

2011-2012 Financial aid. Need-based: 233 full-time freshmen applied for aid; 219 were judged to have need; 219 of these received aid. Average need met was 46%. Average scholarship/grant was $4,142; average loan $3,052. 49% of total undergraduate aid awarded as scholarships/grants, 51% as loans/jobs. Need-based aid available for part-time students. Work-study available nights, weekends and for part-time students. **Non-need-based:** Awarded to 34 full-time undergraduates, including 11 freshmen. Scholarships awarded for academics, alumni affiliation, art, athletics, leadership, minority status, music/drama, ROTC.

Application procedures. Admission: Priority date 8/1; no deadline. $30 fee, may be waived for applicants with need. Admission notification on a rolling basis beginning on or about 10/1. **Financial aid:** Priority date 3/1; no closing date. FAFSA required. Applicants notified on a rolling basis starting 3/15; must reply within 2 week(s) of notification.

Academics. Special study options: Accelerated study, cooperative education, cross-registration, distance learning, double major, dual enrollment of high school students, independent study, internships, liberal arts/career combination, New York semester, study abroad, teacher certification program, Washington semester, weekend college. Bachelor's degree programs available on campus. License preparation in radiology. **Credit/placement by examination:** AP, CLEP, institutional tests. 24 credit hours maximum toward associate degree. **Support services:** Learning center, remedial instruction, study skills assistance, tutoring, writing center.

Honors college/program. 17 students admitted each year. 3.3 GPA and 23 ACT required. Full tuition scholarships awarded; renewable for 1 additional year.

Majors. Business: General, administrative services. **Computer sciences:** Applications programming. **Education:** Elementary. **General:** Horticulture. **Health services:** Health care admin, medical radiologic technology/radiation therapy, nuclear medical technology. **Liberal arts:** Arts/sciences. **Protective services:** Criminal justice.

Most popular majors. Business/marketing 13%, computer/information sciences 11%, education 22%, health sciences 37%, liberal arts 10%.

Computing on campus. 118 workstations in library, computer center. Commuter students can connect to campus network. Online course registration, online library, helpline, student web hosting available.

Student life. Freshman orientation: Available. Preregistration for classes offered. **Activities:** Campus ministries, choral groups, student government, professional business and engineering clubs, art club, nontraditional student club, ski club, Women of Wonder, horticulture, criminal justice club, psychology club.

Athletics. Intramural: Basketball, racquetball, skiing, table tennis, tennis, volleyball. **Team name:** Golden Flashes.

Student services. Adult student services, career counseling, financial aid counseling, personal counseling, placement for graduates, veterans' counselor. **Physically disabled:** Services for visually, hearing impaired. **Transfer:** Transfer adviser for students transferring to 4-year colleges.

Contact. E-mail: ask-us@salem.kent.edu
Phone: (330) 332-0361 Toll-free number: (800) 988-5368
Fax: (330) 332-9256
Michelle Lingenfelter, Director, Enrollment Management and Student Services, Kent State University: Salem, 2491 State Route 45 South, Salem, OH 44460

Kent State University: Stark
Canton, Ohio
www.stark.kent.edu   CB code: 0585

- Public 2-year branch campus college
- Commuter campus in small city

General. Founded in 1946. Regionally accredited. **Enrollment:** 4,651 degree-seeking undergraduates; 217 non-degree-seeking students. **Degrees:** 93 associate awarded. **ROTC:** Army, Air Force. **Location:** 14 miles from Akron, 60 miles from Cleveland. **Calendar:** Semester, limited summer session. **Full-time faculty:** 106 total; 3% minority, 52% women. **Part-time faculty:** 156 total; 3% minority, 49% women. **Class size:** 44% < 20, 47% 20-39, 6% 40-49, 3% 50-99, less than 1% >100.

Student profile. Among degree-seeking undergraduates, 736 enrolled as first-time, first-year students, 438 transferred in from other institutions.

Part-time:	32%	Asian American:	1%
Out-of-state:	1%	Hispanic American:	2%
Women:	60%	25 or older:	36%
African American:	8%		

Basis for selection. Open admission, but selective for some programs. Special requirements for honors college, art, music, education, nursing, business. Essay required for honors college, early admission; audition required for music programs; portfolio required for art programs.

High school preparation. College-preparatory program recommended. 16 units recommended. Recommended units include English 4, mathematics 3, social studies 3, science 3 (laboratory 2), foreign language 2 and visual/performing arts 1. One unit of fine arts may be substituted for 1 unit of foreign language; math units should be in algebra I & II and geometry.

2011-2012 Annual costs. Tuition/fees: $5,288; $13,248 out-of-state. Per-credit charge: $241 in-state; $603 out-of-state. Books/supplies: $1,140. Personal expenses: $2,400.

2011-2012 Financial aid. Need-based: 565 full-time freshmen applied for aid; 505 were judged to have need; 504 of these received aid. Average need met was 49%. Average scholarship/grant was $4,154; average loan $2,842. 48% of total undergraduate aid awarded as scholarships/grants, 52% as loans/jobs. Need-based aid available for part-time students. Work-study available nights, weekends and for part-time students. **Non-need-based:** Awarded to 219 full-time undergraduates, including 56 freshmen. Scholarships awarded for academics, alumni affiliation, art, athletics, leadership, minority status, music/drama, ROTC, state residency.

Application procedures. Admission: No deadline. $30 fee, may be waived for applicants with need. Admission notification on a rolling basis beginning on or about 9/15. Early admission available to high school juniors or seniors in top 15% of class with 24 ACT and 3.4 GPA through Ohio PSEO Program. **Financial aid:** Priority date 3/1; no closing date. FAFSA required. Applicants notified on a rolling basis starting 3/15; must reply within 2 week(s) of notification.

Academics. Special study options: Cross-registration, distance learning, double major, dual enrollment of high school students, independent study, internships, New York semester, student-designed major, Washington semester. Bachelor's degree programs available on campus. **Credit/placement by examination:** AP, CLEP, institutional tests. 24 credit hours maximum toward associate degree, 30 toward bachelor's. **Support services:** Learning center, reduced course load, remedial instruction, study skills assistance, tutoring, writing center.

Honors college/program. 3.2 GPA, essay, 24 ACT required.

Majors. Liberal arts: Arts/sciences. **Protective services:** Criminal justice.

Most popular majors. Liberal arts 85%, security/protective services 14%.

Computing on campus. 145 workstations in library, computer center, student center. Commuter students can connect to campus network. Online course registration, online library, helpline, student web hosting available.

Student life. Freshman orientation: Mandatory. Preregistration for classes offered. **Activities:** Campus ministries, choral groups, drama, literary magazine, music ensembles, musical theater, opera, student government, political science forum, Academy of Life Sciences, student education association, Pan African student alliance.

Athletics. Team name: Golden Flashes.

Student services. Chaplain/spiritual director, career counseling, student employment services, financial aid counseling, personal counseling, veterans' counselor. **Physically disabled:** Services for visually, speech, hearing impaired. **Transfer:** Transfer adviser for students transferring to 4-year colleges.

Contact. E-mail: admit@stark.kent.edu
Phone: (330) 499-9600 Fax: (330) 494-0301
Deborah Speck, Director, Enrollment Management, Kent State University: Stark, 6000 Frank Avenue NW, Canton, OH 44720-7599

Kent State University: Trumbull
Warren, Ohio
www.trumbull.kent.edu   CB code: 0593

- Public 2-year branch campus college
- Commuter campus in small city

General. Founded in 1954. Regionally accredited. **Enrollment:** 3,104 degree-seeking undergraduates; 101 non-degree-seeking students. **Degrees:** 101 associate awarded. **Location:** 2 miles from downtown. **Calendar:** Semester, limited summer session. **Full-time faculty:** 58 total; 3% minority, 45% women. **Part-time faculty:** 70 total; 43% women. **Class size:** 45% < 20, 43% 20-39, 6% 40-49, 6% 50-99.

Student profile. Among degree-seeking undergraduates, 392 enrolled as first-time, first-year students, 232 transferred in from other institutions.

Part-time:	37%	Asian American:	1%
Out-of-state:	1%	Hispanic American:	2%
Women:	64%	25 or older:	51%
African American:	12%		

Basis for selection. Open admission, but selective for some programs. Interview recommended. **Home schooled:** Transcript of courses and grades required.

High school preparation. College-preparatory program recommended. 16 units recommended. Recommended units include English 4, mathematics 3, social studies 3, science 3 (laboratory 2), foreign language 2 and visual/performing arts 1. 1 art recommended.

2011-2012 Annual costs. Tuition/fees: $5,288; $13,248 out-of-state. Per-credit charge: $241 in-state; $603 out-of-state. Books/supplies: $990. Personal expenses: $2,400.

2011-2012 Financial aid. Need-based: 291 full-time freshmen applied for aid; 276 were judged to have need; 276 of these received aid. Average need met was 44%. Average scholarship/grant was $4,810; average loan $3,106. 51% of total undergraduate aid awarded as scholarships/grants, 49% as loans/jobs. Need-based aid available for part-time students. Work-study available nights, weekends and for part-time students. **Non-need-based:** Awarded to 37 full-time undergraduates, including 8 freshmen. Scholarships awarded for academics, alumni affiliation, art, athletics, leadership, minority status, music/drama, ROTC, state residency.

Application procedures. Admission: No deadline. $30 fee, may be waived for applicants with need. Admission notification on a rolling basis beginning on or about 10/1. International students must apply through main campus at Kent. Current high school students eligible for part-time early admission with a 3.5 GPA, 26 ACT, and letter of recommendation. **Financial aid:** Priority date 3/1; no closing date. FAFSA required. Applicants notified on a rolling basis starting 3/15; must reply within 2 week(s) of notification.

Academics. Special study options: Cross-registration, distance learning, double major, dual enrollment of high school students, honors, independent study, internships, New York semester, student-designed major, Washington semester. License preparation in nursing. **Credit/placement by examination:** AP, CLEP, IB, institutional tests. 6 credit hours maximum toward associate degree. **Support services:** Learning center, pre-admission summer program, reduced course load, remedial instruction, tutoring.

Majors. Biology: General. **Business:** General, accounting technology, administrative services, office technology, office/clerical. **Computer sciences:** Applications programming. **Liberal arts:** Arts/sciences. **Protective services:** Criminal justice.

Most popular majors. Business/marketing 34%, computer/information sciences 18%, engineering/engineering technologies 9%, liberal arts 29%, security/protective services 6%.

Computing on campus. 265 workstations in library, computer center. Online course registration, online library, helpline, student web hosting available.

Student life. Freshman orientation: Available. Preregistration for classes offered. **Activities:** Drama, film society, literary magazine, musical theater, nontraditional student and minority student organizations, independent black/minority coalition, Christian Fellowship, environmental council, alcohol, drugs and AIDS awareness programs.

Athletics. NJCAA. **Team name:** Golden Flashes.

Student services. Adult student services, career counseling, student employment services, health services, personal counseling, placement for graduates, veterans' counselor. **Physically disabled:** Services for visually, speech, hearing impaired. **Transfer:** Transfer adviser, college fairs on campus for students transferring to 4-year colleges.

Contact. E-mail: ntreffer@kent.edu
Phone: (330) 847-0571 Toll-free number: (800) 988-5368
Fax: (330) 847-6571
Alison Hoskinson, Assistant Director, Kent State University: Trumbull, 4314 Mahoning Avenue, NW, Warren, OH 44483-1998

Kent State University: Tuscarawas
New Philadelphia, Ohio
www.tusc.kent.edu   CB code: 1434

▶ Public 2-year branch campus college
▶ Commuter campus in large town

General. Founded in 1962. Regionally accredited. **Enrollment:** 2,312 degree-seeking undergraduates; 347 non-degree-seeking students. **Degrees:** 251 associate awarded. **ROTC:** Army, Air Force. **Location:** 80 miles from Cleveland. **Calendar:** Semester, limited summer session. **Full-time faculty:** 54 total; 4% minority, 50% women. **Part-time faculty:** 85 total; 1% minority, 49% women. **Class size:** 39% < 20, 47% 20-39, 7% 40-49, 8% 50-99. **Partnerships:** Formal partnership with Buckeye Career Center engaged in Tech Prep program.

Student profile. Among degree-seeking undergraduates, 401 enrolled as first-time, first-year students, 163 transferred in from other institutions.

Part-time:	38%	Hispanic American:	1%
Out-of-state:	1%	25 or older:	46%
Women:	61%	Live on campus:	1%
African American:	2%		

Basis for selection. Open admission, but selective for some programs and for out-of-state students. Special requirements for nursing program. **Adult students:** Test scores not required for placement if applicant is over 21 years of age.

High school preparation. College-preparatory program recommended. 16 units recommended. Recommended units include English 4, mathematics 3, social studies 3, science 3 (laboratory 2) and foreign language 2. One arts unit recommended.

2011-2012 Annual costs. Tuition/fees: $5,288; $13,248 out-of-state. Per-credit charge: $241 in-state; $603 out-of-state. Books/supplies: $700. Personal expenses: $2,400.

2011-2012 Financial aid. Need-based: 297 full-time freshmen applied for aid; 276 were judged to have need; 275 of these received aid. Average need met was 49%. Average scholarship/grant was $4,275; average loan $2,968. 51% of total undergraduate aid awarded as scholarships/grants, 49% as loans/jobs. Need-based aid available for part-time students. Work-study available nights, weekends and for part-time students. **Non-need-based:** Awarded to 51 full-time undergraduates, including 13 freshmen. Scholarships awarded for academics, alumni affiliation, art, athletics, leadership, minority status, music/drama, ROTC.

Application procedures. Admission: No deadline. $30 fee, may be waived for applicants with need. Admission notification on a rolling basis beginning on or about 9/15. **Financial aid:** Closing date 3/1. FAFSA required. Applicants notified on a rolling basis starting 3/15; must reply within 2 week(s) of notification.

Academics. Special study options: Accelerated study, distance learning, double major, dual enrollment of high school students, honors, independent study, internships, New York semester, student-designed major, Washington semester. License preparation in nursing. **Credit/placement by examination:** AP, CLEP, institutional tests. 15 credit hours maximum toward associate degree, 30 toward bachelor's. **Support services:** Learning center, reduced course load, remedial instruction, study skills assistance, tutoring, writing center.

Majors. Business: General, accounting technology, administrative services. **Computer sciences:** Applications programming. **Education:** Early childhood. **Health services:** Nursing (RN). **Liberal arts:** Arts/sciences. **Protective services:** Criminal justice.

Most popular majors. Business/marketing 7%, computer/information sciences 8%, education 7%, engineering/engineering technologies 14%, health sciences 29%, liberal arts 29%.

Computing on campus. 300 workstations in library, computer center. Online course registration, online library, helpline, student web hosting available.

Student life. Freshman orientation: Mandatory. Preregistration for classes offered. **Activities:** Campus ministries, choral groups, dance, drama, international student organizations, musical theater, student government.

Athletics. Intramural: Basketball M, volleyball. **Team name:** Golden Flashes.

Student services. Career counseling, student employment services, on-campus daycare. **Physically disabled:** Services for visually, hearing impaired. **Transfer:** Transfer adviser for students transferring to 4-year colleges.

Contact. E-mail: info@tusc.kent.edu
Phone: (330) 339-3391 ext. 47425 Fax: (330) 339-3321
Laurie Donley, Director of Enrollment Management, Kent State
University: Tuscarawas, 330 University Drive NE, New Philadelphia, OH
44663-9403

Lakeland Community College
Kirtland, Ohio   CB member
www.lakelandcc.edu   CB code: 1422

- Public 2-year community college
- Commuter campus in large town

General. Founded in 1967. Regionally accredited. **Enrollment:** 9,611
degree-seeking undergraduates. **Degrees:** 938 associate awarded. **Location:**
15 miles from Cleveland. **Calendar:** Semester, extensive summer session.
Full-time faculty: 130 total. **Part-time faculty:** 653 total. **Special facilities:**
Planetarium, observatory, licensed preschool program, laboratory.

Student profile.

Out-of-state: 1%   25 or older: 48%

Transfer out. Colleges most students transferred to 2011: Cleveland
State University, University of Akron, Kent State University, Ohio State
University, John Carroll University.

Basis for selection. Open admission, but selective for some programs.
Admissions to health technology programs based on test scores and school
achievement record.

High school preparation. College-preparatory program recommended.
Recommended units include English 4, mathematics 3, social studies 3,
science 3 and foreign language 2. Health technology programs require algebra,
biology, chemistry.

2011-2012 Annual costs. Tuition/fees: $2,917; $3,766 out-of-district;
$8,053 out-of-state. Per-credit charge: $85 in-district; $113 out-of-district;
$256 out-of-state. Books/supplies: $1,200. Personal expenses: $1,441.

Financial aid. Need-based: Need-based aid available for part-time students. Work-study available nights, weekends and for part-time students.
Non-need-based: Scholarships awarded for academics, art, athletics, job
skills, leadership, minority status, music/drama, state residency. **Additional
information:** Loans available for tuition and books.

Application procedures. Admission: No deadline. $15 fee, may be
waived for applicants with need. Admission notification on a rolling basis.
Financial aid: Closing date 3/1. FAFSA, institutional form required. Applicants notified on a rolling basis starting 5/1.

Academics. Special study options: Accelerated study, cooperative education, cross-registration, distance learning, dual enrollment of high school
students, ESL, independent study, internships, liberal arts/career combination,
weekend college. Bachelor's degree programs available on campus. License
preparation in dental hygiene, nursing, paramedic, radiology, real estate.
Credit/placement by examination: AP, CLEP, institutional tests. 44 credit
hours maximum toward associate degree. **Support services:** Learning center,
reduced course load, remedial instruction, study skills assistance, tutoring.

Majors. Biology: Biotechnology. **Business:** Accounting, administrative services, business admin, e-commerce, hospitality admin, management information systems, small business admin, tourism promotion, tourism/travel. **Computer sciences:** Information systems, LAN/WAN management, programming, web page design. **Education:** Early childhood. **Health services:**
Clinical lab technology, dental hygiene, histologic technology, medical radiologic technology/radiation therapy, nursing (RN), ophthalmic lab technology,
optician, respiratory therapy technology, surgical technology. **Liberal arts:**
Arts/sciences. **Protective services:** Corrections, firefighting, police science,
security services. **Visual/performing arts:** Commercial/advertising art.
Work/family studies: Child care management.

Most popular majors. Business/marketing 10%, engineering/engineering
technologies 6%, health sciences 22%, liberal arts 48%.

Computing on campus. PC or laptop required. 500 workstations in
library, computer center, student center. Commuter students can connect to
campus network. Online course registration, online library, helpline, repair
service, wireless network available.

Student life. Freshman orientation: Available. Preregistration for classes
offered. **Activities:** Bands, choral groups, drama, international student organizations, music ensembles, Model UN, radio station, student government,
student newspaper, TV station, Access Unlimited, minority student union,
Newman Catholic student association, La Tertulia.

Athletics. NJCAA. **Intercollegiate:** Baseball M, basketball, golf M, soccer
M, softball W, volleyball W. **Team name:** Lakers.

Student services. Adult student services, career counseling, student
employment services, financial aid counseling, health services, on-campus
daycare, personal counseling, placement for graduates, veterans' counselor,
women's services. **Physically disabled:** Services for visually, speech, hearing
impaired. **Transfer:** Transfer center, transfer adviser, college fairs on campus
for students transferring to 4-year colleges.

Contact. E-mail: tcooper@lakelandcc.edu
Phone: (440) 525-7100 Toll-free number: (800) 589-8520
Fax: (440) 525-7651
Tracey Cooper, Director of Admissions/Registrar, Lakeland Community
College, 7700 Clocktower Drive, Kirtland, OH 44094-5198

Lincoln College of Technology: Dayton
Dayton, Ohio
www.swcollege.net   CB code: 2483

- For-profit 2-year business college
- Commuter campus in small city

General. Accredited by ACICS. **Degrees:** 133 associate awarded. **Calendar:** Quarter, extensive summer session. **Full-time faculty:** 21 total. **Part-
time faculty:** 11 total. **Class size:** 76% < 20, 24% 20-39.

Basis for selection. Open admission. Applicants not holding high school
diploma or GED must take Wonderlic exam.

2011-2012 Annual costs. Total program costs range from $9,625 up to
$31,000 depending on program. Cost of books and materials included in
tuition. Books/supplies: $825.

Financial aid. All financial aid based on need. Need-based aid available
for part-time students. Work-study available nights, weekends and for part-
time students.

Application procedures. Admission: No deadline. $125 fee. Admission
notification on a rolling basis. **Financial aid:** No deadline. FAFSA required.

Academics. Special study options: Liberal arts/career combination.
Credit/placement by examination: AP, CLEP. **Support services:** GED
preparation, tutoring.

Majors. Business: Business admin. **Computer sciences:** General. **Health
services:** Medical secretary. **Protective services:** Law enforcement admin.

Computing on campus. 44 workstations in library, computer center.

Student life. Freshman orientation: Mandatory. Preregistration for
classes offered.

Student services. Career counseling, financial aid counseling, on-campus
daycare, personal counseling, placement for graduates.

Contact. Phone: (937) 224-0061
Bill Furlong, Director, Lincoln College of Technology: Dayton, 111 West
1st Street, Dayton, OH 45402

Lincoln College of Technology: Franklin
Franklin, Ohio
www.swcollege.net   CB code: 3268

- For-profit 2-year technical and career college
- Large town

General. Accredited by ACICS. **Degrees:** 55 associate awarded. **Calendar:**
Quarter, extensive summer session. **Full-time faculty:** 9 total. **Part-time
faculty:** 7 total.

Basis for selection. Open admission. **Home schooled:** Interview required.

2011-2012 Annual costs. Total program costs range from $9,625 up to
$31,000 depending on program. Cost of books and materials included in
tuition. Books/supplies: $1,000.

Financial aid. Need-based: Work-study available nights, weekends and
for part-time students.

Application procedures. Admission: No deadline. $125 fee. Application must be submitted on paper. Admission notification on a rolling basis.

Academics. Credit/placement by examination: AP, CLEP.

Majors. Business: Business admin, office technology. **Computer sciences:** General. **Health services:** Medical secretary. **Protective services:** Law enforcement admin.

Student life. Activities: Student government, student newspaper.

Student services. Transfer: Re-entry adviser, pre-admission transcript evaluation for new students. Transfer adviser for students transferring to 4-year colleges.

Contact. E-mail: lpaletta@swcollege.net
Phone: (937) 746-6633 ext. 45103 Fax: (937) 746-6754
Laura Paletta, Director of Admissions, Lincoln College of Technology: Franklin, 201 East Second Street, Franklin, OH 45005

Lincoln College of Technology: Tri-County
Cincinnati, Ohio
www.swcollege.net   CB code: 2478

- For-profit 2-year career college
- Commuter campus in large city
- Interview required

General. Accredited by ACICS. **Degrees:** 164 associate awarded. **Calendar:** Quarter, extensive summer session. **Full-time faculty:** 14 total. **Part-time faculty:** 20 total.

Basis for selection. Open admission. **Home schooled:** High school diploma or GED required. Non-high school graduates will be accepted if they pass the Ability-to-Benefit exam; must obtain GED prior to graduation from college.

2011-2012 Annual costs. Total program costs range from $9,625 up to $31,000 depending on program. Cost of books and materials included in tuition. Books/supplies: $900. Personal expenses: $1,701.

Financial aid. All financial aid based on need. Work-study available nights, weekends and for part-time students.

Application procedures. Admission: No deadline. $125 fee. Application must be submitted on paper. Admission notification on a rolling basis. **Financial aid:** No deadline. FAFSA required.

Academics. Credit/placement by examination: AP, CLEP, institutional tests. **Support services:** GED preparation and test center, tutoring.

Majors. Business: Business admin. **Computer sciences:** General. **Health services:** Medical assistant. **Protective services:** Law enforcement admin.

Computing on campus. 80 workstations in library, computer center. Online library available.

Student life. Freshman orientation: Mandatory. Preregistration for classes offered.

Student services. Career counseling, student employment services, financial aid counseling. **Transfer:** Pre-admission transcript evaluation for new students.

Contact. E-mail: rkimble@swcollege.net
Phone: (513) 874-0432
Brandy Sams, Director of Admissions, Lincoln College of Technology: Tri-County, 149 Northland Boulevard, Cincinnati, OH 45246

Lincoln College of Technology: Vine Street Campus
Cincinnati, Ohio
www.swcollege.net   CB code: 3267

- For-profit 2-year business and health science college
- Large city
- Interview required

General. Accredited by ACICS. **Degrees:** 145 associate awarded. **Location:** Downtown. **Calendar:** Quarter, extensive summer session. **Full-time faculty:** 12 total. **Part-time faculty:** 7 total.

Transfer out. Colleges most students transferred to 2011: Southwestern College: Tri-County Campus.

Basis for selection. Open admission. **Home schooled:** Interview required. Applicants without high school diploma or GED must pass an ATB exam. **Learning Disabled:** Recommend applicants with high school IEP to inform Education department, but not required.

2011-2012 Annual costs. Total program costs range from $9,625 up to $31,000 depending on program. Cost of books and materials included in tuition. Books/supplies: $900. Personal expenses: $2,500.

Financial aid. All financial aid based on need. Need-based aid available for part-time students. Work-study available nights, weekends and for part-time students.

Application procedures. Admission: No deadline. $125 fee. **Financial aid:** FAFSA required.

Academics. Special study options: Independent study, internships. **Credit/placement by examination:** AP, CLEP. **Support services:** GED preparation, remedial instruction, study skills assistance, tutoring.

Majors. Business: General. **Health services:** Medical secretary. **Social sciences:** Criminology.

Most popular majors. Business/marketing 33%, health sciences 33%, social sciences 33%.

Computing on campus. 65 workstations in library, computer center. Online library available.

Student life. Freshman orientation: Mandatory. Preregistration for classes offered.

Contact. Phone: (513) 421-3212 Fax: (513) 421-8325
Nicole Schreck, Director of Admission, Lincoln College of Technology: Vine Street Campus, 632 Vine Street, Cincinnati, OH 45202

Lorain County Community College
Elyria, Ohio
www.lorainccc.edu   CB code: 1417

- Public 2-year community college
- Commuter campus in small city

General. Founded in 1963. Regionally accredited. Unique programs serving high school through master's degrees available. Entrepreneurial incubator located on campus. **Enrollment:** 13,147 degree-seeking undergraduates. **Degrees:** 1,059 associate awarded. **Location:** 26 miles south of Cleveland. **Calendar:** Semester, extensive summer session. **Full-time faculty:** 133 total. **Part-time faculty:** 569 total. **Special facilities:** Performing arts center, advanced technologies center, technology park, conference center.

Student profile.

Out-of-state:	1%	25 or older:	44%

Basis for selection. Open admission. **Home schooled:** GED required.

2011-2012 Annual costs. Tuition/fees: $2,679; $3,222 out-of-district; $6,491 out-of-state. Per-credit charge: $97 in-district; $118 out-of-district; $244 out-of-state. Books/supplies: $955. Personal expenses: $1,030.

Financial aid. Need-based: Need-based aid available for part-time students. Work-study available nights, weekends and for part-time students. **Non-need-based:** Scholarships awarded for academics.

Application procedures. Admission: No deadline. No application fee. Admission notification on a rolling basis beginning on or about 4/15. **Financial aid:** Priority date 8/15; no closing date. FAFSA required. Applicants notified on a rolling basis starting 7/1; must reply within 3 week(s) of notification.

Academics. Special study options: Cooperative education, cross-registration, distance learning, dual enrollment of high school students, ESL, independent study, liberal arts/career combination, study abroad, teacher certification program, weekend college. Bachelor's degree programs available on campus. License preparation in dental hygiene, nursing, paramedic, physical therapy, radiology. **Credit/placement by examination:** AP, CLEP, institutional tests. 30 credit hours maximum toward associate degree. **Support services:** GED preparation and test center, learning center, pre-admission summer program, reduced course load, remedial instruction, study skills assistance, tutoring.

Majors. Biology: General. **Business:** General, accounting, administrative services, banking/financial services, business admin, entrepreneurial studies, hotel/motel admin, human resources, tourism/travel. **Computer sciences:** General, information technology, networking, web page design. **Education:** Early childhood, multi-level teacher. **Engineering:** General, electrical, industrial. **Health services:** Athletic training, clinical lab technology, dental hygiene, medical assistant, medical radiologic technology/radiation therapy, medical secretary, nuclear medical technology, nursing (RN), physical therapy assistant, sonography, surgical technology. **Human services:** General, social work. **Liberal arts:** Arts/sciences. **Math:** General. **Parks/recreation:** Sports admin. **Protective services:** Corrections, firefighting, police science. **Social sciences:** General.

Most popular majors. Business/marketing 13%, engineering/engineering technologies 6%, health sciences 29%, liberal arts 39%.

Computing on campus. 250 workstations in library, computer center. Online course registration, online library, helpline, wireless network available.

Student life. Freshman orientation: Mandatory. Preregistration for classes offered. All students enrolled in 12 or fewer credits must take College Experience course. **Activities:** Bands, choral groups, drama, film society, music ensembles, musical theater, radio station, student government, student newspaper, symphony orchestra, TV station, Black Progressives, Los Unidos, student nurses association, Phi Theta Kappa, campus Baptist ministries, Campus Crusades for Christ, student dental hygienist club, early childhood education club.

Athletics. Intramural: Archery, badminton, basketball, bowling, cross-country, golf, racquetball, rifle, soccer, softball, tennis, volleyball. **Team name:** Commodores.

Student services. Adult student services, alcohol/substance abuse counseling, chaplain/spiritual director, career counseling, services for economically disadvantaged, student employment services, financial aid counseling, health services, on-campus daycare, personal counseling, placement for graduates, veterans' counselor, women's services. **Physically disabled:** Services for visually, hearing impaired. **Transfer:** Transfer center, transfer adviser, college fairs on campus for students transferring to 4-year colleges.

Contact. Phone: (440) 366-4032 Toll-free number: (800) 995-5222 Fax: (440) 366-4167
Stephanie Sutton, Dean of Enrollment & Financial Services, Lorain County Community College, 1005 Abbe Road North, Elyria, OH 44035-1691

Marion Technical College
Marion, Ohio
www.mtc.edu   CB code: 0699

‣ Public 2-year community and technical college
‣ Commuter campus in large town

General. Founded in 1971. Regionally accredited. **Enrollment:** 2,392 degree-seeking undergraduates. **Degrees:** 200 associate awarded. **Location:** 45 miles from Columbus. **Calendar:** Semester, limited summer session. **Full-time faculty:** 46 total. **Part-time faculty:** 82 total. **Special facilities:** Center for workforce development, telephone pole farm.

Student profile. Among degree-seeking undergraduates, 15% enrolled in a transfer program, 85% enrolled in a vocational program, 790 enrolled as first-time, first-year students.

Part-time:	51%	Women:	66%
Out-of-state:	1%	25 or older:	48%

Basis for selection. Open admission, but selective for some programs. Additional application required for limited enrollment programs. Interview required for health technologies, human and social services, law enforcement academy. **Adult students:** ACT may be required for limited enrollment programs. **Home schooled:** Transcript of courses and grades required. Appropriate standardized test or other documentation as defined by policy. **Learning Disabled:** Students must meet with Student Resource Center for assessment.

High school preparation. Recommended units include English 4, mathematics 2, social studies 1, science 2 and foreign language 2. Algebra, biology, and chemistry required for health technology applicants. Algebra and physics recommended for engineering applicants.

2011-2012 Annual costs. Tuition/fees: $4,020; $5,928 out-of-state. Per-credit charge: $89 in-state; $142 out-of-state. Books/supplies: $1,200. Personal expenses: $900.

Financial aid. Need-based: Need-based aid available for part-time students. Work-study available nights, weekends and for part-time students.

Non-need-based: Scholarships awarded for academics, leadership, minority status.

Application procedures. Admission: Priority date 5/1; no deadline. $20 fee, may be waived for applicants with need. Admission notification on a rolling basis. **Financial aid:** Closing date 6/1. FAFSA, institutional form required. Applicants notified on a rolling basis.

Academics. Special study options: Accelerated study, cooperative education, cross-registration, distance learning, double major, dual enrollment of high school students, external degree, independent study, internships, liberal arts/career combination, student-designed major, weekend college. License preparation in nursing, occupational therapy, physical therapy, radiology, real estate. **Credit/placement by examination:** AP, CLEP, institutional tests. 48 credit hours maximum toward associate degree. Maximum of 48 quarter hours of credit may be earned through exam, life experience or combination. **Support services:** GED preparation and test center, learning center, reduced course load, remedial instruction, study skills assistance, tutoring.

Majors. Business: General, accounting, accounting technology, administrative services, business admin, executive assistant, human resources, marketing, office management, office technology. **Computer sciences:** General, applications programming, data entry, information technology, LAN/WAN management, networking, programming, vendor certification, web page design, webmaster, word processing. **Health services:** Clinical lab technology, medical radiologic technology/radiation therapy, medical secretary, nursing (RN), occupational therapy assistant, physical therapy assistant. **Protective services:** Law enforcement admin.

Computing on campus. 229 workstations in library, computer center, student center. Commuter students can connect to campus network. Online course registration, online library, helpline, wireless network available.

Student life. Freshman orientation: Available. Preregistration for classes offered. Held 1-2 weeks before classes begin. **Activities:** Campus ministries, choral groups, drama, literary magazine, student government, joint activities committee, Campus Christian Fellowship, program of outdoor pursuits club, cultural arts program, student organized clubs/organizations, indoor rock climbing, wellness and conditioning, aerobics center, Beta Nu Pi honorary society (Phi Theta Kappa local chapter).

Athletics. USCAA. **Intercollegiate:** Basketball, cheerleading M, golf, soccer, volleyball W. **Intramural:** Badminton, basketball, cross-country, football (non-tackle), racquetball, skiing, softball, table tennis, tennis, volleyball.

Student services. Adult student services, career counseling, student employment services, financial aid counseling, personal counseling, placement for graduates, veterans' counselor. **Physically disabled:** Services for visually, speech, hearing impaired. **Transfer:** Pre-admission transcript evaluation for new students. College fairs on campus for students transferring to 4-year colleges.

Contact. E-mail: enroll@mtc.edu
Phone: (740) 389-4636 ext. 334 Fax: (740) 389-6136
Joel Liles, Dean of Enrollment Services, Marion Technical College, 1467 Mt. Vernon Avenue, Marion, OH 43302-5694

Miami University: Hamilton
Hamilton, Ohio
www.ham.muohio.edu   CB code: 1526

‣ Public 2-year branch campus college
‣ Commuter campus in small city

General. Founded in 1968. Regionally accredited. Degrees earned on Hamilton campus conferred by main (Oxford) campus. **Enrollment:** 4,428 degree-seeking undergraduates. **Degrees:** 99 bachelor's, 181 associate awarded. **ROTC:** Naval, Air Force. **Location:** 25 miles from Cincinnati. **Calendar:** Semester, limited summer session. **Full-time faculty:** 84 total. **Part-time faculty:** 140 total. **Class size:** 67% < 20, 24% 20-39, 6% 40-49, 3% 50-99. **Special facilities:** Botanical conservatory.

Basis for selection. Open admission, but selective for some programs. Additional application required for competitive nursing program. **Home schooled:** Applicants must present GED scores or credentials that demonstrate equivalent levels of academic achievement, ability and performance to that of state-chartered diploma at least 8 weeks before classes begin.

High school preparation. 16 units recommended. Recommended units include English 4, mathematics 3, social studies 2, history 1, science 3, foreign language 2 and visual/performing arts 1.

2011-2012 Annual costs. Tuition/fees: $4,793; $13,445 out-of-state. Books/supplies: $730. Personal expenses: $2,025.

Financial aid. Need-based: Need-based aid available for part-time students. Work-study available nights, weekends and for part-time students. **Non-need-based:** Scholarships awarded for academics, athletics, leadership, minority status, state residency. **Additional information:** Special gift funds for needy, multicultural students who enter with appropriate academic record. Separate application required for scholarships; closing date January 31.

Application procedures. Admission: No deadline. $30 fee, may be waived for applicants with need. Admission notification on a rolling basis. Nursing application deadline for Fall admission 2/1. **Financial aid:** Priority date 2/15; no closing date. FAFSA required. Applicants notified on a rolling basis starting 4/1.

Academics. Some graduate coursework available. **Special study options:** Cooperative education, cross-registration, distance learning, double major, dual enrollment of high school students, ESL, honors, independent study, internships, liberal arts/career combination, student-designed major, study abroad, teacher certification program. Bachelor's degree programs available on campus. License preparation in nursing, real estate. **Credit/placement by examination:** AP, CLEP, IB, institutional tests. 32 credit hours maximum toward associate degree, 32 toward bachelor's. **Support services:** Learning center, reduced course load, remedial instruction, study skills assistance, tutoring, writing center.

Majors. Business: Accounting technology, business admin, marketing, office management, real estate. **Computer sciences:** General, networking, support specialist. **Education:** Kindergarten/preschool. **Health services:** Nursing (RN). **Protective services:** Law enforcement admin.

Computing on campus. 300 workstations in library, computer center, student center. Commuter students can connect to campus network. Online course registration, online library, helpline, wireless network available.

Student life. Freshman orientation: Available. Preregistration for classes offered. **Activities:** Choral groups, drama, musical theater, student government, campus activities committee, student nursing association, minority action committee, Campus Crusade for Christ, athletic club, Organization for Wiser and Worldwide Learners.

Athletics. Intramural: Basketball, bowling, skiing, soccer, softball, table tennis, tennis, volleyball, weight lifting. **Team name:** Harriers.

Student services. Career counseling, student employment services, financial aid counseling, minority student services, on-campus daycare, personal counseling, placement for graduates, veterans' counselor. **Physically disabled:** Services for visually, speech, hearing impaired. **Transfer:** Pre-admission transcript evaluation for new students.

Contact. Phone: (513) 785-3111 Fax: (513) 785-1807
Archie Nelson, Director of Admission and Financial Aid, Miami University: Hamilton, 1601 University Boulevard, Hamilton, OH 45011-3399

Miami University: Middletown
Middletown, Ohio
www.mid.muohio.edu   **CB code: 1509**

▸ Public 2-year branch campus and community college
▸ Commuter campus in large town

General. Founded in 1963. Regionally accredited. Degrees earned on Middletown campus conferred by main (Oxford) campus. **Enrollment:** 2,529 degree-seeking undergraduates. **Degrees:** 60 bachelor's, 134 associate awarded. **ROTC:** Naval, Air Force. **Location:** 30 miles from Cincinnati, 20 miles from Dayton. **Calendar:** Semester, extensive summer session. **Full-time faculty:** 60 total. **Special facilities:** Nature trail.

Student profile.

Out-of-state: 1%   25 or older: 28%

Basis for selection. Open admission, but selective for some programs. Special requirements for allied health programs. Interview recommended for nursing program. **Home schooled:** Submit curriculum and description of resources used during last 4 years.

High school preparation. 16 units recommended. Recommended units include English 4, mathematics 3, social studies 3, science 3, foreign language 2 and academic electives 1. One fine arts also recommended.

2011-2012 Annual costs. Tuition/fees: $4,793; $13,445 out-of-state. Books/supplies: $1,195. Personal expenses: $4,088.

Financial aid. All financial aid based on need. Need-based aid available for part-time students. Work-study available nights, weekends and for part-time students.

Application procedures. Admission: Priority date 8/1; no deadline. $30 fee, may be waived for applicants with need. Admission notification on a rolling basis beginning on or about 3/1. **Financial aid:** Priority date 2/15; no closing date. FAFSA required. Applicants notified on a rolling basis.

Academics. Special study options: Cooperative education, cross-registration, distance learning, double major, dual enrollment of high school students, independent study, internships, liberal arts/career combination, student-designed major, study abroad, teacher certification program. Bachelor's degree programs available on campus. License preparation in nursing. **Credit/placement by examination:** AP, CLEP, IB, institutional tests. 30 credit hours maximum toward bachelor's degree. **Support services:** Learning center, pre-admission summer program, reduced course load, remedial instruction, study skills assistance, tutoring, writing center.

Majors. Biology: Molecular, zoology. **Business:** General, accounting, administrative services, business admin, finance, office management, office/clerical. **Communications:** Communications/speech/rhetoric. **Computer sciences:** General, applications programming, systems analysis. **English:** English lit. **Foreign languages:** Spanish. **Health services:** Nursing (RN). **History:** General. **Liberal arts:** Arts/sciences, humanities. **Math:** General. **Philosophy/religion:** Philosophy. **Physical sciences:** Chemistry, physics. **Psychology:** General. **Social sciences:** Anthropology, geography, political science, sociology.

Computing on campus. 170 workstations in library, computer center. Commuter students can connect to campus network. Online course registration, online library, helpline, student web hosting available.

Student life. Freshman orientation: Mandatory. Preregistration for classes offered. Full-day program, choice of 5 days ranging from June 4 through August 11. **Activities:** Drama, literary magazine, student government, student newspaper.

Athletics. Intercollegiate: Baseball M, basketball, golf, tennis, volleyball W. **Intramural:** Basketball, golf, racquetball, soccer, softball, table tennis, volleyball. **Team name:** Thunder Hawks.

Student services. Adult student services, career counseling, student employment services, financial aid counseling, minority student services, on-campus daycare, personal counseling, placement for graduates, veterans' counselor. **Physically disabled:** Services for visually, speech, hearing impaired. **Transfer:** College fairs on campus for students transferring to 4-year colleges.

Contact. E-mail: mlflynn@muohio.edu
Phone: (513) 727-3216 Fax: (513) 727-3223
Archie Nelson, Director of Admission and Financial Aid, Miami University: Middletown, 4200 East University Boulevard, Middletown, OH 45042

Miami-Jacobs Career College: Cincinnati
Sharonville, Ohio
www.miamijacobs.edu

▸ For-profit 2-year business college
▸ Large city

General. Accredited by ACICS. **Calendar:** Quarter.

Annual costs/financial aid. Books/supplies: $1,500.

Contact. Phone: (513) 723-0520
Director of Admissions, Two Crowne Point Court, Suite 100, Sharonville, OH 45241

Miami-Jacobs Career College: Columbus
Columbus, Ohio
www.miamijacobs.edu   **CB code: 3344**

▸ For-profit 2-year junior college
▸ Commuter campus in very large city

General. Accredited by ACICS. **Calendar:** Differs by program.

Annual costs/financial aid. Books/supplies: $1,500.

Contact. Phone: (614) 221-7770
Director of Admissions, 150 East Gay Street, 15th Floor, Columbus, OH 43215

Miami-Jacobs Career College: Dayton
Dayton, Ohio
www.miamijacobs.edu   CB code: 1528

- For-profit 2-year junior college
- Commuter campus in small city
- Application essay, interview required

General. Founded in 1860. Accredited by ACICS. Center for information technology provides high-end software training preparation for certification. **Enrollment:** 530 undergraduates. **Degrees:** 203 associate awarded. **Location:** Downtown. **Calendar:** Quarter, extensive summer session. **Full-time faculty:** 21 total. **Part-time faculty:** 20 total. **Special facilities:** Antique typewriter museum.

Basis for selection. Interview, essay, recommendations most important. Wonderlic exam required.

2011-2012 Annual costs. Personal expenses: $2,500.

Financial aid. All financial aid based on need. Need-based aid available for part-time students. Work-study available nights, weekends and for part-time students.

Application procedures. Admission: No deadline. $20 fee. Admission notification on a rolling basis. **Financial aid:** No deadline. FAFSA, institutional form required. Applicants notified on a rolling basis.

Academics. College has dress code and attendance policy establishing patterns and habits to be carried over into employment setting. **Special study options:** Accelerated study, cross-registration, distance learning, double major, dual enrollment of high school students, independent study, internships, weekend college. **Credit/placement by examination:** AP, CLEP, institutional tests. 45 credit hours maximum toward associate degree. **Support services:** Pre-admission summer program, reduced course load, remedial instruction, tutoring.

Majors. Business: Accounting, administrative services, office management, office technology, office/clerical. **Computer sciences:** General, applications programming, data processing, information systems, information technology, networking, programming. **Engineering:** Software. **Health services:** Massage therapy, medical assistant, medical records technology, medical secretary, medical transcription, respiratory therapy technology, surgical technology. **Protective services:** Law enforcement admin.

Computing on campus. 180 workstations in computer center.

Student life. Freshman orientation: Mandatory. Preregistration for classes offered.

Student services. Adult student services, career counseling, student employment services, financial aid counseling, personal counseling, placement for graduates, veterans' counselor. **Transfer:** Transfer adviser for students transferring to 4-year colleges.

Contact. E-mail: careeradvocate@miamijacobs.edu
Phone: (937) 222-7337
Beth Wilson, Director of Admissions, Miami-Jacobs Career College: Dayton, 110 North Patterson Boulevard, Dayton, OH 45402

National College: Cincinnati
Cincinnati, Ohio
www.national-college.edu

- For-profit 2-year branch campus college
- Large city

General. Regionally accredited; also accredited by ACICS. **Enrollment:** 286 degree-seeking undergraduates. **Degrees:** 84 associate awarded. **Calendar:** Quarter. **Full-time faculty:** 8 total. **Part-time faculty:** 55 total.

Basis for selection. Open admission.

2011-2012 Annual costs. Tuition/fees: $13,770. Per-credit charge: $305. Books/supplies: $1,980.

Financial aid. Need-based: Work-study available nights, weekends and for part-time students.

Application procedures. Admission: No deadline. $50 fee.

Academics. Credit/placement by examination: AP, CLEP.

Majors. Business: Accounting/business management, administrative services, business admin. **Health services:** Pharmacy assistant, surgical technology.

Contact. Phone: (513) 761-1291
Patricia Young, Regional Director of Admissions OH/IN Campuses, National College: Cincinnati, 6871 Steger Drive, Cincinnati, OH 45237

National College: Columbus
Columbus, Ohio
www.ncbt.edu

- For-profit 2-year branch campus college
- Very large city

General. Regionally accredited; also accredited by ACICS. **Enrollment:** 127 degree-seeking undergraduates. **Degrees:** 6 associate awarded. **Calendar:** Quarter. **Full-time faculty:** 8 total. **Part-time faculty:** 29 total.

Basis for selection. Open admission.

2011-2012 Annual costs. Tuition/fees: $13,770. Per-credit charge: $305.

Financial aid. Need-based: Work-study available nights, weekends and for part-time students.

Application procedures. Admission: No deadline. $50 fee.

Academics. Credit/placement by examination: AP, CLEP.

Majors. Health services: Office assistant.

Contact. Patricia Young, Regional Director of Admissions OH/IN Campuses, National College: Columbus, 5665 Forest Hills Boulevard, Columbus, OH 43231

National College: Dayton
Kettering, Ohio
www.national-college.edu

- For-profit 2-year business and technical college
- Large city

General. Accredited by ACICS. **Enrollment:** 271 degree-seeking undergraduates. **Degrees:** 127 associate awarded. **Calendar:** Quarter. **Full-time faculty:** 3 total. **Part-time faculty:** 66 total.

Basis for selection. Open admission.

2011-2012 Annual costs. Tuition/fees: $13,770. Per-credit charge: $305.

Financial aid. Need-based: Work-study available nights, weekends and for part-time students.

Application procedures. Admission: No deadline. $50 fee. **Financial aid:** No deadline.

Academics. Credit/placement by examination: AP, CLEP.

Majors. Business: Business admin. **Computer sciences:** General.

Contact. Phone: (937) 299-9450
Linda Clemons, Director of Admissions, National College: Dayton, 1837 Woodman Center Drive, Kettering, OH 45420

National College: Stow
Stow, Ohio
www.national-college.edu

- For-profit 2-year branch campus college
- Large town

General. Regionally accredited; also accredited by ACICS. **Enrollment:** 211 degree-seeking undergraduates. **Degrees:** 83 associate awarded. **Calendar:** Quarter. **Full-time faculty:** 8 total. **Part-time faculty:** 28 total.

Basis for selection. Open admission.

2011-2012 Annual costs. Tuition/fees: $13,770. Per-credit charge: $305. Books/supplies: $1,980.

Financial aid. Need-based: Work-study available nights, weekends and for part-time students.

Application procedures. Admission: No deadline. $50 fee.

Academics. Credit/placement by examination: AP, CLEP.

Majors. Business: Accounting/business management, administrative services, business admin. **Health services:** Medical assistant, medical records technology, pharmacy assistant.

Contact. Tiffany Bimshas, Director of Admissions, National College: Stow, 3855 Fishercreek Road, Stow, OH 44224

National College: Willoughby Hills
Willoughby Hills, Ohio
www.national-college.edu

▸ For-profit 2-year career college
▸ Small town

General. Accredited by ACICS. **Enrollment:** 85 degree-seeking undergraduates. **Calendar:** Quarter. **Full-time faculty:** 2 total. **Part-time faculty:** 52 total.

Basis for selection. Open admission.

Financial aid. Need-based: Work-study available nights, weekends and for part-time students.

Application procedures. Admission: No deadline. $50 fee.

Academics. Credit/placement by examination: AP, CLEP.

Majors. Business: Accounting. **Computer sciences:** System admin. **Health services:** Medical assistant, medical records technology, pharmacy assistant.

Contact. Phone: (440) 944-0825
Patricia Young, Regional Director of Admissions, OH/IN Campuses, National College: Willoughby Hills, 27557 Chardon Road, Willoughby Hills, OH 44092

National College: Youngstown
Youngstown, Ohio
www.national-college.edu

▸ For-profit 2-year branch campus college
▸ Small city

General. Regionally accredited; also accredited by ACICS. **Enrollment:** 381 degree-seeking undergraduates. **Degrees:** 175 associate awarded. **Calendar:** Quarter. **Full-time faculty:** 9 total. **Part-time faculty:** 43 total.

Basis for selection. Open admission.

2011-2012 Annual costs. Tuition/fees: $13,770. Per-credit charge: $305.

Financial aid. Need-based: Work-study available nights, weekends and for part-time students.

Application procedures. Admission: No deadline. $50 fee. **Financial aid:** No deadline.

Academics. Credit/placement by examination: AP, CLEP.

Majors. Business: Business admin. **Health services:** Medical records technology, office assistant, physical therapy assistant.

Contact. Jolyn Cleland, Director of Admissions, National College: Youngstown, 3487 Belmont Avenue, Youngstown, OH 44505

North Central State College
Mansfield, Ohio
www.ncstatecollege.edu   CB code: 0721

▸ Public 2-year technical college
▸ Commuter campus in small city

General. Founded in 1961. Regionally accredited. **Enrollment:** 3,387 degree-seeking undergraduates. **Degrees:** 395 associate awarded. **Location:** 70 miles from Cleveland and Columbus. **Calendar:** Quarter, limited summer session. **Full-time faculty:** 72 total. **Part-time faculty:** 156 total. **Special facilities:** Wooded hiking trails.

Transfer out. Colleges most students transferred to 2011: Ashland University, Mount Vernon Nazarene College, University of Cincinnati, Franklin University.

Basis for selection. Open admission, but selective for some programs. ACT scores used for admission to physical therapist assistant and radiology programs; score report by September 15. Interview recommended for all health and public service programs.

High school preparation. One algebra and 1 chemistry required for nursing, physical therapist assistant, respiratory therapy, radiologic technology and pharmacy technology programs.

2011-2012 Annual costs. Tuition/fees: $4,090; $8,182 out-of-state. Per-credit charge: $90 in-state; $182 out-of-state. Books/supplies: $1,500. Personal expenses: $501.

Financial aid. All financial aid based on need. Need-based aid available for part-time students. Work-study available nights, weekends and for part-time students.

Application procedures. Admission: No deadline. $25 fee. Admission notification on a rolling basis. **Financial aid:** Priority date 4/1; no closing date. FAFSA required. Applicants notified on a rolling basis starting 5/30; must reply within 1 week(s) of notification.

Academics. Special study options: Distance learning, dual enrollment of high school students, independent study, internships, student-designed major, weekend college. **Credit/placement by examination:** AP, CLEP, institutional tests. **Support services:** Learning center, reduced course load, remedial instruction, study skills assistance, tutoring, writing center.

Majors. Business: General, accounting, administrative services, business admin, operations. **Communications:** Digital media. **Communications technology:** Animation/special effects, radio/TV. **Computer sciences:** General, applications programming, programming. **Education:** Early childhood, teacher assistance. **Health services:** Medical radiologic technology/radiation therapy, mental health services, nursing (RN), physical therapy assistant, radiologic technology/medical imaging, respiratory therapy technology. **Protective services:** Criminal justice, law enforcement admin, police science.

Computing on campus. 144 workstations in library, computer center.

Student life. Freshman orientation: Available. Preregistration for classes offered. Two- or three-hour evening program held prior to beginning of each quarter. **Activities:** Choral groups, student government, student newspaper.

Athletics. Intramural: Basketball, bowling, football (non-tackle), golf, softball, table tennis, tennis, volleyball. **Team name:** Mavericks.

Student services. Career counseling, student employment services, financial aid counseling, on-campus daycare, personal counseling, placement for graduates, veterans' counselor. **Physically disabled:** Services for visually, speech, hearing impaired. **Transfer:** College fairs on campus for students transferring to 4-year colleges.

Contact. E-mail: admissions@ncstatecollege.edu
Phone: (419) 755-4761 Toll-free number: (888) 755-4899
Fax: (419) 755-4757
Nikia Fletcher, Director of Admissions/Enrollment Services, North Central State College, 2441 Kenwood Circle, PO Box 698, Mansfield, OH 44901-0698

Northwest State Community College
Archbold, Ohio
www.northweststate.edu   CB code: 1235

▸ Public 2-year community and technical college
▸ Commuter campus in small town

General. Founded in 1968. Regionally accredited. **Enrollment:** 2,657 degree-seeking undergraduates; 938 non-degree-seeking students. **Degrees:** 373 associate awarded. **Location:** 45 miles from Toledo. **Calendar:** Semester, limited summer session. **Full-time faculty:** 44 total; 14% have terminal degrees, 61% women. **Part-time faculty:** 282 total; 3% have terminal degrees, 1% minority, 58% women. **Class size:** 66% < 20, 31% 20-39, 3% 40-49. **Special facilities:** Childcare center.

Student profile. Among degree-seeking undergraduates, 1% already have a bachelor's degree or higher, 594 enrolled as first-time, first-year students, 69 transferred in from other institutions.

Part-time:	70%	African American:	2%
Out-of-state:	3%	Hispanic American:	6%
Women:	51%	25 or older:	61%

Transfer out. Colleges most students transferred to 2011: University of Toledo, Bowling Green State University, Wright State University, Owens Community College, Rhodes State Community College.

Basis for selection. Open admission, but selective for some programs. Special requirements for nursing program; interview required.

High school preparation. Recommended units include English 4, mathematics 3, social studies 3 and science 3. College-preparatory program preferred.

2011-2012 Annual costs. Tuition/fees: $4,080; $7,980 out-of-state. Per-credit charge: $130 in-state; $260 out-of-state. Books/supplies: $1,000. Personal expenses: $4,100.

2010-2011 Financial aid. Need-based: 42% of total undergraduate aid awarded as scholarships/grants, 58% as loans/jobs. Need-based aid available for part-time students. Work-study available nights, weekends and for part-time students. **Non-need-based:** Scholarships awarded for academics.

Application procedures. Admission: No deadline. $20 fee. Admission notification on a rolling basis. **Financial aid:** Priority date 6/1; no closing date. FAFSA, institutional form required. Applicants notified on a rolling basis starting 4/1.

Academics. Special study options: Cooperative education, distance learning, dual enrollment of high school students, independent study, internships, student-designed major, weekend college. Bachelor's degree programs available on campus. License preparation in nursing, real estate. **Credit/placement by examination:** AP, CLEP, institutional tests. 40 credit hours maximum toward associate degree. **Support services:** Learning center, remedial instruction, tutoring.

Majors. Business: General, accounting, administrative services, banking/financial services, business admin, entrepreneurial studies, executive assistant, international, logistics, marketing, nonprofit/public, office management, office technology, office/clerical, sales/distribution. **Computer sciences:** Programming, security, system admin, web page design. **Education:** General, kindergarten/preschool, teacher assistance. **Engineering:** Computer, mechanical. **Health services:** Medical assistant, medical secretary, nursing (RN). **History:** General. **Human services:** Social work. **Liberal arts:** Arts/sciences. **Protective services:** Corrections, criminal justice, law enforcement admin, police science. **Visual/performing arts:** Design. **Work/family studies:** Child care management, child development.

Most popular majors. Business/marketing 22%, computer/information sciences 7%, engineering/engineering technologies 8%, health sciences 29%, liberal arts 8%, trade and industry 7%.

Computing on campus. 400 workstations in library, computer center. Online library, helpline, wireless network available.

Student life. Freshman orientation: Available. Preregistration for classes offered. **Activities:** Choral groups, international student organizations, student government, Student Nurses Association, Phi Theta Kappa, Campus Crusade for Christ, Student Body Organization, Students for Community Outreach & Awareness, Kappa Beta Delta.

Athletics. Intramural: Basketball, bowling, football (non-tackle), softball, table tennis, volleyball. **Team name:** Pacers.

Student services. Adult student services, career counseling, student employment services, financial aid counseling, on-campus daycare, personal counseling, placement for graduates, veterans' counselor. **Physically disabled:** Services for visually, hearing impaired. **Transfer:** Transfer adviser, college fairs on campus for students transferring to 4-year colleges.

Contact. E-mail: admissions@northweststate.edu
Phone: (419) 267-5511 ext. 320 Fax: (419) 267-5604
Dennis Giacomino, Director of Admissions, Northwest State Community College, 22600 State Route 34, Archbold, OH 43502

Ohio Business College
Sheffield Village, Ohio
www.ohiobusinesscollege.edu   CB code: 2470

- For-profit 2-year branch campus and business college
- Commuter campus in small city

General. Founded in 1903. Accredited by ACICS. **Location:** 35 miles from Cleveland. **Calendar:** Quarter.

Annual costs/financial aid. Books/supplies: $2,640. Need-based financial aid available to full-time and part-time students.

Contact. Phone: (440) 277-0021
Admissions Manager, 5095 Waterford Drive, Sheffield Village, OH 44055

Ohio Business College: Columbus
Columbus, Ohio
www.ohiobusinesscollege.edu

- For-profit 2-year business and health science college
- Very large city

General. Accredited by ACICS. **Calendar:** Differs by program.

Annual costs/financial aid. Books/supplies: $1,160.

Contact. Phone: (614) 891-5030
Admissions Director, 1880 East Dublin-Granville Road, Suite 100, Columbus, OH 43229

Ohio Business College: Sandusky
Sandusky, Ohio
www.ohiobusinesscollege.edu   CB code: 3260

- For-profit 2-year business college
- Commuter campus in small city

General. Accredited by ACICS. **Location:** 60 miles from Cleveland and Toledo. **Calendar:** Quarter.

Annual costs/financial aid. Books/supplies: $1,200. Need-based financial aid available to full-time and part-time students.

Contact. Phone: (419) 627-8345
Director of Admissions, 5202 Timber Commons Drive, Sandusky, OH 44870

Ohio College of Massotherapy
Akron, Ohio
www.ocm.edu   CB code: 2985

- Private 2-year health science college
- Commuter campus in very large city

General. Accredited by ACCSC. **Enrollment:** 121 degree-seeking undergraduates. **Degrees:** 32 associate awarded. **Calendar:** Differs by program. **Part-time faculty:** 15 total. **Special facilities:** Massage and spa clinic.

Basis for selection. Open admission. **Home schooled:** State high school equivalency certificate required.

Financial aid. Need-based: Work-study available nights, weekends and for part-time students.

Application procedures. Admission: Closing date 8/21. $25 fee. **Financial aid:** Priority date 10/1; no closing date.

Academics. Special study options: Distance learning. **Credit/placement by examination:** AP, CLEP. **Support services:** Reduced course load, tutoring.

Majors. Health services: Massage therapy.

Computing on campus. 4 workstations in computer center.

Student life. Freshman orientation: Mandatory. Preregistration for classes offered.

Contact. E-mail: admissions@ocm.edu
Phone: (330) 665-1084 Fax: (330) 665-5021
Margie Martens, Admissions/Marketing Manager, Ohio College of Massotherapy, 225 Heritage Woods Drive, Akron, OH 44321

Ohio State University Agricultural Technical Institute
Wooster, Ohio
www.ati.osu.edu
CB code: 1009

⬧ Public 2-year agricultural and branch campus college
⬧ Residential campus in large town

General. Founded in 1971. Regionally accredited. **Enrollment:** 653 degree-seeking undergraduates; 13 non-degree-seeking students. **Degrees:** 155 associate awarded. **ROTC:** Army, Naval, Air Force. **Location:** 30 miles from Akron, 60 miles from Cleveland. **Calendar:** Quarter, limited summer session. **Full-time faculty:** 26 total; 96% have terminal degrees, 12% minority, 23% women. **Part-time faculty:** 35 total; 6% minority, 40% women. **Class size:** 61% < 20, 33% 20-39, 2% 40-49, 4% 50-99. **Special facilities:** 18 hole public golf course, 1800-acre farm operation/enterprise laboratory, horticulture complex including greenhouses, conservatory and display gardens.

Student profile. Among degree-seeking undergraduates, 278 enrolled as first-time, first-year students, 32 transferred in from other institutions.

Part-time:	10%	African American:	1%
Out-of-state:	2%	25 or older:	8%
Women:	41%	Live on campus:	55%

Transfer out. Colleges most students transferred to 2011: Ohio State University.

Basis for selection. Open admission, but selective for out-of-state students. Out-of-state applicants evaluated on basis of GPA, class rank, curriculum, principal/counselor recommendations, and SAT/ACT scores. **Home schooled:** May be required to provide GED.

High school preparation. College-preparatory program recommended.

2011-2012 Annual costs. Tuition/fees: $6,525; $21,420 out-of-state. Per-credit charge: $181 in-state; $595 out-of-state. Books/supplies: $1,602. Personal expenses: $4,140.

2011-2012 Financial aid. All financial aid based on need. 259 full-time freshmen applied for aid; 213 were judged to have need; 207 of these received aid. Average need met was 48%. Average scholarship/grant was $4,390; average loan $4,099. 35% of total undergraduate aid awarded as scholarships/grants, 65% as loans/jobs. Need-based aid available for part-time students. Work-study available nights, weekends and for part-time students.

Application procedures. Admission: Closing date 7/1 (postmark date). $60 fee, may be waived for applicants with need. Admission notification on a rolling basis beginning on or about 11/15. Must reply by May 1 or within 3 week(s) if notified thereafter. **Financial aid:** Priority date 2/15; no closing date. FAFSA required. Applicants notified on a rolling basis starting 4/1; must reply by 5/1 or within 4 week(s) of notification.

Academics. One-quarter of occupational internship required. **Special study options:** Cross-registration, double major, dual enrollment of high school students, independent study, internships, student-designed major, study abroad. **Credit/placement by examination:** AP, CLEP, institutional tests. 45 credit hours maximum toward associate degree. **Support services:** Learning center, reduced course load, remedial instruction, study skills assistance, tutoring, writing center.

Majors. Business: Business admin, restaurant/food services. **Conservation:** General, environmental science, environmental studies. **Education:** Agricultural. **General:** Agronomy, animal husbandry, business, communications, crop production, dairy, equine science, equipment technology, floriculture, greenhouse operations, horticultural science, horticulture, landscaping, nursery operations, ornamental horticulture, plant sciences, power machinery, products processing, soil science, turf management.

Most popular majors. Agriculture 83%, engineering/engineering technologies 6%, natural resources/environmental science 6%.

Computing on campus. 85 workstations in dormitories, library, computer center. Dormitories wired for high-speed internet access and linked to campus network. Commuter students can connect to campus network. Online course registration, online library, helpline, wireless network available.

Student life. Freshman orientation: Mandatory, $50 fee. Preregistration for classes offered. **Policies:** Resident freshmen under 21 required to live on campus. **Housing:** Coed dorms, apartments available. $200 partly refundable deposit. **Activities:** International student organizations, Phi Theta Kappa, Campus Crusade.

Athletics. Intramural: Basketball, football (tackle), racquetball, softball, volleyball.

Student services. Career counseling, student employment services, financial aid counseling, health services, minority student services, on-campus daycare, personal counseling, placement for graduates. **Physically disabled:** Services for visually, speech, hearing impaired.

Contact. E-mail: ati@osu.edu
Phone: (330) 287-1327 Toll-free number: (800) 647-8283
Fax: (330) 287-1333
David Dietrich, Manager of Enrollment, Ohio State University Agricultural Technical Institute, 1328 Dover Road, Wooster, OH 44691

Ohio Technical College
Cleveland, Ohio
www.ohiotechnicalcollege.com
CB code: 2999

⬧ For-profit 2-year technical college
⬧ Very large city

General. Accredited by ACCSC. **Enrollment:** 725 degree-seeking undergraduates. **Degrees:** 189 associate awarded. **Calendar:** Differs by program, extensive summer session. **Full-time faculty:** 216 total. **Part-time faculty:** 43 total.

Basis for selection. Open admission. Applicants must pass Wonderlic test to be admitted. **Home schooled:** State high school equivalency certificate required.

2011-2012 Annual costs. Tuition for full associate programs range from $26,280 to $29,400. Personal expenses: $1,837.

Financial aid. Need-based: Work-study available nights, weekends and for part-time students.

Application procedures. Admission: No deadline. No application fee. **Financial aid:** No deadline.

Academics. Credit/placement by examination: AP, CLEP.

Student life. Freshman orientation: Mandatory. Preregistration for classes offered. **Activities:** Student newspaper.

Athletics. Team name: Top Techs.

Contact. E-mail: info@ohiotechnicalcollege.com
Phone: (216) 881-1700 Toll-free number: (800) 322-7000
Fax: (216) 881-9145
Tom King, Ohio Technical College, 1374 East 51st Street, Cleveland, OH 44103-1269

Ohio Valley College of Technology
East Liverpool, Ohio
www.ovct.edu
CB code: 5852

⬧ For-profit 2-year junior and technical college
⬧ Commuter campus in large town

General. Founded in 1886. Accredited by ACICS. **Enrollment:** 204 degree-seeking undergraduates. **Degrees:** 110 associate awarded. **Location:** 30 miles from Youngstown, 35 miles from Pittsburgh. **Calendar:** Semester, extensive summer session. **Full-time faculty:** 4 total; 25% minority, 75% women. **Part-time faculty:** 16 total; 6% minority, 81% women. **Class size:** 60% < 20, 40% 20-39.

Student profile. Among degree-seeking undergraduates, 50 enrolled as first-time, first-year students.

Part-time:	22%	African American:	2%
Out-of-state:	13%	25 or older:	75%
Women:	81%		

Basis for selection. Class rank, GPA considered.

2011-2012 Annual costs. Tuition/fees: $10,290. Per-credit charge: $399. Tuition and fees include book rentals.

2010-2011 Financial aid. All financial aid based on need. 57 full-time freshmen applied for aid; 57 were judged to have need; 57 of these received aid. Average scholarship/grant was $4,864; average loan $5,384. 51% of total undergraduate aid awarded as scholarships/grants, 49% as loans/jobs. Need-based aid available for part-time students. Work-study available nights, weekends and for part-time students.

Application procedures. Admission: No deadline. $25 fee. Admission notification on a rolling basis. **Financial aid:** No deadline. FAFSA required. Applicants notified on a rolling basis; must reply within 6 week(s) of notification.

Academics. Special study options: Internships. License preparation in nursing. **Credit/placement by examination:** AP, CLEP, institutional tests. **Support services:** Reduced course load, study skills assistance, tutoring.

Majors. Business: Business admin. **Computer sciences:** Information technology. **Health services:** Dental assistant, medical secretary, office assistant.

Most popular majors. Business/marketing 9%, computer/information sciences 18%, health sciences 80%.

Computing on campus. 20 workstations in computer center. Wireless network available.

Student life. Freshman orientation: Mandatory. Preregistration for classes offered. **Activities:** Student newspaper.

Student services. Career counseling, student employment services, financial aid counseling, placement for graduates. **Transfer:** Transfer adviser for students transferring to 4-year colleges.

Contact. E-mail: info@ovct.edu
Phone: (330) 385-1070 Fax: (330) 385-4606
Chad Baker, Senior Admissions Representative, Ohio Valley College of Technology, 15258 State Route 170, East Liverpool, OH 43920-9585

Owens Community College: Toledo
Toledo, Ohio
www.owens.edu   **CB code: 1643**

- Public 2-year community college
- Commuter campus in very large city

General. Founded in 1966. Regionally accredited. Branch campus in Findlay. **Enrollment:** 13,242 degree-seeking undergraduates; 3,931 non-degree-seeking students. **Degrees:** 1,203 associate awarded. **ROTC:** Army, Air Force. **Location:** 6 miles from downtown. **Calendar:** Semester, limited summer session. **Full-time faculty:** 195 total; 15% have terminal degrees, 6% minority, 54% women. **Part-time faculty:** 1,387 total; 7% have terminal degrees, 8% minority, 51% women. **Class size:** 78% < 20, 22% 20-39, less than 1% 40-49, less than 1% 50-99. **Special facilities:** Center for Emergency Preparedness.

Student profile. Among degree-seeking undergraduates, 2,610 enrolled as first-time, first-year students, 110 transferred in from other institutions.

Part-time:	51%	Asian American:	1%
Out-of-state:	3%	Hispanic American:	7%
Women:	59%	25 or older:	51%
African American:	16%		

Transfer out. Colleges most students transferred to 2011: Bowling Green State University, Lourdes College, University of Findlay, University of Toledo.

Basis for selection. Open admission, but selective for some programs. Admission to health technologies, Peace Officer Academy, and early childhood education requires high school transcripts and test scores.

High school preparation. Recommended units include English 4, mathematics 4, science 3 (laboratory 3), foreign language 2, computer science 1 and academic electives 1.

2011-2012 Annual costs. Tuition/fees: $3,838; $7,222 out-of-state. Per-credit charge: $121 in-state; $242 out-of-state. Books/supplies: $2,000. Personal expenses: $1,800.

2011-2012 Financial aid. Need-based: 1,520 full-time freshmen applied for aid; 1,390 were judged to have need; 1,383 of these received aid. Average need met was 61%. Average scholarship/grant was $4,967; average loan $7,943. 36% of total undergraduate aid awarded as scholarships/grants, 64% as loans/jobs. Need-based aid available for part-time students. Work-study available nights, weekends and for part-time students. **Non-need-based:** Awarded to 533 full-time undergraduates, including 110 freshmen. Scholarships awarded for academics, athletics, job skills, state residency. **Additional information:** Other types of financial aid available: federal family education loan program, private foundation loan (SCHELL).

Application procedures. Admission: No deadline. No application fee. Admission notification on a rolling basis. February 1 application deadline for dental hygiene and physical therapist assistant programs. **Financial aid:** Priority date 3/31; no closing date. FAFSA required.

Academics. Special study options: Accelerated study, cooperative education, distance learning, double major, dual enrollment of high school students, ESL, honors, independent study, internships, study abroad, weekend college. License preparation in dental hygiene, nursing, paramedic, radiology, real estate. **Credit/placement by examination:** AP, CLEP, institutional tests. No limit placed upon number of credit hours student may obtain via proficiency exams as long as student has met graduation residency requirement. **Support services:** GED preparation and test center, learning center, pre-admission summer program, reduced course load, remedial instruction, study skills assistance, tutoring, writing center.

Majors. Area/ethnic studies: Women's. **Biology:** General, biotechnology. **Business:** General, accounting technology, business admin, executive assistant, international, office management, operations, restaurant/food services, retailing, sales/distribution. **Communications:** Communications/speech/rhetoric. **Communications technology:** General. **Computer sciences:** Applications programming, information technology, security. **Education:** General, early childhood, multi-level teacher. **Engineering:** General. **English:** English lit. **Foreign languages:** General. **General:** Landscaping, mechanization. **Health services:** General, dental assistant, dental hygiene, dietetics, health care admin, insurance specialist, licensed practical nurse, management/clinical assistant, massage therapy, medical radiologic technology/radiation therapy, medical records technology, medical secretary, nuclear medical technology, nursing (RN), occupational therapy assistant, physical therapy assistant, radiologic technology/medical imaging, sonography, surgical technology. **History:** General. **Human services:** General, social work. **Math:** General. **Parks/recreation:** Golf management. **Physical sciences:** Chemistry. **Protective services:** Corrections, fire safety technology, firefighting, law enforcement admin, police science. **Visual/performing arts:** Commercial photography, commercial/advertising art, dance, dramatic, industrial design, interior design, music technology, studio arts management.

Most popular majors. Business/marketing 25%, engineering/engineering technologies 13%, health sciences 32%, liberal arts 6%, security/protective services 8%.

Computing on campus. 3,000 workstations in library, computer center. Commuter students can connect to campus network. Online course registration, online library, helpline, wireless network available.

Student life. Freshman orientation: Mandatory, $65 fee. Preregistration for classes offered. **Policies:** Code of Student Conduct provides guidelines for acceptable behavior. **Activities:** Bands, choral groups, dance, drama, international student organizations, literary magazine, music ensembles, musical theater, student government, student newspaper, Bible Study club, Democratic Party club, ski club, Students in Free Enterprise, Rotaract club, Toastmasters International, Student Nurses' Association, hospitality and culinary club, Habitat for Humanity.

Athletics. NJCAA. **Intercollegiate:** Baseball M, basketball, golf M, soccer, softball W, volleyball W. **Intramural:** Basketball, bowling, football (nontackle), golf, skiing, softball, table tennis, tennis, volleyball, weight lifting. **Team name:** Express.

Student services. Adult student services, career counseling, services for economically disadvantaged, student employment services, financial aid counseling, on-campus daycare, placement for graduates, veterans' counselor. **Physically disabled:** Services for visually, hearing impaired. **Transfer:** Pre-admission transcript evaluation for new students. Transfer adviser; college fairs on campus for students transferring to 4-year colleges.

Contact. Phone: (567) 661-7777 Toll-free number: (800) 466-9367 Fax: (567) 661-7418
Cory Stine, Director, Admissions, Owens Community College: Toledo, 30335 Oregon Road, Toledo, OH 43699-1947

PowerSport Institute
North Randall, Ohio
www.psi-now.com

- For-profit 2-year technical college
- Very large city

General. Regionally accredited; also accredited by ACCSC. **Enrollment:** 310 full-time, degree-seeking students. **Degrees:** 34 associate awarded. **Calendar:** Quarter. **Full-time faculty:** 57 total.

Basis for selection. Open admission. Interview required for High Performance, Racing Program.

Financial aid. Need-based: Work-study available nights, weekends and for part-time students.

Application procedures. Admission: No deadline. $100 fee. **Financial aid:** No deadline.

Academics. Credit/placement by examination: AP, CLEP.

Contact. E-mail: admissions@ohiotechnicalcollege.com
Jordan Brenner, Director of Admissions, PowerSport Institute, 21210 Emery Road, North Randall, OH 44128

Remington College: Cleveland
Cleveland, Ohio
www.remingtoncollege.edu/cleveland   CB code: 3154

- For-profit 2-year technical and career college
- Very large city
- Interview required

General. Accredited by ACCSC. **Enrollment:** 593 degree-seeking undergraduates. **Degrees:** 57 associate awarded. **Location:** 8 miles from Cleveland. **Calendar:** Differs by program. **Full-time faculty:** 31 total. **Part-time faculty:** 19 total.

Basis for selection. Wonderlic SLE exam required for some programs. The Wonderlic SLE exam will be used as the sole acceptable entrance exam for all applicants seeking admission. The required passing score for the Wonderlic exam will be 17 or higher for the Computer and Network Administration associate degree program, 13 or higher for all other associate degrees, and 12 or higher for all diploma programs. Applicants will be allowed to take the entrance exam a maximum of three times.

Financial aid. Need-based: Work-study available nights, weekends and for part-time students.

Application procedures. Admission: No deadline. $50 fee. **Financial aid:** No deadline.

Academics. Special study options: Independent study. Externships. **Credit/placement by examination:** AP, CLEP. **Support services:** Learning center.

Majors. Business: Business admin. **Computer sciences:** Networking.

Computing on campus. Online library available.

Student services. Career counseling, financial aid counseling, placement for graduates.

Contact. E-mail: admissions@remingtoncollege.edu
Phone: (216) 475-7520 Fax: (216) 475-6055
Patrick Resetar, Campus President, Remington College: Cleveland, 14445 Broadway Avenue, Cleveland, OH 44125

Remington College: Cleveland West
North Olmsted, Ohio
www.remingtoncollege.edu/clevelandwest   CB code: 4200

- For-profit 2-year technical and career college
- Large town

General. Accredited by ACCSC. **Enrollment:** 336 degree-seeking undergraduates. **Degrees:** 43 associate awarded. **Location:** 10 miles from Cleveland. **Calendar:** Quarter. **Full-time faculty:** 14 total. **Part-time faculty:** 14 total.

Basis for selection. Open admission, but selective for some programs. Selective admissions to allied health programs.

Financial aid. Need-based: Work-study available nights, weekends and for part-time students.

Application procedures. Admission: No deadline. $50 fee. **Financial aid:** No deadline.

Academics. Special study options: Internships. **Credit/placement by examination:** AP, CLEP. **Support services:** GED test center, tutoring.

Majors. Business: Business admin. **Computer sciences:** Networking. **Health services:** Physical therapy assistant. **Protective services:** Criminal justice, law enforcement admin, police science.

Contact. E-mail: admissions@remingtoncollege.edu
Phone: (440) 777-2560
Alicia Chet, Director of Admissions, Remington College: Cleveland West, 26350 Brookpark Road, North Olmsted, OH 44070

Rosedale Bible College
Irwin, Ohio
www.rosedale.edu   CB code: 3936

- Private 2-year Bible and junior college affiliated with Mennonite Church
- Residential campus in rural community

General. Accredited by ABHE. **Enrollment:** 78 degree-seeking undergraduates. **Degrees:** 18 associate awarded. **Location:** 20 miles from Columbus. **Calendar:** Semester. **Full-time faculty:** 2 total. **Part-time faculty:** 16 total; 6% have terminal degrees, 19% women. **Class size:** 65% < 20, 35% 20-39.

Basis for selection. Open admission. **Home schooled:** Transcript of courses and grades required.

2011-2012 Annual costs. Tuition/fees: $8,075. Per-credit charge: $259. Room/board: $5,430. Books/supplies: $650.

Financial aid. Need-based: Need-based aid available for part-time students. Work-study available nights, weekends and for part-time students.

Application procedures. Admission: No deadline. $50 fee. Admission notification on a rolling basis. **Financial aid:** No deadline. FAFSA, institutional form required. Applicants notified on a rolling basis.

Academics. Special study options: Distance learning, double major, dual enrollment of high school students, independent study, study abroad. **Credit/placement by examination:** AP, CLEP. **Support services:** Learning center, reduced course load, tutoring.

Majors. Theology: Bible.

Computing on campus. 17 workstations in dormitories, library, computer center. Wireless network available.

Student life. Freshman orientation: Mandatory. Preregistration for classes offered. **Policies:** Religious observance required. **Housing:** Guaranteed on-campus for all undergraduates. Single-sex dorms, apartments available. **Activities:** Choral groups, drama, music ensembles, student government.

Athletics. Intramural: Basketball, soccer, table tennis, volleyball.

Student services. Chaplain/spiritual director, financial aid counseling, health services. **Transfer:** Pre-admission transcript evaluation for new students.

Contact. E-mail: admissions@rosedale.edu
Phone: (740) 857-1311 Fax: (877) 857-1312
Elizabeth Yoder, Director of Enrollment Services, Rosedale Bible College, 2270 Rosedale Road, Irwin, OH 43029

School of Advertising Art
Kettering, Ohio
www.saa.edu   CB code: 5953

- For-profit 2-year visual arts and technical college
- Commuter campus in small city
- Interview required

General. Accredited by ACCSC. **Enrollment:** 117 degree-seeking undergraduates. **Degrees:** 34 associate awarded. **Location:** 5 miles from Dayton. **Calendar:** Quarter. **Full-time faculty:** 8 total; 38% minority, 25% women. **Part-time faculty:** 1 total; 100% women. **Class size:** 100% 20-39.

Student profile.

Out-of-state:	4%	25 or older:	4%

Transfer out. 10% of students enrolled in the transfer program go on to 4-year colleges. **Colleges most students transferred to 2011:** Art Institute of Pittsburgh, Art Institute of Atlanta, Columbus College of Art and Design, American Inter-Continental University of London, Art Institute of San Francisco.

Basis for selection. Portfolio and creative potential most important with acceptable GPA. SAT or ACT recommended. Portfolio of 8 to 12 pieces of own artwork required. Depending on GPA and attendance, personal essay and 2 letters of recommendation may be required. **Home schooled:** State high school equivalency certificate required. Proof of completion of high school requirements required.

High school preparation. Recommended units include English 4 and visual/performing arts 3. 3 art units recommended.

2011-2012 Annual costs. Tuition/fees: $22,805. Per-credit charge: $360. Books/supplies: $1,580. Personal expenses: $500.

Financial aid. Need-based: Work-study available nights, weekends and for part-time students. **Non-need-based:** Scholarships awarded for academics, art, leadership, minority status.

Application procedures. Admission: No deadline. No application fee. Admission notification on a rolling basis. Students may pay discounted enrollment fee of $50 (normal fee is $100) if they elect to enroll by January 1. **Financial aid:** Priority date 7/1; no closing date. FAFSA required. Applicants notified on a rolling basis starting 4/1; must reply by 7/1 or within 1 week(s) of notification.

Academics. Special study options: Internships. **Credit/placement by examination:** AP, CLEP. **Support services:** Tutoring.

Majors. Communications: Advertising. **Computer sciences:** Computer graphics. **Visual/performing arts:** Commercial/advertising art.

Computing on campus. PC or laptop required. Repair service, student web hosting, wireless network available.

Student life. Freshman orientation: Mandatory. Preregistration for classes offered. Four-hour session held on a Saturday in the summer. **Activities:** Student government.

Student services. Career counseling, financial aid counseling, personal counseling, placement for graduates. **Transfer:** Re-entry adviser, pre-admission transcript evaluation for new students. Transfer adviser for students transferring to 4-year colleges.

Contact. E-mail: admissions@saa.edu
Phone: (937) 294-0592 Toll-free number: (877) 300-9866
Fax: (937) 294-5869
Jessica Barry, President, School of Advertising Art, 1725 East David Road, Kettering, OH 45440-1612

Sinclair Community College
Dayton, Ohio
www.sinclair.edu

CB member
CB code: 1720

- Public 2-year community college
- Commuter campus in small city

General. Founded in 1887. Regionally accredited. Member of the League for Innovation. Institution offers both transfer and technical academic programs. **Enrollment:** 21,314 degree-seeking undergraduates; 3,673 non-degree-seeking students. **Degrees:** 1,731 associate awarded. **ROTC:** Army, Air Force. **Location:** 50 miles from Cincinnati, 70 miles from Columbus. **Calendar:** Semester, extensive summer session. **Full-time faculty:** 407 total; 16% minority, 56% women. **Part-time faculty:** 1,016 total; 12% minority, 56% women. **Class size:** 52% < 20, 47% 20-39, less than 1% 40-49, less than 1% 50-99. **Special facilities:** Art galleries, theater, center for corporate and community events. **Partnerships:** Formal partnerships with eight area high schools.

Student profile. Among degree-seeking undergraduates, 36% enrolled in a transfer program, 51% enrolled in a vocational program, 3,555 enrolled as first-time, first-year students, 634 transferred in from other institutions.

Part-time:	54%	Asian American:	1%
Out-of-state:	2%	Hispanic American:	2%
Women:	59%	25 or older:	53%
African American:	16%		

Transfer out. 35% of students enrolled in the transfer program go on to 4-year colleges. **Colleges most students transferred to 2011:** Wright State University, University of Cincinnati, University of Dayton, Ohio State University, Miami University.

Basis for selection. Open admission, but selective for some programs. Admission to allied health programs, paralegal program, tooling and machining program, early childhood education all based on placement test scores and/or high school grades and specific program criteria. Interview required for some allied health programs. **Adult students:** Accuplacer placement required, if student does not have valid transfer credit or ACT scores.

2011-2012 Annual costs. Tuition/fees: $2,440; $3,858 out-of-district; $7,345 out-of-state. Per-credit charge: $45 in-district; $76 out-of-district; $154 out-of-state. Books/supplies: $1,122. Personal expenses: $1,320.

Financial aid. Need-based: Need-based aid available for part-time students. Work-study available nights, weekends and for part-time students. **Non-need-based:** Scholarships awarded for academics, athletics, state residency.

Application procedures. Admission: No deadline. $20 fee. Admission notification on a rolling basis. **Financial aid:** Priority date 5/1, closing date 8/1. FAFSA, institutional form required. Applicants notified on a rolling basis.

Academics. Special study options: Cooperative education, cross-registration, distance learning, dual enrollment of high school students, ESL, honors, independent study, internships, liberal arts/career combination, student-designed major. License preparation in aviation, dental hygiene, nursing, occupational therapy, paramedic, physical therapy, radiology, real estate. **Credit/placement by examination:** AP, CLEP, institutional tests. 30 credit hours maximum toward associate degree. **Support services:** Learning center, pre-admission summer program, reduced course load, remedial instruction, study skills assistance, tutoring, writing center.

Majors. Area/ethnic studies: African-American. **Business:** General, accounting, business admin, entrepreneurial studies, hotel/motel admin, logistics, office/clerical, real estate, tourism/travel. **Communications:** Communications/speech/rhetoric. **Computer sciences:** General, security. **Education:** Kindergarten/preschool, physical. **Engineering:** General, industrial. **English:** Creative writing, English lit. **Foreign languages:** General, sign language interpretation. **Health services:** Dental hygiene, dietetics, EMT paramedic, medical assistant, medical radiologic technology/radiation therapy, medical records technology, medical secretary, nursing (RN), occupational therapy assistant, physical therapy assistant, respiratory therapy technology, substance abuse counseling, surgical technology, veterinary technology/assistant. **History:** General. **Liberal arts:** Arts/sciences. **Math:** General. **Military:** Geospatial intel. **Philosophy/religion:** Philosophy. **Physical sciences:** Chemistry. **Protective services:** Fire safety technology, infrastructure protection, police science. **Psychology:** General. **Social sciences:** Political science, sociology. **Visual/performing arts:** Art, commercial/advertising art, dramatic, interior design, theater design.

Most popular majors. Business/marketing 15%, computer/information sciences 9%, engineering/engineering technologies 12%, health sciences 26%, liberal arts 13%.

Computing on campus. 1,000 workstations in library, computer center, student center. Commuter students can connect to campus network. Online course registration, helpline, wireless network available.

Student life. Freshman orientation: Available. Preregistration for classes offered. Required for degree- and certificate-seeking students. **Activities:** Bands, campus ministries, choral groups, dance, drama, international student organizations, music ensembles, Model UN, musical theater, opera, student government, student newspaper, African American cultural club, Native American cultural club, Appalachian club, College Democrats, College Republicans, Campus Bible Fellowship, Muslim student association, Phi Theta Kappa (honorary club), global awareness and action club.

Athletics. NJCAA. **Intercollegiate:** Baseball M, basketball, tennis W, volleyball W. **Intramural:** Basketball, football (non-tackle), soccer, volleyball. **Team name:** Tartans.

Student services. Adult student services, alcohol/substance abuse counseling, chaplain/spiritual director, career counseling, services for economically disadvantaged, student employment services, financial aid counseling, minority student services, on-campus daycare, personal counseling, placement for graduates, veterans' counselor, women's services. **Physically disabled:** Services for visually, speech, hearing impaired. **Transfer:** Pre-admission transcript evaluation for new students. Transfer adviser, college fairs on campus for students transferring to 4-year colleges.

Contact. E-mail: admit@sinclair.edu
Phone: (937) 512-3000 Toll-free number: (800) 315-3000
Fax: (937) 512-2393
Dani Stoll, Director of Admissions, Sinclair Community College, 444 West Third Street, Dayton, OH 45402-1460

Southern State Community College
Hillsboro, Ohio
www.sscc.edu
CB code: 1752

◗ Public 2-year community college
◗ Commuter campus in small town

General. Founded in 1975. Regionally accredited. **Enrollment:** 2,777 degree-seeking undergraduates; 573 non-degree-seeking students. **Degrees:** 410 associate awarded. **Location:** 60 miles from Cincinnati, 55 miles from Columbus. **Calendar:** Quarter, limited summer session. **Full-time faculty:** 60 total; 13% have terminal degrees, 47% women. **Part-time faculty:** 144 total; 4% have terminal degrees, 2% minority, 58% women. **Class size:** 66% < 20, 34% 20-39, less than 1% 40-49.

Student profile. Among degree-seeking undergraduates, 52% enrolled in a transfer program, 48% enrolled in a vocational program, 1% already have a bachelor's degree or higher, 443 enrolled as first-time, first-year students, 127 transferred in from other institutions.

Part-time:	35%	Asian American:	1%
Women:	69%	Hispanic American:	1%
African American:	2%	25 or older:	45%

Transfer out. 25% of students enrolled in the transfer program go on to 4-year colleges.

Basis for selection. Open admission, but selective for some programs. Special requirements for nursing, respiratory therapy, EMT programs. Interview required for nursing program. **Learning Disabled:** If modifications requested, appointment with Disabilities Service Coordinator required.

2011-2012 Annual costs. Tuition/fees: $3,633; $6,993 out-of-state. Per-credit charge: $87 in-state; $174 out-of-state. Books/supplies: $2,067.

Financial aid. Need-based: Need-based aid available for part-time students. Work-study available nights, weekends and for part-time students. **Non-need-based:** Scholarships awarded for academics, art, athletics, music/drama.

Application procedures. Admission: No deadline. No application fee. Admission notification on a rolling basis. **Financial aid:** Priority date 7/1, closing date 9/1. FAFSA, institutional form required. Applicants notified by 4/15; must reply within 2 week(s) of notification.

Academics. Special study options: Cross-registration, distance learning, dual enrollment of high school students, liberal arts/career combination, student-designed major. License preparation in nursing, paramedic, real estate. **Credit/placement by examination:** AP, CLEP, institutional tests. 30 credit hours maximum toward associate degree. **Support services:** GED preparation and test center, learning center, remedial instruction, study skills assistance, tutoring.

Majors. Business: General, accounting technology, administrative services, business admin, entrepreneurial studies, real estate. **Computer sciences:** Applications programming, programming, systems analysis. **Education:** Early childhood, teacher assistance. **General:** Food processing. **Health services:** EMT paramedic, medical assistant, nursing (RN), respiratory therapy technology, substance abuse counseling. **Liberal arts:** Arts/sciences. **Protective services:** Corrections, police science.

Most popular majors. Business/marketing 17%, computer/information sciences 7%, health sciences 30%, liberal arts 31%.

Computing on campus. 452 workstations in library, computer center. Commuter students can connect to campus network. Online course registration, online library, helpline, wireless network available.

Student life. Freshman orientation: Mandatory. Preregistration for classes offered. **Activities:** Bands, choral groups, drama.

Athletics. USCAA. **Intercollegiate:** Basketball, soccer M, softball W, volleyball W. **Team name:** Patriots.

Student services. Career counseling, student employment services, financial aid counseling, on-campus daycare, placement for graduates. **Physically disabled:** Services for visually, speech, hearing impaired. **Transfer:** Transfer adviser, college fairs on campus for students transferring to 4-year colleges.

Contact. E-mail: info@sscc.edu
Phone: (937) 393-3431 ext. 2607 Fax: (937) 393-6682
Wendy Johnson, Director of Admissions, Southern State Community College, 100 Hobart Drive, Hillsboro, OH 45133

Stark State College of Technology
North Canton, Ohio
www.starkstate.edu
CB code: 1688

◗ Public 2-year community college
◗ Commuter campus in small city

General. Founded in 1970. Regionally accredited. **Enrollment:** 13,036 degree-seeking undergraduates; 2,496 non-degree-seeking students. **Degrees:** 927 associate awarded. **Location:** 50 miles from Cleveland. **Calendar:** Semester, extensive summer session. **Full-time faculty:** 198 total. **Part-time faculty:** 553 total. **Special facilities:** Rolls Royce fuel cell testing center.

Student profile. Among degree-seeking undergraduates, 3,065 enrolled as first-time, first-year students.

Part-time:	61%	Asian American:	1%
Out-of-state:	1%	Hispanic American:	1%
Women:	61%	Native American:	1%
African American:	21%	25 or older:	54%

Basis for selection. Open admission, but selective for some programs. Special requirements for allied health programs. **Learning Disabled:** All students should meet with disability services coordinator.

High school preparation. College-preparatory program recommended. Recommended units include English 4, mathematics 4, social studies 3, science 3 and foreign language 1.

2011-2012 Annual costs. Tuition/fees: $4,215; $6,465 out-of-state. Per-credit charge: $141 in-state; $216 out-of-state. Books/supplies: $900.

2010-2011 Financial aid. All financial aid based on need. 59% of total undergraduate aid awarded as scholarships/grants, 41% as loans/jobs. Need-based aid available for part-time students. Work-study available nights, weekends and for part-time students.

Application procedures. Admission: Priority date 6/1; no deadline. $65 fee. Admission notification on a rolling basis. **Financial aid:** Priority date 5/1; no closing date. FAFSA, institutional form required. Applicants notified on a rolling basis starting 4/1; must reply within 4 week(s) of notification.

Academics. Special study options: Accelerated study, cooperative education, cross-registration, distance learning, double major, dual enrollment of high school students, independent study, internships, liberal arts/career combination, student-designed major, weekend college. License preparation in dental hygiene, nursing, paramedic. **Credit/placement by examination:** AP, CLEP, institutional tests. 12 credit hours maximum toward associate degree. **Support services:** Learning center, pre-admission summer program, reduced course load, remedial instruction, study skills assistance, tutoring, writing center.

Majors. Architecture: Environmental design, urban/community planning. **Business:** General, accounting, accounting technology, accounting/business management, accounting/finance, administrative services, business admin, communications, construction management, e-commerce, executive assistant, hospitality admin, international, logistics, management information systems, market research, marketing, office management, office technology, operations, sales/distribution, taxation. **Computer sciences:** General, applications programming, computer graphics, computer science, data entry, data processing, database management, information systems, information technology, networking, programming, security, systems analysis, web page design, webmaster, word processing. **Conservation:** Environmental studies. **Education:** Early childhood. **Engineering:** Architectural, civil, electrical, environmental, software. **Health services:** Clinical lab assistant, clinical lab technology, dental hygiene, massage therapy, medical assistant, medical records technology, nursing (RN), occupational therapy assistant, office assistant, physical therapy assistant, respiratory therapy assistant, respiratory therapy technology. **Liberal arts:** Arts/sciences. **Math:** General. **Protective services:** Firefighting. **Social sciences:** General. **Work/family studies:** Aging, child care service.

Computing on campus. 1,875 workstations in computer center, student center. Commuter students can connect to campus network. Online course registration, online library, helpline, wireless network available.

Student life. Freshman orientation: Available. Preregistration for classes offered. Half-day prior to all semesters. Evening sessions are 2 hours. **Activities:** Literary magazine, student newspaper, Bible study group, Minority Awareness Association, Phi Theta Kappa.

Athletics. Team name: Spartans.

Student services. Adult student services, chaplain/spiritual director, career counseling, services for economically disadvantaged, student employment services, financial aid counseling, minority student services, on-campus

daycare, personal counseling, placement for graduates, veterans' counselor. **Physically disabled:** Services for visually, speech, hearing impaired. **Transfer:** Pre-admission transcript evaluation for new students. Transfer adviser, college fairs on campus for students transferring to 4-year colleges.

Contact. E-mail: info@starkstate.edu
Phone: (330) 494-6170 ext. 4228 Toll-free number: (800) 797-8275
Fax: (330) 497-6313
Wallace Hoffer, Dean of Student Services, Stark State College of Technology, 6200 Frank Avenue NW, North Canton, OH 44720

Stautzenberger College
Maumee, Ohio
www.sctoday.edu

CB code: 2487

- For-profit 2-year technical and career college
- Commuter campus in large town

General. Founded in 1928. Accredited by ACICS. **Location:** Suburb of Toledo, 50 miles from Detroit, 120 miles from Cleveland. **Calendar:** Quarter.

Annual costs/financial aid. Tuition ranges from $254 to $375 per credit hour; required fees, $270. Books/supplies: $300. Personal expenses: $2,619. Need-based financial aid available to full-time and part-time students.

Contact. Phone: (419) 866-0261
Director of Admission, 1796 Indian Wood Circle, Maumee, OH 43537-4007

Stautzenberger College: Brecksville
Brecksville, Ohio
www.LearnWhatYouLove.com

- For-profit 2-year career college
- Commuter campus in large town
- Interview required

General. Accredited by ACICS. **Enrollment:** 330 degree-seeking undergraduates. **Degrees:** 82 associate awarded. **Location:** 15 miles from Cleveland. **Calendar:** Quarter, extensive summer session. **Full-time faculty:** 11 total; 36% have terminal degrees, 82% women. **Part-time faculty:** 47 total; 26% have terminal degrees. **Class size:** 85% < 20, 15% 20-39.

Student profile. Among degree-seeking undergraduates, 1% already have a bachelor's degree or higher, 31 enrolled as first-time, first-year students.

Part-time:	68%	Hispanic American:	2%
Women:	89%	25 or older:	48%
African American:	6%		

Transfer out. Colleges most students transferred to 2011: Cuyahoga Community College, Stautzenberger College Toledo, Lorain County Community College.

Basis for selection. Open admission. All incoming students must complete the COMPASS exam with minimum scores. Students who do not meet the minimum threshold are referred to addtional resources outside the College and entrance is deferred until students can meet the minimum threshold. **Home schooled:** Interview required.

High school preparation. College-preparatory program recommended.

2011-2012 Annual costs. Tuition ranges from $254 to $375 per credit hour; required fees, $270. Books/supplies: $1,350.

Financial aid. All financial aid based on need. Need-based aid available for part-time students. Work-study available nights, weekends and for part-time students.

Application procedures. Admission: No deadline. $25 fee. Application must be submitted on paper. Admission notification on a rolling basis. **Financial aid:** No deadline. FAFSA required. Applicants notified on a rolling basis.

Academics. Special study options: Distance learning, independent study, internships. **Credit/placement by examination:** AP, CLEP, institutional tests. **Support services:** Reduced course load, remedial instruction, study skills assistance, tutoring, writing center.

Majors. Business: General. **Health services:** Veterinary technology/assistant.

Most popular majors. Health sciences 90%, legal studies 10%.

Computing on campus. PC or laptop required. 45 workstations in library, computer center. Commuter students can connect to campus network. Online library, wireless network available.

Student life. Freshman orientation: Mandatory. Preregistration for classes offered. **Activities:** Student government.

Student services. Adult student services, career counseling, student employment services, financial aid counseling, personal counseling, placement for graduates. **Physically disabled:** Services for visually, speech, hearing impaired. **Transfer:** Pre-admission transcript evaluation for new students.

Contact. E-mail: lskarcher@LearnWhatYouLove.com
Phone: (440) 838-1999 Fax: (440) 838-0960
Linda Karcher, Director of Admissions, Stautzenberger College: Brecksville, 8001 Katherine Boulevard, Brecksville, OH 44141

Terra State Community College
Fremont, Ohio
www.terra.edu

CB code: 0365

- Public 2-year community and technical college
- Commuter campus in large town

General. Founded in 1968. Regionally accredited. **Enrollment:** 2,623 degree-seeking undergraduates. **Degrees:** 252 associate awarded. **Location:** 33 miles from Toledo, 86 miles from Columbus. **Calendar:** Semester, limited summer session. **Full-time faculty:** 52 total. **Part-time faculty:** 181 total.

Transfer out. Colleges most students transferred to 2011: Bowling Green State University, University of Toledo, Owens Community College, Ohio State University, Tiffin University.

Basis for selection. Open admission.

High school preparation. Recommended units include English 4, mathematics 3, social studies 3 and science 3. Algebra recommended for engineering and computer programming applicants.

2011-2012 Annual costs. Tuition/fees: $4,065; $6,372 out-of-state. Percredit charge: $121 in-state; $198 out-of-state. Books/supplies: $1,350. Personal expenses: $150.

Financial aid. Need-based: Need-based aid available for part-time students. Work-study available nights, weekends and for part-time students. **Non-need-based:** Scholarships awarded for academics.

Application procedures. Admission: No deadline. No application fee. Admission notification on a rolling basis. **Financial aid:** Priority date 5/1; no closing date. FAFSA, institutional form required. Applicants notified on a rolling basis starting 5/15.

Academics. Special study options: Accelerated study, cooperative education, distance learning, double major, dual enrollment of high school students, honors, independent study, internships, student-designed major, weekend college. Bachelor's degree programs available on campus. License preparation in real estate. **Credit/placement by examination:** AP, CLEP, institutional tests. **Support services:** Learning center, reduced course load, remedial instruction, study skills assistance, tutoring, writing center.

Majors. Biology: General. **Business:** General, accounting, banking/financial services, business admin, executive assistant, hospitality admin, marketing, operations, real estate. **Communications technology:** Animation/special effects, desktop publishing. **Computer sciences:** Data processing, networking, programming, web page design. **Education:** General, kindergarten/preschool. **Engineering:** General. **English:** English lit. **Foreign languages:** Translation. **General:** Business. **Health services:** Health care admin, insurance coding, management/clinical assistant, medical assistant, medical records admin, medical records technology, medical secretary, nursing (RN), office assistant. **History:** General. **Human services:** Social work. **Liberal arts:** Arts/sciences, humanities. **Math:** General. **Physical sciences:** Chemistry, physics. **Protective services:** Police science. **Psychology:** General. **Social sciences:** Economics. **Visual/performing arts:** Art history/conservation, music, music management, music performance, studio arts.

Computing on campus. 299 workstations in library, computer center. Online course registration, online library available.

Student life. Freshman orientation: Mandatory. Preregistration for classes offered. **Activities:** Jazz band, choral groups, music ensembles, student government, Phi Theta Kappa, Koinonia, Society of Plastic Engineers.

Athletics. NJCAA. **Intramural:** Basketball, bowling, football (non-tackle) M, softball, table tennis, tennis, volleyball. **Team name:** ThunderCats.

Student services. Career counseling, student employment services, personal counseling, placement for graduates, veterans' counselor. **Physically disabled:** Services for visually, speech, hearing impaired. **Transfer:** Reentry adviser, pre-admission transcript evaluation for new students. Transfer center, transfer adviser, college fairs on campus for students transferring to 4-year colleges.

Contact. E-mail: admissions@terra.edu
Phone: (419) 559-2349 Toll-free number: (866) 288-3772 ext. 2349
Fax: (419) 334-9035
Kristen Taylor, Admissions Director, Terra State Community College, 2830 Napoleon Road, Fremont, OH 43420-9600

Trumbull Business College
Warren, Ohio
www.tbc-trumbullbusiness.com   CB code: 3270

▶ For-profit 2-year business college
▶ Commuter campus in large town

General. Accredited by ACICS. **Enrollment:** 325 degree-seeking undergraduates. **Degrees:** 130 associate awarded. **Calendar:** Quarter.

Basis for selection. Open admission. **Home schooled:** Transcript of courses and grades required.

2011-2012 Annual costs. Tuition/fees: $11,340. Per-credit charge: $252. Books/supplies: $3,500.

Financial aid. **Need-based:** Need-based aid available for part-time students. Work-study available nights, weekends and for part-time students.

Application procedures. **Admission:** No deadline. $75 fee. Admission notification on a rolling basis. **Financial aid:** FAFSA required.

Academics. **Special study options:** Distance learning. **Credit/placement by examination:** AP, CLEP. **Support services:** GED test center, tutoring.

Majors. **Business:** Accounting, business admin, office technology. **Computer sciences:** General. **Health services:** Medical assistant, medical secretary.

Computing on campus. 100 workstations in library, computer center. Online library, wireless network available.

Student life. **Freshman orientation:** Mandatory. Preregistration for classes offered.

Student services. Career counseling, financial aid counseling, placement for graduates.

Contact. E-mail: admissions@tbc-trumbullbusiness.com
Phone: (330) 369-3200
Shawn Swaney, Director of Admissions, Trumbull Business College, 3200 Ridge Road, Warren, OH 44484

University of Akron: Wayne College
Orrville, Ohio
www.wayne.uakron.edu   CB code: 1892

▶ Public 2-year branch campus and junior college
▶ Commuter campus in small town

General. Founded in 1972. Regionally accredited. **Enrollment:** 1,999 degree-seeking undergraduates; 503 non-degree-seeking students. **Degrees:** 82 associate awarded. **ROTC:** Army, Air Force. **Location:** 35 miles from Akron. **Calendar:** Semester, limited summer session. **Full-time faculty:** 27 total; 59% have terminal degrees, 11% minority, 52% women. **Part-time faculty:** 174 total; 13% have terminal degrees, 5% minority, 53% women. **Class size:** 62% < 20, 34% 20-39, 3% 40-49, 1% 50-99. **Special facilities:** Nature trail, arboretum, wetlands, distance learning room.

Student profile. Among degree-seeking undergraduates, 389 enrolled as first-time, first-year students, 68 transferred in from other institutions.

Part-time:	38%	Asian American:	1%
Women:	60%	Hispanic American:	1%
African American:	4%	25 or older:	32%

Transfer out. **Colleges most students transferred to 2011:** Ashland University, Kent State, Cleveland State, Ohio State, Ohio University.

Basis for selection. Open admission. **Adult students:** SAT/ACT scores not required if applicant over 24. **Home schooled:** Recommend completion of GED.

High school preparation. Recommended units include English 4, mathematics 3, social studies 3, science 3 and foreign language 2.

2011-2012 Annual costs. Tuition/fees: $5,910; $13,697 out-of-state. Per-credit charge: $239 in-state; $508 out-of-state. Books/supplies: $600. Personal expenses: $1,465.

Financial aid. **Need-based:** Need-based aid available for part-time students. Work-study available nights, weekends and for part-time students. **Non-need-based:** Scholarships awarded for academics, art, athletics, leadership, minority status, music/drama, state residency. **Additional information:** All financial aid processed through University of Akron.

Application procedures. **Admission:** $40 fee, may be waived for applicants with need. Admission notification on a rolling basis. **Financial aid:** Closing date 3/15. FAFSA, institutional form required. Applicants notified on a rolling basis starting 4/15.

Academics. First 2 years of general bachelor's degree classes available for students who plan to continue at University of Akron or other colleges and universities. Paraprofessional and technical programs (associates and certificates) available in business, industry, public services occupation areas. **Special study options:** Cooperative education, cross-registration, distance learning, dual enrollment of high school students, honors, independent study, internships, liberal arts/career combination, student-designed major, weekend college. **Credit/placement by examination:** AP, CLEP, institutional tests. **Support services:** Learning center, remedial instruction, study skills assistance, tutoring, writing center.

Majors. **Business:** General, accounting, administrative services, business admin, management information systems, marketing, office management, office technology. **Computer sciences:** Applications programming, data processing, networking. **Health services:** Health care admin, medical assistant, medical radiologic technology/radiation therapy, medical secretary, respiratory therapy technology, surgical technology. **Human services:** Social work. **Liberal arts:** Arts/sciences.

Most popular majors. Business/marketing 22%, computer/information sciences 10%, education 11%, health sciences 19%, liberal arts 6%, public administration/social services 12%, security/protective services 13%, social sciences 18%.

Computing on campus. 140 workstations in library, computer center, student center. Commuter students can connect to campus network. Online course registration, helpline, wireless network available.

Student life. **Freshman orientation:** Mandatory. Preregistration for classes offered. **Activities:** Literary magazine, student government, student newspaper.

Athletics. NJCAA. **Intercollegiate:** Basketball, cheerleading M, golf M, volleyball W. **Intramural:** Basketball, racquetball, volleyball W. **Team name:** Warriors.

Student services. Adult student services, career counseling, student employment services, financial aid counseling, personal counseling, placement for graduates, veterans' counselor. **Physically disabled:** Services for visually, speech, hearing impaired. **Transfer:** Pre-admission transcript evaluation for new students. Transfer adviser, college fairs on campus for students transferring to 4-year colleges.

Contact. E-mail: wayneadmissions@uakron.edu
Phone: (330) 683-2010 Toll-free number: (800) 221-8308 ext. 8900
Fax: (330) 684-8989
Alicia Broadus, Coordinator of Admissions, University of Akron: Wayne College, 1901 Smucker Road, Orrville, OH 44667-9758

University of Cincinnati: Clermont College
Batavia, Ohio
www.ucclermont.edu   CB code: 3073

▶ Public 2-year branch campus college
▶ Commuter campus in small town

General. Founded in 1972. Regionally accredited. College serves Clermont, Brown, and eastern Hamilton counties. One of 2 open-access regional campuses of the University of Cincinnati. **Enrollment:** 3,503 degree-seeking

undergraduates; 368 non-degree-seeking students. **Degrees:** 362 associate awarded. **ROTC:** Army. **Location:** 17 miles from Cincinnati. **Calendar:** Quarter, limited summer session. **Full-time faculty:** 98 total. **Part-time faculty:** 150 total. **Partnerships:** Formal partnerships with Sporty's.

Student profile. Among degree-seeking undergraduates, 822 enrolled as first-time, first-year students, 285 transferred in from other institutions.

Part-time:	35%	Asian American:	1%
Women:	57%	Hispanic American:	1%
African American:	3%	25 or older:	28%

Transfer out. Colleges most students transferred to 2011: Northern Kentucky University, University of Cincinnati, Wilmington College.

Basis for selection. Open admission, but selective for some programs. Selective admissions to allied health and police academy. **Home schooled:** Transcript of courses and grades required. All existing school records and formal documentation of high school curriculum required. Course content descriptions, copy of superintendent release form, notarized statement from parent, and precollege curriculum form completed and signed by parent may also be required. Appointment involving student, teacher, and admissions representative may be encouraged.

High school preparation. College-preparatory program recommended. 16 units recommended. Recommended units include English 4, mathematics 3, social studies 2, science 2, foreign language 2 and academic electives 2. 1 fine arts recommended.

2011-2012 Annual costs. Tuition/fees: $5,034; $11,886 out-of-state. Per-credit charge: $119 in-state; $310 out-of-state. Books/supplies: $1,308. Personal expenses: $3,816.

Financial aid. Need-based: Need-based aid available for part-time students. Work-study available nights, weekends and for part-time students. **Non-need-based:** Scholarships awarded for academics, leadership, minority status, state residency. **Additional information:** All financial aid applications and awards administered through Uptown campus except in-house loans and scholarships.

Application procedures. Admission: No deadline. $50 fee, may be waived for applicants with need. Admission notification on a rolling basis. **Financial aid:** No deadline. FAFSA required. Applicants notified on a rolling basis.

Academics. Special study options: Cooperative education, cross-registration, distance learning, double major, dual enrollment of high school students, honors, independent study, internships, student-designed major, study abroad, weekend college. Bachelor's degree programs available on campus. License preparation in aviation, nursing, paramedic, physical therapy, real estate. **Credit/placement by examination:** AP, CLEP, IB, institutional tests. 50% of hours needed for degree may be earned by examination. **Support services:** Learning center, reduced course load, remedial instruction, study skills assistance, tutoring.

Majors. Architecture: Urban/community planning. **Biology:** General. **Business:** General, accounting technology, administrative services, business admin, marketing, office management, office technology. **Computer sciences:** General, applications programming, data entry, data processing, information technology, networking, programming, vendor certification. **Education:** Early childhood, elementary, kindergarten/preschool, middle, secondary. **Health services:** EMT ambulance attendant, EMT paramedic, nursing (RN), physical therapy assistant, predental, premedicine, prenursing, prepharmacy, preveterinary, respiratory therapy technology, surgical technology. **Human services:** Social work. **Liberal arts:** Arts/sciences. **Physical sciences:** Chemistry. **Protective services:** Corrections, criminal justice, forensics, law enforcement admin, security services. **Psychology:** General. **Social sciences:** Urban studies.

Computing on campus. 104 workstations in library, computer center, student center. Commuter students can connect to campus network. Online course registration, online library, helpline, wireless network available.

Student life. Freshman orientation: Mandatory. Preregistration for classes offered. Programs held each quarter for 2-3 hours. **Activities:** Pep band, campus ministries, dance, literary magazine, student government, student newspaper, student tribunal, Christian Fellowship, foreign language club, Young Democrats, Circle K (Kiwanis).

Athletics. USCAA. **Intercollegiate:** Baseball M, basketball, cheerleading M, golf M, softball W, tennis, volleyball W. **Intramural:** Volleyball. **Team name:** Cougars.

Student services. Alcohol/substance abuse counseling, career counseling, services for economically disadvantaged, student employment services, financial aid counseling, personal counseling, placement for graduates, veterans' counselor, women's services. **Physically disabled:** Services for visually, speech, hearing impaired. **Transfer:** Transfer adviser, college fairs on campus for students transferring to 4-year colleges.

Contact. E-mail: clc.admissions@uc.edu
Phone: (513) 732-5294 Toll-free number: (866) 446-2822
Fax: (513) 732-5303
Martha Geiger, Director of Enrollment Services, University of Cincinnati: Clermont College, 4200 Clermont College Drive, Batavia, OH 45103

University of Cincinnati: Raymond Walters College
Cincinnati, Ohio
www.rwc.uc.edu   CB code: 0354

▶ Public 2-year branch campus college
▶ Commuter campus in large city

General. Founded in 1967. Regionally accredited. **Location:** 15 miles from downtown. **Calendar:** Quarter.

Annual costs/financial aid. Tuition/fees (2011-2012): $5,691; $14,025 out-of-state. Books/supplies: $700. Need-based financial aid available to full-time and part-time students.

Contact. Phone: (513) 745-5700
Director, Enrollment Services, 9555 Plainfield Road, Cincinnati, OH 45236-1096

University of Northwestern Ohio
Lima, Ohio
www.unoh.edu   CB code: 0816

▶ Private 2-year business and technical college
▶ Residential campus in large town

General. Founded in 1920. Regionally accredited. **Enrollment:** 4,167 degree-seeking undergraduates. **Degrees:** 142 bachelor's, 1,140 associate awarded; master's offered. **Location:** 75 miles from Toledo, 90 miles from Columbus. **Calendar:** Continuous, extensive summer session. **Full-time faculty:** 109 total. **Part-time faculty:** 51 total.

Student profile.

Out-of-state:	21%	Live on campus:	65%
25 or older:	18%		

Transfer out. Colleges most students transferred to 2011: Lima Technical College, Ohio State University, Wright State University, Bowling Green State University.

Basis for selection. Students with 1.5 GPA or lower admitted conditionally. **Home schooled:** Statement describing home school structure and mission required. **Learning Disabled:** Students must self-disclose personal needs and provide IEP.

2011-2012 Annual costs. Tuition/fees: $9,105. Per-credit charge: $195. Room only: $2,700. Books/supplies: $1,798. Personal expenses: $1,818.

Financial aid. Need-based: Need-based aid available for part-time students. Work-study available nights, weekends and for part-time students. **Non-need-based:** Scholarships awarded for academics, job skills, minority status.

Application procedures. Admission: No deadline. $20 fee. Admission notification on a rolling basis. **Financial aid:** Priority date 4/1; no closing date. FAFSA required. Applicants notified on a rolling basis starting 4/30; must reply within 2 week(s) of notification.

Academics. Students wanting credit for life experience must register for 1-hour course in portfolio development. **Special study options:** Accelerated study, cooperative education, distance learning, double major, weekend college. Bachelor's degree programs available on campus. **Credit/placement by examination:** AP, CLEP, institutional tests. 25 credit hours maximum toward associate degree. **Support services:** Learning center, remedial instruction, tutoring.

Majors. Business: Accounting, administrative services, business admin, marketing, office technology, tourism/travel. **Computer sciences:** General, applications programming. **General:** Business. **Health services:** Medical assistant, medical secretary, pharmacy assistant.

Most popular majors. Business/marketing 6%, trade and industry 73%.

Computing on campus. 212 workstations in library, computer center, student center. Commuter students can connect to campus network. Online course registration available.

Student life. Freshman orientation: Available. Preregistration for classes offered. Held 4 to 6 weeks before quarter or session begins. **Housing:** Guaranteed on-campus for all undergraduates. Single-sex dorms, special housing for disabled, apartments, wellness housing available. $100 deposit. **Activities:** Student government, student newspaper, TV station.

Athletics. Intramural: Bowling, volleyball. **Team name:** Racers.

Student services. Adult student services, career counseling, student employment services, financial aid counseling, minority student services, personal counseling, placement for graduates, veterans' counselor. **Physically disabled:** Services for visually, hearing impaired. **Transfer:** Pre-admission transcript evaluation for new students.

Contact. E-mail: info@unoh.edu
Phone: (419) 998-3120 Fax: (419) 229-6926
Rick Morrison, Director of Admissions, University of Northwestern Ohio, 1441 North Cable Road, Lima, OH 45805

Vatterott College: Cleveland
Broadview Heights, Ohio
www.vatterott-college.edu

- For-profit 2-year technical college
- Commuter campus in large town

General. Accredited by ACCSCT. **Calendar:** Semester.

Annual costs/financial aid. Estimated program costs as of April 2011: diploma (60 weeks) $24,680 - $24,980; associate degree (90 weeks) $36,230 - $36,680. All costs, which include tuition, fees, books and supplies, and taxes, are subject to change. Books/supplies: $1,877.

Contact. Phone: (440) 526-1660
Director of Admissions, 5025 East Royalton Road, Broadview Heights, OH 44147

Virginia Marti College of Art and Design
Lakewood, Ohio
www.vmcad.edu   CB code: 0396

- For-profit 2-year visual arts and business college
- Commuter campus in large city
- Application essay, interview required

General. Founded in 1966. Accredited by ACCSC. **Enrollment:** 50 degree-seeking undergraduates. **Degrees:** 63 associate awarded. **Location:** 7 miles from Cleveland. **Calendar:** Quarter, extensive summer session. **Full-time faculty:** 9 total. **Part-time faculty:** 53 total.

Basis for selection. School achievement record, admission test scores and interview considered. Essay questions and letter of recommendation reviewed. Career Ability Placement Survey (CAPS) required for admission. Portfolio recommended for graphic design, interior design, digital media and fashion design majors; in lieu of portfolio, preliminary art courses required in first quarter. **Home schooled:** Transcript of courses and grades required. **Learning Disabled:** Provide high school IEP for review of special needs.

2011-2012 Annual costs. Tuition/fees: $17,634. Books/supplies: $1,800. Personal expenses: $1,746.

Financial aid. All financial aid based on need. Work-study available nights, weekends and for part-time students.

Application procedures. Admission: Closing date 9/24. $50 fee. Admission notification on a rolling basis. **Financial aid:** No deadline. FAFSA required. Applicants notified on a rolling basis.

Academics. Special study options: Dual enrollment of high school students, independent study, internships, study abroad. **Credit/placement by examination:** AP, CLEP, institutional tests. **Support services:** Remedial instruction, study skills assistance, tutoring.

Majors. Business: Fashion. **Computer sciences:** Computer science. **Visual/performing arts:** Art, art history/conservation, commercial/advertising art, design, fashion design, illustration, interior design, photography.

Computing on campus. 28 workstations in library, computer center. Commuter students can connect to campus network. Online course registration, wireless network available.

Student life. Freshman orientation: Mandatory. Preregistration for classes offered. Two-four hour program held 1 week prior to start of classes. **Policies:** Students participate in yearly fashion shows; competitions; trips to New York, France, and Italy. **Activities:** Student government, student chapters of American Institute of Graphic Artists, Fashion Group International, American Society of Interior Designers.

Student services. Career counseling, student employment services, placement for graduates, veterans' counselor. **Transfer:** Pre-admission transcript evaluation for new students. Transfer adviser for students transferring to 4-year colleges.

Contact. E-mail: qmarti@vmcad.edu
Phone: (216) 221-8584 ext. 106 Toll-free number: (800) 473-4350
Quinn Marti, Director of Admissions, Virginia Marti College of Art and Design, 11724 Detroit Avenue, Lakewood, OH 44107

Washington State Community College
Marietta, Ohio
www.wscc.edu   CB code: 0381

- Public 2-year community college
- Commuter campus in large town

General. Founded in 1971. Regionally accredited. **Enrollment:** 2,211 degree-seeking undergraduates. **Degrees:** 378 associate awarded. **Location:** 112 miles from Columbus. **Calendar:** Quarter, limited summer session. **Full-time faculty:** 61 total. **Part-time faculty:** 129 total.

Student profile.

Out-of-state:	12%	25 or older:	46%

Basis for selection. Open admission, but selective for some programs. Special requirements for medical laboratory technology, nursing, physical therapist assistant, radiology, respiratory therapy programs. ACT required for nursing, radiologic technology programs. Interview required for programs with selective admission.

2011-2012 Annual costs. Tuition/fees: $3,940; $7,732 out-of-state. Per-credit charge: $84 in-state; $169 out-of-state. Books/supplies: $870. Personal expenses: $1,667.

Financial aid. Need-based: Work-study available nights, weekends and for part-time students.

Application procedures. Admission: No deadline. No application fee. Admission notification on a rolling basis. **Financial aid:** No deadline. FAFSA, institutional form required. Applicants notified on a rolling basis starting 5/15; must reply within 2 week(s) of notification.

Academics. Special study options: Distance learning, double major, dual enrollment of high school students, independent study, internships, student-designed major. License preparation in nursing, radiology. **Credit/placement by examination:** AP, CLEP, institutional tests. 60 credit hours maximum toward associate degree. **Support services:** Learning center, pre-admission summer program, reduced course load, remedial instruction, tutoring.

Majors. Business: General, accounting, business admin, e-commerce, marketing. **Communications:** Broadcast journalism, media studies. **Communications technology:** Animation/special effects. **Computer sciences:** Computer graphics, data processing, programming. **Education:** General, elementary, multi-level teacher, secondary. **Engineering:** General, electrical. **Health services:** Clinical lab assistant, medical radiologic technology/radiation therapy, medical transcription, nursing (RN), physical therapy assistant, respiratory therapy technology. **Liberal arts:** Arts/sciences. **Math:** General. **Protective services:** Corrections, law enforcement admin.

Student life. Freshman orientation: Available. Preregistration for classes offered. **Activities:** Choral groups, music ensembles, student government, student newspaper, veterans club, Phi Theta Kappa honor fraternity.

Student services. Adult student services, career counseling, student employment services, financial aid counseling, personal counseling, placement for graduates, veterans' counselor. **Physically disabled:** Services for visually, hearing impaired. **Transfer:** Transfer adviser, college fairs on campus for students transferring to 4-year colleges.

Contact. E-mail: admissions@wscc.edu
Phone: (740) 568-1900 Fax: (740) 373-7496
Paul Wells, Director of Admissions, Washington State Community
College, 710 Colegate Drive, Marietta, OH 45750

Wright State University: Lake Campus
Celina, Ohio
www.wright.edu/lake   CB code: 1947

- Public 2-year branch campus college
- Commuter campus in small town

General. Founded in 1969. Regionally accredited. **Enrollment:** 908 degree-seeking undergraduates; 441 non-degree-seeking students. **Degrees:** 56 bachelor's, 67 associate awarded; master's offered. **Location:** 70 miles from Dayton. **Calendar:** Quarter, limited summer session. **Full-time faculty:** 26 total; 31% women. **Class size:** 65% < 20, 29% 20-39, 6% 40-49.

Student profile. Among degree-seeking undergraduates, 5% enrolled in a transfer program, 6% already have a bachelor's degree or higher, 185 enrolled as first-time, first-year students, 60 transferred in from other institutions.

Part-time:	18%	African American:	2%
Out-of-state:	1%	Hispanic American:	2%
Women:	60%	25 or older:	34%

Basis for selection. Open admission, but selective for some programs. Special requirements for engineering and education programs. SAT/ACT required for all students but only used for placement in selective programs.

High school preparation. College-preparatory program recommended. 16 units recommended. Recommended units include English 4, mathematics 3, social studies 3, science 3 (laboratory 3) and foreign language 2. Math requirement includes 2 algebra. Art, music or theater recommended.

2011-2012 Annual costs. Tuition/fees: $5,424; $12,987 out-of-state. Per-credit charge: $164 in-state; $396 out-of-state.

2011-2012 Financial aid. Need-based: 153 full-time freshmen applied for aid; 142 were judged to have need; 140 of these received aid. Average need met was 55%. Average scholarship/grant was $5,327; average loan $3,436. 33% of total undergraduate aid awarded as scholarships/grants, 67% as loans/jobs. Need-based aid available for part-time students. Work-study available nights, weekends and for part-time students. **Non-need-based:** Awarded to 65 full-time undergraduates, including 11 freshmen. Scholarships awarded for academics, alumni affiliation, art, athletics, leadership, minority status, music/drama, ROTC.

Application procedures. Admission: No deadline. $30 fee. Admission notification on a rolling basis. **Financial aid:** Priority date 2/15; no closing date. FAFSA required. Applicants notified on a rolling basis starting 3/15.

Academics. Special study options: Cooperative education, cross-registration, distance learning, double major, dual enrollment of high school students, honors, independent study, internships, student-designed major. Bachelor's degree programs available on campus. **Credit/placement by examination:** AP, CLEP, IB, institutional tests. **Support services:** Learning center, pre-admission summer program, reduced course load, remedial instruction, tutoring.

Majors. Biology: General. **Business:** General, business admin, management information systems. **Communications:** Communications/speech/rhetoric. **Computer sciences:** Information systems. **History:** General. **Human services:** Social work. **Liberal arts:** Arts/sciences. **Physical sciences:** Chemistry, geology. **Psychology:** General. **Social sciences:** Sociology.

Most popular majors. Business/marketing 37%, computer/information sciences 20%, engineering/engineering technologies 30%, psychology 7%.

Computing on campus. 105 workstations in computer center. Commuter students can connect to campus network. Online course registration, online library, helpline, repair service, wireless network available.

Student life. Freshman orientation: Available. Preregistration for classes offered. **Housing:** $150 fully refundable deposit. **Activities:** Drama, student government, student newspaper, Business Professionals of America, Student Manufacturing Engineers.

Athletics. NCAA. **Intercollegiate:** Basketball, golf M, volleyball W. **Team name:** Raiders.

Student services. Adult student services, career counseling, financial aid counseling, on-campus daycare, personal counseling, placement for graduates, veterans' counselor. **Physically disabled:** Services for visually, hearing impaired.

Contact. E-mail: discoverlakecampus@wright.edu
Phone: (419) 586-0324 Toll-free number: (800) 237-1477
Fax: (419) 586-0358
BJ Hobbler, Student Services Officer, Wright State University: Lake Campus, 7600 State Route 703, Celina, OH 45822-2952

Zane State College
Zanesville, Ohio
www.zanestate.edu   CB code: 1535

- Public 2-year technical college
- Commuter campus in large town

General. Founded in 1969. Regionally accredited. **Location:** 60 miles from Columbus. **Calendar:** Quarter.

Annual costs/financial aid. Tuition/fees (2011-2012): $4,230; $8,460 out-of-state. Books/supplies: $1,500. Need-based financial aid available to full-time and part-time students.

Contact. Phone: (740) 454-2501 ext. 1225
Director of Admissions, 1555 Newark Road, Zanesville, OH 43701-2626

Oklahoma

Carl Albert State College
Poteau, Oklahoma
www.carlalbert.edu
CB code: 1474

- Public 2-year community and junior college
- Commuter campus in large town

General. Founded in 1932. Regionally accredited. **Enrollment:** 2,537 degree-seeking undergraduates. **Degrees:** 450 associate awarded. **Location:** 35 miles from Fort Smith, Arkansas. **Calendar:** Semester, limited summer session. **Full-time faculty:** 45 total. **Part-time faculty:** 8 total.

Transfer out. Colleges most students transferred to 2011: Northeastern State University, University of Arkansas, Southeastern State University, University of Central Oklahoma.

Basis for selection. Open admission, but selective for some programs. Nursing, radiographic technology, and physical therapy assistant programs employ selective enrollment.

High school preparation. 15 units recommended. Recommended units include English 4, mathematics 3, social studies 1, history 2, science 2 (laboratory 2) and academic electives 1. One social science unit should be in American history.

2011-2012 Annual costs. Tuition/fees: $2,490; $5,490 out-of-state. Per-credit charge: $55 in-state; $155 out-of-state. Room/board: $3,840. Books/supplies: $750. Personal expenses: $1,678.

Financial aid. All financial aid based on need. Need-based aid available for part-time students. Work-study available nights, weekends and for part-time students.

Application procedures. Admission: No deadline. No application fee. Admission notification on a rolling basis. **Financial aid:** No deadline. FAFSA, institutional form required. Applicants notified on a rolling basis.

Academics. Special study options: Distance learning, dual enrollment of high school students, honors, independent study, liberal arts/career combination. License preparation in nursing, physical therapy, radiology. **Credit/placement by examination:** AP, CLEP, institutional tests. 18 credit hours maximum toward associate degree. **Support services:** GED test center, learning center, remedial instruction, study skills assistance, tutoring.

Majors. Biology: General, zoology. **Business:** General, accounting, administrative services, business admin. **Communications:** Journalism. **Computer sciences:** Computer science. **Education:** Elementary, secondary. **English:** English lit, rhetoric/composition. **Health services:** Nursing (RN), physical therapy assistant, premedicine, prepharmacy, preveterinary. **Math:** General. **Parks/recreation:** Health/fitness. **Protective services:** Criminal justice. **Psychology:** General. **Social sciences:** General, sociology. **Visual/performing arts:** Art, dramatic, music.

Most popular majors. Business/marketing 17%, education 19%, family/consumer sciences 8%, health sciences 23%, social sciences 13%.

Computing on campus. 50 workstations in library, computer center. Dormitories wired for high-speed internet access. Commuter students can connect to campus network. Online library available.

Student life. Freshman orientation: Mandatory. Preregistration for classes offered. One-day session held at beginning of semester offered online. **Housing:** Single-sex dorms available. $100 deposit. Scholar's housing available. **Activities:** Choral groups, dance, drama, music ensembles, musical theater, radio station, student government, student newspaper, African-American awareness, American Indian student association, Young Democrats, Young Republicans.

Athletics. NJCAA. **Intercollegiate:** Baseball M, basketball M, cheerleading M. **Team name:** Vikings.

Student services. Chaplain/spiritual director, career counseling, services for economically disadvantaged, financial aid counseling, on-campus daycare, veterans' counselor. **Physically disabled:** Services for hearing impaired. **Transfer:** Pre-admission transcript evaluation for new students. Transfer adviser, college fairs on campus for students transferring to 4-year colleges.

Contact. E-mail: ddickerson@carlalbert.edu
Phone: (918) 647-1300 Fax: (918) 647-1306
Dee Ann Dickerson, Registrar, Carl Albert State College, 1507 South McKenna, Poteau, OK 74953-5208

Connors State College
Warner, Oklahoma
www.connorsstate.edu
CB code: 6117

- Public 2-year community and junior college
- Commuter campus in rural community

General. Founded in 1908. Regionally accredited. Main campus in Warner. Branch campus in Muskogee. **Enrollment:** 2,138 degree-seeking undergraduates; 425 non-degree-seeking students. **Degrees:** 315 associate awarded. **Location:** 20 miles from Muskogee, 65 miles from Tulsa. **Calendar:** Semester, extensive summer session. **Full-time faculty:** 47 total. **Part-time faculty:** 45 total. **Class size:** 64% < 20, 32% 20-39, 3% 40-49, 1% 50-99. **Special facilities:** 1,300 acre wetlands and nature preserve.

Student profile. Among degree-seeking undergraduates, 806 enrolled as first-time, first-year students, 759 transferred in from other institutions.

Part-time:	28%	25 or older:	42%
Out-of-state:	4%	Live on campus:	10%
Women:	67%		

Transfer out. Colleges most students transferred to 2011: Northeastern State University, Oklahoma State University.

Basis for selection. Open admission, but selective for some programs. Special requirements for nursing and equine programs; interview required. **Adult students:** Must complete secondary assessment. **Home schooled:** Transcript of courses and grades required. Student's equivalent public high school class must have graduated; must take ACT; proficiency in subject area curricula required. **Learning Disabled:** Students with documented disabilities must complete designated paperwork in the office of the Vice President for Student Services.

High school preparation. College-preparatory program recommended.

2011-2012 Annual costs. Tuition/fees: $2,997; $7,224 out-of-state. Per-credit charge: $70 in-state; $211 out-of-state. Room/board: $5,050. Books/supplies: $1,200.

Financial aid. Need-based: Need-based aid available for part-time students. Work-study available nights, weekends and for part-time students. **Non-need-based:** Scholarships awarded for academics, alumni affiliation, athletics, leadership, state residency.

Application procedures. Admission: No deadline. No application fee. Admission notification on a rolling basis. High school diploma required of applicants younger than 18. **Financial aid:** Closing date 3/1. FAFSA, institutional form required. Applicants notified on a rolling basis starting 4/1; must reply within 2 week(s) of notification.

Academics. Special study options: Distance learning, dual enrollment of high school students, internships, liberal arts/career combination. License preparation in nursing. **Credit/placement by examination:** AP, CLEP, institutional tests. 18 credit hours maximum toward associate degree. **Support services:** Learning center, remedial instruction, tutoring.

Majors. Biology: General. **Business:** General, accounting, business admin. **Communications:** Communications/speech/rhetoric, journalism. **Computer sciences:** General, data processing. **Education:** Early childhood, elementary, physical. **English:** English lit, rhetoric/composition. **General:** Equestrian studies. **Health services:** Nursing (RN), premedicine, preveterinary. **History:** General. **Human services:** Social work. **Liberal arts:** Arts/sciences. **Math:** General. **Physical sciences:** Chemistry, physics. **Protective services:** Police science. **Psychology:** General. **Social sciences:** General, sociology. **Visual/performing arts:** Art. **Work/family studies:** General, business, child care management.

Computing on campus. 217 workstations in dormitories, library, computer center. Dormitories wired for high-speed internet access and linked to campus network. Online library, wireless network available.

Student life. Housing: Single-sex dorms, apartments, wellness housing available. $55 nonrefundable deposit. **Activities:** Campus ministries, drama, student government, student newspaper, Phi Theta Kappa, Aggie club, math and science club, Baptist Collegiate Ministries, behavioral science club, Phi Beta Lambda, President's leadership class.

Athletics. NJCAA. **Intercollegiate:** Baseball M, basketball, cheerleading, rodeo, softball W. **Team name:** Cowboys.

Student services. Adult student services, career counseling, services for economically disadvantaged, student employment services, financial aid counseling, health services, minority student services, veterans' counselor. **Physically disabled:** Services for visually, hearing impaired. **Transfer:** Preadmission transcript evaluation for new students. College fairs on campus for students transferring to 4-year colleges.

Contact. E-mail: cscenroll@connorsstate.edu
Phone: (918) 463-2931 ext. 6300 Fax: (918) 463-6327
Sonya Baker, Registrar, Connors State College, RR 1, Box 1000, Warner, OK 74469-9700

Eastern Oklahoma State College
Wilburton, Oklahoma
www.eosc.edu

CB code: 6189

- Public 2-year community college
- Commuter campus in small town

General. Founded in 1908. Regionally accredited. **Enrollment:** 1,177 full-time, degree-seeking students. **Degrees:** 241 associate awarded. **Location:** 90 miles from Tulsa. **Calendar:** Semester, limited summer session. **Full-time faculty:** 52 total. **Part-time faculty:** 62 total. **Class size:** 22% < 20, 61% 20-39, 16% 40-49, less than 1% 50-99, less than 1% >100. **Special facilities:** Oklahoma Miner Training Institute, Center for Correction Officer Studies.

Student profile.

Out-of-state:	2%	Live on campus:	20%
25 or older:	65%		

Transfer out. Colleges most students transferred to 2011: East Central State University, Northeastern State University, Southeastern Oklahoma State University.

Basis for selection. Open admission, but selective for some programs. Special requirements for nursing program; interview required.

High school preparation. 12 units recommended. Recommended units include English 4, mathematics 3, social studies 2 and science 2. 1 citizenship or government.

2011-2012 Annual costs. Tuition/fees: $3,200; $6,817 out-of-state. Per-credit charge: $79 in-state; $200 out-of-state. Room/board: $4,629. Books/supplies: $578. Personal expenses: $500.

Financial aid. All financial aid based on need. Need-based aid available for part-time students. Work-study available nights, weekends and for part-time students.

Application procedures. Admission: No deadline. $10 fee. Admission notification on a rolling basis. **Financial aid:** Priority date 3/1, closing date 6/30. FAFSA, institutional form required. Applicants notified on a rolling basis starting 5/1; must reply within 2 week(s) of notification.

Academics. Special study options: Cooperative education, distance learning, dual enrollment of high school students, honors, internships. License preparation in nursing. **Credit/placement by examination:** AP, CLEP, institutional tests. 30 credit hours maximum toward associate degree. **Support services:** Learning center, remedial instruction, tutoring.

Majors. Biology: General, bacteriology, entomology. **Business:** General, accounting, administrative services, business admin, management information systems, office/clerical. **Communications:** Journalism. **Computer sciences:** General, computer science, programming, systems analysis. **Conservation:** General, environmental studies, forestry, wildlife/wilderness. **Education:** Agricultural, art, biology, business, chemistry, computer, drama/dance, elementary, health, history, mathematics, music, physical, physics, science, secondary, social science, social studies, speech. **Engineering:** General. **English:** English lit. **General:** Agronomy, animal sciences, business, farm/ranch, food science, horticultural science, horticulture, ornamental horticulture, products processing, soil science. **Health services:** Medical secretary, nursing (RN), predental, premedicine, prenursing, prepharmacy, preveterinary. **History:** General. **Math:** General. **Parks/recreation:** Facilities management, health/fitness. **Physical sciences:** Chemistry, physics. **Protective services:** Criminal justice, law enforcement admin. **Psychology:** General. **Social sciences:** General, sociology. **Visual/performing arts:** Dramatic, music. **Work/family studies:** Child care management.

Most popular majors. Biological/life sciences 6%, business/marketing 9%, education 31%, health sciences 28%, psychology 6%.

Computing on campus. 250 workstations in dormitories, library, computer center. Dormitories linked to campus network. Commuter students can connect to campus network. Online library, helpline, wireless network available.

Student life. Freshman orientation: Mandatory, $12 fee. Preregistration for classes offered. **Housing:** Coed dorms, single-sex dorms, special housing for disabled, apartments available. $50 deposit, deadline 8/15. **Activities:** Choral groups, drama, music ensembles, musical theater, radio station, student government, student newspaper, campus religious organizations, Afro-American and Native American clubs, professional clubs.

Athletics. NJCAA. **Intercollegiate:** Baseball M, basketball, cheerleading, rodeo, softball W. **Intramural:** Basketball, handball, racquetball, softball, swimming, table tennis, tennis, volleyball. **Team name:** Mountaineers.

Student services. Adult student services, chaplain/spiritual director, career counseling, student employment services, financial aid counseling, personal counseling, placement for graduates, veterans' counselor. **Physically disabled:** Services for visually, speech, hearing impaired. **Transfer:** Preadmission transcript evaluation for new students. Transfer adviser, college fairs on campus for students transferring to 4-year colleges.

Contact. Phone: (918) 465-2361 Fax: (918) 465-2431
Victor Woods, Vice President for Student Affairs, Eastern Oklahoma State College, 1301 West Main Street, Wilburton, OK 74578-4999

Murray State College
Tishomingo, Oklahoma
www.mscok.edu

CB code: 6421

- Public 2-year junior college
- Commuter campus in small town

General. Founded in 1908. Regionally accredited. **Enrollment:** 2,527 degree-seeking undergraduates. **Degrees:** 375 associate awarded. **Location:** 32 miles from Ardmore. **Calendar:** Semester, limited summer session. **Full-time faculty:** 51 total. **Part-time faculty:** 56 total.

Basis for selection. Open admission, but selective for some programs. Special requirements for nursing, gunsmithing, and vet tech programs. **Home schooled:** Transcript of courses and grades required.

High school preparation. 15 units recommended. Recommended units include English 4, mathematics 3, social studies 1, history 2, science 2 (laboratory 2) and academic electives 3. Recommend 1 unit in citizenship.

2011-2012 Annual costs. Tuition/fees: $3,200; $7,640 out-of-state. Per-credit charge: $92 in-state; $240 out-of-state. Room/board: $5,600. Books/supplies: $600. Personal expenses: $1,984.

Financial aid. Need-based: Work-study available nights, weekends and for part-time students.

Application procedures. Admission: No deadline. No application fee. Admission notification on a rolling basis beginning on or about 4/15. **Financial aid:** Priority date 4/15, closing date 6/30. Applicants notified on a rolling basis starting 5/1.

Academics. Special study options: Honors. License preparation in nursing. **Credit/placement by examination:** AP, CLEP. **Support services:** Learning center, remedial instruction, tutoring.

Majors. Business: Administrative services, business admin. **Computer sciences:** General, computer science. **Conservation:** General. **Education:** Elementary. **English:** English lit. **Health services:** Preveterinary. **History:** General. **Liberal arts:** Arts/sciences. **Math:** General. **Visual/performing arts:** General. **Work/family studies:** Child care management.

Most popular majors. Business/marketing 11%, health sciences 22%, liberal arts 57%, social sciences 6%.

Computing on campus. Commuter students can connect to campus network. Helpline available.

Student life. Freshman orientation: Mandatory. Preregistration for classes offered. **Housing:** Coed dorms available. $50 deposit. **Activities:** Campus ministries, choral groups, drama, music ensembles, student government.

Athletics. NJCAA. **Intercollegiate:** Baseball M, basketball. **Intramural:** Baseball M, basketball. **Team name:** Aggies.

Student services. Career counseling, veterans' counselor. **Transfer:** College fairs on campus for students transferring to 4-year colleges.

Contact. Phone: (580) 371-2371 ext. 108 Fax: (580) 371-0529
Genna Marten, Registrar and Director of Admissions, Murray State
College, One Murray Campus, Tishomingo, OK 73460

Northeastern Oklahoma Agricultural and Mechanical College
Miami, Oklahoma   CB member
www.neo.edu   CB code: 6484

- Public 2-year community and junior college
- Commuter campus in large town

General. Founded in 1919. Regionally accredited. Extension courses
offered in neighboring towns and online, Reach Higher program for adult
students, bachelor's programs offered on campus through other institutions.
Enrollment: 1,718 full-time, degree-seeking students. **Degrees:** 372 associate awarded. **ROTC:** Air Force. **Location:** 76 miles from Tulsa. **Calendar:**
Semester, extensive summer session. **Full-time faculty:** 71 total; 11% have
terminal degrees, 11% minority, 56% women. **Part-time faculty:** 47 total;
15% minority, 53% women. **Class size:** 56% < 20, 42% 20-39, less than 1%
40-49, less than 1% 50-99. **Special facilities:** College farm, equine center,
music hall, activity center, athletic training facility, student union.

Student profile.

Out-of-state:	17%	Live on campus:	31%

Transfer out. Colleges most students transferred to 2011: Oklahoma
State University, Northeastern State University, University of Central Oklahoma, Missouri Southern State University, Pittsburg State University.

Basis for selection. Open admission. **Adult students:** Students over the
age of 21 must complete placement testing before enrolling in college level
classes. **Home schooled:** Transcript of courses and grades required. **Learning
Disabled:** Applicants should contact director of disabilities services.

High school preparation. College-preparatory program recommended.

2011-2012 Annual costs. Tuition/fees: $2,996; $7,338 out-of-state. Per-
credit charge: $68 in-state; $213 out-of-state. Room/board: $4,492. Books/
supplies: $850. Personal expenses: $1,000.

2010-2011 Financial aid. Need-based: 783 full-time freshmen applied
for aid; 624 were judged to have need; 622 of these received aid. Average
need met was 81%. Average scholarship/grant was $6,552; average loan
$3,001. 72% of total undergraduate aid awarded as scholarships/grants, 28%
as loans/jobs. Need-based aid available for part-time students. Work-study
available nights, weekends and for part-time students. **Non-need-based:**
Awarded to 813 full-time undergraduates, including 388 freshmen. Scholarships awarded for academics, athletics, leadership, music/drama, state residency.

Application procedures. Admission: No deadline. No application fee.
Admission notification on a rolling basis. **Financial aid:** Priority date 4/1;
no closing date. FAFSA required. Applicants notified on a rolling basis
starting 4/1; must reply by 8/30 or within 2 week(s) of notification.

Academics. Special study options: Distance learning, double major, dual
enrollment of high school students, independent study, internships. Bachelor's
degree programs available on campus. License preparation in nursing, physical therapy. **Credit/placement by examination:** AP, CLEP, institutional
tests. 36 credit hours maximum toward associate degree. **Support services:**
GED preparation and test center, learning center, reduced course load, remedial instruction, study skills assistance, tutoring, writing center.

Majors. Area/ethnic studies: Native American. **Biology:** General. **Business:** Accounting, administrative services, business admin, marketing. **Communications:** Radio/TV. **Computer sciences:** General, programming. **Conservation:** Forestry. **Education:** Early childhood. **English:** English lit. **General:** Equestrian studies, farm/ranch. **Health services:** Athletic training,
clinical lab technology, medical secretary, nursing (RN), physical therapy
assistant, predental, premedicine, prenursing, prepharmacy, preveterinary.
Math: General. **Parks/recreation:** Health/fitness, sports admin. **Physical
sciences:** General. **Protective services:** Criminal justice. **Psychology:** General. **Social sciences:** General. **Visual/performing arts:** Art, dramatic, music.

Most popular majors. Business/marketing 10%, education 9%, health
sciences 36%, liberal arts 16%, natural resources/environmental science 11%,
psychology 7%.

Computing on campus. 85 workstations in dormitories, library, computer
center. Dormitories linked to campus network. Commuter students can connect to campus network. Online library, helpline, wireless network available.

Student life. Freshman orientation: Mandatory, $88 fee. Preregistration
for classes offered. **Policies:** Single students under the age of 21 who reside
more than 50 miles away are required to live on-campus. **Housing:** Guaranteed on-campus for all undergraduates. Single-sex dorms, special housing for
disabled, wellness housing available. $75 fully refundable deposit. **Activities:**
Bands, choral groups, dance, drama, music ensembles, musical theater, student government, TV station, Ministerial Alliance, Baptist student union,
Aggie Society, Collegiates for Christ, Young Democrats, Young Republicans,
Phi Theta Kappa, Afro-American Society, Native American student association, Masquers.

Athletics. NJCAA. **Intercollegiate:** Baseball M, basketball, football
(tackle) M, rodeo, soccer, softball W, volleyball W. **Intramural:** Baseball,
basketball, bowling, football (tackle) M, soccer, softball, swimming, volleyball. **Team name:** Norsemen.

Student services. Adult student services, alcohol/substance abuse counseling, career counseling, services for economically disadvantaged, financial
aid counseling, health services, minority student services, personal counseling, veterans' counselor. **Physically disabled:** Services for visually, speech,
hearing impaired. **Transfer:** Transfer adviser, college fairs on campus for
students transferring to 4-year colleges.

Contact. E-mail: neoadmission@neo.edu
Phone: (918) 540-6399 Toll-free number: (888) 464-6636
Fax: (918) 540-6946
Michelle Shackelford, Registrar, Northeastern Oklahoma Agricultural and
Mechanical College, 200 I Street Northeast, Miami, OK 74354-6497

Northern Oklahoma College
Tonkawa, Oklahoma   CB member
www.north-ok.edu   CB code: 6486

- Public 2-year community college
- Commuter campus in small town

General. Founded in 1901. Regionally accredited. **Enrollment:** 5,210
degree-seeking undergraduates. **Degrees:** 627 associate awarded. **Location:**
90 miles from Oklahoma City; 70 miles from Wichita, Kansas. **Calendar:**
Semester, limited summer session. **Full-time faculty:** 65 total. **Part-time
faculty:** 98 total. **Special facilities:** Museum of science and history, observatory, arboretum.

Student profile.

Out-of-state:	1%	Live on campus:	17%

Transfer out. Colleges most students transferred to 2011: Oklahoma
State University, Northwestern Oklahoma State University, Oklahoma University, University of Central Oklahoma.

Basis for selection. Open admission, but selective for out-of-state students. Out-of-state applicants must have high school diploma and rank in
top half of class or have 19 ACT. ACT required for students under 21 years
old for placement. Students with below 19 ACT in English, math, and reading
must take placement tests. **Adult students:** Placement testing required.

High school preparation. High school units mandated by state law may
vary with program.

2011-2012 Annual costs. Tuition/fees: $2,572; $6,495 out-of-state. Per-
credit charge: $62 in-state; $193 out-of-state. Room/board: $4,290. Books/
supplies: $600. Personal expenses: $1,200.

Financial aid. Need-based: Need-based aid available for part-time students. Work-study available nights, weekends and for part-time students.

Application procedures. Admission: No deadline. No application fee.
Application must be submitted on paper. Admission notification on a rolling
basis. **Financial aid:** Priority date 6/1; no closing date. FAFSA, institutional
form required. Applicants notified on a rolling basis starting 4/1.

Academics. Special study options: Distance learning, dual enrollment of
high school students, honors, independent study, internships, liberal arts/
career combination. **Credit/placement by examination:** AP, CLEP, institutional tests. 30 credit hours maximum toward associate degree. **Support
services:** Learning center, remedial instruction, tutoring.

Majors. Area/ethnic studies: Native American. **Biology:** General, zoology.
Business: General, accounting, business admin, office management. **Communications:** Broadcast journalism, journalism, public relations. **Computer
sciences:** General, web page design. **Education:** Elementary, physical, secondary. **English:** English lit. **General:** Agribusiness operations. **Health services:** Medical radiologic technology/radiation therapy, nursing (RN), premedicine, prepharmacy, respiratory therapy technology, surgical technology.

Liberal arts: Arts/sciences. **Math:** General. **Physical sciences:** Chemistry, physics. **Protective services:** Law enforcement admin. **Social sciences:** General. **Visual/performing arts:** Art, music management.

Computing on campus. 200 workstations in dormitories, library, computer center. Dormitories wired for high-speed internet access and linked to campus network. Commuter students can connect to campus network. Online course registration, online library, student web hosting, wireless network available.

Student life. Freshman orientation: Mandatory. Preregistration for classes offered. **Housing:** Single-sex dorms, apartments available. $60 deposit. **Activities:** Bands, choral groups, drama, literary magazine, music ensembles, musical theater, opera, radio station, student government, student newspaper, symphony orchestra, TV station.

Athletics. NJCAA. **Intercollegiate:** Baseball M, basketball, soccer, softball W. **Intramural:** Basketball, racquetball, softball, tennis, volleyball. **Team name:** Mavericks.

Student services. Career counseling, financial aid counseling, health services, personal counseling, veterans' counselor. **Physically disabled:** Services for visually, speech, hearing impaired. **Transfer:** College fairs on campus for students transferring to 4-year colleges.

Contact. E-mail: rick.edgington@north-ok.edu
Phone: (580) 628-6221 Toll-free number: (888) 429-5715
Fax: (580) 628-6371
Rick Edgington, Associate Vice President, Northern Oklahoma College, Box 310, Tonkawa, OK 74653-0310

Oklahoma City Community College
Oklahoma City, Oklahoma   **CB member**
www.occc.edu   **CB code: 0270**

▶ Public 2-year community college
▶ Commuter campus in large city

General. Founded in 1969. Regionally accredited. **Enrollment:** 14,194 degree-seeking undergraduates; 239 non-degree-seeking students. **Degrees:** 1,142 associate awarded. **Calendar:** Semester, extensive summer session. **Full-time faculty:** 148 total; 20% minority, 51% women. **Part-time faculty:** 382 total; 18% minority, 57% women. **Class size:** 54% < 20, 45% 20-39, less than 1% 40-49, less than 1% 50-99. **Special facilities:** Olympic-size swimming pool, diving well.

Student profile. Among degree-seeking undergraduates, 55% enrolled in a transfer program, 45% enrolled in a vocational program, 3% already have a bachelor's degree or higher, 3,330 enrolled as first-time, first-year students, 1,361 transferred in from other institutions.

Part-time:	61%	Hispanic American:	10%
Out-of-state:	2%	Native American:	5%
Women:	59%	International:	3%
African American:	11%	25 or older:	46%
Asian American:	4%		

Transfer out. Colleges most students transferred to 2011: University of Central Oklahoma, University of Oklahoma-OU Health Science Center, Oklahoma State University, University of Oklahoma, Oklahoma City University.

Basis for selection. Open admission, but selective for some programs. Special requirements for nursing, speech language pathology, occupational therapy and physical therapy programs; reading test required. **Home schooled:** If under the age of 21, official high school transcript and ACT required.

High school preparation. 15 units required. Required and recommended units include English 4, mathematics 3, social studies 1, history 2, science 3 (laboratory 1-2) and academic electives 1. History recommendation includes 1 unit of American history and 2 units of citizenship skills or other history. Math must include one semester of Algebra II.

2011-2012 Annual costs. Tuition/fees: $2,851; $7,279 out-of-state. Per-credit charge: $72 in-state; $219 out-of-state. Books/supplies: $1,000. Personal expenses: $1,252.

Financial aid. Need-based: Need-based aid available for part-time students. Work-study available nights, weekends and for part-time students. **Non-need-based:** Scholarships awarded for academics, alumni affiliation, art, leadership, music/drama, state residency.

Application procedures. Admission: No deadline. $25 fee, may be waived for applicants with need. Admission notification on a rolling basis.

Financial aid: Priority date 4/15; no closing date. FAFSA required. Applicants notified on a rolling basis starting 2/15.

Academics. Special study options: Accelerated study, cooperative education, distance learning, double major, dual enrollment of high school students, ESL, honors, independent study, internships, liberal arts/career combination, student-designed major, study abroad, weekend college. License preparation in nursing, occupational therapy, paramedic, physical therapy, real estate. **Credit/placement by examination:** AP, CLEP, IB, institutional tests. 45 credit hours maximum toward associate degree. Credit will not be transcripted until 12 resident hours have been completed. **Support services:** GED preparation and test center, learning center, reduced course load, remedial instruction, study skills assistance, tutoring, writing center.

Majors. Biology: General, bioinformatics, biotechnology. **Business:** General, finance, office/clerical, real estate, tourism promotion, tourism/travel. **Communications:** Broadcast journalism, journalism. **Communications technology:** Desktop publishing, graphics, photo/film/video. **Computer sciences:** General, computer science, data processing, programming, security, systems analysis, web page design. **Education:** General, multi-level teacher, secondary. **Engineering:** General. **Foreign languages:** French, Spanish, translation. **Health services:** EMT paramedic, nursing (RN), occupational therapy assistant, physical therapy assistant. **History:** General. **Liberal arts:** Arts/sciences. **Math:** General. **Physical sciences:** Chemistry, physics. **Psychology:** General. **Social sciences:** Sociology. **Visual/performing arts:** Commercial/advertising art, music, studio arts, theater design. **Work/family studies:** Child care management.

Computing on campus. 2,000 workstations in library, computer center, student center. Commuter students can connect to campus network. Online course registration, online library, helpline, wireless network available.

Student life. Freshman orientation: Available. Preregistration for classes offered. Held the week prior to classes for 3 hours on days, evenings and weekends. **Activities:** Jazz band, campus ministries, choral groups, drama, international student organizations, literary magazine, music ensembles, musical theater, student government, student newspaper, Phi Theta Kappa, Chi Alpha, Christians on Campus, African-American student association, Asian cultural exchange, Native American cultural awareness organization, Young Democrats, deaf student association.

Athletics. Intramural: Baseball M, basketball, golf, soccer, softball, volleyball.

Student services. Career counseling, student employment services, financial aid counseling, on-campus daycare, personal counseling, placement for graduates, veterans' counselor. **Physically disabled:** Services for visually, speech, hearing impaired. **Transfer:** Transfer adviser, college fairs on campus for students transferring to 4-year colleges.

Contact. E-mail: admissions@occc.edu
Phone: (405) 682-6222 Fax: (405) 682-7817
Jon Horinek, Director of Recruitment and Admissions, Oklahoma City Community College, 7777 South May Avenue, Oklahoma City, OK 73159

Oklahoma State University Institute of Technology: Okmulgee
Okmulgee, Oklahoma
www.osuit.edu   **CB code: 3382**

▶ Public 2-year branch campus and technical college
▶ Commuter campus in large town

General. Founded in 1946. Regionally accredited. **Enrollment:** 2,623 degree-seeking undergraduates. **Degrees:** 54 bachelor's, 699 associate awarded. **Location:** 35 miles from Tulsa. **Calendar:** Trimester, extensive summer session. **Full-time faculty:** 167 total. **Part-time faculty:** 42 total.

Student profile.

Out-of-state:	9%	Live on campus:	35%
25 or older:	33%		

Basis for selection. Open admission, but selective for some programs. Special requirements for multimedia and engineering technologies programs.

2011-2012 Annual costs. Tuition/fees: $4,050; $9,360 out-of-state. Per-credit charge: $102 in-state; $279 out-of-state. Room/board: $5,534. Books/supplies: $1,050.

Financial aid. Need-based: Need-based aid available for part-time students. Work-study available nights, weekends and for part-time students.

Additional information: OSUIT Foundation Scholarship application due March 1.

Application procedures. Admission: No deadline. $15 fee. Admission notification on a rolling basis. **Financial aid:** Priority date 4/1; no closing date. FAFSA, institutional form required. Applicants notified on a rolling basis.

Academics. Special study options: Cooperative education, distance learning, double major, dual enrollment of high school students, internships, liberal arts/career combination. Bachelor's degree programs available on campus. License preparation in nursing. **Credit/placement by examination:** AP, CLEP, institutional tests. **Support services:** Learning center, remedial instruction, tutoring.

Majors. Business: General, accounting, administrative services, business admin, hospitality/recreation, management information systems. **Communications technology:** Graphic/printing. **Computer sciences:** General, applications programming, computer graphics, networking, programming. **Education:** General. **Engineering:** Civil, electrical. **General:** Business. **Health services:** Medical secretary, medical transcription, orthotics/prosthetics. **Visual/performing arts:** Commercial/advertising art, photography.

Computing on campus. 50 workstations in dormitories, library, computer center. Dormitories wired for high-speed internet access and linked to campus network. Online library, helpline, repair service, wireless network available.

Student life. Freshman orientation: Available. Preregistration for classes offered. **Housing:** Guaranteed on-campus for all undergraduates. Coed dorms, single-sex dorms, apartments available. $100 deposit. Housing for parents with dependent children available. **Activities:** Film society, student government, student newspaper, Baptist student union, black student society, Native American student association, Junior Ambassadors.

Athletics. NAIA. **Intercollegiate:** Rodeo. **Intramural:** Basketball, bowling, football (non-tackle), handball, racquetball, soccer, softball, table tennis, volleyball. **Team name:** Cowboys.

Student services. Alcohol/substance abuse counseling, career counseling, student employment services, financial aid counseling, health services, on-campus daycare, personal counseling, placement for graduates, veterans' counselor. **Physically disabled:** Services for visually, speech, hearing impaired. **Transfer:** Pre-admission transcript evaluation for new students. College fairs on campus for students transferring to 4-year colleges.

Contact. E-mail: admissions@okstate.edu
Phone: (918) 293-4680 Toll-free number: (800) 722-4471 ext. 4680
Fax: (918) 293-4643
Genie Trammell, Registrar, Oklahoma State University Institute of Technology: Okmulgee, 1801 East Fourth Street, Okmulgee, OK 74447-3901

Oklahoma State University: Oklahoma City
Oklahoma City, Oklahoma
www.osuokc.edu   CB code: 1436

- Public 2-year branch campus and technical college
- Commuter campus in very large city

General. Founded in 1961. Regionally accredited. **Enrollment:** 7,721 degree-seeking undergraduates. **Degrees:** 13 bachelor's, 674 associate awarded. **Location:** 5 miles from downtown. **Calendar:** Semester, extensive summer session. **Full-time faculty:** 81 total. **Part-time faculty:** 323 total. **Special facilities:** Horticulture center, precision driving training center, child development center, golf maintenance training facility, learning resource center, power transmission distribution pole yard.

Transfer out. Colleges most students transferred to 2011: University of Central Oklahoma, Oklahoma State University: Stillwater, University of Oklahoma.

Basis for selection. Open admission, but selective for some programs. Special requirements for nursing program, radiologic technology and emergency responder bachelor program. Interviews required for nursing program.

High school preparation. 15 units recommended. Recommended units include English 4, mathematics 3, social studies 1, history 2, (laboratory 2) and academic electives 3.

2011-2012 Annual costs. Tuition/fees: $3,209; $8,587 out-of-state. Per-credit charge: $85 in-state; $265 out-of-state. Books/supplies: $1,392.

Financial aid. All financial aid based on need. Need-based aid available for part-time students. Work-study available nights, weekends and for part-time students.

Application procedures. Admission: No deadline. No application fee in-state; $15 out-of-state. Admission notification on a rolling basis. **Financial aid:** Priority date 7/19; no closing date. FAFSA required. Applicants notified on a rolling basis starting 8/1; must reply within 2 week(s) of notification.

Academics. Special study options: Cooperative education, distance learning, double major, dual enrollment of high school students, honors, independent study, liberal arts/career combination, weekend college. Fire/police/EMS training available. Bachelor's degree programs available on campus. License preparation in nursing, paramedic, radiology. **Credit/placement by examination:** AP, CLEP, institutional tests. 30 credit hours maximum toward associate degree. Credit granted for Fundamentals of Nursing (6 hours), Adult Nursing (8 hours). **Support services:** GED preparation and test center, learning center, remedial instruction, study skills assistance, tutoring, writing center.

Majors. Business: Accounting technology, accounting/finance, business admin, construction management, management science, office technology. **Computer sciences:** Applications programming, computer graphics. **Education:** Bilingual. **Foreign languages:** Sign language interpretation, sign language linguistics. **General:** Horticulture, turf management. **Health services:** Cardiovascular technology, EMT paramedic, environmental health, health care admin, nursing (RN), radiologic technology/medical imaging, sonography, substance abuse counseling, veterinary technology/assistant. **Protective services:** Firefighting, police science. **Visual/performing arts:** Commercial/advertising art. **Work/family studies:** Child care management.

Computing on campus. 372 workstations in library, computer center, student center. Commuter students can connect to campus network. Online course registration, repair service, wireless network available.

Student life. Freshman orientation: Mandatory. Preregistration for classes offered. **Activities:** Student government, student newspaper, Students Offering Support, Phi Theta Kappa, Project Second Chance, Native American students, Hispanic student association, College Republicans, Young Democrats, deaf/hearing student association, student nursing association.

Student services. Adult student services, career counseling, student employment services, financial aid counseling, on-campus daycare, personal counseling, placement for graduates, veterans' counselor. **Physically disabled:** Services for visually, speech, hearing impaired. **Transfer:** Transfer center, transfer adviser, college fairs on campus for students transferring to 4-year colleges.

Contact. Phone: (405) 945-3224 Toll-free number: (800) 560-4099
Fax: (405) 945-3277
Keila Jarmer, Registrar, Oklahoma State University: Oklahoma City, 900 North Portland, Oklahoma City, OK 73107-6195

Platt College: Moore
Moore, Oklahoma
www.plattcolleges.org

- For-profit 2-year culinary school and health science college
- Large city

General. Regionally accredited; also accredited by ACCSC. **Enrollment:** 138 degree-seeking undergraduates. **Degrees:** 13 associate awarded. **Calendar:** Quarter. **Full-time faculty:** 12 total.

Basis for selection. Open admission, but selective for some programs.

2011-2012 Annual costs. Tuition/fees: $15,100. Costs vary by program.

Financial aid. Need-based: Work-study available nights, weekends and for part-time students.

Application procedures. Admission: No deadline. No application fee.

Academics. Credit/placement by examination: AP, CLEP.

Majors. Health services: Licensed practical nurse, respiratory therapy technology.

Contact. Phone: (405) 912-3260
David Haynes, Director of Admissions, Platt College: Moore, 201 North Eastern, Moore, OK 73160

Platt College: Oklahoma City Central
Oklahoma City, Oklahoma
www.plattcollege.org

- For-profit 2-year branch campus and career college
- Small city
- Interview required

General. Accredited by ACCSC. **Enrollment:** 250 degree-seeking undergraduates. **Degrees:** 70 associate awarded. **Calendar:** Semester. **Full-time faculty:** 17 total. **Part-time faculty:** 7 total.

Basis for selection. Open admission, but selective for some programs. Entrance exam required for placement. **Home schooled:** Transcript of courses and grades required.

2011-2012 Annual costs. Tuition/fees: $15,100. Cost vary by program.

Financial aid. Need-based: Work-study available nights, weekends and for part-time students.

Application procedures. Admission: No deadline. $100 fee. Admission notification on a rolling basis. **Financial aid:** No deadline. FAFSA required.

Academics. Special study options: License preparation in nursing. **Credit/placement by examination:** AP, CLEP. **Support services:** GED preparation, study skills assistance, tutoring.

Majors. Health services: Licensed practical nurse.

Student life. Freshman orientation: Mandatory. Preregistration for classes offered.

Student services. Adult student services, alcohol/substance abuse counseling, career counseling, financial aid counseling, personal counseling, placement for graduates.

Contact. E-mail: klamb@plattcollege.org
Phone: (405) 946-7799 Fax: (405) 943-2150
Kim Lamb, Director of Admissions, Platt College: Oklahoma City Central, 309 South Ann Arbor, Oklahoma City, OK 73128

Platt College: Tulsa
Tulsa, Oklahoma
www.plattcollege.org

- For-profit 2-year culinary school and health science college
- Commuter campus in large city
- Interview required

General. Accredited by ACCSC. **Enrollment:** 600 degree-seeking undergraduates. **Degrees:** 4 bachelor's, 81 associate awarded. **Calendar:** Differs by program. **Full-time faculty:** 28 total. **Part-time faculty:** 11 total. **Class size:** 100% < 20.

Basis for selection. Open admission, but selective for some programs. High school diploma or GED required for some programs. Others require successful completion of entrance exams. Nursing programs require additional interview with Director of Nursing. **Home schooled:** State high school equivalency certificate required.

2011-2012 Annual costs. Tuition/fees: $15,100. Costs vary by program.

Financial aid. All financial aid based on need. Need-based aid available for part-time students. Work-study available nights, weekends and for part-time students.

Application procedures. Admission: No deadline. $100 fee. **Financial aid:** No deadline. FAFSA required.

Academics. Special study options: Liberal arts/career combination. Bachelor's degree programs available on campus. License preparation in nursing. **Credit/placement by examination:** AP, CLEP. **Support services:** Remedial instruction, tutoring.

Majors. Computer sciences: Security. **Health services:** Licensed practical nurse, nursing (RN), respiratory therapy technology.

Computing on campus. 35 workstations in library, computer center. Online library, wireless network available.

Student life. Freshman orientation: Mandatory. Preregistration for classes offered. Held for 5 hours on first day of classes.

Student services. Student employment services, financial aid counseling, placement for graduates. **Transfer:** Pre-admission transcript evaluation for new students.

Contact. E-mail: stephanieh@plattcollege.org
Phone: (918) 663-9000 Fax: (918) 622-1240
Richard Dixon, Admission Director, Platt College: Tulsa, 3801 South Sheridan, Tulsa, OK 74145-1132

Redlands Community College
El Reno, Oklahoma
www.redlandscc.edu   CB code: 7324

- Public 2-year community college
- Commuter campus in large town

General. Founded in 1938. Regionally accredited. **Enrollment:** 1,754 degree-seeking undergraduates; 820 non-degree-seeking students. **Degrees:** 250 associate awarded. **Location:** 25 miles from Oklahoma City. **Calendar:** Semester, limited summer session. **Full-time faculty:** 36 total. **Part-time faculty:** 102 total. **Class size:** 72% < 20, 26% 20-39, less than 1% 40-49, less than 1% 50-99, less than 1% >100. **Special facilities:** Applied agricultural research center, ranch, working farm and equine centers, viticulture and enology programs.

Student profile. Among degree-seeking undergraduates, 70% enrolled in a transfer program, 28% enrolled in a vocational program, 351 enrolled as first-time, first-year students, 229 transferred in from other institutions.

Part-time:	58%	25 or older:	31%
Out-of-state:	5%	Live on campus:	7%
Women:	65%		

Transfer out. Colleges most students transferred to 2011: University of Central Oklahoma, Southwestern Oklahoma State University, Oklahoma State University, University of Oklahoma, University of Science and Arts of Oklahoma.

Basis for selection. Open admission, but selective for some programs. All applicants who have high school diploma or GED are admitted and may be required to take ACT or COMPASS tests. Students without high school diploma or GED must take COMPASS tests. Competitive admissions to nursing and honors programs. Students without ACT or with ACT below 19 required to take COMPASS placement tests offered on campus.

High school preparation. College-preparatory program recommended. Recommended units include English 4, mathematics 3, social studies 2, science 2 and foreign language 1.

2011-2012 Annual costs. Tuition/fees: $3,180; $5,430 out-of-state. Per-credit charge: $106 in-state; $181 out-of-state. Room only: $4,986. Books/supplies: $960.

Financial aid. Need-based: Need-based aid available for part-time students. Work-study available nights, weekends and for part-time students. **Non-need-based:** Scholarships awarded for academics, athletics, leadership.

Application procedures. Admission: No deadline. $25 fee, may be waived for applicants with need. Admission notification on a rolling basis. **Financial aid:** Priority date 7/1; no closing date. FAFSA required. Applicants notified on a rolling basis starting 6/1; must reply within 6 week(s) of notification.

Academics. Special study options: Accelerated study, cooperative education, cross-registration, distance learning, double major, dual enrollment of high school students, external degree, honors, independent study, internships, liberal arts/career combination. License preparation in nursing, paramedic. **Credit/placement by examination:** AP, CLEP, institutional tests. 32 credit hours maximum toward associate degree. **Support services:** Learning center, reduced course load, remedial instruction, study skills assistance, tutoring.

Majors. Business: Business admin. **Computer sciences:** General. **Education:** General. **English:** English lit, rhetoric/composition. **General:** Agronomy, equestrian studies. **Health services:** EMT paramedic, nursing (RN), veterinary technology/assistant. **Math:** General. **Parks/recreation:** Exercise sciences, health/fitness. **Physical sciences:** General. **Protective services:** Police science. **Psychology:** General. **Social sciences:** General. **Visual/performing arts:** Art. **Work/family studies:** Child care management, child development.

Most popular majors. Agriculture 7%, business/marketing 14%, family/consumer sciences 6%, health sciences 19%, liberal arts 30%, security/protective services 9%.

Computing on campus. 300 workstations in dormitories, library, computer center. Dormitories wired for high-speed internet access. Commuter students can connect to campus network. Online course registration, online library, helpline, wireless network available.

Student life. Freshman orientation: Available. Preregistration for classes offered. Class held Thursday and Friday prior to start of Fall semester; charge associated with class is standard tuition rate for one credit hour. **Policies:** Students must abide by policies, regulations, and requirements specified in Student Handbook. **Housing:** Apartments, wellness housing available. $200 partly refundable deposit. Limited housing for agriculture students at working ranch available. **Activities:** Campus ministries, choral groups, Model UN, student government, student nursing association, Aggie club, Phi Theta Kappa, Young Democrats, College Republicans, art club, Students in Free Enterprise, fencing club, photography club.

Athletics. NJCAA. **Intercollegiate:** Baseball M, basketball, golf W, volleyball W. **Intramural:** Basketball, racquetball, swimming, weight lifting. **Team name:** Cougars.

Student services. Adult student services, career counseling, services for economically disadvantaged, student employment services, financial aid counseling, placement for graduates, veterans' counselor. **Transfer:** Transfer adviser, college fairs on campus for students transferring to 4-year colleges.

Contact. E-mail: studentservices@redlandscc.edu
Phone: (405) 262-2552 ext. 1417
Toll-free number: (866) 415-6367 ext. 1417 Fax: (405) 422-1239
Tricia Hobson, Director of Enrollment Management, Redlands Community College, 1300 South Country Club Road, El Reno, OK 73036

Rose State College
Midwest City, Oklahoma
www.rose.edu

CB code: 1462

▶ Public 2-year community college
▶ Commuter campus in small city

General. Founded in 1968. Regionally accredited. **Enrollment:** 7,846 degree-seeking undergraduates; 278 non-degree-seeking students. **Degrees:** 760 associate awarded. **ROTC:** Air Force. **Location:** 5 miles from Oklahoma City. **Calendar:** Semester, extensive summer session. **Full-time faculty:** 122 total; 28% have terminal degrees, 12% minority, 62% women. **Part-time faculty:** 246 total; 11% have terminal degrees, 14% minority, 60% women. **Class size:** 52% < 20, 47% 20-39, 1% 40-49, less than 1% 50-99. **Special facilities:** Regional history center, 1400-seat performing arts theater, wetlands project.

Student profile. Among degree-seeking undergraduates, 64% enrolled in a transfer program, 30% enrolled in a vocational program, 1,651 enrolled as first-time, first-year students, 928 transferred in from other institutions.

Part-time:	60%	Asian American:	2%
Out-of-state:	1%	Hispanic American:	5%
Women:	61%	Native American:	6%
African American:	17%	25 or older:	47%

Transfer out. Colleges most students transferred to 2011: Oklahoma State University, Southwestern Oklahoma State University, University of Oklahoma, University of Central Oklahoma.

Basis for selection. Open admission, but selective for some programs. Interview required for health science programs and possibly for entry into specialized programs. **Adult students:** COMPASS Placement test required. **Home schooled:** Transcript of courses and grades required. Peer class must have graduated.

High school preparation. 15 units required. Required units include English 4, mathematics 3, social studies 1, history 2, science 3 (laboratory 3) and academic electives 2. Electives may include English, lab science, math, history/citizenship skills, computer science or foreign language.

2011-2012 Annual costs. Tuition/fees: $2,779; $8,089 out-of-state. Per-credit charge: $75 in-state; $265 out-of-state. Books/supplies: $1,000.

2010-2011 Financial aid. Need-based: 53% of total undergraduate aid awarded as scholarships/grants, 47% as loans/jobs. Need-based aid available for part-time students. Work-study available nights, weekends and for part-time students. **Non-need-based:** Scholarships awarded for academics, athletics, leadership. **Additional information:** Ticket to Rose grant available to students from Midwest City/Choctaw high schools to cover unmet need in tuition/fees.

Application procedures. Admission: No deadline. No application fee. Admission notification on a rolling basis. **Financial aid:** Priority date 6/1; no closing date. FAFSA required. Applicants notified on a rolling basis starting 3/1; must reply within 4 week(s) of notification.

Academics. Student Success Center available for academic planning. **Special study options:** Accelerated study, cooperative education, cross-registration, distance learning, double major, honors, independent study, internships, liberal arts/career combination, weekend college. Bachelor's degree programs available on campus. License preparation in dental hygiene, nursing, paramedic, radiology. **Credit/placement by examination:** AP, CLEP, IB, institutional tests. 47 credit hours maximum toward associate degree. **Support services:** Learning center, pre-admission summer program, reduced course load, remedial instruction, study skills assistance, tutoring, writing center.

Majors. Area/ethnic studies: African. **Biology:** General. **Business:** General, accounting technology, business admin. **Communications:** Broadcast journalism, journalism, photojournalism. **Computer sciences:** General, LAN/WAN management, networking, web page design, webmaster. **Conservation:** Environmental science. **Education:** Multi-level teacher. **Engineering:** General. **English:** English lit. **Foreign languages:** General. **Health services:** Clinical lab assistant, dental assistant, dental hygiene, EMT paramedic, medical records technology, nursing (RN), predental, premedicine, prenursing, prepharmacy, radiologic technology/medical imaging, respiratory therapy assistant, respiratory therapy technology. **History:** General. **Human services:** Social work. **Liberal arts:** Arts/sciences, library assistant. **Math:** General. **Parks/recreation:** Health/fitness. **Physical sciences:** Chemistry, geology, physics. **Protective services:** Police science. **Psychology:** General. **Social sciences:** General, political science, sociology. **Visual/performing arts:** Multimedia, theater arts management. **Work/family studies:** General, child care management, child development.

Most popular majors. Business/marketing 16%, education 8%, health sciences 26%, liberal arts 29%.

Computing on campus. 150 workstations in library, computer center, student center. Commuter students can connect to campus network. Online course registration, online library, helpline, student web hosting, wireless network available.

Student life. Freshman orientation: Mandatory. Preregistration for classes offered. **Activities:** Jazz band, choral groups, drama, international student organizations, literary magazine, music ensembles, musical theater, student government, student newspaper, Phi Theta Kappa, criminal justice club, black student association, broadcasting club, drama club, Oklahoma Intercollegiate Legislature, American Indian association.

Athletics. NJCAA. **Intercollegiate:** Baseball M, softball W. **Intramural:** Bowling, tennis, volleyball. **Team name:** Raiders.

Student services. Adult student services, alcohol/substance abuse counseling, career counseling, services for economically disadvantaged, student employment services, financial aid counseling, personal counseling, placement for graduates, veterans' counselor. **Physically disabled:** Services for visually, speech, hearing impaired. **Transfer:** Pre-admission transcript evaluation for new students. College fairs on campus for students transferring to 4-year colleges.

Contact. Phone: (405) 733-7312 Toll-free number: (866) 621-0987 Fax: (405) 736-0309
M. Mechelle Aitson-Roessler, Registrar/Director of Admissions, Rose State College, 6420 SE 15th Street, Midwest City, OK 73110-2799

Seminole State College
Seminole, Oklahoma
www.sscok.edu

CB code: 0316

▶ Public 2-year community and junior college
▶ Commuter campus in small town

General. Founded in 1931. Regionally accredited. **Enrollment:** 2,337 degree-seeking undergraduates. **Degrees:** 282 associate awarded. **Location:** 55 miles from Oklahoma City. **Calendar:** Semester, extensive summer session. **Full-time faculty:** 48 total. **Part-time faculty:** 1 total.

Student profile.

Out-of-state:	3%	Live on campus:	3%

Transfer out. Colleges most students transferred to 2011: East Central University, University of Central Oklahoma, Oklahoma State University, Oklahoma University, Oklahoma Baptist University.

Basis for selection. Open admission, but selective for some programs. Additional requirements for admission to A.D. Nursing Program and MLT Program include 19 ACT and score of 15 on Nelson Denny Reading Test. **Learning Disabled:** Documentation from high school, such as IEP or any documentation from physician required.

High school preparation. 15 units recommended. Recommended units include English 4, mathematics 3, social studies 2, history 2, science 2 and academic electives 2.

2011-2012 Annual costs. Tuition/fees: $3,232; $7,625 out-of-state. Per-credit charge: $69 in-state; $215 out-of-state. Room/board: $6,350. Books/supplies: $400. Personal expenses: $920.

Financial aid. Need-based: Work-study available nights, weekends and for part-time students. **Non-need-based:** Scholarships awarded for academics, athletics, state residency.

Application procedures. Admission: No deadline. $15 fee. Application must be submitted on paper. Admission notification on a rolling basis. **Financial aid:** Closing date 1/15. FAFSA, institutional form required. Applicants notified on a rolling basis starting 3/1; must reply within 4 week(s) of notification.

Academics. Special study options: Distance learning, dual enrollment of high school students, honors. **Credit/placement by examination:** AP, CLEP, institutional tests. 30 credit hours maximum toward associate degree. **Support services:** Learning center, remedial instruction, study skills assistance, tutoring, writing center.

Majors. Business: Business admin, office management, office/clerical. **Computer sciences:** Computer science. **Education:** General, elementary. **Health services:** Clinical lab technology, nursing (RN). **Liberal arts:** Arts/sciences. **Math:** General. **Parks/recreation:** Health/fitness. **Social sciences:** General. **Visual/performing arts:** Art.

Most popular majors. Business/marketing 20%, computer/information sciences 10%, health sciences 10%, liberal arts 60%.

Computing on campus. 340 workstations in dormitories, library, computer center, student center. Dormitories wired for high-speed internet access and linked to campus network. Commuter students can connect to campus network. Online library, wireless network available.

Student life. Freshman orientation: Mandatory. Preregistration for classes offered. **Housing:** Coed dorms available. $100 nonrefundable deposit. **Activities:** Campus ministries, dance, international student organizations, student government, student newspaper, Native American student association, Baptist student union, Phi Theta Kappa, Psi Beta psychology honor society, International Honor Society, SSC Veterans, National English Honor Society.

Athletics. NJCAA. Intercollegiate: Baseball M, basketball, golf, softball W, tennis, volleyball. **Intramural:** Baseball M, basketball, bowling, football (non-tackle), racquetball, softball, swimming, table tennis, volleyball. **Team name:** Trojans.

Student services. Adult student services, career counseling, services for economically disadvantaged, financial aid counseling, personal counseling, veterans' counselor. **Physically disabled:** Services for visually, speech, hearing impaired. **Transfer:** Transfer adviser, college fairs on campus for students transferring to 4-year colleges.

Contact. Phone: (405) 382-9950 ext. 230 Fax: (405) 382-9524
Mark Ames, Dean of Student Affairs, Seminole State College, PO Box 351, Seminole, OK 74818

Tulsa Community College

Tulsa, Oklahoma
www.tulsacc.edu

CB member
CB code: 6839

- Public 2-year community college
- Commuter campus in large city

General. Founded in 1968. Regionally accredited. 4 branch campuses located in Tulsa. **Enrollment:** 17,975 degree-seeking undergraduates. **Degrees:** 2,064 associate awarded. **Calendar:** Semester, extensive summer session. **Full-time faculty:** 305 total; 20% have terminal degrees, 12% minority, 61% women. **Part-time faculty:** 843 total; 21% minority, 59% women.

Student profile. Among degree-seeking undergraduates, 60% enrolled in a transfer program, 33% enrolled in a vocational program.

Transfer out. Colleges most students transferred to 2011: University of Oklahoma, Oklahoma State University, Northeastern Oklahoma State University, Tulsa University, University of Central Oklahoma.

Basis for selection. Open admission, but selective for some programs. Special requirements for health-related, legal assistant, and management programs. Interview required for health, legal assistant, and nursing programs. **Adult students:** ACT or Accuplacer CPT required for placement.

2011-2012 Annual costs. Tuition/fees: $3,061; $8,281 out-of-state. Per-credit charge: $73 in-state; $247 out-of-state. Books/supplies: $600. Personal expenses: $900.

Financial aid. Need-based: Need-based aid available for part-time students. Work-study available nights, weekends and for part-time students. **Non-need-based:** Scholarships awarded for academics, art, leadership, music/drama, state residency.

Application procedures. Admission: No deadline. $20 fee. Admission notification on a rolling basis. **Financial aid:** Priority date 8/1; no closing date. FAFSA, institutional form required. Applicants notified on a rolling basis starting 4/1; must reply within 2 week(s) of notification.

Academics. Many short-period intensive courses within conventional semesters. **Special study options:** Cross-registration, distance learning, dual enrollment of high school students, ESL, honors, independent study, internships, weekend college. **Credit/placement by examination:** AP, CLEP, IB, institutional tests. 30 credit hours maximum toward associate degree. **Support services:** Learning center, remedial instruction, study skills assistance, tutoring, writing center.

Majors. Biology: Biotechnology. **Business:** General, accounting, administrative services, business admin, fashion, finance, hospitality admin, hospitality/recreation, human resources, insurance, management information systems, managerial economics, office technology, real estate, tourism/travel. **Communications:** Journalism. **Communications technology:** General. **Computer sciences:** General, applications programming, programming. **Education:** General, physical. **Engineering:** General. **English:** English lit, rhetoric/composition. **Foreign languages:** French, German, Italian, Japanese, Russian, sign language interpretation, Spanish. **General:** Horticultural science. **Health services:** Clinical lab assistant, clinical lab technology, dental hygiene, medical assistant, medical radiologic technology/radiation therapy, medical secretary, occupational therapy assistant, physical therapy assistant, respiratory therapy technology. **History:** General. **Human services:** Social work. **Liberal arts:** Library assistant. **Math:** General. **Parks/recreation:** Sports admin. **Philosophy/religion:** Philosophy. **Physical sciences:** Astronomy, chemistry, geology, physics. **Protective services:** Criminal justice, fire safety technology, police science. **Psychology:** General. **Social sciences:** General, economics, geography, political science, sociology. **Visual/performing arts:** Dramatic, interior design, music. **Work/family studies:** Child care management.

Most popular majors. Business/marketing 20%, education 13%, health sciences 21%, liberal arts 16%, social sciences 11%.

Computing on campus. 2,306 workstations in library, computer center. Online course registration, online library available.

Student life. Freshman orientation: Available. Preregistration for classes offered. **Activities:** Bands, choral groups, drama, music ensembles, student government, student newspaper.

Athletics. Intramural: Basketball, soccer, softball, table tennis, tennis, volleyball.

Student services. Career counseling, student employment services, health services, on-campus daycare, personal counseling, placement for graduates, veterans' counselor. **Physically disabled:** Services for visually, hearing impaired. **Transfer:** College fairs on campus for students transferring to 4-year colleges.

Contact. E-mail: theck@tulsacc.edu
Phone: (918) 595-7000 ext. 3412 Fax: (918) 595-3414
Traci Heck, Dean of Admissions and Records, Tulsa Community College, 6111 East Skelly Drive, Tulsa, OK 74135-6198

Tulsa Welding School

Tulsa, Oklahoma
www.weldingschool.com

CB code: 2958

- For-profit 2-year technical college
- Commuter campus in very large city
- Interview required

Two-Year Colleges

General. Accredited by ACCSC. **Enrollment:** 1,853 degree-seeking undergraduates. **Degrees:** 29 associate awarded. **Calendar:** Differs by program. **Full-time faculty:** 30 total.

Student profile.

Out-of-state:	53%	25 or older:	45%
Women:	4%		

Basis for selection. Open admission. **Home schooled:** Applicants must pass ATB test.

2011-2012 Annual costs. Tuition and fees vary by program from $16,977 to $33,954.

2010-2011 Financial aid. All financial aid based on need. Work-study available nights, weekends and for part-time students.

Application procedures. **Admission:** No deadline. No application fee. Admission notification on a rolling basis. Must have high school diploma or GED or pass Ability To Benefit test. **Financial aid:** FAFSA required.

Academics. **Credit/placement by examination:** AP, CLEP.

Computing on campus. 3 workstations in library.

Student life. **Freshman orientation:** Mandatory. Preregistration for classes offered.

Student services. Career counseling, student employment services, financial aid counseling, personal counseling, placement for graduates. **Physically disabled:** Services for hearing impaired.

Contact. E-mail: tws@ionet.net
Phone: (918) 587-6789 ext. 240
Toll-free number: (800) 331-2934 ext. 221 Fax: (918) 587-8170
Don Smith, Director of Admissions, Tulsa Welding School, 2545 East 11th Street, Tulsa, OK 74104-3909

Vatterott College: Oklahoma City
Oklahoma City, Oklahoma
www.vatterott-college.com   **CB code: 2899**

- For-profit 2-year technical and career college
- Residential campus in very large city

General. Accredited by ACCSCT. **Calendar:** Differs by program.

Annual costs/financial aid. Need-based financial aid available for full-time students.

Contact. Phone: (405) 945-0088
Director of Admissions, 4621 NW 23rd Street, Oklahoma City, OK 73127

Vatterott College: Tulsa
Tulsa, Oklahoma
www.vatterott-college.edu   **CB code: 3637**

- For-profit 2-year branch campus and technical college
- Commuter campus in large city

General. Accredited by ACCSCT. **Calendar:** Differs by program.

Contact. Phone: (918) 835-8288
Director of Admissions, 4343 South 118th East Avenue, Tulsa, OK 74146

Virginia College at Tulsa
Tulsa, Oklahoma
www.tulsa.vc.edu

- For-profit 2-year health science and career college
- Large city

General. Regionally accredited; also accredited by ACICS. **Calendar:** Quarter.

Basis for selection. Open admission.

Financial aid. **Need-based:** Work-study available nights, weekends and for part-time students.

Application procedures. **Admission:** $100 fee.

Academics. **Credit/placement by examination:** AP, CLEP.

Majors. **Business:** Business admin. **Health services:** Medical records admin.

Contact. E-mail: tulsa.info@vc.edu
Virginia College at Tulsa, 5124 South Peoria Avenue, Tulsa, OK 74105

Western Oklahoma State College
Altus, Oklahoma   **CB member**
www.wosc.edu   **CB code: 6020**

- Public 2-year community college
- Commuter campus in large town

General. Founded in 1926. Regionally accredited. **Enrollment:** 932 full-time, degree-seeking students. **Degrees:** 297 associate awarded. **Location:** 55 miles from Lawton, 140 miles from Oklahoma City. **Calendar:** Semester, limited summer session. **Full-time faculty:** 43 total. **Part-time faculty:** 46 total. **Class size:** 78% < 20, 20% 20-39, less than 1% 40-49, 1% 50-99.

Transfer out. **Colleges most students transferred to 2011:** Southwestern Oklahoma State University, Cameron University, Oklahoma State University, University of Central Oklahoma, University of Oklahoma.

Basis for selection. Open admission, but selective for some programs. SAT or ACT required for applicants under 21 for placement; no minimum score required. **Adult students:** COMPASS or ACT required for adults who don't have high school diploma or GED. Must demonstrate proficiency in English, math, science, and reading through COMPASS or ACT subtest scores. **Home schooled:** Transcript of courses and grades required. Must have ACT or SAT. High school class must have graduated and must satisfy curricular requirements.

2011-2012 Annual costs. Tuition/fees: $2,861; $6,701 out-of-state. Per-credit charge: $63 in-state; $191 out-of-state. Room/board: $3,750. Books/supplies: $1,000. Personal expenses: $1,200.

Financial aid. **Need-based:** Need-based aid available for part-time students. Work-study available nights, weekends and for part-time students. **Non-need-based:** Scholarships awarded for academics, alumni affiliation, art, athletics, leadership, music/drama, state residency.

Application procedures. **Admission:** No deadline. $15 fee. Application must be submitted online. Admission notification on a rolling basis. **Financial aid:** Closing date 3/1. FAFSA, institutional form required. Applicants notified on a rolling basis; must reply within 3 week(s) of notification.

Academics. **Special study options:** Cooperative education, distance learning, dual enrollment of high school students, liberal arts/career combination. Cooperative agreements with local technology centers; students may dual-enroll and earn college credits for career tech courses. License preparation in aviation, nursing, radiology. **Credit/placement by examination:** AP, CLEP, IB, institutional tests. 30 credit hours maximum toward associate degree. **Support services:** Learning center, remedial instruction, study skills assistance, tutoring.

Majors. **Biology:** General. **Business:** Administrative services, business admin, office/clerical. **Computer sciences:** General, computer science, information systems, programming. **Education:** Physical. **Engineering:** Engineering science. **English:** English lit. **General:** Agronomy, animal sciences, equipment technology, power machinery. **Health services:** Medical radiologic technology/radiation therapy, medical records admin, medical secretary, nursing (RN). **Liberal arts:** Arts/sciences. **Math:** General. **Parks/recreation:** Health/fitness. **Philosophy/religion:** Religion. **Protective services:** Corrections, firefighting, police science. **Social sciences:** General. **Visual/performing arts:** Art, music. **Work/family studies:** Child care management, child development.

Most popular majors. Business/marketing 9%, family/consumer sciences 6%, health sciences 39%, liberal arts 13%, security/protective services 9%.

Computing on campus. 50 workstations in library. Dormitories wired for high-speed internet access and linked to campus network. Commuter students can connect to campus network. Online course registration, online library, helpline, wireless network available.

Student life. **Freshman orientation:** Mandatory. Preregistration for classes offered. **Housing:** Coed dorms available. $50 fully refundable deposit.

Activities: Bands, choral groups, drama, music ensembles, musical theater, student government, student newspaper, Baptist student union, Wesley Foundation, tutoring club, College Democrats, College Republicans, Fellowship of Christian Athletes.

Athletics. NJCAA. **Intercollegiate:** Baseball M, basketball, softball W. **Intramural:** Basketball, volleyball. **Team name:** Pioneers.

Student services. Career counseling, financial aid counseling, health services, personal counseling, veterans' counselor. **Physically disabled:** Services for visually, hearing impaired. **Transfer:** College fairs on campus for students transferring to 4-year colleges.

Contact. E-mail: lana.scott@wosc.edu
Phone: (580) 477-7717 Fax: (580) 477-7723
Lana Scott, Director of Admissions and Registrar, Western Oklahoma
State College, 2801 North Main Street, Altus, OK 73521

Oregon

Blue Mountain Community College
Pendleton, Oregon
www.bluecc.edu   CB code: 4025

♦ Public 2-year community college
♦ Commuter campus in large town

General. Founded in 1962. Regionally accredited. **Location:** 200 miles from Portland; 200 miles from Boise, Idaho. **Calendar:** Quarter.

Annual costs/financial aid. Tuition/fees (2011-2012): $3,902; $11,102 out-of-state. Students in limited entry programs such as dental and nursing pay additional program fees. Washington state, Idaho, Nevada, California and Montana residents all pay in-state rates. Books/supplies: $1,630. Personal expenses: $1,605. Need-based financial aid available to full-time and part-time students.

Contact. Phone: (541) 278-5759
Director of Admissions, Records and Testing/Registrar, 2411 NW Carden Avenue, Pendleton, OR 97801

Carrington College: Portland
Portland, Oregon
www.carrington.edu

♦ For-profit 2-year career college
♦ Very large city

General. Regionally accredited; also accredited by ACICS. **Enrollment:** 627 degree-seeking undergraduates. **Degrees:** 55 associate awarded. **Calendar:** Differs by program. **Full-time faculty:** 26 total. **Part-time faculty:** 36 total.

Basis for selection. Selective admissions to certain programs.

2011-2012 Annual costs. Tuition/fees: $14,200. Program cost $14,200 (39 weeks). Costs are provided for the largest program. Other programs may vary.

Financial aid. **Need-based:** Work-study available nights, weekends and for part-time students.

Application procedures. **Admission:** No deadline. Admission notification on a rolling basis.

Academics. **Credit/placement by examination:** AP, CLEP.

Majors. **Health services:** Clinical lab science, medical records admin.

Contact. Debra Marcus, Director of Admissions, Carrington College: Portland, 2004 Lloyd Center, Portland, OR 97232-1309

Central Oregon Community College
Bend, Oregon
www.cocc.edu   CB code: 4090

♦ Public 2-year community college
♦ Commuter campus in small city

General. Founded in 1949. Regionally accredited. **Enrollment:** 6,410 degree-seeking undergraduates; 732 non-degree-seeking students. **Degrees:** 505 associate awarded. **ROTC:** Army. **Location:** 150 miles from Portland, 120 miles from Salem. **Calendar:** Quarter, limited summer session. **Full-time faculty:** 111 total; 34% have terminal degrees, 5% minority, 48% women. **Part-time faculty:** 178 total; 4% minority, 57% women. **Class size:** 28% < 20, 69% 20-39, 2% 40-49, less than 1% 50-99. **Special facilities:** Exercise physiology laboratory, dental clinic, Math SMART Lab.

Student profile. Among degree-seeking undergraduates, 46% enrolled in a transfer program, 39% enrolled in a vocational program, 917 enrolled as first-time, first-year students, 459 transferred in from other institutions.

Part-time:	49%	Hispanic American:	7%
Out-of-state:	5%	Native American:	3%
Women:	54%	25 or older:	55%
African American:	1%	Live on campus:	1%
Asian American:	1%		

Transfer out. **Colleges most students transferred to 2011:** Oregon State University, University of Oregon, Southern Oregon University, Portland State University.

Basis for selection. Open admission, but selective for some programs. Special requirements for nursing, emergency medical services. Limited enrollment (first-come first-served basis, with fall term only start date) for medical assistant, dental assistant, and massage therapy. **Home schooled:** High school diploma or GED not required if student is 18 or older.

2011-2012 Annual costs. Tuition/fees: $3,618; $4,743 out-of-district; $9,468 out-of-state. Per-credit charge: $76 in-district; $101 out-of-district; $206 out-of-state. Residents of WA, ID, NV and CA pay the in-state, out-of-district tuition. Room/board: $8,228. Books/supplies: $1,350. Personal expenses: $2,859.

2011-2012 Financial aid. **Need-based:** 424 full-time freshmen applied for aid; 392 were judged to have need; 389 of these received aid. Average need met was 79%. Average scholarship/grant was $5,287; average loan $3,339. 37% of total undergraduate aid awarded as scholarships/grants, 63% as loans/jobs. Need-based aid available for part-time students. Work-study available nights, weekends and for part-time students. **Non-need-based:** Awarded to 24 full-time undergraduates, including 9 freshmen. Scholarships awarded for academics, state residency. **Additional information:** Institution-sponsored short-term loans. Extensive part-time student employment.

Application procedures. **Admission:** Priority date 6/15; no deadline. $25 fee, may be waived for applicants with need. Admission notification on a rolling basis. **Financial aid:** No deadline. FAFSA required. Applicants notified on a rolling basis starting 4/1; must reply within 4 week(s) of notification.

Academics. **Special study options:** Cooperative education, distance learning, double major, dual enrollment of high school students, ESL, independent study, internships, student-designed major, study abroad. Bachelor's degree programs available on campus. License preparation in aviation, nursing, paramedic, physical therapy, radiology. **Credit/placement by examination:** AP, CLEP, IB, institutional tests. Credit for prior training or certification varies by program. **Support services:** GED preparation, learning center, pre-admission summer program, reduced course load, remedial instruction, study skills assistance, tutoring, writing center.

Majors. **Architecture:** Landscape. **Biology:** General. **Business:** Accounting, administrative services, business admin, customer service, hospitality/recreation, management information systems, marketing. **Communications:** Communications/speech/rhetoric. **Computer sciences:** General, computer science, networking, support specialist. **Conservation:** General, forest technology, forestry. **Education:** General. **Engineering:** General. **English:** English lit. **Foreign languages:** General. **General:** Horticultural science. **Health services:** EMT paramedic, massage therapy, medical records technology, nursing (RN), premedicine, prepharmacy, radiologic technology/medical imaging. **History:** General. **Liberal arts:** Arts/sciences, humanities. **Math:** General. **Parks/recreation:** General, health/fitness. **Physical sciences:** General, chemistry, geology, physics. **Protective services:** Criminal justice, firefighting. **Psychology:** General. **Social sciences:** General, anthropology, criminology, economics, GIS/cartography, political science, sociology. **Visual/performing arts:** General, music, studio arts.

Most popular majors. Business/marketing 6%, health sciences 19%, liberal arts 55%, security/protective services 9%.

Computing on campus. 650 workstations in dormitories, library, computer center, student center. Dormitories wired for high-speed internet access and linked to campus network. Commuter students can connect to campus network. Online course registration, online library, helpline, wireless network available.

Student life. **Freshman orientation:** Available, $25 fee. Preregistration for classes offered. **Housing:** Coed dorms, special housing for disabled available. $250 nonrefundable deposit. **Activities:** Bands, campus ministries, choral groups, drama, music ensembles, student government, student newspaper, symphony orchestra.

Athletics. **Intramural:** Basketball, cross-country, football (non-tackle), golf, soccer, softball, table tennis, track and field, volleyball, weight lifting. **Team name:** Bobcats.

Student services. Adult student services, alcohol/substance abuse counseling, career counseling, services for economically disadvantaged, student employment services, financial aid counseling, health services, minority student services, personal counseling, placement for graduates, veterans' counselor, women's services. **Physically disabled:** Services for visually, speech, hearing impaired. **Transfer:** Pre-admission transcript evaluation for new students. Transfer adviser, college fairs on campus for students transferring to 4-year colleges.

Contact. E-mail: welcome@cocc.edu
Phone: (541) 383-7500 Fax: (541) 383-7506
Aimee Metcalf, Director, Admissions and Records, Central Oregon Community College, 2600 Northwest College Way, Bend, OR 97701-5998

Chemeketa Community College
Salem, Oregon
www.chemeketa.edu   CB code: 4745

◗ Public 2-year community and junior college
◗ Commuter campus in small city

General. Founded in 1962. Regionally accredited. **Enrollment:** 9,956 degree-seeking undergraduates. **Degrees:** 1,197 associate awarded. **Location:** 45 miles from Portland. **Calendar:** Quarter, extensive summer session. **Full-time faculty:** 211 total. **Part-time faculty:** 601 total. **Class size:** 45% < 20, 51% 20-39, 3% 40-49, 1% 50-99, less than 1% >100. **Special facilities:** Planetarium, vineyard and winemaking facility. **Partnerships:** Formal partnerships with local high schools.

Student profile.

Out-of-state:	5%	25 or older:	47%

Transfer out. Colleges most students transferred to 2011: University of Oregon, Oregon State University, Western Oregon University, Eastern Oregon University, Portland State University.

Basis for selection. Open admission, but selective for some programs. Limited-enrollment programs may charge admission fee, have application deadlines and require interview; preparatory courses may also be required.

2011-2012 Annual costs. Tuition/fees: $3,915; $11,340 out-of-state. Per-credit charge: $77 in-state; $242 out-of-state. International students have additional required fees. Individual courses may have extra fees. Books/supplies: $1,200. Personal expenses: $300.

Financial aid. All financial aid based on need. Need-based aid available for part-time students. Work-study available nights, weekends and for part-time students.

Application procedures. Admission: No deadline. No application fee. Admission notification on a rolling basis. **Financial aid:** Priority date 4/1; no closing date. FAFSA required. Applicants notified on a rolling basis starting 6/30; must reply within 2 week(s) of notification.

Academics. Special study options: Accelerated study, cooperative education, distance learning, double major, dual enrollment of high school students, ESL, independent study, internships, study abroad, teacher certification program, weekend college. License preparation in dental hygiene, nursing, paramedic. **Credit/placement by examination:** AP, CLEP, IB, institutional tests. 12 credit hours maximum toward associate degree. **Support services:** GED preparation and test center, learning center, pre-admission summer program, remedial instruction, study skills assistance, tutoring, writing center.

Majors. Biology: General, marine, pharmacology, zoology. **Business:** Accounting, administrative services, business admin, hospitality admin, management information systems, management science, office management, office technology, tourism/travel. **Communications:** Journalism. **Communications technology:** Graphic/printing. **Computer sciences:** General. **Conservation:** Forestry. **Education:** Bilingual, early childhood, elementary, secondary. **Engineering:** General, electrical. **English:** English lit, rhetoric/composition. **Foreign languages:** Sign language interpretation. **General:** Agribusiness operations, horticultural science. **Health services:** Dental assistant, dental hygiene, EMT ambulance attendant, EMT paramedic, health care admin, medical records admin, medical secretary, medical transcription, nursing (RN), predental, premedicine, prenursing, prepharmacy, speech-language pathology assistant, substance abuse counseling. **History:** General. **Human services:** Social work. **Liberal arts:** Arts/sciences, humanities. **Math:** General. **Parks/recreation:** Health/fitness. **Philosophy/religion:** Philosophy, religion. **Physical sciences:** Chemistry, geology, physics. **Protective services:** Criminal justice, fire safety technology, firefighting, juvenile corrections, law enforcement admin, police science, security services. **Psychology:** General. **Social sciences:** Anthropology, economics, geography, political science, sociology. **Visual/performing arts:** Art, design, dramatic, film/cinema/video, music, theater design. **Work/family studies:** General, child care management.

Computing on campus. 1,000 workstations in library, computer center. Commuter students can connect to campus network. Online course registration, online library, helpline, wireless network available.

Student life. Freshman orientation: Available. Preregistration for classes offered. **Activities:** Choral groups, dance, literary magazine, student government, student newspaper, TV station, sexual minority students organization, Christian student organization, LDS club, College Republicans, Democratic students, Phi Theta Kappa, Latino development network.

Athletics. NJCAA. **Intercollegiate:** Baseball M, basketball, soccer M, softball W, volleyball W. **Intramural:** Soccer M, softball W, tennis. **Team name:** The Storm.

Student services. Adult student services, alcohol/substance abuse counseling, career counseling, student employment services, financial aid counseling, minority student services, on-campus daycare, placement for graduates. **Physically disabled:** Services for visually, speech, hearing impaired. **Transfer:** Pre-admission transcript evaluation for new students. Transfer adviser, college fairs on campus for students transferring to 4-year colleges.

Contact. E-mail: admissions@chemeketa.edu
Phone: (503) 399-5006 Fax: (503) 399-3918
Melissa Frey, Enrollment Services Coordinator, Chemeketa Community College, Admissions Office, Salem, OR 97309-7070

Clackamas Community College
Oregon City, Oregon
www.clackamas.edu   CB code: 4111

◗ Public 2-year community college
◗ Commuter campus in large town

General. Founded in 1966. Regionally accredited. **Enrollment:** 16,070 undergraduates. **Degrees:** 615 associate awarded. **ROTC:** Air Force. **Location:** 15 miles from Portland. **Calendar:** Quarter, extensive summer session. **Full-time faculty:** 180 total. **Part-time faculty:** 350 total. **Class size:** 67% < 20, 32% 20-39, 1% 40-49. **Special facilities:** Environmental learning center, observatory. **Partnerships:** Formal partnerships with Intel Microelectronics, Portland General Electric/Pacificorps.

Student profile.

Out-of-state:	2%	25 or older:	47%

Transfer out. 10% of students enrolled in the transfer program go on to 4-year colleges. **Colleges most students transferred to 2011:** Portland State University, Oregon State University, University of Oregon.

Basis for selection. Open admission, but selective for some programs. Special prerequisite requirements for Allied Health and Nursing and water quality programs. Special admission process for accelerated degree programs and degree partnership programs.

2012-2013 Annual costs. Tuition/fees (projected): $4,051; $10,846 out-of-state. Per-credit charge: $77 in-state; $228 out-of-state. Books/supplies: $1,800. Personal expenses: $900.

Financial aid. Need-based: Need-based aid available for part-time students. Work-study available nights, weekends and for part-time students. **Non-need-based:** Scholarships awarded for academics, art, athletics, leadership, music/drama. **Additional information:** Institutional tuition rebate guarantee. Frozen tuition rates for new fall students who graduate within 3 years. Any tuition increase levied by college during those 3 years will be refunded to student upon graduation.

Application procedures. Admission: No deadline. No application fee. Admission notification on a rolling basis. **Financial aid:** Priority date 4/10; no closing date. FAFSA, institutional form required. Applicants notified on a rolling basis starting 3/15; must reply within 3 week(s) of notification.

Academics. Some occupational technologies offered as self-paced programs. **Special study options:** Accelerated study, cooperative education, distance learning, double major, dual enrollment of high school students, ESL, independent study, internships. License preparation in nursing, real estate. **Credit/placement by examination:** AP, CLEP, IB, institutional tests. 24 credit hours maximum toward associate degree. **Support services:** GED preparation and test center, learning center, reduced course load, remedial instruction, study skills assistance, tutoring, writing center.

Majors. Business: Accounting, administrative services, business admin, e-commerce, marketing, office management, operations, sales/distribution.

Communications technology: General. **Computer sciences:** Applications programming, networking, web page design, webmaster. **Education:** Early childhood. **Engineering:** Industrial. **General:** Horticulture, landscaping, ornamental horticulture. **Health services:** Nursing (RN). **Human services:** Community org/advocacy, social work. **Liberal arts:** Arts/sciences. **Protective services:** Corrections, firefighting, police science. **Social sciences:** GIS/cartography. **Work/family studies:** Child care management.

Computing on campus. 500 workstations in library, computer center. Commuter students can connect to campus network. Online course registration, online library, helpline, wireless network available.

Student life. Freshman orientation: Available. Preregistration for classes offered. One-day program during week before classes begin. **Activities:** Bands, choral groups, drama, literary magazine, music ensembles, student government, student newspaper, NW Collegiate Ministries, Deutschen Veren (German), French club, Spectrum/Gay/Straight Alliance, International Latter Day Saints Student Association, Spanish club.

Athletics. NJCAA. **Intercollegiate:** Baseball M, basketball, cross-country, soccer W, softball W, track and field, volleyball W, wrestling M. **Team name:** Cougars.

Student services. Adult student services, alcohol/substance abuse counseling, career counseling, student employment services, financial aid counseling, minority student services, on-campus daycare, personal counseling, placement for graduates, veterans' counselor, women's services. **Physically disabled:** Services for visually, speech, hearing impaired. **Transfer:** Transfer adviser, college fairs on campus for students transferring to 4-year colleges.

Contact. E-mail: admissions@clackamas.edu
Phone: (503) 594-6100 Fax: (503) 722-5864
Tara Sprehe, Registrar, Clackamas Community College, 19600 Molalla Avenue, Oregon City, OR 97045

Clatsop Community College
Astoria, Oregon
www.clatsopcollege.com　　　　　　　　　**CB code: 4089**

▸ Public 2-year community college
▸ Commuter campus in large town

General. Founded in 1958. Regionally accredited. Vessel fire fighting training program available. **Enrollment:** 1,249 degree-seeking undergraduates. **Degrees:** 87 associate awarded. **Location:** 100 miles from Portland. **Calendar:** Quarter, limited summer session. **Full-time faculty:** 39 total. **Part-time faculty:** 95 total. **Class size:** 83% < 20, 15% 20-39, less than 1% 40-49, 1% 50-99, less than 1% >100. **Special facilities:** 51-foot commercial fishing vessel.

Student profile.

Out-of-state:　　　　　　13%　　**25 or older:**　　　　42%

Basis for selection. Open admission, but selective for some programs. Special admissions requirements for nursing program applicants and international students.

2011-2012 Annual costs. Tuition/fees: $4,306; $8,131 out-of-state. Per-credit charge: $85 in-state; $170 out-of-state. Books/supplies: $1,200. Personal expenses: $648.

Financial aid. Need-based: Need-based aid available for part-time students. Work-study available nights, weekends and for part-time students. **Non-need-based:** Scholarships awarded for academics.

Application procedures. Admission: No deadline. $15 fee. Admission notification on a rolling basis. **Financial aid:** Priority date 5/1; no closing date. FAFSA, institutional form required. Applicants notified on a rolling basis starting 2/1.

Academics. Special study options: Cooperative education, distance learning, double major, dual enrollment of high school students, student-designed major, teacher certification program. License preparation in nursing. **Credit/placement by examination:** AP, CLEP, institutional tests. 24 credit hours maximum toward associate degree. **Support services:** GED preparation and test center, learning center, reduced course load, remedial instruction, study skills assistance, tutoring, writing center.

Majors. Business: Accounting, business admin, management information systems, office management, office technology. **Computer sciences:** Applications programming, networking. **Health services:** Medical assistant, medical secretary, nursing (RN). **Liberal arts:** Arts/sciences. **Protective services:** Criminal justice, firefighting. **Visual/performing arts:** Music.

Most popular majors. Business/marketing 7%, health sciences 23%, liberal arts 64%.

Computing on campus. 80 workstations in library, computer center, student center.

Student life. Freshman orientation: Mandatory. Preregistration for classes offered. **Activities:** Concert band, dance, drama, student government.

Athletics. Intramural: Volleyball M.

Student services. Career counseling, services for economically disadvantaged, student employment services, financial aid counseling, personal counseling, veterans' counselor. **Physically disabled:** Services for visually, speech, hearing impaired. **Transfer:** Pre-admission transcript evaluation for new students. Transfer center, transfer adviser, college fairs on campus for students transferring to 4-year colleges.

Contact. Phone: (503) 338-2411 Toll-free number: (866) 252-8768 Fax: (503) 325-5738
Amy Magnussen, Recruiting Coordinator, Clatsop Community College, 1653 Jerome Avenue, Astoria, OR 97103

Klamath Community College
Klamath Falls, Oregon
www.klamathcc.edu　　　　　　　　　**CB code: 4127**

▸ Public 2-year community college
▸ Commuter campus in large town

General. Regionally accredited. **Enrollment:** 1,278 degree-seeking undergraduates. **Degrees:** 94 associate awarded. **Calendar:** Quarter, limited summer session. **Full-time faculty:** 28 total. **Part-time faculty:** 82 total.

Basis for selection. Open admission.

2012-2013 Annual costs. Tuition/fees (projected): $3,930; $7,530 out-of-state. Per-credit charge: $75 in-state; $155 out-of-state.

Financial aid. Need-based: Need-based aid available for part-time students. Work-study available nights, weekends and for part-time students.

Application procedures. Admission: No deadline. No application fee. **Financial aid:** No deadline. FAFSA required.

Academics. Special study options: Dual enrollment of high school students. **Credit/placement by examination:** AP, CLEP, IB, institutional tests. 45 credit hours maximum toward associate degree. **Support services:** GED preparation and test center, learning center, remedial instruction, study skills assistance, tutoring, writing center.

Majors. Business: Accounting technology, business admin, marketing. **Conservation:** Environmental science. **Education:** Early childhood, teacher assistance. **General:** Business. **Health services:** Office assistant. **Liberal arts:** Arts/sciences. **Protective services:** Law enforcement admin.

Computing on campus. Commuter students can connect to campus network. Online course registration, online library, wireless network available.

Student life. Freshman orientation: Mandatory. Preregistration for classes offered. **Activities:** Student government.

Athletics. Team name: Badgers.

Student services. Alcohol/substance abuse counseling, career counseling, financial aid counseling, personal counseling. **Physically disabled:** Services for visually, hearing impaired. **Transfer:** College fairs on campus for students transferring to 4-year colleges.

Contact. Phone: (541) 882-3521 Fax: (541) 880-2297
Julie Murray-Jensen, Student Services Offices, Klamath Community College, 7390 South 6th Street, Klamath Falls, OR 97603

Lane Community College
Eugene, Oregon　　　　　　　　　**CB member**
www.lanecc.edu　　　　　　　　　**CB code: 4407**

▸ Public 2-year community college
▸ Commuter campus in small city

General. Founded in 1964. Regionally accredited. Outreach centers in downtown Eugene, Cottage Grove, and Florence. **Enrollment:** 10,096 degree-seeking undergraduates; 2,741 non-degree-seeking students. **Degrees:** 976 associate awarded. **Location:** 110 miles from Portland. **Calendar:** Quarter, extensive summer session. **Full-time faculty:** 217 total; 9% minority, 56% women. **Part-time faculty:** 426 total; 7% minority, 56% women. **Class size:** 28% < 20, 68% 20-39, 3% 40-49, less than 1% 50-99, less than 1% >100. **Partnerships:** Formal partnerships with professional technical advisory groups.

Student profile. Among degree-seeking undergraduates, 1,650 enrolled as first-time, first-year students.

Part-time:	51%	Women:	53%
Out-of-state:	3%	25 or older:	58%

Transfer out. Colleges most students transferred to 2011: University of Oregon, Oregon State University.

Basis for selection. Open admission, but selective for some programs. Special requirements for allied health and flight technology programs.

2011-2012 Annual costs. Tuition/fees: $4,265; $10,519 out-of-state. Per-credit charge: $84 in-state; $213 out-of-state. Books/supplies: $1,086. Personal expenses: $1,035.

2010-2011 Financial aid. Need-based: 55% of total undergraduate aid awarded as scholarships/grants, 45% as loans/jobs. Need-based aid available for part-time students. Work-study available nights, weekends and for part-time students. **Non-need-based:** Scholarships awarded for art, athletics, minority status, music/drama.

Application procedures. Admission: No deadline. No application fee. Admission notification on a rolling basis. **Financial aid:** Closing date 2/15. FAFSA required. Applicants notified on a rolling basis starting 6/1; must reply within 2 week(s) of notification.

Academics. Special study options: Accelerated study, cooperative education, cross-registration, distance learning, double major, dual enrollment of high school students, ESL, independent study, internships, liberal arts/career combination, study abroad, weekend college. License preparation in aviation, dental hygiene, nursing, paramedic. **Credit/placement by examination:** AP, CLEP, institutional tests. **Support services:** GED preparation and test center, learning center, pre-admission summer program, reduced course load, remedial instruction, study skills assistance, tutoring, writing center.

Majors. Business: General, accounting technology, hotel/motel admin, office management, office/clerical, retailing. **Communications:** Broadcast journalism, digital media. **Communications technology:** Animation/special effects. **Computer sciences:** Networking, programming. **Conservation:** Environmental studies, water/wetlands/marine. **Health services:** Dental hygiene, EMT paramedic, nursing (RN), physical therapy assistant, respiratory therapy technology. **Human services:** Community org/advocacy. **Liberal arts:** Arts/sciences. **Parks/recreation:** Sports admin. **Protective services:** Criminal justice. **Visual/performing arts:** Commercial/advertising art. **Work/family studies:** Child care service.

Most popular majors. Business/marketing 6%, health sciences 13%, liberal arts 58%.

Computing on campus. 800 workstations in library, computer center. Commuter students can connect to campus network. Online course registration, online library, helpline available.

Student life. Freshman orientation: Available. Preregistration for classes offered. Each field of study has its own orientation. Program also available for undecided majors. **Activities:** Bands, campus ministries, choral groups, dance, drama, literary magazine, music ensembles, musical theater, radio station, student government, student newspaper, symphony orchestra, women's center.

Athletics. Intercollegiate: Baseball M, basketball, cross-country, track and field, volleyball W. **Intramural:** Badminton, basketball, volleyball. **Team name:** Trojans.

Student services. Adult student services, career counseling, services for economically disadvantaged, student employment services, financial aid counseling, health services, minority student services, on-campus daycare, placement for graduates, veterans' counselor, women's services. **Physically disabled:** Services for visually, speech, hearing impaired. **Transfer:** Pre-admission transcript evaluation for new students. Transfer adviser, college fairs on campus for students transferring to 4-year colleges.

Contact. E-mail: hamblinj@lanecc.edu
Phone: (541) 463-3100 Fax: (541) 463-3995
John Hamblin, Director of Admissions, Lane Community College, 4000 East 30th Avenue, Eugene, OR 97405

Le Cordon Bleu College of Culinary Arts: Portland
Portland, Oregon
www.chefs.edu/Portland

▶ For-profit 2-year culinary school
▶ Commuter campus in very large city

General. Regionally accredited. **Calendar:** Differs by program.

Annual costs/financial aid. Cost of certificate programs in Culinary Arts, and Patisserie and Baking: $17,200 tuition, $300 fees. Fees include cost of textbooks, uniforms, lab fees and tool kits.

Contact. Phone: (888) 848-3202
Admissions Services Coordinator, 600 S.W. 10th Avenue, Suite #500, Portland, OR 97205

Linn-Benton Community College
Albany, Oregon
www.linnbenton.edu
CB member
CB code: 4413

▶ Public 2-year community college
▶ Commuter campus in large town

General. Founded in 1966. Regionally accredited. Courses available at off-campus centers in Corvallis, Lebanon, and Sweet Home. **Enrollment:** 6,922 degree-seeking undergraduates. **Degrees:** 609 associate awarded. **ROTC:** Army, Air Force. **Location:** 70 miles from Portland, 45 miles from Eugene. **Calendar:** Quarter, limited summer session. **Full-time faculty:** 163 total; 9% minority, 45% women. **Part-time faculty:** 369 total; 9% minority, 67% women. **Class size:** 51% < 20, 47% 20-39, 1% 40-49, less than 1% 50-99, less than 1% >100. **Special facilities:** Stables, riding arena.

Student profile. Among degree-seeking undergraduates, 291 transferred in from other institutions.

Out-of-state:	2%	25 or older:	35%

Transfer out. Colleges most students transferred to 2011: Oregon State University, Western Oregon University, University of Oregon, Portland State University, Southern Oregon University.

Basis for selection. Open admission, but selective for some programs. Special requirements for nursing, dental assistant, veterinary technology, pharmacy technology, phlebotomy, public safety dispatcher, and radiologic technology programs. High school diploma or GED required of applicants under 18.

2011-2012 Annual costs. Tuition/fees: $4,095; $8,325 out-of-state. Per-credit charge: $91 in-state; $185 out-of-state. Books/supplies: $1,260. Personal expenses: $1,281.

Financial aid. Need-based: Need-based aid available for part-time students. Work-study available nights, weekends and for part-time students. **Non-need-based:** Scholarships awarded for academics, alumni affiliation, art, athletics, leadership, music/drama.

Application procedures. Admission: Priority date 7/14; deadline 10/4 (receipt date). $30 fee. Admission notification on a rolling basis beginning on or about 7/1. **Financial aid:** Priority date 4/1; no closing date. FAFSA required. Applicants notified on a rolling basis starting 3/30; must reply within 4 week(s) of notification.

Academics. Special study options: Cooperative education, distance learning, ESL, exchange student, independent study, internships, study abroad. Evening degree program. License preparation in nursing, paramedic, radiology, real estate. **Credit/placement by examination:** AP, CLEP, institutional tests. 24 credit hours maximum toward associate degree. **Support services:** GED preparation and test center, learning center, remedial instruction, study skills assistance, tutoring, writing center.

Majors. Biology: General. **Business:** Accounting technology, administrative services, business admin, office management. **Communications:** Journalism. **Computer sciences:** General, applications programming, system admin. **Education:** General, elementary, physical, secondary, teacher assistance. **Engineering:** General. **English:** English lit, rhetoric/composition, technical writing. **Foreign languages:** Spanish. **General:** Animal sciences, business, dairy, equestrian studies, equine science, horticultural science. **Health services:** Medical assistant, medical records admin, medical secretary, nursing (RN), office assistant, predental, premedicine, prenursing, prepharmacy, preveterinary. **History:** General. **Liberal arts:** Arts/sciences. **Math:**

General. **Physical sciences:** Chemistry, physics. **Protective services:** Criminal justice, police science. **Psychology:** General. **Social sciences:** General, anthropology, economics, geography, political science, sociology. **Visual/performing arts:** Art, commercial/advertising art, dramatic, music, photography. **Work/family studies:** General, child care management.

Most popular majors. Business/marketing 11%, engineering/engineering technologies 6%, health sciences 15%, liberal arts 33%, trade and industry 9%.

Computing on campus. 500 workstations in library, computer center, student center. Commuter students can connect to campus network. Online course registration, online library, helpline, wireless network available.

Student life. Freshman orientation: Mandatory. Preregistration for classes offered. 2 hour program; also available on-line. **Activities:** Concert band, choral groups, drama, literary magazine, student government, student newspaper, Pacific party, Campus Crusade for Christ, Baha'i, Christians on Campus, Chi Alpha Radical Reality, Phi Theta Kappa, campus family co-op, student ambassadors, livestock judging.

Athletics. Intercollegiate: Baseball M, basketball, equestrian, volleyball W. **Intramural:** Basketball, bowling, tennis. **Team name:** Roadrunners.

Student services. Adult student services, career counseling, services for economically disadvantaged, student employment services, financial aid counseling, minority student services, on-campus daycare, personal counseling, placement for graduates, veterans' counselor. **Physically disabled:** Services for visually, speech, hearing impaired. **Transfer:** Transfer center, transfer adviser, college fairs on campus for students transferring to 4-year colleges.

Contact. E-mail: admissions@linnbenton.edu
Phone: (541) 917-4811 Fax: (541) 917-4868
Danny Aynes, Admissions Outreach Coordinator, Linn-Benton Community College, 6500 SW Pacific Boulevard, Albany, OR 97321-3779

Mt. Hood Community College
Gresham, Oregon
www.mhcc.cc.or.us

CB member
CB code: 4508

- Public 2-year community college
- Commuter campus in small city

General. Founded in 1965. Regionally accredited. **Enrollment:** 8,686 degree-seeking undergraduates; 558 non-degree-seeking students. **Degrees:** 905 associate awarded. **Location:** 12 miles from Portland. **Calendar:** Quarter, limited summer session. **Full-time faculty:** 158 total; 16% have terminal degrees, 8% minority, 51% women. **Part-time faculty:** 425 total. **Class size:** 48% < 20, 48% 20-39, 2% 40-49, 1% 50-99, less than 1% >100. **Special facilities:** Planetarium, solar observatory. **Partnerships:** Formal partnerships with WorkSource Portland Metro East, Business and Industry Workforce Training-Boeing, Tri-Met, additional small to medium firms.

Student profile. Among degree-seeking undergraduates, 60% enrolled in a transfer program, 40% enrolled in a vocational program, 4% already have a bachelor's degree or higher, 2,401 enrolled as first-time, first-year students, 2,401 transferred in from other institutions.

Part-time:	50%	Hispanic American:	8%
Out-of-state:	5%	Native American:	1%
Women:	54%	International:	1%
African American:	5%	25 or older:	47%
Asian American:	6%		

Transfer out. 36% of students enrolled in the transfer program go on to 4-year colleges. **Colleges most students transferred to 2011:** Portland State University, Oregon State University, University of Oregon, Concordia University, Eastern Oregon University.

Basis for selection. Open admission, but selective for some programs. SAT scores may be used in place of in-house placement test. Special requirements for nursing and graphic design programs. Allied health programs require 2.5 GPA. Interview required for cosmetology and most health services. **Learning Disabled:** Individuals are required to submit documentation to verify eligibility under Sections 504 of the Rehabilitation Act of 1973 and the Americans with Disabilities Act of 1990.

High school preparation. College-preparatory program recommended. Requirements for health programs include 1 algebra, 1 biology, and 1 chemistry.

2011-2012 Annual costs. Tuition/fees: $4,219; $9,844 out-of-state. Per-credit charge: $84 in-state; $209 out-of-state. Books/supplies: $1,560. Personal expenses: $1,035.

Financial aid. Need-based: Need-based aid available for part-time students. Work-study available nights, weekends and for part-time students. **Non-need-based:** Scholarships awarded for academics.

Application procedures. Admission: No deadline. No application fee. Admission notification on a rolling basis. Most health services majors must apply between November 1 and March 30 for fall admission. Application deadlines and priority dates vary by program. **Financial aid:** Closing date 4/1. FAFSA, institutional form required. Applicants notified on a rolling basis starting 4/1; must reply within 4 week(s) of notification.

Academics. Special study options: Accelerated study, cooperative education, distance learning, double major, dual enrollment of high school students, ESL, exchange student, external degree, honors, independent study, internships, liberal arts/career combination, study abroad. Bachelor's degree programs available on campus. License preparation in dental hygiene, nursing, paramedic, physical therapy. **Credit/placement by examination:** AP, CLEP, IB, institutional tests. 45 credit hours maximum toward associate degree. College placement test required for chemistry, math, writing, or reading courses. **Support services:** GED preparation and test center, learning center, pre-admission summer program, reduced course load, remedial instruction, study skills assistance, tutoring.

Majors. Architecture: Technology. **Biology:** General, biochemistry. **Business:** Accounting technology, administrative services, business admin, entrepreneurial studies, executive assistant, hospitality admin, hotel/motel admin, hotel/motel/restaurant management, office technology, office/clerical, resort management, restaurant/food services, small business admin, tourism/travel. **Communications:** Journalism, radio/TV. **Communications technology:** Graphic/printing, photo/film/video, radio/TV. **Computer sciences:** General, applications programming, computer science, database management, information technology, LAN/WAN management, networking, web page design. **Conservation:** General, fisheries, forest technology. **Education:** Early childhood. **English:** English lit. **Health services:** Dental hygiene, EMT paramedic, medical assistant, medical records admin, medical secretary, medical transcription, mental health counseling, nursing (RN), nursing education, occupational therapy assistant, office assistant, physical therapy assistant, prechiropractic, prepharmacy, preveterinary, respiratory therapy technology, surgical technology. **History:** General. **Liberal arts:** Arts/sciences. **Math:** General. **Parks/recreation:** Exercise sciences, facilities management, health/fitness, outdoor education. **Philosophy/religion:** Philosophy. **Physical sciences:** Chemistry, geology, physics. **Protective services:** Firefighting. **Psychology:** General. **Social sciences:** General, economics, geography, political science, sociology. **Visual/performing arts:** Art, art history/conservation, ceramics, commercial/advertising art, design, digital arts, dramatic, drawing, graphic design, painting, printmaking, sculpture, studio arts. **Work/family studies:** Child care service.

Most popular majors. Business/marketing 11%, health sciences 22%, liberal arts 45%.

Computing on campus. Online course registration, online library, wireless network available.

Student life. Freshman orientation: Available. Preregistration for classes offered. **Activities:** Bands, choral groups, dance, drama, international student organizations, music ensembles, musical theater, radio station, student government, student newspaper, symphony orchestra, TV station, campus ambassadors, hotel/tourism/restaurant club, MECHA, veterans association, Rho Theta, student activities board, Japanese club, English conversation club, Student Nurses Association, mental health and human services club.

Athletics. Intercollegiate: Baseball M, basketball, cross-country, track and field, volleyball W. **Intramural:** Basketball, softball, volleyball. **Team name:** Saints.

Student services. Adult student services, career counseling, student employment services, financial aid counseling, health services, minority student services, on-campus daycare, personal counseling, placement for graduates, veterans' counselor. **Physically disabled:** Services for visually, speech, hearing impaired. **Transfer:** Transfer adviser, college fairs on campus for students transferring to 4-year colleges.

Contact. E-mail: admweb@mhcc.edu
Phone: (503) 491-7393 Fax: (503) 491-7388
David Minger, Associate Dean, Enrollment Services, Mt. Hood Community College, 26000 SE Stark Street, Gresham, OR 97030

Pioneer Pacific College
Wilsonville, Oregon
www.pioneerpacific.edu

CB code: 0492

- For-profit 2-year career college
- Commuter campus in large town
- Interview required

General. Accredited by ACICS. Additional campuses include the Health Career Institute in Wilsonville, learning site in Clackamas, branch campus in Springfield. **Enrollment:** 1,100 full-time, degree-seeking students. **Degrees:** 32 bachelor's, 544 associate awarded. **Location:** 20 miles from Portland. **Calendar:** Differs by program, extensive summer session. **Full-time faculty:** 75 total. **Part-time faculty:** 99 total. **Class size:** 94% < 20, 6% 20-39.

Student profile.

Out-of-state: 1% 25 or older: 67%

Transfer out. **Colleges most students transferred to 2011:** University of Phoenix, Clackamas Community College.

Basis for selection. Open admission, but selective for some programs. Selective admissions to practical nursing program.

2011-2012 Annual costs. Personal expenses: $3,619.

Financial aid. All financial aid based on need. Need-based aid available for part-time students. Work-study available nights, weekends and for part-time students.

Application procedures. **Admission:** No deadline. $50 fee. Application must be submitted on paper. Admission notification on a rolling basis. **Financial aid:** No deadline. FAFSA required. Applicants notified on a rolling basis starting 2/27.

Academics. **Special study options:** Accelerated study, honors, internships, liberal arts/career combination. Externships. Bachelor's degree programs available on campus. **Credit/placement by examination:** AP, CLEP, institutional tests. **Support services:** Study skills assistance, tutoring.

Majors. **Business:** Accounting, business admin, marketing. **Computer sciences:** Information systems, webmaster. **Health services:** Health care admin, medical assistant. **Protective services:** Criminal justice.

Most popular majors. Business/marketing 27%, computer/information sciences 15%, health sciences 51%, legal studies 6%, security/protective services 18%.

Computing on campus. 250 workstations in library, computer center. Online library, wireless network available.

Student life. **Freshman orientation:** Mandatory. Preregistration for classes offered.

Student services. Career counseling, student employment services, financial aid counseling, placement for graduates. **Transfer:** Pre-admission transcript evaluation for new students.

Contact. E-mail: inquiries@pioneerpacific.edu
Phone: (503) 682-3903 Toll-free number: (866) 772-4636
Fax: (503) 682-1514
Vickie Church, Director of Admissions, Pioneer Pacific College, 27501 Southwest Parkway Avenue, Wilsonville, OR 97070

Pioneer Pacific College: Springfield
Springfield, Oregon
www.pioneerpacific.edu

- For-profit 2-year branch campus and career college
- Commuter campus in small city

General. Accredited by ACICS. **Location:** 10 miles from Eugene. **Calendar:** Differs by program.

Annual costs/financial aid. Personal expenses: $3,619.

Contact. Phone: (541) 684-4644
Director of Admissions, 3800 Sports Way, Springfield, OR 97477

Portland Community College
Portland, Oregon
www.pcc.edu

CB member
CB code: 4617

- Public 2-year community college
- Commuter campus in very large city

General. Founded in 1961. Regionally accredited. 4 comprehensive campuses; classes offered at several centers throughout district. **Enrollment:** 34,632 degree-seeking undergraduates. **Degrees:** 2,774 associate awarded. **Location:** 5 miles from downtown. **Calendar:** Quarter, extensive summer session. **Full-time faculty:** 459 total; 13% minority, 57% women. **Part-time faculty:** 1,350 total; 12% minority, 56% women.

Student profile. Among degree-seeking undergraduates, 61% enrolled in a transfer program, 39% enrolled in a vocational program.

Transfer out. **Colleges most students transferred to 2011:** Portland State University, University of Oregon, Oregon State University.

Basis for selection. Open admission, but selective for some programs. Enrollment in certain programs or courses may require prerequisite course work or permission by a department representative.

High school preparation. High school diploma required for some allied health programs.

2011-2012 Annual costs. Tuition/fees: $3,891; $9,561 out-of-state. Per-credit charge: $79 in-state; $205 out-of-state. Books/supplies: $1,545. Personal expenses: $1,350.

Financial aid. All financial aid based on need. Need-based aid available for part-time students. Work-study available nights, weekends and for part-time students.

Application procedures. **Admission:** No deadline. No application fee. **Financial aid:** Priority date 3/1; no closing date. FAFSA required. Applicants notified on a rolling basis starting 6/1; must reply within 3 week(s) of notification.

Academics. **Special study options:** Cooperative education, distance learning, double major, dual enrollment of high school students, ESL, honors, internships, study abroad, weekend college. License preparation in aviation, dental hygiene, nursing, paramedic, radiology, real estate. **Credit/placement by examination:** AP, CLEP, institutional tests. 45 credit hours maximum toward associate degree. **Support services:** GED preparation and test center, learning center, reduced course load, remedial instruction, study skills assistance, tutoring, writing center.

Majors. **Biology:** Biotechnology. **Business:** General, accounting technology, administrative services, business admin, management information systems, marketing, office management, retailing. **Computer sciences:** Applications programming, system admin, web page design. **Education:** Early childhood, teacher assistance. **Engineering:** Biomedical. **Foreign languages:** American Sign Language, sign language interpretation. **General:** Landscaping. **Health services:** Clinical lab technology, dental hygiene, dental lab technology, EMT paramedic, medical radiologic technology/radiation therapy, medical records technology, ophthalmic technology, substance abuse counseling, veterinary technology/assistant. **Human services:** General. **Liberal arts:** Arts/sciences. **Parks/recreation:** Health/fitness. **Protective services:** Criminal justice, firefighting. **Visual/performing arts:** Commercial/advertising art, design, interior design. **Work/family studies:** Child care management.

Most popular majors. Business/marketing 9%, health sciences 10%, liberal arts 65%.

Computing on campus. 3,043 workstations in library, computer center, student center. Commuter students can connect to campus network. Online course registration, online library, helpline, wireless network available.

Student life. **Freshman orientation:** Mandatory. Preregistration for classes offered. Online orientation available. **Activities:** Bands, choral groups, dance, drama, international student organizations, literary magazine, music ensembles, musical theater, student government.

Athletics. NJCAA. **Intercollegiate:** Basketball. **Intramural:** Basketball, bowling, cross-country, racquetball, soccer, softball, swimming, tennis, volleyball. **Team name:** Panthers.

Student services. Adult student services, career counseling, services for economically disadvantaged, student employment services, financial aid counseling, minority student services, on-campus daycare, personal counseling, placement for graduates, veterans' counselor, women's services. **Physically disabled:** Services for visually, speech, hearing impaired. **Transfer:** Pre-admission transcript evaluation for new students. Transfer center, transfer adviser, college fairs on campus for students transferring to 4-year colleges.

Contact. Phone: (971) 722-8888 Fax: (971) 722-4988
Veronica Garcia, Dean of Enrollment Services, Portland Community College, Box 19000, Portland, OR 97280-0990

Rogue Community College
Grants Pass, Oregon
www.roguecc.edu
CB code: 4653

- Public 2-year community college
- Commuter campus in large town

General. Founded in 1970. Regionally accredited. Branch campuses in Medford and White City, learning centers in Medford and Cave Junction. **Enrollment:** 4,761 degree-seeking undergraduates; 1,067 non-degree-seeking students. **Degrees:** 385 associate awarded. **Location:** 30 miles from Medford, 240 miles from Portland. **Calendar:** Quarter, limited summer session. **Full-time faculty:** 82 total; 2% minority, 46% women. **Part-time faculty:** 352 total; 3% minority, 53% women. **Class size:** 51% < 20, 46% 20-39, 1% 40-49, 1% 50-99. **Special facilities:** Outdoor concert bowl.

Student profile. Among degree-seeking undergraduates, 83% enrolled in a transfer program, 17% enrolled in a vocational program, 4% already have a bachelor's degree or higher, 880 enrolled as first-time, first-year students, 39 transferred in from other institutions.

Part-time:	51%	Asian American:	2%
Out-of-state:	2%	Hispanic American:	11%
Women:	60%	Native American:	2%
African American:	1%	25 or older:	53%

Transfer out. 25% of students enrolled in the transfer program go on to 4-year colleges. **Colleges most students transferred to 2011:** Southern Oregon University, Oregon State University, Portland State, University of Oregon.

Basis for selection. Open admission, but selective for some programs. Special requirements for nursing, respiratory therapy, emergency medical technology, human services, and mental health technician. Interview recommended for allied health, nursing programs.

2011-2012 Annual costs. Tuition/fees: $4,410; $5,265 out-of-state. Per-credit charge: $85 in-state; $104 out-of-state. Washington, Idaho, Nevada, and California residents pay in-state tuition. Books/supplies: $1,500. Personal expenses: $1,350.

2010-2011 Financial aid. **Need-based:** 458 full-time freshmen applied for aid; 378 were judged to have need; 376 of these received aid. Average need met was 67%. Average scholarship/grant was $4,227; average loan $2,962. 71% of total undergraduate aid awarded as scholarships/grants, 29% as loans/jobs. Need-based aid available for part-time students. Work-study available nights, weekends and for part-time students. **Non-need-based:** Awarded to 335 full-time undergraduates, including 107 freshmen.

Application procedures. **Admission:** No deadline. No application fee. Application must be submitted online. Admission notification on a rolling basis. **Financial aid:** Priority date 5/1; no closing date. FAFSA, institutional form required. Applicants notified on a rolling basis; must reply within 2 week(s) of notification.

Academics. **Special study options:** Cooperative education, distance learning, double major, dual enrollment of high school students, ESL, independent study, liberal arts/career combination, study abroad. License preparation in nursing, paramedic. **Credit/placement by examination:** AP, CLEP, institutional tests. 48 credit hours maximum toward associate degree. **Support services:** GED preparation and test center, learning center, remedial instruction, study skills assistance, tutoring, writing center.

Majors. **Business:** General, accounting technology, business admin, marketing. **Computer sciences:** General. **Health services:** EMT paramedic, nursing (RN), office computer specialist. **Human services:** Social work. **Liberal arts:** Arts/sciences. **Protective services:** Fire safety technology, police science. **Visual/performing arts:** General. **Work/family studies:** Child care management.

Most popular majors. Business/marketing 6%, health sciences 14%, liberal arts 61%, trade and industry 7%.

Computing on campus. 200 workstations in library, computer center. Commuter students can connect to campus network. Online course registration available.

Student life. **Freshman orientation:** Available. Preregistration for classes offered. **Activities:** Bands, choral groups, drama, musical theater, student government, student newspaper, Latino club.

Athletics. **Intramural:** Basketball, volleyball.

Student services. Career counseling, services for economically disadvantaged, student employment services, financial aid counseling, on-campus daycare, personal counseling, placement for graduates, veterans' counselor.

Physically disabled: Services for visually, speech, hearing impaired. **Transfer:** Pre-admission transcript evaluation for new students. Transfer adviser, college fairs on campus for students transferring to 4-year colleges.

Contact. E-mail: csullivan@roguecc.edu
Phone: (541) 956-7427
Claudia Sullivan, Director of Enrollment Services, Rogue Community College, 3345 Redwood Highway, Grants Pass, OR 97527

Southwestern Oregon Community College
Coos Bay, Oregon
www.socc.edu
CB code: 4729

- Public 2-year culinary school and community college
- Commuter campus in large town

General. Founded in 1961. Regionally accredited. **Enrollment:** 1,139 degree-seeking undergraduates. **Degrees:** 315 associate awarded. **Location:** 125 miles from Eugene, 225 miles from Portland. **Calendar:** Quarter, limited summer session. **Full-time faculty:** 59 total. **Part-time faculty:** 167 total. **Special facilities:** Culinary institute, small business development center, university center.

Student profile.

Out-of-state:	17%	Live on campus:	17%
25 or older:	34%		

Transfer out. **Colleges most students transferred to 2011:** Oregon State University, Southern Oregon University, University of Oregon, Linfield College, Eastern Oregon University.

Basis for selection. Open admission, but selective for some programs. Separate application process for nursing students. Background check required for emergency response and EMTs.

2011-2012 Annual costs. Tuition/fees: $4,760; $4,760 out-of-state. Room/board: $6,556. Books/supplies: $1,200. Personal expenses: $540.

Financial aid. **Need-based:** Need-based aid available for part-time students. Work-study available nights, weekends and for part-time students. **Non-need-based:** Scholarships awarded for art, athletics, leadership, music/drama.

Application procedures. **Admission:** No deadline. $40 fee, may be waived for applicants with need. Admission notification on a rolling basis. **Financial aid:** Closing date 3/1. FAFSA required. Applicants notified on a rolling basis starting 5/1; must reply within 3 week(s) of notification.

Academics. **Special study options:** Cooperative education, distance learning, double major, dual enrollment of high school students, ESL, honors, independent study, internships, liberal arts/career combination. Bachelor's degree programs available on campus. License preparation in nursing. **Credit/placement by examination:** AP, CLEP, institutional tests. **Support services:** GED preparation and test center, learning center, reduced course load, remedial instruction, study skills assistance, tutoring, writing center.

Majors. **Business:** Accounting technology, administrative services, banking/financial services, business admin, entrepreneurial studies, management information systems, office management, sales/distribution. **Computer sciences:** Applications programming, computer science, information systems, webmaster. **Conservation:** Environmental studies. **Education:** Teacher assistance. **Engineering:** General. **General:** Turf management. **Health services:** Licensed practical nurse, medical assistant, substance abuse counseling. **Human services:** Social work. **Liberal arts:** Arts/sciences. **Math:** General. **Protective services:** Corrections, criminal justice, firefighting, police science. **Work/family studies:** Child care management, family studies.

Most popular majors. Business/marketing 10%, health sciences 8%, liberal arts 58%, security/protective services 8%.

Computing on campus. 338 workstations in dormitories, library, computer center. Dormitories wired for high-speed internet access and linked to campus network. Commuter students can connect to campus network. Online course registration, online library, helpline, wireless network available.

Student life. **Freshman orientation:** Available. Preregistration for classes offered. **Housing:** Guaranteed on-campus for freshmen. Single-sex dorms, special housing for disabled, apartments, wellness housing available. $250 partly refundable deposit. **Activities:** Bands, choral groups, drama, literary magazine, music ensembles, student government, student newspaper, Rotaract, Phi Theta Kappa, student ambassadors.

Athletics. NJCAA. **Intercollegiate:** Baseball M, basketball, cross-country, golf, soccer, softball W, track and field, volleyball W, wrestling M. **Intramural:** Basketball. **Team name:** Lakers.

Student services. Adult student services, alcohol/substance abuse counseling, career counseling, services for economically disadvantaged, student employment services, financial aid counseling, health services, on-campus daycare, personal counseling, placement for graduates, veterans' counselor. **Physically disabled:** Services for visually, speech, hearing impaired. **Transfer:** Transfer center, college fairs on campus for students transferring to 4-year colleges.

Contact. E-mail: admissions@socc.edu
Phone: (541) 888-7636 Toll-free number: (800) 962-2838 ext. 7636
Fax: (541) 888-7247
Tom Nicholls, Director of Enrollment Management, Southwestern Oregon Community College, 1988 Newmark Avenue, Coos Bay, OR 97420-2956

Treasure Valley Community College
Ontario, Oregon
www.tvcc.cc CB code: 4825

- Public 2-year community college
- Commuter campus in small town

General. Founded in 1961. Regionally accredited. **Enrollment:** 2,344 degree-seeking undergraduates; 215 non-degree-seeking students. **Degrees:** 313 associate awarded. **Location:** 60 miles from Boise, Idaho. **Calendar:** Quarter, extensive summer session. **Full-time faculty:** 53 total; 87% have terminal degrees, 6% minority, 45% women. **Part-time faculty:** 134 total; 2% have terminal degrees, 34% minority, 52% women. **Class size:** 62% < 20, 35% 20-39, 2% 40-49, 2% 50-99.

Student profile. Among degree-seeking undergraduates, 75% enrolled in a transfer program, 25% enrolled in a vocational program, 635 enrolled as first-time, first-year students, 117 transferred in from other institutions.

Part-time:	45%	Hispanic American:	20%
Out-of-state:	65%	Native American:	2%
Women:	60%	25 or older:	45%
African American:	2%	Live on campus:	5%
Asian American:	1%		

Transfer out. Colleges most students transferred to 2011: Eastern Oregon University, Boise State University, Oregon State University, University of Oregon.

Basis for selection. Open admission, but selective for some programs. Special requirements for nursing program. **Home schooled:** Transcript of courses and grades, state high school equivalency certificate required.

High school preparation. College-preparatory program recommended.

2011-2012 Annual costs. Tuition/fees: $4,455; $4,905 out-of-state. Room/board: $6,380. Books/supplies: $1,050. Personal expenses: $1,500.

Financial aid. Need-based: Need-based aid available for part-time students. Work-study available nights, weekends and for part-time students. **Non-need-based:** Scholarships awarded for academics, athletics, leadership, music/drama, state residency.

Application procedures. Admission: No deadline. No application fee. Admission notification on a rolling basis. **Financial aid:** Priority date 4/1; no closing date. FAFSA required. Applicants notified on a rolling basis starting 5/1.

Academics. Special study options: Cooperative education, distance learning, dual enrollment of high school students, ESL, independent study, internships. Elementary education program with Eastern Oregon State College and satellite program with Boise State University. License preparation in nursing, paramedic, real estate. **Credit/placement by examination:** AP, CLEP, institutional tests. 45 credit hours maximum toward associate degree. **Support services:** GED preparation and test center, learning center, pre-admission summer program, reduced course load, remedial instruction, study skills assistance, tutoring, writing center.

Majors. Biology: General. **Business:** General, business admin, management information systems, office management, office/clerical. **Communications:** Communications/speech/rhetoric. **Computer sciences:** General, computer science. **Conservation:** General, wildlife/wilderness. **Education:** Bilingual, elementary, multicultural, physical, secondary, teacher assistance. **Engineering:** General. **English:** English lit. **Foreign languages:** General. **General:** Agronomy, animal sciences, business, economics, equine science, farm/ranch, horticultural science, range science, soil science. **Health services:** Athletic training, dental hygiene, medical radiologic technology/radiation

therapy, medical secretary, medical transcription, nursing (RN), physical therapy, predental, premedicine, prepharmacy, preveterinary. **History:** General. **Human services:** Social work. **Liberal arts:** Arts/sciences. **Math:** General. **Physical sciences:** Chemistry, geology, physics. **Protective services:** Criminal justice, fire safety technology, firefighting, law enforcement admin, police science. **Psychology:** General. **Social sciences:** General, political science. **Visual/performing arts:** General, art, music.

Most popular majors. Business/marketing 8%, education 14%, health sciences 15%, liberal arts 37%.

Computing on campus. 250 workstations in dormitories, library, computer center, student center. Dormitories wired for high-speed internet access and linked to campus network. Commuter students can connect to campus network. Online course registration, online library, helpline, wireless network available.

Student life. Freshman orientation: Available. Preregistration for classes offered. Online orientation available. **Housing:** Coed dorms, wellness housing available. $200 partly refundable deposit. **Activities:** Bands, choral groups, drama, music ensembles, musical theater, student government, Young Republicans, LDS student association.

Athletics. Intercollegiate: Baseball M, basketball, cross-country, rodeo, soccer, tennis, track and field, volleyball. **Intramural:** Basketball, softball, volleyball. **Team name:** Chukars.

Student services. Financial aid counseling, on-campus daycare, personal counseling, veterans' counselor, women's services. **Transfer:** Pre-admission transcript evaluation for new students. Transfer adviser, college fairs on campus for students transferring to 4-year colleges.

Contact. E-mail: admissions@tvcc.cc
Phone: (541) 881-5806 Fax: (541) 881-2721
Stephanie Oester, Director of Admissions, Treasure Valley Community College, 650 College Boulevard, Ontario, OR 97914

Umpqua Community College
Roseburg, Oregon
www.umpqua.edu CB code: 4862

- Public 2-year community college
- Commuter campus in large town

General. Founded in 1964. Regionally accredited. **Enrollment:** 2,210 degree-seeking undergraduates; 1,023 non-degree-seeking students. **Degrees:** 434 associate awarded. **Location:** 70 miles from Eugene. **Calendar:** Quarter, limited summer session. **Full-time faculty:** 63 total; 3% minority, 46% women. **Part-time faculty:** 147 total; 5% minority, 50% women. **Class size:** 54% < 20, 44% 20-39, less than 1% 40-49, 2% 50-99.

Student profile. Among degree-seeking undergraduates, 1% already have a bachelor's degree or higher, 347 enrolled as first-time, first-year students, 434 transferred in from other institutions.

Part-time:	43%	Asian American:	1%
Out-of-state:	1%	Hispanic American:	5%
Women:	58%	Native American:	2%
African American:	1%	25 or older:	60%

Transfer out. Colleges most students transferred to 2011: Oregon State University, University of Oregon, Northwest Christian College, Western Oregon University, Southern Oregon University.

Basis for selection. Open admission, but selective for some programs. Special requirements for nursing program. COMPASS placement test and/or ACT ASSET test used for placement only. **Home schooled:** High school release required.

2011-2012 Annual costs. Tuition/fees: $4,178; $9,413 out-of-state. Per-credit charge: $80 in-state; $206 out-of-state. Books/supplies: $1,500. Personal expenses: $1,200.

Financial aid. Need-based: Need-based aid available for part-time students. Work-study available nights, weekends and for part-time students. **Non-need-based:** Scholarships awarded for academics, athletics.

Application procedures. Admission: No deadline. $25 fee. Application must be submitted on paper. Admission notification on a rolling basis. **Financial aid:** Priority date 3/10; no closing date. FAFSA, institutional form required. Applicants notified on a rolling basis starting 2/9; must reply within 2 week(s) of notification.

Academics. Special study options: Cooperative education, distance learning, dual enrollment of high school students, ESL, honors, independent study,

internships, student-designed major. Bachelor's degree programs available on campus. License preparation in aviation, nursing, paramedic. **Credit/placement by examination:** AP, CLEP, SAT, institutional tests. 45 credit hours maximum toward associate degree. 24 hours of credit by exam may be counted toward 1-year certificate program. **Support services:** GED preparation and test center, learning center, remedial instruction, study skills assistance, tutoring.

Majors. Business: General, accounting, accounting technology, administrative services, business admin, executive assistant, management information systems, marketing. **Computer sciences:** Information systems. **Education:** General, early childhood. **Health services:** EMT paramedic, medical secretary, nursing (RN), staff services technology. **Liberal arts:** Arts/sciences. **Protective services:** Firefighting, police science. **Work/family studies:** Child care management.

Most popular majors. Business/marketing 20%, computer/information sciences 6%, engineering/engineering technologies 6%, health sciences 16%, liberal arts 48%.

Computing on campus. 200 workstations in library, computer center, student center. Commuter students can connect to campus network. Online course registration, helpline, wireless network available.

Student life. Freshman orientation: Available. Preregistration for classes offered. Held the Thursday or Friday prior to beginning of term. **Activities:** Bands, choral groups, drama, music ensembles, musical theater, student government, student newspaper.

Athletics. Intercollegiate: Basketball, volleyball W. **Team name:** River Hawks.

Student services. Adult student services, career counseling, services for economically disadvantaged, student employment services, financial aid counseling, on-campus daycare, personal counseling, placement for graduates, veterans' counselor. **Physically disabled:** Services for visually, hearing impaired. **Transfer:** Transfer center, transfer adviser, college fairs on campus for students transferring to 4-year colleges.

Contact. E-mail: lavera.noland@umpqua.edu
Phone: (541) 440-7743 Toll-free number: (800) 820-5161
Fax: (541) 440-4612
David Farrington, Director of Enrollment Services, Umpqua Community College, 1140 College Road, Roseburg, OR 97470-0226

Pennsylvania

Antonelli Institute of Art and Photography
Erdenheim, Pennsylvania
www.antonelli.edu
CB code: 0971

- For-profit 2-year visual arts and junior college
- Commuter campus in large town
- Interview required

General. Founded in 1938. Accredited by ACCSC. **Enrollment:** 203 degree-seeking undergraduates. **Degrees:** 85 associate awarded. **Location:** 1 mile from Philadelphia. **Calendar:** Semester, limited summer session. **Full-time faculty:** 6 total. **Part-time faculty:** 6 total. **Class size:** 100% < 20. **Special facilities:** Wet black and white darkroom, computer graphics labs, digital photo labs.

Student profile.

Out-of-state:	21%	Live on campus:	48%
25 or older:	4%		

Transfer out. Colleges most students transferred to 2011: Brooks Institute, Arcadia University, Chestnut Hill College.

Basis for selection. Emphasis placed on interview, recommendations, and samples of art and photography. Although not required, student portfolios will be evaluated. **Home schooled:** Transcript of courses and grades, interview required. Documentation of high school graduation/equivalency from local school district, state department of education or recognized home school organization required. If these items are not available, a GED will be required.

2011-2012 Annual costs. Books/supplies: $5,900. Personal expenses: $2,210.

Financial aid. All financial aid based on need. Need-based aid available for part-time students. Work-study available nights, weekends and for part-time students.

Application procedures. Admission: No deadline. $50 fee, may be waived for applicants with need. Admission notification on a rolling basis. **Financial aid:** No deadline. FAFSA required. Applicants notified on a rolling basis; must reply within 2 week(s) of notification.

Academics. Credit/placement by examination: AP, CLEP.

Majors. Visual/performing arts: Commercial photography, commercial/advertising art, design, photography.

Computing on campus. 60 workstations in library, computer center. Online library, wireless network available.

Student life. Freshman orientation: Mandatory. Preregistration for classes offered. **Housing:** Coed dorms, apartments, wellness housing available. $375 fully refundable deposit. Dormitory facilities available from local apartments.

Athletics. Intramural: Volleyball.

Student services. Career counseling, student employment services, financial aid counseling, personal counseling, placement for graduates. **Transfer:** Pre-admission transcript evaluation for new students. Transfer adviser for students transferring to 4-year colleges.

Contact. E-mail: admissions@antonelli.edu
Phone: (800) 722-7871 Toll-free number: (800) 722-7871
Fax: (215) 836-2794
Nancy Awot, Director of Admissions, Antonelli Institute of Art and Photography, 300 Montgomery Avenue, Erdenheim, PA 19038-8242

Art Institute of York
York, Pennsylvania
www.artinstitutes.edu/york
CB code: 1548

- For-profit 2-year visual arts and technical college
- Commuter campus in large town
- Application essay, interview required

General. Founded in 1952. Accredited by ACCSC. **Enrollment:** 584 degree-seeking undergraduates. **Degrees:** 1 bachelor's, 153 associate awarded. **Location:** 20 miles from Harrisburg, 90 miles from Philadelphia. **Calendar:** Quarter, extensive summer session. **Full-time faculty:** 26 total. **Part-time faculty:** 38 total. **Class size:** 75% < 20, 25% 20-39.

Basis for selection. High school diploma or GED, 1.5 GPA for associate degree students, 2.0 GPA for bachelor's students, essay and interview. Portfolio required for Media Arts and Animation program.

2011-2012 Annual costs. Tuition/fees: $21,555. Per-credit charge: $479. Books/supplies: $1,250. Personal expenses: $3,500.

Financial aid. All financial aid based on need. Work-study available nights, weekends and for part-time students.

Application procedures. Admission: No deadline. $50 fee, may be waived for applicants with need. Admission notification on a rolling basis. **Financial aid:** Priority date 8/1; no closing date. FAFSA required. Applicants notified on a rolling basis starting 6/1.

Academics. Special study options: Internships. Bachelor's degree programs available on campus. **Credit/placement by examination:** AP, CLEP, institutional tests. 15 credit hours maximum toward associate degree, 30 toward bachelor's. **Support services:** Learning center, reduced course load, remedial instruction, study skills assistance, tutoring, writing center.

Majors. Business: Fashion. **Communications technology:** Animation/special effects. **Visual/performing arts:** Commercial/advertising art, graphic design, interior design.

Most popular majors. Business/marketing 15%, visual/performing arts 85%.

Computing on campus. 175 workstations in library, computer center, student center. Dormitories wired for high-speed internet access. Online course registration, repair service, wireless network available.

Student life. Freshman orientation: Mandatory. Preregistration for classes offered. Half-day program, 3-6 days before school starts. **Housing:** Single-sex dorms available. $125 partly refundable deposit. **Activities:** Student government, student newspaper.

Student services. Alcohol/substance abuse counseling, career counseling, student employment services, financial aid counseling, personal counseling, placement for graduates. **Transfer:** Pre-admission transcript evaluation for new students.

Contact. Phone: (800) 864-7725 Fax: (717) 840-1951
Scott Vukoder, Senior Director of Admissions, Art Institute of York, 1409 Williams Road, York, PA 17402

Berks Technical Institute
Wyomissing, Pennsylvania
www.berks.edu
CB code: 3198

- For-profit 2-year business and technical college
- Commuter campus in small city

General. Accredited by ACCSCT. **Location:** 64 miles from Philadelphia. **Calendar:** Quarter.

Annual costs/financial aid. Approximate cost for diploma program, $9,000 to $11,000; for degree program, $12,000 to $14,000. Books/supplies: $992. Need-based financial aid available to full-time and part-time students.

Contact. Phone: (610) 372-1722
Director of Admissions, 2205 Ridgewood Road, Wyomissing, PA 19610

Bidwell Training Center
Pittsburgh, Pennsylvania
www.bidwell-training.org
CB code: 3199

- Private 1-year business and health science college
- Commuter campus in large city

General. Accredited by ACCSCT. **Calendar:** Differs by program.

Annual costs/financial aid. Need-based financial aid available for full-time students.

Contact. Phone: (412) 323-4000 ext. 156
Senior Director of Operations, 1815 Metropolitan Street, Pittsburgh, PA 15233

Bradford School: Pittsburgh
Pittsburgh, Pennsylvania
www.bradfordpittsburgh.edu   **CB code: 2206**

- For-profit 2-year junior college
- Commuter campus in very large city
- Interview required

General. Accredited by ACICS. **Enrollment:** 582 degree-seeking undergraduates. **Degrees:** 262 associate awarded. **Calendar:** Semester. **Full-time faculty:** 10 total. **Part-time faculty:** 9 total.

Basis for selection. High school record, class rank, recommendations, interview most important.

Financial aid. Need-based: Work-study available nights, weekends and for part-time students.

Application procedures. Admission: No deadline. $50 fee. Admission notification on a rolling basis. **Financial aid:** FAFSA required.

Academics. Credit/placement by examination: AP, CLEP.

Majors. Business: Accounting, administrative services, hospitality admin, sales/distribution, tourism/travel. **Computer sciences:** General, programming. **Health services:** Dental assistant, medical assistant. **Visual/performing arts:** Commercial/advertising art.

Most popular majors. Business/marketing 35%, health sciences 38%, legal studies 6%, visual/performing arts 18%.

Computing on campus. 150 workstations in library.

Student life. Housing: Coed dorms available.

Student services. Financial aid counseling, placement for graduates.

Contact. Phone: (412) 391-6710 Toll-free number: (800) 391-6810 Fax: (412) 471-6714
John Enright, Director of Admissions, Bradford School: Pittsburgh, 125 West Station Square Drive, Pittsburgh, PA 15219

Bucks County Community College
Newtown, Pennsylvania   **CB member**
www.bucks.edu   **CB code: 2066**

- Public 2-year community college
- Commuter campus in large town

General. Founded in 1964. Regionally accredited. Credit courses available at several off-campus locations. **Enrollment:** 10,063 degree-seeking undergraduates; 642 non-degree-seeking students. **Degrees:** 818 associate awarded. **Location:** 35 miles from Philadelphia. **Calendar:** Semester, limited summer session. **Full-time faculty:** 175 total; 28% have terminal degrees, 9% minority, 53% women. **Part-time faculty:** 440 total; 12% have terminal degrees, 6% minority, 56% women. **Class size:** 67% < 20, 33% 20-39, less than 1% 40-49, less than 1% 50-99. **Partnerships:** Formal partnerships with Bucks County Technical High School, Eastern Center for Arts and Technology, Middle Bucks Institute of Technology, Northern Montgomery County Technical Career Center, Upper Bucks County Area Vocational Technical High School, Western Center for Technical Studies.

Student profile. Among degree-seeking undergraduates, 72% enrolled in a transfer program, 22% enrolled in a vocational program, 2,720 enrolled as first-time, first-year students, 197 transferred in from other institutions.

Part-time:	58%	**Asian American:**	3%
Out-of-state:	1%	**Hispanic American:**	4%
Women:	55%	**Native American:**	1%
African American:	5%	**25 or older:**	36%

Transfer out. 45% of students enrolled in the transfer program go on to 4-year colleges. **Colleges most students transferred to 2011:** Temple University, Pennsylvania State University, West Chester University, Drexel University, La Salle University.

Basis for selection. Open admission, but selective for some programs. Admission to nursing, fine arts, chef apprenticeship and fine woodworking programs based on satisfaction of prerequisites. Placement test administered after admission. Admission to paralegal certificate program is restricted. Proof of specific previous college study is required. Interview required for chef apprentice, fine arts, fine woodworking, and nursing programs. Audition required for music program; portfolio required for art, fine woodworking programs; essay required for chef apprentice program. **Adult students:** Students over 65 exempt from placement tests, except in mathematics for proper placement. **Home schooled:** Final official transcript certified by state required. **Learning Disabled:** Special testing accommodations for the entrance assessment test for students with learning disabilities.

High school preparation. College-preparatory program recommended.

2011-2012 Annual costs. Tuition/fees: $4,279; $7,609 out-of-district; $10,939 out-of-state. Per-credit charge: $111 in-district; $222 out-of-district; $333 out-of-state. $949 required fee included above are for in-county students. Out-of-county students pay additional $300 capital fee; out-of-state students pay additional $600 capital fee. Books/supplies: $1,350. Personal expenses: $1,350.

2010-2011 Financial aid. Need-based: 70% of total undergraduate aid awarded as scholarships/grants, 30% as loans/jobs. Need-based aid available for part-time students. Work-study available nights, weekends and for part-time students. **Non-need-based:** Scholarships awarded for academics, art, music/drama.

Application procedures. Admission: Closing date 5/1 (postmark date). No application fee. Admission notification on a rolling basis. **Financial aid:** Closing date 5/1. FAFSA required. Applicants notified on a rolling basis starting 6/1; must reply within 2 week(s) of notification.

Academics. Special study options: Cooperative education, distance learning, dual enrollment of high school students, ESL, external degree, honors, independent study, internships, student-designed major, weekend college. License preparation in nursing, occupational therapy, physical therapy, radiology, real estate. **Credit/placement by examination:** AP, CLEP, institutional tests. 30 credit hours maximum toward associate degree. **Support services:** GED preparation and test center, learning center, reduced course load, remedial instruction, study skills assistance, tutoring, writing center.

Majors. Area/ethnic studies: American, Latin American. **Biology:** Biotechnology. **Business:** General, accounting technology, banking/financial services, business admin, hotel/motel admin, office management, retailing, small business admin, tourism/travel, travel services. **Communications:** Communications/speech/rhetoric, journalism. **Computer sciences:** General, information systems, LAN/WAN management, networking, programming, system admin. **Conservation:** Environmental science. **Education:** General, biology, chemistry, early childhood, health, history, kindergarten/preschool, mathematics, physical. **Engineering:** General. **Health services:** Clinical research coordinator, medical assistant, nursing (RN), office assistant. **Human services:** Social work. **Liberal arts:** Arts/sciences, humanities. **Math:** General. **Parks/recreation:** Sports admin. **Physical sciences:** Chemistry. **Protective services:** Correctional facilities, corrections, criminal justice, fire safety technology, law enforcement admin. **Psychology:** General. **Social sciences:** General. **Visual/performing arts:** General, cinematography, commercial/advertising art, dramatic, graphic design, music. **Work/family studies:** Child care service, family studies, institutional food production.

Most popular majors. Business/marketing 23%, education 14%, health sciences 15%, liberal arts 15%, visual/performing arts 7%.

Computing on campus. 450 workstations in library, computer center. Commuter students can connect to campus network. Online course registration, online library, helpline, wireless network available.

Student life. Freshman orientation: Available. Preregistration for classes offered. **Activities:** Bands, choral groups, dance, drama, film society, literary magazine, music ensembles, student government, student newspaper, TV station, variety of service, social, and recreational programs, including Phi Theta Kappa, Inter-Varsity Christian Fellowship, Habitat for Humanity, Future Teacher's Organization.

Athletics. NJCAA. **Intercollegiate:** Baseball M, basketball M, equestrian, golf, soccer, tennis, volleyball W. **Intramural:** Baseball M, basketball M, bowling W, equestrian, skiing, softball, volleyball. **Team name:** Centurions.

Student services. Adult student services, alcohol/substance abuse counseling, career counseling, services for economically disadvantaged, student employment services, financial aid counseling, minority student services, on-campus daycare, personal counseling, veterans' counselor, women's services. **Physically disabled:** Services for visually, speech, hearing impaired. **Transfer:** Pre-admission transcript evaluation for new students. Transfer center, transfer adviser, college fairs on campus for students transferring to 4-year colleges.

Contact. E-mail: admissions@bucks.edu
Phone: (215) 968-8100 Fax: (215) 968-8110
Marlene Barlow, Director of Admissions, Bucks County Community
College, 275 Swamp Road, Newtown, PA 18940

Butler County Community College
Butler, Pennsylvania
www.bc3.edu   **CB code: 2069**

- Public 2-year community college
- Commuter campus in small city

General. Founded in 1965. Regionally accredited. Classes offered in Cranberry township, Mercer, and Lawrence counties. **Enrollment:** 4,163 degree-seeking undergraduates. **Degrees:** 373 associate awarded. **Location:** 35 miles from Pittsburgh. **Calendar:** Semester, limited summer session. **Full-time faculty:** 67 total; 15% have terminal degrees, 58% women. **Part-time faculty:** 279 total; 1% have terminal degrees, 47% women. **Special facilities:** Cultural center/theater, meteorology lab, computer forensics lab. **Partnerships:** Formal partnerships with American Management Association, Workforce & Economic Development Network of PA, Backflow Management, Inc., Carnegie Mellon University, 13 regional fire schools, 12 local high schools.

Student profile. Among degree-seeking undergraduates, 70% enrolled in a transfer program, 30% enrolled in a vocational program.

Out-of-state:	1%	25 or older:	37%

Transfer out. 75% of students enrolled in the transfer program go on to 4-year colleges. **Colleges most students transferred to 2011:** Slippery Rock University of Pennsylvania, Clarion University of Pennsylvania, Indiana University of Pennsylvania.

Basis for selection. Open admission, but selective for some programs. Admission to nursing, medical assistant, physical therapist assistant, massage therapy, and metrology programs based on high school record.

2011-2012 Annual costs. Tuition/fees: $3,564; $5,940 out-of-district; $8,580 out-of-state. Per-credit charge: $88 in-district; $176 out-of-district; $252 out-of-state.

Financial aid. Need-based: Need-based aid available for part-time students. Work-study available nights, weekends and for part-time students. **Non-need-based:** Scholarships awarded for academics, state residency.

Application procedures. Admission: No deadline. $25 fee, may be waived for applicants with need. Application must be submitted on paper. Admission notification on a rolling basis. **Financial aid:** Priority date 4/15; no closing date. FAFSA required. Applicants notified on a rolling basis starting 5/1; must reply within 2 week(s) of notification.

Academics. Special study options: Cooperative education, distance learning, independent study, internships. License preparation in nursing, physical therapy. **Credit/placement by examination:** AP, CLEP, institutional tests. 45 credit hours maximum toward associate degree. **Support services:** GED preparation, learning center, pre-admission summer program, reduced course load, remedial instruction, study skills assistance, tutoring, writing center.

Majors. Biology: General. **Business:** Accounting technology, administrative services, business admin, human resources, marketing, sales/distribution, tourism promotion. **Communications:** Digital media, organizational. **Computer sciences:** Applications programming, security, web page design. **Education:** General, kindergarten/preschool. **Engineering:** General. **English:** English lit. **Health services:** EMT paramedic, health care admin, massage therapy, nursing (RN), office assistant, physical therapy assistant, radiologic technology/medical imaging. **Math:** General. **Parks/recreation:** General, sports admin. **Physical sciences:** General. **Protective services:** Homeland security, law enforcement admin, police science. **Psychology:** General. **Visual/performing arts:** Graphic design, photography. **Work/family studies:** Institutional food production.

Most popular majors. Business/marketing 24%, engineering/engineering technologies 9%, health sciences 21%, liberal arts 7%, psychology 7%, security/protective services 6%.

Computing on campus. 108 workstations in library, computer center. Online course registration available.

Student life. Freshman orientation: Available. Preregistration for classes offered. **Activities:** Drama, literary magazine, student government, student newspaper, Christian outreach organization.

Athletics. NJCAA. **Intercollegiate:** Baseball M, basketball, cheerleading, golf M, softball W, volleyball W. **Intramural:** Basketball, golf, table tennis, volleyball, weight lifting. **Team name:** Pioneers.

Student services. Adult student services, career counseling, services for economically disadvantaged, student employment services, financial aid counseling, on-campus daycare, personal counseling, placement for graduates, veterans' counselor. **Physically disabled:** Services for visually, hearing impaired. **Transfer:** Pre-admission transcript evaluation for new students. Transfer adviser, college fairs on campus for students transferring to 4-year colleges.

Contact. E-mail: pattie.bajuszik@bc3.edu
Phone: (724) 287-8711 ext. 8346 Toll-free number: (888) 826-2829
Fax: (724) 287-3460
Pattie Bajuszik, Director of Admissions, Butler County Community
College, PO Box 1203, Butler, PA 16003-1203

Cambria-Rowe Business College
Johnstown, Pennsylvania
www.crbc.net   **CB code: 2210**

- For-profit 2-year business and career college
- Commuter campus in small city

General. Founded in 1891. Accredited by ACICS. **Enrollment:** 139 degree-seeking undergraduates; 3 non-degree-seeking students. **Degrees:** 88 associate awarded. **Location:** 60 miles from Pittsburgh. **Calendar:** Quarter, limited summer session. **Full-time faculty:** 11 total; 18% have terminal degrees, 91% women.

Student profile. Among degree-seeking undergraduates, 46 enrolled as first-time, first-year students.

Part-time:	3%	Asian American:	1%
Women:	76%	Hispanic American:	3%
African American:	13%	25 or older:	45%

Transfer out. Colleges most students transferred to 2011: Saint Francis University, Mount Aloysius College.

Basis for selection. Open admission. Interview recommended. **Home schooled:** Transcript of courses and grades required.

2012-2013 Annual costs. Tuition/fees (projected): $11,705. Per-credit charge: $300.

Financial aid. Need-based: Need-based aid available for part-time students. Work-study available nights, weekends and for part-time students. **Non-need-based:** Scholarships awarded for academics, leadership.

Application procedures. Admission: No deadline. $30 fee. Students notified within 2 weeks of receipt of application. **Financial aid:** Closing date 8/1. FAFSA required. Applicants notified on a rolling basis.

Academics. Special study options: Accelerated study. **Credit/placement by examination:** AP, CLEP, institutional tests. **Support services:** Tutoring.

Majors. Business: General, accounting, administrative services, business admin. **Computer sciences:** Support specialist. **Health services:** Medical secretary, medical transcription.

Most popular majors. Business/marketing 43%, computer/information sciences 11%, health sciences 45%.

Computing on campus. PC or laptop required. Online library, repair service, wireless network available.

Student life. Freshman orientation: Mandatory. Preregistration for classes offered. Usually held 3 weeks prior to start date.

Student services. Adult student services, career counseling, student employment services, financial aid counseling, personal counseling, placement for graduates.

Contact. E-mail: admissions@crbc.net
Phone: (814) 536-5168 Toll-free number: (800) 639-2273
Fax: (814) 536-5160
Amanda Artim, Director of Admissions, Cambria-Rowe Business College,
221 Central Avenue, Johnstown, PA 15902

Cambria-Rowe Business College: Indiana
Indiana, Pennsylvania
www.crbc.net   **CB code: 3274**

- For-profit 2-year business and career college
- Commuter campus in small town
- Interview required

Two-Year Colleges

General. Accredited by ACICS. **Enrollment:** 101 degree-seeking undergraduates. **Degrees:** 40 associate awarded. **Calendar:** Quarter. **Full-time faculty:** 8 total; 25% have terminal degrees, 100% women.

Student profile. Among degree-seeking undergraduates, 20 enrolled as first-time, first-year students.

Part-time:	2%	**Hispanic American:**	1%
Women:	87%	**25 or older:**	45%

Basis for selection. Admissions based on high school transcript or GED scores and passing grade on entrance examination administered by school.

2012-2013 Annual costs. Tuition/fees (projected): $11,705. Per-credit charge: $300.

Financial aid. Need-based: Need-based aid available for part-time students. Work-study available nights, weekends and for part-time students. **Non-need-based:** Scholarships awarded for academics, leadership.

Application procedures. Admission: No deadline. $30 fee. Admission notification on a rolling basis. **Financial aid:** Closing date 8/1. FAFSA required. Applicants notified on a rolling basis.

Academics. Credit/placement by examination: AP, CLEP, institutional tests. **Support services:** Tutoring.

Majors. Business: Accounting, administrative services, business admin, management information systems. **Computer sciences:** Support specialist. **Health services:** Medical secretary.

Most popular majors. Business/marketing 45%, computer/information sciences 8%, health sciences 45%.

Computing on campus. PC or laptop required. Online library, repair service, wireless network available.

Student life. Freshman orientation: Mandatory. Preregistration for classes offered.

Student services. Adult student services, career counseling, financial aid counseling, personal counseling, placement for graduates. **Transfer:** Pre-admission transcript evaluation for new students.

Contact. E-mail: sbell-leger@crbc.net
Phone: (724) 463-0222 Toll-free number: (800) 639-2273
Stacey Bell-Leger, Admissions Representative, Cambria-Rowe Business College: Indiana, 422 South 13th Street, Indiana, PA 15701

Career Training Academy
New Kensington, Pennsylvania
www.careerta.edu　　　　　　　　　**CB code: 3205**

▶ For-profit 2-year career college
▶ Commuter campus in small town

General. Accredited by ACCSCT. **Location:** 18 miles from Pittsburgh. **Calendar:** Differs by program.

Annual costs/financial aid. Need-based financial aid available for full-time students.

Contact. Phone: (724) 337-1000
Director of Admissions, 950 Fifth Avenue, New Kensington, PA 15068

Career Training Academy: Monroeville
Monroeville, Pennsylvania
www.careerta.edu　　　　　　　　　**CB code: 3207**

▶ For-profit 2-year branch campus college
▶ Commuter campus in small city

General. Accredited by ACCSCT. **Location:** 10 miles from Pittsburgh. **Calendar:** Differs by program.

Annual costs/financial aid. Personal expenses: $2,889. Need-based financial aid available to full-time and part-time students.

Contact. Phone: (412) 372-3900
Director of Admissions, 4314 Old William Penn Highway #103, Monroeville, PA 15146

Career Training Academy: Pittsburgh
Pittsburgh, Pennsylvania
www.careerta.edu

▶ For-profit 2-year branch campus college
▶ Commuter campus in small city

General. Regionally accredited. **Calendar:** Differs by program.

Contact. Phone: (412) 367-4000
Admissions, 1500 Shoppes at Northway, Pittsburgh, PA 15237

CHI Institute: Broomall
Broomall, Pennsylvania
www.chitraining.com　　　　　　　**CB code: 3398**

▶ For-profit 2-year career college
▶ Commuter campus in large town

General. Accredited by ACCSCT. **Location:** 7 miles from Philadelphia. **Calendar:** Quarter.

Annual costs/financial aid. Need-based financial aid available to full-time and part-time students.

Contact. Phone: (610) 355-3300
Director of Admissions, 1991 Sproul Road, Suite 42, Broomall, PA 19008

CHI Institute: Franklin Mills
Philadelphia, Pennsylvania
www.chitraining.com　　　　　　　**CB code: 3386**

▶ For-profit 2-year technical college
▶ Commuter campus in large town

General. Founded in 1981. Accredited by ACCSCT. **Location:** 5 miles from Philadelphia. **Calendar:** Differs by program.

Annual costs/financial aid. Books/supplies: $765.

Contact. Phone: (215) 357-5100
Admissions Director, 125 Franklin Mills Boulevard, Philadelphia, PA 19154

Commonwealth Technical Institute
Johnstown, Pennsylvania
www.hgac.org　　　　　　　　　　　**CB code: 3125**

▶ Private 2-year technical college
▶ Residential campus in small city

General. Accredited by ACCSCT. **Calendar:** Semester.

Annual costs/financial aid. Tuition/fees (2011-2012): $22,448. Room/board: $9,516. Books/supplies: $300. Need-based financial aid available to full-time and part-time students.

Contact. Phone: (814) 255-8237
Director of Admissions, 727 Goucher Street, Johnstown, PA 15905-3902

Community College of Allegheny County
Pittsburgh, Pennsylvania　　　　　**CB member**
www.ccac.edu　　　　　　　　　　　　**CB code: 2156**

▶ Public 2-year community college
▶ Commuter campus in very large city

General. Founded in 1966. Regionally accredited. Campuses located in and around Pittsburgh. **Enrollment:** 19,233 degree-seeking undergraduates; 1,139 non-degree-seeking students. **Degrees:** 1,796 associate awarded. **Calendar:** Semester, extensive summer session. **Full-time faculty:** 273 total. **Part-time faculty:** 1,547 total. **Class size:** 55% < 20, 44% 20-39, less than 1% 40-49, less than 1% 50-99.

Student profile. Among degree-seeking undergraduates, 4,538 enrolled as first-time, first-year students.

Part-time:	59%	Women:	58%
Out-of-state:	2%	25 or older:	46%

Transfer out. Colleges most students transferred to 2011: University of Pittsburgh, Robert Morris University, Duquesne University, Point Park University, Carlow College.

Basis for selection. Open admission, but selective for some programs. Special requirements for some health-related, culinary arts, and automotive programs. COMPASS used for placement. Audition recommended for music program.

2011-2012 Annual costs. Tuition/fees: $2,824; $5,267 out-of-district; $7,710 out-of-state. Per-credit charge: $87 in-district; $175 out-of-district; $262 out-of-state. Books/supplies: $1,000.

Financial aid. Need-based: Need-based aid available for part-time students. Work-study available nights, weekends and for part-time students. **Non-need-based:** Scholarships awarded for academics, minority status.

Application procedures. Admission: No deadline. No application fee. Admission notification on a rolling basis. **Financial aid:** Priority date 5/1; no closing date. FAFSA required. Applicants notified on a rolling basis starting 5/1.

Academics. Special study options: Cooperative education, cross-registration, distance learning, dual enrollment of high school students, ESL, honors, independent study, internships, liberal arts/career combination. License preparation in nursing. **Credit/placement by examination:** AP, CLEP, institutional tests. 30 credit hours maximum toward associate degree. **Support services:** GED preparation and test center, learning center, reduced course load, remedial instruction, study skills assistance, tutoring, writing center.

Majors. Biology: General. **Business:** Accounting technology, administrative services, banking/financial services, business admin, entrepreneurial studies, human resources, management information systems, marketing. **Communications:** Journalism. **Education:** Elementary, teacher assistance. **Foreign languages:** General. **General:** Horticulture, landscaping, turf management. **Health services:** Cardiovascular technology, clinical lab technology, medical assistant, medical radiologic technology/radiation therapy, medical records technology, mental health services, nuclear medical technology, nursing (RN), occupational therapy assistant, pharmacy assistant, physical therapy assistant, respiratory therapy technology, sonography, surgical technology. **Human services:** Social work. **Liberal arts:** Arts/sciences, humanities. **Math:** General. **Parks/recreation:** Health/fitness. **Physical sciences:** Chemistry, physics. **Protective services:** Corrections, fire safety technology, police science. **Psychology:** General. **Social sciences:** General, sociology. **Visual/performing arts:** Art, commercial/advertising art, music. **Work/family studies:** Child development.

Most popular majors. Business/marketing 17%, health sciences 38%, liberal arts 23%.

Computing on campus. 3,700 workstations in library, computer center. Commuter students can connect to campus network. Helpline available.

Student life. Freshman orientation: Available. Preregistration for classes offered. **Activities:** Dance, drama, international student organizations, student government, student newspaper.

Athletics. NJCAA. **Intercollegiate:** Baseball M, basketball, bowling, golf, ice hockey M, softball W, tennis, volleyball W.

Student services. Adult student services, career counseling, student employment services, health services, on-campus daycare, personal counseling, placement for graduates, veterans' counselor. **Physically disabled:** Services for visually, speech, hearing impaired. **Transfer:** Transfer adviser for students transferring to 4-year colleges.

Contact. E-mail: admissions@ccac.edu
Phone: (412) 237-2511 Fax: (412) 237-4581
Mary Lou Kennedy, Director of Admissions, Community College of Allegheny County, 808 Ridge Avenue, Pittsburgh, PA 15212

Community College of Beaver County
Monaca, Pennsylvania
www.ccbc.edu

CB member
CB code: 2126

❯ Public 2-year community college
❯ Commuter campus in small town

General. Founded in 1966. Regionally accredited. **Location:** 30 miles from Pittsburgh. **Calendar:** Semester.

Annual costs/financial aid. Tuition/fees (2011-2012): $3,660; $6,510 out-of-district; $9,360 out-of-state. Academic enhancement fees, ranging from $25 to $900 per course, apply in programs requiring specialized technology and equipment; $10 per-credit-hour fee for courses that include a lab. Additional per-credit-hour capital fee: $20 for out-of-county residents, $40 for out-of-state residents. Books/supplies: $1,000. Personal expenses: $1,200. Need-based financial aid available to full-time and part-time students.

Contact. Phone: (724) 480-3500
Registrar, One Campus Drive, Monaca, PA 15061-2588

Community College of Philadelphia
Philadelphia, Pennsylvania
www.ccp.edu

CB member
CB code: 2682

❯ Public 2-year community college
❯ Commuter campus in very large city

General. Founded in 1965. Regionally accredited. Regional centers located in northeast, northwest, and west Philadelphia. Many additional temporary facilities located throughout city. **Enrollment:** 19,756 degree-seeking undergraduates. **Degrees:** 1,673 associate awarded. **ROTC:** Army. **Calendar:** Semester, extensive summer session. **Full-time faculty:** 413 total; 25% minority, 48% women. **Part-time faculty:** 771 total; 30% minority, 48% women. **Class size:** 35% < 20, 65% 20-39, less than 1% 40-49.

Student profile. Among degree-seeking undergraduates, 77% enrolled in a transfer program, 23% enrolled in a vocational program, 4,155 enrolled as first-time, first-year students, 596 transferred in from other institutions.

Part-time:	72%	Women:	65%
Out-of-state:	3%	25 or older:	50%

Transfer out. Colleges most students transferred to 2011: Temple University, Drexel University, University of Phoenix, Delaware County Community College, Penn State University.

Basis for selection. Open admission, but selective for some programs. Special requirements for health, music, art and some technical programs. Audition required for music program; portfolio required for art program.

High school preparation. One chemistry, 2 math required of health program applicants.

2011-2012 Annual costs. Tuition/fees: $5,100; $9,240 out-of-district; $13,380 out-of-state. Per-credit charge: $138 in-district; $276 out-of-district; $414 out-of-state. Books/supplies: $1,000. Personal expenses: $856.

2010-2011 Financial aid. All financial aid based on need. 765 full-time freshmen applied for aid; 732 were judged to have need; 728 of these received aid. Average need met was 14%. Average scholarship/grant was $2,626. 56% of total undergraduate aid awarded as scholarships/grants, 44% as loans/jobs. Need-based aid available for part-time students. Work-study available nights, weekends and for part-time students.

Application procedures. Admission: No deadline. $20 fee. Admission notification on a rolling basis. **Financial aid:** Closing date 5/1. FAFSA, institutional form required. Applicants notified on a rolling basis.

Academics. Special study options: Accelerated study, distance learning, dual enrollment of high school students, ESL, honors, internships, study abroad, weekend college. License preparation in dental hygiene, nursing, radiology, real estate. **Credit/placement by examination:** AP, CLEP, institutional tests. 30 credit hours maximum toward associate degree. **Support services:** GED preparation and test center, learning center, pre-admission summer program, reduced course load, remedial instruction, tutoring.

Majors. Area/ethnic studies: Women's. **Business:** General, accounting, administrative services, banking/financial services, business admin, fashion, international marketing, logistics, office/clerical, operations, real estate, sales/distribution. **Communications technology:** Recording arts. **Computer sciences:** General, applications programming, data processing, networking, programming, security, system admin, webmaster. **Education:** General, business, secondary. **Engineering:** General. **English:** Rhetoric/composition. **Foreign languages:** Sign language interpretation. **Health services:** Clinical lab technology, dental hygiene, health services admin, medical assistant, medical radiologic technology/radiation therapy, medical records technology, mental health services, nursing (RN), respiratory therapy technology. **Liberal arts:** Arts/sciences. **Math:** General. **Physical sciences:** General. **Protective services:** Fire safety technology, forensics, police science. **Social sciences:**

Geography. **Visual/performing arts:** Art, commercial photography, commercial/advertising art, dramatic, music, music performance. **Work/family studies:** Child care management, institutional food production.

Most popular majors. Business/marketing 13%, health sciences 12%, liberal arts 41%.

Computing on campus. 994 workstations in library, student center. Commuter students can connect to campus network. Online course registration, helpline, wireless network available.

Student life. Freshman orientation: Available. Preregistration for classes offered. **Activities:** Jazz band, choral groups, dance, drama, film society, music ensembles, radio station, student government, student newspaper, TV station, Christian Coalition, Newman club, Black Student Congress, Latin American student organization, Phi Theta Kappa, Muslim student association, Vietnamese student organization, Asian-American association.

Athletics. Intercollegiate: Baseball M, basketball, cross-country, soccer M, softball W, volleyball W. **Intramural:** Basketball, soccer, softball, tennis, track and field, volleyball. **Team name:** Colonials.

Student services. Adult student services, career counseling, student employment services, financial aid counseling, health services, on-campus daycare, personal counseling, placement for graduates, veterans' counselor, women's services. **Physically disabled:** Services for visually, speech, hearing impaired. **Transfer:** Transfer adviser, college fairs on campus for students transferring to 4-year colleges.

Contact. E-mail: admissions@ccp.edu
Phone: (215) 751-8010
Jeri Draper, Director of Recruitment and Admissions, Community College of Philadelphia, 1700 Spring Garden Street, Philadelphia, PA 19130-3991

Consolidated School of Business: Lancaster
Lancaster, Pennsylvania
www.csb.edu   CB code: 2240

- For-profit 2-year career college
- Commuter campus in small city
- Interview required

General. Founded in 1986. Accredited by ACICS. Additional campus in York. **Enrollment:** 165 undergraduates. **Degrees:** 47 associate awarded. **Location:** 85 miles from Philadelphia, 35 miles from Harrisburg. **Calendar:** Differs by program. **Full-time faculty:** 8 total. **Part-time faculty:** 2 total.

Basis for selection. Open admission.

High school preparation. Recommended computer application coursework for accelerated or advanced placement.

2011-2012 Annual costs. Tuition/fees: $12,450. Fees vary by program and range from $120 to $600 for a full program. Optional laptop computer program: $900. Books/supplies: $1,500.

Financial aid. Need-based: Need-based aid available for part-time students. Work-study available nights, weekends and for part-time students. **Non-need-based:** Scholarships awarded for academics, leadership, minority status.

Application procedures. Admission: No deadline. No application fee. Admission notification on a rolling basis. **Financial aid:** No deadline. FAFSA required. Applicants notified on a rolling basis.

Academics. Programs consist of 3 core elements: business English, computer applications and approximately 34 credit hours of specialty courses. Curriculum developed with area employer's input to maximize job placement. **Special study options:** Accelerated study, internships. **Credit/placement by examination:** AP, CLEP. **Support services:** Study skills assistance, tutoring.

Majors. Business: Accounting, accounting technology, administrative services, business admin, executive assistant, office technology. **Computer sciences:** Data entry, data processing, web page design, webmaster, word processing. **Health services:** Insurance coding, insurance specialist, management/clinical assistant, medical records admin, medical secretary, medical transcription, office admin, office assistant, office computer specialist, receptionist.

Computing on campus. PC or laptop required. 125 workstations in library. Wireless network available.

Student life. Freshman orientation: Mandatory. Preregistration for classes offered. **Activities:** Student newspaper.

Student services. Adult student services, career counseling, student employment services, financial aid counseling, placement for graduates. **Physically disabled:** Services for speech, hearing impaired. **Transfer:** Pre-admission transcript evaluation for new students.

Contact. E-mail: admissions@csb.edu
Phone: (717) 394-6211 Toll-free number: (800) 541-8298
Fax: (717) 394-6213
Director of Admissions, Consolidated School of Business: Lancaster, 2124 Ambassador Circle, Lancaster, PA 17603

Consolidated School of Business: York
York, Pennsylvania
www.csb.edu   CB code: 2242

- For-profit 2-year career college
- Commuter campus in small city
- Interview required

General. Founded in 1986. Accredited by ACICS. Additional campus in Lancaster. **Enrollment:** 170 undergraduates. **Degrees:** 76 associate awarded. **Location:** 28 miles from Harrisburg, 33 miles from Baltimore. **Calendar:** Differs by program, extensive summer session. **Full-time faculty:** 7 total. **Part-time faculty:** 5 total.

Basis for selection. Open admission. Interview and tour must be completed before acceptance issued. All financial aid matters must be satisfied before classes begin.

2012-2013 Annual costs. Tuition/fees (projected): $13,050. Program fees vary by program. Tuition and fees include laptop computer. Books/supplies: $1,500.

Financial aid. Need-based: Need-based aid available for part-time students. Work-study available nights, weekends and for part-time students.

Application procedures. Admission: No deadline. No application fee. Admission notification on a rolling basis. **Financial aid:** No deadline. FAFSA required. Applicants notified on a rolling basis.

Academics. Programs consist of 3 core elements: business English, computer applications and approximately 34 credit hours of specialty courses. Curriculum developed with area employers' input to maximize job placement. **Special study options:** Accelerated study, internships. **Credit/placement by examination:** AP, CLEP. **Support services:** Study skills assistance, tutoring.

Majors. Business: Accounting, accounting technology, administrative services, business admin, executive assistant, office technology. **Computer sciences:** Data processing, LAN/WAN management, web page design, webmaster, word processing. **Health services:** Insurance coding, insurance specialist, management/clinical assistant, medical secretary, medical transcription, office computer specialist, receptionist.

Computing on campus. PC or laptop required. Wireless network available.

Student life. Freshman orientation: Mandatory. Preregistration for classes offered. **Activities:** Student newspaper.

Student services. Adult student services, career counseling, student employment services, financial aid counseling, placement for graduates. **Transfer:** Pre-admission transcript evaluation for new students.

Contact. E-mail: admissions@csb.edu
Phone: (717) 764-9550 Toll-free number: (800) 520-0691
Director of Admissions, Consolidated School of Business: York, York City Business and Industry Park, York, PA 17404

Dean Institute of Technology
Pittsburgh, Pennsylvania
www.deantech.edu   CB code: 2199

- For-profit 2-year technical college
- Commuter campus in large city

General. Founded in 1948. Accredited by ACCSCT. **Location:** 2 miles from downtown. **Calendar:** Quarter.

Annual costs/financial aid. Tuition varies according to area of study and credentials awarded. Examples of entire program costs, tuition only, include electrical technician ($19,800, occupational associate degree) and

building maintenance ($8,845, diploma). Books/supplies: $709. Personal expenses: $1,440. Need-based financial aid available to full-time and part-time students.

Contact. Phone: (412) 531-4433
Admissions Director, 1501 West Liberty Avenue, Pittsburgh, PA 15226

Delaware County Community College
Media, Pennsylvania
www.dccc.edu

CB member
CB code: 2125

- Public 2-year community college
- Commuter campus in large town

General. Founded in 1967. Regionally accredited. **Enrollment:** 13,248 degree-seeking undergraduates. **Degrees:** 1,054 associate awarded. **Location:** 20 miles from Philadelphia. **Calendar:** Semester, limited summer session. **Full-time faculty:** 146 total; 19% minority, 58% women. **Part-time faculty:** 660 total; 14% minority, 51% women. **Special facilities:** Fitness center, advanced technology center, science, technology, education and mathematics complex. **Partnerships:** Formal partnerships with many local businesses.

Student profile. Among degree-seeking undergraduates, 58% enrolled in a transfer program, 41% enrolled in a vocational program, 1,106 transferred in from other institutions.

Out-of-state:	1%	25 or older:	36%

Transfer out. 47% of students enrolled in the transfer program go on to 4-year colleges.

Basis for selection. Open admission, but selective for some programs. The following students, programs have special admissions requirements: non-high school graduates over the age of 19, nursing, paramedic, plumbing apprenticeship, police academy, respiratory therapy, surgical technology. **Home schooled:** Placement testing is done for most first-time students.

2011-2012 Annual costs. Tuition/fees: $3,090; $6,120 out-of-district; $9,150 out-of-state. Per-credit charge: $101 in-district; $202 out-of-district; $303 out-of-state. Books/supplies: $2,000. Personal expenses: $500.

Financial aid. Need-based: Need-based aid available for part-time students. Work-study available nights, weekends and for part-time students. **Non-need-based:** Scholarships awarded for academics, job skills. **Additional information:** An international work study program is available for students on an F1 visa in the fall and spring semesters. DCCC provides federal, college-funded and international work study. Approximately $20,000,000 of financial aid is awarded annually at DCCC.

Application procedures. Admission: No deadline. $25 fee, may be waived for applicants with need. Admission notification on a rolling basis. **Financial aid:** Closing date 7/1. FAFSA required. Applicants notified on a rolling basis.

Academics. Special student support and tutoring programs offered if the students meet particular criteria for admission to the support programs. **Special study options:** Accelerated study, cooperative education, distance learning, double major, dual enrollment of high school students, ESL, independent study, internships, student-designed major, study abroad. License preparation in nursing, physical therapy. **Credit/placement by examination:** AP, CLEP, institutional tests. 16 credit hours maximum toward associate degree. **Support services:** GED preparation and test center, learning center, pre-admission summer program, reduced course load, remedial instruction, study skills assistance, tutoring, writing center.

Majors. Business: Accounting technology, banking/financial services, business admin, construction management, e-commerce, entrepreneurial studies, hotel/motel admin, management information systems, office management. **Communications:** Communications/speech/rhetoric, journalism. **Communications technology:** Animation/special effects. **Computer sciences:** General, applications programming, data entry, information systems, networking, web page design, webmaster. **Education:** Early childhood, multi-level teacher, teacher assistance. **Engineering:** General. **Health services:** EMT paramedic, insurance specialist, medical assistant, nursing (RN), respiratory therapy technology, surgical technology, ward supervisor. **Liberal arts:** Arts/sciences. **Protective services:** Police science. **Psychology:** General. **Social sciences:** Anthropology, sociology. **Visual/performing arts:** Commercial/advertising art, studio arts.

Most popular majors. Business/marketing 18%, education 16%, health sciences 8%, interdisciplinary studies 7%, liberal arts 25%.

Computing on campus. 1,300 workstations in library, computer center, student center. Online course registration, online library, helpline, repair service, wireless network available.

Student life. Freshman orientation: Available. Preregistration for classes offered. Held at the beginning of each semester. **Housing:** Host family housing. **Activities:** Drama, literary magazine, radio station, student government, student newspaper, art and design club, Campus Bible Fellowship, criminal justice club, contemporary band, Delaware Valley computer-aided design club, engineering club, Future Financial Professionals, Gay Straight Alliance, hotel/restaurant management club, literature club, multicultural club, political science club, social dance club.

Athletics. Intercollegiate: Baseball M, basketball, golf, soccer M, softball W, tennis, volleyball W. **Intramural:** Basketball, volleyball. **Team name:** Phantoms.

Student services. Adult student services, alcohol/substance abuse counseling, career counseling, services for economically disadvantaged, student employment services, financial aid counseling, health services, minority student services, personal counseling, placement for graduates, veterans' counselor, women's services. **Physically disabled:** Services for visually, speech, hearing impaired. **Transfer:** Transfer center, transfer adviser, college fairs on campus for students transferring to 4-year colleges.

Contact. Phone: (610) 359-5050 Fax: (610) 723-1530
Hope Diehl, Director of Admissions and Enrollment Services, Delaware County Community College, 901 South Media Line Road, Media, PA 19063

Douglas Education Center
Monessen, Pennsylvania
www.dec.edu

CB code: 3288

- For-profit 2-year visual arts and business college
- Residential campus in small town
- Interview required

General. Accredited by ACICS. **Enrollment:** 250 degree-seeking undergraduates. **Degrees:** 166 associate awarded. **Location:** 30 miles from Pittsburgh. **Calendar:** Semester, extensive summer session. **Full-time faculty:** 10 total. **Part-time faculty:** 13 total.

Basis for selection. Open admission. Successful completion of the Wonderlic Scholastic Level Examination. Portfolios recommended. **Adult students:** SAT/ACT scores not required.

2011-2012 Annual costs. All-inclusive associate and diploma programs in art, business, cosmetology and medical fields are available. Tuition ranges from $4,650 to $32,000. Books and supplies range from $520 to $6,625.

Financial aid. All financial aid based on need. Need-based aid available for part-time students. Work-study available nights, weekends and for part-time students.

Application procedures. Admission: No deadline. $50 fee. Application must be submitted on paper. Admission notification on a rolling basis. **Financial aid:** No deadline. FAFSA required. Applicants notified on a rolling basis.

Academics. Special study options: Accelerated study, double major, internships, liberal arts/career combination. **Credit/placement by examination:** AP, CLEP. **Support services:** Learning center, remedial instruction, tutoring.

Majors. Business: Business admin, office technology. **Health services:** Medical secretary, office admin. **Visual/performing arts:** Graphic design, illustration.

Most popular majors. Business/marketing 72%, health sciences 6%, visual/performing arts 21%.

Computing on campus. Commuter students can connect to campus network. Online library, wireless network available.

Student life. Freshman orientation: Mandatory. Preregistration for classes offered. **Housing:** Apartments available.

Student services. Adult student services, career counseling, student employment services, financial aid counseling, placement for graduates. **Transfer:** Pre-admission transcript evaluation for new students.

Contact. E-mail: dec@dec.edu
Phone: (724) 684-3684 ext. 100
Toll-free number: (800) 413-6013 ext. 100
Sherry Lee Walters, Director of Admissions, Douglas Education Center, 130 Seventh Street, Monessen, PA 15062

DuBois Business College
DuBois, Pennsylvania
www.dbcollege.com

CB code: 3886

- For-profit 2-year business and technical college
- Commuter campus in large town
- Interview required

General. Founded in 1885. Accredited by ACICS. **Enrollment:** 200 degree-seeking undergraduates. **Degrees:** 126 associate awarded. **Location:** 100 miles from Pittsburgh. **Calendar:** Quarter, extensive summer session. **Full-time faculty:** 15 total. **Part-time faculty:** 4 total. **Partnerships:** Formal partnerships with 32 Tech Prep high schools.

Student profile.

Out-of-state:	1%	Live on campus:	40%
25 or older:	40%		

Basis for selection. Open admission.

High school preparation. Courses in shorthand, accounting, computer, typing, law, psychology, and speech recommended.

2011-2012 Annual costs. Books/supplies: $2,500.

Financial aid. Need-based: Work-study available nights, weekends and for part-time students.

Application procedures. Admission: No deadline. $25 fee, may be waived for applicants with need. Admission notification on a rolling basis. Must reply by May 1 or within 5 week(s) if notified thereafter. **Financial aid:** Closing date 8/1. FAFSA required. Applicants notified on a rolling basis.

Academics. Special study options: Cooperative education, double major, internships, liberal arts/career combination, study abroad. **Credit/placement by examination:** AP, CLEP, institutional tests. **Support services:** Reduced course load, remedial instruction, tutoring.

Majors. Business: General, accounting, administrative services, business admin. **Health services:** Medical secretary.

Computing on campus. 100 workstations in library, computer center.

Student life. Freshman orientation: Mandatory. Preregistration for classes offered. **Housing:** Single-sex dorms available. $225 deposit. **Activities:** Student government, student newspaper, student association.

Athletics. Intercollegiate: Volleyball. **Intramural:** Volleyball.

Student services. Adult student services, career counseling, student employment services, financial aid counseling, personal counseling, placement for graduates, veterans' counselor. **Physically disabled:** Services for visually, speech, hearing impaired. **Transfer:** Transfer adviser for students transferring to 4-year colleges.

Contact. E-mail: admissions@dbcollege.com
Phone: (814) 371-6920 Toll-free number: (800) 692-6213
Fax: (814) 371-3974
Lisa Doty, Director of Admissions, DuBois Business College, One Beaver Drive, DuBois, PA 15801

DuBois Business College: Huntingdon
Huntingdon, Pennsylvania
www.dbcollege.com

CB code: 3290

- For-profit 2-year business college
- Small town

General. Accredited by ACICS. **Enrollment:** 73 degree-seeking undergraduates. **Degrees:** 19 associate awarded. **Calendar:** Differs by program. **Full-time faculty:** 3 total. **Part-time faculty:** 3 total.

Basis for selection. Open admission.

2011-2012 Annual costs. Books/supplies: $2,500.

Financial aid. Need-based: Work-study available nights, weekends and for part-time students.

Application procedures. Admission: No deadline. $25 fee. Admission notification on a rolling basis. **Financial aid:** Closing date 8/1.

Academics. Credit/placement by examination: AP, CLEP.

Majors. Business: Accounting/business management, business admin, executive assistant. **Computer sciences:** Support specialist, webmaster. **Health services:** Medical assistant, medical secretary.

Most popular majors. Business/marketing 35%, health sciences 11%, legal studies 54%.

Contact. Phone: (814) 641-0440 Toll-free number: (800) 692-6213
Terry Khoury, Director of Admission, DuBois Business College: Huntingdon, 1001 Moore Street, Huntingdon, PA 16652

DuBois Business College: Oil City
Oil City, Pennsylvania
www.dbcollege.com

CB code: 3292

- For-profit 2-year branch campus and business college
- Large town

General. Accredited by ACICS. **Location:** 90 miles from Pittsburgh. **Calendar:** Quarter.

Annual costs/financial aid. Books/supplies: $2,500.

Contact. Phone: (814) 677-1322
Director of Admissions, 701 East Third Street, Oil City, PA 16301

Erie Business Center
Erie, Pennsylvania
www.eriebc.edu

CB code: 2215

- For-profit 2-year business college
- Commuter campus in small city

General. Founded in 1884. Accredited by ACICS. **Enrollment:** 267 degree-seeking undergraduates. **Degrees:** 88 associate awarded. **Location:** 95 miles from Cleveland. **Calendar:** Trimester, extensive summer session. **Full-time faculty:** 11 total. **Part-time faculty:** 24 total.

Basis for selection. Secondary school GPA and rank recommended.

2011-2012 Annual costs. Tuition/fees: $11,680. Per-credit charge: $353. Books/supplies: $800.

Financial aid. Need-based: Need-based aid available for part-time students. Work-study available nights, weekends and for part-time students.

Application procedures. Admission: No deadline. $25 fee, may be waived for applicants with need. Admission notification on a rolling basis. **Financial aid:** No deadline. FAFSA required.

Academics. Credit/placement by examination: AP, CLEP. **Support services:** Reduced course load, study skills assistance, tutoring.

Majors. Business: Accounting, administrative services, marketing, tourism/travel. **Computer sciences:** Computer graphics, networking, programming. **Health services:** Medical assistant, medical secretary, medical transcription.

Most popular majors. Business/marketing 53%, computer/information sciences 13%, health sciences 25%, legal studies 9%.

Computing on campus. Online library available.

Student life. Freshman orientation: Mandatory, $25 fee. Preregistration for classes offered. **Activities:** Drama, musical theater.

Student services. Student employment services, financial aid counseling, placement for graduates.

Contact. E-mail: admissions@eriebc.edu
Phone: (814) 456-7504 ext. 102
Toll-free number: (800) 352-3743 ext. 102 Fax: (814) 459-3701
Gretchen Reinard, Director of Admissions, Erie Business Center, 246 West Ninth Street, Erie, PA 16501

Erie Business Center South
New Castle, Pennsylvania
www.eriebc.edu/newcastle

CB code: 2577

- For-profit 2-year branch campus and business college
- Commuter campus in small city
- Application essay, interview required

General. Accredited by ACICS. **Enrollment:** 70 degree-seeking undergraduates. **Degrees:** 25 associate awarded. **Location:** 60 miles from Pittsburgh. **Calendar:** Trimester. **Full-time faculty:** 3 total. **Part-time faculty:** 3 total. **Partnerships:** Formal partnerships with Laurel HIgh School, Lincoln High School, Neshannock High School, West Middlesex High School, Beaver Falls High School, Union High School, Seneca Valley High School.

Transfer out. Colleges most students transferred to 2011: Thiel College, Slippery Rock University, Edinboro University.

Basis for selection. Open admission. **Home schooled:** Transcript of courses and grades, state high school equivalency certificate, interview required.

2011-2012 Annual costs. Tuition/fees: $6,540. Per-credit charge: $199. Books/supplies: $1,800. Personal expenses: $1,107.

Financial aid. Need-based: Work-study available nights, weekends and for part-time students.

Application procedures. Admission: No deadline. $25 fee. **Financial aid:** No deadline.

Academics. Special study options: Internships. **Credit/placement by examination:** AP, CLEP. **Support services:** Reduced course load, tutoring.

Majors. Business: Accounting, business admin, marketing, tourism/travel. **Computer sciences:** General. **Health services:** Medical records admin, medical transcription.

Computing on campus. Online library available.

Student life. Freshman orientation: Mandatory. Preregistration for classes offered. **Activities:** Student government, student newspaper.

Student services. Career counseling, student employment services, financial aid counseling, placement for graduates. **Transfer:** Pre-admission transcript evaluation for new students. Transfer adviser for students transferring to 4-year colleges.

Contact. E-mail: musolinok@eriebcs.com
Phone: (724) 658-9066 Toll-free number: (800) 722-6227
Fax: (724) 658-3083
Karen Musolino, Admissions Coordinator, Erie Business Center South, 170 Cascade Galleria, New Castle, PA 16101

Erie Institute of Technology
Erie, Pennsylvania
www.erieit.org

CB code: 2284

- For-profit 2-year technical college
- Small city

General. Accredited by ACCSCT. **Calendar:** Semester.

Annual costs/financial aid. Books/supplies: $1,380. Personal expenses: $30.

Contact. Phone: (814) 868-9900
Director of Admissions, 940 Millcreek Mall, Erie, PA 16565

Fortis Institute: Erie
Erie, Pennsylvania
www.fortis.edu

CB code: 2502

- For-profit 2-year business college
- Small city

General. Accredited by ACICS. **Calendar:** Quarter.

Annual costs/financial aid. Tuition ranges from $8,600 to $14,214; required fees, including books, from $892 to $2,316 per academic year, depending on program.

Contact. Phone: (814) 838-7673
Enrollment Coordinator, 5757 West Twenty-Sixth Street, Erie, PA 16506

Fortis Institute: Forty Fort
Forty Fort, Pennsylvania
www.fortis.edu

CB code: 3190

- For-profit 2-year technical college
- Small town

General. Regionally accredited. **Calendar:** Differs by program.

Annual costs/financial aid. Cost of full programs ranges from $13,500 to $22,240 depending on program.

Contact. Phone: (570) 288-8400
Admissions Director, 166 Slocum Avenue, Forty Fort, PA 18704-2936

Harcum College
Bryn Mawr, Pennsylvania
www.harcum.edu

CB member
CB code: 2287

- Private 2-year junior college
- Commuter campus in large town
- Application essay required

General. Founded in 1915. Regionally accredited. **Enrollment:** 1,527 degree-seeking undergraduates. **Degrees:** 268 associate awarded. **Location:** 10 miles from Philadelphia. **Calendar:** Semester, limited summer session. **Full-time faculty:** 168 total. **Part-time faculty:** 250 total. **Class size:** 87% < 20, 12% 20-39, less than 1% 40-49. **Special facilities:** Veterinary services building, physical therapist assistant lab, dental clinic, nursing lab, radiology lab.

Student profile.

Out-of-state:	10%	Live on campus:	17%
25 or older:	40%		

Transfer out. Colleges most students transferred to 2011: Cabrini College, West Chester University, Temple University, Rosemont College, Widener University.

Basis for selection. School record of primary importance. Writing sample required. 750 SAT (exclusive of Writing) and/or 2.0 GPA required. Nursing, dental hygiene, physical therapy assistant, veterinary technology require 900 SAT (exclusive of Writing) and 2.5 GPA. ACCUPLACER exam used for placement. Interview required of dental hygiene, radiology technician, nursing and neurodiognostic technician programs; recommended for all others. **Adult students:** SAT/ACT scores not required if out of high school 3 year(s) or more. **Learning Disabled:** Must provide documentation of disability to ensure proper accommodations are made.

High school preparation. Recommended units include English 4, mathematics 2, social studies 2, history 2, science 2 and academic electives 2. Required units for veterinary technnology, dental hygiene, and physical therapy assistant programs include 2 algebra, geometry, biology, chemistry. 1 unit biology and algebra required for dental assisting program. 2 algebra, biology, and chemistry required for medical laboratory technology.

2011-2012 Annual costs. Tuition/fees: $19,820. Per-credit charge: $630. Room/board: $8,400. Books/supplies: $1,200. Personal expenses: $2,792.

Financial aid. Need-based: Need-based aid available for part-time students. Work-study available nights, weekends and for part-time students. **Non-need-based:** Scholarships awarded for academics, leadership.

Application procedures. Admission: Closing date 2/15. $50 fee, may be waived for applicants with need. Admission notification on a rolling basis. **Financial aid:** Priority date 4/15, closing date 5/1. FAFSA, institutional form required. Applicants notified on a rolling basis starting 3/1; must reply within 3 week(s) of notification.

Academics. 86% of academic programs offered have internship/practicum component. **Special study options:** Accelerated study, cooperative education, distance learning, double major, dual enrollment of high school students, ESL, independent study, internships, liberal arts/career combination, study

abroad. License preparation in dental hygiene, nursing, physical therapy, radiology. **Credit/placement by examination:** AP, CLEP, institutional tests. 20 credit hours maximum toward associate degree. Maximum of 30 credits total for transfer credits, life experience, challenge examination, and CLEP. **Support services:** Learning center, pre-admission summer program, reduced course load, remedial instruction, study skills assistance, tutoring.

Majors. Business: General, business admin, fashion, sales/distribution. **Education:** Early childhood. **General:** Animal sciences. **Health services:** Clinical lab technology, dental assistant, dental hygiene, physical therapy assistant, radiologic technology/medical imaging, veterinary technology/assistant. **Liberal arts:** Arts/sciences. **Protective services:** Law enforcement admin. **Psychology:** General. **Visual/performing arts:** Fashion design, interior design.

Most popular majors. Business/marketing 8%, education 9%, health sciences 63%, visual/performing arts 14%.

Computing on campus. 86 workstations in dormitories, library, computer center, student center. Dormitories wired for high-speed internet access. Commuter students can connect to campus network. Online course registration, online library, helpline, repair service, wireless network available.

Student life. Freshman orientation: Available. Preregistration for classes offered. One-day introduction to campus services, separate evening orientation for Lifelong Learners. **Housing:** Guaranteed on-campus for all undergraduates. Coed dorms, special housing for disabled available. $200 deposit. **Activities:** International student organizations, literary magazine, student government, student newspaper, Ebony Club, Campus Ambassadors, animal technician student organization, Phi Theta Kappa, peer mentors, community service club, dental assisting club, Association for the Education of Young Children, physical therapy assistant club.

Athletics. NJCAA. **Intercollegiate:** Basketball, volleyball W. **Team name:** Bears.

Student services. Adult student services, alcohol/substance abuse counseling, career counseling, services for economically disadvantaged, student employment services, financial aid counseling, health services, minority student services, on-campus daycare, personal counseling, placement for graduates, veterans' counselor, women's services. **Physically disabled:** Services for visually, speech, hearing impaired. **Transfer:** Re-entry adviser, pre-admission transcript evaluation for new students. Transfer center, transfer adviser, college fairs on campus for students transferring to 4-year colleges.

Contact. E-mail: journey@harcum.edu
Phone: (610) 526-6050 Toll-free number: (800) 345-2600
Fax: (610) 526-6147
Rachel Bowen, Dean of Admissions, Harcum College, 750 Montgomery Avenue, Bryn Mawr, PA 19010-3476

Harrisburg Area Community College

Harrisburg, Pennsylvania   **CB member**
www.hacc.edu   **CB code: 2309**

▶ Public 2-year community college
▶ Commuter campus in small city

General. Founded in 1964. Regionally accredited. County high schools utilized for credit-course offerings. Availability varies by semester. **Enrollment:** 14,164 degree-seeking undergraduates; 8,431 non-degree-seeking students. **Degrees:** 1,847 associate awarded. **ROTC:** Army. **Location:** 90 miles from Philadelphia, 180 miles from New York City. **Calendar:** Semester, limited summer session. **Full-time faculty:** 370 total; 18% have terminal degrees, 17% minority, 60% women. **Part-time faculty:** 707 total; 11% have terminal degrees, 7% minority, 57% women. **Class size:** 53% < 20, 45% 20-39, 1% 40-49, less than 1% 50-99.

Student profile. Among degree-seeking undergraduates, 24% enrolled in a transfer program, 76% enrolled in a vocational program, 2,143 enrolled as first-time, first-year students, 1,554 transferred in from other institutions.

Part-time:	70%	Asian American:	2%
Out-of-state:	2%	Hispanic American:	9%
Women:	67%	International:	2%
African American:	12%	25 or older:	44%

Transfer out. 68% of students enrolled in the transfer program go on to 4-year colleges. **Colleges most students transferred to 2011:** Penn State University, Shippensburg University, Millersville University, Elizabethtown College, York College.

Basis for selection. Open admission, but selective for some programs. Special requirements for allied health programs and chef apprenticeship. ACT required for allied health programs, score report by February 1. Interview

required for allied health, and chef apprenticeship programs; essay required for chef apprenticeship program. **Home schooled:** Statement describing home school structure and mission, transcript of courses and grades, letter of recommendation (nonparent) required.

2011-2012 Annual costs. Tuition/fees: $4,950; $6,675 out-of-district; $9,660 out-of-state. Fees vary based on student type (in-district, out-of-district, out-of-state). Tuition reported includes additional required fees for out-of-district ($150), and out-of-state ($300) students. Books/supplies: $1,820. Personal expenses: $1,600.

2010-2011 Financial aid. Need-based: 1,106 full-time freshmen applied for aid; 888 were judged to have need; 861 of these received aid. Average need met was 53%. Average scholarship/grant was $2,363; average loan $2,961. 29% of total undergraduate aid awarded as scholarships/grants, 71% as loans/jobs. Need-based aid available for part-time students. Work-study available nights, weekends and for part-time students. **Non-need-based:** Awarded to 65 full-time undergraduates, including 6 freshmen. Scholarships awarded for academics. **Additional information:** Federal work study community service positions available.

Application procedures. Admission: No deadline. $35 fee, may be waived for applicants with need. Admission notification on a rolling basis. Must reply by May 1 or within 5 week(s) if notified thereafter. **Financial aid:** Priority date 3/15; no closing date. FAFSA, institutional form required. Applicants notified on a rolling basis starting 6/1.

Academics. Special study options: Distance learning, dual enrollment of high school students, ESL, honors, independent study, internships, study abroad. Albright College (Reading Campus and Harrisburg Campus), Drexel University (Behavioral & Addictions Counseling Sciences Programs only), Eastern University (St. Davids campus and Central PA campus), Elizabethtown College, Elizabethtown College Accelerated Program, Lebanon Valley College, Millersville University, Penn State Harrisburg, Peirce College (Paralegal Studies only), Shippensburg University, Susquehanna University, Temple University, Wilson College. License preparation in dental hygiene, nursing, paramedic, radiology, real estate. **Credit/placement by examination:** AP, CLEP, IB, institutional tests. 30 credit hours maximum toward associate degree. **Support services:** GED preparation and test center, learning center, remedial instruction, study skills assistance, tutoring, writing center.

Majors. Architecture: Architecture. **Biology:** General. **Business:** General, accounting technology, accounting/business management, administrative services, banking/financial services, business admin, hospitality admin, hotel/motel admin, real estate, sales/distribution, small business admin, tourism/travel. **Communications:** Media studies. **Computer sciences:** General, computer science, networking, security, web page design. **Conservation:** Environmental science, environmental studies. **Education:** Early childhood, secondary. **Engineering:** General, robotics. **General:** Agribusiness operations, landscaping, viticulture. **Health services:** Cardiovascular technology, clinical lab technology, dental hygiene, dietetics, EMT paramedic, health care admin, health services admin, medical assistant, nuclear medical technology, nursing (RN), radiologic technology/medical imaging, respiratory therapy technology, sonography, surgical technology. **Human services:** Social work. **Math:** General. **Philosophy/religion:** Philosophy. **Physical sciences:** General, chemistry. **Protective services:** Criminalistics, firefighting, law enforcement admin, police science. **Psychology:** General. **Social sciences:** General, GIS/cartography, international relations. **Visual/performing arts:** General, art, crafts, design, dramatic, graphic design, music management, photography. **Work/family studies:** Institutional food production.

Most popular majors. Business/marketing 23%, education 6%, health sciences 24%, liberal arts 11%.

Computing on campus. 350 workstations in library, computer center, student center. Online course registration, helpline, wireless network available.

Student life. Freshman orientation: Mandatory. Preregistration for classes offered. Varies by campus. **Activities:** Choral groups, drama, literary magazine, musical theater, student government, student newspaper, Allies, African American Student Association, Christian Student Fellowship, International Awareness, Student Environmental Action Coalition, Phi Beta Lambda, psychology club, Mosaico club, bilingual club.

Athletics. Intercollegiate: Basketball, golf M, soccer M, tennis, volleyball. **Intramural:** Football (non-tackle) M.

Student services. Career counseling, student employment services, financial aid counseling, minority student services, veterans' counselor. **Physically disabled:** Services for visually, hearing impaired. **Transfer:** Pre-admission transcript evaluation for new students. Transfer adviser, college fairs on campus for students transferring to 4-year colleges.

Contact. E-mail: admit@hacc.edu
Phone: (717) 780-2400 Toll-free number: (800) 222-4222
Fax: (717) 236-7674
Tisa Riley, Director of Enrollment Services, Harrisburg Area Community College, One HACC Drive, Cooper 206, Harrisburg, PA 17110-2999

Hussian School of Art
Philadelphia, Pennsylvania
www.hussianart.edu
CB code: 7309

- For-profit 2-year visual arts and technical college
- Commuter campus in very large city
- Interview required

General. Founded in 1946. Accredited by ACCSC. Located on Independence Mall, within The Historic Bourse Building. **Enrollment:** 138 degree-seeking undergraduates. **Degrees:** 28 associate awarded. **Calendar:** Semester. **Part-time faculty:** 29 total. **Class size:** 31% < 20, 69% 20-39. **Special facilities:** Computer graphics facilities.

Student profile.

Out-of-state: 10%   25 or older: 2%

Basis for selection. Personal interview and portfolio review required for acceptance; talent, ability, communication skills and potential most important. Portfolio of original art samples required.

High school preparation. High school art or other art training required.

2011-2012 Annual costs. Tuition/fees: $14,550. Supply costs estimated at $395 for required freshman supply kit; consumable supply estimate of $350 additional for the freshman year. Books/supplies: $800. Personal expenses: $2,538.

Financial aid. Need-based: Work-study available nights, weekends and for part-time students.

Application procedures. Admission: No deadline. $25 fee, may be waived for applicants with need, free for online applicants. Admission notification on a rolling basis. **Financial aid:** No deadline. FAFSA, institutional form required. Applicants notified on a rolling basis starting 2/15; must reply within 3 week(s) of notification.

Academics. Second-semester freshmen must earn GPA of 2.0 or above to continue in good standing. **Special study options:** Internships. **Credit/placement by examination:** AP, CLEP. Proficiency credit for special aptitude/experience on an individualized basis. **Support services:** Pre-admission summer program.

Majors. Visual/performing arts: Commercial/advertising art, graphic design.

Computing on campus. PC or laptop required. 60 workstations in computer center. Wireless network available.

Student life. Freshman orientation: Available. Preregistration for classes offered. Morning program held 2 weeks prior to official start of classes. **Housing:** No housing offered. Suggestions available for local housing options.

Student services. Career counseling, financial aid counseling, placement for graduates. **Transfer:** Pre-admission transcript evaluation for new students.

Contact. E-mail: info@hussianart.edu
Phone: (215) 574-9600 ext. 201 Fax: (215) 574-9800
Lynne Wartman, Admissions Director, Hussian School of Art, The Bourse, Suite 300, 111 South Independence Mall East, Philadelphia, PA 19106

ITT Technical Institute: King of Prussia
King of Prussia, Pennsylvania
www.itt-tech.edu

- For-profit 2-year visual arts and technical college
- Commuter campus in large town

General. Accredited by ACICS. **Enrollment:** 572 undergraduates. **Degrees:** 156 associate awarded. **Calendar:** Quarter. **Full-time faculty:** 9 total. **Part-time faculty:** 70 total.

Basis for selection. Must pass admissions test or have scored, within previous five years, minimum of 17 ACT or 800 SAT (exclusive of Writing), or have earned either 36 quarter credit hours (or 24 semester or trimester credit hours) with overall cumulative GPA of 2.0 from accredited institution. Meeting with a representative of ITT Tech and arranging a time to tour the school is required.

2011-2012 Annual costs. Estimated costs as of June 2011: per-credit-hour charge, $493, depending upon level and course of study; academic fee, $200. Certain programs of study require purchase of tools, which could cost an additional $100 to $500. All costs are subject to change.

Financial aid. Need-based: Work-study available nights, weekends and for part-time students.

Application procedures. Admission: No application fee.

Academics. Credit/placement by examination: AP, CLEP.

Majors. Computer sciences: Networking, web page design. **Protective services:** Law enforcement admin.

Most popular majors. Computer/information sciences 55%, engineering/engineering technologies 44%, security/protective services 6%.

Student services. Career counseling, student employment services, placement for graduates.

Contact. Toll-free number: (866) 902-8324
ITT Technical Institute: King of Prussia, 760 Moore Road, Suite 150, King of Prussia, PA 19406-1212

ITT Technical Institute: Pittsburgh
Pittsburgh, Pennsylvania
www.itt-tech.edu
CB code: 2745

- For-profit 2-year technical college
- Commuter campus in large city
- Interview required

General. Accredited by ACICS. **Enrollment:** 389 undergraduates. **Degrees:** 130 associate awarded. **Calendar:** Quarter, extensive summer session. **Full-time faculty:** 9 total. **Part-time faculty:** 21 total.

Basis for selection. Satisfactory scores from on-site tests in English and mathematics required.

2011-2012 Annual costs. Estimated costs as of June 2011: per-credit-hour charge, $493, depending upon level and course of study; academic fee, $200. Certain programs of study require purchase of tools, which could cost an additional $100 to $500. All costs are subject to change.

Financial aid. Need-based: Work-study available nights, weekends and for part-time students.

Application procedures. Admission: No deadline. No application fee. Admission notification on a rolling basis. **Financial aid:** No deadline. FAFSA, institutional form required. Applicants notified on a rolling basis.

Academics. Credit/placement by examination: AP, CLEP. **Support services:** Learning center, tutoring.

Majors. Computer sciences: Networking, web page design. **Protective services:** Law enforcement admin. **Visual/performing arts:** Design.

Most popular majors. Computer/information sciences 53%, engineering/engineering technologies 41%, security/protective services 6%.

Computing on campus. Online library available.

Student life. Freshman orientation: Available. Preregistration for classes offered.

Student services. Career counseling, student employment services, placement for graduates.

Contact. Phone: (412) 937-9150 Toll-free number: (800) 353-8324
Fax: (412) 937-9425
Robert Burnfield, Director of Recruitment, ITT Technical Institute: Pittsburgh, 10 Parkway Center, Pittsburgh, PA 15220

JNA Institute of Culinary Arts
Philadelphia, Pennsylvania
www.culinaryarts.edu
CB code: 3049

- For-profit 2-year technical college
- Commuter campus in very large city

General. Accredited by ACCSC. **Enrollment:** 78 degree-seeking undergraduates. **Degrees:** 24 associate awarded. **Calendar:** Quarter, extensive summer session. **Full-time faculty:** 10 total. **Part-time faculty:** 3 total. **Special facilities:** Student-operated restaurant and catering services.

Student profile.

Out-of-state: 12%   25 or older: 38%

Basis for selection. Open admission.

2011-2012 Annual costs. Tuition for 15-month associate program, $20,000; 6-month professional cooking diploma program, $10,000. Required fees $75 for both programs. Books and supplies are $325 for the diploma program and $1,050 for the associate program.

Financial aid. Need-based: Work-study available nights, weekends and for part-time students.

Application procedures. Admission: No deadline. No application fee. **Financial aid:** No deadline. FAFSA required.

Academics. Special study options: Internships. **Credit/placement by examination:** AP, CLEP.

Student life. Freshman orientation: Mandatory. Preregistration for classes offered.

Student services. Alcohol/substance abuse counseling, career counseling, student employment services, financial aid counseling, legal services, placement for graduates.

Contact. E-mail: admissions@culinaryarts.edu
Phone: (215) 468-8800 Toll-free number: (877) 872-3197
John English, Director of Admissions, JNA Institute of Culinary Arts, 1212 South Broad Street, Philadelphia, PA 19146

Johnson College
Scranton, Pennsylvania
www.johnson.edu
CB member
CB code: 1542

- Private 2-year technical college
- Commuter campus in small city

General. Founded in 1912. Accredited by ACCSCT. **Location:** 117 miles from Philadelphia, 125 miles from New York City. **Calendar:** Semester.

Annual costs/financial aid. Tuition/fees (2011-2012): $16,362. Required fees for HVAC students is $1,130; for RAD students $1,430. Other expenses: cost of tools vary by program. Room/board: $5,683. Books/supplies: $1,500. Need-based financial aid available to full-time and part-time students.

Contact. Phone: (570) 702-8911
Director of Enrollment Management, 3427 North Main Avenue, Scranton, PA 18508

Kaplan Career Institute: Harrisburg
Harrisburg, Pennsylvania
www.kaplancareerinstitute.com
CB code: 3212

- For-profit 2-year health science and technical college
- Commuter campus in small city
- Application essay, interview required

General. Accredited by ACICS. Formerly known as Thompson Institute. **Degrees:** 103 associate awarded. **Calendar:** Continuous, extensive summer session. **Full-time faculty:** 17 total. **Part-time faculty:** 17 total.

Student profile.

25 or older: 45%   Live on campus: 10%

Basis for selection. Open admission, but selective for some programs. Students must achieve passing score on assessment exam. Criminal Justice entrants must undergo criminal background check. **Home schooled:** Interview required. Must have Commonwealth diploma.

2011-2012 Annual costs. Books/supplies: $2,040. Personal expenses: $2,862.

Financial aid. Need-based: Need-based aid available for part-time students. Work-study available nights, weekends and for part-time students.

Application procedures. Admission: No deadline. $10 fee. Application must be submitted on paper. Admission notification on a rolling basis. **Financial aid:** No deadline. FAFSA, institutional form required.

Academics. Special study options: Internships. **Credit/placement by examination:** AP, CLEP. Credits in any combination (CLEP, experiential, examination, transfer) may not exceed 50% of the program. **Support services:** Study skills assistance, tutoring.

Majors. Business: Business admin. **Computer sciences:** LAN/WAN management, networking, web page design, webmaster. **Health services:** Medical assistant. **Protective services:** Corrections, criminal justice, law enforcement admin.

Computing on campus. 30 workstations in library, computer center. Commuter students can connect to campus network. Online library, helpline, student web hosting available.

Student life. Freshman orientation: Mandatory. Preregistration for classes offered. **Housing:** Apartments available.

Student services. Adult student services, career counseling, services for economically disadvantaged, student employment services, financial aid counseling, placement for graduates.

Contact. E-mail: mhale@kaplan.edu
Phone: (717) 558-1300 Toll-free number: (888) 532-7645
Fax: (717) 558-1342
Mark Hale, Director of Admissions, Kaplan Career Institute: Harrisburg, 5650 Derry Street, Harrisburg, PA 17111-4112

Kaplan Career Institute: Pittsburgh
Pittsburgh, Pennsylvania
www.kaplancareerinstitute.com
CB code: 3823

- For-profit 2-year business and health science college
- Commuter campus in large city
- Application essay, interview required

General. Accredited by ACICS. **Degrees:** 4 associate awarded. **Calendar:** Quarter, extensive summer session. **Full-time faculty:** 8 total. **Part-time faculty:** 24 total. **Special facilities:** Firearms training simulator.

Basis for selection. Wonderlic required. Students are required to achieve a minimum score on an independently developed entrance examination and, under the Kaplan Commitment undergraduate students must show a minimum level of academic performance in their initial classes before they will be fully accepted into their programs.

2011-2012 Annual costs. Books/supplies: $789.

Financial aid. All financial aid based on need. Need-based aid available for part-time students. Work-study available nights, weekends and for part-time students.

Application procedures. Admission: No deadline. $10 fee, may be waived for applicants with need. Admission notification on a rolling basis. **Financial aid:** Closing date 4/30. FAFSA, institutional form required. Applicants notified on a rolling basis.

Academics. Special study options: Double major, internships. License preparation in occupational therapy. **Credit/placement by examination:** AP, CLEP. 11 credit hours maximum toward associate degree. **Support services:** Reduced course load, study skills assistance, tutoring.

Majors. Business: Accounting, administrative services, business admin, fashion. **Computer sciences:** General, applications programming, information technology, LAN/WAN management, programming, security, systems analysis, webmaster. **Engineering:** Computer. **Health services:** Medical assistant, medical secretary, occupational therapy assistant. **Protective services:** Corrections, criminal justice, law enforcement admin, police science, security services.

Computing on campus. 225 workstations in library, computer center. Online library, helpline, repair service available.

Student life. Freshman orientation: Mandatory, $20 fee. Preregistration for classes offered.

Student services. Career counseling, student employment services, financial aid counseling, personal counseling, placement for graduates.

Contact. E-mail: lglaser@kaplan.edu
Phone: (412) 261-2647 Toll-free number: (800) 441-5222
Fax: (412) 261-0998
Thomas Driscoll, Director of Admissions, Kaplan Career Institute: Pittsburgh, 10 Wood Street, Pittsburgh, PA 15222

Keystone Technical Institute
Harrisburg, Pennsylvania
www.kti.edu   CB code: 3188

▶ For-profit 2-year culinary school and technical college
▶ Commuter campus in small city
▶ Interview required

General. Accredited by ACCSC. **Enrollment:** 300 degree-seeking undergraduates. **Location:** 206 miles from Philadelphia, 200 miles from Washington, DC. **Calendar:** Differs by program. **Full-time faculty:** 25 total. **Part-time faculty:** 13 total.

Basis for selection. Open admission. **Home schooled:** For state grants, applicants must submit either accredited diploma or certification from local superintendent of compliance with Home Education Act. **Learning Disabled:** Provide copy of independent educational program.

2011-2012 Annual costs. Books/supplies: $2,800. Personal expenses: $1,200.

Financial aid. All financial aid based on need. Need-based aid available for part-time students. Work-study available nights, weekends and for part-time students.

Application procedures. Admission: No deadline. $50 fee. Admission notification on a rolling basis. **Financial aid:** Closing date 8/1. FAFSA required. Applicants notified on a rolling basis.

Academics. Special study options: Dual enrollment of high school students, honors, internships. License preparation in radiology. **Credit/placement by examination:** AP, CLEP. **Support services:** Study skills assistance, tutoring.

Majors. Computer sciences: Data entry, data processing. **Health services:** Asian bodywork therapy, Chinese medicine/herbology, dental assistant, massage therapy, medical assistant, medical records admin, medical records technology, medical secretary, medical transcription, movement therapy. **Work/family studies:** Child care management.

Most popular majors. Health sciences 76%, legal studies 15%.

Computing on campus. 65 workstations in library. Online library, helpline, repair service available.

Student life. Freshman orientation: Mandatory. Preregistration for classes offered. Held first day of class for all new students.

Student services. Adult student services, alcohol/substance abuse counseling, career counseling, services for economically disadvantaged, student employment services, financial aid counseling, on-campus daycare, placement for graduates. **Transfer:** Re-entry adviser, pre-admission transcript evaluation for new students. Transfer adviser, college fairs on campus for students transferring to 4-year colleges.

Contact. E-mail: info@kti.edu
Phone: (717) 545-4747 Toll-free number: (800) 400-3322
David Snyder, Admissions Director, Keystone Technical Institute, 2301 Academy Drive, Harrisburg, PA 17112-1012

Lackawanna College
Scranton, Pennsylvania
www.lackawanna.edu   CB code: 2373

▶ Private 2-year junior college
▶ Commuter campus in small city
▶ Interview required

General. Founded in 1894. Regionally accredited. **Enrollment:** 1,490 degree-seeking undergraduates; 77 non-degree-seeking students. **Degrees:** 260 associate awarded. **ROTC:** Army. **Location:** 125 miles from New York City, 125 miles from Philadelphia. **Calendar:** Semester, limited summer session. **Full-time faculty:** 31 total; 6% have terminal degrees, 45% women. **Part-time faculty:** 185 total; 3% have terminal degrees. **Special facilities:** Environmental institute, police academy. **Partnerships:** Formal partnerships

with Tobyhanna Army Depot and Cinram Corporation; IT Security Pipeline Program and Misericordia University.

Student profile. Among degree-seeking undergraduates, 443 enrolled as first-time, first-year students, 274 transferred in from other institutions.

Part-time:	23%	Asian American:	1%
Out-of-state:	11%	Hispanic American:	5%
Women:	46%	25 or older:	25%
African American:	18%	Live on campus:	21%

Transfer out. Colleges most students transferred to 2011: Marywood University, Keystone College, College Misericordia, East Stroudsburg University, Bloomsburg University.

Basis for selection. Open admission. **Adult students:** SAT/ACT scores not required. **Home schooled:** Transcript of courses and grades, state high school equivalency certificate, interview required. **Learning Disabled:** Submit current documentation of disability for arrangement of accommodations.

High school preparation. 11 units recommended. Recommended units include English 4, mathematics 3, social studies 1 and science 3.

2011-2012 Annual costs. Tuition/fees: $11,770. Per-credit charge: $395. Room/board: $7,400. Books/supplies: $1,400. Personal expenses: $1,540.

2011-2012 Financial aid. Need-based: 382 full-time freshmen applied for aid; 373 were judged to have need; 366 of these received aid. Average need met was 53%. Average scholarship/grant was $7,320; average loan $3,504. 44% of total undergraduate aid awarded as scholarships/grants, 56% as loans/jobs. Need-based aid available for part-time students. Work-study available nights, weekends and for part-time students. **Non-need-based:** Awarded to 26 full-time undergraduates, including 15 freshmen. Scholarships awarded for academics, athletics.

Application procedures. Admission: No deadline. $30 fee, may be waived for applicants with need. Admission notification on a rolling basis. Must reply by May 1 or within 4 week(s) if notified thereafter. **Financial aid:** Priority date 5/1; no closing date. FAFSA, institutional form required. Applicants notified on a rolling basis starting 5/1.

Academics. Peer and professional tutoring available upon request, in addition to online tutoring, evenings and weekends. **Special study options:** Cooperative education, distance learning, double major, dual enrollment of high school students, honors, independent study, internships. License preparation in nursing, paramedic, real estate. **Credit/placement by examination:** AP, CLEP, institutional tests. 30 credit hours maximum toward associate degree. **Support services:** GED preparation and test center, learning center, pre-admission summer program, reduced course load, remedial instruction, tutoring, writing center.

Majors. Biology: General. **Business:** General, accounting, administrative services, banking/financial services, business admin, management information systems. **Computer sciences:** Security. **Conservation:** Environmental science, environmental studies. **Education:** General. **Health services:** Medical secretary, sonography, surgical technology. **Liberal arts:** Arts/sciences. **Protective services:** Criminal justice, police science. **Social sciences:** General. **Work/family studies:** Child care service.

Most popular majors. Business/marketing 26%, education 8%, engineering/engineering technologies 6%, health sciences 24%, liberal arts 10%, security/protective services 14%.

Computing on campus. 202 workstations in library, computer center. Dormitories wired for high-speed internet access and linked to campus network. Online library, helpline available.

Student life. Freshman orientation: Mandatory. Preregistration for classes offered. Two day program, scheduled the weekend before the start of classes. **Housing:** Guaranteed on-campus for freshmen. Coed dorms, single-sex dorms available. $250 fully refundable deposit. **Activities:** Drama, literary magazine, student government, student newspaper, spiritual study group, student government association, diversity club and social justice center.

Athletics. NJCAA. **Intercollegiate:** Baseball M, basketball, cheerleading M, cross-country, football (tackle) M, golf M, soccer W, softball W, volleyball W. **Team name:** Falcons.

Student services. Adult student services, career counseling, services for economically disadvantaged, student employment services, financial aid counseling, personal counseling, placement for graduates, veterans' counselor. **Transfer:** Re-entry adviser, pre-admission transcript evaluation for new students. Transfer adviser, college fairs on campus for students transferring to 4-year colleges.

Contact. E-mail: adminfo@lackawanna.edu
Phone: (570) 961-7814 Toll-free number: (877) 346-3552
Fax: (570) 961-7843
Brian Costanzo, Dean of Enrollment Management, Lackawanna College,
501 Vine Street, Scranton, PA 18509

Lansdale School of Business
North Wales, Pennsylvania
www.lsb.edu   CB code: 5853

- For-profit 2-year career college
- Commuter campus in small town

General. Accredited by ACICS. **Location:** 25 miles from Philadelphia.
Calendar: Semester.

Contact. Phone: (215) 699-5700
Director of Admissions, 290 Wissahickon Avenue, North Wales, PA
19454-4114

Laurel Business Institute
Uniontown, Pennsylvania
www.laurel.edu   CB code: 2329

- For-profit 2-year technical and career college
- Commuter campus in large town
- Application essay, interview required

General. Founded in 1985. Accredited by ACICS. **Enrollment:** 223 degree-seeking undergraduates. **Degrees:** 50 associate awarded. **Location:** 50 miles from Pittsburgh. **Calendar:** Trimester, extensive summer session. **Full-time faculty:** 18 total. **Part-time faculty:** 15 total. **Class size:** 95% < 20, 5% 20-39. **Special facilities:** Microsoft testing center, Prometric testing site. **Partnerships:** Formal partnership with Nemacolin Woodlands resort.

Student profile.

Out-of-state: 1%   25 or older: 85%

Transfer out. Colleges most students transferred to 2011: University of Phoenix, Central Penn.

Basis for selection. All applicants must take Wonderlic for skill assessment and placement.

2011-2012 Annual costs. Books/supplies: $970.

Financial aid. All financial aid based on need. Need-based aid available for part-time students. Work-study available nights, weekends and for part-time students.

Application procedures. Admission: No deadline. $50 fee. Application must be submitted on paper. Admission notification on a rolling basis. **Financial aid:** Closing date 8/1. FAFSA, institutional form required. Applicants notified on a rolling basis; must reply within 4 week(s) of notification.

Academics. Special study options: Accelerated study, double major, dual enrollment of high school students, honors, internships. **Credit/placement by examination:** AP, CLEP, institutional tests. 24 credit hours maximum toward associate degree. **Support services:** Reduced course load, tutoring.

Majors. Business: Accounting, business admin. **Education:** Early childhood. **Health services:** Massage therapy, office assistant, respiratory therapy technology.

Most popular majors. Business/marketing 23%, computer/information sciences 14%, education 12%, family/consumer sciences 6%, health sciences 28%, personal/culinary services 19%.

Computing on campus. 50 workstations in library, computer center. Online library available.

Student life. Freshman orientation: Mandatory. Preregistration for classes offered. Orientation takes place prior to the first day of each term. **Policies:** Attendance required in all classes. Excessive absences will result in points being deducted from final grade. **Activities:** Student newspaper, Phi Beta Lambda.

Student services. Student employment services, placement for graduates. **Physically disabled:** Services for visually, speech impaired. **Transfer:** Pre-admission transcript evaluation for new students.

Contact. E-mail: admission@laurel.edu
Phone: (724) 439-4900 Fax: (724) 439-3607
Douglas Decker, Admissions Director, Laurel Business Institute, 11 East
Penn Street, Uniontown, PA 15401

Laurel Technical Institute
Sharon, Pennsylvania
www.laurel.edu   CB code: 2466

- For-profit 2-year business and technical college
- Commuter campus in large town
- Interview required

General. Accredited by ACICS. Branch campus located in Meadville. **Enrollment:** 278 degree-seeking undergraduates. **Degrees:** 90 associate awarded. **Location:** 50 miles from Pittsburgh; 15 miles from Youngstown, Ohio. **Calendar:** Quarter, extensive summer session. **Full-time faculty:** 20 total. **Part-time faculty:** 10 total. **Class size:** 76% < 20, 24% 20-39.

Student profile.

Out-of-state: 7%   25 or older: 45%

Basis for selection. All applicants must take CPAt for skill assessment and placement. If SAT or ACT submitted, CPAt requirement may be waived.

High school preparation. Recommended units include English 3, mathematics 3 and science 2. Accounting, business, computer and English preferred.

2011-2012 Annual costs. Books/supplies: $1,500.

Financial aid. Need-based: Work-study available nights, weekends and for part-time students. **Non-need-based:** Scholarships awarded for academics.

Application procedures. Admission: No deadline. $50 fee. Admission notification on a rolling basis. **Financial aid:** No deadline. Institutional form required.

Academics. Special study options: Internships. **Credit/placement by examination:** AP, CLEP, institutional tests. 15 credit hours maximum toward associate degree. **Support services:** Study skills assistance.

Majors. Business: Business admin. **Health services:** Medical records technology, respiratory therapy assistant.

Most popular majors. Business/marketing 15%, computer/information sciences 15%.

Computing on campus. 35 workstations in computer center.

Student life. Freshman orientation: Mandatory. Preregistration for classes offered. Orientation takes place prior to the first day of each term. **Activities:** Student government, student newspaper.

Student services. Career counseling, financial aid counseling, placement for graduates. **Transfer:** Pre-admission transcript evaluation for new students.

Contact. E-mail: lti.admission@laurel.edu
Phone: (724) 983-0700 Fax: (724) 983-8355
Doug Decker, Director of Admissions, Laurel Technical Institute, 200
Sterling Avenue, Sharon, PA 16146

Le Cordon Bleu College of Culinary Arts: Pittsburgh
Pittsburgh, Pennsylvania
www.paculinary.com   CB code: 2440

- For-profit 2-year culinary school and technical college
- Residential campus in large city

General. Founded in 1986. Regionally accredited. **Location:** 300 miles from Philadelphia. **Calendar:** Semester.

Annual costs/financial aid. Books/supplies: $3,374. Need-based financial aid available for full-time students.

Contact. Phone: (412) 566-2433
Director of Admissions, 717 Liberty Avenue, Pittsburgh, PA 15222

Lehigh Carbon Community College
Schnecksville, Pennsylvania
www.lccc.edu   CB code: 2381

- Public 2-year community college
- Commuter campus in small town

General. Founded in 1966. Regionally accredited. 3 campuses serve both rural and urban students. **Enrollment:** 6,275 degree-seeking undergraduates; 1,435 non-degree-seeking students. **Degrees:** 721 associate awarded. **ROTC:** Army. **Location:** 8 miles from Allentown, 50 miles from Philadelphia. **Calendar:** Semester, limited summer session. **Full-time faculty:** 91 total; 16% have terminal degrees, 2% minority, 63% women. **Part-time faculty:** 353 total; 1% have terminal degrees, 9% minority, 46% women. **Class size:** 49% < 20, 51% 20-39, less than 1% 40-49, less than 1% 50-99.

Student profile. Among degree-seeking undergraduates, 65% enrolled in a transfer program, 35% enrolled in a vocational program, 1% already have a bachelor's degree or higher, 1,294 enrolled as first-time, first-year students, 546 transferred in from other institutions.

Part-time:	57%	25 or older:	33%
Women:	61%		

Transfer out. 69% of students enrolled in the transfer program go on to 4-year colleges. **Colleges most students transferred to 2011:** Kutztown University, DeSales University, Cedar Crest College, Albright College, Penn State University.

Basis for selection. Open admission, but selective for some programs. Special requirements for aviation, allied health, nursing and veterinary technician programs. COMPASS used for course placement. High school diploma or GED required of applicants to allied health and professional pilot programs, and applicants under the age of 18. Interview required for allied health, aviation, medical assistant, veterinary technician programs. **Home schooled:** Personal interview encouraged.

High school preparation. Special requirements for allied health programs and nursing.

2011-2012 Annual costs. Tuition/fees: $3,240; $6,240 out-of-district; $9,240 out-of-state. Per-credit charge: $91 in-district; $191 out-of-district; $291 out-of-state. Books/supplies: $2,000. Personal expenses: $1,200.

2010-2011 Financial aid. **Need-based:** 828 full-time freshmen applied for aid; 656 were judged to have need; 620 of these received aid. Average scholarship/grant was $4,008; average loan $2,856. 68% of total undergraduate aid awarded as scholarships/grants, 32% as loans/jobs. Need-based aid available for part-time students. Work-study available nights, weekends and for part-time students. **Non-need-based:** Awarded to 20 full-time undergraduates, including 10 freshmen. Scholarships awarded for academics, job skills.

Application procedures. **Admission:** No deadline. No application fee. Admission notification on a rolling basis. **Financial aid:** Priority date 5/1; no closing date. FAFSA required. Applicants notified on a rolling basis starting 1/1; must reply within 2 week(s) of notification.

Academics. **Special study options:** Cooperative education, cross-registration, distance learning, dual enrollment of high school students, ESL, external degree, honors, independent study, internships, study abroad. Bachelor's degree programs available on campus. License preparation in aviation, nursing, occupational therapy, physical therapy. **Credit/placement by examination:** AP, CLEP, institutional tests. 26 credit hours maximum toward associate degree. **Support services:** GED preparation and test center, learning center, pre-admission summer program, reduced course load, remedial instruction, study skills assistance, tutoring, writing center.

Honors college/program. Top 10% of sponsoring school district, with 1200 SAT (exclusive of Writing), skills assessment score of 90 or above in reading and writing, and 70 or above in algebra required.

Majors. **Biology:** General, biotechnology. **Business:** General, accounting technology, business admin, human resources, resort management. **Communications:** Communications/speech/rhetoric. **Communications technology:** Animation/special effects, radio/TV, recording arts. **Computer sciences:** General, applications programming, networking, programming, security, web page design. **Education:** General, early childhood, special ed, teacher assistance. **Engineering:** General. **General:** Horticultural science. **Health services:** Medical assistant, medical records technology, nursing (RN), occupational therapy assistant, physical therapy assistant, veterinary technology/assistant. **Liberal arts:** Arts/sciences, humanities. **Math:** General. **Parks/recreation:** Sports admin. **Physical sciences:** General. **Protective services:** Criminal justice, law enforcement admin. **Psychology:** General. **Social sciences:** GIS/cartography. **Visual/performing arts:** Art, fashion design, game design, graphic design, interior design.

Most popular majors. Business/marketing 16%, education 14%, health sciences 19%, liberal arts 14%, security/protective services 7%.

Computing on campus. 1,100 workstations in library, computer center. Commuter students can connect to campus network. Online course registration, online library, wireless network available.

Student life. **Freshman orientation:** Available. Preregistration for classes offered. Traditional orientation for new students takes place in June and July for durations of aproximately 5 hours; all new students are expected to attend. **Policies:** Must follow student bill of rights and responsibilities. **Activities:** Choral groups, drama, radio station, student government, business honor society, education honor society, Students in Free Enterprise, student chapter National Kitchen and Bath Association, ANIME club, veterans club, political society, Phi Theta Kappa.

Athletics. **Intercollegiate:** Baseball, basketball, cheerleading, golf, soccer M, volleyball W. **Intramural:** Baseball M, basketball, bowling, golf, soccer, softball, volleyball. **Team name:** Cougars.

Student services. Adult student services, career counseling, student employment services, financial aid counseling, minority student services, on-campus daycare, personal counseling, placement for graduates, veterans' counselor. **Physically disabled:** Services for visually, speech, hearing impaired. **Transfer:** Pre-admission transcript evaluation for new students. Transfer adviser, college fairs on campus for students transferring to 4-year colleges.

Contact. E-mail: tellme@lccc.edu
Phone: (610) 799-1575 Toll-free number: (800) 414-3975
Fax: (610) 799-1629
Louis Hegyes, Director of Recruitment/Admissions, Lehigh Carbon Community College, 4525 Education Park Drive, Schnecksville, PA 18078

Lincoln Technical Institute: Allentown
Allentown, Pennsylvania
www.lincolntech.com   CB code: 2741

- For-profit 2-year technical college
- Commuter campus in small city
- Interview required

General. Founded in 1946. Accredited by ACCSC. **Degrees:** 44 associate awarded. **Location:** 60 miles from Philadelphia. **Calendar:** Differs by program. **Full-time faculty:** 19 total. **Part-time faculty:** 3 total.

Basis for selection. Open admission.

2011-2012 Annual costs. Total program costs range from $13,275 up to $29,795 depending on program. Cost of books and materials included in tuition.

Financial aid. **Need-based:** Work-study available nights, weekends and for part-time students.

Application procedures. **Admission:** No deadline. $150 fee, may be waived for applicants with need. **Financial aid:** No deadline.

Academics. **Credit/placement by examination:** AP, CLEP.

Most popular majors. Engineering/engineering technologies 34%, trade and industry 66%.

Student life. **Freshman orientation:** Mandatory. Preregistration for classes offered. **Housing:** Wellness housing available. **Activities:** TV station.

Contact. Phone: (610) 398-5300 Toll-free number: (877) 533-2592
Fax: (610) 395-2706
Mark Garner, Director of Admissions, Lincoln Technical Institute: Allentown, 5151 Tilghman Street, Allentown, PA 18104

Lincoln Technical Institute: Northeast Philadelphia
Philadelphia, Pennsylvania
www.lincolntech.com

- For-profit 2-year technical college
- Very large city

Two-Year Colleges

General. Accredited by ACICS. **Degrees:** 2 associate awarded. **Calendar:** Differs by program. **Full-time faculty:** 12 total. **Part-time faculty:** 9 total.

Basis for selection. Open admission.

2011-2012 Annual costs. Total program costs range from $13,362 up to $26,058 depending on program. Cost of books and materials included in tuition.

Financial aid. Need-based: Work-study available nights, weekends and for part-time students.

Application procedures. Admission: No deadline. $150 fee.

Academics. Credit/placement by examination: AP, CLEP. **Support services:** Tutoring.

Majors. Health services: Office assistant.

Computing on campus. Online library available.

Student life. Freshman orientation: Mandatory. Preregistration for classes offered.

Contact. Phone: (215) 969-0869 Toll-free number: (877) 453-5151 Fax: (215) 969-3457
Paula Little, Director of Admissions, Lincoln Technical Institute: Northeast Philadelphia, 2180 Hornig Road, Philadelphia, PA 19116

Lincoln Technical Institute: Philadelphia
Philadelphia, Pennsylvania
www.lincolntech.com   **CB code: 9010**

- For-profit 2-year technical college
- Commuter campus in very large city

General. Accredited by ACCSC. **Degrees:** 108 associate awarded. **Calendar:** Quarter. **Full-time faculty:** 17 total.

Basis for selection. Open admission.

2011-2012 Annual costs. Total program costs range from $12,650 up to $30,778 depending on program. Cost of books and materials included in tuition.

Financial aid. Need-based: Work-study available nights, weekends and for part-time students.

Application procedures. Admission: No deadline. $150 fee. Admission notification on a rolling basis.

Academics. Credit/placement by examination: AP, CLEP.

Contact. E-mail: dcunningham@lincolntech.com
Phone: (215) 335-0800 Toll-free number: (877) 606-6581
Fax: (215) 335-1443
Pat Fittipaldi, Director of Admissions, Lincoln Technical Institute: Philadelphia, 9191 Torresdale Avenue, Philadelphia, PA 19136

Luzerne County Community College
Nanticoke, Pennsylvania
www.luzerne.edu   **CB code: 2382**

- Public 2-year community college
- Commuter campus in large town

General. Founded in 1966. Regionally accredited. **Enrollment:** 6,525 degree-seeking undergraduates; 254 non-degree-seeking students. **Degrees:** 914 associate awarded. **ROTC:** Air Force. **Location:** 8 miles from Wilkes-Barre. **Calendar:** Semester, extensive summer session. **Full-time faculty:** 111 total. **Part-time faculty:** 479 total.

Student profile. Among degree-seeking undergraduates, 52% enrolled in a transfer program, 48% enrolled in a vocational program, 1,841 enrolled as first-time, first-year students.

Part-time:	47%	Asian American:	1%
Women:	59%	Hispanic American:	7%
African American:	4%	25 or older:	38%

Transfer out. 64% of students enrolled in the transfer program go on to 4-year colleges. **Colleges most students transferred to 2011:** Bloomsburg University, Wilkes University, King's College, College Misericordia.

Basis for selection. Open admission, but selective for some programs. High school record, college record, test scores considered for admission to health sciences programs. Diagnostic Entrance Test required of nursing applicants. Interview recommended for health sciences program. **Home schooled:** Transcript of courses and grades, state high school equivalency certificate required. **Learning Disabled:** Comprehensive services for special needs students at no cost providing the students present the required documentation.

High school preparation. One algebra, 1 chemistry, 1 biology required of nursing, respiratory therapy, surgical technology, and dental hygiene applicants.

2011-2012 Annual costs. Tuition/fees: $3,150; $5,970 out-of-district; $8,790 out-of-state. Per-credit charge: $84 in-district; $168 out-of-district; $252 out-of-state. Books/supplies: $1,500. Personal expenses: $1,400.

Financial aid. Need-based: Need-based aid available for part-time students. Work-study available nights, weekends and for part-time students.

Application procedures. Admission: No deadline. No application fee. Admission notification on a rolling basis. **Financial aid:** Priority date 4/15; no closing date. FAFSA, institutional form required. Applicants notified on a rolling basis starting 7/1.

Academics. Special study options: Cooperative education, distance learning, dual enrollment of high school students, ESL, external degree, honors, independent study, internships, liberal arts/career combination, weekend college. **Credit/placement by examination:** AP, CLEP, institutional tests. 30 credit hours maximum toward associate degree. **Support services:** GED preparation and test center, learning center, pre-admission summer program, reduced course load, remedial instruction, study skills assistance, tutoring, writing center.

Majors. Business: General, accounting, accounting technology, administrative services, banking/financial services, business admin, management information systems, real estate. **Communications:** Advertising, journalism. **Communications technology:** Recording arts. **Computer sciences:** General, applications programming, computer graphics, security, web page design. **Education:** General, teacher assistance. **General:** Landscaping. **Health services:** Dental assistant, dental hygiene, EMT paramedic, insurance specialist, medical transcription, nursing (RN), prechiropractic, preoptometry, prepharmacy, respiratory therapy technology, surgical technology. **Liberal arts:** Arts/sciences, humanities. **Math:** General. **Parks/recreation:** Health/fitness. **Protective services:** Criminal justice, fire safety technology. **Social sciences:** General. **Visual/performing arts:** Graphic design, illustration, photography. **Work/family studies:** Institutional food production.

Most popular majors. Business/marketing 14%, education 8%, health sciences 26%, liberal arts 11%, security/protective services 6%, trade and industry 7%.

Computing on campus. 150 workstations in library, computer center, student center. Commuter students can connect to campus network. Online course registration, online library, helpline, student web hosting, wireless network available.

Student life. Freshman orientation: Mandatory. Preregistration for classes offered. **Activities:** Drama, international student organizations, literary magazine, radio station, student government, student newspaper, TV station, Circle K, Brothers and Sisters in Christ, ACLU, NAACP, Amnesty International, NOW, GLBTA.

Athletics. Intercollegiate: Baseball M, basketball, cross-country, golf, softball W, volleyball W. **Intramural:** Badminton, basketball, football (non-tackle), volleyball. **Team name:** Trailblazers.

Student services. Adult student services, career counseling, student employment services, health services, personal counseling, placement for graduates, veterans' counselor. **Physically disabled:** Services for visually, hearing impaired. **Transfer:** Pre-admission transcript evaluation for new students. Transfer adviser, college fairs on campus for students transferring to 4-year colleges.

Contact. E-mail: admissions@luzerne.edu
Phone: (570) 740-0337 Toll-free number: (800) 377-5222 ext. 337
Fax: (570) 740-0238
Francis Curry, Director of Admissions, Luzerne County Community College, 1333 South Prospect Street, Nanticoke, PA 18634-3899

Manor College
Jenkintown, Pennsylvania
www.manor.edu

CB code: 2260

- Private 2-year junior college affiliated with Ukrainian Catholic Church
- Commuter campus in small town
- SAT or ACT with writing required

General. Founded in 1947. Regionally accredited. **Enrollment:** 868 degree-seeking undergraduates; 72 non-degree-seeking students. **Degrees:** 166 associate awarded. **Location:** 15 miles from Philadelphia. **Calendar:** Semester, limited summer session. **Full-time faculty:** 24 total; 33% have terminal degrees, 4% minority, 79% women. **Part-time faculty:** 104 total; 31% have terminal degrees, 12% minority, 62% women. **Class size:** 77% < 20, 23% 20-39. **Special facilities:** Ukrainian heritage studies center and museum, dental health center, law library, veterinary technology radiology lab, surgical suite, Civil War library.

Student profile. Among degree-seeking undergraduates, 57% enrolled in a transfer program, 43% enrolled in a vocational program, 2% already have a bachelor's degree or higher, 221 enrolled as first-time, first-year students, 173 transferred in from other institutions.

Part-time:	38%	Asian American:	2%
Out-of-state:	2%	Hispanic American:	5%
Women:	78%	25 or older:	37%
African American:	31%	Live on campus:	4%

Transfer out. 64% of students enrolled in the transfer program go on to 4-year colleges. **Colleges most students transferred to 2011:** Holy Family University, LaSalle University, Temple University, Drexel University, Thomas Jefferson University.

Basis for selection. Class rank, GPA, course selection; institutional entrance test required of all applicants except those holding bachelor's degree. **Adult students:** SAT/ACT scores not required. SAT/ACT scores not required if applicant over 21. **Home schooled:** Statement describing home school structure and mission required. **Learning Disabled:** IEP required of all with diagnosed disability.

High school preparation. College-preparatory program recommended. 16 units required. Required and recommended units include English 4, mathematics 2, social studies 2, science 1-2 (laboratory 1-2) and academic electives 6. Biology with laboratory; chemistry with laboratory; 3 math courses required of all Allied Health Science applicants.

2012-2013 Annual costs. Tuition/fees (projected): $14,506. Per-credit charge: $299. Tuition for Allied Health program $14,774; $399 per-credit hour. Room/board: $6,270. Books/supplies: $1,170. Personal expenses: $2,812.

2011-2012 Financial aid. All financial aid based on need. 198 full-time freshmen applied for aid; 198 were judged to have need; 198 of these received aid. Average need met was 33%. Average scholarship/grant was $4,800; average loan $3,522. 61% of total undergraduate aid awarded as scholarships/grants, 39% as loans/jobs. Need-based aid available for part-time students. Work-study available nights, weekends and for part-time students.

Application procedures. Admission: Closing date 8/15 (postmark date). No application fee. Application must be submitted online. Admission notification by 9/11. Admission notification on a rolling basis. Must reply by May 1 or within 2 week(s) if notified thereafter. **Financial aid:** Priority date 3/15; no closing date. FAFSA required. Applicants notified on a rolling basis starting 3/1; must reply within 2 week(s) of notification.

Academics. Special study options: Accelerated study, distance learning, double major, dual enrollment of high school students, ESL, honors, independent study, internships. License preparation in dental hygiene, real estate. **Credit/placement by examination:** AP, CLEP, institutional tests. 30 credit hours maximum toward associate degree. **Support services:** Learning center, pre-admission summer program, reduced course load, remedial instruction, study skills assistance, tutoring, writing center.

Majors. Business: Accounting, business admin, international, marketing. **Communications:** Communications/speech/rhetoric. **Computer sciences:** Applications programming. **Education:** Early childhood, elementary. **Health services:** Dental assistant, dental hygiene, prenursing, preveterinary, veterinary technology/assistant. **Liberal arts:** Arts/sciences. **Psychology:** General.

Most popular majors. Business/marketing 14%, health sciences 55%, legal studies 8%, liberal arts 7%, psychology 8%.

Computing on campus. 121 workstations in dormitories, library, computer center. Dormitories wired for high-speed internet access and linked to campus network. Commuter students can connect to campus network. Online library, helpline, wireless network available.

Student life. Freshman orientation: Mandatory, $35 fee. Preregistration for classes offered. 3 one-day orientations in January and August. **Policies:** Alcohol and drug policy strictly enforced; mandatory meningitis vaccines and completed health record forms to live in residence hall. **Housing:** Coed dorms, wellness housing available. $100 fully refundable deposit, deadline 9/11. **Activities:** Campus ministries, dance, drama, international student organizations, literary magazine, music ensembles, Model UN, student government, student newspaper, Students United for Nature, Black Cultural Awareness, Rotaract, Music Ministry, Admissions Ambassadors, Orientation Leaders, Student Senate.

Athletics. NJCAA. **Intercollegiate:** Basketball, soccer, volleyball W. **Team name:** Blue Jays.

Student services. Adult student services, alcohol/substance abuse counseling, chaplain/spiritual director, career counseling, services for economically disadvantaged, student employment services, financial aid counseling, health services, personal counseling, placement for graduates. **Physically disabled:** Services for hearing impaired. **Transfer:** Pre-admission transcript evaluation for new students. Transfer center, transfer adviser, college fairs on campus for students transferring to 4-year colleges.

Contact. E-mail: ftadmiss@manor.edu
Phone: (215) 884-2216 Fax: (215) 576-6564
Jeffrey Levine, Director of Admissions, Manor College, 700 Fox Chase Road, Jenkintown, PA 19046-3319

McCann School of Business and Technology: Dickson City
Dickson City, Pennsylvania
www.mccann.edu

- For-profit 2-year business and technical college
- Commuter campus in small city
- Interview required

General. Accredited by ACICS. **Enrollment:** 563 degree-seeking undergraduates. **Degrees:** 119 associate awarded. **Calendar:** Quarter, extensive summer session. **Full-time faculty:** 10 total. **Part-time faculty:** 44 total.

Basis for selection. Evidence of high school diploma or equivalent required; interview; must earn certain score on entrance examination.

2011-2012 Annual costs. Costs vary by program of study; average annual tuition, $9,000; per-credit-hour charge, $250.

Financial aid. Need-based: Work-study available nights, weekends and for part-time students.

Application procedures. Admission: No deadline. $40 fee, may be waived for applicants with need. Admission notification on a rolling basis. **Financial aid:** No deadline. FAFSA required.

Academics. Credit/placement by examination: AP, CLEP. **Support services:** Reduced course load, remedial instruction, tutoring.

Majors. Business: Marketing. **Computer sciences:** General, networking. **Education:** Early childhood, teacher assistance. **Health services:** Massage therapy, medical assistant, medical secretary, receptionist, surgical technology.

Student life. Freshman orientation: Mandatory. Preregistration for classes offered. **Activities:** Student council, business club, medical club, early childhood club.

Student services. Career counseling, student employment services, financial aid counseling, placement for graduates.

Contact. Phone: (570) 307-2000 Toll-free number: (888) 513-5868
Judie Roccograndi, Director of Admissions, McCann School of Business and Technology: Dickson City, 2227 Scranton Carbondale Highway, Dickson City, PA 18519

McCann School of Business and Technology: Hazleton
Hazleton, Pennsylvania
www.mccannschool.edu

CB code: 3887

- For-profit 2-year business and technical college
- Commuter campus in large town

General. Founded in 1897. Accredited by ACICS. **Location:** 35 miles from Wilkes Barre. **Calendar:** Quarter.

Annual costs/financial aid. Costs vary by program of study; average annual tuition, $9,000; per-credit-hour charge, $250. Books/supplies: $1,500. Personal expenses: $1,600.

Contact. Phone: (570) 454-6172
Director of Admissions, 370 Maplewood Drive, Hazleton, PA 18202

McCann School of Business and Technology: Pottsville
Pottsville, Pennsylvania
www.mccann.edu   CB code: 3296

- For-profit 2-year branch campus and technical college
- Commuter campus in small town
- Interview required

General. Accredited by ACICS. **Enrollment:** 543 degree-seeking undergraduates. **Degrees:** 143 associate awarded. **Location:** One hour from Harrisburg. **Calendar:** Quarter, extensive summer session. **Full-time faculty:** 8 total. **Part-time faculty:** 40 total. **Special facilities:** On-site massage therapy training center.

Basis for selection. Open admission. Students must achieve a score of 15 on the Wonderlic Basic Skills Assessment, must possess a GED or high school diploma.

2011-2012 Annual costs. Costs vary by program of study; average annual tuition, $9,000; per-credit-hour charge, $250.

Financial aid. Need-based: Work-study available nights, weekends and for part-time students.

Application procedures. Admission: No deadline. $40 fee.

Academics. Special study options: Distance learning, dual enrollment of high school students, internships. **Credit/placement by examination:** AP, CLEP. **Support services:** Reduced course load, remedial instruction, tutoring.

Majors. Business: Accounting, administrative services, business admin. **Computer sciences:** General. **Education:** Early childhood. **Protective services:** Criminal justice, police science, security services.

Computing on campus. 125 workstations in library, computer center. Commuter students can connect to campus network. Online library, helpline, repair service, wireless network available.

Student life. Freshman orientation: Mandatory. Preregistration for classes offered.

Student services. Adult student services, career counseling, student employment services, financial aid counseling, placement for graduates.

Contact. Phone: (570) 622-7622 Toll-free number: (888) 781-3025
Fax: (570) 622-7770
Emmanuel Vlastos, Director of Admission, McCann School of Business and Technology: Pottsville, 2650 Woodglen Road, Pottsville, PA 17901

McCann School of Business and Technology: Sunbury
Sunbury, Pennsylvania
www.mccann.edu   CB code: 3298

- For-profit 2-year branch campus and technical college
- Commuter campus in small town

General. Accredited by ACICS. **Calendar:** Quarter.

Annual costs/financial aid. Costs vary by program of study; average annual tuition, $9,000; per-credit-hour charge, $250.

Contact. Phone: (570) 286-3058
Director of Admissions, 1147 North 4th Street, Sunbury, PA 17801

Metropolitan Career Center Computer Technology Institute
Philadelphia, Pennsylvania
www.careersinit.org

- Private 2-year technical college
- Very large city

General. Accredited by ACCSCT. **Calendar:** Differs by program.

Annual costs/financial aid. Full program cost is $23,994; does not include all fees and supplies. Per-credit-hour charge, $387. Books/supplies: $1,400. Personal expenses: $1,640. Need-based financial aid available to full-time and part-time students.

Contact. Phone: (215) 568-9215
Admissions Director, 100 South Broad Street, Suite 830, Philadelphia, PA 19110

Montgomery County Community College
Blue Bell, Pennsylvania   CB member
www.mc3.edu   CB code: 2445

- Public 2-year community college
- Commuter campus in large town

General. Founded in 1964. Regionally accredited. Campus in Pottstown serves students in western part of the county. Off-campus site: Lansdale (automotive). **Enrollment:** 13,819 degree-seeking undergraduates; 166 non-degree-seeking students. **Degrees:** 1,236 associate awarded. **Location:** 20 miles from Philadelphia. **Calendar:** Semester, extensive summer session. **Full-time faculty:** 185 total; 9% minority, 56% women. **Part-time faculty:** 569 total; 9% minority, 54% women. **Class size:** 50% < 20, 50% 20-39. **Special facilities:** Dental hygiene clinic; observatory and observational deck.

Student profile. Among degree-seeking undergraduates, 61% enrolled in a transfer program, 39% enrolled in a vocational program, 4,370 enrolled as first-time, first-year students, 428 transferred in from other institutions.

Part-time:	60%	Asian American:	5%
Out-of-state:	1%	Hispanic American:	5%
Women:	56%	International:	2%
African American:	14%	25 or older:	37%

Transfer out. 68% of students enrolled in the transfer program go on to 4-year colleges. **Colleges most students transferred to 2011:** Temple University, Gwynedd-Mercy College, West Chester University, Penn State, Kutztown University.

Basis for selection. Open admission, but selective for some programs. Special requirements for allied health and automotive technology programs. ACT or SAT required for allied health applicants; report score by August 1. County residents given priority. High school transcript required for students less than 5 years out of high school. **Home schooled:** Transcript of courses and grades required. Must provide approved curriculum and portfolio. **Learning Disabled:** Recommend meeting with Director of Services for Students with Disabilities. Require current documentation from students of accommodations needed.

High school preparation. Biology, chemistry, and algebra required of nursing and medical laboratory technician applicants, chemistry of dental hygiene applicants.

2011-2012 Annual costs. Tuition/fees: $3,750; $7,140 out-of-district; $10,530 out-of-state. Per-credit charge: $103 in-district; $206 out-of-district; $309 out-of-state. Books/supplies: $1,300. Personal expenses: $1,640.

2010-2011 Financial aid. Need-based: 1,258 full-time freshmen applied for aid; 1,091 were judged to have need; 985 of these received aid. Average need met was 22%. Average scholarship/grant was $2,941; average loan $1,665. 64% of total undergraduate aid awarded as scholarships/grants, 36% as loans/jobs. Need-based aid available for part-time students. Work-study available nights, weekends and for part-time students. **Non-need-based:** Awarded to 1,673 full-time undergraduates, including 670 freshmen. Scholarships awarded for academics.

Application procedures. Admission: No deadline. $25 fee, may be waived for applicants with need, free for online applicants. Admission notification on a rolling basis. **Financial aid:** Priority date 5/1; no closing date. FAFSA required. Applicants notified on a rolling basis starting 2/1.

Academics. Special study options: Accelerated study, cooperative education, distance learning, dual enrollment of high school students, ESL, honors,

independent study, internships, student-designed major, study abroad, teacher certification program, weekend college. Bachelor's degree programs available on campus. License preparation in dental hygiene, nursing, radiology, real estate. **Credit/placement by examination:** AP, CLEP, institutional tests. 30 credit hours maximum toward associate degree. **Support services:** GED preparation and test center, learning center, pre-admission summer program, reduced course load, remedial instruction, study skills assistance, tutoring.

Majors. Biology: Biotechnology. **Business:** General, accounting technology, administrative services, business admin, communications, hospitality/recreation, real estate, sales/distribution, travel services. **Communications:** Communications/speech/rhetoric, digital media. **Communications technology:** Recording arts. **Computer sciences:** Computer science, information systems, information technology, system admin, web page design, webmaster. **Education:** Elementary, music, physical, secondary, teacher assistance. **Engineering:** Engineering science, nuclear, software. **Health services:** Clinical lab technology, dental hygiene, mental health services, nursing (RN), office admin, radiologic technology/medical imaging, substance abuse counseling, surgical technology. **Liberal arts:** Arts/sciences, humanities. **Math:** General. **Parks/recreation:** Health/fitness. **Physical sciences:** General. **Protective services:** Fire safety technology, police science, security management. **Psychology:** General. **Social sciences:** General. **Visual/performing arts:** Acting, art, dance, graphic design. **Work/family studies:** Child care management.

Most popular majors. Business/marketing 13%, education 6%, health sciences 17%, liberal arts 41%.

Computing on campus. 1,064 workstations in library, student center. Commuter students can connect to campus network. Online course registration, online library, helpline, wireless network available.

Student life. Freshman orientation: Available. Preregistration for classes offered. One day, week before semester starts. 3 days offered at Central campus. 2 days offered at West campus. **Activities:** Jazz band, choral groups, dance, drama, film society, international student organizations, literary magazine, music ensembles, radio station, student government, student newspaper, TV station, African-American club, Christian fellowship club, Gay-Straight Alliance, political science club, Muslim student association, African student association.

Athletics. NJCAA. **Intercollegiate:** Baseball M, basketball, soccer, softball W, volleyball W. **Intramural:** Badminton, basketball, bowling, cross-country, football (non-tackle) M, racquetball, soccer, table tennis, tennis, volleyball, weight lifting. **Team name:** Mustangs.

Student services. Adult student services, career counseling, services for economically disadvantaged, student employment services, financial aid counseling, health services, minority student services, on-campus daycare, personal counseling, placement for graduates, veterans' counselor, women's services. **Physically disabled:** Services for visually, speech, hearing impaired. **Transfer:** Pre-admission transcript evaluation for new students. Transfer center, transfer adviser, college fairs on campus for students transferring to 4-year colleges.

Contact. E-mail: admissionsregistration@mc3.edu
Phone: (215) 641-6551 Fax: (215) 641-6681
Penny Sawyer, Director of Admissions, Montgomery County Community College, 340 DeKalb Pike, Blue Bell, PA 19422

New Castle School of Trades
Pulaski, Pennsylvania
www.ncstrades.com   CB code: 2404

▶ For-profit 2-year technical college
▶ Commuter campus in rural community

General. Accredited by ACCSCT. **Location:** 10 miles from Youngstown, Ohio. **Calendar:** Continuous.

Annual costs/financial aid. Tution varies by program from $5,775 to $19,270 including fees. Books and tool expenses up to $3,245. Need-based financial aid available to full-time and part-time students.

Contact. Phone: (724) 964-8811
Director of Admissions, 4164 US 422, Pulaski, PA 16143-9721

Newport Business Institute: Lower Burrell
Lower Burrell, Pennsylvania
www.nbi.edu   CB code: 2413

▶ For-profit 2-year business college
▶ Commuter campus in small town

General. Accredited by ACICS. **Location:** 15 miles from Pittsburgh. **Calendar:** Quarter.

Annual costs/financial aid. Tuition/fees (2011-2012): $11,775. Books/supplies: $1,275. Need-based financial aid available to full-time and part-time students.

Contact. Phone: (724) 339-7542
Assistant Director of Admissions, 945 Greensburg Road, Lower Burrell, PA 15068

Newport Business Institute: Williamsport
Williamsport, Pennsylvania
www.nbi.edu   CB code: 2551

▶ For-profit 2-year business and career college
▶ Commuter campus in small city
▶ Interview required

General. Accredited by ACICS. **Enrollment:** 120 degree-seeking undergraduates. **Degrees:** 40 associate awarded. **Calendar:** Quarter. **Full-time faculty:** 6 total. **Part-time faculty:** 10 total.

Student profile. Among degree-seeking undergraduates, 21 transferred in from other institutions.

Basis for selection. Open admission.

2011-2012 Annual costs. Books/supplies: $1,228.

Financial aid. Need-based: Work-study available nights, weekends and for part-time students.

Application procedures. Admission: No deadline. $25 fee. Admission notification on a rolling basis. **Financial aid:** No deadline. FAFSA required. Applicants notified on a rolling basis.

Academics. Special study options: Distance learning, internships. **Credit/placement by examination:** AP, CLEP.

Majors. Business: Business admin. **Health services:** Medical secretary.

Most popular majors. Business/marketing 45%, health sciences 44%, legal studies 11%.

Computing on campus. PC or laptop required. Wireless network available.

Student life. Freshman orientation: Mandatory. Preregistration for classes offered. **Activities:** Student government.

Student services. Financial aid counseling, personal counseling, placement for graduates. **Transfer:** Pre-admission transcript evaluation for new students.

Contact. E-mail: admissions1_nbi@comcast.net
Phone: (570) 326-2869 Toll-free number: (800) 962-6971
Fax: (570) 326-2136
John Kiernan, Director, Newport Business Institute: Williamsport, 941 West Third Street, Williamsport, PA 17701

Northampton Community College
Bethlehem, Pennsylvania   CB member
www.northampton.edu   CB code: 2573

▶ Public 2-year community college
▶ Commuter campus in small city

General. Founded in 1966. Regionally accredited. Branch campus at Monroe County. Off-campus sites in southside Bethlehem, Hawley (Pike County), and Tobyhanna. Individualized transfer study program. **Enrollment:** 10,951 degree-seeking undergraduates; 399 non-degree-seeking students. **Degrees:** 1,156 associate awarded. **Location:** 60 miles from Philadelphia, 90 miles from New York City. **Calendar:** Semester, limited summer session. **Full-time faculty:** 118 total; 46% have terminal degrees, 17% minority, 59% women. **Part-time faculty:** 603 total; 15% have terminal degrees, 9% minority, 56% women. **Special facilities:** ISO Class 7 clean room facility, electro-technology applications center, kindergarten, student-run restaurant. **Partnerships:** Formal partnerships with General Motors and Chrysler.

Two-Year Colleges

Student profile. Among degree-seeking undergraduates, 58% enrolled in a transfer program, 42% enrolled in a vocational program, 5% already have a bachelor's degree or higher, 2,436 enrolled as first-time, first-year students, 1,102 transferred in from other institutions.

Part-time:	55%	Hispanic American:	18%
Out-of-state:	2%	International:	1%
Women:	60%	25 or older:	36%
African American:	11%	Live on campus:	2%
Asian American:	2%		

Transfer out. 76% of students enrolled in the transfer program go on to 4-year colleges. **Colleges most students transferred to 2011:** East Stroudsburg University, Kutztown University, DeSales University, Pennsylvania State University, Cedar Crest College.

Basis for selection. Open admission, but selective for some programs. Special requirements for allied health, veterinary technician, and culinary arts programs. Interview required for radiography, veterinary technology, and diagnostic medical sonography programs; portfolio required for communication design, fine arts programs; audition required for theater program.

High school preparation. Biology, chemistry, and algebra requirements for allied health programs.

2011-2012 Annual costs. Tuition/fees: $3,420; $7,500 out-of-district; $11,130 out-of-state. Per-credit charge: $82 in-district; $164 out-of-district; $246 out-of-state. Room/board: $7,404. Books/supplies: $1,400. Personal expenses: $1,300.

2011-2012 Financial aid. **Need-based:** 78% of total undergraduate aid awarded as scholarships/grants, 22% as loans/jobs. Need-based aid available for part-time students. Work-study available nights, weekends and for part-time students. **Non-need-based:** Scholarships awarded for academics, alumni affiliation, art, leadership, minority status, music/drama, state residency.

Application procedures. **Admission:** No deadline. $25 fee, may be waived for applicants with need. Admission notification on a rolling basis. **Financial aid:** Priority date 3/31; no closing date. FAFSA, institutional form required. Applicants notified on a rolling basis starting 6/1.

Academics. **Special study options:** Distance learning, dual enrollment of high school students, ESL, honors, independent study, internships, student-designed major, study abroad, teacher certification program. License preparation in dental hygiene, nursing, radiology, real estate. **Credit/placement by examination:** AP, CLEP, institutional tests. 30 credit hours maximum toward associate degree. **Support services:** GED preparation and test center, learning center, reduced course load, remedial instruction, study skills assistance, tutoring, writing center.

Majors. **Biology:** General, biotechnology. **Business:** General, accounting technology, administrative services, business admin, construction management, hotel/motel admin, marketing, restaurant/food services. **Communications:** Communications/speech/rhetoric, journalism. **Communications technology:** Radio/TV. **Computer sciences:** Computer science, networking, programming, security, web page design. **Education:** Early childhood, middle, secondary, teacher assistance. **Engineering:** General. **Health services:** Athletic training, dental hygiene, medical secretary, nursing (RN), radiologic technology/medical imaging, sonography, surgical technology, veterinary technology/assistant. **Human services:** Social work. **Liberal arts:** Arts/sciences. **Math:** General. **Parks/recreation:** Sports admin. **Physical sciences:** Chemistry, physics. **Protective services:** Criminal justice, fire services admin, firefighting. **Visual/performing arts:** Acting, graphic design, interior design, studio arts.

Most popular majors. Business/marketing 16%, health sciences 15%, liberal arts 18%, security/protective services 7%.

Computing on campus. 1,400 workstations in dormitories, library, computer center, student center. Dormitories wired for high-speed internet access and linked to campus network. Commuter students can connect to campus network. Online course registration, online library, helpline, student web hosting, wireless network available.

Student life. **Freshman orientation:** Mandatory. Preregistration for classes offered. 1/2 day program offered throughout the summer. **Housing:** Coed dorms, apartments available. $150 deposit. **Activities:** Campus ministries, choral groups, dance, drama, film society, international student organizations, literary magazine, Model UN, radio station, student government, student newspaper, Black Brothers Union, Christian fellowship club, Hispanic American cultural club, Muslim student association, Phi Theta Kappa, political science club, South Asian student organization.

Athletics. NJCAA. **Intercollegiate:** Baseball M, basketball, bowling, golf, soccer M, softball W, tennis, volleyball W. **Intramural:** Basketball, football (non-tackle), soccer, volleyball. **Team name:** Spartans.

Student services. Adult student services, alcohol/substance abuse counseling, career counseling, services for economically disadvantaged, financial aid counseling, health services, minority student services, on-campus daycare, personal counseling, placement for graduates. **Physically disabled:** Services for visually, speech, hearing impaired. **Transfer:** Pre-admission transcript evaluation for new students. Transfer center, transfer adviser, college fairs on campus for students transferring to 4-year colleges.

Contact. E-mail: adminfo@northampton.edu
Phone: (610) 861-5500 Fax: (610) 861-4560
James McCarthy, Director of Admissions, Northampton Community College, 3835 Green Pond Road, Bethlehem, PA 18020-7599

Oakbridge Academy of Arts
Lower Burrell, Pennsylvania
www.oaa.edu   CB code: 2984

- For-profit 2-year visual arts college
- Commuter campus in large town
- Interview required

General. Accredited by ACCSC. **Enrollment:** 65 degree-seeking undergraduates. **Degrees:** 13 associate awarded. **Location:** 21 miles from Pittsburgh. **Calendar:** Quarter, extensive summer session. **Full-time faculty:** 3 total. **Part-time faculty:** 7 total.

Transfer out. **Colleges most students transferred to 2011:** Art Institute of Pittsburgh.

Basis for selection. Open admission. Portfolio review recommended for visual design and photography programs. **Home schooled:** Transcript of courses and grades, state high school equivalency certificate required. **Learning Disabled:** Reading test.

2011-2012 Annual costs. Tuition/fees: $11,475. Books/supplies: $1,000. Personal expenses: $4,123.

Financial aid. All financial aid based on need. Need-based aid available for part-time students. Work-study available nights, weekends and for part-time students.

Application procedures. **Admission:** No deadline. $50 fee. Application must be submitted on paper. Admission notification on a rolling basis. **Financial aid:** Closing date 5/1. FAFSA required. Applicants notified on a rolling basis.

Academics. **Special study options:** Internships. **Credit/placement by examination:** AP, CLEP. **Support services:** Tutoring.

Majors. **Communications:** Advertising. **Visual/performing arts:** General, commercial photography, commercial/advertising art, design, drawing, graphic design, painting, photography.

Computing on campus. PC or laptop required. 20 workstations in computer center. Wireless network available.

Student life. **Freshman orientation:** Mandatory. Preregistration for classes offered. **Activities:** Student government.

Student services. Placement for graduates. **Transfer:** Pre-admission transcript evaluation for new students.

Contact. E-mail: admissions@oaa.edu
Phone: (724) 335-5336 Toll-free number: (800) 734-5601
Fax: (724) 335-5336
Sharon Panaia, Admissions Director, Oakbridge Academy of Arts, 1250 Greensburg Road, Lower Burrell, PA 15068

Orleans Technical Institute
Philadelphia, Pennsylvania
www.orleanstech.edu   CB code: 3127

- Private 2-year technical and career college
- Commuter campus in very large city

General. Regionally accredited. **Calendar:** Differs by program.

Annual costs/financial aid. Books/supplies: $810. Personal expenses: $1,320. Need-based financial aid available to full-time and part-time students.

Contact. Phone: (215) 728-4426
Director of Admissions, 2770 Red Lion Road, Philadelphia, PA 19114

Pace Institute
Reading, Pennsylvania
www.paceinstitute.com   CB code: 2438

▶ For-profit 2-year junior college
▶ Large city

General. Accredited by ACICS. **Calendar:** Differs by program.

Annual costs/financial aid. Tuition/fees (2011-2012): $7,464. Books/supplies: $888.

Contact. Phone: (610) 375-1212
Vice President of Enrollment Resources, 606 Court Street, Reading, PA 19601

Penn Commercial Business and Technical School
Washington, Pennsylvania
www.penncommercial.edu   CB code: 3300

▶ For-profit 2-year business and technical college
▶ Commuter campus in small city

General. Accredited by ACICS. **Enrollment:** 203 degree-seeking undergraduates. **Degrees:** 106 associate awarded. **Calendar:** Differs by program. **Full-time faculty:** 19 total. **Part-time faculty:** 12 total.

Basis for selection. Open admission, but selective for some programs.

2011-2012 Annual costs. Books/supplies: $945. Personal expenses: $2,438.

Financial aid. Need-based: Work-study available nights, weekends and for part-time students.

Application procedures. Admission: No deadline. $25 fee. Admission notification on a rolling basis. **Financial aid:** Closing date 5/15.

Academics. Credit/placement by examination: AP, CLEP.

Majors. Business: General, administrative services, business admin. **Computer sciences:** Information technology, networking. **Health services:** Medical secretary, office assistant.

Contact. E-mail: pcadmissions@penncommercial.edu
Phone: (724) 222-5330 ext. 1 Fax: (724) 225-3561
Jayme Tuite, Admissions Director, Penn Commercial Business and Technical School, 242 Oak Spring Road, Washington, PA 15301

Pennco Tech
Bristol, Pennsylvania
www.penncotech.com   CB code: 0380

▶ For-profit 2-year technical college
▶ Large town

General. Founded in 1973. Accredited by ACCSC. Branch campus in Blackwood, New Jersey. **Enrollment:** 90 degree-seeking undergraduates. **Degrees:** 85 associate awarded. **Location:** 18 miles from Philadelphia. **Calendar:** Modular, year-round calendar. Limited summer session. **Full-time faculty:** 70 total. **Part-time faculty:** 14 total.

Basis for selection. Open admission.

2011-2012 Annual costs. Books/supplies: $850.

Financial aid. Need-based: Work-study available nights, weekends and for part-time students.

Application procedures. Admission: No deadline. $100 fee. Admission notification on a rolling basis. **Financial aid:** No deadline. Applicants notified on a rolling basis.

Academics. Credit/placement by examination: AP, CLEP, institutional tests. 30 credit hours maximum toward associate degree. **Support services:** Tutoring.

Majors. Business: Hospitality admin. **Computer sciences:** Programming. **Engineering:** Electrical.

Student life. Housing: Single-sex dorms available. **Activities:** Choral groups, TV station.

Student services. Career counseling, student employment services, on-campus daycare, personal counseling, placement for graduates.

Contact. E-mail: admissions@penncotech.com
Phone: (215) 824-3200 Toll-free number: (800) 575-9399
John Keenan, Director of Admissions, Pennco Tech, 3815 Otter Street, Bristol, PA 19007

Pennsylvania Highlands Community College
Johnstown, Pennsylvania
www.pennhighlands.edu   CB code: 2484

▶ Public 2-year community college
▶ Commuter campus in large town

General. Regionally accredited. **Enrollment:** 1,601 undergraduates. **Degrees:** 221 associate awarded. **Location:** 70 miles from Pittsburgh. **Calendar:** Semester, extensive summer session. **Full-time faculty:** 26 total. **Part-time faculty:** 95 total.

Transfer out. Colleges most students transferred to 2011: University of Pittsburgh at Johnstown, Indiana University of Pennsylvania, Mount Aloysius College, Penn State University, Saint Francis University.

Basis for selection. Open admission.

High school preparation. College-preparatory program recommended.

2011-2012 Annual costs. Tuition/fees: $4,160; $7,060 out-of-district; $9,960 out-of-state. Per-credit charge: $96 in-district; $192 out-of-district; $288 out-of-state. Students in Blair, Bedford, Fulton, Huntingdon, and Somerset counties pay a special regional tuition of $5,100. Books/supplies: $1,000.

Financial aid. Need-based: Need-based aid available for part-time students. Work-study available nights, weekends and for part-time students. Non-need-based: Scholarships awarded for academics, state residency.

Application procedures. Admission: No deadline. No application fee. Admission notification on a rolling basis. **Financial aid:** Closing date 4/1. FAFSA required. Applicants notified on a rolling basis; must reply by 8/1.

Academics. Special study options: Cooperative education, distance learning, dual enrollment of high school students, honors, independent study, internships. **Credit/placement by examination:** AP, CLEP, institutional tests. **Support services:** Learning center, reduced course load, remedial instruction, study skills assistance, tutoring.

Majors. Biology: Biotechnology, cell/histology. **Business:** General, accounting, accounting technology, administrative services. **Communications:** Communications/speech/rhetoric. **Computer sciences:** General, networking. **Education:** General, teacher assistance. **Health services:** EMT paramedic, office assistant, radiologic technology/medical imaging. **Protective services:** Law enforcement admin. **Work/family studies:** Child care service.

Computing on campus. 250 workstations in library, computer center, student center. Online course registration, online library, helpline, wireless network available.

Student life. Freshman orientation: Available. Preregistration for classes offered. **Activities:** Literary magazine, student government.

Athletics. NJCAA. **Intercollegiate:** Basketball M, volleyball W. **Team name:** Black Bears.

Student services. Career counseling, services for economically disadvantaged, student employment services, financial aid counseling, placement for graduates. **Transfer:** Pre-admission transcript evaluation for new students. College fairs on campus for students transferring to 4-year colleges.

Contact. E-mail: jmaul@pennhighlands.edu
Phone: (814) 262-6446 Toll-free number: (888) 385-7325
Fax: (814) 262-6420
Jeff Maul, Director of Admissions, Pennsylvania Highlands Community College, 101 Community College Way, Johnstown, PA 15904

Pennsylvania Institute of Health and Technology
Mount Braddock, Pennsylvania
www.piht.edu   CB code: 3214

- For-profit 2-year business college
- Small town

General. Accredited by ACICS. **Calendar:** Differs by program.

Annual costs/financial aid. Cost of entire associate degree program: $22,470; diploma program: $14,200.

Contact. Phone: (724) 437-4600
Director of Student Services, Route 119 North and Mount Braddock Road, Mount Braddock, PA 15465

Pennsylvania Institute of Technology
Media, Pennsylvania
www.pit.edu   CB code: 2675

- Private 2-year technical college
- Commuter campus in small town
- Application essay, interview required

General. Founded in 1953. Regionally accredited. **Enrollment:** 841 degree-seeking undergraduates. **Degrees:** 163 associate awarded. **Location:** 13 miles from Philadelphia, 15 miles from Wilmington, Delaware. **Calendar:** Semester, extensive summer session. **Full-time faculty:** 25 total. **Part-time faculty:** 73 total. **Class size:** 99% < 20, less than 1% 20-39. **Partnerships:** Formal partnerships with Tech Prep in high schools.

Basis for selection. Open admission, but selective for some programs. Selective admissions to Practical Nursing program. Interview and essay used for placement purposes only.

2011-2012 Annual costs. Tuition/fees: $10,800. Per-credit charge: $330. Books/supplies: $900.

Financial aid. Need-based: Need-based aid available for part-time students. Work-study available nights, weekends and for part-time students. **Non-need-based:** Scholarships awarded for academics, leadership. **Additional information:** Application deadline of May 1st for PHEAA and Philadelphia State Grant aid.

Application procedures. Admission: No deadline. $25 fee, may be waived for applicants with need. Admission notification on a rolling basis. **Financial aid:** No deadline. FAFSA, institutional form required. Applicants notified on a rolling basis starting 7/1.

Academics. Curricula designed to prepare students for positions in industry through combination of general education and job specific courses. **Special study options:** Accelerated study, cooperative education, double major, dual enrollment of high school students, independent study, internships. **Credit/placement by examination:** AP, CLEP, institutional tests. 60 credit hours maximum toward associate degree. **Support services:** Learning center, pre-admission summer program, reduced course load, remedial instruction, tutoring.

Majors. Business: Administrative services, business admin. **Computer sciences:** Computer science, networking. **Health services:** Medical secretary.

Most popular majors. Business/marketing 11%, computer/information sciences 14%, engineering/engineering technologies 16%, health sciences 59%.

Computing on campus. 80 workstations in library, computer center, student center. Commuter students can connect to campus network. Online library available.

Student life. Freshman orientation: Mandatory. Preregistration for classes offered. Held 1 week before start of classes. **Activities:** Student government, amateur radio club.

Athletics. Intramural: Basketball M, softball M, volleyball.

Student services. Adult student services, career counseling, student employment services, personal counseling, placement for graduates, veterans' counselor. **Physically disabled:** Services for speech, hearing impaired. **Transfer:** Transfer adviser, college fairs on campus for students transferring to 4-year colleges.

Contact. E-mail: info@pit.edu
Phone: (610) 565-7900 Toll-free number: (800) 422-0025
Fax: (610) 892-1510
John DeTurris, Director of Admissions, Pennsylvania Institute of Technology, 800 Manchester Avenue, Media, PA 19063-4098

Pennsylvania School of Business
Allentown, Pennsylvania
www.psb.edu   CB code: 3044

- For-profit 2-year Career college with programs in three areas: business, medical, and technical.
- Commuter campus in small city

General. Accredited by ACCSC. **Enrollment:** 115 degree-seeking undergraduates; 157 non-degree-seeking students. **Degrees:** 56 associate awarded. **Location:** 50 miles north of Philadelphia; 90 miles west of New York City. **Calendar:** Semester, extensive summer session. **Full-time faculty:** 17 total. **Part-time faculty:** 14 total.

Student profile. Among degree-seeking undergraduates, 59 enrolled as first-time, first-year students.

Part-time:	55%	Women:	62%

Basis for selection. Open admission, but selective for some programs.

2012-2013 Annual costs. Tuition/fees (projected): $9,275. Books/supplies: $1,000. Personal expenses: $2,069.

2010-2011 Financial aid. Need-based: 81 full-time freshmen applied for aid; 81 were judged to have need; 81 of these received aid. Average scholarship/grant was $4,500. Need-based aid available for part-time students. Work-study available nights, weekends and for part-time students.

Application procedures. Admission: No deadline. No application fee. Admission notification on a rolling basis. **Financial aid:** No deadline. FAFSA required. Applicants notified on a rolling basis.

Academics. Special study options: Only Medical Assistant program offers internship. **Credit/placement by examination:** AP, CLEP. **Support services:** Reduced course load, tutoring.

Majors. Business: Business admin. **Computer sciences:** General. **Health services:** Office admin.

Most popular majors. Business/marketing 50%, computer/information sciences 20%, health sciences 30%.

Computing on campus. Repair service, wireless network available.

Student life. Freshman orientation: Mandatory. Preregistration for classes offered.

Contact. E-mail: sjarvis@psb.edu
Phone: (610) 841-3333 Fax: (610) 841-3334
Sam Jarvis, Director of Admissions, Pennsylvania School of Business, 265 Lehigh Street, Allentown, PA 18102

Pittsburgh Institute of Aeronautics
Pittsburgh, Pennsylvania
www.pia.edu   CB code: 0652

- Private 2-year technical college
- Commuter campus in large city

General. Founded in 1929. Regionally accredited; also accredited by ACCSC. Located in active county airport. **Enrollment:** 200 degree-seeking undergraduates; 93 non-degree-seeking students. **Degrees:** 405 associate awarded. **Location:** 8 miles from Pittsburgh. **Calendar:** Quarter, extensive summer session. **Full-time faculty:** 20 total; 10% minority, 10% women. **Part-time faculty:** 2 total. **Special facilities:** Fleet of over 8 aircraft, modern aviation maintenance, aviation electronics, electronic systems shops and labs.

Student profile. Among degree-seeking undergraduates, 100% enrolled in a vocational program.

Out-of-state:	35%	25 or older:	25%
Women:	6%		

Basis for selection. Open admission. School visit required before classes begin. **Adult students:** SAT/ACT scores not required.

2011-2012 Annual costs. Tuition/fees: $14,715. Books/supplies: $1,320. Personal expenses: $400.

Financial aid. Need-based: Work-study available nights, weekends and for part-time students.

Application procedures. Admission: No deadline. $150 fee. Admission notification on a rolling basis. **Financial aid:** Priority date 5/1; no closing date. FAFSA required. Applicants notified on a rolling basis.

Academics. Special study options: License preparation in aviation. **Credit/placement by examination:** AP, CLEP, institutional tests. **Support services:** Remedial instruction, tutoring.

Majors. Engineering: Electrical.

Computing on campus. 35 workstations in computer center. Commuter students can connect to campus network.

Student life. Housing: Referral housing available. **Activities:** Student government, student newspaper.

Athletics. Intramural: Bowling, golf.

Student services. Adult student services, career counseling, student employment services, financial aid counseling, placement for graduates, veterans' counselor. **Transfer:** Pre-admission transcript evaluation for new students.

Contact. E-mail: admissions@pia.edu
Phone: (412) 346-2100 Toll-free number: (800) 444-1440
Fax: (412) 466-0513
Steven Sabold, Supervisor of Admissions and Recruitment, Pittsburgh Institute of Aeronautics, Box 10897, Pittsburgh, PA 15236-0897

Pittsburgh Institute of Mortuary Science
Pittsburgh, Pennsylvania
www.pims.edu   CB code: 7030

- Private 2-year technical college
- Commuter campus in large city
- Application essay required

General. Founded in 1939. Accredited by American Board of Funeral Services Education, Inc. **Enrollment:** 217 degree-seeking undergraduates. **Degrees:** 41 associate awarded. **Calendar:** Trimester, extensive summer session. **Full-time faculty:** 2 total. **Part-time faculty:** 18 total. **Special facilities:** Preparation center, specialized library.

Transfer out. Colleges most students transferred to 2011: Point Park University.

Basis for selection. Rolling admissions based on combination of requisite high school grade point average, 300 word essay, and receipt of all required documents. **Home schooled:** Transcript of courses and grades, state high school equivalency certificate, letter of recommendation (nonparent) required. 300 word essay required. High School grade point average minimum of 2.0 out of 4. **Learning Disabled:** Diagnosis documentation within 3 years of enrollment required.

High school preparation. College-preparatory program recommended.

2011-2012 Annual costs. Tuition/fees: $16,730. Per-credit charge: $250. Books/supplies: $866.

Financial aid. Need-based: Need-based aid available for part-time students. Work-study available nights, weekends and for part-time students.

Application procedures. Admission: Priority date 9/1; no deadline. $40 fee. Admission notification on a rolling basis. **Financial aid:** Closing date 9/17. FAFSA required. Applicants notified on a rolling basis.

Academics. Four-pronged approach to funeral service management via natural sciences, social sciences, mortuary sciences, and business studies.

Students with previous associate degrees will earn diploma or another associate degree in embalming and funeral directing. **Special study options:** Distance learning. **Credit/placement by examination:** AP, CLEP, institutional tests. 48 credit hours maximum toward associate degree. **Support services:** Reduced course load, tutoring.

Computing on campus. 10 workstations in library, computer center.

Student life. Freshman orientation: Mandatory. Preregistration for classes offered. Generally held week before start of classes. **Housing:** Housing available at local funeral homes. **Activities:** Student government.

Student services. Alcohol/substance abuse counseling, career counseling, student employment services, financial aid counseling, personal counseling, placement for graduates, veterans' counselor. **Transfer:** Pre-admission transcript evaluation for new students. Transfer adviser for students transferring to 4-year colleges.

Contact. E-mail: pims5808@aol.com
Phone: (412) 362-8500 Toll-free number: (800) 933-5808
Fax: (412) 362-1684
Karen Rocco, Registrar, Pittsburgh Institute of Mortuary Science, 5808 Baum Boulevard, Pittsburgh, PA 15206-3706

Prism Career Institute
Upper Darby, Pennsylvania
www.prismcareerinstitute.edu   CB code: 2887

- For-profit 2-year business and career college
- Commuter campus in very large city

General. Location: 4 miles from Philadelphia. **Calendar:** Semester.

Annual costs/financial aid. Personal expenses: $2,067. Need-based financial aid available to full-time and part-time students.

Contact. Phone: (610) 789-6700
Director of Admissions, 6800 Market Street, Upper Darby, PA 19082

Reading Area Community College
Reading, Pennsylvania
www.racc.edu   CB code: 2743

- Public 2-year community college
- Commuter campus in small city

General. Founded in 1971. Regionally accredited. **Enrollment:** 4,580 degree-seeking undergraduates. **Degrees:** 398 associate awarded. **Location:** 55 miles from Philadelphia. **Calendar:** Semester, limited summer session. **Full-time faculty:** 64 total. **Part-time faculty:** 194 total. **Class size:** 44% < 20, 56% 20-39, less than 1% 40-49, less than 1% 50-99. **Special facilities:** Performing arts center, training and technology center.

Student profile.

Out-of-state:	1%	25 or older:	47%

Transfer out. Colleges most students transferred to 2011: Albright College, Kutztown University, Alvernia College, West Chester University, Penn State-Berks.

Basis for selection. Open admission, but selective for some programs. Special admissions criteria for culinary arts, electic utility technology, medical laboratory technician, nursing, practical nursing, respiratory care programs. Interview suggested. **Home schooled:** Transcript of courses and grades, state high school equivalency certificate required. **Learning Disabled:** Students must submit necessary documentation prior to accommodations being made.

High school preparation. 16 units required for nursing program, including 4 English, 3 social studies, 2 math (1 must be algebra), and 2 science with related laboratory or equivalent.

2011-2012 Annual costs. Books/supplies: $1,800. Personal expenses: $1,200.

Financial aid. Need-based: Work-study available nights, weekends and for part-time students.

Application procedures. Admission: No deadline. No application fee. Admission notification on a rolling basis. **Financial aid:** No deadline. FAFSA, institutional form required. Applicants notified on a rolling basis starting 4/15; must reply within 2 week(s) of notification.

Academics. Special study options: Cooperative education, cross-registration, distance learning, dual enrollment of high school students, ESL, honors, independent study, internships, student-designed major. License preparation in nursing. **Credit/placement by examination:** AP, CLEP, institutional tests. 45 credit hours maximum toward associate degree. **Support services:** GED preparation and test center, learning center, pre-admission summer program, reduced course load, remedial instruction, study skills assistance, tutoring.

Majors. Biology: General. **Business:** General, accounting, administrative services, business admin, office management, office technology, office/clerical, operations. **Communications:** General. **Computer sciences:** Data processing, networking, programming, web page design, webmaster. **Education:** General, business, early childhood, elementary, middle, secondary. **Engineering:** General, electrical. **Health services:** Clinical lab science, medical secretary, nursing (RN), predental, premedicine, prepharmacy, respiratory therapy technology. **Human services:** Social work. **Liberal arts:** Arts/sciences. **Protective services:** Law enforcement admin, police science. **Psychology:** General. **Social sciences:** General, criminology. **Work/family studies:** Child care management.

Most popular majors. Business/marketing 16%, education 6%, health sciences 25%, liberal arts 23%, security/protective services 7%, trade and industry 7%.

Computing on campus. 90 workstations in library, computer center. Online course registration, online library, helpline, wireless network available.

Student life. Freshman orientation: Mandatory. Preregistration for classes offered. Half-day program designed to introduce new students to important policies and procedures, campus resources, college success skills. **Activities:** Choral groups, dance, international student organizations, literary magazine, student government, student newspaper.

Athletics. Intercollegiate: Basketball M, soccer. **Intramural:** Basketball M. **Team name:** Ravens.

Student services. Career counseling, services for economically disadvantaged, student employment services, on-campus daycare, personal counseling, placement for graduates, veterans' counselor. **Physically disabled:** Services for visually, hearing impaired. **Transfer:** Transfer center, transfer adviser, college fairs on campus for students transferring to 4-year colleges.

Contact. E-mail: admissions@racc.edu
Phone: (610) 607-6224 Toll-free number: (800) 626-1665
Fax: (610) 607-6238
Calley Stevens Taylor, Director of Enrollment Services, Reading Area Community College, 10 South Second Street, Reading, PA 19603-1706

Rosedale Technical Institute
Pittsburgh, Pennsylvania
www.rosedaletech.org   CB code: 3025

- Private 2-year technical and career college
- Commuter campus in large city
- Interview required

General. Accredited by ACCSC. **Enrollment:** 251 degree-seeking undergraduates. **Degrees:** 122 associate awarded. **Calendar:** Differs by program, extensive summer session. **Full-time faculty:** 22 total. **Part-time faculty:** 6 total.

Basis for selection. Open admission, but selective for some programs. High school diploma or equivalency required. General knowledge test used in admissions process, and interview is required. Applicants to automotive and diesel programs must be eligible for valid driver's license prior to graduation. Wonderlic exam required for admissions.

2011-2012 Annual costs. Tuition/fees: $12,230. Cost of total program: $24,160 for tuition plus books (vary based on program) and tools (vary based on program). Books/supplies: $2,400.

Financial aid. Need-based: Work-study available nights, weekends and for part-time students.

Application procedures. Admission: No deadline. $20 fee. Admission notification on a rolling basis. **Financial aid:** Closing date 8/1. FAFSA required.

Academics. Credit/placement by examination: AP, CLEP. **Support services:** Learning center, study skills assistance, tutoring.

Computing on campus. 25 workstations in library, computer center. Online library, wireless network available.

Student life. Freshman orientation: Mandatory. Preregistration for classes offered. Held 2 weeks prior to start of classes. **Activities:** Student newspaper.

Student services. Career counseling, student employment services, financial aid counseling, legal services, personal counseling, placement for graduates.

Contact. E-mail: admissions@rosedaletech.org
Phone: (412) 521-6200 Toll-free number: (800) 521-6262
Fax: (412) 521-2520
Debbie Bier, Director of Admissions, Rosedale Technical Institute, 215 Beecham Drive, Pittsburgh, PA 15205-9791

Sanford-Brown Institute: Monroeville
Pittsburgh, Pennsylvania
www.sanfordbrown.edu   CB code: 2939

- For-profit 2-year health science and career college
- Commuter campus in large town
- Interview required

General. Accredited by ACCSC. **Degrees:** 165 associate awarded. **Calendar:** Differs by program. **Full-time faculty:** 25 total. **Part-time faculty:** 8 total.

Basis for selection. Open admission, but selective for some programs. Assessment test and additional requirements relative to program. **Home schooled:** Statement describing home school structure and mission, transcript of courses and grades, state high school equivalency certificate, interview required.

Financial aid. Need-based: Need-based aid available for part-time students. Work-study available nights, weekends and for part-time students.

Application procedures. Admission: No deadline. $25 fee. Admission notification on a rolling basis. **Financial aid:** No deadline. Applicants notified on a rolling basis.

Academics. Special study options: Distance learning, internships. License preparation in paramedic. **Credit/placement by examination:** AP, CLEP. **Support services:** Learning center, study skills assistance, tutoring.

Majors. Health services: EMT ambulance attendant, office computer specialist, pharmacy assistant, respiratory therapy technology, surgical technology.

Computing on campus. 75 workstations in library, computer center. Online course registration available.

Contact. Phone: (412) 373-6400 Toll-free number: (800) 622-1394
Fax: (412) 374-0863
Jason Stack, Director of Admission, Sanford-Brown Institute: Monroeville, 777 Penn Center Boulevard, Pittsburgh, PA 15235

Sanford-Brown Institute: Pittsburgh
Pittsburgh, Pennsylvania
www.westernschoolpitt.com   CB code: 2933

- For-profit 2-year technical college
- Very large city

General. Accredited by ACCSCT. **Location:** Downtown. **Calendar:** Differs by program.

Annual costs/financial aid. Need-based financial aid available for full-time students.

Contact. Phone: (800) 333-6607
Director of Admissions, 421 Seventh Avenue, Pittsburgh, PA 15219

South Hills School of Business & Technology
State College, Pennsylvania
www.southhills.edu   CB code: 2467

- For-profit 2-year business and technical college
- Commuter campus in large town

General. Founded in 1970. Regionally accredited. **Location:** 125 miles from Pittsburgh, 200 miles from Philadelphia. **Calendar:** Quarter.

Annual costs/financial aid. Tuition/fees (2011-2012): $14,961. Diagnostic Medical Sonography tuition: first year $14,856; 2nd year $15,936; 3rd yr $17,886. Engineering Technology tuition $15,456 per year. Activity fee $35 per term. Books/supplies: $2,400. Need-based financial aid available to full-time and part-time students.

Contact. Phone: (814) 234-7755
Director of Admissions, 480 Waupelani Drive, State College, PA 16801-4516

Thaddeus Stevens College of Technology
Lancaster, Pennsylvania
www.stevenscollege.edu   CB code: 0560

▶ Public 2-year technical and career college
▶ Residential campus in small city

General. Founded in 1905. Regionally accredited. **Location:** 60 miles from Philadelphia, 30 miles from Harrisburg. **Calendar:** Semester.

Annual costs/financial aid. Tuition/fees (2011-2012): $6,830; $6,830 out-of-state. Room/board: $7,900. Books/supplies: $500. Personal expenses: $300.

Contact. Phone: (717) 299-7701
Director of Enrollment Services, 750 East King Street, Lancaster, PA 17602

Triangle Tech: Bethlehem
Bethlehem, Pennsylvania
www.triangle-tech.edu

▶ For-profit 2-year branch campus and technical college
▶ Commuter campus in small city
▶ Interview required

General. Regionally accredited; also accredited by ACCSC. **Enrollment:** 116 degree-seeking undergraduates. **Degrees:** 69 associate awarded. **Calendar:** Semester, extensive summer session. **Full-time faculty:** 11 total; 9% women. **Part-time faculty:** 1 total. **Class size:** 89% < 20, 11% 20-39.

Student profile. Among degree-seeking undergraduates, 100% enrolled in a vocational program, 1% already have a bachelor's degree or higher, 63 enrolled as first-time, first-year students.

Out-of-state:	12%	Asian American:	1%
Women:	2%	Hispanic American:	13%
African American:	10%	25 or older:	24%

Transfer out. 5% of students enrolled in the transfer program go on to 4-year colleges.

Basis for selection. Open admission. School tour required. **Home schooled:** State high school equivalency certificate required.

High school preparation. Recommended units include mathematics 3.

2010-2011 Financial aid. Need-based: 102 full-time freshmen applied for aid; 102 were judged to have need; 102 of these received aid. Average need met was 72%. Average scholarship/grant was $6,663; average loan $4,186. 53% of total undergraduate aid awarded as scholarships/grants, 47% as loans/jobs. Need-based aid available for part-time students. Work-study available nights, weekends and for part-time students. **Non-need-based:** Awarded to 32 full-time undergraduates, including 22 freshmen.

Application procedures. Admission: No deadline. No application fee. Admission notification on a rolling basis. **Financial aid:** No deadline. FAFSA required. Applicants notified on a rolling basis.

Academics. Credit/placement by examination: AP, CLEP, institutional tests. **Support services:** Learning center, remedial instruction, study skills assistance, tutoring.

Computing on campus. 55 workstations in library, computer center.

Student life. Freshman orientation: Mandatory. Preregistration for classes offered.

Student services. Career counseling, financial aid counseling. **Transfer:** Re-entry adviser, pre-admission transcript evaluation for new students. Transfer center, transfer adviser, college fairs on campus for students transferring to 4-year colleges.

Contact. Phone: (610) 266-2910 Toll-free number: (800) 874-8324 Fax: (610) 266-2911
Jason Vallozzi, Executive Director of Admissions, Triangle Tech: Bethlehem, 3184 Airport Road, Bethlehem, PA 18017

Triangle Tech: DuBois
DuBois, Pennsylvania
www.triangle-tech.edu   CB code: 7133

▶ For-profit 2-year technical college
▶ Commuter campus in large town
▶ Interview required

General. Accredited by ACCSC. **Enrollment:** 217 degree-seeking undergraduates. **Degrees:** 229 associate awarded. **Location:** 145 miles from Pittsburgh. **Calendar:** Semester, extensive summer session. **Full-time faculty:** 19 total; 32% women. **Class size:** 100% < 20.

Student profile. Among degree-seeking undergraduates, 100% enrolled in a vocational program, 1% already have a bachelor's degree or higher, 98 enrolled as first-time, first-year students, 1 transferred in from other institutions.

Women:	3%	25 or older:	36%

Transfer out. 1% of students enrolled in the transfer program go on to 4-year colleges.

Basis for selection. Open admission. **Home schooled:** State high school equivalency certificate required.

High school preparation. Recommended units include English 4 and mathematics 4.

2012-2013 Annual costs. Tuition/fees (projected): $16,437. Per-credit charge: $446. Books/supplies: $1,431. Personal expenses: $5,010.

2010-2011 Financial aid. All financial aid based on need. 86 full-time freshmen applied for aid; 83 were judged to have need; 83 of these received aid. Average need met was 24%. Average scholarship/grant was $3,248; average loan $1,582. 48% of total undergraduate aid awarded as scholarships/grants, 52% as loans/jobs. Need-based aid available for part-time students. Work-study available nights, weekends and for part-time students.

Application procedures. Admission: No deadline. No application fee. Admission notification on a rolling basis. **Financial aid:** No deadline. FAFSA, institutional form required. Applicants notified on a rolling basis.

Academics. Special study options: Dual enrollment of high school students. **Credit/placement by examination:** AP, CLEP. **Support services:** Learning center, remedial instruction, study skills assistance, tutoring.

Most popular majors. Engineering/engineering technologies 7%, trade and industry 92%.

Computing on campus. 55 workstations in library, computer center.

Student life. Freshman orientation: Mandatory. Preregistration for classes offered. Held the Thursday before classes begin, approximately 1-1/2 hours. **Activities:** Student government.

Student services. Career counseling, student employment services, financial aid counseling, placement for graduates. **Transfer:** Pre-admission transcript evaluation for new students.

Contact. E-mail: scraig@triangle-tech.edu
Phone: (814) 371-2090 Toll-free number: (800) 874-8324 Fax: (814) 371-9227
Terry Kucic, Director of Admissions, Triangle Tech: DuBois, PO Box 551, DuBois, PA 15801-0551

Triangle Tech: Erie
Erie, Pennsylvania
www.triangle-tech.edu   CB code: 1572

▶ For-profit 2-year technical and career college
▶ Commuter campus in small city
▶ Interview required

General. Founded in 1976. Accredited by ACCSC. **Enrollment:** 104 degree-seeking undergraduates. **Degrees:** 114 associate awarded. **Location:** 100 miles from Pittsburgh, Cleveland, and Buffalo. **Calendar:** Semester, extensive summer session. **Full-time faculty:** 14 total; 14% women. **Part-time faculty:** 14 total; 14% women.

Student profile. Among degree-seeking undergraduates, 100% enrolled in a vocational program, 31 enrolled as first-time, first-year students.

Out-of-state:	3%	African American:	14%
Women:	3%	25 or older:	51%

Basis for selection. Open admission.

2011-2012 Annual costs. Books/supplies: $1,150. Personal expenses: $1,608.

2010-2011 Financial aid. All financial aid based on need. 143 full-time freshmen applied for aid; 135 were judged to have need; 135 of these received aid. 55% of total undergraduate aid awarded as scholarships/grants, 45% as loans/jobs. Need-based aid available for part-time students. Work-study available nights, weekends and for part-time students.

Application procedures. Admission: No deadline. $75 fee. Admission notification on a rolling basis. **Financial aid:** No deadline. FAFSA required. Applicants notified on a rolling basis.

Academics. Credit/placement by examination: AP, CLEP, institutional tests. **Support services:** Remedial instruction, study skills assistance, tutoring.

Most popular majors. Engineering/engineering technologies 18%, trade and industry 82%.

Computing on campus. 63 workstations in computer center.

Student life. Freshman orientation: Mandatory. Preregistration for classes offered. **Activities:** Student government, student newspaper.

Student services. Career counseling, student employment services, financial aid counseling, personal counseling, placement for graduates. **Transfer:** Re-entry adviser, pre-admission transcript evaluation for new students. Transfer adviser for students transferring to 4-year colleges.

Contact. Phone: (814) 453-6016 Fax: (814) 454-2818
Jason Vallozzi, Executive Director of Admissions, Triangle Tech: Erie, 2000 Liberty Street, Erie, PA 16502-2594

Triangle Tech: Greensburg
Greensburg, Pennsylvania
www.triangle-tech.edu   **CB code: 0658**

- For-profit 2-year technical college
- Commuter campus in large town
- Interview required

General. Founded in 1944. Accredited by ACCSC. **Enrollment:** 198 degree-seeking undergraduates. **Degrees:** 181 associate awarded. **Location:** 40 miles from Pittsburgh. **Calendar:** Semester, extensive summer session. **Full-time faculty:** 19 total; 10% women. **Class size:** 100% < 20.

Student profile. Among degree-seeking undergraduates, 100% enrolled in a vocational program, 1% already have a bachelor's degree or higher, 135 enrolled as first-time, first-year students.

Women:	2%	25 or older:	40%
African American:	3%		

Transfer out. 1% of students enrolled in the transfer program go on to 4-year colleges.

Basis for selection. Open admission.

2011-2012 Annual costs. Books/supplies: $1,176. Personal expenses: $1,608.

2010-2011 Financial aid. Need-based: 165 full-time freshmen applied for aid; 157 were judged to have need; 157 of these received aid. Average need met was 15%. Average scholarship/grant was $5,636; average loan $3,635. 52% of total undergraduate aid awarded as scholarships/grants, 48% as loans/jobs. Need-based aid available for part-time students. Work-study available nights, weekends and for part-time students. **Non-need-based:** Awarded to 3 full-time undergraduates, including 1 freshmen.

Application procedures. Admission: No deadline. No application fee. Admission notification on a rolling basis. **Financial aid:** No deadline. FAFSA, institutional form required. Applicants notified on a rolling basis starting 1/1.

Academics. Credit/placement by examination: AP, CLEP, institutional tests. **Support services:** Learning center, remedial instruction, study skills assistance, tutoring.

Most popular majors. Engineering/engineering technologies 37%, trade and industry 63%.

Computing on campus. 52 workstations in library, computer center.

Student life. Freshman orientation: Mandatory. Preregistration for classes offered. **Activities:** Student government.

Student services. Career counseling, student employment services, personal counseling, placement for graduates, veterans' counselor. **Transfer:** Re-entry adviser, pre-admission transcript evaluation for new students. Transfer adviser for students transferring to 4-year colleges.

Contact. Phone: (724) 832-1050 Toll-free number: (800) 874-8324
Fax: (724) 834-0325
Jason Vallozzi, Director of Admissions, Triangle Tech: Greensburg, 222 East Pittsburgh Street, Suite A, Greensburg, PA 15601-3304

Triangle Tech: Pittsburgh
Pittsburgh, Pennsylvania
www.triangle-tech.edu   **CB code: 0734**

- For-profit 2-year technical college
- Commuter campus in large city
- Interview required

General. Founded in 1944. Accredited by ACCSC. **Enrollment:** 281 degree-seeking undergraduates; 5 non-degree-seeking students. **Degrees:** 165 associate awarded. **Location:** 5 miles from downtown. **Calendar:** Semester, extensive summer session. **Full-time faculty:** 23 total; 4% minority. **Class size:** 90% < 20, 10% 20-39.

Student profile. Among degree-seeking undergraduates, 1% already have a bachelor's degree or higher, 102 enrolled as first-time, first-year students.

Out-of-state:	2%	African American:	25%
Women:	4%	25 or older:	41%

Transfer out. Colleges most students transferred to 2011: Point Park University, Robert Morris University, Edinboro University, Slippery Rock University, University of Pittsburgh.

Basis for selection. Open admission, but selective for some programs. Must have high school diploma or GED. Applicants must take TABE test for placement. **Home schooled:** Transcript of courses and grades, state high school equivalency certificate required.

2011-2012 Annual costs. Books/supplies: $1,315. Personal expenses: $1,608.

2010-2011 Financial aid. Need-based: 184 full-time freshmen applied for aid; 178 were judged to have need; 178 of these received aid. Average need met was 15%. Average scholarship/grant was $6,769; average loan $3,904. 52% of total undergraduate aid awarded as scholarships/grants, 48% as loans/jobs. Need-based aid available for part-time students. Work-study available nights, weekends and for part-time students. **Non-need-based:** Awarded to 41 full-time undergraduates, including 32 freshmen. Scholarships awarded for academics, state residency.

Application procedures. Admission: No deadline. $75 fee. Admission notification on a rolling basis. **Financial aid:** No deadline. FAFSA, institutional form required. Applicants notified on a rolling basis.

Academics. Credit/placement by examination: AP, CLEP, institutional tests. 36 credit hours maximum toward associate degree. **Support services:** Learning center, remedial instruction, study skills assistance, tutoring.

Computing on campus. 46 workstations in library, computer center. Online library available.

Student life. Freshman orientation: Mandatory. Preregistration for classes offered. Held approximately 5 days prior to start; about 2-1/2 hours long. **Activities:** Student government.

Student services. Career counseling, student employment services, financial aid counseling, personal counseling, placement for graduates. **Transfer:** Pre-admission transcript evaluation for new students. College fairs on campus for students transferring to 4-year colleges.

Contact. E-mail: info@triangle-tech.edu
Phone: (412) 359-1000 Toll-free number: (800) 874-8324
Fax: (412) 359-1012
Jason Vallozzi, Director of Admissions, Triangle Tech: Pittsburgh, 1940 Perrysville Avenue, Pittsburgh, PA 15214-3897

Triangle Tech: Sunbury
Sunbury, Pennsylvania
www.triangle-tech.edu

- For-profit 2-year technical college
- Commuter campus in large town
- Interview required

General. Accredited by ACCSC. **Enrollment:** 110 degree-seeking undergraduates. **Degrees:** 121 associate awarded. **Calendar:** Semester. **Full-time faculty:** 12 total; 17% women. **Class size:** 100% < 20.

Student profile. Among degree-seeking undergraduates, 100% enrolled in a vocational program, 63 enrolled as first-time, first-year students.

Women:	1%	25 or older:	41%

Basis for selection. Open admission.

2011-2012 Annual costs. Books/supplies: $1,034. Personal expenses: $1,608.

2010-2011 Financial aid. Need-based: 119 full-time freshmen applied for aid; 113 were judged to have need; 113 of these received aid. Average need met was 98%. Average scholarship/grant was $6,658; average loan $3,974. 49% of total undergraduate aid awarded as scholarships/grants, 51% as loans/jobs. Need-based aid available for part-time students. Work-study available nights, weekends and for part-time students. **Non-need-based:** Awarded to 31 full-time undergraduates, including 28 freshmen.

Application procedures. Admission: No deadline. No application fee. Admission notification on a rolling basis. **Financial aid:** No deadline. FAFSA, institutional form required. Applicants notified on a rolling basis.

Academics. Credit/placement by examination: AP, CLEP, institutional tests. **Support services:** Tutoring.

Computing on campus. 27 workstations in library, computer center.

Student life. Freshman orientation: Mandatory. Preregistration for classes offered.

Student services. Adult student services, student employment services, financial aid counseling, placement for graduates.

Contact. E-mail: jdrumm@triangle-tech.edu
Phone: (570) 988-0700 Toll-free number: (800) 874-8324
Fax: (570) 988-4641
Jason Vallozzi, Vice President of Admissions, Triangle Tech: Sunbury, 191 Performance Road, Sunbury, PA 17801

University of Pittsburgh at Titusville
Titusville, Pennsylvania
www.upt.pitt.edu   CB code: 2937

- Public 2-year branch campus and liberal arts college
- Residential campus in small town
- SAT or ACT (ACT writing optional) required

General. Founded in 1963. Regionally accredited. **Enrollment:** 446 degree-seeking undergraduates; 17 non-degree-seeking students. **Degrees:** 59 associate awarded. **Location:** 100 miles from Pittsburgh, 50 miles from Erie. **Calendar:** Semester, limited summer session. **Full-time faculty:** 20 total. **Part-time faculty:** 40 total. **Class size:** 61% < 20, 36% 20-39, 3% 40-49.

Student profile. Among degree-seeking undergraduates, 181 enrolled as first-time, first-year students, 30 transferred in from other institutions.

Part-time:	13%	Asian American:	2%
Out-of-state:	12%	Hispanic American:	3%
Women:	62%	Live on campus:	55%
African American:	22%		

Transfer out. Colleges most students transferred to 2011: Clarion University, Edinboro University, Indiana University of Pennsylvania, Penn State University, Slippery Rock University of Pennsylvania.

Basis for selection. Decisions based on academic performance. Applicants deserving additional consideration referred to Admissions Committee. SAT recommended. Essay, interview recommended. **Adult students:** SAT/ACT scores not required if out of high school 1 year(s) or more. **Home schooled:** Math/English placement tests required. **Learning Disabled:** Students with disabilities asked to provide comprehensive documentation to Disability Resources and Services representative to establish eligibility for accommodations.

High school preparation. College-preparatory program recommended. 15 units required. Required and recommended units include English 4, mathematics 2, science 1 (laboratory 1), foreign language 3 and academic electives 7. One unit lab science required.

2011-2012 Annual costs. Tuition/fees: $11,118; $20,308 out-of-state. Per-credit charge: $430 in-state; $813 out-of-state. Room/board: $8,922. Books/supplies: $1,110. Personal expenses: $1,660.

2010-2011 Financial aid. Need-based: 171 full-time freshmen applied for aid; 159 were judged to have need; 159 of these received aid. Average need met was 80%. Average scholarship/grant was $6,763; average loan $3,071. 45% of total undergraduate aid awarded as scholarships/grants, 55% as loans/jobs. Need-based aid available for part-time students. Work-study available nights, weekends and for part-time students. **Non-need-based:** Awarded to 447 full-time undergraduates, including 170 freshmen. Scholarships awarded for academics, athletics, state residency.

Application procedures. Admission: No deadline. $45 fee, may be waived for applicants with need. Admission notification on a rolling basis beginning on or about 11/1. **Financial aid:** Priority date 3/1; no closing date. FAFSA required. Applicants notified on a rolling basis starting 4/1; must reply within 2 week(s) of notification.

Academics. Special study options: Cross-registration, distance learning, dual enrollment of high school students, independent study, internships. Bachelor's degree programs available on campus. License preparation in nursing. **Credit/placement by examination:** AP, CLEP, SAT, ACT, institutional tests. 6 credit hours maximum toward associate degree. **Support services:** Learning center, reduced course load, remedial instruction, study skills assistance, tutoring.

Majors. Business: General, accounting, management information systems. **Health services:** Nursing (RN), physical therapy assistant. **Liberal arts:** Arts/sciences. **Work/family studies:** General.

Most popular majors. Biological/life sciences 17%, business/marketing 15%, health sciences 51%, liberal arts 14%.

Computing on campus. 62 workstations in dormitories, library, computer center, student center. Dormitories wired for high-speed internet access and linked to campus network. Commuter students can connect to campus network. Online course registration, online library, helpline, student web hosting, wireless network available.

Student life. Freshman orientation: Mandatory, $60 fee. Preregistration for classes offered. Held weekend (Thursday through Sunday) prior to start of fall semester; includes freshman services, projects, activities. **Policies:** Organizations must complete 1 community service and fundraising activity per year to receive student activity funding. **Housing:** Guaranteed on-campus for all undergraduates. Coed dorms, special housing for disabled available. $100 nonrefundable deposit. Townhouse apartments without cooking facilities available. **Activities:** Campus ministries, student government, diversity club, Students in Free Enterprise, commuter student association, Alpha Omega Christian fellowship, Phi Theta Kappa, student activities board, chemistry club, student physical therapy association, College Republicans.

Athletics. USCAA. **Intercollegiate:** Basketball. **Intramural:** Basketball, bowling, football (tackle), golf, racquetball, skiing, soccer, softball, table tennis, tennis, volleyball. **Team name:** Panthers.

Student services. Adult student services, alcohol/substance abuse counseling, career counseling, student employment services, financial aid counseling, health services, minority student services, personal counseling, placement for graduates, veterans' counselor. **Physically disabled:** Services for visually impaired. **Transfer:** Pre-admission transcript evaluation for new students. Transfer adviser, college fairs on campus for students transferring to 4-year colleges.

Contact. E-mail: uptadm@pitt.edu
Phone: (814) 827-4509 Toll-free number: (888) 878-0462
Fax: (814) 827-4519
John Mumford, Executive Director of Enrollment Management, University of Pittsburgh at Titusville, UPT Admissions Office, Titusville, PA 16354-0287

Valley Forge Military Academy and College
Wayne, Pennsylvania   **CB member**
www.vfmac.edu   **CB code: 2955**

- Private 2-year junior and military college
- Residential campus in small city
- SAT or ACT (ACT writing optional) required

General. Founded in 1928. Regionally accredited. One of only 5 military junior colleges in nation offering Army ROTC early commissioning program leading to commission as second lieutenant in U.S. Army Reserve at end of second year. Regimental marching band, drum and bugle corps, regimental choir. **Enrollment:** 248 degree-seeking undergraduates; 79 non-degree-seeking students. **Degrees:** 47 associate awarded. **ROTC:** Army, Air Force. **Location:** 15 miles from Philadelphia. **Calendar:** Semester, limited summer session. **Full-time faculty:** 18 total. **Part-time faculty:** 4 total. **Special facilities:** Motorized artillery unit, mounted cavalry troop, aviation training.

Student profile. Among degree-seeking undergraduates, 248 enrolled as first-time, first-year students.

Out-of-state:	69%	Live on campus:	100%
Women:	15%		

Transfer out. Colleges most students transferred to 2011: Lehigh University, Villanova University, Drexel University, The Citadel, George Mason University.

Basis for selection. School achievement record, test scores, and personal character most important. 2.0 GPA or higher and SAT score of 800 or higher or ACT score of 17 or higher required for admission. TOEFL score accepted in lieu of SAT or ACT scores for international students. Interview recommended. **Home schooled:** Statement describing home school structure and mission, transcript of courses and grades, interview, letter of recommendation (nonparent) required.

High school preparation. College-preparatory program recommended. Required and recommended units include English 4, mathematics 3, science 3 and foreign language 2.

2012-2013 Annual costs. Tuition/fees (projected): $31,355. Room/board: $11,145. Books/supplies: $1,000.

2011-2012 Financial aid. Need-based: Average need met was 66%. Average scholarship/grant was $18,463; average loan $3,718. 78% of total undergraduate aid awarded as scholarships/grants, 22% as loans/jobs. Work-study available nights, weekends and for part-time students. **Non-need-based:** Scholarships awarded for academics, alumni affiliation, athletics, music/drama, ROTC. **Additional information:** Students enrolled in advanced military science program can receive up to $5,000 from the Army. In addition, competitively awarded ROTC scholarships pay average of another $14,100 per school year for direct educational expenses.

Application procedures. Admission: No deadline. $25 fee, may be waived for applicants with need. Admission notification on a rolling basis. Must reply by May 1 or within 2 week(s) if notified thereafter. **Financial aid:** Closing date 5/1. FAFSA required. Applicants notified on a rolling basis starting 5/15; must reply within 2 week(s) of notification.

Academics. Special study options: Cross-registration, dual enrollment of high school students, ESL, study abroad. **Credit/placement by examination:** AP, CLEP, SAT, ACT, institutional tests. 15 credit hours maximum toward associate degree. **Support services:** Reduced course load, remedial instruction, writing center.

Majors. Business: General. **Engineering:** General, engineering science. **Liberal arts:** Arts/sciences. **Protective services:** Criminal justice.

Most popular majors. Business/marketing 26%, health sciences 9%, history 6%, legal studies 32%, liberal arts 17%, physical sciences 6%.

Computing on campus. PC or laptop required. 44 workstations in library, computer center. Dormitories wired for high-speed internet access and linked to campus network. Helpline, repair service, wireless network available.

Student life. Freshman orientation: Mandatory. Preregistration for classes offered. 3-day orientation with placement testing. **Policies:** Religious observance required. **Housing:** Guaranteed on-campus for all undergraduates. Single-sex dorms, wellness housing available. $1,000 partly refundable deposit, deadline 5/1. **Activities:** Bands, choral groups, drama, music ensembles, radio station, student government, student newspaper, Catholic Fellowship, Jewish Fellowship, Christian Fellowship, Muslim Fellowship, Young Republicans.

Athletics. Intercollegiate: Basketball M, cross-country M, equestrian M, football (tackle) M, lacrosse M, rifle M, soccer M, tennis M, wrestling M.

Intramural: Baseball M, basketball M, fencing M, football (tackle) M, golf M, judo M, rugby M, soccer M, softball M, volleyball M, water polo M, weight lifting M. **Team name:** Trojans.

Student services. Chaplain/spiritual director, career counseling, financial aid counseling, health services, personal counseling, placement for graduates. **Transfer:** Pre-admission transcript evaluation for new students. Transfer adviser for students transferring to 4-year colleges.

Contact. E-mail: admission@vfmac.edu
Phone: (610) 989-1300 Toll-free number: (800) 234-8362
Fax: (610) 688-1545
Mark Osborn, Director of Admissions, Valley Forge Military Academy and College, 1001 Eagle Road, Wayne, PA 19087

Vet Tech Institute
Pittsburgh, Pennsylvania
www.vettechinstitute.edu   **CB code: 7134**

- For-profit 2-year health science and technical college
- Commuter campus in large city

General. Accredited by ACCSC. Veterinary technician AVMA accredited. **Enrollment:** 340 degree-seeking undergraduates. **Degrees:** 171 associate awarded. **Calendar:** Semester. **Full-time faculty:** 9 total. **Part-time faculty:** 5 total. **Special facilities:** Animal tech rooms, on-site kennel.

Transfer out. Colleges most students transferred to 2011: Point Park College.

Basis for selection. Satisfactory performance on school admission test required. Essay, interview recommended.

2012-2013 Annual costs. Tuition/fees (projected): $14,116. Books/supplies: $750.

Financial aid. Need-based: Work-study available nights, weekends and for part-time students. **Non-need-based:** Scholarships awarded for academics.

Application procedures. Admission: No deadline. $50 fee. Admission notification on a rolling basis. **Financial aid:** No deadline. FAFSA required. Applicants notified on a rolling basis.

Academics. Special study options: Internships. **Credit/placement by examination:** AP, CLEP. **Support services:** Tutoring.

Majors. Health services: Veterinary technology/assistant.

Computing on campus. 38 workstations in library, computer center.

Student life. Freshman orientation: Mandatory. Preregistration for classes offered.

Student services. Career counseling, student employment services, financial aid counseling, placement for graduates.

Contact. E-mail: admissions@vettechinstitute.edu
Phone: (412) 391-7021 Toll-free number: (800) 570-0693
Fax: (412) 232-4348
Terry Taylor, Senior Admissions Coordinator, Vet Tech Institute, 125 Seventh Street, Pittsburgh, PA 15222-3400

Westmoreland County Community College
Youngwood, Pennsylvania
www.wccc.edu   **CB code: 2968**

- Public 2-year community college
- Commuter campus in small town

General. Founded in 1970. Regionally accredited. **Enrollment:** 6,249 degree-seeking undergraduates; 694 non-degree-seeking students. **Degrees:** 658 associate awarded. **Location:** 30 miles from Pittsburgh. **Calendar:** Semester, limited summer session. **Full-time faculty:** 90 total; 4% minority, 53% women. **Part-time faculty:** 459 total; 2% minority, 54% women. **Class size:** 69% < 20, 31% 20-39. **Special facilities:** Culinary arts kitchens, greenhouse, student lounges, theater.

Student profile. Among degree-seeking undergraduates, 20% enrolled in a transfer program, 80% enrolled in a vocational program, 1,746 enrolled as first-time, first-year students.

Part-time:	49%	Asian American:	1%
Women:	63%	Hispanic American:	1%
African American:	4%	25 or older:	40%

Transfer out. Colleges most students transferred to 2011: University of Pittsburgh, Indiana University of Pennsylvania, California University of Pennsylvania, Seton Hill University, St. Vincent College.

Basis for selection. Open admission, but selective for some programs. Allied Health program applicants required to take Comparative Guidance and Placement test, submit application by November 30 of the year prior to enrollment, and satisfactory results from pre-entrance physicals. Interview recommended.

2011-2012 Annual costs. Tuition/fees: $2,910; $5,310 out-of-district; $7,710 out-of-state. Per-credit charge: $80 in-district; $160 out-of-district; $240 out-of-state. Books/supplies: $1,300. Personal expenses: $1,300.

Financial aid. Need-based: Need-based aid available for part-time students. Work-study available nights, weekends and for part-time students. **Non-need-based:** Scholarships awarded for academics.

Application procedures. Admission: No deadline. $15 fee, may be waived for applicants with need. Admission notification on a rolling basis. **Financial aid:** No deadline. FAFSA, institutional form required. Applicants notified on a rolling basis starting 5/1.

Academics. Special study options: Accelerated study, cooperative education, cross-registration, distance learning, double major, dual enrollment of high school students, honors, independent study, internships, student-designed major, study abroad. License preparation in dental hygiene, nursing, radiology, real estate. **Credit/placement by examination:** AP, CLEP, institutional tests. 30 credit hours maximum toward associate degree. **Support services:** GED preparation and test center, learning center, remedial instruction, study skills assistance, tutoring, writing center.

Majors. Business: Accounting technology, administrative services, banking/financial services, business admin, executive assistant, hotel/motel admin, human resources, marketing, real estate, tourism/travel. **Communications technology:** Photo/film/video. **Computer sciences:** Computer science, database management, networking, programming, security, web page design. **General:** Floriculture, horticulture, turf management. **Health services:** Dental hygiene, dietetic technician, medical secretary, nursing (RN), radiologic technology/medical imaging. **Liberal arts:** Arts/sciences. **Protective services:** Criminal justice, fire safety technology. **Visual/performing arts:** Commercial/advertising art. **Work/family studies:** Child care service.

Most popular majors. Business/marketing 26%, computer/information sciences 10%, family/consumer sciences 6%, health sciences 43%, security/protective services 9%.

Computing on campus. 620 workstations in library, computer center. Commuter students can connect to campus network. Online course registration, online library, helpline, student web hosting, wireless network available.

Student life. Freshman orientation: Available. Preregistration for classes offered. **Policies:** All clubs required to complete 10 hours of community service per semester and send two representatives to each student government meeting twice monthly. **Activities:** Bands, choral groups, drama, literary magazine, musical theater, student government, student newspaper, symphony orchestra, cultural awareness coalition, Reach Out club, Republican club, human services club, Veteran's club.

Athletics. NJCAA. **Intercollegiate:** Baseball M, basketball, bowling, golf, softball W, volleyball W. **Intramural:** Baseball M, basketball, bowling, golf, skiing, soccer, softball, table tennis, volleyball. **Team name:** Wolfpack.

Student services. Career counseling, services for economically disadvantaged, student employment services, financial aid counseling, on-campus daycare, personal counseling, placement for graduates, veterans' counselor. **Physically disabled:** Services for visually, speech, hearing impaired. **Transfer:** Pre-admission transcript evaluation for new students. Transfer adviser, college fairs on campus for students transferring to 4-year colleges.

Contact. E-mail: admissions@wccc.edu
Phone: (724) 925-4077 Toll-free number: (800) 262-2103 ext. 4077
Fax: (724) 925-4292
Janice Grabowski, Director of Admissions, Westmoreland County Community College, 145 Pavilion Lane, Youngwood, PA 15697

Williamson Free School of Mechanical Trades
Media, Pennsylvania
www.williamson.edu   CB code: 0765

- Private 2-year technical college for men affiliated with nondenominational tradition
- Residential campus in large town
- Interview required

General. Founded in 1888. Accredited by ACCSC. Discipline-oriented school that prepares students through academic instruction and hands-on training in a structured environment; scholarship-only students. **Enrollment:** 260 degree-seeking undergraduates. **Degrees:** 76 associate awarded. **Location:** 14 miles from Philadelphia, 14 miles from Wilmington, Delaware. **Calendar:** Semester. **Full-time faculty:** 18 total. **Part-time faculty:** 15 total. **Class size:** 100% < 20. **Special facilities:** Natural arboretum.

Student profile.

Out-of-state:	25%	Live on campus:	100%

Basis for selection. Family financial need, average or better performance on entrance exam, and exceptional interview score. Applicants must be male US citizens and may not turn 20 years old prior to June 1st of year of admission. Armed Services Vocational Aptitude Battery required by application deadline. Essay recommended.

High school preparation. Math units must include algebra I and geometry. Science units should include chemistry and physics.

2012-2013 Annual costs. All students receive full scholarships covering tuition, room and board, and textbooks for the three-year program. Required fees for personal clothing and tools for the freshman year average $1,200.

Financial aid. Need-based: Work-study available nights, weekends and for part-time students.

Application procedures. Admission: Closing date 2/28 (postmark date). No application fee. Must reply by 5/14. **Financial aid:** No deadline.

Academics. Special study options: Cooperative education, internships. **Credit/placement by examination:** AP, CLEP, institutional tests. **Support services:** Pre-admission summer program, tutoring.

Majors. General: Horticulture, landscaping, turf management.

Most popular majors. Agriculture 14%, trade and industry 61%.

Computing on campus. 165 workstations in dormitories, library, computer center. Wireless network available.

Student life. Freshman orientation: Mandatory. Preregistration for classes offered. Takes place during the first 4 days of school and includes shop orientation, rules, classroom schedules, math testing. **Policies:** Student life carefully structured, including a standard daily schedule, dress code, required chapel, and clearly defined student responsibilities. Religious observance required. **Housing:** Guaranteed on-campus for all undergraduates. **Activities:** Jazz band, campus ministries, choral groups, student government, student newspaper, Fellowship of Christian Athletes, Campus Crusade for Christ, Bible study groups.

Athletics. NJCAA, USCAA. **Intercollegiate:** Baseball M, basketball M, cross-country M, football (tackle) M, lacrosse M, soccer M, tennis M, wrestling M. **Intramural:** Archery M. **Team name:** Mechanics.

Student services. Alcohol/substance abuse counseling, chaplain/spiritual director, career counseling, services for economically disadvantaged, student employment services, health services, personal counseling, placement for graduates.

Contact. E-mail: jmerillat@williamson.edu
Phone: (610) 566-1776 ext. 235 Fax: (610) 566-6502
Jay Merillat, Dean of Enrollments, Williamson Free School of Mechanical Trades, 106 South New Middletown Road, Media, PA 19063

Yorktowne Business Institute
York, Pennsylvania
www.ybi.edu   CB code: 2553

- For-profit 2-year business and health science college
- Commuter campus in small city

General. Founded in 1976. Accredited by ACICS. **Location:** 100 miles from Philadelphia, 50 miles from Baltimore. **Calendar:** Trimester.

Annual costs/financial aid. Books/supplies: $2,900. Personal expenses: $1,656. Need-based financial aid available to full-time and part-time students.

Contact. Phone: (717) 846-5000
Director of Admissions, West 7th Avenue, York, PA 17404-2034

YTI Career Institute: Altoona
Altoona, Pennsylvania
www.yti.edu

- For-profit 2-year technical and career college
- Commuter campus in small city

General. Regionally accredited; also accredited by ACCSC. **Enrollment:** 195 degree-seeking undergraduates; 102 non-degree-seeking students. **Degrees:** 49 associate awarded. **Calendar:** Quarter. **Full-time faculty:** 16 total; 69% women. **Part-time faculty:** 21 total; 19% women. **Special facilities:** Dental lab, medical assistant lab, pharmacy technician lab. **Partnerships:** Formal partnerships with local businesses to participate in a 12-week externship and/or a 4-5 week externship.

Student profile.

Women: 74%   **25 or older:** 5%

Basis for selection. Open admission, but selective for some programs. **Home schooled:** Transcript of courses and grades required.

Financial aid. Need-based: Work-study available nights, weekends and for part-time students.

Application procedures. Admission: No deadline. $50 fee. Application must be submitted on paper.

Academics. Credit/placement by examination: AP, CLEP.

Majors. Business: Business admin. **Health services:** Medical assistant. **Protective services:** Criminal justice.

Most popular majors. Health sciences 53%.

Contact. E-mail: altoonaadmission@yti.edu
Phone: (814) 944-5643 Toll-free number: (800) 795-0971
Fax: (814) 944-5309
Natalie Lombardo, Director of Admissions, YTI Career Institute: Altoona, 2900 Fairway Drive, Altoona, PA 16602

YTI Career Institute: Capital Region
Mechanicsburg, Pennsylvania
www.yti.edu

- For-profit 2-year career college
- Small town

General. Regionally accredited; also accredited by ACCSC. **Enrollment:** 97 degree-seeking undergraduates. **Degrees:** 53 associate awarded. **Calendar:** Differs by program. **Full-time faculty:** 22 total. **Part-time faculty:** 22 total.

Basis for selection. Open admission, but selective for some programs.

2011-2012 Annual costs. Tuition/fees: $12,050. Per-credit charge: $260. Books/supplies: $1,700. Personal expenses: $2,850.

Financial aid. Need-based: Work-study available nights, weekends and for part-time students.

Application procedures. Admission: $50 fee.

Academics. Credit/placement by examination: AP, CLEP. **Support services:** Learning center, study skills assistance, tutoring.

Majors. Computer sciences: Security. **Health services:** Medical assistant.

Contact. Phone: (800) 338-8037 Fax: (717) 761-0558
David Profita, Director of Admissions, YTI Career Institute: Capital Region, 401 East Winding Hill Road, Suite 101, Mechanicsburg, PA 17055

YTI Career Institute: Lancaster
Lancaster, Pennsylvania
www.yti.edu

- For-profit 2-year technical and career college
- Commuter campus in small city
- Interview required

General. Accredited by ACCSC. **Enrollment:** 531 degree-seeking undergraduates. **Degrees:** 268 associate awarded. **Calendar:** Quarter. **Full-time faculty:** 47 total. **Part-time faculty:** 22 total. **Class size:** 77% < 20, 23% 20-39.

Basis for selection. Open admission, but selective for some programs. Medical Assistant programs require criminal background check and health information form completed by certified physician to include documentation for Hepatitis B and TB immunizations. Dental Assisting Program requires verification of Hepatitis B vaccination. Criminal Justice and First Response program requires background/record check, valid driver's license, and applicants must be at least 18 years of age at time of matriculation. COMPASS used for placement.

2011-2012 Annual costs. Diploma programs: $13,464 to $20,000; associate degree programs: $25,620 to $35,000. Additional supply costs of $1,400 to $3,500 may apply, depending on program. Books/supplies: $1,800. Personal expenses: $899.

Financial aid. Need-based: Work-study available nights, weekends and for part-time students.

Application procedures. Admission: No deadline. $50 fee.

Academics. Special study options: Internships. License preparation in radiology. **Credit/placement by examination:** AP, CLEP. **Support services:** Learning center, tutoring.

Majors. Health services: Medical assistant. **Protective services:** Law enforcement admin.

Contact. Phone: (717) 295-1100 Toll-free number: (866) 984-5262
Fax: (717) 295-1135
Diane Merino, Director of Admissions, YTI Career Institute: Lancaster, 3050 Hempland Road, Lancaster, PA 17601

YTI Career Institute: York
York, Pennsylvania
www.yti.edu   CB code: 2943

- For-profit 2-year technical and career college
- Commuter campus in small city

General. Candidate for regional accreditation; also accredited by ACCSC. **Enrollment:** 665 degree-seeking undergraduates. **Degrees:** 281 associate awarded. **Calendar:** Quarter. **Full-time faculty:** 56 total. **Part-time faculty:** 15 total.

Basis for selection. Open admission, but selective for some programs. Medical Assistant programs require criminal background check and health information form completed by certified physician to include documentation for Hepatitis B and TB immunizations. Heating, Air Conditioning & Refrigeration Technology and Electrical Technology programs must pass a preliminary criminal background check and possess a valid driver's license. Motorsports Technology program must have a valid motorcycle license or permit. COMPASS used for placement.

2011-2012 Annual costs. Diploma programs: $13,500 to $16,640; associate degree programs: $25,000 to $35,000. Additional supply costs of $1,700 to $3,400 may apply, depending on program. Personal expenses: $2,097.

Financial aid. Need-based: Work-study available nights, weekends and for part-time students.

Application procedures. Admission: No deadline. $50 fee. Admission notification on a rolling basis.

Academics. Special study options: Internships. **Credit/placement by examination:** AP, CLEP, institutional tests. **Support services:** Remedial instruction, study skills assistance, tutoring.

Majors. Business: Accounting, business admin, hospitality admin, marketing. **Computer sciences:** Systems analysis. **Health services:** Medical assistant. **Parks/recreation:** Golf management. **Protective services:** Law enforcement admin, police science, security services.

Computing on campus. 250 workstations in library, computer center. Commuter students can connect to campus network. Helpline, repair service, wireless network available.

Student life. Freshman orientation: Mandatory. Preregistration for classes offered. **Housing:** Apartments available.

Student services. Adult student services, career counseling, student employment services, financial aid counseling, placement for graduates. **Transfer:** Re-entry adviser, pre-admission transcript evaluation for new students. Transfer adviser for students transferring to 4-year colleges.

Contact. E-mail: todd.harlow@yti.edu
Phone: (717) 757-1100 Toll-free number: (800) 227-9675
Fax: (717) 757-4964
Todd Harlow, Director of Admissions, YTI Career Institute: York, 1405 Williams Road, York, PA 17402

Puerto Rico

Centro de Estudios Multidisciplinarios
San Juan, Puerto Rico
www.cempr.edu

- Private 2-year health science college
- Large city

General. Accredited by ACCSC. **Enrollment:** 1,260 full-time, degree-seeking students. **Degrees:** 191 associate awarded. **Calendar:** Quarter. **Full-time faculty:** 6 total. **Part-time faculty:** 85 total.

Basis for selection. Open admission.

Financial aid. Need-based: Work-study available nights, weekends and for part-time students.

Application procedures. Admission: No deadline. $30 fee.

Academics. Credit/placement by examination: AP, CLEP.

Majors. Health services: Nursing (RN), pharmacy assistant, respiratory therapy technology.

Contact. E-mail: jmrestotorres@yahoo.com
Phone: (787) 765-4210 Toll-free number: (787) 765-4210
Fax: (787) 765-4277
Juan Resto, Director of Admissions, Centro de Estudios Multidisciplinarios, PO Box 191317, San Juan, PR 00926-1931

Colegio de Cinematograflf8a, Artes y Televisión
San Juan, Puerto Rico
www.ccat.edu

- Private 2-year liberal arts and technical college
- Commuter campus in small city

General. Accredited by ACCSC. **Enrollment:** 649 undergraduates. **Degrees:** 55 associate awarded. **Location:** 5 miles from San Juan. **Calendar:** Semester, limited summer session. **Full-time faculty:** 2 total. **Part-time faculty:** 28 total. **Class size:** 27% < 20, 73% 20-39.

Transfer out. Colleges most students transferred to 2011: University of the Sacred Heart, University of Puerto Rico.

Basis for selection. Open admission. **Home schooled:** Statement describing home school structure and mission required. College Board results.

2011-2012 Annual costs. Books/supplies: $360.

Financial aid. Need-based: Work-study available nights, weekends and for part-time students. **Non-need-based:** Scholarships awarded for alumni affiliation, art, athletics, job skills, leadership, minority status, music/drama, religious affiliation, ROTC, state residency.

Application procedures. Admission: Closing date 9/3 (receipt date). $25 fee, may be waived for applicants with need. Admission notification on a rolling basis. **Financial aid:** No deadline. FAFSA required. Applicants notified on a rolling basis.

Academics. Special study options: Internships. **Credit/placement by examination:** AP, CLEP. **Support services:** Reduced course load, study skills assistance, tutoring.

Majors. Communications: Radio/TV. **Communications technology:** Recording arts. **Visual/performing arts:** Cinematography.

Computing on campus. 50 workstations in library, computer center. Commuter students can connect to campus network.

Student life. Freshman orientation: Available. Preregistration for classes offered.

Student services. Career counseling, financial aid counseling.

Contact. E-mail: admissions@ccat.edu
Phone: (787) 779-2500 Fax: (787) 995-2525
Nydia Alvaranza, Admissions Officer, Colegio de Cinematografía, Artes y Televisión, PO Box 10774, San Juan, PR 00922

Columbia Centro Universitario: Yauco
Yauco, Puerto Rico
www.columbiaco.edu   CB code: 3215

- For-profit 2-year business and health science college
- Commuter campus in large town
- Interview required

General. Regionally accredited. **Enrollment:** 430 degree-seeking undergraduates. **Degrees:** 51 bachelor's, 82 associate awarded. **Calendar:** Differs by program. **Full-time faculty:** 10 total; 10% have terminal degrees, 80% women. **Part-time faculty:** 48 total; 17% have terminal degrees. **Class size:** 100% 50-99.

Student profile. Among degree-seeking undergraduates, 71 enrolled as first-time, first-year students, 298 transferred in from other institutions.

Part-time: 50%   **Women:** 73%

Transfer out. 18% of students enrolled in the transfer program go on to 4-year colleges. **Colleges most students transferred to 2011:** Inter American University of Puerto Rico.

Basis for selection. Open admission, but selective for some programs. **Home schooled:** Transcript of courses and grades, state high school equivalency certificate, interview required.

2011-2012 Annual costs. Books/supplies: $862. Personal expenses: $1,500.

2010-2011 Financial aid. All financial aid based on need. 54 full-time freshmen applied for aid; 49 were judged to have need; 49 of these received aid. 99% of total undergraduate aid awarded as scholarships/grants, 1% as loans/jobs. Need-based aid available for part-time students. Work-study available nights, weekends and for part-time students.

Application procedures. Admission: $50 fee. Application must be submitted on paper. **Financial aid:** FAFSA, institutional form required.

Academics. Special study options: Bachelor's degree programs available on campus. License preparation in nursing. **Credit/placement by examination:** AP, CLEP. **Support services:** Learning center, study skills assistance, tutoring.

Majors. Business: Business admin, office technology. **Computer sciences:** Programming. **Health services:** Nursing (RN).

Computing on campus. 13 workstations in library. Repair service, wireless network available.

Student life. Freshman orientation: Mandatory. Preregistration for classes offered.

Student services. Alcohol/substance abuse counseling, student employment services, financial aid counseling, personal counseling, placement for graduates. **Transfer:** Pre-admission transcript evaluation for new students.

Contact. E-mail: rpadilla@columbiaco.edu
Phone: (787) 856-0930 Toll-free number: (800) 981-4877
Fax: (787) 856-0945
Diriee Rodriquez, Columbia Centro Universitario: Yauco, Box 3062, Yauco, PR 00698-3062

EDIC College
Caguas, Puerto Rico
www.ediccollege.com

- For-profit 2-year health science and technical college
- Large city
- Interview required

General. Regionally accredited; also accredited by ACICS. **Enrollment:** 1,036 degree-seeking undergraduates. **Degrees:** 106 associate awarded. **Calendar:** Semester. **Full-time faculty:** 18 total. **Part-time faculty:** 62 total.

Basis for selection. Open admission, but selective for some programs. For associate degree program, 2.3 GPA required.

2011-2012 Annual costs. Degree-program tuition and administrative fees for students beginning Fall 2011: diploma, $6,350, associate degree, $6,350. Costs may vary by program. Certain programs of study require purchase of special supplies, which could cost an additional $500 to $1,900.

Financial aid. All financial aid based on need. Need-based aid available for part-time students. Work-study available nights, weekends and for part-time students.

Application procedures. Admission: $25 fee. Application must be submitted on paper. **Financial aid:** No deadline. FAFSA, institutional form required. Applicants notified on a rolling basis.

Academics. Special study options: Distance learning. **Credit/placement by examination:** AP, CLEP. **Support services:** Tutoring.

Majors. Health services: Radiologic technology/medical imaging, sonography. **Physical sciences:** Optics.

Computing on campus. 1 workstations in library. Online course registration available.

Student services. Transfer: Pre-admission transcript evaluation for new students.

Contact. E-mail: admisiones@ediccollege.edu
Phone: (787) 744-8519 ext. 229 Fax: (787) 258-6300
Virginia Cartagena, Admissions Director, EDIC College, Box 9120, Caguas, PR 00726-9120

Huertas Junior College
Caguas, Puerto Rico
www.huertas.edu
CB member
CB code: 3406

- For-profit 2-year junior and technical college ·
- Commuter campus in large city

General. Founded in 1945. **Enrollment:** 1,805 degree-seeking undergraduates. **Degrees:** 396 associate awarded. **Location:** 25 miles from San Juan, 32 miles from Naranjito. **Calendar:** Semester, extensive summer session. **Full-time faculty:** 23 total. **Part-time faculty:** 102 total. **Special facilities:** Simulation clinic for health-related programs.

Transfer out. Colleges most students transferred to 2011: Banca Institute, EDIC College, Liceo of Arts and Technology, Mech Tech.

Basis for selection. Open admission. **Learning Disabled:** Students with learning disabilities referred to counseling office for assistance.

High school preparation. Required units include science 3. Students with work experience present a letter from their employer indicating domain of knowledge and skills related to program.

2011-2012 Annual costs. Books/supplies: $700.

Financial aid. All financial aid based on need. Need-based aid available for part-time students. Work-study available nights, weekends and for part-time students.

Application procedures. Admission: No deadline. $25 fee. Application must be submitted on paper. Admission notification on a rolling basis. **Financial aid:** No deadline. FAFSA, institutional form required. Applicants notified on a rolling basis.

Academics. Special study options: Accelerated study, cooperative education. **Credit/placement by examination:** AP, CLEP. **Support services:** Learning center, study skills assistance, tutoring.

Majors. Business: Accounting, administrative services, business admin. **Computer sciences:** Computer science. **Health services:** Dental assistant, medical records admin, medical records technology, pharmacy assistant, respiratory therapy technology.

Computing on campus. 50 workstations in library, computer center. Wireless network available.

Student life. Freshman orientation: Mandatory. Preregistration for classes offered. Program held in first 2 weeks of classes.

Student services. Career counseling, student employment services, health services, on-campus daycare, personal counseling, placement for graduates,

---

veterans' counselor. **Physically disabled:** Services for hearing impaired. **Transfer:** Transfer adviser for students transferring to 4-year colleges.

Contact. E-mail: admisiones@huertas.edu
Phone: (787) 743-1242 Fax: (787) 743-0203
Barbara Hassim, Director of Admissions, Huertas Junior College, PO Box 8429, Caguas, PR 00726

Humacao Community College
Humacao, Puerto Rico
www.humacaocommunitycollege.com
CB code: 2313

- Private 2-year business and community college
- Commuter campus in small city
- Interview required

General. Founded in 1956. Accredited by ACICS. **Enrollment:** 474 full-time, degree-seeking students. **Degrees:** 205 associate awarded. **Location:** 42 miles from San Juan. **Calendar:** Trimester, extensive summer session. **Full-time faculty:** 11 total. **Part-time faculty:** 20 total. **Class size:** 62% < 20, 38% 20-39.

Transfer out. Colleges most students transferred to 2011: Turabo University, University of Puerto Rico (all campuses), Inter American University of Puerto Rico (all campuses), Huertas Junior College.

Basis for selection. Open admission. **Home schooled:** Transcript of courses and grades, state high school equivalency certificate required.

High school preparation. 15 units recommended. Recommended units include English 3, mathematics 3, social studies 3, science 3 and academic electives 3.

2011-2012 Annual costs. Books/supplies: $1,152. Personal expenses: $1,350.

Financial aid. All financial aid based on need. Need-based aid available for part-time students. Work-study available nights, weekends and for part-time students.

Application procedures. Admission: No deadline. $15 fee. Application must be submitted on paper. Admission notification on a rolling basis. **Financial aid:** Priority date 1/1, closing date 6/30. FAFSA, institutional form required. Applicants notified on a rolling basis starting 3/4.

Academics. Special study options: Internships. **Credit/placement by examination:** AP, CLEP. 9 credit hours maximum toward associate degree. **Support services:** Learning center, remedial instruction, tutoring.

Majors. Business: Administrative services, business admin. **Computer sciences:** Information systems. **Health services:** Dental assistant, medical records technology, medical secretary, pharmacy assistant.

Most popular majors. Business/marketing 25%, computer/information sciences 10%, engineering/engineering technologies 15%, health sciences 50%.

Computing on campus. 242 workstations in library, computer center, student center. Online library available.

Student life. Freshman orientation: Mandatory. Preregistration for classes offered. **Activities:** Student government.

Student services. Adult student services, alcohol/substance abuse counseling, career counseling, student employment services, financial aid counseling, personal counseling, placement for graduates, veterans' counselor. **Transfer:** Re-entry adviser, pre-admission transcript evaluation for new students. Transfer adviser for students transferring to 4-year colleges.

Contact. Phone: (787) 285-2525 Fax: (787) 850-1577
Carmen Rivera, Admissions Director, Humacao Community College, PO Box 9139, Humacao, PR 00792-9139

ICPR Junior College
San Juan, Puerto Rico
www.icprjc.edu
CB member
CB code: 7315

- For-profit 2-year business and junior college
- Commuter campus in very large city

General. Founded in 1946. Regionally accredited. Multicampus institution with main campus in Hato Rey, extension campus in Bayamón, branch campuses in Arecibo, Mayaüez, and Manatí. **Enrollment:** 1,691 degree-seeking undergraduates. **Degrees:** 126 associate awarded. **Calendar:** Semester, extensive summer session. **Full-time faculty:** 29 total. **Part-time faculty:** 59 total.

Student profile. Among degree-seeking undergraduates, 10% enrolled in a transfer program, 72% enrolled in a vocational program, 2% already have a bachelor's degree or higher, 874 enrolled as first-time, first-year students.

Part-time:	19%	Hispanic American:	100%
Women:	59%		

Transfer out. 10% of students enrolled in the transfer program go on to 4-year colleges.

Basis for selection. Open admission. **Home schooled:** Transcript of courses and grades, state high school equivalency certificate required.

High school preparation. Recommended units include English 4, mathematics 4, social studies 4, history 4, science 4 (laboratory 4), foreign language 4, computer science 4, visual/performing arts 4 and academic electives 4.

2011-2012 Annual costs. Tuition/fees: $6,330. Books/supplies: $1,026. Personal expenses: $2,067.

2011-2012 Financial aid. Need-based: 74% of total undergraduate aid awarded as scholarships/grants, 26% as loans/jobs. Work-study available nights, weekends and for part-time students. **Non-need-based:** Scholarships awarded for state residency.

Application procedures. Admission: No deadline. No application fee. Admission notification on a rolling basis. **Financial aid:** Closing date 4/15. FAFSA, institutional form required. Applicants notified on a rolling basis starting 11/15.

Academics. Credit/placement by examination: AP, CLEP. **Support services:** Tutoring.

Majors. Business: Accounting, administrative services, business admin, hotel/motel admin, management information systems, marketing, office technology, tourism/travel. **Computer sciences:** General, applications programming. **Health services:** Medical secretary.

Computing on campus. 500 workstations in library, computer center, student center. Wireless network available.

Student life. Freshman orientation: Available. Preregistration for classes offered.

Student services. Alcohol/substance abuse counseling, career counseling, student employment services, financial aid counseling, personal counseling, placement for graduates, veterans' counselor. **Physically disabled:** Services for hearing impaired. **Transfer:** Re-entry adviser for new students.

Contact. E-mail: acalderon@icprjc.edu
Phone: (787) 763-1010 ext. 255 Toll-free number: (877) 751-4277
Fax: (787) 763-7249
Isander Velazquez, Director of Admission and Marketing, ICPR Junior College, PO Box 190304, San Juan, PR 00919-0304

Ponce Paramedical College
Coto Laurel, Puerto Rico
www.popac.edu

- For-profit 2-year health science and career college
- Small city

General. Accredited by ACCSC. **Enrollment:** 3,514 degree-seeking undergraduates. **Degrees:** 253 associate awarded. **Calendar:** Continuous, extensive summer session. **Full-time faculty:** 81 total. **Part-time faculty:** 171 total.

Basis for selection. Open admission. **Home schooled:** Transcript of courses and grades, state high school equivalency certificate, interview required.

Financial aid. Need-based: Work-study available nights, weekends and for part-time students.

Application procedures. Admission: No deadline. $25 fee. Admission notification on a rolling basis. **Financial aid:** No deadline.

Academics. Credit/placement by examination: AP, CLEP. **Support services:** Tutoring.

Majors. Health services: Nursing (RN), respiratory therapy technology.

Computing on campus. Online library available.

Student life. Freshman orientation: Available. Preregistration for classes offered. **Activities:** Student newspaper.

Athletics. Team name: POPAC.

Student services. Financial aid counseling, health services, personal counseling, placement for graduates.

Contact. E-mail: admisiones@popac.edu
Phone: (787) 848-1589 ext. 413 Toll-free number: (800) 981-7184
Ruth Negron, Director of Admissions, Ponce Paramedical College, Calle Acacia 1213, Urb. Villa Flores, Ponce, PR 00780-0106

Universal Career Community College: Humacao
Humacao, Puerto Rico
www.universalcareer.org

- Private 2-year career college
- Small city

General. Regionally accredited. **Calendar:** Semester.

Contact. Phone: (787) 285-0746
PO Box 9022888, San Juan, PR 00902-2888

Universal Career Community College: Manati
Manati, Puerto Rico
www.universalcareer.org

- Private 2-year career college
- Small city

General. Regionally accredited. **Calendar:** Semester.

Contact. Phone: (787) 854-1636
PO Box 9022888, San Juan, PR 00902-2888

Universal Career Community College: San Juan
Santurce, Puerto Rico
www.universalcareer.org

- Private 2-year career college
- Very large city

General. Regionally accredited. **Calendar:** Semester.

Contact. Phone: (787) 728-7299
PO Box 9022888, San Juan, PR 00902-2888

Universal Technology College of Puerto Rico
Aguadilla, Puerto Rico
www.unitecpr.edu/

- Private 2-year health science and career college
- Commuter campus in small city

General. Accredited by ACCSC. **Enrollment:** 1,348 full-time, degree-seeking students. **Degrees:** 213 associate awarded. **Calendar:** Semester, limited summer session. **Full-time faculty:** 26 total. **Part-time faculty:** 55 total. **Class size:** 10% < 20, 90% 20-39. **Special facilities:** Art gallery, peace gallery (commemorating winners of Nobel Prize).

Basis for selection. Open admission. **Home schooled:** State high school equivalency certificate required.

2011-2012 Annual costs. Books/supplies: $450. Personal expenses: $250.

Financial aid. All financial aid based on need. Need-based aid available for part-time students. Work-study available nights, weekends and for part-time students.

Two-Year Colleges

Application procedures. Admission: No deadline. $20 fee. Application must be submitted on paper. Admission notification on a rolling basis. **Financial aid:** Priority date 4/30, closing date 6/30. FAFSA, institutional form required. Applicants notified on a rolling basis starting 2/1; must reply by 6/30.

Academics. Special study options: Weekend college. License preparation in nursing, paramedic. **Credit/placement by examination:** AP, CLEP. **Support services:** Reduced course load, study skills assistance, tutoring.

Majors. Business: Administrative services. **Computer sciences:** Programming. **Health services:** Nursing (RN).

Most popular majors. Business/marketing 30%, health sciences 70%.

Student life. Freshman orientation: Mandatory. Preregistration for classes offered. **Activities:** Student newspaper.

Athletics. Team name: Delfines.

Student services. Financial aid counseling, on-campus daycare, placement for graduates, veterans' counselor. **Transfer:** Re-entry adviser, pre-admission transcript evaluation for new students.

Contact. E-mail: admisiones@unitecpr.net
Phone: (787) 882-2065 ext. 308
Toll-free number: (188) 864-8322 ext. 308 Fax: (787) 891-2370
Teresita Rivera, Admissions Coordinator, Universal Technology College of Puerto Rico, Apartado 1955, Victoria Station, Aguadilla, PR 00605

Rhode Island

Community College of Rhode Island
Warwick, Rhode Island
www.ccri.edu

CB member
CB code: 3733

◗ Public 2-year community college
◗ Commuter campus in small city

General. Founded in 1964. Regionally accredited. Additional campuses in Lincoln, Providence, and Newport. **Enrollment:** 16,981 degree-seeking undergraduates; 912 non-degree-seeking students. **Degrees:** 1,378 associate awarded. **ROTC:** Army. **Location:** 10 miles from Providence. **Calendar:** Semester, extensive summer session. **Full-time faculty:** 325 total. **Part-time faculty:** 488 total. **Class size:** 35% < 20, 65% 20-39, less than 1% 40-49. **Special facilities:** Observatory.

Student profile. Among degree-seeking undergraduates, 3,757 enrolled as first-time, first-year students, 516 transferred in from other institutions.

Part-time:	64%	Asian American:	3%
Out-of-state:	4%	Hispanic American:	16%
Women:	61%	Native American:	1%
African American:	9%	25 or older:	37%

Transfer out. Colleges most students transferred to 2011: Rhode Island College, University of Rhode Island, New England Institute of Technology, Johnson and Wales University, Roger Williams University, Bryant University.

Basis for selection. Open admission, but selective for some programs. Placement testing in mathematics and English required; testing in chemistry may be required for programs with limited enrollment.

High school preparation. College-preparatory program required. Some programs may require mathematics and science background. Special considerations for nursing and allied health applicants.

2011-2012 Annual costs. Tuition/fees: $3,676; $9,816 out-of-state. Per-credit charge: $153 in-state; $454 out-of-state. Books/supplies: $1,200. Personal expenses: $2,745.

Financial aid. Need-based: Need-based aid available for part-time students. Work-study available nights, weekends and for part-time students. **Non-need-based:** Scholarships awarded for athletics.

Application procedures. Admission: No deadline. $20 fee, may be waived for applicants with need. Admission notification on a rolling basis beginning on or about 1/1. Application closing date and admitted student reply deadline is the first week of fall semester in September and first week of spring semester in January. After the first week of each semester, applicants are processed for the following semester. **Financial aid:** Priority date 3/1; no closing date. FAFSA, institutional form required. Applicants notified on a rolling basis starting 5/1; must reply within 2 week(s) of notification.

Academics. Special study options: Cooperative education, cross-registration, distance learning, double major, dual enrollment of high school students, ESL, honors, independent study, internships, study abroad, weekend college. License preparation in dental hygiene, nursing, occupational therapy, physical therapy, radiology, real estate. **Credit/placement by examination:** AP, CLEP. 30 credit hours maximum toward associate degree. **Support services:** GED preparation and test center, learning center, reduced course load, remedial instruction, study skills assistance, tutoring, writing center.

Majors. Business: General, accounting, administrative services, banking/financial services, business admin, customer service, marketing. **Computer sciences:** General, applications programming, networking, webmaster. **Education:** Kindergarten/preschool, special ed. **Engineering:** General, surveying. **Health services:** Clinical lab technology, dental hygiene, histologic assistant, massage therapy, medical secretary, mental health counseling, nursing (RN), occupational therapy assistant, optician, physical therapy assistant, radiologic technology/medical imaging, respiratory therapy technology, sonography, substance abuse counseling. **Human services:** Social work. **Liberal arts:** Arts/sciences. **Protective services:** Disaster management, firefighting, police science. **Visual/performing arts:** Art, dramatic, jazz, music. **Work/family studies:** Aging.

Most popular majors. Business/marketing 12%, health sciences 29%, liberal arts 39%, security/protective services 8%.

Computing on campus. 1,200 workstations in library, computer center, student center. Commuter students can connect to campus network. Online course registration, online library, helpline, wireless network available.

Student life. Freshman orientation: Mandatory. Preregistration for classes offered. **Activities:** Bands, choral groups, dance, drama, international student organizations, music ensembles, student government, student newspaper, TV station, Black American student association, Latin American student organization, Spanish club, Asian club, Christian club, American Sign Language club & deaf students union, Bible study club, cultural alliance club, Muslim student association, Students for Environmental Action.

Athletics. NJCAA. **Intercollegiate:** Baseball M, basketball, cross-country, golf, soccer, softball W, tennis, track and field, volleyball W. **Intramural:** Table tennis. **Team name:** Knights.

Student services. Adult student services, alcohol/substance abuse counseling, career counseling, services for economically disadvantaged, student employment services, financial aid counseling, health services, minority student services, on-campus daycare, personal counseling, placement for graduates, veterans' counselor, women's services. **Physically disabled:** Services for visually, speech, hearing impaired. **Transfer:** Re-entry adviser, pre-admission transcript evaluation for new students. Transfer adviser, college fairs on campus for students transferring to 4-year colleges.

Contact. E-mail: webadmission@ccri.edu
Phone: (401) 825-2003 Fax: (401) 825-2394
Terri Kless, Director of Enrollment Services, Community College of Rhode Island, 400 East Avenue, Warwick, RI 02886-1807

South Carolina

Aiken Technical College
Aiken, South Carolina
www.atc.edu   CB code: 5037

▶ Public 2-year community and technical college
▶ Commuter campus in small city

General. Founded in 1972. Regionally accredited. **Enrollment:** 2,995 degree-seeking undergraduates; 50 non-degree-seeking students. **Degrees:** 285 associate awarded. **Location:** 9 miles from Aiken, 12 miles from Augusta, Georgia. **Calendar:** Semester, extensive summer session. **Full-time faculty:** 47 total. **Part-time faculty:** 102 total. **Class size:** 66% < 20, 34% 20-39.

Student profile. Among degree-seeking undergraduates, 587 enrolled as first-time, first-year students.

Part-time:	56%	Asian American:	1%
Out-of-state:	12%	Hispanic American:	2%
Women:	64%	Native American:	1%
African American:	33%	25 or older:	42%

Transfer out. Colleges most students transferred to 2011: Augusta State University, Lander University, University of South Carolina.

Basis for selection. Open admission, but selective for some programs. Test scores considered if submitted. Special requirements for all health programs. **Adult students:** SAT/ACT scores not required.

High school preparation. 18 units recommended. Recommended units include English 4, mathematics 4, social studies 2, history 2, science 2, foreign language 2 and academic electives 2.

2011-2012 Annual costs. Tuition/fees: $3,806; $4,066 out-of-district; $10,140 out-of-state. Books/supplies: $900. Personal expenses: $1,500.

2010-2011 Financial aid. Need-based: Average need met was 59%. Average scholarship/grant was $2,547; average loan $1,351. 82% of total undergraduate aid awarded as scholarships/grants, 18% as loans/jobs. Need-based aid available for part-time students. Work-study available nights, weekends and for part-time students. **Non-need-based:** Scholarships awarded for academics, athletics, leadership, minority status, state residency.

Application procedures. Admission: Priority date 7/1; no deadline. No application fee. Admission notification on a rolling basis. **Financial aid:** Priority date 5/1, closing date 6/1. FAFSA required. Applicants notified on a rolling basis starting 4/1; must reply within 2 week(s) of notification.

Academics. Special study options: Accelerated study, cooperative education, cross-registration, distance learning, double major, dual enrollment of high school students, independent study, internships, liberal arts/career combination. License preparation in nursing, radiology. **Credit/placement by examination:** AP, CLEP, institutional tests. **Support services:** Learning center, pre-admission summer program, reduced course load, remedial instruction, study skills assistance, tutoring, writing center.

Majors. Business: Accounting, administrative services, business admin, sales/distribution. **Computer sciences:** Data processing. **Education:** Voc/tech. **Engineering:** Computer, electrical. **Health services:** Medical radiologic technology/radiation therapy, nursing (RN). **Human services:** Social work. **Liberal arts:** Arts/sciences. **Protective services:** Criminal justice.

Most popular majors. Business/marketing 16%, health sciences 33%, interdisciplinary studies 8%, liberal arts 22%, public administration/social services 7%.

Computing on campus. 1,005 workstations in library, computer center, student center. Online course registration, online library, helpline, repair service, wireless network available.

Student life. Freshman orientation: Available. Preregistration for classes offered. Online orientation available at http://orientation.atc.edu/. **Activities:** Campus ministries, student government, Phi Theta Kappa Honor Society.

Athletics. NJCAA. **Intercollegiate:** Basketball M, softball W. **Intramural:** Basketball, softball, table tennis, volleyball. **Team name:** Knights.

Student services. Adult student services, alcohol/substance abuse counseling, career counseling, services for economically disadvantaged, student employment services, financial aid counseling, minority student services, personal counseling, placement for graduates, veterans' counselor. **Physically disabled:** Services for visually, speech, hearing impaired. **Transfer:** Pre-admission transcript evaluation for new students. Transfer adviser, college fairs on campus for students transferring to 4-year colleges.

Contact. Phone: (803) 593-9954 ext. 1247 Fax: (803) 593-6526 Dawn Butts, Director of Admissions and Records, Aiken Technical College, PO Drawer 696, Aiken, SC 29802

Central Carolina Technical College
Sumter, South Carolina
www.cctech.edu   CB code: 5665

▶ Public 2-year community and technical college
▶ Commuter campus in large town

General. Founded in 1963. Regionally accredited. Branch campuses in Clarendon, Kershaw, and Lee Counties. Additional facility located at Shaw Air Force Base. **Enrollment:** 4,268 degree-seeking undergraduates; 260 non-degree-seeking students. **Degrees:** 206 associate awarded. **Location:** 45 miles from Columbia. **Calendar:** Semester, extensive summer session. **Full-time faculty:** 101 total. **Part-time faculty:** 142 total. **Special facilities:** South Carolina Environmental Training Center.

Student profile. Among degree-seeking undergraduates, 916 enrolled as first-time, first-year students.

Part-time:	63%	25 or older:	49%
Women:	71%		

Transfer out. Colleges most students transferred to 2011: University of South Carolina, Clemson University, Lander University, Limestone, Francis Marion University.

Basis for selection. Open admission, but selective for some programs. Test scores required for placement. Associate degree nursing program: TEAS minimum of 74 composite. LPN program: minimum TEAS 67. Interview required for nursing program. **Adult students:** SAT/ACT scores not required.

High school preparation. Required units include English 4, mathematics 4, social studies 1, history 1, science 3, foreign language 1, computer science 1 and academic electives 7. Economics .5, US Government .5.

2011-2012 Annual costs. Tuition/fees: $3,476; $4,046 out-of-district; $6,042 out-of-state. Books/supplies: $1,100. Personal expenses: $1,030.

Financial aid. Need-based: Need-based aid available for part-time students. Work-study available nights, weekends and for part-time students.

Application procedures. Admission: No deadline. No application fee. Admission notification on a rolling basis. **Financial aid:** No deadline. FAFSA required. Applicants notified on a rolling basis starting 4/11; must reply within 2 week(s) of notification.

Academics. Special study options: Distance learning, dual enrollment of high school students, weekend college. License preparation in nursing, paramedic. **Credit/placement by examination:** AP, CLEP, IB, institutional tests. **Support services:** Remedial instruction, study skills assistance, tutoring, writing center.

Majors. Business: Accounting, administrative services, management science. **Computer sciences:** Programming. **Conservation:** Management/policy. **Health services:** Nursing (RN), surgical technology. **Liberal arts:** Arts/sciences.

Most popular majors. Business/marketing 22%, computer/information sciences 7%, family/consumer sciences 8%, health sciences 28%, liberal arts 14%, security/protective services 6%.

Computing on campus. 125 workstations in library, computer center. Commuter students can connect to campus network. Online course registration, online library, helpline available.

Student life. Freshman orientation: Available. Preregistration for classes offered. **Activities:** Phi Theta Kappa, Earth club, computer club.

Student services. Career counseling, services for economically disadvantaged, student employment services, financial aid counseling, personal counseling, placement for graduates, veterans' counselor, women's services. **Physically disabled:** Services for visually, speech, hearing impaired. **Transfer:** Pre-admission transcript evaluation for new students. College fairs on campus for students transferring to 4-year colleges.

Contact. E-mail: admissions@cctech.edu
Phone: (803) 778-6605 Toll-free number: (800) 221-8711 ext. 205
Fax: (803) 778-6696
Barbara Wright, Director of Admissions and Student Services, Central
Carolina Technical College, 506 North Guignard Drive, Sumter, SC
29150-2499

Clinton Junior College
Rock Hill, South Carolina
www.clintonjuniorcollege.edu   **CB code: 5743**

- Private 2-year junior and liberal arts college
- Residential campus in small city

General. Regionally accredited; also accredited by TRACS. **Enrollment:**
174 degree-seeking undergraduates. **Degrees:** 32 associate awarded. **Calendar:** Semester. **Full-time faculty:** 8 total. **Part-time faculty:** 26 total.

Student profile.

Out-of-state:	10%	Live on campus:	90%
25 or older:	4%		

Basis for selection. Open admission. **Home schooled:** Statement describing home school structure and mission, transcript of courses and grades required.

2011-2012 Annual costs. Tuition/fees: $4,185. Room/board: $7,253. Books/supplies: $400.

Financial aid. Need-based: Work-study available nights, weekends and for part-time students.

Application procedures. Admission: No deadline. $25 fee. Institutional placement test given after enrollment. **Financial aid:** No deadline.

Academics. Credit/placement by examination: AP, CLEP.

Majors. Business: General. **Education:** Early childhood. **Liberal arts:** Arts/sciences. **Physical sciences:** General. **Theology:** Bible.

Student life. Activities: Choral groups, student government.

Athletics. NJCAA. **Intercollegiate:** Basketball M. **Team name:** Golden Bulls.

Contact. E-mail: rcopeland@clintonjuniorcollege.edu
Phone: (803) 327-7402 ext. 242
Robert Copeland, Vice President for Student Affairs, Clinton Junior
College, 1029 Crawford Road, Rock Hill, SC 29730

Denmark Technical College
Denmark, South Carolina
www.denmarktech.edu   **CB code: 5744**

- Public 2-year technical college
- Residential campus in small town

General. Founded in 1948. Regionally accredited. **Enrollment:** 1,607 degree-seeking undergraduates. **Degrees:** 66 associate awarded. **Location:** 55 miles from Columbia. **Calendar:** Semester, extensive summer session. **Full-time faculty:** 36 total. **Part-time faculty:** 19 total.

Student profile.

Out-of-state:	4%	Live on campus:	33%

Basis for selection. Open admission. Interview recommended.

High school preparation. Recommended units include English 4, mathematics 4, social studies 2, science 2 and foreign language 2. College preparatory program required for AA and AS transfer college programs.

2011-2012 Annual costs. Tuition/fees: $2,590; $4,870 out-of-state. Room/board: $3,666. Books/supplies: $1,100.

Financial aid. Need-based: Need-based aid available for part-time students. Work-study available nights, weekends and for part-time students.

Application procedures. Admission: No deadline. $10 fee, may be waived for applicants with need. Admission notification on a rolling basis.

Financial aid: No deadline. FAFSA required. Applicants notified on a rolling basis starting 6/1; must reply within 2 week(s) of notification.

Academics. Special study options: Cooperative education, cross-registration, independent study, internships. License preparation in nursing. **Credit/placement by examination:** AP, CLEP, institutional tests. **Support services:** GED preparation, learning center, reduced course load, remedial instruction, tutoring.

Majors. Business: General. **Liberal arts:** Arts/sciences.

Computing on campus. 85 workstations in library, computer center. Dormitories wired for high-speed internet access and linked to campus network. Commuter students can connect to campus network. Wireless network available.

Student life. Freshman orientation: Mandatory. Preregistration for classes offered. **Housing:** Single-sex dorms available. **Activities:** Choral groups, student government, student newspaper, Student Christian Association.

Athletics. Intercollegiate: Basketball. **Intramural:** Basketball. **Team name:** Panthers and Lady Panthers.

Student services. Career counseling, student employment services, health services, personal counseling, placement for graduates, veterans' counselor. **Transfer:** College fairs on campus for students transferring to 4-year colleges.

Contact. E-mail: spellsf@denmarktech.edu
Phone: (803) 793-5176 Fax: (803) 793-5290
Denmark Technical College, 1126 Solomon Blatt Boulevard, Denmark, SC 29042

Florence-Darlington Technical College
Florence, South Carolina
www.fdtc.edu   **CB code: 5207**

- Public 2-year community and technical college
- Commuter campus in small city

General. Founded in 1964. Regionally accredited. **Enrollment:** 6,011 degree-seeking undergraduates. **Degrees:** 603 associate awarded. **Location:** 80 miles from Columbia, 50 miles from Myrtle Beach. **Calendar:** Semester, extensive summer session. **Full-time faculty:** 105 total. **Part-time faculty:** 195 total. **Partnerships:** Formal partnerships with local, regional, and national corporations which enhance student opportunities for training.

Transfer out. Colleges most students transferred to 2011: Francis Marion University, Clemson University, University of South Carolina.

Basis for selection. Open admission, but selective for some programs. Computerized Placement Test administered as alternative to SAT or ACT for placement for most programs. NLN, HOAE or HOBET required for some allied health programs. **Home schooled:** GED may be required.

High school preparation. Recommended units include English 4, mathematics 3, social studies 2, history 1, science 2 (laboratory 2), foreign language 2 and academic electives 2. Algebra I, algebra II, biology, and chemistry required for most health programs.

2011-2012 Annual costs. Tuition/fees: $3,526; $3,798 out-of-district; $5,692 out-of-state. Books/supplies: $900. Personal expenses: $2,338.

Financial aid. Need-based: Need-based aid available for part-time students. Work-study available nights, weekends and for part-time students. **Non-need-based:** Scholarships awarded for academics.

Application procedures. Admission: Priority date 7/15; deadline 8/10. No application fee. Admission notification on a rolling basis beginning on or about 1/1. **Financial aid:** Priority date 5/1; no closing date. FAFSA required. Applicants notified on a rolling basis starting 7/1; must reply within 2 week(s) of notification.

Academics. Special study options: Cooperative education, cross-registration, distance learning, double major, dual enrollment of high school students, independent study, internships, liberal arts/career combination. Cooperative program with Greenville Technical College for physical therapy, Fayetteville Technical College for funeral services. License preparation in dental hygiene, nursing, physical therapy. **Credit/placement by examination:** AP, CLEP, IB, institutional tests. Student may receive credit for up to 50% of the course work required by his or her major. **Support services:** GED preparation, learning center, reduced course load, remedial instruction, study skills assistance, tutoring, writing center.

Majors. Business: Accounting, administrative services, entrepreneurial studies, sales/distribution. **Computer sciences:** Data processing. **Education:** Voc/tech. **Health services:** Clinical lab technology, dental hygiene, medical radiologic technology/radiation therapy, medical records technology, nursing (RN), physical therapy assistant, respiratory therapy technology. **Human services:** Social work. **Liberal arts:** Arts/sciences. **Physical sciences:** General. **Protective services:** Criminal justice.

Computing on campus. 128 workstations in library, computer center. Commuter students can connect to campus network. Online course registration, wireless network available.

Student life. Freshman orientation: Available. Preregistration for classes offered. **Activities:** Music ensembles, student government, student newspaper.

Athletics. NJCAA. **Intercollegiate:** Baseball M, softball W. **Team name:** Stingers.

Student services. Career counseling, services for economically disadvantaged, student employment services, financial aid counseling, on-campus daycare, personal counseling, placement for graduates, veterans' counselor. **Physically disabled:** Services for hearing impaired. **Transfer:** Transfer adviser for students transferring to 4-year colleges.

Contact. E-mail: admissions@fdtc.edu
Phone: (843) 661-8324 Toll-free number: (800) 228-5745
Fax: (843) 661-8041
Elaine Hodges, Director of Admissions, Florence-Darlington Technical College, PO Box 100548, Florence, SC 29501-0548

Forrest Junior College
Anderson, South Carolina
www.forrestcollege.edu
CB code: 7138

- For-profit 2-year business college
- Commuter campus in large town
- Application essay, interview required

General. Accredited by ACICS. Majority of students are working adults with children. Free child care provided. **Enrollment:** 121 degree-seeking undergraduates. **Degrees:** 42 associate awarded. **Location:** 30 miles from Greenville. **Calendar:** Quarter, extensive summer session. **Full-time faculty:** 3 total. **Part-time faculty:** 20 total.

Student profile. Among degree-seeking undergraduates, 121 enrolled as first-time, first-year students.

Transfer out. Colleges most students transferred to 2011: Greenville Technical College, Piedmont Technical College, Lander University, Strayer University, Webster University.

Basis for selection. Open admission, but selective for some programs. Special program requirements will vary depending upon the area of study. Each applicant is given individual consideration for admission. Audition, portfolio recommended. **Home schooled:** Transcript of courses and grades, state high school equivalency certificate required.

2011-2012 Annual costs. Tuition/fees: $12,975. Per-credit charge: $245.

Financial aid. All financial aid based on need. Need-based aid available for part-time students. Work-study available nights, weekends and for part-time students.

Application procedures. Admission: No deadline. $50 fee. Admission notification on a rolling basis. **Financial aid:** Closing date 4/1. FAFSA required. Applicants notified on a rolling basis starting 4/30; must reply by 5/31 or within 4 week(s) of notification.

Academics. Special study options: Double major, independent study, internships, liberal arts/career combination, weekend college. **Credit/placement by examination:** AP, CLEP, institutional tests. **Support services:** GED preparation, reduced course load, remedial instruction, tutoring.

Majors. Business: General, accounting, administrative services, business admin, communications, human resources, managerial economics, marketing, office management, office technology, office/clerical. **Computer sciences:** General, information systems. **Education:** Early childhood, sales/marketing, teacher assistance. **Health services:** Clinical lab assistant, clinical lab technology, medical assistant, medical records admin, medical records technology, medical secretary, medical transcription. **Work/family studies:** Child care management.

Computing on campus. PC or laptop required. 52 workstations in library, computer center. Online library, repair service available.

Student life. Freshman orientation: Mandatory. Preregistration for classes offered. **Activities:** Literary magazine, student government, student newspaper.

Student services. Adult student services, career counseling, student employment services, financial aid counseling, on-campus daycare, placement for graduates. **Transfer:** Pre-admission transcript evaluation for new students.

Contact. E-mail: janieturmon@forrestcollege.edu
Phone: (864) 225-7653 ext. 2210 Fax: (864) 261-7471
Janie Turmon, Admissions Officer, Forrest Junior College, 601 East River Street, Anderson, SC 29624

Golf Academy of America: The Carolinas
Myrtle Beach, South Carolina
www.golfacademy.edu
CB code: 3223

- For-profit 2-year golf academy
- Large town

General. Accredited by ACICS. **Enrollment:** 291 degree-seeking undergraduates. **Degrees:** 224 associate awarded. **Calendar:** Differs by program. **Full-time faculty:** 12 total. **Part-time faculty:** 8 total.

Basis for selection. Open admission.

2011-2012 Annual costs. Tuition/fees: $16,443. Cost for three semesters, $24,650, covers tuition, fees, and textbooks. Typically, students enroll for the calendar year and attend classes for three semesters consecutively. Books/supplies: $700. Personal expenses: $1,552.

Financial aid. Need-based: Work-study available nights, weekends and for part-time students.

Application procedures. Admission: No deadline. $50 fee.

Academics. Credit/placement by examination: AP, CLEP.

Majors. Parks/recreation: Golf management.

Contact. E-mail: sdga@sdgagolf.com
Phone: (480) 905-9288 Toll-free number: (800) 342-7342
Fax: (480) 905-8705
Valerie Pimentel, Admissions Director, Golf Academy of America: The Carolinas, 7373 North Scottsdale Road, Suite B-100, Scottsdale, AZ 82253

Greenville Technical College
Greenville, South Carolina
www.gvltec.edu
CB code: 5278

- Public 2-year community and technical college
- Commuter campus in large city

General. Founded in 1962. Regionally accredited. Classes and some programs offered at satellite campuses in Greenville County. **Enrollment:** 13,204 degree-seeking undergraduates; 1,249 non-degree-seeking students. **Degrees:** 1,194 associate awarded. **ROTC:** Army. **Calendar:** Semester, extensive summer session. **Full-time faculty:** 337 total; 9% have terminal degrees, 10% minority, 58% women. **Part-time faculty:** 456 total; 13% have terminal degrees, 14% minority, 64% women.

Student profile. Among degree-seeking undergraduates, 2,312 enrolled as first-time, first-year students, 509 transferred in from other institutions.

Part-time:	53%	Women:	63%
Out-of-state:	1%	Live on campus:	3%

Transfer out. 84% of students enrolled in the transfer program go on to 4-year colleges.

Basis for selection. Open admission, but selective for some programs. Weighted admissions requirements for registered nursing, licensed practical nursing, certain allied health programs. Interview required for allied health sciences, nursing, photography, and aircraft mechanic applicants and recommended for all others. Portfolio required for visual arts program. **Home schooled:** Applicants who are members of South Carolina Home School

Association must provide current copy of membership card. **Learning Disabled:** Contact Student Disability Services early in admission process for appropriate accommodations. Self-identification and documentation required.

High school preparation. Algebra, biology, and chemistry are required for most health care program applicants.

2011-2012 Annual costs. Tuition/fees: $3,748; $4,160 out-of-district; $7,760 out-of-state. Books/supplies: $1,075. Personal expenses: $723.

2010-2011 Financial aid. Need-based: 46% of total undergraduate aid awarded as scholarships/grants, 54% as loans/jobs. Need-based aid available for part-time students. Work-study available nights, weekends and for part-time students. **Non-need-based:** Scholarships awarded for academics, state residency.

Application procedures. Admission: Priority date 8/1; deadline 8/1. $35 fee. Admission notification on a rolling basis. **Financial aid:** Priority date 5/1; no closing date. FAFSA required. Applicants notified on a rolling basis starting 6/15; must reply within 2 week(s) of notification.

Academics. Special study options: Accelerated study, cooperative education, distance learning, dual enrollment of high school students, ESL, honors, independent study, internships, liberal arts/career combination, teacher certification program, weekend college. License preparation in aviation, dental hygiene, nursing, occupational therapy, paramedic, physical therapy, radiology, real estate. **Credit/placement by examination:** AP, CLEP, IB, institutional tests. Department heads require portfolio for prior learning through work experience. **Support services:** Learning center, reduced course load, remedial instruction, study skills assistance, tutoring, writing center.

Honors college/program. Require 3.5 GPA and interview with head of department.

Majors. Biology: Biotechnology. **Business:** Accounting, administrative services, business admin, purchasing, sales/distribution. **Computer sciences:** Data processing. **Health services:** Clinical lab technology, dental hygiene, EMT paramedic, medical radiologic technology/radiation therapy, medical records technology, nursing (RN), occupational therapy assistant, physical therapy assistant, respiratory therapy technology, sonography. **Human services:** Social work. **Liberal arts:** Arts/sciences. **Protective services:** Criminal justice, firefighting. **Social sciences:** GIS/cartography. **Work/family studies:** Child care management.

Most popular majors. Business/marketing 14%, health sciences 37%, liberal arts 20%.

Computing on campus. 1,683 workstations in library, computer center. Dormitories wired for high-speed internet access. Commuter students can connect to campus network. Online library, helpline, wireless network available.

Student life. Freshman orientation: Mandatory. Preregistration for classes offered. **Housing:** Coed dorms, special housing for disabled available. $150 fully refundable deposit, deadline 8/1. College-affiliated housing available on Barton campus. **Activities:** Campus ministries, choral groups, drama, international student organizations, student government, student newspaper, Baptist collegiate ministry, human services organization, Spanish club, National Technical Honor Society, Phi Theta Kappa, ROTARACT, Tech Warriors, Associated General Contractors, International Association of Administrative Professionals.

Athletics. Intramural: Badminton, basketball, bowling, football (non-tackle), table tennis, tennis, volleyball.

Student services. Adult student services, alcohol/substance abuse counseling, chaplain/spiritual director, career counseling, services for economically disadvantaged, student employment services, financial aid counseling, on-campus daycare, personal counseling, placement for graduates, veterans' counselor. **Physically disabled:** Services for visually, speech, hearing impaired. **Transfer:** Re-entry adviser, pre-admission transcript evaluation for new students. Transfer adviser for students transferring to 4-year colleges.

Contact. E-mail: greenvilletech@gvltec.edu
Phone: (864) 250-8109 Toll-free number: (800) 922-1183
Fax: (864) 250-8534
Carolyn Watkins, Dean of Admissions, Greenville Technical College, P.O. Box 5616, Greenville, SC 29606-5616

Horry-Georgetown Technical College
Conway, South Carolina
www.hgtc.edu   **CB code: 5305**

- Public 2-year community and technical college
- Commuter campus in large town

General. Founded in 1965. Regionally accredited. **Enrollment:** 6,837 degree-seeking undergraduates; 650 non-degree-seeking students. **Degrees:** 735 associate awarded. **Location:** 4 miles from Conway, 8 miles from Myrtle Beach. **Calendar:** Semester, extensive summer session. **Full-time faculty:** 141 total. **Part-time faculty:** 225 total. **Special facilities:** Golf course, culinary arts center.

Student profile. Among degree-seeking undergraduates, 60% enrolled in a transfer program, 40% enrolled in a vocational program, 1,208 enrolled as first-time, first-year students.

Part-time:	56%	African American:	24%
Out-of-state:	10%	Asian American:	1%
Women:	66%	Hispanic American:	3%

Transfer out. Colleges most students transferred to 2011: Coastal Carolina University.

Basis for selection. Open admission, but selective for some programs. Special requirements and background checks for engineering technology, all health science programs, early care and education, human services, cosmetology, aesthetics, massage therapy, and nail technician.

2011-2012 Annual costs. Tuition/fees: $3,530; $4,444 out-of-district; $5,808 out-of-state. Books/supplies: $1,500. Personal expenses: $1,615.

Financial aid. Need-based: Need-based aid available for part-time students. Work-study available nights, weekends and for part-time students. **Non-need-based:** Scholarships awarded for academics, state residency. **Additional information:** Participates in South Carolina lottery tuition assistance program. Full-time technical college students who are state residents receive assistance for tuition not covered by federal or need-based grants.

Application procedures. Admission: No deadline. $30 fee ($30 out-of-state), may be waived for applicants with need. Admission notification on a rolling basis. **Financial aid:** Priority date 4/1, closing date 6/30. FAFSA required. Applicants notified on a rolling basis starting 4/1.

Academics. Special study options: Accelerated study, distance learning, double major, dual enrollment of high school students, exchange student, independent study, internships. License preparation in dental hygiene, nursing, radiology, real estate. **Credit/placement by examination:** AP, CLEP, institutional tests. **Support services:** Learning center, reduced course load, remedial instruction, study skills assistance, tutoring.

Majors. Business: General, accounting, administrative services, hotel/motel admin. **Computer sciences:** Data processing. **Conservation:** Forest technology. **Education:** Voc/tech. **Engineering:** Electrical. **General:** Horticulture, turf management. **Health services:** Dental hygiene, EMT paramedic, medical radiologic technology/radiation therapy, nursing (RN), pharmacy assistant. **Human services:** Social work. **Liberal arts:** Arts/sciences. **Protective services:** Criminal justice. **Visual/performing arts:** Design. **Work/family studies:** Child care management.

Most popular majors. Business/marketing 16%, engineering/engineering technologies 6%, family/consumer sciences 11%, health sciences 26%, liberal arts 17%, security/protective services 6%.

Computing on campus. 1,000 workstations in library, computer center, student center. Commuter students can connect to campus network. Online course registration, online library, helpline, wireless network available.

Student life. Freshman orientation: Available. Preregistration for classes offered. **Activities:** Choral groups.

Student services. Career counseling, financial aid counseling, on-campus daycare, personal counseling, placement for graduates, veterans' counselor.

Contact. E-mail: admissions@hgtc.edu
Phone: (843) 349-5277 ext. 5277 Fax: (843) 349-7501
George Swindoll, Assistant Vice President for Enrollment Development and Registration, Horry-Georgetown Technical College, PO Box 261966, Conway, SC 29528-6066

Midlands Technical College
Columbia, South Carolina   **CB member**
www.midlandstech.edu   **CB code: 5584**

- Public 2-year technical college
- Commuter campus in large city

General. Founded in 1974. Regionally accredited. Additional campuses include Airport Campus, Beltline Campus, Batesburg-Leesville Center, Northeast/Enterprise Campus, Fort Jackson and Harbison Campus. **Enrollment:** 12,080 undergraduates. **Degrees:** 1,006 associate awarded. **ROTC:**

Army, Naval, Air Force. **Location:** 10 miles from Columbia. **Calendar:** Semester, limited summer session. **Full-time faculty:** 215 total. **Part-time faculty:** 513 total. **Class size:** 49% < 20, 51% 20-39. **Partnerships:** Formal partnerships with middle schools.

Student profile.

Out-of-state:	2%	**25 or older:**		38%

Transfer out. Colleges most students transferred to 2011: University of South Carolina.

Basis for selection. Open admission, but selective for some programs. High school record, SAT/ACT or college placement test scores, and interviews considered for nursing/health science applicants. National League for Nursing Test required of nursing applicants. Admission cut-off scores established for full admission into each program. Students falling below cut-off scores may enter in developmental studies. Interview, orientation required for health science and nursing programs. **Home schooled:** Must be an approved Home School Association in South Carolina. If student is applying for concurrent admission they must have a letter of permission from the home school association and a letter of permission from their parent/guardian.

2011-2012 Annual costs. Tuition/fees: $3,756; $4,644 out-of-district; $10,764 out-of-state. Books/supplies: $1,240. Personal expenses: $1,200.

Financial aid. Need-based: Need-based aid available for part-time students. Work-study available nights, weekends and for part-time students.

Application procedures. Admission: Priority date 7/20; no deadline. $35 fee. Admission notification on a rolling basis. **Financial aid:** Priority date 4/15; no closing date. FAFSA required. Applicants notified on a rolling basis; must reply within 2 week(s) of notification.

Academics. Special study options: Cooperative education, distance learning, dual enrollment of high school students, ESL, liberal arts/career combination. License preparation in nursing, physical therapy, radiology. **Credit/placement by examination:** AP, CLEP, institutional tests. **Support services:** GED preparation, learning center, remedial instruction, study skills assistance, tutoring, writing center.

Majors. Business: Accounting, administrative services, business admin. **Communications technology:** Graphic/printing. **Computer sciences:** Computer science, data processing, information systems. **Health services:** Clinical lab technology, dental assistant, dental hygiene, medical radiologic technology/radiation therapy, medical records technology, nuclear medical technology, nursing (RN), pharmacy assistant, physical therapy assistant, respiratory therapy assistant, respiratory therapy technology. **Liberal arts:** Arts/sciences. **Protective services:** Criminal justice. **Visual/performing arts:** Commercial/advertising art. **Work/family studies:** Child development.

Most popular majors. Business/marketing 14%, health sciences 23%, interdisciplinary studies 6%, liberal arts 34%.

Computing on campus. 46 workstations in library, computer center, student center. Commuter students can connect to campus network. Online course registration, online library, helpline, wireless network available.

Student life. Freshman orientation: Available. Preregistration for classes offered. **Activities:** Campus ministries, drama, international student organizations, literary magazine, student government, student newspaper, Campus Crusade for Christ, student human services organization, African American student organization.

Athletics. Intramural: Baseball, bowling, equestrian, football (non-tackle), softball, volleyball.

Student services. Adult student services, career counseling, services for economically disadvantaged, student employment services, financial aid counseling, placement for graduates, veterans' counselor. **Physically disabled:** Services for visually, speech, hearing impaired. **Transfer:** Re-entry adviser, pre-admission transcript evaluation for new students. Transfer adviser, college fairs on campus for students transferring to 4-year colleges.

Contact. E-mail: mtcinfo@midlandstech.edu
Phone: (803) 738-8324 Toll-free number: (800) 922-8038
Fax: (803) 738-7784
Derrah Cassidy, Director of Admissions, Midlands Technical College, PO Box 2408, Columbia, SC 29202

Miller-Motte Technical College
North Charleston, South Carolina
www.miller-motte.net

- For-profit 2-year branch campus and technical college
- Small city

General. Accredited by ACICS. **Enrollment:** 900 degree-seeking undergraduates. **Degrees:** 199 associate awarded. **Calendar:** Quarter. **Full-time faculty:** 12 total. **Part-time faculty:** 46 total.

Basis for selection. Open admission. **Adult students:** SAT/ACT scores not required. **Home schooled:** Transcript of courses and grades, interview required.

Financial aid. Need-based: Work-study available nights, weekends and for part-time students.

Application procedures. Admission: No deadline. $40 fee. **Financial aid:** FAFSA, institutional form required. Applicants notified on a rolling basis.

Academics. Credit/placement by examination: AP, CLEP. **Support services:** Tutoring.

Majors. Business: Accounting/business management, business admin. **Health services:** Massage therapy, medical assistant, surgical technology.

Contact. Phone: (843) 574-0101 Toll-free number: (877) 617-4740
Fax: (843) 329-4992
Elaine Que, Director of Admissions, Miller-Motte Technical College, 8085 Rivers Avenue, Suite E, North Charleston, SC 29406

Miller-Motte Technical College: Conway
Conway, South Carolina
www.miller-motte.edu

- For-profit 2-year health science and career college
- Small city

General. Regionally accredited. **Calendar:** Quarter.

Contact. Phone: (843) 591-1102
Director of Admissions, 2451 Highway 501 East, Conway, SC 29526

Northeastern Technical College
Cheraw, South Carolina
www.netc.edu   CB code: 5095

- Public 2-year community and technical college
- Commuter campus in small town

General. Founded in 1969. Regionally accredited. **Enrollment:** 1,230 degree-seeking undergraduates. **Degrees:** 163 associate awarded. **Location:** 89 miles from Columbia. **Calendar:** Semester, extensive summer session. **Full-time faculty:** 30 total; 7% have terminal degrees, 3% minority, 57% women. **Part-time faculty:** 100 total; 3% have terminal degrees, 20% minority, 53% women.

Student profile.

Out-of-state:	1%	**25 or older:**		87%

Transfer out. Colleges most students transferred to 2011: Francis Marion University, Clemson University, Coastal Carolina University, Florence-Darlington Technical College, University of South Carolina.

Basis for selection. Open admission, but selective for some programs. Special requirements for nursing program, including high school math and science courses and SAT (exclusive of Writing) combined score of 960. Interview recommended. **Home schooled:** Must be under auspices of school district or an approved homeschool agency.

High school preparation. Algebra I and II, chemistry with laboratory required for nursing applicants.

2011-2012 Annual costs. Tuition/fees: $3,438; $3,654 out-of-district; $5,982 out-of-state. Books/supplies: $1,200. Personal expenses: $1,800.

Financial aid. Need-based: Work-study available nights, weekends and for part-time students.

Application procedures. Admission: No deadline. $25 fee, may be waived for applicants with need. Admission notification on a rolling basis. **Financial aid:** No deadline. FAFSA required. Applicants notified on a rolling basis; must reply within 8 week(s) of notification.

Academics. Special study options: Cross-registration, distance learning, dual enrollment of high school students, independent study, liberal arts/career

Two-Year Colleges

combination. **Credit/placement by examination:** AP, CLEP, IB, institutional tests. Credit by examination limited to 50% of semester hours required for degree. ASSET and English language proficiency required for placement. **Support services:** Remedial instruction, tutoring, writing center.

Majors. Business: Accounting, administrative services, business admin, office technology, office/clerical. **Computer sciences:** Data processing. **Education:** General. **Health services:** Licensed practical nurse, nursing (RN). **Liberal arts:** Arts/sciences.

Most popular majors. Business/marketing 30%, engineering/engineering technologies 11%, liberal arts 30%, public administration/social services 7%, trade and industry 27%.

Computing on campus. 125 workstations in library, computer center. Online library, wireless network available.

Student life. Freshman orientation: Available. Preregistration for classes offered. Four early orientations held in the summer. **Activities:** Student government, student newspaper, service-leadership organization.

Student services. Career counseling, student employment services, personal counseling, placement for graduates, veterans' counselor. **Transfer:** Transfer adviser for students transferring to 4-year colleges.

Contact. E-mail: mpace@netc.edu
Phone: (843) 921-6900 Fax: (843) 921-1476
Danielle Pace, Director of Enrollment Management, Northeastern Technical College, Drawer 1007, Cheraw, SC 29520

Orangeburg-Calhoun Technical College
Orangeburg, South Carolina
www.octech.edu   CB code: 5527

- Public 2-year community and technical college
- Commuter campus in large town

General. Founded in 1968. Regionally accredited. **Enrollment:** 3,000 undergraduates. **Degrees:** 217 associate awarded. **ROTC:** Army. **Location:** 75 miles from Charleston, 45 miles from Columbia. **Calendar:** Semester, extensive summer session. **Full-time faculty:** 76 total. **Part-time faculty:** 88 total.

Basis for selection. Open admission, but selective for some programs. COMPASS and ASSET are used for placement. SAT or ACT may be submitted in place of ASSET or COMPASS. Admission to nursing and allied health programs based on school achievement record and test scores. **Adult students:** ACT and SAT test scores are only valid for us for 5 years. Students may also take the COMPASS placement test if they do not have ACT or SAT scores or if their scores do not meet admissions criteria.

High school preparation. 24 units recommended. Recommended units include English 4, mathematics 4, social studies 3, history 1, science 3, foreign language 1, computer science 1 and academic electives 7.

2011-2012 Annual costs. Tuition/fees: $3,554; $4,394 out-of-district; $6,518 out-of-state. Books/supplies: $800. Personal expenses: $2,123.

Financial aid. All financial aid based on need. Need-based aid available for part-time students. Work-study available nights, weekends and for part-time students.

Application procedures. Admission: No deadline. $25 fee, may be waived for applicants with need. Admission notification on a rolling basis beginning on or about 1/1. **Financial aid:** Priority date 6/4; no closing date. FAFSA, institutional form required. Applicants notified on a rolling basis starting 5/1; must reply within 2 week(s) of notification.

Academics. Special study options: Cooperative education, cross-registration, distance learning, double major, dual enrollment of high school students, independent study, liberal arts/career combination. License preparation in nursing, radiology, real estate. **Credit/placement by examination:** AP, CLEP, institutional tests. 60% of hours needed for degree may be earned by examination. **Support services:** GED preparation and test center, learning center, pre-admission summer program, reduced course load, remedial instruction, study skills assistance, tutoring, writing center.

Majors. Business: General, accounting, administrative services. **Computer sciences:** Data processing, programming. **Conservation:** Forest resources. **Health services:** Clinical lab assistant, clinical lab technology, medical radiologic technology/radiation therapy, nursing (RN). **Liberal arts:** Arts/sciences. **Protective services:** Criminal justice.

Computing on campus. 100 workstations in library, computer center, student center. Commuter students can connect to campus network. Online course registration, online library, helpline, repair service, wireless network available.

Student life. Freshman orientation: Available. Preregistration for classes offered. **Activities:** Student government, honor fraternities, curriculum clubs.

Athletics. Intramural: Basketball M, cheerleading M, football (tackle) M.

Student services. Adult student services, career counseling, services for economically disadvantaged, student employment services, financial aid counseling, minority student services, personal counseling, placement for graduates, veterans' counselor. **Physically disabled:** Services for visually, speech, hearing impaired. **Transfer:** Pre-admission transcript evaluation for new students. Transfer adviser, college fairs on campus for students transferring to 4-year colleges.

Contact. E-mail: askme@octech.edu
Phone: (803) 535-1224 Fax: (803) 535-1388
Sernetta Quick, Director of Admissions and Recruitment, Orangeburg-Calhoun Technical College, 3250 St. Matthews Road, Orangeburg, SC 29118-8222

Piedmont Technical College
Greenwood, South Carolina
www.ptc.edu   CB code: 5550

- Public 2-year community and technical college
- Commuter campus in small city

General. Founded in 1966. Regionally accredited. Serves 7-county region of the state (satellite campus in each county offering Internet classes, traditional classes and interactive televised classes with main campus). **Enrollment:** 5,247 degree-seeking undergraduates; 975 non-degree-seeking students. **Degrees:** 515 associate awarded. **Location:** 75 miles from Columbia, 50 miles from Greenville. **Calendar:** Semester, extensive summer session. **Full-time faculty:** 100 total. **Part-time faculty:** 145 total. **Class size:** 72% < 20, 28% 20-39, less than 1% 40-49, less than 1% 50-99. **Special facilities:** Engineering lab, South Carolina Center for Funeral Service Education, technologically advanced nursing labs equipped with SIMS man Bruce.

Student profile. Among degree-seeking undergraduates, 11% enrolled in a transfer program, 32% enrolled in a vocational program, 2% already have a bachelor's degree or higher, 1,038 enrolled as first-time, first-year students.

Part-time:	52%	African American:	42%
Out-of-state:	1%	Hispanic American:	1%
Women:	67%	25 or older:	55%

Transfer out. Colleges most students transferred to 2011: Lander University, Clemson University, University of South Carolina, South Carolina State University.

Basis for selection. Open admission, but selective for some programs. Students with SAT Verbal of at least 480 and SAT Math of at least 440 or ACT Composite of at least 20 do not need to take institutional placement tests.

2011-2012 Annual costs. Tuition/fees: $3,622; $4,030 out-of-district; $5,232 out-of-state. Books/supplies: $900. Personal expenses: $250.

2010-2011 Financial aid. All financial aid based on need. Need-based aid available for part-time students. Work-study available nights, weekends and for part-time students.

Application procedures. Admission: No deadline. No application fee. Admission notification on a rolling basis. **Financial aid:** Priority date 5/1; no closing date. FAFSA required. Applicants notified on a rolling basis starting 6/1; must reply within 2 week(s) of notification.

Academics. Special study options: Cooperative education, distance learning, double major, dual enrollment of high school students, independent study, internships, liberal arts/career combination. Bachelor's degree programs available on campus. License preparation in nursing, real estate. **Credit/placement by examination:** AP, CLEP, IB, institutional tests. 24 credit hours maximum toward associate degree. **Support services:** GED preparation, learning center, pre-admission summer program, reduced course load, remedial instruction, study skills assistance, tutoring, writing center.

Majors. Business: General, administrative services. **Computer sciences:** Data processing. **Education:** Voc/tech. **Health services:** Cardiovascular technology, medical radiologic technology/radiation therapy, nursing (RN), respiratory therapy technology. **Human services:** Social work. **Liberal arts:** Arts/sciences. **Protective services:** Criminal justice.

Most popular majors. Business/marketing 25%, engineering/engineering technologies 9%, health sciences 13%, liberal arts 13%, security/protective services 10%, trade and industry 26%.

Computing on campus. 250 workstations in computer center, student center. Commuter students can connect to campus network. Online library, helpline, repair service available.

Student life. Freshman orientation: Available. Preregistration for classes offered. **Activities:** Alpha Delta Omega, Christian sudent union, computer club, horticulture club, Kappa Beta Delta, Lambda Chi Nu, Phi Theta Kappa, psychology club, rad tech club, student nurses association.

Student services. Adult student services, career counseling, services for economically disadvantaged, student employment services, financial aid counseling, minority student services, personal counseling, placement for graduates, veterans' counselor. **Transfer:** Pre-admission transcript evaluation for new students. Transfer adviser, college fairs on campus for students transferring to 4-year colleges.

Contact. E-mail: Latimer.T@ptc.edu
Phone: (864) 941-8369 Toll-free number: (800) 868-5528
Fax: (864) 941-8555
Tanisha Latimer, Dean of Enrollment Management, Piedmont Technical College, PO Box 1467, Greenwood, SC 29648

Spartanburg Community College
Spartanburg, South Carolina
www.sccsc.edu   CB code: 5668

- Public 2-year community and technical college
- Commuter campus in small city
- Interview required

General. Founded in 1961. Regionally accredited. Satellite campuses located in Greer and Gaffney. Limited courses available on-site in Union. **Enrollment:** 6,008 degree-seeking undergraduates. **Degrees:** 433 associate awarded. **Location:** 4 miles from downtown. **Calendar:** Semester, limited summer session. **Full-time faculty:** 118 total. **Part-time faculty:** 239 total. **Class size:** 64% < 20, 36% 20-39. **Special facilities:** Horticultural arboretum. **Partnerships:** Formal partnership with Ford Asset Program (auto mechanic training program).

Student profile. Among degree-seeking undergraduates, 26% enrolled in a transfer program, 67% enrolled in a vocational program, 7% already have a bachelor's degree or higher, 1,205 enrolled as first-time, first-year students.

Part-time:	51%	Asian American:	3%
Out-of-state:	2%	Hispanic American:	3%
Women:	62%	25 or older:	38%
African American:	25%		

Transfer out. 82% of students enrolled in the transfer program go on to 4-year colleges. **Colleges most students transferred to 2011:** Clemson University, University of South Carolina Upstate, University of South Carolina at Columbia, Wofford College, Spartanburg Methodist College.

Basis for selection. Open admission, but selective for some programs. Test of Adult Basic Education required for admissions. Programmer's Aptitude Test required for computer programming and data processing. Admission to some health science programs limited usually based on size of class. Essay recommended. **Home schooled:** Transcript of courses and grades required. State Department approval of the applicable home school association.

High school preparation. College-preparatory program recommended. 21 units required. Required units include English 4, mathematics 2, social studies 2, history 2, science 2 (laboratory 2), foreign language 1 and academic electives 6. One biology and/or chemistry and 1 algebra required for most health programs. Algebra required for all engineering and computer programs.

2011-2012 Annual costs. Tuition/fees: $3,740; $4,650 out-of-district; $7,616 out-of-state. Books/supplies: $1,000. Personal expenses: $2,763.

2010-2011 Financial aid. Need-based: 99% of total undergraduate aid awarded as scholarships/grants, 1% as loans/jobs. Need-based aid available for part-time students. Work-study available nights, weekends and for part-time students. **Non-need-based:** Scholarships awarded for academics. **Additional information:** Participates in South Carolina lottery tuition assistance program. Full-time technical college students who are state residents receive assistance for tuition not covered by federal or need-based grants.

Application procedures. Admission: No deadline. $25 fee. Admission notification on a rolling basis. **Financial aid:** Priority date 2/28, closing date 5/1. FAFSA required. Applicants notified on a rolling basis starting 5/1.

Academics. Special study options: Cooperative education, distance learning, double major, dual enrollment of high school students, independent study. License preparation in dental hygiene, nursing, occupational therapy, physical therapy, radiology. **Credit/placement by examination:** AP, CLEP, IB, institutional tests. Students must complete 25% of core courses in their program of study through instruction offered by the college. **Support services:** GED preparation and test center, learning center, remedial instruction, study skills assistance, tutoring, writing center.

Majors. Business: Accounting, administrative services, business admin, hospitality admin, hotel/motel admin, marketing, restaurant/food services. **Computer sciences:** Data processing. **Education:** Voc/tech. **General:** Horticulture. **Health services:** Clinical lab technology, medical radiologic technology/radiation therapy, nursing (RN), predental, respiratory therapy technology. **Liberal arts:** Arts/sciences.

Most popular majors. Business/marketing 17%, health sciences 25%, interdisciplinary studies 14%, liberal arts 26%, trade and industry 14%.

Computing on campus. 2,000 workstations in library, computer center, student center. Commuter students can connect to campus network. Online course registration, helpline, repair service, wireless network available.

Student life. Freshman orientation: Mandatory. Preregistration for classes offered. Approximately two-hour long session held on campus prior to the start of each semester. **Activities:** Campus ministries, drama, student government, Campus Crusade for Christ.

Student services. Adult student services, career counseling, services for economically disadvantaged, student employment services, financial aid counseling, personal counseling, placement for graduates, veterans' counselor, women's services. **Physically disabled:** Services for visually, speech, hearing impaired. **Transfer:** Transfer adviser, college fairs on campus for students transferring to 4-year colleges.

Contact. E-mail: Admissions, SCC@sccsc.edu
Phone: (864) 592-4800 Toll-free number: (866) 592-4700
Fax: (864) 592-4642
Lynn Dale, Director of Enrollment Services, Spartanburg Community College, Box 4386, Spartanburg, SC 29305-4386

Spartanburg Methodist College
Spartanburg, South Carolina   CB member
www.smcsc.edu   CB code: 5627

- Private 2-year junior and liberal arts college affiliated with United Methodist Church
- Residential campus in small city
- SAT or ACT (ACT writing optional) required

General. Founded in 1911. Regionally accredited. **Enrollment:** 797 degree-seeking undergraduates; 6 non-degree-seeking students. **Degrees:** 175 associate awarded. **ROTC:** Army. **Location:** 30 miles from Greenville, 60 miles from Charlotte, NC. **Calendar:** Semester, limited summer session. **Full-time faculty:** 27 total; 41% have terminal degrees, 11% minority, 52% women. **Part-time faculty:** 43 total; 14% have terminal degrees, 12% minority, 46% women. **Class size:** 22% < 20, 76% 20-39, 2% 40-49.

Student profile. Among degree-seeking undergraduates, 100% enrolled in a transfer program, 475 enrolled as first-time, first-year students, 32 transferred in from other institutions.

Part-time:	2%	Hispanic American:	5%
Out-of-state:	4%	Native American:	1%
Women:	45%	25 or older:	1%
African American:	31%	Live on campus:	76%
Asian American:	1%		

Transfer out. 81% of students enrolled in the transfer program go on to 4-year colleges. **Colleges most students transferred to 2011:** University of South Carolina Upstate, Clemson University, University of South Carolina, Lander University, College of Charleston.

Basis for selection. High school GPA, SAT/ACT scores, and class rank very important. Audition, essay, interview recommended. **Adult students:** SAT/ACT scores not required if applicant over 21. **Home schooled:** Applicants need complete high school academic transcript. Recommend students be supervised through accredited home school association to provide curriculum and academic oversight throughout high school program.

High school preparation. College-preparatory program recommended. 24 units recommended. Recommended units include English 4, mathematics 4, social studies 2, history 1, science 3, foreign language 1, computer science 1 and academic electives 7. 1 unit of Physical Education or Junior ROTC.

Two-Year Colleges

2011-2012 Annual costs. Tuition/fees: $14,058. Per-credit charge: $375. Room/board: $7,918. Books/supplies: $1,200.

2011-2012 Financial aid. Need-based: Average need met was 76%. Average scholarship/grant was $2,250; average loan $1,750. 74% of total undergraduate aid awarded as scholarships/grants, 26% as loans/jobs. Need-based aid available for part-time students. Work-study available nights, weekends and for part-time students. **Non-need-based:** Scholarships awarded for academics, athletics, religious affiliation.

Application procedures. Admission: No deadline. $20 fee, may be waived for applicants with need. Admission notification on a rolling basis beginning on or about 9/1. Housing deposit refundable until June 1. Applicant notified of decision within a week. **Financial aid:** Priority date 6/30, closing date 8/22. FAFSA required. Applicants notified on a rolling basis starting 3/1; must reply within 2 week(s) of notification.

Academics. Special study options: Dual enrollment of high school students, ESL, honors, independent study, liberal arts/career combination, study abroad. **Credit/placement by examination:** AP, CLEP, SAT, ACT, institutional tests. 15 credit hours maximum toward associate degree. **Support services:** Learning center, pre-admission summer program, reduced course load, remedial instruction, study skills assistance, tutoring, writing center.

Majors. Business: Business admin. **Liberal arts:** Arts/sciences. **Protective services:** Law enforcement admin. **Visual/performing arts:** General.

Most popular majors. Security/protective services 6%.

Computing on campus. 45 workstations in dormitories, library, computer center, student center. Dormitories wired for high-speed internet access and linked to campus network. Commuter students can connect to campus network. Online library, helpline, wireless network available.

Student life. Freshman orientation: Mandatory, $25 fee. Preregistration for classes offered. One session in mid-July, one session in early August, one session on move-in weekend (mid August). **Policies:** No alcohol, drugs, or firearms allowed on campus. All campus buildings smoke free. **Housing:** Guaranteed on-campus for all undergraduates. Coed dorms, single-sex dorms, special housing for disabled, wellness housing available. $100 fully refundable deposit, deadline 11/30. **Activities:** Jazz band, campus ministries, choral groups, dance, drama, literary magazine, music ensembles, student government, student newspaper, computer programming club, Psi Omega Theatre Fraternity, People Organizing People Successfully, Presbyterian Student Association, Wesley Fellowship, Campus Crusade for Christ, Sigma Kappa Delta, Phi Theta Kappa, Psi Beta.

Athletics. NJCAA. **Intercollegiate:** Baseball M, basketball, cheerleading, cross-country, golf, soccer, softball W, tennis, volleyball W, wrestling M. **Intramural:** Basketball, football (non-tackle) M, softball, table tennis, tennis, volleyball. **Team name:** Pioneers.

Student services. Adult student services, alcohol/substance abuse counseling, chaplain/spiritual director, career counseling, services for economically disadvantaged, student employment services, financial aid counseling, health services, personal counseling, placement for graduates, veterans' counselor. **Physically disabled:** Services for visually, speech, hearing impaired. **Transfer:** Pre-admission transcript evaluation for new students. Transfer center, transfer adviser, college fairs on campus for students transferring to 4-year colleges.

Contact. E-mail: admiss@smcsc.edu
Phone: (864) 587-4213 Toll-free number: (800) 772-7286
Fax: (864) 587-4355
Michael Queen, Director of Admissions, Spartanburg Methodist College, 1000 Powell Mill Road, Spartanburg, SC 29301-5899

Technical College of the Lowcountry
Beaufort, South Carolina
www.tcl.edu
CB code: 5047

- Public 2-year community and technical college
- Commuter campus in small city

General. Founded in 1972. Regionally accredited. **Enrollment:** 2,392 degree-seeking undergraduates; 235 non-degree-seeking students. **Degrees:** 173 associate awarded. **Location:** 45 miles from Savannah, GA. **Calendar:** Semester, extensive summer session. **Full-time faculty:** 48 total. **Part-time faculty:** 117 total.

Student profile. Among degree-seeking undergraduates, 503 enrolled as first-time, first-year students.

Part-time:	67%	**Women:**	73%

Basis for selection. Open admission, but selective for some programs. SAT or ACT required for placement and counseling. Nursing students are encouraged to have a personal interview and must submit NET test results. Interview recommended for nursing program. **Adult students:** After admission all students take either COMPASS or ASSET for placement.

2011-2012 Annual costs. Tuition/fees: $3,604; $7,852 out-of-state.

Financial aid. All financial aid based on need. Need-based aid available for part-time students. Work-study available nights, weekends and for part-time students. **Additional information:** State lottery aid may be available to South Carolina residents who take 6 credit hours or more.

Application procedures. Admission: No deadline. $25 fee. Admission notification on a rolling basis. **Financial aid:** No deadline. FAFSA required.

Academics. Special study options: Cooperative education, cross-registration, distance learning, double major, dual enrollment of high school students, ESL, independent study, internships. **Credit/placement by examination:** AP, CLEP, institutional tests. **Support services:** GED preparation and test center, learning center, pre-admission summer program, reduced course load, remedial instruction, study skills assistance, tutoring, writing center.

Majors. Business: General, administrative services. **Computer sciences:** Data processing. **Health services:** Medical radiologic technology/radiation therapy, nursing (RN), physical therapy assistant. **Liberal arts:** Arts/sciences. **Protective services:** Criminal justice. **Work/family studies:** Child care service.

Computing on campus. 400 workstations in library, computer center, student center. Online library, helpline available.

Student life. Freshman orientation: Available. Preregistration for classes offered. One-day session at start of fall semester. **Activities:** Student government, Phi Theta Kappa, Rotaract Club, professional societies.

Student services. Career counseling, student employment services, financial aid counseling, personal counseling, placement for graduates, veterans' counselor.

Contact. E-mail: bthomas@tcl.edu
Phone: (843) 525-8208 Toll-free number: (800) 768-8252
Fax: (843) 525-8285
Brad Thomas, Director of Admissions, Technical College of the Lowcountry, 921 South Ribaut Road, Beaufort, SC 29901-1288

Tri-County Technical College
Pendleton, South Carolina
www.tctc.edu
CB code: 5789

- Public 2-year community and technical college
- Commuter campus in small town

General. Founded in 1962. Regionally accredited. **Enrollment:** 6,950 undergraduates. **Degrees:** 601 associate awarded. **ROTC:** Army, Air Force. **Location:** 5 miles from Clemson. **Calendar:** Semester, limited summer session. **Full-time faculty:** 130 total. **Part-time faculty:** 200 total.

Student profile. 495 transferred in from other institutions.

Out-of-state:	2%	**25 or older:**	85%

Transfer out. Colleges most students transferred to 2011: Clemson University, University of South Carolina, Lander University, Anderson University, Southern Wesleyan University.

Basis for selection. Open admission, but selective for some programs. **Home schooled:** Documentation of home-schooled diploma can be supplied by a state department of education or a regional accrediting organization.

2011-2012 Annual costs. Tuition/fees: $3,570; $4,434 out-of-district; $7,944 out-of-state. Books/supplies: $900. Personal expenses: $1,920.

Financial aid. Need-based: Need-based aid available for part-time students. Work-study available nights, weekends and for part-time students. **Non-need-based:** Scholarships awarded for academics, state residency. **Additional information:** Deadline for application to institutional scholarships April 2.

Application procedures. Admission: Closing date 7/20 (postmark date). $30 fee. Admission notification on a rolling basis. **Financial aid:** Priority date 4/1, closing date 7/30. FAFSA required. Applicants notified on a rolling basis starting 6/15; must reply within 2 week(s) of notification.

Academics. Special study options: Cooperative education, distance learning, dual enrollment of high school students, internships, liberal arts/career combination. License preparation in nursing, real estate. **Credit/placement by examination:** AP, CLEP, IB, institutional tests. Credit available from documented work experience, course waiver, noncollective organization training programs, technical advanced placement. **Support services:** Learning center, reduced course load, remedial instruction, study skills assistance, tutoring, writing center.

Majors. Business: Accounting, administrative services, business admin. **Communications technology:** Radio/TV. **Computer sciences:** Data processing. **Health services:** Clinical lab technology, nursing (RN), respiratory therapy assistant, veterinary technology/assistant. **Liberal arts:** Arts/sciences. **Protective services:** Criminal justice. **Work/family studies:** Child care service, clothing/textiles.

Computing on campus. 800 workstations in library, computer center. Commuter students can connect to campus network. Online course registration, online library, helpline, wireless network available.

Student life. Freshman orientation: Mandatory. Preregistration for classes offered. **Activities:** Choral groups, drama, international student organizations, student government, Minority Student Association, criminal justice club, Tri-County Voices (chorus), Student Veterinary Technician Association, Student Nurses Association, Future Lab Professionals, environmental club, international student association, Spanish club, book discussion group.

Athletics. NJCAA. **Intercollegiate:** Basketball W, golf M, soccer. **Team name:** Hawks.

Student services. Career counseling, services for economically disadvantaged, student employment services, financial aid counseling, minority student services, placement for graduates, veterans' counselor. **Physically disabled:** Services for visually, speech, hearing impaired. **Transfer:** Pre-admission transcript evaluation for new students. Transfer adviser, college fairs on campus for students transferring to 4-year colleges.

Contact. E-mail: info@tctc.edu
Phone: (864) 646-1550 Fax: (864) 646-5080
Renae Frazier, Director of Recruitment & Admissions, Tri-County Technical College, PO Box 587, Pendleton, SC 29670

Trident Technical College
Charleston, South Carolina
www.tridenttech.edu

CB member
CB code: 5049

- Public 2-year community and technical college
- Commuter campus in large city

General. Founded in 1964. Regionally accredited. 4 campuses: Palmer Campus in downtown Charleston, Main Campus in North Charleston, Mount Pleasant Campus in Mount Pleasant and Berkeley Campus in Moncks Corner. **Enrollment:** 15,412 degree-seeking undergraduates; 1,369 non-degree-seeking students. **Degrees:** 1,203 associate awarded. **Location:** 15 miles from downtown. **Calendar:** Semester, extensive summer session. **Full-time faculty:** 315 total; 14% minority, 53% women. **Part-time faculty:** 505 total; 15% minority, 61% women. **Class size:** 37% < 20, 59% 20-39, 2% 40-49, 1% 50-99, less than 1% >100.

Student profile. Among degree-seeking undergraduates, 3,133 enrolled as first-time, first-year students, 869 transferred in from other institutions.

Part-time:	52%	Asian American:	1%
Out-of-state:	3%	Hispanic American:	4%
Women:	62%	Native American:	1%
African American:	31%	25 or older:	44%

Basis for selection. Open admission, but selective for some programs. Special requirements for nursing students. **Learning Disabled:** Student should provide current medical, psychological, and/or psychiatric documentation providing a diagnosis and describing how his/her disability affects his/her ability to function in a collegiate, adult learning environment. Documentation indicating what accommodations the student received in high school and/or at another college may also be helpful.

2011-2012 Annual costs. Tuition/fees: $3,600; $3,994 out-of-district; $6,814 out-of-state. Books/supplies: $1,150. Personal expenses: $1,226.

Financial aid. Need-based: Need-based aid available for part-time students. Work-study available nights, weekends and for part-time students.

Application procedures. Admission: Closing date 8/6 (postmark date). $30 fee. Admission notification on a rolling basis. Applicants to early admissions program must rank in upper half of high school class and must have combined SAT score (exclusive of Writing) of 800 or ACT composite score

of 17. **Financial aid:** No deadline. FAFSA required. Applicants notified on a rolling basis; must reply within 6 week(s) of notification.

Academics. Special study options: Accelerated study, cooperative education, cross-registration, distance learning, double major, dual enrollment of high school students, ESL, independent study, internships, weekend college. License preparation in aviation, dental hygiene, nursing, paramedic, radiology. **Credit/placement by examination:** AP, CLEP, IB, institutional tests. **Support services:** GED preparation, learning center, reduced course load, remedial instruction, study skills assistance, tutoring, writing center.

Majors. Business: General, accounting, administrative services, business admin, customer service, e-commerce, entrepreneurial studies, hospitality admin, hotel/motel admin, logistics, marketing, office management, restaurant/food services, tourism/travel, transportation. **Communications:** Broadcast journalism. **Communications technology:** General. **Computer sciences:** Data processing, information systems, programming. **Education:** Voc/tech. **General:** Horticultural science, horticulture. **Health services:** Clinical lab technology, dental hygiene, medical radiologic technology/radiation therapy, nursing (RN), occupational therapy assistant, physical therapy assistant, respiratory therapy technology. **Liberal arts:** Arts/sciences. **Physical sciences:** General. **Protective services:** Fire services admin, law enforcement admin. **Visual/performing arts:** Commercial/advertising art, graphic design. **Work/family studies:** Child care management.

Most popular majors. Business/marketing 10%, health sciences 26%, interdisciplinary studies 6%, liberal arts 30%, public administration/social services 6%.

Computing on campus. 3,000 workstations in library, computer center, student center. Online library, wireless network available.

Student life. Freshman orientation: Available. Preregistration for classes offered. 45-minute ongoing service. **Activities:** Drama, international student organizations, radio station, student government, student newspaper, Phi Theta Kappa international honor society, Alpha Mu Gamma, Asian Studies, Black Student Association, Campus Crusade for Christ, La Sociedad Hispanoamericana, Society of Student Leaders.

Student services. Adult student services, alcohol/substance abuse counseling, career counseling, services for economically disadvantaged, student employment services, financial aid counseling, personal counseling, placement for graduates, veterans' counselor. **Physically disabled:** Services for visually, hearing impaired. **Transfer:** Pre-admission transcript evaluation for new students. Transfer adviser, college fairs on campus for students transferring to 4-year colleges.

Contact. E-mail: admissions@tridenttech.edu
Phone: (843) 574-6125 Toll-free number: (877) 349-7184
Fax: (843) 574-6483
Clara Martin, Director of Admissions, Trident Technical College, Box 118067, AM-M, Charleston, SC 29423-8067

University of South Carolina: Lancaster
Lancaster, South Carolina
usclancaster.sc.edu

CB code: 5849

- Public 2-year branch campus and junior college
- Commuter campus in large town

General. Founded in 1959. Regionally accredited. **Enrollment:** 1,092 degree-seeking undergraduates. **Degrees:** 129 associate awarded. **ROTC:** Army. **Location:** 50 miles from Columbia, 40 miles from Charlotte, North Carolina. **Calendar:** Semester, limited summer session. **Full-time faculty:** 55 total. **Part-time faculty:** 29 total. **Special facilities:** Health sciences facilities, diabetic education center.

Student profile.

Out-of-state:	2%	25 or older:	19%

Transfer out. Colleges most students transferred to 2011: University of South Carolina-Columbia, Winthrop University, Clemson University, York Technical College.

Basis for selection. Open admission. SAT or ACT required in admissions process but applicants with scores below required levels will be admitted provisionally. **Adult students:** SAT/ACT scores not required if applicant over 21. **Home schooled:** Transcript of courses and grades required.

High school preparation. College-preparatory program recommended. 23 units recommended. Recommended units include English 4, mathematics 3, social studies 3, history 1, science 3 (laboratory 3), foreign language 2 and academic electives 4. One unit physical education/ ROTC required.

Two-Year Colleges

2011-2012 Annual costs. Tuition/fees: $6,092; $14,696 out-of-state. Per-credit charge: $238 in-state; $596 out-of-state. Books/supplies: $1,036. Personal expenses: $950.

Financial aid. Need-based: Work-study available nights, weekends and for part-time students.

Application procedures. Admission: Priority date 7/30; no deadline. $40 fee, may be waived for applicants with need. Admission notification on a rolling basis. **Financial aid:** Priority date 4/15; no closing date. FAFSA required. Applicants notified on a rolling basis starting 6/1; must reply within 2 week(s) of notification.

Academics. Special study options: Accelerated study, cross-registration, distance learning, dual enrollment of high school students, honors, independent study, internships, liberal arts/career combination. Bachelor's degree programs available on campus. License preparation in nursing. **Credit/placement by examination:** AP, CLEP, IB, institutional tests. 30 credit hours maximum toward associate degree. **Support services:** Learning center, study skills assistance, tutoring, writing center.

Majors. Business: Administrative services, business admin. **Health services:** Nursing (RN). **Liberal arts:** Arts/sciences. **Protective services:** Criminal justice. **Visual/performing arts:** Art.

Computing on campus. 110 workstations in library, computer center, student center. Commuter students can connect to campus network. Online course registration, repair service, wireless network available.

Student life. Freshman orientation: Mandatory, $35 fee. Preregistration for classes offered. 2-day program. **Activities:** Campus ministries, drama, literary magazine, student government, student newspaper, Black awareness group, adult group for education, Campus Crusade for Christ.

Athletics. NJCAA. **Intercollegiate:** Baseball M, golf M, soccer W, tennis. **Intramural:** Basketball, table tennis, volleyball. **Team name:** Lancers.

Student services. Adult student services, career counseling, student employment services, financial aid counseling, health services, personal counseling, veterans' counselor. **Transfer:** Pre-admission transcript evaluation for new students. College fairs on campus for students transferring to 4-year colleges.

Contact. Phone: (803) 313-7073 Fax: (803) 313-7116
Karen Faile, Director of Enrollment Management, University of South Carolina: Lancaster, Box 889, Lancaster, SC 29721

University of South Carolina: Salkehatchie
Allendale, South Carolina
uscsalkehatchie.sc.edu   **CB code: 5847**

▶ Public 2-year branch campus college
▶ Commuter campus in rural community
▶ SAT or ACT required

General. Founded in 1965. Regionally accredited. **Enrollment:** 810 degree-seeking undergraduates. **Degrees:** 121 associate awarded. **ROTC:** Army, Naval, Air Force. **Location:** 75 miles from Columbia, 75 miles from Charleston. **Calendar:** Semester, limited summer session. **Full-time faculty:** 25 total. **Part-time faculty:** 40 total.

Student profile.

Out-of-state:	1%	**25 or older:**	26%

Transfer out. Colleges most students transferred to 2011: University of South Carolina-Columbia, University of South Carolina-Aiken.

Basis for selection. Secondary school record and class rank most important. Standardized test scores also important. **Adult students:** SAT/ACT scores not required if applicant over 25.

High school preparation. College-preparatory program required. Required units include English 4, mathematics 3, social studies 3, history 1, science 2 (laboratory 2), foreign language 2 and academic electives 2.

2011-2012 Annual costs. Tuition/fees: $6,092; $14,696 out-of-state. Per-credit charge: $238 in-state; $596 out-of-state. Books/supplies: $1,036. Personal expenses: $1,746.

Financial aid. Need-based: Need-based aid available for part-time students. Work-study available nights, weekends and for part-time students. **Non-need-based:** Scholarships awarded for academics.

Application procedures. Admission: Priority date 8/19; no deadline. $40 fee, may be waived for applicants with need. Admission notification on a rolling basis. **Financial aid:** Priority date 4/30; no closing date. FAFSA required. Applicants notified on a rolling basis starting 6/1.

Academics. Special study options: Cross-registration, dual enrollment of high school students, independent study, student-designed major, study abroad. Bachelor's degree programs available on campus. **Credit/placement by examination:** AP, CLEP, IB, institutional tests. 15 credit hours maximum toward associate degree. **Support services:** Learning center, pre-admission summer program, reduced course load, tutoring.

Majors. Liberal arts: Arts/sciences.

Computing on campus. 102 workstations in library, computer center.

Student life. Freshman orientation: Mandatory. Preregistration for classes offered. **Activities:** Student government, minority student organization.

Athletics. NJCAA. **Intercollegiate:** Baseball M, basketball M, soccer, softball W. **Team name:** Indians.

Student services. Career counseling, financial aid counseling, personal counseling, veterans' counselor. **Physically disabled:** Services for visually, hearing impaired.

Contact. Phone: (803) 584-3446 Toll-free number: (800) 922-5500
Fax: (803) 584-3884
Jane Brewer, Dean for Student Services, University of South Carolina: Salkehatchie, PO Box 617, Allendale, SC 29810

University of South Carolina: Sumter
Sumter, South Carolina
www.uscsumter.edu   **CB code: 5821**

▶ Public 2-year branch campus college
▶ Commuter campus in small city
▶ SAT or ACT (ACT writing optional) required

General. Founded in 1966. Regionally accredited. **Enrollment:** 691 degree-seeking undergraduates. **Degrees:** 91 associate awarded. **ROTC:** Army. **Location:** 40 miles from Columbia, 98 miles from Charleston. **Calendar:** Semester, limited summer session. **Full-time faculty:** 50 total. **Part-time faculty:** 38 total. **Class size:** 68% < 20, 30% 20-39, 2% 40-49. **Partnerships:** Formal partnerships with high schools (college-level courses for eligible high school students.).

Student profile.

Out-of-state:	1%	**25 or older:**	20%

Transfer out. Colleges most students transferred to 2011: Central Carolina Technical College, College of Charleston, Midlands Technical College.

Basis for selection. Entering freshmen must have 2.25 GPA. Class rank and test scores also important. All freshmen required to take foreign language tests. Placement in mathematics may require additional testing. Interview required for academically marginal. **Adult students:** SAT/ACT scores not required if applicant over 23. **Home schooled:** Official transcripts, SAT/ACT and a GPR converted to the South Carolina Uniform grading scale if home schooled in South Carolina. **Learning Disabled:** Must submit recent documentation.

High school preparation. College-preparatory program required. 20 units required. Required and recommended units include English 4, mathematics 3-4, social studies 3, history 2, science 3 (laboratory 3), foreign language 2-3 and academic electives 4. 1 physical education required, 1 computer science recommended.

2011-2012 Annual costs. Tuition/fees: $6,142; $14,746 out-of-state. Per-credit charge: $238 in-state; $596 out-of-state. Books/supplies: $932. Personal expenses: $2,053.

Financial aid. All financial aid based on need. Need-based aid available for part-time students. Work-study available nights, weekends and for part-time students.

Application procedures. Admission: Priority date 8/1; no deadline. $40 fee, may be waived for applicants with need. Admission notification on a rolling basis. **Financial aid:** Priority date 4/15; no closing date. FAFSA required. Applicants notified on a rolling basis starting 4/16; must reply within 2 week(s) of notification.

Academics. Special study options: Cross-registration, distance learning, dual enrollment of high school students, independent study, liberal arts/career combination, student-designed major, teacher certification program. Bachelor's degree programs available on campus. **Credit/placement by examination:** AP, CLEP, institutional tests. 30 credit hours maximum toward associate degree. **Support services:** Learning center, remedial instruction, study skills assistance, tutoring, writing center.

Majors. Liberal arts: Arts/sciences.

Computing on campus. 195 workstations in library, computer center, student center. Commuter students can connect to campus network. Online course registration, online library, student web hosting, wireless network available.

Student life. Freshman orientation: Mandatory. Preregistration for classes offered. **Activities:** Choral groups, drama, literary magazine, music ensembles, student government, student newspaper, African-American club, Baptist Student clubs, campus activities board, Circle K, student art guild, student education association, student nursing organization, environmental club.

Athletics. NJCAA. Intercollegiate: Baseball M, soccer, softball W. **Intramural:** Baseball M, basketball, bowling, football (non-tackle), golf, handball, racquetball, soccer M, softball, table tennis, tennis, volleyball, weight lifting. **Team name:** Fire Ants.

Student services. Adult student services, chaplain/spiritual director, career counseling, services for economically disadvantaged, student employment services, financial aid counseling, personal counseling, placement for graduates, veterans' counselor. **Physically disabled:** Services for visually, speech, hearing impaired.

Contact. E-mail: kbritton@uscsumter.edu
Phone: (803) 938-3762 Fax: (803) 938-3901
Keith Britton, Director of Admissions, University of South Carolina: Sumter, 200 Miller Road, Sumter, SC 29150-2498

University of South Carolina: Union
Union, South Carolina
uscunion.sc.edu   **CB code: 5846**

▶ Public 2-year branch campus and liberal arts college
▶ Commuter campus in small town
▶ SAT or ACT required

General. Founded in 1965. Regionally accredited. Off-campus site at Laurens offers full range of courses. **Enrollment:** 310 degree-seeking undergraduates. **Degrees:** 49 associate awarded. **Location:** 30 miles from Spartanburg, 60 miles from Columbia. **Calendar:** Semester, limited summer session. **Full-time faculty:** 8 total. **Part-time faculty:** 15 total.

Student profile. Among degree-seeking undergraduates, 75 transferred in from other institutions.

| **Out-of-state:** | 1% | **25 or older:** | 40% |

Transfer out. 75% of students enrolled in the transfer program go on to 4-year colleges.

Basis for selection. Secondary school record most important. Standardized test scores and class rank also important. Students with high school diploma or GED but without required high school curriculum units may be admitted into Opportunity Program based on school achievement record and SAT or ACT scores. Institutional placement tests in mathematics and writing required of all freshmen. **Adult students:** SAT/ACT scores not required.

High school preparation. College-preparatory program required. 20 units required. Required units include English 4, mathematics 3, social studies 3, science 3 (laboratory 3), foreign language 2 and academic electives 4.

2011-2012 Annual costs. Tuition/fees: $6,122; $14,726 out-of-state. Per-credit charge: $238 in-state; $596 out-of-state. Books/supplies: $744. Personal expenses: $1,307.

2011-2012 Financial aid. All financial aid based on need. Work-study available nights, weekends and for part-time students.

Application procedures. Admission: No deadline. $40 fee, may be waived for applicants with need. Admission notification on a rolling basis beginning on or about 6/1. **Financial aid:** Priority date 4/15; no closing date. FAFSA required. Applicants notified on a rolling basis starting 7/15; must reply within 2 week(s) of notification.

Academics. Upper division courses leading to bachelor's degree in interdisciplinary studies available. Degree awarded by Columbia campus. **Special study options:** Cross-registration, distance learning, dual enrollment of high school students, independent study, internships, student-designed major. Bachelor's degree programs available on campus. **Credit/placement by examination:** AP, CLEP, institutional tests. **Support services:** Pre-admission summer program, reduced course load, remedial instruction, tutoring, writing center.

Majors. Liberal arts: Arts/sciences.

Student life. Freshman orientation: Mandatory. Preregistration for classes offered. **Activities:** Drama, literary magazine, student government, student newspaper, Afro-American and political groups, student media association, computer club, history club, art club, travel club, music club, biology club.

Athletics. Intercollegiate: Basketball M, softball W. **Intramural:** Baseball M, basketball, bowling, gymnastics, racquetball, skiing, softball, table tennis, tennis, volleyball.

Student services. Adult student services, career counseling, student employment services, on-campus daycare, personal counseling. **Transfer:** College fairs on campus for students transferring to 4-year colleges.

Contact. Phone: (864) 429-8728 Fax: (864) 427-3682
Brad Greer, Director of Enrollment Services, University of South Carolina: Union, PO Drawer 729, Union, SC 29379

Virginia College at Charleston
North Charleston, South Carolina
www.charleston.vc.edu

▶ For-profit 2-year health science and career college
▶ Large city

General. Regionally accredited; also accredited by ACICS. **Enrollment:** 500 degree-seeking undergraduates. **Degrees:** 1 bachelor's, 3 associate awarded. **Calendar:** Quarter. **Full-time faculty:** 16 total. **Part-time faculty:** 26 total.

Basis for selection. Open admission.

Financial aid. Need-based: Work-study available nights, weekends and for part-time students.

Application procedures. Admission: $100 fee.

Academics. Credit/placement by examination: AP, CLEP.

Majors. Business: Business admin. **Health services:** Medical records admin, surgical technology.

Contact. E-mail: charleston.info@vc.edu
Phone: (843) 614-4300
Virginia College at Charleston, 6185 Rivers Avenue, North Charleston, SC 29406

Virginia College at Columbia
Columbia, South Carolina
www.columbia.vc.edu

▶ For-profit 2-year health science and career college
▶ Large city

General. Regionally accredited; also accredited by ACICS. **Enrollment:** 750 degree-seeking undergraduates. **Calendar:** Quarter.

Basis for selection. Open admission.

Financial aid. Need-based: Work-study available nights, weekends and for part-time students.

Application procedures. Admission: $100 fee.

Academics. Credit/placement by examination: AP, CLEP.

Majors. Business: Business admin. **Health services:** Medical records admin, surgical technology.

Contact. E-mail: columbia.info@vc.edu
Phone: (803) 509-7100
Virginia College at Columbia, 7201 Two Notch Road, Columbia, SC 29223

Virginia College at Greenville
Greenville, South Carolina
www.greenville.vc.edu

- For-profit 2-year business and career college
- Very large city

General. Regionally accredited; also accredited by ACICS. **Enrollment:** 780 degree-seeking undergraduates. **Degrees:** 53 associate awarded. **Calendar:** Quarter. **Full-time faculty:** 19 total. **Part-time faculty:** 21 total.

Basis for selection. Open admission.

Financial aid. Need-based: Work-study available nights, weekends and for part-time students.

Application procedures. Admission: $100 fee.

Academics. Credit/placement by examination: AP, CLEP.

Majors. Business: Business admin. **Health services:** Medical records admin, surgical technology.

Contact. E-mail: greenville.info@vc.edu
Phone: (864) 679-4900
Virginia College at Greenville, 78 Global Drive, Greenville, SC 29607

Virginia College at Spartanburg
Spartanburg, South Carolina
www.spartanburg.vc.edu

- For-profit 2-year technical and career college
- Large city

General. Regionally accredited; also accredited by ACICS. **Enrollment:** 450 degree-seeking undergraduates. **Calendar:** Quarter.

Basis for selection. Open admission.

Financial aid. Need-based: Work-study available nights, weekends and for part-time students.

Application procedures. Admission: $100 fee.

Academics. Credit/placement by examination: AP, CLEP.

Majors. Business: Business admin. **Health services:** Medical records admin, surgical technology.

Contact. E-mail: spartanburg.info@vc.edu
Phone: (864) 504-3200
Virginia College at Spartanburg, 8150 Warren H. Abernathy Highway, Spartanburg, SC 29301

Williamsburg Technical College
Kingstree, South Carolina
www.wiltech.edu   CB code: 5892

- Public 2-year community and technical college
- Commuter campus in small town

General. Founded in 1969. Regionally accredited. **Enrollment:** 633 degree-seeking undergraduates; 28 non-degree-seeking students. **Degrees:** 69 associate awarded. **Location:** 75 miles from Charleston, 40 miles from Florence. **Calendar:** Semester, extensive summer session. **Full-time faculty:** 20 total. **Part-time faculty:** 25 total. **Class size:** 90% < 20, 10% 20-39. **Partnerships:** Formal partnerships with Tupperware, Firestone and Williamsburg County school district.

Student profile. Among degree-seeking undergraduates, 195 enrolled as first-time, first-year students.

Part-time:	58%	African American:	70%
Women:	68%	25 or older:	52%

Transfer out. Colleges most students transferred to 2011: Francis Marion University, Coker College, Limestone College, University of South Carolina, Coastal Carolina University.

Basis for selection. Open admission. Academically weak students must enroll in Applied Studies Program.

High school preparation. 25 units recommended. Recommended units include English 4, mathematics 4, social studies 3, history 1, science 3, foreign language 1 and academic electives 7. Recommend one unit physical education/JROTC. 1 unit computer technology, 6 or more units in occupational area will substitute for one science.

2011-2012 Annual costs. Tuition/fees: $3,438; $3,558 out-of-district; $6,642 out-of-state. Books/supplies: $1,000. Personal expenses: $3,780.

Financial aid. Need-based: Need-based aid available for part-time students. Work-study available nights, weekends and for part-time students. **Non-need-based:** Scholarships awarded for academics, leadership, minority status, state residency. **Additional information:** Tuition waivers for children of war veterans.

Application procedures. Admission: No deadline. $10 fee, may be waived for applicants with need. Admission notification on a rolling basis. **Financial aid:** Priority date 4/15; no closing date. FAFSA required. Applicants notified on a rolling basis starting 7/1; must reply within 4 week(s) of notification.

Academics. Special study options: Distance learning, double major, dual enrollment of high school students, honors, independent study, internships, liberal arts/career combination, student-designed major. License preparation in nursing. **Credit/placement by examination:** AP, CLEP, institutional tests. 18 credit hours maximum toward associate degree. **Support services:** Learning center, pre-admission summer program, remedial instruction, study skills assistance, tutoring.

Majors. Business: General, administrative services, information resources management, office management. **Computer sciences:** General. **Education:** Early childhood, teacher assistance. **Engineering:** Electrical. **Liberal arts:** Arts/sciences.

Computing on campus. 60 workstations in library, computer center. Online library, wireless network available.

Student life. Freshman orientation: Available. Preregistration for classes offered. **Activities:** Student government.

Student services. Career counseling, services for economically disadvantaged, financial aid counseling, personal counseling, placement for graduates, veterans' counselor. **Physically disabled:** Services for hearing impaired. **Transfer:** Pre-admission transcript evaluation for new students. College fairs on campus for students transferring to 4-year colleges.

Contact. E-mail: dubosec@wiltech.edu
Phone: (843) 355-4162 Toll-free number: (800) 768-2021 ext. 4162
Fax: (843) 355-4289
Alexis Wright, Admissions Director, Williamsburg Technical College, 601 Martin Luther King Jr. Avenue, Kingstree, SC 29556-4197

York Technical College
Rock Hill, South Carolina
www.yorktech.edu   CB code: 5989

- Public 2-year community and technical college
- Commuter campus in large town

General. Founded in 1962. Regionally accredited. Member of Charlotte Area Consortium of Colleges and Universities. **Enrollment:** 4,971 degree-seeking undergraduates; 650 non-degree-seeking students. **Degrees:** 503 associate awarded. **Location:** 70 miles from Columbia, 14 miles from Charlotte, NC. **Calendar:** Semester, extensive summer session. **Full-time faculty:** 127 total. **Part-time faculty:** 225 total. **Special facilities:** Center for Manufacturing Productivity. **Partnerships:** Formal partnerships with 3D Systems, Okuma Corporation.

Student profile. Among degree-seeking undergraduates, 23% enrolled in a transfer program, 77% enrolled in a vocational program, 10% already have a bachelor's degree or higher, 1,201 enrolled as first-time, first-year students.

Part-time:	47%	Women:	63%
Out-of-state:	5%	25 or older:	65%

Transfer out. Colleges most students transferred to 2011: Winthrop University, Clemson University, University of South Carolina.

Basis for selection. Open admission, but selective for some programs. COMPASS, SAT, or ACT scores may be used for admission and placement. Additional qualification criteria required for admission to limited enrollment Health Science programs. **Home schooled:** Applicants must have graduated from approved South Carolina homeschool association or a homeschool recognized by the Department of Education in its home state to be classified as a high school graduate. **Learning Disabled:** Students with disabilities who wish to receive special testing accommodations should contact Special Resources Office in Student Services.

High school preparation. College prep chemistry required for Dental Hygiene and Nursing (RN) program.

2011-2012 Annual costs. Tuition/fees: $3,628; $4,016 out-of-district; $8,216 out-of-state. Books/supplies: $1,200.

Financial aid. Need-based: Need-based aid available for part-time students. Work-study available nights, weekends and for part-time students. **Non-need-based:** Scholarships awarded for academics, leadership, state residency.

Application procedures. Admission: No deadline. No application fee. Application must be submitted online. Admission notification on a rolling basis. **Financial aid:** Priority date 6/1; no closing date. FAFSA required. Applicants notified on a rolling basis starting 4/1; must reply within 2 week(s) of notification.

Academics. Special study options: Cooperative education, distance learning, dual enrollment of high school students, liberal arts/career combination. License preparation in dental hygiene, nursing, paramedic, radiology, real estate. **Credit/placement by examination:** AP, CLEP, institutional tests. At least 25% of semester credit hours required for program completion must be earned through instruction at York Technical College. **Support services:** Learning center, reduced course load, remedial instruction, study skills assistance, tutoring, writing center.

Majors. Business: General, accounting, administrative services, business admin, human resources, logistics. **Computer sciences:** Applications programming, LAN/WAN management, programming. **Education:** Early childhood. **Health services:** Clinical lab technology, dental hygiene, medical radiologic technology/radiation therapy, nursing (RN), radiologic technology/medical imaging. **Liberal arts:** Arts/sciences. **Protective services:** Fire services admin, police science.

Most popular majors. Business/marketing 34%, engineering/engineering technologies 10%, family/consumer sciences 9%, health sciences 16%, liberal arts 15%.

Computing on campus. 180 workstations in library, computer center. Commuter students can connect to campus network. Online library, helpline, wireless network available.

Student life. Freshman orientation: Mandatory. Preregistration for classes offered. Held by department of study before classes begin. **Activities:** Jacobin Society, Phi Theta Kappa, Christian Fellowship, Students With Vision.

Student services. Career counseling, student employment services, financial aid counseling, on-campus daycare, personal counseling, placement for graduates, veterans' counselor. **Physically disabled:** Services for visually, hearing impaired. **Transfer:** Transfer adviser, college fairs on campus for students transferring to 4-year colleges.

Contact. E-mail: admissionsoffice@yorktech.com
Phone: (803) 327-8008 Toll-free number: (800) 922-8324
Fax: (803) 981-7237
Kenny Aldridge, Admissions Department Manager, York Technical College, 452 South Anderson Road, Rock Hill, SC 29730

South Dakota

Globe University: Sioux Falls
Sioux Falls, South Dakota
www.globeuniversity.edu

- For-profit 2-year university and career college
- Small city

General. Regionally accredited; also accredited by ACICS. **Enrollment:** 262 degree-seeking undergraduates. **Degrees:** 3 bachelor's, 57 associate awarded. **Calendar:** Quarter. **Full-time faculty:** 10 total. **Part-time faculty:** 28 total.

Basis for selection. Open admission.

Financial aid. Need-based: Work-study available nights, weekends and for part-time students.

Application procedures. Admission: $50 fee.

Academics. Credit/placement by examination: AP, CLEP.

Majors. Business: Business admin. **Health services:** Massage therapy, medical secretary, veterinary technology/assistant. **Protective services:** Police science.

Contact. Les Remp, Admissions Team Lead, Globe University: Sioux Falls, 5101 South Broadband Lane, Sioux Falls, SD 57108

Kilian Community College
Sioux Falls, South Dakota
www.kilian.edu   CB code: 6149

- Private 2-year community college
- Commuter campus in small city

General. Founded in 1976. Regionally accredited. **Enrollment:** 308 degree-seeking undergraduates; 27 non-degree-seeking students. **Degrees:** 37 associate awarded. **Location:** 180 miles from Omaha, NE; 240 miles from Minneapolis-St. Paul. **Calendar:** Trimester, limited summer session. **Full-time faculty:** 5 total; 60% have terminal degrees, 60% women. **Part-time faculty:** 45 total; 69% have terminal degrees, 20% minority, 44% women. **Class size:** 89% < 20, 11% 20-39.

Student profile. Among degree-seeking undergraduates, 52 enrolled as first-time, first-year students, 38 transferred in from other institutions.

Part-time:	87%	Women:	71%
Out-of-state:	1%	25 or older:	61%

Transfer out. Colleges most students transferred to 2011: Presentation College, University of Sioux Falls, Colorado Technical University, University of South Dakota, South Dakota State University.

Basis for selection. Open admission. **Learning Disabled:** Students must provide documentation to Dean of Student Services/Counselor prior to enrolling.

2011-2012 Annual costs. Tuition/fees: $8,080. Per-credit charge: $262. Books/supplies: $1,020. Personal expenses: $725.

2010-2011 Financial aid. Need-based: 13 full-time freshmen applied for aid; 13 were judged to have need; 13 of these received aid. Average need met was 33%. Average scholarship/grant was $4,500; average loan $3,500. 29% of total undergraduate aid awarded as scholarships/grants, 71% as loans/jobs. Need-based aid available for part-time students. Work-study available nights, weekends and for part-time students. **Non-need-based:** Awarded to 3 full-time undergraduates, including 1 freshmen. Scholarships awarded for academics, leadership, minority status.

Application procedures. Admission: No deadline. $25 fee. Admission notification on a rolling basis. **Financial aid:** No deadline. FAFSA, institutional form required. Applicants notified on a rolling basis starting 7/1; must reply within 2 week(s) of notification.

Academics. Special study options: Cross-registration, distance learning, double major, dual enrollment of high school students, ESL, independent study, internships. Bachelor's degree programs available on campus. **Credit/placement by examination:** AP, CLEP, institutional tests. 18 credit hours maximum toward associate degree. **Support services:** Learning center, remedial instruction, study skills assistance, tutoring, writing center.

Majors. Area/ethnic studies: Native American. **Business:** Accounting, business admin, executive assistant, financial planning. **Computer sciences:** General. **Education:** General, early childhood. **Health services:** Medical secretary, substance abuse counseling. **History:** General. **Human services:** Social work. **Liberal arts:** Arts/sciences. **Protective services:** Criminal justice. **Psychology:** General. **Social sciences:** Sociology.

Most popular majors. Business/marketing 18%, education 8%, health sciences 15%, liberal arts 15%, public administration/social services 33%, security/protective services 6%.

Computing on campus. 48 workstations in computer center, student center. Online library available.

Student life. Freshman orientation: Available. Preregistration for classes offered. 2-3 hour program held the week before classes begin. **Activities:** Student newspaper.

Student services. Adult student services, career counseling, financial aid counseling, personal counseling. **Transfer:** Pre-admission transcript evaluation for new students. Transfer adviser for students transferring to 4-year colleges.

Contact. E-mail: mklockman@kilian.edu
Phone: (605) 221-3100 Toll-free number: (800) 888-1147
Fax: (605) 336-2606
Mary Klockman, Director of Admissions, Kilian Community College, 300 East 6th Street, Sioux Falls, SD 57103-7020

Lake Area Technical Institute
Watertown, South Dakota
www.lakeareatech.edu   CB code: 0717

- Public 2-year technical college
- Commuter campus in large town

General. Founded in 1965. Regionally accredited. **Enrollment:** 1,600 degree-seeking undergraduates. **Degrees:** 340 associate awarded. **Location:** 90 miles from Sioux Falls. **Calendar:** Semester, limited summer session. **Full-time faculty:** 95 total. **Part-time faculty:** 15 total.

Basis for selection. Open admission, but selective for some programs. Testing requirements vary by program. Entrance exam required for Nursing. Writing sample required for Occupational Therapy Assistant, and Physical Therapist Assistant programs. Photography requires a portfolio including digital image photography, and essays on each image.

High school preparation. 3 units math/science recommended. 1 Latin and typing recommended.

2011-2012 Annual costs. Program costs vary from $5,094 - $8,870 per year, depending on course of study; includes tuition, books and supplies. Books/supplies: $550. Personal expenses: $750.

Financial aid. All financial aid based on need. Need-based aid available for part-time students. Work-study available nights, weekends and for part-time students.

Application procedures. Admission: No deadline. $20 fee. Admission notification on a rolling basis. **Financial aid:** Priority date 4/15; no closing date. FAFSA required. Applicants notified on a rolling basis starting 5/1.

Academics. Special study options: Internships. **Credit/placement by examination:** AP, CLEP, institutional tests. **Support services:** Learning center, pre-admission summer program, reduced course load, tutoring.

Majors. Business: Accounting, banking/financial services, business admin, finance. **Computer sciences:** General, data processing, programming. **Engineering:** Civil, mechanical. **General:** Agribusiness operations. **Health services:** Clinical lab technology, nursing (RN), occupational therapy assistant, physical therapy assistant.

Computing on campus. 70 workstations in library, computer center, student center.

Student life. Freshman orientation: Available. Preregistration for classes offered. **Activities:** Student government, student newspaper.

Athletics. Intercollegiate: Rodeo. **Intramural:** Basketball, bowling, softball, volleyball.

Student services. Career counseling, student employment services, health services, on-campus daycare, personal counseling, placement for graduates, veterans' counselor. **Transfer:** Transfer adviser for students transferring to 4-year colleges.

Contact. Phone: (605) 882-5284 Toll-free number: (800) 657-4344
Fax: (605) 882-6299
LuAnn Strait, Director of Institutional Relations, Lake Area Technical Institute, PO Box 730, Watertown, SD 57201

Mitchell Technical Institute
Mitchell, South Dakota
www.mitchelltech.edu   CB code: 7038

◗ Public 2-year technical college
◗ Commuter campus in large town

General. Founded in 1968. Regionally accredited. **Enrollment:** 935 degree-seeking undergraduates; 120 non-degree-seeking students. **Degrees:** 281 associate awarded. **Location:** 70 miles from Sioux Falls. **Calendar:** Semester, limited summer session. **Full-time faculty:** 68 total; 2% minority, 35% women. **Part-time faculty:** 10 total; 70% women. **Class size:** 31% < 20, 66% 20-39, 3% 40-49. **Special facilities:** Satellite communications earth station, day care center, indoor utilities field, wind turbine.

Student profile. Among degree-seeking undergraduates, 100% enrolled in a vocational program, 1% already have a bachelor's degree or higher, 321 enrolled as first-time, first-year students, 104 transferred in from other institutions.

Part-time:	3%	Hispanic American:	1%
Out-of-state:	10%	Native American:	5%
Women:	31%	25 or older:	25%

Basis for selection. Additional application, job shadow essay, interviews, and weighting of GPA and ACT required for radiologic technology and radiation therapy. ACT recommended. COMPASS and TABE used for placement for students without ACT. Interviews required for selected programs. **Adult students:** COMPASS or TABE scores in place of the ACT. **Home schooled:** Statement describing home school structure and mission, transcript of courses and grades required.

High school preparation. 16 units recommended. Recommended units include English 4, mathematics 2, social studies 2, science 2 and computer science 1.

2011-2012 Annual costs. Tuition/fees: $5,310; $5,310 out-of-state. Books/supplies: $1,330. Personal expenses: $1,900.

2010-2011 Financial aid. Need-based: 45% of total undergraduate aid awarded as scholarships/grants, 55% as loans/jobs. Need-based aid available for part-time students. Work-study available nights, weekends and for part-time students.

Application procedures. Admission: No deadline. No application fee. Admission notification on a rolling basis. **Financial aid:** No deadline. FAFSA required. Applicants notified on a rolling basis; must reply within 3 week(s) of notification.

Academics. Special study options: Distance learning, double major, dual enrollment of high school students, independent study, internships. License preparation in radiology. **Credit/placement by examination:** AP, CLEP, ACT, institutional tests. 12 credit hours maximum toward associate degree. **Support services:** Learning center, reduced course load, remedial instruction, study skills assistance, tutoring.

Majors. Business: Accounting/business management, office technology. **Computer sciences:** Support specialist, system admin. **General:** Equipment technology, production. **Health services:** Clinical lab technology, medical assistant, medical radiologic technology/radiation therapy, office assistant, radiologic technology/medical imaging, speech-language pathology assistant. **Social sciences:** GIS/cartography.

Most popular majors. Business/marketing 14%, computer/information sciences 10%, engineering/engineering technologies 10%, health sciences 16%, trade and industry 32%.

Computing on campus. PC or laptop required. 100 workstations in library, computer center. Helpline, repair service, wireless network available.

Student life. Freshman orientation: Mandatory. Preregistration for classes offered. **Activities:** Student government.

Athletics. Intercollegiate: Rodeo. **Intramural:** Basketball, bowling, volleyball. **Team name:** Mavericks.

Student services. Adult student services, career counseling, services for economically disadvantaged, student employment services, financial aid counseling, on-campus daycare, personal counseling, placement for graduates, veterans' counselor, women's services. **Physically disabled:** Services for visually, speech, hearing impaired. **Transfer:** Transfer adviser for students transferring to 4-year colleges.

Contact. E-mail: questions@mitchelltech.edu
Phone: (605) 995-3025 Toll-free number: (800) 684-1969
Fax: (605) 996-3299
Clayton Deuter, Director of Admission, Mitchell Technical Institute, 1800 E Spruce Street, Mitchell, SD 57301

Sisseton Wahpeton College
Sisseton, South Dakota
www.swc.tc   CB code: 3403

◗ Public 2-year community and technical college
◗ Commuter campus in large town

General. Founded in 1979. Regionally accredited. Member of American Indian Higher Education Consortium. Dakota language and culture resource. **Enrollment:** 264 degree-seeking undergraduates. **Degrees:** 24 associate awarded. **Location:** 48 miles from Watertown; 85 miles from Fargo, ND. **Calendar:** Semester, limited summer session. **Full-time faculty:** 7 total; 14% have terminal degrees, 29% minority, 71% women. **Part-time faculty:** 13 total; 8% have terminal degrees, 38% minority, 54% women. **Special facilities:** Indians in North America book collection, Song to the Great Spirit building, Institute for Excellence in Dakota language.

Student profile.

Part-time:	34%	Women:	72%
Out-of-state:	5%		

Transfer out. Colleges most students transferred to 2011: University of Minnesota, North Dakota State University, University of North Dakota, South Dakota State University, University of South Dakota.

Basis for selection. Open admission. If student is member of recognized Native American tribe, must submit certification of tribal membership. **Home schooled:** State high school equivalency certificate required.

High school preparation. 16 units recommended. Recommended units include English 4, mathematics 4 and science 8.

2011-2012 Annual costs. Tuition/fees: $3,790. Per-credit charge: $110. Tuition rate shown is for Native American students. Non-Native American students pay a different rate. Books/supplies: $600. Personal expenses: $1,680.

Financial aid. Need-based: Work-study available nights, weekends and for part-time students.

Application procedures. Admission: Closing date 7/1. No application fee. Admission notification on a rolling basis. **Financial aid:** No deadline. FAFSA required. Applicants notified on a rolling basis.

Academics. Special study options: Double major, dual enrollment of high school students, independent study, internships, liberal arts/career combination. **Credit/placement by examination:** AP, CLEP, institutional tests. **Support services:** GED preparation and test center, learning center, remedial instruction, tutoring.

Majors. Area/ethnic studies: Native American. **Business:** Accounting, business admin, hospitality admin. **Computer sciences:** General. **Education:** Early childhood. **Health services:** Nursing (RN), substance abuse counseling. **Liberal arts:** Arts/sciences. **Physical sciences:** Planetary.

Most popular majors. Business/marketing 25%, health sciences 42%, liberal arts 17%.

Computing on campus. 136 workstations in library, computer center, student center. Wireless network available.

Student life. Freshman orientation: Mandatory. Preregistration for classes offered. Two-day program. **Activities:** Student government.

Student services. Career counseling, personal counseling. **Transfer:** Transfer adviser for students transferring to 4-year colleges.

Two-Year Colleges

Contact. E-mail: dredday@swc.tc
Phone: (605) 698-3966 Fax: (605) 698-3132
Darlene Redday, Admissions Officer/Registrar, Sisseton Wahpeton
College, BIA 700, Box 689, Sisseton, SD 57262-0689

Southeast Technical Institute
Sioux Falls, South Dakota
www.southeasttech.edu

CB code: 7054

▸ Public 2-year technical college
▸ Commuter campus in small city

General. Founded in 1969. Regionally accredited. **Enrollment:** 2,439
degree-seeking undergraduates; 68 non-degree-seeking students. **Degrees:**
596 associate awarded. **Location:** 220 miles from Minneapolis-St. Paul; 200
miles from Omaha, NE. **Calendar:** Semester, limited summer session. **Full-
time faculty:** 82 total; 2% have terminal degrees, 48% women. **Part-time
faculty:** 98 total; 4% have terminal degrees.

Student profile. Among degree-seeking undergraduates, 100% enrolled in
a vocational program, 5% already have a bachelor's degree or higher, 596
enrolled as first-time, first-year students, 429 transferred in from other institutions.

Part-time:	22%	Hispanic American:	2%
Out-of-state:	9%	Native American:	2%
Women:	51%	25 or older:	27%
African American:	2%	Live on campus:	2%
Asian American:	1%		

Transfer out. Colleges most students transferred to 2011: University
of Sioux Falls, Bellevue University, Colorado Technical University, South
Dakota State University, University of South Dakota.

Basis for selection. Open admission, but selective for some programs.
Additional testing and background checks required for all health and criminal
justice programs. ACT recommended for selective programs. **Home
schooled:** Statement describing home school structure and mission, transcript
of courses and grades, interview required. ACT and institutional entrance
exam required.

High school preparation. 22 units recommended. Recommended units
include English 4, mathematics 3, social studies 3, science 3, computer science
1, visual/performing arts 1 and academic electives 6. Physical Education -
.5, Economics or Personal Finance - .5.

2011-2012 Annual costs. Tuition/fees: $4,830; $4,830 out-of-state. Per-
credit charge: $95 in-state; $95 out-of-state. Mandatory laptop fee of $1340
covers all required software and hardware needed, as well as a 3 year warranty.
Books/supplies: $1,200. Personal expenses: $1,500.

Financial aid. All financial aid based on need. Need-based aid available
for part-time students. Work-study available nights, weekends and for part-
time students.

Application procedures. Admission: No deadline. No application fee.
Admission notification on a rolling basis. Must reply by May 1 or within 4
week(s) if notified thereafter. **Financial aid:** Priority date 5/1; no closing
date. FAFSA required. Applicants notified on a rolling basis starting 5/1;
must reply within 3 week(s) of notification.

Academics. Special study options: Double major. Bachelor's degree programs available on campus. License preparation in nursing, real estate. **Credit/
placement by examination:** AP, CLEP, IB, institutional tests. 30 credit
hours maximum toward associate degree. **Support services:** GED preparation
and test center, learning center, reduced course load, remedial instruction,
study skills assistance, tutoring.

Majors. Architecture: Technology. **Biology:** Biomedical sciences. **Business:** Accounting, banking/financial services, business admin, construction
management, entrepreneurial studies, human resources, insurance, marketing.
Communications: Advertising. **Communications technology:** Animation/
special effects, graphic/printing. **Computer sciences:** General, applications
programming, LAN/WAN management, networking, programming. **General:** Greenhouse operations, horticulture, landscaping, nursery operations,
turf management. **Health services:** Cardiovascular technology, electroencephalograph technology, nuclear medical technology, nursing (RN), sonography, ward clerk. **Protective services:** Law enforcement admin. **Visual/
performing arts:** Commercial/advertising art. **Work/family studies:** Child
care management.

Most popular majors. Business/marketing 40%, health sciences 25%,
trade and industry 23%.

Computing on campus. PC or laptop required. 88 workstations in library,
computer center, student center. Commuter students can connect to campus
network. Online course registration, online library, helpline, repair service,
student web hosting, wireless network available.

Student life. Freshman orientation: Available. Preregistration for classes
offered. Held 8 times throughout the summer, about 4 hours. **Housing:**
Apartments available. $100 fully refundable deposit, deadline 7/1. **Activities:**
Student government.

Athletics. Intramural: Basketball, bowling, football (non-tackle), volleyball.

Student services. Career counseling, student employment services, financial aid counseling, on-campus daycare, personal counseling, placement for
graduates. **Physically disabled:** Services for visually, speech, hearing
impaired. **Transfer:** Pre-admission transcript evaluation for new students.
College fairs on campus for students transferring to 4-year colleges.

Contact. E-mail: admissions@southeasttech.edu
Phone: (605) 367-6040 Toll-free number: (800) 247-0789
Fax: (605) 367-4372
Jim Rokusek, Director of Student Services, Southeast Technical Institute,
2320 North Career Avenue, Sioux Falls, SD 57107

Western Dakota Technical Institute
Rapid City, South Dakota
www.wdt.edu

CB code: 6393

▸ Public 2-year technical college
▸ Commuter campus in small city

General. Founded in 1978. Regionally accredited. **Location:** 3 miles from
downtown. **Calendar:** Semester.

Annual costs/financial aid. Tuition/fees (2011-2012): $5,040; $5,040
out-of-state. Total program cost ranges from $7,792 to $18,640, depending
on course of study. Books/supplies: $816. Personal expenses: $1,353. Need-
based financial aid available to full-time and part-time students.

Contact. Phone: (605) 718-2411
Admissions Coordinator, 800 Mickelson Drive, Rapid City, SD 57703

Tennessee

Anthem Career College: Memphis
Nashville, Tennessee
www.anthem.edu

▶ For-profit 2-year career college
▶ Large city

General. Regionally accredited; also accredited by ACICS. **Enrollment:** 439 degree-seeking undergraduates. **Degrees:** 385 associate awarded. **Calendar:** Differs by program. **Full-time faculty:** 15 total. **Part-time faculty:** 8 total.

Basis for selection. Open admission.

Financial aid. Need-based: Work-study available nights, weekends and for part-time students.

Application procedures. Admission: No deadline. $20 fee.

Academics. Credit/placement by examination: AP, CLEP.

Majors. Business: Business admin. **Health services:** Medical assistant.

Contact. Samantha Coz, Director of Admissions, Anthem Career College: Memphis, 560 Royal Parkway, Nashville, TN 38134

Anthem Career College: Nashville
Nashville, Tennessee
www.anthem.edu

▶ For-profit 2-year technical and career college
▶ Very large city

General. Regionally accredited. **Calendar:** Differs by program.

Contact. Phone: (615) 232-3700
Director of Admissions, 560 Royal Parkway, Nashville, TN 37214

Chattanooga College
Chattanooga, Tennessee
www.ecpconline.com   CB code: 2267

▶ For-profit 2-year technical college
▶ Large city

General. Regionally accredited. **Calendar:** Quarter.

Contact. Phone: (423) 624-0077
Director of Admissions, 3805 Brainerd Road, Chattanooga, TN 37411

Chattanooga State Community College
Chattanooga, Tennessee
www.chattanoogastate.edu   CB code: 1084

▶ Public 2-year community and technical college
▶ Commuter campus in small city

General. Founded in 1963. Regionally accredited. Credit-bearing courses offered at various off-campus locations. **Enrollment:** 8,615 degree-seeking undergraduates; 1,823 non-degree-seeking students. **Degrees:** 843 associate awarded. **Location:** 129 miles from Nashville. **Calendar:** Semester, limited summer session. **Full-time faculty:** 224 total; 12% minority, 56% women. **Part-time faculty:** 421 total.

Student profile. Among degree-seeking undergraduates, 31% enrolled in a transfer program, 55% enrolled in a vocational program, 1,586 enrolled as first-time, first-year students, 3,247 transferred in from other institutions.

Part-time:	48%	**Women:**	62%
Out-of-state:	9%	**25 or older:**	41%

Transfer out. Colleges most students transferred to 2011: Austin Peay State University, East Tennessee State University, Middle Tennessee State University, Tennessee Tech University, University of Tennessee at Chattanooga.

Basis for selection. Open admission, but selective for some programs. Special requirements for allied health program. National standardized dental assisting and dental hygiene tests required of applicants to these programs. Interview required for allied health, nursing programs. **Adult students:** Placement test required. **Home schooled:** Transcript of courses and grades required. Students must register with local department/board of education or present affiliation with accredited homeschool agency.

High school preparation. 19 units recommended. Recommended units include English 4, mathematics 3, social studies 1, history 1, science 2 (laboratory 1), foreign language 2 and visual/performing arts 1. College preparatory program required for students choosing transfer majors.

2011-2012 Annual costs. Tuition/fees: $3,567; $13,671 out-of-state. Per-credit charge: $129 in-state; $530 out-of-state. Books/supplies: $1,800.

Financial aid. Need-based: Need-based aid available for part-time students. Work-study available nights, weekends and for part-time students. **Non-need-based:** Scholarships awarded for state residency.

Application procedures. Admission: Priority date 8/15; no deadline. $15 fee. Admission notification on a rolling basis. **Financial aid:** Priority date 6/1; no closing date. FAFSA required. Applicants notified on a rolling basis starting 4/1; must reply within 2 week(s) of notification.

Academics. Special study options: Accelerated study, cooperative education, cross-registration, distance learning, double major, dual enrollment of high school students, honors, independent study, internships, student-designed major. Bachelor's degree programs available on campus. License preparation in dental hygiene, nursing, occupational therapy, paramedic, physical therapy, radiology, real estate. **Credit/placement by examination:** AP, CLEP, IB, institutional tests. Final 20 hours must be taken in residency; maximun of 40 hours may be awarded by combination of credit by exam and credit for experience. **Support services:** GED preparation and test center, learning center, pre-admission summer program, reduced course load, remedial instruction, study skills assistance, tutoring, writing center.

Honors college/program. 25 ACT/1130-1160 SAT and 3.5 GPA required.

Majors. Business: Accounting technology, administrative services, business admin, management information systems, office/clerical. **Communications:** Advertising. **Computer sciences:** Web page design. **Education:** General. **English:** Technical writing. **Foreign languages:** Sign language interpretation. **Health services:** Dental hygiene, environmental health, medical radiologic technology/radiation therapy, medical records technology, nursing (RN), physical therapy assistant, respiratory therapy technology, veterinary technology/assistant. **Human services:** Community org/advocacy. **Liberal arts:** Arts/sciences. **Protective services:** Firefighting. **Visual/performing arts:** Commercial/advertising art. **Work/family studies:** Food/nutrition.

Most popular majors. Business/marketing 11%, engineering/engineering technologies 10%, health sciences 27%, liberal arts 38%.

Computing on campus. 1,200 workstations in library, computer center, student center. Commuter students can connect to campus network. Online course registration, online library, helpline, wireless network available.

Student life. Freshman orientation: Mandatory, $10 fee. Preregistration for classes offered. 5-hour sessions held July-August. **Activities:** Jazz band, choral groups, drama, music ensembles, radio station, student government, student newspaper, TV station, Baptist student union.

Athletics. NJCAA. **Intercollegiate:** Baseball M, basketball. **Intramural:** Racquetball, soccer, softball, table tennis, tennis. **Team name:** Tigers.

Student services. Adult student services, alcohol/substance abuse counseling, career counseling, services for economically disadvantaged, student employment services, financial aid counseling, minority student services, on-campus daycare, personal counseling, placement for graduates, veterans' counselor. **Physically disabled:** Services for visually, speech, hearing impaired. **Transfer:** Transfer adviser, college fairs on campus for students transferring to 4-year colleges.

Two-Year Colleges

Contact. Phone: (423) 697-4401 Fax: (423) 697-4709
Brad McCormick, Director Admissions and Records, Chattanooga State
Community College, 4501 Amnicola Highway, Chattanooga, TN 37406

Cleveland State Community College
Cleveland, Tennessee
www.clevelandstatecc.edu   **CB code: 2848**

- Public 2-year community college
- Commuter campus in small city

General. Founded in 1967. Regionally accredited. **Enrollment:** 2,817
degree-seeking undergraduates; 997 non-degree-seeking students. **Degrees:**
356 associate awarded. **Location:** 30 miles from Chattanooga, 80 miles from
Knoxville. **Calendar:** Semester, limited summer session. **Full-time faculty:**
71 total; 16% have terminal degrees, 8% minority, 51% women. **Part-time
faculty:** 117 total; 12% have terminal degrees, 4% minority, 63% women.
Class size: 41% < 20, 52% 20-39, 1% 40-49, 6% 50-99. **Special facilities:** Observatory.

Student profile. Among degree-seeking undergraduates, 39% enrolled in
a transfer program, 45% enrolled in a vocational program, 704 enrolled as
first-time, first-year students, 180 transferred in from other institutions.

Part-time:	33%	Women:	64%
Out-of-state:	1%	25 or older:	39%

Transfer out. 29% of students enrolled in the transfer program go on to
4-year colleges. **Colleges most students transferred to 2011:** University
of Tennessee-Chattanooga, University of Tennessee-Knoxville, Tennessee
Technological University, Lee University.

Basis for selection. Open admission, but selective for some programs.
Program admission required for nursing and medical office assistant. **Home
schooled:** Transcript of courses and grades required.

High school preparation. 14 units required. Required units include
English 4, mathematics 3, social studies 1, history 1, science 2 (laboratory
1), foreign language 2 and visual/performing arts 1. Recommended units
listed are required for transfer programs.

2011-2012 Annual costs. Tuition/fees: $3,521; $13,625 out-of-state. Per-
credit charge: $129 in-state; $530 out-of-state. Books/supplies: $900. Personal
expenses: $500.

2011-2012 Financial aid. Need-based: Average need met was 64%. Average scholarship/grant was $2,735; average loan $1,597. 70% of total undergraduate aid awarded as scholarships/grants, 30% as loans/jobs. Need-based
aid available for part-time students. Work-study available nights, weekends
and for part-time students. **Non-need-based:** Scholarships awarded for athletics, minority status.

Application procedures. Admission: No deadline. $10 fee. Admission
notification on a rolling basis. **Financial aid:** Priority date 5/15; no closing
date. FAFSA, institutional form required. Applicants notified on a rolling
basis starting 7/1; must reply within 2 week(s) of notification.

Academics. Special study options: Cooperative education, cross-
registration, distance learning, double major, dual enrollment of high school
students, honors, independent study, internships, study abroad. License preparation in nursing. **Credit/placement by examination:** AP, CLEP, institutional tests. 15 credit hours maximum toward associate degree. Students
scoring above 32 on the English portion of the enhanced ACT receive 6
credits of English composition. AP credit awarded is determined on an
individual basis by the relevant department for grades of 3 or higher. **Support
services:** GED test center, learning center, reduced course load, remedial
instruction, study skills assistance, tutoring.

Majors. Business: Administrative services, business admin. **Education:**
General. **Health services:** Nursing (RN). **Human services:** General. **Liberal
arts:** Arts/sciences. **Work/family studies:** Child development.

Most popular majors. Business/marketing 15%, engineering/engineering
technologies 8%, family/consumer sciences 6%, health sciences 15%, liberal
arts 52%.

Computing on campus. 864 workstations in library, computer center,
student center. Commuter students can connect to campus network. Online
course registration, online library, helpline, wireless network available.

Student life. Freshman orientation: Available. Preregistration for classes
offered. Half-day program includes campus tour, career and academic counseling, placement assessment, and registration. **Activities:** Campus ministries,
choral groups, literary magazine, student government, student newspaper,

Baptist Student Union, Circle-K, Phi Theta Kappa, Professional Secretaries
International, Adult Student League.

Athletics. NJCAA. **Intercollegiate:** Baseball M, basketball, cheerleading,
softball W. **Intramural:** Badminton, bowling, golf, table tennis, tennis, volleyball. **Team name:** Cougars.

Student services. Adult student services, career counseling, student
employment services, financial aid counseling, minority student services,
personal counseling, placement for graduates, veterans' counselor. **Physically
disabled:** Services for visually, speech, hearing impaired. **Transfer:** Re-
entry adviser, pre-admission transcript evaluation for new students. Transfer
adviser, college fairs on campus for students transferring to 4-year colleges.

Contact. E-mail: mburnette@clevelandstatecc.edu
Phone: (423) 472-7141 ext. 213 Toll-free number: (800) 604-2722
Fax: (423) 478-6255
Midge Burnette, Director of Admissions and Records, Cleveland State
Community College, 3535 Adkisson Drive, Cleveland, TN 37320-3570

Columbia State Community College
Columbia, Tennessee
www.columbiastate.edu   **CB code: 1081**

- Public 2-year community college
- Commuter campus in large town

General. Founded in 1966. Regionally accredited. **Enrollment:** 4,714
degree-seeking undergraduates. **Degrees:** 540 associate awarded. **Location:**
40 miles from Nashville. **Calendar:** Semester, limited summer session. **Full-
time faculty:** 97 total. **Part-time faculty:** 205 total. **Class size:** 34% < 20,
21% 20-39, 9% 40-49, 16% 50-99, 20% >100.

Basis for selection. Open admission, but selective for some programs.
Special requirements for allied health sciences.

High school preparation. Recommended units include English 4, mathematics 3, social studies 1, history 1, science 2 (laboratory 1) and foreign
language 2. One visual and performing arts recommended.

2011-2012 Annual costs. Tuition/fees: $3,523; $13,627 out-of-state. Per-
credit charge: $129 in-state; $530 out-of-state. Books/supplies: $1,000. Per-
sonal expenses: $1,586.

Financial aid. Need-based: Need-based aid available for part-time students. Work-study available nights, weekends and for part-time students.
Non-need-based: Scholarships awarded for academics, athletics, state residency.

Application procedures. Admission: Closing date 8/18. $10 fee. Admis-
sion notification on a rolling basis. **Financial aid:** Closing date 7/31. FAFSA,
institutional form required. Applicants notified on a rolling basis starting
5/15; must reply within 2 week(s) of notification.

Academics. Special study options: Cooperative education, distance learning, dual enrollment of high school students, study abroad. License preparation in nursing, radiology. **Credit/placement by examination:** AP, CLEP,
institutional tests. 42 credit hours maximum toward associate degree. **Support
services:** GED test center, learning center, remedial instruction, study skills
assistance, tutoring.

Majors. Business: Business admin, management information systems.
Computer sciences: Web page design. **Education:** General. **Health services:**
Medical radiologic technology/radiation therapy, nursing (RN), respiratory
therapy technology, veterinary technology/assistant. **Liberal arts:** Arts/sci-
ences. **Math:** General. **Protective services:** Police science.

Computing on campus. 60 workstations in library, computer center.
Commuter students can connect to campus network. Online course registration, online library, helpline, wireless network available.

Student life. Freshman orientation: Available. Preregistration for classes
offered. **Activities:** Choral groups, drama, international student organizations,
literary magazine, student government, student newspaper, Phi Theta Kappa,
Student Nursing Association, Student Tennessee Education Association, student radiographer organization, North American Veterinary Technician Association, Pulmonary Pit Club.

Athletics. NJCAA. **Intercollegiate:** Baseball M, basketball, softball W.
Intramural: Basketball, softball M. **Team name:** Chargers, Lady Chargers.

Student services. Career counseling, student employment services, financial aid counseling, minority student services, personal counseling, placement
for graduates, veterans' counselor. **Physically disabled:** Services for visually,

hearing impaired. **Transfer:** College fairs on campus for students transferring to 4-year colleges.

Contact. E-mail: admissions@columbiastate.edu
Phone: (931) 540-2790 Fax: (931) 560-4125
David Ogden, Director of Admissions and Registrar, Columbia State Community College, 1665 Hampshire Pike, Columbia, TN 38401

Daymar Institute: Clarksville
Clarksville, Tennessee
www.daymarinstitute.edu   CB code: 3225

- For-profit 2-year business and career college
- Small city

General. Regionally accredited. **Calendar:** Differs by program.

Annual costs/financial aid. Tuition/fees (2011-2012): $15,850. Per-credit-hour charge (tuition only): $325 per quarter credit hour for most courses. $390 per quarter credit hour for 300-400 level courses. $365 per quarter credit hour for LAW specific courses. $410 per quarter credit hour for Information Technology and Personal Fitness Training specific courses. $475 per quarter credit hour for Associate Degree in Nursing specific courses. Books/supplies: $2,250.

Contact. Phone: (931) 552-7600
Campus Director, 1860 Wilma Rudolph Boulevard, Clarksville, TN 37040

Daymar Institute: Murfreesboro
Murfreesboro, Tennessee
www.daymarinstitute.edu

- For-profit 2-year junior college
- Commuter campus in very large city

General. Regionally accredited. **Location:** 25 miles from Nashville. **Calendar:** Quarter.

Annual costs/financial aid. Tuition/fees (2011-2012): $15,850. Per-credit-hour charge (tuition only): $325 per quarter credit hour for most courses. $390 per quarter credit hour for 300-400 level courses. $365 per quarter credit hour for LAW specific courses. $410 per quarter credit hour for Information Technology and Personal Fitness Training specific courses. $475 per quarter credit hour for Associate Degree in Nursing specific courses. Books/supplies: $2,250.

Contact. Phone: (615) 217-9347
Director of Admissions, 415 Golden Bear Court, Murfreesboro, TN 37128

Daymar Institute: Nashville
Nashville, Tennessee
www.daymarinstitute.edu   CB code: 7325

- For-profit 2-year career college
- Commuter campus in very large city

General. Founded in 1884. Regionally accredited. **Location:** 2 miles from downtown. **Calendar:** Quarter.

Annual costs/financial aid. Tuition/fees (2011-2012): $15,850. Per-credit-hour charge (tuition only): $325 per quarter credit hour for most courses. $390 per quarter credit hour for 300-400 level courses. $365 per quarter credit hour for LAW specific courses. $410 per quarter credit hour for Information Technology and Personal Fitness Training specific courses. $475 per quarter credit hour for Associate Degree in Nursing specific courses. Books/supplies: $2,500. Need-based financial aid available to full-time and part-time students.

Contact. Phone: (615) 361-7555
Director of Admissions, 340 & 283 Plus Park at Pavilion Boulevard, Nashville, TN 37217

Dyersburg State Community College
Dyersburg, Tennessee
www.dscc.edu   CB code: 7323

- Public 2-year community college
- Commuter campus in large town

General. Founded in 1967. Regionally accredited. **Enrollment:** 2,943 degree-seeking undergraduates; 808 non-degree-seeking students. **Degrees:** 261 associate awarded. **Location:** 78 miles from Memphis. **Calendar:** Semester, limited summer session. **Full-time faculty:** 53 total; 15% minority, 62% women. **Part-time faculty:** 138 total; 4% minority, 64% women. **Class size:** 34% < 20, 64% 20-39, 1% 40-49, less than 1% 50-99.

Student profile. Among degree-seeking undergraduates, 37% enrolled in a transfer program, 41% enrolled in a vocational program, 864 enrolled as first-time, first-year students, 2,021 transferred in from other institutions.

Part-time:	43%	African American:	26%
Out-of-state:	1%	Hispanic American:	2%
Women:	72%	25 or older:	37%

Transfer out. 41% of students enrolled in the transfer program go on to 4-year colleges. **Colleges most students transferred to 2011:** University of Tennessee-Martin, University of Memphis, Middle Tennessee State University.

Basis for selection. Open admission, but selective for some programs. Admission into nursing program based on point system that includes preadmission examination test score, GPA, science courses taken with grade of "B" or above, and prior health care experience. High school students who meet specific admission requirements may enroll as first time freshmen. **Learning Disabled:** Students with disabilities encouraged to inform the college of any needed assistance during application process.

High school preparation. College-preparatory program recommended. 22 units required. Required and recommended units include English 4, mathematics 4, social studies 3, history 1, science 3, foreign language 2, visual/performing arts 1 and academic electives 3. Physical education and wellness 1.5 units, personal finance .5 units.

2011-2012 Annual costs. Tuition/fees: $3,533; $13,918 out-of-state. Per-credit charge: $157 in-state; $488 out-of-state. Books/supplies: $1,100. Personal expenses: $1,080.

Financial aid. Need-based: Need-based aid available for part-time students. Work-study available nights, weekends and for part-time students. **Non-need-based:** Scholarships awarded for academics, alumni affiliation, athletics, job skills, leadership, minority status, music/drama, state residency.

Application procedures. Admission: Priority date 8/1; deadline 8/19 (receipt date). $10 fee. Admission notification on a rolling basis. **Financial aid:** Priority date 3/1; no closing date. FAFSA required. Applicants notified on a rolling basis starting 3/1; must reply within 2 week(s) of notification.

Academics. Special study options: Accelerated study, cooperative education, distance learning, dual enrollment of high school students, honors, independent study, internships, liberal arts/career combination, study abroad, teacher certification program. License preparation in nursing, paramedic. **Credit/placement by examination:** AP, CLEP, institutional tests. 24 credit hours maximum toward associate degree. **Support services:** GED preparation and test center, learning center, reduced course load, remedial instruction, study skills assistance, tutoring.

Majors. Biology: General. **Business:** Business admin. **Computer sciences:** Information systems. **Education:** General. **Health services:** Medical records technology, nursing (RN). **History:** General. **Liberal arts:** Arts/sciences. **Math:** General. **Protective services:** Police science. **Psychology:** General. **Social sciences:** General. **Work/family studies:** Child development.

Most popular majors. Business/marketing 14%, education 10%, health sciences 41%, liberal arts 14%.

Computing on campus. 860 workstations in library, computer center, student center. Commuter students can connect to campus network. Online course registration, online library, helpline, wireless network available.

Student life. Freshman orientation: Available. Preregistration for classes offered. Half-day programs. **Activities:** Campus ministries, choral groups, drama, music ensembles, student government, student newspaper, American Chemical Society Affiliates, business and office systems association, student nurses association, Minority Association for Successful Students, astronomy club, advanced technology association, music club, Phi Theta Kappa, psychology club.

Athletics. NJCAA. **Intercollegiate:** Baseball M, basketball, cheerleading, softball W. **Intramural:** Basketball, soccer, softball, volleyball. **Team name:** Eagles.

Student services. Adult student services, alcohol/substance abuse counseling, career counseling, services for economically disadvantaged, student employment services, financial aid counseling, minority student services, personal counseling, placement for graduates, veterans' counselor, women's services. **Physically disabled:** Services for visually, speech, hearing impaired. **Transfer:** Pre-admission transcript evaluation for new students. Transfer

adviser, college fairs on campus for students transferring to 4-year colleges.

Contact. E-mail: enroll@dscc.edu
Phone: (731) 286-3330 Fax: (731) 286-3325
J. Dan Gullett, Assistant Vice President for Academic Affairs, Dyersburg State Community College, 1510 Lake Road, Dyersburg, TN 38024

Fountainhead College of Technology
Knoxville, Tennessee
www.fountainheadcollege.edu   CB code: 0446

- For-profit 2-year technical and career college
- Commuter campus in large city

General. Founded in 1947. Accredited by ACCSCT. **Location:** 200 miles from Nashville, 200 miles from Atlanta. **Calendar:** Semester.

Annual costs/financial aid. Tuition/fees (2011-2012): $15,620. Additional $1,300-$2,000 fee for mandatory purchase of computer. Cost varies by program. Books/supplies: $1,500.

Contact. Phone: (865) 688-9422
Director of Administration, 3203 Tazewell Pike, Knoxville, TN 37918

Huntington College of Health Sciences
Knoxville, Tennessee
www.hchs.edu   CB code: 3945

- For-profit 2-year virtual health science college
- Small city

General. Accredited by DETC. **Calendar:** Differs by program.

Annual costs/financial aid. Books/supplies: $1,350.

Contact. Phone: (865) 524-8079
Director of Administration, 1204D Kenesaw, Knoxville, TN 37919-7736

Jackson State Community College
Jackson, Tennessee
www.jscc.edu   CB code: 2266

- Public 2-year community college
- Commuter campus in small city

General. Founded in 1965. Regionally accredited. **Enrollment:** 4,928 degree-seeking undergraduates. **Degrees:** 603 associate awarded. **ROTC:** Army. **Location:** 80 miles from Memphis, 130 miles from Nashville. **Calendar:** Semester, limited summer session. **Full-time faculty:** 95 total; 17% have terminal degrees, 6% minority, 67% women. **Part-time faculty:** 179 total. **Class size:** 25% < 20, 70% 20-39, 4% 40-49, less than 1% 50-99.

Student profile.

Out-of-state:	1%	25 or older:	39%

Transfer out. Colleges most students transferred to 2011: Union University, University of Memphis, University of Tennessee at Martin, Middle Tennessee State University, Lambuth University.

Basis for selection. Open admission, but selective for some programs. Special requirements for nursing, medical laboratory technology, radiology, respiratory care, physical therapy assistant, and emergency medical technician programs. Interview required for allied health, nursing programs. **Adult students:** Students 21 years or older take COMPASS placement test. **Home schooled:** Transcript of courses and grades required.

High school preparation. 22 units recommended. Recommended units include English 4, mathematics 4, social studies 3, science 3, foreign language 2, visual/performing arts 1 and academic electives 3. 2 units wellness studies.

2011-2012 Annual costs. Tuition/fees: $3,529; $13,633 out-of-state. Per-credit charge: $129 in-state; $530 out-of-state. Books/supplies: $1,200. Personal expenses: $4,544.

Financial aid. Need-based: Need-based aid available for part-time students. Work-study available nights, weekends and for part-time students. **Non-need-based:** Scholarships awarded for academics, art, athletics, job skills, leadership, minority status, music/drama.

Application procedures. Admission: No deadline. $10 fee. Admission notification on a rolling basis. **Financial aid:** Priority date 3/15; no closing date. FAFSA, institutional form required. Applicants notified on a rolling basis starting 6/1; must reply within 2 week(s) of notification.

Academics. Special study options: Cooperative education, distance learning, double major, dual enrollment of high school students, honors, internships, liberal arts/career combination, weekend college. Bachelor's degree programs available on campus. License preparation in nursing, paramedic, physical therapy, radiology, real estate. **Credit/placement by examination:** AP, CLEP, institutional tests. 21 credit hours maximum toward associate degree. Must complete additional 15 college credit hours before credit by examination is awarded. **Support services:** GED test center, learning center, reduced course load, remedial instruction, study skills assistance, tutoring, writing center.

Majors. Biology: General. **Business:** Accounting, business admin, management information systems. **Communications:** Communications/speech/rhetoric. **Education:** General. **Engineering:** General. **English:** English lit. **General:** Business. **Health services:** Clinical lab technology, medical radiologic technology/radiation therapy, nursing (RN), physical therapy assistant, pre-medicine, prenursing, respiratory therapy technology. **History:** General. **Human services:** General, social work. **Liberal arts:** Arts/sciences. **Math:** General. **Parks/recreation:** Health/fitness. **Philosophy/religion:** Philosophy. **Physical sciences:** General, chemistry. **Protective services:** Police science. **Psychology:** General. **Social sciences:** Political science, sociology. **Visual/performing arts:** Art. **Work/family studies:** Child development.

Most popular majors. Business/marketing 9%, health sciences 44%, liberal arts 33%.

Computing on campus. 1,000 workstations in library, student center. Commuter students can connect to campus network. Online course registration, online library, helpline, wireless network available.

Student life. Freshman orientation: Available. Preregistration for classes offered. **Activities:** Choral groups, literary magazine, student government, Baptist Collegiate Ministries, Phi Theta Kappa, Science Ambassadors, student veteran's association.

Athletics. NJCAA. **Intercollegiate:** Baseball M, basketball, softball W. **Team name:** Generals.

Student services. Career counseling, student employment services, financial aid counseling, personal counseling, placement for graduates, veterans' counselor. **Physically disabled:** Services for visually, speech, hearing impaired. **Transfer:** College fairs on campus for students transferring to 4-year colleges.

Contact. E-mail: awinchester@jscc.edu
Phone: (731) 425-8844 Fax: (731) 425-9559
Andrea Winchester, Director of Admissions, Jackson State Community College, 2046 North Parkway, Jackson, TN 38301-3797

John A. Gupton College
Nashville, Tennessee
www.guptoncollege.com   CB code: 0539

- Private 2-year school of mortuary science
- Commuter campus in large city

General. Founded in 1946. Regionally accredited. **Enrollment:** 148 degree-seeking undergraduates. **Degrees:** 34 associate awarded. **Calendar:** Semester, limited summer session. **Full-time faculty:** 4 total; 50% women. **Part-time faculty:** 9 total; 56% have terminal degrees, 11% minority, 22% women. **Class size:** 42% 20-39, 58% 50-99.

Student profile.

Out-of-state:	26%	Live on campus:	11%
25 or older:	37%		

Transfer out. Colleges most students transferred to 2011: Middle Tennessee State University, Western Kentucky University, Jackson State Community College.

Basis for selection. Open admission, but selective for some programs. 2 letters of recommendation are needed. **Home schooled:** Transcript of courses and grades, state high school equivalency certificate, letter of recommendation (nonparent) required.

High school preparation. 10 units recommended. Recommended units include English 4, mathematics 3 and science 3.

2011-2012 Annual costs. Tuition/fees: $9,050. Per-credit charge: $283. Room only: $3,600. Books/supplies: $1,000.

Financial aid. All financial aid based on need. Need-based aid available for part-time students. Work-study available nights, weekends and for part-time students.

Application procedures. Admission: No deadline. $20 fee. Application must be submitted on paper. Admission notification on a rolling basis. **Financial aid:** No deadline. FAFSA required. Applicants notified on a rolling basis.

Academics. Credit/placement by examination: AP, CLEP. **Support services:** Reduced course load, tutoring.

Computing on campus. 8 workstations in library, computer center. Wireless network available.

Student life. Freshman orientation: Mandatory. Preregistration for classes offered. **Housing:** Apartments, wellness housing available. $450 fully refundable deposit.

Student services. Career counseling. **Transfer:** Pre-admission transcript evaluation for new students.

Contact. E-mail: purcell@guptoncollege.edu
Phone: (615) 327-3927 Fax: (615) 321-4518
Terri Purcell, Director of Admissions, John A. Gupton College, 1616 Church Street, Nashville, TN 37203-2920

Miller-Motte Technical College: Chattanooga
Chattanooga, Tennessee
www.miller-motte.com/chattanoogawelcome.html

- For-profit 2-year technical college
- Commuter campus in large city

General. Accredited by ACICS. **Calendar:** Quarter.

Contact. Phone: (423) 510-9675
Director of Admissions, 6020 Shallowford Road, Suite 100, Chattanooga, TN 37421

Miller-Motte Technical College: Clarksville
Clarksville, Tennessee
www.miller-motte.com   CB code: 3228

- For-profit 2-year business and health science college
- Commuter campus in small city

General. Accredited by ACICS. **Location:** 45 miles from Nashville. **Calendar:** Quarter.

Annual costs/financial aid. Books/supplies: $1,200. Personal expenses: $1,350. Need-based financial aid available to full-time and part-time students.

Contact. Phone: (931) 553-0071
Director of Admissions, 1820 Business Park Drive, Clarksville, TN 37040

Motlow State Community College
Lynchburg, Tennessee
www.mscc.edu   CB code: 1543

- Public 2-year community college
- Commuter campus in rural community

General. Founded in 1969. Regionally accredited. **Enrollment:** 4,821 degree-seeking undergraduates. **Degrees:** 529 associate awarded. **Location:** 65 miles from Nashville. **Calendar:** Semester, limited summer session. **Full-time faculty:** 79 total. **Part-time faculty:** 184 total.

Student profile. Among degree-seeking undergraduates, 1,164 enrolled as first-time, first-year students.

Part-time:	60%	**Women:**	62%
Out-of-state:	1%		

Transfer out. Colleges most students transferred to 2011: Middle Tennessee State University, Tennessee Technological University.

Basis for selection. Open admission, but selective for some programs. Students entering into the college's Nursing Program have different admissions criteria. Interview required for nursing program. **Home schooled:** Transcript of courses and grades required.

High school preparation. 16 units recommended. Recommended units include English 4, mathematics 3, social studies 2, history 1, science 2 (laboratory 1) and foreign language 2.

2011-2012 Annual costs. Tuition/fees: $3,528; $13,632 out-of-state. Per-credit charge: $129 in-state; $530 out-of-state. Books/supplies: $1,200. Personal expenses: $1,000.

Financial aid. Need-based: Need-based aid available for part-time students. Work-study available nights, weekends and for part-time students. **Non-need-based:** Scholarships awarded for academics, alumni affiliation, art, athletics, leadership, music/drama.

Application procedures. Admission: $25 fee. Admission notification on a rolling basis. **Financial aid:** Priority date 2/15; no closing date. FAFSA, institutional form required. Applicants notified on a rolling basis starting 3/15.

Academics. Special study options: Accelerated study, cooperative education, distance learning, double major, dual enrollment of high school students, honors, independent study, internships, study abroad, weekend college. License preparation in nursing. **Credit/placement by examination:** AP, CLEP, institutional tests. Maximum number of credits by examination that may be earned is limited to 25% of total number of credits needed for graduation. **Support services:** Reduced course load, remedial instruction, study skills assistance, tutoring.

Majors. Business: Business admin. **Education:** General, elementary, secondary. **Health services:** Nursing (RN). **Liberal arts:** Arts/sciences.

Computing on campus. 250 workstations in library, computer center. Commuter students can connect to campus network. Online course registration, online library, helpline, repair service, wireless network available.

Student life. Freshman orientation: Mandatory. Preregistration for classes offered. **Activities:** Campus ministries, choral groups, drama, international student organizations, literary magazine, music ensembles, student government, Baptist student union, African American student association, outing club, communications club, law and government club, literary club, Phi Theta Kappa, psychology club, Tennessee Association of Student Nurses.

Athletics. NJCAA. **Intercollegiate:** Baseball M, basketball, softball W. **Intramural:** Baseball M, basketball, bowling, softball. **Team name:** Bucks.

Student services. Adult student services, alcohol/substance abuse counseling, career counseling, student employment services, financial aid counseling, health services, personal counseling, placement for graduates, veterans' counselor. **Physically disabled:** Services for visually impaired. **Transfer:** Pre-admission transcript evaluation for new students. College fairs on campus for students transferring to 4-year colleges.

Contact. E-mail: galsup@mscc.edu
Phone: (931) 393-1529 Toll-free number: (800) 654-4877
Fax: (931) 393-1971
Greer Alsup, Director of Admissions and Records, Motlow State Community College, Box 8500, Lynchburg, TN 37352-8500

Nashville Auto-Diesel College
Nashville, Tennessee
www.nadcedu.com   CB code: 3098

- For-profit 1-year technical college
- Commuter campus in large city
- Interview required

General. Accredited by ACCSC. **Degrees:** 59 associate awarded. **Calendar:** Differs by program, extensive summer session. **Full-time faculty:** 67 total. **Class size:** 100% 20-39.

Student profile.

Out-of-state:	90%	**Live on campus:**	30%
25 or older:	1%		

Basis for selection. Secondary school record, interview, test scores most important. State proficiency tests used in admission decisions.

2011-2012 Annual costs. Full program costs range from $24,500 to $35,700 for diploma programs; $30,800 to $36,300 for degree programs. Books/supplies: $987.

Financial aid. All financial aid based on need. Work-study available nights, weekends and for part-time students.

Application procedures. Admission: No deadline. $100 fee. Admission notification on a rolling basis. **Financial aid:** No deadline. FAFSA required. Applicants notified on a rolling basis.

Academics. Credit/placement by examination: AP, CLEP, institutional tests. **Support services:** Study skills assistance, tutoring.

Computing on campus. 46 workstations in library, computer center. Dormitories wired for high-speed internet access. Online library available.

Student life. Freshman orientation: Mandatory. Preregistration for classes offered. **Housing:** Single-sex dorms available. $200 deposit.

Student services. Career counseling, student employment services, financial aid counseling, placement for graduates, veterans' counselor. **Physically disabled:** Services for visually impaired.

Contact. E-mail: admissions@nadcedu.com
Phone: (615) 226-3990 Toll-free number: (800) 228-6232
Fax: (615) 262-8466
Shayne Pulver, Director of Admissions, Nashville Auto-Diesel College, 1524 Gallatin Road, Nashville, TN 37206

Nashville State Community College
Nashville, Tennessee
www.nscc.edu   CB code: 0850

- Public 2-year community and technical college
- Commuter campus in very large city

General. Founded in 1969. Regionally accredited. **Enrollment:** 8,273 degree-seeking undergraduates. **Degrees:** 548 associate awarded. **Location:** 6 miles from Nashville, 200 miles from Memphis. **Calendar:** Semester, limited summer session. **Full-time faculty:** 160 total. **Part-time faculty:** 362 total. **Special facilities:** Television production studio.

Student profile. Among degree-seeking undergraduates, 58% enrolled in a transfer program, 42% enrolled in a vocational program, 4,015 transferred in from other institutions.

Out-of-state: 2%   **25 or older:**   51%

Transfer out. Colleges most students transferred to 2011: Middle Tennessee University, Tennessee State University, Tennessee Technical University.

Basis for selection. Open admission, but selective for some programs. Test scores used for placement. Interview required for automotive services technology, occupational therapy assistant, surgical technology and nursing programs. **Adult students:** Degree-seeking students over 21 with no previous college-level English and/or math required to take COMPASS placement exam. **Home schooled:** Transcript should be official copy from organization as defined by state law and must have certification of registration with superintendent of local education agency where student would have attended.

High school preparation. Recommended units include English 4, mathematics 3, social studies 2, history 2, science 2 (laboratory 1), foreign language 2 and visual/performing arts 1. 1 visual/performing art recommended. Business technologies majors: 1 unit bookkeeping or accounting recommended. Engineering technologies majors: additional math and science recommended.

2011-2012 Annual costs. Tuition/fees: $3,477; $13,581 out-of-state. Per-credit charge: $129 in-state; $530 out-of-state. Books/supplies: $1,200. Personal expenses: $465.

Financial aid. Need-based: Need-based aid available for part-time students. Work-study available nights, weekends and for part-time students. **Non-need-based:** Scholarships awarded for academics, minority status.

Application procedures. Admission: No deadline. $20 fee. Automotive services technology applicants must have automobile dealer sponsorship prior to acceptance. **Financial aid:** Priority date 3/1, closing date 7/1. FAFSA, institutional form required. Applicants notified on a rolling basis starting 6/1; must reply within 2 week(s) of notification.

Academics. Special study options: Cooperative education, distance learning, double major, dual enrollment of high school students, ESL, honors, internships, student-designed major, study abroad. **Credit/placement by examination:** AP, CLEP, institutional tests. 20 credit hours maximum toward associate degree. **Support services:** GED preparation, learning center, reduced course load, remedial instruction, study skills assistance, tutoring, writing center.

Majors. Business: Accounting, business admin. **Communications technology:** General. **Computer sciences:** General. **Education:** Early childhood. **Foreign languages:** Sign language interpretation. **Health services:** Medical secretary. **Protective services:** Police science. **Visual/performing arts:** Commercial/advertising art, photography.

Computing on campus. 518 workstations in library, computer center. Commuter students can connect to campus network. Online course registration, online library, helpline, wireless network available.

Student life. Freshman orientation: Available. Preregistration for classes offered. **Activities:** International student organizations, literary magazine, student government, student newspaper, black student organization.

Student services. Adult student services, career counseling, student employment services, personal counseling, placement for graduates, veterans' counselor. **Physically disabled:** Services for visually, hearing impaired. **Transfer:** Pre-admission transcript evaluation for new students. College fairs on campus for students transferring to 4-year colleges.

Contact. Phone: (615) 353-3215 Toll-free number: (800) 272-7363
Fax: (615) 353-3243
Laura Potter, Director of Admissions, Nashville State Community College, 120 White Bridge Road, Nashville, TN 37209-4515

National College of Business and Technology: Bartlett
Bartlett, Tennessee
www.ncbt.edu

- For-profit 2-year branch campus college
- Large town

General. Regionally accredited; also accredited by ACICS. **Enrollment:** 195 degree-seeking undergraduates. **Degrees:** 77 associate awarded. **Calendar:** Quarter. **Full-time faculty:** 2 total. **Part-time faculty:** 30 total.

Basis for selection. Open admission.

2011-2012 Annual costs. Tuition/fees: $13,770. Per-credit charge: $305.

Financial aid. Need-based: Work-study available nights, weekends and for part-time students.

Application procedures. Admission: No deadline. $50 fee. **Financial aid:** No deadline.

Academics. Credit/placement by examination: AP, CLEP.

Majors. Business: Accounting/business management, administrative services, business admin. **Health services:** Medical assistant, medical records technology, pharmacy assistant.

Contact. Phone: (901) 213-1681
Erica Lawrence, Director of Admissions, National College of Business and Technology: Bartlett, 5760 Stage Road, Bartlett, TN 38134

National College of Business and Technology: Bristol
Bristol, Tennessee
www.ncbt.edu   CB code: 3247

- For-profit 2-year business college
- Commuter campus in large town

General. Accredited by ACICS. Eight campuses in Virginia. **Enrollment:** 266 degree-seeking undergraduates. **Degrees:** 65 associate awarded. **Calendar:** Quarter, limited summer session. **Full-time faculty:** 2 total. **Part-time faculty:** 19 total.

Basis for selection. Open admission. Interview recommended.

2011-2012 Annual costs. Tuition/fees: $13,770. Per-credit charge: $305. Books/supplies: $1,200.

Financial aid. All financial aid based on need. Need-based aid available for part-time students. Work-study available nights, weekends and for part-time students.

Application procedures. Admission: No deadline. $50 fee, may be waived for applicants with need. Admission notification on a rolling basis. **Financial aid:** No deadline. FAFSA required. Applicants notified on a rolling basis starting 9/1.

Academics. Special study options: Double major, internships. **Credit/ placement by examination:** AP, CLEP, institutional tests. **Support services:** Tutoring.

Majors. Business: Accounting, administrative services, business admin, office management. **Computer sciences:** Computer science. **Health services:** Medical assistant.

Computing on campus. 35 workstations in library, computer center.

Student life. Freshman orientation: Mandatory. Preregistration for classes offered.

Student services. Career counseling, personal counseling.

Contact. E-mail: market@educorp.edu
Phone: (423) 878-4440
Dana Hutton, Director of Admissions, National College of Business and Technology: Bristol, 1328 Highway 11W, Bristol, TN 37620

National College of Business and Technology: Knoxville
Knoxville, Tennessee
www.ncbt.edu

▶ For-profit 2-year business and technical college
▶ Large city

General. Accredited by ACICS. **Enrollment:** 246 degree-seeking undergraduates. **Degrees:** 81 associate awarded. **Calendar:** Quarter. **Full-time faculty:** 9 total. **Part-time faculty:** 18 total.

Basis for selection. Open admission. Interview recommended.

2011-2012 Annual costs. Tuition/fees: $13,770. Per-credit charge: $305.

Financial aid. Need-based: Work-study available nights, weekends and for part-time students.

Application procedures. Admission: No deadline. $50 fee. **Financial aid:** No deadline.

Academics. Credit/placement by examination: AP, CLEP.

Majors. Business: Accounting, administrative services, business admin. **Health services:** Medical assistant, medical records admin, pharmacy assistant, surgical technology.

Contact. Phone: (865) 539-2011
Teresa Neubert, Director of Admissions, National College of Business and Technology: Knoxville, 8415 Kingston Pike, Knoxville, TN 37919

National College of Business and Technology: Madison
Madison, Tennessee
www.ncbt.edu

▶ For-profit 2-year branch campus college
▶ Large town

General. Regionally accredited; also accredited by ACICS. **Enrollment:** 266 degree-seeking undergraduates. **Degrees:** 73 associate awarded. **Calendar:** Quarter. **Full-time faculty:** 2 total. **Part-time faculty:** 29 total.

Basis for selection. Open admission.

2011-2012 Annual costs. Tuition/fees: $13,770. Per-credit charge: $305.

Financial aid. Need-based: Work-study available nights, weekends and for part-time students.

Application procedures. Admission: No deadline. $50 fee. **Financial aid:** No deadline.

Academics. Credit/placement by examination: AP, CLEP.

Majors. Business: Accounting/business management, administrative services, business admin, hospitality admin, tourism/travel. **Health services:** Medical assistant, medical records technology, pharmacy assistant.

Contact. Phone: (615) 612-3015
Danavan Hylton, Director of Admissions, National College of Business and Technology: Madison, 900 Madison Square, Madison, TN 37115

National College of Business and Technology: Memphis
Memphis, Tennessee
www.ncbt.edu

▶ For-profit 2-year branch campus college
▶ Very large city

General. Regionally accredited; also accredited by ACICS. **Enrollment:** 255 degree-seeking undergraduates. **Degrees:** 89 associate awarded. **Calendar:** Quarter. **Full-time faculty:** 4 total. **Part-time faculty:** 48 total.

Basis for selection. Open admission.

2011-2012 Annual costs. Tuition/fees: $13,770. Per-credit charge: $305. Books/supplies: $1,980.

Financial aid. Need-based: Work-study available nights, weekends and for part-time students.

Application procedures. Admission: No deadline. $50 fee. **Financial aid:** No deadline.

Academics. Credit/placement by examination: AP, CLEP.

Majors. Business: Accounting/business management, administrative services, business admin. **Health services:** Medical assistant, medical records technology, pharmacy assistant, surgical technology.

Contact. Phone: (901) 363-9046
Shelly Burrow, Director of Admissions, National College of Business and Technology: Memphis, 3545 Lamar Avenue, Suite 1, Memphis, TN 38118

National College of Business and Technology: Nashville
Nashville, Tennessee
www.ncbt.edu   CB code: 3227

▶ For-profit 2-year business and technical college
▶ Commuter campus in large city

General. Accredited by ACICS. **Enrollment:** 248 degree-seeking undergraduates. **Degrees:** 67 associate awarded. **Calendar:** Quarter. **Full-time faculty:** 2 total. **Part-time faculty:** 35 total.

Basis for selection. Open admission. Interview recommended.

2011-2012 Annual costs. Tuition/fees: $13,770. Per-credit charge: $305. Books/supplies: $900. Personal expenses: $3,259.

Financial aid. All financial aid based on need. Need-based aid available for part-time students. Work-study available nights, weekends and for part-time students.

Application procedures. Admission: No deadline. $50 fee. **Financial aid:** No deadline. FAFSA required.

Academics. Special study options: Liberal arts/career combination. **Credit/placement by examination:** AP, CLEP.

Majors. Business: Accounting, administrative services, business admin. **Computer sciences:** General. **Health services:** Medical assistant, medical secretary.

Student life. Freshman orientation: Mandatory. Preregistration for classes offered.

Contact. E-mail: market@educorp.edu
Phone: (615) 333-3344
Dana Hutton, Director of Admissions, National College of Business and Technology: Nashville, PO Box 6400, Roanoke, VA 24017

Northeast State Community College
Blountville, Tennessee
www.NortheastState.edu   CB code: 0453

- Public 2-year community and technical college
- Commuter campus in small city

General. Founded in 1965. Regionally accredited. **Enrollment:** 6,478 degree-seeking undergraduates. **Degrees:** 703 associate awarded. **Location:** 12 miles from Johnson City, 10 miles from Kingsport. **Calendar:** Semester, limited summer session. **Full-time faculty:** 110 total. **Part-time faculty:** 230 total.

Student profile.

Part-time:	45%	**Women:**	54%
Out-of-state:	2%		

Transfer out. Colleges most students transferred to 2011: East Tennessee State University, Milligan College, Tennessee Tech, University of Tennessee.

Basis for selection. Open admission, but selective for some programs. Special requirements for health related professions division. **Adult students:** COMPASS placement test required for applicants 21 and older without math or English transfer credit.

High school preparation. Recommended units include English 4, mathematics 3, social studies 1, history 1, science 2, foreign language 2 and visual/performing arts 1.

2011-2012 Annual costs. Tuition/fees: $3,533; $13,637 out-of-state. Per-credit charge: $129 in-state; $530 out-of-state. Books/supplies: $1,500.

Financial aid. Need-based: Need-based aid available for part-time students. Work-study available nights, weekends and for part-time students. **Non-need-based:** Scholarships awarded for academics, alumni affiliation, art, job skills, leadership, minority status, music/drama, religious affiliation.

Application procedures. Admission: No deadline. $10 fee. Admission notification on a rolling basis beginning on or about 6/1. **Financial aid:** Priority date 3/31; no closing date. FAFSA required. Applicants notified on a rolling basis starting 3/1; must reply within 3 week(s) of notification.

Academics. Special study options: Accelerated study, cooperative education, distance learning, double major, dual enrollment of high school students, honors, independent study, study abroad, weekend college. License preparation in paramedic. **Credit/placement by examination:** AP, CLEP, institutional tests. 15 credit hours maximum toward associate degree. **Support services:** GED test center, reduced course load, remedial instruction, tutoring.

Majors. Business: Administrative services, business admin. **Computer sciences:** General, webmaster. **Health services:** Cardiovascular technology, clinical lab assistant, dental lab technology, medical assistant. **Liberal arts:** Arts/sciences. **Protective services:** Criminal justice, forensics, police science. **Social sciences:** General. **Work/family studies:** Child development, family studies.

Most popular majors. Business/marketing 9%, engineering/engineering technologies 12%, health sciences 12%, liberal arts 49%, trade and industry 9%.

Computing on campus. 900 workstations in library, computer center. Commuter students can connect to campus network. Online library, wireless network available.

Student life. Freshman orientation: Mandatory. Preregistration for classes offered. Offered online; takes place prior to registration. **Activities:** Drama, literary magazine, student government.

Student services. Career counseling, services for economically disadvantaged, student employment services, financial aid counseling, health services, minority student services, personal counseling, placement for graduates, veterans' counselor. **Physically disabled:** Services for visually, speech, hearing impaired. **Transfer:** Transfer adviser, college fairs on campus for students transferring to 4-year colleges.

Contact. E-mail: jgstarling@northeaststate.edu
Phone: (423) 323-0253 Toll-free number: (800) 836-7822
Fax: (423) 323-0215
Jennifer Starling, Dean of Enrollment Management, Northeast State Community College, Box 246, Blountville, TN 37617-0246

Nossi College of Art
Goodlettsville, Tennessee
www.nossi.edu   CB code: 3118

- For-profit 2-year visual arts and technical college
- Commuter campus in large town
- Interview required

General. Accredited by ACCSC. **Enrollment:** 425 degree-seeking undergraduates. **Degrees:** 21 bachelor's, 84 associate awarded. **Location:** 20 miles from Nashville. **Calendar:** Semester, extensive summer session. **Full-time faculty:** 6 total. **Part-time faculty:** 31 total.

Basis for selection. Interview and talent most important. Portfolio required for commercial art program.

2011-2012 Annual costs. Tuition for first year (3 semesters) $14,100; required fees $700. Books/supplies: $700.

Financial aid. Need-based: Need-based aid available for part-time students. Work-study available nights, weekends and for part-time students.

Application procedures. Admission: No deadline. $100 fee.

Academics. Credit/placement by examination: AP, CLEP.

Majors. Visual/performing arts: General, commercial photography, commercial/advertising art.

Computing on campus. 40 workstations in library, computer center.

Student life. Freshman orientation: Mandatory. Preregistration for classes offered.

Student services. Alcohol/substance abuse counseling, career counseling, student employment services, financial aid counseling, personal counseling, placement for graduates.

Contact. E-mail: admissions@nossi.edu
Phone: (615) 851-1088 ext. 17 Toll-free number: (887) 860-1601
Fax: (615) 851-1087
Mary Alexander, Director of Admissions, Nossi College of Art, 907 Rivergate Parkway, Building E-6, Goodlettsville, TN 37072

Pellissippi State Community College
Knoxville, Tennessee
www.pstcc.edu   CB code: 0319

- Public 2-year community and technical college
- Commuter campus in small city

General. Founded in 1974. Regionally accredited. **Enrollment:** 11,259 degree-seeking undergraduates. **Degrees:** 932 associate awarded. **ROTC:** Army. **Location:** 178 miles from Nashville, 388 miles from Memphis. **Calendar:** Semester, extensive summer session. **Full-time faculty:** 201 total. **Part-time faculty:** 248 total. **Class size:** 46% < 20, 52% 20-39, 2% 40-49, less than 1% 50-99, less than 1% >100.

Student profile.

Out-of-state:	1%	**25 or older:**	40%

Transfer out. Colleges most students transferred to 2011: University of Tennessee in Knoxville, East Tennessee State University, Tennessee Technological University, Maryville College, Middle Tennessee State University.

Basis for selection. Open admission. **Adult students:** Institutional placement test required of students 21 and older who have not had college-level math or English. **Learning Disabled:** Accommodations for testing/programs provided on case-by-case basis with supporting documentation.

High school preparation. 14 units recommended. Recommended units include English 4, mathematics 3, social studies 1, history 1, science 1 (laboratory 1) and foreign language 2. 1 U.S. history and one visual and performing arts required.

2011-2012 Annual costs. Tuition/fees: $3,570; $13,992 out-of-state. Per-credit charge: $129 in-state; $401 out-of-state. Books/supplies: $800. Personal expenses: $1,500.

Financial aid. Need-based: Need-based aid available for part-time students. Work-study available nights, weekends and for part-time students.

Non-need-based: Scholarships awarded for academics, art, minority status, music/drama.

Application procedures. Admission: Closing date 8/20 (postmark date). $10 fee, may be waived for applicants with need. Admission notification on a rolling basis beginning on or about 9/1. **Financial aid:** Priority date 5/1; no closing date. FAFSA required. Applicants notified on a rolling basis starting 7/15; must reply within 2 week(s) of notification.

Academics. Special study options: Cooperative education, distance learning, double major, dual enrollment of high school students, ESL, honors, independent study, internships, liberal arts/career combination, weekend college. **Credit/placement by examination:** AP, CLEP, IB, institutional tests. 36 credit hours maximum toward associate degree. **Support services:** GED preparation and test center, learning center, pre-admission summer program, reduced course load, remedial instruction, study skills assistance, tutoring, writing center.

Majors. Business: Accounting technology, administrative services, business admin, e-commerce. **Computer sciences:** Computer science, information systems, web page design. **Human services:** Community org/advocacy. **Liberal arts:** Arts/sciences. **Social sciences:** GIS/cartography. **Visual/performing arts:** Cinematography, commercial/advertising art, interior design. **Work/family studies:** Child development.

Most popular majors. Business/marketing 9%, liberal arts 59%, visual/performing arts 9%.

Computing on campus. 1,290 workstations in library, computer center, student center. Commuter students can connect to campus network. Online course registration, online library, helpline, repair service, wireless network available.

Student life. Freshman orientation: Available. Preregistration for classes offered. **Activities:** Jazz band, campus ministries, choral groups, drama, international student organizations, literary magazine, music ensembles, musical theater, student government, student newspaper, Association of Information Technology Professionals, Institute of Electrical and Electronics Engineers, paralegal association, active black students association, Students In Free Enterprise, Phi Theta Kappa.

Athletics. Intramural: Archery, basketball, football (non-tackle), golf, soccer, softball, tennis, volleyball.

Student services. Career counseling, student employment services, personal counseling, placement for graduates, veterans' counselor. **Physically disabled:** Services for visually, speech, hearing impaired. **Transfer:** Transfer adviser, college fairs on campus for students transferring to 4-year colleges.

Contact. E-mail: latouzeau@pstcc.edu
Phone: (865) 694-6570 Fax: (865) 539-7217
Leigh Anne Touzeau, Assistant Vice President, Enrollment Services, Pellissippi State Community College, Box 22990, Knoxville, TN 37933-0990

Remington College: Memphis
Memphis, Tennessee
www.remingtoncollege.edu/memphis   CB code: 3159

▶ For-profit 2-year business and technical college
▶ Commuter campus in very large city
▶ Interview required

General. Accredited by ACCSC. **Enrollment:** 938 degree-seeking undergraduates. **Degrees:** 125 associate awarded. **Calendar:** Quarter, extensive summer session. **Full-time faculty:** 35 total. **Part-time faculty:** 7 total. **Class size:** 81% < 20, 19% 20-39.

Basis for selection. All applicants must pass college administered entrance exam prior to acceptance.

Financial aid. All financial aid based on need. Need-based aid available for part-time students. Work-study available nights, weekends and for part-time students.

Application procedures. Admission: No deadline. $50 fee. Admission notification on a rolling basis. **Financial aid:** No deadline. FAFSA, institutional form required. Applicants notified on a rolling basis; must reply within 2 week(s) of notification.

Academics. Special study options: Cooperative education, independent study, liberal arts/career combination. Bachelor's degree programs available on campus. **Credit/placement by examination:** AP, CLEP, institutional

tests. 48 credit hours maximum toward associate degree, 96 toward bachelor's. **Support services:** Tutoring.

Majors. Business: Office technology. **Computer sciences:** LAN/WAN management. **Protective services:** Criminal justice.

Computing on campus. Commuter students can connect to campus network. Helpline, repair service, wireless network available.

Student life. Freshman orientation: Mandatory. Preregistration for classes offered. 3-hour session held Saturday two weeks before quarter begins. **Activities:** Student newspaper.

Student services. Adult student services, career counseling, student employment services, financial aid counseling, placement for graduates. **Transfer:** Pre-admission transcript evaluation for new students.

Contact. E-mail: admissions@remingtoncollege.edu
Phone: (901) 345-1000 Fax: (901) 396-8310
Marc Wright, Director of Admissions, Remington College: Memphis, 2710 Nonconnah Boulevard, Memphis, TN 38132

Remington College: Nashville
Nashville, Tennessee
www.remingtoncollege.edu/nashville

▶ For-profit 2-year technical and career college
▶ Very large city

General. Accredited by ACCSC. **Enrollment:** 373 degree-seeking undergraduates. **Degrees:** 20 associate awarded. **Calendar:** Quarter, extensive summer session. **Full-time faculty:** 20 total. **Part-time faculty:** 13 total. **Special facilities:** Forensics lab, crime scene lab, courtroom, laser shot range, 3 medical office labs, dental lab, salon.

Basis for selection. Open admission, but selective for some programs. Selective admissions to allied health programs.

Financial aid. Need-based: Work-study available nights, weekends and for part-time students.

Application procedures. Admission: No deadline. $50 fee. **Financial aid:** No deadline.

Academics. Credit/placement by examination: AP, CLEP.

Majors. Protective services: Law enforcement admin.

Contact. E-mail: admissions@remingtoncollege.edu
Phone: (615) 889-5520
Larry Collins, Campus President, Remington College: Nashville, 441 Donelson Pike, Suite 150, Nashville, TN 37214

Roane State Community College
Harriman, Tennessee
www.roanestate.edu   CB code: 1656

▶ Public 2-year community and junior college
▶ Commuter campus in small town

General. Founded in 1971. Regionally accredited. **Enrollment:** 5,321 degree-seeking undergraduates; 1,480 non-degree-seeking students. **Degrees:** 783 associate awarded. **Location:** 40 miles from Knoxville. **Calendar:** Semester, limited summer session. **Full-time faculty:** 133 total; 12% minority, 53% women. **Part-time faculty:** 215 total; 5% minority, 56% women. **Class size:** 40% < 20, 57% 20-39, 2% 40-49, less than 1% 50-99. **Special facilities:** Observatory, agricultural exposition center.

Student profile. Among degree-seeking undergraduates, 36% enrolled in a transfer program, 64% enrolled in a vocational program, 1,273 enrolled as first-time, first-year students, 334 transferred in from other institutions.

Part-time:	45%	Hispanic American:	2%
Out-of-state:	1%	Native American:	1%
Women:	66%	25 or older:	39%
African American:	3%		

Transfer out. Colleges most students transferred to 2011: University of Tennessee-Knoxville, Tennessee Technological University, Middle Tennessee State University, East Tennessee State University.

Basis for selection. Open admission, but selective for some programs. All health science programs require 20 ACT and 2.5 GPA for 8 hours general course work. Additional requirements for nursing program. Interview required for some health programs; audition required for some music programs. **Adult students:** Placement assessment may be required. **Home schooled:** State high school equivalency certificate required.

High school preparation. 20 units recommended. Recommended units include English 4, mathematics 3, social studies 1, history 1, science 2 and foreign language 2.

2011-2012 Annual costs. Tuition/fees: $3,537; $13,641 out-of-state. Per-credit charge: $129 in-state; $530 out-of-state. Books/supplies: $1,500.

Financial aid. Need-based: Need-based aid available for part-time students. Work-study available nights, weekends and for part-time students. **Non-need-based:** Scholarships awarded for academics, art, athletics, leadership, music/drama, state residency.

Application procedures. Admission: No deadline. $10 fee. Admission notification on a rolling basis. **Financial aid:** Priority date 4/1; no closing date. FAFSA, institutional form required. Applicants notified on a rolling basis starting 5/1.

Academics. Online academic support services available evenings and weekends. **Special study options:** Accelerated study, cooperative education, distance learning, double major, dual enrollment of high school students, ESL, honors, independent study, internships, liberal arts/career combination, study abroad, teacher certification program, weekend college. License preparation in dental hygiene, nursing, occupational therapy, paramedic, physical therapy, radiology. **Credit/placement by examination:** AP, CLEP, IB, institutional tests. 18 credit hours maximum toward associate degree. **Support services:** GED preparation and test center, learning center, remedial instruction, study skills assistance, tutoring, writing center.

Majors. Business: Business admin, management science. **Computer sciences:** Web page design. **Education:** General, early childhood. **Health services:** Dental hygiene, environmental health, medical radiologic technology/radiation therapy, medical records technology, nursing (RN), occupational therapy assistant, optician, physical therapy assistant, respiratory therapy technology. **Liberal arts:** Arts/sciences. **Protective services:** Police science. **Social sciences:** GIS/cartography.

Most popular majors. Business/marketing 12%, education 6%, health sciences 34%, liberal arts 32%, science technologies 9%.

Computing on campus. 600 workstations in library, computer center, student center. Commuter students can connect to campus network. Online course registration, online library, helpline, wireless network available.

Student life. Freshman orientation: Mandatory. Preregistration for classes offered. One half-day orientation. **Activities:** Jazz band, campus ministries, choral groups, dance, drama, international student organizations, music ensembles, musical theater, student government, American Chemical Society, Baptist collegiate ministry, International Association of Administrative Professionals, Oak Ridge Institute for Continued Learning, occupational therapy student club, Phi Theta Kappa, physical therapy student association, Playmakers, psychology and sociology club, respiratory therapy student association.

Athletics. NJCAA. **Intercollegiate:** Baseball M, basketball, softball W. **Intramural:** Basketball, softball. **Team name:** Raiders.

Student services. Career counseling, student employment services, financial aid counseling, minority student services, personal counseling, placement for graduates, veterans' counselor. **Physically disabled:** Services for visually, speech, hearing impaired. **Transfer:** Transfer adviser, college fairs on campus for students transferring to 4-year colleges.

Contact. E-mail: admissions@roanestate.edu
Phone: (865) 882-4523 Toll-free number: (866) 462-7722 ext. 4523
Fax: (865) 882-4527
Brenda Rector, Director of Admissions and Records, Roane State Community College, 276 Patton Lane, Harriman, TN 37748

Southwest Tennessee Community College
Memphis, Tennessee
www.southwest.tn.edu   CB code: 0274

- Public 2-year community college
- Commuter campus in very large city

General. Founded in 1970. Regionally accredited. **Enrollment:** 11,682 degree-seeking undergraduates; 1,276 non-degree-seeking students. **Degrees:** 846 associate awarded. **ROTC:** Army, Air Force. **Calendar:** Semester, extensive summer session. **Full-time faculty:** 208 total; 36% minority, 58% women. **Part-time faculty:** 486 total; 43% minority, 39% women. **Class size:** 45% < 20, 55% 20-39, less than 1% 40-49.

Student profile. Among degree-seeking undergraduates, 19% enrolled in a transfer program, 2,901 enrolled as first-time, first-year students, 884 transferred in from other institutions.

Part-time:	51%	**Hispanic American:**	3%
Women:	65%	**International:**	1%
African American:	63%	**25 or older:**	43%
Asian American:	2%		

Transfer out. Colleges most students transferred to 2011: University of Memphis, Middle Tennessee State University, Tennessee State University, University of Tennessee at Martin.

Basis for selection. Open admission, but selective for some programs. Special requirements for admission to nursing, dietetic technician, laboratory phlebotomy, medical assistant, medical laboratory technician, physical therapist assistant, radiologic technology, paramedic programs. **Adult students:** ACT COMPASS exam required for placement. **Learning Disabled:** Require documentation of disability to be shown to disability counselor.

High school preparation. 15 units required. Required units include English 4, mathematics 3, social studies 1, history 1, science 2 (laboratory 1), foreign language 2 and visual/performing arts 1.

2011-2012 Annual costs. Tuition/fees: $3,666; $13,290 out-of-state. Per-credit charge: $129 in-state; $530 out-of-state. Books/supplies: $1,000. Personal expenses: $1,400.

Financial aid. Need-based: Need-based aid available for part-time students. Work-study available nights, weekends and for part-time students. **Non-need-based:** Scholarships awarded for academics, athletics, minority status, music/drama, state residency. **Additional information:** State grants available to eligible students who apply by 4/1.

Application procedures. Admission: No deadline. $10 fee. Admission notification on a rolling basis. **Financial aid:** Priority date 3/15; no closing date. FAFSA required. Applicants notified on a rolling basis starting 6/1; must reply within 4 week(s) of notification.

Academics. Special study options: Cooperative education, distance learning, double major, dual enrollment of high school students, ESL, honors, independent study, internships, liberal arts/career combination, student-designed major, study abroad, weekend college. On-site extension courses at business, industry and government installations. License preparation in nursing, paramedic, physical therapy, radiology, real estate. **Credit/placement by examination:** AP, CLEP, institutional tests. **Support services:** GED preparation and test center, learning center, pre-admission summer program, reduced course load, remedial instruction, study skills assistance, tutoring.

Majors. Biology: Biotechnology. **Business:** General, accounting technology, administrative services, business admin, hotel/motel admin, management information systems. **Computer sciences:** General, web page design. **Education:** General. **General:** Horticulture. **Health services:** Clinical lab technology, dietician assistant, EMT paramedic, medical radiologic technology/radiation therapy, nursing (RN), physical therapy assistant. **Liberal arts:** Arts/sciences. **Protective services:** Police science. **Visual/performing arts:** Commercial/advertising art. **Work/family studies:** Child development.

Most popular majors. Business/marketing 14%, engineering/engineering technologies 6%, health sciences 19%, liberal arts 42%.

Computing on campus. 500 workstations in library, computer center. Commuter students can connect to campus network. Online course registration, online library, helpline, wireless network available.

Student life. Freshman orientation: Available. Preregistration for classes offered. **Activities:** Bands, choral groups, drama, music ensembles, student government, student newspaper, NAACP, Baptist student union, Human Key Society, National Student Support Council for Africa, black student association, Phi Theta Kappa honor society, police science association, science club, radiologic technology student association, Collegiate Secretaries.

Athletics. NJCAA. **Intercollegiate:** Baseball M, basketball, softball W. **Team name:** Saluqis.

Student services. Adult student services, career counseling, services for economically disadvantaged, student employment services, financial aid counseling, on-campus daycare, personal counseling, placement for graduates, veterans' counselor. **Physically disabled:** Services for visually, speech, hearing impaired. **Transfer:** Re-entry adviser, pre-admission transcript evaluation for new students. Transfer center, transfer adviser, college fairs on campus for students transferring to 4-year colleges.

Contact. Phone: (901) 333-5924 Toll-free number: (877) 717-7822 Fax: (901) 333-4473
Vanessa Dowdy, Director, Southwest Tennessee Community College, PO Box 780, Memphis, TN 38101-0780

Vatterott College: Memphis
Memphis, Tennessee
www.vatterott-college.edu

▶ For-profit 2-year technical college
▶ Commuter campus in large city

General. Accredited by ACCSCT. **Calendar:** Differs by program.

Annual costs/financial aid. Estimated program costs as of April 2011: diploma (50 weeks) $18,660, (60 weeks) $18,660 - $24,970; associate degree (90 weeks) $35,450 - $37,120. All costs, which include tuition, fees, books and supplies, and taxes, are subject to change. Books/supplies: $1,050.

Contact. Phone: (901) 761-5730
Director of Admissions, 2655 Dividend Drive, Memphis, TN 38132

Virginia College School of Business and Health
Chattanooga, Tennessee
www.chattanooga.vc.edu

▶ For-profit 2-year business and career college
▶ Large city

General. Regionally accredited; also accredited by ACICS. **Enrollment:** 600 degree-seeking undergraduates. **Degrees:** 2 bachelor's, 22 associate awarded. **Calendar:** Quarter. **Full-time faculty:** 20 total. **Part-time faculty:** 22 total.

Basis for selection. Open admission.

Financial aid. Need-based: Work-study available nights, weekends and for part-time students.

Application procedures. Admission: $100 fee.

Academics. Credit/placement by examination: AP, CLEP.

Majors. Business: Business admin. **Health services:** Medical records admin, surgical technology.

Contact. E-mail: chattanooga.info@vc.edu
Virginia College School of Business and Health, 721 Eastgate Loop, Chattanooga, TN 37411

Volunteer State Community College
Gallatin, Tennessee
www.volstate.edu   **CB code: 1881**

▶ Public 2-year community and junior college
▶ Commuter campus in small city

General. Founded in 1970. Regionally accredited. **Enrollment:** 7,217 degree-seeking undergraduates; 1,436 non-degree-seeking students. **Degrees:** 723 associate awarded. **Location:** 25 miles from Nashville. **Calendar:** Semester, limited summer session. **Full-time faculty:** 155 total; 21% have terminal degrees, 14% minority, 50% women. **Part-time faculty:** 232 total; 5% have terminal degrees, 11% minority, 59% women. **Class size:** 41% < 20, 56% 20-39, 3% 40-49. **Special facilities:** Community garden. **Partnerships:** Formal partnership with GAP Incorporated.

Student profile. Among degree-seeking undergraduates, 45% enrolled in a transfer program, 55% enrolled in a vocational program, 1,621 enrolled as first-time, first-year students, 662 transferred in from other institutions.

Part-time:	45%	African American:	10%
Out-of-state:	1%	Asian American:	1%
Women:	62%	Hispanic American:	3%

Transfer out. Colleges most students transferred to 2011: Middle Tennessee State University, Austin Peay State University, Tennessee State University, Tennessee Technical University.

Basis for selection. Open admission, but selective for some programs. Allied health students admitted based on GPA and interview after completing designated amount of college coursework. Test scores, when required in selective programs, must be received by 8/30. Interview required for allied health program. **Adult students:** Unless exempt by ACT, ASSET placement test required. **Home schooled:** Transcript must be official copy from affiliated organization as defined by state law or be accompanied by certification of registration with superintendent of local education agency where student would otherwise attend.

High school preparation. 14 units recommended. Recommended units include English 4, mathematics 3, social studies 1, history 1, science 2 (laboratory 1), foreign language 2 and visual/performing arts 1.

2011-2012 Annual costs. Tuition/fees: $3,519; $13,623 out-of-state. Per-credit charge: $129 in-state; $530 out-of-state. Books/supplies: $950. Personal expenses: $400.

2010-2011 Financial aid. Need-based: 1,203 full-time freshmen applied for aid; 990 were judged to have need; 990 of these received aid. Average need met was 54%. Average scholarship/grant was $4,984; average loan $2,635. 76% of total undergraduate aid awarded as scholarships/grants, 24% as loans/jobs. Need-based aid available for part-time students. Work-study available nights, weekends and for part-time students. **Non-need-based:** Awarded to 1,473 full-time undergraduates, including 687 freshmen. Scholarships awarded for academics, art, athletics, leadership, minority status, music/drama, state residency.

Application procedures. Admission: Priority date 7/31; deadline 8/28 (receipt date). $20 fee. Admission notification on a rolling basis. **Financial aid:** Priority date 4/15; no closing date. FAFSA, institutional form required. Applicants notified on a rolling basis; must reply within 2 week(s) of notification.

Academics. Special study options: Accelerated study, cooperative education, distance learning, double major, dual enrollment of high school students, ESL, honors, independent study, internships, study abroad. Bachelor's degree programs available on campus. License preparation in dental hygiene, paramedic, physical therapy, radiology, real estate. **Credit/placement by examination:** AP, CLEP, institutional tests. 36 credit hours maximum toward associate degree. Maximum 12 hours of credit by examination in specific allied health programs. **Support services:** GED test center, learning center, pre-admission summer program, reduced course load, remedial instruction, study skills assistance, tutoring, writing center.

Majors. Business: Business admin. **Computer sciences:** Web page design. **Education:** General. **Health services:** Clinical lab technology, medical radiologic technology/radiation therapy, medical records technology, ophthalmic technology, physical therapy assistant, respiratory therapy technology. **Human services:** Community org/advocacy. **Liberal arts:** Arts/sciences. **Protective services:** Firefighting, police science. **Work/family studies:** Child development.

Most popular majors. Business/marketing 11%, health sciences 20%, liberal arts 60%.

Computing on campus. 800 workstations in library, computer center. Commuter students can connect to campus network. Online course registration, online library, helpline, wireless network available.

Student life. Freshman orientation: Mandatory. Preregistration for classes offered. One-day program held multiple times prior to registration both on campus and online. **Activities:** Campus ministries, choral groups, drama, literary magazine, radio station, student government, student newspaper, TV station, African-American student union, returning women's organization, College Democrats, College Republicans.

Athletics. NJCAA. **Intercollegiate:** Baseball M, basketball, softball W. **Team name:** Pioneers.

Student services. Career counseling, services for economically disadvantaged, financial aid counseling, health services, minority student services, personal counseling, placement for graduates, veterans' counselor. **Physically disabled:** Services for visually, speech, hearing impaired. **Transfer:** Pre-admission transcript evaluation for new students. Transfer adviser, college fairs on campus for students transferring to 4-year colleges.

Contact. E-mail: admissions@volstate.edu
Phone: (615) 452-8600 ext. 3688
Toll-free number: (888) 335-8722 ext. 3688 Fax: (615) 230-4875
Tim Amyx, Director of Admissions & Registration, Volunteer State Community College, 1480 Nashville Pike, Gallatin, TN 37066

Walters State Community College
Morristown, Tennessee
www.ws.edu
CB code: 1893

- Public 2-year culinary school and community college
- Commuter campus in small city

General. Founded in 1970. Regionally accredited. Degree programs and courses held at sites throughout 10-county service delivery area; campus facilities located in Morristown, Greeneville, Sevierville, and Tazewell. **Enrollment:** 5,795 degree-seeking undergraduates; 1,164 non-degree-seeking students. **Degrees:** 722 associate awarded. **ROTC:** Army. **Location:** 45 miles from Knoxville. **Calendar:** Semester, limited summer session. **Full-time faculty:** 155 total; 28% have terminal degrees, 6% minority, 55% women. **Part-time faculty:** 260 total; 16% have terminal degrees, less than 1% minority, 60% women. **Special facilities:** Observatory, training restaurant, exposition center, industrial technology manufacturing laboratory with complete computer integrated manufacturing (CIM), work center and coordinate measuring machine, public safety law enforcement training center, greenhouse, production horticulture lab, arboretum, center for workforce education, clean energy laboratory, fire science/EMT training.

Student profile. Among degree-seeking undergraduates, 50% enrolled in a transfer program, 50% enrolled in a vocational program, 1% already have a bachelor's degree or higher, 1,602 enrolled as first-time, first-year students.

Part-time:	33%	Asian American:	1%
Women:	63%	Hispanic American:	2%
African American:	3%	25 or older:	36%

Transfer out. 45% of students enrolled in the transfer program go on to 4-year colleges. **Colleges most students transferred to 2011:** University of Tennessee-Knoxville, East Tennessee State University, Carson Newman College, Tusculum College, Lincoln Memorial University.

Basis for selection. Open admission, but selective for some programs. Special requirements for education, allied health and public safety programs. **Adult students:** Placement assessment required.

High school preparation. College-preparatory program recommended. 14 units required. Required units include English 4, mathematics 3, social studies 1, history 1, science 2 (laboratory 1), foreign language 2 and visual/performing arts 1. College-preparatory program required for 2-year transfer program: 1 unit biological science, 4 English, 2 foreign language, 3 mathematics, 1 physical science, 2 social science, 1 visual or performing arts. Same preparation recommended for all students.

2011-2012 Annual costs. Tuition/fees: $3,531; $13,635 out-of-state. Per-credit charge: $129 in-state; $530 out-of-state. Books/supplies: $1,200. Personal expenses: $1,400.

2010-2011 Financial aid. **Need-based:** 80% of total undergraduate aid awarded as scholarships/grants, 20% as loans/jobs. Need-based aid available for part-time students. Work-study available nights, weekends and for part-time students. **Non-need-based:** Scholarships awarded for academics, athletics, minority status, music/drama, state residency.

Application procedures. **Admission:** No deadline. $10 fee. Admission notification on a rolling basis. **Financial aid:** Priority date 5/1; no closing date. FAFSA required. Applicants notified on a rolling basis.

Academics. Instructional alternatives include interactive television, web-based, video streaming, telecourses, and mobilized campus. **Special study options:** Accelerated study, distance learning, dual enrollment of high school students, ESL, honors, internships, liberal arts/career combination, weekend college. Bachelor's degree programs available on campus. License preparation in nursing, paramedic, physical therapy. **Credit/placement by examination:** AP, CLEP, institutional tests. 42 credit hours maximum toward associate degree. **Support services:** GED test center, learning center, reduced course load, remedial instruction, study skills assistance, tutoring, writing center.

Honors college/program. 24 ACT and completion of honors core program required. Students over 21 without required ACT score must submit scores of 68 on writing portion and 50 on algebra portion of COMPASS.

Majors. **Business:** Business admin, management information systems. **Computer sciences:** Web page design. **Education:** General. **General:** Ornamental horticulture. **Health services:** EMT paramedic, medical records technology, nursing (RN), physical therapy assistant, respiratory therapy technology. **Liberal arts:** Arts/sciences. **Protective services:** Police science. **Work/family studies:** Child development.

Most popular majors. Business/marketing 11%, health sciences 29%, liberal arts 49%.

Computing on campus. 1,405 workstations in library, computer center, student center. Commuter students can connect to campus network. Online course registration, online library, helpline, wireless network available.

Student life. **Freshman orientation:** Mandatory. Preregistration for classes offered. **Activities:** Bands, campus ministries, choral groups, dance, drama, international student organizations, literary magazine, music ensembles, musical theater, student government, student newspaper, Baptist collegiate ministry, Methodist student group, international club, Sevierville Collegiate Ministry, Service Learners of WSGC, Sevier Couny Ambassadors, Senators Pages, Phi Theta Kappa.

Athletics. NJCAA. **Intercollegiate:** Baseball M, basketball, cheerleading, golf, softball W. **Intramural:** Basketball, football (tackle), soccer, softball. **Team name:** Senators.

Student services. Adult student services, alcohol/substance abuse counseling, chaplain/spiritual director, career counseling, student employment services, financial aid counseling, health services, minority student services, personal counseling, placement for graduates, veterans' counselor. **Physically disabled:** Services for visually, speech, hearing impaired. **Transfer:** Re-entry adviser for new students. Transfer center, transfer adviser, college fairs on campus for students transferring to 4-year colleges.

Contact. E-mail: mike.campbell@ws.edu
Phone: (423) 585-2685 Toll-free number: (800) 225-4770
Fax: (423) 585-6786
Mike Campbell, Assistant Vice President for Student Affairs, Walters State Community College, 500 South Davy Crockett Parkway, Morristown, TN 37813-6899

West Tennessee Business College
Jackson, Tennessee
www.wtbc.edu

- For-profit 2-year career college
- Commuter campus in small city
- Interview required

General. Accredited by ACICS. **Enrollment:** 355 degree-seeking undergraduates. **Degrees:** 5 associate awarded. **Location:** 80 miles from Memphis. **Calendar:** Differs by program. **Full-time faculty:** 20 total.

Student profile. Among degree-seeking undergraduates, 100% enrolled in a vocational program, 1% already have a bachelor's degree or higher.

Basis for selection. Applicants required to take the CPAt in-house test by ACT.

2011-2012 Annual costs. Total cost of medical/clinical assistant diploma program: $15,770. Tuition includes books, labs, and supplies.

Financial aid. **Need-based:** Work-study available nights, weekends and for part-time students.

Application procedures. **Admission:** No deadline. $50 fee. Admission notification on a rolling basis. **Financial aid:** No deadline.

Academics. Credit/placement by examination: AP, CLEP.

Majors. **Business:** Administrative services, business admin. **Health services:** Medical secretary.

Computing on campus. 130 workstations in computer center, student center. Online library, wireless network available.

Student life. **Freshman orientation:** Mandatory. Preregistration for classes offered.

Student services. Career counseling, student employment services, financial aid counseling, placement for graduates.

Contact. E-mail: ann.record@wtbc.edu
Phone: (731) 668-7240 Toll-free number: (800) 737-9822
Ann Record, Admissions Director, West Tennessee Business College, 1186 Highway 45 Bypass, Jackson, TN 38301

Texas

speech, hearing impaired. **Transfer:** Transfer adviser, college fairs on campus for students transferring to 4-year colleges.

Contact. E-mail: info@alvincollege.edu
Phone: (281) 756-3531 Fax: (281) 756-3843
Stephanie Stockstill, Director of Admissions/Academic Advising, Alvin Community College, 3110 Mustang Road, Alvin, TX 77511-4898

Alvin Community College
Alvin, Texas
www.alvincollege.edu   CB code: 6005

- Public 2-year community and liberal arts college
- Commuter campus in large town

General. Founded in 1948. Regionally accredited. **Enrollment:** 5,082 degree-seeking undergraduates. **Degrees:** 410 associate awarded. **ROTC:** Army. **Location:** 32 miles from Houston. **Calendar:** Semester, extensive summer session. **Full-time faculty:** 109 total. **Part-time faculty:** 218 total. **Special facilities:** Radio station, recording studio, indoor firing range for law enforcement program, Nolan Ryan exhibit.

Transfer out. Colleges most students transferred to 2011: University of Houston-Clear Lake, University of Houston, Texas A&M, Sam Houston State University, Southwest Texas State University.

Basis for selection. Open admission, but selective for some programs. Texas Academic Skills Program test required by Texas law. Special requirements for nursing, respiratory therapy, criminal justice, court reporting, musical theater, EMT, diagnostic cardiovascular sonography programs. Interview required for court reporting, medical laboratory technology, nursing, respiratory therapy programs; audition required for music, musical theater programs.

High school preparation. 25 units recommended. Recommended units include English 4, mathematics 4, social studies 4, science 3, foreign language 3 and academic electives 7.

2011-2012 Annual costs. Tuition/fees: $1,714; $2,974 out-of-district; $4,354 out-of-state. Per-credit charge: $42 in-district; $84 out-of-district; $130 out-of-state. Books/supplies: $1,575.

Financial aid. All financial aid based on need. Need-based aid available for part-time students. Work-study available nights, weekends and for part-time students.

Application procedures. Admission: No deadline. No application fee. Admission notification on a rolling basis. **Financial aid:** No deadline. FAFSA required. Applicants notified on a rolling basis; must reply within 2 week(s) of notification.

Academics. Special study options: Cooperative education, cross-registration, distance learning, dual enrollment of high school students, ESL, honors, internships, liberal arts/career combination, study abroad. License preparation in nursing, paramedic. **Credit/placement by examination:** AP, CLEP, institutional tests. **Support services:** GED preparation and test center, learning center, reduced course load, remedial instruction, study skills assistance, tutoring, writing center.

Majors. Biology: General. **Business:** General, business admin, executive assistant. **Communications:** Radio/TV. **Computer sciences:** Programming. **Education:** Early childhood, physical. **Health services:** Cardiovascular technology, EMT paramedic, mental health services, nursing (RN), respiratory therapy technology. **Liberal arts:** Arts/sciences. **Math:** General. **Parks/recreation:** Health/fitness. **Physical sciences:** General. **Protective services:** Corrections, criminal justice. **Visual/performing arts:** Art, dramatic, music performance. **Work/family studies:** Child development.

Computing on campus. 600 workstations in library, computer center. Online course registration, online library, wireless network available.

Student life. Freshman orientation: Mandatory. Preregistration for classes offered. **Housing:** Housing provided for scholarship athletes. **Activities:** Bands, choral groups, dance, drama, literary magazine, music ensembles, musical theater, radio station, student government, student newspaper, TV station, Newman Association, Phi Theta Kappa, Pan American College Forum, Baptist student union.

Athletics. NJCAA. **Intercollegiate:** Baseball M, softball W. **Team name:** Dolphins.

Student services. Career counseling, student employment services, financial aid counseling, on-campus daycare, personal counseling, placement for graduates, veterans' counselor. **Physically disabled:** Services for visually,

---

Amarillo College
Amarillo, Texas
www.actx.edu   CB code: 6006

- Public 2-year community college
- Commuter campus in small city

General. Founded in 1929. Regionally accredited. In addition to traditional population pursuing courses for credit, institution serves 12,000 workforce development and leisure studies students. **Enrollment:** 8,579 degree-seeking undergraduates. **Degrees:** 904 associate awarded. **Location:** 300 miles from Dallas, 300 miles from Denver. **Calendar:** Semester, extensive summer session. **Full-time faculty:** 226 total. **Part-time faculty:** 254 total. **Class size:** 53% < 20, 38% 20-39, 4% 40-49, 4% 50-99, less than 1% >100. **Special facilities:** Art museum, natural science museum, children's theater.

Student profile.

Out-of-state: 1%   Live on campus: 1%

Transfer out. Colleges most students transferred to 2011: West Texas A&M University, Texas Tech University.

Basis for selection. Open admission.

High school preparation. 18 units recommended. Recommended units include English 4, mathematics 2, social studies 2, history 2, science 2, foreign language 3 and academic electives 3.

2011-2012 Annual costs. Tuition/fees: $1,988; $2,858 out-of-district; $4,358 out-of-state. Books/supplies: $996. Personal expenses: $1,302.

Financial aid. Need-based: Work-study available nights, weekends and for part-time students. **Non-need-based:** Scholarships awarded for academics, state residency.

Application procedures. Admission: Priority date 8/1; no deadline. No application fee. Admission notification on a rolling basis. **Financial aid:** Priority date 6/15; no closing date. FAFSA, institutional form required. Applicants notified on a rolling basis starting 6/15; must reply within 2 week(s) of notification.

Academics. Special study options: Accelerated study, cooperative education, distance learning, dual enrollment of high school students, ESL, honors, internships, weekend college. License preparation in nursing, real estate. **Credit/placement by examination:** AP, CLEP, institutional tests. 15 credit hours maximum toward associate degree. **Support services:** GED preparation and test center, learning center, remedial instruction, study skills assistance, tutoring, writing center.

Majors. Biology: General. **Business:** General, accounting, administrative services, finance, office/clerical, real estate, tourism promotion. **Communications:** Advertising, broadcast journalism, communications/speech/rhetoric, journalism. **Communications technology:** General. **Computer sciences:** General, computer graphics, information systems, programming. **Education:** General, elementary, music, physical. **Engineering:** General, computer. **English:** English lit, rhetoric/composition. **Health services:** Clinical lab science, clinical lab technology, dental hygiene, EMT paramedic, medical radiologic technology/radiation therapy, medical records technology, nuclear medical technology, nursing (RN), occupational therapy assistant, physical therapy assistant, predental, premedicine, prepharmacy, preveterinary, respiratory therapy technology, substance abuse counseling, surgical technology. **Human services:** Social work. **Liberal arts:** Arts/sciences. **Math:** General. **Parks/recreation:** Health/fitness. **Philosophy/religion:** Religion. **Physical sciences:** General, chemistry, geology, physics. **Protective services:** Corrections, fire safety technology, police science. **Psychology:** General. **Social sciences:** General. **Visual/performing arts:** Art, commercial photography, commercial/advertising art, design, dramatic, interior design, music, photography. **Work/family studies:** Child care management.

Computing on campus. Online course registration, online library, helpline available.

Student life. Freshman orientation: Mandatory. Preregistration for classes offered. **Housing:** Apartments available. **Activities:** Bands, choral groups, dance, drama, literary magazine, music ensembles, musical theater, opera, radio station, student government, student newspaper, TV station.

Athletics. Intramural: Basketball, tennis, volleyball.

Student services. Adult student services, career counseling, student employment services, on-campus daycare, personal counseling, placement for graduates, veterans' counselor. **Physically disabled:** Services for visually, speech, hearing impaired. **Transfer:** Transfer adviser, college fairs on campus for students transferring to 4-year colleges.

Contact. E-mail: AskAC@actx.edu
Phone: (806) 371-5030 Fax: (806) 371-5066
Diane Brice, Registrar and Director of Admissions, Amarillo College, Box 447, Amarillo, TX 79178

Angelina College
Lufkin, Texas
www.angelina.edu   **CB code: 6025**

- Public 2-year community college
- Commuter campus in large town

General. Founded in 1966. Regionally accredited. Teaching centers located in 5 contiguous counties. Branch campuses located in Jasper, Crockett and Nacogdoches. **Enrollment:** 5,849 degree-seeking undergraduates. **Degrees:** 341 associate awarded. **ROTC:** Army. **Location:** 125 miles from Houston. **Calendar:** Semester, extensive summer session. **Full-time faculty:** 110 total; 9% have terminal degrees, 6% minority, 58% women. **Part-time faculty:** 239 total; 5% have terminal degrees, 9% minority, 59% women. **Class size:** 70% < 20, 30% 20-39. **Special facilities:** Computer-aided design laboratory, performing arts center.

Student profile. Among degree-seeking undergraduates, 1,857 enrolled as first-time, first-year students, 337 transferred in from other institutions.

Part-time:	66%	Asian American:	1%
Women:	64%	Hispanic American:	11%
African American:	15%	Native American:	1%

Transfer out. Colleges most students transferred to 2011: Stephen F. Austin State University, Sam Houston State University.

Basis for selection. Open admission, but selective for some programs. Special requirements for nursing, respiratory care, EMS, pharmacy, surgery technology, diagnostic medical sonography and radiologic technology programs; interview required. General Aptitude Test Battery required of nursing applicants. All students must take Texas Higher Education Assessment Test or ACCUPLACER before enrolling. **Adult students:** Physical education requirements waived for veterans. **Home schooled:** Transcript of courses and grades required. **Learning Disabled:** May have to take different test based on disability.

2011-2012 Annual costs. Tuition/fees: $1,710; $2,490 out-of-district; $3,420 out-of-state. Room/board: $3,400. Books/supplies: $1,120. Personal expenses: $2,005.

2010-2011 Financial aid. Need-based: 1,244 full-time freshmen applied for aid; 1,189 were judged to have need; 1,178 of these received aid. Average need met was 93%. Average scholarship/grant was $3,866. 99% of total undergraduate aid awarded as scholarships/grants, 1% as loans/jobs. Need-based aid available for part-time students. Work-study available nights, weekends and for part-time students. **Non-need-based:** Awarded to 908 full-time undergraduates, including 669 freshmen. Scholarships awarded for academics, art, athletics, job skills, leadership, music/drama, state residency.

Application procedures. Admission: No deadline. No application fee. Admission notification on a rolling basis. **Financial aid:** Priority date 7/15; no closing date. FAFSA, institutional form required. Applicants notified on a rolling basis starting 7/15.

Academics. Special study options: Accelerated study, cooperative education, distance learning, dual enrollment of high school students, internships, liberal arts/career combination. License preparation in nursing, paramedic, radiology, real estate. **Credit/placement by examination:** AP, CLEP, IB, institutional tests. 15 credit hours maximum toward associate degree. **Support services:** GED preparation and test center, learning center, reduced course load, remedial instruction, study skills assistance, tutoring.

Majors. Biology: General. **Business:** General, accounting, administrative services, business admin. **Communications:** Communications/speech/rhetoric. **Communications technology:** Recording arts. **Computer sciences:** General, data processing, networking. **Education:** Health. **Engineering:** General. **English:** Rhetoric/composition. **Health services:** Clinical lab technology, EMT paramedic, nursing (RN), predental, premedicine, prepharmacy, preveterinary, radiologic technology/medical imaging, respiratory therapy technology, sonography, substance abuse counseling. **Math:** General. **Physical sciences:** Physics. **Protective services:** Criminal justice. **Visual/performing**

arts: Art, design, dramatic, music. **Work/family studies:** Child development.

Most popular majors. Business/marketing 13%, engineering/engineering technologies 8%, health sciences 41%, liberal arts 6%.

Computing on campus. 60 workstations in library, student center. Commuter students can connect to campus network. Online course registration, online library, wireless network available.

Student life. Freshman orientation: Mandatory. Preregistration for classes offered. **Housing:** Coed dorms, wellness housing available. $100 fully refundable deposit, deadline 7/15. Apartments for single parents. **Activities:** Bands, choral groups, dance, drama, music ensembles, musical theater, student government, student newspaper, Baptist student union.

Athletics. NJCAA. **Intercollegiate:** Baseball M, basketball, cheerleading, softball W. **Intramural:** Golf, volleyball. **Team name:** Roadrunners.

Student services. Adult student services, career counseling, services for economically disadvantaged, student employment services, financial aid counseling, placement for graduates, veterans' counselor. **Physically disabled:** Services for visually, speech, hearing impaired. **Transfer:** Preadmission transcript evaluation for new students. Transfer adviser, college fairs on campus for students transferring to 4-year colleges.

Contact. E-mail: registrar@angelina.edu
Phone: (936) 639-5212 Fax: (936) 633-5455
Jeremy Thomas, Director of Admissions & Enrollment Services, Angelina College, PO Box 1768, Lufkin, TX 75902-1768

ATI Career Training Center: Dallas
Dallas, Texas
www.aticareertraining.edu

- For-profit 2-year technical college
- Very large city

General. Accredited by ACCSCT. **Calendar:** Semester.

Annual costs/financial aid. Need-based financial aid available for full-time students.

Contact. Phone: (214) 902-8191
Director of Admissions, 10003 Technology Boulevard, West, Dallas, TX 75220

Austin Community College
Austin, Texas   **CB member**
www.austincc.edu   **CB code: 6759**

- Public 2-year community college
- Commuter campus in very large city

General. Founded in 1972. Regionally accredited. 8 campuses serving greater Austin, 11 instructional centers in surrounding towns. **Enrollment:** 36,854 degree-seeking undergraduates. **Degrees:** 1,507 associate awarded. **ROTC:** Army, Air Force. **Location:** 85 miles from San Antonio. **Calendar:** Semester, extensive summer session. **Full-time faculty:** 620 total; 28% have terminal degrees, 28% minority, 57% women. **Part-time faculty:** 1,487 total; 18% have terminal degrees, 22% minority, 48% women. **Class size:** 40% < 20, 60% 20-39, less than 1% 40-49, less than 1% 50-99. **Special facilities:** Water-quality monitoring well. **Partnerships:** Formal partnerships with Sustainability Project, Semiconductor Manufacturing Program, Seton Health.

Transfer out. Colleges most students transferred to 2011: University of Texas at Austin, Texas State University.

Basis for selection. Open admission, but selective for some programs. Special requirements for health sciences programs. Students may submit SAT or ACT test scores for exemption from Texas Success Initiative (TSI). **Adult students:** SAT/ACT scores not required. Texas Success Initiative test may be required.

2011-2012 Annual costs. Tuition/fees: $2,115; $6,375 out-of-district; $9,495 out-of-state. Books/supplies: $1,200. Personal expenses: $2,200.

2010-2011 Financial aid. Need-based: 1,219 full-time freshmen applied for aid; 989 were judged to have need; 873 of these received aid. 61% of total undergraduate aid awarded as scholarships/grants, 39% as loans/jobs. Need-based aid available for part-time students. Work-study available nights, weekends and for part-time students.

Application procedures. Admission: No deadline. No application fee. No notification. Applications accepted at all times for any future semester enrollment. **Financial aid:** Closing date 4/1. FAFSA, institutional form required. Applicants notified on a rolling basis starting 6/1; must reply within 2 week(s) of notification.

Academics. Special study options: Accelerated study, distance learning, dual enrollment of high school students, ESL, honors, independent study, internships, study abroad, teacher certification program, weekend college. License preparation in dental hygiene, nursing, occupational therapy, paramedic, physical therapy, radiology, real estate. **Credit/placement by examination:** AP, CLEP, IB, institutional tests. 30 credit hours maximum toward associate degree. **Support services:** GED preparation and test center, learning center, reduced course load, remedial instruction, study skills assistance, tutoring.

Majors. Biology: General. **Business:** General, accounting technology, administrative services, banking/financial services, business admin, hospitality admin, international, marketing, real estate. **Communications:** Journalism, radio/TV. **Communications technology:** Animation/special effects. **Computer sciences:** General, networking, programming. **Education:** Early childhood, health, middle, secondary. **Engineering:** General. **English:** Creative writing, rhetoric/composition, technical writing, writing. **Foreign languages:** General, French, German, Japanese, Latin, Russian, sign language interpretation, Spanish. **Health services:** Clinical lab technology, dental hygiene, EMT paramedic, medical records technology, nursing (RN), occupational therapy assistant, physical therapy assistant, predental, premedicine, prepharmacy, preveterinary, radiologic technology/medical imaging, recreational therapy, sonography, substance abuse counseling, surgical technology. **History:** General. **Human services:** Social work. **Math:** General. **Parks/recreation:** Health/fitness. **Philosophy/religion:** Philosophy. **Physical sciences:** General, chemistry, geology, physics. **Protective services:** Corrections, fire safety technology, police science. **Psychology:** General. **Social sciences:** Anthropology, economics, geography, GIS/cartography, political science, sociology. **Visual/performing arts:** Art, commercial photography, commercial/advertising art, dance, dramatic, music, music management. **Work/family studies:** Child development.

Most popular majors. Business/marketing 13%, engineering/engineering technologies 8%, health sciences 29%, visual/performing arts 9%.

Computing on campus. 637 workstations in library, computer center. Commuter students can connect to campus network. Online course registration, online library, helpline, wireless network available.

Student life. Freshman orientation: Mandatory. Preregistration for classes offered. **Policies:** No alcohol, no drugs, no hazing. **Activities:** Jazz band, dance, drama, literary magazine, music ensembles, student government, student newspaper, Phi Theta Kappa, Hispanic student association, Biomass, Peer Players, Austin Society for Semi-Conductor Electronics Technicians, Campus Crusade for Christ, Toastmasters, American Drafting Design Association, associate degree student nursing association, black student alliance.

Student services. Alcohol/substance abuse counseling, career counseling, services for economically disadvantaged, student employment services, financial aid counseling, minority student services, on-campus daycare, placement for graduates, veterans' counselor. **Physically disabled:** Services for visually, speech, hearing impaired. **Transfer:** Transfer center, transfer adviser, college fairs on campus for students transferring to 4-year colleges.

Contact. E-mail: admission@austincc.edu
Phone: (512) 223-7503 Fax: (512) 223-7175
Linda Kluck, Director of Admissions and Records, Austin Community College, PO Box 15306, Austin, TX 78761-5306

Blinn College
Brenham, Texas
www.blinn.edu
CB code: 6043

- Public 2-year community college
- Commuter campus in large town

General. Founded in 1883. Regionally accredited. Campuses located at Brenham, Bryan, Sealy and Schulenburg. **Enrollment:** 18,186 degree-seeking undergraduates. **Degrees:** 875 associate awarded. **Location:** 79 miles from Houston, 90 miles from Austin. **Calendar:** Semester, limited summer session. **Full-time faculty:** 371 total. **Part-time faculty:** 495 total. **Special facilities:** College-operated museum, state park, city-operated historical museums, observatory, ice cream factory, George Bush library, children's museum, natural science center, art museums.

Student profile.

Out-of-state:	1%	Live on campus:	10%
25 or older:	14%		

Transfer out. Colleges most students transferred to 2011: Texas A&M-College Station, Sam Houston State University, Texas State University, University of Texas at Austin, University of Houston.

Basis for selection. Open admission, but selective for some programs. Special requirements for registered nursing program, dental hygiene, physical therapy, various other allied health and some technology-based programs. TASP test required for all per Texas state law. **Home schooled:** Transcript of courses and grades required.

2011-2012 Annual costs. Tuition/fees: $2,160; $3,390 out-of-district; $5,730 out-of-state. Per-credit charge: $40 in-district; $81 out-of-district; $159 out-of-state. Room/board: $5,750. Books/supplies: $1,018. Personal expenses: $1,350.

Financial aid. Need-based: Need-based aid available for part-time students. Work-study available nights, weekends and for part-time students.

Application procedures. Admission: No deadline. No application fee. Admission notification on a rolling basis. **Financial aid:** Priority date 6/1; no closing date. FAFSA, institutional form required. Applicants notified on a rolling basis starting 7/1.

Academics. All campuses offer academic support services. **Special study options:** Cross-registration, distance learning, dual enrollment of high school students, ESL, liberal arts/career combination, teacher certification program. License preparation in dental hygiene, nursing, paramedic, physical therapy, radiology, real estate. **Credit/placement by examination:** AP, CLEP, IB, institutional tests. 12 credit hours maximum toward associate degree. THEA (Texas Higher Education Assessment) test used for placement; students submitting sufficient score on TAKS, SAT or ACT exempt (Education students must take THEA). **Support services:** GED preparation and test center, learning center, pre-admission summer program, reduced course load, remedial instruction, study skills assistance, tutoring, writing center.

Majors. Biology: General. **Business:** Accounting, office/clerical, small business admin. **Computer sciences:** System admin. **Education:** Multi-level teacher. **English:** English lit, rhetoric/composition. **Foreign languages:** General, French, German, sign language interpretation, Spanish. **Health services:** Medical radiologic technology/radiation therapy, nursing (RN). **History:** General. **Liberal arts:** Arts/sciences. **Math:** General. **Parks/recreation:** Exercise sciences. **Philosophy/religion:** Philosophy. **Physical sciences:** Chemistry, physics. **Protective services:** Criminal justice, firefighting. **Psychology:** General. **Social sciences:** General. **Visual/performing arts:** Design, dramatic, music. **Work/family studies:** Child care management.

Most popular majors. Biological/life sciences 10%, business/marketing 20%, English 7%, health sciences 15%, liberal arts 7%, security/protective services 7%.

Computing on campus. 500 workstations in library, computer center. Dormitories wired for high-speed internet access and linked to campus network. Commuter students can connect to campus network. Online course registration, online library, helpline, wireless network available.

Student life. Freshman orientation: Available. Preregistration for classes offered. Held 3-4 times during summer, parents welcome. **Policies:** Student classroom attendance policy, full-time student status for residence halls. **Housing:** Single-sex dorms, special housing for disabled, apartments, wellness housing available. $200 fully refundable deposit. **Activities:** Bands, campus ministries, choral groups, dance, drama, international student organizations, music ensembles, musical theater, student government, College Republicans, Young Democrats, Bahai Club, Baptist Student Ministries, Catholic Student Organization, Wesley Foundation, Blinn College Lion's Club, Ebony and Ivory, Hispanic Organization, Kappa Kappa Psi, Chi Alpha.

Athletics. NJCAA. **Intercollegiate:** Baseball M, basketball, cheerleading, football (tackle) M, softball W, volleyball W. **Intramural:** Basketball, softball, volleyball. **Team name:** Buccaneers.

Student services. Career counseling, financial aid counseling, personal counseling, veterans' counselor. **Physically disabled:** Services for visually, speech, hearing impaired. **Transfer:** Transfer adviser, college fairs on campus for students transferring to 4-year colleges.

Contact. E-mail: recruit@blinn.edu
Phone: (979) 830-4140 Fax: (979) 830-4009
Julie Maass, Dean of Admissions/Registrar, Blinn College, 902 College Avenue, Brenham, TX 77833

Brazosport College
Lake Jackson, Texas
www.brazosport.edu
CB code: 6054

- Public 2-year community college
- Commuter campus in large town

General. Founded in 1948. Regionally accredited. **Enrollment:** 4,105 degree-seeking undergraduates. **Degrees:** 25 bachelor's, 269 associate awarded. **Location:** 50 miles from Houston. **Calendar:** Semester, extensive summer session. **Full-time faculty:** 86 total; 23% have terminal degrees, 14% minority, 42% women. **Part-time faculty:** 94 total; 15% minority, 37% women. **Class size:** 53% < 20, 46% 20-39, less than 1% 40-49, less than 1% 50-99. **Special facilities:** Chemical unit operations laboratory, music performance hall, child care center, center for business and industry training.

Student profile. Among degree-seeking undergraduates, 654 enrolled as first-time, first-year students, 143 transferred in from other institutions.

Part-time:	79%	Asian American:	1%
Out-of-state:	1%	Hispanic American:	19%
Women:	51%	25 or older:	30%
African American:	6%		

Transfer out. 40% of students enrolled in the transfer program go on to 4-year colleges. **Colleges most students transferred to 2011:** University of Houston, Sam Houston State University, Texas A&M University, Stephen F. Austin State University, University of Texas.

Basis for selection. Open admission, but selective for some programs. Special requirements for nursing and applied technology programs. **Home schooled:** Transcript of courses and grades required.

2012-2013 Annual costs. Tuition/fees (projected): $1,977; $2,847 out-of-district; $4,257 out-of-state. Per-credit charge: $50 in-district; $79 out-of-district; $126 out-of-state. Books/supplies: $1,500. Personal expenses: $2,725.

2010-2011 Financial aid. **Need-based:** Average scholarship/grant was $4,093. 97% of total undergraduate aid awarded as scholarships/grants, 3% as loans/jobs. Need-based aid available for part-time students. Work-study available nights, weekends and for part-time students. **Non-need-based:** Scholarships awarded for academics, art, job skills, leadership, music/drama, state residency.

Application procedures. **Admission:** Closing date 8/28 (receipt date). No application fee. Admission notification on a rolling basis. **Financial aid:** Priority date 7/1; no closing date. FAFSA, institutional form required. Applicants notified on a rolling basis starting 5/1.

Academics. **Special study options:** Cooperative education, distance learning, dual enrollment of high school students, ESL, honors, internships. Bachelor's degree programs available on campus. License preparation in nursing, paramedic. **Credit/placement by examination:** AP, CLEP, institutional tests. 24 credit hours maximum toward associate degree. Minimum of 6 semester credit hours must be earned in residence before credit posted on transcript. **Support services:** GED preparation and test center, learning center, remedial instruction, study skills assistance, tutoring.

Majors. **Biology:** General. **Business:** General, accounting, administrative services, business admin, finance, purchasing. **Communications:** Communications/speech/rhetoric. **Computer sciences:** General, programming. **Education:** General, elementary, health, secondary. **Engineering:** General. **English:** English lit, rhetoric/composition. **Foreign languages:** General. **Health services:** Nursing (RN). **History:** General. **Human services:** General. **Liberal arts:** Arts/sciences, library assistant. **Math:** General. **Physical sciences:** General, chemistry, physics, planetary. **Protective services:** Police science. **Psychology:** General. **Social sciences:** Economics, political science, sociology. **Theology:** Theology. **Visual/performing arts:** Art, dramatic, music. **Work/family studies:** General, child care management.

Most popular majors. Business/marketing 6%, engineering/engineering technologies 13%, health sciences 7%, liberal arts 54%, science technologies 9%.

Computing on campus. 40 workstations in library, computer center. Online course registration, wireless network available.

Student life. **Freshman orientation:** Mandatory. Preregistration for classes offered. **Activities:** Bands, choral groups, drama, music ensembles, student government, student newspaper, Baptist student ministry, Phi Theta Kappa.

Athletics. **Intramural:** Archery, basketball, bowling, fencing, football (non-tackle), golf, soccer, softball, table tennis, tennis, volleyball.

Student services. Career counseling, student employment services, financial aid counseling, on-campus daycare, personal counseling, placement for graduates, veterans' counselor. **Physically disabled:** Services for visually impaired. **Transfer:** Transfer adviser, college fairs on campus for students transferring to 4-year colleges.

Contact. Phone: (979) 230-3216 Fax: (979) 230-3376 Carrie Streeter, Student Admissions and Registrar, Brazosport College, 500 College Drive, Lake Jackson, TX 77566

Brookhaven College
Farmers Branch, Texas
www.brookhavencollege.edu

CB code: 6070

◗ Public 2-year community college
◗ Commuter campus in large town

General. Founded in 1965. Regionally accredited. **Enrollment:** 11,495 degree-seeking undergraduates; 2,210 non-degree-seeking students. **Degrees:** 535 associate awarded. **Location:** 12 miles from downtown Dallas. **Calendar:** Semester, limited summer session. **Full-time faculty:** 129 total; 30% minority, 58% women. **Part-time faculty:** 670 total.

Student profile. Among degree-seeking undergraduates, 5% already have a bachelor's degree or higher, 1,648 enrolled as first-time, first-year students.

Part-time:	77%	Asian American:	12%
Women:	59%	Hispanic American:	29%
African American:	20%	International:	1%

Transfer out. **Colleges most students transferred to 2011:** Universtiy of Texas at Dallas, University of North Texas, University of Texas at Arlington, Texas A&M-Commerce.

Basis for selection. Open admission, but selective for some programs. Observes TASP guidelines. Admission to Nursing program based on a point system consisting of three parts: HESI score, GPA of prerequisite courses, and completion of support courses.

2011-2012 Annual costs. Tuition/fees: $1,350; $2,490 out-of-district; $3,960 out-of-state. Per-credit charge: $45 in-district; $83 out-of-district; $132 out-of-state. For out-of-state students, $200 minimum charge for 1 semester hour. Books/supplies: $1,200. Personal expenses: $920.

Financial aid. **Need-based:** Work-study available nights, weekends and for part-time students. **Non-need-based:** Scholarships awarded for academics, leadership, music/drama. **Additional information:** Some tuition waivers available based upon state residency and veteran status.

Application procedures. **Admission:** No deadline. No application fee. Admission notification on a rolling basis. **Financial aid:** Priority date 6/1; no closing date. FAFSA required. Applicants notified on a rolling basis.

Academics. **Special study options:** Cooperative education, distance learning, dual enrollment of high school students, ESL, honors, internships, study abroad, weekend college. License preparation in nursing, paramedic, radiology. **Credit/placement by examination:** AP, CLEP, IB. At least 25% of credit hours required for graduation must be taken by instruction and not by credit-by-exam. **Support services:** GED preparation, remedial instruction, study skills assistance, tutoring, writing center.

Majors. **Business:** General, accounting, business admin, e-commerce, executive assistant, marketing, office management. **Communications:** Communications/speech/rhetoric. **Computer sciences:** Information systems, programming. **Education:** Early childhood, multi-level teacher, secondary. **Health services:** EMT paramedic, nursing (RN), radiologic technology/medical imaging. **Liberal arts:** Arts/sciences, humanities. **Social sciences:** GIS/cartography. **Visual/performing arts:** Design, graphic design, music. **Work/family studies:** Child development.

Most popular majors. Business/marketing 9%, health sciences 20%, liberal arts 65%.

Computing on campus. Commuter students can connect to campus network. Online library, helpline, wireless network available.

Student life. **Freshman orientation:** Mandatory. Preregistration for classes offered. **Activities:** Jazz band, campus ministries, choral groups, dance, drama, film society, international student organizations, music ensembles, Model UN, musical theater, student government, student newspaper, Phi Theta Kappa, SERVE, International Movement for Peace Among People.

Athletics. NJCAA. **Intercollegiate:** Baseball M, basketball M, soccer W, volleyball W. **Team name:** Bears.

Student services. Adult student services, career counseling, student employment services, health services, personal counseling, placement for graduates, veterans' counselor. **Physically disabled:** Services for visually, speech, hearing impaired. **Transfer:** College fairs on campus for students transferring to 4-year colleges.

Contact. E-mail: bhcAdmissions@dcccd.edu
Phone: (972) 860-4883 Fax: (972) 860-4886
Thoa Vo, Director of Admissions, Brookhaven College, 3939 Valley View Lane, Farmers Branch, TX 75244-4997

Cedar Valley College
Lancaster, Texas
www.cedarvalleycollege.edu   CB code: 6148

- Public 2-year community college
- Commuter campus in large town

General. Founded in 1974. Regionally accredited. One of seven colleges in the Dallas County Community College District. **Enrollment:** 6,802 degree-seeking undergraduates. **Degrees:** 317 associate awarded. **Location:** 10 miles from Dallas. **Calendar:** Semester, limited summer session. **Full-time faculty:** 65 total. **Part-time faculty:** 227 total. **Special facilities:** LEEDS certified veterinary technology building, commercial music facilities. **Partnerships:** Formal partnerships with IBM, Gate Foundation, Texas A&M University, Vartec, Owens Corning, University of North Texas, Upward Bound.

Transfer out. Colleges most students transferred to 2011: University of Texas at Arlington, Texas A&M at Commerce, University of North Texas.

Basis for selection. Open admission. Student must be a graduate of an accredited high school, or at least 18 years of age, or be admitted by individual approval. **Home schooled:** Interview required.

2011-2012 Annual costs. Tuition/fees: $1,350; $2,490 out-of-district; $3,960 out-of-state. Per-credit charge: $45 in-district; $83 out-of-district; $132 out-of-state. For out-of-state students, $200 minimum charge for 1 semester hour. Books/supplies: $800. Personal expenses: $1,045.

Financial aid. Need-based: Work-study available nights, weekends and for part-time students.

Application procedures. Admission: No deadline. No application fee. Application must be submitted on paper. Admission notification on a rolling basis. **Financial aid:** Priority date 5/1; no closing date. FAFSA required. Applicants notified on a rolling basis.

Academics. Special study options: Accelerated study, cooperative education, distance learning, dual enrollment of high school students, ESL, liberal arts/career combination, student-designed major, study abroad, weekend college. License preparation in real estate. **Credit/placement by examination:** AP, CLEP, institutional tests. 45 credit hours maximum toward associate degree. **Support services:** GED preparation and test center, learning center, reduced course load, remedial instruction, study skills assistance, tutoring, writing center.

Majors. Business: Accounting/business management, administrative services, business admin, management information systems, marketing, office management, office technology, real estate. **Communications technology:** Recording arts. **Computer sciences:** Data processing, networking, programming. **Health services:** Veterinary technology/assistant. **Protective services:** Law enforcement admin. **Visual/performing arts:** Design, music performance.

Computing on campus. 400 workstations in library, computer center, student center. Commuter students can connect to campus network. Online course registration, online library, helpline, repair service, wireless network available.

Student life. Freshman orientation: Mandatory. Preregistration for classes offered. 1-day program includes assessment testing. **Activities:** Jazz band, choral groups, dance, drama, literary magazine, music ensembles, musical theater, student government, student newspaper, Sierra club, Christian student union, Latin American student organization, Phi Theta Kappa, student ambassadors, pre-professional club, art club, veterinary technology club.

Athletics. NJCAA. **Intercollegiate:** Baseball M, basketball M, soccer W, volleyball W. **Intramural:** Football (non-tackle) M, soccer W, volleyball W. **Team name:** Suns.

Student services. Adult student services, career counseling, services for economically disadvantaged, student employment services, financial aid counseling, health services, minority student services, personal counseling, placement for graduates, veterans' counselor. **Physically disabled:** Services for visually, speech, hearing impaired. **Transfer:** Pre-admission transcript evaluation for new students. College fairs on campus for students transferring to 4-year colleges.

Contact. E-mail: ljohnson@dcccd.edu
Phone: (972) 860-8201 Fax: (972) 860-8001
Lucia Johnson, Director of Admissions and Registrar, Cedar Valley College, 3030 North Dallas Avenue, Lancaster, TX 75134

Central Texas College
Killeen, Texas
www.ctcd.edu   CB code: 6130

- Public 2-year community and technical college
- Commuter campus in small city

General. Founded in 1965. Regionally accredited. **Enrollment:** 20,809 degree-seeking undergraduates; 6,499 non-degree-seeking students. **Degrees:** 2,472 associate awarded. **ROTC:** Army. **Location:** 60 miles from Austin. **Calendar:** Semester, extensive summer session. **Full-time faculty:** 175 total. **Part-time faculty:** 850 total. **Special facilities:** Planetarium, space theater. **Partnerships:** Formal partnerships with Killeen and Copperas Cove ISDs (school to career facilitator program).

Student profile. Among degree-seeking undergraduates, 66% enrolled in a transfer program, 34% enrolled in a vocational program, 4,776 enrolled as first-time, first-year students, 3,210 transferred in from other institutions.

Part-time:	76%	Hispanic American:	16%
Out-of-state:	58%	Native American:	1%
Women:	45%	25 or older:	66%
African American:	28%	Live on campus:	1%
Asian American:	3%		

Transfer out. Colleges most students transferred to 2011: University of Mary Hardin-Baylor, Texas A&M Central Texas, Texas State University, University of North Texas, Texas Tech University.

Basis for selection. Open admission, but selective for some programs. Special admission requirements for nursing, paramedic, EMT, and aviation science programs. Interview required for medical laboratory technician, nursing programs; audition recommended for music; portfolio recommended for art. **Home schooled:** Transcript of courses and grades required.

High school preparation. College-preparatory program recommended. 22 units recommended. Recommended units include English 4, mathematics 3, social studies 1.5, history 1, science 2 (laboratory 1), computer science 1, visual/performing arts 1 and academic electives 1. 0.5 economics, 0.5 speech, 4.5 electives, 0.5 health, 1.5 physical education recommended.

2011-2012 Annual costs. Tuition/fees: $1,770; $2,280 out-of-district; $5,250 out-of-state. Per-credit charge: $59 in-district; $76 out-of-district; $175 out-of-state. Room/board: $3,700. Books/supplies: $1,500. Personal expenses: $500.

Financial aid. All financial aid based on need. Need-based aid available for part-time students. Work-study available nights, weekends and for part-time students.

Application procedures. Admission: No deadline. No application fee. Admission notification on a rolling basis. **Financial aid:** Closing date 6/1. FAFSA, institutional form required. Applicants notified on a rolling basis starting 3/1; must reply within 4 week(s) of notification.

Academics. Special study options: Cross-registration, distance learning, dual enrollment of high school students, ESL, independent study, internships, liberal arts/career combination. License preparation in aviation, nursing, paramedic, real estate. **Credit/placement by examination:** AP, CLEP, IB, institutional tests. 48 credit hours maximum toward associate degree. **Support services:** GED preparation and test center, learning center, reduced course load, remedial instruction, study skills assistance, tutoring.

Majors. Biology: General. **Business:** Administrative services, business admin, hospitality admin, office management, real estate. **Communications:** Broadcast journalism, radio/TV. **Communications technology:** Graphic/printing. **Computer sciences:** General, information technology, networking, programming, security, system admin. **Conservation:** Environmental science. **Education:** General. **Engineering:** General. **Foreign languages:** General. **General:** Equestrian studies, farm/ranch, horticulture. **Health services:** Clinical lab assistant, clinical lab technology, nursing (RN), premedicine, substance abuse counseling. **Human services:** Social work. **Liberal arts:** Arts/sciences. **Math:** General. **Physical sciences:** Chemistry, geology, physics. **Protective services:** Corrections, homeland security, law enforcement admin, police science. **Social sciences:** General. **Visual/performing arts:** Art, music. **Work/family studies:** Child care management.

Computing on campus. 600 workstations in library, computer center. Online course registration, online library, wireless network available.

Student life. Freshman orientation: Available. Preregistration for classes offered. **Housing:** Coed dorms, apartments available. $100 nonrefundable deposit, deadline 8/1. **Activities:** Jazz band, choral groups, international student organizations, radio station, student government, TV station.

Athletics. Intramural: Basketball, soccer, softball, volleyball.

Two-Year Colleges

Student services. Adult student services, alcohol/substance abuse counseling, career counseling, services for economically disadvantaged, student employment services, financial aid counseling, on-campus daycare, personal counseling, placement for graduates, veterans' counselor. **Physically disabled:** Services for visually, speech, hearing impaired. **Transfer:** Re-entry adviser, pre-admission transcript evaluation for new students. Transfer center, transfer adviser, college fairs on campus for students transferring to 4-year colleges.

Contact. E-mail: admissions@ctcd.edu
Phone: (254) 526-1696 Toll-free number: (800) 792-3348 ext. 1696
Fax: (254) 526-1481
Stephen O'Donovan, Director, Admissions and Recruitment, Central Texas College, Box 1800, Killeen, TX 76540

Cisco College
Cisco, Texas
www.cisco.edu   CB code: 6096

▶ Public 2-year community college
▶ Commuter campus in small town

General. Founded in 1940. Regionally accredited. Cisco College operates from 2 campuses, one in Cisco and the other in Abilene. **Enrollment:** 3,699 degree-seeking undergraduates; 664 non-degree-seeking students. **Degrees:** 229 associate awarded. **Location:** 100 miles from Fort Worth. **Calendar:** Semester, limited summer session. **Full-time faculty:** 86 total. **Part-time faculty:** 106 total. **Class size:** 51% < 20, 44% 20-39, 3% 40-49, 2% 50-99.

Student profile. Among degree-seeking undergraduates, 36% enrolled in a transfer program, 3% enrolled in a vocational program, 1% already have a bachelor's degree or higher, 1,498 enrolled as first-time, first-year students.

Part-time:	64%	**Women:**	61%
Out-of-state:	8%	**Live on campus:**	28%

Transfer out. Colleges most students transferred to 2011: Hardin Simmons University, Tarleton State University, University of North·Texas, Angelo State University, Texas Tech University.

Basis for selection. Open admission.

2012-2013 Annual costs. Tuition/fees (projected): $2,440; $3,070 out-of-district; $4,050 out-of-state. Room/board: $3,700. Books/supplies: $1,500. Personal expenses: $3,021.

2011-2012 Financial aid. Need-based: Work-study available nights, weekends and for part-time students. **Additional information:** Financial aid application deadline July 1 for Fall semester, November 1 for Spring semester.

Application procedures. Admission: No deadline. No application fee. Admission notification on a rolling basis. **Financial aid:** FAFSA required. Applicants notified on a rolling basis starting 8/15.

Academics. Special study options: Dual enrollment of high school students. Bachelor's degree programs available on campus. License preparation in nursing, real estate. **Credit/placement by examination:** AP, CLEP. 22 credit hours maximum toward associate degree. **Support services:** GED test center, remedial instruction, tutoring.

Majors. Biology: General. **Business:** General, accounting. **Communications:** Communications/speech/rhetoric. **Computer sciences:** General. **Education:** General. **Engineering:** General. **Foreign languages:** French, Spanish. **General:** Animal sciences, business. **Health services:** Medical records technology. **History:** General. **Human services:** Social work. **Math:** General. **Physical sciences:** Chemistry. **Psychology:** General. **Social sciences:** General, economics, sociology. **Visual/performing arts:** Art, dramatic.

Most popular majors. Health sciences 35%, liberal arts 55%.

Computing on campus. Wireless network available.

Student life. Freshman orientation: Available. Preregistration for classes offered. **Housing:** Single-sex dorms available. **Activities:** Bands, choral groups, music ensembles, student government.

Athletics. NJCAA. **Intercollegiate:** Baseball W, basketball, football (tackle) M, soccer, volleyball W. **Team name:** Wranglers.

Contact. E-mail: admissions@cisco.edu
Phone: (254) 442-5000 Fax: (254) 442-5000
Olin Odom, Dean of Enrollment Management, Cisco College, 101 College Heights, Cisco, TX 76437

Clarendon College
Clarendon, Texas
www.clarendoncollege.edu   CB code: 6097

▶ Public 2-year community college
▶ Residential campus in rural community

General. Founded in 1898. Regionally accredited. **Enrollment:** 1,348 degree-seeking undergraduates. **Degrees:** 119 associate awarded. **Location:** 60 miles from Amarillo. **Calendar:** Semester, limited summer session. **Full-time faculty:** 35 total. **Part-time faculty:** 38 total. **Class size:** 73% < 20, 24% 20-39, 1% 40-49, less than 1% 50-99, less than 1% >100. **Partnerships:** Formal partnership with Tech Prep.

Student profile.

Out-of-state:	8%	**Live on campus:**	24%

Transfer out. Colleges most students transferred to 2011: West Texas A&M University, Texas Tech University, Texas A&M University, Tarleton State University, Midwestern State University.

Basis for selection. Open admission, but selective for some programs. Special requirements for certain technical programs. Interview before May 1 required for ranch and feedlot operations program. 3 personal references, interview required for vocational nursing program. **Home schooled:** Transcript of courses and grades required. A request for admission by Individual Approval should be submitted to the Admissions Office.

High school preparation. 24 units recommended. Recommended units include English 4, mathematics 4, social studies 2, history 2, science 4, foreign language 2, academic electives 3.5. 0.5 health, 0.5 economics, 1 computer, 0.5 speech recommended.

2011-2012 Annual costs. Tuition/fees: $2,610; $3,210 out-of-district; $4,140 out-of-state. Room/board: $4,176. Books/supplies: $1,000. Personal expenses: $3,894.

Financial aid. Need-based: Need-based aid available for part-time students. Work-study available nights, weekends and for part-time students. **Non-need-based:** Scholarships awarded for academics, art, athletics, leadership, music/drama, state residency.

Application procedures. Admission: Priority date 8/15; no deadline. No application fee. Admission notification on a rolling basis. **Financial aid:** Priority date 8/1; no closing date. FAFSA, institutional form required. Applicants notified on a rolling basis starting 5/15; must reply by 8/15 or within 2 week(s) of notification.

Academics. Special study options: Cross-registration, distance learning, dual enrollment of high school students, internships, liberal arts/career combination, student-designed major. License preparation in nursing. **Credit/placement by examination:** AP, CLEP. 30 credit hours maximum toward associate degree. **Support services:** GED test center, remedial instruction, tutoring.

Majors. Biology: General. **Business:** General, accounting, finance, management science, marketing, office technology. **Communications:** Communications/speech/rhetoric. **Computer sciences:** General. **Conservation:** Environmental science. **Education:** General, elementary, secondary. **Engineering:** General. **English:** English lit, rhetoric/composition. **Foreign languages:** General. **General:** Agronomy, animal sciences, business, economics, equestrian studies, farm/ranch. **Health services:** EMT paramedic, nursing (RN), predental, premedicine, prepharmacy, preveterinary. **History:** General. **Human services:** Social work. **Liberal arts:** Arts/sciences. **Math:** General. **Parks/recreation:** General, exercise sciences, health/fitness. **Philosophy/religion:** Religion. **Physical sciences:** Chemistry, geology, physics. **Protective services:** Criminal justice. **Psychology:** General. **Social sciences:** Economics, political science, sociology. **Visual/performing arts:** Art, commercial/advertising art, dramatic, music.

Most popular majors. Agriculture 16%, business/marketing 18%, computer/information sciences 10%, education 8%, health sciences 10%, liberal arts 18%, security/protective services 7%.

Computing on campus. 221 workstations in library, computer center. Dormitories wired for high-speed internet access. Commuter students can connect to campus network. Online course registration, online library, wireless network available.

Student life. Freshman orientation: Mandatory. Preregistration for classes offered. Full-semester, two-hour hybrid course with both in-class and on-line components. **Housing:** Guaranteed on-campus for freshmen. Coed dorms, single-sex dorms, special housing for disabled available. $100 partly refundable deposit. **Activities:** Jazz band, choral groups, drama, music ensembles, student government, multicultural club, student ambassadors, Block & Bridle, rodeo club.

Athletics. NJCAA. **Intercollegiate:** Baseball M, basketball, cheerleading, cross-country, rodeo, softball W, volleyball W. **Intramural:** Basketball, football (non-tackle), golf, rodeo, table tennis, volleyball. **Team name:** Bulldogs.

Student services. Career counseling, financial aid counseling. **Physically disabled:** Services for visually, speech, hearing impaired. **Transfer:** College fairs on campus for students transferring to 4-year colleges.

Contact. E-mail: admissions@clarendoncollege.edu
Phone: (806) 874-3571 Toll-free number: (800) 687-9737
Fax: (806) 874-5080
Martha Smith, Director of Admissions, Clarendon College, PO Box 968, Clarendon, TX 79226

Coastal Bend College
Beeville, Texas
www.coastalbend.edu CB code: 6055

- Public 2-year community college
- Commuter campus in large town

General. Founded in 1965. Regionally accredited. In addition to main campus in Beeville, there are campuses in Alice, Kingsville, and Pleasanton. **Enrollment:** 3,936 degree-seeking undergraduates. **Degrees:** 274 associate awarded. **Location:** 60 miles from Corpus Christi, 90 miles from San Antonio. **Calendar:** Semester, limited summer session. **Full-time faculty:** 105 total. **Part-time faculty:** 101 total. **Partnerships:** Formal partnerships with national corporations to provide truck driver training, with local businesses to provide training for employees, and with high schools and tech prep programs.

Student profile.

Out-of-state:	1%	Live on campus:	5%
25 or older:	60%		

Transfer out. Colleges most students transferred to 2011: Texas A&M-Corpus Christi, Texas A&M-Kingsville, Southwest Texas State University, Texas A&M-College Station, University of Texas.

Basis for selection. Open admission, but selective for some programs. Texas requires that all students satisfy Texas THEA test requirements before being enrolled in college-level courses in public college or university. Scores not used in admission decisions. Special requirements for dental hygiene and vocational nursing programs. **Adult students:** SAT/ACT scores not required. **Home schooled:** Transcript of courses and grades required. Transcript must be notarized.

2011-2012 Annual costs. Tuition/fees: $2,100; $3,870 out-of-district; $4,320 out-of-state. Room/board: $4,581. Books/supplies: $600. Personal expenses: $1,500.

Financial aid. Need-based: Need-based aid available for part-time students. Work-study available nights, weekends and for part-time students. **Non-need-based:** Scholarships awarded for academics, leadership.

Application procedures. Admission: No deadline. No application fee. Admission notification on a rolling basis. **Financial aid:** Priority date 4/1; no closing date. FAFSA, institutional form required. Applicants notified on a rolling basis starting 5/1; must reply within 2 week(s) of notification.

Academics. Special study options: Cooperative education, cross-registration, distance learning, dual enrollment of high school students, independent study, internships, liberal arts/career combination, weekend college. License preparation in dental hygiene, nursing, radiology. **Credit/placement by examination:** AP, CLEP, institutional tests. 30 credit hours maximum toward associate degree. ACCUPLACER, ASSET, COMPASS, MAPS tests may be used instead of THEA. **Support services:** GED preparation and test center, learning center, remedial instruction, study skills assistance, tutoring.

Majors. Biology: General. **Business:** General, accounting, administrative services, business admin, office technology, office/clerical. **Communications:** Communications/speech/rhetoric. **Computer sciences:** General, computer science, data processing, programming. **Conservation:** General. **Education:** General, elementary, secondary. **Engineering:** General. **English:** English lit, rhetoric/composition. **Foreign languages:** Spanish. **Health services:** Dental hygiene, medical records technology, medical secretary, nursing (RN), predental, premedicine, prepharmacy, preveterinary. **History:** General. **Liberal arts:** Arts/sciences. **Math:** General. **Physical sciences:** Chemistry, geology, physics. **Protective services:** Corrections, criminal justice, police science. **Psychology:** General. **Social sciences:** Political science, sociology. **Visual/performing arts:** General, commercial/advertising art, music, studio arts. **Work/family studies:** General, child care management.

Computing on campus. 700 workstations in library, computer center. Dormitories wired for high-speed internet access and linked to campus network. Commuter students can connect to campus network. Online course registration, online library, helpline, wireless network available.

Student life. Freshman orientation: Mandatory. Preregistration for classes offered. Half-day program, parents welcome. **Housing:** Single-sex dorms, apartments available. $250 partly refundable deposit, deadline 8/15. **Activities:** Student government, Baptist student union, Newman Club.

Athletics. NJCAA. **Intercollegiate:** Basketball, volleyball W. **Intramural:** Archery, badminton, basketball, bowling, cross-country, golf, soccer, softball, swimming, table tennis, tennis, track and field, volleyball, weight lifting. **Team name:** Cougars.

Student services. Career counseling, services for economically disadvantaged, student employment services, financial aid counseling, on-campus daycare, personal counseling, placement for graduates, veterans' counselor. **Physically disabled:** Services for visually, speech, hearing impaired. **Transfer:** Pre-admission transcript evaluation for new students. Transfer adviser, college fairs on campus for students transferring to 4-year colleges.

Contact. E-mail: register@coastalbend.edu
Phone: (361) 354-2254 Toll-free number: (800) 722-2838 ext. 2254
Fax: (361) 354-2554
Alicia Ulloa, Registrar and Director Admissions, Coastal Bend College, 3800 Charco Road, Beeville, TX 78102

College of the Mainland
Texas City, Texas
www.com.edu CB code: 6133

- Public 2-year community and technical college
- Commuter campus in large town

General. Founded in 1966. Regionally accredited. **Enrollment:** 3,370 degree-seeking undergraduates. **Degrees:** 351 associate awarded. **Location:** 25 miles from Houston. **Calendar:** Semester, extensive summer session. **Full-time faculty:** 109 total. **Part-time faculty:** 102 total.

Student profile.

Out-of-state:	1%	25 or older:	44%

Transfer out. Colleges most students transferred to 2011: University of Houston-Clear Lake.

Basis for selection. Open admission, but selective for some programs. Special requirements for nursing program.

2011-2012 Annual costs. Tuition/fees: $1,623; $2,673 out-of-district; $3,873 out-of-state. Per-credit charge: $240 in-district; $450 out-of-district; $690 out-of-state. Books/supplies: $833. Personal expenses: $1,087.

Financial aid. All financial aid based on need. Need-based aid available for part-time students. Work-study available nights, weekends and for part-time students.

Application procedures. Admission: No deadline. No application fee. Admission notification on a rolling basis. **Financial aid:** No deadline. FAFSA, institutional form required. Applicants notified on a rolling basis.

Academics. Special study options: Cooperative education, cross-registration, distance learning, double major, dual enrollment of high school students, ESL, independent study, internships, teacher certification program, weekend college. License preparation in nursing, paramedic, real estate. **Credit/placement by examination:** AP, CLEP, institutional tests. 24 credit hours maximum toward associate degree. **Support services:** GED preparation and test center, learning center, remedial instruction, study skills assistance, tutoring, writing center.

Majors. Biology: General. **Business:** General, accounting, administrative services, banking/financial services, business admin, labor relations, marketing, office management, office technology, office/clerical, real estate. **Communications:** Journalism. **Computer sciences:** General, programming. **Education:** Elementary, secondary. **Engineering:** General. **Health services:** Licensed practical nurse. **History:** General. **Human services:** General, social work. **Liberal arts:** Arts/sciences. **Math:** General. **Physical sciences:** Chemistry, planetary. **Protective services:** Fire safety technology, police science. **Psychology:** General. **Social sciences:** General, economics, political science, sociology. **Visual/performing arts:** General, dramatic, music, studio arts. **Work/family studies:** Child care management.

Computing on campus. 100 workstations in library, computer center. Online course registration, online library, helpline, wireless network available.

Student life. Freshman orientation: Mandatory. Preregistration for classes offered. **Activities:** Bands, choral groups, drama, literary magazine, music ensembles, musical theater, student government, Phi Beta Kappa, Students for Christ, COM Amigos, Organization of African-American Culture, biology club.

Athletics. Intramural: Basketball, football (non-tackle) M, racquetball, soccer, softball, tennis, volleyball. **Team name:** Ducks.

Student services. Career counseling, student employment services, financial aid counseling, on-campus daycare, personal counseling, placement for graduates, veterans' counselor. **Physically disabled:** Services for visually, speech, hearing impaired. **Transfer:** Transfer adviser, college fairs on campus for students transferring to 4-year colleges.

Contact. E-mail: kmusik@com.edu
Phone: (409) 933-8264 Toll-free number: (888) 258-8859 ext. 8264
Fax: (409) 938-3126
Kelly Musick, Director of Admissions and Records, College of the Mainland, 1200 Amburn Road, Texas City, TX 77591

Collin County Community College District
McKinney, Texas　　　　　　　　**CB member**
www.collin.edu　　　　　　　　**CB code: 1951**

▶ Public 2-year community college
▶ Commuter campus in large city

General. Founded in 1985. Regionally accredited. **Enrollment:** 27,534 degree-seeking undergraduates; 59 non-degree-seeking students. **Degrees:** 1,565 associate awarded. **ROTC:** Army. **Location:** 25 miles from Dallas. **Calendar:** Semester, extensive summer session. **Full-time faculty:** 358 total; 39% have terminal degrees, 15% minority, 58% women. **Part-time faculty:** 755 total; 19% have terminal degrees, 20% minority, 58% women. **Class size:** 18% < 20, 81% 20-39, less than 1% 40-49, less than 1% 50-99. **Special facilities:** Regional fire training facility. **Partnerships:** Formal partnership with Cisco to provide Certified Network Professional Certification.

Student profile. Among degree-seeking undergraduates, 4,893 enrolled as first-time, first-year students, 1,165 transferred in from other institutions.

Part-time:	64%	Asian American:	8%
Out-of-state:	2%	Hispanic American:	15%
Women:	57%	International:	4%
African American:	11%	25 or older:	36%

Transfer out. Colleges most students transferred to 2011: University of Texas at Dallas, University of North Texas, Texas A&M University, University of Texas at Austin, Texas Tech University.

Basis for selection. Open admission, but selective for some programs. Special requirements for programs in nursing, dental hygiene, emergency medical services, firefighter, respiratory care, interpreter prep, honors institute, center for advanced study in mathematics and natural sciences. **Home schooled:** If under 18 years must provide written parental/guardian permission.

High school preparation. 17 units recommended. Recommended units include English 4, mathematics 3, social studies 2, history 2, science 2 (laboratory 2) and foreign language 2.

2011-2012 Annual costs. Tuition/fees: $1,020; $2,040 out-of-district; $3,690 out-of-state. Per-credit charge: $27 in-district; $61 out-of-district; $116 out-of-state. Books/supplies: $1,300. Personal expenses: $1,775.

Financial aid. Need-based: Need-based aid available for part-time students. Work-study available nights, weekends and for part-time students. **Non-need-based:** Scholarships awarded for academics, art, athletics, job skills, leadership, minority status, music/drama, state residency.

Application procedures. Admission: No deadline. No application fee. Admission notification on a rolling basis. **Financial aid:** Priority date 6/1, closing date 6/30. FAFSA, institutional form required. Applicants notified on a rolling basis starting 5/1; must reply within 2 week(s) of notification.

Academics. Special study options: Cooperative education, distance learning, dual enrollment of high school students, ESL, honors, internships, weekend college. Learning communities, service learning opportunities, dual admissions agreements with University of North Texas, University of Texas at Dallas, Southern Methodist University, Texas Woman's University, Texas Tech University, Texas A&M University-Commerce, Baylor University, Texas A&M, Dallas Baptist University, Austin College, Texas A&M University-College Station. License preparation in dental hygiene, nursing. **Credit/placement by examination:** AP, CLEP, institutional tests. 18 credit hours maximum toward associate degree. 6 hours traditional credit must be

completed in residence before examination credit awarded. **Support services:** Learning center, remedial instruction, study skills assistance, tutoring, writing center.

Honors college/program. Students with GPA of 3.5 or over admitted to Honors Institute.

Majors. Business: Business admin, hospitality admin, office technology, real estate, sales/distribution. **Communications technology:** Animation/special effects. **Computer sciences:** General, networking, programming, web page design. **Foreign languages:** Sign language interpretation. **Health services:** Dental hygiene, EMT paramedic, nursing (RN), respiratory therapy technology. **Protective services:** Fire safety technology. **Visual/performing arts:** Commercial/advertising art, interior design, music management. **Work/family studies:** Child development.

Most popular majors. Health sciences 11%, liberal arts 74%.

Computing on campus. 1,980 workstations in library, computer center. Online course registration, helpline, repair service, wireless network available.

Student life. Freshman orientation: Available. Preregistration for classes offered. One-day program; online section available for distance learning students. **Activities:** Jazz band, campus ministries, choral groups, dance, drama, international student organizations, literary magazine, music ensembles, Model UN, musical theater, student government, American Sign Language club, black student association, nursing student association, hospitality and culinary arts student society, Latter-day Saints student association, Muslim student association, College Republicans.

Athletics. NJCAA. **Intercollegiate:** Basketball, tennis. **Team name:** Cougars.

Student services. Adult student services, alcohol/substance abuse counseling, career counseling, student employment services, financial aid counseling, on-campus daycare, personal counseling, placement for graduates. **Physically disabled:** Services for visually, speech, hearing impaired. **Transfer:** Transfer adviser, college fairs on campus for students transferring to 4-year colleges.

Contact. E-mail: tfields@collin.edu
Phone: (972) 881-5710 Fax: (972) 881-5175
Stephanie Meinhardt, Registrar/ Director of Admissions, Collin County Community College District, 2800 East Spring Creek Parkway, Plano, TX 75074

Commonwealth Institute of Funeral Service
Houston, Texas
www.commonwealthinst.org　　　　　　**CB code: 7031**

▶ Private 2-year school of mortuary science
▶ Commuter campus in very large city

General. Founded in 1988. Accredited by American Board of Funeral Service Education, Inc. **Enrollment:** 155 degree-seeking undergraduates. **Degrees:** 48 associate awarded. **Location:** 15 miles from downtown. **Calendar:** Quarter. **Full-time faculty:** 2 total. **Part-time faculty:** 6 total. **Class size:** 50% < 20, 50% 50-99.

Student profile.

Out-of-state:	20%	25 or older:	49%

Basis for selection. Class rank and standardized test scores most important. SAT or ACT recommended. TASP required.

2011-2012 Annual costs. Tuition/fees: $10,904. Reported tuition is for associate degree program. Includes cost of textbooks and clinical supplies. Personal expenses: $1,102.

Financial aid. All financial aid based on need. Need-based aid available for part-time students. Work-study available nights, weekends and for part-time students.

Application procedures. Admission: No deadline. $50 fee. Admission notification on a rolling basis beginning on or about 8/28. Application deadline is within 72 hours of enrollment deadline. **Financial aid:** Priority date 8/31; no closing date. FAFSA required. Applicants notified on a rolling basis starting 7/12.

Academics. Credit/placement by examination: AP, CLEP. **Support services:** Tutoring.

Computing on campus. 15 workstations in library, computer center.

Student life. Housing: Some local funeral homes provide student employees accommodations while attending college. **Activities:** Student government.

Student services. Career counseling, student employment services, financial aid counseling, personal counseling, placement for graduates, veterans' counselor. **Transfer:** Re-entry adviser, pre-admission transcript evaluation for new students. Transfer adviser for students transferring to 4-year colleges.

Contact. Phone: (281) 873-0262 Fax: (281) 873-5232
Patricia Moreno, Registrar, Commonwealth Institute of Funeral Service, 415 Barren Springs Drive, Houston, TX 77090-5913

Court Reporting Institute of Dallas
Dallas, Texas
www.crid.com   CB code: 3231

- For-profit 2-year technical and career college
- Very large city

General. Accredited by ACICS. **Calendar:** Quarter.

Annual costs/financial aid. Tuition and fee ranges: $38,067 to $48,067 (associate degree). Books/supplies: $700.

Contact. Phone: (214) 350-9722
Director, 1341 West Mockingbird Lane, Suite 200E, Dallas, TX 75247

Court Reporting Institute of Houston
Houston, Texas
www.crid.com

- For-profit 2-year technical college
- Commuter campus in very large city

General. Accredited by ACICS. **Calendar:** Quarter.

Annual costs/financial aid. Cost of entire Associate of Applied Science, Court Reporting program: $37,259 for 2-1/2 year program for full-time on-campus students; $38,463, 2-1/2 year program for full-time online students; $46,323 for 5-1/2 year program for part-time on-campus students; $47,783, 5-1/2 year program for part-time online students.

Contact. Phone: (713) 996-8300
Director of Admissions, 13101 Northwest Freeway, Suite 100, Houston, TX 77040

Culinary Institute LeNotre
Houston, Texas
www.culinaryinstitute.edu

- For-profit 2-year culinary school and junior college
- Commuter campus in very large city
- Application essay, interview required

General. Regionally accredited; also accredited by ACCSC. **Enrollment:** 276 degree-seeking undergraduates. **Degrees:** 43 associate awarded. **Calendar:** Five 10-week terms. **Full-time faculty:** 11 total; 9% women. **Part-time faculty:** 14 total; 14% have terminal degrees, 14% minority, 50% women.

Basis for selection. Open admission.

2010-2011 Financial aid. Need-based: Work-study available nights, weekends and for part-time students.

Application procedures. Admission: No deadline. $50 fee.

Academics. Special study options: Accelerated study, double major, internships. **Credit/placement by examination:** AP, CLEP. **Support services:** Learning center, remedial instruction.

Computing on campus. 19 workstations in library, computer center. Online library, wireless network available.

Student life. Freshman orientation: Mandatory. Preregistration for classes offered.

Student services. Career counseling, financial aid counseling, placement for graduates, veterans' counselor.

Contact. E-mail: admission@culinaryinstitute.edu
Phone: (713) 692-0077 Toll-free number: (888) 536-6873
Fax: (713) 692-7399
Bob Jeffords, Compliance Director, Culinary Institute LeNotre, 7070 Allensby Street, Houston, TX 77022

Dallas Institute of Funeral Service
Dallas, Texas
www.dallasinstitute.edu   CB code: 7032

- Private 2-year school of mortuary science
- Commuter campus in very large city

General. Regionally accredited. 15-month AAS in funeral service program and 6-month funeral director's program (Texas, Louisiana, and Missouri students only). **Enrollment:** 153 degree-seeking undergraduates. **Degrees:** 76 associate awarded. **Calendar:** Quarter, limited summer session. **Full-time faculty:** 5 total. **Part-time faculty:** 3 total. **Special facilities:** On-campus embalming facilities.

Basis for selection. Open admission.

2011-2012 Annual costs. Tuition is $3,000 per quarter, which includes required textbooks, laboratory supplies, activities fees, graduation fee, Practice National Board Exam, and National Board Exam (or State Board Exam for FDs) fee. AAS degree is 5 quarters long. Funeral Directors program is 2 quarters long. Personal expenses: $1,190.

Financial aid. Need-based: Work-study available nights, weekends and for part-time students.

Application procedures. Admission: Closing date 8/15. $50 fee. Admission notification on a rolling basis. Application deadline is 30 days prior to enrollment. **Financial aid:** No deadline. Applicants notified on a rolling basis.

Academics. Special study options: Distance learning. **Credit/placement by examination:** AP, CLEP, IB. **Support services:** Study skills assistance, tutoring.

Computing on campus. 25 workstations in library, computer center. Wireless network available.

Student services. Physically disabled: Services for visually, hearing impaired.

Contact. Phone: (214) 388-5466 Fax: (214) 388-0316
Terry Parrish, Director of Admissions, Dallas Institute of Funeral Service, 3909 South Buckner Boulevard, Dallas, TX 75227-4314

Del Mar College
Corpus Christi, Texas
www.delmar.edu   CB code: 6160

- Public 2-year community college
- Commuter campus in large city

General. Founded in 1935. Regionally accredited. Courses taught at multiple off-campus sites in the Coastal Bend Region. Center for Early Learning provides day-care on campus. Collegiate High School operated on-campus in cooperation with Corpus Christi Independent School District. **Enrollment:** 12,071 degree-seeking undergraduates. **Degrees:** 1,122 associate awarded. **ROTC:** Army. **Location:** 155 miles from San Antonio. **Calendar:** Semester, extensive summer session. **Full-time faculty:** 296 total. **Part-time faculty:** 539 total. **Partnerships:** Formal partnerships with Corpus Christi Army Depot, University of the Incarnate Word.

Student profile. Among degree-seeking undergraduates, 55% enrolled in a transfer program, 45% enrolled in a vocational program, 2% already have a bachelor's degree or higher, 12,071 enrolled as first-time, first-year students.

Out-of-state:	1%	Hispanic American:	55%
African American:	4%	Native American:	1%
Asian American:	2%	25 or older:	38%

Transfer out. Colleges most students transferred to 2011: Texas A&M University (College Station, Corpus Christi, Kingsville); University of Texas (Austin, San Antonio).

Basis for selection. Open admission, but selective for some programs. Admissions criteria for health science programs vary by program. Interview required for health science programs. **Home schooled:** Transcript of courses and grades required. Must provide notarized transcript with date of graduation.

High school preparation. 24 units recommended. Recommended units include English 4, mathematics 3, social studies 1, history 2, science 2, foreign language 2 and academic electives 10.

2011-2012 Annual costs. Tuition/fees: $2,700; $4,200 out-of-district; $5,310 out-of-state. Per-credit charge: $51 in-district; $101 out-of-district; $138 out-of-state. Books/supplies: $1,215. Personal expenses: $1,044.

Financial aid. All financial aid based on need. Need-based aid available for part-time students. Work-study available nights, weekends and for part-time students.

Application procedures. Admission: No deadline. No application fee. Admission notification on a rolling basis. **Financial aid:** Priority date 5/1; no closing date. FAFSA required. Applicants notified on a rolling basis starting 7/1; must reply within 2 week(s) of notification.

Academics. Short semester courses, accelerated associate degree program. **Special study options:** Accelerated study, cooperative education, distance learning, double major, dual enrollment of high school students, ESL, honors, independent study, internships, teacher certification program, weekend college. License preparation in aviation, dental hygiene, nursing, occupational therapy, paramedic, physical therapy, radiology, real estate. **Credit/placement by examination:** AP, CLEP, IB, institutional tests. 30 credit hours maximum toward associate degree. Credit may not be earned by examination for most performance-oriented courses. **Support services:** GED preparation and test center, learning center, remedial instruction, study skills assistance, tutoring, writing center.

Majors. Biology: General. **Business:** General, accounting technology, administrative services, business admin, finance, hotel/motel admin, logistics, management information systems, marketing. **Communications:** Advertising, journalism, radio/TV. **Communications technology:** Desktop publishing, photo/film/video, recording arts. **Computer sciences:** Applications programming, security. **Education:** Art, bilingual, Deaf/hearing impaired, developmentally delayed, early childhood, early childhood special, elementary, English, foreign languages, health, history, mathematics, middle, music, secondary, social studies, special ed. **Engineering:** Electrical. **English:** English lit, rhetoric/composition. **Foreign languages:** General, sign language interpretation. **Health services:** Clinical lab technology, dental assistant, dental hygiene, EMT paramedic, marriage/family therapy, medical records technology, medical secretary, mental health services, nuclear medical technology, nursing (RN), occupational therapy assistant, pharmacy assistant, physical therapy assistant, prenursing, prepharmacy, radiologic technology/medical imaging, respiratory therapy technology, sonography, substance abuse counseling, surgical technology. **History:** General. **Human services:** Social work. **Liberal arts:** Arts/sciences. **Math:** General. **Parks/recreation:** Health/fitness. **Physical sciences:** Chemical physics, chemistry, geology, physics. **Protective services:** Corrections, criminal justice, fire safety technology, firefighting, police science. **Psychology:** General. **Social sciences:** Political science, sociology. **Visual/performing arts:** Art, dramatic, music performance, music theory/composition. **Work/family studies:** Child care management, child development.

Most popular majors. Business/marketing 9%, education 16%, health sciences 19%, trade and industry 9%.

Computing on campus. 2,570 workstations in library, computer center, student center. Commuter students can connect to campus network. Online course registration, online library, helpline, wireless network available.

Student life. Freshman orientation: Available. Preregistration for classes offered. 2-hour session held 6 weeks prior to scheduled registration. **Activities:** Bands, campus ministries, choral groups, dance, drama, international student organizations, literary magazine, music ensembles, opera, student government, student newspaper, Catholic Newman association, Latter-day Saints student association, Baptist student ministry, LULAC, student veteran's association, College Republicans, black student union.

Athletics. Intramural: Badminton, basketball, bowling, cross-country, football (non-tackle), golf, racquetball, swimming, table tennis, tennis, volleyball. **Team name:** Vikings.

Student services. Adult student services, career counseling, student employment services, financial aid counseling, on-campus daycare, personal counseling, placement for graduates, veterans' counselor. **Physically disabled:** Services for visually, speech, hearing impaired. **Transfer:** College fairs on campus for students transferring to 4-year colleges.

Contact. E-mail: reginfo@delmar.edu
Phone: (361) 698-1255 Toll-free number: (800) 652-3357
Fax: (361) 698-1595
Gilbert Becerra, Dean of Outreach and Enrollment Services, Del Mar College, 101 Baldwin Boulevard, Corpus Christi, TX 78404-3897

Eastfield College
Mesquite, Texas
www.efc.dcccd.edu　　　　　　　　　　　**CB code: 6201**

▶ Public 2-year community and liberal arts college
▶ Commuter campus in small city

General. Founded in 1970. Regionally accredited. **Enrollment:** 9,993 degree-seeking undergraduates. **Degrees:** 568 associate awarded. **Location:** 1 mile from Dallas. **Calendar:** Semester, limited summer session. **Full-time faculty:** 121 total; 39% minority, 45% women. **Part-time faculty:** 361 total. **Class size:** 79% < 20, 20% 20-39, less than 1% 40-49, less than 1% 50-99, less than 1% >100. **Special facilities:** Automotive diagnostic center.

Student profile.

| Out-of-state: | 1% | **25 or older:** | 37% |

Transfer out. Colleges most students transferred to 2011: University of Texas-Arlington, University of Texas-Dallas, University of North Texas, Texas A&M-Commerce, Southern Methodist University.

Basis for selection. Open admission. Interview recommended for international students.

High school preparation. 22 units recommended. Recommended units include English 4, mathematics 3, social studies 1, history 1, science 2, academic electives 5.5. 0.5 health education; 0.5 speech; 1 history, geography or science; 1 technical applications; 1 history or geography recommended.

2011-2012 Annual costs. Tuition/fees: $1,350; $2,490 out-of-district; $3,960 out-of-state. Per-credit charge: $45 in-district; $83 out-of-district; $132 out-of-state. For out of state students, $200 minimum charge for 1 semester hour. Books/supplies: $400. Personal expenses: $935.

Financial aid. Need-based: Need-based aid available for part-time students. Work-study available nights, weekends and for part-time students.

Application procedures. Admission: No deadline. No application fee. Admission notification on a rolling basis. **Financial aid:** Priority date 5/1; no closing date. FAFSA, institutional form required. Applicants notified on a rolling basis starting 4/15.

Academics. Special study options: Cooperative education, distance learning, dual enrollment of high school students, ESL, honors, independent study, weekend college. **Credit/placement by examination:** AP, CLEP, IB, institutional tests. 15 credit hours maximum toward associate degree. **Support services:** GED preparation, learning center, pre-admission summer program, remedial instruction, tutoring.

Majors. Business: Accounting, business admin, e-commerce, executive assistant, office management, office technology. **Communications technology:** Graphic/printing. **Computer sciences:** General, applications programming, computer science, data processing, networking, programming. **Health services:** Substance abuse counseling. **Human services:** Social work. **Liberal arts:** Arts/sciences. **Protective services:** Criminal justice. **Work/family studies:** Child development.

Most popular majors. Business/marketing 11%, liberal arts 68%, trade and industry 6%.

Computing on campus. 152 workstations in library, computer center. Online library available.

Student life. Freshman orientation: Available. Preregistration for classes offered. Online and on-campus orientations offered. **Policies:** Student code of conduct in effect. **Activities:** Bands, choral groups, dance, drama, literary magazine, music ensembles, student government, student newspaper, Fellowship of Christian Athletes, Latter-day Saint student association, multicultural club, Vital Signers, piano club, poetry club, automotive club, jazz dance club.

Athletics. NJCAA. **Intercollegiate:** Baseball M, basketball M, golf M, soccer W, volleyball W. **Intramural:** Basketball M, bowling, golf M, gymnastics, tennis, volleyball. **Team name:** Harvesters.

Student services. Career counseling, student employment services, health services, on-campus daycare, personal counseling, placement for graduates, veterans' counselor. **Physically disabled:** Services for visually, speech, hearing impaired. **Transfer:** College fairs on campus for students transferring to 4-year colleges.

Contact. E-mail: efc@dcccd.edu
Phone: (972) 860-7100 Fax: (972) 860-8306
Linda Richardson, Dean of Admissions and Testing, Eastfield College, 3737 Motley Drive, Mesquite, TX 75150

El Centro College
Dallas, Texas
www.elcentrocollege.edu

CB member
CB code: 6199

♦ Public 2-year community college
♦ Commuter campus in very large city

General. Founded in 1966. Regionally accredited. **Enrollment:** 9,252 degree-seeking undergraduates; 1,329 non-degree-seeking students. **Degrees:** 654 associate awarded. **ROTC:** Army. **Calendar:** Semester, limited summer session. **Full-time faculty:** 134 total; 9% have terminal degrees, 35% minority, 66% women. **Part-time faculty:** 369 total; 9% have terminal degrees, 41% minority, 58% women. **Class size:** 58% < 20, 41% 20-39, less than 1% 40-49, less than 1% 50-99. **Special facilities:** Outdoor amphitheater, art studios, interior design and fashion design studios, allied health laboratories, culinary labs. **Partnerships:** Formal partnerships with regional CISCO training center, many local businesses, and area high schools.

Student profile. Among degree-seeking undergraduates, 80% enrolled in a transfer program, 20% enrolled in a vocational program, 4% already have a bachelor's degree or higher, 1,599 enrolled as first-time, first-year students, 497 transferred in from other institutions.

Part-time:	76%	Hispanic American:	35%
Out-of-state:	1%	Native American:	1%
Women:	68%	International:	2%
African American:	35%	25 or older:	49%
Asian American:	4%		

Transfer out. Colleges most students transferred to 2011: University of Texas at Arlington, University of North Texas, University of Texas at Dallas, Southern Methodist University.

Basis for selection. Open admission, but selective for some programs. Specific application requirements for nursing, some allied health, and food and hospitality programs. Interview recommended for international students.

2011-2012 Annual costs. Tuition/fees: $1,350; $2,490 out-of-district; $3,960 out-of-state. Per-credit charge: $45 in-district; $83 out-of-district; $132 out-of-state. For out-of-state students, $200 minimum charge for 1 semester hour. Books/supplies: $1,400. Personal expenses: $1,758.

Financial aid. Need-based: Need-based aid available for part-time students. Work-study available nights, weekends and for part-time students. **Additional information:** Interview required for financial aid applicants.

Application procedures. Admission: No deadline. No application fee. Admission notification on a rolling basis beginning on or about 6/1. **Financial aid:** Priority date 5/1; no closing date. FAFSA required. Applicants notified on a rolling basis; must reply within 2 week(s) of notification.

Academics. Special study options: Accelerated study, cooperative education, cross-registration, distance learning, double major, dual enrollment of high school students, ESL, external degree, honors, internships, liberal arts/career combination, teacher certification program. License preparation in nursing, paramedic, radiology. **Credit/placement by examination:** AP, CLEP, IB, institutional tests. 45 credit hours maximum toward associate degree. **Support services:** GED preparation, learning center, reduced course load, remedial instruction, study skills assistance, tutoring.

Majors. Business: Accounting, business admin, executive assistant, management information systems. **Computer sciences:** Data processing, information systems, programming. **Education:** Teacher assistance. **Health services:** Cardiovascular technology, clinical lab technology, medical radiologic technology/radiation therapy, medical records admin, medical records technology, nursing (RN), respiratory therapy technology, sonography. **Liberal arts:** Arts/sciences. **Visual/performing arts:** Fashion design, interior design.

Most popular majors. Health sciences 57%, legal studies 9%, liberal arts 20%.

Computing on campus. 832 workstations in library, computer center, student center. Commuter students can connect to campus network. Online course registration, online library, helpline, wireless network available.

Student life. Freshman orientation: Mandatory. Preregistration for classes offered. **Activities:** Choral groups, drama, music ensembles, musical theater, student government, Phi Theta Kappa, organization of Latin American students, El Centro computer society, international college association, Disabled and Realizing Excellence, teacher education preparatory program, Circle-K, association of black college students.

Athletics. Intercollegiate: Basketball M.

Student services. Adult student services, career counseling, services for economically disadvantaged, student employment services, financial aid counseling, health services, minority student services, personal counseling, placement for graduates, veterans' counselor. **Physically disabled:** Services for visually, hearing impaired. **Transfer:** Transfer adviser, college fairs on campus for students transferring to 4-year colleges.

Contact. E-mail: rgarza@dcccd.edu
Phone: (214) 860-2311 Fax: (214) 860-2233
Rebecca Garza, Director of Admissions/Registrar, El Centro College, 801 Main Street, Dallas, TX 75202

El Paso Community College
El Paso, Texas
www.epcc.edu

CB member
CB code: 6203

♦ Public 2-year community college
♦ Commuter campus in very large city

General. Founded in 1969. Regionally accredited. Comprised of five campuses in greater El Paso. **Enrollment:** 29,177 degree-seeking undergraduates; 1,546 non-degree-seeking students. **Degrees:** 2,975 associate awarded. **ROTC:** Army. **Location:** 240 miles from Albuquerque, New Mexico. **Calendar:** Semester, extensive summer session. **Full-time faculty:** 387 total. **Part-time faculty:** 1,113 total. **Special facilities:** Advanced technology center. **Partnerships:** Formal partnerships with local high schools for Tech Prep programs and with hospitals for health programs.

Student profile. Among degree-seeking undergraduates, 5,451 enrolled as first-time, first-year students.

Part-time:	60%	Asian American:	1%
Out-of-state:	6%	Hispanic American:	86%
Women:	57%	International:	2%
African American:	2%	25 or older:	37%

Transfer out. Colleges most students transferred to 2011: University of Texas at El Paso, New Mexico State University.

Basis for selection. Open admission, but selective for some programs. Observes TASP requirements. Nelson-Denny Reading Test, institutional math test and minimum GPA required for admission to health programs.

2012-2013 Annual costs. Tuition/fees (projected): $2,088; $2,736 out-of-state. Per-credit charge: $67 in-state; $94 out-of-state. Books/supplies: $545. Personal expenses: $1,223.

Financial aid. Need-based: Work-study available nights, weekends and for part-time students. **Non-need-based:** Scholarships awarded for academics, athletics.

Application procedures. Admission: No deadline. No application fee. Admission notification on a rolling basis. **Financial aid:** Priority date 5/1; no closing date. FAFSA, institutional form required. Applicants notified on a rolling basis starting 7/1; must reply within 2 week(s) of notification.

Academics. Special study options: Cooperative education, cross-registration, distance learning, double major, dual enrollment of high school students, ESL, honors, independent study, internships, teacher certification program, weekend college. License preparation in dental hygiene, nursing, physical therapy, radiology. **Credit/placement by examination:** AP, CLEP, IB, institutional tests. 45 credit hours maximum toward associate degree. **Support services:** GED preparation and test center, learning center, remedial instruction, study skills assistance, tutoring, writing center.

Majors. Area/ethnic studies: Women's. **Biology:** General. **Business:** General, accounting, administrative services, business admin, fashion, finance, hospitality/recreation, international, management science, office/clerical, operations, real estate, tourism promotion, tourism/travel. **Communications:** Communications/speech/rhetoric, journalism. **Communications technology:** General. **Computer sciences:** General, computer science, information systems, programming, systems analysis. **Education:** Elementary, physical, secondary, special ed, technology/industrial arts. **Engineering:** General. **English:** English lit, rhetoric/composition. **Foreign languages:** General, sign language interpretation. **Health services:** Clinical lab technology, dental assistant, dental hygiene, dietetics, medical assistant, medical radiologic technology/radiation therapy, medical records technology, mental health services, nursing (RN), optician, physical therapy assistant, predental, premedicine, prepharmacy, preveterinary, respiratory therapy technology, substance abuse counseling, surgical technology. **History:** General. **Liberal arts:** Arts/sciences. **Math:** General. **Parks/recreation:** Health/fitness. **Physical sciences:** Chemistry, geology, physics. **Protective services:** Corrections, criminal justice, fire safety technology. **Psychology:** General. **Social sciences:** General, political science, sociology. **Visual/performing arts:** Art, cinematography, commercial photography, commercial/advertising art, dramatic, fashion design, interior design, music, photography. **Work/family studies:** Child care management, family studies, institutional food production.

Computing on campus. 2,000 workstations in library, computer center. Wireless network available.

Student life. Freshman orientation: Mandatory. Preregistration for classes offered. **Activities:** Jazz band, choral groups, dance, drama, film society, literary magazine, music ensembles, radio station, student government, student newspaper, TV station, Phi Theta Kappa, African-American coalition, art student society, architecture club, social science club.

Athletics. NJCAA. **Intercollegiate:** Baseball M, softball W. **Intramural:** Basketball, bowling, cross-country, soccer, softball, table tennis, tennis, track and field, volleyball, weight lifting. **Team name:** Tejanos/Tejanas.

Student services. Career counseling, student employment services, health services, personal counseling, placement for graduates, veterans' counselor, women's services. **Physically disabled:** Services for visually, speech, hearing impaired. **Transfer:** Transfer adviser, college fairs on campus for students transferring to 4-year colleges.

Contact. Phone: (915) 831-2580 Fax: (915) 831-2161
Daryle Hendry, Director of Admissions, El Paso Community College, Box 20500, El Paso, TX 79998

Frank Phillips College
Borger, Texas
www.fpctx.edu   CB code: 6222

- Public 2-year community and junior college
- Commuter campus in large town

General. Founded in 1948. Regionally accredited. Guaranteed transfer program. Contract training provided on site or at on-campus location for Occupational Safety and Health Administration mandated certification. **Enrollment:** 533 degree-seeking undergraduates. **Degrees:** 69 associate awarded. **Location:** 60 miles from Amarillo. **Calendar:** Semester, extensive summer session. **Full-time faculty:** 31 total. **Part-time faculty:** 36 total. **Class size:** 31% < 20, 68% 20-39, 1% 40-49.

Student profile.

Out-of-state:	5%	Live on campus:	20%
25 or older:	22%		

Transfer out. Colleges most students transferred to 2011: West Texas A&M University, Texas A&M University, Texas Tech University.

Basis for selection. Open admission. SAT/ACT, COMPASS, ASSET, TAKS, or ACCUPLACER may be used in lieu of THEA. Veterans receive preferential admission. Texas Success Initiative guidelines followed. **Home schooled:** Transcript of courses and grades required.

2011-2012 Annual costs. Tuition/fees: $2,526; $3,216 out-of-district; $3,398 out-of-state. Room/board: $4,545. Books/supplies: $605. Personal expenses: $985.

Financial aid. Need-based: Need-based aid available for part-time students. Work-study available nights, weekends and for part-time students. **Non-need-based:** Scholarships awarded for academics, athletics, music/drama, state residency. **Additional information:** Some Texas fire department and police department personnel, active duty military personnel, children of military missing in action may qualify for reduced or waived tuition. Out-of-state tuition waived for students living in Oklahoma counties adjacent to Texas.

Application procedures. Admission: No deadline. No application fee. Admission notification on a rolling basis. **Financial aid:** Closing date 7/1. FAFSA, institutional form required. Applicants notified on a rolling basis; must reply within 2 week(s) of notification.

Academics. Special study options: Cooperative education, distance learning, dual enrollment of high school students, internships, liberal arts/career combination. License preparation in nursing. **Credit/placement by examination:** AP, CLEP, IB, institutional tests. 24 credit hours maximum toward associate degree. **Support services:** GED preparation and test center, learning center, pre-admission summer program, reduced course load, remedial instruction, study skills assistance, tutoring, writing center.

Majors. Biology: General. **Business:** General, accounting, administrative services, business admin. **Computer sciences:** General. **Education:** General, elementary, secondary. **English:** English lit. **General:** Equestrian studies, farm/ranch, range science. **Health services:** Medical secretary. **History:** General. **Liberal arts:** Arts/sciences. **Math:** General. **Philosophy/religion:** Philosophy. **Physical sciences:** Chemistry, physics. **Psychology:** General. **Social sciences:** General, political science, sociology. **Visual/performing arts:** Music.

Computing on campus. 59 workstations in dormitories, library, student center. Dormitories wired for high-speed internet access. Online course registration, wireless network available.

Student life. Freshman orientation: Mandatory. Preregistration for classes offered. Session available at start of and during semester. **Housing:** Single-sex dorms, apartments, wellness housing available. $150 fully refundable deposit, deadline 8/1. **Activities:** Choral groups, drama, music ensembles, student government, rodeo club, agriculture club, Phi Theta Kappa, cosmetology club, licensed vocational nursing club, Circle K, business club, art club, computer club, Future Educators Association.

Athletics. NJCAA. **Intercollegiate:** Baseball M, basketball, softball W, volleyball W. **Intramural:** Basketball, bowling, cheerleading, racquetball, softball, table tennis, tennis, volleyball. **Team name:** Plainsmen.

Student services. Adult student services, alcohol/substance abuse counseling, career counseling, services for economically disadvantaged, student employment services, financial aid counseling, personal counseling, placement for graduates, veterans' counselor. **Transfer:** Re-entry adviser, pre-admission transcript evaluation for new students. Transfer adviser, college fairs on campus for students transferring to 4-year colleges.

Contact. E-mail: admissions@fpctx.edu
Phone: (806) 457-4200 ext. 707 Fax: (806) 457-4225
Michele Stevens, Director of Enrollment Management, Frank Phillips College, Box 5118, Borger, TX 79008-5118

Galveston College
Galveston, Texas
www.gc.edu   CB code: 6255

- Public 2-year community college
- Commuter campus in small city

General. Founded in 1967. Regionally accredited. **Enrollment:** 2,222 degree-seeking undergraduates. **Degrees:** 204 associate awarded. **Location:** 50 miles from Houston. **Calendar:** Semester, limited summer session. **Full-time faculty:** 52 total. **Part-time faculty:** 69 total. **Class size:** 61% < 20, 37% 20-39, 1% 40-49, less than 1% 50-99, less than 1% >100. **Special facilities:** Center for health related technology. **Partnerships:** Formal partnership with UTMB in health career profession.

Student profile.

Out-of-state:	4%	25 or older:	44%

Transfer out. Colleges most students transferred to 2011: University of Houston at Clear Lake, University of Texas Medical Branch at Galveston, Texas A&M University at Galveston.

Basis for selection. Open admission, but selective for some programs. Health occupations majors have special admission requirements.

2011-2012 Annual costs. Tuition/fees: $1,900; $4,150 out-of-state. Per-credit charge: $37 in-state; $100 out-of-state. Books/supplies: $878. Personal expenses: $1,560.

Financial aid. All financial aid based on need. Need-based aid available for part-time students. Work-study available nights, weekends and for part-time students.

Application procedures. Admission: No deadline. No application fee. Application must be submitted on paper. Admission notification on a rolling basis. **Financial aid:** Priority date 6/9; no closing date. FAFSA required. Applicants notified on a rolling basis starting 6/1.

Academics. Special study options: Cooperative education, distance learning, dual enrollment of high school students, independent study, internships, weekend college. License preparation in dental hygiene, nursing, paramedic, radiology, real estate. **Credit/placement by examination:** AP, CLEP. 24 credit hours maximum toward associate degree. **Support services:** GED test center, learning center, remedial instruction, tutoring.

Majors. Biology: General, marine. **Business:** Accounting, administrative services, business admin, entrepreneurial studies, marketing, office/clerical. **Computer sciences:** General, computer science, information systems, programming. **Education:** Elementary, physical. **Engineering:** General. **English:** English lit, rhetoric/composition. **Foreign languages:** Spanish. **Health services:** EMT paramedic, health care admin, medical radiologic technology/radiation therapy, medical records technology, medical secretary, nuclear medical technology, nursing (RN), predental, premedicine, preveterinary. **History:** General. **Human services:** Social work. **Liberal arts:** Arts/sciences. **Math:** General. **Physical sciences:** Chemistry, geology, physics. **Protective services:** Criminal justice, fire safety technology. **Psychology:**

General. **Social sciences:** Anthropology, economics, geography, political science, sociology. **Visual/performing arts:** Art, dramatic, music. **Work/family studies:** Family studies.

Most popular majors. Health sciences 43%, liberal arts 48%.

Computing on campus. 170 workstations in library, computer center, student center. Commuter students can connect to campus network. Online library, helpline, wireless network available.

Student life. Freshman orientation: Mandatory. Preregistration for classes offered. **Housing:** Special housing for scholarship athletes available. **Activities:** Choral groups, drama, music ensembles, student government, student newspaper, student activities council, journalism club, African American club, Campus Crusade for Christ, Hispanic student organization, single parents organization, environmental awareness club, Phi Theta Kappa, nuclear medicine club, student nurses association.

Athletics. NJCAA. **Intercollegiate:** Baseball M, softball W, volleyball W. **Intramural:** Bowling, golf, tennis. **Team name:** Whitecaps.

Student services. Career counseling, student employment services, financial aid counseling, on-campus daycare, personal counseling, placement for graduates, veterans' counselor. **Physically disabled:** Services for visually, speech, hearing impaired. **Transfer:** Transfer adviser, college fairs on campus for students transferring to 4-year colleges.

Contact. E-mail: calcala@gc.edu
Phone: (409) 944-1230 Fax: (409) 944-1501
Kimberly Ellis, Director of Admissions/Registrar, Galveston College, 4015 Avenue Q, Galveston, TX 77550-7447

Grayson County College
Denison, Texas
www.grayson.edu

CB member
CB code: 6254

- Public 2-year community and technical college
- Commuter campus in large town

General. Founded in 1963. Regionally accredited. **Enrollment:** 4,536 degree-seeking undergraduates. **Degrees:** 555 associate awarded. **Location:** 7 miles from Sherman, 75 miles from Dallas. **Calendar:** Semester, limited summer session. **Full-time faculty:** 100 total. **Part-time faculty:** 187 total. **Special facilities:** Vineyard.

Student profile.

Out-of-state:	2%	Live on campus:	6%

Basis for selection. Open admission, but selective for some programs. Special requirements for nursing, radiology, medical lab tech, vocational nursing certificate, EMT/paramedic programs. Observes TASP requirements. **Home schooled:** Transcript of courses and grades required.

2011-2012 Annual costs. Tuition/fees: $1,560; $2,520 out-of-district; $3,990 out-of-state. Per-credit charge: $52 in-district; $84 out-of-district; $210 out-of-state. Room/board: $4,143. Books/supplies: $594. Personal expenses: $1,412.

Financial aid. Need-based: Need-based aid available for part-time students. Work-study available nights, weekends and for part-time students. **Additional information:** Short term loans available.

Application procedures. Admission: No deadline. No application fee. Application must be submitted online. Admission notification on a rolling basis. Priority date for receipt of applications vary. Dates are published in the schedule of classes. **Financial aid:** Priority date 6/1; no closing date. FAFSA required. Applicants notified on a rolling basis; must reply within 5 week(s) of notification.

Academics. Special study options: Distance learning, dual enrollment of high school students, ESL, honors. Bachelor's degree programs available on campus. License preparation in nursing, paramedic, radiology. **Credit/placement by examination:** AP, CLEP, institutional tests. 24 credit hours maximum toward associate degree. **Support services:** GED preparation and test center, learning center, reduced course load, remedial instruction, study skills assistance, tutoring.

Majors. Biology: General. **Business:** General, accounting, administrative services, office management, office technology, office/clerical. **Computer sciences:** General, programming. **Education:** General, elementary, secondary. **Engineering:** General. **English:** Rhetoric/composition. **Health services:** Clinical lab science, EMT paramedic, nursing (RN), substance abuse counseling. **Liberal arts:** Arts/sciences. **Math:** General. **Physical sciences:** Chemistry, geology, physics. **Protective services:** Law enforcement admin, police

science. **Psychology:** General. **Social sciences:** Sociology. **Visual/performing arts:** Art, commercial/advertising art, dramatic, music.

Computing on campus. 150 workstations in library, computer center. Dormitories wired for high-speed internet access and linked to campus network. Online course registration, online library, helpline, wireless network available.

Student life. Freshman orientation: Mandatory. Preregistration for classes offered. Web-based program. Dates vary. **Housing:** Coed dorms, special housing for disabled, wellness housing available. $175 fully refundable deposit. **Activities:** Bands, campus ministries, choral groups, drama, international student organizations, music ensembles, Model UN, student government.

Athletics. NJCAA. **Intercollegiate:** Baseball M, basketball, softball W. **Intramural:** Baseball M, basketball, softball W. **Team name:** Vikings.

Student services. Adult student services, career counseling, services for economically disadvantaged, financial aid counseling, personal counseling, veterans' counselor. **Physically disabled:** Services for visually, speech, hearing impaired. **Transfer:** College fairs on campus for students transferring to 4-year colleges.

Contact. Phone: (903) 465-8604 Fax: (903) 463-8758
Kim Faris, Director of Admissions and Records, Grayson County College, 6101 Grayson Drive, Denison, TX 75020

Hallmark College of Aeronautics
San Antonio, Texas
www.hallmarkcollege.edu

CB code: 3166

- For-profit 2-year technical and career college
- Commuter campus in very large city
- Interview required

General. Accredited by ACCSC. Hallmark College of Aeronautics is located on the grounds of San Antonio International Airport. **Enrollment:** 206 degree-seeking undergraduates. **Degrees:** 123 associate awarded. **Location:** 80 miles from Austin. **Calendar:** Differs by program, extensive summer session. **Full-time faculty:** 17 total; 29% minority, 12% women. **Part-time faculty:** 2 total. **Class size:** 51% < 20, 49% 20-39. **Partnerships:** Formal partnership with Alamo Area Aerospace Academy.

Student profile. Among degree-seeking undergraduates, 100% enrolled in a vocational program. Of all enrolled students, 1% already have a bachelor's degree or higher.

Transfer out. Colleges most students transferred to 2011: Texas State Technical College, Palo Alto College, St. Philips College.

Basis for selection. Student must pass the entrance assessment and tour the facilities. **Home schooled:** Transcript of courses and grades, interview required.

High school preparation. Distribution of high school units not required or recommended for admissions.

2012-2013 Annual costs. Tuition/fees (projected): $30,502. Reported tuition is for the combined AAS Airframe Technology/AAS Powerplant Technology program. AAS Airframe Technology program is $19,630; AAS Powerplant Technology program is $19,932; Aviation Technician Diploma program is $27,784. Cost includes books, equipment and supplies. Security fee is $95. International students: 8% added to the total charge of the program.

Financial aid. Need-based: Work-study available nights, weekends and for part-time students.

Application procedures. Admission: No deadline. $110 fee. Admission notification on a rolling basis. Completed admissions process accepted by Acceptance Committee up to the time term begins and orientation for new students. **Financial aid:** No deadline. FAFSA required. Applicants notified on a rolling basis.

Academics. Special study options: Accelerated study, liberal arts/career combination. License preparation in aviation. **Credit/placement by examination:** AP, CLEP, institutional tests. 49 credit hours maximum toward associate degree. **Support services:** Remedial instruction, study skills assistance, tutoring.

Computing on campus. Online library available.

Student life. Freshman orientation: Mandatory. Preregistration for classes offered. **Activities:** Student newspaper.

Student services. Career counseling, student employment services, financial aid counseling, placement for graduates. **Transfer:** Pre-admission transcript evaluation for new students.

Contact. E-mail: slross@hallmarkcollege.edu
Phone: (210) 826-1000 ext. 106 Toll-free number: (888) 656-9300
Fax: (210) 699-1807
Slava Ross, Vice President of Admissions, Hallmark College of Aeronautics, 8901 Wetmore Road, San Antonio, TX 78230-4229

Hallmark College of Technology
San Antonio, Texas
www.hallmarkcollege.edu   CB code: 2307

- For-profit 2-year technical and career college
- Commuter campus in very large city
- Interview required

General. Founded in 1969. Accredited by ACCSC. Additional campus focusing on aeronautics (Hallmark College of Aeronautics) located on property of San Antonio International Airport offers day/evening certificate/degree programs in aviation maintenance: airframe and powerplant technology. **Enrollment:** 379 degree-seeking undergraduates. **Degrees:** 8 bachelor's, 135 associate awarded. **Location:** 80 miles from Austin. **Calendar:** Differs by program, extensive summer session. **Full-time faculty:** 23 total. **Part-time faculty:** 10 total. **Class size:** 91% < 20, 9% 20-39. **Special facilities:** Megacomputer laboratory.

Student profile. Among degree-seeking undergraduates, 100% enrolled in a vocational program. Of all enrolled students, 2% already have a bachelor's degree or higher.

Transfer out. 1% of students enrolled in the transfer program go on to 4-year colleges. **Colleges most students transferred to 2011:** University of Phoenix, UTSA, San Antonio College, DeVry University.

Basis for selection. High school diploma or GED required. Hybrid Readiness Assessment for certificate and associate degrees. Competitive selection process for AAS Nursing. Entrance exam, tour of facilities required for all. ACT/SAT used only for admission to bachelor's program. Test scores must be within 12 years of the time of application. Student exempt from the ACT/SAT requirement if one of following requirements is met: student holds associate degree from accredited college/university; student has completed minimum of 30 college credits earning cumulative GPA of 2.5 on 4.0 scale and is determined to be college ready; student has passed the ACCUPLACER. Interviews required for all programs, essay/personal statement required for bachelor's degree program. **Home schooled:** Transcript of courses and grades, interview required. Student must be approved by the Acceptance Committee for admissions after meeting all entrance requirements. Hybrid Readiness Assessment required. **Learning Disabled:** Request for accommodations evaluated on a case-by-case basis by the Dean of Education or the Campus President. Committed to providing reasonable accommodations and individual attention to qualified disabled students.

2012-2013 Annual costs. Tuition/fees (projected): $12,600. Reported cost is for the Accounting Certificate program. Medical Assistant Certificate and Healthcare Information Specialist (Billing/Coding) Certificate program is $13,400. AAS in Medical Assistant is $19,850. AAS in Computer Network Systems Technology is $30,800. AAS in Nursing is $31,680 and the Bachelor of Science degree program is $55,000. All Allied Health programs have a $100 lab fee. Nursing program has a $4,800 program fee. International students: 8% added to the total charge of the program. Tuition includes books, equipment and supplies.

Financial aid. **Need-based:** Work-study available nights, weekends and for part-time students.

Application procedures. **Admission:** No deadline. $110 fee. Admission notification on a rolling basis. Application fee for nursing is $25. Application process for admissions must be completed and student accepted by the Acceptance Committee before the new term begins. **Financial aid:** No deadline. FAFSA required. Applicants notified on a rolling basis.

Academics. **Special study options:** Accelerated study, distance learning, internships. Bachelor's degree programs available on campus. License preparation in nursing. **Credit/placement by examination:** AP, CLEP, SAT, ACT, institutional tests. 36 credit hours maximum toward associate degree. **Support services:** Remedial instruction, study skills assistance, tutoring.

Majors. **Computer sciences:** Networking. **Health services:** Medical assistant, nursing (RN).

Computing on campus. 127 workstations in computer center. Online library, wireless network available.

Student life. **Freshman orientation:** Mandatory. Preregistration for classes offered. **Activities:** Student newspaper.

Student services. Career counseling, student employment services, financial aid counseling, placement for graduates. **Transfer:** Pre-admission transcript evaluation for new students.

Contact. E-mail: slross@hallmarkcollege.edu
Phone: (210) 690-9000 ext. 214 Toll-free number: (800) 880-6600
Fax: (210) 697-8225
Slava Ross, Vice President of Admissions, Hallmark College of Technology, Hallmark College of Technology, San Antonio, TX 78230-1736

Hill College
Hillsboro, Texas
www.hillcollege.edu   CB code: 6285

- Public 2-year community college
- Commuter campus in small town

General. Founded in 1923. Regionally accredited. **Enrollment:** 4,322 degree-seeking undergraduates. **Degrees:** 284 associate awarded. **Location:** 32 miles from Waco, 64 miles from Dallas. **Calendar:** Semester, limited summer session. **Full-time faculty:** 82 total. **Part-time faculty:** 141 total. **Special facilities:** Texas Heritage Museum.

Student profile.

Part-time:	63%	Women:	60%
Out-of-state:	1%	Live on campus:	14%

Transfer out. **Colleges most students transferred to 2011:** Tarleton State University, Tarrant County Junior College, University of Texas at Arlington.

Basis for selection. Open admission, but selective for some programs. Observes TASP guidelines. THEA Test or Approved State Alternative Test required for academic students unless exempted by state. Special requirements for nursing program. **Home schooled:** Transcript of courses and grades required.

2011-2012 Annual costs. Tuition/fees: $1,980; $2,670 out-of-district; $3,070 out-of-state. Johnson County residents pay $5 per credit hour differential, or $2,130 annual tuition. Room/board: $3,550. Books/supplies: $2,443. Personal expenses: $1,763.

Financial aid. **Need-based:** Need-based aid available for part-time students. Work-study available nights, weekends and for part-time students. **Non-need-based:** Scholarships awarded for academics, athletics, music/drama.

Application procedures. **Admission:** No deadline. No application fee. Application must be submitted online. Admission notification on a rolling basis. **Financial aid:** Closing date 7/1. FAFSA, institutional form required. Applicants notified on a rolling basis.

Academics. **Special study options:** Cooperative education, distance learning, dual enrollment of high school students, honors, independent study, internships, liberal arts/career combination. Bachelor's degree programs available on campus. **Credit/placement by examination:** AP, CLEP. 24 credit hours maximum toward associate degree. **Support services:** GED test center, learning center, reduced course load, remedial instruction, study skills assistance, tutoring.

Majors. **Biology:** General, botany. **Business:** Administrative services, business admin, office management, office technology, office/clerical, real estate. **Communications:** Communications/speech/rhetoric, journalism. **Computer sciences:** General, applications programming, computer science, data processing, programming. **Education:** General. **Engineering:** General. **English:** English lit. **Foreign languages:** General. **General:** Business. **Health services:** Licensed practical nurse. **Liberal arts:** Arts/sciences. **Math:** General. **Parks/recreation:** Health/fitness. **Physical sciences:** Chemistry, geology, physics. **Protective services:** Criminal justice, fire services admin, law enforcement admin, police science, security services. **Psychology:** General. **Visual/performing arts:** General, art, commercial/advertising art, music. **Work/family studies:** Institutional food production.

Computing on campus. Dormitories wired for high-speed internet access. Commuter students can connect to campus network. Online course registration, online library, helpline, wireless network available.

Student life. **Freshman orientation:** Mandatory. Preregistration for classes offered. **Housing:** Single-sex dorms, wellness housing available. $300 partly refundable deposit. **Activities:** Bands, choral groups, drama, music

ensembles, student government, Circle K, Young Democrats, Young Republicans, Baptist student union, student council.

Athletics. NJCAA. **Intercollegiate:** Baseball M, basketball, golf, rodeo, soccer, softball W, volleyball W. **Intramural:** Volleyball. **Team name:** Rebels.

Student services. Adult student services, career counseling, services for economically disadvantaged, student employment services, financial aid counseling, personal counseling, placement for graduates, veterans' counselor. **Physically disabled:** Services for visually, speech, hearing impaired. **Transfer:** Transfer adviser, college fairs on campus for students transferring to 4-year colleges.

Contact. E-mail: enrollmentinfo@hillcollege.edu
Phone: (254) 659-7600 Fax: (254) 582-7591
Sherry Davis, Director of Student Records and Registration, Hill College, 112 Lamar Drive, Hillsboro, TX 76645

Houston Community College System
Houston, Texas   **CB member**
www.hccs.edu   **CB code: 0929**

▶ Public 2-year community college
▶ Commuter campus in very large city

General. Founded in 1971. Regionally accredited. Multi-campus college enrolling a large number of international students. Students may attend the campus of their choice. **Enrollment:** 53,333 degree-seeking undergraduates; 9,682 non-degree-seeking students. **Degrees:** 3,606 associate awarded. **ROTC:** Army, Air Force. **Location:** 51 miles from Galveston, 164 miles from Austin. **Calendar:** Semester, extensive summer session. **Full-time faculty:** 772 total; 26% have terminal degrees, 41% minority, 52% women. **Part-time faculty:** 1,780 total; 16% have terminal degrees, 53% minority, 54% women. **Class size:** 25% < 20, 75% 20-39, less than 1% 40-49, less than 1% 50-99. **Special facilities:** 300-seat Heinen Theatre, a registered National Landmark, HCC Public Safety Institute. **Partnerships:** Formal partnerships with local high schools for tech-prep and school-to-work programs; contract training agreements with industry.

Student profile. Among degree-seeking undergraduates, 10,450 enrolled as first-time, first-year students, 4,318 transferred in from other institutions.

Part-time:	67%	Asian American:	10%
Out-of-state:	10%	Hispanic American:	29%
Women:	59%	International:	9%
African American:	33%	25 or older:	40%

Basis for selection. Open admission, but selective for some programs. High school transcript, assessment, personal interview required for admission to some health programs. According to Texas state law, students must take TASP (Texas Academic Skills Program) test or TASP alternative. Some students may qualify for TASP exemptions. International students must demonstrate English proficiency by taking TASP (or accepted alternative) and CELSA. Interview required for health careers. **Adult students:** If a student has not previously taken an approved Texas State Initiative (TSI) test or other required placement test and is not exempt or waived from testing requirements, they must test prior to enrollment.

2011-2012 Annual costs. Tuition/fees: $2,022; $4,032 out-of-district; $4,527 out-of-state. Books/supplies: $2,800. Personal expenses: $6,130.

Financial aid. Need-based: Need-based aid available for part-time students. Work-study available nights, weekends and for part-time students. **Additional information:** Although financial aid applications can be submitted at any time during the academic year, FAFSA's received after priority filing date of April 15 will be considered for funding only after all on-time filers have been awarded and then only if funds are available.

Application procedures. Admission: No deadline. No application fee. Admission notification on a rolling basis. **Financial aid:** FAFSA required.

Academics. Special study options: Cooperative education, distance learning, dual enrollment of high school students, ESL, honors, independent study, internships, study abroad, weekend college. Cross-cultural studies. License preparation in aviation, dental hygiene, nursing, occupational therapy, paramedic, physical therapy, radiology, real estate. **Credit/placement by examination:** AP, CLEP, IB, SAT, ACT, institutional tests. 24 credit hours maximum toward associate degree. **Support services:** GED preparation and test center, learning center, remedial instruction, tutoring.

Majors. Business: Accounting, banking/financial services, business admin, communications, fashion, hotel/motel admin, international, logistics, marketing, office technology, real estate, tourism/travel. **Communications technology:** Animation/special effects, graphic/printing, radio/TV. **Computer sciences:** Applications programming, networking, programming, system admin.

Foreign languages: Sign language interpretation. **General:** Horticulture, turf management. **Health services:** Cardiovascular technology, clinical lab technology, dental hygiene, EMT paramedic, histologic assistant, medical records technology, mental health services, nuclear medical technology, nursing (RN), occupational therapy assistant, radiologic technology/medical imaging, respiratory therapy technology. **Human services:** General. **Parks/recreation:** Health/fitness. **Protective services:** Fire safety technology, police science. **Social sciences:** GIS/cartography. **Visual/performing arts:** Cinematography, fashion design, interior design, music management, music performance, music theory/composition. **Work/family studies:** Child development.

Most popular majors. Business/marketing 11%, health sciences 9%, liberal arts 68%.

Computing on campus. 4,121 workstations in library, computer center. Online course registration, helpline available.

Student life. Freshman orientation: Mandatory. Preregistration for classes offered. **Activities:** Bands, campus ministries, choral groups, drama, international student organizations, music ensembles, musical theater, student government, student newspaper, TV station, international student association, Vietnamese student association, United Student Council, black student union, Association of Latin American Students, Phi Theta Kappa.

Athletics. Intramural: Basketball M, football (non-tackle) M, golf, soccer, softball, volleyball W.

Student services. Alcohol/substance abuse counseling, career counseling, services for economically disadvantaged, student employment services, financial aid counseling, minority student services, on-campus daycare, personal counseling, placement for graduates, veterans' counselor, women's services. **Physically disabled:** Services for visually, speech, hearing impaired. **Transfer:** College fairs on campus for students transferring to 4-year colleges.

Contact. E-mail: admissions@hccs.edu
Phone: (713) 718-8500
Mary Lemburg, Registrar, Houston Community College System, PO Box 667517, MC 1136, Houston, TX 77266-7517

Howard College
Big Spring, Texas
www.howardcollege.edu   **CB code: 6277**

▶ Public 2-year community college
▶ Commuter campus in large town

General. Founded in 1945. Regionally accredited. **Enrollment:** 2,812 degree-seeking undergraduates. **Degrees:** 290 associate awarded. **Location:** 105 miles from Lubbock, 40 miles from Midland. **Calendar:** Semester, limited summer session. **Full-time faculty:** 143 total. **Part-time faculty:** 113 total. **Special facilities:** Rodeo arena, arts center, coliseum.

Student profile.

Out-of-state:	8%	Live on campus:	8%
25 or older:	28%		

Transfer out. Colleges most students transferred to 2011: Texas Tech University, Angelo State University, Tarleton State University, University of Texas-Permian Basin, Texas A&M University.

Basis for selection. Open admission, but selective for some programs. Special requirements for health, cosmetology programs. Interview required for dental hygiene, degree and licensed vocational nursing, cosmetology programs.

2011-2012 Annual costs. Tuition/fees: $2,012; $2,942 out-of-district; $4,332 out-of-state. Room/board: $4,071. Books/supplies: $800. Personal expenses: $1,330.

Financial aid. Need-based: Need-based aid available for part-time students. Work-study available nights, weekends and for part-time students. **Non-need-based:** Scholarships awarded for academics, art, athletics, leadership, music/drama.

Application procedures. Admission: No deadline. No application fee. Admission notification on a rolling basis. **Financial aid:** Priority date 4/1; no closing date. FAFSA, institutional form required. Applicants notified on a rolling basis starting 7/15; must reply within 2 week(s) of notification.

Academics. Special study options: Cooperative education, cross-registration, distance learning, dual enrollment of high school students, ESL,

liberal arts/career combination, weekend college. License preparation in dental hygiene, nursing, occupational therapy, paramedic, physical therapy, radiology, real estate. **Credit/placement by examination:** AP, CLEP, institutional tests. 18 credit hours maximum toward associate degree. **Support services:** GED preparation and test center, learning center, pre-admission summer program, reduced course load, remedial instruction, study skills assistance, tutoring, writing center.

Majors. Architecture: Landscape. **Biology:** General. **Business:** General, accounting, office/clerical. **Communications:** Journalism. **Computer sciences:** General. **Education:** General. **English:** English lit. **Foreign languages:** General, sign language interpretation. **General:** Business. **Health services:** Athletic training, dental hygiene, dental lab technology, EMT ambulance attendant, medical assistant, medical records admin, medical records technology, nursing (RN), physical therapy assistant, predental, premedicine, respiratory therapy technology, substance abuse counseling. **Liberal arts:** Arts/sciences. **Math:** General. **Parks/recreation:** Health/fitness. **Physical sciences:** Chemistry, physics. **Protective services:** Corrections, forensics, law enforcement admin. **Psychology:** General. **Social sciences:** General. **Visual/performing arts:** General, art, dramatic, music. **Work/family studies:** Child care management.

Most popular majors. Business/marketing 19%, computer/information sciences 7%, health sciences 21%, liberal arts 43%, security/protective services 6%.

Computing on campus. 100 workstations in dormitories, library, computer center. Dormitories wired for high-speed internet access and linked to campus network. Commuter students can connect to campus network. Online course registration, online library, helpline, wireless network available.

Student life. Freshman orientation: Available. Preregistration for classes offered. **Housing:** Single-sex dorms, wellness housing available. **Activities:** Bands, choral groups, dance, drama, music ensembles, musical theater, student government.

Athletics. NJCAA. **Intercollegiate:** Baseball M, basketball, cheerleading, rodeo, softball W. **Intramural:** Basketball, bowling, golf, handball, racquetball, softball, table tennis, tennis, volleyball. **Team name:** Hawks.

Student services. Adult student services, alcohol/substance abuse counseling, career counseling, services for economically disadvantaged, student employment services, financial aid counseling, health services, on-campus daycare, personal counseling, placement for graduates, veterans' counselor. **Physically disabled:** Services for hearing impaired. **Transfer:** Transfer adviser, college fairs on campus for students transferring to 4-year colleges.

Contact. E-mail: dmerrick@howardcollege.edu
Phone: (432) 264-5000 Fax: (432) 264-5072
Donna Merrick, Registrar, Howard College, 1001 Birdwell Lane, Big Spring, TX 79720

International Academy of Design and Technology: San Antonio
San Antonio, Texas
www.iadtsanantonio.com

» For-profit 2-year technical college
» Very large city

General. Regionally accredited; also accredited by ACICS. **Enrollment:** 650 degree-seeking undergraduates. **Degrees:** 113 associate awarded. **Calendar:** Quarter. **Full-time faculty:** 9 total. **Part-time faculty:** 50 total.

Basis for selection. Open admission.

2011-2012 Annual costs. Tuition/fees: $11,700. Per-credit charge: $325.

Financial aid. Need-based: Work-study available nights, weekends and for part-time students.

Application procedures. Admission: No deadline. **Financial aid:** No deadline.

Academics. Special study options: Bachelor's degree programs available on campus. **Credit/placement by examination:** AP, CLEP.

Majors. Business: Fashion, merchandising. **Visual/performing arts:** Graphic design.

Contact. E-mail: ngarcia@iadtsanantonio.com
Phone: (210) 530-9449
International Academy of Design and Technology: San Antonio, 4511 Horizon Hill Boulevard, San Antonio, TX 78229

ITT Technical Institute: Arlington
Arlington, Texas
www.itt-tech.edu   CB code: 3572

» For-profit 2-year technical college
» Commuter campus in large city
» Interview required

General. Founded in 1982. Accredited by ACICS. **Enrollment:** 855 undergraduates. **Degrees:** 36 bachelor's, 199 associate awarded. **Location:** 11 miles from Fort Worth, 18 miles from Dallas. **Calendar:** Quarter, extensive summer session. **Full-time faculty:** 10 total. **Part-time faculty:** 65 total.

Basis for selection. Satisfactory score from on-site English and mathematics tests required.

2011-2012 Annual costs. Estimated costs as of June 2011: per-credit-hour charge, $493, depending upon level and course of study; academic fee, $200. Certain programs of study require purchase of tools, which could cost an additional $100 to $500. All costs are subject to change.

Financial aid. Need-based: Work-study available nights, weekends and for part-time students.

Application procedures. Admission: No deadline. No application fee. Admission notification on a rolling basis. **Financial aid:** No deadline. FAFSA, institutional form required. Applicants notified on a rolling basis.

Academics. Credit/placement by examination: AP, CLEP. **Support services:** Learning center, tutoring.

Majors. Business: General. **Computer sciences:** LAN/WAN management, networking, programming, web page design. **Visual/performing arts:** Design, graphic design.

Computing on campus. Online library available.

Student life. Freshman orientation: Available. Preregistration for classes offered.

Student services. Career counseling, student employment services, placement for graduates.

Contact. Phone: (817) 794-5100 Toll-free number: (888) 288-4950
Fax: (817) 275-8446
Ed Leal, Director of Recruitment, ITT Technical Institute: Arlington, 551 Ryan Plaza Drive, Arlington, TX 76011

ITT Technical Institute: Austin
Austin, Texas
www.itt-tech.edu   CB code: 2692

» For-profit 2-year technical college
» Commuter campus in large city
» Interview required

General. Accredited by ACICS. **Enrollment:** 798 undergraduates. **Degrees:** 47 bachelor's, 187 associate awarded. **Calendar:** Quarter, extensive summer session. **Full-time faculty:** 12 total. **Part-time faculty:** 61 total.

Basis for selection. Satisfactory scores from on-site tests in English and mathematics required.

2011-2012 Annual costs. Estimated costs as of June 2011: per-credit-hour charge, $493, depending upon level and course of study; academic fee, $200. Certain programs of study require purchase of tools, which could cost an additional $100 to $500. All costs are subject to change.

Financial aid. Need-based: Work-study available nights, weekends and for part-time students.

Application procedures. Admission: No deadline. No application fee. Admission notification on a rolling basis. **Financial aid:** No deadline. FAFSA, institutional form required. Applicants notified on a rolling basis.

Academics. Credit/placement by examination: AP, CLEP. **Support services:** Learning center, tutoring.

Majors. Business: Accounting technology. **Computer sciences:** Networking, programming, web page design. **Visual/performing arts:** Design.

Computing on campus. Online library available.

Student life. Freshman orientation: Available. Preregistration for classes offered.

Student services. Career counseling, student employment services, placement for graduates.

Contact. Phone: (512) 467-6800 Toll-free number: (800) 431-0677 Fax: (512) 467-6677
Jim Branham, Director of Recruitment, ITT Technical Institute: Austin, 6330 Highway 290 East, Suite 150, Austin, TX 78723

ITT Technical Institute: Houston North
Houston, Texas
www.itt-tech.edu   CB code: 2712

- For-profit 2-year technical college
- Commuter campus in very large city
- Interview required

General. Accredited by ACICS. **Enrollment:** 1,007 undergraduates. **Degrees:** 19 bachelor's, 304 associate awarded. **Calendar:** Quarter, extensive summer session.

Basis for selection. Satisfactory scores from on-site tests in English and mathematics required.

2011-2012 Annual costs. Estimated costs as of June 2011: per-credit-hour charge, $493, depending upon level and course of study; academic fee, $200. Certain programs of study require purchase of tools, which could cost an additional $100 to $500. All costs are subject to change.

Financial aid. Need-based: Work-study available nights, weekends and for part-time students.

Application procedures. Admission: No deadline. Admission notification on a rolling basis. **Financial aid:** No deadline. FAFSA, institutional form required. Applicants notified on a rolling basis.

Academics. Credit/placement by examination: AP, CLEP. **Support services:** Learning center, tutoring.

Majors. Computer sciences: Networking, programming. **Visual/performing arts:** Design.

Computing on campus. Online library available.

Student services. Career counseling, student employment services, placement for graduates.

Contact. Phone: (281) 873-0512 Toll-free number: (800) 879-6486
Benjamin Moore, Director of Recruitment, ITT Technical Institute: Houston North, 15651 North Freeway, Houston, TX 77090

ITT Technical Institute: Houston West
Houston, Texas
www.itt-tech.edu   CB code: 3573

- For-profit 2-year technical college
- Commuter campus in very large city
- Interview required

General. Founded in 1983. Accredited by ACICS. **Enrollment:** 1,007 undergraduates. **Degrees:** 19 bachelor's, 304 associate awarded. **Calendar:** Quarter, extensive summer session. **Full-time faculty:** 15 total. **Part-time faculty:** 62 total.

Basis for selection. Satisfactory score from on-site English and mathematics tests required.

2011-2012 Annual costs. Estimated costs as of June 2011: per-credit-hour charge, $493, depending upon level and course of study; academic fee, $200. Certain programs of study require purchase of tools, which could cost an additional $100 to $500. All costs are subject to change.

Financial aid. Need-based: Work-study available nights, weekends and for part-time students.

Application procedures. Admission: No deadline. Admission notification on a rolling basis. **Financial aid:** No deadline. FAFSA, institutional form required. Applicants notified on a rolling basis.

Academics. Credit/placement by examination: AP, CLEP. **Support services:** Learning center, tutoring.

Majors. Business: General. **Computer sciences:** LAN/WAN management, networking, programming. **Visual/performing arts:** Design, graphic design.

Computing on campus. Online library available.

Student life. Freshman orientation: Available. Preregistration for classes offered.

Student services. Career counseling, student employment services, placement for graduates.

Contact. Phone: (713) 952-2294 Toll-free number: (800) 235-4787
Fax: (713) 952-2393
Johnny Jackson, Director of Recruitment, ITT Technical Institute: Houston West, 2950 South Gessner, Houston, TX 77063-3751

ITT Technical Institute: Richardson
Richardson, Texas
www.itt-tech.edu   CB code: 2747

- For-profit 2-year technical college
- Commuter campus in small city
- Interview required

General. Accredited by ACICS. **Enrollment:** 706 undergraduates. **Degrees:** 32 bachelor's, 174 associate awarded. **Location:** 12 miles from Dallas. **Calendar:** Quarter, extensive summer session. **Full-time faculty:** 12 total. **Part-time faculty:** 43 total.

Basis for selection. Satisfactory scores from on-site tests in English and mathematics required.

2011-2012 Annual costs. Estimated costs as of June 2011: per-credit-hour charge, $493, depending upon level and course of study; academic fee, $200. Certain programs of study require purchase of tools, which could cost an additional $100 to $500. All costs are subject to change.

Financial aid. Need-based: Work-study available nights, weekends and for part-time students.

Application procedures. Admission: No deadline. Admission notification on a rolling basis. **Financial aid:** No deadline. FAFSA, institutional form required. Applicants notified on a rolling basis.

Academics. Credit/placement by examination: AP, CLEP. **Support services:** Learning center, tutoring.

Majors. Business: General, accounting technology. **Computer sciences:** LAN/WAN management, networking, programming. **Health services:** Nursing (RN). **Visual/performing arts:** Design.

Student services. Career counseling, student employment services, placement for graduates.

Contact. Phone: (972) 690-9100 Toll-free number: (888) 488-5761
Fax: (972) 690-0853
Nate Wallace, Director of Recruitment, ITT Technical Institute: Richardson, 2101 Waterview Parkway, Richardson, TX 75080

ITT Technical Institute: San Antonio
San Antonio, Texas
www.itt-tech.edu   CB code: 2328

- For-profit 2-year technical college
- Commuter campus in very large city
- Interview required

General. Founded in 1988. Accredited by ACICS. **Enrollment:** 767 undergraduates. **Degrees:** 35 bachelor's, 163 associate awarded. **Location:** 200 miles from Houston, 75 miles from Austin. **Calendar:** Quarter, extensive summer session. **Full-time faculty:** 8 total. **Part-time faculty:** 62 total.

Basis for selection. Satisfactory scores from on-site tests in English and mathematics required.

2011-2012 Annual costs. Estimated costs as of June 2011: per-credit-hour charge, $493, depending upon level and course of study; academic fee,

$200. Certain programs of study require purchase of tools, which could cost an additional $100 to $500. All costs are subject to change.

Financial aid. Need-based: Work-study available nights, weekends and for part-time students.

Application procedures. Admission: No deadline. Admission notification on a rolling basis. **Financial aid:** No deadline. FAFSA, institutional form required. Applicants notified on a rolling basis.

Academics. Credit/placement by examination: AP, CLEP. **Support services:** Learning center, tutoring.

Majors. Business: General, accounting technology. **Computer sciences:** Networking, programming, web page design. **Visual/performing arts:** Design, graphic design.

Computing on campus. Online library available.

Student life. Freshman orientation: Available. Preregistration for classes offered.

Student services. Career counseling, student employment services, placement for graduates.

Contact. Phone: (210) 694-4612 Toll-free number: (800) 880-0570 Fax: (210) 694-4651
Michell "Buddy" Hoyt, Director of Recruitment, ITT Technical Institute: San Antonio, 5700 Northwest Parkway, San Antonio, TX 78249-3303

ITT Technical Institute: Webster
Webster, Texas
www.itt-tech.edu   CB code: 2715

- For-profit 2-year technical college
- Commuter campus in very large city
- Interview required

General. Accredited by ACICS. **Degrees:** 17 bachelor's, 123 associate awarded. **Calendar:** Quarter, extensive summer session.

Basis for selection. Satisfactory scores from on-site tests in English and mathematics required.

2011-2012 Annual costs. Estimated costs as of June 2011: per-credit-hour charge, $493, depending upon level and course of study; academic fee, $200. Certain programs of study require purchase of tools, which could cost an additional $100 to $500. All costs are subject to change.

Financial aid. Need-based: Work-study available nights, weekends and for part-time students.

Application procedures. Admission: No deadline. Admission notification on a rolling basis. **Financial aid:** No deadline. Institutional form required. Applicants notified on a rolling basis.

Academics. Credit/placement by examination: AP, CLEP. **Support services:** Learning center, tutoring.

Majors. Computer sciences: LAN/WAN management, programming. **Visual/performing arts:** Design.

Computing on campus. Online library available.

Student life. Freshman orientation: Available. Preregistration for classes offered.

Student services. Career counseling, student employment services, placement for graduates.

Contact. Toll-free number: (888) 488-9347
Derric Sutton, Director of Recruitment, ITT Technical Institute: Webster, 1001 Magnolia Avenue, Webster, TX 77598

Jacksonville College
Jacksonville, Texas
www.jacksonville-college.edu   CB code: 6317

- Private 2-year junior and liberal arts college affiliated with Baptist faith
- Commuter campus in large town

General. Founded in 1899. Regionally accredited. Owned and operated by the Baptist Missionary Association of Texas and affiliated with the Southern Baptists of Texas Convention. **Enrollment:** 457 undergraduates. **Degrees:** 36 associate awarded. **Location:** 120 miles from Dallas, 25 miles from Tyler. **Calendar:** Semester, limited summer session. **Full-time faculty:** 11 total. **Part-time faculty:** 10 total. **Class size:** 67% < 20, 32% 20-39, 1% >100.

Student profile.

Out-of-state:	6%	Live on campus:	32%

Transfer out. Colleges most students transferred to 2011: University of Texas at Tyler, Stephen F. Austin State University, Dallas Baptist University, East Texas Baptist University.

Basis for selection. Open admission. Interview recommended. **Home schooled:** Must take ACT, SAT, or THEA due to no Texas Assessment of Knowledge and Skills (TAKS) testing.

2011-2012 Annual costs. Tuition/fees: $6,920. Per-credit charge: $210. Room/board: $3,258. Books/supplies: $1,000. Personal expenses: $1,310.

Financial aid. Need-based: Need-based aid available for part-time students. Work-study available nights, weekends and for part-time students. **Non-need-based:** Scholarships awarded for academics, athletics, leadership, music/drama, religious affiliation, state residency.

Application procedures. Admission: Priority date 8/15; no deadline. $15 fee. Application must be submitted on paper. Admission notification on a rolling basis beginning on or about 1/15. **Financial aid:** Priority date 8/1; no closing date. FAFSA, institutional form required. Applicants notified on a rolling basis.

Academics. Special study options: Dual enrollment of high school students. **Credit/placement by examination:** AP, CLEP, institutional tests. **Support services:** Reduced course load, remedial instruction, tutoring, writing center.

Majors. Liberal arts: Arts/sciences.

Computing on campus. 45 workstations in dormitories, library, computer center. Dormitories wired for high-speed internet access and linked to campus network. Commuter students can connect to campus network. Wireless network available.

Student life. Freshman orientation: Available. Preregistration for classes offered. **Housing:** Single-sex dorms, apartments available. $80 deposit. **Activities:** Concert band, campus ministries, choral groups, drama, music ensembles, student government, student newspaper, ministerial alliance, mission band.

Athletics. NJCAA. **Intercollegiate:** Basketball. **Intramural:** Basketball, football (non-tackle), softball, table tennis, tennis, volleyball. **Team name:** Jaguars.

Student services. Chaplain/spiritual director, career counseling, financial aid counseling, health services, personal counseling. **Transfer:** Transfer adviser, college fairs on campus for students transferring to 4-year colleges.

Contact. E-mail: admissions@jacksonville-college.edu
Phone: (903) 586-2518 Toll-free number: (800) 256-8522
Fax: (903) 586-0743
Danny Morris, Director of Admissions, Jacksonville College, 105 B.J. Albritton Drive, Jacksonville, TX 75766-4759

Kilgore College
Kilgore, Texas
www.kilgore.edu   CB code: 6341

- Public 2-year community college
- Commuter campus in large town

General. Founded in 1935. Regionally accredited. **Enrollment:** 6,391 degree-seeking undergraduates. **Degrees:** 648 associate awarded. **Location:** 60 miles from Shreveport, Louisiana, 120 miles from Dallas. **Calendar:** Semester, extensive summer session. **Full-time faculty:** 161 total; 9% have terminal degrees, 6% minority, 52% women. **Part-time faculty:** 233 total; 3% have terminal degrees, 8% minority, 54% women. **Class size:** 48% < 20, 48% 20-39, 3% 40-49, 1% 50-99. **Special facilities:** East Texas oil museum, rangerette museum.

Student profile. Among degree-seeking undergraduates, 53% enrolled in a transfer program, 47% enrolled in a vocational program, 1% already have a bachelor's degree or higher, 1,279 enrolled as first-time, first-year students.

Part-time:	53%	Hispanic American:	11%
Out-of-state:	3%	Native American:	1%
Women:	63%	International:	1%
African American:	20%	25 or older:	33%
Asian American:	1%	Live on campus:	7%

Transfer out. 19% of students enrolled in the transfer program go on to 4-year colleges. **Colleges most students transferred to 2011:** University of Texas at Tyler, University of North Texas, Stephen F. Austin State University, Texas A&M University, University of Texas at Austin.

Basis for selection. Open admission, but selective for some programs. For health occupation programs and some public service programs, standardized test scores, secondary school record, essay used as admissions criteria.

2011-2012 Annual costs. Tuition/fees: $1,590; $3,420 out-of-district; $4,740 out-of-state. Per-credit charge: $27 in-district; $88 out-of-district; $132 out-of-state. Room/board: $4,270. Books/supplies: $1,680. Personal expenses: $1,200.

Financial aid. Need-based: Need-based aid available for part-time students. Work-study available nights, weekends and for part-time students. **Non-need-based:** Scholarships awarded for academics, alumni affiliation, art, athletics, job skills, leadership, music/drama, state residency. **Additional information:** State of Texas grants and loans available for honor graduates with unmet needs and for non-traditional students.

Application procedures. Admission: Priority date 8/15; no deadline. No application fee. Admission notification on a rolling basis. **Financial aid:** Priority date 6/1, closing date 7/15. FAFSA, institutional form required. Applicants notified on a rolling basis starting 3/1; must reply within 2 week(s) of notification.

Academics. Special study options: Cooperative education, distance learning, dual enrollment of high school students, ESL, internships. License preparation in nursing. **Credit/placement by examination:** AP, CLEP, institutional tests. 14 credit hours maximum toward associate degree. **Support services:** GED preparation and test center, learning center, pre-admission summer program, reduced course load, remedial instruction, study skills assistance, tutoring, writing center.

Majors. Biology: General. **Business:** General, accounting, business admin, e-commerce, executive assistant, management information systems, operations. **Communications:** Communications/speech/rhetoric, journalism. **Computer sciences:** General, programming, systems analysis. **Education:** General, art, biology, chemistry, health, health occupations, history, social science. **Engineering:** General, chemical, civil. **English:** English lit. **Foreign languages:** Spanish. **Health services:** Clinical lab technology, EMT paramedic, medical radiologic technology/radiation therapy, nursing (RN), physical therapy assistant, surgical technology. **History:** General. **Liberal arts:** Arts/sciences. **Math:** General. **Parks/recreation:** Health/fitness. **Physical sciences:** Chemistry, physics. **Protective services:** Criminal justice, law enforcement admin, police science. **Psychology:** General. **Social sciences:** Sociology. **Visual/performing arts:** Art, commercial photography, commercial/advertising art, dance, dramatic, music. **Work/family studies:** Child care management.

Most popular majors. Business/marketing 10%, education 8%, engineering/engineering technologies 8%, health sciences 33%, liberal arts 13%, visual/performing arts 6%.

Computing on campus. 350 workstations in library, computer center, student center. Dormitories wired for high-speed internet access and linked to campus network. Commuter students can connect to campus network. Online course registration, online library, helpline, wireless network available.

Student life. Freshman orientation: Mandatory, $40 fee. Preregistration for classes offered. **Housing:** Single-sex dorms available. $200 deposit, deadline 8/15. **Activities:** Bands, choral groups, dance, drama, music ensembles, musical theater, radio station, student government, student newspaper, TV station, church organizations, rodeo club, physical therapy club.

Athletics. NJCAA. **Intercollegiate:** Basketball, football (tackle) M. **Intramural:** Badminton, bowling, handball, racquetball, softball, swimming, tennis, volleyball. **Team name:** Rangers.

Student services. Career counseling, student employment services, financial aid counseling, health services, on-campus daycare, personal counseling, placement for graduates, veterans' counselor. **Physically disabled:** Services for visually, speech, hearing impaired. **Transfer:** Pre-admission transcript evaluation for new students. College fairs on campus for students transferring to 4-year colleges.

Contact. Phone: (903) 983-8209 Fax: (903) 983-8607
Eloise Ashley, Associate Director of Admissions and Recruitment, Kilgore College, 1100 Broadway, Kilgore, TX 75662-3299

Lamar Institute of Technology
Beaumont, Texas
www.lit.edu
CB code: 4239

- Public 2-year technical college
- Commuter campus in small city

General. Enrollment: 2,670 degree-seeking undergraduates. **Degrees:** 410 associate awarded. **Location:** 80 miles from Houston. **Calendar:** Semester, limited summer session. **Full-time faculty:** 68 total. **Part-time faculty:** 94 total. **Class size:** 63% < 20, 35% 20-39, 1% 40-49, less than 1% 50-99. **Special facilities:** Stand-alone Process Distillation Unit for petro-chemical majors.

Student profile.

Out-of-state:	2%	Live on campus:	3%
25 or older:	35%		

Basis for selection. Open admission, but selective for some programs. Special requirements for various allied health programs (dental hygiene, sonography, health information technology, radiology, respiratory care).

2011-2012 Annual costs. Tuition/fees: $4,251; $13,641 out-of-state. Per-credit charge: $94 in-state; $407 out-of-state.

Financial aid. Need-based: Work-study available nights, weekends and for part-time students.

Application procedures. Admission: No deadline. No application fee. Admission notification on a rolling basis. **Financial aid:** Priority date 4/1; no closing date.

Academics. Credit/placement by examination: AP, CLEP, IB, SAT, ACT, institutional tests.

Majors. Business: Accounting technology, administrative services, business admin, real estate. **Computer sciences:** General. **Health services:** Dental hygiene, EMT paramedic, medical radiologic technology/radiation therapy, medical records technology, respiratory therapy technology, sonography. **Human services:** General. **Protective services:** Fire safety technology, forensics. **Social sciences:** GIS/cartography. **Work/family studies:** Child care service.

Most popular majors. Business/marketing 17%, computer/information sciences 6%, engineering/engineering technologies 26%, health sciences 26%, science technologies 13%.

Computing on campus. 150 workstations in library, computer center. Dormitories wired for high-speed internet access and linked to campus network. Online course registration, online library, wireless network available.

Student life. Freshman orientation: Available. Preregistration for classes offered. **Housing:** Single-sex dorms, wellness housing available. Access to dormitories located on Lamar University campus.

Student services. Alcohol/substance abuse counseling, career counseling, services for economically disadvantaged, student employment services, financial aid counseling, health services, placement for graduates, veterans' counselor. **Physically disabled:** Services for visually, hearing impaired.

Contact. Phone: (409) 880-8321 Toll-free number: (800) 950-6989 Fax: (409) 880-1711
Vivian Jefferson, Dean of Student Services, Lamar Institute of Technology, PO Box 10043, Beaumont, TX 77705

Lamar State College at Orange
Orange, Texas
www.lsco.edu
CB code: 1694

- Public 2-year junior and liberal arts college
- Commuter campus in small city

General. Regionally accredited. **Enrollment:** 2,204 degree-seeking undergraduates; 556 non-degree-seeking students. **Degrees:** 179 associate awarded. **Location:** 92 miles from Houston. **Calendar:** Semester, limited summer session. **Full-time faculty:** 49 total. **Part-time faculty:** 66 total. **Partnerships:** Formal partnership with CISCO.

Student profile. Among degree-seeking undergraduates, 30% enrolled in a transfer program, 70% enrolled in a vocational program, 1% already have a bachelor's degree or higher, 444 enrolled as first-time, first-year students.

Part-time:	48%	Asian American:	1%
Out-of-state:	9%	Hispanic American:	5%
Women:	75%	25 or older:	35%
African American:	22%		

Basis for selection. Open admission, but selective for some programs. Nursing program competitive; high school record and test scores may be evaluated for admission. Interview required for students without high school diploma or GED, to determine if applicant can benefit from available educational programs.

High school preparation. 12 units recommended. Recommended units include English 4, mathematics 3, history 2 and science 3.

2011-2012 Annual costs. Tuition/fees: $3,865; $13,255 out-of-state. Per-credit charge: $94 in-state; $407 out-of-state. Books/supplies: $650. Personal expenses: $1,592.

Financial aid. All financial aid based on need. Need-based aid available for part-time students. Work-study available nights, weekends and for part-time students.

Application procedures. Admission: No deadline. No application fee. Admission notification on a rolling basis. **Financial aid:** Priority date 4/1; no closing date. FAFSA, institutional form required. Applicants notified on a rolling basis starting 5/15; must reply within 2 week(s) of notification.

Academics. Special study options: Distance learning, dual enrollment of high school students, internships, liberal arts/career combination, teacher certification program. License preparation in nursing, paramedic. **Credit/placement by examination:** AP, CLEP. 15 credit hours maximum toward associate degree. **Support services:** GED test center, learning center, remedial instruction, study skills assistance, tutoring.

Majors. Biology: General. **Business:** General, accounting technology, administrative services, business admin. **Computer sciences:** General, data processing, programming. **Education:** General. **English:** Rhetoric/composition, writing. **Health services:** Clinical lab technology, EMT paramedic, medical secretary, nursing (RN). **Liberal arts:** Arts/sciences. **Math:** General. **Protective services:** Corrections, criminal justice. **Psychology:** General. **Social sciences:** Sociology.

Computing on campus. 150 workstations in library, computer center, student center. Commuter students can connect to campus network. Online library, helpline, wireless network available.

Student life. Freshman orientation: Available. Preregistration for classes offered. **Activities:** Student government.

Athletics. Intramural: Basketball, racquetball, volleyball.

Student services. Career counseling, financial aid counseling, placement for graduates, veterans' counselor. **Physically disabled:** Services for visually, hearing impaired.

Contact. Phone: (409) 882-3364 Fax: (409) 882-3055
Kerry Olson, Director of Admissions and Financial Aid, Lamar State College at Orange, 410 Front Street, Orange, TX 77630

Lamar State College at Port Arthur
Port Arthur, Texas
www.lamarpa.edu   **CB code: 6589**

- Public 2-year community and technical college
- Commuter campus in small city

General. Regionally accredited. **Enrollment:** 2,534 degree-seeking undergraduates. **Degrees:** 178 associate awarded. **Location:** 90 miles from Houston. **Calendar:** Semester, limited summer session. **Full-time faculty:** 60 total. **Part-time faculty:** 55 total. **Partnerships:** Formal partnerships with Microsoft and Novell (authorized training center).

Student profile. Among degree-seeking undergraduates, 8% enrolled in a transfer program, 37% enrolled in a vocational program, 2% already have a bachelor's degree or higher.

Transfer out. Colleges most students transferred to 2011: Lamar University, Texas A&M University.

Basis for selection. Open admission. **Adult students:** SAT/ACT scores not required. **Home schooled:** Transcript of courses and grades required.

2011-2012 Annual costs. Tuition/fees: $4,414; $13,714 out-of-state. Per-credit charge: $94 in-state; $404 out-of-state. Books/supplies: $1,379. Personal expenses: $2,457.

Financial aid. All financial aid based on need. Need-based aid available for part-time students. Work-study available nights, weekends and for part-time students.

Application procedures. Admission: No deadline. No application fee. Admission notification on a rolling basis beginning on or about 2/1. **Financial aid:** Priority date 4/1; no closing date. FAFSA, institutional form required. Applicants notified on a rolling basis starting 4/15; must reply within 2 week(s) of notification.

Academics. Special study options: Distance learning, double major, dual enrollment of high school students, internships, liberal arts/career combination. License preparation in nursing. **Credit/placement by examination:** AP, CLEP. SAT used for math placement if submitted. **Support services:** Learning center, pre-admission summer program, reduced course load, remedial instruction, study skills assistance, tutoring.

Majors. Business: Accounting, administrative services, business admin. **Computer sciences:** General. **Health services:** Medical secretary, nursing (RN), substance abuse counseling, surgical technology. **Protective services:** Criminal justice. **Visual/performing arts:** Music. **Work/family studies:** General, child care management.

Most popular majors. Business/marketing 17%, health sciences 36%, liberal arts 22%, visual/performing arts 9%.

Computing on campus. 50 workstations in library. Commuter students can connect to campus network. Online course registration, online library, wireless network available.

Student life. Freshman orientation: Available. Preregistration for classes offered. Held 1 day in July and 1 in August. **Activities:** Choral groups, drama, music ensembles, musical theater, student government, diversity club, Phi Theta Kappa, criminal justice association, Gamma Phi Gamma, professional cosmetologist association, speech and debate club, tech club, Chi Alpha, allied health sciences society.

Athletics. NJCAA. **Intercollegiate:** Basketball M, softball W. **Team name:** Seahawks.

Student services. Career counseling, services for economically disadvantaged, student employment services, financial aid counseling, personal counseling, placement for graduates, veterans' counselor. **Physically disabled:** Services for visually, speech, hearing impaired. **Transfer:** Pre-admission transcript evaluation for new students. College fairs on campus for students transferring to 4-year colleges.

Contact. E-mail: Nichoca@lamarpa.edu
Phone: (409) 984-6168 Toll-free number: (800) 477-5872 ext. 6168
Fax: (409) 984-6025
Connie Nicholas, Registrar, Lamar State College at Port Arthur, Box 310, Port Arthur, TX 77641-0310

Laredo Community College
Laredo, Texas   **CB member**
www.laredo.edu   **CB code: 6362**

- Public 2-year community college
- Commuter campus in large city

General. Founded in 1946. Regionally accredited. Two-campus institution. **Enrollment:** 8,875 degree-seeking undergraduates. **Degrees:** 742 associate awarded. **ROTC:** Army. **Location:** 150 miles from San Antonio, 140 miles from Corpus Christi. **Calendar:** Semester, extensive summer session. **Full-time faculty:** 197 total. **Part-time faculty:** 122 total. **Special facilities:** Environmental science center, special collections relating to regional history.

Student profile.

Out-of-state:	8%	Live on campus:	2%
25 or older:	30%		

Transfer out. Colleges most students transferred to 2011: Texas A&M International University, University of Texas at San Antonio.

Basis for selection. Open admission, but selective for some programs. Special requirements for nursing and allied health programs.

2011-2012 Annual costs. Tuition/fees: $2,706; $3,966 out-of-district; $5,286 out-of-state. Books/supplies: $1,250. Personal expenses: $1,288.

Financial aid. Need-based: Work-study available nights, weekends and for part-time students.

Application procedures. Admission: No deadline. No application fee. Admission notification on a rolling basis. **Financial aid:** Priority date 5/1; no closing date. FAFSA, institutional form required. Applicants notified on a rolling basis.

Academics. Mandatory assessment program provides effective educational services for students. **Special study options:** Accelerated study, cooperative education, cross-registration, distance learning, dual enrollment of high school students, ESL, exchange student, honors, liberal arts/career combination, teacher certification program, weekend college. License preparation in nursing, occupational therapy, paramedic, physical therapy, radiology, real estate. **Credit/placement by examination:** AP, CLEP, institutional tests. 30 credit hours maximum toward associate degree. **Support services:** GED preparation and test center, learning center, remedial instruction, tutoring.

Majors. Biology: General, bacteriology, botany, marine. **Business:** General, accounting, administrative services, fashion, finance, marketing, office management, office technology, office/clerical, real estate, sales/distribution. **Communications:** Broadcast journalism, communications/speech/rhetoric. **Computer sciences:** General, computer science, information systems, programming. **Education:** General, agricultural, art, bilingual, biology, business, chemistry, computer, early childhood, elementary, English, family/consumer sciences, foreign languages, health, history, mathematics, music, physical, physics, reading, Spanish, special ed, speech. **Engineering:** General, agricultural, architectural, electrical, petroleum. **English:** English lit. **Foreign languages:** General, Spanish. **Health services:** Clinical lab technology, EMT paramedic, medical assistant, medical radiologic technology/radiation therapy, medical secretary, mental health services, nursing (RN), occupational health, occupational therapy assistant, physical therapy assistant, predental, premedicine, prepharmacy, preveterinary. **History:** General. **Human services:** Social work. **Liberal arts:** Arts/sciences. **Math:** General. **Philosophy/religion:** Philosophy. **Physical sciences:** Chemistry, geology, physics. **Protective services:** Criminal justice, fire safety technology. **Psychology:** General. **Social sciences:** General, economics, political science, sociology. **Visual/performing arts:** Art, dramatic, music. **Work/family studies:** General, child care management.

Computing on campus. 514 workstations in library, computer center. Dormitories wired for high-speed internet access. Online course registration, online library, repair service available.

Student life. Freshman orientation: Available. Preregistration for classes offered. **Housing:** Coed dorms available. $100 fully refundable deposit. **Activities:** Bands, choral groups, dance, drama, literary magazine, music ensembles, musical theater, opera, student government, student newspaper, symphony orchestra, TV station.

Athletics. NJCAA. **Intercollegiate:** Baseball M, tennis, volleyball W. **Intramural:** Baseball M, basketball, bowling, football (tackle) M, golf, handball, racquetball, softball, tennis, volleyball. **Team name:** Palominos.

Student services. Alcohol/substance abuse counseling, chaplain/spiritual director, career counseling, services for economically disadvantaged, student employment services, financial aid counseling, health services, on-campus daycare, personal counseling, placement for graduates, veterans' counselor. **Physically disabled:** Services for visually, speech, hearing impaired. **Transfer:** Transfer adviser, college fairs on campus for students transferring to 4-year colleges.

Contact. E-mail: admissions@laredo.edu
Phone: (956) 721-5117 Fax: (956) 721-5493
Felix Gamez, Director of Admissions and Records, Laredo Community College, West End Washington Street, Laredo, TX 78040-4395

Le Cordon Bleu College of Culinary Arts: Austin
Austin, Texas
www.chefs.edu/austin   CB code: 4188

▸ For-profit 2-year culinary school
▸ Very large city

General. Regionally accredited. **Calendar:** Semester.

Annual costs/financial aid. Cost of associate degree program in Culinary Arts, $38,625; certificate program in Culinary Arts, $17,200; certificate in Patisserie and Baking, $17,200. Books/supplies: $3,355.

Contact. Phone: (512) 837-2665
Director of Admissions, 3110 Esperanza Crossing, Suite 100, Austin, TX 78758-3641

Lee College
Baytown, Texas   CB member
www.lee.edu   CB code: 6363

▸ Public 2-year community college
▸ Commuter campus in small city

General. Founded in 1934. Regionally accredited. **Enrollment:** 5,515 degree-seeking undergraduates. **Degrees:** 729 associate awarded. **Location:** 25 miles from Houston. **Calendar:** Semester, limited summer session. **Full-time faculty:** 161 total. **Part-time faculty:** 198 total.

Basis for selection. Open admission, but selective for some programs. Observes TASP guidelines. Special requirements for allied health programs.

2011-2012 Annual costs. Tuition/fees: $1,812; $2,712 out-of-district; $4,362 out-of-state. Per-credit charge: $42 in-district; $72 out-of-district; $127 out-of-state. Books/supplies: $1,200. Personal expenses: $1,354.

Financial aid. Need-based: Need-based aid available for part-time students. Work-study available nights, weekends and for part-time students. **Non-need-based:** Scholarships awarded for academics, art, athletics, job skills, music/drama.

Application procedures. Admission: No deadline. No application fee. Admission notification on a rolling basis. **Financial aid:** Priority date 4/1; no closing date. FAFSA required. Applicants notified on a rolling basis starting 6/1.

Academics. Special study options: Cooperative education, distance learning, dual enrollment of high school students, ESL, honors, independent study, internships, weekend college. **Credit/placement by examination:** AP, CLEP, institutional tests. 30 credit hours maximum toward associate degree. **Support services:** GED preparation and test center, learning center, remedial instruction, tutoring.

Majors. Business: Accounting, administrative services, business admin, office/clerical. **Communications technology:** Graphic/printing. **Computer sciences:** General, data processing, information systems, programming. **English:** English lit, technical writing. **Foreign languages:** General. **Health services:** EMT paramedic, medical records technology, substance abuse counseling. **Liberal arts:** Arts/sciences. **Math:** General. **Parks/recreation:** Health/fitness. **Physical sciences:** General. **Protective services:** Police science. **Visual/performing arts:** Dramatic, music.

Computing on campus. 500 workstations in library, computer center, student center. Online course registration, online library, helpline, wireless network available.

Student life. Freshman orientation: Available. Preregistration for classes offered. **Activities:** Bands, choral groups, drama, literary magazine, music ensembles, student government, Baptist student union, awareness club, Phi Theta Kappa, nursing students association, environmental science club, cosmetology club, digital information society, student honors council.

Athletics. NJCAA. **Intercollegiate:** Basketball M, tennis W, volleyball W. **Intramural:** Basketball, bowling, football (non-tackle), softball, table tennis, volleyball. **Team name:** Rebels.

Student services. Adult student services, career counseling, student employment services, financial aid counseling, personal counseling, placement for graduates, veterans' counselor. **Physically disabled:** Services for hearing impaired. **Transfer:** Transfer adviser for students transferring to 4-year colleges.

Contact. E-mail: admissions@lee.edu
Phone: (281) 425-6393 Fax: (281) 425-6831
Becki Griffith, Registrar, Lee College, Box 818, Baytown, TX 77522

Lincoln College of Technology: Grand Prairie
Grand Prairie, Texas
www.lincolntech.com   CB code: 3059

▸ For-profit 2-year technical college
▸ Large city

General. Regionally accredited; also accredited by ACCSC. **Degrees:** 23 associate awarded. **Calendar:** Semester. **Full-time faculty:** 72 total. **Part-time faculty:** 10 total.

Basis for selection. Open admission.

2011-2012 Annual costs. Total program costs range from $19,018 up to $31,929 depending on program. Cost of books and materials included in tuition.

Financial aid. Need-based: Work-study available nights, weekends and for part-time students.

Application procedures. Admission: No deadline. $100 fee.

Academics. Credit/placement by examination: AP, CLEP.

Contact. Toll-free number: (877) 533-2598
Joe Hernandez, Director of Admissions, Lincoln College of Technology: Grand Prairie, 2915 Alouette Drive, Grand Prairie, TX 75052

Lon Morris College
Jacksonville, Texas
www.lonmorris.edu

CB code: 6369

- Private 2-year junior and liberal arts college affiliated with United Methodist Church
- Residential campus in large town
- SAT or ACT (ACT writing optional) required

General. Founded in 1873. Regionally accredited. Over 30 majors in three divisions of studies. Our mission is to offer a strong liberal arts education within a Christian community. **Enrollment:** 552 degree-seeking undergraduates. **Degrees:** 87 associate awarded. **ROTC:** Army, Naval, Air Force. **Location:** 100 miles from Dallas, 25 miles from Tyler. **Calendar:** Semester, limited summer session. **Full-time faculty:** 54 total. **Part-time faculty:** 37 total. **Class size:** 39% < 20, 58% 20-39, 3% 40-49.

Student profile.

Out-of-state:	32%	**Live on campus:**	90%

Transfer out. Colleges most students transferred to 2011: Stephen F. Austin State University, University of Texas at Tyler, Sam Houston State University.

Basis for selection. School achievement record, minimum GPA of 2.0, recommendation, ACT/SAT scores important. Audition required for choral, drama; interview recommended for academically weak; portfolio recommended for art. **Home schooled:** Transcript of courses and grades required. **Learning Disabled:** Students with learning disabilities exempt from SAT/ACT requirements.

High school preparation. College-preparatory program recommended. 9 units recommended. Recommended units include English 4, social studies 2, science 2 and foreign language 1.

2011-2012 Annual costs. Tuition/fees: $15,000. Room/board: $6,830. Books/supplies: $617. Personal expenses: $2,295.

Financial aid. All financial aid based on need. Need-based aid available for part-time students. Work-study available nights, weekends and for part-time students.

Application procedures. Admission: No deadline. $35 fee, may be waived for applicants with need. Admission notification on a rolling basis. **Financial aid:** Priority date 5/1; no closing date. FAFSA, institutional form required. Applicants notified on a rolling basis starting 2/15; must reply within 2 week(s) of notification.

Academics. Special study options: Distance learning, dual enrollment of high school students, ESL, independent study, study abroad. **Credit/placement by examination:** AP, CLEP, IB, SAT, ACT, institutional tests. 30 credit hours maximum toward associate degree. **Support services:** Learning center, pre-admission summer program, reduced course load, remedial instruction, study skills assistance, tutoring, writing center.

Majors. Biology: General. **Business:** General, accounting. **Computer sciences:** Computer science. **Education:** General. **English:** English lit, rhetoric/composition. **Foreign languages:** Spanish. **Health services:** Predental, premedicine, prenursing, prepharmacy, preveterinary. **History:** General. **Liberal arts:** Arts/sciences. **Math:** General. **Philosophy/religion:** Philosophy, religion. **Physical sciences:** Astronomy, chemistry, physics. **Protective services:** Criminal justice. **Psychology:** General. **Social sciences:** General, economics, political science, sociology. **Visual/performing arts:** General, art, art history/conservation, dramatic, music, music history, music performance, music theory/composition, piano/keyboard, studio arts, theater design, voice/opera.

Computing on campus. 50 workstations in library, computer center. Dormitories wired for high-speed internet access and linked to campus network. Commuter students can connect to campus network. Online course registration, online library, wireless network available.

Student life. Freshman orientation: Mandatory. Preregistration for classes offered. Held the week before classes begin. **Housing:** Single-sex dorms, wellness housing available. $100 partly refundable deposit. **Activities:** Bands, choral groups, dance, drama, international student organizations, literary magazine, music ensembles, musical theater, student government, ecology club, poetry and literary group, midnight club, Christian service organization, Disciples on Campus, Christian worship group, LMC Chamber, student activity association.

Athletics. NJCAA. **Intercollegiate:** Baseball M, basketball, cheerleading, cross-country, football (tackle) M, golf M, soccer, softball W. **Intramural:** Baseball M, basketball, football (non-tackle), soccer, softball, swimming, table tennis, tennis, volleyball. **Team name:** Bearcats.

Student services. Chaplain/spiritual director, career counseling, student employment services, financial aid counseling, health services, personal counseling. **Physically disabled:** Services for visually, speech, hearing impaired. **Transfer:** Pre-admission transcript evaluation for new students. Transfer adviser, college fairs on campus for students transferring to 4-year colleges.

Contact. E-mail: kmarquis@lonmorris.edu
Phone: (903) 589-4005 Toll-free number: (800) 259-5753
Fax: (903) 589-4006
Kris Marquis, Director of Admissions/Student Financial Aid, Lon Morris College, 800 College Avenue, Jacksonville, TX 75766

Lone Star College System
The Woodlands, Texas
www.lonestar.edu/

CB member
CB code: 6508

- Public 2-year community college
- Commuter campus in very large city

General. Founded in 1972. Regionally accredited. Includes 6 colleges: LSC-CyFair, LSC-Kingwood, LSC-North Harris, LSC-Montgomery, LSC-Tomball, LSC-University Park. **Enrollment:** 75,680 degree-seeking undergraduates. **Degrees:** 3,249 associate awarded. **ROTC:** Army, Air Force. **Location:** 40 miles from Houston. **Calendar:** Semester, extensive summer session. **Full-time faculty:** 808 total; 20% have terminal degrees, 21% minority, 58% women. **Part-time faculty:** 2,863 total; 30% minority, 57% women. **Class size:** 28% < 20, 70% 20-39, less than 1% 40-49, 1% 50-99, less than 1% >100.

Student profile. Among degree-seeking undergraduates, 13,684 enrolled as first-time, first-year students.

Part-time:	66%	**25 or older:**	38%
Women:	61%		

Transfer out. Colleges most students transferred to 2011: University of Houston, Sam Houston State University, Texas A&M-College Station, University of Texas-Austin, University of Houston-Downtown.

Basis for selection. Open admission, but selective for some programs. Placement testing required in reading, writing, and math. Special requirements for nursing, respiratory therapy, occupational therapy, physical therapist assistant program, veterinary technician, diagnostic medical imagery, cosmetology.

2011-2012 Annual costs. Tuition/fees: $1,744; $3,844 out-of-district; $4,294 out-of-state. Per-credit charge: $40 in-district; $110 out-of-district; $125 out-of-state. Books/supplies: $600. Personal expenses: $1,692.

2011-2012 Financial aid. Need-based: 4,290 full-time freshmen applied for aid; 3,878 were judged to have need; 3,518 of these received aid. Average need met was 72%. Average scholarship/grant was $4,832; average loan $3,290. 74% of total undergraduate aid awarded as scholarships/grants, 26% as loans/jobs. Need-based aid available for part-time students. Work-study available nights, weekends and for part-time students. **Non-need-based:** Awarded to 513 full-time undergraduates, including 177 freshmen. Scholarships awarded for academics.

Application procedures. Admission: No deadline. No application fee. Admission notification on a rolling basis. **Financial aid:** Priority date 5/10; no closing date. FAFSA required. Applicants notified on a rolling basis starting 4/1.

Academics. Special study options: Cooperative education, cross-registration, distance learning, dual enrollment of high school students, ESL, external degree, honors, independent study, internships, study abroad, teacher

certification program, weekend college. Bachelor's degree programs available on campus. License preparation in dental hygiene, nursing, occupational therapy, paramedic, physical therapy, radiology, real estate. **Credit/placement by examination:** AP, CLEP, IB, institutional tests. 42 credit hours maximum toward associate degree. **Support services:** GED preparation and test center, learning center, pre-admission summer program, reduced course load, remedial instruction, study skills assistance, tutoring, writing center.

Majors. Architecture: Technology. **Business:** Accounting, administrative services, business admin, hospitality admin. **Computer sciences:** General. **Education:** Educational technology, kindergarten/preschool, middle. **Foreign languages:** Sign language interpretation. **Health services:** Dental hygiene, EMT paramedic, medical radiologic technology/radiation therapy, medical records technology, medical secretary, nursing (RN), occupational therapy assistant, pharmacy assistant, physical therapy assistant, respiratory therapy technology, sonography, substance abuse counseling, veterinary technology/assistant. **Liberal arts:** Arts/sciences. **Protective services:** Firefighting. **Social sciences:** GIS/cartography. **Visual/performing arts:** Interior design, music. **Work/family studies:** Child care management.

Most popular majors. Business/marketing 6%, health sciences 14%, liberal arts 52%, trade and industry 9%.

Computing on campus. 500 workstations in library, computer center, student center. Commuter students can connect to campus network. Online course registration, online library, helpline, wireless network available.

Student life. Freshman orientation: Available. Preregistration for classes offered. Available on campus and online. **Activities:** Bands, campus ministries, choral groups, dance, drama, international student organizations, literary magazine, music ensembles, Model UN, opera, student government, student newspaper, symphony orchestra, TV station, Phi Theta Kappa, honors student association, student nurses association, African American society, Latin American student association, Asian student association, Campus Crusade for Christ, Muslim student organization, Show of Hands (deaf students).

Athletics. Intercollegiate: Baseball M. **Intramural:** Badminton, basketball, bowling, football (non-tackle), golf, racquetball, soccer, softball, table tennis, tennis, volleyball.

Student services. Adult student services, career counseling, services for economically disadvantaged, student employment services, financial aid counseling, minority student services, on-campus daycare, personal counseling, placement for graduates, veterans' counselor. **Physically disabled:** Services for visually, speech, hearing impaired. **Transfer:** Transfer adviser, college fairs on campus for students transferring to 4-year colleges.

Contact. Phone: (832) 813-6500
Connie Garrick, Director of Records and Reporting, Lone Star College System, 5000 Research Forest Drive, The Woodlands, TX 77381-4356

McLennan Community College
Waco, Texas   **CB member**
www.mclennan.edu   **CB code: 6429**

▶ Public 2-year community and junior college
▶ Commuter campus in small city

General. Founded in 1965. Regionally accredited. **Enrollment:** 4,634 full-time, degree-seeking students. **Degrees:** 325 associate awarded. **ROTC:** Air Force. **Location:** 100 miles from Dallas and Austin. **Calendar:** Semester, extensive summer session. **Full-time faculty:** 191 total; 19% have terminal degrees, 60% women. **Part-time faculty:** 326 total; 13% have terminal degrees, 57% women. **Class size:** 43% < 20, 51% 20-39, 4% 40-49, 2% 50-99, less than 1% >100.

Student profile. Among full-time, degree-seeking students, 5,588 transferred in from other institutions.

African American:	18%	Hispanic American:	21%
Asian American:	1%	Native American:	1%

Basis for selection. Open admission, but selective for some programs. Observes TASP guidelines in testing for placement. Admission to health careers programs is competitive. **Adult students:** SAT/ACT scores not required.

High school preparation. College-preparatory program recommended.

2011-2012 Annual costs. Tuition/fees: $3,210; $3,690 out-of-district; $5,400 out-of-state. Per-credit charge: $98 in-district; $114 out-of-district; $171 out-of-state. Books/supplies: $1,149. Personal expenses: $1,962.

2011-2012 Financial aid. Need-based: Need-based aid available for part-time students. Work-study available nights, weekends and for part-time students. **Non-need-based:** Scholarships awarded for athletics.

Application procedures. Admission: No deadline. No application fee. Admission notification on a rolling basis. **Financial aid:** Priority date 6/1; no closing date. FAFSA required. Applicants notified on a rolling basis starting 5/1.

Academics. Special study options: Distance learning, dual enrollment of high school students, honors, internships, study abroad, teacher certification program. Bachelor's degree programs available on campus. License preparation in nursing, paramedic, physical therapy, radiology, real estate. **Credit/placement by examination:** AP, CLEP, institutional tests. 24 credit hours maximum toward associate degree. **Support services:** Learning center, reduced course load, remedial instruction, tutoring, writing center.

Majors. Business: General, accounting, office technology, real estate. **Communications:** Communications/speech/rhetoric. **Computer sciences:** General, data processing, programming. **Foreign languages:** Sign language interpretation. **Health services:** Clinical lab technology, EMT paramedic, medical radiologic technology/radiation therapy, medical records technology, medical secretary, mental health services, respiratory therapy technology, substance abuse counseling. **Protective services:** Law enforcement admin. **Work/family studies:** Child care management.

Computing on campus. 900 workstations in library, computer center, student center. Commuter students can connect to campus network. Online library, helpline, wireless network available.

Student life. Freshman orientation: Mandatory. Preregistration for classes offered. **Activities:** Concert band, campus ministries, choral groups, dance, drama, international student organizations, literary magazine, music ensembles, musical theater, student government.

Athletics. NJCAA. **Intercollegiate:** Baseball M, basketball, golf M, softball W. **Team name:** Highlanders/Highlassies.

Student services. Adult student services, career counseling, student employment services, financial aid counseling, health services, on-campus daycare, personal counseling, placement for graduates, veterans' counselor. **Physically disabled:** Services for visually, hearing impaired. **Transfer:** Transfer adviser, college fairs on campus for students transferring to 4-year colleges.

Contact. Phone: (254) 299-8628 Fax: (254) 299-8694
Karen Clark, Director of Admissions, McLennan Community College, 1400 College Drive, Waco, TX 76708

Midland College
Midland, Texas
www.midland.edu   **CB code: 6459**

▶ Public 2-year community college
▶ Commuter campus in small city

General. Founded in 1969. Regionally accredited. **Enrollment:** 3,932 degree-seeking undergraduates; 2,415 non-degree-seeking students. **Degrees:** 13 bachelor's, 380 associate awarded. **Location:** 300 miles from El Paso, 300 miles from Dallas. **Calendar:** Semester, extensive summer session. **Full-time faculty:** 139 total; 19% have terminal degrees, 14% minority, 49% women. **Part-time faculty:** 198 total; 8% minority, 58% women. **Class size:** 29% < 20, 71% 20-39.

Student profile. Among degree-seeking undergraduates, 847 enrolled as first-time, first-year students.

Part-time:	59%	Asian American:	1%
Out-of-state:	1%	Hispanic American:	33%
Women:	60%	25 or older:	60%
African American:	5%	Live on campus:	2%

Transfer out. Colleges most students transferred to 2011: University of Texas of the Permian Basin, Texas A&M University, Angelo State University, West Texas A&M University, Texas Tech University.

Basis for selection. Open admission, but selective for some programs. Observes TASP requirements. Special requirements for allied health science programs.

2011-2012 Annual costs. Tuition/fees: $2,160; $3,180 out-of-district; $4,350 out-of-state. Room/board: $4,340. Books/supplies: $1,059. Personal expenses: $1,816.

Financial aid. Need-based: Need-based aid available for part-time students. Work-study available nights, weekends and for part-time students. **Non-need-based:** Scholarships awarded for academics, athletics, minority status, music/drama, state residency.

Application procedures. Admission: Priority date 9/1; no deadline. No application fee. Admission notification on a rolling basis. **Financial aid:** Priority date 4/2, closing date 6/1. FAFSA required. Applicants notified on a rolling basis starting 5/15; must reply within 2 week(s) of notification.

Academics. Special study options: Cooperative education, cross-registration, distance learning, dual enrollment of high school students, ESL, honors, internships, liberal arts/career combination, Washington semester. Bachelor's degree programs available on campus. License preparation in aviation, nursing, paramedic, radiology, real estate. **Credit/placement by examination:** AP, CLEP, IB, institutional tests. 12 credit hours maximum toward associate degree. **Support services:** GED preparation and test center, learning center, reduced course load, remedial instruction, study skills assistance, tutoring, writing center.

Majors. Biology: General. **Business:** General, accounting, administrative services, business admin, entrepreneurial studies, management information systems, management science, managerial economics, office technology, office/clerical. **Communications:** Communications/speech/rhetoric, journalism. **Communications technology:** Graphic/printing. **Computer sciences:** General, computer graphics, data processing, information systems, programming. **Conservation:** Environmental science. **Education:** Physical, teacher assistance. **Engineering:** Petroleum. **Foreign languages:** General, French, Spanish. **Health services:** EMT ambulance attendant, EMT paramedic, medical radiologic technology/radiation therapy, medical records technology, nursing (RN), premedicine, prepharmacy, substance abuse counseling, veterinary technology/assistant. **History:** General. **Human services:** Social work. **Math:** General. **Parks/recreation:** Exercise sciences. **Protective services:** Fire safety technology, firefighting, law enforcement admin, police science. **Social sciences:** General. **Visual/performing arts:** Art, dramatic, music, music performance. **Work/family studies:** Child care management.

Most popular majors. Business/marketing 13%, health sciences 29%, liberal arts 29%, trade and industry 7%.

Computing on campus. 274 workstations in library, computer center, student center. Dormitories wired for high-speed internet access and linked to campus network. Online course registration, repair service, wireless network available.

Student life. Freshman orientation: Available. Preregistration for classes offered. 3-hour session held 5 times throughout year. **Housing:** Coed dorms, single-sex dorms, apartments available. $100 deposit, deadline 7/1. **Activities:** Bands, choral groups, drama, literary magazine, music ensembles, student government, student newspaper, several religious groups, ethnic and service clubs, clubs related to majors.

Athletics. NJCAA. **Intercollegiate:** Basketball, golf M, softball W. **Intramural:** Basketball, bowling, football (non-tackle), soccer M, table tennis, tennis, volleyball. **Team name:** Chaparrals.

Student services. Career counseling, student employment services, on-campus daycare, personal counseling, placement for graduates, veterans' counselor. **Physically disabled:** Services for visually, speech, hearing impaired. **Transfer:** Transfer center, transfer adviser, college fairs on campus for students transferring to 4-year colleges.

Contact. E-mail: jmartinez@midland.edu
Phone: (432) 685-4502 Fax: (432) 685-4623
Jeremy Martinez, Admissions Director, Midland College, 3600 North Garfield, Midland, TX 79705

Mountain View College
Dallas, Texas
www.mvc.dcccd.edu
CB code: 6438

- Public 2-year community college
- Commuter campus in very large city

General. Founded in 1970. Regionally accredited. College campus designated as Urban Wildlife Sanctuary by the Humane Society of the United States. **Enrollment:** 7,043 degree-seeking undergraduates. **Degrees:** 584 associate awarded. **Location:** 8 miles from downtown Dallas. **Calendar:** Semester, extensive summer session. **Full-time faculty:** 77 total. **Part-time faculty:** 274 total. **Partnerships:** Formal partnerships with many local businesses and local offices of national/international corporations.

Student profile.

Out-of-state:	1%	25 or older:	38%

Transfer out. Colleges most students transferred to 2011: University of Texas at Arlington, University of North Texas, Texas A&M University.

Basis for selection. Open admission. Observes state of Texas TSI guidelines. High school students accepted if principal recommends enrollment. **Home schooled:** Transcript of courses and grades required.

2011-2012 Annual costs. Tuition/fees: $1,350; $2,490 out-of-district; $3,960 out-of-state. Per-credit charge: $45 in-district; $83 out-of-district; $132 out-of-state. For out-of-state students, $200 minimum charge for 1 semester hour. Books/supplies: $1,200. Personal expenses: $1,664.

Financial aid. Need-based: Need-based aid available for part-time students. Work-study available nights, weekends and for part-time students.

Application procedures. Admission: No deadline. No application fee. Admission notification on a rolling basis. **Financial aid:** Priority date 5/1; no closing date. FAFSA, institutional form required. Applicants notified on a rolling basis starting 6/1.

Academics. Special study options: Accelerated study, distance learning, dual enrollment of high school students, ESL, honors, liberal arts/career combination, teacher certification program, weekend college. License preparation in aviation, nursing. **Credit/placement by examination:** AP, CLEP, IB, institutional tests. 45 credit hours maximum toward associate degree. Test scores or local assessment must show ability to enroll in college level classes. **Support services:** Learning center, reduced course load, remedial instruction, study skills assistance, tutoring, writing center.

Majors. Business: General, accounting, business admin. **Computer sciences:** Computer science, data processing, LAN/WAN management, networking, programming, web page design. **Education:** Early childhood, kindergarten/preschool, middle. **Health services:** Nursing (RN). **Liberal arts:** Arts/sciences. **Math:** General. **Protective services:** Criminal justice. **Visual/performing arts:** Music, studio arts.

Most popular majors. Business/marketing 9%, education 9%, liberal arts 75%.

Computing on campus. 700 workstations in library, computer center, student center. Commuter students can connect to campus network. Online course registration, online library, helpline, wireless network available.

Student life. Freshman orientation: Available. Preregistration for classes offered. **Activities:** Concert band, campus ministries, choral groups, dance, drama, international student organizations, music ensembles, musical theater, student government, LULAC, Black student club, Campus Crusade for Christ.

Athletics. NJCAA. **Intercollegiate:** Baseball M, basketball, soccer, softball W, volleyball W. **Intramural:** Basketball, soccer, volleyball. **Team name:** Lions.

Student services. Adult student services, career counseling, services for economically disadvantaged, student employment services, financial aid counseling, health services, minority student services, personal counseling, placement for graduates, veterans' counselor. **Physically disabled:** Services for visually, speech, hearing impaired. **Transfer:** Transfer center, transfer adviser, college fairs on campus for students transferring to 4-year colleges.

Contact. E-mail: gmh9782@dcccd.edu
Phone: (214) 860-8600 Fax: (214) 860-8570
Glenda Hall, Director of Admissions, Mountain View College, 4849 West Illinois Avenue, Dallas, TX 75211-6599

Navarro College
Corsicana, Texas
www.navarrocollege.edu
CB code: 6465

- Public 2-year community and junior college
- Commuter campus in large town

General. Founded in 1946. Regionally accredited. **Enrollment:** 10,433 degree-seeking undergraduates. **Degrees:** 627 associate awarded. **Location:** 50 miles from Dallas. **Calendar:** Semester, extensive summer session. **Full-time faculty:** 126 total. **Part-time faculty:** 436 total. **Special facilities:** Arts, science and technology center; IMAX theater.

Student profile. Among degree-seeking undergraduates, 64% enrolled in a transfer program, 36% enrolled in a vocational program, 2,072 enrolled as first-time, first-year students.

Part-time:	53%	Women:	61%
Out-of-state:	1%	Live on campus:	8%

Basis for selection. Open admission, but selective for some programs. Special requirements for health professions programs. Portfolio required for art.

2011-2012 Annual costs. Tuition/fees: $1,602; $2,622 out-of-district; $3,972 out-of-state. Room/board: $4,939. Books/supplies: $1,446. Personal expenses: $2,339.

2010-2011 Financial aid. Need-based: 64% of total undergraduate aid awarded as scholarships/grants, 36% as loans/jobs. Work-study available nights, weekends and for part-time students.

Application procedures. Admission: No deadline. No application fee. Admission notification on a rolling basis. **Financial aid:** Priority date 6/1; no closing date. FAFSA required. Applicants notified on a rolling basis starting 7/1; must reply within 2 week(s) of notification.

Academics. Special study options: Distance learning, dual enrollment of high school students, ESL, honors, independent study, internships, liberal arts/career combination, weekend college. Bachelor's degree programs available on campus. License preparation in nursing, occupational therapy, paramedic. **Credit/placement by examination:** AP, CLEP, institutional tests. 30 credit hours maximum toward associate degree. CLEP credit awarded only after successful completion of 12 credit hours in residence. **Support services:** GED preparation and test center, learning center, reduced course load, remedial instruction, tutoring.

Majors. Biology: General. **Business:** General, accounting, administrative services, business admin, office technology. **Communications:** Communications/speech/rhetoric. **Communications technology:** Graphic/printing. **Computer sciences:** General. **Education:** General, elementary, physical, secondary. **Engineering:** General. **English:** English lit, rhetoric/composition. **Foreign languages:** Linguistics. **General:** Business, farm/ranch. **Health services:** Licensed practical nurse, predental, premedicine, prepharmacy, preveterinary. **Liberal arts:** Arts/sciences. **Math:** General. **Physical sciences:** Chemistry, physics. **Protective services:** Criminal justice, fire safety technology, police science. **Psychology:** General. **Social sciences:** General. **Visual/performing arts:** Art, commercial/advertising art, dramatic, music, music performance, voice/opera. **Work/family studies:** Child care management.

Computing on campus. Dormitories wired for high-speed internet access and linked to campus network. Online course registration, wireless network available.

Student life. Freshman orientation: Available. Preregistration for classes offered. **Housing:** Single-sex dorms available. $210 deposit. **Activities:** Bands, choral groups, drama, international student organizations, music ensembles, student government, religious organizations, honorary and special interest clubs.

Athletics. NJCAA. **Intercollegiate:** Baseball M, basketball M, cheerleading, football (tackle) M, soccer W, softball W, volleyball W. **Intramural:** Softball. **Team name:** Bulldogs.

Student services. Career counseling, student employment services, personal counseling, placement for graduates, veterans' counselor. **Transfer:** Pre-admission transcript evaluation for new students. Transfer adviser, college fairs on campus for students transferring to 4-year colleges.

Contact. E-mail: admissions@navarrocollege.edu
Phone: (903) 875-7348 Toll-free number: (800) 628-2776
Fax: (903) 875-7353
David Edwards, Registrar, Navarro College, 3200 West Seventh Avenue, Corsicana, TX 75110

North Central Texas College
Gainesville, Texas
www.nctc.edu   CB code: 6245

▶ Public 2-year community college
▶ Commuter campus in large city

General. Founded in 1924. Regionally accredited. **Enrollment:** 9,944 undergraduates. **Degrees:** 571 associate awarded. **ROTC:** Air Force. **Location:** 70 miles from main campus to Dalla. 35 miles from largest campus to Dallas. **Calendar:** Semester, extensive summer session. **Full-time faculty:** 122 total; 13% have terminal degrees, 6% minority, 59% women. **Part-time faculty:** 281 total; 8% have terminal degrees, 12% minority, 59% women. **Special facilities:** Planetarium, experimental farm, cattle center, horse arena.

Student profile.

Out-of-state:	3%	Live on campus:	2%
25 or older:	28%		

Basis for selection. Open admission, but selective for some programs. Observes TASP guidelines. Special requirements for some health professions programs.

High school preparation. 16 units recommended. Recommended units include English 4, mathematics 2, social studies 2 and science 2.

2011-2012 Annual costs. Tuition/fees: $1,470; $2,700 out-of-district; $4,200 out-of-state. Per-credit charge: $36 in-district; $77 out-of-district; $127 out-of-state. Room/board: $3,040. Books/supplies: $1,410. Personal expenses: $1,620.

Financial aid. All financial aid based on need. Need-based aid available for part-time students. Work-study available nights, weekends and for part-time students.

Application procedures. Admission: No deadline. No application fee. Admission notification on a rolling basis. High school transcript, proof of state residency, pre-TASP placement required for certain courses of study. **Financial aid:** Priority date 5/1; no closing date. FAFSA required. Applicants notified on a rolling basis starting 6/1; must reply within 4 week(s) of notification.

Academics. Special study options: Cross-registration, distance learning, dual enrollment of high school students. **Credit/placement by examination:** AP, CLEP, institutional tests. 18 credit hours maximum toward associate degree. **Support services:** GED preparation and test center, learning center, remedial instruction, study skills assistance, tutoring, writing center.

Majors. Business: General, administrative services, office technology, office/clerical. **Computer sciences:** General, data processing. **General:** Equestrian studies, farm/ranch. **Health services:** EMT paramedic, nursing (RN), occupational health, occupational therapy assistant. **Protective services:** Criminal justice, police science. **Social sciences:** Criminology. **Visual/performing arts:** Commercial photography.

Computing on campus. 60 workstations in dormitories, library, computer center, student center. Dormitories linked to campus network. Commuter students can connect to campus network. Online course registration, online library, helpline available.

Student life. Freshman orientation: Mandatory. Preregistration for classes offered. One-day program throughout summer and when classes commence. **Housing:** Coed dorms, special housing for disabled, wellness housing available. $150 deposit. **Activities:** Choral groups, dance, drama, literary magazine, music ensembles, student government, Baptist student union, Future Farmers of America, honor society, Young Republicans, nursing student association, criminal justice club, Methodist student organization, computer club.

Athletics. NJCAA. **Intercollegiate:** Baseball M, rodeo, tennis W, volleyball W. **Intramural:** Badminton, basketball, bowling, equestrian, golf, racquetball, softball, table tennis, tennis, track and field, volleyball. **Team name:** Lions.

Student services. Adult student services, career counseling, student employment services, personal counseling, veterans' counselor, women's services. **Transfer:** Transfer adviser for students transferring to 4-year colleges.

Contact. E-mail: admissions@nctc.edu
Phone: (940) 668-4222 ext. 222 Fax: (940) 668-6049
Kari Ford, Director of Admissions, North Central Texas College, 1525 West California Street, Gainesville, TX 76240

North Lake College
Irving, Texas   CB member
www.northlakecollege.edu   CB code: 6519

▶ Public 2-year community and liberal arts college
▶ Commuter campus in large city

General. Founded in 1977. Regionally accredited. **Enrollment:** 9,151 degree-seeking undergraduates. **Degrees:** 951 associate awarded. **Location:** 15 miles from Dallas. **Calendar:** Semester, limited summer session. **Full-time faculty:** 104 total. **Part-time faculty:** 351 total. **Class size:** 59% < 20, 36% 20-39, 3% 40-49, less than 1% 50-99, less than 1% >100. **Special facilities:** Natatorium, pool.

Student profile.

Out-of-state:	3%	25 or older:	40%

Transfer out. Colleges most students transferred to 2011: University of Texas at Arlington, University of North Texas, University of Texas at Dallas.

Basis for selection. Open admission. **Home schooled:** Transcript of courses and grades, interview required. Must take placement test.

High school preparation. College-preparatory program recommended.

2011-2012 Annual costs. Tuition/fees: $1,350; $2,490 out-of-district; $3,960 out-of-state. Per-credit charge: $45 in-district; $83 out-of-district; $132 out-of-state. For out-of-state students, $200 minimum charge for 1 semester hour. Books/supplies: $600.

Financial aid. Need-based: Need-based aid available for part-time students. Work-study available nights, weekends and for part-time students. **Non-need-based:** Scholarships awarded for academics, minority status, state residency.

Application procedures. Admission: No deadline. No application fee. Admission notification on a rolling basis. **Financial aid:** Priority date 3/1, closing date 5/1. FAFSA required. Applicants notified on a rolling basis starting 7/1.

Academics. Special study options: Accelerated study, cooperative education, cross-registration, distance learning, double major, dual enrollment of high school students, ESL, honors, independent study, internships, liberal arts/career combination, study abroad, teacher certification program. License preparation in nursing, real estate. **Credit/placement by examination:** AP, CLEP, institutional tests. 15 credit hours maximum toward associate degree. **Support services:** GED preparation and test center, learning center, pre-admission summer program, reduced course load, remedial instruction, study skills assistance, tutoring, writing center.

Majors. Architecture: Technology. **Business:** Accounting, administrative services, business admin, management science, office management, office technology, real estate. **Communications:** Communications/speech/rhetoric. **Communications technology:** Graphics, photo/film/video. **Computer sciences:** General, applications programming, computer science, information systems, information technology, networking, programming, security, systems analysis, web page design. **Education:** Elementary, ESL, kindergarten/preschool, music, teacher assistance. **English:** American lit, English lit. **Liberal arts:** Arts/sciences. **Math:** General, computational, statistics. **Psychology:** General. **Visual/performing arts:** Cinematography.

Computing on campus. 1,200 workstations in library, computer center, student center. Online course registration, online library, helpline, wireless network available.

Student life. Freshman orientation: Mandatory. Preregistration for classes offered. **Activities:** Bands, choral groups, dance, drama, film society, international student organizations, literary magazine, music ensembles, musical theater, opera, student government, student newspaper, association of black collegians, environmental club, Christians on Campus, Phi Theta Kappa, single parents association, Estamos Unidos, South Asian student organization, student ambassadors, anime club.

Athletics. NJCAA. **Intercollegiate:** Baseball, basketball, cheerleading M, gymnastics, swimming, volleyball, weight lifting. **Intramural:** Baseball, basketball, cheerleading W, soccer, swimming. **Team name:** Blazers.

Student services. Adult student services, alcohol/substance abuse counseling, career counseling, services for economically disadvantaged, student employment services, financial aid counseling, health services, minority student services, personal counseling, placement for graduates, veterans' counselor. **Physically disabled:** Services for visually, hearing impaired. **Transfer:** Pre-admission transcript evaluation for new students. Transfer center, transfer adviser, college fairs on campus for students transferring to 4-year colleges.

Contact. Phone: (972) 273-3183 Fax: (972) 273-3112
Francyenne Maynard, Dean, Student Support Services, North Lake College, 5001 North MacArthur Boulevard, Irving, TX 75038-3899

Northeast Texas Community College
Mount Pleasant, Texas
www.ntcc.edu
CB code: 6531

◆ Public 2-year community college
◆ Commuter campus in large town

General. Founded in 1984. Regionally accredited. **Enrollment:** 2,634 degree-seeking undergraduates. **Degrees:** 282 associate awarded. **Location:** 60 miles from Texarkana, 118 miles from Dallas. **Calendar:** Semester, extensive summer session. **Full-time faculty:** 72 total. **Part-time faculty:** 120 total.

Basis for selection. Open admission, but selective for some programs. Special requirements for health science programs, cosmetology, some criminal justice programs. **Home schooled:** Statement describing home school structure and mission, transcript of courses and grades, state high school equivalency certificate, letter of recommendation (nonparent) required.

High school preparation. 0.5 fine arts recommended.

2011-2012 Annual costs. Tuition/fees: $2,076; $3,306 out-of-district; $4,696 out-of-state. Room/board: $5,200. Books/supplies: $1,150. Personal expenses: $2,163.

Financial aid. Need-based: Need-based aid available for part-time students. Work-study available nights, weekends and for part-time students.

Application procedures. Admission: No deadline. No application fee. Application must be submitted online. Admission notification on a rolling basis. **Financial aid:** Priority date 6/1; no closing date. FAFSA, institutional form required. Applicants notified on a rolling basis starting 6/1.

Academics. Special study options: Cooperative education, distance learning, dual enrollment of high school students, ESL, honors, liberal arts/career combination. Bachelor's degree programs available on campus. License preparation in dental hygiene, nursing, paramedic, physical therapy, radiology, real estate. **Credit/placement by examination:** AP, CLEP. 15 credit hours maximum toward associate degree. **Support services:** GED preparation and test center, learning center, remedial instruction, study skills assistance, tutoring, writing center.

Majors. Biology: General. **Business:** Administrative services, banking/financial services, business admin, office technology, real estate. **Computer sciences:** Programming. **Engineering:** Applied physics. **English:** English lit. **Foreign languages:** Spanish. **General:** Business. **Health services:** Clinical lab technology, dental hygiene, EMT paramedic, medical assistant, medical radiologic technology/radiation therapy, medical secretary, nursing (RN), physical therapy assistant. **History:** General. **Liberal arts:** Arts/sciences. **Math:** General. **Parks/recreation:** Health/fitness. **Physical sciences:** Chemistry. **Protective services:** Police science. **Psychology:** General. **Social sciences:** Political science, sociology. **Visual/performing arts:** Art, dramatic, music.

Computing on campus. 150 workstations in dormitories, library, computer center. Dormitories wired for high-speed internet access. Commuter students can connect to campus network. Online course registration, online library, wireless network available.

Student life. Freshman orientation: Mandatory, $30 fee. Preregistration for classes offered. **Housing:** Single-sex dorms available. **Activities:** Jazz band, choral groups, drama, music ensembles, musical theater, student government, student newspaper, student coordinating board, Baptist student union, student nurses, Phi Theta Kappa, computer club, career opportunities in protective services.

Athletics. NJCAA. **Intercollegiate:** Baseball M, rodeo, softball W. **Intramural:** Basketball M, soccer M, softball, tennis, volleyball. **Team name:** Eagles.

Student services. Adult student services, career counseling, services for economically disadvantaged, student employment services, financial aid counseling, minority student services, placement for graduates, veterans' counselor. **Transfer:** Pre-admission transcript evaluation for new students. College fairs on campus for students transferring to 4-year colleges.

Contact. E-mail: admrec@ntcc.edu
Phone: (903) 434-8354 Toll-free number: (800) 870-0142 ext. 8354
Fax: (903) 572-6712
Sonya Woods, Director of Admissions, Northeast Texas Community College, PO Box 1307, Mount Pleasant, TX 75456-1307

Northwest Vista College
San Antonio, Texas
www.alamo.edu/nvc
CB code: 6517

◆ Public 2-year community college
◆ Commuter campus in very large city

General. Regionally accredited. **Enrollment:** 12,999 degree-seeking undergraduates. **Degrees:** 941 associate awarded. **Location:** 16 miles from downtown. **Calendar:** Semester, extensive summer session. **Full-time faculty:** 127 total. **Part-time faculty:** 270 total.

Transfer out. Colleges most students transferred to 2011: University of Texas at San Antonio, Texas State University, Palo Alto College, San Antonio College, St. Philip's College.

Two-Year Colleges

Basis for selection. Open admission. **Home schooled:** Transcript of courses and grades required.

High school preparation. 22 units recommended. Recommended units include English 4, mathematics 3, social studies 5, history 1, science 3, foreign language 2 and academic electives 3.

2011-2012 Annual costs. Tuition/fees: $1,980; $3,660 out-of-district; $7,020 out-of-state. Per-credit charge: $56 in-district; $112 out-of-district; $224 out-of-state.

Financial aid. **Need-based:** Need-based aid available for part-time students. Work-study available nights, weekends and for part-time students. **Non-need-based:** Scholarships awarded for academics, leadership.

Application procedures. **Admission:** Priority date 4/23; deadline 8/19. No application fee. **Financial aid:** Priority date 4/1; no closing date. FAFSA required. Applicants notified on a rolling basis starting 5/15; must reply within 2 week(s) of notification.

Academics. **Special study options:** Cross-registration, distance learning, dual enrollment of high school students, ESL, internships, liberal arts/career combination, teacher certification program, weekend college. **Credit/placement by examination:** AP, CLEP, institutional tests. 32 credit hours maximum toward associate degree. **Support services:** Learning center, remedial instruction, study skills assistance, tutoring, writing center.

Majors. **Biology:** General. **Business:** Business admin. **Communications:** Communications/speech/rhetoric, journalism, media studies. **Communications technology:** General. **Computer sciences:** General, computer science, networking, programming. **Education:** General. **English:** English lit, rhetoric/composition. **Foreign languages:** General. **History:** General. **Human services:** Social work. **Liberal arts:** Arts/sciences. **Math:** General. **Parks/recreation:** Exercise sciences, health/fitness. **Physical sciences:** Chemistry. **Psychology:** General. **Social sciences:** General, economics, political science, sociology.

Computing on campus. 3,500 workstations in library, computer center, student center. Commuter students can connect to campus network. Online course registration, online library, helpline, wireless network available.

Student life. **Freshman orientation:** Mandatory. Preregistration for classes offered. **Activities:** Campus ministries, dance, drama, film society, literary magazine, student government, student newspaper.

Athletics. **Team name:** Wildcats.

Student services. Career counseling, student employment services, financial aid counseling, health services, personal counseling, placement for graduates, veterans' counselor. **Physically disabled:** Services for visually, speech, hearing impaired. **Transfer:** Pre-admission transcript evaluation for new students. Transfer center, transfer adviser, college fairs on campus for students transferring to 4-year colleges.

Contact. E-mail: nvc-admissions@mail.accd.edu
Phone: (210) 486-4700 Fax: (210) 486-4170
Robin Carrillo, Director of Enrollment Management, Northwest Vista College, 3535 North Ellison Drive, San Antonio, TX 78251-4217

Odessa College
Odessa, Texas
www.odessa.edu   CB code: 6540

- Public 2-year community college
- Commuter campus in small city

General. Founded in 1946. Regionally accredited. Extension centers in Pecos, Monahans, Andrews, Crane, Kermit, McCamey, Seminole. **Enrollment:** 5,128 undergraduates. **Degrees:** 345 associate awarded. **Location:** 140 miles from Lubbock, 290 miles from El Paso. **Calendar:** Semester, extensive summer session. **Full-time faculty:** 126 total. **Part-time faculty:** 150 total.

Student profile.

Out-of-state:	1%	Live on campus:	5%
25 or older:	33%		

Basis for selection. Open admission, but selective for some programs. Allied health programs require successful completion of placement exams, supporting applications, and interviews. Requirements for other selective programs vary. **Home schooled:** Transcript of courses and grades required.

2011-2012 Annual costs. Tuition/fees: $1,965; $3,015 out-of-district; $4,065 out-of-state. Per-credit charge: $55 in-district; $90 out-of-district;

$125 out-of-state. Room/board: $4,700. Books/supplies: $1,400. Personal expenses: $1,234.

2010-2011 Financial aid. **Need-based:** 466 full-time freshmen applied for aid; 402 were judged to have need; 383 of these received aid. Average need met was 54%. Average scholarship/grant was $2,757; average loan $2,351. 89% of total undergraduate aid awarded as scholarships/grants, 11% as loans/jobs. Need-based aid available for part-time students. Work-study available nights, weekends and for part-time students. **Non-need-based:** Awarded to 622 full-time undergraduates, including 291 freshmen. Scholarships awarded for academics, athletics, music/drama.

Application procedures. **Admission:** No deadline. No application fee. Admission notification on a rolling basis. **Financial aid:** Priority date 5/1; no closing date. FAFSA required. Applicants notified on a rolling basis starting 6/1.

Academics. **Special study options:** Cooperative education, cross-registration, distance learning, dual enrollment of high school students, independent study, internships, liberal arts/career combination. License preparation in nursing, paramedic, physical therapy, radiology. **Credit/placement by examination:** AP, CLEP, institutional tests. 30 credit hours maximum toward associate degree. **Support services:** GED preparation and test center, learning center, reduced course load, remedial instruction, study skills assistance, tutoring, writing center.

Majors. **Biology:** General. **Business:** General, administrative services, business admin. **Computer sciences:** Computer science, information systems, programming. **Education:** General, teacher assistance. **Foreign languages:** General. **Health services:** Clinical lab science, EMT paramedic, medical radiologic technology/radiation therapy, medical secretary, nursing (RN), physical therapy assistant, respiratory therapy technology, substance abuse counseling, surgical technology. **Liberal arts:** Arts/sciences. **Math:** General. **Physical sciences:** Chemistry, geology. **Protective services:** Fire safety technology, firefighting, police science. **Psychology:** General. **Social sciences:** General. **Visual/performing arts:** Art, commercial photography, music. **Work/family studies:** Child care management.

Computing on campus. 775 workstations in dormitories, library, computer center, student center. Dormitories wired for high-speed internet access and linked to campus network. Commuter students can connect to campus network. Online course registration, online library, helpline, student web hosting, wireless network available.

Student life. **Freshman orientation:** Mandatory. Preregistration for classes offered. **Housing:** Apartments available. $200 partly refundable deposit. **Activities:** Bands, choral groups, drama, music ensembles, opera, radio station, student government, Baptist student union, veterans organization, Black organization of successful students, student alliance of Latinos succeeding academically.

Athletics. NJCAA. **Intercollegiate:** Baseball M, basketball, cross-country, golf M, rodeo, softball W. **Intramural:** Racquetball, softball, table tennis, tennis, volleyball. **Team name:** Wranglers.

Student services. Career counseling, student employment services, financial aid counseling, on-campus daycare, personal counseling, placement for graduates, veterans' counselor. **Physically disabled:** Services for visually, hearing impaired. **Transfer:** Pre-admission transcript evaluation for new students. Transfer adviser, college fairs on campus for students transferring to 4-year colleges.

Contact. E-mail: admissions@odessa.edu
Phone: (432) 335-6432 Fax: (432) 335-6636
Tracy Hilliard, Associate Director of Admissions, Odessa College, 201 West University, Odessa, TX 79764-7127

Palo Alto College
San Antonio, Texas   CB member
www.alamo.edu/pac   CB code: 3730

- Public 2-year community college
- Commuter campus in very large city

General. Founded in 1987. Regionally accredited. **Enrollment:** 9,163 undergraduates. **Degrees:** 861 associate awarded. **ROTC:** Army. **Calendar:** Semester, limited summer session. **Full-time faculty:** 137 total. **Part-time faculty:** 150 total. **Special facilities:** Stinson Airport FAA aviation education resource center, veterinary computer and clinical labs, outdoor animal pen.

Transfer out. **Colleges most students transferred to 2011:** University of Texas at San Antonio, St. Mary's University, Our Lady of the Lake University, University of the Incarnate Word.

Basis for selection. Open admission.

2011-2012 Annual costs. Tuition/fees: $1,980; $3,660 out-of-district; $7,020 out-of-state. Per-credit charge: $56 in-district; $112 out-of-district; $224 out-of-state. Books/supplies: $1,900.

Financial aid. All financial aid based on need. Need-based aid available for part-time students. Work-study available nights, weekends and for part-time students.

Application procedures. Admission: No deadline. No application fee. Application must be submitted online. Admission notification on a rolling basis. **Financial aid:** Priority date 4/1, closing date 6/1. FAFSA required. Applicants notified on a rolling basis starting 5/31.

Academics. Special study options: Accelerated study, distance learning, dual enrollment of high school students, ESL, internships, liberal arts/career combination, study abroad, weekend college. License preparation in aviation. **Credit/placement by examination:** AP, CLEP, institutional tests. 32 credit hours maximum toward associate degree. **Support services:** GED preparation, learning center, remedial instruction, study skills assistance, tutoring, writing center.

Majors. Biology: General. **Business:** Accounting, administrative services, banking/financial services, business admin, logistics, office management, office technology. **Communications:** Advertising, communications/speech/rhetoric, journalism. **Computer sciences:** General, computer science, information systems, programming. **Conservation:** Environmental science. **Education:** General. **Engineering:** General, environmental. **English:** English lit. **Foreign languages:** General. **General:** Agribusiness operations, animal sciences, horticultural science, landscaping, turf management. **Health services:** Nursing assistant. **History:** General. **Human services:** Social work. **Liberal arts:** Arts/sciences. **Math:** General. **Parks/recreation:** Exercise sciences. **Philosophy/religion:** Philosophy. **Physical sciences:** General, chemistry, physics. **Protective services:** Law enforcement admin. **Psychology:** General. **Social sciences:** Anthropology, economics, political science, sociology. **Visual/performing arts:** Art, music, studio arts. **Work/family studies:** Food/nutrition.

Computing on campus. Commuter students can connect to campus network. Online course registration, online library, wireless network available.

Student life. Freshman orientation: Mandatory. Preregistration for classes offered. **Activities:** Jazz band, campus ministries, choral groups, dance, drama, music ensembles, student government, student newspaper, international club, veterinary technician association, Phi Theta Kappa.

Athletics. Team name: Palominos.

Student services. Adult student services, alcohol/substance abuse counseling, career counseling, services for economically disadvantaged, student employment services, financial aid counseling, on-campus daycare, personal counseling, veterans' counselor. **Physically disabled:** Services for visually, speech, hearing impaired. **Transfer:** Transfer center, transfer adviser, college fairs on campus for students transferring to 4-year colleges.

Contact. Phone: (210) 486-3700
Elizabeth Villarreal, Director of Enrollment Management, Palo Alto College, 1400 West Villaret Blvd., San Antonio, TX 78224-2499

Panola College
Carthage, Texas
www.panola.edu

CB code: 6572

▶ Public 2-year community and junior college
▶ Commuter campus in small town

General. Founded in 1947. Regionally accredited. Additional campuses in Marshall and Center, Texas. Panola offers a variety of online and interactive television classes on its campuses as well as at area high schools. **Enrollment:** 2,562 degree-seeking undergraduates; 2 non-degree-seeking students. **Degrees:** 230 associate awarded. **Location:** 40 miles from Shreveport, Louisiana; 150 miles from Dallas. **Calendar:** Semester, limited summer session. **Full-time faculty:** 61 total; 7% have terminal degrees, 8% minority, 59% women. **Part-time faculty:** 71 total; 4% have terminal degrees, 8% minority, 65% women. **Class size:** 68% < 20, 29% 20-39, less than 1% 40-49, 2% 50-99, less than 1% >100.

Student profile. Among degree-seeking undergraduates, 471 enrolled as first-time, first-year students, 282 transferred in from other institutions.

Part-time:	56%	**Hispanic American:**	7%
Out-of-state:	8%	**Native American:**	1%
Women:	70%	**International:**	1%
African American:	21%	**25 or older:**	34%
Asian American:	1%	**Live on campus:**	8%

Transfer out. Colleges most students transferred to 2011: Stephen F. Austin State University, University of Texas at Tyler, Texas A&M Commerce, East Texas Baptist University.

Basis for selection. Open admission, but selective for some programs. Institution observes Texas Success Initiative guidelines. Departmental admission required prior to registration for some occupational/vocational programs of study. Dual credit/early admissions high school enrollment offers high school students an opportunity to earn credits toward a college degree while completing requirements for high school graduation. Interview required for some health program applicants. Auditions required for some fine arts scholarships.

High school preparation. 22 units required; 26 recommended. Required and recommended units include English 4, mathematics 3-4, social studies 3-4, science 2-4, foreign language 2, visual/performing arts .5-1.5 and academic electives 1. 1 physical ed course.

2011-2012 Annual costs. Tuition/fees: $2,010; $3,210 out-of-district; $4,050 out-of-state. Per-credit charge: $67 in-district; $107 out-of-district; $135 out-of-state. Room/board: $4,586. Books/supplies: $1,833. Personal expenses: $3,298.

2010-2011 Financial aid. Need-based: 262 full-time freshmen applied for aid; 234 were judged to have need; 226 of these received aid. Average need met was 32%. Average scholarship/grant was $2,207. 99% of total undergraduate aid awarded as scholarships/grants, 1% as loans/jobs. Need-based aid available for part-time students. Work-study available nights, weekends and for part-time students. **Non-need-based:** Awarded to 298 full-time undergraduates, including 129 freshmen. Scholarships awarded for academics, alumni affiliation, art, athletics, leadership, music/drama.

Application procedures. Admission: No deadline. No application fee. **Financial aid:** Priority date 6/1; no closing date. FAFSA, institutional form required. Applicants notified on a rolling basis starting 6/1.

Academics. Special study options: Distance learning, dual enrollment of high school students, liberal arts/career combination. License preparation in nursing, occupational therapy, paramedic. **Credit/placement by examination:** AP, CLEP. 12 credit hours maximum toward associate degree. **Support services:** GED preparation and test center, learning center, remedial instruction, study skills assistance, tutoring.

Majors. Business: General, office management. **Computer sciences:** General. **Education:** General, early childhood. **Health services:** Medical records technology, nursing (RN), occupational therapy assistant, office admin. **Liberal arts:** Arts/sciences.

Most popular majors. Education 8%, engineering/engineering technologies 6%, health sciences 45%, liberal arts 36%.

Computing on campus. 509 workstations in dormitories, library, computer center, student center. Dormitories wired for high-speed internet access and linked to campus network. Commuter students can connect to campus network. Online course registration, online library, helpline, wireless network available.

Student life. Freshman orientation: Available. Preregistration for classes offered. **Housing:** Coed dorms, apartments, wellness housing available. $200 partly refundable deposit, deadline 7/15. **Activities:** Bands, campus ministries, choral groups, dance, drama, literary magazine, music ensembles, musical theater, student government, student newspaper, student government association, forensic/drama club, chemistry club, Phi Theta Kappa, computer club, gaming club, nursing club, biology club, health technology club, occupational therapy assistant club, Green Jackets service club.

Athletics. NJCAA. **Intercollegiate:** Baseball M, basketball, rodeo, volleyball W. **Intramural:** Basketball, football (non-tackle), racquetball, softball, volleyball. **Team name:** Ponies and Fillies.

Student services. Alcohol/substance abuse counseling, career counseling, services for economically disadvantaged, financial aid counseling, personal counseling, veterans' counselor. **Physically disabled:** Services for visually, speech, hearing impaired. **Transfer:** Pre-admission transcript evaluation for new students. College fairs on campus for students transferring to 4-year colleges.

Contact. E-mail: jdorman@panola.edu
Phone: (903) 693-2038 Fax: (903) 693-2031
Jeremy Dorman, Registrar/Director of Admissions, Panola College, 1109 West Panola Street, Carthage, TX 75633

Paris Junior College
Paris, Texas
www.parisjc.edu

CB member
CB code: 6573

- Public 2-year community and junior college
- Commuter campus in large town

General. Founded in 1924. Regionally accredited. **Enrollment:** 5,936 degree-seeking undergraduates. **Degrees:** 410 associate awarded. **Location:** 110 miles from Dallas. **Calendar:** Semester, limited summer session. **Full-time faculty:** 91 total. **Part-time faculty:** 161 total. **Special facilities:** Collection of historical documents and artifacts of region.

Student profile.

Out-of-state:	4%	Live on campus:	5%
25 or older:	33%		

Basis for selection. Open admission, but selective for some programs. Special admission to nursing program; interview required.

2011-2012 Annual costs. Tuition/fees: $1,560; $2,490 out-of-district; $3,840 out-of-state. Per-credit charge: $135 in-district; $197 out-of-district; $287 out-of-state. Room/board: $4,820. Books/supplies: $500.

Financial aid. Need-based: Need-based aid available for part-time students. Work-study available nights, weekends and for part-time students. **Non-need-based:** Scholarships awarded for athletics, music/drama.

Application procedures. Admission: No deadline. No application fee. Admission notification on a rolling basis. **Financial aid:** No deadline. FAFSA required. Applicants notified on a rolling basis starting 6/1.

Academics. Special study options: Accelerated study, cross-registration, distance learning, dual enrollment of high school students. License preparation in nursing, paramedic, radiology. **Credit/placement by examination:** AP, CLEP, institutional tests. **Support services:** GED preparation and test center, learning center, reduced course load, remedial instruction, tutoring, writing center.

Majors. Biology: General. **Business:** General, accounting, administrative services, business admin, office management, office technology. **Communications:** Journalism. **Computer sciences:** General, LAN/WAN management. **Education:** General, multi-level teacher. **Engineering:** General. **English:** English lit. **Foreign languages:** General, French, German, Spanish. **Health services:** EMT paramedic, nursing (RN), predental, premedicine, prepharmacy, preveterinary, radiologic technology/medical imaging. **History:** General. **Liberal arts:** Arts/sciences. **Math:** General. **Parks/recreation:** Health/fitness. **Physical sciences:** General, chemistry, physics. **Protective services:** Criminal justice. **Psychology:** General. **Social sciences:** Criminology, political science, sociology. **Visual/performing arts:** Dramatic, metal/jewelry, music, studio arts.

Computing on campus. Dormitories wired for high-speed internet access and linked to campus network. Commuter students can connect to campus network.

Student life. Freshman orientation: Mandatory. Preregistration for classes offered. **Housing:** Single-sex dorms, apartments available. **Activities:** Campus ministries, choral groups, drama, music ensembles, student government, student newspaper, Baptist student union, Afro-American club, honorary business fraternity, honorary scholastic fraternity.

Athletics. NJCAA. **Intercollegiate:** Baseball M, basketball, golf M, softball W, volleyball W. **Team name:** Dragons.

Student services. Career counseling, services for economically disadvantaged, student employment services, financial aid counseling, health services, personal counseling, placement for graduates, veterans' counselor.

Contact. Phone: (903) 785-7661 Fax: (903) 784-9370
Amie Cato, Director of Admissions, Paris Junior College, 2400 Clarksville Street, Paris, TX 75460

Platt College: Dallas
Dallas, Texas
www.plattcolleges.edu

- For-profit 1-year career college
- Very large city

General. Regionally accredited. **Calendar:** Quarter.

Contact. 2974 LBJ Freeway, Suite 300, Dallas, TX 75234

Ranger College
Ranger, Texas
www.rangercollege.edu

CB code: 6608

- Public 2-year junior college
- Rural community

General. Founded in 1926. Regionally accredited. **Enrollment:** 773 degree-seeking undergraduates. **Degrees:** 38 associate awarded. **Location:** 85 miles from Fort Worth, 65 miles from Abilene. **Calendar:** Semester, limited summer session. **Full-time faculty:** 38 total. **Part-time faculty:** 71 total.

Basis for selection. Open admission, but selective for some programs. Observe all TSI guidelines. Special requirements for vocational nursing program candidates include additional applications and testing.

2011-2012 Annual costs. Tuition/fees: $2,175; $3,255 out-of-district; $4,215 out-of-state. Per-credit charge: $50 in-district; $86 out-of-district; $118 out-of-state. Room/board: $3,698.

Financial aid. All financial aid based on need. Need-based aid available for part-time students. Work-study available nights, weekends and for part-time students.

Application procedures. Admission: No deadline. No application fee. Application must be submitted on paper. Candidates accepted into the vocational nursing program will receive notification and must reply by the date indicated. **Financial aid:** Priority date 6/1, closing date 7/24. FAFSA required. Applicants notified on a rolling basis; must reply within 2 week(s) of notification.

Academics. Special study options: Distance learning, dual enrollment of high school students, honors. 2-2 programs in education, business administration, computer systems, and information sciences with Tarleton State University. License preparation in nursing. **Credit/placement by examination:** AP, CLEP, institutional tests. 12 credit hours maximum toward associate degree. **Support services:** GED test center, learning center, reduced course load, remedial instruction.

Majors. Business: Administrative services. **Computer sciences:** General. **Liberal arts:** Arts/sciences.

Computing on campus. 30 workstations in library, computer center.

Student life. Freshman orientation: Mandatory. Preregistration for classes offered. **Housing:** Single-sex dorms available. **Activities:** Bands, dance, music ensembles, student government, student newspaper.

Athletics. NJCAA. **Intercollegiate:** Baseball M, basketball, cheerleading, golf, rodeo, soccer, softball W, volleyball W. **Team name:** Rangers.

Student services. Career counseling, student employment services, health services, personal counseling, placement for graduates, veterans' counselor. **Transfer:** Transfer adviser for students transferring to 4-year colleges.

Contact. Phone: (254) 647-3234 ext. 215 Fax: (254) 647-3739
John Slaughter, Registrar, Ranger College, 1100 College Circle, Ranger, TX 76470

Remington College: Dallas
Garland, Texas
www.remingtoncollege.edu/dallas

CB code: 3232

- For-profit 2-year junior and technical college
- Small city

General. Regionally accredited; also accredited by ACCSC. **Enrollment:** 1,212 degree-seeking undergraduates. **Degrees:** 183 associate awarded. **Calendar:** Differs by program. **Full-time faculty:** 44 total. **Part-time faculty:** 10 total.

Basis for selection. Open admission.

2011-2012 Annual costs. Personal expenses: $3,360.

Financial aid. Need-based: Work-study available nights, weekends and for part-time students.

Application procedures. Admission: No deadline. $50 fee. **Financial aid:** No deadline.

Academics. Credit/placement by examination: AP, CLEP.

Majors. Business: Business admin. **Computer sciences:** Networking. **Health services:** Medical assistant. **Protective services:** Law enforcement admin.

Contact. E-mail: admissions@remingtoncollege.edu
Phone: (972) 686-7878
Shonda Whisenhunt, Director of Admissions, Remington College: Dallas, 1800 Eastgate Drive, Garland, TX 75041

Remington College: Fort Worth
Fort Worth, Texas
www.remingtoncollege.edu/ftworth   CB code: 3151

- For-profit 2-year technical and career college
- Commuter campus in large city
- Interview required

General. Accredited by ACCSC. **Enrollment:** 574 degree-seeking undergraduates. **Degrees:** 43 associate awarded. **Location:** 7 miles from downtown. **Calendar:** Differs by program. **Full-time faculty:** 21 total. **Part-time faculty:** 17 total.

Basis for selection. Open admission. Programs offered on a monthly basis. **Home schooled:** Transcript of courses and grades required.

Financial aid. Need-based: Work-study available nights, weekends and for part-time students.

Application procedures. Admission: No deadline. $50 fee. **Financial aid:** No deadline.

Academics. Credit/placement by examination: AP, CLEP.

Majors. Business: Business admin. **Computer sciences:** Computer graphics, networking. **Protective services:** Criminal justice.

Student services. Career counseling, financial aid counseling, placement for graduates.

Contact. E-mail: admissions@remingtoncollege.edu
Phone: (817) 451-0017 Fax: (817) 496-1257
Ty Vaughn, Director of Admissions, Remington College: Fort Worth, 300 East Loop 820, Fort Worth, TX 76112

Remington College: Houston
Houston, Texas
www.remingtoncollege.edu/houston   CB code: 3152

- For-profit 2-year technical college
- Commuter campus in very large city

General. Accredited by ACCSC. **Enrollment:** 382 degree-seeking undergraduates. **Degrees:** 64 associate awarded. **Calendar:** Quarter. **Full-time faculty:** 26 total. **Part-time faculty:** 11 total.

Basis for selection. Open admission. ASSET used as admissions exams for degree programs.

2011-2012 Annual costs. Personal expenses: $1,764.

Financial aid. Need-based: Need-based aid available for part-time students. Work-study available nights, weekends and for part-time students. **Non-need-based:** Scholarships awarded for state residency.

Application procedures. Admission: No deadline. $50 fee. Application must be submitted on paper. Admission notification on a rolling basis. **Financial aid:** No deadline. FAFSA, institutional form required. Applicants notified on a rolling basis.

Academics. Special study options: Internships. **Credit/placement by examination:** AP, CLEP. **Support services:** Tutoring.

Majors. Computer sciences: General, applications programming, networking, programming, systems analysis. **Engineering:** Electrical, software.

Computing on campus. 200 workstations in library, computer center. Online library, helpline, repair service available.

Student services. Adult student services, career counseling, student employment services, financial aid counseling. **Transfer:** Pre-admission transcript evaluation for new students.

Contact. Phone: (281) 899-1240 Fax: (281) 597-8466
Mark Donahue, Director of Admissions, Remington College: Houston, 3110 Hayes Road, Suite 380, Houston, TX 77082

Remington College: North Houston
Houston, Texas
www.remingtoncollege.edu/northhouston

- For-profit 2-year health science and technical college
- Commuter campus in very large city

General. Accredited by ACCSC. **Enrollment:** 596 degree-seeking undergraduates. **Degrees:** 57 associate awarded. **Calendar:** Quarter. **Full-time faculty:** 25 total. **Part-time faculty:** 9 total.

Basis for selection. Open admission.

Financial aid. Need-based: Work-study available nights, weekends and for part-time students.

Application procedures. Admission: No deadline. $50 fee. Admission notification on a rolling basis. **Financial aid:** No deadline.

Academics. Credit/placement by examination: AP, CLEP.

Majors. Business: Business admin. **Health services:** Insurance coding, medical assistant, pharmacy assistant. **Protective services:** Law enforcement admin.

Contact. E-mail: admissions@remingtoncollege.edu
Phone: (281) 885-4450
Edmund Flores, Director of Admissions, Remington College: North Houston, 11310 Greens Crossing, Suite 200, Houston, TX 77067

Richland College
Dallas, Texas
www.rlc.dcccd.edu   CB code: 6607

- Public 2-year community college
- Commuter campus in very large city

General. Founded in 1972. Regionally accredited. **Enrollment:** 16,391 degree-seeking undergraduates. **Degrees:** 951 associate awarded. **Location:** 15 miles from downtown. **Calendar:** Semester, extensive summer session. **Full-time faculty:** 137 total. **Part-time faculty:** 689 total. **Special facilities:** Planetarium, laser light theater, horticulture demonstration garden, meditation labyrinth.

Student profile.

Out-of-state:	2%	**25 or older:**	39%

Basis for selection. Open admission. Students required by legislative mandate to take TASP test or alternative assessment before enrolling in college-level courses. **Home schooled:** Require completed application, concurrent enrollment permission form, student information profile sheet, student health history form, authorization to release test scores, official home school transcripts.

2011-2012 Annual costs. Tuition/fees: $1,350; $2,490 out-of-district; $3,960 out-of-state. Per-credit charge: $45 in-district; $83 out-of-district; $132 out-of-state. For out-of-state students, $200 minimum charge for 1 semester hour. Books/supplies: $350. Personal expenses: $935.

Financial aid. Need-based: Need-based aid available for part-time students. Work-study available nights, weekends and for part-time students. **Non-need-based:** Scholarships awarded for art, leadership, music/drama.

Application procedures. Admission: No deadline. No application fee. Admission notification on a rolling basis. **Financial aid:** Priority date 5/11; no closing date. FAFSA required. Applicants notified on a rolling basis starting 6/1; must reply within 2 week(s) of notification.

Academics. Special study options: Cooperative education, cross-registration, distance learning, dual enrollment of high school students, ESL,

honors, independent study, internships, study abroad, teacher certification program, weekend college. License preparation in real estate. **Credit/placement by examination:** AP, CLEP, institutional tests. 45 credit hours maximum toward associate degree. **Support services:** Learning center, remedial instruction, study skills assistance, tutoring.

Majors. Business: Accounting, administrative services, business admin, entrepreneurial studies, management information systems, real estate, tourism/travel. **Communications technology:** General. **Computer sciences:** General, applications programming. **Education:** Bilingual, teacher assistance. **General:** Horticultural science, horticulture. **Health services:** Insurance coding, medical informatics, medical records technology. **Liberal arts:** Arts/sciences.

Computing on campus. 210 workstations in library, computer center. Commuter students can connect to campus network. Online course registration, online library, wireless network available.

Student life. Freshman orientation: Mandatory. Preregistration for classes offered. Sessions held online with alternative optional on-campus orientation. **Activities:** Bands, campus ministries, choral groups, dance, drama, music ensembles, musical theater, student government, student newspaper, TV station, Spanish heritage association, arts club, Educators of America, Sierra Student Coalition, German film club.

Athletics. NJCAA. **Intercollegiate:** Baseball M, basketball M, soccer, volleyball W. **Intramural:** Basketball, bowling, cross-country, football (nontackle), golf, soccer, softball, tennis, volleyball. **Team name:** Thunder Ducks.

Student services. Adult student services, career counseling, services for economically disadvantaged, student employment services, financial aid counseling, health services, minority student services, personal counseling, placement for graduates, veterans' counselor, women's services. **Physically disabled:** Services for visually, speech, hearing impaired. **Transfer:** Transfer adviser, college fairs on campus for students transferring to 4-year colleges.

Contact. Phone: (972) 238-6106 Fax: (972) 238-6346
Rebecca Witherspoon, Director of Admissions, Richland College, 12800 Abrams Road, Dallas, TX 75243-2199

San Antonio College
San Antonio, Texas
www.alamo.edu/sac

CB member
CB code: 6645

♦ Public 2-year community college
♦ Commuter campus in very large city

General. Founded in 1925. Regionally accredited. **Enrollment:** 22,085 degree-seeking undergraduates. **Degrees:** 1,030 associate awarded. **ROTC:** Army, Air Force. **Location:** Downtown. **Calendar:** Semester, extensive summer session. **Full-time faculty:** 422 total. **Part-time faculty:** 618 total. **Special facilities:** Planetarium.

Transfer out. Colleges most students transferred to 2011: University of Texas at San Antonio.

Basis for selection. Open admission, but selective for some programs. Nursing requires 2.5 GPA, satisfactory completion of human anatomy/physiology and ethics. Mortuary science program requires admissions interview, proof of complete hepatitis B vaccination series (or submit a waiver/declination form), and counseling card. Dental assisting requires complete dental assisting technology program application, proof of advisement, formal admission to college, and counseling card. **Adult students:** Texas Higher Education Assessment required.

2011-2012 Annual costs. Tuition/fees: $1,980; $3,660 out-of-district; $7,020 out-of-state. Per-credit charge: $56 in-district; $112 out-of-district; $224 out-of-state. Books/supplies: $1,200. Personal expenses: $2,571.

Financial aid. All financial aid based on need. Need-based aid available for part-time students. Work-study available nights, weekends and for part-time students. **Additional information:** Leveraging Educational Assistance Partnership (LEAP), public student incentive grant, towards excellence access and success grants (Texas and Texas II grants) available.

Application procedures. Admission: Closing date 8/25. No application fee. Application must be submitted online. Admission notification on a rolling basis. Nursing applicants must apply by January 15. **Financial aid:** Priority date 3/1; no closing date. FAFSA required.

Academics. Special study options: Cooperative education, cross-registration, distance learning, double major, dual enrollment of high school students, ESL, honors, internships, liberal arts/career combination, study abroad, teacher certification program, weekend college. Internet courses,

premedical/predental program, alternative teacher certification program, basic skills enrichment program, distance education through Virtual College of Texas, teaching academy program. License preparation in dental hygiene, nursing, paramedic, real estate. **Credit/placement by examination:** AP, CLEP, IB, institutional tests. 32 credit hours maximum toward associate degree. Student must earn 6 credits at college before credit by examination may be posted on transcript. No credit by examination may be earned for course already completed in classroom. **Support services:** GED preparation and test center, learning center, reduced course load, remedial instruction, study skills assistance, tutoring, writing center.

Majors. Business: Accounting technology, business admin. **Communications:** Journalism, radio/TV. **Computer sciences:** Programming, security. **Education:** Teacher assistance. **Engineering:** General. **Foreign languages:** Sign language interpretation. **Health services:** Medical assistant, nursing (RN), substance abuse counseling. **Human services:** General. **Math:** General. **Protective services:** Corrections, criminal justice, fire safety technology, police science, security management. **Psychology:** General. **Visual/performing arts:** Graphic design. **Work/family studies:** Child development.

Computing on campus. 325 workstations in library, computer center, student center. Commuter students can connect to campus network. Online course registration, online library, helpline, wireless network available.

Student life. Freshman orientation: Mandatory. Preregistration for classes offered. **Housing:** Special program places students in homes of elderly residents who have spare rooms and need assistance. **Activities:** Bands, choral groups, dance, drama, film society, international student organizations, literary magazine, music ensembles, musical theater, radio station, student government, student newspaper, symphony orchestra, TV station, Baptist student center, Catholic student center, Methodist student center, Church of Christ student center, black student alliance, United Mexican-American Students, College Republicans, Young Democrats, Young Socialist Alliance.

Athletics. Intramural: Basketball, bowling, cheerleading, cross-country, fencing, golf, racquetball, soccer, softball, swimming, table tennis, tennis, triathlon, volleyball, water polo. **Team name:** Rangers.

Student services. Adult student services, alcohol/substance abuse counseling, chaplain/spiritual director, career counseling, services for economically disadvantaged, student employment services, financial aid counseling, health services, on-campus daycare, personal counseling, placement for graduates, veterans' counselor, women's services. **Physically disabled:** Services for visually, speech, hearing impaired. **Transfer:** Pre-admission transcript evaluation for new students. Transfer center, transfer adviser, college fairs on campus for students transferring to 4-year colleges.

Contact. E-mail: sac-ar@mail.accd.edu
Phone: (210) 486-0700 Toll-free number: (800) 944-7575
Fax: (210) 486-1543
J. Martin Ortega, Director of Admissions and Records, San Antonio College, 1300 San Pedro Avenue, San Antonio, TX 78212-4299

San Jacinto College
Pasadena, Texas
www.sanjac.edu

CB code: 6694

♦ Public 2-year community and technical college
♦ Commuter campus in very large city

General. Founded in 1960. Regionally accredited. Campuses in Houston and Pasadena and multiple extension centers. Aerospace and Biotechnology Academy (NASA-Johnson Space Center). **Enrollment:** 27,856 degree-seeking undergraduates; 1,536 non-degree-seeking students. **Degrees:** 2,489 associate awarded. **ROTC:** Air Force. **Location:** 20 miles from Houston. **Calendar:** Semester, limited summer session. **Full-time faculty:** 495 total; 16% have terminal degrees, 25% minority, 54% women. **Part-time faculty:** 702 total; 10% have terminal degrees, 32% minority, 57% women. **Class size:** 32% < 20, 64% 20-39, 1% 40-49, less than 1% 50-99, 3% >100. **Special facilities:** Nature preserve (North Campus). **Partnerships:** Formal partnerships with NASA Space Center Houston, Partnership for Innovation in Biotechnology and Life Sciences, Boeing for Reduced Gravity Student Flight Program, University of Houston-College of Engineering for Aerospace Workforce Innovation Network.

Student profile. Among degree-seeking undergraduates, 27% enrolled in a transfer program, 27% enrolled in a vocational program, 5,198 enrolled as first-time, first-year students, 1,623 transferred in from other institutions.

Part-time:	68%	Hispanic American:	41%
Out-of-state:	1%	Native American:	1%
Women:	57%	International:	2%
African American:	10%	25 or older:	30%
Asian American:	5%		

Transfer out. Colleges most students transferred to 2011: University of Houston, University of Houston-Clear Lake, Houston Community College, Texas A&M University, University of Texas at Austin.

Basis for selection. Open admission, but selective for some programs. Special requirements for health science program. Psychological Services Bureau test and interview required of nursing applicants. SAT or ACT score used for nursing, medical laboratory technology, radiography, and respiratory programs. In some selective programs, specific courses taken successfully within San Jacinto district may obviate need for qualifying SAT/ACT scores. Interview recommended for nursing program, and EMT programs. **Learning Disabled:** Students should meet with Special Populations counselor after registering for classes.

High school preparation. College-preparatory program recommended.

2011-2012 Annual costs. Tuition/fees: $1,680; $2,430 out-of-district; $3,930 out-of-state. Per-credit charge: $38 in-district; $63 out-of-district; $113 out-of-state. Books/supplies: $700.

2010-2011 Financial aid. All financial aid based on need. 1,933 full-time freshmen applied for aid; 1,513 were judged to have need; 1,482 of these received aid. Average need met was 1%. Average scholarship/grant was $4,038; average loan $2,820. 69% of total undergraduate aid awarded as scholarships/grants, 31% as loans/jobs. Need-based aid available for part-time students. Work-study available nights, weekends and for part-time students.

Application procedures. Admission: No deadline. No application fee. Application must be submitted online. Admission notification on a rolling basis. **Financial aid:** Priority date 7/1; no closing date. FAFSA, institutional form required. Applicants notified on a rolling basis starting 4/1; must reply within 4 week(s) of notification.

Academics. Special study options: Accelerated study, cooperative education, cross-registration, distance learning, double major, dual enrollment of high school students, ESL, honors, internships, teacher certification program, weekend college. License preparation in aviation, nursing, paramedic, radiology, real estate. **Credit/placement by examination:** AP, CLEP, institutional tests. Freshman College Composition CLEP subject examination must be accompanied by essay. **Support services:** GED preparation and test center, learning center, pre-admission summer program, remedial instruction, study skills assistance, tutoring, writing center.

Majors. Area/ethnic studies: Chicano/Hispanic-American/Latino. **Biology:** General, biotechnology. **Business:** General, accounting, administrative services, business admin, international, management information systems, office technology, real estate. **Communications:** Journalism. **Communications technology:** Radio/TV. **Computer sciences:** General, LAN/WAN management, programming, security, webmaster. **Conservation:** Environmental science. **Education:** Elementary, kindergarten/preschool, middle, science, secondary. **Engineering:** Engineering mechanics. **English:** English lit. **Foreign languages:** General. **General:** Agribusiness operations. **Health services:** Clinical lab science, clinical lab technology, EMT paramedic, licensed practical nurse, medical records technology, medical secretary, mental health counseling, nursing (RN), optometric assistant, physical therapy assistant, radiologic technology/medical imaging, respiratory therapy technology, sonography, surgical technology. **History:** General. **Math:** General. **Parks/recreation:** Health/fitness. **Philosophy/religion:** Philosophy. **Physical sciences:** General, chemistry, geology, physics. **Protective services:** Fire safety technology, firefighting, police science. **Psychology:** General. **Social sciences:** General, political science, sociology. **Visual/performing arts:** Art, commercial/advertising art, dance, design, dramatic, film/cinema/video, interior design, music. **Work/family studies:** Child development, institutional food production.

Most popular majors. Biological/life sciences 6%, business/marketing 14%, health sciences 20%, liberal arts 23%.

Computing on campus. 200 workstations in library, computer center. Online course registration, helpline, repair service, wireless network available.

Student life. Freshman orientation: Mandatory. Preregistration for classes offered. Choice of on-campus or online orientation. 4-hour sessions scheduled several times prior to beginning of semester. **Policies:** Student conduct code. **Activities:** Jazz band, choral groups, dance, drama, literary magazine, music ensembles, musical theater, student government, student newspaper, Phi Theta Kappa honor society, Latin American student organization, College Republicans, College Democrats, Phi Beta Lambda, Texas student education association, student government association.

Athletics. NJCAA. **Intercollegiate:** Baseball M, basketball, volleyball W. **Intramural:** Badminton, basketball, racquetball, softball, swimming, tennis, volleyball, weight lifting. **Team name:** Ravens / Gators / Coyotes.

Student services. Alcohol/substance abuse counseling, career counseling, student employment services, financial aid counseling, on-campus daycare, personal counseling, placement for graduates, veterans' counselor. **Transfer:**

Transfer adviser, college fairs on campus for students transferring to 4-year colleges.

Contact. E-mail: information@sjcd.edu
Phone: (281) 998-6150 Fax: (281) 478-2720
Wanda Munson, Dean of Enrollment Management & College Registrar, San Jacinto College, 8060 Spencer Highway, Pasadena, TX 77505-5999

Sanford-Brown College: Houston
Houston, Texas
www.sanfordbrown.edu/Houston

⦁ For-profit 2-year health science and career college
⦁ Commuter campus in very large city

General. Regionally accredited; also accredited by ACICS. **Enrollment:** 1,200 degree-seeking undergraduates. **Calendar:** Semester. **Full-time faculty:** 52 total. **Part-time faculty:** 40 total.

Basis for selection. Open admission.

Financial aid. Need-based: Work-study available nights, weekends and for part-time students.

Academics. Credit/placement by examination: AP, CLEP.

Majors. Health services: Anesthesiologist assistant, cardiovascular technology, clinical lab technology, sonography.

Contact. E-mail: vsmith@sbhouston.com
Phone: (713) 779-1110 Toll-free number: (855) 525-9444
William Harris, Director of Admissions, Sanford-Brown College: Houston, 9999 Richmond Avenue, Houston, TX 77042

South Plains College
Levelland, Texas
www.southplainscollege.edu   CB code: 6695

⦁ Public 2-year community and junior college
⦁ Commuter campus in large town

General. Founded in 1957. Regionally accredited. **Enrollment:** 8,335 degree-seeking undergraduates; 1,885 non-degree-seeking students. **Degrees:** 614 associate awarded. **Location:** 30 miles from Lubbock. **Calendar:** Semester, extensive summer session. **Full-time faculty:** 263 total. **Part-time faculty:** 197 total. **Special facilities:** Audio/video recording studio, fine art gallery.

Student profile. Among degree-seeking undergraduates, 75% enrolled in a transfer program, 25% enrolled in a vocational program, 1% already have a bachelor's degree or higher, 1,574 enrolled as first-time, first-year students.

Part-time:	51%	Hispanic American:	36%
Out-of-state:	3%	Native American:	1%
Women:	54%	International:	1%
African American:	6%	25 or older:	21%
Asian American:	1%	Live on campus:	10%

Transfer out. 42% of students enrolled in the transfer program go on to 4-year colleges. **Colleges most students transferred to 2011:** Texas Tech University, Angelo State University, West Texas A&M University, Eastern New Mexico State University.

Basis for selection. Open admission, but selective for some programs. State law requires THEA exam before student may enroll in college-level course work. Special requirements for allied health, cosmetology, law enforcement academy programs. Interview required for health care.

2011-2012 Annual costs. Tuition/fees: $2,312; $2,966 out-of-district; $3,452 out-of-state. Room/board: $3,100. Books/supplies: $580. Personal expenses: $1,100.

Financial aid. Need-based: Need-based aid available for part-time students. Work-study available nights, weekends and for part-time students. **Non-need-based:** Scholarships awarded for academics, art, athletics, leadership, music/drama, state residency.

Application procedures. Admission: No deadline. No application fee. Admission notification on a rolling basis. **Financial aid:** Priority date 6/1; no closing date. FAFSA required. Applicants notified on a rolling basis starting 6/30; must reply within 2 week(s) of notification.

Academics. Special study options: Distance learning, dual enrollment of high school students, internships. License preparation in nursing, occupational therapy, paramedic, physical therapy, radiology, real estate. **Credit/placement by examination:** AP, CLEP, institutional tests. 15 credit hours maximum toward associate degree. **Support services:** GED preparation, learning center, remedial instruction, study skills assistance, tutoring.

Majors. Biology: General. **Business:** Accounting, administrative services, business admin, fashion, office management, real estate. **Communications:** Broadcast journalism, communications/speech/rhetoric, journalism. **Communications technology:** Graphic/printing. **Computer sciences:** General, computer science, data processing. **Education:** General. **Engineering:** General. **English:** English lit. **Foreign languages:** French, Spanish. **General:** Business. **Health services:** Athletic training, EMT paramedic, medical radiologic technology/radiation therapy, medical records technology, medical secretary, nursing (RN), predental, premedicine, prenursing, preop/surgical nursing, prepharmacy, preveterinary, respiratory therapy technology. **History:** General. **Liberal arts:** Arts/sciences. **Math:** General. **Parks/recreation:** Health/fitness. **Physical sciences:** Chemistry, geology, physics. **Protective services:** Fire safety technology, firefighting, law enforcement admin. **Psychology:** General. **Social sciences:** Criminology, political science, sociology. **Visual/performing arts:** Cinematography, commercial/advertising art, design, dramatic, music. **Work/family studies:** General, child care management.

Most popular majors. Business/marketing 12%, education 11%, health sciences 16%, liberal arts 33%, trade and industry 6%.

Computing on campus. 2,000 workstations in dormitories, library, computer center, student center. Dormitories linked to campus network. Commuter students can connect to campus network. Online course registration, online library, wireless network available.

Student life. Freshman orientation: Mandatory. Preregistration for classes offered. **Housing:** Single-sex dorms, special housing for disabled, apartments available. $100 deposit. **Activities:** Bands, campus ministries, choral groups, dance, drama, international student organizations, literary magazine, music ensembles, musical theater, opera, radio station, student government, student newspaper, symphony orchestra, TV station.

Athletics. NJCAA. **Intercollegiate:** Basketball, cheerleading, cross-country, rodeo, track and field. **Intramural:** Basketball, football (non-tackle), golf, racquetball, soccer, softball, table tennis, tennis, volleyball. **Team name:** Texans/Lady Texans.

Student services. Career counseling, student employment services, financial aid counseling, health services, minority student services, personal counseling, placement for graduates, veterans' counselor. **Physically disabled:** Services for visually, hearing impaired. **Transfer:** Transfer adviser, college fairs on campus for students transferring to 4-year colleges.

Contact. E-mail: arangel@southplainscollege.edu
Phone: (806) 894-9611 ext. 2373 Fax: (806) 897-3167
Andrea Rangel, Dean of Admissions and Records, South Plains College, 1401 South College Avenue, Levelland, TX 79336

South Texas College
McAllen, Texas
www.southtexascollege.edu   **CB code: 6654**

- Public 2-year community and technical college
- Commuter campus in very large city

General. Regionally accredited. Virtual campus with full online student services and student learning support. **Enrollment:** 29,562 degree-seeking undergraduates. **Degrees:** 113 bachelor's, 2,077 associate awarded. **Location:** 250 miles from San Antonio. **Calendar:** Semester, extensive summer session. **Full-time faculty:** 525 total; 19% have terminal degrees, 60% minority, 43% women. **Part-time faculty:** 418 total; 6% have terminal degrees, 81% minority, 53% women. **Class size:** 37% < 20, 61% 20-39, less than 1% 40-49, less than 1% 50-99, less than 1% >100.

Student profile. Among degree-seeking undergraduates, 4,518 enrolled as first-time, first-year students, 813 transferred in from other institutions.

Part-time:	63%	**Hispanic American:**	91%
Women:	57%	**25 or older:**	22%
Asian American:	1%		

Transfer out. 48% of students enrolled in the transfer program go on to 4-year colleges. **Colleges most students transferred to 2011:** University of Texas-Pan American.

Basis for selection. Open admission, but selective for some programs. Nursing and allied health programs determine admissions based on an internal ranking system which factors GPA for all coursework including prequisite

courses, GPA for all non-native coursework, and test scores including college entrance exams and college placement tests. **Home schooled:** Transcript of courses and grades required. **Learning Disabled:** Accommodations made for ADA students upon request and documentation of services needed. No special admission requirements.

2012-2013 Annual costs. Tuition/fees (projected): $3,150; $3,423 out-of-district; $7,200 out-of-state. Books/supplies: $1,200. Personal expenses: $1,200.

2010-2011 Financial aid. Need-based: 99% of total undergraduate aid awarded as scholarships/grants, 1% as loans/jobs. Need-based aid available for part-time students. Work-study available nights, weekends and for part-time students. **Non-need-based:** Scholarships awarded for academics.

Application procedures. Admission: No deadline. No application fee. Admission notification on a rolling basis. **Financial aid:** Priority date 3/1; no closing date. FAFSA required. Applicants notified on a rolling basis starting 4/15.

Academics. Special study options: Accelerated study, cooperative education, distance learning, double major, dual enrollment of high school students, ESL, honors, independent study, internships, study abroad, weekend college. Bachelor's degree programs available on campus. **Credit/placement by examination:** AP, CLEP, IB, institutional tests. **Support services:** GED test center, learning center, remedial instruction, study skills assistance, tutoring, writing center.

Majors. Architecture: Technology. **Area/ethnic studies:** Chicano/Hispanic-American/Latino. **Biology:** General. **Business:** Accounting, banking/financial services, business admin, logistics, marketing, office management. **Computer sciences:** General, applications programming, computer science, networking, security, support specialist, web page design, webmaster. **Education:** Early childhood, elementary, middle, secondary. **Engineering:** General. **English:** English lit. **Foreign languages:** Sign language interpretation, Spanish. **Health services:** EMT paramedic, medical records technology, nursing assistant, occupational therapy assistant, office assistant, pharmacy assistant, physical therapy assistant, radiologic technology/medical imaging. **History:** General. **Liberal arts:** Arts/sciences. **Math:** General. **Parks/recreation:** Exercise sciences. **Philosophy/religion:** Philosophy. **Physical sciences:** Chemistry, physics. **Protective services:** Law enforcement admin. **Psychology:** General. **Social sciences:** General, political science. **Visual/performing arts:** General, music, studio arts. **Work/family studies:** Child development.

Most popular majors. Biological/life sciences 7%, business/marketing 10%, education 20%, health sciences 14%, liberal arts 10%, psychology 6%.

Computing on campus. Online course registration, online library, helpline, wireless network available.

Student life. Freshman orientation: Mandatory. Preregistration for classes offered. **Activities:** Campus ministries, drama, film society, literary magazine, musical theater, student government.

Athletics. Intramural: Basketball, football (non-tackle), football (tackle), softball, volleyball. **Team name:** Jaguars.

Student services. Adult student services, career counseling, services for economically disadvantaged, student employment services, financial aid counseling, minority student services, on-campus daycare, personal counseling, placement for graduates, veterans' counselor, women's services. **Physically disabled:** Services for visually, speech, hearing impaired. **Transfer:** Pre-admission transcript evaluation for new students. Transfer center, transfer adviser, college fairs on campus for students transferring to 4-year colleges.

Contact. Phone: (956) 872-8311 Toll-free number: (800) 742-7822
Fax: (956) 872-8321
Matthew Hebbard, Director of Admissions and Registrar, South Texas College, 3201 West Pecan Boulevard, McAllen, TX 78502

Southwest Institute of Technology
Austin, Texas
www.switaustin.com   **CB code: 2471**

- For-profit 2-year technical college
- Commuter campus in large city

General. Accredited by ACCSCT. **Calendar:** Quarter.

Annual costs/financial aid. Books/supplies: $1,526. Need-based financial aid available for full-time students.

Contact. Phone: (512) 892-2640
Director of Admissions, 5424 Highway 290 West, Suite 200, Austin, TX 78735

Southwest Texas Junior College
Uvalde, Texas
www.swtjc.edu   CB code: 6666

- Public 2-year community and junior college
- Commuter campus in large town

General. Founded in 1946. Regionally accredited. **Enrollment:** 2,043 full-time, degree-seeking students. **Degrees:** 489 associate awarded. **Location:** 80 miles from San Antonio, 70 miles from Del Rio. **Calendar:** Semester, limited summer session. **Full-time faculty:** 115 total. **Part-time faculty:** 86 total.

Student profile.

Out-of-state: 10%   Live on campus: 9%

Basis for selection. Open admission.

2011-2012 Annual costs. Tuition/fees: $2,291; $3,746 out-of-district; $4,241 out-of-state. Per-credit charge: $55 in-district; $104 out-of-district; $120 out-of-state. Required fees specified apply to Uvalde campus; the amount for the Del Rio and Eagle Pass campuses is $922.50; for all other sites, $735. Room/board: $3,600. Books/supplies: $1,680. Personal expenses: $2,400.

Financial aid. Need-based: Need-based aid available for part-time students. Work-study available nights, weekends and for part-time students.

Application procedures. Admission: No deadline. No application fee. Admission notification on a rolling basis. **Financial aid:** Priority date 6/15; no closing date. FAFSA required. Applicants notified on a rolling basis starting 5/1; must reply within 2 week(s) of notification.

Academics. Special study options: Dual enrollment of high school students. License preparation in aviation, nursing. **Credit/placement by examination:** AP, CLEP. TASP required of all students for placement and counseling. **Support services:** GED preparation and test center, learning center, remedial instruction, study skills assistance, tutoring, writing center.

Majors. Business: Administrative services, management information systems, office technology. **Computer sciences:** General, data processing. **Education:** General. **General:** Agribusiness operations, business, farm/ranch. **Health services:** Licensed practical nurse, nursing (RN). **Liberal arts:** Arts/sciences.

Computing on campus. 150 workstations in dormitories, library, computer center. Dormitories wired for high-speed internet access and linked to campus network. Commuter students can connect to campus network. Online library, helpline available.

Student life. Freshman orientation: Mandatory. Preregistration for classes offered. **Housing:** Coed dorms, single-sex dorms available. **Activities:** Drama, literary magazine, radio station, student government, student newspaper.

Athletics. Intercollegiate: Rodeo. **Intramural:** Baseball M, basketball, golf, racquetball, softball, swimming, tennis, volleyball.

Student services. Adult student services, chaplain/spiritual director, career counseling, services for economically disadvantaged, student employment services, financial aid counseling, health services, minority student services, on-campus daycare, personal counseling, placement for graduates, veterans' counselor. **Physically disabled:** Services for visually, hearing impaired. **Transfer:** Pre-admission transcript evaluation for new students. Transfer adviser, college fairs on campus for students transferring to 4-year colleges.

Contact. E-mail: luana.rodriguez@swtjc.cc.tx.us
Phone: (830) 278-4401 Fax: (830) 591-7396
Joe Barker, Dean of Admissions/Student Services, Southwest Texas Junior College, 2401 Garner Field Road, Uvalde, TX 78801

St. Philip's College
San Antonio, Texas
www.alamo.edu/spc   CB member   CB code: 6642

- Public 2-year community college
- Commuter campus in very large city

General. Founded in 1898. Regionally accredited. Some courses held at off-campus sites throughout San Antonio. **Enrollment:** 8,267 degree-seeking undergraduates. **Degrees:** 614 associate awarded. **ROTC:** Army. **Location:** 1 mile from downtown. **Calendar:** Semester, extensive summer session. **Full-time faculty:** 188 total; 11% have terminal degrees, 47% minority, 45% women. **Part-time faculty:** 249 total; 7% have terminal degrees, 49% minority, 45% women. **Class size:** 50% < 20, 46% 20-39, less than 1% 40-49, 3% 50-99. **Special facilities:** Restaurant on campus run by hospitality students, human patient simulator, diesel lab. **Partnerships:** Formal partnerships with Boeing and Dee Howard for aircraft technology training.

Student profile. Among degree-seeking undergraduates, 49% enrolled in a transfer program, 51% enrolled in a vocational program.

Out-of-state: 1%   **25 or older:**   46%

Transfer out. Colleges most students transferred to 2011: University of Texas at San Antonio, Texas State University.

Basis for selection. Open admission, but selective for some programs. Special requirements for nursing and certain allied health programs. **Adult students:** Students age 65 and older do not have to test if they are auditing classes. **Home schooled:** Transcript of courses and grades required.

2011-2012 Annual costs. Tuition/fees: $1,980; $3,660 out-of-district; $7,020 out-of-state. Per-credit charge: $56 in-district; $112 out-of-district; $224 out-of-state. Books/supplies: $1,350. Personal expenses: $2,185.

2011-2012 Financial aid. All financial aid based on need. 75% of total undergraduate aid awarded as scholarships/grants, 25% as loans/jobs. Need-based aid available for part-time students. Work-study available nights, weekends and for part-time students.

Application procedures. Admission: No deadline. No application fee. **Financial aid:** No deadline. FAFSA required.

Academics. Special study options: Accelerated study, cooperative education, cross-registration, distance learning, double major, dual enrollment of high school students, ESL, honors, independent study, internships, study abroad, weekend college. License preparation in aviation, nursing, occupational therapy, physical therapy, radiology, real estate. **Credit/placement by examination:** AP, CLEP, institutional tests. 32 credit hours maximum toward associate degree. **Support services:** GED preparation and test center, learning center, pre-admission summer program, reduced course load, remedial instruction, study skills assistance, tutoring, writing center.

Majors. Architecture: Interior. **Biology:** General, biomedical sciences. **Business:** Accounting, accounting technology, administrative services, business admin, construction management, hospitality admin, tourism/travel. **Communications technology:** General. **Computer sciences:** Data entry, data processing, information systems, LAN/WAN management, programming, webmaster. **Conservation:** General. **Education:** General, teacher assistance. **Engineering:** General. **English:** Rhetoric/composition, writing. **Foreign languages:** General, Spanish. **Health services:** Clinical lab technology, medical radiologic technology/radiation therapy, medical records admin, medical records technology, medical secretary, occupational therapy assistant, physical therapy assistant, predental, premedicine, prenursing, respiratory therapy technology. **History:** General. **Human services:** Social work. **Liberal arts:** Arts/sciences. **Math:** General. **Parks/recreation:** Health/fitness. **Philosophy/religion:** Philosophy. **Physical sciences:** Chemistry, geology. **Protective services:** Law enforcement admin. **Psychology:** General. **Social sciences:** Economics, political science, sociology, urban studies. **Visual/performing arts:** Art, dramatic, music, studio arts. **Work/family studies:** Child care management, institutional food production.

Most popular majors. Business/marketing 7%, engineering/engineering technologies 7%, health sciences 39%, liberal arts 11%, personal/culinary services 7%, trade and industry 11%.

Computing on campus. 2,623 workstations in library, computer center. Commuter students can connect to campus network. Online course registration, online library, helpline, repair service available.

Student life. Freshman orientation: Mandatory. Preregistration for classes offered. **Activities:** Jazz band, campus ministries, choral groups, dance, drama, international student organizations, literary magazine, music ensembles, musical theater, student government, student newspaper, Black Educational Network, Los Unidos, African-American Men on the Move, Campus Crusade for Christ.

Athletics. Intramural: Basketball, swimming, table tennis, tennis, volleyball, weight lifting. **Team name:** Tigers.

Student services. Adult student services, chaplain/spiritual director, career counseling, services for economically disadvantaged, student employment services, financial aid counseling, health services, on-campus daycare, personal counseling, placement for graduates, veterans' counselor, women's

services. **Physically disabled:** Services for visually, hearing impaired. **Transfer:** Transfer center, transfer adviser, college fairs on campus for students transferring to 4-year colleges.

Contact. E-mail: angarza2@alamo.edu
Phone: (210) 486-2300 Fax: (210) 486-2836
Ana Garza, Director of Enrollment Management, St. Philip's College, 1801 Martin Luther King Drive, San Antonio, TX 78203

Tarrant County College
Fort Worth, Texas
www.tccd.edu

CB member
CB code: 6834

▶ Public 2-year community college
▶ Commuter campus in very large city

General. Founded in 1965. Regionally accredited. Five campuses located within Tarrant County: South, Northwest, and Trinity River Campuses in Fort Worth; Northeast Campus in Hurst; and Southeast Campus in Arlington. **Enrollment:** 50,089 degree-seeking undergraduates. **Degrees:** 3,355 associate awarded. **ROTC:** Army, Air Force. **Calendar:** Semester, extensive summer session. **Full-time faculty:** 648 total; 18% have terminal degrees, 30% minority, 56% women. **Part-time faculty:** 1,168 total; 14% have terminal degrees, 22% minority, 51% women.

Student profile.

Out-of-state:	1%	25 or older:	37%

Transfer out. Colleges most students transferred to 2011: University of Texas at Arlington, University of North Texas, Texas Woman's University, Texas Tech University, Texas State University.

Basis for selection. Open admission, but selective for some programs. Special requirements for nursing and allied health programs, and certain automotive programs; must submit separate application and meet highly selective admission criteria. Placement testing required of all first-time college students and for those entering certain English, math, and reading-based courses. Interview and essay may be required for selective admission programs. **Home schooled:** Transcript of courses and grades required.

2012-2013 Annual costs. Tuition/fees (projected): $1,560; $2,280 out-of-district; $5,130 out-of-state. Per-credit charge: $52 in-district; $76 out-of-district; $171 out-of-state. Books/supplies: $1,426. Personal expenses: $1,843.

2010-2011 Financial aid. Need-based: 82% of total undergraduate aid awarded as scholarships/grants, 18% as loans/jobs. Need-based aid available for part-time students. Work-study available nights, weekends and for part-time students. **Non-need-based:** Scholarships awarded for academics.

Application procedures. Admission: Closing date 8/15 (receipt date). No application fee. Admission notification on a rolling basis. There is a deadline for International applicants. Applicants 18 years of age or older without high school diploma may be admitted on individual basis. **Financial aid:** Priority date 5/1; no closing date. FAFSA, institutional form required. Applicants notified on a rolling basis starting 5/1; must reply within 2 week(s) of notification.

Academics. Core curriculum guaranteed to transfer to any Texas public university. **Special study options:** Distance learning, double major, dual enrollment of high school students, ESL, honors, liberal arts/career combination. Limited Saturday classes available. License preparation in aviation, dental hygiene, nursing, paramedic, physical therapy, radiology, real estate. **Credit/placement by examination:** AP, CLEP, institutional tests. 18 credit hours maximum toward associate degree. **Support services:** GED preparation and test center, learning center, reduced course load, remedial instruction, study skills assistance, tutoring, writing center.

Majors. Business: General, accounting technology, administrative services, business admin, operations, real estate, tourism/travel. **Communications technology:** Graphic/printing, radio/TV. **Computer sciences:** General, networking, programming. **Education:** Early childhood, middle, secondary. **Foreign languages:** Sign language interpretation. **General:** Horticulture. **Health services:** Dental hygiene, dietician assistant, EMT paramedic, medical records technology, mental health services, nursing (RN), physical therapy assistant, radiologic technology/medical imaging, respiratory therapy technology. **Human services:** General. **Protective services:** Criminal justice, fire safety technology. **Social sciences:** GIS/cartography. **Work/family studies:** Child development.

Computing on campus. 3,000 workstations in library, computer center, student center. Commuter students can connect to campus network. Online course registration, online library, wireless network available.

Student life. Freshman orientation: Available. Preregistration for classes offered. 1-2 hours, held intermittently. **Activities:** Bands, choral groups, dance, drama, literary magazine, music ensembles, student government, student newspaper.

Athletics. Intramural: Basketball M, table tennis.

Student services. Adult student services, career counseling, services for economically disadvantaged, student employment services, financial aid counseling, health services, personal counseling, placement for graduates. **Physically disabled:** Services for visually, speech, hearing impaired. **Transfer:** College fairs on campus for students transferring to 4-year colleges.

Contact. Phone: (817) 515-8223 Fax: (817) 515-5283
Assistant Director for Admissions Services, Tarrant County College, 1500 Houston Street, Fort Worth, TX 76102-6599

Temple College
Temple, Texas
www.templejc.edu

CB code: 6818

▶ Public 2-year community college
▶ Commuter campus in small city

General. Founded in 1926. Regionally accredited. **Enrollment:** 5,464 degree-seeking undergraduates. **Degrees:** 404 associate awarded. **Location:** 65 miles from Austin. **Calendar:** Semester, limited summer session. **Full-time faculty:** 119 total. **Part-time faculty:** 182 total. **Class size:** 51% < 20, 48% 20-39, less than 1% 40-49, 1% 50-99. **Special facilities:** Health sciences simulation center. **Partnerships:** Formal partnerships with area high schools for tech prep programs.

Student profile.

Out-of-state:	1%	25 or older:	38%

Transfer out. Colleges most students transferred to 2011: Texas A&M University, Tarleton State University, Texas State University, University of Texas at Austin, University of Mary Hardin-Baylor.

Basis for selection. Open admission, but selective for some programs. Limited enrollment in allied health programs; interview required. **Home schooled:** Transcript of courses and grades required.

High school preparation. College-preparatory program recommended. 23 units recommended. Recommended units include English 4, mathematics 3, social studies 2, history 2, science 3, foreign language 2 and academic electives 7.

2011-2012 Annual costs. Tuition/fees: $2,640; $4,620 out-of-district; $7,020 out-of-state. Per-credit charge: $88 in-district; $154 out-of-district; $234 out-of-state. Books/supplies: $1,329. Personal expenses: $1,658.

Financial aid. All financial aid based on need. Need-based aid available for part-time students. Work-study available nights, weekends and for part-time students.

Application procedures. Admission: No deadline. No application fee. Admission notification on a rolling basis. **Financial aid:** Priority date 6/1; no closing date. FAFSA required. Applicants notified on a rolling basis starting 5/1; must reply within 4 week(s) of notification.

Academics. Special study options: Accelerated study, cooperative education, distance learning, dual enrollment of high school students, ESL, honors, internships. License preparation in dental hygiene, nursing, paramedic. **Credit/placement by examination:** AP, CLEP, IB, institutional tests. 32 credit hours maximum toward associate degree. Last 18 hours or total 32 hours earned in residence may not be earned through credit by examination. **Support services:** GED preparation, learning center, remedial instruction, study skills assistance, tutoring, writing center.

Majors. Biology: General. **Business:** General, office management. **Computer sciences:** General, data entry, LAN/WAN management, programming, system admin, webmaster. **Education:** Elementary, teacher assistance. **Engineering:** General. **Health services:** Dental hygiene, EMT paramedic, nursing (RN), respiratory therapy technology, sonography. **Human services:** Social work. **Liberal arts:** Arts/sciences. **Math:** General. **Protective services:** Criminal justice. **Social sciences:** GIS/cartography. **Visual/performing arts:** Art, music. **Work/family studies:** Child development.

Most popular majors. Business/marketing 14%, health sciences 26%, liberal arts 39%.

Computing on campus. 150 workstations in dormitories, library, computer center, student center. Dormitories wired for high-speed internet access

Two-Year Colleges

and linked to campus network. Commuter students can connect to campus network. Online library, helpline, repair service, wireless network available.

Student life. Freshman orientation: Available. Preregistration for classes offered. Held prior to fall semester; 4 hours over 2 days. **Housing:** Apartments available. Privately run student apartments on campus. **Activities:** Bands, campus ministries, choral groups, dance, drama, literary magazine, music ensembles, musical theater, student government, symphony orchestra, Black American Cultural Club, Society of Latin American Cultures, College Republicans, Young Democrats, Literary Club, Baptist Student Ministries.

Athletics. NJCAA. Intercollegiate: Baseball M, basketball, softball W, tennis, volleyball W. **Intramural:** Basketball, bowling, football (non-tackle), golf, racquetball, soccer, softball, swimming, table tennis, tennis, volleyball. **Team name:** Leopards.

Student services. Adult student services, career counseling, services for economically disadvantaged, student employment services, financial aid counseling, personal counseling, placement for graduates, veterans' counselor. **Physically disabled:** Services for visually, hearing impaired. **Transfer:** Preadmission transcript evaluation for new students. Transfer adviser, college fairs on campus for students transferring to 4-year colleges.

Contact. E-mail: carey.rose@templejc.edu
Phone: (254) 298-8300 Toll-free number: (800) 460-4636
Fax: (254) 298-8288
Carey Rose, Director of Admission and Records, Temple College, 2600 South First Street, Temple, TX 76504-7435

Texarkana College
Texarkana, Texas
www.texarkanacollege.edu   CB code: 6819

♦ Public 2-year community college
♦ Commuter campus in small city

General. Founded in 1927. Regionally accredited. **Enrollment:** 4,484 undergraduates. **Degrees:** 275 associate awarded. **Location:** 80 miles from Shreveport, Louisiana; 120 miles from Little Rock, Arkansas; 180 miles from Dallas. **Calendar:** Semester, limited summer session. **Full-time faculty:** 103 total. **Part-time faculty:** 282 total. **Special facilities:** 365-acre farm.

Student profile.

Out-of-state:	30%	Live on campus:	3%
25 or older:	38%		

Transfer out. Colleges most students transferred to 2011: Texas A&M at Texarkana, Southern Arkansas University.

Basis for selection. Open admission. Interview recommended for nursing program.

2011-2012 Annual costs. Tuition/fees: $1,830; $3,090 out-of-district; $4,260 out-of-state. Per-credit charge: $39 in-district; $81 out-of-district; $120 out-of-state. Arkansas and Oklahoma residents pay out-of-district rates. Books/supplies: $1,962. Personal expenses: $1,200.

Financial aid. Need-based: Need-based aid available for part-time students. Work-study available nights, weekends and for part-time students. **Non-need-based:** Scholarships awarded for academics, athletics.

Application procedures. Admission: No deadline. No application fee. Admission notification on a rolling basis. **Financial aid:** Priority date 6/1; no closing date. FAFSA, institutional form required. Applicants notified on a rolling basis starting 3/1.

Academics. Special study options: Cooperative education, cross-registration, distance learning, dual enrollment of high school students, honors, internships, liberal arts/career combination. License preparation in nursing, paramedic. **Credit/placement by examination:** AP, CLEP. 14 credit hours maximum toward associate degree. **Support services:** GED test center, learning center, remedial instruction, study skills assistance, tutoring.

Majors. Biology: General. **Business:** General, administrative services, business admin, marketing. **Communications:** Journalism. **Computer sciences:** General. **Engineering:** General. **Foreign languages:** General. **Health services:** EMT paramedic, nursing (RN), substance abuse counseling. **History:** General. **Liberal arts:** Humanities. **Math:** General. **Physical sciences:** Chemistry, physics. **Protective services:** Criminal justice, law enforcement admin. **Social sciences:** General, political science. **Visual/performing arts:** Art, dramatic, music. **Work/family studies:** Child development.

Most popular majors. Business/marketing 8%, health sciences 24%, liberal arts 41%.

Computing on campus. 500 workstations in library, computer center. Dormitories wired for high-speed internet access. Online course registration, online library, wireless network available.

Student life. Freshman orientation: Available, $137 fee. Preregistration for classes offered. **Housing:** Coed dorms available. $150 fully refundable deposit, deadline 5/1. Pets allowed in dorm rooms. **Activities:** Concert band, choral groups, drama, literary magazine, musical theater, radio station, student government, student newspaper, Baptist student union, Black student association, 21st century Democrats, Young Republicans, Earth club.

Athletics. NJCAA. Intercollegiate: Baseball M, golf, softball W. **Intramural:** Archery, badminton, basketball, bowling, football (non-tackle), handball, racquetball, soccer, softball, swimming, tennis, volleyball. **Team name:** Bulldogs.

Student services. Career counseling, student employment services, personal counseling, veterans' counselor. **Physically disabled:** Services for visually, speech, hearing impaired. **Transfer:** College fairs on campus for students transferring to 4-year colleges.

Contact. E-mail: admissions@texarkanacollege.edu
Phone: (903) 832-5565 ext. 3358 Fax: (903) 832-5030
Tom Elder, Director of Admissions and Registrar, Texarkana College, 2500 North Robison Road, Texarkana, TX 75599

Texas State Technical College: Harlingen
Harlingen, Texas
www.harlingen.tstc.edu   CB code: 6843

♦ Public 2-year technical college
♦ Commuter campus in small city

General. Founded in 1969. Regionally accredited. **Enrollment:** 3,002 degree-seeking undergraduates; 2,805 non-degree-seeking students. **Degrees:** 364 associate awarded. **Location:** 25 miles from Brownsville, 30 miles from South Padre Island. **Calendar:** Semester, extensive summer session. **Full-time faculty:** 148 total; 5% have terminal degrees, 60% minority, 38% women. **Part-time faculty:** 54 total; 63% minority, 22% women. **Class size:** 49% < 20, 46% 20-39, 2% 40-49, 3% 50-99, less than 1% >100. **Special facilities:** Motors lab for aviation technology, aviation hangars, agricultural pavilion, industrial labs.

Student profile. Among degree-seeking undergraduates, 563 enrolled as first-time, first-year students.

Part-time:	51%	African American:	1%
Out-of-state:	1%	Asian American:	1%
Women:	51%	Hispanic American:	88%

Transfer out. Colleges most students transferred to 2011: University of Texas at Brownsville, University of Texas-Pan American, University of Texas-San Antonio, South Texas College, Texas Southmost College.

Basis for selection. Open admission, but selective for some programs. Competitive admissions for dental assisting, surgical technology, dental hygiene, and health information technology programs. Associate degree candidates required to take state-mandated Texas Academic Skills Program. Results used only for placement. SAT/ACT scores may be substituted. **Home schooled:** Statement describing home school structure and mission required.

2012-2013 Annual costs. Tuition/fees (projected): $6,098; $13,500 out-of-state. Room/board: $7,340. Books/supplies: $1,441. Personal expenses: $2,624.

2011-2012 Financial aid. Need-based: Average scholarship/grant was $3,842; average loan $1,113. 85% of total undergraduate aid awarded as scholarships/grants, 15% as loans/jobs. Need-based aid available for part-time students. Work-study available nights, weekends and for part-time students.

Application procedures. Admission: No deadline. No application fee. Admission notification on a rolling basis. **Financial aid:** Priority date 3/1; no closing date. FAFSA, institutional form required.

Academics. Special study options: Cooperative education, distance learning, dual enrollment of high school students, ESL, independent study, internships, liberal arts/career combination, teacher certification program, weekend college. License preparation in aviation, dental hygiene, nursing, paramedic. **Credit/placement by examination:** AP, CLEP, institutional tests. **Support services:** GED preparation and test center, learning center, remedial instruction, study skills assistance, tutoring.

Majors. Biology: General. **Business:** General, administrative services, executive assistant. **Computer sciences:** Information technology, networking,

programming. **Education:** Teacher assistance. **Engineering:** General. **General:** Business technology. **Health services:** Dental hygiene, dental lab technology, EMT paramedic, medical assistant, medical records technology, surgical technology. **Math:** General. **Visual/performing arts:** Commercial/advertising art.

Most popular majors. Business/marketing 6%, computer/information sciences 10%, education 11%, engineering/engineering technologies 22%, health sciences 22%, trade and industry 13%.

Computing on campus. 1,750 workstations in library, computer center, student center. Online library, helpline available.

Student life. Freshman orientation: Mandatory. Preregistration for classes offered. **Housing:** Guaranteed on-campus for all undergraduates. Coed dorms, special housing for disabled, apartments, wellness housing available. $100 deposit. **Activities:** Campus ministries, dance, literary magazine, student government, student newspaper, Baptist student union, Hispanic club.

Athletics. Intramural: Baseball, basketball, football (tackle), racquetball, soccer, softball, table tennis, volleyball, weight lifting.

Student services. Alcohol/substance abuse counseling, career counseling, student employment services, financial aid counseling, health services, on-campus daycare, personal counseling, placement for graduates, veterans' counselor, women's services. **Physically disabled:** Services for visually, speech, hearing impaired. **Transfer:** Transfer adviser, college fairs on campus for students transferring to 4-year colleges.

Contact. E-mail: paula.arredondo@harlingen.tstc.edu
Phone: (956) 364-4320 Toll-free number: (800) 852-8784
Fax: (956) 364-5117
Paula Arredondo, Registrar, Texas State Technical College: Harlingen, 1902 North Loop 499, Harlingen, TX 78550-3697

Texas State Technical College: Marshall
Marshall, Texas
www.marshall.tstc.edu

- Public 2-year technical college
- Large town

General. Regionally accredited. **Enrollment:** 524 degree-seeking undergraduates. **Degrees:** 183 associate awarded. **Location:** 150 miles from Dallas, 230 miles from Houston. **Calendar:** Semester, extensive summer session. **Full-time faculty:** 40 total. **Part-time faculty:** 13 total.

Basis for selection. Open admission. Admission tests used only for placement.

2011-2012 Annual costs. Tuition/fees: $4,200; $9,000 out-of-state. Room only: $2,410.

Financial aid. Need-based: Work-study available nights, weekends and for part-time students.

Application procedures. Admission: Closing date 8/2. No application fee. Admission notification on a rolling basis. **Financial aid:** Priority date 6/1; no closing date. FAFSA required.

Academics. Credit/placement by examination: AP, CLEP.

Majors. Business: E-commerce. **Communications technology:** General. **Computer sciences:** Artificial intelligence, LAN/WAN management, networking. **Health services:** Environmental health.

Student life. Freshman orientation: Mandatory, $15 fee. Preregistration for classes offered. **Activities:** Student newspaper.

Contact. Phone: (903) 935-1010
Patricia Robbins, Director of Admissions, Texas State Technical College: Marshall, 2650 East End Boulevard South, Marshall, TX 75672

Texas State Technical College: Waco
Waco, Texas
www.waco.tstc.edu CB code: 6328

- Public 2-year technical college
- Residential campus in small city

General. Founded in 1965. Regionally accredited. **Enrollment:** 5,090 degree-seeking undergraduates. **Degrees:** 736 associate awarded. **Location:** 90 miles from Dallas, 99 miles from Austin. **Calendar:** Semester, extensive summer session. **Full-time faculty:** 252 total. **Part-time faculty:** 24 total. **Special facilities:** Advanced manufacturing center, 8,600-foot runway at TSTC-Waco airport, institutionally owned and operated 18-hole golf course.

Basis for selection. Open admission. Accuplacer or THEA test required prior to enrollment; used for placement purposes only. Aircraft pilot training, dental assistant technology, and pharmacy technician students must provide updated immunization data to be admitted and to register. Aircraft pilot training students must provide a current Class II Medical certificate to be eligible to register; fall start only. Interview required for students who indicate felony charges. **Home schooled:** Transcript of courses and grades required.

2011-2012 Annual costs. Tuition/fees: $4,200; $9,000 out-of-state. Room/board: $5,290. Books/supplies: $751. Personal expenses: $1,899.

Financial aid. All financial aid based on need. Need-based aid available for part-time students. Work-study available nights, weekends and for part-time students.

Application procedures. Admission: No deadline. No application fee. Admission notification on a rolling basis. **Financial aid:** Priority date 6/1; no closing date. FAFSA required. Applicants notified on a rolling basis starting 5/15.

Academics. Special study options: Cooperative education, distance learning, double major, dual enrollment of high school students. License preparation in aviation, dental hygiene. **Credit/placement by examination:** AP, CLEP, IB, institutional tests. 24 credit hours maximum toward associate degree. **Support services:** GED test center, learning center, remedial instruction, study skills assistance, tutoring.

Majors. Communications technology: Animation/special effects. **Computer sciences:** LAN/WAN management, programming, security, system admin, web page design. **Education:** Educational technology. **General:** Turf management. **Visual/performing arts:** Game design, graphic design.

Computing on campus. 1,000 workstations in library, computer center, student center. Dormitories wired for high-speed internet access and linked to campus network. Commuter students can connect to campus network. Helpline, student web hosting, wireless network available.

Student life. Freshman orientation: Mandatory. Preregistration for classes offered. Held prior to semester. **Housing:** Coed dorms, special housing for disabled, apartments, wellness housing available. $150 fully refundable deposit. Duplexes and houses available to married students or students with families. **Activities:** Campus ministries, student government, student newspaper.

Athletics. Intramural: Basketball, football (non-tackle), golf, racquetball, softball, volleyball. **Team name:** Tornadoes.

Student services. Adult student services, career counseling, student employment services, financial aid counseling, health services, on-campus daycare, personal counseling, placement for graduates, veterans' counselor, women's services. **Physically disabled:** Services for visually, speech, hearing impaired. **Transfer:** Pre-admission transcript evaluation for new students. Transfer adviser for students transferring to 4-year colleges.

Contact. Phone: (254) 867-2361
Toll-free number: (800) 792-8784 ext. 2361 Fax: (254) 867-2250
Mary Daniel, Director of Admissions and Records/Registrar, Texas State Technical College: Waco, 3801 Campus Drive, Waco, TX 76705

Texas State Technical College: West Texas
Sweetwater, Texas
www.westtexas.tstc.edu CB code: 3137

- Public 2-year technical college
- Commuter campus in large town

General. Founded in 1970. Regionally accredited. **Enrollment:** 600 degree-seeking undergraduates. **Degrees:** 276 associate awarded. **Location:** 50 miles from Abilene. **Calendar:** Semester, limited summer session. **Full-time faculty:** 93 total. **Part-time faculty:** 26 total. **Special facilities:** Robotics lab, Cisco Academy, Microsoft Academy. **Partnerships:** Formal partnership with Florida Power & Light Energy for development of TSTC West Texas' Wind Energy Technology Program.

Student profile.

Out-of-state:	1%	Live on campus:	16%
25 or older:	44%		

Two-Year Colleges

Basis for selection. Open admission, but selective for some programs. Standardized test scores, if submitted, may be used in placement and counseling. SAT and ACT scores, if high enough, may exempt applicant from THEA testing requirements. Base score on placement test considered for nursing program.

2011-2012 Annual costs. Tuition/fees: $4,200; $9,000 out-of-state. Room/board: $4,655. Books/supplies: $1,100. Personal expenses: $650.

Financial aid. Need-based: Need-based aid available for part-time students. Work-study available nights, weekends and for part-time students. **Non-need-based:** Scholarships awarded for academics, leadership.

Application procedures. Admission: No application fee. Admission notification on a rolling basis. Application deadline is 45 days prior to start of semester. **Financial aid:** Priority date 5/1; no closing date. FAFSA, institutional form required. Applicants notified on a rolling basis starting 7/1.

Academics. Special study options: Cooperative education, cross-registration, distance learning, dual enrollment of high school students, internships, liberal arts/career combination. 1-1 and 1-1-2 electronics technology programs with numerous area institutions. License preparation in aviation, nursing, paramedic. **Credit/placement by examination:** AP, CLEP, institutional tests. Varies per program and individual student. **Support services:** GED test center, learning center, reduced course load, remedial instruction, study skills assistance, tutoring.

Majors. Business: Management information systems. **Communications technology:** General. **Computer sciences:** Networking, programming, web page design. **Conservation:** Environmental science. **Health services:** EMT paramedic, licensed practical nurse, medical records technology, substance abuse counseling. **Visual/performing arts:** Design.

Computing on campus. 50 workstations in library, student center. Dormitories wired for high-speed internet access. Commuter students can connect to campus network. Online library, helpline, wireless network available.

Student life. Freshman orientation: Mandatory. Preregistration for classes offered. Held day before start of classes. **Housing:** Coed dorms, special housing for disabled, apartments, wellness housing available. $150 deposit. Pets allowed in dorm rooms. **Activities:** Student government, student newspaper, Mexican American club, Baptist student union, technical students association, data processing management association, Business Professionals of America, society of manufacturing engineers, Vocational Industrial Clubs of America.

Athletics. Intramural: Basketball, bowling, golf, softball, swimming, table tennis, tennis, volleyball W.

Student services. Career counseling, services for economically disadvantaged, student employment services, financial aid counseling, health services, personal counseling, placement for graduates, veterans' counselor, women's services. **Physically disabled:** Services for hearing impaired. **Transfer:** Transfer adviser, college fairs on campus for students transferring to 4-year colleges.

Contact. E-mail: maria.aguirre@tstc.edu
Phone: (325) 235-7300 Toll-free number: (800) 592-8784
Fax: (325) 235-7416
Maria Aguirre-Acuna, Director of Admissions & Records, Texas State Technical College: West Texas, 300 Homer K Taylor Drive, Sweetwater, TX 79556

Trinity Valley Community College
Athens, Texas
www.tvcc.edu   CB code: 6271

- Public 2-year community college
- Commuter campus in large town

General. Founded in 1946. Regionally accredited. 3 extension centers in state. **Enrollment:** 7,480 degree-seeking undergraduates. **Degrees:** 823 associate awarded. **Location:** 70 miles from Dallas. **Calendar:** Semester, limited summer session. **Full-time faculty:** 154 total. **Part-time faculty:** 96 total. **Special facilities:** 2 operating ranches with more than 500 acres.

Student profile.

Out-of-state:	3%	Live on campus:	10%

Basis for selection. Open admission, but selective for some programs. Institution observes all TASP requirements. Special requirements for nursing program.

2011-2012 Annual costs. Tuition/fees: $1,920; $3,360 out-of-district; $4,200 out-of-state. Per-credit charge: $30 in-district; $78 out-of-district; $106 out-of-state. Room/board: $4,320. Books/supplies: $435. Personal expenses: $980.

Financial aid. Need-based: Need-based aid available for part-time students. Work-study available nights, weekends and for part-time students. **Non-need-based:** Scholarships awarded for academics, athletics.

Application procedures. Admission: No deadline. No application fee. Admission notification on a rolling basis. **Financial aid:** Closing date 7/1. FAFSA, institutional form required. Applicants notified on a rolling basis starting 7/1; must reply within 2 week(s) of notification.

Academics. Special study options: Distance learning, dual enrollment of high school students, honors, internships, liberal arts/career combination, weekend college. **Credit/placement by examination:** AP, CLEP. 18 credit hours maximum toward associate degree. **Support services:** GED preparation and test center, learning center, remedial instruction, tutoring.

Majors. Biology: General. **Business:** Accounting, administrative services, business admin, office technology. **Communications:** Communications/ speech/rhetoric, journalism. **Computer sciences:** General, computer graphics, data processing, programming. **Education:** General, early childhood, elementary, middle. **Engineering:** General, polymer. **English:** English lit, rhetoric/composition. **Foreign languages:** Spanish. **General:** Business, farm/ ranch, horticulture. **Health services:** Nursing (RN), predental, premedicine, prenursing, prepharmacy, preveterinary. **Liberal arts:** Arts/sciences. **Math:** General. **Parks/recreation:** Health/fitness. **Physical sciences:** Chemistry, physics. **Protective services:** Firefighting, law enforcement admin. **Psychology:** General. **Social sciences:** General, sociology. **Visual/performing arts:** General, art, dramatic, music. **Work/family studies:** Child care management.

Student life. Freshman orientation: Available, $20 fee. Preregistration for classes offered. **Housing:** Single-sex dorms available. **Activities:** Bands, campus ministries, choral groups, dance, drama, international student organizations, music ensembles, student government, student newspaper, Baptist student union, nontraditional student organization, Phi Beta Kappa, criminal justice fraternity.

Athletics. NJCAA. **Intercollegiate:** Basketball, football (tackle) M. **Intramural:** Basketball, bowling, handball M, racquetball, soccer M, softball, table tennis, tennis, volleyball. **Team name:** Cardinals.

Student services. Career counseling, student employment services, personal counseling, placement for graduates, veterans' counselor. **Physically disabled:** Services for speech impaired. **Transfer:** Pre-admission transcript evaluation for new students. Transfer adviser, college fairs on campus for students transferring to 4-year colleges.

Contact. Phone: (903) 675-6357 Fax: (903) 675-6209
Colette Hilliard, Dean of Enrollment, Trinity Valley Community College, 100 Cardinal Drive, Athens, TX 75751

Tyler Junior College
Tyler, Texas
www.tjc.edu   CB code: 6833

- Public 2-year community and junior college
- Commuter campus in small city

General. Founded in 1926. Regionally accredited. **Enrollment:** 11,056 degree-seeking undergraduates; 822 non-degree-seeking students. **Degrees:** 1,126 associate awarded. **Location:** 85 miles from Dallas, 85 miles from Shreveport, Louisiana. **Calendar:** Semester, extensive summer session. **Full-time faculty:** 269 total; 9% minority, 57% women. **Part-time faculty:** 268 total; 10% minority, 60% women. **Class size:** 40% < 20, 48% 20-39, 10% 40-49, 3% 50-99, less than 1% >100. **Special facilities:** Planetarium, conservatory.

Student profile. Among degree-seeking undergraduates, 2,640 enrolled as first-time, first-year students, 956 transferred in from other institutions.

Part-time:	41%	25 or older:	29%
Out-of-state:	4%	Live on campus:	8%
Women:	59%		

Transfer out. Colleges most students transferred to 2011: Stephen F. Austin State University, Texas A&M University, University of Texas at Tyler.

Basis for selection. Open admission, but selective for some programs. Admission to allied health programs based on test scores. High school units mandated by state law may vary by program. Texas Higher Education Assessment (THEA) required by Texas law for all incoming students. Interview

required for some allied health programs, recommended for others. **Home schooled:** Must complete equivalent of accepted high school diploma.

2011-2012 Annual costs. Tuition/fees: $2,262; $3,642 out-of-district; $4,242 out-of-state. Per-credit charge: $30 in-district; $76 out-of-district; $96 out-of-state. Room/board: $5,017. Books/supplies: $1,130. Personal expenses: $3,083.

2010-2011 Financial aid. Need-based: 65% of total undergraduate aid awarded as scholarships/grants, 35% as loans/jobs. Need-based aid available for part-time students. Work-study available nights, weekends and for part-time students. **Non-need-based:** Scholarships awarded for academics, alumni affiliation, art, athletics, leadership, music/drama.

Application procedures. Admission: No deadline. No application fee. Admission notification on a rolling basis. **Financial aid:** Priority date 6/1; no closing date. FAFSA, institutional form required. Applicants notified on a rolling basis starting 3/1; must reply within 2 week(s) of notification.

Academics. Special study options: Accelerated study, cooperative education, cross-registration, distance learning, dual enrollment of high school students, ESL, honors, internships, liberal arts/career combination, weekend college. License preparation in dental hygiene, nursing, paramedic, radiology, real estate. **Credit/placement by examination:** AP, CLEP, IB, institutional tests. **Support services:** GED preparation and test center, learning center, remedial instruction, study skills assistance, tutoring.

Honors college/program. SAT 1070 (exclusive of Writing), minimum 500 Math and Verbal; ACT 23, minimum 19 in each area.

Majors. Biology: General. **Business:** General, accounting technology, administrative services, business admin, managerial economics, marketing, office management. **Communications:** Journalism. **Communications technology:** Graphic/printing. **Computer sciences:** General, applications programming, information systems, web page design. **Conservation:** Environmental science. **Education:** General, early childhood, special ed. **Engineering:** General. **English:** Rhetoric/composition. **Foreign languages:** General, sign language interpretation. **General:** Farm/ranch. **Health services:** Clinical lab assistant, dental hygiene, EMT ambulance attendant, EMT paramedic, medical radiologic technology/radiation therapy, medical records technology, medical secretary, nursing (RN), office admin, ophthalmic lab technology, predental, premedicine, prenursing, prepharmacy, preveterinary, radiologic technology/medical imaging, respiratory therapy technology, sonography, substance abuse counseling, surgical technology. **History:** General. **Human services:** General, social work. **Liberal arts:** Arts/sciences. **Math:** General. **Parks/recreation:** Exercise sciences, health/fitness. **Physical sciences:** Chemistry, geology, physics. **Protective services:** Criminal justice, fire safety technology, police science. **Psychology:** General. **Social sciences:** Sociology. **Visual/performing arts:** General, art, commercial/advertising art, dance, dramatic, music, music performance, studio arts. **Work/family studies:** Child care management.

Most popular majors. Business/marketing 10%, education 7%, health sciences 21%, liberal arts 26%.

Computing on campus. 95 workstations in library, computer center, student center. Dormitories wired for high-speed internet access. Commuter students can connect to campus network. Online course registration, online library, helpline, repair service, student web hosting, wireless network available.

Student life. Freshman orientation: Mandatory, $50 fee. Preregistration for classes offered. 2-day orientation program in summer. **Housing:** Single-sex dorms available. $200 partly refundable deposit. **Activities:** Bands, campus ministries, choral groups, dance, drama, international student organizations, literary magazine, music ensembles, musical theater, student government, student newspaper, symphony orchestra, TV station, Wesleyan Ministries, Phi Theta Kappa, Hispanic student organization.

Athletics. NAIA, NJCAA. **Intercollegiate:** Baseball M, basketball, cheerleading, football (tackle) M, golf, soccer, tennis, volleyball W. **Intramural:** Badminton, basketball, football (tackle) M, handball, racquetball, softball, table tennis, tennis, volleyball M. **Team name:** Apaches.

Student services. Adult student services, alcohol/substance abuse counseling, chaplain/spiritual director, career counseling, services for economically disadvantaged, student employment services, financial aid counseling, health services, personal counseling, placement for graduates, veterans' counselor, women's services. **Physically disabled:** Services for visually, speech, hearing impaired. **Transfer:** College fairs on campus for students transferring to 4-year colleges.

Contact. E-mail: admissions@tjc.edu
Phone: (903) 510-2523 Toll-free number: (800) 687-5680
Fax: (903) 510-2161
Nidia Hassan, Director of Admissions, Tyler Junior College, Box 9020, Tyler, TX 75711-9020

Vernon College
Vernon, Texas
www.vernoncollege.edu   CB code: 6913

- Public 2-year community and junior college
- Commuter campus in large town

General. Founded in 1970. Regionally accredited. **Enrollment:** 2,655 degree-seeking undergraduates. **Degrees:** 238 associate awarded. **Location:** 50 miles from Wichita Falls. **Calendar:** Semester, extensive summer session. **Full-time faculty:** 81 total. **Part-time faculty:** 81 total.

Student profile.

Out-of-state:	5%	Live on campus:	6%
25 or older:	49%		

Basis for selection. Open admission, but selective for some programs. Additional requirements for nursing and cosmetology applicants.

2011-2012 Annual costs. Tuition/fees: $2,730; $3,900 out-of-district; $5,850 out-of-state. Room/board: $3,552. Books/supplies: $1,000. Personal expenses: $1,238.

Financial aid. All financial aid based on need. Need-based aid available for part-time students. Work-study available nights, weekends and for part-time students.

Application procedures. Admission: No deadline. $10 fee. Admission notification on a rolling basis. **Financial aid:** Priority date 7/1; no closing date. FAFSA required. Applicants notified on a rolling basis starting 4/1.

Academics. Special study options: Cooperative education, distance learning, dual enrollment of high school students, internships. License preparation in aviation, nursing, paramedic, real estate. **Credit/placement by examination:** AP, CLEP, IB, institutional tests. **Support services:** GED test center, learning center, reduced course load, remedial instruction, study skills assistance, tutoring, writing center.

Majors. Business: General, accounting, administrative services, human resources, marketing, office technology. **Computer sciences:** Data processing. **General:** Farm/ranch. **Health services:** Nursing (RN). **Liberal arts:** Arts/sciences. **Protective services:** Criminal justice.

Computing on campus. 60 workstations in library, computer center. Dormitories wired for high-speed internet access. Online course registration available.

Student life. Freshman orientation: Available. Preregistration for classes offered. **Housing:** Single-sex dorms available. **Activities:** Choral groups, drama, music ensembles, musical theater, student government.

Athletics. NJCAA. **Intercollegiate:** Baseball M, rodeo, softball W, volleyball W. **Intramural:** Archery, badminton, baseball M, basketball, football (non-tackle), golf, handball, racquetball, softball, swimming, table tennis, tennis, track and field, volleyball. **Team name:** Chaparral.

Student services. Adult student services, career counseling, services for economically disadvantaged, student employment services, financial aid counseling, health services, personal counseling, placement for graduates, veterans' counselor. **Physically disabled:** Services for visually, speech, hearing impaired. **Transfer:** Transfer adviser for students transferring to 4-year colleges.

Contact. E-mail: sdavenport@vernoncollege.edu
Phone: (940) 552-6291 Fax: (940) 553-1753
Joe Hite, Dean of Admissions and Financial Aid/Registrar, Vernon College, 4400 College Drive, Vernon, TX 76384-4092

Vet Tech Institute of Houston
Houston, Texas
www.bradfordschools.com

- For-profit 2-year technical college
- Very large city
- Interview required

General. Regionally accredited; also accredited by ACICS. **Enrollment:** 348 degree-seeking undergraduates. **Degrees:** 74 associate awarded. **Calendar:** Semester. **Full-time faculty:** 10 total. **Part-time faculty:** 3 total.

Basis for selection. Interviews required.

Financial aid. Need-based: Work-study available nights, weekends and for part-time students.

Application procedures. Admission: No deadline. $50 fee.

Academics. Credit/placement by examination: AP, CLEP. **Support services:** Learning center, tutoring.

Majors. Business: Accounting. **Health services:** Veterinary technology/assistant.

Contact. E-mail: mortiz@bradfordschoolhouston.edu
Phone: (713) 629-1500
Mike SanFilipo, Director of Admissions, Vet Tech Institute of Houston, 4669 Southwest Freeway, Houston, TX 77027

Victoria College
Victoria, Texas
www.victoriacollege.edu
CB code: 6915

- Public 2-year community college
- Commuter campus in small city

General. Founded in 1925. Regionally accredited. **Enrollment:** 4,583 degree-seeking undergraduates. **Degrees:** 210 associate awarded. **Location:** 110 miles from San Antonio, 125 miles from Austin. **Calendar:** Semester, limited summer session. **Full-time faculty:** 101 total. **Part-time faculty:** 81 total.

Student profile. Among degree-seeking undergraduates, 57% enrolled in a transfer program, 43% enrolled in a vocational program, 1% already have a bachelor's degree or higher, 926 enrolled as first-time, first-year students, 414 transferred in from other institutions.

Part-time:	63%	Asian American:	1%
Women:	67%	Hispanic American:	34%
African American:	5%	Native American:	1%

Basis for selection. Open admission, but selective for some programs. Special requirements for allied health programs; interview required.

High school preparation. 24 units recommended. Recommended units include English 4, mathematics 3, social studies 2.5, history 1, science 3, foreign language 2, academic electives 3.5. 0.5 economics, 1 fine arts, 0.5 speech, 1 technical applications recommended.

2011-2012 Annual costs. Tuition/fees: $2,400; $3,810 out-of-district; $4,110 out-of-state. Books/supplies: $2,090. Personal expenses: $2,502.

Financial aid. Need-based: Work-study available nights, weekends and for part-time students. **Non-need-based:** Scholarships awarded for academics, art, minority status, music/drama.

Application procedures. Admission: No deadline. No application fee. Admission notification on a rolling basis beginning on or about 7/1. **Financial aid:** Priority date 4/15; no closing date. FAFSA, institutional form required. Applicants notified on a rolling basis.

Academics. Special study options: Distance learning, dual enrollment of high school students. 2+2 plans with University of Texas-San Antonio, University of Houston-Victoria, Texas A&M-Corpus Christi, University of Texas-Brownsville. License preparation in nursing, paramedic, physical therapy. **Credit/placement by examination:** AP, CLEP, IB, institutional tests. **Support services:** GED preparation and test center, learning center, remedial instruction, tutoring.

Majors. Business: Administrative services, business admin. **Computer sciences:** General, information systems, networking, programming, system admin, web page design, webmaster. **Health services:** Clinical lab technology, EMT paramedic, nursing (RN), respiratory therapy technology. **Liberal arts:** Arts/sciences.

Most popular majors. Business/marketing 7%, engineering/engineering technologies 7%, health sciences 35%, liberal arts 34%, science technologies 8%.

Computing on campus. 500 workstations in library, computer center, student center. Commuter students can connect to campus network. Online course registration, online library, helpline, wireless network available.

Student life. Freshman orientation: Mandatory. Preregistration for classes offered. Students required to enroll in EDUC 1300 class. **Activities:** Bands, campus ministries, choral groups, dance, drama, international student organizations, literary magazine, music ensembles, student government, student newspaper.

Athletics. Intramural: Baseball M, basketball, tennis, volleyball. **Team name:** Pirates.

Student services. Career counseling, services for economically disadvantaged, student employment services, financial aid counseling, personal counseling, veterans' counselor. **Physically disabled:** Services for visually impaired. **Transfer:** College fairs on campus for students transferring to 4-year colleges.

Contact. E-mail: registrar@victoriacollege.edu
Phone: (361) 572-6408 Fax: (361) 582-2525
Missy Klimitchek, Registrar, Victoria College, 2200 East Red River, Victoria, TX 77901

Virginia College at Austin
Austin, Texas
www.vc.edu/austin

- For-profit 2-year business and health science college
- Commuter campus in very large city

General. Accredited by ACICS. **Enrollment:** 688 degree-seeking undergraduates. **Degrees:** 116 associate awarded. **Calendar:** Differs by program.

Basis for selection. Open admission, but selective for some programs.

2011-2012 Annual costs. Tuition/fees: $21,900.

Financial aid. Need-based: Work-study available nights, weekends and for part-time students.

Application procedures. Admission: $100 fee.

Academics. Credit/placement by examination: AP, CLEP.

Majors. Business: Office management. **Education:** Bilingual. **Health services:** Office assistant, surgical technology.

Contact. Phone: (512) 371-3500 Toll-free number: (888) 420-2048
Fax: (512) 371-3502
Tyka Booker, Director of Admissions, Virginia College at Austin, 6301 East Highway 290, Austin, TX 78723

Wade College
Dallas, Texas
www.wadecollege.edu
CB code: 1537

- For-profit 2-year career college
- Commuter campus in very large city
- Application essay, interview required

General. Founded in 1965. Regionally accredited. **Enrollment:** 270 degree-seeking undergraduates. **Degrees:** 99 associate awarded. **Location:** 2 miles from downtown Dallas. **Calendar:** Trimester, extensive summer session. **Full-time faculty:** 11 total; 36% have terminal degrees, 9% minority, 54% women. **Part-time faculty:** 11 total; 9% have terminal degrees, 64% women.

Transfer out. 10% of students enrolled in the transfer program go on to 4-year colleges.

Basis for selection. Open admission, but selective for some programs. Special requirements for students seeking BA degree in Merchandising and Design.

High school preparation. College-preparatory program required.

2011-2012 Annual costs. Tuition/fees: $11,710. Room only: $5,000. Books/supplies: $1,350.

Financial aid. All financial aid based on need. Need-based aid available for part-time students. Work-study available nights, weekends and for part-time students.

Application procedures. Admission: No deadline. $25 fee. Application must be submitted on paper. Admission notification on a rolling basis. **Financial aid:** No deadline. FAFSA required. Applicants notified on a rolling basis; must reply within 4 week(s) of notification.

Academics. Special study options: Accelerated study, double major, liberal arts/career combination. Weekend classes offered but cannot complete degree attending weekends only. Bachelor's degree programs available on

campus. **Credit/placement by examination:** AP, CLEP, IB, institutional tests. **Support services:** Pre-admission summer program, reduced course load, remedial instruction, tutoring.

Majors. Business: Sales/distribution. **Visual/performing arts:** Design.

Most popular majors. Business/marketing 50%, visual/performing arts 50%.

Computing on campus. 80 workstations in library, computer center. Dormitories wired for high-speed internet access. Online library, wireless network available.

Student life. Freshman orientation: Mandatory. Preregistration for classes offered. **Housing:** Apartments available. $200 fully refundable deposit. **Activities:** Student newspaper, Phi Theta Kappa, Golden Key Honor Society, Kappa Omicron Nu, concentration-specific clubs in graphic design, interior design, fashion design, merchandising and design.

Student services. Adult student services, career counseling, student employment services, financial aid counseling, placement for graduates, veterans' counselor. **Transfer:** Re-entry adviser, pre-admission transcript evaluation for new students. Transfer adviser for students transferring to 4-year colleges.

Contact. E-mail: admissions@wadecollege.edu
Phone: (214) 658-8800 Toll-free number: (800) 624-4850
Fax: (214) 637-0827
Julia Andalman, Director of Admissions and Marketing, Wade College, Dallas Market Center, PO Box 421149, Dallas, TX 75342

Weatherford College
Weatherford, Texas
www.wc.edu   **CB code: 6931**

▶ Public 2-year community college
▶ Commuter campus in large town

General. Founded in 1869. Regionally accredited. Off-campus courses held in Aledo, Bridgeport, Jacksboro, Springtown, Azle. Satellite campus in Mineral Wells, Granbury and Decatur. **Enrollment:** 5,530 undergraduates. **ROTC:** Air Force. **Location:** 25 miles from Fort Worth. **Calendar:** Semester, extensive summer session. **Full-time faculty:** 98 total. **Part-time faculty:** 104 total. **Special facilities:** 300-acre college farm. **Partnerships:** Formal partnerships with tech prep program and dual credit articulation agreements.

Student profile.

Out-of-state:	3%	Live on campus:	5%
25 or older:	50%		

Transfer out. Colleges most students transferred to 2011: Tarleton State University, University of North Texas, University of Texas at Arlington, Texas Tech University.

Basis for selection. Open admission, but selective for some programs. Nursing school, fire science requires entrance examination. Peace officer requires physical, drug testing, background check.

2011-2012 Annual costs. Tuition/fees: $2,130; $3,210 out-of-district; $4,860 out-of-state. Room/board: $7,130. Books/supplies: $1,000. Personal expenses: $1,297.

Financial aid. All financial aid based on need. Work-study available nights, weekends and for part-time students.

Application procedures. Admission: No deadline. No application fee. Admission notification on a rolling basis. **Financial aid:** Priority date 7/3; no closing date. FAFSA required. Applicants notified on a rolling basis; must reply within 2 week(s) of notification.

Academics. Special study options: Cooperative education, distance learning, dual enrollment of high school students, ESL, honors, internships, liberal arts/career combination, teacher certification program, weekend college. License preparation in nursing, occupational therapy, paramedic, radiology, real estate. **Credit/placement by examination:** AP, CLEP, institutional tests. 30 credit hours maximum toward associate degree. Credit earned by examination does not reduce resident requirement of 15 semester hours of class completed at college. **Support services:** GED preparation and test center, learning center, remedial instruction, study skills assistance, tutoring.

Majors. Business: General, accounting, administrative services, human resources, marketing, office/clerical, operations. **Communications:** Communications/speech/rhetoric. **Computer sciences:** General, data processing, programming. **General:** Business, farm/ranch. **Health services:** EMT paramedic, licensed practical nurse, medical radiologic technology/radiation therapy, occupational therapy assistant, pharmacy assistant, predental, premedicine, prenursing, prepharmacy, radiologic technology/medical imaging, radiologist assistant, respiratory therapy assistant, respiratory therapy technology, sonography, veterinary technology/assistant. **Liberal arts:** Arts/sciences. **Protective services:** Corrections, firefighting, law enforcement admin, police science. **Social sciences:** Sociology. **Work/family studies:** Child care service.

Computing on campus. 300 workstations in dormitories, library, computer center. Dormitories wired for high-speed internet access and linked to campus network. Commuter students can connect to campus network. Online course registration, wireless network available.

Student life. Freshman orientation: Mandatory. Preregistration for classes offered. Half-day sessions held before registration. **Housing:** Special housing for disabled, apartments, wellness housing available. $250 deposit, deadline 8/15. **Activities:** Jazz band, choral groups, dance, drama, music ensembles, musical theater, student government, black awareness student organization, Hispanic student organization, Baptist student union, international student organization, Wesleyan foundation, Baptist student ministries, A Better Life Through Education, disabled club.

Athletics. NJCAA. **Intercollegiate:** Baseball M, basketball, cheerleading, rodeo, softball W. **Intramural:** Badminton, basketball, softball, tennis, volleyball. **Team name:** Coyotes.

Student services. Adult student services, career counseling, services for economically disadvantaged, student employment services, financial aid counseling, personal counseling, placement for graduates, veterans' counselor. **Physically disabled:** Services for visually, speech, hearing impaired. **Transfer:** Pre-admission transcript evaluation for new students. Transfer adviser, college fairs on campus for students transferring to 4-year colleges.

Contact. Phone: (817) 598-6241 Toll-free number: (800) 287-5471
Fax: (817) 598-6205
Ralph Willingham, Director of Admissions, Weatherford College, 225 College Park Drive, Weatherford, TX 76086

Western Technical College
El Paso, Texas
www.westerntech.edu   **CB code: 2941**

▶ For-profit 2-year technical college
▶ Commuter campus in very large city

General. Accredited by ACCSC. Two campuses: main campus East, branch campus in NE section. **Enrollment:** 684 degree-seeking undergraduates. **Degrees:** 224 associate awarded. **Calendar:** Differs by program. **Full-time faculty:** 46 total. **Part-time faculty:** 9 total.

Basis for selection. Open admission, but selective for some programs. Some programs require CPAT or other entrance requirements.

2011-2012 Annual costs. Tuition varies by program: Automotive Technology (1,500 clock hours), $23,865; Refrigeration/HVAC Technology (1,500 clock hours), $23,865; Diesel Technology (1,400 clock hours), $22,274; Advanced Welding Technology (1,500 clock hours), $26,850; Medical/Clinical Assistant, (1,000 clock hours), $12,580. Registration fee, $100.

Financial aid. All financial aid based on need. Need-based aid available for part-time students. Work-study available nights, weekends and for part-time students.

Application procedures. Admission: No deadline. $100 fee. **Financial aid:** No deadline. FAFSA required. Applicants notified on a rolling basis.

Academics. Credit/placement by examination: AP, CLEP. **Support services:** GED preparation, remedial instruction, tutoring.

Computing on campus. 200 workstations in library, computer center, student center. Online library, wireless network available.

Student life. Freshman orientation: Mandatory. Preregistration for classes offered.

Student services. Financial aid counseling, on-campus daycare, placement for graduates.

Contact. Phone: (915) 532-3737 Toll-free number: (800) 225-5984 Laura Pena, Director of Admissions, Western Technical College, 9624 Plaza Circle, El Paso, TX 79927

Western Technical College: Diana Drive
El Paso, Texas
www.westerntech.edu

♦ For-profit 2-year branch campus and technical college
♦ Commuter campus in very large city
♦ Interview required

General. Accredited by ACCSC. **Enrollment:** 499 degree-seeking undergraduates. **Degrees:** 119 associate awarded. **Calendar:** Differs by program. **Full-time faculty:** 16 total; 56% minority, 31% women. **Part-time faculty:** 11 total; 64% minority, 73% women.

Basis for selection. Open admission, but selective for some programs. Assessment test and various minimum scores required for following programs: medical clinical assistant, health information technology, information systems and security, electronic engineering technology, massage therapy, and physical therapist assistant.

2011-2012 Annual costs. Tuition varies by program: Information Systems and Security (1,800 clock hours), $27,810; Electronics Engineering Technology (1,800 clock hours), $27,810; Massage Therapy (900 clock hours), $10,629; Health Information Technology (1,000 clock hours), $13,680; Medical/Clinical Assistant (1,000 clock hours), $12,580; Physical Therapist Assistant (1,732 clock hours), $31,176. Registration fee, $100.

Financial aid. **Need-based:** Work-study available nights, weekends and for part-time students.

Application procedures. **Admission:** No deadline. $100 fee. **Financial aid:** No deadline.

Academics. **Credit/placement by examination:** AP, CLEP. **Support services:** GED preparation, remedial instruction, tutoring.

Majors. **Computer sciences:** General. **Health services:** Physical therapy assistant.

Computing on campus. Online library, wireless network available.

Student life. **Freshman orientation:** Mandatory. Preregistration for classes offered.

Student services. Financial aid counseling, placement for graduates.

Contact. Phone: (915) 566-9621 Toll-free number: (800) 522-2072 Fax: (915) 565-9903 Bill Terrell, Director of Admissions, Western Technical College: Diana Drive, 9451 Diana Drive, El Paso, TX 79924

Western Texas College
Snyder, Texas
www.wtc.edu   **CB code: 6951**

♦ Public 2-year community and junior college
♦ Commuter campus in large town

General. Founded in 1969. Regionally accredited. **Enrollment:** 2,287 undergraduates. **Degrees:** 171 associate awarded. **Location:** 80 miles from Lubbock. **Calendar:** Semester, extensive summer session. **Full-time faculty:** 44 total; 18% have terminal degrees, 36% women. **Part-time faculty:** 59 total; 70% women. **Class size:** 80% < 20, 19% 20-39, less than 1% 40-49, less than 1% 50-99.

Student profile. 10% already have a bachelor's degree or higher, 391 enrolled as first-time, first-year students, 630 transferred in from other institutions.

Out-of-state:	3%	**Live on campus:**	10%
25 or older:	32%		

Transfer out. **Colleges most students transferred to 2011:** Texas Tech University, Angelo State University, University of Texas, Texas A&M University.

Basis for selection. Open admission, but selective for some programs. Institutional placement tests may be submitted in place of SAT/ACT. Special

requirements for nursing program. Interview recommended. **Home schooled:** Transcript of courses and grades required.

2011-2012 Annual costs. Tuition/fees: $2,370; $2,995 out-of-district; $3,750 out-of-state. Per-credit charge: $52 in-district; $73 out-of-district; $98 out-of-state. Room/board: $5,100. Books/supplies: $500. Personal expenses: $900.

Financial aid. **Need-based:** Need-based aid available for part-time students. Work-study available nights, weekends and for part-time students. **Non-need-based:** Scholarships awarded for academics, art, athletics, leadership, music/drama, state residency.

Application procedures. **Admission:** No deadline. No application fee. Application must be submitted on paper. Admission notification on a rolling basis beginning on or about 11/5. **Financial aid:** Priority date 8/1; no closing date. FAFSA, institutional form required. Applicants notified on a rolling basis starting 5/1; must reply within 2 week(s) of notification.

Academics. **Special study options:** Distance learning, dual enrollment of high school students, honors, internships. License preparation in nursing, paramedic. **Credit/placement by examination:** AP, CLEP, institutional tests. 12 credit hours maximum toward associate degree. **Support services:** GED preparation and test center, learning center, pre-admission summer program, reduced course load, remedial instruction, tutoring.

Majors. **Biology:** General. **Business:** General, accounting, administrative services, business admin. **Communications:** Journalism. **Communications technology:** Radio/TV. **Computer sciences:** General, computer science, data processing, LAN/WAN management, programming. **Education:** General, early childhood. **Engineering:** General. **English:** English lit. **Foreign languages:** General. **General:** Animal sciences, greenhouse operations, horticulture, landscaping, nursery operations. **Health services:** EMT paramedic, predental, premedicine, prenursing, prepharmacy, preveterinary. **History:** General. **Liberal arts:** Arts/sciences. **Math:** General. **Parks/recreation:** Facilities management, health/fitness. **Philosophy/religion:** Philosophy. **Physical sciences:** Chemistry, geology, physics. **Psychology:** General. **Social sciences:** General, economics, geography, international relations, political science, sociology. **Visual/performing arts:** Art, ceramics, dramatic, drawing, metal/jewelry, painting, photography, sculpture.

Computing on campus. 70 workstations in dormitories, library, computer center, student center. Dormitories wired for high-speed internet access and linked to campus network. Online course registration, online library available.

Student life. **Freshman orientation:** Available. Preregistration for classes offered. **Housing:** Guaranteed on-campus for all undergraduates. Single-sex dorms, apartments available. $50 deposit. **Activities:** Drama, literary magazine, musical theater, student government, TV station, Baptist student union, Phi Theta Kappa.

Athletics. NJCAA. **Intercollegiate:** Baseball M, basketball, cross-country, golf, rodeo, soccer, softball W, track and field, volleyball W. **Intramural:** Basketball, cheerleading W, golf, handball, racquetball, volleyball, weight lifting. **Team name:** Westerners.

Student services. Adult student services, alcohol/substance abuse counseling, career counseling, services for economically disadvantaged, student employment services, financial aid counseling, personal counseling, placement for graduates, veterans' counselor. **Transfer:** Pre-admission transcript evaluation for new students. Transfer adviser, college fairs on campus for students transferring to 4-year colleges.

Contact. E-mail: nleatherwood@wtc.edu Phone: (325) 573-7918 Toll-free number: (888) 468-6982 Fax: (325) 573-9321 Nellie Leatherwood, Director of Admissions, Western Texas College, 6200 College Avenue, Snyder, TX 79549

Westwood College: Dallas
Dallas, Texas
www.westwood.edu/locations/texas/dallas-campus

♦ For-profit 2-year technical college
♦ Commuter campus in very large city

General. Regionally accredited. **Calendar:** Differs by program.

Annual costs/financial aid. Tuition/fees (2011-2012): $15,020. Books/supplies: $1,106.

Contact. Phone: (214) 570-0100 Director of Admissions, 8390 LBJ Freeway, Dallas, TX 75243

Westwood College: Fort Worth
Fort Worth, Texas
www.westwood.edu/locations/texas/fort-worth-campus

▶ For-profit 2-year health science and technical college
▶ Commuter campus in very large city

General. Regionally accredited. **Calendar:** Differs by program.

Annual costs/financial aid. Tuition/fees (2011-2012): $15,020. Books/supplies: $1,106.

Contact. Phone: (817) 547-9600
Director of Admissions, 4232 North Freeway, Fort Worth, TX 76137

Westwood College: Houston South
Houston, Texas
www.westwood.edu

▶ For-profit 2-year technical college
▶ Commuter campus in very large city

General. Regionally accredited. **Calendar:** Differs by program.

Annual costs/financial aid. Tuition/fees (2011-2012): $15,020. Books/supplies: $1,106. Need-based financial aid available to full-time and part-time students.

Contact. Phone: (866) 340-3677
Director of Admissions, 7322 Southwest Freeway, Houston, TX 77074

Wharton County Junior College
Wharton, Texas
www.wcjc.edu   **CB code: 6939**

▶ Public 2-year community and junior college
▶ Commuter campus in small town

General. Founded in 1946. Regionally accredited. **Enrollment:** 6,998 degree-seeking undergraduates. **Degrees:** 436 associate awarded. **Location:** 60 miles from Houston. **Calendar:** Semester, limited summer session. **Full-time faculty:** 162 total; 17% have terminal degrees, 19% minority, 61% women. **Part-time faculty:** 134 total; 8% have terminal degrees, 23% minority, 52% women. **Class size:** 44% < 20, 54% 20-39, 1% 40-49, less than 1% 50-99, less than 1% >100.

Student profile. Among degree-seeking undergraduates, 66% enrolled in a transfer program, 34% enrolled in a vocational program, 2% already have a bachelor's degree or higher, 1,518 enrolled as first-time, first-year students, 478 transferred in from other institutions.

Part-time:	59%	**25 or older:**	24%
Out-of-state:	2%	**Live on campus:**	3%
Women:	57%		

Transfer out. Colleges most students transferred to 2011: Texas A&M University, University of Houston, Sam Houston State University, Texas State University, University of Texas.

Basis for selection. Open admission, but selective for some programs. Test scores and school achievement record important factors for admission into nursing, dental hygiene, physical therapy, and radiology programs. Audition required for music scholarship applicants.

High school preparation. College-preparatory program recommended. Recommended units include English 4, mathematics 3, science 3 and foreign language 2.

2011-2012 Annual costs. Tuition/fees: $2,580; $4,920 out-of-state. Per-credit charge: $32 in-state; $64 out-of-state. Room/board: $3,600. Books/supplies: $1,000. Personal expenses: $2,655.

Financial aid. Need-based: Need-based aid available for part-time students. Work-study available nights, weekends and for part-time students. **Non-need-based:** Scholarships awarded for academics, athletics, music/drama.

Application procedures. Admission: Priority date 7/1; no deadline. No application fee. Application must be submitted on paper. Admission notification on a rolling basis beginning on or about 2/1. **Financial aid:** Priority date 6/1; no closing date. FAFSA, institutional form required. Applicants notified on a rolling basis starting 3/1; must reply within 8 week(s) of notification.

Academics. Special study options: Cooperative education, cross-registration, distance learning, dual enrollment of high school students, internships, teacher certification program. License preparation in dental hygiene, nursing, paramedic, physical therapy, radiology. **Credit/placement by examination:** AP, CLEP, institutional tests. 16 credit hours maximum toward associate degree. **Support services:** GED preparation and test center, learning center, remedial instruction, tutoring.

Majors. Biology: General. **Business:** Business admin. **Computer sciences:** General, networking. **Education:** Early childhood, elementary. **English:** English lit. **General:** Business technology. **Health services:** Dental hygiene, EMT paramedic, medical records technology, nursing (RN), physical therapy assistant, radiologic technology/medical imaging. **History:** General. **Liberal arts:** Arts/sciences. **Math:** General. **Parks/recreation:** Exercise sciences. **Physical sciences:** Chemistry, physics. **Protective services:** Police science. **Psychology:** General. **Social sciences:** Criminology, sociology. **Visual/performing arts:** Art, dramatic, music. **Work/family studies:** Child development.

Most popular majors. Health sciences 19%, liberal arts 47%, science technologies 10%.

Computing on campus. 500 workstations in library, computer center, student center. Commuter students can connect to campus network. Online course registration, online library available.

Student life. Freshman orientation: Available. Preregistration for classes offered. **Housing:** Single-sex dorms available. $100 deposit, deadline 7/1. **Activities:** Bands, choral groups, drama, music ensembles, musical theater, student government.

Athletics. NJCAA. **Intercollegiate:** Baseball M, rodeo, volleyball W. **Team name:** Pioneers.

Student services. Career counseling, services for economically disadvantaged, financial aid counseling, personal counseling. **Physically disabled:** Services for visually, speech, hearing impaired. **Transfer:** Transfer adviser, college fairs on campus for students transferring to 4-year colleges.

Contact. E-mail: registrar@wcjc.edu
Phone: (979) 532-4560 ext. 6303 Toll-free number: (800) 561-9252
Fax: (979) 532-6494
Karen Preisler, Director of Admissions/Registrar, Wharton County Junior College, 911 Boling Highway, Wharton, TX 77488-0080

Utah

Two-Year Colleges

Broadview Entertainment Arts University
Salt Lake City, Utah
www.broadviewuniversity.edu

- For-profit 2-year university and visual arts college
- Small city

General. Regionally accredited; also accredited by ACICS. **Enrollment:** 47 degree-seeking undergraduates. **Calendar:** Quarter. **Full-time faculty:** 4 total. **Part-time faculty:** 6 total.

Basis for selection. Open admission.

Financial aid. Need-based: Work-study available nights, weekends and for part-time students.

Application procedures. Admission: $50 fee.

Academics. Credit/placement by examination: AP, CLEP.

Contact. Phone: (801) 300-4300
Broadview Entertainment Arts University, 240 East Morris Avenue, Salt Lake City, UT 84115

Broadview University: Layton
Layton, Utah
www.broadviewuniversity.edu

- For-profit 2-year university and career college
- Small city

General. Regionally accredited; also accredited by ACICS. **Enrollment:** 302 degree-seeking undergraduates. **Degrees:** 4 bachelor's, 45 associate awarded. **Calendar:** Quarter. **Full-time faculty:** 6 total. **Part-time faculty:** 23 total.

Basis for selection. Open admission.

Financial aid. Need-based: Work-study available nights, weekends and for part-time students.

Application procedures. Admission: $50 fee.

Academics. Credit/placement by examination: AP, CLEP.

Majors. Business: Business admin. **Health services:** Massage therapy, medical secretary, veterinary technology/assistant. **Protective services:** Police science.

Contact. Rachel Baxter, Director of Admissions, Broadview University: Layton, 869 West Hill Field Road, Layton, UT 84041

Broadview University: West Jordan
West Jordan, Utah
www.broadviewuniversity.edu **CB code: 2892**

- For-profit 2-year technical and career college
- Commuter campus in small city
- Interview required

General. Regionally accredited; also accredited by ACICS. **Enrollment:** 496 degree-seeking undergraduates. **Degrees:** 5 bachelor's, 153 associate awarded. **Location:** 8 miles from Salt Lake City. **Calendar:** Quarter, extensive summer session. **Full-time faculty:** 15 total. **Part-time faculty:** 28 total.

Transfer out. Colleges most students transferred to 2011: Salt Lake Community College.

Basis for selection. Open admission, but selective for some programs. Interview and institutional testing required for placement. Application fee

for nursing program is $100. **Home schooled:** GED certificate and documentation required.

2011-2012 Annual costs. Tuition/fees: $18,450. Per-credit charge: $410. Nursing program courses $565 per-credit-hour.

Financial aid. All financial aid based on need. Need-based aid available for part-time students. Work-study available nights, weekends and for part-time students.

Application procedures. Admission: No deadline. $50 fee. Application must be submitted online. Admission notification on a rolling basis. **Financial aid:** No deadline. FAFSA, institutional form required. Applicants notified on a rolling basis starting 7/1; must reply within 2 week(s) of notification.

Academics. Special study options: Distance learning, liberal arts/career combination. Bachelor's degree programs available on campus. **Credit/placement by examination:** AP, CLEP. Credits for prior work experience and examination may not exceed 75% of total credits required to complete student's program. **Support services:** Reduced course load, tutoring.

Majors. Business: Accounting, business admin. **Computer sciences:** Information technology. **Health services:** Licensed practical nurse, massage therapy, medical assistant, medical records admin, pharmacy assistant, veterinary technology/assistant. **Parks/recreation:** Exercise sciences.

Most popular majors. Health sciences 43%, legal studies 16%.

Computing on campus. 90 workstations in library, computer center. Online library, wireless network available.

Student life. Freshman orientation: Mandatory. Preregistration for classes offered. **Policies:** Drug and alcohol-free campus.

Student services. Career counseling, student employment services, financial aid counseling, placement for graduates. **Transfer:** Re-entry adviser for new students.

Contact. E-mail: admissions@utahcollege.edu
Phone: (801) 304-4224 Toll-free number: (866) 304-4224
Fax: (801) 304-4229
Aaron Escher, Director of Admissions, Broadview University: West Jordan, 1902 West 7800 South, West Jordan, UT 84088

Careers Unlimited
Orem, Utah
www.ucdh.edu/

- For-profit 2-year health science college
- Commuter campus in large city

General. Accredited by ACCSCT. **Location:** 45 miles from Salt Lake City. **Calendar:** Trimester.

Annual costs/financial aid. Estimated cost for entire bachelor's degree program in dental hygiene: $50,950 including fees.

Contact. Phone: (801) 426-8234
Director of Admissions, 1176 South 1480 West, Orem, UT 84058

Eagle Gate College: Layton
Layton, Utah
www.eaglegatecollege.edu

- For-profit 2-year career college
- Commuter campus in small city

General. Accredited by ACICS. **Enrollment:** 398 degree-seeking undergraduates. **Degrees:** 20 bachelor's, 117 associate awarded. **Location:** 20 miles from Salt Lake City, 10 miles from Ogden. **Calendar:** Quarter, extensive summer session. **Full-time faculty:** 13 total; 77% have terminal degrees, 54% women. **Part-time faculty:** 33 total; 21% have terminal degrees, 3% minority, 33% women. **Class size:** 90% < 20, 10% 20-39.

Basis for selection. Open admission. **Home schooled:** Statement describing home school structure and mission, state high school equivalency certificate required.

2011-2012 Annual costs. Tuition/fees: $13,977. Full-time tuition and fees vary according to program of study.

Financial aid. Need-based: Work-study available nights, weekends and for part-time students.

Application procedures. Admission: No deadline. No application fee. **Financial aid:** No deadline.

Academics. Special study options: Accelerated study, distance learning. Bachelor's degree programs available on campus. **Credit/placement by examination:** AP, CLEP. 45 credit hours maximum toward associate degree, 90 toward bachelor's. **Support services:** Learning center, reduced course load, tutoring, writing center.

Majors. Business: Accounting, business admin. **Computer sciences:** Web page design. **Health services:** Insurance coding, medical assistant, pharmacy assistant. **Protective services:** Law enforcement admin. **Visual/performing arts:** Graphic design.

Most popular majors. Business/marketing 25%, computer/information sciences 10%, health sciences 35%, legal studies 14%, security/protective services 28%, visual/performing arts 17%.

Computing on campus. 54 workstations in library, computer center. Commuter students can connect to campus network. Wireless network available.

Student life. Freshman orientation: Mandatory. Preregistration for classes offered.

Student services. Adult student services, career counseling, student employment services, financial aid counseling, placement for graduates.

Contact. E-mail: admissions@eaglegatecollege.edu
Phone: (801) 546-7500 ext. 7512 Toll-free number: (800) 429-4513
Fax: (801) 593-6654
David Moser, Director of Admissions, Eagle Gate College: Layton, 915 North 400 West Layton, Layton, UT 84041

Eagle Gate College: Murray
Murray, Utah
www.eaglegatecollege.edu

▶ For-profit 2-year business and technical college
▶ Large town

General. Accredited by ACICS. **Enrollment:** 360 degree-seeking undergraduates. **Degrees:** 17 bachelor's, 349 associate awarded. **Calendar:** Five ten-week terms. **Full-time faculty:** 14 total. **Part-time faculty:** 42 total.

Basis for selection. Open admission.

2011-2012 Annual costs. Tuition/fees: $13,977. Full-time tuition and fees vary according to program of study.

2010-2011 Financial aid. Need-based: Work-study available nights, weekends and for part-time students.

Application procedures. Admission: No deadline. $40 fee. Admission notification on a rolling basis. **Financial aid:** No deadline.

Academics. Special study options: Bachelor's degree programs available on campus. **Credit/placement by examination:** AP, CLEP.

Majors. Business: Accounting/finance, business admin. **Computer sciences:** General. **Health services:** Dental assistant, insurance coding, medical assistant, pharmacy assistant. **Protective services:** Law enforcement admin. **Visual/performing arts:** Graphic design.

Contact. Phone: (801) 281-7700 Toll-free number: (866) 284-8680
Raymond Johnson, Director of Admissions, Eagle Gate College: Murray, 5588 South Green Street, Murray, UT 84123

LDS Business College
Salt Lake City, Utah
www.ldsbc.edu   **CB code: 4412**

▶ Private 2-year business and junior college affiliated with Church of Jesus Christ of Latter-day Saints
▶ Commuter campus in large city
▶ Interview required

General. Founded in 1886. Regionally accredited. **Enrollment:** 1,979 degree-seeking undergraduates; 7 non-degree-seeking students. **Degrees:** 446 associate awarded. **ROTC:** Army, Air Force. **Calendar:** Semester, limited summer session. **Full-time faculty:** 21 total; 19% have terminal degrees, 24% women. **Part-time faculty:** 111 total; 5% have terminal degrees, 2% minority, 47% women. **Class size:** 33% < 20, 62% 20-39, 4% 40-49, less than 1% 50-99, less than 1% >100.

Student profile. Among degree-seeking undergraduates, 31% enrolled in a transfer program, 69% enrolled in a vocational program, 487 enrolled as first-time, first-year students, 249 transferred in from other institutions.

Part-time:	27%	Hispanic American:	11%
Out-of-state:	35%	International:	14%
Women:	48%	25 or older:	26%
Asian American:	1%		

Transfer out. Colleges most students transferred to 2011: Brigham Young University, University of Utah, Utah State University.

Basis for selection. Open admission, but selective for some programs. Students in interior design program must submit color board. Non-native speakers must pass an English proficiency test. SAT/ACT recommended for counseling; used as pre-test and placement in English or math. **Adult students:** Students who have not taken ACT or SAT must take COMPASS for placement in English and math. **Home schooled:** Students must submit ACT or GED if not from accredited program. Students qualify for admission after reaching age 17. **Learning Disabled:** Must submit documentation under ADA.

2012-2013 Annual costs. Tuition/fees: $3,060. Per-credit charge: $128. Books/supplies: $1,060. Personal expenses: $2,000.

Financial aid. Need-based: Need-based aid available for part-time students. Work-study available nights, weekends and for part-time students. **Non-need-based:** Scholarships awarded for academics, leadership.

Application procedures. Admission: Closing date 8/31 (receipt date). $35 fee. Application must be submitted online. Admission notification on a rolling basis beginning on or about 10/15. **Financial aid:** Priority date 7/1; no closing date. FAFSA required. Applicants notified on a rolling basis starting 3/1; must reply by 7/1 or within 3 week(s) of notification.

Academics. Special study options: Dual enrollment of high school students, internships. **Credit/placement by examination:** AP, CLEP, IB, institutional tests. 30 credit hours maximum toward associate degree. **Support services:** Reduced course load, study skills assistance, tutoring.

Majors. Business: General, accounting, business admin, entrepreneurial studies, executive assistant, office management, selling. **Computer sciences:** General. **Health services:** Medical records admin, medical secretary, office admin, office assistant. **Visual/performing arts:** Interior design, photography.

Most popular majors. Business/marketing 39%, liberal arts 49%, visual/performing arts 8%.

Computing on campus. 350 workstations in library, computer center. Commuter students can connect to campus network. Online course registration, helpline, wireless network available.

Student life. Freshman orientation: Available. Preregistration for classes offered. Full-day session held Friday before start of classes, Saturday half-day activity, Sunday evening activity. **Policies:** Religious observance required. **Activities:** Choral groups, dance, student government, service-learning council.

Athletics. Team name: Lions.

Student services. Career counseling, student employment services, financial aid counseling, health services, personal counseling, placement for graduates. **Transfer:** Transfer adviser, college fairs on campus for students transferring to 4-year colleges.

Contact. E-mail: admissions@ldsbc.edu
Phone: (801) 524-8145 Toll-free number: (800) 999-5767
Fax: (801) 524-1900
Dawn Fellows, Assistant Director of Admission, LDS Business College, 95 North 300 West, Salt Lake City, UT 84101-3500

Provo College
Provo, Utah
www.provocollege.edu   **CB code: 3021**

▶ For-profit 2-year junior college
▶ Small city

General. Accredited by ACCSC. **Enrollment:** 270 degree-seeking undergraduates. **Degrees:** 152 associate awarded. **Calendar:** Quarter, extensive summer session. **Full-time faculty:** 60 total. **Part-time faculty:** 20 total.

Basis for selection. Open admission, but selective for some programs.

2011-2012 Annual costs. Estimated cost of associate degree programs: $27,070-$48,644. Cost vary by program and are subject to change. Books/supplies: $600. Personal expenses: $2,088.

Financial aid. **Need-based:** Work-study available nights, weekends and for part-time students.

Application procedures. **Admission:** No deadline. $40 fee. Admission notification on a rolling basis.

Academics. **Credit/placement by examination:** AP, CLEP. **Support services:** Learning center, tutoring.

Majors. **Business:** Accounting, administrative services, business admin, hospitality/recreation. **Computer sciences:** General, programming. **Health services:** Dental assistant, medical secretary, physical therapy assistant. **Protective services:** Law enforcement admin. **Visual/performing arts:** General, commercial/advertising art.

Most popular majors. Business/marketing 7%, health sciences 61%, visual/performing arts 16%.

Contact. Phone: (801) 375-1861 Toll-free number: (800) 748-4834
Fax: (801) 375-9728
Jeff Moss, Director of Admissions, Provo College, 1450 West 820 North, Provo, UT 84601

Salt Lake Community College
Salt Lake City, Utah
www.slcc.edu

CB member
CB code: 4864

- Public 2-year community and technical college
- Commuter campus in very large city

General. Founded in 1948. Regionally accredited. 5 campus locations, 8 teaching centers. **Enrollment:** 25,279 degree-seeking undergraduates; 6,720 non-degree-seeking students. **Degrees:** 3,413 associate awarded. **ROTC:** Army, Air Force. **Location:** 5 miles from downtown. **Calendar:** Semester, extensive summer session. **Full-time faculty:** 345 total; 47% women. **Part-time faculty:** 909 total; 44% women. **Class size:** 37% < 20, 61% 20-39, 2% 40-49, less than 1% 50-99.

Student profile. Among degree-seeking undergraduates, 69% enrolled in a transfer program, 31% enrolled in a vocational program, 3,387 enrolled as first-time, first-year students, 739 transferred in from other institutions.

Part-time:	65%	Hispanic American:	12%
Out-of-state:	5%	Native American:	1%
Women:	51%	International:	1%
African American:	2%	25 or older:	37%
Asian American:	4%		

Transfer out. **Colleges most students transferred to 2011:** University of Utah, Utah State University, Weber State University, Westminster College.

Basis for selection. Open admission, but selective for some programs. Admission for flight technology programs based on testing; admissions for health sciences based on school records, testing and prerequisite courses.

High school preparation. 27 units recommended. Recommended units include English 4, mathematics 2, social studies 3, science 2 and academic electives 11. Biological science recommended for health science programs. Algebra recommended for preengineering and electronics.

2011-2012 Annual costs. Tuition/fees: $3,052; $9,604 out-of-state. Per-credit charge: $110 in-state; $383 out-of-state. Books/supplies: $1,680. Personal expenses: $2,970.

2010-2011 Financial aid. **Need-based:** 98% of total undergraduate aid awarded as scholarships/grants, 2% as loans/jobs. Need-based aid available for part-time students. Work-study available nights, weekends and for part-time students. **Non-need-based:** Scholarships awarded for academics, alumni affiliation, art, athletics, leadership, minority status, music/drama.

Application procedures. **Admission:** No deadline. $40 fee. Admission notification on a rolling basis. **Financial aid:** Priority date 5/1; no closing date. FAFSA, institutional form required. Applicants notified on a rolling basis starting 5/1; must reply within 4 week(s) of notification.

Academics. **Special study options:** Cooperative education, distance learning, dual enrollment of high school students, ESL, exchange student, study abroad. Bachelor's degree programs available on campus. License preparation in aviation, dental hygiene, nursing. **Credit/placement by examination:** AP, CLEP, IB, SAT, ACT, institutional tests. 50 credit hours maximum toward associate degree. **Support services:** GED preparation and test center, learning center, pre-admission summer program, reduced course load, remedial instruction, study skills assistance, tutoring, writing center.

Majors. **Biology:** General. **Business:** General, accounting technology, business admin, finance, marketing, restaurant/food services. **Communications:** Communications/speech/rhetoric, digital media. **Communications technology:** Animation/special effects, photo/film/video, radio/TV. **Computer sciences:** General, computer science. **Education:** Early childhood special, kindergarten/preschool. **Engineering:** Electrical, manufacturing, materials, mechanical. **English:** English lit. **Foreign languages:** Sign language interpretation. **Health services:** Dental hygiene, medical radiologic technology/radiation therapy, nursing (RN), occupational therapy assistant, physical therapy assistant. **History:** General. **Human services:** Social work. **Liberal arts:** Humanities. **Math:** General. **Parks/recreation:** Sports admin. **Physical sciences:** Chemistry, geology, physics. **Protective services:** Criminal justice. **Psychology:** General. **Social sciences:** Economics, geography, political science, sociology. **Visual/performing arts:** Design, music, photography, theater design. **Work/family studies:** Family studies.

Most popular majors. Business/marketing 8%, health sciences 12%, liberal arts 54%.

Computing on campus. 2,400 workstations in library, computer center, student center. Commuter students can connect to campus network. Online course registration, helpline, wireless network available.

Student life. **Freshman orientation:** Available. Preregistration for classes offered. One-day program. **Activities:** Bands, choral groups, dance, drama, literary magazine, radio station, student government, student newspaper, TV station, Circle-K, Latter-Day Saints student association, Hispanos Unidos, African-American student association, American Indian club, Asian club, Polynesian club, American Sign Language club, professional societies.

Athletics. NJCAA. **Intercollegiate:** Baseball M, basketball, softball W, volleyball W. **Team name:** Bruins.

Student services. Alcohol/substance abuse counseling, career counseling, services for economically disadvantaged, student employment services, financial aid counseling, health services, minority student services, on-campus daycare, personal counseling, placement for graduates, veterans' counselor. **Physically disabled:** Services for visually, speech, hearing impaired. **Transfer:** Transfer center, transfer adviser, college fairs on campus for students transferring to 4-year colleges.

Contact. E-mail: futurestudents@slcc.edu
Phone: (801) 957-4298 Fax: (801) 957-4961
Eric Weber, Dean of Student Enrollment Services, Salt Lake Community College, 4600 South Redwood Road, Salt Lake City, UT 84130-0808

Snow College
Ephraim, Utah
www.snow.edu

CB code: 4727

- Public 2-year community and junior college
- Residential campus in small town

General. Founded in 1888. Regionally accredited. Collaborative program with Julliard in music, theater arts, and dance. Classes, conferences, and workshops hosted by Great Basin Environmental Education Center, offering students outdoor and environmental-service friendly education. **Enrollment:** 4,465 degree-seeking undergraduates. **Degrees:** 748 associate awarded. **Location:** 120 miles from Salt Lake City, 70 miles from Provo. **Calendar:** Semester, limited summer session. **Full-time faculty:** 117 total. **Part-time faculty:** 156 total. **Class size:** 60% < 20, 34% 20-39, 3% 40-49, 2% 50-99, less than 1% >100.

Student profile.

Out-of-state:	3%	Live on campus:	5%
25 or older:	10%		

Transfer out. **Colleges most students transferred to 2011:** Utah State University, Salt Lake Community College, Utah Valley State College, Southern Utah University.

Basis for selection. Open admission. Auditions recommended for fine arts. **Home schooled:** State high school equivalency certificate required.

High school preparation. 15 units recommended. Recommended units include English 4, mathematics 2, social studies 3, science 3 (laboratory 3).

2011-2012 Annual costs. Tuition/fees: $2,910; $9,586 out-of-state. Declining balance meal plan available. Room only: $1,200. Books/supplies: $530. Personal expenses: $900.

Financial aid. **Need-based:** Work-study available nights, weekends and for part-time students. **Non-need-based:** Scholarships awarded for academics, alumni affiliation, athletics, leadership, music/drama, state residency.

Application procedures. **Admission:** Priority date 6/1; no deadline. $30 fee. Application must be submitted on paper. Admission notification on a rolling basis beginning on or about 12/1. Applications received after May 15 will be on a space-available basis. **Financial aid:** Priority date 3/1, closing date 6/1. FAFSA, institutional form required. Applicants notified on a rolling basis starting 8/1; must reply within 1 week(s) of notification.

Academics. **Special study options:** Cooperative education, distance learning, dual enrollment of high school students, ESL, honors, independent study. **Credit/placement by examination:** AP, CLEP, institutional tests. 45 credit hours maximum toward associate degree. **Support services:** GED test center, learning center, reduced course load, remedial instruction, study skills assistance, tutoring, writing center.

Majors. **Biology:** General, bacteriology, botany, physiology, zoology. **Business:** General, accounting, business admin, managerial economics. **Communications:** Journalism. **Computer sciences:** General, computer science, information systems. **Conservation:** General, forestry, management/policy, wildlife/wilderness. **Education:** General, business, early childhood, elementary, ESL, family/consumer sciences, health, physical, secondary, special ed. **Engineering:** General. **English:** English lit, writing. **Foreign languages:** General, French, Japanese, Spanish. **General:** Agribusiness operations, animal sciences, business, farm/ranch. **Health services:** Clinical lab science, EMT paramedic, licensed practical nurse, pharmacy assistant, predental, premedicine, prenursing, prepharmacy, preveterinary, veterinary technology/assistant. **History:** General. **Human services:** Social work. **Math:** General, statistics. **Parks/recreation:** General, health/fitness. **Philosophy/religion:** Philosophy. **Physical sciences:** Chemistry, geology, physics. **Protective services:** Law enforcement admin. **Psychology:** General. **Social sciences:** General, anthropology, economics, geography, political science, sociology. **Visual/performing arts:** General, art, dance, music. **Work/family studies:** General, child care management, clothing/textiles, family/community services, food/nutrition.

Most popular majors. Business/marketing 8%, education 10%, health sciences 10%, liberal arts 38%, visual/performing arts 8%.

Computing on campus. 450 workstations in library, computer center, student center. Dormitories wired for high-speed internet access and linked to campus network. Online course registration, online library, helpline, wireless network available.

Student life. **Freshman orientation:** Available. Preregistration for classes offered. Begins 2 days prior to fall semester. **Housing:** Coed dorms, single-sex dorms, apartments available. $200 partly refundable deposit, deadline 6/1. **Activities:** Bands, choral groups, dance, drama, literary magazine, music ensembles, musical theater, radio station, student government, student newspaper, symphony orchestra, Latter-Day Saints student association, associated women students, associated men students, Badgers Against Alcohol & Drugs, Polynesian club, ski club, Spanish club, international club.

Athletics. NJCAA. **Intercollegiate:** Basketball, football (tackle) M, softball W, volleyball W. **Intramural:** Basketball, bowling, football (non-tackle) M, golf, racquetball, rugby M, soccer, softball, tennis, volleyball. **Team name:** Badgers.

Student services. Adult student services, alcohol/substance abuse counseling, career counseling, services for economically disadvantaged, financial aid counseling, health services, on-campus daycare, personal counseling, veterans' counselor. **Physically disabled:** Services for visually, hearing impaired. **Transfer:** Pre-admission transcript evaluation for new students. Transfer adviser, college fairs on campus for students transferring to 4-year colleges.

Contact. E-mail: hsrelations@snow.edu
Phone: (435) 283-7150 Toll-free number: (800) 848-3399
Fax: (435) 283-6879
Greg Dart, Director of Admissions, Snow College, 150 East College Avenue, Ephraim, UT 84627

Vista College
Clearfield, Utah
www.vistacollege.edu

◗ For-profit 2-year career college
◗ Small city

General. Regionally accredited. **Calendar:** Quarter.

Annual costs/financial aid. Cost of diploma programs: $18,500 - $19,500; associate degree programs: $26,500; all costs inclusive of books, fees and supplies.

Contact. Phone: (801) 774-9900
775 South 2000 East, Clearfield, UT 84015

Vermont

Community College of Vermont
Montpelier, Vermont
www.ccv.edu

CB member
CB code: 3286

- Public 2-year community and liberal arts college
- Commuter campus in small town

General. Founded in 1970. Regionally accredited. **Enrollment:** 4,883 degree-seeking undergraduates. **Degrees:** 426 associate awarded. **Calendar:** Semester, extensive summer session. **Part-time faculty:** 737 total; 12% have terminal degrees, 60% women.

Student profile. Among degree-seeking undergraduates, 504 transferred in from other institutions.

Transfer out. Colleges most students transferred to 2011: University of Vermont, Johnson State College, Champlain College, Vermont Technical College.

Basis for selection. Open admission. **Learning Disabled:** Students must meet with Americans with Disabilities coordinator and bring appropriate documentation.

2011-2012 Annual costs. Tuition/fees: $6,520; $12,940 out-of-state. Per-credit charge: $214 in-state; $428 out-of-state. New England Board of Higher Education rate for students from other New England states: 150% of Vermont resident tuition. Available to degree candidates in academic areas not offered by educational institutions in their home states. Books/supplies: $1,000.

2010-2011 Financial aid. All financial aid based on need. 55% of total undergraduate aid awarded as scholarships/grants, 45% as loans/jobs. Need-based aid available for part-time students. Work-study available nights, weekends and for part-time students.

Application procedures. Admission: No deadline. No application fee. Admission notification on a rolling basis. **Financial aid:** No deadline. FAFSA, institutional form required. Applicants notified on a rolling basis starting 9/1; must reply within 3 week(s) of notification.

Academics. Special study options: Cross-registration, distance learning, double major, dual enrollment of high school students, external degree, independent study, internships, student-designed major, study abroad. **Credit/placement by examination:** AP, CLEP, IB, institutional tests. 45 credit hours maximum toward associate degree. **Support services:** Learning center, reduced course load, remedial instruction, study skills assistance, tutoring, writing center.

Majors. Business: General, accounting, hospitality admin, tourism/travel. **Communications:** Media studies. **Computer sciences:** General, system admin. **Conservation:** Environmental science. **Education:** General, early childhood. **Liberal arts:** Arts/sciences. **Protective services:** Criminal justice, disaster management. **Visual/performing arts:** General, graphic design.

Most popular majors. Business/marketing 24%, education 10%, liberal arts 43%, public administration/social services 9%.

Computing on campus. 800 workstations in library, computer center. Commuter students can connect to campus network. Online course registration, online library, helpline, wireless network available.

Student life. Freshman orientation: Available. Preregistration for classes offered. **Activities:** Choral groups, student government.

Student services. Adult student services, career counseling, services for economically disadvantaged, financial aid counseling, placement for graduates, veterans' counselor. **Physically disabled:** Services for visually, speech, hearing impaired. **Transfer:** Transfer adviser, college fairs on campus for students transferring to 4-year colleges.

Contact. E-mail: inquire@ccv.edu
Phone: (802) 828-2800 Toll-free number: (800) 228-6686
Fax: (802) 828-2805
Adam Warrington, Director of Admissions, Community College of Vermont, PO Box 489, Montpelier, VT 05601

Landmark College
Putney, Vermont
www.landmark.edu

CB code: 0081

- Private 2-year liberal arts college
- Residential campus in small town
- Application essay, interview required

General. Founded in 1983. Regionally accredited. College exclusively for bright students with dyslexia, attention disorders, or specific learning disabilities. Professional development workshops and consultancies offered. **Enrollment:** 488 degree-seeking undergraduates. **Degrees:** 97 associate awarded. **Location:** 8 miles from Brattleboro; 23 miles from Keene, NH. **Calendar:** Semester, limited summer session. **Full-time faculty:** 78 total; 13% have terminal degrees, 1% minority, 63% women. **Part-time faculty:** 3 total. **Class size:** 100% < 20. **Special facilities:** Fine arts building, ropes course.

Student profile. Among degree-seeking undergraduates, 100% enrolled in a transfer program, 154 enrolled as first-time, first-year students, 84 transferred in from other institutions.

Out-of-state:	94%	Hispanic American:	4%
Women:	33%	International:	1%
African American:	6%	25 or older:	4%
Asian American:	2%	Live on campus:	95%

Basis for selection. Successful applicants are highly motivated, have average-to-superior intellectual ability and diagnosis of dyslexia, attentional disorder (ADHD), or specific learning disability. WAIS III or Woodcock Johnson Cognitive assessment required. Nelson-Denny reading scores required.

High school preparation. College-preparatory program recommended. Recommended units include English 4, mathematics 3, social studies 3, history 3, science 3, foreign language 1, visual/performing arts 1 and academic electives 1.

2011-2012 Annual costs. Tuition/fees: $48,710. Room/board: $8,620. Books/supplies: $1,200. Personal expenses: $750.

2010-2011 Financial aid. Need-based: Average need met was 42%. Average scholarship/grant was $20,000; average loan $3,500. 78% of total undergraduate aid awarded as scholarships/grants, 22% as loans/jobs. Need-based aid available for part-time students. Work-study available nights, weekends and for part-time students. **Non-need-based:** Scholarships awarded for academics, art, leadership, minority status, music/drama. **Additional information:** Students encouraged to apply to their state departments of vocational rehabilitation for additional financial assistance.

Application procedures. Admission: Priority date 5/15; no deadline. $75 fee, may be waived for applicants with need. Application must be submitted on paper. Admission notification on a rolling basis beginning on or about 12/1. **Financial aid:** Priority date 3/1; no closing date. FAFSA required. Applicants notified on a rolling basis starting 3/15; must reply within 2 week(s) of notification.

Academics. Special study options: Internships, study abroad. **Credit/placement by examination:** AP, CLEP, SAT, ACT, institutional tests. **Support services:** Learning center, pre-admission summer program, reduced course load, remedial instruction, study skills assistance, writing center.

Majors. Business: Business admin. **Liberal arts:** Arts/sciences.

Most popular majors. Business/marketing 7%, liberal arts 93%.

Computing on campus. PC or laptop required. 50 workstations in dormitories, library, student center. Dormitories wired for high-speed internet access and linked to campus network. Online library, helpline, repair service, wireless network available.

Student life. Freshman orientation: Mandatory. Preregistration for classes offered. **Policies:** Alcohol not permitted on-campus. All new students must live on-campus. **Housing:** Guaranteed on-campus for all undergraduates. Coed dorms, special housing for disabled, wellness housing available. **Activities:** Jazz band, choral groups, dance, drama, literary magazine, music ensembles, radio station, student government, student newspaper, Phi Theta Kappa honor society, community service club.

Athletics. Intercollegiate: Basketball, equestrian, soccer. **Intramural:** Basketball. **Team name:** Landsharks.

Student services. Adult student services, alcohol/substance abuse counseling, career counseling, financial aid counseling, health services, personal counseling, placement for graduates, women's services. **Transfer:** Transfer center, transfer adviser, college fairs on campus for students transferring to 4-year colleges.

Contact. E-mail: admissions@landmark.edu
Phone: (802) 387-6718 Fax: (802) 387-6868
Dale Herold, Vice President for Enrollment Management, Landmark
College, River Road South, Putney, VT 05346

New England Culinary Institute
Montpelier, Vermont
www.neci.edu   CB code: 3405

▶ For-profit 2-year culinary school
▶ Residential campus in small town

General. Founded in 1980. Accredited by ACCSCT. **Location:** 39 miles
from Burlington. **Calendar:** Continuous.

Annual costs/financial aid. Tuition/fees (2011-2012): $26,425. Room/
board: $7,450. Books/supplies: $1,375. Personal expenses: $2,223. Need-
based financial aid available for full-time students.

Contact. Phone: (802) 223-6324
Director of Admissions, 56 College Street, Montpelier, VT 05602

Virginia

Advanced Technology Institute
Virginia Beach, Virginia
www.auto.edu

- For-profit 2-year technical college
- Commuter campus in large city

General. Accredited by ACCSCT. **Calendar:** Differs by program.

Contact. Phone: (757) 490-1241
Director of Admissions, 5700 Southern Boulevard, Virginia Beach, VA 23462

Aviation Institute of Maintenance: Virginia Beach
Chesapeake, Virginia
www.aviationmaintenance.edu

- For-profit 2-year technical college
- Commuter campus in large city

General. Accredited by ACCSCT. **Calendar:** Continuous.

Contact. Phone: (757) 363-2121
Director of Admissions, 2211 South Military Highway, Chesapeake, VA 23320

Blue Ridge Community College
Weyers Cave, Virginia
www.brcc.edu   **CB code: 5083**

- Public 2-year community college
- Commuter campus in large town

General. Founded in 1965. Regionally accredited. **Enrollment:** 4,836 degree-seeking undergraduates. **Degrees:** 556 associate awarded. **Location:** 12 miles from Harrisonburg, 15 miles from Staunton. **Calendar:** Semester, limited summer session. **Full-time faculty:** 67 total. **Part-time faculty:** 376 total. **Special facilities:** Arboretum, fine arts center. **Partnerships:** Formal partnership with Tech Prep Consortium.

Student profile.

Out-of-state: 2%   25 or older: 24%

Transfer out. Colleges most students transferred to 2011: James Madison University, Mary Baldwin College, Old Dominion University, Eastern Mennonite University, Bridgewater College.

Basis for selection. Open admission, but selective for some programs. Special requirements for commercial driving, veterinary assistant technology and nursing programs (also has residency requirement); interview required.

High school preparation. College-preparatory program recommended. 8 units recommended. Recommended units include English 4, mathematics 2, social studies 1 and science 1.

2011-2012 Annual costs. Tuition/fees: $4,098; $9,396 out-of-state. Per-credit charge: $112 in-state; $288 out-of-state. Out-of-state students pay an additional $450 capital outlay fee. Books/supplies: $600. Personal expenses: $900.

Financial aid. Need-based: Need-based aid available for part-time students. Work-study available nights, weekends and for part-time students. **Non-need-based:** Scholarships awarded for academics, job skills, leadership, minority status.

Application procedures. Admission: No deadline. No application fee. Admission notification on a rolling basis. Closing date for veterinary assistant technology is January 1. Nursing clinical component application deadline is January 31. **Financial aid:** Priority date 5/1; no closing date. FAFSA, institutional form required. Applicants notified on a rolling basis starting 5/30; must reply within 2 week(s) of notification.

Academics. Special study options: Accelerated study, cross-registration, distance learning, double major, dual enrollment of high school students, honors, independent study, internships, study abroad, teacher certification program. Bachelor's degree programs available on campus. License preparation in nursing, real estate. **Credit/placement by examination:** AP, CLEP, IB, institutional tests. 25 credit hours maximum toward associate degree. Credit cannot duplicate earned course credits, nor courses audited or failed. **Support services:** Learning center, remedial instruction, study skills assistance, tutoring, writing center.

Majors. Business: Accounting, administrative services, business admin. **Computer sciences:** General, information systems, programming, systems analysis. **General:** Animal sciences. **Health services:** Nursing (RN), veterinary technology/assistant. **Liberal arts:** Arts/sciences.

Computing on campus. 285 workstations in library, computer center, student center. Commuter students can connect to campus network. Online course registration, online library, helpline, wireless network available.

Student life. Freshman orientation: Available. Preregistration for classes offered. Held week before classes begin, open to parents. **Activities:** Drama, international student organizations, student government, Phi Theta Kappa, Christian Fellowship, Students in Free Enterprise, Vet Tech Club, Alpha Beta Gamma, Buddies Club, Collegiate FFA, Environmental Awareness, SPECTRUM Multicultural.

Athletics. Intramural: Basketball M.

Student services. Adult student services, career counseling, services for economically disadvantaged, student employment services, financial aid counseling, minority student services, placement for graduates, veterans' counselor, women's services. **Physically disabled:** Services for visually, speech, hearing impaired. **Transfer:** Pre-admission transcript evaluation for new students. Transfer adviser, college fairs on campus for students transferring to 4-year colleges.

Contact. Phone: (540) 453-2287
Toll-free number: (888) 750-2722 ext. 2287 Fax: (540) 453-2437
Mary Wayland, Dean of Academic Support Services, Blue Ridge Community College, Box 80, Weyers Cave, VA 24486-9989

Bryant & Stratton College: Richmond
Richmond, Virginia
www.bryantstratton.edu   **CB code: 4762**

- For-profit 2-year career college
- Commuter campus in small city

General. Enrollment: 1,012 degree-seeking undergraduates. **Degrees:** 22 bachelor's, 162 associate awarded. **Calendar:** Trimester, extensive summer session. **Full-time faculty:** 22 total. **Part-time faculty:** 55 total. **Class size:** 100% 20-39.

Basis for selection. Open admission, but selective for some programs. **Adult students:** SAT/ACT scores not required. **Home schooled:** Interview required.

2011-2012 Annual costs. Tuition/fees: $15,570. Books/supplies: $1,000. Personal expenses: $2,610.

Financial aid. All financial aid based on need. Need-based aid available for part-time students. Work-study available nights, weekends and for part-time students.

Application procedures. Admission: No deadline. $35 fee. Application must be submitted on paper. Admission notification on a rolling basis. **Financial aid:** No deadline. FAFSA required.

Academics. Special study options: Distance learning, double major, independent study, internships. Bachelor's degree programs available on campus. License preparation in nursing. **Credit/placement by examination:** AP, CLEP, institutional tests. 30 credit hours maximum toward associate degree, 60 toward bachelor's. Up to 50% of total credit hours required for graduation, including 50% of the total required hours in major study areas, may be earned through combination of transfer credits and proficiency evaluations. **Support services:** Learning center, study skills assistance, tutoring.

Majors. Business: Accounting, administrative services, business admin, human resources. **Computer sciences:** Information technology. **Health services:** Medical assistant, medical secretary. **Protective services:** Criminal justice.

Computing on campus. 250 workstations in library, computer center. Commuter students can connect to campus network. Online course registration, online library, helpline, wireless network available.

Student life. Freshman orientation: Mandatory. Preregistration for classes offered. Day and evening sessions, the day before classes begin. **Activities:** Student government.

Student services. Career counseling, student employment services, financial aid counseling, placement for graduates, veterans' counselor. **Physically disabled:** Services for hearing impaired.

Contact. Phone: (804) 745-2444 Toll-free number: (800) 735-2420 Fax: (804) 745-6884
David Mayle, Director of Admissions, Bryant & Stratton College: Richmond, 8141 Hull Street Road, Richmond, VA 23235

Bryant & Stratton College: Virginia Beach
Virginia Beach, Virginia
www.bryantstratton.edu   **CB code: 4761**

♦ For-profit 2-year business and junior college
♦ Commuter campus in large city
♦ Interview required

General. Founded in 1952. Regionally accredited. **Enrollment:** 424 degree-seeking undergraduates. **Degrees:** 23 bachelor's, 156 associate awarded. **Location:** 10 miles from Norfolk. **Calendar:** Semester, extensive summer session. **Full-time faculty:** 18 total. **Part-time faculty:** 65 total. **Class size:** 89% < 20, 11% 20-39.

Transfer out. Colleges most students transferred to 2011: Tidewater Community College, Strayer University, University of Phoenix.

Basis for selection. Open admission, but selective for some programs. Personal interview most important. TOEFL used for non-native English speakers.

High school preparation. Recommended units include English 4, mathematics 2, social studies 3, science 2, foreign language 2 and academic electives 1.

2011-2012 Annual costs. Tuition/fees: $15,570. Books/supplies: $1,600. Personal expenses: $2,785.

Financial aid. Need-based: Need-based aid available for part-time students. Work-study available nights, weekends and for part-time students.

Application procedures. Admission: No deadline. $35 fee, may be waived for applicants with need. Admission notification on a rolling basis. **Financial aid:** No deadline. FAFSA required. Applicants notified on a rolling basis.

Academics. Free tutoring and extensive academic advising available. Portfolio projects in all classes. **Special study options:** Cooperative education, double major, independent study, internships, liberal arts/career combination, weekend college. **Credit/placement by examination:** AP, CLEP, institutional tests. 30 credit hours maximum toward associate degree, 60 toward bachelor's. **Support services:** Learning center, reduced course load, remedial instruction, study skills assistance, tutoring, writing center.

Majors. Business: Accounting, administrative services, business admin, human resources. **Computer sciences:** General. **Health services:** Medical assistant, office assistant. **Protective services:** Law enforcement admin.

Most popular majors. Business/marketing 51%, computer/information sciences 11%, health sciences 15%, legal studies 23%, security/protective services 16%.

Computing on campus. 150 workstations in library, computer center. Online library, wireless network available.

Student life. Freshman orientation: Mandatory. Preregistration for classes offered. Held week classes start, 2 to 3 hours. **Activities:** Student government, student newspaper, Alpha Beta Gamma, Phi Beta Lambda, law society, medical club, computer club, Society for the Advancement of Management.

Student services. Adult student services, career counseling, student employment services, on-campus daycare, personal counseling, placement for graduates, veterans' counselor. **Transfer:** Pre-admission transcript evaluation for new students.

Contact. E-mail: dmsoutherland@bryantstratton.edu
Phone: (757) 499-7900 Fax: (757) 499-9977
Deana Southerland, Director of Admissions, Bryant & Stratton College: Virginia Beach, 301 Centre Pointe Drive, Virginia Beach, VA 23462-4417

Central Virginia Community College
Lynchburg, Virginia   **CB member**
www.cvcc.va.us   **CB code: 5141**

♦ Public 2-year community college
♦ Commuter campus in small city

General. Founded in 1966. Regionally accredited. **Enrollment:** 5,461 degree-seeking undergraduates. **Degrees:** 367 associate awarded. **Location:** 120 miles from Richmond. **Calendar:** Semester, limited summer session. **Full-time faculty:** 61 total. **Part-time faculty:** 268 total.

Transfer out. Colleges most students transferred to 2011: Lynchburg College, Virginia Polytechnic Institute and State University, Longwood College, Old Dominion University.

Basis for selection. Open admission, but selective for some programs. Allied health program applicants must have 2 interviews with program head and meet specific criteria. Only 15 applicants accepted into each program each year. Interview required for health program.

2011-2012 Annual costs. Tuition/fees: $3,705; $9,003 out-of-state. Per-credit charge: $112 in-state; $288 out-of-state. Out of state students pay an additional $450 capital outlay fee. Books/supplies: $600. Personal expenses: $1,550.

Financial aid. Need-based: Work-study available nights, weekends and for part-time students. **Non-need-based:** Scholarships awarded for academics, alumni affiliation. **Additional information:** Payment plan available.

Application procedures. Admission: Priority date 9/5; no deadline. No application fee. Admission notification on a rolling basis. **Financial aid:** Priority date 3/15; no closing date. FAFSA required. Applicants notified on a rolling basis starting 5/1; must reply within 2 week(s) of notification.

Academics. GPA of 2.0 required to graduate. System-wide core curriculum to ensure ease of transfer. **Special study options:** Cooperative education, distance learning, dual enrollment of high school students, ESL, independent study, internships, study abroad, weekend college. Bachelor's degree programs available on campus. License preparation in dental hygiene, paramedic, radiology, real estate. **Credit/placement by examination:** AP, CLEP, IB, institutional tests. 45 credit hours maximum toward associate degree. **Support services:** Learning center, reduced course load, remedial instruction, study skills assistance, tutoring.

Majors. Business: General, accounting, administrative services, business admin, finance, management information systems. **Computer sciences:** Information systems. **Education:** General. **Health services:** Clinical lab technology, physics/radiologic health. **Liberal arts:** Arts/sciences. **Protective services:** Law enforcement admin. **Visual/performing arts:** Commercial/advertising art.

Computing on campus. 230 workstations in library, computer center. Commuter students can connect to campus network. Online library available.

Student life. Freshman orientation: Mandatory, $65 fee. Preregistration for classes offered. **Activities:** Drama, literary magazine, student government, student newspaper, Black Student Union, art club, honor society, Students Together For Environmental Protection, data processing management association, Spanish club, medical lab club, respiratory club, radiology club.

Athletics. Intramural: Softball, volleyball.

Student services. Career counseling, student employment services, financial aid counseling, personal counseling, placement for graduates, veterans' counselor. **Physically disabled:** Services for visually, speech, hearing impaired. **Transfer:** Transfer adviser, college fairs on campus for students transferring to 4-year colleges.

Contact. Toll-free number: (800) 562-3060 Fax: (434) 832-7793
Geoffrey Hicks, Chief Academic Officer, Central Virginia Community College, 3506 Wards Road, Lynchburg, VA 24502-2498

Two-Year Colleges

Dabney S. Lancaster Community College
Clifton Forge, Virginia
www.dslcc.edu   CB code: 5139

- Public 2-year community and technical college
- Commuter campus in small town

General. Founded in 1967. Regionally accredited. Virginia Governor's School on campus. **Enrollment:** 1,000 degree-seeking undergraduates. **Degrees:** 101 associate awarded. **Location:** 55 miles from Roanoke. **Calendar:** Semester, extensive summer session. **Full-time faculty:** 20 total. **Part-time faculty:** 90 total. **Class size:** 88% < 20, 11% 20-39, less than 1% 40-49. **Special facilities:** Wood harvesting lab, forestry lab, wind turbine service technician lab.

Basis for selection. Open admission, but selective for some programs. Special requirements for nursing program. High school diploma or GED required of applicants under 18. Interview required for nursing program.

High school preparation. Course recommendations vary according to planned curriculum.

2011-2012 Annual costs. Tuition/fees: $3,645; $8,943 out-of-state. Per-credit charge: $112 in-state; $288 out-of-state. Out-of-state students pay an additional $450 capital outlay fee. Books/supplies: $580. Personal expenses: $1,680.

Financial aid. All financial aid based on need. Need-based aid available for part-time students. Work-study available nights, weekends and for part-time students.

Application procedures. Admission: No deadline. No application fee. Admission notification on a rolling basis beginning on or about 2/1. **Financial aid:** Priority date 3/15; no closing date. FAFSA, institutional form required. Applicants notified on a rolling basis starting 4/15; must reply within 2 week(s) of notification.

Academics. Special study options: Cooperative education, distance learning, double major, dual enrollment of high school students, independent study, internships. **Credit/placement by examination:** AP, CLEP, institutional tests. **Support services:** GED preparation, learning center, pre-admission summer program, reduced course load, remedial instruction, study skills assistance, tutoring, writing center.

Majors. Business: Administrative services, business admin, communications, office management, office/clerical. **Communications technology:** Graphic/printing. **Computer sciences:** General. **Conservation:** Forestry. **Liberal arts:** Arts/sciences. **Protective services:** Criminal justice, police science.

Most popular majors. Education 11%, health sciences 43%, liberal arts 14%, natural resources/environmental science 18%, science technologies 6%, security/protective services 6%.

Computing on campus. 60 workstations in library, computer center, student center. Commuter students can connect to campus network. Online library, helpline, wireless network available.

Student life. Freshman orientation: Mandatory. Preregistration for classes offered. **Activities:** Choral groups, literary magazine, student government, student newspaper, various social, religious and service clubs available.

Athletics. Intramural: Basketball, bowling, football (non-tackle), table tennis. **Team name:** Roadrunners.

Student services. Career counseling, student employment services, financial aid counseling, personal counseling, placement for graduates, veterans' counselor. **Physically disabled:** Services for visually, speech, hearing impaired. **Transfer:** Transfer adviser, college fairs on campus for students transferring to 4-year colleges.

Contact. Phone: (540) 863-2815 Toll-free number: (877) 133-7522
Fax: (540) 863-2915
Matt McGraw, Director of Student Services, Dabney S. Lancaster Community College, Box 1000, Clifton Forge, VA 24422

Danville Community College
Danville, Virginia
www.dcc.vccs.edu   CB code: 5163

- Public 2-year community college
- Commuter campus in small city

General. Founded in 1967. Regionally accredited. **Enrollment:** 4,390 degree-seeking undergraduates. **Degrees:** 224 associate awarded. **Location:** 45 miles from Greensboro, North Carolina. **Calendar:** Semester, limited summer session. **Full-time faculty:** 59 total. **Part-time faculty:** 228 total. **Class size:** 71% < 20, 28% 20-39, 1% 50-99.

Student profile.

Out-of-state:	2%	**25 or older:**	52%

Transfer out. Colleges most students transferred to 2011: Averett University, Virginia Polytechnic Institute, Radford University.

Basis for selection. Open admission, but selective for some programs. Special requirements for nursing program.

High school preparation. Recommended units include English 4 and mathematics 1.

2011-2012 Annual costs. Tuition/fees: $3,600; $8,898 out-of-state. Per-credit charge: $112 in-state; $288 out-of-state. Out-of-state students pay an additional $450 capital outlay fee. Books/supplies: $700. Personal expenses: $1,328.

Financial aid. All financial aid based on need. Need-based aid available for part-time students. Work-study available nights, weekends and for part-time students.

Application procedures. Admission: Priority date 8/20; no deadline. No application fee. Admission notification on a rolling basis beginning on or about 1/15. **Financial aid:** Priority date 6/1; no closing date. FAFSA required. Applicants notified on a rolling basis starting 5/1; must reply within 2 week(s) of notification.

Academics. System-wide core curriculum to ensure ease of transfer. **Special study options:** Accelerated study, cooperative education, distance learning, double major, dual enrollment of high school students, honors, independent study, internships. Bachelor's degree programs available on campus. License preparation in dental hygiene, nursing, real estate. **Credit/placement by examination:** AP, CLEP, institutional tests. **Support services:** GED preparation and test center, learning center, pre-admission summer program, reduced course load, remedial instruction, study skills assistance, tutoring.

Majors. Business: General, accounting, administrative services, business admin, executive assistant, receptionist. **Communications technology:** Graphic/printing. **Computer sciences:** General, computer science, programming. **Engineering:** General. **Health services:** Dental hygiene, medical secretary, office assistant, respiratory therapy assistant. **Liberal arts:** Arts/sciences, humanities. **Protective services:** Law enforcement admin. **Work/family studies:** Child development.

Most popular majors. Business/marketing 45%, education 17%, liberal arts 37%, security/protective services 11%.

Computing on campus. 425 workstations in library, computer center. Online course registration, online library available.

Student life. Freshman orientation: Mandatory. Preregistration for classes offered. Two 1-day summer sessions to choose from. **Activities:** Choral groups, student government, African-American culture club, Christian Students Fellowship, graphics club, International Association of Administrative Professionals, Phi Theta Kappa, National Vocational-Technical Honor Society, gospel club, Lambda Alpha Epsilon.

Athletics. Team name: Knights.

Student services. Adult student services, chaplain/spiritual director, career counseling, student employment services, financial aid counseling, on-campus daycare, personal counseling, placement for graduates, veterans' counselor, women's services. **Physically disabled:** Services for visually, speech, hearing impaired. **Transfer:** College fairs on campus for students transferring to 4-year colleges.

Contact. E-mail: ethornton@dcc.vccs.edu
Phone: (434) 797-8467 Toll-free number: (800) 560-4291
Fax: (434) 797-8451
Janet Laughlin, Dean of Student Success and Academic Advancement, Danville Community College, 1008 South Main Street, Danville, VA 24541

Eastern Shore Community College
Melfa, Virginia
www.es.vccs.edu   CB code: 5844

- Public 2-year community college
- Commuter campus in rural community

General. Founded in 1971. Regionally accredited. **Enrollment:** 1,025 undergraduates. **Degrees:** 50 associate awarded. **Location:** 70 miles from Norfolk. **Calendar:** Semester, limited summer session. **Full-time faculty:** 68 total; 10% minority, 52% women. **Part-time faculty:** 46 total; 9% minority, 50% women.

Student profile. 40% enrolled in a transfer program, 30% enrolled in a vocational program.

Transfer out. 40% of students enrolled in the transfer program go on to 4-year colleges. **Colleges most students transferred to 2011:** Old Dominion University, University of Virginia, Virginia Polytechnic Institute.

Basis for selection. Open admission, but selective for some programs. Practical Nursing program has prerequisites for admission. Students must take the PSB nursing aptitude test and meet state requirements for screening. **Learning Disabled:** ESCC honors all reasonable, documented requests for accommodations. In order to obtain special accommodations, a student must meet with a counselor prior to classes.

High school preparation. College-preparatory program required. 18 units recommended. Recommended units include English 4, mathematics 3, social studies 2 and science 2.

2011-2012 Annual costs. Tuition/fees: $3,630; $8,928 out-of-state. Per-credit charge: $112 in-state; $288 out-of-state. Out-of-state students pay an additional $450 capital outlay fee. Books/supplies: $900. Personal expenses: $1,500.

Financial aid. All financial aid based on need. Need-based aid available for part-time students. Work-study available nights, weekends and for part-time students. **Additional information:** ESCC is a member of the Servicemembers Opportunity Colleges program.

Application procedures. Admission: No deadline. No application fee. Admission notification on a rolling basis. **Financial aid:** Priority date 5/1; no closing date. FAFSA required. Applicants notified on a rolling basis starting 6/1; must reply within 2 week(s) of notification.

Academics. Special study options: Cross-registration, distance learning, dual enrollment of high school students. Bachelor's degree programs available on campus. License preparation in nursing, real estate. **Credit/placement by examination:** AP, CLEP, institutional tests. 30 credit hours maximum toward associate degree. Students who do not achieve minimum scores on institutional placement tests must enroll in developmental courses. **Support services:** GED preparation and test center, learning center, reduced course load, remedial instruction, study skills assistance, tutoring, writing center.

Majors. Business: Business admin, office/clerical. **Computer sciences:** General. **Education:** General, science. **Engineering:** Electrical. **Liberal arts:** Arts/sciences.

Computing on campus. 53 workstations in library, computer center. Online course registration, online library, helpline, wireless network available.

Student life. Freshman orientation: Available. Preregistration for classes offered. **Activities:** Campus ministries, literary magazine, student government, Phi Theta Kappa, Phi Beta Lambda, ACTS.

Student services. Adult student services, career counseling, student employment services, financial aid counseling, personal counseling, placement for graduates, veterans' counselor. **Physically disabled:** Services for visually, hearing impaired. **Transfer:** Transfer adviser, college fairs on campus for students transferring to 4-year colleges.

Contact. E-mail: bsmith@es.vccs.edu
Phone: (757) 789-1731 Toll-free number: (877) 871-8455
Fax: (757) 789-1737
P Smith, Dean of Student Services, Eastern Shore Community College, 29300 Lankford Highway, Melfa, VA 23410-9755

Germanna Community College
Locust Grove, Virginia
www.germanna.edu   CB code: 5276

- Public 2-year community college
- Commuter campus in rural community

General. Founded in 1969. Regionally accredited. Off-campus sites in high schools; dual enrollment courses offered at area high schools. **Enrollment:** 7,779 degree-seeking undergraduates. **Degrees:** 617 associate awarded. **Location:** 15 miles from Culpeper, 18 miles from Fredericksburg. **Calendar:** Semester, limited summer session. **Full-time faculty:** 74 total. **Part-time**

faculty: 327 total. **Class size:** 40% < 20, 60% 20-39, less than 1% 50-99. **Special facilities:** Art exhibits, local history collection.

Student profile.

Out-of-state:	1%	**25 or older:**	29%

Transfer out. Colleges most students transferred to 2011: University of Mary Washington, Old Dominion University, Radford University, Virginia Commonwealth University, Virginia Tech.

Basis for selection. Open admission, but selective for some programs. Special requirements for nursing program with local applicants given preference. **Adult students:** SAT scores, GCC placement tests, or proof of college transcripts required. **Home schooled:** Transcript of courses and grades required. Provide current copy of signed home school agreement between appropriate school system and authorizing parent or guardian. Provide written recommendation from home school teacher or tutor.

2011-2012 Annual costs. Tuition/fees: $3,618; $8,916 out-of-state. Per-credit charge: $112 in-state; $288 out-of-state. Out-of-state students pay additional $450 capital outlay fee. Books/supplies: $800. Personal expenses: $2,770.

Financial aid. Need-based: Need-based aid available for part-time students. Work-study available nights, weekends and for part-time students. **Non-need-based:** Scholarships awarded for academics.

Application procedures. Admission: No deadline. No application fee. Admission notification on a rolling basis. Nursing program applications must be completed by February 1. **Financial aid:** Priority date 4/1; no closing date. FAFSA required. Applicants notified on a rolling basis starting 5/15; must reply within 2 week(s) of notification.

Academics. System-wide core curriculum to ensure ease of transfer. **Special study options:** Accelerated study, distance learning, double major, dual enrollment of high school students, ESL, independent study, internships, liberal arts/career combination. Bachelor's degree programs available on campus. License preparation in dental hygiene, nursing. **Credit/placement by examination:** AP, CLEP, institutional tests. 8 credit hours maximum toward associate degree. **Support services:** GED test center, reduced course load, remedial instruction, study skills assistance, tutoring.

Majors. Biology: General. **Business:** General, business admin. **Computer sciences:** Information technology. **Education:** General, elementary. **Health services:** Dental hygiene, nursing (RN), radiologic technology/medical imaging. **Liberal arts:** Arts/sciences. **Protective services:** Police science. **Psychology:** General.

Most popular majors. Biological/life sciences 10%, business/marketing 22%, education 7%, health sciences 16%, liberal arts 41%.

Computing on campus. 90 workstations in library, computer center. Online course registration, online library, helpline, wireless network available.

Student life. Freshman orientation: Mandatory. Preregistration for classes offered. **Activities:** Student government, Black studies, student Christian associations.

Athletics. Team name: Grizzly Bears.

Student services. Career counseling, student employment services, financial aid counseling, personal counseling, placement for graduates, veterans' counselor. **Physically disabled:** Services for visually, hearing impaired. **Transfer:** Transfer adviser, college fairs on campus for students transferring to 4-year colleges.

Contact. Phone: (540) 423-9122 Fax: (540) 423-9158
Rita Dunston, Registrar, Germanna Community College, 2130 Germanna Highway, Locust Grove, VA 22508-2102

J. Sargeant Reynolds Community College
Richmond, Virginia
www.reynolds.edu   CB code: 5340

- Public 2-year community college
- Commuter campus in very large city

General. Founded in 1972. Regionally accredited. **Enrollment:** 11,261 degree-seeking undergraduates; 2,109 non-degree-seeking students. **Degrees:** 193 associate awarded. **ROTC:** Army. **Location:** Downtown. **Calendar:** Semester, extensive summer session. **Full-time faculty:** 134 total. **Part-time faculty:** 495 total. **Special facilities:** Hospitality development center, distance education center. **Partnerships:** Formal partnerships with local medical facilities.

Two-Year Colleges

Student profile. Among degree-seeking undergraduates, 2,180 enrolled as first-time, first-year students.

Part-time:	65%	Women:	61%
Out-of-state:	3%	25 or older:	44%

Transfer out. **Colleges most students transferred to 2011:** Virginia Commonwealth University, Old Dominion University.

Basis for selection. Open admission, but selective for some programs. Special requirements for nursing, health technology, engineering, legal assisting programs; interview recommended.

High school preparation. College preparatory units recommended for applicants to college transfer programs. Recommended units vary per program of study and include up to 4 English, 4 mathematics, 2 lab science, 2 foreign language, 2 social studies.

2011-2012 Annual costs. Tuition/fees: $3,873; $9,171 out-of-state. Per-credit charge: $114 in-state; $290 out-of-state. Out-of-state students pay additional $450 capital outlay fee. Books/supplies: $1,000. Personal expenses: $900.

2010-2011 Financial aid. Need-based: 76% of total undergraduate aid awarded as scholarships/grants, 24% as loans/jobs. Need-based aid available for part-time students. Work-study available nights, weekends and for part-time students. **Non-need-based:** Scholarships awarded for academics.

Application procedures. Admission: No deadline. No application fee. Admission notification on a rolling basis beginning on or about 1/15. **Financial aid:** Priority date 4/15; no closing date. FAFSA required. Applicants notified on a rolling basis starting 7/15; must reply within 2 week(s) of notification.

Academics. Special study options: Cooperative education, distance learning, double major, dual enrollment of high school students, ESL, independent study, internships, weekend college. License preparation in dental hygiene, nursing, paramedic, real estate. **Credit/placement by examination:** AP, CLEP, IB, institutional tests. 53 credit hours maximum toward associate degree. Essay required for composition and literature subject exams (CLEP). **Support services:** Learning center, pre-admission summer program, reduced course load, remedial instruction, study skills assistance, tutoring, writing center.

Majors. Architecture: Technology. **Business:** Accounting, business admin, hospitality admin, office technology, office/clerical. **Computer sciences:** General, computer science, information systems, programming. **Education:** Early childhood, teacher assistance. **Engineering:** General. **General:** Horticulture, landscaping, turf management. **Health services:** Clinical lab technology, dental lab technology, nursing (RN), occupational therapy assistant, optician, respiratory therapy technology. **Human services:** Community org/advocacy. **Liberal arts:** Arts/sciences. **Math:** General. **Protective services:** Criminal justice, firefighting. **Social sciences:** General. **Visual/performing arts:** Music. **Work/family studies:** Child care management, institutional food production.

Computing on campus. 1,100 workstations in library, computer center, student center. Commuter students can connect to campus network. Online course registration, helpline, repair service, wireless network available.

Student life. Freshman orientation: Available. Preregistration for classes offered. **Activities:** Campus ministries, music ensembles, student government, TV station, culinary arts, horticultural club, music club, PAVE club, Phi Beta Lambda, Phi Theta Kappa, photography club, sign language club, Student Virginia Education Association, sustainable agriculture club.

Student services. Career counseling, student employment services, financial aid counseling, veterans' counselor. **Physically disabled:** Services for visually, speech, hearing impaired. **Transfer:** Transfer adviser, college fairs on campus for students transferring to 4-year colleges.

Contact. E-mail: kpettis-walden@reynolds.edu
Phone: (804) 523-5029 Fax: (804) 371-3650
Karen Pettis-Walden, Director of Admissions and Records, J. Sargeant Reynolds Community College, Box 85622, Richmond, VA 23285-5622

John Tyler Community College
Chester, Virginia
www.jtcc.edu
CB member
CB code: 5342

- Public 2-year community college
- Commuter campus in small city

General. Founded in 1965. Regionally accredited. **Enrollment:** 6,753 degree-seeking undergraduates; 4,045 non-degree-seeking students. **Degrees:** 599 associate awarded. **ROTC:** Army. **Location:** 16 miles from Richmond. **Calendar:** Semester, extensive summer session. **Full-time faculty:** 103 total; 58% women. **Part-time faculty:** 445 total; 58% women.

Student profile. Among degree-seeking undergraduates, 1,387 enrolled as first-time, first-year students.

Part-time:	57%	Women:	62%

Basis for selection. Open admission, but selective for some programs. Special requirements for nursing, funeral services and police science programs. **Home schooled:** Parents of students must provide written permission to enroll their children and meet with the dean of student services prior to applying. Placement tests required.

High school preparation. Required units include English 4 and mathematics 4. Biology and/or chemistry required for allied health programs.

2011-2012 Annual costs. Tuition/fees: $3,620; $8,917 out-of-state. Per-credit charge: $112 in-state; $288 out-of-state. Students pay additional $450 capital outlay fee.

Financial aid. Need-based: Need-based aid available for part-time students. Work-study available nights, weekends and for part-time students. **Non-need-based:** Scholarships awarded for academics, state residency.

Application procedures. Admission: Priority date 8/1; no deadline. No application fee. Admission notification on a rolling basis. High school students may attend with written approval of school principal. **Financial aid:** Priority date 5/15, closing date 7/15. FAFSA required. Applicants notified on a rolling basis starting 6/15.

Academics. Students seeking associate degree must complete 25 percent of core courses at college. **Special study options:** Cooperative education, distance learning, dual enrollment of high school students, internships, weekend college. 2-2 transfer programs in various engineering technology disciplines and business education; 1-3 transfer certificate in art. License preparation in nursing. **Credit/placement by examination:** AP, CLEP, IB, institutional tests. **Support services:** Learning center, remedial instruction, study skills assistance, tutoring.

Majors. Architecture: Technology. **Business:** Business admin. **Computer sciences:** General. **Engineering:** General. **Health services:** Nursing (RN). **Liberal arts:** Arts/sciences, humanities. **Protective services:** Law enforcement admin. **Visual/performing arts:** General. **Work/family studies:** Child care service.

Most popular majors. Business/marketing 6%, health sciences 16%, liberal arts 64%.

Computing on campus. 2,115 workstations in library, student center. Commuter students can connect to campus network. Online course registration, online library available.

Student life. Freshman orientation: Mandatory. Preregistration for classes offered. **Activities:** Drama, student government, Nursing Students Association, Human Services Club, Funeral Services Club, Biology Club, Art Club, Elements of Life Club, Chemistry Club, Future Teachers Club, Phi Theta Kappa, Disciples of Christ Club.

Student services. Adult student services, alcohol/substance abuse counseling, career counseling, financial aid counseling, personal counseling, veterans' counselor. **Physically disabled:** Services for visually, speech, hearing impaired. **Transfer:** Transfer adviser, college fairs on campus for students transferring to 4-year colleges.

Contact. E-mail: admissionsandrecords@jtcc.edu
Phone: (804) 706-5220 Toll-free number: (800) 552-3490
Fax: (804) 796-4362
Joy James, Director of Admission, John Tyler Community College, 13101 Jefferson Davis Highway, Chester, VA 23831-5316

Lord Fairfax Community College
Middletown, Virginia
www.lfcc.edu
CB code: 5381

- Public 2-year community college
- Commuter campus in small town

General. Founded in 1969. Regionally accredited. Locations in Fauquier, Middletown and the Luray-Page County Center. **Enrollment:** 7,301 degree-seeking undergraduates. **Degrees:** 520 associate awarded. **Calendar:** Semester, limited summer session. **Full-time faculty:** 67 total. **Part-time faculty:** 289 total.

Transfer out. Colleges most students transferred to 2011: George Mason University, James Madison University, Old Dominion University, Shenandoah University, University of Mary Washington.

Basis for selection. Open admission, but selective for some programs. Selective admission for health profession. **Adult students:** SAT/ACT scores not required.

2011-2012 Annual costs. Tuition/fees: $3,659; $8,957 out-of-state. Per-credit charge: $112 in-state; $288 out-of-state. Out-of-state students pay an additional $450 capital outlay fee. Books/supplies: $800.

Financial aid. All financial aid based on need. Need-based aid available for part-time students. Work-study available nights, weekends and for part-time students.

Application procedures. Admission: No deadline. No application fee. Admission notification on a rolling basis. **Financial aid:** Priority date 5/1; no closing date. FAFSA required. Applicants notified on a rolling basis starting 6/1.

Academics. Special study options: Distance learning, double major, dual enrollment of high school students, ESL, honors, independent study. Bachelor's degree programs available on campus. License preparation in dental hygiene, nursing, paramedic, real estate. **Credit/placement by examination:** AP, CLEP, institutional tests. **Support services:** GED test center, learning center, reduced course load, remedial instruction, study skills assistance, tutoring.

Majors. Business: Accounting, administrative services, business admin, management information systems, marketing, office management. **Communications:** Communications/speech/rhetoric. **Computer sciences:** General, database management, networking, webmaster. **Education:** General. **Engineering:** General, civil, electrical, mechanical. **Health services:** Dental hygiene, nursing (RN). **Liberal arts:** Arts/sciences. **Philosophy/religion:** Philosophy, religion.

Computing on campus. Online course registration, online library available.

Student life. Freshman orientation: Mandatory. Preregistration for classes offered. **Activities:** Dance, drama, international student organizations, musical theater, student government, student newspaper, special interest and program-related organizations, ambassadors club, honor society.

Athletics. Intercollegiate: Basketball, soccer. **Team name:** Cannons.

Student services. Adult student services, career counseling, services for economically disadvantaged, financial aid counseling, veterans' counselor. **Physically disabled:** Services for visually, speech, hearing impaired. **Transfer:** Transfer center, transfer adviser, college fairs on campus for students transferring to 4-year colleges.

Contact. E-mail: admissions@lfcc.edu
Toll-free number: (800) 906-5322 Fax: (540) 868-7005
Karen Bucher, Dean of Students, Lord Fairfax Community College, 173 Skirmisher Lane, Middletown, VA 22645

Miller-Motte Technical College: Lynchburg
Lynchburg, Virginia
www.miller-motte.com

▶ For-profit 2-year technical college
▶ Commuter campus in small city

General. Accredited by ACICS. **Location:** 60 miles from Charlottesville, 180 miles from Richmond. **Calendar:** Quarter.

Annual costs/financial aid. Need-based financial aid available to full-time and part-time students.

Contact. Phone: (434) 239-5222
1011 Creekside Lane, Lynchburg, VA 24502

Mountain Empire Community College
Big Stone Gap, Virginia
www.mecc.edu   **CB code: 5451**

▶ Public 2-year community college
▶ Commuter campus in small town

General. Founded in 1970. Regionally accredited. **Enrollment:** 1,474 full-time, degree-seeking students. **Degrees:** 250 associate awarded. **Location:** 40 miles from Bristol. **Calendar:** Semester, limited summer session. **Full-time faculty:** 42 total. **Part-time faculty:** 158 total.

Student profile.

Out-of-state:	4%	**25 or older:**	40%

Transfer out. Colleges most students transferred to 2011: University of Virginia's College at Wise, Radford University, Virginia Polytechnic Institute and State University, East Tennessee State University.

Basis for selection. Open admission, but selective for some programs. Nursing students must meet admission test score, plus biology, chemistry and algebra I required. Respiratory therapy students must meet admission test score, plus algebra I and biology required. High school diploma or GED required for practical nursing, nursing and respiratory care programs.

High school preparation. Recommended units include English 4, mathematics 1 and social studies 2. 1 algebra, 1 biology, 1 chemistry required for nursing program; 1 algebra, 1 biology required for respiratory care program.

2011-2012 Annual costs. Tuition/fees: $3,660; $8,958 out-of-state. Per-credit charge: $112 in-state; $288 out-of-state. Out-of-state students pay additional $450 capital outlay fee. Books/supplies: $860.

Financial aid. Need-based: Need-based aid available for part-time students. Work-study available nights, weekends and for part-time students. **Non-need-based:** Scholarships awarded for academics, state residency. **Additional information:** The college does not participate in loan programs. All financial aid is in form of grants, scholarships, or work study.

Application procedures. Admission: No deadline. No application fee. Admission notification on a rolling basis beginning on or about 1/1. **Financial aid:** Priority date 5/1; no closing date. FAFSA required. Applicants notified on a rolling basis starting 1/1.

Academics. System-wide core curriculum to ensure ease of transfer. **Special study options:** Accelerated study, distance learning, double major, dual enrollment of high school students, independent study, internships, liberal arts/career combination, student-designed major. Bachelor's degree programs available on campus. **Credit/placement by examination:** AP, CLEP, IB, institutional tests. 16 credit hours maximum toward associate degree. Maximum 25% of credits awarded for work and/or life experience. **Support services:** Learning center, pre-admission summer program, reduced course load, remedial instruction, tutoring.

Majors. Biology: General. **Business:** General, accounting, business admin, office management, office/clerical. **Computer sciences:** General, information systems, information technology, networking, word processing. **Conservation:** General, environmental science, forestry. **Education:** General. **Engineering:** Electrical, manufacturing. **General:** Soil science. **Health services:** EMT paramedic, medical secretary, medical transcription, nursing (RN), predental, premedicine, prepharmacy, preveterinary, respiratory therapy technology. **Human services:** Social work. **Liberal arts:** Arts/sciences. **Math:** General. **Protective services:** Corrections, criminal justice, law enforcement admin.

Most popular majors. Business/marketing 17%, computer/information sciences 16%, education 12%, health sciences 10%, legal studies 6%, liberal arts 26%.

Computing on campus. 400 workstations in library, computer center.

Student life. Freshman orientation: Mandatory. Preregistration for classes offered. **Activities:** Drama, student government, student newspaper, service, business, nursing organizations available.

Athletics. Intramural: Archery, badminton, basketball, bowling, softball, table tennis, tennis, volleyball. **Team name:** Red Fox Fliers.

Student services. Career counseling, student employment services, financial aid counseling, health services, personal counseling, placement for graduates, veterans' counselor. **Transfer:** Pre-admission transcript evaluation for new students. Transfer adviser for students transferring to 4-year colleges.

Contact. E-mail: khall@me.vccs.edu
Phone: (276) 523-2400 Fax: (276) 523-8297
Kristy Hall, Director of Enrollment Services, Mountain Empire Community College, 3441 Mountain Empire Road, Big Stone Gap, VA 24219

National College: Charlottesville
Charlottesville, Virginia
www.ncbt.edu   CB code: 3248

- For-profit 2-year business college
- Commuter campus in small city
- Interview required

General. Accredited by ACICS. **Enrollment:** 129 degree-seeking undergraduates. **Degrees:** 46 associate awarded. **Calendar:** Quarter, limited summer session. **Full-time faculty:** 5 total. **Part-time faculty:** 14 total.

Basis for selection. Open admission.

2011-2012 Annual costs. Tuition/fees: $13,770. Per-credit charge: $305. Books/supplies: $1,200.

Financial aid. All financial aid based on need. Need-based aid available for part-time students. Work-study available nights, weekends and for part-time students.

Application procedures. Admission: No deadline. $50 fee, may be waived for applicants with need. Admission notification on a rolling basis. **Financial aid:** No deadline. FAFSA required. Applicants notified on a rolling basis.

Academics. Special study options: Double major, internships, liberal arts/career combination. **Credit/placement by examination:** AP, CLEP, institutional tests. **Support services:** Tutoring.

Majors. Business: Accounting, administrative services, business admin. **Computer sciences:** Computer science. **Health services:** Medical assistant.

Computing on campus. 35 workstations in library, computer center.

Student life. Freshman orientation: Mandatory. Preregistration for classes offered.

Contact. Phone: (804) 295-0136 Toll-free number: (800) 664-1886 Fax: (804) 979-8061
Larry Steele, Regional Director of Admissions, National College: Charlottesville, PO Box 6400, Roanoke, VA 24017

National College: Danville
Danville, Virginia
www.ncbt.edu   CB code: 3249

- For-profit 2-year branch campus and business college
- Commuter campus in small city

General. Accredited by ACICS. **Enrollment:** 319 degree-seeking undergraduates. **Degrees:** 12 bachelor's, 78 associate awarded. **Calendar:** Quarter, limited summer session. **Full-time faculty:** 6 total. **Part-time faculty:** 66 total.

Basis for selection. Open admission. Interview recommended.

2011-2012 Annual costs. Tuition/fees: $13,770. Per-credit charge: $305. Books/supplies: $1,200.

Financial aid. All financial aid based on need. Need-based aid available for part-time students. Work-study available nights, weekends and for part-time students.

Application procedures. Admission: No deadline. $50 fee, may be waived for applicants with need. Admission notification on a rolling basis. **Financial aid:** No deadline. FAFSA required. Applicants notified on a rolling basis starting 9/1.

Academics. Special study options: Double major, internships. **Credit/placement by examination:** AP, CLEP, institutional tests. **Support services:** Tutoring.

Majors. Business: Accounting, administrative services, business admin. **Computer sciences:** Computer science. **Health services:** Medical assistant.

Computing on campus. 35 workstations in library, computer center.

Student life. Freshman orientation: Mandatory. Preregistration for classes offered.

Student services. Career counseling, student employment services, personal counseling, placement for graduates.

Contact. E-mail: market@educorp.edu
Phone: (804) 793-6822
Jeff Moore, Director of Admissions, National College: Danville, PO Box 6400, Roanoke, VA 24017

National College: Harrisonburg
Harrisonburg, Virginia
www.national-college.edu   CB code: 3173

- For-profit 2-year business college
- Commuter campus in large town

General. Accredited by ACICS. **Enrollment:** 322 degree-seeking undergraduates. **Degrees:** 14 bachelor's, 79 associate awarded. **Calendar:** Quarter, limited summer session. **Full-time faculty:** 8 total. **Part-time faculty:** 19 total.

Basis for selection. Open admission, but selective for some programs. Interview recommended.

2011-2012 Annual costs. Tuition/fees: $13,770. Per-credit charge: $305. Books/supplies: $1,200.

Financial aid. All financial aid based on need. Need-based aid available for part-time students. Work-study available nights, weekends and for part-time students.

Application procedures. Admission: No deadline. $50 fee, may be waived for applicants with need. Admission notification on a rolling basis. **Financial aid:** No deadline. FAFSA required. Applicants notified on a rolling basis starting 9/1.

Academics. Special study options: Double major, internships. **Credit/placement by examination:** AP, CLEP, institutional tests. **Support services:** Tutoring.

Majors. Business: Accounting, administrative services, business admin, office management. **Computer sciences:** Computer science. **Health services:** Medical assistant.

Computing on campus. 35 workstations in library, computer center.

Student life. Freshman orientation: Mandatory. Preregistration for classes offered.

Student services. Career counseling, personal counseling.

Contact. E-mail: market@national-college.edu
Phone: (540) 432-0943 Fax: (540) 432-1133
Shara Graham, Director of Admissions, National College: Harrisonburg, PO Box 6400, Roanoke, VA 24017

National College: Lynchburg
Lynchburg, Virginia
www.national-college.edu   CB code: 3172

- For-profit 2-year business college
- Commuter campus in small city

General. Accredited by ACICS. **Enrollment:** 274 degree-seeking undergraduates. **Degrees:** 7 bachelor's, 51 associate awarded. **Calendar:** Quarter, limited summer session. **Full-time faculty:** 2 total. **Part-time faculty:** 27 total.

Basis for selection. Open admission. Interview recommended.

2011-2012 Annual costs. Tuition/fees: $13,770. Per-credit charge: $305. Books/supplies: $1,200.

Financial aid. All financial aid based on need. Need-based aid available for part-time students. Work-study available nights, weekends and for part-time students.

Application procedures. Admission: No deadline. $50 fee, may be waived for applicants with need. Admission notification on a rolling basis. **Financial aid:** No deadline. FAFSA required. Applicants notified on a rolling basis starting 9/1.

Academics. Special study options: Double major, internships. **Credit/placement by examination:** AP, CLEP, institutional tests. **Support services:** Tutoring.

Majors. Business: Accounting, administrative services, business admin. **Computer sciences:** General, computer science. **Health services:** Medical assistant.

Computing on campus. 35 workstations in library, computer center.

Student life. Freshman orientation: Mandatory. Preregistration for classes offered.

Student services. Career counseling, student employment services, financial aid counseling, personal counseling, placement for graduates, veterans' counselor.

Contact. E-mail: market@national-college.edu
Phone: (804) 239-3500 Toll-free number: (800) 664-1886
Crystal Souder, Director of Admissions, National College: Lynchburg, PO Box 6400, Roanoke, VA 24017

National College: Martinsville
Martinsville, Virginia
www.national-college.edu   CB code: 3171

- For-profit 2-year business and junior college
- Commuter campus in small city

General. Accredited by ACICS. **Enrollment:** 374 degree-seeking undergraduates. **Calendar:** Quarter, limited summer session. **Full-time faculty:** 6 total. **Part-time faculty:** 24 total.

Basis for selection. Open admission.

2011-2012 Annual costs. Tuition/fees: $13,770. Per-credit charge: $305. Books/supplies: $1,200.

Financial aid. All financial aid based on need. Need-based aid available for part-time students. Work-study available nights, weekends and for part-time students.

Application procedures. Admission: No deadline. $50 fee, may be waived for applicants with need. Admission notification on a rolling basis. **Financial aid:** No deadline. FAFSA required. Applicants notified on a rolling basis.

Academics. Special study options: Double major, internships. **Credit/placement by examination:** AP, CLEP, institutional tests. **Support services:** Tutoring.

Majors. Business: Accounting, administrative services, business admin. **Computer sciences:** Computer science.

Computing on campus. 35 workstations in library, computer center.

Student life. Freshman orientation: Mandatory. Preregistration for classes offered.

Student services. Career counseling, student employment services, personal counseling.

Contact. Phone: (540) 632-5621
Barbara Rakes, Director of Admissions, National College: Martinsville, PO Box 6400, Roanoke, VA 24017

New River Community College
Dublin, Virginia
www.nr.edu   CB code: 5513

- Public 2-year community college
- Commuter campus in rural community

General. Founded in 1966. Regionally accredited. **Enrollment:** 3,186 degree-seeking undergraduates. **Degrees:** 445 associate awarded. **ROTC:** Naval. **Location:** 50 miles from Roanoke. **Calendar:** Semester, limited summer session. **Full-time faculty:** 55 total. **Part-time faculty:** 136 total. **Class size:** 57% < 20, 36% 20-39, 5% 40-49, 1% 50-99, less than 1% >100.

Transfer out. Colleges most students transferred to 2011: Radford University, Virginia Tech, Old Dominion University.

Basis for selection. Open admission. Interview required for nursing program. **Adult students:** SAT/ACT scores not required.

2011-2012 Annual costs. Tuition/fees: $3,632; $8,930 out-of-state. Per-credit charge: $112 in-state; $288 out-of-state. Out-of-state students pay additional $450 capital outlay fee. Books/supplies: $700. Personal expenses: $1,200.

Financial aid. Need-based: Need-based aid available for part-time students. Work-study available nights, weekends and for part-time students.

Application procedures. Admission: No deadline. No application fee. Admission notification on a rolling basis. **Financial aid:** Closing date 4/15. FAFSA, institutional form required. Applicants notified on a rolling basis starting 6/1.

Academics. Special study options: Cooperative education, distance learning, dual enrollment of high school students, teacher certification program. License preparation in real estate. **Credit/placement by examination:** AP, CLEP, IB, institutional tests. **Support services:** GED preparation and test center, learning center, remedial instruction, study skills assistance, tutoring, writing center.

Majors. Business: Accounting, administrative services, business admin, logistics, office technology. **Computer sciences:** Computer graphics, information technology, programming. **Education:** General, early childhood. **Engineering:** General, computer. **Health services:** Medical secretary. **Liberal arts:** Arts/sciences. **Protective services:** Forensics, law enforcement admin. **Visual/performing arts:** Game design.

Computing on campus. Commuter students can connect to campus network. Online course registration, online library, repair service, wireless network available.

Student life. Freshman orientation: Available. Preregistration for classes offered. **Activities:** Concert band, choral groups, literary magazine, music ensembles, TV station, Black Awareness Association, Phi Beta Lambda, Phi Theta Kappa.

Athletics. Intramural: Baseball M, basketball, cheerleading, soccer, softball, table tennis, tennis, volleyball. **Team name:** Knights.

Student services. Career counseling, student employment services, financial aid counseling, on-campus daycare, personal counseling, placement for graduates, veterans' counselor. **Physically disabled:** Services for visually, speech, hearing impaired. **Transfer:** Transfer adviser, college fairs on campus for students transferring to 4-year colleges.

Contact. E-mail: nrtaylm@nr.edu
Phone: (540) 674-3603 Toll-free number: (866) 462-6722
Fax: (540) 674-3644
Margaret Taylor, Coordinator of Admissions and Records, New River Community College, Drawer 1127, Dublin, VA 24084

Northern Virginia Community College
Annandale, Virginia   CB member
www.nvcc.edu   CB code: 5515

- Public 2-year community college
- Commuter campus in small city

General. Founded in 1965. Regionally accredited. 6 campuses in Alexandria, Annandale, Loudoun County, Manassas, Springfield (medical education), Woodbridge. **Enrollment:** 50,044 degree-seeking undergraduates. **Degrees:** 4,695 associate awarded. **Location:** 12 miles from Washington, DC. **Calendar:** Semester, limited summer session. **Full-time faculty:** 635 total. **Part-time faculty:** 1,454 total.

Transfer out. Colleges most students transferred to 2011: George Mason University.

Basis for selection. Open admission, but selective for some programs. Admission to health and veterinary technology programs based on academic prerequisites, placement tests, and space availability. Interview recommended for allied health, animal science, dental hygiene, nursing programs.

2011-2012 Annual costs. Tuition/fees: $4,283; $9,660 out-of-state. Per-credit charge: $129 in-state; $308 out-of-state. Out of state students pay an additional $450 capital outlay fee. Books/supplies: $850. Personal expenses: $2,159.

Financial aid. Need-based: Work-study available nights, weekends and for part-time students. **Non-need-based:** Scholarships awarded for academics, state residency.

Application procedures. Admission: No deadline. No application fee. Admission notification on a rolling basis. **Financial aid:** Priority date 3/1; no closing date. FAFSA, institutional form required. Applicants notified on a rolling basis starting 5/15; must reply within 2 week(s) of notification.

Academics. System-wide core curriculum to ensure ease of transfer. **Special study options:** Cooperative education, distance learning, double major, dual enrollment of high school students, ESL, honors, independent study, internships, liberal arts/career combination, student-designed major, study abroad, weekend college. Old Dominion University Teletechnet degree programs. **Credit/placement by examination:** AP, CLEP, IB, institutional tests. Maximum of 75% of credit hours required for program may be awarded through CLEP. 25% of requirements must be completed at institution. **Support services:** Learning center, reduced course load, remedial instruction, tutoring, writing center.

Majors. Business: Accounting, business admin, international, management information systems, office management, purchasing, real estate, tourism/travel. **Communications:** Communications/speech/rhetoric. **Computer sciences:** General, computer science, programming. **Education:** Art, early childhood. **Engineering:** Civil. **General:** Horticultural science. **Health services:** Clinical lab assistant, clinical lab technology, dental hygiene, EMT paramedic, medical radiologic technology/radiation therapy, medical records technology, physical therapy assistant, respiratory therapy technology, substance abuse counseling, veterinary technology/assistant. **Liberal arts:** Arts/sciences. **Math:** General. **Parks/recreation:** Facilities management. **Protective services:** Fire safety technology, fire services admin, law enforcement admin, security services. **Psychology:** General. **Visual/performing arts:** Commercial photography, commercial/advertising art, interior design, music, photography, studio arts. **Work/family studies:** Institutional food production.

Computing on campus. 2,000 workstations in library, computer center.

Student life. Activities: Bands, choral groups, dance, drama, international student organizations, music ensembles, musical theater, student government, student newspaper, symphony orchestra, TV station, honor societies, African American student organizations, religious groups, Korean and Vietnamese student organizations, data processing management club, art association, physical therapist assistants club, Omega Engineering Students.

Athletics. Intramural: Basketball, football (tackle), soccer, volleyball.

Student services. Career counseling, veterans' counselor. **Physically disabled:** Services for visually, hearing impaired. **Transfer:** Transfer adviser, college fairs on campus for students transferring to 4-year colleges.

Contact. Phone: (703) 323-3000
Northern Virginia Community College, 4001 Wakefield Chapel Road, Annandale, VA 22003-3796

Patrick Henry Community College
Martinsville, Virginia
www.ph.vccs.edu   **CB code: 5549**

- Public 2-year community college
- Commuter campus in large town

General. Founded in 1962. Regionally accredited. **Enrollment:** 2,650 degree-seeking undergraduates; 710 non-degree-seeking students. **Degrees:** 260 associate awarded. **Location:** 50 miles from Roanoke, 50 miles from Greensboro, North Carolina. **Calendar:** Semester, limited summer session. **Full-time faculty:** 50 total. **Part-time faculty:** 113 total. **Special facilities:** Southern history collection, Virginia literature collection, fine arts theater.

Student profile. Among degree-seeking undergraduates, 635 enrolled as first-time, first-year students.

| Part-time: | 45% | 25 or older: | 50% |
| Women: | 62% | | |

Basis for selection. Open admission. High school diploma or GED required for some programs.

2011-2012 Annual costs. Tuition/fees: $3,625; $8,923 out-of-state. Per-credit charge: $112 in-state; $288 out-of-state. Out-of-state students pay additional $450 capital outlay fee. Books/supplies: $500. Personal expenses: $840.

2010-2011 Financial aid. Need-based: 97% of total undergraduate aid awarded as scholarships/grants, 3% as loans/jobs. Need-based aid available for part-time students. Work-study available nights, weekends and for part-time students.

Application procedures. Admission: Priority date 8/1; no deadline. No application fee. Admission notification on a rolling basis beginning on or about 2/1. Deadline for nursing applicants March 1. **Financial aid:** Priority date 6/1; no closing date. FAFSA required. Applicants notified on a rolling basis starting 6/15.

Academics. System-wide core curriculum to ensure ease of transfer. **Special study options:** Cooperative education, distance learning, double major, dual enrollment of high school students, independent study, internships, teacher certification program, weekend college. Bachelor's degree programs available on campus. License preparation in nursing. **Credit/placement by examination:** AP, CLEP, institutional tests. 12 credit hours maximum toward associate degree. **Support services:** Learning center, pre-admission summer program, reduced course load, remedial instruction, study skills assistance, tutoring, writing center.

Majors. Business: Accounting, business admin. **Computer sciences:** General, programming. **Liberal arts:** Arts/sciences.

Computing on campus. 500 workstations in library, computer center, student center. Commuter students can connect to campus network. Online library, helpline, repair service, wireless network available.

Student life. Freshman orientation: Available. Preregistration for classes offered. **Activities:** Choral groups, drama, musical theater, student government, student newspaper, TV station, Black student association, Phi Theta Kappa, campus awareness network, nurses association.

Athletics. NJCAA. **Intercollegiate:** Baseball M, basketball, cheerleading, soccer, softball. **Intramural:** Basketball, soccer, softball, table tennis, tennis, volleyball. **Team name:** Patriots.

Student services. Adult student services, career counseling, student employment services, personal counseling, placement for graduates, veterans' counselor. **Physically disabled:** Services for visually, speech, hearing impaired. **Transfer:** Transfer adviser, college fairs on campus for students transferring to 4-year colleges.

Contact. E-mail: ttisdale@ph.vccs.edu
Phone: (276) 656-0325 Toll-free number: (800) 232-7997
Fax: (276) 656-0352
Travis Tisdale, Admissions, Patrick Henry Community College, 645 Patriot Avenue, Martinsville, VA 24115-5311

Paul D. Camp Community College
Franklin, Virginia
www.pdc.edu   **CB code: 5557**

- Public 2-year community college
- Commuter campus in small town

General. Founded in 1970. Regionally accredited. Campuses in Franklin and Suffolk, site in Smithfield. **Enrollment:** 836 degree-seeking undergraduates. **Degrees:** 120 associate awarded. **Location:** 50 miles from Norfolk. **Calendar:** Semester, limited summer session. **Full-time faculty:** 19 total; 10% have terminal degrees, 42% minority, 58% women. **Part-time faculty:** 60 total. **Class size:** 87% < 20, 11% 20-39, 2% 40-49.

Transfer out. Colleges most students transferred to 2011: Old Dominion University, Christopher Newport University, Norfolk State University.

Basis for selection. Open admission, but selective for some programs. Limited enrollment to nursing programs. **Home schooled:** Letter of recommendation (nonparent) required. Student must provide Admissions and Records Office current copy of signed home school agreement between appropriate school system and authorizing parent or guardian.

High school preparation. Recommended units include English 4, mathematics 2, social studies 2, history 2, science 2 (laboratory 2) and foreign language 1.

2011-2012 Annual costs. Tuition/fees: $3,623; $8,923 out-of-state. Per-credit charge: $112 in-state; $288 out-of-state. Out-of-state students pay additional $450 capital outlay fee. Books/supplies: $1,353.

2011-2012 Financial aid. Need-based: 98% of total undergraduate aid awarded as scholarships/grants, 2% as loans/jobs. Need-based aid available for part-time students. Work-study available nights, weekends and for part-time students.

Application procedures. Admission: Priority date 8/1; no deadline. No application fee. Admission notification on a rolling basis. **Financial aid:** Priority date 6/1; no closing date. FAFSA required. Applicants notified on a rolling basis starting 8/1; must reply within 2 week(s) of notification.

Academics. **Special study options:** Cross-registration, distance learning, dual enrollment of high school students, honors, independent study, internships. License preparation in nursing, real estate. **Credit/placement by examination:** AP, CLEP, institutional tests. 52 credit hours maximum toward associate degree. **Support services:** Learning center, pre-admission summer program, reduced course load, remedial instruction, study skills assistance, tutoring.

Majors. **Business:** Administrative services, business admin, office management. **Computer sciences:** General. **Education:** General. **Health services:** Nursing (RN). **Protective services:** Police science.

Computing on campus. 100 workstations in library, computer center. Online course registration, online library available.

Student life. **Freshman orientation:** Mandatory. Preregistration for classes offered. **Activities:** Student government, student newspaper, honor societies, Circle K.

Student services. Career counseling, student employment services, personal counseling, placement for graduates, veterans' counselor. **Transfer:** Pre-admission transcript evaluation for new students. College fairs on campus for students transferring to 4-year colleges.

Contact. Phone: (757) 569-6700 Fax: (757) 569-6795
Renee Felts, Dean, Paul D. Camp Community College, 100 North College Drive, Franklin, VA 23851-0737

Piedmont Virginia Community College
Charlottesville, Virginia
www.pvcc.edu   **CB code: 5561**

▶ Public 2-year community college
▶ Commuter campus in large town

General. Founded in 1969. Regionally accredited. **Enrollment:** 3,901 degree-seeking undergraduates. **Degrees:** 388 associate awarded. **ROTC:** Army, Air Force. **Location:** 70 miles from Richmond. **Calendar:** Semester, limited summer session. **Full-time faculty:** 65 total. **Part-time faculty:** 240 total. **Class size:** 48% < 20, 51% 20-39, 1% 40-49, less than 1% 50-99. **Partnerships:** Formal partnerships with local businesses, including nursing/retirement home and hospitals.

Student profile. Among degree-seeking undergraduates, 50% enrolled in a transfer program, 19% enrolled in a vocational program, 8% already have a bachelor's degree or higher, 378 transferred in from other institutions.

Out-of-state:	1%	**25 or older:**	36%

Transfer out. 50% of students enrolled in the transfer program go on to 4-year colleges. **Colleges most students transferred to 2011:** University of Virginia, Virginia Commonwealth University, James Madison University, Virginia Tech, Old Dominion University.

Basis for selection. Open admission, but selective for some programs. Special requirements for nursing, radiography, sonography, surgical technology, EMS, and LPN programs; interview recommended. **Home schooled:** Students must meet with counselor prior to enrolling and test into college level courses.

2011-2012 Annual costs. Tuition/fees: $3,665; $8,963 out-of-state. Per-credit charge: $112 in-state; $288 out-of-state. Out-of-state students pay additional $450 capital outlay fee. Books/supplies: $1,077. Personal expenses: $1,908.

Financial aid. **Need-based:** Need-based aid available for part-time students. Work-study available nights, weekends and for part-time students. **Non-need-based:** Scholarships awarded for academics.

Application procedures. **Admission:** No deadline. No application fee. Application must be submitted online. Admission notification on a rolling basis. Accepted applicants to nursing program must reply within 10 days. **Financial aid:** No deadline. FAFSA required. Applicants notified on a rolling basis starting 4/1.

Academics. System-wide core curriculum to ensure ease of transfer. **Special study options:** Accelerated study, cooperative education, distance learning, dual enrollment of high school students, ESL, honors, independent study, internships, weekend college. License preparation in nursing, paramedic, radiology. **Credit/placement by examination:** AP, CLEP, institutional tests. Must obtain 25% of degree requirement credits at PVCC. **Support services:** Learning center, pre-admission summer program, reduced course load, remedial instruction, study skills assistance, tutoring, writing center.

Majors. **Business:** Accounting technology, business admin. **Computer sciences:** General. **Education:** General. **Engineering:** General. **Health services:** EMT paramedic, nursing (RN), radiologic technology/medical imaging, sonography. **Liberal arts:** Arts/sciences. **Protective services:** Police science. **Visual/performing arts:** General.

Most popular majors. Business/marketing 20%, engineering/engineering technologies 6%, health sciences 20%, liberal arts 33%.

Computing on campus. 306 workstations in library, computer center. Online course registration, online library, helpline, wireless network available.

Student life. **Freshman orientation:** Mandatory. Preregistration for classes offered. **Activities:** Choral groups, dance, drama, international student organizations, literary magazine, music ensembles, student government, student newspaper, black student alliance, Phi Theta Kappa, Christian Fellowship, investment club, engineering club, Masquers club, volunteer club, student ambassadors.

Athletics. **Intramural:** Basketball, golf, lacrosse W, soccer, table tennis, tennis, volleyball, weight lifting.

Student services. Adult student services, career counseling, services for economically disadvantaged, student employment services, financial aid counseling, personal counseling, placement for graduates, veterans' counselor. **Physically disabled:** Services for visually, speech, hearing impaired. **Transfer:** Pre-admission transcript evaluation for new students. Transfer center, transfer adviser, college fairs on campus for students transferring to 4-year colleges.

Contact. E-mail: admissions@pvcc.edu
Phone: (434) 961-6551 Fax: (434) 961-5425
Lorraine Conca, Registrar, Piedmont Virginia Community College, 501 College Drive, Charlottesville, VA 22902-7589

Rappahannock Community College
Glenns, Virginia
www.rappahannock.edu   **CB code: 5590**

▶ Public 2-year community college
▶ Commuter campus in rural community

General. Founded in 1970. Regionally accredited. **Enrollment:** 1,907 degree-seeking undergraduates. **Degrees:** 197 associate awarded. **Location:** 50 miles from Richmond, VA. **Calendar:** Semester, limited summer session. **Full-time faculty:** 24 total. **Part-time faculty:** 127 total.

Transfer out. **Colleges most students transferred to 2011:** Old Dominion University.

Basis for selection. Open admission, but selective for some programs. Placement test in reading/writing and one in math required. There is an application process for ADN, PN, and EMS programs.

2011-2012 Annual costs. Tuition/fees: $3,666; $8,964 out-of-state. Per-credit charge: $112 in-state; $288 out-of-state. Out-of-state students pay additional $450 capital outlay fee. Books/supplies: $690. Personal expenses: $1,500.

2010-2011 Financial aid. **Need-based:** 99% of total undergraduate aid awarded as scholarships/grants, 1% as loans/jobs. Need-based aid available for part-time students. Work-study available nights, weekends and for part-time students.

Application procedures. **Admission:** No deadline. No application fee. Admission notification on a rolling basis. **Financial aid:** Priority date 4/15; no closing date. FAFSA, institutional form required. Applicants notified on a rolling basis starting 6/30.

Academics. **Special study options:** Cooperative education, cross-registration, distance learning, double major, dual enrollment of high school students, independent study, internships, liberal arts/career combination. License preparation in nursing. **Credit/placement by examination:** AP, CLEP, institutional tests. **Support services:** Learning center, reduced course load, remedial instruction, study skills assistance, tutoring.

Majors. **Business:** Accounting, accounting/business management, business admin. **Health services:** Nursing (RN). **Liberal arts:** Arts/sciences. **Protective services:** Law enforcement admin.

Computing on campus. 60 workstations in library, computer center. Online course registration, online library, helpline, wireless network available.

Student life. Freshman orientation: Mandatory. Preregistration for classes offered. **Activities:** Student government, student newspaper, Phi Theta Kappa Honors Society.

Athletics. Intramural: Baseball M, basketball M, bowling, softball W, table tennis, tennis, volleyball. **Team name:** Gulls.

Student services. Adult student services, career counseling, services for economically disadvantaged, student employment services, financial aid counseling, personal counseling, placement for graduates, veterans' counselor. **Physically disabled:** Services for visually, speech, hearing impaired. **Transfer:** Transfer adviser, college fairs on campus for students transferring to 4-year colleges.

Contact. Phone: (804) 758-6700 Fax: (804) 758-3852
Felicia Packett, Registrar, Rappahannock Community College, 12745 College Drive, Glenns, VA 23149-2616

Richard Bland College
Petersburg, Virginia
www.rbc.edu

CB member
CB code: 5574

- Public 2-year junior and liberal arts college
- Commuter campus in small city
- Application essay required

General. Founded in 1960. Regionally accredited. Affiliated with The College of William and Mary. Only two-year residential college in Virginia. **Enrollment:** 1,303 degree-seeking undergraduates; 325 non-degree-seeking students. **Degrees:** 198 associate awarded. **ROTC:** Army. **Location:** 3 miles from Petersburg, 25 miles from Richmond. **Calendar:** Semester, limited summer session. **Full-time faculty:** 33 total. **Part-time faculty:** 35 total. **Class size:** 32% < 20, 52% 20-39, 8% 40-49, 8% 50-99. **Special facilities:** Nature trail, Civil War sites.

Student profile. Among degree-seeking undergraduates, 100% enrolled in a transfer program, 520 enrolled as first-time, first-year students, 76 transferred in from other institutions.

Part-time:	22%	Asian American:	1%
Out-of-state:	2%	Hispanic American:	2%
Women:	63%	25 or older:	9%
African American:	34%	Live on campus:	15%

Transfer out. 85% of students enrolled in the transfer program go on to 4-year colleges. **Colleges most students transferred to 2011:** Virginia Commonwealth University, College of William and Mary, James Madison University, Longwood University, Virginia Tech.

Basis for selection. Academic record most important; test scores, essay also important; recommendations, extracurricular activities, interview considered. 2.0 GPA required for all commuter students, 2.5 GPA for residential students. Students who wish to live on campus must have at least a 2.5 GPA to be considered. Commuter students must have a 2.0 GPA or higher to be considered. SAT or ACT recommended. All incoming students who have not completed college-level course work in English and/or mathematics must take the COMPASS placement tests. Interview recommended depending on GPA. **Home schooled:** Transcript of courses and grades required. GED or SAT required. SAT scores must be equal to or greater than the mean score for current RBC students. **Learning Disabled:** Students eligible for ADA should contact the Division of Student Affairs one month prior to the start of classes to request services.

High school preparation. 13 units required. Required units include English 4, mathematics 3, history 2, science 2 and foreign language 2.

2012-2013 Annual costs. Tuition/fees (projected): $3,742; $13,114 out-of-state. Per-credit charge: $128 in-state; $545 out-of-state. Room only: $9,270. Books/supplies: $1,200. Personal expenses: $1,996.

2011-2012 Financial aid. Need-based: Average need met was 25%. Average scholarship/grant was $4,000; average loan $3,500. 71% of total undergraduate aid awarded as scholarships/grants, 29% as loans/jobs. Need-based aid available for part-time students. Work-study available nights, weekends and for part-time students. **Non-need-based:** Scholarships awarded for academics.

Application procedures. Admission: Priority date 5/15; deadline 8/15 (receipt date). $25 fee, may be waived for applicants with need. Application must be submitted on paper. Admission notification on a rolling basis beginning on or about 2/1. Students are admitted before completing high school, cannot be considered as full-time first-time. They are considered as part of the dual enrollment program. **Financial aid:** Priority date 4/1; no closing date. FAFSA, institutional form required. Applicants notified by 6/1; must reply within 2 week(s) of notification.

Academics. Special study options: Dual enrollment of high school students. Educational trips abroad during spring break and summer session for academic credit. **Credit/placement by examination:** AP, CLEP, institutional tests. 30 credit hours maximum toward associate degree. **Support services:** Reduced course load, remedial instruction, study skills assistance, tutoring, writing center.

Majors. Liberal arts: Arts/sciences.

Computing on campus. 100 workstations in dormitories, library, student center. Dormitories wired for high-speed internet access and linked to campus network. Commuter students can connect to campus network. Online library, wireless network available.

Student life. Freshman orientation: Available. Preregistration for classes offered. Half day program to include a separate orientation for parents and meetings with advisors. **Policies:** Campus-wide honor code observed. **Housing:** Coed dorms available. $500 nonrefundable deposit, deadline 5/15. **Activities:** Choral groups, dance, drama, international student organizations, literary magazine, music ensembles, student government, student newspaper, Spanish club, Gay Lesbian Bisexual Transgender Alliance, Student Ambassadors, wellness club, biology club, dance club.

Athletics. Intramural: Basketball, bowling, cheerleading W, cross-country, football (non-tackle), golf, soccer, tennis. **Team name:** Statesman.

Student services. Career counseling, financial aid counseling, health services. **Physically disabled:** Services for visually, speech, hearing impaired. **Transfer:** Pre-admission transcript evaluation for new students. Transfer adviser, college fairs on campus for students transferring to 4-year colleges.

Contact. E-mail: admit@rbc.edu
Phone: (804) 862-6249 Fax: (804) 862-6490
Randy Dean, Assistant Provost for Student Activities, Richard Bland College, 11301 Johnson Road, Petersburg, VA 23805

Skyline College: Roanoke
Roanoke, Virginia
www.skyline.edu

CB code: 3147

- For-profit 2-year technical college
- Commuter campus in small city
- Interview required

General. Regionally accredited; also accredited by ACCSC. **Enrollment:** 274 degree-seeking undergraduates. **Degrees:** 14 bachelor's, 75 associate awarded. **Calendar:** Differs by program, extensive summer session. **Full-time faculty:** 21 total; 19% minority, 62% women. **Part-time faculty:** 25 total; 12% minority, 84% women.

Basis for selection. Interview important; program-specific admissions tests required. No special considerations given.

Financial aid. Need-based: Need-based aid available for part-time students. Work-study available nights, weekends and for part-time students.

Application procedures. Admission: No deadline. $45 fee. Admission notification on a rolling basis. **Financial aid:** No deadline. FAFSA required. Applicants notified on a rolling basis.

Academics. Special study options: Accelerated study, distance learning. Bachelor's degree programs available on campus. **Credit/placement by examination:** AP, CLEP. 15 credit hours maximum toward associate degree, 30 toward bachelor's. **Support services:** Remedial instruction, tutoring.

Majors. Computer sciences: Security. **Engineering:** Electrical. **Health services:** Health care admin, medical assistant.

Computing on campus. 180 workstations in library, computer center. Online library available.

Student life. Freshman orientation: Available. Preregistration for classes offered.

Student services. Career counseling, student employment services, financial aid counseling, placement for graduates, veterans' counselor.

Contact. Phone: (540) 563-8080
Walter Merchant, Director, Skyline College: Roanoke, 5234 Airport Road, Roanoke, VA 24012

Southside Virginia Community College
Alberta, Virginia
www.sv.vccs.edu   CB code: 5660

▶ Public 2-year community college
▶ Commuter campus in rural community
▶ Interview required

General. Founded in 1970. Regionally accredited. Additional campuses at John H. Daniel Campus, Keysville, VA; Campus Without Walls, Emporia, VA. **Enrollment:** 3,355 degree-seeking undergraduates. **Degrees:** 456 associate awarded. **ROTC:** Army. **Location:** 70 miles from Richmond. **Calendar:** Semester, limited summer session. **Full-time faculty:** 79 total. **Part-time faculty:** 266 total. **Special facilities:** Nature trail, fitness trail.

Student profile.

Out-of-state: 1%   25 or older: 36%

Transfer out. Colleges most students transferred to 2011: Longwood University, Old Dominion University, Saint Paul's College, Virginia Commonwealth University.

Basis for selection. Open admission, but selective for some programs. National League for Nursing Pre-Admissions Examination required for nursing applicants. Psychological Services Bureau Revised Aptitude for Practical Nursing Examination required for practical nursing applicants. **Home schooled:** If not enrolled in program leading to completion credential, student should obtain GED.

2011-2012 Annual costs. Tuition/fees: $3,645; $8,943 out-of-state. Per-credit charge: $112 in-state; $288 out-of-state. Out-of-state students pay additional $450 capital outlay fee. Books/supplies: $1,040. Personal expenses: $2,340.

Financial aid. Need-based: Need-based aid available for part-time students. Work-study available nights, weekends and for part-time students. **Non-need-based:** Scholarships awarded for academics.

Application procedures. Admission: No deadline. No application fee. Admission notification on a rolling basis. **Financial aid:** Priority date 6/1, closing date 8/1. FAFSA required. Applicants notified on a rolling basis starting 6/15.

Academics. System-wide core curriculum to ensure ease of transfer. **Special study options:** Cross-registration, distance learning, dual enrollment of high school students, honors, internships, study abroad. Cooperative programs in respiratory therapy with J. Sargeant Reynolds Community College, medical laboratory program with Central Virginia Community College. Bachelor's degree programs available on campus. License preparation in nursing. **Credit/placement by examination:** AP, CLEP, institutional tests. 45 credit hours maximum toward associate degree. **Support services:** GED preparation and test center, reduced course load, remedial instruction, study skills assistance, tutoring.

Majors. Business: Administrative services, business admin, management science. **Computer sciences:** General. **Education:** General. **Health services:** Clinical lab technology, nursing (RN), respiratory therapy technology. **Liberal arts:** Arts/sciences. **Protective services:** Police science.

Most popular majors. Business/marketing 18%, health sciences 22%, liberal arts 47%, security/protective services 10%.

Computing on campus. 200 workstations in library, computer center.

Student life. Freshman orientation: Mandatory, $78 fee. Preregistration for classes offered. **Activities:** Choral groups, drama, music ensembles, student government, Phi Theta Kappa, Criminal Justice Organization, Phi Beta Lambda, Lambda Alpha Epsilon, Alpha Delta Omega.

Athletics. Intramural: Basketball, softball, table tennis, tennis, volleyball.

Student services. Career counseling, financial aid counseling, personal counseling, veterans' counselor. **Transfer:** Pre-admission transcript evaluation for new students. College fairs on campus for students transferring to 4-year colleges.

Contact. E-mail: rhina.jones@sv.vccs.edu
Phone: (434) 949-1000 Fax: (434) 949-7863
Shannon Feinman, Director of Admissions, Southside Virginia Community College, 109 Campus Drive, Alberta, VA 23821

Southwest Virginia Community College
Richlands, Virginia
www.sw.edu   CB code: 5659

▶ Public 2-year community college
▶ Commuter campus in small town

General. Founded in 1967. Regionally accredited. **Enrollment:** 2,061 degree-seeking undergraduates. **Degrees:** 414 associate awarded. **Location:** 45 miles from Bluefield and Bristol. **Calendar:** Semester, extensive summer session. **Full-time faculty:** 46 total; 44% women. **Part-time faculty:** 200 total. **Class size:** 75% < 20, 20% 20-39, 2% 40-49, 2% 50-99. **Special facilities:** Community center, arts center.

Student profile. Among degree-seeking undergraduates, 39% enrolled in a transfer program, 61% enrolled in a vocational program, 1% already have a bachelor's degree or higher.

Out-of-state: 3%   25 or older: 40%

Transfer out. 54% of students enrolled in the transfer program go on to 4-year colleges. **Colleges most students transferred to 2011:** Virginia Tech, Radford University, University of Virginia at Wise, East Tennessee State University.

Basis for selection. Open admission, but selective for some programs. Special requirements for engineering and health programs. Students are required to take COMPASS, ASSET or some other placement test with the scores used to determine if students will need to take developmental English, mathematics or reading. Interview required for full-time.

High school preparation. Subject and unit requirements vary with degree programs.

2011-2012 Annual costs. Tuition/fees: $3,615; $8,913 out-of-state. Per-credit charge: $112 in-state; $288 out-of-state. Out-of-state students pay an additional $450 capital outlay fee. Books/supplies: $1,000. Personal expenses: $1,700.

2011-2012 Financial aid. All financial aid based on need. Need-based aid available for part-time students. Work-study available nights, weekends and for part-time students.

Application procedures. Admission: No deadline. No application fee. Admission notification on a rolling basis. Applicants for nursing and allied health programs must apply by January 15 and reply within 2 weeks of acceptance. No deferred admission for these programs. **Financial aid:** Priority date 5/30; no closing date. FAFSA, institutional form required. Applicants notified on a rolling basis starting 7/1.

Academics. Special study options: Accelerated study, cooperative education, distance learning, double major, dual enrollment of high school students, honors, independent study, internships. Bachelor's degree programs available on campus. **Credit/placement by examination:** AP, CLEP. **Support services:** Learning center, pre-admission summer program, reduced course load, remedial instruction, study skills assistance, tutoring, writing center.

Majors. Business: General, accounting, administrative services, business admin, managerial economics. **Computer sciences:** General, LAN/WAN management. **Conservation:** Environmental studies. **Education:** General, early childhood. **Engineering:** General, electrical. **Health services:** EMT paramedic, medical secretary, nursing (RN), occupational therapy assistant, radiologic technology/medical imaging, respiratory therapy assistant. **Liberal arts:** Arts/sciences. **Protective services:** Corrections, police science.

Most popular majors. Health sciences 32%, liberal arts 40%.

Computing on campus. 150 workstations in library, computer center. Commuter students can connect to campus network. Online course registration, online library, helpline, wireless network available.

Student life. Freshman orientation: Available, $121 fee. Preregistration for classes offered. **Activities:** Jazz band, choral groups, international student organizations, literary magazine, music ensembles, student government, Intervoice Club, Black Student Union, Phi Theta Kappa, Lion's Club, Phi Beta Lambda, Lambda Alpha Epsilon, Helping Minds, Campus Crusade for Christ, Young Republicans, Young Democrats.

Athletics. Intramural: Racquetball. **Team name:** Eagles.

Student services. Career counseling, services for economically disadvantaged, student employment services, financial aid counseling, health services, minority student services, personal counseling, placement for graduates, veterans' counselor. **Physically disabled:** Services for visually, speech, hearing impaired. **Transfer:** Transfer adviser, college fairs on campus for students transferring to 4-year colleges.

Contact. E-mail: admissions@sw.edu
Phone: (276) 964-7238 Toll-free number: (800) 822-7822
Fax: (276) 964-7716
Jim Farris, Coordinator of Admissions and Counseling, Southwest
Virginia Community College, PO Box SVCC, Richlands, VA 24641-1101

Thomas Nelson Community College
Hampton, Virginia
www.tncc.edu   CB code: 5793

- Public 2-year community college
- Commuter campus in small city

General. Founded in 1967. Regionally accredited. **Enrollment:** 9,245
degree-seeking undergraduates. **Degrees:** 742 associate awarded. **Location:**
20 miles from Norfolk, 35 miles from Virginia Beach. **Calendar:** Semester,
limited summer session. **Full-time faculty:** 111 total. **Part-time faculty:**
494 total.

Transfer out. Colleges most students transferred to 2011: Christopher
Newport University, Old Dominion University, Norfolk State University,
Hampton University.

Basis for selection. Open admission, but selective for some programs.
Special requirements for nursing program. **Home schooled:** Must be 18 or
have GED.

High school preparation. Nursing program requires specific high
school units.

2011-2012 Annual costs. Tuition/fees: $3,611; $8,909 out-of-state. Per-
credit charge: $112 in-state; $288 out-of-state. Out-of-state students pay
additional $450 capital outlay fee. Books/supplies: $800. Personal
expenses: $1,600.

Financial aid. Need-based: Need-based aid available for part-time students. Work-study available nights, weekends and for part-time students.

Application procedures. Admission: No deadline. No application fee.
Application must be submitted online. Admission notification on a rolling
basis. **Financial aid:** Priority date 5/1; no closing date. FAFSA, institutional
form required. Applicants notified on a rolling basis starting 6/1; must reply
within 2 week(s) of notification.

Academics. System-wide core curriculum to ensure ease of transfer, 2+2
program available. **Special study options:** Accelerated study, cooperative
education, cross-registration, distance learning, dual enrollment of high school
students, ESL, honors, independent study, internships. License preparation
in nursing, paramedic, real estate. **Credit/placement by examination:** AP,
CLEP, institutional tests. SAT Critical Reading or ACT English tests may
be substituted for institutional placement examinations if scores high enough.
Support services: Learning center, remedial instruction, study skills assistance, tutoring, writing center.

Majors. Business: Accounting, business admin, management science, office
management. **Computer sciences:** General, computer graphics, computer
science, information systems, networking, programming. **Education:** Early
childhood. **Engineering:** General, electrical. **Health services:** Licensed practical nurse. **Human services:** General, social work. **Liberal arts:** Arts/sci-
ences. **Protective services:** Fire services admin, law enforcement admin.
Social sciences: General. **Visual/performing arts:** Commercial/advertising
art, photography, studio arts.

Computing on campus. Online library, wireless network available.

Student life. Freshman orientation: Available. Preregistration for classes
offered. **Activities:** Choral groups, dance, drama, international student organizations, student government, Digital Arts Society, philosophy and religion
club, science club, Phi Theta Kappa.

Athletics. Intramural: Baseball M, basketball. **Team name:** Gators.

Student services. Career counseling, student employment services, financial aid counseling, personal counseling, placement for graduates, veterans'
counselor. **Physically disabled:** Services for visually, speech, hearing
impaired. **Transfer:** Transfer center, transfer adviser, college fairs on campus
for students transferring to 4-year colleges.

Contact. E-mail: admissions@tncc.edu
Phone: (757) 825-2800 Fax: (757) 825-2763
Vicki Richmond, Associate Vice President for Enrollment Services,
Thomas Nelson Community College, PO Box 9407, Hampton, VA 23670

Tidewater Community College
Norfolk, Virginia   CB member
www.tcc.edu   CB code: 5032

- Public 2-year community college
- Commuter campus in large city

General. Founded in 1968. Regionally accredited. Multi-location institution
with campuses at Portsmouth, Virginia Beach, Chesapeake, and Norfolk.
Enrollment: 29,043 degree-seeking undergraduates. **Degrees:** 2,660 associate awarded. **ROTC:** Army, Naval. **Calendar:** Semester, extensive summer
session. **Full-time faculty:** 346 total. **Part-time faculty:** 1,161 total. **Class
size:** 36% < 20, 63% 20-39, less than 1% 40-49, less than 1% 50-99. **Special
facilities:** Visual arts center, automotive center.

Student profile. Among degree-seeking undergraduates, 47% enrolled in
a transfer program, 43% enrolled in a vocational program.

Out-of-state:	10%	Hispanic American:	4%
African American:	38%	Native American:	1%
Asian American:	4%	25 or older:	53%

Transfer out. Colleges most students transferred to 2011: Old Dominion
University, Norfolk State University, Virginia Wesleyan College, Christopher
Newport University.

Basis for selection. Open admission, but selective for some programs.
Special requirements for health professions programs. Placement testing
required for English or mathematics courses. Interview required for medical
technologies and other limited enrollment programs.

2011-2012 Annual costs. Tuition/fees: $4,376; $9,674 out-of-state. Per-
credit charge: $112 in-state; $288 out-of-state. Out-of-state students pay
additional $450 capital outlay fee. Books/supplies: $1,500. Personal
expenses: $2,500.

Financial aid. Need-based: Need-based aid available for part-time students. Work-study available nights, weekends and for part-time students.

Application procedures. Admission: No deadline. No application fee.
Admission notification on a rolling basis. **Financial aid:** Priority date 4/1;
no closing date. FAFSA required. Applicants notified on a rolling basis
starting 4/1.

Academics. System-wide core curriculum to ensure ease of transfer. **Special study options:** Cooperative education, cross-registration, distance learning, double major, dual enrollment of high school students, ESL, honors,
independent study, internships, study abroad. Member Virginia Tidewater
Consortium of Higher Education. License preparation in nursing, occupational
therapy, paramedic, physical therapy, radiology, real estate. **Credit/place-
ment by examination:** AP, CLEP, institutional tests. **Support services:**
Learning center, reduced course load, remedial instruction, study skills assistance, tutoring, writing center.

Majors. Business: Accounting, administrative services, banking/financial
services, business admin, hospitality admin, real estate, sales/distribution.
Computer sciences: General, networking, systems analysis. **Conservation:**
Environmental studies. **Education:** General, early childhood, teacher assistance. **Engineering:** General, industrial. **Foreign languages:** American Sign
Language. **General:** Business technology, horticulture. **Health services:**
EMT paramedic, medical radiologic technology/radiation therapy, medical
records technology, nursing (RN), occupational therapy assistant, physical
therapy assistant, respiratory therapy technology. **Human services:** General.
Liberal arts: Arts/sciences. **Parks/recreation:** General, facilities management. **Protective services:** Firefighting. **Social sciences:** General. **Visual/
performing arts:** Commercial/advertising art, graphic design, interior design,
multimedia, photography, studio arts.

Most popular majors. Biological/life sciences 8%, business/marketing
21%, engineering/engineering technologies 8%, health sciences 11%, liberal
arts 22%, social sciences 14%.

Computing on campus. Commuter students can connect to campus network. Online course registration, online library, helpline, wireless network
available.

Student life. Freshman orientation: Available. Preregistration for classes
offered. **Activities:** Choral groups, drama, music ensembles, student government, student newspaper, Phi Theta Kappa, Black Student Union, Christian
Fellowship, business club, science fiction and astronomy club, student nurses
association, military and veterans student association, computer club.

Athletics. Intercollegiate: Basketball, soccer M. **Team name:** Storm.

Student services. Adult student services, career counseling, student
employment services, financial aid counseling, on-campus daycare, personal

Two-Year Colleges

counseling, placement for graduates, veterans' counselor, women's services. **Physically disabled:** Services for visually, speech, hearing impaired. **Transfer:** Transfer adviser, college fairs on campus for students transferring to 4-year colleges.

Contact. E-mail: info@tcc.edu
Phone: (757) 822-1100 Toll-free number: (800) 371-0898
Daniel DeMarte, Vice President for Student Learning and Chief Academic Officer, Tidewater Community College, 1700 College Crescent, Virginia Beach, VA 23453

Virginia College at Richmond
Richmond, Virginia
www.richmond.vc.edu

‣ For-profit 2-year culinary school and career college
‣ Very large city

General. Regionally accredited; also accredited by ACICS. **Enrollment:** 800 degree-seeking undergraduates. **Calendar:** Quarter.

Basis for selection. Open admission.

Financial aid. Need-based: Work-study available nights, weekends and for part-time students.

Application procedures. Admission: $100 fee.

Academics. Credit/placement by examination: AP, CLEP.

Majors. Business: Business admin. **Health services:** Medical records admin, surgical technology.

Contact. E-mail: richmond.info@vc.edu
Phone: (804) 977-5100
Virginia College at Richmond, 7200 Midlothian Turnpike, Richmond, VA 23225

Virginia Highlands Community College
Abingdon, Virginia
www.vhcc.edu   CB code: 5927

‣ Public 2-year community college
‣ Commuter campus in small town

General. Founded in 1967. Regionally accredited. **Enrollment:** 1,923 degree-seeking undergraduates. **Degrees:** 237 associate awarded. **Location:** 120 miles from Roanoke. **Calendar:** Semester, extensive summer session. **Full-time faculty:** 47 total. **Part-time faculty:** 177 total. **Special facilities:** Greenhouse, regional artisan center.

Student profile.

Out-of-state:	11%	25 or older:	36%

Transfer out. Colleges most students transferred to 2011: East Tennessee State University, Virginia Tech, Radford University, Old Dominion University, University of Virginia at Wise.

Basis for selection. Open admission, but selective for some programs. COMPASS required for placement. Paramedic, nursing, radiography, physical therapy, dental hygiene, and medical laboratory technology programs have special requirements. **Learning Disabled:** Developmental courses are to be taken by students who test below set standards on COMPASS and/or ASSET test.

High school preparation. 12 units recommended. Recommended units include English 4, mathematics 2, social studies 4, science 1 (laboratory 1).

2011-2012 Annual costs. Tuition/fees: $3,630; $8,928 out-of-state. Per-credit charge: $112 in-state; $288 out-of-state. Out-of-state students pay additional $450 capital outlay fee. Books/supplies: $750. Personal expenses: $1,272.

Financial aid. Need-based: Work-study available nights, weekends and for part-time students.

Application procedures. Admission: No deadline. No application fee. Admission notification on a rolling basis. **Financial aid:** No deadline. FAFSA, institutional form required. Applicants notified on a rolling basis starting 5/1.

Academics. Special study options: Cooperative education, distance learning, double major, dual enrollment of high school students, independent study, internships, liberal arts/career combination. License preparation in nursing, paramedic, real estate. **Credit/placement by examination:** AP, CLEP, institutional tests. 45 credit hours maximum toward associate degree. **Support services:** Learning center, pre-admission summer program, reduced course load, remedial instruction, tutoring.

Majors. Business: Accounting, administrative services, business admin, office management. **Computer sciences:** General, data processing. **Education:** General, drama/dance. **General:** Farm/ranch. **Health services:** Clinical lab assistant, dental hygiene, medical radiologic technology/radiation therapy, nursing (RN), physical therapy assistant. **Human services:** Social work. **Liberal arts:** Arts/sciences. **Protective services:** Police science.

Computing on campus. 230 workstations in library, computer center, student center. Online course registration, wireless network available.

Student life. Freshman orientation: Mandatory, $68 fee. Preregistration for classes offered. **Activities:** Choral groups, drama, music ensembles, musical theater, student government, IMPACT club, law enforcement club, Roteract club, College Republicans, College Democrats, Aanglers' club, VATNP (nursing) club, National Honors Society, Christian club, SIFE.

Athletics. Intramural: Basketball. **Team name:** Wolves.

Student services. Career counseling, services for economically disadvantaged, student employment services, financial aid counseling, personal counseling, placement for graduates, veterans' counselor. **Physically disabled:** Services for visually, speech, hearing impaired. **Transfer:** Transfer adviser, college fairs on campus for students transferring to 4-year colleges.

Contact. E-mail: dbarrett@vhcc.edu
Phone: (276) 739-2460 Fax: (276) 739-2591
Karen Cheers, Director of Admissions, Records and Financial Aid, Virginia Highlands Community College, PO Box 828, Abingdon, VA 24212-0828

Virginia Western Community College
Roanoke, Virginia
www.virginiawestern.edu   CB code: 5868

‣ Public 2-year community college
‣ Commuter campus in small city

General. Founded in 1966. Regionally accredited. **Enrollment:** 5,584 degree-seeking undergraduates; 2,973 non-degree-seeking students. **Degrees:** 560 associate awarded. **Location:** 3 miles from downtown. **Calendar:** Semester, extensive summer session. **Full-time faculty:** 85 total. **Part-time faculty:** 370 total. **Special facilities:** Community arboretum; dental hygiene clinic.

Student profile. Among degree-seeking undergraduates, 44% enrolled in a transfer program, 56% enrolled in a vocational program, 1,421 enrolled as first-time, first-year students.

Part-time:	56%	Asian American:	3%
Out-of-state:	1%	Hispanic American:	2%
Women:	57%	Native American:	1%
African American:	15%		

Transfer out. Colleges most students transferred to 2011: Virginia Tech, Radford University, Old Dominion University, Roanoke College, Hollins University.

Basis for selection. Open admission, but selective for some programs. Special requirements for health programs and communication design program. Interview required for health technologies. **Adult students:** SAT/ACT scores not required. **Learning Disabled:** Student Support Services/REACH program provides accommodations for students with learning disabilities.

2011-2012 Annual costs. Tuition/fees: $3,873; $9,171 out-of-state. Per-credit charge: $112 in-state; $288 out-of-state. Out-of-state students pay additional $450 capital outlay fee. Books/supplies: $550. Personal expenses: $1,200.

Financial aid. Need-based: Need-based aid available for part-time students. Work-study available nights, weekends and for part-time students. **Non-need-based:** Scholarships awarded for academics, state residency.

Application procedures. Admission: No deadline. No application fee. Application must be submitted online. Admission notification on a rolling basis. **Financial aid:** No deadline. FAFSA required. Applicants notified on a rolling basis starting 4/1.

Academics. Special study options: Distance learning, dual enrollment of high school students, external degree, honors, independent study, internships, liberal arts/career combination, study abroad, weekend college. License preparation in dental hygiene, nursing, radiology. **Credit/placement by examination:** AP, CLEP, IB, institutional tests. **Support services:** Learning center, reduced course load, remedial instruction, study skills assistance, tutoring, writing center.

Majors. Biology: Biotechnology. **Business:** General, accounting, administrative services, business admin, management information systems, office technology. **Communications technology:** General. **Computer sciences:** General. **Education:** General, early childhood, social science. **Engineering:** General, surveying. **General:** Horticulture. **Health services:** Dental hygiene, mental health services, nursing (RN), radiologic technology/medical imaging. **Liberal arts:** Arts/sciences, humanities. **Math:** General. **Protective services:** Criminal justice, police science. **Social sciences:** General. **Visual/performing arts:** Commercial/advertising art, studio arts. **Work/family studies:** Child care management.

Most popular majors. Business/marketing 15%, engineering/engineering technologies 10%, health sciences 19%, interdisciplinary studies 8%, liberal arts 23%, social sciences 11%.

Computing on campus. 100 workstations in library, computer center. Online course registration, online library, helpline, wireless network available.

Student life. Freshman orientation: Mandatory. Preregistration for classes offered. **Activities:** Choral groups, drama, student government, student newspaper, minority student alliance, Christian Fellowship.

Athletics. Intramural: Basketball, cheerleading W, softball, tennis.

Student services. Adult student services, alcohol/substance abuse counseling, career counseling, services for economically disadvantaged, student employment services, financial aid counseling, minority student services, personal counseling, placement for graduates, veterans' counselor. **Physically disabled:** Services for visually, speech, hearing impaired. **Transfer:** Transfer center, transfer adviser, college fairs on campus for students transferring to 4-year colleges.

Contact. E-mail: mpatterson@virginiawestern.edu
Phone: (540) 857-7231 Fax: (540) 857-6102
Meg Patterson, Admissions and Records Coordinator/Registrar, Virginia Western Community College, Box 14007, Roanoke, VA 24038

Wytheville Community College
Wytheville, Virginia
www.wcc.vccs.edu
CB code: 5917

▸ Public 2-year community college
▸ Commuter campus in small town

General. Founded in 1962. Regionally accredited. **Enrollment:** 2,485 degree-seeking undergraduates. **Degrees:** 368 associate awarded. **Location:** 74 miles from Roanoke. **Calendar:** Semester, limited summer session. **Full-time faculty:** 41 total. **Part-time faculty:** 179 total.

Student profile.

Out-of-state:	5%	25 or older:	32%

Transfer out. 64% of students enrolled in the transfer program go on to 4-year colleges. **Colleges most students transferred to 2011:** Radford University, Old Dominion University, Virginia Tech, James Madison University.

Basis for selection. Open admission, but selective for some programs. Limited admissions to allied health programs. High school transcripts required of all allied health applicants. Interview required for allied health, police science. **Home schooled:** Statement describing home school structure and mission required.

High school preparation. College-preparatory program recommended.

2011-2012 Annual costs. Tuition/fees: $3,630; $8,928 out-of-state. Per-credit charge: $112 in-state; $288 out-of-state. Out-of-state students pay additional $450 capital outlay fee. Books/supplies: $840. Personal expenses: $250.

Financial aid. All financial aid based on need. Need-based aid available for part-time students. Work-study available nights, weekends and for part-time students.

Application procedures. Admission: No deadline. No application fee. Admission notification on a rolling basis. **Financial aid:** Priority date 4/1;

no closing date. FAFSA, institutional form required. Applicants notified on a rolling basis starting 5/1; must reply within 4 week(s) of notification.

Academics. Special study options: Distance learning, dual enrollment of high school students, honors, independent study, internships. License preparation in dental hygiene, nursing, physical therapy, radiology. **Credit/placement by examination:** AP, CLEP, institutional tests. **Support services:** Remedial instruction, tutoring, writing center.

Majors. Business: Accounting, administrative services, business admin, managerial economics. **Computer sciences:** Information systems. **Education:** General. **Health services:** Clinical lab technology, dental hygiene, nursing (RN), physical therapy assistant, radiologic technology/medical imaging, respiratory therapy technology. **Liberal arts:** Arts/sciences. **Protective services:** Police science. **Work/family studies:** Child care management.

Most popular majors. Computer/information sciences 7%, education 12%, health sciences 44%, liberal arts 15%, physical sciences 9%, security/protective services 13%.

Computing on campus. 133 workstations in library, computer center, student center. Online course registration, wireless network available.

Student life. Freshman orientation: Available. Preregistration for classes offered. **Activities:** Bands, drama, student government, student newspaper.

Athletics. NJCAA. **Intercollegiate:** Basketball M, volleyball W. **Intramural:** Basketball, soccer M, softball, table tennis, tennis, volleyball. **Team name:** Wildcats.

Student services. Career counseling, services for economically disadvantaged, student employment services, financial aid counseling, personal counseling, placement for graduates, veterans' counselor. **Physically disabled:** Services for visually, hearing impaired. **Transfer:** College fairs on campus for students transferring to 4-year colleges.

Contact. E-mail: wcterrs@wcc.vccs.edu
Phone: (276) 223-4701 Toll-free number: (800) 468-1195
Fax: (276) 223-4860
Sabrina Terry, Registrar, Wytheville Community College, 1000 East Main Street, Wytheville, VA 24382

Washington

Bates Technical College
Tacoma, Washington
www.bates.ctc.edu
CB code: 4152

◗ Public 2-year technical college
◗ Commuter campus in small city

General. Two additional campuses in Tacoma. **Enrollment:** 1,441 degree-seeking undergraduates. **Degrees:** 203 associate awarded. **Calendar:** Quarter, extensive summer session. **Full-time faculty:** 113 total; less than 1% have terminal degrees, 7% minority, 43% women. **Part-time faculty:** 36 total; 19% minority, 58% women.

Student profile. Among degree-seeking undergraduates, 1% enrolled in a transfer program, 100% enrolled in a vocational program.

Out-of-state:	12%	25 or older:	76%

Transfer out. 1% of students enrolled in the transfer program go on to 4-year colleges. **Colleges most students transferred to 2011:** University of Washington.

Basis for selection. Open admission. COMPASS required for admission. **Adult students:** SAT/ACT scores not required.

2011-2012 Annual costs. Tuition/fees: $4,085; $9,320 out-of-state. Books/supplies: $1,020.

Financial aid. All financial aid based on need. Need-based aid available for part-time students. Work-study available nights, weekends and for part-time students.

Application procedures. Admission: No deadline. $50 fee. **Financial aid:** No deadline. FAFSA, institutional form required. Applicants notified on a rolling basis starting 9/7.

Academics. Special study options: Cooperative education, distance learning, dual enrollment of high school students, ESL, independent study, internships, teacher certification program. License preparation in dental hygiene, nursing, occupational therapy. **Credit/placement by examination:** AP, CLEP, IB. **Support services:** GED preparation and test center, learning center, reduced course load, remedial instruction, study skills assistance, tutoring.

Majors. Business: Administrative services, marketing. **Communications technology:** Radio/TV. **Computer sciences:** Database management, networking, programming, web page design, webmaster. **Health services:** Dental assistant, dental lab technology, hearing instrument specialist, licensed practical nurse, occupational therapy assistant. **Protective services:** Fire systems technology, firefighting. **Work/family studies:** Child care service.

Computing on campus. Commuter students can connect to campus network. Online library, repair service, wireless network available.

Student life. Freshman orientation: Available. Preregistration for classes offered. **Activities:** International student organizations, student government, TV station.

Student services. Adult student services, career counseling, services for economically disadvantaged, student employment services, financial aid counseling, minority student services, on-campus daycare. **Transfer:** Pre-admission transcript evaluation for new students.

Contact. E-mail: registration@bates.ctc.edu
Phone: (253) 680-7002
Patrick Brown, Registrar, Bates Technical College, 1101 South Yakima Avenue, Tacoma, WA 98405

Bellevue College
Bellevue, Washington
www.bellevuecollege.edu
CB code: 4029

◗ Public 2-year community college
◗ Commuter campus in small city

General. Founded in 1965. Regionally accredited. **Enrollment:** 5,139 degree-seeking undergraduates. **Degrees:** 47 bachelor's, 1,898 associate awarded. **Location:** 12 miles from Seattle. **Calendar:** Quarter, limited summer session. **Full-time faculty:** 170 total. **Part-time faculty:** 592 total. **Special facilities:** Planetarium, National Workforce Center for Emerging Technologies, greenhouses, observatory, scanning electron microscope.

Transfer out. Colleges most students transferred to 2011: University of Washington, Washington State University, Central Washington University, Seattle University, Western Washington University.

Basis for selection. Open admission, but selective for some programs. Interview, essay, 2 letters of recommendation, transcripts required of applicants to allied health programs, including radiologic technology, diagnostic ultrasound, radiation therapy. **Home schooled:** Must be at least 18 years old. **Learning Disabled:** Student may request reasonable classroom accommodations through Disability Support Services Office. Student must provide documentation from appropriate professional.

High school preparation. Allied health programs have special requirements.

2011-2012 Annual costs. Tuition/fees: $3,782; $9,017 out-of-state. Per-credit charge: $79 in-state; $195 out-of-state. Books/supplies: $924. Personal expenses: $1,968.

Financial aid. Need-based: Need-based aid available for part-time students. Work-study available nights, weekends and for part-time students. **Non-need-based:** Scholarships awarded for academics, athletics.

Application procedures. Admission: No deadline. $34 fee. Admission notification on a rolling basis. **Financial aid:** Priority date 4/16; no closing date. FAFSA, institutional form required. Applicants notified on a rolling basis starting 8/1.

Academics. Special study options: Distance learning, dual enrollment of high school students, ESL, honors, independent study, internships, study abroad. Bachelor's degree programs available on campus. **Credit/placement by examination:** AP, CLEP, institutional tests. 15 credit hours maximum toward associate degree. **Support services:** GED preparation and test center, learning center, remedial instruction, tutoring, writing center.

Majors. Business: Accounting, accounting technology, administrative services, business admin, marketing, office management, real estate. **Computer sciences:** General, computer graphics, database management, networking, programming, security, web page design. **Education:** Early childhood. **Health services:** Medical radiologic technology/radiation therapy, nuclear medical technology, nursing (RN), sonography. **Liberal arts:** Arts/sciences. **Parks/recreation:** General. **Protective services:** Fire safety technology, fire services admin, firefighting, law enforcement admin. **Visual/performing arts:** Interior design.

Most popular majors. Business/marketing 12%, computer/information sciences 8%, health sciences 8%, liberal arts 64%.

Computing on campus. 244 workstations in library, computer center. Commuter students can connect to campus network. Online course registration, online library, helpline, student web hosting, wireless network available.

Student life. Freshman orientation: Available. Preregistration for classes offered. Quarterly, prior to start of term. **Activities:** Jazz band, choral groups, dance, drama, literary magazine, music ensembles, musical theater, radio station, student government, student newspaper, TV station.

Athletics. NAIA, NJCAA. **Intercollegiate:** Baseball M, basketball, cross-country, golf M, soccer, softball W, tennis, track and field, volleyball W. **Intramural:** Badminton, basketball, racquetball, soccer W, softball W, table tennis, tennis, volleyball. **Team name:** Bulldogs.

Student services. Career counseling, services for economically disadvantaged, student employment services, financial aid counseling, health services, minority student services, on-campus daycare, personal counseling, placement for graduates, veterans' counselor, women's services. **Physically disabled:** Services for visually, speech, hearing impaired. **Transfer:** Transfer center, transfer adviser, college fairs on campus for students transferring to 4-year colleges.

Contact. E-mail: admissions@bellevuecollege.edu
Phone: (425) 564-2222 Fax: (425) 564-4065
Catherine Kwong, Director, Registrar Services & Evaluations, Bellevue College, 3000 Landerholm Circle SE, Bellevue, WA 98007-6484

Bellingham Technical College
Bellingham, Washington
www.btc.ctc.edu

CB member
CB code: 3499

- Public 2-year technical college
- Commuter campus in small city

General. Regionally accredited. **Enrollment:** 2,131 degree-seeking undergraduates. **Degrees:** 348 associate awarded. **Location:** 90 miles from Seattle. **Calendar:** Quarter, limited summer session. **Full-time faculty:** 66 total. **Part-time faculty:** 114 total. **Class size:** 84% < 20, 15% 20-39, less than 1% 40-49, less than 1% 50-99.

Student profile.

Out-of-state:	1%	25 or older:	52%

Basis for selection. Open admission, but selective for some programs. Specific admission criteria such as completion of prerequisites required for Dental Assisting, Civil Engineering, Mechanical Engineering, Surveying & Mapping, Instrumentation & Control, Electronics, Process Technology, Practical Nursing, Radiologic Technology, Registered Nursing, Surgery Technology, and Veterinary Technician programs. Selective admission is applicable to Dental Hygiene only.

2011-2012 Annual costs. Tuition/fees: $3,374; $8,209 out-of-state. Per-credit charge: $71 in-state; $179 out-of-state. Books/supplies: $2,110. Personal expenses: $1,623.

Financial aid. All financial aid based on need. Need-based aid available for part-time students. Work-study available nights, weekends and for part-time students.

Application procedures. Admission: No deadline. No application fee. Application must be submitted on paper. Admission notification on a rolling basis. **Financial aid:** Closing date 4/1. FAFSA required. Applicants notified on a rolling basis starting 7/1; must reply within 2 week(s) of notification.

Academics. Special study options: Distance learning, ESL, internships. License preparation in nursing, paramedic, real estate. **Credit/placement by examination:** AP, CLEP, institutional tests. **Support services:** GED preparation and test center, learning center, remedial instruction, study skills assistance, tutoring.

Majors. Business: Accounting technology, executive assistant, human resources, marketing, operations. **Computer sciences:** Data entry, networking. **Conservation:** Fisheries. **Education:** Voc/tech. **Health services:** Dental assistant, dental hygiene, EMT paramedic, insurance coding, medical radiologic technology/radiation therapy, nursing (RN), radiologic technology/medical imaging, surgical technology, veterinary technology/assistant.

Most popular majors. Computer/information sciences 9%, engineering/engineering technologies 15%, health sciences 28%, trade and industry 38%.

Computing on campus. 14 workstations in library. Commuter students can connect to campus network. Online course registration, online library, wireless network available.

Student life. Freshman orientation: Available. Preregistration for classes offered. Orientation is held quarterly for new students within the month prior to students' start date. **Activities:** Student government.

Student services. Adult student services, career counseling, services for economically disadvantaged, financial aid counseling, minority student services, veterans' counselor. **Physically disabled:** Services for visually, speech, hearing impaired. **Transfer:** Pre-admission transcript evaluation for new students.

Contact. E-mail: admissions@btc.ctc.edu
Phone: (360) 752-8345 Fax: (360) 676-2798
Erin Runestrand, Director of Admissions, Bellingham Technical College, 3028 Lindbergh Avenue, Bellingham, WA 98225-1599

Big Bend Community College
Moses Lake, Washington
www.bigbend.edu

CB code: 4024

- Public 2-year community college
- Commuter campus in large town

General. Founded in 1962. Regionally accredited. **Enrollment:** 1,563 degree-seeking undergraduates; 621 non-degree-seeking students. **Degrees:** 393 associate awarded. **Location:** 107 miles from Spokane, 170 miles from Seattle. **Calendar:** Quarter, limited summer session. **Full-time faculty:** 51 total; 10% have terminal degrees, 6% minority, 33% women. **Part-time faculty:** 86 total; 2% have terminal degrees, 17% minority, 63% women. **Partnerships:** Formal partnership with high schools for Tech Prep programs.

Student profile. Among degree-seeking undergraduates, 58% enrolled in a transfer program, 42% enrolled in a vocational program, 1% already have a bachelor's degree or higher, 329 enrolled as first-time, first-year students, 251 transferred in from other institutions.

Part-time:	22%	Asian American:	1%
Out-of-state:	5%	Hispanic American:	32%
Women:	58%	25 or older:	47%
African American:	2%	Live on campus:	5%

Transfer out. Colleges most students transferred to 2011: Central Washington University, Eastern Washington University, Washington State University.

Basis for selection. Open admission, but selective for some programs. Special admission criteria for aviation and nursing programs.

2011-2012 Annual costs. Tuition/fees: $3,692; $8,927 out-of-state. Per-credit charge: $96 in-state; $268 out-of-state. Room only: $2,520. Books/supplies: $984. Personal expenses: $2,040.

2011-2012 Financial aid. All financial aid based on need. 69% of total undergraduate aid awarded as scholarships/grants, 31% as loans/jobs. Need-based aid available for part-time students. Work-study available nights, weekends and for part-time students.

Application procedures. Admission: No deadline. $30 fee. Admission notification on a rolling basis. **Financial aid:** Priority date 4/1; no closing date. FAFSA, institutional form required. Applicants notified on a rolling basis starting 5/15; must reply within 2 week(s) of notification.

Academics. Special study options: Cooperative education, distance learning, dual enrollment of high school students, liberal arts/career combination. Bachelor's degree programs available on campus. License preparation in aviation, nursing. **Credit/placement by examination:** AP, CLEP, institutional tests. 45 credit hours maximum toward associate degree. **Support services:** GED preparation and test center, learning center, reduced course load, remedial instruction, study skills assistance, tutoring, writing center.

Majors. Business: General, accounting technology, office management. **Education:** Early childhood, teacher assistance. **General:** Production. **Health services:** Medical assistant, nursing (RN), office admin. **Liberal arts:** Arts/sciences. **Physical sciences:** General.

Most popular majors. Business/marketing 6%, health sciences 11%, liberal arts 71%, trade and industry 7%.

Computing on campus. 432 workstations in dormitories, library, computer center, student center. Online course registration, online library, helpline, student web hosting, wireless network available.

Student life. Freshman orientation: Available. Preregistration for classes offered. Half-day fall student advising and registration sessions held throughout the summer. Full-day student orientation held in September. **Housing:** Coed dorms, wellness housing available. $200 partly refundable deposit. **Activities:** Choral groups, music ensembles, student government.

Athletics. Intercollegiate: Baseball M, basketball, softball W, volleyball W. **Team name:** Vikings.

Student services. Career counseling, services for economically disadvantaged, student employment services, financial aid counseling, minority student services, on-campus daycare, personal counseling, placement for graduates, veterans' counselor. **Physically disabled:** Services for visually, speech, hearing impaired. **Transfer:** Transfer adviser, college fairs on campus for students transferring to 4-year colleges.

Contact. E-mail: admissions@bigbend.edu
Phone: (509) 793-2061 Toll-free number: (877) 745-1212
Fax: (509) 762-6243
Candy Lacher, Associate Vice President of Student Services, Big Bend Community College, 7662 Chanute Street, Moses Lake, WA 98837-3299

Carrington College: Spokane
Spokane, Washington
www.carrington.edu

- For-profit 2-year career college
- Very large city

General. Regionally accredited; also accredited by ACICS. **Enrollment:** 588 degree-seeking undergraduates. **Degrees:** 37 associate awarded. **Calendar:** Differs by program. **Full-time faculty:** 10 total. **Part-time faculty:** 22 total.

Basis for selection. Applicants must be at least 18 in Washington by the first day of classes, have a high school diploma or its equivalent, interview with an Enrollment Services Representative, complete admission testing, and fulfill additional program-specific requirements.

Financial aid. **Need-based:** Work-study available nights, weekends and for part-time students.

Application procedures. **Financial aid:** No deadline.

Academics. **Credit/placement by examination:** AP, CLEP.

Majors. **Health services:** Medical radiologic technology/radiation therapy, office admin.

Contact. Phone: (888) 720-5014
Lisa Heide, Director of Admissions, Carrington College: Spokane, 10102 East Knox Avenue, Spokane, WA 99206-4187

Cascadia Community College
Bothell, Washington
www.cascadia.edu   CB code: 2859

- Public 2-year community college
- Commuter campus in large town

General. Commitment to themes of global perspective and sustainability infused into most courses. **Enrollment:** 1,765 degree-seeking undergraduates; 932 non-degree-seeking students. **Degrees:** 452 associate awarded. **Location:** 15 miles from Seattle. **Calendar:** Quarter, extensive summer session. **Full-time faculty:** 37 total. **Part-time faculty:** 106 total; 68% women.

Student profile. Among degree-seeking undergraduates, 76% enrolled in a transfer program, 9% enrolled in a vocational program, 3% already have a bachelor's degree or higher, 336 enrolled as first-time, first-year students.

Part-time:	46%	**Women:**	46%

Basis for selection. Open admission. All students taking credit classes required to assess their current skill levels in English and Math with the COMPASS placement test.

2011-2012 Annual costs. Tuition/fees: $3,662; $8,897 out-of-state. Per-credit charge: $79 in-state; $195 out-of-state.

Financial aid. **Need-based:** Work-study available nights, weekends and for part-time students.

Application procedures. **Admission:** No deadline. $35 fee. **Financial aid:** Priority date 4/15; no closing date. FAFSA, institutional form required.

Academics. **Special study options:** Distance learning, dual enrollment of high school students, ESL, independent study, internships, study abroad. **Credit/placement by examination:** AP, CLEP, IB, institutional tests. 45 credit hours maximum toward associate degree. **Support services:** GED preparation, learning center, remedial instruction, study skills assistance, tutoring, writing center.

Majors. **Biology:** General. **Computer sciences:** General. **Conservation:** Environmental science. **Education:** Elementary. **Physical sciences:** Chemistry, geology, physics.

Computing on campus. Commuter students can connect to campus network. Online library, helpline, wireless network available.

Student life. **Freshman orientation:** Mandatory. Preregistration for classes offered. Orientation, advising, and registration sessions last approximately two hours and are offered several times before each quarter begins. Students given assistance in selecting courses, building schedules, registering for classes, and are also introduced to web registration as well as other online services. **Activities:** Film society, international student organizations, literary magazine, music ensembles, student government, student newspaper, Students in Service, Campus Crusade for Christ, Access Futures.

Athletics. **Team name:** Kodiaks.

Student services. Adult student services, career counseling, services for economically disadvantaged, student employment services, financial aid counseling, personal counseling, veterans' counselor. **Physically disabled:** Services for visually, speech, hearing impaired. **Transfer:** Pre-admission

transcript evaluation for new students. Transfer center, transfer adviser, college fairs on campus for students transferring to 4-year colleges.

Contact. E-mail: admissions@cascadia.edu
Phone: (425) 352-8860 Fax: (425) 352-8137
Erin Blakeney, Associate Dean for Admissions and Retention, Cascadia Community College, 18345 Campus Way, NE, Bothell, WA 98011

Centralia College
Centralia, Washington
www.centralia.edu   CB code: 4045

- Public 2-year community college
- Commuter campus in large town

General. Founded in 1925. Regionally accredited. Home to the Pacific Northwest Center of Excellence for Clean Energy. **Enrollment:** 2,545 degree-seeking undergraduates. **Degrees:** 399 associate awarded. **Location:** 90 miles from Seattle, 90 miles from Portland, Oregon. **Calendar:** Quarter, extensive summer session. **Full-time faculty:** 63 total; 3% minority, 52% women. **Part-time faculty:** 150 total; 5% minority, 53% women. **Class size:** 50% < 20, 43% 20-39, 5% 40-49, 2% 50-99. **Special facilities:** Kiser Natural Outdoor Learning Lab, River Heights Nature Preserve.

Student profile. Among degree-seeking undergraduates, 47% enrolled in a transfer program, 53% enrolled in a vocational program.

Out-of-state:	1%	**25 or older:**	.	53%

Transfer out. **Colleges most students transferred to 2011:** Western Washington University, Washington State University, The Evergreen State College, Saint Martin's College, Central Washington University.

Basis for selection. Open admission, but selective for some programs. Special requirements for nursing program, includes prerequisites and grade point average criteria. **Home schooled:** Transcript of courses and grades required. **Learning Disabled:** Students with learning disabilities desiring accomodations must register with Disability Services to receive accomodations.

High school preparation. College-preparatory program recommended. 16 units recommended. Recommended units include English 4, mathematics 3, social studies 2, history 1, science 2 (laboratory 1), foreign language 2 and academic electives 1.

2012-2013 Annual costs. Tuition/fees (projected): $4,316; $9,551 out-of-state. Per-credit charge: $87 in-state; $265 out-of-state. Books/supplies: $924. Personal expenses: $3,030.

Financial aid. **Need-based:** Need-based aid available for part-time students. Work-study available nights, weekends and for part-time students. **Non-need-based:** Scholarships awarded for academics, alumni affiliation, art, athletics, leadership, minority status, music/drama.

Application procedures. **Admission:** Priority date 9/1; no deadline. No application fee. Admission notification on a rolling basis beginning on or about 12/1. **Financial aid:** Priority date 5/1, closing date 9/1. FAFSA, institutional form required. Applicants notified on a rolling basis starting 7/10; must reply within 2 week(s) of notification.

Academics. Online tutoring available 24/7. **Special study options:** Cooperative education, cross-registration, distance learning, double major, dual enrollment of high school students, ESL, honors, independent study, internships, liberal arts/career combination, student-designed major, study abroad, teacher certification program, weekend college. Bachelor's degree programs available on campus. License preparation in nursing, paramedic, real estate. **Credit/placement by examination:** AP, CLEP, IB, institutional tests. 45 credit hours maximum toward associate degree. **Support services:** GED preparation and test center, learning center, reduced course load, remedial instruction, study skills assistance, tutoring, writing center.

Honors college/program. Selective application process after completion of 30 college credits. Limited to 20 students per year.

Majors. **Biology:** General, botany. **Business:** General, accounting, business admin, marketing, office technology, office/clerical, receptionist, sales/distribution. **Communications:** Broadcast journalism, journalism, radio/TV. **Communications technology:** Graphics, radio/TV. **Computer sciences:** General, computer science, data processing, information systems, LAN/WAN management, networking, programming. **Conservation:** Wildlife/wilderness. **Education:** General, early childhood, teacher assistance. **Engineering:** General. **English:** English lit. **Foreign languages:** General, French, German,

Spanish. **Health services:** Nursing (RN), polarity therapy, sonography. **History:** General. **Liberal arts:** Arts/sciences. **Math:** General. **Parks/recreation:** Health/fitness. **Physical sciences:** General, chemistry, geology, physics, planetary. **Protective services:** Forensics, law enforcement admin, police science. **Psychology:** General. **Social sciences:** General, anthropology, economics, political science, sociology. **Visual/performing arts:** General, art, commercial/advertising art, dramatic, graphic design, music, music theory/composition, studio arts. **Work/family studies:** Child care service.

Computing on campus. 160 workstations in library, computer center, student center. Online course registration, online library, helpline, wireless network available.

Student life. Freshman orientation: Available, $20 fee. Preregistration for classes offered. Held 2 days prior to fall quarter. **Activities:** Bands, choral groups, drama, international student organizations, literary magazine, music ensembles, musical theater, radio station, student government, student newspaper, TV station, honors club, international student club, Rotaract.

Athletics. Intercollegiate: Baseball M, basketball, golf W, softball W, volleyball W. **Team name:** Trailblazers.

Student services. Adult student services, career counseling, services for economically disadvantaged, student employment services, financial aid counseling, minority student services, on-campus daycare, personal counseling, placement for graduates, veterans' counselor. **Physically disabled:** Services for visually, speech, hearing impaired. **Transfer:** Re-entry adviser, pre-admission transcript evaluation for new students. Transfer center, transfer adviser, college fairs on campus for students transferring to 4-year colleges.

Contact. E-mail: admissions@centralia.edu
Phone: (360) 736-9391 ext. 221 Fax: (360) 330-7503
Qy-Ana Manning, Registrar, Centralia College, 600 Centralia College Boulevard, Centralia, WA 98531

Clark College
Vancouver, Washington
www.clark.edu   CB code: 4055

▸ Public 2-year community college
▸ Commuter campus in small city

General. Founded in 1933. Regionally accredited. **Enrollment:** 9,518 degree-seeking undergraduates; 3,226 non-degree-seeking students. **Degrees:** 1,528 associate awarded. **ROTC:** Army, Air Force. **Location:** 8 miles from Portland, Oregon. **Calendar:** Quarter, extensive summer session. **Full-time faculty:** 207 total; 14% have terminal degrees, 6% minority, 60% women. **Part-time faculty:** 504 total; 11% have terminal degrees, 10% minority, 58% women. **Class size:** 48% < 20, 49% 20-39, 2% 40-49, less than 1% 50-99, less than 1% >100. **Special facilities:** Environmental education center, arboretum. **Partnerships:** Formal partnerships with Toyota T-10 and Cisco; industry partnerships to train students in specific equipment use.

Student profile. Among degree-seeking undergraduates, 1,764 enrolled as first-time, first-year students, 379 transferred in from other institutions.

Part-time:	46%	Asian American:	4%
Out-of-state:	3%	Hispanic American:	7%
Women:	58%	Native American:	1%
African American:	3%	25 or older:	38%

Transfer out. Colleges most students transferred to 2011: Washington State University-Vancouver, Portland State University, University of Washington, Western Washington University, Central Washington.

Basis for selection. Open admission, but selective for some programs. GPA requirements vary by program. COMPASS required for placement in math and English. Interview required for dental hygiene, nursing, and pharmacy technician applicants.

2011-2012 Annual costs. Tuition/fees: $3,743; $8,978 out-of-state. Books/supplies: $972. Personal expenses: $1,530.

2010-2011 Financial aid. Need-based: Need-based aid available for part-time students. Work-study available nights, weekends and for part-time students. **Non-need-based:** Scholarships awarded for academics, alumni affiliation, art, athletics, leadership, minority status, music/drama, state residency.

Application procedures. Admission: Closing date 9/7. $20 fee. Admission notification on a rolling basis. **Financial aid:** No deadline. FAFSA, institutional form required. Applicants notified on a rolling basis starting 6/1; must reply within 2 week(s) of notification.

Academics. Special study options: Accelerated study, cooperative education, distance learning, dual enrollment of high school students, ESL, independent study, internships, liberal arts/career combination, weekend college. Bachelor's degree programs available on campus. License preparation in dental hygiene, nursing, radiology. **Credit/placement by examination:** AP, CLEP, IB, institutional tests. 30 credit hours maximum toward associate degree. **Support services:** GED preparation and test center, learning center, reduced course load, remedial instruction, study skills assistance, tutoring, writing center.

Majors. Business: Accounting technology, business admin, executive assistant, human resources, office technology. **Communications technology:** Graphics. **Computer sciences:** Data entry, networking, programming, webmaster. **Education:** Early childhood. **General:** Horticulture, landscaping. **Health services:** Dental hygiene, EMT paramedic, medical assistant, medical secretary, nursing (RN), radiologic technology/medical imaging, substance abuse counseling. **Liberal arts:** Arts/sciences. **Parks/recreation:** Sports admin.

Most popular majors. Business/marketing 10%, health sciences 16%, liberal arts 61%.

Computing on campus. 923 workstations in library, computer center, student center. Online course registration, online library, helpline, wireless network available.

Student life. Freshman orientation: Available. Preregistration for classes offered. Sessions held during quarterly registration period. Online orientation option available. **Activities:** Bands, choral groups, drama, international student organizations, literary magazine, Model UN, musical theater, student government, student newspaper, symphony orchestra, American Sign Language, Clark College Feminists, manga anime club, club for social action, Generation for Truth prayer club, international club, Japanese language club, Queer Penguins and Allies, multicultural student union, Students for Political Action Now.

Athletics. Intercollegiate: Basketball, cross-country, soccer, track and field, volleyball W. **Intramural:** Basketball, fencing, football (non-tackle), soccer, softball, table tennis, volleyball. **Team name:** Penguins.

Student services. Adult student services, alcohol/substance abuse counseling, career counseling, services for economically disadvantaged, student employment services, financial aid counseling, health services, legal services, minority student services, on-campus daycare, personal counseling, placement for graduates, veterans' counselor. **Physically disabled:** Services for visually, speech, hearing impaired. **Transfer:** Transfer adviser, college fairs on campus for students transferring to 4-year colleges.

Contact. E-mail: admissions@clark.edu
Phone: (360) 992-2107 Fax: (360) 992-2867
Sheryl Anderson, Director of Admissions, Clark College, Welcome Center, MS PUB002, Vancouver, WA 98663

Clover Park Technical College
Lakewood, Washington
www.cptc.edu   CB code: 3971

▸ Public 2-year technical college
▸ Commuter campus in small city

General. Regionally accredited. **Enrollment:** 1,560 degree-seeking undergraduates. **Degrees:** 415 associate awarded. **Location:** 10 miles from Tacoma, 40 miles from Seattle. **Calendar:** Quarter, extensive summer session. **Full-time faculty:** 92 total. **Part-time faculty:** 104 total. **Class size:** 70% < 20, 27% 20-39, 2% 40-49, 1% 50-99.

Basis for selection. Open admission, but selective for some programs. Some programs have test score minimums and/or course prerequisite requirements.

2011-2012 Annual costs. Tuition/fees: $4,020; $8,828 out-of-state. Per-credit charge: $89 in-state; $196 out-of-state. Books/supplies: $1,200. Personal expenses: $1,950.

Financial aid. All financial aid based on need. Need-based aid available for part-time students. Work-study available nights, weekends and for part-time students.

Application procedures. Admission: No deadline. $50 fee. Admission notification on a rolling basis. **Financial aid:** Priority date 6/15, closing date 7/20. FAFSA, institutional form required. Applicants notified on a rolling basis.

Academics. Special study options: Cooperative education, distance learning, dual enrollment of high school students, ESL, internships. License preparation in aviation, nursing. **Credit/placement by examination:** AP, CLEP, institutional tests. 15 credit hours maximum toward associate degree. 25 percent of total approved hours may be awarded for prior work and/or life experience. **Support services:** GED preparation and test center, tutoring.

Majors. Business: Accounting technology, marketing, office management. **Communications technology:** Graphic/printing, radio/TV. **Computer sciences:** LAN/WAN management, networking, programming, security, web page design. **Education:** Early childhood, teacher assistance. **General:** Landscaping. **Health services:** Clinical lab assistant, dental assistant, licensed practical nurse, massage therapy, pharmacy assistant, surgical technology. **Visual/performing arts:** Interior design.

Most popular majors. Computer/information sciences 14%, education 8%, health sciences 34%, trade and industry 15%.

Computing on campus. 94 workstations in library. Online library available.

Student life. Freshman orientation: Available. Preregistration for classes offered. **Activities:** Student government.

Student services. Adult student services, career counseling, services for economically disadvantaged, student employment services, financial aid counseling, minority student services, on-campus daycare, veterans' counselor. **Physically disabled:** Services for visually, speech, hearing impaired.

Contact. Phone: (253) 589-5678 Fax: (253) 589-5852
Judy MacDougall, Director of Enrollment Services, Clover Park Technical College, 4500 Steilacoom Boulevard, SW, Lakewood, WA 98499-4098

Columbia Basin College
Pasco, Washington
www.columbiabasin.edu   CB code: 4077

- Public 2-year community college
- Commuter campus in small city

General. Founded in 1955. Regionally accredited. **Enrollment:** 5,128 degree-seeking undergraduates. **Degrees:** 1,004 associate awarded. **Location:** 135 miles from Spokane, 225 miles from Seattle. **Calendar:** Quarter, limited summer session. **Full-time faculty:** 130 total. **Part-time faculty:** 186 total. **Special facilities:** Performing arts theater, health science center, observatory, math and science working atrium, regional medical library, tutor and writing center, research farm.

Student profile.

Out-of-state: 1%   25 or older: 58%

Transfer out. Colleges most students transferred to 2011: Washington State University.

Basis for selection. Open admission, but selective for some programs. Special application process and requirements for nursing, dental hygiene, radiologic technology, paramedic, medical assistant, automotive technology, nuclear technology, and surgical technician programs. Applicants not graduates of regionally accredited high schools or those without a GED must submit Washington Pre-College Test, SAT, or ACT scores.

High school preparation. College-preparatory program required. 11 units recommended. Recommended units include English 3, mathematics 2, social studies 3, science 2 and foreign language 1.

2011-2012 Annual costs. Tuition/fees: $3,932; $9,167 out-of-state. Books/supplies: $924. Personal expenses: $1,524.

Financial aid. Need-based: Need-based aid available for part-time students. Work-study available nights, weekends and for part-time students. **Non-need-based:** Scholarships awarded for academics, athletics, state residency.

Application procedures. Admission: $29 fee, may be waived for applicants with need. Application must be submitted on paper. Admission notification on a rolling basis. **Financial aid:** Closing date 4/15. FAFSA, institutional form required. Applicants notified on a rolling basis starting 6/15; must reply within 2 week(s) of notification.

Academics. Special study options: Cross-registration, distance learning, dual enrollment of high school students, ESL, internships, liberal arts/career combination, weekend college. Bachelor's degree programs available on campus. License preparation in dental hygiene, nursing, paramedic, radiology. **Credit/placement by examination:** AP, CLEP, IB, institutional tests. 30

credit hours maximum toward associate degree. **Support services:** GED preparation and test center, learning center, reduced course load, remedial instruction, study skills assistance, tutoring, writing center.

Majors. Business: Accounting, administrative services, business admin, management information systems, office management, purchasing, sales/distribution. **Computer sciences:** General, computer science, data processing, programming. **Education:** General, early childhood. **General:** Agribusiness operations, business. **Health services:** Clinical lab technology, dental hygiene, EMT paramedic, licensed practical nurse, medical records admin, medical transcription. **Liberal arts:** Arts/sciences. **Physical sciences:** General. **Protective services:** Firefighting, law enforcement admin, police science. **Visual/performing arts:** General, commercial/advertising art. **Work/family studies:** Child care management.

Most popular majors. Health sciences 7%, liberal arts 77%.

Computing on campus. 680 workstations in library, computer center. Online course registration, online library, wireless network available.

Student life. Freshman orientation: Mandatory. Preregistration for classes offered. **Activities:** Bands, choral groups, drama, music ensembles, musical theater, student government, student newspaper.

Athletics. NJCAA. **Intercollegiate:** Baseball M, basketball, golf, soccer, softball W, volleyball W. **Intramural:** Basketball, bowling, soccer M, softball, volleyball. **Team name:** Hawks.

Student services. Adult student services, career counseling, student employment services, minority student services, personal counseling, placement for graduates, veterans' counselor, women's services. **Physically disabled:** Services for visually, speech, hearing impaired. **Transfer:** Transfer adviser, college fairs on campus for students transferring to 4-year colleges.

Contact. E-mail: admissions@columbiabasin.edu
Phone: (509) 547-0511 Fax: (509) 546-0401
Patricia Campbell, Director of Admissions and Registration, Columbia Basin College, 2600 North 20th Avenue, Pasco, WA 99301

Edmonds Community College
Lynnwood, Washington
www.edcc.edu   CB code: 4307

- Public 2-year community college
- Commuter campus in small city

General. Founded in 1967. Regionally accredited. **Location:** 15 miles from Seattle. **Calendar:** Quarter.

Annual costs/financial aid. Tuition/fees (2011-2012): $3,997; $9,232 out-of-state. Books/supplies: $900. Personal expenses: $1,824. Need-based financial aid available to full-time and part-time students.

Contact. Phone: (425) 640-1459
Office Manager, Enrollment Services, 20000 68th Avenue West, Lynnwood, WA 98036-5912

Everett Community College
Everett, Washington
www.everettcc.edu   CB code: 4303

- Public 2-year community college
- Commuter campus in small city

General. Founded in 1941. Regionally accredited. **Enrollment:** 5,088 degree-seeking undergraduates. **Degrees:** 889 associate awarded. **Location:** 30 miles from Seattle. **Calendar:** Quarter, limited summer session. **Full-time faculty:** 117 total. **Part-time faculty:** 200 total. **Class size:** 37% < 20, 60% 20-39, 3% 40-49, less than 1% 50-99. **Partnerships:** Formal partnership with Boeing.

Student profile.

Out-of-state: 2%   25 or older: 41%

Transfer out. Colleges most students transferred to 2011: Western Washington University, University of Washington, Central Washington University, Washington State University.

Basis for selection. Open admission, but selective for some programs. Special requirements for nursing, fire science, and criminal justice. Interview recommended for nursing.

Two-Year Colleges

High school preparation. College-preparatory program recommended. 16 units recommended. Recommended units include English 4, mathematics 3, social studies 3, history 2, science 2 and foreign language 2.

2011-2012 Annual costs. Tuition/fees: $3,601; $8,836 out-of-state. Per-credit charge: $78 in-state; $194 out-of-state. Books/supplies: $924. Personal expenses: $1,590.

Financial aid. Need-based: Need-based aid available for part-time students. Work-study available nights, weekends and for part-time students. **Non-need-based:** Scholarships awarded for academics, alumni affiliation, art, athletics, job skills, leadership, minority status, music/drama, state residency.

Application procedures. Admission: No deadline. No application fee. Admission notification on a rolling basis. **Financial aid:** Priority date 5/5; no closing date. FAFSA, institutional form required. Applicants notified on a rolling basis starting 4/15; must reply within 4 week(s) of notification.

Academics. Offers direct-transfer associate degrees that assure full transfer to most Washington and Oregon universities. Transfer degrees for specific majors at designated universities can be designed by the student and faculty advisor. **Special study options:** Cooperative education, distance learning, dual enrollment of high school students, ESL, independent study, internships, study abroad. Bachelor's degree programs available on campus. License preparation in aviation, nursing, paramedic. **Credit/placement by examination:** AP, CLEP, IB, institutional tests. 45 credit hours maximum toward associate degree. **Support services:** GED preparation and test center, learning center, reduced course load, remedial instruction, study skills assistance, tutoring, writing center.

Majors. Area/ethnic studies: Asian. **Biology:** General. **Business:** General, accounting, administrative services, business admin, management information systems, office/clerical. **Communications:** Advertising, communications/speech/rhetoric, journalism. **Computer sciences:** General, computer graphics, computer science, information systems, networking, programming, webmaster. **Conservation:** General, environmental science. **Education:** General, early childhood. **Engineering:** General. **English:** American lit, creative writing, English lit, rhetoric/composition, technical writing, writing. **Foreign languages:** General, comparative lit, French, German, Japanese, Russian, Spanish. **General:** Animal sciences. **Health services:** Dental hygiene, medical assistant, nursing (RN), predental, premedicine, prepharmacy, preveterinary. **History:** General. **Liberal arts:** Arts/sciences. **Math:** General. **Philosophy/religion:** Philosophy. **Physical sciences:** Astronomy, atmospheric science, chemistry, geology, oceanography, physics. **Protective services:** Corrections, firefighting, law enforcement admin. **Psychology:** General. **Social sciences:** General, anthropology, economics, geography, political science, sociology. **Visual/performing arts:** General, art, commercial/advertising art, dramatic, music, music performance, photography, studio arts.

Most popular majors. Business/marketing 17%, health sciences 11%, liberal arts 54%.

Computing on campus. 900 workstations in library, computer center, student center. Online course registration, wireless network available.

Student life. Freshman orientation: Mandatory. Preregistration for classes offered. One-day program of placement testing, orientation and advising sessions. **Housing:** Housing in private homes available for foreign students. **Activities:** Choral groups, drama, literary magazine, music ensembles, musical theater, student government, student newspaper, 25 student clubs.

Athletics. Intercollegiate: Baseball M, basketball, cross-country, soccer, softball W, volleyball W. **Intramural:** Basketball, bowling, golf, soccer, softball, tennis, volleyball, weight lifting. **Team name:** Trojans.

Student services. Adult student services, career counseling, services for economically disadvantaged, student employment services, financial aid counseling, minority student services, on-campus daycare, personal counseling, placement for graduates, veterans' counselor, women's services. **Physically disabled:** Services for visually, speech, hearing impaired. **Transfer:** Transfer adviser, college fairs on campus for students transferring to 4-year colleges.

Contact. E-mail: admissions@everettcc.edu
Phone: (425) 388-9219 Fax: (425) 388-9173
Laurie Franklin, Dean of Enrollment/Student Financial Services, Everett Community College, 2000 Tower Street, Everett, WA 98201-1352

General. Founded in 1930. Regionally accredited. **Enrollment:** 1,450 full-time, degree-seeking students. **Degrees:** 333 associate awarded. **Location:** 100 miles from Seattle. **Calendar:** Quarter, limited summer session. **Full-time faculty:** 60 total. **Part-time faculty:** 52 total. **Class size:** 77% < 20, 22% 20-39, less than 1% 40-49, less than 1% 50-99. **Special facilities:** 4-acre lake linked to Grays Harbor estuary and fish hatcheries, 440 seat theater. **Partnerships:** Formal partnerships with local businesses for internships and short-term training.

Transfer out. Colleges most students transferred to 2011: Washington State University, Evergreen State College, Western Washington University, Central Washington University, Eastern Washington University.

Basis for selection. Open admission, but selective for some programs. High school diploma or GED required of applicants under 18 years of age. Limited admission to nursing program.

2011-2012 Annual costs. Tuition/fees: $3,930; $9,165 out-of-state. Books/supplies: $972. Personal expenses: $2,178.

Financial aid. Need-based: Need-based aid available for part-time students. Work-study available nights, weekends and for part-time students. **Non-need-based:** Scholarships awarded for academics, art, athletics, music/drama.

Application procedures. Admission: Priority date 9/1; no deadline. No application fee. Admission notification on a rolling basis. **Financial aid:** Closing date 5/1. FAFSA, institutional form required. Applicants notified on a rolling basis starting 5/15.

Academics. Special study options: Accelerated study, cooperative education, distance learning, double major, dual enrollment of high school students, ESL, independent study, internships, study abroad. Bachelor's degree programs available on campus. License preparation in nursing. **Credit/placement by examination:** AP, CLEP, institutional tests. 45 credit hours maximum toward associate degree. **Support services:** GED preparation and test center, learning center, reduced course load, remedial instruction, study skills assistance, tutoring, writing center.

Majors. Business: Accounting technology, business admin, office management. **Computer sciences:** Data processing. **Conservation:** General, wildlife/wilderness. **Education:** Teacher assistance. **Health services:** Nursing (RN). **Liberal arts:** Arts/sciences. **Physical sciences:** General. **Protective services:** Police science.

Most popular majors. Business/marketing 8%, health sciences 16%, liberal arts 53%, trade and industry 14%.

Computing on campus. 382 workstations in library, computer center, student center. Online course registration, online library, student web hosting, wireless network available.

Student life. Freshman orientation: Mandatory. Preregistration for classes offered. Offered online or face to face. **Activities:** Bands, campus ministries, choral groups, drama, music ensembles, musical theater, student government, student newspaper, symphony orchestra, Native American student association, Tyee honorary service club, human services student association, Hispanic/Latino club, student nurses association, non-traditional students community, natural resources club, gay, lesbian, bisexual, transgender and straight students club.

Athletics. Intercollegiate: Baseball M, basketball, golf, softball W, volleyball W. **Team name:** Chokers.

Student services. Adult student services, career counseling, services for economically disadvantaged, student employment services, financial aid counseling, minority student services, on-campus daycare, personal counseling, placement for graduates, veterans' counselor. **Physically disabled:** Services for visually, speech, hearing impaired. **Transfer:** Pre-admission transcript evaluation for new students. Transfer adviser, college fairs on campus for students transferring to 4-year colleges.

Contact. E-mail: admissions@ghc.edu
Phone: (360) 538-4026 Toll-free number: (800) 562-4830
Fax: (360) 538-4293
Nancy DeVerse, Associate Dean for Student Services/Registrar, Grays Harbor College, 1620 Edward P Smith Drive, Aberdeen, WA 98520

Grays Harbor College
Aberdeen, Washington
www.ghc.edu   **CB code: 4332**

- Public 2-year community college
- Commuter campus in large town

Green River Community College
Auburn, Washington
www.greenriver.edu   **CB code: 4337**

- Public 2-year community college
- Commuter campus in large town

General. Founded in 1965. Regionally accredited. **Enrollment:** 5,413 degree-seeking undergraduates. **Degrees:** 1,391 associate awarded. **Location:** 35 miles from Seattle. **Calendar:** Quarter, limited summer session. **Full-time faculty:** 143 total. **Part-time faculty:** 321 total. **Class size:** 17% < 20, 80% 20-39, 4% 40-49.

Basis for selection. Open admission, but selective for some programs. Special requirements for health occupation programs. Interview required for occupational therapy.

2011-2012 Annual costs. Tuition/fees: $3,970; $9,205 out-of-state. Books/supplies: $939. Personal expenses: $1,170.

Financial aid. All financial aid based on need. Need-based aid available for part-time students. Work-study available nights, weekends and for part-time students.

Application procedures. Admission: No deadline. $10 fee. Admission notification on a rolling basis. **Financial aid:** Closing date 4/15. FAFSA, institutional form required. Applicants notified on a rolling basis starting 6/30; must reply within 2 week(s) of notification.

Academics. Special study options: Cooperative education, cross-registration, distance learning, dual enrollment of high school students, ESL, independent study, internships, study abroad. **Credit/placement by examination:** AP, CLEP, institutional tests. **Support services:** GED preparation and test center, learning center, reduced course load, remedial instruction, tutoring, writing center.

Majors. Business: Accounting, marketing, office technology, office/clerical, real estate. **Computer sciences:** Database management, networking, security, system admin. **Conservation:** Water/wetlands/marine. **Education:** Early childhood, teacher assistance. **Health services:** Medical secretary, occupational therapy assistant, physical therapy assistant. **Liberal arts:** Arts/sciences. **Protective services:** Police science. **Visual/performing arts:** General.

Computing on campus. 210 workstations in library, computer center.

Student life. Freshman orientation: Available. Preregistration for classes offered. **Housing:** Apartments available. **Activities:** Jazz band, choral groups, dance, drama, music ensembles, radio station, student government, student newspaper, Asian Student Union, Black Student Union, Native American Student Association, Los Latinos Unidos, Phi Theta Kappa, Teachers of Tomorrow, Skills USA, forestry club, court reporting club, American Society of Mechanical Engineers.

Athletics. NJCAA. **Intercollegiate:** Baseball M, basketball, golf, soccer, softball W, tennis, volleyball W. **Intramural:** Badminton, baseball M, basketball, soccer, softball, tennis, volleyball. **Team name:** Gators.

Student services. Career counseling, services for economically disadvantaged, student employment services, financial aid counseling, health services, minority student services, on-campus daycare, personal counseling, placement for graduates, veterans' counselor, women's services. **Physically disabled:** Services for visually, hearing impaired. **Transfer:** Transfer center, transfer adviser, college fairs on campus for students transferring to 4-year colleges.

Contact. E-mail: EnrollmentServices@greenriver.edu
Phone: (253) 833-9111 ext. 2500 Fax: (253) 288-3454
Denise Bennatts, Registrar, Green River Community College, 12401 SE 320th Street, Auburn, WA 98092

Highline Community College
Des Moines, Washington
www.highline.edu   CB code: 4348

- Public 2-year community college
- Commuter campus in small city

General. Founded in 1961. Regionally accredited. Over 60% students of color; representing the diversity of the community. More than 50 countries represented with well over 100 languages spoken among students. **ROTC:** Army, Air Force. **Location:** 18 miles from Seattle. **Calendar:** Quarter, limited summer session. **Full-time faculty:** 150 total. **Part-time faculty:** 185 total. **Special facilities:** Sleep study laboratory, respiratory care patient care simulator, marine and science technology center.

Basis for selection. Open admission, but selective for some programs. School achievement record considered for health programs. College and work experience also considered for nursing.

High school preparation. Health occupation programs require chemistry and algebra.

2011-2012 Annual costs. Tuition/fees: $3,617; $8,852 out-of-state. Per-credit charge: $79 in-state; $195 out-of-state. Books/supplies: $618. Personal expenses: $1,644.

Financial aid. Need-based: Need-based aid available for part-time students. Work-study available nights, weekends and for part-time students.

Application procedures. Admission: No deadline. $24 fee. Admission notification on a rolling basis. **Financial aid:** Priority date 6/1; no closing date. FAFSA required. Applicants notified on a rolling basis starting 6/1.

Academics. Special study options: Accelerated study, cooperative education, cross-registration, distance learning, double major, dual enrollment of high school students, ESL, honors, independent study, internships, student-designed major. Bachelor's degree programs available on campus. **Credit/placement by examination:** AP, CLEP, institutional tests. **Support services:** GED preparation and test center, learning center, pre-admission summer program, reduced course load, remedial instruction, tutoring.

Majors. Business: General, accounting, administrative services, business admin, fashion, hospitality/recreation, international, office/clerical, sales/distribution, tourism/travel. **Communications:** Communications/speech/rhetoric, journalism. **Computer sciences:** General. **Education:** General, teacher assistance. **Engineering:** General. **English:** English lit. **Foreign languages:** General, French, German, linguistics. **Health services:** Dental assistant, health care admin, medical assistant, medical transcription, nursing (RN), respiratory therapy technology. **History:** General. **Liberal arts:** Arts/sciences, library assistant. **Math:** General. **Parks/recreation:** Health/fitness. **Physical sciences:** Astronomy, geology. **Psychology:** General. **Social sciences:** General, anthropology, economics, geography, sociology. **Visual/performing arts:** General, art, commercial/advertising art, dramatic, multimedia, music. **Work/family studies:** General, child care management, food/nutrition.

Most popular majors. Business/marketing 6%, computer/information sciences 6%, health sciences 9%, liberal arts 66%.

Computing on campus. 100 workstations in library, computer center, student center.

Student life. Activities: Bands, choral groups, drama, literary magazine, music ensembles, student government, student newspaper, TV station, Indian and international student clubs, political forum, paralegal and arts societies, respiratory care club, academic honor society, campus crusade for Christ.

Athletics. NJCAA. **Intercollegiate:** Basketball, cross-country, soccer, softball W, track and field, volleyball W, wrestling M. **Team name:** Thunderbirds.

Student services. Adult student services, career counseling, student employment services, health services, minority student services, on-campus daycare, personal counseling, placement for graduates, veterans' counselor, women's services. **Physically disabled:** Services for visually, speech, hearing impaired. **Transfer:** Transfer adviser, college fairs on campus for students transferring to 4-year colleges.

Contact. E-mail: mkuwasaki@highline.edu
Phone: (206) 878-3710 ext. 3559 Fax: (206) 870-3782
Debbie Faison, Assistant Registrar, Highline Community College, 2400 South 240th Street, Des Moines, WA 98198-9800

Lake Washington Institute of Technology
Kirkland, Washington
www.lwtech.edu   CB code: 1453

- Public 2-year technical college
- Commuter campus in large town

General. Founded in 1949. Regionally accredited. **Enrollment:** 2,481 degree-seeking undergraduates. **Degrees:** 14 bachelor's, 556 associate awarded. **Location:** 10 miles from Seattle. **Calendar:** Quarter, extensive summer session. **Full-time faculty:** 77 total. **Part-time faculty:** 271 total. **Class size:** 3% < 20, 97% 20-39. **Partnerships:** High Tech Center at local high school.

Basis for selection. Open admission, but selective for some programs. Limited admissions to nursing, dental hygiene, physical therapist assistant, Bachelor of Technology in Applied Design. The Bachelor of Technology program has a $50 application fee.

2011-2012 Annual costs. Tuition/fees: $3,929; $9,164 out-of-state. Per-credit charge: $79 in-state; $195 out-of-state. Books/supplies: $1,911. Personal expenses: $1,590.

Financial aid. Need-based: Need-based aid available for part-time students. Work-study available nights, weekends and for part-time students.

Application procedures. Admission: No application fee. Admission notification on a rolling basis. **Financial aid:** Closing date 4/15. FAFSA, institutional form required. Applicants notified on a rolling basis.

Academics. Special study options: Cooperative education, distance learning, dual enrollment of high school students, ESL, internships, liberal arts/career combination, weekend college. Bachelor's degree programs available on campus. License preparation in dental hygiene, nursing, occupational therapy, physical therapy. **Credit/placement by examination:** AP, CLEP, IB. **Support services:** GED preparation and test center, learning center, reduced course load, remedial instruction, study skills assistance, tutoring, writing center.

Majors. Business: Accounting, administrative services, hospitality/recreation. **Computer sciences:** Data processing. **General:** Horticulture. **Health services:** Dental assistant, dental hygiene, licensed practical nurse, medical assistant. **Work/family studies:** Child care management.

Most popular majors. Computer/information sciences 17%, engineering/engineering technologies 13%, health sciences 38%, trade and industry 14%.

Computing on campus. 1,200 workstations in library, computer center. Online course registration, online library, wireless network available.

Student life. Freshman orientation: Available. Preregistration for classes offered. **Activities:** Student government.

Student services. Adult student services, career counseling, student employment services, on-campus daycare, personal counseling, placement for graduates. **Physically disabled:** Services for visually, speech, hearing impaired. **Transfer:** Pre-admission transcript evaluation for new students. Transfer adviser, college fairs on campus for students transferring to 4-year colleges.

Contact. E-mail: admissions@lwtech.edu
Phone: (425) 739-8104 Fax: (425) 739-8110
Cindy Mowry, Director of Enrollment Services, Lake Washington Institute of Technology, 11605 132nd Avenue, NE, Kirkland, WA 98034

Lower Columbia College
Longview, Washington
www.lowercolumbia.edu   CB code: 4402

- Public 2-year community college
- Commuter campus in small city

General. Founded in 1934. Regionally accredited. **Enrollment:** 2,021 degree-seeking undergraduates; 2,231 non-degree-seeking students. **Degrees:** 550 associate awarded. **Location:** 50 miles from Portland, Oregon, 120 miles from Seattle. **Calendar:** Quarter, limited summer session. **Full-time faculty:** 70 total; 44% women. **Part-time faculty:** 153 total. **Class size:** 60% < 20, 36% 20-39, 2% 40-49, 2% 50-99, less than 1% >100. **Special facilities:** Fine and performing arts center.

Student profile. Among degree-seeking undergraduates, 29% enrolled in a transfer program, 48% enrolled in a vocational program, 2% already have a bachelor's degree or higher, 388 enrolled as first-time, first-year students.

Part-time:	30%	Women:	61%
Out-of-state:	2%	25 or older:	55%

Transfer out. 50% of students enrolled in the transfer program go on to 4-year colleges. **Colleges most students transferred to 2011:** Washington State University-Vancouver, Washington State University-Pullman, Central Washington University, Eastern Washington University, Western Washington University.

Basis for selection. Open admission, but selective for some programs. Special requirements for nursing program and medical assistant program.

2011-2012 Annual costs. Tuition/fees: $3,790; $9,025 out-of-state. Books/supplies: $1,185. Personal expenses: $1,800.

2010-2011 Financial aid. Need-based: 4% of total undergraduate aid awarded as scholarships/grants, 96% as loans/jobs. Need-based aid available for part-time students. Work-study available nights, weekends and for part-time students.

Application procedures. Admission: No deadline. $30 fee. Admission notification on a rolling basis. **Financial aid:** Priority date 5/1; no closing date. FAFSA, institutional form required. Applicants notified on a rolling basis starting 4/21; must reply within 2 week(s) of notification.

Academics. Comprehensive tutoring and other support services available in LCC's Learning Commons. **Special study options:** Cooperative education, cross-registration, distance learning, dual enrollment of high school students, ESL, independent study, internships, liberal arts/career combination, student-designed major, teacher certification program. Bachelor's degree programs available on campus. License preparation in nursing. **Credit/placement by examination:** AP, CLEP, institutional tests. **Support services:** GED preparation and test center, learning center, reduced course load, remedial instruction, study skills assistance, tutoring, writing center.

Majors. Business: Accounting, accounting technology, administrative services, business admin, office technology, office/clerical. **Computer sciences:** General, computer science, data entry, data processing, networking, programming. **Education:** Elementary, teacher assistance. **Engineering:** General. **English:** English lit. **Health services:** Licensed practical nurse, medical assistant, medical secretary, nursing (RN), nursing assistant, substance abuse counseling. **Liberal arts:** Arts/sciences. **Protective services:** Law enforcement admin. **Work/family studies:** Child development.

Most popular majors. Business/marketing 8%, health sciences 27%, liberal arts 45%, trade and industry 13%.

Computing on campus. 450 workstations in library, computer center, student center. Online course registration, online library, wireless network available.

Student life. Freshman orientation: Available. Preregistration for classes offered. **Housing:** Apartments normally available in local community. **Activities:** Bands, choral groups, dance, drama, international student organizations, literary magazine, music ensembles, musical theater, student government, theater club, student nurses organization, services and relations club, campus entertainment, diesel mechanics club, Phi Theta Kappa.

Athletics. NJCAA. **Intercollegiate:** Baseball M, basketball, soccer W, softball W, volleyball W. **Team name:** Red Devils.

Student services. Adult student services, career counseling, services for economically disadvantaged, student employment services, financial aid counseling, on-campus daycare, personal counseling, placement for graduates, veterans' counselor. **Physically disabled:** Services for visually, speech, hearing impaired. **Transfer:** Re-entry adviser, pre-admission transcript evaluation for new students. Transfer center, transfer adviser, college fairs on campus for students transferring to 4-year colleges.

Contact. E-mail: entry@lowercolumbia.edu
Phone: (360) 442-2311 Toll-free number: (866) 900-2311
Fax: (360) 442-2379
Lynn Lawrence, Registrar, Lower Columbia College, 1600 Maple Street, Longview, WA 98632-0310

North Seattle Community College
Seattle, Washington
www.northseattle.edu   CB code: 4554

- Public 2-year community college
- Commuter campus in very large city

General. Founded in 1970. Regionally accredited. Associate degree and certificate programs available via elearning; college is committed to sustainability and environmentally responsible practices. **Enrollment:** 2,178 degree-seeking undergraduates; 4,099 non-degree-seeking students. **Degrees:** 694 associate awarded. **Location:** 8 miles from downtown. **Calendar:** Quarter, limited summer session. **Full-time faculty:** 89 total; 7% have terminal degrees, 32% minority, 56% women. **Part-time faculty:** 216 total; less than 1% have terminal degrees, 12% minority, 66% women. **Class size:** 16% < 20, 83% 20-39, less than 1% 40-49, less than 1% 50-99, less than 1% >100. **Special facilities:** Wetlands, wellness center, observatory. **Partnerships:** Formal partnerships with Rolex Watch USA, Comcast, Lennox / HVAC, Northwest Hospital, City of Seattle Municipal Court.

Student profile. Among degree-seeking undergraduates, 64% enrolled in a transfer program, 36% enrolled in a vocational program, 29% already have a bachelor's degree or higher, 549 enrolled as first-time, first-year students.

Part-time:	52%	Asian American:	12%
Out-of-state:	2%	Hispanic American:	7%
Women:	51%	Native American:	2%
African American:	6%	25 or older:	63%

Transfer out. Colleges most students transferred to 2011: University of Washington, Seattle University, Seattle Pacific University, Washington State University, Western Washington University.

Basis for selection. Open admission. Applicants with deficient English or Math skills are required to take remedial courses to qualify for college level work.

2011-2012 Annual costs. Tuition/fees: $3,676; $8,911 out-of-state. Books/supplies: $1,000. Personal expenses: $1,570.

2010-2011 Financial aid. Need-based: Need-based aid available for part-time students. Work-study available nights, weekends and for part-time students.

Application procedures. Admission: No deadline. No application fee. Admission notification on a rolling basis. **Financial aid:** Priority date 3/15, closing date 7/31. FAFSA, institutional form required. Applicants notified on a rolling basis starting 7/1; must reply within 2 week(s) of notification.

Academics. Special study options: Cooperative education, cross-registration, distance learning, dual enrollment of high school students, ESL, independent study, internships, liberal arts/career combination, study abroad. Bachelor's degree programs available on campus. License preparation in nursing, paramedic, real estate. **Credit/placement by examination:** AP, CLEP, IB, institutional tests. 45 credit hours maximum toward associate degree. **Support services:** GED preparation and test center, learning center, reduced course load, remedial instruction, study skills assistance, tutoring, writing center.

Majors. Business: General, accounting technology, administrative services, office management, office technology, office/clerical, real estate. **Communications technology:** General. **Computer sciences:** Networking. **Education:** General, early childhood. **Health services:** Licensed practical nurse, medical assistant, nursing (RN), office assistant, pharmacy assistant. **Visual/performing arts:** General, art, dramatic, music, studio arts.

Most popular majors. Business/marketing 21%, engineering/engineering technologies 6%, health sciences 19%, liberal arts 44%.

Computing on campus. 2,000 workstations in library, computer center, student center. Commuter students can connect to campus network. Online course registration, online library, helpline, student web hosting, wireless network available.

Student life. Freshman orientation: Available. Preregistration for classes offered. Students can select from in-person or on-line orientations. **Activities:** Bands, choral groups, drama, international student organizations, literary magazine, music ensembles, radio station, student government, symphony orchestra, TV station, Phi Theta Kappa, Black student union, Indonesian community club, Vietnamese student association, art group, student leadership council, Muslim student association, bio-med club, golf club, investment club.

Athletics. Intercollegiate: Basketball. **Intramural:** Basketball. **Team name:** Storm.

Student services. Adult student services, career counseling, services for economically disadvantaged, student employment services, financial aid counseling, minority student services, on-campus daycare, personal counseling, placement for graduates, veterans' counselor, women's services. **Physically disabled:** Services for visually, speech, hearing impaired. **Transfer:** Transfer adviser, college fairs on campus for students transferring to 4-year colleges.

Contact. E-mail: ARRC@sccd.ctc.edu
Phone: (206) 934-3663 Fax: (206) 934-3671
Betsy Abts, Registrar / Director of Admissions, North Seattle Community College, 9600 College Way North, Seattle, WA 98103-3599

Northwest Aviation College
Auburn, Washington
www.NorthwestAviationCollege.edu   CB code: 3115

- For-profit 2-year technical college
- Commuter campus in large town

General. Accredited by ACCSCT. **Location:** 7 miles from Seattle. **Calendar:** Quarter.

Annual costs/financial aid. Program costs for Associate program in Aviation Flight Technology range from $6,283 to $77,476; Ceriticate programs for Professional Pilot 1: $66,603; Professional Pilot 2: $72,328; Professional Pilot 3: $74,100. All costs include tuition, books, materials, aircraft rental.

Contact. Phone: (253) 854-4960
Director of Education, 506 23rd Street, NE, Auburn, WA 98002

Northwest Indian College
Bellingham, Washington
www.nwic.edu   CB code: 3973

- Public 2-year Tribal college
- Commuter campus in small town

General. Regionally accredited. **Enrollment:** 551 degree-seeking undergraduates. **Degrees:** 3 bachelor's, 69 associate awarded. **Location:** 8 miles from Bellingham. **Calendar:** Quarter, limited summer session. **Full-time faculty:** 22 total. **Part-time faculty:** 45 total.

Transfer out. Colleges most students transferred to 2011: Western Washington University, University of Washington, Lewis-Clark State College.

Basis for selection. Open admission. **Adult students:** SAT/ACT scores not required.

2012-2013 Annual costs. Tuition/fees (projected): $3,720; $9,588 out-of-state. Per-credit charge: $95 in-state; $258 out-of-state. Books/supplies: $960. Personal expenses: $1,725.

2010-2011 Financial aid. Need-based: 98% of total undergraduate aid awarded as scholarships/grants, 2% as loans/jobs. Need-based aid available for part-time students. Work-study available nights, weekends and for part-time students. **Non-need-based:** Scholarships awarded for academics.

Application procedures. Admission: Priority date 5/1; no deadline. No application fee. Application must be submitted on paper. Admission notification on a rolling basis. **Financial aid:** No deadline. FAFSA, institutional form required. Applicants notified on a rolling basis.

Academics. Special study options: Cooperative education, distance learning, dual enrollment of high school students, independent study, internships, student-designed major. Bachelor's degree programs available on campus. **Credit/placement by examination:** AP, CLEP, institutional tests. **Support services:** GED preparation and test center, learning center, reduced course load, remedial instruction, study skills assistance, tutoring, writing center.

Majors. Area/ethnic studies: Native American. **Business:** Business admin. **Computer sciences:** Information technology. **Education:** Early childhood, Native American.

Most popular majors. Area/ethnic studies 25%, health sciences 10%, liberal arts 65%.

Computing on campus. 90 workstations in dormitories, library, computer center, student center. Dormitories wired for high-speed internet access and linked to campus network. Online course registration, helpline, repair service, wireless network available.

Student life. Freshman orientation: Available. Preregistration for classes offered. First days of fall quarter. **Housing:** Guaranteed on-campus for all undergraduates. Coed dorms, wellness housing available. $200 fully refundable deposit. Family housing available. **Activities:** Drama, student government, student newspaper, service learning center, culture club.

Athletics. Intercollegiate: Basketball. **Intramural:** Basketball. **Team name:** Eagles.

Student services. Adult student services, alcohol/substance abuse counseling, career counseling, services for economically disadvantaged, student employment services, financial aid counseling, minority student services, on-campus daycare. **Transfer:** Pre-admission transcript evaluation for new students. Transfer adviser, college fairs on campus for students transferring to 4-year colleges.

Contact. E-mail: admissions@nwic.edu
Phone: (360) 676-2772 ext. 4269
Toll-free number: (866) 676-2772 ext. 4269 Fax: (360) 392-4333
Crystal Bagby, Associate Dean of Student Services, Northwest Indian College, 2522 Kwina Road, Bellingham, WA 98226-9217

Northwest School of Wooden Boatbuilding
Port Hadlock, Washington
www.nwboatschool.org   CB code: 3116

- Private 1-year technical and maritime college
- Commuter campus in large town

General. Accredited by ACCSC. Institution teaches traditional and contemporary wooden boatbuilding, including woodworking, drafting, lofting, repair and restoration, and yacht interiors. Supplemental courses are available in sailmaking, blacksmithing, rigging, boat design, and systems and wiring. **Enrollment:** 44 degree-seeking undergraduates. **Degrees:** 6 associate awarded. **Location:** 60 miles from Seattle. **Calendar:** Quarter, limited summer session. **Full-time faculty:** 4 total. **Part-time faculty:** 2 total. **Special facilities:** Campus located on the Puget Sound. Classes take place in boathouses over the water.

Student profile.

Out-of-state:	80%	25 or older:	75%

Basis for selection. Open admission.

2011-2012 Annual costs. Twelve month AOS degree programs offered at a cost of $17,400. Estimated cost of tools $1,300-$1,500; nine month diploma programs range from $11,925 to $13,050; registration fee cost $100. Books/supplies: $1,000.

Financial aid. Need-based: Work-study available nights, weekends and for part-time students.

Application procedures. Admission: No deadline. $100 fee. Application must be submitted on paper. Admission notification on a rolling basis.

Academics. Credit/placement by examination: AP, CLEP.

Computing on campus. 1 workstations in library.

Student life. Freshman orientation: Mandatory. Preregistration for classes offered.

Contact. E-mail: info@nwboatschool.org
Phone: (360) 385-4948 Fax: (360) 385-5089
Laura Allen, Director of Admissions, Northwest School of Wooden Boatbuilding, 42 North Water Street, Port Hadlock, WA 98339

Olympic College
Bremerton, Washington
www.olympic.edu

CB member
CB code: 4583

- Public 2-year community and liberal arts college
- Commuter campus in large town

General. Founded in 1946. Regionally accredited. Campuses at Shelton and Poulsbo. Classes also offered off-campus at Naval Base Kitsap and Westsound Technical Skills Center. **Enrollment:** 8,503 undergraduates. **Degrees:** 8 bachelor's, 1,064 associate awarded. **Calendar:** Quarter, extensive summer session. **Full-time faculty:** 124 total. **Part-time faculty:** 385 total. **Partnerships:** Formal partnerships with Puget Sound Naval Shipyard, West Sound Technical, US Navy, Service Corps of Retired Executives, the NW Women's Business Center, Apprentice, and the Navy College Program Distance Learning Partnership.

Student profile. 68% enrolled in a transfer program, 32% enrolled in a vocational program.

Transfer out. Colleges most students transferred to 2011: University of Washington, Central Washington University, Washington State University, Western Washington University.

Basis for selection. Open admission, but selective for some programs. Admission to associate degree nursing, physical therapy assistant, licensed practical nursing, medical office assistant program based on several requirements which may include: completion of pre-requisite courses, course grade or cumulative academic GPA, test scores, basic first aid certification. English and Math placement assessment administered to degree/certificate-seeking applicants or for those who wish to enroll in English or Math classes. Nursing and health occupation programs require students to attend a pre-application orientation. The PTA program requires an essay. **Adult students:** SAT/ACT scores not required. All students, including international students, must complete an English and mathematics skills level test upon arrival for placement at the appropriate level. **Home schooled:** Transcript of courses and grades required. Home school applicants who have not yet completed high school graduation must provide a transcript. **Learning Disabled:** Students with learning disabilities may self-identify and access services such as special testing, note-taking, counseling, course selection, sign language interpreters, materials in alternate format, specialized equipment and adaptive technology and other similar accommodations.

2011-2012 Annual costs. Tuition/fees: $3,737; $8,972 out-of-state. Books/supplies: $972. Personal expenses: $1,524.

Financial aid. Need-based: Need-based aid available for part-time students. Work-study available nights, weekends and for part-time students. **Non-need-based:** Scholarships awarded for academics, state residency. **Additional information:** Waivers available for select groups including Fallen Veterans, Children of Deceased or Disabled Law Enforcement Officers, and others.

Application procedures. Admission: No deadline. No application fee. Admission notification on a rolling basis. **Financial aid:** Priority date 3/1; no closing date. FAFSA, institutional form required. Applicants notified on a rolling basis starting 6/1; must reply within 2 week(s) of notification.

Academics. Special study options: Cooperative education, cross-registration, distance learning, dual enrollment of high school students, ESL, independent study, internships, liberal arts/career combination, student-designed major. 2+2 program with Old Dominion University and Western Washington University for BA on Bremerton Olympic College campus. Dual enrollment Running Start Program available for high school juniors/seniors. Dual admission for International students. Bachelor's degree programs available on campus. License preparation in nursing, physical therapy. **Credit/placement by examination:** AP, CLEP, IB, institutional tests. Credit awarded by exam, experiential credit, or CLEP varies by degree program. **Support services:** GED preparation and test center, learning center, reduced course load, remedial instruction, study skills assistance, tutoring, writing center.

Majors. Biology: General, marine. **Business:** Accounting technology, business admin, hospitality admin, organizational leadership. **Communications technology:** Animation/special effects. **Computer sciences:** Networking, programming. **Conservation:** General. **Education:** Early childhood, teacher assistance. **Health services:** Medical assistant, nursing (RN), physical therapy assistant, substance abuse counseling. **Math:** General. **Physical sciences:** Chemistry, geology, physics. **Protective services:** Firefighting, police science. **Psychology:** General. **Visual/performing arts:** General, art, digital arts, dramatic, game design, multimedia, music.

Computing on campus. 500 workstations in library, computer center, student center. Commuter students can connect to campus network. Online library, helpline, student web hosting, wireless network available.

Student life. Freshman orientation: Available. Preregistration for classes offered. In-person or online. In-person orientation takes place before advising. **Policies:** Student code of conduct. **Housing:** Apartments available for out-of-region students. International students may choose Homestay. **Activities:** Bands, choral groups, drama, international student organizations, music ensembles, musical theater, opera, student government, student newspaper, symphony orchestra, American Sign Language club, engineering club, Eskrima, gay straight alliance, international student club, MESA, clay club, Phi Theta Kappa.

Athletics. Intercollegiate: Baseball M, basketball, cross-country, golf, soccer, softball W, volleyball W. **Intramural:** Basketball, table tennis, volleyball, weight lifting. **Team name:** Rangers.

Student services. Adult student services, career counseling, services for economically disadvantaged, student employment services, financial aid counseling, minority student services, on-campus daycare, personal counseling, placement for graduates, veterans' counselor, women's services. **Physically disabled:** Services for visually, speech, hearing impaired. **Transfer:** Re-entry adviser for new students. Transfer adviser, college fairs on campus for students transferring to 4-year colleges.

Contact. E-mail: prospect@olympic.edu
Phone: (360) 475-7479 Toll-free number: (800) 259-6718 ext. 7479
Fax: (360) 475-7202
Jennifer Fyllingness, Director of Admissions and Outreach, Olympic College, 1600 Chester Avenue, Bremerton, WA 98337-1699

Peninsula College
Port Angeles, Washington
www.pencol.edu

CB code: 4615

- Public 2-year community college
- Commuter campus in large town

General. Founded in 1961. Regionally accredited. **Enrollment:** 1,310 degree-seeking undergraduates. **Degrees:** 9 bachelor's, 330 associate awarded. **Location:** 75 miles from Seattle. **Calendar:** Quarter, limited summer session. **Full-time faculty:** 57 total. **Part-time faculty:** 187 total. **Class size:** 82% < 20, 17% 20-39, less than 1% 40-49, less than 1% 50-99. **Special facilities:** Marine laboratory, dam removal project.

Student profile.

Out-of-state:	1%	25 or older:	41%

Basis for selection. Open admission, but selective for some programs. Special requirements for nursing program. COMPASS/ASSET required for full-time applicants for placement only. Admission to college does not guarantee admission to all courses or vocational education programs. Additional applications may be necessary. **Adult students:** SAT/ACT scores not required.

2011-2012 Annual costs. Tuition/fees: $3,892; $9,127 out-of-state. Books/supplies: $972. Personal expenses: $1,679.

Financial aid. Need-based: Need-based aid available for part-time students. Work-study available nights, weekends and for part-time students. **Non-need-based:** Scholarships awarded for academics, athletics, job skills.

Application procedures. Admission: No deadline. No application fee. Admission notification on a rolling basis. **Financial aid:** Closing date 4/1. FAFSA, institutional form required. Applicants notified on a rolling basis starting 6/1; must reply within 2 week(s) of notification.

Academics. Special study options: Distance learning, double major, dual enrollment of high school students, ESL, honors, internships, liberal arts/career combination, study abroad. Bachelor's degree programs available on campus. License preparation in dental hygiene, nursing. **Credit/placement by examination:** AP, CLEP, institutional tests. 10 credit hours maximum toward associate degree. Must complete minimum 30 quarter hours of credit in residency with 2.75 GPA. **Support services:** GED preparation and test center, learning center, reduced course load, remedial instruction, study skills assistance, tutoring, writing center.

Majors. Business: Accounting, accounting technology, administrative services, business admin, marketing, office management. **Communications:** Journalism. **Computer sciences:** General, applications programming, data processing, networking, vendor certification, web page design. **Conservation:** Fisheries. **Education:** Early childhood. **Health services:** Home attendant, medical assistant, medical secretary, nursing (RN), substance abuse counseling. **Liberal arts:** Arts/sciences. **Protective services:** Corrections, law enforcement admin. **Work/family studies:** Child care management, child care service.

Most popular majors. Health sciences 17%, liberal arts 64%, natural resources/environmental science 7%.

Computing on campus. 79 workstations in library, computer center, student center. Online course registration, online library, wireless network available.

Student life. Freshman orientation: Available. Preregistration for classes offered. **Activities:** Jazz band, choral groups, dance, drama, literary magazine, music ensembles, student government, student newspaper, Christian collegiate fellowship, communications careers club, Native American Nations, Phi Theta Kappa, Phi Beta Lambda, IT club, basketball club, German club.

Athletics. Intercollegiate: Basketball, soccer. **Intramural:** Basketball, soccer, tennis, volleyball. **Team name:** Pirates.

Student services. Adult student services, career counseling, services for economically disadvantaged, student employment services, financial aid counseling, on-campus daycare, personal counseling, placement for graduates, veterans' counselor. **Physically disabled:** Services for visually, hearing impaired. **Transfer:** Pre-admission transcript evaluation for new students. Transfer adviser, college fairs on campus for students transferring to 4-year colleges.

Contact. E-mail: admissions@pencol.edu
Phone: (877) 452-9277 Toll-free number: (877) 452-9277
Fax: (360) 417-6581
Krista Francis, Enrollment Service Manager, Peninsula College, 1502 East Lauridsen Boulevard, Port Angeles, WA 98362

Pierce College
Lakewood, Washington
www.pierce.ctc.edu   CB code: 4103

◗ Public 2-year community college
◗ Commuter campus in small city

General. Founded in 1967. Regionally accredited. Colleges in Puyallup and Lakewood. Education centers at Jointbase Lewis McChord (JBLM), McNeil Island, Cedar Creek, Western State Hospital and Rainier School. **Enrollment:** 9,392 degree-seeking undergraduates. **Degrees:** 1,507 associate awarded. **ROTC:** Army. **Location:** 10 miles from downtown. **Calendar:** Quarter, limited summer session. **Full-time faculty:** 124 total. **Part-time faculty:** 303 total. **Special facilities:** Bird refuge, international house (video conferencing center for international/cross-cultural communications).

Transfer out. Colleges most students transferred to 2011: University of Washington, Evergreen State College, Central Washington University, St. Martin's University, Western Washington University.

Basis for selection. Open admission, but selective for some programs. Admissions to dental hygiene and veterinary technology programs based on college course work, high school GPA, and/or related work experience. Running Start students must test at college level in English prior to admission. Students required to take ASSET or COMPASS placement tests to register for math, English, or reading courses. **Adult students:** SAT/ACT scores not required. Placement testing required for English and Quantitative courses. **Learning Disabled:** Accommodations for placement testing.

High school preparation. Algebra, biology, and chemistry required of veterinary technology applicants. Dental hygiene applicants have special mathematics/science requirements.

2011-2012 Annual costs. Tuition/fees: $3,883; $9,118 out-of-state.

Financial aid. Need-based: Need-based aid available for part-time students. Work-study available nights, weekends and for part-time students. **Non-need-based:** Scholarships awarded for academics, athletics, music/drama.

Application procedures. Admission: No deadline. $25 fee. Admission notification on a rolling basis. March 1 closing date for veterinary technology applications, February 1 for dental hygiene. High school students admitted early through Running Start Program. Must test at college level prior to admission. **Financial aid:** Closing date 5/1. FAFSA, institutional form required. Applicants notified on a rolling basis starting 4/15.

Academics. Special study options: Cooperative education, cross-registration, distance learning, double major, dual enrollment of high school students, ESL, independent study, internships, student-designed major, study abroad, weekend college. License preparation in dental hygiene, nursing. **Credit/placement by examination:** AP, CLEP, institutional tests. 25 credit hours maximum toward associate degree. Credit by exam does not count toward degree residency requirement. **Support services:** GED preparation and test center, learning center, pre-admission summer program, reduced course load, remedial instruction, study skills assistance, tutoring, writing center.

Majors. Business: General, accounting, administrative services, business admin, office management, office/clerical. **Computer sciences:** Data processing, programming. **Education:** Business, early childhood, teacher assistance. **Foreign languages:** Translation. **General:** Animal sciences. **Health services:** Clinical lab assistant, dental hygiene, medical secretary, mental health services, substance abuse counseling, veterinary technology/assistant. **Liberal arts:** Arts/sciences. **Protective services:** Criminal justice, fire safety technology. **Visual/performing arts:** Commercial/advertising art. **Work/family studies:** Child care management.

Computing on campus. Online course registration, online library, helpline, wireless network available.

Student life. Freshman orientation: Mandatory. Preregistration for classes offered. Orientation offered quarterly and throughout summer. **Activities:** Bands, choral groups, drama, literary magazine, music ensembles, musical theater, student government, student newspaper, ethnic and foreign student associations, religious organizations, special interest clubs, Phi Theta Kappa.

Athletics. Intercollegiate: Baseball M, basketball, soccer M, softball W, volleyball W. **Intramural:** Cheerleading. **Team name:** Raiders.

Student services. Adult student services, career counseling, services for economically disadvantaged, student employment services, financial aid counseling, minority student services, on-campus daycare, personal counseling, veterans' counselor, women's services. **Physically disabled:** Services for visually, speech, hearing impaired. **Transfer:** Transfer center, transfer adviser, college fairs on campus for students transferring to 4-year colleges.

Contact. E-mail: admiss1@pierce.ctc.edu
Phone: (253) 964-6501 Fax: (253) 964-6427
Maggie Segesser, Director of Admissions, Pierce College, 9401 Farwest Drive SW, Lakewood, WA 98498-1999

Renton Technical College
Renton, Washington
www.RTC.edu   CB code: 0790

◗ Public 2-year technical college
◗ Commuter campus in large town

General. Founded in 1942. Regionally accredited. **Enrollment:** 1,337 degree-seeking undergraduates. **Degrees:** 439 associate awarded. **Location:** 10 miles from Seattle. **Calendar:** Quarter, extensive summer session. **Full-time faculty:** 67 total. **Part-time faculty:** 121 total. **Special facilities:** Technology resource center.

Basis for selection. Open admission. ACT, ASSET and SLEP scores required for all applicants for placement purposes. Interview recommended. **Adult students:** Students must complete on-campus assessment.

2011-2012 Annual costs. Tuition/fees: $3,895; $7,750 out-of-state. Books/supplies: $972. Personal expenses: $1,530.

Financial aid. All financial aid based on need. Need-based aid available for part-time students. Work-study available nights, weekends and for part-time students.

Application procedures. **Admission:** No deadline. $30 fee. Application must be submitted on paper. Admission notification on a rolling basis. **Financial aid:** Priority date 5/1; no closing date. FAFSA, institutional form required. Applicants notified on a rolling basis.

Academics. Many programs have co-op component. **Special study options:** Cooperative education, distance learning, dual enrollment of high school students, ESL, external degree, internships, liberal arts/career combination, student-designed major. License preparation in nursing, real estate. **Credit/placement by examination:** AP, CLEP. 30 credit hours maximum toward associate degree. **Support services:** GED preparation and test center, learning center, remedial instruction, study skills assistance, tutoring.

Majors. **Business:** Accounting, administrative services, office management, office/clerical. **Computer sciences:** Applications programming, computer science, networking, programming. **Education:** Business, early childhood, teacher assistance, voc/tech. **Engineering:** Electrical. **Health services:** Dental assistant, insurance coding, licensed practical nurse, massage therapy, medical assistant, medical records admin, medical secretary, pharmacy assistant, surgical technology. **Work/family studies:** Child care management.

Computing on campus. 150 workstations in library, computer center, student center. Online library available.

Student life. **Freshman orientation:** Available. Preregistration for classes offered. **Activities:** Student newspaper.

Student services. Career counseling, student employment services, financial aid counseling, on-campus daycare, personal counseling, placement for graduates. **Physically disabled:** Services for visually, speech, hearing impaired. **Transfer:** Pre-admission transcript evaluation for new students. Transfer adviser for students transferring to 4-year colleges.

Contact. E-mail: briverman@rtc.edu
Phone: (425) 235-5840 Fax: (425) 235-7832
Becky Riverman, Director of Admission, Renton Technical College, 3000 NE Fourth Street, Renton, WA 98056-4195

Seattle Central Community College
Seattle, Washington
www.seattlecentral.edu
CB code: 4033

- Public 2-year community college
- Commuter campus in very large city

General. Founded in 1966. Regionally accredited. **Enrollment:** 9,859 degree-seeking undergraduates. **Degrees:** 16 bachelor's, 1,039 associate awarded. **Calendar:** Quarter, limited summer session. **Full-time faculty:** 157 total. **Part-time faculty:** 321 total.

Basis for selection. Open admission, but selective for some programs. Limited admission to health sciences and vocational programs. Essay, interview recommended for all; audition recommended for music; portfolio required for art, photography.

2011-2012 Annual costs. Tuition/fees: $3,773; $9,008 out-of-state. Books/supplies: $924. Personal expenses: $1,896.

Financial aid. All financial aid based on need. Need-based aid available for part-time students. Work-study available nights, weekends and for part-time students. **Additional information:** Currently enrolled international students can apply for institutional scholarship in second year of study.

Application procedures. **Admission:** No deadline. No application fee. Admission notification on a rolling basis. **Financial aid:** Closing date 7/27. FAFSA, institutional form required. Applicants notified on a rolling basis; must reply within 2 week(s) of notification.

Academics. **Special study options:** Cooperative education, distance learning, dual enrollment of high school students, independent study, internships, study abroad. **Credit/placement by examination:** AP, CLEP, institutional tests. **Support services:** GED preparation, learning center, remedial instruction, tutoring.

Majors. **Biology:** Biotechnology. **Business:** Accounting, administrative services, fashion. **Communications:** Advertising, communications/speech/rhetoric. **Communications technology:** Graphic/printing, graphics, photo/film/video, printing management. **Computer sciences:** General, applications programming, information technology, programming. **Education:** General. **Foreign languages:** Sign language interpretation. **Health services:** Mental health services, preop/surgical nursing, respiratory therapy technology. **Liberal arts:** Arts/sciences. **Visual/performing arts:** Commercial photography.

Computing on campus. 190 workstations in library, computer center, student center.

Student life. **Freshman orientation:** Mandatory. Preregistration for classes offered. **Activities:** Choral groups, dance, drama, student government, student newspaper, numerous ethnic/minority, socio-political, cultural clubs available.

Athletics. **Intramural:** Baseball M, basketball, soccer, volleyball.

Student services. Career counseling, student employment services, financial aid counseling, minority student services, on-campus daycare, personal counseling, veterans' counselor, women's services. **Physically disabled:** Services for visually, speech, hearing impaired. **Transfer:** Transfer adviser, college fairs on campus for students transferring to 4-year colleges.

Contact. E-mail: admiss@sccd.ctc.edu
Phone: (206) 587-5450 Fax: (206) 587-6321
Diane Coleman, Associate Dean of Enrollment Services, Seattle Central Community College, 1701 Broadway, Seattle, WA 98122

Shoreline Community College
Shoreline, Washington
www.shoreline.edu
CB code: 4738

- Public 2-year community college
- Commuter campus in small city

General. Founded in 1964. Regionally accredited. **Enrollment:** 2,435 degree-seeking undergraduates. **Degrees:** 824 associate awarded. **Location:** 10 miles from Seattle. **Calendar:** Quarter, limited summer session. **Full-time faculty:** 111 total. **Part-time faculty:** 244 total.

Transfer out. **Colleges most students transferred to 2011:** University of Washington, Western Washington University.

Basis for selection. Open admission, but selective for some programs. SAT, ACT, or ASSET required for English and math placement unless student has taken college-level English or math with grades of C or better. Nursing and dental hygiene programs use competitive admissions process.

2011-2012 Annual costs. Tuition/fees: $3,999; $9,234 out-of-state. Books/supplies: $924. Personal expenses: $3,516.

Financial aid. **Need-based:** Work-study available nights, weekends and for part-time students. **Additional information:** Tuition and/or fee waiver for students with need on space-available basis.

Application procedures. **Admission:** No deadline. No application fee. Admission notification on a rolling basis. **Financial aid:** Closing date 3/31. FAFSA, institutional form required. Applicants notified on a rolling basis starting 8/1; must reply within 3 week(s) of notification.

Academics. **Special study options:** Cooperative education, cross-registration, distance learning, dual enrollment of high school students, ESL, independent study, internships, study abroad. Senior College for senior citizens. **Credit/placement by examination:** AP, CLEP, IB. **Support services:** GED preparation and test center, learning center, remedial instruction, tutoring.

Majors. **Biology:** Biotechnology. **Business:** Accounting technology, business admin, fashion, international, logistics, marketing, sales/distribution, small business admin. **Communications:** Broadcast journalism. **Communications technology:** Graphic/printing. **Computer sciences:** General, data processing, database management, networking, web page design. **Education:** Early childhood, special ed, teacher assistance. **Engineering:** General, civil, mechanical. **Health services:** Clinical lab assistant, dental hygiene, dietetics, medical records technology, nursing (RN). **Liberal arts:** Arts/sciences. **Physical sciences:** General, oceanography. **Protective services:** Law enforcement

admin. **Visual/performing arts:** Cinematography, commercial/advertising art, design, music management, music performance, photography, theater design. **Work/family studies:** Food/nutrition.

Most popular majors. Business/marketing 10%, liberal arts 86%.

Computing on campus. 450 workstations in library, computer center. Commuter students can connect to campus network. Online library, helpline, wireless network available.

Student life. Freshman orientation: Mandatory. Preregistration for classes offered. Two to three hours, prior to each quarter. **Activities:** Bands, choral groups, drama, international student organizations, literary magazine, music ensembles, musical theater, opera, student government, student newspaper, black student union, arts and entertainment board, women's club, Cambodian club, Vietnamese club, DEC, Phi Theta Kappa.

Athletics. NJCAA. **Intercollegiate:** Baseball M, basketball, soccer, softball W, tennis, volleyball W. **Intramural:** Archery, basketball, bowling, diving, fencing, golf, racquetball, skiing, soccer, softball W, swimming, tennis, volleyball. **Team name:** Dolphins.

Student services. Adult student services, career counseling, student employment services, financial aid counseling, minority student services, on-campus daycare, personal counseling, placement for graduates, veterans' counselor, women's services. **Physically disabled:** Services for visually, hearing impaired. **Transfer:** Transfer adviser, college fairs on campus for students transferring to 4-year colleges.

Contact. E-mail: sccadmis@ctc.edu
Phone: (206) 546-4621 Fax: (206) 546-5835
Chris Melton, Registrar, Shoreline Community College, 16101 Greenwood Avenue North, Seattle, WA 98133

Skagit Valley College
Mount Vernon, Washington
www.skagit.edu   CB code: 4699

- Public 2-year community college
- Commuter campus in large town

General. Founded in 1926. Regionally accredited. 2 campuses: Mount Vernon (main campus) and Oak Harbor on Whidbey Island. **Enrollment:** 5,763 degree-seeking undergraduates. **Degrees:** 607 associate awarded. **Location:** 60 miles from Seattle, 90 miles from Vancouver, British Columbia. **Calendar:** Quarter, extensive summer session. **Full-time faculty:** 114 total. **Part-time faculty:** 179 total. **Partnerships:** Contract programs with Washington businesses, Tech Prep, College in the High School.

Transfer out. Colleges most students transferred to 2011: Everett Community College, Whatcom Community College, Western Washington University, Edmonds Community College, University of Washington.

Basis for selection. Open admission. High school diploma required for some programs.

2011-2012 Annual costs. Tuition/fees: $3,797; $9,032 out-of-state. Room only: $3,870. Books/supplies: $900.

Financial aid. All financial aid based on need. Need-based aid available for part-time students. Work-study available nights, weekends and for part-time students.

Application procedures. Admission: No deadline. No application fee. Admission notification on a rolling basis. **Financial aid:** Priority date 5/1; no closing date. FAFSA, institutional form required. Applicants notified on a rolling basis starting 7/1; must reply within 2 week(s) of notification.

Academics. Special study options: Cooperative education, cross-registration, distance learning, dual enrollment of high school students, ESL, external degree, honors, independent study, internships. License preparation in nursing. **Credit/placement by examination:** AP, CLEP, IB, institutional tests. 15 credit hours maximum toward associate degree. **Support services:** GED preparation and test center, learning center, pre-admission summer program, reduced course load, remedial instruction, study skills assistance, tutoring, writing center.

Majors. Business: Accounting, administrative services, business admin, hospitality/recreation. **Communications:** Communications/speech/rhetoric. **Computer sciences:** General, applications programming, information systems, programming. **Conservation:** Environmental science. **Education:** Early childhood. **Engineering:** Electrical. **General:** Business, dairy, horticulture. **Health services:** Licensed practical nurse, nursing (RN), prenursing.

Liberal arts: Arts/sciences. **Protective services:** Firefighting, law enforcement admin. **Visual/performing arts:** Commercial/advertising art.

Computing on campus. 250 workstations in library, computer center. Commuter students can connect to campus network. Online course registration, helpline, repair service, student web hosting available.

Student life. Freshman orientation: Available. Preregistration for classes offered. Orientation/registration/testing before start of each quarter. Evening and day orientation at beginning of each quarter. **Housing:** Apartments available. $180 deposit. **Activities:** Bands, choral groups, dance, drama, literary magazine, music ensembles, musical theater, radio station, student government, student newspaper, symphony orchestra, Calling All Color, nurses club, firefighters club, Campus Christian Fellowship, sailing club, Delta Epsilon Chi, ski club, horticultural club, Phi Theta Kappa, international club.

Athletics. Intercollegiate: Baseball M, basketball, golf, soccer, softball W, tennis, volleyball W. **Intramural:** Badminton, baseball M, basketball, bowling, golf, sailing, soccer, softball, tennis, volleyball. **Team name:** Cardinals.

Student services. Adult student services, career counseling, services for economically disadvantaged, student employment services, financial aid counseling, health services, minority student services, on-campus daycare, personal counseling, placement for graduates, veterans' counselor, women's services. **Physically disabled:** Services for visually, speech, hearing impaired. **Transfer:** Re-entry adviser, pre-admission transcript evaluation for new students. Transfer center, transfer adviser, college fairs on campus for students transferring to 4-year colleges.

Contact. E-mail: admissions@skagit.edu
Phone: (360) 416-7697 Toll-free number: (877) 385-5360
Fax: (360) 416-7890
Karen Bade, Recruitment & Admissions Coordinator, Skagit Valley College, 2405 East College Way, Mount Vernon, WA 98273

South Puget Sound Community College
Olympia, Washington   CB member
www.spscc.ctc.edu   CB code: 4578

- Public 2-year community college
- Commuter campus in small city

General. Founded in 1962. Regionally accredited. **Enrollment:** 3,635 degree-seeking undergraduates. **Degrees:** 1,007 associate awarded. **ROTC:** Air Force. **Location:** 60 miles from Seattle. **Calendar:** Quarter, limited summer session. **Full-time faculty:** 96 total. **Part-time faculty:** 258 total.

Student profile.

Out-of-state:	3%	**25 or older:**	41%

Transfer out. Colleges most students transferred to 2011: Evergreen State College, St. Martin University, University of Washington, Washington State University, Western Washington State University.

Basis for selection. Open admission, but selective for some programs. Special requirements for nursing, dental assisting, fire protection. **Adult students:** CASAS required for Adult Basic Education.

2011-2012 Annual costs. Tuition/fees: $3,585; $8,820 out-of-state. Books/supplies: $904. Personal expenses: $3,018.

Financial aid. Need-based: Need-based aid available for part-time students. Work-study available nights, weekends and for part-time students. **Non-need-based:** Scholarships awarded for academics, athletics.

Application procedures. Admission: Closing date 9/5. No application fee. Admission notification on a rolling basis beginning on or about 12/1. Early applicants register in mid-July for fall quarter. **Financial aid:** Priority date 5/1, closing date 6/27. FAFSA, institutional form required. Applicants notified on a rolling basis starting 7/10; must reply within 2 week(s) of notification.

Academics. Special study options: Cooperative education, cross-registration, distance learning, dual enrollment of high school students, ESL, honors, independent study, internships, study abroad, weekend college. License preparation in nursing. **Credit/placement by examination:** AP, CLEP, IB, institutional tests. 45 credit hours maximum toward associate degree. **Support services:** GED preparation and test center, learning center, remedial instruction, study skills assistance, tutoring, writing center.

Majors. Business: General, accounting, administrative services, hospitality admin, office/clerical. **Computer sciences:** Applications programming, data

processing, information systems. **Education:** Early childhood. **General:** Horticulture, ornamental horticulture. **Health services:** Dental assistant, medical assistant, medical secretary, nursing assistant. **Liberal arts:** Arts/sciences. **Protective services:** Firefighting.

Most popular majors. Business/marketing 7%, health sciences 14%, liberal arts 66%.

Computing on campus. 117 workstations in library, computer center, student center. Commuter students can connect to campus network. Online course registration, online library, wireless network available.

Student life. Freshman orientation: Available. Preregistration for classes offered. **Activities:** Choral groups, drama, international student organizations, music ensembles, musical theater, student government, student newspaper.

Athletics. Intercollegiate: Basketball, soccer M, softball W. **Team name:** Clippers.

Student services. Adult student services, career counseling, services for economically disadvantaged, student employment services, financial aid counseling, minority student services, on-campus daycare, personal counseling, placement for graduates, veterans' counselor. **Physically disabled:** Services for visually, speech, hearing impaired. **Transfer:** Transfer adviser, college fairs on campus for students transferring to 4-year colleges.

Contact. E-mail: enrollmentservices@spscc.ctc.edu
Phone: (360) 754-7711 ext. 5241 Fax: (360) 596-5907
Lyn Sharp, Director of Admissions and Registration, South Puget Sound Community College, 2011 Mottman Road, SW, Olympia, WA 98512-6218

South Seattle Community College
Seattle, Washington
www.southseattle.edu   **CB code: 4759**

▶ Public 2-year community college
▶ Commuter campus in very large city

General. Founded in 1969. Regionally accredited. Culturally diverse campus with over 35 languages spoken. **Enrollment:** 4,213 degree-seeking undergraduates. **Degrees:** 20 bachelor's, 529 associate awarded. **Location:** 10 minutes from downtown. **Calendar:** Quarter, limited summer session. **Full-time faculty:** 75 total; 11% have terminal degrees, 28% minority, 40% women. **Part-time faculty:** 214 total; 15% minority, 58% women. **Special facilities:** College operates a bakery and restaurants; arboretum, Seattle Chinese garden.

Transfer out. Colleges most students transferred to 2011: University of Washington.

Basis for selection. Open admission, but selective for some programs. COMPASS, ESL COMPASS tests used for placement and counseling. **Learning Disabled:** Referred to Educational Support Services Office.

High school preparation. College-preparatory program required.

2011-2012 Annual costs. Tuition/fees: $3,707; $8,942 out-of-state. Books/supplies: $972. Personal expenses: $4,230.

Financial aid. Need-based: Need-based aid available for part-time students. Work-study available nights, weekends and for part-time students. **Non-need-based:** Scholarships awarded for academics, state residency.

Application procedures. Admission: No deadline. No application fee. Admission notification on a rolling basis. **Financial aid:** Priority date 4/16; no closing date. FAFSA, institutional form required. Applicants notified on a rolling basis starting 7/1.

Academics. Special study options: Cross-registration, distance learning, dual enrollment of high school students, ESL, independent study, internships, study abroad. Concurrent enrollment agreements with other colleges. Bachelor's degree programs available on campus. License preparation in aviation, nursing. **Credit/placement by examination:** AP, CLEP, IB, institutional tests. Credit awarded for CLEP applies only to electives category of Associate of Arts degree. **Support services:** GED preparation and test center, learning center, reduced course load, remedial instruction, study skills assistance, tutoring, writing center.

Majors. Biology: General. **Business:** General, accounting, hospitality admin, office management, office technology, restaurant/food services. **Computer sciences:** LAN/WAN management, system admin, web page design, webmaster. **Engineering:** General, software. **General:** Horticultural science,

---

landscaping. **Health services:** Licensed practical nurse, premedicine, prenursing, prepharmacy. **Liberal arts:** Arts/sciences. **Physical sciences:** Atmospheric science, chemistry.

Computing on campus. 700 workstations in library, computer center, student center. Online course registration, online library, wireless network available.

Student life. Freshman orientation: Available. Preregistration for classes offered. **Policies:** Enrollment in 10 or more credits and 2.5 cumulative GPA required to serve as student government representative. **Activities:** Choral groups, international student organizations, literary magazine, student government, Vietnamese student association, Black student union, Phi Theta Kappa, Students for Sustainability, engineering club, international student club, Muslim student association, business club, Christian club, MECHA, Multiculture Alliance, Vetern's club.

Athletics. Intramural: Basketball. **Team name:** Storm.

Student services. Adult student services, career counseling, services for economically disadvantaged, student employment services, financial aid counseling, minority student services, on-campus daycare, placement for graduates, veterans' counselor, women's services. **Physically disabled:** Services for visually, speech, hearing impaired. **Transfer:** Re-entry adviser, pre-admission transcript evaluation for new students. Transfer adviser, college fairs on campus for students transferring to 4-year colleges.

Contact. E-mail: admission.SSCC@seattlecolleges.edu
Phone: (206) 934-6691 Fax: (206) 934-7947
Vanessa Reed, Director of Student Outreach, Admissions and Recruitment, South Seattle Community College, 6000 16th Avenue, SW, Seattle, WA 98106-1499

Spokane Community College
Spokane, Washington
www.scc.spokane.edu   **CB code: 4739**

▶ Public 2-year community college
▶ Commuter campus in small city

General. Founded in 1963. Regionally accredited. **Enrollment:** 5,114 degree-seeking undergraduates. **Degrees:** 1,087 associate awarded. **ROTC:** Army, Naval, Air Force. **Location:** 2 miles from downtown. **Calendar:** Quarter, limited summer session. **Full-time faculty:** 189 total. **Part-time faculty:** 175 total. **Special facilities:** Nursery, floral shop, automotive repair service center, cosmetology center.

Student profile.

Out-of-state:	4%	25 or older:	54%

Transfer out. Colleges most students transferred to 2011: Eastern Washington University, Washington State University.

Basis for selection. Open admission, but selective for some programs. Admission to college does not guarantee acceptance into every program. ASSET used for placement. Our admissions deadline is now three weeks prior to the start of a quarter. **Home schooled:** If under 18, must be deemed able to benefit from curricular offerings of college. Required to take ASSET or COMPASS tests and must place at college level.

2011-2012 Annual costs. Tuition/fees: $3,765; $9,000 out-of-state. Books/supplies: $780. Personal expenses: $3,012.

Financial aid. Need-based: Work-study available nights, weekends and for part-time students. **Non-need-based:** Scholarships awarded for athletics.

Application procedures. Admission: Closing date 8/31. $25 fee, may be waived for applicants with need. Admission notification on a rolling basis beginning on or about 1/1. **Financial aid:** Priority date 5/13; no closing date. FAFSA, institutional form required. Applicants notified on a rolling basis; must reply within 2 week(s) of notification.

Academics. Special study options: Cooperative education, cross-registration, distance learning, dual enrollment of high school students, ESL, independent study, internships, student-designed major, study abroad. License preparation in nursing, paramedic. **Credit/placement by examination:** AP, CLEP, institutional tests. 60 credit hours maximum toward associate degree. **Support services:** Learning center, reduced course load, remedial instruction, study skills assistance, tutoring, writing center.

Majors. Business: General, accounting, administrative services, banking/financial services, business admin, management information systems, marketing, office management, office technology, office/clerical, selling, vehicle

parts marketing. **Computer sciences:** Applications programming, data processing, information systems. **Conservation:** Forest resources, forestry, water/wetlands/marine, wildlife/wilderness. **General:** Business, greenhouse operations, horticulture, nursery operations, soil science, turf management. **Health services:** Cardiovascular technology, clinical lab technology, dental assistant, EMT paramedic, medical secretary, optician, pharmacy assistant, recreational therapy, respiratory therapy technology, surgical technology, ward clerk. **Liberal arts:** Arts/sciences. **Parks/recreation:** Facilities management. **Protective services:** Corrections, fire services admin, law enforcement admin, police science, security services.

Computing on campus. 913 workstations in library, computer center, student center. Online course registration available.

Student life. Freshman orientation: Available. Preregistration for classes offered. **Activities:** Drama, literary magazine, student government, student newspaper.

Athletics. Intercollegiate: Baseball M, basketball, cross-country, golf, soccer, softball W, tennis, track and field, volleyball W. **Team name:** Big Foot.

Student services. Adult student services, career counseling, services for economically disadvantaged, student employment services, financial aid counseling, minority student services, on-campus daycare, personal counseling, placement for graduates, veterans' counselor. **Physically disabled:** Services for visually, speech, hearing impaired. **Transfer:** College fairs on campus for students transferring to 4-year colleges.

Contact. E-mail: AdmissionsInfo@scc.spokane.edu
Phone: (509) 533-8860 Toll-free number: (800) 248-5644
Fax: (509) 533-8860
Sherry Carroll, Manager, Admissions/Student Entry & Success, Spokane Community College, 1810 North Greene Street, Spokane, WA 99217-5399

Spokane Falls Community College
Spokane, Washington
www.spokanefalls.edu   CB code: 4752

▶ Public 2-year community college
▶ Commuter campus in small city

General. Founded in 1967. Regionally accredited. **Location:** 4 miles from downtown. **Calendar:** Quarter.

Annual costs/financial aid. Tuition/fees (2011-2012): $3,645; $8,880 out-of-state. Books/supplies: $924. Personal expenses: $3,110. Need-based financial aid available to full-time and part-time students.

Contact. Phone: (509) 533-3305
Dean of Enrollment Services and Student Development, 3410 West Fort George Wright Drive, Spokane, WA 99224

Tacoma Community College
Tacoma, Washington   CB member
www.tacomacc.edu   CB code: 4826

▶ Public 2-year community college
▶ Commuter campus in small city

General. Founded in 1965. Regionally accredited. Programs offered at Tacoma Campus and Gig Harbor Center. **Enrollment:** 3,900 degree-seeking undergraduates. **Degrees:** 771 associate awarded. **Location:** 30 miles from Seattle, 30 miles from Olympia. **Calendar:** Quarter, limited summer session. **Full-time faculty:** 137 total. **Part-time faculty:** 341 total.

Student profile.

Out-of-state:	1%	25 or older:	49%

Transfer out. Colleges most students transferred to 2011: University of Washington.

Basis for selection. Open admission, but selective for some programs. **Adult students:** Accuplacer assessment required for students intending to enroll in 6 or more credits; students taking math or English; students enrolling in a degree or certificate program. **Learning Disabled:** Students who wish to receive accommodations need to present documentation to the college.

High school preparation. College-preparatory program recommended. 23 units recommended. Recommended units include English 4, mathematics

3, social studies 4, history 3, science 3 (laboratory 1), foreign language 2, computer science 1, visual/performing arts 1 and academic electives 1.

2011-2012 Annual costs. Tuition/fees: $3,745; $8,980 out-of-state. Books/supplies: $800.

Financial aid. All financial aid based on need. Need-based aid available for part-time students. Work-study available nights, weekends and for part-time students.

Application procedures. Admission: No deadline. No application fee. Admission notification on a rolling basis. **Financial aid:** Priority date 3/26; no closing date. FAFSA, institutional form required. Applicants notified on a rolling basis starting 7/20; must reply within 4 week(s) of notification.

Academics. Special study options: Distance learning, dual enrollment of high school students, ESL, internships, study abroad. Concurrent enrollment with nearby community colleges. Bachelor's degree programs available on campus. License preparation in nursing, paramedic, radiology. **Credit/placement by examination:** AP, CLEP, IB, institutional tests. 45 credit hours maximum toward associate degree. **Support services:** GED preparation and test center, learning center, reduced course load, remedial instruction, study skills assistance, tutoring, writing center.

Majors. Computer sciences: General. **Education:** Teacher assistance. **Health services:** EMT paramedic. **Liberal arts:** Arts/sciences. **Protective services:** Corrections.

Computing on campus. 185 workstations in library, computer center, student center. Commuter students can connect to campus network. Online course registration, online library, helpline, wireless network available.

Student life. Freshman orientation: Mandatory. Preregistration for classes offered. **Housing:** Homestay Program available for international students. **Activities:** Jazz band, choral groups, international student organizations, literary magazine, music ensembles, student government, student newspaper.

Athletics. Intercollegiate: Baseball M, basketball, soccer, volleyball W. **Team name:** Titans.

Student services. Adult student services, career counseling, services for economically disadvantaged, student employment services, financial aid counseling, minority student services, on-campus daycare, personal counseling, veterans' counselor. **Physically disabled:** Services for visually, speech, hearing impaired. **Transfer:** Pre-admission transcript evaluation for new students. Transfer adviser, college fairs on campus for students transferring to 4-year colleges.

Contact. E-mail: admit@tacomacc.edu
Phone: (253) 566-5001 Fax: (253) 566-6011
Steve Ashpole, Director of Enrollment Services/Registrar, Tacoma Community College, 6501 South 19th Street, Tacoma, WA 98466-9971

Walla Walla Community College
Walla Walla, Washington
www.wwcc.edu   CB code: 4963

▶ Public 2-year community and technical college
▶ Commuter campus in large town

General. Founded in 1967. Regionally accredited. Academic and vocational courses offered at educational center at Clarkston, Washington and Department of Corrections at the Washington State Penitentiary. **Degrees:** 728 associate awarded. **Location:** 158 miles from Spokane, 262 miles from Seattle. **Calendar:** Quarter, limited summer session. **Full-time faculty:** 120 total. **Part-time faculty:** 210 total. **Class size:** 78% < 20, 19% 20-39, less than 1% 40-49, 2% 50-99. **Special facilities:** Enology (winemaking), viticulture, culinary and John Deere facilities. **Partnerships:** Formal partnerships with John Deere & Company training center, Cisco Corporation.

Student profile.

Out-of-state:	20%	25 or older:	45%

Transfer out. Colleges most students transferred to 2011: Washington State University, Lewis & Clark College, Walla Walla University, Eastern Washington University, University of Idaho.

Basis for selection. Open admission, but selective for some programs. Special requirements for health science and vocational programs. COMPASS or ASSET placement tests used for English, reading, math. TOEFL score of 500 or higher needed to demonstrate English proficiency. **Learning Disabled:** Flexible procedures; early registration.

High school preparation. Recommended units include English 4, mathematics 4 and science 3.

2011-2012 Annual costs. Tuition/fees: $3,917; $9,152 out-of-state. Books/supplies: $924. Personal expenses: $1,800.

Financial aid. Need-based: Need-based aid available for part-time students. Work-study available nights, weekends and for part-time students. **Non-need-based:** Scholarships awarded for academics, athletics, leadership, music/drama.

Application procedures. Admission: No deadline. No application fee. Admission notification on a rolling basis. **Financial aid:** Priority date 3/1; no closing date. FAFSA, institutional form required. Applicants notified on a rolling basis starting 6/1; must reply within 2 week(s) of notification.

Academics. Special study options: Cooperative education, distance learning, dual enrollment of high school students, ESL, external degree, honors, independent study, internships, liberal arts/career combination. License preparation in nursing, paramedic. **Credit/placement by examination:** AP, CLEP, institutional tests. 23 credit hours maximum toward associate degree. **Support services:** GED preparation and test center, learning center, pre-admission summer program, reduced course load, remedial instruction, study skills assistance, tutoring, writing center.

Majors. Business: Accounting technology, banking/financial services, business admin, executive assistant, office management, retailing. **Communications technology:** Desktop publishing. **Computer sciences:** Data entry, data processing, information systems, networking, web page design, webmaster. **Education:** Early childhood, teacher assistance. **General:** Business, equipment technology, mechanization, production, turf management. **Health services:** Medical secretary, nursing (RN). **Liberal arts:** Arts/sciences. **Parks/recreation:** Facilities management. **Protective services:** Corrections, criminal justice, firefighting.

Most popular majors. Agriculture 10%, business/marketing 6%, health sciences 22%, liberal arts 39%, trade and industry 10%.

Computing on campus. 716 workstations in library, computer center, student center. Commuter students can connect to campus network. Online course registration, online library, helpline, repair service, student web hosting, wireless network available.

Student life. Freshman orientation: Mandatory. Preregistration for classes offered. **Activities:** Jazz band, choral groups, dance, drama, international student organizations, music ensembles, musical theater, student government, student newspaper, Warriors for Christ, ecology club.

Athletics. NJCAA. **Intercollegiate:** Baseball M, basketball, cheerleading W, golf, rodeo, soccer, softball W, volleyball W. **Intramural:** Basketball, softball, volleyball. **Team name:** Warriors.

Student services. Adult student services, career counseling, services for economically disadvantaged, student employment services, financial aid counseling, minority student services, on-campus daycare, personal counseling, placement for graduates, veterans' counselor, women's services. **Physically disabled:** Services for visually, speech, hearing impaired. **Transfer:** Reentry adviser, pre-admission transcript evaluation for new students. Transfer center, transfer adviser, college fairs on campus for students transferring to 4-year colleges.

Contact. E-mail: admissions@wwcc.edu
Phone: (509) 527-4283 Toll-free number: (877) 992-9922
Fax: (509) 527-3661
Carlos Delgadillo, Director of Admissions and Registrar, Walla Walla Community College, 500 Tausick Way, Walla Walla, WA 99362-9972

Wenatchee Valley College
Wenatchee, Washington
www.wvc.edu
CB code: 4942

- Public 2-year community college
- Commuter campus in large town

General. Founded in 1939. Regionally accredited. Central Washington University has branch facilities on campus. **Enrollment:** 2,888 degree-seeking undergraduates. **Degrees:** 617 associate awarded. **Location:** 145 miles from Seattle, 170 miles from Spokane. **Calendar:** Quarter, limited summer session. **Full-time faculty:** 68 total. **Part-time faculty:** 160 total. **Class size:** 55% < 20, 43% 20-39, 1% 40-49, less than 1% 50-99, less than 1% >100.

Student profile.

Out-of-state:	3%	Live on campus:	2%
25 or older:	51%		

Transfer out. Colleges most students transferred to 2011: Central Washington University, Washington State University, Eastern Washington University, University of Washington, Western Washington University.

Basis for selection. Open admission, but selective for some programs. Allied health applicants must submit supplemental application form that details work completed in specific program prerequisites. **Home schooled:** Applicants must be affiliated with their local school district. **Learning Disabled:** Students are encouraged to meet with Special Populations Coordinator.

2011-2012 Annual costs. Tuition/fees: $3,647; $8,882 out-of-state. Books/supplies: $972. Personal expenses: $1,674.

Financial aid. Need-based: Need-based aid available for part-time students. Work-study available nights, weekends and for part-time students. **Non-need-based:** Scholarships awarded for academics, athletics.

Application procedures. Admission: No deadline. No application fee. Admission notification on a rolling basis. **Financial aid:** Closing date 3/1. FAFSA required. Applicants notified by 7/2; must reply within 3 week(s) of notification.

Academics. Special study options: Accelerated study, cooperative education, cross-registration, distance learning, double major, dual enrollment of high school students, ESL, independent study, internships, liberal arts/career combination, student-designed major. Bachelor's degree programs available on campus. License preparation in nursing, paramedic, radiology. **Credit/placement by examination:** AP, CLEP, institutional tests. 15 credit hours maximum toward associate degree. At least 15 credits must be completed in residence before credits earned by examination will be applied. **Support services:** GED preparation and test center, remedial instruction, study skills assistance, tutoring, writing center.

Majors. Business: Accounting technology, business admin, office management. **Computer sciences:** Networking. **Conservation:** General. **Education:** Early childhood. **General:** Production, products processing. **Health services:** Clinical lab assistant, nursing (RN), radiologic technology/medical imaging, sonography, substance abuse counseling. **Liberal arts:** Arts/sciences. **Protective services:** Police science.

Most popular majors. Health sciences 20%, liberal arts 70%.

Computing on campus. 75 workstations in library, computer center, student center. Dormitories wired for high-speed internet access. Online course registration, online library, helpline, student web hosting, wireless network available.

Student life. Freshman orientation: Available. Preregistration for classes offered. **Housing:** Coed dorms available. Housing available nearby. **Activities:** Jazz band, choral groups, dance, drama, music ensembles, student government, professional associations, Inter-Varsity Fellowship.

Athletics. NJCAA. **Intercollegiate:** Baseball M, basketball, soccer, softball W, volleyball W. **Intramural:** Basketball. **Team name:** Knights.

Student services. Adult student services, career counseling, services for economically disadvantaged, student employment services, financial aid counseling, minority student services, on-campus daycare, personal counseling, veterans' counselor. **Physically disabled:** Services for visually, speech, hearing impaired. **Transfer:** Pre-admission transcript evaluation for new students. College fairs on campus for students transferring to 4-year colleges.

Contact. Phone: (509) 682-6806 Toll-free number: (877) 982-4698
Fax: (509) 682-6801
William Maxwell, Registrar, Wenatchee Valley College, 1300 Fifth Street, Wenatchee, WA 98801-1799

Whatcom Community College
Bellingham, Washington
www.whatcom.ctc.edu
CB member
CB code: 1275

- Public 2-year community college
- Commuter campus in small city

General. Founded in 1970. Regionally accredited. **Enrollment:** 3,733 degree-seeking undergraduates. **Degrees:** 877 associate awarded. **Location:** 90 miles from Seattle, 60 miles from Vancouver, Canada. **Calendar:** Quarter, limited summer session. **Full-time faculty:** 74 total. **Part-time faculty:** 217 total. **Class size:** 28% < 20, 70% 20-39, 2% 40-49.

Transfer out. Colleges most students transferred to 2011: Western Washington University, University of Washington, Washington State University, Central Washington University, Eastern Washington University.

Basis for selection. Open admission.

High school preparation. College-preparatory program recommended. Recommended units include English 4, mathematics 4, social studies 3, science 2 (laboratory 1), foreign language 3, visual/performing arts 1 and academic electives 1.

2011-2012 Annual costs. Tuition/fees: $3,722; $8,957 out-of-state. Books/supplies: $1,080. Personal expenses: $2,238.

Financial aid. Need-based: Need-based aid available for part-time students. Work-study available nights, weekends and for part-time students. **Non-need-based:** Scholarships awarded for academics, athletics, state residency.

Application procedures. Admission: Priority date 6/23; no deadline. No application fee. Admission notification on a rolling basis. **Financial aid:** Priority date 3/1; no closing date. FAFSA, institutional form required. Applicants notified on a rolling basis starting 7/1; must reply within 3 week(s) of notification.

Academics. Special study options: Accelerated study, cooperative education, distance learning, dual enrollment of high school students, ESL, honors, independent study, internships, student-designed major, study abroad. License preparation in nursing. **Credit/placement by examination:** AP, CLEP, IB, institutional tests. 15 credit hours maximum toward associate degree. **Support services:** GED preparation and test center, learning center, reduced course load, remedial instruction, study skills assistance, tutoring, writing center.

Majors. Business: General, accounting. **Computer sciences:** Computer science, data processing, systems analysis. **Education:** General, early childhood, teacher assistance. **Health services:** Massage therapy, medical assistant, nursing (RN), physical therapy assistant. **Liberal arts:** Arts/sciences. **Protective services:** Police science. **Visual/performing arts:** Commercial/advertising art.

Most popular majors. Health sciences 13%, liberal arts 79%.

Computing on campus. 294 workstations in library, computer center, student center. Online course registration, online library, wireless network available.

Student life. Freshman orientation: Available. Preregistration for classes offered. Prior to fall, winter and spring quarters, new student orientation sessions held for students along with a separate parent track. Students take campus tour, attend workshops, meet faculty. **Activities:** Jazz band, choral groups, drama, film society, international student organizations, student government, student newspaper, Phi Theta Kappa, Japanese Anime, Deaf Students Fellowship, health and wellness club, international friendship club, snow club, Gay-Straight Alliance, multicultural club.

Athletics. Intercollegiate: Basketball, soccer, volleyball W. **Intramural:** Badminton, basketball, soccer, tennis, volleyball. **Team name:** Orcas.

Student services. Adult student services, alcohol/substance abuse counseling, career counseling, student employment services, financial aid counseling, on-campus daycare, personal counseling, veterans' counselor. **Physically disabled:** Services for visually, speech, hearing impaired. **Transfer:** Reentry adviser for new students. Transfer center, transfer adviser, college fairs on campus for students transferring to 4-year colleges.

Contact. E-mail: admit@whatcom.ctc.edu
Phone: (360) 383-3080 Fax: (360) 383-4000
Michael Singletary, Registrar, Whatcom Community College, 237 West Kellogg Road, Bellingham, WA 98226

Yakima Valley Community College
Yakima, Washington
www.yvcc.edu   **CB code: 4993**

◗ Public 2-year community college
◗ Commuter campus in small city

General. Founded in 1928. Regionally accredited. Additional campus in Grandview. **Location:** 150 miles from Seattle. **Calendar:** Quarter, extensive summer session. **Full-time faculty:** 106 total. **Part-time faculty:** 186 total.

Student profile.

Out-of-state:	10%	Live on campus:	2%
25 or older:	49%		

Transfer out. Colleges most students transferred to 2011: Central Washington University, Washington State University.

Basis for selection. Open admission, but selective for some programs. Special requirements for allied health programs. ACT/ASSET required for placement and advising of degree seeking students and for math/English placement. Previous college/university transcripts showing successful completion of English and math courses may replace ASSET. Essay required for radiologic technology.

High school preparation. College-preparatory program recommended.

2011-2012 Annual costs. Tuition/fees: $3,850; $9,085 out-of-state. Room only: $3,050.

2010-2011 Financial aid. Need-based: 80% of total undergraduate aid awarded as scholarships/grants, 20% as loans/jobs. Need-based aid available for part-time students. Work-study available nights, weekends and for part-time students. **Non-need-based:** Scholarships awarded for athletics.

Application procedures. Admission: Closing date 8/11 (receipt date). $20 fee. Admission notification on a rolling basis. **Financial aid:** Closing date 4/15. FAFSA required. Applicants notified on a rolling basis starting 8/1; must reply within 2 week(s) of notification.

Academics. Special study options: Cooperative education, distance learning, dual enrollment of high school students, ESL, independent study, internships, liberal arts/career combination, weekend college. Bachelor's degree programs available on campus. License preparation in dental hygiene, nursing, radiology. **Credit/placement by examination:** AP, CLEP, IB, institutional tests. 45 credit hours maximum toward associate degree. **Support services:** GED preparation and test center, learning center, remedial instruction, study skills assistance, tutoring, writing center.

Majors. Business: General, accounting, accounting technology, administrative services, business admin, e-commerce, entrepreneurial studies, marketing, office management. **Communications technology:** Graphic/printing. **Computer sciences:** General, information systems, web page design. **Education:** General, early childhood. **Engineering:** General. **General:** Business, food processing, products processing, supplies. **Health services:** Dental hygiene, insurance coding, licensed practical nurse, medical assistant, medical radiologic technology/radiation therapy, medical secretary, nursing (RN), pharmacy assistant, substance abuse counseling, surgical technology, veterinary technology/assistant. **Liberal arts:** Arts/sciences. **Protective services:** Criminal justice, fire services admin, firefighting, law enforcement admin. **Visual/performing arts:** Design. **Work/family studies:** Child care management.

Most popular majors. Business/marketing 15%, health sciences 14%, liberal arts 43%.

Computing on campus. 300 workstations in dormitories, library, computer center, student center. Dormitories wired for high-speed internet access. Online course registration, wireless network available.

Student life. Freshman orientation: Mandatory. Preregistration for classes offered. Held three weeks prior to the beginning of each quarter. Includes faculty powerpoint presentation, online registration, student satisfaction survey, campus tour; student ID's and parking permits distributed. **Housing:** Single-sex dorms, wellness housing available. $250 partly refundable deposit. **Activities:** Jazz band, choral groups, drama, music ensembles, musical theater, student government, student newspaper, Mecha, Veterans, Tiin Ma, International Club, Phi Theta Kappa, Action, Auto, allied health clubs.

Athletics. NJCAA. **Intercollegiate:** Baseball M, basketball, soccer W, softball W, volleyball W, wrestling. **Intramural:** Basketball. **Team name:** Yaks.

Student services. Career counseling, services for economically disadvantaged, financial aid counseling, health services, minority student services, on-campus daycare, personal counseling, veterans' counselor, women's services. **Physically disabled:** Services for visually, speech, hearing impaired. **Transfer:** Transfer adviser, college fairs on campus for students transferring to 4-year colleges.

Contact. E-mail: admis@yvcc.edu
Phone: (509) 574-4712 Fax: (509) 574-4649
Denise Anderson, Registrar and Director for Enrollment Services, Yakima Valley Community College, PO Box 22520, Yakima, WA 98907-2520

West Virginia

Blue Ridge Community and Technical College
Martinsburg, West Virginia   **CB member**
www.blueridgectc.edu   **CB code: 4892**

- Public 2-year community and technical college
- Commuter campus in small city

General. Regionally accredited. **Enrollment:** 1,896 degree-seeking undergraduates; 2,421 non-degree-seeking students. **Degrees:** 181 associate awarded. **Location:** Downtown. **Calendar:** Semester, limited summer session. **Full-time faculty:** 27 total; 4% minority, 70% women. **Part-time faculty:** 64 total; 12% have terminal degrees, 58% women. **Class size:** 77% < 20, 19% 20-39, 3% 40-49, 1% 50-99, less than 1% >100.

Student profile. Among degree-seeking undergraduates, 12% already have a bachelor's degree or higher, 403 enrolled as first-time, first-year students.

Part-time:	40%	Women:	66%
Out-of-state:	7%	25 or older:	40%

Transfer out. Colleges most students transferred to 2011: Shepherd University.

Basis for selection. Open admission. **Adult students:** Students without ACT/SAT may take the ACCUPLACER in-house. **Home schooled:** Transcript of courses and grades, state high school equivalency certificate required.

High school preparation. Recommended units include English 4, mathematics 4, social studies 2, history 1, science 3 (laboratory 3), foreign language 2 and visual/performing arts 1.

2011-2012 Annual costs. Tuition/fees: $3,120; $5,616 out-of-state. Per-credit charge: $130 in-state; $234 out-of-state. Books/supplies: $1,000. Personal expenses: $2,000.

Financial aid. Need-based: Need-based aid available for part-time students. Work-study available nights, weekends and for part-time students.

Application procedures. Admission: No deadline. $25 fee, may be waived for applicants with need. Application must be submitted on paper. Admission notification on a rolling basis. **Financial aid:** Closing date 4/15. FAFSA required. Applicants notified on a rolling basis starting 6/10; must reply within 2 week(s) of notification.

Academics. Special study options: Dual enrollment of high school students, ESL, independent study, internships, liberal arts/career combination. License preparation in dental hygiene, nursing, paramedic, real estate. **Credit/placement by examination:** AP, CLEP, institutional tests. **Support services:** Learning center, reduced course load, remedial instruction, tutoring, writing center.

Majors. Business: General, business admin, office technology. **Computer sciences:** Information systems. **Health services:** EMT paramedic, medical assistant, nursing (RN), surgical technology. **Liberal arts:** Arts/sciences. **Protective services:** Criminal justice, fire safety technology, firefighting.

Most popular majors. Business/marketing 14%, engineering/engineering technologies 7%, health sciences 21%, liberal arts 39%, security/protective services 7%.

Computing on campus. 106 workstations in library, computer center, student center. Online course registration, online library, helpline, student web hosting, wireless network available.

Student life. Freshman orientation: Available. Preregistration for classes offered. **Activities:** Campus ministries, drama, student government.

Athletics. Team name: Bruins.

Student services. Adult student services, career counseling, student employment services, financial aid counseling, placement for graduates, veterans' counselor. **Physically disabled:** Services for visually, speech, hearing impaired. **Transfer:** Pre-admission transcript evaluation for new students. College fairs on campus for students transferring to 4-year colleges.

Contact. E-mail: bneal@blueridgectc.edu
Phone: (304) 260-4380 ext. 2109 Fax: (304) 260-4376
Brenda Neal, Director of Access, Blue Ridge Community and Technical College, 400 West Stephen Street, Martinsburg, WV 25401

Bridgemont Community and Technical College
Montgomery, West Virginia
www.bridgemont.edu   **CB code: 5786**

- Public 2-year community and technical college
- Commuter campus in small town

General. Regionally accredited. **Enrollment:** 940 undergraduates. **Degrees:** 142 associate awarded. **Location:** 25 miles from Charleston. **Calendar:** Semester, limited summer session. **Full-time faculty:** 38 total. **Part-time faculty:** 36 total. **Partnerships:** Formal partnership with Toyota for work/study program in electrical/mechanical instrumentation.

Basis for selection. Open admission, but selective for some programs. Selective admissions to dental hygiene, respiratory therapy, veterinarian technology, and blasting technology programs. **Adult students:** If adults have not taken the SAT or ACT, they may take the compass or accuplacer test. **Home schooled:** Transcript of courses and grades required.

2011-2012 Annual costs. Tuition/fees: $3,794; $8,810 out-of-state. Per-credit charge: $146 in-state; $354 out-of-state. Room/board: $7,310.

Financial aid. Need-based: Work-study available nights, weekends and for part-time students.

Application procedures. Admission: No deadline. No application fee. Admission notification on a rolling basis.

Academics. Special study options: Accelerated study, dual enrollment of high school students. License preparation in dental hygiene. **Credit/placement by examination:** AP, CLEP, institutional tests. **Support services:** GED preparation, learning center, remedial instruction, study skills assistance, tutoring.

Majors. Business: Accounting, business admin, executive assistant, hospitality admin, hospitality/recreation, office management. **Computer sciences:** General. **Health services:** Dental hygiene, facilities admin, medical assistant, medical records admin, medical secretary, office admin, office assistant, receptionist, respiratory therapy assistant, respiratory therapy technology, veterinary technology/assistant.

Computing on campus. Dormitories wired for high-speed internet access and linked to campus network. Commuter students can connect to campus network. Wireless network available.

Student life. Freshman orientation: Mandatory. Preregistration for classes offered. Held the weekend before the beginning of the fall semester. **Housing:** Coed dorms, single-sex dorms available. $100 fully refundable deposit, deadline 8/1. **Activities:** Student government, student newspaper.

Student services. Student employment services, financial aid counseling, placement for graduates, veterans' counselor. **Physically disabled:** Services for hearing impaired. **Transfer:** Pre-admission transcript evaluation for new students.

Contact. E-mail: admissions@bridgemont.edu
Phone: (304) 734-6603
Joyce Surbaugh, Director of Enrollment Management, Bridgemont Community and Technical College, 619 Second Avenue, Montgomery, WV 25136

Eastern West Virginia Community and Technical College
Moorefield, West Virginia
www.eastern.wvnet.edu   **CB code: 3837**

- Public 2-year community and technical college
- Commuter campus in rural community

General. Regionally accredited. **Enrollment:** 735 degree-seeking undergraduates. **Degrees:** 40 associate awarded. **Location:** 55 miles from Winchester, VA. **Calendar:** Semester, limited summer session. **Part-time faculty:** 36 total.

Transfer out. Colleges most students transferred to 2011: Shepherd College, West Virginia University, Potomac State College.

Basis for selection. Open admission. Degree-seeking students required to take ACCUPLACER. **Home schooled:** Transcript of courses and grades required. Applicants advised to take GED.

2011-2012 Annual costs. Tuition/fees: $2,184; $6,816 out-of-state. Per-credit charge: $91 in-state; $284 out-of-state.

Financial aid. Need-based: Need-based aid available for part-time students. Work-study available nights, weekends and for part-time students.

Application procedures. Admission: No deadline. No application fee. Admission notification on a rolling basis. **Financial aid:** Priority date 6/1; no closing date. FAFSA, institutional form required. Applicants notified on a rolling basis; must reply within 2 week(s) of notification.

Academics. Special study options: Distance learning, double major, dual enrollment of high school students, external degree, internships, student-designed major. License preparation in nursing. **Credit/placement by examination:** AP, CLEP, institutional tests. **Support services:** GED preparation and test center, reduced course load, remedial instruction, study skills assistance, tutoring.

Majors. Business: Administrative services, business admin. **Computer sciences:** Information systems. **Liberal arts:** Arts/sciences. **Work/family studies:** Child care service.

Computing on campus. Online course registration, online library available.

Student life. Freshman orientation: Mandatory. Preregistration for classes offered. General orientation program is 3 hours long. Second program required for students taking online courses.

Student services. Adult student services, career counseling, services for economically disadvantaged, financial aid counseling, veterans' counselor. **Physically disabled:** Services for visually, hearing impaired. **Transfer:** Pre-admission transcript evaluation for new students. College fairs on campus for students transferring to 4-year colleges.

Contact. E-mail: askeast@eastern.wvnet.edu
Phone: (304) 434-8000 Toll-free number: (877) 982-2322
Fax: (304) 434-7000
Robert Eagle, Dean of Academics and Learner Support Services, Eastern West Virginia Community and Technical College, 316 Eastern Drive, Moorefield, WV 26836

Huntington Junior College
Huntington, West Virginia
www.huntingtonjuniorcollege.edu   **CB code: 7310**

- For-profit 2-year junior college
- Commuter campus in small city

General. Founded in 1936. Regionally accredited. **Enrollment:** 947 undergraduates. **Degrees:** 168 associate awarded. **Location:** 45 miles from Charleston. **Calendar:** Quarter, extensive summer session. **Full-time faculty:** 25 total. **Part-time faculty:** 13 total.

Basis for selection. Open admission. Interview recommended.

2011-2012 Annual costs. Tuition/fees: $6,900. Includes books.

Financial aid. Need-based: Work-study available nights, weekends and for part-time students.

Application procedures. Admission: No deadline. No application fee. Admission notification on a rolling basis. **Financial aid:** No deadline. Applicants notified on a rolling basis.

Academics. Special study options: Distance learning, honors, internships. **Credit/placement by examination:** AP, CLEP, institutional tests. **Support services:** Learning center, reduced course load, remedial instruction, study skills assistance, tutoring.

Majors. Business: General, accounting, administrative services. **Computer sciences:** General, database management, programming, web page design. **Foreign languages:** Classics. **Health services:** Dental assistant, insurance coding, medical assistant.

Computing on campus. 117 workstations in library, computer center. Online course registration, online library, helpline available.

Student life. Freshman orientation: Mandatory. Preregistration for classes offered. 3 hour program held during the first day of class.

Student services. Career counseling, student employment services, financial aid counseling, personal counseling, placement for graduates, veterans' counselor. **Physically disabled:** Services for visually, hearing impaired. **Transfer:** Pre-admission transcript evaluation for new students. Transfer center for students transferring to 4-year colleges.

Contact. E-mail: admissions@huntingtonjuniorcollege.edu
Phone: (304) 697-7550 Toll-free number: (800) 344-4522
Fax: (304) 697-7554
James Garrett, Director of Marketing and Education Services, Huntington Junior College, 900 Fifth Avenue, Huntington, WV 25701

Kanawha Valley Community and Technical College
Institute, West Virginia
www.kvctc.edu

- Public 2-year community and technical college
- Commuter campus in small town
- Interview required

General. Regionally accredited. Campus is moving to a new location in South Charleston, WV in Summer 2012. **Enrollment:** 1,612 degree-seeking undergraduates; 73 non-degree-seeking students. **Degrees:** 277 associate awarded. **Location:** 8 miles from Charleston. **Calendar:** Semester, limited summer session. **Full-time faculty:** 39 total. **Part-time faculty:** 44 total. **Partnerships:** Formal partnerships with Charleston Area Medical Center, American Electric Power and Adult Basic Education.

Student profile. Among degree-seeking undergraduates, 136 enrolled as first-time, first-year students.

Part-time:	38%	Asian American:	1%
Women:	69%	Native American:	1%
African American:	15%		

Basis for selection. Open admission, but selective for some programs. Nursing requirements include 3.0 GPA and 21 ACT or 1000 SAT (exclusive of Writing). Nuclear medicine technology requires interview with the program director or clinical coordinator and submission of ACT or SAT scores. Interviews required for admissions to the Nuclear Medicine program. **Home schooled:** Statement describing home school structure and mission, transcript of courses and grades required. Must provide detailed description of home school curriculum.

High school preparation. Recommended units include English 4, mathematics 4, social studies 4, science 3 (laboratory 2) and foreign language 2.

2011-2012 Annual costs. Tuition/fees: $3,082; $8,764 out-of-state. Room/board: $6,602. Books/supplies: $1,009.

Financial aid. Need-based: Work-study available nights, weekends and for part-time students. **Non-need-based:** Scholarships awarded for academics, state residency. **Additional information:** All students may apply for tuition waivers. Financial aid deadline enforced only if Federal financial aid is the only source of payment.

Application procedures. Admission: No deadline. No application fee. Admission notification on a rolling basis. **Financial aid:** Closing date 6/30.

Academics. Special study options: Cooperative education, double major, dual enrollment of high school students, internships. License preparation in nursing, occupational therapy, paramedic, real estate. **Credit/placement by examination:** AP, CLEP, institutional tests. **Support services:** GED preparation and test center, remedial instruction, study skills assistance, tutoring, writing center.

Majors. Business: Accounting, accounting technology, administrative services, banking/financial services, business admin, finance, sales/distribution. **Communications:** Communications/speech/rhetoric. **Computer sciences:** Computer science, information systems. **Health services:** EMT paramedic, mental health services, nuclear medical technology, nursing (RN). **Liberal arts:** Arts/sciences. **Physical sciences:** Meteorology. **Protective services:** Police science.

Most popular majors. Business/marketing 18%, engineering/engineering technologies 15%, health sciences 22%, interdisciplinary studies 9%, liberal arts 29%.

Computing on campus. Commuter students can connect to campus network. Online course registration, online library, helpline, wireless network available.

Student life. Freshman orientation: Mandatory. Preregistration for classes offered. **Activities:** Literary magazine, student government.

Student services. Alcohol/substance abuse counseling, career counseling, financial aid counseling, health services, personal counseling, veterans' counselor. **Physically disabled:** Services for visually, speech, hearing impaired. **Transfer:** College fairs on campus for students transferring to 4-year colleges.

Contact. E-mail: admissions@kvctc.edu
Phone: (304) 205-6700 Toll-free number: (800) 987-2112
Fax: (304) 205-6700
Michelle Wicks, Director of Admissions, Kanawha Valley Community and Technical College, PO Box 1000, Institute, WV 25112-1000

Mountain State College
Parkersburg, West Virginia
www.msc.edu   CB code: 2389

▸ For-profit 2-year junior and career college
▸ Commuter campus in large town
▸ Interview required

General. Founded in 1888. Accredited by ACICS. All program can be taken online. **Enrollment:** 191 degree-seeking undergraduates. **Degrees:** 32 associate awarded. **Location:** 81 miles from Charleston. **Calendar:** Quarter. **Full-time faculty:** 7 total. **Part-time faculty:** 6 total. **Special facilities:** Legal resource center, dependency resource center.

Basis for selection. Open admission. CPAT required for placement.

2011-2012 Annual costs. Tuition/fees: $8,215. Books/supplies: $1,100.

Financial aid. Need-based: Work-study available nights, weekends and for part-time students.

Application procedures. Admission: No deadline. $115 fee. Admission notification on a rolling basis. **Financial aid:** No deadline. FAFSA required. Applicants notified on a rolling basis.

Academics. Special study options: Accelerated study, cooperative education, distance learning, double major, internships. **Credit/placement by examination:** AP, CLEP. **Support services:** Tutoring.

Majors. Business: Accounting, administrative services, hospitality/recreation, tourism promotion, tourism/travel. **Computer sciences:** General, applications programming. **Health services:** Medical assistant, medical transcription, mental health services, substance abuse counseling.

Most popular majors. Computer/information sciences 10%, health sciences 90%.

Computing on campus. 25 workstations in library, computer center. Commuter students can connect to campus network. Online library, helpline, wireless network available.

Student life. Freshman orientation: Mandatory. Preregistration for classes offered. Held the week prior to beginning of quarter. **Activities:** Student government, student newspaper.

Student services. Career counseling, student employment services, financial aid counseling, personal counseling, placement for graduates.

Contact. E-mail: adm@msc.edu
Phone: (304) 485-5487 Toll-free number: (800) 841-0201
Fax: (304) 485-3524
Pamela Russell, Director of Admissions, Mountain State College, 1508 Spring Street, Parkersburg, WV 26101-3993

National College: Parkersburg
Parkersburg, West Virginia
www.national-college.edu

▸ For-profit 2-year career college
▸ Small city

General. Accredited by ACICS. **Enrollment:** 78 degree-seeking undergraduates. **Calendar:** Quarter. **Full-time faculty:** 3 total. **Part-time faculty:** 10 total.

Basis for selection. Open admission.

Financial aid. Need-based: Work-study available nights, weekends and for part-time students.

Application procedures. Admission: $50 fee.

Academics. Credit/placement by examination: AP, CLEP.

Majors. Business: Business admin. **Computer sciences:** Information systems. **Health services:** Health care admin, office assistant.

Contact. Phone: (304) 699-3005
Hope Harrell, Director of Admissions, National College: Parkersburg, 110 Park Center Drive, Parkersburg, WV 26101

National College: Princeton
Princeton, West Virginia
www.ncbt.edu   CB code: 3246

▸ For-profit 2-year business college
▸ Commuter campus in small city

General. Accredited by ACICS. **Enrollment:** 150 degree-seeking undergraduates. **Degrees:** 3 bachelor's, 28 associate awarded. **Calendar:** Quarter. **Full-time faculty:** 10 total. **Part-time faculty:** 7 total.

Basis for selection. Open admission. Interview recommended.

2011-2012 Annual costs. Tuition/fees: $13,770. Per-credit charge: $305. Books/supplies: $1,200.

Financial aid. All financial aid based on need. Need-based aid available for part-time students. Work-study available nights, weekends and for part-time students.

Application procedures. Admission: No deadline. $50 fee, may be waived for applicants with need. Admission notification on a rolling basis. **Financial aid:** No deadline. FAFSA required. Applicants notified on a rolling basis starting 9/1.

Academics. Special study options: Double major, internships, liberal arts/career combination. **Credit/placement by examination:** AP, CLEP, institutional tests. **Support services:** Tutoring.

Majors. Business: Accounting, administrative services, business admin, office management. **Computer sciences:** Computer science. **Health services:** Medical assistant.

Computing on campus. 35 workstations in computer center.

Student life. Freshman orientation: Mandatory. Preregistration for classes offered.

Student services. Career counseling, personal counseling.

Contact. E-mail: tharris@national-college.edu
Phone: (540) 326-3621
Tonya Elmore, Director of Admissions, National College: Princeton, PO Box 6400, Roanoke, VA 24017

New River Community and Technical College
Beckley, West Virginia
www.newriver.edu   CB code: 5943

▸ Public 2-year community and technical college
▸ Commuter campus in large town

General. Regionally accredited. **Enrollment:** 2,193 degree-seeking undergraduates; 724 non-degree-seeking students. **Degrees:** 160 associate awarded. **Calendar:** Semester, limited summer session. **Full-time faculty:** 49 total; 22% have terminal degrees, 6% minority, 49% women. **Part-time faculty:** 126 total; 3% minority, 51% women.

Student profile. Among degree-seeking undergraduates, 539 enrolled as first-time, first-year students, 315 transferred in from other institutions.

| Part-time: | 21% | Women: | 71% |
| Out-of-state: | 1% | 25 or older: | 50% |

Basis for selection. Open admission. **Adult students:** COMPASS required for placement.

2011-2012 Annual costs. Tuition/fees: $3,080; $7,672 out-of-state. Per-credit charge: $128 in-state; $320 out-of-state. Books/supplies: $600.

Financial aid. Need-based: Work-study available nights, weekends and for part-time students.

Application procedures. Admission: No deadline. No application fee.

Academics. Special study options: Distance learning, double major, dual enrollment of high school students, internships, weekend college. License preparation in nursing, paramedic. **Credit/placement by examination:** AP, CLEP. **Support services:** GED preparation, remedial instruction, tutoring, writing center.

Majors. Business: General, accounting, banking/financial services, hospitality admin, marketing, tourism/travel. **Communications technology:** General. **Computer sciences:** General, information technology, LAN/WAN management. **Conservation:** Environmental science. **Education:** General, teacher assistance. **General:** Aquaculture. **Health services:** Medical assistant. **Protective services:** Corrections, law enforcement admin.

Most popular majors. Business/marketing 27%, health sciences 9%, legal studies 14%, liberal arts 36%, physical sciences 11%.

Student life. Freshman orientation: Available. Preregistration for classes offered. **Activities:** Student government, student newspaper.

Student services. Career counseling, financial aid counseling. **Physically disabled:** Services for visually, speech, hearing impaired.

Contact. E-mail: admissions@newriver.edu
Phone: (866) 349-3739 Fax: (304) 929-5484
Tracy Evans, Director of Enrollment Services, New River Community and Technical College, 167 Dye Drive, Beckley, WV 25801

Potomac State College of West Virginia University
Keyser, West Virginia
www.potomacstatecollege.edu   **CB code: 5539**

▶ Public 2-year branch campus and junior college
▶ Commuter campus in small town

General. Founded in 1901. Regionally accredited. **Enrollment:** 1,483 degree-seeking undergraduates; 319 non-degree-seeking students. **Degrees:** 19 bachelor's, 199 associate awarded. **Location:** 80 miles from Morgantown, 150 miles from Baltimore. **Calendar:** Semester, limited summer session. **Full-time faculty:** 41 total; 34% have terminal degrees, 5% minority, 51% women. **Part-time faculty:** 58 total; 3% have terminal degrees, 2% minority, 52% women. **Class size:** 44% < 20, 45% 20-39, 7% 40-49, 4% 50-99, less than 1% >100. **Special facilities:** 3 fully operational farms and a 27,500 sq foot indoor riding arena to support agriculture and forestry programs; demonstration kitchen for hospitality.

Student profile. Among degree-seeking undergraduates, 79% enrolled in a transfer program, 15% enrolled in a vocational program, 720 enrolled as first-time, first-year students, 60 transferred in from other institutions.

Part-time:	6%	Native American:	1%
Out-of-state:	23%	International:	1%
Women:	49%	25 or older:	23%
African American:	15%	Live on campus:	29%
Hispanic American:	3%		

Transfer out. Colleges most students transferred to 2011: West Virginia University, Fairmont State College, Frostburg State University.

Basis for selection. Open admission, but selective for out-of-state students. Due to enrollment growth, out-of-state applicants are occasionally waitlisted or denied. **Adult students:** SAT/ACT not required for placement if applicant is out of high school 5 years or more.

2011-2012 Annual costs. Tuition/fees: $3,058; $8,990 out-of-state. Per-credit charge: $129 in-state; $376 out-of-state. Tuition for students residing in border counties is $5,294. Room/board: $7,290. Books/supplies: $750.

2010-2011 Financial aid. Need-based: Need-based aid available for part-time students. Work-study available nights, weekends and for part-time students. **Non-need-based:** Scholarships awarded for academics, athletics, leadership.

Application procedures. Admission: No deadline. No application fee. Admission notification on a rolling basis beginning on or about 9/15. English ACT used in conjunction with high school GPA to place students in either

college-level or remedial composition courses. Scores also used for math placement. **Financial aid:** Priority date 3/1; no closing date. FAFSA required. Applicants notified on a rolling basis starting 3/15; must reply within 2 week(s) of notification.

Academics. Special study options: Distance learning, double major, dual enrollment of high school students, honors, internships, study abroad. Bachelor's degree programs available on campus. **Credit/placement by examination:** AP, CLEP, institutional tests. 30 credit hours maximum toward associate degree. **Support services:** Learning center, reduced course load, remedial instruction, tutoring.

Majors. Biology: General. **Business:** Administrative services, business admin, fashion, hospitality admin, managerial economics, restaurant/food services. **Communications:** Journalism. **Computer sciences:** General, applications programming, data processing, information technology, programming. **Conservation:** General, forest management, forest resources, management/policy, wildlife/wilderness, wood science. **Education:** General, elementary, physical, secondary. **Engineering:** Civil, electrical, mechanical. **English:** English lit. **Foreign languages:** General. **General:** Agronomy, animal sciences, business technology, education services, equestrian studies, horticultural science. **Health services:** Athletic training, nursing practice, occupational therapy, physical therapy, predental, premedicine, prenursing, prepharmacy, preveterinary. **History:** General. **Human services:** Social work. **Liberal arts:** Arts/sciences. **Math:** General. **Parks/recreation:** Facilities management. **Physical sciences:** Chemistry, geology, physics. **Protective services:** Correctional facilities, criminal justice, law enforcement admin. **Psychology:** General. **Social sciences:** Economics, political science, sociology.

Most popular majors. Agriculture 17%, business/marketing 15%, education 12%, health sciences 9%, liberal arts 19%, security/protective services 10%.

Computing on campus. 100 workstations in library, computer center, student center. Dormitories wired for high-speed internet access. Helpline, repair service, wireless network available.

Student life. Freshman orientation: Mandatory, $50 fee. Preregistration for classes offered. **Housing:** Coed dorms, single-sex dorms available. $200 fully refundable deposit, deadline 8/15. Dorm for agriculture and agricultural-related majors. **Activities:** Bands, campus ministries, choral groups, drama, music ensembles, musical theater, student government, student newspaper, agriculture and forestry club, Circle K, equestrian club, criminal justice club, engineering club, peer advocates, life sciences club, campus and community ministry.

Athletics. NJCAA. **Intercollegiate:** Baseball M, basketball, golf, soccer, softball W, volleyball W. **Intramural:** Basketball. **Team name:** Catamounts.

Student services. Alcohol/substance abuse counseling, career counseling, services for economically disadvantaged, student employment services, financial aid counseling, health services, minority student services, on-campus daycare, personal counseling, placement for graduates, veterans' counselor, women's services. **Physically disabled:** Services for visually, hearing impaired. **Transfer:** Pre-admission transcript evaluation for new students. Transfer adviser, college fairs on campus for students transferring to 4-year colleges.

Contact. E-mail: go2psc@mail.wvu.edu
Phone: (304) 788-6820 Toll-free number: (800) 262-7332
Fax: (304) 788-6939
Beth Little, Director of Enrollment Services, Potomac State College of West Virginia University, 75 Arnold Street, Keyser, WV 26726

Southern West Virginia Community and Technical College
Mount Gay, West Virginia   **CB member**
www.southernwv.edu   **CB code: 0770**

▶ Public 2-year community college
▶ Commuter campus in small town

General. Founded in 1971. Regionally accredited. Additional campuses in Williamson, Saulsville, and Madison. **Enrollment:** 2,457 degree-seeking undergraduates. **Degrees:** 209 associate awarded. **Location:** 60 miles from Charleston. **Calendar:** Trimester, limited summer session. **Full-time faculty:** 70 total. **Part-time faculty:** 79 total. **Special facilities:** Allied health and technology building.

Transfer out. Colleges most students transferred to 2011: Marshall University, West Virginia University, West Virginia State University, Mountain State University, Concord University.

Basis for selection. Open admission, but selective for some programs. Limited admissions to nursing, medical laboratory, radiologic technology, dental hygiene, respiratory technology, and surgical technology programs. Application and criteria are posted on web page by October 1 and deadline to submit application is January 31. **Adult students:** Adult students may take ACCUPLACER to determine placement in English and math. **Home schooled:** Transcript of courses and grades required. **Learning Disabled:** Meeting with disability counselor recommended.

2011-2012 Annual costs. Tuition/fees: $2,304; $6,816 out-of-state. Per-credit charge: $96 in-state; $284 out-of-state. Books/supplies: $1,200. Personal expenses: $900.

Financial aid. Need-based: Need-based aid available for part-time students. Work-study available nights, weekends and for part-time students.

Application procedures. Admission: No deadline. No application fee. Admission notification on a rolling basis. **Financial aid:** No deadline. FAFSA required. Applicants notified on a rolling basis.

Academics. Special study options: Distance learning, dual enrollment of high school students, independent study, teacher certification program. Fast Track courses. Bachelor's degree programs available on campus. License preparation in dental hygiene, nursing, paramedic, radiology. **Credit/placement by examination:** AP, CLEP, institutional tests. **Support services:** GED preparation, learning center, reduced course load, remedial instruction, tutoring.

Majors. Business: Accounting, business admin, executive assistant. **Computer sciences:** Information technology. **Health services:** Clinical lab technology, dental hygiene, EMT paramedic, health aide, medical radiologic technology/radiation therapy, nursing (RN), respiratory therapy technology, surgical technology. **Liberal arts:** Arts/sciences. **Protective services:** Criminal justice. **Work/family studies:** Child care management.

Most popular majors. Business/marketing 17%, health sciences 50%, liberal arts 22%, security/protective services 14%.

Computing on campus. Online course registration, online library, helpline, wireless network available.

Student life. Freshman orientation: Available. Preregistration for classes offered. Offered to first-time freshman, or students with less than 30 credit hours. **Activities:** Drama, musical theater, student government, special interest clubs.

Student services. Adult student services, career counseling, student employment services, financial aid counseling, on-campus daycare, personal counseling, placement for graduates, veterans' counselor. **Physically disabled:** Services for visually, speech, hearing impaired. **Transfer:** Transfer adviser, college fairs on campus for students transferring to 4-year colleges.

Contact. Phone: (304) 896-7443 Toll-free number: (866) 798-2821 Fax: (304) 792-7056
Teri Wells, Student Records Assistant, Southern West Virginia Community and Technical College, PO Box 2900, Mount Gay, WV 25637

Valley College
Martinsburg, West Virginia
www.vct.edu
CB code: 3176

- For-profit 2-year business and career college
- Commuter campus in large town
- Interview required

General. Accredited by ACICS. Additional campuses in Princeton and Beckley. Distance Education available at sister campus (Valley College, Beckley). **Enrollment:** 26 degree-seeking undergraduates. **Degrees:** 2 associate awarded. **Location:** 20 miles from Winchester, Virginia; 20 miles from Hagerstown, Maryland. **Calendar:** Differs by program, extensive summer session. **Full-time faculty:** 2 total. **Part-time faculty:** 1 total.

Transfer out. Colleges most students transferred to 2011: Mountain State University, Shepherd University, Blue Ridge Community and Technical College.

Basis for selection. Open admission. **Home schooled:** Transcript of courses and grades, state high school equivalency certificate required.

2011-2012 Annual costs. Tuition/fees: $9,150. Per-credit charge: $275. Books/supplies: $1,385. Personal expenses: $9,279.

Financial aid. Need-based: Need-based aid available for part-time students. Work-study available nights, weekends and for part-time students.

Application procedures. Admission: No deadline. No application fee. Application must be submitted on paper. Admission notification on a rolling basis. Institutional placement test administered for students without ACT or SAT. **Financial aid:** No deadline. FAFSA, institutional form required. Applicants notified on a rolling basis.

Academics. Credit/placement by examination: AP, CLEP. 29 credit hours maximum toward associate degree. **Support services:** Remedial instruction, study skills assistance.

Majors. Business: General, business admin, small business admin.

Computing on campus. 42 workstations in computer center.

Student life. Freshman orientation: Mandatory. Preregistration for classes offered. Orientation held during first week of classes.

Student services. Career counseling, student employment services, financial aid counseling, placement for graduates. **Transfer:** Pre-admission transcript evaluation for new students.

Contact. E-mail: martinsburg@vct.edu
Phone: (304) 263-0979 Fax: (304) 263-2413
Matthew Jenkins, Director of Admissions, Valley College, 287 Aikens Center, Martinsburg, WV 25404

West Virginia Business College: Nutter Fort
Wheeling, West Virginia
www.wvbc.edu
CB code: 2546

- For-profit 2-year business college
- Commuter campus in small city

General. Accredited by ACICS. **Location:** 35 miles from Morgantown. **Calendar:** Quarter.

Annual costs/financial aid. Tuition/fees (2011-2012): $9,000. Need-based financial aid available to full-time and part-time students.

Contact. Phone: (304) 232-0361
Director, 1052 Main Street, Wheeling, WV 26003

West Virginia Business College: Wheeling
Wheeling, West Virginia
www.wvbc.edu

- For-profit 2-year business and career college
- Commuter campus in small city
- Interview required

General. Accredited by ACICS. **Enrollment:** 125 degree-seeking undergraduates. **Degrees:** 64 associate awarded. **Location:** 50 miles from Pittsburgh. **Calendar:** Quarter, extensive summer session. **Part-time faculty:** 20 total. **Class size:** 97% < 20, 3% 20-39.

Basis for selection. Open admission. **Home schooled:** State high school equivalency certificate required.

2011-2012 Annual costs. Tuition/fees: $9,000. Books/supplies: $1,800.

Financial aid. Need-based: Work-study available nights, weekends and for part-time students.

Application procedures. Admission: No deadline. $50 fee. Application must be submitted on paper. Admission notification on a rolling basis.

Academics. Credit/placement by examination: AP, CLEP. 8 credit hours maximum toward associate degree. **Support services:** Study skills assistance, tutoring.

Majors. Business: Administrative services, business admin. **Computer sciences:** General, support specialist, word processing. **Health services:** Clinical lab technology, health aide, health care admin, home attendant, insurance coding, insurance specialist, medical assistant, medical records technology, medical transcription, office admin, office assistant, receptionist, sterile processing technology, surgical technology.

Most popular majors. Business/marketing 25%, computer/information sciences 13%, health sciences 25%, legal studies 13%.

Computing on campus. Online library, wireless network available.

Student life. **Activities:** Student government, student newspaper.

Student services. Career counseling, financial aid counseling, placement for graduates.

Contact. E-mail: jweir@wvbc.edu
Phone: (304) 232-0631 ext. 13 Fax: (304) 232-0363
Brandy Kuri, Director of Admissions, West Virginia Business College: Wheeling, 1052 Main Street, Wheeling, WV 26003

West Virginia Junior College
Morgantown, West Virginia
www.wvjcmorgantown.edu   CB code: 3179

⬥ For-profit 2-year junior college
⬥ Large town

General. Accredited by ACICS. **Enrollment:** 170 degree-seeking undergraduates. **Degrees:** 72 associate awarded. **Calendar:** Quarter. **Full-time faculty:** 4 total. **Part-time faculty:** 5 total.

Basis for selection. Open admission.

2011-2012 Annual costs. Estimated program costs: associate degree, $21,800-$43,545; diploma, $14,567. Includes fees and supplies. Personal expenses: $2,529.

Financial aid. **Need-based:** Need-based aid available for part-time students. Work-study available nights, weekends and for part-time students.

Application procedures. **Admission:** No deadline. $25 fee. Admission notification on a rolling basis. Prospective students meet with admissions counselor as part of application process. **Financial aid:** No deadline. FAFSA required. Applicants notified on a rolling basis.

Academics. **Credit/placement by examination:** AP, CLEP.

Majors. **Business:** Business admin, office technology. **Computer sciences:** Information systems, information technology. **Health services:** Insurance coding, medical assistant.

Contact. E-mail: info@wvjc.edu
Phone: (304) 296-8282
Leann Cardozo, Academic Director, West Virginia Junior College, 148 Willey Street, Morgantown, WV 26505

West Virginia Junior College: Bridgeport
Bridgeport, West Virginia
www.wvjcinfo.net

⬥ For-profit 2-year health science and junior college
⬥ Commuter campus in large town
⬥ Interview required

General. Accredited by ACICS. **Enrollment:** 350 degree-seeking undergraduates. **Degrees:** 117 associate awarded. **Location:** 40 miles from Morgantown. **Calendar:** Quarter. **Full-time faculty:** 7 total. **Part-time faculty:** 11 total.

Basis for selection. Open admission, but selective for some programs. Applicants are required to meet with an Admissions Representative. Specific programs have additional admissions requirements; Medical programs must have on file evidence of student liability insurance and Hepatitis B immunization prior to performing externships. **Adult students:** SAT/ACT scores not required. **Home schooled:** State high school equivalency certificate required.

2011-2012 Annual costs. Cost of programs range from $16,004 to $23,869, including fees and supplies.

Financial aid. **Need-based:** Need-based aid available for part-time students. Work-study available nights, weekends and for part-time students.

Application procedures. **Admission:** No deadline. No application fee. Application must be submitted on paper. Admission notification on a rolling basis. **Financial aid:** FAFSA required.

Academics. **Special study options:** Distance learning, internships. **Credit/placement by examination:** AP, CLEP. **Support services:** Study skills assistance, tutoring.

Majors. **Business:** Business admin. **Computer sciences:** Information technology. **Health services:** Dental assistant, medical assistant, medical secretary.

Computing on campus. 100 workstations in library, computer center. Online course registration, online library, repair service, wireless network available.

Student life. **Freshman orientation:** Mandatory. Preregistration for classes offered.

Student services. Adult student services, career counseling, student employment services, financial aid counseling, placement for graduates, veterans' counselor. **Physically disabled:** Services for visually, speech, hearing impaired. **Transfer:** Pre-admission transcript evaluation for new students.

Contact. E-mail: admissions@wvjcinfo.net
Phone: (304) 842-4007 Toll-free number: (800) 470-5627 ext. 110
Fax: (304) 842-8191
Darin Webster, Director of Admissions, West Virginia Junior College: Bridgeport, 176 Thompson Drive, Bridgeport, WV 26330

West Virginia Junior College: Charleston
Charleston, West Virginia
www.wvjc.edu   CB code: 3180

⬥ For-profit 2-year junior and technical college
⬥ Commuter campus in small city

General. Accredited by ACICS. **Calendar:** Quarter.

Annual costs/financial aid. Tuition/fees (2011-2012): $11,725. Need-based financial aid available to full-time and part-time students.

Contact. Phone: (304) 345-2820
Executive Director, 1000 Virginia Street East, Charleston, WV 25301

West Virginia Northern Community College
Wheeling, West Virginia
www.wvncc.edu   CB code: 0674

⬥ Public 2-year community and technical college
⬥ Commuter campus in large town

General. Founded in 1972. Regionally accredited. Additional campuses in New Martinsville and Weirton. **Enrollment:** 2,535 degree-seeking undergraduates; 459 non-degree-seeking students. **Degrees:** 338 associate awarded. **Location:** 45 miles from Pittsburgh. **Calendar:** Semester, limited summer session. **Full-time faculty:** 62 total; 8% have terminal degrees, 6% minority, 66% women. **Part-time faculty:** 143 total; 4% have terminal degrees, less than 1% minority. **Partnerships:** Formal agreements with Northern Panhandle Technical Education and Training Partnership, Oglebay Institute Partnership, RESA 6, West Virginia Rehabilitation Center, National Retail Federation, Northern Panhandle Workforce Investment Board.

Student profile. Among degree-seeking undergraduates, 502 enrolled as first-time, first-year students, 314 transferred in from other institutions.

Part-time:	44%	African American:	5%
Out-of-state:	24%	25 or older:	51%
Women:	71%		

Transfer out. **Colleges most students transferred to 2011:** West Liberty State College, Wheeling Jesuit University, West Virginia University, Bethany College, Ohio Eastern University.

Basis for selection. Open admission, but selective for some programs. Special requirements for health programs. Students without high school diploma or GED must submit ACT. **Learning Disabled:** Students who would like to receive accommodations must contact Student Disabilities coordinator.

High school preparation. Strong science and math background recommended for health science applicants.

2011-2012 Annual costs. Tuition/fees: $2,478; $7,254 out-of-state. Tuition for students residing in bordering counties is $4,750. Books/supplies: $600. Personal expenses: $1,153.

Financial aid. **Need-based:** Need-based aid available for part-time students. Work-study available nights, weekends and for part-time students.

Application procedures. **Admission:** No deadline. No application fee. Application must be submitted online. Admission notification on a rolling basis. Health science applicants must apply by January 10; late applicants evaluated after June 30 if space available. **Financial aid:** Priority date 3/15; no closing date. FAFSA, institutional form required. Applicants notified on a rolling basis starting 3/10.

Academics. **Special study options:** Accelerated study, distance learning, double major, dual enrollment of high school students, independent study, internships, liberal arts/career combination. 2+2 in education, business administration, criminal justice at West Liberty State College. 2+2 mental health and human services, social work, accounting/business administration, business studies, business administration option, and transfer agreement in early childhood education with Franciscan University of Steubenville. 2+2 in social work with West Virginia University. License preparation in nursing. **Credit/placement by examination:** AP, CLEP, institutional tests. 45 credit hours maximum toward associate degree. **Support services:** Learning center, remedial instruction, study skills assistance, tutoring.

Majors. **Business:** Accounting technology, administrative services, business admin, hospitality admin. **Computer sciences:** Programming. **Health services:** Medical radiologic technology/radiation therapy, nursing (RN), respiratory therapy technology, surgical technology. **Human services:** Social work. **Liberal arts:** Arts/sciences. **Protective services:** Police science.

Most popular majors. Business/marketing 9%, health sciences 47%, liberal arts 23%, public administration/social services 8%.

Computing on campus. 215 workstations in library, computer center. Commuter students can connect to campus network. Online course registration, online library, wireless network available.

Student life. **Freshman orientation:** Mandatory. Preregistration for classes offered. Held during spring and early fall for about 3.5-4 hours. **Activities:** Student government, student newspaper, African American/multicultural organization, COOP.

Athletics. **Intramural:** Badminton, basketball, bowling, football (non-tackle), golf, soccer, softball, volleyball. **Team name:** Thundering Chickens.

Student services. Career counseling, student employment services, financial aid counseling, placement for graduates, veterans' counselor. **Physically disabled:** Services for visually, speech, hearing impaired. **Transfer:** Transfer adviser, college fairs on campus for students transferring to 4-year colleges.

Contact. E-mail: info@wvncc.edu
Phone: (304) 233-5900 ext. 8848 Fax: (304) 232-8187
Richard McCray, Associate Director of Admissions, West Virginia Northern Community College, 1704 Market Street, Wheeling, WV 26003

West Virginia University at Parkersburg
Parkersburg, West Virginia
www.wvup.edu

CB member
CB code: 5932

- Public 2-year community college
- Commuter campus in large town

General. Founded in 1971. Regionally accredited. **Enrollment:** 4,000 degree-seeking undergraduates. **Degrees:** 176 bachelor's, 560 associate awarded. **Location:** 80 miles from Charleston; 110 miles from Columbus, Ohio. **Calendar:** Semester, limited summer session. **Full-time faculty:** 96 total. **Part-time faculty:** 203 total. **Class size:** 56% < 20, 40% 20-39, 2% 40-49, 1% 50-99.

Student profile.

Out-of-state:	3%	25 or older:	44%

Basis for selection. Open admission, but selective for some programs. Special requirements for nursing, surgical technology, paramedic science and bachelor's degree programs. SAT or ACT (ACT preferred) required but not used in admission decisions. Interview required for nursing program.

High school preparation. 16 units recommended. Recommended units include English 4, mathematics 3, social studies 4, science 3 (laboratory 2). Social studies recommendations may be fulfilled with history units.

2011-2012 Annual costs. Tuition/fees: $2,276; $8,052 out-of-state. Per-credit charge: $95 in-state; $335 out-of-state. Associate degree tuition and fees shown above; baccalaureate program tuition: $3,118, in-state and $8,236, out-of-state. Books/supplies: $1,000. Personal expenses: $1,400.

Financial aid. **Need-based:** Need-based aid available for part-time students. Work-study available nights, weekends and for part-time students. **Non-need-based:** Scholarships awarded for academics, leadership, state residency.

Application procedures. **Admission:** No deadline. No application fee. Admission notification on a rolling basis. **Financial aid:** Priority date 3/1; no closing date. FAFSA required. Applicants notified on a rolling basis; must reply within 2 week(s) of notification.

Academics. **Special study options:** Cooperative education, cross-registration, distance learning, dual enrollment of high school students, ESL, external degree, honors, independent study, internships, teacher certification program, weekend college. License preparation in nursing, paramedic. **Credit/placement by examination:** AP, CLEP, IB, institutional tests. **Support services:** Learning center, reduced course load, remedial instruction, study skills assistance, tutoring.

Majors. **Business:** Executive assistant, management information systems. **Communications:** Journalism. **Computer sciences:** Information systems. **Education:** Elementary, teacher assistance. **Health services:** Nursing (RN). **Liberal arts:** Arts/sciences. **Protective services:** Criminal justice.

Most popular majors. Business/marketing 20%, health sciences 16%, liberal arts 41%, security/protective services 6%.

Computing on campus. 435 workstations in library, computer center. Online course registration, online library, helpline, wireless network available.

Student life. **Freshman orientation:** Mandatory. Preregistration for classes offered. **Activities:** Choral groups, drama, literary magazine, music ensembles, musical theater, student government, student newspaper, reading association, environmental action group, multicultural awareness coalition, psychology club, Campus Christian Fellowship, criminal justice organization, Spark (community volunteers), student nursing association, American Welding Society.

Athletics. **Intramural:** Basketball, bowling, golf, softball, table tennis, volleyball. **Team name:** Riverhawks.

Student services. Adult student services, career counseling, services for economically disadvantaged, student employment services, financial aid counseling, on-campus daycare, personal counseling, placement for graduates, veterans' counselor. **Physically disabled:** Services for visually, speech, hearing impaired. **Transfer:** Pre-admission transcript evaluation for new students. Transfer adviser, college fairs on campus for students transferring to 4-year colleges.

Contact. E-mail: info@mail.wvup.edu
Phone: (304) 424-8220 Fax: (304) 424-8332
Christine Post, Assistant Dean for Enrollment Management, West Virginia University at Parkersburg, 300 Campus Drive, Parkersburg, WV 26104-8647

Wisconsin

Blackhawk Technical College
Janesville, Wisconsin
www.blackhawk.edu
CB code: 7319

- Public 2-year technical college
- Commuter campus in small city

General. Founded in 1912. Regionally accredited. **Enrollment:** 3,278 degree-seeking undergraduates. **Degrees:** 359 associate awarded. **Location:** 75 miles from Milwaukee and Chicago. **Calendar:** Semester, limited summer session. **Full-time faculty:** 109 total; 3% have terminal degrees, 6% minority, 57% women. **Part-time faculty:** 279 total; 6% minority, 47% women. **Class size:** 74% < 20, 26% 20-39.

Student profile. Among degree-seeking undergraduates, 100% enrolled in a vocational program, 3% already have a bachelor's degree or higher, 634 enrolled as first-time, first-year students.

Part-time:	57%	African American:	7%
Out-of-state:	1%	Asian American:	1%
Women:	61%	Hispanic American:	6%

Basis for selection. Open admission, but selective for some programs. Applicants to nursing, dental hygiene, radiography, sonography, and physical therapist assistant programs must meet additional testing and course requirements.

2011-2012 Annual costs. Tuition/fees: $3,528; $5,208 out-of-state. Per-credit charge: $112 in-state; $168 out-of-state. Material fees vary by program; minimum $4 per course. $10 per credit fee for online courses. Books/supplies: $1,399. Personal expenses: $2,053.

2010-2011 Financial aid. **Need-based:** 62% of total undergraduate aid awarded as scholarships/grants, 38% as loans/jobs. Need-based aid available for part-time students. Work-study available nights, weekends and for part-time students.

Application procedures. **Admission:** Priority date 9/1; no deadline. $30 fee. Admission notification on a rolling basis beginning on or about 10/1. **Financial aid:** Priority date 4/30; no closing date. FAFSA required. Applicants notified on a rolling basis starting 3/15.

Academics. **Special study options:** Accelerated study, distance learning, dual enrollment of high school students, ESL, independent study, internships, student-designed major. License preparation in nursing, physical therapy, radiology. **Credit/placement by examination:** AP, CLEP. 30 credit hours maximum toward associate degree. **Support services:** GED preparation and test center, learning center, pre-admission summer program, reduced course load, remedial instruction, study skills assistance, tutoring.

Majors. **Business:** Accounting, administrative services, marketing, office management, operations, training/development. **Computer sciences:** LAN/WAN management, security, web page design. **Engineering:** Electrical. **Health services:** Clinical lab assistant, medical radiologic technology/radiation therapy, medical secretary, nursing (RN), physical therapy assistant, sonography. **Protective services:** Fire safety technology, police science. **Work/family studies:** Institutional food production.

Most popular majors. Security/protective services 14%.

Computing on campus. 75 workstations in library, computer center. Online course registration, helpline, wireless network available.

Student life. **Freshman orientation:** Available. Preregistration for classes offered. **Activities:** Student government, student newspaper.

Student services. Alcohol/substance abuse counseling, career counseling, services for economically disadvantaged, student employment services, financial aid counseling, minority student services, on-campus daycare, personal counseling, placement for graduates, veterans' counselor. **Physically disabled:** Services for visually, speech, hearing impaired.

Contact. Phone: (608) 757-7665 Fax: (608) 743-4407 Edward Robinson, Vice President Student Services, Blackhawk Technical College, Box 5009, Janesville, WI 53547-5009

Bryant & Stratton College: Milwaukee
Milwaukee, Wisconsin
www.bryantstratton.edu
CB code: 3617

- For-profit 2-year business and junior college
- Commuter campus in very large city
- Application essay, interview required

General. Founded in 1854. Regionally accredited. **Enrollment:** 1,089 degree-seeking undergraduates. **Degrees:** 2 bachelor's, 113 associate awarded. **Location:** 75 miles from Chicago. **Calendar:** Trimester, extensive summer session. **Full-time faculty:** 15 total. **Part-time faculty:** 79 total. **Class size:** 75% < 20, 25% 20-39.

Basis for selection. School achievement record, test scores, interview important. SAT/ACT scores can take place of school's entrance exam.

2011-2012 Annual costs. Tuition/fees: $15,570. Tuition and fees may vary by program. Books/supplies: $750.

Financial aid. All financial aid based on need. Work-study available nights, weekends and for part-time students.

Application procedures. **Admission:** No deadline. $25 fee. Admission notification on a rolling basis. **Financial aid:** No deadline. FAFSA required. Applicants notified on a rolling basis; must reply within 2 week(s) of notification.

Academics. **Special study options:** Distance learning, double major, internships. License preparation on campus provided for Medical Coding and Certified Secretary, and Medical Assisting (exam given on campus). Bachelor's degree programs available on campus. **Credit/placement by examination:** AP, CLEP, institutional tests. 30 credit hours maximum toward associate degree. **Support services:** Reduced course load, remedial instruction, study skills assistance, tutoring.

Majors. **Business:** General, accounting, administrative services. **Computer sciences:** Information systems, information technology, systems analysis. **Health services:** Medical assistant, medical secretary, nursing (RN). **Protective services:** Law enforcement admin. **Visual/performing arts:** Graphic design.

Most popular majors. Business/marketing 45%, computer/information sciences 31%, health sciences 22%.

Computing on campus. 100 workstations in library, computer center.

Student life. **Freshman orientation:** Mandatory. Preregistration for classes offered. **Housing:** Nearby dormitories available through St. Catherine's Residence for Women. **Activities:** Student government, student newspaper, Association for Information Technology Professionals, Collegiate Secretaries International, Allied Health Association, Phi Beta Lambda, student board.

Athletics. **Team name:** Bobcats.

Student services. Career counseling, student employment services, financial aid counseling, personal counseling, placement for graduates, veterans' counselor. **Transfer:** Re-entry adviser, pre-admission transcript evaluation for new students. Transfer adviser for students transferring to 4-year colleges.

Contact. Phone: (414) 276-5200 Fax: (414) 276-3930 Kathryn Cotey, Director of Admissions, Bryant & Stratton College: Milwaukee, 310 West Wisconsin Avenue, Suite 500, Milwaukee, WI 53203

Chippewa Valley Technical College
Eau Claire, Wisconsin
www.cvtc.edu
CB code: 0786

- Public 2-year technical college
- Commuter campus in small city

General. Founded in 1912. Regionally accredited. **Enrollment:** 5,042 degree-seeking undergraduates; 998 non-degree-seeking students. **Degrees:** 512 associate awarded. **Location:** 90 miles from Minneapolis-St. Paul. **Calendar:** Semester, limited summer session. **Special facilities:** Health education center with lab facilities, NanoRite facility. **Partnerships:** Formal partnerships with University of Wisconsin Family Medicine Clinic, University of Wisconsin-Marquette, Haas Manufacturing, Eau Claire Area School District Technology Charter, NanoRite, University of Wisconsin-Stout, NWMOC,

Workforce Resource, Job Service, ECAEDC- SmarttNet, Districts Mutual Insurance.

Student profile. Among degree-seeking undergraduates, 1,968 enrolled as first-time, first-year students.

Part-time:	45%	Hispanic American:	2%
Women:	59%	Native American:	1%
African American:	1%	25 or older:	43%
Asian American:	4%		

Basis for selection. Open admission, but selective for some programs. Additional testing and course requirements for applicants to nursing, dental hygiene, radiography, surgical technologist, medical assistant and physical therapist assistant programs.

High school preparation. Algebra and science requirements for some degree programs.

2011-2012 Annual costs. Tuition/fees: $3,575; $5,255 out-of-state. Per-credit charge: $112 in-state; $168 out-of-state. Material fees vary by program; minimum $4 per course. $10 per credit fee for online courses.

Financial aid. Need-based: Need-based aid available for part-time students. Work-study available nights, weekends and for part-time students.

Application procedures. Admission: No deadline. $30 fee, may be waived for applicants with need. Admission notification on a rolling basis. **Financial aid:** Priority date 3/15; no closing date. FAFSA required. Applicants notified on a rolling basis starting 6/1; must reply within 2 week(s) of notification.

Academics. Special study options: Distance learning, double major, dual enrollment of high school students, ESL, external degree, independent study, internships, liberal arts/career combination, student-designed major. License preparation in dental hygiene, nursing, paramedic, radiology. **Credit/placement by examination:** AP, CLEP, institutional tests. 34 credit hours maximum toward associate degree. 50% of semester hours needed for degree may be earned as credit by examination. **Support services:** GED preparation and test center, learning center, reduced course load, remedial instruction, study skills assistance, tutoring.

Majors. Business: Accounting, administrative services, business admin, human resources, marketing. **Computer sciences:** General, applications programming, networking, programming. **Education:** Early childhood. **Engineering:** Civil. **Health services:** Clinical lab technology, dental hygiene, EMT paramedic, medical radiologic technology/radiation therapy, medical records technology, nursing (RN), physical therapy assistant, respiratory therapy technology, sonography, substance abuse counseling. **Liberal arts:** Arts/sciences. **Protective services:** Firefighting, police science. **Work/family studies:** Child care service.

Most popular majors. Business/marketing 25%, computer/information sciences 7%, engineering/engineering technologies 7%, health sciences 42%.

Computing on campus. Commuter students can connect to campus network. Online course registration, helpline, wireless network available.

Student life. Freshman orientation: Mandatory. Preregistration for classes offered. **Activities:** Student government, student newspaper, Student Impact, Diversity Student Organization, Pride Alliance.

Student services. Career counseling, services for economically disadvantaged, student employment services, financial aid counseling, health services, minority student services, personal counseling, placement for graduates, veterans' counselor. **Physically disabled:** Services for visually, speech, hearing impaired. **Transfer:** Pre-admission transcript evaluation for new students. Transfer center, college fairs on campus for students transferring to 4-year colleges.

Contact. E-mail: infocenter@cvtc.edu
Phone: (715) 833-6200 Toll-free number: (800) 547-2882
Fax: (715) 833-6470
Paige Wegner, Director of Enrollment Services, Chippewa Valley Technical College, 620 West Clairemont Avenue, Eau Claire, WI 54701-6162

College of Menominee Nation
Keshena, Wisconsin
www.menominee.edu   CB code: 3974

♦ Private 2-year community college
♦ Commuter campus in rural community

General. Regionally accredited. **Enrollment:** 601 degree-seeking undergraduates. **Degrees:** 6 bachelor's, 74 associate awarded. **Location:** 150 miles from Madison, 35 miles from Green Bay. **Calendar:** Semester, limited summer session. **Full-time faculty:** 31 total. **Part-time faculty:** 22 total. **Class size:** 77% < 20, 23% 20-39.

Transfer out. Colleges most students transferred to 2011: University of Wisconsin-Green Bay, University of Wisconsin-Oshkosh, Silver Lake College.

Basis for selection. Open admission, but selective for some programs. ACCUPLACER required of all students for placement. **Home schooled:** Must present state certification of completion of requirements. **Learning Disabled:** Students should meet with disability advisor upon registration.

2011-2012 Annual costs. Tuition/fees: $7,350. Per-credit charge: $240. Books/supplies: $1,072. Personal expenses: $1,452.

Financial aid. All financial aid based on need. Need-based aid available for part-time students. Work-study available nights, weekends and for part-time students.

Application procedures. Admission: Closing date 8/30 (receipt date). No application fee. Admission notification on a rolling basis. **Financial aid:** FAFSA required. Applicants notified on a rolling basis.

Academics. Some courses are offered off-site via broadcasting. **Special study options:** Double major, independent study, internships, liberal arts/career combination. Bachelor's degree programs available on campus. **Credit/placement by examination:** AP, CLEP, institutional tests. **Support services:** Reduced course load, remedial instruction, study skills assistance, tutoring.

Majors. Biology: General. **Business:** Accounting, administrative services, business admin. **Computer sciences:** General. **Conservation:** General. **Education:** Early childhood, kindergarten/preschool. **Health services:** Prenursing. **Liberal arts:** Arts/sciences. **Math:** General. **Social sciences:** General. **Work/family studies:** Food/nutrition.

Computing on campus. 65 workstations in library, computer center. Commuter students can connect to campus network. Online library, wireless network available.

Student life. Freshman orientation: Mandatory. Preregistration for classes offered. Held for 3 hours approximately 1 week prior to classes. **Activities:** Student government, Circle K, Young Democrats.

Student services. Adult student services, alcohol/substance abuse counseling, career counseling, services for economically disadvantaged, financial aid counseling, minority student services, personal counseling, veterans' counselor. **Physically disabled:** Services for visually, speech, hearing impaired. **Transfer:** Pre-admission transcript evaluation for new students. College fairs on campus for students transferring to 4-year colleges.

Contact. E-mail: tjames@menominee.edu
Phone: (715) 799-5600 ext. 3053
Toll-free number: (800) 567-2344 ext. 3053 Fax: (715) 799-4392
Tessa James, Admissions Representative, College of Menominee Nation, N 172 State Highway 47/55, Keshena, WI 54135

Fox Valley Technical College
Appleton, Wisconsin   **CB member**
www.fvtc.edu   **CB code: 0747**

♦ Public 2-year technical college
♦ Commuter campus in small city

General. Founded in 1967. Regionally accredited. **Enrollment:** 8,084 degree-seeking undergraduates; 2,607 non-degree-seeking students. **Degrees:** 1,019 associate awarded. **Location:** 100 miles from Milwaukee. **Calendar:** Semester, limited summer session. **Full-time faculty:** 325 total; 43% women. **Part-time faculty:** 725 total; 46% women.

Student profile. Among degree-seeking undergraduates, 1,089 enrolled as first-time, first-year students.

Part-time:	63%	Asian American:	3%
Out-of-state:	1%	Hispanic American:	3%
Women:	52%	Native American:	1%
African American:	2%	25 or older:	51%

Basis for selection. Open admission, but selective for some programs.

2011-2012 Annual costs. Tuition/fees: $3,729; $5,409 out-of-state. Per-credit charge: $112 in-state; $168 out-of-state. Material fees vary by program;

minimum $4 per course. $10 per credit fee for online courses. Books/supplies: $1,355. Personal expenses: $1,700.

2010-2011 Financial aid. All financial aid based on need. 43% of total undergraduate aid awarded as scholarships/grants, 57% as loans/jobs. Need-based aid available for part-time students. Work-study available nights, weekends and for part-time students.

Application procedures. Admission: Closing date 8/15 (receipt date). $30 fee, may be waived for applicants with need. Admission notification on a rolling basis. **Financial aid:** Priority date 4/15; no closing date. FAFSA required. Applicants notified on a rolling basis.

Academics. Special study options: Accelerated study, distance learning, double major, dual enrollment of high school students, ESL, internships, student-designed major. License preparation in aviation, dental hygiene, nursing, occupational therapy, paramedic, physical therapy. **Credit/placement by examination:** AP, CLEP, institutional tests. 45 credit hours maximum toward associate degree. **Support services:** GED preparation and test center, reduced course load, remedial instruction, tutoring.

Majors. Business: Accounting, administrative services, banking/financial services, business admin, hospitality admin, human resources, logistics, marketing, operations. **Communications:** Radio/TV. **Communications technology:** Graphic/printing, graphics. **Computer sciences:** Networking, programming, systems analysis, webmaster. **Conservation:** General. **Education:** Early childhood. **General:** Mechanization, supplies. **Health services:** Dental hygiene, EMT paramedic, medical records technology, nursing (RN), occupational therapy assistant, office admin, substance abuse counseling. **Parks/recreation:** Facilities management. **Protective services:** Fire safety technology, forensics, forest/wildland firefighting, police science. **Visual/performing arts:** Interior design.

Computing on campus. 275 workstations in library, computer center, student center. Commuter students can connect to campus network. Online course registration, online library, helpline, repair service, wireless network available.

Student life. Freshman orientation: Mandatory. Preregistration for classes offered. Held on various dates 2 months prior to beginning of semester. **Activities:** Student government, student newspaper, over 40 curriculumn-related clubs.

Athletics. NJCAA. **Intercollegiate:** Basketball, volleyball W. **Intramural:** Basketball, football (non-tackle), soccer, softball, table tennis, volleyball. **Team name:** Foxes.

Student services. Adult student services, alcohol/substance abuse counseling, career counseling, services for economically disadvantaged, student employment services, financial aid counseling, health services, minority student services, on-campus daycare, personal counseling, placement for graduates, veterans' counselor, women's services. **Physically disabled:** Services for visually, speech, hearing impaired.

Contact. E-mail: admissions@fvtc.edu
Phone: (920) 735-5645 Toll-free number: (800) 735-3882
Fax: (920) 735-2484
Elizabeth Burns, Director of Admissions, Fox Valley Technical College, 1825 North Bluemound Drive, Appleton, WI 54912-2277

Gateway Technical College
Kenosha, Wisconsin
www.gtc.edu

CB member
CB code: 0761

- Public 2-year technical college
- Commuter campus in small city

General. Founded in 1911. Regionally accredited. Campuses at Burlington, Elkhorn, Kenosha and Racine. **Enrollment:** 8,291 degree-seeking undergraduates. **Degrees:** 844 associate awarded. **Location:** 30 miles from Milwaukee, 60 miles from Chicago. **Calendar:** Semester, limited summer session. **Full-time faculty:** 300 total. **Part-time faculty:** 100 total.

Student profile.

Out-of-state:	3%	25 or older:	60%

Basis for selection. Open admission, but selective for some programs. **Home schooled:** Letter from student confirming completion of the equivalent of 12th grade through a home-schooling program.

High school preparation. Chemistry and biology required for nursing and other health-care program applicants.

2011-2012 Annual costs. Tuition/fees: $3,629; $5,309 out-of-state. Per-credit charge: $112 in-state; $168 out-of-state. Material fees vary by program; minimum $4 per course. $10 per credit fee for online courses. Books/supplies: $910. Personal expenses: $1,461.

Financial aid. Need-based: Need-based aid available for part-time students. Work-study available nights, weekends and for part-time students. **Non-need-based:** Scholarships awarded for state residency.

Application procedures. Admission: No deadline. $30 fee. Admission notification on a rolling basis. **Financial aid:** Priority date 7/1; no closing date. FAFSA, institutional form required. Applicants notified on a rolling basis starting 5/1; must reply within 2 week(s) of notification.

Academics. Special study options: Accelerated study, cooperative education, cross-registration, distance learning, dual enrollment of high school students, ESL, independent study, internships, student-designed major. License preparation in aviation, nursing, paramedic, physical therapy, radiology. **Credit/placement by examination:** AP, CLEP, institutional tests. 48 credit hours maximum toward associate degree. Institutional biology and chemistry test required for nursing applicants. **Support services:** GED preparation and test center, learning center, remedial instruction, tutoring.

Majors. Business: Accounting, administrative services, hotel/motel admin, marketing, operations. **Communications technology:** Radio/TV. **Computer sciences:** Networking, programming, support specialist, webmaster. **Education:** Early childhood, teacher assistance. **English:** Technical writing. **General:** Horticulture. **Health services:** Clinical lab technology, medical radiologic technology/radiation therapy, medical records technology, nursing (RN), physical therapy assistant, surgical technology. **Protective services:** Firefighting, police science. **Visual/performing arts:** Graphic design, interior design. **Work/family studies:** Child care management.

Computing on campus. 270 workstations in library, computer center, student center. Online course registration, wireless network available.

Student life. Freshman orientation: Available. Preregistration for classes offered. **Activities:** International student organizations, radio station, student government, student newspaper, wide variety of occupationally-oriented and community-related organizations available.

Student services. Adult student services, alcohol/substance abuse counseling, career counseling, services for economically disadvantaged, student employment services, financial aid counseling, minority student services, personal counseling, placement for graduates, veterans' counselor. **Physically disabled:** Services for visually, speech, hearing impaired. **Transfer:** Transfer adviser, college fairs on campus for students transferring to 4-year colleges.

Contact. E-mail: admissionsgroup@gtc.edu
Phone: (262) 741-8168 Fax: (262) 741-8115
Susan Roberts, Director of Admissions, Gateway Technical College, 3520 30th Avenue, Kenosha, WI 53144-1690

Globe University: Appleton
Grand Chute, Wisconsin
www.globeuniversity.edu

- For-profit 2-year university and career college
- Large town

General. Regionally accredited; also accredited by ACICS. **Enrollment:** 264 degree-seeking undergraduates. **Calendar:** Quarter. **Full-time faculty:** 4 total. **Part-time faculty:** 4 total.

Basis for selection. Open admission.

Financial aid. Need-based: Work-study available nights, weekends and for part-time students.

Application procedures. Admission: $50 fee.

Academics. Credit/placement by examination: AP, CLEP.

Majors. Business: Business admin. **Health services:** Massage therapy, medical secretary, veterinary technology/assistant. **Protective services:** Police science.

Contact. Jordan Klein, Director of Admissions, Globe University: Appleton, 5045 West Grande Market Drive, Grand Chute, WI 54913

Globe University: Eau Claire
Eau Claire, Wisconsin
www.globeuniversity.edu

- For-profit 2-year university and career college
- Small city

General. Regionally accredited; also accredited by ACICS. **Enrollment:** 509 degree-seeking undergraduates. **Degrees:** 17 bachelor's, 125 associate awarded. **Calendar:** Quarter. **Full-time faculty:** 11 total. **Part-time faculty:** 36 total.

Basis for selection. Open admission.

Financial aid. Need-based: Work-study available nights, weekends and for part-time students.

Application procedures. Admission: $50 fee.

Academics. Credit/placement by examination: AP, CLEP.

Majors. Business: Business admin. **Health services:** Massage therapy, medical secretary, veterinary technology/assistant. **Protective services:** Police science.

Contact. Phone: (715) 855-6600
Josh Kampa, Director of Admissions, Globe University: Eau Claire, 4955 Bullis Farm Road, Eau Claire, WI 54701

Globe University: La Crosse
Onalaska, Wisconsin
www.globeuniversity.edu

- For-profit 2-year university and career college
- Large town

General. Regionally accredited; also accredited by ACICS. **Enrollment:** 436 degree-seeking undergraduates. **Degrees:** 3 bachelor's, 45 associate awarded. **Calendar:** Quarter. **Full-time faculty:** 10 total. **Part-time faculty:** 42 total.

Basis for selection. Open admission.

Financial aid. Need-based: Work-study available nights, weekends and for part-time students.

Application procedures. Admission: $50 fee.

Academics. Credit/placement by examination: AP, CLEP.

Majors. Business: Business admin. **Health services:** Massage therapy, medical secretary, veterinary technology/assistant. **Protective services:** Police science.

Contact. Cory Simonson, Director of Admissions, Globe University: La Crosse, 2651 Midwest Drive, Onalaska, WI 54650

Globe University: Madison East
Madison, Wisconsin
www.globeuniversity.edu

- For-profit 2-year university and career college
- Small city

General. Accredited by ACICS. **Enrollment:** 342 degree-seeking undergraduates. **Degrees:** 3 bachelor's, 6 associate awarded. **Calendar:** Quarter. **Full-time faculty:** 11 total. **Part-time faculty:** 30 total.

Basis for selection. Open admission.

Financial aid. Need-based: Work-study available nights, weekends and for part-time students.

Application procedures. Admission: $50 fee.

Academics. Credit/placement by examination: AP, CLEP.

Majors. Business: Business admin. **Health services:** Massage therapy, medical secretary, veterinary technology/assistant. **Protective services:** Police science.

Contact. Brittany Knutson, Director of Admissions, Globe University: Madison East, 4901 Eastpark Boulevard, Madison, WI 53718

Globe University: Wausau
Rothschild, Wisconsin
www.globeuniversity.edu

- For-profit 2-year university and career college
- Small town

General. Regionally accredited; also accredited by ACICS. **Enrollment:** 393 degree-seeking undergraduates. **Degrees:** 5 bachelor's, 6 associate awarded. **Calendar:** Quarter. **Full-time faculty:** 9 total. **Part-time faculty:** 37 total.

Basis for selection. Open admission.

Financial aid. Need-based: Work-study available nights, weekends and for part-time students.

Application procedures. Admission: $50 fee.

Academics. Credit/placement by examination: AP, CLEP.

Majors. Business: Business admin. **Health services:** Massage therapy, medical secretary, veterinary technology/assistant. **Protective services:** Police science.

Contact. Phone: (715) 301-1300
Andrea Palas, Director of Admissions, Globe University: Wausau, 1480 Country Road XX, Rothschild, WI 54474

Lac Courte Oreilles Ojibwa Community College
Hayward, Wisconsin
www.lco.edu   **CB code: 7351**

- Public 2-year community college
- Commuter campus in small town

General. Regionally accredited. **Calendar:** Semester.

Annual costs/financial aid. Tuition/fees (2011-2012): $4,825; $4,825 out-of-state. Books/supplies: $300. Need-based financial aid available for full-time students.

Contact. Phone: (715) 634-4790 ext. 104
Registrar, 13466 West Trepania Road, Hayward, WI 54843

Lakeshore Technical College
Cleveland, Wisconsin   **CB member**
www.gotoltc.edu   **CB code: 0618**

- Public 2-year technical college
- Commuter campus in rural community

General. Founded in 1912. Regionally accredited. **Enrollment:** 2,344 degree-seeking undergraduates; 783 non-degree-seeking students. **Degrees:** 400 associate awarded. **Location:** 15 miles from Sheboygan, 65 miles from Milwaukee. **Calendar:** Semester, limited summer session. **Full-time faculty:** 115 total. **Part-time faculty:** 276 total. **Special facilities:** Five wind turbines, rescue tower, emergency vehicle obstacle driving course, old-growth forest. **Partnerships:** Formal partnerships with all public schools and employers in Manitowoc and Sheboygan counties for Tech Prep.

Student profile. Among degree-seeking undergraduates, 3% already have a bachelor's degree or higher, 267 enrolled as first-time, first-year students.

Part-time:	60%	Asian American:	4%
Out-of-state:	1%	Hispanic American:	2%
Women:	57%	Native American:	1%
African American:	1%	25 or older:	75%

Transfer out. Colleges most students transferred to 2011: Silver Lake College, Lakeland College, Marian College.

Basis for selection. Open admission, but selective for some programs. All health-related, public safety and child care programs require background checks and physical examinations. **Home schooled:** State high school equivalency certificate required.

2011-2012 Annual costs. Tuition/fees: $3,545; $5,225 out-of-state. Per-credit charge: $112 in-state; $168 out-of-state. Material fees vary by program; minimum $4 per course. $10 per credit fee for online courses. Books/supplies: $1,265. Personal expenses: $1,639.

Financial aid. All financial aid based on need. Need-based aid available for part-time students. Work-study available nights, weekends and for part-time students.

Application procedures. Admission: No deadline. $30 fee, may be waived for applicants with need. Admission notification on a rolling basis. Financial aid: Priority date 6/1; no closing date. FAFSA, institutional form required. Applicants notified on a rolling basis starting 6/1; must reply within 3 week(s) of notification.

Academics. Special study options: Accelerated study, cooperative education, cross-registration, distance learning, double major, dual enrollment of high school students, ESL, exchange student, honors, independent study, internships, student-designed major. License preparation in nursing, paramedic, real estate. Credit/placement by examination: AP, CLEP, institutional tests. Support services: GED preparation and test center, learning center, pre-admission summer program, reduced course load, remedial instruction, study skills assistance, tutoring.

Majors. Business: Accounting, administrative services, business admin, hotel/motel admin, human resources, logistics, marketing, operations, warehousing. Computer sciences: Computer graphics, networking, support specialist. Education: Early childhood. Health services: Clinical lab technology, EMT paramedic, medical radiologic technology/radiation therapy, medical secretary, nursing (RN), pharmacy assistant. Protective services: Fire safety technology, police science.

Most popular majors. Business/marketing 34%, computer/information sciences 14%, engineering/engineering technologies 9%, health sciences 19%, legal studies 12%, security/protective services 7%.

Computing on campus. 950 workstations in library, computer center, student center. Online course registration, online library, helpline, wireless network available.

Student life. Freshman orientation: Available. Preregistration for classes offered. Activities: Student government, student newspaper.

Student services. Adult student services, alcohol/substance abuse counseling, career counseling, services for economically disadvantaged, student employment services, financial aid counseling, health services, minority student services, on-campus daycare, personal counseling, placement for graduates, veterans' counselor. Physically disabled: Services for visually, speech, hearing impaired. Transfer: Re-entry adviser, pre-admission transcript evaluation for new students. Transfer adviser, college fairs on campus for students transferring to 4-year colleges.

Contact. E-mail: enroll@gotoltc.edu
Phone: (920) 693-1162 Toll-free number: (888) 468-6582
Fax: (920) 693-3561
Doug Gossen, Vice President Student Services, Lakeshore Technical College, 1290 North Avenue, Cleveland, WI 53015-9761

Madison Area Technical College
Madison, Wisconsin
www.matcmadison.edu   CB code: 1536

- Public 2-year community and technical college
- Commuter campus in small city

General. Founded in 1912. Regionally accredited. Campuses in Fort Atkinson, Portage, Reedsburg, and Watertown. Enrollment: 16,845 degree-seeking undergraduates; 3,701 non-degree-seeking students. Degrees: 1,246 associate awarded. Calendar: Semester, limited summer session. Full-time faculty: 397 total. Part-time faculty: 1,333 total. Special facilities: Satellite downlink.

Student profile. Among degree-seeking undergraduates, 3,932 enrolled as first-time, first-year students.

Part-time:	50%	Women:	63%
Out-of-state:	2%	25 or older:	10%

Basis for selection. Open admission, but selective for some programs. School achievement record, class rank, test scores considered for all health occupation programs.

High school preparation. High school academic subject requirements for health and technical programs.

2011-2012 Annual costs. Tuition/fees: $3,578; $5,258 out-of-state. Per-credit charge: $112 in-state; $168 out-of-state. Material fees vary by program; minimum $4 per course. $10 per credit fee for online courses. Books/supplies: $760. Personal expenses: $1,340.

Financial aid. Need-based: Work-study available nights, weekends and for part-time students.

Application procedures. Admission: Closing date 8/30. $30 fee, may be waived for applicants with need. Admission notification on a rolling basis. Early application recommended for programs with limited enrollment. Financial aid: Priority date 4/15; no closing date. FAFSA required. Applicants notified on a rolling basis starting 4/15.

Academics. College transfer program, advanced technical certificates, apprenticeships, English as a Second Language, adult continuing education and basic skills education available. Special study options: Accelerated study, cross-registration, distance learning, dual enrollment of high school students, ESL, external degree, internships. Bachelor's degree programs available on campus. License preparation in nursing. Credit/placement by examination: AP, CLEP, institutional tests. 32 credit hours maximum toward associate degree. Support services: GED preparation, learning center, reduced course load, remedial instruction, study skills assistance, tutoring.

Majors. Business: Accounting, administrative services, business admin, communications, fashion, finance, hospitality admin, hospitality/recreation, insurance, office management, real estate, tourism/travel. Communications technology: Graphic/printing. Computer sciences: General, programming. General: Animal sciences, horticulture. Health services: Clinical lab technology, dental hygiene, EMT paramedic, medical assistant, medical radiologic technology/radiation therapy, medical records admin, medical secretary, mental health services, nursing (RN), occupational therapy assistant, respiratory therapy technology, veterinary technology/assistant. Liberal arts: Arts/sciences. Protective services: Police science. Visual/performing arts: Commercial photography, commercial/advertising art, design, interior design. Work/family studies: Child care management, food/nutrition.

Most popular majors. Business/marketing 28%, computer/information sciences 7%, family/consumer sciences 6%, health sciences 19%, trade and industry 12%, visual/performing arts 7%.

Computing on campus. 470 workstations in library, computer center.

Student life. Freshman orientation: Available. Preregistration for classes offered. Policies: Student life department promotes a variety of cultural diversity and activities and plays an active role in student government activities. Activities: Jazz band, choral groups, drama, music ensembles, student government, student newspaper.

Athletics. NJCAA. Intercollegiate: Baseball M, basketball, bowling, cross-country M, golf M, softball W, volleyball W, wrestling M. Intramural: Basketball, racquetball, soccer, swimming, table tennis, tennis, volleyball. Team name: Wolf Pack.

Student services. Career counseling, student employment services, health services, on-campus daycare, personal counseling, placement for graduates, veterans' counselor. Physically disabled: Services for visually, speech, hearing impaired. Transfer: Transfer adviser for students transferring to 4-year colleges.

Contact. Phone: (608) 246-6205 Fax: (608) 258-2329
Jennifer Hoege, Admissions Administrator, Madison Area Technical College, 3350 Anderson Street, Madison, WI 53704-2599

Madison Media Institute
Madison, Wisconsin   CB member
www.madisonmedia.edu

- For-profit 2-year visual arts and music college
- Large city

General. Accredited by ACCSCT. Calendar: Trimester.

Annual costs/financial aid. Tuition for associate degree program in Recording and Music Technology: $38,560. Costs vary by programs. Books/supplies: $420.

Contact. Phone: (800) 236-4997
Director of Admissions, 2702 Agriculture Drive, Madison, WI 53718

Mid-State Technical College
Wisconsin Rapids, Wisconsin
www.mstc.edu

CB member
CB code: 0635

▸ Public 2-year technical college
▸ Commuter campus in large town

General. Founded in 1967. Regionally accredited. Branch campuses in Marshfield and Stevens Point, outreach center in Adams Friendship. **Enrollment:** 3,005 degree-seeking undergraduates; 425 non-degree-seeking students. **Degrees:** 456 associate awarded. **Location:** 20 miles from Stevens Point, 115 miles from Madison. **Calendar:** Semester, limited summer session. **Full-time faculty:** 91 total; 10% have terminal degrees, 1% minority, 56% women. **Part-time faculty:** 131 total; 3% have terminal degrees, 2% minority, 53% women.

Student profile. Among degree-seeking undergraduates, 100% enrolled in a vocational program, 563 enrolled as first-time, first-year students.

Part-time:	54%	Asian American:	3%
Out-of-state:	1%	Hispanic American:	1%
Women:	57%	Native American:	1%
African American:	1%	25 or older:	50%

Basis for selection. Open admission, but selective for some programs. Students must take ACCUPLACER entrance exam for placement. Certain programs have additional admission requirements. **Home schooled:** Transcript of courses and grades required. Proof of completion of 12th grade required.

High school preparation. College-preparatory program recommended. Recommended units include English 4, mathematics 4, science 4 and computer science 1. Biology, anatomy, physiology, chemistry, medical terminology recommended for health programs. Information processing, general business, business law, economics, accounting recommended for business programs. Geometry, drafting, chemistry, advanced math recommended for technical and industrial programs.

2011-2012 Annual costs. Tuition/fees: $3,528; $5,208 out-of-state. Per-credit charge: $112 in-state; $168 out-of-state. Material fees vary by program; minimum $4 per course. $10 per credit fee for online courses. Books/supplies: $1,036. Personal expenses: $1,774.

2010-2011 Financial aid. **Need-based:** 2,535 full-time freshmen applied for aid; 2,079 were judged to have need; 2,079 of these received aid. Average loan was $2,925. 60% of total undergraduate aid awarded as scholarships/grants, 40% as loans/jobs. Need-based aid available for part-time students. Work-study available nights, weekends and for part-time students. **Non-need-based:** Scholarships awarded for academics, leadership.

Application procedures. Admission: No deadline. $30 fee, may be waived for applicants with need. Admission notification on a rolling basis. **Financial aid:** Priority date 4/15; no closing date. FAFSA required. Applicants notified on a rolling basis starting 5/30; must reply within 2 week(s) of notification.

Academics. Special study options: Accelerated study, distance learning, double major, dual enrollment of high school students, ESL, independent study, internships, student-designed major. Online programs. License preparation in nursing, paramedic. **Credit/placement by examination:** AP, CLEP, institutional tests. **Support services:** GED preparation and test center, learning center, reduced course load, remedial instruction, study skills assistance, tutoring.

Majors. Biology: Bioinformatics. **Business:** Accounting, administrative services, business admin, human resources, marketing, operations. **Computer sciences:** Networking, programming. **Conservation:** Urban forestry. **Education:** Early childhood. **Engineering:** Transportation. **Health services:** Clinical research coordinator, EMT paramedic, nursing (RN), respiratory therapy technology. **Physical sciences:** Atmospheric science. **Protective services:** Corrections, police science.

Most popular majors. Business/marketing 31%, computer/information sciences 11%, engineering/engineering technologies 8%, health sciences 22%, trade and industry 11%.

Computing on campus. 600 workstations in library, computer center, student center. Online course registration, online library, helpline, wireless network available.

Student life. Freshman orientation: Available. Preregistration for classes offered. **Activities:** Student government, Association for Information Technology Professionals, automotive & diesel tech club, Campus Crusade for Christ, civil technology club, criminal justice-corrections club, cosmetology and barbering club, early childhood education club, electronics club, law enforcement organization, Mid-State Renewable Energy Society.

Student services. Adult student services, alcohol/substance abuse counseling, career counseling, services for economically disadvantaged, student employment services, financial aid counseling, minority student services, personal counseling, placement for graduates, veterans' counselor, women's services. **Physically disabled:** Services for visually, speech, hearing impaired. **Transfer:** Pre-admission transcript evaluation for new students. Transfer adviser, college fairs on campus for students transferring to 4-year colleges.

Contact. E-mail: enrollment@mstc.edu
Phone: (715) 422-5444 Toll-free number: (888) 575-6782
Fax: (715) 422-5440
Amanda Lang, Director of Enrollment Management, Mid-State Technical College, 500 32nd Street North, Wisconsin Rapids, WI 54494

Milwaukee Area Technical College
Milwaukee, Wisconsin
www.matc.edu

CB member
CB code: 1475

▸ Public 2-year junior and technical college
▸ Commuter campus in very large city

General. Founded in 1912. Regionally accredited. Campuses in Milwaukee, Oak Creek, Mequon, and West Allis. **Enrollment:** 19,055 degree-seeking undergraduates; 425 non-degree-seeking students. **Degrees:** 1,632 associate awarded. **Location:** 85 miles from Chicago. **Calendar:** Semester, limited summer session. **Full-time faculty:** 563 total; 9% have terminal degrees, 28% minority, 50% women. **Part-time faculty:** 771 total; 6% have terminal degrees, 20% minority, 49% women. **Class size:** 66% < 20, 33% 20-39, less than 1% 40-49.

Student profile. Among degree-seeking undergraduates, 14% enrolled in a transfer program, 86% enrolled in a vocational program, 2% already have a bachelor's degree or higher, 2,557 enrolled as first-time, first-year students, 276 transferred in from other institutions.

Part-time:	67%	Asian American:	4%
Out-of-state:	1%	Hispanic American:	10%
Women:	55%	Native American:	2%
African American:	29%	25 or older:	62%

Transfer out. 12% of students enrolled in the transfer program go on to 4-year colleges. **Colleges most students transferred to 2011:** University of Wisconsin-Milwaukee, Waukesha County Technical College, Cardinal Stritch University, Gateway Technical College, Alverno College.

Basis for selection. Open admission, but selective for some programs. Special requirements for health programs. **Home schooled:** Must complete ACCUPLACER testing.

High school preparation. Specific subject requirements for some programs.

2011-2012 Annual costs. Tuition/fees: $3,803; $5,483 out-of-state. Per-credit charge: $112 in-state; $168 out-of-state. Material fees vary by program; minimum $4 per course. $10 per credit fee for online courses. Books/supplies: $1,399. Personal expenses: $2,102.

2010-2011 Financial aid. **Need-based:** 1,520 full-time freshmen applied for aid; 1,312 were judged to have need; 1,312 of these received aid. Average need met was 59%. Average scholarship/grant was $9,027; average loan $4,851. 44% of total undergraduate aid awarded as scholarships/grants, 56% as loans/jobs. Need-based aid available for part-time students. Work-study available nights, weekends and for part-time students. **Non-need-based:** Scholarships awarded for academics.

Application procedures. Admission: Closing date 8/3 (postmark date). $30 fee. Admission notification on a rolling basis. **Financial aid:** Priority date 3/15; no closing date. FAFSA required. Applicants notified on a rolling basis starting 4/15.

Academics. Special study options: Accelerated study, cooperative education, distance learning, double major, dual enrollment of high school students, ESL, honors, independent study, internships, liberal arts/career combination, weekend college. Teacher education program with guaranteed admission to University of Wisconsin-Milwaukee. License preparation in aviation, dental hygiene, nursing. **Credit/placement by examination:** AP, CLEP, institutional tests. **Support services:** GED preparation and test center, learning center, reduced course load, remedial instruction, study skills assistance, tutoring, writing center.

Majors. Architecture: Technology. **Business:** Accounting, administrative services, banking/financial services, business admin, fashion, hotel/motel admin, logistics, marketing, operations, real estate, tourism/travel. **Communications technology:** Graphic/printing, graphics, radio/TV. **Computer sciences:** Computer graphics, networking, programming, support specialist,

webmaster. **Education:** Early childhood. **Foreign languages:** Sign language interpretation. **General:** Landscaping. **Health services:** Anesthesiologist assistant, cardiovascular technology, clinical lab technology, dental hygiene, dental lab technology, dietetic technician, electroencephalograph technology, medical radiologic technology/radiation therapy, medical secretary, occupational therapy, occupational therapy assistant, office admin, physical therapy assistant, respiratory therapy assistant, respiratory therapy technology, surgical technology. **Liberal arts:** Arts/sciences. **Protective services:** Firefighting, police science. **Visual/performing arts:** Commercial photography, game design, graphic design, interior design, music technology.

Most popular majors. Business/marketing 19%, computer/information sciences 9%, engineering/engineering technologies 14%, health sciences 21%, security/protective services 9%, visual/performing arts 9%.

Computing on campus. 275 workstations in library, computer center, student center. Online course registration, online library, helpline, wireless network available.

Student life. Freshman orientation: Mandatory. Preregistration for classes offered. **Housing:** Certified housing available at nearby colleges and other facilities. **Activities:** Literary magazine, student government, student newspaper, TV station, student senate, student life committee, African American student club, American Culinary Federation, architectural technology club, Association of Information Technology Professionals, campus Bible fellowship, criminal justice student organization, environmental club, Phi Theta Kappa Honor Society, paralegal association.

Athletics. NJCAA. **Intercollegiate:** Baseball M, basketball M, golf, soccer M, softball W, volleyball W. **Intramural:** Basketball, table tennis, volleyball. **Team name:** Stormers.

Student services. Adult student services, alcohol/substance abuse counseling, career counseling, services for economically disadvantaged, student employment services, financial aid counseling, health services, legal services, minority student services, on-campus daycare, personal counseling, placement for graduates, veterans' counselor, women's services. **Physically disabled:** Services for visually, speech, hearing impaired. **Transfer:** Transfer center, transfer adviser, college fairs on campus for students transferring to 4-year colleges.

Contact. E-mail: adamss4@matc.edu
Phone: (414) 297-6370 Fax: (414) 297-7800
Sarah Adams, Registrar, Director, Enrollment Services, Milwaukee Area Technical College, 700 West State Street, Milwaukee, WI 53233-1443

Moraine Park Technical College
Fond du Lac, Wisconsin
www.morainepark.edu
CB member
CB code: 0667

- Public 2-year technical college
- Commuter campus in large town

General. Founded in 1967. Regionally accredited. Campus locations in Beaver Dam and West Bend. **Enrollment:** 3,671 degree-seeking undergraduates; 3,063 non-degree-seeking students. **Degrees:** 467 associate awarded. **Location:** 60 miles from Milwaukee. **Calendar:** Semester, limited summer session. **Full-time faculty:** 144 total. **Part-time faculty:** 212 total.

Student profile. Among degree-seeking undergraduates, 100% enrolled in a vocational program, 6% already have a bachelor's degree or higher, 395 enrolled as first-time, first-year students.

Part-time:	68%	25 or older:	71%
Women:	65%		

Basis for selection. Open admission, but selective for some programs. Students without high school diploma may be admitted to certain limited job-entry preparation programs.

High school preparation. 16 units recommended. Recommended units include English 3, mathematics 2, social studies 2 and science 2.

2011-2012 Annual costs. Tuition/fees: $3,543; $5,223 out-of-state. Per-credit charge: $112 in-state; $168 out-of-state. Material fees vary by program; minimum $4 per course. $10 per credit fee for online courses. Books/supplies: $1,265. Personal expenses: $2,845.

2010-2011 Financial aid. Need-based: Need-based aid available for part-time students. Work-study available nights, weekends and for part-time students. **Non-need-based:** Scholarships awarded for academics, job skills, leadership, minority status, state residency.

Application procedures. Admission: No deadline. $30 fee, may be waived for applicants with need. Admission notification on a rolling basis.

Limited enrollment health care programs have varying application deadlines. **Financial aid:** Priority date 5/1; no closing date. FAFSA, institutional form required. Applicants notified on a rolling basis starting 5/15; must reply within 2 week(s) of notification.

Academics. Special study options: Accelerated study, distance learning, double major, dual enrollment of high school students, ESL, independent study, internships, student-designed major, weekend college. License preparation in real estate. **Credit/placement by examination:** AP, CLEP, institutional tests. 30 credit hours maximum toward associate degree. **Support services:** GED preparation and test center, learning center, pre-admission summer program, reduced course load, remedial instruction, tutoring.

Majors. Business: Accounting, administrative services, marketing, office management, office technology, sales/distribution. **Communications technology:** Graphic/printing. **Computer sciences:** Applications programming, data processing. **Health services:** EMT paramedic, medical records technology, medical secretary, nursing (RN), substance abuse counseling. **Protective services:** Corrections, fire safety technology, police science. **Work/family studies:** Child care management, family studies.

Most popular majors. Business/marketing 25%, computer/information sciences 7%, education 6%, engineering/engineering technologies 14%, health sciences 32%, security/protective services 7%.

Computing on campus. Commuter students can connect to campus network. Online library, helpline, wireless network available.

Student life. Freshman orientation: Mandatory. Preregistration for classes offered. **Activities:** Student government.

Student services. Career counseling, student employment services, health services, on-campus daycare, personal counseling, placement for graduates, veterans' counselor. **Physically disabled:** Services for visually, hearing impaired. **Transfer:** College fairs on campus for students transferring to 4-year colleges.

Contact. Phone: (920) 924-3408 Toll-free number: (800) 472-4554
Fax: (920) 924-3421
Bonita Bauer, Dean of Admissions and Retention, Moraine Park Technical College, 235 North National Avenue, Fond du Lac, WI 54935-1940

Nicolet Area Technical College
Rhinelander, Wisconsin
www.nicoletcollege.edu
CB code: 0713

- Public 2-year community and technical college
- Commuter campus in small town

General. Founded in 1967. Regionally accredited. **Location:** 225 miles from Milwaukee, 200 miles from Madison. **Calendar:** Semester.

Annual costs/financial aid. Tuition/fees (2011-2012): $3,528; $5,208 out-of-state. Material fees vary by program; minimum $4 per course. $10 per credit fee for online courses. Books/supplies: $1,352. Personal expenses: $1,700.

Contact. Phone: (715) 365-4451
Director of Admissions/PK-16 Pathways, Box 518, Rhinelander, WI 54501

Northcentral Technical College
Wausau, Wisconsin
www.ntc.edu
CB member
CB code: 0735

- Public 2-year community and technical college
- Commuter campus in small city

General. Founded in 1911. Regionally accredited. Regional campuses located in Antigo, Medford, Merrill, Phillips, Spencer and Wittenberg. **Enrollment:** 3,317 degree-seeking undergraduates. **Degrees:** 495 associate awarded. **Location:** 200 miles from Milwaukee and Minneapolis-St. Paul, 150 miles from Madison. **Calendar:** Semester, limited summer session. **Full-time faculty:** 151 total. **Part-time faculty:** 10 total.

Basis for selection. Open admission, but selective for some programs. Special requirements for health programs including application portfolio. ACCUPLACER or ACT required for placement. **Home schooled:** Transcript of courses and grades required.

2011-2012 Annual costs. Tuition/fees: $3,628; $5,308 out-of-state. Per-credit charge: $112 in-state; $168 out-of-state. Material fees vary by program; minimum $4 per course. $10 per credit fee for online courses. Books/supplies: $1,200.

Financial aid. Need-based: Need-based aid available for part-time students. Work-study available nights, weekends and for part-time students.

Application procedures. Admission: No deadline. $30 fee, may be waived for applicants with need. Admission notification on a rolling basis. **Financial aid:** No deadline. FAFSA required. Applicants notified on a rolling basis.

Academics. Special study options: Accelerated study, distance learning, double major, dual enrollment of high school students, ESL, internships, student-designed major, weekend college. Bachelor's degree programs available on campus. License preparation in dental hygiene, nursing, paramedic, radiology. **Credit/placement by examination:** AP, CLEP, IB, institutional tests. 24 credit hours maximum toward associate degree. **Support services:** GED preparation and test center, learning center, pre-admission summer program, reduced course load, remedial instruction, study skills assistance, tutoring, writing center.

Majors. Architecture: Technology. **Business:** Accounting, administrative services, business admin, marketing. **Communications technology:** Graphic/printing. **Computer sciences:** Data entry, networking, programming, support specialist, web page design. **Education:** Early childhood. **Engineering:** Electrical, engineering mechanics. **Foreign languages:** Sign language interpretation. **General:** Agribusiness operations, business, dairy. **Health services:** Clinical lab assistant, clinical lab technology, dental hygiene, EMT paramedic, nursing (RN), radiologic technology/medical imaging. **Protective services:** Firefighting, police science. **Work/family studies:** Child care service.

Computing on campus. Commuter students can connect to campus network. Online course registration, online library, helpline, repair service, wireless network available.

Student life. Freshman orientation: Available. Preregistration for classes offered. **Housing:** Coed dorms available. **Activities:** Student government, student newspaper.

Athletics. Intercollegiate: Soccer M, volleyball W. **Intramural:** Basketball, football (non-tackle), softball, volleyball. **Team name:** Timberwolves.

Student services. Adult student services, career counseling, services for economically disadvantaged, student employment services, financial aid counseling, health services, minority student services, on-campus daycare, personal counseling, placement for graduates. **Physically disabled:** Services for visually, speech, hearing impaired. **Transfer:** Pre-admission transcript evaluation for new students. Transfer adviser, college fairs on campus for students transferring to 4-year colleges.

Contact. E-mail: admissions@ntc.edu
Toll-free number: (888) 682-7144
Sarah Dillon, Director of Enrollment, Northcentral Technical College, 1000 West Campus Drive, Wausau, WI 54401

Northeast Wisconsin Technical College
Green Bay, Wisconsin   **CB member**
www.nwtc.edu   **CB code: 4190**

‣ Public 2-year community and technical college
‣ Commuter campus in small city
‣ Application essay required

General. Founded in 1913. Regionally accredited. **Enrollment:** 5,965 degree-seeking undergraduates. **Degrees:** 1,066 associate awarded. **Location:** 129 miles from Milwaukee, 150 miles from Madison. **Calendar:** Semester, limited summer session. **Full-time faculty:** 272 total; 4% minority, 48% women. **Part-time faculty:** 1,158 total; 5% minority, 54% women. **Special facilities:** Horticultural Learning Center. **Partnerships:** Formal partnership with Snap-on Incorporated.

Transfer out. Colleges most students transferred to 2011: University of Wisconsin-Green Bay, University of Wisconsin-Oshkosh.

Basis for selection. Open admission, but selective for some programs. Special requirements for health programs. **Home schooled:** State high school equivalency certificate required.

High school preparation. College-preparatory program required.

2011-2012 Annual costs. Tuition/fees: $3,608; $5,288 out-of-state. Per-credit charge: $112 in-state; $168 out-of-state. Material fees vary by program; minimum $4 per course. $10 per credit fee for online courses. Books/supplies: $1,148. Personal expenses: $1,920.

Financial aid. Need-based: Need-based aid available for part-time students. Work-study available nights, weekends and for part-time students.

Application procedures. Admission: Closing date 9/5 (receipt date). $30 fee, may be waived for applicants with need. Admission notification on a rolling basis beginning on or about 9/15. **Financial aid:** Priority date 4/15; no closing date. FAFSA required. Applicants notified on a rolling basis starting 6/1; must reply within 2 week(s) of notification.

Academics. Special study options: Accelerated study, distance learning, double major, dual enrollment of high school students, ESL, honors, independent study, internships, liberal arts/career combination, study abroad, weekend college. License preparation in dental hygiene, nursing, paramedic, physical therapy, radiology, real estate. **Credit/placement by examination:** AP, CLEP, institutional tests. 48 credit hours maximum toward associate degree. **Support services:** GED preparation and test center, learning center, reduced course load, remedial instruction, study skills assistance, tutoring, writing center.

Majors. Architecture: Technology. **Business:** Accounting, administrative services, business admin, hospitality/recreation, logistics, sales/distribution. **Computer sciences:** General, networking. **Education:** Early childhood. **General:** Business, farm/ranch, food science. **Health services:** Dental hygiene, geriatric nursing, health care admin, medical records admin, medical secretary, nursing (RN), physical therapy assistant, respiratory therapy technology. **Protective services:** Fire safety technology, police science. **Work/family studies:** Child care management.

Computing on campus. Online course registration, online library, helpline, wireless network available.

Student life. Freshman orientation: Available. Preregistration for classes offered. 2-hour program in conjunction with registration. **Activities:** International student organizations, student government, Asian American student association, African American student association, Native American student association, Hispanic student association, Students Taking Responsibility in Drug Education, Phi Theta Kappa International Honor Society.

Athletics. Intramural: Basketball, football (non-tackle), volleyball.

Student services. Adult student services, alcohol/substance abuse counseling, career counseling, services for economically disadvantaged, student employment services, financial aid counseling, health services, minority student services, personal counseling, placement for graduates, veterans' counselor. **Physically disabled:** Services for visually, speech, hearing impaired. **Transfer:** Re-entry adviser for new students. Transfer adviser, college fairs on campus for students transferring to 4-year colleges.

Contact. Phone: (920) 498-5444
Toll-free number: (800) 422-6982 ext. 5444 Fax: (920) 498-6882
Christine Lemerande, Program Enrollment Supervisor, Northeast Wisconsin Technical College, 2740 West Mason Street, Green Bay, WI 54307-9042

Rasmussen College: Green Bay
Green Bay, Wisconsin
www.rasmussen.edu

‣ For-profit 2-year technical college
‣ Small city

General. Regionally accredited. **Enrollment:** 647 degree-seeking undergraduates. **Degrees:** 105 associate awarded. **Calendar:** Quarter. **Full-time faculty:** 7 total. **Part-time faculty:** 33 total.

Basis for selection. Open admission, but selective for some programs.

2011-2012 Annual costs. Tuition/fees: $15,750. Per-credit charge: $350. Full-time tuition varies according to program of study. Examples of per-credit-hour charges include Early Childhood Education ($310), Medical Lab Technician, Surgical Technician, Practical Nursing ($395), Professional Nursing, Information Systems Mgmt, Multemedia Technician ($395). Personal expenses: $2,214.

Financial aid. Need-based: Work-study available nights, weekends and for part-time students.

Application procedures. Admission: No deadline. $40 fee.

Academics. Credit/placement by examination: AP, CLEP.

Majors. Business: Accounting, business admin, management information systems, office management. **Computer sciences:** Webmaster. **Education:** Early childhood. **Health services:** Clinical lab assistant, massage therapy, medical assistant, medical records technology, medical transcription, office admin, pharmacy assistant. **Protective services:** Police science.

Contact. Phone: (920) 593-8400
Susan Hammerstrom, Director of Admissions, Rasmussen College: Green Bay, 904 South Taylor Street, Suite 100, Green Bay, WI 54303-2349

Rasmussen College: Wausau
Wausau, Wisconsin
www.rasmussen.edu

- For-profit 2-year career college
- Large town

General. Regionally accredited. **Enrollment:** 522 degree-seeking undergraduates. **Calendar:** Quarter. **Part-time faculty:** 5 total.

Basis for selection. Open admission, but selective for some programs.

2011-2012 Annual costs. Tuition/fees: $15,750. Per-credit charge: $350. Full-time tuition varies according to program of study. Examples of per-credit-hour charges include Early Childhood Education ($310), Medical Lab Technician, Surgical Technician, Practical Nursing ($395), Professional Nursing, Information Systems Mgmt, Multemedia Technician ($395).

Financial aid. Need-based: Work-study available nights, weekends and for part-time students.

Application procedures. Admission: No deadline. $40 fee.

Academics. Credit/placement by examination: AP, CLEP.

Majors. Health services: Medical assistant.

Contact. Susan Hammerstrom, Director of Admissions, Rasmussen College: Wausau, 1101 Westwood Drive, Wausau, WI 54401

Southwest Wisconsin Technical College
Fennimore, Wisconsin
www.swtc.edu   **CB code: 0900**

- Public 2-year technical college
- Commuter campus in rural community

General. Founded in 1967. Regionally accredited. **Location:** 75 miles from Madison. **Calendar:** Semester.

Annual costs/financial aid. Tuition/fees (2011-2012): $3,565; $5,245 out-of-state. Material fees vary by program; minimum $4 per course. $10 per credit fee for online courses. Books/supplies: $1,200. Personal expenses: $1,800.

Contact. Phone: (608) 822-3262 ext. 2354
Director of Student Services, 1800 Bronson Boulevard, Fennimore, WI 53809

University of Wisconsin-Baraboo/Sauk County
Baraboo, Wisconsin
www.baraboo.uwc.edu   **CB code: 1996**

- Public 2-year branch campus and liberal arts college
- Commuter campus in large town
- SAT or ACT (ACT writing optional) required

General. Founded in 1968. Regionally accredited. **Enrollment:** 617 degree-seeking undergraduates. **Degrees:** 90 associate awarded. **Location:** 40 miles from Madison. **Calendar:** Semester, limited summer session. **Full-time faculty:** 18 total. **Part-time faculty:** 18 total. **Class size:** 57% < 20, 42% 20-39, less than 1% 40-49.

Student profile.

Out-of-state: 1%   25 or older: 17%

Transfer out. Colleges most students transferred to 2011: University of Wisconsin-Madison, University of Wisconsin-LaCrosse, University of Wisconsin-Stevens Point, University of Wisconsin-Whitewater, University of Wisconsin-Platteville.

Basis for selection. High school courses, rank in upper 75% of class, ACT or SAT most important. Students in bottom 25% may be admitted based on individual record and circumstances. Students not admitted may be deferred and admitted the following semester. Special attention given to returning adult, homeschooled, learning disabled, and minority students. ACT or SAT used for advisory purposes only for most students. Interview required for those with borderline academic records and class rank. **Adult students:** SAT/ACT scores not required if applicant over 21. Placement test required of students without college credit English and/or math courses. **Home schooled:** Transcript of courses and grades, interview required. Interview, portfolio of curriculum, method of assessment, work samples and experiences recommended. **Learning Disabled:** Interview recommended; recent professional testing required to create program accommodations.

High school preparation. 17 units required. Required and recommended units include English 4, mathematics 3-4, social studies 3, science 3-4 (laboratory 3-4), foreign language 2 and academic electives 4. Math must be college preparatory.

2011-2012 Annual costs. Tuition/fees: $4,906; $11,889 out-of-state. Per-credit charge: $188 in-state; $479 out-of-state. Minnesota reciprocity tuition: $190 per-credit-hour. Books/supplies: $680. Personal expenses: $1,690.

Financial aid. All financial aid based on need. Need-based aid available for part-time students. Work-study available nights, weekends and for part-time students.

Application procedures. Admission: Priority date 6/1; deadline 8/31 (receipt date). $45 fee, may be waived for applicants with need. Admission notification on a rolling basis beginning on or about 9/15. **Financial aid:** Priority date 4/15; no closing date. FAFSA, institutional form required. Applicants notified on a rolling basis starting 4/15; must reply within 3 week(s) of notification.

Academics. Required courses for associate degree available evenings over 4-year period. Bachelor's degree available on campus through University of Wisconsin Milwaukee. **Special study options:** Cross-registration, distance learning, dual enrollment of high school students, external degree, honors, independent study, internships, liberal arts/career combination, study abroad. Bachelor's degree programs available on campus. **Credit/placement by examination:** AP, CLEP, IB, institutional tests. **Support services:** Learning center, reduced course load, remedial instruction, study skills assistance, tutoring, writing center.

Majors. Liberal arts: Arts/sciences.

Computing on campus. 60 workstations in library, computer center, student center. Commuter students can connect to campus network. Online course registration, online library, wireless network available.

Student life. Freshman orientation: Mandatory, $200 fee. Preregistration for classes offered. Orientation in 3 parts over summer. **Policies:** Students participate actively in campus governance and committee work with faculty and staff. **Housing:** Privately owned apartments adjacent to campus. **Activities:** Bands, choral groups, drama, literary magazine, music ensembles, student government, student newspaper, Campus Crusade for Christ, Phi Theta Kappa, Wellness Alliance, business club, Native American club, cine club, UWB Ambassadors, green club, art club, Future Educators.

Athletics. NJCAA. **Intercollegiate:** Basketball M, soccer, tennis, volleyball W. **Intramural:** Basketball, cross-country, racquetball, softball, volleyball. **Team name:** Fighting Spirits.

Student services. Adult student services, alcohol/substance abuse counseling, career counseling, financial aid counseling, minority student services, personal counseling, veterans' counselor. **Physically disabled:** Services for visually, speech, hearing impaired. **Transfer:** Pre-admission transcript evaluation for new students. Transfer adviser, college fairs on campus for students transferring to 4-year colleges.

Contact. E-mail: apply@wisconsin.edu
Phone: (608) 355-5230 Fax: (608) 355-5289
Ruth Joyce, Assistant Dean for Student Services, University of Wisconsin-Baraboo/Sauk County, 1006 Connie Road, Baraboo, WI 53913-1098

University of Wisconsin-Barron County
Rice Lake, Wisconsin
www.barron.uwc.edu   CB code: 1772

- Public 2-year branch campus and junior college
- Commuter campus in small town
- SAT or ACT (ACT writing optional) required

General. Founded in 1966. Regionally accredited. **Enrollment:** 706 degree-seeking undergraduates. **Degrees:** 65 associate awarded. **Location:** 80 miles from Minneapolis-St. Paul, 50 miles from Eau Claire. **Calendar:** Semester, limited summer session. **Full-time faculty:** 26 total. **Part-time faculty:** 19 total. **Special facilities:** Observatory, amphitheater.

Student profile.

Out-of-state: 2%   25 or older: 21%

Basis for selection. Rank in upper 75% of class ensures admission. Students in bottom 25% or those submitting GED scores evaluated on individual basis. ACT preferred. **Adult students:** SAT/ACT scores not required if applicant over 21.

High school preparation. 16 units required. Required units include English 4, mathematics 3, social studies 3 and science 2.

2011-2012 Annual costs. Tuition/fees: $5,020; $12,003 out-of-state. Per-credit charge: $188 in-state; $479 out-of-state. Minnesota reciprocity tuition: $190 per-credit-hour. Books/supplies: $780. Personal expenses: $1,690.

Financial aid. Need-based: Need-based aid available for part-time students. Work-study available nights, weekends and for part-time students.

Application procedures. Admission: Priority date 7/1; no deadline. $44 fee, may be waived for applicants with need. Admission notification on a rolling basis. **Financial aid:** Priority date 4/15; no closing date. FAFSA required. Applicants notified on a rolling basis starting 6/1.

Academics. Special study options: Cross-registration, dual enrollment of high school students, internships. **Credit/placement by examination:** AP, CLEP, institutional tests. **Support services:** Learning center, pre-admission summer program, reduced course load, remedial instruction, tutoring.

Majors. Liberal arts: Arts/sciences.

Computing on campus. 24 workstations in library, computer center.

Student life. Freshman orientation: Available, $50 fee. Preregistration for classes offered. **Activities:** Bands, choral groups, drama, music ensembles, musical theater, student government, student newspaper, Phi Theta Kappa.

Athletics. NJCAA. **Intercollegiate:** Baseball M, basketball, golf, soccer, volleyball W. **Intramural:** Basketball, table tennis, volleyball. **Team name:** Chargers.

Student services. Adult student services, career counseling, student employment services, health services, personal counseling, veterans' counselor. **Physically disabled:** Services for visually, speech, hearing impaired. **Transfer:** Transfer adviser, college fairs on campus for students transferring to 4-year colleges.

Contact. Phone: (715) 234-8024 Fax: (715) 234-8024
Dale Fenton, Director of Student Services, University of Wisconsin-Barron County, 1800 College Drive, Rice Lake, WI 54868

University of Wisconsin-Fond du Lac
Fond du Lac, Wisconsin
www.fdl.uwc.edu   CB code: 1942

- Public 2-year junior college
- Commuter campus in large town
- SAT or ACT (ACT writing optional) required

General. Founded in 1968. Regionally accredited. **Enrollment:** 747 degree-seeking undergraduates. **Degrees:** 122 associate awarded. **Location:** 70 miles from Milwaukee. **Calendar:** Semester, limited summer session. **Full-time faculty:** 22 total. **Part-time faculty:** 18 total. **Class size:** 31% < 20, 65% 20-39, 5% 40-49. **Special facilities:** Nature preserve, arboretum.

Student profile.

Out-of-state: 1%   25 or older: 28%

Transfer out. Colleges most students transferred to 2011: University of Wisconsin-Oshkosh, University of Wisconsin-Milwaukee, University of Wisconsin-Madison, University of Wisconsin-Stevens Point, University of Wisconsin-Green Bay.

Basis for selection. Rank in upper 75% of class ensures admission. Students in bottom 25% will be considered. Applicants with Wisconsin GED score of 250 or higher ensured admission. Applicants admitted who rank in bottom 25% of class may have course credit restrictions during first semester or may be required to participate in summer school classes as condition of continued enrollment. ACT preferred. **Adult students:** SAT/ACT scores not required if applicant over 21. **Home schooled:** Transcript of courses and grades required.

High school preparation. College-preparatory program recommended. 17 units required. Required units include English 4, mathematics 3, social studies 3, science 3 and academic electives 4.

2011-2012 Annual costs. Tuition/fees: $4,854; $11,837 out-of-state. Per-credit charge: $188 in-state; $479 out-of-state. Minnesota reciprocity tuition: $190 per-credit-hour. Books/supplies: $950. Personal expenses: $1,690.

Financial aid. Need-based: Need-based aid available for part-time students. Work-study available nights, weekends and for part-time students. **Non-need-based:** Scholarships awarded for academics, leadership, music/drama.

Application procedures. Admission: Priority date 6/30; no deadline. $44 fee, may be waived for applicants with need. Admission notification on a rolling basis beginning on or about 9/15. **Financial aid:** Priority date 4/15; no closing date. FAFSA required. Applicants notified on a rolling basis starting 6/1; must reply within 2 week(s) of notification.

Academics. Special study options: Accelerated study, cross-registration, distance learning, dual enrollment of high school students, independent study, liberal arts/career combination, study abroad. Bachelor's degree programs available on campus. **Credit/placement by examination:** AP, CLEP, IB, institutional tests. 18 credit hours maximum toward associate degree. **Support services:** Learning center, pre-admission summer program, reduced course load, remedial instruction, study skills assistance, tutoring.

Majors. Liberal arts: Arts/sciences.

Computing on campus. 60 workstations in library, computer center. Commuter students can connect to campus network. Online course registration, online library, wireless network available.

Student life. Freshman orientation: Mandatory, $85 fee. Preregistration for classes offered. **Housing:** Student housing available at nearby Marian College. **Activities:** Bands, choral groups, drama, literary magazine, music ensembles, musical theater, student government, student newspaper, symphony orchestra.

Athletics. NJCAA. **Intercollegiate:** Basketball, golf, soccer, tennis, volleyball W. **Intramural:** Basketball M, bowling, volleyball. **Team name:** Falcons.

Student services. Career counseling, financial aid counseling, personal counseling, veterans' counselor. **Physically disabled:** Services for visually, speech, hearing impaired. **Transfer:** Transfer adviser for students transferring to 4-year colleges.

Contact. Phone: (920) 929-1122 Fax: (920) 929-3626
Joyce Atkins, University of Wisconsin-Fond du Lac, 400 University Drive, Fond du Lac, WI 54935-2950

University of Wisconsin-Fox Valley
Menasha, Wisconsin
www.uwfox.uwc.edu   CB code: 1889

- Public 2-year liberal arts college
- Commuter campus in small city
- SAT or ACT (ACT writing optional) required

General. Founded in 1933. Regionally accredited. **Enrollment:** 1,833 degree-seeking undergraduates. **Degrees:** 197 associate awarded. **Location:** 90 miles from Milwaukee. **Calendar:** Semester, limited summer session. **Full-time faculty:** 50 total. **Part-time faculty:** 36 total. **Class size:** 100% < 20. **Special facilities:** Observatory, planetarium, earth science museum, communication arts center.

Student profile. Among degree-seeking undergraduates, 100% enrolled in a transfer program, 255 transferred in from other institutions.

African American:	2%	Native American:	1%
Asian American:	6%	25 or older:	30%
Hispanic American:	2%		

Transfer out. 90% of students enrolled in the transfer program go on to 4-year colleges.

Basis for selection. Rank in upper 75% of class ensures admission. Students in bottom 25% may be placed on waiting list and SAT/ACT may be considered. Course unit requirements must be met. Interview required for those in bottom 25% of class and those submitting GED scores. **Adult students:** SAT/ACT scores not required if applicant over 21. **Home schooled:** Transcript of courses and grades required.

High school preparation. College-preparatory program recommended. 17 units required. Required and recommended units include English 4, mathematics 3, social studies 3, science 3, foreign language 2 and academic electives 4. Math units must be in algebra, geometry, and higher level.

2011-2012 Annual costs. Tuition/fees: $4,775; $11,758 out-of-state. Per-credit charge: $188 in-state; $479 out-of-state. Minnesota reciprocity tuition: $190 per-credit-hour. Books/supplies: $500. Personal expenses: $810.

Financial aid. Need-based: Need-based aid available for part-time students. Work-study available nights, weekends and for part-time students. **Non-need-based:** Scholarships awarded for academics, leadership.

Application procedures. Admission: Priority date 5/1; no deadline. $44 fee, may be waived for applicants with need. Admission notification on a rolling basis. **Financial aid:** Priority date 4/15; no closing date. FAFSA required. Applicants notified on a rolling basis starting 6/1; must reply within 3 week(s) of notification.

Academics. Enrollment includes admissions to all University of Wisconsin campuses. **Special study options:** Accelerated study, distance learning, dual enrollment of high school students, honors, independent study, internships, study abroad. **Credit/placement by examination:** AP, CLEP, institutional tests. **Support services:** Learning center, pre-admission summer program, reduced course load, remedial instruction, study skills assistance, tutoring, writing center.

Majors. Liberal arts: Arts/sciences.

Computing on campus. 100 workstations in library, computer center. Commuter students can connect to campus network. Online course registration, online library, student web hosting, wireless network available.

Student life. Freshman orientation: Mandatory, $140 fee. Preregistration for classes offered. Day-long program. **Activities:** Bands, choral groups, dance, drama, film society, literary magazine, music ensembles, musical theater, radio station, student government, student newspaper, symphony orchestra, TV station.

Athletics. NJCAA. **Intercollegiate:** Basketball, golf, soccer, tennis, volleyball. **Team name:** Cyclones.

Student services. Adult student services, alcohol/substance abuse counseling, career counseling, services for economically disadvantaged, financial aid counseling, minority student services, on-campus daycare, personal counseling, veterans' counselor. **Physically disabled:** Services for visually, speech, hearing impaired. **Transfer:** Transfer adviser, college fairs on campus for students transferring to 4-year colleges.

Contact. Phone: (920) 832-2620 Fax: (920) 832-2850
Carla Rabe, Assistant Campus Dean for Student Services, University of Wisconsin-Fox Valley, 1478 Midway Road, Menasha, WI 54952-2850

University of Wisconsin-Manitowoc
Manitowoc, Wisconsin
www.manitowoc.uwc.edu   CB code: 1890

- Public 2-year branch campus and liberal arts college
- Commuter campus in large town
- SAT or ACT required

General. Founded in 1933. Regionally accredited. **Enrollment:** 666 degree-seeking undergraduates. **Degrees:** 95 associate awarded. **Location:** 45 miles from Green Bay. **Calendar:** Semester, limited summer session. **Full-time faculty:** 20 total; 5% minority. **Part-time faculty:** 20 total.

Student profile.

Out-of-state:	1%	25 or older:	30%

Transfer out. Colleges most students transferred to 2011: University of Wisconsin-Green Bay, University of Wisconsin-Oshkosh, University of Wisconsin-Madison, University of Wisconsin-Milwaukee, University of Wisconsin-Stevens Point.

Basis for selection. Rank in top 75% of high school class and 19 ACT ensures admission. Students in bottom 25% or ACT below 19 will be considered but may be admitted in the high risk category. Interview may be required for applicants in bottom quarter of class. **Adult students:** SAT/ACT scores not required if applicant over 21. **Home schooled:** Transcript of courses and grades required. 19 ACT required. **Learning Disabled:** Students must meet with campus coordinator for students with disabilities for information about support programs.

High school preparation. College-preparatory program recommended. 17 units required. Required units include English 4, mathematics 3, social studies 3, science 3 and academic electives 4.

2011-2012 Annual costs. Tuition/fees: $5,050; $12,033 out-of-state. Per-credit charge: $188 in-state; $479 out-of-state. Tuition and fees above include book rental. Minnesota reciprocity tuition: $190 per-credit-hour. Books/supplies: $910. Personal expenses: $1,720.

Financial aid. All financial aid based on need. Need-based aid available for part-time students. Work-study available nights, weekends and for part-time students.

Application procedures. Admission: Priority date 7/1; no deadline. $44 fee, may be waived for applicants with need. Admission notification on a rolling basis beginning on or about 9/15. **Financial aid:** Priority date 3/1; no closing date. FAFSA required. Applicants notified on a rolling basis starting 5/1; must reply within 2 week(s) of notification.

Academics. Special study options: Cross-registration, dual enrollment of high school students, honors, independent study. Bachelor's degree programs available on campus. **Credit/placement by examination:** AP, CLEP, IB, institutional tests. 18 credit hours maximum toward associate degree. **Support services:** Learning center, reduced course load, remedial instruction, tutoring, writing center.

Majors. Liberal arts: Arts/sciences.

Computing on campus. 60 workstations in library, computer center. Commuter students can connect to campus network. Online course registration, online library, helpline, wireless network available.

Student life. Freshman orientation: Mandatory, $75 fee. Preregistration for classes offered. One-day program. **Activities:** Bands, choral groups, drama, literary magazine, music ensembles, student government, student newspaper, symphony orchestra.

Athletics. NAIA, NJCAA. **Intercollegiate:** Basketball, golf, tennis, volleyball W. **Intramural:** Badminton, football (non-tackle). **Team name:** Blue Devils.

Student services. Adult student services, career counseling, financial aid counseling, personal counseling, veterans' counselor. **Physically disabled:** Services for visually, speech, hearing impaired. **Transfer:** Re-entry adviser for new students. Transfer adviser for students transferring to 4-year colleges.

Contact. E-mail: manadmit@uwc.edu
Phone: (920) 683-4707 Fax: (920) 683-4776
Julie DeZeeuw, Assistant Dean for Student Services, University of Wisconsin-Manitowoc, 705 Viebahn Street, Manitowoc, WI 54220-6699

University of Wisconsin-Marathon County
Wausau, Wisconsin
www.uwmc.uwc.edu   CB code: 1995

- Public 2-year liberal arts college
- Commuter campus in small city
- SAT or ACT (ACT writing optional) required

General. Founded in 1933. Regionally accredited. Guaranteed transfer program to University of Wisconsin 4-year schools. **Enrollment:** 1,366 degree-seeking undergraduates. **Degrees:** 123 associate awarded. **Location:** 180 miles from Milwaukee, 180 miles from Minneapolis-St. Paul. **Calendar:** Semester, limited summer session. **Full-time faculty:** 33 total. **Part-time faculty:** 48 total. **Special facilities:** Planetarium, hiking and cross-country ski trails, indoor skating and curling rinks.

Two-Year Colleges

Student profile.

Out-of-state:	3%	**Live on campus:**	12%
25 or older:	28%		

Basis for selection. Rank in upper 75% of class ensures admission. Students in bottom 25% and those with GED admitted on basis of interview. **Adult students:** SAT/ACT scores not required if applicant over 21. **Learning Disabled:** Must provide official documentation for review of accommodations 90 days in advance.

High school preparation. 17 units required. Required and recommended units include English 4, mathematics 3-4, social studies 3-4, science 3-4 and foreign language 4. Math units must be algebra, geometry or other courses leading to calculus.

2011-2012 Annual costs. Tuition/fees: $4,841; $11,824 out-of-state. Per-credit charge: $188 in-state; $479 out-of-state. Minnesota reciprocity tuition: $190 per-credit-hour. Room/board: $4,273. Books/supplies: $700. Personal expenses: $900.

Financial aid. All financial aid based on need. Need-based aid available for part-time students. Work-study available nights, weekends and for part-time students.

Application procedures. Admission: Priority date 8/1; no deadline. $44 fee, may be waived for applicants with need. Admission notification on a rolling basis. **Financial aid:** Priority date 4/15; no closing date. FAFSA, institutional form required. Applicants notified on a rolling basis starting 6/1; must reply within 3 week(s) of notification.

Academics. Special study options: Cross-registration, dual enrollment of high school students, honors, independent study, internships, liberal arts/career combination, study abroad. Bachelor's degree programs available on campus. **Credit/placement by examination:** AP, CLEP, IB, institutional tests. 18 credit hours maximum toward associate degree. **Support services:** Learning center, pre-admission summer program, reduced course load, remedial instruction, study skills assistance, tutoring, writing center.

Majors. Liberal arts: Arts/sciences.

Computing on campus. 92 workstations in dormitories, library, computer center. Dormitories wired for high-speed internet access and linked to campus network. Online library, helpline available.

Student life. Freshman orientation: Available, $100 fee. Preregistration for classes offered. One-day program held week before start of fall classes. **Policies:** Zero tolerance alcohol and drug policy in residence hall. **Housing:** Coed dorms available. $100 deposit. **Activities:** Bands, choral groups, drama, literary magazine, music ensembles, musical theater, student government, student newspaper, symphony orchestra, Christian Fellowship, business club, computer club, drama club, international relations club, biology club, gay/lesbian/bisexual student association.

Athletics. NJCAA. **Intercollegiate:** Basketball, golf, soccer, tennis, volleyball W. **Intramural:** Archery, badminton, basketball, bowling, fencing, golf, handball, racquetball, skiing, skin diving, softball, swimming, table tennis, tennis, volleyball. **Team name:** Huskies.

Student services. Adult student services, career counseling, student employment services, personal counseling, veterans' counselor. **Physically disabled:** Services for visually, hearing impaired. **Transfer:** Transfer adviser, college fairs on campus for students transferring to 4-year colleges.

Contact. E-mail: uwmc@uwe.edu
Phone: (715) 261-6241 Toll-free number: (888) 367-8962
Fax: (715) 261-6331
Franklyn Taylor, Admissions Director, University of Wisconsin-Marathon County, 518 South Seventh Avenue, Wausau, WI 54401-5396

University of Wisconsin-Marinette
Marinette, Wisconsin
www.marinette.uwc.edu   **CB code: 1891**

- Public 2-year branch campus and liberal arts college
- Commuter campus in large town
- SAT or ACT (ACT writing optional), application essay required

General. Founded in 1946. Regionally accredited. **Enrollment:** 461 degree-seeking undergraduates. **Degrees:** 95 associate awarded. **Location:** 50 miles from Green Bay, 170 miles from Milwaukee. **Calendar:** Semester, limited summer session. **Full-time faculty:** 19 total; 90% have terminal degrees, 10% minority, 42% women. **Part-time faculty:** 20 total; 10% have terminal degrees, 45% women.

Student profile.

Out-of-state:	20%	**25 or older:**	23%

Transfer out. Colleges most students transferred to 2011: University of Wisconsin-Green Bay, University of Wisconsin-Oshkosh, University of Wisconsin-Stevens Point, University of Wisconsin-Madison, Northern Michigan University.

Basis for selection. Class rank, GPA, courses, ACT scores, and involvement important. Applicants not meeting minimum standards may be accepted but required to take reduced course load and/or noncredit courses to remedy deficiencies. **Adult students:** SAT/ACT scores not required if applicant over 21. **Home schooled:** Transcript of courses and grades required.

High school preparation. 17 units required. Required units include English 4, mathematics 3, social studies 3 and science 3. 4 electives of computer science, business, foreign language and/or fine arts required.

2011-2012 Annual costs. Tuition/fees: $4,848; $11,831 out-of-state. Per-credit charge: $188 in-state; $479 out-of-state. Minnesota reciprocity tuition: $190 per-credit-hour. Books/supplies: $860. Personal expenses: $1,690.

Financial aid. All financial aid based on need. Need-based aid available for part-time students. Work-study available nights, weekends and for part-time students.

Application procedures. Admission: Priority date 7/1; no deadline. $44 fee, may be waived for applicants with need. Admission notification on a rolling basis. Students may be conditionally admitted prior to receipt of ACT scores, but may not register for classes until scores are received. **Financial aid:** Priority date 4/15; no closing date. FAFSA required. Applicants notified on a rolling basis.

Academics. Special study options: Accelerated study, cross-registration, distance learning, dual enrollment of high school students, ESL, independent study, study abroad. Bachelor's degree programs available on campus. **Credit/placement by examination:** AP, CLEP, institutional tests. **Support services:** Reduced course load, remedial instruction, study skills assistance, tutoring, writing center.

Majors. Area/ethnic studies: Women's. **Liberal arts:** Arts/sciences.

Computing on campus. 80 workstations in library, computer center, student center. Online course registration, online library, helpline, wireless network available.

Student life. Freshman orientation: Mandatory, $60 fee. Preregistration for classes offered. **Activities:** Bands, choral groups, drama, international student organizations, literary magazine, music ensembles, musical theater, student government, student newspaper, Phi Theta Kappa.

Athletics. NJCAA. **Intercollegiate:** Basketball, volleyball W. **Intramural:** Basketball, bowling, football (non-tackle), skiing, table tennis, volleyball. **Team name:** Buccaneers.

Student services. Adult student services, career counseling, services for economically disadvantaged, student employment services, financial aid counseling, minority student services, personal counseling, veterans' counselor. **Physically disabled:** Services for visually, speech, hearing impaired. **Transfer:** Transfer adviser, college fairs on campus for students transferring to 4-year colleges.

Contact. E-mail: ssinfo@uwc.edu
Phone: (715) 735-4301 Fax: (715) 735-4304
Cynthia Bailey, Assistant Campus Dean for Student Services, University of Wisconsin-Marinette, 750 West Bay Shore Street, Marinette, WI 54143

University of Wisconsin-Marshfield/Wood County
Marshfield, Wisconsin
www.marshfield.uwc.edu   **CB code: 1997**

- Public 2-year branch campus college
- Commuter campus in large town
- SAT or ACT (ACT writing optional) required

General. Founded in 1964. Regionally accredited. Two-year transfer program prepares students for any four-year program in Wisconsin system. **Enrollment:** 715 degree-seeking undergraduates. **Degrees:** 50 associate awarded. **Location:** 138 miles from Madison. **Calendar:** Semester, limited summer session. **Full-time faculty:** 19 total. **Part-time faculty:** 20 total. **Class size:** 30% < 20, 67% 20-39, 1% 40-49, 2% 50-99.

Student profile.

Out-of-state:	1%	**25 or older:**	28%

Transfer out. Colleges most students transferred to 2011: University of Wisconsin-Steven's Point, University of Wisconsin-Eau Claire, University of Wisconsin-Madison.

Basis for selection. Rank in top 75% of class and 17 specified high school academic units ensures admission. Students in bottom 25% and/or with missing units may be placed on waiting list. Students not admitted may be admitted to a following semester. Placement tests required in math and English. **Adult students:** SAT/ACT scores not required if applicant over 21 or out of high school 3 years or more.

High school preparation. 17 units required. Required and recommended units include English 4, mathematics 3-4, social studies 3, science 3-4 and academic electives 4.

2011-2012 Annual costs. Tuition/fees: $4,846; $11,829 out-of-state. Per-credit charge: $188 in-state; $479 out-of-state. Minnesota reciprocity tuition: $190 per-credit-hour. Books/supplies: $500. Personal expenses: $1,690.

Financial aid. All financial aid based on need. Need-based aid available for part-time students. Work-study available nights, weekends and for part-time students.

Application procedures. Admission: No deadline. $44 fee. Admission notification on a rolling basis. **Financial aid:** Closing date 4/15. FAFSA required. Applicants notified on a rolling basis starting 5/15; must reply within 3 week(s) of notification.

Academics. Special study options: Cross-registration, distance learning, dual enrollment of high school students, independent study, internships, study abroad. **Credit/placement by examination:** AP, CLEP, institutional tests. **Support services:** Pre-admission summer program, reduced course load, remedial instruction, study skills assistance, tutoring.

Majors. Liberal arts: Arts/sciences.

Computing on campus. 40 workstations in library, computer center, student center. Commuter students can connect to campus network. Online course registration available.

Student life. Freshman orientation: Mandatory, $55 fee. Preregistration for classes offered. 1-day session held in late August. **Activities:** Bands, choral groups, drama, literary magazine, music ensembles, musical theater, student government, student newspaper, symphony orchestra, Inter-Varsity Christian Fellowship, business club, nursing associaton, program board, honor fraternity, student education association.

Athletics. NJCAA. **Intercollegiate:** Basketball, golf, tennis, volleyball W. **Intramural:** Basketball, bowling, football (tackle) M, soccer, softball, tennis, volleyball. **Team name:** Marauders.

Student services. Adult student services, alcohol/substance abuse counseling, career counseling, student employment services, financial aid counseling, personal counseling, veterans' counselor. **Physically disabled:** Services for visually, speech, hearing impaired. **Transfer:** Transfer adviser, college fairs on campus for students transferring to 4-year colleges.

Contact. E-mail: msfadmit@uwc.edu
Phone: (715) 389-6500 Fax: (715) 384-1718
Jeffrey Meece, Assistant Campus Dean for Student Services, University of Wisconsin-Marshfield/Wood County, 2000 West Fifth Street, Marshfield, WI 54449

University of Wisconsin-Richland
Richland Center, Wisconsin
www.richland.uwc.edu   CB code: 1662

♦ Public 2-year liberal arts college
♦ Commuter campus in small town
♦ SAT or ACT (ACT writing optional) required

General. Founded in 1967. Regionally accredited. **Enrollment:** 476 degree-seeking undergraduates. **Degrees:** 80 associate awarded. **Location:** 60 miles from Madison, 60 miles from LaCrosse. **Calendar:** Semester, limited summer session. **Full-time faculty:** 15 total. **Part-time faculty:** 18 total. **Class size:** 57% < 20, 43% 20-39.

Student profile. Among degree-seeking undergraduates, 100% enrolled in a transfer program.

Out-of-state:	1%	**Live on campus:**	40%
25 or older:	18%		

Transfer out. 95% of students enrolled in the transfer program go on to 4-year colleges. **Colleges most students transferred to 2011:** University of Wisconsin-LaCrosse, University of Wisconsin-Stevens Point, University of Wisconsin-Platteville, University of Wisconsin-Madison, University of Wisconsin-Eau Claire,.

Basis for selection. Rank in upper 75% of class ensures admission. Students in bottom 25% may be admitted on discretionary category basis. Qualified students denied admission will be admitted at later date. Test scores for matriculating students must be received prior to enrollment. Interview required for applicants in bottom 25% of class; recommended for all others. **Adult students:** SAT/ACT scores not required if applicant over 21. **Home schooled:** 19 ACT required.

High school preparation. 17 units required. Required units include English 4, mathematics 3, social studies 3, science 3 and academic electives 4. 4 of the required units may be in foreign language, fine arts, computer science or other academic areas.

2011-2012 Annual costs. Tuition/fees: $5,014; $11,998 out-of-state. Per-credit charge: $188 in-state; $479 out-of-state. Minnesota reciprocity tuition: $190 per-credit-hour. Books/supplies: $860. Personal expenses: $1,650.

2011-2012 Financial aid. All financial aid based on need. 61% of total undergraduate aid awarded as scholarships/grants, 39% as loans/jobs. Need-based aid available for part-time students. Work-study available nights, weekends and for part-time students.

Application procedures. Admission: No deadline. $44 fee, may be waived for applicants with need. Admission notification on a rolling basis. **Financial aid:** Priority date 4/1; no closing date. FAFSA required. Applicants notified on a rolling basis starting 5/15; must reply within 3 week(s) of notification.

Academics. Associate of arts and science degree accepted throughout University of Wisconsin System as transfer tool; satisfies general education requirements of any system campus. Online writing lab available to students at all times. **Special study options:** Cross-registration, distance learning, dual enrollment of high school students, independent study, study abroad, teacher certification program. Bachelor's degree programs available on campus. **Credit/placement by examination:** AP, CLEP, IB, institutional tests. **Support services:** Reduced course load, remedial instruction, study skills assistance, tutoring, writing center.

Majors. Liberal arts: Arts/sciences.

Computing on campus. 60 workstations in dormitories, library, computer center. Dormitories wired for high-speed internet access and linked to campus network. Commuter students can connect to campus network. Online library, wireless network available.

Student life. Freshman orientation: Mandatory, $35 fee. Preregistration for classes offered. Held during the first week of fall classes. **Housing:** Coed dorms, apartments available. $200 deposit. **Activities:** Concert band, choral groups, drama, international student organizations, literary magazine, music ensembles, musical theater, student government, student newspaper, Educators of the Future, Gay-Straight Alliance, Campus Democrats, College Republicans, gamers club, InterVarsity Christian Fellowship, history club, community service association.

Athletics. Intercollegiate: Basketball, volleyball W. **Intramural:** Basketball, football (non-tackle), racquetball, softball, swimming, tennis, volleyball. **Team name:** Roadrunners.

Student services. Adult student services, alcohol/substance abuse counseling, career counseling, student employment services, financial aid counseling, personal counseling. **Transfer:** Transfer adviser, college fairs on campus for students transferring to 4-year colleges.

Contact. E-mail: rlninfo@uwc.edu
Phone: (608) 647-6186 ext. 3 Fax: (608) 647-2275
John Poole, Director of Student Services, University of Wisconsin-Richland, 1200 Highway 14 West, Richland Center, WI 53581

University of Wisconsin-Rock County
Janesville, Wisconsin
www.rock.uwc.edu   **CB code: 1998**

- Public 2-year branch campus and liberal arts college
- Commuter campus in small city
- SAT or ACT (ACT writing optional) required

General. Founded in 1966. Regionally accredited. **Enrollment:** 1,289 degree-seeking undergraduates. **Degrees:** 100 associate awarded. **Location:** 40 miles from Madison. **Calendar:** Semester, limited summer session. **Full-time faculty:** 33 total. **Part-time faculty:** 23 total. **Class size:** 51% < 20, 46% 20-39, 2% 40-49, less than 1% 50-99.

Student profile.

Out-of-state: 1%   **25 or older:**   25%

Transfer out. Colleges most students transferred to 2011: University of Wisconsin-Whitewater, University of Wisconsin-Madison.

Basis for selection. Rank in upper 75% of class ensures admission. Students in bottom 25% and those with GED admitted under special conditions. SAT or ACT scores used for students with GED or in bottom 25% of class. Essays considered. **Adult students:** SAT/ACT scores not required if applicant over 21. **Home schooled:** Transcript of courses and grades required.

High school preparation. 17 units recommended. Recommended units include English 4, mathematics 3, social studies 3, science 3 and academic electives 4.

2011-2012 Annual costs. Tuition/fees: $4,849; $11,832 out-of-state. Per-credit charge: $188 in-state; $479 out-of-state. Minnesota reciprocity tuition: $190 per-credit-hour. Books/supplies: $500. Personal expenses: $810.

Financial aid. All financial aid based on need. Need-based aid available for part-time students. Work-study available nights, weekends and for part-time students.

Application procedures. Admission: No deadline. $44 fee. Admission notification on a rolling basis. **Financial aid:** Closing date 3/15. FAFSA, institutional form required. Applicants notified on a rolling basis starting 6/1; must reply within 3 week(s) of notification.

Academics. Special study options: Cross-registration, distance learning, dual enrollment of high school students, independent study, study abroad. Bachelor's degree programs available on campus. **Credit/placement by examination:** AP, CLEP, institutional tests. **Support services:** Learning center, reduced course load, remedial instruction, study skills assistance, tutoring, writing center.

Majors. Liberal arts: Arts/sciences.

Computing on campus. 50 workstations in library, computer center. Commuter students can connect to campus network.

Student life. Freshman orientation: Mandatory, $95 fee. Preregistration for classes offered. 3-hour sessions held in May, June, July, and August. **Activities:** Bands, choral groups, dance, drama, literary magazine, music ensembles, student government, student newspaper, symphony orchestra, Future Educators, adult student organization.

Athletics. NJCAA. **Intercollegiate:** Soccer, tennis, volleyball W. **Intramural:** Badminton, basketball, soccer, softball, tennis, volleyball. **Team name:** Rattlers.

Student services. Adult student services, alcohol/substance abuse counseling, career counseling, services for economically disadvantaged, student employment services, financial aid counseling, minority student services, personal counseling, veterans' counselor. **Physically disabled:** Services for visually, hearing impaired. **Transfer:** Re-entry adviser for new students. Transfer adviser, college fairs on campus for students transferring to 4-year colleges.

Contact. E-mail: rckinfo@uwc.edu
Phone: (608) 758-6523 Fax: (608) 758-6579
Kristin Fillhouer, Assistant Campus Dean for Student Services, University of Wisconsin-Rock County, 2909 Kellogg Avenue, Janesville, WI 53546-5699

University of Wisconsin-Sheboygan
Sheboygan, Wisconsin
www.sheboygan.uwc.edu   **CB code: 1994**

- Public 2-year community and junior college
- Commuter campus in small city
- SAT or ACT (ACT writing optional) required

General. Founded in 1933. Regionally accredited. Several collaborative degrees with 4-year institutions so students can earn bachelor's degree. **Enrollment:** 896 degree-seeking undergraduates. **Degrees:** 77 associate awarded. **Location:** 60 miles from Milwaukee, 50 miles from Green Bay. **Calendar:** Semester, limited summer session. **Full-time faculty:** 22 total. **Part-time faculty:** 25 total.

Student profile.

Out-of-state: 1%   **25 or older:**   24%

Transfer out. Colleges most students transferred to 2011: University of Wisconsin-Milwaukee, University of Wisconsin-Green Bay, University of Wisconsin-Whitewater, University of Wisconsin-Madison, University of Wisconsin-Oshkosh.

Basis for selection. Admissions based on secondary school record and class rank. Standardized test scores also important. ACT preferred. Interview recommended. **Adult students:** SAT/ACT scores not required if applicant over 21.

High school preparation. 17 units required. Required units include English 4, mathematics 3, social studies 3 and science 3. Additional 4 units required from English, social science, math, natural science, foreign language, fine arts, or computer science.

2011-2012 Annual costs. Tuition/fees: $4,814; $11,797 out-of-state. Per-credit charge: $188 in-state; $479 out-of-state. Minnesota reciprocity tuition: $190 per-credit-hour. Books/supplies: $470. Personal expenses: $1,690.

Financial aid. Need-based: Need-based aid available for part-time students. Work-study available nights, weekends and for part-time students. **Non-need-based:** Scholarships awarded for academics, leadership, music/drama.

Application procedures. Admission: Priority date 6/30; no deadline. $45 fee, may be waived for applicants with need. Admission notification on a rolling basis. **Financial aid:** Priority date 4/15; no closing date. FAFSA, institutional form required. Applicants notified on a rolling basis starting 6/1; must reply within 2 week(s) of notification.

Academics. Special study options: Distance learning, dual enrollment of high school students, exchange student, honors, independent study, study abroad. Bachelor's degree programs available on campus. **Credit/placement by examination:** AP, CLEP, IB, institutional tests. **Support services:** GED test center, learning center, reduced course load, remedial instruction, study skills assistance, tutoring, writing center.

Majors. Liberal arts: Arts/sciences.

Computing on campus. 80 workstations in library, computer center. Commuter students can connect to campus network. Helpline available.

Student life. Freshman orientation: Mandatory, $75 fee. Preregistration for classes offered. **Activities:** Bands, choral groups, drama, film society, literary magazine, musical theater, student government, student newspaper, TV station, Intervarsity Christian Fellowship, Circle K, 10% Society, Zoomers Club.

Athletics. NJCAA. **Intercollegiate:** Basketball, golf, tennis, volleyball W. **Intramural:** Badminton, basketball, football (tackle) M, soccer, softball, volleyball. **Team name:** Wombats.

Student services. Adult student services, career counseling, financial aid counseling, personal counseling, veterans' counselor. **Physically disabled:** Services for visually, speech, hearing impaired. **Transfer:** Pre-admission transcript evaluation for new students. Transfer center, transfer adviser, college fairs on campus for students transferring to 4-year colleges.

Contact. Phone: (920) 459-6633 Fax: (920) 459-6662
Connie Christensen, Assistant Campus Dean for Student Services, University of Wisconsin-Sheboygan, One University Drive, Sheboygan, WI 53081

University of Wisconsin-Washington County
West Bend, Wisconsin
www.washington.uwc.edu   **CB code: 1993**

▶ Public 2-year branch campus and liberal arts college
▶ Commuter campus in large town
▶ SAT or ACT (ACT writing optional) required

General. Founded in 1968. Regionally accredited. **Enrollment:** 1,033 degree-seeking undergraduates. **Degrees:** 160 associate awarded. **Location:** 70 miles from Madison, 35 miles from Milwaukee. **Calendar:** Semester, limited summer session. **Full-time faculty:** 26 total. **Part-time faculty:** 32 total. **Special facilities:** Observatory.

Student profile.

Out-of-state:	2%	**25 or older:**	17%

Transfer out. Colleges most students transferred to 2011: University of Wisconsin-Milwaukee, University of Wisconsin-Oshkosh, University of Wisconsin-Whitewater, University of Wisconsin-Madison.

Basis for selection. Rank in top 75% of class ensures admission. Students in bottom 25% placed in discretionary category. Qualified students not admitted for specific semester applied for will be admitted at later date. ACT preferred. Interview required for applicants with GED or those ranking in bottom 25% of high school class. **Adult students:** SAT/ACT scores not required if applicant over 21. **Home schooled:** Transcript of courses and grades required.

High school preparation. 17 units required. Required units include English 4, mathematics 3, social studies 3, science 3 and academic electives 4.

2011-2012 Annual costs. Tuition/fees: $4,829; $11,812 out-of-state. Per-credit charge: $188 in-state; $479 out-of-state. Minnesota reciprocity tuition: $190 per-credit-hour. Books/supplies: $552. Personal expenses: $930.

Financial aid. Need-based: Need-based aid available for part-time students. Work-study available nights, weekends and for part-time students. **Non-need-based:** Scholarships awarded for academics.

Application procedures. Admission: Priority date 8/1; no deadline. $44 fee, may be waived for applicants with need. Admission notification on a rolling basis beginning on or about 11/1. **Financial aid:** Priority date 4/15; no closing date. FAFSA required. Applicants notified on a rolling basis starting 4/30; must reply within 3 week(s) of notification.

Academics. Special study options: Cross-registration, distance learning, dual enrollment of high school students, honors, independent study, internships, study abroad. Collaborative B.A. degree programs in organizational administration, information resources, communications, BSN in nursing, all in cooperation with University of Wisconsin-Milwaukee. Bachelor's degree programs available on campus. **Credit/placement by examination:** AP, CLEP, IB, institutional tests. **Support services:** Learning center, pre-admission summer program, reduced course load, remedial instruction, study skills assistance, tutoring, writing center.

Majors. Liberal arts: Arts/sciences.

Computing on campus. 78 workstations in library, computer center. Commuter students can connect to campus network. Wireless network available.

Student life. Freshman orientation: Mandatory, $75 fee. Preregistration for classes offered. **Activities:** Bands, choral groups, dance, drama, literary magazine, music ensembles, musical theater, student government, student newspaper, symphony orchestra, Phi Theta Kappa honorary society, Literary Guild, business club, Student Impact.

Athletics. NAIA. **Intercollegiate:** Basketball, golf, soccer, tennis, volleyball W. **Intramural:** Basketball, softball, volleyball. **Team name:** Wildcats.

Student services. Adult student services, career counseling, financial aid counseling, personal counseling, veterans' counselor. **Physically disabled:** Services for hearing impaired. **Transfer:** Pre-admission transcript evaluation for new students. Transfer center, transfer adviser, college fairs on campus for students transferring to 4-year colleges.

Contact. Phone: (262) 335-5201 Fax: (262) 335-5274
Kathleen Kissling, University of Wisconsin-Washington County, 400 University Drive, West Bend, WI 53095

University of Wisconsin-Waukesha
Waukesha, Wisconsin
www.waukesha.uwc.edu   **CB code: 1999**

▶ Public 2-year branch campus and junior college
▶ Commuter campus in small city
▶ SAT or ACT (ACT writing optional) required

General. Founded in 1966. Regionally accredited. **Enrollment:** 1,937 degree-seeking undergraduates; 297 non-degree-seeking students. **Degrees:** 188 associate awarded. **Location:** 17 miles from Milwaukee. **Calendar:** Semester, limited summer session. **Full-time faculty:** 63 total; 97% have terminal degrees, 18% minority, 43% women. **Part-time faculty:** 29 total; 72% have terminal degrees, 31% women. **Special facilities:** 98-acre environmental studies field station.

Student profile. Among degree-seeking undergraduates, 1,364 enrolled as first-time, first-year students, 216 transferred in from other institutions.

Part-time:	42%	**Women:**	45%
Out-of-state:	1%	**25 or older:**	28%

Transfer out. Colleges most students transferred to 2011: University of Wisconsin-Milwaukee, University of Wisconsin-Whitewater, University of Wisconsin-Madison.

Basis for selection. Rank in top 75% of class or 19 ACT ensures admission. Students in bottom 25% and those with GED considered based on recommended interview. **Adult students:** SAT/ACT scores not required if applicant over 21.

High school preparation. 17 units required. Required and recommended units include English 4, mathematics 3, social studies 3, science 3, foreign language 2 and academic electives 4.

2011-2012 Annual costs. Tuition/fees: $4,821; $11,804 out-of-state. Per-credit charge: $188 in-state; $479 out-of-state. Minnesota reciprocity tuition: $190 per-credit-hour. Books/supplies: $980. Personal expenses: $1,690.

2011-2012 Financial aid. Need-based: 38% of total undergraduate aid awarded as scholarships/grants, 62% as loans/jobs. Need-based aid available for part-time students. Work-study available nights, weekends and for part-time students. **Non-need-based:** Scholarships awarded for academics, alumni affiliation, art, leadership, minority status, music/drama, state residency.

Application procedures. Admission: Priority date 4/1; no deadline. $44 fee, may be waived for applicants with need. Admission notification on a rolling basis beginning on or about 9/15. **Financial aid:** Priority date 4/15; no closing date. FAFSA required. Applicants notified on a rolling basis starting 5/15; must reply within 3 week(s) of notification.

Academics. Special study options: Accelerated study, cross-registration, distance learning, dual enrollment of high school students, honors, independent study, study abroad. Bachelor's degree programs available on campus. **Credit/placement by examination:** AP, CLEP, IB, institutional tests. CLEP general exams must be taken before 16 degree credits completed. **Support services:** Learning center, pre-admission summer program, reduced course load, remedial instruction, study skills assistance, tutoring, writing center.

Majors. Liberal arts: Arts/sciences.

Computing on campus. 90 workstations in library, computer center, student center. Commuter students can connect to campus network. Online course registration, wireless network available.

Student life. Freshman orientation: Mandatory, $225 fee. Preregistration for classes offered. Sessions held periodically throughout summer. **Activities:** Bands, choral groups, dance, drama, literary magazine, music ensembles, musical theater, student government, student newspaper, diversity club, philosophy council, Phi Theta Kappa honor society, Campus Crusade for Christ, College Democrats, College Republicans, Circle K, African American Union, Organization of Latin American Leaders.

Athletics. NJCAA. **Intercollegiate:** Basketball, cheerleading M, golf, soccer, tennis, volleyball W. **Team name:** Cougars.

Student services. Adult student services, career counseling, financial aid counseling, on-campus daycare, personal counseling, veterans' counselor. **Physically disabled:** Services for visually, speech, hearing impaired. **Transfer:** Transfer adviser, college fairs on campus for students transferring to 4-year colleges.

Contact. E-mail: wakadmit@uwc.edu
Phone: (262) 521-5041 Toll-free number: (888) 289-9285
Fax: (262) 521-5530
Deb Kusick, Admission Specialist, University of Wisconsin-Waukesha, 1500 North University Drive, Waukesha, WI 53188

Waukesha County Technical College
Pewaukee, Wisconsin
www.wctc.edu
CB code: 0724

▶ Public 2-year technical college
▶ Commuter campus in large town

General. Founded in 1923. Regionally accredited. **Enrollment:** 5,935 degree-seeking undergraduates; 3,514 non-degree-seeking students. **Degrees:** 629 associate awarded. **Location:** 15 miles from Milwaukee. **Calendar:** Semester, limited summer session. **Full-time faculty:** 190 total. **Part-time faculty:** 704 total. **Special facilities:** Green energy training facilities, wind turbine, green roofs.

Student profile. Among degree-seeking undergraduates, 100% enrolled in a vocational program, 517 enrolled as first-time, first-year students.

Part-time:	65%	25 or older:	50%
Women:	52%		

Basis for selection. Open admission, but selective for some programs. Individual programs may have additional requirements or prerequisites, and some programs may have wait lists. Some health occupations programs may require interviews and a general college preparatory background of prerequisites. **Home schooled:** Transcript of courses and grades required.

2011-2012 Annual costs. Tuition/fees: $3,561; $5,241 out-of-state. Per-credit charge: $112 in-state; $168 out-of-state. Materials fees vary by program; minimum $4 per course. $10 per credit fee for online courses. Books/supplies: $1,400. Personal expenses: $1,780.

2010-2011 Financial aid. Need-based: Work-study available nights, weekends and for part-time students. **Non-need-based:** Scholarships awarded for academics.

Application procedures. Admission: No deadline. $30 fee, may be waived for applicants with need. Admission notification on a rolling basis. **Financial aid:** Priority date 3/31; no closing date. FAFSA required. Applicants notified on a rolling basis.

Academics. Special study options: Cooperative education, distance learning, double major, dual enrollment of high school students, ESL, independent study, internships, student-designed major, study abroad. License preparation in dental hygiene, nursing, paramedic, real estate. **Credit/placement by examination:** AP, CLEP, institutional tests. **Support services:** GED preparation and test center, learning center, reduced course load, remedial instruction, study skills assistance, tutoring, writing center.

Majors. Business: Accounting, administrative services, business admin, hotel/motel/restaurant management, international marketing, marketing, operations, real estate. **Communications technology:** Graphics. **Computer sciences:** Programming, support specialist. **Education:** Early childhood, teacher assistance. **Health services:** Dental hygiene, EMT paramedic, medical radiologic technology/radiation therapy, medical records technology, nursing (RN), physical therapy assistant, surgical technology. **Protective services:** Fire safety technology, police science. **Visual/performing arts:** Digital arts, graphic design, interior design.

Most popular majors. Business/marketing 32%, computer/information sciences 15%, engineering/engineering technologies 6%, health sciences 17%, visual/performing arts 6%.

Computing on campus. Online course registration, online library, helpline, wireless network available.

Student life. Freshman orientation: Available. Preregistration for classes offered. **Activities:** Student government.

Student services. Adult student services, career counseling, services for economically disadvantaged, student employment services, financial aid counseling, minority student services, on-campus daycare, personal counseling, placement for graduates. **Physically disabled:** Services for visually, speech, hearing impaired. **Transfer:** Pre-admission transcript evaluation for new students. College fairs on campus for students transferring to 4-year colleges.

Contact. Phone: (262) 691-5275 Fax: (262) 691-5593
Kathleen Kazda, Manager, Admissions and Assessment, Waukesha County Technical College, 800 Main Street, Pewaukee, WI 53072

Western Technical College
La Crosse, Wisconsin
www.westerntc.edu
CB code: 1087

▶ Public 2-year community and technical college
▶ Commuter campus in small city

General. Founded in 1912. Regionally accredited. **Enrollment:** 5,122 degree-seeking undergraduates. **Degrees:** 627 associate awarded. **Location:** 200 miles from Milwaukee, 150 miles from Minneapolis-St. Paul. **Calendar:** Semester, limited summer session. **Full-time faculty:** 217 total. **Part-time faculty:** 155 total.

Student profile. Among degree-seeking undergraduates, 1,054 enrolled as first-time, first-year students.

Part-time:	59%	Asian American:	3%
Women:	54%	Hispanic American:	1%
African American:	2%	Native American:	1%

Basis for selection. Open admission, but selective for some programs. Standardized test scores required for admission into selected programs. COMPASS required for placement if ACT scores not available. Interviews recommended for placement, portfolios recommended for commercial art applicants for placement.

High school preparation. Recommended units include English 3, mathematics 2, social studies 3 and science 2.

2011-2012 Annual costs. Tuition/fees: $3,750; $5,430 out-of-state. Per-credit charge: $112 in-state; $168 out-of-state. Material fees vary by program; minimum $4 per course. $10 per credit fee for online courses. Room/board: $5,200. Books/supplies: $1,400. Personal expenses: $1,774.

Financial aid. Need-based: Need-based aid available for part-time students. Work-study available nights, weekends and for part-time students.

Application procedures. Admission: No deadline. $30 fee, may be waived for applicants with need. Admission notification on a rolling basis. **Financial aid:** Priority date 3/1; no closing date. FAFSA, institutional form required. Applicants notified on a rolling basis starting 4/1.

Academics. Special study options: Accelerated study, cooperative education, distance learning, double major, dual enrollment of high school students, ESL, honors, independent study, internships. License preparation in nursing, occupational therapy, paramedic, physical therapy, radiology, real estate. **Credit/placement by examination:** AP, CLEP, institutional tests. 45 credit hours maximum toward associate degree. **Support services:** GED preparation and test center, learning center, reduced course load, remedial instruction, study skills assistance, tutoring, writing center.

Majors. Architecture: Technology. **Business:** Accounting, administrative services, business admin, customer service support, finance, human resources, operations, sales/distribution. **Communications:** Media studies. **Communications technology:** General, desktop publishing. **Computer sciences:** Applications programming, data entry, data processing, LAN/WAN management, networking. **Education:** Teacher assistance. **General:** Business technology. **Health services:** Clinical lab technology, dental hygiene, electroencephalograph technology, medical radiologic technology/radiation therapy, medical records technology, nursing (RN), occupational therapy assistant, physical therapy assistant, respiratory therapy technology. **Human services:** Community org/advocacy. **Protective services:** Fire safety technology, police science. **Visual/performing arts:** Design, graphic design, interior design. **Work/family studies:** Child care management.

Most popular majors. Business/marketing 26%, communications/journalism 6%, computer/information sciences 7%, health sciences 32%, security/protective services 7%.

Computing on campus. 145 workstations in dormitories, library, computer center. Dormitories wired for high-speed internet access and linked to campus network. Commuter students can connect to campus network. Online course registration, online library, helpline, repair service, wireless network available.

Student life. Freshman orientation: Mandatory. Preregistration for classes offered. General school orientation held in August. **Housing:** Coed dorms available. **Activities:** Student government, multicultural club, Campus Crusade for Christ.

Athletics. NJCAA. **Intercollegiate:** Baseball M, basketball, volleyball W. **Intramural:** Badminton, basketball, bowling, volleyball. **Team name:** Cavaliers.

Student services. Adult student services, alcohol/substance abuse counseling, career counseling, services for economically disadvantaged, student

employment services, financial aid counseling, health services, minority student services, on-campus daycare, personal counseling, placement for graduates, veterans' counselor, women's services. **Physically disabled:** Services for visually, speech, hearing impaired. **Transfer:** Pre-admission transcript evaluation for new students.

Contact. E-mail: wellsj@westerntc.edu
Phone: (608) 785-9476 Toll-free number: (800) 322-9982
Fax: (608) 785-9148
Jayne Wells, Admissions, Registration and Records, Western Technical College, PO Box 908, La Crosse, WI 54602-0908

Wisconsin Indianhead Technical College
Shell Lake, Wisconsin
www.witc.edu CB code: 1580

▶ Public 2-year technical college
▶ Commuter campus in small town
▶ Interview required

General. Founded in 1972. Regionally accredited. 4 campuses and 2 outreach centers covering 11 county area. **Enrollment:** 3,201 degree-seeking undergraduates; 410 non-degree-seeking students. **Degrees:** 466 associate awarded. **Calendar:** Semester, limited summer session. **Full-time faculty:** 153 total. **Part-time faculty:** 633 total.

Student profile. Among degree-seeking undergraduates, 692 enrolled as first-time, first-year students.

Part-time:	52%	Hispanic American:	1%
Out-of-state:	7%	Native American:	2%
Women:	61%	25 or older:	48%
African American:	1%		

Transfer out. Colleges most students transferred to 2011: University of Wisconsin.

Basis for selection. Open admission, but selective for some programs. ACCUPLACER used for skills assessment and placement. Developmental coursework required if scores below established range. **Home schooled:** Must pass ability to benefit assessment.

High school preparation. College-preparatory program recommended.

2011-2012 Annual costs. Tuition/fees: $3,642; $5,322 out-of-state. Per-credit charge: $112 in-state; $168 out-of-state. Material fees vary by program; minimum $4 per course. $10 per credit fee for online courses. Books/supplies: $1,400. Personal expenses: $1,774.

2010-2011 Financial aid. All financial aid based on need. Need-based aid available for part-time students. Work-study available nights, weekends and for part-time students.

Application procedures. Admission: No deadline. $30 fee. Admission notification on a rolling basis. **Financial aid:** Priority date 4/15; no closing date. FAFSA required. Applicants notified on a rolling basis starting 5/10; must reply by 9/1 or within 4 week(s) of notification.

Academics. Special study options: Accelerated study, distance learning, double major, internships. License preparation in dental hygiene, nursing, occupational therapy, paramedic, real estate. **Credit/placement by examination:** AP, CLEP, institutional tests. **Support services:** GED preparation and test center, learning center, pre-admission summer program, reduced course load, remedial instruction, study skills assistance, tutoring.

Majors. Business: Accounting, administrative services, business admin, finance, operations. **Computer sciences:** General, programming. **Health services:** EMT paramedic, nursing (RN), occupational therapy assistant. **Work/family studies:** Child care management.

Most popular majors. Business/marketing 41%, computer/information sciences 7%, engineering/engineering technologies 6%, family/consumer sciences 8%, health sciences 30%, security/protective services 8%.

Computing on campus. 1,900 workstations in library, computer center, student center. Online course registration, online library, helpline, repair service, wireless network available.

Student life. Freshman orientation: Available. Preregistration for classes offered. **Housing:** Apartments available. **Activities:** Student government, student newspaper, technical student organizations, vocational student organizations.

Student services. Adult student services, career counseling, services for economically disadvantaged, student employment services, financial aid counseling, health services, minority student services, personal counseling, placement for graduates, veterans' counselor. **Physically disabled:** Services for visually, speech, hearing impaired. **Transfer:** College fairs on campus for students transferring to 4-year colleges.

Contact. Phone: (715) 468-2815 Toll-free number: (800) 243-9482
Fax: (715) 468-2819
Laura Sullivan, Director of Enrollment, Wisconsin Indianhead Technical College, 505 Pine Ridge Drive, Shell Lake, WI 54871

Wyoming

Casper College
Casper, Wyoming
www.caspercollege.edu

CB code: 4043

- Public 2-year community college
- Commuter campus in small city

General. Founded in 1945. Regionally accredited. **Enrollment:** 2,998 degree-seeking undergraduates; 1,308 non-degree-seeking students. **Degrees:** 598 associate awarded. **Location:** 280 miles from Denver. **Calendar:** Semester, limited summer session. **Full-time faculty:** 151 total; 30% have terminal degrees, 5% minority, 41% women. **Part-time faculty:** 113 total; 5% have terminal degrees, less than 1% minority, 47% women. **Class size:** 70% < 20, 27% 20-39, 1% 40-49, 1% 50-99. **Special facilities:** Wildlife museum, geological museum, family resource center, fitness center, Western history center.

Student profile. Among degree-seeking undergraduates, 74% enrolled in a transfer program, 24% enrolled in a vocational program, 674 enrolled as first-time, first-year students, 257 transferred in from other institutions.

Part-time:	32%	Hispanic American:	4%
Out-of-state:	7%	Native American:	1%
Women:	61%	International:	1%
African American:	2%	25 or older:	43%
Asian American:	1%	Live on campus:	10%

Transfer out. Colleges most students transferred to 2011: University of Wyoming, University of North Dakota, Colorado State University, Montana State University, Black Hills State University.

Basis for selection. Open admission, but selective for some programs and for out-of-state students. 2.0 GPA required for out-of-state applicants. Selective admission for nursing, respiratory therapy, radiology; requirements vary by program. Audition recommended for music, theater, athletics and forensics; portfolio recommended for art. **Home schooled:** Program must be accredited and recognized by state department of education as being equivalent to high school diploma.

High school preparation. College-preparatory program recommended. Recommended units include English 4, mathematics 4, social studies 3, science 4 and foreign language 2.

2011-2012 Annual costs. Tuition/fees: $2,136; $5,544 out-of-state. Per-credit charge: $71 in-state; $216 out-of-state. Western Undergraduate Exchange students pay $107 per credit-hour. Room/board: $5,300. Books/supplies: $888. Personal expenses: $2,250.

Financial aid. Need-based: Need-based aid available for part-time students. Work-study available nights, weekends and for part-time students. **Non-need-based:** Scholarships awarded for academics, art, athletics, leadership, music/drama, state residency.

Application procedures. Admission: Priority date 8/1; deadline 8/15 (postmark date). No application fee. Admission notification on a rolling basis beginning on or about 2/1. **Financial aid:** Priority date 3/15; no closing date. FAFSA required. Applicants notified on a rolling basis starting 4/1.

Academics. Special study options: Cooperative education, cross-registration, distance learning, dual enrollment of high school students, honors, independent study, internships. Bachelor's degree programs available on campus. License preparation in nursing, paramedic, radiology. **Credit/placement by examination:** AP, CLEP, IB, institutional tests. 30 credit hours maximum toward associate degree. **Support services:** GED preparation and test center, learning center, remedial instruction, study skills assistance, tutoring, writing center.

Majors. Area/ethnic studies: Women's. **Biology:** General. **Business:** Accounting, accounting technology, administrative services, business admin, construction management, entrepreneurial studies, hospitality admin, management information systems, marketing, office technology, retailing. **Communications:** Communications/speech/rhetoric, journalism, media studies. **Computer sciences:** Information technology, programming, web page design, webmaster. **Conservation:** Environmental science, wildlife/wilderness. **Education:** Art, elementary, kindergarten/preschool, music, physical, social studies, teacher assistance, technology/industrial arts. **Engineering:** General. **English:** English lit. **Foreign languages:** General. **General:** Animal husbandry, business, range science. **Health services:** Athletic training, clinical lab technology, EMT paramedic, nursing (RN), occupational therapy assistant, pharmacy assistant, predental, premedicine, preoccupational therapy, preoptometry, prepharmacy, prephysical therapy, preveterinary, radiologic technology/medical imaging, respiratory therapy technology, substance abuse counseling. **History:** General. **Human services:** Social work. **Liberal arts:** Arts/sciences. **Math:** General. **Physical sciences:** Chemistry, geology, physics. **Protective services:** Criminal justice, disaster management, firefighting, forensics. **Psychology:** General. **Social sciences:** Anthropology, economics, GIS/cartography, international relations, political science, sociology. **Visual/performing arts:** Acting, art, dance, graphic design, music, music performance, musical theater, photography, studio arts, theater design.

Most popular majors. Education 9%, health sciences 25%, liberal arts 12%, security/protective services 9%, trade and industry 6%.

Computing on campus. 120 workstations in library, computer center. Dormitories wired for high-speed internet access and linked to campus network. Commuter students can connect to campus network. Helpline, wireless network available.

Student life. Freshman orientation: Mandatory. Preregistration for classes offered. One day new student orientation held the week before classes begin. **Housing:** Coed dorms, apartments, wellness housing available. $200 fully refundable deposit. **Activities:** Bands, campus ministries, choral groups, dance, drama, international student organizations, literary magazine, music ensembles, musical theater, student government, student newspaper, Latter-day Saints student association, Baptist student union, Phi Theta Kappa, Phi Rho Pi, student nurses association, Students in Free Enterprise, AG club, student activities board, Bakkai.

Athletics. NJCAA. **Intercollegiate:** Basketball, rodeo, volleyball W. **Intramural:** Basketball, bowling, football (non-tackle), racquetball, soccer, softball, tennis, volleyball. **Team name:** Thunderbirds.

Student services. Adult student services, alcohol/substance abuse counseling, career counseling, student employment services, financial aid counseling, health services, legal services, on-campus daycare, personal counseling, placement for graduates, veterans' counselor. **Physically disabled:** Services for visually, speech, hearing impaired. **Transfer:** Transfer adviser, college fairs on campus for students transferring to 4-year colleges.

Contact. E-mail: kfoltz@caspercollege.edu
Phone: (307) 268-2458 Toll-free number: (800) 442-2963
Fax: (307) 268-2611
Kyla Foltz, Director of Admissions, Casper College, 125 College Drive, Casper, WY 82601

Central Wyoming College
Riverton, Wyoming
www.cwc.edu

CB code: 4115

- Public 2-year community college
- Commuter campus in large town

General. Founded in 1966. Regionally accredited. Partnership with the National Outdoor Leadership School (NOLS). **Enrollment:** 1,484 degree-seeking undergraduates; 758 non-degree-seeking students. **Degrees:** 233 associate awarded. **Location:** 120 miles from Casper, 240 miles from Billings, MT. **Calendar:** Semester, limited summer session. **Full-time faculty:** 49 total; 74% have terminal degrees, 8% minority, 37% women. **Part-time faculty:** 103 total; 33% have terminal degrees, 8% minority, 53% women. **Class size:** 85% < 20, 14% 20-39, less than 1% 40-49. **Special facilities:** Rodeo arena, fine arts center, Microsoft training laboratory, Cisco training laboratory, Native American artifacts, canyon center, Wyoming PBS station. **Partnerships:** Formal partnerships with Microsoft, Cisco (training labs, software), National Outdoor Leadership School (NOLS).

Student profile. Among degree-seeking undergraduates, 61% enrolled in a transfer program, 39% enrolled in a vocational program, 376 enrolled as first-time, first-year students, 159 transferred in from other institutions.

Part-time:	45%	Hispanic American:	7%
Out-of-state:	15%	Native American:	13%
Women:	61%	International:	1%
African American:	1%	25 or older:	42%
Asian American:	1%	Live on campus:	11%

Transfer out. Colleges most students transferred to 2011: University of Wyoming, Colorado State University, Montana State University, University of Utah, Chadron.

Basis for selection. Open admission, but selective for some programs. Special admission to nursing program; minimum GPA and test scores required. Certain music courses require audition.

2011-2012 Annual costs. Tuition/fees: $2,208; $5,616 out-of-state. Per-credit charge: $71 in-state; $252 out-of-state. Western Undergraduate Exchange students pay $107 per credit hour. Room/board: $4,175. Books/supplies: $1,000. Personal expenses: $1,500.

2011-2012 Financial aid. Need-based: 207 full-time freshmen applied for aid; 157 were judged to have need; 150 of these received aid. Need-based aid available for part-time students. Work-study available nights, weekends and for part-time students. **Non-need-based:** Awarded to 379 full-time undergraduates, including 122 freshmen. Scholarships awarded for academics, alumni affiliation, art, athletics, leadership, minority status, music/drama, state residency.

Application procedures. Admission: No deadline. No application fee. Admission notification on a rolling basis beginning on or about 1/1. **Financial aid:** Priority date 4/15; no closing date. FAFSA, institutional form required. Applicants notified on a rolling basis starting 5/1; must reply within 2 week(s) of notification.

Academics. Special study options: Cooperative education, cross-registration, distance learning, double major, dual enrollment of high school students, external degree, honors, independent study, student-designed major, teacher certification program. Bachelor's degree programs available on campus. License preparation in dental hygiene, nursing, paramedic. **Credit/placement by examination:** AP, CLEP, institutional tests. 32 credit hours maximum toward associate degree. Some DANTES and APE exams accepted. **Support services:** GED preparation and test center, learning center, reduced course load, remedial instruction, study skills assistance, tutoring, writing center.

Majors. Area/ethnic studies: Native American. **Biology:** General. **Business:** General, accounting, accounting technology, administrative services, business admin, customer service support, hotel/motel admin. **Communications:** Radio/TV. **Computer sciences:** Computer science. **Conservation:** Environmental science. **Education:** Early childhood, elementary, secondary, teacher assistance. **Engineering:** General, environmental. **English:** English lit. **General:** Business, equestrian studies, range science. **Health services:** Athletic training, nursing (RN), office assistant. **Math:** General. **Parks/recreation:** General, facilities management. **Physical sciences:** General, geology. **Protective services:** Firefighting, homeland security, law enforcement admin. **Psychology:** General. **Social sciences:** General. **Visual/performing arts:** Acting, art, commercial photography, dramatic, graphic design, music, theater design. **Work/family studies:** Child care management.

Most popular majors. Business/marketing 6%, education 7%, health sciences 15%, liberal arts 30%, visual/performing arts 9%.

Computing on campus. 450 workstations in dormitories, library, computer center, student center. Dormitories wired for high-speed internet access and linked to campus network. Commuter students can connect to campus network. Online course registration, online library, wireless network available.

Student life. Freshman orientation: Mandatory. Preregistration for classes offered. **Housing:** Coed dorms, apartments available. $225 partly refundable deposit, deadline 5/1. **Activities:** Bands, choral groups, dance, drama, music ensembles, musical theater, radio station, student government, student newspaper, TV station, American Indian club, multicultural club, social science club, veterans club, Hispanic club, law and justice club, science club, Phi Theta Kappa, American Indian science and engineering society.

Athletics. NJCAA. **Intercollegiate:** Basketball, rodeo, volleyball W. **Intramural:** Badminton, basketball, skiing, soccer, softball, swimming, table tennis, tennis, volleyball, weight lifting. **Team name:** Rustlers.

Student services. Adult student services, alcohol/substance abuse counseling, career counseling, services for economically disadvantaged, student employment services, financial aid counseling, personal counseling, placement for graduates, veterans' counselor. **Physically disabled:** Services for visually, hearing impaired. **Transfer:** College fairs on campus for students transferring to 4-year colleges.

Contact. E-mail: admit@cwc.edu
Phone: (307) 855-2119 Toll-free number: (800) 865-0193
Fax: (307) 855-2065
Mikal Dalley, Admissions Office Assistant, Central Wyoming College, 2660 Peck Avenue, Riverton, WY 82501

Eastern Wyoming College
Torrington, Wyoming
www.ewc.wy.edu   CB code: 4700

▶ Public 2-year community college
▶ Commuter campus in small town

General. Founded in 1948. Regionally accredited. **Enrollment:** 822 degree-seeking undergraduates; 827 non-degree-seeking students. **Degrees:** 144 associate awarded. **Location:** 190 miles from Denver. **Calendar:** Semester, limited summer session. **Full-time faculty:** 44 total; 18% have terminal degrees. **Part-time faculty:** 45 total. **Special facilities:** Veterinarian technology facility.

Student profile. Among degree-seeking undergraduates, 63% enrolled in a transfer program, 37% enrolled in a vocational program, 264 enrolled as first-time, first-year students.

Part-time:	37%	Hispanic American:	6%
Out-of-state:	13%	Native American:	3%
Women:	63%	International:	1%
African American:	1%	25 or older:	33%

Transfer out. Colleges most students transferred to 2011: University of Wyoming, Chadron State College.

Basis for selection. Open admission. **Home schooled:** Transcript of courses and grades required. ACT recommended but not required. Signed statement that student was homeschooled required for financial aid.

2011-2012 Annual costs. Tuition/fees: $2,280; $5,688 out-of-state. Room/board: $4,640. Books/supplies: $1,200. Personal expenses: $1,532.

Financial aid. Need-based: Need-based aid available for part-time students. Work-study available nights, weekends and for part-time students. **Non-need-based:** Scholarships awarded for academics, alumni affiliation, art, athletics, leadership, music/drama. **Additional information:** Installment payment plan on room and board contracts offered.

Application procedures. Admission: No deadline. No application fee. Admission notification on a rolling basis. **Financial aid:** Priority date 3/15; no closing date. FAFSA, institutional form required. Applicants notified on a rolling basis starting 1/1.

Academics. Special study options: Cross-registration, distance learning, dual enrollment of high school students, ESL, honors, independent study, internships. License preparation on campus for welding and joining, veterinary technology, and cosmetology. Bachelor's degree programs available on campus. **Credit/placement by examination:** AP, CLEP, IB, institutional tests. 16 credit hours maximum toward associate degree. **Support services:** GED preparation and test center, learning center, reduced course load, remedial instruction, study skills assistance, tutoring.

Majors. Biology: General, environmental. **Business:** Accounting, administrative services, business admin, office management. **Communications:** Communications/speech/rhetoric. **Computer sciences:** Networking. **Conservation:** Wildlife/wilderness. **Education:** Agricultural, business, early childhood, elementary, mathematics, music, physical, secondary. **English:** English lit. **Foreign languages:** General. **General:** Agribusiness operations, animal sciences, economics, farm/ranch, range science. **Health services:** Predental, premedicine, prenursing, prepharmacy, preveterinary, veterinary technology/assistant. **History:** General. **Liberal arts:** Arts/sciences. **Math:** General, statistics. **Protective services:** Correctional facilities, criminal justice, law enforcement admin, police science. **Psychology:** General. **Social sciences:** Economics, political science, sociology. **Visual/performing arts:** Art, music.

Computing on campus. 120 workstations in dormitories, library, student center. Dormitories wired for high-speed internet access. Online course registration available.

Student life. Freshman orientation: Available. Preregistration for classes offered. Held in fall 1 day prior to first day of classes. **Housing:** Coed dorms, wellness housing available. $100 fully refundable deposit. **Activities:** Campus ministries, choral groups, musical theater, student government, student newspaper.

Athletics. NJCAA. **Intercollegiate:** Basketball, golf M, rodeo, volleyball W. **Intramural:** Basketball, bowling, handball, racquetball, rodeo, softball, tennis, volleyball, weight lifting. **Team name:** Lancers.

Student services. Adult student services, alcohol/substance abuse counseling, career counseling, student employment services, financial aid counseling, health services, personal counseling, placement for graduates, veterans' counselor. **Physically disabled:** Services for visually, speech, hearing impaired. **Transfer:** Re-entry adviser, pre-admission transcript evaluation

for new students. Transfer adviser, college fairs on campus for students transferring to 4-year colleges.

Contact. E-mail: rex.cogdill@ewc.wy.edu
Phone: (307) 532-8230 Toll-free number: (800) 658-3195
Fax: (307) 532-8222
Rex Cogdill, Vice President for Student Services, Eastern Wyoming College, 3200 West C Street, Torrington, WY 82240

Laramie County Community College
Cheyenne, Wyoming
www.lccc.wy.edu   **CB code: 0360**

▶ Public 2-year community college
▶ Commuter campus in small city

General. Founded in 1968. Regionally accredited. Additional campus in Laramie, outreach centers in Pine Bluffs, and at FE Warren AFB. **Enrollment:** 4,029 degree-seeking undergraduates; 498 non-degree-seeking students. **Degrees:** 474 associate awarded. **ROTC:** Army, Air Force. **Location:** 4 miles from downtown, 100 miles from Denver. **Calendar:** Semester, limited summer session. **Full-time faculty:** 96 total; 14% have terminal degrees, 1% minority, 53% women. **Part-time faculty:** 246 total; 6% minority, 57% women. **Class size:** 67% < 20, 31% 20-39, less than 1% 40-49, less than 1% 50-99, less than 1% >100. **Special facilities:** Bureau of Land Management park, indoor arena.

Student profile. Among degree-seeking undergraduates, 60% enrolled in a transfer program, 40% enrolled in a vocational program, 476 enrolled as first-time, first-year students, 310 transferred in from other institutions.

Part-time:	47%	25 or older:	39%
Out-of-state:	11%	Live on campus:	6%
Women:	58%		

Transfer out. Colleges most students transferred to 2011: University of Wyoming.

Basis for selection. Open admission, but selective for some programs. Special requirements for Dental Hygiene, Diagnostic Medical Sonography, Equine Studies, Nursing, Physical Therapist Assistant, Radiography, Surgical Technology, Wind Energy. Interview required for equine studies. **Home schooled:** Students must complete institutional home schooler form and attach to transcript. **Learning Disabled:** Interview with Disability Resource Center coordinator to arrange accommodations.

2011-2012 Annual costs. Tuition/fees: $2,544; $5,952 out-of-state. Per-credit charge: $71 in-state; $213 out-of-state. Room/board: $7,740. Books/supplies: $1,650. Personal expenses: $1,548.

2010-2011 Financial aid. Need-based: 246 full-time freshmen applied for aid; 131 were judged to have need; 131 of these received aid. 61% of total undergraduate aid awarded as scholarships/grants, 39% as loans/jobs. Need-based aid available for part-time students. Work-study available nights, weekends and for part-time students. **Non-need-based:** Awarded to 132 full-time undergraduates, including 33 freshmen. Scholarships awarded for academics, art, athletics, music/drama.

Application procedures. Admission: No deadline. $20 fee. Admission notification on a rolling basis. Deadline for housing deposit: at time of housing application. Refundable: in full - until May 1; in part - May 2-July 1; Non-Refundable - July 2 or after. Nursing, Radiology, and Dental Hygiene applications must be received by February 1. Diagnostic Medical Sonography applications must be received by March 1. Wind Energy Technology applications must be received by July 31. **Financial aid:** Priority date 4/1; no closing date. FAFSA, institutional form required. Applicants notified on a rolling basis starting 4/1; must reply within 2 week(s) of notification.

Academics. Special study options: Cooperative education, distance learning, double major, dual enrollment of high school students, ESL, independent study, internships. License preparation in dental hygiene, nursing, paramedic, radiology. **Credit/placement by examination:** AP, CLEP, IB, institutional tests. 15 credit hours maximum toward associate degree. **Support services:** GED preparation and test center, learning center, remedial instruction, study skills assistance, tutoring, writing center.

Majors. Biology: General. **Business:** General, accounting, business admin, entrepreneurial studies. **Communications:** Communications/speech/rhetoric, digital media, media studies. **Computer sciences:** Computer science, programming. **Conservation:** Wildlife/wilderness. **Education:** General, early childhood, physical. **Engineering:** General. **English:** English lit. **Foreign languages:** Spanish. **General:** Agribusiness operations, business technology, equestrian studies, production. **Health services:** Dental hygiene, EMT paramedic, nursing (RN), physical therapy assistant, prepharmacy, radiologic

technology/medical imaging, sonography, surgical technology. **History:** General. **Human services:** General. **Liberal arts:** Humanities. **Math:** General. **Philosophy/religion:** Religion. **Physical sciences:** Chemistry. **Protective services:** Corrections, firefighting, law enforcement admin. **Psychology:** General. **Social sciences:** General, anthropology, economics, political science, sociology. **Visual/performing arts:** Art, music.

Computing on campus. 1,090 workstations in dormitories, library, computer center, student center. Dormitories wired for high-speed internet access and linked to campus network. Commuter students can connect to campus network. Online course registration, online library, helpline, repair service, student web hosting, wireless network available.

Student life. Freshman orientation: Available. Preregistration for classes offered. **Housing:** Coed dorms, wellness housing available. $100 deposit. **Activities:** Bands, choral groups, drama, international student organizations, literary magazine, music ensembles, musical theater, student government, student newspaper.

Athletics. NJCAA. **Intercollegiate:** Basketball M, equestrian, rodeo, soccer, volleyball W. **Team name:** Golden Eagles.

Student services. Adult student services, alcohol/substance abuse counseling, career counseling, services for economically disadvantaged, student employment services, financial aid counseling, health services, on-campus daycare, personal counseling, placement for graduates, veterans' counselor. **Physically disabled:** Services for visually, speech, hearing impaired. **Transfer:** College fairs on campus for students transferring to 4-year colleges.

Contact. E-mail: learnmore@lccc.wy.edu
Phone: (307) 778-1357 Toll-free number: (800) 522-2993 ext. 1357
Fax: (307) 778-1350
Holly Allison, Director of Admissions, Laramie County Community College, 1400 East College Drive, Cheyenne, WY 82007-3299

Northwest College
Powell, Wyoming
www.northwestcollege.edu   **CB code: 4542**

▶ Public 2-year community college
▶ Residential campus in small town

General. Founded in 1946. Regionally accredited. **Enrollment:** 1,802 degree-seeking undergraduates; 256 non-degree-seeking students. **Degrees:** 374 associate awarded. **Location:** 90 miles from Billings, MT. **Calendar:** Semester, limited summer session. **Full-time faculty:** 79 total; 39% women. **Part-time faculty:** 75 total. **Special facilities:** Field station, observatory.

Student profile. Among degree-seeking undergraduates, 418 enrolled as first-time, first-year students.

Part-time:	31%	Hispanic American:	8%
Out-of-state:	24%	Native American:	2%
Women:	60%	International:	3%
Asian American:	1%	25 or older:	31%

Transfer out. Colleges most students transferred to 2011: University of Wyoming, Montana State University-Billings, Valley City State University, Montana State University-Bozeman.

Basis for selection. Open admission, but selective for some programs and for out-of-state students. Admissions for out-of-state applicants based on high school GPA and placement test scores. Nursing and Equine Riding and Training programs require extra applications and qualifications. Placement tests in math and English required for all first-time freshmen. **Adult students:** COMPASS placement test on-campus can substitute for SAT/ACT scores. **Home schooled:** Home schooled applicants must also submit the Home School Transcript Evaluation Form. **Learning Disabled:** Individuals must identify needs in order to procure services.

High school preparation. College-preparatory program recommended. 17 units recommended. Recommended units include English 4, mathematics 4, social studies 3, science 4 (laboratory 3) and foreign language 2.

2011-2012 Annual costs. Tuition/fees: $2,330; $5,738 out-of-state. Per-credit charge: $71 in-state; $213 out-of-state. Western Undergraduate Exchange students pay $107 per credit-hour. Room/board: $4,460. Books/supplies: $1,000. Personal expenses: $1,500.

Financial aid. Need-based: Need-based aid available for part-time students. Work-study available nights, weekends and for part-time students. **Non-need-based:** Scholarships awarded for academics, alumni affiliation, art, athletics, leadership, music/drama, state residency.

Application procedures. Admission: No deadline. No application fee. Admission notification on a rolling basis. **Financial aid:** Priority date 3/1; no closing date. FAFSA, institutional form required. Applicants notified on a rolling basis; must reply within 2 week(s) of notification.

Academics. Special study options: Accelerated study, cooperative education, distance learning, double major, dual enrollment of high school students, ESL, independent study, internships, liberal arts/career combination, study abroad. License preparation in aviation, nursing. **Credit/placement by examination:** AP, CLEP, institutional tests. **Support services:** GED preparation and test center, learning center, reduced course load, remedial instruction, study skills assistance, tutoring, writing center.

Majors. Biology: General. **Business:** General, accounting, administrative services, business admin. **Communications:** Broadcast journalism, communications/speech/rhetoric, journalism, radio/TV. **Communications technology:** Desktop publishing, graphic/printing. **Conservation:** Management/policy. **Education:** Agricultural, elementary, kindergarten/preschool, secondary. **Engineering:** General. **English:** English lit. **Foreign languages:** French, Spanish. **General:** Agribusiness operations, animal sciences, communications, crop production, equestrian studies, farm/ranch, production, range science. **Health services:** Athletic training, nursing (RN), predental, premedicine, preoccupational therapy, preoptometry, prepharmacy, prephysical therapy, preveterinary, veterinary technology/assistant. **History:** General. **Liberal arts:** Arts/sciences. **Math:** General. **Parks/recreation:** General, health/fitness. **Physical sciences:** Chemistry, physics. **Protective services:** Law enforcement admin. **Psychology:** General. **Social sciences:** General, anthropology, archaeology, international relations, political science, sociology. **Visual/performing arts:** Art, cinematography, commercial photography, commercial/advertising art, music, play/screenwriting.

Most popular majors. Agriculture 11%, business/marketing 8%, education 10%, health sciences 13%, liberal arts 21%, visual/performing arts 12%.

Computing on campus. 500 workstations in dormitories, library, computer center, student center. Dormitories wired for high-speed internet access and linked to campus network. Commuter students can connect to campus network. Online library, helpline, repair service, wireless network available.

Student life. Freshman orientation: Available, $30 fee. Preregistration for classes offered. Held the Thursday through Sunday prior to fall semester. **Housing:** Guaranteed on-campus for freshmen. Coed dorms, single-sex dorms, apartments available. $125 partly refundable deposit. **Activities:** Bands, campus ministries, choral groups, dance, drama, film society, international student organizations, literary magazine, music ensembles, musical theater, opera, radio station, student government, student newspaper, symphony orchestra, TV station.

Athletics. NJCAA. **Intercollegiate:** Basketball, rodeo, soccer, volleyball W, wrestling M. **Intramural:** Basketball, football (non-tackle), golf, skiing, softball, volleyball. **Team name:** Trappers.

Student services. Adult student services, alcohol/substance abuse counseling, career counseling, services for economically disadvantaged, financial aid counseling, health services, minority student services, on-campus daycare, personal counseling, veterans' counselor. **Physically disabled:** Services for visually, speech, hearing impaired. **Transfer:** Pre-admission transcript evaluation for new students. Transfer adviser, college fairs on campus for students transferring to 4-year colleges.

Contact. E-mail: west.hernandez@northwestcollege.edu
Phone: (307) 754-6101 Toll-free number: (800) 560-4692
Fax: (307) 754-6249
West Hernandez, Admissions Manager, Northwest College, Orendorff Building, Powell, WY 82435-1898

Sheridan College
Sheridan, Wyoming
www.sheridan.edu   CB code: 4536

▶ Public 2-year community college
▶ Commuter campus in large town

General. Founded in 1948. Regionally accredited. **Enrollment:** 2,016 degree-seeking undergraduates; 2,060 non-degree-seeking students. **Degrees:** 344 associate awarded. **Location:** 130 miles from Casper; 130 miles from Billings, Montana. **Calendar:** Semester, limited summer session. **Full-time faculty:** 95 total; 19% have terminal degrees, 1% minority, 50% women. **Part-time faculty:** 103 total; 7% have terminal degrees, 39% women. **Class size:** 72% < 20, 28% 20-39, less than 1% 40-49. **Special facilities:** Geological museum, federal depository for government publications, observatory.

Student profile. Among degree-seeking undergraduates, 50% enrolled in a transfer program, 46% enrolled in a vocational program, 511 enrolled as first-time, first-year students, 153 transferred in from other institutions.

Part-time:	36%	Hispanic American:	4%
Out-of-state:	14%	Native American:	3%
Women:	62%	International:	1%
African American:	2%	25 or older:	37%
Asian American:	1%	Live on campus:	11%

Transfer out. Colleges most students transferred to 2011: University of Wyoming, Chadron State College, Black Hills State University, Montana State University.

Basis for selection. Open admission, but selective for some programs. Special admissions for nursing, dental hygiene, massage therapy; requirements vary by program.

High school preparation. One chemistry required of dental hygiene applicants.

2011-2012 Annual costs. Tuition/fees: $2,544; $5,952 out-of-state. Per-credit charge: $71 in-state; $213 out-of-state. Room/board: $4,900. Books/supplies: $1,250. Personal expenses: $1,800.

Financial aid. Need-based: Need-based aid available for part-time students. Work-study available nights, weekends and for part-time students. **Non-need-based:** Scholarships awarded for academics, art, athletics, leadership, music/drama, state residency.

Application procedures. Admission: No deadline. No application fee. Admission notification on a rolling basis. **Financial aid:** Priority date 3/1; no closing date. FAFSA, institutional form required. Applicants notified on a rolling basis; must reply within 3 week(s) of notification.

Academics. Special study options: Cooperative education, distance learning, double major, dual enrollment of high school students, ESL, independent study, internships, liberal arts/career combination. Bachelor's degree programs available on campus. License preparation in dental hygiene, nursing. **Credit/placement by examination:** AP, CLEP, institutional tests. 18 credit hours maximum toward associate degree. **Support services:** GED preparation and test center, learning center, reduced course load, remedial instruction, study skills assistance, tutoring, writing center.

Majors. Biology: General. **Business:** General, administrative services, hospitality admin. **Communications:** General. **Computer sciences:** General, information systems, security, webmaster. **Education:** Early childhood, elementary, secondary, teacher assistance. **Engineering:** General. **English:** English lit. **Foreign languages:** General. **General:** Business, horticultural science, range science, turf management. **Health services:** Dental hygiene, massage therapy, nursing (RN). **History:** General. **Math:** General. **Parks/recreation:** Exercise sciences, health/fitness. **Protective services:** Criminal justice. **Psychology:** General. **Social sciences:** General. **Visual/performing arts:** Art, dramatic, music.

Most popular majors. Business/marketing 8%, education 6%, health sciences 21%, liberal arts 32%, trade and industry 8%.

Computing on campus. 500 workstations in dormitories, library, student center. Dormitories wired for high-speed internet access and linked to campus network. Commuter students can connect to campus network. Online library, helpline, student web hosting, wireless network available.

Student life. Freshman orientation: Mandatory. Preregistration for classes offered. All-day event the first day of the semester. **Policies:** Non-smoking campus. **Housing:** Coed dorms, single-sex dorms, special housing for disabled, apartments available. $125 fully refundable deposit. Apartments available for single parents. **Activities:** Bands, choral groups, drama, music ensembles, student government, student newspaper, TV station, art club, nursing clubs, dental auxiliary, multidiversity club.

Athletics. NJCAA. **Intercollegiate:** Basketball, cross-country, rodeo, volleyball W. **Intramural:** Basketball, bowling, soccer, softball, tennis, volleyball. **Team name:** Generals.

Student services. Adult student services, career counseling, student employment services, financial aid counseling, health services, personal counseling, placement for graduates. **Physically disabled:** Services for visually, speech, hearing impaired. **Transfer:** Pre-admission transcript evaluation for new students. Transfer adviser, college fairs on campus for students transferring to 4-year colleges.

Contact. E-mail: admissions@sheridan.edu
Phone: (307) 674-6446 ext. 2002
Toll-free number: (800) 913-9139 ext. 2002 Fax: (307) 674-3373
Zane Garstad, Director of Admissions, Sheridan College, PO Box 1500, Sheridan, WY 82801-1500

Western Wyoming Community College
Rock Springs, Wyoming
www.wwcc.wy.edu　　　　　　　**CB code: 4957**

▶ Public 2-year community college
▶ Commuter campus in large town

General. Founded in 1959. Regionally accredited. **Enrollment:** 2,926 degree-seeking undergraduates; 1,086 non-degree-seeking students. **Degrees:** 330 associate awarded. **Location:** 180 miles from Salt Lake City. **Calendar:** Semester, limited summer session. **Full-time faculty:** 75 total. **Part-time faculty:** 150 total. **Class size:** 82% < 20, 18% 20-39. **Special facilities:** Dinosaur museum, natural history museum, wildlife exhibit.

Student profile. Among degree-seeking undergraduates, 38% enrolled in a transfer program, 16% enrolled in a vocational program, 1% already have a bachelor's degree or higher, 746 enrolled as first-time, first-year students.

Part-time:	57%	Hispanic American:	10%
Out-of-state:	55%	Native American:	1%
Women:	60%	International:	1%
African American:	1%	25 or older:	52%
Asian American:	1%	Live on campus:	10%

Transfer out. Colleges most students transferred to 2011: University of Wyoming, Utah State University, Idaho State University.

Basis for selection. Open admission, but selective for some programs. Admissions to nursing program based on academic performance, pre-entrance exam and prerequisite course completion. **Home schooled:** If home school is not through an accredited institution, student needs to obtain GED.

High school preparation. Recommended units include English 4, mathematics 3, social studies 2, science 3 (laboratory 1) and foreign language 2.

2011-2012 Annual costs. Tuition/fees: $2,142; $5,550 out-of-state. Per-credit charge: $71 in-state; $213 out-of-state. Room/board: $4,106. Books/supplies: $1,200. Personal expenses: $1,200.

Financial aid. Need-based: Need-based aid available for part-time students. Work-study available nights, weekends and for part-time students. **Non-need-based:** Scholarships awarded for academics, art, athletics, music/drama, state residency.

Application procedures. Admission: No deadline. No application fee. Application must be submitted online. Admission notification on a rolling basis. **Financial aid:** Priority date 4/1; no closing date. FAFSA required. Applicants notified on a rolling basis starting 2/15; must reply within 2 week(s) of notification.

Academics. Online tutoring provided through Smart Thinking at no charge to students. **Special study options:** Cooperative education, distance learning, dual enrollment of high school students, ESL, external degree, honors, independent study, internships. Bachelor's degree programs available on campus. License preparation in nursing. **Credit/placement by examination:** AP, CLEP, IB, institutional tests. 40 credit hours maximum toward associate degree. **Support services:** GED preparation and test center, learning center, remedial instruction, study skills assistance, tutoring.

Honors college/program. Competitive program, open to 20 students a year. Students participate in challenging courses and travel to cultural and educational events at the expense of the institution.

Majors. Biology: General, ecology, wildlife. **Business:** Accounting, administrative services, business admin, marketing, office technology. **Communications:** Communications/speech/rhetoric, journalism. **Computer sciences:** General, computer science, data processing, information systems. **Conservation:** General, environmental studies, water/wetlands/marine, wildlife/wilderness. **Education:** General, elementary, multi-level teacher, secondary. **Engineering:** General. **English:** English lit. **Foreign languages:** Spanish. **Health services:** Licensed practical nurse, medical assistant, medical secretary, predental, premedicine, prenursing, prepharmacy, preveterinary. **History:** General. **Human services:** Social work. **Math:** General. **Parks/recreation:** Exercise sciences. **Physical sciences:** Chemistry, geology. **Protective services:** Law enforcement admin. **Psychology:** General. **Social sciences:** General, anthropology, archaeology, criminology, international relations, political science, sociology. **Visual/performing arts:** General, art, ceramics, dance, dramatic, music, studio arts, theater design.

Most popular majors. Business/marketing 7%, education 13%, health sciences 13%, liberal arts 24%, trade and industry 7%, visual/performing arts 6%.

Computing on campus. 210 workstations in dormitories, library, computer center, student center. Dormitories wired for high-speed internet access and linked to campus network. Commuter students can connect to campus network. Online course registration, online library, helpline, wireless network available.

Student life. Freshman orientation: Mandatory. Preregistration for classes offered. Program for students and parents. **Housing:** Coed dorms, special housing for disabled, apartments available. $150 partly refundable deposit. **Activities:** Bands, campus ministries, choral groups, dance, drama, international student organizations, music ensembles, musical theater, radio station, student government, student newspaper, Phi Theta Kappa, outdoor club, ambassadors, Students Without Borders.

Athletics. NJCAA. **Intercollegiate:** Basketball, cheerleading, soccer, volleyball W, wrestling M. **Intramural:** Basketball, football (non-tackle), softball, table tennis, tennis, volleyball. **Team name:** Mustangs.

Student services. Adult student services, alcohol/substance abuse counseling, career counseling, student employment services, financial aid counseling, on-campus daycare, personal counseling, placement for graduates, veterans' counselor. **Physically disabled:** Services for visually, hearing impaired. **Transfer:** Pre-admission transcript evaluation for new students. Transfer adviser, college fairs on campus for students transferring to 4-year colleges.

Contact. E-mail: admissions@wwcc.wy.edu
Phone: (307) 382-1648 Toll-free number: (800) 226-1181
Fax: (307) 382-1636
Joe Mueller, Director of Admissions, Western Wyoming Community College, Box 428, Rock Springs, WY 82902-0428

Two-Year Colleges

American Samoa

Guam

American Samoa Community College
Pago Pago, American Samoa CB member
www.amsamoa.edu CB code: 0020

◗ Public 2-year community college
◗ Commuter campus in large town

General. Founded in 1970. Regionally accredited. Only institution of higher education in American Samoa and only land grant institution in the South Pacific. Students seeking 4-year degrees often transfer to colleges in Hawaii or mainland United States. **Enrollment:** 2,042 degree-seeking undergraduates. **Degrees:** 249 associate awarded. **ROTC:** Army. **Location:** 9 miles from downtown. **Calendar:** Semester, limited summer session. **Full-time faculty:** 56 total. **Part-time faculty:** 57 total.

Transfer out. Colleges most students transferred to 2011: University of Hawaii, Manoa; University of Hawaii, Hilo; Chaminade University of Honolulu; Hawaii Pacific University.

Basis for selection. Open admission. Institutional placement exam may be required for applicants without SAT/ACT scores.

2011-2012 Annual costs. Books/supplies: $1,200. Personal expenses: $900.

Financial aid. All financial aid based on need. Need-based aid available for part-time students. Work-study available nights, weekends and for part-time students.

Application procedures. Admission: No deadline. No application fee. **Financial aid:** No deadline. FAFSA required. Applicants notified on a rolling basis; must reply within 3 week(s) of notification.

Academics. Special study options: Distance learning, independent study, teacher certification program. License preparation in nursing. **Credit/placement by examination:** AP, CLEP, institutional tests. Credit by examination for course credit may be taken only once. "E" grades for credit by examination will not be counted toward overall grade point average and cumulative grade point average. Credits earned by examination are not covered under federal financial aid. **Support services:** GED preparation, learning center, reduced course load, remedial instruction, study skills assistance, tutoring.

Majors. Business: Accounting, business admin, office management. **Conservation:** Management/policy. **Education:** General, multi-level teacher. **General:** Business. **Health services:** Nursing assistant. **Liberal arts:** Arts/sciences. **Protective services:** Criminal justice, forensics. **Social sciences:** Political science. **Visual/performing arts:** Art, music. **Work/family studies:** General.

Most popular majors. Security/protective services 10%.

Computing on campus. 104 workstations in library, computer center. Helpline, repair service available.

Student life. Freshman orientation: Mandatory. Preregistration for classes offered. **Activities:** Bands, choral groups, dance, music ensembles, musical theater, student government, student newspaper, Phi Theta Kappa, Polynesian club, Christian club, You Are Not Alone Coalition (emotional support for young people).

Athletics. Intramural: Basketball, golf, tennis, volleyball, weight lifting. **Team name:** Chiefs.

Student services. Alcohol/substance abuse counseling, career counseling, services for economically disadvantaged, student employment services, financial aid counseling, health services, personal counseling, veterans' counselor. **Transfer:** Pre-admission transcript evaluation for new students. Transfer adviser for students transferring to 4-year colleges.

Contact. E-mail: admissions@amsamoa.edu
Phone: (684) 699-9155 ext. 411 Fax: (684) 699-1083
James Sutherland, Admissions Officer, American Samoa Community College, PO Box 2609, Pago Pago, AS 96799-2609

Guam Community College
Barrigada, Guam
www.guamcc.edu CB code: 2302

◗ Public 2-year community and technical college
◗ Commuter campus in small city

General. Founded in 1977. Regionally accredited. Multicultural U.S. territory with island setting. **Enrollment:** 2,011 degree-seeking undergraduates; 537 non-degree-seeking students. **Degrees:** 126 associate awarded. **ROTC:** Army. **Location:** 1,500 miles from Manila, Philippines; 3,600 miles from Honolulu. **Calendar:** Semester, limited summer session. **Full-time faculty:** 116 total; 6% have terminal degrees, 80% minority. **Part-time faculty:** 85 total; 1% have terminal degrees, 79% minority. **Class size:** 39% < 20, 61% 20-39. **Special facilities:** Rare book collection of more than 400 volumes devoted to the history of Guam, Micronesia, and the Pacific.

Student profile. Among degree-seeking undergraduates, 75% enrolled in a transfer program, 25% enrolled in a vocational program, 459 enrolled as first-time, first-year students, 59 transferred in from other institutions.

Part-time:	62%	Asian American:	2%
Women:	57%	International:	1%
African American:	1%	25 or older:	26%

Transfer out. Colleges most students transferred to 2011: University of Guam.

Basis for selection. Open admission. **Home schooled:** Official high school transcript required.

High school preparation. Recommended units include English 4, mathematics 3, social studies 3, science 2 and academic electives 9.

2011-2012 Annual costs. Tuition/fees: $4,386; $5,136 out-of-state. Per-credit charge: $130 in-state; $155 out-of-state. Books/supplies: $1,200. Personal expenses: $2,250.

2011-2012 Financial aid. Need-based: 181 full-time freshmen applied for aid; 181 were judged to have need; 181 of these received aid. Average need met was 100%. Average scholarship/grant was $2,775. 99% of total undergraduate aid awarded as scholarships/grants, 1% as loans/jobs. Work-study available nights, weekends and for part-time students. **Additional information:** Tuition assistance available for students in nontraditional courses.

Application procedures. Admission: No deadline. No application fee. Application must be submitted on paper. Admission notification on a rolling basis. **Financial aid:** Priority date 5/1; no closing date. FAFSA, institutional form required. Applicants notified on a rolling basis starting 8/28; must reply within 2 week(s) of notification.

Academics. Special study options: Cooperative education, cross-registration, double major, dual enrollment of high school students, independent study, internships. **Credit/placement by examination:** AP, CLEP, institutional tests. 48 credit hours maximum toward associate degree. **Support services:** GED preparation and test center, learning center, remedial instruction, study skills assistance, tutoring.

Majors. Business: Accounting, office management, office technology, sales/distribution, tourism/travel. **Computer sciences:** Computer science. **Education:** Early childhood, teacher assistance. **Health services:** Medical assistant. **Liberal arts:** Arts/sciences. **Protective services:** Law enforcement admin. **Visual/performing arts:** Graphic design. **Work/family studies:** Institutional food production.

Most popular majors. Business/marketing 20%, computer/information sciences 8%, education 24%, health sciences 9%.

Computing on campus. 79 workstations in library, computer center, student center. Online library, repair service available.

Student life. Freshman orientation: Available. Preregistration for classes offered. Held one week before start of semester. **Activities:** Student government, Habitat for Humanity, Health Occupational Students of America, Phi Theta Kappa, Postsecondary Tourism Association.

Student services. Adult student services, alcohol/substance abuse counseling, career counseling, services for economically disadvantaged, student employment services, financial aid counseling, health services, personal counseling, placement for graduates, veterans' counselor. **Physically disabled:** Services for visually, speech, hearing impaired. **Transfer:** Re-entry adviser for new students.

Contact. E-mail: patrick.clymer@guamcc.edu
Phone: (671) 735-5531 Fax: (671) 734-5238
Patrick Clymer, Coordinator of Admissions and Registration, Guam Community College, PO Box 23069 GMF, Barrigada, GU 96921

Marshall Islands

College of the Marshall Islands
Majuro, Marshall Islands
www.cmi.edu   **CB code: 7142**

◗ Public 2-year community and junior college
◗ Commuter campus in large town

General. Regionally accredited. Vocational education and research center in Arrak operated by College of the Marshall Islands. **Enrollment:** 998 undergraduates. **Degrees:** 68 associate awarded. **Location:** 2,280 miles from Honolulu. **Calendar:** Semester, limited summer session. **Full-time faculty:** 47 total; 8% have terminal degrees, 38% minority, 53% women. **Part-time faculty:** 20 total; 75% minority. **Special facilities:** Nuclear institute, research and extension science station, public policy institute.

Student profile. 1% enrolled in a vocational program.

Transfer out. Colleges most students transferred to 2011: University of Hawaii - Hilo, Brigham Young University Hawaii, University of Hawaii - Manoa.

Basis for selection. Completed applications reviewed with consideration for CMI placement test scores, high school transcript, GED/RMI equivalency test scores. Interviews and essays optional depending on the requirements of the admissions committee.

2011-2012 Annual costs. Tuition/fees: $4,745; $4,745 out-of-state. Per-credit charge: $130 in-state; $130 out-of-state. Room only: $740. Books/supplies: $800.

2010-2011 Financial aid. All financial aid based on need. 365 full-time freshmen applied for aid; 365 were judged to have need; 365 of these received aid. Average scholarship/grant was $1,000. Need-based aid available for part-time students. Work-study available nights, weekends and for part-time students.

Application procedures. Admission: Closing date 6/30 (receipt date). $30 fee. Admission notification on a rolling basis. **Financial aid:** Closing date 6/30. FAFSA required. Applicants notified on a rolling basis.

Academics. Special study options: Distance learning, double major, dual enrollment of high school students, independent study, internships, teacher certification program. **Credit/placement by examination:** AP, CLEP, institutional tests. **Support services:** GED test center, learning center, remedial instruction, study skills assistance, tutoring, writing center.

Majors. Business: Business admin. **Education:** Elementary. **Health services:** Nursing (RN). **Liberal arts:** Arts/sciences.

Most popular majors. Business/marketing 20%, education 22%, health sciences 22%, liberal arts 36%.

Computing on campus. 300 workstations in dormitories, library, computer center, student center. Commuter students can connect to campus network. Online library, helpline, wireless network available.

Student life. Freshman orientation: Available. Preregistration for classes offered. Two-day orientation held the week before classes start. **Housing:** Single-sex dorms available. $40 fully refundable deposit. **Activities:** Student government, student newspaper.

Athletics. Intramural: Basketball, table tennis, volleyball. **Team name:** Navigators.

Student services. Alcohol/substance abuse counseling, career counseling, financial aid counseling, health services, personal counseling. **Transfer:** Transfer center, transfer adviser for students transferring to 4-year colleges.

Contact. E-mail: cmiadmissions@cmi.edu
Phone: (692) 625-3394 ext. 227 Fax: (692) 625-7203
Rosita Capelle, Director of Admissions and Records, College of the Marshall Islands, Box 1258, Majuro, MH 96960

Micronesia

College of Micronesia-FSM
Kolonia, Micronesia
www.comfsm.fm   **CB code: 0115**

◗ Public 2-year branch campus and community college
◗ Commuter campus in small city

General. Founded in 1963. Regionally accredited. **Enrollment:** 2,913 degree-seeking undergraduates. **Degrees:** 228 associate awarded. **Calendar:** Semester, limited summer session. **Full-time faculty:** 96 total. **Part-time faculty:** 35 total.

Student profile.

Out-of-state:	7%	Live on campus:	20%
25 or older:	16%		

Transfer out. Colleges most students transferred to 2011: University of Hawaii at Hilo, University of Guam, Southwestern Adventist University, Chaminade University, Durham Community College.

Basis for selection. Minimum 2.0 GPA and passing institutional test scores required. **Home schooled:** Transcript of courses and grades, letter of recommendation (nonparent) required.

2011-2012 Annual costs. Books/supplies: $850. Personal expenses: $1,250.

Financial aid. All financial aid based on need. Work-study available nights, weekends and for part-time students.

Application procedures. Admission: Closing date 6/30. $10 fee. Admission notification on a rolling basis. **Financial aid:** No deadline. FAFSA, institutional form required. Applicants notified on a rolling basis.

Academics. Special study options: Cooperative education, distance learning, independent study, internships, liberal arts/career combination, teacher certification program. Bachelor's degree programs available on campus. **Credit/placement by examination:** AP, CLEP. **Support services:** Learning center, remedial instruction, study skills assistance, tutoring, writing center.

Majors. Biology: Marine. **Business:** General, accounting. **Computer sciences:** General, computer science. **Education:** Elementary, multi-level teacher, special ed. **Liberal arts:** Arts/sciences.

Computing on campus. 6 workstations in dormitories, library, computer center, student center. Dormitories linked to campus network. Online library, repair service, wireless network available.

Student life. Freshman orientation: Mandatory. Preregistration for classes offered. Week-long orientation held beginning of fall semester. **Housing:** Single-sex dorms available. $50 nonrefundable deposit, deadline 6/15. On-campus housing for all undergraduates on space available basis. **Activities:** Choral groups, dance, drama, radio station, student government.

Athletics. Intercollegiate: Basketball, softball, track and field, volleyball. **Intramural:** Basketball, softball, volleyball. **Team name:** Sharks.

Student services. Alcohol/substance abuse counseling, career counseling, financial aid counseling, health services, personal counseling. **Transfer:** Pre-admission transcript evaluation for new students. Transfer center, transfer adviser for students transferring to 4-year colleges.

Contact. E-mail: oar@comfsm.fm
Phone: (691) 320-2480 ext. 150 Fax: (691) 320-2479
Joey Oducado, Admissions Coordinator, College of Micronesia-FSM, PO Box 159, Kolonia, FM 96941

Palau

Palau Community College
Koror, Palau
www.palau.edu

CB code: 7329

❥ Public 2-year community and technical college
❥ Commuter campus in large town

General. Founded in 1969. Regionally accredited. **Enrollment:** 733 degree-seeking undergraduates; 9 non-degree-seeking students. **Degrees:** 73 associate awarded. **Location:** 800 miles from Guam, 600 miles from Manila. **Calendar:** Semester, limited summer session. **Full-time faculty:** 30 total; 7% have terminal degrees, 60% women. **Part-time faculty:** 28 total; 64% women. **Special facilities:** Land grant-funded agriculture/aquaculture research and development center, tourism and hospitality building.

Student profile. Among degree-seeking undergraduates, 124 enrolled as first-time, first-year students, 5 transferred in from other institutions.

Part-time:	31%	Women:	57%
Out-of-state:	96%		

Basis for selection. Open admission, but selective for some programs and for out-of-state students. Associate of applied science applicants must be high school graduates with 2.0 GPA or have GED; standardized tests (SAT or ACT) recommended for placement in English grammar, reading, and mathematics. **Adult students:** SAT/ACT scores not required. Must take COMPASS to fulfill Ability To Benefit (ATB) requirements to qualify for federal financial aid.

2011-2012 Annual costs. Books/supplies: $1,200. Personal expenses: $800.

Financial aid. Need-based: Work-study available nights, weekends and for part-time students.

Application procedures. Admission: Priority date 5/15; no deadline. $10 fee. Application must be submitted on paper. Admission notification on a rolling basis beginning on or about 7/1. Must reply by May 1 or within 2 week(s) if notified thereafter. **Financial aid:** Priority date 4/1; no closing date. FAFSA required. Applicants notified on a rolling basis starting 5/1.

Academics. Special study options: Accelerated study, distance learning, double major, dual enrollment of high school students, independent study, internships, liberal arts/career combination, student-designed major, weekend college. Adult high school. Bachelor's degree programs available on campus. License preparation in nursing. **Credit/placement by examination:** AP, CLEP, institutional tests. **Support services:** Learning center, remedial instruction, study skills assistance, tutoring.

Majors. Business: Accounting/business management, administrative services, business admin, hospitality admin, hotel/motel/restaurant management, restaurant/food services, tourism/travel. **Computer sciences:** Information technology. **Conservation:** Environmental science. **Education:** Early childhood, elementary, secondary, special ed. **Health services:** Nursing education. **Liberal arts:** Arts/sciences, library science. **Protective services:** Police science.

Most popular majors. Agriculture 7%, business/marketing 34%, education 7%, trade and industry 36%.

Computing on campus. 57 workstations in dormitories, library, computer center, student center. Dormitories linked to campus network. Commuter students can connect to campus network. Online library, repair service, wireless network available.

Student life. Freshman orientation: Mandatory. Preregistration for classes offered. Week-long program held prior to first week of classes; includes placement tests, academic advising, and registration. **Policies:** Possession, consumption, and storage of alcoholic beverages and illegal drugs prohibited. **Housing:** Coed dorms, single-sex dorms available. **Activities:** Student government, student newspaper, Associated Students of PCC, Republic of Palau student organization, RMI student organization, Pohnpei students organization, Pacific writers club, agriculture science majors club, canoe club.

Athletics. Intramural: Basketball M, softball, swimming, table tennis, volleyball. **Team name:** Mesekiu.

Student services. Alcohol/substance abuse counseling, career counseling, student employment services, financial aid counseling, health services, on-campus daycare, personal counseling, placement for graduates. **Transfer:** Pre-admission transcript evaluation for new students. Transfer adviser for students transferring to 4-year colleges.

Contact. E-mail: dahliapcc@palaunet.com
Phone: (680) 488-2470 ext. 235 Fax: (680) 488-4468
Dahlia Katosang, Director of Admissions & Financial Aid, Palau Community College, PO Box 9, Koror, PW 96940

Early Decision and Early Action table

The following table lists early decision and early action policies at 462 colleges, which are listed alphabetically by state or country. Colleges were asked to supply the deadline for student applications and the date by which the college will notify the applicant of a decision to admit, deny admission, or defer the application to the regular admission cycle. If a college offers two early decision cycles, both sets of dates are listed.

Some colleges support both a binding early decision plan and a nonbinding early action plan and report dates for both. Colleges with binding early decision plans were asked to give the number of students who applied for early decision and the number of those applicants admitted to the fall 2011 freshman class.

Institution	Early Applicants		Early Decision		Early Action	
	Number Applied	Number admitted	Apply by	Notified by	Apply by	Notified by
Alabama						
Auburn University					10/1	10/15
Arizona						
Prescott College	13	13	12/1	12/15		
Arkansas						
Hendrix College					11/15	12/15
Lyon College					10/31	11/15
University of Arkansas					11/15	12/15
California						
Azusa Pacific University					11/15	1/15
Biola University	3861	2994			11/15	1/15
California Baptist University					12/15	1/31
California Institute of Technology					11/1	12/15
California Lutheran University					11/15	1/15
California Polytechnic State University: San Luis Obispo	3639	812	10/31	12/15		
California State University: Sacramento					11/30	
Chapman University	3610	1332			11/15	1/10
Claremont McKenna College	419	139	11/15 1/2	12/15 2/15		
Concordia University					12/1	12/15
Harvey Mudd College	261	56	11/15 1/2	12/15 2/15		
Loyola Marymount University	2557	1698			11/1	12/20
Menlo College					12/1	12/15
Mills College	1008	405			11/15	12/1
Mount St. Mary's College					12/1	1/1
Notre Dame de Namur University					12/1	12/15
Occidental College	233	106	11/15 1/2	12/15 2/1		

Institution	Early Applicants		Early Decision		Early Action	
	Number Applied	Number admitted	Apply by	Notified by	Apply by	Notified by
Pitzer College			11/15	1/1		
Point Loma Nazarene University					11/15	12/20
Pomona College	643	132	11/1 12/28	12/15 2/15		
Santa Clara University	3729	2431	11/1	12/15	11/1	12/23
Scripps College	123	70	11/15 1/2	12/15 2/15		
Soka University of America	66	24			10/15	12/1
St. Mary's College of California	1307	1151			11/15	1/15
Stanford University	5928	749			11/1	12/15
The Master's College					11/15	12/22
University of San Diego	4036	2541			11/15	1/31
University of San Francisco	2862	1951			11/15	1/16
University of the Pacific					11/15	1/15
Westmont College					11/1	12/20
Whittier College					12/1	12/30

Colorado

Institution	Number Applied	Number admitted	Apply by	Notified by	Apply by	Notified by
Colorado College	1981	767	11/15 1/1	12/15 2/10	11/15	12/20
Colorado State University					12/1	2/1
University of Colorado Boulder					12/1	1/15
University of Denver	3555	2977			11/1	1/15

Connecticut

Institution	Number Applied	Number admitted	Apply by	Notified by	Apply by	Notified by
Connecticut College	395	235	11/15 1/1	12/15 2/15		
Fairfield University	3811	2524	1/1	2/1	11/1	1/1
Mitchell College			11/15	12/1		
Quinnipiac University			10/15	12/1		
Sacred Heart University	222	167	12/1	12/15		
Trinity College	493	335	11/15 1/1	12/15 2/15		
United States Coast Guard Academy	1017	196			11/1	1/15
University of Connecticut					12/1	2/1
University of Hartford					11/15	12/1
University of New Haven					11/15	12/15
Wesleyan University	918	380	11/15 1/1	12/15 2/15		
Yale University	5257	761			11/1	12/15

Delaware

Institution	Number Applied	Number admitted	Apply by	Notified by	Apply by	Notified by
Delaware College of Art and Design					12/1	12/23

District of Columbia

Institution	Number Applied	Number admitted	Apply by	Notified by	Apply by	Notified by
Catholic University of America					11/15	12/15
George Washington University	2318	838	11/10 1/10	12/15 2/1		
Georgetown University	6657	1594			11/1	12/15
Howard University					11/1	12/24
Trinity Washington University					12/1	1/1

Florida

Institution	Number Applied	Number admitted	Apply by	Notified by	Apply by	Notified by
Eckerd College					11/15	12/15
Flagler College	729	393	12/1 1/15	12/15 2/1		
Florida Southern College	150	112	12/1	12/15		
Jacksonville University					12/1	12/15
Palm Beach Atlantic University					12/1	12/15

Institution	Early Applicants		Early Decision		Early Action	
	Number Applied	Number admitted	Apply by	Notified by	Apply by	Notified by
Rollins College	327	206	11/15 1/15	12/15 2/1		
Stetson University	44	37	11/1	11/15		
University of Miami	11144	5375	11/1	12/15	11/1	2/1
University of Tampa	10457	6351			5/1	12/15

Georgia

Institution	Number Applied	Number admitted	Apply by	Notified by	Apply by	Notified by
Abraham Baldwin Agricultural College			3/1			
Agnes Scott College	1016	487			11/15	12/15
Emory University	1404	574	11/1 1/1	12/15 2/15		
Georgia College and State University					11/1	12/1
Georgia Institute of Technology					10/1	11/20
Georgia Southwestern State University			12/15	1/15		
Georgia State University					11/1	1/8
LaGrange College					12/31	
Mercer University					11/1	11/15
Morehouse College	254	177	11/1	12/15	11/1	12/15
Oglethorpe University					11/15	12/5
Oxford College of Emory University	578	486	11/1 1/1			
Spelman College	1927	1032	11/1	12/15	11/15	12/31
University of Georgia					10/15	12/1
Wesleyan College			11/15 1/15	12/15 2/15	2/15	3/15

Idaho

Institution	Number Applied	Number admitted	Apply by	Notified by	Apply by	Notified by
College of Idaho	261	207			11/15	11/15
Northwest Nazarene University					12/15	1/15

Illinois

Institution	Number Applied	Number admitted	Apply by	Notified by	Apply by	Notified by
DePaul University					11/15	1/15
Illinois College					12/15	12/23
Illinois Institute of Technology					12/1	2/28
Illinois Wesleyan University					11/15	1/15
Knox College	1179	811			12/1	12/31
Lake Forest College	1294	835	12/1		12/1	1/20
Lakeview College of Nursing						
Moody Bible Institute			12/1	1/15		
Northwestern University	2115	730	11/1	12/15		
School of the Art Institute of Chicago					1/3	2/15
Trinity College of Nursing and Health Sciences	14	9		12/20		
University of Chicago					11/1	12/17
Wheaton College	1086	622			11/1	12/31

Indiana

Institution	Number Applied	Number admitted	Apply by	Notified by	Apply by	Notified by
Butler University	7457	5522			11/1	12/15
DePauw University			11/1	1/1	12/1	2/15
Earlham College	727	627	12/1	12/15	1/1	2/1
Grace College					12/1	12/20
Hanover College	2355	1743			12/1	12/20
Saint Mary's College	89	73	11/15	12/15		
Taylor University					12/1	12/20
University of Evansville	3048	2558			12/1	12/15
University of Notre Dame	5294	1940			11/1	12/19
Wabash College	69	60	11/15	12/1	12/1	12/22

Institution	Early Applicants		Early Decision		Early Action	
	Number Applied	Number admitted	Apply by	Notified by	Apply by	Notified by
Iowa						
Coe College					12/10	1/20
Cornell College	1557	688	11/1 2/1	12/15 3/1	12/1	2/1
Grinnell College	286	144	11/15 1/2	12/15 2/1		
Kansas						
Central Christian College of Kansas			9/30	10/15		
Kentucky						
Bellarmine University					11/1	11/15
Centre College					12/1	1/15
Georgetown College			10/15		10/15	
Transylvania University					12/1	1/15
Louisiana						
Centenary College of Louisiana					12/15	1/15
Dillard University					12/1	12/30
Tulane University					11/15	12/15
Xavier University of Louisiana					1/15	2/15
Maine						
Bates College	542	232	11/15 1/1	12/20 2/14		
Bowdoin College	826	225	11/15 1/1	12/15 2/15		
Colby College			11/15 1/1	12/15 2/1		
College of the Atlantic	38	28	12/1 1/10	12/15 1/25		
Maine College of Art					12/15	12/24
Maine Maritime Academy			12/20	1/1		
Saint Joseph's College of Maine					11/15	12/17
Thomas College	481	215			12/15	12/31
Unity College in Maine	502	240			12/15	1/15
University of Maine					12/15	1/31
University of Maine at Farmington					11/15	1/15
University of Maine at Machias					12/15	12/31
University of New England					12/1	12/31
Maryland						
Goucher College	1523	1253	11/15 1/15	12/15 2/15	12/1	2/1
Hood College	25	10	11/1	11/15	11/1	11/15
Johns Hopkins University	1327	517	11/1	12/15		
Loyola University Maryland	6054	4585			11/1	1/15
Maryland Institute College of Art			11/15	12/15		
McDaniel College					12/1	12/21
Mount St. Mary's University	409	323			12/1	12/25
Salisbury University	3798	2408			12/1	1/15
St. Mary's College of Maryland	282	150	11/1 12/1	11/20 12/20		
University of Maryland: Baltimore County					11/1	12/1
University of Maryland: Eastern Shore					11/15	12/1
Washington College	50	34	11/1	12/1	12/1	1/15

Institution	Early Applicants		Early Decision		Early Action	
	Number Applied	Number admitted	Apply by	Notified by	Apply by	Notified by
Massachusetts						
Amherst College	447	149	11/15	12/15		
Assumption College	1900	1693			11/1	12/15
Babson College	1539	685	11/1	12/15	11/1	1/1
Bay Path College					12/15	1/2
Becker College					11/15	12/15
Bentley University	2747	1610			11/15	1/15
Berklee College of Music					11/1	1/31
Boston College	6210	2712			11/1	12/25
Boston University	897	395	11/1	12/15		
Brandeis University	483	201	11/15 1/1	12/15 2/1		
Bridgewater State University					11/15	12/15
Clark University	1105	874			11/15	12/23
College of the Holy Cross	512	347	12/15	1/15		
Curry College	1647	878			12/1	12/15
Emerson College	2072	1282			11/1	12/15
Emmanuel College	1326	1086	11/1	12/1	11/15	1/20
Framingham State University	645	286			11/15	12/15
Gordon College			11/15	12/1	11/15	12/15
Hampshire College	513	452	11/15	12/15	12/1	2/1
Harvard College					11/1	12/16
Lesley University					12/1	12/31
Massachusetts College of Art and Design	233	166			12/1	1/5
Massachusetts College of Liberal Arts					12/1	12/15
Massachusetts College of Pharmacy and Health Sciences					11/15	12/25
Massachusetts Institute of Technology	6403	772			11/1	12/20
Massachusetts Maritime Academy					11/1	12/15
Merrimack College			11/15	1/1	11/30	1/1
Montserrat College of Art	125	50			12/1	12/15
Mount Holyoke College	292	161	11/15 1/1	1/1 2/1		
Northeastern University					11/1	12/31
Regis College					12/1	12/20
Salem State University					11/15	12/15
Simmons College					12/1	1/15
Smith College	330	177	11/15 1/2	12/15 1/31		
Springfield College			12/1	2/1		
Stonehill College	2197	1577	11/1	12/15	11/1	1/15
Suffolk University	2178	1418			11/15	12/20
Tufts University			11/1 1/1	12/15 2/15		
University of Massachusetts Amherst	10680	8102			11/1	12/30
University of Massachusetts Dartmouth					11/15	12/15
University of Massachusetts Lowell					12/1	1/15
Wellesley College	275	124	11/1	12/15		
Wheaton College	128	108	11/15	12/15	11/15	1/15
Wheelock College	350	325			12/1	12/20
Williams College	574	216	11/10	12/15		
Worcester Polytechnic Institute	3628	2440			11/10	12/10

Institution	Early Applicants		Early Decision		Early Action	
	Number Applied	Number admitted	Apply by	Notified by	Apply by	Notified by
Michigan						
Hillsdale College	1234	581	11/15	12/1	12/15	2/15
Kalamazoo College	31	30	11/1	11/20	11/20	12/20
Michigan State University					10/7	11/11
Olivet College					12/1	1/15
University of Michigan					11/1	12/23
Minnesota						
Carleton College	416	211	11/15 1/15	12/15 2/15		
College of St. Benedict	1540	1260			11/15	12/15
Gustavus Adolphus College					11/1	11/20
Hamline University	1746	1279			12/1	12/20
Macalester College	227	115	11/15 1/3	12/15 2/7		
Minneapolis College of Art and Design					12/1	12/15
St. John's University	1132	918			11/15	12/15
St. Olaf College	317	252	11/15 1/15	12/15 2/15		
Mississippi						
Millsaps College	1082	490	11/15	12/1	12/1	
Mississippi College			12/1	12/15		
Missouri						
Stephens College			11/15	12/1	1/1	1/15
Washington University in St. Louis			11/15	12/15		
Nebraska						
Nebraska Wesleyan University	376	360			11/15	12/15
New Hampshire						
Dartmouth College			11/1	12/15		
Rivier College					11/15	12/1
Saint Anselm College					11/15	1/15
Southern New Hampshire University					11/15	12/15
University of New Hampshire	7806	6614			11/15	1/15
New Jersey						
Bloomfield College	903	596			12/15	12/23
Caldwell College					12/1	1/1
Drew University	88	66	11/1 1/15	1/15	1/15	
Georgian Court University					11/15	12/30
Monmouth University	2975	2400			12/1	1/15
Princeton University					11/1	12/15
Ramapo College of New Jersey					11/15	12/15
Rider University	1534	1499			11/15	12/15
Seton Hall University					11/15	12/31
Stevens Institute of Technology	515	322	11/15 1/15	12/15 2/15		
The College of New Jersey	523	322	11/15	12/15		
William Paterson University of New Jersey					12/1	1/15
New York						
Adelphi University	1977	1622			12/1	12/31
Albany College of Pharmacy and Health Sciences			11/1	12/10		
Alfred University	44	43	12/1	12/15		

Institution	Early Applicants		Early Decision		Early Action	
	Number Applied	Number admitted	Apply by	Notified by	Apply by	Notified by
Bard College	562	403			11/1	1/1
Barnard College	550	240	11/15	12/15		
Clarkson University	155	121	12/1	1/1		
Colgate University	660	348	11/15 1/15	12/15		
College of Mount St. Vincent					11/15	12/15
College of New Rochelle			11/1	12/15		
Columbia University	3274	629	11/1	12/15		
Concordia College	94	84			11/15	12/15
Cooper Union for the Advancement of Science and Art	719	70	12/1 12/1	12/23 2/1		
Cornell University	3479	1227	11/1			
Dowling College					12/31	1/31
Elmira College	94	33	11/15 1/15	12/15 1/31		
Eugene Lang College The New School for Liberal Arts			11/1	12/1		
Five Towns College	8	5	10/15 12/1	11/1 1/15		
Fordham University	10247	5323			11/1	12/25
Hamilton College	598	249	11/15 1/1	12/15 2/15		
Hartwick College	63	55	11/1	12/1		
Hobart and William Smith Colleges	332	280	11/15 1/1	12/15 2/1		
Hofstra University	11025	5649			11/15	12/15
Iona College	3314	2763			12/1	12/21
Ithaca College	242	223	11/1	12/15		
Jewish Theological Seminary of America			11/15 1/15	12/15 2/15		
LIM College					11/15	12/15
Lebanese American University	1680	690			1/31	3/1
Manhattan College	87	50	11/15	12/15		
Manhattanville College			12/1	12/31		
Marist College	261	199	11/1	12/15	11/15	1/31
Mercy College					12/1	1/2
Nazareth College	60	49	11/15	12/15	12/15	1/15
New York University	5333	1414	11/1 1/1	12/15 3/15		
Niagara University					10/1	12/1
North Country Community College			11/15	12/15		
Pace University	4056	3393			11/30	1/1
Pace University: Pleasantville/Briarcliff					11/30	1/1
Parsons The New School for Design					11/1	1/1
Pratt Institute					11/1	12/22
Rensselaer Polytechnic Institute	1141	364	11/1 12/15	12/10 1/14		
Rochester Institute of Technology			12/1	1/15		
Russell Sage College	165	152			12/1	12/15
SUNY College at Buffalo	97	58	11/15	12/15		
SUNY College at Cortland					11/15	1/1
SUNY College at Fredonia			11/1	12/1		
SUNY College at Geneseo			11/15	12/15		
SUNY College at New Paltz					11/15	12/15
SUNY College at Old Westbury			11/1	12/15		
SUNY College at Oneonta					11/15	12/15
SUNY College at Oswego	215	100	11/15	12/15		
SUNY College at Plattsburgh	55	28	11/15	12/15		

Institution	Early Applicants		Early Decision		Early Action	
	Number Applied	Number admitted	Apply by	Notified by	Apply by	Notified by
SUNY College at Purchase	485	309			11/15	12/15
SUNY College of Environmental Science and Forestry			12/1	1/2		
SUNY Institute of Technology at Utica/ Rome	125	84			11/15	12/15
SUNY University at Albany					11/15	1/15
SUNY University at Binghamton	8220	3657			11/15	1/15
SUNY University at Buffalo	444	282	11/1	12/15		
Sage College of Albany	188	149			12/1	12/15
Sarah Lawrence College			11/1 1/1	12/15 2/15		
Siena College	536	89	12/1	12/15	12/1	1/1
Skidmore College	398	287	11/15 1/15	12/15 2/15		
St. John Fisher College	167	111	12/1	1/15		
St. Joseph's College of Nursing			11/15	12/15		
St. Lawrence University	246	212	11/1			
Syracuse University	1107	853	11/15	12/16		
The King's College					11/15	12/15
Union College	318	242	11/15 1/15	12/15 2/1		
University of Rochester			11/1	12/15		
Vassar College	703	266	11/15 1/1	12/15 2/1		
Wagner College	100	86	12/15	1/15		
Webb Institute	19	6	10/15	12/15		
Wells College			12/15	1/15	12/15	2/1
North Carolina						
Carolinas College of Health Sciences			12/1	1/15		
Davidson College	547	238	11/15 1/2	12/15 2/1		
Duke University	2227	645	11/1	12/15		
Elon University	5767	2977	11/1	12/1	11/10	12/20
Greensboro College					12/15	1/15
High Point University	3424	3034	11/1	11/23	11/8	12/12
Meredith College	108	55	10/30	11/15		
North Carolina State University					11/1	1/31
Pfeiffer University						
Piedmont International University			11/1	12/1	11/1	12/1
University of North Carolina at Asheville					11/15	12/15
University of North Carolina at Chapel Hill	14111	5716			10/15	1/31
University of North Carolina at Charlotte					10/15	12/15
University of North Carolina at Wilmington					11/1	1/20
Wake Forest University	762	323	1/1			
Warren Wilson College			11/15	12/1		
Western Carolina University	8620	3652			11/15	12/15
Ohio						
Case Western Reserve University	2482	1798			11/1	12/15
Cleveland Institute of Art	42	40			12/1	12/15
College of Wooster	2480	1777	11/15	12/1	12/15	12/31
Denison University			11/15 1/15			
Kenyon College	405	221	11/15 1/15	12/15 2/1		

Institution	Early Applicants		Early Decision		Early Action	
	Number Applied	Number admitted	Apply by	Notified by	Apply by	Notified by
Miami University: Oxford	12362	10541	11/15	12/15	12/1	2/1
Oberlin College	431	245	11/15 1/2	12/15 2/1		
Ohio Wesleyan University					12/15	1/15
University of Dayton	8976	7804			12/15	2/1
Ursuline College	1	1			11/15	2/15
Wittenberg University	2911	2637	11/15	12/15	12/1	1/1
Oklahoma						
University of Tulsa					11/7	11/22
Oregon						
Eastern Oregon University					12/1	1/15
George Fox University	1634	1333			12/1	12/15
Lewis & Clark College					11/1	1/15
Linfield College	644	625			11/15	1/15
Oregon State University					11/1	12/15
Reed College			11/15 12/20	12/15 2/1		
University of Oregon					11/1	12/15
Willamette University	4815	2788			12/1	1/15
Pennsylvania						
Allegheny College	122	59	11/15	12/15		
Bryn Mawr College	92	88	11/15 1/1	12/15 2/1		
Bucknell University	761	419	11/15 1/15	12/15 2/15		
Carnegie Mellon University	885	308	11/1 12/1	12/15 1/15		
Dickinson College	3001	1458	11/15 1/15	12/15 2/15	12/1	2/1
Duquesne University	1733	950	11/1	12/15	12/1	
Franklin & Marshall College	455	356	11/15 1/15	12/15 2/15		
Gettysburg College	442	339	11/15 1/15	12/15 2/15		
Grove City College	439	289	11/15	12/15		
Haverford College	270	129	11/15	12/15		
Juniata College	1218	999	11/15 2/1	12/23		
La Salle University	2141	1790			11/15	12/15
Lafayette College	488	317	1/15			
Lehigh University	878	561	11/15 1/15	12/15 2/15		
Moravian College	824	745	2/1		12/1	12/15
Muhlenberg College	413	310	2/15			
Pennsylvania Academy of the Fine Arts	26	20	12/1			
Saint Joseph's University	4015	3604			11/15	12/25
Susquehanna University			11/15	12/1		
Swarthmore College	533	156	11/15 1/1	12/15 2/15		
University of Pennsylvania	4571	1192	11/1	12/15		
University of Scranton	4199	3572			11/15	12/15
Ursinus College			1/15	2/15	12/1	1/1
Villanova University	6986	2875			11/1	12/20
Washington & Jefferson College	2497	1444	12/1	12/15	1/15	2/15
Westminster College					11/15	12/1

Institution	Early Applicants		Early Decision		Early Action	
	Number Applied	Number admitted	Apply by	Notified by	Apply by	Notified by
Puerto Rico						
University of Puerto Rico: Aguadilla					1/15	1/30
University of Puerto Rico: Mayaguez					1/30	2/15
Rhode Island						
Brown University	2803	572	11/1	12/15		
Bryant University	2478	1548	11/15 1/16	12/15 2/16	12/1	1/15
Providence College					11/1	1/1
Rhode Island School of Design			11/1	12/1		
Roger Williams University					11/1	1/15
Salve Regina University	1619	1178			11/1	12/25
University of Rhode Island	13509	11307			12/1	2/3
South Carolina						
College of Charleston	5678	4737			11/1	12/15
Erskine College					11/1	11/15
Furman University	715	621	11/1	12/1	11/15	2/1
Medical University of South Carolina						
Presbyterian College	612	562	11/1	12/1	11/15	12/15
University of South Carolina: Columbia	7733	4517			10/15	12/20
Wofford College	872	635	11/15	12/5		
Tennessee						
Fisk University					12/1	12/31
Rhodes College	99	30	11/1 1/1	12/1 2/1	11/15	1/15
University of the South	105	80	11/15 1/2	12/17 2/8		
Vanderbilt University	5122	1328	11/1 1/3	12/15 2/15		
Texas						
Abilene Christian University					11/1	12/1
Austin College					1/15	3/1
Baylor University					11/1	1/15
Rice University	1036	298	11/1	12/15		
Southern Methodist University					11/1	12/31
Southwestern University			11/1	12/15	12/1	2/1
Texas Christian University	9048	4476			11/1	1/1
Texas Southern University	23	23				
Trinity University	2023	1645	11/1	12/1	12/1	2/1
University of Dallas					12/1	1/15
University of St. Thomas					11/1	11/15
Utah						
Neumont University					11/24	1/1
Vermont						
Bennington College	325	273	11/15 1/3	12/20 2/1	12/1	2/1
Champlain College	221	193	11/15 1/15	12/15 2/15		
Lyndon State College					11/1	12/15
Marlboro College	128	94	11/15	12/1	1/15	2/1
Middlebury College	988	282	11/1 1/1	12/15 2/15		
Norwich University			11/15	12/31		
St. Michael's College	2676	2019			11/1	1/1

Institution	Early Applicants		Early Decision		Early Action	
	Number Applied	Number admitted	Apply by	Notified by	Apply by	Notified by
Sterling College					12/15	1/15
University of Vermont	4639	3690			11/1	12/15
Virginia						
Christendom College	182	162			12/1	12/15
Christopher Newport University			11/15	12/15	12/1	1/15
College of William and Mary	1076	535	11/1	12/1		
Emory & Henry College					12/1	1/1
George Mason University	3816	2735			11/1	12/19
Hampden-Sydney College	142	51	11/15	12/15	1/15	2/15
Hampton University					12/1	12/15
Hollins University	47	43	12/1	12/15		
James Madison University	8011	5178			11/1	1/15
Longwood University	1707	868			12/1	1/15
Lynchburg College	301	129	11/15	12/15		
Mary Baldwin College			11/15	12/1		
Old Dominion University	4799	3959			12/1	1/15
Patrick Henry College					11/1	12/1
Radford University	2220	2195			12/1	1/15
Randolph College					12/1	1/1
Randolph-Macon College					11/15	1/1
Roanoke College	81	44	11/15	12/15		
University of Mary Washington					11/15	1/31
University of Richmond	758	292	11/15 1/15	12/15 2/15		
University of Virginia					11/1	1/31
University of Virginia's College at Wise					12/1	12/15
Virginia Military Institute	478	257	11/15	12/15		
Virginia Polytechnic Institute and State University	2024	1031	11/1	12/15		
Washington and Lee University	511	224	11/15 1/2	12/21 2/1		
Washington						
Gonzaga University	3272	2180			11/15	1/15
Northwest University	460	299			11/15	12/15
Seattle Pacific University					11/15	1/5
Seattle University	1845	1364			11/15	12/23
University of Puget Sound	149	104	11/15 1/2	12/15 2/15		
Whitman College	135	93	11/15 1/1	12/19 1/27		
Whitworth University					12/1	12/20
West Virginia						
Shepherd University	639	605			11/15	12/15
Wisconsin						
Beloit College					12/1	1/15
Lawrence University	842	580	11/15	12/1	12/1	1/30
Milwaukee Institute of Art & Design					11/15	12/1
Ripon College					12/1	12/15
Canada						
Simon Fraser University					2/28	4/15
Lebanon						
American University of Beirut	380	379			11/30	1/30

Institution	Early Applicants		Early Decision		Early Action	
	Number Applied	Number admitted	Apply by	Notified by	Apply by	Notified by
Mexico						
Universidad Anahuac						
Morocco						
Al Akhawayn University	617	322	3/31	5/15		
Switzerland						
Ecole Hoteliere de Lausanne	350	80			12/1	2/15
Franklin College Switzerland	384	267			12/1	1/15

Tables and Indexes

Wait list table

Students who are wait listed have met a college's admission requirements, but will only be offered a place in the freshman class if space becomes available. The table that follows shows wait list outcomes for students who applied for admission to the freshman class of 2011-2012 at 317 colleges, which are listed alphabetically by state.

Tables and Indexes

Institution	Total applied	Number placed on wait list	Number accepting place on wait list	Number on wait list admitted
Arkansas				
Phillips Community College of the University of Arkansas		50	50	46
California				
Azusa Pacific University	8187	195	71	15
California Institute of Technology	5225	556	366	40
California State University: Monterey Bay	11607	0		
Chapman University	9616	1050	209	1
Claremont McKenna College	4481	1066	447	0
Deep Springs College	140	2	1	1
Dominican University of California	3093	146	25	25
Harvey Mudd College	2957	432	202	46
Loyola Marymount University	11309	1280	1256	522
Occidental College	6120	1019	425	48
Pepperdine University	9384	1734	988	113
Point Loma Nazarene University	3671	209	71	58
Pomona College	7207	899	369	31
Santa Clara University	13342	2532	1022	218
Scripps College	2163	366	196	0
Soka University of America	364	27	0	
Southern California Institute of Architecture	43	14	14	7
St. Mary's College of California	4874	394	219	38
Stanford University	34348	1078	784	13
Thomas Aquinas College	171	27	27	11
University of California: Davis	45806	6077	2220	871
University of California: Irvine	49287	1570	820	0
University of California: Riverside	28101	2538	1580	1014
University of California: Santa Barbara	49008	3384	2063	0
University of San Diego	13867	1610	628	28
Colorado				
Colorado College	4916	1066	431	14
Colorado School of Mines	10145	1472	249	19
University of Denver	10504	1024	445	47
Connecticut				
Fairfield University	8486	1434	492	60
Quinnipiac University	18642	1640	990	180
Trinity College	6967	2449	765	255
United States Coast Guard Academy	2374	479	400	54
University of Connecticut	27247	5768	2067	1000
Wesleyan University	9658	1866	843	0

Institution	Total applied	Number placed on wait list	Number accepting place on wait list	Number on wait list admitted
Yale University	27283	996	671	104
Delaware				
University of Delaware	23647	1932	857	285
District of Columbia				
George Washington University	21591	2477	564	112
Georgetown University	19254	2170	1246	2
Florida				
Flagler College	3933	677	181	33
New College of Florida	1272	103	47	26
Rollins College	4416	210	73	0
University of Central Florida	33968	3229	1168	90
Georgia				
Agnes Scott College	2284	29	9	2
Emory University	17027	5249	2960	133
Georgia Institute of Technology	14088	1219	704	303
Georgia State University	12869	872	338	285
Spelman College	5864	567	82	31
University of Georgia	17569	899	615	11
Illinois				
Illinois State University	13156	0		
Illinois Wesleyan University	3319	290	58	16
Knox College	2385	41	15	5
McKendree University	1359	15	11	3
Northwestern University	30926	3537	1605	0
Robert Morris University: Chicago	3132	0	0	0
University of Chicago	21762	4888	3203	105
University of Illinois at Urbana-Champaign	28751	1159	680	140
Wheaton College	2050	389	147	23
Indiana				
Butler University	9518	208	191	180
Earlham College	1620	73	66	12
Hanover College	3015	0		
Purdue University	29513	190	190	0
Rose-Hulman Institute of Technology	4298	163	93	16
University of Notre Dame	16548	1893	951	7
Wabash College	1456	69	53	2
Iowa				
Cornell College	3202	152	91	33
Grinnell College	2613	541	273	14
Northwest Iowa Community College	1928	239	239	12
St. Luke's College	18	6	6	2
University of Iowa	18939	0	0	0
Wartburg College	2346	0		
Kentucky				
Centre College	2413	192	45	9
Louisiana				
Tulane University	37767	3745	1009	15
Xavier University of Louisiana	4463	91	21	13
Maine				
Bates College	5196	1305	302	12
Colby College	5186	1198	611	18

Institution	Total applied	Number placed on wait list	Number accepting place on wait list	Number on wait list admitted
College of the Atlantic	400	23	8	7
Husson University	1560	39	20	15
Unity College in Maine	737	0		

Maryland

Institution	Total applied	Number placed on wait list	Number accepting place on wait list	Number on wait list admitted
Goucher College	3763	170	96	16
Hood College	1686	47	46	0
Johns Hopkins University	19391	2725	2364	19
Loyola University Maryland	12066	1854	625	143
McDaniel College	2754	79	32	8
Mount St. Mary's University	5166	75	34	8
St. Mary's College of Maryland	2398	254	153	40
University of Maryland: Baltimore County	8099	530	530	487
University of Maryland: College Park	26310	969	0	0

Massachusetts

Institution	Total applied	Number placed on wait list	Number accepting place on wait list	Number on wait list admitted
Amherst College	8461	1219	564	29
Assumption College	4380	361	129	2
Babson College	5079	981	395	34
Bard College at Simon's Rock	290	0		
Becker College	2509	75	19	9
Bentley University	6695	1400	550	83
Berklee College of Music	4956	300	248	21
Boston College	32974	6441	2589	367
Boston University	41802	3329	1402	329
Brandeis University	8917	1321	303	87
Bridgewater State University	7039	690	355	130
Clark University	4127	97	34	9
College of the Holy Cross	7353	1556	440	0
Curry College	5063	129	80	65
Endicott College	3477	32	32	2
Franklin W. Olin College of Engineering	768	34	25	5
Hampshire College	2517	214	98	53
Lesley University	2763	10	9	1
Massachusetts College of Art and Design	1418	0		
Massachusetts Institute of Technology	17909	1068	967	27
Montserrat College of Art	404	10	7	1
Mount Holyoke College	3416	750	503	0
New England Conservatory of Music	1092	142	106	6
Northeastern University	43255	5729	2859	85
Smith College	4128	475	240	0
Springfield Technical Community College	3189	43	43	20
Stonehill College	7200	713	275	265
Suffolk University	9137	468	182	85
University of Massachusetts Amherst	32564	5062	1261	125
Wellesley College	4400	1162	551	87
Wheaton College	3448	198	125	38
Williams College	7030	1352	584	14
Worcester Polytechnic Institute	7049	1571	484	0

Michigan

Institution	Total applied	Number placed on wait list	Number accepting place on wait list	Number on wait list admitted
Hillsdale College	2207	45	35	5
Hope College	3575	0	0	0
Kalamazoo College	2225	178	107	11
Michigan State University	28416	900	600	350
University of Michigan	39584	14659	4498	42

Institution	Total applied	Number placed on wait list	Number accepting place on wait list	Number on wait list admitted
Minnesota				
Bethel University	2314	63	4	4
Carleton College	4988	1397	165	64
College of St. Benedict	1972	75	30	10
College of Visual Arts	153	0		
Dakota County Technical College	3138	280	280	106
Dunwoody College of Technology	693	17	17	12
Gustavus Adolphus College	4818	10	10	0
Hamline University	2982	0		
Macalester College	6111	508	196	196
Saint Cloud State University	5256	0		
St. Olaf College	4181	740	212	53
University of St. Thomas	5250	0		
Missouri				
College of the Ozarks	3299	734	734	39
Lindenwood University	3335	193	97	97
Linn State Technical College	1184	86	86	42
Saint Louis University	13389	160	160	111
Nebraska				
Creighton University	5104	12	1	0
New Hampshire				
Dartmouth College	22385	1891	1047	86
Saint Anselm College	4134	700	398	0
New Jersey				
Princeton University	27189	1248	869	19
Rider University	7947	44	44	13
Saint Peter's College	2779	105	35	30
New York				
Albany College of Pharmacy and Health Sciences	1437	59	23	23
Bard College	5670	264	79	16
Barnard College	5153	896	576	7
Clarkson University	4686	124	5	3
Colgate University	7835	1525	712	33
Cooper Union for the Advancement of Science and Art	3415	70	60	10
Cornell University	36387	2982	1846	0
Daemen College	2372	0		
Dominican College of Blauvelt	1594	12	12	0
Elmira College	2424	35	33	1
Finger Lakes Community College		101	101	11
Fordham University	31792	5944	1637	607
Hamilton College	5265	1136	542	34
Hartwick College	4897	487	89	89
Hobart and William Smith Colleges	4454	505	165	7
Hofstra University	21376	836	264	55
Ithaca College	13436	1633	587	95
Juilliard School	2566	44	35	12
Le Moyne College	5772	92	31	16
Lebanese American University	3617	80	80	58
Manhattan College	6253	211	80	30
Maria College	341	30	30	10
Marist College	11399	3823	1051	0
Marymount Manhattan College	3664	0		

Institution	Total applied	Number placed on wait list	Number accepting place on wait list	Number on wait list admitted
Nazareth College	2976	164	18	18
Phillips Beth Israel School of Nursing	135	15	10	5
Pratt Institute	4247	580	150	30
Rensselaer Polytechnic Institute	14584	3584	2280	82
SUNY College at Brockport	8575	318	90	43
SUNY College at Oneonta	12338	0		
SUNY College at Plattsburgh	7368	129	46	37
SUNY College of Environmental Science and Forestry	1865	260	83	20
SUNY College of Technology at Alfred	3890	270	152	36
SUNY Maritime College	1348	25	25	5
SUNY University at Binghamton	28101	1299	519	20
SUNY University at Buffalo	21357	639	188	155
SUNY University at Stony Brook	27822	2495	1096	32
Siena College	9723	1350	187	37
Skidmore College	5780	1256	966	2
St. Elizabeth College of Nursing	42	14	13	13
St. Lawrence University	4273	351	101	18
Syracuse University	25884	4875	1983	521
Union College	5151	908	328	11
Vassar College	7985	1460	600	19
Wagner College	3001	83	74	18

North Carolina

Institution	Total applied	Number placed on wait list	Number accepting place on wait list	Number on wait list admitted
Appalachian State University	12959	725	161	0
Elon University	9079	2334	948	83
Guilford College	3054	127	28	4
High Point University	6866	402	288	161
North Carolina Agricultural and Technical State University	6692	210	210	86
University of North Carolina School of the Arts	624	23	23	8
University of North Carolina at Chapel Hill	22652	2015	1066	192
Wayne Community College	1704	59	26	21
William Peace University	1071	0		

Ohio

Institution	Total applied	Number placed on wait list	Number accepting place on wait list	Number on wait list admitted
Art Institute of Cincinnati	57	0	0	0
Case Western Reserve University	13543	2233	929	419
College of Wooster	4893	347	120	49
Franciscan University of Steubenville	1739	74	43	19
Kenyon College	4272	1152	376	15
Mercy College of Ohio	87	8	6	1
Miami University: Oxford	18482	1282	317	32
Oberlin College	7395	1223	448	141
Ohio State University: Columbus Campus	26100	814	249	4
Ohio University	13251	233	118	96
Xavier University	9783	139	29	13

Oklahoma

Institution	Total applied	Number placed on wait list	Number accepting place on wait list	Number on wait list admitted
University of Oklahoma	11456	2607	2607	1719
University of Tulsa	6257	318	318	71

Oregon

Institution	Total applied	Number placed on wait list	Number accepting place on wait list	Number on wait list admitted
Lewis & Clark College	5901	598	167	4
University of Oregon	23012	2481	1087	947

Pennsylvania

Institution	Total applied	Number placed on wait list	Number accepting place on wait list	Number on wait list admitted
Allegheny College	4770	340	340	25
Bloomsburg University of Pennsylvania	11423	69	69	6

Institution	Total applied	Number placed on wait list	Number accepting place on wait list	Number on wait list admitted
Bryn Athyn College of the New Church	833	5	0	
Bryn Mawr College	2335	645	352	7
Bucknell University	7940	2198	914	19
Carlow University	1072	55	55	55
Carnegie Mellon University	16527	5003	642	6
Curtis Institute of Music	279	5	5	0
Dickinson College	6063	1150	469	2
East Stroudsburg University of Pennsylvania	6520	0		
Elizabethtown College	3665	167	113	39
Franklin & Marshall College	5105	1820	647	28
Gannon University	3633	100	95	0
Grove City College	1592	302	105	70
Haverford College	3470	811	370	0
Lafayette College	5716	1559	608	0
Lehigh University	11578	3684	1514	1
Messiah College	3154	1	1	0
Millersville University of Pennsylvania	6974	862	405	65
Misericordia University	2013	50	50	15
Moravian College	1940	81	23	14
Mount Aloysius College	1323	0		
Muhlenberg College	4876	1670	345	21
Neumann University	2660	0		
Penn State DuBois	433	0		
Penn State University Park	44502	1159	1140	1138
Pennsylvania Academy of the Fine Arts	90	10	0	0
Saint Joseph's University	7401	546	191	51
Susquehanna University	3610	243	39	19
Temple University	18977	1421	648	264
University of Pennsylvania	31663	2417	1385	56
University of Pittsburgh	23409	1125	315	15
University of Pittsburgh at Bradford	961	0		
University of Scranton	9047	1060	323	29
University of the Sciences in Philadelphia	3723	0	0	0
Ursinus College	3851	142	68	38
Villanova University	15394	4950	2272	152
Washington & Jefferson College	6643	45	17	2
West Chester University of Pennsylvania	15080	2861	745	10
Widener University	5336	64	2	1
Williamson Free School of Mechanical Trades	361	35	35	11

Rhode Island

Institution	Total applied	Number placed on wait list	Number accepting place on wait list	Number on wait list admitted
Bryant University	5177	210	80	19
Providence College	9873	2204	447	160
Roger Williams University	9202	250	101	15
Salve Regina University	4686	277	239	3
University of Rhode Island	20012	1385	526	28

South Carolina

Institution	Total applied	Number placed on wait list	Number accepting place on wait list	Number on wait list admitted
College of Charleston	11086	391	367	17
Furman University	4888	67	13	4
Wofford College	2871	77	17	5

South Dakota

Institution	Total applied	Number placed on wait list	Number accepting place on wait list	Number on wait list admitted
Mitchell Technical Institute	945	23	23	14

Institution	Total applied	Number placed on wait list	Number accepting place on wait list	Number on wait list admitted
Tennessee				
Belmont University	3878	0	0	0
University of the South	2920	426	106	43
Vanderbilt University	24837	5518	1831	212
Texas				
Rice University	13816	2342	1493	1
Southern Methodist University	10338	504	196	42
Southwestern University	2613	28	4	0
St. Edward's University	3886	342	342	82
Texas A&M University	25949	8044	3901	995
Texas Christian University	19168	2986	1014	201
Texas Tech University	17569	344	317	241
Trinity University	4507	363	168	24
University of Texas at Austin	32589	456	318	92
Vermont				
Bennington College	1145	80	12	3
Champlain College	2587	21	16	10
Middlebury College	8533	2114	1006	20
Norwich University	3131	14	3	0
St. Michael's College	4474	235	99	17
University of Vermont	22341	3269	1027	572
Virginia				
Christendom College	288	6	6	2
Christopher Newport University	7351	1005	394	66
College of William and Mary	12825	3248	1496	18
George Mason University	17548	1894	817	54
Hollins University	813	0		
James Madison University	22864	3406	1568	165
Jefferson College of Health Sciences	447	20	17	0
Radford University	7596	978	978	174
Randolph-Macon College	4249	250	66	6
Roanoke College	4184	283	80	36
University of Mary Washington	4807	378	143	120
University of Richmond	9431	3577	1192	83
University of Virginia	23587	4326	2726	177
Virginia Military Institute	2095	480	185	20
Washington and Lee University	6487	1980	727	50
Washington				
Gonzaga University	6851	579	225	50
Seattle Pacific University	4211	645	645	24
Seattle University	6317	1385	1385	341
University of Puget Sound	7194	522	186	96
University of Washington	24540	2519	1412	284
University of Washington Tacoma	854	0		
Western Washington University	9083	1329	836	643
Whitman College	3086	520	186	0
Whitworth University	7040	560	560	39
Wisconsin				
Beloit College	2107	76	35	16
Lawrence University	2666	483	128	93
Marquette University	22354	3311	1058	431
Northeast Wisconsin Technical College	9044	1077	1042	481
University of Wisconsin-Green Bay	3471	39	39	27

Institution	Total applied	Number placed on wait list	Number accepting place on wait list	Number on wait list admitted
University of Wisconsin-Stevens Point	5571	616	616	0
Morocco				
Al Akhawayn University	1192	22	11	11
Switzerland				
Ecole Hoteliere de Lausanne	1360	77	50	20

Indexes

College type

Liberal arts colleges

Four-year

Alabama

Athens State University
Birmingham-Southern College
Concordia College
Faulkner University
Huntingdon College
Judson College
Miles College
New Charter University
Oakwood University
Spring Hill College
Stillman College
Talladega College
University of Mobile
University of Montevallo

Alaska

Alaska Pacific University
University of Alaska
    Southeast

Arizona

Arizona Christian University
Harrison Middleton University
Prescott College

Arkansas

Arkansas Baptist College
Arkansas Tech University
Ecclesia College
Henderson State University
Hendrix College
John Brown University
Lyon College
Ouachita Baptist University
Philander Smith College
University of the Ozarks
Williams Baptist College

California

American Jewish University
Antioch University
    Los Angeles
    Santa Barbara
California Institute of Integral
    Studies
California Lutheran University
California State University
    Bakersfield
    Chico
    Monterey Bay
    San Bernardino
    Stanislaus
Chapman University
Claremont McKenna College
Concordia University
Fresno Pacific University
Harvey Mudd College
Hope International University
Horizon College of San Diego
Humboldt State University
Humphreys College
La Sierra University
The Master's College
Menlo College
Mills College
Mount St. Mary's College
NewSchool of Architecture &
    Design
Notre Dame de Namur
    University
Occidental College
Pacific Union College
Patten University
Pepperdine University
Pitzer College
Point Loma Nazarene University
Pomona College
Providence Christian College
St. Mary's College of California
San Diego Christian College
San Jose State University
Scripps College
Simpson University
Soka University of America
Sonoma State University
Stanford University
Thomas Aquinas College
Touro College Los Angeles
University of La Verne
University of Redlands
University of the West
Vanguard University of
    Southern California
Westmont College
Whittier College
William Jessup University

Colorado

Adams State College
Colorado Christian University
Colorado College
Colorado Heights University
Colorado Mesa University
Fort Lewis College
Metropolitan State College of
    Denver
Naropa University
Regis University
United States Air Force
    Academy
Western State College of
    Colorado

Connecticut

Albertus Magnus College
Charter Oak State College
Connecticut College
Eastern Connecticut State
    University
Holy Apostles College and
    Seminary
Mitchell College
Sacred Heart University
Saint Joseph College
Trinity College
Wesleyan University

Delaware

Wesley College
Wilmington University

District of Columbia

Gallaudet University
Trinity Washington University
University of the District of
    Columbia

Florida

Ave Maria University
Beacon College
Bethune-Cookman University
Clearwater Christian College
Eckerd College
Edward Waters College
Everglades University
    Orlando
Flagler College
Florida College
Florida Memorial University
Florida Southern College
Jacksonville University
New College of Florida
Palm Beach Atlantic University
Rollins College
St. John Vianney College
    Seminary
Southeastern University
University of Tampa
Warner University

Georgia

Agnes Scott College
Augusta State University
Berry College
Brenau University
Brewton-Parker College
Chorter University
    Shorter University
Clayton State University
Columbus State University
Covenant College
Dalton State College
Emmanuel College
Fort Valley State University
Georgia College and State
    University
Georgia Gwinnett College
Georgia Southwestern State
    University
LaGrange College
Macon State College
Morehouse College
Oglethorpe University
Paine College
Piedmont College
Point University
Reinhardt University
Savannah State University
Spelman College
Thomas University
Toccoa Falls College
Truett-McConnell College
Wesleyan College

Hawaii

Brigham Young University-
    Hawaii
Hawaii Pacific University
University of Hawaii
    Hilo
    West Oahu

Idaho

College of Idaho
Lewis-Clark State College
New Saint Andrews College

Illinois

Augustana College
Benedictine University
Blackburn College
Columbia College Chicago
Concordia University Chicago
Dominican University
Elmhurst College
Eureka College
Greenville College
Hebrew Theological College
Illinois College
Illinois Wesleyan University
Judson University
Knox College
Lake Forest College
MacMurray College
McKendree University
Monmouth College
North Central College
North Park University
Olivet Nazarene University
Principia College
Quincy University
Rockford College
St. Augustine College
Shimer College
Trinity Christian College
Trinity International University
University of Chicago
University of Illinois
    Springfield
University of St. Francis
Wheaton College

Indiana

Anderson University
Bethel College
Calumet College of St. Joseph
DePauw University
Earlham College
Franklin College
Goshen College
Grace College
Hanover College
Holy Cross College
Huntington University
Indiana Wesleyan University
Manchester College
Marian University
Martin University
Oakland City University
Saint Joseph's College
Saint Mary's College
St. Mary-of-the-Woods College
Taylor University
University of Evansville
University of Indianapolis
University of St. Francis
University of Southern Indiana
Wabash College

Iowa

Briar Cliff University
Buena Vista University
Central College
Clarke University
Coe College
Cornell College
Divine Word College
Dordt College
Graceland University
Grand View University
Grinnell College
Iowa Wesleyan College
Loras College
Luther College
Maharishi University of
    Management
Morningside College
Mount Mercy University
Northwestern College
St. Ambrose University
Simpson College
Upper Iowa University
Waldorf College
Wartburg College
William Penn University

Kansas

Baker University
Benedictine College
Bethany College
Bethel College
Central Christian College of
    Kansas
Friends University
Kansas Wesleyan University
McPherson College
MidAmerica Nazarene
    University
Newman University
Ottawa University
Southwestern College
Sterling College
Tabor College

Kentucky

Alice Lloyd College
Asbury University
Bellarmine University
Berea College
Brescia University
Centre College
Georgetown College
Kentucky Christian University
Kentucky Wesleyan College
Lindsey Wilson College
Mid-Continent University
Midway College
St. Catharine College
Thomas More College
Transylvania University
Union College
University of Pikeville
University of the Cumberlands

Louisiana

Centenary College of Louisiana
Dillard University
Louisiana College
Loyola University New Orleans
Our Lady of Holy Cross
    College

Maine

Bates College
Bowdoin College
Colby College
College of the Atlantic
Saint Joseph's College of Maine
Thomas College
Unity College in Maine
University of Maine
    Farmington
    Machias
University of Southern Maine

Maryland

Coppin State University
Goucher College
Hood College
McDaniel College
Morgan State University
Mount St. Mary's University
National Labor College
Notre Dame of Maryland
    University
St. John's College
St. Mary's College of Maryland
Salisbury University
Sojourner-Douglass College
University of Baltimore
Washington Adventist
    University
Washington College

Massachusetts

American International College
Amherst College
Anna Maria College
Assumption College
Bard College at Simon's Rock
Bay Path College
Becker College
Cambridge College
Clark University
College of the Holy Cross
Curry College
Eastern Nazarene College
Elms College
Emmanuel College
Endicott College
Fitchburg State University
Framingham State University
Gordon College
Hampshire College

Harvard College
Hellenic College/Holy Cross
Lasell College
Lesley University
Massachusetts College of
  Liberal Arts
Merrimack College
Mount Holyoke College
Mount Ida College
Newbury College
Nichols College
Pine Manor College
Regis College
Simmons College
Smith College
Springfield College
Stonehill College
Wellesley College
Wheaton College
Wheelock College
Williams College
Worcester State University

Michigan

Adrian College
Albion College
Alma College
Aquinas College
Calvin College
Concordia University
Cornerstone University
Finlandia University
Grace Bible College
Griggs University
Hillsdale College
Hope College
Kalamazoo College
Kuyper College
Madonna University
Marygrove College
Michigan Jewish Institute
Olivet College
Robert B. Miller College
Rochester College
Siena Heights University
Spring Arbor University

Minnesota

Augsburg College
Bethany Lutheran College
Bethel University
Brown College: Mendota
  Heights
Carleton College
College of St. Benedict
College of St. Scholastica
Concordia College: Moorhead
Crown College
Gustavus Adolphus College
Hamline University
Macalester College
Northwestern College
St. Catherine University
St. John's University
St. Olaf College
Southwest Minnesota State
  University
University of Minnesota
  Morris
University of St. Thomas

Mississippi

Belhaven University
Blue Mountain College
Millsaps College
Mississippi University for
  Women
Mississippi Valley State
  University
Rust College
Tougaloo College
William Carey University

Missouri

Avila University
Central Methodist University
College of the Ozarks
Columbia College

Culver-Stockton College
Drury University
Evangel University
Fontbonne University
Hannibal-LaGrange University
Lincoln University
Lindenwood University
Missouri Baptist University
Missouri Southern State
  University
Missouri Valley College
Missouri Western State
  University
Rockhurst University
Stephens College
Truman State University
Westminster College
William Jewell College

Montana

Carroll College
Rocky Mountain College
Salish Kootenai College
University of Great Falls
University of Montana
University of Montana: Western

Nebraska

Chadron State College
College of Saint Mary
Doane College
Hastings College
Midland University
Nebraska Wesleyan University
Peru State College
Union College
Wayne State College
York College

Nevada

Nevada State College
Sierra Nevada College

New Hampshire

Chester College of New
  England
Colby-Sawyer College
College of St. Mary Magdalen
Dartmouth College
Franklin Pierce University
Granite State College
Keene State College
New England College
Rivier College
Saint Anselm College
Thomas More College of
  Liberal Arts
University of New Hampshire at
  Manchester

New Jersey

Bloomfield College
Caldwell College
Centenary College
The College of New Jersey
College of St. Elizabeth
Drew University
Felician College
Georgian Court University
Kean University
Ramapo College of New Jersey
Richard Stockton College of
  New Jersey
Saint Peter's College
Somerset Christian College
Thomas Edison State College
William Paterson University of
  New Jersey

New Mexico

Institute of American Indian
  Arts
New Mexico Institute of Mining
  and Technology
St. John's College
University of the Southwest

New York

Bard College
Barnard College
Boricua College
Canisius College
Cazenovia College
City University of New York
  Baruch College
  Brooklyn College
  College of Staten Island
  Hunter College
  Lehman College
  Medgar Evers College
  Queens College
  York College
Colgate University
College of Mount St. Vincent
College of New Rochelle
College of Saint Rose
Columbia University
  School of General Studies
Concordia College
D'Youville College
Daemen College
Dominican College of Blauvelt
Dowling College
Elmira College
Eugene Lang College The New
  School for Liberal Arts
Excelsior College
Five Towns College
Hamilton College
Hartwick College
Hilbert College
Hobart and William Smith
  Colleges
Houghton College
Iona College
Ithaca College
Keuka College
The King's College
Le Moyne College
Long Island University
  Brooklyn Campus
  C. W. Post Campus
Manhattan College
Manhattanville College
Marist College
Marymount Manhattan College
Medaille College
Medaille College: Amherst
Medaille College: Rochester
Mercy College
Metropolitan College of New
  York
Molloy College
Mount Saint Mary College
Nazareth College
Nyack College
Paul Smith's College
Roberts Wesleyan College
Russell Sage College
Sage College of Albany
St. Francis College
St. John Fisher College
St. Joseph's College, New York
St. Joseph's College: Suffolk
  Campus
St. Lawrence University
St. Thomas Aquinas College
Sarah Lawrence College
Siena College
Skidmore College
SUNY
  College at Brockport
  College at Buffalo
  College at Cortland
  College at Fredonia
  College at Geneseo
  College at New Paltz
  College at Old Westbury
  College at Oneonta
  College at Plattsburgh
  College at Potsdam
  Empire State College
Touro College
Union College

Utica College
Vassar College
Wagner College
Wells College

North Carolina

Barton College
Belmont Abbey College
Bennett College for Women
Brevard College
Campbell University
Catawba College
Chowan University
Davidson College
Elizabeth City State University
Elon University
Gardner-Webb University
Greensboro College
Guilford College
High Point University
Johnson C. Smith University
Lees-McRae College
Lenoir-Rhyne University
Livingstone College
Mars Hill College
Meredith College
Methodist University
Montreat College
Mount Olive College
North Carolina Wesleyan
  College
Pfeiffer University
St. Andrews University
St. Augustine's College
Salem College
Shaw University
University of North Carolina
  Asheville
  Pembroke
Warren Wilson College
William Peace University

North Dakota

Jamestown College
Minot State University
Valley City State University

Ohio

Ashland University
Baldwin-Wallace College
Bluffton University
Cedarville University
Central State University
College of Mount St. Joseph
College of Wooster
Defiance College
Denison University
Heidelberg University
Hiram College
Kenyon College
Lake Erie College
Laura and Alvin Siegal College
  of Judaic Studies
Lourdes University
Marietta College
Muskingum University
Notre Dame College
Oberlin College
Ohio Dominican University
Ohio Mid-Western College
Ohio Wesleyan University
Otterbein University
Pontifical College Josephinum
Tiffin University
University of Rio Grande
Urbana University
Ursuline College
Walsh University
Wilberforce University
Wilmington College
Wittenberg University

Oklahoma

Bacone College
Hillsdale Free Will Baptist
  College
Langston University

Mid-America Christian
  University
Oklahoma Baptist University
Oklahoma Christian University
Oklahoma City University
Oklahoma Panhandle State
  University
Oklahoma Wesleyan University
Oral Roberts University
St. Gregory's University
Southeastern Oklahoma State
  University
Southern Nazarene University
Southwestern Christian
  University
University of Science and Arts
  of Oklahoma

Oregon

Art Institute of Portland
Concordia University
Corban University
Eastern Oregon University
Gutenberg College
Lewis & Clark College
Linfield College
Marylhurst University
Reed College
Southern Oregon University
Warner Pacific College
Western Oregon University
Willamette University

Pennsylvania

Albright College
Allegheny College
Alvernia University
Bloomsburg University of
  Pennsylvania
Bryn Athyn College of the New
  Church
Bryn Mawr College
Cabrini College
Carlow University
Cedar Crest College
Chatham University
Chestnut Hill College
Delaware Valley College
Dickinson College
Elizabethtown College
Franklin & Marshall College
Geneva College
Gettysburg College
Gratz College
Grove City College
Gwynedd-Mercy College
Haverford College
Immaculata University
Juniata College
Keystone College
King's College
La Roche College
La Salle University
Lafayette College
Lebanon Valley College
Lincoln University
Lock Haven University of
  Pennsylvania
Lycoming College
Mercyhurst University
Messiah College
Millersville University of
  Pennsylvania
Misericordia University
Moravian College
Mount Aloysius College
Muhlenberg College
Rosemont College
St. Francis University
St. Vincent College
Seton Hill University
Susquehanna University
Swarthmore College
Thiel College
University of Pittsburgh
  Greensburg
  Johnstown
University of Scranton

Ursinus College
Valley Forge Christian College
Washington & Jefferson College
Waynesburg University
Westminster College
Wilson College
York College of Pennsylvania

Puerto Rico

Atlantic College
Inter American University of
 Puerto Rico
 Aguadilla Campus
 Arecibo Campus
Universidad Adventista de las
 Antillas
Universidad del Este
Universidad Metropolitana
University of Puerto Rico
 Aguadilla
 Cayey University College
 Humacao
University of the Sacred Heart

Rhode Island

Brown University
Bryant University
Providence College
Rhode Island College
Roger Williams University
Salve Regina University

South Carolina

Allen University
Benedict College
Bob Jones University
Charleston Southern University
Claflin University
Coker College
College of Charleston
Columbia College
Converse College
Erskine College
Francis Marion University
Furman University
Lander University
Limestone College
Morris College
Newberry College
North Greenville University
Presbyterian College
Southern Wesleyan University
University of South Carolina
 Aiken
 Beaufort
Voorhees College
Wofford College

South Dakota

Augustana College
Black Hills State University
Dakota Wesleyan University
Mount Marty College
Northern State University
Oglala Lakota College
Sinte Gleska University
University of Sioux Falls

Tennessee

Aquinas College
Austin Peay State University
Bethel University
Bryan College
Carson-Newman College
Cumberland University
Fisk University
Freed-Hardeman University
King College
Lane College
Lee University
LeMoyne-Owen College
Lincoln Memorial University
Lipscomb University
Martin Methodist College
Maryville College
Milligan College
Rhodes College
South College

Southern Adventist University
Tennessee Wesleyan College
Trevecca Nazarene University
Tusculum College
Union University
Victory University
Williamson Christian College

Texas

Austin College
College of Saint Thomas More
Concordia University Texas
East Texas Baptist University
Houston Baptist University
Huston-Tillotson University
Jarvis Christian College
Lubbock Christian University
McMurry University
Midwestern State University
Paul Quinn College
St. Edward's University
St. Mary's University
Schreiner University
Southwestern Adventist
 University
Southwestern Christian College
Southwestern University
Texas College
Texas Lutheran University
Trinity University
University of Dallas
University of St. Thomas
Wayland Baptist University
Wiley College

Utah

Dixie State College
Stevens-Henager College
 Ogden
Westminster College

Vermont

Bennington College
Burlington College
Castleton State College
Champlain College
College of St. Joseph in
 Vermont
Goddard College
Green Mountain College
Johnson State College
Lyndon State College
Marlboro College
Middlebury College
St. Michael's College
Southern Vermont College
Sterling College

Virginia

Averett University
Bluefield College
Bridgewater College
Christendom College
Christopher Newport University
Eastern Mennonite University
Emory & Henry College
Ferrum College
Hampden-Sydney College
Hollins University
Lynchburg College
Mary Baldwin College
Patrick Henry College
Randolph College
Randolph-Macon College
Roanoke College
St. Paul's College
Southern Virginia University
Sweet Briar College
University of Richmond
University of Virginia's College
 at Wise
Virginia Intermont College
Virginia Military Institute
Virginia Union University
Virginia University of
 Lynchburg
Virginia Wesleyan College
Washington and Lee University

Washington

Antioch University
 Seattle
Evergreen State College
Gonzaga University
Heritage University
Northwest University
Trinity Lutheran College
University of Puget Sound
Walla Walla University
Whitman College
Whitworth University

West Virginia

Alderson-Broaddus College
Bethany College
Bluefield State College
Concord University
Davis and Elkins College
Glenville State College
Ohio Valley University
Salem International University
University of Charleston
West Virginia State University
West Virginia University
 Institute of Technology
West Virginia Wesleyan College
Wheeling Jesuit University

Wisconsin

Alverno College
Beloit College
Carroll University
Carthage College
Concordia University Wisconsin
Edgewood College
Lakeland College
Lawrence University
Maranatha Baptist Bible College
Marian University
Mount Mary College
Northland College
Ripon College
St. Norbert College
Silver Lake College of the Holy
 Family
University of Wisconsin
 Green Bay
 River Falls
 Superior
Viterbo University
Wisconsin Lutheran College

**Commonwealth of The
Marianas**

Northern Marianas College

France

American University of Paris

Italy

The American University of
 Rome
John Cabot University

Kuwait

American University of Kuwait

Lebanon

Notre Dame University: Louaize

Morocco

Al Akhawayn University

Pakistan

Forman Christian College

Switzerland

Franklin College
 Switzerland

United Kingdom

Richmond, The American
 International University in
 London

Two-year

Arkansas

Arkansas State University
 Newport
National Park Community
 College

California

Antelope Valley College
Deep Springs College
Feather River College
Fresno City College
Marymount College
 Palos Verdes California

Colorado

Colorado Mountain College

Florida

Edison State College

Georgia

Andrew College
College of Coastal Georgia
Georgia Highlands College
Georgia Perimeter College
Oxford College of Emory
 University
Waycross College
Young Harris College

Hawaii

Hawaii Tokai International
 College

Illinois

Lincoln College

Indiana

Ancilla College

Iowa

Kaplan University
 Cedar Rapids

Kansas

Donnelly College
Hesston College

Massachusetts

Dean College
Fisher College

Michigan

Montcalm Community College
Wayne County Community
 College

Minnesota

Itasca Community College

Missouri

Cottey College
Crowder College
Missouri State University: West
 Plains
Stevens Institute of Business &
 Arts

New Jersey

Assumption College for Sisters
Gloucester County College

New Mexico

Luna Community College

New York

Maria College
SUNY
 College of Technology at
 Alfred
 College of Technology at
 Delhi

Ohio

Chatfield College

Pennsylvania

University of Pittsburgh
 Titusville

Puerto Rico

Colegio de Cinematografía,
 Artes y Televisión

South Carolina

Clinton Junior College
Spartanburg Methodist College
University of South Carolina
 Union

Texas

Alvin Community College
Eastfield College
Jacksonville College
Lamar State College at Orange
Lon Morris College
North Lake College

Vermont

Community College of Vermont
Landmark College

Virginia

Richard Bland College

Washington

Olympic College

Wisconsin

University of Wisconsin
 Baraboo/Sauk County
 Fox Valley
 Manitowoc
 Marathon County
 Marinette
 Richland
 Rock County
 Washington County

**Upper-division
colleges**

Alabama

Athens State University
United States Sports Academy

California

Alliant International University
Antioch University
 Los Angeles
 Santa Barbara
California Institute of Integral
 Studies
John F. Kennedy University
Pacific Oaks College
Samuel Merritt University

Georgia

Georgia Health Sciences
 University

Illinois

Governors State University
Lakeview College of Nursing
Resurrection University
Rush University
Saint Anthony College of
 Nursing
St. Francis Medical Center
 College of Nursing
St. John's College

Kansas

University of Kansas Medical
 Center

Louisiana

Louisiana State University
 Health Sciences Center

Maryland

University of Maryland
 Baltimore

Michigan

Walsh College of Accountancy
 and Business Administration

Agricultural colleges

Arts/music colleges

Bible colleges

Hobe Sound Bible College, FL
Horizon College of San Diego, CA
Huntsville Bible College, AL
International Baptist College, AZ
Johnson University, TN
Kentucky Christian University, KY
Kentucky Mountain Bible College, KY
The King's University, CA
Lancaster Bible College, PA
Laurel University, NC
Life Pacific College, CA
Lincoln Christian University, IL
Manhattan Christian College, KS
Maranatha Baptist Bible College, WI
Mid-Atlantic Christian University, NC
Mid-Continent University, KY
Moody Bible Institute, IL
Multnomah University, OR
Nazarene Bible College, CO
Nebraska Christian College, NE
New Hope Christian College, OR
New Orleans Baptist Theological Seminary: Leavell College, LA
North Central University, MN
Northland International University, WI
Oak Hills Christian College, MN
Ohio Christian University, OH
Ozark Christian College, MO
Philadelphia Biblical University, PA
Piedmont International University, NC
Point University, GA
St. Louis Christian College, MO
School of Urban Missions: Oakland, CA
Shasta Bible College and Graduate School, CA
Somerset Christian College, NJ
Southeastern Baptist College, MS
Southeastern Baptist Theological Seminary, NC
Southeastern Bible College, AL
Southern California Seminary, CA
Southwestern Assemblies of God University, TX
Southwestern Baptist Theological Seminary, TX
Southwestern Christian College, TX
Theological University of the Caribbean, PR
Toccoa Falls College, GA
Tri-State Bible College, OH
Trinity Baptist College, FL
Trinity Bible College, ND
Trinity College of Florida, FL
Trinity Lutheran College, WA
Universidad Pentecostal Mizpa, PR
Virginia Baptist College, VA
Visible Music College, TN
W.L. Bonner Bible College, SC
Washington Bible College, MD
William Jessup University, CA
World Mission University, CA
Zion Bible College, MA

Two-year

Epic Bible College, CA
Rosedale Bible College, OH

Business colleges

Four-year

American University of Puerto Rico, PR
Babson College, MA
Baker College
  of Allen Park, MI
  of Auburn Hills, MI
  of Cadillac, MI
  of Clinton Township, MI
  of Flint, MI
  of Jackson, MI
  of Muskegon, MI
  of Owosso, MI
  of Port Huron, MI
Beckfield College, KY
Bellevue University, NE
Bentley University, MA
Berkeley College, NY
Berkeley College, NJ
Berkeley College of New York City, NY
Briarcliffe College, NY
Brown College: Mendota Heights, MN
Bryant & Stratton College Eastlake, OH
Bryant University, RI
California College San Diego, CA
California State University Stanislaus, CA
California University of Management and Sciences, CA
Capitol College, MD
Chadron State College, NE
City College
  Fort Lauderdale, FL
City University of New York Baruch College, NY
Clarion University of Pennsylvania, PA
Cleary University, MI
Colorado Heights University, CO
Columbia Centro Universitario: Caguas, PR
Concordia College: Moorhead, MN
Daniel Webster College, NH
Davenport University, MI
DeVry College of New York Midtown Campus, NY
Dowling College, NY
Ecole Hoteliere de Lausanne, CH
Electronic Data Processing College of Puerto Rico, PR
Electronic Data Processing College: San Sebastian, PR
Fashion Institute of Technology, NY
Franklin University, OH
Globe Institute of Technology, NY
Globe University
  Woodbury, MN
Goldey-Beacom College, DE
Herzing University
  Atlanta, GA
  Birmingham, AL
  Brookfield, WI
  Kenosha, WI
  Madison, WI
  Toledo, OH
Hesser College, NH
Hickey College, MO
Hodges University, FL
Humphreys College, CA
Husson University, ME
Huston-Tillotson University, TX
Indiana Institute of Technology, IN

Instituto Tecnologico Autonomo de Mexico, MX
Instituto Tecnologico y de Estudios Superiores de Occidente, MX
International Business College, IN
Iona College, NY
ITT Technical Institute
  Owings Mills, MD
  Tulsa, OK
Jones College, FL
King's College, PA
LA College International, CA
Lasell College, MA
Lexington College, IL
Lincoln University, CA
Mayville State University, ND
Menlo College, CA
Metropolitan College of New York, NY
Michigan Jewish Institute, MI
Midstate College, IL
Millsaps College, MS
Minnesota School of Business
  Blaine, MN
  Plymouth, MN
  Richfield, MN
  Shakopee, MN
Missouri Western State University, MO
Monroe College, NY
Morrison University, NV
Mount Ida College, MA
Mount Olive College, NC
Mt. Sierra College, CA
National American University
  Bloomington, MN
  Rapid City, SD
  Rio Rancho, NM
National College
  Salem, VA
Newbury College, MA
Nichols College, MA
Northwestern Polytechnic University, CA
Northwood University
  Florida, FL
  Michigan, MI
  Texas, TX
Parsons Paris School of Design, FR
Peirce College, PA
Pittsburg State University, KS
Post University, CT
Potomac College, VA
Potomac College, DC
Presentation College, SD
Restaurant School at Walnut Hill College, PA
Rockhurst University, MO
Sage College of Albany, NY
Sanford-Brown College
  Milwaukee, WI
  Vienna, VA
Savannah State University, GA
Silicon Valley University, CA
Southeastern Baptist College, MS
Southern California Institute of Technology, CA
Stevens-Henager College
  Logan, UT
  Murray, UT
SUNY
  College at Old Westbury, NY
  Institute of Technology at Utica/Rome, NY
Thomas College, ME
University of Phoenix
  Indianapolis, IN
  West Michigan, MI
University of the West, CA
Virginia College
  Huntsville, AL

Walsh College of Accountancy and Business Administration, MI
Webber International University, FL
Western International University, AZ
Westwood College
  Inland Empire, CA

Two-year

AIB College of Business, IA
Berks Technical Institute, PA
Bidwell Training Center, PA
Bradford School, OH
Brown Mackie College
  Akron, OH
  Atlanta, GA
  Cincinnati, OH
  Findlay, OH
  Fort Wayne, IN
  Hopkinsville, KY
  Merrillville, IN
  Miami, FL
  North Kentucky, KY
Bryant & Stratton College
  Albany, NY
  Amherst, NY
  Buffalo, NY
  Henrietta, NY
  Milwaukee, WI
  Rochester, NY
  Southtowns, NY
  Syracuse, NY
  Virginia Beach, VA
Business Informatics Center, NY
Cambria-Rowe Business College, PA
Cambria-Rowe Business College: Indiana, PA
City College
  Gainesville, FL
  Miami, FL
College of Business and Technology: Hialeah, FL
College of Court Reporting, IN
College of Westchester, NY
Columbia Centro Universitario: Yauco, PR
Concorde Career College
  Kansas City, MO
Daymar College
  Chillicothe, OH
  Louisville, KY
  Owensboro, KY
Daymar Institute: Clarksville, TN
Delta School of Business & Technology, LA
Douglas Education Center, PA
DuBois Business College, PA
DuBois Business College
  Huntingdon, PA
  Oil City, PA
Duluth Business University, MN
Eagle Gate College: Murray, UT
Elmira Business Institute, NY
Elmira Business Institute: Vestal, NY
Empire College, CA
Erie Business Center, PA
Erie Business Center South, PA
Fashion Careers College, CA
Fashion Institute of Design and Merchandising
  Los Angeles, CA
  San Diego, CA
  San Francisco, CA
Fisher College, MA
Florida Career College: Miami, FL
Florida Career College: Pembroke Pines, FL
Florida Technical College
  Lakeland, FL

Forrest Junior College, SC
Fortis College
  Orange Park, FL
  Ravenna, OH
Fortis Institute
  Erie, PA
Gallipolis Career College, OH
Harrison College
  Anderson, IN
Herzing University
  Winter Park, FL
Humacao Community College, PR
ICPR Junior College, PR
International Business College: Indianapolis, IN
ITT Technical Institute
  Canton, MI
  Hilliard, OH
  Kansas City, MO
  Kennesaw, GA
  Newburgh, IN
Jamestown Business College, NY
Kaplan Career Institute: Pittsburgh, PA
Kaplan College: Hammond, IN
Kaplan College: Sacramento, CA
Kaplan College: San Diego, CA
Kaplan University
  Hagerstown, MD
  South Portland, ME
Keiser Career College: Greenacres, FL
Keiser Career College: Miami Lakes, FL
Key College, FL
Laurel Technical Institute, PA
LDS Business College, UT
Lincoln College of New England: Suffield, CT
Lincoln College of Technology Dayton, OH
Long Island Business Institute, NY
McCann School of Business and Technology
  Dickson City, PA
  Hazleton, PA
Metro Business College, MO
  Jefferson City, MO
  Rolla, MO
Miami-Jacobs Career College: Cincinnati, OH
Miller-Motte Technical College: Clarksville, TN
Minneapolis Business College, MN
MTI College, CA
National College
  Charlottesville, VA
  Danville, VA
  Danville, KY
  Dayton, OH
  Florence, KY
  Harrisonburg, VA
  Lexington, KY
  Louisville, KY
  Lynchburg, VA
  Martinsville, VA
  Pikeville, KY
  Princeton, WV
  Richmond, KY
National College of Business and Technology
  Bristol, TN
  Knoxville, TN
  Nashville, TN
New England College of Business and Finance, MA
Newport Business Institute: Lower Burrell, PA
Newport Business Institute: Williamsport, PA
Northwest Florida State College, FL

Ohio Business College, OH
Ohio Business College:
   Columbus, OH
Ohio Business College:
   Sandusky, OH
Olean Business Institute, NY
Penn Commercial Business and
   Technical School, PA
Pennsylvania Institute of Health
   and Technology, PA
Plaza College, NY
Prism Career Institute, PA
Professional Business College,
   NY
Remington College
   Memphis, TN
Sanford-Brown College, MO
South Coast College, CA
South Hills School of Business
   & Technology, PA
Southwestern College
   Lincoln College of
      Technology: Vine Street
      Campus, OH
Stenotype Institute: Jacksonville,
   FL
Stevens Institute of Business &
   Arts, MO
Taylor Business Institute, IL
Trumbull Business College, OH
University of Northwestern
   Ohio, OH
Utica School of Commerce, NY
Valley College, WV
Virginia College
   Austin, TX
   Greenville, SC
   Gulf Coast, MS
   Pensacola, FL
   School of Business and
      Health, TN
Virginia Marti College of Art
   and Design, OH
West Virginia Business College:
   Nutter Fort, WV
West Virginia Business College:
   Wheeling, WV
Yorktowne Business Institute,
   PA

Culinary schools

Four-year

Art Institute of Atlanta, GA
Art Institute of California:
   Hollywood, CA
Art Institute of California:
   Inland Empire, CA
Art Institute of California:
   Orange County, CA
Art Institute of California:
   Sacramento, CA
Art Institute of California: San
   Francisco, CA
The Art Institute of Colorado,
   CO
Art Institute of Houston, TX
Art Institute of Las Vegas, NV
Art Institute of Phoenix, AZ
Art Institute of Pittsburgh, PA
Art Institute of Seattle, WA
Art Institute of Tucson, AZ
Art Institute of Washington, VA
Art Institutes International
   Minnesota, MN
Culinary Institute of America,
   NY
Kendall College, IL
Lexington College, IL
Restaurant School at Walnut
   Hill College, PA
Southern New Hampshire
   University, NH

Two-year

Art Institute of California:
   Sunnyvale, CA
Art Institute of New York City,
   NY
Art Institute of Ohio:
   Cincinnati, OH
Atlantic Cape Community
   College, NJ
California Culinary Academy,
   CA
Culinary Institute LeNotre, TX
Institute of Technology: Clovis,
   CA
Keystone Technical Institute,
   PA
L'Ecole Culinaire, MO
Le Cordon Bleu College of
   Culinary Arts
   Austin, TX
   Chicago, IL
   Los Angeles, CA
   Miami, FL
   Minneapolis-St. Paul, MN
   Orlando, FL
   Pittsburgh, PA
   Portland, OR
   Scottsdale, AZ
Lincoln College of New
   England: Suffield, CT
New England Culinary Institute,
   VT
Platt College
   Moore, OK
   Tulsa, OK
Southwestern Oregon
   Community College, OR
Virginia College
   Richmond, VA
   Savannah, GA
Walters State Community
   College, TN

Engineering colleges

Four-year

Capitol College, MD
Clemson University, SC
Cogswell Polytechnical College,
   CA
Colorado School of Mines, CO
Cooper Union for the
   Advancement of Science and
   Art, NY
Daniel Webster College, NH
DigiPen Institute of Technology,
   WA
Franklin W. Olin College of
   Engineering, MA
Harvey Mudd College, CA
Illinois Institute of Technology,
   IL
Indiana Institute of Technology,
   IN
Instituto Tecnologico Autonomo
   de Mexico, MX
Instituto Tecnologico y de
   Estudios Superiores de
   Occidente, MX
Inter American University of
   Puerto Rico
   Bayamon Campus, PR
Kettering University, MI
Lafayette College, PA
Lake Superior State University,
   MI
Manhattan College, NY
Massachusetts Maritime
   Academy, MA
Missouri Technical School, MO
Montana Tech of the University
   of Montana, MT
Neumont University, UT

New Mexico Institute of Mining
   and Technology, NM
Northwestern Polytechnic
   University, CA
Rose-Hulman Institute of
   Technology, IN
Silicon Valley University, CA
Southern California Institute of
   Technology, CA
Stevens Institute of Technology,
   NJ
SUNY
   Institute of Technology at
      Utica/Rome, NY
Trine University, IN
Union College, NY
United States Coast Guard
   Academy, CT
Universidad Politecnica de
   Puerto Rico, PR
University of Pittsburgh
   Johnstown, PA
University of Puerto Rico
   Mayaguez, PR
Vaughn College of Aeronautics
   and Technology, NY
Warsaw University of
   Technology, PL
Webb Institute, NY
Wentworth Institute of
   Technology, MA
West Virginia University
   Institute of Technology, WV

Maritime colleges

Four-year

California Maritime Academy,
   CA
Maine Maritime Academy, ME
Massachusetts Maritime
   Academy, MA
SUNY
   Maritime College, NY
United States Merchant Marine
   Academy, NY

Two-year

Northwest School of Wooden
   Boatbuilding, WA
Northwestern Michigan College,
   MI

Military colleges

Four-year

The Citadel, SC
North Georgia College & State
   University, GA
Norwich University, VT
United States Air Force
   Academy, CO
United States Coast Guard
   Academy, CT
United States Merchant Marine
   Academy, NY
United States Military
   Academy, NY
United States Naval Academy,
   MD
Virginia Military Institute, VA

Two-year

Georgia Military College, GA
Marion Military Institute, AL
New Mexico Military Institute,
   NM
Valley Forge Military Academy
   and College, PA
Wentworth Military Junior
   College, MO

Nursing and health science colleges

Four-year

Albany College of Pharmacy
   and Health Sciences, NY
Allen College, IA
Aquinas College, TN
Baker College
   of Allen Park, MI
   of Cadillac, MI
Baptist College of Health
   Sciences, TN
Bastyr University, WA
Beckfield College, KY
Bellin College, WI
Blessing-Rieman College of
   Nursing, IL
Bloomfield College, NJ
BryanLGH College of Health
   Sciences, NE
Bryant & Stratton College
   Parma, OH
Cabarrus College of Health
   Sciences, NC
California College San Diego,
   CA
Chamberlain College of Nursing
   Addison, IL
   Chicago, IL
   Columbus, OH
   Jacksonville, FL
   Phoenix, AZ
   St. Louis, MO
Chamberlain College Of
   Nursing
   Miramar, FL
Charles Drew University of
   Medicine and Science, CA
Clarkson College, NE
Coe College, IA
College of New Rochelle, NY
CollegeAmerica
   Fort Collins, CO
Columbia College of Nursing,
   WI
Cox College, MO
Curry College, MA
D'Youville College, NY
Denver School of Nursing, CO
Dominican College of Blauvelt,
   NY
ECPI University, VA
Electronic Data Processing
   College: San Sebastian, PR
Florida Hospital College of
   Health Sciences, FL
Globe University
   Woodbury, MN
Goldfarb School of Nursing at
   Barnes-Jewish College, MO
Gwynedd-Mercy College, PA
Herzing University
   Omaha School of Massage
      Therapy and Healthcare,
      NE
Husson University, ME
Independence University, UT
Ithaca College, NY
Jefferson College of Health
   Sciences, VA
Kettering College of Medical
   Arts, OH
King College, TN
Lakeview College of Nursing,
   IL
Loma Linda University, CA
Louisiana State University
   Health Sciences Center, LA
Massachusetts College of
   Pharmacy and Health
   Sciences, MA
Medcenter One College of
   Nursing, ND
Mercy College of Health
   Sciences, IA

Mercy College of Ohio, OH
Misericordia University, PA
Monroe College, NY
Mount Carmel College of
   Nursing, OH
Mount Marty College, SD
Mountain State University, WV
National American University
   Bloomington, MN
National University of Health
   Sciences, IL
Nebraska Methodist College of
   Nursing and Allied Health,
   NE
New York Institute of
   Technology, NY
Northwestern Health Sciences
   University, MN
Oregon Health & Science
   University, OR
Our Lady of the Lake College,
   LA
Platt College
   Aurora, CO
Presentation College, SD
Regis College, MA
Research College of Nursing,
   MO
Resurrection University, IL
Rivier College, NH
Rush University, IL
Russell Sage College, NY
Saint Anselm College, NH
Saint Anthony College of
   Nursing, IL
St. Catharine College, KY
St. Catherine University, MN
St. Francis Medical Center
   College of Nursing, IL
St. John's College, IL
St. Luke's College, MO
Samuel Merritt University, CA
Sanford-Brown College
   Milwaukee, WI
Simmons College, MA
Springfield College, MA
Stevens-Henager College
   Logan, UT
   Murray, UT
   Orem, UT
SUNY
   Downstate Medical Center,
      NY
   Upstate Medical University,
      NY
Texas A&M University
   Baylor College of Dentistry,
      TX
Thomas Jefferson University:
   College of Health
   Professions, PA
Trinity College of Nursing and
   Health Sciences, IL
University of Arkansas
   for Medical Sciences, AR
University of Findlay, OH
University of Kansas Medical
   Center, KS
University of Maryland
   Baltimore, MD
University of Medicine and
   Dentistry of New Jersey
   School of Health Related
      Professions, NJ
   School of Nursing, NJ
University of Minnesota
   Rochester, MN
University of Mississippi
   Medical Center, MS
University of Nebraska
   Medical Center, NE
University of Phoenix
   Central Florida, FL
   North Florida, FL
   West Florida, FL
University of Tennessee
   Health Science Center, TN

University of Texas
  Health Science Center at
    Houston, TX
  Health Science Center at
    San Antonio, TX
  Medical Branch at
    Galveston, TX
University of the Sciences in
  Philadelphia, PA
Vermont Technical College, VT
West Coast University, CA
Winston-Salem State University,
  NC

Two-year

Anthem College
  Atlanta, GA
  Orlando, FL
ATI College of Health, FL
ATS Institute of Technology,
  OH
Aultman College of Nursing and
  Health Sciences, OH
Bainbridge College, GA
Bidwell Training Center, PA
Boulder College of Massage
  Therapy, CO
Brown Mackie College
  Atlanta, GA
  Cincinnati, OH
  North Kentucky, KY
Bryman School of Arizona, AZ
Careers Unlimited, UT
Carolinas College of Health
  Sciences, NC
Carrington College
  Citrus Heights, CA
  Pleasant Hill, CA
  Reno, NV
  Sacramento, CA
  San Leandro, CA
Central Maine Medical Center
  College of Nursing and
  Health Professions, ME
Centro de Estudios
  Multidisciplinarios, PR
City College
  Gainesville, FL
  Miami, FL
Cochran School of Nursing, NY
Colorado Technical University
  North Kansas City, MO
Columbia Centro Universitario:
  Yauco, PR
Concorde Career College
  Aurora, CO
  Garden Grove, CA
  Kansas City, MO
  North Hollywood, CA
  San Diego, CA
Dakota College at Bottineau,
  ND
Eastern International College,
  NJ
EDIC College, PR
Florida College of Natural
  Health
  Bradenton, FL
  Maitland, FL
Florida Keys Community
  College, FL
Fortis College
  Cuyahoga, OH
  Orange Park, FL
Good Samaritan College of
  Nursing and Health Science,
  OH
Goodwin College, CT
Harrison College
  Anderson, IN
Helene Fuld College of Nursing,
  NY
Herzing University
  Winter Park, FL
Hondros College, OH
Huntington College of Health
  Sciences, TN

Jefferson Davis Community
  College, AL
Kaplan Career Institute:
  Harrisburg, PA
Kaplan Career Institute:
  Pittsburgh, PA
Kaplan College: Indianapolis,
  IN
Kaplan College: Palm Springs,
  CA
Kaplan College: Salida, CA
Kaplan College: San Diego, CA
Keiser Career College:
  Greenacres, FL
Keiser Career College: Miami
  Lakes, FL
Keiser University, FL
Laboure College, MA
Lebanon College, NH
Lincoln College of Technology
  Florence, KY
Los Angeles County College of
  Nursing and Allied Health,
  CA
Maria College, NY
Metro Business College
  Jefferson City, MO
Miller-Motte Technical College:
  Clarksville, TN
Miller-Motte Technical College:
  Conway, SC
Myotherapy Institute, NE
Ohio Business College:
  Columbus, OH
Ohio College of Massotherapy,
  OH
Pacific College of Oriental
  Medicine: San Diego, CA
Phillips Beth Israel School of
  Nursing, NY
Platt College
  Moore, OK
  Tulsa, OK
Ponce Paramedical College, PR
Remington College
  North Houston, TX
St. Elizabeth College of
  Nursing, NY
St. Joseph's College of Nursing,
  NY
St. Luke's College, IA
St. Vincent's College, CT
Sanford-Brown College, MO
  Houston, TX
Sanford-Brown Institute
  Jacksonville, FL
  Monroeville, PA
  Tampa, FL
South College, NC
Southeast Missouri Hospital
  College of Nursing and
  Health Sciences, MO
Southwestern College
  Lincoln College of
    Technology: Vine Street
    Campus, OH
State College of Florida,
  Manatee-Sarasota, FL
Swedish Institute, NY
Texas County Technical
  Institute, MO
Universal Technology College
  of Puerto Rico, PR
University of Rochester School
  of Nursing, NY
Vatterott College
  Des Moines, IA
Vet Tech Institute, PA
Virginia College
  Augusta, GA
  Austin, TX
  Baton Rouge, LA
  Charleston, SC
  Columbia, SC
  Columbus, GA
  Gulf Coast, MS
  Macon, GA
  Montgomery, AL
  Pensacola, FL
  Tulsa, OK

Wallace State Community
  College at Hanceville, AL
West Virginia Junior College:
  Bridgeport, WV
Westwood College
  Fort Worth, TX
Yorktowne Business Institute,
  PA

Schools of mortuary science

Two-year

American Academy McAllister
  Institute of Funeral Service,
  NY
Cincinnati College of Mortuary
  Science, OH
Commonwealth Institute of
  Funeral Service, TX
Dallas Institute of Funeral
  Service, TX
John A. Gupton College, TN
Mid-America College of Funeral
  Service, IN

Seminary/rabbinical colleges

Four-year

Austin Graduate School of
  Theology, TX
Baptist Bible College, MO
Baptist Missionary Association
  Theological Seminary, TX
Beis Medrash Heichal Dovid,
  NY
Beth Hamedrash Shaarei Yosher
  Institute, NY
Beth Hatalmud Rabbinical
  College, NY
Beth Medrash Govoha, NJ
Calvary Bible College and
  Theological Seminary, MO
Central Yeshiva Tomchei
  Tmimim-Lubavitch, NY
Conception Seminary College,
  MO
Criswell College, TX
Divine Word College, IA
Earlham College, IN
Erskine College, SC
Faith Baptist Bible College and
  Theological Seminary, IA
Faith Evangelical Seminary,
  WA
George Fox University, OR
Global University, MO
Hebrew Theological College, IL
Hellenic College/Holy Cross,
  MA
Holy Apostles College and
  Seminary, CT
Holy Trinity Orthodox
  Seminary, NY
International Baptist College,
  AZ
Jewish Theological Seminary of
  America, NY
Kehilath Yakov Rabbinical
  Seminary, NY
The King's University, CA
Luther Rice University, GA
Machzikei Hadath Rabbinical
  College, NY
The Master's College, CA
Mesivta Torah Vodaath
  Seminary, NY
Midwest University, MO
Mirrer Yeshiva Central Institute,
  NY
Moody Bible Institute, IL

Mount Angel Seminary, OR
Multnomah University, OR
Ner Israel Rabbinical College,
  MD
New Orleans Baptist
  Theological Seminary:
  Leavell College, LA
Ohr Somayach Tanenbaum
  Education Center, NY
Piedmont International
  University, NC
Pontifical College Josephinum,
  OH
Rabbi Jacob Joseph School, NJ
Rabbinical Academy Mesivta
  Rabbi Chaim Berlin, NY
Rabbinical College Beth Shraga,
  NY
Rabbinical College Bobover
  Yeshiva B'nei Zion, NY
Rabbinical College Ch'san Sofer
  of New York, NY
Rabbinical College of America,
  NJ
Rabbinical College of Long
  Island, NY
Rabbinical College of Ohr
  Shimon Yisroel, NY
Rabbinical College of Telshe,
  OH
Rabbinical Seminary of
  America, NY
Sacred Heart Major Seminary,
  MI
St. Charles Borromeo Seminary
  - Overbrook, PA
St. John Vianney College
  Seminary, FL
St. Joseph Seminary College,
  LA
Shasta Bible College and
  Graduate School, CA
Shor Yoshuv Rabbinical
  College, NY
Southeastern Baptist Theological
  Seminary, NC
Southern California Seminary,
  CA
Southwestern Baptist
  Theological Seminary, TX
Talmudic College of Florida, FL
Talmudical Academy of New
  Jersey, NJ
Talmudical Institute of Upstate
  New York, NY
Talmudical Seminary Oholei
  Torah, NY
Talmudical Yeshiva of
  Philadelphia, PA
Telshe Yeshiva-Chicago, IL
Tennessee Temple University,
  TN
Theological University of the
  Caribbean, PR
Torah Temimah Talmudical
  Seminary, NY
U.T.A. Mesivta-Kiryas Jocl, NY
United Talmudical Seminary,
  NY
University of Dubuque, IA
Virginia University of
  Lynchburg, VA
Washington Bible College, MD
World Mission University, CA
Yeshiva and Kolel Bais
  Medrash Elyon, NY
Yeshiva and Kollel Harbotzas
  Torah, NY
Yeshiva Beth Yehuda-Yeshiva
  Gedolah of Greater Detroit,
  MI
Yeshiva College of the Nations
  Capital, MD
Yeshiva D'Monsey Rabbinical
  College, NY
Yeshiva Derech Chaim, NY

Yeshiva Gedolah Imrei Yosef
  D'Spinka, NY
Yeshiva Gedolah Rabbinical
  College, FL
Yeshiva Gedolah Zichron
  Moshe, NY
Yeshiva Karlin Stolin, NY
Yeshiva of Nitra, NY
Yeshiva of the Telshe Alumni,
  NY
Yeshiva Ohr Elchonon Chabad/
  West Coast Talmudical
  Seminary, CA
Yeshiva Shaar Hatorah, NY
Yeshiva Shaarei Torah of
  Rockland, NY
Yeshivas Novominsk, NY
Yeshivat Mikdash Melech, NY
Yeshivath Beth Moshe, PA
Yeshivath Viznitz, NY

Two-year

Salvation Army College for
  Officer Training at
  Crestmont, CA
Shepherds Theological
  Seminary, NC

Teacher's colleges

Four-year

American Indian College of the
  Assemblies of God, AZ
Arlington Baptist College, TX
Athens State University, AL
Augusta State University, GA
Austin College, TX
Baker University, KS
Baptist Bible College of
  Pennsylvania, PA
Baptist College of Florida, FL
Black Hills State University, SD
Bluefield College, VA
Bridgewater State University,
  MA
California State University
  Monterey Bay, CA
Cambridge College, MA
Canisius College, NY
City University of New York
  Queens College, NY
Clarion University of
  Pennsylvania, PA
College of St. Joseph in
  Vermont, VT
College of Saint Rose, NY
Concordia University, OR
Concordia University, MI
Dalton State College, GA
Eastern Illinois University, IL
Emmanuel College, GA
Fitchburg State University, MA
Florida Christian College, FL
Fort Valley State University,
  GA
Framingham State University,
  MA
Free Will Baptist Bible College,
  TN
Frostburg State University, MD
Glenville State College, WV
Great Basin College, NV
Heritage University, WA
Howard Payne University, TX
Jarvis Christian College, TX
Jones College, FL
Keene State College, NH
Kendall College, IL
Lander University, SC
Laura and Alvin Siegal College
  of Judaic Studies, OH
Lesley University, MA
Louisiana State University
  Shreveport, LA

Lyndon State College, VT
Macon State College, GA
Manhattanville College, NY
Mayville State University, ND
National-Louis University, IL
Nevada State College, NV
New England College, NH
Northwestern Oklahoma State University, OK
Oglala Lakota College, SD
Pacific Oaks College, CA
Peru State College, NE
Piedmont College, GA
Plymouth State University, NH
Rabbinical College of Long Island, NY
Rabbinical College of Telshe, OH
Rasmussen College
    Mokena/Tinley Park, IL
Reinhardt University, GA
Rust College, MS
St. Joseph's College, New York, NY
St. Joseph's College: Suffolk Campus, NY
Southeastern Oklahoma State University, OK
Southeastern University, FL
SUNY
    College at Buffalo, NY
    College at Cortland, NY
    College at Plattsburgh, NY
    College at Potsdam, NY
Tennessee Wesleyan College, TN
Trinity Baptist College, FL
Union College, KY
University of Hawaii
    West Oahu, HI
University of Maine
    Farmington, ME
University of Mary Washington, VA
University of Montana:
    Western, MT
University of the Southwest, NM
Valley City State University, ND
VanderCook College of Music, IL
Virginia Intermont College, VA
Wayne State College, NE
West Virginia State University, WV
Western Oregon University, OR
Wheelock College, MA
William Woods University, MO
Worcester State University, MA
York College, NE

Two-year

Gordon College, GA

Technical and career colleges

Four-year

Art Institute of Fort Lauderdale, FL
Baker College
    of Auburn Hills, MI
    of Clinton Township, MI
    of Flint, MI
    of Jackson, MI
    of Muskegon, MI
    of Owosso, MI
    of Port Huron, MI
Bluefield State College, WV
Briarcliffe College, NY
Carrington College
    Emeryville, CA

Central Pennsylvania College, PA
Charter College, AK
City College
    Fort Lauderdale, FL
City University of New York
    New York City College of Technology, NY
Clayton State University, GA
Coleman University, CA
CollegeAmerica
    Fort Collins, CO
Collins College, AZ
Colorado Technical University, CO
Columbia Centro Universitario:
    Caguas, PR
DeVry College of New York
    Midtown Campus, NY
ECPI University, VA
Electronic Data Processing College of Puerto Rico, PR
Ex'pression College for Digital Arts, CA
Florida Career College: Boynton Beach, FL
Florida Career College:
    Jacksonville, FL
Florida Career College:
    Lauderdale Lakes, FL
Florida Career College:
    Riverview, FL
Hamilton Technical College, IA
Herzing University
    Atlanta, GA
    Birmingham, AL
    Brookfield, WI
    Kenner, LA
    Kenosha, WI
    Toledo, OH
Hickey College, MO
International Academy of Design and Technology
    Chicago, IL
    Detroit, MI
    Henderson, NV
    Sacramento, CA
International Academy of Design and Technology:
    Tampa, FL

ITT Technical Institute
    Albuquerque, NM
    Arnold, MO
    Birmingham, AL
    Boise, ID
    Chantilly, VA
    Duluth, GA
    Earth City, MO
    Everett, WA
    Fort Wayne, IN
    Ft. Lauderdale, FL
    Green Bay, WI
    Greenfield, WI
    Greenville, SC
    Henderson, NV
    Indianapolis, IN
    Jacksonville, FL
    Knoxville, TN
    Lake Mary, FL
    Lathrop, CA
    Little Rock, AR
    Louisville, KY
    Memphis, TN
    Miami, FL
    Mount Prospect, IL
    Murray, UT
    Nashville, TN
    Norfolk, VA
    Omaha, NE
    Owings Mills, MD
    Oxnard, CA
    Portland, OR
    Rancho Cordova, CA
    Richmond, VA
    St. Rose, LA
    San Bernardino, CA
    San Diego, CA
    Seattle, WA
    Spokane, WA
    Springfield, VA
    Sylmar, CA
    Tampa, FL
    Tempe, AZ
    Torrance, CA
    Tucson, AZ
    Tulsa, OK
    Westminster, CO
LA College International, CA
Lewis-Clark State College, ID
Miller-Motte College:
    Wilmington, NC
Minnesota School of Business
    Plymouth, MN
    Richfield, MN
    Shakopee, MN
Missouri Technical School, MO
Montana State University
    Billings, MT
Montana Tech of the University of Montana, MT
National American University
    Rapid City, SD
Neumont University, UT
New England Institute of Art, MA
New England Institute of Technology, RI
Peirce College, PA
Pennsylvania College of Technology, PA
Platt College
    Ontario, CA
    San Diego, CA
Rasmussen College
    Fort Myers, FL
    Lake Elmo/Woodbury, MN
    Mokena/Tinley Park, IL
Remington College
    Tampa, FL
Sanford-Brown College
    Vienna, VA
Spartan College of Aeronautics and Technology, OK
Stanbridge College, CA
Stevens-Henager College
    Logan, UT

SUNY
    Farmingdale State College, NY
University of Arkansas
    Monticello, AR
University of Puerto Rico
    Aguadilla, PR
    Bayamon University College, PR
Utah Valley University, UT
Vermont Technical College, VT
Virginia College
    Birmingham, AL
    Huntsville, AL
Warsaw University of Technology, PL
Wentworth Institute of Technology, MA
Westwood College
    Anaheim, CA
    Atlanta Midtown, GA
    Chicago Loop, IL
    Denver North, CO
    Denver South, CO
    DuPage, IL
    Inland Empire, CA
    Northlake, GA
    O'Hare Airport, IL
    South Bay, CA
World College, VA

Two-year

Advanced Technology Institute, VA
Aiken Technical College, SC
Albany Technical College, GA
Alexandria Technical and Community College, MN
Altamaha Technical College, GA
Anoka Technical College, MN
Antelope Valley College, CA
Anthem Career College
    Nashville, TN
Anthem College
    Aurora, CO
    Kansas City, MO
    Minneapolis, MN
    Orlando, FL
    Phoenix, AZ
Antonelli College
    Cincinnati, OH
    Hattiesburg, MS
    Jackson, MS
Arizona Automotive Institute, AZ
Arkansas State University
    Mountain Home, AR
Art Institute of California:
    Sunnyvale, CA
Art Institute of New York City, NY
Art Institute of York, PA
ASA Institute of Business and Computer Technology, NY
Asheville-Buncombe Technical Community College, NC
Asnuntuck Community College, CT
Athens Technical College, GA
ATI Career Training Center
    Dallas, TX
    Ft. Lauderdale, FL
    Oakland Park, FL
ATI College of Health, FL
Atlanta Technical College, GA
ATS Institute of Technology, OH
Augusta Technical College, GA
Aviation Institute of Maintenance: Virginia Beach, VA
Bates Technical College, WA
Baton Rouge School of Computers, LA
Bel-Rea Institute of Animal Technology, CO

Bellingham Technical College, WA
Belmont Technical College, OH
Benjamin Franklin Institute of Technology, MA
Berks Technical Institute, PA
Big Sandy Community and Technical College, KY
Black River Technical College, AR
Blackhawk Technical College, WI
Blue Cliff College
    Metairie, LA
    Shreveport, LA
Blue Ridge Community and Technical College, WV
Blue Ridge Community College, NC
Bluegrass Community and Technical College, KY
Bolivar Technical College, MO
Bradford School, OH
Bramson ORT College, NY
Bridgemont Community and Technical College, WV
Broadview University
    West Jordan, UT
Brown Mackie College
    Louisville, KY
    South Bend, IN
Bryan College
    Sacramento, CA
    Topeka, KS
Bryant & Stratton College
    Cleveland, OH
Caldwell Community College and Technical Institute, NC
Capital Community College, CT
Carrington College
    Antioch, CA
    Citrus Heights, CA
    Pleasant Hill, CA
    Sacramento, CA
    San Jose, CA
    San Leandro, CA
    Stockton, CA
Carteret Community College, NC
Central Carolina Technical College, SC
Central Community College, NE
Central Georgia Technical College, GA
Central Lakes College, MN
Central Maine Community College, ME
Central New Mexico Community College, NM
Central Ohio Technical College, OH
Central Texas College, TX
Century College, MN
Chattahoochee Technical College, GA
Chattanooga College, TN
Chattanooga State Community College, TN
CHI Institute: Franklin Mills, PA
Chippewa Valley Technical College, WI
Cincinnati State Technical and Community College, OH
Cleveland Institute of Electronics, OH
Clover Park Technical College, WA
Coffeyville Community College, KS
Colegio de Cinematografía, Artes y Televisión, PR
Coleman College: San Marcos, CA
College of Business and Technology
    Cutler Bay, FL

Tables and Indexes

Special characteristics

Colleges for men

Four-year

Beis Medrash Heichal Dovid, NY
Beth Hamedrash Shaarei Yosher Institute, NY
Beth Hatalmud Rabbinical College, NY
Beth Medrash Govoha, NJ
Central Yeshiva Tomchei Tmimim-Lubavitch, NY
Conception Seminary College, MO
Hampden-Sydney College, VA
Holy Trinity Orthodox Seminary, NY
Kehilath Yakov Rabbinical Seminary, NY
Machzikei Hadath Rabbinical College, NY
Mesivta Torah Vodaath Seminary, NY
Mirrer Yeshiva Central Institute, NY
Morehouse College, GA
Mount Angel Seminary, OR
Ner Israel Rabbinical College, MD
Ohr Somayach Tanenbaum Education Center, NY
Pontifical College Josephinum, OH
Rabbinical Academy Mesivta Rabbi Chaim Berlin, NY
Rabbinical College Beth Shraga, NY
Rabbinical College Bobover Yeshiva B'nei Zion, NY
Rabbinical College Ch'san Sofer of New York, NY
Rabbinical College of America, NJ
Rabbinical College of Long Island, NY
Rabbinical College of Ohr Shimon Yisroel, NY
Rabbinical College of Telshe, OH
Rabbinical Seminary of America, NY
St. Charles Borromeo Seminary - Overbrook, PA
St. John Vianney College Seminary, FL
St. John's University, MN
St. Joseph Seminary College, LA
Shor Yoshuv Rabbinical College, NY
Talmudic College of Florida, FL
Talmudical Academy of New Jersey, NJ
Talmudical Institute of Upstate New York, NY
Talmudical Seminary Oholei Torah, NY
Talmudical Yeshiva of Philadelphia, PA
Telshe Yeshiva-Chicago, IL
Torah Temimah Talmudical Seminary, NY
U.T.A. Mesivta-Kiryas Jocl, NY
United Talmudical Seminary, NY
Wabash College, IN

Yeshiva and Kolel Bais Medrash Elyon, NY
Yeshiva and Kollel Harbotzas Torah, NY
Yeshiva Beth Yehuda-Yeshiva Gedolah of Greater Detroit, MI
Yeshiva College of the Nations Capital, MD
Yeshiva D'Monsey Rabbinical College, NY
Yeshiva Derech Chaim, NY
Yeshiva Gedolah Imrei Yosef D'Spinka, NY
Yeshiva Gedolah Rabbinical College, FL
Yeshiva Gedolah Zichron Moshe, NY
Yeshiva Karlin Stolin, NY
Yeshiva of Nitra, NY
Yeshiva of the Telshe Alumni, NY
Yeshiva Ohr Elchonon Chabad/West Coast Talmudical Seminary, CA
Yeshiva Shaar Hatorah, NY
Yeshiva Shaarei Torah of Rockland, NY
Yeshivas Novominsk, NY
Yeshivat Mikdash Melech, NY
Yeshivath Beth Moshe, PA
Yeshivath Viznitz, NY

Two-year

Deep Springs College, CA
Williamson Free School of Mechanical Trades, PA

Colleges for women

Four-year

Agnes Scott College, GA
Alverno College, WI
Barnard College, NY
Bay Path College, MA
Bennett College for Women, NC
Brenau University, GA
Bryn Mawr College, PA
Cedar Crest College, PA
Chatham University, PA
College of New Rochelle, NY
College of St. Benedict, MN
College of St. Elizabeth, NJ
College of Saint Mary, NE
Columbia College, SC
Converse College, SC
Georgian Court University, NJ
Hollins University, VA
Judson College, AL
Lexington College, IL
Mary Baldwin College, VA
Meredith College, NC
Midway College, KY
Mills College, CA
Moore College of Art and Design, PA
Mount Holyoke College, MA
Mount Mary College, WI
Mount St. Mary's College, CA
Notre Dame of Maryland University, MD
Pine Manor College, MA
Russell Sage College, NY
St. Catherine University, MN
Saint Joseph College, CT
Saint Mary's College, IN
St. Mary-of-the-Woods College, IN
Salem College, NC
Scripps College, CA
Simmons College, MA
Smith College, MA
Spelman College, GA

Stephens College, MO
Sweet Briar College, VA
Ursuline College, OH
Wellesley College, MA
Wesleyan College, GA
Wilson College, PA

Two-year

Assumption College for Sisters, NJ
Cottey College, MO

Affiliated with a religion

African Methodist Episcopal Church

Four-year

Allen University, SC
Edward Waters College, FL
Paul Quinn College, TX
Wilberforce University, OH

African Methodist Episcopal Zion Church

Four-year

Livingstone College, NC

American Baptist Churches in the USA

Four-year

Alderson-Broaddus College, WV
Arkansas Baptist College, AR
Bacone College, OK
Benedict College, SC
Eastern University, PA
Franklin College, IN
Judson University, IL
Keuka College, NY
Linfield College, OR
Ottawa University, KS
University of Sioux Falls, SD

Assemblies of God

Four-year

American Indian College of the Assemblies of God, AZ
Central Bible College, MO
Evangel University, MO
Global University, MO
North Central University, MN
Northwest University, WA
School of Urban Missions: Oakland, CA
Southeastern University, FL
Southwestern Assemblies of God University, TX
Trinity Bible College, ND
Valley Forge Christian College, PA
Vanguard University of Southern California, CA
Zion Bible College, MA

Baptist faith

Four-year

Arlington Baptist College, TX
Baptist Bible College, MO
Baptist Bible College of Pennsylvania, PA
Baptist Missionary Association Theological Seminary, TX
Baptist University of the Americas, TX
Baylor University, TX
Bluefield College, VA
Campbell University, NC
Campbellsville University, KY
Cedarville University, OH

Central Baptist College, AR
Corban University, OR
Dallas Baptist University, TX
East Texas Baptist University, TX
Georgetown College, KY
Hardin-Simmons University, TX
Houston Baptist University, TX
Howard Payne University, TX
International Baptist College, AZ
Judson College, AL
Liberty University, VA
Maranatha Baptist Bible College, WI
Mars Hill College, NC
Mercer University, GA
Missouri Baptist University, MO
Morris College, SC
Northland International University, WI
Ohio Mid-Western College, OH
Piedmont International University, NC
Selma University, AL
Shasta Bible College and Graduate School, CA
Shaw University, NC
Southeastern Baptist College, MS
University of Mary Hardin-Baylor, TX
University of Mobile, AL
University of the Cumberlands, KY
Virginia Intermont College, VA
Virginia Union University, VA

Two-year

Jacksonville College, TX

Baptist General Conference

Four-year

Bethel University, MN
Oakland City University, IN

Brethren Church

Four-year

Ashland University, OH
Emmaus Bible College, IA
Grace College, IN

Christian and Missionary Alliance

Four-year

Crown College, MN
Nyack College, NY
Simpson University, CA
Toccoa Falls College, GA

Christian Church

Four-year

Bethesda University of California, CA
Cincinnati Christian University, OH
Crossroads College, MN
Hope International University, CA
Johnson University, TN
Lincoln Christian University, IL
Manhattan Christian College, KS
Milligan College, TN
Patrick Henry College, VA
Point University, GA
St. Louis Christian College, MO
Visible Music College, TN

Two-year

Shepherds Theological Seminary, NC

Christian Church (Disciples of Christ)

Four-year

Barton College, NC
Bethany College, WV
Chapman University, CA
Columbia College, MO
Culver-Stockton College, MO
Eureka College, IL
Hiram College, OH
Jarvis Christian College, TX
Lynchburg College, VA
Midway College, KY
Northwest Christian University, OR
Texas Christian University, TX
Transylvania University, KY
William Woods University, MO

Christian Methodist Episcopal Church

Four-year

Lane College, TN
Miles College, AL
Paine College, GA
Texas College, TX

Christian Reformed Church

Four-year

Calvin College, MI
Dordt College, IA
Kuyper College, MI

Church of Christ

Four-year

Abilene Christian University, TX
Amridge University, AL
Austin Graduate School of Theology, TX
Faulkner University, AL
Freed-Hardeman University, TN
Harding University, AR
Heritage Christian University, AL
Kentucky Christian University, KY
Lipscomb University, TN
Lubbock Christian University, TX
Mid-Atlantic Christian University, NC
Ohio Valley University, WV
Oklahoma Christian University, OK
Pepperdine University, CA
Rochester College, MI
Southwestern Christian College, TX
York College, NE

Two-year

Crowley's Ridge College, AR

Church of God

Four-year

Anderson University, IN
Lee University, TN
Mid-America Christian University, OK
University of Findlay, OH
Warner Pacific College, OR
Warner University, FL

Church of Jesus Christ of Latter-day Saints

Four-year

Brigham Young University, UT
Brigham Young University-Hawaii, HI

Tables and Indexes

Brigham Young University-
Idaho, ID
Southern Virginia University,
VA

Two-year

LDS Business College, UT

Church of the Brethren

Four-year

Bridgewater College, VA
Elizabethtown College, PA
Manchester College, IN
McPherson College, KS

Church of the Nazarene

Four-year

Eastern Nazarene College, MA
MidAmerica Nazarene
University, KS
Mount Vernon Nazarene
University, OH
Nazarene Bible College, CO
Northwest Nazarene University,
ID
Olivet Nazarene University, IL
Point Loma Nazarene
University, CA
Southern Nazarene University,
OK
Trevecca Nazarene University,
TN

Cumberland Presbyterian Church

Four-year

Bethel University, TN

Episcopal Church

Four-year

Bard College, NY
Clarkson College, NE
St. Augustine College, IL
St. Augustine's College, NC
St. Luke's College, MO
St. Paul's College, VA
University of the South, TN
Voorhees College, SC

Evangelical Covenant Church of America

Four-year

North Park University, IL

Evangelical Free Church of America

Four-year

Trinity International University,
IL

Evangelical Lutheran Church in America

Four-year

Augustana College, IL
Augustana College, SD
Bethany College, KS
California Lutheran University,
CA
Capital University, OH
Carthage College, WI
Concordia College: Moorhead,
MN
Finlandia University, MI
Gettysburg College, PA
Grand View University, IA
Gustavus Adolphus College,
MN
Lenoir-Rhyne University, NC
Luther College, IA
Muhlenberg College, PA
Newberry College, SC

Pacific Lutheran University,
WA
Roanoke College, VA
St. Olaf College, MN
Susquehanna University, PA
Texas Lutheran University, TX
Thiel College, PA
Waldorf College, IA
Wartburg College, IA
Wittenberg University, OH

Evangelical Lutheran Synod

Four-year

Bethany Lutheran College, MN

Free Methodist Church of North America

Four-year

Central Christian College of
Kansas, KS
Greenville College, IL
Roberts Wesleyan College, NY
Seattle Pacific University, WA
Spring Arbor University, MI

Free Will Baptists

Four-year

California Christian College,
CA
Free Will Baptist Bible College,
TN
Mount Olive College, NC

General Association of Regular Baptist Churches

Four-year

Faith Baptist Bible College and
Theological Seminary, IA

interdenominational tradition

Four-year

Asbury University, KY
Azusa Pacific University, CA
Belmont University, TN
Beulah Heights University, GA
Biola University, CA
Bryan College, TN
College of the Ozarks, MO
Cornerstone University, MI
Ecclesia College, AR
Grace University, NE
Hobe Sound Bible College, FL
John Brown University, AR
Laurel University, NC
Messiah College, PA
Moody Bible Institute, IL
Multnomah University, OR
Oak Hills Christian College,
MN
Patten University, CA
Regent University, VA
Taylor University, IN
Trinity College of Florida, FL
Williamson Christian College,
TN

Jewish faith

Four-year

American Jewish University,
CA
Beis Medrash Heichal Dovid,
NY
Beth Hamedrash Shaarei Yosher
Institute, NY
Beth Hatalmud Rabbinical
College, NY
Beth Medrash Govoha, NJ

Central Yeshiva Tomchei
Tmimim-Lubavitch, NY
Gratz College, PA
Hebrew Theological College, IL
Jewish Theological Seminary of
America, NY
Kehilath Yakov Rabbinical
Seminary, NY
Machzikei Hadath Rabbinical
College, NY
Mesivta Torah Vodaath
Seminary, NY
Mirrer Yeshiva Central Institute,
NY
Ner Israel Rabbinical College,
MD
Ohr Somayach Tanenbaum
Education Center, NY
Rabbinical Academy Mesivta
Rabbi Chaim Berlin, NY
Rabbinical College Beth Shraga,
NY
Rabbinical College Bobover
Yeshiva B'nei Zion, NY
Rabbinical College Ch'san Sofer
of New York, NY
Rabbinical College of America,
NJ
Rabbinical College of Long
Island, NY
Rabbinical College of Telshe,
OH
Rabbinical Seminary of
America, NY
Shor Yoshuv Rabbinical
College, NY
Talmudic College of Florida, FL
Talmudical Academy of New
Jersey, NJ
Talmudical Institute of Upstate
New York, NY
Talmudical Seminary Oholei
Torah, NY
Talmudical Yeshiva of
Philadelphia, PA
Telshe Yeshiva-Chicago, IL
Torah Temimah Talmudical
Seminary, NY
U.T.A. Mesivta-Kiryas Jocl, NY
United Talmudical Seminary,
NY
Yeshiva and Kolel Bais
Medrash Elyon, NY
Yeshiva and Kollel Harbotzas
Torah, NY
Yeshiva Beth Yehuda-Yeshiva
Gedolah of Greater Detroit,
MI
Yeshiva College of the Nations
Capital, MD
Yeshiva D'Monsey Rabbinical
College, NY
Yeshiva Derech Chaim, NY
Yeshiva Gedolah Imrei Yosef
D'Spinka, NY
Yeshiva Gedolah Rabbinical
College, FL
Yeshiva Gedolah Zichron
Moshe, NY
Yeshiva Karlin Stolin, NY
Yeshiva of Nitra, NY
Yeshiva of the Telshe Alumni,
NY
Yeshiva Ohr Elchonon Chabad/
West Coast Talmudical
Seminary, CA
Yeshiva Shaar Hatorah, NY
Yeshiva Shaarei Torah of
Rockland, NY
Yeshivas Novominsk, NY
Yeshivat Mikdash Melech, NY
Yeshivath Beth Moshe, PA

Two-year

Bramson ORT College, NY

Lutheran Church

Four-year

Trinity Lutheran College, WA
Valparaiso University, IN

Lutheran Church - Missouri Synod

Four-year

Concordia College, NY
Concordia University, CA
Concordia University, OR
Concordia University, MI
Concordia University, NE
Concordia University Chicago,
IL
Concordia University St. Paul,
MN
Concordia University Texas, TX
Concordia University
Wisconsin, WI

Lutheran Church in America

Four-year

Wagner College, NY

Mennonite Brethren Church

Four-year

Fresno Pacific University, CA
Tabor College, KS

Mennonite Church

Four-year

Bethel College, KS
Bluffton University, OH
Eastern Mennonite University,
VA
Goshen College, IN

Two-year

Hesston College, KS
Rosedale Bible College, OH

Missionary Church

Four-year

Bethel College, IN

Moravian Church in America

Four-year

Moravian College, PA
Salem College, NC

nondenominational tradition

Four-year

Alaska Bible College, AK
Amberton University, TX
Appalachian Bible College, WV
Arizona Christian University,
AZ
Bob Jones University, SC
Boise Bible College, ID
Calvary Bible College and
Theological Seminary, MO
Carolina Christian College, NC
Clearwater Christian College,
FL
Colorado Christian University,
CO
Dallas Christian College, TX
Davis College, NY
Friends University, KS
Gordon College, MA

Horizon College of San Diego,
CA
Kenyon College, OH
The King's College, NY
The King's University, CA
Lancaster Bible College, PA
LeTourneau University, TX
New Hope Christian College,
OR
Northwestern College, MN
Occidental College, CA
Oral Roberts University, OK
Palm Beach Atlantic University,
FL
San Diego Christian College,
CA
Southeastern Bible College, AL
Washington Bible College, MD
Westmont College, CA
Wheaton College, IL
William Jessup University, CA
World Mission University, CA

Two-year

Williamson Free School of
Mechanical Trades, PA

Pentecostal Holiness Church

Four-year

Emmanuel College, GA
Southwestern Christian
University, OK
Universidad Pentecostal Mizpa,
PR

Presbyterian Church (USA)

Four-year

Agnes Scott College, GA
Alma College, MI
Arcadia University, PA
Austin College, TX
Belhaven University, MS
Blackburn College, IL
Bloomfield College, NJ
Buena Vista University, IA
Carroll University, WI
Centre College, KY
Coe College, IA
Davidson College, NC
Davis and Elkins College, WV
Eckerd College, FL
Forman Christian College, PK
Grove City College, PA
Hampden-Sydney College, VA
Hanover College, IN
Hastings College, NE
Jamestown College, ND
King College, TN
Lees-McRae College, NC
Lindenwood University, MO
Lyon College, AR
Macalester College, MN
Mary Baldwin College, VA
Maryville College, TN
Millikin University, IL
Missouri Valley College, MO
Monmouth College, IL
Muskingum University, OH
Presbyterian College, SC
Queens University of Charlotte,
NC
Rhodes College, TN
Rocky Mountain College, MT
St. Andrews University, NC
Schreiner University, TX
Sterling College, KS
Stillman College, AL
Trinity University, TX
Tusculum College, TN
University of Dubuque, IA
University of Pikeville, KY
University of the Ozarks, AR
University of Tulsa, OK

Warren Wilson College, NC
Waynesburg University, PA
Westminster College, MO
Westminster College, PA
Whitworth University, WA
William Peace University, NC
Wilson College, PA

Reformed Church in America

Four-year

Central College, IA
Hope College, MI
Northwestern College, IA

Reformed Presbyterian Church of North America

Four-year

Geneva College, PA

Roman Catholic Church

Four-year

Albertus Magnus College, CT
Alvernia University, PA
Alverno College, WI
Anna Maria College, MA
Aquinas College, MI
Aquinas College, TN
Assumption College, MA
Ave Maria University, FL
Avila University, MO
Barry University, FL
Bayamon Central University, PR
Bellarmine University, KY
Belmont Abbey College, NC
Benedictine College, KS
Benedictine University, IL
Boston College, MA
Brescia University, KY
Briar Cliff University, IA
Cabrini College, PA
Caldwell College, NJ
Calumet College of St. Joseph, IN
Canisius College, NY
Cardinal Stritch University, WI
Carlow University, PA
Carroll College, MT
Catholic Distance University, VA
Catholic University of America, DC
Chaminade University of Honolulu, HI
Chestnut Hill College, PA
Christendom College, VA
Christian Brothers University, TN
Clarke University, IA
College of Mount St. Joseph, OH
College of Mount St. Vincent, NY
College of New Rochelle, NY
College of St. Benedict, MN
College of St. Elizabeth, NJ
College of St. Joseph in Vermont, VT
College of Saint Mary, NE
College of St. Mary Magdalen, NH
College of St. Scholastica, MN
College of Saint Thomas More, TX
College of the Holy Cross, MA
Conception Seminary College, MO
Creighton University, NE
DePaul University, IL
DeSales University, PA
Divine Word College, IA
Dominican University, IL

Duquesne University, PA
Edgewood College, WI
Elms College, MA
Emmanuel College, MA
Fairfield University, CT
Felician College, NJ
Fontbonne University, MO
Fordham University, NY
Franciscan University of Steubenville, OH
Gannon University, PA
Georgetown University, DC
Georgian Court University, NJ
Gonzaga University, WA
Gwynedd-Mercy College, PA
Hilbert College, NY
Holy Apostles College and Seminary, CT
Holy Cross College, IN
Holy Family University, PA
Holy Names University, CA
Immaculata University, PA
Instituto Tecnologico y de Estudios Superiores de Occidente, MX
Iona College, NY
John Carroll University, OH
King's College, PA
La Roche College, PA
La Salle University, PA
Le Moyne College, NY
Lewis University, IL
Lexington College, IL
Loras College, IA
Lourdes University, OH
Loyola Marymount University, CA
Loyola University Chicago, IL
Loyola University Maryland, MD
Loyola University New Orleans, LA
Madonna University, MI
Manhattan College, NY
Marian University, IN
Marian University, WI
Marquette University, WI
Marygrove College, MI
Marylhurst University, OR
Marymount University, VA
Marywood University, PA
Mercy College of Health Sciences, IA
Mercy College of Ohio, OH
Mercyhurst University, PA
Merrimack College, MA
Misericordia University, PA
Molloy College, NY
Mount Aloysius College, PA
Mount Angel Seminary, OR
Mount Carmel College of Nursing, OH
Mount Marty College, SD
Mount Mary College, WI
Mount Mercy University, IA
Mount Saint Mary College, NY
Mount St. Mary's College, CA
Mount St. Mary's University, MD
Neumann University, PA
Newman University, KS
Niagara University, NY
Notre Dame College, OH
Notre Dame de Namur University, CA
Notre Dame of Maryland University, MD
Ohio Dominican University, OH
Our Lady of Holy Cross College, LA
Our Lady of the Lake College, LA
Our Lady of the Lake University of San Antonio, TX
Pontifical Catholic University of Puerto Rico, PR

Pontifical College Josephinum, OH
Providence College, RI
Quincy University, IL
Regis College, MA
Regis University, CO
Resurrection University, IL
Rivier College, NH
Rockhurst University, MO
Rosemont College, PA
Sacred Heart Major Seminary, MI
Sacred Heart University, CT
St. Ambrose University, IA
Saint Anselm College, NH
Saint Anthony College of Nursing, IL
Saint Bonaventure University, NY
St. Catharine College, KY
St. Catherine University, MN
St. Charles Borromeo Seminary - Overbrook, PA
St. Edward's University, TX
St. Francis College, NY
St. Francis Medical Center College of Nursing, IL
St. Francis University, PA
St. Gregory's University, OK
St. John Fisher College, NY
St. John Vianney College Seminary, FL
St. John's College, IL
St. John's University, NY
St. John's University, MN
Saint Joseph College, CT
St. Joseph Seminary College, LA
Saint Joseph's College, IN
Saint Joseph's College of Maine, ME
Saint Joseph's University, PA
Saint Leo University, FL
Saint Louis University, MO
Saint Louis University: Madrid, ES
Saint Martin's University, WA
Saint Mary's College, IN
St. Mary's College of California, CA
St. Mary's University, TX
St. Mary's University of Minnesota, MN
St. Mary-of-the-Woods College, IN
St. Michael's College, VT
St. Norbert College, WI
Saint Peter's College, NJ
Saint Thomas University, FL
St. Vincent College, PA
Saint Xavier University, IL
Salve Regina University, RI
Santa Clara University, CA
Seattle University, WA
Seton Hall University, NJ
Seton Hill University, PA
Siena College, NY
Siena Heights University, MI
Silver Lake College of the Holy Family, WI
Spalding University, KY
Spring Hill College, AL
Stonehill College, MA
Thomas Aquinas College, CA
Thomas More College, KY
Thomas More College of Liberal Arts, NH
Trinity Washington University, DC
Universidad Anahuac, MX
University of Dallas, TX
University of Dayton, OH
University of Detroit Mercy, MI
University of Great Falls, MT
University of Mary, ND
University of Notre Dame, IN
University of Portland, OR

University of St. Francis, IN
University of St. Francis, IL
University of St. Mary, KS
University of St. Thomas, TX
University of St. Thomas, MN
University of San Diego, CA
University of San Francisco, CA
University of Scranton, PA
University of the Incarnate Word, TX
University of the Sacred Heart, PR
Ursuline College, OH
Villanova University, PA
Viterbo University, WI
Walsh University, OH
Wheeling Jesuit University, WV
Xavier University, OH
Xavier University of Louisiana, LA

Two-year

Ancilla College, IN
Assumption College for Sisters, NJ
Benedictine University at Springfield, IL
Chatfield College, OH
Donnelly College, KS
Good Samaritan College of Nursing and Health Science, OH
Laboure College, MA
Marian Court College, MA
Marymount College Palos Verdes California, CA
St. Elizabeth College of Nursing, NY
St. Joseph's College of Nursing, NY
Trocaire College, NY
Villa Maria College of Buffalo, NY

Seventh-day Adventists

Four-year

Andrews University, MI
Florida Hospital College of Health Sciences, FL
Kettering College of Medical Arts, OH
La Sierra University, CA
Loma Linda University, CA
Oakwood University, AL
Pacific Union College, CA
Southern Adventist University, TN
Southwestern Adventist University, TX
Union College, NE
Universidad Adventista de las Antillas, PR
Walla Walla University, WA
Washington Adventist University, MD

Society of Friends (Quaker)

Four-year

Barclay College, KS
Earlham College, IN
George Fox University, OR
Guilford College, NC
William Penn University, IA
Wilmington College, OH

Southern Baptist Convention

Four-year

Anderson University, SC
Baptist College of Florida, FL
Blue Mountain College, MS
Brewton-Parker College, GA

California Baptist University, CA
Carson-Newman College, TN
Charleston Southern University, SC
Chorter University Shorter University, GA
Chowan University, NC
Clear Creek Baptist Bible College, KY
Criswell College, TX
Gardner-Webb University, NC
Hannibal-LaGrange University, MO
Louisiana College, LA
Mid-Continent University, KY
Mississippi College, MS
New Orleans Baptist Theological Seminary: Leavell College, LA
North Greenville University, SC
Oklahoma Baptist University, OK
Ouachita Baptist University, AR
Samford University, AL
Southeastern Baptist Theological Seminary, NC
Southwest Baptist University, MO
Truett-McConnell College, GA
Union University, TN
Wayland Baptist University, TX
Williams Baptist College, AR

Ukrainian Catholic Church

Two-year

Manor College, PA

United Brethren in Christ

Four-year

Huntington University, IN

United Church of Christ

Four-year

Catawba College, NC
Chamberlain College of Nursing St. Louis, MO
Defiance College, OH
Doane College, NE
Drury University, MO
Elmhurst College, IL
Fisk University, TN
Heidelberg University, OH
Lakeland College, WI
LeMoyne-Owen College, TN
Northland College, WI
Olivet College, MI
Pacific University, OR
Piedmont College, GA
Talladega College, AL

United Methodist Church

Four-year

Adrian College, MI
Albion College, MI
Albright College, PA
Allegheny College, PA
American University, DC
Baker University, KS
Baldwin-Wallace College, OH
Bennett College for Women, NC
Bethune-Cookman University, FL
Birmingham-Southern College, AL
Brevard College, NC
BryanLGH College of Health Sciences, NE
Centenary College, NJ

Tables and Indexes

Centenary College of Louisiana, LA
Central Methodist University, MO
Claflin University, SC
Clark Atlanta University, GA
Columbia College, SC
Cornell College, IA
Dakota Wesleyan University, SD
DePauw University, IN
Drew University, NJ
Duke University, NC
Emory & Henry College, VA
Emory University, GA
Ferrum College, VA
Florida Southern College, FL
Green Mountain College, VT
Greensboro College, NC
Hamline University, MN
Hendrix College, AR
High Point University, NC
Huntingdon College, AL
Iowa Wesleyan College, IA
Kansas Wesleyan University, KS
Kentucky Wesleyan College, KY
LaGrange College, GA
Lebanon Valley College, PA
Lindsey Wilson College, KY
Lycoming College, PA
MacMurray College, IL
Martin Methodist College, TN
McKendree University, IL
McMurry University, TX
Methodist University, NC
Millsaps College, MS
Morningside College, IA
Nebraska Methodist College of Nursing and Allied Health, NE
Nebraska Wesleyan University, NE
North Carolina Wesleyan College, NC
North Central College, IL
Ohio Northern University, OH
Ohio Wesleyan University, OH
Oklahoma City University, OK
Otterbein University, OH
Pfeiffer University, NC
Philander Smith College, AR
Randolph College, VA
Randolph-Macon College, VA
Reinhardt University, GA
Rust College, MS
Shenandoah University, VA
Simpson College, IA
Southern Methodist University, TX
Southwestern College, KS
Southwestern University, TX
Tennessee Wesleyan College, TN
Texas Wesleyan University, TX
Union College, KY
University of Evansville, IN
University of Indianapolis, IN
University of Mount Union, OH
Virginia Wesleyan College, VA
Wesley College, DE
Wesleyan College, GA
West Virginia Wesleyan College, WV
Wiley College, TX
Willamette University, OR
Wofford College, SC

Two-year

Andrew College, GA
Lon Morris College, TX
Louisburg College, NC
Oxford College of Emory University, GA

Spartanburg Methodist College, SC
Young Harris College, GA

Wesleyan Church

Four-year

Houghton College, NY
Indiana Wesleyan University, IN
Oklahoma Wesleyan University, OK

Wisconsin Evangelical Lutheran Synod

Four-year

Martin Luther College, MN
Wisconsin Lutheran College, WI

Historically Black colleges

Four-year

Alabama Agricultural and Mechanical University, AL
Alabama State University, AL
Albany State University, GA
Alcorn State University, MS
Allen University, SC
Arkansas Baptist College, AR
Benedict College, SC
Bennett College for Women, NC
Bluefield State College, WV
Bowie State University, MD
Central State University, OH
Cheyney University of Pennsylvania, PA
Claflin University, SC
Clark Atlanta University, GA
Coppin State University, MD
Delaware State University, DE
Dillard University, LA
Edward Waters College, FL
Elizabeth City State University, NC
Fisk University, TN
Florida Agricultural and Mechanical University, FL
Fort Valley State University, GA
Grambling State University, LA
Hampton University, VA
Harris-Stowe State University, MO
Howard University, DC
Huston-Tillotson University, TX
Jackson State University, MS
Jarvis Christian College, TX
Johnson C. Smith University, NC
Kentucky State University, KY
Lane College, TN
Langston University, OK
LeMoyne-Owen College, TN
Lincoln University, MO
Livingstone College, NC
Miles College, AL
Mississippi Valley State University, MS
Morehouse College, GA
Morgan State University, MD
Morris College, SC
Norfolk State University, VA
North Carolina Agricultural and Technical State University, NC
North Carolina Central University, NC
Oakwood University, AL
Paine College, GA
Paul Quinn College, TX

Philander Smith College, AR
Prairie View A&M University, TX
Rust College, MS
St. Augustine's College, NC
St. Paul's College, VA
Savannah State University, GA
Selma University, AL
Shaw University, NC
South Carolina State University, SC
Southern University New Orleans, LA
Southern University and Agricultural and Mechanical College, LA
Southwestern Christian College, TX
Spelman College, GA
Stillman College, AL
Talladega College, AL
Tennessee State University, TN
Texas College, TX
Texas Southern University, TX
Tougaloo College, MS
Tuskegee University, AL
University of Arkansas Pine Bluff, AR
University of Maryland Eastern Shore, MD
University of the District of Columbia, DC
University of the Virgin Islands, VI
Virginia State University, VA
Voorhees College, SC
West Virginia State University, WV
Wilberforce University, OH
Wiley College, TX
Winston-Salem State University, NC
Xavier University of Louisiana, LA

Two-year

Bishop State Community College, AL
Coahoma Community College, MS
Denmark Technical College, SC
Hinds Community College, MS
Lawson State Community College, AL
St. Philip's College, TX
Southern University Shreveport, LA

Hispanic serving colleges

Four-year

Adams State College, CO
American University of Puerto Rico, PR
Angelo State University, TX
Antioch University Santa Barbara, CA
Atlantic College, PR
Baptist University of the Americas, TX
Bayamon Central University, PR
Boricua College, NY
California Christian College, CA
California State Polytechnic University: Pomona, CA

California State University Bakersfield, CA
Dominguez Hills, CA
Fresno, CA
Fullerton, CA
Long Beach, CA
Los Angeles, CA
Monterey Bay, CA
Northridge, CA
San Bernardino, CA
San Marcos, CA
Stanislaus, CA
Calumet College of St. Joseph, IN
Caribbean University, PR
Carlos Albizu University, FL
Carlos Albizu University: San Juan, PR
City University of New York City College, NY
John Jay College of Criminal Justice, NY
Lehman College, NY
New York City College of Technology, NY
College of Biblical Studies-Houston, TX
College of Mount St. Vincent, NY
Colorado Heights University, CO
Conservatory of Music of Puerto Rico, PR
Dominican University, IL
Eastern New Mexico University, NM
Electronic Data Processing College: San Sebastian, PR
Escuela de Artes Plasticas de Puerto Rico, PR
Florida International University, FL
Fresno Pacific University, CA
Hodges University, FL
Houston Baptist University, TX
Humphreys College, CA
Inter American University of Puerto Rico
Aguadilla Campus, PR
Arecibo Campus, PR
Barranquitas Campus, PR
Bayamon Campus, PR
Fajardo Campus, PR
Guayama Campus, PR
Metropolitan Campus, PR
Ponce Campus, PR
San German Campus, PR
La Sierra University, CA
Lexington College, IL
Mercy College, NY
Mount Angel Seminary, OR
Mount St. Mary's College, CA
New Jersey City University, NJ
New Mexico Highlands University, NM
New Mexico Institute of Mining and Technology, NM
New Mexico State University, NM
Northeastern Illinois University, IL
Northwood University Texas, TX
Notre Dame de Namur University, CA
Nova Southeastern University, FL
Our Lady of the Lake University of San Antonio, TX
Pacific Oaks College, CA
Pontifical Catholic University of Puerto Rico, PR
St. Augustine College, IL
St. Edward's University, TX
St. John Vianney College Seminary, FL

St. Mary's University, TX
Saint Peter's College, NJ
Saint Thomas University, FL
San Diego State University, CA
Sul Ross State University, TX
Texas A&M International University, TX
Texas A&M University Corpus Christi, TX
Kingsville, TX
Texas State University: San Marcos, TX
Turabo University, PR
Universidad Adventista de las Antillas, PR
Universidad Central del Caribe, PR
Universidad del Este, PR
Universidad Metropolitana, PR
Universidad Pentecostal Mizpa, PR
Universidad Politecnica de Puerto Rico, PR
University College of San Juan, PR
University of California Merced, CA
Riverside, CA
University of Houston, TX
Clear Lake, TX
Downtown, TX
Victoria, TX
University of La Verne, CA
University of New Mexico, NM
University of Puerto Rico
Aguadilla, PR
Arecibo, PR
Bayamon University College, PR
Carolina Regional College, PR
Cayey University College, PR
Mayaguez, PR
Medical Sciences, PR
Ponce, PR
Rio Piedras, PR
Utuado, PR
University of St. Thomas, TX
University of Texas
Brownsville - Texas Southmost College, TX
El Paso, TX
Health Science Center at San Antonio, TX
Pan American, TX
San Antonio, TX
of the Permian Basin, TX
University of the Incarnate Word, TX
University of the Sacred Heart, PR
University of the Southwest, NM
Vaughn College of Aeronautics and Technology, NY
Whittier College, CA
Woodbury University, CA

Two-year

Allan Hancock College, CA
Amarillo College, TX
Antelope Valley College, CA
Arizona Western College, AZ
Bakersfield College, CA
Barstow Community College, CA
Bergen Community College, NJ
Big Bend Community College, WA
Brazosport College, TX
Brookhaven College, TX
Broward College, FL
Cabrillo College, CA
Canada College, CA
Capital Community College, CT
Central Arizona College, AZ

Central New Mexico
  Community College, NM
Centro de Estudios
  Multidisciplinarios, PR
Cerritos College, CA
Chabot College, CA
Chaffey College, CA
Citrus College, CA
City College
  Casselberry, FL
City Colleges of Chicago
    Harold Washington College,
    IL
    Harry S. Truman College,
    IL
    Malcolm X College, IL
    Richard J. Daley College,
    IL
    Wilbur Wright College, IL
City University of New York
    Borough of Manhattan
    Community College, NY
    Bronx Community College,
    NY
    Hostos Community College,
    NY
    LaGuardia Community
    College, NY
    Queensborough Community
    College, NY
Clarendon College, TX
Clovis Community College, NM
Coastal Bend College, TX
Cochise College, AZ
College of the Canyons, CA
College of the Desert, CA
College of the Sequoias, CA
Contra Costa College, CA
Crafton Hills College, CA
Cuyamaca College, CA
Cypress College, CA
Del Mar College, TX
Dodge City Community
  College, KS
Dona Ana Community College
  of New Mexico State
  University, NM
Donnelly College, KS
East Los Angeles College, CA
Eastern New Mexico University:
  Roswell, NM
Eastfield College, TX
El Camino College, CA
El Centro College, TX
El Paso Community College,
  TX
Elgin Community College, IL
Estrella Mountain Community
  College, AZ
Evergreen Valley College, CA
Fresno City College, CA
Fullerton College, CA
Galveston College, TX
Garden City Community
  College, KS
GateWay Community College,
  AZ
Gavilan College, CA
Glendale Community College,
  AZ
Hartnell College, CA
Houston Community College
  System, TX
Howard College, TX
Hudson County Community
  College, NJ
Humacao Community College,
  PR
Imperial Valley College, CA
Laredo Community College, TX
Lee College, TX
Lone Star College System, TX
Long Beach City College, CA
Los Angeles City College, CA
Los Angeles County College of
  Nursing and Allied Health,
  CA

Los Angeles Harbor College,
  CA
Los Angeles Mission College,
  CA
Los Angeles Pierce College, CA
Los Angeles Trade and
  Technical College, CA
Los Angeles Valley College,
  CA
Los Medanos College, CA
Luna Community College, NM
Marian Court College, MA
Merced College, CA
Mesalands Community College,
  NM
Miami Dade College, FL
Midland College, TX
Modesto Junior College, CA
Monterey Peninsula College,
  CA
Morton College, IL
Mount San Antonio College,
  CA
Mount San Jacinto College, CA
Mountain View College, TX
Napa Valley College, CA
New Mexico Junior College,
  NM
New Mexico State University
    Alamogordo, NM
    Carlsbad, NM
    Grants, NM
North Lake College, TX
Northern Essex Community
  College, MA
Northern New Mexico College,
  NM
Northwest Vista College, TX
Norwalk Community College,
  CT
Odessa College, TX
Otero Junior College, CO
Oxnard College, CA
Palo Alto College, TX
Palo Verde College, CA
Palomar College, CA
Pasadena City College, CA
Passaic County Community
  College, NJ
Phoenix College, AZ
Pima Community College, AZ
Porterville College, CA
Professional Business College,
  NY
Pueblo Community College, CO
Reedley College, CA
Rio Hondo College, CA
Riverside Community College,
  CA
St. Philip's College, TX
San Antonio College, TX
San Bernardino Valley College,
  CA
San Diego City College, CA
San Diego Mesa College, CA
San Jacinto College, TX
San Joaquin Delta College, CA
San Jose City College, CA
Santa Ana College, CA
Santa Barbara City College, CA
Santa Fe Community College,
  NM
Santa Monica College, CA
Santiago Canyon College, CA
Seward County Community
  College, KS
South Mountain Community
  College, AZ
South Plains College, TX
South Texas College, TX
Southwest Texas Junior College,
  TX
Southwestern College, CA
Taft College, CA
Texas State Technical College
  Harlingen, TX

Trinidad State Junior College,
  CO
Triton College, IL
Union County College, NJ
Universal Technology College
  of Puerto Rico, PR
Urban College of Boston, MA
Valencia College, FL
Ventura College, CA
Victor Valley College, CA
Victoria College, TX
Waubonsee Community
  College, IL
West Hills College: Coalinga,
  CA
West Hills College: Lemoore,
  CA
West Los Angeles College, CA
Western Texas College, TX
Wharton County Junior College,
  TX
Yakima Valley Community
  College, WA

Tribal colleges

Four-year

Haskell Indian Nations
  University, KS
Institute of American Indian
  Arts, NM

Two-year

Aaniiih Nakoda College, MT
Bay Mills Community College,
  MI
Blackfeet Community College,
  MT
Cankdeska Cikana Community
  College, ND
Chief Dull Knife College, MT
College of Menominee Nation,
  WI
Dine College, AZ
Fond du Lac Tribal and
  Community College, MN
Fort Berthold Community
  College, ND
Fort Peck Community College,
  MT
Little Big Horn College, MT
Little Priest Tribal College, NE
Nebraska Indian Community
  College, NE
Sisseton Wahpeton College, SD
Sitting Bull College, ND
Southwestern Indian Polytechnic
  Institute, NM
Stone Child College, MT
United Tribes Technical
  College, ND

Undergraduate enrollment size

Very small (fewer than 750)

Four-year

Alabama

Amridge University
Heritage Christian University
Judson College
Southeastern Bible College
United States Sports Academy
Virginia College
    Huntsville

Alaska

Alaska Bible College

Arizona

Dunlap-Stone University
International Baptist College
ITT Technical Institute
    Tucson
Northcentral University
Prescott College
Southwest University of Visual
    Arts

Arkansas

ITT Technical Institute
    Little Rock
Lyon College
Philander Smith College
University of the Ozarks
Williams Baptist College

California

American Jewish University
Antioch University
    Los Angeles
    Santa Barbara
Bethesda University of
    California
California Christian College
California Institute of Integral
    Studies
California Miramar University
California National University
    for Advanced Studies
California University of
    Management and Sciences
Charles Drew University of
    Medicine and Science
Cogswell Polytechnical College
Coleman University
Design Institute of San Diego
Golden Gate University
Holy Names University
Horizon College of San Diego
Interior Designers Institute
International Academy of
    Design and Technology
    Sacramento
ITT Technical Institute
    Lathrop
    Oxnard
LA College International
Laguna College of Art and
    Design
Life Pacific College
Menlo College
Mt. Sierra College
NewSchool of Architecture &
    Design
Northwestern Polytechnic
    University
Pacific States University

Platt College
    Ontario
    San Diego
Providence Christian College
Samuel Merritt University
San Diego Christian College
San Francisco Art Institute
San Francisco Conservatory of
    Music
School of Urban Missions:
    Oakland
Shasta Bible College and
    Graduate School
Soka University of America
Southern California Institute of
    Architecture
Southern California Institute of
    Technology
Southern California Seminary
Stanbridge College
Thomas Aquinas College
Touro College Los Angeles
University of the West
World Mission University
Yeshiva Ohr Elchonon Chabad/
    West Coast Talmudical
    Seminary

Colorado

Aspen University
CollegeAmerica
    Fort Collins
ITT Technical Institute
    Westminster
Naropa University
Rocky Mountain College of Art
    & Design

Connecticut

Holy Apostles College and
    Seminary
Lyme Academy College of Fine
    Arts
Paier College of Art

Delaware

Goldey-Beacom College

Florida

Baptist College of Florida
Carlos Albizu University
Clearwater Christian College
Digital Media Arts College
Florida College
ITT Technical Institute
    Jacksonville
    Lake Mary
Jones College
Northwood University
    Florida
Remington College
    Tampa
St. John Vianney College
    Seminary
Schiller International University
South University: Tampa
Trinity College of Florida
Webber International University

Georgia

Beulah Heights University
Brewton-Parker College
Emmanuel College
Georgia Health Sciences
    University
Wesleyan College

Idaho

Boise Bible College
ITT Technical Institute
    Boise
New Saint Andrews College
University of Phoenix
    Idaho

Illinois

Harrington College of Design
Lexington College
Lincoln Christian University

Principia College
St. Francis Medical Center
    College of Nursing
Shimer College
Trinity College of Nursing and
    Health Sciences
VanderCook College of Music
Westwood College
    DuPage
    O'Hare Airport
    River Oaks

Indiana

Holy Cross College

Iowa

Allen College
Divine Word College
Emmaus Bible College
Faith Baptist Bible College and
    Theological Seminary
Iowa Wesleyan College
Maharishi University of
    Management

Kansas

Barclay College
Bethany College
Bethel College
Central Christian College of
    Kansas
Manhattan Christian College
Ottawa University
Sterling College
Tabor College
University of Kansas Medical
    Center
University of St. Mary

Kentucky

Brescia University
Clear Creek Baptist Bible
    College
Kentucky Christian University
Kentucky Wesleyan College

Louisiana

St. Joseph Seminary College

Maine

College of the Atlantic
Maine College of Art
New England School of
    Communications
Unity College in Maine

Maryland

Johns Hopkins University:
    Peabody Conservatory of
    Music
National Labor College
Notre Dame of Maryland
    University
St. John's College
University of Maryland
    Baltimore
University of Phoenix
    Maryland

Massachusetts

Bard College at Simon's Rock
Boston Architectural College
Boston Conservatory
Franklin W. Olin College of
    Engineering
Hellenic College/Holy Cross
Montserrat College of Art
New England Conservatory of
    Music
Pine Manor College
School of the Museum of Fine
    Arts
Zion Bible College

Michigan

Cleary University
Concordia University
Kuyper College

Robert B. Miller College
Sacred Heart Major Seminary

Minnesota

Bethany Lutheran College
College of Visual Arts
Martin Luther College
Minneapolis College of Art and
    Design
Northwestern Health Sciences
    University
Oak Hills Christian College
University of Minnesota
    Rochester

Mississippi

Blue Mountain College
Southeastern Baptist College
University of Mississippi
    Medical Center

Missouri

Baptist Bible College
Calvary Bible College and
    Theological Seminary
Central Bible College
Conception Seminary College
Culver-Stockton College
Goldfarb School of Nursing at
    Barnes-Jewish College
Research College of Nursing
St. Louis Christian College
St. Luke's College
Stephens College

Nebraska

Creative Center
ITT Technical Institute
    Omaha
Nebraska Christian College
Nebraska Methodist College of
    Nursing and Allied Health
Union College

Nevada

Roseman University of Health
    Sciences
Sierra Nevada College

New Hampshire

College of St. Mary Magdalen
Daniel Webster College

New Jersey

Somerset Christian College
University of Medicine and
    Dentistry of New Jersey
    School of Health Related
    Professions
    School of Nursing
University of Phoenix
    Jersey City

New Mexico

Institute of American Indian
    Arts
St. John's College
University of the Southwest

New York

Beis Medrash Heichal Dovid
Berkeley College
Davis College
Eastman School of Music of the
    University of Rochester
Holy Trinity Orthodox Seminary
Jewish Theological Seminary of
    America
Juilliard School
Kehilath Yakov Rabbinical
    Seminary
The King's College
Machzikei Hadath Rabbinical
    College
Manhattan School of Music
Mannes College The New
    School for Music
Medaille College: Amherst
Medaille College: Rochester

Mesivta Torah Vodaath
    Seminary
Mirrer Yeshiva Central Institute
New York School of Interior
    Design
Ohr Somayach Tanenbaum
    Education Center
Rabbinical Academy Mesivta
    Rabbi Chaim Berlin
Rabbinical College Beth Shraga
Rabbinical College Bobover
    Yeshiva B'nei Zion
Rabbinical College of Long
    Island
Rabbinical College of Ohr
    Shimon Yisroel
Rabbinical Seminary of America
Shor Yoshuv Rabbinical College
SUNY
    Downstate Medical Center
    Upstate Medical University
Talmudical Institute of Upstate
    New York
Torah Temimah Talmudical
    Seminary
Webb Institute
Wells College
Yeshiva and Kolel Bais
    Medrash Elyon
Yeshiva D'Monsey Rabbinical
    College
Yeshiva Derech Chaim
Yeshiva Gedolah Imrei Yosef
    D'Spinka
Yeshiva Gedolah Zichron
    Moshe
Yeshiva Karlin Stolin
Yeshiva Shaar Hatorah
Yeshiva Shaarei Torah of
    Rockland
Yeshivas Novominsk
Yeshivat Mikdash Melech

North Carolina

Apex School of Theology
Bennett College for Women
Brevard College
Cabarrus College of Health
    Sciences
Carolina Christian College
Laurel University
Mid-Atlantic Christian
    University
Montreat College
Piedmont International
    University
St. Andrews University
Southeastern Baptist
    Theological Seminary
William Peace University

North Dakota

Medcenter One College of
    Nursing
Trinity Bible College

Ohio

Antioch University
    Midwest
Cincinnati Christian University
Cleveland Institute of Art
Pontifical College Josephinum

Oklahoma

ITT Technical Institute
    Tulsa
Mid-America Christian
    University
St. Gregory's University

Oregon

Mount Angel Seminary
Multnomah University
New Hope Christian College
Northwest Christian University
Oregon College of Art & Craft
Pacific Northwest College of
    Art

Pennsylvania

Baptist Bible College of
  Pennsylvania
Bryn Athyn College of the New
  Church
Chatham University
Curtis Institute of Music
Harrisburg University of
  Science and Technology
Moore College of Art and
  Design
Penn State
  Beaver
  DuBois
  Greater Allegheny
  New Kensington
  Shenango
  Wilkes-Barre
Pennsylvania Academy of the
  Fine Arts
Pennsylvania College of Art and
  Design
Rosemont College
St. Charles Borromeo Seminary
  - Overbrook
Talmudical Yeshiva of
  Philadelphia
Wilson College

Puerto Rico

Carlos Albizu University: San
  Juan
Conservatory of Music of
  Puerto Rico
Escuela de Artes Plasticas de
  Puerto Rico
Universidad Central del Caribe
Universidad Pentecostal Mizpa
University of Puerto Rico
  Medical Sciences

South Carolina

Allen University
Columbia International
  University
Converse College
ITT Technical Institute
  Greenville
Medical University of South
  Carolina

South Dakota

Dakota Wesleyan University

Tennessee

Fisk University
Free Will Baptist Bible College
Memphis College of Art
O'More College of Design
University of Tennessee
  Health Science Center
Watkins College of Art, Design
  & Film

Texas

Amberton University
Arlington Baptist College
Austin Graduate School of
  Theology
Baptist University of the
  Americas
College of Biblical Studies-
  Houston
Jarvis Christian College
Paul Quinn College
Southwestern Adventist
  University
Southwestern Christian College
Texas A&M University
  Baylor College of Dentistry
University of Texas
  Health Science Center at
    Houston
  Medical Branch at
    Galveston

Utah

Neumont University
Stevens-Henager College
  Logan

Vermont

Bennington College
Burlington College
College of St. Joseph in
  Vermont
Goddard College
Green Mountain College
Marlboro College
Southern Vermont College
Sterling College

Virginia

Bluefield College
Catholic Distance University
Christendom College
Hollins University
ITT Technical Institute
  Chantilly
Patrick Henry College
Potomac College
Randolph College
Stratford University:
  Woodbridge
Sweet Briar College
University of Phoenix
  Northern Virginia
Virginia Intermont College
Virginia University of
  Lynchburg
World College

Washington

Bastyr University
International Academy of
  Design and Technology
    Seattle
ITT Technical Institute
  Everett
  Spokane
Northwest College of Art

West Virginia

Alderson-Broaddus College
Ohio Valley University

Wisconsin

Columbia College of Nursing
Milwaukee Institute of Art &
  Design
Northland College
Northland International
  University
Silver Lake College of the Holy
  Family

Wyoming

University of Phoenix
  Cheyenne

France

American University of Paris
Parsons Paris School of Design

Italy

The American University of
  Rome

Spain

Saint Louis University: Madrid

Switzerland

Franklin College
  Switzerland

Two-year

Alabama

Marion Military Institute
Prince Institute of Professional
  Studies

Alaska

Ilisagvik College

Arizona

Golf Academy of America:
  Phoenix
Kaplan College: Phoenix
Refrigeration School
Tohono O'odham Community
  College

Arkansas

Bryan College
  Rogers
Rich Mountain Community
  College

California

American Academy of Dramatic
  Arts: West
Coleman College: San Marcos
Concorde Career College
  North Hollywood
Deep Springs College
Empire College
Epic Bible College
Fashion Institute of Design and
  Merchandising
    San Diego
Fremont College: Cerritos
Kaplan College: Palm Springs
Los Angeles County College of
  Nursing and Allied Health
Pacific College of Oriental
  Medicine: San Diego
Platt College
  Los Angeles
Professional Golfers Career
  College
South Coast College

Colorado

Boulder College of Massage
  Therapy
Colorado School of Healing
  Arts
Colorado School of Trades
Concorde Career College
  Aurora
IntelliTec College
Kaplan College: Denver
Prince Institute
Redstone College

Connecticut

St. Vincent's College

Delaware

Delaware College of Art and
  Design

Florida

City College
  Gainesville
College of Business and
  Technology: Flagler
College of Business and
  Technology: Hialeah
College of Business and
  Technology: Kendall
Florida College of Natural
  Health
    Maitland
Herzing University
  Winter Park
Key College

Georgia

Andrew College
Gupton Jones College of
  Funeral Service

Hawaii

Hawaii Tokai International
  College
Remington College
  Honolulu

Illinois

Illinois Eastern Community
  Colleges
    Frontier Community
      College
    Lincoln Trail College
Rockford Career College
Taylor Business Institute

Indiana

Ancilla College
ITT Technical Institute
  Newburgh
Kaplan College: Merrillville

Iowa

St. Luke's College

Kansas

Colby Community College
Northwest Kansas Technical
  College

Kentucky

Daymar College
  Owensboro
Spencerian College: Lexington
Sullivan College of Technology
  and Design

Louisiana

Baton Rouge School of
  Computers
Blue Cliff College
  Metairie
  Shreveport
Delta College of Arts &
  Technology
ITI Technical College

Maine

Central Maine Medical Center
  College of Nursing and
  Health Professions
Landing School of Boatbuilding
  and Design
Washington County Community
  College

Maryland

Garrett College
Kaplan University
  Hagerstown

Massachusetts

Benjamin Franklin Institute of
  Technology
ITT Technical Institute
  Norwood
  Wilmington
Laboure College
Marian Court College
New England College of
  Business and Finance

Michigan

Saginaw Chippewa Tribal
  College

Minnesota

Duluth Business University
Institute of Production and
  Recording
ITT Technical Institute
  Eden Prairie
Leech Lake Tribal College
Rainy River Community
  College

Missouri

Cottey College
Metropolitan Community
  College: Business &
  Technology
Vatterott College
  St. Joseph

Montana

Dawson Community College
Miles Community College
Stone Child College

Nebraska

Little Priest Tribal College
Nebraska College of Technical
  Agriculture

New Hampshire

Lebanon College

New Jersey

Assumption College for Sisters

New Mexico

Southwestern Indian Polytechnic
  Institute

New York

American Academy McAllister
  Institute of Funeral Service
American Academy of Dramatic
  Arts
Bryant & Stratton College
  Amherst
Cochran School of Nursing
Helene Fuld College of Nursing
Institute of Design and
  Construction
Island Drafting and Technical
  Institute
ITT Technical Institute
  Albany
  Getzville
  Liverpool
Jamestown Business College
Long Island Business Institute
Mildred Elley
Phillips Beth Israel School of
  Nursing
St. Elizabeth College of Nursing
St. Joseph's College of Nursing
Utica School of Commerce
Villa Maria College of Buffalo

North Carolina

Carolinas College of Health
  Sciences
King's College
Louisburg College
Martin Community College
Miller-Motte College: Cary
Miller-Motte College:
  Fayetteville
Montgomery Community
  College
Shepherds Theological Seminary

North Dakota

Fort Berthold Community
  College
Lake Region State College

Ohio

Art Institute of Cincinnati
Aultman College of Nursing and
  Health Sciences
Cincinnati College of Mortuary
  Science
Davis College
ETI Technical College of Niles
ITT Technical Institute
  Dayton
  Hilliard
  Norwood
  Strongsville
Kaplan College: Dayton
Miami-Jacobs Career College:
  Dayton
Ohio State University
  Agricultural Technical
  Institute
Ohio Valley College of
  Technology
Stautzenberger College:
  Brecksville

Oklahoma

Platt College
  Moore
  Tulsa

Pennsylvania

Cambria-Rowe Business College
Cambria-Rowe Business
  College: Indiana
Consolidated School of Business
  Lancaster
  York
ITT Technical Institute
  King of Prussia
  Pittsburgh
JNA Institute of Culinary Arts
Pennsylvania School of
  Business
Pittsburgh Institute of
  Aeronautics
Triangle Tech
  Bethlehem
  DuBois
  Erie
  Greensburg
  Pittsburgh
  Sunbury
University of Pittsburgh
  Titusville
Valley Forge Military Academy
  and College
YTI Career Institute
  Altoona

Puerto Rico

Colegio de Cinematografía,
  Artes y Televisión
Columbia Centro Universitario:
  Yauco
Humacao Community College

South Carolina

Forrest Junior College
Williamsburg Technical College

South Dakota

Kilian Community College
Sisseton Wahpeton College

Tennessee

West Tennessee Business
  College

Texas

Culinary Institute LeNotre
International Academy of
  Design and Technology
  San Antonio
ITT Technical Institute
  Richardson
Jacksonville College
Lon Morris College
Texas State Technical College
  Marshall
Wade College
Western Technical College

Vermont

Landmark College

Virginia

Bryant & Stratton College
  Virginia Beach
Skyline College: Roanoke

West Virginia

West Virginia Junior College:
  Bridgeport

Wisconsin

University of Wisconsin
  Richland

Palau

Palau Community College

Small (750–1,999)

Four-year

Alabama

Birmingham-Southern College
Huntingdon College
ITT Technical Institute
  Birmingham
Spring Hill College
University of Mobile

Alaska

University of Alaska
  Southeast

Arizona

Art Institute of Phoenix
Brown Mackie College
  Tucson
Collins College
Embry-Riddle Aeronautical
  University: Prescott Campus
ITT Technical Institute
  Tempe
University of Advancing
  Technology

Arkansas

Arkansas Baptist College
Central Baptist College
Hendrix College
John Brown University
Ouachita Baptist University

California

Art Center College of Design
Art Institute of California:
  Inland Empire
Art Institute of California: San
  Francisco
Brooks Institute
California College of the Arts
California College San Diego
California Institute of
  Technology
California Institute of the Arts
California Maritime Academy
Claremont McKenna College
Concordia University
Dominican University of
  California
Ex'pression College for Digital
  Arts
Harvey Mudd College
Hope International University
Humphreys College
ITT Technical Institute
  Rancho Cordova
  San Bernardino
  San Diego
  Sylmar
  Torrance
La Sierra University
Loma Linda University
The Master's College
Mills College
Notre Dame de Namur
  University
Otis College of Art and Design
Pacific Union College
Patten University
Pitzer College
Pomona College
Scripps College
Simpson University
West Coast University
Westmont College
Whittier College
William Jessup University
Woodbury University

Colorado

American Sentinel University
Johnson & Wales University:
  Denver
Nazarene Bible College
University of Phoenix
  Denver
Western State College of
  Colorado

Connecticut

Albertus Magnus College
Connecticut College
Mitchell College
Post University
Saint Joseph College
United States Coast Guard
  Academy

Delaware

Wesley College

District of Columbia

Gallaudet University

Florida

Eckerd College
Edward Waters College
Florida Career College: Boynton
  Beach
Florida Career College:
  Jacksonville
Florida Career College:
  Lauderdale Lakes
Florida Career College:
  Riverview
ITT Technical Institute
  Ft. Lauderdale
  Miami
Lynn University
New College of Florida
Ringling College of Art and
  Design
Rollins College
Saint Leo University
Saint Thomas University
University of Phoenix
  Central Florida
  North Florida
  South Florida
Warner University

Georgia

Agnes Scott College
Berry College
Brenau University
Chorter University
  Shorter University
Covenant College
LaGrange College
Life University
Oglethorpe University
Paine College
Piedmont College
Point University
Reinhardt University
Thomas University
Toccoa Falls College

Hawaii

Chaminade University of
  Honolulu
University of Hawaii
  West Oahu

Idaho

College of Idaho
Northwest Nazarene University

Illinois

Concordia University Chicago
Dominican University
East-West University
Greenville College
Illinois College
Illinois Institute of Art:
  Schaumburg
Judson University
Knox College

Lake Forest College
Monmouth College
National-Louis University
Quincy University
Rockford College
St. Augustine College
Trinity Christian College
University of St. Francis

Indiana

Bethel College
Calumet College of St. Joseph
Earlham College
Franklin College
Goshen College
Grace College
Hanover College
Huntington University
ITT Technical Institute
  Fort Wayne
Manchester College
Martin University
Oakland City University
Rose-Hulman Institute of
  Technology
Saint Joseph's College
Saint Mary's College
St. Mary-of-the-Woods College
Taylor University
Trine University
University of St. Francis
Wabash College

Iowa

Briar Cliff University
Buena Vista University
Central College
Clarke University
Coe College
Cornell College
Dordt College
Graceland University
Grinnell College
Loras College
Mercy College of Health
  Sciences
Morningside College
Mount Mercy University
Northwestern College
Simpson College
University of Dubuque
Waldorf College
Wartburg College

Kansas

Baker University
Benedictine College
Friends University
Haskell Indian Nations
  University
MidAmerica Nazarene
  University
Newman University
Southwestern College

Kentucky

Asbury University
Berea College
Centre College
Georgetown College
ITT Technical Institute
  Louisville
Spalding University
Thomas More College
Transylvania University
Union College
University of Pikeville
University of the Cumberlands

Louisiana

Centenary College of Louisiana
Dillard University
ITT Technical Institute
  St. Rose
Louisiana College
Louisiana State University
  Health Sciences Center

New Orleans Baptist
  Theological Seminary:
  Leavell College
Our Lady of the Lake College

Maine

Bates College
Bowdoin College
Colby College
Maine Maritime Academy
Thomas College
University of Maine
  Fort Kent
  Machias
  Presque Isle

Maryland

Goucher College
Hood College
ITT Technical Institute
  Owings Mills
Maryland Institute College of
  Art
McDaniel College
Mount St. Mary's University
St. Mary's College of Maryland
Washington Adventist
  University
Washington College

Massachusetts

American International College
Amherst College
Anna Maria College
Bay Path College
Becker College
Cambridge College
Eastern Nazarene College
Gordon College
Hampshire College
Lasell College
Lesley University
Massachusetts College of Art
  and Design
Massachusetts College of
  Liberal Arts
Massachusetts Maritime
  Academy
Mount Ida College
Newbury College
Nichols College
Regis College
Simmons College
Wheaton College
Wheelock College

Michigan

Albion College
Alma College
Andrews University
Art Institute of Michigan
Baker College
  of Cadillac
  of Port Huron
College for Creative Studies
Hillsdale College
Kalamazoo College
Kettering University
Lawrence Technological
  University
Northwood University
  Michigan
Olivet College

Minnesota

Art Institutes International
  Minnesota
Concordia University St. Paul
Crown College
Hamline University
Macalester College
Northwestern College
St. John's University
University of Minnesota
  Crookston
  Morris

Mississippi

Millsaps College
Rust College

Missouri

Avila University
Central Methodist University
College of the Ozarks
Columbia College
Drury University
Evangel University
Fontbonne University
Harris-Stowe State University
Missouri Baptist University
Missouri Valley College
Park University
Rockhurst University
Westminster College
William Jewell College
William Woods University

Montana

Carroll College
Montana State University
  Northern
Rocky Mountain College
University of Great Falls
University of Montana: Western

Nebraska

Clarkson College
College of Saint Mary
Concordia University
Doane College
Nebraska Wesleyan University
Peru State College
University of Nebraska
  Medical Center

Nevada

ITT Technical Institute
  Henderson

New Hampshire

Colby-Sawyer College
Granite State College
New England College
Rivier College
Saint Anselm College
University of New Hampshire at
  Manchester

New Jersey

Caldwell College
Centenary College
College of St. Elizabeth
Drew University
Felician College
Georgian Court University

New Mexico

ITT Technical Institute
  Albuquerque
New Mexico Institute of Mining
  and Technology

New York

Albany College of Pharmacy
  and Health Sciences
Alfred University
Bard College
Boricua College
Briarcliffe College
Cazenovia College
City University of New York
  CUNY Online
College of Mount St. Vincent
College of New Rochelle
Columbia University
  School of General Studies
Concordia College
Cooper Union for the
  Advancement of Science and
  Art
D'Youville College
Daemen College
Dominican College of Blauvelt
Elmira College

Eugene Lang College The New
  School for Liberal Arts
Five Towns College
Hamilton College
Hartwick College
Hilbert College
Houghton College
Keuka College
Manhattanville College
Marymount Manhattan College
Medaille College
Metropolitan College of New
  York
Paul Smith's College
Polytechnic Institute of New
  York University
Roberts Wesleyan College
Russell Sage College
Sage College of Albany
Saint Bonaventure University
St. Joseph's College, New York
St. Thomas Aquinas College
SUNY
  College of Environmental
    Science and Forestry
  Institute of Technology at
    Utica/Rome
  Maritime College
U.T.A. Mesivta-Kiryas Jocl
United States Merchant Marine
  Academy
United Talmudical Seminary
Vaughn College of Aeronautics
  and Technology
Wagner College

North Carolina

Art Institute of Charlotte
Barton College
Belmont Abbey College
Catawba College
Chowan University
Davidson College
Greensboro College
Johnson C. Smith University
Lees-McRae College
Lenoir-Rhyne University
Livingstone College
Mars Hill College
Meredith College
Miller-Motte College:
  Wilmington
North Carolina Wesleyan
  College
Pfeiffer University
Queens University of Charlotte
St. Augustine's College
University of North Carolina
  School of the Arts
Warren Wilson College
Wingate University

North Dakota

Jamestown College
Mayville State University
University of Mary
Valley City State University

Ohio

Bluffton University
Bryant & Stratton College
  Parma
College of Mount St. Joseph
College of Wooster
Columbus College of Art and
  Design
Defiance College
Kenyon College
Kettering College of Medical
  Arts
Lake Erie College
Lourdes University
Malone University
Marietta College
Mercy College of Ohio
Mount Carmel College of
  Nursing

Mount Vernon Nazarene
  University
Muskingum University
Notre Dame College
Ohio Dominican University
Ohio State University
  Lima Campus
  Mansfield Campus
  Marion Campus
Ohio University
  Zanesville Campus
Ohio Wesleyan University
Union Institute & University
University of Rio Grande
Ursuline College
Wilmington College
Wittenberg University

Oklahoma

Oklahoma Baptist University
Oklahoma Christian University
Oklahoma Panhandle State
  University
Oklahoma Wesleyan University
Southern Nazarene University
Spartan College of Aeronautics
  and Technology
University of Science and Arts
  of Oklahoma

Oregon

Corban University
ITT Technical Institute
  Portland
Linfield College
Marylhurst University
Pacific University
Reed College
Willamette University

Pennsylvania

Bryn Mawr College
Cabrini College
Carlow University
Cedar Crest College
Central Pennsylvania College
Chestnut Hill College
Cheyney University of
  Pennsylvania
Delaware Valley College
Geneva College
Haverford College
Juniata College
Keystone College
La Roche College
Lancaster Bible College
Lebanon Valley College
Lycoming College
Moravian College
Mount Aloysius College
Penn State
  Brandywine
  Fayette, The Eberly Campus
  Hazleton
  Lehigh Valley
  Mont Alto
  Schuylkill
  Worthington Scranton
  York
Philadelphia Biblical University
St. Francis University
St. Vincent College
Seton Hill University
Swarthmore College
Thiel College
University of Pittsburgh
  Bradford
  Greensburg
University of the Arts
Ursinus College
Valley Forge Christian College
Washington & Jefferson College
Waynesburg University

Puerto Rico

Atlantic College
Bayamon Central University

Columbia Centro Universitario:
  Caguas
Electronic Data Processing
  College: San Sebastian
National University College:
  Arecibo
National University College:
  Ponce
National University College:
  Rio Grande
Universidad Adventista de las
  Antillas
University College of San Juan
University of Puerto Rico
  Utuado

Rhode Island

Rhode Island School of Design

South Carolina

Claflin University
Coker College
Columbia College
Limestone College
Morris College
Newberry College
North Greenville University
Presbyterian College
University of South Carolina
  Beaufort
Wofford College

South Dakota

Augustana College
Dakota State University
Mount Marty College
Northern State University
South Dakota School of Mines
  and Technology
University of Sioux Falls

Tennessee

Bryan College
Carson-Newman College
Christian Brothers University
Cumberland University
Freed-Hardeman University
ITT Technical Institute
  Knoxville
  Memphis
  Nashville
King College
LeMoyne-Owen College
Lincoln Memorial University
Martin Methodist College
Maryville College
Milligan College
Rhodes College
Tennessee Wesleyan College
Trevecca Nazarene University
Tusculum College
University of the South

Texas

Austin College
Concordia University Texas
East Texas Baptist University
Hardin-Simmons University
Howard Payne University
Huston-Tillotson University
Lubbock Christian University
McMurry University
Our Lady of the Lake
  University of San Antonio
Schreiner University
Southwestern University
Texas A&M University
  Galveston
  Texarkana
Texas College
Texas Lutheran University
Texas Tech University Health
  Sciences Center
Texas Wesleyan University
University of Dallas
University of St. Thomas

University of Texas
  Health Science Center at
    San Antonio
Wayland Baptist University

Utah

ITT Technical Institute
  Murray

Vermont

Castleton State College
Johnson State College
Lyndon State College
St. Michael's College
Vermont Technical College

Virginia

Averett University
Bridgewater College
Eastern Mennonite University
Emory & Henry College
Ferrum College
Hampden-Sydney College
ITT Technical Institute
  Norfolk
  Richmond
Jefferson College of Health
  Sciences
Mary Baldwin College
Randolph-Macon College
Roanoke College
Shenandoah University
Southern Virginia University
University of Virginia's College
  at Wise
Virginia Military Institute
Virginia Union University
Virginia Wesleyan College
Washington and Lee University

Washington

Art Institute of Seattle
City University of Seattle
Cornish College of the Arts
DigiPen Institute of Technology
ITT Technical Institute
  Seattle
Northwest University
Saint Martin's University
Whitman College

West Virginia

Bethany College
Bluefield State College
Davis and Elkins College
Glenville State College
University of Charleston
West Virginia University
  Institute of Technology
West Virginia Wesleyan College
Wheeling Jesuit University

Wisconsin

Beloit College
Edgewood College
ITT Technical Institute
  Green Bay
  Greenfield
Lawrence University
Maranatha Baptist Bible College
Marian University
Mount Mary College
Ripon College

Italy

John Cabot University

Kuwait

American University of Kuwait

Morocco

Al Akhawayn University

Switzerland

Ecole Hoteliere de Lausanne

Two-year

Alabama

Chattahoochee Valley
  Community College

Medium to large (2,000-7,499)

Four-year

Delaware

Delaware State University
Wilmington University

District of Columbia

American University
Catholic University of America
Georgetown University
University of the District of
Columbia

Florida

Art Institute of Fort Lauderdale
Barry University
Bethune-Cookman University
Embry-Riddle Aeronautical
University
Flagler College
Florida Institute of Technology
Florida Southern College
Hodges University
Jacksonville University
Johnson & Wales University:
North Miami
Miami International University
of Art and Design
Nova Southeastern University
Palm Beach Atlantic University
Southeastern University
Stetson University
University of Tampa

Georgia

Albany State University
Armstrong Atlantic State
University
Augusta State University
Clark Atlanta University
Clayton State University
Columbus State University
Dalton State College
Emory University
Fort Valley State University
Georgia College and State
University
Georgia Southwestern State
University
Macon State College
Mercer University
Morehouse College
North Georgia College & State
University
Savannah State University
Southern Polytechnic State
University
Spelman College

Hawaii

Brigham Young University-
Hawaii
Hawaii Pacific University
University of Hawaii
Hilo

Idaho

Lewis-Clark State College

Illinois

Augustana College
Benedictine University
Bradley University
Chicago State University
Elmhurst College
Governors State University
Illinois Institute of Art: Chicago
Illinois Institute of Technology
Illinois Wesleyan University
Lewis University
McKendree University
Millikin University
Moody Bible Institute
North Central College
North Park University
Olivet Nazarene University
Robert Morris University:
Chicago
Roosevelt University
Saint Xavier University

School of the Art Institute of
Chicago
University of Chicago
University of Illinois
Springfield
Wheaton College

Indiana

Anderson University
Butler University
DePauw University
Indiana Institute of Technology
Indiana University
East
Kokomo
Northwest
South Bend
Southeast
Indiana Wesleyan University
ITT Technical Institute
Indianapolis
Marian University
Purdue University
North Central
University of Evansville
University of Indianapolis
Valparaiso University

Iowa

Drake University
Grand View University
Luther College
St. Ambrose University
Upper Iowa University

Kansas

Emporia State University
Pittsburg State University
Washburn University

Kentucky

Bellarmine University
Campbellsville University
Kentucky State University
Lindsey Wilson College
Mid-Continent University
Morehead State University

Louisiana

Grambling State University
Louisiana State University
Shreveport
Loyola University New Orleans
McNeese State University
Nicholls State University
Northwestern State University
Southern University and
Agricultural and Mechanical
College
University of Louisiana at
Monroe
Xavier University of Louisiana

Maine

Husson University
University of Maine
Augusta
Farmington
University of New England

Maryland

Bowie State University
Coppin State University
Frostburg State University
Johns Hopkins University
Loyola University Maryland
Morgan State University
Stevenson University
United States Naval Academy
University of Maryland
Eastern Shore

Massachusetts

Assumption College
Babson College
Bentley University
Berklee College of Music
Brandeis University
Clark University

College of the Holy Cross
Curry College
Emerson College
Emmanuel College
Endicott College
Fitchburg State University
Framingham State University
Harvard College
Massachusetts College of
Pharmacy and Health
Sciences
Massachusetts Institute of
Technology
Merrimack College
Mount Holyoke College
Salem State University
Smith College
Springfield College
Stonehill College
Suffolk University
Tufts University
University of Massachusetts
Dartmouth
Wellesley College
Wentworth Institute of
Technology
Western New England
University
Westfield State University
Williams College
Worcester Polytechnic Institute
Worcester State University

Michigan

Aquinas College
Baker College
of Allen Park
of Auburn Hills
of Clinton Township
of Flint
of Jackson
of Muskegon
of Owosso
Calvin College
Cornerstone University
Hope College
Lake Superior State University
Madonna University
Michigan Technological
University
Siena Heights University
Spring Arbor University
University of Detroit Mercy
University of Michigan
Dearborn
Flint

Minnesota

Bemidji State University
Bethel University
Capella University
Carleton College
College of St. Benedict
College of St. Scholastica
Concordia College: Moorhead
Gustavus Adolphus College
Metropolitan State University
Minnesota State University
Moorhead
St. Catherine University
St. Mary's University of
Minnesota
St. Olaf College
Southwest Minnesota State
University
University of St. Thomas

Mississippi

Alcorn State University
Belhaven University
Delta State University
Jackson State University
Mississippi College
Mississippi Valley State
University

Missouri

Global University
Lincoln University
Lindenwood University
Maryville University of Saint
Louis
Missouri Southern State
University
Missouri University of Science
and Technology
Missouri Western State
University
Northwest Missouri State
University
Southwest Baptist University
Truman State University
Washington University in St.
Louis
Webster University

Montana

Montana State University
Billings
Montana Tech of the University
of Montana

Nebraska

Bellevue University
Creighton University
University of Nebraska
Kearney
Wayne State College

Nevada

Great Basin College

New Hampshire

Dartmouth College
Hesser College
Keene State College
Plymouth State University
Southern New Hampshire
University

New Jersey

Bloomfield College
The College of New Jersey
Fairleigh Dickinson University
College at Florham
Metropolitan Campus
Monmouth University
New Jersey City University
New Jersey Institute of
Technology
Princeton University
Ramapo College of New Jersey
Richard Stockton College of
New Jersey
Rider University
Rutgers, The State University of
New Jersey
Camden Regional Campus
Newark Regional Campus
Saint Peter's College
Seton Hall University
Stevens Institute of Technology

New Mexico

Eastern New Mexico University
New Mexico Highlands
University

New York

Adelphi University
Barnard College
Berkeley College of New York
City
Canisius College
City University of New York
Medgar Evers College
York College
Clarkson University
Colgate University
College of Saint Rose
Columbia University
Culinary Institute of America
Dowling College

Hobart and William Smith
Colleges
Hofstra University
Iona College
Ithaca College
Le Moyne College
Lebanese American University
Long Island University
Brooklyn Campus
C. W. Post Campus
Manhattan College
Marist College
Mercy College
Molloy College
Monroe College
Mount Saint Mary College
Nazareth College
New York Institute of
Technology
Niagara University
Nyack College
Parsons The New School for
Design
Pratt Institute
Rensselaer Polytechnic Institute
St. Francis College
St. John Fisher College
St. Joseph's College: Suffolk
Campus
St. Lawrence University
School of Visual Arts
Siena College
Skidmore College
SUNY
College at Brockport
College at Cortland
College at Fredonia
College at Geneseo
College at New Paltz
College at Old Westbury
College at Oneonta
College at Oswego
College at Plattsburgh
College at Potsdam
College at Purchase
Farmingdale State College
Union College
United States Military Academy
University of Rochester
Utica College
Vassar College
Yeshiva University

North Carolina

Campbell University
Duke University
Elizabeth City State University
Elon University
Fayetteville State University
Gardner-Webb University
Guilford College
High Point University
Johnson & Wales University:
Charlotte
Mount Olive College
North Carolina Central
University
Shaw University
University of North Carolina
Asheville
Pembroke
Wake Forest University
Western Carolina University
Winston-Salem State University

Ohio

Ashland University
Baldwin-Wallace College
Capital University
Case Western Reserve
University
Cedarville University
Central State University
Denison University
Franciscan University of
Steubenville
John Carroll University
Oberlin College

Ohio Christian University
Ohio State University
 Newark Campus
Ohio University
 Chillicothe Campus
 Lancaster Campus
 Southern Campus at Ironton
Otterbein University
Shawnee State University
Tiffin University
University of Findlay
University of Mount Union
Walsh University
Xavier University

Oklahoma

Cameron University
East Central University
Langston University
Northwestern Oklahoma State
 University
Oklahoma City University
Oral Roberts University
Rogers State University
Southeastern Oklahoma State
 University
Southwestern Oklahoma State
 University
University of Tulsa

Oregon

Eastern Oregon University
George Fox University
Lewis & Clark College
Oregon Institute of Technology
Southern Oregon University
University of Portland
Western Oregon University

Pennsylvania

Albright College
Allegheny College
Alvernia University
Arcadia University
Art Institute of Pittsburgh
Bucknell University
California University of
 Pennsylvania
Carnegie Mellon University
Clarion University of
 Pennsylvania
DeSales University
Dickinson College
Duquesne University
East Stroudsburg University of
 Pennsylvania
Eastern University
Edinboro University of
 Pennsylvania
Elizabethtown College
Franklin & Marshall College
Gannon University
Gettysburg College
Grove City College
Gwynedd-Mercy College
Holy Family University
Immaculata University
King's College
La Salle University
Lafayette College
Lehigh University
Lock Haven University of
 Pennsylvania
Mansfield University of
 Pennsylvania
Marywood University
Mercyhurst University
Messiah College
Misericordia University
Muhlenberg College
Neumann University
Peirce College
Penn State
 Abington
 Altoona
 Berks
 Erie, The Behrend College
 Harrisburg

Pennsylvania College of
 Technology
Philadelphia University
Point Park University
Robert Morris University
Saint Joseph's University
Shippensburg University of
 Pennsylvania
Susquehanna University
University of Pittsburgh
 Johnstown
University of Scranton
University of the Sciences in
 Philadelphia
Villanova University
Westminster College
Widener University
Wilkes University
York College of Pennsylvania

Puerto Rico

Caribbean University
Inter American University of
 Puerto Rico
 Aguadilla Campus
 Barranquitas Campus
 Bayamon Campus
 Fajardo Campus
 Guayama Campus
 Metropolitan Campus
 Ponce Campus
 San German Campus
National University College:
 Bayamon
Pontifical Catholic University of
 Puerto Rico
Universidad Politecnica de
 Puerto Rico
University of Puerto Rico
 Aguadilla
 Arecibo
 Bayamon University
 College
 Carolina Regional College
 Cayey University College
 Humacao
 Ponce
University of the Sacred Heart

Rhode Island

Brown University
Bryant University
New England Institute of
 Technology
Providence College
Rhode Island College
Roger Williams University
Salve Regina University

South Carolina

Anderson University
Bob Jones University
The Citadel
Francis Marion University
Furman University
South Carolina State University
University of South Carolina
 Aiken
 Upstate
Winthrop University

South Dakota

Black Hills State University
University of South Dakota

Tennessee

Belmont University
Lane College
Lee University
Lipscomb University
Southern Adventist University
Tennessee State University
Union University
University of Tennessee
 Martin
Vanderbilt University

Texas

Abilene Christian University
Angelo State University
Art Institute of Houston
Dallas Baptist University
Houston Baptist University
LeTourneau University
Midwestern State University
Prairie View A&M University
St. Edward's University
St. Mary's University
Southern Methodist University
Southwestern Assemblies of
 God University
Sul Ross State University
Texas A&M International
 University
Texas A&M University
 Kingsville
Texas Southern University
Trinity University
University of Houston
 Clear Lake
University of Mary Hardin-
 Baylor
University of Texas
 Tyler
 of the Permian Basin
University of the Incarnate
 Word
West Texas A&M University

Utah

Southern Utah University
Westminster College

Vermont

Champlain College
Middlebury College
Norwich University

Virginia

Christopher Newport University
College of William and Mary
Longwood University
Lynchburg College
Marymount University
Norfolk State University
Regent University
University of Mary Washington
University of Richmond
Virginia State University

Washington

Evergreen State College
Gonzaga University
Pacific Lutheran University
Seattle Pacific University
Seattle University
University of Puget Sound
University of Washington
 Bothell
University of Washington
 Tacoma
Whitworth University

West Virginia

Concord University
Fairmont State University
Mountain State University
Shepherd University
West Liberty University
West Virginia State University

Wisconsin

Alverno College
Cardinal Stritch University
Carroll University
Carthage College
Concordia University Wisconsin
Milwaukee School of
 Engineering
St. Norbert College
University of Wisconsin
 Green Bay
 Parkside
 Platteville
 Superior

Guam

University of Guam

Virgin Islands

University of the Virgin Islands

Egypt

American University in Cairo

France

Institut D'Etudes Politiques de
 Paris

Lebanon

American University of Beirut
Notre Dame University: Louaize

Mexico

Instituto Tecnologico Autonomo
 de Mexico

Pakistan

Forman Christian College

Singapore

Singapore Management
 University

United Arab Emirates

American University in Dubai

Two-year

Alabama

Bevill State Community College
Central Alabama Community
 College
Enterprise State Community
 College
Faulkner State Community
 College
Gadsden State Community
 College
Lawson State Community
 College
Northwest-Shoals Community
 College
Southern Union State
 Community College
Wallace State Community
 College at Hanceville

Arizona

Cochise College
Coconino County Community
 College
Dine College
Eastern Arizona College
GateWay Community College
Mohave Community College
Northland Pioneer College
Scottsdale Community College
South Mountain Community
 College
Universal Technical Institute

Arkansas

Arkansas Northeastern College
Arkansas State University -
 Beebe
 Newport
Black River Technical College
Mid-South Community College
North Arkansas College
University of Arkansas
 Community College at
 Morrilton

California

Art Institute of California: Los
 Angeles
Barstow Community College
Berkeley City College
Canada College
Cerro Coso Community College
College of Alameda
College of Marin
College of the Redwoods
College of the Siskiyous
Copper Mountain College

Crafton Hills College
Fashion Institute of Design and
 Merchandising
 Los Angeles
Lake Tahoe Community College
Lassen Community College
Le Cordon Bleu College of
 Culinary Arts
 Los Angeles
Mendocino College
Merritt College
Napa Valley College
Oxnard College
Palo Verde College
Porterville College
West Hills College: Coalinga
West Hills College: Lemoore

Colorado

Aims Community College
Community College of Aurora
Pueblo Community College

Connecticut

Capital Community College
Gateway Community College
Goodwin College
Housatonic Community College
Manchester Community College
Middlesex Community College
Naugatuck Valley Community
 College
Norwalk Community College
Three Rivers Community
 College
Tunxis Community College

Delaware

Delaware Technical and
 Community College
 Dover
 Owens
 Stanton/Wilmington

Florida

Florida Gateway College
Florida National College
Gulf Coast State College
Lake-Sumter Community
 College
Saint Johns River State College
South Florida Community
 College

Georgia

Abraham Baldwin Agricultural
 College
Albany Technical College
Athens Technical College
Atlanta Technical College
Augusta Technical College
Bainbridge College
Central Georgia Technical
 College
College of Coastal Georgia
Columbus Technical College
Darton College
Georgia Highlands College
Georgia Military College
Georgia Northwestern Technical
 College
Georgia Piedmont Technical
 College
Gordon College
Gwinnett Technical College
Middle Georgia Technical
 College
North Georgia Technical
 College
Savannah Technical College
South Georgia College
Southern Crescent Technical
 College
West Georgia Technical College
Wiregrass Georgia Technical
 College

Hawaii

University of Hawaii
  Hawaii Community College
  Honolulu Community
    College
  Maui College
  Windward Community
    College

Idaho

North Idaho College

Illinois

Black Hawk College
Danville Area Community
  College
Heartland Community College
Highland Community College
Illinois Valley Community
  College
John Wood Community College
Kaskaskia College
Kishwaukee College
Lincoln Land Community
  College
McHenry County College
Morton College
Prairie State College
Rend Lake College
Richland Community College
Sauk Valley Community
  College
Shawnee Community College

Indiana

Ivy Tech Community College
  Bloomington
  Columbus
  Kokomo
  Lafayette
  Richmond
  South Central
  Southeast
  Southwest
  Wabash Valley

Iowa

Hawkeye Community College
Iowa Lakes Community College
Iowa Western Community
  College
Muscatine Community College
North Iowa Area Community
  College
Northeast Iowa Community
  College
Scott Community College
Southeastern Community
  College
  North Campus
Western Iowa Tech Community
  College

Kansas

Allen County Community
  College
Barton County Community
  College
Cowley County Community
  College
Highland Community College
Hutchinson Community College
Kansas City Kansas Community
  College
Wichita Area Technical College

Kentucky

Gateway Community and
  Technical College
Hopkinsville Community
  College
Maysville Community and
  Technical College
Southeast Kentucky Community
  and Technical College
West Kentucky Community and
  Technical College

Louisiana

Bossier Parish Community
  College
Louisiana State University
  Eunice

Maine

Central Maine Community
  College
Eastern Maine Community
  College
Southern Maine Community
  College

Maryland

Carroll Community College
Cecil College
Chesapeake College
Frederick Community College
Hagerstown Community College
Harford Community College
Wor-Wic Community College

Massachusetts

Berkshire Community College
Cape Cod Community College
Greenfield Community College
Holyoke Community College
Massachusetts Bay Community
  College
Mount Wachusett Community
  College
North Shore Community
  College
Northern Essex Community
  College
Quincy College
Roxbury Community College
Springfield Technical
  Community College

Michigan

Jackson Community College
Lake Michigan College
Mid Michigan Community
  College
Monroe County Community
  College
Muskegon Community College
North Central Michigan College
Northwestern Michigan College
St. Clair County Community
  College
Southwestern Michigan College

Minnesota

Alexandria Technical and
  Community College
Anoka Technical College
Central Lakes College
Dakota County Technical
  College
Hennepin Technical College
Inver Hills Community College
Lake Superior College
Minnesota State College -
  Southeast Technical
Minnesota State Community and
  Technical College
Minnesota West Community
  and Technical College
North Hennepin Community
  College
Northland Community &
  Technical College
Riverland Community College
Rochester Community and
  Technical College
St. Cloud Technical and
  Community College
St. Paul College
South Central College

Mississippi

Copiah-Lincoln Community
  College
Pearl River Community College

Missouri

Crowder College
East Central College
Jefferson College
Metropolitan Community
  College: Blue River
Metropolitan Community
  College: Longview
Metropolitan Community
  College: Maple Woods
Metropolitan Community
  College: Penn Valley
Ranken Technical College
St. Charles Community College
Three Rivers Community
  College

Nebraska

Central Community College
Northeast Community College

Nevada

Western Nevada College

New Hampshire

Great Bay Community College
Manchester Community College
NHTI-Concord's Community
  College

New Jersey

Atlantic Cape Community
  College
County College of Morris
Cumberland County College
Gloucester County College
Raritan Valley Community
  College
Warren County Community
  College

New Mexico

Clovis Community College
Eastern New Mexico
  University: Roswell
New Mexico Junior College
New Mexico State University
  Alamogordo
San Juan College
Santa Fe Community College

New York

ASA Institute of Business and
  Computer Technology
Broome Community College
Cayuga Community College
City University of New York
  Hostos Community College
Corning Community College
Finger Lakes Community
  College
Fulton-Montgomery Community
  College
Genesee Community College
Herkimer County Community
  College
Jamestown Community College
Jefferson Community College
Mohawk Valley Community
  College
Niagara County Community
  College
North Country Community
  College
Orange County Community
  College
Rockland Community College
Schenectady County
  Community College
SUNY
  College of Agriculture and
    Technology at Morrisville
  College of Technology at
    Alfred
  College of Technology at
    Canton
  College of Technology at
    Delhi

Technical Career Institutes
Tompkins Cortland Community
  College
Ulster County Community
  College

North Carolina

Alamance Community College
Asheville-Buncombe Technical
  Community College
Blue Ridge Community College
Caldwell Community College
  and Technical Institute
Catawba Valley Community
  College
Cleveland Community College
Coastal Carolina Community
  College
College of the Albemarle
Craven Community College
Durham Technical Community
  College
Gaston College
Haywood Community College
Johnston Community College
Lenoir Community College
Mitchell Community College
Nash Community College
Piedmont Community College
Richmond Community College
Rockingham Community
  College
Rowan-Cabarrus Community
  College
South Piedmont Community
  College
Southwestern Community
  College
Wayne Community College
Wilkes Community College

North Dakota

Bismarck State College
North Dakota State College of
  Science

Ohio

Central Ohio Technical College
Clark State Community College
Eastern Gateway Community
  College
Edison State Community
  College
James A. Rhodes State College
Kent State University
  Ashtabula
  Geauga
  Stark
  Trumbull
  Tuscarawas
Marion Technical College
Northwest State Community
  College
Southern State Community
  College
Terra State Community College
University of Cincinnati
  Clermont College

Oklahoma

Connors State College
Eastern Oklahoma State College
Northeastern Oklahoma
  Agricultural and Mechanical
  College
Seminole State College

Oregon

Central Oregon Community
  College
Rogue Community College
Treasure Valley Community
  College
Umpqua Community College

Pennsylvania

Butler County Community
  College

Lehigh Carbon Community
  College
Luzerne County Community
  College
Westmoreland County
  Community College

Puerto Rico

Ponce Paramedical College

South Carolina

Aiken Technical College
Central Carolina Technical
  College
Florence-Darlington Technical
  College
Horry-Georgetown Technical
  College
Orangeburg-Calhoun Technical
  College
Piedmont Technical College
Spartanburg Community College
Technical College of the
  Lowcountry
Tri-County Technical College
York Technical College

South Dakota

Southeast Technical Institute

Tennessee

Cleveland State Community
  College
Dyersburg State Community
  College
Motlow State Community
  College
Northeast State Community
  College
Roane State Community College
Volunteer State Community
  College
Walters State Community
  College

Texas

Alvin Community College
Angelina College
Brazosport College
Cisco College
College of the Mainland
Galveston College
Grayson County College
Hill College
Howard College
Kilgore College
Lamar Institute of Technology
Lamar State College at Orange
Lamar State College at Port
  Arthur
Lee College
Midland College
Northeast Texas Community
  College
Odessa College
Panola College
Paris Junior College
Southwest Texas Junior College
Texarkana College
Texas State Technical College
  Harlingen
Vernon College
Victoria College
Weatherford College
Western Texas College
Wharton County Junior College

Vermont

Community College of Vermont

Virginia

Blue Ridge Community College
Central Virginia Community
  College
Danville Community College
John Tyler Community College
Mountain Empire Community
  College

Patrick Henry Community
  College
Piedmont Virginia Community
  College
Rappahannock Community
  College
Southwest Virginia Community
  College
Virginia Western Community
  College
Wytheville Community College

Washington

Bates Technical College
Centralia College
Columbia Basin College
Grays Harbor College
Lower Columbia College
North Seattle Community
  College
Shoreline Community College
Skagit Valley College
South Puget Sound Community
  College

West Virginia

New River Community and
  Technical College
West Virginia Northern
  Community College
West Virginia University at
  Parkersburg

Wisconsin

Blackhawk Technical College
Chippewa Valley Technical
  College
Lakeshore Technical College
Mid-State Technical College
Moraine Park Technical College
University of Wisconsin
  Fox Valley
Waukesha County Technical
  College
Western Technical College
Wisconsin Indianhead Technical
  College

Wyoming

Casper College
Laramie County Community
  College
Sheridan College
Western Wyoming Community
  College

Guam

Guam Community College

Large (7,500-14,499)

Four-year

Alabama

Columbia Southern University
Jacksonville State University
University of Alabama
  Birmingham
University of South Alabama

Alaska

University of Alaska
  Anchorage

Arkansas

Arkansas State University
Arkansas Tech University
University of Arkansas
  Little Rock
University of Central Arkansas

California

Academy of Art University
California State University
  Chico
  Dominguez Hills
  East Bay
  San Bernardino
  San Marcos
  Stanislaus
National University
Sonoma State University

Colorado

University of Colorado
  Colorado Springs
  Denver
University of Northern Colorado

Connecticut

Central Connecticut State
  University
Southern Connecticut State
  University

District of Columbia

George Washington University

Florida

Embry-Riddle Aeronautical
  University: Worldwide
  Campus
Florida Agricultural and
  Mechanical University
Florida Gulf Coast University
University of Miami
University of North Florida
University of West Florida

Georgia

Georgia Gwinnett College
Georgia Institute of Technology
Savannah College of Art and
  Design
University of West Georgia
Valdosta State University

Hawaii

University of Hawaii
  Manoa

Idaho

Idaho State University
University of Idaho

Illinois

Columbia College Chicago
Eastern Illinois University
Loyola University Chicago
Northeastern Illinois University
Northwestern University
Southern Illinois University
  Carbondale
Southern Illinois University
  Edwardsville
Western Illinois University

Indiana

Indiana State University
Indiana University-Purdue
  University Fort Wayne
Purdue University
  Calumet
University of Notre Dame
University of Southern Indiana

Iowa

University of Northern Iowa

Kansas

Fort Hays State University
Wichita State University

Kentucky

Murray State University
Northern Kentucky University
University of Louisville

Louisiana

Southeastern Louisiana
  University

Tulane University
University of Louisiana at
  Lafayette
University of New Orleans

Maine

University of Maine

Maryland

Salisbury University
University of Maryland
  Baltimore County

Massachusetts

Boston College
Bridgewater State University
University of Massachusetts
  Boston
  Lowell

Michigan

Davenport University
Ferris State University
Northern Michigan University
Saginaw Valley State University

Minnesota

Minnesota State University
  Mankato
Saint Cloud State University
University of Minnesota
  Duluth
Walden University
Winona State University

Mississippi

University of Southern
  Mississippi

Missouri

Saint Louis University
Southeast Missouri State
  University
University of Central Missouri
University of Missouri
  Kansas City
  St. Louis

Montana

Montana State University

Nebraska

University of Nebraska
  Omaha

Nevada

University of Nevada
  Reno

New Hampshire

University of New Hampshire

New Jersey

Kean University
Montclair State University
Rowan University
William Paterson University of
  New Jersey

New Mexico

New Mexico State University

New York

City University of New York
  Baruch College
  Brooklyn College
  City College
  College of Staten Island
  John Jay College of
    Criminal Justice
  Lehman College
Cornell University
Fashion Institute of Technology
Fordham University
Pace University
Rochester Institute of
  Technology
St. John's University

SUNY
  College at Buffalo
  Empire State College
  University at Albany
  University at Binghamton
Syracuse University

North Carolina

North Carolina Agricultural and
  Technical State University
University of North Carolina
  Greensboro
  Wilmington

North Dakota

North Dakota State University
University of North Dakota

Ohio

Bowling Green State University
Cleveland State University
Miami University
  Oxford
University of Dayton
Wright State University
Youngstown State University

Oklahoma

Northeastern State University

Pennsylvania

Bloomsburg University of
  Pennsylvania
Drexel University
Indiana University of
  Pennsylvania
Kutztown University of
  Pennsylvania
Millersville University of
  Pennsylvania
Slippery Rock University of
  Pennsylvania
University of Pennsylvania
West Chester University of
  Pennsylvania

Puerto Rico

Turabo University
Universidad del Este
Universidad Metropolitana
University of Puerto Rico
  Mayaguez
  Rio Piedras

Rhode Island

Johnson & Wales University:
  Providence
University of Rhode Island

South Carolina

Coastal Carolina University
College of Charleston

South Dakota

South Dakota State University

Tennessee

Austin Peay State University
East Tennessee State University
Tennessee Technological
  University
University of Tennessee
  Chattanooga

Texas

Baylor University
Lamar University
Sam Houston State University
Stephen F. Austin State
  University
Tarleton State University
Texas A&M University
  Corpus Christi
Texas Christian University
Texas Woman's University
University of Houston
  Downtown
University of Texas
  Dallas

Utah

Dixie State College

Vermont

University of Vermont

Virginia

Liberty University
Radford University
University of Virginia

Washington

Eastern Washington University
Western Washington University

West Virginia

Marshall University

Wisconsin

Marquette University
University of Wisconsin
  Eau Claire
  La Crosse
  Oshkosh
  Stevens Point
  Stout

Wyoming

University of Wyoming

Canada

Queen's University

Mexico

Universidad Anahuac

United Kingdom

King's College London

Two-year

Alabama

Calhoun Community College
Jefferson State Community
  College

Arizona

Arizona Western College
Estrella Mountain Community
  College
Glendale Community College
Paradise Valley Community
  College
Phoenix College
Rio Salado College
Yavapai College

Arkansas

Northwest Arkansas Community
  College

California

Allan Hancock College
Antelope Valley College
Butte College
Cabrillo College
Citrus College
Coastline Community College
College of San Mateo
College of the Canyons
College of the Desert
College of the Sequoias
Contra Costa College
Cosumnes River College
Cuesta College
Evergreen Valley College
Folsom Lake College
Gavilan College
Golden West College
Hartnell College
Imperial Valley College
Irvine Valley College
Laney College
Las Positas College
Los Angeles Harbor College
Los Angeles Mission College
Los Angeles Southwest College
Los Medanos College
Merced College
Mission College

Monterey Peninsula College
Moorpark College
Moreno Valley College
Norco College
Ohlone College
Reedley College
San Bernardino Valley College
San Diego Miramar College
San Jose City College
Santiago Canyon College
Shasta College
Solano Community College
Taft College
Ventura College
Victor Valley College
West Los Angeles College
West Valley College
Yuba Community College
District

Colorado

Arapahoe Community College
Community College of Denver
Pikes Peak Community College
Red Rocks Community College

Florida

Brevard Community College
College of Central Florida
Daytona State College
Indian River Community
College
Indian River State College
Northwest Florida State College
Pasco-Hernando Community
College
Pensacola State College
Polk State College
Santa Fe College
State College of Florida,
Manatee-Sarasota
Tallahassee Community College

Georgia

Chattahoochee Technical
College
Gainesville State College

Hawaii

University of Hawaii
Kapiolani Community
College

Idaho

College of Western Idaho

Illinois

College of Lake County
Elgin Community College
Harper College
Illinois Central College
Lake Land College
Lewis and Clark Community
College
Moraine Valley Community
College
Parkland College
Rock Valley College
South Suburban College of
Cook County
Southwestern Illinois College
Triton College
Waubonsee Community College

Indiana

Ivy Tech Community College
East Central
North Central
Northeast
Northwest

Kentucky

Bluegrass Community and
Technical College
Elizabethtown Community and
Technical College
Somerset Community College

Louisiana

Baton Rouge Community
College

Maryland

College of Southern Maryland
Howard Community College
Prince George's Community
College

Massachusetts

Bristol Community College
Middlesex Community College
Quinsigamond Community
College

Michigan

Delta College
Macomb Community College
Mott Community College
Washtenaw Community College

Minnesota

Anoka-Ramsey Community
College
Century College
Minneapolis Community and
Technical College
Normandale Community
College

Missouri

St. Louis Community College
Meramec

New Jersey

Brookdale Community College
Burlington County College
Camden County College
Essex County College
Hudson County Community
College
Mercer County Community
College
Middlesex County College
Ocean County College
Passaic County Community
College
Union County College

New Mexico

Dona Ana Community College
of New Mexico State
University

New York

City University of New York
Bronx Community College
Kingsborough Community
College
Dutchess Community College
Erie Community College
Onondaga Community College
Westchester Community College

North Carolina

Cape Fear Community College
Fayetteville Technical
Community College
Forsyth Technical Community
College
Guilford Technical Community
College

Ohio

Cincinnati State Technical and
Community College
Lakeland Community College
Owens Community College
Toledo
Stark State College of
Technology

Oklahoma

Oklahoma City Community
College
Rose State College

Oregon

Lane Community College
Mt. Hood Community College

Pennsylvania

Bucks County Community
College
Delaware County Community
College
Harrisburg Area Community
College
Montgomery County
Community College
Northampton Community
College

South Carolina

Greenville Technical College
Midlands Technical College

Tennessee

Chattanooga State Community
College
Nashville State Community
College
Southwest Tennessee
Community College

Texas

Amarillo College
Brookhaven College
Del Mar College
Eastfield College
El Centro College
Laredo Community College
McLennan Community College
Mountain View College
Navarro College
North Central Texas College
North Lake College
Northwest Vista College
Palo Alto College
St. Philip's College
South Plains College
Tyler Junior College

Virginia

Germanna Community College
J. Sargeant Reynolds
Community College

Washington

Clark College
Olympic College
Pierce College
South Seattle Community
College

Wisconsin

Fox Valley Technical College

Very large (15,000 or more)

Four-year

Alabama

Auburn University
Troy University
University of Alabama

Arizona

Arizona State University
Grand Canyon University
Northern Arizona University
University of Arizona

Arkansas

University of Arkansas

California

California Polytechnic State
University: San Luis Obispo
California State Polytechnic
University: Pomona

California State University
Fresno
Fullerton
Long Beach
Los Angeles
Northridge
Sacramento
San Diego State University
San Francisco State University
San Jose State University
University of California
Berkeley
Davis
Irvine
Los Angeles
Riverside
San Diego
Santa Barbara
Santa Cruz
University of Southern
California

Colorado

Colorado State University
Metropolitan State College of
Denver
University of Colorado
Boulder

Connecticut

University of Connecticut

Delaware

University of Delaware

Florida

Florida Atlantic University
Florida International University
Florida State University
University of Central Florida
University of Florida
University of South Florida

Georgia

Georgia Southern University
Georgia State University
Kennesaw State University
University of Georgia

Idaho

Boise State University
Brigham Young University-
Idaho

Illinois

DePaul University
Illinois State University
Northern Illinois University
University of Illinois
Chicago
Urbana-Champaign

Indiana

Ball State University
Indiana University
Bloomington
Indiana University-Purdue
University Indianapolis
Purdue University

Iowa

Iowa State University
University of Iowa

Kansas

Kansas State University
University of Kansas

Kentucky

University of Kentucky
Western Kentucky University

Louisiana

Louisiana State University and
Agricultural and Mechanical
College

Maryland

Towson University
University of Maryland
College Park
University College

Massachusetts

Boston University
Northeastern University
University of Massachusetts
Amherst

Michigan

Central Michigan University
Eastern Michigan University
Grand Valley State University
Michigan State University
Oakland University
University of Michigan
Wayne State University
Western Michigan University

Minnesota

University of Minnesota
Twin Cities

Mississippi

Mississippi State University
University of Mississippi

Missouri

Missouri State University
University of Missouri
Columbia

Nebraska

University of Nebraska
Lincoln

Nevada

University of Nevada
Las Vegas

New Jersey

Rutgers, The State University of
New Jersey
New Brunswick/Piscataway
Campus
Thomas Edison State College

New York

City University of New York
Hunter College
New York City College of
Technology
Queens College
New York University
SUNY
University at Buffalo
University at Stony Brook

North Carolina

Appalachian State University
East Carolina University
North Carolina State University
University of North Carolina
Chapel Hill
Charlotte

Ohio

Kent State University
Ohio State University
Columbus Campus
Ohio University
University of Akron
University of Cincinnati
University of Toledo

Oklahoma

Oklahoma State University
University of Central Oklahoma
University of Oklahoma

Oregon

Portland State University
University of Oregon

Pennsylvania

Penn State
University Park

Temple University
University of Pittsburgh

South Carolina

University of South Carolina
    Columbia

Tennessee

Middle Tennessee State
    University
University of Memphis
University of Tennessee
    Knoxville

Texas

Texas A&M University
Texas State University: San
    Marcos
Texas Tech University
University of Houston
University of North Texas
University of Texas
    Arlington
    Austin
    Brownsville - Texas
      Southmost College
    El Paso
    Pan American
    San Antonio

Utah

Brigham Young University
University of Utah
Utah State University
Utah Valley University
Weber State University
Western Governors University

Virginia

George Mason University
James Madison University
Old Dominion University
Virginia Commonwealth
    University
Virginia Polytechnic Institute
    and State University

Washington

University of Washington
Washington State University

West Virginia

American Public University
    System
West Virginia University

Wisconsin

University of Wisconsin
    Madison
    Milwaukee

Canada

Simon Fraser University
University of Alberta
University of British Columbia
University of Toronto

Two-year

Arizona

Mesa Community College
Penn Foster College

California

American River College
Bakersfield College
Cerritos College
Chabot College
Chaffey College
City College of San Francisco
Cypress College
De Anza College
Diablo Valley College
East Los Angeles College
El Camino College
Foothill College
Fresno City College
Fullerton College
Glendale Community College
Grossmont College

Long Beach City College
Los Angeles City College
Los Angeles Pierce College
Los Angeles Trade and
    Technical College
Los Angeles Valley College
MiraCosta College
Modesto Junior College
Mount San Antonio College
Mount San Jacinto College
Orange Coast College
Palomar College
Pasadena City College
Rio Hondo College
Riverside Community College
Sacramento City College
Saddleback College
San Diego City College
San Diego Mesa College
San Joaquin Delta College
Santa Ana College
Santa Barbara City College
Santa Monica College
Santa Rosa Junior College
Sierra College
Southwestern College

Colorado

Front Range Community
    College

Florida

Broward College
Florida State College at
    Jacksonville
Hillsborough Community
    College
Keiser University
Miami Dade College
Palm Beach State College
St. Petersburg College
Seminole State College of
    Florida
Valencia College

Georgia

Georgia Perimeter College

Illinois

College of DuPage
Joliet Junior College

Indiana

Ivy Tech Community College
    Central Indiana
Vincennes University

Iowa

Des Moines Area Community
    College
Kirkwood Community College

Kansas

Johnson County Community
    College

Louisiana

Delgado Community College

Maryland

Anne Arundel Community
    College
Community College of
    Baltimore County
Montgomery College

Michigan

Grand Rapids Community
    College
Lansing Community College
Oakland Community College
Wayne County Community
    College

Nevada

College of Southern Nevada

New Jersey

Bergen Community College

New Mexico

Central New Mexico
    Community College

New York

City University of New York
    Borough of Manhattan
      Community College
    LaGuardia Community
      College
    Queensborough Community
      College
Monroe Community College
Suffolk County Community
    College

North Carolina

Central Piedmont Community
    College
Wake Technical Community
    College

Ohio

Columbus State Community
    College
Cuyahoga Community College
    Metropolitan
Sinclair Community College

Oklahoma

Tulsa Community College

Oregon

Clackamas Community College
Portland Community College

Pennsylvania

Community College of
    Allegheny County
Community College of
    Philadelphia

Rhode Island

Community College of Rhode
    Island

South Carolina

Trident Technical College

Texas

Austin Community College
Blinn College
Central Texas College
Collin County Community
    College District
El Paso Community College
Houston Community College
    System
Lone Star College System
San Antonio College
San Jacinto College
South Texas College
Tarrant County College

Utah

Salt Lake Community College

Virginia

Northern Virginia Community
    College
Tidewater Community College

Wisconsin

Madison Area Technical
    College
Milwaukee Area Technical
    College

Admission selectivity

Admit under 50% of applicants

Four-year

Alabama

Alabama State University
Spring Hill College
Stillman College
University of Alabama
University of West Alabama

Arizona

Grand Canyon University

California

Art Institute of California:
Sacramento
Art Institute of California: San
Diego
Azusa Pacific University
California Institute of
Technology
California Institute of the Arts
California Lutheran University
California Polytechnic State
University: San Luis Obispo
California State University
East Bay
Fullerton
Long Beach
Monterey Bay
Chapman University
Claremont McKenna College
Fresno Pacific University
Harvey Mudd College
Humphreys College
La Sierra University
Laguna College of Art and
Design
Menlo College
Mt. Sierra College
Occidental College
Pacific Union College
Pepperdine University
Pitzer College
Pomona College
Providence Christian College
San Diego Christian College
San Diego State University
San Francisco Conservatory of
Music
Scripps College
Soka University of America
Stanford University
University of California
Berkeley
Davis
Irvine
Los Angeles
San Diego
Santa Barbara
University of La Verne
University of San Diego
University of Southern
California
University of the Pacific

Colorado

Colorado College
Colorado School of Mines
United States Air Force
Academy

Connecticut

Connecticut College
Trinity College

United States Coast Guard
Academy
University of Connecticut
Wesleyan University
Yale University

Delaware

Delaware State University

District of Columbia

American University
George Washington University
Georgetown University
University of the District of
Columbia

Florida

Art Institute of Fort Lauderdale
Ave Maria University
Baptist College of Florida
Edward Waters College
Flagler College
Florida Agricultural and
Mechanical University
Florida Atlantic University
Florida Christian College
Florida International University
Jacksonville University
Miami International University
of Art and Design
Northwood University
Florida
Saint Thomas University
Trinity College of Florida
University of Central Florida
University of Florida
University of Miami
University of North Florida
University of South Florida

Georgia

Agnes Scott College
Albany State University
Brenau University
Clayton State University
Dalton State College
Emory University
Fort Valley State University
Georgia Southern University
Point University
Spelman College

Hawaii

Brigham Young University-
Hawaii

Illinois

Chicago State University
Illinois Institute of Art:
Schaumburg
Lexington College
National-Louis University
North Park University
Northwestern University
Robert Morris University:
Chicago
Rockford College
Shimer College
Southern Illinois University
Carbondale
University of Chicago
University of St. Francis

Indiana

Calumet College of St. Joseph
Purdue University
Calumet
University of Notre Dame

Iowa

Cornell College
Maharishi University of
Management

Kansas

Central Christian College of
Kansas

Haskell Indian Nations
University
Newman University

Kentucky

Alice Lloyd College
Berea College
Brescia University
Kentucky State University
Northern Kentucky University

Louisiana

Louisiana State University
Shreveport
Tulane University

Maine

Bates College
Bowdoin College
Colby College

Maryland

Coppin State University
Johns Hopkins University
Johns Hopkins University:
Peabody Conservatory of
Music
United States Naval Academy
University of Maryland
College Park
Eastern Shore

Massachusetts

Amherst College
Babson College
Bentley University
Berklee College of Music
Boston College
Boston Conservatory
Boston University
Brandeis University
College of the Holy Cross
Emerson College
Franklin W. Olin College of
Engineering
Gordon College
Harvard College
Massachusetts Institute of
Technology
New England Conservatory of
Music
Northeastern University
Simmons College
Smith College
Tufts University
Wellesley College
Williams College

Michigan

Andrews University
College for Creative Studies
Hillsdale College
Marygrove College
University of Michigan

Minnesota

Carleton College
Macalester College
University of Minnesota
Twin Cities

Mississippi

Alcorn State University
Blue Mountain College
Mississippi College
Mississippi University for
Women
Rust College
Tougaloo College

Missouri

College of the Ozarks
Columbia College
St. Louis Christian College
Washington University in St.
Louis

Montana

University of Great Falls

Nebraska

College of Saint Mary
Nebraska Methodist College of
Nursing and Allied Health
Peru State College

New Hampshire

Dartmouth College
University of New Hampshire at
Manchester

New Jersey

The College of New Jersey
New Jersey City University
Princeton University
Stevens Institute of Technology

New York

Bard College
Barnard College
City University of New York
Baruch College
Brooklyn College
City College
Hunter College
John Jay College of
Criminal Justice
Lehman College
Queens College
Colgate University
Columbia University
School of General Studies
Cooper Union for the
Advancement of Science and
Art
Cornell University
Eastman School of Music of the
University of Rochester
Fashion Institute of Technology
Fordham University
Hamilton College
Juilliard School
Manhattan School of Music
Mannes College The New
School for Music
Marist College
New York School of Interior
Design
New York University
Rensselaer Polytechnic Institute
St. John's University
St. Lawrence University
Siena College
Skidmore College
SUNY
College at Brockport
College at Cortland
College at Geneseo
College at New Paltz
College at Old Westbury
College at Oneonta
College at Oswego
College at Plattsburgh
College at Purchase
College of Environmental
Science and Forestry
Farmindale State College
Institute of Technology at
Utica/Rome
University at Binghamton
University at Stony Brook
Syracuse University
Union College
United States Merchant Marine
Academy
United States Military Academy
University of Rochester
Vassar College
Webb Institute

North Carolina

Campbell University
Catawba College
Davidson College
Duke University

Johnson C. Smith University
Laurel University
Mid-Atlantic Christian
University
Shaw University
University of North Carolina
Chapel Hill
School of the Arts
Wake Forest University
Western Carolina University

Ohio

Central State University
Cleveland State University
Denison University
Kenyon College
Kettering College of Medical
Arts
Oberlin College

Oklahoma

University of Science and Arts
of Oklahoma
University of Tulsa

Oregon

Corban University
New Hope Christian College
Reed College

Pennsylvania

Albright College
Bryn Athyn College of the New
Church
Bryn Mawr College
Bucknell University
Carnegie Mellon University
Central Pennsylvania College
Curtis Institute of Music
Dickinson College
Franklin & Marshall College
Gettysburg College
Harrisburg University of
Science and Technology
Haverford College
Lafayette College
Lehigh University
Muhlenberg College
Pennsylvania College of Art and
Design
Seton Hill University
Swarthmore College
University of Pennsylvania
University of the Arts
Villanova University
Washington & Jefferson College
West Chester University of
Pennsylvania

Puerto Rico

Bayamon Central University
Inter American University of
Puerto Rico
Bayamon Campus
Fajardo Campus
Metropolitan Campus
Ponce Campus
Turabo University
Universidad Metropolitana
University of Puerto Rico
Bayamon University
College
Humacao
Rio Piedras
University of the Sacred Heart

Rhode Island

Brown University
Rhode Island School of Design

South Carolina

Claflin University
Coker College
Lander University
University of South Carolina
Aiken

Tennessee

Christian Brothers University
Cumberland University
Lane College
LeMoyne-Owen College
Memphis College of Art
O'More College of Design
Vanderbilt University

Texas

Baylor University
Dallas Baptist University
Houston Baptist University
Northwood University
    Texas
Prairie View A&M University
Rice University
Southwestern Adventist
    University
Southwestern Assemblies of
    God University
Texas A&M International
    University
Texas A&M University
    Commerce
Texas Christian University
Texas Southern University
University of Houston
    Victoria
University of Mary Hardin-
    Baylor
University of Texas
    Austin

Vermont

Middlebury College

Virginia

Bluefield College
College of William and Mary
Hampton University
Jefferson College of Health
    Sciences
Mary Baldwin College
University of Richmond
University of Virginia
Virginia Military Institute
Washington and Lee University

Washington

DigiPen Institute of Technology
Whitworth University

West Virginia

Bluefield State College
Ohio Valley University
West Virginia University
    Institute of Technology

Wisconsin

Cardinal Stritch University

Canada

University of British Columbia

France

Parsons Paris School of Design

Switzerland

Ecole Hoteliere de Lausanne

Two-year

California

American Academy of Dramatic
    Arts: West
Deep Springs College
Marymount College
    Palos Verdes California

Georgia

Andrew College
Gordon College
Oxford College of Emory
    University

Iowa

St. Luke's College

Massachusetts

Laboure College

Minnesota

Dunwoody College of
    Technology

New Mexico

New Mexico Military Institute

New York

Clinton Community College
Columbia-Greene Community
    College
Maria College
Phillips Beth Israel School of
    Nursing
Plaza College

Ohio

Hondros College

Pennsylvania

Williamson Free School of
    Mechanical Trades

South Dakota

Mitchell Technical Institute

Admit 50 to 75% of applicants

Four-year

Alabama

Alabama Agricultural and
    Mechanical University
Auburn University
Auburn University at
    Montgomery
Birmingham-Southern College
Faulkner University
Huntingdon College
Judson College
Troy University
Tuskegee University
University of Alabama
    Birmingham
    Huntsville

Alaska

University of Alaska
    Southeast

Arizona

Arizona Christian University
Northern Arizona University
University of Arizona

Arkansas

Arkansas State University
Central Baptist College
Harding University
Henderson State University
John Brown University
Lyon College
Ouachita Baptist University
Philander Smith College
Southern Arkansas University
University of Arkansas
    Little Rock
Williams Baptist College

California

Art Institute of California:
    Hollywood
Art Institute of California:
    Inland Empire
Bethesda University of
    California
California Baptist University
California State Polytechnic
    University: Pomona

California State University
    Bakersfield
    Channel Islands
    Fresno
    Los Angeles
    Northridge
    Sacramento
    San Bernardino
    San Marcos
Cogswell Polytechnical College
Dominican University of
    California
Holy Names University
The King's University
Loyola Marymount University
The Master's College
Mills College
Mount St. Mary's College
Notre Dame de Namur
    University
Otis College of Art and Design
Point Loma Nazarene University
St. Mary's College of California
San Francisco State University
Santa Clara University
University of California
    Riverside
    Santa Cruz
University of Redlands
University of San Francisco
Vanguard University of
    Southern California
West Coast University
Westmont College
Whittier College
William Jessup University
Woodbury University
World Mission University
Yeshiva Ohr Elchonon Chabad/
    West Coast Talmudical
    Seminary

Colorado

Adams State College
Colorado Christian University
Fort Lewis College
Johnson & Wales University:
    Denver
Metropolitan State College of
    Denver
University of Colorado
    Colorado Springs
    Denver
University of Denver
University of Northern Colorado

Connecticut

Albertus Magnus College
Central Connecticut State
    University
Eastern Connecticut State
    University
Fairfield University
Paier College of Art
Post University
Quinnipiac University
Sacred Heart University
Southern Connecticut State
    University
University of Bridgeport
University of Hartford
University of New Haven
Western Connecticut State
    University

Delaware

Goldey-Beacom College
University of Delaware
Wesley College

District of Columbia

Gallaudet University
Howard University
Trinity Washington University

Florida

Barry University
Bethune-Cookman University

Carlos Albizu University
Clearwater Christian College
Eckerd College
Florida Gulf Coast University
Florida Institute of Technology
Florida Southern College
Florida State University
Johnson & Wales University:
    North Miami
Lynn University
New College of Florida
Nova Southeastern University
Ringling College of Art and
    Design
Rollins College
Southeastern University
Stetson University
University of Tampa
University of West Florida
Webber International University

Georgia

Augusta State University
Berry College
Chorter University
    Shorter University
Clark Atlanta University
Columbus State University
Covenant College
Emmanuel College
Georgia College and State
    University
Georgia Institute of Technology
Georgia Southwestern State
    University
Georgia State University
Kennesaw State University
LaGrange College
Life University
Morehouse College
North Georgia College & State
    University
Paine College
Piedmont College
Reinhardt University
Savannah College of Art and
    Design
Southern Polytechnic State
    University
University of Georgia
University of West Georgia
Valdosta State University
Wesleyan College

Hawaii

Hawaii Pacific University
University of Hawaii
    Hilo
    West Oahu

Idaho

College of Idaho
Lewis-Clark State College
University of Idaho

Illinois

Augustana College
Aurora University
Blackburn College
Bradley University
Concordia University Chicago
DePaul University
Dominican University
Eastern Illinois University
Elmhurst College
Eureka College
Greenville College
Illinois College
Illinois Institute of Technology
Illinois State University
Illinois Wesleyan University
Judson University
Knox College
Lake Forest College
Lewis University
Lincoln Christian University
Loyola University Chicago
MacMurray College

McKendree University
Millikin University
Monmouth College
North Central College
Northeastern Illinois University
Northern Illinois University
Trinity College of Nursing and
    Health Sciences
University of Illinois
    Chicago
    Springfield
    Urbana-Champaign
Western Illinois University
Wheaton College

Indiana

Anderson University
Ball State University
Bethel College
Butler University
DePauw University
Earlham College
Franklin College
Goshen College
Hanover College
Indiana Institute of Technology
Indiana State University
Indiana University
    Bloomington
    East
    Kokomo
    South Bend
Indiana University-Purdue
    University Indianapolis
Indiana Wesleyan University
Manchester College
Marian University
Oakland City University
Purdue University
Purdue University
    North Central
Rose-Hulman Institute of
    Technology
Saint Joseph's College
Trine University
University of St. Francis
University of Southern Indiana
Valparaiso University
Wabash College

Iowa

Briar Cliff University
Buena Vista University
Central College
Clarke University
Coe College
Drake University
Faith Baptist Bible College and
    Theological Seminary
Graceland University
Grinnell College
Iowa Wesleyan College
Luther College
Mercy College of Health
    Sciences
Morningside College
Mount Mercy University
Northwestern College
Upper Iowa University
Waldorf College
William Penn University

Kansas

Benedictine College
Bethany College
Bethel College
Friends University
Kansas Wesleyan University
McPherson College
Sterling College
University of St. Mary

Kentucky

Asbury University
Bellarmine University
Campbellsville University
Centre College
Eastern Kentucky University

Kentucky Wesleyan College
Midway College
Union College
University of Kentucky
University of Louisville
University of the Cumberlands

Louisiana

Centenary College of Louisiana
Grambling State University
Louisiana College
Loyola University New Orleans
McNeese State University
University of Louisiana at
Lafayette
University of New Orleans
Xavier University of Louisiana

Maine

College of the Atlantic
New England School of
Communications
Unity College in Maine
University of Maine
Fort Kent

Maryland

Capitol College
Frostburg State University
Goucher College
Loyola University Maryland
Maryland Institute College of
Art
Morgan State University
Mount St. Mary's University
Notre Dame of Maryland
University
St. Mary's College of Maryland
Salisbury University
Stevenson University
Towson University
University of Maryland
Baltimore County
Washington College

Massachusetts

Anna Maria College
Bay Path College
Becker College
Bridgewater State University
Clark University
Curry College
Eastern Nazarene College
Emmanuel College
Endicott College
Fitchburg State University
Framingham State University
Hampshire College
Lasell College
Lesley University
Massachusetts College of Art
and Design
Massachusetts College of
Liberal Arts
Mount Holyoke College
Mount Ida College
Newbury College
Salem State University
School of the Museum of Fine
Arts
Springfield College
Stonehill College
University of Massachusetts
Amherst
Boston
Dartmouth
Lowell
Wentworth Institute of
Technology
Westfield State University
Wheaton College
Wheelock College
Worcester Polytechnic Institute
Worcester State University

Michigan

Adrian College
Alma College

Central Michigan University
Concordia University
Cornerstone University
Eastern Michigan University
Kalamazoo College
Kettering University
Kuyper College
Lawrence Technological
University
Madonna University
Michigan State University
Northern Michigan University
Northwood University
Michigan
Oakland University
Olivet College
Rochester College
Siena Heights University
Spring Arbor University
University of Detroit Mercy
University of Michigan
Dearborn
Flint

Minnesota

College of St. Benedict
Concordia University St. Paul
Gustavus Adolphus College
Hamline University
Minneapolis College of Art and
Design
Minnesota State University
Moorhead
North Central University
Oak Hills Christian College
St. Catherine University
St. John's University
St. Mary's University of
Minnesota
St. Olaf College
University of Minnesota
Crookston
Morris
Winona State University

Mississippi

Belhaven University
Delta State University
Jackson State University
Millsaps College
Mississippi State University
University of Southern
Mississippi

Missouri

Avila University
Central Methodist University
Culver-Stockton College
Drury University
Evangel University
Fontbonne University
Hannibal-LaGrange University
Kansas City Art Institute
Lindenwood University
Maryville University of Saint
Louis
Missouri Baptist University
Saint Louis University
Southwest Baptist University
Stephens College
University of Missouri
Kansas City
St. Louis
Webster University
Westminster College
William Jewell College

Montana

Carroll College
Montana State University
Northern
Rocky Mountain College

Nebraska

Concordia University
Grace University
Hastings College
Union College

University of Nebraska
Lincoln

Nevada

Nevada State College
Sierra Nevada College

New Hampshire

Daniel Webster College
Keene State College
Plymouth State University
Saint Anselm College
University of New Hampshire

New Jersey

Bloomfield College
College of St. Elizabeth
Fairleigh Dickinson University
College at Florham
Metropolitan Campus
Georgian Court University
Kean University
Monmouth University
Montclair State University
New Jersey Institute of
Technology
Ramapo College of New Jersey
Richard Stockton College of
New Jersey
Rider University
Rowan University
Rutgers, The State University of
New Jersey
Camden Regional Campus
New Brunswick/Piscataway
Campus
Newark Regional Campus
Saint Peter's College
William Paterson University of
New Jersey

New Mexico

Eastern New Mexico University
New Mexico Institute of Mining
and Technology
University of New Mexico

New York

Adelphi University
Albany College of Pharmacy
and Health Sciences
Alfred University
Canisius College
Cazenovia College
College of Mount St. Vincent
College of Saint Rose
Concordia College
Daemen College
Davis College
Dominican College of Blauvelt
Five Towns College
Hilbert College
Hobart and William Smith
Colleges
Hofstra University
Houghton College
Iona College
Ithaca College
Jewish Theological Seminary of
America
The King's College
Le Moyne College
LIM College
Manhattan College
Manhattanville College
Medaille College
Mercy College
Molloy College
Monroe College
Nazareth College
New York Institute of
Technology
Parsons The New School for
Design
Paul Smith's College
Polytechnic Institute of New
York University
Pratt Institute

Roberts Wesleyan College
Rochester Institute of
Technology
Russell Sage College
Sage College of Albany
St. Francis College
St. John Fisher College
St. Joseph's College, New York
School of Visual Arts
SUNY
College at Fredonia
College at Potsdam
Maritime College
University at Albany
University at Buffalo
Wagner College
Yeshiva University

North Carolina

Appalachian State University
Barton College
Belmont Abbey College
Bennett College for Women
Brevard College
Cabarrus College of Health
Sciences
Chowan University
East Carolina University
Elizabeth City State University
Elon University
Fayetteville State University
Gardner-Webb University
Greensboro College
Guilford College
High Point University
Johnson & Wales University:
Charlotte
Livingstone College
Mars Hill College
Meredith College
Methodist University
Montreat College
Mount Olive College
North Carolina Agricultural and
Technical State University
North Carolina Central
University
North Carolina State University
North Carolina Wesleyan
College
Pfeiffer University
Piedmont International
University
Queens University of Charlotte
St. Andrews University
St. Augustine's College
Salem College
University of North Carolina
Asheville
Charlotte
Pembroke
Wilmington
William Peace University
Winston-Salem State University

North Dakota

Jamestown College
University of North Dakota

Ohio

Ashland University
Baldwin-Wallace College
Bluffton University
Case Western Reserve
University
Cincinnati Christian University
Cleveland Institute of Art
College of Mount St. Joseph
College of Wooster
Columbus College of Art and
Design
Defiance College
Hiram College
Lake Erie College
Lourdes University
Marietta College
Mercy College of Ohio

Miami University
Oxford
Mount Vernon Nazarene
University
Ohio Christian University
Ohio Dominican University
Ohio State University
Columbus Campus
Ohio Wesleyan University
Tiffin University
University of Akron
University of Cincinnati
University of Findlay
University of Mount Union
Ursuline College
Xavier University

Oklahoma

Langston University
Oklahoma Baptist University
Oklahoma Christian University
Oklahoma City University
Oklahoma Wesleyan University
Oral Roberts University
Rogers State University

Oregon

Eastern Oregon University
Lewis & Clark College
Marylhurst University
Multnomah University
Northwest Christian University
Pacific Northwest College of
Art
Portland State University
University of Oregon
University of Portland
Warner Pacific College
Willamette University

Pennsylvania

Allegheny College
Arcadia University
Bloomsburg University of
Pennsylvania
Cabrini College
California University of
Pennsylvania
Carlow University
Cedar Crest College
Chatham University
Chestnut Hill College
Clarion University of
Pennsylvania
Delaware Valley College
DeSales University
Drexel University
Duquesne University
Eastern University
Elizabethtown College
Holy Family University
Indiana University of
Pennsylvania
Juniata College
King's College
Kutztown University of
Pennsylvania
La Roche College
La Salle University
Lebanon Valley College
Lock Haven University of
Pennsylvania
Lycoming College
Marywood University
Messiah College
Millersville University of
Pennsylvania
Misericordia University
Moore College of Art and
Design
Penn State
Shenango
University Park
Philadelphia Biblical University
Philadelphia University
Point Park University
Rosemont College
St. Vincent College

Slippery Rock University of
Pennsylvania
Susquehanna University
Talmudical Yeshiva of
Philadelphia
Temple University
Thiel College
University of Pittsburgh
University of Pittsburgh
Bradford
University of Scranton
University of the Sciences in
Philadelphia
Ursinus College
Waynesburg University
Westminster College
Widener University
Wilson College
York College of Pennsylvania

Puerto Rico

Conservatory of Music of
Puerto Rico
Escuela de Artes Plasticas de
Puerto Rico
Inter American University of
Puerto Rico
Aguadilla Campus
Arecibo Campus
Guayama Campus
San German Campus
Pontifical Catholic University of
Puerto Rico
University of Puerto Rico
Aguadilla
Mayaguez
Utuado

Rhode Island

Providence College
Rhode Island College
Salve Regina University

South Carolina

Allen University
Anderson University
Charleston Southern University
Clemson University
Coastal Carolina University
College of Charleston
Columbia College
Columbia International
University
Converse College
Erskine College
Francis Marion University
Limestone College
Newberry College
North Greenville University
Presbyterian College
University of South Carolina
Beaufort
Columbia
Upstate
Voorhees College
Winthrop University
Wofford College

South Dakota

Mount Marty College

Tennessee

Bryan College
Carson-Newman College
King College
Lee University
Lincoln Memorial University
Lipscomb University
Maryville College
Middle Tennessee State
University
Milligan College
Rhodes College
Tennessee State University
Tusculum College
University of Memphis

University of Tennessee
Chattanooga
Knoxville
Martin
University of the South

Texas

Abilene Christian University
Austin College
Dallas Christian College
East Texas Baptist University
Hardin-Simmons University
Howard Payne University
Lamar University
Lubbock Christian University
McMurry University
Midwestern State University
Our Lady of the Lake
University of San Antonio
St. Edward's University
St. Mary's University
Schreiner University
Southern Methodist University
Southwestern University
Stephen F. Austin State
University
Texas A&M University
Galveston
Texas Lutheran University
Texas Tech University
Texas Wesleyan University
Trinity University
University of Houston
University of North Texas
University of Texas
Arlington
Dallas
Pan American
Tyler
West Texas A&M University

Utah

Brigham Young University
Southern Utah University
Westminster College

Vermont

Bennington College
College of St. Joseph in
Vermont
Green Mountain College
Marlboro College
Norwich University
Vermont Technical College

Virginia

Averett University
Bridgewater College
Christopher Newport University
Eastern Mennonite University
Emory & Henry College
George Mason University
Hampden-Sydney College
James Madison University
Longwood University
Lynchburg College
Norfolk State University
Randolph College
Randolph-Macon College
Roanoke College
Virginia Commonwealth
University
Virginia Polytechnic Institute
and State University
Virginia State University
Virginia Union University

Washington

Cornish College of the Arts
Gonzaga University
Northwest University
Saint Martin's University
Seattle University
Trinity Lutheran College
University of Puget Sound
University of Washington

University of Washington
Bothell
Whitman College

West Virginia

Alderson-Broaddus College
Appalachian Bible College
Bethany College
Concord University
Davis and Elkins College
Fairmont State University
University of Charleston
Wheeling Jesuit University

Wisconsin

Beloit College
Carthage College
Concordia University Wisconsin
Edgewood College
Lawrence University
Marquette University
Milwaukee Institute of Art &
Design
Milwaukee School of
Engineering
Mount Mary College
Northland College
Silver Lake College of the Holy
Family
University of Wisconsin
Green Bay
Madison
Milwaukee
Parkside
Stevens Point
Superior
Wisconsin Lutheran College

Canada

Simon Fraser University
University of Toronto
University of Waterloo

Egypt

American University in Cairo

Lebanon

American University of Beirut

Morocco

Al Akhawayn University

Pakistan

Forman Christian College

Switzerland

Franklin College
Switzerland

Two-year

Alabama

Marion Military Institute

Alaska

Ilisagvik College

California

Art Institute of California:
Sunnyvale

Delaware

Delaware College of Art and
Design

Georgia

Abraham Baldwin Agricultural
College
Georgia Perimeter College
Young Harris College

Idaho

North Idaho College

Iowa

AIB College of Business

Maine

Central Maine Medical Center
College of Nursing and
Health Professions

Maryland

Garrett College

Massachusetts

Dean College
Fisher College

Missouri

Cottey College

New York

American Academy of Dramatic
Arts
Bryant & Stratton College
Albany
Long Island Business Institute
St. Elizabeth College of Nursing
SUNY
College of Agriculture and
Technology at Morrisville
College of Technology at
Alfred
College of Technology at
Canton
College of Technology at
Delhi
Villa Maria College of Buffalo

North Carolina

Louisburg College

Ohio

Art Institute of Cincinnati
Aultman College of Nursing and
Health Sciences

Pennsylvania

Art Institute of York
Manor College

South Carolina

Spartanburg Methodist College

Vermont

Landmark College

Admit over 75% of applicants

Four-year

Alabama

Jacksonville State University
Samford University
Southeastern Bible College
University of Mobile
University of Montevallo
University of North Alabama
University of South Alabama

Alaska

University of Alaska
Anchorage
Fairbanks

Arizona

Arizona State University
Embry-Riddle Aeronautical
University: Prescott Campus
Prescott College
Southwest University of Visual
Arts
University of Advancing
Technology

Arkansas

Arkansas Tech University
Ecclesia College
Hendrix College
University of Central Arkansas

California

American Jewish University
Biola University
California College of the Arts

California State University
Chico
Dominguez Hills
Stanislaus
Concordia University
Ex'pression College for Digital
Arts
Humboldt State University
Life Pacific College
San Francisco Art Institute
San Jose State University
Simpson University
Sonoma State University
Southern California Institute of
Architecture
Thomas Aquinas College
University of California
Merced

Colorado

Colorado State University
Naropa University
Regis University
University of Colorado
Boulder
Western State College of
Colorado

Connecticut

Saint Joseph College

District of Columbia

Catholic University of America

Florida

Embry-Riddle Aeronautical
University
Florida College
Florida Hospital College of
Health Sciences
Hodges University
Palm Beach Atlantic University
St. John Vianney College
Seminary
Saint Leo University

Georgia

Armstrong Atlantic State
University
Brewton-Parker College
Georgia Gwinnett College
Mercer University
Oglethorpe University
Truett-McConnell College

Hawaii

Chaminade University of
Honolulu
University of Hawaii
Manoa

Idaho

Boise Bible College
Boise State University
Brigham Young University-
Idaho
Idaho State University
New Saint Andrews College

Illinois

Benedictine University
Blessing-Rieman College of
Nursing
Kendall College
Moody Bible Institute
Olivet Nazarene University
Principia College
Quincy University
Roosevelt University
School of the Art Institute of
Chicago
Southern Illinois University
Edwardsville
Trinity Christian College
Trinity International University

Indiana

Grace College
Holy Cross College

Huntington University
Indiana University
   Northwest
   Southeast
Indiana University-Purdue
   University Fort Wayne
Saint Mary's College
Taylor University
University of Evansville
University of Indianapolis

Iowa

Allen College
Ashford University
Divine Word College
Dordt College
Emmaus Bible College
Grand View University
Iowa State University
Loras College
St. Ambrose University
Simpson College
University of Dubuque
University of Iowa
University of Northern Iowa
Wartburg College

Kansas

Baker University
Barclay College
Emporia State University
Kansas State University
MidAmerica Nazarene
   University
Pittsburg State University
Southwestern College
Tabor College
University of Kansas
Wichita State University

Kentucky

Georgetown College
Kentucky Christian University
Mid-Continent University
Morehead State University
Murray State University
Thomas More College
Transylvania University
Western Kentucky University

Louisiana

Dillard University
Louisiana State University and
   Agricultural and Mechanical
   College
Nicholls State University
Northwestern State University
St. Joseph Seminary College
University of Louisiana at
   Monroe

Maine

Husson University
Maine College of Art
Thomas College
University of Maine
University of Maine
   Farmington
   Machias
   Presque Isle
University of New England
University of Southern Maine

Maryland

Hood College
McDaniel College
Ner Israel Rabbinical College
St. John's College
Washington Bible College

Massachusetts

American International College
Assumption College
Bard College at Simon's Rock
Hellenic College/Holy Cross
Massachusetts College of
   Pharmacy and Health
   Sciences
Merrimack College

Montserrat College of Art
Nichols College
Regis College
Suffolk University
Western New England
   University
Zion Bible College

Michigan

Albion College
Aquinas College
Calvin College
Davenport University
Grand Valley State University
Hope College
Lake Superior State University
Michigan Technological
   University
Sacred Heart Major Seminary
Saginaw Valley State University
Wayne State University
Western Michigan University

Minnesota

Bemidji State University
Bethany Lutheran College
Bethel University
College of St. Scholastica
College of Visual Arts
Concordia College: Moorhead
Crown College
Martin Luther College
Minnesota State University
   Mankato
Northwestern College
Saint Cloud State University
Southwest Minnesota State
   University
University of Minnesota
   Duluth
University of St. Thomas

Mississippi

University of Mississippi

Missouri

Calvary Bible College and
   Theological Seminary
Conception Seminary College
Missouri Southern State
   University
Missouri State University
Missouri University of Science
   and Technology
Northwest Missouri State
   University
Park University
Rockhurst University
Southeast Missouri State
   University
Truman State University
University of Central Missouri
University of Missouri
   Columbia
William Woods University

Montana

Montana State University
   Billings
Montana Tech of the University
   of Montana
University of Montana

Nebraska

Creative Center
Creighton University
Doane College
Nebraska Wesleyan University
University of Nebraska
   Kearney
   Omaha

Nevada

University of Nevada
   Las Vegas
   Reno

New Hampshire

Colby-Sawyer College
College of St. Mary Magdalen
Franklin Pierce University
New England College
Rivier College
Southern New Hampshire
   University

New Jersey

Caldwell College
Centenary College
Drew University
Felician College
Seton Hall University

New Mexico

New Mexico State University
St. John's College
Southwest University of Visual
   Arts

New York

Clarkson University
Culinary Institute of America
D'Youville College
Dowling College
Elmira College
Eugene Lang College The New
   School for Liberal Arts
Hartwick College
Holy Trinity Orthodox Seminary
Keuka College
Lebanese American University
Long Island University
   Brooklyn Campus
   C. W. Post Campus
Marymount Manhattan College
Mount Saint Mary College
Niagara University
Pace University
Saint Bonaventure University
St. Joseph's College: Suffolk
   Campus
St. Thomas Aquinas College
SUNY
   Empire State College
Utica College
Vaughn College of Aeronautics
   and Technology
Wells College

North Carolina

Lees-McRae College
Lenoir-Rhyne University
Warren Wilson College
Wingate University

North Dakota

North Dakota State University
University of Mary

Ohio

Bowling Green State University
Capital University
Cedarville University
Franciscan University of
   Steubenville
John Carroll University
Kent State University
Malone University
Mount Carmel College of
   Nursing
Muskingum University
Notre Dame College
Ohio Northern University
Ohio University
Otterbein University
Pontifical College Josephinum
University of Dayton
Walsh University
Wilmington College
Wittenberg University
Wright State University

Oklahoma

Cameron University
East Central University

Northwestern Oklahoma State
   University
Oklahoma Panhandle State
   University
Oklahoma State University
Southeastern Oklahoma State
   University
Southwestern Christian
   University
Southwestern Oklahoma State
   University
Spartan College of Aeronautics
   and Technology
University of Central Oklahoma
University of Oklahoma

Oregon

George Fox University
Linfield College
Mount Angel Seminary
Oregon College of Art & Craft
Oregon Institute of Technology
Oregon State University
Pacific University
Southern Oregon University
Western Oregon University

Pennsylvania

Alvernia University
Baptist Bible College of
   Pennsylvania
Cheyney University of
   Pennsylvania
East Stroudsburg University of
   Pennsylvania
Edinboro University of
   Pennsylvania
Gannon University
Geneva College
Grove City College
Gwynedd-Mercy College
Immaculata University
Keystone College
Mansfield University of
   Pennsylvania
Mercyhurst University
Moravian College
Mount Aloysius College
Neumann University
Penn State
   Abington
   Altoona
   Beaver
   Berks
   Brandywine
   DuBois
   Erie, The Behrend College
   Fayette, The Eberly Campus
   Greater Allegheny
   Harrisburg
   Hazleton
   Lehigh Valley
   Mont Alto
   New Kensington
   Schuylkill
   Wilkes-Barre
   Worthington Scranton
   York
Pennsylvania Academy of the
   Fine Arts
Robert Morris University
St. Charles Borromeo Seminary
   - Overbrook
St. Francis University
Saint Joseph's University
Shippensburg University of
   Pennsylvania
University of Pittsburgh
   Greensburg
   Johnstown
Valley Forge Christian College
Wilkes University

Puerto Rico

Electronic Data Processing
   College: San Sebastian
National University College:
   Arecibo

National University College:
   Bayamon
National University College:
   Rio Grande
Universidad Pentecostal Mizpa
Universidad Politecnica de
   Puerto Rico
University of Puerto Rico
   Arecibo
   Carolina Regional College
   Cayey University College
   Ponce

Rhode Island

Bryant University
Johnson & Wales University:
   Providence
Roger Williams University
University of Rhode Island

South Carolina

Bob Jones University
The Citadel
Furman University
Morris College
South Carolina State University

South Dakota

Augustana College
Black Hills State University
Dakota State University
Dakota Wesleyan University
Northern State University
South Dakota School of Mines
   and Technology
South Dakota State University
University of Sioux Falls
University of South Dakota

Tennessee

Austin Peay State University
Belmont University
East Tennessee State University
Fisk University
Freed-Hardeman University
Tennessee Technological
   University
Tennessee Wesleyan College
Trevecca Nazarene University
Union University
Watkins College of Art, Design
   & Film

Texas

Angelo State University
Concordia University Texas
Huston-Tillotson University
Sam Houston State University
Tarleton State University
Texas A&M University
   Corpus Christi
Texas State University: San
   Marcos
Texas Woman's University
University of Dallas
University of St. Thomas
University of Texas
   San Antonio
   of the Permian Basin
University of the Incarnate
   Word
Wayland Baptist University

Utah

Neumont University
University of Utah
Utah State University

Vermont

Burlington College
Castleton State College
Champlain College
Johnson State College
Lyndon State College
St. Michael's College
Southern Vermont College
Sterling College
University of Vermont

Tables and Indexes

Virginia

Christendom College
Hollins University
Marymount University
Old Dominion University
Patrick Henry College
Radford University
Regent University
St. Paul's College
Shenandoah University
Southern Virginia University
Sweet Briar College
University of Mary Washington
University of Virginia's College
 at Wise
Virginia Intermont College
Virginia Wesleyan College

Washington

Eastern Washington University
Evergreen State College
Pacific Lutheran University
Seattle Pacific University
University of Washington
 Tacoma
Washington State University
Western Washington University

West Virginia

Glenville State College
Marshall University
Shepherd University
West Virginia State University
West Virginia University
West Virginia Wesleyan College

Wisconsin

Alverno College
Carroll University
Lakeland College
Maranatha Baptist Bible College
Marian University
Ripon College
St. Norbert College
University of Wisconsin
 Eau Claire
 La Crosse
 Platteville
 Stout
Viterbo University

Wyoming

University of Wyoming

Virgin Islands

University of the Virgin Islands

France

American University of Paris

Kuwait

American University of Kuwait

United Arab Emirates

American University in Dubai

Two-year

California

Concorde Career College
 North Hollywood
Epic Bible College
Fashion Institute of Design and
 Merchandising
 San Francisco

Georgia

Georgia Highlands College
ITT Technical Institute
 Kennesaw

Hawaii

Hawaii Tokai International
 College

Illinois

Taylor Business Institute

Kentucky

Sullivan College of Technology
and Design

Massachusetts

Bay State College

New Jersey

Assumption College for Sisters

New York

American Academy McAllister
 Institute of Funeral Service
Jamestown Business College

Ohio

Cincinnati College of Mortuary
 Science
Davis College
Good Samaritan College of
 Nursing and Health Science

Pennsylvania

Bradford School: Pittsburgh
University of Pittsburgh
 Titusville

Virginia

Richard Bland College

Wisconsin

University of Wisconsin
 Fox Valley

Open admission

Four-year

Alabama

Amridge University
Columbia Southern University
Huntsville Bible College
Miles College
Selma University
Talladega College
United States Sports Academy
University of Phoenix
 Birmingham
Virginia College
 Birmingham
 Huntsville

Alaska

Alaska Bible College

Arizona

Argosy University: Online
Argosy University: Phoenix
Brown Mackie College
 Tucson
Collins College
Dunlap-Stone University
International Baptist College
Northcentral University
University of Phoenix
 Phoenix-Hohokam
 Southern Arizona
Western International University

Arkansas

Arkansas Baptist College
University of Arkansas
 Fort Smith
 Monticello
University of Phoenix
 Little Rock
 Northwest Arkansas

California

Academy of Art University
Alliant International University
Antioch University
 Los Angeles
Argosy University: Inland
 Empire
Argosy University: Los Angeles
Argosy University: Orange
 County
Argosy University: San Diego
Argosy University: San
 Francisco Bay Area

Art Institute of California:
 Orange County
Bergin University of Canine
 Studies
California Christian College
California Coast University
California College San Diego
California Miramar University
Charles Drew University of
 Medicine and Science
Coleman University
Horizon College of San Diego
Interior Designers Institute
International Academy of
 Design and Technology
 Sacramento
LA College International
National Hispanic University
National University
Pacific States University
Patten University
Platt College
 San Diego
School of Urban Missions:
 Oakland
Southern California Institute of
 Technology
Southern California Seminary
Stanbridge College
Trident University International
University of Phoenix
 Bay Area
 Central Valley
 Sacramento Valley
 San Diego
 Southern California

Colorado

American Sentinel University
Argosy University: Denver
Aspen University
CollegeAmerica
 Fort Collins
Colorado Technical University
Nazarene Bible College
Platt College
 Aurora
Rocky Mountain College of Art
 & Design
University of Phoenix
 Denver
 Southern Colorado

Connecticut

University of Phoenix
 Fairfield County

Delaware

University of Phoenix
 Delaware
Wilmington University

District of Columbia

Potomac College
University of Phoenix
 Washington DC

Florida

Argosy University: Sarasota
Argosy University: Tampa
Digital Media Arts College
Florida Career College: Boynton
 Beach
Florida Career College:
 Jacksonville
Florida Career College:
 Lauderdale Lakes
Florida Career College:
 Riverview
International Academy of
 Design and Technology
 Orlando
Jones College
Rasmussen College
 Fort Myers
 Ocala
 Pasco County
 Tampa/Brandon

Schiller International University
University of Phoenix
 Central Florida
 North Florida
 South Florida
 West Florida

Georgia

Argosy University: Atlanta
Bauder College
Beulah Heights University
Luther Rice University
Macon State College
Thomas University
University of Phoenix
 Atlanta
 Augusta
 Columbus Georgia
 Savannah

Hawaii

Argosy University: Hawaii
University of Phoenix
 Hawaii

Idaho

University of Phoenix
 Idaho

Illinois

American Academy of Art
Argosy University: Schaumburg
Columbia College Chicago
East-West University
Governors State University
Harrington College of Design
Midstate College
Saint Anthony College of
 Nursing
St. Augustine College
St. John's College
Saint Xavier University
University of Phoenix
 Chicago

Indiana

International Business College
Martin University
University of Phoenix
 Indianapolis

Iowa

Hamilton Technical College
Kaplan University
 Cedar Falls
 Des Moines
 Mason City
University of Phoenix
 Des Moines

Kansas

University of Phoenix
 Wichita
Washburn University

Kentucky

Beckfield College
Clear Creek Baptist Bible
 College
Lindsey Wilson College
St. Catharine College
University of Phoenix
 Louisville
University of Pikeville

Louisiana

Southwest University
University of Phoenix
 Baton Rouge
 Lafayette
 Louisiana
 Shreveport

Maine

University of Maine
 Augusta

Maryland

National Labor College
University of Maryland
 University College
University of Phoenix
 Maryland

Massachusetts

Boston Architectural College
Cambridge College
University of Phoenix
 Boston

Michigan

Baker College
 of Allen Park
 of Auburn Hills
 of Cadillac
 of Clinton Township
 of Flint
 of Jackson
 of Muskegon
 of Owosso
 of Port Huron
Cleary University
Ferris State University
Finlandia University
University of Phoenix
 Metro Detroit
 West Michigan

Minnesota

Argosy University: Twin Cities
Art Institutes International
 Minnesota
Capella University
Globe University
 Minneapolis
 Woodbury
Minnesota School of Business
 Blaine
 Elk River
 Lakeville
 Moorhead
 Richfield
Northwestern Health Sciences
 University
Rasmussen College
 Blaine
 Lake Elmo/Woodbury
 Moorhead
University of Phoenix
 Minneapolis-St. Paul
Walden University

Mississippi

Southeastern Baptist College
University of Mississippi
 Medical Center
University of Phoenix
 Jackson

Missouri

Baptist Bible College
Global University
Grantham University
Harris-Stowe State University
Hickey College
Lincoln University
Missouri Western State
 University
National American University
 Kansas City
 Lee's Summit
University of Phoenix
 Kansas City
 St. Louis
 Springfield

Montana

University of Montana: Western

Nebraska

Bellevue University
Chadron State College
Clarkson College
University of Phoenix
 Omaha

Wayne State College

Nevada

Art Institute of Las Vegas
Great Basin College
Morrison University
University of Phoenix
Las Vegas
Northern Nevada

New Hampshire

Granite State College
Hesser College

New Jersey

Thomas Edison State College
University of Phoenix
Jersey City

New Mexico

New Mexico Highlands
University
University of Phoenix
New Mexico
University of the Southwest

New York

City University of New York
CUNY Online
Medgar Evers College
New York City College of
Technology
Excelsior College
Globe Institute of Technology
Yeshivat Mikdash Melech

North Carolina

Apex School of Theology
Art Institute of Charlotte
Carolina Christian College
Miller-Motte College:
Wilmington
Southeastern Baptist
Theological Seminary
University of Phoenix
Charlotte
Raleigh

North Dakota

Dickinson State University
Mayville State University
Rasmussen College
Fargo

Ohio

Bryant & Stratton College
Eastlake
Parma
Franklin University
Ohio Mid-Western College
Ohio State University
Lima Campus
Mansfield Campus
Marion Campus
Newark Campus
Ohio University
Chillicothe Campus
Eastern Campus
Lancaster Campus
Southern Campus at Ironton
Zanesville Campus
Shawnee State University
Tri-State Bible College
University of Phoenix
Cincinnati
Cleveland
Columbus Ohio
University of Rio Grande
University of Toledo
Youngstown State University

Oklahoma

Mid-America Christian
University
University of Phoenix
Oklahoma City
Tulsa

Oregon

University of Phoenix
Oregon

Pennsylvania

Peirce College
Pennsylvania College of
Technology
University of Phoenix
Harrisburg
Philadelphia
Pittsburgh
Yeshivath Beth Moshe

Puerto Rico

Atlantic College
Caribbean University
Columbia Centro Universitario:
Caguas
Universidad Adventista de las
Antillas
Universidad del Este
University of Phoenix
Puerto Rico

Rhode Island

New England Institute of
Technology

South Carolina

University of Phoenix
Columbia

Tennessee

Argosy University: Nashville
Free Will Baptist Bible College
International Academy of
Design and Technology
Nashville
University of Phoenix
Chattanooga
Knoxville
Memphis
Nashville
Williamson Christian College

Texas

Argosy University: Dallas
Arlington Baptist College
Art Institute of Dallas
Baptist Missionary Association
Theological Seminary
Baptist University of the
Americas
College of Biblical Studies-
Houston
Jarvis Christian College
Southwestern Christian College
Texas College
University of Houston
Downtown
University of Phoenix
Austin
Dallas Fort Worth
Houston Westside
San Antonio
University of Texas
Brownsville - Texas
Southmost College
Wiley College

Utah

Argosy University: Salt Lake
City
Broadview University
Orem
Dixie State College
Independence University
Stevens-Henager College
Logan
University of Phoenix
Utah
Utah Valley University
Weber State University
Western Governors University

Virginia

Argosy University: Washington
D.C.

Catholic Distance University
National College
Salem
Potomac College
Stratford University: Falls
Church
Stratford University:
Woodbridge
University of Management and
Technology
University of Phoenix
Northern Virginia
Richmond
Virginia University of
Lynchburg
World College

Washington

Argosy University: Seattle
Art Institute of Seattle
City University of Seattle
University of Phoenix
Western Washington

West Virginia

American Public University
System
Mountain State University

Wisconsin

Globe University
Green Bay
Herzing University
Madison
Northland International
University
Rasmussen College
Appleton
University of Phoenix
Madison
Milwaukee

Guam

University of Guam

Lebanon

Notre Dame University: Louaize

Mexico

Instituto Tecnologico y de
Estudios Superiores de
Occidente

Two-year

Alabama

Alabama Southern Community
College
Bevill State Community College
Bishop State Community
College
Calhoun Community College
Central Alabama Community
College
Chattahoochee Valley
Community College
Enterprise State Community
College
Faulkner State Community
College
Gadsden State Community
College
George C. Wallace Community
College at Dothan
George C. Wallace State
Community College at Selma
Jefferson Davis Community
College
Jefferson State Community
College
Lawson State Community
College
Lurleen B. Wallace Community
College
Northeast Alabama Community
College
Northwest-Shoals Community
College

Prince Institute of Professional
Studies
Remington College
Mobile
Shelton State Community
College
Snead State Community College
Southern Union State
Community College
Virginia College
Mobile
Wallace State Community
College at Hanceville

Alaska

Prince William Sound
Community College

Arizona

Anthem College
Phoenix
Arizona Automotive Institute
Arizona Western College
Brookline College
Phoenix
Tempe
Tucson
Bryman School of Arizona
Carrington College
Mesa
Phoenix Westside
Tucson
Carrington College: Phoenix
Central Arizona College
Chandler-Gilbert Community
College
Cochise College
Coconino County Community
College
Dine College
Eastern Arizona College
Estrella Mountain Community
College
GateWay Community College
Glendale Community College
Kaplan College: Phoenix
Le Cordon Bleu College of
Culinary Arts
Scottsdale
Mesa Community College
Mohave Community College
Northland Pioneer College
Paradise Valley Community
College
Paralegal Institute
Penn Foster College
Phoenix College
Pima Community College
Refrigeration School
Rio Salado College
Scottsdale Community College
Sessions College for
Professional Design
South Mountain Community
College
Tohono O'odham Community
College
Universal Technical Institute
Yavapai College

Arkansas

Arkansas Northeastern College
Arkansas State University
Beebe
Mountain Home
Black River Technical College
Bryan College
Rogers
College of the Ouachitas
Cossatot Community College of
the University of Arkansas
Crowley's Ridge College
East Arkansas Community
College
Mid-South Community College
National Park Community
College
North Arkansas College

Northwest Arkansas Community
College
Ozarka College
Phillips Community College of
the University of Arkansas
Pulaski Technical College
Remington College
Little Rock
Rich Mountain Community
College
South Arkansas Community
College
Southeast Arkansas College
Southern Arkansas University
Tech
University of Arkansas
Community College at
Batesville
Community College at
Hope
Community College at
Morrilton

California

Allan Hancock College
American River College
Antelope Valley College
Bakersfield College
Barstow Community College
Berkeley City College
Bryan College
Sacramento
Bryan University: Los Angeles
Butte College
Cabrillo College
Canada College
Carrington College
Antioch
Cerritos College
Cerro Coso Community College
Chabot College
Chaffey College
Citrus College
City College of San Francisco
Coastline Community College
Coleman College: San Marcos
College of Alameda
College of Marin
College of San Mateo
College of the Canyons
College of the Desert
College of the Redwoods
College of the Sequoias
College of the Siskiyous
Columbia College
Contra Costa College
Copper Mountain College
Cosumnes River College
Crafton Hills College
Cuesta College
Cuyamaca College
Cypress College
De Anza College
Diablo Valley College
East Los Angeles College
El Camino College
Empire College
Evergreen Valley College
Feather River College
Folsom Lake College
Foothill College
Fremont College: Cerritos
Fresno City College
Fullerton College
Gavilan College
Glendale Community College
Golden West College
Golf Academy of America: San
Diego
Grossmont College
Hartnell College
Imperial Valley College
Irvine Valley College
Kaplan College: Palm Springs
Kaplan College: Panorama City
Kaplan College: Sacramento
Kaplan College: Salida

Butler Community College
Cloud County Community
College
Coffeyville Community College
Colby Community College
Cowley County Community
College
Dodge City Community College
Donnelly College
Fort Scott Community College
Garden City Community
College
Hesston College
Highland Community College
Hutchinson Community College
Independence Community
College
Johnson County Community
College
Kansas City Kansas Community
College
Labette Community College
Manhattan Area Technical
College
Neosho County Community
College
North Central Kansas Technical
College
Northwest Kansas Technical
College
Pratt Community College
Seward County Community
College
Wichita Area Technical College

Kentucky

Ashland Community and
Technical College
Big Sandy Community and
Technical College
Bluegrass Community and
Technical College
Daymar College
Bowling Green
Owensboro
Paducah
Elizabethtown Community and
Technical College
Gateway Community and
Technical College
Hazard Community and
Technical College
Henderson Community College
Hopkinsville Community
College
Lincoln College of Technology
Florence
Madisonville Community
College
Maysville Community and
Technical College
National College
Danville
Florence
Lexington
Louisville
Pikeville
Richmond
Owensboro Community and
Technical College
Somerset Community College
Southeast Kentucky Community
and Technical College
Spencerian College
Spencerian College: Lexington
West Kentucky Community and
Technical College

Louisiana

Baton Rouge Community
College
Baton Rouge School of
Computers
Blue Cliff College
Metairie
Shreveport
Bossier Parish Community
College

Delgado Community College
Delta College of Arts &
Technology
Gretna Career College
ITI Technical College
Louisiana State University
Eunice
Nunez Community College
Remington College
Baton Rouge
Lafayette
Shreveport
River Parishes Community
College
South Louisiana Community
College
Southern University
Shreveport
Virginia College
Baton Rouge

Maine

Beal College
Central Maine Community
College
Eastern Maine Community
College
Kaplan University
South Portland
Kennebec Valley Community
College
Landing School of Boatbuilding
and Design
Southern Maine Community
College
Washington County Community
College
York County Community
College

Maryland

Allegany College of Maryland
Anne Arundel Community
College
Baltimore City Community
College
Carroll Community College
Cecil College
Chesapeake College
College of Southern Maryland
Community College of
Baltimore County
Frederick Community College
Hagerstown Community College
Harford Community College
Howard Community College
Kaplan University
Hagerstown
Montgomery College
Prince George's Community
College
TESST College of Technology
Baltimore
Beltsville
Towson
Wor-Wic Community College

Massachusetts

Berkshire Community College
Bristol Community College
Bunker Hill Community College
Cape Cod Community College
Greenfield Community College
Holyoke Community College
Massachusetts Bay Community
College
Massasoit Community College
Middlesex Community College
Mount Wachusett Community
College
New England College of
Business and Finance
North Shore Community
College
Northern Essex Community
College
Quincy College

Quinsigamond Community
College
Roxbury Community College
Springfield Technical
Community College
Urban College of Boston

Michigan

Alpena Community College
Bay de Noc Community College
Bay Mills Community College
Delta College
Glen Oaks Community College
Gogebic Community College
Grand Rapids Community
College
Henry Ford Community College
Jackson Community College
Kalamazoo Valley Community
College
Kellogg Community College
Kirtland Community College
Lake Michigan College
Lansing Community College
Macomb Community College
Mid Michigan Community
College
Monroe County Community
College
Montcalm Community College
Mott Community College
Muskegon Community College
North Central Michigan College
Northwestern Michigan College
Oakland Community College
Saginaw Chippewa Tribal
College
St. Clair County Community
College
Schoolcraft College
Southwestern Michigan College
Washtenaw Community College
Wayne County Community
College
West Shore Community College

Minnesota

Academy College
Alexandria Technical and
Community College
Anoka Technical College
Anoka-Ramsey Community
College
Anthem College
Minneapolis
Central Lakes College
Century College
Dakota County Technical
College
Fond du Lac Tribal and
Community College
Hennepin Technical College
Herzing University
Minneapolis
Hibbing Community College
Inver Hills Community College
Itasca Community College
Lake Superior College
Le Cordon Bleu College of
Culinary Arts
Minneapolis-St. Paul
Leech Lake Tribal College
Mesabi Range Community and
Technical College
Minneapolis Business College
Minneapolis Community and
Technical College
Minnesota State College -
Southeast Technical
Minnesota State Community and
Technical College
Minnesota West Community
and Technical College
Normandale Community
College
North Hennepin Community
College

Northland Community &
Technical College
Northwest Technical College
Pine Technical College
Rainy River Community
College
Rasmussen College
Bloomington
Brooklyn Park
Eagan
Mankato
St. Cloud
Riverland Community College
Rochester Community and
Technical College
St. Cloud Technical and
Community College
St. Paul College
South Central College
Vermilion Community College

Mississippi

Antonelli College
Jackson
Coahoma Community College
Copiah-Lincoln Community
College
East Mississippi Community
College
Hinds Community College
Holmes Community College
Itawamba Community College
Meridian Community College
Mississippi Delta Community
College
Mississippi Gulf Coast
Community College
Northeast Mississippi
Community College
Pearl River Community College
Southwest Mississippi
Community College

Missouri

Anthem College
Kansas City
Bolivar Technical College
Crowder College
East Central College
Jefferson College
Linn State Technical College
Metro Business College
Jefferson City
Rolla
Metropolitan Community
College: Blue River
Metropolitan Community
College: Business &
Technology
Metropolitan Community
College: Longview
Metropolitan Community
College: Maple Woods
Metropolitan Community
College: Penn Valley
Mineral Area College
Missouri State University: West
Plains
Moberly Area Community
College
North Central Missouri College
Ozarks Technical Community
College
Pinnacle Career Institute:
Kansas City
Ranken Technical College
St. Charles Community College
St. Louis Community College
Florissant Valley
Meramec
State Fair Community College
Stevens Institute of Business &
Arts
Texas County Technical
Institute
Three Rivers Community
College

Vatterott College
O'Fallon
St. Joseph
Wentworth Military Junior
College

Montana

Aaniiih Nakoda College
Blackfeet Community College
Chief Dull Knife College
Dawson Community College
Flathead Valley Community
College
Fort Peck Community College
Little Big Horn College
Miles Community College
Montana State University
Great Falls College of
Technology
Stone Child College
University of Montana: Helena
College of Technology

Nebraska

Central Community College
Kaplan University
Lincoln
Omaha
Little Priest Tribal College
Metropolitan Community
College
Mid-Plains Community College
Area
Nebraska College of Technical
Agriculture
Nebraska Indian Community
College
Northeast Community College
Southeast Community College
Western Nebraska Community
College

Nevada

College of Southern Nevada
Kaplan College: Las Vegas
Truckee Meadows Community
College
Western Nevada College

New Hampshire

Great Bay Community College
Lakes Region Community
College
Lebanon College
Manchester Community College
Nashua Community College
NHTI-Concord's Community
College
River Valley Community
College
White Mountains Community
College

New Jersey

Atlantic Cape Community
College
Bergen Community College
Brookdale Community College
Burlington County College
Camden County College
County College of Morris
Cumberland County College
Eastern International College
Essex County College
Gloucester County College
Hudson County Community
College
Mercer County Community
College
Middlesex County College
Ocean County College
Passaic County Community
College
Raritan Valley Community
College
Salem Community College
Sussex County Community
College

Union County College
Warren County Community
College

New Mexico

Brookline College
Albuquerque
Central New Mexico
Community College
Clovis Community College
Dona Ana Community College
of New Mexico State
University
Eastern New Mexico
University: Roswell
Luna Community College
Mesalands Community College
Navajo Technical College
New Mexico Junior College
New Mexico State University
Alamogordo
Carlsbad
Grants
Northern New Mexico College
San Juan College
Santa Fe Community College
Southwestern Indian Polytechnic
Institute

New York

Adirondack Community College
Art Institute of New York City
ASA Institute of Business and
Computer Technology
Broome Community College
Bryant & Stratton College
Buffalo
Southtowns
Syracuse
Business Informatics Center
Cayuga Community College
City University of New York
Borough of Manhattan
Community College
Bronx Community College
Hostos Community College
Kingsborough Community
College
LaGuardia Community
College
Queensborough Community
College
Corning Community College
Dutchess Community College
Elmira Business Institute
Elmira Business Institute: Vestal
Erie Community College
Finger Lakes Community
College
Fulton-Montgomery Community
College
Genesee Community College
Herkimer County Community
College
Hudson Valley Community
College
Institute of Design and
Construction
Island Drafting and Technical
Institute
Jamestown Community College
Jefferson Community College
Mildred Elley
Mohawk Valley Community
College
Monroe Community College
Nassau Community College
New York Career Institute
Niagara County Community
College
North Country Community
College
Onondaga Community College
Orange County Community
College
Rockland Community College
Schenectady County
Community College

Suffolk County Community
College
Sullivan County Community
College
Technical Career Institutes
Tompkins Cortland Community
College
Trocaire College
Ulster County Community
College
Utica School of Commerce
Westchester Community College

North Carolina

Alamance Community College
Asheville-Buncombe Technical
Community College
Beaufort County Community
College
Bladen Community College
Blue Ridge Community College
Brunswick Community College
Caldwell Community College
and Technical Institute
Cape Fear Community College
Carolinas College of Health
Sciences
Carteret Community College
Catawba Valley Community
College
Central Carolina Community
College
Central Piedmont Community
College
Cleveland Community College
Coastal Carolina Community
College
College of the Albemarle
Craven Community College
Davidson County Community
College
Durham Technical Community
College
Edgecombe Community College
Fayetteville Technical
Community College
Forsyth Technical Community
College
Gaston College
Guilford Technical Community
College
Halifax Community College
Haywood Community College
Isothermal Community College
James Sprunt Community
College
Johnston Community College
Lenoir Community College
Martin Community College
Mayland Community College
McDowell Technical
Community College
Miller-Motte College: Cary
Mitchell Community College
Montgomery Community
College
Nash Community College
Pamlico Community College
Piedmont Community College
Pitt Community College
Randolph Community College
Richmond Community College
Roanoke-Chowan Community
College
Robeson Community College
Rockingham Community
College
Rowan-Cabarrus Community
College
Sampson Community College
Sandhills Community College
Shepherds Theological Seminary
South College
South Piedmont Community
College
Southeastern Community
College

Southwestern Community
College
Stanly Community College
Surry Community College
Tri-County Community College
Vance-Granville Community
College
Wake Technical Community
College
Wayne Community College
Western Piedmont Community
College
Wilkes Community College
Wilson Community College

North Dakota

Bismarck State College
Cankdeska Cikana Community
College
Dakota College at Bottineau
Fort Berthold Community
College
Lake Region State College
North Dakota State College of
Science
Rasmussen College
Bismarck
Sitting Bull College
United Tribes Technical College
Williston State College

Ohio

Belmont Technical College
Bowling Green State University:
Firelands College
Bradford School
Bryant & Stratton College
Cleveland
Central Ohio Technical College
Chatfield College
Cincinnati State Technical and
Community College
Clark State Community College
Cleveland Institute of
Electronics
Columbus State Community
College
Cuyahoga Community College
Metropolitan
Eastern Gateway Community
College
Edison State Community
College
ETI Technical College of Niles
Fortis College
Centerville
Hocking College
International College of
Broadcasting
James A. Rhodes State College
Kaplan College: Columbus
Kaplan College: Dayton
Kent State University
Ashtabula
East Liverpool
Geauga
Salem
Stark
Trumbull
Tuscarawas
Lakeland Community College
Lincoln College of Technology
Dayton
Franklin
Tri-County
Lorain County Community
College
Marion Technical College
Miami University
Hamilton
Middletown
National College
Cincinnati
Columbus
Dayton
Stow
Willoughby Hills
Youngstown

North Central State College
Northwest State Community
College
Ohio College of Massotherapy
Ohio State University
Agricultural Technical
Institute
Ohio Technical College
Owens Community College
Toledo
PowerSport Institute
Remington College
Cleveland West
Rosedale Bible College
Sinclair Community College
Southern State Community
College
Southwestern College
Lincoln College of
Technology: Vine Street
Campus
Stark State College of
Technology
Stautzenberger College:
Brecksville
Terra State Community College
Trumbull Business College
University of Akron: Wayne
College
University of Cincinnati
Clermont College
Washington State Community
College
Wright State University: Lake
Campus

Oklahoma

Carl Albert State College
Connors State College
Eastern Oklahoma State College
Murray State College
Northeastern Oklahoma
Agricultural and Mechanical
College
Northern Oklahoma College
Oklahoma City Community
College
Oklahoma State University
Institute of Technology:
Okmulgee
Oklahoma City
Platt College
Moore
Oklahoma City Central
Tulsa
Redlands Community College
Rose State College
Seminole State College
Tulsa Community College
Tulsa Welding School
Virginia College
Tulsa
Western Oklahoma State
College

Oregon

Central Oregon Community
College
Chemeketa Community College
Clackamas Community College
Clatsop Community College
Klamath Community College
Lane Community College
Linn-Benton Community
College
Mt. Hood Community College
Pioneer Pacific College
Portland Community College
Rogue Community College
Southwestern Oregon
Community College
Treasure Valley Community
College
Umpqua Community College

Pennsylvania

Bucks County Community
College

Butler County Community
College
Cambria-Rowe Business College
Community College of
Allegheny County
Community College of
Philadelphia
Consolidated School of Business
Lancaster
York
Delaware County Community
College
Douglas Education Center
DuBois Business College
DuBois Business College
Huntingdon
Erie Business Center South
Harrisburg Area Community
College
JNA Institute of Culinary Arts
Kaplan Career Institute:
Harrisburg
Keystone Technical Institute
Lackawanna College
Lehigh Carbon Community
College
Lincoln Technical Institute:
Allentown
Lincoln Technical Institute:
Northeast Philadelphia
Lincoln Technical Institute:
Philadelphia
Luzerne County Community
College
McCann School of Business and
Technology
Pottsville
Montgomery County
Community College
Newport Business Institute:
Williamsport
Northampton Community
College
Oakbridge Academy of Arts
Penn Commercial Business and
Technical School
Pennco Tech
Pennsylvania Highlands
Community College
Pennsylvania Institute of
Technology
Pennsylvania School of
Business
Pittsburgh Institute of
Aeronautics
Reading Area Community
College
Rosedale Technical Institute
Sanford-Brown Institute
Monroeville
Triangle Tech
Bethlehem
DuBois
Erie
Greensburg
Pittsburgh
Sunbury
Westmoreland County
Community College
YTI Career Institute
Altoona
Capital Region
Lancaster
York

Puerto Rico

Centro de Estudios
Multidisciplinarios
Colegio de Cinematografía,
Artes y Televisión
Columbia Centro Universitario:
Yauco
EDIC College
Huertas Junior College
Humacao Community College
ICPR Junior College
Ponce Paramedical College

Universal Technology College
of Puerto Rico

Rhode Island

Community College of Rhode
Island

South Carolina

Aiken Technical College
Central Carolina Technical
College
Clinton Junior College
Denmark Technical College
Florence-Darlington Technical
College
Forrest Junior College
Golf Academy of America: The
Carolinas
Greenville Technical College
Horry-Georgetown Technical
College
Midlands Technical College
Miller-Motte Technical College
Northeastern Technical Service
Orangeburg-Calhoun Technical
College
Piedmont Technical College
Spartanburg Community College
Technical College of the
Lowcountry
Tri-County Technical College
Trident Technical College
University of South Carolina
Lancaster
Virginia College
Charleston
Columbia
Greenville
Spartanburg
Williamsburg Technical College
York Technical College

South Dakota

Globe University
Sioux Falls
Kilian Community College
Lake Area Technical Institute
Sisseton Wahpeton College
Southeast Technical Institute

Tennessee

Anthem Career College
Memphis
Chattanooga State Community
College
Cleveland State Community
College
Columbia State Community
College
Dyersburg State Community
College
Jackson State Community
College
John A. Gupton College
Motlow State Community
College
Nashville State Community
College
National College of Business
and Technology
Bartlett
Bristol
Knoxville
Madison
Memphis
Nashville
Northeast State Community
College
Pellissippi State Community
College
Remington College
Nashville
Roane State Community College
Southwest Tennessee
Community College
Virginia College
School of Business and
Health

Volunteer State Community
College
Walters State Community
College

Texas

Alvin Community College
Amarillo College
Angelina College
Austin Community College
Blinn College
Brazosport College
Brookhaven College
Cedar Valley College
Central Texas College
Cisco College
Clarendon College
Coastal Bend College
College of the Mainland
Collin County Community
College District
Culinary Institute LeNotre
Dallas Institute of Funeral
Service
Del Mar College
Eastfield College
El Centro College
El Paso Community College
Frank Phillips College
Galveston College
Grayson County College
Hill College
Houston Community College
System
Howard College
International Academy of
Design and Technology
San Antonio
Jacksonville College
Kilgore College
Lamar Institute of Technology
Lamar State College at Orange
Lamar State College at Port
Arthur
Laredo Community College
Lee College
Lincoln College of Technology:
Grand Prairie
Lone Star College System
McLennan Community College
Midland College
Mountain View College
Navarro College
North Central Texas College
North Lake College
Northeast Texas Community
College
Northwest Vista College
Odessa College
Palo Alto College
Panola College
Paris Junior College
Ranger College
Remington College
Dallas
Fort Worth
Houston
North Houston
Richland College
St. Philip's College
San Antonio College
San Jacinto College
Sanford-Brown College
Houston
South Plains College
South Texas College
Southwest Texas Junior College
Tarrant County College
Temple College
Texarkana College
Texas State Technical College
Harlingen
Marshall
Waco
West Texas
Trinity Valley Community
College

Tyler Junior College
Vernon College
Victoria College
Virginia College
Austin
Wade College
Weatherford College
Western Technical College
Western Technical College:
Diana Drive
Western Texas College
Wharton County Junior College

Utah

Broadview University
Broadview Entertainment
Arts University
Layton
West Jordan
Eagle Gate College: Layton
Eagle Gate College: Murray
LDS Business College
Provo College
Salt Lake Community College
Snow College

Vermont

Community College of Vermont

Virginia

Blue Ridge Community College
Bryant & Stratton College
Richmond
Virginia Beach
Central Virginia Community
College
Dabney S. Lancaster
Community College
Danville Community College
Eastern Shore Community
College
Germanna Community College
J. Sargeant Reynolds
Community College
John Tyler Community College
Lord Fairfax Community
College
Mountain Empire Community
College
National College
Charlottesville
Danville
Harrisonburg
Lynchburg
Martinsville
New River Community College
Northern Virginia Community
College
Patrick Henry Community
College
Paul D. Camp Community
College
Piedmont Virginia Community
College
Rappahannock Community
College
Southside Virginia Community
College
Southwest Virginia Community
College
Thomas Nelson Community
College
Tidewater Community College
Virginia College
Richmond
Virginia Highlands Community
College
Virginia Western Community
College
Wytheville Community College

Washington

Bates Technical College
Bellevue College
Bellingham Technical College
Big Bend Community College
Cascadia Community College
Centralia College

Clark College
Clover Park Technical College
Columbia Basin College
Everett Community College
Grays Harbor College
Green River Community
College
Highline Community College
Lake Washington Institute of
Technology
Lower Columbia College
North Seattle Community
College
Northwest Indian College
Northwest School of Wooden
Boatbuilding
Olympic College
Peninsula College
Pierce College
Renton Technical College
Seattle Central Community
College
Shoreline Community College
Skagit Valley College
South Puget Sound Community
College
South Seattle Community
College
Spokane Community College
Tacoma Community College
Walla Walla Community
College
Wenatchee Valley College
Whatcom Community College
Yakima Valley Community
College

West Virginia

Blue Ridge Community and
Technical College
Bridgemont Community and
Technical College
Eastern West Virginia
Community and Technical
College
Huntington Junior College
Kanawha Valley Community
and Technical College
Mountain State College
National College
Parkersburg
Princeton
New River Community and
Technical College
Potomac State College of West
Virginia University
Southern West Virginia
Community and Technical
College
Valley College
West Virginia Business College:
Wheeling
West Virginia Junior College
West Virginia Junior College:
Bridgeport
West Virginia Northern
Community College
West Virginia University at
Parkersburg

Wisconsin

Blackhawk Technical College
Chippewa Valley Technical
College
College of Menominee Nation
Fox Valley Technical College
Gateway Technical College
Globe University
Appleton
Eau Claire
La Crosse
Madison East
Wausau
Lakeshore Technical College
Madison Area Technical
College
Mid-State Technical College

Milwaukee Area Technical
College
Moraine Park Technical College
Northcentral Technical College
Northeast Wisconsin Technical
College
Rasmussen College
Green Bay
Wausau
Waukesha County Technical
College
Western Technical College
Wisconsin Indianhead Technical
College

Wyoming

Casper College
Central Wyoming College
Eastern Wyoming College
Laramie County Community
College
Northwest College
Sheridan College
Western Wyoming Community
College

American Samoa

American Samoa Community
College

Guam

Guam Community College

Palau

Palau Community College

Admission/ placement policies

No closing date

Four-year

Alabama

Amridge University
Athens State University
Birmingham-Southern College
Columbia Southern University
Faulkner University
Herzing University
    Birmingham
ITT Technical Institute
    Birmingham
Jacksonville State University
Judson College
Oakwood University
Samford University
Selma University
South University: Montgomery
Southeastern Bible College
Stillman College
Talladega College
Troy University
United States Sports Academy
University of Alabama
University of Alabama
    Birmingham
University of North Alabama
University of Phoenix
    Birmingham
University of West Alabama
Virginia College
    Birmingham
    Huntsville

Arizona

American Indian College of the
    Assemblies of God
Art Institute of Tucson
Brown Mackie College
    Tucson
Chamberlain College of Nursing
    Phoenix
Collins College
DeVry University
    Phoenix
Dunlap-Stone University
Embry-Riddle Aeronautical
    University: Prescott Campus
Grand Canyon University
International Baptist College
ITT Technical Institute
    Tempe
    Tucson
Northcentral University
Northern Arizona University
Southwest University of Visual
    Arts
University of Advancing
    Technology
University of Phoenix
    Phoenix-Hohokam
    Southern Arizona
Western International University

Arkansas

Arkansas Baptist College
Arkansas Tech University
Harding University
ITT Technical Institute
    Little Rock
John Brown University
Lyon College

Ouachita Baptist University
University of Arkansas
    Fort Smith
    Monticello
    Pine Bluff
University of Central Arkansas
University of Phoenix
    Little Rock
    Northwest Arkansas
University of the Ozarks
Williams Baptist College

California

Academy of Art University
Alliant International University
Antioch University
    Santa Barbara
Art Center College of Design
Art Institute of California:
    Hollywood
Art Institute of California:
    Orange County
Art Institute of California:
    Sacramento
Art Institute of California: San
    Diego
Art Institute of California: San
    Francisco
Biola University
Brooks Institute
California Baptist University
California Christian College
California Coast University
California College of the Arts
California College San Diego
California National University
    for Advanced Studies
California State University
    Dominguez Hills
    San Bernardino
Carrington College
    Emeryville
Charles Drew University of
    Medicine and Science
Cogswell Polytechnical College
Coleman University
Concordia University
Design Institute of San Diego
DeVry University
    Pomona
Dominican University of
    California
Ex'pression College for Digital
    Arts
Golden Gate University
Humphreys College
Interior Designers Institute
International Academy of
    Design and Technology
    Sacramento
ITT Technical Institute
    Lathrop
    Oxnard
    Rancho Cordova
    San Bernardino
    San Diego
    Sylmar
    Torrance
The King's University
LA College International
La Sierra University
Laguna College of Art and
    Design
Lincoln University
Loma Linda University
The Master's College
Menlo College
Mount St. Mary's College
Mt. Sierra College
National Hispanic University
National University
NewSchool of Architecture &
    Design
Notre Dame de Namur
    University
Otis College of Art and Design
Pacific Oaks College

Pacific States University
Pacific Union College
Platt College
    Ontario
    San Diego
Providence Christian College
Samuel Merritt University
San Francisco Art Institute
Simpson University
Southern California Institute of
    Technology
Southern California Seminary
Thomas Aquinas College
Trident University International
University of La Verne
University of Phoenix
    Central Valley
    Sacramento Valley
    San Diego
    Southern California
University of San Francisco
University of the West
West Coast University
Westmont College
Whittier College
Woodbury University
World Mission University
Yeshiva Ohr Elchonon Chabad/
    West Coast Talmudical
    Seminary

Colorado

Adams State College
American Sentinel University
The Art Institute of Colorado
Aspen University
CollegeAmerica
    Fort Collins
Colorado Heights University
Colorado Mesa University
Colorado Technical University
DeVry University
    Westminster
ITT Technical Institute
    Westminster
Johnson & Wales University:
    Denver
Naropa University
Nazarene Bible College
Platt College
    Aurora
Rocky Mountain College of Art
    & Design
University of Colorado
    Colorado Springs
University of Phoenix
    Denver
    Southern Colorado
Western State College of
    Colorado
Westwood College
    Denver North
    Denver South

Connecticut

Albertus Magnus College
Charter Oak State College
Eastern Connecticut State
    University
Holy Apostles College and
    Seminary
Lyme Academy College of Fine
    Arts
Mitchell College
Paier College of Art
Post University
Sacred Heart University
Saint Joseph College
University of Bridgeport
University of Hartford
University of New Haven
University of Phoenix
    Fairfield County
Western Connecticut State
    University

Delaware

Delaware State University
Goldey-Beacom College
University of Phoenix
    Delaware
Wesley College
Wilmington University

District of Columbia

Gallaudet University
Potomac College
University of Phoenix
    Washington DC

Florida

Art Institute of Fort Lauderdale
Ave Maria University
Barry University
Bethune-Cookman University
Carlos Albizu University
Chamberlain College of Nursing
    Jacksonville
DeVry University
    Miramar
    Orlando
Eckerd College
Edward Waters College
Embry-Riddle Aeronautical
    University
Embry-Riddle Aeronautical
    University: Worldwide
    Campus
Florida Career College: Boynton
    Beach
Florida Career College:
    Jacksonville
Florida Career College:
    Lauderdale Lakes
Florida Career College:
    Riverview
Florida Institute of Technology
Florida Southern College
Hodges University
International Academy of
    Design and Technology
    Orlando
ITT Technical Institute
    Ft. Lauderdale
    Jacksonville
    Miami
    Tampa
Jacksonville University
Johnson & Wales University:
    North Miami
Jones College
Lynn University
Miami International University
    of Art and Design
Northwood University
    Florida
Palm Beach Atlantic University
Rasmussen College
    Fort Myers
    Ocala
    Pasco County
Remington College
    Tampa
Ringling College of Art and
    Design
Saint Thomas University
Schiller International University
South University: Tampa
South University: West Palm
    Beach
Stetson University
Talmudic College of Florida
University of North Florida
University of Phoenix
    Central Florida
    North Florida
    South Florida
    West Florida
University of Tampa
Warner University

Georgia

Augusta State University
Bauder College
Beulah Heights University
Brenau University
Carver Bible College
Chorter University
    Shorter University
Clayton State University
Covenant College
DeVry University
    Decatur
Herzing University
    Atlanta
LaGrange College
Luther Rice University
Oglethorpe University
Reinhardt University
South University: Savannah
Thomas University
University of Phoenix
    Atlanta
    Augusta
    Columbus Georgia
    Savannah

Hawaii

Chaminade University of
    Honolulu
Hawaii Pacific University
University of Phoenix
    Hawaii

Idaho

Idaho State University
ITT Technical Institute
    Boise
Lewis-Clark State College
University of Phoenix
    Idaho

Illinois

American Academy of Art
Argosy University: Schaumburg
Augustana College
Benedictine University
Blackburn College
Blessing-Rieman College of
    Nursing
Bradley University
Chamberlain College of Nursing
    Addison
    Chicago
Chicago State University
Columbia College Chicago
Concordia University Chicago
DeVry University
    Chicago
    Online
Dominican University
East-West University
Elmhurst College
Governors State University
Greenville College
Harrington College of Design
Hebrew Theological College
Illinois College
Illinois Institute of Art: Chicago
Illinois Institute of Art:
    Schaumburg
Illinois Institute of Technology
Illinois Wesleyan University
ITT Technical Institute
    Mount Prospect
Judson University
Kendall College
Lake Forest College
Lewis University
Lexington College
Lincoln Christian University
Loyola University Chicago
MacMurray College
McKendree University
Midstate College
Millikin University
Monmouth College
National-Louis University

North Central College
Principia College
Quincy University
Robert Morris University:
  Chicago
Rockford College
Roosevelt University
St. Augustine College
St. John's College
Saint Xavier University
Shimer College
Southern Illinois University
  Carbondale
Telshe Yeshiva-Chicago
Trinity Christian College
Trinity College of Nursing and
  Health Sciences
Trinity International University
University of Illinois
  Springfield
University of Phoenix
  Chicago
VanderCook College of Music
Western Illinois University
Westwood College
  DuPage
  O'Hare Airport
  River Oaks

Indiana

Calumet College of St. Joseph
Franklin College
Indiana Institute of Technology
Indiana University
  East
  Northwest
  South Bend
  Southeast
Indiana Wesleyan University
International Business College
ITT Technical Institute
  Fort Wayne
  Indianapolis
Manchester College
Martin University
Purdue University
Purdue University
  Calumet
  North Central
Saint Joseph's College
Saint Mary's College
St. Mary-of-the-Woods College
Taylor University
University of Phoenix
  Indianapolis
University of St. Francis
Valparaiso University
Wabash College

Iowa

Briar Cliff University
Buena Vista University
Clarke University
Drake University
Emmaus Bible College
Graceland University
Hamilton Technical College
Iowa Wesleyan College
Kaplan University
  Cedar Falls
  Des Moines
  Mason City
Loras College
Luther College
Morningside College
Northwestern College
St. Ambrose University
University of Dubuque
University of Phoenix
  Des Moines
Upper Iowa University
Waldorf College
Wartburg College
William Penn University

Kansas

Baker University
Benedictine College

Bethany College
Bethel College
Central Christian College of
  Kansas
Emporia State University
Fort Hays State University
Friends University
Kansas State University
Kansas Wesleyan University
McPherson College
Newman University
Ottawa University
Pittsburg State University
Sterling College
Tabor College
University of Kansas Medical
  Center
University of Phoenix
  Wichita
University of St. Mary
Wichita State University

Kentucky

Alice Lloyd College
Asbury University
Beckfield College
Brescia University
Campbellsville University
ITT Technical Institute
  Louisville
Kentucky Christian University
Kentucky Mountain Bible
  College
Kentucky State University
Kentucky Wesleyan College
Lindsey Wilson College
Mid-Continent University
Midway College
Morehead State University
St. Catharine College
Spalding University
Sullivan University
Union College
University of Phoenix
  Louisville

Louisiana

Herzing University
  Kenner
ITT Technical Institute
  St. Rose
Louisiana Tech University
Loyola University New Orleans
New Orleans Baptist
  Theological Seminary:
  Leavell College
Nicholls State University
Our Lady of Holy Cross
  College
St. Joseph Seminary College
Southern University
  New Orleans
Southwest University
University of Louisiana at
  Lafayette
University of Louisiana at
  Monroe
University of New Orleans
University of Phoenix
  Baton Rouge
  Lafayette
  Louisiana
  Shreveport

Maine

Maine College of Art
New England School of
  Communications
Saint Joseph's College of Maine
Thomas College
University of Maine
University of Maine
  Farmington
  Fort Kent
  Presque Isle
University of Southern Maine

Maryland

Bowie State University
Capitol College
Frostburg State University
Mount St. Mary's University
National Labor College
Ner Israel Rabbinical College
Notre Dame of Maryland
  University
St. John's College
Stevenson University
University of Maryland
  University College
University of Phoenix
  Maryland
Washington College

Massachusetts

American International College
Anna Maria College
Bay Path College
Becker College
Bridgewater State University
Cambridge College
Curry College
Eastern Nazarene College
Elms College
Fitchburg State University
Framingham State University
Gordon College
Lesley University
Massachusetts College of
  Liberal Arts
Massachusetts College of
  Pharmacy and Health
  Sciences
Massachusetts Maritime
  Academy
Montserrat College of Art
Mount Ida College
New England Conservatory of
  Music
New England Institute of Art
Newbury College
Nichols College
Pine Manor College
School of the Museum of Fine
  Arts
University of Massachusetts
  Dartmouth
University of Phoenix
  Boston
Wentworth Institute of
  Technology
Western New England
  University
Wheelock College
Zion Bible College

Michigan

Alma College
Andrews University
Aquinas College
Baker College
  of Allen Park
  of Auburn Hills
  of Cadillac
  of Clinton Township
  of Flint
  of Jackson
  of Muskegon
  of Owosso
  of Port Huron
Cornerstone University
Davenport University
Eastern Michigan University
Hope College
Kettering University
Kuyper College
Lawrence Technological
  University
Madonna University
Michigan State University
Michigan Technological
  University
Northern Michigan University

Northwood University
  Michigan
Oakland University
Olivet College
Rochester College
Saginaw Valley State University
Siena Heights University
University of Michigan
  Dearborn
  Flint
University of Phoenix
  Metro Detroit
  West Michigan
Wayne State University
Western Michigan University
Yeshiva Beth Yehuda-Yeshiva
  Gedolah of Greater Detroit

Minnesota

Art Institutes International
  Minnesota
Bemidji State University
Bethel University
Capella University
College of St. Benedict
College of St. Scholastica
Concordia College: Moorhead
Globe University
  Minneapolis
  Woodbury
Hamline University
Minnesota School of Business
  Blaine
  Plymouth
  Richfield
  Rochester
  St. Cloud
  Shakopee
Northwestern Health Sciences
  University
Oak Hills Christian College
Rasmussen College
  Blaine
  Lake Elmo/Woodbury
  Moorhead
St. Catherine University
St. John's University
University of Minnesota
  Crookston
  Rochester
  Twin Cities
University of Phoenix
  Minneapolis-St. Paul
University of St. Thomas
Walden University
Winona State University

Mississippi

Alcorn State University
Belhaven University
Blue Mountain College
Delta State University
Mississippi College
Mississippi State University
Mississippi University for
  Women
Rust College
Tougaloo College
University of Southern
  Mississippi

Missouri

Avila University
Baptist Bible College
Central Bible College
Chamberlain College of Nursing
  St. Louis
College of the Ozarks
DeVry University
  Kansas City
Evangel University
Fontbonne University
Global University
Goldfarb School of Nursing at
  Barnes-Jewish College
Grantham University
Hickey College

ITT Technical Institute
  Arnold
  Earth City
Lindenwood University
Missouri Baptist University
Missouri Southern State
  University
Missouri Valley College
National American University
  Kansas City
Northwest Missouri State
  University
Research College of Nursing
Rockhurst University
Southwest Baptist University
Stephens College
Truman State University
University of Central Missouri
University of Missouri
  Columbia
  Kansas City
University of Phoenix
  Kansas City
  St. Louis
  Springfield
Westminster College
William Woods University

Montana

Montana State University
  Billings
  Northern
Montana Tech of the University
  of Montana
Rocky Mountain College
University of Montana
University of Montana: Western

Nebraska

Bellevue University
Chadron State College
Clarkson College
College of Saint Mary
Creative Center
Doane College
Grace University
Hastings College
ITT Technical Institute
  Omaha
Nebraska Methodist College of
  Nursing and Allied Health
Peru State College
University of Nebraska
  Kearney
University of Phoenix
  Omaha

Nevada

Art Institute of Las Vegas
Great Basin College
ITT Technical Institute
  Henderson
Morrison University
University of Nevada
  Reno
University of Phoenix
  Las Vegas
  Northern Nevada

New Hampshire

Colby-Sawyer College
Daniel Webster College
Franklin Pierce University
Granite State College
Hesser College
New England College
Rivier College
Southern New Hampshire
  University
Thomas More College of
  Liberal Arts

New Jersey

Berkeley College
Caldwell College
Centenary College
DeVry University
  North Brunswick

Fairleigh Dickinson University
  College at Florham
  Metropolitan Campus
Felician College
Rider University
Saint Peter's College
Seton Hall University
Talmudical Academy of New
  Jersey
Thomas Edison State College
University of Medicine and
  Dentistry of New Jersey
  School of Health Related
  Professions

New Mexico

Eastern New Mexico University
ITT Technical Institute
  Albuquerque
New Mexico Highlands
  University
New Mexico State University
St. John's College
Southwest University of Visual
  Arts
University of New Mexico
University of Phoenix
  New Mexico
University of the Southwest

New York

Adelphi University
Albany College of Pharmacy
  and Health Sciences
Beis Medrash Heichal Dovid
Berkeley College
Berkeley College of New York
  City
Beth Hamedrash Shaarei Yosher
  Institute
Boricua College
Briarcliffe College
Cazenovia College
Central Yeshiva Tomchei
  Tmimim-Lubavitch
City University of New York
  Brooklyn College
  College of Staten Island
College of Mount St. Vincent
College of New Rochelle
College of Saint Rose
Concordia College
Culinary Institute of America
D'Youville College
Daemen College
Davis College
DeVry College of New York
  Midtown Campus
Dominican College of Blauvelt
Dowling College
Excelsior College
Five Towns College
Globe Institute of Technology
Hartwick College
Hofstra University
Houghton College
Kehilath Yakov Rabbinical
  Seminary
Keuka College
The King's College
Le Moyne College
LIM College
Long Island University
  C. W. Post Campus
Manhattan College
Marymount Manhattan College
Medaille College
Medaille College: Amherst
Medaille College: Rochester
Mercy College
Mesivta Torah Vodaath
  Seminary
Mirrer Yeshiva Central Institute
Molloy College
Monroe College
New York School of Interior
  Design
Nyack College

Ohr Somayach Tanenbaum
  Education Center
Paul Smith's College
Polytechnic Institute of New
  York University
Rabbinical Academy Mesivta
  Rabbi Chaim Berlin
Rabbinical College Beth Shraga
Rabbinical College Bobover
  Yeshiva B'nei Zion
Rabbinical College of Long
  Island
Rabbinical College of Ohr
  Shimon Yisroel
Rochester Institute of
  Technology
Russell Sage College
Sage College of Albany
St. Francis College
St. John Fisher College
St. John's University
St. Thomas Aquinas College
School of Visual Arts
Shor Yoshuv Rabbinical College
SUNY
  College at Brockport
  College at Buffalo
  College at Cortland
  College at Fredonia
  College at Old Westbury
  College at Oneonta
  College at Oswego
  College at Plattsburgh
  College at Potsdam
  College of Environmental
    Science and Forestry
  Empire State College
  Farmingdale State College
  Maritime College
  University at Binghamton
  University at Buffalo
  Upstate Medical University
Talmudical Seminary Oholei
  Torah
Torah Temimah Talmudical
  Seminary
Touro College
U.T.A. Mesivta-Kiryas Jocl
United Talmudical Seminary
Utica College
Vaughn College of Aeronautics
  and Technology
Yeshiva and Kolel Bais
  Medrash Elyon
Yeshiva and Kollel Harbotzas
  Torah
Yeshiva D'Monsey Rabbinical
  College
Yeshiva Derech Chaim
Yeshiva Gedolah Zichron
  Moshe
Yeshiva Karlin Stolin
Yeshiva of Nitra
Yeshiva of the Telshe Alumni
Yeshiva Shaar Hatorah
Yeshiva Shaarei Torah of
  Rockland
Yeshiva University
Yeshivas Novominsk
Yeshivat Mikdash Melech
Yeshivath Viznitz

North Carolina

Apex School of Theology
Appalachian State University
Art Institute of Charlotte
Barton College
Bennett College for Women
Brevard College
Cabarrus College of Health
  Sciences
Campbell University
Carolina Christian College
Catawba College
Chowan University
Gardner-Webb University
Greensboro College

Johnson & Wales University:
  Charlotte
Johnson C. Smith University
Lees-McRae College
Lenoir-Rhyne University
Livingstone College
Mars Hill College
Methodist University
Mid-Atlantic Christian
  University
Miller-Motte College:
  Wilmington
North Carolina Agricultural and
  Technical State University
North Carolina Central
  University
North Carolina Wesleyan
  College
Pfeiffer University
Piedmont International
  University
Queens University of Charlotte
St. Andrews University
St. Augustine's College
Salem College
Southeastern Baptist
  Theological Seminary
University of North Carolina
  School of the Arts
University of Phoenix
  Charlotte
  Raleigh
William Peace University
Wingate University

North Dakota

Dickinson State University
Jamestown College
Mayville State University
Medcenter One College of
  Nursing
Minot State University
Rasmussen College
  Fargo
Trinity Bible College
University of Mary
University of North Dakota
Valley City State University

Ohio

Ashland University
Baldwin-Wallace College
Bryant & Stratton College
  Parma
Cedarville University
Central State University
Chamberlain College of Nursing
  Columbus
Cleveland Institute of Art
Columbus College of Art and
  Design
Defiance College
DeVry University
  Columbus
Franciscan University of
  Steubenville
Franklin University
Hiram College
John Carroll University
Kent State University
Kettering College of Medical
  Arts
Lourdes University
Malone University
Notre Dame College
Ohio Christian University
Ohio Dominican University
Ohio Mid-Western College
Ohio University
  Chillicothe Campus
  Eastern Campus
  Lancaster Campus
  Southern Campus at Ironton
  Zanesville Campus
Otterbein University
Pontifical College Josephinum
Shawnee State University
Tiffin University

Union Institute & University
University of Mount Union
University of Phoenix
  Cincinnati
  Cleveland
  Columbus Ohio
University of Rio Grande
University of Toledo
Wittenberg University
Wright State University

Oklahoma

Bacone College
Cameron University
East Central University
Hillsdale Free Will Baptist
  College
ITT Technical Institute
  Tulsa
Mid-America Christian
  University
Northeastern State University
Northwestern Oklahoma State
  University
Oklahoma Christian University
Oklahoma Panhandle State
  University
Oklahoma State University
Oklahoma Wesleyan University
Oral Roberts University
Rogers State University
St. Gregory's University
Southeastern Oklahoma State
  University
Southwestern Christian
  University
Southwestern Oklahoma State
  University
Spartan College of Aeronautics
  and Technology
University of Central Oklahoma
University of Phoenix
  Oklahoma City
  Tulsa
University of Tulsa

Oregon

George Fox University
ITT Technical Institute
  Portland
Linfield College
Marylhurst University
Northwest Christian University
Oregon College of Art & Craft
Pacific Northwest College of
  Art
Portland State University
Southern Oregon University
University of Phoenix
  Oregon
Warner Pacific College
Western Oregon University
Willamette University

Pennsylvania

Albright College
Alvernia University
Art Institute of Philadelphia
Art Institute of Pittsburgh
Bloomsburg University of
  Pennsylvania
Cabrini College
California University of
  Pennsylvania
Carlow University
Cedar Crest College
Central Pennsylvania College
Chestnut Hill College
Clarion University of
  Pennsylvania
DeVry University
  Fort Washington
Eastern University
Edinboro University of
  Pennsylvania
Elizabethtown College
Gannon University
Geneva College

Gratz College
Harrisburg University of
  Science and Technology
Holy Family University
Immaculata University
Indiana University of
  Pennsylvania
King's College
Kutztown University of
  Pennsylvania
La Roche College
La Salle University
Lancaster Bible College
Lebanon Valley College
Lock Haven University of
  Pennsylvania
Mansfield University of
  Pennsylvania
Marywood University
Mercyhurst University
Messiah College
Millersville University of
  Pennsylvania
Misericordia University
Mount Aloysius College
Neumann University
Peirce College
Penn State
  Abington
  Altoona
  Beaver
  Berks
  Brandywine
  DuBois
  Erie, The Behrend College
  Fayette, The Eberly Campus
  Greater Allegheny
  Harrisburg
  Hazleton
  Lehigh Valley
  Mont Alto
  New Kensington
  Schuylkill
  Shenango
  University Park
  Wilkes-Barre
  Worthington Scranton
  York
Pennsylvania Academy of the
  Fine Arts
Pennsylvania College of Art and
  Design
Philadelphia Biblical University
Philadelphia University
Point Park University
Restaurant School at Walnut
  Hill College
Robert Morris University
Rosemont College
Shippensburg University of
  Pennsylvania
Slippery Rock University of
  Pennsylvania
Talmudical Yeshiva of
  Philadelphia
Thiel College
University of Phoenix
  Harrisburg
  Philadelphia
  Pittsburgh
University of Pittsburgh
University of Pittsburgh
  Bradford
  Greensburg
  Johnstown
University of the Arts
University of the Sciences in
  Philadelphia
Waynesburg University
West Chester University of
  Pennsylvania
Widener University
Wilkes University
Yeshivath Beth Moshe
York College of Pennsylvania

Puerto Rico

American University of Puerto Rico
Atlantic College
Caribbean University
Columbia Centro Universitario: Caguas
Electronic Data Processing College: San Sebastian
Inter American University of Puerto Rico
  Arecibo Campus
  Barranquitas Campus
  Guayama Campus
Turabo University
Universidad Adventista de las Antillas
Universidad del Este
Universidad Pentecostal Mizpa
Universidad Politecnica de Puerto Rico
University of Phoenix
  Puerto Rico
University of Puerto Rico
  Utuado

Rhode Island

Johnson & Wales University: Providence
New England Institute of Technology
Salve Regina University

South Carolina

Anderson University
Benedict College
Charleston Southern University
The Citadel
Columbia College
Converse College
Erskine College
Francis Marion University
ITT Technical Institute
  Greenville
Lander University
Morris College
Newberry College
South University: Columbia
University of Phoenix
  Columbia
University of South Carolina
  Beaufort
  Upstate
Voorhees College

South Dakota

Augustana College
Dakota State University
Northern State University
South Dakota School of Mines and Technology
South Dakota State University
University of Sioux Falls
University of South Dakota

Tennessee

Aquinas College
Bethel University
Bryan College
Christian Brothers University
Cumberland University
East Tennessee State University
Fisk University
Free Will Baptist Bible College
Freed-Hardeman University
International Academy of Design and Technology
  Nashville
ITT Technical Institute
  Knoxville
  Nashville
King College
Lincoln Memorial University
Lipscomb University
Maryville College
Memphis College of Art
Middle Tennessee State University

Rhodes College
South College
Southern Adventist University
Tusculum College
University of Phoenix
  Chattanooga
  Memphis
  Nashville
Williamson Christian College

Texas

Amberton University
Arlington Baptist College
Art Institute of Dallas
Art Institute of Houston
Austin Graduate School of Theology
Baptist University of the Americas
Baylor University
College of Biblical Studies-Houston
College of Saint Thomas More
Criswell College
Dallas Baptist University
DeVry University
  Houston
  Irving
Hardin-Simmons University
Houston Baptist University
Howard Payne University
Jarvis Christian College
LeTourneau University
Northwood University
  Texas
Our Lady of the Lake University of San Antonio
St. Mary's University
Southwestern Assemblies of God University
Southwestern Baptist Theological Seminary
Stephen F. Austin State University
Sul Ross State University
Tarleton State University
Texas A&M University
  Commerce
  Kingsville
  Texarkana
Texas College
Texas Wesleyan University
University of Mary Hardin-Baylor
University of Phoenix
  Austin
  Dallas Fort Worth
  Houston Westside
  San Antonio
University of Texas
  Arlington
  Tyler
University of the Incarnate Word
Wayland Baptist University
West Texas A&M University
Wiley College

Utah

Broadview University
  Orem
Independence University
ITT Technical Institute
  Murray
Neumont University
Stevens-Henager College
  Logan
University of Phoenix
  Utah
Utah State University
Western Governors University

Vermont

Castleton State College
College of St. Joseph in Vermont
Green Mountain College
Johnson State College

Lyndon State College
Marlboro College
Norwich University
Southern Vermont College
Sterling College
Vermont Technical College

Virginia

Bridgewater College
Catholic Distance University
Christendom College
DeVry University
  Arlington
Eastern Mennonite University
Emory & Henry College
Hollins University
ITT Technical Institute
  Chantilly
  Norfolk
  Richmond
Jefferson College of Health Sciences
Liberty University
Longwood University
Lynchburg College
Mary Baldwin College
Marymount University
Potomac College
St. Paul's College
Southern Virginia University
Stratford University: Falls Church
Stratford University: Woodbridge
University of Phoenix
  Northern Virginia
  Richmond
Virginia Baptist College
Virginia Intermont College
Virginia Union University
Virginia University of Lynchburg
Virginia Wesleyan College
World College

Washington

Art Institute of Seattle
City University of Seattle
DeVry University
  Federal Way
DigiPen Institute of Technology
Evergreen State College
International Academy of Design and Technology
  Seattle
ITT Technical Institute
  Seattle
  Spokane
Northwest College of Art
Pacific Lutheran University
Saint Martin's University
Seattle University
University of Phoenix
  Western Washington
University of Washington
  Bothell
Walla Walla University
Washington State University

West Virginia

Alderson-Broaddus College
American Public University System
Appalachian Bible College
Bethany College
Bluefield State College
Concord University
Davis and Elkins College
Glenville State College
Marshall University
Mountain State University
Ohio Valley University
Salem International University
Shepherd University
University of Charleston
West Liberty University
West Virginia State University

West Virginia University Institute of Technology
West Virginia Wesleyan College
Wheeling Jesuit University

Wisconsin

Alverno College
Beloit College
Carroll University
Carthage College
Herzing University
  Madison
Lakeland College
Maranatha Baptist Bible College
Marian University
Milwaukee Institute of Art & Design
Milwaukee School of Engineering
Mount Mary College
Northland College
Northland International University
Rasmussen College
  Appleton
Ripon College
St. Norbert College
Silver Lake College of the Holy Family
University of Phoenix
  Madison
  Milwaukee
University of Wisconsin
  Eau Claire
  Green Bay
  La Crosse
  Oshkosh
  Platteville
  River Falls
  Stevens Point
  Stout
Wisconsin Lutheran College

Wyoming

University of Phoenix
  Cheyenne

France

American University of Paris

Italy

The American University of Rome

Mexico

Instituto Tecnologico Autonomo de Mexico

Switzerland

Franklin College
  Switzerland

United Kingdom

Richmond, The American International University in London

Two-year

Alabama

Alabama Southern Community College
Bevill State Community College
Bishop State Community College
Calhoun Community College
Central Alabama Community College
Chattahoochee Valley Community College
Community College of the Air Force
Enterprise State Community College
Faulkner State Community College
Gadsden State Community College

George C. Wallace Community College at Dothan
George C. Wallace State Community College at Selma
Jefferson Davis Community College
Jefferson State Community College
Lawson State Community College
Lurleen B. Wallace Community College
Northeast Alabama Community College
Northwest-Shoals Community College
Prince Institute of Professional Studies
Remington College
  Mobile
Shelton State Community College
Southern Union State Community College
Virginia College
  Mobile
Wallace State Community College at Hanceville

Alaska

Prince William Sound Community College

Arizona

Anthem College
  Phoenix
Arizona Automotive Institute
Arizona Western College
Brookline College
  Phoenix
  Tempe
  Tucson
Bryman School of Arizona
Carrington College
  Mesa
  Phoenix Westside
  Tucson
Carrington College: Phoenix
Central Arizona College
Chandler-Gilbert Community College
Cochise College
Coconino County Community College
Dine College
Eastern Arizona College
Estrella Mountain Community College
GateWay Community College
Glendale Community College
Kaplan College: Phoenix
Le Cordon Bleu College of Culinary Arts
  Scottsdale
Mesa Community College
Mohave Community College
Northland Pioneer College
Paradise Valley Community College
Paralegal Institute
Penn Foster College
Phoenix College
Pima Community College
Refrigeration School
Rio Salado College
Scottsdale Community College
Sessions College for Professional Design
South Mountain Community College
Tohono O'odham Community College
Universal Technical Institute
Yavapai College

Arkansas

Arkansas Northeastern College
Arkansas State University
  Beebe
  Newport

Indiana

Ancilla College
Fortis College
    Indianapolis
Harrison College
    Anderson
International Business College:
    Indianapolis
Ivy Tech Community College
    Bloomington
    Central Indiana
    Columbus
    East Central
    Kokomo
    Lafayette
    North Central
    Northeast
    Northwest
    Richmond
    South Central
    Southeast
    Southwest
    Wabash Valley
Kaplan College: Hammond
Kaplan College: Indianapolis
Kaplan College: Merrillville
Lincoln College of Technology:
    Indianapolis
Mid-America College of
    Funeral Service
National College
    Indianapolis
Vincennes University

Iowa

Clinton Community College
Des Moines Area Community
    College
Ellsworth Community College
Hawkeye Community College
Iowa Central Community
    College
Iowa Lakes Community College
Iowa Western Community
    College
Kaplan University
    Cedar Rapids
Kirkwood Community College
Marshalltown Community
    College
Muscatine Community College
North Iowa Area Community
    College
Northeast Iowa Community
    College
Northwest Iowa Community
    College
Scott Community College
Southeastern Community
    College
    North Campus
Southwestern Community
    College
Western Iowa Tech Community
    College

Kansas

Allen County Community
    College
Barton County Community
    College
Butler Community College
Cloud County Community
    College
Coffeyville Community College
Colby Community College
Cowley County Community
    College
Dodge City Community College
Donnelly College
Fort Scott Community College
Garden City Community
    College
Hesston College
Highland Community College
Hutchinson Community College

Independence Community
    College
Johnson County Community
    College
Kansas City Kansas Community
    College
Labette Community College
Manhattan Area Technical
    College
Neosho County Community
    College
North Central Kansas Technical
    College
Pratt Community College
Seward County Community
    College

Kentucky

Ashland Community and
    Technical College
Big Sandy Community and
    Technical College
Daymar College
    Bowling Green
    Owensboro
    Paducah
Elizabethtown Community and
    Technical College
Gateway Community and
    Technical College
Hazard Community and
    Technical College
Hopkinsville Community
    College
Lincoln College of Technology
    Florence
Maysville Community and
    Technical College
National College
    Danville
    Florence
    Lexington
    Louisville
    Pikeville
    Richmond
Somerset Community College
Southeast Kentucky Community
    and Technical College
Spencerian College
Spencerian College: Lexington
Sullivan College of Technology
    and Design
West Kentucky Community and
    Technical College

Louisiana

Baton Rouge School of
    Computers
Blue Cliff College
    Metairie
    Shreveport
Delgado Community College
Delta College of Arts &
    Technology
ITI Technical College
Nunez Community College
Remington College
    Baton Rouge
    Lafayette
    Shreveport
South Louisiana Community
    College
Southern University
    Shreveport

Maine

Beal College
Central Maine Community
    College
Eastern Maine Community
    College
Kaplan University
    South Portland
Kennebec Valley Community
    College
Landing School of Boatbuilding
    and Design

Northern Maine Community
    College
Southern Maine Community
    College
York County Community
    College

Maryland

Allegany College of Maryland
Anne Arundel Community
    College
Carroll Community College
Cecil College
Chesapeake College
College of Southern Maryland
Community College of
    Baltimore County
Frederick Community College
Garrett College
Hagerstown Community College
Harford Community College
Howard Community College
Kaplan University
    Hagerstown
Montgomery College
Prince George's Community
    College
TESST College of Technology
    Baltimore
    Towson
Wor-Wic Community College

Massachusetts

Bay State College
Benjamin Franklin Institute of
    Technology
Berkshire Community College
Bristol Community College
Bunker Hill Community College
Cape Cod Community College
Fisher College
Greenfield Community College
Holyoke Community College
ITT Technical Institute
    Norwood
Laboure College
Marian Court College
Massachusetts Bay Community
    College
Massasoit Community College
Middlesex Community College
Mount Wachusett Community
    College
New England College of
    Business and Finance
North Shore Community
    College
Northern Essex Community
    College
Quincy College
Quinsigamond Community
    College
Roxbury Community College
Springfield Technical
    Community College
Urban College of Boston

Michigan

Alpena Community College
Delta College
Glen Oaks Community College
Gogebic Community College
Grand Rapids Community
    College
Henry Ford Community College
ITT Technical Institute
    Troy
Jackson Community College
Kalamazoo Valley Community
    College
Kellogg Community College
Kirtland Community College
Lake Michigan College
Macomb Community College
Mid Michigan Community
    College
Monroe County Community
    College

Montcalm Community College
Mott Community College
Muskegon Community College
North Central Michigan College
Northwestern Michigan College
Oakland Community College
Saginaw Chippewa Tribal
    College
St. Clair County Community
    College
Schoolcraft College
Southwestern Michigan College
Washtenaw Community College
Wayne County Community
    College
West Shore Community College

Minnesota

Academy College
Alexandria Technical and
    Community College
Anoka Technical College
Anoka-Ramsey Community
    College
Anthem College
    Minneapolis
Central Lakes College
Century College
Dakota County Technical
    College
Duluth Business University
Fond du Lac Tribal and
    Community College
Hennepin Technical College
Herzing University
    Minneapolis
Hibbing Community College
Institute of Production and
    Recording
Inver Hills Community College
Lake Superior College
Le Cordon Bleu College of
    Culinary Arts
    Minneapolis-St. Paul
Mesabi Range Community and
    Technical College
Minneapolis Business College
Minneapolis Community and
    Technical College
Minnesota School of Business
    Brooklyn Center
Minnesota State College -
    Southeast Technical
Minnesota West Community
    and Technical College
North Hennepin Community
    College
Northland Community &
    Technical College
Northwest Technical College
Pine Technical College
Rainy River Community
    College
Rasmussen College
    Bloomington
    Brooklyn Park
    Eagan
    Mankato
    St. Cloud
Riverland Community College
St. Paul College
South Central College
Vermilion Community College

Mississippi

Antonelli College
    Jackson
Coahoma Community College
Copiah-Lincoln Community
    College
East Mississippi Community
    College
Hinds Community College
Holmes Community College
Itawamba Community College
Meridian Community College
Mississippi Delta Community
    College

Mississippi Gulf Coast
    Community College
Northeast Mississippi
    Community College
Pearl River Community College
Southwest Mississippi
    Community College
Virginia College
    Gulf Coast
    Jackson

Missouri

Anthem College
    Kansas City
Bolivar Technical College
Cottey College
Crowder College
East Central College
Jefferson College
Linn State Technical College
Metro Business College
    Jefferson City
    Rolla
Metropolitan Community
    College: Blue River
Metropolitan Community
    College: Business &
    Technology
Metropolitan Community
    College: Longview
Metropolitan Community
    College: Maple Woods
Metropolitan Community
    College: Penn Valley
Mineral Area College
Moberly Area Community
    College
Ozarks Technical Community
    College
Pinnacle Career Institute:
    Kansas City
Ranken Technical College
St. Charles Community College
St. Louis Community College
    Florissant Valley
    Meramec
State Fair Community College
Stevens Institute of Business &
    Arts
Texas County Technical
    Institute
Three Rivers Community
    College
Vatterott College
    St. Joseph
Wentworth Military Junior
    College

Montana

Aaniiih Nakoda College
Blackfeet Community College
Chief Dull Knife College
Dawson Community College
Flathead Valley Community
    College
Fort Peck Community College
Little Big Horn College
Miles Community College
Montana State University
    Great Falls College of
    Technology
Stone Child College

Nebraska

Central Community College
Kaplan University
    Lincoln
    Omaha
Little Priest Tribal College
Metropolitan Community
    College
Mid-Plains Community College
    Area
Nebraska College of Technical
    Agriculture
Nebraska Indian Community
    College
Northeast Community College

Consolidated School of Business
Lancaster
York
Delaware County Community
College
Douglas Education Center
DuBois Business College
DuBois Business College
Huntingdon
Erie Business Center
Erie Business Center South
Harrisburg Area Community
College
Hussian School of Art
ITT Technical Institute
Pittsburgh
JNA Institute of Culinary Arts
Kaplan Career Institute:
Harrisburg
Kaplan Career Institute:
Pittsburgh
Keystone Technical Institute
Lackawanna College
Laurel Business Institute
Laurel Technical Institute
Lehigh Carbon Community
College
Lincoln Technical Institute:
Allentown
Lincoln Technical Institute:
Northeast Philadelphia
Lincoln Technical Institute:
Philadelphia
Luzerne County Community
College
McCann School of Business and
Technology
Dickson City
Pottsville
Montgomery County
Community College
Newport Business Institute:
Williamsport
Northampton Community
College
Oakbridge Academy of Arts
Penn Commercial Business and
Technical School
Pennco Tech
Pennsylvania Highlands
Community College
Pennsylvania Institute of
Technology
Pennsylvania School of
Business
Pittsburgh Institute of
Aeronautics
Pittsburgh Institute of Mortuary
Science
Reading Area Community
College
Rosedale Technical Institute
Sanford-Brown Institute
Monroeville
Triangle Tech
Bethlehem
DuBois
Erie
Greensburg
Pittsburgh
Sunbury
University of Pittsburgh
Titusville
Valley Forge Military Academy
and College
Vet Tech Institute
Westmoreland County
Community College
YTI Career Institute
Altoona
Lancaster
York

Puerto Rico

Centro de Estudios
Multidisciplinarios
Huertas Junior College

Humacao Community College
ICPR Junior College
Ponce Paramedical College
Universal Technology College
of Puerto Rico

Rhode Island

Community College of Rhode
Island

South Carolina

Aiken Technical College
Central Carolina Technical
College
Clinton Junior College
Denmark Technical College
Forrest Junior College
Golf Academy of America: The
Carolinas
Horry-Georgetown Technical
College
Midlands Technical College
Miller-Motte Technical College
Northeastern Technical College
Orangeburg-Calhoun Technical
College
Piedmont Technical College
Spartanburg Community College
Spartanburg Methodist College
Technical College of the
Lowcountry
University of South Carolina
Lancaster
Salkehatchie
Sumter
Union
Williamsburg Technical College
York Technical College

South Dakota

Kilian Community College
Lake Area Technical Institute
Mitchell Technical Institute
Southeast Technical Institute

Tennessee

Anthem Career College
Memphis
Chattanooga State Community
College
Cleveland State Community
College
Jackson State Community
College
John A. Gupton College
Nashville Auto-Diesel College
Nashville State Community
College
National College of Business
and Technology
Bartlett
Bristol
Knoxville
Madison
Memphis
Nashville
Northeast State Community
College
Nossi College of Art
Remington College
Memphis
Nashville
Roane State Community College
Southwest Tennessee
Community College
Walters State Community
College
West Tennessee Business
College

Texas

Alvin Community College
Amarillo College
Angelina College
Austin Community College
Blinn College
Brookhaven College
Cedar Valley College

Central Texas College
Cisco College
Clarendon College
Coastal Bend College
College of the Mainland
Collin County Community
College District
Commonwealth Institute of
Funeral Service
Culinary Institute LeNotre
Del Mar College
Eastfield College
El Centro College
El Paso Community College
Frank Phillips College
Galveston College
Grayson County College
Hallmark College of
Aeronautics
Hallmark College of
Technology
Hill College
Houston Community College
System
Howard College
International Academy of
Design and Technology
San Antonio
ITT Technical Institute
Arlington
Austin
Houston North
Houston West
Richardson
San Antonio
Webster
Jacksonville College
Kilgore College
Lamar Institute of Technology
Lamar State College at Orange
Lamar State College at Port
Arthur
Laredo Community College
Lee College
Lincoln College of Technology:
Grand Prairie
Lon Morris College
Lone Star College System
McLennan Community College
Midland College
Mountain View College
Navarro College
North Central Texas College
North Lake College
Northeast Texas Community
College
Odessa College
Palo Alto College
Panola College
Paris Junior College
Ranger College
Remington College
Dallas
Fort Worth
Houston
North Houston
Richland College
St. Philip's College
San Jacinto College
South Plains College
South Texas College
Southwest Texas Junior College
Temple College
Texarkana College
Texas State Technical College
Harlingen
Waco
Trinity Valley Community
College
Tyler Junior College
Vernon College
Vet Tech Institute of Houston
Victoria College
Wade College
Weatherford College
Western Technical College

Western Technical College:
Diana Drive
Western Texas College
Wharton County Junior College

Utah

Broadview University
West Jordan
Eagle Gate College: Layton
Eagle Gate College: Murray
Provo College
Salt Lake Community College
Snow College

Vermont

Community College of Vermont
Landmark College

Virginia

Blue Ridge Community College
Bryant & Stratton College
Richmond
Virginia Beach
Central Virginia Community
College
Dabney S. Lancaster
Community College
Danville Community College
Eastern Shore Community
College
Germanna Community College
J. Sargeant Reynolds
Community College
John Tyler Community College
Lord Fairfax Community
College
Mountain Empire Community
College
National College
Charlottesville
Danville
Harrisonburg
Lynchburg
Martinsville
New River Community College
Northern Virginia Community
College
Patrick Henry Community
College
Paul D. Camp Community
College
Piedmont Virginia Community
College
Rappahannock Community
College
Skyline College: Roanoke
Southside Virginia Community
College
Southwest Virginia Community
College
Thomas Nelson Community
College
Tidewater Community College
Virginia Highlands Community
College
Virginia Western Community
College
Wytheville Community College

Washington

Bates Technical College
Bellevue College
Bellingham Technical College
Big Bend Community College
Cascadia Community College
Centralia College
Clover Park Technical College
Everett Community College
Grays Harbor College
Green River Community
College
Highline Community College
Lower Columbia College
North Seattle Community
College
Northwest Indian College
Northwest School of Wooden
Boatbuilding

Olympic College
Peninsula College
Pierce College
Renton Technical College
Seattle Central Community
College
Shoreline Community College
Skagit Valley College
South Seattle Community
College
Tacoma Community College
Walla Walla Community
College
Wenatchee Valley College
Whatcom Community College

West Virginia

Blue Ridge Community and
Technical College
Bridgemont Community and
Technical College
Eastern West Virginia
Community and Technical
College
Huntington Junior College
Kanawha Valley Community
and Technical College
Mountain State College
National College
Princeton
New River Community and
Technical College
Potomac State College of West
Virginia University
Southern West Virginia
Community and Technical
College
Valley College
West Virginia Business College:
Wheeling
West Virginia Junior College
West Virginia Junior College:
Bridgeport
West Virginia Northern
Community College
West Virginia University at
Parkersburg

Wisconsin

Blackhawk Technical College
Bryant & Stratton College
Milwaukee
Chippewa Valley Technical
College
Gateway Technical College
Lakeshore Technical College
Mid-State Technical College
Moraine Park Technical College
Northcentral Technical College
Rasmussen College
Green Bay
Wausau
University of Wisconsin
Barron County
Fond du Lac
Fox Valley
Manitowoc
Marathon County
Marinette
Marshfield/Wood County
Richland
Rock County
Sheboygan
Washington County
Waukesha
Waukesha County Technical
College
Western Technical College
Wisconsin Indianhead Technical
College

Wyoming

Central Wyoming College
Eastern Wyoming College
Laramie County Community
College
Northwest College
Sheridan College

Western Wyoming Community
College

American Samoa

American Samoa Community
College

Guam

Guam Community College

Palau

Palau Community College

SAT Subject Tests
required for
admission

Four-year

California

California Institute of
Technology
Fresno Pacific University*
Harvey Mudd College
Pomona College*

Connecticut

Wesleyan University*
Yale University*

Kansas

Newman University*

Massachusetts

Amherst College*
Boston College*
Boston University
Franklin W. Olin College of
Engineering
Harvard College
Massachusetts Institute of
Technology
Tufts University*
Wellesley College*
Williams College

Missouri

Missouri Southern State
University

New Hampshire

Dartmouth College

New Jersey

Princeton University

New York

Barnard College*
Columbia University
Hamilton College*
SUNY
College at Buffalo
Vassar College*
Webb Institute

North Carolina

Duke University*
North Carolina Agricultural and
Technical State University

Pennsylvania

Bryn Mawr College*
Carnegie Mellon University
Haverford College*
Swarthmore College*
University of Pennsylvania*

Rhode Island

Brown University*

Texas

Rice University*

West Virginia

Alderson-Broaddus College*

Canada

University of Toronto

United Kingdom

King's College London

SAT Subject Tests
recommended for
admission

Four-year

Alabama

University of Mobile

California

California Baptist University*
Chapman University
Mills College
Occidental College
Simpson University*
Stanford University
University of California
Berkeley
Irvine
Santa Barbara
University of the Pacific

Delaware

University of Delaware

District of Columbia

American University
Catholic University of America
George Washington University*
Georgetown University
Howard University
Trinity Washington University*

Florida

Florida International University

Illinois

DePaul University*
Northwestern University

Indiana

Indiana University
Bloomington

Kansas

Friends University*

Maine

University of Maine*
Fort Kent

Maryland

Johns Hopkins University

Massachusetts

Babson College

Michigan

Calvin College
Hillsdale College
Michigan State University*

Minnesota

Carleton College

Montana

University of Great Falls

New York

City University of New York
Queens College
Clarkson University
Eastman School of Music of the
University of Rochester*

Fordham University
Hofstra University
Mercy College
Skidmore College
SUNY
College at Old Westbury
University at Stony Brook

North Carolina

Davidson College*
North Carolina Central
University*

Ohio

Cedarville University*
Oberlin College

Oregon

Reed College

Pennsylvania

Cheyney University of
Pennsylvania
Lafayette College
Moravian College*
St. Francis University

Virginia

George Mason University*
Hampden-Sydney College
University of Virginia
Washington and Lee University

Canada

University of Alberta

France

Institut D'Etudes Politiques de
Paris

Switzerland

Franklin College
Switzerland

Two-year

California

Deep Springs College

Georgia

Gordon College

New York

St. Elizabeth College of Nursing

---

* ACT accepted as an alternative to SAT Subject Tests

Colleges that offer ROTC

Air Force ROTC

Four-year

Alabama

Alabama State University
Auburn University
Auburn University at
 Montgomery
Birmingham-Southern College
Faulkner University
Huntingdon College
Miles College
Samford University
Spring Hill College
Stillman College
Troy University
Tuskegee University
University of Alabama
University of Alabama
 Birmingham
University of Mobile
University of Montevallo
University of South Alabama
University of West Alabama

Alaska

University of Alaska
 Anchorage

Arizona

Arizona Christian University
Arizona State University
DeVry University
 Phoenix
Embry-Riddle Aeronautical
 University: Prescott Campus
Northern Arizona University
University of Arizona

Arkansas

John Brown University
University of Arkansas
 Fort Smith

California

Azusa Pacific University
Biola University
California Baptist University
California Institute of
 Technology
California Lutheran University
California State University
 Dominguez Hills
 Fresno
 Los Angeles
 Northridge
 Sacramento
 San Bernardino
 San Marcos
Chapman University
Claremont McKenna College
Harvey Mudd College
Holy Names University
Loyola Marymount University
The Master's College
Menlo College
National University
Notre Dame de Namur
 University
Occidental College
Pepperdine University
Pitzer College
Point Loma Nazarene University
Pomona College
Samuel Merritt University
San Diego Christian College
San Diego State University

San Francisco State University
San Jose State University
Santa Clara University
Scripps College
Sonoma State University
Stanford University
University of California
 Berkeley
 Davis
 Irvine
 Los Angeles
 Riverside
 Santa Cruz
University of Redlands
University of San Diego
University of San Francisco
University of Southern
 California
University of the Pacific
Vanguard University of
 Southern California
Westmont College

Colorado

Colorado Christian University
Colorado School of Mines
Colorado State University
Metropolitan State College of
 Denver
University of Colorado
 Boulder
 Denver
University of Denver
University of Northern Colorado

Connecticut

Central Connecticut State
 University
Eastern Connecticut State
 University
Fairfield University
Quinnipiac University
Southern Connecticut State
 University
University of Connecticut
University of Hartford
University of New Haven
Wesleyan University
Western Connecticut State
 University
Yale University

Delaware

Delaware State University
Goldey-Beacom College
University of Delaware
Wilmington University

District of Columbia

American University
Catholic University of America
George Washington University
Georgetown University
Howard University
University of the District of
 Columbia

Florida

Barry University
Bethune-Cookman University
Clearwater Christian College
Eckerd College
Embry-Riddle Aeronautical
 University
Florida Agricultural and
 Mechanical University
Florida Atlantic University
Florida College
Florida International University
Florida Southern College
Florida State University
Lynn University
Saint Leo University
University of Central Florida
University of Florida
University of Miami
University of South Florida

University of Tampa
University of West Florida

Georgia

Agnes Scott College
Clayton State University
Emory University
Georgia Institute of Technology
Georgia State University
Kennesaw State University
Morehouse College
Oglethorpe University
Southern Polytechnic State
 University
Spelman College
University of Georgia
University of West Georgia
Valdosta State University

Hawaii

Brigham Young University-
 Hawaii
Chaminade University of
 Honolulu
Hawaii Pacific University
University of Hawaii
 Manoa
 West Oahu

Idaho

Lewis-Clark State College
Northwest Nazarene University
University of Idaho

Illinois

Elmhurst College
Illinois Institute of Technology
Lewis University
Loyola University Chicago
McKendree University
North Central College
North Park University
Northeastern Illinois University
Northwestern University
Saint Xavier University
Shimer College
Southern Illinois University
 Carbondale
Southern Illinois University
 Edwardsville
University of Chicago
University of Illinois
 Chicago
 Urbana-Champaign
Wheaton College

Indiana

Bethel College
Butler University
DePauw University
Holy Cross College
Indiana State University
Indiana University
 Bloomington
 South Bend
 Southeast
Indiana University-Purdue
 University Indianapolis
Purdue University
Rose-Hulman Institute of
 Technology
Saint Mary's College
St. Mary-of-the-Woods College
Trine University
University of Notre Dame
Valparaiso University

Iowa

Coe College
Drake University
Grand View University
Iowa State University
University of Iowa

Kansas

Baker University
Haskell Indian Nations
 University
Kansas State University

Manhattan Christian College
MidAmerica Nazarene
 University
University of Kansas
University of St. Mary
Washburn University

Kentucky

Asbury University
Bellarmine University
Centre College
Georgetown College
Kentucky State University
Midway College
Northern Kentucky University
Spalding University
Thomas More College
Transylvania University
University of Kentucky
University of Louisville
Western Kentucky University

Louisiana

Dillard University
Grambling State University
Louisiana State University and
 Agricultural and Mechanical
 College
Loyola University New Orleans
Northwestern State University
Our Lady of Holy Cross
 College
Our Lady of the Lake College
Southern University
 New Orleans
Southern University and
 Agricultural and Mechanical
 College
Tulane University
University of New Orleans
Xavier University of Louisiana

Maine

University of Maine
 Augusta
University of Southern Maine

Maryland

Bowie State University
Johns Hopkins University
Loyola University Maryland
Salisbury University
Stevenson University
Towson University
University of Maryland
 Baltimore County
 College Park

Massachusetts

American International College
Amherst College
Anna Maria College
Assumption College
Babson College
Bay Path College
Bentley University
Boston College
Boston University
Brandeis University
Bridgewater State University
Clark University
College of the Holy Cross
Curry College
Eastern Nazarene College
Elms College
Harvard College
Massachusetts College of
 Pharmacy and Health
 Sciences
Massachusetts Institute of
 Technology
Massachusetts Maritime
 Academy
Merrimack College
Mount Holyoke College
Nichols College
Northeastern University
Pine Manor College

Salem State University
Smith College
Springfield College
Tufts University
University of Massachusetts
 Amherst
 Boston
 Lowell
Wellesley College
Wentworth Institute of
 Technology
Western New England
 University
Westfield State University
Williams College
Worcester Polytechnic Institute
Worcester State University

Michigan

Central Michigan University
Concordia University
Eastern Michigan University
Finlandia University
Lawrence Technological
 University
Michigan State University
Michigan Technological
 University
Oakland University
Olivet College
Spring Arbor University
University of Michigan
University of Michigan
 Dearborn
Wayne State University

Minnesota

Bethel University
College of St. Scholastica
Concordia College: Moorhead
Concordia University St. Paul
Hamline University
Macalester College
Minnesota State University
 Moorhead
North Central University
Northwestern College
St. Catherine University
University of Minnesota
 Crookston
 Duluth
 Twin Cities
University of St. Thomas

Mississippi

Belhaven University
Jackson State University
Millsaps College
Mississippi College
Mississippi State University
Mississippi University for
 Women
University of Mississippi
University of Southern
 Mississippi

Missouri

Central Bible College
Central Methodist University
Columbia College
Fontbonne University
Harris-Stowe State University
Lincoln University
Missouri University of Science
 and Technology
Saint Louis University
Southeast Missouri State
 University
Stephens College
University of Central Missouri
University of Missouri
 Columbia
 St. Louis
Washington University in St.
 Louis
Webster University
Westminster College
William Woods University

Montana

Montana State University

Nebraska

Bellevue University
Clarkson College
College of Saint Mary
Concordia University
Creighton University
Doane College
Grace University
Nebraska Wesleyan University
University of Nebraska
  Lincoln
  Medical Center
  Omaha
York College

Nevada

University of Nevada
  Las Vegas

New Hampshire

Colby-Sawyer College
Daniel Webster College
Franklin Pierce University
Granite State College
Keene State College
New England College
Plymouth State University
Rivier College
University of New Hampshire
University of New Hampshire at
  Manchester

New Jersey

The College of New Jersey
Fairleigh Dickinson University
  College at Florham
    Metropolitan Campus
Felician College
Kean University
Monmouth University
Montclair State University
New Jersey Institute of
  Technology
Princeton University
Ramapo College of New Jersey
Rutgers, The State University of
  New Jersey
  Camden Regional Campus
  New Brunswick/Piscataway
    Campus
  Newark Regional Campus
Saint Peter's College
Stevens Institute of Technology
William Paterson University of
  New Jersey

New Mexico

New Mexico State University
University of New Mexico

New York

Adelphi University
Albany College of Pharmacy
  and Health Sciences
Barnard College
Cazenovia College
Clarkson University
College of Mount St. Vincent
College of Saint Rose
Columbia University
  School of General Studies
Cornell University
Dowling College
Elmira College
Fordham University
Hamilton College
Iona College
Ithaca College
Jewish Theological Seminary of
  America
Le Moyne College
Manhattan College
Mercy College
Mesivta Torah Vodaath
  Seminary

Nazareth College
New York Institute of
  Technology
New York University
Pace University
Polytechnic Institute of New
  York University
Rensselaer Polytechnic Institute
Roberts Wesleyan College
Rochester Institute of
  Technology
Russell Sage College
Sage College of Albany
St. Francis College
St. John Fisher College
St. Lawrence University
St. Thomas Aquinas College
Siena College
Skidmore College
SUNY
  College at Brockport
  College at Cortland
  College at Geneseo
  College at Old Westbury
  College at Oswego
  College at Potsdam
  College of Environmental
    Science and Forestry
  University at Albany
  University at Binghamton
  University at Stony Brook
Syracuse University
Union College
University of Rochester
Utica College
Vaughn College of Aeronautics
  and Technology
Wells College

North Carolina

Belmont Abbey College
Bennett College for Women
Davidson College
Duke University
East Carolina University
Elon University
Fayetteville State University
Gardner-Webb University
Greensboro College
High Point University
Johnson C. Smith University
Lenoir-Rhyne University
Meredith College
Methodist University
Mount Olive College
North Carolina Agricultural and
  Technical State University
North Carolina Central
  University
North Carolina State University
Queens University of Charlotte
Shaw University
University of North Carolina
  Chapel Hill
  Charlotte
  Greensboro
  Pembroke
William Peace University
Wingate University

North Dakota

Mayville State University
North Dakota State University
University of North Dakota

Ohio

Baldwin-Wallace College
Bowling Green State University
Capital University
Case Western Reserve
  University
Cedarville University
Central State University
Cleveland Institute of Art
Cleveland State University
College of Mount St. Joseph
Franciscan University of
  Steubenville

Heidelberg University
Kent State University
Lourdes University
Malone University
Miami University
  Oxford
Mount Carmel College of
  Nursing
Ohio Northern University
Ohio State University
  Columbus Campus
  Lima Campus
  Mansfield Campus
  Marion Campus
  Newark Campus
Ohio University
Ohio University
  Lancaster Campus
Ohio Wesleyan University
Otterbein College
Tiffin University
University of Akron
University of Cincinnati
University of Dayton
University of Findlay
University of Mount Union
University of Toledo
Wilberforce University
Wittenberg University
Wright State University
Xavier University
Youngstown State University

Oklahoma

Langston University
Oklahoma Baptist University
Oklahoma Christian University
Oklahoma City University
Oklahoma State University
Oral Roberts University
St. Gregory's University
Southern Nazarene University
University of Oklahoma
University of Tulsa

Oregon

Concordia University
Corban University
George Fox University
Linfield College
Oregon State University
Pacific University
Portland State University
University of Oregon
University of Portland
Warner Pacific College
Western Oregon University
Willamette University

Pennsylvania

Bloomsburg University of
  Pennsylvania
Bryn Athyn College of the New
  Church
Bryn Mawr College
Cabrini College
Carlow University
Carnegie Mellon University
Chatham University
Drexel University
Duquesne University
East Stroudsburg University of
  Pennsylvania
Eastern University
Keystone College
King's College
La Roche College
La Salle University
Marywood University
Misericordia University
Penn State
  Abington
  Altoona
  Brandywine
  Hazleton
  New Kensington
  University Park
  Wilkes-Barre
  Worthington Scranton

Philadelphia Biblical University
Point Park University
Robert Morris University
Rosemont College
Saint Joseph's University
St. Vincent College
Swarthmore College
Temple University
University of Pennsylvania
University of Pittsburgh
University of Pittsburgh
  Greensburg
University of Scranton
University of the Sciences in
  Philadelphia
Villanova University
Washington & Jefferson College
West Chester University of
  Pennsylvania
Westminster College
Widener University
Wilkes University

Puerto Rico

Bayamon Central University
Caribbean University
Inter American University of
  Puerto Rico
  Aguadilla Campus
  Bayamon Campus
  Fajardo Campus
  Metropolitan Campus
  San German Campus
Pontifical Catholic University of
  Puerto Rico
Universidad Metropolitana
Universidad Politecnica de
  Puerto Rico
University of Puerto Rico
  Mayaguez
  Rio Piedras

South Carolina

Anderson University
Benedict College
Charleston Southern University
The Citadel
Claflin University
Clemson University
College of Charleston
South Carolina State University
University of South Carolina
  Columbia

South Dakota

Augustana College
Dakota State University
South Dakota State University
University of Sioux Falls

Tennessee

Austin Peay State University
Belmont University
Carson-Newman College
Christian Brothers University
Free Will Baptist Bible College
LeMoyne-Owen College
Lipscomb University
Middle Tennessee State
  University
Rhodes College
Tennessee State University
Tennessee Technological
  University
Tennessee Wesleyan College
University of Memphis
University of Tennessee
  Knoxville
Vanderbilt University

Texas

Angelo State University
Baylor University
College of Saint Thomas More
Concordia University Texas
Dallas Baptist University
Houston Baptist University
Lubbock Christian University

Midwestern State University
Our Lady of the Lake
  University of San Antonio
Rice University
St. Edward's University
St. Mary's University
Southern Methodist University
Texas A&M University
Texas Christian University
Texas Lutheran University
Texas State University: San
  Marcos
Texas Tech University
Texas Wesleyan University
Texas Woman's University
Trinity University
University of Dallas
University of Houston
  Downtown
  Victoria
University of Mary Hardin-
  Baylor
University of North Texas
University of St. Thomas
University of Texas
  Arlington
  Austin
  Dallas
  El Paso
  San Antonio
University of the Incarnate
  Word
Wayland Baptist University

Utah

Brigham Young University
University of Utah
Utah State University
Utah Valley University
Weber State University
Westminster College

Vermont

Lyndon State College
Norwich University
St. Michael's College

Virginia

George Mason University
James Madison University
Liberty University
Mary Baldwin College
University of Virginia
Virginia Military Institute
Virginia Polytechnic Institute
  and State University

Washington

Saint Martin's University
Seattle Pacific University
Seattle University
University of Washington
University of Washington
  Bothell
University of Washington
  Tacoma
Washington State University

West Virginia

Fairmont State University
Shepherd University
West Virginia University

Wisconsin

Alverno College
Carroll University
Carthage College
Maranatha Baptist Bible College
Marquette University
Milwaukee School of
  Engineering
University of Wisconsin
  Madison
  Milwaukee
  Stout
  Superior
  Whitewater
Wisconsin Lutheran College

Wyoming

University of Wyoming

Two-year

Alabama

Bishop State Community
College
Jefferson State Community
College
Marion Military Institute
Shelton State Community
College

Arizona

Coconino County Community
College
Estrella Mountain Community
College
GateWay Community College
Mesa Community College
Phoenix College
Pima Community College
Yavapai College

Arkansas

Northwest Arkansas Community
College

California

Canada College
Chabot College
College of San Mateo
College of the Sequoias
Cuyamaca College
De Anza College
Foothill College
Fresno City College
Irvine Valley College
Los Angeles City College
Los Angeles Mission College
MiraCosta College
Mission College
Mount San Antonio College
Ohlone College
Riverside Community College
Sacramento City College
San Diego City College
Solano Community College
West Valley College

Colorado

Arapahoe Community College
Front Range Community
College
Red Rocks Community College

Connecticut

Capital Community College
Tunxis Community College

Delaware

Delaware Technical and
Community College
Stanton/Wilmington

Florida

Brevard Community College
Broward College
Daytona State College
Miami Dade College
Santa Fe College
Tallahassee Community College
Valencia College

Hawaii

University of Hawaii
Honolulu Community
College
Leeward Community
College

Illinois

John A. Logan College
Lincoln Land Community
College
Parkland College
Shawnee Community College
Southwestern Illinois College

Indiana

Vincennes University

Iowa

Hawkeye Community College
Iowa Western Community
College

Maryland

Anne Arundel Community
College
Prince George's Community
College

Massachusetts

Holyoke Community College
Middlesex Community College
Quinsigamond Community
College

Michigan

Lansing Community College

Minnesota

Anoka-Ramsey Community
College
Century College
Inver Hills Community College
Normandale Community
College
North Hennepin Community
College

Missouri

St. Louis Community College
Meramec

New Jersey

Brookdale Community College
Raritan Valley Community
College
Union County College

New Mexico

Central New Mexico
Community College
Dona Ana Community College
of New Mexico State
University
New Mexico State University
Alamogordo

New York

Hudson Valley Community
College
Maria College
Mohawk Valley Community
College
Monroe Community College
Onondaga Community College
Schenectady County
Community College
SUNY
College of Technology at
Canton

North Carolina

Catawba Valley Community
College

Ohio

Columbus State Community
College
Cuyahoga Community College
Metropolitan
Hocking College
Kent State University
Stark
Tuscarawas
Miami University
Hamilton
Middletown
Ohio State University
Agricultural Technical
Institute
Owens Community College
Toledo
Sinclair Community College

University of Akron: Wayne
College

Oklahoma

Northeastern Oklahoma
Agricultural and Mechanical
College
Rose State College

Oregon

Clackamas Community College
Linn-Benton Community
College

Pennsylvania

Luzerne County Community
College
Valley Forge Military Academy
and College

South Carolina

Midlands Technical College
Tri-County Technical College
University of South Carolina
Salkehatchie

Tennessee

Southwest Tennessee
Community College

Texas

Austin Community College
Houston Community College
System
Lon Morris College
Lone Star College System
McLennan Community College
North Central Texas College
San Antonio College
San Jacinto College
Tarrant County College
Weatherford College

Utah

LDS Business College
Salt Lake Community College

Virginia

Piedmont Virginia Community
College

Washington

Clark College
Highline Community College
South Puget Sound Community
College
Spokane Community College

Wyoming

Laramie County Community
College

Army ROTC

Four-year

Alabama

Alabama Agricultural and
Mechanical University
Alabama State University
Auburn University
Auburn University at
Montgomery
Birmingham-Southern College
Faulkner University
Huntingdon College
Jacksonville State University
Judson College
Miles College
Samford University
Spring Hill College
Stillman College
Talladega College
Troy University
Tuskegee University
University of Alabama

University of Alabama
Birmingham
Huntsville
University of Mobile
University of Montevallo
University of North Alabama
University of South Alabama
University of West Alabama

Alaska

University of Alaska
Anchorage
Fairbanks

Arizona

Arizona State University
Embry-Riddle Aeronautical
University: Prescott Campus
Grand Canyon University
Northern Arizona University
Southwest University of Visual
Arts
University of Arizona

Arkansas

Arkansas State University
Arkansas Tech University
Central Baptist College
Henderson State University
Hendrix College
John Brown University
Ouachita Baptist University
University of Arkansas
Fort Smith
Little Rock
Monticello
Pine Bluff
University of Central Arkansas
Williams Baptist College

California

Azusa Pacific University
Biola University
California Baptist University
California Institute of
Technology
California Lutheran University
California Polytechnic State
University: San Luis Obispo
California State Polytechnic
University: Pomona
California State University
Dominguez Hills
Fresno
Fullerton
Long Beach
Los Angeles
Northridge
Sacramento
San Bernardino
San Marcos
Chapman University
Claremont McKenna College
Concordia University
Harvey Mudd College
Holy Names University
Loyola Marymount University
The Master's College
Menlo College
Mills College
National University
Occidental College
Pepperdine University
Pitzer College
Point Loma Nazarene University
Pomona College
St. Mary's College of California
Samuel Merritt University
San Diego Christian College
San Diego State University
San Francisco State University
San Jose State University
Santa Clara University
Scripps College
Simpson University
Sonoma State University
Stanford University

University of California
Berkeley
Davis
Irvine
Los Angeles
Riverside
Santa Barbara
Santa Cruz
University of La Verne
University of Redlands
University of San Diego
University of San Francisco
University of Southern
California
Vanguard University of
Southern California
Westmont College
Whittier College

Colorado

Colorado Christian University
Colorado College
Colorado School of Mines
Colorado State University
Colorado State University
Pueblo
Colorado Technical University
Metropolitan State College of
Denver
Regis University
University of Colorado
Boulder
Colorado Springs
Denver
University of Denver
University of Northern Colorado

Connecticut

Central Connecticut State
University
Eastern Connecticut State
University
Fairfield University
Quinnipiac University
Sacred Heart University
Southern Connecticut State
University
Trinity College
University of Bridgeport
University of Connecticut
University of Hartford
University of New Haven
Wesleyan University
Western Connecticut State
University
Yale University

Delaware

Delaware State University
University of Delaware
Wesley College
Wilmington University

District of Columbia

American University
Catholic University of America
George Washington University
Georgetown University
Howard University
Trinity Washington University
University of the District of
Columbia

Florida

Barry University
Bethune-Cookman University
Clearwater Christian College
Eckerd College
Embry-Riddle Aeronautical
University
Florida Agricultural and
Mechanical University
Florida Atlantic University
Florida College
Florida Institute of Technology
Florida International University
Florida Southern College
Florida State University

Lynn University
Palm Beach Atlantic University
Saint Leo University
Southeastern University
Stetson University
University of Central Florida
University of Florida
University of Miami
University of North Florida
University of South Florida
University of Tampa
University of West Florida

Georgia

Agnes Scott College
Albany State University
Armstrong Atlantic State University
Augusta State University
Clark Atlanta University
Clayton State University
Columbus State University
Covenant College
Emory University
Fort Valley State University
Georgia College and State University
Georgia Gwinnett College
Georgia Institute of Technology
Georgia Southern University
Georgia State University
Kennesaw State University
Mercer University
Morehouse College
North Georgia College & State University
Paine College
Savannah College of Art and Design
Savannah State University
Southern Polytechnic State University
Spelman College
University of Georgia

Hawaii

Brigham Young University-Hawaii
Chaminade University of Honolulu
Hawaii Pacific University
University of Hawaii
Manoa
West Oahu

Idaho

Boise State University
Brigham Young University-Idaho
College of Idaho
Idaho State University
Lewis-Clark State College
Northwest Nazarene University
University of Idaho

Illinois

Aurora University
Benedictine University
Bradley University
Chicago State University
DePaul University
Eastern Illinois University
Elmhurst College
Illinois Institute of Technology
Illinois State University
Illinois Wesleyan University
Judson University
Lewis University
Loyola University Chicago
McKendree University
Monmouth College
North Central College
North Park University
Northeastern Illinois University
Northern Illinois University
Northwestern University
Olivet Nazarene University

Robert Morris University: Chicago
Shimer College
Southern Illinois University Carbondale
Southern Illinois University Edwardsville
University of Chicago
University of Illinois Chicago
Urbana-Champaign
University of St. Francis
Western Illinois University
Wheaton College

Indiana

Ball State University
Bethel College
Butler University
DePauw University
Franklin College
Holy Cross College
Indiana Institute of Technology
Indiana State University
Indiana University
Bloomington
Kokomo
Northwest
South Bend
Southeast
Indiana University-Purdue University Fort Wayne
Indiana University-Purdue University Indianapolis
Indiana Wesleyan University
Marian University
Purdue University
Rose-Hulman Institute of Technology
Saint Mary's College
St. Mary-of-the-Woods College
University of Evansville
University of Indianapolis
University of Notre Dame
University of St. Francis
University of Southern Indiana
Valparaiso University

Iowa

Allen College
Briar Cliff University
Buena Vista University
Clarke University
Coe College
Drake University
Grand View University
Iowa State University
Loras College
Morningside College
University of Dubuque
University of Iowa
University of Northern Iowa

Kansas

Baker University
Benedictine College
Kansas State University
Manhattan Christian College
MidAmerica Nazarene University
Pittsburg State University
University of Kansas
University of St. Mary
Washburn University

Kentucky

Asbury University
Bellarmine University
Campbellsville University
Centre College
Eastern Kentucky University
Georgetown College
Kentucky Christian University
Kentucky State University
Kentucky Wesleyan College
Midway College
Morehead State University
Murray State University

Northern Kentucky University
Spalding University
Thomas More College
Transylvania University
Union College
University of Kentucky
University of Louisville
University of Pikeville
University of the Cumberlands
Western Kentucky University

Louisiana

Dillard University
Grambling State University
Louisiana College
Louisiana State University
Alexandria
Shreveport
Louisiana State University and Agricultural and Mechanical College
Louisiana Tech University
Loyola University New Orleans
Northwestern State University
Our Lady of Holy Cross College
Our Lady of the Lake College
Southern University New Orleans
Southern University and Agricultural and Mechanical College
Tulane University
University of Louisiana at Lafayette
University of Louisiana at Monroe
University of New Orleans
Xavier University of Louisiana

Maine

Colby College
Husson University
Maine Maritime Academy
New England School of Communications
Saint Joseph's College of Maine
Thomas College
University of Maine
University of Maine Augusta
University of New England
University of Southern Maine

Maryland

Bowie State University
Capitol College
Coppin State University
Goucher College
Hood College
Johns Hopkins University
Loyola University Maryland
Maryland Institute College of Art
McDaniel College
Morgan State University
Mount St. Mary's University
Notre Dame of Maryland University
Salisbury University
Stevenson University
Towson University
University of Maryland Baltimore County
College Park

Massachusetts

American International College
Amherst College
Assumption College
Babson College
Bay Path College
Becker College
Bentley University
Boston College
Boston University
Brandeis University
Bridgewater State University

Clark University
College of the Holy Cross
Curry College
Eastern Nazarene College
Elms College
Emmanuel College
Endicott College
Fitchburg State University
Gordon College
Hampshire College
Harvard College
Massachusetts College of Pharmacy and Health Sciences
Massachusetts Institute of Technology
Massachusetts Maritime Academy
Mount Holyoke College
Nichols College
Northeastern University
Pine Manor College
Regis College
Salem State University
Smith College
Springfield College
Stonehill College
Suffolk University
Tufts University
University of Massachusetts
Amherst
Boston
Dartmouth
Lowell
Wellesley College
Wentworth Institute of Technology
Western New England University
Westfield State University
Wheaton College
Worcester Polytechnic Institute
Worcester State University

Michigan

Adrian College
Alma College
Aquinas College
Calvin College
Central Michigan University
Concordia University
Eastern Michigan University
Ferris State University
Finlandia University
Hope College
Kalamazoo College
Kuyper College
Madonna University
Michigan State University
Michigan Technological University
Northern Michigan University
Spring Arbor University
University of Michigan
University of Michigan Dearborn
Flint
Wayne State University
Western Michigan University

Minnesota

Bethany Lutheran College
Bethel University
College of St. Benedict
Concordia College: Moorhead
Concordia University St. Paul
Crown College
Gustavus Adolphus College
Hamline University
Macalester College
Minnesota State University Mankato
Moorhead
North Central University
Northwestern College
St. Catherine University
Saint Cloud State University
St. John's University

St. Mary's University of Minnesota
University of Minnesota Twin Cities
University of St. Thomas
Winona State University

Mississippi

Alcorn State University
Belhaven University
Delta State University
Jackson State University
Millsaps College
Mississippi College
Mississippi State University
Mississippi University for Women
Mississippi Valley State University
Tougaloo College
University of Mississippi
University of Southern Mississippi

Missouri

Avila University
Calvary Bible College and Theological Seminary
Central Bible College
Central Methodist University
College of the Ozarks
Columbia College
Drury University
Evangel University
Fontbonne University
Harris-Stowe State University
Lincoln University
Lindenwood University
Maryville University of Saint Louis
Missouri Baptist University
Missouri State University
Missouri University of Science and Technology
Missouri Valley College
Missouri Western State University
Northwest Missouri State University
Park University
Research College of Nursing
Rockhurst University
Saint Louis University
Southwest Baptist University
Stephens College
Truman State University
University of Central Missouri
University of Missouri Columbia
Kansas City
St. Louis
Washington University in St. Louis
Webster University
Westminster College
William Jewell College
William Woods University

Montana

Carroll College
Montana State University Billings
Rocky Mountain College
University of Montana

Nebraska

Bellevue University
BryanLGH College of Health Sciences
Chadron State College
Clarkson College
College of Saint Mary
Concordia University
Creighton University
Doane College
Nebraska Methodist College of Nursing and Allied Health
Nebraska Wesleyan University

Tables and Indexes

University of Nebraska
  Kearney
  Lincoln
  Medical Center
  Omaha
Wayne State College
York College

Nevada

University of Nevada
  Las Vegas
  Reno

New Hampshire

Colby-Sawyer College
Daniel Webster College
Dartmouth College
Franklin Pierce University
Granite State College
New England College
Plymouth State University
Rivier College
Saint Anselm College
Southern New Hampshire
  University
University of New Hampshire
University of New Hampshire at
  Manchester

New Jersey

Bloomfield College
Caldwell College
The College of New Jersey
Fairleigh Dickinson University
  College at Florham
  Metropolitan Campus
Felician College
Kean University
Monmouth University
Montclair State University
New Jersey Institute of
  Technology
Princeton University
Rider University
Rowan University
Rutgers, The State University of
  New Jersey
  Camden Regional Campus
  New Brunswick/Piscataway
    Campus
  Newark Regional Campus
Saint Peter's College
Seton Hall University
Stevens Institute of Technology

New Mexico

New Mexico State University
Southwest University of Visual
  Arts
University of New Mexico

New York

Adelphi University
Albany College of Pharmacy
  and Health Sciences
Alfred University
Canisius College
Cazenovia College
City University of New York
  Baruch College
  Lehman College
  Queens College
  York College
Clarkson University
Colgate University
College of New Rochelle
College of Saint Rose
Columbia University
  School of General Studies
Cornell University
D'Youville College
Daemen College
Dowling College
Elmira College
Fordham University
Hamilton College
Hilbert College
Hofstra University

Houghton College
Iona College
Ithaca College
Jewish Theological Seminary of
  America
The King's College
Le Moyne College
Long Island University
  C. W. Post Campus
Manhattan College
Marist College
Medaille College
Mercy College
Molloy College
Monroe College
Nazareth College
New York Institute of
  Technology
New York University
Niagara University
Pace University
Pace University: Pleasantville/
  Briarcliff
Polytechnic Institute of New
  York University
Rensselaer Polytechnic Institute
Roberts Wesleyan College
Rochester Institute of
  Technology
Russell Sage College
Sage College of Albany
Saint Bonaventure University
St. Francis College
St. John Fisher College
St. John's University
St. Lawrence University
Siena College
Skidmore College
SUNY
  College at Brockport
  College at Buffalo
  College at Cortland
  College at Fredonia
  College at Geneseo
  College at Old Westbury
  College at Oswego
  College at Plattsburgh
  College of Potsdam
  College of Environmental
    Science and Forestry
  Institute of Technology at
    Utica/Rome
  Maritime College
  University at Albany
  University at Binghamton
  University at Buffalo
  University at Stony Brook
  Upstate Medical University
Syracuse University
Talmudical Seminary Oholei
  Torah
Union College
University of Rochester
Utica College
Vaughn College of Aeronautics
  and Technology
Wagner College
Wells College

North Carolina

Appalachian State University
Belmont Abbey College
Bennett College for Women
Campbell University
Catawba College
Davidson College
Duke University
East Carolina University
Elizabeth City State University
Elon University
Fayetteville State University
Gardner-Webb University
Greensboro College
High Point University
Johnson C. Smith University
Lenoir-Rhyne University
Livingstone College

Meredith College
Methodist University
Mid-Atlantic Christian
  University
North Carolina Agricultural and
  Technical State University
North Carolina Central
  University
North Carolina State University
North Carolina Wesleyan
  College
Pfeiffer University
Queens University of Charlotte
St. Augustine's College
Salem College
Shaw University
University of North Carolina
  Chapel Hill
  Charlotte
  Greensboro
  Pembroke
Wake Forest University
William Peace University
Wingate University
Winston-Salem State University

North Dakota

Mayville State University
North Dakota State University
University of North Dakota

Ohio

Baldwin-Wallace College
Bowling Green State University
Capital University
Case Western Reserve
  University
Cedarville University
Central State University
Cleveland Institute of Art
Cleveland State University
College of Mount St. Joseph
Denison University
DeVry University
  Columbus
Franciscan University of
  Steubenville
Franklin University
Heidelberg University
John Carroll University
Kent State University
Lourdes University
Malone University
Miami University
  Oxford
Mount Carmel College of
  Nursing
Notre Dame College
Ohio Dominican University
Ohio Northern University
Ohio State University
  Columbus Campus
  Lima Campus
  Mansfield Campus
  Marion Campus
  Newark Campus
Ohio University
Ohio University
  Lancaster Campus
Ohio Wesleyan University
Otterbein University
Tiffin University
University of Akron
University of Cincinnati
University of Dayton
University of Findlay
University of Mount Union
University of Toledo
Ursuline College
Wilberforce University
Wittenberg University
Wright State University
Xavier University
Youngstown State University

Oklahoma

Cameron University
Langston University

Northeastern State University
Oklahoma Christian University
Oklahoma City University
Oklahoma State University
Southern Nazarene University
Southwestern Christian
  University
University of Central Oklahoma
University of Oklahoma

Oregon

Corban University
Eastern Oregon University
Oregon Institute of Technology
Oregon State University
Pacific University
Portland State University
Southern Oregon University
University of Oregon
University of Portland
Warner Pacific College
Western Oregon University
Willamette University

Pennsylvania

Albright College
Alvernia University
Arcadia University
Baptist Bible College of
  Pennsylvania
Bloomsburg University of
  Pennsylvania
Bryn Athyn College of the New
  Church
Bucknell University
Cabrini College
California University of
  Pennsylvania
Carlow University
Carnegie Mellon University
Cedar Crest College
Chatham University
Cheyney University of
  Pennsylvania
Clarion University of
  Pennsylvania
DeSales University
Dickinson College
Drexel University
Duquesne University
East Stroudsburg University of
  Pennsylvania
Eastern University
Edinboro University of
  Pennsylvania
Gannon University
Geneva College
Gettysburg College
Immaculata University
Indiana University of
  Pennsylvania
Keystone College
King's College
Kutztown University of
  Pennsylvania
La Roche College
La Salle University
Lafayette College
Lebanon Valley College
Lehigh University
Lock Haven University of
  Pennsylvania
Lycoming College
Mansfield University of
  Pennsylvania
Marywood University
Mercyhurst University
Millersville University of
  Pennsylvania
Misericordia University
Moravian College
Muhlenberg College
Neumann University

Penn State
  Abington
  Altoona
  Berks
  Brandywine
  Erie, The Behrend College
  Fayette, The Eberly Campus
  Harrisburg
  Hazleton
  Lehigh Valley
  Mont Alto
  University Park
  Wilkes-Barre
  Worthington Scranton
Pennsylvania College of
  Technology
Point Park University
Robert Morris University
Rosemont College
St. Francis University
Saint Joseph's University
St. Vincent College
Seton Hill University
Shippensburg University of
  Pennsylvania
Slippery Rock University of
  Pennsylvania
Susquehanna University
Swarthmore College
Temple University
University of Pennsylvania
University of Pittsburgh
University of Pittsburgh
  Bradford
  Greensburg
University of Scranton
University of the Sciences in
  Philadelphia
Villanova University
Washington & Jefferson College
Waynesburg University
West Chester University of
  Pennsylvania
Westminster College
Widener University
Wilkes University
Wilson College
York College of Pennsylvania

Puerto Rico

American University of Puerto
  Rico
Bayamon Central University
Caribbean University
Inter American University of
  Puerto Rico
  Aguadilla Campus
  Arecibo Campus
  Bayamon Campus
  Guayama Campus
  Metropolitan Campus
  San German Campus
Pontifical Catholic University of
  Puerto Rico
Turabo University
Universidad del Este
Universidad Metropolitana
Universidad Politecnica de
  Puerto Rico
University of Puerto Rico
  Aguadilla
  Arecibo
  Bayamon University
    College
  Cayey University College
  Mayaguez
  Ponce
  Rio Piedras
  Utuado

Rhode Island

Brown University
Bryant University
Johnson & Wales University:
  Providence
Providence College
Rhode Island College
Roger Williams University

Salve Regina University
University of Rhode Island

South Carolina

Allen University
Anderson University
Benedict College
Charleston Southern University
The Citadel
Claflin University
Clemson University
Coastal Carolina University
Columbia College
Converse College
Francis Marion University
Furman University
Lander University
Limestone College
Morris College
Newberry College
North Greenville University
Presbyterian College
South Carolina State University
University of South Carolina
    Columbia
    Upstate
Voorhees College
Winthrop University
Wofford College

South Dakota

Augustana College
Black Hills State University
Dakota Wesleyan University
Mount Marty College
South Dakota School of Mines
    and Technology
South Dakota State University
University of South Dakota

Tennessee

Austin Peay State University
Belmont University
Carson-Newman College
Christian Brothers University
Cumberland University
East Tennessee State University
Fisk University
Free Will Baptist Bible College
King College
LeMoyne-Owen College
Lincoln Memorial University
Lipscomb University
Middle Tennessee State
    University
Milligan College
Rhodes College
Tennessee Technological
    University
Tennessee Wesleyan College
Trevecca Nazarene University
Union University
University of Memphis
University of Tennessee
    Chattanooga
    Knoxville
    Martin
Vanderbilt University

Texas

Baylor University
College of Saint Thomas More
Concordia University Texas
Dallas Baptist University
Houston Baptist University
Huston-Tillotson University
Lubbock Christian University
Our Lady of the Lake
    University of San Antonio
Prairie View A&M University
Rice University
St. Edward's University
St. Mary's University
Sam Houston State University
Southern Methodist University
Southwestern Assemblies of
    God University

Stephen F. Austin State
    University
Tarleton State University
Texas A&M International
    University
Texas A&M University
    Corpus Christi
    Kingsville
Texas Christian University
Texas Lutheran University
Texas Southern University
Texas State University: San
    Marcos
Texas Tech University
Texas Wesleyan University
Texas Woman's University
University of Dallas
University of Houston
    Downtown
University of Mary Hardin-
    Baylor
University of North Texas
University of St. Thomas
University of Texas
    Arlington
    Austin
    Brownsville - Texas
        Southmost College
    Dallas
    El Paso
    Pan American
    San Antonio
University of the Incarnate
    Word
Wayland Baptist University

Utah

Brigham Young University
Dixie State College
Southern Utah University
University of Utah
Utah State University
Utah Valley University
Weber State University
Westminster College

Vermont

Castleton State College
Champlain College
Johnson State College
Middlebury College
Norwich University
St. Michael's College
University of Vermont
Vermont Technical College

Virginia

Christopher Newport University
College of William and Mary
George Mason University
Hampden-Sydney College
Hampton University
James Madison University
Liberty University
Longwood University
Mary Baldwin College
Marymount University
Norfolk State University
Old Dominion University
Radford University
Randolph-Macon College
Regent University
St. Paul's College
Southern Virginia University
University of Mary Washington
University of Richmond
University of Virginia
University of Virginia's College
    at Wise
Virginia Commonwealth
    University
Virginia Military Institute
Virginia Polytechnic Institute
    and State University
Virginia State University
Virginia Union University
Virginia Wesleyan College
Washington and Lee University

Washington

DeVry University
    Federal Way
Eastern Washington University
Gonzaga University
Northwest University
Pacific Lutheran University
Saint Martin's University
Seattle Pacific University
Seattle University
University of Puget Sound
University of Washington
University of Washington
    Bothell
University of Washington
    Tacoma
Walla Walla University
Washington State University
Whitworth University

West Virginia

Fairmont State University
Glenville State College
Marshall University
University of Charleston
West Virginia State University
West Virginia University
West Virginia University
    Institute of Technology

Wisconsin

Alverno College
Carroll University
Carthage College
Edgewood College
Maranatha Baptist Bible College
Marquette University
Milwaukee School of
    Engineering
Mount Mary College
Ripon College
St. Norbert College
University of Wisconsin
    Eau Claire
    Green Bay
    La Crosse
    Madison
    Milwaukee
    Oshkosh
    Parkside
    Platteville
    River Falls
    Stevens Point
    Stout
    Whitewater
Viterbo University
Wisconsin Lutheran College

Wyoming

University of Wyoming

Guam

University of Guam

Virgin Islands

University of the Virgin Islands

Two-year

Alabama

Bishop State Community
    College
Chattahoochee Valley
    Community College
Gadsden State Community
    College
Jefferson State Community
    College
Marion Military Institute
Shelton State Community
    College

Arizona

Coconino County Community
    College
GateWay Community College
Mesa Community College

Paradise Valley Community
    College
Phoenix College
Pima Community College
Yavapai College

Arkansas

Arkansas State University
    Beebe
College of the Ouachitas
Northwest Arkansas Community
    College

California

Canada College
Chabot College
City College of San Francisco
College of San Mateo
De Anza College
Diablo Valley College
Foothill College
Fresno City College
Los Angeles City College
Los Angeles Mission College
MiraCosta College
Riverside Community College
Sacramento City College
San Diego City College
West Valley College

Colorado

Arapahoe Community College
Community College of Denver
Front Range Community
    College
Red Rocks Community College

Connecticut

Capital Community College
Tunxis Community College

Florida

Brevard Community College
Broward College
Daytona State College
Florida State College at
    Jacksonville
Hillsborough Community
    College
Miami Dade College
Northwest Florida State College
Pasco-Hernando Community
    College
Pensacola State College
Polk State College
Santa Fe College
Tallahassee Community College
Valencia College

Georgia

East Georgia College
Georgia Military College

Hawaii

University of Hawaii
    Honolulu Community
        College
    Leeward Community
        College
    Windward Community
        College

Idaho

North Idaho College

Illinois

Carl Sandburg College
John A. Logan College
Kankakee Community College
Kishwaukee College
Lewis and Clark Community
    College
Lincoln Land Community
    College
Parkland College
Shawnee Community College
Southwestern Illinois College
Spoon River College
Waubonsee Community College

Indiana

Vincennes University

Iowa

Hawkeye Community College
Iowa Western Community
    College

Kentucky

Elizabethtown Community and
    Technical College

Maine

Eastern Maine Community
    College

Maryland

Allegany College of Maryland
Anne Arundel Community
    College
Prince George's Community
    College

Massachusetts

Fisher College
Holyoke Community College
Middlesex Community College
Quinsigamond Community
    College
Roxbury Community College

Michigan

Lansing Community College
Washtenaw Community College

Minnesota

Anoka-Ramsey Community
    College
Inver Hills Community College
Normandale Community
    College
North Hennepin Community
    College

Mississippi

Hinds Community College

Missouri

St. Louis Community College
    Florissant Valley
    Meramec
State Fair Community College
Wentworth Military Junior
    College

Nevada

College of Southern Nevada
Truckee Meadows Community
    College

New Jersey

Brookdale Community College
Middlesex County College
Raritan Valley Community
    College

New Mexico

Central New Mexico
    Community College
Dona Ana Community College
    of New Mexico State
    University
New Mexico Military Institute

New York

Erie Community College
Herkimer County Community
    College
Hudson Valley Community
    College
Maria College
Mohawk Valley Community
    College
Monroe Community College
Niagara County Community
    College
Onondaga Community College
Orange County Community
    College

SUNY
College of Agriculture and
Technology at Morrisville
College of Technology at
Alfred
College of Technology at
Canton

North Carolina
Louisburg College
Pitt Community College
Wake Technical Community
College

Ohio
Cincinnati State Technical and
Community College
Columbus State Community
College
Hocking College
Kent State University
Stark
Tuscarawas
Ohio State University
Agricultural Technical
Institute
Owens Community College
Toledo
Sinclair Community College
University of Akron: Wayne
College
University of Cincinnati
Clermont College

Oregon
Central Oregon Community
College
Linn-Benton Community
College

Pennsylvania
Community College of
Philadelphia
Harrisburg Area Community
College
Lackawanna College
Lehigh Carbon Community
College
Valley Forge Military Academy
and College

Rhode Island
Community College of Rhode
Island

South Carolina
Greenville Technical College
Midlands Technical College
Orangeburg-Calhoun Technical
College
Spartanburg Methodist College
Tri-County Technical College
University of South Carolina
Lancaster
Salkehatchie
Sumter

Tennessee
Jackson State Community
College
Pellissippi State Community
College
Southwest Tennessee
Community College
Walters State Community
College

Texas
Alvin Community College
Angelina College
Austin Community College
Central Texas College
Collin County Community
College District
Del Mar College
El Centro College
El Paso Community College
Houston Community College
System

Laredo Community College
Lon Morris College
Lone Star College System
Palo Alto College
St. Philip's College
San Antonio College
Tarrant County College

Utah
LDS Business College
Salt Lake Community College

Virginia
J. Sargeant Reynolds
Community College
John Tyler Community College
Piedmont Virginia Community
College
Richard Bland College
Southside Virginia Community
College
Tidewater Community College

Washington
Clark College
Highline Community College
Pierce College
Spokane Community College

Wyoming
Laramie County Community
College

American Samoa
American Samoa Community
College

Guam
Guam Community College

Naval ROTC

Four-year

Alabama
Auburn University
Stillman College

Arizona
Arizona State University
University of Arizona

California
California Maritime Academy
California State University
San Marcos
Loyola Marymount University
National University
Point Loma Nazarene University
Samuel Merritt University
San Diego Christian College
San Diego State University
Sonoma State University
Stanford University
University of California
Berkeley
Davis
Los Angeles
Santa Cruz
University of Redlands
University of San Diego
University of Southern
California

Colorado
University of Colorado
Boulder

Connecticut
Quinnipiac University
Yale University

District of Columbia
Catholic University of America
George Washington University
Georgetown University

University of the District of
Columbia

Florida
Clearwater Christian College
Embry-Riddle Aeronautical
University
Florida Agricultural and
Mechanical University
Florida State University
Jacksonville University
University of Florida
University of North Florida
University of South Florida
University of Tampa

Georgia
Armstrong Atlantic State
University
Clark Atlanta University
Clayton State University
Emory University
Georgia Institute of Technology
Georgia State University
Morehouse College
Savannah State University
Southern Polytechnic State
University
Spelman College

Hawaii
Brigham Young University-
Hawaii

Idaho
Lewis-Clark State College
University of Idaho

Illinois
Illinois Institute of Technology
Loyola University Chicago
Northwestern University
Shimer College
University of Illinois
Chicago
Urbana-Champaign

Indiana
Indiana University
South Bend
Purdue University
Saint Mary's College
University of Notre Dame

Iowa
Iowa State University

Kansas
University of Kansas
Washburn University

Louisiana
Dillard University
Louisiana State University and
Agricultural and Mechanical
College
Louisiana Tech University
Loyola University New Orleans
Our Lady of Holy Cross
College
Southern University
New Orleans
Southern University and
Agricultural and Mechanical
College
Tulane University
University of New Orleans
Xavier University of Louisiana

Maine
Husson University
Maine Maritime Academy
University of Maine
University of Maine
Augusta

Maryland
University of Maryland
College Park

Massachusetts
Boston College
Boston University
Clark University
College of the Holy Cross
Harvard College
Massachusetts College of
Pharmacy and Health
Sciences
Massachusetts Institute of
Technology
Massachusetts Maritime
Academy
Northeastern University
Tufts University
University of Massachusetts
Boston
Worcester Polytechnic Institute
Worcester State University

Michigan
Eastern Michigan University
Finlandia University
University of Michigan
University of Michigan
Dearborn
Wayne State University

Minnesota
Concordia University St. Paul
Macalester College
University of Minnesota
Twin Cities
University of St. Thomas

Mississippi
Tougaloo College
University of Mississippi

Missouri
Columbia College
Lincoln University
Stephens College
University of Missouri
Columbia
William Woods University

Nebraska
BryanLGH College of Health
Sciences
University of Nebraska
Lincoln
York College

New Hampshire
Rivier College

New Jersey
Montclair State University

New Mexico
University of New Mexico

New York
Albany College of Pharmacy
and Health Sciences
City University of New York
Queens College
College of New Rochelle
College of Saint Rose
Columbia University
School of General Studies
Cornell University
Eastman School of Music of the
University of Rochester
Fordham University
Jewish Theological Seminary of
America
Mesivta Torah Vodaath
Seminary
Molloy College
Rensselaer Polytechnic Institute
Rochester Institute of
Technology
Russell Sage College
St. John Fisher College
Siena College

SUNY
College at Brockport
Maritime College
Talmudical Seminary Oholei
Torah
Union College
University of Rochester

North Carolina
Belmont Abbey College
Duke University
North Carolina State University
University of North Carolina
Chapel Hill
William Peace University

Ohio
Cleveland Institute of Art
Miami University
Oxford
Ohio State University
Columbus Campus
Lima Campus
Mansfield Campus
Marion Campus
Newark Campus
Ohio University
Lancaster Campus

Oklahoma
University of Oklahoma

Oregon
Oregon State University
Warner Pacific College
Western Oregon University

Pennsylvania
Carlow University
Carnegie Mellon University
Chatham University
Drexel University
Duquesne University
Penn State
University Park
Saint Joseph's University
Swarthmore College
Temple University
University of Pennsylvania
University of Pittsburgh
Villanova University
Westminster College
Widener University

Puerto Rico
Caribbean University
Inter American University of
Puerto Rico
Bayamon Campus
Ponce Campus
Universidad Metropolitana

South Carolina
Allen University
The Citadel
University of South Carolina
Columbia

Tennessee
Belmont University
Christian Brothers University
Fisk University
Tennessee Wesleyan College
University of Memphis
Vanderbilt University

Texas
Houston Baptist University
Prairie View A&M University
Rice University
Texas A&M University
Galveston
University of Houston
University of Texas
Austin

Utah
University of Utah
Weber State University
Westminster College

Tables and Indexes

Vermont

Norwich University

Virginia

Hampton University
Mary Baldwin College
Norfolk State University
Old Dominion University
University of Virginia
Virginia Military Institute
Virginia Polytechnic Institute
and State University

Washington

Seattle Pacific University
Seattle University
University of Washington
University of Washington
Bothell
University of Washington
Tacoma
Washington State University

Wisconsin

Marquette University
Milwaukee School of
Engineering
Mount Mary College
University of Wisconsin
Madison
Milwaukee
Wisconsin Lutheran College

Two-year

Arizona

GateWay Community College
Mesa Community College
Pima Community College

California

Contra Costa College
Diablo Valley College
Foothill College
Fullerton College
Los Angeles City College
MiraCosta College
Mission College
Riverside Community College
Sacramento City College

Connecticut

Capital Community College
Tunxis Community College

Florida

Florida State College at
Jacksonville
Pasco-Hernando Community
College
Tallahassee Community College

Hawaii

University of Hawaii
Hawaii Community College

Illinois

Lincoln Land Community
College
Parkland College
Shawnee Community College

Iowa

Hawkeye Community College

Minnesota

Anoka-Ramsey Community
College
Normandale Community
College
North Hennepin Community
College

Mississippi

East Mississippi Community
College

New Mexico

Central New Mexico
Community College

New York

Maria College
Monroe Community College

Ohio

Cuyahoga Community College
Metropolitan
Miami University
Hamilton
Middletown
Ohio State University
Agricultural Technical
Institute

South Carolina

Midlands Technical College
University of South Carolina
Salkehatchie

Texas

Lon Morris College

Virginia

New River Community College
Tidewater Community College

Washington

Spokane Community College

Colleges with NCAA sports

Baseball Division I

Alabama

Alabama Agricultural and
 Mechanical University M
Alabama State University M
Auburn University M
Jacksonville State University M
Samford University M
Troy University M
University of Alabama M
University of Alabama
 Birmingham M
University of South Alabama M

Arizona

Arizona State University M
University of Arizona M

Arkansas

Arkansas State University M
University of Arkansas M
 Little Rock M
 Pine Bluff M
University of Central Arkansas
 M

California

California Polytechnic State
 University: San Luis Obispo
 M
California State University
 Bakersfield M
 Fresno M
 Fullerton M
 Long Beach M
 Northridge M
 Sacramento M
Loyola Marymount University
 M
Pepperdine University M
St. Mary's College of California
 M
San Diego State University M
San Jose State University M
Santa Clara University M
Stanford University M
University of California
 Berkeley M
 Davis M
 Irvine M
 Los Angeles M
 Riverside M
 Santa Barbara M
University of San Diego M
University of San Francisco M
University of Southern
 California M
University of the Pacific M

Colorado

United States Air Force
 Academy M
University of Northern Colorado
 M

Connecticut

Central Connecticut State
 University M
Fairfield University M
Quinnipiac University M
Sacred Heart University M
University of Connecticut M
University of Hartford M
Yale University M

Delaware

Delaware State University M
University of Delaware M

District of Columbia

George Washington University
 M
Georgetown University M

Florida

Bethune-Cookman University M
Florida Agricultural and
 Mechanical University M
Florida Atlantic University M
Florida Gulf Coast University M
Florida International University
 M
Florida State University M
Jacksonville University M
Stetson University M
University of Central Florida M
University of Florida M
University of Miami M
University of North Florida M
University of South Florida M

Georgia

Georgia Institute of Technology
 M
Georgia Southern University M
Georgia State University M
Kennesaw State University M
Mercer University M
Savannah State University M
University of Georgia M

Hawaii

University of Hawaii
 Manoa M

Illinois

Bradley University M
Chicago State University M
Eastern Illinois University M
Illinois State University M
Northern Illinois University M
Northwestern University M
Southern Illinois University
 Carbondale M
Southern Illinois University
 Edwardsville M
University of Illinois
 Chicago M
 Urbana-Champaign M
Western Illinois University M

Indiana

Ball State University M
Butler University M
Indiana State University M
Indiana University
 Bloomington M
Indiana University-Purdue
 University Fort Wayne M
Purdue University M
University of Evansville M
University of Notre Dame M
Valparaiso University M

Iowa

University of Iowa M

Kansas

Kansas State University M
University of Kansas M
Wichita State University M

Kentucky

Eastern Kentucky University M
Morehead State University M
Murray State University M
University of Kentucky M
University of Louisville M
Western Kentucky University M

Louisiana

Grambling State University M
Louisiana State University and
 Agricultural and Mechanical
 College M
Louisiana Tech University M
McNeese State University M
Nicholls State University M

Northwestern State University
 M
Southeastern Louisiana
 University M
Southern University and
 Agricultural and Mechanical
 College M
Tulane University M
University of Louisiana at
 Lafayette M
University of Louisiana at
 Monroe M

Maine

University of Maine M

Maryland

Coppin State University M
Mount St. Mary's University M
Towson University M
United States Naval Academy
 M
University of Maryland
 Baltimore County M
 College Park M
 Eastern Shore M

Massachusetts

Boston College M
College of the Holy Cross M
Harvard College M
Northeastern University M
University of Massachusetts
 Amherst M

Michigan

Central Michigan University M
Eastern Michigan University M
Michigan State University M
Oakland University M
University of Michigan M
Western Michigan University M

Minnesota

University of Minnesota
 Twin Cities M

Mississippi

Alcorn State University M
Jackson State University M
Mississippi State University M
Mississippi Valley State
 University M
University of Mississippi M
University of Southern
 Mississippi M

Missouri

Missouri State University M
Saint Louis University M
Southeast Missouri State
 University M
University of Missouri
 Columbia M

Nebraska

Creighton University M
University of Nebraska
 Lincoln M
 Omaha M

Nevada

University of Nevada
 Las Vegas M
 Reno M

New Hampshire

Dartmouth College M

New Jersey

Fairleigh Dickinson University
 Metropolitan Campus M
Monmouth University M
New Jersey Institute of
 Technology M
Princeton University M
Rider University M

Rutgers, The State University of
 New Jersey
 New Brunswick/Piscataway
 Campus M
Saint Peter's College M
Seton Hall University M

New Mexico

New Mexico State University M
University of New Mexico M

New York

Canisius College M
Columbia University M
Cornell University M
Fordham University M
Hofstra University M
Iona College M
Long Island University
 Brooklyn Campus M
Manhattan College M
Marist College M
Niagara University M
Saint Bonaventure University M
St. John's University M
Siena College M
SUNY
 University at Albany M
 University at Binghamton
 M
 University at Buffalo M
 University at Stony Brook
 M
United States Military Academy
 M
Wagner College M

North Carolina

Appalachian State University M
Campbell University M
Davidson College M
Duke University M
East Carolina University M
Elon University M
Gardner-Webb University M
High Point University M
North Carolina Agricultural and
 Technical State University M
North Carolina Central
 University M
North Carolina State University
 M
University of North Carolina
 Asheville M
 Chapel Hill M
 Charlotte M
 Greensboro M
 Wilmington M
Wake Forest University M
Western Carolina University M

North Dakota

North Dakota State University
 M
University of North Dakota M

Ohio

Bowling Green State University
 M
Kent State University M
Miami University
 Oxford M
Ohio State University
 Columbus Campus M
Ohio University M
University of Akron M
University of Cincinnati M
University of Dayton M
University of Toledo M
Wright State University M
Xavier University M
Youngstown State University M

Oklahoma

Oklahoma State University M
Oral Roberts University M
University of Oklahoma M

Oregon

Oregon State University M
University of Oregon M
University of Portland M

Pennsylvania

Bucknell University M
La Salle University M
Lafayette College M
Lehigh University M
Penn State
 University Park M
Saint Joseph's University M
Temple University M
University of Pennsylvania M
University of Pittsburgh M
Villanova University M

Rhode Island

Brown University M
Bryant University M
University of Rhode Island M

South Carolina

Charleston Southern University
 M
The Citadel M
Clemson University M
Coastal Carolina University M
College of Charleston M
Furman University M
Presbyterian College M
University of South Carolina
 Columbia M
 Upstate M
Winthrop University M
Wofford College M

South Dakota

South Dakota State University
 M

Tennessee

Austin Peay State University M
Belmont University M
East Tennessee State University
 M
Lipscomb University M
Middle Tennessee State
 University M
Tennessee Technological
 University M
University of Memphis M
University of Tennessee
 Knoxville M
 Martin M
Vanderbilt University M

Texas

Baylor University M
Dallas Baptist University M
Houston Baptist University M
Lamar University M
Prairie View A&M University
 M
Rice University M
Sam Houston State University
 M
Stephen F. Austin State
 University M
Texas A&M University M
 Corpus Christi M
Texas Christian University M
Texas Southern University M
Texas State University: San
 Marcos M
Texas Tech University M
University of Houston M
University of Texas
 Arlington M
 Austin M
 Pan American M
 San Antonio M

Utah

Brigham Young University M
Southern Utah University M

University of Utah M
Utah Valley University M

Virginia

College of William and Mary M
George Mason University M
James Madison University M
Liberty University M
Longwood University M
Norfolk State University M
Old Dominion University M
Radford University M
University of Richmond M
University of Virginia M
Virginia Commonwealth
　University M
Virginia Military Institute M
Virginia Polytechnic Institute
　and State University M

Washington

Gonzaga University M
Seattle University M
University of Washington M
Washington State University M

West Virginia

Marshall University M
West Virginia University M

Wisconsin

University of Wisconsin
　Milwaukee M

Baseball Division II

Alabama

Miles College M
Stillman College M
Tuskegee University M
University of Alabama
　Huntsville M
University of Montevallo M
University of North Alabama M
University of West Alabama M

Arizona

Grand Canyon University M

Arkansas

Arkansas Tech University M
Harding University M
Henderson State University M
Ouachita Baptist University M
Southern Arkansas University M
University of Arkansas
　Fort Smith M
　Monticello M

California

Academy of Art University M
Azusa Pacific University M
California Baptist University M
California State Polytechnic
　University: Pomona M
California State University
　Chico M
　Dominguez Hills M
　East Bay M
　Los Angeles M
　Monterey Bay M
　San Bernardino M
　Stanislaus M
Fresno Pacific University M
Point Loma Nazarene
　University M
San Francisco State University
　M
Sonoma State University M
University of California
　San Diego M

Colorado

Colorado Christian University
　M
Colorado Mesa University M
Colorado School of Mines M

Colorado State University
　Pueblo M
Metropolitan State College of
　Denver M
Regis University M

Connecticut

Post University M
Southern Connecticut State
　University M
University of Bridgeport M
University of New Haven M

Delaware

Wilmington University M

Florida

Barry University M
Eckerd College M
Flagler College M
Florida Institute of Technology
　M
Florida Southern College M
Lynn University M
Nova Southeastern University M
Palm Beach Atlantic University
　M
Rollins College M
Saint Leo University M
University of Tampa M
University of West Florida M

Georgia

Albany State University M
Armstrong Atlantic State
　University M
Augusta State University M
Chorter University
　Shorter University M
Clark Atlanta University M
Columbus State University M
Georgia College and State
　University M
Georgia Southwestern State
　University M
Morehouse College M
North Georgia College & State
　University M
Paine College M
University of West Georgia M
Valdosta State University M
Young Harris College M

Hawaii

Hawaii Pacific University M
University of Hawaii
　Hilo M

Idaho

Northwest Nazarene University
　M

Illinois

Lewis University M
McKendree University M
Quincy University M
University of Illinois
　Springfield M

Indiana

Oakland City University M
Saint Joseph's College M
University of Indianapolis M
University of Southern Indiana
　M

Iowa

Upper Iowa University M

Kansas

Emporia State University M
Fort Hays State University M
Newman University M
Pittsburg State University M
Washburn University M

Kentucky

Bellarmine University M
Kentucky State University M

Northern Kentucky University
　M

Louisiana

University of New Orleans M

Maryland

Washington Adventist
　University M

Massachusetts

American International College
　M
Assumption College M
Bentley University M
Merrimack College M
Stonehill College M
University of Massachusetts
　Lowell M

Michigan

Grand Valley State University
　M
Hillsdale College M
Northwood University
　Michigan M
Saginaw Valley State University
　M
Wayne State University M

Minnesota

Bemidji State University M
Concordia University St. Paul
　M
Minnesota State University
　Mankato M
Saint Cloud State University M
Southwest Minnesota State
　University M
University of Minnesota
　Crookston M
　Duluth M
Winona State University M

Mississippi

Delta State University M

Missouri

Drury University M
Lincoln University M
Lindenwood University M
Maryville University of Saint
　Louis M
Missouri Southern State
　University M
Missouri University of Science
　and Technology M
Missouri Western State
　University M
Northwest Missouri State
　University M
Rockhurst University M
Southwest Baptist University M
Truman State University M
University of Central Missouri
　M
University of Missouri
　St. Louis M
William Jewell College M

Montana

Montana State University
　Billings M

Nebraska

University of Nebraska
　Kearney M
Wayne State College M

New Hampshire

Franklin Pierce University M
Saint Anselm College M
Southern New Hampshire
　University M

New Jersey

Bloomfield College M
Caldwell College M
Felician College M

New Mexico

Eastern New Mexico University
　M
New Mexico Highlands
　University M

New York

Adelphi University M
City University of New York
　Queens College M
College of Saint Rose M
Concordia College M
Dominican College of Blauvelt
　M
Dowling College M
Le Moyne College M
Long Island University
　C. W. Post Campus M
Mercy College M
Molloy College M
New York Institute of
　Technology M
Nyack College M
Pace University M
St. Thomas Aquinas College M

North Carolina

Barton College M
Belmont Abbey College M
Brevard College M
Catawba College M
Chowan University M
Elizabeth City State University
　M
Lenoir-Rhyne University M
Mars Hill College M
Mount Olive College M
Pfeiffer University M
St. Augustine's College M
Shaw University M
University of North Carolina
　Pembroke M
Wingate University M
Winston-Salem State University
　M

North Dakota

Minot State University M
University of Mary M

Ohio

Ashland University M
Cedarville University M
Lake Erie College M
Malone University M
Notre Dame College M
Ohio Dominican University M
Tiffin University M
University of Findlay M
Walsh University M

Oklahoma

Cameron University M
East Central University M
Northeastern State University M
Oklahoma Panhandle State
　University M
Southeastern Oklahoma State
　University M
Southern Nazarene University
　M
Southwestern Oklahoma State
　University M
University of Central Oklahoma
　M

Oregon

Western Oregon University M

Pennsylvania

Bloomsburg University of
　Pennsylvania M
California University of
　Pennsylvania M
Chestnut Hill College M
Clarion University of
　Pennsylvania M

East Stroudsburg University of
　Pennsylvania M
Gannon University M
Indiana University of
　Pennsylvania M
Kutztown University of
　Pennsylvania M
Lock Haven University of
　Pennsylvania M
Mansfield University of
　Pennsylvania M
Mercyhurst University M
Millersville University of
　Pennsylvania M
Philadelphia University M
Seton Hill University M
Shippensburg University of
　Pennsylvania M
Slippery Rock University of
　Pennsylvania M
University of Pittsburgh
　Johnstown M
University of the Sciences in
　Philadelphia M
West Chester University of
　Pennsylvania M

Puerto Rico

University of Puerto Rico
　Mayaguez M

South Carolina

Anderson University M
Benedict College M
Claflin University M
Coker College M
Erskine College M
Francis Marion University M
Lander University M
Limestone College M
Newberry College M
North Greenville University M
University of South Carolina
　Aiken M

South Dakota

Augustana College M
Northern State University M
University of Sioux Falls M

Tennessee

Carson-Newman College M
Christian Brothers University M
King College M
Lane College M
LeMoyne-Owen College M
Lincoln Memorial University M
Trevecca Nazarene University
　M
Tusculum College M
Union University M

Texas

Abilene Christian University M
Angelo State University M
McMurry University M
St. Edward's University M
St. Mary's University M
Tarleton State University M
Texas A&M International
　University M
Texas A&M University
　Kingsville M
University of Texas
　of the Permian Basin M
University of the Incarnate
　Word M
West Texas A&M University M

Utah

Dixie State College M

Vermont

St. Michael's College M

Virginia

Virginia State University M

Washington

Saint Martin's University M

West Virginia

Alderson-Broaddus College M
Bluefield State College M

Concord University M
Davis and Elkins College M
Fairmont State University M
Glenville State College M
Ohio Valley University M
Salem International University M
Shepherd University M
University of Charleston M
West Liberty University M
West Virginia State University M
West Virginia Wesleyan College M
Wheeling Jesuit University M

Wisconsin

University of Wisconsin Parkside M

Baseball Division III

Alabama

Birmingham-Southern College M
Huntingdon College M

Arkansas

Hendrix College M
University of the Ozarks M

California

California Institute of Technology M
California Lutheran University M
Chapman University M
Claremont McKenna College M
Occidental College M
Pomona College M
University of La Verne M
University of Redlands M
Whittier College M

Connecticut

Albertus Magnus College M
Eastern Connecticut State University M
Mitchell College M
Trinity College M
United States Coast Guard Academy M
Wesleyan University M
Western Connecticut State University M

Delaware

Wesley College M

District of Columbia

Catholic University of America M
Gallaudet University M

Georgia

Berry College M
Covenant College M
Emory University M
LaGrange College M
Oglethorpe University M
Piedmont College M

Illinois

Augustana College M
Aurora University M
Benedictine University M
Blackburn College M
Concordia University Chicago M
Dominican University M
Elmhurst College M
Eureka College M
Greenville College M
Illinois College M
Illinois Wesleyan University M
Knox College M
MacMurray College M

Millikin University M
Monmouth College M
North Central College M
North Park University M
Principia College M
Rockford College M
University of Chicago M
Wheaton College M

Indiana

Anderson University M
DePauw University M
Earlham College M
Franklin College M
Hanover College M
Manchester College M
Rose-Hulman Institute of Technology M
Trine University M
Wabash College M

Iowa

Buena Vista University M
Central College M
Coe College M
Cornell College M
Grinnell College M
Loras College M
Luther College M
Simpson College M
University of Dubuque M
Wartburg College M

Kentucky

Centre College M
Kentucky Wesleyan College M
Spalding University M
Thomas More College M
Transylvania University M

Louisiana

Centenary College of Louisiana M
Louisiana College M

Maine

Bates College M
Bowdoin College M
Colby College M
Husson University M
Saint Joseph's College of Maine M
Thomas College M
University of Maine
    Farmington M
    Presque Isle M
University of Southern Maine M

Maryland

Frostburg State University M
Johns Hopkins University M
McDaniel College M
St. Mary's College of Maryland M
Salisbury University M
Washington College M

Massachusetts

Amherst College M
Anna Maria College M
Babson College M
Becker College M
Brandeis University M
Bridgewater State University M
Clark University M
Curry College M
Eastern Nazarene College M
Elms College M
Emerson College M
Endicott College M
Fitchburg State University M
Framingham State University M
Gordon College M
Lasell College M
Lesley University M
Massachusetts College of Liberal Arts M
Massachusetts Institute of Technology M

Massachusetts Maritime Academy M
Newbury College M
Nichols College M
Salem State University M
Springfield College M
Suffolk University M
Tufts University M
University of Massachusetts
    Boston M
    Dartmouth M
Wentworth Institute of Technology M
Western New England University M
Westfield State University M
Wheaton College M
Williams College M
Worcester Polytechnic Institute M
Worcester State University M

Michigan

Adrian College M
Albion College M
Alma College M
Calvin College M
Finlandia University M
Hope College M
Kalamazoo College M
Olivet College M

Minnesota

Bethany Lutheran College M
Bethel University M
Carleton College M
College of St. Scholastica M
Concordia College: Moorhead M
Crown College M
Gustavus Adolphus College M
Hamline University M
Macalester College M
Martin Luther College M
North Central University M
Northwestern College M
St. John's University M
St. Mary's University of Minnesota M
St. Olaf College M
University of Minnesota Morris M
University of St. Thomas M

Mississippi

Millsaps College M
Mississippi College M
Rust College M

Missouri

Fontbonne University M
Washington University in St. Louis M
Webster University M
Westminster College M

Nebraska

Nebraska Wesleyan University M

New Hampshire

Colby-Sawyer College M
Daniel Webster College M
Keene State College M
New England College M
Plymouth State University M
Rivier College M

New Jersey

Centenary College M
The College of New Jersey M
Drew University M
Fairleigh Dickinson University College at Florham M
Kean University M
Montclair State University M
New Jersey City University M
Ramapo College of New Jersey M

Richard Stockton College of New Jersey M
Rowan University M
Rutgers, The State University of New Jersey
    Camden Regional Campus M
    Newark Regional Campus M
Stevens Institute of Technology M
William Paterson University of New Jersey M

New York

Cazenovia College M
City University of New York
    Baruch College M
    City College M
    College of Staten Island M
    John Jay College of Criminal Justice M
    Lehman College M
Clarkson University M
College of Mount St. Vincent M
D'Youville College M
Hamilton College M
Hilbert College M
Ithaca College M
Keuka College M
Manhattanville College M
Medaille College M
Mount Saint Mary College M
Polytechnic Institute of New York University M
Rensselaer Polytechnic Institute M
Rochester Institute of Technology M
St. John Fisher College M
St. Joseph's College, New York M
St. Joseph's College: Suffolk Campus M
St. Lawrence University M
Skidmore College M
SUNY
    College at Brockport M
    College at Cortland M
    College at Fredonia M
    College at New Paltz M
    College at Old Westbury M
    College at Oneonta M
    College at Oswego M
    College at Plattsburgh M
    College at Purchase M
    Farmingdale State College M
    Institute of Technology at Utica/Rome M
    Maritime College M
Union College M
United States Merchant Marine Academy M
University of Rochester M
Utica College M
Vassar College M
Yeshiva University M

North Carolina

Greensboro College M
Guilford College M
Methodist University M
North Carolina Wesleyan College M

Ohio

Baldwin-Wallace College M
Bluffton University M
Capital University M
Case Western Reserve University M
College of Mount St. Joseph M
College of Wooster M
Defiance College M
Denison University M
Heidelberg University M
Hiram College M
John Carroll University M

Kenyon College M
Marietta College M
Muskingum University M
Oberlin College M
Ohio Northern University M
Ohio Wesleyan University M
Otterbein University M
University of Mount Union M
Wilmington College M
Wittenberg University M

Oregon

George Fox University M
Lewis & Clark College M
Linfield College M
Pacific University M
Willamette University M

Pennsylvania

Albright College M
Allegheny College M
Alvernia University M
Arcadia University M
Baptist Bible College of Pennsylvania M
Delaware Valley College M
DeSales University M
Dickinson College M
Eastern University M
Elizabethtown College M
Franklin & Marshall College M
Geneva College M
Gettysburg College M
Grove City College M
Gwynedd-Mercy College M
Haverford College M
Immaculata University M
Juniata College M
Keystone College M
King's College M
La Roche College M
Lancaster Bible College M
Lebanon Valley College M
Marywood University M
Messiah College M
Misericordia University M
Moravian College M
Mount Aloysius College M
Muhlenberg College M
Neumann University M
Penn State
    Abington M
    Altoona M
    Berks M
    Erie, The Behrend College M
    Harrisburg M
Philadelphia Biblical University M
St. Vincent College M
Susquehanna University M
Swarthmore College M
Thiel College M
University of Pittsburgh
    Bradford M
    Greensburg M
University of Scranton M
Ursinus College M
Washington & Jefferson College M
Waynesburg University M
Westminster College M
Widener University M
Wilkes University M
York College of Pennsylvania M

Rhode Island

Johnson & Wales University: Providence M
Rhode Island College M
Roger Williams University M
Salve Regina University M

Tennessee

Maryville College M
Rhodes College M
University of the South M

Texas

Austin College M
Concordia University Texas M
East Texas Baptist University M
Hardin-Simmons University M
Howard Payne University M
LeTourneau University M
Schreiner University M
Southwestern University M
Sul Ross State University M
Texas Lutheran University M
Trinity University M
University of Dallas M
University of Mary Hardin-
    Baylor M
University of Texas
    Dallas M
    Tyler M

Vermont

Castleton State College M
Lyndon State College M
Middlebury College M
Norwich University M
Southern Vermont College M

Virginia

Averett University M
Bridgewater College M
Christopher Newport University
    M
Eastern Mennonite University M
Emory & Henry College M
Ferrum College M
Hampden-Sydney College M
Lynchburg College M
Randolph-Macon College M
Roanoke College M
Shenandoah University M
University of Mary Washington
    M
Virginia Wesleyan College M
Washington and Lee University
    M

Washington

Pacific Lutheran University M
University of Puget Sound M
Whitman College M
Whitworth University M

West Virginia

Bethany College M

Wisconsin

Beloit College M
Carroll University M
Carthage College M
Concordia University Wisconsin
    M
Edgewood College M
Lakeland College M
Lawrence University M
Maranatha Baptist Bible College
    M
Marian University M
Milwaukee School of
    Engineering M
Northland College M
Ripon College M
St. Norbert College M
University of Wisconsin
    La Crosse M
    Oshkosh M
    Platteville M
    Stevens Point M
    Stout M
    Superior M
    Whitewater M
Wisconsin Lutheran College M

Basketball Division I

Alabama

Alabama Agricultural and
    Mechanical University

Alabama State University
Auburn University
Jacksonville State University
Samford University
Troy University
University of Alabama
University of Alabama
    Birmingham
University of South Alabama

Arizona

Arizona State University
Northern Arizona University
University of Arizona

Arkansas

Arkansas State University
University of Arkansas
    Little Rock
    Pine Bluff
University of Central Arkansas

California

California Polytechnic State
    University: San Luis Obispo
California State University
    Bakersfield
    Fresno
    Fullerton
    Long Beach
    Northridge
    Sacramento
Loyola Marymount University
Pepperdine University
St. Mary's College of California
San Diego State University
San Jose State University
Santa Clara University
Stanford University
University of California
    Berkeley
    Davis
    Irvine
    Los Angeles
    Riverside
    Santa Barbara
University of San Diego
University of San Francisco
University of Southern
    California
University of the Pacific

Colorado

Colorado State University
United States Air Force
    Academy
University of Colorado
    Boulder
University of Denver
University of Northern Colorado

Connecticut

Central Connecticut State
    University
Fairfield University
Quinnipiac University
Sacred Heart University
University of Connecticut
University of Hartford
Yale University

Delaware

Delaware State University
University of Delaware

District of Columbia

American University
George Washington University
Georgetown University
Howard University

Florida

Bethune-Cookman University
Florida Agricultural and
    Mechanical University
Florida Atlantic University
Florida Gulf Coast University
Florida International University
Florida State University

Jacksonville University
Stetson University
University of Central Florida
University of Florida
University of Miami
University of North Florida
University of South Florida

Georgia

Georgia Institute of Technology
Georgia Southern University
Georgia State University
Kennesaw State University
Mercer University
Savannah State University
University of Georgia

Hawaii

University of Hawaii
    Manoa

Idaho

Boise State University
Idaho State University
University of Idaho

Illinois

Bradley University
Chicago State University
DePaul University
Eastern Illinois University
Illinois State University
Loyola University Chicago
Northern Illinois University
Northwestern University
Southern Illinois University
    Carbondale
Southern Illinois University
    Edwardsville
University of Illinois
    Chicago
    Urbana-Champaign
Western Illinois University

Indiana

Ball State University
Butler University
Indiana State University
Indiana University
    Bloomington
Indiana University-Purdue
    University Fort Wayne
Indiana University-Purdue
    University Indianapolis
Purdue University
University of Evansville
University of Notre Dame
Valparaiso University

Iowa

Drake University
Iowa State University
University of Iowa
University of Northern Iowa

Kansas

Kansas State University
University of Kansas
Wichita State University

Kentucky

Eastern Kentucky University
Morehead State University
Murray State University
University of Kentucky
University of Louisville
Western Kentucky University

Louisiana

Grambling State University
Louisiana State University and
    Agricultural and Mechanical
    College
Louisiana Tech University
McNeese State University
Nicholls State University
Northwestern State University
Southeastern Louisiana
    University

Southern University and
    Agricultural and Mechanical
    College
Tulane University
University of Louisiana at
    Lafayette
University of Louisiana at
    Monroe

Maine

University of Maine

Maryland

Coppin State University
Loyola University Maryland
Morgan State University
Mount St. Mary's University
Towson University
United States Naval Academy
University of Maryland
    Baltimore County
    College Park
    Eastern Shore

Massachusetts

Boston College
Boston University
College of the Holy Cross
Harvard College
Northeastern University
University of Massachusetts
    Amherst

Michigan

Central Michigan University
Eastern Michigan University
Michigan State University
Oakland University
University of Detroit Mercy
University of Michigan
Western Michigan University

Minnesota

University of Minnesota
    Twin Cities

Mississippi

Alcorn State University
Jackson State University
Mississippi State University
Mississippi Valley State
    University
University of Mississippi
University of Southern
    Mississippi

Missouri

Missouri State University
Saint Louis University
Southeast Missouri State
    University
University of Missouri
    Columbia
    Kansas City

Montana

Montana State University
University of Montana

Nebraska

Creighton University
University of Nebraska
    Lincoln
    Omaha

Nevada

University of Nevada
    Las Vegas
    Reno

New Hampshire

Dartmouth College
University of New Hampshire

New Jersey

Fairleigh Dickinson University
    Metropolitan Campus
Monmouth University
New Jersey Institute of
    Technology

Princeton University
Rider University
Rutgers, The State University of
    New Jersey
    New Brunswick/Piscataway
    Campus
Saint Peter's College
Seton Hall University

New Mexico

New Mexico State University
University of New Mexico

New York

Barnard College F
Canisius College
Colgate University
Columbia University
Cornell University
Fordham University
Hofstra University
Iona College
Long Island University
    Brooklyn Campus
Manhattan College
Marist College
Niagara University
Saint Bonaventure University
St. Francis College
St. John's University
Siena College
SUNY
    University at Albany
    University at Binghamton
    University at Buffalo
    University at Stony Brook
Syracuse University
United States Military Academy
Wagner College

North Carolina

Appalachian State University
Campbell University
Davidson College
Duke University
East Carolina University
Elon University
Gardner-Webb University
High Point University
North Carolina Agricultural and
    Technical State University
North Carolina Central
    University
North Carolina State University
University of North Carolina
    Asheville
    Chapel Hill
    Charlotte
    Greensboro
    Wilmington
Wake Forest University
Western Carolina University

North Dakota

North Dakota State University
University of North Dakota

Ohio

Bowling Green State University
Cleveland State University
Kent State University
Miami University
    Oxford
Ohio State University
    Columbus Campus
Ohio University
University of Akron
University of Cincinnati
University of Dayton
University of Toledo
Wright State University
Xavier University
Youngstown State University

Oklahoma

Oklahoma State University
Oral Roberts University
University of Oklahoma
University of Tulsa

Oregon

Oregon State University
Portland State University
University of Oregon
University of Portland

Pennsylvania

Bucknell University
Drexel University
Duquesne University
La Salle University
Lafayette College
Lehigh University
Penn State
University Park
Robert Morris University
St. Francis University
Saint Joseph's University
Temple University
University of Pennsylvania
University of Pittsburgh
Villanova University

Rhode Island

Brown University
Bryant University
Providence College
University of Rhode Island

South Carolina

Charleston Southern University
The Citadel M
Clemson University
Coastal Carolina University
College of Charleston
Furman University
Presbyterian College
South Carolina State University
University of South Carolina
Columbia
Upstate
Winthrop University
Wofford College

South Dakota

South Dakota State University
University of South Dakota

Tennessee

Austin Peay State University
Belmont University
East Tennessee State University
Lipscomb University
Middle Tennessee State
University
Tennessee State University
Tennessee Technological
University
University of Memphis
University of Tennessee
Chattanooga
Knoxville
Martin
Vanderbilt University

Texas

Baylor University
Houston Baptist University
Lamar University
Prairie View A&M University
Rice University
Sam Houston State University
Southern Methodist University
Stephen F. Austin State
University
Texas A&M University
Corpus Christi
Texas Christian University
Texas Southern University
Texas State University: San
Marcos
Texas Tech University
University of Houston
University of North Texas

University of Texas
Arlington
Austin
El Paso
Pan American
San Antonio

Utah

Brigham Young University
Southern Utah University
University of Utah
Utah State University
Utah Valley University
Weber State University

Vermont

University of Vermont

Virginia

College of William and Mary
George Mason University
Hampton University
James Madison University
Liberty University
Longwood University
Norfolk State University
Old Dominion University
Radford University
University of Richmond
University of Virginia
Virginia Commonwealth
University
Virginia Military Institute M
Virginia Polytechnic Institute
and State University

Washington

Eastern Washington University
Gonzaga University
Seattle University
University of Washington
Washington State University

West Virginia

Marshall University
West Virginia University

Wisconsin

Marquette University
University of Wisconsin
Green Bay
Madison
Milwaukee

Wyoming

University of Wyoming

Basketball Division II

Alabama

Miles College
Stillman College
Tuskegee University
University of Alabama
Huntsville
University of Montevallo
University of North Alabama
University of West Alabama

Alaska

University of Alaska
Anchorage
Fairbanks

Arizona

Grand Canyon University

Arkansas

Arkansas Tech University
Harding University
Henderson State University
Ouachita Baptist University
Southern Arkansas University
University of Arkansas
Fort Smith
Monticello

California

Academy of Art University
Azusa Pacific University
California Baptist University
California State Polytechnic
University: Pomona
California State University
Chico
Dominguez Hills
East Bay
Los Angeles
Monterey Bay
San Bernardino
Stanislaus
Dominican University of
California
Fresno Pacific University
Humboldt State University
Notre Dame de Namur
University
Point Loma Nazarene University
San Francisco State University
Sonoma State University
University of California
San Diego

Colorado

Adams State College
Colorado Christian University
Colorado Mesa University
Colorado School of Mines
Colorado State University
Pueblo
Fort Lewis College
Metropolitan State College of
Denver
Regis University
University of Colorado
Colorado Springs
Western State College of
Colorado

Connecticut

Post University
Southern Connecticut State
University
University of Bridgeport
University of New Haven

Delaware

Goldey-Beacom College
Wilmington University

District of Columbia

University of the District of
Columbia

Florida

Barry University
Eckerd College
Flagler College
Florida Institute of Technology
Florida Southern College
Lynn University
Nova Southeastern University
Palm Beach Atlantic University
Rollins College
Saint Leo University
University of Tampa
University of West Florida

Georgia

Albany State University
Armstrong Atlantic State
University
Augusta State University
Chorter University
Shorter University
Clark Atlanta University
Clayton State University
Columbus State University
Fort Valley State University
Georgia College and State
University
Georgia Southwestern State
University
Morehouse College M

North Georgia College & State
University
Paine College
University of West Georgia
Valdosta State University
Young Harris College

Hawaii

Brigham Young University-
Hawaii
Chaminade University of
Honolulu
Hawaii Pacific University
University of Hawaii
Hilo

Idaho

Northwest Nazarene University

Illinois

Lewis University
McKendree University
Quincy University
University of Illinois
Springfield

Indiana

Oakland City University
Saint Joseph's College
University of Indianapolis
University of Southern Indiana

Iowa

Upper Iowa University

Kansas

Emporia State University
Fort Hays State University
Newman University
Pittsburg State University
Washburn University

Kentucky

Bellarmine University
Kentucky State University
Northern Kentucky University

Louisiana

University of New Orleans

Maryland

Bowie State University
Washington Adventist
University

Massachusetts

American International College
Assumption College
Bentley University
Merrimack College
Stonehill College
University of Massachusetts
Lowell

Michigan

Ferris State University
Grand Valley State University
Hillsdale College
Lake Superior State University
Michigan Technological
University
Northern Michigan University
Northwood University
Michigan
Saginaw Valley State University
Wayne State University

Minnesota

Bemidji State University
Concordia University St. Paul
Minnesota State University
Mankato
Moorhead
Saint Cloud State University
Southwest Minnesota State
University
University of Minnesota
Crookston
Duluth
Winona State University

Mississippi

Delta State University

Missouri

Drury University
Lincoln University
Lindenwood University
Maryville University of Saint
Louis
Missouri Southern State
University
Missouri University of Science
and Technology
Missouri Western State
University
Northwest Missouri State
University
Rockhurst University
Southwest Baptist University
Truman State University
University of Central Missouri
University of Missouri
St. Louis
William Jewell College

Montana

Montana State University
Billings

Nebraska

Chadron State College
University of Nebraska
Kearney
Wayne State College

New Hampshire

Franklin Pierce University
Saint Anselm College
Southern New Hampshire
University

New Jersey

Bloomfield College
Caldwell College
Felician College
Georgian Court University F

New Mexico

Eastern New Mexico University
New Mexico Highlands
University

New York

Adelphi University
City University of New York
Queens College
College of Saint Rose
Concordia College
Dominican College of Blauvelt
Dowling College
Le Moyne College
Long Island University
C. W. Post Campus
Mercy College
Molloy College
New York Institute of
Technology
Nyack College
Pace University
Roberts Wesleyan College
St. Thomas Aquinas College

North Carolina

Barton College
Belmont Abbey College
Brevard College
Catawba College
Chowan University
Elizabeth City State University
Fayetteville State University
Johnson C. Smith University
Lees-McRae College
Lenoir-Rhyne University
Livingstone College
Mars Hill College
Mount Olive College
Pfeiffer University
Queens University of Charlotte
St. Augustine's College

Shaw University
University of North Carolina Pembroke
Wingate University
Winston-Salem State University

North Dakota
Minot State University
University of Mary

Ohio
Ashland University
Cedarville University
Central State University
Lake Erie College
Malone University
Notre Dame College
Ohio Dominican University
Tiffin University
University of Findlay
Ursuline College F
Walsh University

Oklahoma
Cameron University
East Central University
Northeastern State University
Oklahoma Panhandle State University
Southeastern Oklahoma State University
Southern Nazarene University
Southwestern Oklahoma State University
University of Central Oklahoma

Oregon
Western Oregon University

Pennsylvania
Bloomsburg University of Pennsylvania
California University of Pennsylvania
Chestnut Hill College
Cheyney University of Pennsylvania
Clarion University of Pennsylvania
East Stroudsburg University of Pennsylvania
Edinboro University of Pennsylvania
Gannon University
Holy Family University
Indiana University of Pennsylvania
Kutztown University of Pennsylvania
Lock Haven University of Pennsylvania
Mansfield University of Pennsylvania
Mercyhurst University
Millersville University of Pennsylvania
Philadelphia University
Seton Hill University
Shippensburg University of Pennsylvania
Slippery Rock University of Pennsylvania
University of Pittsburgh Johnstown
University of the Sciences in Philadelphia
West Chester University of Pennsylvania

Puerto Rico
University of Puerto Rico Bayamón University College Mayaguez Rio Piedras

South Carolina
Anderson University
Benedict College

Claflin University
Coker College
Converse College F
Erskine College
Francis Marion University
Lander University
Limestone College
Newberry College
North Greenville University
University of South Carolina Aiken

South Dakota
Augustana College
Black Hills State University
Northern State University
South Dakota School of Mines and Technology
University of Sioux Falls

Tennessee
Carson-Newman College
Christian Brothers University
King College
Lane College
LeMoyne-Owen College
Lincoln Memorial University
Trevecca Nazarene University
Tusculum College
Union University

Texas
Abilene Christian University
Angelo State University
Dallas Baptist University M
McMurry University
Midwestern State University
St. Edward's University
St. Mary's University
Tarleton State University
Texas A&M International University
Texas A&M University Commerce Kingsville
Texas Woman's University F
University of Texas of the Permian Basin
University of the Incarnate Word
West Texas A&M University

Utah
Dixie State College

Vermont
St. Michael's College

Virginia
Virginia State University
Virginia Union University

Washington
Saint Martin's University
Seattle Pacific University
Western Washington University

West Virginia
Alderson-Broaddus College
Bluefield State College
Concord University
Davis and Elkins College
Fairmont State University
Glenville State College
Ohio Valley University
Salem International University
Shepherd University
University of Charleston
West Liberty University
West Virginia State University
West Virginia Wesleyan College
Wheeling Jesuit University

Wisconsin
University of Wisconsin Parkside

Canada
Simon Fraser University

Basketball Division III

Alabama
Birmingham-Southern College
Huntingdon College

Arkansas
Hendrix College
University of the Ozarks

California
California Institute of Technology
California Lutheran University
Chapman University
Claremont McKenna College
Occidental College
Pitzer College
Pomona College
University of California Santa Cruz
University of La Verne
University of Redlands
Whittier College

Colorado
Colorado College

Connecticut
Albertus Magnus College
Connecticut College
Eastern Connecticut State University
Mitchell College
Saint Joseph College F
Trinity College
United States Coast Guard Academy
Wesleyan University
Western Connecticut State University

Delaware
Wesley College

District of Columbia
Catholic University of America
Gallaudet University
Trinity Washington University F

Georgia
Agnes Scott College F
Berry College
Covenant College
Emory University
LaGrange College
Oglethorpe University
Piedmont College
Spelman College F
Wesleyan College F

Illinois
Augustana College
Aurora University
Benedictine University
Blackburn College
Concordia University Chicago
Dominican University
Elmhurst College
Eureka College
Greenville College
Illinois College
Illinois Wesleyan University
Knox College
Lake Forest College
MacMurray College
Millikin University
Monmouth College
North Central College
North Park University
Principia College
Rockford College

University of Chicago
Wheaton College

Indiana
Anderson University
DePauw University
Earlham College
Franklin College
Hanover College
Manchester College
Rose-Hulman Institute of Technology
Saint Mary's College F
Trine University
Wabash College M

Iowa
Buena Vista University
Central College
Coe College
Cornell College
Grinnell College
Loras College
Luther College
Simpson College
University of Dubuque
Wartburg College

Kentucky
Centre College
Kentucky Wesleyan College
Spalding University
Thomas More College
Transylvania University

Louisiana
Centenary College of Louisiana
Louisiana College

Maine
Bates College
Bowdoin College
Colby College
Husson University
Maine Maritime Academy
Saint Joseph's College of Maine
Thomas College
University of Maine Farmington
University of Maine Presque Isle
University of New England
University of Southern Maine

Maryland
Frostburg State University
Goucher College
Hood College
Johns Hopkins University
McDaniel College
Notre Dame of Maryland University F
St. Mary's College of Maryland
Salisbury University
Stevenson University
Washington College

Massachusetts
Amherst College
Anna Maria College
Babson College
Bay Path College F
Becker College
Brandeis University
Bridgewater State University
Clark University
Curry College
Eastern Nazarene College
Elms College
Emerson College
Emmanuel College
Endicott College
Fitchburg State University
Framingham State University
Gordon College
Lasell College
Lesley University
Massachusetts College of Liberal Arts

Massachusetts Institute of Technology
Mount Holyoke College F
Mount Ida College
Newbury College
Nichols College
Pine Manor College F
Regis College
Salem State University
Simmons College F
Smith College F
Springfield College
Suffolk University
Tufts University
University of Massachusetts Boston
Dartmouth
Wellesley College F
Wentworth Institute of Technology
Western New England University
Westfield State University
Wheaton College
Wheelock College
Williams College
Worcester Polytechnic Institute
Worcester State University

Michigan
Adrian College
Albion College
Alma College
Calvin College
Finlandia University
Hope College
Kalamazoo College
Olivet College

Minnesota
Bethany Lutheran College
Bethel University
Carleton College
College of St. Benedict F
College of St. Scholastica
Concordia College: Moorhead
Crown College
Gustavus Adolphus College
Hamline University
Macalester College
Martin Luther College
North Central University
Northwestern College
St. Catherine University F
St. John's University M
St. Mary's University of Minnesota
St. Olaf College
University of Minnesota Morris
University of St. Thomas

Mississippi
Millsaps College
Mississippi College
Rust College

Missouri
Baptist Bible College F
Fontbonne University
Washington University in St. Louis
Webster University
Westminster College

Nebraska
Nebraska Wesleyan University

New Hampshire
Colby-Sawyer College
Daniel Webster College
Keene State College
New England College
Plymouth State University
Rivier College

New Jersey
Centenary College
The College of New Jersey

College of St. Elizabeth F
Drew University
Fairleigh Dickinson University
College at Florham
Kean University
Montclair State University
New Jersey City University
Ramapo College of New Jersey
Richard Stockton College of
New Jersey
Rowan University
Rutgers, The State University of
New Jersey
Camden Regional Campus
Newark Regional Campus
Stevens Institute of Technology
William Paterson University of
New Jersey

New York

Alfred University
Bard College
Cazenovia College
City University of New York
Baruch College
Brooklyn College
City College
College of Staten Island
Hunter College
John Jay College of
Criminal Justice
Lehman College
Medgar Evers College
York College
Clarkson University
College of Mount St. Vincent
College of New Rochelle F
D'Youville College
Elmira College
Hamilton College
Hartwick College
Hilbert College
Hobart and William Smith
Colleges
Ithaca College
Keuka College
Manhattanville College
Medaille College
Mount Saint Mary College
Nazareth College
New York University
Polytechnic Institute of New
York University
Rensselaer Polytechnic Institute
Rochester Institute of
Technology
Sage College of Albany
St. John Fisher College
St. Joseph's College, New York
M
St. Joseph's College: Suffolk
Campus
St. Lawrence University
Skidmore College
SUNY
College at Brockport
College at Buffalo
College at Cortland
College at Fredonia
College at Geneseo
College at New Paltz
College at Old Westbury
College at Oneonta
College at Oswego
College at Plattsburgh
College at Potsdam
College at Purchase
College of Agriculture and
Technology at Cobleskill
College of Agriculture and
Technology at Morrisville
Farmindale State College
Institute of Technology at
Utica/Rome M
Maritime College M
Union College

United States Merchant Marine
Academy
University of Rochester
Utica College
Vassar College
Wells College
Yeshiva University

North Carolina

Greensboro College
Guilford College
Meredith College F
Methodist University
North Carolina Wesleyan
College
Salem College F
William Peace University

Ohio

Baldwin-Wallace College
Bluffton University
Capital University
Case Western Reserve
University
College of Mount St. Joseph
College of Wooster
Defiance College
Denison University
Franciscan University of
Steubenville
Heidelberg University
Hiram College
John Carroll University
Kenyon College
Marietta College
Muskingum University
Oberlin College
Ohio Northern University
Ohio Wesleyan University
Otterbein University
University of Mount Union
Wilmington College
Wittenberg University

Oregon

George Fox University
Lewis & Clark College
Linfield College
Pacific University
Willamette University

Pennsylvania

Albright College
Allegheny College
Alvernia University
Arcadia University
Baptist Bible College of
Pennsylvania M
Bryn Mawr College F
Cabrini College
Carnegie Mellon University
Cedar Crest College F
Chatham University F
Delaware Valley College
DeSales University
Dickinson College
Eastern University
Elizabethtown College
Franklin & Marshall College
Geneva College
Gettysburg College
Grove City College
Gwynedd-Mercy College
Haverford College
Immaculata University
Juniata College
Keystone College
King's College
La Roche College
Lancaster Bible College
Lebanon Valley College
Lycoming College
Marywood University
Messiah College
Misericordia University
Moravian College
Mount Aloysius College
Muhlenberg College

Neumann University
Penn State
Abington
Altoona
Berks
Erie, The Behrend College
Harrisburg
Philadelphia Biblical University
Rosemont College
St. Vincent College
Susquehanna University
Swarthmore College
Thiel College
University of Pittsburgh
Bradford
Greensburg
University of Scranton
Ursinus College
Washington & Jefferson College
Waynesburg University
Westminster College
Widener University
Wilkes University
Wilson College F
York College of Pennsylvania

Rhode Island

Johnson & Wales University:
Providence
Rhode Island College
Roger Williams University
Salve Regina University

Tennessee

Maryville College
Rhodes College
University of the South

Texas

Austin College
Concordia University Texas
East Texas Baptist University
Hardin-Simmons University
Howard Payne University
LeTourneau University
Schreiner University
Southwestern University
Sul Ross State University
Texas Lutheran University
Trinity University
University of Dallas
University of Mary Hardin-
Baylor
University of Texas
Dallas
Tyler

Vermont

Castleton State College
Green Mountain College
Johnson State College
Lyndon State College
Middlebury College
Norwich University
Southern Vermont College

Virginia

Averett University
Bridgewater College
Christopher Newport University
Eastern Mennonite University
Emory & Henry College
Ferrum College
Hampden-Sydney College M
Hollins University F
Lynchburg College
Mary Baldwin College F
Marymount University
Randolph College
Randolph-Macon College
Roanoke College
Shenandoah University
University of Mary Washington
Virginia Wesleyan College
Washington and Lee University

Washington

Pacific Lutheran University
University of Puget Sound

Whitman College
Whitworth University

West Virginia

Bethany College

Wisconsin

Alverno College F
Beloit College
Carroll University
Carthage College
Concordia University Wisconsin
Edgewood College
Lakeland College
Lawrence University
Maranatha Baptist Bible College
Marian University
Milwaukee School of
Engineering
Mount Mary College F
Northland College
Ripon College
St. Norbert College
University of Wisconsin
Eau Claire
La Crosse
Oshkosh
Platteville
River Falls
Stevens Point
Stout
Superior
Whitewater
Wisconsin Lutheran College

Bowling Division I

Alabama

Alabama Agricultural and
Mechanical University F
Alabama State University F
University of Alabama
Birmingham F

Arkansas

Arkansas State University F
University of Arkansas
Pine Bluff F

Connecticut

Sacred Heart University F

Delaware

Delaware State University F

District of Columbia

Howard University F

Florida

Bethune-Cookman University F
Florida Agricultural and
Mechanical University F

Indiana

Valparaiso University F

Louisiana

Grambling State University F
Louisiana Tech University F
Southern University and
Agricultural and Mechanical
College F
Tulane University F

Maryland

Coppin State University F
Morgan State University F
University of Maryland
Eastern Shore F

Mississippi

Jackson State University F
Mississippi Valley State
University F

Nebraska

University of Nebraska
Lincoln F

New Jersey

Fairleigh Dickinson University
Metropolitan Campus F
Monmouth University F
Saint Peter's College F

New York

Long Island University
Brooklyn Campus F
St. Francis College F

North Carolina

North Carolina Agricultural and
Technical State University F
North Carolina Central
University F

Pennsylvania

St. Francis University F

South Carolina

South Carolina State University
F

Tennessee

Vanderbilt University F

Texas

Prairie View A&M University F
Sam Houston State University F
Stephen F. Austin State
University F
Texas Southern University F

Virginia

Hampton University F
Norfolk State University F

Bowling Division II

Maryland

Bowie State University F

Missouri

University of Central Missouri F

New York

Adelphi University F

North Carolina

Chowan University F
Elizabeth City State University
F
Fayetteville State University F
Johnson C. Smith University F
Livingstone College F
St. Augustine's College F
Shaw University F
Winston-Salem State University
F

Ohio

Ursuline College F

Pennsylvania

Cheyney University of
Pennsylvania F
Kutztown University of
Pennsylvania F

Virginia

Virginia State University F
Virginia Union University F

West Virginia

Salem International University F

Bowling Division III

Illinois

Elmhurst College F

Kentucky

Spalding University F

Michigan

Adrian College F
Alma College F

Missouri

Fontbonne University F

New Jersey

New Jersey City University F

New York

Medaille College F

Pennsylvania

Penn State
Altoona F

Wisconsin

University of Wisconsin
Whitewater F

Cross-country Division I

Alabama

Alabama Agricultural and
Mechanical University F
Alabama State University
Auburn University
Jacksonville State University
Samford University
Troy University
University of Alabama
University of Alabama
Birmingham F
University of South Alabama

Arizona

Arizona State University
Northern Arizona University
University of Arizona

Arkansas

Arkansas State University
University of Arkansas
Little Rock
Pine Bluff
University of Central Arkansas

California

California Polytechnic State
University: San Luis Obispo
California State University
Bakersfield F
Fresno
Fullerton
Long Beach M
Northridge
Sacramento
Loyola Marymount University
Pepperdine University
St. Mary's College of California
San Diego State University F
San Jose State University
Santa Clara University
Stanford University
University of California
Berkeley
Davis
Irvine
Los Angeles
Riverside
Santa Barbara
University of San Diego
University of San Francisco
University of Southern
California F
University of the Pacific F

Colorado

Colorado State University
United States Air Force
Academy
University of Colorado
Boulder
University of Northern Colorado

Connecticut

Central Connecticut State
University
Fairfield University

Quinnipiac University
Sacred Heart University
University of Connecticut
University of Hartford
Yale University

Delaware

Delaware State University
University of Delaware F

District of Columbia

American University
George Washington University
Georgetown University
Howard University

Florida

Bethune-Cookman University
Florida Agricultural and
Mechanical University
Florida Atlantic University
Florida Gulf Coast University
Florida International University
Florida State University
Jacksonville University
Stetson University
University of Central Florida F
University of Florida
University of Miami
University of North Florida
University of South Florida

Georgia

Georgia Institute of Technology
Georgia Southern University F
Georgia State University
Kennesaw State University
Mercer University
Savannah State University
University of Georgia

Hawaii

University of Hawaii
Manoa F

Idaho

Boise State University
Idaho State University
University of Idaho

Illinois

Bradley University
Chicago State University
DePaul University
Eastern Illinois University
Illinois State University
Loyola University Chicago
Northern Illinois University F
Northwestern University F
Southern Illinois University
Carbondale
Southern Illinois University
Edwardsville
University of Illinois
Chicago
Urbana-Champaign
Western Illinois University

Indiana

Ball State University F
Butler University
Indiana State University
Indiana University
Bloomington
Indiana University-Purdue
University Fort Wayne
Indiana University-Purdue
University Indianapolis
Purdue University
University of Evansville
University of Notre Dame
Valparaiso University

Iowa

Drake University
Iowa State University
University of Iowa
University of Northern Iowa

Kansas

Kansas State University
University of Kansas
Wichita State University

Kentucky

Eastern Kentucky University
Morehead State University
Murray State University
University of Kentucky
University of Louisville
Western Kentucky University

Louisiana

Grambling State University
Louisiana State University and
Agricultural and Mechanical
College
Louisiana Tech University
McNeese State University
Nicholls State University
Northwestern State University
Southeastern Louisiana
University
Southern University and
Agricultural and Mechanical
College
Tulane University
University of Louisiana at
Lafayette
University of Louisiana at
Monroe

Maine

University of Maine

Maryland

Coppin State University
Loyola University Maryland
Morgan State University
Mount St. Mary's University
Towson University F
United States Naval Academy
University of Maryland
Baltimore County
College Park
Eastern Shore

Massachusetts

Boston College
Boston University
College of the Holy Cross
Harvard College
Northeastern University
University of Massachusetts
Amherst

Michigan

Central Michigan University
Eastern Michigan University
Michigan State University
Oakland University
University of Detroit Mercy
University of Michigan
Western Michigan University F

Minnesota

University of Minnesota
Twin Cities

Mississippi

Alcorn State University
Jackson State University
Mississippi State University
Mississippi Valley State
University
University of Mississippi
University of Southern
Mississippi F

Missouri

Missouri State University F
Saint Louis University
Southeast Missouri State
University
University of Missouri
Columbia
Kansas City

Montana

Montana State University
University of Montana

Nebraska

Creighton University
University of Nebraska
Lincoln
Omaha F

Nevada

University of Nevada
Las Vegas F
Reno F

New Hampshire

Dartmouth College
University of New Hampshire

New Jersey

Fairleigh Dickinson University
Metropolitan Campus
Monmouth University
New Jersey Institute of
Technology
Princeton University
Rider University
Rutgers, The State University of
New Jersey
New Brunswick/Piscataway
Campus
Saint Peter's College
Seton Hall University

New Mexico

New Mexico State University
University of New Mexico

New York

Barnard College F
Canisius College
Colgate University
Columbia University
Cornell University
Fordham University
Hofstra University
Iona College
Long Island University
Brooklyn Campus
Manhattan College
Marist College
Niagara University
Saint Bonaventure University
St. Francis College
St. John's University F
Siena College
SUNY
University at Albany
University at Binghamton
University at Buffalo
University at Stony Brook
Syracuse University
United States Military Academy
Wagner College

North Carolina

Appalachian State University
Campbell University
Davidson College
Duke University
East Carolina University
Elon University
Gardner-Webb University
High Point University
North Carolina Agricultural and
Technical State University
North Carolina Central
University
North Carolina State University
University of North Carolina
Asheville
Chapel Hill
Charlotte
Greensboro
Wilmington
Wake Forest University
Western Carolina University

North Dakota

North Dakota State University
University of North Dakota

Ohio

Bowling Green State University
Cleveland State University F
Kent State University
Miami University
Oxford
Ohio State University
Columbus Campus
Ohio University
University of Akron
University of Cincinnati
University of Dayton
University of Toledo
Wright State University
Xavier University
Youngstown State University

Oklahoma

Oklahoma State University
Oral Roberts University
University of Oklahoma
University of Tulsa

Oregon

Oregon State University F
Portland State University
University of Oregon
University of Portland

Pennsylvania

Bucknell University
Duquesne University
La Salle University
Lafayette College
Lehigh University
Penn State
University Park
Robert Morris University
St. Francis University
Saint Joseph's University
Temple University
University of Pennsylvania
University of Pittsburgh
Villanova University

Rhode Island

Brown University
Bryant University
Providence College
University of Rhode Island

South Carolina

Charleston Southern University
The Citadel
Clemson University
Coastal Carolina University
College of Charleston
Furman University
Presbyterian College
South Carolina State University
University of South Carolina
Columbia F
Upstate
Winthrop University
Wofford College

South Dakota

South Dakota State University
University of South Dakota

Tennessee

Austin Peay State University
Belmont University
East Tennessee State University
Lipscomb University
Middle Tennessee State
University
Tennessee State University
Tennessee Technological
University
University of Memphis
University of Tennessee
Chattanooga
Knoxville
Martin

Vanderbilt University

Texas

Baylor University
Houston Baptist University
Lamar University
Prairie View A&M University
Rice University
Sam Houston State University
Southern Methodist University F
Stephen F. Austin State
  University
Texas A&M University
  Corpus Christi
Texas Christian University
Texas Southern University
Texas State University: San
  Marcos
Texas Tech University
University of Houston
University of North Texas
University of Texas
  Arlington
  Austin
  El Paso
  Pan American
  San Antonio

Utah

Brigham Young University
Southern Utah University
University of Utah F
Utah State University
Utah Valley University
Weber State University

Vermont

University of Vermont

Virginia

College of William and Mary
George Mason University
Hampton University
James Madison University F
Liberty University
Longwood University
Norfolk State University
Radford University
University of Richmond
University of Virginia
Virginia Commonwealth
  University
Virginia Military Institute
Virginia Polytechnic Institute
  and State University

Washington

Eastern Washington University
Gonzaga University
Seattle University
University of Washington
Washington State University

West Virginia

Marshall University
West Virginia University F

Wisconsin

Marquette University
University of Wisconsin
  Green Bay
  Madison
  Milwaukee

Wyoming

University of Wyoming

**Cross-country
Division II**

Alabama

Miles College
Stillman College
Tuskegee University
University of Alabama
  Huntsville
University of Montevallo

University of North Alabama
University of West Alabama

Alaska

University of Alaska
  Anchorage
  Fairbanks

Arizona

Grand Canyon University

Arkansas

Arkansas Tech University F
Harding University
Henderson State University F
Ouachita Baptist University F
Southern Arkansas University
University of Arkansas
  Fort Smith
  Monticello

California

Academy of Art University
Azusa Pacific University
California Baptist University
California State Polytechnic
  University: Pomona
California State University
  Chico
  Dominguez Hills F
  East Bay
  Los Angeles F
  Monterey Bay
  San Bernardino F
  Stanislaus
Dominican University of
  California M
Fresno Pacific University
Humboldt State University
Notre Dame de Namur
  University
Point Loma Nazarene University
San Francisco State University
Sonoma State University F
University of California
  San Diego

Colorado

Adams State College
Colorado Christian University
Colorado Mesa University
Colorado School of Mines
Colorado State University
  Pueblo F
Fort Lewis College
Metropolitan State College of
  Denver
Regis University
University of Colorado
  Colorado Springs
Western State College of
  Colorado

Connecticut

Post University
Southern Connecticut State
  University
University of Bridgeport
University of New Haven

Delaware

Goldey-Beacom College
Wilmington University

District of Columbia

University of the District of
  Columbia

Florida

Flagler College
Florida Institute of Technology
Florida Southern College
Nova Southeastern University
Palm Beach Atlantic University
  F
Rollins College
Saint Leo University
University of Tampa
University of West Florida

Georgia

Albany State University
Armstrong Atlantic State
  University M
Augusta State University
Chorter University
  Shorter University
Clark Atlanta University
Clayton State University
Columbus State University
Fort Valley State University
Georgia College and State
  University
Georgia Southwestern State
  University F
Morehouse College M
Paine College
University of West Georgia
Valdosta State University
Young Harris College

Hawaii

Brigham Young University-
  Hawaii
Chaminade University of
  Honolulu
Hawaii Pacific University
University of Hawaii
  Hilo F

Idaho

Northwest Nazarene University

Illinois

Lewis University
McKendree University
Quincy University

Indiana

Oakland City University
Saint Joseph's College
University of Indianapolis
University of Southern Indiana

Kansas

Emporia State University
Fort Hays State University
Newman University
Pittsburg State University

Kentucky

Bellarmine University
Kentucky State University
Northern Kentucky University

Louisiana

University of New Orleans

Maryland

Bowie State University
Washington Adventist
  University

Massachusetts

American International College
Assumption College
Bentley University
Merrimack College
Stonehill College
University of Massachusetts
  Lowell

Michigan

Ferris State University
Grand Valley State University
Hillsdale College
Lake Superior State University
Michigan Technological
  University
Northern Michigan University F
Northwood University
  Michigan
Saginaw Valley State University
Wayne State University

Minnesota

Bemidji State University F
Concordia University St. Paul

Minnesota State University
  Mankato
  Moorhead
Saint Cloud State University
University of Minnesota
  Duluth
Winona State University

Mississippi

Delta State University F

Missouri

Drury University
Lincoln University F
Lindenwood University M
Maryville University of Saint
  Louis
Missouri Southern State
  University
Missouri University of Science
  and Technology
Northwest Missouri State
  University
Southwest Baptist University
Truman State University
University of Central Missouri
William Jewell College

Montana

Montana State University
  Billings

Nebraska

University of Nebraska
  Kearney
Wayne State College

New Hampshire

Franklin Pierce University F
Saint Anselm College
Southern New Hampshire
  University

New Jersey

Bloomfield College
Caldwell College F
Felician College
Georgian Court University F

New Mexico

Eastern New Mexico University
New Mexico Highlands
  University

New York

Adelphi University
City University of New York
  Queens College
College of Saint Rose
Concordia College
Dominican College of Blauvelt
  F
Dowling College
Le Moyne College
Long Island University
  C. W. Post Campus
Molloy College
New York Institute of
  Technology
Nyack College
Pace University
Roberts Wesleyan College
St. Thomas Aquinas College

North Carolina

Barton College
Belmont Abbey College
Brevard College
Catawba College
Elizabeth City State University
Fayetteville State University
Johnson C. Smith University
Lees-McRae College
Lenoir-Rhyne University
Livingstone College
Mars Hill College
Mount Olive College
Pfeiffer University
Queens University of Charlotte

St. Augustine's College
Shaw University
University of North Carolina
  Pembroke
Wingate University
Winston-Salem State University

North Dakota

Minot State University
University of Mary

Ohio

Ashland University
Cedarville University
Central State University
Lake Erie College
Malone University
Notre Dame College
Ohio Dominican University
Tiffin University
University of Findlay
Ursuline College F
Walsh University

Oklahoma

Cameron University M
East Central University
Oklahoma Panhandle State
  University
Southeastern Oklahoma State
  University F
Southern Nazarene University
Southwestern Oklahoma State
  University F
University of Central Oklahoma
  F

Oregon

Western Oregon University

Pennsylvania

Bloomsburg University of
  Pennsylvania
California University of
  Pennsylvania
Chestnut Hill College
Cheyney University of
  Pennsylvania
Clarion University of
  Pennsylvania F
East Stroudsburg University of
  Pennsylvania
Edinboro University of
  Pennsylvania
Gannon University
Holy Family University
Indiana University of
  Pennsylvania
Kutztown University of
  Pennsylvania
Lock Haven University of
  Pennsylvania
Mansfield University of
  Pennsylvania
Mercyhurst University
Millersville University of
  Pennsylvania
Philadelphia University
Seton Hill University
Shippensburg University of
  Pennsylvania
Slippery Rock University of
  Pennsylvania
University of Pittsburgh
  Johnstown F
University of the Sciences in
  Philadelphia
West Chester University of
  Pennsylvania

Puerto Rico

University of Puerto Rico
  Bayamon University
    College
  Mayaguez
  Rio Piedras

South Carolina

Anderson University
Benedict College
Claflin University
Coker College
Converse College F
Erskine College
Francis Marion University
Limestone College
Newberry College
North Greenville University
University of South Carolina
Aiken F

South Dakota

Augustana College
Black Hills State University
Northern State University
South Dakota School of Mines
and Technology
University of Sioux Falls

Tennessee

Carson-Newman College
Christian Brothers University
King College
Lane College
LeMoyne-Owen College
Lincoln Memorial University
Trevecca Nazarene University
Tusculum College
Union University

Texas

Abilene Christian University
Angelo State University
Dallas Baptist University
McMurry University
Midwestern State University F
St. Mary's University F
Tarleton State University
Texas A&M International
University
Texas A&M University
Commerce
Kingsville
University of Texas
of the Permian Basin
University of the Incarnate
Word
West Texas A&M University

Utah

Dixie State College

Vermont

St. Michael's College

Virginia

Virginia State University
Virginia Union University

Washington

Saint Martin's University
Seattle Pacific University
Western Washington University

West Virginia

Alderson-Broaddus College
Bluefield State College
Concord University
Davis and Elkins College
Fairmont State University
Glenville State College
Ohio Valley University
Salem International University
University of Charleston F
West Liberty University
West Virginia Wesleyan College
Wheeling Jesuit University

Wisconsin

University of Wisconsin
Parkside

Canada

Simon Fraser University

Cross-country Division III

Alabama

Birmingham-Southern College
Huntingdon College

Arkansas

Hendrix College
University of the Ozarks

California

California Institute of
Technology
California Lutheran University
Chapman University
Claremont McKenna College
Mills College F
Occidental College
Pitzer College
Pomona College
University of California
Santa Cruz
University of La Verne
University of Redlands
Whittier College

Colorado

Colorado College

Connecticut

Albertus Magnus College
Connecticut College
Eastern Connecticut State
University
Mitchell College
Saint Joseph College F
Trinity College
United States Coast Guard
Academy
Wesleyan University

Delaware

Wesley College

District of Columbia

Catholic University of America
Gallaudet University

Georgia

Berry College
Covenant College
Emory University
LaGrange College
Oglethorpe University
Piedmont College
Spelman College F
Wesleyan College F

Illinois

Augustana College
Aurora University
Benedictine University
Blackburn College
Concordia University Chicago
Dominican University
Elmhurst College
Eureka College
Greenville College
Illinois College
Illinois Wesleyan University
Knox College
Lake Forest College
Millikin University
Monmouth College
North Central College
North Park University
Principia College
Rockford College
University of Chicago
Wheaton College

Indiana

Anderson University
DePauw University
Earlham College
Franklin College
Hanover College
Manchester College
Rose-Hulman Institute of
Technology
Saint Mary's College F
Trine University
Wabash College M

Iowa

Buena Vista University
Central College
Coe College
Cornell College
Grinnell College
Loras College
Luther College
Simpson College
University of Dubuque
Wartburg College

Kentucky

Centre College
Kentucky Wesleyan College
Spalding University
Thomas More College
Transylvania University

Louisiana

Centenary College of Louisiana
Louisiana College

Maine

Bates College
Bowdoin College
Colby College
Husson University F
Maine Maritime Academy
Saint Joseph's College of Maine
Thomas College
University of Maine
Farmington
Presque Isle
University of New England
University of Southern Maine

Maryland

Frostburg State University
Goucher College
Hood College
Johns Hopkins University
McDaniel College
St. Mary's College of Maryland
M
Salisbury University
Stevenson University

Massachusetts

Amherst College
Anna Maria College M
Babson College
Bay Path College F
Brandeis University
Bridgewater State University
Clark University
Curry College F
Eastern Nazarene College
Elms College
Emerson College
Emmanuel College
Endicott College
Fitchburg State University
Framingham State University
Gordon College
Lasell College
Lesley University
Massachusetts College of
Liberal Arts
Massachusetts Institute of
Technology
Massachusetts Maritime
Academy
Mount Holyoke College F
Mount Ida College

Newbury College
Pine Manor College F
Salem State University
Simmons College F
Smith College F
Springfield College
Suffolk University
Tufts University
University of Massachusetts
Boston M
Dartmouth
Wellesley College F
Western New England
University
Westfield State University
Wheaton College
Wheelock College
Williams College
Worcester Polytechnic Institute
Worcester State University

Michigan

Adrian College
Albion College
Alma College
Calvin College
Finlandia University
Hope College
Kalamazoo College
Olivet College

Minnesota

Bethany Lutheran College
Bethel University
Carleton College
College of St. Benedict F
College of St. Scholastica
Concordia College: Moorhead
Crown College
Gustavus Adolphus College
Hamline University
Macalester College
Martin Luther College
North Central University
Northwestern College
St. Catherine University F
St. John's University M
St. Mary's University of
Minnesota
St. Olaf College
University of Minnesota
Morris
University of St. Thomas

Mississippi

Millsaps College
Mississippi College
Rust College

Missouri

Fontbonne University
Washington University in St.
Louis
Webster University
Westminster College

Nebraska

Nebraska Wesleyan University

New Hampshire

Colby-Sawyer College
Daniel Webster College
Keene State College
New England College
Rivier College

New Jersey

Centenary College
The College of New Jersey
College of St. Elizabeth F
Drew University
Fairleigh Dickinson University
College at Florham
New Jersey City University
Ramapo College of New Jersey
Richard Stockton College of
New Jersey
Rowan University

Rutgers, The State University of
New Jersey
Camden Regional Campus
Newark Regional Campus
Stevens Institute of Technology

New York

Alfred University
Bard College
Cazenovia College
City University of New York
Baruch College
Brooklyn College
City College
College of Staten Island
Hunter College
John Jay College of
Criminal Justice
Lehman College
Medgar Evers College
York College
Clarkson University
College of Mount St. Vincent
College of New Rochelle F
D'Youville College
Hamilton College
Hartwick College
Hilbert College
Hobart and William Smith
Colleges M
Ithaca College
Keuka College
Manhattanville College
Medaille College
Mount Saint Mary College
Nazareth College
New York University
Polytechnic Institute of New
York University
Rensselaer Polytechnic Institute
Rochester Institute of
Technology
Sage College of Albany M
St. John Fisher College
St. Joseph's College, New York
St. Joseph's College: Suffolk
Campus M
St. Lawrence University
SUNY
College at Brockport
College at Buffalo
College at Cortland
College at Fredonia
College at Geneseo
College at New Paltz
College at Old Westbury
College at Oneonta
College at Oswego
College at Plattsburgh
College at Potsdam
College at Purchase
College of Agriculture and
Technology at Cobleskill
College of Agriculture and
Technology at Morrisville
Farmingdale State College
Institute of Technology at
Utica/Rome
Maritime College
Union College
United States Merchant Marine
Academy
University of Rochester
Utica College
Vassar College
Wells College
Yeshiva University

North Carolina

Greensboro College
Guilford College
Meredith College F
Methodist University
Salem College F
William Peace University

Ohio

Baldwin-Wallace College
Bluffton University
Capital University
Case Western Reserve
    University
College of Mount St. Joseph
College of Wooster
Defiance College
Denison University
Franciscan University of
    Steubenville
Heidelberg University
Hiram College
John Carroll University
Kenyon College
Marietta College
Muskingum University
Oberlin College
Ohio Northern University
Ohio Wesleyan University
Otterbein University
University of Mount Union
Wilmington College
Wittenberg University

Oregon

George Fox University
Lewis & Clark College
Linfield College
Pacific University
Willamette University

Pennsylvania

Albright College
Allegheny College
Alvernia University
Baptist Bible College of
    Pennsylvania
Bryn Mawr College F
Cabrini College
Carnegie Mellon University
Cedar Crest College F
Chatham University F
Delaware Valley College
DeSales University
Dickinson College
Eastern University
Elizabethtown College
Franklin & Marshall College
Geneva College
Gettysburg College
Grove City College
Gwynedd-Mercy College
Haverford College
Immaculata University
Juniata College
Keystone College
King's College
La Roche College
Lancaster Bible College
Lebanon Valley College
Lycoming College
Marywood University
Messiah College
Misericordia University
Moravian College
Mount Aloysius College
Muhlenberg College
Neumann University
Penn State
    Abington
    Altoona
    Berks
    Erie, The Behrend College
    Harrisburg
Philadelphia Biblical University
Rosemont College
St. Vincent College
Susquehanna University
Swarthmore College
Thiel College
University of Pittsburgh
    Bradford
    Greensburg
University of Scranton
Ursinus College

Washington & Jefferson College
Waynesburg University
Westminster College
Widener University
Wilkes University
York College of Pennsylvania

Rhode Island

Johnson & Wales University:
    Providence
Rhode Island College
Roger Williams University
Salve Regina University

Tennessee

Maryville College
Rhodes College
University of the South

Texas

Concordia University Texas
East Texas Baptist University
Hardin-Simmons University
Howard Payne University
LeTourneau University
Schreiner University
Southwestern University
Sul Ross State University
Texas Lutheran University F
Trinity University
University of Dallas
University of Texas
    Dallas
    Tyler

Vermont

Castleton State College
Green Mountain College
Johnson State College
Lyndon State College
Middlebury College
Norwich University
Southern Vermont College

Virginia

Averett University
Bridgewater College
Christopher Newport University
Eastern Mennonite University
Emory & Henry College
Ferrum College
Hampden-Sydney College M
Lynchburg College
Mary Baldwin College F
Marymount University
Randolph College
Roanoke College
Shenandoah University
University of Mary Washington
Virginia Wesleyan College
Washington and Lee University

Washington

Pacific Lutheran University
University of Puget Sound
Whitman College
Whitworth University

West Virginia

Bethany College

Wisconsin

Alverno College F
Beloit College
Carroll University
Carthage College
Concordia University Wisconsin
Edgewood College
Lakeland College
Lawrence University
Maranatha Baptist Bible College
Marian University
Milwaukee School of
    Engineering
Mount Mary College F
Northland College
Ripon College
St. Norbert College

University of Wisconsin
    Eau Claire
    La Crosse
    Oshkosh
    Platteville
    River Falls
    Stevens Point
    Stout
    Superior
    Whitewater
Wisconsin Lutheran College

Fencing Division I

California

Stanford University

Colorado

United States Air Force
    Academy

Connecticut

Sacred Heart University
Yale University

Illinois

Northwestern University F

Indiana

University of Notre Dame

Massachusetts

Boston College
Harvard College

Michigan

University of Detroit Mercy

New Jersey

Fairleigh Dickinson University
    Metropolitan Campus F
New Jersey Institute of
    Technology
Princeton University

New York

Barnard College F
Columbia University
Cornell University F
St. John's University

North Carolina

Duke University
University of North Carolina
    Chapel Hill

Ohio

Cleveland State University
Ohio State University
    Columbus Campus

Pennsylvania

Lafayette College M
Penn State
    University Park
Temple University F
University of Pennsylvania

Rhode Island

Brown University

Fencing Division II

California

University of California
    San Diego

Michigan

Wayne State University

New York

City University of New York
    Queens College F

Fencing Division III

California

California Institute of
    Technology

Maryland

Johns Hopkins University

Massachusetts

Brandeis University
Massachusetts Institute of
    Technology
Tufts University F
Wellesley College F

New Jersey

Drew University
Stevens Institute of Technology

New York

City University of New York
    City College F
    Hunter College
New York University
Vassar College
Yeshiva University

Pennsylvania

Haverford College

Wisconsin

Lawrence University

Field hockey Division I

California

Stanford University F
University of California
    Berkeley F
    Davis F
University of the Pacific F

Connecticut

Fairfield University F
Quinnipiac University F
Sacred Heart University F
University of Connecticut F
Yale University F

Delaware

University of Delaware F

District of Columbia

American University F
Georgetown University F

Illinois

Northwestern University F

Indiana

Ball State University F
Indiana University
    Bloomington F

Iowa

University of Iowa F

Kentucky

University of Louisville F

Maine

University of Maine F

Maryland

Towson University F
University of Maryland
    College Park F

Massachusetts

Boston College F
Boston University F
College of the Holy Cross F
Harvard College F
Northeastern University F
University of Massachusetts
    Amherst F

Michigan

Central Michigan University F
Michigan State University F
University of Michigan F

Missouri

Missouri State University F
Saint Louis University F

New Hampshire

Dartmouth College F
University of New Hampshire F

New Jersey

Monmouth University F
Princeton University F
Rider University F
Rutgers, The State University of
    New Jersey
        New Brunswick/Piscataway
        Campus F

New York

Barnard College F
Colgate University F
Columbia University F
Cornell University F
Hofstra University F
Siena College F
SUNY
    University at Albany F
Syracuse University F

North Carolina

Appalachian State University F
Davidson College F
Duke University F
University of North Carolina
    Chapel Hill F
Wake Forest University F

Ohio

Kent State University F
Miami University
    Oxford F
Ohio State University
    Columbus Campus F
Ohio University F

Pennsylvania

Bucknell University F
Drexel University F
La Salle University F
Lafayette College F
Lehigh University F
Lock Haven University of
    Pennsylvania F
Penn State
    University Park F
Robert Morris University F
St. Francis University F
Saint Joseph's University F
Temple University F
University of Pennsylvania F
Villanova University F

Rhode Island

Brown University F
Bryant University F
Providence College F

Vermont

University of Vermont F

Virginia

College of William and Mary F
James Madison University F
Longwood University F
Old Dominion University F
Radford University F
University of Richmond F
University of Virginia F
Virginia Commonwealth
    University F

Field hockey Division II

Connecticut

Southern Connecticut State University F

Kentucky

Bellarmine University F

Massachusetts

American International College F
Assumption College F
Bentley University F
Merrimack College F
Stonehill College F
University of Massachusetts Lowell F

Missouri

Lindenwood University F

New Hampshire

Franklin Pierce University F
Saint Anselm College F

New York

Adelphi University F
Long Island University C. W. Post Campus F
Mercy College F

Pennsylvania

Bloomsburg University of Pennsylvania F
East Stroudsburg University of Pennsylvania F
Indiana University of Pennsylvania F
Kutztown University of Pennsylvania F
Mansfield University of Pennsylvania F
Mercyhurst University F
Millersville University of Pennsylvania F
Seton Hill University F
Shippensburg University of Pennsylvania F
Slippery Rock University of Pennsylvania F
West Chester University of Pennsylvania F

South Carolina

Limestone College F

Vermont

St. Michael's College F

Field hockey Division III

Arkansas

Hendrix College F

Connecticut

Connecticut College F
Eastern Connecticut State University F
Trinity College F
Wesleyan University F
Western Connecticut State University F

Delaware

Wesley College F

District of Columbia

Catholic University of America F

Indiana

DePauw University F
Earlham College F
Trine University F

Kentucky

Centre College F
Transylvania University F

Maine

Bates College F
Bowdoin College F
Colby College F
Husson University F
Saint Joseph's College of Maine F
Thomas College F
University of Maine Farmington F
University of New England F
University of Southern Maine F

Maryland

Frostburg State University F
Goucher College F
Hood College F
Johns Hopkins University F
McDaniel College F
Notre Dame of Maryland University F
St. Mary's College of Maryland F
Salisbury University F
Stevenson University F
Washington College F

Massachusetts

Amherst College F
Anna Maria College F
Babson College F
Bay Path College F
Becker College F
Bridgewater State University F
Clark University F
Elms College F
Endicott College F
Fitchburg State University F
Framingham State University F
Gordon College F
Lasell College F
Massachusetts Institute of Technology F
Mount Holyoke College F
Nichols College F
Regis College F
Salem State University F
Simmons College F
Smith College F
Springfield College F
Tufts University F
University of Massachusetts Dartmouth F
Wellesley College F
Western New England University F
Westfield State University F
Wheaton College F
Wheelock College F
Williams College F
Worcester Polytechnic Institute F
Worcester State University F

New Hampshire

Daniel Webster College F
Keene State College F
New England College F
Plymouth State University F
Rivier College F

New Jersey

The College of New Jersey F
Drew University F
Fairleigh Dickinson University College at Florham F
Kean University F
Montclair State University F
Ramapo College of New Jersey F
Richard Stockton College of New Jersey F
Rowan University F

Stevens Institute of Technology F
William Paterson University of New Jersey F

New York

Elmira College F
Hamilton College F
Hartwick College F
Hobart and William Smith Colleges F
Ithaca College F
Manhattanville College F
Nazareth College F
Rensselaer Polytechnic Institute F
St. Lawrence University F
Skidmore College F
SUNY
    College at Brockport F
    College at Cortland F
    College at Geneseo F
    College at New Paltz F
    College at Oneonta F
    College at Oswego F
    College of Agriculture and Technology at Morrisville F
Union College F
University of Rochester F
Utica College F
Vassar College F
Wells College F

Ohio

College of Wooster F
Denison University F
Kenyon College F
Oberlin College F
Ohio Wesleyan University F
Wittenberg University F

Pennsylvania

Albright College F
Alvernia University F
Arcadia University F
Bryn Mawr College F
Cabrini College F
Cedar Crest College F
Delaware Valley College F
DeSales University F
Dickinson College F
Eastern University F
Elizabethtown College F
Franklin & Marshall College F
Gettysburg College F
Gwynedd-Mercy College F
Haverford College F
Immaculata University F
Juniata College F
Keystone College F
King's College F
Lebanon Valley College F
Marywood University F
Messiah College F
Misericordia University F
Moravian College F
Muhlenberg College F
Neumann University F
St. Vincent College F
Susquehanna University F
Swarthmore College F
University of Scranton F
Ursinus College F
Washington & Jefferson College F
Widener University F
Wilkes University F
Wilson College F
York College of Pennsylvania F

Rhode Island

Salve Regina University F

Tennessee

Rhodes College F
University of the South F

Vermont

Castleton State College F
Middlebury College F

Virginia

Bridgewater College F
Christopher Newport University F
Eastern Mennonite University F
Lynchburg College F
Randolph-Macon College F
Roanoke College F
Shenandoah University F
Sweet Briar College F
University of Mary Washington F
Virginia Wesleyan College F
Washington and Lee University F

Football (tackle) Division IA

Alabama

Auburn University M
Troy University M
University of Alabama M
University of Alabama Birmingham M
University of South Alabama M

Arizona

Arizona State University M
University of Arizona M

Arkansas

Arkansas State University M
University of Arkansas M

California

California State University Fresno M
San Diego State University M
San Jose State University M
Stanford University M
University of California Berkeley M
    Los Angeles M
University of Southern California M

Colorado

Colorado State University M
United States Air Force Academy M
University of Colorado Boulder M

Connecticut

University of Connecticut M

Florida

Florida Atlantic University M
Florida International University M
Florida State University M
University of Central Florida M
University of Florida M
University of Miami M
University of South Florida M

Georgia

Georgia Institute of Technology M
University of Georgia M

Hawaii

University of Hawaii Manoa M

Idaho

Boise State University M
University of Idaho M

Illinois

Northern Illinois University M
Northwestern University M

University of Illinois Urbana-Champaign M

Indiana

Ball State University M
Indiana University Bloomington M
Purdue University M
University of Notre Dame M

Iowa

Iowa State University M
University of Iowa M

Kansas

Kansas State University M
University of Kansas M

Kentucky

University of Kentucky M
University of Louisville M
Western Kentucky University M

Louisiana

Louisiana State University and Agricultural and Mechanical College M
Louisiana Tech University M
Tulane University M
University of Louisiana at Lafayette M
University of Louisiana at Monroe M

Maryland

United States Naval Academy M
University of Maryland College Park M

Massachusetts

Boston College M
University of Massachusetts Amherst M

Michigan

Central Michigan University M
Eastern Michigan University M
Michigan State University M
University of Michigan M
Western Michigan University M

Minnesota

University of Minnesota Twin Cities M

Mississippi

Mississippi State University M
University of Mississippi M
University of Southern Mississippi M

Missouri

University of Missouri Columbia M

Nebraska

University of Nebraska Lincoln M

Nevada

University of Nevada
    Las Vegas M
    Reno M

New Jersey

Rutgers, The State University of New Jersey New Brunswick/Piscataway Campus M

New Mexico

New Mexico State University M
University of New Mexico M

New York

SUNY
    University at Buffalo M
Syracuse University M
United States Military Academy M

North Carolina

Duke University M
East Carolina University M
North Carolina State University
    M
University of North Carolina
    Chapel Hill M
Wake Forest University M

Ohio

Bowling Green State University
    M
Kent State University M
Miami University
    Oxford M
Ohio State University
    Columbus Campus M
Ohio University M
University of Akron M
University of Cincinnati M
University of Toledo M

Oklahoma

Oklahoma State University M
University of Oklahoma M
University of Tulsa M

Oregon

Oregon State University M
University of Oregon M

Pennsylvania

Penn State
    University Park M
Temple University M
University of Pittsburgh M

South Carolina

Clemson University M
University of South Carolina
    Columbia M

Tennessee

Middle Tennessee State
    University M
University of Memphis M
University of Tennessee
    Knoxville M
Vanderbilt University M

Texas

Baylor University M
Rice University M
Southern Methodist University
    M
Texas A&M University M
Texas Christian University M
Texas State University: San
    Marcos M
Texas Tech University M
University of Houston M
University of North Texas M
University of Texas
    Austin M
    El Paso M
    San Antonio M

Utah

Brigham Young University M
University of Utah M
Utah State University M

Virginia

University of Virginia M
Virginia Polytechnic Institute
    and State University M

Washington

University of Washington M
Washington State University M

West Virginia

Marshall University M
West Virginia University M

Wisconsin

University of Wisconsin
    Madison M

Wyoming

University of Wyoming M

**Football (tackle)
Division IAA**

Alabama

Alabama Agricultural and
    Mechanical University M
Alabama State University M
Jacksonville State University M
Samford University M

Arizona

Northern Arizona University M

Arkansas

University of Arkansas
    Pine Bluff M
University of Central Arkansas
    M

California

California Polytechnic State
    University: San Luis Obispo
    M
California State University
    Sacramento M
University of California
    Davis M
University of San Diego M

Colorado

University of Northern Colorado
    M

Connecticut

Central Connecticut State
    University M
Sacred Heart University M
Yale University M

Delaware

Delaware State University M
University of Delaware M

District of Columbia

Georgetown University M
Howard University M

Florida

Bethune-Cookman University M
Florida Agricultural and
    Mechanical University M
Jacksonville University M

Georgia

Georgia Southern University M
Georgia State University M
Savannah State University M

Idaho

Idaho State University M

Illinois

Eastern Illinois University M
Illinois State University M
Southern Illinois University
    Carbondale M
Western Illinois University M

Indiana

Butler University M
Indiana State University M
Valparaiso University M

Iowa

Drake University M
University of Northern Iowa M

Kentucky

Eastern Kentucky University M
Morehead State University M
Murray State University M

Louisiana

Grambling State University M
McNeese State University M

Nicholls State University M
Northwestern State University
    M
Southeastern Louisiana
    University M
Southern University and
    Agricultural and Mechanical
    College M

Maine

University of Maine M

Maryland

Morgan State University M
Towson University M

Massachusetts

College of the Holy Cross M
Harvard College M

Mississippi

Alcorn State University M
Jackson State University M
Mississippi Valley State
    University M

Missouri

Missouri State University M
Southeast Missouri State
    University M

Montana

Montana State University M
University of Montana M

New Hampshire

Dartmouth College M
University of New Hampshire
    M

New Jersey

Monmouth University M
Princeton University M

New York

Colgate University M
Columbia University M
Cornell University M
Fordham University M
Marist College M
SUNY
    University at Albany M
    University at Stony Brook
    M
Wagner College M

North Carolina

Appalachian State University M
Campbell University M
Davidson College M
Elon University M
Gardner-Webb University M
North Carolina Agricultural and
    Technical State University M
North Carolina Central
    University M
Western Carolina University M

North Dakota

North Dakota State University
    M
University of North Dakota M

Ohio

University of Dayton M
Youngstown State University M

Oregon

Portland State University M

Pennsylvania

Bucknell University M
Duquesne University M
Lafayette College M
Lehigh University M
Robert Morris University M
St. Francis University M
University of Pennsylvania M
Villanova University M

Rhode Island

Brown University M
Bryant University M
University of Rhode Island M

South Carolina

Charleston Southern University
    M
The Citadel M
Coastal Carolina University M
Furman University M
Presbyterian College M
South Carolina State University
    M
Wofford College M

South Dakota

South Dakota State University
    M
University of South Dakota M

Tennessee

Austin Peay State University M
Tennessee State University M
Tennessee Technological
    University M
University of Tennessee
    Chattanooga M
    Martin M

Texas

Lamar University M
Prairie View A&M University
    M
Sam Houston State University
    M
Stephen F. Austin State
    University M
Texas Southern University M

Utah

Southern Utah University M
Weber State University M

Virginia

College of William and Mary M
Hampton University M
James Madison University M
Liberty University M
Norfolk State University M
Old Dominion University M
University of Richmond M
Virginia Military Institute M

Washington

Eastern Washington University
    M

**Football (tackle)
Division II**

Alabama

Miles College M
Stillman College M
Tuskegee University M
University of North Alabama M
University of West Alabama M

Arkansas

Arkansas Tech University M
Harding University M
Henderson State University M
Ouachita Baptist University M
Southern Arkansas University M
University of Arkansas
    Monticello M

California

Azusa Pacific University M
Humboldt State University M

Colorado

Adams State College M
Colorado Mesa University M
Colorado School of Mines M
Colorado State University
    Pueblo M

Fort Lewis College M
Western State College of
    Colorado M

Connecticut

Southern Connecticut State
    University M
University of New Haven M

Georgia

Albany State University M
Chorter University
    Shorter University M
Clark Atlanta University M
Fort Valley State University M
Morehouse College M
University of West Georgia M
Valdosta State University M

Illinois

McKendree University M
Quincy University M

Indiana

Saint Joseph's College M
University of Indianapolis M

Iowa

Upper Iowa University M

Kansas

Emporia State University M
Fort Hays State University M
Pittsburg State University M
Washburn University M

Kentucky

Kentucky State University M

Maryland

Bowie State University M

Massachusetts

American International College
    M
Assumption College M
Bentley University M
Merrimack College M
Stonehill College M

Michigan

Ferris State University M
Grand Valley State University
    M
Hillsdale College M
Michigan Technological
    University M
Northern Michigan University
    M
Northwood University
    Michigan M
Saginaw Valley State University
    M
Wayne State University M

Minnesota

Bemidji State University M
Concordia University St. Paul
    M
Minnesota State University
    Mankato M
    Moorhead M
Saint Cloud State University M
Southwest Minnesota State
    University M
University of Minnesota
    Crookston M
    Duluth M
Winona State University M

Mississippi

Delta State University M

Missouri

Lincoln University M
Lindenwood University M
Missouri Southern State
    University M
Missouri University of Science
    and Technology M

Missouri Western State University M
Northwest Missouri State University M
Southwest Baptist University M
Truman State University M
University of Central Missouri M
William Jewell College M

Nebraska

Chadron State College M
University of Nebraska Kearney M
Wayne State College M

New Hampshire

Saint Anselm College M

New Mexico

Eastern New Mexico University M
New Mexico Highlands University M

New York

Long Island University C. W. Post Campus M
Pace University M

North Carolina

Brevard College M
Catawba College M
Chowan University M
Elizabeth City State University M
Fayetteville State University M
Johnson C. Smith University M
Lenoir-Rhyne University M
Livingstone College M
Mars Hill College M
St. Augustine's College M
Shaw University M
University of North Carolina Pembroke M
Wingate University M
Winston-Salem State University M

North Dakota

Minot State University M
University of Mary M

Ohio

Ashland University M
Central State University M
Lake Erie College M
Malone University M
Notre Dame College M
Ohio Dominican University M
Tiffin University M
University of Findlay M
Walsh University M

Oklahoma

East Central University M
Northeastern State University M
Oklahoma Panhandle State University M
Southeastern Oklahoma State University M
Southern Nazarene University M
Southwestern Oklahoma State University M
University of Central Oklahoma M

Oregon

Western Oregon University M

Pennsylvania

Bloomsburg University of Pennsylvania M
California University of Pennsylvania M
Cheyney University of Pennsylvania M
Clarion University of Pennsylvania M

East Stroudsburg University of Pennsylvania M
Edinboro University of Pennsylvania M
Gannon University M
Indiana University of Pennsylvania M
Kutztown University of Pennsylvania M
Lock Haven University of Pennsylvania M
Mercyhurst University M
Millersville University of Pennsylvania M
Seton Hill University M
Shippensburg University of Pennsylvania M
Slippery Rock University of Pennsylvania M
West Chester University of Pennsylvania M

South Carolina

Benedict College M
Newberry College M
North Greenville University M

South Dakota

Augustana College M
Black Hills State University M
Northern State University M
South Dakota School of Mines and Technology M
University of Sioux Falls M

Tennessee

Carson-Newman College M
Lane College M
Tusculum College M

Texas

Abilene Christian University M
Angelo State University M
McMurry University M
Midwestern State University M
Tarleton State University M
Texas A&M University Commerce M
Texas A&M University Kingsville M
University of the Incarnate Word M
West Texas A&M University M

Utah

Dixie State College M

Virginia

Virginia State University M
Virginia Union University M

West Virginia

Concord University M
Fairmont State University M
Glenville State College M
Shepherd University M
University of Charleston M
West Liberty University M
West Virginia State University M
West Virginia Wesleyan College M

Canada

Simon Fraser University M

Football (tackle) Division III

Alabama

Birmingham-Southern College M
Huntingdon College M

California

California Lutheran University M
Chapman University M

Claremont McKenna College M
Occidental College M
Pitzer College M
Pomona College M
University of La Verne M
University of Redlands M
Whittier College M

Connecticut

Trinity College M
United States Coast Guard Academy M
Wesleyan University M
Western Connecticut State University M

Delaware

Wesley College M

District of Columbia

Catholic University of America M
Gallaudet University M

Georgia

LaGrange College M

Illinois

Augustana College M
Aurora University M
Benedictine University M
Concordia University Chicago M
Elmhurst College M
Eureka College M
Greenville College M
Illinois College M
Illinois Wesleyan University M
Knox College M
Lake Forest College M
MacMurray College M
Millikin University M
Monmouth College M
North Central College M
North Park University M
Rockford College M
University of Chicago M
Wheaton College M

Indiana

Anderson University M
DePauw University M
Earlham College M
Franklin College M
Hanover College M
Manchester College M
Rose-Hulman Institute of Technology M
Trine University M
Wabash College M

Iowa

Buena Vista University M
Central College M
Coe College M
Cornell College M
Grinnell College M
Loras College M
Luther College M
Simpson College M
University of Dubuque M
Wartburg College M

Kentucky

Centre College M
Kentucky Wesleyan College M
Thomas More College M

Louisiana

Louisiana College M

Maine

Bates College M
Bowdoin College M
Colby College M
Husson University M
Maine Maritime Academy M

Maryland

Frostburg State University M
Johns Hopkins University M
McDaniel College M
Salisbury University M
Stevenson University M

Massachusetts

Amherst College M
Anna Maria College M
Becker College M
Bridgewater State University M
Curry College M
Endicott College M
Fitchburg State University M
Framingham State University M
Massachusetts Institute of Technology M
Massachusetts Maritime Academy M
Mount Ida College M
Nichols College M
Springfield College M
Tufts University M
University of Massachusetts Dartmouth M
Western New England University M
Westfield State University M
Williams College M
Worcester Polytechnic Institute M
Worcester State University M

Michigan

Adrian College M
Albion College M
Alma College M
Hope College M
Kalamazoo College M
Olivet College M

Minnesota

Bethel University M
Carleton College M
College of St. Scholastica M
Concordia College: Moorhead M
Crown College M
Gustavus Adolphus College M
Hamline University M
Macalester College M
Martin Luther College M
Northwestern College M
St. John's University M
St. Olaf College M
University of Minnesota Morris M
University of St. Thomas M

Mississippi

Millsaps College M
Mississippi College M

Missouri

Washington University in St. Louis M
Westminster College M

Nebraska

Nebraska Wesleyan University M

New Hampshire

Plymouth State University M

New Jersey

The College of New Jersey M
Fairleigh Dickinson University College at Florham M
Kean University M
Montclair State University M
Rowan University M
William Paterson University of New Jersey M

New York

Alfred University M
Hamilton College M

Hartwick College M
Hobart and William Smith Colleges M
Ithaca College M
Rensselaer Polytechnic Institute M
St. John Fisher College M
St. Lawrence University M
SUNY
College at Brockport M
College at Buffalo M
College at Cortland M
College of Agriculture and Technology at Morrisville M
Maritime College M
Union College M
United States Merchant Marine Academy M
University of Rochester M
Utica College M

North Carolina

Greensboro College M
Guilford College M
Methodist University M
North Carolina Wesleyan College M

Ohio

Baldwin-Wallace College M
Bluffton University M
Capital University M
Case Western Reserve University M
College of Mount St. Joseph M
College of Wooster M
Defiance College M
Denison University M
Heidelberg University M
Hiram College M
John Carroll University M
Kenyon College M
Marietta College M
Muskingum University M
Oberlin College M
Ohio Northern University M
Ohio Wesleyan University M
Otterbein University M
University of Mount Union M
Wilmington College M
Wittenberg University M

Oregon

Lewis & Clark College M
Linfield College M
Pacific University M
Willamette University M

Pennsylvania

Albright College M
Allegheny College M
Carnegie Mellon University M
Delaware Valley College M
Dickinson College M
Franklin & Marshall College M
Geneva College M
Gettysburg College M
Grove City College M
Juniata College M
King's College M
Lebanon Valley College M
Lycoming College M
Moravian College M
Muhlenberg College M
St. Vincent College M
Susquehanna University M
Thiel College M
Ursinus College M
Washington & Jefferson College M
Waynesburg University M
Westminster College M
Widener University M
Wilkes University M

Rhode Island

Salve Regina University M

Tennessee

Maryville College M
Rhodes College M
University of the South M

Texas

Austin College M
East Texas Baptist University M
Hardin-Simmons University M
Howard Payne University M
Sul Ross State University M
Texas Lutheran University M
Trinity University M
University of Mary Hardin-
   Baylor M

Vermont

Castleton State College M
Middlebury College M
Norwich University M

Virginia

Averett University M
Bridgewater College M
Christopher Newport University
   M
Emory & Henry College M
Ferrum College M
Hampden-Sydney College M
Randolph-Macon College M
Shenandoah University M
Washington and Lee University
   M

Washington

Pacific Lutheran University M
University of Puget Sound M
Whitworth University M

West Virginia

Bethany College M

Wisconsin

Beloit College M
Carroll University M
Carthage College M
Concordia University Wisconsin
   M
Lakeland College M
Lawrence University M
Maranatha Baptist Bible College
   M
Ripon College M
St. Norbert College M
University of Wisconsin
   Eau Claire M
   La Crosse M
   Oshkosh M
   Platteville M
   River Falls M
   Stevens Point M
   Stout M
   Whitewater M
Wisconsin Lutheran College M

Golf Division I

Alabama

Alabama Agricultural and
   Mechanical University M
Alabama State University
Auburn University
Jacksonville State University
Samford University
Troy University
University of Alabama
University of Alabama
   Birmingham
University of South Alabama

Arizona

Arizona State University
Northern Arizona University F
University of Arizona

Arkansas

Arkansas State University
University of Arkansas
   Little Rock
   Pine Bluff
University of Central Arkansas

California

California Polytechnic State
   University: San Luis Obispo
California State University
   Bakersfield
   Fresno
   Fullerton
   Long Beach
   Northridge
   Sacramento
Loyola Marymount University
   M
Pepperdine University
St. Mary's College of California
   M
San Diego State University
San Jose State University
Santa Clara University
Stanford University
University of California
   Berkeley
   Davis
   Irvine
   Los Angeles
   Riverside
   Santa Barbara M
University of San Diego M
University of San Francisco
University of Southern
   California
University of the Pacific M

Colorado

Colorado State University
United States Air Force
   Academy M
University of Colorado
   Boulder
University of Denver
University of Northern Colorado

Connecticut

Central Connecticut State
   University
Fairfield University
Quinnipiac University F
Sacred Heart University
University of Connecticut M
University of Hartford
Yale University

Delaware

University of Delaware

District of Columbia

George Washington University
   M
Georgetown University

Florida

Bethune-Cookman University
Florida Agricultural and
   Mechanical University M
Florida Atlantic University
Florida Gulf Coast University
Florida International University
   F
Florida State University
Jacksonville University
Stetson University
University of Central Florida
University of Florida
University of Miami F
University of North Florida
University of South Florida

Georgia

Augusta State University
Georgia Institute of Technology
   M
Georgia Southern University M
Georgia State University
Kennesaw State University
Mercer University
Savannah State University
University of Georgia

Hawaii

University of Hawaii
   Manoa

Idaho

Boise State University
Idaho State University F
University of Idaho

Illinois

Bradley University
Chicago State University
DePaul University M
Eastern Illinois University
Illinois State University
Loyola University Chicago
Northern Illinois University
Northwestern University
Southern Illinois University
   Carbondale
Southern Illinois University
   Edwardsville
University of Illinois
   Urbana-Champaign
Western Illinois University

Indiana

Ball State University
Butler University
Indiana State University F
Indiana University
   Bloomington
Indiana University-Purdue
   University Fort Wayne
Indiana University-Purdue
   University Indianapolis
Purdue University
University of Evansville
University of Notre Dame
Valparaiso University

Iowa

Drake University
Iowa State University
University of Iowa
University of Northern Iowa

Kansas

Kansas State University
University of Kansas
Wichita State University

Kentucky

Eastern Kentucky University
Morehead State University
Murray State University
University of Kentucky
University of Louisville
Western Kentucky University

Louisiana

Louisiana State University and
   Agricultural and Mechanical
   College
Louisiana Tech University M
McNeese State University
Nicholls State University M
Southeastern Louisiana
   University M
Tulane University F
University of Louisiana at
   Lafayette M
University of Louisiana at
   Monroe

Maryland

Loyola University Maryland M
Mount St. Mary's University

Towson University
United States Naval Academy
   M
University of Maryland
   College Park
   Eastern Shore M

Massachusetts

Boston College
Boston University F
College of the Holy Cross
Harvard College

Michigan

Eastern Michigan University
Michigan State University
Oakland University
University of Detroit Mercy
University of Michigan
Western Michigan University F

Minnesota

University of Minnesota
   Twin Cities

Mississippi

Alcorn State University
Jackson State University
Mississippi State University
Mississippi Valley State
   University
University of Mississippi
University of Southern
   Mississippi

Missouri

Missouri State University
University of Missouri
   Columbia
   Kansas City

Montana

Montana State University F
University of Montana F

Nebraska

Creighton University
University of Nebraska
   Lincoln
   Omaha

Nevada

University of Nevada
   Las Vegas
   Reno

New Hampshire

Dartmouth College

New Jersey

Fairleigh Dickinson University
   Metropolitan Campus
Monmouth University
Princeton University
Rider University M
Rutgers, The State University of
   New Jersey
   New Brunswick/Piscataway
   Campus
Saint Peter's College M
Seton Hall University

New Mexico

New Mexico State University
University of New Mexico

New York

Canisius College M
Colgate University M
Columbia University
Cornell University M
Fordham University M
Hofstra University
Iona College M
Long Island University
   Brooklyn Campus
Manhattan College M
Niagara University
Saint Bonaventure University M
St. Francis College

St. John's University
Siena College
SUNY
   University at Albany F
   University at Binghamton
   M
United States Military Academy
   M
Wagner College

North Carolina

Appalachian State University
Campbell University
Davidson College M
Duke University
East Carolina University
Elon University
Gardner-Webb University
High Point University
North Carolina Central
   University M
North Carolina State University
University of North Carolina
   Chapel Hill
   Charlotte M
   Greensboro
   Wilmington
Wake Forest University
Western Carolina University

North Dakota

North Dakota State University
University of North Dakota

Ohio

Bowling Green State University
Cleveland State University
Kent State University
Miami University
   Oxford M
Ohio State University
   Columbus Campus
Ohio University
University of Akron
University of Cincinnati
University of Dayton
University of Toledo
Wright State University M
Xavier University
Youngstown State University

Oklahoma

Oklahoma State University
Oral Roberts University
University of Oklahoma
University of Tulsa

Oregon

Oregon State University
Portland State University F
University of Oregon

Pennsylvania

Bucknell University
Drexel University M
La Salle University M
Lafayette College M
Lehigh University
Penn State
   University Park
Robert Morris University
St. Francis University
Saint Joseph's University M
Temple University M
University of Pennsylvania
Villanova University M

Rhode Island

Brown University
Bryant University M
University of Rhode Island M

South Carolina

Charleston Southern University
The Citadel F
Clemson University M
Coastal Carolina University
College of Charleston M
Francis Marion University M

Furman University
Presbyterian College
South Carolina State University F
University of South Carolina
   Columbia
   Upstate
Winthrop University
Wofford College

South Dakota

South Dakota State University
University of South Dakota

Tennessee

Austin Peay State University
Belmont University
East Tennessee State University
Lipscomb University
Middle Tennessee State University
Tennessee State University
Tennessee Technological University
University of Memphis
University of Tennessee
   Chattanooga
   Knoxville
   Martin M
Vanderbilt University

Texas

Baylor University
Houston Baptist University
Lamar University
Prairie View A&M University
Rice University M
Sam Houston State University
Southern Methodist University
Stephen F. Austin State University
Texas A&M University
   Corpus Christi F
Texas Christian University
Texas Southern University
Texas State University: San Marcos
Texas Tech University
University of Houston M
University of North Texas
University of Texas
   Arlington M
   Austin
   El Paso
   Pan American
   San Antonio

Utah

Brigham Young University
Southern Utah University
University of Utah M
Utah State University M
Utah Valley University
Weber State University

Virginia

College of William and Mary
George Mason University M
Hampton University
James Madison University
Liberty University M
Longwood University
Old Dominion University
Radford University
University of Richmond
University of Virginia
Virginia Commonwealth University M
Virginia Polytechnic Institute and State University M

Washington

Eastern Washington University F
Gonzaga University
Seattle University
University of Washington
Washington State University

West Virginia

Marshall University

Wisconsin

Marquette University M
University of Wisconsin
   Green Bay
   Madison

Wyoming

University of Wyoming

Golf Division II

Alabama

University of Montevallo
University of North Alabama M

Arizona

Grand Canyon University

Arkansas

Arkansas Tech University
Harding University
Henderson State University
Ouachita Baptist University
Southern Arkansas University
University of Arkansas
   Fort Smith
   Monticello

California

Academy of Art University
California Baptist University
California State University
   Chico
   Dominguez Hills M
   East Bay
   Monterey Bay
   San Bernardino M
   Stanislaus M
Dominican University of California
Notre Dame de Namur University M
Point Loma Nazarene University
Sonoma State University
University of California
   San Diego M

Colorado

Adams State College
Colorado Christian University
Colorado Mesa University
Colorado School of Mines M
Colorado State University
   Pueblo
Fort Lewis College M
Regis University
University of Colorado
   Colorado Springs M

Connecticut

Post University M

Delaware

Goldey-Beacom College M
Wilmington University M

Florida

Barry University
Eckerd College
Flagler College
Florida Institute of Technology
Florida Southern College
Lynn University
Nova Southeastern University
Rollins College
Saint Leo University
University of Tampa
University of West Florida

Georgia

Armstrong Atlantic State University
Chorter University
   Shorter University

Clayton State University M
Columbus State University
Georgia College and State University M
Georgia Southwestern State University M
Morehouse College M
North Georgia College & State University
Paine College M
University of West Georgia
Valdosta State University M
Young Harris College

Hawaii

Brigham Young University-Hawaii M
Chaminade University of Honolulu M
Hawaii Pacific University M
University of Hawaii
   Hilo

Idaho

Northwest Nazarene University M

Illinois

Lewis University
McKendree University
Quincy University
University of Illinois
   Springfield

Indiana

Oakland City University
Saint Joseph's College
University of Indianapolis
University of Southern Indiana

Iowa

Upper Iowa University

Kansas

Fort Hays State University
Newman University
Pittsburg State University M
Washburn University M

Kentucky

Bellarmine University
Kentucky State University M
Northern Kentucky University

Louisiana

University of New Orleans

Massachusetts

American International College M
Assumption College M
Bentley University M
University of Massachusetts
   Lowell M

Michigan

Ferris State University
Grand Valley State University
Lake Superior State University
Northern Michigan University M
Northwood University
   Michigan
Saginaw Valley State University M
Wayne State University M

Minnesota

Bemidji State University
Concordia University St. Paul
Minnesota State University
   Mankato
   Moorhead F
Saint Cloud State University
Southwest Minnesota State University F
University of Minnesota
   Crookston
Winona State University

Mississippi

Delta State University M

Missouri

Drury University
Lincoln University
Lindenwood University
Maryville University of Saint Louis
Missouri Southern State University M
Missouri Western State University
Northwest Missouri State University F
Rockhurst University
Southwest Baptist University M
Truman State University F
University of Central Missouri M
University of Missouri
   St. Louis
William Jewell College

Montana

Montana State University
   Billings

Nebraska

Chadron State College F
University of Nebraska
   Kearney
Wayne State College

New Hampshire

Franklin Pierce University M
Saint Anselm College M
Southern New Hampshire University M

New Jersey

Felician College M

New York

Adelphi University M
College of Saint Rose M
Concordia College M
Dominican College of Blauvelt M
Dowling College M
Le Moyne College
Nyack College M
Pace University M
Roberts Wesleyan College M
St. Thomas Aquinas College M

North Carolina

Barton College
Belmont Abbey College
Brevard College
Catawba College
Chowan University M
Elizabeth City State University M
Fayetteville State University M
Johnson C. Smith University M
Lenoir-Rhyne University
Livingstone College M
Mars Hill College
Mount Olive College
Pfeiffer University
Queens University of Charlotte
St. Augustine's College M
University of North Carolina
   Pembroke
Wingate University
Winston-Salem State University M

North Dakota

Minot State University

Ohio

Ashland University
Cedarville University M
Lake Erie College
Malone University
Notre Dame College
Ohio Dominican University

Tiffin University
University of Findlay
Ursuline College F
Walsh University

Oklahoma

Cameron University
East Central University
Northeastern State University
Oklahoma Panhandle State University
Southeastern Oklahoma State University M
Southern Nazarene University M
Southwestern Oklahoma State University
University of Central Oklahoma

Pennsylvania

California University of Pennsylvania
Clarion University of Pennsylvania
East Stroudsburg University of Pennsylvania F
Gannon University
Holy Family University M
Indiana University of Pennsylvania M
Kutztown University of Pennsylvania F
Mercyhurst University
Millersville University of Pennsylvania
Philadelphia University M
Seton Hill University F
University of Pittsburgh
   Johnstown
University of the Sciences in Philadelphia M
West Chester University of Pennsylvania

South Carolina

Anderson University
Benedict College
Coker College
Erskine College
Lander University
Limestone College
Newberry College
North Greenville University
University of South Carolina
   Aiken M

South Dakota

Augustana College
Black Hills State University F
Northern State University M
South Dakota School of Mines and Technology
University of Sioux Falls

Tennessee

Carson-Newman College
Christian Brothers University
King College
LeMoyne-Owen College M
Lincoln Memorial University
Trevecca Nazarene University
Tusculum College
Union University

Texas

Abilene Christian University M
Angelo State University F
Dallas Baptist University
McMurry University
Midwestern State University
St. Edward's University
St. Mary's University
Tarleton State University F
Texas A&M International University
Texas A&M University
   Commerce
   Kingsville F

University of the Incarnate
  Word
West Texas A&M University

Utah

Dixie State College

Vermont

St. Michael's College M

Virginia

Virginia State University M
Virginia Union University M

Washington

Saint Martin's University
Western Washington University

West Virginia

Bluefield State College M
Concord University
Davis and Elkins College M
Fairmont State University
Glenville State College
Ohio Valley University
Shepherd University M
University of Charleston M
West Liberty University
West Virginia State University
West Virginia Wesleyan College
Wheeling Jesuit University

Wisconsin

University of Wisconsin
  Parkside M

Canada

Simon Fraser University

Golf Division III

Alabama

Birmingham-Southern College
Huntingdon College

Arkansas

Hendrix College

California

California Lutheran University
Chapman University M
Claremont McKenna College
Occidental College
Pitzer College M
Pomona College
University of California
  Santa Cruz F
University of La Verne M
University of Redlands
Whittier College M

Connecticut

Mitchell College M
Trinity College M
Wesleyan University M

Delaware

Wesley College M

Georgia

Berry College
Covenant College
Emory University M
LaGrange College M
Oglethorpe University
Piedmont College

Illinois

Augustana College
Aurora University
Benedictine University
Blackburn College M
Dominican University M
Elmhurst College
Eureka College M
Illinois College
Illinois Wesleyan University
Knox College

MacMurray College
Millikin University
Monmouth College
North Central College
North Park University
Rockford College M
Wheaton College

Indiana

Anderson University
DePauw University
Franklin College
Hanover College
Manchester College
Rose-Hulman Institute of
  Technology
Saint Mary's College F
Trine University
Wabash College M

Iowa

Buena Vista University
Central College
Coe College
Cornell College
Grinnell College
Loras College
Luther College
Simpson College
University of Dubuque
Wartburg College

Kentucky

Centre College
Kentucky Wesleyan College
Spalding University
Thomas More College
Transylvania University

Louisiana

Centenary College of Louisiana
Louisiana College M

Maine

Bates College
Bowdoin College
Husson University M
Maine Maritime Academy M
Saint Joseph's College of Maine
  M
University of Maine
  Farmington M
  Presque Isle M
University of New England M

Maryland

Hood College M
McDaniel College
Stevenson University

Massachusetts

Amherst College
Anna Maria College M
Babson College M
Becker College M
Elms College M
Emmanuel College M
Endicott College M
Massachusetts College of
  Liberal Arts M
Mount Holyoke College F
Newbury College M
Nichols College M
Salem State University M
Springfield College M
Suffolk University M
Tufts University M
University of Massachusetts
  Dartmouth M
Wellesley College F
Wentworth Institute of
  Technology M
Western New England
  University M
Westfield State University
Williams College
Worcester State University M

Michigan

Adrian College
Albion College
Alma College
Calvin College
Finlandia University
Hope College
Kalamazoo College
Olivet College

Minnesota

Bethany Lutheran College
Bethel University
Carleton College
College of St. Benedict F
Concordia College: Moorhead
Crown College M
Gustavus Adolphus College
Macalester College
Martin Luther College M
North Central University
Northwestern College
St. Catherine University F
St. John's University M
St. Mary's University of
  Minnesota
St. Olaf College
University of Minnesota
  Morris
University of St. Thomas

Mississippi

Millsaps College
Mississippi College M

Missouri

Fontbonne University
Washington University in St.
  Louis F
Webster University M
Westminster College

Nebraska

Nebraska Wesleyan University

New Hampshire

Daniel Webster College M

New Jersey

Centenary College M
Fairleigh Dickinson University
  College at Florham
New Jersey City University M
Rutgers, The State University of
  New Jersey
  Camden Regional Campus
  M
Stevens Institute of Technology
  M
William Paterson University of
  New Jersey M

New York

Cazenovia College M
Clarkson University M
D'Youville College M
Elmira College
Hamilton College M
Hilbert College M
Hobart and William Smith
  Colleges M
Ithaca College F
Keuka College M
Manhattanville College M
Nazareth College
New York University
Polytechnic Institute of New
  York University M
Rensselaer Polytechnic Institute
  M
Sage College of Albany M
St. John Fisher College
St. Joseph's College: Suffolk
  Campus M
St. Lawrence University
Skidmore College M

SUNY
  College at Cortland F
  College at Old Westbury M
  College at Oswego M
  College at Potsdam M
  College at Purchase M
  College of Agriculture and
    Technology at Cobleskill
    M
  Farmindale State College M
United States Merchant Marine
  Academy M
University of Rochester M
Utica College M
Vassar College F

North Carolina

Greensboro College
Guilford College M
Methodist University
North Carolina Wesleyan
  College M
William Peace University M

Ohio

Baldwin-Wallace College
Capital University
College of Mount St. Joseph
College of Wooster
Defiance College
Denison University
Heidelberg University
Hiram College
John Carroll University
Kenyon College M
Muskingum University
Oberlin College M
Ohio Northern University
Ohio Wesleyan University
Otterbein University
University of Mount Union
Wilmington College
Wittenberg University

Oregon

George Fox University
Lewis & Clark College
Linfield College
Pacific University
Willamette University

Pennsylvania

Albright College
Allegheny College
Alvernia University
Arcadia University M
Baptist Bible College of
  Pennsylvania M
Cabrini College M
Carnegie Mellon University M
Delaware Valley College M
DeSales University M
Dickinson College
Eastern University
Elizabethtown College M
Franklin & Marshall College
Gettysburg College
Grove City College
Immaculata University M
Keystone College M
King's College M
La Roche College M
Lebanon Valley College M
Lycoming College M
Marywood University M
Messiah College M
Misericordia University
Moravian College M
Mount Aloysius College M
Muhlenberg College
Neumann University M
Penn State
  Abington M
  Altoona
  Berks M
  Erie, The Behrend College
  Harrisburg M

Philadelphia Biblical University
  M
Rosemont College M
St. Vincent College
Susquehanna University
Swarthmore College M
Thiel College
University of Pittsburgh
  Bradford M
  Greensburg M
University of Scranton M
Ursinus College
Washington & Jefferson College
Waynesburg University
Westminster College
Widener University M
Wilkes University M
York College of Pennsylvania
  M

Rhode Island

Johnson & Wales University:
  Providence M
Rhode Island College

Tennessee

Maryville College
Rhodes College
University of the South

Texas

Concordia University Texas
Hardin-Simmons University
LeTourneau University
Schreiner University
Southwestern University
Texas Lutheran University
Trinity University
University of Dallas M
University of Mary Hardin-
  Baylor
University of Texas
  Dallas
  Tyler

Vermont

Castleton State College M
Johnson State College M
Middlebury College

Virginia

Averett University M
Bridgewater College M
Christopher Newport University
  M
Ferrum College M
Hampden-Sydney College M
Hollins University F
Lynchburg College M
Marymount University M
Randolph-Macon College M
Roanoke College M
Shenandoah University M
Virginia Wesleyan College M
Washington and Lee University
  M

Washington

Pacific Lutheran University
University of Puget Sound
Whitman College
Whitworth University

West Virginia

Bethany College

Wisconsin

Beloit College M
Carroll University
Carthage College
Concordia University Wisconsin
Edgewood College
Lakeland College
Lawrence University M
Marian University
Milwaukee School of
  Engineering M
Ripon College
St. Norbert College

University of Wisconsin
  Eau Claire
  Oshkosh F
  Platteville F
  River Falls F
  Stevens Point F
  Stout
  Whitewater F
Wisconsin Lutheran College

Gymnastics Division I

Alabama
Auburn University F
University of Alabama F

Alaska
University of Alaska
  Anchorage F

Arizona
Arizona State University F
University of Arizona F

Arkansas
University of Arkansas F

California
California State University
  Sacramento F
San Jose State University F
Stanford University
University of California
  Berkeley
  Davis F
  Los Angeles F

Colorado
United States Air Force
  Academy
University of Denver F

Connecticut
Yale University F

District of Columbia
George Washington University
  F

Florida
University of Florida F

Georgia
University of Georgia F

Idaho
Boise State University F

Illinois
Illinois State University F
Northern Illinois University F
University of Illinois
  Chicago
  Urbana-Champaign

Indiana
Ball State University F

Iowa
Iowa State University F
University of Iowa

Kentucky
University of Kentucky F

Louisiana
Louisiana State University and
  Agricultural and Mechanical
  College F

Maryland
Towson University F
United States Naval Academy
  M
University of Maryland
  College Park F

Michigan
Central Michigan University F
Eastern Michigan University F
Michigan State University F
University of Michigan
Western Michigan University F

Minnesota
University of Minnesota
  Twin Cities

Missouri
Southeast Missouri State
  University F
University of Missouri
  Columbia F

Nebraska
University of Nebraska
  Lincoln

New Hampshire
University of New Hampshire F

New Jersey
Rutgers, The State University of
  New Jersey
  New Brunswick/Piscataway
  Campus F

New York
Cornell University F
United States Military Academy
  M

North Carolina
North Carolina State University
  F
University of North Carolina
  Chapel Hill F

Ohio
Bowling Green State University
  F
Kent State University F
Ohio State University
  Columbus Campus F

Oklahoma
University of Oklahoma

Oregon
Oregon State University F

Pennsylvania
Penn State
  University Park
Temple University
University of Pennsylvania F
University of Pittsburgh F

Rhode Island
Brown University F

Utah
Brigham Young University F
Southern Utah University F
University of Utah F
Utah State University F

Virginia
College of William and Mary

Washington
University of Washington F

West Virginia
West Virginia University F

Gymnastics Division II

California
Azusa Pacific University F

Connecticut
Southern Connecticut State
  University F
University of Bridgeport F

Missouri
Lindenwood University F

Pennsylvania
West Chester University of
  Pennsylvania F

Texas
Texas Woman's University F

Washington
Seattle Pacific University F

Gymnastics Division III

Louisiana
Centenary College of Louisiana
  F

Massachusetts
Springfield College

Minnesota
Gustavus Adolphus College F
Hamline University F
Winona State University F

New York
Ithaca College F
SUNY
  College at Brockport F
  College at Cortland F

Pennsylvania
Ursinus College F
Wilson College F

Rhode Island
Rhode Island College F

Wisconsin
University of Wisconsin
  Eau Claire F
  La Crosse F
  Oshkosh F
  Stout F
  Whitewater F

Ice Hockey Division I

Alabama
University of Alabama
  Huntsville M

Alaska
University of Alaska
  Anchorage M
  Fairbanks M

Colorado
Colorado College M
United States Air Force
  Academy M
University of Denver M

Connecticut
Quinnipiac University M
Sacred Heart University M
University of Connecticut M
Yale University M

Indiana
University of Notre Dame M

Maine
University of Maine M

Massachusetts
American International College
  M
Bentley University M
Boston College M
Boston University M
College of the Holy Cross M
Harvard College M

Merrimack College M
Northeastern University M
University of Massachusetts
  Amherst M
  Lowell M

Michigan
Ferris State University M
Lake Superior State University
  M
Michigan State University M
Michigan Technological
  University M
Northern Michigan University
  M
University of Michigan M
Western Michigan University M

Minnesota
Bemidji State University M
Minnesota State University
  Mankato
Saint Cloud State University M
University of Minnesota
  Duluth
  Twin Cities M

Nebraska
University of Nebraska
  Omaha M

New Hampshire
Dartmouth College M
University of New Hampshire
  M

New Jersey
Princeton University M

New York
Canisius College M
Clarkson University M
Colgate University M
Cornell University M
Niagara University M
Rensselaer Polytechnic Institute
  M
Rochester Institute of
  Technology M
St. Lawrence University M
Union College M
United States Military Academy
  M

North Dakota
University of North Dakota M

Ohio
Bowling Green State University
  M
Miami University
  Oxford M
Ohio State University
  Columbus Campus M

Pennsylvania
Mercyhurst University M
Robert Morris University M

Rhode Island
Brown University M
Providence College M

Vermont
University of Vermont M

Wisconsin
University of Wisconsin
  Madison M

Ice Hockey Division II

Massachusetts
Assumption College M
Stonehill College M

New Hampshire
Franklin Pierce University M
Saint Anselm College M
Southern New Hampshire
  University M

Vermont
St. Michael's College M

Ice Hockey Division III

Connecticut
Connecticut College M
Trinity College M
Wesleyan University M

Illinois
Lake Forest College M

Maine
Bowdoin College M
Colby College M
University of New England M
University of Southern Maine M

Massachusetts
Amherst College M
Babson College M
Becker College M
Curry College M
Fitchburg State University M
Framingham State University M
Nichols College M
Salem State University M
Suffolk University M
Tufts University M
University of Massachusetts
  Boston M
  Dartmouth M
Wentworth Institute of
  Technology M
Western New England
  University M
Westfield State University M
Williams College M
Worcester State University M

Michigan
Adrian College M
Finlandia University M

Minnesota
Bethel University M
College of St. Scholastica M
Concordia College: Moorhead
  M
Gustavus Adolphus College M
Hamline University M
St. John's University M
St. Mary's University of
  Minnesota M
St. Olaf College M
University of St. Thomas M

New Hampshire
New England College M
Plymouth State University M

New York
Elmira College M
Hamilton College M
Hobart and William Smith
  Colleges M
Manhattanville College M
Skidmore College M
SUNY
  College at Brockport M
  College at Buffalo M
  College at Cortland M
  College at Fredonia M
  College at Geneseo M
  College at Oswego M
  College at Plattsburgh M
  College at Potsdam M
  College of Agriculture and
  Technology at Morrisville
  M

Tables and Indexes

Utica College M

Pennsylvania

Neumann University M

Rhode Island

Johnson & Wales University:
   Providence M
Salve Regina University M

Vermont

Castleton State College M
Middlebury College M
Norwich University M

Wisconsin

Concordia University Wisconsin
   M
Lawrence University M
Marian University M
Milwaukee School of
   Engineering M
Northland College M
St. Norbert College M
University of Wisconsin
   Eau Claire M
   River Falls M
   Stevens Point M
   Stout M
   Superior M

California

California State University
   Fresno F
St. Mary's College of California
   F
San Diego State University F
Stanford University F
University of California
   Berkeley F
   Davis F
University of Southern
   California F

Colorado

United States Air Force
   Academy M
University of Denver

Connecticut

Central Connecticut State
   University F
Fairfield University
Quinnipiac University
Sacred Heart University
University of Connecticut F
University of Hartford M
Yale University

Delaware

University of Delaware

District of Columbia

American University F
George Washington University
   F
Georgetown University
Howard University F

Florida

Jacksonville University
University of Florida F

Georgia

Mercer University M

Illinois

Northwestern University F

Indiana

University of Notre Dame

Kentucky

Bellarmine University M
University of Louisville F

Maryland

Johns Hopkins University
Loyola University Maryland
Mount St. Mary's University
Towson University
United States Naval Academy
University of Maryland
   Baltimore County
   College Park

Massachusetts

Boston College F
Boston University F
College of the Holy Cross
Harvard College
University of Massachusetts
   Amherst

Michigan

University of Detroit Mercy
University of Michigan M

New Hampshire

Dartmouth College
University of New Hampshire F

New Jersey

Monmouth University F
Princeton University
Rutgers, The State University of
   New Jersey
   New Brunswick/Piscataway
   Campus

New York

Barnard College F
Canisius College
Colgate University
Columbia University F
Cornell University
Hobart and William Smith
   Colleges M
Hofstra University
Iona College F
Long Island University
   Brooklyn Campus F
Manhattan College
Marist College
Niagara University F
Saint Bonaventure University F
St. John's University M
Siena College
SUNY
   University at Albany
   University at Binghamton
   University at Stony Brook
Syracuse University
United States Military Academy
   M
Wagner College

North Carolina

Davidson College F
Duke University
High Point University F
University of North Carolina
   Chapel Hill

Ohio

Ohio State University
   Columbus Campus
University of Cincinnati F

Oregon

University of Oregon F

Pennsylvania

Bucknell University
Drexel University
Duquesne University F
La Salle University F
Lafayette College
Lehigh University
Penn State
   University Park
Robert Morris University
St. Francis University F
Saint Joseph's University
Temple University F

University of Pennsylvania
Villanova University

Rhode Island

Brown University
Bryant University
Providence College M

South Carolina

Presbyterian College

Tennessee

Vanderbilt University F

Vermont

University of Vermont

Virginia

College of William and Mary F
George Mason University F
James Madison University F
Longwood University F
Old Dominion University F
University of Richmond F
University of Virginia
Virginia Military Institute M
Virginia Polytechnic Institute
   and State University F

California

Dominican University of
   California M
Notre Dame de Namur
   University M

Colorado

Adams State College
Colorado Mesa University
Fort Lewis College F
Regis University F

Connecticut

Post University F
Southern Connecticut State
   University F
University of Bridgeport F
University of New Haven F

Delaware

Wilmington University F

Florida

Florida Institute of Technology
   M
Florida Southern College
Rollins College
Saint Leo University M
University of Tampa M

Georgia

Chorter University
   Shorter University

Massachusetts

American International College
Assumption College
Bentley University
Merrimack College
Stonehill College F

Michigan

Grand Valley State University F

Missouri

Lindenwood University

New Hampshire

Franklin Pierce University
Saint Anselm College
Southern New Hampshire
   University

New Jersey

Georgian Court University F

New York

Adelphi University
City University of New York
   Queens College F
College of Saint Rose M
Dominican College of Blauvelt
Dowling College
Le Moyne College
Long Island University
   C. W. Post Campus
Mercy College
Molloy College
New York Institute of
   Technology M
Pace University M
St. Thomas Aquinas College F

North Carolina

Belmont Abbey College
Catawba College M
Lees-McRae College
Lenoir-Rhyne University
Mars Hill College M
Pfeiffer University
Queens University of Charlotte
Wingate University M

Ohio

Lake Erie College
Notre Dame College F
Tiffin University F

Pennsylvania

Bloomsburg University of
   Pennsylvania F
Chestnut Hill College
East Stroudsburg University of
   Pennsylvania F
Edinboro University of
   Pennsylvania F
Gannon University F
Holy Family University F
Indiana University of
   Pennsylvania F
Kutztown University of
   Pennsylvania F
Lock Haven University of
   Pennsylvania F
Mercyhurst University
Millersville University of
   Pennsylvania F
Philadelphia University F
Seton Hill University
Shippensburg University of
   Pennsylvania F
Slippery Rock University of
   Pennsylvania F
West Chester University of
   Pennsylvania F

South Carolina

Coker College M
Converse College F
Erskine College F
Limestone College
Newberry College F

Vermont

St. Michael's College

West Virginia

Ohio Valley University M
Shepherd University F
West Virginia Wesleyan
   College F
Wheeling Jesuit University M

Alabama

Birmingham-Southern College
Huntingdon College M

Arkansas

Hendrix College M

California

Claremont McKenna College F
Occidental College F
Pitzer College F
Pomona College F
University of Redlands F
Whittier College

Colorado

Colorado College

Connecticut

Connecticut College
Eastern Connecticut State
   University
Mitchell College M
Saint Joseph College F
Trinity College
Wesleyan University
Western Connecticut State
   University

Delaware

Wesley College

District of Columbia

Catholic University of America
Trinity Washington University F

Georgia

Agnes Scott College F
Berry College
LaGrange College F
Oglethorpe University M
Piedmont College M

Illinois

Augustana College
Aurora University M
North Central College F

Indiana

Hanover College M
Trine University

Kentucky

Centre College

Maine

Bates College
Bowdoin College
Colby College
Husson University
Maine Maritime Academy M
Saint Joseph's College of Maine
Thomas College
University of Maine
   Farmington
University of New England
University of Southern Maine

Maryland

Frostburg State University
Goucher College
Hood College
McDaniel College
Notre Dame of Maryland
   University F
St. Mary's College of Maryland
Salisbury University
Stevenson University
Washington College

Massachusetts

Amherst College
Anna Maria College
Babson College
Becker College
Bridgewater State University F
Clark University M
Curry College
Elms College F
Emerson College
Emmanuel College
Endicott College
Fitchburg State University F
Framingham State University F

Gordon College
Lasell College
Massachusetts Institute of
Technology
Massachusetts Maritime
Academy
Mount Holyoke College F
Mount Ida College
Nichols College
Pine Manor College F
Regis College
Salem State University
Simmons College F
Smith College F
Springfield College
Tufts University
University of Massachusetts
Boston M
Dartmouth
Wellesley College F
Wentworth Institute of
Technology M
Western New England
University
Westfield State University F
Wheaton College
Wheelock College
Williams College
Worcester State University F

Michigan

Adrian College
Albion College
Alma College
Olivet College F

Mississippi

Millsaps College

Missouri

Fontbonne University

New Hampshire

Colby-Sawyer College F
Daniel Webster College
Keene State College
New England College
Plymouth State University
Rivier College

New Jersey

Centenary College
The College of New Jersey F
College of St. Elizabeth F
Drew University
Fairleigh Dickinson University
College at Florham
Kean University
Montclair State University
Ramapo College of New Jersey
F
Richard Stockton College of
New Jersey M
Rowan University F
Rutgers, The State University of
New Jersey
Camden Regional Campus
F
Stevens Institute of Technology

New York

Alfred University
Bard College
Cazenovia College
Clarkson University
College of Mount St. Vincent
Elmira College
Hamilton College
Hartwick College
Hilbert College M
Hobart and William Smith
Colleges F
Ithaca College
Keuka College
Manhattanville College
Medaille College
Mount Saint Mary College
Nazareth College

Polytechnic Institute of New
York University F
Rensselaer Polytechnic Institute
Rochester Institute of
Technology
Sage College of Albany F
St. John Fisher College
St. Lawrence University
Skidmore College
SUNY
College at Brockport
College at Buffalo F
College at Cortland
College at Fredonia F
College at Geneseo
College at New Paltz F
College at Oneonta
College at Oswego
College at Plattsburgh M
College at Potsdam
College of Agriculture and
Technology at Cobleskill
M
College of Agriculture and
Technology at Morrisville
Farmingdale State College
Institute of Technology at
Utica/Rome M
Maritime College
Union College
United States Merchant Marine
Academy M
University of Rochester F
Utica College
Vassar College
Wells College

North Carolina

Greensboro College
Guilford College
Methodist University F
North Carolina Wesleyan
College F

Ohio

College of Mount St. Joseph
College of Wooster
Denison University
Kenyon College
Oberlin College
Ohio Wesleyan University
Otterbein University
Wittenberg University

Oregon

Linfield College F
Pacific University F

Pennsylvania

Allegheny College F
Alvernia University
Arcadia University F
Bryn Mawr College F
Cabrini College
Cedar Crest College F
DeSales University M
Dickinson College
Eastern University
Elizabethtown College
Franklin & Marshall College
Gettysburg College
Gwynedd-Mercy College
Haverford College
Immaculata University
King's College
La Roche College M
Lancaster Bible College F
Lebanon Valley College
Lycoming College
Marywood University
Messiah College
Misericordia University
Muhlenberg College
Neumann University
Penn State
Abington
Rosemont College
St. Vincent College

Susquehanna University
Swarthmore College
Thiel College
University of Scranton
Ursinus College
Washington & Jefferson College
Waynesburg University F
Widener University
Wilkes University F
Wilson College F
York College of Pennsylvania

Rhode Island

Rhode Island College F
Roger Williams University
Salve Regina University

Tennessee

Rhodes College M
University of the South

Texas

Southwestern University M
University of Dallas

Vermont

Castleton State College
Green Mountain College
Johnson State College M
Lyndon State College M
Middlebury College
Norwich University

Virginia

Bridgewater College F
Christopher Newport University
Ferrum College
Hampden-Sydney College M
Hollins University F
Lynchburg College
Marymount University
Randolph College M
Randolph-Macon College
Roanoke College
Shenandoah University
Sweet Briar College F
University of Mary Washington
Virginia Wesleyan College
Washington and Lee University

Washington

University of Puget Sound F

West Virginia

Bethany College M

Wisconsin

Beloit College
Carthage College
Concordia University Wisconsin
Milwaukee School of
Engineering M

Rifle Division I

Alabama

Jacksonville State University M
University of Alabama
Birmingham F

Colorado

United States Air Force
Academy

Kentucky

Morehead State University
Murray State University
University of Kentucky

Maryland

United States Naval Academy

Mississippi

University of Mississippi F

Nebraska

University of Nebraska
Lincoln F

Nevada

University of Nevada
Reno

New York

United States Military Academy

North Carolina

North Carolina State University

Ohio

Ohio State University
Columbus Campus
University of Akron

South Carolina

The Citadel
Wofford College

Tennessee

University of Memphis
University of Tennessee
Martin

Texas

Texas Christian University F
University of Texas
El Paso F

Virginia

Virginia Military Institute

West Virginia

West Virginia University

Rifle Division II

Alaska

University of Alaska
Fairbanks

Georgia

Columbus State University
North Georgia College & State
University

Pennsylvania

University of the Sciences in
Philadelphia

Rifle Division III

Connecticut

United States Coast Guard
Academy

Indiana

Rose-Hulman Institute of
Technology

Massachusetts

Massachusetts Institute of
Technology
Massachusetts Maritime
Academy
Wentworth Institute of
Technology

New York

City University of New York
John Jay College of
Criminal Justice
SUNY
Maritime College

**Rowing (crew)
Division I**

Alabama

University of Alabama F

California

California State University
Sacramento F

Loyola Marymount University F
St. Mary's College of California
F
San Diego State University F
Santa Clara University F
Stanford University F
University of California
Berkeley F
Los Angeles F
University of San Diego F
University of Southern
California F

Connecticut

Fairfield University F
Sacred Heart University F
University of Connecticut F
Yale University F

Delaware

University of Delaware F

District of Columbia

George Washington University
F
Georgetown University F

Florida

Jacksonville University F
Stetson University F
University of Central Florida F
University of Miami F

Indiana

Indiana University
Bloomington F
University of Notre Dame F

Iowa

Drake University F
University of Iowa F

Kansas

Kansas State University F
University of Kansas F

Kentucky

University of Louisville F

Maryland

Loyola University Maryland F
United States Naval Academy F

Massachusetts

Boston College F
Boston University F
College of the Holy Cross F
Harvard College F
Massachusetts Institute of
Technology F
Northeastern University F
University of Massachusetts
Amherst F

Michigan

Eastern Michigan University F
Michigan State University F
University of Michigan F

Minnesota

University of Minnesota
Twin Cities F

Nebraska

Creighton University F

New Hampshire

Dartmouth College F

New Jersey

Princeton University F
Rutgers, The State University of
New Jersey
New Brunswick/Piscataway
Campus F

New York

Barnard College F
Canisius College F
Colgate University F
Columbia University F

Cornell University F
Fordham University F
Iona College F
Marist College F
SUNY
    University at Buffalo F
Syracuse University F

North Carolina
Duke University F
University of North Carolina
    Chapel Hill F

Ohio
Ohio State University
    Columbus Campus F
University of Dayton F

Oklahoma
University of Oklahoma F
University of Tulsa F

Oregon
Oregon State University F

Pennsylvania
Bucknell University F
Drexel University F
Duquesne University F
La Salle University F
Lehigh University F
Robert Morris University F
Saint Joseph's University F
Temple University F
University of Pennsylvania F
Villanova University F

Rhode Island
Brown University F
University of Rhode Island F

South Carolina
Clemson University F

Tennessee
University of Tennessee
    Knoxville F

Texas
Southern Methodist University F
University of Texas
    Austin F

Virginia
George Mason University F
Old Dominion University F
University of Virginia F

Washington
Gonzaga University F
University of Washington F
Washington State University F

West Virginia
West Virginia University F

Wisconsin
University of Wisconsin
    Madison F

Rowing (crew) Division II

California
Humboldt State University F
University of California
    San Diego F

Florida
Barry University F
Florida Institute of Technology
    F
Nova Southeastern University F
Rollins College F
University of Tampa F

Massachusetts
Assumption College F
Merrimack College F

New Hampshire
Franklin Pierce University F

New York
Dowling College F

Oklahoma
University of Central Oklahoma
    F

Pennsylvania
Mercyhurst University F
Philadelphia University F

Washington
Seattle Pacific University F
Western Washington University
    F

West Virginia
University of Charleston F

Rowing (crew) Division III

California
Chapman University F
Mills College F

Connecticut
Connecticut College F
Trinity College F
United States Coast Guard
    Academy F
Wesleyan University F

Illinois
North Park University F

Maine
Bates College F
Colby College F

Maryland
Washington College F

Massachusetts
Clark University F
Massachusetts Maritime
    Academy F
Mount Holyoke College F
Simmons College F
Smith College F
Tufts University F
Wellesley College F
Williams College F
Worcester Polytechnic Institute
    F

New Jersey
Richard Stockton College of
    New Jersey F
Rutgers, The State University of
    New Jersey
        Camden Regional Campus
            F

New York
D'Youville College F
Hamilton College F
Hobart and William Smith
    Colleges F
Ithaca College F
Rochester Institute of
    Technology F
St. Lawrence University F
Skidmore College F
SUNY
    Maritime College F
Union College F
United States Merchant Marine
    Academy F
University of Rochester F

Ohio
Marietta College F

Oregon
Lewis & Clark College F
Willamette University F

Pennsylvania
Bryn Mawr College F
Franklin & Marshall College F

Virginia
University of Mary Washington
    F

Washington
Pacific Lutheran University F
University of Puget Sound F

Skiing Division I

Colorado
University of Colorado
    Boulder
University of Denver

Massachusetts
Boston College
Harvard College

Montana
Montana State University

New Hampshire
Dartmouth College
University of New Hampshire

New Mexico
University of New Mexico

Rhode Island
Brown University F

Utah
University of Utah

Vermont
University of Vermont

Wisconsin
University of Wisconsin
    Green Bay

Skiing Division II

Alaska
University of Alaska
    Anchorage
    Fairbanks

Michigan
Michigan Technological
    University
Northern Michigan University

Minnesota
Saint Cloud State University F

New Hampshire
Saint Anselm College

Vermont
St. Michael's College

Skiing Division III

Maine
Bates College
Bowdoin College
Colby College
University of Maine
    Presque Isle

Massachusetts
Babson College
Massachusetts Institute of
    Technology
Williams College

Michigan
Finlandia University

Minnesota
College of St. Scholastica
Gustavus Adolphus College
St. Olaf College

Nebraska
Clarkson College M

New Hampshire
Colby-Sawyer College
Plymouth State University

New York
Clarkson University F
St. Lawrence University

Vermont
Middlebury College

Soccer Division I

Alabama
Alabama Agricultural and
    Mechanical University F
Alabama State University F
Auburn University F
Jacksonville State University F
Samford University F
Troy University F
University of Alabama F
University of Alabama
    Birmingham
University of South Alabama F

Arizona
Arizona State University F
Northern Arizona University F
University of Arizona F

Arkansas
Arkansas State University F
University of Arkansas F
    Little Rock F
    Pine Bluff F
University of Central Arkansas

California
California Polytechnic State
    University: San Luis Obispo
California State University
    Bakersfield
    Fresno F
    Fullerton
    Long Beach F
    Northridge
    Sacramento
Loyola Marymount University
Pepperdine University F
St. Mary's College of California
San Diego State University
San Jose State University
Santa Clara University
Stanford University
University of California
    Berkeley
    Davis
    Irvine
    Los Angeles
    Riverside
    Santa Barbara
University of San Diego
University of San Francisco
University of Southern
    California F
University of the Pacific F

Colorado
Colorado College F
United States Air Force
    Academy
University of Colorado
    Boulder F
University of Denver
University of Northern Colorado
    F

Connecticut
Central Connecticut State
    University
Fairfield University
Quinnipiac University
Sacred Heart University
University of Connecticut
University of Hartford
Yale University

Delaware
Delaware State University F
University of Delaware

District of Columbia
American University
George Washington University
Georgetown University
Howard University

Florida
Florida Atlantic University
Florida Gulf Coast University
Florida International University
Florida State University F
Jacksonville University
Stetson University
University of Central Florida
University of Florida F
University of Miami F
University of North Florida
University of South Florida

Georgia
Georgia Southern University
Georgia State University
Kennesaw State University F
Mercer University
University of Georgia F

Hawaii
University of Hawaii
    Manoa F

Idaho
Boise State University F
Idaho State University F
University of Idaho F

Illinois
Bradley University M
DePaul University
Eastern Illinois University
Illinois State University F
Loyola University Chicago
Northern Illinois University
Northwestern University
Southern Illinois University
    Edwardsville
University of Illinois
    Chicago M
    Urbana-Champaign F
Western Illinois University

Indiana
Ball State University F
Butler University
Indiana State University F
Indiana University
    Bloomington
Indiana University-Purdue
    University Fort Wayne
Indiana University-Purdue
    University Indianapolis
Purdue University F
University of Evansville
University of Notre Dame
Valparaiso University

Iowa

Drake University
Iowa State University F
University of Iowa F
University of Northern Iowa F

Kansas

University of Kansas F

Kentucky

Eastern Kentucky University F
Morehead State University F
Murray State University F
University of Kentucky
University of Louisville
Western Kentucky University F

Louisiana

Grambling State University F
Louisiana State University and
　Agricultural and Mechanical
　College F
Louisiana Tech University F
McNeese State University F
Nicholls State University F
Northwestern State University F
Southeastern Louisiana
　University F
Southern University and
　Agricultural and Mechanical
　College F
University of Louisiana at
　Lafayette F
University of Louisiana at
　Monroe F

Maine

University of Maine F

Maryland

Loyola University Maryland
Mount St. Mary's University
Towson University
United States Naval Academy
University of Maryland
　Baltimore County
　College Park

Massachusetts

Boston College
Boston University
College of the Holy Cross
Harvard College
Northeastern University
University of Massachusetts
　Amherst

Michigan

Central Michigan University F
Eastern Michigan University F
Michigan State University
Oakland University
University of Detroit Mercy
University of Michigan
Western Michigan University

Minnesota

University of Minnesota
　Twin Cities F

Mississippi

Alcorn State University F
Jackson State University F
Mississippi State University F
Mississippi Valley State
　University F
University of Mississippi F
University of Southern
　Mississippi F

Missouri

Missouri State University
Saint Louis University
Southeast Missouri State
　University F
University of Missouri
　Columbia F
　Kansas City

Montana

University of Montana F

Nebraska

Creighton University
University of Nebraska
　Lincoln F
　Omaha

Nevada

University of Nevada
　Las Vegas
　Reno F

New Hampshire

Dartmouth College
University of New Hampshire

New Jersey

Fairleigh Dickinson University
　Metropolitan Campus
Monmouth University
New Jersey Institute of
　Technology
Princeton University
Rider University
Rutgers, The State University of
　New Jersey
　New Brunswick/Piscataway
　Campus
Saint Peter's College
Seton Hall University

New Mexico

New Mexico State University F
University of New Mexico

New York

Adelphi University M
Barnard College F
Canisius College
Colgate University
Columbia University
Cornell University
Fordham University
Hartwick College M
Hofstra University
Iona College
Long Island University
　Brooklyn Campus
Manhattan College
Marist College
Niagara University
Saint Bonaventure University
St. Francis College M
St. John's University
Siena College
SUNY
　University at Albany
　University at Binghamton
　University at Buffalo
　University at Stony Brook
Syracuse University
United States Military Academy
Wagner College F

North Carolina

Appalachian State University
Campbell University
Davidson College
Duke University
East Carolina University F
Elon University
Gardner-Webb University
High Point University
North Carolina State University
University of North Carolina
　Asheville
　Chapel Hill
　Charlotte
　Greensboro
　Wilmington
Wake Forest University
Western Carolina University F

North Dakota

North Dakota State University F
University of North Dakota F

Ohio

Bowling Green State University
Cleveland State University
Kent State University F
Miami University
　Oxford F
Ohio State University
　Columbus Campus
Ohio University F
University of Akron
University of Cincinnati
University of Dayton
University of Toledo F
Wright State University
Xavier University
Youngstown State University F

Oklahoma

Oklahoma State University F
Oral Roberts University
University of Oklahoma F
University of Tulsa

Oregon

Oregon State University
Portland State University F
University of Oregon F
University of Portland

Pennsylvania

Bucknell University
Drexel University
Duquesne University
La Salle University
Lafayette College
Lehigh University
Penn State
　University Park
Robert Morris University
St. Francis University
Saint Joseph's University
Temple University
University of Pennsylvania
University of Pittsburgh
Villanova University

Rhode Island

Brown University
Bryant University
Providence College
University of Rhode Island

South Carolina

Charleston Southern University
　F
The Citadel F
Clemson University
Coastal Carolina University
College of Charleston
Francis Marion University F
Furman University
Presbyterian College
South Carolina State University
　F
University of South Carolina
　Columbia
　Upstate
Winthrop University
Wofford College

South Dakota

South Dakota State University F
University of South Dakota F

Tennessee

Austin Peay State University F
Belmont University
East Tennessee State University
Lipscomb University
Middle Tennessee State
　University F
Tennessee Technological
　University F
University of Memphis
University of Tennessee
　Chattanooga F
　Knoxville F
　Martin F

Vanderbilt University F

Texas

Baylor University F
Houston Baptist University
Lamar University F
Prairie View A&M University F
Rice University F
Sam Houston State University F
Southern Methodist University
Stephen F. Austin State
　University F
Texas A&M University F
Texas Christian University F
Texas Southern University F
Texas State University: San
　Marcos F
Texas Tech University F
University of Houston F
University of North Texas F
University of Texas
　Austin F
　El Paso F
　San Antonio F

Utah

Brigham Young University F
Southern Utah University F
University of Utah F
Utah State University F
Utah Valley University F
Weber State University F

Vermont

University of Vermont

Virginia

College of William and Mary
George Mason University
James Madison University
Liberty University
Longwood University
Old Dominion University
Radford University
University of Richmond
University of Virginia
Virginia Commonwealth
　University
Virginia Military Institute
Virginia Polytechnic Institute
　and State University

Washington

Eastern Washington University
　F
Gonzaga University
Seattle University
University of Washington
Washington State University F

West Virginia

Marshall University
West Virginia University

Wisconsin

Marquette University
University of Wisconsin
　Green Bay
　Madison
　Milwaukee

Wyoming

University of Wyoming F

Soccer Division II

Alabama

University of Alabama
　Huntsville
University of Montevallo
University of North Alabama F

Arizona

Grand Canyon University

Arkansas

Harding University
Ouachita Baptist University

California

Academy of Art University
Azusa Pacific University
California Baptist University
California State Polytechnic
　University: Pomona
California State University
　Chico
　Dominguez Hills
　East Bay
　Los Angeles
　Monterey Bay
　San Bernardino
　Stanislaus
Dominican University of
　California
Fresno Pacific University
Humboldt State University
Notre Dame de Namur
　University
Point Loma Nazarene University
San Francisco State University
Sonoma State University
University of California
　San Diego

Colorado

Adams State College
Colorado Christian University
Colorado Mesa University
Colorado School of Mines
Colorado State University
　Pueblo
Fort Lewis College
Metropolitan State College of
　Denver
Regis University
University of Colorado
　Colorado Springs

Connecticut

Post University
Southern Connecticut State
　University
University of Bridgeport
University of New Haven

Delaware

Goldey-Beacom College
Wilmington University

District of Columbia

University of the District of
　Columbia M

Florida

Barry University
Eckerd College
Flagler College
Florida Institute of Technology
Florida Southern College
Lynn University
Nova Southeastern University
Palm Beach Atlantic University
Rollins College
Saint Leo University
University of Tampa
University of West Florida

Georgia

Armstrong Atlantic State
　University F
Chorter University
　Shorter University
Clayton State University
Columbus State University F
Georgia College and State
　University F
Georgia Southwestern State
　University
North Georgia College & State
　University
University of West Georgia F
Valdosta State University F
Young Harris College

Hawaii

Brigham Young University-
Hawaii
Chaminade University of
Honolulu
Hawaii Pacific University
University of Hawaii
Hilo

Idaho

Northwest Nazarene University

Illinois

Lewis University
McKendree University
Quincy University
University of Illinois
Springfield

Indiana

Oakland City University
Saint Joseph's College
University of Indianapolis
University of Southern Indiana

Iowa

Upper Iowa University

Kansas

Emporia State University F
Fort Hays State University
Newman University
Washburn University F

Kentucky

Bellarmine University
Northern Kentucky University

Maryland

Washington Adventist
University

Massachusetts

American International College
Assumption College
Bentley University
Merrimack College
Stonehill College
University of Massachusetts
Lowell

Michigan

Ferris State University F
Grand Valley State University F
Michigan Technological
University F
Northern Michigan University F
Northwood University
Michigan
Saginaw Valley State University

Minnesota

Bemidji State University F
Concordia University St. Paul F
Minnesota State University
Mankato F
Moorhead F
Saint Cloud State University F
Southwest Minnesota State
University F
University of Minnesota
Crookston F
Duluth F
Winona State University F

Mississippi

Delta State University

Missouri

Drury University
Lindenwood University
Maryville University of Saint
Louis
Missouri Southern State
University F
Missouri University of Science
and Technology
Missouri Western State
University F

Northwest Missouri State
University F
Rockhurst University
Southwest Baptist University F
Truman State University
University of Central Missouri F
University of Missouri
St. Louis
William Jewell College

Montana

Montana State University
Billings

Nebraska

Wayne State College F

New Hampshire

Franklin Pierce University
Saint Anselm College
Southern New Hampshire
University

New Jersey

Bloomfield College
Caldwell College
Felician College
Georgian Court University F

New Mexico

Eastern New Mexico University
New Mexico Highlands
University F

New York

Adelphi University F
City University of New York
Queens College
College of Saint Rose
Concordia College
Dominican College of Blauvelt
Dowling College
Le Moyne College
Long Island University
C. W. Post Campus
Mercy College
Molloy College
New York Institute of
Technology
Nyack College
Pace University F
Roberts Wesleyan College
St. Thomas Aquinas College

North Carolina

Barton College
Belmont Abbey College
Brevard College
Catawba College
Chowan University
Lees-McRae College
Lenoir-Rhyne University
Mars Hill College
Mount Olive College
Pfeiffer University
Queens University of Charlotte
University of North Carolina
Pembroke
Wingate University

North Dakota

Minot State University F
University of Mary

Ohio

Ashland University
Cedarville University
Lake Erie College
Malone University
Notre Dame College
Ohio Dominican University
Tiffin University
University of Findlay
Ursuline College F
Walsh University

Oklahoma

East Central University F
Northeastern State University
Southern Nazarene University

Southwestern Oklahoma State
University F
University of Central Oklahoma
F

Oregon

Western Oregon University F

Pennsylvania

Bloomsburg University of
Pennsylvania
California University of
Pennsylvania
Chestnut Hill College
Clarion University of
Pennsylvania F
East Stroudsburg University of
Pennsylvania
Edinboro University of
Pennsylvania F
Gannon University
Holy Family University
Indiana University of
Pennsylvania F
Kutztown University of
Pennsylvania F
Lock Haven University of
Pennsylvania
Mansfield University of
Pennsylvania F
Mercyhurst University
Millersville University of
Pennsylvania
Philadelphia University
Seton Hill University
Shippensburg University of
Pennsylvania
Slippery Rock University of
Pennsylvania
University of Pittsburgh
Johnstown
West Chester University of
Pennsylvania

Puerto Rico

University of Puerto Rico
Mayaguez M

South Carolina

Anderson University
Coker College
Converse College F
Erskine College
Francis Marion University M
Lander University
Limestone College
Newberry College
North Greenville University
University of South Carolina
Aiken

South Dakota

Augustana College F
Northern State University F
University of Sioux Falls

Tennessee

Carson-Newman College
Christian Brothers University
King College
Lincoln Memorial University
Trevecca Nazarene University
Tusculum College
Union University

Texas

Abilene Christian University F
Angelo State University F
Dallas Baptist University F
McMurry University
Midwestern State University
St. Edward's University
St. Mary's University
Texas A&M International
University
Texas A&M University
Commerce F
Texas Woman's University F

University of Texas
of the Permian Basin
University of the Incarnate
Word
West Texas A&M University

Utah

Dixie State College

Vermont

St. Michael's College

Washington

Saint Martin's University
Seattle Pacific University
Western Washington University

West Virginia

Alderson-Broaddus College
Concord University
Davis and Elkins College
Ohio Valley University
Salem International University
Shepherd University
University of Charleston
West Virginia Wesleyan College
Wheeling Jesuit University

Wisconsin

University of Wisconsin
Parkside

Canada

Simon Fraser University

Soccer Division III

Alabama

Birmingham-Southern College
Huntingdon College

Arkansas

Hendrix College
University of the Ozarks

California

California Institute of
Technology M
California Lutheran University
Chapman University
Claremont McKenna College
Mills College F
Occidental College
Pitzer College F
Pomona College
University of California
Santa Cruz
University of La Verne
University of Redlands
Whittier College

Colorado

Colorado College M

Connecticut

Albertus Magnus College
Connecticut College
Eastern Connecticut State
University
Mitchell College
Saint Joseph College F
Trinity College
United States Coast Guard
Academy
Wesleyan University
Western Connecticut State
University

Delaware

Wesley College

District of Columbia

Catholic University of America
Gallaudet University
Trinity Washington University F

Georgia

Agnes Scott College F
Berry College
Covenant College
Emory University
LaGrange College
Oglethorpe University
Piedmont College
Spelman College F
Wesleyan College F

Illinois

Augustana College
Aurora University
Benedictine University
Blackburn College
Concordia University Chicago
Dominican University
Elmhurst College
Eureka College
Greenville College
Illinois College
Illinois Wesleyan University
Knox College
Lake Forest College
MacMurray College
Millikin University
Monmouth College
North Central College
North Park University
Principia College
Rockford College
University of Chicago
Wheaton College

Indiana

Anderson University
DePauw University
Earlham College
Franklin College
Hanover College
Manchester College
Rose-Hulman Institute of
Technology
Saint Mary's College F
Trine University
Wabash College M

Iowa

Buena Vista University
Central College
Coe College
Cornell College
Grinnell College
Loras College
Luther College
Simpson College
University of Dubuque
Wartburg College

Kentucky

Centre College
Kentucky Wesleyan College
Spalding University
Thomas More College
Transylvania University

Louisiana

Centenary College of Louisiana
Louisiana College

Maine

Bates College
Bowdoin College
Colby College
Husson University
Maine Maritime Academy
Saint Joseph's College of Maine
Thomas College
University of Maine
Farmington
Presque Isle
University of New England
University of Southern Maine

Maryland

Frostburg State University
Goucher College

Hood College
Johns Hopkins University
McDaniel College
Notre Dame of Maryland
  University F
St. Mary's College of Maryland
Salisbury University
Stevenson University
Washington College

Massachusetts

Amherst College
Anna Maria College
Babson College
Bay Path College F
Becker College
Brandeis University
Bridgewater State University
Clark University
Curry College
Eastern Nazarene College
Elms College
Emerson College
Emmanuel College
Endicott College
Fitchburg State University
Framingham State University
Gordon College
Lasell College
Lesley University
Massachusetts College of
  Liberal Arts
Massachusetts Institute of
  Technology
Massachusetts Maritime
  Academy
Mount Holyoke College F
Mount Ida College
Newbury College
Nichols College
Pine Manor College F
Regis College
Salem State University
Simmons College F
Smith College F
Springfield College
Suffolk University
Tufts University
University of Massachusetts
  Boston
  Dartmouth
Wellesley College F
Wentworth Institute of
  Technology
Western New England
  University
Westfield State University
Wheaton College
Wheelock College
Williams College
Worcester Polytechnic Institute
Worcester State University

Michigan

Adrian College
Albion College
Alma College
Calvin College
Finlandia University
Hope College
Kalamazoo College
Olivet College

Minnesota

Bethany Lutheran College
Bethel University
Carleton College
College of St. Benedict F
College of St. Scholastica
Concordia College: Moorhead
Crown College
Gustavus Adolphus College
Hamline University
Macalester College
Martin Luther College
North Central University
Northwestern College
St. Catherine University F

St. John's University M
St. Mary's University of
  Minnesota
St. Olaf College
University of Minnesota
  Morris
University of St. Thomas

Mississippi

Millsaps College
Mississippi College

Missouri

Baptist Bible College
Fontbonne University
Washington University in St.
  Louis
Webster University
Westminster College

Nebraska

Nebraska Wesleyan University

New Hampshire

Colby-Sawyer College
Daniel Webster College
Keene State College
New England College
Plymouth State University
Rivier College

New Jersey

Centenary College
The College of New Jersey
College of St. Elizabeth F
Drew University
Fairleigh Dickinson University
  College at Florham
Kean University
Montclair State University
New Jersey City University
Ramapo College of New Jersey
Richard Stockton College of
  New Jersey
Rowan University
Rutgers, The State University of
  New Jersey
  Camden Regional Campus
  Newark Regional Campus
Stevens Institute of Technology
William Paterson University of
  New Jersey

New York

Alfred University
Bard College
Cazenovia College
City University of New York
  Baruch College M
  Brooklyn College M
  City College
  College of Staten Island
  Hunter College M
  John Jay College of
    Criminal Justice
  Lehman College M
  Medgar Evers College
  York College M
Clarkson University
College of Mount St. Vincent
D'Youville College
Elmira College
Hamilton College
Hartwick College F
Hilbert College
Hobart and William Smith
  Colleges
Ithaca College
Keuka College
Manhattanville College
Medaille College
Mount Saint Mary College
Nazareth College
New York University
Polytechnic Institute of New
  York University
Rensselaer Polytechnic Institute
Rochester Institute of
  Technology

Sage College of Albany
St. John Fisher College
St. Joseph's College, New York
  M
St. Joseph's College: Suffolk
  Campus
St. Lawrence University
Skidmore College
SUNY
  College at Brockport
  College at Buffalo
  College at Cortland
  College at Fredonia
  College at Geneseo
  College at New Paltz
  College at Old Westbury
  College at Oneonta
  College at Oswego
  College at Plattsburgh
  College at Potsdam
  College at Purchase
  College of Agriculture and
    Technology at Cobleskill
  College of Agriculture and
    Technology at Morrisville
  Farmingdale State College
  Institute of Technology at
    Utica/Rome
  Maritime College
Union College
United States Merchant Marine
  Academy M
University of Rochester
Utica College
Vassar College
Wells College
Yeshiva University

North Carolina

Greensboro College
Guilford College
Meredith College F
Methodist University
North Carolina Wesleyan
  College
Salem College F
William Peace University F

Ohio

Baldwin-Wallace College
Bluffton University
Capital University
Case Western Reserve
  University
College of Mount St. Joseph
College of Wooster
Defiance College
Denison University
Franciscan University of
  Steubenville
Heidelberg University
Hiram College
John Carroll University
Kenyon College
Marietta College
Muskingum University
Oberlin College
Ohio Northern University
Ohio Wesleyan University
Otterbein University
University of Mount Union
Wilmington College
Wittenberg University

Oregon

George Fox University
Lewis & Clark College F
Linfield College
Pacific University
Willamette University

Pennsylvania

Albright College
Allegheny College
Alvernia University
Arcadia University
Bryn Mawr College F
Cabrini College

Carnegie Mellon University
Cedar Crest College F
Chatham University F
Delaware Valley College
DeSales University
Dickinson College
Eastern University
Elizabethtown College
Franklin & Marshall College
Geneva College
Gettysburg College
Grove City College
Gwynedd-Mercy College
Haverford College
Immaculata University
Juniata College
Keystone College
King's College
La Roche College
Lancaster Bible College
Lebanon Valley College
Lycoming College
Marywood University
Messiah College
Misericordia University
Moravian College
Mount Aloysius College
Muhlenberg College
Neumann University
Penn State
  Abington M
  Altoona
  Berks
  Erie, The Behrend College
  Harrisburg
Philadelphia Biblical University
Rosemont College
St. Vincent College
Susquehanna University
Swarthmore College
Thiel College
University of Pittsburgh
  Bradford
  Greensburg
University of Scranton
Ursinus College
Washington & Jefferson College
Waynesburg University
Westminster College
Widener University
Wilkes University
Wilson College F
York College of Pennsylvania

Rhode Island

Johnson & Wales University:
  Providence
Rhode Island College
Roger Williams University
Salve Regina University

Tennessee

Maryville College
Rhodes College
University of the South

Texas

Austin College
Concordia University Texas
East Texas Baptist University
Hardin-Simmons University
Howard Payne University
LeTourneau University
Schreiner University
Southwestern University
Texas Lutheran University
Trinity University
University of Dallas
University of Mary Hardin-
  Baylor
University of Texas
  Dallas
  Tyler

Vermont

Castleton State College
Green Mountain College
Johnson State College

Lyndon State College
Middlebury College
Norwich University
Southern Vermont College

Virginia

Averett University
Bridgewater College
Christopher Newport University
Eastern Mennonite University
Emory & Henry College
Ferrum College
Hampden-Sydney College M
Hollins University F
Lynchburg College
Mary Baldwin College F
Marymount University
Randolph College
Randolph-Macon College
Roanoke College
Shenandoah University
Sweet Briar College F
University of Mary Washington
Virginia Wesleyan College
Washington and Lee University

Washington

Pacific Lutheran University
University of Puget Sound
Whitman College
Whitworth University

West Virginia

Bethany College

Wisconsin

Alverno College F
Beloit College
Carroll University
Carthage College
Concordia University Wisconsin
Edgewood College
Lakeland College
Lawrence University
Maranatha Baptist Bible College
Marian University
Milwaukee School of
  Engineering
Mount Mary College F
Northland College
Ripon College
St. Norbert College
University of Wisconsin
  Eau Claire F
  La Crosse F
  Oshkosh
  Platteville
  River Falls F
  Stevens Point F
  Stout F
  Superior
  Whitewater
Wisconsin Lutheran College

Softball Division I

Alabama

Alabama Agricultural and
  Mechanical University F
Alabama State University F
Auburn University F
Jacksonville State University F
Samford University F
Troy University F
University of Alabama F
University of Alabama
  Birmingham F
University of South Alabama F

Arizona

Arizona State University F
University of Arizona F

Arkansas

University of Arkansas F
  Pine Bluff F

University of Central Arkansas F

California

California Polytechnic State
   University: San Luis Obispo
   F
California State University
   Bakersfield F
   Fresno F
   Fullerton F
   Long Beach F
   Northridge F
   Sacramento F
Loyola Marymount University F
St. Mary's College of California
   F
San Diego State University F
San Jose State University F
Santa Clara University F
Stanford University F
University of California
   Berkeley F
   Davis F
   Los Angeles F
   Riverside F
   Santa Barbara F
University of San Diego F
University of the Pacific F

Colorado

Colorado State University F
University of Northern Colorado
   F

Connecticut

Central Connecticut State
   University F
Fairfield University F
Quinnipiac University F
Sacred Heart University F
University of Connecticut F
University of Hartford F
Yale University F

Delaware

Delaware State University F
University of Delaware F

District of Columbia

George Washington University
   F
Georgetown University F
Howard University F

Florida

Bethune-Cookman University F
Florida Agricultural and
   Mechanical University F
Florida Atlantic University F
Florida Gulf Coast University F
Florida International University
   F
Florida State University F
Jacksonville University F
Stetson University F
University of Central Florida F
University of Florida F
University of North Florida F
University of South Florida F

Georgia

Georgia Institute of Technology
   F
Georgia Southern University F
Georgia State University F
Kennesaw State University F
Mercer University F
Savannah State University F
University of Georgia F

Hawaii

University of Hawaii
   Manoa F

Idaho

Boise State University F
Idaho State University F

Illinois

Bradley University F
DePaul University F
Eastern Illinois University F
Illinois State University F
Loyola University Chicago F
Northern Illinois University F
Northwestern University F
Southern Illinois University
   Carbondale F
Southern Illinois University
   Edwardsville F
University of Illinois
   Chicago F
   Urbana-Champaign F
Western Illinois University F

Indiana

Ball State University F
Butler University F
Indiana State University F
Indiana University
   Bloomington F
Indiana University-Purdue
   University Fort Wayne F
Indiana University-Purdue
   University Indianapolis F
Purdue University F
University of Evansville F
University of Notre Dame F
Valparaiso University F

Iowa

Drake University F
Iowa State University F
University of Iowa F
University of Northern Iowa F

Kansas

University of Kansas F
Wichita State University F

Kentucky

Eastern Kentucky University F
Morehead State University F
Murray State University F
University of Kentucky F
University of Louisville F
Western Kentucky University F

Louisiana

Grambling State University F
Louisiana State University and
   Agricultural and Mechanical
   College F
Louisiana Tech University F
McNeese State University F
Nicholls State University F
Northwestern State University F
Southeastern Louisiana
   University F
Southern University and
   Agricultural and Mechanical
   College F
University of Louisiana at
   Lafayette F
University of Louisiana at
   Monroe F

Maine

University of Maine F

Maryland

Coppin State University F
Morgan State University F
Mount St. Mary's University F
Towson University F
University of Maryland
   Baltimore County F
   College Park F
   Eastern Shore F

Massachusetts

Boston College F
Boston University F
College of the Holy Cross F
Harvard College F
University of Massachusetts
   Amherst F

Michigan

Central Michigan University F
Eastern Michigan University F
Michigan State University F
Oakland University F
University of Detroit Mercy F
University of Michigan F
Western Michigan University F

Minnesota

University of Minnesota
   Twin Cities F

Mississippi

Alcorn State University F
Jackson State University F
Mississippi State University F
Mississippi Valley State
   University F
University of Mississippi F
University of Southern
   Mississippi F

Missouri

Missouri State University F
Saint Louis University F
Southeast Missouri State
   University F
University of Missouri
   Columbia F
   Kansas City F

Nebraska

Creighton University F
University of Nebraska
   Lincoln F
   Omaha F

Nevada

University of Nevada
   Las Vegas F
   Reno F

New Hampshire

Dartmouth College F

New Jersey

Fairleigh Dickinson University
   Metropolitan Campus F
Monmouth University F
Princeton University F
Rider University F
Rutgers, The State University of
   New Jersey
   New Brunswick/Piscataway
   Campus F
Saint Peter's College F
Seton Hall University F

New Mexico

New Mexico State University F
University of New Mexico F

New York

Barnard College F
Canisius College F
Colgate University F
Columbia University F
Cornell University F
Fordham University F
Hofstra University F
Iona College F
Long Island University
   Brooklyn Campus F
Manhattan College F
Marist College F
Niagara University F
Saint Bonaventure University F
St. John's University F
Siena College F
SUNY
   University at Albany F
   University at Binghamton F
   University at Buffalo F
   University at Stony Brook F
Syracuse University F
United States Military Academy
   F
Wagner College F

North Carolina

Appalachian State University F
Campbell University F
East Carolina University F
Elon University F
Gardner-Webb University F
North Carolina Agricultural and
   Technical State University F
North Carolina Central
   University F
North Carolina State University
   F
University of North Carolina
   Chapel Hill F
   Charlotte F
   Greensboro F
   Wilmington F
Western Carolina University F

North Dakota

North Dakota State University F
University of North Dakota F

Ohio

Bowling Green State University
   F
Cleveland State University F
Kent State University F
Miami University
   Oxford F
Ohio State University
   Columbus Campus F
Ohio University F
University of Akron F
University of Dayton F
University of Toledo F
Wright State University F
Youngstown State University F

Oklahoma

Oklahoma State University F
University of Oklahoma F
University of Tulsa F

Oregon

Oregon State University F
Portland State University F
University of Oregon F

Pennsylvania

Bucknell University F
Drexel University F
La Salle University F
Lafayette College F
Lehigh University F
Penn State
   University Park F
Robert Morris University F
St. Francis University F
Saint Joseph's University F
Temple University F
University of Pennsylvania F
University of Pittsburgh F
Villanova University F

Rhode Island

Brown University F
Bryant University F
Providence College F
University of Rhode Island F

South Carolina

Charleston Southern University
   F
Coastal Carolina University F
College of Charleston F
Furman University F
Presbyterian College F
South Carolina State University
   F
University of South Carolina
   Columbia F
   Upstate F
Winthrop University F

South Dakota

South Dakota State University F
University of South Dakota F

Tennessee

Austin Peay State University F
Belmont University F
East Tennessee State University
   F
Lipscomb University F
Middle Tennessee State
   University F
Tennessee State University F
Tennessee Technological
   University F
University of Memphis F
University of Tennessee
   Chattanooga F
   Knoxville F
   Martin F

Texas

Baylor University F
Houston Baptist University F
Prairie View A&M University F
Sam Houston State University F
Stephen F. Austin State
   University F
Texas A&M University
   Corpus Christi F
Texas Southern University F
Texas State University: San
   Marcos F
Texas Tech University F
University of Houston F
University of North Texas F
University of Texas
   Arlington F
   Austin F
   El Paso F
   San Antonio F

Utah

Brigham Young University F
Southern Utah University F
University of Utah F
Utah State University F
Utah Valley University F
Weber State University F

Virginia

George Mason University F
Hampton University F
James Madison University F
Liberty University F
Longwood University F
Norfolk State University F
Radford University F
University of Virginia F
Virginia Polytechnic Institute
   and State University F

Washington

Seattle University F
University of Washington F

West Virginia

Marshall University F

Wisconsin

University of Wisconsin
   Green Bay F
   Madison F

Softball Division II

Alabama

Miles College F
Stillman College F
Tuskegee University F
University of Alabama
   Huntsville F
University of North Alabama F
University of West Alabama F

Arizona

Grand Canyon University F

Arkansas

Arkansas Tech University F
Henderson State University F

Tables and Indexes

Ouachita Baptist University F
Southern Arkansas University F
University of Arkansas
Monticello F

California

Academy of Art University F
Azusa Pacific University F
California Baptist University F
California State University
Chico F
Dominguez Hills F
East Bay F
Monterey Bay F
San Bernardino F
Stanislaus F
Dominican University of
California F
Humboldt State University F
Notre Dame de Namur
University F
San Francisco State University
F
Sonoma State University F
University of California
San Diego F

Colorado

Adams State College F
Colorado Mesa University F
Colorado School of Mines F
Colorado State University
Pueblo F
Fort Lewis College F
Metropolitan State College of
Denver F
Regis University F
University of Colorado
Colorado Springs F

Connecticut

Post University F
Southern Connecticut State
University F
University of Bridgeport F
University of New Haven F

Delaware

Goldey-Beacom College F
Wilmington University F

Florida

Barry University F
Eckerd College F
Flagler College F
Florida Institute of Technology
F
Florida Southern College F
Lynn University F
Nova Southeastern University F
Palm Beach Atlantic University
F
Rollins College F
Saint Leo University F
University of Tampa F
University of West Florida F

Georgia

Albany State University F
Armstrong Atlantic State
University F
Augusta State University F
Chorter University
Shorter University F
Clark Atlanta University F
Columbus State University F
Fort Valley State University F
Georgia College and State
University F
Georgia Southwestern State
University F
North Georgia College & State
University F
Paine College F
University of West Georgia F
Valdosta State University F
Young Harris College F

Hawaii

Brigham Young University-
Hawaii F
Chaminade University of
Honolulu F
Hawaii Pacific University F
University of Hawaii
Hilo F

Idaho

Northwest Nazarene University
F

Illinois

Lewis University F
McKendree University F
Quincy University F
University of Illinois
Springfield F

Indiana

Oakland City University F
Saint Joseph's College F
University of Indianapolis F
University of Southern Indiana
F

Iowa

Upper Iowa University F

Kansas

Emporia State University F
Fort Hays State University F
Newman University F
Pittsburg State University F
Washburn University F

Kentucky

Bellarmine University F
Kentucky State University F
Northern Kentucky University F

Maryland

Bowie State University F
Washington Adventist
University F

Massachusetts

American International College
F
Assumption College F.
Bentley University F
Merrimack College F
Stonehill College F
University of Massachusetts
Lowell F

Michigan

Ferris State University F
Grand Valley State University F
Hillsdale College F
Lake Superior State University
F
Northwood University
Michigan F
Saginaw Valley State University
F
Wayne State University F

Minnesota

Bemidji State University F
Concordia University St. Paul F
Minnesota State University
Mankato F
Moorhead F
Saint Cloud State University F
Southwest Minnesota State
University F
University of Minnesota
Crookston F
Duluth F
Winona State University F

Mississippi

Delta State University F

Missouri

Drury University F
Lincoln University F
Lindenwood University F

Maryville University of Saint
Louis F
Missouri Southern State
University F
Missouri University of Science
and Technology F
Missouri Western State
University F
Northwest Missouri State
University F
Rockhurst University F
Southwest Baptist University F
Truman State University F
University of Central Missouri F
University of Missouri
St. Louis F
William Jewell College F

Montana

Montana State University
Billings F

Nebraska

Chadron State College F
University of Nebraska
Kearney F
Wayne State College F

New Hampshire

Franklin Pierce University F
Saint Anselm College F
Southern New Hampshire
University F

New Jersey

Bloomfield College F
Caldwell College F
Felician College F
Georgian Court University F

New Mexico

Eastern New Mexico University
F
New Mexico Highlands
University F

New York

Adelphi University F
City University of New York
Queens College F
College of Saint Rose F
Concordia College F
Dominican College of Blauvelt
F
Dowling College F
Le Moyne College F
Long Island University
C. W. Post Campus F
Mercy College F
Molloy College F
New York Institute of
Technology F
Nyack College F
Pace University F
St. Thomas Aquinas College F

North Carolina

Barton College F
Belmont Abbey College F
Brevard College F
Catawba College F
Chowan University F
Elizabeth City State University
F
Fayetteville State University F
Johnson C. Smith University F
Lees-McRae College F
Lenoir-Rhyne University F
Livingstone College F
Mars Hill College F
Mount Olive College F
Pfeiffer University F
Queens University of Charlotte
F
St. Augustine's College F
Shaw University F
University of North Carolina
Pembroke F
Wingate University F

Winston-Salem State University
F

North Dakota

Minot State University F
University of Mary F

Ohio

Ashland University F
Cedarville University F
Lake Erie College F
Malone University F
Notre Dame College F
Ohio Dominican University F
Tiffin University F
University of Findlay F
Ursuline College F
Walsh University F

Oklahoma

Cameron University F
East Central University F
Northeastern State University F
Oklahoma Panhandle State
University F
Southeastern Oklahoma State
University F
Southern Nazarene University F
Southwestern Oklahoma State
University F
University of Central Oklahoma
F

Oregon

Western Oregon University F

Pennsylvania

Bloomsburg University of
Pennsylvania F
California University of
Pennsylvania F
Chestnut Hill College F
Clarion University of
Pennsylvania F
East Stroudsburg University of
Pennsylvania F
Edinboro University of
Pennsylvania F
Gannon University F
Holy Family University F
Indiana University of
Pennsylvania F
Kutztown University of
Pennsylvania F
Lock Haven University of
Pennsylvania F
Mansfield University of
Pennsylvania F
Mercyhurst University F
Millersville University of
Pennsylvania F
Philadelphia University F
Seton Hill University F
Shippensburg University of
Pennsylvania F
Slippery Rock University of
Pennsylvania F
University of the Sciences in
Philadelphia F
West Chester University of
Pennsylvania F

Puerto Rico

University of Puerto Rico
Mayaguez F

South Carolina

Anderson University F
Benedict College F
Claflin University F
Coker College F
Erskine College F
Francis Marion University F
Lander University F
Limestone College F
Newberry College F
North Greenville University F
University of South Carolina
Aiken F

South Dakota

Augustana College F
Black Hills State University F
Northern State University F
University of Sioux Falls F

Tennessee

Carson-Newman College F
Christian Brothers University F
King College F
Lane College F
LeMoyne-Owen College F
Lincoln Memorial University F
Trevecca Nazarene University F
Tusculum College F
Union University F

Texas

Abilene Christian University F
Angelo State University F
Midwestern State University F
St. Edward's University F
St. Mary's University F
Tarleton State University F
Texas A&M International
University F
Texas A&M University
Kingsville F
Texas Woman's University F
University of Texas
of the Permian Basin F
University of the Incarnate
Word F
West Texas A&M University F

Utah

Dixie State College F

Vermont

St. Michael's College F

Virginia

Virginia State University F
Virginia Union University F

Washington

Saint Martin's University F
Western Washington University
F

West Virginia

Alderson-Broaddus College F
Bluefield State College F
Concord University F
Davis and Elkins College F
Fairmont State University F
Glenville State College F
Ohio Valley University F
Salem International University F
Shepherd University F
University of Charleston F
West Liberty University F
West Virginia State University
F
West Virginia Wesleyan
College F
Wheeling Jesuit University F

Wisconsin

University of Wisconsin
Parkside F

Canada

Simon Fraser University F

Softball Division III

Alabama

Birmingham-Southern College F
Huntingdon College F

Arkansas

Hendrix College F
University of the Ozarks F

California

California Lutheran University F
Chapman University F
Claremont McKenna College F
Occidental College F
Pitzer College F
Pomona College F
University of La Verne F
University of Redlands F
Whittier College F

Connecticut

Albertus Magnus College F
Eastern Connecticut State
  University F
Mitchell College F
Saint Joseph College F
Trinity College F
United States Coast Guard
  Academy F
Wesleyan University F
Western Connecticut State
  University F

Delaware

Wesley College F

District of Columbia

Catholic University of America
  F
Gallaudet University F

Georgia

Agnes Scott College F
Berry College F
Covenant College F
Emory University F
LaGrange College F
Piedmont College F
Spelman College F
Wesleyan College F

Illinois

Augustana College F
Aurora University F
Benedictine University F
Blackburn College F
Concordia University Chicago F
Dominican University F
Elmhurst College F
Eureka College F
Greenville College F
Illinois College F
Illinois Wesleyan University F
Knox College F
Lake Forest College F
MacMurray College F
Millikin University F
Monmouth College F
North Central College F
North Park University F
Principia College F
Rockford College F
University of Chicago F
Wheaton College F

Indiana

Anderson University F
DePauw University F
Franklin College F
Hanover College F
Manchester College F
Rose-Hulman Institute of
  Technology F
Saint Mary's College F
Trine University F

Iowa

Buena Vista University F
Central College F
Coe College F
Cornell College F
Grinnell College F
Loras College F
Luther College F
Simpson College F
University of Dubuque F
Wartburg College F

Kentucky

Centre College F
Kentucky Wesleyan College F
Spalding University F
Thomas More College F
Transylvania University F

Louisiana

Centenary College of Louisiana
  F
Louisiana College F

Maine

Bates College F
Bowdoin College F
Colby College F
Husson University F
Maine Maritime Academy F
Saint Joseph's College of Maine
  F
Thomas College F
University of Maine
  Farmington F
  Presque Isle F
University of New England F
University of Southern Maine F

Maryland

Frostburg State University F
Hood College F
McDaniel College F
Notre Dame of Maryland
  University F
Salisbury University F
Stevenson University F
Washington College F

Massachusetts

Amherst College F
Anna Maria College F
Babson College F
Bay Path College F
Becker College F
Brandeis University F
Bridgewater State University F
Clark University F
Curry College F
Eastern Nazarene College F
Elms College F
Emerson College F
Emmanuel College F
Endicott College F
Fitchburg State University F
Framingham State University F
Gordon College F
Lasell College F
Lesley University F
Massachusetts College of
  Liberal Arts F
Massachusetts Institute of
  Technology F
Massachusetts Maritime
  Academy F
Mount Ida College F
Newbury College F
Nichols College F
Pine Manor College F
Regis College F
Salem State University F
Simmons College F
Smith College F
Springfield College F
Suffolk University F
Tufts University F
University of Massachusetts
  Boston F
  Dartmouth F
Wellesley College F
Wentworth Institute of
  Technology F
Western New England
  University F
Westfield State University F
Wheaton College F
Wheelock College F
Williams College F

Michigan

Worcester Polytechnic Institute
  F
Worcester State University F

Michigan

Adrian College F
Albion College F
Alma College F
Calvin College F
Finlandia University F
Hope College F
Kalamazoo College F
Olivet College F

Minnesota

Bethany Lutheran College F
Bethel University F
Carleton College F
College of St. Benedict F
College of St. Scholastica F
Concordia College: Moorhead F
Crown College F
Gustavus Adolphus College F
Hamline University F
Macalester College F
Martin Luther College F
North Central University F
Northwestern College F
St. Catherine University F
St. Mary's University of
  Minnesota F
St. Olaf College F
University of Minnesota
  Morris F
University of St. Thomas F

Mississippi

Millsaps College F
Mississippi College F
Rust College F

Missouri

Fontbonne University F
Washington University in St.
  Louis F
Webster University F
Westminster College F

Nebraska

Nebraska Wesleyan University
  F

New Hampshire

Daniel Webster College F
Keene State College F
New England College F
Plymouth State University F
Rivier College F

New Jersey

Centenary College F
The College of New Jersey F
College of St. Elizabeth F
Drew University F
Fairleigh Dickinson University
  College at Florham F
Kean University F
Montclair State University F
New Jersey City University F
Ramapo College of New Jersey
  F
Richard Stockton College of
  New Jersey F
Rowan University F
Rutgers, The State University of
  New Jersey
    Camden Regional Campus
      F
    Newark Regional Campus F
Stevens Institute of Technology
  F
William Paterson University of
  New Jersey F

New York

Alfred University F
Cazenovia College F

City University of New York

City University of New York
  Baruch College F
  Brooklyn College F
  College of Staten Island F
  Hunter College F
  John Jay College of
    Criminal Justice F
  Lehman College F
  York College F
College of Mount St. Vincent F
College of New Rochelle F
D'Youville College F
Elmira College F
Hamilton College F
Hilbert College F
Ithaca College F
Keuka College F
Manhattanville College F
Medaille College F
Mount Saint Mary College F
Nazareth College F
Polytechnic Institute of New
  York University F
Rensselaer Polytechnic Institute
  F
Rochester Institute of
  Technology F
Russell Sage College F
Sage College of Albany F
St. John Fisher College F
St. Joseph's College, New York
  F
St. Joseph's College: Suffolk
  Campus F
St. Lawrence University F
Skidmore College F
SUNY
  College at Brockport F
  College at Buffalo F
  College at Cortland F
  College at Fredonia F
  College at Geneseo F
  College at New Paltz F
  College at Old Westbury F
  College at Oneonta F
  College at Oswego F
  College at Plattsburgh F
  College at Potsdam F
  College at Purchase F
  College of Agriculture and
    Technology at Cobleskill
    F
  College of Agriculture and
    Technology at Morrisville
    F
  Farmindale State College F
  Institute of Technology at
    Utica/Rome F
Union College F
United States Merchant Marine
  Academy F
University of Rochester F
Utica College F
Wells College F

North Carolina

Greensboro College F
Guilford College F
Meredith College F
Methodist University F
North Carolina Wesleyan
  College F
William Peace University F

Ohio

Baldwin-Wallace College F
Bluffton University F
Capital University F
Case Western Reserve
  University F
College of Mount St. Joseph F
College of Wooster F
Defiance College F
Denison University F
Franciscan University of
  Steubenville F
Heidelberg University F
Hiram College F

John Carroll University F
Kenyon College F
Marietta College F
Muskingum University F
Oberlin College F
Ohio Northern University F
Ohio Wesleyan University F
Otterbein University F
University of Mount Union F
Wilmington College F
Wittenberg University F

Oregon

George Fox University F
Lewis & Clark College F
Linfield College F
Pacific University F
Willamette University F

Pennsylvania

Albright College F
Allegheny College F
Alvernia University F
Arcadia University F
Baptist Bible College of
  Pennsylvania F
Cabrini College F
Cedar Crest College F
Chatham University F
Delaware Valley College F
DeSales University F
Dickinson College F
Eastern University F
Elizabethtown College F
Franklin & Marshall College F
Geneva College F
Gettysburg College F
Grove City College F
Gwynedd-Mercy College F
Haverford College F
Immaculata University F
Juniata College F
Keystone College F
King's College F
La Roche College F
Lebanon Valley College F
Lycoming College F
Marywood University F
Messiah College F
Misericordia University F
Moravian College F
Mount Aloysius College F
Muhlenberg College F
Neumann University F
Penn State
  Abington F
  Altoona F
  Berks F
  Erie, The Behrend College
    F
  Harrisburg F
Philadelphia Biblical University
  F
Rosemont College F
St. Vincent College F
Susquehanna University F
Swarthmore College F
Thiel College F
University of Pittsburgh
  Bradford F
  Greensburg F
University of Scranton F
Ursinus College F
Washington & Jefferson College
  F
Waynesburg University F
Westminster College F
Widener University F
Wilkes University F
Wilson College F
York College of Pennsylvania F

Rhode Island

Johnson & Wales University:
  Providence F
Rhode Island College F
Roger Williams University F
Salve Regina University F

Tennessee

Maryville College F
Rhodes College F
University of the South F

Texas

Austin College F
Concordia University Texas F
East Texas Baptist University F
Hardin-Simmons University F
Howard Payne University F
LeTourneau University F
Schreiner University F
Southwestern University F
Sul Ross State University F
Texas Lutheran University F
Trinity University F
University of Dallas F
University of Mary Hardin-
  Baylor F
University of Texas
  Dallas F
  Tyler F

Vermont

Castleton State College F
Green Mountain College F
Johnson State College F
Lyndon State College F
Middlebury College F
Norwich University F
Southern Vermont College F

Virginia

Averett University F
Bridgewater College F
Christopher Newport University
  F
Eastern Mennonite University F
Emory & Henry College F
Ferrum College F
Lynchburg College F
Mary Baldwin College F
Randolph College F
Randolph-Macon College F
Roanoke College F
Shenandoah University F
Sweet Briar College F
University of Mary Washington
  F
Virginia Wesleyan College F

Washington

Pacific Lutheran University F
University of Puget Sound F
Whitworth University F

West Virginia

Bethany College F

Wisconsin

Alverno College F
Beloit College F
Carroll University F
Carthage College F
Concordia University Wisconsin
  F
Edgewood College F
Lakeland College F
Lawrence University F
Maranatha Baptist Bible College
  F
Marian University F
Milwaukee School of
  Engineering F
Mount Mary College F
Northland College F
Ripon College F
St. Norbert College F
University of Wisconsin
  Eau Claire F
  La Crosse F
  Oshkosh F
  Platteville F
  River Falls F
  Stevens Point F
  Stout F
  Superior F
  Whitewater F

Wisconsin Lutheran College F

Swimming and diving Division I

Alabama

Auburn University
University of Alabama

Arizona

Arizona State University
Northern Arizona University F
University of Arizona

Arkansas

University of Arkansas F
  Little Rock F

California

California Polytechnic State
  University: San Luis Obispo
California State University
  Bakersfield
  Fresno F
Loyola Marymount University F
Pepperdine University F
San Diego State University F
San Jose State University F
Stanford University
University of California
  Berkeley
  Davis F
  Los Angeles F
  Santa Barbara
University of San Diego F
University of Southern
  California
University of the Pacific

Colorado

Colorado State University F
United States Air Force
  Academy
University of Denver
University of Northern Colorado
  F

Connecticut

Central Connecticut State
  University F
Fairfield University
Sacred Heart University F
University of Connecticut
Yale University

Delaware

University of Delaware

District of Columbia

American University
George Washington University
Georgetown University
Howard University

Florida

Florida Agricultural and
  Mechanical University
Florida Atlantic University
Florida Gulf Coast University F
Florida International University
  F
Florida State University
University of Florida
University of Miami
University of North Florida F

Georgia

Georgia Institute of Technology
Georgia Southern University F
University of Georgia

Hawaii

University of Hawaii
  Manoa

Idaho

Boise State University F
University of Idaho F

Illinois

Eastern Illinois University
Illinois State University F
Northwestern University
Southern Illinois University
  Carbondale
University of Illinois
  Chicago
  Urbana-Champaign F
Western Illinois University

Indiana

Ball State University
Butler University F
Indiana University
  Bloomington
Indiana University-Purdue
  University Indianapolis
Purdue University
University of Evansville
University of Notre Dame
Valparaiso University

Iowa

Iowa State University F
University of Iowa
University of Northern Iowa F

Kansas

University of Kansas F

Kentucky

University of Kentucky
University of Louisville
Western Kentucky University

Louisiana

Louisiana State University and
  Agricultural and Mechanical
  College
Tulane University F

Maine

University of Maine

Maryland

Loyola University Maryland
Mount St. Mary's University F
Towson University
United States Naval Academy
University of Maryland
  Baltimore County
  College Park

Massachusetts

Boston College
Boston University
College of the Holy Cross
Harvard College
Northeastern University F
University of Massachusetts
  Amherst

Michigan

Eastern Michigan University
Michigan State University
Oakland University
University of Michigan

Minnesota

University of Minnesota
  Twin Cities

Missouri

Missouri State University
Saint Louis University
University of Missouri
  Columbia

Nebraska

University of Nebraska
  Lincoln F
  Omaha F

Nevada

University of Nevada
  Las Vegas
  Reno F

New Hampshire

Dartmouth College
University of New Hampshire F

New Jersey

New Jersey Institute of
  Technology M
Princeton University
Rider University
Rutgers, The State University of
  New Jersey
  New Brunswick/Piscataway
    Campus F
Saint Peter's College
Seton Hall University

New Mexico

New Mexico State University F
University of New Mexico F

New York

Barnard College F
Canisius College
Colgate University
Columbia University
Cornell University
Fordham University
Iona College
Manhattan College
Marist College
Niagara University
Saint Bonaventure University
St. Francis College
Siena College F
SUNY
  University at Binghamton
  University at Buffalo
  University at Stony Brook
United States Military Academy
Wagner College F

North Carolina

Campbell University F
Davidson College
Duke University
East Carolina University
Gardner-Webb University
North Carolina Agricultural and
  Technical State University F
North Carolina State University
University of North Carolina
  Chapel Hill
  Wilmington

North Dakota

University of North Dakota

Ohio

Bowling Green State University
  F
Cleveland State University
Miami University
  Oxford
Ohio State University
  Columbus Campus
Ohio University F
University of Akron F
University of Cincinnati
University of Toledo F
Wright State University
Xavier University
Youngstown State University F

Oregon

Oregon State University F

Pennsylvania

Bucknell University
Drexel University
Duquesne University F
La Salle University
Lafayette College
Lehigh University
Penn State
  University Park
St. Francis University F
University of Pennsylvania
University of Pittsburgh
Villanova University

Rhode Island

Brown University
Bryant University
Providence College
University of Rhode Island F

South Carolina

Clemson University
College of Charleston
University of South Carolina
  Columbia

South Dakota

South Dakota State University
University of South Dakota

Tennessee

University of Tennessee
  Knoxville
Vanderbilt University F

Texas

Rice University F
Southern Methodist University
Texas A&M University
Texas Christian University
University of Houston F
University of North Texas F
University of Texas
  Austin

Utah

Brigham Young University
University of Utah

Vermont

University of Vermont F

Virginia

College of William and Mary
George Mason University
James Madison University F
Liberty University F
Old Dominion University
Radford University F
University of Richmond F
University of Virginia
Virginia Military Institute
Virginia Polytechnic Institute
  and State University

Washington

Seattle University
Washington State University F

West Virginia

Marshall University F
West Virginia University

Wisconsin

University of Wisconsin
  Green Bay
  Madison
  Milwaukee

Wyoming

University of Wyoming

Swimming and diving Division II

Alaska

University of Alaska
  Fairbanks F

Arizona

Grand Canyon University

Arkansas

Henderson State University
Ouachita Baptist University

California

California Baptist University
California State University
  East Bay F
Fresno Pacific University

University of California
San Diego

Colorado

Adams State College
Colorado Mesa University
Colorado School of Mines

Connecticut

Post University
Southern Connecticut State
University
University of Bridgeport

Florida

Florida Institute of Technology
Florida Southern College
Nova Southeastern University
Rollins College
Saint Leo University
University of Tampa

Illinois

Lewis University

Indiana

University of Indianapolis

Massachusetts

Assumption College F
Bentley University

Michigan

Grand Valley State University
Hillsdale College F
Northern Michigan University F
Wayne State University

Minnesota

Minnesota State University
Mankato F
Moorhead F
Saint Cloud State University

Mississippi

Delta State University

Missouri

Drury University
Lindenwood University
Missouri University of Science
and Technology M
Truman State University
William Jewell College

Nebraska

University of Nebraska
Kearney F

New York

Adelphi University
City University of New York
Queens College
College of Saint Rose
Le Moyne College
Long Island University
C. W. Post Campus F
Pace University

North Carolina

Catawba College
Lenoir-Rhyne University
Mars Hill College
Pfeiffer University
Queens University of Charlotte
Wingate University

Ohio

Ashland University
Lake Erie College
Malone University
Notre Dame College
University of Findlay
Ursuline College F

Pennsylvania

Bloomsburg University of
Pennsylvania
California University of
Pennsylvania F

Clarion University of
Pennsylvania
East Stroudsburg University of
Pennsylvania F
Edinboro University of
Pennsylvania
Gannon University
Indiana University of
Pennsylvania
Kutztown University of
Pennsylvania F
Lock Haven University of
Pennsylvania F
Mansfield University of
Pennsylvania F
Millersville University of
Pennsylvania F
Shippensburg University of
Pennsylvania
West Chester University of
Pennsylvania

Puerto Rico

University of Puerto Rico
Mayaguez
Rio Piedras

South Carolina

Converse College F
Limestone College

South Dakota

Northern State University F

Tennessee

King College

Texas

McMurry University
University of Texas
of the Permian Basin
University of the Incarnate
Word

Vermont

St. Michael's College

West Virginia

Davis and Elkins College
Fairmont State University
West Virginia Wesleyan College
Wheeling Jesuit University

Canada

Simon Fraser University

Swimming and diving Division III

Arkansas

Hendrix College

California

California Institute of
Technology
California Lutheran University
Chapman University F
Claremont McKenna College
Mills College F
Occidental College
Pitzer College M
Pomona College
University of California
Santa Cruz
University of La Verne
University of Redlands
Whittier College

Colorado

Colorado College
Regis University M

Connecticut

Connecticut College
Eastern Connecticut State
University F
Saint Joseph College F

Trinity College
United States Coast Guard
Academy
Wesleyan University
Western Connecticut State
University F

District of Columbia

Catholic University of America
Gallaudet University

Georgia

Berry College
Emory University
LaGrange College F

Illinois

Augustana College
Eureka College
Illinois College
Illinois Wesleyan University
Knox College
Lake Forest College
Millikin University
Monmouth College
North Central College
Principia College
University of Chicago
Wheaton College

Indiana

DePauw University
Franklin College
Rose-Hulman Institute of
Technology
Saint Mary's College F
Wabash College M

Iowa

Coe College
Grinnell College
Loras College
Luther College
Simpson College

Kentucky

Centre College
Transylvania University

Louisiana

Centenary College of Louisiana

Maine

Bates College
Bowdoin College
Colby College
Husson University F
Saint Joseph's College of Maine
University of New England F

Maryland

Frostburg State University
Goucher College
Hood College
Johns Hopkins University
McDaniel College
Notre Dame of Maryland
University F
St. Mary's College of Maryland
Salisbury University
Washington College

Massachusetts

Amherst College
Babson College
Bridgewater State University
Clark University
Elms College
Gordon College
Massachusetts Institute of
Technology
Mount Holyoke College F
Regis College F
Simmons College F
Smith College F
Springfield College
Tufts University
University of Massachusetts
Dartmouth
Wellesley College F

Western New England
University F
Westfield State University F
Wheaton College
Williams College
Worcester Polytechnic Institute

Michigan

Albion College
Alma College
Calvin College
Hope College
Kalamazoo College
Olivet College

Minnesota

Carleton College
College of St. Benedict F
Concordia College: Moorhead F
Gustavus Adolphus College
Hamline University
Macalester College
St. Catherine University F
St. John's University M
St. Mary's University of
Minnesota
St. Olaf College
University of Minnesota
Morris F
University of St. Thomas

Missouri

Washington University in St.
Louis

New Hampshire

Colby-Sawyer College
Keene State College
Plymouth State University F

New Jersey

The College of New Jersey
College of St. Elizabeth F
Drew University
Fairleigh Dickinson University
College at Florham
Montclair State University
Ramapo College of New Jersey
Rowan University
Stevens Institute of Technology
William Paterson University of
New Jersey

New York

Alfred University
Cazenovia College
City University of New York
Baruch College
Brooklyn College M
College of Staten Island
Hunter College F
John Jay College of
Criminal Justice F
Lehman College
York College
Clarkson University
College of Mount St. Vincent
College of New Rochelle F
Hamilton College
Hartwick College
Hobart and William Smith
Colleges F
Ithaca College
Mount Saint Mary College
Nazareth College
New York University
Rensselaer Polytechnic Institute
Rochester Institute of
Technology
St. Joseph's College, New York
F
St. Lawrence University
Skidmore College

SUNY

College at Brockport
College at Buffalo
College at Cortland
College at Fredonia
College at Geneseo
College at New Paltz
College at Old Westbury
College at Oneonta
College at Oswego
College at Potsdam
College at Purchase
College of Agriculture and
Technology at Cobleskill
Maritime College
Union College
United States Merchant Marine
Academy
University of Rochester
Utica College
Vassar College
Wells College

North Carolina

Greensboro College
Guilford College F

Ohio

Baldwin-Wallace College
Case Western Reserve
University
College of Wooster
Defiance College
Denison University
Hiram College
John Carroll University
Kenyon College
Oberlin College
Ohio Northern University
Ohio Wesleyan University
University of Mount Union
Wilmington College
Wittenberg University

Oregon

Lewis & Clark College
Linfield College
Pacific University
Willamette University

Pennsylvania

Albright College
Allegheny College
Arcadia University
Bryn Mawr College F
Cabrini College
Carnegie Mellon University
Chatham University F
Dickinson College
Elizabethtown College
Franklin & Marshall College
Gettysburg College
Grove City College
Juniata College F
King's College
Lebanon Valley College
Lycoming College
Marywood University
Messiah College
Misericordia University
Penn State
Altoona
Erie, The Behrend College
St. Vincent College
Susquehanna University
Swarthmore College
University of Pittsburgh
Bradford
University of Scranton
Ursinus College
Washington & Jefferson College
Westminster College
Widener University
York College of Pennsylvania

Rhode Island

Rhode Island College F
Roger Williams University

Tennis

Tennis

Tennis

Tennis

Tennis

Tennessee

Rhodes College
University of the South

Texas

Austin College
Southwestern University
Trinity University

Vermont

Middlebury College
Norwich University

Virginia

Bridgewater College F
Emory & Henry College F
Hollins University F
Marymount University
Randolph-Macon College
Sweet Briar College F
University of Mary Washington
Washington and Lee University

Washington

Pacific Lutheran University
University of Puget Sound
Whitman College
Whitworth University

West Virginia

Bethany College

Wisconsin

Beloit College
Carroll University
Carthage College
Lawrence University
Ripon College
University of Wisconsin
  Eau Claire
  La Crosse
  Oshkosh
  River Falls
  Stevens Point
  Whitewater

Tennis Division I

Alabama

Alabama Agricultural and
  Mechanical University
Alabama State University
Auburn University
Jacksonville State University
Samford University
Troy University
University of Alabama
University of Alabama
  Birmingham
University of South Alabama

Arizona

Arizona State University F
Northern Arizona University
University of Arizona

Arkansas

Arkansas State University F
University of Arkansas
  Little Rock F
  Pine Bluff
University of Central Arkansas
  F

California

California Polytechnic State
  University: San Luis Obispo
California State University
  Bakersfield F
  Fresno
  Fullerton F
  Long Beach F
  Northridge F
  Sacramento
Loyola Marymount University
Pepperdine University
St. Mary's College of California

San Diego State University
San Jose State University F
Santa Clara University
Stanford University
University of California
  Berkeley
  Davis
  Irvine
  Los Angeles
  Riverside
  Santa Barbara
University of San Diego
University of San Francisco
University of Southern
  California
University of the Pacific

Colorado

Colorado State University F
United States Air Force
  Academy
University of Colorado
  Boulder F
University of Denver
University of Northern Colorado

Connecticut

Fairfield University
Quinnipiac University
Sacred Heart University
University of Connecticut
University of Hartford
Yale University

Delaware

Delaware State University F
University of Delaware

District of Columbia

George Washington University
Georgetown University
Howard University

Florida

Bethune-Cookman University
Florida Agricultural and
  Mechanical University
Florida Atlantic University
Florida Gulf Coast University
Florida International University
  F
Florida State University
Jacksonville University
Stetson University
University of Central Florida
University of Florida
University of Miami
University of North Florida
University of South Florida

Georgia

Georgia Institute of Technology
Georgia Southern University
Georgia State University
Kennesaw State University
Mercer University
Savannah State University F
University of Georgia

Hawaii

University of Hawaii
  Manoa

Idaho

Boise State University
Idaho State University
University of Idaho

Illinois

Bradley University
Chicago State University
DePaul University
Eastern Illinois University
Illinois State University
Northern Illinois University
Northwestern University
Southern Illinois University
  Carbondale

Southern Illinois University
  Edwardsville
University of Illinois
  Chicago
  Urbana-Champaign
Western Illinois University

Indiana

Ball State University
Butler University
Indiana University
  Bloomington
Indiana University-Purdue
  University Fort Wayne
Indiana University-Purdue
  University Indianapolis
Purdue University
University of Evansville F
University of Notre Dame
Valparaiso University

Iowa

Drake University
Iowa State University F
University of Iowa
University of Northern Iowa F

Kansas

Kansas State University F
University of Kansas F
Wichita State University

Kentucky

Eastern Kentucky University
Morehead State University
Murray State University
University of Kentucky
University of Louisville
Western Kentucky University

Louisiana

Grambling State University F
Louisiana State University and
  Agricultural and Mechanical
  College
Louisiana Tech University F
McNeese State University F
Nicholls State University
Northwestern State University F
Southeastern Louisiana
  University F
Southern University and
  Agricultural and Mechanical
  College F
Tulane University
University of Louisiana at
  Lafayette
University of Louisiana at
  Monroe F

Maryland

Coppin State University
Loyola University Maryland
Morgan State University
Mount St. Mary's University
Towson University F
United States Naval Academy
University of Maryland
  Baltimore County
  College Park
  Eastern Shore

Massachusetts

Boston College
Boston University
College of the Holy Cross
Harvard College
University of Massachusetts
  Amherst F

Michigan

Eastern Michigan University F
Michigan State University
Oakland University F
University of Detroit Mercy
University of Michigan
Western Michigan University

Minnesota

University of Minnesota
  Twin Cities

Mississippi

Alcorn State University
Jackson State University
Mississippi State University
Mississippi Valley State
  University
University of Mississippi
University of Southern
  Mississippi

Missouri

Saint Louis University
Southeast Missouri State
  University F
University of Missouri
  Columbia F
  Kansas City

Montana

Montana State University
University of Montana

Nebraska

Creighton University
University of Nebraska
  Lincoln
  Omaha

Nevada

University of Nevada
  Las Vegas
  Reno

New Hampshire

Dartmouth College

New Jersey

Fairleigh Dickinson University
  Metropolitan Campus
Monmouth University
New Jersey Institute of
  Technology
Princeton University
Rider University
Rutgers, The State University of
  New Jersey
  New Brunswick/Piscataway
  Campus F
Saint Peter's College
Seton Hall University F

New Mexico

New Mexico State University
University of New Mexico

New York

Barnard College F
Colgate University
Columbia University
Cornell University
Fordham University
Hofstra University
Long Island University
  Brooklyn Campus F
Manhattan College F
Marist College
Niagara University
Saint Bonaventure University
St. Francis College
St. John's University
Siena College
SUNY
  University at Albany F
  University at Binghamton
  University at Buffalo
  University at Stony Brook
Syracuse University F
United States Military Academy
Wagner College

North Carolina

Appalachian State University
Campbell University
Davidson College
Duke University

East Carolina University
Elon University
Gardner-Webb University
North Carolina Agricultural and
  Technical State University F
North Carolina Central
  University
North Carolina State University
University of North Carolina
  Asheville
  Chapel Hill
  Charlotte
  Greensboro
  Wilmington
Wake Forest University
Western Carolina University F

North Dakota

University of North Dakota F

Ohio

Bowling Green State University
  F
Cleveland State University
Miami University
  Oxford F
Ohio State University
  Columbus Campus
University of Akron F
University of Cincinnati F
University of Dayton
University of Toledo
Wright State University
Xavier University
Youngstown State University

Oklahoma

Oklahoma State University
Oral Roberts University
University of Oklahoma
University of Tulsa

Oregon

Portland State University
University of Oregon
University of Portland

Pennsylvania

Bucknell University
Drexel University
Duquesne University
La Salle University
Lafayette College
Lehigh University
Penn State
  University Park
Robert Morris University
St. Francis University
Saint Joseph's University
Temple University
University of Pennsylvania
University of Pittsburgh F
Villanova University

Rhode Island

Brown University
Bryant University
Providence College F
University of Rhode Island F

South Carolina

Charleston Southern University
  F
The Citadel M
Clemson University
Coastal Carolina University
College of Charleston
Furman University
Presbyterian College
South Carolina State University
University of South Carolina
  Columbia
  Upstate
Winthrop University
Wofford College

South Dakota

South Dakota State University
University of South Dakota F

Tennessee

Austin Peay State University
Belmont University
East Tennessee State University
Lipscomb University
Middle Tennessee State
University
Tennessee State University
Tennessee Technological
University M
University of Memphis
University of Tennessee
Chattanooga
Knoxville
Martin F
Vanderbilt University

Texas

Baylor University
Lamar University
Prairie View A&M University
Rice University
Sam Houston State University F
Southern Methodist University
Stephen F. Austin State
University F
Texas A&M University
Corpus Christi
Texas Christian University
Texas State University: San
Marcos F
Texas Tech University
University of Houston F
University of North Texas F
University of Texas
Arlington
Austin
El Paso F
Pan American
San Antonio

Utah

Brigham Young University
Southern Utah University F
University of Utah
Utah State University
Weber State University

Virginia

College of William and Mary
George Mason University
Hampton University
James Madison University
Liberty University
Longwood University
Norfolk State University
Old Dominion University
Radford University
University of Richmond
University of Virginia
Virginia Commonwealth
University
Virginia Polytechnic Institute
and State University

Washington

Eastern Washington University
Gonzaga University
Seattle University
University of Washington
Washington State University F

West Virginia

Marshall University F
West Virginia University F

Wisconsin

Marquette University
University of Wisconsin
Green Bay
Madison
Milwaukee F

Wyoming

University of Wyoming F

Tennis Division II

Alabama

Stillman College
Tuskegee University
University of Alabama
Huntsville
University of Montevallo F
University of North Alabama
University of West Alabama

Arizona

Grand Canyon University

Arkansas

Arkansas Tech University F
Harding University
Henderson State University F
Ouachita Baptist University
Southern Arkansas University F
University of Arkansas
Fort Smith

California

Academy of Art University F
Azusa Pacific University M
California State Polytechnic
University: Pomona F
California State University
Los Angeles F
Stanislaus F
Dominican University of
California F
Fresno Pacific University
Notre Dame de Namur
University F
Point Loma Nazarene University
Sonoma State University
University of California
San Diego

Colorado

Colorado Christian University
Colorado Mesa University
Colorado State University
Pueblo
Metropolitan State College of
Denver

Connecticut

Post University
University of New Haven F

Delaware

Goldey-Beacom College F

District of Columbia

University of the District of
Columbia

Florida

Barry University
Eckerd College
Flagler College
Florida Institute of Technology
Florida Southern College
Lynn University
Nova Southeastern University F
Palm Beach Atlantic University
Rollins College
Saint Leo University
University of Tampa F
University of West Florida

Georgia

Albany State University F
Armstrong Atlantic State
University
Augusta State University
Chorter University
Shorter University
Clark Atlanta University F
Clayton State University F
Columbus State University

Fort Valley State University
Georgia College and State
University
Georgia Southwestern State
University
Morehouse College M
North Georgia College & State
University
University of West Georgia F
Valdosta State University
Young Harris College

Hawaii

Brigham Young University-
Hawaii
Chaminade University of
Honolulu F
Hawaii Pacific University
University of Hawaii
Hilo

Illinois

Lewis University
McKendree University
Quincy University
University of Illinois
Springfield

Indiana

Oakland City University
Saint Joseph's College
University of Indianapolis
University of Southern Indiana

Iowa

Upper Iowa University F

Kansas

Emporia State University
Fort Hays State University F
Newman University
Washburn University

Kentucky

Bellarmine University
Northern Kentucky University

Louisiana

University of New Orleans

Maryland

Bowie State University F

Massachusetts

American International College
Assumption College
Bentley University
Merrimack College
Stonehill College

Michigan

Ferris State University
Grand Valley State University
Hillsdale College F
Lake Superior State University
Michigan Technological
University
Northwood University
Michigan
Saginaw Valley State University
F
Wayne State University

Minnesota

Bemidji State University F
Minnesota State University
Mankato F
Moorhead F
Saint Cloud State University
Southwest Minnesota State
University F
University of Minnesota
Crookston F
Duluth F
Winona State University F

Mississippi

Delta State University

Missouri

Drury University
Lincoln University F

Lindenwood University
Maryville University of Saint
Louis
Missouri Southern State
University F
Missouri Western State
University F
Northwest Missouri State
University
Rockhurst University
Southwest Baptist University
Truman State University
University of Missouri
St. Louis
William Jewell College

Montana

Montana State University
Billings

Nebraska

University of Nebraska
Kearney

New Hampshire

Franklin Pierce University
Saint Anselm College
Southern New Hampshire
University

New Jersey

Bloomfield College M
Caldwell College
Georgian Court University F

New York

Adelphi University
City University of New York
Queens College
College of Saint Rose F
Concordia College
Dowling College
Le Moyne College
Long Island University
C. W. Post Campus F
Molloy College F
New York Institute of
Technology M
Pace University
Roberts Wesleyan College
St. Thomas Aquinas College

North Carolina

Barton College
Belmont Abbey College
Brevard College
Catawba College
Chowan University
Elizabeth City State University
F
Fayetteville State University F
Johnson C. Smith University
Lees-McRae College
Lenoir-Rhyne University
Livingstone College F
Mars Hill College
Mount Olive College
Pfeiffer University
Queens University of Charlotte
St. Augustine's College
Shaw University
University of North Carolina
Pembroke F
Wingate University
Winston-Salem State University

North Dakota

University of Mary F

Ohio

Ashland University F
Cedarville University
Central State University
Lake Erie College
Malone University
Ohio Dominican University
Tiffin University
University of Findlay

Ursuline College F
Walsh University

Oklahoma

Cameron University
East Central University
Northeastern State University F
Southeastern Oklahoma State
University
Southern Nazarene University F
University of Central Oklahoma
F

Pennsylvania

Bloomsburg University of
Pennsylvania
California University of
Pennsylvania F
Chestnut Hill College
Cheyney University of
Pennsylvania F
Clarion University of
Pennsylvania F
East Stroudsburg University of
Pennsylvania F
Edinboro University of
Pennsylvania
Holy Family University F
Indiana University of
Pennsylvania F
Kutztown University of
Pennsylvania
Mercyhurst University
Millersville University of
Pennsylvania
Philadelphia University
Seton Hill University F
Shippensburg University of
Pennsylvania F
Slippery Rock University of
Pennsylvania F
University of the Sciences in
Philadelphia
West Chester University of
Pennsylvania

Puerto Rico

University of Puerto Rico
Bayamon University
College
Mayaguez
Rio Piedras

South Carolina

Anderson University
Benedict College
Coker College
Converse College F
Erskine College
Francis Marion University
Lander University
Limestone College
Newberry College
North Greenville University
University of South Carolina
Aiken

South Dakota

Augustana College
Northern State University F
University of Sioux Falls F

Tennessee

Carson-Newman College
Christian Brothers University
King College
Lane College
LeMoyne-Owen College
Lincoln Memorial University
Tusculum College

Texas

Abilene Christian University
Dallas Baptist University
McMurry University
Midwestern State University
St. Edward's University
St. Mary's University
Tarleton State University F

Texas A&M University
Kingsville F
University of Texas
of the Permian Basin
University of the Incarnate
Word

Utah

Dixie State College F

Vermont

St. Michael's College

Virginia

Virginia State University
Virginia Union University

West Virginia

Bluefield State College
Concord University
Davis and Elkins College
Fairmont State University
Shepherd University
University of Charleston
West Liberty University
West Virginia State University
West Virginia Wesleyan College

Tennis Division III

Alabama

Birmingham-Southern College
Huntingdon College

Arkansas

Hendrix College
University of the Ozarks

California

California Institute of
Technology
California Lutheran University
Chapman University
Claremont McKenna College
Mills College F
Occidental College
Pitzer College M
Pomona College
University of California
Santa Cruz
University of La Verne F
University of Redlands
Whittier College

Colorado

Colorado College

Connecticut

Albertus Magnus College
Connecticut College
Mitchell College
Saint Joseph College F
Trinity College
United States Coast Guard
Academy M
Wesleyan University
Western Connecticut State
University

Delaware

Wesley College

District of Columbia

Catholic University of America
Trinity Washington University F

Georgia

Agnes Scott College F
Berry College
Covenant College
Emory University
LaGrange College
Oglethorpe University
Piedmont College
Spelman College F
Wesleyan College F

Illinois

Augustana College
Aurora University
Benedictine University F
Blackburn College F
Concordia University Chicago
Dominican University
Elmhurst College
Eureka College
Greenville College
Illinois College
Illinois Wesleyan University
Knox College
Lake Forest College
Millikin University F
Monmouth College
North Central College
Principia College
Rockford College
University of Chicago
Wheaton College

Indiana

Anderson University
DePauw University
Earlham College
Franklin College
Hanover College
Manchester College
Rose-Hulman Institute of
Technology
Saint Mary's College F
Trine University
Wabash College M

Iowa

Buena Vista University
Central College
Coe College
Cornell College
Grinnell College
Loras College
Luther College
Simpson College
University of Dubuque
Wartburg College

Kentucky

Centre College
Kentucky Wesleyan College F
Thomas More College
Transylvania University

Louisiana

Centenary College of Louisiana
Louisiana College

Maine

Bates College
Bowdoin College
Colby College
Thomas College
University of Southern Maine

Maryland

Frostburg State University
Goucher College
Hood College
Johns Hopkins University
McDaniel College
Notre Dame of Maryland
University F
St. Mary's College of Maryland
Salisbury University
Stevenson University
Washington College

Massachusetts

Amherst College
Anna Maria College
Babson College
Bay Path College F
Becker College
Brandeis University
Bridgewater State University
Clark University
Curry College
Eastern Nazarene College

Emerson College
Emmanuel College F
Endicott College
Gordon College
Lesley University
Massachusetts College of
Liberal Arts
Massachusetts Institute of
Technology
Mount Holyoke College F
Mount Ida College F
Newbury College
Nichols College
Regis College
Salem State University
Simmons College F
Smith College F
Springfield College
Suffolk University
Tufts University
University of Massachusetts
Boston
Dartmouth
Wellesley College F
Wentworth Institute of
Technology
Western New England
University
Wheaton College
Wheelock College M
Williams College
Worcester State University F

Michigan

Adrian College
Albion College
Alma College
Calvin College
Hope College
Kalamazoo College
Olivet College F

Minnesota

Bethany Lutheran College
Bethel University
Carleton College
College of St. Benedict F
College of St. Scholastica
Concordia College: Moorhead
Gustavus Adolphus College
Hamline University
Macalester College
Martin Luther College
North Central University M
Northwestern College
St. Catherine University F
St. John's University M
St. Mary's University of
Minnesota
St. Olaf College
University of Minnesota
Morris
University of St. Thomas

Mississippi

Millsaps College
Mississippi College
Rust College

Missouri

Fontbonne University
Washington University in St.
Louis
Webster University
Westminster College

Nebraska

Nebraska Wesleyan University

New Hampshire

Colby-Sawyer College
Plymouth State University F

New Jersey

The College of New Jersey
College of St. Elizabeth F
Drew University
Fairleigh Dickinson University
College at Florham

Kean University F
Ramapo College of New Jersey
Richard Stockton College of
New Jersey F
Rutgers, The State University of
New Jersey
Camden Regional Campus
Newark Regional Campus
Stevens Institute of Technology
William Paterson University of
New Jersey F

New York

Alfred University
Bard College
City University of New York
Baruch College
Brooklyn College
City College
College of Staten Island
Hunter College
John Jay College of
Criminal Justice
Lehman College
Medgar Evers College F
York College
College of New Rochelle F
D'Youville College
Elmira College
Hamilton College
Hartwick College
Hobart and William Smith
Colleges
Ithaca College
Keuka College
Manhattanville College
Medaille College F
Mount Saint Mary College
Nazareth College
New York University
Polytechnic Institute of New
York University
Rensselaer Polytechnic Institute
Rochester Institute of
Technology
Russell Sage College F
Sage College of Albany
St. John Fisher College
St. Joseph's College, New York
M
St. Joseph's College: Suffolk
Campus
St. Lawrence University
Skidmore College
SUNY
College at Brockport F
College at Cortland F
College at Fredonia F
College at Geneseo F
College at New Paltz F
College at Oneonta
College at Oswego
College at Plattsburgh F
College at Purchase
Farmingdale State College
Union College
United States Merchant Marine
Academy M
University of Rochester
Utica College
Vassar College
Wells College F
Yeshiva University

North Carolina

Greensboro College
Guilford College
Meredith College F
Methodist University
North Carolina Wesleyan
College
Salem College F
William Peace University F

Ohio

Baldwin-Wallace College
Bluffton University M
Capital University

Case Western Reserve
University
College of Mount St. Joseph
College of Wooster
Defiance College
Denison University
Franciscan University of
Steubenville
Heidelberg University
Hiram College F
John Carroll University
Kenyon College
Marietta College
Muskingum University
Oberlin College
Ohio Northern University
Ohio Wesleyan University
Otterbein University
University of Mount Union
Wilmington College
Wittenberg University

Oregon

George Fox University
Lewis & Clark College
Linfield College
Pacific University
Willamette University

Pennsylvania

Albright College
Allegheny College
Alvernia University
Arcadia University
Baptist Bible College of
Pennsylvania
Bryn Mawr College F
Cabrini College
Carnegie Mellon University
Cedar Crest College F
Chatham University F
DeSales University F
Dickinson College
Eastern University
Elizabethtown College
Franklin & Marshall College
Geneva College F
Gettysburg College
Grove City College
Gwynedd-Mercy College
Haverford College
Immaculata University
Juniata College
Keystone College
King's College
La Roche College F
Lancaster Bible College
Lebanon Valley College
Lycoming College
Marywood University
Messiah College
Misericordia University
Moravian College
Mount Aloysius College
Muhlenberg College
Neumann University
Penn State
Abington
Altoona
Berks
Erie, The Behrend College
Harrisburg
Philadelphia Biblical University
F
Rosemont College
St. Vincent College
Susquehanna University
Swarthmore College
Thiel College M
University of Pittsburgh
Bradford
Greensburg
University of Scranton
Ursinus College
Washington & Jefferson College
Waynesburg University
Westminster College

Wilkes University
York College of Pennsylvania

Rhode Island

Johnson & Wales University:
   Providence
Rhode Island College
Roger Williams University
Salve Regina University

Tennessee

Maryville College
Rhodes College
University of the South

Texas

Austin College
Concordia University Texas F
East Texas Baptist University
Hardin-Simmons University
Howard Payne University
LeTourneau University
Schreiner University
Southwestern University
Sul Ross State University
Texas Lutheran University
Trinity University
University of Mary Hardin-
   Baylor
University of Texas
   Dallas
   Tyler

Vermont

Castleton State College
Johnson State College
Lyndon State College
Middlebury College
Norwich University M

Virginia

Averett University
Bridgewater College
Christopher Newport University
Emory & Henry College
Ferrum College
Hampden-Sydney College M
Hollins University F
Lynchburg College
Mary Baldwin College F
Randolph College
Randolph-Macon College
Roanoke College
Shenandoah University
Sweet Briar College F
University of Mary Washington
Virginia Wesleyan College
Washington and Lee University

Washington

Pacific Lutheran University
University of Puget Sound
Whitman College
Whitworth University

West Virginia

Bethany College

Wisconsin

Beloit College
Carroll University
Carthage College
Concordia University Wisconsin
Edgewood College
Lakeland College
Lawrence University
Marian University
Milwaukee School of
   Engineering
Mount Mary College F
Ripon College
St. Norbert College
University of Wisconsin
   Eau Claire
   La Crosse
   Oshkosh
   River Falls F
   Stevens Point F
   Stout F
   Whitewater

Wisconsin Lutheran College

Track, indoor Division I

Alabama

Alabama Agricultural and
   Mechanical University
Alabama State University
Auburn University
Jacksonville State University F
Samford University
Troy University F
University of Alabama
University of Alabama
   Birmingham F
University of South Alabama

Arizona

Arizona State University
Northern Arizona University
University of Arizona

Arkansas

Arkansas State University
University of Arkansas
   Little Rock
   Pine Bluff
University of Central Arkansas

California

California Polytechnic State
   University: San Luis Obispo
   F
California State University
   Bakersfield
   Fresno F
   Fullerton F
   Long Beach
   Northridge
   Sacramento
Loyola Marymount University
St. Mary's College of California
   M
San Diego State University F
Stanford University
University of California
   Berkeley
   Davis F
   Irvine F
   Los Angeles
   Riverside
   Santa Barbara F
University of San Francisco
University of Southern
   California

Colorado

Colorado State University
United States Air Force
   Academy
University of Colorado
   Boulder
University of Northern Colorado

Connecticut

Central Connecticut State
   University
Quinnipiac University
Sacred Heart University
University of Connecticut
University of Hartford
Yale University

Delaware

Delaware State University
University of Delaware F

District of Columbia

American University
Georgetown University
Howard University

Florida

Bethune-Cookman University
Florida Agricultural and
   Mechanical University

Florida Atlantic University F
Florida International University
Florida State University
Jacksonville University F
University of Central Florida F
University of Florida
University of Miami
University of North Florida
University of South Florida

Georgia

Georgia Institute of Technology
Georgia Southern University F
Georgia State University
Kennesaw State University
Savannah State University
University of Georgia

Hawaii

University of Hawaii
   Manoa F

Idaho

Boise State University
Idaho State University
University of Idaho

Illinois

Bradley University F
Chicago State University
DePaul University
Eastern Illinois University
Illinois State University
Loyola University Chicago
Northern Illinois University F
Southern Illinois University
   Carbondale
Southern Illinois University
   Edwardsville
University of Illinois
   Chicago
   Urbana-Champaign
Western Illinois University

Indiana

Ball State University F
Butler University
Indiana State University
Indiana University
   Bloomington
Indiana University-Purdue
   University Fort Wayne F
Purdue University
University of Notre Dame
Valparaiso University

Iowa

Drake University
Iowa State University
University of Iowa
University of Northern Iowa

Kansas

Kansas State University
University of Kansas
Wichita State University

Kentucky

Eastern Kentucky University
Murray State University F
University of Kentucky
University of Louisville
Western Kentucky University

Louisiana

Grambling State University
Louisiana State University and
   Agricultural and Mechanical
   College
Louisiana Tech University
McNeese State University
Nicholls State University F
Northwestern State University
Southeastern Louisiana
   University
Southern University and
   Agricultural and Mechanical
   College
Tulane University F

University of Louisiana at
   Lafayette
University of Louisiana at
   Monroe

Maine

University of Maine

Maryland

Coppin State University
Loyola University Maryland F
Morgan State University
Mount St. Mary's University
Towson University F
United States Naval Academy
University of Maryland
   Baltimore County
   College Park
   Eastern Shore

Massachusetts

Boston College
Boston University
College of the Holy Cross
Harvard College
Northeastern University
University of Massachusetts
   Amherst

Michigan

Central Michigan University
Eastern Michigan University
Michigan State University
Oakland University
University of Detroit Mercy
University of Michigan
Western Michigan University F

Minnesota

University of Minnesota
   Twin Cities

Mississippi

Jackson State University
Mississippi State University
Mississippi Valley State
   University
University of Mississippi
University of Southern
   Mississippi

Missouri

Missouri State University F
Saint Louis University
Southeast Missouri State
   University
University of Missouri
   Columbia
   Kansas City

Montana

Montana State University
University of Montana

Nebraska

University of Nebraska
   Lincoln
   Omaha F

Nevada

University of Nevada
   Las Vegas F
   Reno F

New Hampshire

Dartmouth College
University of New Hampshire

New Jersey

Fairleigh Dickinson University
   Metropolitan Campus
Monmouth University
New Jersey Institute of
   Technology
Princeton University
Rider University
Rutgers, The State University of
   New Jersey
   New Brunswick/Piscataway
   Campus

Saint Peter's College

New Mexico

New Mexico State University F
University of New Mexico

New York

Barnard College F
Colgate University
Columbia University
Cornell University
Fordham University
Iona College
Long Island University
   Brooklyn Campus
Manhattan College
Marist College
St. Francis College
St. John's University F
SUNY
   University at Albany
   University at Binghamton
   University at Buffalo
   University at Stony Brook
Syracuse University
United States Military Academy
Wagner College

North Carolina

Appalachian State University
Campbell University
Davidson College
Duke University
East Carolina University
Elon University F
Gardner-Webb University
High Point University
North Carolina Agricultural and
   Technical State University
North Carolina Central
   University
North Carolina State University
University of North Carolina
   Asheville
   Chapel Hill
   Charlotte
   Greensboro M
   Wilmington
Wake Forest University
Western Carolina University

North Dakota

North Dakota State University
University of North Dakota

Ohio

Bowling Green State University
   F
Cleveland State University F
Kent State University
Miami University
   Oxford F
Ohio State University
   Columbus Campus
Ohio University F
University of Akron
University of Cincinnati
University of Dayton F
University of Toledo F
Wright State University F
Xavier University
Youngstown State University

Oklahoma

Oklahoma State University
Oral Roberts University
University of Oklahoma
University of Tulsa

Oregon

Oregon State University
Portland State University
University of Oregon
University of Portland

Pennsylvania

Bucknell University
Duquesne University F
La Salle University

Lafayette College
Lehigh University
Penn State
University Park
Robert Morris University
St. Francis University
Saint Joseph's University
Temple University
University of Pennsylvania
University of Pittsburgh
Villanova University

Rhode Island

Brown University
Bryant University
Providence College
University of Rhode Island

South Carolina

Charleston Southern University
The Citadel
Clemson University
Coastal Carolina University F
College of Charleston F
Furman University
South Carolina State University
University of South Carolina
Columbia
Upstate
Winthrop University
Wofford College

South Dakota

South Dakota State University
University of South Dakota

Tennessee

Austin Peay State University F
Belmont University
East Tennessee State University
Lipscomb University
Middle Tennessee State
University
Tennessee State University
Tennessee Technological
University F
University of Memphis
University of Tennessee
Chattanooga
Knoxville
Vanderbilt University F

Texas

Baylor University
Houston Baptist University
Lamar University
Prairie View A&M University
Rice University
Sam Houston State University
Southern Methodist University F
Stephen F. Austin State
University
Texas A&M University
Corpus Christi
Texas Christian University
Texas Southern University
Texas State University: San
Marcos
Texas Tech University
University of Houston
University of North Texas
University of Texas
Arlington
Austin
El Paso
Pan American
San Antonio

Utah

Brigham Young University
Southern Utah University
University of Utah F
Utah State University
Utah Valley University
Weber State University

Vermont

University of Vermont

Virginia

College of William and Mary
George Mason University
Hampton University
James Madison University F
Liberty University
Norfolk State University
Radford University
University of Richmond
University of Virginia
Virginia Commonwealth
University
Virginia Military Institute
Virginia Polytechnic Institute
and State University

Washington

Eastern Washington University
Gonzaga University
Seattle University
University of Washington
Washington State University

West Virginia

Marshall University F
West Virginia University F

Wisconsin

Marquette University
University of Wisconsin
Madison
Milwaukee

Wyoming

University of Wyoming

**Track, indoor
Division II**

Alabama

University of Alabama
Huntsville

Arizona

Grand Canyon University

Arkansas

Harding University

California

Academy of Art University
Azusa Pacific University
California Baptist University
California State University
Dominguez Hills F
Los Angeles F
Stanislaus F
San Francisco State University
F

Colorado

Adams State College
Colorado Mesa University
Colorado School of Mines
Colorado State University
Pueblo F
Metropolitan State College of
Denver
University of Colorado
Colorado Springs
Western State College of
Colorado

Connecticut

Southern Connecticut State
University
University of New Haven

District of Columbia

University of the District of
Columbia F

Georgia

Chorter University
Shorter University
Clayton State University

Idaho

Northwest Nazarene University

Illinois

Lewis University
McKendree University

Indiana

Saint Joseph's College
University of Indianapolis
University of Southern Indiana

Kansas

Emporia State University
Fort Hays State University
Pittsburg State University

Kentucky

Bellarmine University
Kentucky State University
Northern Kentucky University

Maryland

Bowie State University

Massachusetts

American International College
Assumption College
Bentley University
Merrimack College M
Stonehill College
University of Massachusetts
Lowell

Michigan

Ferris State University
Grand Valley State University
Hillsdale College
Lake Superior State University
Northern Michigan University F
Northwood University
Michigan
Saginaw Valley State University

Minnesota

Bemidji State University F
Concordia University St. Paul
Minnesota State University
Mankato
Moorhead
Saint Cloud State University
University of Minnesota
Duluth
Winona State University F

Missouri

Drury University
Lincoln University
Lindenwood University
Maryville University of Saint
Louis
Missouri Southern State
University
Missouri University of Science
and Technology
Northwest Missouri State
University
Southwest Baptist University
Truman State University
University of Central Missouri
William Jewell College

Montana

Montana State University
Billings

Nebraska

Chadron State College
University of Nebraska
Kearney
Wayne State College

New Jersey

Georgian Court University F

New Mexico

New Mexico Highlands
University F

New York

Adelphi University
City University of New York
Queens College
College of Saint Rose
Mercy College F
Molloy College
Roberts Wesleyan College
St. Thomas Aquinas College

North Carolina

Johnson C. Smith University
Lees-McRae College
Lenoir-Rhyne University
Livingstone College
Mars Hill College
Mount Olive College
Queens University of Charlotte
St. Augustine's College
Winston-Salem State University

North Dakota

Minot State University
University of Mary

Ohio

Ashland University
Cedarville University
Central State University
Lake Erie College
Malone University
Notre Dame College
Ohio Dominican University
Tiffin University
University of Findlay
Ursuline College F
Walsh University

Oklahoma

Southern Nazarene University
University of Central Oklahoma
F

Oregon

Western Oregon University

Pennsylvania

Bloomsburg University of
Pennsylvania
California University of
Pennsylvania
Cheyney University of
Pennsylvania
Clarion University of
Pennsylvania F
East Stroudsburg University of
Pennsylvania
Edinboro University of
Pennsylvania F
Indiana University of
Pennsylvania
Kutztown University of
Pennsylvania
Lock Haven University of
Pennsylvania
Mansfield University of
Pennsylvania
Millersville University of
Pennsylvania
Seton Hill University
Shippensburg University of
Pennsylvania
Slippery Rock University of
Pennsylvania
University of Pittsburgh
Johnstown F
West Chester University of
Pennsylvania

South Carolina

Anderson University
Benedict College

Claflin University
Limestone College

South Dakota

Augustana College
Black Hills State University
Northern State University
South Dakota School of Mines
and Technology
University of Sioux Falls

Tennessee

Carson-Newman College
King College

Texas

Abilene Christian University
Angelo State University F
Dallas Baptist University
McMurry University
Texas A&M University
Kingsville
University of the Incarnate
Word
West Texas A&M University

Virginia

Virginia State University
Virginia Union University

Washington

Saint Martin's University
Seattle Pacific University
Western Washington University

West Virginia

Alderson-Broaddus College
Concord University
Shepherd University F
West Virginia State University
Wheeling Jesuit University

Wisconsin

University of Wisconsin
Parkside

Canada

Simon Fraser University

**Track, indoor
Division III**

Alabama

Birmingham-Southern College

Arkansas

Hendrix College M

California

University of La Verne

Colorado

Colorado College F

Connecticut

Connecticut College
Eastern Connecticut State
University
Trinity College
United States Coast Guard
Academy
Wesleyan University

Delaware

Wesley College

District of Columbia

Catholic University of America

Georgia

Emory University

Illinois

Augustana College
Aurora University
Benedictine University
Concordia University Chicago
Elmhurst College
Greenville College

Illinois College
Illinois Wesleyan University
Knox College
Millikin University
Monmouth College
North Central College
North Park University
Principia College
Rockford College
University of Chicago
Wheaton College F

Indiana

Anderson University
DePauw University
Earlham College
Franklin College
Hanover College
Manchester College
Rose-Hulman Institute of
   Technology
Trine University
Wabash College M

Iowa

Buena Vista University
Central College
Coe College
Cornell College
Grinnell College
Loras College
Luther College
Northwestern College F
Simpson College
University of Dubuque
Wartburg College

Kentucky

Centre College
Spalding University
Transylvania University

Maine

Bates College
Bowdoin College
Colby College
University of Southern Maine

Maryland

Frostburg State University
Goucher College
Hood College
Johns Hopkins University
McDaniel College
Salisbury University
Stevenson University

Massachusetts

Amherst College
Brandeis University
Bridgewater State University
Emmanuel College
Fitchburg State University
Gordon College
Lasell College
Lesley University
Massachusetts Institute of
   Technology
Mount Holyoke College F
Regis College
Smith College F
Springfield College
Tufts University
University of Massachusetts
   Boston
   Dartmouth
Wellesley College F
Westfield State University
Wheaton College
Williams College
Worcester Polytechnic Institute
Worcester State University

Michigan

Adrian College
Albion College
Alma College
Calvin College
Olivet College M

Minnesota

Bethel University
Carleton College
College of St. Benedict F
College of St. Scholastica
Concordia College: Moorhead
Gustavus Adolphus College
Hamline University
Macalester College
North Central University M
Northwestern College M
St. Catherine University F
St. John's University M
St. Mary's University of
   Minnesota
St. Olaf College
University of Minnesota
   Morris
University of St. Thomas

Mississippi

Mississippi College

Missouri

Fontbonne University
Washington University in St.
   Louis

Nebraska

Nebraska Wesleyan University

New Hampshire

Keene State College
New England College M

New Jersey

The College of New Jersey
Montclair State University
Ramapo College of New Jersey
Richard Stockton College of
   New Jersey
Rowan University
Rutgers, The State University of
   New Jersey
      Camden Regional Campus
      Newark Regional Campus
Stevens Institute of Technology

New York

Alfred University
City University of New York
   City College
   Hunter College
   Lehman College
   Medgar Evers College
   York College
Hamilton College
Ithaca College
Manhattanville College
Mount Saint Mary College M
Nazareth College
New York University
Rensselaer Polytechnic Institute
Rochester Institute of
   Technology
St. John Fisher College
St. Joseph's College: Suffolk
   Campus
St. Lawrence University
SUNY
   College at Brockport
   College at Buffalo
   College at Cortland
   College at Fredonia
   College at Geneseo
   College at Oneonta
   College at Oswego
   College at Plattsburgh
   College of Agriculture and
      Technology at Cobleskill
   Farmindale State College
Union College
United States Merchant Marine
   Academy
University of Rochester
Utica College

North Carolina

Guilford College
Methodist University

Ohio

Baldwin-Wallace College
Bluffton University
Capital University
Case Western Reserve
   University
College of Mount St. Joseph
College of Wooster
Defiance College
Denison University
Heidelberg University
John Carroll University
Kenyon College
Marietta College
Muskingum University
Oberlin College
Ohio Northern University
Ohio Wesleyan University
Otterbein University
University of Mount Union
Wilmington College
Wittenberg University

Oregon

George Fox University F
Lewis & Clark College
Linfield College
Willamette University

Pennsylvania

Albright College
Allegheny College
Alvernia University
Bryn Mawr College F
Carnegie Mellon University
Delaware Valley College
DeSales University
Dickinson College
Elizabethtown College
Franklin & Marshall College
Geneva College
Gettysburg College
Gwynedd-Mercy College
Haverford College
Immaculata University
Juniata College
Keystone College
Lebanon Valley College
Messiah College
Misericordia University
Moravian College
Muhlenberg College
Neumann University M
Penn State
   Erie, The Behrend College
Susquehanna University
Swarthmore College
Thiel College
Ursinus College
Washington & Jefferson College
Waynesburg University
Westminster College
Widener University
York College of Pennsylvania

Rhode Island

Rhode Island College

Tennessee

Rhodes College
University of the South

Texas

Hardin-Simmons University
Texas Lutheran University F
Trinity University
University of Dallas M

Vermont

Middlebury College

Virginia

Bridgewater College
Christopher Newport University
Eastern Mennonite University
Lynchburg College
Roanoke College
Shenandoah University
University of Mary Washington
Virginia Wesleyan College
Washington and Lee University

Washington

University of Puget Sound
Whitworth University

West Virginia

Bethany College

Wisconsin

Beloit College
Carroll University
Carthage College
Concordia University Wisconsin
Edgewood College
Lakeland College
Lawrence University
Milwaukee School of
   Engineering
Ripon College
St. Norbert College
University of Wisconsin
   Eau Claire
   La Crosse
   Oshkosh
   Platteville
   River Falls
   Stevens Point
   Stout
   Superior
   Whitewater
Wisconsin Lutheran College

Track, outdoor Division I

Alabama

Alabama Agricultural and
   Mechanical University
Alabama State University
Auburn University
Jacksonville State University F
Samford University
Troy University
University of Alabama
University of Alabama
   Birmingham F
University of South Alabama

Arizona

Arizona State University
Northern Arizona University
University of Arizona

Arkansas

Arkansas State University
University of Arkansas
   Little Rock
   Pine Bluff
University of Central Arkansas

California

California Polytechnic State
   University: San Luis Obispo
California State University
   Bakersfield
   Fresno
   Fullerton
   Long Beach
   Northridge
   Sacramento
Loyola Marymount University
Pepperdine University
San Diego State University F
Santa Clara University
Stanford University
University of California
   Berkeley
   Davis
   Irvine
   Los Angeles
   Riverside
   Santa Barbara

University of San Diego F
University of San Francisco
University of Southern
   California

Colorado

Colorado State University
United States Air Force
   Academy
University of Colorado
   Boulder
University of Northern Colorado

Connecticut

Central Connecticut State
   University
Quinnipiac University F
Sacred Heart University
University of Connecticut
University of Hartford
Yale University

Delaware

Delaware State University
University of Delaware F

District of Columbia

American University
Georgetown University
Howard University

Florida

Bethune-Cookman University
Florida Agricultural and
   Mechanical University
Florida Atlantic University F
Florida International University
Florida State University
Jacksonville University F
University of Central Florida F
University of Florida
University of Miami
University of North Florida
University of South Florida

Georgia

Georgia Institute of Technology
Georgia Southern University F
Georgia State University
Kennesaw State University
Savannah State University
University of Georgia M

Hawaii

University of Hawaii
   Manoa F

Idaho

Boise State University
Idaho State University
University of Idaho

Illinois

Bradley University
Chicago State University
DePaul University
Eastern Illinois University
Illinois State University
Loyola University Chicago
Northern Illinois University F
Southern Illinois University
   Carbondale
Southern Illinois University
   Edwardsville
University of Illinois
   Chicago
   Urbana-Champaign
Western Illinois University

Indiana

Ball State University F
Butler University
Indiana State University
Indiana University
   Bloomington
Indiana University-Purdue
   University Fort Wayne F
Indiana University-Purdue
   University Indianapolis M
Purdue University

University of Notre Dame
Valparaiso University

Iowa

Drake University
Iowa State University
University of Iowa
University of Northern Iowa

Kansas

Kansas State University
University of Kansas
Wichita State University

Kentucky

Eastern Kentucky University
Morehead State University
Murray State University F
University of Kentucky
University of Louisville
Western Kentucky University

Louisiana

Grambling State University
Louisiana State University and
    Agricultural and Mechanical
    College
Louisiana Tech University
McNeese State University
Nicholls State University F
Northwestern State University
Southeastern Louisiana
    University
Southern University and
    Agricultural and Mechanical
    College
Tulane University
University of Louisiana at
    Lafayette
University of Louisiana at
    Monroe

Maine

University of Maine

Maryland

Coppin State University
Loyola University Maryland F
Morgan State University
Mount St. Mary's University
Towson University F
United States Naval Academy
University of Maryland
    Baltimore County
    College Park
    Eastern Shore

Massachusetts

Boston College
Boston University
College of the Holy Cross
Harvard College
Northeastern University
University of Massachusetts
    Amherst

Michigan

Central Michigan University
Eastern Michigan University
Michigan State University
Oakland University
University of Detroit Mercy
University of Michigan
Western Michigan University F

Minnesota

University of Minnesota
    Twin Cities

Mississippi

Alcorn State University
Jackson State University
Mississippi State University
Mississippi Valley State
    University
University of Mississippi
University of Southern
    Mississippi

Missouri

Missouri State University F
Saint Louis University
Southeast Missouri State
    University
University of Missouri
    Columbia
    Kansas City

Montana

Montana State University
University of Montana

Nebraska

University of Nebraska
    Lincoln
    Omaha F

Nevada

University of Nevada
    Las Vegas F
    Reno F

New Hampshire

Dartmouth College
University of New Hampshire

New Jersey

Fairleigh Dickinson University
    Metropolitan Campus
Monmouth University
New Jersey Institute of
    Technology
Princeton University
Rider University
Rutgers, The State University of
    New Jersey
    New Brunswick/Piscataway
        Campus
Saint Peter's College

New Mexico

New Mexico State University F
University of New Mexico

New York

Colgate University
Columbia University
Cornell University
Fordham University
Iona College
Long Island University
    Brooklyn Campus
Manhattan College
Marist College
St. Francis College
St. John's University F
SUNY
    University at Albany
    University at Binghamton
    University at Buffalo
    University at Stony Brook
Syracuse University
United States Military Academy
Wagner College

North Carolina

Appalachian State University
Campbell University
Davidson College
Duke University
East Carolina University
Elon University F
Gardner-Webb University
High Point University
North Carolina Agricultural and
    Technical State University
North Carolina Central
    University
North Carolina State University
University of North Carolina
    Asheville
    Chapel Hill
    Charlotte
    Greensboro
    Wilmington
Wake Forest University
Western Carolina University

North Dakota

North Dakota State University
University of North Dakota

Ohio

Bowling Green State University
    F
Cleveland State University F
Kent State University
Miami University
    Oxford
Ohio State University
    Columbus Campus
Ohio University F
University of Akron
University of Cincinnati
University of Dayton F
University of Toledo F
Wright State University F
Xavier University
Youngstown State University

Oklahoma

Oklahoma State University
Oral Roberts University
University of Oklahoma
University of Tulsa

Oregon

Oregon State University
Portland State University
University of Oregon
University of Portland

Pennsylvania

Bucknell University
Duquesne University
La Salle University
Lafayette College
Lehigh University
Penn State
    University Park
Robert Morris University
St. Francis University
Saint Joseph's University
Temple University
University of Pennsylvania
University of Pittsburgh
Villanova University

Rhode Island

Brown University
Bryant University M
Providence College
University of Rhode Island

South Carolina

Charleston Southern University
The Citadel
Clemson University
Coastal Carolina University
College of Charleston F
Furman University
South Carolina State University
University of South Carolina
    Columbia
    Upstate
Winthrop University
Wofford College

South Dakota

South Dakota State University
University of South Dakota

Tennessee

Austin Peay State University F
Belmont University
East Tennessee State University
Lipscomb University
Middle Tennessee State
    University
Tennessee State University
Tennessee Technological
    University F
University of Memphis
University of Tennessee
    Chattanooga
    Knoxville
Vanderbilt University F

Texas

Baylor University
Houston Baptist University
Lamar University
Prairie View A&M University
Rice University
Sam Houston State University
Southern Methodist University F
Stephen F. Austin State
    University
Texas A&M University
    Corpus Christi
Texas Christian University
Texas Southern University
Texas State University: San
    Marcos
Texas Tech University
University of Houston
University of North Texas
University of Texas
    Arlington
    Austin
    El Paso
    Pan American
    San Antonio

Utah

Brigham Young University
Southern Utah University
University of Utah F
Utah State University
Utah Valley University
Weber State University

Vermont

University of Vermont

Virginia

College of William and Mary
George Mason University
Hampton University
James Madison University F
Liberty University
Norfolk State University
Radford University
University of Richmond
University of Virginia
Virginia Commonwealth
    University
Virginia Military Institute
Virginia Polytechnic Institute
    and State University

Washington

Eastern Washington University
Gonzaga University
Seattle University
University of Washington
Washington State University

West Virginia

Marshall University F
West Virginia University F

Wisconsin

Marquette University
University of Wisconsin
    Madison
    Milwaukee

Wyoming

University of Wyoming

Track, outdoor Division II

Alabama

Miles College
Stillman College
Tuskegee University
University of Alabama
    Huntsville

Alaska

University of Alaska
    Anchorage

Arizona

Grand Canyon University

Arkansas

Harding University

California

Academy of Art University
Azusa Pacific University
California Baptist University
California State Polytechnic
    University: Pomona
California State University
    Chico
    Dominguez Hills F
    East Bay
    Los Angeles
    Stanislaus
Fresno Pacific University
Humboldt State University
Point Loma Nazarene University
San Francisco State University
    F
University of California
    San Diego

Colorado

Adams State College
Colorado Mesa University
Colorado School of Mines
Colorado State University
    Pueblo F
Metropolitan State College of
    Denver
University of Colorado
    Colorado Springs
Western State College of
    Colorado

Connecticut

Southern Connecticut State
    University
University of New Haven

District of Columbia

University of the District of
    Columbia F

Florida

Florida Institute of Technology
Florida Southern College
Nova Southeastern University
University of Tampa

Georgia

Albany State University
Chorter University
    Shorter University
Clark Atlanta University
Clayton State University
Columbus State University
Fort Valley State University
Morehouse College M
Paine College

Idaho

Northwest Nazarene University

Illinois

Lewis University
McKendree University M

Indiana

Saint Joseph's College
University of Indianapolis
University of Southern Indiana

Kansas

Emporia State University
Fort Hays State University
Pittsburg State University

Kentucky

Bellarmine University
Kentucky State University
Northern Kentucky University

Maryland

Bowie State University
Washington Adventist
University

Massachusetts

American International College
Assumption College
Bentley University
Merrimack College
Stonehill College
University of Massachusetts
Lowell

Michigan

Ferris State University
Grand Valley State University
Hillsdale College
Lake Superior State University
Michigan Technological
University
Northern Michigan University F
Northwood University
Michigan
Saginaw Valley State University

Minnesota

Bemidji State University F
Concordia University St. Paul
Minnesota State University
Mankato
Moorhead
Saint Cloud State University
University of Minnesota
Duluth
Winona State University F

Missouri

Drury University
Lincoln University
Lindenwood University
Maryville University of Saint
Louis
Missouri Southern State
University
Missouri University of Science
and Technology
Northwest Missouri State
University
Southwest Baptist University
Truman State University
University of Central Missouri
William Jewell College

Montana

Montana State University
Billings

Nebraska

Chadron State College
University of Nebraska
Kearney
Wayne State College

New Jersey

Caldwell College F
Georgian Court University F

New Mexico

Eastern New Mexico University
New Mexico Highlands
University F

New York

Adelphi University
City University of New York
Queens College
College of Saint Rose
Dominican College of Blauvelt
F
Molloy College
Pace University
Roberts Wesleyan College
St. Thomas Aquinas College

North Carolina

Barton College
Belmont Abbey College
Brevard College

Johnson C. Smith University
Lees-McRae College
Lenoir-Rhyne University
Livingstone College
Mars Hill College
Mount Olive College
Queens University of Charlotte
St. Augustine's College
Shaw University
University of North Carolina
Pembroke
Wingate University
Winston-Salem State University

North Dakota

Minot State University
University of Mary

Ohio

Ashland University
Cedarville University
Central State University
Lake Erie College
Malone University
Notre Dame College
Ohio Dominican University
Tiffin University
University of Findlay
Ursuline College F
Walsh University

Oklahoma

Southern Nazarene University
University of Central Oklahoma
F

Oregon

Western Oregon University

Pennsylvania

Bloomsburg University of
Pennsylvania
California University of
Pennsylvania
Cheyney University of
Pennsylvania
Clarion University of
Pennsylvania F
East Stroudsburg University of
Pennsylvania
Edinboro University of
Pennsylvania
Indiana University of
Pennsylvania
Kutztown University of
Pennsylvania
Lock Haven University of
Pennsylvania
Mansfield University of
Pennsylvania
Millersville University of
Pennsylvania
Philadelphia University
Seton Hill University
Shippensburg University of
Pennsylvania
Slippery Rock University of
Pennsylvania
University of Pittsburgh
Johnstown F
West Chester University of
Pennsylvania

Puerto Rico

University of Puerto Rico
Bayamon University
College
Mayaguez
Rio Piedras

Rhode Island

Bryant University F

South Carolina

Anderson University M
Benedict College
Claflin University
Francis Marion University

Limestone College
North Greenville University

South Dakota

Augustana College
Black Hills State University
Northern State University
South Dakota School of Mines
and Technology
University of Sioux Falls

Tennessee

Carson-Newman College
King College
Lane College

Texas

Abilene Christian University
Angelo State University
Dallas Baptist University
McMurry University
Tarleton State University
Texas A&M University
Commerce
Kingsville
University of the Incarnate
Word
West Texas A&M University

Virginia

Virginia State University
Virginia Union University

Washington

Saint Martin's University
Seattle Pacific University
Western Washington University

West Virginia

Alderson-Broaddus College
Concord University
Glenville State College
University of Charleston F
West Liberty University
West Virginia State University
West Virginia Wesleyan College
Wheeling Jesuit University

Wisconsin

University of Wisconsin
Parkside

Canada

Simon Fraser University

Track, outdoor Division III

Alabama

Birmingham-Southern College
Huntingdon College F

Arkansas

Hendrix College

California

California Institute of
Technology
California Lutheran University
Chapman University F
Claremont McKenna College
Mills College F
Occidental College
Pitzer College M
Pomona College
University of La Verne
University of Redlands
Whittier College

Colorado

Colorado College

Connecticut

Connecticut College
Eastern Connecticut State
University
Trinity College

United States Coast Guard
Academy
Wesleyan University

Delaware

Wesley College

District of Columbia

Catholic University of America
Gallaudet University

Georgia

Berry College
Emory University
Oglethorpe University

Illinois

Augustana College
Aurora University
Benedictine University
Concordia University Chicago
Elmhurst College
Eureka College
Greenville College
Illinois College
Illinois Wesleyan University
Knox College
Millikin University
Monmouth College
North Central College
North Park University
Principia College
Rockford College
University of Chicago
Wheaton College

Indiana

Anderson University
DePauw University
Earlham College
Franklin College
Hanover College
Manchester College
Rose-Hulman Institute of
Technology
Trine University
Wabash College M

Iowa

Buena Vista University
Central College
Coe College
Cornell College
Grinnell College
Loras College
Luther College
Simpson College
University of Dubuque
Wartburg College

Kentucky

Centre College
Spalding University
Thomas More College
Transylvania University

Maine

Bates College
Bowdoin College
Colby College
Saint Joseph's College of Maine
M
University of Southern Maine

Maryland

Frostburg State University
Goucher College
Hood College
Johns Hopkins University
McDaniel College
Salisbury University
Stevenson University M

Massachusetts

Amherst College
Babson College
Brandeis University
Bridgewater State University
Emmanuel College
Fitchburg State University

Gordon College
Lesley University
Massachusetts Institute of
Technology
Mount Holyoke College F
Regis College
Salem State University F
Smith College F
Springfield College
Tufts University
University of Massachusetts
Boston
Dartmouth
Wellesley College F
Westfield State University
Wheaton College
Williams College
Worcester Polytechnic Institute
Worcester State University

Michigan

Adrian College
Albion College
Alma College
Calvin College
Hope College
Olivet College

Minnesota

Bethel University
Carleton College
College of St. Benedict F
College of St. Scholastica
Concordia College: Moorhead
Gustavus Adolphus College
Hamline University
Macalester College
Martin Luther College
North Central University
Northwestern College
St. Catherine University F
St. John's University M
St. Mary's University of
Minnesota
St. Olaf College
University of Minnesota
Morris
University of St. Thomas

Mississippi

Millsaps College
Mississippi College
Rust College

Missouri

Fontbonne University
Washington University in St.
Louis
Webster University

Nebraska

Nebraska Wesleyan University

New Hampshire

Colby-Sawyer College
Keene State College
New England College

New Jersey

The College of New Jersey
Montclair State University
Ramapo College of New Jersey
Richard Stockton College of
New Jersey
Rowan University
Rutgers, The State University of
New Jersey
Camden Regional Campus
Newark Regional Campus
Stevens Institute of Technology

New York

Alfred University
Bard College
City University of New York
City College
Hunter College
Lehman College
Medgar Evers College
York College

Hamilton College
Ithaca College
Manhattanville College
Mount Saint Mary College F
Nazareth College
New York University
Rensselaer Polytechnic Institute
Rochester Institute of
Technology
St. John Fisher College
St. Joseph's College: Suffolk
Campus
St. Lawrence University
SUNY
College at Brockport
College at Buffalo
College at Cortland
College at Fredonia
College at Geneseo
College at Oneonta
College at Oswego
College at Plattsburgh
College of Agriculture and
Technology at Cobleskill
Farmindale State College
Union College
United States Merchant Marine
Academy
University of Rochester
Utica College
Vassar College

North Carolina

Guilford College
Methodist University

Ohio

Baldwin-Wallace College
Bluffton University
Capital University
Case Western Reserve
University
College of Mount St. Joseph
College of Wooster
Defiance College
Denison University
Franciscan University of
Steubenville
Heidelberg University
John Carroll University
Kenyon College
Marietta College
Muskingum University
Oberlin College
Ohio Northern University
Ohio Wesleyan University
Otterbein University
University of Mount Union
Wilmington College
Wittenberg University

Oregon

George Fox University
Lewis & Clark College
Linfield College
Pacific University
Willamette University

Pennsylvania

Albright College
Allegheny College
Alvernia University
Bryn Mawr College F
Carnegie Mellon University
Delaware Valley College
DeSales University
Dickinson College
Elizabethtown College
Franklin & Marshall College
Geneva College
Gettysburg College
Grove City College
Gwynedd-Mercy College
Haverford College
Immaculata University
Juniata College
Keystone College
Lebanon Valley College

Messiah College
Misericordia University
Moravian College
Muhlenberg College
Neumann University
Penn State
Erie, The Behrend College
St. Vincent College M
Susquehanna University
Swarthmore College
Thiel College
Ursinus College
Washington & Jefferson College
Waynesburg University
Westminster College
Widener University
York College of Pennsylvania

Rhode Island

Rhode Island College
Roger Williams University
Salve Regina University F

Tennessee

Rhodes College
University of the South

Texas

Concordia University Texas
Hardin-Simmons University
Southwestern University
Sul Ross State University
Texas Lutheran University F
Trinity University
University of Dallas
University of Texas
Tyler

Vermont

Middlebury College

Virginia

Bridgewater College
Christopher Newport University
Eastern Mennonite University
Lynchburg College
Roanoke College
Shenandoah University
University of Mary Washington
Virginia Wesleyan College
Washington and Lee University

Washington

Pacific Lutheran University
University of Puget Sound
Whitworth University

West Virginia

Bethany College

Wisconsin

Beloit College
Carroll University
Carthage College
Concordia University Wisconsin
Edgewood College
Lakeland College
Lawrence University
Milwaukee School of
Engineering
Ripon College
St. Norbert College
University of Wisconsin
Eau Claire
La Crosse
Oshkosh
Platteville
River Falls
Stevens Point
Stout
Superior
Whitewater
Wisconsin Lutheran College

Volleyball Division I

Alabama

Alabama Agricultural and
Mechanical University F

Alabama State University F
Auburn University F
Jacksonville State University F
Samford University F
Troy University F
University of Alabama F
University of Alabama
Birmingham F
University of South Alabama F

Arizona

Arizona State University F
Northern Arizona University F
University of Arizona F

Arkansas

Arkansas State University F
University of Arkansas F
Little Rock F
Pine Bluff F
University of Central Arkansas
F

California

California Polytechnic State
University: San Luis Obispo
F
California State University
Bakersfield F
Fresno F
Fullerton F
Long Beach F
Northridge F
Sacramento F
Loyola Marymount University F
Pepperdine University F
St. Mary's College of California
F
San Diego State University F
San Jose State University F
Santa Clara University F
Stanford University F
University of California
Berkeley F
Davis F
Irvine F
Los Angeles F
Riverside F
Santa Barbara F
University of San Diego F
University of San Francisco F
University of Southern
California F
University of the Pacific F

Colorado

Colorado State University F
United States Air Force
Academy F
University of Colorado
Boulder F
University of Denver F
University of Northern Colorado
F

Connecticut

Central Connecticut State
University F
Fairfield University F
Quinnipiac University F
Sacred Heart University F
University of Connecticut F
University of Hartford F
Yale University F

Delaware

Delaware State University F
University of Delaware F

District of Columbia

American University F
George Washington University
F
Georgetown University F
Howard University F

Florida

Bethune-Cookman University F
Florida Agricultural and
Mechanical University F
Florida Atlantic University F
Florida Gulf Coast University F
Florida International University
F
Florida State University F
Jacksonville University F
Stetson University F
University of Central Florida F
University of Florida F
University of Miami F
University of North Florida F
University of South Florida F

Georgia

Georgia Institute of Technology
F
Georgia Southern University F
Georgia State University F
Kennesaw State University F
Mercer University F
Savannah State University F
University of Georgia F

Hawaii

University of Hawaii
Manoa F

Idaho

Boise State University F
Idaho State University F
University of Idaho F

Illinois

Bradley University F
Chicago State University F
DePaul University F
Eastern Illinois University F
Illinois State University F
Loyola University Chicago F
Northern Illinois University F
Northwestern University F
Southern Illinois University
Carbondale F
Southern Illinois University
Edwardsville F
University of Illinois
Chicago F
Urbana-Champaign F
Western Illinois University F

Indiana

Ball State University F
Butler University F
Indiana State University F
Indiana University
Bloomington F
Indiana University-Purdue
University Fort Wayne F
Indiana University-Purdue
University Indianapolis F
Purdue University F
University of Evansville F
University of Notre Dame F
Valparaiso University F

Iowa

Drake University F
Iowa State University F
University of Iowa F
University of Northern Iowa F

Kansas

Kansas State University F
University of Kansas F
Wichita State University F

Kentucky

Eastern Kentucky University F
Morehead State University F
Murray State University F
University of Kentucky F
University of Louisville F
Western Kentucky University F

Louisiana

Grambling State University F
Louisiana State University and
Agricultural and Mechanical
College F
Louisiana Tech University F
McNeese State University F
Nicholls State University F
Northwestern State University F
Southeastern Louisiana
University F
Southern University and
Agricultural and Mechanical
College F
Tulane University F
University of Louisiana at
Lafayette F
University of Louisiana at
Monroe F

Maine

University of Maine F

Maryland

Coppin State University F
Loyola University Maryland F
Morgan State University F
Towson University F
United States Naval Academy F
University of Maryland
Baltimore County F
College Park F
Eastern Shore F

Massachusetts

Boston College F
College of the Holy Cross F
Harvard College F
Northeastern University F

Michigan

Central Michigan University F
Eastern Michigan University F
Michigan State University F
Oakland University F
University of Michigan F
Western Michigan University F

Minnesota

University of Minnesota
Twin Cities F

Mississippi

Alcorn State University F
Jackson State University F
Mississippi State University F
Mississippi Valley State
University F
University of Mississippi F
University of Southern
Mississippi F

Missouri

Missouri State University F
Saint Louis University F
Southeast Missouri State
University F
University of Missouri
Columbia F
Kansas City F

Montana

Montana State University F
University of Montana F

Nebraska

Creighton University F
University of Nebraska
Lincoln F
Omaha F

Nevada

University of Nevada
Las Vegas F
Reno F

New Hampshire

Dartmouth College F
University of New Hampshire F

New Jersey

Fairleigh Dickinson University
Metropolitan Campus F
New Jersey Institute of
Technology F
Princeton University F
Rider University F
Rutgers, The State University of
New Jersey
New Brunswick/Piscataway
Campus F
Saint Peter's College F
Seton Hall University F

New Mexico

New Mexico State University F
University of New Mexico F

New York

Barnard College F
Canisius College F
Colgate University F
Columbia University F
Cornell University F
Fordham University F
Hofstra University F
Iona College F
Long Island University
Brooklyn Campus F
Manhattan College F
Marist College F
Niagara University F
St. Francis College F
St. John's University F
Siena College F
SUNY
University at Albany F
University at Binghamton F
University at Buffalo F
University at Stony Brook F
Syracuse University F
United States Military Academy
F

North Carolina

Appalachian State University F
Campbell University F
Davidson College F
Duke University F
East Carolina University F
Elon University F
Gardner-Webb University F
High Point University F
North Carolina Agricultural and
Technical State University F
North Carolina Central
University F
North Carolina State University
F
University of North Carolina
Asheville F
Chapel Hill F
Charlotte F
Greensboro F
Wilmington F
Wake Forest University F
Western Carolina University F

North Dakota

North Dakota State University F
University of North Dakota F

Ohio

Bowling Green State University
F
Cleveland State University F
Kent State University F
Miami University
Oxford F
Ohio State University
Columbus Campus F
Ohio University F
University of Akron F
University of Cincinnati F
University of Dayton F
University of Toledo F
Wright State University F

Xavier University F
Youngstown State University F

Oklahoma

Oral Roberts University F
University of Oklahoma F
University of Tulsa F

Oregon

Oregon State University F
Portland State University F
University of Oregon F
University of Portland F

Pennsylvania

Bucknell University F
Duquesne University F
La Salle University F
Lafayette College F
Lehigh University F
Penn State
University Park F
Robert Morris University F
St. Francis University F
Temple University F
University of Pennsylvania F
University of Pittsburgh F
Villanova University F

Rhode Island

Brown University F
Bryant University F
Providence College F
University of Rhode Island F

South Carolina

Charleston Southern University
F
The Citadel F
Clemson University F
Coastal Carolina University F
College of Charleston F
Furman University F
Presbyterian College F
South Carolina State University
F
University of South Carolina
Columbia F
Upstate F
Winthrop University F
Wofford College F

South Dakota

South Dakota State University F
University of South Dakota F

Tennessee

Austin Peay State University F
Belmont University F
East Tennessee State University
F
Lipscomb University F
Middle Tennessee State
University F
Tennessee State University F
Tennessee Technological
University F
University of Memphis F
University of Tennessee
Chattanooga F
Knoxville F
Martin F

Texas

Baylor University F
Houston Baptist University F
Lamar University F
Prairie View A&M University F
Rice University F
Sam Houston State University F
Southern Methodist University F
Stephen F. Austin State
University F
Texas A&M University F
Corpus Christi F
Texas Christian University F
Texas Southern University F
Texas State University: San
Marcos F

Texas Tech University F
University of Houston F
University of North Texas F
University of Texas
Arlington F
Austin F
El Paso F
Pan American F
San Antonio F

Utah

Brigham Young University F
Southern Utah University F
University of Utah F
Utah State University F
Utah Valley University F
Weber State University F

Virginia

College of William and Mary F
George Mason University F
Hampton University F
James Madison University F
Liberty University F
Norfolk State University F
Radford University F
University of Virginia F
Virginia Commonwealth
University F
Virginia Polytechnic Institute
and State University F

Washington

Eastern Washington University
F
Gonzaga University F
Seattle University F
University of Washington F
Washington State University F

West Virginia

Marshall University F
West Virginia University F

Wisconsin

Marquette University F
University of Wisconsin
Green Bay F
Madison F
Milwaukee F

Wyoming

University of Wyoming F

| **Volleyball Division II** |

Alabama

Miles College F
Stillman College F
Tuskegee University F
University of Alabama
Huntsville F
University of Montevallo F
University of North Alabama F
University of West Alabama F

Alaska

University of Alaska
Anchorage F
Fairbanks F

Arizona

Grand Canyon University F

Arkansas

Arkansas Tech University F
Harding University F
Henderson State University F
Ouachita Baptist University F
Southern Arkansas University F
University of Arkansas
Fort Smith F
Monticello F

California

Academy of Art University F
Azusa Pacific University F

California Baptist University F
California State Polytechnic
University: Pomona F
California State University
Chico F
Dominguez Hills F
East Bay F
Los Angeles F
Monterey Bay F
San Bernardino F
Stanislaus F
Dominican University of
California F
Fresno Pacific University F
Humboldt State University F
Notre Dame de Namur
University F
Point Loma Nazarene
University F
San Francisco State University
F
Sonoma State University F
University of California
San Diego F

Colorado

Adams State College F
Colorado Christian University F
Colorado Mesa University F
Colorado School of Mines F
Colorado State University
Pueblo F
Fort Lewis College F
Metropolitan State College of
Denver F
Regis University F
University of Colorado
Colorado Springs F
Western State College of
Colorado F

Connecticut

Post University F
Southern Connecticut State
University F
University of Bridgeport F
University of New Haven F

Delaware

Goldey-Beacom College F
Wilmington University F

District of Columbia

University of the District of
Columbia F

Florida

Barry University F
Eckerd College F
Flagler College F
Florida Institute of Technology
F
Florida Southern College F
Lynn University F
Nova Southeastern University F
Palm Beach Atlantic University
F
Rollins College F
Saint Leo University F
University of Tampa F
University of West Florida F

Georgia

Albany State University F
Armstrong Atlantic State
University F
Augusta State University F
Chorter University
Shorter University F
Clark Atlanta University F
Fort Valley State University F
Paine College F
University of West Georgia F
Valdosta State University F

Hawaii

Brigham Young University-
Hawaii F

Chaminade University of
Honolulu F
Hawaii Pacific University F
University of Hawaii
Hilo F

Idaho

Northwest Nazarene University
F

Illinois

Lewis University F
McKendree University F
Quincy University F
University of Illinois
Springfield F

Indiana

Oakland City University F
Saint Joseph's College F
University of Indianapolis F
University of Southern Indiana
F

Iowa

Upper Iowa University F

Kansas

Emporia State University F
Fort Hays State University F
Newman University F
Pittsburg State University F
Washburn University F

Kentucky

Bellarmine University F
Kentucky State University F
Northern Kentucky University F

Louisiana

University of New Orleans F

Maryland

Bowie State University F
Washington Adventist
University F

Massachusetts

American International College
F
Assumption College F
Bentley University F
Merrimack College F
Stonehill College F
University of Massachusetts
Lowell F

Michigan

Ferris State University F
Grand Valley State University F
Hillsdale College F
Lake Superior State University
F
Michigan Technological
University F
Northern Michigan University F
Northwood University
Michigan F
Saginaw Valley State University
F
Wayne State University F

Minnesota

Bemidji State University F
Concordia University St. Paul F
Minnesota State University
Mankato F
Moorhead F
Saint Cloud State University F
Southwest Minnesota State
University F
University of Minnesota
Crookston F
Duluth F
Winona State University F

Missouri

Drury University F
Lindenwood University F

Maryville University of Saint
  Louis F
Missouri Southern State
  University F
Missouri University of Science
  and Technology F
Missouri Western State
  University F
Northwest Missouri State
  University F
Rockhurst University F
Southwest Baptist University F
Truman State University F
University of Central Missouri F
University of Missouri
  St. Louis F
William Jewell College F

Montana

Montana State University
  Billings F

Nebraska

Chadron State College F
University of Nebraska
  Kearney F
Wayne State College F

New Hampshire

Franklin Pierce University F
Saint Anselm College F
Southern New Hampshire
  University F

New Jersey

Bloomfield College F
Caldwell College F
Felician College F
Georgian Court University F

New Mexico

Eastern New Mexico University
  F
New Mexico Highlands
  University F

New York

Adelphi University F
City University of New York
  Queens College F
College of Saint Rose F
Concordia College F
Dominican College of Blauvelt
  F
Dowling College F
Le Moyne College F
Long Island University
  C. W. Post Campus F
Mercy College F
Molloy College F
New York Institute of
  Technology F
Nyack College F
Pace University F
Roberts Wesleyan College F

North Carolina

Barton College F
Belmont Abbey College F
Brevard College F
Catawba College F
Chowan University F
Elizabeth City State University
  F
Fayetteville State University F
Johnson C. Smith University F
Lees-McRae College F
Lenoir-Rhyne University F
Livingstone College F
Mars Hill College F
Mount Olive College F
Pfeiffer University F
Queens University of Charlotte
  F
St. Augustine's College F
Shaw University F
University of North Carolina
  Pembroke F
Wingate University F

Winston-Salem State University
  F

North Dakota

Minot State University F
University of Mary F

Ohio

Ashland University F
Cedarville University F
Central State University F
Lake Erie College F
Malone University F
Notre Dame College F
Ohio Dominican University F
Tiffin University F
University of Findlay F
Ursuline College F
Walsh University F

Oklahoma

Cameron University F
East Central University F
Oklahoma Panhandle State
  University F
Southeastern Oklahoma State
  University F
Southern Nazarene University F
Southwestern Oklahoma State
  University F
University of Central Oklahoma
  F

Oregon

Western Oregon University F

Pennsylvania

California University of
  Pennsylvania F
Chestnut Hill College F
Cheyney University of
  Pennsylvania F
Clarion University of
  Pennsylvania F
East Stroudsburg University of
  Pennsylvania F
Edinboro University of
  Pennsylvania F
Gannon University F
Holy Family University F
Indiana University of
  Pennsylvania F
Kutztown University of
  Pennsylvania F
Lock Haven University of
  Pennsylvania F
Mercyhurst University F
Millersville University of
  Pennsylvania F
Philadelphia University F
Seton Hill University F
Shippensburg University of
  Pennsylvania F
Slippery Rock University of
  Pennsylvania F
University of Pittsburgh
  Johnstown F
University of the Sciences in
  Philadelphia F
West Chester University of
  Pennsylvania F

Puerto Rico

University of Puerto Rico
  Bayamon University
    College F
  Mayaguez F
  Rio Piedras F

South Carolina

Anderson University F
Benedict College F
Claflin University F
Coker College F
Converse College F
Erskine College F
Francis Marion University F
Lander University F
Limestone College F

Newberry College F
North Greenville University F
University of South Carolina
  Aiken F

South Dakota

Augustana College F
Black Hills State University F
Northern State University F
South Dakota School of Mines
  and Technology F
University of Sioux Falls F

Tennessee

Carson-Newman College F
Christian Brothers University F
King College F
Lane College F
LeMoyne-Owen College F
Lincoln Memorial University F
Trevecca Nazarene University F
Tusculum College F
Union University F

Texas

Abilene Christian University F
Angelo State University F
Dallas Baptist University F
McMurry University F
Midwestern State University F
St. Edward's University F
St. Mary's University F
Tarleton State University F
Texas A&M International
  University F
Texas A&M University
  Commerce F
  Kingsville F
Texas Woman's University F
University of Texas
  of the Permian Basin F
University of the Incarnate
  Word F
West Texas A&M University F

Utah

Dixie State College F

Vermont

St. Michael's College F

Virginia

Virginia State University F
Virginia Union University F

Washington

Saint Martin's University F
Seattle Pacific University F
Western Washington University
  F

West Virginia

Alderson-Broaddus College F
Bluefield State College F
Concord University F
Davis and Elkins College F
Fairmont State University F
Glenville State College F
Ohio Valley University F
Shepherd University F
University of Charleston F
West Liberty University F
West Virginia State University
  F
West Virginia Wesleyan
  College F
Wheeling Jesuit University F

Wisconsin

University of Wisconsin
  Parkside F

Canada

Simon Fraser University F

Volleyball Division III

Alabama

Birmingham-Southern College F
Huntingdon College F

Arkansas

Hendrix College F

California

California Institute of
  Technology F
California Lutheran University F
Chapman University F
Claremont McKenna College F
Mills College F
Occidental College F
Pomona College F
University of California
  Santa Cruz F
University of La Verne F
University of Redlands F
Whittier College F

Colorado

Colorado College F

Connecticut

Albertus Magnus College F
Connecticut College F
Eastern Connecticut State
  University F
Mitchell College F
Saint Joseph College F
Trinity College F
United States Coast Guard
  Academy F
Wesleyan University F
Western Connecticut State
  University F

Delaware

Wesley College F

District of Columbia

Catholic University of America
  F
Gallaudet University F
Trinity Washington University F

Georgia

Agnes Scott College F
Berry College F
Covenant College F
Emory University F
LaGrange College F
Oglethorpe University F
Piedmont College F
Spelman College F

Illinois

Augustana College F
Aurora University F
Benedictine University F
Blackburn College F
Concordia University Chicago F
Dominican University F
Elmhurst College F
Eureka College F
Greenville College F
Illinois College F
Illinois Wesleyan University F
Knox College F
Lake Forest College F
MacMurray College F
Millikin University F
Monmouth College F
North Central College F
North Park University F
Principia College F
Rockford College F
University of Chicago F
Wheaton College F

Indiana

Anderson University F
DePauw University F
Earlham College F
Franklin College F
Hanover College F
Manchester College F
Rose-Hulman Institute of
  Technology F
Saint Mary's College F
Trine University F

Iowa

Buena Vista University F
Central College F
Coe College F
Cornell College F
Grinnell College F
Loras College F
Luther College F
Simpson College F
University of Dubuque F
Wartburg College F

Kentucky

Centre College F
Kentucky Wesleyan College F
Spalding University F
Thomas More College F
Transylvania University F

Louisiana

Centenary College of Louisiana
  F

Maine

Bates College F
Bowdoin College F
Colby College F
Husson University F
Maine Maritime Academy F
Saint Joseph's College of Maine
  F
University of Maine
  Farmington F
  Presque Isle F
University of New England F
University of Southern Maine F

Maryland

Frostburg State University F
Goucher College F
Hood College F
Johns Hopkins University F
McDaniel College F
Notre Dame of Maryland
  University F
St. Mary's College of Maryland
  F
Salisbury University F
Stevenson University F
Washington College F

Massachusetts

Amherst College F
Anna Maria College F
Babson College F
Bay Path College F
Becker College F
Brandeis University F
Bridgewater State University F
Clark University F
Curry College F
Eastern Nazarene College F
Elms College F
Emerson College F
Emmanuel College F
Endicott College F
Framingham State University F
Gordon College F
Lasell College F
Lesley University F
Massachusetts College of
  Liberal Arts F
Massachusetts Institute of
  Technology F
Massachusetts Maritime
  Academy F
Mount Holyoke College F
Mount Ida College F
Newbury College F
Pine Manor College F
Regis College F
Salem State University F
Simmons College F
Smith College F
Springfield College F
Suffolk University F
Tufts University F

University of Massachusetts
 Boston F
 Dartmouth F
Wellesley College F
Wentworth Institute of
 Technology F
Western New England
 University F
Westfield State University F
Wheaton College F
Williams College F
Worcester Polytechnic Institute
 F
Worcester State University F

Michigan

Adrian College F
Albion College F
Alma College F
Calvin College F
Finlandia University F
Hope College F
Kalamazoo College F
Olivet College F

Minnesota

Bethany Lutheran College F
Bethel University F
Carleton College F
College of St. Benedict F
College of St. Scholastica F
Concordia College: Moorhead F
Crown College F
Gustavus Adolphus College F
Hamline University F
Macalester College F
Martin Luther College F
North Central University F
Northwestern College F
St. Catherine University F
St. Mary's University of
 Minnesota F
St. Olaf College F
University of Minnesota
 Morris F
University of St. Thomas F

Mississippi

Millsaps College F
Mississippi College F
Rust College F

Missouri

Fontbonne University F
Washington University in St.
 Louis F
Webster University F
Westminster College F

Nebraska

Nebraska Wesleyan University
 F

New Hampshire

Colby-Sawyer College F
Daniel Webster College F
Keene State College F
Plymouth State University F
Rivier College F

New Jersey

Centenary College F
College of St. Elizabeth F
Fairleigh Dickinson University
 College at Florham F
Kean University F
Montclair State University F
New Jersey City University F
Ramapo College of New Jersey
 F
Richard Stockton College of
 New Jersey F
Rowan University F
Rutgers, The State University of
 New Jersey
 Camden Regional Campus
 F
 Newark Regional Campus F

Stevens Institute of Technology
 F
William Paterson University of
 New Jersey F

New York

Alfred University F
Bard College F
Cazenovia College F
City University of New York
 Baruch College F
 Brooklyn College F
 City College F
 College of Staten Island F
 Hunter College F
 John Jay College of
 Criminal Justice F
 Lehman College F
 Medgar Evers College F
 York College F
Clarkson University F
College of Mount St. Vincent F
College of New Rochelle F
D'Youville College F
Elmira College F
Hamilton College F
Hartwick College F
Hilbert College F
Ithaca College F
Keuka College F
Manhattanville College F
Medaille College F
Mount Saint Mary College F
Nazareth College F
New York University F
Polytechnic Institute of New
 York University F
Rochester Institute of
 Technology F
Russell Sage College F
Sage College of Albany F
St. John Fisher College F
St. Joseph's College, New York
 F
St. Joseph's College: Suffolk
 Campus F
St. Lawrence University F
Skidmore College F
SUNY
 College at Brockport F
 College at Buffalo F
 College at Cortland F
 College at Fredonia F
 College at Geneseo F
 College at New Paltz F
 College at Old Westbury F
 College at Oneonta F
 College at Oswego F
 College at Plattsburgh F
 College at Potsdam F
 College at Purchase F
 College of Agriculture and
 Technology at Cobleskill
 F
 College of Agriculture and
 Technology at Morrisville
 F
 Farmingdale State College F
 Institute of Technology at
 Utica/Rome F
 Maritime College F
Union College F
United States Merchant Marine
 Academy F
University of Rochester F
Utica College F
Vassar College F
Wells College F
Yeshiva University F

North Carolina

Greensboro College F
Guilford College F
Meredith College F
Methodist University F
North Carolina Wesleyan
 College F

Salem College F
William Peace University F

Ohio

Baldwin-Wallace College F
Bluffton University F
Capital University F
Case Western Reserve
 University F
College of Mount St. Joseph F
College of Wooster F
Defiance College F
Denison University F
Franciscan University of
 Steubenville F
Heidelberg University F
Hiram College F
John Carroll University F
Kenyon College F
Marietta College F
Muskingum University F
Oberlin College F
Ohio Northern University F
Ohio Wesleyan University F
Otterbein University F
University of Mount Union F
Wilmington College F
Wittenberg University F

Oregon

George Fox University F
Lewis & Clark College F
Linfield College F
Pacific University F
Willamette University F

Pennsylvania

Albright College F
Allegheny College F
Alvernia University F
Arcadia University F
Baptist Bible College of
 Pennsylvania F
Bryn Mawr College F
Cabrini College F
Carnegie Mellon University F
Cedar Crest College F
Chatham University F
Delaware Valley College F
DeSales University F
Dickinson College F
Eastern University F
Elizabethtown College F
Franklin & Marshall College F
Geneva College F
Gettysburg College F
Grove City College F
Gwynedd-Mercy College F
Haverford College F
Immaculata University F
Juniata College F
Keystone College F
King's College F
La Roche College F
Lancaster Bible College F
Lebanon Valley College F
Lycoming College F
Marywood University F
Messiah College F
Misericordia University F
Moravian College F
Mount Aloysius College F
Muhlenberg College F
Neumann University F
Penn State
 Abington F
 Altoona F
 Berks F
 Erie, The Behrend College
 F
 Harrisburg F
Philadelphia Biblical University
 F
Rosemont College F
St. Vincent College F
Susquehanna University F
Swarthmore College F
Thiel College F

University of Pittsburgh
 Bradford F
 Greensburg F
University of Scranton F
Ursinus College F
Washington & Jefferson College
 F
Waynesburg University F
Westminster College F
Widener University F
Wilkes University F
York College of Pennsylvania F

Rhode Island

Johnson & Wales University:
 Providence F
Rhode Island College F
Roger Williams University F
Salve Regina University F

Tennessee

Maryville College F
Rhodes College F
University of the South F

Texas

Austin College F
Concordia University Texas F
East Texas Baptist University F
Hardin-Simmons University F
Howard Payne University F
LeTourneau University F
Schreiner University F
Southwestern University F
Sul Ross State University F
Texas Lutheran University F
Trinity University F
University of Dallas F
University of Mary Hardin-
 Baylor F
University of Texas
 Dallas F
 Tyler F

Vermont

Castleton State College F
Green Mountain College F
Johnson State College F
Lyndon State College F
Middlebury College F
Norwich University F
Southern Vermont College F

Virginia

Averett University F
Bridgewater College F
Christopher Newport University
 F
Eastern Mennonite University F
Emory & Henry College F
Ferrum College F
Hollins University F
Lynchburg College F
Mary Baldwin College F
Marymount University F
Randolph College F
Randolph-Macon College F
Roanoke College F
Shenandoah University F
Sweet Briar College F
University of Mary Washington
 F
Virginia Wesleyan College F
Washington and Lee University
 F

Washington

Pacific Lutheran University F
University of Puget Sound F
Whitman College F
Whitworth University F

West Virginia

Bethany College F

Wisconsin

Alverno College F
Beloit College F
Carroll University F

Carthage College F
Concordia University Wisconsin
 F
Edgewood College F
Lakeland College F
Lawrence University F
Maranatha Baptist Bible College
 F
Marian University F
Milwaukee School of
 Engineering F
Mount Mary College F
Northland College F
Ripon College F
St. Norbert College F
University of Wisconsin
 Eau Claire F
 La Crosse F
 Oshkosh F
 Platteville F
 River Falls F
 Stevens Point F
 Stout F
 Superior F
 Whitewater F
Wisconsin Lutheran College F

Water polo Division I

California

California State University
 Long Beach M
Loyola Marymount University
 M
Pepperdine University M
Santa Clara University M
Stanford University M
University of California
 Berkeley M
 Davis M
 Irvine M
 Los Angeles M
 Santa Barbara M
University of Southern
 California M
University of the Pacific M

Colorado

United States Air Force
 Academy M

District of Columbia

George Washington University
 M

Maryland

United States Naval Academy
 M

Massachusetts

Harvard College M

New Jersey

Princeton University M

New York

Fordham University M
Iona College M
St. Francis College M

Pennsylvania

Bucknell University M

Rhode Island

Brown University M

Water polo Division II

California

California Baptist University M
Fresno Pacific University M
University of California
 San Diego M

Ohio

Notre Dame College M

Pennsylvania

Gannon University M
Mercyhurst University M

West Virginia

Salem International University
M

Water polo Division III

California

California Institute of
Technology M
California Lutheran University
M
Chapman University M
Claremont McKenna College M
Occidental College M
Pitzer College M
Pomona College M
University of La Verne M
University of Redlands M
Whittier College M

Connecticut

Connecticut College M

Maryland

Johns Hopkins University M

Massachusetts

Massachusetts Institute of
Technology M

Pennsylvania

Penn State
Erie, The Behrend College
M
Washington & Jefferson College
M

Wrestling Division I

Arizona

Arizona State University M

California

California Polytechnic State
University: San Luis Obispo
M
California State University
Bakersfield M
Stanford University M

Colorado

United States Air Force
Academy M
University of Northern Colorado
M

Connecticut

Sacred Heart University M

District of Columbia

American University M

Idaho

Boise State University M

Illinois

Northern Illinois University M
Northwestern University M
Southern Illinois University
Edwardsville M
University of Illinois
Urbana-Champaign M

Indiana

Indiana University
Bloomington M
Purdue University M

Iowa

Iowa State University M
University of Iowa M
University of Northern Iowa M

Maryland

United States Naval Academy
M
University of Maryland
College Park M

Massachusetts

Boston University M
Harvard College M

Michigan

Central Michigan University M
Eastern Michigan University M
Michigan State University M
University of Michigan M

Minnesota

University of Minnesota
Twin Cities M

Missouri

University of Missouri
Columbia M

Nebraska

University of Nebraska
Lincoln M

New Jersey

Princeton University M
Rider University M
Rutgers, The State University of
New Jersey
New Brunswick/Piscataway
Campus M

New York

Columbia University M
Cornell University M
Hofstra University M
SUNY
University at Binghamton
M
University at Buffalo M
United States Military Academy
M

North Carolina

Appalachian State University M
Campbell University M
Davidson College M
Duke University M
Gardner-Webb University M
North Carolina State University
M
University of North Carolina
Chapel Hill M

North Dakota

North Dakota State University
M

Ohio

Cleveland State University M
Kent State University M
Ohio State University
Columbus Campus M
Ohio University M

Oklahoma

Oklahoma State University M
University of Oklahoma M

Oregon

Oregon State University M

Pennsylvania

Bloomsburg University of
Pennsylvania M
Bucknell University M
Clarion University of
Pennsylvania M
Drexel University M
Edinboro University of
Pennsylvania M

Franklin & Marshall College M
Lehigh University M
Lock Haven University of
Pennsylvania M
Millersville University of
Pennsylvania M
Penn State
University Park M
University of Pennsylvania M
University of Pittsburgh M

Rhode Island

Brown University M

South Carolina

The Citadel M

South Dakota

South Dakota State University
M

Tennessee

University of Tennessee
Chattanooga M

Utah

Utah Valley University M

Virginia

George Mason University M
Old Dominion University M
University of Virginia M
Virginia Military Institute M
Virginia Polytechnic Institute
and State University M

West Virginia

West Virginia University M

Wisconsin

University of Wisconsin
Madison M

Wyoming

University of Wyoming M

Wrestling Division II

Arizona

Grand Canyon University M

Arkansas

Ouachita Baptist University M

California

California Baptist University M
San Francisco State University
M

Colorado

Adams State College M
Colorado Mesa University M
Colorado School of Mines M
Colorado State University
Pueblo M
Western State College of
Colorado M

Georgia

Chorter University
Shorter University M

Illinois

McKendree University M

Indiana

University of Indianapolis M

Iowa

Upper Iowa University M

Kansas

Fort Hays State University M
Newman University M

Massachusetts

American International College
M

Minnesota

Minnesota State University
Mankato M
Moorhead M
Saint Cloud State University M
Southwest Minnesota State
University M

Missouri

Lindenwood University M
Maryville University of Saint
Louis M
Truman State University M
University of Central Missouri
M

Nebraska

Chadron State College M
University of Nebraska
Kearney M

New Mexico

New Mexico Highlands
University M

North Carolina

Belmont Abbey College M
University of North Carolina
Pembroke M

North Dakota

Minot State University M
University of Mary M

Ohio

Ashland University M
Lake Erie College M
Notre Dame College M
Tiffin University M
University of Findlay M

Oklahoma

University of Central Oklahoma
M

Pennsylvania

East Stroudsburg University of
Pennsylvania M
Gannon University M
Kutztown University of
Pennsylvania M
Mercyhurst University M
Seton Hill University M
Shippensburg University of
Pennsylvania M
University of Pittsburgh
Johnstown M

Puerto Rico

University of Puerto Rico
Mayaguez M

South Carolina

Anderson University M
Limestone College M
Newberry College M

South Dakota

Augustana College M
Northern State University M

Tennessee

King College M

West Virginia

Ohio Valley University M
West Liberty University M

Wisconsin

University of Wisconsin
Parkside M

Canada

Simon Fraser University M

Wrestling Division III

Connecticut

Trinity College M
United States Coast Guard
Academy M
Wesleyan University M

Illinois

Augustana College M
Elmhurst College M
Knox College M
North Central College M
University of Chicago M
Wheaton College M

Indiana

Manchester College M
Trine University M
Wabash College M

Iowa

Buena Vista University M
Central College M
Coe College M
Cornell College M
Loras College M
Luther College M
Simpson College M
University of Dubuque M
Wartburg College M

Maine

University of Southern Maine M

Maryland

Johns Hopkins University M
McDaniel College M

Massachusetts

Bridgewater State University M
Springfield College M
Western New England
University M
Williams College M
Worcester Polytechnic Institute
M

Michigan

Alma College M
Olivet College M

Minnesota

Concordia College: Moorhead
M
St. John's University M
St. Olaf College M

New Hampshire

Plymouth State University M

New Jersey

Centenary College M
The College of New Jersey M
Stevens Institute of Technology
M

New York

City University of New York
Hunter College M
Ithaca College M
New York University M
Rochester Institute of
Technology M
SUNY
College at Brockport M
College at Cortland M
College at Oneonta M
College at Oswego M
United States Merchant Marine
Academy M
Yeshiva University M

Ohio

Baldwin-Wallace College M
Case Western Reserve
  University M
College of Mount St. Joseph M
Heidelberg University M
John Carroll University M
Muskingum University M
Ohio Northern University M
University of Mount Union M
Wilmington College M

Oregon

Pacific University M

Pennsylvania

Delaware Valley College M
Elizabethtown College M
Gettysburg College M
King's College M
Lycoming College M
Messiah College M
Muhlenberg College M
Thiel College M
University of Scranton M
Ursinus College M
Washington & Jefferson College
  M
Waynesburg University M
Wilkes University M
York College of Pennsylvania
  M

Rhode Island

Johnson & Wales University:
  Providence M
Rhode Island College M
Roger Williams University M

Vermont

Norwich University M

Virginia

Washington and Lee University
  M

Wisconsin

Concordia University Wisconsin
  M
Lakeland College M
Maranatha Baptist Bible College
  M
Milwaukee School of
  Engineering M
University of Wisconsin
    Eau Claire M
    La Crosse M
    Oshkosh M
    Platteville M
    Stevens Point M
    Whitewater M

Alphabetical index of colleges

Applying to College?

Remove the anxiety with these newly revised guides.

Campus Visits & College Interviews, 3rd Edition

By Zola Dincin Schneider & Norman G. Schneider

176 pages, paperback
ISBN: 978-0-87447-988-1

Price: $14.99

The College Application Essay, 5th Edition

By Sarah Myers McGinty

176 pages, paperback
ISBN: 978-0-87447-987-4

Price: $15.99

CollegeBoard

More College Planning Resources
from the College Board

College Handbook 2013

The only guide listing all accredited universities, two-year and four-year colleges, and technical schools in the United States — more than 3,900 in total.

2,200 pages, paperback
ISBN: 978-0-87447-980-5
$29.99

The Official SAT Study Guide™: Second Edition

The Official SAT Study Guide™ is the only book that features 10 official practice tests created by the test maker. The No. 1 best-selling guide is packed with valuable test-taking approaches and focused sets of practice questions — just like those on the actual SAT® — to help students get ready for the test.

998 pages, trade paper
ISBN: 978-0-87447-852-5
$21.99

Book of Majors 2013

Explore in-depth descriptions of 200 majors, and see where over 1,100 majors are offered at colleges nationwide.

1,350 pages, paperback
ISBN: 978-0-87447-981-2
$27.99

Get It Together for College, 2nd Edition

Take advantage of expert tips that help students stay on top of the college admission process.

240 pages, paperback
ISBN: 978-0-87447-974-4
$15.99

PAYING FOR COLLEGE

Getting Financial Aid 2013

A must-have book in today's economy, this is the perfect resource for families managing the high cost of college. This easy step-by-step guide shows why, when and how to apply for financial aid.

1,050 pages, paperback
978-0-87447-982-9
$22.99

Scholarship Handbook 2013

The most complete and comprehensive guide to help families tap into the more than 1.7 million scholarships, internships and loans available to students each year.

624 pages, paperback
ISBN: 978-0-87447-983-6
$29.99

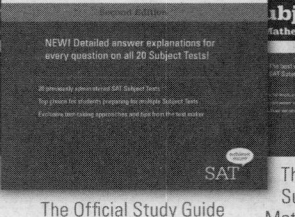